NOT FOR SALE

(7.1.66)

YOU'RE GONNA' LOVE MY BABY
(McNair—Miller—Perkinson)
BARBARA McNAIR
Producer: Berry Gordy, Jr.

E.M.I. RECORDS LIMITED

THE LIBERTINES

TMG 544

STEREO
ILPS-9105

RARE
RECORD
PRICE
GUIDE
2014

Over 100,000 listings and values.
Available in softback, hardback,
online and as a download
on the iBookstore.

See **www.rarerecordpriceguide.com** for details

LONDON

THE WHO
My Generation
•
Shout and Shimmy

tamla motown

M-G-M

DEREK
LAWRENCE
MUSIC LTD.

EARTH ROCKER

Acknowledgements

Thanks go to all the people who have reviewed sections of this book. Their helpful comments have helped to shape this tome. These people include Dr Gillian Marshman, Dr Carmine de Pasquale, Dr Sandy Craig, Dr David Ross, Dr Jeff Barbara, Dr David Schultz, Dr Peter Tamblyn, Dr Michael Briffa, Dr Steve Stranks, and Dr Alan Stapleton.

Debbie Marriott is the consummate professional—focused, affable, and meticulous. Her work on the manuscript (and everything else that continues at the same time) is simply remarkable.

Without the unbelievable support of Rosemary, most weeks I wouldn't get out of bed on Monday morning. It is not easy living in a world of disorganized papers.

How could one man be so tolerant? Paul keeps the coffee flowing and computers working with an equanimity which defies belief.

This book is the result.

Preface

Palliative and supportive care is a rich and challenging area of clinical practice. Clinicians need to have a clear understanding of the life-limiting illness, the comorbid illnesses that impact so greatly on the population we serve, and the knowledge of both disease-modifying and symptomatic measures that ultimately optimize comfort and function.

Comprehensive assessment will help this person to realize their priorities at a time of life that can be challenging for everyone involved. We hope that this book will provide a simple but thorough framework for quality day-to-day clinical care dealing with unexpected changes in the clinical condition of someone with a life-limiting illness.

An emergency is subjective. Emergencies are so often dictated by their life-threatening nature and the potential for improved outcomes. In clinical practice, we tend to think of emergencies as life and death situations. Until we as clinicians know whether it is a life and death situation, any unexpected change is an emergency to the person with the life-limiting illness, their family, and to us until we have more information.

In patient-centred palliative and supportive care, emergencies also need to be defined by the potential distress that a particular clinical issue raises for that person and their family, together with the symptoms that herald this unexpected change. With the background of a life-limiting illness, many people quite reasonably interpret unexpected change as the harbinger of death.

Therefore, the unexpected onset of new symptoms in someone with a life-limiting illness is a very challenging part of clinical practice.

- How aggressively should this person be investigated?
- What treatment options are reasonable?

Good palliative and supportive care relies on the full range of clinical skills in order to deliver outcomes appropriate to *this* person with *their* life-limiting illness. Through careful history, physical examination, and the judicious use of investigations, clinicians can negotiate treatment choices best tailored to this person's needs. For many people with a life-limiting illness, the best symptom control remains treatment of the underlying pathology causing the new symptom.

This book is for practice in emergency departments, acute care hospitals, patients in in-patient palliative care units including hospices, residential aged care facilities, and when people are still in their own homes. It attempts to select medications and routes of administration of available medications to deal with the acute problem at hand, and while more definitive measures are being put in place.

Knowing the tempo of this person's life-limiting illness will allow health professionals to give appropriate advice. Guiding this decision-making process is an understanding of where this person is on their disease trajectory. This book uses three categories which consider how this person's needs are changing as their disease progresses:

- in the terminal stages of their life-limiting illness with poor level of function
- deteriorating, and needing increasing support
- stable with a good level of function.

These three categories broadly reflect the natural history of the disease with no intervening complications. The first generally equates to an expected prognosis of days or hours, the second to weeks, and the third to at least months or years (or in the case of many people receiving supportive care, a prognosis otherwise not limited by the disease).

An acute deterioration in someone who is otherwise stable may become a terminal event if it is not treated. Clinically, this unexpected deterioration needs to be distinguished from the terminal stage of an advanced illness where the life-limiting illness is now expected to lead rapidly to death. Such distinctions do not override individual choice where, despite a good level of function, fully informed people may choose a less active option.

Assessment includes a comprehensive overview of:

- where this person is on the disease trajectory of their life-limiting illness (rate of weight loss, presence of fatigue or anorexia, and the rate of functional decline)
- the natural history of this life-limiting illness and the comorbid illnesses that this person has
- how this person sees their future emotionally and existentially.

Knowing how their disease is manifesting itself systemically provides insight into future expected decline. It is the *unexpected* change in condition that this book addresses.

Section 1 is designed to help clinicians **make the diagnosis** of the cause of an unexpected change. It is presented as a series of symptoms which may present without warning, and where there may be potentially reversible causes that need to be excluded before the symptom should be labelled 'refractory' or 'intractable'. Looking for treatable problems that mimic the untreatable in people with life-limiting illnesses forms the basis of differential diagnoses in palliative and supportive care. The interventions considered need to be appropriate to the severity of the symptom, the stage of disease, and the likelihood of improving that symptom through the clinical path proposed. In palliative and supportive care, a symptom can only be considered refractory when:

- easily reversible causes have been excluded

or

- by agreement; a fully informed person with a life-limiting illness chooses not to define further any underlying pathology even if it is simply reversible.

Section 2 focuses on **detailed evaluation and treatment options** tailored to the needs of people with a life-limiting illness. It looks at the underlying reversible clinical pathology that can cause symptoms and the treatment options, ranging from attempting full reversal of the new pathology through to symptom support. This range of options will need to be discussed with people who have a life-limiting illness to inform their decision-making, particularly if they are relatively well.

Symptom control includes an adequate assessment for **all people** with a new symptom. Optimizing level of comfort and level of function is pivotal for **all people**, irrespective of their stage of disease.

For **some people** with a good or reasonable level of function and prognosis, discussions are needed to determine whether the more intensive investigation, treatments, and interventions should be pursued. This is not always a simple decision and will require input from a number of health professionals in advising the person and their family about the potential benefits and burdens of the proposed intervention.

This book provides guidance for all members of the multidisciplinary team—doctors, nurses, allied health practitioners—in assessing this person in the context of a sudden or unexpected change in their clinical condition while facing a life-limiting illness.

David Currow
Katherine Clark

Key to the book

Section 1 Frequently encountered symptoms

Symptoms

Symptom: e.g. shortness of breath and fever
Timeframe for onset: acute, subacute, acute-on-chronic
Possible causes: e.g. community-acquired pneumonia—go to relevant part of Section 2

Reversibility

- Factors which are likely to have a reversible component and may require prompt intervention. The best symptom control remains, where possible, to treat the underlying cause of the symptom.
- Factors unlikely to have an easily reversible component will need symptomatic treatment.

Symptomatic treatment for this clinical presentation

- Non-pharmacological interventions
- Pharmacological interventions

Section 2 Specific clinical conditions

Having made the clinical diagnosis from the presenting symptom, obtain more detailed information from 'specific clinical conditions'.

Assessment

- Key history to help distinguish likely (reversible) causes
- Key physical examination

Investigations and treatment

Potential investigations (and how they will help clinical decision-making) and treatment options including symptom control by prognosis/current global functional status *before* this acute change. Prognosis estimated as:

- Hours or days or needing a great deal of support and spending most of his/her time in bed. (symptom control is covered here)
- Weeks to months *or* starting to need support, with limited energy, spending more time at home. This should be read in addition to the section where people's prognosis is estimated as hours to days
- Months to years *or* still playing golf. This section adds to the sections 'Hours to days' and 'Weeks to months' for people with a better prognosis.

Books for additional information

Oxford Textbook of Medicine (4th edition)
D. Warrell, T. Cox, J. Firth, and E. Benz J
Oxford University Press, 2003

Oxford Textbook of Palliative Medicine (3rd edition)
D. Doyle, G. Hanks, N. Cherny, and K. Calman
Oxford University Press, 2004

Oxford Handbook of Palliative Care
M. Watson, C. Lucas, A. Hoy, and I. Back
Oxford University Press, 2005

Oxford Handbook of Oncology
J. Cassidy, D. Bissett, and R.A.J. Spence
Oxford University Press, 2002

Contents

List of abbreviations

AAA	abdominal aortic aneurysm
ABG	arterial blood gas
ACE	angiotensin-converting enzyme
ACTH	adrenocorticotrophic hormone
ADH	antidiuretic hormone
ALT	alanine transaminase
AMI	acute myocardial infarction
AML	acute myeloid leukaemia
ANCA	anti-neutrophilic cytoplasmic antibodies
APTT	activated partial thromboplastin time
AST	aspartate transaminase
AV	atrioventricular
BP	blood pressure
BGL	blood glucose level
Ca	calcium
CLL	chronic lymphocytic leukaemia
CML	chronic myelocytic leukaemia
CNS	central nervous system
CN	cranial nerve
Coags	coagulation
COPD	chronic obstructive pulmonary disease
CrCl	creatinine clearance
CRH	corticotrophin-releasing hormone
CRP	C-reactive protein
CSF	cerebrospinal fluid
CT	computerized tomography
CTPA	computed tomography pulmonary angiogram
CVA	cerebrovascular accident
CXR	chest X-ray
DIC	disseminated intravascular coagulation
DVT	deep vein thrombosis
ECG	electrocardiogram
EEG	electroencephalogram
ERCP	endoscopic retrograde cholangiopancreatography
ESR	erythrocyte sedimentation rate
EUC	electrolytes, urea and creatinine

FBC	full blood count
FFP	fresh frozen plasma
GCS	Glasgow Coma Score
G-CSF	granulocyte colony-stimulating factor
GFR	glomerular filtration rate
GM-CSF	granulocyte–macrophage colony-stimulating factor
GGT	gamma glutamyl transpeptidase
GIT	gastrointestinal tract
HAE	hereditary angio oedema
H_2	histamine 2
Hb	haemoglobin
HUS	haemolytic uraemic syndrome
IDC	indwelling catheter
IE	infective endocarditis
IM	intramuscular
INH	Isoniazid
INR	international normalized ratio
ITP	idiopathic thrombocytopaenic purpura
IV	intravenous
JVP	jugular venous pressure
LDH	lactate dehydrogenase
LFT	liver function tests
LP	lumbar puncture
LMW	low molecular weight
MAOI	monoamine oxidase inhibitor
MCV	mean corpuscular volume
MRI	magnetic resonance imaging
MSU	mid stream urine
NaCl	sodium chloride
NG	nasogastric
NSAID	non-steriodal anti-inflammatory drugs
PCA	patient controlled analgesia
PE	pulmonary embolus
PLA	platelets
PND	paroxysmal nocturnal dyspnoea
PO	per oral
PPI	proton pump inhibitor
PR	per rectum/progesterone receptor/pulse rate
PT	prothrombin time
RA	rheumatoid arthritis
RDW	red cell distribution width

RTOG	Radiation Therapy Oncology Group
SC	subcutaneous
SIADH	syndrome of inappropriate antidiuretic hormone secretion
SL	sublingual
SLE	systemic lupus erythematosus
SNRI	serotonin and noradrenaline reuptake inhibitor
SSRI	selective serotonin reuptake inhibitor
SVC	superior vena cava
T_3	tri-iodothyronine
T_4	Thyroxine
TFT	thyroid function test
TPN	total parenteral nutrition
TSH	thyroid-stimulating hormone
TTP	thrombotic thrombocytopaenic purpura
VP	ventriculo-peritoneal
VTED	venous thromboembolic disease
WCC	white cell count
WHO	World Health Organization

Section 1

Frequently encountered symptoms

Frequently encountered symptoms

The 'WHY' framework*

Clinical decision-making in palliative care—fundamental questions that underlie good palliative practice for health professionals.

Does this person have a life-limiting illness?

Every health professional involved in the care of this person should satisfy themselves that this person has a progressive life-limiting illness. Admission to a palliative care service without a life-limiting illness has occurred, at times with disastrous consequences. There have also been examples where, in the presence of a life-limiting illness, a new intercurrent problem has been wrongly attributed to the life-limiting illness.

The supportive care needs of people who are seriously unwell with a potential life-limiting illness are also considered in this book.

The question 'Why?' arises when someone's clinical course does not reflect the known course of the illness. Therefore, knowing the natural history of this illness is the foundation on which the answer to this question is built. Is today's new symptom:

- an expected manifestation of the disease?
- an unexpected manifestation of the disease?
- an exacerbation of an intercurrent problem?
- a new intercurrent problem?

When there is deterioration, the following question will need to be asked:

'Is this person unwell today because of overall progression in (maximally) treated disease?'

OR

'Is this person unwell today because of the effects of an acute problem with an easily reversible cause?'

Another way to approach the assessment is to ask **'Is this an expected or an unexpected deterioration?'**

For most people with cancer and end-stage organ failure, death is a result of shutdown of the whole body, not simply where the cancer is growing or which organ is failing. Uncontrolled cancer or end-stage organ failure are systemic diseases where most changes are 'expected', leading to a gradual and predictable global decline. Unexpected changes need to be carefully evaluated (including the possibility that the problem is iatrogenic).

Screening questions that need to be included if you are to have an overview of all that is going on for this person include:

Why has a change in condition occurred?
What is the timeframe for the change? (acute changes often have a potentially reversible cause)
What else has changed in or around the same time period?

---

* We are grateful to the academic team at Flinders University Department of Palliative and Supportive Services for their input into this section.

Throughout the course of an illness, these questions need to be asked explicitly with each and every change encountered.

'Can we do something about the problem?' 'Yes' does not mean that we start to treat. We need to consider:
- this presenting problem
- the underlying life-limiting illness and its current systemic manifestations (fatigue, weight loss, anorexia)
- whether the problem is likely to be reversible or not
- the person's wishes under these circumstances.

(Therefore, we also need to assess the person's testamentary capacity. If the person is unable to give guidance because of their illness, ask the next-of-kin/guardian/significant person/medical power of attorney what *this person* would want to be done (or not done) in these circumstances.)

Although this level of questioning may seem excessive, most people at the end-of-life want to be included in decision-making about their care and ensure that simple things to improve their level of function and comfort are discussed.

Where possible, the best treatment of any symptom is still to treat the cause of the problem.

What can we reasonably do to maintain or improve comfort or function for this person?

Global assessment of the person with palliative or supportive care needs

Five key considerations

The life-limiting illness

- Each life-limiting illness has its own natural history. Being aware of how it affects someone, where it manifests itself, and how it limits life are crucial. What is the median, 1 year, and 5 year survival with this person's extent of disease?

Intercurrent illnesses

- What are the intercurrent illnesses that are actively contributing to the symptoms this person is experiencing?
- Can the treatment of any active intercurrent problems improve this person's prognosis, level of function, or level of comfort?
- What are the intercurrent illnesses that are inactive and not limiting prognosis, function, or comfort?

Response to disease- or prognosis-modifying therapies

- How has the person responded to therapy for their life-limiting illness in the past?
- How is the person responding to current therapies?
- Can the course of the illness be modified (with therapies that are acceptable and reasonable given the person's overall level of function and prognosis)?
- Will such interventions predictably improve prognosis, or help maintain or improve function or comfort?

Change in functional status over time

- Is global functioning stable or changing over months, weeks, days, or hours? (This is a key index for the future course of the life-limiting illness if nothing else can be modified). (See Appendix 1.)
- How quickly are systemic indices including level of function, energy levels, appetite, and weight changing? (See Appendix 2.)

The person's perception of their future

- Always listen carefully to the goals, dreams, and fears of the person with a life-limiting illness—they have a great deal of insight. What does this person most need in order to live life fully at this time?

Further reading

Oxford Handbook of Palliative Care, pp. xxx–xxxi, 4–5.

Chest pain

Onset of symptom

Acute onset (less than 24 hs) of chest pain

- **Retrosternal and heavy**, associated with shortness of breath, radiation of pain to the jaw, neck, or either hand, and an impending sense of doom is typical of myocardial ischaemic pain (p.110). Identical pain may be experienced with oesophagitis or oesophageal spasm.
- **Sharp and central**, worsens with respiration, and relieved by sitting forward is typical of pericarditis (p.102). This is often associated with fevers, increasing shortness of breath, and a pericardial rub.
- **Radiating to the back, has a sudden onset, and with a retrosternal component**, very distressing and associated with nausea and shortness of breath is typical of aortic dissection (p.116). This is usually associated with hypertension.
- **Worse with respiration, sharp, and well localized** is typical of pleural pain. This may be associated with acute onset of breathlessness, fever, and cough. The differential diagnosis includes pulmonary embolism (p.106), pleurisy secondary to infection (p.264), pneumothorax (p.272), costochondritis, rib fracture, and local trauma.
- **Arising from the scapula and radiating anteriorly to the chest**, associated with fever, sweats, and tachycardia is suggestive of mediastinitis (p.276). These people may be very unwell. The association of recent oesophageal surgery or stenting raises this as a differential.
- **Associated with abdominal pain** may indicate pancreatitis (p.150), oesophageal disorders (spasm, oesophagitis, ulceration, reflux, mucositis), or biliary disorders (gallstones, malignant obstruction, sepsis (p.148).)
- **Associated with anxiety**: normal physical examination may indicate an emotional cause of acute chest pain. This is not uncommon, although physical causes must first be excluded.

Subacute onset (1–3 days) of chest pain

- **Difficult to localize** but described as a deep aching discomfort in cancer patients may be due to malignant pericardial invasion (p.102).
- **More gradual onset of pleuritic pain** may represent malignant invasion of the pleura, rib fractures or infiltration, chest wall invasion, or zoster infection.
- **Dermatomal in distribution** may occur because of intercostal nerve damage (malignant infiltration, post-thoracotomy, or post-pleurodesis), or may be due to a radiculopathy (acute herpes zoster, malignant thoracic cord disease). (See Appendix 3.)

Acute-on-chronic chest pain

Chronic chest pain may develop from local trauma (including instrumentation) or because of neuropathy. Promptly diagnose and treat in people with a good prognosis.

Can you modify anything contributing to the symptom?

The pain of an **acute coronary syndrome**, regardless of the person's estimated prognosis, may be modified by the administration of oxygen, sublingual or topical nitrates (with sufficient blood pressure), and morphine (IV or SC 2.5–5 mg as required in opioid-naïve people), with the aim of limiting ischaemia. If the prognosis of the individual prior to the onset of this problem is considered greater than weeks, anti-platelet treatment (aspirin 100 mg daily) and antithrombin treatment (LMW heparin) should be initiated. For people with a longer prognosis, promptly consider reperfusion therapy (thrombolysis, stenting).

The pain of **pericarditis**, regardless of prognosis, may be modified by the use of NSAIDs (p.102).

An **aortic dissection** may propagate and lead to aortic rupture if associated hypertension is not managed. The aim in all but the terminal stages of an illness is to prevent this complication. The initial antihypertensive agent must be a beta-blocker. Failure to treat initially with a beta-blocker may provoke catecholamine release and exacerbation of hypertension (p.120).

All people with a **pulmonary embolus** (p.106) require oxygen to maintain O_2 saturation greater than 92 per cent. This is to improve chest pain and dyspnoea that occurs because of hypoxaemia, increased pulmonary artery pressures, and pulmonary vascular resistance. In people with longer prognosis, mortality is lessened by treatment and, unless there are contraindications, anticoagulation should be initiated.

Acute onset of unilateral chest pain and absence of air entry associated with shortness of breath may indicate a **pneumothorax** (p.272). The most important step is to consider whether the pneumothorax is under tension.

Acute mediastinitis (p.276) occurs most commonly as the result of a ruptured trachea or oesophagus, or a serious infection (pleura, lung, sternum, or descending from the neck or oropharynx). If the rupture is not limited to the mediastinum or is between the visceral pleura and the mediastinum, surgical advice should be sought.

Pericardial effusions (p.100) in people with a prognosis of greater than weeks are best palliated with pericardiacentesis. If this is a recurrent problem, consideration of a surgical pericardial window is indicated.

Chest infections causing pleuritic chest pain will usually respond to antibiotics. This may be regardless of prognosis (p.264).

The pain of **herpes zoster** may precede the rash. When the rash occurs it is vesicular and later crusts. Promptly commencing antiviral medications may not prevent post-herpetic neuralgia (oral famciclovir 250 mg three times daily in people who are not immunocompromised and 500 mg three times daily in those who are immunocompromised for 7 days, or aciclovir 800 mg five times daily for 7 days, both requiring dose modification in people with impaired renal function) but duration or intensity of episodes of pain may be lessened. Concomitant administration of corticosteroids with antiviral treatment may improve acute herpetic pain and healing of vesicles, without preventing post-herpetic neuralgia. (Corticosteroids must not be prescribed in the acute phase without antivirals.)

The onset of chest and back pain secondary to a threatened **cord compression** (p.204) is a vitally important diagnosis to consider. The first sign of a cord compression is often back pain, usually in the absence of a neurological deficit. Dexamethasone (16 mg in 24 hs) may limit cord damage, regardless of prognosis. Early imaging in someone who is otherwise mobile is necessary.

Malignant bone disease requires combinations of interventions, including opioid analgesia, paracetamol, anti-inflammatory agents (dexamethasone, NSAIDS, COX-II inhibitors), bisphosphonates, and, if symptoms are not settling or with a pathological fracture, radiotherapy.

Chest pain arising from **oesophageal spasm** may respond to calcium-channel blockers or nitrates. Additionally, **oesophagitis** secondary to any cause should prompt prescription of proton pump inhibitors, metoclopramide 10 mg three or four times daily, and sucralfate 1 g four times daily. Opioid analgesia may still be required. A similar approach may be taken in pain occurring secondary to peptic ulcer disease.

Post-thoracotomy pain is difficult to predict and to modify. Failure to improve using a systematic approach with stepwise addition of analgesia prompts consideration of interventional pain relief such as an intercostal block. (See Appendix 3.)

What underlying factors cannot be improved?

People with a large or **saddle pulmonary embolus**, who present with shock, have a grave prognosis. The groups at risk include people with cancer, immobile people, and the elderly. This is the group who are least likely to tolerate aggressive interventions with thrombolysis, which carries its own risks of morbidity and mortality.

People who develop **descending necrotic mediastinitis** have a very poor prognosis with a high incidence of septic deaths.

Symptomatic treatment

Non-pharmacological intervention

People with ischaemic chest pain may require a combined approach to management that includes rest and oxygen.

People with rib fractures or malignant bone disease may benefit from review by a physiotherapist to teach them how to support the affected region while still performing breathing exercises to avoid secondary chest infections.

People with bone metastases causing chest pain or cord compression should promptly receive a radiotherapy consultation.

Pharmacological intervention

All people with chest pain require the correct strength of analgesia for the severity of the pain they are experiencing. Individuals with strong pain require opioids. The most widely recommended initial opioid, except when a true history of allergy exists, remains morphine. True contraindications to morphine are rare, and must be excluded on history. When initiating opioids, low doses administered 'around the clock', always with breakthrough or rescue analgesia available, should be used. An appropriate dose to start with is 2.5–5.0 mg of oral morphine given every 4 hs with a similar dose used for breakthrough analgesia as necessary. Modifications to this depend upon the individual's past exposure to opioids, their frailty, and review of their most recent renal function.

People with ischaemic chest pain may additionally benefit from a nitrate (sublingual, oral or transdermal), a calcium-channel blocker and opioids. The starting doses of the medications depend upon the haemodynamic state of the person.

People with pleuritic pain may be treated with an opioid in severe cases and an anti-inflammatory agent, either steroidal or non-steroidal.

People with chest pain secondary to malignant disease require the prescription of opioids and appropriate adjuvant analgesia. In malignant bone disease, this includes regular paracetamol (1 g four times daily), except when there is a past history of heavy alcohol use, in the very frail elderly, or in the malnourished. Other useful adjuvant agents include NSAIDs and bisphosphonates (IV pamidronate 60–90 mg zeledronic acid 4 mg iv).

Neuropathic pain also requires the use of adjuvant agents. Recommended agents include tricyclic antidepressants (amitriptyline, doxepin) or anticonvulsants (carbamazepine, sodium valproate, clonazepam, gabapentin, pregabalin). Another agent to consider is ketamine.

Further reading
Oxford Textbook of Palliative Medicine, p. 611.

Abdominal pain

Onset of symptom

Acute onset (less than 24 hs) of abdominal pain

- **Guarding**, worse with palpation or coughing, suggests inflammation. Fever, confusion, nausea, and vomiting suggest infection. Infections include peritonitis (primary, secondary), cholecystitis, or cholangitis (p.148), pancreatitis (p.150), appendicitis, lower lobe pneumonia (p.264), or myocardial ischaemia (p.110). A rigid abdomen suggests a ruptured viscus.
- **Left lower quadrant pain** associated with loose bowel actions and a low grade fever suggests diverticulitis. Bright rectal blood loss can be caused by mucositis (p.126), colitis (p.130), diverticulitis, colon cancer, polyp, or angiodysplasia. Consider torrential gut bleeding as a cause of shock. Generalized lower abdominal pain associated with loose bowel actions suggests colitis or enteritis (p.130).
- **Pain with few physical findings** is typical of gut ischaemia secondary to obstruction of the mesenteric vessels (p.131). Later changes include GI bleeding, abdominal distension, and a rigid tender abdomen with guarding. These people may be shocked.
- **Cramping, associated with altered bowel habits** (constipation progressing to obstipation, nausea, and vomiting) may be due to GIT obstruction (p.140). This pain may initially be intermittent but becomes more severe and constant with progressive obstruction. Obstructive pain may develop secondary to constipation, functional obstruction, adhesions, tumours, strangulated hernia, volvulus or gallstone ileus. Distal large bowel obstruction is less frequently associated with vomiting.
- **Sudden-onset upper quadrant pain** may represent splenic or renal infarction, usually associated with fever, nausea, and vomiting. It is seen in people with haematological disorders (sickle cell anaemia, lymphoma, or leukaemia), embolic disorders (cardiac arrhythmias, septic emboli, antiphospholipid disorders), vascular disorders (aortic dissection, vasculitis), or splenic torsion.
- **Severe right upper quadrant pain** may represent a subcapsular hepatic bleed (relieved by sitting forward).

Subacute onset (1–3 days) of abdominal pain

- **In the upper abdomen and associated with back pain, nausea, vomiting, and fever**, may be due to acute pancreatitis (p.150). The presence of hypotension, tachycardia, and associated sepsis indicates severity. The associated signs of periumbilical and flank bruising reflect haemorrhagic pancreatitis.
- **Epigastric pain** may indicate peptic ulcer disease (*Helicobacter pylori*, NSAIDs, corticosteroids, delayed gastric emptying, smoking) or gastritis.
- **Localized to the right upper quadrant**, associated with jaundice and an encephalopathy, may indicate acute liver failure. This occurs most commonly in the context of previous cirrhosis of the liver, but may occur *de novo* (p.154).

Acute-on-chronic onset of abdominal pain

- **Acute worsening in the right upper quadrant** radiating around to the back or across the epigastrium in a person with a liver malignancy (either primary or metastatic) may represent capsule stretch or a bleed into a metastasis. This pain may be severe and worsen with respiration. The liver will be tender to palpation.
- **Epigastric pain radiating through to the back** in a person with a past history of pancreatitis may indicate a pancreatic cyst, pancreatic necrosis, chronic pancreatitis, or pain from cancer of the pancreas.
- **Epigastric pain** in individuals with known dyspepsia may represent development of an ulcer, ulcer perforation, or an underlying malignancy.
- **Poor localization of pain that occurs 30–60 min after meals** may be due to mesenteric angina. This may be due to vascular disease or secondary to malignant compression of more than two branches of the mesenteric artery.

Can you modify anything contributing to the symptom?

Peritonitis may be **primary** (spontaneous bacterial peritonitis) or **secondary** (peritoneal dialysis, ruptured viscus including appendicitis). Spontaneous bacterial peritonitis is suggested in people with cirrhosis and decompensated liver disease. A diagnostic tap for white cell count (polymorphs), LDH, glucose, and protein should be performed.

Secondary peritonitis due to perforation or transmural ischaemia has a very high mortality rate untreated. Otherwise well people require surgical intervention and broad-spectrum antibiotics.

Epigastric pain radiating to the right upper quadrant and right shoulder tip is characteristic of **cholecystitis** (p.148). These people should receive hydration, analgesia, and antibiotics. In critically unwell people, percutaneous drainage of the gall bladder may provide relief of pain and reduce mortality.

The most important complication of impacted gallstones is **acute pancreatitis**. Consideration of ERCP must be made in order to relieve the obstruction. Complications include a pseudocyst, abscess, or chronic pancreatitis.

In right lower quadrant pain, consider **appendicitis**.

There are multiple causes of **colitis** (infectious, ischaemic, ulcerative, granulomatosis) (p.130). The most likely cause will be identified on history. The most common cause is secondary to *Clostridium difficile* toxin. If diarrhoea persists, cholestyramine 4 g may reduce symptoms.

Mucositis occurring secondary to radiotherapy or chemotherapy may improve with supportive hydration and, in cases that fail to resolve, regular octreotide.

Simple **diverticulitis** requires adequate hydration and antibiotics. A perforated diverticulum may lead to peritonitis or an abscess. A surgical review may be indicated.

In the case of **peptic ulcer disease**, symptoms may be improved by decreasing acid secretion (ranitidine 300 mg daily or omeprazole 20 mg daily), reducing contact of acid with the ulcer to promote healing (sucralfate 1 g four times daily). Treat *H. pylori* if present and stop contributing medications if possible.

Acute liver failure (p.154) requires discontinuation of hepatotoxic medications. Treat reversible causes (paracetamol overdose), maintain blood glucose with a 5 per cent dextrose infusion, and restrict protein intake and protein absorption (lactulose 20 ml two to three times daily).

What underlying factors cannot be improved?

Catastrophic intra-abdominal events carry a very poor prognosis and are unlikely to be reversible in this patient population. These include gut necrosis secondary to **mesenteric infarction** and **ruptured aortic aneurysm**. Although the symptoms of a bowel obstruction can be palliated, a multilevel obstruction cannot be surgically reversed and is also likely to lead to a rapid decline.

Further reading

Oxford Textbook of Palliative Medicine, pp. 452–455.

Pelvic pain

Onset of symptom

Pelvic disease causes several different types of pain (visceral, neuropathic, and musculoskeletal).

Acute onset (less than 24 hs) of pelvic pain

- **Abrupt onset, severe, associated with guarding, worse with palpation and coughing** may represent an inflammatory cause of pain, such as peritonitis (primary, secondary) (p.13).
- **In women** the differential diagnosis of acute onset of pain which is difficult to localize, and which may be associated with nausea and vomiting includes a ruptured ovarian cyst or uterus, ovarian torsion, or pelvic inflammatory disease (PID). This diagnosis is often missed and must be considered in people with pelvic pain and fevers. Other diagnoses to consider include fallopian tube disorders (torsion, salpingitis) or haemorrhage into an ovarian cyst.
- **In men or women, better localized pain** leads to consideration of appendicitis, with pain originating in the right lower quadrant, diverticulitis with pain localized to left lower quadrant, pain associated with loose bowel actions and a low-grade fever, pain localized in the midline or either iliac fossa with incarcerated inguinal or abdominal hernias, or generalized discomfort from colitis (p.130), colorectal cancer, polyp or angiodysplasia (p.138) when this presentation is associated with bright rectal blood loss.
- **Abrupt onset and associated with flank pain** raises the possibility of a pyelonephritis (p.288), renal infarct (p.296), ruptured renal papillae (p.292), or renal colic (p.288). The association with flank to loin pain suggests the passage of stones, blood clot, or tissue along the ureter. All these conditions may occur with fever, haematuria, and nausea and vomiting.
- **Distressing and in the midline suprapubic region associated with a palpable mass** may be due to acute urinary retention (p.294). A history of dysuria, difficulty voiding, frequency, haematuria, and fever should be sought. Similar pain occurring more laterally, also associated with a palpable mass, may be due to ovarian cysts, ovarian malignancy, or a pelvic abscess.
- **In men, acute onset of scrotal pain may be due to primary problems in the scrotum,** which may include torsion of the testis (in young men), trauma, and acute epididymitis. An uncommon but very severe problem in debilitated or immunocompromised people is necrotizing fasciitis. Acute onset of scrotal pain may be referred pain from the prostate, prostatic urethra, bladder neck, or seminal vesicles. Very rarely, pain may be referred from a ruptured aortic aneurysm.

- In men, acute onset of penile pain may also be due to localized problems or referred pain. Painful localized problems include phimosis (with urinary retention), ischaemic priapism complicating sickle cell anaemia (p.180), vasculitis (p.90), or polycythaemia. These people must be examined neurologically to exclude spinal cord compression and a full drug history collected. Referred pain may be due to ureteric colic, renal pathology, and spinal cord compromise (p.204).

Subacute onset (1–3 days) of pelvic pain
- Dull, aching, poorly localized at rest, but more defined with movement, may represent bony invasion. Prostate cancer metastasizes commonly to bones but so do cancers originating in breast, lung, kidney, thyroid, and GIT. Other gynaecological malignancies and pelvic cancers may be associated with bony problems due to local expansion and pressure.
- Dull, aching, and associated with a dragging sensation when standing may be due to visceral pelvic pain. Infiltration of the uterus (cancer, adenomas, endometriosis, and stretching of the broad ligament) tends to lead to pain that is felt in the midline of the hypogastrium. Cervix pain (cancer, infections) is usually perceived in the lower back, sacrum, and hypogastrium. Ovarian pain tends to be the most poorly localized due to interconnection of ovarian nerves with other pelvic nerves. It is usually perceived towards the edge of the pelvis.
- Prostate pain tends to be the experienced in the perineum, scrotum, and penis. Prostate discomfort may result from malignant infiltration or prostatitis. People with prostatitis present with perineal pain and may have urinary retention that has been preceded by dysuria and fevers. For people with pelvic cancers there is often a mixed picture of nociceptive, neuropathic, and somatic pain.

Acute-on-chronic onset of pelvic pain
- Chronic pelvic pain with acute exacerbations in women is a clinical challenge.
There are numerous proposed aetiologies for chronic pelvic pain in women, which include gynaecological, urological, GIT, and musculoskeletal causes. An acute exacerbation of pelvic pain is most commonly due to endometriosis, pelvic inflammatory disease, adhesions, or irritable bowel syndrome.
- Chronic pelvic pain in men with acute exacerbations may be due to chronic prostatitis.
These people present with chronic perineal pain associated with low back pain and dysuria. This may be due to chronic infection, inflammation of the prostate, or chronic pelvic pain syndrome in men.

Can you modify anything contributing to the symptom?

People with a **ruptured ovarian cyst** or **ovarian torsion** require pelvic ultrasound to confirm the diagnosis. Most pain from a ruptured cyst will settle with rest and analgesia.

Torsion of an ovary or other adnexal structure requires laparoscopy to ascertain if the structure can be saved or requires surgical resection.

Generalized abdominal pain that localises to the right lower quadrant is typical of **appendicitis**. Escalating pain that suddenly lessens may reflect a ruptured appendix. This is predominantly a clinical diagnosis. If a rupture is suspected, antibiotics and surgical opinion are indicated.

There are multiple causes of **colitis** (p.130).

Ischaemic colitis occurs because of impaired blood supply to the gut wall. The best intervention is surgical resection of the affected area if the person is well enough. People with colitis secondary to **inflammatory bowel disease** require immunosuppressive therapy to be recommended.

Mucositis (p.126) occurring secondary to radiotherapy or chemotherapy may improve with hydration and either IV ranitidine or a PPI such as omeprazole 40 mg IV daily.

Diverticulitis (p.13).

People with **pyelonephritis** (p.288) will appear unwell with fever, rigor, and renal angle tenderness. They often have associated dysuria and haematuria. If the person fails to settle, consider complications including papillary necrosis, renal calculi, or a fungal infection.

Acute disruption to the arterial blood supply to the kidney may result in a **renal infarct** associated with pain, fever and haematuria. The most important steps are rapid diagnosis and initiation of anticoagulation (p.296).

Papillary necrosis and subsequent rupture and sloughing off of debris occurs secondary to a variety of disorders including urinary tract infections (especially fungal) and medications (NSAIDs, COX-II inhibitors, paracetamol). This is most likely to complicate urinary tract infections in diabetics and a person with sickle cell anaemia. It is important to stop medications that may be contributing, and ensure adequate hydration and appropriate antibiotics.

Renal calculi may cause extremely severe pain. These people require hydration and adequate analgesia. Renal function must be checked and blood collected for blood and urine cultures. Appropriate antibiotics should be initiated (p.292).

Acute urinary retention requires urinary catheterization (p.294). Initially, a urethral catheter should be considered. Consult a urologist if catheterisation is difficult. Heavily blood-stained urine should prompt bladder irrigation through a three-way catheter. Send a specimen of sterile urine for culture. Once the catheter has been placed, a full neurological examination is indicated to exclude a spinal cord or cauda equina lesion (p.204).

Acute scrotal pain in young men is a surgical emergency as it may herald torsion of the testis.

Epididymitis is most probably due to infection, and urine cultures must be collected and broad-spectrum antibiotics commenced immediately. Trimethoprim/Sulfamethoxazole 1BD for 2/52 or ciprofloxacin 500mg BD 2/52.

Necrotizing fasciitis is diagnosed by the appearance of the perineum which has early erythema followed by desquamation with underlying dark necrotic areas. These people require fluid resuscitation, antibiotics, and surgical debridement.

Phimosis may lead to urinary retention. Topical steroids may provide temporary relief. A surgical consultation is indicated.

Ischaemic priapism is a medical emergency. If this is due to sickle cell anaemia commence hydration, analgesia, and oxygen. Other causes require an urgent urology consultation.

Pain due to **bony metastases in the pelvis** may be improved by combinations of medications (opioids, NSAIDs, paracetamol, dexamethasone, bisphosphonates). Plain X-rays and a bone scan will help exclude a fracture. A radiotherapy consultation should be sought.

Malignant visceral pain responds well to opioid analgesia. With pelvic metastases, there is often a neuropathic component that will require the addition of appropriate adjuvant analgesia. For all people with cancer pain, consider modifying symptoms with chemotherapy, hormone therapy or radiotherapy.

Prostate pain may be due to acute prostatitis, acute-on-chronic prostatitis, or prostate cancer. The pain of acute prostatitis should settle with antibiotics. More chronic pain should prompt a search for prostate cancer. Chronic prostatitis is a more difficult pain to settle.

What underlying factors cannot be improved?

Pre-existing long-term pelvic pain may not be modifiable in the face of a life-limiting illness.

Symptomatic treatment

Non-pharmacological intervention

In some cases, people with pelvic pain may have a long history of pain that worsens with their deteriorating condition. These people require comprehensive support that addresses their psychological, social, and emotional concerns.

Pharmacological intervention

A measured approach to pain control is required. Prescribe medications according to the severity and type of pain. This needs to be approached in a systematic manner with appropriate use of adjuvant analgesia depending upon the type(s) of pain experienced. It is likely that people with advanced cancer will require opioid analgesia as part of their analgesic regime. It is reasonable to start with low doses of short-acting medications, given around the clock.

Further reading

Oxford Textbook of Medicine, Vol. 3, p. 450.
Oxford Handbook of Palliative Care, pp. 320–323.

Low back pain

Onset of symptom

Chronic low back pain is a major cause of long-term comorbidity in the community. It will often worsen at the end-of-life. The palliative dictum that pain can be relieved is often challenged in people who have had significant long-term back pain.

Acute onset (less than 24 hs) of low back pain and ...
- **A history of osteoporosis or metastatic bone disease**: vertebral crush fractures can occur at any time without obvious trauma. In addition to the pain of the fracture, there may be significant neuropathic pain with entrapment of the nerve at the level of the fracture.
- **A history of prolonged glucocorticoid use**: consider accelerated osteoporosis with crush fracture.
- **Known metastatic malignancy in the CNS**: other sites of disease may become clinically apparent with cauda equina involvement (radicular pain involving the buttocks, decreased saddle sensation, and impaired sphincter control) or the lower cord (epidural, subdural, or intrathecal disease).
- **Fever (neutropenia, vascular access lines or epidural or intrathecal lines)**: consider epidural abscess or meningitis, and urgent initiation of systemic antibiotics and removal of the catheter line (depending upon the life expectancy).
- **Coagulopathy or thrombocytopaenia**: exclude a local epidural bleed.
- **Sudden loss of mobility**: exclude a cord compression from direct tumour effects, vertebral collapse impinging on the cord, or local bleeding compromising the cord.
- **Atrial fibrillation and neurological deficits**: consider anterior spinal artery occlusion.

Subacute onset of low back pain (1–3 days)
- **Bed-bound**: people may often experience increasing low back pain when they are bed-bound (without neurological deficit) at the end-of-life. Repositioning and alternating pressure mattresses may help in this.
- **Pressure areas**: extreme pain is often experienced as skin breaks down over the sacrum. Always inspect for compromised skin.
- **Metastatic bone disease (or a malignancy such as prostate, non-small cell lung, or breast cancer that has a propensity for bone metastases)**: back pain is a common presentation of bone disease. (Back pain also precedes most episodes of cord compression, often by weeks.)

Acute-on-chronic low back pain
- **Cachexia**: people will often have worsening of long-term back pain as muscle bulk is lost (including paravertebral muscles). Although potentially pain free for many years, people with previous significant back pain may find that it worsens significantly if they become deconditioned.
- **Spondyloarthropathy**: at the end-of-life, decreasing mobility may worsen long-term back pain.

Can you modify anything contributing to the symptom?

Sepsis (epidural or intrathecal) requires urgent intervention (especially if it is iatrogenic) (p.205).

Cord compression requires urgent introduction of dexamethasone while the cause of the compression is defined (p.204).

For most people with metastatic bone disease, radiotherapy (or chemotherapy in people with chemosensitive tumours) will be of benefit.

Careful management (including pressure-alternating mattresses) of people, whether in the community or in hospital, will help avoid pressure damage to skin. Programmes to maintain mobility (even in bed) are important so that people can shift their weight in bed.

What underlying factors cannot be improved?

People with **deconditioning and cachexia** at the end-of-life will derive limited benefit from mobility interventions.

Long-term back pain will not suddenly be treatable just because the person has a life-limiting illness. Other clinicians will also have tried opioids and antineuropathic agents over a much longer period of time.

Symptomatic treatment

Non-pharmacological intervention

For people who are mobile, maintaining mobility with tailored physical therapy is very important. For those who can manage it, gentle strengthening exercises will be important both currently and in future care.

Pharmacological intervention

Data support the use of opioids, NSAIDs, and muscle relaxants such as diazepam 2.5 mg–5 mg tds PO (when there is muscle spasm) when there is an acute exacerbation of low back pain.

Further reading

Oxford Textbook of Medicine, Vol 3. pp. 23–29.
Oxford Textbook of Palliative Medicine, pp. 714–715.
Oxford Handbook of Palliative Care, p. 174.

Pain in the setting of previous substance misuse

Onset of symptom

People with a history of substance misuse may have a life-limiting illness. Managing symptoms such as pain or anxiety in this clinical setting requires the same level of careful assessment and therapy as with any other person.

Distinguish between someone who is still using substances illicitly and those who may have had a history at some time earlier in life.

Carefully assess for the cause of pain in the same systematic way as one would for anyone else.

Acute onset (less than 24 hs)

- **Fever and substance misuse**: consider recent IV drug use and the possibility of sepsis including infective endocarditis (p.104), osteomyelitis, or cerebral abscess.
- **Fever, tachycardia, or hypertension**: exclude drug withdrawal as a cause for diaphoretic signs.
- **Confusion and a history of alcohol use**: ensure that this person is not developing Wernicke's encephalopathy. Administer thiamine (100 mg daily IV or orally) to people with a history of excessive alcohol use and cognitive decompensation.

Can you modify anything contributing to the symptom?

Careful evaluation of current users of illicit drugs is crucial to their ongoing care whether in the community or in hospital. Acute withdrawal needs to recognized early and treated actively. Treatment depends on the substance which is being used.

What underlying factors cannot be improved?

In the setting of a life-limiting illness it is unlikely that there can be a significant improvement in drug misuse patterns.

Symptomatic treatment

Non-pharmacological intervention

A supportive environment is important. Although it may seem obvious, a non-judgemental approach to the person and their support network is needed by all the staff who come into contact with them. This can be difficult in an in-patient setting when, for example, substance misuse is continuing.

Pharmacological intervention

Medications for symptom control should be chosen as they would be for any other person. The doses of opioids in people with opioid-responsive pain who have recently used recreational opioids may need to be higher and dose intervals even reduced to obtain the same therapeutic benefit.

Opioid-enhancing agents such as NSAIDs and paracetamol should be used as adjuvants for opioid-responsive pain. For pain with a neuropathic component, tricyclic antidepressants, membrane stabilizers, and steroids have a continuing role.

For people who have used benzodiazepines for non-therapeutic indications, tolerance is likely to be a significant problem and benzodiazepines (except in alcohol withdrawal) are likely to be of very limited benefit.

Further reading

Oxford Textbook of Medicine, Vol. 3, pp. 1340–1341.
Oxford Textbook of Palliative Medicine, p. 857.

Breathlessness

Onset of symptom

Dyspnoea is one of the few symptoms which generally worsens as death approaches in a life-limiting illness.

Acute onset (less than 24 hs) of dyspnoea and ...
- **Fever**: **community-acquired pneumonia** (p.264), **empyema** (p.270), or **mediastinitis** (p.276) (which most often present with a history of thoracic instrumentation) or a history of **valvular heart disease** with septic/inflammatory damage to the valve (p.104).
- **Asymmetrical signs on chest examination**: a **pneumothorax** (p.272) may be spontaneous but more frequently follows recent fine-needle biopsy of a chest mass.
- **Normal examination**: **acute pulmonary thromboembolism** (p.106), or **acute pancreatitis** (p.150) which can cause significant desaturation and can occur with malignant obstruction of the common bile duct.
- **History of chest pain**: **acute myocardial infarction** (including those with no chest symptoms) can present with cardiac decompensation (p.110). Other causes of chest pain and dyspnoea include **dissecting thoracic aneurysm** (p.116) and **pericarditis** (p.102).
- **Acute bleeding**: is likely to be obvious except in people on anticoagulation who have GIT (p.134) or **retroperitoneal bleeding**.
- **Following a fall or fracture**: consider **fat embolus syndrome**. Examine for a rash and increasing confusion (p.232).

Subacute onset of dyspnoea (1–3 days)
- **With fever**: **atypical pneumonias** (p. 264) often have a prodrome of a few days with influenza-like symptoms and low-grade fever. A productive cough and low-grade fever suggest **bronchitis**.
- **Relatively normal examination**: **lymphangitis carcinomatosis** (p.284) can present with a subtle sub-acute onset but, once established, breathlessness often worsens quickly. Exacerbations of underlying COPD will often have an onset spread over several days.
- **Asymmetrical signs on chest examination**: people with progressive **tracheal obstruction** (p.278) notice increasing shortness of breath and often a fixed wheeze as the lumen diameter diminishes. Obstruction of the more distal airways may also occur. Consider this in people presenting with dyspnoea and a wheeze.
- **Fluid overload** which can develop with either **cardiac decompensation** due to silent ischaemia/infarction (p.110) or end-stage renal failure. This may also be iatrogenic, particularly in frail people with life-threatening disease.
- **Clinical stigmata of anaemia**: rapid loss of haemoglobin may occur with either **bleeding** (p.168, p.170) or **haemolysis** (p.174). This is usually associated with fatigue, headache, impaired concentration, and chest tightness.
- **Unexplained hypotension, increasing fatigue, and cough** may be due to **cardiac tamponade** (p.100). This is most likely to occur in people with end-stage renal failure or cancer.

CONTENTS

EDITOR
Ian Shirley

DESIGN & PRODUCTION MANAGEMENT
Abdul Rauf
Val Cutts

ADVERTISING MANAGER
Bill Edwards

PUBLISHER
Andy McDuff

Published in the United Kingdom 2012 by
Diamond Publishing Ltd. Room 101, 140 Wales Farm Road, London W3 6UG

Founded by Sean O'Mahony in 1987.

ISBN 978-0-9560639-4-6

THE ULTIMATE COLLECTOR'S GUIDE

Welcome to the twelfth edition of the *Rare Record Price Guide*, the largest and most comprehensive book of its kind. Like its predecessors, this volume has been compiled by the expert research team of *Record Collector*, the world's leading magazine in the field.

The goal of this book is simple: to list and value every collectable pop and rock record issued in the UK since 1950. As regular readers will already know, the *Rare Record Price Guide* doesn't just include vinyl singles, EPs and LPs, although they are still very heavily featured. It also provides information about every other way in which recorded music has been sold to the public over the last 60 years or more, from the brittle 78rpm shellac singles of the 1950s, to the latest permutations of digital sound on compact discs and even memory sticks. The only format we don't cover is digital downloads!

Musically, the coverage is equally diverse and thorough. Although the majority of items listed in this book could be at least vaguely described as 'rock' or 'pop', every aspect of music-making outside the specialist classical field is featured in these pages. For over 35 years, record collecting itself has expanded enormously, both in terms of the number of people taking part and the types of music that they are interested in.

Rest assured that no matter how obscure your tastes, you'll find the most sought-after items here whether your particular obsession is 50s rockabilly, 60s MOR, 70s jazz-funk, house, 80s post-punk, hip-hop, reggae, NWOBHM, Northern soul, British jazz, folk, progressive or today's indie bands. If it's collectable, and it was released in the UK, then you'll find it in the *Rare Record Price Guide*.

WHO SAYS HOW MUCH IT'S WORTH?

The question we're always asked about the prices listed in this book is how we calculate them. The answer is a mix of our 33 years of experience in the field; our ongoing research into the latest prices at record fairs and shops, and in sales both via mail order and online; and the invaluable help of a dedicated and extremely knowledgeable team of consultants and experts, who themselves regularly buy and sell items in their specialist areas.

As we always say, however, there is no *fixed* price for a second-hand record, no matter how rare it is. There are still bargains to be found out there, while in other situations like a feverishly competitive online auction particularly sought-after items can fetch prices way above their 'book' value. The price of a rare record is purely determined by what people are prepared to pay for it.

That said, our close scrutiny of the collecting market since the start of the 1980s allows us to make the best possible judgement about the records in this book. Prices may vary from one part of the country to another, or depending whether a disc is being sold in a shop, via an advert in *Record Collector*, at a major international fair, or on internet sites like 991.com, GEMM, Music Stack or eBay. But we believe that the guide values we list are the most accurate and realistic you'll find anywhere.

The other important point, which can't be repeated often enough, is that anyone selling records to a professional dealer can't expect to raise more than 50% of the prices listed here, except in very unusual cases. It doesn't matter whether you're selling rock'n'roll or jewellery, the same basic mark-up applies right across the collecting field, to cover the dealer's costs and profit margin. If you're selling directly to another collector, however, face-to-face or, as many collectors are now doing, over the internet, you can obviously hope to obtain the prices we list or even more, though please remember that all the values in this book are for records in absolutely perfect (or 'Mint') condition. To find out what you should be paying or charging, for a record in less than perfect condition, check the Ready Reckoner printed at the back of this book.

ACROSS THE AGES

Although many of the most valuable items listed in the *Rare Record Price Guide* date back to the 1950s, 1960s, 1970s, 1980s and 1990s, don't be fooled into thinking that record collecting is all about the distant past. As you turn the pages, you'll find plenty of releases from the last decade and the latest collectables by major artists like Radiohead, for example, alongside limited edition singles by hot new artists like Marina and The Diamonds and other rarities which were on sale one day and then became fiendishly hard to track a few months later.

Check the details of those brand-new collectables, and you'll get some idea which of tomorrow's releases are likely to be sought-after in the future. But there are some things you can't predict, like the next 60s or 70s 7" that is worth £6 today but will be worth £60 in three months time. Or bands who were hot and collectable one year and saw their prices tumbling the next. Also, don't forget that virtually every record listed in this book, even the ones worth thousands of pounds, were once available for a few pounds, or even pence. For all those thousands of releases which have already become collector's items, however, the *Rare Record Price Guide* tells you what they are, what they look like, and how much they're going to cost.

ACKNOWLEDGEMENTS

CONSULTANTS Billy Albert, Keith Ashford, Alan Barndale John Barnjum, Rob Barrs, Neil Baylis, Mikael Billborn, Marco Bonacchi Greg Brooks, Andy Brooksbank, Nick Brown, Mark Burgess, Ian Clark, Nigel Cook, Augusto Croce, Peter Croxson, Brian Davis, Nick Farmer, Les Hare, Michael De Koningh, Jason Draper, James Ellis, Steve Elphick, John Esplen, Mark Evetts, Leo Feigin, John Fisher, Sean Forbes, Joe Geesin, Roger Gobell, Kevin Goulding, Paul Green, Tim Greenhall, Steve Guntrip, Lenny Helsing, Marco Henning, Rob Henson, Sam Hobden, John Hodgson, Dizzy Holmes, Justin Huntley, Max Hooley, Dudley Jaynes, Gordon Johnson, Michael Johnson, Damien Jones, Mark Jones, Freek Kinkelaar, Jake Kennedy, Ben Legge, Dave Lewis, Graeme McLagen, John Manship, Haaken Eric Mathiesen, Ian McCann, Joel McIver, Lee Medhurst, Richard Morton-Jack, Mike at Elista, Howie Moxon, Pete Nash, Pol O' Maoleoin, Greg Moffitt, Chas Pearson, Derek Penny, Edwin Pouncey, Laurence Prangell, Andy Price, Jay Rathbone, John Reed, Reg @ Beatles 64, Ian Roberts, Dave Sallis, Mike Savage, Barry Smith, Bob Solly, Bob Stoat, Torbjorn Stuhre, Brian Strong, Mitchell Thompson, Jonny Trunk, Audun Tylden, Peter Vickers, J Walton, Jamie Ward, Ben Watkins, Garry Warren, Martin Webb, Alan Whitaker, Eric White, Robin Wills, Alan Woodburn, Conrad Zimmer. Special thanks to all those users of the Online site and readers of Record Collector who also submitted corrections, amendments or new additions. **FINALLY, SPECIAL THANKS** to previous editors, contributors and the vast numbers of fanzines, websites and fan clubs whose hard work and expertise has helped - and continues - to make the Guide what it is today.

HOW TO USE THE GUIDE

PRICING YOUR RECORDS

Although the *Rare Record Price Guide 2014* contains a comprehensive listing of collectable UK releases, it does NOT list all the recordings made by the artists we've included. More detailed discographies of important artists can be found every month in *Record Collector* magazine.

MINIMUM VALUES FOR INCLUSION

ONLY THOSE RELEASES WHICH ARE CURRENTLY SOLD AT THE MINIMUM VALUES LISTED BELOW HAVE BEEN INCLUDED.

Any other releases obviously sell for less than these prices.

7" SINGLES, MAXI-SINGLES, CASSETTE SINGLES, DOUBLE PACKS **£5**
78s, FLEXIDISCS & CD SINGLES **£10**
10" SINGLES **£8**
EPs, 12" SINGLES & CASSETTE EPs **£8**
LPs **£12**
DOUBLE-LPs **£15**
CD ALBUMS **£18**

NOTE: EPs from the 1950s and 1960s usually sold at around twice the retail price of a 7" single. But most so-called EPs released since 1976 actually retailed at the same price as 7" singles. These records have been included in the Guide if they are worth £5 or more.

CURRENT MINT VALUES

The prices listed in this book are for the original issues of records, cassettes and CDs in MINT condition. Bear in mind that most records which turn up from the 1950s, 60s, 70s, 80s & 90s are NOT in Mint condition and their value will be affected accordingly. To find out the value of any item which is in less than Mint condition, consult our Grading System and the Ready Reckoner located at the back of this Guide.

ALPHABETICAL ORDER

The artists in this Guide are listed in alphabetical order, from A to Z. After the alphabetical listings, there is a section of Various Artists compilation releases, divided into several sections covering singles and 50s & 60s EPs, 70s, 80s & 90s EPs, LPs, film soundtrack LPs, original cast recordings from theatrical shows and library music.

The alphabetical order within the Guide has been determined by the first letter of a group name or an artist's surname. The word 'The' has not been taken into account when placing artists in alphabetical order; for instance, The Beatles' are listed under 'B', rather than 'T'.

The order follows the usual alphabetical principle of 'reading through' an artist's name or title, so that (for example) 'Peter Gabriel' is listed before 'Gabriel's Angels', and 'Generation X' is listed before 'Gen X'. Names and titles which include numbers appear as if the number was spelt out in full; e.g. the band '23 Skidoo' are listed as if their name was 'Twenty Three Skidoo'.

CHRONOLOGICAL ORDER

Within each artist entry, records are listed in chronological order of release. Singles (including 7", 10", 12", CD, cassette, and double packs) are listed first; then EPs; and finally LPs (including cassette and CD albums).

In the case of long entries, different formats of releases have also been grouped together under separate headers to make them easier to find.

PACKAGING AND INSERTS

All prices refer to records with all their original packaging and inserts (where applicable) intact. Wherever possible, we have provided details of inserts and special items of packaging for each entry – pointing out gatefold sleeves, lyric sheets and other bonus items like posters, for example.

Any record with some or all of these additional items missing will obviously be worth less than the values listed here. The level of depreciation depends on the missing items: in some cases, the value of an album can be dramatically reduced without its collectable insert (as in the case of the Who's *The Who Sell Out* LP, for example), while in others, it is the record itself that is desirable, and the insert is only of secondary importance (as with the Picadilly Line LP, *The Huge World Of Emily Small*).

DOUBLE PRICES: PICTURE SLEEVES

Since 1978, all U.K. 7", 10" and 12" singles have usually been issued in picture sleeves. Before 1978, however, picture covers were the exception rather than the rule.

All those singles which originally appeared in a picture sleeve are listed with the abbreviation '(p/s)'. Where the picture sleeve was only available with the first batch of singles, there are two prices listed: the first refers to the record with its picture sleeve, the second without. If only one price is listed, then the single has to have its picture sleeve intact and in Mint condition to qualify for this value.

Most singles from the 1950s, 1960s and early 1970s were issued in 'company' sleeves, carrying the name and logo of the label which issued the record. Unless a picture sleeve is indicated, the prices listed in this guide are for singles with their company sleeves intact and, like the records themselves, in Mint condition. Many collectors are not too concerned about company sleeves - although in isolated cases (like the cult 60s label Planet), the company sleeves can be harder to find than the records themselves.

Company sleeves don't usually have much effect on a record's value. For example, an original Creation single from 1966, valued at £45, may only be worth £35 without its Planet company sleeve. At the other extreme, no doo-wop collector is going to be bothered if a copy of a rarity like The Penguins' Earth Angel, valued at £1750, comes in a plain sleeve, or indeed, no sleeve at all - what matters here is that the record is in Mint condition.

DOUBLE PRICES: FREEBIES & INSERTS

Two prices have been listed for those items which were available in more than one form. 'Freebie' singles given away with newspapers and magazines have two values: the first for the record with the publication, the second for the disc itself. Records which were issued only briefly with an insert, like a poster or lyric sheet, are often priced both with and without the extra packaging.

DOUBLE PRICES: CHANGES IN DESIGN

Two or more prices have been given for records which were released more than once with the same catalogue number, but in slightly different form - with a change of label colour or sleeve design (for instance, the substitution of triangular centres by round centres on late 1950s singles), or the manufacture of more recent singles in a variety of different coloured vinyls.

These variations of packaging and presentation can make an enormous difference to the value of a record, which is why we have documented them here. They help collectors identify the first pressing or edition of each release, which is almost always more sought-after than later issues of the same record. One notable example is the first edition of the Beatles' *Please Please Me* LP, which featured the black-and-gold Parlophone label for a few weeks, before the introduction of the more modern-looking yellow-and-black label. Black-and-gold copies of the stereo version of this LP are worth up to £5000, whilst standard yellow and black label later pressings are worth between £2800 and £350.

Occasionally, second pressings can be worth more than the originals, as is the case with early Shadows and Cliff Richard singles. Green label copies of these 45s sold in their millions, while later re-pressings on black labels are much scarcer. So always check which pressing of any record you are buying before parting with your money.

MONO AND STEREO

In the case of EPs and LPs from the 1950s and 1960s, mono and stereo releases often have different values – and different catalogue numbers. Both prices are listed, together with the separate catalogue numbers for the two versions of each release (mono first, then stereo). Where the mono and stereo editions are worth the same amount, only one price has been listed.

The last few years have seen a polarisation in the prices between mono and stereo pressings – increasingly so for those late mono releases from 1968 to 1970, when the single-channelled format was being phased out in favour of the twin-tracked stereo. Similarly, early stereo copies have proved to be sound investments.

UK RELEASES AND EXPORT ISSUES

Only UK releases are included in the *Rare Record Price Guide*, not overseas issues. The exceptions to this rule are a handful of folk releases and U2 singles, all from the Irish Republic, which were heavily imported into Britain, but not officially issued here. The other exceptions are 'Export Releases'. These were manufactured in the UK in the 1950s and 1960s by companies like EMI and Decca for distribution to countries which didn't have their own pressing plants. Because they were pressed in very small quantities, and then distributed to the furthest corners of the globe, export records by artists like the Beatles and the Rolling Stones are often worth many times the values of similar items pressed for the UK.

UK RELEASES PRESSED OVERSEAS

Although the great majority of the records we've listed were manufactured in the UK, not all UK releases were made in this country – or vice versa. For example, a large proportion of the Rolling Stones' US singles on the London label in the 1960s were actually manufactured in Britain. More recently, many British releases by major labels – notably Warners –

have been made in Europe, and sent in identical form to Britain and many other countries. In these cases, the record sleeves often carry many different catalogue numbers, to cater for every country where the records are being distributed.

The problem of identifying the country where a particular record has been issued has grown more difficult with the advent of CDs. In these cases, it is the packaging that helps you identify the origin of a particular CD, rather than the disc itself.

78 rpm RELEASES

The common misconception about 78s is that they are more valuable than 7" singles. In fact, the opposite is true in most cases, as far more 78s were sold in the 1950s than 45 rpm 7" singles.

The last batches of 78s issued from 1958 to 1960 are the main exception to this rule (see Eddie Cochran's entry, for example). As these were often only available in small quantities (as the public switched to 45s), or even by special order, they can prove to be much harder to find than their 45 rpm equivalents.

COMMERCIAL RELEASES, NOT PROMOS

In general, this Guide only includes records which were manufactured for commercial release, or for distribution in some way to the public – as a freebie with a magazine, for example.

Promotional records, demos, acetates and test pressings have not usually been included, apart from exceptional cases where these items actually reached the public, or where (as with artists like the pre-Iron Maiden act, Urchin) one promo single has become so famous among collectors that it would have been misleading for it not to be mentioned. The major exceptions to this rule are artists like the Beatles, and modern artists like The Pet Shop Boys, Kylie Minogue, Depeche Mode and Madonna whose promos – often with extended hard to find remixes – are sometimes more valuable than their commercial releases and highly sought after by their fans. Also, although we have included some CD-R promo releases in this Guide the value of these items usually fluctuate wildly upwards before release and then fall alarmingly once the official album or single is in the shops. Some collectors do want them – especially completists – but we should state that the sale of watermarked and numbered CD-R's is illegal.

Full details of the values of non-commercial rarities like promos, demos, acetates and test pressings can be found in the articles and discographies in *Record Collector* every month.

THE HISTORY OF THE
RARE RECORD PRICE GUIDE

RECORD COLLECTOR MAGAZINE

Record Collector was first published in 1979, and the magazine quickly established itself as the bible of pop and rock history. When the magazine was born, record collecting was a small, rather disorganised business, which wasn't making much effort to encourage new people to get involved.

From the start, *Record Collector* set out to provide the information that collectors needed, whether they'd been buying and selling records for years, or were just starting to build up a collection. There were two vital things they wanted to know: what records had been released by their favourite artists, and how much were they worth?

Every issue of *Record Collector* has provided complete discographies (lists of record releases, complete with full catalogue numbers, release dates and current Mint values) for an amazing variety of performers, from pre-rock stars like Frank Sinatra to the latest chart-bound arrivals and cult indie bands, via every imaginable style and genre along the way. Our in-depth features have provided the essential information to help readers get the most out of their music – by explaining the history of the artists and the records.

THE CHANGING FACE OF THE
RARE RECORD PRICE GUIDE

In 1987, we published our first price guide - a slim volume which was designed as a quick and easy reference source to records by around 2,000 important artists.

That was only the beginning, though. We soon began work on the first edition of the book you're holding. Published in late 1992, the first *Rare Record Price Guide* filled 960 pages and listed 60,000 rare and collectable records.

The response to that book was tremendous, but we quickly realised that the collecting market was changing so fast that we couldn't rest on our laurels. Every year, thousands of new records reach the shops, in a bewildering variety of formats - everything from 7" singles and cassettes to expensive multi-CD box sets.

A small but sizeable proportion of these new releases became instant collector's items. Over the last 20 years, it's been common for record companies to issue special limited editions – anything from a few hundred to a few thousand copies – which sell out in a few days. The most sought-after of these records can triple or quadruple their value within a few months.

At the same time, interest in vinyl from the past continues to grow. As collectors track down all the records they want in a particular genre, they start to broaden their horizons. As a result, obscure items from the 50s, 60s, 70s and 80s become much-wanted treasures on the collectors' market – and their prices rise to reflect the new demand.

That's why we published a second edition, a year later, which grew to 1152 pages, with 70,000 records listed. And this was expanded again for the 1995 edition (over 75,000 entries and 1252 pages) and 1997/98 edition (85,000 entries and 1440 pages), to take in all the latest collectable releases.

The Millennium Edition ran to 1504 pages; another two years on, the *Rare Record Price Guide 2002* was bigger than ever, the 2004 edition was 1536 pages the RRPG 2006 1504 pages, RRPG 2008 and 2010 1408 pages and RRPG 2012 1440 pages. Now you're holding the latest edition covering more than 60 years of rare and collectable records.

THE BIRTH OF COLLECTING

When the collecting scene was in its infancy in the 1970s, the market was focused on particular artists or genres. All the early attention was concentrated on 1950s rock'n'roll, and 1960s beat music. In addition, major artists like the Beatles, the Rolling Stones, Elvis Presley and David Bowie began to attract specialist collectors. But the whole collecting scene blossomed during the 1980s and it's now true to say that there aren't any musical styles which *aren't* collectable. Folk, jazz, techno, hip-hop, blues, heavy metal, punk, psychedelia, progressive rock, film soundtracks, soul, funk, reggae, disco, mainstream rock and pop, even easy listening - each genre boasts its share of in-demand rarities.

LIMITED EDITIONS

In the late 1970s, the arrival of punk spawned scores of new, independent record labels, which had fresh views about the way to market their releases. It became common for singles to appear in picture sleeves, as they had done overseas since the 1960s.

Records also began to appear on coloured vinyl or as picture discs, in an attempt to attract more buyers. Never slow to cash in on a marketing trend, the major record companies soon joined in. By the early 1980s, they were issuing a bewildering variety of editions of the same record in slightly different formats.

This sudden change in marketing techniques helped to trigger an entirely new development on the collecting scene. For the first time, records were becoming instant collector's items. A limited-edition single could be released one week, and sell for twice its retail price a fortnight later.

That opened the floodgates. No longer were 1950s and 1960s records the only things you'd find in the collector's shops. Now, it was open season, for anything and everything from Tubby Hayes to U2.

COMPACT DISCS

The arrival of CDs in the mid-1980s was greeted with doom and gloom in some quarters. But extensive remastering and reissue programs on CD have helped to increase the market for old vinyl releases.

If you grew up in the 1960s, you probably remember that it was difficult to find records that had been hits only a few years earlier. Now, you can go into most record stores and buy compilations and original albums with bonus tracks from every era of music history. For thousands of collectors, however, owning the music on CD or via download isn't enough – and they track down the original releases of music made and released before they were born.

The CD is now well established as a collectable format – particularly for promotional items, limited edition singles, and some original 80s albums which have yet to be remastered. Although more music is sold through digital downloading than any other format the CD still remains the dominant physical format on which music is released and bought worldwide.

STATE OF THE MARKET

We have always stated that the value of a rare record is determined purely by what someone is prepared to pay for it. Saying that, these days this should be amended to state that the value of a rare record is determined purely by what someone is prepared to pay for it on any particular day. Although there are still record shops out there and dealers trading at fairs ranging from the regular Spitalfields market in London to the massive Utrecht fair the main outlet for rare and collectable records is the internet. Although there are a number of sites catering for collectors from Discogs.com to online dealers like 991.com the main litmus remains eBay. Although there are gripes and groans about charges most record collectors and dealers know that if you have a rare and collectable record in excellent condition or above and if you don't have a known customer lined up, then the place to achieve the best price is eBay. Thus, in the weeks after the Queen celebrated her Diamond Jubilee a copy of the rare Sex Pistols LTS acetate from 1977 *God Save The Queen/No Feelings* sold for a whopping £12,600 and earlier in 2012 what was described as an excellent copy of the 1963 Beatles demo 7" *Love Me Do/PS I Love You* sold for £12,100. Of course, as eBay is an online auction site the final electronic hammer price can vary greatly on a rare 7", EP or LP in the same condition on any given day. Thus in 2012 a Mint copy of *London Calling* from 1979 by The Clash sold for £156. Other copies of this seminal punk double LP have sold for £128, £111 as well as £31 and £41. Now, one thing that forces up the price of rare and collectable records on eBay is not only the depths of the pockets of international bidders from Manchester to Manchuria but other factors come into play including the care, attention and detail that sellers put into their descriptions, the number and clarity of their photographs, sound clips as well as the sellers online reputation. But variations in price are fascinating although they do make our job in setting guide prices harder especially when dealers and collectors check prices on Popsike to see the highest price that a rare record has sold for and subconsciously use that as a comparison for the record that they want to sell themselves. Returning to the Clash LP, acting on evidence from online sources like Popsike alone would suggest that a guide price in the region of £60-£70 would seem reasonable but many contributors to the guide sell this LP in shops and at fairs in the U.K. briskly for prices between £20 and £40 and so the guide price in this new edition is £40. Of course, on any given day...

With regards to market conditions the internet has had a big impact upon the amount of stock that dealers are able to buy. Many collectors have become dealers themselves; selling records online and therefore dealers are finding it tougher to find collections. The online market has also led to the further erosion of record shops across the country and even Intoxica in Portobello road is closing its doors to go online. But shops that are managing to keep their doors open from Sounds Original in Ealing to Rubber Soul in Stoke On Trent and Across The Tracks in Brighton are to be commended and supported as they offer the personal touch that is so important in record collecting. Despite certain areas and records seemingly only being in the reach of wealthy collectors the bread and butter of record collecting remains 7" singles, EPs, 12" singles and LPs that can be picked up for anywhere between £4 and £40 ranging from Jo Stafford at one end of the spectrum to Madness at the other. As with books, there is no better place to buy records than a shop and some like Ben's in Guildford do not sell records online which means that collectors who come down to his shop are going to be able to look at new stock as it is priced and put into the racks rather than wonder what is in the back and being listed on eBay. Other shops like Flashback in London augment physical selling with their own online catalogue which gives them and collectors the best of both worlds. Ironically, shops like HMV are retreating from the high streets in the face of competition from internet sellers like Amazon who can beat them on the price of a new CD and the fact that many people now buy music through downloads. Saying that, shops like Rough Trade East in London are flourishing due to diversification that not only sees them selling vinyl and CDs but also having live bands, a coffee shop and a vibrant web presence and mail order arm. As all readers will know the annual Record Store Day acts as a shot in the arm to independent retailers although in 2012 there seemed to be too many releases which meant that whilst some records by artists like Morrissey became instant (online) collectables others remained in store for weeks and months after.

When it comes to pricing entries in the 2014 Guide we have tried to remain impartial. That means that if tough decisions have to be taken to reduce prices then we have done so. Thus, areas like some 78rpm singles and some artists from the 50s and early 60s have seen some amendments which has seen entries being removed from the Guide (although they remain in our online version) or downgraded in price. This is no reflection on the quality of the music but the current marketplace where a generation that used to seek out every London release or the entire output of Dean Martin and Fats Domino are dwindling in numbers. It must be stressed that there remains a market for rare records from this period but some prices for common records from artists from Elvis Presley to Brenda Lee have remained static or have fallen. We have been told by some that a reduction in prices reduces market confidence. The issue is, however, that if records are not selling at the prices in this guide then this means that demand is not there or that the records are selling at lower prices or not at all. The issue is that if you are a 50s or early 60s collector these are good hunting times as records by artists from Cliff Richard to Slim Whitman in excellent or even Mint condition can be had at reasonable prices at fairs or online. This also applies to some 80s pop, dance and hip-hop 12" singles. At the other end of the scale there have been some massive increases in prices of red hot collectable. It seems that some records from the late 60s and early 70s LPs have moved into the realms of 'scarities' rather than rarities with prices for rare albums on labels like Vertigo, Harvest, Neon, Deram-Nova, Island, Mushroom, Nepentha, Middle Earth, Deram, Stable and others gaining even more traction than before and mint albums for rare psychedelic or progressive artists from The Open Mind to Cressida are going through the roof. Private pressings, Acid folk and rare jazz pressings also remain scarce and in demand. The same applies to mint records by blue chip artists like the Beatles, The Rolling Stones, Jimi Hendrix, Pink Floyd, Deep Purple, Black Sabbath and many others. The market for freak beat, psych, soul, Northern soul and mod 7"singles remain strong and vibrant. As always the market for reggae and ska is robust in some areas especially for in demand records like Lee Perry's *Jungle Lion* 7" from 1973 and new territory is being broken every week with records from the 70s, 80s and 90s from Mad Professor to Wayne Smith securing decent prices. The same applies to punk and new wave records with Mario Panciera's seminal *45 Revolutions* book that documented punk, mod, powerpop, NWOBHM and indie singles released in the UK and Ireland between 1976 and 1979 acting as an invaluable tool and has even seen some collectors look to collect ever record that is in the book! On the other hand vital sites like 45.cat and Discogs are fantastic resources for collectors offering invaluable information on UK and international releases.

Another area where interest and prices seem to be growing is 80s and 90s independent music as well as areas like obscure cold wave 7" singles. Even without their reformation, the records of the Stone Roses would have continued to sell and rise in value and the Brit-pop generation has developed a keen archaeological instinct for mint vinyl from Blur to Oasis and beyond. Two areas that really are shooting up in price are albums from the 90s and 00s. As we have stated before the rise of the CD saw a fall and at times near extinction of vinyl pressings. This not only affected artists like Pulp, Mazzy Star, Porcupine Tree and Primal Scream but also blue chip artists like David Bowie, Bob Dylan, Tom Waits and others whose albums may have only been pressed in limited numbers of 1000 to 2000 copies. We have investigated this area in greater detail and include 90s and 00s LPs as diverse as OMD and The Cult.

As for the core of the RRPG, as well as adding and subtracting records and reviewing and revising prices we have also tried to add more detail. The David Bowie section has been overhauled to incorporate demos, variations as well as Irish pressings. We have also taken a good look at the Beatles which not only goes into forensic detail over albums like *Please Please Me* but also every known variations on singles from label typography to known solid centre pressings. Aware that this entry is probably the most poured over section of the Guide if you see any errors or have any additional information please let us know! There has also been extensive work in many areas of the Guide with more detail on what to look out for to determine a first pressing as well as extensive additions from soul to metal being upgraded and augmented. We have also reflected interest in independent labels from Factory to Postcard with attendant information and price uplifts. What is interesting is to see artists like The Fall and Nick Cave joining the likes of The Cure and Joy Division as sought after collectables.

Finally, you will have noticed that we have increased the entry price for CD singles and flexi discs. From what we can see, prices in these formats have fallen and so we have raised the entry level to £10 so that only collectables in these formats are in this Guide. As always, we have worked hard to do our best to offer you a comprehensive overview of Guide prices for records released in the U.K. since the 50s. And don't forget, we are also online which features not only the records in the guide but those that have fallen beneath the entry level for this printed version.

As always, with the publication of this guide we will start work working hard to update the database in preparation for the next edition!

USING THE GUIDE
A BRIEF SUMMARY

ALL PRICES REFER TO RECORDS
AND PACKAGING IN MINT CONDITION
(See pages 1439-40 for Grading System and Ready Reckoner)

ARTISTS AND GROUPS are listed in alphabetical order.
Numerical names (e.g. 2.3) are listed as if the numbers are spelt in full
(i.e. Two.Three).

ALL RECORDS LISTED ARE
U.K. COMMERCIAL RELEASES
with the following exceptions:

> (1) Records pressed in the U.K. for export overseas.
>
> (2) Important demo or promo releases.
>
> (3) Records or flexidiscs included as freebies with magazines,
> books and other records.

**In general, promo and demo editions are not included, except when
these records contain unique material and/or packaging, or are
by major collectable artists.**

EACH ENTRY includes:

> SINGLES (7" 45s & cassettes) valued at £5 or more
>
> 78 rpm, CD singles and flexidiscs singles valued at £10 or more
>
> 10" singles valued at £8 or more
>
> EPs, 12" singles valued at £8 or more
>
> LPs valued at £12 or more
>
> DOUBLE-LPs valued at £15 or more
>
> CD ALBUMS valued at £18 or more
>
> Records worth less than these prices have not been included.

WITHIN EACH ENTRY, records are listed in chronological order of
release, within each of the following categories (where applicable):
78s, SINGLES, EPs, LPs, CDs, PROMOS. The exceptions are major artists like
the Beatles, the Rolling Stones and Elvis Presley, where the entry is further
divided into originals, reissues and label variations.

Where TWO PRICES are listed for a single item, they refer to

> (a) the record with and without a special insert or piece of packaging
>
> (b) mono and stereo editions of EPs and LPs
>
> (c) versions of the same record with different artwork, vinyl colour, etc.

ABBREVIATIONS
USED IN THIS GUIDE

act.................actually	mag..............magazine
alt...............alternative	no.................number
b&w........black and white	no'd..............numbered
cass...............cassette	p/s...........picture sleeve
cat. no.....catalogue number	pic disc........picture disc
CD............compact disc	pt(s)...............part(s)
co................company	sl..................sleeve
d/pack.........double pack	st.................stereo
dble...............double	stkr...............sticker
diff..............different	t/p............test pressing
edn................edition	vers..............version
EP.....extended-play record	vol...............volume
ext...............extended	w/..................with
flexi.............flexidisc	w/l...........white label
g/f(old).....gatefold sleeve	2-CD or 2xCD....double CD
inst..........instrumental	2-LP or 2xLP.....double LP
intl...........international	2 x 45.....two 45rpm singles
LP.....long-playing record	3-LP.............triple LP
m/s...........mono/stereo	78............78rpm single

IMPORTANT RECORD COMPANY ABBREVIATIONS

Amalgam.................................Amalgamated
B. Banquet............................Beggars Banquet
B'full/Brains.........................Bucketfull Of Brains
Col.......................................Columbia
Elek.......................................Elektra
Font..Fontana
L.T.T. Slaughter.....................Lambs To The Slaughter
M. For Nations.......................Music For Nations
MFP....................................Music For Pleasure
M. Minor..............................Major Minor
Parl......................................Parlophone
PSI...........................Phil Spector International
Pye Intl............................Pye International
R. Digest...........................Readers Digest
Regal Zono............................Regal Zonophone
R. Stones...............................Rolling Stones
S'side.....................................Stateside
St. Tones...............................Street Tones
Sweet Folk & C.................Sweet Folk And Country
T. Motown............................Tamla Motown
UA..................................United Artists
W. Bros............................Warner Brothers
WRC...........................World Record Club

IMPORTANT TERMS
USED IN THIS GUIDE

acetate	one-off disc cut by hand in a mastering studio, used for demonstration purposes
adaptor	plastic outer disc clipped onto 3" CDs to make them compatible with 5" CD players
art sleeve	pictorial cover using graphics rather than photographs or drawings
artwork	original design for sleeves or labels
audiophile pressing	high quality pressing for hi-fi enthusiasts
blister pack	shaped outer PVC packaging, usually for 3" CDs
bonus disc	disc given away free with another disc
bootleg	illegal pressing of material
box set	records or CDs in presentation case
budget release	pressing which retailed below full-price
catalogue number	manufacturer's reference number on record labels and sleeves
CD-R	one-off CD, digital equivalent of acetate
CD-ROM	audio/visual computer-compatible CD
CD Video	5" CD containing several audio tracks and (usually) one video track; now obsolete
company sleeve	standard non-picture sleeve for singles, printed with name or logo of label
counterfeit	illegal reproduction of official release (a.k.a. pirates)
DAT	digital audio tape
deleted	no longer commercially available
demo	record issued for demonstration purposes; not commercially available
die-cut sleeve	sleeve with circular hole cut into the centre
digipak	gatefold CD sleeve with plastic inner tray
DJ-only	record issued for radio airplay only
double groove	record with two grooves pressed concentrically on same side
double pack	two singles issued together as one package
DVDAC	digital versatile disc Audio
DVD	digital versatile disc
8-track cartridge	1970s tape format, popular for in-car entertainment; now obsolete
EP	extended play disc, with four or more tracks, usually in a picture sleeve
EPK	electronic press kit; i.e. short promo-only documentary available on video
envelope p/s	large mailing-type cover with envelope-style foldover flap
etched disc	one-sided vinyl record with laser-etched graphics (e.g. group's signatures) on other side
export issue	record or CD pressed in the UK for sale exclusively overseas
factory custom pressing	unofficial record pressed after hours (usually on coloured vinyl) at official pressing plant
flexidisc	thin, flexible record, usually issued free with magazine, etc.
flipback sleeve	LP or EP cover glued together with card flaps from the front folded over onto the back
foldaround/foldout/ foldover sleeve	sleeve which opens out as a poster, etc.
freebie	record given away free of charge
gatefold sleeve	double-size sleeve opening out like a book
import	record or CD pressed abroad but sold in the UK
inlay	printed paper booklet with CD packaging
inner sleeve	protective sleeve inside main cover
insert	loose item included as part of a record's packaging, e.g. postcard, poster, lyric sheet, etc.
interview album	spoken word record, often used as promo

jewel case	standard clear plastic case for cassettes and CDs
jukebox centre	plastic centre inserted into record with large centre hole
jukebox issue	record issued exclusively to jukebox franchise holders
laminated sleeve	cover with high-gloss plastic coating
large centre hole	1.5 inch (3.8 cm) hole in singles
long box	tall, rectangular outer card packaging for CDs
LP	long playing vinyl record; standard album format superseded by CDs
matrix number	master tape number, scratched into the 'land' or run-off groove area; sometimes also found on the record label
maxi-single	early 70s term for an EP, featuring more than two tracks, often in a picture sleeve
megamix	medley of different tracks, often linked by dance beats
mid-price release	record which retails at a discount
mispressing	record or CD pressed with incorrect material
mono	one-channelled playback system
numbered (no'd)	individually numbered, limited edition release
obi	sealed paper strip wrapped around sleeve of disc; originated in Japan where obis were printed with Japanese translations of foreign titles
one-sided	vinyl record which plays on one side only
picture disc	novelty record made by sealing a picture within clear vinyl
picture sleeve	pictorial paper or card sleeve, used specifically for one particular record
plain sleeve	single sleeve without special printing or artwork
premium	record available via a special offer with another product e.g. food or drink
press kit	information pack with photos and biography, used by record companies to promote new releases
private pressing	record issued and distributed by private individuals rather than a company
promo	promotional record or item sent out to the media for publicity purposes
push-out centre	centre of a single connected to the rest of the disc at 3 or 4 points, so it can be pushed out for use on jukeboxes, etc.
quadrophonic	1970s four-channelled playback system, now obsolete
reel-to-reel tape	1960s tape format, superseded by cassette
reissue	re-release of a deleted disc
remix	different version of existing track created by rearranging its component parts
removeable/ age replaceable centre	centre which can be removed from a record without damage and later replaced (not to be confused with jukebox or 'spider' centres)
re-pressing	a second run of a record or CD which hasn't been deleted
run-off groove	groove between end of playing surface and record label
sampler	compilation showcasing an artist or label
sealed/shrinkwrapped	machine-wrapped in cellophane
shaped disc	any non-circular record
shellac	brittle material used for 78s
slipcase	small card cover used for some CDs and cassette singles
solid centre	centre of record which cannot be removed, as on LPs
stickered sleeve	sleeve with sticker as an integral part of its packaging
stereo	two-channelled playback system
test pressing	manufacturer's sample record, pressed for quality control
tri-centre	push-out triangular centre on some 1950s singles/EPs
tri-fold	triple fold-out sleeve
uncut picture disc	shaped disc not yet trimmed to proper shape
unissued/unreleased	disc not made commercially available; may or may not have been pressed
vinyl	material from which records are made
warp	buckle in vinyl caused by heat
white label	usually blank, perhaps printed or handwritten labels, often for promo purposes; term also used for demo, promo or test pressing
withdrawn	record deliberately removed from sale by its manufacturer

AARDVARK
70	Deram Nova SDN 17	AARDVARK (LP, mono)	300
70	Deram Nova DN 17	AARDVARK (LP, stereo)	250

(see also Home)

A-AUSTR
70	Holy Ground HG 113	A-AUSTR - MUSICS FROM HOLY GROUND (LP, with booklet, 99 only)	400
89	Magic Mixture MM 1	A-AUSTR (LP, reissue, 450 only)	40
95	Holy Ground 010101LP	A-AUSTR (LP, second reissue, foldover gatefold sleeve)	20

(see also Bill Nelson)

ABACUS
74	York YR 207	Indian Dancer/Be That Way	20
72	Polydor 2371 215	ABACUS (LP)	50

ABBA
73	Epic EPC 1793	Ring Ring/Rock'N'Roll Band (yellow label)	30
74	Epic EPC 2848	So Long/I've Been Waiting For You (yellow label)	10
79	Epic EPC 7499	Voulez Vous/Angel Eyes (red or yellow vinyl, p/s)	400
80	Epic EPC 12-8835	The Winner Takes It All/Elaine (12", gatefold pop-up p/s)	10
81	Epic EPCA 11-1740	One Of Us/Should I Laugh Or Cry (picture disc)	6
82	Epic EPCA 11-2971	Under Attack/You Owe Me One (picture disc)	20
82	Epic EPCA 2618	GREATEST ORIGINAL HITS (EP)	8
83	Epic A 3894	Thank You For The Music/Our Last Summer (poster p/s)	5
83	Epic WA 3894	Thank You For The Music/Our Last Summer (shaped picture disc)	25
84	Epic ABBA 26	ANNIVERSARY BOXED SET (26 x blue vinyl 7", numbered, 2,000 only)	300
84	Epic ABBA 26	ANNIVERSARY BOXED SET (26 x black vinyl 7")	100
93	Polydor 859 085-2	MORE ABBA GOLD (4-track CD, promo only)	25
94	Polydor 853 891-2	DREAM WORLD (CD, 4-track sampler, promo only)	40
99	Polydor 563 286-2	ABBA Singles Collection 1974-1982 (29 CD singles in card sleeves & 1-track CD picture disc, with booklet, in silver tin, 20,000 only)	50
04	Polydor 982054-1	Waterloo/Watch Out (picture disc, 2,000 only, numbered)	15
74	Epic EPC 80179	WATERLOO (LP, yellow label)	12
75	Epic EPC 80835	ABBA (LP, yellow label)	12
76	Epic EPC 69218	GREATEST HITS (LP, gatefold sleeve, yellow label, some with "Fernando" sticker)	12
78	Epic EPC 86002	THE ALBUM (LP, gatefold with sticker)	12
79	Epic EPC 11-86086	VOULEZ VOUS (LP, picture disc)	60
80	Epic ABBOX 1	SUPER TROUPER (LP, box set with book & poster)	15
83	Epic ABBOX 11-2/ABBA-11-10	THE SINGLES - THE FIRST TEN YEARS (2-LP, picture discs, with poster, ticket & booklet in box)	40
83	Epic CDEPC 10022	SUPER TROUPER (CD, original issue)	20
83	Epic CDEPC 10032	THE VISITORS (CD, original issue)	18
84	St. Michael 1361/5704	THE HIT COLLECTION (cassette, with 64-page book Their Story, available via Marks & Spencer)	25
92	Polydor 517007	GOLD (2-LP)	20
99	Simply Vinyl SVLP103	ABBA (LP, 180 gram pressing)	15
05	Polar POLS 252	COMPLETE STUDIO RECORDINGS (12-CD box set, 2 booklets)	100

(see also Hep Stars, Hootenanny Singers, Agnetha Faltskog, Frida, Northern Lights)

ABBASANI
91	Roots Rock RR 001	Revelation Time/Version	40
91	Roots Rock RR 009	REVELATION TIME (LP)	30

BILLY ABBOTT & JEWELS
63	Cameo Parkway P 874	Groovy Baby/Come On And Dance With Me	35

ABERDEEN
94	Sarah SARAH 93	Bryon/Toy Tambourine (p/s, insert)	18
95	Sarah SARAH 97	Fireworks/When It Doesn't Matter/Sunny Summer (p/s, insert)	18

A.B.H.
78	Music Bank BECK 694	Geoffrey/Colt 45 Rock (no p/s)	20

SHIRLEY ABICAIR
56	Parlophone MSP 6224	Willie Can/Happy Trails	5
64	Piccadilly 7N 35364	I Will Be There/Am I Losing You	5

ABNORMAL/BARBED WIRE
87	Oi Records OIR 010	SKINS 'N' PUNKS VOL. 4 (LP)	12

ABRACADABRA
72	RCA 2252	Maggie McGhee/Turn On To Me	6

MICK ABRAHAMS (BAND)
71	Chrysalis ILPS 9147	(A MUSICAL EVENING WITH) THE MICK ABRAHAMS BAND (LP, g/fold sleeve)	20
72	Chrysalis CHR 1005	AT LAST (LP, first pressing, circular foldout sleeve, Island logo and address in white on green label)	60
75	SRT SRTM 73313	HAVE FUN LEARNING THE GUITAR WITH MICK ABRAHAMS (LP, solo, with typed insert)	15

(see also Blodwyn Pig, Jethro Tull, Mighty Flyers)

ABRASIVE WHEELS
81	Abrasive ABW 1	Army Song/Juvenile/So Low (p/s)	10
82	Riot City RIOT 9	Army Song/Juvenile/So Slow (p/s, reissue, red vinyl)	6
82	Riot City RIOT 16	Burn The Schools/Urban Rebels/Burn 'Em Down (p/s)	6
82	Riot City CITY 001	WHEN THE PUNKS GO MARCHING IN (LP)	20
84	Clay CLAY 9	BLACK LEATHER GIRL (LP)	18

ABS
87	Shed 001	GREASE YOUR RALPH (EP, fold-out p/s)	12

| 89 | Link MLP 100 | MENTAL ENENA (LP) | 12 |
| 90 | Blasting Youth | NAIL IT DOWN (LP, with insert) | 12 |

MIKE ABSALOM
60s	Sportsdisc ILP 1081	THE MIGHTY ABSALOM SINGS BATHROOM BLUES (LP)	20
69	Saydisc SDL 162	SAVE THE LAST GHERKIN FOR ME (LP)	70
71	Vertigo 6360 053	MIKE ABSALOM (LP, swirl label, poster sleeve)	200
72	Philips 6308 131	HECTOR AND OTHER PECCADILLOS (LP)	40

ABSENT FRIENDS
| 85 | Zebra 1 | Stand Up And Fight/Drift Apart (p/s) | 30 |

ABSOLUTE
85	Reset 7REST 5	TV Glare/At The Third Stroke (p/s)	10
85	Reset 12 REST 5	TV Glare/At The Third Stroke (12", p/s)	20
87	Reset 7REST 8	Can't You See/Love In My Heart (release cancelled)	60

(see also Erasure)

ABSOLUTE ELSEWHERE
| 76 | Warner Bros K 16697 | Earthbound/Gold Of The Gods (p/s) | 5 |
| 76 | Warner Bros K 56192 | IN SEARCH OF ANCIENT GODS (LP, gatefold, die-cut, with booklet) | 20 |

(see also Bill Bruford)

ABSTRAC & LADY PENELOPE
| 97 | Confetti Records COEP 03 | Love In Dub/Dub In Love/Peeper (Part 1) (12") | 8 |
| 97 | Confetti Records COEP 12 | 10 TIMES A DAY E.P. (12", Promo) | 12 |

ABYSSINIAN BAPTIST CHOIR
| 63 | Philips 847095 BY | ABYSSINIAN BAPTIST CHOIR (LP) | 15 |

ABYSSINIANS
73	Harry J. HJ 6652	Yim Mas Gan/JOHN CROW GENERATION: Crank Shaft	20
75	Grounation GR 2029	Love Comes And Goes/(Version)	6
75	Soundtracs SK1	Tenayistillin Wandimae/Tenayistillin	8
76	Tropical S'tracks TST 109	African Race/Satta A Massagana	12
76	Nationwide NW009	Sweet Feelings/Version	8
77	Klik KL 631	Forward On To Zion/Satta A Massagana	10
78	Different HAVED 7	Satte A Massagana/I & I (12")	30
79	Different HAVE 18	Declaration Of Rights/African Race	8
78	Different GETL 100	FORWARD ON TO ZION (LP)	35
78	Virgin Front Line FL1019	ARISE (LP, with lyric sheet)	15

ACADEMY
| 69 | Morgan Bluetown BTS 2 | Rachel's Dream/Munching The Candy (as Academy featuring Polly Perkins) | 25 |
| 69 | Morgan Bluetown BT 5001 | POP-LORE ACCORDING TO THE ACADEMY (LP) | 175 |

(see also Polly Perkins)

ACCENT (1)
| 67 | Decca F 12679 | Red Sky At Night/Wind Of Change | 250 |

(see also Rick Hayward)

ACCENT (2)
| 84 | Motion | We Are Lost/Blue And Royal Line (p/s with insert) | 8 |

ACCENTS
| 59 | Coral Q 72351 | Wiggle, Wiggle/Dreamin' And Schemin' | 20 |
| 59 | Coral Q 72351 | Wiggle, Wiggle/Dreamin' And Schemin' (78) | 10 |

ACCESS
| 81 | Ellie Jay EJSP 9674 STA001-7 | AUDACITY EP (EP, p/s) | 25 |

ACCIDENT
| 84 | Flicknife SHARP 016 | A CLOCKWORK LEGION (LP) | 20 |
| 87 | Link LP 12 | CRAZY! (LP) | 15 |

(see also Major Accident)

ACCIDENT ON THE EAST LANCS.
| 80 | Roach RR 1 | The Back End Of Nowhere/Rat Race (p/s) | 75 |
| 80 | Roach SPLIFF 001 | We Want It Legalised/Tell Me What You Want (no p/s) | 50 |

ACCIDENTS
80	H. Line 'n' Sinker HOOK 1	Blood Spattered With Guitars/Curtains For You (p/s)	20
80	Hook Line 'n' Sinker	KISS ME ON THE APOCALYPSE (LP, unreleased; test pressings only, White handwritten labels)	150
90s	Detour DRLP04	KISS ME ON THE APOCALYPSE (LP)	15

ACCOLADE
70	Columbia DB 8688	Natural Day/Prelude To A Dawn	12
70	Columbia SCX 6405	ACCOLADE (LP)	40
72	Regal Zono. SLRZ 1024	ACCOLADE 2 (LP)	80

(see also Gordon Giltrap, Wizz Jones, Pauline Filby, Don Partridge)

ACCURSED
80s	Wrek 'EM ACC 3	Going Down (p/s)	8
83	Wrek 'EM ACC 1	AGGRESSIVE PUNK (LP)	20
83	Wrek 'EM ACC 3	UP WITH THE PUNKS (LP)	15
84	Wrek 'EM ACC 4	LAUGHING AT YOU (LP)	15

ACCUSED
| 87 | Children Of The Revolution/ Earache GURT 17/MOSH 1 | THE RETURN OF MARTHA SPLATTERHEAD (LP, insert) | 12 |

AC/DC
SINGLES
76	Atlantic K 10745	It's A Long Way To The Top (If You Wanna Rock'N'Roll)/ Can I Sit Next To You, Girl? (no p/s)	20
76	Atlantic K 10805	Jailbreak/Fling Thing (original issue with running times on label, dark label, heavy print, no p/s)	22
76	Atlantic K 10860	High Voltage/Live Wire (in p/s)	120
76	Atlantic K 10860	High Voltage/Live Wire (no p/s)	15

77	Atlantic K 10899	Dirty Deeds Done Dirt Cheap/Big Balls/The Jack (maxi-single, 'schoolboy' p/s)	100
77	Atlantic K 11018	Let There Be Rock (edit)/Problem Child (small label lettering & 3.06 timing, no p/s)	12
77	Atlantic K 11018	Let There Be Rock (edit)/Problem Child (without small label lettering & 3.06 timing, no p/s)	7
78	Atlantic K 11142	Rock'N'Roll Damnation/Sin City (initially with small label lettering & 3.05 timing, no p/s)	6
78	Atlantic K 11142T	Rock'N'Roll Damnation/Sin City (12", p/s)	15
78	Atlantic K 11207	Whole Lotta Rosie (live)/Hell Ain't A Bad Place To Be (live) (dark labels; later reissued with lighter labels (worth less) no p/s)	5
78	Atlantic K 11207T	Whole Lotta Rosie (live)/Hell Ain't A Bad Place To Be (live) (12", no p/s)	15
79	Atlantic K 11321	Highway To Hell/If You Want Blood (You've Got It) ('1979' on p/s)	5
79	Atlantic K 11406	Girl's Got Rhythm/Get It Hot (p/s, initial pressing without 'Elephant Head' motif)	6
79	Atlantic K 11406	Girl's Got Rhythm/Get It Hot (p/s, without 'Elephant Head' motif)	5
79	Atlantic K 11406E	Girl's Got Rhythm/If You Want Blood (You've Got It)/Hell Ain't A Bad Place To Be (live)/Rock'N'Roll Damnation (EP, gatefold envelope p/s)	12
80	Atlantic K 11435	Touch Too Much/Live Wire (live)/Shot Down In Flames (live) (p/s)	5
80	Atlantic K 11435	Touch Too Much/Live Wire (live)/Shot Down In Flames (live) (p/s, misprinted back-to-front)	15
80	Atlantic K 10805	Jailbreak/Fling Thing (reissue, light label, fine print; first pressing initially without 'Elephant Head' motif on p/s)	15
80	Atlantic K 10805	Jailbreak/Fling Thing (reissue, light label, fine print; with 'Elephant Head' motif on p/s)	10
80	Atlantic K 11142	Rock'N'Roll Damnation/Sin City (reissue, initially without 'Elephant Head' motif on p/s)	8
80	Atlantic K 11321	Highway To Hell/If You Want Blood (You've Got It) (reissue, '1980' on p/s)	5
80	Atlantic HM 1	High Voltage/Live Wire (reissue, p/s)	6
80	Atlantic HM 2	Dirty Deeds Done Dirt Cheap/Big Balls/The Jack (reissue, p/s)	6
80	Atlantic HM 3	It's A Long Way To The Top (If You Wanna Rock'N'Roll)/ Can I Sit Next To You? (p/s, reissue)	6
80	Atlantic HM 4	Whole Lotta Rosie (live)/Hell Ain't A Bad Place To Be (live) (p/s, reissue)	6
80	Atlantic K 11600	You Shook Me All Night Long/Have A Drink With Me (p/s)	5
80	Atlantic K 11600	You Shook Me All Night Long/Have A Drink With Me (p/s, mispressing, A-side plays "Shake A Leg")	100
80	Atlantic K 11630T	Rock'N'Roll Ain't Noise Pollution/Hell's Bells (12", p/s, with badge)	8
82	Atlantic SAM 143	For Those About To Rock (We Salute You)/C.O.D. (12", p/s, promo only)	40
83	Atlantic A 9774P	Guns For Hire/Landslide (logo-shaped picture disc)	10
84	Atlantic A 9651P	Nervous Shakedown/Rock'N'Roll Ain't Noise Pollution (live) (shaped picture disc)	15
85	Atlantic A 9532W	Danger/Back In Business (poster p/s)	6
85	Atlantic A 9532P	Danger/Back In Business (fly-shaped picture disc)	20
86	Atlantic A 9474P	Shake Your Foundations/Stand Up (Angus-shaped picture disc)	20
86	Atlantic A 9425P	Who Made Who/Guns For Hire (live) (shaped picture disc)	20
86	Atlantic A 9425TW	Who Made Who (remix)/Guns For Hire (live) (12", stickered p/s & poster)	15
86	Atlantic A 9377P	You Shook Me All Night Long/She's Got Balls (live) (shaped picture disc)	20
88	Atlantic A 9136TP	Heatseeker/Go Zone/Snake Eye (12", picture disc)	15
88	Atlantic A 9098TP	That's The Way I Wanna Rock'N'Roll/Kissin' Dynamite/Borrowed Time (12", picture disc)	8
88	Atlantic A 9098CD	That's The Way I Wanna Rock'N'Roll/Kissin' Dynamite/Shoot To Thrill/ Whole Lotta Rosie (3" CD with adaptor, 5" case)	15
90	Atco B8907T	Thunderstruck/Fire Your Guns/DT/Chase The Ace (12" poster p/s)	8
90	Atco B8907T	Thunderstruck/Fire Your Guns/DT/Chase The Ace (12" coloured test pressings, white, blue, red, clear, yellow, green & marbled swirl pattern	300
91	Atco B8886T	Money Talks/Mistress For Christmas/Borrowed Time (12" poster p/s)	20
91	Atco 8830X	Are You Ready/Got You By The Balls (numbered p/s, with patch)	8
91	Atco 8830W	Are You Ready/Got You By The Balls (numbered 'satchel' p/s)	5
92	Atco B8479CD/X	Highway To Hell (Bonny Intro)/Hell's Bells/The Jack/Highway To Hell/ Hell Ain't A Bad Place To Be/High Voltage (2 x CD, digipak)	12
93	Atco B6073T	Dirty Deeds Done Cheap/Shoot To Thrill (live)/Dirty Deeds Done Cheap (live) (12")	10
93	Atco B8396T	Big Gun/Back To Black/For Those About To Rock (12", p/s)	8
95	East West 3BALLCD	Hail Caesar/Hard As A Rock/Ballbreaker (CD, no'd hologram p/s, promo only)	15
95	East West A4368X	Hard As A Rock/Caught With Your Pants Down (p/s, yellow vinyl, numbered)	8

ALBUMS

76	Atlantic K50257	HIGH VOLTAGE (LP, cartoon sleeve)	15
77	Atlantic K50483	LET THERE BE ROCK (LP, etched matrix numbers K50366 A-1/B-2)	15
77	Atlantic K 50366	LET THERE BE ROCK (LP, mispressing, both sides play Side 1)	200
79	Atlantic K50625	HIGHWAY TO HELL (LP)	12
79	Atlantic K 50628	HIGHWAY TO HELL (LP, test pressing in alternative "live" proof sleeve)	300
80	Atlantic K50735	BACK IN BLACK (LP, embossed sleeve, with inner, A1/B1 Matrixes)	20
81	K50851	FOR THOSE ABOUT TO ROCK (LP)	12
81	Atlantic SAM 155	JAPAN TOUR '81 (LP, picture disc, promo only, clear rim)	150
81	Atlantic SAM 155	JAPAN TOUR '81 (LP, picture disc, promo only, black rim)	120
81	Atlantic 60149	BOX SET (3-LP, including "High Voltage", "Dirty Deeds Done Cheap" & Powerage, promo 7" & poster; export issue)	45
91	Atco WX 364P	THE RAZOR'S EDGE (LP, picture disc with inlay card)	15
95	East West SAM 1693	BALLBREAKER (CD, promo only compilation)	30
95	East West 7559 61780-1	BALLBREAKER (LP)	25
97	East West 7559 62162 2	BONFIRE (CD boxed set)	30
03	Epic 509298-7	ACDCROCKS.com BOX (15 x CD box set)	150
09	Columbia 38377	BLACK ICE (2-LP, gatefold, inner sleeves)	18

(see also Geordie, A II Z, Home)

ACE

| 71 | Decca F13216 | Speed Freak/Ace Of Spades | 6 |

C ACE & INSWINGS

| 74 | Tropical AL 026 | Hot Butter Dub/Pits And Pieces | 30 |

BUDDY ACE

| 68 | Action ACT 4504 | Got To Get Myself Together/Darling Depend On Me | 25 |
| 64 | Vocalion VEP 1-70164 | BUDDY ACE (EP) | 100 |

CHARLIE ACE

70	High Note HS 051	Creation (Version)/GAYTONES: Creation (Version Three)	12
70	Punch PH 49	Silver And Gold/PHILL PRATT ALLSTARS: Bump And Bore	12
70	Punch PH 53	Book Of Books/WINSTON HARRIS: Musical Dove	10
70	Punch PH 62	Love I Madly/Especially For You (A-side by Charley & Lloyd)	10
70	Punch PH 67	Do Something/MAYTONES: Run Babylon	10

71	G.G. GG 4507	Ontarius Version/G.G. ALL STARS: Ontarius Version 2	10
71	G.G. GG 4518	Do Something/MAYTONES: Groove Me	10
71	Upsetter US 359	The Creeper/UPSETTERS: The Creeper (Version)	18
71	Smash SMA 2325	Need No Whip/Grine Grine	10

(see also Charles, Paulette & Gee, Gaytones, Phil Pratt Allstars, Maytones, G.G. Allstars, Upsetters, Gaby Wilton & Charlie Ace)

JOHNNY ACE

61	Vogue V 9180	Pledging My Love/Anymore	60
61	Vocalion V 9180	Pledging My Love/Anymore (reissue)	15
62	Vogue VE 1-70150	JOHNNY ACE (EP)	125
61	Vocalion VA 160177	THE MEMORIAL ALBUM (LP)	150
61	Vogue VA 160177	THE MEMORIAL ALBUM (LP, reissue)	40

RICHARD ACE (& SOUND DIMENSIONS)

67	Coxsone CS 7031	Don't Let The Sun Catch You Crying/VICEROYS: Magadown	50
67	Studio One SO 2022	I Need You/SOUL VENDORS: Cool Shade	120
69	Studio One SO 2072	More Reggae (with Sound Dimensions)/GLADIATORS: Hello Carol	35
69	Trojan TR 654	Hang 'Em High (with Sound Dimensions)/BLACK & GEORGE: Candy Lady	70
70	Sugar SU 104	Sound Of The Reggae/Got To Build A Wall	35

(see also Viceroys, Soul Vendors, Gladiators, Ken Boothe)

ACE LANE

83	Expulsion EXIT3	SEE YOU IN HEAVEN (LP)	15

ACEN

92	Production House PNT 034	Close Your Eyes (XXX mix)/Close Your Eyes (vitamin 'E' mix) (12")	20
92	Production House PNT 034 R	Close Your Eyes (Remix I: Optikonfusion!)/ Close Your Eyes (Remix II: The Sequel) (12")	20
93	Production House PNT 034 R-A, PNT 051 A-2	Close Your Eyes (Non Beatles Version Mispress) (12")	90
92	Production House PNT 042	Trip II The Moon (Part 1)/Obsessed (12", die-cut p/s)	25
92	Production House PNT 042	Trip II The Moon - Part 2 (12", Promo 100 copies)	60
92	Production House PNT 042 R	Trip II The Moon (Part 2, The Darkside)/The Life And Crimes Of A Ruffneck (12", die-cut p/s)	25
92	Production House PNT 042 RX	Trip II The Moon (Part 3, kaleidoscopiklimax)/Obsessed (Part 2, Pictures Of Silence) (12", die-cut p/s)	25
92	Production House PNC 042	Trip II The Moon/Obsessed/Close Your Eyes (XXX Mix) (CD)	15
92	Production House PNC 042R	Trip II The Moon (The Darkside)/The Life And Crimes Of A Ruffneck/ Close Your Eyes (Optikonfusion!) (CD)	15
92	Production House PNC 042RX	Trip II The Moon (Kaleidoscopiklimax)/Obsessed II (Picture Of Silence) (CD)	15
93	Production House PNT 051R	Window In The Sky (DMS Remix)/Window In The Sky (Nino's Night Remix) (white label 12")	15
93	Production House PNT 051	Krystal Fairground (12", Promo, one-sided)	50
93	Production House PNC 051	Window In The Sky (Kingdom Of Light - Radio Edit)/Window In The Sky (Monolythikmaniak)/Window In The Sky (Krystal Fairground)/Window In The Sky (Kingdom Of Light) (CD)	20

A CERTAIN RATIO

79	Factory FAC 5	All Night Party/The Thin Boys (p/s, 5,000 only, 1,000 with sticker stating ltd. edition on poor quality vinyl)	25
79	Factory FAC 5	All Night Party/The Thin Boys (p/s, 5,000 only, 4,000 without sticker stating ltd. edition on poor quality vinyl)	20
80	Factory FAC 22	Blown Away/Flight/And Then Again (12", p/s, with inner sleeve)	12
81	Factory FAC 52	Waterline/Funaezekea (12", p/s)	8
82	Factory FAC 62-7	Knife Slits Water/Tumba Rumba (p/s)	5
83	Factory FAC 72-7	I Need Someone Tonite (edit)/Don't You Worry 'Bout A Thing (edit) (promo)	5
84	Factory FAC 112P	Life's A Scream (edit)/There's Only This (edit) (promo pack including 7", photo & biography in custom ACR envelope)	10
80	Factory FACT 16C	THE GRAVEYARD & THE BALLROOM (cassette in plastic wallet, first 400 in orange, then later blue, green, brown, red and grey. 1000 only)	20
81	Factory FACT 35	TO EACH (LP)	12
82	Factory FACT 55	SEXTET (LP, textured sleeve with insert)	12
82	Factory FACT 65	I'D LIKE TO SEE YOU AGAIN (LP)	12
85	private label	A CERTAIN RATIO LIVE IN AMERICA (cassette, sold at gigs)	12
85	Factory FACT 16C	THE GRAVEYARD AND THE BALLROOM (reissue, cassette, in box with insert)	25
86	Factory FACT 135c	THE OLD AND THE NEW (cassette, in box with insert)	25
86	Factory FACT 166	FORCE (LP)	12
86	Factory FACT 166c	FORCE (cassette, in box with insert)	25
02	Soul Jazz SJRLP60	EARLY (2-LP)	15

(see also Sir Horatio)

ACES (1)

63	Parlophone R 5094	Wait Until Tomorrow/The Last One	12
64	Parlophone R 5108	I Count The Tears/But Say It Isn't So	12

ACES (2)

81	Etc ETC 01	One Way Street/Why Should It Be Mine (p/s)	15

(see also Menace)

ACHES & PAINS

66	Page One POF 008	There's No Other Like Your Mother/Again And Again	6

ACHILLES & HIS HEELS

61	Fontana H 340	Brigitte Bardot/Acapulco	6

ACHOR

76	Cedar CEDAR 1	END OF MY DAY (LP)	15
78	Dove Tail DOVE 54	HOSANNA TO THE SON OF DAVID (LP)	12

(see also Wine Of Lebanon, Valley Of Achor)

ACID GALLERY

69	CBS 4608	Dance Around The Maypole/Right Toe Blues	70

(see also Christie, Epics, Carl Wayne & Vikings, Roy Wood, Outer Limits)

ACID MOTHERS TEMPLE AND THE MELTING PARAISO UFO

00	Staticresonance 2	MONSTER OF THE UNIVERSE (Monster Of The Universe/Wholly Weary Flashback/Surfin' Paris-Texas/Midnight Mountain Dew (EP, 500 only, p/s 2 x 7" sold on tour, 500 only)	20
01	Staticresonance 5	My Guitar Wants To Kiss Your Mother/NISHINIHON: Super Station (Hell In A Cell Version) (red vinyl, p/s)	10

MINT VALUE £

00s	Ochre OCH 057	Hello Good Child/You're My Boy (300 on purple vinyl)	6
01	Swordfish SFAM CD 2	LA NOVIA (CD)	20
01	Staticresonance 1	ABSOLUTELY FREAKOUT, (ZAP YOUR MIND) (LP, 1000 only)	30
02	Staticresonance 4	ABSOLUTE FREAK OUT (ZAP YOUR MIND) (2xCD, gatefold card sleeve)	20

(See also Cotton Casino)

ACKEE
86	Heavyweight HW 003	Call Me Rambo/Rambo Gun Salute (12", as Ackie)	25
87	Route One RO 004	Ragamuffin Boogie Rock/Lick Them (Dance Hall Style) (12")	100
87	Route One RO 005	Roughneck Time/Version (12")	100

DAVID ACKLES
68	Elektra EKSN 45039	La Route A Chicago/Down River	5
69	Elektra EKSN 45054	Laissez Faire/Blue Ribbons	5
70	Elektra EKSN 45079	Subway To The Country/That's No Reason To Cry	5
68	Elektra EKL 4022	DAVID ACKLES (LP, orange label, mono)	40
68	Electra EKS74022	DAVID ACKLES (LP, orange label, stereo)	30
70	Elektra EKS 74060	SUBWAY TO THE COUNTRY (LP, orange label)	20
72	Elektra K 42112	AMERICAN GOTHIC (LP)	15
73	CBS 32466	FIVE AND DIME (LP)	15

BARBARA ACKLIN
68	MCA MU 1038	Love Makes A Woman/Come And See Me Baby	10
69	MCA MU 1071	Am I The Same Girl/Be By My Side (DJ Copy)	50
69	MCA MU 1071	Am I The Same Girl/Be By My Side	10
69	MCA MU 1102	Love Makes A Woman/Come And See Me Baby (reissue)	7
69	MCA MU 1103	Am I The Same Girl/Be By My Side (reissue)	5
69	MCA MUP(S) 366	LOVE MAKES A WOMAN (LP)	25
71	MCA MUPS 410	SEVEN DAYS OF NIGHT (LP)	20
71	MCA MUPS 416	SOMEONE ELSE'S ARMS (LP)	20

(see also Gene Chandler & Barbara Acklin)

ACME ATTRACTIONS
| 80 | A Trax KICK 007 | Anyway/Never Again (p/s) | 40 |
| 81 | Orchid OR1 | Eve Of Destruction/It's OK (p/s, with Bonnie Parker) | 20 |

A CRAZE
| 83 | Respond KOB 706 | Wearing Your Jumper/She Is So (p/s, produced by Paul Weller) | 7 |

SEPH ACRE & PETS
| 58 | Pye International 7N 25001 | You Are My Love/Rock And Roll Cha Cha | 6 |

(see also Pets)

ACRYLIC TONES
| 90s | Detour DR010 | Girl/Theme From.../Rainbow Song (p/s) | 5 |

ACT (1)
67	Columbia DB 8179	Cobbled Streets/One Heart	25
67	Columbia DB 8261	Here Come Those Tears Again/Without You	15
68	Columbia DB 8331	Just A Little Bit/The Remedies Of Doctor Brohnicoy	65

ACT (2)
| 81 | Act ACT 001 | Dance To Despair/Who Let The Flowers Fall? (p/s and lyric sheet) | 7 |

ACT (3)
87	ZTT 12ACT 28	Snobbery And Decay (Naked Civil Remix)/Strong Poison/Theme From Snobbery And Decay (12", gatefold p/s, with poster)	10
87	ZTT CT 01	Snobbery And Decay (Moonlighting Mix)/Instant 1/Instant 2 (12" promo, plain black die-cut sleeve)	30
87	ZTT VIMM 1	Absolutely Immune 2/Bloodrush/States Of Logic (12", p/s)	10
88	ZTT BET 1	Chance/Winner '88 (p/s, withdrawn)	30
88	ZTT BETT 1	Chance (12 To 1 Mix)/Winner '88/Chance (We Give You Another Chance) (12", p/s, withdrawn)	80
88	ZTT BETCD 1	Chance (12 To 1 Mix)/Winner '88/Chance (We Give You Another Chance) (CD, existence unconfirmed)	0
88	ZTT ZQCD 1	LAUGHTER, TEARS AND RAGE (CD)	30

(see also Propaganda, Claudia Brucken, Glenn Gregory & Claudia Brucken, Thomas Leer)

ACTION
65	Parlophone R 5354	Land Of 1000 Dances/In My Lonely Room	60
66	Parlophone R 5410	I'll Keep Holding On/Hey Sah-Lo-Ney	65
66	Parlophone R 5474	Baby You've Got It/Since I Lost My Baby	90
67	Parlophone R 5572	Never Ever/Twenty Fourth Hour	80
67	Parlophone R 5610	Shadows And Reflections/Something Has Hit Me	100
67	Parlophone R 5410	Shadows And Reflections/Something Has Hit Me (p/s for export to Holland)	150
81	Edsel E 5001	I'll Keep Holding On/Wasn't It You? (p/s)	10
81	Edsel E 5002	Since I Lost My Baby/Never Ever/Wasn't It You (p/s)	10
82	Edsel E 5003	Shadows And Reflections/Something Has Hit Me (p/s)	10
84	Edsel E 5008	Hey Sah-Lo-Ney/Come On, Come With Me (p/s)	10
80	Edsel ED 101	THE ULTIMATE ACTION (LP, with inner sleeve, first presing with extra tracks)	20
84	Carnaby CY 004	16 SLICES OF (LP)	12
85	Castle DOJO LP 3	ACTION SPEAK LOUDER THAN... (mini-LP)	15
95	Dig The Fuzz DIG 005	BRAIN - THE LOST RECORDINGS (LP, insert, booklet)	15
98	Dig The Fuzz DIG 025	ROLLED GOLD (LP)	15

(see also Boys, Sandra Barry & Boys, Mighty Baby, Reg King, Stone's Masonry)

ACTION PACT
81	Subversive ANARCHO 1	HEATHROW TOUCHDOWN (EP, 1 side by Dead Man's Shadow)	20
82	Fallout FALL 003	Suicide Bag/Stanwell/Blue Blood (p/s)	10
83	Fallout FALL 010	People/Times Must Change/Sixties Flix (p/s)	10
83	Fallout FALL 019	Question Of Choice/Hook Line & Sinker (p/s)	10
83	Fallout FALL 013	MERCURY THEATRE ON THE AIR (LP)	12
84	Fallout FALL 030	SURVIVAL OF THE FATTEST (LP)	12

ACTION PAINTING!
90	Sarah SARAH 028	These Things Happen/Boy Meets World (wraparound p/s, with insert)	10
93	Sarah SARAH 73	Classical Music/Sensation No. 5/Hip To Hate (p/s, insert)	12
93	Sarah SARAH 87	Mustard Gas/Art Student/Collapsing Cloud (p/s, insert)	12

ACTIVES
83	Quiet Records QS001	RIOT (EP)	35
84	Quiet Records QS 004	WAIT & SEE (EP" 12")	25
83	Quiet Records QLP 4	KICK IT DOWN (LP, with insert)	50

ACTRESS
69	CBS 4016	It's What You Give/Good Job With Prospects	160

ROY ACUFF & SMOKY MOUNTAIN BOYS
57	Brunswick 05635	I Like Mountain Music/It's Hard To Love (And Not To Be In Love)	8

ACUTE LOGIC
81	Illogical EJSP 9589	Morroccan Nights/The Obsession/The Balcony (p/s, insert)	30

ADAM & THE ANTS
78	Decca F 13803	Young Parisians/Lady (in p/s, original with paper labels)	12
78	Decca F13803	Young Parisians/Lady (company sleeve)	6
79	Do It DUN8	Zerox/Whip In My Valise	5
79	Want 1	Cartrouble Part 1/Cartrouble Part 2/Kick (1-sided promo)	15
79	Do It RIDE 3	DIRK WEARS WHITE SOX (LP)	12
79	Do It RIDE 3M	DIRK WEARS WHITE SOX (cassette with insert)	15
80	CBS 4025361	DIRK WEARS WHITE SOX (cassette reissue)	20
90	Strange Fruit SFRLP 115	PEEL SESSIONS (LP)	15
00	Sony ANTBOX 5007822	ANTBOX (3-CD with book in 7" sized box)	35
06	Sony 88697009032	ADAM & THE ANTS - REMASTERED (7-CD, box set)	40

(see also Adam Ant, Maneaters, Models, Danny & Nogoodniks)

ADAM, MIKE & TIM
64	Decca F 12040	Little Baby/You're The Reason Why	6
65	Decca F 12221	Little Pictures/Summers Here Again	8
66	Columbia DB 7836	Flowers On The Wall/Give That Girl A Break	6
66	Columbia DB 7902	A Most Peculiar Man/Wedding Day	5

(see also Mike Sedgewick)

ADAM AND DEE
69	Tangerine DP 0002	Question Of Childhood/Run To Her	120

ADAMO
63	HMV 7EG 8860	BELGIUMS TOP RECORDING STAR (EP)	8

ALICIA ADAMS
61	Capitol CL 15195	Love Bandit/Oom Dooby Doom Lovey Dovey Sh' Boom	10

ARTHUR ADAMS
81	RCA RCAT 146	You Got The Floor/Stay With Me Tonight (12")	15

ARTHUR K. ADAMS
68	Blue Horizon 57-3136	She Drives Me Out Of My Mind/Gimme Some Of Your Lovin'	25

BILLY ADAMS (1)
60	Capitol CL 15107	Count Every Star/Peggy's Party	8

BILLY ADAMS (2)
69	London 10258	I Need Your Love/Why Don't You Believe Me (DJ Copy)	20
69	London HL 10258	I Need Your Love/Why Don't You Believe Me	8

ADAMS (CHRIS AND PAULINE)
75	Charisma CB 244	If Only The Good Die Young/The City At Night	8

DANNY ADAMS & CHALLENGERS
64	Philips BF 1346	Bye Bye Baby, Bye Bye/I'm So Proud Of You	7

DERROLL ADAMS
67	Ace Of Clubs ACL 1227	PORTLAND TOWN (LP)	70
72	Village Thing VTS 17	FEELIN' FINE (LP, with inner sleeve)	70
72	Village Thing VTS 17	FEELIN' FINE (LP, without inner sleeve)	40

(see also Ramblin' Jack Elliott)

EVE ADAMS
61	Qualition PSP 7131	Kookie Talk/My Love Dear	7

FAYE ADAMS
56	London HLU 8339	I'll Be True/Happiness To My Soul (Gold Tri label)	700
56	London HLU 8339	I'll Be True/Happiness To My Soul (78)	35

GAYLE ADAMS
82	Epic A 2167	Baby I Need Your Loving/Don't Jump To Conclusions	10
82	Epic A13 2167	Baby I Need Your Loving/Don't Jump To Conclusions (12")	15

GLADSTON ADAMS
69	Trojan TR 659	Dollars And Cents/TOMMY McCOOK: Popcorn Reggay	20

(see also Gladstone Anderson)

GLEN ADAMS
67	Island WI 3072	Silent Lover/I Remember	60
67	Island WI 3083	She (actually titled "I'm Shocking")/SONNY BURKE: Some Other Time	60
67	Island WI 3099	Grab A Girl/DELROY WILSON: This Heart Of Mine	50
67	Island WI 3100	Hold Down Miss Winey/VINCENT GORDON: Sounds And Soul	70
67	Island WI 3120	She's So Fine/ROY SHIRLEY: Girlie	50
68	Blue Cat BS 126	She Is Leaving/UNIQUES: Girls Like Dirt	30
68	Trojan TR 621	Rent Too High/Every Time	25
68	Duke DU 58	My Girl/GLADIATORS: You Were To Be	20
68	Bullet BU 414	Cat Woman/PETER TOUCH: Selassie Serenade (B-side actually by Peter Tosh)	20
68	Collins Downbeat CR 010	King Sized/I'm Gonna Take You Back (B-side actually by Owen Gray)	75
68	Collins Downbeat CR 006	Cool Cool Rock Steady (as Glen Addams & Collins Band)/OWEN GRAY & COLLINS BAND: Girl I Will Be Leaving	125
68	Giant GN 33	Lonely Girl/ROY SHIRLEY: Warming Up The Scene	40
69	Amalgamated AMG 837	She's So Fine/ERNEST WILSON: Private Number	20
69	Crab CRAB 21	Mighty Organ/ERNEST WILSON: Just Once	25
69	Sound Systems SS 105	Down To Earth Reggae/Reggae From Mankind	20

70	Gas GAS 141	Leaving On A Jet Plane/REGGAE BOYS: Phrases	25
70	Junior JR 110	Sound In/Sound & Pleasure	20
71	Big BG 321	Weary Version 3/TONY BREVETT: Hills And Valleys	18
71	Explosion EX 2048	Never Fall In Love/JET SCENE: Jet 747	12
71	Upsetter US 367	Never Had A Dream/UPSETTERS: Version	45

(see also Glen Adams, Reggae Boys, Roy Shirley, Maxie & Glen, Delroy Wilson, Derrick Morgan, Ernest Wilson, Owen Gray)

JOHNNY ADAMS (& GONDOLIERS)
59	Top Rank JAR 192	Come On/Nowhere To Go (as Johnny Adams & Gondoliers)	5

JUNE ADAMS
66	King KG 1038	River Keep Movin'/Heavenly Father	20

LLOYD ADAMS
62	Wasp W001	I Wish Your Picture Was You/Pleading For Love (Possibly unreleased)	35
62	Wasp W009	I Wish Your Picture Was You/Pleading For Love	25

MARIE ADAMS
59	Capitol CL 14963	A Fool In Love/What Do You Want To Make Those Eyes At Me For	40
59	Capitol CL 14964	A Fool In Love/What Do You Want To Make Those Eyes At Me For (promo copy in picture sleeve)	50

(see also Johnny Otis)

PAUL & LINDA ADAMS
75	Sweet Folk & Country SFA 27	FAR OVER THE FELL (LP)	15
76	Sweet Folk & Country SFA 053	COUNTRY HIRINGS (LP)	12

PEPPER ADAMS
58	Vogue LAE 12134	CRITICS CHOICE (LP)	20
59	Pye NLP 28007	COOL SOUND (LP)	18

RAY ADAMS
62	Decca F 11507	Venus In Blue Jeans/He's Got My Sympathy	5

RITCHIE ADAMS
60	London HLU 9200	Back To School/Don't Go My Love, Don't Go	30

RUSH ADAMS
54	Parlophone MSP 6101	I'm Sorry Dear/No One To Cry To	10
55	Parlophone CMSP 33	Then I'll Be Happy/Arizona (with Ace Dooley & Son) (export issue)	5
56	MGM SP 1162	Love Plays The Strings Of My Banjo/Kiss! Kiss! Kiss!	5
56	MGM SP 1176	The Birds And The Bees (with Loulie Jean Norman)/My Buddy's Girl	5

(see also David Rose)

RYAN ADAMS
00	Cooking Vinyl COOK 205	HEARTBREAKER (LP, with inner)	30
08	Lost Highway 02517872608	CARDINOLOGY (2-LP)	20

STEVE ADAMS
77	Mind's Ear MER 2010	STEVE ADAMS (LP)	15

WOODROW ADAMS
65	Blue Horizon BH 1001	Baby You Just Don't Know/Wine Head Woman (99 copies only)	250

ZAYNE ADAMS
69	NEMS 56 4473	Can't You See Me/If You Were My Woman	15

BRYAN ADAMS
81	AMLH 64864	YOU WANT IT YOU GOT IT (LP)	12
87	AMA 3907	INTO THE FIRE (LP)	12

ADAM'S APPLES
77	Brunswick BR 42	Don't Take It Out On This World/Don't You Want To Take Me Home	10

ADAMS FAMILY
93	Loose LOOSE 02	Frustration/Timewaster (p/s)	6

BARRY ADAMSON
92	Mute STUMM 105	SOUL MURDER (LP)	12
93	Mute STUMM 120	THE NEGRO INSIDE ME (LP)	12
96	Mute STUMM 134	OEDIPUS SCHMOEDIPUS (LP)	15
98	Mute STUMM 161	AS ABOVE SO BELOW (LP)	12

AD CONSPIRACY
79	Diamond	AD CONSPIRACY (LP)	25

CANNONBALL ADDERLEY
61	Riverside RIV 33457	African Waltz/Kelly Blue	7
61	Riverside 45414	Things Are Getting Better/Sidewalks Of New York	5
63	Riverside 106911 RIF	Jive Samba/Lillie	6
63	Riverside 10691R RIF	Tengo Tango/Brother Dix	5
67	Capitol CL 15489	Mercy Mercy Mercy/Games	12
59	Riverside 12-30333	CANNONBALL TAKES CHARGE (LP)	20
62	Riverside RLP 12-311	THE CANNONBALL ADDERLEY QUINTET IN SAN FRANCISCO (LP)	15
62	Riverside RLP 12-318	WORK SONG (LP, actually by Nat Adderley)	20
63	Riverside RLP 433	KNOW WHAT I MEAN (LP, with BILL EVANS)	20
65	Fontana FJL 107	WOW (LP)	15
65	Fontana FJL 117	WHAM! (LP)	15
67	Capitol T2617	WHY AM I TREATED SO BAD? (LP)	20
68	Capitol T 2987	ACCENT ON AFRICA (LP)	15
68	Capitol ST2822	74 MILES AWAY (LP)	15

(see also Nancy Wilson, Miles Davis, John Coltrane)

NAT ADDERLEY
56	London LTZC 15018	NAT ADDERLEY (LP)	20
62	Riverside RLP 12-318	WORK SONG (LP)	20
65	Fontana FJL 118	NATURALLY (LP)	20

ADDICTION
92	Vicious Pumpin' OBS 002	ADDICTION EP (12", stamped white label)	20
92	Vicious Pumpin' VIC 003	MIND PENETRATION EP (12", stamped white label)	25

92	Vicious Pumpin' VIC 003R	MIND PENETRATION (THE REMIXES) EP (12", stamped white label)	40
92	Vicious Vinyl VIC 001	THE CREATIVE DUB EP (12")	15
93	Vicious Pumpin' VIC 013	Wildstyle/Untitled (12")	10

ADDICTS
| 64 | Decca F 11902 | That's My Girl/Here She Comes | 40 |

ADDIX
| 79 | Zig Zag ZZ 22002 | Too Blind To See/(No Such Thing As A) Bad Boy (p/s) | 15 |

ADD N TO X
| 98 | Satellite STL010 | ON THE WIRES OF OUR NERVES (2-LP) | 15 |
| 99 | Mute STUMM 170 | AVANT HARD (2-LP, gatefold) | 15 |

ADDRISSI BROTHERS
59	London HL 8922	Cherrystone/Lilies Grow High (some copies have tri-centre)	20
59	London HL 8973	Un Jarro/Saving My Kisses	5
59	Columbia DB 4370	Back To The Old Salt Mine/It's Love	30

JEAN ADEBAMBO
| 79 | Ade J ADE 101 | Say That You Love Me/Dance Of Love | 15 |

ADELE
| 08 | XL XLS 393 | Make You Feel My Love/Painting Pictures (p/s, 500 only) | 15 |
| 07 | Pacemaker 1 | Hometown Glory/Best For Last (7", 500 only) | 15 |

BOBBY ADENO
| 66 | Vocalion V 9279 | The Hands Of Time/It's A Sad World (DJ copy) | 50 |
| 66 | Vocalion V 9279 | The Hands Of Time/It's A Sad World | 30 |

ADICTS
81	Dining Out TUX 1	LUNCH WITH THE ADICTS (EP, with insert & screen-printed p/s)	50
82	Fall Out FALL 002	Viva La Revolution/Steamroller (p/s)	20
82	Razor RZS 101	Chinese Takeaway/You'll Never Walk Alone (p/s)	7
83	Razor RZS 104	Bad Boy/Shake, Rattle, Bang Your Head (p/s)	10
83	Razor RZLP 104	Bad Boy/Shake, Rattle, Bang Your Head (shaped picture disc)	12
81	Dwed SMT 008	SONGS OF PRAISE (LP)	40
81	Fall Out FALL LP 006	SONGS OF PRAISE (LP, reissue, yellow vinyl, 2,000 only)	20
81	Fall Out FALL LP 006P	SONGS OF PRAISE (LP, reissue, picture disc)	20
82	Razor RAZ 2	SOUND OF MUSIC (LP)	20
85	Razor RAZ15	SMART ALEX (LP)	15
87	Fall Out FALLLP021	THIS IS YOUR LIFE (LP)	18

(see also ADX)

BETH ADLAM WITH BUZZ & BOYS
| 60 | Starlite ST45 024 | Seventeen/I'll Walk Into The Sea | 20 |

LARRY ADLER
| 56 | Columbia SCH 5217 | Rififi/Halaguena | 5 |

PETER ADLER
| 64 | Decca 12394 | I'm Gonna Turn My Life Around/But I Was Cool | 25 |
| 65 | Decca F 12262 | Love And Not Hate/You Especially | 5 |

ADLIBS (U.K.)
| 65 | Fontana TF 584 | Neighbour Neighbour/Lovely Ladies | 50 |

AD-LIBS (U.S.)
66	Red Bird RB 10-102	The Boy From New York City/Kicked Around (DJ Copy)	50
66	Red Bird RB 10-102	The Boy From New York City/Kicked Around	40
69	Deep Soul DS 9102	Giving Up/Appreciation	35
75	Contempo CS 9029	The Boy From New York City/Johnny My Boy	10
79	Inferno HEAT 1	New York In The Dark/The Boy From New York City (p/s, coloured vinyl)	5

ADMIRAL SIR CLOUDESLEY SHOVELL
| 10 | Rise Above RISE 7 123 | Return To Zero/Day After (p/s, 300 only) | 10 |

ADMIRALS
| 65 | Fontana TF 597 | Promised Land/Palisades Park | 25 |
| 75 | Angen ANG 102 | Natty Should Be Free/ANSEL COLLINS: Far East Special | 10 |

ADMIRAL TIBET
86	Redman Intl. RED 4	New Tactics/RED DRAGON: Ease Off (12")	20
86	Rix RIZ 006	Permission/Sixth Commandment Dub/Version (12")	30
80s	Live & Love LLD301	Victim of Babylon/GREGORY PECK: Wah Do You (12")	15

(see also Red Dragon)

ADMIT YOU'RE SHIT
| 86 | Mortarhate MORT 27 | 12 INCHES OF AYS (12" EP) | 10 |
| 81 | Mortarhate MORT 17 | EXPECT NO MERCY (EP) | 25 |

AD NAUSEUM
| 83 | Flicknife FLS 12 | BRAINSTORM (EP, p/s) | 10 |
| 87 | | THE GREATEST SHOW ON EARTH (Mini-LP) | 20 |

A.D. 1984
79	Voyage VOY 005	The Russians Are Coming/New Moon Falling (p/s)	15
80	Grand Prix 001/002	Race To Nowhere/Leisure Crime (with lyric sheet)	15
81	Grand Prix GP 003	The Clockwork Generation/Melody In The Key Of Time (p/s)	10

AD VANCE VS GESCOM
| 98 | Fat Cat 12FAT 009 | Viral/FOEHN: Shrouded/Funeral In Space (12", p/s) | 10 |

ADVENTURERS
| 60 | Capitol CL 15108 | Trail Blazer/Rip Van Winkle | 30 |

ADVENTURES
| 61 | Philips BBL 7548 | CAN'T STOP TWISTIN' (LP) | 30 |

ANTHONY ADVERSE
| 86 | él GPO 13 | Our Fairy Tale/Eine Symphonie Des Grauens (p/s) | 5 |
| 87 | él GPO 29 | Imperial Violets/Fountain (p/s) | 5 |

| 85 | El ACME 11 | RED SHOES (LP) | 20 |

ADVERTISING

| 77 | EMI EMI 2710 | Lipstick/Lonely Guys (p/s) | 5 |
| 77 | EMI EMI 2754 | Stolen Love/Suspender Fun (p/s) | 5 |

(see also Secret Affair, Innocents, Simon Boswell)

ADVERTS

77	Stiff BUY 13	One Chord Wonders/Quickstep (p/s, 1st pressing with push-out centre)	20
77	Stiff BUY 13	One Chord Wonders/Quickstep (p/s, re-pressing with solid centre)	10
77	Anchor ANC 1043	Gary Gilmore's Eyes/Bored Teenagers (p/s)	8
77	Anchor ANC 1047	Safety In Numbers/We Who Wait (p/s)	8
78	Bright BR 1	No Time To Be 21/New Day Dawning (p/s)	7
78	RCA PB 5128	Television's Over/Back From The Dead (p/s)	6
79	RCA 5160	My Place/New Church (p/s)	6
83	Bright BULB 1	Gary Gilmore's Eyes/We Who Wait/New Day Dawning (p/s)	10
78	Bright BRL 201	CROSSING THE RED SEA WITH THE ADVERTS (LP, red vinyl, 5,000 only)	25
78	Bright BULB 1	CROSSING THE RED SEA WITH THE ADVERTS (LP, black vinyl second pressing)	15
79	RCA PL 25246	CAST OF THOUSANDS (LP)	15
81	Butt/Bright ALSO 002	CROSSING THE RED SEA WITH THE ADVERTS (LP, reissue, red vinyl)	15
87	Strange Fruit SFPS 034	PEEL SESSIONS (12", metallic finish)	10

ADVOCATES

| 73 | Dovetail DOVE 1 | ADVOCATES (LP) | 30 |
| 75 | Dovetail DOVE 7 | HERE I REST MY CASE (LP) | 30 |

ADX

| 85 | Sire U 9070 | Falling In Love Again/Come Along (p/s) | 5 |

(see also Adicts)

AERIAL FIX

| 80 | Square SQS 3 | So Hard/It's About Time | 7 |
| 81 | Island WIP 6698 | Take It From Here/Somewhere | 10 |

AEROPHONE

| 71 | RPM 357 | Sweet Sweet Suzie/Of Tomorrow | 15 |

AEROSMITH

73	CBS 1898	Dream On/Somebody	10
76	CBS 4000	Dream On/Somebody (reissue)	5
76	CBS 4452	Last Child/Combination	5
77	CBS 4878	Walk This Way/Uncle Salty	5
77	CBS S AR 2	Draw The Line/Bright, Light, Fright (p/s)	5
78	CBS 6584	Come Together/Kings And Queens	5
80	CBS 8220	Remember (Walking In The Sand)/Bone To Bone (p/s)	5
87	Geffen GEF 29TP	Dude (Looks Like A Lady)/Simoriah/Once Is Enough (12", picture disc)	10
88	Geffen GEF 34TP	Angel/Girl Keeps Coming Apart (12", picture disc)	8
89	Geffen GEF 68P	Janie's Got A Gun/Voodoo Medicine Man (shaped picture disc)	10
90	Geffen GEF 72P	Dude (Looks Like A Lady)/Monkey On My Back (shaped picture disc)	8
97	Columbia 664501-7	Hole In My Soul/Nine Lives (live) (picture disc, card insert)	5
98	Columbia 6664087	I Don't Want To Miss A Thing/Taste Of India (picture disc)	10
01	Columbia 670931-7	Jaded (shaped picture disc)	8
73	CBS 32005	AEROSMITH (LP)	12

(see also Run DMC, Flame)

AEROVONS

| 69 | Parlophone R 5790 | The Train/A Song For Jane | 40 |
| 69 | Parlophone R 5804 | World Of You/Say Georgia | 120 |

A FAIR SET

| 65 | Decca F 12168 | Honey And Wine/Run Around | 18 |

PETER AFENDOULIS

| 78 | Folkland FL 1018 | THERE'S ONLY ONE F IN AFENDOULIS (LP, mail-order only) | 40 |

AFEX

| 67 | King KG 1058 | She Got The Time/I Never Knew Love Was Like This | 140 |

AFFAIRS OF THE HEART

| 83 | Heartbeat PULSE 100 | Waterloo Sunset/Waterloo Version (p/s) | 10 |

AFFINITY

| 70 | Vertigo 6059 007 | I Wonder If I Care As Much/Three Sisters | 35 |
| 70 | Vertigo 6360 004 | AFFINITY (LP, gatefold sleeve, large swirl label) | 300 |

(see also Linda Hoyle, Jeff Beck Group, Queen, Ice)

AFFLICTED

81	Bonk AFF 1	I'm Afflicted/Be Aware (rubber-stamped white labels, p/s, with insert)	70
81	Bonk AFF 1	I'm Afflicted/Be Aware (rubber-stamped white labels, p/s, without insert)	30
82	Bonk AFF 2	All Right Boy/Who Can Tell (with p/s, stamped white labels)	60
82	Bonk AFF 2	All Right Boy/Who Can Tell (without p/s, stamped white labels)	10
82	Bonk AFF 4	One Forty Two/Senseless Whale Stalker (untitled single in stamped striped bag)	20
82	Bonk AFF 3	THE AFFLICTED MAN'S MUSICAL BAG (LP, stamped white label in stamped bag sleeve)	25
82	Bonk AFF 6	HIGH SPEED AND THE AFFLICTED MAN - GET STONED (LP)	12

AFFLICTED MAN

| 80 | Human HUM1 | I'M OFF MI HEAD (LP) | 20 |

AFI

99	Nitro ADELINE 002	A FIRE INSIDE EP (ps, insert)	10
01	Nitro 15843-2	The Days Of The Phoenix/A Winter's Tale/Wester (CD, 500 only)	25
03	Nitro 450 460-2	Girl's Not Grey/The Hanging Garden (p/s, grey vinyl)	8
03	Nitro 450 462-6	The Leaving Song Pt. II/The Great Disappointment (Demo) (p/s, green vinyl)	8
09	DGC/Interscope 2721645/7	Medicate/Carcinogen Crush//Medicate/Ether (2 x 7", stickered sleeves, 1000 only, numbered)	7
10	Polydor 2736938	Beautiful Thieves (1-sided 7", etched B-side, p/s, 500 only)	8
03	Nitro 65522300261	SING THE SORROW (2-LP, red vinyl, inner sleeves)	25
03	Universal	SING THE SORROW (CD, with DVD in black harback book 500 only, sold on tour)	40

AFRICAN
72	Sioux SI 006	Cock Mouth Kill Cock/ERROL T: I Need To Know 15

AFRICAN BEAVERS
65	RCA RCA 1447	Find My Baby/Jungle Fever 25

AFRICAN BROTHER (ACTUALLY MATUMBI)
77	Mainline ML 1	Gimme Gimmie African Love/PURE ROOTS: Dub 15
79	Greensleeves GRED 14	A Di System/Gimme Gimme African Love (12") 12

AFRICAN HEAD CHARGE
81	ON-U LP13	MY LIFE IN A HOLE IN THE GROUND (LP) 20
82	ON-U LP 19	ENVIRONMENTAL STUDIES (LP) 20
83	ON-U LP 27	DRASTIC SEASON (LP) 20
86	On-U ONULP 40	OFF THE BEATEN TRACK (LP) 15

AFRICAN MESSENGERS
64	Page One P04043	Highlife Picadilly/Blues For The Messengers...8

AFRICAN MUSIC MACHINE
72	Mojo 2092 046	Black Water Gold (Pearl)/Making Nassau Fruit Drink 15
73	Contempo CR 13	Tropical/The Girl In France 8
73	Contempo CR 25	Never Name A Baby/Dapp 8
74	Contempo CS 2025	Mr Brown/Camel Time 8

AFRICAN PRINCESS
81	Jah Shaka Shaka 809	Jah Jah Children Cry/Jah Jah Dub (12")..40

AFRICAN STONE
76	K & B	Run Rasta Run/Version 20

AFRIQUE
73	Pye International 7N 25616	Soul Makossa/Hot Mud 8
74	Mainstream MSL 1018	SOUL MAKOSSA (LP) 20

AFRO
71	Punch PH 89	Lonely World/ALTON ELLIS ALL STARS: Put It On 15

AFRO AKINO
74	Afrodesia 1001	Hwe Anna/Maria 10

AFRO DIMENSIONS
72	Ackee 535	Dance With Me/Lonely Nights 15
72	Jay Boy BOY 84	If You Don't Want My Love/Just Because 20

AFRO ENCHANTERS
63	Island WI 071	Peace And Love/Wayward African 30

AFRO FUNK
75	Kabana KAB 1	Obanya Special/Try And Try 15
75	Kabana BSC 01	BODY MUSIC (LP) 50

AFROTONES
69	Trojan TR 655	Things I Love/ERIC FATTER: Since You've Been Gone 20
69	Duke DU 19	Freedom Sound/BOYS: Easy Sound 20
69	High Note HS 023	All For One/BELTONES: Broken Heart 15

(see also Delroy Wilson)

AFTER DARK
81	After Dark AD 001	Evil Woman/Johnny/Lucy (p/s) 35
83	Lazer PROMO 1	Deathbringer/Call Of The Wild (picture disc, promo only) 30
83	Lazer PROMO 1	Deathbringer/Call Of The Wild (white label test pressing) 60

AFTERMATH
87	Moshroom MOSH 2001	DON'T CHEER ME UP (LP) 12

AFTERMATH (U.K.)
81	Red Star AFTERMATH 0001	The Freedom Fighter/All The Others/1980 (p/s)..15

AFTERSHAVE
73	Splendid SPS 401	Warmaker/One Of The Best 150

AFTER TEA
68	Ace Of Clubs SCL-R 1251	AFTER TEA (LP)...50

(see also Ray Fenwick)

AFTER THE FIRE
80	Epic EPC 8394	Love Will Always Make You Cry/Every Mother's Son (p/s, withdrawn) 5
75	Rapid RR 001	SIGNS OF CHANGE (LP, with insert) 25
82	Epic EPC 85135	BATTERIES NOT INCLUDED (LP, withdrawn version with different sleeve) 12

(see also Narnia, Waiting For The Sun)

A FURTHER ROOM
80	Test Pressing Records TP2	Would You Wanna Die For England/Animals 12

AGATHOCLES
90	Deaf DEAF 01	SUPPOSE IT WAS YOU (split LP with DRUDGE)..20

YASUKO AGAWA
86	Blue Bird BRT 26	L.A. Nights/New York Afternoon (12")..15

AGENT ORANGE
92	Dog Tag AO 001	Sounds Flakey To Me (Jungle Mix)/Only You Have The Bass/ Sounds Flakey To Me (Original Mix) (12") 30
93	Dog Tag AO 002	TECNOSKA EP: The Nuttiest Ska/Gettin' Rougher (Ska Mix)/ Gettin' Rougher (Kaos Remix) (12") 20

AGENTS
79	Grapevine GRP 142	Trouble/The Love I Hold 18

AGGRESSORS
70	Pye 17889	Whisky And Soda/Soul Of The Jungle...15
70	Marble Arch 1260	REGGAE STEADIE GO (LP) 12

AGGROVATORS

70	Jackpot JP 751	Sex Machine/You Left Me And Gone (both act. by Dave Barker & Aggrovators)................20
70	Smash SMA 2302	Big Red Ball Parts 1 & 2 (A-side actually "Big Red Bumble" by Lloyd Tyrell; B-side actually "Big Bumble Version" by Lloyd & Devon) 20
71	Smash SMA 2312	One More Bottle Of Beer/Beer Version 10
73	Smash SMA 2339	Straight To Jackson Head/You Are My Angel 12
73	Downtown DT 500	Dreadlocks Man/Rasta Want Peace (both actually by Rasta Twins) 12
76	Grounation GROL 507	RASTA DUB '76 (LP) 40
78	Live & Love LAP 04	JAMMIES IN A LION STYLE DUB (LP) 35
78	Third World TWS 939	KAYA DUB (LP) 30
78	Conflict COLP 2006	RASTA DUB 2000 (LP) 30

(see also Dave Barker, Dennis Alcapone, Jerry Lewis [Jamaica], Delroy Wilson, John Holt, Alton Ellis, Cornell Campbell)

AGGROVATORS AND THE REVOLUTIONARIES

| 77 | Third World TWS 900 | THE AGGROVATORS MEET THE REVOLUTIONARIES AT CHANNEL ONE (LP) ....25 |
| 78 | Burning Sounds BS 1028 | GUERILLA DUB (LP) ....30 |

AGINCOURT

| 70 | Merlin HF 3 | FLY AWAY (LP, with insert) ....900 |

(see also Friends, Ithaca, Alice Through The Looking Glass, Tomorrow Come Someday)

AGNES STRANGE

75	Birdsnest BN 1	Give Yourself A Chance/Clever Fool 12
77	Baal BDN 38048	Can't Make Up My Mind/Johnny B. Goode 10
75	Birdsnest BRL 9000	STRANGE FLAVOUR (LP) 150

AGNOSTIC FRONT

| 85 | Rough Justice JUST 3 | CAUSE FOR ALARM (LP) ....15 |

AGONY BAG

| 80 | Monza MON 2 | Rabies Is A Killer/Never Never Never (p/s) ....10 |

(see also Pesky Gee, Black Widow)

AGONY COLUMN

| 79 | Tyger TYG 2 | I Had It All Worked Out/Good Grief (p/s) ....10 |

AGORA

| 94 | Z Records ZEDD 010 | LATIN CONNECTION EP (12") ....10 |

AGROS

| 71 | Punch PH 56 | What Do You Fall In Love For/SLICKERS: Too Much ....20 |
| 70 | Pye 17889 | Whisky & Soda/Soul Of The Jungle ....15 |

CHRISTINA AGUILERA

| 06 | RCA 82876 82639 | BACK TO BASICS (3-LP, numbered) ....70 |

A GUY CALLED GERALD

88	Rham RX 8804	Voodoo Ray/Escape/Rhapsody In Acid/Blow Your House Down (12", p/s) 25
90	Columbia XPR 1535	Emotions Electric (Frankie Foncett Remix 1)/Emotions Electric (Frankie Foncett Remix 2)(12", promo in stickered plain sleeve) 15
92	Juice Box JBOX 001	Digital Bad Boy/Let It Move You/A Storm Is Coming/Could You Understand? (12", tracks 1and 4 vocals by MC Tunes) 12
92	Juice Box JBOX 003	Cops/The Trak/28 Gun Bad Boy/Paranoia (12") 40
92	Juice Box JBOX 004	Ses Makes You Wise/Sunshine/King Of The Jungle/Boase up (12") 15
92	Juice Box JBOX 005	The Musical Magical Midi Machine/Let It Go/Like A Drug/Free Africa (12") 15
92	Columbia XPR 1684	Cops/The Track/Paranoia/28 Gun Bad Boy (12" white label promo) 40
93	Juice Box JBOX 009	Too Fucked To Dance/Darker Than I Should Be/Anything v2.1/Is The Right Time (12") 12
93	Juice Box JBOX 014	The Glok Track/Gerald's Bassline/Ease The Pressure/Take Me (12") 12
94	Juice Box JBOX 019	Darker Than I Should Be (Ladies mix)/Gloc (Remix) (12") 12

A-HA

84	Warner Bros W 9146	Take On Me/And You Tell Me (silver/blue p/s) 40
84	Warner Bros W 9146T	Take On Me (Extended)/And You Tell Me/Stop And Make Your Mind Up (12", silver/blue p/s, with poster & stickers) 100
84	Warner Bros W 9146T	Take On Me (Extended)/And You Tell Me/Stop And Make Your Mind Up (12", silver/blue p/s, without poster & stickers) 50
85	Warner Bros W 9006T	Take On Me/Love Is The Reason (12", black & white p/s) 10
85	Warner Bros W 9006	Take On Me/Love Is The Reason (reissue, colour p/s with gatefold booklet)............5
86	Warner Bros W 8736P	Train Of Thought (Remix)/And You Tell Me (train-shaped picture disc) 8
86	Warner Bros W 8663TP	Hunting High And Low (Extended)/Hunting High And Low (Remix)/ The Blue Sky (Demo) (12", picture disc) 10
86	Warner Bros W 8500TP	Cry Wolf (Extended)/Cry Wolf (7" Version)/Maybe Maybe (12", picture disc)..................10
87	Warner Bros W 8405TP	Manhattan Skyline (Extended Remix)/Manhattan Skyline (LP Version)/ We're Looking For The Whales (12", picture disc)..8
87	Warner Bros W 8305TP	The Living Daylights (Extended)/(7" Remix)/(Instrumental) (12", picture disc) 10
88	Warner Bros W 7936TP	Stay On These Roads (Extended Remix)/Soft Rains Of April (Original Mix) (12", picture disc) 8
88	Warner Bros W 7840TP	The Blood That Moves The Body (Extended)/The Blood That Moves The Body (LP Version)/There's Never A Forever Thing (12", picture disc)..................................10
88	Warner Bros. W7749W	Touchy!/Hurry Home ('felt' p/s) 20
88	Warner Bros W 7636TP	You're The One (12" Remix)/You're The One (Instrumental)/ Out Of The Blue Comes Green (12", picture disc) 8
91	Warner Bros. W001213	Early Morning/East Of The Sun (7" box set with 3 postcards) 8

(see also Phenomena)

AHAB

| 82 | Chicken Jazz JAZZ 5 | Party Girl/Don't Give Up On Us (p/s)..5 |

(see also Another Pretty Face, Waterboys)

AHAB & WAILERS

| 63 | Pye 7N 15553 | Cleopatra's Needle/Neb's Tune ....15 |

A HEADS

| 82 | TW Records HIT 107 | Dying Man/Hell Cell/Changing Places (p/s) ....12 |
| 82 | Bluurg FISH 03 | Forgotten Hero ....8 |

AIKEN'S DRUM

| 81 | Private Pressing SRTX/CUS 1134 | AIKEN'S DRUM (LP) ....40 |

AIL SYMUDIAD

80	Sain 765	Ad Drefnu/Whisgi A Soda (p/s)	10
81	Fflach RF 001	Twristiaid Yn Y Dre/Modur Sanctaiddy/Hyfyed Bingo (500 only, first 100 in dayglo sleeve)	10
81	Fflach RF AS 002	Geiriau/Annwyl Rhywun/Cura Dy Law (p/s)	10
81	Fflach RF AS 003	Garej Paradwys/Ffarwel L'e Fyddin (p/s)	10
82	Fflach 4	Lleisau O'r Gorffennol/Dilyn Y Sebon (p/s)	10
82	Fflach RF AS 005	Edrych Trwy Y Camerau/ANGYLION STANLI: Emyn Roc A Roi (split single, p/s)	10

AIM (1)

94	Detour DR 018	Call Your Name/Out On The Streets (p/s,1,000 only, 100 on blue vinyl)	8
94	Detour DR 018	Call Your Name/Out On The Streets (p/s,1,000 only, black vinyl)	6

AIM (2)

99	Grand Central GCLP 105	COLD WATER MUSIC (2-LP)	20

AIR (1)

71	Atlantic 2400 148	AIR (LP)	20

AIR (2)

98	Source V 2848	MOON SAFARI (LP)	15
07	EMI V 3032	POCKET SYMPHONY (LP, white vinyl)	12

AIRBORNE

83	Clubland SJP 844	Burn In Hell/Lord Satan/Temple Of Metal (p/s)	12

AIRCRAFT

80	Square SQS 3	Move In Rhythm/Pumping iron	20

DEBRAH AIRE

67	Polydor 56180	This Land Is Mine/What The World Needs Now Is Love	40

(see also Sharon Tandy)

AIRHEAD

92	Korova 9030 74679 2	BOING! (LP)	20

AIRKRAFT

79	Lathe TSR1	Here Comes That Sound/Video Romance/White Boys (EP)	12

AIRMAIL

79	Graffiti GIT 001	No Human Feeling/In A Moment	8

AIRSHIP

79	Decca FR 13856	Get Out, Take Your Mother With You/Gimme A Can Of Spray Paint	40

AIR SUPPLY

80	Arista ARIST 362	All Out Of Love/Old Habits Die Hard	5

AIRTO

71	Buddah 2318 040	SEEDS ON THE GROUND - THE NATURAL SOUNDS OF AIRTO (LP, gatefold)	20
73	CTI CTI 18	FINGERS (LP)	18
74	CTI CTI 21	IN CONCERT (LP, with Deodato)	15
74	CTI CTI 23	VIRGIN LAND (LP)	15

(see also Deodato)

AIR TRAFFIC CONTROL

77	Epic S EPS 5667	Gotta Get A Message Back To You/Move On Up	8

AISHA

86	Ariwa ARI 060	Prophecy/Dub (12")	20
94	Ariwa ARI 153	Only Jah Works/Crisis (12")	15

AITCH

71	Decca F13150	Let It Be Me/Let Me Say This	6

BOBBY AITKEN (& CARIBBEATS)

62	Island WI 028	Baby Baby (actually with Patsy)/Lonely Boy	18
62	Blue Beat BB 93	Never Never (South Virginia)/Isabella (as Bobby Aitken & Buster's Group)	18
63	Blue Beat BB 146	Don't Leave Me/Mom And Dad (as Bobby Aitken & Tinse)	18
63	Rio R 14	I've Told You/Please Go Back	18
63	Rio R 15	It Takes A Friend/LAUREL AITKEN: Sunshine	18
64	Rio R 34	Rolling Stone/LESTER STERLING'S GROUP: Man About Town	40
64	Rio R 40	Garden Of Eden/Whiplash	20
64	Rio R 50	Little Girl/Together	10
65	Rio R 52	Rain Came Tumbling Down/SHENLEY & LUNAN: Something Is On Your Mind	15
65	Rio R 64	Mr Judge/BINZ: Times Have Changed	18
65	Black Swan WI 441	Jerico/LESTER STERLING: Lunch Time	25
66	Ska Beat JB 252	Thunderball/ORIGINATORS: Chelip Chelip	200
67	Doctor Bird DB 1071	Keep On Pushing/You Won't Regret It	30
67	Doctor Bird DB 1072	Let Them Have A Home/Temptation (with Caribbeats)	30
67	Doctor Bird DB 1077	Sweets For My Sweet/How Sweet It Is (with Caribbeats)	50
67	Island WI 3028	Kiss Bam Bam/CYNTHIA RICHARDS: How Could I	70
67	Giant GN 11	What A Fool/Curfew (with Caribbeats)	50

(see also Caribbeats, Laurel Aitken, Frank Cosmo, Lloyd & Glen)

LAUREL AITKEN (& BLUE BEATS)

59	Kalypso XX 15	Sweet Chariot/Nebuchnezer	30
59	Kalypso XX 16	Aitken's Boogie/Cherrie	30
60	Kalypso XX 19	Baba Kill Me Goat/Tribute To Collie Smith	20
60	Starlite ST45 011	Boogie In My Bones/Little Sheila	40
60	Starlite ST45 014	Honey Girl (with Caribs)/Drinkin' Whisky (with Bluebeats)	40
60	Melodisc M 1570	Mary Lee/Lonesome Lover (with Bluebeats)	30
60	Blue Beat B 1	Boogie Rock/Heavenly Angel (with the BOOGIE CATS) (white label)	50
60	Blue Beat BB 1	Boogie Rock/Heavenly Angel (with the BOOGIE CATS) (blue label)	30
60	Blue Beat BB 10	Jeannie Is Back/If It's Money You Need	30
60	Blue Beat BB 14	Judgment Day/Yea Yea Baby	15
60	Blue Beat BB 22	Railroad Track/Tell Me Darling (with the Blue Beats)	20
60	Blue Beat BB 25	More Whisky/LLOYD CLARKE: Parapinto Boogie	20
61	Starlite ST45 034	Love Me Baby/Stars Were Made	30

Laurel AITKEN (& BLUE BEATS)

61	Blue Beat BB 40	Bartender/Mash Potato Boogie	20
61	Blue Beat BB 52	Bouncing Woman/Nursery Rhyme Boogie (with Blue Beats)	30
61	Blue Beat BB 70	Mighty Redeemer/Please Don't Leave Me	15
62	Blue Beat BB 84	Brother David/Back To New Orleans (with Blue Beats)	15
62	Blue Beat BB 109	Lucille/I Love You More Everyday	15
62	Blue Beat BB 120	Sixty Days And Sixty Nights/Going To Kansas City (with Les Dawson Trio)	40
62	Blue Beat BB 142	Jenny Jenny/Weary Wanderer (with Bandits and Ruddy & Sketto)	20
62	Dice CC 1	Mabel/You Got Me Rocking (with Hyacinth)	25
63	Dice CC 13	Sweet Jamaica/Bossa Nova Hop	25
63	Blue Beat BB 164	Zion/Swing Low Sweet Chariot	25
63	Blue Beat BB 194	Little Girl/Daniel Saw The Stone (with Ruddy and Sketto)	20
63	Duke DK 1002	Low Down Dirty Girl/Pink Lane Shuffle	30
63	Island WI 092	I Shall Remove/We Got To Move	40
63	Island WI 095	What A Weeping/Zion City Wall	25
63	Island WI 099	In My Soul/One More River To Cross	40
63	Rio R 11	Adam & Eve/BOBBY AITKEN: Devil Woman	20
63	Rio R 12	Mary/Hometown	20
63	Rio R 13	Bad Minded Woman/Life	20
63	Rio R 17	Devil Or Angel/Fire	20
63	Rio R 18	Freedom Train/Peace Perfect Peace	20
64	Rio R 35	Rock Of Ages/The Mule	20
64	Rio R 36	Leave Me Standing/Bagaboo (Bug-A-Boo)	20
64	Rio R 37	John Saw Them Coming/Jericho	20
64	R&B JB 167	Yes Indeed/You Can't Stop Me From Loving You	20
64	R&B JB 170	Pick Up Your Bundle And Go/Let My People Go	20
64	R&B JB 171	Bachelor Life/You Was Up	20
64	Columbia DB 7280	Be Mine/Don't Stay Out Late	15
64	Blue Beat BB 249	This Great Day/I May Never See My Baby	25
64	J.N.A.C. 1	West Indian Cricket Test/3 Cheers For Worrell	25
64	Black Swan WI 401	Lion Of Judah/Remember My Darling (B-side with Cynthia Richards)	40
64	Black Swan WI 411	The Saint/Go Gal Go	40
64	Dice CC 28	Jamaica/I Don't Want No More	25
65	Dice CC 31	We Shall Overcome/You Left Me Standing	25
65	Rio R 53	Mary Don't You Weep/I Believe	20
65	Rio R 54	Mary Lou/Jump And Shout	20
65	Rio R 56	One More Time/Ring Don't Mean A Thing	20
65	Rio R 60	Come And Let Us Go/Lonely Nights	25
65	Rio R 65	Let's Be Lovers/I Need You	25
65	Venus VE 4	How Can I Forget You?/Weeping And Crying	10
65	Island WI 198	Boogie In My Bones/Little Sheila	25
65	Island WI 252	How Can I Forget You/Weeping And Crying (white label, existence unconfirmed)	0
66	Blue Beat BB 340	Clementine/Bongo Jerk	30
66	Blue Beat BB 369	Shame And Scandal/Coconut Woman	30
66	Ska Beat JB 232	Jamboree/Looking For My Baby	40
66	Ska Beat JB 236	Propaganda/Shake	35
66	Ska Beat JB 239	Green Banana/Darling	35
66	Rio R 91	How Can I Forget You/I've Been Weeping And Crying	15
66	Rio R 92	Baby Don't Do It/That Girl	15
66	Rio R 97	We Shall Overcome/Street Of Glory	15
66	Rio R 99	Clap Your Hands/Revival	15
66	Rainbow RAI 101	Don't Break Your Promises/Last Night (with Soulmen)	40
66	Rainbow RAI 106	Voodoo Woman/Bewildered And Blue (B-side with Carols)	40
67	Rainbow RAI 111	Sweet Precious Love/I Want To Love You Forever (with Carols)	40
67	Columbia Blue Beat DB 102	Rock Steady/Blowin' In The Wind	30
67	Columbia Blue Beat DB 106	I'm Still In Love With You Girl/Blue Rhythm	30
67	Fab FAB 5	Never You Hurt/I Need You (as Laurel Aitken & Soulmen)	50
68	Fab FAB 45	For Sentimental Reasons/Last Waltz (as Laurel Aitken & Rainbows)	30
68	Doctor Bird DB 1160	Mr Lee/Birmingham Girl	30
68	Doctor Bird DB 1161	La La La (Means I Love You)/DETOURS: Sunnyside	25
69	Ackee ACK 105	Skinheads Are Wrecking The Town (white label only, unissued)	250
69	Doctor Bird DB 1187	Fire In Your Wire/Quando Quando	30
69	Doctor Bird DB 1190	Rice And Peas/CLASSICS: Worried Over Me	40
69	Doctor Bird DB 1196	Reggae Prayer/Deliverance Will Come	40
69	Doctor Bird/J.J. DB 1197	The Rise And Fall (Of Laurel)/If You're Not Black	40
69	Doctor Bird DB 1202	Haile Haile (The Lion)/SEVEN LETTERS: Call Collect	50
69	Doctor Bird DB 1203	Carolina/Kingston Town	40
69	Junior JR 105	Think Me No Know/RECO: Trombone Man	30
69	Nu Beat NB 024	Woppi King/Mr Soul	25
69	Nu Beat NB 025	Suffering Still (with Girlie)/Reggae '69	25
69	Nu Beat NB 032	Haile Selassie/Blues Dance	25
69	Nu Beat NB 033	Lawd Doctor (with Girlie)/Big Fight In Hell Stadium	25
69	Nu Beat NB 035	Run Powell Run/RICO RODRIGUEZ: A Message To You	30
69	Nu Beat NB 039	Save The Last Dance/Walk Right Back	20
69	Nu Beat NB 040	Don't Be Cruel/John B.	20
69	Nu Beat NB 043	Shoo Be Doo/Babylon Gone	20
69	Nu Beat NB 044	Landlords And Tenants/Everybody Sufferin'	20
69	Nu Beat NB 045	Jesse James/Freedom	20
69	Nu Beat NB 046	Pussy Price Gone Up/Gimme Back Me Dollar	20
69	Junior JR 106	River Nile (existence unconfirmed, white labels only)	40
69	Nu Beat NB 047	Skinhead Train/GRUVY BEATS: Kent People	65
70	Nu Beat NB 048	Skinhead Invasion/Benwood Dick (unissued, blank white label demos only)	125
70	Nu Beat NB 048	Mr Popcorn/GRUVY BEATS: Share Your Popcorn	18
70	Nu Beat NB 049	I've Got Your Love/GRUVY BEATS: Blue Mink	15
70	Nu Beat NB 050	Scandal In Brixton Market/Soul Grinder (both sides with Girlie)	20
70	New Beat NB 054	Nobody But Me/Baby Please Don't Go	12
70	New Beat NB 056	I'll Never Love Any Girl/The Best I Can	12
70	New Beat NB 057	Reggae Popcorn/Take Me Back	20
70	New Beat NB 063	Baby I Need Your Loving/Think It Over	20
70	New Beat NB 065	Sex Machine/Since You Left	20
70	New Beat NB 072	Pachanga/Version	20
70	Ackee ACK 104	Pussy Got Thirteen Life/Single Man	25

70	Ackee ACK 106	Sin Pon You/Everynight	80
70	Bamboo BAM 16	Moon Rock/Cut Up Munno (apparantly, white labels only)	80
70	Pama PM 818	Mary's Boy Child/RUPIE EDWARDS ALLSTARS: Version	12
70	Pama Supreme PS 300	Why Can't I Touch You/Can't Turn Your Back On Me	12
71	Trojan TR 7826	It's Too Late/AITKEN'S BAND: Slow Rock	10
71	New Beat NB 078	True Love/The Best I Can	6
71	New Beat NB 089	I Can't Stop Loving You/El Paso	6
71	Black Swan BW 1408	If It's Hell Below/Just A Little Bit Of Love	40
71	Big Shot BI 595	Dancing With My Baby/Do The Boogaloo	20
72	Big Shot BI 605	Take Me In Your Arms/Two-Timing Woman	8
72	Camel CA 90	Africa Arise/GI GINGRI: Holy Mount Zion	12
72	Columbia DB 8914	Pretty Face In The Market Place/Come Back To My Lonely World	6
75	Camel CA 2007	La Vien En Rose/Spanish Eyes	8
75	Punch PU 121	Fattie Bum Bum/Fattie Bum Bum	5
80	I-Spy SEE 4	Big Fat Man/It's Too Late (as Laurel Aitken & Unitone)	5
80	I-Spy SEE 6	Rudi Got Married/Honey Come Back To Me	5
66	Rio LR 1	SKA WITH LAUREL (LP)	200
67	Doctor Bird DLM 5012	SAYS FIRE (LP)	120
69	Pama PSP 1012	THE HIGH PRIEST OF REGGAE (LP)	100
69	Pama ECO 8	SCANDAL IN BRIXTON MARKET (LP, with Girlie)	100
69	J.J.	RISE AND FALL (LP)	120
73	Count Shelly CSLP1	MORIA SOPHIA (LP)	40

(see also Laurel & Owen, Girlie, King Horror, Lorenzo, Ruts, Bobby Aitken, Classics, Beresford Ricketts, Duke Reid, Tommy McCook)

A-JAES

| 64 | Oak RGJ 132 | I'm Leaving You/Kansas City | 1000 |

AKA & CHARLATANS

| 78 | Vanity VANE 1 | Heroes Are Losers/Lady Of The Night/Perhaps One Day (12", various screen-printed die-cut p/s) | 12 |

AKAPEL

| 92 | Phlange AK001 | Pick It Up (vocal)/(Instrumental)/Stick Your Big Dinky In/Background Beats/Let Me Hear You Say/Keep On/They Won't Believe Me (12") | 12 |

JEWEL AKENS

65	London HLN 9954	The Birds And The Bees/Tic Tac Toe	6
65	London HLN 9969	Georgie Porgie/Around The Corner	7
66	Ember EMB S 219	Dancin' Jenny/A Wee Bit More of Your Lovin'	15
65	London HA-N 8234	THE BIRDS AND THE BEES (LP)	25

AKERCOCKE

| 05 | Earache 7MOSH 322 | Eyes Of The Dawn (Demo)/The Fulcrum (transluscent red vinyl, no p/s) | 15 |

AK 47

| 81 | Output ORR 202 | Stop! Dance!/Autobiography/Hilversum-Ao (p/s) | 10 |
| 91 | Rugger Bugger SEEP 004 | DON'T CALL ME VANILLA (LP) | 12 |

(see also AK Process, File Under Pop)

TOSHIKO AKIYOSHI

| 58 | Columbia 33CX 101101 | NEWPORT JAZZ FESTIVAL 1957 (LP) | 15 |

JAN AKKERMAN

73	Harvest HAR 5069	Blue Boy/Minstrel-Farmers Dance	6
73	Harvest SHSP 4026	PROFILE (LP)	20
73	Atlantic K40522	TABERNAKEL (LP, gatefold)	15

(see also Hunters [Holland], Brainbox, Focus)

AK PROCESS

| 79 | Output OPR 101 | Electronic Music: After All Love/Post Town (p/s, white labels) | 6 |

(see also AK 47)

AKRYLYKZ

80	Double R RED 2	Spyderman/Smart Boy (p/s)	6
80	Polydor POSP 128	Spyderman/Smart Boy (reissue, p/s)	5
80	Polydor 2059 253	J.D./Ska'd For Life (p/s)	5

AL ET ALL

| 80 | Arny's Shack As 047 | STRANGE AFFAIR (LP) | 200 |

AL & VIBRATORS

67	Doctor Bird DB 1085	Move Up/Lone Lover	20
69	High Note HS 005	Check Up/I'll Come Back	20
69	High Note HS 007	Move Up Calypso/PATSY: Fire In Your Wire	20

(see also Vibrators, Patsy Todd, Lord Power)

STEVE ALAIMO

62	Pye International 7N 25161	My Friends/Going Back To Marty	5
63	Pye International 7N 25174	Every Day I Have To Cry/(Please Take A Chance On Me) Little Girl (DJ Copy)	50
63	Pye International 7N 25174	Every Day I Have To Cry/(Please Take A Chance On Me) Little Girl	30
63	Pye International 7N 25199	It's A Long Long Way To Happiness/A Lifetime Of Loneliness	6
66	HMV POP 1531	So Much Love/Truer Than True (DJ Copy)	30
66	HMV POP 1531	So Much Love/Truer Than True	20
68	Atlantic 588 227	Watching The Trains Go By/Thank You For The Sunshine Days	10

ALARM

81	White Cross W 3/4	Unsafe Buildings/Up For Murder (gatefold p/s)	25
82	Illegal ILS 0032	Marching On/Across The Border/Lie Of The Land (p/s)	5
83	I.R.S. PFPC 1023	68 Guns Parts 1 & 2 (p/s, with free cassette: The Stand/Across The Border/Marching On/Lie Of The Land/For Freedom" (all live) [CS 70504])	5
84	I.R.S. IRS 103	The Deceiver/Reason 41 (p/s, clear vinyl)	5
84	I.R.S. IRS 103	The Deceiver/Reason 41 (p/s, mispress on mustard vinyl)	45
84	I.R.S. IRSD 103/103A	The Deceiver/Reason 41//Lie Of The Land/Legal Matter (double pack, g/fold p/s)	5

(see also Seventeen)

ALASKA

| 82 | Kingdom KV 8025 | Bailando/Red Rum | 5 |

ALBA
77	Rubber RUB 021	ALBA (LP)	12

DAMON ALBARN
03	Honest Johns HJP10	DEMOCRAZY (2x10" white vinyl, picture disc, 5,000 only)	12

(see also Blur, Gorillaz, Monkey, GB & TQ)

ALBATROSS
74	Mooncrest Moon 29	Rock 'N' Roll Boogie Man/Witchy Witchy Lady	5
74	Mooncrest Moon 28	Anything I Want To/Bournemouth Rock	6
75	Gull GULS. 16	Tobacco Road/Let It Roll	5

Prices fine

BILLY ALBERT "THE KID"
56	Vogue Coral Q 72214	Black Jack/The Golden Touch	5

EDDIE ALBERT
55	London HL 8136	I'm In Favour Of Friendship/Come Pretty Little Girl	15
56	London HLU 8241	Little Child (Daddy Dear) (with Sondra Lee)/Jenny Kissed Me	15

MEL ALBERT
59	Top Rank JAR 178	Sugar Plum/Never Let Me Go	10

ALBERT EMBANKMENT
71	Decca F23152	As Tears Go By/Cover Me	5

ALBERTO & RICARDO
64	RCA RCA 1376	Love's Made A Fool Of You/I'll Do It To You	6

ALBERTO Y LOST TRIOS PARANOIAS
76	Big T BIG 541	Dread Jaws/De Version	6
77	Stiff LAST 2	SNUFF ROCK EP (12" promo, only 50 pressed)	200
78	Logo GO(D) 323	Heads Down No Nonsense Mindless Boogie/Thank You Fuck You/Dead Meat (double pack, gatefold p/s)	5
78	Logo GO 340	Juan Lopez (The Lonely Goatherd)/Teenage Paradise/Dead Meat Part III	6
76	Transatlantic TRA 316	ALBERTO Y LOST TRIOS PARANOIAS (LP, with insert)	12
77	Transatlantic TRA 349	ITALIANS FROM OUTER SPACE (LP)	12
78	Logo LOGO 1009	SKITE (LP)	12
80	Logo MOGO 4008	THE WORST OF THE BERTS (LP)	12

(see also Mothmen, Charlie Parkas)

ALBIANS
79	K & K 003	Princess/Princess Dub (12", with Ranking Neville)	12
80	K & K KK 0012	Who Is Going To Love Me/VIN GORDON: Who Is Going To Rock Me Tonight (12")	20

(See also N. McCoy & Albians)

ALBINO GORILLA
71	Ember EMBS321	Shake Me, Wake Me/Going To A Go Go	6

ALBION BAND
76	Harvest HAR 5113	Hopping Down In Kent/Merry Sherwood Rangers (as Albion Dance Band)	5
77	Harvest HAR 5128	The Postman's Knock/La Sexte Estample Real (as Albion Dance Band)	5
78	Harvest HAR 5156	Poor Old Horse/Ragged Heroes (p/s)	5
79	Harvest HAR 5175	Pain And Paradise/Lay Me Low (p/s)	5
73	Island HELP 25	BATTLE OF THE FIELD (LP, as Albion Country Band)	20
77	Harvest SHSP 4059	THE PROSPECT BEFORE US (LP, as Albion Dance Band)	12
78	Harvest SHSP 4092	RISE UP LIKE THE SUN (LP, textured sleeve)	15

(see also Shirley Collins, Fairport Convention, Keith Dewhurst & Albion Band)

MICHAEL ALBUQUERQUE
69	United Artists UP 35037	Better Men Than Me/Burn Burn Burn	10
70	United Artists UP 35098	Roll Him Over/Blind Man	8

(see also Michael D'Albuquerque, E.L.O.)

DENNIS ALCAPONE
70	Explosion EX 2039	Revelation Version/Marka Version	15
70	Supreme SUP 214	You Must Believe Me (with Niney)/RUPIE EDWARDS ALLSTARS: Funk The Funk	12
70	Big Shot BI 565	Shades Of Hudson/Spanish Amigo	30
71	Treasure Isle TI 7069	The Great Woggie/TOMMY McCOOK & SUPERSONICS: Buttercup Version	20
71	Banana BA 328	Duppy Serenade (as Innkeeper)/Sunshine Version	18
71	Banana BA 341	(Love Me) Forever Version/I Don't Want To See You Cry	25
71	Upsetter US 373	Well Dread/UPSETTERS: Dread Version	12
71	Upsetter US 377	Alpha And Omega/JUNIOR BYLES: Beat Down Babylon	15
71	Duke DU 125	Medley Version/Version Two	8
71	Prince Buster PB 8	Sons Of Zion/ANSELL COLLINS: Short Circuit	12
71	Prince Buster PB 12	Let It Roll (with Max Romeo)/ANSELL COLLINS: Clear Blue	15
71	Jackpot JP 773	Jumping Jack (with John Holt)/AGGROVATORS: King Of The Track	8
71	Jackpot JP 775	Togetherness (Black & White) (with John Holt)/DELROY WILSON: Live Good	8
71	Jackpot JP 776	Tell It Like It Is/DELROY WILSON : Come Along	8
71	Dynamic DYN 421	Horse And Buggy/ROLAND ALPHONSO & DENZIL LAING: Buggy And Horse	12
71	Dynamic DYN 422	Ripe Cherry/INNER CIRCLE: Red Cherry	10
71	Dynamic DYN 427	Alcapones Guns Don't Bark/Alcapones Guns Don't Bark Version	15
71	Camel CA 74	This A Butter/PHIL PRATT ALLSTARS: Version	12
71	Tropical AL 003	False Prophet/MAX ROMEO: Rude Medley	12
72	Tropical AL 019	Worldwide Love (with Twinkle Brothers)/CARL MASTERS: Gable Up	12
72	Ackee ACK 146	Power Version/BLUESBLASTERS: Martie (B-side actually titled "Margie")	18
72	Prince Buster PB 24	Giant/PRINCE BUSTER: Science	20
72	Upsetter US 381	Wonderman (with Dave Barker, actually by Dave Barker)/ Place Called Africa (with Dave Barker & Junior Byles)	20
72	Upsetter US 388	Master Key/UPSETTERS: Keyhole	20
72	Grape GR 3035	Rasta Dub/UPSETTERS: Rasta Version	20
72	Attack ATT 8027	Fine Style/WINSTON SCOTLAND: On The Track	15
72	Duke DU 131	The Sky's The Limit/HUDSON'S ALLSTARS: Limit Version	12
72	Duke DU 147	Get In The Groove (with Dennis Brown)/DYNAMITES: Version	12
72	Techniques TE 918	Look Into Yourself/TECHNIQUES ALLSTARS: Yourself Version	15
72	Green Door GD 4041	Rub Up A Daughter/TONY'S ALLSTARS: Daughter Version	15
72	Bullet BU 509	Dub Up A Daughter/PRINCE TONY ALL STARS: Version	15

73	Prince Buster PB51	Kings And Castles/Version	10
73	Downtown DT 508	You Don't Say/TONY'S ALLSTARS: Version	10
73	Treasure Isle TI 7074	Wake Up Jamaica/Version (with Tommy McCook)	18
73	Jackpot JP 808	Cassius Clay/SLIM SMITH: Love And Affection	18
73	Bread BR 1121	Musical Liquidator/Lorna Banana (B-side with Prince Jazzbo)	15
73	G.G. GG 4538	Musical Alphabet/BUCKLEY ALLSTARS: Things Gonna Change (B-side actually by Maytones)	12
73	Pyramid PYR 7008	Belch It Off/Jack Horner	8
74	Harry J HJ 6666	Sorry Harry/Party Time	8
76	Ethnic Fight EF 001	Pressure In A Babylon/ETHNIC FIGHT BAND: Pressure Dub	6
71	Trojan TBL 187	GUNS DON'T ARGUE (LP)	25
73	Magnet MGT 001	KING OF THE TRACK (LP)	30
74	Attack ATLP 1005	BELCH IT OFF (LP)	15
75	Live And Love LALP 104	DREAD CAPONE (LP)	30
77	Third World TWS 801	SIX MILLION DOLLAR MAN (LP)	15
77	Third World TWS 911	INVESTIGATOR ROCK (LP)	15

(see also El Paso, Dennis & Lizzy, Mad Roy, D. Smith, Wailing Souls, Innkeepers, GG Allstars, Stranger Cole, Lizzy & Dennis, Lee)

CRAIG ALDEN
60	London HLW 9224	Crazy Little Horn/Goggle-Eye'd	56

STEVE ALDO (& CHALLENGERS)
64	Decca F 12041	Can I Get A Witness/Baby What You Want Me To Do (with Challengers)	45
66	Parlophone R 5432	Everybody Has To Cry/You're Absolutely Right (solo)	200
66	Parlophone R 5432	Everybody Has To Cry/You're Absolutely Right (solo) (DJ Copy)	150

RONNIE ALDRICH
54	Decca F 10248	Coach Call Boogie/Donegal Cradle Song	10
54	Decca F 10274	Wolf On The Prowl/Mudhopper	10
55	Decca F 10494	Ko Ko Mo (I Love You So)/Rock Love (with Squads)	10
55	Decca F 10544	Rock Candy/Boom, Boom Boomerang (with Squads)	12
55	Decca F 10564	Rhythm 'N Blues/Where Ya Gone, Baby? (with Squads)	12
57	Columbia DB 3882	Right Now, Right Now/Rock And Roll Boogie (with Squadronaires)	12
57	Columbia DB 3945	Crazy Bear/The Big Band Beat (with Squadronaires)	8
69	Decca F 12909	Ride My See-Saw/Romance On The North Sea (with London Festival Orch.)	5

(see also Squadronaires, Joan Regan)

URIE ALDRIDGE
71	Harry J. HJ 6634	Set Me Free/LLOYD WILLIS: Free Version	8

(see also John Holt)

ALEANNA
78	Inchecronin INC 7421	ALEANNA (LP)	40

ALEEM
84	Streetwave MKHAN 26	Release Yourself/Dub (12")	20
84	Streetwave MKHAN 61	Get Loose/Release Yourself (12")	15

AKI ALEONG (& HIS LICORICE TWISTERS)
61	Reprise R 20021	Trade Winds, Trade Winds/Without Your Love	5
61	Reprise R 20042	Moon River (Twist)/Tonight (Twist)	6
61	Reprise R 6011	TWISTIN' THE HITS (LP)	12

ALETHIANS
73	Myrrh Gold MYR 1002	R.S.V.P. (LP)	40
70s	Myrrh Gold MST 6506	ONE WAY (LP)	30

ARTHUR ALEXANDER
62	London HLD 9523	You Better Move On/A Shot Of Rhythm And Blues	40
63	London HLD 9566	Where Have You Been/Soldier Of Love	30
63	London HLD 9641	Anna/I Hang My Head And Cry	30
63	London HLD 9667	Go Home Girl/You're The Reason	35
64	London HLD 9899	Black Night/Ole John Amos	35
66	London HLU 10023	(Baby) For You/The Other Woman	30
76	Buddah BDS 439	Everyday I Have To Cry/Everybody Needs Somebody To Love	20
63	London RE-D 1364	ALEXANDER THE GREAT (EP)	90
63	London RE-D 1401	ARTHUR ALEXANDER (EP)	100
62	London HA-D 2457	YOU BETTER MOVE ON (LP)	150

DAVID ALEXANDER
74	Rare Earth RES112	Love, Love, Love/Missy	6

GOLDIE ALEXANDER
81	Project PRJ 1	Show You My Love/Get Back	5

JEFF ALEXANDER & HIS ORCHESTRA
58	London HA-P 2130	ALFRED HITCHCOCK PRESENTS - MUSIC TO BE MURDERED BY (LP, mono)	20
58	London SH-P 6012	ALFRED HITCHCOCK PRESENTS - MUSIC TO BE MURDERED BY (LP, stereo)	40

LLOYD ALEXANDER REAL ESTATE
68	President PT 157	Gonna Live Again/Watcha Gonna Do	80

LUCIEN ALEXANDER
67	Polydor 56205	Baby, You've Been On My Mind/Play Along (Miss R)	20

TEXAS ALEXANDER
61	Fontana 467 136TE	TREASURES OF NORTH AMERICAN NEGRO MUSIC VOLUME 7 (EP)	10

ALEXISONFIRE
04	Sorepoint	Counterparts And Number Them/THE BLED: Ruth Buzzi Better Watch Her Back (die-cut sleeve, purple vinyl)	10
05	Sorepoint SORE 0398	Accidents/No Transitory (p/s, green vinyl)	8

ALFI & HARRY
56	London HLU 8242	Trouble With Harry/A Little Beauty (triangular centre, gold lettering on label)	25

(see also David Seville)

ALFIE
01	Regal (no cat. no.)	Zoom (p/s, 1-track square, 300 only)	10

MINT VALUE £

CLEM ALFORD
74	Columbia SCX 6571	MIRROR IMAGE - THE ELECTRONIC SITAR OF CLEM ALFORD (LP)	60
75	KPM KPM 1183	INDIA (LP, music library issue, side 2 only)	40

(see also Sagram, Magic Carpet)

ALFRED & MELMOTH
68	Island WI 3130	I Want Someone/ALFRED BROWN: One Scotch One Bourbon One Beer	20

SANDRA ALFRED
58	Oriole CB 1408	Rocket And Roll/Six Day Rock	75
58	Oriole CB 1408	Rocket And Roll/Six Day Rock (78)	20

(see also Sandra Barry, Slack Alice)

AUGUSTO ALGUERO & HIS ORCHESTRA
68	Polydor 184 21	HEY JUDE (LP)	12
71	Polydor 2489 034	LAUGH! LAUGH! (LP)	15

LYNN ALICE
76	K&B KB 5520	(You Keep Me) Hanging On/(You Keep Me) Hanging On	7

ALICE THROUGH THE LOOKING GLASS
69	H&F Recording/SNP (no cat. no.)	ALICE THROUGH THE LOOKING GLASS (LP, private pressing, handmade sleeve, actually by Peter Howell & John Ferdinando)	800
97	Tenth Planet TP 032	ALICE THROUGH THE LOOKING GLASS (LP, reissue, no'd, 1,000 only)	20

(see also Ithaca, Friends, Agincourt, Tomorrow Come Someday, BBC Radiophonic Workshop/Peter Howell)

ALICE IN CHAINS
92	Columbia 658 888-7	Would?/Man In The Box (picture disc, numbered, PVC sleeve)	10
92	Columbia 658 888-6	Would?/Man In The Box/Brother/Right Turn (12", green vinyl, no'd die-cut slv.)	8
93	Columbia 659 090-6	Them Bones/We Die Young/Got Me Wrong/Am I Inside (12", no'd, blue vinyl)	8
93	Columbia 659 090-7	Them Bones/We Die Young (p/s, numbered poster)	5
93	Columbia 659 365-7	Angry Chair/I Know Somethin' About You (snakeskin wallet sleeve)	5
93	Columbia 659 751-7	Down In A Hole/Rooster (picture disc)	10
93	Columbia 659365-6	Angry Chair/I Know Somethin' ('Bout You)/Bleed The Freak/It Ain't Like That (12", stickered, die-cut p/s)	8
93	Columbia 659 751-6	Down In A Hole/A Little Bitter/Rooster/Love Hate Love (12", die cut p/s)	8
93	Columbia 659751-6	Down In A Hole/A Little Bitter/Love, Hate, Love (12", die-cut p/s)	8
95	Columbia 662 623-7	Grind/Nutshell (green vinyl, numbered card)	8
96	Columbia 662893-7	Heaven Beside You/Would? (live) (white vinyl, foldover p/s in stickered PVC sleeve)	5
91	Columbia 467201-1	FACELIFT (LP)	15
92	Columbia 472330-1	DIRT (LP)	15
94	Columbia 475713-1	JAR OF FLIES/SAP (LP, yellow vinyl with blue vinyl, 1-sided, etched 12" EP)	40
95	Columbia 481114-1	ALICE IN CHAINS (double LP, gatefold sleeve, inners)	25
10	Music On Vinyl MOVLP 086	JAR OF FLIES/SAP (2-LP, reissue, gatefold, orange and blue vinyl)	25

ALICE ISLAND BAND
74	Warren WAR 341	SPLENDID ISOLATION (LP, with insert)	200

ALIEN KULTURE
81	RAR LRAR 1	Asian Youth/Culture Crossover (p/s)	40

ALIEN SEX FIEND
84	Anagram 11 ANA 25	E.S.T. (Trip To The Moon)/Boneshaker Baby/I Am A Product (live) (11", PVC sleeve with insert)	10
90	Windsong 02	ASF BOX (box set, export issue, 4,000 only, with 3 coloured vinyl singles [12", 11" & 10"], poster, T-shirt & imitation dog turd)	25
93	Anagram GRAM 69	LEGENDARY BATCAVE TAPES (LP)	15

(see also Demon Preacher, Demons)

ALIENS
06	EMI PETROCK 12 001	ALIENOID STARMONICA EP (12")	8
07	EMI 9463868181	ASTRONOMY FOR DOGS (2-LP)	18
08	Petrock LP 002	LUNA (2-LP)	15

(see also Beta Band)

NUSRAT FATEH ALI KHAN
89	Real World RWLP3	SHAHEN-SHAH (LP)	12

ALIMANTADO (DR.)
73	Atra ATRA 007	Return Of Muhummad Ali/Black Love	12
75	Sun & Star ST 003	Best Dress Chicken/She Wreng-Ep	15
77	Greensleeves GRE 002	Born For A Purpose/Reason For Living (with the Rebels)	10
78	Virgin VOLE 1	Slavery Let I Go/Find The One (12")	8
78	Greensleeves GRE 5	Still Alive/Life All Over (with the Rebels)	6
78	Greensleeves GRE 13	Best Dressed Chicken In Town/Can't Conquer Natty Dreadlocks (yellow vinyl)	15
79	Greensleeves GRED 10	Born For A Purpose/Reason For Living/Still Alive/Life All Over (12", with the Rebels)	20
79	Greensleeves GRED 17	Sitting In The Park/Skanking In The Park (12", with the Rebels)	10
80	Isda SUS 11	It Cold In A Babylon/Version (12")	8
78	Greensleeves GREL 1	BEST DRESSED CHICKEN IN TOWN (LP)	20
81	Greensleeves GREL 22	SONS OF THUNDER (LP)	20

ALISON, ANN, KEN, BLUE & TAF
72	TEB SLE 50	SONGS FROM AN OLD BARN (EP)	25

ALKALINE TRIO
02	B-Unique BUN 0167	Stupid Kid/Metro (7" picture disc, stickered PVC sleeve)	8
02	B-Unique BUN 013-7	Private Eye/Private Eye (original) (picture disc, stickered PVC sleeve)	5
03	Universal 9809024	We've Had Enough/Blue In The Face (live) (picture disc, stickered PVC sleeve)	6
03	Universal 9811507	All On Black/This Could Be Love (Acoustic SBN Session) (picture disc)	6
05	Vagrant VRUK 012LP	CRIMSON (LP, red vinyl, stickered sleeve, inner)	15

ALKATRAZ
76	Rockfield UAS 30001	DOING A MOONLIGHT (LP)	20

(see also Man, Quicksand)

ALL ABOUT EVE
85	Eden EDEN 1	D For Desire/Don't Follow Me (12", p/s)	12

(see also Ghost Dance, Gene Loves Jezebel)

ALL BECAUSE THE LADY LOVES
80	Sweet	IF YOU RISK EVERYTHING (EP, with insert) 25

ALL SORTS OF FOLK
72	Private Pressing CH 101	ALL SORTS OF FOLK (LP) 150

ALL SOUNDBWOY OUT
07	ASBO 001	ASBO (1-sided white label 12") 30

(see also Loefa)

ALLAH & MR. LONELY
73	Fab FAB 190	Hide & Seek/CANCER ALL STARS : Version (actually by Allen & Mr. Lonely) 8

JOHNNIE ALLAN
74	Oval 1001	Promised Land/SHELTON DUNAWAY: Betty And Dupree 8
78	Oval Still LOT 1	Promised Land/PETE FOWLER: One Heart, One Song (p/s) 5

RICHARD ALLAN
60	Parlophone R 4634	As Time Goes By/Only One 20
60	Parlophone R 4711	Don't Ever Say You're Gonna Leave Me/Poetry In Motion 5

STEVE ALLAN
79	Creole CR 164	Together We Are Beautiful/All Mine 6
74	M & M FFM10025	Villa Katrina/Singers Song 6

ALL DAY
73	private pressing	YORK POP MUSIC PROJECT (LP) 150

ANNISTEEN ALLEN
55	Capitol CL 14264	Fujiyama Mama/Wheels Of Love 250
55	Capitol CL 14264	Fujiyama Mama/Wheels Of Love (78) 30
57	Brunswick 05639	Don't Nobody Move/The Money Tree 30

BOBBY ALLEN (& COMMANCHES)
62	Fontana 267252 TF	Your Cheatin' Heart/I'll Forget About You 5
63	Fontana TF 401	Here Comes The Bride/Nothing's Impossible 5
64	Fontana TF 429	Half As Much As You/So In Love With You (with Commanches) 5

(see also Commanches)

CLAY ALLEN
62	Starlite ST45 086	This Time It's Really Goodbye/Broken Home 5
63	Starlite ST45 096	I Can't Stop The Blues From Moving/You've Got The Cleanest Mind 5
63	Starlite ST45 106	Crazy Crazy World/Just A Stone's Throw Away 5

DAEVID ALLEN
75	Virgin VS 123	Fred The Fish/It's The Time Of Your Life (p/s, promo only) 8
79	Charly CY 51056	Much Too Old/I Am A Freud (with New York Gong, p/s with insert) 5
83	Charly CY 2101	ALIEN IN NEW YORK (12" EP) 8
75	Caroline C 1512	BANANA MOON (LP, black and white 'Twins' label, ends in a continuous loop) 20
76	Virgin V 5024	GOOD MORNING! (LP, by Daevid Allen & Euterpe) 20
77	Affinity AFF3	NOW IS THE HAPPIEST TIME OF YOUR LIFE (LP) 12
79	Charly CRL 5015	N'EXISTE PAS! (LP, with lyric insert) 12

(see also Gong, Planet Gong, Soft Machine)

DEAN ALLEN
58	London HLM 8698	Rock Me To Sleep/Ooh-Ooh Baby Baby 25
58	London HLM 8698	Rock Me To Sleep/Ooh-Ooh Baby Baby (78) 10

EDGAR J ALLEN
73	Spark SRL 1102	Happiness Corner/Got You On The Run 6

JEFF ALLEN
57	HMV JO 477	That'll Be The Day/Guilty Mind (export issue) 25

JERRY ALLEN & HIS TRIO
54	Decca F 10248	S'Posin'/When I Needed You Most 5
55	Decca F 10443	Kind/Delaunay's Dilemma 5

(see also Excursion)

LEE ALLEN (& HIS BAND)
58	HMV POP 452	Walkin' With Mr. Lee/Promenade 40
58	HMV POP 452	Walkin' With Mr. Lee/Promenade (78) 10
59	Top Rank JAR 265	Cat Walk/Creole Alley 10
59	Top Rank JKR 8020	WALKIN' WITH MR LEE (EP) 30
62	Ember ELR 3312	MOOD MUSIC LIBRARY (LP, uncredited library issue, generic sleeve) 50

(see also Huey 'Piano' Smith & Clowns)

LILY ALLEN
06	No Label LILY 001	LDN/Knock Em Down (500 only, jukebox centre) 12
06	Regal 3694931	ALRIGHT, STILL (LP, approx 200 pressed) 20

MAURICE ALLEN
58	Pye Nixa 7N 15128	Ooh Baby/Rockhearted 30
58	Pye 7N 15128	Ooh Baby/Rockhearted (78) 10

PATRICK ALLEN
77	Kab KB 5540	Groovy Feeling/Instrumental 20

PETER ALLEN
77	A&M AMLH 63706	IT IS TIME FOR (2 x LP) 40

REX ALLEN
54	Brunswick 05341	This Ole House/They Were Doin' The Mambo (with Tex Williams) 15
57	Brunswick 05675	The Little White Horses/Drango 6
57	Brunswick 05677	Wringle Wrangle/Westward Ho The Wagons 7
57	Brunswick 05699	Flower Of San Antone/Money, Marbles And Chalk 7
59	Top Rank JAR 188	One More Sunrise (Morgen)/The Little Old Church In The Valley 5
62	Mercury AMT 1191	Don't Go Near The Indians/Touched So Deeply 5

(see also Tex Williams, Patti Page)

STEVE ALLEN (& HIS ORCHESTRA)
56	Vogue Coral Q 72118	The Ballad Of Davy Crockett/Very Square Dance	5

(see also George Cates)

TONY ALLEN (1)
00	Strut STRUTAALP001	JEALOUSY (LP, reissue with Africa 70)	15
00	Strut STRUTAALP002	NO DISCRIMINATION (LP, reissue with Afro Messengers)	15
00	Strut STRUTALP 002	NO ACCOMODATION FOR LAGOS (LP, reissue with Africa 70)	15

TONY ALLEN (2)
84	Earthworks MWKS 3001	NEPA (LP)	30

VERNON ALLEN
64	R&B JB 169	Far I Come/Babylon	250

(VERNON) ALLEN & (MILTON) HAMILTON
66	Blue Beat BB 348	It Is I/Baby What's More	15
66	Blue Beat BB 353	You're The Angel/Someone Like You	15

ALLENS
75	Mowest MW 3029	High Tide/California Music	6

ALLEY CATS
59	Vogue V 9155	Last Night/Snap-Crackle And Pop	25
59	Vogue V 9155	Last Night/Snap-Crackle And Pop (78)	20

ALLIES
79	Harp HSP 1025	Plush Living/Computer (p/s, 500 only despite numbering)	8

ALLISON
94	Twinkle NG 544	WAILING (LP)	15

BOBBY ALLISON
64	Solar SRP 103	You've Got Everything/Change Your Mind	5

GENE ALLISON
58	London HLU 8605	Hey, Hey, I Love You/You Can Make It If You Try	150
58	London HLU 8605	Hey, Hey, I Love You/You Can Make It If You Try (78)	40

JERRY ALLISON & CRICKETS
65	Liberty LIB 10196	Now Hear This/Everybody's Got A Little Problem	20

(see also Crickets, Ivan)

LUTHER ALLISON
71	Delmark DS 625	LOVE ME MAMA (LP, blue label)	15

LYNN ALLISON
57	Columbia DB 3867	Mama From The Train (A Kiss, A Kiss)/Song Of The Sparrow	5

MOSE ALLISON
61	Fontana H 292	Baby Please Don't Go/Deed I Do	30
64	Columbia DB 7330	I Love The Life I Live/Life Is Suicide	7
59	Esquire EP 214	PARCHMAN FARM (EP)	30
59	Esquire EP 221	BACK COUNTRY SUITE (EP)	25
60	Esquire EP 224	BLUEBERRY HILL (EP)	20
61	Esquire EP 231	THAT MAN MOSE AGAIN (EP)	20
64	Columbia SEG 8353	ALLISON SINGS THE BLUES (EP)	20
59	Esquire 32-051	BACK COUNTRY SUITE (LP)	25
59	Esquire 32-071	LOCAL COLOUR (LP)	25
59	Esquire 32-083	YOUNG MAN MOSE (LP)	25
60	Esquire 32-094	CREEK BANK (LP)	25
61	Esquire 32-131	AUTUMN SONG (LP)	25
62	Esquire 32-171	RAMBLIN' WITH MOSE (LP)	25
63	London HA-K 8083	SWINGIN' MACHINE (LP, as Mose Allison Jazz Group)	20
64	Columbia SX 6058	V-8 FORD (LP)	20
64	Stateside SL 10106	MOSE ALLISON SINGS (LP)	20
66	Atlantic 587/588 007	MOSE ALIVE (LP, plum and orange label)	15
66	CBS Realm RM(S) 52318	I LOVE THE LIFE I LIVE (LP)	15
66	Atlantic 587/588 031	WILD MAN ON THE LOOSE (LP)	12
67	Transatlantic PR 7189	AUTUMN SONG (LP)	12
68	Transatlantic PR 7279	MOSE ALLISON (LP)	12

ALLISONS (U.K.)
61	Fontana H 304	Words/Blue Tears	5
61	Fontana H 336	What A Mess!/Lorraine (p/s)	15
61	Fontana H 362	Lesson In Love/Oh, My Love	5
62	Fontana 267 231TF	Sweet And Lovely/Sugar Love	5
62	Fontana 267 255TF	I'll Cross My Fingers/You Should Be Sorry	5
61	Fontana TFE 17339	THE ALLISONS (EP)	18
61	Fontana TFL 5135	ARE YOU SURE (LP, mono)	20
61	Fontana STFL 558	ARE YOU SURE (LP, stereo)	22

ALLISONS (U.S.)
64	Stateside SS 289	Surfer Street/Money (vocal: Darlene Love)	35

(see also Blossoms, Darlene Love)

ALL LIVING FEAR
94	FEAR 002CD	JESSICA (CD single, 460 copies)	15

ALLMAN BROTHERS BAND
69	Atco 228 033	THE ALLMAN BROTHERS BAND (LP, gatefold sleeve)	50
71	Atco 2400 032	IDLEWILD SOUTH (LP)	60
71	Atlantic 2402 035	AT FILLMORE EAST (2-LP, gatefold sleeve)	40
72	Capricorn K67501	EAT A PEACH (2-LP, gatefold sleeve with insert)	25
73	Capricorn K47507	BROTHERS AND SISTERS (LP, gatefold sleeve with insert)	15

(see also Gregg Allman, Duane & Gregg Allman, Allman Joys, Hour Glass)

DUANE & GREGG ALLMAN
73	Polydor 2310 235	DUANE & GREGG ALLMAN (LP, laminated sleeve)	12

(see also Allman Brothers, Gregg Allman)

GREGG ALLMAN
73	Capricorn K 47508/CP0116	LAID BACK (LP)	12

(see also Allman Brothers, Duane & Gregg Allman)

ALLMAN JOYS
73	Mercury 6398 005	ALLMAN JOYS (LP)	20

ALL NIGHT BAND
79	Contact CON 5	Lovely Ladies/It's My Life	15

ALL NIGHT LONG
62	Fontana H 365	Muy Rapido/Skin Fever	12

TOMMY ALLSUP
65	London HA-U 8218	BUDDY HOLLY SONG BOOK (LP)	40

ALL THE RAGE
82	Rage RR 001	Concrete City/Emergency (p/s)	150

JOHNNY ALMOND MUSIC MACHINE
69	Deram DM 266	Solar Level/To R.K.	35
69	Deram DML/SML 1043	PATENT PENDING (LP)	50
70	Deram SML 1057	HOLLYWOOD BLUES (LP)	60

(see also Alan Price Set, Zoot Money, Paul Williams Set, John Mayall & Bluesbreakers, Mark-Almond, Jon Mark)

ALMOND LETTUCE
68	Columbia DB 8442	The Tree Dog Song/To Henry With Hope	6
69	Philips BF 1764	Magic Circle/Twenty Weary Miles	10

MARC ALMOND
82	Lyntone LYN 12505	Discipline (as 'Marc Almond & Friends', pink flexidisc with Flexipop issue 23. Friends are Throbbing Gristle)	20
84	Some Bizzare BZS 2310	The Boy Who Came Back (Extended)/Joey Demento (Extended) (10", p/s)	8
84	Some Bizzare BZS 2410	You Have (Ext.)/Black Mountain Blues/Split Lip (Ext.) (10", p/s, with lyric sheet)	8
84	Some Bizzare BZS 2510	Tenderness Is A Weakness (Extended)/Love For Sale/Pink Shack Blues (live)/ The Heel (live) (10", p/s, with lyric insert)	8
84	Gutter Hearts LYN 14210	My Death (fan club flexidisc)	12
84	Gutter Hearts GH 1	BITE BACK + BLUES (fan club-only LP, credited to "Raoul & The Ruined")	30
86	Some Bizzare GLOWY 2-10	A Woman's Story/The Heel/A Salty Dog/The Plague/ The Little White Cloud That Cried/For One Moment/Just Good Friends (10" picture disc, stickered PVC sleeve)	8
87	Some Bizzare GLOWD 4	Melancholy Rose/Gyp The Blood//Pirate Jenny/Surabaya Johnny (double pack, gatefold p/s)	6
88	Parlophone PSR 500	Kept Boy (1-sided 7" with etched reverse - intended to be free with THE STARS WE ARE LP - but plans scrapped)	20
92	WEA YZ 638T	Extract From "Trois Chanson De Bilitis"/The Days Of Pearly Spencer/ Dancing In A Golden Cage/Dancing In A Golden Cage	0
04	Theatre Of Dreams 005	Sheherezade (Turkish Delight Mix)/Sheherezade (Seven Veils Mix) (p/s, pink vinyl, only available online)	8
05	Theatre Of Dreams 006	Delirious (Demented Deluded Delirious)/Theatre Of Dreams (p/s, blue vinyl, only available online)	8
95	EMI CDMATBOX 1	TREASURE BOX 1 (2-CD, box set)	15
84	Some Bizarre 822 832-2	VERMIN IN ERMINE (CD)	15
85	Some Bizarre CD FAITH 1	STORIES OF JOHNNY (CD)	15
87	Some Bizarre CD FAITH 2	MOTHER FIST ANF HER FIVE DAUGHTERS (CD)	15
97	Some Bizarre SBZ 029CD	VERMIN IN ERMINE (CD, 3rd issue, video enhanced)	15
97	Some Bizarre SBZ 030CD	STORIES OF JOHNNY (CD, 2nd issue, video enhanced)	15
97	Some Bizarre SBZ 031CD	MOTHER FIST AND HER FIVE DAUGHTERS (CD, 2nd issue, video enhanced)	15
97	Some Bizarre SBZCD 022	VIOLENT SILENCE/FLESH VOLCANO (CD, withdrawn)	15

(see also Soft Cell, Marc & Mambas, Burmoe Brothers, Vicious Pink Phenomena, Flesh Volcano, Annie Hogan, Sally Timms, Gene Pitney)

ALMOND MARZIPAN
70	Trend TNT 53	Open Up Your Heart/Summer Love	15
70	Trend TNT 55	Marie Take A Chance/I'll Forget You	6

ALONE AGAIN OR
84	All One ALG 1	Drum The Beat (In My Soul)/Smartie Edit (p/s)	5

(see also Shamen)

HERB ALPERT (& TIJUANA BRASS)
67	Pye International 7N 25419	Casino Royale (From The Film)/The Wall Street Rag (unissued)	0
68	A&M AMS 700	Casino Royale (From The Film)/The Wall Street Rag (p/s)	6

ALPHA & OMEGA
92	A&O 09	KING & QUEEN (LP)	25
90s	A&O 18	OVERSTANDING (LP)	20
90s	A&O 27	WATCH AND PRAY (LP)	20
90s	A&O 93	EVERYDAY LIFE (LP)	15

ORVILLE ALPHANSO
65	Caribou CRC 1	Bellylick/Inspiration	35

ALPHASTONE
90s	Enraptured RAPTLP 33	LIFE IS A MOTORWAY EP (2 x 12", gatefold sleeve, limited issue)	10
90s	Enraptured RAPTLP 18	ELASTICATED WAVEBAND (LP, clear vinyl, 100 only)	15

CARLTON ALPHONSO
67	Pama PM 700	Where In This World/Peace Makers	40
69	Grape GR 3000	Belittle Me/Keep Your Love	30

CLYDE ALPHONSO
69	Studio One SO 2076	Good Enough/Let The Music Play	130

PANCHO ALPHONSO AND THE REVOLUTIONARIES
79	Attack ATT TACK 8	Never Give Up In A Babylon/Love Is A Pleasure (12")	20
78	Trojan TRLS 165	NEVER GET TO ZION (LP)	18

(see also Alphonso Pancho)

ROLAND ALPHONSO (ALIAS ROLAND AL)
61	Blue Beat BB 58	Blackberry Brandy/ALVIN & CECIL: Marjorie	25

MINT VALUE £

62	Blue Beat BB 112	Four Corners Of The World (with Alley Cats)/SHINERS: Romantic Shuffle	30
64	R&B JB 161	Mr President/The MAYTALS: A Man Who Knows	25
64	R&B JB 164	Crime Wave/MAYTALS: Hello Honey	45
65	Island WI 217	El Pussy Cat/LORD BRYNNER: Tiger In Your Tank	30
65	Ska Beat JB 210	Nimble Foot/ANDY & JOEY: Love Is Stronger	60
65	Ska Beat JB 216	Nuclear Weapon (with Baba Brooks)/STRANGER COLE: Love Thy Neighbour	40
65	Rio R 5804	Jazz Ska/HYACINTH: Oh Gee	50
66	Blue Beat BB 356	Just A Closer Walk/Jericho Train	175
66	Island WI 259	James Bond/LEE PERRY: Just Keep It Up	150
66	Doctor Bird DB 1010	From Russia With Love/Cleopatra (with Soul Brothers)	80
66	Doctor Bird DB 1011	Sufferer's Choice (with Soul Brothers)/SOULETTES: I Want To Be	50
66	Doctor Bird DB 1013	WAILERS: Rude Boy/ROLANDO AL & SOUL BROTHERS: Ringo's Theme (This Boy)	90
66	Doctor Bird DB 1017	Sugar And Spice/Get Out Of My Life (with Soul Brothers)	25
66	Doctor Bird DB 1020	Phoenix City (with Soul Brothers)/DEACONS: Men Alone	30
66	Doctor Bird DB 1023	Doctor Ring-A-Ding/FREDDIE & HEARTACHES: Here Is My Heart	80
66	Doctor Bird DB 1035	I Love You/Song Of Love	25
66	Doctor Bird DB 1039	WAILERS: Rasta Put It On/ROLAND AL & SOUL BROTHERS: Ska With Ringo	150
66	Ska Beat JB 231	Rinky Dink (So Good) (with Studio One Orchestra)/ SCRATCH & DYNAMITES: Deacon Johnson	45
67	Pyramid PYR 6003	Middle East/Wise Man	30
67	Pyramid PYR 6005	Women Of The World (& Beverley's Allstars)/SPANISHTONIANS: Kisses	30
67	Pyramid PYR 6006	On The Move (& Beverley's Allstars)/DESMOND DEKKER & ACES: It's A Shame	25
67	Pyramid PYR 6007	Jungle Bit (& Beverley's Allstars)/NORMAN GRANT: Somebody Please Help Me	25
67	Pyramid PYR 6008	The Cat/DESMOND DEKKER & ACES: Rudy Got Soul	30
67	Pyramid PYR 6009	Guantanamera Ska (& Beverley's Allstars)/SPANISHTONIANS: Suffer Me Not	30
67	Pyramid PYR 6011	Nothing For Nothing/DESMOND DEKKER & ACES: Rude Boy Train	25
67	Pyramid PYR 6018	Sock It To Me (& Beverley's Allstars)/SPANISHTONIANS: Rudie Gets Plenty	100
68	Pyramid PYR 6022	Whiter Shade Of Pale/On The Move	80
68	Pyramid PYR 6030	Dreamland/MAYTALS: 54-46, That's My Number	30
68	Pyramid PYR 6043	Stream Of Life/MAYTALS: Struggle	45
68	Coxsone CS 7077	Reggae In The Grass/ROY RICHARDS: Get Smart	45
69	Gas GAS 112	A Thousand Tons Of Megaton (actually by Derrick Morgan)/Musical Resurrection	25
70	Punch PH 39	Roll On (& Upsetters)/CARL DAWKINS: True Love	45
71	Banana BA 340	Mellow Mood (Way To My Heart)/MAYTALS: Marching On	20
68	Hi Note BSLP 5001	ABC ROCK STEADY (with the Originals Orchestra)	100

ALPHORAS
| 78 | Junior JR 107 | Running Out Of Love/It Pains Me (actually by LEROY SMART) | 15 |

ALPINES
| 68 | Double D DD 110 | Get Ready/CARIBBEATS: Come Back Charlie | 25 |

AL QUAFA QUINTETO
| 76 | Pablo PAB 12 | LEBLON BEACH (LP) | 12 |

ALQUIN
| 73 | Polydor 2480 152 | MARKS (LP) | 15 |

ALSATIANS
| 80 | SRT SRTS/80/CUS-629 | Teen Romance/Our Man In Marrakesh (no p/s, 1000 only) | 40 |

RITA ALSTON
| 70 | Trojan TR 7751 | Popcorn Funky Reggae/NAT COLE: My Love | 15 |
| 70 | Trojan TR 7752 | All Kinds Of Everything/CARL LEVEY: Instrumental Version | 6 |

(see also Rita, Nat Cole)

SHIRLEY ALSTON
| 75 | London HLA 10506 | I'd Rather Not Be Loving You/Can't Stop Singin' (Bout The Boy I Love) | 15 |
| 75 | London SHA 8491 | WITH A LITTLE HELP FROM MY FRIENDS (LP) | 25 |

(see also Shirelles)

ALTECS
| 61 | London HLU 9387 | Easy/Recess | 19 |

(see also The Black Dog)

ALTERATIONS
| 78 | Bead Records BEAD 9 | CUSACK/BERESFORD/DAY/TOOP (LP) | 30 |

ALTERED STATES
| 88 | Red Rhino CALC 31 | IS ANYONE OUT THERE? (LP) | 60 |

ALTERN 8
91	Network NWKTR 34	Frequency (12")	8
92	Network ST-8	Full On...Mask Hysteria Megamix (12")	8
92	Network E-VAPO 38DJ	Evapor 8 (12" Special DJ Edition)	8
93	Network NWKT 73	Everybody (12")	8
93	Network NWKTR 73	Everybody Remix (12")	8
91	Network NWKT 24	VERTIGO EP (12")	8
92	Network Records A8 PIC 1	FULL ON...MASK HYSTERIA (LP)	15
92	Network TOP LP1	FULL ON...MASK HYSTERIA (LP & 12")	20

ALTERNATIVE
| 82 | Crass Records 221984/8 | IN NOMINE PATRI (EP) | 10 |
| 83 | Corpus Christi CHRIST 13 | IF THEY TREAT YOU LIKE SHIT - ACT LIKE MANURE (LP, with lyric insert) | 50 |

ALTERNATIVE TV
77	Sniffing Glue SG 75 RPS	Love Lies Limp (1-sided flexidisc with Sniffing Glue fanzine issue 12)	20
77	Deptford Fun City DFC 02	How Much Longer/You Bastard (p/s)	7
77	Deptford Fun City DFC 02	How Much Longer/You Bastard (p/s, labelled 'alternate versions')	7
78	Deptford Fun City DFC 04	Life After Life/Life After Dub (p/s)	6
78	Deptford Fun City DFC 05	Life/Love Lies Limp (p/s)	7
78	Deptford Fun City DFC 07	Action Time Vision/Another Coke (live p/s)	10
79	Deptford Fun City DFC 10	The Force Is Blind/Lost In Room (Vibing Up The Senile Man) (p/s, last track uncredited)	5
78	Deptford Fun City DLP 01	THE IMAGE HAS CRACKED (LP)	18
78	Deptford Fun City DLP 02	WHAT YOU SEE IS ... WHAT YOU ARE (LP, 1 side by Here & Now)	12
79	Crystal CLP 01	LIVE AT THE RAT CLUB (LP)	15

80	Deptford Fun City DLP 05	ACTION TIME VISION (LP, with inner sleeve)	15

(see also Mark Perry, Good Missionaries, The Door & The Window, Reflections, Jools Holland, Alex Fergusson, Rat & Whale)

ALTERNATORS
78	Energy NRG 001	No Answers/The Kid Don't Know (no p/s)	60

ALTERNOMEN UNLIMITED
79	Object OM 06	Facade/Connections (p/s)	5

(see also Spherical Objects)

ALTON (ELLIS) & EDDY
60	Blue Beat BB 17	Muriel/CLUE J. & HIS BLUES BLASTERS: Silky	15
62	Island WI 009	My Love Divine/Let Me Dream	20

(see also Alton Ellis)

ALVARO
77	Squeaky Shoes SSRM 1	DRINKING MY OWN SPERM (LP)	20

(see also 101'ers)

ALVYN
69	Morgan Bluetown MR 18S	You've Gotta Have An Image/Mind The Gap	15

AMALGAM (1)
69	Transatlantic TRA 196	A PRAYER FOR PEACE (LP)	50
73	A Records A 002	PLAY BLACKWELL & HIGGINS (LP)	35
74	Goodwill WS 1	JUST OTHERS (LP, with insert, 250 only)	700

AMALGAM (2)
80	Impetus IMPLP 47901	WIPE OUT (4-LP box set with booklet)	50

GLEN AMAMS
69	Escort ES 804	Rich In Love/WOODPECKERS: Zumbelly	15

(see also Glen Adams)

A MAN CALLED ADAM
89	Acid Jazz JAZID 15T	Earthly Powers/Techno Powers (12", p/s)	10

(see also Leftfield)

AMAZIAH
74	Sunrise SR 001	STRAIGHT TALKER (LP, private pressing with insert)	75

AMAZING BLONDEL
72	Island WIP 6153	Alleluia (Cantus Firmus To Counterpoint)/Safety In God Alone	5
70	Bell SBLL 131	THE AMAZING BLONDEL AND A FEW FACES (LP, blue/silver label)	200
70	Island ILPS 9136	EVENSONG (LP, gatefold sleeve)	25
71	Island ILPS 9156	FANTASIA LINDUM (LP, with inner lyric sleeve)	30
71	Island ILPS 9156	FANTASIA LINDUM (LP, without inner lyric sleeve)	15
72	Island ILPS 9327	ENGLAND (LP, gatefold)	25
73	Island ILPS 9257	BLONDEL (LP, gatefold sleeve)	20
74	DJM DJF 20442	MULGRAVE STREET (LP)	15
75	DJM DJF 20446	INSPIRATION (LP)	15
76	DJM DJLPS 472	BAD DREAMS (LP)	12

(see also Dimples, Gospel Garden, Methusilah)

AMAZING DANCING BAND
68	Verve VS 567	Deep Blue Train/Simon Smith & His Amazing Dancing Bear	15
67	Verve SVLP 9214	AMAZING DANCING BAND (LP)	20

AMAZING FRIENDLY APPLE
69	Decca F 12887	Water Woman/Magician	125

AMAZING SPACE FROGS
79	Ribbett RIB 1	THE DIRTY HABITS EP	300

AMAZON TRUST
70	Polydor 2058065	Run Baby Run/Sheila Lee	50

AMBASSADOR 277
88	El GPUT37	Pop Up Man/Malediction (10" p/s)	10

AMBASSADORS OF SWING
92	Kold Sweat KSEP 204	RAP GAME EP	6

AMBER ASYLUM
96	Elfenblut SAG 1	FROZEN IN AMBER (LP, inner)	15

AMBER SQUAD
80	Sound Of Leicester ST 1	(I Can't) Put My Finger On You/Tell You A Lie (p/s)	25
80	Dead Good DEAD 17	Can We Go Dancing?/You Should See (What I Do To You In My Dreams) (p/s)	20

AMBERGRIS
70	Paramount SPFL 262	AMBERGRIS (LP)	12

AMBOY DUKES (U.K.)
68	Polydor 56228	Judy In Disguise/Who's Foolin' Who	15
68	Polydor 56243	Simon Says/The Marquis	15

(AMERICAN) AMBOY DUKES
68	Fontana TF 971	Let's Go Get Stoned/It's Not True	20
67	Fontana (S)TL 5468	THE AMBOY DUKES (LP)	75
69	London HA-T/SH-T 8378	JOURNEY TO THE CENTER OF THE MIND (LP, as American Amboy Dukes)	50
69	London HA-T/SH-T 8392	MIGRATION (LP, as American Amboy Dukes)	45
74	Discreet DS 2203	TOOTH, FANG AND CLAW (LP)	15

(see also Ted Nugent)

SAMMY AMBROSE
65	Stateside SS 385	This Diamond Ring/Bad Night	110
65	Stateside SS 399	Monkey See Monkey Do/Welcome To Dreamsville (DJ Copy)	350
65	Stateside SS 399	Monkey See Monkey Do/Welcome To Dreamsville	200
87	Kent 6T3	Welcome To Dreamsville/PLATTERS: Not My Girl	25

AMBROSE SLADE

69	Fontana TF 1015	Genesis/Roach Daddy	300
69	Fontana STL 5492	BEGINNINGS (LP, laminated sleeve, black label with silver print; beware of counterfeits with matt sleeve & black & white label)	700
75	Contour 6870 678	BEGINNINGS OF SLADE (LP, reissue, different cover & running order, withdrawn)	70
10	Morgan Blue Town BT5006	BEGINNINGS (LP, reissue, 750 only with insert & signed certificate)	20

(see also Slade, 'N Betweens)

AMBROSETTI QUARTET

55	Columbia SEG 7595	AMBROSETTI QUARTET (EP, company sleeve, no p/s)	8

AMEBIX

82	Spiderleg SDL 6	Who's The Enemy/Carnage/No Gods No Masters (p/s)	30
83	Spiderleg SDL 10	Winter/Beginning Of The End (p/s)	25
82	Spiderleg SDLP 14	NO SANCTUARY (LP)	30
85	Alternative Tentacles VIRUS46	ARISE (LP)	20
87	Heavy Metal HMRLP 99	MONOLITH (LP)	25

LOLA AMECHE

53	Oriole CB 1143	Rock The Joint/Don't Let The Stars Get In Your Eyes (78)	15

AMEN CORNER

67	Deram DM 136	Gin House Blues/I Know (early copies entitled "Gin House" on label)	6
67	Deram DM 151	The World Of Broken Hearts/Nema	7
68	Deram DM 172	Bend Me, Shape Me/Satisnek The Jobsworth	6
68	Deram DM 197	High In The Sky/Run Run Run	6
69	Deram 228	The World Of Broken Hearts/Gin House Blues	6
69	Immediate IM 073	(If Paradise Is) Half As Nice/Hey Hey Girl	6
69	Immediate IM 081	Hello Susie/Evil Man's Gonna Win	5
69	Immediate IM 084	Get Back/Farewell To The Real Magnificent Seven	5
69	Immediate AS 3	So Fine (promo only 'single sampler' for IMSP 023)	20
68	Deram DML/SML 1021	ROUND AMEN CORNER (LP)	20
69	Immediate IMSP 023	THE NATIONAL WELSH COAST LIVE EXPLOSION COMPANY (LP, g/fold sleeve, pink label)	20
69	Immediate IMSP 028	FAREWELL TO THE REAL MAGNIFICENT SEVEN (LP, gatefold sleeve)	20

(see also Andy Fairweather-Low, Fairweather, Mayfield's Mule, Judas Jump)

AMERICAN BREED

67	CBS 2888	Step Out Of Your Mind/The Same Old Thing	10
67	CBS 2972	Step Out Of Your Mind/The Same Old Thing (reissue)	5
68	Stateside SS 2078	Bend Me Shape Me/Mindrocker	8
68	Dot DOT 101	Green Light/Don't It Make You Cry	15
68	Dot DOT 106	Ready, Willing And Able/Take Me If You Want Me	7
67	Dot DOLP 255	AMERICAN BREED (LP)	15
68	Dot (S)LPD 502	BEND ME, SHAPE ME (LP)	15
68	Dot (S)LPD 507	NO WAY TO TREAT A LADY (LP, soundtrack)	20
68	Dot (S)LPD 518	PUMPKIN, POWDER, SCARLET AND GREEN (LP)	15
69	Dot (S)LPD 526	THE LONELY SIDE OF THE CITY (LP)	12

AMERICAN GYPSY

71	CBS 7027	Gypsy Queen Pt 1/Dead & Gone	12
75	BTM SBT 101	Angel Eyes/Lady Eleanor	15
70	CBS 64276	AMERICAN GYPSY (2-LP)	30
75	BTM BTM 1001	AMERICAN GYPSY (LP)	20

AMERICAN JAM (BAND)

72	Parlophone R5971	American Jam/Natures Child	15
74	Young Blood YB 1056	Jam Jam/Back On The Road	18

(see also Kansas Hook)

AMERICAN MUSIC CLUB

87	Zippo ZONG 0202	ENGINE (LP, with inner sleeve)	15
88	Demon FIEND 134	CALIFORNIA (LP)	12
89	Demon FIEND 151	UNITED KINGDON (LP)	12
93	Virgin V2708	MERCURY	15

AMERICAN POETS

66	London HLC 10037	She Blew A Good Thing/Out To Lunch (as American Poets) (DJ copy)	200
66	London HLC 10037	She Blew A Good Thing/Out To Lunch (as American Poets)	100
71	United Artists UP 35308	She Blew A Good Thing/Out To Lunch (reissue, as Poets]	20

AMERICAN SPRING

72	United Artists UP 35376	Good Time/Sweet Mountain	15
72	United Artists UP 35421	Mama Said/Tennessee Waltz	15
73	CBS CBS 1590	Shyin' Away/Falling In Love	20
72	United Artists UAG 29363	AMERICAN SPRING (LP, "Tree" cover)	45
72	United Artists UAG 29363	AMERICAN SPRING (LP, "Tree" gatefold cover with picture of group)	60

(see also Beach Boys, Honeys)

AMERICAN YOUTH CHOIR

71	Polydor 2066 013	Together We Can Make It/Keep Your Fine Self Near Me	40

AMES BROTHERS

53	HMV 7M 153	You, You, You/My Life, My Love, My Happiness	6
54	HMV 7M 179	I Can't Believe That You're In Love/Boogie Woogie Maxine	30

ED AMES

67	RCA 1577	My Cup Runneth Over/Climb Ev'ry Mountain	5

NANCY AMES

66	Columbia DB 7809	Friends And Lovers Forever/I've Got A Lot Of Love (Left In Me)	20
66	Columbia DB 8039	Cry Softly/I Don't Want To Talk About It (DJ copy)	150
66	Columbia DB 8039	Cry Softly/I Don't Want To Talk About It	100

AMIGO

76	Lucky LY 6015	Judas A No Rasta/Version	50

AMITY

76	Red Rag RRR 001	AMITY (LP)	150

AMM

66	Incus EP 1	AT THE ROUNDHOUSE (EP)	80
67	Elektra EUKS 7256	AMM MUSIC (LP)	140
87	Matchless MR13	INEXHAUSTABLE DOCUMENT (LP)	20

(see also Eddie Provost Band)

ALBERT AMMONS

55	Vogue EPV 1071	ALBERT AMMONS (EP)	20
57	Brunswick OE 9325	BOOGIE WOOGIE STOMP (EP)	20
54	Mercury MG 25012	ALBERT AMMONS (10" LP)	30
62	Storyville SLP 184	BOOGIE WOOGIE TRIO (LP)	20

(see also [Big] Joe Turner)

ALBERT AMMONS & PETE JOHNSON

55	HMV DLP 1011	EIGHT TO THE BAR (10" LP)	25

ALBERT AMMONS, PETE JOHNSON & MEADE 'LUX' LEWIS

55	Columbia SEG 7528	SHOUT FOR JOY (EP)	10

(see also Pete Johnson, Meade 'Lux' Lewis)

GENE AMMONS (BAND)

60	Starlite ST45 017	Echo Chamber Blues/Ammons' Boogie	40
63	Starlite ST45 097	Anna/Cae' Cae'	10
59	Esquire 32-047	HI FI JAM SESSION (LP)	20
59	Esquire 32-077	FUNKY (LP)	25
60	Esquire 32-097	JAMMIN' WITH GENE (LP)	25
62	Esquire 32-147	BLUE GENE (LP)	20
63	Esquire 32-177	BOSS TENOR (LP)	25
63	Esquire 32-178	BAD! BOSSA NOVA (LP)	25
72	Prestige PR 24021	JUG & DODO (LP, with Dodo Marmarosa)	15
73	Prestige PR 10019	YOU TALK THAT TALK (LP)	15
73	Prestige PR 10021	BROTHER JUG (LP)	20

AMON DÜÜL

81	Illuminated JAMS 24	HAWK MEETS PENGUIN (LP)	15
85	Illuminated JAMS 27	MEETINGS WITH MENMACHINES (LP)	15

AMON DÜÜL II

70	Liberty LBF 15355	Archangel's Thunderbird/Burning Sister	25
69	Liberty LBS 83279	PHALLUS DEI (LP)	200
70	Liberty LSP 101/LBS 83359	YETI (2-LP, gatefold sleeve)	60
71	United Artists UAD 60003/4	DANCE OF THE LEMMINGS (2-LP, laminated gatefold sleeve)	50
72	Sunset SLS 50257	PHALLUS DEI (LP, reissue)	20
72	United Artists UAG 23927	CARNIVAL IN BABYLON (LP, gatefold sleeve)	30
72	United Artists UAG 29406	WOLF CITY (LP, gatefold sleeve)	25
73	United Artists USP 102	LIVE IN LONDON (LP)	20
73	United Artists UAS 29504	VIVE LA TRANCE (LP, with inner sleeve)	20
74	United Artists UA 29723 G	LEMMINGMANIA (LP)	15
74	Atlantic K 50136	HIJACK (LP)	15

(see also Utopia)

GLADYS AMONI

76	Untouchable UT 002	Your Best Friend/Your Best Dub	8

AMORPHOUS ANDROGYNOUS

93	Quigley LPEBV 1	TALES OF EPHIDRINA (LP)	15

(see also Future Sound Of London)

AMORY KANE

68	MCA MU 1036	Reflections Of Your Face/Four Ravens	25
70	CBS 5111	Him Or Me/Forever Waiting	10

ADAM AMOS & NOEL ROCKS

60s	Celtic Music CM 011	CASUAL ON THE BALCONY (LP)	35
60s	Celtic Music CM 026	ADAM AMOS & NOEL ROCKS (LP)	30

AMOS & SARA

82	It's War Boys	Go Home Soldier/Enough Is Enough/Surveillance O.H.M.S. (12", screenprint p/s)	8

(see also Homosexuals)

TORI AMOS

91	East West YZ 618T	ME AND A GUN EP (12")	8
91	East West YZ 618T	Silent All These Years/Upside Down/Me And A Gun/Thoughts (12", p/s)	8
92	East West A 7531T	China/Sugar/Flying Dutchman/Humpty Dumpty (12", p/s)	8
92	East West A7504DJ	Winter (radio edit)/The Pool (promo 7" in p/s)	15
92	East West A 7479CDX	CRUCIFY LIVE EP (CD, box set, with art prints, sealed)	30
92	East West A 7479CDX	CRUCIFY LIVE EP (CD, box set, with art prints, unsealed)	20
92	East West A 7433	Silent All These Years/Ode To The Banana King Part 1 (p/s)	5
92	East West A 7433CDX	Silent All These Years/Ode To The Banana King Part 1/Song For Eric/ Happy Phantom (CD, digipak, sealed)	35
92	East West A 7433CDX	Silent All These Years/Ode To The Banana King Part 1/Song For Eric/ Happy Phantom (CD, digipak, unsealed)	20
94	East West A 7281CDX	Cornflake Girl/A Case Of You/If 6 Were 9/Strange Fruit (CD, digipak, sealed)	30
94	East West A 7281CDX	Cornflake Girl/A Case Of You/If 6 Were 9/Strange Fruit (CD, picture disc digipak, unsealed)	20
94	East West SAM 1418	God - Carl Craig and C.J. Bolland remixes (12" promo)	12
96	East West SAM 1867	Professional Widow (Armand's Star Trunk Funkin' Mix)/(Just Da Funk Dub) (12")	8
98	East West AT 0045C	Raspberry Swirl (Lip Gloss Version)/(Sticky Extended Vocal Mix)/ (Scarlet Spectrum Feels) (CD, withdrawn)	10
99	Atlantic AT 0077CD2	GLORY OF THE 80s EP (CD, part 2 of 2-CD set, mispressing, plays CD-1 tracks)	12
92	East West 7567 82358-1	LITTLE EARTHQUAKES (LP)	20
92	East West 7567-82358-2	LITTLE EARTHQUAKES ('Wooden box' CD set)	50
96	East West 7567-82862-1	BOYS FOR PELE (2-LP)	20
98	East West 7567 83095-1	FROM THE CHOIRGIRL HOTEL (LP)	20
06	Epic (No cat no)	THE ORIGINAL BOOTLEGS (12 CD box set, 6 stickers)	150

AMPHETAMEANIES
99	F&J Records SHAG024	Last Night/Suzie The Muppet Ltd (7" p/s 600 pressed)	8

(see also Belle and Sebastian, Franz Ferdinand)

CURTIS AMY
61	Vogue LA12287	GROOVIN' BLUE (LP, with Frank Butler)	30
60s	Fontana 688136ZL	KATANGA (LP)	25
60s	Vogue	THE BLUE MESSAGE (LP, with Paul Bryant)	15
60s	Vogue	MEETIN' HERE (LP, with Paul Bryant)	15

ANACRUSIS
91	Metal Blade ZORRO 23	MANIC IMPRESSIONS (LP)	18

ANAL FLEAS
82	Rectal FLEA 45	Psych/Over the Edge/Landlord/Go Down (p/s, with insert)	80

ANALYSIS
81	Survival SUR 003	Surface Tension/Connections (p/s)	40

ANAN
68	Pye 7N 17571	Haze Woman/I Wonder Where My Sister's Gone	45
68	Pye 7N 17642	Madena/Standing Still	20

PETER ANATHAN
66	Fontana TF 705	You Can't Stop Me Loving You/Feel I'm Falling	15

ANATHEMA
90	Private Pressing	AN ILLIAD OF WOES EP (4 track demo cassette)	30
91	Private Pressing	ALL FAITH IS LOST EP (4 track demo cassette)	30
92	Peaceville VILE 36T	THE CRESTFALLEN EP (12", p/s)	30
94	Peaceville CC 6	WE ARE THE BIBLE EP (purple vinyl, p/s)	25
93	Peaceville VILE 34	SERENADES (LP)	30
95	Peaceville VILE 52	THE SILENT ENIGMA (LP)	25
96	Peaceville VILE 64	ETERNITY (LP)	25
99	Music For Nations MFN 250	JUDGEMENT (LP)	35
01	Music For Nations MFN 260	A FINE DAY TO EXIT (LP)	25
02	Peaceville LPVILE 73	ALTERNATIVE 4 (LP, first issued on CD in 1998)	30
10	Peaceville VILELP 305	A NATURAL DISASTER (2-LP, first issued on CD in 2003)	20
10	Kscope 812	WE'RE HERE BECAUSE WE'RE HERE (2-LP, 2000 only)	20

ANCIENT GREASE
71	Mercury 6338 033	WOMAN AND CHILDREN FIRST (LP, black/silver labels)	200

(see also Eyes Of Blue, Big Sleep, Man, Gary Pickford-Hopkins, Gentle Giant)

AND ALSO THE TREES
84	Reflex RE 3	The Secret Sea/Secrecy (p/s)	8
84	Reflex 12 RE 6	The Secret Sea/Secrecy/There Were No Bounds/The Tease The Tear/ Midnight Garden/Wallpaper Dying (12", p/s)	10
84	Reflex FS 9	Shantell/Wallpaper Dying (p/s)	5
83	Reflex (no cat. no.)	AND ALSO THE TREES (EP, cassette only)	15
84	Reflex LEX 1	AND ALSO THE TREES (LP)	18

ERIC ANDERSEN
65	Fontana TFL 6061	TODAY IS THE HIGHWAY (LP)	60
68	Fontana STFL 6068	'BOUT CHANGES AND THINGS TAKE 2 (LP, black/silver label)	40

LALE ANDERSEN
56	HMV 7EG 8277	THE ORIGINAL LILI MARLENE (EP)	10

BILL ANDERSON
63	Brunswick 05893	8 x 10/One Mile Over Two Mules Back	5

CAROL ANDERSON
79	Grapevine GRP 133	Sad Girl/I'll Get Off At The Next Stop	10

CHRISTIAN ANDERSON
74	DJM DJS 330	Supergirl/My Imagination (DJ Copy)	15
74	DJM DJS 330	Supergirl/My Imagination	6

ERNESTINE ANDERSON
60	Mercury AMT 1103	A Kiss To Build A Dream On/Come On, Baby, Let's Go	5
61	Mercury AMT 1137	A Lover's Question/That's All I Want From You	15
64	Sue WI 309	Keep An Eye On Love/Continental Mind	100
65	Stateside SS 455	Somebody Told You/How Many Times	15
65	Mercury MF 912	Jerk & Twine/You Can't Buy Love	30
61	Mercury MMC 14062	MOANIN' (LP)	15
64	Sue ILP 911	THE NEW SOUND OF ERNESTINE ANDERSON (LP, unissued)	150

GLADSTONE ANDERSON (& FOLLOWERS)
69	Blue Cat BS 172	Judas/The World Come To An End (with Followers)	30
74	Ashanti ASH 413	It May Sound Silly/Gladdy's Workshop	6
73	Ashanti SHAN 103	IT MAY SOUND SILLY (LP)	20

(see also Stranger & Gladdy, Tommy McCook)

HALEY ANDERSON
83	Magnet 12 MID 5	All To Myself (Dance Mix)/(7" Version)/(Instrumental) (12")	30

IAN (A.) ANDERSON
71	Village Thing VTSX 1002	One More Chance/Policeman's Ball	18
69	Saydisc EP SD 134	ALMOST THE COUNTRY BLUES (EP, with Elliot Jackson)	50
68	Saydisc Matchbox SDM 159	THE INVERTED WORLD (LP, with Mike Cooper)	70
69	Liberty LBS 83242E	STEREO DEATH BREAKDOWN (LP, blue label, as Ian Anderson Country Blues Band)	60
70	Fontana STL 5542	BOOK OF CHANGES (LP, black/silver labels)	120
70	Village Thing VTS 3	ROYAL YORK CRESCENT (LP, with lyric insert)	35
72	Village Thing VTS 9	A VULTURE IS NOT A BIRD YOU CAN TRUST (LP, laminated front cover)	35
72	Village Thing VTS 18	SINGER SLEEPS ON AS BLAZE RAGES (LP)	60

(see also Mike Cooper, Anderson Jones Jackson)

JAMES ANDERSON
71	Atlantic 2091-055	Mama Mama/Muskatel Muskatel	20

JON ANDERSON

76	Atlantic K 10840	Flight Of The Moorglade/To The Runner	5
80	Atlantic K 11619	Some Are Born/Days (p/s)	5

(see also Hans Christian, Warriors, Yes, Mike Oldfield, Jon & Vangelis)

KIP ANDERSON

67	President PT 163	You'll Lose A Good Thing/I'm Out Of Love	10

LEROY ANDERSON

57	Brunswick OE 9356	POPS CONCERT PART 1 (EP)	8
57	Brunswick OE 9357	POPS CONCERT PART 2 (EP)	8

MILLER ANDERSON

71	Deram DM 337	Bright City/Another Time, Another Place	12
71	Deram SDL 3	BRIGHT CITY (LP, gatefold sleeve)	90

(see also Voice, At Last The 1958 Rock'n'Roll Show, Keef Hartley Band, Hemlock, Dog Soldier, Lyn Dobson)

MOIRA ANDERSON

69	Decca F12989	The Holy City/Ave Maria	8

REUBEN ANDERSON

66	Doctor Bird DB 1045	Christmas Time Again/DESMOND TUCKER: Oh Holy Night	25

SONNY ANDERSON

60	London HLP 9036	Lonely Lonely Train/Yes, I'm Gonna Love You	60

UDELL T. ANDERSON

69	Direction 58-4212	Love Ain't Love/Funky Walk	15
69	Direction 58-4459	Keep On Loving Me/Rainmaker	8

VICKI ANDERSON

71	Mojo 2001 150	Super Good Part 1/Super Good Part 2	10
73	Mojo 2093 005	I'm Too Tough For Mr Big Stuff (Hot Pants)/Sound Funky	15
74	Mojo 2093 028	Don't Throw Your Love In The Garbage Can/Land Of Milk And Honey/ BOBBY BYRD: Sayin' It And Doin' It Are Two Different Things	10

(see also Bobby Byrd, James Brown)

ANDERSON, JONES, JACKSON

68	Saydisc 33 SD 125	ANDERSON, JONES, JACKSON (EP)	35

(see also Ian A. Anderson, Al Jones)

ANDERSON'S ALLSTARS

68	Blue Cat BS 133	Intensified Girls/Jump And Shout	150

PETER ANDREOLII

77	20th Century BTC 2342	Mind Excursion/When I Open Up My Eyes	5

BARBARA ANDREWS

70	Escort ERT 838	Lonesome Feeling/RAINY BOP: Hop Scotch	20

BARRY ANDREWS

80	Virgin VS 378	Rossmore Road (NW1)/Win A Night Out With A Well Known Paranoiac (p/s)	6

(see also XTC, Shriekback, Robert Fripp)

CATHERINE ANDREWS

80	Cat Tracks PURR LP 2	FRUITS (LP, with lyric sheet & poster sleeve)	50

(see also Gordon Giltrap, Inner City Unit)

CHRIS ANDREWS

66	Decca F 22365	Something On My Mind/I'll Do The Best I Can	5
66	Decca F 22404	Whatcha Gonna Do Now?/Lady Oh Lady	6
67	Decca F 22668	Hold On/Easy	40
69	Pye International 17727	Pretty Belinda/Make No Mistakes	7

(see also Chris Ravel & Ravers)

DAVE ANDREWS & SUGAR

68	Jewel JL 04	I'm On My Way/Beatin' Of My Heart	60

(see also Heinz)

ERNIE ANDREWS

60	Vogue V 9166	'Round Midnight/Lover Come Back To Me	6
65	Capitol CL 15407	Where Were You/What Do I See In The Girl	20
76	Capitol CL 15873	Fine Young Girl/Then I'll Know	8

HARVEY ANDREWS

72	Cube BUG 20	Soldier/In The Darkness	5
72	Cube BUG 26	Learning The Game/Don't Know The Time	5
65	Transatlantic TRAEP 133	HARVEY ANDREWS (EP)	35
75	Transatlantic BIG 525	(I'm Resigning) From Today/Darby And Joan (with Graham Cooper)	6
70	Decca Nova SDN 9	PLACES AND FACES (LP)	40
72	Cube HIFLY 10	WRITER OF SONGS (LP, with lyric insert)	20
73	Fly HIFLY 15	FRIENDS OF MINE (LP, gatefold sleeve)	20

INEZ ANDREWS & ANDREWETTES

65	Vogue EDVP 1283	INEZ ANDREWS & ANDREWETTES (EP)	40

JOHN ANDREWS & LONELY ONES

66	Parlophone R 5455	A Rose Growing In The Ruins/It's Just Love (DJ copy)	250
66	Parlophone R 5455	A Rose Growing In The Ruins/It's Just Love	175

LEE ANDREWS (& HEARTS)

57	London HL 7031	Teardrops/Girl Around The Corner (solo, export issue)	300
58	London HLM 8546	Teardrops/Girl Around The Corner (solo)	300
58	London HLM 8546	Teardrops/Girl Around The Corner (solo)	40
58	London HLU 8661	Try The Impossible/Nobody's Home (as Lee Andrews & Hearts)	300
58	London HLU 8661	Try The Impossible/Nobody's Home (as Lee Andrews & Hearts)	40

PATTY ANDREWS

55	Capitol CL 14324	Without Love/Where To My Love?	6
55	Capitol CL 14374	Suddenly There's A Valley/Booga Da Woog	6

(see also Bing Crosby, Jimmy Durante)

RUBY ANDREWS
76	ABC 4156	I Got A Bone To Pick With You/I Don't Know How To Love You	20

ANDREWS SISTERS
57	Capitol CL 14705	Rum And Coca-Cola/No, Baby	8

TIM ANDREWS
67	Parlophone R 5656	Sad Simon Lives Again/You Won't Be Seeing Me Anymore	30
68	Parlophone R 5695	(Something About) Suburbia/Your Tea Is Strong	30
70	Parlophone R 5824	Tiny Goddess/Josephine	40

(see also Fleur De Lys, Rupert's People)

TIM ANDREWS & PAUL KORDA
68	Parlophone R 5714	Smile If You Want To/Makin' Love To Him	20

(see also Paul Korda)

ANDROIDS
79	Android AND 001	Robot Riot/Andwellas Dream (p/s)	15

ANDROMEDA
69	RCA RCA 1854	Go Your Way/Keep Out 'Cos I'm Dying	30
69	RCA SF 8031	ANDROMEDA (LP)	700
90	Reflection MM 06	SEVEN, LONELY STREET (LP, with numbered & signed booklet, 500 only)	25
95	Kissing Spell KSLP 9497	LIVE 1967 (LP)	12

(see also Attack, Five Day Week Straw People, Hard Stuff, Atomic Rooster, John Du Cann, Fuzzy Duck)

AND SO TO BED
78	Stonehouse SH004	THE EP	12

AND THE INDIAN LOGIC
00s	Logic KJR 01	Beggar Man/The Change (p/s)	10

AND THE NATIVE HIPSTERS
79	Heater Volume HVR 003	There Goes Concorde Again.../Stands, Still The Building.../ I Wanna Be Around (several different coloured photocopied foldaround sleeves with insert in ploythene bag)	20
82	Illuminated/Glass HIP 1	TENDERLY HURT ME (Poor Prince/Hang Ten/Tenderly Hurt Me/Stuck) (12" EP, p/s)	15

ANDWELLA('S DREAM)
69	CBS 4301	Sunday/Midday Sun (as Andwella's Dream)	35
69	CBS 4469	Mrs. Man/Felix (as Andwella's Dream)	80
69	CBS 4634	Mr. Sunshine/Shades Of Grey (as Andwella's Dream)	50
70	Reflection RS 1	Every Little Minute/Michael Fitzhenry (as Andwellas Dream)	15
70	Reflection RS 3	Hold Onto Your Mind/Shadow Of The Night (as Andwella)	30
71	Reflection RS 6	People's People/Are You Ready (as Andwella)	10
69	CBS 63673	LOVE AND POETRY (LP, as Andwella's Dream)	700
70	Reflection REFL 10	WORLD'S END (LP, as Andwella, stickered sleeve with poster)	120
70	Reflection REFL 10	WORLD'S END (LP, without poster)	60
71	Reflection REF 1010	PEOPLE'S PEOPLE (LP, as Andwella)	70

(see also David Lewis, David Baxter)

BOB ANDY
67	Island WI 3040	I've Got To Get Back Home/SONNY BURKE: Rudy Girl	70
68	Studio One SO 2063	Too Experienced/Let Them Stay	50
68	Coxsone CS 7074	Born A Man/MARCIA GRIFFITHS: Mark My Word	50
69	Doctor Bird DB 1183	The Way I Feel/ETHIOPIANS: Long Time Now	60
69	Doctor Bird DB 1191	Games People Play/The Sun Shines For Me	25
69	Studio One SO 2075	I'm Going Home/SOUND DIMENSION: Straight Flush	40
70	Harry J. HJ 6612	Peace Of Mine/Weep	8
71	Trojan TR 7809	Green Green Valley/Peace Of Mind	6
71	Trojan TR 7821	One Woman/You Don't Know (B-side actually "Save Me Version" by Bob Andy Band)	6
71	Trojan TR 7840	One Woman/You Don't Know	6
71	London HLJ 7127	Games People Play/GAYLETTES: Son Of A Preacher Man (export issue)	10
72	Sioux SI 019	Baby I Need Your Loving/CIRCLES: Mammy Blue	10
72	Sioux SI 020	Everyday People/HONG GANG: Smoking Wild	10
72	Green Door GD 4047	Life/HARRY J. ALL STARS: Version	15
73	Green Door GD 4059	You Don't Know/The Border Song	30
73	Horse HOSS 31	One Woman/Second Hand Love	6
75	Fab FAB 241	Feeling Soul/SOUND DIMENSION: Part 2	15
75	Sound Tracs SK2 8	Nyah/Nyah Dub	8
76	Tropical TST 110	Feeling Soul/Rock It Down	10
86	L ANKA AV0025TLP	RETROSPECTIVE (LP)	12

(see also Bob & Marcia, Larry & Alvin)

ANDY & CLYDE
65	Rio R 62	Never Be A Slave/Magic Is Love	12
65	Rio R 69	I'm So Lonesome/WINSTON STEWART: Day After Day	12
65	Rio R 71	We All Have To Part/UPSETTERS: Scandalizing	80

HORACE ANDY
72	Count Shelley 2	Cha Cha Children/Version	8
72	Attack ATT 8026	Feel Good All Over/PHIL PRATT ALLSTARS: Feel Good (Version)	6
73	Bread BR 1170	Don't Try To Use Me/Goddess Of Love	12
73	Randy's RAN 533	Don't Think About Me (with Earl Flute)/DINO PERKINS: Skin Him Alive	20
73	Atra ATRA 008	Children Of Israel/Part 2	8
74	Ackee ACK 530	Til/IMPACT ALLSTARS: Version	6
75	Attack ATT 8117	Nice And Easy/Version	10
75	Fab FAB 260	Oh Lord Why Lord/SOUND DIMENSION: Part 2	10
75	Morpheus MOR 1010	Got To Get You	6
76	Venture VEN 7706	Skylarking/Version	10
76	Terminal TM 105	Thank The Lord/Part Two (actually the SUNSHOT BAND)	10
77	Serious Business SB 02	Rock To Sleep/Version	35
79	Sufferer's Height SUFF 005	Pure Ranking/The Return Of Jammy's Hi-Fi (Round One)/TREVOR RANKING: Whip Them Jah Jah (12")	30
84	Music Hawk MHD 13	Confusion/Version (12")	15

85	Rough Trade RTT 172	Get Down/RHYTHM POSSE : Get Down Deeper (12")	50
72	Trojan TBL 197	YOU ARE MY ANGEL (LP)	25
78	Solid Groove SGL 107	EXCLUSIVELY (LP)	40
84	Music Hawk MHLP001	CONFUSION (LP)	20
99	Virgin SADLP 9	LIVING IN THE FLOOD (LP)	15

(see also Jon Cuno, Big Youth)

HORACE ANDY & FREDDIE MCKAY
| 75 | Treble 7 | Talking Love/Dub | 8 |

ANDY & JOEY
62	Island WI 056	Have You Ever/Cross My Heart	20
64	Port-O-Jam PJ 4009	I Want To Know/My Love Has Gone	40
64	Ska Beat JB 162	You're Wondering Now/You'll Never (copies also exist on R&B label)	30

(see also Roland Alphonso)

PATRICK ANDY
| 78 | Grove Music GMDM 3 | Woman, Woman, Woman/TOMMY MCCOOK: Lamb's Bread (12") | 30 |

JOHNNY ANGEL
60	Parlophone R 4642	Chinese Butterfly/My Very Good Friend The Milkman	8
60	Parlophone R 4679	Too Young To Go Steady/You're Thrilling	8
61	Parlophone R 4750	What Happens To Love/Luna Luna Luna Lu	8
61	Parlophone R 4795	Web Of Love/Trocadero-Double-Nine-One-O	8
62	Parlophone R 4874	Look, Look Little Angel/Jenny From Missouri	8
62	Parlophone R 4948	Better Luck Next Time/The Power Of You	5
63	Parlophone R 5026	A Touch Of Venus/The Two Together	5

MARIAN ANGEL
65	Columbia DB 7537	It's Gonna Be Alright/Tomorrow's Fool	15
65	Columbia DB 7705	You Can't Buy My Love/One Way Only	10
66	CBS 202391	Little Bit Of Sunshine/All The Time In The World	15

ANGEL PAVEMENT
| 69 | Fontana TF 1059 | Baby You've Gotta Stay/Green Mello Hill | 18 |
| 70 | Fontana TF 1072 | Tell Me What I've Got To Do/When Will I See June Again | 25 |

(see also Fortes Mentum, Pussy)

ANGEL STREET
| 79 | Ellie Jay EJSP 9290 | Done It Again/Song For You (500 only) | 200 |

ANGEL WITCH
80	EMI EMI 5064	Sweet Danger/Flight Nineteen (p/s)	10
80	EMI 12EMI 5064	Sweet Danger/Flight Nineteen/Hades Paradise (12", p/s)	20
80	Bronze BRO 108	Angel Witch/Gorgon (p/s)	8
81	Bronze BRO 121	Loser/Suffer/Dr Phibes (p/s)	10
85	Killerwatt KIL 3001	Goodbye/Reawakening (no p/s)	6
80	Bronze BRON 532	ANGELWITCH (LP)	20
85	Killerwatt KILP 4001	SCREAMIN' N' BLEEDIN' (LP)	15

(see also Tytan)

ANGEL (1)
| 74 | Cube BUG 41 | Little Boy Blue/Tragedy Queen | 10 |
| 74 | Cube BUG 51 | Good Time Fanny/Who D'Ya Think Your Fooling | 10 |

ANGEL (2)
77	Casablanca CBC 104	Magic Touch/Big Boy	5
76	Casablanca CBC 4007	ANGEL (LP, with insert)	15
76	Casablanca CBC 4010	HELLUVA BAND (LP)	12

ANGELA & HER FANS
| 66 | Pye 7N 17108 | Love Ya Illya/I Know You | 10 |

(see also Alma Cogan)

ANGELETTES
| 72 | Decca F 13284 | Don't Let Him Touch You/Rainy Day | 5 |

ANGELIC UPSTARTS
78	Dead IS/AU/1024	Murder Of Liddle Towers/Police Oppression (p/s, 1,000 only)	50
78	Rough Trade RT/SW 001	Murder Of Liddle Towers/Police Oppression (reissue, p/s)	6
79	Warner Bros K 17354	I'm An Upstart/Leave Me Alone (green vinyl, no p/s)	5
79	Warner Bros K 17354T	I'm An Upstart/Leave Me Alone (12", p/s)	8
79	Warner Bros K 17426C	Teenage Warning/The Young Ones (red vinyl, no p/s)	5
80	Zonophone Z 7	Last Night Another Soldier/The Man Who Came In From The Beano (p/s)	5
81	Zonophone Z 12	England/Stick's Diary (p/s)	12
83	Anagram ANA 12	The Burglar (p/s, unissued)	0
85	Gas GM 3010	Brighton Bomb/Thin Red Line/Soldier (12", banned 'Maggie Thatcher' p/s)	15
79	Warner Bros K 56717	TEENAGE WARNING (LP)	15
80	Warner Bros K 56806	WE GOTTA GET OUT OF THIS PLACE (LP)	12
81	Zonophone ZEM 102	LIVE (LP, with free live flexidisc: "We're Gonna Take The World"/ Leave Me Alone/"The Young Ones"/"White Riot" [no cat. no.])	15
81	Zonophone ZEM 102	LIVE (LP)	12
83	Anagram GRAM 007	ANGEL DUST (LP)	12
85	Gas GLP 4012	THE POWER OF THE PRESS (LP)	12
85	Razor RAZM 32	LIVE IN YUGOSLAVIA (LP)	15
85	Anagram GRAM004	REASONS WHY (LP, with inner sleeve)	12
90	Link LP 140	LOST & FOUND (LP)	15

ANGELINA
| 65 | Fontana TF 648 | I Just Don't Know How/Wishing My Life Away | 5 |

BOBBY ANGELO & TUXEDOS
| 61 | HMV POP 892 | Baby Sitting/Skinny Lizzie | 20 |
| 61 | HMV POP 982 | I Gotta Have You/Don't Stop | 30 |

(see also Innocents [UK], End)

JERRY ANGELO
| 59 | Parlophone R 4548 | Crush Me/Mary Lou | 10 |

59	Parlophone R 4561	If You Change Your Mind/I Love You My Love	5
60	Parlophone R 4656	Maria Elena/Old Man River	10
62	Palette PG 9031	Lonely Hill/Make Her Mine	5
62	Palette PG 9034	Innocent Angel/The Boy Who Walks Alone	10

MICHAEL ANGELO & HIS ORCHESTRA
| 61 | Columbia DB 4705 | Rocco's Theme/Spinneree | 6 |

(see also John Barry)

MAYA ANGELOU
| 57 | London HA-U 2062 | MISS CALYPSO (LP) | 12 |

ANGELS
62	Pye International 7N 25150	Everybody Loves A Lover/Blow Joe	20
63	Mercury AMT 1211	My Boyfriend's Back/(Love Me) Now	20
63	Mercury AMT 1215	I Adore Him/Thank You And Goodnight	10
64	Philips BF 1312	Wow Wee Wee/Snowflakes And Teardrops	10

(see also Beach-Nuts)

ANGELS & AIRWAVES
06	Geffen 1702866	It Hurts/The Gift (live) (Picture disc in stickered PVC sleeve)	12
06	Geffen MCS 40461	The Adventure (1-sided picture disc in stickered PVC sleeve)	12
07	Geffen 1751195	Everything's Magic/Do It For Me Now (Acoustic) (picture disc in stickered PVC sleeve)	10

(see also Blink 182, Box Car Racer)

ANGELS AND EIGHTEEN
| 72 | RAK 137 | Midnight Flight/Flight 2 | 100 |

GUY ANGIER
| 70 | (No label or cat no) | GUITAR AND BANANAS (LP, with insert) | 50 |

ANGLIANS
| 67 | CBS 202489 | A Friend Of Mine/Daytime Lover | 15 |

(see also Moving Finger)

ANGLOS
65	Brit WI 004	Incense/You're Fooling Me	50
65	Fontana TF 589	Incense/You're Fooling Me (reissue)	25
67	Sue WI 4033	Incense/You're Fooling Me (unissued)	200
69	Island WIP 6061	Incense/You're Fooling Me (2nd reissue)	10

(see also Spencer Davis Group, Stevie Winwood)

ANGOR WAT
| 85 | Children Of The Revolution GURT8 | GENERAL STRIKE (LP) | 15 |

ANGRY YOUNG MEN
| 59 | Fontana H 187 | Big Daddy/Ciribiribin | 8 |

ANIMAL COLLECTIVE
04	Paw Tracks PAW 003	Wastered/Wastered (12" one side BLACK DICE, 1,000 only)	20
04	Fat Cat 7FAT 15	Who Could Win A Rabbit/Baby Day (p/s)	15
05	Fat Cat 7FAT 19	Grass/Must Be Treeman/Ficle Cycle (p/s)	15
06	No label or Cat. No.)	Purple Bottle/Polly (tour 7", white label, plain white die-cut sleeve. Later pressings have track info on sleeve)	20
06	Fat Cat 12FAT 060	People/Tikwid/My Favourite Colours/People (live) (12")	20
07	Domino RUG 270T	Fireworks (1-sided pink vinyl other side etched 10", stickered, die-cut pink sleeve)	10
04	Fat Cat FATSPLP 08	SUNG TONGS (LP)	20
05	Fat Cat FATSLP 11	FEELS (2-LP)	18
06	Domino WIGLP199	STRAWBERRY JAM (2-LP, gatefold with inners)	20
09	Fat Cat FATSP08LPX	SUNG TONGS (2-LP, reissue, 180 gm vinyl)	15
09	Fat Cat FATSP11LPX	FEELS (2-LP, gatefold, reissue 180gm vinyl)	15
09	Domino WIGLP216	MERRIWEATHER POST PAVILION (2-LP, gatefold)	15

(see also Panda Bear, Avey Tare)

ANIMAL FARM
| 84 | Rot Records ASS 7 | Model Soldier/John And Julie (p/s) | 10 |

ANIMALS
64	Columbia DB 7247	Baby Let Me Take You Home/Gonna Send You Back To Walker	10
64	Columbia DB 7301	The House Of The Rising Sun/Talkin' 'Bout You	6
64	Columbia DB 7354	I'm Crying/Take It Easy	6
65	Columbia DB 7445	Don't Let Me Be Misunderstood/Club-A-Go Go (standard issue, matrix: '2N')	7
65	Columbia DB 7445	Don't Let Me Be Misunderstood/Club-A-Go Go (mispressing, with 'demo' version of A-side, matrix: '1N')	10
65	Columbia DB 7539	Bring It On Home To Me/For Miss Caulker	7
65	Columbia DB 7639	We've Gotta Get Out Of This Place/I Can't Believe It	8
65	Columbia DB 7741	It's My Life/I'm Going To Change The World	6
66	Decca F 12332	Inside Looking Out/Outcast	10
66	Decca F 12407	Don't Bring Me Down/Cheating	10
82	Rak RRP 1	The House Of The Rising Sun/Don't Let Me Be Misunderstood/I'm Crying (picture disc)	5
63	Graphic Sound ALO 10867	I JUST WANNA MAKE LOVE TO YOU (12" EP, 1-sided, 99 only, as Alan Price Rhythm & Blues Group or as Animals, private pressing, blank white cover, typed label)	450
64	Columbia SEG 8374	THE ANIMALS IS HERE (EP)	25
65	Columbia SEG 8400	THE ANIMALS (EP)	20
65	Columbia SEG 8439	THE ANIMALS NO. 2 (EP)	25
65	Columbia SEG 8452	THE ANIMALS ARE BACK (EP)	30
65	Decca DFE 8643	IN THE BEGINNING THERE WAS EARLY ANIMALS (EP, reissue of Graphic Sound EP)	35
66	Columbia SEG 8499	ANIMAL TRACKS (EP)	35
64	Columbia 33SX 1669	THE ANIMALS (LP, blue/black label with "sold in the U.K..." label text)	80
64	EMI Regal SREG 1104	THE ANIMALS (LP, export issue)	60
65	Columbia 33SX 1708	ANIMAL TRACKS (LP, first pressing with 33SX on label)	100
66	Columbia SX 6035	THE MOST OF THE ANIMALS (LP)	25
66	Decca LK 4797	ANIMALISMS (LP)	45
76	DJM DJSL 069	IN CONCERT FROM NEWCASTLE (LP)	15
77	BARN 2314 104	BEFORE WE WERE RUDELY INTERRUPTED (LP)	15

(see also Eric Burdon & Animals, Alan Price, Danny McCullough)

ANIMALS & MEN
80	Strange Days DAYS 1	The Terraplane Fixation/Shell Shock (p/s)	7
80	TW HIT 101	Don't Misbehave In The New Age/Machines (p/s)	5

ANIMATED EGG
69	Marble Arch MAL 890	ANIMATED EGG (LP)	30

ANITA & TH' SO AND SO'S
62	RCA RCA 1278	Joey Baby/Rinky Tinky Rhythm	5

PAUL ANKA
SINGLES
57	Columbia DB 3980	Diana/Don't Gamble With Love (mauve label)	10
57	Columbia DB 3980	Diana/Don't Gamble With Love (re-pressings on green or black label)	5
57	Columbia DB 4022	I Love You, Baby/Tell Me That You Love Me (mauve label)	5
58	Columbia DB 4063	You Are My Destiny/When I Stop Loving You (mauve label)	5
58	Columbia DB 4110	Crazy Love/Let The Bells Keep Ringing (mauve label)	5
58	Columbia DB 4199	Just Young/So It's Goodbye	5
59	Columbia DB 4241	(All Of A Sudden) My Heart Sings/That's Love	6
59	Columbia DB 4355	Put Your Head On My Shoulder/Don't Ever Leave Me	5
63	RCA RCA 1340	Remember Diana/At Night (p/s)	5
68	RCA RCA 1676	Can't Get You Out Of My Mind/When We Get There	40
68	RCA RCA 1676	Can't Get You Out Of My Mind/When We Get There (DJ copy)	50
75	RCA RCA 2498	I Can't Help Loving You/Can't Get Along Very Well Without Her	12

EPs
57	Columbia SEG 7747	DIANA (EP)	15
58	Columbia SEG 7801	ANKA AGAIN (EP)	15
59	Columbia SEG 7890	SING SING SING (EP)	15
60	Columbia SEG 7985	SINGS SONGS FROM 'GIRLS' TOWN' AND OTHER SUCCESSES (EP)	15
64	RCA RCX 7127	FLY ME TO THE MOON (EP)	8
64	RCA RCX 7170	SYLVIE (EP)	10

ALBUMS
58	Columbia 33SX 1092	PAUL ANKA (LP, green label)	20

(see also Micki Marlo & Paul Anka, Neil Sedaka)

ANNABEL DREAM
60s	Oak (no cat no)	My Last Date With You/Gary, Won't You Marry Me (Unreleased - acetate only)	50

ANNALISE
99	Boss Tunage BOSTAGE 701	Signposts And Alleyways/Empire Builder (p/s, 1-sided green vinyl with free CD, numbered, 250 copies only)	10

ANNETTE (& AFTERBEATS)
59	Top Rank JAR 137	Lonely Guitar/Wild Willie	6
59	Top Rank JAR 233	First Name Initial/My Heart Became Of Age (with Afterbeats)	8
60	Top Rank JAR 343	It Took Dreams/O Dio Mio	5
60	Pye International 7N 25061	Pineapple Princess/Luau Cha Cha Cha (with Afterbeats)	8
64	HMV POP 1270	Muscle Beach Party/I Dream About Frankie	30
64	HMV POP 1322	Scrambled Egghead/Merlin Jones	12
65	HMV POP 1447	The Monkey's Uncle (with The Beach Boys)/How Will I Know My Love	40
59	Gala 45XP 1046	TALL PAUL (EP)	20
61	Buena Vista BV 3305	DANCE ANNETTE (LP)	25
64	HMV CLP 1782	ANNETTE'S BEACH PARTY (LP)	30
64	Buena Vista BV 3325	PAJAMA PARTY (LP)	25

ANNETTE & KEYMEN
64	King KG 1006	Look Who's Blue/How Can I Tell Him	5

ANNIS
79	GTO GT 266	Don't Play Your Games/After Me	10

ANNIVERSARY
78	Aerco AERE 102	GIVE ME A SMILE (EP)	20

ANN-MARGRET
61	RCA RCA 1245	I Just Don't Understand/I Don't Hurt Anymore	10
64	RCA RCX 7148	THE VIVACIOUS ONE (EP)	15
62	RCA RD 27239/SF 5116	AND HERE SHE IS (LP, mono/stereo)	15
64	RCA Victor RD/SF 7649	BACHELORS' PARADISE (LP, mono/stereo)	12

ANNO DOMINO
71	Deram SML-R 1085	ON THIS NEW DAY (LP)	300

ANONYMOUSLY YOURS
69	Trojan TR 680	Get Back/ERNIE SMITH : Not For Sale	15
69	Trojan TR 681	It's Your Thing/69 (B-side actually by Wallace Wilson)	15
69	Duke DU 40	Organism/Itch	12

ANOREXIA
80	Slim SJP 812	Rapist In The Park/I'm A Square/Pets	35

ANOTHER MAN'S POISON
92	Tick Tock TT 2	I Spit On My Fist/Wallop (p/s)	7
92	Tick Tock TT1	Alf Garnet's Heart Attack/Now That's What I Call (hand stamped die cut paper sleeve)	10

ANOTHER PRETTY FACE
79	New Pleasure Z1	All The Boys Love Carrie/That's Not Enough (green and white foldout p/s)	18
79	New Pleasure Z2	All The Boys Love Carrie/That's Not Enough (red and white p/s)	10
80	Chicken Jazz JAZZ 1	Heaven Gets Closer Every Day/Live Forever (p/s)	7
80	Virgin VS 320	Whatever Happened To The West?/Goodbye 1970's (p/s)	10
80	Chicken Jazz JAZZ 1	I'M SORRY THAT I BEAT YOU, I'M SORRY THAT I SCREAMED, FOR A MOMENT THERE I REALLY LOST CONTROL (8-track cassette with fanzine and badge. Some copies exist with tracks of DNV single taped onto the end)	30
81	Chicken Jazz JAZZ 2	Soul To Soul/A Woman's Place/God On The Screen (foldout p/s)	15

MINT VALUE £

ANOTHER SUNNY DAY
88	Sarah SARAH 003	Anorak City (flexidisc free with Are You Scared To Get Happy fanzine (SARAH 004, 1,500 only – must be together)	30
88	Sarah SARAH 007	I'm In Love With A Girl Who Doesn't Know I Exist/Things Will Be Nice/ The Centre Of My Little World (14" x 10" foldout poster p/s)	25
89	Caff CAFF 7	Genetic Engineering/Kilburn Towers (p/s, with inner)	30
89	Sarah SARAH 016	What's happened?/Can't You Tell It's True?/Impossible (foldover p/s in poly bag, insert)	10
89	Sarah SARAH 022	You Should All Be Murdered/Horseriding/Green (foldover p/s in poly bag, insert)	15
90	Sarah SARAH 035	Rio/The Very Beginning (p/s, insert)	10
92	Sarah SARAH 060	New Year's Honours/I Don't Suppose I'll Get A Second Chance (p/s, insert)	10
92	Sarah SARAH 613	LONDON WEEKEND (LP)	25

ANSEL SCANDAL
76	Dynamic DYN 105	Roots Food/Roots Food - Dub	6

BRETT ANSELL
62	Oriole CB 1701	That's Where Lonesome Lives/The Door Is Open	20
62	Oriole CB 1725	Rosalita/The Outsider	15

ANSELL (COLLINS) & ELAINE
72	Camel CA 98	Presenting Cheater/RON WILSON: Official Trombone	15

MARK ANSLEY
70	Mother MOT 2	909/Venus	30

ANSWER
05	Albert JASUK 015	Keep On Believin'/New Day Rising	8
05	Albert JAS UK 017	Never Too Late/Some Unity (stickered p/s)	7

ANSWERS (1)
66	Columbia DB 7847	It's Just A Fear/You've Gotta Believe Me	200
66	Columbia DB 7953	That's What You're Doing To Me/Got A Letter From My Baby	70

(see also Misunderstood, High Tide)

ANSWERS (2)
71	Spark SRL 1058	Give Me All That I Need/Tawny Wood	12

ANT
74	Pye 7N 45332	Banana Pie/No Road Goes Your Way	15

ADAM ANT
85	CBS A 6367	Vive Le Rock/Greta X (p/s, mispressing, both sides play "Vive Le Rock")	5
85	CBS CD 26583	VIVE LE ROCK (CD, with extra track "Human Bondage Den")	20
95	EMI CDEMS370	Beautiful Dream (single version)/Let's Have A Fight/Billy Boy/Wonderful (acoustic) (CD withdrawn, 7 known copies)	100
85	EMI CDEM370	Beautiful Dream (single version)/Shake Your Hips/Antmusic (Acoustic)/Beautiful Dream (Lucas Full Length Mix) (CD, withdrawn, 2 known copies)	150

(see also Adam & The Ants, Maneaters)

ANTEEEKS
66	Philips BF 1471	I Don't Want You/Ball And Chain	200

PETER ANTELL
65	Pye International 7N 25329	The Times They Are A-Changin'/Yesterday And Tomorrow	5

ANTENA
82	Operation Twilight OPT 02	The Boy From Ipanema/Spiral Staircase (p/s)	5

ANTHEM (1)
71	Buddah 2359017	ANTHEM (LP)	40

ANTHEM (2)
81	EJSP9576	England/Some Like It Hot/Do You Mind (EP, p/s, 500 only)	100

ANTHILL MOB (1)
92	Anthill ANT 1T	Penelope's Theme (12" white label)	35
93	Anthill ANT 2T	Antology/Black Rushin'/The hooded claw (tango mix) (12")	30
93	Anthill ANT 3T	Antology (The Top Buzz Stonehenge Remix)/Black Rushin' (Anthill Remix) (12")	20

ANTHILL MOB (2)
95	Confetti MK 01	Feel It/Deep Down/Untitled/Untitled (white label 12")	30
95	Confetti MK001	MAKESHIFT EP (12")	90
96	Confetti COEP 01	Promise Of... /Was She Ever Mine?/So In Love/Got To Do It (12")	35
96	Confetti COEP 02	Feel The Groove/ANTHILL MOB FEATURING P. PITSTOP - Do You Know?/P. PITSTOP - I Know How To Love! (12")	25
97	Confetti COEP 05	Why (Inside The Rise)/Things Just Started (12")	25
97	Confetti COEP 06	Cloudy Day/Agitator (12")	15
97	Confetti COEP 01	Missing/Player/X2C/Flava/Sound/Cuts (2 x 12")	70
97	Confetti COEP 08	Higher/How Ya Feeling (12")	15
97	Love Peace & Unity LOVE 03	Burning (The Original Mix) (10" picture disc, 500 only, same track both sides)	35
97	Makeshift MR 001	Set You Free/In The Name/Shake The House/Heaven Knows (12")	15
98	Makeshift MR 002	Never Ever Time/Time To Move/Don't Know/Give Me (12")	20
98	Quench QUE 14	Don't Leave Me/Listen (12")	30
00	Confetti COEP 19	ANTHILL MOB EP (12")	25
97	Love Peace & Unity LOVE 04	A SPECIAL COLLECTION OF ENCHANTED RHYTHMS (2 x LP)	40

(see also Mystic matt And The Anthill Mob)

BILLIE ANTHONY
54	Columbia SCM 5143	This Ole House/Oh, What A Dream	10
54	Columbia SCM 5155	Teach Me Tonight/Don't Let The Kiddygeddin	6
55	Columbia SCM 5164	Butterscotch Hop/No More	12
55	Columbia SCM 5174	Tweedlee Dee/Shake The Hand Of A Stranger	10
55	Columbia SCM 5184	Something's Gotta Give/Boom Boom Boomerang	6
55	Columbia SCM 5191	The Banjo's Back In Town (with Big Ben Banjo Band)/Ten Little Kisses	6
55	Columbia SCM 5210	Bring Me A Bluebird/The Old Pi-anna Rag	6
57	Columbia DB 3874	I Dreamed/The Charge Of The Light Brigade (B-side with ex-R.S.M. Brittain)	5
57	Columbia DB 3935	Rock-A-Billy/A Needle And Thread	10
57	Columbia DB 3970	One/It's Fun Finding Out About London (with Big Ben Banjo Band)	6
56	Columbia SCM 5286	Sweet Old Fashioned Girl/The Treasure Of Love	5

(see also Big Ben Banjo Band)

DAVID ANTHONY
68	Island WI 3148	All Night/Out Of My Mind	40

(see also Dave Anthony's Moods)

JIM ANTHONY
72	Satril SAT 4	Sasha/White Rose	5

MARC ANTHONY
63	Stateside SS 210	Let's All Cheer Again/Why Do I Love You	12

MARK ANTHONY & JETS
70	Unity UN 565	More Balls/TONY KING: Bum Ball (Chapter II)	5

MARKE ANTHONY
60	Decca F11242	Why Didn't You Tell Me/Foolishly	6

RAY ANTHONY (1)
55	Capitol CL 14205	I Don't Hurt Anymore/Woman's World	5
55	Capitol CL 14243	Juke Box Special/Heat Wave	5
55	Capitol CL 14275	Baby You/Happy Hornblowers (with Dick Stabile Orchestra)	5
55	Capitol CL 14306	Sluefoot/Something's Gotta Give	5
55	Capitol CL 14321	Learnin' The Blues/Mmmm Mamie	5
55	Capitol CL 14345	Pete Kelly's Blues/DC-7	5
55	Capitol CL 14354	Hernando's Hideaway/The Bunny Hop	10
56	Capitol CL 14525	Flip-Flop/Hurricane Anthony	10
56	Capitol CL 14670	Love Is Just Around The Corner/Dancing Lovers	5
57	Capitol CL 14689	Rock Around The Rock Pile/The Girl Can't Help It	20
57	Capitol CL 14703	Plymouth Rock/Calypso Dance	5
57	Capitol CL 14769	The Bunny Hop/The Hokey Pokey	5
57	Capitol CL 14775	Drive-In/Show Me The Way To Go Home	5
58	Capitol CL 14929	Peter Gunn/Tango For Two (Mmm Shall We Dance?)	8
59	Capitol CL 15019	The Bunny Hop Rock/Walkin' To Mother's	6
57	Capitol EAP 1-823	THE GIRL CAN'T HELP IT (EP)	35
57	Capitol EAP 1-958	ROCK AND ROLL WITH RAY ANTHONY (EP)	35

(see also Gordon MacRae & Ray Anthony)

RAY ANTHONY (2)
79	Mango Media 23	The Arabian Funk/Time	20

RAYBURN ANTHONY
60	London HLS 9167	Who's Gonna Shoe Your Pretty Little Feet/There's No Tomorrow	25

VAL ANTHONY
53	Columbia SCM 5079	Walk With The Wind/No Tears, No Regrets	5
54	Columbia SCM 5103	The Heart Of A Fool/The Portuguese Fishermen	5

DAVE ANTHONY'S MOODS
66	Parlophone R 5438	New Directions/Give It A Chance	75

(see also David Anthony)

ANTHRAX (U.K.)
83	Small Wonder SMALL 27	THEY'VE GOT IT ALL WRONG (EP, p/s)	10
83	Crass 221984/9	CAPITALISM IS CANNIBALISM (EP, foldout p/s)	20

ANTHRAX (U.S.)
86	Island 12ISP 285	Madhouse/Air/God Save The Queen (12", picture disc)	18
86	Island 12IS 285	Madhouse/Air/God Save The Queen (12", p/s with patch)	12
87	Island ISP 338	I'm The Man/Caught In The Mosh (Live) (Anthrax logo shaped picture disc)	7
87	Island ISX 316	I Am The Law (live)/Bud E. Luvbomm And Satan's Lougne Band/Madhouse (live) (red vinyl, p/s)	18
87	Island ISP 325	Indians/Sabbath Bloody Sabbath (picture disc with sticker)	8
89	Island IS 409	Anti Social/Parasite (p/s)	7
91	Island 12 IS 490	Bring The Noise (featuring Chuck D)/Keep It In The Family (live)/I Am The Law '91 (12", p/s)	8
86	Music For Nations MFN62P	SPREADING THE DISEASE (LP, picture disc)	20
87	Music For Nations MFN14P	FISTFUL OF METAL (LP, picture disc)	20
87	Island PILPS 9865	AMONG THE LIVING (LP, picture disc)	20

ANTI ESTABLISHMENT
80	Charnel House CADAV 1	1980/Mechanical Man (p/s)	10
82	Glass GLASS 022	Future Girl/No Trust (p/s)	5
83	Glass GLASS 023	Anti Men/Misunderstood (p/s)	5

ANTILLES
83	Creole CR 12-51	I've Got To Have You/Latin Dream (12")	30

ANTI NOWHERE LEAGUE
81	WXYZ ABCD1	Streets Of London (1-sided test pressing)	35
82	WXYZ ABCD 1	So What/Streets Of London (p/s, withdrawn)	8
82	WXYZ ABCD 2	I Hate ... People/Let's Break The Law (p/s)	6
82	WXYZ ABCD 4	Woman/Rocker (picture disc)	6
87	GWR A1	Crime/Working For The Company (Unreleased Test Pressing)	20
82	WXYZ LMNOP1	WE ARE...THE LEAGUE (LP)	15

ANTI PASTI
90	Dose DOSE1	FORE SORE POINTS (EP, 500 only)	18
81	Rondelet ABOUT 5	LAST CALL (LP)	12

ANTI SECT
84	Endangered Music EDR 4	Out From The Void/Hope Future Poisoned By Fear	25
11	Anti Sect ANTI 010	4 Minutes Past Midnight/Out From The Void (Part 2) (10", gig only, limited edition of 300)	10
83	Spiderleg SDL 16	IN DARKNESS THERE IS NO CHOICE (LP)	30
84	Big Top	LIVE IN THE DARKNESS (LP, splattered grey vinyl with insert, 1,000 only)	20
94	Vinyl Japan	PEACE IS BETTER THAN A PLACE IN HISTORY (LP)	20

ANTI-SOCIAL WORKERS & MAD PROFESSOR
83	Ariwa ARI008LP	POSITIVE STYLE PUNKY REGGAE PARTY (LP)	20

MINT VALUE £

ANTI SOCIAL (1)
77	Dynamite DRO 1	Traffic Lights/Teacher Teacher (no p/s)	500
82	Beat The System BTS 2	Battle Scarred Skinheads/Sewer Rat/Official Hooligan (p/s)	18
82	Beat The System FIT 2	Too Many People/Let's Have Some (p/s)	10

ANTI SOCIAL (2)
82	Lightbeat SOCIAL 1	MADE IN ENGLAND (EP)	20

ANTI STATE CONTROL
83	Asc Records ASC1	Glue Sniffing Blues/M.U.S.E/Third World Bomb	200

ANTI SYSTEM
83	Reconcilliation RECONCILE 3	Strangelove/So Long As/MORBID HUMOUR: Oh My God (Parts 1 and 2)	25
83	Paragon/Pax PAX 11	DEFENCE OF THE REALM (EP)	25
86	Reconcilliation RECONCILE 4	A LOOK AT LIFE (12" EP)	20
85	Reconcilliation RECONCILE 1	NO LAUGHING MATTER (LP)	30

ANTOINE
66	Vogue VRS 7009	Les Elucubrations D'Antoine/J'ai Oublié La Nuit	5
66	Vogue VRS 7017	Before The Good Thing/Elephants Looking At Me	5
66	Vogue VRS 7022	Ma Fete Forraine/Only These Few Snowflakes	5
68	Vogue VRS 7028	La Tramontana/Io Voglie Andaré In Guerra	5
69	Vogue VRS 7031	The Football Match/Where Did Everyone Go To	5
66	Vogue VRE 5024	LA GUERRE (LP)	12
68	Vogue VRL 3032	ANTOINE (LP)	15

ANTOINETTE
64	Decca F 11820	Jenny Let Him Go/Please Don't Hurt Me Anymore	10
64	Piccadilly 7N 35201	There He Goes (The Boy I Love)/Little Things Mean A Lot	10
65	Piccadilly 7N 35223	Thank You For Loving Me/If You Really Love Me	5
65	Piccadilly 7N 35252	Our House/What's A-Happening To Me	5
66	Piccadilly 7N 35293	Why Don't I Run Away From You/There's No-One In The Whole Wide World	30
66	Piccadilly 7N 35310	Lullaby Of Love/I'm For You	20

(see also Toni Daly)

ANTON
75	Spark 1120	Shot Down In Action/Mine All Mine	12

REY ANTON
62	Oriole CB 1722	As If I Care/After The Laughter	15
62	Oriole CB 1771	Hey Good Looking/Mary Lou	15
63	Oriole CB 1811	Peppermint Man/Can't Say More Than That (with Batons)	15
63	Oriole CB 1843	How Long Can This Last/If You Don't Want Me Now	20
64	Parlophone R 5132	You Can't Judge A Book By The Cover/It's Cold Outside (with Peppermint Men)	35
64	Parlophone R 5172	Heard It All Before/I Want You (with Peppermint Men)	20
65	Parlophone R 5245	Wishbone/Kingsway (with Peppermint Men)	20
65	Parlophone R 5274	Girl You Don't Know Me/Don't Treat Me Bad (with Peppermint Men)	30
65	Parlophone R 5310	Nothing Comes Easy/Breakout (with Peppermint Men)	15
65	Parlophone R 5358	Premeditation/Now That It's Over (with Pro Form)	30
66	Parlophone R 5420	Don't You Worry Boy/Hold It Babe (with Pro Formula)	15
66	Parlophone R 5487	Things Get Better/Newsboy (with Pro Form)	15

ANTONIOU
82	Elite DAZZ 17	Sound On Sound/Street Sound (12" stickered plain sleeve)	8

(see also Atmosfear)

TONY ANTONIU
84	Spartan 12 SP 12	Send In The Night/(Extender Version) (12")	30

DAVE ANTONY
68	Mercury MF 1031	Race With The Wind/Hide And Seek	20

(see also Dave Anthony['s Moods])

MARK ANTONY & AVENGERS
60s	Malconi MCD LP 17	MARK ANTONY & THE AVENGERS (LP, private pressing, plain sleeve)	100

MIKI ANTONY
70	RCA 1906	Cinnamon/Easy Rider	7
71	Columbia DB 8759	Sally Sunshine/It's Good To See You	8
72	Bell 1275	If It Wasn't For The Reason That I Love You/Try It, You'll Like It	6

ANTS
63	Parlophone R 5082	Christmas Star/Wandering	8

ANVIL FLUTES & CAPRICORN VOICES
68	Deram DML/SML 1026	SOMETHING NEW IS COMING (LP)	20

ANNIE ANXIETY
81	Crass Records 32984/3	BARBED WIRE HALO: Cyanide Tears/Hello Horror (7")	8
84	Corpus Christi CHRIST 10	SOUL POSSESSION (LP)	12

(see also Crass)

ANY TROUBLE
79	Pennine PSS 7165	Yesterdays Love/Nice Girls, (1000 only, 100 with 'sewn' p/s)	20
79	Pennine PSS 7165	Yesterdays Love/Nice Girls, (1000 only, p/s)	15

(see also Clive Gregson)

AOA
85	COR COR 4	WHO ARE THEY TRYING TO CON (EP, 12", comes with 7" sleeve with lyrics)	20
86	COR GURT 12	UNLIMITED GENOCIDE (Split LP with OI POLLOI, insert)	20
88	ENDANGERED EDR LP 2	SATISFACTORY ARRANGEMENT (LP)	30

APARTMENT
80	Heartbeat PULSE 7	The Car/Winter (p/s)	20

APATCHI BAND
73	President PT 392	Issmak/Crashpad	30

APES
72	Leicester Recording Co LRS LS 1	APES (LP)	50

APEX RHYTHM & BLUES ALLSTARS

59	John Lever AP 100	Yorkshire Relish/Caravan	40
60s	John Lever JLEP 1	APEX RHYTHM & BLUES ALLSTARS (EP, no p/s)	350

(see also Ian Hunter)

APHEX TWIN

91	Mighty Force 01	ANALOGUE BUBBLEBATH VOL. 1 (12" EP, label on 1 side only, other side has white label, some stamped)	20
91	Rabbit City CUT 002	ANALOGUE BUBBLEBATH VOL. 2 (12" EP, stamped white label)	40
92	R&S RSUK 12	Didgeridoo/Analogue Bubblebath 1/Flaphead/Isoprophlex (12", stickered R&S sleeve, 'Isoprophlex' is actually 'Phloam')	10
92	R&S RSUK 12CD	Didgeridoo/Analogue Bubblebath 1/Flaphead/Isoprophlex (CD, 'Isoprophlex' is actually 'Phloam')	50
93	Rephlex CAT 008	ANALOGUE BUBBLEBATH VOL. 3 (12" EP, paper bag sleeve)	15
93	Rephlex CAT 008	ANALOGUE BUBBLEBATH VOL. 3 (CD, bubble wrap sleeve)	18
93	Warp WAP 39	On/73-Yips/D-Scape/Xepha (12", p/s)	8
93	Warp WAP 39R	On (D-Scape Mix)/On (Reload Mix)/On (μ-Ziq Mix)/On (28 Mix) (12", p/s)	10
93	Warp WAP 60	VENTOLIN EP (12", p/s)	15
93	Warp WAP 60R	VENTOLIN EP (THE REMIXES) (12", p/s)	15
93	Warp WAP 60/WAP 60R	VENTOLIN EP (2 x 12", includes both above 12"s, stickered gatefold p/s)	25
94	Rephlex CAT 019 EP	ANALOGUE BUBBLEBATH VOL. 4 (12" EP, p/s with insert, as AFX)	10
94	Rephlex CAT 019 CD	ANALOGUE BUBBLEBATH VOL. 4 (CD, as AFX)	20
95	Warp WAP 63	Donkey Rhubarb/Vaz Deferenz/Icct Hedral (Philip Glass Orchestration)/ Pancake Lizard (12", p/s)	12
95	Warp WAP 67	HANGABLE AUTO BULB EP (12",as AFX)	40
95	Warp WAP 69	HANGABLE AUTO BULB 2 EP (12", as AFX)	40
97	Warp WAP 94P/WAP 94RP	Come To Daddy(Pappy Mix)/Flim/Come To Daddy (Little Lord Faulteroy Mix)/Bucephalus Bouncing Ball/To Cure A Weakling Child (Contour Regard)/Funny Little Man/Come To Daddy (Mummy Mix)/IZ-US (2 x promo 12", 500 only)	40
99	Warp WAP105	Windowlicker/(Impossible to title)/Nanno (12", inner)	12
01	Warp DRUKQS 01 54	Cymru Beats (Argonaut Mix)/Cock 10 (Delco Freedom Mix) (12", stickered black sleeve)	10
05	Rephlex ANALORD 10	Fenix Funk 5/XMD 5a (12" in PVC binder with 12 sleeves for the Analord series)	180
05	Rephlex ANALORD 10	Fenix Funk 5/XMD 5a (12", picture disc)	8
92	R&S/Apollo AMBLP 3922	SELECTED AMBIENT WORKS 85-92 (2-LP, 1st issue with no barcode)	35
94	Warp WARPLP 21	SELECTED AMBIENT WORKS VOL. 2 (3-LP, brown vinyl, black and white sleeve with numbered sticker)	60
94	Warp WARPLP 21	SELECTED AMBIENT WORKS VOL. 2 (3-LP, black vinyl, stickered colour sleeve)	35
95	Warp WARPLP 30	I CARE BECAUSE YOU DO (2-LP, stickered sleeve)	30
96	Warp WARPLP 43	RICHARD D. JAMES (LP)	25
02	Warp WARPLP 92X	DRUKQS (4-LP in 12" x 17" numbered box, 1,000 only)	80

(see also Caustic Window, Polygon Window, Q-Chastic, Kosmic Kommando)

APHRODITE'S CHILD

68	Mercury MF 1039	Rain & Tears/Don't Try To Catch A River	20
69	Mercury MF 1079	End Of The World/You Always Stand In My Way	15
69	Polydor 56769	I Want To Live/Magic Mirror	20
69	Polydor 56785	Let Me Love, Let Me Live/Marie Jolie	5
70	Polydor 56791	It's Five O'Clock/Funky Mary	5
72	Vertigo 6032 900	Break/Babylon	15
68	Mercury SMCL 20140	END OF THE WORLD/RAIN AND TEARS (LP, black/silver label, laminated sleeve)	35
69	Polydor 2384 005	IT'S FIVE O'CLOCK (LP, gatefold sleeve)	40
72	Vertigo 6673 001	666 - THE APOCALYPSE OF JOHN (2-LP, swirl labels, gatefold, red laminated sleeve. NB. Sleeve has catalogue number 6673 001 whilst albums have 6333500/6333501 on labels)	800
75	Philips 6483025	RAIN & TEARS (LP)	12
77	Vertigo 6641 581	666 (2-LP, reissue, as Aphrodite's Child with Demis Roussos & Vangelis, different sleeve, 'spaceship' labels)	30

(see also Vangelis, Forminx)

APOCALYPSE

82	Gate GATE 2	Storm Child/Chosen Few (p/s)	125

APOLLO XI

91	Wau! Mr. Modo APOLLO 11	Peace (In The Middle East) (7" Mix 2)/Peace (Sea Of Tranquility Mix)/ Peace (Is This Really The Orb? Mix) (12")	10

(see also Orb)

APOLLOS

60	Mercury AMT 1096	Rockin' Horses/Just Dreaming	10

A POPULAR HISTORY OF SIGNS

80	Melodia M1	Justice Not Vengeance/Possession (p/s)	5
81	Melodia M2	Crowds/Crossing The Border (p/s, insert)	5

APOSTLES

82	No Label	BLOW IT UP BURN IT DOWN KICK IT TILL IT BREAKS EP (fold out p/s)	15
83	Scum SCUM 2	RISING FROM THE ASHES EP	10
83	Scum SCUM 3	THE CURSE OF THE CREATURE EP	10
84	Scum SCUM 4	THE GIVING OF LOVE COSTS NOTHING EP	10
86	Fight Back FIGHT 9	DEATH TO WACKY POP (Split EP with THE JOY OF LIVING)	8
85	Mortarhate MORT 9	SMASH THE SPECTACLE! EP	10
86	Children Of The Revolution GURT 11	THE LIVES AND TIMES OF THE APOSTLES (LP)	12
86	Mortarhate MORT 23	PUNK OBITUARY (LP, gatefold, insert, lyric sheet)	15

APOSTOLIC INTERVENTION

67	Immediate IM 043	(Tell Me) Have You Ever Seen Me/Madame Garcia	220

(see also Small Faces, Humble Pie)

APPALACHIANS

63	HMV POP 1158	Bony Moronie/It Takes A Man	20
65	Mercury MF 930	Look Away/My Broken Heart (this is a different band)	12

APPALOOSA

94	Recoil RCL 003	UNPLUGGED EP (12", 3-track, die-cut sleeve)	15

(see also Global Communications)

DAVE APPELL (& APPLEJACKS)

55	Brunswick 05396	Smarter/My Heart Will Wait For You (as Dave Appell & Applejacks)	6
57	Columbia DB 3894	Country Dance/Applejack (as Dave Appell & Applejacks)	6
62	Columbia DB 4763	Happy Jose/Noivous (as Dave Appell & Orchestra)	5

(see also Applejacks [U.S.], John Zacherle)

APPLE

68	Page One POF 101	Let's Take A Trip Down The Rhine/Buffalo Billy Can	100
68	Page One POF 110	Doctor Rock/The Other Side	90
69	Page One POLS 016	AN APPLE A DAY (LP, textured sleeve, blue/silver labels with 'apple' insert)	1200
69	Page One POLS 016	AN APPLE A DAY (LP, without 'apple' insert)	800

APPLE PIE AND CUSTARD

74	Philips 6006439	Five Sisters/Doctor Fantastic	6

GEOFF APPLEBY

76	Virgin VS157	Hey Sadie/Move On Down The Road	6

APPLEJACKS (U.K.)

64	Decca F 11833	Tell Me When/Baby Jane	5
64	Decca F 11916	Like Dreamers Do/Everybody Fall Down	5
64	Decca F 11981	Three Little Words/You're The One For Me	5
65	Decca F 12050	Chim Chim Chiree/It's Not A Game Anymore (export, unissued)	20
65	Decca F 12106	It's Not A Game Anymore/Bye Bye Girl	10
65	Decca F 12216	I Go To Sleep/Make Up Or Break Up	20
65	Decca F 12301	I'm Through/We Gotta Get Together	8
67	CBS 202615	You've Been Cheating/Love Was In My Eyes	40
64	Decca LK 4635	THE APPLEJACKS (LP)	150

APPLEJACKS (U.S.)

58	London HLU 8753	Mexican Hat Rock/Stop, Stop Red Light	8
58	London HL 7063	Mexican Hat Rock/Stop, Stop Red Light (export issue)	10
59	London HLU 8806	Rocka-Conga/Am I Blue	10

(see also Dave Appell)

APPLETREE THEATRE

68	Verve (S)VLP 6018	PLAYBACK (LP)	50

CHARLIE APPLEWHITE

54	Brunswick 05358	No One But You/Parade	5
55	Brunswick 05411	Prize Of Gold/Mister Publisher (Have I Got A Song For You)	5
55	Brunswick 05416	Blue Star - The Medic Theme/A Prayer Was Born	10

APPOLINAIRES

80s	Two Tone 20 TT	Feelings Gone/Feelings Back (paper labels)	10

APPRECIATIONS

77	Destiny 1016	I Can't Hide It/Instrumental Version (2 acetates only)	100

APPROACHING FOOTSTEPS

82	Sanctuary HEH 001	Autumn/Fire And Ashes	25

APRIL SHOWERS

84	Chrysalis CHS 122787	Abandon Ship/Everytime We Say Goodbye (12", p/s)	70

APRIL WINE

72	Pye 7N 45145	You Could Have Been A Lady/Teacher	25
72	Pye 7N 45163	Bad Side Of The Moon/Believe In Me	10
73	Pye 7N 45624	Weeping Widow/Just Like That	6
76	London HLU 10549	You Won't Dance With Me/Shot Down	6
81	Capitol CL 16184	Just Between You And Me/Big City Girls (P/S)	5

AQUA LEVI & THE ROOTS IMENSION

92	Roots RI 7002	Babylon Must Set Me Free/Freedom Dub	35
91	Roots RI 001	His Foundation/His Dub (12")	60
92	Roots RI 003	Gather My Children/Gather My Dub (12")	40

AQUARIAN AGE

68	Parlophone R 5700	10,000 Words In A Cardboard Box/Good Wizard Meets Naughty Wizard	500

(see also Twink, Tomorrow, Clem Cattini Ork, Nicky Hopkins)

AQUARIAN DREAM

79	Buddah BDSL 488	Phoenix/East 6th Street (12")	40
76	Buddah DISC 008	NORMAN CONNORS PRESENTS AQUARIAN DREAM (LP)	50

(see also Norman Connors)

AQUARIANS

71	Ackee ACK 135	Circy Cap/Circy Version	12
71	Ackee ACK 137	Rebel/Invasion Version	35

(see also Augustus Pablo, Herman)

AQUATONES

58	London HLO 8631	You/She's The One For Me	45
58	London HLO 8631	You/She's The One For Me (78)	20

AQUILA

70	RCA SF 8126	THE AQUILA SUITE (LP, gatefold sleeve, orange labels)	60

(see also Patrick Campbell-Lyons)

ARABESQUE

72	Polydor 2058-237	Fairytale/Solace And Jamboree	12

ARABIS

69	Doctor Bird DB 1204	Jump High Jump Low/TONY SHABAZZ: Stool Pigeon	18

ARABS

78	Hit Run APLP 9002	CRY TUFF - DUB ENCOUNTER CHAPTER 1	55

(see also Prince Far I)

ARAB STRAP

96	Chemikal U'nd CHEM 007	The First Big Weekend/Gilded (700 only)	20
97	Chemikal U'nd CHEM 017	Hey! Fever/Girls Of Summer (p/s)	15
98	Too Many Cooks BROTH 001	Live: Packs Of Three/Blood	18
03	Chemikal U'nd CHEM 0677	THE SHY RETIRER EP : Radio Edit, Ditry Hospital Remix, Why Can't This Be Love, Good Part, New Saturday (12")	10
96	Chemikal U'nd CHEM 010	THE WEEK NEVER STARTS AROUND HERE (LP)	25
98	Chemikal U'nd CHEM 021	PHILOPHOBIA (2-LP)	25
99	Go! Beat 547387	MAD FOR SADNESS (LP, 1000 only)	25
99	Go! Beat 547387 2	MAD FOR SADNESS (CD, 3000 only)	20
99	Go! Beat 5478051	ELEPHANT SHOE (LP)	25
01	Chemikal Underground CHEM 050	THE RED THREAD (LP)	20
02	Private Pressing	QUIET VIOLENCE (LP)	35
05	Chemikal Underground CHEM 082	THE LAST ROMANCE (LP)	25
10	Chemikal Underground CHEM 135	SCENES OF A SEXUAL NATURE (3-CD, CD Rom, 4-LP& cassette, 1000 only, numbered with certificate)	100

ARAGORN

81	Neat NEAT 07	Black Ice/Noonday (p/s)	15

A RAINCOAT

76	EMI EMI 2393	It Came In The Night/Morocco	10

ARANBEE POP SYMPHONY ORCHESTRA

66	Immediate IMLP/IMSP 003	TODAY'S POP SYMPHONY (LP, lilac labels)	125

(see also Andrew Oldham Orchestra, Keith Richard[s])

ARBITRATER

93	Cyclone CYCLONE 2	DARKENED REALITY (CD)	100

ARBORS

69	CBS 4137	The Letter/Most Of It	7
69	CBS 4640	Motel Overture/Touch Me	7

ARBRE

75	DJM DJS 397	Fallin'/Doin' Alright	10
76	DJM DJS 10716	Senorita/Zero To Four (with promo p/s)	12

A.R.C. ROCKBAND

79	Rock Records	Homemade Wine/The Chase (p/s)	80

ARC (1)

71	Decca SKL-R 5077	ARC . . . AT THIS (LP, blue/silver "boxed" Decca labels)	140

(see also Heavy Jelly, Skip Bifferty, Bell & Arc, Blockheads)

ARC (2)

80	Orchrist ORC 1	Tribute To Mike Hailwood/For My Next Kick (p/s)	50
81	Slipped Disc SD001	War Of The Ring/Ice Cream Theme (p/s)	100

ARCADE FIRE

03	Private Pressing	ARCADE FIRE DEMO EP (CD, p/s Known as Us Kids Now)	35
05	Rough Trade RTRADS225	Neighbourhood #2/My Buddy	5
05	Rough Trade RTRADS232	Neighbourhood #2/My Buddy (luminous vinyl, p/s)	5
05	Rough Trade RTRADSX 232	Neighbourhood #3 (live)/Power Out (Live)/This Must Be The Place (Live, featuring David Byrne) (p/s)	7
05	Rough Trade RTRADS 252	Rebellion (Lies)/Rebellion (Lies) (Live) (p/s, white vinyl)	6
05	Rough Trade RTRADS 254	Cold Wind/Brazil (clear vinyl, poly sleeve, stickered, PVC insert)	7
07	Sonovox 1736028	No Cars Go/Surf City Easter Bloc (p/s)	5
10	Rough Trade	We Used To Wait (1-sided promo, white label 1000 only)	10
05	Rough Trade RTRADLP 219	FUNERAL (LP)	25
06	Universal 1724447	NEON BIBLE (2-LP, 4th side etched, stickered sleeve)	20
10	Universal 2743427	THE SUBURBS (2-LP)	15

ARCADIA

85	EMI 12 NSR 1	Election Day (Consensus Mix)/Election Day (7" Version)/ She's Moody And Grey She's Mean And She's Restless 12" promo in foil sleeve, sealed)	20
85	EMI 12 NSR 1	Election Day (Consensus Mix)/Election Day (7" Version)/ She's Moody And Grey She's Mean And She's Restless 12" promo in foil sleeve, unsealed)	15
85	EMI 12 NSRA 1	Election Day (Cryptic Cut No Voice Mix)/Election Day (7" Mix)/ Election Day (Consensus Mix) (12", p/s)	8
85	EMI 12 NSRX 1	Election Day (The Fact And Story Mix) (12", 1-sided, white label, plain black black sleeve, promo only)	35
85	EMI 12 NSR 2	The Promise (Extended Remix)/Rose Arcana/The Promise 7" version (12" gold cover with sticker and poster insert)	30
86	EMI 12 NSR 3	The Flame (Extended Remix)/Yo Homeboy Mix/Election Day - Early Rough Mix (12" p/s)	12

(see also Duran Duran)

ARCADIUM

69	Middle Earth MDS 102	Sing My Song/Riding Alone	120
69	Middle Earth MDLS 302	BREATHE AWHILE (LP, laminated sleeve)	900

(see also Kingdom Come, 'Middle Earth Sampler' in Various Artists)

ARCH CRIMINALS

86	Fight Back FIGHT 8	HANG (12" EP, with insert)	10

DON ARCHELL

63	Decca F 11749	When I Fall In Love/Stay Away	6

ELIZABETH ARCHER & THE EQUATORS

77	Lightning TRO 9011	Feel Like Making Love/Version	30

ARCHIE WHITEWATER

70	Pye Intl. NSPL 28143	ARCHIE WHITEWATER (LP)	120

ARCTIC MONKEYS

05	Bang Bang BANGB 71	FIVE MINUTES WITH EP (500 only, p/s)	70
05	Bang Bang BANGBCD	FIVE MINUTES WITH EP (CD, 1000 only)	70
05	Domino RUG 212	I Bet You Look Good On The Dancefloor/Bigger Boys And Stolen Sweethearts (p/s)	8
06	Domino RUG 236	Leave Before The Lights Come On/Baby I'm Yours (p/s)	6

MINT VALUE £

06	Domino RUG 216	When The Sun Goes Down/Settle For A Draw (p/s) 5
07	Domino RUG 258	Matador/Deframe2r (die-cut p/s, white vinyl, 1000 only) 10
07	Domino RUF 279	Death Ramps/Nettles (As DEATH RAMPS, 250 only, stamped labels) 20
06	Domino FAKE 1P	Fake Tales Of San Francisco/From The Ritz To The Rubble [white label promo]................15
09	Domino RUG349CDP2	Cornerstone/Catapult/Sketched/Fright Lined Dining Room (CD promo, jewel case) 15
11	Domino RUG 422	The Hellcat Spangled Shalala/Little Illusion Machine (Wirrel Riddler) (p/s, with download card, heavyweight vinyl, most destroyed in PIAS distribution fire, 500 later repressed on thinner vinyl) 7
06	Domino WIG 162	WHATEVER PEOPLE SAY I AM THATS WHAT I'M NOT (LP)...15
08	Domino DOMDVD005X	AT THE APOLLO (LP, box set with poster, DVD & stickered sleeve)................................35
07	Domino WIGLP 188	FAVOURITE WORST NIGHTMARE (LP)..12

ARCTURUS
| 97 | Music For Nations MFN 230 | LA MASQUERADE INFENALE (LP, 1000 only) ....60 |
| 96 | Ancient Lore Creations ALC 002 PLP | ASPERA HIEMS SYMFONIA (LP, picture disc, 1000 only) ....40 |

ARCWELDER
| 92 | Duophonic DS 45 03 | Favor/Plastic (orange vinyl, p/s, 300 only) ....12 |
| 92 | Duophonic DS 45 03 | Favor/Plastic (p/s, 1000 only)...8 |

TONI ARDEN
55	HMV 7M 314	Beware/I'll Step Aside...5
57	Brunswick 05645	Little By Little/Without Love (There Is Nothing) 10
57	Brunswick 05679	My Empty Heart/Like A Baby 10

NEIL ARDLEY
79	Decca FR 13847	Leap In The Dark/Summer Ice 5
65	Decca SKL 4690	WESTERN UNION (LP) 150
70	Columbia SCX 6414	GREEK VARIATIONS (LP, with Ian Carr & Don Rendell) 250
72	Regal Zono. SLRZ 1028	A SYMPHONY OF AMARANTHS (LP, red/silver labels) 200
74	Argo ZDA 164/5	WILL POWER (2-LP, with Ian Carr, Stan Tracey & Mike Gibbs) 125
75	Gull GULP 1018	KALEIDOSCOPE OF RAINBOWS (LP) 18
78	Decca TXS-R 133	HARMONY OF THE SPHERES (LP, featuring John Martyn) 20
09	Gull/Pure Pleasure GULP 1018	KALEIDOSCOPE OF RAINBOWS (2-LP, reissue)..18

(see also Ian Carr, Don Rendell, New Jazz Orchestra, Michael Gibbs)

A.R.E. WEAPONS
| 01 | Rough Trade RTRADES 022 | Street Gang (p/s) ....6 |

AREA CODE 615
| 70 | Polydor 2066 249 | Stone Fox Chase/Always The Same (first issue on paper labels, later moulded labels are second pressing) ....6 |

COLIN AREETY
| 72 | Deram DM 370 | Holy Cow/Can't Do It For You ....8 |
| 73 | Deram 383 | (If Loving You Is Wrong) I Don't Want To Be Right/One Night Affair ....7 |

ARENA TWINS
| 59 | London HL 7071 | Mama, Care Mama/Little Pig (export issue) ....20 |

ARGENT
71	Epic EPC 5423	Celebration/Kingdom...15
71	Epic EPC 9135	Hold Your Head Up/Closer To Heaven/Keep On Rollin' (33rpm EP, p/s)..........................12
72	Epic S EPC 7786	Hold Your Head Up/Keep On Rollin' 5
72	Epic EPC 8115	Tragedy/Rejoice 7
73	Epic EPC 1243	God Gave Rock And Roll To You/Christmas For The Free...5
73	Epic EPC 1628	It's Only Money Part 2/Candles On The River 5
74	Epic EPC 2147	Thunder And Lightning/Keeper Of The Flame 8
74	Epic EPC 2448	Man For All Reasons/Music From The Spheres 8
75	Epic EPC 80691	Highwire/Circus 5
74	Epic SEPC 2849	Keep On Rollin'/I Am The Dance Of Ages..10
70	CBS 63781	ARGENT (LP, gatefold sleeve)..50
71	Epic EPC 64190	RING OF HANDS (LP, gatefold sleeve) 35
72	Epic EPC 64962	ALL TOGETHER NOW (LP, gatefold sleeve, with booklet)...25
73	Epic EPC 65475	IN DEEP (LP) 12
74	Epic EQ 32195/Q 65475	IN DEEP (LP, quadrophonic)..25
74	Epic EPC 88063	ENCORE (2-LP) 15
75	Epic EPC 80691	CIRCUS (LP, with lyric insert) 12
75	RCA RS 1020	COUNTERPOINTS (LP) 15

(see also Zombies, Unit 4 + 2, Roulettes, John Verity Band, Phoenix)

ARGONAUTS
| 85 | Lyntone LYN 18249/50 | Apeman/Under My Thumb (signed white label, no p/s)..60 |

(see also Madness)

ARGOSY
| 69 | DJM DJS 214 | Mr. Boyd/Imagine ....100 |

(see also Elton John, Supertramp)

ARGUS
| 84 | ABS SRT 4KS258 | Holocaust/The Widow (title sleeve) ....100 |

(see also People Like Us)

ARIEL
74	Harvest HAR 5085	Jamaican Farewel/And I'm Blue 7
74	Harvest HAR 5088	Yeah Tonite/Laughing Man...10
73	Harvest SHSP 4028	A STRANGE FANTASTIC DREAM (LP, textured sleeve) 20
75	Harvest SHSP 4039	ROCK AND ROLL SCARS (LP) 15

ARIEL PINK'S HAUNTED GRAFFITI
| 10 | 4AD AD3X24 | Round And Round/Mistaken Wedding (p/s) ....8 |

ARIZONA SWAMP COMPANY
| 70 | Parlophone R 5841 | Train Keeps Rollin'/Tennessee Woman ....40 |

(see also Nashville Teens)

DEE ARLEN
| 59 | Philips PB 950 | Stay/Why Should We Wait Any Longer..5 |

STEVE ARLEN
58	Melodisc M 1458	That's Love/Easy 'N' Free	5
62	HMV POP 1021	They Took John Away/Down In The Valley	10

DEKE ARLON (& OFFBEATS)
64	HMV POP 1340	I Need You/I Must Go And Tell Her	5
64	Columbia DB 7194	I'm Just A Boy/Can't Make Up My Mind	12
65	Columbia DB 7487	If I Didn't Have A Dime/Gotta Little Girl	5
65	Columbia DB 7753	Little Piece Of Paper/I've Been Away (solo)	5
66	Columbia DB 7841	Hard Times For Young Lovers/Little Boy (solo)	8

ARMAGEDDON
75	A&M AMLH 64513	ARMAGEDDON (LP, with lyric inner sleeve, silver labels)	60

(see also Keith Relf, Steamhammer, Captain Beyond)

ARMANDO
00	Trax UK DJTRX 002	New World Order (Remix) (12", promo)	8

JOAN ARMATRADING
72	Cube HIFLY 12	WHATEVER'S FOR US (LP)	15

ARMED FORCE
80	Armed Forces AF1	Popstar/Attack (p/s, 500 only)	20

ARMENIAN JAZZ QUARTET
57	London HLR 8454	Pretty Girl/Harem Dance	10

ARMENTA
83	Savoir Faire FAIT 005	I Wanna Be With You/Part 2/Part 3 (12")	15

ARMPIT JUG BAND
75	Cottage COT 201/R	NO SWEAT (LP)	12

ARMS & LEGS
76	MAM MAM 140	Janice/She'll Surprise You	8
76	MAM MAM 147	Heat Of The Night/Good Times	8
77	MAM MAM 156	Is There Any More Wine/She'll Surprise You	8

(see also Joe Jackson)

RUSSELL ARMS
57	London HLB 8406	Cinco Robles (Five Oaks)/The World Is Made Of Lisa (gold label)	25
57	London HLB 8406	Cinco Robles (Five Oaks)/The World Is Made Of Lisa (silver label)	12
57	London HL 7018	Cinco Robles (Five Oaks)/The World Is Made Of Lisa (export issue)	12

CHUCK ARMSTRONG
73	Action ACT 4620	God Bless The Children/Black Foxy Woman	15

FRANKIE ARMSTRONG (& FRIENDS)
79	Action Against Corrie RRFA 001	We Must Choose/RED RINSE: A Woman's Right To Choose (private pressing)	30
72	Topic 12TS 216	LOVELY ON THE WATER (LP)	30
75	Topic 12TS 273	SONGS AND BALLADS (LP)	18

(see also A.L. Lloyd)

JACK ARMSTRONG
57	Beltona SEP 43	NORTHUMBRIAN PIPE MUSIC (EP)	8
74	Saydisc SDL 252	CELEBRATED MINSTREL (LP)	20

LORNA ARMSTRONG
74	Ackee 535	Dance With Me/Lonely Nights	15

LOUIS ARMSTRONG
SINGLES
53	Columbia SCM 5061	King Of The Zulus/Lonesome Blues	5
54	Columbia SCM 5118	Chicago Breakdown/Twelfth Street Rag	5
54	Columbia SCM 5142	I'm Not Rough/Put 'Em Down Blues	5
54	Brunswick 05303	Basin Street Blues (Parts 1 & 2)	5
54	Brunswick 05332	Skokiaan (Parts 1 & 2)	5
54	Brunswick 05347	Muskrat Ramble/Someday You'll Be Sorry (B-side with Commanders)	5
55	Brunswick 05364	Trees/Spooks	5
55	Brunswick 05400	Ko Ko Mo (I Love You So)/Struttin' With Some Barbecue (with Gary Crosby)	6
59	Philips PB 967	Mack The Knife/The Faithful Hussar	6
69	United Artists UP 35059	We Have All The Time In The World/Pretty Little Missy	12
69	United Artists UA 3172	We Have All The Time In The World/Pretty Little Missy (reissue, p/s)	8

ALBUMS
54	HMV DLP 1036	LAUGHIN' LOUIS (10")	12
54	Columbia 33S 1041	LOUIS ARMSTRONG AND HIS HOT SEVEN (10")	12
54	Brunswick LA 8679	SATCHMO SERENADES (10")	12

(see also Danny Kaye, Ella Fitzgerald & Louis Armstrong, Nina & Frederik, Bing Crosby,

HERBIE ARMSTRONG
80	Avatar 108	Real Real Gone/Blackout	10

GINNY ARNELL
63	MGM MGM 1217	Dumb Head/How Many Times Can One Heart Break	20
63	MGM MGM 1243	I Wish I Knew What Dress To Wear/He's My Little Devil	20
65	MGM MGM 1270	Just Like A Boy/Portrait Of A Fool	15
65	MGM MGM 1283	Little Bit Of Love/B-I-I-I-Why	20

CHICO ARNEZ (& HIS LATIN AMERICAN ORCHESTRA)
59	Pye N 15196	Yashmak/Ain't She Sweet	8
69	Columbia DB 8642	Hippy Parade/Tina	5
69	Columbia DB 8597	Eso Beso/One For Pancho	5
71	Gemini GMS 019	Leg Box/Reggae Deck	5
68	Columbia SCX6265	FROM CHICO...WITH LOVE (LP)	15
69	Studio 2 TWO 279	CHICO (LP)	18
71	Gemini GM 2006	THIS IS CHICO (LP)	18
72	Contour 2870 153	NEW SOUNDS OF CHICO ARNEZ (LP)	12

MINT VALUE £

CALVIN ARNOLD
68	MGM MGM 1378	Funky Way/Snatchin' Back	20
68	MGM MGM 1449	Mama In Law/Mini Skirt	20

EDDY ARNOLD
54	HMV 7MC 10	Prayer/Robe Of Calvary (export issue)	7
54	HMV 7MC 16	Free Home Demonstration/If I Never Get To Heaven (export issue)	7
54	HMV 7MC 19	Second Fling/My Everything (export issue)	7
54	HMV 7MC 22	Hep Cat Baby/This Is The Thanks I Get (For Loving You) (export issue)	20
55	HMV 7MC 32	In Time/Two Kinds Of Love (export issue)	10
55	HMV 7M 339	I Walked Alone Last Night/The Richest Man (In The World)	8
57	RCA RCA 1008	Gonna Find Me A Bluebird/Little Bit	5
59	RCA RCA 1138	Tennessee Stud/What's The Good (Of All This Love)	10
60	RCA RCA 1212	Just Out Of Reach/Before This Day Ends	5
66	RCA 1519	I Want To Go With You/Mary Claire Melvina Rebecca Jane	5
66	RCA 1529	If You Were Mine, Mary/Molly Darling	5
54	HMV 7EG 8020	EDDY ARNOLD (EP)	10

KOKOMO ARNOLD
69	Saydisc Matchbox SDR 163	KOKOMO ARNOLD (LP)	25

PAUL ARNOLD
67	Pye 7N 17317	Somewhere In A Rainbow/Got A Feeling	7

(see also Overlanders)

P.P. ARNOLD
66	Immediate IM 040	Everything's Gonna Be Alright/Life Is But Nothin'	150
66	Immediate IM 040	Everything's Gonna Be Alright/Life Is But Nothin' (DJ copy)	250
67	Immediate IM 047	The First Cut Is The Deepest/Speak To Me	25
67	Immediate IM 055	The Time Has Come/If You See What I Mean	18
68	Immediate IM 061	(If You Think You're) Groovy/Though It Hurts Me Badly	18
68	Immediate IM 067	Angel Of The Morning/Life Is But Nothin'	8
69	Immediate IM 079	The First Cut Is The Deepest/The Time Has Come	8
69	Polydor 56350	Bury Me Down The River/Give A Hand, Take A Hand	8
70	Polydor 2058 061	Likely Piece Of Work/May The Winds Blow	5
80	Virgin/NEMS SV 103	Angel Of The Morning/Everything's Gonna Be Alright/The First Cut Is The Deepest/Groovy/The Time Has Come (doublepack, gatefold p/s)	15
75	Immediate IM 109	First Cut Is The Deepest/King Of Kings (re-issue)	10
67	Immediate IMLP/IMSP 011	THE FIRST LADY OF IMMEDIATE (LP, withdrawn)	400
68	Immediate IMSP 017	KAFUNTA (LP, gatefold sleeve)	75

(see also Ikettes, Nice, Small Faces, Spectrum, P.P. & Primes)

P.P. ARNOLD & THE JEFF WAYNE SINGERS
60s	Pepsi Lyntone 2498	We've Got Pepsi (1-sided with Pepsi Company sleeve)	15

AROVANE
99	City Centre Offices BLOCK 1	Occer (plain black sleeve, with inserts, 850 only)	6

ARPADYS
77	Polydor 2933802	ARPADYS (LP)	40

ARRIVAL
69	Decca F 12986	Friends/Don't Turn His Love Away	6
70	Decca F 13026	I Will Survive/See The Lord	6
71	CBS S 7617	Family Tree/Part Of My Dream	10
70	Decca SKL 5055	ARRIVAL (LP, blue/silver with 'boxed' Decca logo)	20

ARRIVALS
69	Pye 7N 17761	Scooby Doo/She's About A Mover	12

ARROGANT
80	Rocket XPRES 43	Ego/So Near So Far (p/s)	12

DON ARROL
61	Decca F 11318	Ev'rybody Likes It/It's All Happening Here	6

ARROWS (U.S.)
65	Capitol CL 15386	Apache '65/Blue Guitar	5

ARROWS (1) (U.K.)
69	Pye 7N 17756	Mercy/See Saw	5

ARROWS (2) (U.K.)
75	RAK RAK 205	I Love Rock 'n' Roll/Broken Down Heart	10

CLIVE ARROWSMITH
74	Scratchy CHS 2027	Desire/Almost Gone	8

ARSENAL 1ST TEAM SQUAD
71	Pye 7N 46067	Good Old Arsenal/The Boys From Highbury (in p/s)	7

ARS NOVA
68	Elektra EKSN 45029	Zoroaster/Pavan For My Lady	12
68	Elektra EKSN 45034	Fields Of People/Song To The City	12
68	Elektra EKS 74020	ARS NOVA (LP, orange label, gatefold sleeve)	30
69	Atlantic 588 196	SUNSHINE AND SHADOWS (LP)	30

ART
75	Island WIP 6048	What's That Sound (For What It's Worth)/Flying Anchors (with promo Art sleeve)	30
67	Island WIP 6019	What's That Sound (For What It's Worth)/Rome Take Away Three	20
69	Island WIP 6048	Room With A View/SPOOKY TOOTH: Nobody There At All (promo only)	50
75	Island WIP 6224	What's That Sound (For What It's Worth)/Flying Anchors	7
67	Island ILP 967	SUPERNATURAL FAIRY TALES (LP, first pressing, pink label with black/orange circle logo, laminated sleeve)	300
70	Island ILP 967	SUPERNATURAL FAIRY TALES (LP, second pressing, pink label with 'i' logo and factory stamped matrix numbers, those with hand written matrixes are bootlegs, laminated sleeve)	200
75	Island ILP 967	SUPERNATURAL FAIRY TALES (LP, reissue, matt sleeve, 'palm tree' label)	35

(see also V.I.P.'s, Baron With His Pounding Piano, Spooky Tooth, Luther Grosvenor, Hapshash & Coloured Coat)

ART BRUT
04	Fierce Panda NING 164	Modern Art/My Little Brother (hand-painted, die cut p/s)	5

ART ZOYD
82	Recommended RR 14.15	Ménage (12.59) (1-sided, other side printed, foldout sleeve in PVC sleeve, existence unconfirmed)	10
82	Recommended RR 14/15	PHASE V (2-LP with booklet, inserts and free 1-sided 7" Maege (RR 14.5))	20

ART ATTACKS
78	Albatross TIT 1	I'm A Dalek/Neutron Bomb (p/s)	20
79	Fresh FRESH 3	First And Last: Punk Rock Stars/Rat City/First And Last (p/s)	20
96	Overground OVER 58	OUTRAGE AND HORROR (LP, 600 only, pressed in U.K. for export to Japan)	25

(see also Monochrome Set, Tagmemics, Kray Cherubs)

ART BEARS
79	Recommended RR 7904	Rats & Monkeys/Collapse	5
81	Recommended RE 6622	CODA TO "MAN AND BOY" (EP, live, 1-sided clear vinyl, silk-screened p/s, 1,750 only, this price for 500 signed & numbered for subscribers)	12
78	Recommended REC 2188	HOPES AND FEARS (LP, gatefold sleeve with poster & booklet)	20
79	Recommended REC 0618	WINTER SONGS (LP, with booklet)	20
81	Recommended RE 6622	THE WORLD AS IT IS TODAY (LP, 45rpm, with booklet)	12

(see also Henry Cow, Slapp Happy)

ARTERY
79	Limited Edition TAKE 1	Mother Moon/Pretends/Heinz (p/s)	10
80	Aardvark STEAL 3	Unbalanced/The Slide (p/s, with EP [Perhaps/Turtle/Toytown/Heinz])	8
81	Aardvark AARD 5	Cars In Motion/Life And Death (p/s)	6
81	Armageddon AS 026	Afterwards/Into The Garden (p/s)	6
83	Red Flame RFB25	Alabama Song/A Song For Lena (p/s)	7
82	Red Flame RFM 4	OCEANS (LP, with insert)	12
83	Red Flame RF 18	ONE AFTERNOON IN A HOT AIR BALOON (LP)	18
84	Golden Dawn GDLP 01	SECOND COMING (LP)	15
85	Golden Dawn GDLP 02	NUMBER FOUR (LP)	15

(see also Mission)

DAVE & TONI ARTHUR
70	Trailer LER 1	Bushes And Briars/Lazio Feher	8
67	Transatlantic TRA 154	MORNING STANDS ON TIPTOE (LP)	75
69	Topic 12T 190	THE LARK IN THE MORNING (LP, blue label)	40
71	Trailer LER 2017	HEARKEN TO THE WITCHES' RUNE (LP, red label)	30

ARTHUR'S MOTHER
71	Polydor 2058093	On The Dole/Butterfly	8

ANDY ARTHURS
77	EMI 2618	Listen To My Brain (Kapounding)/Come To The Party (p/s)	5
78	Radar ADA 7	I Can Detect You (For 1000 Miles)/I Am A Machine (p/s, withdrawn)	10
78	TDS TDS 3	I Can Detect You (For 1000 Miles)/I Am A Machine (p/s, reissue)	5
79	TDS TDS 6	I Feel Flat/Play The Music (p/s)	7

ARTICLE 58
81	Rational RATE 4	Event To Come/Echoes/Lost And Found (p/s)	8

ART INTERFACE
83	ART ART 2	Secretaries From Heaven (Radio Version)/Secretaries From Heaven (Real Version) (p/s)	10

ARTISTICS
66	Coral Q 72488	I'm Gonna Miss You/Hope We Have	70
66	Coral Q 72488	I'm Gonna Miss You/Hope We Have (DJ Copy)	100
67	Coral Q 72492	Girl I Need You/I'm Glad I Met You	40
67	Coral Q 72492	Girl I Need You/I'm Glad I Met You (DJ Copy)	100
70	MCA MU 1117	I'm Gonna Miss You/Hope We Have (reissue)	5
76	Brunswick BR 39	I'm Gonna Miss You/GENE CHANDLER: There Was A Time	8
66	Columbia	GET MY HANDS ON SOME LOVIN' (LP, unconfirmed existence)	250

ART MOVEMENT
68	Decca F 12768	I Love Being In Love With You/The Game Of Love	10
68	Decca F 12836	Loving Touch/Happy Song	7
69	Columbia DB 8602	Yes Sir . . . No Sir/Sally Goes Round The Moon	5
70	Columbia DB 8651	For As Long As You Need Me/Nice 'n' Easy	5
70	Columbia DB 8697	The Sooner I Get To You/Morning Girl	5

ART NOUVEAU
79	Gimpy Dak DAK 1	Fear Machine/Animal Instincts (p/s)	50

ART NOUVEAUX
64	Fontana TF 483	Extra Terrestrial Visitations/The Way To Play It	30

ART OBJECTS
80	Heartbeat PULSE 10	Showing Off To Impress The Girls/Our Silver Sister (live) (p/s)	12
81	Fried Egg EGG 007	Hard Objects/Bibliotheque/Fit Of Pique (p/s)	10
81	Heartbeat HB 5	BAGPIPE MUSIC (LP)	18

ART OF NOISE
83	ZTT ZTIS 100	INTO BATTLE WITH THE ART OF NOISE (12" EP)	8
83	ZTT 100	Beatbox/Moments In Love (12")	8
84	ZTT P ZTPS 01	Close (To The Edit)/A Time To Hear (Who's Listening) (picture disc)	5
84	ZTT 12 P ZTPS 01	Edited/A Time To Clear (It Up) (12", picture disc)	8
85	ZTT 12 ZTPS 1	CLOSE TO THE EDIT (12", stamped green label, unreleased)	10
85	ZTT P ZTPS 02	Moments In Love/Beatbox (tortoise-shaped picture disc)	6
86	China WOKP 9	Paranoimia/Why Me (shaped picture disc)	15
91	China CHINX 23	Art Of Love/(Ambience Of Love Mix) (12", p/s)	10
84	ZTT ZCID Q2	DAFT (CD)	18

ART SCIENCE TECHNOLOGY
90	Debut DEBTX 3100	A.S.T./Esus Flow (2 mixes) (12", p/s)	12

(see also Future Sound Of London, Stakker)

ARTWOODS

64	Decca F 12015	Sweet Mary/If I Ever Get My Hands On You	70
65	Decca F 12091	Oh My Love/Big City	60
65	Decca F 12206	Goodbye Sisters/She Knows What To Do	60
66	Decca F 12384	I Take What I Want/I'm Looking For A Saxophonist Doubling French Horn Wearing Size 37 Boots	80
66	Decca F 12465	I Feel Good/Molly Anderson's Cookery Book	90
67	Parlophone R 5590	What Shall I Do/In The Deep End	140
66	Decca DFE 8654	JAZZ IN JEANS (EP)	600
66	Decca LK 4830	ART GALLERY (LP, red/silver label with 'unboxed' Decca logo and 'FFrr" laminated front sleeve)	700
70	Decca Eclipse ECM 2025	ART GALLERY (LP, reissue in different sleeve, also stereo [ECS 2025])	120
73	Spark SRLM 2006	THE ARTWOODS (LP)	40

(see also St. Valentine's Day Massacre, Keef Hartley Band, Jon Lord, Dog Soldier, Lucas & Mike Cotton Sound)

ARTWORK

02	Big Apple BAM 001	RED EP (12")	15
02	Big Apple BAM 001	RED EP (12", red vinyl)	20

ARZACHEL

69	Evolution Z 1003	ARZACHEL (LP, blue label, laminated front sleeve)	800

(see also Egg, Steve Hillage, Khan, Hatfield & the North, National Health, Gong)

ARZENBOYS

75	DJM DJS 370	Bump On My Head/Instrumental Version	6

ASGARD

72	Threshold TH 10	Friends/Children Of A New Born Age	6
73	Threshold TH 15	In The Realm Of Asgard/Town Cryer	6
72	Threshold THS 6	IN THE REALM OF ASGARD (LP, white/blue label, gatefold sleeve)	100

ASH

94	La La Land LA LA 001	Jack Names The Planets/Don't Know (wraparound p/s in poly bag, 5,000 only)	10
94	Infectious INFECT 13S	Petrol/The Little Pond/A Message From Oscar Wilde And Patrick The Brewer (p/s, 500 only)	15
94	Infectious INFECT 16S	Uncle Pat/Different Today (p/s, 1,000 only)	12
95	Infectious INFECT 21J	Kung Fu/Day Of The Triffids (p/s, 'Japanese' wraparound no'd p/s in poly bag)	8
95	Infectious INFECT 21C	Kung Fu/Kung Fu (red vinyl promo)	6
95	Fantastic Plastic FP 004	Get Ready/Zero Zero Zero (red vinyl, 1,000 only, mail order only)	18
95	Infectious INFECT 24S	Girl From Mars/Astral (Conversations With Toulouse Lautrec)/Cantina Band (p/s)	8
96	Infectious INFECT 39S/41X	Goldfinger/Oh Yeah (p/s)	5
97	Barbie Records KEN 1	I Only Want To Be With You/Kung Fu (Live) (silver speckled vinyl p/s, fan club 7")	40
94	Infectious INFECT 14LP	TRAILER (LP, with yellow vinyl 7", "Silver Surfer"/"Jazz '59" [INFECT 14S])	20
96	Infectious INFECT 40LP	1977 (LP, gatefold)	20
98	Infectious INFECT60LP	NU-CLEAR SOUNDS (LP, gatefold, clear vinyl)	18
01	Infectious INFECT 100LP	FREE ALL ANGELS (LP, gatefold)	15

VIC ASH QUARTET

56	Tempo A 135	Blue Lou/Doxy	10
56	Tempo A 137	Early Morning/Just One Of Those Things	10
55	Jazz Today JTE 100	SESSION FOR FOUR (EP)	20
56	Nixa NJE 1002	HOAGY (EP)	15
56	Nixa NJE 1032	VIC ASH & FOUR (EP)	20
56	Columbia SEG 7634	CLARINET VIRTUOSO (EP)	15
56	Tempo EXA 44	MODERN JAZZ SCENE (EP)	45

(see also Maxine Sullivan, Jazz Five)

HAROLD ASHBY

61	Columbia 33SX 1379	TENOR STUFF (LP, with Paul Gonsalves)	50

IRVING ASHBY & HIS COMBO

58	London HLP 8578	Big Guitar/Motatin'	20
58	London HLP 8578	Big Guitar/Motatin' (78)	10

ASH CAN SCHOOL

86	Unit Two TWO 01	She's Only Sleeping/A Day Out Of Paris (p/s)	30

JOHNNY ASHCROFT

59	Felsted AF 118	A Pub With No Beer/Bouquet For The Bride	5
60	HMV POP 759	Little Boy Lost/My Love Is A River	5

PEGGY ASHCROFT & MARTIN BEST

72	Argo ZSW 532	SENSE AND NONSENSE (LP)	30

DOUG ASHDOWN

66	CBS 202083	Guess I'm Doing Fine/I Sure Ain't Standing Still	8

ASHER D & DADDY FREDDY

87	Music Of Life NOTE 005	RAGAMUFFIN HIP HOP EP (12")	8

RAFMRA ASHER

78	Maccabees FG1	Fourth Generation/Version	20

ASHFORD & SIMPSON

74	Warner Bros. K16373	Have You Ever Tried It/Time	7
77	Warner Bros. K17679 (T)	Love Don't Make It Right/Bourgie Bourgie (with incorrect mastering) (12")	20
77	Warner Bros. K17679 (T)	Love Don't Make It Right/Bourgie Bourgie (with correct mastering) (12")	50
78	Warner Brothers 12K 17096	Don't Cost You Nothing/Let Love Use Me (12")	15

(see also Valerie Simpson)

ASHKAN

70	Decca Nova DN-R 1	IN FROM THE COLD (LP, mono)	150
70	Decca Nova SDN-R 1	IN FROM THE COLD (LP, stereo)	80

(see also Fleetwood Mac)

MICKEY ASHMAN

60	Pye Jazz NJL 25	TAKING THE MICKEY (LP)	40
61	Pye Jazz NJL 29	THROUGH DARKEST ASHMAN (LP)	60

ASHRA
77	Virgin V 2080	NEW AGE OF EARTH (LP)	15
77	Virgin V 2091	BLACKOUTS (LP)	12

BUD ASHTON (& HIS GROUP)
60	Embassy WB 409	Because They're Young/Apache	5

(see also Typhoons, Jaybirds)

ASHTON, GARDNER & DYKE
69	Polydor 56306	Maiden Voyage/See The Sun In My Eyes	80
70	Capitol CL 15665	The Resurrection Shuffle/Hymn To Everyone	5
69	Polydor 583 081	ASHTON, GARDNER & DYKE (LP)	25
70	Capitol E-ST 563	THE WORST OF ASHTON, GARDNER AND DYKE (LP)	20
72	Capitol EA-ST 22862	WHAT A BLOODY LONG DAY IT'S BEEN (LP, gatefold sleeve)	20

(see also Ashton & Lord, Remo Four, Creation, Birds, Mike Hurst & Method, Badger, Medicine Head, Family)

MARK ASHTON
72	United Artists UP 353390	Get Up And Groove/Barking Dogs	15

ASHTON ON RIBBLE HIGH SCHOOL MUSIC SOCIETY
74	(No label or cat no)	ASHTON SOUND 74 (LP, with inserts)	100

(TONY) ASHTON & (JON) LORD
72	Purple PUR 109	Celebration/Sloeback	7
74	Purple PUR 121	We're Gonna Make It/Band Of The Salvation Army Band	7
74	Oyster OYR 101	TONY ASHTON: The Resurrection Shuffle/Ballad Of Mr Giver	6
74	Purple TPS 3507	FIRST OF THE BIG BANDS (LP)	20

(see also Ashton Gardner & Dyke, Paice Ashton & Lord, Jon Lord, Deep Purple, Green Bullfrog)

ASIA
82	Geffen GEFA 2228	Only Time Will Tell/Ride Easy (picture disc)	5
82	Geffen WA 3580	Don't Cry/True Colours (blue or green logo-shaped picture disc)	10
92	IRS 951.959	AQUA (LP, gatefold sleeve)	15

(see also Yes, Emerson Lake & Palmer, Steve Howe)o

ASIA FIELDS
90	Frank FRANK 2	Friction/Jack-knifed (12", test pressing only, plain white die-cut sleeve)	25

ASIAN DUB FOUNDATION
98	LONDON FFRR 556 066	RAFI'S REVENGE (2-LP)	25
00	Virgin 724384911218	COMMUNITY MUSIC (2-LP)	15
03	LP VIR 201	ENEMY OF THE ENEMY	0

ED ASKEW
69	Fontana	ED ASKEW (LP)	30

ASLAN
76	Profile GMOR 006	PAWS FOR THOUGHT (LP)	70
77	Profile GMOR 144	SECOND HELPINGS (LP)	70

AS ONE
95	New Electronica Elec 23LP	REFLECTIONS ON REFLECTIONS (2xLP)	25
95	New Electronica Elec 26LP	CELESTIAL SOUL (2xLP)	20

ASPECTS
01	Hombre MEX033	We Get Fowl/Correct English (remix) (12")	8
99	Hombre MEX 010	REVENGE OF THE NERDS (EP)	10
98	Hombre MEX007	2012 (EP)	15

MONICA ASPELUND
77	RCA PB 9044	Lapponia/La-La, Sing A Song	8

RON ASPERY
72	Blakey BLP5989	BACK DOOR (LP)	50

GARY & VERA ASPEY
76	Topic 12TS 299	A TASTE OF HOT POT (LP)	25

ASPHALT RIBBONS
88	Tigerlily LILY 002	DOWNSIDE EP (12", p/s)	30
89	In Tape IT 063	THE ORCHARD EP (p/s)	25
89	In Tape ITTI 063	THE ORCHARD EP (12", p/s)	30
89	In Tape ITTI 063	THE ORCHARD EP (12", p/s + T-Shirt inset)	35
89	In Tape ITTI 063	THE ORCHARD EP (12", 200 pressed at 48rpm and withdrawn)	30
89	In Tape IT 068	Good Love/Long Lost Uncle/The Day I Turned Bad (p/s)	35
89	In Tape ITTI 068	Good Love/Long Lost Uncle/The Day I Turned Bad (12", p/s)	20
89	In Tape IT 6545 1	Over Again/EVA: Unquenchable (p/s, promo only)	25
91	ETT 101-1	OLD HORSE (LP)	30
91	ETT 101-2	OLD HORSE (CD)	30

(see also Tindersticks)

MARY ASQUITH
78	Mother Earth MUM 1204	CLOSING TIME (LP)	30

ASSAGAI
71	Vertigo 6059 034	Telephone Girl/I'll Wait For You	40
71	Vertigo 6360 030	ASSAGAI (LP, gatefold sleeve, large swirl label)	150
72	Philips 6308 079	ZIMBABWE (LP, black/silver labels)	90
72	Contour 2870 394	ASSAGAI (LP)	15
70s	Sounds Superb SPR 90054	AFRO ROCK (LP) (Same as Vertigo 6360030)	12

LYS ASSIA
57	Decca F 10930	Through The Eyes Of Love/Scusami	6
57	Decca DFE 6383	FOUR CONTINENTAL HITS (EP)	10

ASSOCIATES
79	Double Hip DHR 1	Boys Keep Swinging/Mona Property Girl (no p/s, 500 only)	80
79	MCA MCA 537	Boys Keep Swinging/Mona Property Girl (no p/s, demos more common, £15)	25
80	Fiction FICS 11	The Affectionate Punch/You Were Young (p/s)	5
81	Fiction FICSX 13	A/Would I ... Bounce Back (p/s)	5

MINT VALUE £

81	RSO RSO 78	Kites/A Girl Named Property (p/s, band on A-side credited as "39 Lyon St.")....................5
81	RSO RSOX 78	Kites/A Girl Named Property (12", p/s, A-side credited as "39 Lyon St.")...........................8
82	Lyntone LYN 11649	Even Dogs In The Wild (clear 1-sided flexi free with Flexipop mag, issue 20) 12
82	Beggars Banquet BEG 86	Tell Me Easter's On Friday/Straw Towels (unreleased, white labels only)........................30
85	WEA YX 47TE	Take Me To The Girl/Perhaps/God Bless The Child (live)/Even Dogs In The Wild (live)/The Boy That Santa Claus Forgot (live) (10", p/s)...10
88	WEA YZ 329T	Country Boy/Heart Of Glass (Dub Mix)/Just Can't Say Goodbye (12" Mix) (12", p/s, unissued, white labels only)..50
88	WEA YZ 329CD	Country Boy/Just Can't Say Goodbye (12" Mix)/Take Me To The Girl/ Heart Of Glass (Dub Mix) (3" CD with adaptor in jewel case, unissued)...50
90	Circa YRCDT 46	Fever (single version)/Groovin' With Mr. Bloe/Fever In The Shadows (CD) 15
90	WEA YZ 534T	POPERETTA (EP) (12", p/s)..10
90	WEA YZ 534CD	POPERETTA (EP) (CD)..10
80	Fiction FIX 05	THE AFFECTIONATE PUNCH (LP) 10
90	Circa CIRCD 11	WILD AND LONELY (CD) 30
82	Beggars Banquet BEGA 43	FOURTH DRAWER DOWN (LP, gatefold sleeve with poster, label credits SITU 2) 15
88	WEA WX 222C	THE GLAMOUR CHASE (unreleased advance cassette only: with extra track Take Me To The Girl)..30

(see also Billy MacKenzie, Jih)

ASSOCIATION

66	London HLT 10054	Along Comes Mary/Your Own Love..10
66	London HLT 10074	Cherish/Don't Blame It On Me...10
66	London HLT 10098	Pandora's Golden Heebie Jeebies/Standing Still..15
67	London HLT 10118	No Fair At All/Looking Glass..10
67	London HLT 10140	Windy/Sometime...10
67	London HLT 10157	Never My Love/Requiem For The Masses..8
68	Warner Bros WB 6113	Everything That Touches You/Requiem For The Masses..6
68	Warner Bros WB 7163	Everything That Touches You/We Love Us..6
68	Warner Bros WB 7195	Time For Livin'/Birthday Morning...5
68	Warner Bros WB 7229	Six Man Band/Like Always...5
69	Warner Bros WB 7267	Goodbye Columbus/The Time It Is Today...8
69	Warner Bros WB 7119	Windy/Never My Love...7
70	Warner Bros WB 7372	Just About The Same/Look At Me, Look At You...6
72	CBS S 8062	Darling Be Home Soon/Indian Wells Woman..6
67	London HA-T 8305	AND THEN . . . ALONG COMES THE ASSOCIATION (LP)..40
67	London HA-T 8313	RENAISSANCE (LP)..35
67	London HA-T/SH-T 8342	INSIGHT OUT (LP)...35
68	Warner Bros W(S) 1733	BIRTHDAY (LP)..30
69	Warner Bros W(S) 1767	GREATEST HITS (LP) 20
69	Warner Bros W(S) 1786	GOODBYE COLUMBUS (LP, soundtrack)...18
69	Warner Bros W(S) 1800	THE ASSOCIATION (LP)..20

FRED ASTAIRE

| 57 | HMV POP 337 | Funny Face/AUDREY HEPBURN: How Long Has This Been Going On.............................5 |
| 57 | MGM MGM 964 | The Ritz Roll And Rock/JANIS PAIGE: Satin And Silk..5 |

(see also Judy Garland, Bing Crosby)

A STATE OF MIND

| 85 | Mind Matters NO THOUGHT 4 | What's The Difference?/Animal Human Exploitation (fold out p/s) ....15 |

ASTERIX

| 70 | Decca F 13075 | Everybody/If I Could Fly ....20 |

EDWIN/TED ASTLEY (ORCHESTRA)

63	Oriole CB 1880	The World Ten Times Over/Soho..10
65	RCA RCA 1492	Danger Man Theme/Saint Theme...40
66	Decca F 12389	The Baron/Drop Head (as Ted Astley)...20

VIRGINIA ASTLEY

82	Why Fi WFI 001	Love's A Lonely Place To Be/Soaring (p/s with lyric insert) 5
82	Why Fi WHY 08	A BAO A QU (10" EP)...10
87	Warner Bros. WEA YZ 107	Some Small Hope/A Summer Long Since Passed (P/s, featuring David Sylvian).............6

(see also David Sylvian)

ANN ASTON

| 74 | Pye 7N 45403 | I Can't Stop Myself From Loving You Babe/Freedom Train..5 |

ASTON HALL

| 80 | Tamebeat TAME 001 | The Daily Sun/Popular People (p/s) ....15 |

ASTON VILLA F.C.

| 75 | Polydor 2058 563 | We're Going Up/THE VILLAINS: We're Going Up...6 |

ASTON & YEN

| 66 | Doctor Bird DB 1064 | Skillamy/BABA BROOKS & BAND: Party Time..30 |

ASTORS

65	Atlantic AT 4037	Candy/I Found Out 80
65	Atlantic AT 4037	Candy/I Found Out (DJ Copy)..120
69	Atlantic 584 245	Candy/I Found Out (reissue)...15

ASTRA

| 10 | Rise Above RISE 127 FREE | Empty Spaces/DIAGONAL: Stop (300 only, gig freebie)...12 |

ASTRA NOVA ORCHESTRA

| 74 | Alaska ALA 26 | Ev'ry Little Beat Of Your Heart/Soul Sleeper ....30 |

ASTRAL NAVIGATIONS

71	Holyground HG 114/ NSR 172	ASTRAL NAVIGATIONS (LP, actually by Lightyears Away & Thundermother, poster cover & booklet, 250 copies only, some numbered) 425
89	Magic Mixture MM 2	ASTRAL NAVIGATIONS (LP, reissue with booklet, 425 copies only)..............................35
90s	Holyground HBG 122/1 CD	ASTRAL NAVIGATIONS (CD) 20

(see also Bill Nelson, David John & Mood)

ASTRONAUTS (U.K.)

| 79 | Bugle BLAST 1 | THE ASTRONAUTS EP (All Night Party/Back Soon/ Everything Stops The Baby/Survivors) (p/s)..15 |
| 82 | Stiff BUY DJ 145 | I'm Your Astronaut (Promo only, p/s) ....10 |

Rare Record Price Guide 2014

80	Bugle BLAST 5	PRANKSTERS IN REVOLT (EP)	20
81	Bugle GENIUS 001	PETER PAN HITS THE SUBURBS (LP)	50
82	Bugle GENIUS 002	IT'S ALL DONE BY MIRRORS (LP)	40
86	All The Madmen MAD 5	IT'S ALL DONE BY MIRRORS (LP, reissue)	15
86	All The Madmen MAD 11	SOON (LP)	12

(see also Restricted Hours, Syndicate)

ASTRONAUTS (1)
| 63 | RCA Victor RCA 1349 | Baja/Kuk | 12 |
| 63 | RCA Victor RD 7662 | ORBIT KAMPUS (LP) | 30 |

ASTRONAUTS (2)
| 66 | Hala Gala HG 9 | Before You Leave/Syncopate | 5 |

ASWAD
76	Island WIP 6312	Back to Africa/Africa	8
76	Island WIP 6338	Three Babylon/Ire Woman	8
78	Grove Music GMDM 9	It's Not Our Wish (That We Should Fight)/Stranger (green vinyl)	20
80	Grove Music 12WIP 6575	Rainbow Culture/Covenant (dub) (12")	18
81	Grove Music 12WIP 6693	Babylon/Behold (12")	12
81	Grove Music IPR 2037	Warrior Charge/Dub Charge (12")	35
81	CBS CBSA 13-1653	Ways Of The Lord/Lords Of The Dub (12", p/s)	8
82	CBS XPS 148	Unsatisfied/Oh Jah (Dub) (10")	12
84	Simba SIM 014	Hooked On You/Version	8
79	Grove Music GMLP 6	HULET (LP)	20
81	Island ASWAD 1	SHOWCASE (LP)	15
82	Island ILPS 9711	NEW CHAPTER OF DUB (LP)	15

ASYLUM
| 74 | Wax SR 2073 | It's My Destiny - Lazy Love/Suzy's Back (p/s) | 100 |

ASYLUM CHOIR
| 68 | Mercury SMCL 21041 | A LOOK INSIDE THE ASYLUM CHOIR (LP) | 25 |

(see also Leon Russell)

ATACAMA
| 71 | Charisma CAS 1039 | ATACAMA (LP, pink/white 'scroll' label) | 30 |
| 72 | Charisma CAS 1060 | THE SUN BURNS UP ABOVE (LP, large 'mad hatter' label) | 25 |

ATAVISTIC
| 87 | Loony Tunes TUNE 7 | EQUILIBRIUM EP (p/s) | 8 |
| 87 | Peaceville WARP 3 | LIFE DURING WARTIME EP (p/s) | 10 |

ATGYFODIAD
| 74 | Sain SAIN 41 | DISGYN MAE'R GLAW (EP) | 12 |

ATHENIANS
64	ESC ESC 1	You Tell Me/Little Queenie (custom sleeve)	50
64	Waverley SLP 532	I've Got Love If You Want It/I'm A Lover Not A Fighter (p/s)	120
64	Waverley SLP 532	I've Got Love If You Want It/I'm A Lover Not A Fighter	60
65	Waverley SLP 533	Thinking Of Your Love/Mercy Mercy (in custom sleeve)	60
65	Waverley SLP 533	Thinking Of Your Love/Mercy Mercy (not in custom sleeve)	30

GLENN ATHENS & TROJANS
| 65 | Spot 7E 1018 | GLENN ATHENS & TROJANS (EP) | 200 |

JUAN ATKINS
| 91 | ULR ULRT 3001 | THE FUTURE SOUND EP (12") | 20 |

PETE ATKIN
70	Philips 6006 050	Be Careful When They Offer You The Moon/Master Of The Revels	5
67	Private pressing	WHILE THE MUSIC LASTS (LP, 99 copies, with Julie Covington)	100
67	Private pressing	THE PARTY'S MOVING ON (LP, 160 copies, with Julie Covington)	150
70	Fontana 6309 011	BEWARE THE BEAUTIFUL STRANGER (LP, black/silver labels)	30
71	Philips 6308 070	DRIVING THROUGH MYTHICAL AMERICA (LP)	30
73	RCA SF 8336	A KING AT NIGHTFALL (LP, with insert)	15
74	RCA LPL1 5014	THE ROAD OF SILK (LP, with insert)	12

BENNY ATKINS
| 60 | Mercury AMT 1113 | Lipstick On Your Lips/I'm Following You | 15 |

CHET ATKINS
59	RCA Victor RCA 1153	Boo Boo Stick Beat/Django's Castle	5
59	RCA Victor RCA 1153	Boo Boo Stick Beat/Django's Castle (78)	12
60	RCA Victor RCA 1174	Teensville/One Mint Julep	8
60	RCA Victor RCA 1209	The Dark At The Top Of The Stairs Theme/Hocus Pocus	6
64	RCA Victor RCA 1382	Susie Q/Windy & Warm	10
65	RCA Victor RCA 1441	Cloudy And Cool/Travelin'	5
65	RCA Victor RCA 1464	Yakety Axe/Letter Edged In Black	5
66	RCA Victor RCA 1515	From Nashville With Love/Rhythm Guitar	5
63	RCA Victor RCX 7118	GUITAR GENIUS (EP)	10
60	RCA Victor RD 27168	TEENSVILLE (LP)	20
63	RCA Victor SF 7529	OUR MAN IN NASHVILLE (LP, stereo)	12
63	RCA Victor RD/SF 7602	TEENSCENE (LP, mono/stereo)	12
63	RCA Victor SF 7647	PROGRESSIVE PICKING (LP, stereo)	12

(see also Country Hams, Hank Snow, Mark Knopfler, Jerry Reid)

DAVE ATKINSON
| 76 | (No label or cat no) | THE BEGGAR & THE SAND (LP) | 50 |

ATLANTIC BRIDGE
| 71 | Dawn DNX 2507 | I Can't Lie To You/Hilary Dickson/Childhood Room (p/s) | 10 |
| 70 | Dawn DNLS 3014 | ATLANTIC BRIDGE (LP, gatefold sleeve, red/black labels) | 50 |

ATLANTICS
| 64 | Windsor WPS 129 | Don't Say No/Send Him To Me | 20 |
| 64 | Oriole CB-1963 | Bombora/Greensleeves | 12 |

ATLANTIS
72	Fury FY 302	I Ain't Got Time/Teddy Boyd's Rock 'N' Roll Show	50
73	Vertigo 6360 609	ATLANTIS (LP, small swirl label, sleeve printed in Germany)	40

(see also Rocking Horse)

ATLANTIS RISING
83	CMI CMI700	Tightrope/Reverie: A Vision	20

ATLAS
78	Emerging WIL 001	AGAINST ALL THE ODDS (LP, private pressing)	25

ATLAS SOUND
11	4AD AD3141	Parallax/Parallax (demo)/Oh Ricky/Quark Part 1 (each side has 2 concentric grooves, only 2 tracks listed on p/s)	6

(see also Deerhunter)

AT LAST THE 1958 ROCK & ROLL SHOW
68	CBS 3349	I Can't Drive/Working On The Railroad	25

(see also Ian Hunter, Mott The Hoople, Freddie 'Fingers' Lee, Miller Anderson, Charles Woolfe)

ATMOSFEAR
79	Elite DAZZ 1	Dancing In Outer Space/Dancing In Outer Space (Version) (12")	15
79	MCA 12 MCA 543	Dancing In Outer Space/Dancing In Outer Space (Version) (12", co. sleeve)	15
82	Elite/City Sounds LDAZZ 12	Xtra Speical (Dry Mix)/(Wet Mix) (12")	15
81	MCA MCF 3110	ENTRANCE (LP)	15
84	Elite ATM 33-1	FIRST/FOURMOST (mini-LP)	15

(see also Antoniou)

ATMOSPHERES
59	London HLW 8977	Kabalo/The Fickle Chicken	15
59	London HLW 8977	Kabalo/The Fickle Chicken (78)	10
60	London HLW 9091	Telegraph/Caravan	15

ATOMIC ROOSTER
70	B&C CB 121	Friday The 13th/Banstead (initial copies in p/s)	15
70	B&C CB 121	Friday The 13th/Banstead	8
72	Dawn DNS 1027	Stand By Me/Never To Lose	6
72	Dawn DNS 1029	Save Me/Close Your Eyes	8
74	Decca FR 13503	Tell Your Story (Sing Your Song)/O.D. (as Vincent Crane's Atomic Rooster)	8
80	EMI EMI 5084	Do You Know Who's Looking For You/Throw Your Life Away (p/s)	6
80	EMI 12EMI 5084	Do You Know Who's Looking For You (Ext.)/Throw Your Life Away (12", p/s)	10
81	Polydor POSP 334	Play It Again/Start To Live (p/s)	5
81	Polydor POSPX 334	Play It Again/Start To Live/Devil's Answer (live) (12", p/s)	5
82	Polydor POSP 408	End Of The Day/Living Underground (p/s)	5
82	Polydor POSPX 408	End Of The Day/Living Underground/Tomorrow Night (live) (12", p/s)	8
70	B&C CAS 1010	ATOMIC ROOSTER (LP, Matrix CAS +1010 + A/CAS + 1010 + B (Flute Mix)	150
70	B&C CAS 1010	ATOMIC ROOSTER (LP, Matrix CAS +1010 + A2/CAS + 1010 + B2 (Flute Mix)	100
70	B&C CAS 1010	ATOMIC ROOSTER (LP, Matrix CAS +1010 + A1U/CAS + 1010 + B1U (Guitar mix)	50
70	B&C CAS 1026	DEATH WALKS BEHIND YOU (LP, gatefold sleeve)	70
71	Pegasus PEG 1	IN HEARING OF ATOMIC ROOSTER (LP, gatefold sleeve)	35
72	Dawn DNLS 3038	MADE IN ENGLAND (LP, limited 'denim' cover, gatefold, with poster, lilac label)	100
73	Dawn DNLS 3038	MADE IN ENGLAND (LP, re-pressing, standard cover, gatefold insert, lilac label)	30
73	Dawn DNLS 3049	NICE'N'GREASY (LP, lilac label)	40
80	EMI EMC3341	ATOMIC ROOSTER (LP)	15
83	Towerbell TOW LP 4	HEADLINE NEWS (LP)	15

(see also Cactus, Crane/Farlowe, Chris Farlowe, Crazy World Of Arthur Brown, Hard Stuff, Leaf Hound, Andromeda, John Du Cann)

ATOMS
79	Rinka R 23	Max Bygraves Killed My Mother/Beatles Jacket (colour silk-screened p/s in poly bag with inserts)	12

ATORIE
89	Conscious CON001	It's My Time/Peace Of Mind (12")	90

A II Z
81	Polydor POSP 243	No Fun After Midnight/Treason (no p/s)	10
81	Polydor POSPX 243	No Fun After Midnight/Treason/Valhalla's Force (12", p/s, red vinyl)	15
81	Polydor POSP 314	I'm The One Who Loves You/Ringside Seat (p/s)	12
80	Polydor 2383 587	THE WITCH OF BERKELEY - LIVE (LP, initially sealed with sew-on patch)	20
80	Polydor 2383 587	THE WITCH OF BERKELEY - LIVE (LP)	15

(see also AC/DC)

ATTACK (U.K.)
67	Decca F 12550	Try It/We Don't Know	150
67	Decca F 12578	Any More Than I Do/Hi-Ho Silver Lining	45
67	Decca F 12631	Created By Clive/Colour Of My Mind	100
67	Decca F 12631	Created By Clive/Colour Of My Mind (p/s for export to Holland)	200
68	Decca F 12725	Neville Thumbcatch/Lady Orange Peel	175
72	Decca F 13353	Hi-Ho Silver Lining/Any More Than I Do (reissue, unissued)	0
90	Reflection MM 08	MAGIC IN THE AIR (LP)	15

(see also Andromeda, Five Day Week Straw People, Nice)

ATTACK (U.S.)
67	Philips BF 1585	Washington Square/Please Phil Spector	18

ATTACK WAVE PESTREPELLER
98	Prescription DRUG 4	NUG YAR (LP, hand-made sleeve, label, with insert 99 copies only)	18

ATTAK
82	No Future OI 17	Today's Generation: Murder In The Subway/Future Dreams (p/s)	8
83	No Future PUNK 6	THEY WILL EAT YOU WHEN YOU MEAT YOU (LP)	15

ATTEMPTED MOUSTACHE
78	Skeleton SKL 003	Superman/No Way Out (folded p/s)	8

ATTENDANTS
80	Black & White BW 2	Happy Families/Deadbeats & Knowones (p/s)	20

AT THE DRIVE IN
00	Virgin VUS 189	Rolodex Propaganda (Album Version)/Extracurricular/One Armed Scissor (Lamacq Version) (p/s)	6
00	Virgin VUS 193	Invalid Litter Dept/Initiation (Lamacq Version) (p/s, yellow vinyl)	6

AT THE GATES
94	Peaceville CC7	Gardens Of Grief (yellow vinyl, members only release)	15
94	Peaceville CC 7	Souls Of The Evil Departed/All Life Ends (yellow vinyl, p/s)	30
92	Deaf DEAF 10	THE RED IN THE SKY IS OURS (LP)	25
93	Deaf DEAF 14	WITH FEAR I KISS THE BURNING DARKNESS (LP)	25
94	Peaceville VILE 47	TERMINAL SPIRIT DISEASE (LP, inner)	50
95	Earache MOSH 143	SLAUGHTER OF THE SOUL (LP, no inner)	40
02	Earache MOSH 143	SLAUGHTER OF THE SOUL (LP, reissue, inner)	25
02	Earache MOSH 143	SLAUGHTER OF THE SOUL (LP, orange vinyl reissue)	25
06	Earache MOSH 143 PD	SLAUGHTER OF THE SOUL (LP, 2nd reissue, picture disc)	20

AT THE SIGNE OF THE BULL
72	Guildhall/Boston Sound GHS 7	AT THE SIGNE OF THE BULL (LP)	25

ATTRACTION
66	Columbia DB 7936	Stupid Girl/Please Tell Me	50
66	Columbia DB 8010	Party Line/She's A Girl	160

ATTRITION
85	Third Mind TMS 04	Shrinkwrap/Pendulum Turns (12", p/s with insert)	10
82	Private AC 001	DEATH HOUSE (cassette)	25
83	Third Mind TMT 06	ONSLAUGHT (cassette)	15
83	Adventures In Reality ARR 12	ACTION AND REACTION (Cassette)	15
83	Adventures In Reality ARR 11	DEATH HOUSE (cassette)	15
83	Rabbit RR 003	DEUX DEMOS (cassette)	15
84	Third Mind TMLP 06	THE ATTRITION OF REASON (LP)	15

ATTRIX
78	Attrix RB 01	Lost Lenore/Hard Times (p/s, stamped white labels)	15
81	Scoff DT 011	Procession/11th Hour (p/s)	10

AU GO-GO SINGERS
65	Columbia DB 7493	San Francisco Bay Blues/Pink Polemoniums	8
64	Columbia 33SX 1696	THEY CALL US AU GO-GO SINGERS (LP)	40

(see also Buffalo Springfield, Stephen Stills, Poco)

AU PAIRS
80	Human OTO 2	You/Domestic Departure/Kerb Crawler	8
80	Human OTO 4	It's Obvious/Diet	8
81	Human HUM 8	Inconvenience/Pretty Boys (p/s)	8
81	Human HUM 8-12	Inconvenience/Pretty Boys/Headache (For Michelle) (12")	10
81	Human HUMAN 1	PLAYING WITH A DIFFERENT SEX (LP, with iron-on transfer)	20
81	Human HUMAN 1	PLAYING WITH A DIFFERENT SEX (LP, without iron-on transfer)	12
82	Kamera KAM 010	SENSE AND SENSUALITY (LP, with insert)	15
83	AKA AKA 6	LIVE IN BERLIN (LP)	12

AUBREY SMALL
72	Polydor 2058 204	Loser/Oh What A Day It's Been	15
71	Polydor 2383 048	AUBREY SMALL (LP, with gatefold insert)	120

(see also Sons Of Man)

AUDIENCE
71	Charisma CB 126	Belladonna Moonshine/The Big Spell	6
71	Charisma CB 141	Indian Summer/It Brings A Tear/Priestess (p/s)	10
71	Charisma CB 156	You're Not Smiling/Eye To Eye	10
71	Charisma CB 156	Eye To Eye/Eye To Eye (double B side mispressing)	25
72	Charisma CB 185	Stand By The Door/Thunder And Lightnin'	5
72	Charisma CB 196	Raviole/Hard Cruel World	5
69	Polydor 583 065	AUDIENCE (LP)	250
70	Charisma CAS 1012	FRIEND'S FRIEND'S FRIEND (LP, pink label with 'scroll' logo)	40
71	Charisma CAS 1032	THE HOUSE ON THE HILL (LP, pink scroll label, gatefold sleeve with lyric inner sleeve)	30
72	Charisma CAS 1054	LUNCH (LP, gatefold sleeve, with lyric inner sleeve)	30

(see also Howard Werth & Moonbeams, Stackridge, Hot Chocolate)

AUDIO ACTIVE
94	On U Sound ONULP 73	WE ARE AUDIO ACTIVE (TOKYO SPACE COWBOYS) (LP)	18

AUDREY
69	Downtown DT 414	Love Me Tonight/BROTHER DAN ALLSTARS: Show Them Amigo	12
69	Downtown DT 418	Lover's Concerto/HERBIE GREY & RUDIES Along Came Roy	12
69	Downtown DT 436	You'll Lose A Good Thing/DESMOND RILEY: If I Had Wings	10
70	Downtown DT 452	Sweeter Than Sugar/The Way You Move	10
70	Downtown DT 454	Oh I Was Wrong/Let's Try It Again (B-side with Dandy)	10
70	Downtown DT 457	Someday We'll Be Together/MUSIC DOCTORS: Sunset Rock	12
70	Downtown DT 463	How Glad I Am/DANDY & AUDREY: I'm So Glad	8
70	Trend 6099 006	Getting Ready For A Heartache/M Y O B: Leave Me Alone	10
81	Jah Skaka 826	English Girl/African Queen (12")	20

(see also Dandy)

MIKE AUDSLEY
72	Sonet SNTF 641	DARK AND DEVIL WATERS (LP, with insert)	18
74	Sonet SNTF 659	STORYBOARD (LP)	12

LOREN AUERBACH
84	Christabel CRL 001	AFTER THE LONG NIGHT (LP)	40
85	Christabel CRL 002	LAYING THE GAME (LP)	40

HUGHES AUFRAY
66	Fontana TL 5419	EN DIRECT DE L'OLYMPIA (LP)	12

BRIAN AUGER (&) TRINITY
65	Columbia DB 7590	Fool Killer/Let's Do It Tonight (as Brian Auger Trinity)	50

MINT VALUE £

65	Columbia DB 7715	Green Onions '65/Kiko (as Brian Auger Trinity)	75
67	Columbia DB 8163	Tiger/Oh Baby, Won't You Come Back Home To Croydon, Where Everybody Beedle's And Bo's (solo)	60
67	Marmalade 598 003	Red Beans And Rice Pts 1 & 2	40
68	Marmalade 598 006	I Don't Know Where You Are/A Kind Of Love In (with Julie Driscoll, unissued in favour of "This Wheel's On Fire")	0
69	Marmalade 598 015	What You Gonna Do/Bumpin' On Sunset	18
70	RCA RCA 1947	I Want To Take You Higher/Just Me Just You	10
71	Polydor 2058 119	This Wheel's On Fire/Road To Cairo (as Brian Auger & Julie Driscoll)	8
71	Polydor 2058 133	Marie's Wedding/Tomorrow City (as Brian Auger's Oblivion Express)	6
73	CBS 1444	Inner City Blues/Light Of The Path (as Brian Auger's Oblivion Express)	10
74	CBS 2309	Straight Ahead/Change	6
68	Marmalade 608 004	DON'T SEND ME NO FLOWERS (LP, with Jimmy Page & Sonny Boy Williamson)	120
69	Marmalade 607/608 003	DEFINITELY WHAT! (LP)	100
69	Polydor 2334 004	THE BEST OF BRIAN AUGER, JULIE DRISCOLL & THE TRINITY (LP)	20
70	RCA SF 8101	BEFOUR (LP)	35
71	RCA SF 8170	OBLIVION EXPRESS (LP)	25
71	Polydor 2383 062	BETTER LAND (LP, as Brian Auger's Oblivion Express)	30
72	Polydor 2383 104	SECOND WIND (LP, as Brian Auger's Oblivion Express)	30
73	CBS 65625	CLOSER TO IT (LP)	15
74	CBS 80058	STRAIGHT AHEAD (LP)	18

(see also Julie Driscoll Brian Auger & Trinity, Shotgun Express, Jimmy Page, Sonny Boy Williamson)

NAT AUGUSTIN
83	Debut DEBT 12 6	All Of My Love/Summer Is Here Again (12")	80

AUM
69	London HA-K/SH-K 8401	BLUESVIBES (LP)	45

CLIFF AUNGIER
68	Polydor 56250	Time/Fisherboy	30
68	RCA RCA 1730	My Love And I/Abigail	10
69	Pye 7N 17753	Lady From Baltimore/Back On The Road Again	10
69	Pye NSPL 18294	THE LADY FROM BALTIMORE (LP)	20

(see also Royd Rivers & Cliff Aungier)

AUNTIEPUS
79	Septic AUNT 1	Half-Way To Venezuela/Marmalade Freak (p/s)	6

(see also Damned)

AURORA
83	Aurora RAM 9	I'll Be Your Fantasy/If I Really Knew Her (no p/s)	40

(see also AC/DC)

AURRA
82	Battersea BATTL 1	A Little Love/Make Up Your Mind (12")	10

AUSTIN
93	Suburban Base SUBBASE 18	THE AUSTIN EP (12", stamped white label)	30

PATTI AUSTIN
69	United Artists UP 35018	The Family Tree/Magical Boy	5
71	CBS 7180	Are We Ready For Love/Now That I Know What Loneliness Is	25
74	Probe PRO 608	Music To My Heart/Love 'Em And Leave 'Em Kind Of Love	15

PETER AUSTIN
68	Caltone TONE 125	Your Love/Time Is Getting Harder	120
75	Terminal 108	When You Are Near/Dub	7

(see also Little Freddy, Mr. Foundation)

REG AUSTIN
65	Pye 7N 15885	My Saddest Day/I'll Find Her	50

SIL AUSTIN
58	Mercury 7MT 220	Don't You Just Know It/Rainstorm	15
58	Mercury 7MT 225	Hey, Eula/The Last Time	10
58	Mercury MEP 9540	THE BAND WITH THE BEAT (EP)	35
58	Mercury MEP 9541	GO SIL GO (EP)	35
58	Mercury MPL 6534	SLOW WALK ROCK (LP)	40

AUSTRA
11	Domino RUG 429T	SPARKLE (12" remix EP, most destroyed in PIAS warehouse fire)	8

AUSTRALIAN CRICKET TEAM
72	Penny Farthing PEN 739	Bowl, Ball, Swing, Bat/Here Come The Aussies	7

AUSTRALIAN PLAYBOYS
67	Immediate IM 054	Black Sheep R.I.P./Sad	800

(see also Procession, Manfred Mann Earth Band)

AUTECHRE
91	Hardcore HARD 003	Cavity Job/Accelera 1 + 2 (12", 1,000 only)	40
94	Warp WAP 54	ANTI EP (12", p/s sealed with sticker)	15
94	Warp 10WAP 44	BASSCADET EP (3 x 10" p/s in box)	18
95	Warp WAP64r	ANVIL VAPRE EP (12")	12
95	Warp WAP 58	GARBAGE EP (12")	15
96	Warp WAP 72	We R Are Why/Are Y Are We (12, p/s, mail order only)	25
97	Warp WAP96r	CICHLISUITE EP (12")	12
97	Warp WAP 89	Goz Quarter/Latent Quarter (12")	8
97	Warp WAP 89X	EVANE: Laughing Quarter/Draun Quarter (12")	10
99	Warp WAP 124	SPLTRMX: Weissensee Against Im Gluck/At Drowning In A Sea Of Independence (12", 3000 only)	18
99	Warp WAPEP7.1	EP 7.1 (12")	10
99	Warp WAPE7.2	EP 7.2 (12")	10
99	Warp WAP 112	PEEL SESSION (12")	12
93	Warp LP 17LTD	INCUNABULA (2-LP set, silver vinyl)	35
94	Warp WARPL 25	AMBER (2-LP)	30
95	Warp WARPLP 38	TRI REPETAE (2-LP)	30

97	Warp WARPLP 49	CHIASTIC SLIDE (2-LP)	15
98	Warp WARPLP66	LP5 (2-LP)	15
01	Warp WARPLP 128	CONFIELD (2-LP)	15
08	Warp WARPCD 333X	QUARISTICE (2-CD metal sleeve)	70

(see also Gescom)

AUTEURS

93	Rough trade 45REV15	Housebreaker/Valet Parking	5
92	Hut PM 264	NEW WAVE (LP with free 7")	25
94	Hut Recordings HUTLPX 16	NOW I'M A COWBOY (LP, with free 1-sided 7")	25
96	Hut HUT LP33	AFTER MURDER PARK (LP)	25
99	Hut HUT LP53	HOW I LEARNED TO LOVE THE BOOTBOYS (LP)	25

AUTO DA FÉ (IRELAND)

82	Auto dafé A.D.F. 003	November November/For Rich People (p/s)	10
82	Auto Dafé A.D.F. 004	Bad Experience/Lot 3 (Live Instrumental)	10
82	Rewind REWIND 13	November November/For Rich People	8

AUTOGRAPHS

| 78 | RAK RAK 281 | While I'm Still Young/Fabulous (p/s) | 15 |
| 78 | Strawberry Mastering | While I'm Still Young (different version, acetate only) | 30 |

AUTOMATIC DLAMINI

87	D For Drum DLAM 2	I Don't Know You But... /I've Never Seen That Colour Anywhere Before (p/s, with insert)	5
87	Idea IDEA 009	Me And My Conscience (p/s)	5
87	Idea IDEAT 009	Me And My Conscience (12", p/s)	8
87	Idea IDEALP 001	THE D IS FOR DRUM (LP)	12
92	Big Intl. BOT 04	FROM A DIVA TO A DIVER (LP)	12

(see also P.J. Harvey)

AUTOMATIC FINE TUNING

| 76 | Charisma CAS 1122 | A.F.T (LP) | 25 |

AUTOMATICS

| 78 | Island WIP 6433 | Wakin' With The Radio On/Watch Her Now (unissued) | 0 |
| 78 | Island WIP 6439 | When Tanks Roll Over Poland Again/Watch Her Now (p/s) | 15 |

AUTOPSY

| 89 | Peaceville VILE 12 | SEVERED SURVIVAL (LP, picture disc) | 25 |
| 91 | Peaceville VILE 25 | MENTAL FUNERAL (LP, picture disc) | 25 |

AUTOSALVAGE

| 88 | Edsel ED 286 | AUTOSALVAGE (LP, reissue) | 25 |

GENE AUTRY

| 70 | CBS 4739 | Rudolph The Red Nosed Reindeer/Frost The Snow Man | 5 |

AUTUMN

| 71 | Pye 7N 45090 | My Little Girl/Sun Sunshine | 7 |
| 72 | Pye 7N45144 | Stood Up/Not The Way She Looks | 20 |

AUTUMN VINE

| 70 | Evolution E 2447 | He Ain't No Superman/Maxi Baby | 12 |

AVALANCHE (1)

| 71 | Parlophone R 5890 | Finding My Way Home/Rabbits | 40 |

(see also Norman Haines Band)

AVALANCHE (2)

| 80 | Childers AVA 1 | The Preacher/Mean Lady (no p/s) | 90 |

AVALANCHES

| 01 | XL Recordings XLLP 138 | SINCE I LEFT YOU (2-LP) | 30 |

AVALON

| 82 | SRTS 82/CUS/1296 | Going Thru'/Gypsey Secret (not released in p/s) | 130 |

FRANKIE AVALON

58	HMV POP 453	Dede Dinah/Ooh-La-La	15
58	London HL 8636	You Excite Me/Darlin'	30
58	London HL 8636	You Excite Me/Darlin'	10
58	HMV POP 517	Ginger Bread/Blue Betty	12
59	HMV POP 569	I'll Wait For You/What Little Girl?	12
59	HMV POP 603	Venus/I'm Broke	5
59	HMV POP 636	Bobby Sox To Stockings/A Boy Without A Girl	5
59	HMV POP 658	Just Ask Your Heart/Two Fools	5
60	HMV POP 742	The Faithful Kind/Gee Whizz - Whilikins - Golly Gee	5
60	HMV POP 766	Where Are You/Tuxedo Junction	5
61	HMV POP 879	Gotta Get A Girl/Who Else But You	5
62	Pye Int. 7N 25171	Dance The Bossa Nova/Welcome Home Baby	5
63	Pye Int. 7N 25183	My Ex-Best Friend/First Love Never Dies	5
63	Pye Int. 7N 25203	Cleopatra/Heartbeats	5
58	HMV 7EG 8471	FRANKIE AVALON (EP)	10
58	HMV 7EG 8482	FRANKIE AVALON NO. 2 (EP)	10
58	HMV 7EG 8507	FRANKIE AVALON NO. 3 (EP)	10
60	HMV 7EG 8632	SONGS OF THE ALAMO (EP)	10
59	HMV CLP 1346	SWINGIN' ON A RAINBOW (LP)	12
60	HMV CLP 1423	SUMMER SCENE (LP)	12
60	HMV CLP 1440	YOUNG AND IN LOVE (LP, mono)	12
60	HMV CSD 1358	YOUNG AND IN LOVE (LP, stereo)	15
64	United Artists ULP 1078	MUSCLE BEACH PARTY (LP)	40

AVALONS

| 66 | Island WI 263 | Everyday/I Love You | 15 |

AVANT-GARDE

| 68 | CBS 3704 | Naturally Stoned/Honey And Gall | 12 |

AVANT GARDENER(S)
80	Appaloosa AP 013	DIG IT (LP)	12

AVAVA
91	A5 AVA 5555	AVAVA (LP, 500 only)	12

AVENGER
83	Neat NEAT 31	Too Wild To Tame/On The Rocks (p/s, with insert)	10
84	Neat NEAT 1018	BLOOD SPORTS (LP)	15
85	Neat NEAT 1026	KILLER ELITE (LP, with lyric insert)	15

AVENGERS (1)
68	Parlophone R 5661	Everyone's Gonna Wonder/Take My Hand	15

(see also Vanity Fair)

AVENGERS (2)
72	Bullet BU 521	Highjack Plane/Shower Of Rain	5

AVERAGE WHITE BAND
80	RCA XC 1152	Let's Go Round Again/A Love Of Your Own (12")	8
73	MCA MUPS 486	SHOW YOUR HAND (LP, black/silver labels)	25

AVIATOR
79	Harvest SHSP 4096	AVIATOR (LP)	12
80	Harvest SHSP 4107	TURBULENCE (LP)	15

AVO-8
80	Stroppo STROP 1	Gone Wrong/Target One/No Hesitation (p/s)	7

ALAN AVON & TOY SHOP
70	Concord CON 005	These Are The Reasons/Night To Remember	150

(see also Hedgehoppers Anonymous)

AVON CITIES' JAZZ BAND
56	Tempo A 151	Shim-Me Sha-Me Wabble/Hawaiian War Chant	5
60	Tempo A 169	Upper Set/American Patrol	5
56	Tempo LAP 10	AVON CITIES JAZZ BAND (LP)	15
58	Tempo TAP 18	AVON CITIES JAZZ (LP, with Ray Bush)	15

(see also Ray Bush)

VALERIE AVON
67	Columbia DB 8201	He Knows I Love Him Too Much/To Be Let	10

(see also Avons)

AVONS
59	Columbia DB 4363	Seven Little Girls Sitting In The Back Seat/Alone At Eight	5
60	Columbia DB 4413	Pickin' Petals/We Fell In Love	7
60	Columbia DB 4461	We're Only Young Once/I Keep Dreaming	5
61	Columbia DB 4700	Skin Divin'/Little Bo Peep	5
62	Columbia DB 4899	A Wonderful Dream/Tonight You Belong To Me	5
63	Decca F 11588	Hey Paula/I Wanna Do It	5
63	Decca F 11641	Love Should Be True/All About You	5
64	Fontana TF 442	I Am The Girl/Once Upon A Summer's Day	5

(see also Valerie Avon, Avon Sisters)

AVON SISTERS
59	Columbia DB 4236	Jerri-Lee (I Love Him So)/Baby-O	12
59	Columbia DB 4236	Jerri-Lee (I Love Him So)/Baby-O (78)	10

AWAY FROM THE SAND
73	Beaujangle DV 003	AWAY FROM THE SAND (LP, allegedly only 50 copies)	100

A WITNESS
86	Ron johnson ZRON 12	I AM JOHNS PANCREAS (LP)	12

AXEGRINDER
89	Peaceville VILE 7	RISE OF THE SERPENT MEN (LP)	30

DAVID AXELROD
68	Capitol ST 2982	SONG OF INNOCENCE (LP, 'Sold in the U.K...' on label)	45
71	RCA LSP 4636	MESSIAH (LP)	40
73	MCA MUPS 472	THE AUCTION (LP, black/blue hexagon label)	40

(see also Electric Prunes)

AXIS
80	Metal Minded ISAX 1047	Lady/Messiah (p/s)	8
81	Axis	When You Hold Me	8
81	Neat NEAT 13	You Got It/One Step Ahead (p/s)	5

HOYT AXTON
63	Saga SS503	Greenback Dollar/The Crawdad Song	8
69	CBS 4316	It's All Right Now/Way Before The Time Of Towns	12
79	Young Blood YB 32	Della And The Dealer/Gotta Keep Rollin'	5
64	Stateside SL 10082	GREENBACK DOLLAR (LP)	20
64	Stateside SL 10096	THUNDER 'N' LIGHTNIN' (LP)	20
66	London HA-F/SH-F 8276	THE BEST OF HOYT AXTON (LP)	20

AXXESS
83	Lamborghini LMGLP 100	NOVELS FOR THE MOONS (LP)	30

AYERS, CALE, NICO & ENO
74	Island ILPS 9291	JUNE 1ST, 1974 (LP)	18

(see also Kevin Ayers, John Cale, Nico, Brian Eno)

KEVIN AYERS (& WHOLE WORLD)
70	Harvest HAR 5011	Singing A Song In The Morning/Eleanor's Cake Which Ate Her	20
70	Harvest HAR 5027	Butterfly Dance/Puis-Je? (with Whole World)	25
71	Harvest HAR 5042	Stranger In Blue Suede Shoes/Stars (with Whole World)	10
72	Harvest HAR 5064	Oh! Wot A Dream/Connie On A Rubber Band	10
73	Harvest HAR 5071	Caribbean Moon/Take Me To Tahiti (p/s)	20

74	Island WIP 6194	The Up Song/Everybody's Sometimes & Some People's All The Time Blues	6
74	Island WIP 6201	After The Show/Thank You Very Much	6
75	Harvest HAR 5100	Caribbean Moon/Take Me To Tahiti	6
76	Island WIP 6271	Falling In Love Again/Everyone Knows The Song	6
76	Harvest HAR 5107	Stranger In Blue Suede Shoes/Fake Mexican Tourist Blues (possibly in p/s)	20
76	Harvest HAR 5107	Stranger In Blue Suede Shoes/Fake Mexican Tourist Blues	5
76	Harvest HAR 5109	Caribbean Moon/Take Me To Tahiti (reissue)	5
76	Harvest HAR 5109	Caribbean Moon/Take Me To Tahiti (reissue, in different p/s)	20
77	Harvest HAR 5124	Star/The Owl	6
80	Harvest HAR 5198	Money, Money, Money/Stranger In Blue Suede Shoes (p/s)	6
83	Charly/Celluloid CYZ 7107	My Speeding Heart/Champagne & Valium (p/s)	10
86	Illuminated LEV 71	Stepping Out/Only Heaven Knows (no p/s)	10
70	Harvest SHVL 763	JOY OF A TOY (LP, gatefold sleeve, 1st pressing with no EMI box)	80
70	Harvest SHSP 4005	SHOOTING AT THE MOON (LP, with Whole World)	50
72	Harvest SHVL 800	WHATEVERSHEBRINGSWESING (LP, gatefold sleeve)	40
73	Harvest SHVL 807	BANANAMOUR (LP, gatefold sleeve, with booklet)	100
73	Harvest SHVL 807	BANANAMOUR (LP, gatefold sleeve, without booklet)	30
74	Island ILPS 9263	THE CONFESSIONS OF DR. DREAM AND OTHER STORIES (LP, with inner)	30
75	Island ILPS 9322	SWEET DECEIVER (LP, with inner sleeve)	15
75	Harvest SHDW 407	JOY OF A TOY/SHOOTING AT THE MOON (2-LP, reissue, gatefold sleeve)	25
76	Harvest SHSP 2005	ODD DITTIES (LP)	18
76	Harvest SHSP 4057	YES WE HAVE NO MAÑANAS (LP, textured sleeve, with inner sleeve)	20
78	Harvest SHSP 4085	RAINBOW TAKEAWAY (LP)	15
86	Illuminated AMA 25	AS CLOSE AS YOU THINK (LP)	25
86	Harvest Black EMS 1124	BANANAMOUR (LP, reissue)	15
92	Permanent PERM LP 5	STILL LIFE WITH GUITAR (LP)	15
80	Harvest SHSP 4106	THAT'S WHAT YOU GET BABE (LP)	12

(see also Soft Machine, Lady June, Lol Coxhill, David Bedford, Mike Oldfield, Bridget St. John)

ROY AYERS (UBIQUITY)

77	Polydor 2066 842	Running Away/Cincinnati Growl (as Roy Ayers' Ubiquity)	5
80	Polydor POSP 135	Running Away/Can't You See Me	5
80	Polydor POSPX 135	Running Away/Can't You See Me (12")	10
80	Polydor POSPX 186	Sometimes, Believe In Yourself (12")	8
83	Polydor UM 1T	Silver Vibrations/Fast Money (12")	8
87	Urban URBX 6	Can't You See Me/Love Will Bring Us Back Together/Sweet Tears (12", p/s)	15
83	Uno Melodic UMLP 2	DRIVIN' ON UP (LP)	20

(see also Jack Wilson Quartet)

ALBERT AYLER

64	Transatlantic TRA 130	SPIRITS (LP)	40
64	Fontana Jazz SFJL 925	GHOSTS (LP)	40
64	Fontana Jazz STJL 927	MY NAME IS (LP)	40
65	Fontana 933 SFJL	SPIRITUAL UNITY (LP)	40
65	Fontana SFJL 925	GHOSTS (LP, reissue)	30
65	Fontana Jazz SFJL 927	MY NAME IS (LP, reissue)	30
67	Polydor 2383089	WITCHES & DEVILS (LP)	25
68	Impulse IMPL 8022	NEW GRASS (LP, gatefold sleeve)	25
69	Impulse SIPL 519	NEW GRASS (LP, reissue, single sleeve)	20
69	Sonet SNTF 604	FIRST RECORDINGS (LP)	15
70s	Freedom 41000 FLP	VIBRATIONS (LP)	15

J AYRES

| 77 | Hawkeye HE 004 | Pretty Looks/THE REVOLUTIONARIES - Ugly | 6 |

AYRSHIRE FOLK

| 74 | Deroy DER 1052 | AYRSHIRE FOLK (LP, private pressing) | 50 |

AYSHEA

65	Fontana TF 627	Eeny Meeny/Peep My Love	20
68	Polydor 56276	Celebration Of The Year/Only Love Can Save Me Now	35
69	Polydor 56302	Another Night/Taking The Sun From My Eyes	12
70	Polydor 2001 029	Mr White's White Flying Machine/Ship Of The Line	10
70	Polydor 2058 074	Who's Gonna Rescue Jesus/The Flowers Are Mine	5
71	MAM MAM 59	Old Fashioned Love Song/Family Of A Man	5
73	Harvest HAR 5073	Farewell/The Best Years Of My Life	8
74	DJM DJS 339	Another Without You Day/Moonbeam	6
70	Polydor 2384 026	AYSHEA (LP)	30

(see also Ayshea Brough, Roy Wood)

CHARLES AZNAVOUR

| 56 | London DEP 95014 | AZNAVOUR INVADES | 20 |

AZTEC CAMERA

81	Postcard 81-3	Just Like Gold/We Could Send Letters (die-cut sleeve, with card)	50
81	Postcard 81-3	Just Like Gold/We Could Send Letters (die-cut sleeve, without card)	20
81	Postcard 81-8	Mattress Of Wire/Lost Outside The Tunnel (p/s)	30
82	Rough Trade RT 112	Pillar To Post/Queen's Tattoos (p/s)	5
82	Rough Trade RT 112P	Pillar To Post/Queen's Tattoos (picture disc)	8
83	Rainhill ACFC 1	Oblivious (Langer/Winstanley Remix)/Oblivious (Colin Fairley Remix) (fan club issue, no p/s)	20
94	Windsong WHISCD 006	LIVE ON THE TEST (CD)	20

(see also French Impressionists)

AZUL

| 77 | Venture VEN7778 | Babylon Special/Version | 10 |

AZYMUTH

| 79 | Milestone MRC 101 | Jazz Carnival/Fly Over The Horizon (12") | 10 |
| 80 | Milestone MRC 102 | Dear Limmertz/Papasong (12") | 15 |

IKE B & CRYSTALS
68   Island WI 3151   Try A Little Merriness/Patricia...25

JOHN B
72   Decca F 13362   Take A Look Around/Run Run Run 6

B TROOP
81   iluminated JAMS 6   EUROPEANS (LP) 15

MEHER BABA
70   Univ. Spiritual League 1   HAPPY BIRTHDAY (LP, with booklet and lyric sheet 6 Pete Townshend tracks, 100 only) 200
70   Univ. Spiritual League 2   I AM (LP, with inserts, features 5 Pete Townshend tracks) 100
76   Univ. Spiritual League 3   WITH LOVE (LP, features 3 Pete Townshend tracks) 100
70s   MBO MBO 1   STAR OF THE SILENT SCREEN . . . MEHER BABA (LP, reissue of "Happy Birthday" without inserts) 20
70s   MBO MBO 2   I AM (LP, reissue, without inserts) 20
(see also Pete Townshend)

BABE RUTH
71   Decca F13234   Rupert's Magic Feather/Flood 6
71   Capitol CL 15869   Elusive/Say No More...5
71   Capitol CL 15869   Elusive/Say No More (DJ Copy)..6
72   Harvest HAR 5087   Wells Fargo/Theme From A Few Dollars More...5
75   Harvest HAR 5090   Private Number/Somebody's Nobody...5
72   Harvest SHSP 4022   FIRST BASE (LP, 1st pressing with 'Sympathy Music Ltd' credit for 'Wells Fargo' with lyric insert)..30
72   Harvest SHSP 4022   FIRST BASE (LP, 2nd pressing with 'Tone Music' credit for 'Wells Fargo' with lyric insert) 20
74   Harvest SHVL 812   AMAR CABALLERO (LP, gatefold sleeve) 20
75   Harvest SHSP 4038   BABE RUTH (LP, inner lyric sleeve)..20
77   Harvest SHSM 2019   THE BEST OF BABE RUTH (LP) 12
(see also Jenny Haan, Bernie Marsden, Wild Turkey, Elias Hulk, Liquid Gold)

BABES IN TOYLAND
92   Southern 18503-7   Bruise Violet/Magick Flute Gone (purple vinyl, p/s) 6

ALICE BABS
63   Fontana TF 409   After You've Gone/St. Louis Blues Twist 5
64   Oriole CB1955   Drip Drop (Droppen Drip Och Droppen Drapp)/Brevet Fran Lillian 5

MONTY BABSON
61   Palette PG 9010   Utopia/Brand New Feeling 5
61   Palette PG 9016   My Faith/The Moon Will Weep 5
61   Palette PG 9021   Blue Trumpet/Square Feet..5
61   Palette PG 9028   Mama Darling/It All Began WIth You 5
59   London HLJ 8877   All Night Long/The Things Money Cannot Buy 5
67   CBS 2996   If My Friends Could See Me Now/Here Today Gone Tomorrow 5
68   CBS 3313   Get Out Of My Heart/I Smoke Too Much I Drink Too Much And I Cry....................5
63   Pye Int. NEP 44020   MONTY BABSON (EP) 8
60   London HAJ 2212   ALL NIGHT LONG (LP) 12

BABY
69   Spark SRL 1030   Heartbreaker/Michael Blues 20

BABY BIRD
95   Baby Bird LP 1   IF I WAS BORN A MAN (LP, 500 only)..15
95   Baby Bird LP 2   BAD SHAVE (LP, 500 only)...15
02   Essential CD7   ORIGINAL LO FI (5-CD box set)..20

BABY D
92   Production House PNT 043RX   Let Me Be Your Fantasy (Acen In Wonderland)/Fantasy (Ray Keith Remix)(12")...................15
95   Systematic SYSX 11   I Need Your Loving/Neil McLelland MIx)/T.S.O.B. Mix)/(Masters Of House Mix) (12") 8
96   Systematic 828683 1   DELIVERANCE (3-LP) 20

BABY DOLLS
60   Warner Bros WB 16   Quiet!/Hey, Baby! 20

BABY GRUNTING
71   United Artists UP 35258   Keep The Circle Turning/Way Down The Line 6

BABY HUEY
71   Buddah 2365 001   LIVING LEGEND - THE BABY HUEY STORY (LP) 40

BABY JANE & ROCKABYES
63   United Artists UP 1010   How Much Is That Doggie In The Window/My Boy John 15

BABY LEMONADE
87   Narodnik NRK 004   The Secret Goldfish/Real World (p/s) 8

BABYLON
69   Polydor 56356   Into The Promised Land/Nobody's Fault But Mine (p/s) 35
69   Polydor 56356   Into The Promised Land/Nobody's Fault But Mine (no p/s) 20
(see also Carole Grimes)

BABYLON TIMEWARP
93   Subliminal TENSE 001   Durban Poison/Durban Poison (-32Hz And Dropping Mix)/ Durban Poison (The Kashmir Mix)(12") 40

BABYSHAMBLES
05   Rough Trade RTRADS 260   Albion/Wolfman (p/s) 6
04   High Society (no cat no)   What Katie Did (Demo) (1,000 numbered copies of clear flexi, with Annelise's Magazine. With magazine)..50

04	High Society (no cat no)	What Katie Did (Demo) (1,000 numbered copies of clear flexi, with Annelise's Magazine. Without magazine)	30
04	High Society HS7IN011	Babyshambles/At The Flophouse (p/s, 1000 only)	40
04	High Society HSCDS003	Babyshambles/At The Flophouse (CD, 1,000 only)	40
06	B Unique BUN 116-7	Janie Jones/Janie Jones (Statik Remix) (p/s, as Babyshambles And Friends)	6
10	Parlophone	Side Of The Road (jukebox centre, die cut sleeve, 1000 only)	10
05	Rough Trade RTRADLP240	DOWN IN ALBION (2xLP with side 4 etched)	25

(see also Libertines, Wolfman)

BABY SUNSHINE
75	Deroy DER 1301	BABY SUNSHINE (LP, with insert)	100

(see also Fairy's Moke)

BACCA
73	Grape GR 3048	George Foreman/Version	5

BURT BACHARACH
65	London HLR 9958	Don't Go Breaking My Heart/24 Hours From Tulsa	5
65	London HLR 9968	Trains And Boats And Planes/Wives And Lovers	5
65	London HLR 9983	What's New Pussycat/My Little Red Book (B-side with Tony Middleton)	30
65	London HLR 9958	24 Hours From Tulsa/Don't Go Breaking My Heart	7
69	A&M AMS 702	Bond Street/Alfie	5
67	RCA Victor RD 7874	CASINO ROYALE (LP, soundtrack, mono)	30
67	RCA Victor SF 7874	CASINO ROYALE (LP, soundtrack, stereo)	40

(see also Tony Middleton, Breakaways)

BACHDENKEL
77	Initial IRC 001	LEMMINGS (LP, stickered gatefold sleeve, with bonus EP)	50
77	Initial IRL 001	LEMMINGS (LP)	15
77	Initial IRL 002	STALINGRAD (LP, numbered with lyric insert)	40

JOHNNY BACHELOR
60	London HLN 9074	Mumbles/Arabella Jean	80

BACHELOR PAD
87	Sha La La Ba Ba Ba Ba Ba 003	Girl Of Your Dreams/BABY LEMONADE: Jiffy Neckware Creation (p/s, flexi with Are You Scared To Get Happy or Simply Thrilled 3 fanzines)	10

BACHELORS (U.K.)
58	Parlophone R 4454	Platter Party/Love Is A Two Way Street	25
59	Parlophone R 4547	Please Don't Touch/Ding Dong	20
60	Decca F 11300	Lovin' Babe/Why Can't It Be Me	15

BACHMAN TURNER OVERDRIVE
74	MERCURY 9100007	NOT FRAGILE (LP)	12

BACH TWO BACH
71	Mushroom 100 MR 10	BACH TWO BACH (LP)	20

BACK O TOWN SYNCOPATORS
64	Columbia DB 7358	Manhattan Spiritual/Colonel Bogey	6

BACK TO ZERO
79	Fiction FICS 004	Your Side Of Heaven/Back To Back	10

BACK ALLEY CHOIR
72	York SYK 517	Smile Born Of Courtesy/Why Are You Here	40
73	York FYK 406	BACK ALLEY CHOIR (LP, 500 only)	400

BACKBEAT PHILHARMONIC
61	Top Rank JAR 576	Rock And Roll Symphony Parts 1 & 2	8

BACK DOOR
72	Blakey BLP 5989	BACK DOOR (LP, sold at gigs)	50
73	Warner Bros. K 46231	BACK DOOR (LP)	18
76	Warner Bros. K56243	ACTIVATE (LP)	15

(see also Whitesnake)

BACKHOUSE JAMES BLUES BAND
68	private pressing	BACKHOUSE JAMES BLUES BAND	400

MIRIAM BACKHOUSE
77	Mother Earth MUM 1203	GYPSY WITHOUT A ROAD (LP)	120

BACKLASH
80	Gargoyle GRGL 777	OFF WITH HIS HEAD (EP)	50

BACK PORCH MAJORITY
65	Columbia DB 7627	Ramblin' Man/Good Time Joe	8

BACKSEAT ROMEOS
80	Future Earth FER 007	Zero Ambition/In The Night (p/s)	35

BACK STREET BAND
69	Ember EMBS 277	This Ain't The Road/Daybreak (p/s)	8

JIM BACKUS
58	London HLJ 8674	Delicious (The Laughing Song)/I Need A Vacation	5

BACKYARD BABIES
98	Bad Afro FROO 12	(Is It) Still Alright To Smile/B. Babylon (featuring Ginger from Wildhearts) (p/s, yellow vinyl)	10
09	Spinefarm 2701938	Degenerated/SUPERSHIT 666: Star War Jr. (hand-numbered p/s, blue vinyl, 500 only)	7
98	Coalition COLA 046	Look At You/Powderhead/Can't Find The Door/Wireless Mind (gatefold p/s)	8
98	Coalition COLA 051	Bombed (Out Of My Mind)/Rocker (featuring Michael Monroe) (yellow vinyl, fully-autographed numbered (apart from promos) gatefold p/s, 2000 only)	10
99	Coalition COLA 073	Babylon (featuring "Wildhearted Ginger")/Stars (red vinyl, foldover p/s & insert in poly bag, 1000 copies sold at gigs only)	10

(see also Hanoi Rocks, Super$hit666, Wildhearts)

BACKYARD HEAVIES
73	Action ACT 4616	Just Keep On Truckin'/Never Can Say Goodbye	25

BACON FAT

70	Blue Horizon 57-3171	Nobody But You/Small's On 53rd	18
70	Blue Horizon 57-3181	Evil/Blues Feeling	25
70	Blue Horizon 7-63858	GREASE ONE FOR ME (LP)	70
71	Blue Horizon 2431 001	TOUGH DUDE (LP)	90

(see also Dirty Blues Band, George 'Harmonica' Smith)

GAR BACON

58	Felsted AF 107	Mary Jane/Chains Of Love	20
58	Felsted AF 107	Mary Jane/Chains Of Love (78)	40
59	Fontana H 196	Marshal, Marshal/Too Young To Love	30
59	Fontana H 196	Marshal, Marshal/Too Young To Love (78)	40

BAD ACTORS

| 80 | Sophist. Noise SONO 1 | Strange Love/Energy Society (p/s) | 10 |
| 80 | Plastic Speech | Love Song/Are They Hostile (p/s) | 5 |

BAD BOYS

| 64 | Piccadilly 7N 35208 | The Owl And The Pussycat/That's What I'll Do | 10 |

BAD BRAINS

82	Alt. Tentacles VIRUS 13	I Luv Jah/Sailin' On/Big Takeover (12", p/s)	8
83	Food For Thought YUMT101	I And I Survive (An' T'ing)/Destroy Babylon (12", insert, p/s)	20
83	Abstract ABT 007	ROCK FOR LIGHT (LP)	20

BAD COMPANY (1)

| 74 | Island ILPS 9279 | BAD COMPANY (LP) | 12 |

BAD COMPANY (2)

98	BC Recordings BCR 001	The Nine/The Bridge (company p/s)	20
99	BC R'dings BCR 002	THE FEAR EP: 4 days/Refuge/The Fear/Jellyfish (2 x 12", p/s)	8
99	Prototype PROUK 001	The Pulse/China Cup (12", die-cut p/s)	10
00	BC R'dings BCRUKLPS 001	DIGITAL NATION ALBUM SAMPLER: Flashback (Tumpa)/Spacewalk (promo 12", stickered black die-cut sleeve, A-side with Trace)	12
01	BC R'dings BCRUKEP 001	BOOK OF THE BAD VOL. 1 EP: The Voice/Numbers/Spide/Believe (2 x 12", p/s)	10
01	BC R'dings BCRUKEP 002	BOOK OF THE BAD VOL. 2 EP: Dogs On The Moon/Grunge/Ladies of Spain/ The Running Man (2 x 12", p/s)	10
01	BC R'dings BCRUKEP 003	BOOK OF TH BAD VOL. 3 EP: Mindgames/Rodeo/Miami flashback/ Storyteller (2 x 12", p/s)	10
01	Prototype PROUK 003	Planet Dust/Speedball (12", p/s)	10
00	BC R'dings BCRLP 001	INSIDE THE MACHINE (5 x 12")	35
00	BC R'dings BCRUKLP 001	DIGITAL NATION (5 x 12")	25

BADFINGER

70	Apple APPLE 20	Come And Get It/Rock Of All Ages (p/s)	10
70	Apple APPLE 31	No Matter What/Better Days (p/s)	15
71	Apple APPLE 35	Name Of The Game/Suitcase (unreleased)	0
72	Apple APPLE 40	Day After Day/Sweet Tuesday Morning (p/s)	15
72	Apple APPLE 42	Baby Blue/Flying (unreleased in U.K.)	0
74	Apple APPLE 49	Apple Of My Eye/Blind Owl	50
70	Apple SAPCOR 12	MAGIC CHRISTIAN MUSIC (LP)	50
70	Apple SAPCOR 16	NO DICE (LP, gatefold sleeve)	50
72	Apple SAPCOR 19	STRAIGHT UP (LP)	50
73	Warner Bros K 56023	BADFINGER (LP, with insert)	30
74	Apple SAPCOR 27	ASS (LP, with inner sleeve)	60
74	Warner Bros K 56076	WISH YOU WERE HERE (LP, withdrawn)	100
79	Elektra K52129	AIRWAVES (LP, with lyric inner sleeve)	20
91	Apple SAPCOR 12	MAGIC CHRISTIAN MUSIC (LP, reissue, gatefold sleeve with bonus 12" [Sapcor 121])	25
92	Apple SAPCOR 16	NO DICE (LP, reissue, gatefold sleeve with bonus 12" [SAPCOR 161])	25
93	Apple SAPCOR 19	STRAIGHT UP (LP, reissue, gatefold sleeve with bonus 12" [SAPCOR 191])	25
95	Apple SAPCOR 28	COME AND GET IT - THE BEST OF BADFINGER (2-LP, gatefold sleeve)	30

(see also Iveys, Masterminds, Gary Walker & Rain, Natural Gas, Blue Goose)

BADGE

| 81 | Metal Minded MM 2 | Silver Woman/Something I've Lost (p/s) | 25 |

BADGER BELL BAND

| 85 | Noize Gate SETT 001 | Nothing Left/Rock The Vicar (no p/s) | 40 |

(see also Badger)

BADGER (1)

74	Epic EPC 2326	White Lady/Don't Pull The Trigger	5
73	Atlantic K 40473	ONE LIVE BADGER (LP, gatefold pop-up sleeve)	40
74	Epic EPC 80009	WHITE LADY (LP)	15

(see also Ashton Gardner & Dyke, Jackie Lomax, Yes, Flash)

BADGER (2)

| 81 | Noize Gate NG 02 | Over The Wall/Faceless Gang (p/s) | 40 |

BADGEWEARER

| 90 | Grugg GRUGG 002 | THIS BAG IS NOT A TOY (EP) | 5 |

HENK BADINGS

| 60 | Philips SABL 206 | ELECTRONIC MUSIC (LP, gatefold) | 15 |

BADLY DRAWN BOY

97	Mo Wax (no cat no)	Nursery Rhyme (with UNKLE, 5" promo 150 only)	60
98	Twisted Nerve TNXL001	Roadmovie/My Friend Cubilas (feat. Doves) (die-cut sleeve, with insert)	8
90s	Twisted Nerve (no cat. no.)	I Love You All (one-track musical box, 150 only)	90
98	Twisted Nerve TNXMS1	Donna And Blitzen (1 track on 5 track one-sided red vinyl 7", 195 copies, p/s)	50
97	Twisted Nerve TN 001	EP1 (EP, 500 only)	60
98	Twisted Nerve TN 002	EP2: I Love You All/The Treeclimber/ I Love You All (I Loop You All Andy Votel Mix)/Thinking Of You (EP, 1,000 only)	30
98	Twisted Nerve XL TN 001T	EP3 (EP, 1,000 only)	8
06	EMI (no cat no)	BORN IN THE UK (3 x 7" 200 of each red, blue, green in "chip bag" with Wooden fork, stickered, price is same for each)	5
11	One Last Fruit BDBX10	LOST FOR WORDS (EP, signed photo insert)	15

00	Twisted Nerve TNXLCD 133	THE HOUR OF THE BEWILDERBEAST (LP, 1st pressing, withdrawn, with version of 'Magic In The Air' with the line "Love Is Contagious", and Woody Allen on sleeve	25
00	Twisted Nerve TNXLLP133	THE HOUR OF THE BEWILDERBEAST (LP)	15

(see also Doves)

BAD NEWS
87	EMI EMC 3535	BAD NEWS (LP, gatefold sleeve)	12
88	EMI EMC 3542	BOOTLEG (LP, 1 track produced by Brian May)	12

(see also Brian May)

BADOO
80	KG IImperial KG 001	Rocking Of The Five Thousand/BADOO & TOYAN: Reaching To Be Free (12")	20

BAD TASTE
88	Newgate SRT8KS 1554	Rockin' Girl (p/s, with insert)	30
88	Newgate SRT8KS 1554	Rockin' Girl (p/s, without insert)	10

JOAN BAEZ
62	Fontana TF 428	We Shall Overcome/What Have They Done To The Rain	5
63	Fontana TF 564	We Shall Overcome/Don't Think Twice It's All Right	5

(see also Earl Scruggs, Bob Dylan)

DOC BAGBY
58	Fontana H 106	Dumplin's/Sylvia's Calling (78)	10

BAGGA
77	Matumbi MAT 002	Daughter Of Zion/Version	50

DON BAGLEY
58	Pye NPL 28008	JAZZ ON THE ROCKS (LP)	20

BAG-O-WIRE
75	Klik KLP 9007	BAG-O-WIRE (LP)	40
77	Epic 82133	BAG-O-WIRE (LP)	30

BURR BAILEY (& SIX SHOOTERS)
63	Decca F 11686	San Francisco Bay/Like A Bird Without Feathers (with Six Shooters)	25
64	Decca F 11846	Chahawki/You Made Me Cry	50

CLIVE BAILEY & RICO'S GROUP
62	Blue Beat BB 92	Evening Train/Take Me Home	15
68	Double D DD104	Drink & Drive/Oh Oh Sugar	20

DEREK BAILEY
70	Incus INCUS 2	SOLO GUITAR (LP)	60
71	Incus INCUS 2R	SOLO GUITAR (LP)	60
74	Incus INCUS 12	LOT 74 (LP)	50
80	Incus INCUS 40	AIDA (LP)	60
85	Incus INCUS 48	NOTES (LP)	25
04	Organ Of Corti 10	TAPS (LP, 220gm vinyl, limited issue)	15

(see also Tony Oxley, Springboard, Steve Lacy & Derek Bailey, Anthony Braxton & Derek Bailey, Jamie Muir & Derek Bailey)

DEREK BAILEY, BARRY GUY & PAUL RUTHERFORD
70	Incus INCUS 3/4	ISKRA 1903 (LP)	45

(see also Barry Guy)

DEREK BAILEY & HAN BENNINK
72	Incus INCUS 9	SELECTIONS FROM LIVE PERFORMANCES AT VERITY'S PLACE (LP)	40
76	Incus INCUS 25	COMPANY 3 (LP)	35

DEREK BAILEY, ANTHONY BRAXTON & EVAN PARKER
76	Incus INCUS 23	COMPANY 2 (LP)	40

DEREK BAILEY & TONY COE
79	Incus INCUS 34	TIME (LP)	40

DEREK BAILEY, HUGH DAVIES, JAMIE MUIR, EVAN PARKER
70s	Incus INCUS 17	THE MUSIC IMPROVISATION COMPANY 1968-1971 (LP)	30

DEREK BAILEY & TRISTAN HONSINGER
76	Incus INCUS 20	DUO (LP)	40

DEREK BAILEY & EVAN PARKER
75	Incus INCUS 16	THE LONDON CONCERT (LP)	35
85	Incus INCUS 50	COMPATIBLES (LP)	35

(see also Evan Parker)

DEREK BAILEY, EVAN PARKER & HAN BENNINK
70	Incus INCUS 1	THE TOPOGRAPHY OF THE LUNGS (LP)	100

MILDRED BAILEY
57	Parlophone GEP 8600	MILDRED BAILEY AND HER ALLEY CATS (EP)	10
54	Brunswick LA 8692	THE ROCKIN' CHAIR LADY (10" LP)	15

PEARL BAILEY
56	London HLN 8354	That Certain Feeling/Hit The Road To Dreamland	8
56	London REU 1104	THAT CERTAIN FEELING (EP)	10

ROY BAILEY (U.K.)
71	Trailer LER 3021	ROY BAILEY (LP)	15
76	Fuse AC 262	NEW BELL AWAKE (LP)	15
82	Fuse CF 382	HARD TIMES (LP, with insert)	15

(see also Leon Rosselson)

ROY BAILEY (JAMAICA)
72	Duke DU 146	Run Away Child/Wedding March	7

ZEDDIE BAILEY
73	Grape GR 3037	Babylon Gone/TONY KING: Speak No Evil	7

ALY BAIN & MIKE WHELLANS
70s	Trailer LER 2022	ALY BAIN & MIKE WHELLANS (LP)	15

BOB BAIN & HIS MUSIC
58	Capitol CL 14912	Wagon Wheels/Strollin' Home	5
58	Capitol T965	ROCKIN' ROLLIN' AND STROLLIN' (LP)	40

ARTHUR BAIRD SKIFFLE GROUP
56	Beltona BL 2669	Union Train/Union Maid	30
56	Beltona BL 2669	Union Train/Union Maid (78)	10

EDDIE BAIRD
76	DJM DJLP 467	HARD GRAFT (LP)	12

(see also Amazing Blondel)

CARROLL BAKER
76	RCA PB 9056	It's My Party/Loves Golden Rule	6
78	RCA PB 9370	I'm Getting High Remembering/If It Wasn't For You	6

CHET BAKER (QUARTET)
56	Vogue V 2377	My Funny Valentine/But Not For Me	5
56	Vogue V 2381	Just Friends/Daybreak	5
56	Vogue V 2232	Winter Wonderland/This Time The Dream's On Me	5
56	Vogue V 2309	Long Ago And Far Away/Bea's Flat	5
54	Vogue LDE 045	CHET BAKER QUARTET (10" LP)	25
55	Philips BBL 7022	CHET BAKER AND STRINGS (LP)	20
55	Vogue LDE 116	CHET BAKER QUARTET (10" LP)	20
56	Vogue LAE 12018	CHET BAKER SINGS (LP)	20
56	Vogue LDE 159	CHET BAKER SEXTET (10" LP)	25
56	Vogue LDE 163	CHET BAKER ENSEMBLE (10" LP)	25
56	Vogue LDE 182	CHET BAKER SINGS (10" LP)	20
56	Felsted PDL 85008	CHET BAKER QUARTET VOL. 1 (LP)	25
56	Felsted PDL 85013	CHET BAKER QUARTET VOL. 2 (LP)	20
57	Felsted PDL 85036	I GET CHET (LP, as Chet Baker & His Combo)	20
57	Vogue LAE 12044	CHET BAKER QUARTET AT ANN ARBOR (LP)	20
57	Vogue LAE 12076	CHET BAKER AND HIS CREW (LP, mono)	20
58	Vogue LAE 12109	CHET BAKER - PHIL'S BLUES (LP)	20
59	Vogue SEA 5005	CHET BAKER AND HIS CREW (LP, stereo)	20
59	Vogue LAE 12164	CHET BAKER SINGS (LP)	20
59	Vogue LAE 12183	CHET BAKER AND ART PEPPER SEXTET - PLAYBOYS! (LP)	35

(see also Art Pepper, Russ Freeman & Chet Baker Quartet, Gerry Mulligan)

DESMOND BAKER & CLAREDONIANS
66	Island WI 295	Rude Boy Gonna Jail/SHARKS: Don't Fool Me	25

(see also Claredonians)

DOROTHY BAKER
63	Parlophone R5040	A Little Like Lovin'/Try Being Nice To Me	5

ERNEST BAKER
00	Grapevine 2000 110	Alone Again/Do It With Feeling	15

(see also Graham Bond Organisation, Cream, Blind Faith, Fela Ransome-Kuti [& Africa '70], Harold McNair, Griffin, Denny Laine)

GEORGE BAKER SELECTION
70	Penny Farthing 717	Little Green Bag/Pretty Little Dreamer	15

GINGER BAKER('S AIRFORCE)
70	Polydor 56380	Man Of Constant Sorrow/Doin' It	5
71	Polydor 2058 107	Atunde! (We Are Here)/Part 2 (as Ginger Baker Drum Choir)	5
70	Polydor 2662 001	GINGER BAKER'S AIRFORCE (LP, gatefold sleeve)	50
70	Polydor 2383 029	AIRFORCE II (LP, gatefold sleeve, with insert)	30
72	Polydor 2383 133	STRATAVARIOUS (LP)	20

GLEN BAKER
85	The Stand THE STAND 3	BRIEF ENCOUNTER (LP)	20

(see also Enid)

HYLDA BAKER
59	Decca F 11186	She Knows Y'know/Makin' Love	5
69	Columbia DB 8936	Nearest And Dearest/The More You Laugh	5

JEANETTE BAKER
59	Vogue Pop V 9143	Everything Reminds Me Of You/JEANETTE & DECKY: Crazy With You	250
59	Vogue Pop V 9143	Everything Reminds Me Of You/JEANETTE & DECKY: Crazy With You (78)	30

JOHN BAKER
08	Trunk JBH 030 LP	THE JOHN BAKER TAPES (LP, 500 only)	20

KENNY BAKER
53	Parlophone MSP 6019	Round About Midnight/Afternoon In Paris	5
53	Parlophone MSP 6057	Hayfoot, Strawfoot/The Continental	5
61	Palette PG 9012	Jacqueline/Blue Ice	5
55	Jazz Today JTL 1	OPERATION JAM SESSION (10" LP, with The Jazz Today Unit)	60
55	Jazz Today JTL 4	KENNY BAKER QUARTET/AFTER HOURS GROUP (10" LP)	40
55	Jazz Today JTL 5	TRIBUTE TO BENNY CARTER (10" LP, with The Jazz Today Unit, one side by Bertie King Jazz Group)	20
57	Pye Nixa NJL 10	PRESENTS THE HALF DOZEN (LP)	15
57	Pye Nixa NJT 517	BAKER PLAYS McHUGH (LP)	15
59	Columbia 33S1140	BLOWIN' UP A STORM (10" LP)	25
78	77 77S 56	BAKER'S JAM (LP)	20

LAVERN BAKER (& GLIDERS)
55	Columbia SCM 5172	Tweedle Dee/Tomorrow Night (with Gliders)	400
55	Columbia DB 3591	Tweedle Dee/Tomorrow Night (with Gliders) (78)	40
55	London HLA 8199	Play It Fair/That Old Lucky Sun (with Gliders)	300
55	London HLA 8199	Play It Fair/That Old Lucky Sun (with Gliders) (78)	30
56	London HLE 8260	My Happiness Forever (with Gliders)/Get Up! Get Up! (You Sleepy Head)	300
56	London HLE 8260	My Happiness Forever (with Gliders)/Get Up! Get Up! (You Sleepy Head) (78)	25
57	Columbia DB 3879	Jim Dandy/Tra La La (with Gliders)	350
57	Columbia DB 3879	Jim Dandy/Tra La La (with Gliders) (78)	25
57	London HLE 8396	I Can't Love You Enough/Still	150

57	London HLE 8396	I Can't Love You Enough/Still (78)..25
57	London HLE 8442	Game Of Love/Jim Dandy Got Married 250
57	London HLE 8442	Game Of Love/Jim Dandy Got Married (78) 20
57	London HLE 8524	Humpty Dumpty Heart/Love Me Right..150
57	London HLE 8524	Humpty Dumpty Heart/Love Me Right (78)..20
58	London HLE 8638	Learning To Love/Substitute...100
58	London HLE 8638	Learning To Love/Substitute (78)...15
58	London HLE 8672	Whipper Snapper/Harbour Lights 100
58	London HLE 8672	Whipper Snapper/Harbour Lights (78) 20
59	London HLE 8790	I Cried A Tear/St. Louis Blues..50
59	London HLE 8790	I Cried A Tear/St. Louis Blues (78)..20
59	London HLE 8871	I Waited Too Long/You're Teasing Me..30
59	London HLE 8871	I Waited Too Long/You're Teasing Me (78)...25
59	London HLE 8945	So High So Low/If You Love Me (I Won't Care)..30
59	London HLE 8945	So High So Low/If You Love Me (I Won't Care) (78).......................................25
60	London HLE 9023	Tiny Tim/For Love Of You 35
60	London HLE 9252	Bumble Bee/My Turn Will Come 25
61	London HLE 9300	You're The Boss/I'll Never Be Free (with Jimmy Ricks) 45
61	London HLK 9343	Saved/Don Juan...30
61	London HLK 9468	Hey, Memphis/Voodoo Voodoo 50
63	London HLK 9649	See See Rider/The Story Of My Love (I Had A Dream) 25
65	Atlantic AET 6009	THE BEST OF LAVERN BAKER (EP) 80
58	London HA-E 2107	ROCK 'N' ROLL WITH LAVERN BAKER (LP, with thin card cover)....................400
58	London Jazz LTZK 15139	SINGS BESSIE SMITH (LP)..75
61	London HA-K 2422	SAVED (LP)...60
63	London HA-K 8074	SEE SEE RIDER (LP) 50
64	Atlantic ATL 5002	THE BEST OF LAVERN BAKER (LP, plum label)...60
68	Atlantic 587/588 133	SEE SEE RIDER (LP, reissue)...20

MICKEY BAKER

70	Major Minor SMLP 67	IN BLUNDERLAND (LP) 35

(see also Mighty Flea, Champion Jack Dupree, Mickey & Sylvia)

SALLY BAKER

70s	Old Dog PUP 1	IN THE SPOTLIGHT (LP)...50

SAM BAKER

68	Monument MON 1009	I Believe In You/I'm Number One 25

TOM BAKER

79	Argo ZDSW 722/3	THE STRANGE CASE OF DR. JEKYLL & MR. HYDE (2-LP) 15

TWO-TON BAKER

55	London HL 8121	Clink, Clank (In My Piggy Bank)/Mr. Froggie (Went A Courtin') 40
55	London HL 8121	Clink, Clank (In My Piggy Bank)/Mr. Froggie (Went A Courtin') (78) 10

VICKY BAKER

64	London HLU 9856	No More Foolish Stories/Darling Say The Word..15

YVONNE BAKER

77	London HLU 10553	You Didn't Say A Word/BOBBY PARIS: Night Owl 10

(see also Sensations, Bobby Paris)

DAVE BAKER

80	Black Jack BJD 4507	Glow Of Love/Version (12") 20

BAKER-GURVITZ ARMY

75	Mountain TOP 4	The Gambler/Time...5
74	Vertigo 9103 201	BAKER-GURVITZ ARMY (LP, with lyric insert) 18

(see also Ginger Baker, Three Man Army, Parrish & Gurvitz, Gun, Sharks)

BAKERLOO

69	Harvest HAR 5004	Driving Backwards/Once Upon A Time..25
69	Harvest SHVL 762	BAKERLOO (LP, gatefold sleeve, no EMI on label) 250

(see also Colosseum, Uriah Heep, Humble Pie)

BAKER STREET PHILHARMONIC

71	Pye International 7N 25540	The Last One/Theme From 'Love Story' 5
70	Pye Intl. NSPL 28131	BY THE LIGHT OF THE MOON (LP)..15

(see also Mike Vickers)

BAKER TWINS

64	Pye 7N 15628	He's No Good/Words Written On Water..20

BALANCE

81	Portrait PRTA 1477	Breaking Away/It's So Strange 8
73	Incus INCUS 11	BALANCE (LP)..70
73	private pressing	IN FOR THE COUNT (LP)...20
81	Portrait	BALANCE (LP, reissue)...12
82	Portrait	IN FOR THE COUNT (LP, reissue) 12

BALDHEAD GROWLER

67	Jump Up JU 531	Sausage/Bingo Woman 8

CHRIS BALDO

68	Vogue VRS 7029	Living For Your Love/Arretez - Vous A Saint Michel.......................................15

LONG JOHN BALDRY

64	United Artists UP 1056	You'll Be Mine (with Rod Stewart)/Up Above My Head (I Hear Music In The Air)................50
65	United Artists UP 1078	I'm On To You Baby/Goodbye Baby 12
65	United Artists UP 1107	How Long Will It Last/House Next Door 35
66	United Artists UP 1124	Unseen Hands/Turn On Your Lovelight 10
66	United Artists UP 1136	The Drifter/Only A Fool Breaks His Own Heart 50
66	United Artists UP 1158	Cuckoo/Bring My Baby Back To Me 25
67	United Artists UP 1204	Only A Fool Breaks His Own Heart/Let Him Go (And Let Me Love You) 20
65	United Artists UEP 1013	LONG JOHN'S BLUES (EP, with Hoochie Coochie Men) 80
64	United Artists ULP 1081	LONG JOHN'S BLUES (LP, with Hoochie Coochie Men) 70
66	United Artists (S)ULP 1146	LOOKING AT LONG JOHN (LP)...50

MINT VALUE £

68	Pye N(S)PL 18228	LET THERE BE LONG JOHN (LP, unissued)	0
69	Pye N(S)PL 18306	WAIT FOR ME (LP)	15
72	Warner Bros. K46160	EVERYTHING STOPS FOR TEA (LP, gatefold sleeve, green label)	20

(see also Rod Stewart, Alexis Korner, Bluesology)

THOR BALDURSSON
| 67 | Decca F12653 | Arlene Chateau/Painter | 10 |

BALDWIN
| 67 | Decca F22624 | The Land At Rainbows end/Beautiful Butterfly | 45 |

KEITH BALFOUR
| 69 | Studio One SO 2079 | Dreaming/Tired Of Waiting | 20 |

BALIL
| 93 | Rising High RSN 72 | Parasignt/Island/Rosary Pilots/Avidya (12") | 20 |
| 95 | Pure Plastic PP 005 | Nine Open/ RUE EAST: Endless Filters (12") | 8 |

CANNON BALL (CARL BRYAN) & JOHNNY MELODY (MOORE)
| 69 | Big Shot BI 518 | Parapinto/Cool Hand Luke | 25 |

ED BALL
| 95 | Creation CRELP 183 | WELCOME TO THE WONDERFUL WORLD OF (2-LP) | 15 |

(see also Times, O Level, TV Personalities, Teenage Filmstars)

DAVE BALLANTYNE
| 66 | Columbia DB 7807 | I Can't Express It/Ginger Eyes | 8 |
| 66 | Columbia DB 7896 | Love Around The World/World Full Of Women | 8 |

(see also Just Plain Jones, Esprit De Corps)

FLORENCE BALLARD
| 68 | Stateside SS 2113 | It Doesn't Matter How I Say It (It's What I Say That Matters)/ Goin' Out Of My Head | 75 |
| 68 | Stateside SS 2113 | It Doesn't Matter How I Say It (It's What I Say That Matters)/ Goin' Out Of My Head (DJ Copy) | 100 |

(see also Supremes)

HANK BALLARD (& MIDNIGHTERS)
59	Parlophone R 4558	The Twist/Kansas City	30
60	Parlophone R 4682	Finger Poppin' Time/I Love You, I Love You So-o-o	30
60	Parlophone R 4688	The Twist/Teardrops On Your Letter	30
60	Parlophone R 4707	Let's Go, Let's Go, Let's Go/If You'd Forgive Me	30
61	Parlophone R 4728	The Hoochie Coochie Coo/LITTLE WILLIE JOHN: Walk Slow	20
61	Parlophone R 4762	Let's Go Again/Deep Blue Sea	50
61	Parlophone R 4771	The Continental Walk/What Is This I See	20
72	Mojo 2093 010	Annie Had A Baby/Teardrops On Your Letter	10
80s	Urban	From The Loveside/FOSTER SYLVERS: Misdemeanor	10
61	Parlophone PMC 1158	SPOTLIGHT ON HANK BALLARD (LP)	200
63	London HA 8101	THE JUMPIN' HANK BALLARD (LP)	100

(see also Midnighters)

KAYE BALLARD
| 55 | Brunswick 05376 | Triumph Of Love/Where Were You Last Night? | 5 |
| 55 | Brunswick 05436 | Don't You Tell Pa/In Love And Out Again | 5 |

RUSS BALLARD
74	Epic EPC 2670	Fly Away/Danger Zone Part 2	5
74	Epic EPC 3122	Loose Women/Danger Zone Part 1	5
74	Epic SEPC 4995	Some Kinda Hurricane/You Can Do Voodoo	6
75	Epic EPC 3925	Since You've Been GOne/Venus (Shine Your Light)	5

BALLOON BUSTERS
| 69 | Pye 7N 17748 | Alcock And Brown/Bluer Than Blue (p/s) | 10 |
| 69 | Pye 7N 17748 | Alcock And Brown/Bluer Than Blue | 5 |

BALLOON CORPS
| 69 | Stateside SS8034 | Make It Right/Muddy Water | 20 |

BALLOON FARM
| 68 | London HLP 10185 | A Question Of Temperature/Hurtin' For Your Love | 100 |

BALLS
| 71 | Wizard WIZ 101 | Fight For My Country/Janie Slow Down | 30 |

(see also Denny Laine, Lemon Tree, Trevor Burton, Uglys, Wizzard)

LORI BALMER
| 68 | Polydor 56293 | Treacle Brown/Four Faces West | 40 |

BALTIMORE & OHIO MARCHING BAND
67	Stateside SS 2065	Lapland/Condition Red	60
67	Stateside SS 2065	Lapland/Condition Red (DJ copy)	200
68	Stateside (S)SL 10231	LAPLAND (LP)	35

BAMA WINDS
| 69 | Island ILPS 9096 | WINDY (LP) | 22 |

BAM BAM
| 88 | Desire Records WANTX 7 | Where's Your Child/Spend The Night (12") | 10 |

BAMBI
| 76 | Sol-Doon SDR 019 | Lady Of Lies/Somebody Told Me | 15 |

BAMBIS
| 64 | Oriole CB 1965 | Not Wrong/Handle With Care | 45 |
| 65 | CBS 201778 | Baby Blue/If This Is Love | 45 |

BAMBOO FRINGE
| 82 | Probe Plus PP 4 | Dorian Grey/How Do I Dance To This Music (p/s) | 8 |
| 85 | Skysaw SAW 2 | LIFE AND TIMES OF (LP, with inner) | 12 |

BAMBOO SHOOT
| 68 | Columbia DB 8370 | The Fox Has Gone To Ground/There And Back Again Lane | 200 |

BAMBOO ZOO
81	Phoney Gram PH 45 01	Ghost Party/Binding Wire (p/s) 12
81	Phoney Gram PHOG 8101	LOOK! LISTEN! CONSUME! (LP) 18

BAMBOOS OF JAMAICA
70	Pye Intl. 7N 25515	Reggae Man/Candy...8

BANANA BUNCH
71	DJM DJS 252	Tra-La-La Song/Season Of The Rain 15
70	Page One POF 183	Tra-La-La Song/Funky Hoe 20

(see also Nite People)

BANANAMEN
83	Big Beat NS 88	The Crusher/Love Me/Surfin' Bird (p/s) 5

BANANARAMA
85	London NANPD 9	Do Not Disturn (3- shaped picture discs with plinth) 15
86	London NAN PD 11	More Than Physical/Venus/Scarlett (picture disc, PVC sleeve)..................................15

BANBARRA
76	United Artists UP 36113	Shack Up Parts 1 & 2...10
85	Stateside 12STATES 1	Shack Up (Extended)/Shack Up (Part 1)/Shack Up (Part II) (12" p/s) 10

BANCO DE GAIA
95	Bark L 011 S	LAST TRAIN TO LHASA (4-LP, limited edition)..18

THE BAND
68	Capitol CL 15559	The Weight/I Shall Be Released..8
69	Capitol CL 15613	Up On Cripple Creek/The Night They Drove Old Dixie Down 8
69	Capitol CL 15629	Rag Mama Rag/The Unfaithful Servant 5
73	Capitol CL 15767	Ain't Got No Home/Get Up Jake...5
78	Warner Bros K 17187	Theme From The Last Waltz/Out Of The Blue..5
68	Capitol T 2955	MUSIC FROM BIG PINK (LP, black/rainbow label, mono) 50
68	ST 2955	MUSIC FROM BIG PINK (LP, black/rainbow label, stereo) 35

(see also Levon & The Hawks, Bob Dylan, Ronnie Hawkins, Robbie Robertson)

BAND AKA
81	Epic EPC A13 2376	Grace/Instrumental (12")..12

BANDITS
85	Hosspig HPG1	Treasure Trove/Right In The Head (p/s)..25

BANDITZ
80	Phaeton SPIN 2	JCB/Damage Your Health (p/s) 15

BAND OF ANGELS
64	United Artists UP 1049	Not True As Yet/Me 15
64	United Artists UP 1066	She'll Never Be You/Gonna Make A Woman Of You 15
66	Piccadilly 7N 35279	Leave It To Me/Too Late My Love 15
66	Piccadilly 7N 35292	Invitation/Cheat And Lie 70

(see also Mike D'Abo, Manfred Mann)

BAND OF HORSES
07	Kids KIDS 014	Funeral/The Ends Not Near (p/s, 750 only, no'd, with download card) 8

BAND OF JOY
78	Poydor 2310588	BAND OF JOY (LP, with lyric insert) 25

BAND OF MERCY & SALVATION
69	Duke DU 20	Suffering Stink/BOB MELODY: The Break (B-side actually by Winston Francis).....................50

BANDOGGS
78	Transatlantic LTRA 504	BANDOGGS (LP, cream label) 18

(see also Peter & Chris Coe)

BANDY LEGS
74	WWW WWS 01	Ride Ride/Don't Play Games 20
76	Jet JET 783	Bet You Can't Dance/Circles 20

(see also Quartz)

BANG (1)
72	EST 11015	BANG (LP) 60

(see also Quartz)

BANG (2)
72	Capitol CL15722	Questions/Future Shock 20

ED BANGER
78	Rabid TOSH 106	Kinnel Tommy/Baby Was A Baby (p/s) 7
78	EMI International INT 571	Kinnel Tommy/Baby Was A Baby (reissue, numbered p/s)...7
81	Spiv DIV 1	I've Just Had My Car Nicked/P.C. Plod/Sponge (p/s, with photo insert) 8
83	Cloud Nine CNS 01	Poor People/Vicars In The Dark (p/s) 7

(see also Nosebleeds, Slaughter & The Dogs)

BANGOR FLYING CIRCUS
70	Stateside-Dunhill SSL 5022	BANGOR FLYING CIRCUS (LP)..25

DEVENDRA BANHART
04	XL XLS 184H	HERE ARE FOUR SONGS FROM REJOICING IN THE HANDS OF THE GOLDEN EMPRESS (2x7")..8
05	XL XLLP 185	REJOICING IN THE HANDS/NINO ROJO (2-LP) 20
06	XL XLLP 192C	CRIPPLE CROW (2-LP)...15

BANISHED
93	Peaceville CC 3	Altered Minds/Cast Out THe Flesh (blue vinyl, p/s) 15
93	Deaf DEAF 13	DELIVER ME UNTO PAIN (LP) 25

(see also Baphomet)

BESSIE BANKS
64	Red Bird BC 106	Go Now/Sounds Like My Baby 80
64	Red Bird BC 106	Go Now/Sounds Like My Baby(DJ Copy)...100
67	Verve VS 563	I Can't Make It (Without You Baby)/Need You..100

MINT VALUE £

67	Verve VS 563	I Can't Make It (Without You Baby)/Need You (DJ Copy)	100
68	Soul City SC 105	Go Now/Sounds Like My Baby (reissue)	25
75	Contempo CS 2070	Baby You Sure Know How To Get To Me/Try To Leave Me If You Can	35

DARRELL BANKS
66	London HL 10070	Open The Door To Your Heart/Our Love (Is In The Pocket) (demo only)	800
66	Stateside SS 536	Open The Door To Your Heart/Our Love (Is In The Pocket) (1st pressing demo with white/red label)	200
66	Stateside SS 536	Open The Door To Your Heart/Our Love (Is In The Pocket) (1st pressing)	40
66	Stateside SS 536	Open The Door To Your Heart/Our Love (Is In The Pocket) (2st pressing demo with green/white label)	90
66	Stateside SS 536	Open The Door To Your Heart/Our Love (Is In The Pocket) (2nd pressing)	20
67	Atlantic 584 120	Angel Baby (Don't You Ever Leave Me)/Look Into The Eyes Of A Fool	55
69	Stax STAX 124	Just Because Your Love Is Gone/I'm The One Who Loves You	100
77	Atlantic K 10879	Angel Baby (Don't You Ever Leave Me)/Look Into The Eyes Of A Fool (reissue)	10
69	Stax SXATS 1011	HERE TO STAY (LP)	50

HOMER BANKS
66	Liberty LIB 12028	A Lot Of Love/Fighting To Win	30
66	Liberty LIB 12028	A Lot Of Love/Fighting To Win (DJ Copy)	60
67	Liberty LIB 12047	60 Minutes Of Your Love/Do You Know What	30
67	Liberty LIB 12047	60 Minutes Of Your Love/Do You Know What (DJ Copy)	60
67	Liberty LIB 12060	Hooked By Love/Lady Of Stone	40
67	Liberty LIB 12060	Hooked By Love/Lady Of Stone (DJ Copy)	75
68	Minit MLF 11004	Round The Clock Lover Man/Foolish Hearts Break Fast	15
68	Minit MLF 11007	60 Minutes Of Your Love/A Lot Of Love	15
69	Minit MLF 11015	Me Or Your Mama/I Know You Know I Know You Know	10
70	Liberty LBF 15392	60 Minutes Of Your Love/I Know You Know I Know You Know	15
72	United Artists UP 35360	Hooked By Love/Lady Of Stone (reissue)	8

LARRY BANKS
67	Stateside SS 579	I Don't Wanna Do It/I'm Coming Home	60
67	Stateside SS 579	I Don't Wanna Do It/I'm Coming Home (DJ Copy)	75
09	Kent 6T 25	My Life Is No Better/JACKIE DAY: Get To Steppin	20

LLOYD BANKS
| 66 | Reaction 591 008 | We'll Meet Again/Look Out Girl | 20 |

PETER BANKS
| 73 | Sovereign SVNA 7256 | PETER BANKS (LP, gatefold sleeve) | 30 |

(see also Syndicats, Syn, Neat Change, Yes, Flash, Jan Akkerman, Phil Collins, Steve Hackett)o

BANNED
77	Can't Eat EAT 1 UP	Little Girl/CPGJ's (stamped white labels, in handmade p/s)	50
77	Can't Eat EAT 1 UP	Little Girl/CPGJ's (stamped white labels)	12
78	Harvest HAR 5149	Him Or Me/You Dirty Rat	5

(see also Gryphon)

BANSHEES
64	Columbia DB 7361	I Got A Woman/Don't Say Goodnight And Mean Goodbye	25
65	Columbia DB 7530	Big Buildin'/Mockingbird	20
65	Columbia DB 7752	I'm Gonna Keep On Loving You/Yes Indeed	15

PATO BANTON
| 85 | Ariwa ARI LP 023 | MAD PROFESSOR CAPTURES PATO BANTON (LP) | 15 |

BAPHOMET
| 92 | Peaceville VILE 31 | THE DEAD SHALL INHERIT (LP) | 25 |

(see also Banished)

SELWYN BAPTISTE
| 70 | Black Swan BW 1402 | Mo' Bay/RECO'S ALL STARS: Going West | 12 |

BARBARA & ERNIE
| 71 | Atlantic 2466 015 | PRELUDE TO (LP) | 60 |

BARBARA AND THE BROWNS
| 08 | Kent Select CITY 008 | I'm Gonna Start A War/OTIS REDDING: Love By The Pound | 10 |

BARBARA & BRENDA
| 68 | Direction 58-3799 | Never Love A Robin/Sally's Party | 15 |

BARBARA & WINSTON
| 64 | Island WI 418 | The Dream/I Love You | 18 |

BARBARA ANN
| 65 | Piccadilly 7N 35221 | You've Lost That Loving Feeling/Till The Summer Time | 20 |
| 65 | Piccadilly 7N 35244 | Black Is The Colour Of My True Love's Hair/Since You've Loved Me | 6 |

BARBARIANS
| 65 | Stateside SS 449 | Are You A Boy Or Are You A Girl/Take It Or Leave It | 25 |
| 66 | Stateside SS 497 | Moulty/I'll Keep On Seeing You | 30 |

BARBECUE BOB
| 67 | Kokomo K 1002 | GEORGIA BLUES NO. 1 (LP, 99 copies only) | 100 |

BARBED WIRE
| 86 | Oi Records OIR 006 | THE AGE THAT DIDN'T CARE (LP) | 20 |

JOHN HENRY BARBEE
| 65 | Storyville 616 013 | I AIN'T GONNA PICK NO MORE COTTON (LP) | 20 |
| 65 | Storyville 670 171 | PORTRAITS IN BLUES VOLUME 9 (LP) | 25 |

CHRIS BARBER('S JAZZ BAND)
SINGLES
54	Columbia SCMC 10	White Christmas/On A Christmas Day (with Lonn e Donegan, export issue)	15
55	Decca F 10492	Bobby Shafto/The Martinique	8
55	Decca F 10666	It's Tight Like That/All The Girls Go Crazy About The Way I Walk	8
56	Tempo A 116	Precious Lord, Lead Me On (with Lonnie Donegan)/Tiger Rag	8
56	Tempo A 132	Saratoga Swing/Ice Cream	5

| 57 | Tempo A 160 | Ice Cream/Down By The Riverside ....5 |

EPs

| 55 | Columbia SEG 7568 | PLAYS SPIRITUALS ....8 |
| 62 | Columbia SEG 8214 | BARBER'S BLUES BOOK VOL. 1 ....8 |

ALBUMS

54	Decca LF 1198	NEW ORLEANS JOYS (10", with Lonnie Donegan's Skiffle Group) 25
55	Nixa Jazz Today NJL 1	ECHOES OF HARLEM (with Ottilie Patterson) 20
55	Jazz Today JTL 3	CHRIS BARBER PLAYS VOL. 1 (10") 20
56	Nixa Jazz Today NJT 500	CHRIS BARBER PLAYS VOL. 1 (10", reissue) 15
56	Nixa Jazz Today NJT 502	CHRIS BARBER PLAYS VOL. 2 (10") 15
57	Nixa Jazz Today NJT 505	CHRIS BARBER PLAYS VOL. 3 (10") 15
57	Nixa Jazz Today NJT 508	CHRIS BARBER PLAYS VOL. 4 (10") 15
57	Columbia 33S 1112	JAZZ SACRED AND SECULAR (10", with Lonnie Donegan).....................................15
57	Nixa Jazz Today NJL 6	CHRIS BARBER'S JAZZ BAND WITH OTTILIE PATTERSON, JOHNNY DUNCAN AND THE SKIFFLE GROUP (LP)...15
58	Pye Nixa Jazz NJL 15	CHRIS BARBER IN CONCERT VOL. 2 (with Ottilie Patterson) 15
58	Pye Nixa Jazz NJL 17	CHRIS BARBER IN CONCERT VOL. 3 (with Ottilie Patterson) 15
58	Decca LK 4246	BARBER'S BEST 15
59	Columbia 33SX 1158	BAND BOX VOL. 1 15
59	Columbia 33SX 1189	BARBER IN BERLIN VOL. 1 (with Ottilie Patterson) 15
59	Columbia 33SX	BARBER IN BERLIN VOL. 2 (with Ottilie Patterson) 15
60	Columbia 33SX 1245	BAND BOX VOL. 2 - ELITE SYNCOPATIONS (stereo SCX 3319)................................15
61	Columbia 33SX 1321	CHRIS BARBER'S AMERICAN JAZZ BAND (also stereo SCX 3376)..............................15
61	Columbia 33SX 1333	BLUES BOOK (with Ottilie Patterson, also stereo SCX 3384) 15
61	Columbia 33SX 1346	AT THE LONDON PALLADIUM (also stereo [SCX 3392]) 15
61	Columbia 33SX 1401	BEST YET!...15
65	Columbia 33SX 1657	GOOD MORNIN' BLUES 25
65	Decca LK 4742	FOLK BARBER STYLE (mono)...15
65	Phase 4 Stereo PFS 4070	FOLK BARBER STYLE (as Chris Barber & His Jazz Band).....................................15

(see also Ottilie Patterson, Lonnie Donegan, Sonny Terry & Brownie McGhee, Kenneth Washington & Chris Barber, Dickie Bishop & Sidekicks)

CHRIS BARBER'S SKIFFLE GROUP
58	Pye Jazz 7NJ 2014	Doin' My Time/Where Could I Go? (with Johnny Duncan) 15
58	Pye Jazz 7NJ 2017	Can't You Line 'Em/Gipsy Dave (with Dickie Bishop) 15
57	Pye Jazz NJE 1025	CHRIS BARBER SKIFFLE GROUP (EP) 20

(see also Lonnie Donegan, Johnny Duncan & Blue Grass Boys)

CHRIS BARBER AND HIS BAND
67	Marmalade 598 005	Catcall/Mercy Mercy Mercy 60
69	Marmalade 558 013	Battersea Rain Dance/Sleepy Joe 25
69	Marmalade 608 009	BATTERSEA RAIN DANCE (LP, as Chris Barber & His Band)................................40
69	Polydor 2384 020	BATTERSEA RAIN DANCE (LP) (2nd Pressing) 20

CHRIS BARBER SOUL BAND
| 65 | Columbia DB 7461 | Finishing Straight/Morning Train ....30 |

(see also Louis Jordan & Chris Barber)

FRANK BARBER FIVE
| 62 | Ember JBS 709 | Flyover/Golden Shadows ....5 |
| 66 | Columbia DB 7886 | Busy Lizzie/Theme From "Mr Broadway" ....5 |

(see also Frank & Barbarians)

JOHN BARBER
| 71 | Sentinel SENS 1008 | CORNWALL IS CALLING (LP as Joh Barber and the St. Ives Minstrels) ....12 |

DAVE BARBOUR & HIS ORCHESTRA
| 59 | Oriole CB 1507 | Tough/Bu Bam ....5 |

KEITH BARBOUR
| 69 | CBS 4606 | Echo Park/Here I Am Losing You...6 |

EDDIE BARCLAY & HIS ORCHESTRA
| 57 | Felsted ESD 3041 | JAMES DEAN - MUSIC FROM HIS FILMS (EP) ....15 |

EDDIE BARCLAY & QUINCY JONES
| 58 | Felsted PDL 85056 | EDDIE AND QUINCY (LP)..15 |

RUE BARCLAY & PEGGY DUNCAN
| 54 | London HL 8033 | Tongue Tied Boy/River Of Tears ....40 |

TIMOTHY BARCLAY
| 70 | Penny Farthing PEN 740 | Catch The Wind/The Girl From Indiana ....12 |

BARCLAY JAMES HARVEST
68	Parlophone R 5693	Early Morning/Mr. Sunshine 35
69	Harvest HAR 5003	Brother Thrush/Poor Wages 15
70	Harvest HAR 5025	Taking Some Time On/The Iron Maiden 15
71	Harvest HAR 5034	Mocking Bird/Vanessa Simmons 10
72	Harvest HAR 5051	I'm Over You/Child Of Man 10
72	Harvest HAR 5058	Thank You/Medicine Man 10
73	Harvest HAR 5068	Rock And Roll Woman/The Joker (BJH logo p/s) 12
74	Polydor 2058 474	Poor Boy Blues/Crazy City 7
74	Polydor (matrix: SH 1041/2)	Negative Earth/RARE BIRD: Diamonds (33rpm flexidisc free with Sounds magazine)......10
75	Harvest HAR 5094	Mocking Bird/Galadriel 5
70	Harvest SHVL 770	BARCLAY JAMES HARVEST (LP, gatefold sleeve, no EMI box on label).....................50
71	Harvest SHVL 788	ONCE AGAIN (LP, gatefold sleeve, no EMI box on label)...............................30
71	Harvest SHVL 794	BARCLAY JAMES HARVEST AND OTHER SHORT STORIES (LP, gatefold sleeve) 25
72	Harvest Q4SHVL 788	ONCE AGAIN (LP, quadrophonic) 40
73	Harvest SHSP 4023	BABY JAMES HARVEST (LP)..20
76	Harvest SHVL 770	BARCLAY JAMES HARVEST (LP, gatefold sleeve, repressing EMI box on label)............15

(see also Bombadil, John Lees, Woolly Wolstenholme)

PETER BARDENS
| 70 | Transatlantic TRA 222 | THE ANSWER (LP, white/lilac label with 't' logo)...................................100 |
| 71 | Transatlantic TRA 243 | PETER BARDENS (LP, gatefold sleeve, side one label is multi-coloured)...............50 |

BARDO POND

| 76 | Transatlantic TRASAM 36 | VINTAGE '69 (LP, featuring Peter Green, clear vinyl) | 20 |
| 76 | Transatlantic TRASAM 36 | VINTAGE '69 (LP, featuring Peter Green) | 15 |

(see also Cheynes, Peter B's, Shotgun Express, Them, Village, Camel, Steve Tilston)

BARDO POND
| 03 | STP STPRLP6 | ON THE ELLIPSE (2-LP, gatefold) | 18 |

BRIGITTE BARDOT
66	Vogue VRS 7018	Mister Sun/Gang Gang (p/s)	100
66	Vogue VRS 7018	Mister Sun/Gang Gang	30
68	Pye International 7N 25450	Harley-Davidson/Contact (p/s)	100
68	Pye International 7N 25450	Harley-Davidson/Contact	30
63	Philips BL 7561	BRIGITTE BARDOT (LP)	120
64	Philips B 77 984	'BB'	100
07	Ilith LR 146	SINGS (LP, reissue, inner, print)	15

BARDS (1)
| 68 | Capitol CL 15536 | The Owl And The Pussycat/Light Of Love | 25 |

BARDS (2)
| 71 | Folk Heritage FHR 019M | TIME FOR THE BARDS (LP) | 120 |

BARDS OF BARLEYCORN
| 77 | Beet Music BMR 101 | WHEN GRANDMA USED TO CALL (LP) | 20 |

BOBBY BARE
| 63 | RCA RCA 1352 | Detroit City/Heart Of Ice | 5 |

(see also Bill Parsons, Skeeter Davis & Bobby Bare)

BARE FOOT
| 71 | Pye 7N 45110 | Frightened/Girl Are You A Woman Now (Promo copies say "Bear Foot") | 15 |

BAREFOOT BLUES BAND
70	Beacon BEA 163	Can't You See/Sunday Morning Barefoot Blues	25
72	Deram DM 353	The Spirit Of Joe Hill/I Believe In Music	8
73	Deram DM 372	Getting Better All The Time/Half Of Me	6

MINOUCHE BARELLI
| 67 | CBS 2806 | Boum Badaboum/Let Me Take You | 15 |

MARK BARKAN
| 67 | Stateside SS 2064 | A Great Day For The Clown/Pity The Woman | 40 |

BAR-KAYS
67	Stax 601 014	Soul Finger/Knucklehead	8
68	Stax 601 036	A Hard Day's Night/I Want Someone	8
69	Atlantic 584 244	Soul Finger/Knucklehead (reissue)	5
69	Stax STAX 135	Midnight Cowboy/A.J. The House Fly	5
70	Stax STAX 146	Sing And Dance/I Thank You	5
78	Stax 12 STAX 505	Holy Ghost/Monster (12")	15
69	Atco 228 030	SOUL FINGER (LP)	30
69	Stax SXATS 1009	GOTTA GROOVE (LP)	25
71	Stax 2362 003	BLACK ROCK (LP)	20
73	Stax 2325 087	DO YOU SEE WHAT I SEE? (LP)	20
76	Stax STX 1033	COLD BLOODED (LP)	15

(see also Otis Redding)

DAVE BARKER
70	Duke DU 74	Funkey Reggae/TOMMY McCOOK & SUPERSONICS: I Love You My Baby (B-side actually by Versatiles)	25
70	Punch PH 20	Prisoner Of Love/BUSTY & UPSETTERS: Soul Juice	20
70	Punch PH 22	You Betray Me/Will You Still Love Me Tomorrow?	20
70	Punch PH 25	Shocks Of Mighty Parts 1 & 2	12
70	Punch PH 42	Reggae Meeting/MARTIN ALL STARS: Soul Bone	20
70	Jackpot JP 736	The Fastest Man Alive/NORMAN GRANT: Bloodshot Eyes	15
70	Jackpot JP 742	Wet Version/I Got To Get Away	15
70	Jackpot JP 745	Girl Of My Dreams/On Broadway	20
70	High Note HS 049	She Want It/FIRST GENERATION: Give Him Up	15
70	Randy's RAN 503	October/RANDY'S ALLSTARS: Time Out	70
70	Unity UN 567	Blessed Are The Meek (with Slim Smith)/JEFF BARNES & UNIQUES: The People's Voice	20
70	Techniques TE915	Karatae/Version	12
70	Upsetter US 331	Shocks Of Mighty/Set Me Free (with Upsetters)	15
70	Upsetter US 344	Some Sympathy/UNTOUCHABLES: Tender Love	30
70	Upsetter US 347	Sound Underground/Don't Let The Sun Catch You Crying (features the Wailers)	50
71	Upsetter US 358	Shocks '71/HURRICANES: You've Got To Be Mine	20
71	Upsetter US 362	Groove Me/UPSETTERS: Screwdriver	30
71	Upsetter US 364	What A Confusion/UPSETTERS: Confusion - Version 2	25
71	Ackee ACK 113	Johnny Dollar/Version	30
71	Ackee ACK 119	Life Of A Millionaire/Version	30
71	Trojan TR 7851	Sex Machine/You Left Me And Gone (both sides with Aggrovators)	20
71	Punch PH 69	What A Confusion/BOB MARLEY: Small Axe	45
71	Supreme SUP 228	Double Heavy/Johnny Dollar	30
71	Downtown DT 482	Only The Strong Survive/Only The Strong - Version	15
72	Jackpot JP 803	You'll Be Sorry/Green Grow The Lilacs	8
72	Big Shot BI 614	Are You Sure/I Don't Know Why (B-side actually by Sensations)	6
72	Fab FAB 25	Green Grow The Lilacs/JIMMY RILEY: Keep An Eye (On Your Closest Friend) (white label)	12
76	Trojan TRL 127	PRISONER OF LOVE (LP)	40

(see also Glen & Dave, Dave & Ansell Collins, Bobby & Dave, Aggrovators, David Crooks, Dennis Alcapone, Don Drummond, Owen Gary, Lizzy & Dennis, Bob Marley, Lester Sterling, Busty Brown)

STAN BARKER
| 79 | Nelson N1001 | VOLUME 1 (LP) | 40 |

WARREN BARKER
| 60 | Warner Bros. WEP 6036 | 77 SUNSET STRIP (EP) | 8 |

BARK PSYCHOSIS
| 90 | Cheree CHEREE 6T | All Different Things/By-Blow (12", p/s) | 8 |

90	Cheree CHEREE 10T	Nothing Feels/I Know (12", p/s) 8
91	3rd Stone STONE 004T	Manman/Blood Rush/Tooled Up (12", p/s) 8
92	3rd Stone STONE 006T	Scum (1-sided etched 12", p/s) 12
94	Circa CIRCA 29	HEX (LP) 50
04	Fire FIRELP 90	CODENAME: DUSTSUCKER (LP, inner) 30

BARLASTON DOWN
| 73 | Decca F13321 | Always/Mean Woman Mambo ....7 |

BARLEY BREE
| 67 | Piccadilly 7N 35393 | Sometime In The Morning/Save Your Love..10 |

BARNABY RUDGE
| 68 | CBS 3262 | Joe, Organ & Co./Railway Jim ....10 |

(see also Will Malone)

BARNES/ADAMS
| 60s | Lyntone LYN 1021 | When It Comes To The Crunch (It's Smiths Time)/Rhythm And Crunch (flexi, p/s) ....15 |

BARNEY J. BARNES & INTRO.
| 67 | Decca F 12662 | It Must Be Love/Can't Stand The Pain ....80 |

BENNY BARNES
| 60 | Mercury AMT 1094 | Token Of Love/That-A-Boy Willie ....20 |

DENA BARNES
| 80 | Grapevine GRP 141 | If You Ever Walked Out Of My Life/Who Am I...15 |

JEFF BARNES
70	Jackpot JP 735	Get In The Groove/JOHN HOLT: A Little Tear...8
70	Unity UN 568	1,000 Tons Of Version/Wake The Nation (B-side with Hugh Roy) 25
70	Pama PM 802	Jeff Barnes Thing/LENNOX BROWN: Lover's Mood 8
71	Smash SMA 2313	Wake The Nation (with Hugh Roy)/1,000 Tons Of Version 20
71	Gas 163	Peoples Version (work Out) (with PAT KELLY)/TONY LEE & PAT KELLY: Too Late 30

(see also Hugh Roy, Dave Barker, Darker Shade Of Blue, Delroy Wilson)

J.J. BARNES
67	Polydor 56722	Day Tripper/Deeper In Love 35
69	Stax STAX 130	Baby Please Come Back Home/Easy Living 35
73	Tamla Motown TMG 870	Real Humdinger/Please Let Me In/I Ain't Gonna Do It..12
74	Contempo CS 2009	To An Early Grave/To An Early Grave (Instrumental Version) 5
78	Contempo 2105	She's Mine/Erroll Flynn 20
75	Contempo CLP 520	THE GROOVESVILLE MASTERS (LP) 15
77	Contempo CLP 604	SARA SMILE (LP) 20

J.J. BARNES/STEVE MANCHA
| 69 | Stax SXATS 1012 | RARE STAMPS (LP) ....50 |

LLOYD BARNES
| 64 | Blue Beat BB 235 | Time Is Hard/BUSTER'S ALLSTARS: Reincarnation ....30 |

RICHARD BARNES
| 70 | Philips BF 1840 | Take To The Mountains/But It's Now I Need Your Love..8 |
| 70 | Philips 630 8027 | RICHARD BARNES (LP, black/silver label)..45 |

(see also Quiet Five, Tony Hazzard)

SIDNEY BARNES
| 76 | Charly CYS 1007 | I Hurt On The Other Side/Good Lovin' (as Sid Barnes) ....18 |

BARRY BARNETT
58	HMV POP 487	The Book Of Love/All I Have To Do Is Dream 10
58	HMV POP 511	When/Secretly...5
58	HMV POP 521	My Lucky Love/Too Young To Love 5
58	HMV POP 532	Susie Darlin'/Just A Dream..5
59	HMV POP 579	The Diary/Only A Memory 5
59	HMV POP 627	Cuckoo Girl/I'll String Along With You 10
63	HMV POP 1126	The Hit Of The Week/If You Ever Leave Me 6
66	Mercury MF 945	How Can You Explain/If There Wasn't Any You 6

ERIC BARNET(T)
68	Gas GAS 100	The Horse (actually by Theo Beckford & Group)/Action Line (actually by Versatiles)...12
69	Gas GAS 106	Te Ta Toe (act. by Theo Beckford & Group)/MILTON BOOTHE: Lonely And Blue 12
69	Crab CRAB 37	Quaker City/Double Up (both actually by Theo Beckford & Group) 12
70	Gas GAS 130	Pink Shark/Swing Free (both actually by Theo Beckford & Group, white labels only)...........20
70	Gas GAS 147	Bumper To Bumper/Fat Turkey (both actually by Theo Beckford & Group) 18

(see also Theo[philus] Beckford)

BARNFATHER
| 73 | Bell BLL 1341 | Clock On The Wall/Hollywood Girls..5 |

BARNSTORMERS SPASM BAND
58	Parlophone R 4416	Whistling Rufus/Won't You Come Home, Bill Bailey? 8
58	Parlophone R 4416	Whistling Rufus/Won't You Come Home, Bill Bailey? (78) 15
59	Tempo A 168	Stormin' The Barn/That's All There Is (There Ain't No More) 10
59	Tempo A 168	Stormin' The Barn/That's All There Is (There Ain't No More) (78)......................................15

(see also Original Barnstormers Spasm Band)

H.B. BARNUM
61	Fontana H 299	Lost Love/Hallelujah 15
65	Capitol CL 15391	The Record (Baby I Love You)/I'm A Man...40
65	Capitol CL 15391	The Record (Baby I Love You)/I'm A Man (DJ Copy) 80
76	Capitol CL 15851	Heartbreaker/Searchin' For My Soul 10
79	Capitol CL 16067	Heartbreaker/BOBBY PARIS: I Walked Away 15
64	RCA Victor RCX 7147	THE GREAT H.B. BARNUM (EP) 100
62	RCA Victor RD/SF 7500	THE BIG VOICE OF BARNUM . . . H.B., THAT IS (LP, mono/stereo).................................15
63	RCA Victor RD/SF 7543	EVERYBODY LOVES H.B. (LP, mono/stereo)..15

(see also Robins)

MINT VALUE £

CARL BARON & CHEETAHS
63	Columbia DB 7162	This Is Only The Beginning/Beg Borrow Or Steal	15

RIKKY BARON
| 60 | Parlophone R 4706 | Angry Young Man/My Lonely Heart | 10 |
| 63 | Parlophone R 4754 | Everybody/You're Breaking My Heart | 5 |

BARON WITH HIS POUNDING PIANO
| 65 | Sue WI 398 | Is A Blue Bird Blue/In The Mood | 50 |

(see also V.I.P.'s)

BARONS (U.K.)
| 61 | Oriole CB 1608 | Cossack/Summertime | 6 |
| 61 | Oriole CB 1620 | Samurai/Whirlwind | 6 |

BARONS (U.S.)
57	London HLP 8391	Don't Walk Out/Once In A Lifetime	1500
57	London HLP 8391	Don't Walk Out/Once In A Lifetime (78)	100
71	Jay Boy BOY 45	No More Baby Love/Society Don't Let Us Down	10

BARRABAS
| 73 | RCA RCA 2339 | Wild Safari/Woman | 12 |

BARRACUDA
| 73 | EMI EMI 2027 | Summer Girls/I Feel So Down | 8 |

BARRACUDAS
79	Cells CELLOUT 1	I Want My Woody Back/Subway Surfin' (p/s)	15
80	Zonophone Z 5	Summer Fun/Chevy Baby (p/s, with stickers)	15
80	Zonophone Z 5	Summer Fun/Chevy Baby (p/s, without stickers)	6
80	Zonophone Z 8	His Last Summer/Barracuda Waver/Surfers Are Back (p/s)	6
80	Zonophone Z 11	(I Wish It Could Be) 1965 Again/Rendezvous (p/s)	5
81	Zonophone Z 17	I Can't Pretend/The KGB (Made A Man Out Of Me) (p/s)	5
80	Zonophone ZONO 103	DROP OUT WITH THE BARRACUDAS (LP)	12

DICKIE BARRETT
| 58 | MGM MGM 976 | Smoke Gets In Your Eyes/Remember Me | 50 |

JOE BARRETT
| 55 | Brunswick 05432 | I'm Sincere/Why Did You Break My Heart? | 5 |

RICHARD BARRETT & CHANTELS
| 59 | HMV POP 609 | Come Softly To Me/Walking Through Dreamland | 30 |

(see also Chantels)

RICHIE BARRETT
| 62 | London HLK 9552 | Some Other Guy/Tricky Dicky | 75 |

'SWEET EMMA' BARRETT
| 60s | Riverside RLP 364 | THE BELL GAL AND HER DIXIELAND BOYS (LP) | 15 |

SYD BARRETT
69	Harvest HAR 5009	Octopus/Golden Hair	250
69	Harvest HAR 5009	Octopus/Golden Hair (Promo with mispelt 'Barratt' and release date 14.11.69)	350
88	Strange Fruit SFPS 043	THE PEEL SESSIONS (12", EP, initial pressing with metallic sleeve)	15
88	Strange Fruit SFPS 043	THE PEEL SESSIONS (12", EP)	15
88	Strange Fruit SFPSCD 043	THE PEEL SESSIONS (CD EP)	10
70	Harvest SHVL 765	THE MADCAP LAUGHS (LP, laminated sleeve, no EMI box on label)	150
70	Harvest SHVL 765	THE MADCAP LAUGHS (LP, matt gatefold sleeve, no EMI box on label)	70
70	Harvest SHSP 4007	BARRETT (LP, laminated sleeve, first pressing with no EMI boxed label)	200
70	Harvest SHSP 4007	BARRETT (LP, textured flipback sleeve, no EMI logo)	45
72	Harvest SHSP 4007	BARRETT (LP, textured non-flipback sleeve, second pressing with EMI boxed logo)	20
74	Harvest SHDW 404	SYD BARRETT (2-LP, reissue of "Madcap" & "Barrett", gatefold sleeve)	35
88	Harvest SHSP 4126	OPEL (LP, gatefold sleeve)	18
93	EMI SYD BOX 1	CRAZY DIAMOND (3-CD box set, with booklet)	25
97	Harvest 7423 855663 18	THE MADCAP LAUGHS (LP, 180gm reissue, heavy quality sleeve)	20
97	Harvest 7423 821450 11	BARRETT (LP, 180gm reissue, heavy quality sleeve)	20
99	Harvest SVLP 153	OPEL (2-LP, 180gm reissue, heavy quality sleeve)	25
99	Simply Vinyl SVLP 153	OPEL (LP 180gm reissue, heavy quality gatefold sleeve)	25
00	Simply Vinyl SVLP 281	BARRETT (LP, 180gm reissue, heavy quality gatefold sleeve)	20
00	Simply Vinyl SVLP 289	THE MADCAP LAUGHS (LP, 180gm reissue, heavy quality gatefold sleeve)	20

(see also Pink Floyd)

WILD WILLY BARRETT
77	Logo GO 105	Return Of Kong/Nice To Know You're My Friend (p/s)	5
79	Polydor 2059 067	Let's Playd Schools/I Did It Otway (p/s)	5
86	Galvanised DIP 1	ORGANIC BONDAGE (LP, with Stephen Two Names; in wooden sleeve)	15

(see also John Otway/Wild Willy Barrett)

RAY BARRETTO
63	Columbia DB 7051	El Watusi/Ritmo Sabroso	20
65	Columbia DB 7684	El Watusi/Swingin' Shepherd Blues	20
69	London HL 10262	Acid/Mercy Mercy Baby (withdrawn)	50
67	Island ILP 946	EL WATUSI (LP)	40
69	London HA/SH 8383	ACID (LP)	50

BARRIER
68	Eyemark EMS 1013	Georgie Brown/Dawn Breaks Through (in handmade p/s)	450
68	Eyemark EMS 1013	Georgie Brown/Dawn Breaks Through	250
68	Philips BF 1692	The Tide Is Turning/Place In Your Heart	15
68	Philips BF 1731	Spot The Lights/Uh	70

BARRINO BROTHERS
| 72 | Invictus INV 523 | I Shall Not Be Moved/When Love Was A Child | 15 |

BARRON KNIGHTS
62	Fontana H 368	Let's Face It/Never Miss A Chance	8
63	Columbia DB 7108	Jo-Anne/That's My Girl	5
64	Columbia DB 7188	Comin' Home Baby/Peanut Butter	20

64	Columbia DB 7375	Come To The Dance/Choose Me Tonight	5
64	Columbia DB 7427	The House Of Johann Strauss/She's The One	5
65	Columbia DB 7698	It Was A Very Good Year/Worry And Wonder	5
66	Columbia DB 7884	Round The World Rhythm & Blues/Where There's A Will	5
66	Columbia DB 7933	Doing What She's Not Supposed To Do/Every Night	5
66	Columbia DB 8071	Under New Management Medley (both sides)	5
67	Columbia DB 8161	Lazy Fat People/In The Night	5
67	Columbia DB 8280	Here Come The Bees/It's A Sin	5
68	Columbia DB 8423	I Never Will Marry/Cold In My Nose	5
68	Columbia DB 8485	An Olympic Record/An Olympic Record	5
69	Columbia DB 8612	Love And The World Loves With You/Along Come Those Summer Days	5
69	Columbia DB 8679	Traces/Awake	5
72	Penny Farthing PEN 786	You're All I Need/Nothin' Doin'	12
64	Columbia SEG 8425	GUYING THE TOP POPS (EP)	8
66	Columbia SEG 8526	THOSE VERSATILE BARRON KNIGHTS (EP)	10
64	Columbia 33SX 1648	CALL UP THE GROUPS (LP)	20
66	Columbia SX 6007	BARRON KNIGHTS (LP)	20
67	Columbia SX 6176	SCRIBED (LP)	20
72	Penny Farthing PELS 536	ONE MAN'S MEAT (LP)	12

BARROW POETS

68	Fontana TF 939	Letter In A Bottle (Music "Sleepy Lagoon")/Dynamite Barbee (Music "Barbee Song")	5
67	Barrow BR 1	AT THE PRINTER'S DEVIL (EP, private pressing)	20
63	Argo PLP 1072	PRESENT AN ENTERTAINMENT OF POETRY AND MUSIC (LP)	20
68	Fontana STL 5479	FOLK RHYMES TUNES AND VERSES (LP)	15
68	Fontana 6857 003	FINEST FOLK (LP)	18
70	RCA SF 8110	JOKER (LP)	20
72	Argo ZSW 508	OUTPATIENTS (LP)	15
72	Argo ZSW 511	MAGIC EGG (LP)	22

AL BARRY

70	Duke DU 81	Ooh Wee/Hold It Baby	5
70	Doctor Bird DB 1502	Morning Sun/MARKONIANS: Over And Over	100
71	Creole 1005	Down We Go/It Pays To Do Good	20

(see also Desmond Dekker & Aces)

DAVE BARRY & SARA BERNER

56	London HLU 8324	Out Of This World With Flying Saucers Parts 1 & 2 (Tri Gold)	70
56	London HLU 8324	Out Of This World With Flying Saucers Parts 1 & 2 (Tri Silver)	30

DAWN BARRY

71	Phoenix NIX 118	My World Keeps Getting Smaller Evry Day/No Love At All	6

GENE BARRY

65	Pye 7N 15873	I'll Remember You/I've Got Your Number)	5

JOE BARRY

61	Mercury AMT 1149	I'm A Fool To Care/I Got A Feeling	10
68	Stateside SS 2127	I Started Loving You Again/California Bound	15
62	Mercury ZEP 10130	A FOOL TO CARE (EP)	100

JOHN BARRY (SEVEN)

SINGLES

57	Parlophone R 4363	Zip Zip/Three Little Fishes (as John Barry & The Seven)	40
57	Parlophone R 4363	Zip Zip/Three Little Fishes (as John Barry & The Seven) (78)	15
58	Parlophone R 4394	Every Which Way/You've Gotta Way (as John Barry Seven)	40
58	Parlophone R 4394	Every Which Way/You've Gotta Way (as John Barry Seven) (78)	15
58	Parlophone R 4418	Big Guitar/Rodeo (as John Barry Seven)	25
58	Parlophone R 4418	Big Guitar/Rodeo (as John Barry Seven) (78)	10
58	Parlophone R 4453	Pancho/Hideaway (as John Barry Seven)	10
58	Parlophone R 4488	Farrago/Bee's Knees (as John Barry Seven)	5
59	Parlophone R 4530	Long John/Snap 'n' Whistle (as John Barry Seven)	5
59	Parlophone R 4560	Little John/For Pete's Sake (as John Barry Seven)	5
59	Parlophone R 4582	Twelfth Street Rag/Christella (as John Barry Seven)	6
60	Columbia DB 4414	Hit And Miss/Rockin' Already (as John Barry Seven)	10
60	Columbia DB 4446	Beat For Beatniks/Big Fella (as John Barry Orchestra)	10
60	Columbia DB 4480	Blueberry Hill/Never Let Go (as John Barry Orchestra)	10
60	Columbia DB 4505	Walk Don't Run/I'm Movin' On (as John Barry Seven)	5
60	Columbia DB 4554	Black Stockings/Get Lost Jack Frost (as John Barry Seven)	5
61	Columbia DB 4598	The Magnificent Seven/Skid Row (as John Barry Seven)	5
61	Columbia DB 4659	The Menace/Rodeo (as John Barry Orchestra)	5
61	Columbia DB 4699	Starfire/A Matter Of Who (as John Barry Seven)	5
61	Columbia DB 4746	Watch Your Step/Twist It (as John Barry Seven)	5
62	Columbia DB 4806	Cutty Sark/Lost Patrol (as John Barry Seven & Orchestra)	5
62	Columbia DB 4898	The James Bond Theme/The Blacksmith Blues (with Orchestra) (green or black labels)	10
62	Columbia DB 4941	The Lolly Theme/March Of The Mandarins (as John Barry Seven & Orchestra)	5
63	Columbia DB 7003	The Human Jungle/Onward, Christian Spacemen (in p/s)	8
63	Columbia DB 7003	The Human Jungle/Onward, Christian Spacemen	5
64	Columbia DB 7414	Twenty-Four Hours Ago/Seven Faces	10
63	Ember EMB S 178	Kinky/Fancy Dance	5
63	Ember EMB S 181	007/From Russia With Love (in p/s)	18
63	Ember EMB S 181	007/From Russia With Love	5
63	Ember EMB S 183	Elizabeth/The London Theme	5
63	Ember EMB S 185	Zulu Stamp/Monkey Feathers (mauve/grey or red/yellow label; in p/s)	10
63	Ember EMB S 185	Zulu Stamp/Monkey Feathers (mauve/grey or red/yellow label)	5
63	Lyntone LYN 378	Theme Music From The Ingersoll Trendsetters T.V. Commercial flexidisc with 8-page A4 promo booklet)	20
64	United Artists UP 1060	Seance On A Wet Afternoon/Oublie Ça	5
64	United Artists UP 1068	Goldfinger/Troubador	5
64	Stateside SS 296	Barney's Blues/Theme From The Film "Man In The Middle" (No More)	5
65	CBS 201747	A Man Alone (Ipcress File Theme)/Barbara's Theme	5
65	CBS 201822	The Syndicate/What A Question	5
66	CBS 202390	Vendetta/The Danny Scipio Theme	5
67	CBS 202451	Wednesday's Child (Quiller Memorandum)/Sleep Well My Darling	5

Len BARRY

67	CBS 2825	You Only Live Twice/The Girl With The Sun In Her Hair	5
67	Ember EMB S 243	007/The Loneliness Of Autumn (in p/s)	10
69	CBS 3935	The Lion In Winter Parts 1 & 2	5
69	CBS 4468	Midnight Cowboy/Fun City	5
69	CBS 4680	On Her Majesty's Secret Service/We Have All The Time In The World	5
70	Probe PRO 518	The Last Valley/Main Title Theme	5
71	CBS 7469	Theme From "The Persuaders"/The Girl With The Sun In Her Hair	5
72	Polydor 2058 216	This Way Mary/Diamonds Are Forever	5
72	Polydor 2058 275	The Adventurer/Follow Follow	5
80	United Artists UP 634	Midnight Cowboy/Fun City (p/s)	5

EPs

58	Parlophone GEP 8737	THE BIG BEAT (as John Barry Seven)	40
61	Columbia SEG 8069	THE JOHN BARRY SOUND (as John Barry Seven)	20
62	Columbia SEG 8138	BEAT GIRL (as John Barry Seven, with Adam Faith)	20
63	Columbia SEG 8255	JOHN BARRY THEME SUCCESSES	10
63	United Artists UEP 1011	FROM RUSSIA WITH LOVE (soundtrack)	10
64	Ember EMB EP 4544	LONELINESS OF AUTUMN	10
64	United Artists UEP 1012	GOLDFINGER (soundtrack)	10
65	Ember EMB EP 4551	JAMES BOND IS BACK	25
65	United Artists UEP 1015	THUNDERBALL: Thunderball/Death Of Fiona/Bond Below Disco Volante/ Mr Kiss Kiss Bang Bang (soundtrack)	10
67	CBS WEP 1126	THEMES FROM JAMES BOND FILMS (mail order via Carr's Sport biscuits)	10
67	CBS WEP 1129	BIG THEMES FROM THE BIG SCREEN (mail order via Wall's)	10
67	CBS WEP 1131	GREAT SCREEN THEMES (mail order via Lyon's Bakery)	10

ALBUMS

60	Columbia 33SX 1225	BEAT GIRL (soundtrack, with Adam Faith)	50
61	Columbia 33SX 1358	STRINGBEAT (mono)	30
61	Columbia SCX 3401	STRINGBEAT (stereo)	35
63	United Artists (S)ULP 1052	FROM RUSSIA WITH LOVE (soundtrack, mono)	25
63	United Artists (S)ULP 1052	FROM RUSSIA WITH LOVE (soundtrack, stereo)	25
63	Colpix PXL 459	ELIZABETH TAYLOR IN LONDON (mono)	30
63	Colpix PXL 459	ELIZABETH TAYLOR IN LONDON (stereo)	35
64	Ember NR 5012	ZULU (soundtrack, yellow/orange label, flipback sleeve)	20
64	Stateside S(S)L 10087	MAN IN THE MIDDLE (soundtrack, with Lionel Bart)	15
64	United Artists (S)ULP 1076	GOLDFINGER (soundtrack, mono)	25
64	United Artists (S)ULP 1076	GOLDFINGER (soundtrack, stereo)	25
65	Ember NR 5025	JOHN BARRY PLAYS 007	20
65	Ember NR 56088	FOUR IN THE MORNING (soundtrack, mono)	15
65	Ember NR 56088	FOUR IN THE MORNING (soundtrack, stereo)	15
65	CBS BPG 62530	THE IPCRESS FILE (soundtrack, mono only)	60
65	United Artists ULP 1104	THE KNACK (AND HOW TO GET IT) (soundtrack)	50
65	United Artists (S)ULP 1110	THUNDERBALL (soundtrack, mono)	25
65	United Artists (S)ULP 1110	THUNDERBALL (soundtrack, stereo)	25
66	Fontana STL 5387	THE WRONG BOX (soundtrack, release cancelled)	0
66	CBS (S)BPG 62665	THE CHASE (soundtrack, mono)	15
66	CBS (S)BPG 62665	THE CHASE (soundtrack, stereo)	15
66	CBS (S)BPG 62869	THE QUILLER MEMORANDUM (soundtrack, mono)	15
66	CBS (S)BPG 62869	THE QUILLER MEMORANDUM (soundtrack, stereo)	15
67	United Artists (S)ULP 1168	THE WHISPERERS (soundtrack)	15
67	United Artists (S)ULP 1171	YOU ONLY LIVE TWICE (soundtrack)	20
67	United Artists LAS 29021	THE BEST OF BOND (mono)	15
68	Stateside S(S)L 10263	DEADFALL (soundtrack, Shirley Bassey on 1 track)	35
69	United Artists UAS 29020	ON HER MAJESTY'S SECRET SERVICE (soundtrack, foldout sleeve)	25
69	MCA MUPS 360	BOOM! (soundtrack, with Georgie Fame)	30
71	United Artists UAS 29216	DIAMONDS ARE FOREVER (soundtrack)	30
71	Probe SPB 1027	THE LAST VALLEY (soundtrack, with insert)	15
71	Probe SPB 1027	THE LAST VALLEY (soundtrack, without insert)	15
72	Ember SE 8008	JOHN BARRY REVISITED (foldout sleeve, initial pressing in 'nude' gatefold sleeve)	30
74	United Artists UAS 29671	THE MAN WITH THE GOLDEN GUN (soundtrack)	15
83	A&M 394 967-2	OCTOPUSSY (CD, soundtrack, withdrawn)	50

(see also Alan Bown, Chad & Jeremy, Adam Faith, Elizabeth Taylor, Desmond Lane, Johnny Pearson, Tony Bennett, Jim Lowe, Lyn Paul, Russ Conway, Lance Fortune, Alan Haven, Countdowns, Johnny De Little, Marion Ryan, Dick Kallman)

LEN BARRY

65	Cameo Parkway P 969	Hearts Are Trump/Little White House	30
65	Brunswick 05942	1-2-3/Bullseye	5
65	Brunswick 05942	1-2-3/Bullseye (DJ Copy)	30
66	Brunswick 05949	Like A Baby/Happiness (Is A Girl Like You)	10
66	Brunswick 05949	Like A Baby/Happiness (DJ Copy)	30
66	Brunswick 05955	Somewhere/It's A Crying Shame	10
66	Brunswick 05955	Somewhere/It's A Crying Shame (DJ Copy)	30
66	Brunswick 05962	It's That Time Of The Year/Happily Ever After	10
66	Brunswick 05962	It's That Time Of The Year/Happily Ever After (DJ Copy)	30
66	Brunswick 05966	I Struck It Rich/Love Is	20
66	Brunswick 05966	I Struck It Rich/Love Is (DJ Copy)	40
67	RCA RCA 1588	The Moving Finger Writes/Our Love	20
67	RCA RCA 1588	The Moving Finger Writes/Our Love (DJ Copy)	30
68	Bell BLL 1022	4-5-6 Now I'm Alone/Funky Night	5
71	Now! NOW 1003	Now I'm Alone/Funky Night	5
72	MCA MU 1172	1-2-3/You Baby	8
73	Paramount PARA 3031	Heaven And Earth/I'm Marching To The Music	15
73	Paramount PARA 3039	It's Time To Fall In Love/Touching, Holding, Feeling	5
66	Cameo Parkway CPE 556	HAVIN' A GOOD TIME (EP)	30
65	Brunswick LAT 8637	1-2-3 (LP)	25
66	Brunswick LAT 8656	IT'S THAT TIME OF YEAR (LP, unreleased, sleeve may not exist)	900
66	Cameo Parkway C 1082	LEN BARRY AND THE DOVELLS (LP)	30
69	Bulldog BDL 1013	MORE FROM THE 1-2-3 MAN (LP)	20
69	RCA Intl. INTS 1027	MY KIND OF SOUL (LP)	15

(see also Dovells, Electric Indian)

MARGARET BARRY
60	Top Rank 251020	IRELAND'S QUEEN OF THE TINKERS SINGS (LP)	20

MARGARET BARRY (& MICHAEL GORMAN)
58	Topic 10T 6	STREET SONGS AND FIDDLE TUNES OF IRELAND (10" LP, mid-blue label, later buff/black or dark blue/silver labels)	15

SANDRA BARRY (& THE BOYS)
64	Decca F 11851	Really Gonna Shake/When We Get Married (as Sandra Barry & Boys)	100
65	Pye 7N 15753	The End Of The Line/We Were Lovers	15
65	Pye 7N 15840	Question/You Can Take It From Me	15
66	Pye 7N 17102	Stop! Thief/I Won't Try To Change Your Mind	15

(see also Boys, Sandra Alfred, Slack Alice)

BARRY & THE TAMERLANES
63	Warner Bros WB 116	I Wonder What She's Doing Tonight/Don't Go	25
64	Warner Bros WB 124	Roberta/Butterfly	15
64	Warner Bros WM 8145	I WONDER WHAT SHE'S DOING TONIGHT (LP)	60

(see also Barry De Vorzon)

BARRY SISTERS (U.S.)
56	London HLA 8248	Cha Cha Joe/Baby Come A Little Closer	40
56	London HLA 8304	Till You Come Back To Me/Intrigue	70
56	Columbia DB 3843	Sing Me A Sentimental Love Song/The Italian Theme	5
58	Columbia DB 4215	I Hear Bells/I Get Up Ev'ry Morning	5
60	Columbia DB 4562	Misty/Why Don't You Do Right?	5
60	Columbia 33SX 1309	SIDE BY SIDE (LP)	12

(see also Three Barry Sisters)

LIONEL BART
61	Decca F11405	Give Us A Kiss For Christmas/How Now Brown Cow	5
68	Deram DM 212	Isn't This Where We Came In/May A Man Be Merry	10
59	Decca LF 1324	BART FOR BART'S SAKE (10" LP)	20
68	Deram SML 1028	ISN'T THIS WHERE WE CAME IN (LP, stereo, gatefold sleeve)	40

CHRIS BARTLEY
67	Cameo Parkway P 101	The Sweetest Thing This Side Of Heaven/Love Me Baby	70
67	Cameo Parkway P 101	The Sweetest Thing This Side Of Heaven/Love Me Baby (DJ Copy)	100
68	Bell BLL 1031	I Found A Goodie/Be Mine Forever	30
75	Right On RO 105	I See Your Name/I See Your Name (Instrumental)	10
86	Move MIS 4	Baby I'm For Real/I've Found A Goodie/Truer Words Were Never Spoken/ The Sweetest Thing This Side Of Heaven (12", p/s)	15

BARTOK
82	On ON 1	Insanity/I Am The Bomb (p/s)	12

(see also Jah Wobble, Damned)

EILEEN BARTON
55	Vogue Coral Q 72060	The Year We Fell In Love/I Don't Want To Mambo Polka	5
55	Vogue Coral Q 72075	Fujiyama Mama/I'd've Baked A Cake	100
55	Vogue Coral Q 72075	Fujiyama Mama/I'd've Baked A Cake (78)	10
56	Vogue Coral Q 72122	Cry Me A River/Come Home	20
56	Vogue Coral Q 72122	Cry Me A River/Come Home (78)	10
56	Vogue Coral Q 72148	Teenage Heart/My Social Hot Dog	20
56	Vogue Coral Q 72205	Spring It Was/I Have To Tell You	5
57	Vogue Coral Q 72250	Too Close For Comfort/Here I Am In Love Again	5
57	Vogue Coral Q 72270	Without Love/The Scene Of The Crime	5

MARIA BARTON
80	Airship AP 56	RAINFUL DAYS (LP)	100

ROD BARTON (& THE LINCOLNAIRES)
62	Salvo SLO 1812	Dear Old San Francisco/NERVOUS NORVOUS: Does A Chinese Chicken Have A Pigtail	40

DAVE BARTRAM
83	Utopia UTO 2	Black Ice/Excitement (p/s)	5

BASCZAX
79	Pipeline ICI ONE	Madison Fallout/Auto Mekanik Destruktor (4 single sided 7" pages as sleeve)	25

BASELINE
81	Extrabit EX 1	Suspended Animation/Truth About The Lies (with p/s)	125
81	Extrabit EX 1	Suspended Animation/Truth About The Lies (without p/s)	50

BASEMENT 5
80	Island ILPS9641	1965-80 (LP, with inner, poster and embossed sleeve)	15

BASEMENT JAXX
01	XL XLLP 143X	ROOTY (LP, picture disc, 1000 only)	12

BASEMENT PHIL
91	Basement BRSS 001	Take Me Up (Part 1)/(Part 2)/(Part 3) (12" promo)	25
92	Basement BRSS 002	Bachbeat (Part 1)/I Love You/Bachbeat (Part 2) (12" promo)	12
92	Basement BRSS 009	WE CAN ROCK IT EP (12", as Basement Phil And The Engineers)	10

BASHERS
76	Virgin VS 154	The Womble Bashers/Womble Bashers Wock	20

(see also Mike McGear)

BASHFUL ALLEY
82	Ellie Jay BA 001	Running Blind/My, My, My (p/s, black-and-white or black-and-yellow sleeve)	50
82	Graffiti BA 001	Running Blind/My, My, My (p/s, reissue)	35

ROBBIE BASHO
69	Sonet SNTF 612	FALCONERS ARMS VOL 1. (LP)	20

BASIC BLACK AND PEARL
75	Bus Stop BUS 1030	There'll Come A Time, There'll Come A Day/Right On Baby	15

COUNT BASIE & HIS ORCHESTRA
67	Coral Q 72497	Green Onions/Hang On Sloopy	15

BASIES

68	MCA MCA 1014	For Your Precious Love/Uptight (with Jackie Wilson)..5
68	Decca AD 1008	For Your Precious Love/Uptight (with Jackie Wilson, export issue) 5
53	Brunswick LA 8589	BASIE'S BEST (10" LP) 12
53	Mercury MG 25015	KANSAS CITY 7/LESTER YOUNG QUARTET (LP, 1 side each) 15
54	Oriole/Mercury MG 25015	COUNT BASIE/LESTER YOUNG (10" LP, 1 side each) 15
55	Columbia 33S 1054	THE COUNT (10" LP)..15
55	Philips BBR 8036	THE OLD AND THE NEW COUNT (10" LP) 15
55	Columbia Clef 33C 9010	THE COUNT BASIE SEXTET (10" LP) 15
61	Columbia SX 1332	STRING ALONG WITH BASIE (LP) 15
65	Verve VLP/SVLP 9082	BASIELAND (LP)..15
66	United Artists (S)ULP 1127	BASIE MEETS BOND (LP)...20
70	Philips 6369 408	AFRIQUE (LP) 15

(see also Joe Williams, Jackie Wilson, Tony Bennett, Lester Young, Ella Fitzgerald)

BASIES

| 67 | Coxsone CS 7030 | River Jordan/SOUL VENDORS: Swing Easy ....35 |

BASKIN & COPPERFIELD

| 70 | Decca F 13053 | The Long And Winding Road/Beautiful Blue Eyes ....10 |
| 70 | Decca F 23079 | I Never See The Sun/Stranger On The Ground ....8 |

BASKING SHARKS

83	Fin FON 01	Diamond Age/New Industry (p/s, insert) 15
83	SRR SRR 0013	THRILL OF THE GAME EP 20
83	RS 001	SHARK ISLAND (LP) 30

BILLY BASS

| 69 | Pama PM 761 | I Need Your Love So Bad/I'm Coming To ....50 |

FONTELLA BASS

65	Chess CRS 8007	Don't Mess Up A Good Thing (with Bobby McClure)/OLIVER SAIN: Jerk Loose 30
65	Chess CRS 8007	Don't Mess Up A Good Thing/Baby What You Want Me To Do (different B-side, existence unconfirmed) 0
65	Chess CRS 8023	Rescue Me/Soul Of The Man...10
65	Chess CRS 8023	Rescue Me/Soul Of The Man (DJ Copy) 40
66	Chess CRS 8027	Recovery/Leave It In The Hands Of Love 15
66	Chess CRS 8027	Recovery/Leave It In The Hands Of Love (DJ Copy) 35
66	Chess CRS 8032	I Can't Rest/Surrender..30
66	Chess CRS 8032	I Can't Rest/Surrender (DJ Copy) 70
66	Chess CRS 8042	Safe And Sound/You'll Never Know..10
66	Chess CRS 8042	Safe And Sound/You'll Never Know (DJ Copy) 35
69	Chess CRS 8090	Rescue Me/I Can't Rest..10
69	Chess CRS 8090	Rescue Me/I Can't Rest (DJ Copy)..25
69	Chess CRS 8023	Rescue Me/Soul Of The Man (reissue) 5
72	Mojo 2092 032	Who You Gonna Blame/Hold On This Time 5
72	Mojo 2092 045	I Want Everyone To Know/I Need To Be Loved 5
66	Chess CRE 6015	FONTELLA'S HITS (EP) 25
66	Chess CRE 6020	I CAN'T REST (EP) 40
66	Chess CRE 6025	FONTELLA BASS AND BOBBY McCLURE (EP) 40
66	Chess CRL 4517	THE NEW LOOK (LP) 40

(see also Bobby McClure)

SHIRLEY BASSEY

57	Philips JK 1006	The Banana Boat Song/Tra La La (jukebox issue) 10
57	Philips JK 1018	If I Had A Needle And Thread/Tonight My Heart She Is Crying (jukebox issue)..........10
57	Philips JK 1034	Puh-leeze! Mister Brown/Take My Love, Take My Love (jukebox issue) 10
58	Philips PB 845	As I Love You/Hands Across The Sea 5
58	Philips PB 860	Kiss Me, Honey Honey, Kiss Me/There's Never Been A Night..5
59	Philips PB 917	Love For Sale/Crazy Rhythm...5
59	Philips PB 919	My Funny Valentine/How About You?...5
59	Philips PB 975	Night And Day/The Gypsy In My Soul...5
66	United Artists UP 1134	Don't Take The Lovers From The World/Takeaway 15

(see also Yello, Nelson Riddle Orchestra, John Barry)

BAS-SHEVA

| 55 | Capitol CL 14218 | Flame Of Love/I Just Wanna Be Your Loving Baby ....10 |

JOE BATAAN

75	RCA RCA 2457	Latin Strut/Peace, Friendship And Solidarity 12
75	RCA RCA 2553	The Bottle/When You're Down 12
69	London HA/SH 8386	RIOT! (LP)..40

JUNE BATEMAN

| 64 | Sue WI 347 | I Don't Wanna/NOBLE 'THIN MAN' WATTS & HIS BAND: Noble's Theme ....70 |

COLLIN BATES TRIO

| 68 | Fontana SFJL 913 | BREW (LP) ....200 |

JON BATES

| 65 | CBS 202818 | Where Were You Last Night/If Anything Goes Wrong ....5 |

MARTYN BATES

| 82 | Cherry Red TRED 38 | LETTERS WRITTEN (10" EP) ....10 |
| 80s | Ambivalent Scale | IMAGINATION FEELS LIKE POISON (CD, with book, 500 only)....................................20 |

(see also Eyeless In Gaza)

BATFINKS

| 89 | Link LINK LP 082 | WAZZED 'N' BLASTED (LP) ....12 |

BAT FOR LASHES

| 04 | No label or Cat. No. | WHO STOLE PETRETSKI'S THUNDER? (CD-R tour only EP) ....20 |
| 06 | Echo EC 185 | The Wizard/I Saw A Light (demo) ....8 |

BATHORY

84	Under One Flag FLAG 8	BATHORY (LP) 20
85	Under One Flag FLAG 9	THE RETURN... (LP, inner) 40
87	Under One Flag FLAG 11	UNDER THE SIGN OF THE BLACK MARK (LP) 20
88	Under One Flag FLAG 26	BLOOD FIRE DEATH (LP, gatefold sleeve, insert)..30

| 88 | Under One Flag FLAG 26 P | BLOOD FIRE DEATH (LP, picture disc) | 35 |

BATMAN THEME
| 88 | Bam Caruso NRIC 107 | Batman Theme/Batman Theme (Instrumental Mix) (p/s) | 15 |

(see also Jan & Dean)

STIV BATORS
| 79 | London/Bomp HLZ 10575 | It's Cold Outside/The Last Year (p/s) | 15 |
| 03 | TRY 001 | King Of The Brats/Young Don't Cry (p/s) | 5 |

(see also Dead Boys, Lords Of The New Church, Wanderers)

BATS
64	Columbia DB 7429	Accept It/Lovers Lie Sleeping	10
66	Decca F 22534	Listen To My Heart/Stop Don't Do It	25
67	Decca F 22568	You Will Now, Won't You?/You Look Good Together	20
67	Decca F 22616	Hard To Get Up In The Morning/Take Me As I Am	10

MIKE BATT
68	Liberty LBF 15093	Mister Poem/Fading Yellow	30
68	Liberty LBF 15122	I See Wonderful Things In You/Mary Goes Round	25
69	Liberty LBF 15210	Your Mother Should Know/Suddenly	20
75	Epic EPC 3460	Summertime City/Children Of The Storm	5
70	Midland Counties Ice Cream RMS1	Liberate A Lolly	10
77	Epic A 3957	Railway Hotel/The Ride To Agadir	8
70	Penny Farthing PAGS 534	BATT TRACKS (LP)	15
72	DJM DJSL 020	PORTRAIT OF SIMON & GARFUNKEL (LP)	12
72	DJM DJSL 022	PORTRAIT OF BOB DYLAN (LP)	12
72	DJM DJSL 023	PORTRAIT OF CAT STEVENS (LP)	12
74	DJM DJSL 038	PORTRAIT OF MIKE BATT (LP)	12

(see also Hapshash & Coloured Coat, Anderson Harley & Batt)

BATTERED ORNAMENTS
| 70 | Harvest HAR 5013 | Goodbye We Loved You (Madly)/CHRIS SPEDDING: Rock'n'Roll Band | 10 |
| 69 | Harvest SHVL 758 | MANTLE-PIECE (LP, gatefold sleeve, no EMI box on label) | 300 |

(see also Pete Brown & His Battered Ornaments, Chris Spedding, People Band)

BATTERSEA
| 78 | Rak RK 1013 | Bord And Bred/Summer Rain (no p/s) | 20 |

SKIP BATTIN
| 72 | Signpost SGP 756 | Central Park/St. Louis Browns | 6 |
| 72 | Signpost SG 4255 | SKIP (LP) | 18 |

(see also Skip & Flip, Byrds, Flying Burrito Brothers, Evergreen Blueshoes)

BATTLEAXE
82	Guardian GRC 132	Burn This Town/Battleaxe (no p/s)	40
83	Music For Nations MFN8	BURN THIS TOWN (LP)	15
84	Music For Nations MFN 25	POWER FROM THE UNIVERSE (LP)	12

BATWING CHAPS
| 84 | Full Moon FM 01 | I Won't Change/Crave (p/s) | 6 |

BAUHAUS
79	Small Wonder TEENY 2	Bela Lugosi's Dead/Boys/Dark Entries (not listed on sleeve) (12")	12
79	Small Wonder TEENY 2	Bela Lugosi's Dead/Boys/Dark Entries (12", p/s, white vinyl, 5000 only)	25
80	Axis AXIS 3	Dark Entries/Untitled (brown label, p/s)	18
80	Axis AD 3	Dark Entries/Untitled (blue label, p/s)	15
80	4AD BEG 37	Dark Entries/Untitled (p/s, blue 4AD labels, lists BEG 37 on sleeve)	10
80	Beggars Banquet BEG 37	Dark Entries/Untitled (p/s, red Beggars Banquet labels)	10
80	4AD AD 7	Terror Couple Kill Colonel/Scopes/Terror Couple Kill Colonel II (version) (mispressed with 'rejected' version of third track, p/s)	15
81	Beggars Banquet BEG 54T	Kick In The Eye/Satori (12", white label in stamped plain sleeve)	15
81	Beggars Banquet BEG 59	The Passion Of Lovers/1.2.3.4 (card sleeve with lyric insert)	6
81	Beggars Banquet BEG 59	The Passion Of Lovers/1.2.3.4 (paper sleeve, mispressing with A side label on both sides)	8
82	Beggars Banquet BEG 79	Spirit/Terror Couple Kill Colonel (live in Paris) (Beggars logo labels and sleeve titles)	5
82	Beggars Banquet AD 3	Dark Entries/Untitled (reissue, 'nudes wrestling' label, no contact address on p/s)	8
82	Beggars Banquet BEG 79	Spirit/Terror Couple Kill Colonel (live in Paris) (Beggars logo labels and no sleeve titles)	7
82	Beggars Banquet BEG 74T	Kick In The Eye/Poison Pen/Harry/Earwax (12" mispressing, p/s, matrix: A1)	25
82	Beggars Banquet BEG 79	Spirit/Terror Couple Kill Colonel (live) (p/s, mispressed, A-side plays Gary Numan's "We Take Mystery [To Bed]")	25
82	Beggars Banquet BEG 79P	Spirit/Terror Couple Kill Colonel (live) (picture disc in printed PVC sleeve)	7
82	Lyntone LYN 12106	A God In An Alcove (Early Version) (hard vinyl test pressing)	15
82	Beggars Banquet BEG 83	Ziggy Stardust/Third Uncle (original glossy card sleeve)	5
82	Beggars Banquet BEG 83	Ziggy Stardust/Third Uncle (original glossy card sleeve, signed by band for record company staff)	30
82	Beggars Banquet BEG 83	Ziggy Stardust/Third Uncle (Beggars Banquet labels no picture sleeve)	8
82	Beggars Banquet BEG 83T	Ziggy Stardust/Party Of The First Part/Third Uncle/Waiting For The Man, 12" p/s, with stickered poster p/s)	8
82	Beggars Banquet BEG 83T	Ziggy Stardust/Party Of The First Part/Third Uncle/Waiting For The Man, (12", repressing in thin spineless sleeve with reversed artwork)	10
82	Beggars Banquet BEG 83T	Ziggy Stardust/Party Of The First Part/Third Uncle/Waiting For The Man, 12" glossy card p/s, no poster, signed for record company staff)	30
82	Beggars Banquet BH 1	SATORI IN PARIS : Hair Of The Dog (live in Paris)/Double Dare (live in Paris)	5
83	Lyntone LYN 13777/8	The Sanity Assassin/Spirit In The Sky (fan club freebie, 320 only)	300
84	Beggars Banquet BEG 91P	She's In Parties/Departure (picture disc in PVC sleeve)	8
88	Small Wonder TEENY 2P	Bela Lugosi's Dead/Boys/Dark Entries (12", reissue, luminous picture disc in PVC sleeve)	25
89	Small Wonder TEENY 2	Bela Lugosi's Dead/Boys/Dark Entries (12", reissue, green vinyl, p/s)	25
89	Small Wonder TEENY 2	Bela Lugosi's Dead/Boys/Dark Entries (12", reissue, blue vinyl, p/s)	25
90	Beggars Banquet BEG 74T	Kick In the Eye/In Fear Of Dub/Harry/Earwax (Searching For Satori EP) (12", reissue, black sleeve lettering, green/gold labels)	15
91	Small Wonder TEENY 2	Bela Lugosi's Dead/Boys/Dark Entries (12", reissue, pink, clear or purple vinyl, in corresponding coloured p/s)	25
80	4AD CAD 13	IN THE FLAT FIELD (LP, 8 Hogarth Road address on rear sleeve)	12

MINT VALUE £

82	Beggars Banquet BEGA 38	PRESS THE EJECT AND GIVE ME THE TAPE (LP, with bonus 45 "Satori In Paris" [BH 1] & poster) 25
82	Beggars Banquet BEGA 42	THE SKY'S GONE OUT (LP, with bonus LP "Press The Eject And Give Me The Tape" [BEGA 38] inner sleeves & stickered sleeve) 20
83	Beggars Banquet BEGA 45P	BURNING FROM THE INSIDE (LP, picture disc) 20
83	Beggars Banquet BEGA 45P	BURNING FROM THE INSIDE (LP, with 5" die cut and BEGA 45P cat number on sleeve) ...15
85	Beggars Banquet BEGA 64	1979-1983 (2-LP, with inserts, 50,000 copies, numbered) 25
88	Beggars Banquet BAUCDBOX1	1979-1983 (2-CD box set with 64 page book and enamel badge, exclusive silver card sleeves) 50
92	Nemo 1 CD	REST IN PEACE - THE FINAL CONCERT (2-CD, mis-press with Nirvana album on disc 1) 25

(see also Sinister Ducks, Tones On Tail, David J, Bubblemen)

PETER BAUMANN
76	Virgin V 2069	ROMANCE '76 (LP) 12

JOAN BAXTER & BEAT MEN
64	Embassy WB 661	Baby Love/GERRY GLEN: Tokto Melody 5

ART BAXTER
56	Philips PB 652	Jingle Rock/Rock And Roll Rag (78) 10
57	Philips PB 666	Don't Knock The Rock/Rock Rock Rock (78) 10
57	Philips BBR 8107	ROCK YOU SINNERS (10" LP) 150

DAVID BAXTER
70	Reflection REFL 9	GOODBYE DAVE (LP, white/brown label) 80

(see also David Lewis, Andwella)

LES BAXTER & HIS ORCHESTRA
54	Capitol CL 14166	I Love Paris/Manhattan 5
55	Capitol CL 14239	Earth Angel/Happy Baby (as Les Baxter & Bombers) 30
55	Capitol CL 14249	I Ain't Mad At You (with Bombers)/Blue Mirage 5
55	Capitol CL 14257	Unchained Melody/Blue Star (The Medic Theme) 5

(see also Leonard Pennario)

RONNIE BAXTER
60	Top Rank JAR 293	I Finally Found You/Is It Because? 5

B.B. BLUNDER
71	United Artists UP 35203	Sticky Living/Rocky Yagbatee Yagbag 10
71	United Artists UP 35204	Little Boy/10,000 Miles 20
71	United Artists UAG 29156	WORKERS' PLAYTIME (LP, gatefold sleeve) 50

(see also Reg King & B.B. Blunder, Action, Julie Driscoll Brian Auger & Trinity, Kevin Westlake, Mark Charig, Blossom Toes)

BBC RADIOPHONIC WORKSHOP/PETER HOWELL
64	Decca F 11837	Doctor Who/BRENDA & JOHNNY: This Can't Be Love (unboxed Decca logo) 30
72	Decca F 11837	Doctor Who/BRENDA & JOHNNY: This Can't Be Love (reissue, boxed logo) 10
73	BBC RESL 11	Doctor Who/Reg (blue label, credits 'Delia Derbyshire', 'TARDIS' p/s) 10
73	BBC RESL 11	Doctor Who/Reg (white label, credits 'Delia Derbyshire', 'TARDIS' p/s) 6
76	BBC RESL 11	Doctor Who/Reg (reissue, no p/s, silver label) 6
78	BBC RESL 11	Doctor Who/Reg (2nd reissue, in 'TARDIS' p/s, blue label, white rim) 6
80	PRT RESL 80	Doctor Who/The Astronauts ('Tom Baker' p/s, as 'Peter Howell & BBC Radiophonic Workshop') 8
82	PRT RESL 80	Doctor Who/The Astronauts (reissue, 'Peter Davison' p/s) 8
84	PRT RESL 80	Doctor Who/The Astronauts (2nd reissue, 'Colin Baker' p/s) 5
72	BBC REC 93S	TEST CARD MUSIC (LP) 20
73	BBC RED 93 S	FOURTH DIMENSION (LP) 15
76	BBC REC 225	OUT OF THIS WORLD (LP) 15
70	BBC REC 25 M	BBC RADIOPHONIC MUSIC - WORK BY DELIA DERBYSHIRE (LP) 20
78	BBC REC 307	THROUGH A GLASS DARKLY (LP) 30
78	BBC REC 316	DOCTOR WHO SOUND EFFECTS No. 19 (LP) 12
04	Rephlex 147 LP	MUSIC FROM THE BBC RADIOPHONIC WORKSHOP (4 x 10") 30

(see also Dr. Who, Jon Pertwee, Ray Cathode, Radiophonic Workshop, Ithaca, Alice Through The Looking Glass, Agincourt, Blossom Toes, Dudley Simpson & Brian Hodgson)

BEA & DEE
59	Capitol CL 15066	Jerry/Wishing Time 5

BEACH BOYS
SINGLES
62	Capitol CL 15273	Surfin' Safari/409 40
63	Capitol CL 15285	Ten Little Indians/County Fair 90
63	Capitol CL 15305	Surfin' USA/Shut Down 20
64	Capitol CL 15339	Fun, Fun, Fun/Why Do Fools Fall In Love 25
64	Capitol CL 15350	I Get Around/Don't Worry Baby (First pressing with purple labels) 8
64	Capitol CL 15361	When I Grow Up (To Be A Man)/She Knows Me Too Well 8
65	Capitol CL 15370	Dance, Dance, Dance/The Warmth Of The Sun 10
65	Capitol CL 15384	All Summer Long/Do You Wanna Dance 10
65	Capitol CL 15392	Help Me Rhonda/Kiss Me Baby 10
65	Capitol CL 15409	California Girls/Let Him Run Wild 10
65	Capitol CL 15425	The Little Girl I Once Knew/There's No Other (Like My Baby) 15
66	Capitol CL 15432	Barbara Ann/Girl Don't Tell Me 7
66	Capitol CL 15441	Sloop John B/You're So Good To Me 8
66	Capitol CL 15459	God Only Knows/Wouldn't It Be Nice 8
66	Capitol CL 15475	Good Vibrations/Wendy 6
67	Capitol CL 15502	Then I Kissed Her/Mountain Of Love 7
67	Capitol CL 15510	Heroes And Villains/You're Welcome 7
67	Capitol CL 15521	Wild Honey/Wind Chimes 8
68	Capitol CL 15527	Darlin'/Country Air 6
68	Capitol CL 15545	Friends/Little Bird 6
68	Capitol CL 15554	Do It Again/Wake The World 6
68	Capitol CL 15572	Bluebirds Over The Mountain/Never Learn Not To Love 6
69	Capitol CL 15598	Break Away/Celebrate The News 6
70	Capitol CL 15640	Cottonfields/The Nearest Faraway Place (black label) 5
70	Stateside SS 2181	Tears In The Morning/It's About Time 5
71	Stateside SS 2190	Long Promised Road/Deirdre 6
71	Stateside SS 2194	Don't Go Near The Water/Student Demonstration Time (demos in p/s £20) 6

72	Reprise K 14173	You Need A Mess Of Help To Stand Alone/Cuddle Up (p/s) 10
72	Capitol CMS 1	Wouldn't It Be Nice/Fun Fun Fun/California Girls (printed sleeve) 6
72	Capitol CMS 2	Barbara Ann/Dance Dance Dance/You're So Good To Me (printed sleeve) 6
74	Reprise K 14346	California Saga: California/Sail On Sailor/Marcella/I'm The Pied Piper (printed sleeve) 5
76	Reprise K 14411	Child Of Winter/Susie Cincinnati (withdrawn) 125
76	Reprise K 14440	Rock And Roll Music/The T.M. Song (p/s) 5
76	EMI PSR 402	Commercial for "20 Golden Greats"/Good Vibrations/Carl Wilson Interview (promo)............8
77	Reprise K 14481	Mona/Rock And Roll Music/Sail On Sailor/Marcella (p/s) 5
77	Capitol CL 15954	Little Saint Nick/Little Saint Nick (Instr.)/Santa Claus Is Coming To Town 7
78	Capitol CL 15969	Little Deuce Coupe/SUNRAYS: I Live For The Sun/SUPERSTOCKS: Hot Rod High (p/s)............5
79	Caribou 12-7204	Here Comes The Night/(Disco Version)/Baby Blue (12", p/s, blue vinyl) 10
79	Capitol BBP 26	SINGLES COLLECTION (26 x 7" box set) 50

EPs

63	Capitol EAP 1-20540	SURFIN' USA 30
64	Capitol EAP 1-20603	FUN, FUN, FUN 30
64	Capitol EAP 5267	FOUR BY THE BEACH BOYS 25
64	Capitol EAP 4-2198	BEACH BOYS CONCERT 25
64	Capitol EAP 1-20781	THE BEACH BOYS HITS 15
67	Capitol EAP 6-2458	GOD ONLY KNOWS 20

ALBUMS

62	Capitol T 1808	SURFIN' SAFARI (mono only) 45
63	Capitol (S)T 1890	SURFIN' USA (mono) 35
63	Capitol (S)T 1890	SURFIN' USA (stereo) 45
63	Capitol (S)T 1981	SURFER GIRL (mono) 25
63	Capitol (S)T 1981	SURFER GIRL (stereo) 35
63	Capitol (S)T 1998	LITTLE DEUCE COUPE (mono) 25
63	Capitol (S)T 1998	LITTLE DEUCE COUPE (stereo) 35
63	Capitol (S)T 2027	SHUT DOWN VOLUME 2 (mono) 25
63	Capitol (S)T 2027	SHUT DOWN VOLUME 2 (stereo) 35
64	Capitol (S)T 2164	THE BEACH BOYS' CHRISTMAS ALBUM (mono)..30
64	Capitol (S)T 2164	THE BEACH BOYS' CHRISTMAS ALBUM (stereo) 25
64	Capitol (S)T 2198	BEACH BOYS CONCERT (mono) 20
64	Capitol (S)T 2198	BEACH BOYS CONCERT (stereo) 25
64	Capitol (S)T 2110	ALL SUMMER LONG (mono) 20
64	Capitol (S)T 2110	ALL SUMMER LONG (stereo) 25
65	Capitol (S)T 2398	BEACH BOYS' PARTY! (mono) 20
65	Capitol (S)T 2398	BEACH BOYS' PARTY! (stereo) 25
65	Capitol (S)T 2269	BEACH BOYS TODAY! (mono) 20
65	Capitol (S)T 2269	BEACH BOYS TODAY! (stereo) 25
65	Capitol (S)T 2354	SUMMER DAYS (AND SUMMER NIGHTS!!) (mono) 20
65	Capitol (S)T 2354	SUMMER DAYS (AND SUMMER NIGHTS!!) (stereo) 25
66	Capitol (S)T 2458	PET SOUNDS 60
66	Capitol (S)T 20856	THE BEST OF THE BEACH BOYS 12
67	Capitol (S)T 1981	SURFER GIRL (reissue, non-flipback sleeve) 12
67	Capitol (S)T 20956	THE BEST OF THE BEACH BOYS VOL. 2 12
67	Capitol (S)T 9001	SMILEY SMILE 45
68	Capitol (S)T 2859	WILD HONEY (mono) 40
68	Capitol (S)T 2859	WILD HONEY (stereo) 20
68	Capitol (S)T 2895	FRIENDS (mono) 30
68	Capitol (S)T 2895	FRIENDS (stereo) 18
69	Capitol (S)T 21142	THE BEST OF THE BEACH BOYS VOL. 3 (mono) 15
69	Capitol (S)T 21142	THE BEST OF THE BEACH BOYS VOL. 3 (stereo) 12
69	Capitol E-T/E-ST 133	20/20 (mono, gatefold sleeve) 22
69	Capitol E-T/E-ST 133	20/20 (stereo, gatefold sleeve)..18

(The above LPs were originally issued with flipback sleeves & rainbow-rim black labels; later orange or yellow label copies are worth half-to-two-thirds the value.)

70	Stateside SSLA 8251	SUNFLOWER (gatefold sleeve)...25
71	Stateside SSL 10313	SURF'S UP (textured sleeve, with gatefold insert) 20
71	Stateside SSL 10313	SURF'S UP (textured sleeve, without gatefold insert) 15
73	Reprise/Brother K 54008	HOLLAND (with insert & bonus EP "Mount Vernon And Fairway" [K 54008/7] in p/s)..........30
73	Reprise/Brother K 54008	HOLLAND 12
81	WRC SM 651-657	THE CAPITOL YEARS (7-LP box set) 25
99	Simply Vinyl SVLP 149	PET SOUNDS (LP, reissue, 180gm vinyl) 18
00	Simply Vinyl SVLP 219	SMILEY SMILE (LP, reissue, 180gm vinyl) 15

(see also Brian Wilson, Dennis Wilson, Bruce Johnston, Legendary Masked Surfers, American Spring, Annette, Flame, Flames, California Music, Rutles, Moon, Murry Wilson, Survivors)

BEACH HOUSE

| 10 | Bella Union BELLAU 229 | Norway/Baby (red vinyl, p/s) ....8 |

BEACHCOMBER

| 70 | Parlophone R 5850 | Surfin' Soul/Nothing To Say..10 |

BEACHCOMBERS

| 63 | Columbia DB 7124 | Mad Goose/You Can't Sit Down ....30 |
| 64 | Columbia DB 7200 | Night Train/The Keel Row ....35 |

(see also Pat Wayne)

BEACH-NUTS

| 65 | London HL 9988 | Out In The Sun (Hey-O)/Someday Soon...35 |

(see also Angels, Strangeloves)

BEACON STREET UNION

| 68 | MGM MGM 1416 | Blue Suede Shoes/Four Hundred And Five ....25 |
| 68 | MGM MGM-C(S) 8069 | THE EYES OF THE BEACON STREET UNION (LP) ....80 |

BEADS

| 71 | Decca F13244 | Eeo Eio/Sweetie Peetie ....8 |

BEADY EYE

| 10 | Beady Eye EYE 1 | Bring The Light/Sons Of The Stage (4,000 only) ....20 |
| 10 | Beady Eye EYE 3 | Four Letter Word/World Outside My Room (4,000 only) ....20 |

11	Beady Eye EYE 4	The Roller/Two Of A Kind (unnumbered) 5
11	Beady Eye EYE 4	The Roller/Two Of A Kind (heavyweight vinyl sold via website, numbered)..............10
11	Beady Eye EYE 5	Millionaire/Man Of Misery 5

CARL BEAN
| 78 | Motown TMG 1108 | I Was Born This Way/Instrumental ....6 |
| 78 | Tamla Motown TMG 1108-12 | I Was Born This Way (Remix)/Instrumental (12") ....12 |

GEORGE BEAN
63	Decca F 11762	Secret Love/Lonely Weekends 25
64	Decca F 11808	Will You Be My Lover Tonight?/It Should Be You 15
64	Decca F 11922	A Sad Story/Er Um Er 10
65	Decca F 12228	She Belongs To Me/Why Must They Criticise? (as George Bean & Runners)...............15
67	CBS 2801	The Candy Shop Is Closed/Smile From Sequin 25
68	CBS 3374	Bring Back Lovin'/Floatin' 35

(see also Trifle, Bean & Loopy's Lot)

BEAN & LOOPY'S LOT
| 66 | Parlophone R 5458 | A Stitch In Time/Haywire ....60 |

(see also Alan Bown Set)

BEANO
| 75 | Deram DM 427 | Little Cinderalla/Bye And Bye ....7 |
| 77 | Decca F 13690 | Everybody Knows/Clowns Painted Smile (p/s) ....6 |

BEANS
| 62 | Starlite ST45 071 | Jumping Beans/Salute To Fitz ....10 |
| 62 | Starlite ST45 076 | Hey Janey/Crazy Dog ....15 |

BEAR
| 68 | Verve FTS 3059 | GREETINGS CHILDREN OF PARADISE (LP) ....35 |

EDWARD BEAR
| 72 | Capitol CL 15727 | Masquerade/Pirate King ....6 |

DEAN BEARD & CREW CATS
| 57 | London HLE 8463 | Rakin' And Scrapin'/On My Mind Again ....300 |
| 57 | London HLE 8463 | Rakin' And Scrapin'/On My Mind Again (78) ....50 |

BEARDED LADY
| 74 | Young Blood YB 1018 | Rock Star/Country Lady ....15 |

BEARS
79	Good Vibrations Intl. GVI 1	Insane/Decisions (p/s) 15
79	Waldo's JS 001	On Me/Wot's Up Mate (p/s, various designs, with insert) 12
86	Tigerbeat GROWL 001	INSANE!! (LP) 20

BEARZ
| 80 | Axis AXIS 2 | She's My Girl/Girls Will Do (p/s) ....20 |
| 84 | Occult OCC 1 | Darwin/Julie (p/s) ....12 |

BEAS
| 68 | Pama PM 744 | Dr. Goldfoot And His Bikini Machine/Where Do I Go From You ....50 |

BEAST
| 83 | I.D. EYE 3 | New Moone/Guardian (p/s, insert) ....5 |
| 83 | I.D. EYE T3 | New Moone/Guardian (12". p/s) ....10 |

(see also the Cramps)

BEASTIE BOYS
86	Def Jam A 7055	Hold It, Now Hit It/Acapulco (p/s)..5
86	Def Jam TA 7055	Hold It, Now Hit It/Acapulco (12", p/s)..10
86	Def Jam 650 114 7	She's On It/Slow'n'Low (p/s with 3 badges) 10
86	Def Jam 650 114 6	She's On It/Slow'n'Low/Hold On, Now Hit It (12", p/s)...10
87	Def Jam 650 169 7	It's The New Style/Paul Revere (p/s)...5
87	Def Jam 650 169 6	It's The New Style/It's The New Style (Instrumental)/Paul Revere/ Paul Revere (Instrumental) (12", p/s)...10
87	Def Jam 650 418 7	(You Gotta) Fight For Your Right (To Party)/Time To Get III (p/s) 6
87	Def Jam 650 418 6	(You Gotta) Fight For Your Right (To Party)/Time To Get III (12", p/s) 10
87	Def Jam BEASTP 1	No Sleep Till Brooklyn/Posse In Effect (plane-shaped picture disc) 15
87	Def Jam BEASTT 1	No Sleep Till Brooklyn/Posse In Effect (12", p/s)...10
87	Def Jam BEASTQ 3	Girls/She's Crafty (logo shaped picture disc)...8
89	Capitol 12CL 540	HEY LADIES (LOVE AMERICAN STYLE EP) (12", p/s) 15
92	Capitol CDCL 665	Jimmy James (Single Version)/The Blue Nun/Jimmy James (Original Original Version)/Drinkin' Wine (CD, slimline jewel case)...12
92	Capitol CDCLS 665	Frozen Metal Head/Jimmy James (Single Version)/So What'cha Want (All The Way Live Freestyle Version)/Jimmy James (Original Original Version) Drinkin' Wine (CD) 12
94	Capitol CL 716	Get It Together/Sabotage/Dope Little Song (green vinyl, p/s)...................................6
94	Capitol 10CL716	Get It Together/(Buck Wild Remix)/(Intrumental)/Sabotage (10" p/s)........................8
94	Capitol 7243 8 8173476	Sure Shot/Mullet Head/Sure Shot (Caldato Mix) (red vinyl, p/s)................................6
94	Capitol 10CL726	Sure Shot/Mullet Head/Sure Shot (Caldato Mix) (10" p/s) 8
99	Capitol 10CL818	Alive/Start/Alive Bra Remix) (10" p/s) 6
92	Capitol CDCL 653	PASS THE MIC (Netty's Girl/Something's Got To Give/Pass The Mic [Pt. 2, Skills To Pay The Bills]) (CD, slimline jewel case)..12
87	Def Jam 450 062 1	LICENSED TO ILL (LP, with poster) 15
89	Capitol EST2102	PAUL'S BOUTIQUE (LP) 20
92	Grand Royal EST 2171	CHECK YOUR HEAD (2-LP) 25
98	Grand Royal GR062	HELLO NASTY (2-LP, orange vinyl) 25
04	Capitol 7243 4 73397	TO THE 5 BOROUGHS (2-LP) 20

(see also Money Mark)

BEAT
79	2-Tone CHS TT 6	Tears Of A Clown/Ranking Full Stop (paper label, company sleeve) 8
79	2-Tone TT 6	Tears Of A Clown/Ranking Full Stop (later pressing, moulded label, company sleeve) 5
83	Go-Feet FEET 1217	Can't Get Used To Losing You (1983 Remix Version)/Mirror In The Bathroom/ Spar Wid Me (12", p/s)...8
80	Go-Feet BEAT 001	JUST CAN'T STOP IT (LP, with inner)..12

(see also Fine Young Cannibals)

NICKY BEAT & THE BEATNICKS
78   Rigid IS BEAT 1033   I Can Hear Voices/Split Second Love/Starstruck (p/s) 10

BEAT BOYS
63   Decca F 11730   That's My Plan/Third Time Lucky 30
(see also Rats)

BEAT BROTHERS
63   Polydor NH 52185   Nick Nack Hully Gully/Lantern Hully Gully 25
(see also Tony Sheridan & Beat Brothers, Bobby Patrick Big Six)

BEAT CHICS
64   Decca F 12016   Skinny Minnie/Now I Know 25

BEATHOVEN
88   CBS 651 626-7   Socrates/Socrates (withdrawn) 30

THE BEATLES
SINGLES : 1962
(Original Parlophone Beatles singles came in a variety of company sleeves which are referred to here as "Type X" etc. and are depicted in the illustrations at the back of this Guide.) (With "The Parlophone Co. Ltd." in upper or lower case & "Recording first published 1962," label text, without "Sold in UK ...". All Beatles 7" singles issued before 1967 have push-out centres unless otherwise stated)

62   Parlophone 45-R 4949   Love Me Do/P.S. I Love You (First pressing, red label, 'Ringo on drums & no tambourine' version; with or without "Made In Great Britain" credit, Matrix 7XCE 17144-1N/7XCE 17145-1N, in sleeve Type A, B or C) 150
62   Parlophone 45-R 4983   Love Me Do/P.S. I Love You (First pressing, red label, 'Ringo on drums & no tambourine' version; label variation with "Made In Great Britain" credit on only one side, Matrix 7XCE 17144-1N/7XCE 17145-1N, in sleeve Type A, B, or C) 130

SINGLES : 1963
(with "The Parlophone Co. Ltd." in either upper or lower case & "Recording first published 1963" label text without "Sold in the UK..." unless otherwise stated)

63   Parlophone 45-R 4983   Please Please Me/Ask Me Why (First pressing, red label; with or without "Made In Great Britain"credit, Matrix 7XCE 17217-1N/&XCE 17218-1N, in sleeve Type A, B or C) 200
63   Parlophone R 5015   From Me To You/Thank You Girl (First pressing, Matrixes: 7XCE 17329 - 1N/7XCE 17330 - 1N, in Type 1 sleeve) 15
63   Parlophone R5055   She Loves You/I'll Get You (First pressing, Matrix numbers: 7XCE 17395-1N/7XCE 17396-1N in Type 1 sleeve) 15
63   Parlophone R 5055   She Loves You/I'll Get You (First pressing, label variation, with elongated "Northern Songs Ltd" and different typography for "7XCEE. 17395" and "Recording First Published 1963" Matrix numbers: 7XCE 17395-1N/7XCE 17396-1N, in Type 1 sleeve) 15
63   Parlophone R 5055   She Loves You/I'll Get You (First pressing, second label variation, smaller "She Love You" typography and "Northern Songs Ltd" on three lines; Matrix numbers: 7XCE 17395-1N/7XCE 17396-1N, in Type 1 sleeve) 15
63   Parlophone R 5084   I Want To Hold Your Hand/This Boy (First pressing, with "The Parlophone Co. Ltd" in upper-case only, Matrixes: 7XCE 17559-1N/7XCE 17560-1N, in Type 1 sleeve) 15
63   Parlophone R 5084   I Want To Hold Your Hand/This Boy (First pressing, label variation with "N.C.B." after "Northern Songs Mus Ltd" with "The Parlophone Co. Ltd" in upper-case only, Matrixes: 7XCE 17559-1N/7XCE 17560-1N) 15
63   Parlophone R 4949   Love Me Do/P.S. I Love You (Second pressing, black label, with "The Parlophone Co. Ltd in upper-lower case, matrix suffixed with '1N' indicating 'Ringo on drums & no tambourine' version) 150
63   Parlophone 45-R 4983   Please Please Me/Ask Me Why (Second pressing, black label, with "The Parlophone Co. Ltd" in upper-lower case, with "45" prefix, Matrixes: 7XCE 17217-1N/7XCE 17218-1N) 20
63   Parlophone R 4983   Please Please Me/Ask Me Why (Third pressing, black label, with "The Parlophone Co. Ltd" in upper-lower case, without "45" prefix) 20

SINGLES : 1964
(with "The Parlophone Co. Ltd." in either upper or lower case & "Recording first published 1964" label text with "Sold in the UK..." unless otherwise stated)

64   Parlophone R 5114   Can't Buy Me Love/You Can't Do That (First pressing, with "The Parlophone Co. Ltd" in upper case, in Type 1 sleeve) 15
64   Parlophone R 5114   Can't Buy Me Love/You Can't Do That (First pressing with label variation, with "The Parlophone Co. Ltd" in upper case but "NCB" added after "Northern Songs") 20
64   Parlophone R 5160   A Hard Day's Night/Things We Said Today (First pressing in Type 1B sleeve) 15
64   Parlophone R 5200   I Feel Fine/She's A Woman (First pressing, with "The Parlophone Co. Ltd" in upper case, in Type 1B sleeve) 15
64   Parlophone R 5200   I Feel Fine/She's A Woman (First pressing, label variation, different "Northern Songs NCB" layout and "Recording First Published 1964" below Maxtrix number) 15
64   Parlophone R 5084   I Want To Hold Your Hand/This Boy (Second pressing) 60
64   Parlophone R 4949   Love Me Do/P.S. I Love You (Third pressing, black label, with "The Parlophone Co. Ltd" in upper case, matrix suffixed with 1N' indicating 'Ringo on drums & no tambourine' version) 80

(with "The Parlophone Co. Ltd.", "Recording first published 1962" & Sold in UK ... label text)
64   Parlophone R 4983   Please Please Me/Ask Me Why (Fourth pressing, with "The Parlophone Co. Ltd" in upper/lower case and "Sold in the U.K." label text) 80

SINGLES : 1965
(with "The Parlophone Co. Ltd." in upper case & "Sold in the UK...". 2nd and other pressings from 1965 have "The Gramophone Co. Ltd" unless otherwise stated)

65   Parlophone DP 562   If I Fell/Tell Me Why (First U.K. pressing of 1964 export single, Matrixes: &XCE 17756-1N/7XCE 17757-1N, in Type 1B sleeve) 100
65   Parlophone R 5265   Ticket To Ride/Yes It Is (First pressing, in Type 2 sleeve) 15
65   Parlophone R 5265   Ticket To Ride/Yes It Is (First pressing, label variation, smaller "Sold In U.K..." text, larger "Northern Songs NCB" type and (Lennon-McCartney) credit longer than "Ticket To Ride" song title) 15
65   Parlophone R 5265   Ticket To Ride/Yes It Is (First pressing, label variation, smaller "Northern Songs NCB" type, brackets around matrix number, larger "Trade Mark" and "Parlophone" logos and "T" in "Gt Britain" is in upper (T), not lower case (t)) 15
65   Parlophone R 5305   Help!/I'm Down (First pressing, in Type 2 sleeve) 15
65   Parlophone R 5305   Help!/I'm Down (Second pressing, with "The Gramophone Co Ltd" label text) 15
65   Parlophone R 5389   We Can Work It Out/Day Tripper (First pressing, in Type 3 sleeve) 15
65   Parlophone R 5389   We Can Work It Out/Day Tripper (Second pressing, with "The Gramophone Co Ltd" label text) 15
65   Parlophone R 5389   We Can Work It Out/Day Tripper (Second pressing, label variation with different type for "Sold In U.K..." "Northern Songs NCB", matrix number and date. Comma "," separates "Lennon, McCartney" rather than a dash "-") 15

65	Parlophone R 4949	Love Me Do/P.S. I Love You (Fourth pressing, black label, with "The Parlophone Co. Ltd" in upper case, "T" in "Gt Britain" now upper case to read "GT. Britain" "Recorded first published" also now in lower case: matrix suffixed with 1N' indicating 'Ringo on drums & no tambourine' version)	100

SINGLES : 1966

(with "The Gramophone Co. Ltd." in upper case & "Sold in the UK...". label text, unless otherwise stated)

66	Parlophone R 5452	Paperback Writer/Rain (First pressing, in Type 4 or 5 sleeve)	15
66	Parlophone R 5452	Paperback Writer/Rain (First pressing, label variation, with larger "Northern Songs, NCB" credit and larger "P" before "1966")	15
66	Parlophone R 5493	Yellow Submarine/Eleanor Rigby (First pressing, in Type 5 or 6 sleeve)	15
66	Parlophone R 5493	Yellow Submarine/Eleanor Rigby (First pressing, label variation with larger "Northern Songs, NCB", no brackets on Matrix number, larger circled "P" and larger typeface for "Eleanor Rigby")	15
66	Parlophone R 5493	Yellow Submarine/Eleanor Rigby (First pressing, label variation with mid-size "Northern Songs, NCB", no brackets on Matrix number, with comma "," separating "Lennon, McCartney" rather than a "-" "Lennon-McCartney", larger typeface for "Eleanor Rigby" and "Sold In U.K...")	15
66	Parlophone R5493	Yellow Submarine/Eleanor Rigby (Second pressing, solid centre, label variation, larger "Northern Songs, NCB" text, smaller "Lennon-McCartney" credit and larger circled "P")	20
66	Parlophone R 5493	Yellow Submarine/Eleanor Rigby (Second pressing, solid centre label variation, larger "Northern Songs, NCB" text, no brackets on Matrix number and larger typeface on "Eleanor Rigby")	15
66	Parlophone R 5084	I Want To Hold Your Hand/This Boy (Third pressing, solid centre, "The Parlophone Co" rim text)	80
66	Parlophone R 5114	Can't Buy Me Love/You Can't Do That (Second pressing, solid centre, with "The Parlophone Co. Ltd" label text)	150
66	Parlophone R 5200	I Feel Fine/She's A Woman (Second pressing, solid centre)	150

SINGLES : 1967

(All pressings after 1967 have push-out or solid centres with "The Gramophone Co. Ltd." in upper case & "Sold in the UK..." label text, unless otherwise stated)

67	Parlophone R 5570	Strawberry Fields Forever/Penny Lane (First pressing, 250,000 only in p/s)	70
67	Parlophone R 5570	Strawberry Fields Forever/Penny Lane (Second pressing, in Type 5,6 or 7 sleeve)	15
67	Parlophone R 5655	Hello, Goodbye/I Am The Walrus (First pressing, company sleeve, with "7/- to 50/- " on reverse)	12
67	Parlophone R 5655	Hello Goodbye/I Am The Walrus (First pressing, label variation with "Northern Songs NCB" on three lines not two, different typeface and matrix number appearing beneath date of "1967", smaller typeface for "Hello, Goodbye" and "Lennon, McCartney" separated by a "," rather than a "-", "Lennon-McCartney")	15
67	Parlophone R 5620	All You Need Is Love/Baby You're A Rich Man (First pressing, solid or pushout centre, with no reference to "Live World Television Transmission")	70
67	Parlophone R 5620	All You Need Is Love/Baby You're A Rich Man (Second pressing, with reference to "Live WorldTelevision Transmission")	15
67	Parlophone R 5620	All You Need Is Love/Baby You're A Rich Man (Second pressing, label variation, push-out/solid centre with reference to "Live World Television Transmission" and "Northern Songs NCB" on three lines rather than two, brackets around matrix number, "1967" above Matrix number and "Recorded during 'Live;..." text starts after Lennon-McCartney credit rather than beneath it)	25
67	Parlophone R 5452	Paperback Writer/Rain (Second pressing, solid centre only)	80
67	Parlophone R 5493	Yellow Submarine/Eleanor Rigby (Second pressing, solid centre only)	15
67	Parlophone R5305	Help/I'm Down (Third pressing, solid centre, "The Gramophone Co. Ltd" and "Sold in U.K...." label text)	100
67	Parlophone R5305	Help/I'm Down (Third pressing, solid centre, "The Parlophone Co. Ltd" and "Sold in U.K...." label text)	80

SINGLES : 1968

(All Apple pressings except for early issues of "Let It Be" come in black glossy 'Apple' sleeves)

68	Parlophone R 5675	Lady Madonna/The Inner Light (First pressing, with Fan Club insert; sleeve with 7/- to 50/- on reverse)	55
68	Apple R 5722	Hey Jude/Revolution (First pressing, push-out or solid centre)	20
68	Parlophone R 5675	Lady Madonna/The Inner Light (Second pressing, no insert)	15
68	Parlophone R 5084	I Want To Hold Your Hand/This Boy (Fourth pressing, solid centre, with "The Gramophone Co" rim text)	200

SINGLES : 1969

(All Apple pressings except for early issues of "Let It Be" come in black gloss "Apple" sleeves)

69	Apple R 5777	Get Back/Don't Let Me Down (First pressing, push-out or solid centre, as "The Beatles with Billy Preston")	20
69	Apple R 5777	Get Back/Don't Let Me Down (First pressing, label variation with "Northern Songs/NCB" rather than "Northern Songs" solid centre or push-out centre, as "The Beatles with Billy Preston")	20
69	Apple R 5777	Get Back/Don't Let Me Down (Second pressing, solid centre or push-out centre as "The Beatles with Billy Preston", without "Sold in UK..." label text)	20
69	Apple R 5786	Ballad Of John And Yoko/Old Brown Shoe (First pressing, solid or push-out centre)	20
69	Apple R 5786	Ballad Of John And Yoko/Old Brown Shoe (Second pressing, solid centre or push-out centre without "Sold in UK..." label text)	18
69	Apple R 5814	Something/Come Together (First pressing, solid centre or push-out centre without "Sold in UK..." label text)	45
69	Apple R 5722	Hey Jude/Revolution (Second pressing, without "Sold in UK..." label text)	15
69	Parlophone R 5305	Help!/I'm Down (Fourth pressing, with "The Parlophone Co. Ltd" but no "Sold In U.K..." label text)	40
69	Parlophone R 5389	We Can Work It Out/Day Tripper (Third pressing, solid centre, no "sold in U.K..." label text)	80
69	Parlophone R 5452	Paperback Writer/Rain (Third pressing, no "Sold in U.K...." label text)	40
69	Parlophone R 5570	Strawberry Fields Forever/Penny Lane (Third pressing, no "Sold In U.K..." label text)	35
69	Parlophone R 5493	Yellow Submarine/Eleanor Rigby (Third pressing, no "Sold In U.K...." label text)	40
69	Parlophone R 5620	All You Need Is Love/Baby You're A Rich Man (Third pressing, no "Sold In U.K..." label text, push-out centre)	40
69	Parlophone R5675	Lady Madonna/The inner Burning Light (Third pressing, with "pip" in centre of label, no "Sold UN U.K..." label text)	35
69	Parlophone R5675	Lady Madonna/The Inner Burning Light (Fourth pressing, with no "Sold In U.K..." label text)	35

SINGLES : 1970

70	Apple R 5833	Let It Be/You Know My Name (Look Up The Number) (First pressing, scratched-out B-side matrix: APPLES 1002, p/s)	30
70	Apple R 5833	Let It Be/You Know My Name (Look Up The Number) (Second pressing, scratched-out B-side matrix: APPLES 1002, no p/s)	15
70	Apple R 5833	Let It Be/You Know My Name (Look Up The Number) (Third pressing, B-side matrix: 7YCE 21408, no p/s)	15

SINGLES : 70S, 80S, 90S & 00S SINGLES: REISSUES AND PICTURE DISCS

(Please note that 1970s Parlophone copies of Beatles singles with EMI boxed logos are of nominal value. Add £10 to the value for any single with a red & white 'Factory Sample Not For Sale' sticker.)

78	Parlophone R 6022	Sgt. Pepper's Lonely Hearts Club Band/With A Little Help From My Friends/A Day In The Life (p/s)	8
78	Parlophone R 6022	Sgt. Peppers Lonely Hearts Club Band/With A Little Help From My Friends/A Day In The Life (p/s)	6
82	Parlophone R 4949	Love Me Do/P.S. I Love You (p/s, red label reissue, with "mono" notice &publishing miscredited to "Ardmore & Beechwood" -4 Matrix, Andy White version)	10
82	Parlophone RP 4949	Love Me Do/P.S. I Love You (7" picture disc, with/without publishing miscredit)	10
82	Parlophone 12R 4949	Love Me Do/P.S. I Love You/Love Me Do (Original Single Version) (12", p/s)	10
83	Parlophone RP 4983	Please Please Me/Ask Me Why (picture disc)	7
83	Parlophone RP 5015	From Me To You/Thank You Girl (picture disc, some with Souvenir From Abbey Road Studios sticker on sleeve)	10
83	Parlophone RP 5015	From Me To You/Thank You Girl (picture disc, some with Souvenir From Abbey Road Studios sticker on sleeve)	10
83	Parlophone RP 5015	From Me To You/Thank You Girl (picture disc, some with Souvenir From Abbey Road Studios sticker on sleeve)	7
83	Parlophone RP 5055	She Loves You/I'll Get You (picture disc)	12
	(Issued in PVC sleeve)		
83	Parlophone RP 5084	I Want To Hold Your Hand/This Boy (picture disc)	7
83	Parlophone R 5570	Penny Lane/Strawberry Fields Forever	8
84	Parlophone RP 5114	Can't Buy Me Love/You Can't Do That (picture disc)	7
84	Parlophone RP 5160	A Hard Day's Night/Things We Said Today (picture disc)	15
84	Parlophone RP 5200	I Feel Fine/She's A Woman (picture disc)	7
85	Parlophone RP 5265	Ticket To Ride/Yes It Is (picture disc)	7
85	Parlophone RP 5305	Help!/I'm Down (picture disc)	7
85	Parlophone RP 5389	We Can Work It Out/Day Tripper (picture disc)	7
86	Parlophone RP 5452	Paperback Writer/Rain (picture disc)	15
86	Parlophone RP 5493	Yellow Submarine/Eleanor Rigby (picture disc)	8
87	Parlophone RP 5570	Strawberry Fields Forever/Penny Lane (picture disc, later with slightly larger picture on disc)	8
87	Parlophone RP 5620	All You Need Is Love/Baby You're A Rich Man (picture disc)	8
87	Parlophone 12R 5620	All You Need Is Love/Baby You're A Rich Man (12", p/s)	10
87	Parlophone RP 5655	Hello, Goodbye/I Am The Walrus (picture disc)	7
88	Parlophone RP 5675	Lady Madonna/The Inner Light (picture disc, with "Past Masters" insert)	7
88	Apple RP 5722	Hey Jude/Revolution (picture disc, with "Apple" insert)	7
	(Issued in PVC sleeve)		
88	Apple 12R 5722	Hey Jude/Revolution (12", p/s)	25
88	Apple 12RP 5722	Hey Jude/Revolution (12", picture disc with "Apple" insert)	12
89	Apple RP 5777	Get Back/Don't Let Me Down (with Billy Preston,picture disc, with "20th Anniversary" insert)	7
89	Apple RP 5786	Ballad Of John And Yoko/Old Brown Shoe (picture disc, with "20th Anniversary" insert)	7
89	Apple RP 5814	Something/Come Together (picture disc, with "20th Anniversary" insert)	7
	(Issued in PVC sleeve)		
90	Apple RP 5833	Let It Be/You Know My Name (Look Up The Number) (picture disc, with "20th Anniversary" insert)	7
95	Apple R 6422	Free As A Bird/Christmastime Is Here Again (7", p/s)	8
95	Apple CDR 6422	Free As A Bird/I Saw Her Standing There/ This Boy/Christmastime Is Here (5" CD)	10
96	Apple R 6425	Real Love/Baby's In Black (7", p/s)	8
96	Apple CDR 6425	Real Love/Baby's In Black/Yellow Submarine/Here There And Everywhere (5" CD)	10
10	Parlophone 5099964163970	Paperback Writer/Rain (jukebox centre)	40

SINGLES : CONTRACT PRESSINGS: SINGLES

(Records were often pressed by non-EMI companies under contract, owing to overwhelming demand for Beatles records. Subtle differences indicating their origin can be detected. Philips pressings (the 'Hey Jude' single only) are the easiest to spot as they alone have three-pronged centres. All the others had four except for the French Pathe-Marconi pressings of 'Hello Goodbye' which have solid centres and 'Made In France' at the foot of the label. The centre of a Decca contract pressing has a ridge 3mm from the perimeter. Pre-1966 EMI pressings have flat push-out centres. Thereafter many records were produced with a mix of push-out and solid centres. EMI always pressed stamper letters into the vinyl, positioned at 3 o'clock to the matrix number. Up to three letters from the code 'GRAMOPHLTD' were used each representing a number. EMI stamper letters are seldom seen on contract pressings. Great controversy has surrounded the origin of the only other known style of pre-1965 Beatles' contract pressings. Previously thought to have been made by Pye they are now believed to have been pressed at the ORIOLE pressing plant before their September 1964 aquisition by CBS. The centres of these pressings have no ridge and are finished with rough edges. They are also thicker and heavier than any of the other pressings. Although released in November 1964 'I Feel Fine' also has these characteristics and is assumed to have come from this source. CBS using the old ORIOLE presses. However, it is thought that PYE actually pressed one Beatles 45 and one EP after 1964. The centres of these two pressings look very similar to those made by DECCA but have a less prominent ridge. The edges of records made by PHILIPS, ORIOLE and PYE are not straight-cut but are tapered off. The edges of EMI, DECCA and Pathe-Marconi pressings are all straight-cut. (Decca contract pressings have no stamper letters (G or D) positioned at 3 o'clock to the matrix number; the centre has a ridge 3mm from the perimeter. Pye pressings have no stamper letters (G or D) at 3 o'clock to the matrix number; the centre has no ridge, and is finished with rough edges. They are also thicker and heavier than any of the other pressings. The edges of records made by PHILIPS, ORIOLE and PYE are not straight-cut but are tapered off. The edges of EMI, DECCA and Pathe-Marconi pressings are all straight-cut. (Decca contract pressings have no stamper letters (G or D) positioned at 3 o'clock to the matrix number; the centre has no ridge, and is finished with rough edges. Pye pressings between 1973 and 1979 are a dark, translucent red when held up to a strong light.) Let us hope that the online community of Beatles fans and collectors worldwide will one day solve the magical mystery tour of Beatles contract pressings. Until that day, the following is where we at Record Collector stand at the present time)

63	Parlophone R 5055	She Loves You/I'll Get You (Decca pressing)	25
63	Parlophone R 5055	She Loves You/I'll Get You (Decca pressing, variation, "Parlophone Co.Ltd" in upper case, different typography for "Northern Songs" Matrix number and "Recording First Published 1963")	25
63	Parlophone R 5084	I Want To Hold Your Hand/This Boy (Decca pressing)	25
63	Parlophone R 5084	I Want To Hold Your Hand/This Boy (Decca pressing, label variation with "N.C.B." after "Northern Songs Mus. Ltd.")	25

(Records pressed by non-EMI companies on contract, owing to overwhelming demand; Decca contract pressings have no stamper letters (G or D) positioned at 3 o'clock to the matrix number; the centre has a ridge 3mm from the perimeter. Pye pressings have no stamper letters (G or D) at 3 o'clock to the matrix number; the centre has no ridge, and is finished with rough edges. Pye pressings are thicker and heavier than EMI and Decca pressings)

63	Parlophone R 5084	I Want To Hold Your Hand/This Boy (Pye pressing)	30
63	Parlohone R 5084	I Want To Hold Your Hand/This Boy (Pye pressing, label variant with differnt typography and "N.C.B." after "Northern Songs Mus Ltd.")	25
64	Parlophone R 5114	Can't Buy Me Love/You Can't Do That (Pye pressing)	22
64	Parlophone R5114	Can't Buy Me Love/You Can't Do That (Pye contract pressing with solid centre, side 1, matrix 7XCE 17657-1N)	40
64	Parlophone R 5114	Can't Buy Me Love/You Can't Do That (Pye pressing label variation with "NCB" out of alignment with the "N" and "S" of "Northern Songs")	25
64	Parlophone R 5200	I Feel Fine/She's A Woman (Pye pressing)	25
64	Parlophone R 5200	I Feel Fine/She's A Woman (Decca pressing)	25

65	Parlophone R 5305	Help!/I'm Down (Decca contract pressing)	25
67	Parlophone R 5655	Hello Goodbye/I Am The Walrus (Decca pressing)	25
67	Parlophone R 5655	Hello Goodbye/I Am The Walrus (Decca contract pressing, label variation, with "Northern Songs NCB" on three lines not two, "1967" above not below matrix number and "Lennon, McCartney" separated by a comma ',' rather than a "-", "Lennon-McCartney")	25
68	Apple R 5722	Hey Jude/Revolution (Decca contract pressing)	38
68	Apple R 5722	Hey Jude/Revolution (Pye contract pressing)	40
68	Apple R 5722	Hey Jude/Revolution (Philips contract pressing, three-pronged push-out centre)	70

SINGLES : DEMO SINGLES

(Beatles demo singles between 1962 and 1966 have a red "A" on the A side unless otherwise stated. Demos from All You Need Is Love (1967) to Something (1969) have a white "A" on a green label. Finally, demos with the centre's missing are worth half these values)

62	Parlophone 45-R 4949	Love Me Do/P.S. I Love You (Demo copy, McCartney misspelt "McArtney", 250 only)	5000
63	Parlophone 45-R 4983	Please Please Me/Ask Me Why (demo copy)	1500
63	Parlophone (45-)R 5015	From Me To You/Thank You Girl (Demo copy, with or without '45-' prefix)	750
63	Parlophone R 5055	She Loves You/I'll Get You (Demo copy)	750
63	Parlophone R 5084	I Want To Hold Your Hand/This Boy (Demo copy)	750
64	Parlophone R 5114	Can't Buy Me Love/You Can't Do That (Demo copy)	750
64	Parlophone R 5160	A Hard Day's Night/Things We Said Today (Demo copy, red "A" on both sides)	750
64	Parlophone R 5200	I Feel Fine/She's A Woman (Demo single, existence unconfirmed)	0
65	Parlophone R 5265	Ticket To Ride/Yes It Is (Demo copy)	650
65	Parlophone R 5305	Help!/I'm Down (Demo copy, existence unconfirmed)	0
65	Parlophone R 5389	We Can Work It Out/Day Tripper (Demo copy, red "A" on both sides)	500
66	Parlophone R 5452	Paperback Writer/Rain (Demo copy)	450
66	Parlophone R 5493	Yellow Submarine/Eleanor Rigby (Demo copy, existence unconfirmed)	0
67	Parlophone R 5570	Strawberry Fields Forever/Penny Lane (existence unconfirmed)	0
67	Parlophone R 5655	Hello, Goodbye/I Am The Walrus	500
67	Parlophone R 5620	All You Need Is Love/Baby You're A Rich Man (Demo copy)	450
68	Apple (no cat. no.)	Hey Jude/Revolution (Demo copy, green & white Apple 'custom' label, handwritten details)	450
69	Apple R 5777	Get Back/Don't Let Me Down (Demo copy, green and white Apple 'custom' label test pressing,typed details)	400
69	Parlophone R 5786	Ballad Of John And Yoko/Old Brown Shoe (Demo copy, existence unconfirmed)	0
68	Parlophone R 5675	Lady Madonna/The Inner Light (Demo copy)	500
69	Parlophone R 5814	Something/Come Together (Demo copy)	600
70	Parlophone R 5833	Let It Be/You Know My Name (Look Up The Number) (existence unconfirmed)	0
76	Parlophone R 6013	Yesterday/I Should Have Known Better (Demo, silver/black paer label with a silver "A", green generic p/s)	25
76	Parlophone R 6016	Back In The U.S.S.R./Twist And Shout (silver/black paper label with a silver "A",green generic p/s)	25
78	Parlophone R 6022	Sgt. Pepper's Lonely Hearts Club Band/With A Little Help From My Friends/A Day In The Life (silver/black paper label with a silver "A", p/s)	25

SINGLES : FRENCH PRESSINGS - SINGLES

| 67 | Parlophone R 5655 | Hello Goodbye/I Am The Walrus (Pathé Marconi pressing, alleged push-out centre version) | 100 |
| 67 | Parlophone R 5655 | Hello Goodbye/I Am The Walrus (Pathé Marconi pressing) | 25 |

SINGLES : POLYDOR RECORDINGS

(With push-out centres & orange labels)

62	Polydor NH 66833	My Bonnie/The Saints (When The Saints Go Marching In) (as Tony Sheridan & The Beatles; 1st pressing, 'broad' title& "Made In England" label text)	100
63	Polydor NH 66833	My Bonnie/The Saints (When The Saints Go Marching In) (as Tony Sheridan & The Beatles, push-out or solid centre,'narrow' title & "Made In England" label text)	65
64	Polydor NH 52275	Cry For A Shadow (A-side credited to 'Beatles')/TONY SHERIDAN & THE BEATLES: Why (Can't You Love Me Again) ('scroll' label, with "Made In England" text)	50
64	Polydor NH 52317	Ain't She Sweet (A-side as 'The Beatles, vocal: John Lennon')/If You Love Me, Baby (B-side credited to 'The Beatles with Tony Sheridan, vocal'; 1st pressing, 'scroll' label with "Made In England" label text)	45
64	Polydor NH 52317	Ain't She Sweet/If You Love Me, Baby (2nd pressing, red label, with "Made In England" text)	20
64	Polydor NH 52906	Sweet Georgia Brown/Nobody's Child (German import only, unissued in U.K.)	40

SINGLES : SINGLES BOX SETS

76	Parlophone/Apple BS 24	THE BEATLES' SINGLES COLLECTION 1962-1970 (24 x 7", each in green p/s, green & white stickered box set)	45
76	Parlophone/Apple/ World Record Club	THE BEATLES' COLLECTION (24 x 7", mail-order black box set; later copies with "Sgt. Pepper's Lonely Hearts Club Band" [R 6022])	45
78	Parlophone/Apple BSC 1	THE BEATLES' SINGLES COLLECTION (26 x 7" blue box set, with insert; some copies include mispressing of "Get Back" [Apple R 5777])	40
82	Parlophone/Apple BSCP 1	THE BEATLES' SINGLES COLLECTION (27 x 7" blue box set, with bonus picture disc "Love Me Do" [RP 4949], export issue)	45
82	Parlophone/Apple BSCP 1	THE BEATLES' SINGLES COLLECTION (27 x 7" blue box set, with mispressed picture disc Love Me Do/"Love Me Do" [RP 4949], export issue)	50
89	Parlophone/Apple CDBSC 1	THE BEATLES' SINGLES COLLECTION (22 x 3" CD single box set)	75
89	Parlophone/Apple CDBSCP 1	THE BEATLES' SINGLES COLLECTION (22 x 5" CD single box set)	65

SINGLES : UNIQUE PROMO SINGLES

68	Apple (no cat. no.)	OUR FIRST FOUR (4 x 7" in presentation pack, including "Hey Jude" [R 5722] & "Those Were The Days" by Mary Hopkin [APPLE 2], "Sour Milk Sea" by Jackie Lomax [APPLE 3] & "Thingumybob" by Black Dyke Mills Band [APPLE 4]; each mounted in PVC pocket on printe.	2500
68	Apple (no cat. no.)	OUR FIRST FOUR (4 x 7" in presentation pack, including "Hey Jude" [R 5722] & "Those Were The Days" by Mary Hopkin [APPLE 2], "Sour Milk Sea" by Jackie Lomax [APPLE 3] & "Thingumybob" by Black Dyke Mills Band [APPLE 4]; each mounted in PVC pocket on printe.	1000
76	EMI SPSR 401	Medley Of Songs For "Rock'n'Roll Music" (excerpts)	500

EXPORT SINGLES

64	Parlophone DP 562	If I Fell/Tell Me Why (First pressing, export single without "Sold in UK..." label text)	65
65	Parlophone DP 563	Yesterday/Dizzy Miss Lizzy (export single)	90
66	Parlophone DP 564	Michelle/Drive My Car (export single)	150
68	Parlophone DP 570	Hey Jude/Revolution (Export copy with Swedish p/s)	60
68	Parlophone DP 570	Hey Jude/Revolution (Export copy without Swedish p/s)	45
70	Parlophone P-R 5833	Let It Be/You Know My Name (Look Up The Number) (Export copy, no p/s)	60

("Let It Be" was pressed with "Parlophone" label text on one side & "Gramophone" on the other)

| 70 | Apple P-R 5833 | Let It Be/You Know My Name (Look Up The Number) (Export copy, no p/s) ....300 |

EPS : 1963

(With "The Parlophone Co. Ltd" and "Recording first published 1963" label text. Unless otherwise stated, all 60s EPs have push-out centres and laminated flipback sleeves.)

63	Parlophone GEP 8882	TWIST AND SHOUT (EP, First pressing)...12
63	Parlophone GEP 8880	THE BEATLES' HITS (EP, First pressing, without "Recording first published 1963" label text)..12
63	Parlophone GEP 8883	THE BEATLES (No. 1) (EP, first pressing, without "Recording first published 1963" label text)...12
63	Parlophone GEP 8880	THE BEATLES' HITS (EP, Second pressing) 12

EPS : 1964

(With "The Parlophone Co. Ltd." & "Recording first published 1964" label text & "Sold in the UK..." unless otherwise stated)

64	Parlophone GEP 8891	ALL MY LOVING (EP, First pressing without "Sold in UK" label text) 15
64	Parlophone GEP 8891	ALL MY LOVING (EP, Second pressing, with "Sold in U.K...." label text) 12
64	Parlophone GEP 8899	GOLDEN DISCS (unreleased, 2 x 1-sided test pressings [matrices: 7TCE-1N & 7TCE-1N] & 1 set of label proofs only;price does not include labels)........................2500
64	Parlophone GEP 8913	LONG TALL SALLY (EP, First pressing)...20
64	Parlophone GEP 8920	EXTRACTS FROM THE FILM "A HARD DAY'S NIGHT" (EP)................................20
64	Parlophone GEP 8924	EXTRACTS FROM THE ALBUM "A HARD DAY'S NIGHT" (EP) 30
64	Parlophone GEP 8882	TWIST AND SHOUT (EP, Second pressing) 12

EPS : 1965

(With "The Parlophone Co. Ltd", & "Sold in UK.." label text, unless otherwise stated.)

65	Parlophone GEP 8931	BEATLES FOR SALE (EP, First pressing)...25
65	Parlophone GEP 8938	BEATLES FOR SALE (No. 2) (EP, first pressing) 35
65	Parlophone GEP 8946	THE BEATLES MILLION SELLERS (EP, with 'Golden Discs' text on labels)................20
65	Parlophone GEP 8883	THE BEATLES (No. 1) (EP, Second pressing, with "The Gramophone Co Ltd" & "Sold in UK..." label text)...10
65	Parlophone GEP 8880	THE BEATLES' HITS (EP, Third pressing, with "The Gramophone Co Ltd" & "Sold in UK..." label text)...10
65	Parlophone GEP 8882	TWIST AND SHOUT (Third pressing, with "The Gramophone Co Ltd" & "Sold in UK..." label text)...10

EPS : 1966

(With "The Gramophone Co. Ltd" & "Sold in UK..." label text unless otherwise stated.)

66	Parlophone GEP 8948	YESTERDAY (EP, First pressing)..75
66	Parlophone GEP 8952	NOWHERE MAN (EP, first pressing) 120
66	Parlophone GEP 8946	THE BEATLES' MILLION SELLERS (EP, Second pressing, with "Million Sellers" label text) 15

EPS : 1967 (EPS)

(With "The Gramophone Co. Ltd" & "Sold in UK..." label text unless otherwise stated. Please note that any EP titles with "The Gramophone Co Ltd" but without "Sold in UK..." are 70s re-pressings and are worth half these listed values. Later copies with EMI label text & varnished sleeves are worth around one-third of the listed values).

67	Parlophone MMT-1	MAGICAL MYSTERY TOUR (2-EP, gatefold sleeve, first pressing with booklet & blue lyric sheet; push-out or solid centre; mono) 50
67	Parlophone SMMT-1	MAGICAL MYSTERY TOUR (2-EP, gatefold sleeve, first pressing with booklet & blue lyric sheet; stereo)...70
67	Parlophone GEP 8931	BEATLES FOR SALE (EP, Second pressing with "The Parlophone Co. Ltd" label text; solid centre) 25
67	Parlophone GEP 8952	NOWHERE MAN (EP, Second pressing solid centre) 35

EPS : CONTRACT PRESSINGS : EPS

| 66 | GEP 8946 | THE BEATLES MILLION SELLERS (EP, Pye contract pressing, with 'Golden Discs' text on labels)..50 |

EPS : EPS REISSUES AND BOXED SETS

73	Parlophone SMMT-1	MAGICAL MYSTERY TOUR (2-EP, gatefold sleeve, stereo only, with booklet & yellow lyric sheet)..15
81	Parlophone BEP 14	THE BEATLES EP COLLECTION (14-EP box set, with bonus stereo EP [SGE 1])..............120
95	Apple R 6406	Baby It's You/I'll Follow The Sun/Devil In Her Heart/Boys (7" EP)...........................15
95	Apple CDR 6406	Baby It's You/I'll Follow The Sun/Devil In Her Heart/Boys (5" CD EP)......................10

EPS : POLYDOR RECORDINGS : EPS

| 64 | Polydor EPH 21 610 | TONY SHERIDAN WITH THE BEATLES (1st pressing, German import in U.K. p/s, orange 'scroll' label; Why songwriting credit as 'Sheridan' or 'Sheridan-Crompton')....................100 |
| 64 | Polydor EPH 21 610 | TONY SHERIDAN WITH THE BEATLES (2nd pressing, German import in U.K. p/s, red label;Why songwriting credit as 'Sheridan' or 'Sheridan-Crompton') ....40 |

ALBUMS : 1963

(With "The Parlophone Co Ltd" label text but without "Sold in UK..." label text, unless otherwise stated. First pressings of PLEASE PLEASE ME and WITH THE BEATLES have polythene-lined "Use Emitex" die-cut inners. Flipback sleeves).

63	Parlophone PMC 1202	PLEASE PLEASE ME (First pressing, black & gold label, with "Dick James Mus. Co." publishing credit for "I Saw Her Standing There", "Misery", Do You Want To Know A Secret & "There's A Place"; "Made by Ernest J Day" sleeve with printers credit on right hand side rear of sleeve; Front photo credited to "Angus McBean" at bottom far right of front cover of sleeve less than 5mm from edge. "A" of Angus starting under second letter "S" in the word "songs" in the album title: large mono in top right corner. Research estimates that around 25,000 pressed) 1000
63	Parlophone PCS 3042	PLEASE PLEASE ME (First pressing, black & gold label, with "Dick James Mus. Co." publishing credit for "Please Please Me", "I Saw Her Standing There", "Misery", Do You Want To Know A Secret & "There's A Place"; E.J. Day sleeve; stereo) 5000
63	Parlophone PMC 1202	PLEASE PLEASE ME (Second pressing, black & gold label, with "Dick James Mus. Co." publishing credit for "I Saw Her Standing There", "Misery", Do You Want To Know A Secret & "There's A Place"; Made by Ernest J Day Ltd" sleeve with printers credit on right hand side rear of sleeve; Front photo credited to "Angus McBean" at bottom far right of front cover of sleeve less than 5mm from edge. "A" of Angus starting under second letter "S" in the word "songs" in the album title: large mono in top right corner. Research estimates that around 12,000 pressed) 1000
63	Parlophone PCS 3042	PLEASE PLEASE ME (Second pressing, black & gold label, with "Northern Songs" publishing credit for "Please Please Me", "I Saw Her Standing There", "Misery", Do You Want To Know A Secret & "There's A Place"; E. J. Day sleeve; stereo) 4500
63	Parlophone PMC 1202	PLEASE PLEASE ME (Third pressing, black & yellow label with 33 1/3 RPM on label next to matrix number. Many of these records have LOWER stamper numbers than some black and gold second pressings (with Northern Songs credit) suggesting that these records were being pressed at the same time. Made by Ernest J Day Ltd" sleeve with printers credit on right hand side rear of sleeve; Front photo credited to "Angus McBean" at bottom far right of front cover of

MINT VALUE £

		sleeve less than 5mm from edge. "A" of Angus starting under second letter "S" in the word "songs" in the album title: large mono in top right corner. Research estimates that around 5,000 pressed)	500
63	Parlophone PCS 3042	PLEASE PLEASE ME (Third pressing, black & yellow label with 33 1/3 on label, stereo)	2800
63	Parlophone PMC 1202	PLEASE PLEASE ME (Fourth pressing, black/yellow label Made by Ernest J Day Ltd" sleeve with printers credit on right hand side rear of sleeve; Front photo credited to "Angus McBean" at bottom far right of front cover of sleeve less than 5mm from edge. "A" of Angus starting under second letter "S" in the word "songs" in the album title: large mono in top right corner. Research estimates that around 25,000 pressed. Please note that there are some in sleeves with the Angus McBean credit around 20mm from the edge with the "A" of Angus starting under the letter "G" in "songs".)	120
63	Parlophone PCS 3042	PLEASE PLEASE ME (Fourth pressing, with large "stereo" on front cover; E. J. Day sleeve; stereo)	200
63	Parlophone PMC 1202	PLEASE PLEASE ME (Fifth pressing, "Recording first published 1963" added below matrix number. Research estimates around 184,000 pressed. E. J. Day sleeve with medium mono and "A" of "Angus" starting under the letter "G" in "Songs" or Garrod & Lofthouse Ltd sleeve with large mono and McBean credit around 20mm from edge with "A" of "Angus" starting under letter "G" in "Songs." Large "mono"on front cover; mono)	80
63	Parlophone PCS 3042	PLEASE PLEASE ME (Fifth pressing, G & L or E. J. Day sleeve, with large "stereo"on front cover; stereo)	120
63	Parlophone PMC 1206	WITH THE BEATLES (First pressing, black & yellow label, with "Recording first published", & "Jobete" publishing credit for "Money"; G&L or E.J. Day sleeve, with large "Mono" on front cover; mono)	150
63	Parlophone PCS 3045	WITH THE BEATLES (First pressing black & yellow label, with "Recording first published", & "Jobete" publishing credit for "Money"; G & L or E. J. Day sleeve, with large "stereo" on front cover; stereo)	200
63	Parlophone PMC 1206	WITH THE BEATLES (Second pressing, black & yellow label, with "Recording first published",& "Dominion, Belinda" publishing credit for "Money"; G & L or E. J. Day sleeve, with large "mono" on front cover; mono)	100
63	Parlophone PCS 3045	WITH THE BEATLES (Second pressing, black & yellow label, with "Recording first published",& "Dominion, Belinda" publishing credit for "Money"; G & L or E. J. Day sleeve,with large "stereo" on front cover; stereo)	175

ALBUMS : 1964

(With "The Parlophone Co. Ltd", "Recording first published 1963" & "Sold in UK..." label text, flipback sleeves)

64	Parlophone PMC 1230	A HARD DAY'S NIGHT (First pressing, G & L or E. J. Day sleeve, mid-sized "mono" on front cover; mono)	80
64	Parlophone PCS 3058	A HARD DAY'S NIGHT (First pressing, G & L or E. J. Day sleeve, mid-sized "stereo"on front cover; stereo)	200
64	Parlophone PMC 1240	BEATLES FOR SALE (First pressing, G & L gatefold sleeve with visible flaps inside gatefold sleeve, with outline "mono"on front cover; mono)	80
64	Parlophone PCS 3062	BEATLES FOR SALE (First pressing, G & L gatefold sleeve with visible flaps inside gatefold, with outline "stereo" on front cover; stereo)	150
64	Parlophone PCS 3042	PLEASE PLEASE ME (sixth pressing, G & L sleeve, with large "stereo" on front cover; stereo)	60

ALBUMS : 1965

(With "The Gramophone Co Ltd" & "Sold in UK..." label text. Flipback sleeves)

65	Parlophone PMC 1255	HELP! (LP, first pressing, G & L sleeve, with outline "mono" on front cover; mono)	80
65	Parlophone PCS 3071	HELP! (LP, first pressing, G & L sleeve, with outline "stereo" on front cover; stereo)	120
65	Parlophone PMC 1267	RUBBER SOUL (First pressing, G & L or E. J. Day sleeve; mono, "loud cut" with XEX 571-9 and EXE 580-1 matrixes)	200
65	Parlophone PCS 3075	RUBBER SOUL (First pressing, G & L or E. J. Day sleeve; stereo)	200
65	Parlophone PMC 1267	RUBBER SOUL (Second pressing, matrix: [XEX 579-4 or 5]; mono)	70
65	Parlophone PCS 3062	BEATLES FOR SALE (First pressing, outline "stereo" on front gatefold sleeve; stereo)	60
65	Parlophone PCS 1202	PLEASE PLEASE ME (sixth pressing, from July 1965 until August 1969 "Sold in U.K. subject to resale price conditions, see price lists." printed on centre of all labels. In February 1965 "Recording first published" replaced with (P) in a circle 1963. Records with (P) 1963 start with side 2 matrix XEX 422 - 2N: Research suggests that 250,000 copies pressed. G & L sleeve, with large or small "mono" with McBean credit around 20mm from edge with "A" of "Angus" starting under letter "G" in "Songs; mono)	50
65	Parlophone PCS 3042	PLEASE PLEASE ME (Seventh pressing, stereo, with small "stereo" on front cover)	50
65	Parlophone PCS 3045	WITH THE BEATLES (Third pressing, small "stereo" on front cover; stereo)	50
65	Parlophone PMC 1230	A HARD DAY'S NIGHT (Second pressing, small "mono" on front cover; mono)	50
65	Parlophone PCS 3058	A HARD DAY'S NIGHT (Second pressing, small "stereo" on front cover; stereo)	60
65	Parlophone PCS 3058	A HARD DAY'S NIGHT (Second pressing, outline "stereo" on front cover; stereo)	200

ALBUMS : 1966

(With "The Gramophone Co. Ltd", & "Sold in UK..." label text.)

66	Parlophone PMC 7009	REVOLVER (First pressing, Side Two matrix [XEX 606-1], (G & L or E. J. Day sleeve; mono)	400
66	Parlophone PMC 7009	REVOLVER (First pressing, G & L or E. J. Day sleeve; mono)	100
66	Parlophone PMC 7009	REVOLVER (First pressing, G & L or E. J. Day sleeve; mono)	100
66	Parlophone PMC 7009	REVOLVER (Second pressing, G & L or E. J. Day sleeve, plain white or sepia "LP advertising" inner sleeves mono)	
66	Parlophone PMC 7016	A COLLECTION OF BEATLES OLDIES (First pressing, G & L or E. J. Day sleeve; mono)	65
66	Parlophone PCS 7016	A COLLECTION OF BEATLES OLDIES (First pressing, G & L or E. J. Day sleeve; stereo)	75
66	Parlophone PMC 1255	HELP! (LP, second pressing, G & L sleeve, plain white or sepia "LP advertising" inner sleeves; mono, with small solid black "mono" on front cover)	50
66	Parlophone PCS 3071	HELP! (LP, second pressing, G & L sleeve, plain white or sepia "LP advertising" inner sleeves; stereo, with small solid black "stereo" on front cover)	60

ALBUMS : 1967

(With "The Gramophone Co. Ltd" & "Sold in UK..." label text)

67	Parlophone PMC 7027	SGT. PEPPER'S LONELY HEARTS CLUB BAND (First pressing, G & L laminated gatefold sleeve, visible flaps inside gatefold sleeve, with red & white inner & cut-out insert; mono)	150
67	Parlophone PCS 7027	SGT. PEPPER'S LONELY HEARTS CLUB BAND (First pressing, G & L laminated gatefold sleeve, visible flaps inside gatefold sleeve, with red & white inner & cut-out insert; stereo)	175

ALBUMS : 1968

(With top-opening G&L gatefold sleeves, black inners, poster & 4 colour prints. Dark green labels with "Sold in UK..." text, visible flaps inside gatefold sleeve)

68	Apple PMC/PCS 7067/8	THE BEATLES (WHITE ALBUM) (First pressing, mono or stereo, numbered below 0000010) 7000
68	Apple PMC/PCS 7067/8	THE BEATLES (WHITE ALBUM) (First pressing, 2-LP, mono or stereo, numbered between 0000011 & 0001000) 2000
68	Apple PMC/PCS 7067/8	THE BEATLES (WHITE ALBUM) (First pressing, 2-LP, mono or stereo, numbered between 0001001 & 0010000) 800
68	Apple PMC 7067/8	THE BEATLES (WHITE ALBUM) (First pressing, 2-LP, mono, numbered above 0010000) 250
68	Apple PCS 7067/8	THE BEATLES (WHITE ALBUM) (First pressing, 2-LP, stereo, numbered above 0010000) 200

ALBUMS : 1969

(Apple LPs have G&L sleeves & black inners. Dark green labels with "Sold in UK..." text unless otherwise stated. Parlophone repressings are in G&L sleeves with "The Gramophone Co. Ltd." but without "Sold in UK..." label text unless otherwise stated. These pressings also have plain white or sepia "LP advertising" inners.)

69	Apple PMC 7070	YELLOW SUBMARINE (LP, first pressing with red lines above & below rear sleevenote; mono) 225
69	Apple PCS 7070	YELLOW SUBMARINE (LP, first pressing with red lines above & below rear sleevenote; stereo) 80
69	Apple PCS 7070	YELLOW SUBMARINE (LP, second pressing with red lines above & below rear sleevenote; stereo) 35
69	Apple PCS 7080	GET BACK (LP, unreleased, acetates only) 0
69	Apple PCS 7088	ABBEY ROAD (LP, first pressing, black or plain white inner sleeve, with Apple logo aligned to Side 1 track listing on rear sleeve; with "Her Majesty" credit on label) 60
69	Parlophone PMC 1202	PLEASE PLEASE ME (Seventh pressing, pressed between August to December 1969, "Sold in U.K. .." text removed mono, with small "mono" on front cover made by Garrod & Lofthouse Ltd. Angus McBean credit 20mm from the edge with the "A" of "Angus" starting under the letter "G" in "Songs". Research estimates than only 1000 copies pressed) 350
69	Parlophone PCS 3042	PLEASE PLEASE ME (Eigth pressing, small "stereo" on front cover; stereo) 40
69	Parlophone PCS 3045	WITH THE BEATLES (Fourth pressing, small "stereo" on front cover; stereo) 50
69	Parlophone PMC 1230	A HARD DAY'S NIGHT (Third pressing, small "mono" on front cover; mono) 50
69	Parlophone PCS 3058	A HARD DAY'S NIGHT (Third pressing, small "stereo" on front cover; stereo) 50
69	Parlophone PCS 3062	BEATLES FOR SALE (Third pressing, gatefold sleeve; stereo) 40
69	Parlophone PMC 1255	HELP! (LP, third pressing, small solid black "mono" on front cover; mono) 50
69	Parlophone PCS 3071	HELP! (LP, third pressing, small solid black "stereo" on front cover; stereo) 45
69	Parlophone PCS 3075	RUBBER SOUL (Second pressing, some with E. J. Day sleeve; stereo) 35
69	Parlophone PMC 1267	RUBBER SOUL (Third pressing, mono) 40
69	Parlophone PMC 7009	REVOLVER (Third pressing, mono) 50
69	Parlophone PCS 7009	REVOLVER (Second pressing, stereo) 50
69	Parlophone PMC 7016	A COLLECTION OF BEATLES OLDIES (Second pressing, mono) 40
69	Parlophone PCS 7016	A COLLECTION OF BEATLES OLDIES (Second pressing, stereo) 35
69	Parlophone PCS 7027	SGT. PEPPER'S LONELY HEARTS CLUB BAND (Second pressing, gatefold sleeve, with white inner and cut-out insert, stereo) 35
69	Parlophone PMC 7027	SGT. PEPPER'S LONELY HEARTS CLUB BAND (Third pressing, laminated gatefold sleeve,& cut-out insert; mono) 60
69	Apple PCS 7067/8	THE BEATLES (WHITE ALBUM) (Second pressing, 2-LP, top-opening, numbered g/fold sl., poster & 4 colour prints; stereo) 100

ALBUMS : 1970

(With G&L sleeves and dark green labels, unless otherwise stated)

70	Apple PXS 1	LET IT BE (LP box set, first pressing dark green label red Apple logo on rear sleeve & white inner, with Get Back book housed in black card tray ['PXS 1' not listed on package], with rare Apple mini poster) 800
70	Apple PXS 1	LET IT BE (LP box set, first pressing dark green label red Apple logo on rear sleeve & white inner, with Get Back book housed in black card tray ['PXS 1' not listed on package], without rare Apple mini poster) 700
70	Apple/Lyntone LYN 2154	FROM THEN TO YOU (The Beatles' Christmas Album) 400
70	Parlophone PMC 1202	PLEASE PLEASE ME (Eigth pressing, black and silver label, single boxed EMI logo at 6 'o' clock, with G & L sleeve & sepia "LP advertising" inner. Label has "The Gramophone Co. Ltd." but no "Sold in UK ..." small "mono" on front cover made by Garrod & Lofthouse Ltd. Angus McBean credit 20mm from the edge with the "A" of "Angus" starting under the letter "G" in "Songs". Research suggests that around 1000 copies pressed; mono) 300

ALBUMS : ALBUM BOX SETS

78	Parlophone BC 13	THE BEATLES COLLECTION (13 x LP, stereo, some with poster) 150
80	World Record Club SM 701/708	THE BEATLES BOX (8-LP, mail order only) 80
82	Parlophone BMC 10	THE BEATLES MONO COLLECTION (10 x LP, red box) 350

ALBUMS : CD ALBUMS AND BOX SETS

87	HMV BEACD 25/1	PLEASE PLEASE ME/WITH THE BEATLES/A HARD DAY'S NIGHT/BEATLES FOR SALE (4 x CD, numbered 12" black box set withBook Of Beatles Lists paperback book) 100
87	HMV BEACD 25/2	HELP!/RUBBER SOUL/REVOLVER (3 x CD, numbered 12" red box set with insert & reprint of Beatles Book Monthly, issue 12) 50
87	HMV BEACD 25/4	THE BEATLES (2-CD, numbered 12" box set with booklet & badge) 30
87	HMV BEACD 25/5	YELLOW SUBMARINE (CD, numbered 12" box set with insert, cut-outs & badge) 50
87	HMV BEACD 25/6	MAGICAL MYSTERY TOUR (CD, numbered 12" box set with booklet, poster & badge) 20
87	HMV BEACD 25/7	ABBEY ROAD (CD, numbered 12" box set with 2 posters, booklet & badge) 18
87	HMV BEACD 25/8	LET IT BE (CD, numbered 12" box set with booklet & badge) 18
87	HMV BEACD 25/3	SGT. PEPPER'S LONELY HEARTS CLUB BAND (CD, numbered 12" box set with booklet, cut-outs & badge) 18

ALBUMS : CONTRACT PRESSINGS : LPS

(Records were often pressed by non-EMI companies under contract, owing to overwhelming demand for Beatles records. Subtle differences indicating their origin can be detected. Philips pressings (the 'Hey Jude' single only) are the easiest to spot as they alone have three-pronged centres. All the others had four except for the French Pathe-Marconi pressings of 'Hello Goodbye' which have solid centres and 'Made In France' at the foot of the label. The centre of a Decca contract pressing has a ridge 3mm from the perimeter. Pre-1966 EMI pressings have flat push-out centres. Thereafter many records were produced with a mix of push-out and solid centres. EMI always pressed stamper letters into the vinyl, positioned at 3 o' clock to the matrix number. Up to three letters from the code 'GRAMOPHLTD' were used each representing a number. EMI stamper letters are seldom seen on contract pressings. Great controversy has surrounded the origin of the only other known style of pre-1965 Beatles' contract pressings. Previously thought to have been made by Pye they are now believed to have been pressed at the ORIOLE pressing plant before their September 1964 aquisition by CBS. The centres of these pressings have no ridge and rough edges. They are also thicker and heavier than any of the other pressings. Although released in November 1964 'I Feel Fine' also has these characteristics and is assumed to have come from this source. CBS using the old ORIOLE presses. However, it is thought that PYE actually pressed one Beatles 45 and one EP after 1964. The centres of these two pressings look very similar to those made by DECCA but have a less prominent ridge. The edges of records made by PHILIPS, ORIOLE and PYE are not straight-cut but are tapered off. The edges of EMI, DECCA and Pathe-Marconi pressings are all straight-cut. (Decca contract pressings have no stamper letters (G or D) positioned at 3 o'clock to the matrix number; the label has a

circularimpression 15mm from the outer edge. Pye pressings between 1973 and 1979 are a dark, translucent red when held up to a strong light.)
Let us hope that the online community of Beatles fans and collectors worldwide will one day solve the magical mystery tour of Beatles contract pressings. Until that day, the following is where we at Record Collector stand at the present time)

63	Parlophone PMC 1202	PLEASE PLEASE ME (Decca contract pressing)	150
63	Parlophone PMC 1206	WITH THE BEATLES (Pye contract pressing)	135
63	Parlophone PMC 1206	WITH THE BEATLES (Decca contract pressing)	120
68	Parlophone P-PCS 7067/8	THE BEATLES (WHITE ALBUM) (2-LP, Decca contract pressing, yellow & black labels)	3000

(Decca contract pressings have no stamper letters (G or D) positioned at 3 o'clock to the matrix number; the label has a circularimpression 15mm from the outer edge. Pye pressings are a dark, translucent red when held up to a strong light.)

69	Parlophone P-PCS 7088	ABBEY ROAD (LP, contract pressing export issue, yellow & black labels, Decca pressing)	1000
69	Parlophone P-PCS 7099	ABBEY ROAD (LP, contract pressing, export issue, silver & black labels, Decca pressing)	500
70s	Apple PCSP 717	THE BEATLES 1962-1966 (2-LP, gatefold sleeve with lyric inners, Pye pressing)	50
84	Parlophone/Nimbus PCS 7027	SGT. PEPPER'S LONELY HEARTS CLUB BAND (mail-order only, from Practical Hi-Fi Magazine, Nimbus pressing)	600

ALBUMS : EXPORT LPS : ORIGINALS

(with black/yellow labels unless otherwise stated)

65	Parlophone CPCS 101	SOMETHING NEW (LP, export 1st pressing, with "Parlophone Co. Ltd." label text)	500
65	Parlophone CPCS 101	SOMETHING NEW (LP, export 2nd pressing, with "Gramophone Co. Ltd." label text)	350
66	Parlophone CPCS 103	THE BEATLES' SECOND ALBUM (LP, export, first pressing with yellow/black labels)	400
66	Parlophone CPCS 104	BEATLES VI (LP, first export pressing with yellow/black labels)	400
68	Parlophone P-PCS 7067/8	THE BEATLES (WHITE ALBUM) (2-LP, export pressing, yellow/black labels, numbered, top opening 'mono' gatefold sleeve with "stereo" sticker & black inners, poster & 4 colour prints)	800
69	Odeon PPCS 7070	YELLOW SUBMARINE (LP, export pressing Odeon sticker on rear of Apple sleeve)	2000

(with yellow/black labels)

69	Parlophone P-PCS 7088	ABBEY ROAD (LP, export pressing, Parlophone sticker on rear of Apple sleeve, Apple logo on label)	800
70	Parlophone P-PCS 7096	LET IT BE (LP, first export pressing with yellow/black labels)	700
70	Parlophone CPCS 106	HEY JUDE (silver/black label, large boxed Parlophone label at top and small EMI boxed logo at bottom, laminated sleeve)	600

ALBUMS : EXPORT LPS : REISSUES

69	Parlophone P-PCS 7088	ABBEY ROAD (LP, export copy reissue, Parlophone sticker on rear of Apple sleeve; one EMI boxed logo)	125
69	Apple CPCS 106	HEY JUDE (2nd reissue, dark green label)	75
69	Parlophone CPCS 101	SOMETHING NEW (one EMI boxed logo)	150
69	Parlophone CPCS 103	THE BEATLES' SECOND ALBUM (LP, export, second pressing with sliver/black labels, one EMI boxed logo)	150
69	Parlophone CPCS 104	BEATLES VI (LP, second export pressing with silver/black labels, one EMI boxed logo)	150
70	Parlophone P-PCS 7096	LET IT BE (LP, second export pressing with silver/black labels, one EMI boxed logo)	150
70	Parl./Apple (P-)PCS 7096	LET IT BE (LP, export pressing second reissue, Apple label [PCS 7096] in Parlophone sleeve)	35

(with silver/black labels)

70	Parlophone CPCS 103	THE BEATLES' SECOND ALBUM (LP, export, 2nd reissue, silver/black labels two EMI boxed logos)	100
73	Apple CPCS 106	HEY JUDE (3rd reissue, light green label)	25
78	Apple PCS 7067/8	THE BEATLES (WHITE ALBUM) (2-LP, export pressing, white vinyl, gatefold sleeve)	40
78	Parlophone PCTC 255	MAGICAL MYSTERY TOUR (LP, transparent yellow vinyl)	40

(with silver/black labels)

78	Apple PCS 7088	ABBEY ROAD (LP, green vinyl)	40
78	Apple PCS 7096	LET IT BE (LP white vinyl)	40
70s	Parl./Apple (P-)CPCS 106	HEY JUDE (Apple label [CPCS 106] in Parlophone sleeve [P-CPSC 106])	35

ALBUMS : FRENCH PRESSINGS

(Parlophone label LPs have 'Made in France' on EMI rim copy. Apple label LPs have 'Made in France by Pathe Marconi EMI' rim copy. All albums are in British-printed sleeves bearing 'Made in France' stickers.)

73	Parlophone PCS 3042	PLEASE PLEASE ME	12
73	Parlophone PCS 3045	WITH THE BEATLES	12
73	Parlophone PCS 3058	A HARD DAY'S NIGHT	12
73	Parlophone PCS 3062	BEATLES FOR SALE (gatefold sleeve)	12
73	Parlophone PCS 3071	HELP!	12
73	Parlophone PCS 3075	RUBBER SOUL	12
73	Parlophone PCS 7009	REVOLVER	12
73	Parlophone PCS 7016	A COLLECTION OF BEATLES OLDIES (LP, French pressing)	12
73	Parlophone PCS 7027	SGT. PEPPER'S LONELY HEARTS CLUB BAND (French pressing, gatefold sleeve with cut-out insert, some copies with banded vinyl)	15
73	Apple PCS 7067/8	THE BEATLES (WHITE ALBUM) (2-LP, French pressing, un-numbered, laminated, side-opening gatefold sleeve, with four colour prints & poster)	25
73	Apple PCS 7070	YELLOW SUBMARINE (LP, French pressing)	15
73	Apple PCS 7088	ABBEY ROAD (some copies with banded vinyl)	15
73	Apple PCS 7096	LET IT BE	12
73	Apple PCSP 717	THE BEATLES 1962-1966 (2-LP, gatefold sleeve with lyric inners)	20

ALBUMS : LPS : 1980S RE-PRESSINGS

80	Parlophone PMC 7009	REVOLVER (mono, pressed between 1980 and 1982,Black label with two white-black EMI logos and silver print. Matrix numbers: Side 1: YEX 605-3; Side 2: YEX 606-4)	15
82	Parlophone PMC 1202	PLEASE PLEASE ME (mono)	15
82	Parlophone PMC 1206	WITH THE BEATLES (mono)	15
82	Parlophone PMC 1230	A HARD DAY'S NIGHT (mono)	15
82	Parlophone PMC 1240	BEATLES FOR SALE (gatefold sleeve, mono)	12
82	Parlophone PMC 1255	HELP! (mono)	12
82	Parlophone PMC 1267	RUBBER SOUL (mono)	12

(lightweight vinyl with yellow/black labels listing "mono")

82	Apple PMC 7070	YELLOW SUBMARINE (LP, light green Apple label; mono)	12
82	Parlophone PMC 7027	SGT. PEPPER'S LONELY HEARTS CLUB BAND (gatefold sleeve with cut-out inserts, mono)	12

(lightweight vinyl with yellow/black labels listing "mono")

82	Apple PMC 7067/8	THE BEATLES (WHITE ALBUM) (2-LP, un-numbered, side-opening gatefold sleeve, with poster & 4 prints, light green Apple label; mono)	30

ALBUMS : LPS : RETROSPECTIVES

73	Apple PCSP 717	THE BEATLES 1962-1966 (2-LP, labels state PCS 7171 and PCS 7172)	40
73	Apple PCSP 718	THE BEATLES 1967-1970 (2-LP, labels state 7131 and 7182)	40

76	Parlophone PLSP 719	ROCK N ROLL MUSIC (2-LP, gatefold)	30
76	Parlophone PCTC 255	MAGICAL MYSTERY TOUR (LP, gatefold sleeve with 24-page stapled insert)	12
76	Polydor 2683 068	THE BEATLES TAPES (2-LP)	30
77	EMI EMTV 4	THE BEATLES AT THE HOLLYWOOD BOWL (gatefold sleeve, with inner)	15
77	Lingasong LNS 1	LIVE AT THE STAR CLUB 1962 (2-LP)	30
77	Parlophone PCSP 721	LOVE SONGS (2-LP, gatefold)	30
77	EMI HRL 026	HISTORY OF ROCK VOL.26 THE BEATLES (2-LP gatefold sleeve)	30
78	Apple PCSPR 717	THE BEATLES 1962-1966 (2-LP, red vinyl, gatefold stickered sleeve with lyric inners)	20
78	Apple PCSPB 718	THE BEATLES 1967-1970 (2-LP, blue vinyl, gatefold stickered sleeve with lyric inners)	20
79	Parlophone PCM 1001	RARITIES (LP)	30
79	Parlophone PCS 7184	HEY JUDE (black/silver label with two boxed EMI logos)	12
82	Parlophone EMTVS 34	THE BEATLES' GREATEST HITS (2-LP, unreleased)	0
82	Parlophone PCS 7218	REEL MUSIC (with inner & 12-page insert)	12
88	HMV BPM 1	PAST MASTERS VOLUME 1 & 2 (2-LP, gatefold sleeve)	45
94	Apple PCSP 726	LIVE AT THE BBC (2-LP, gatefold sleeve, with inners)	30
95	Apple PCSP 727	ANTHOLOGY 1 (3-LP, gatefold sleeve, with inners)	50
96	Apple PCSP 728	ANTHOLOGY 2 (3-LP, gatefold sleeve, with inners)	50
96	Apple PCSP 729	ANTHOLOGY 3 (3-LP, gatefold sleeve, with inners)	50
99	Apple 521 4811	YELLOW SUBMARINE SONGTRACK (yellow vinyl, gatefold stickered sleeve)	35
99	Apple 521 4811	YELLOW SUBMARINE SONGTRACK (LP, gatefold stickered sleeve)	30
00	Apple 529 3251	THE BEATLES 1 (2-LP, gatefold sleeve, with poster & 4 prints)	40
03	Apple 595 4380	LET IT BE...NAKED (LP, gatefold sleeve PLUS "Fly On The Wall" 7" EP)	40
07	Apple 379 8081	LOVE (2-LP, gatefold sleeve, with inners)	30

ALBUMS : LPS: 1969 RE-PRESSINGS

69	Parlophone PMC 1202	PLEASE PLEASE ME (Re-pressing 1969, mono)	50
69	Parlophone PCS 3042	PLEASE PLEASE ME (1969 re-pressing, stereo, with one boxed EMI logo on label)	35
69	Parlophone PCS 3045	WITH THE BEATLES (1969 re-pressing, stereo only)	30
69	Parlophone PMC 1255	HELP! (LP, 1969 repressing, mono)	150
69	Parlophone PCS 3071	HELP! (LP, 1969 repressing, stereo)	30
69	Parlophone PCS 3058	A HARD DAY'S NIGHT (1969 re-pressing, stereo only)	30
69	Parlophone PCS 3062	BEATLES FOR SALE (1969 repressing - gatefold sleeve, stereo only)	30
69	Parlophone PCS 3075	RUBBER SOUL (1969 repressing, stereo only)	40
69	Parlophone PCS 7009	REVOLVER (1969 repressing, stereo only)	50
69	Parlophone PCS 7016	A COLLECTION OF BEATLES OLDIES (stereo only)	25
69	Parlophone PMC 7027	SGT. PEPPER'S LONELY HEARTS CLUB BAND (1969 repressing, laminated gatefold sleeve, with cut-out insert, mono)	60
69	Parlophone PCS 7027	SGT. PEPPER'S LONELY HEARTS CLUB BAND (1969 repressing, laminated gatefold sleeve, with cut-out insert, stereo)	30

(with laminated flipback sleeves & silver/black labels with one boxed EMI logo)

73	Apple PCS 7067/8	THE BEATLES (WHITE ALBUM) (2-LP, un-numbered, laminated, side-opening gatefold sleeve, with poster & 4 soft card colour prints, stereo only)	35

ALBUMS : POLYDOR RECORDINGS : LPS

64	Polydor Hi-Fi 46 432	THE BEATLES' FIRST (purple/black sleeve, Germany only, unissued in U.K.)	100
67	Polydor Special 236 201	THE BEATLES' FIRST (as Tony Sheridan & The Beatles, 1st pressing, without 'stereo' on label or sleeve, 'pop art' sleeve)	50
67	Polydor Special 236 201	THE BEATLES' FIRST (later pressings with 'stereo' on label & sleeve, minor label variations, 'pop art' sleeve)	30

MISPRESSINGS

63	Parlophone R 4983	Please Please Me/Ask Me Why (Mispressing, A-side actually plays 'Quiet Morning' by the Brian Fahey Orchestra)	50
64	Parlophone GEP 8882	TWIST AND SHOUT (label error: "Do You Want A Know A Secret")	20
64	Parlophone PCS 3062	BEATLES FOR SALE (label error: "I'm A Losser")	200
65	Parlophone GEP 8946	THE BEATLES' MILLION SELLERS (label error: "Beatles Golden Discs")	20
65	Parlophone PCS 3075	RUBBER SOUL (label error: "Norweigian Wood")	350
65	Parlophone CPCS 101	SOMETHING NEW (LP, export issue, label misprint error: "Sold in UK")	500
66	Parlophone PMC 7009	REVOLVER (copies with side 2 matrix no.: XEX 606-1 have 'Remix 11' of Tomorrow Never Knows, G & L or E. J. Day sleeve; mono only)	200
66	Parlophone CPCS 106	BEATLES VI (LP, export issue, label error: "Sold in UK")	500
67	Parlophone PMC 7027	SGT. PEPPER'S LONELY HEARTS CLUB BAND (First pressing with label misprint omits "A Day In The Life" credit; G & L laminated gatefold sleeve, with plain white inner & insert,; mono only)	200

With "The Gramophone Co Ltd" & "Sold in the UK..." label text

68	Apple PCS 7067/8	THE BEATLES (WHITE ALBUM) (2-LP label misprinting error: "Rocky Racoon")	200
69	Apple PCS 7088	ABBEY ROAD (LP, first pressing Apple logo misaligned to Side 1 track listing on rear sleeve; with or without "Her Majesty" credit on label; black or plain white inner sleeve)	60
69	Apple PCS 7088	ABBEY ROAD (label omits "Her Majesty")	35
69	Apple CPCS 106	HEY JUDE (label misprint error: "Revolutions")	250
69	Parlophone PCS 7009	REVOLVER (1969 repressing, stereo only with misprint "I Got To Get You Into My Life" on side 2)	70

(with laminated flipback sleeves & silver/black labels with one boxed EMI logo)

69	Parlophone PMC 7027	SGT. PEPPER'S LONELY HEARTS CLUB BAND (1969 Mispressing, mono; matrix YEX 637/8; plays stereo)	200
99	Parlophone PCS 3075	RUBBER SOUL (label error: pressed on Apple)	100

FLEXIDISCS

(Fan club flexidiscs are worth around £20 less without newsletters and half the listed values without picture sleeves.)

63	Lyntone LYN 492	The Beatles' Christmas Record (Flexidisc, gatefold p/s)	120
64	Lyntone LYN 757	Another Beatles Christmas Record (Flexidisc, p/s, with gatefold newsletter insert)	100
65	Lyntone LYN 948	The Beatles' Third Christmas Record (Flexidisc, p/s, with gatefold newsletter insert)	100
66	Lyntone LYN 1145	Pantomime: Everywhere It's Christmas (Flexidisc, p/s, with 7" x 7" newsletter insert)	100
67	Lyntone LYN 1360	Christmas Time (Is Here Again) (Flexidisc, p/s, with 7" x 7" newsletter insert)	100
68	Lyntone LYN 1743/4	The Beatles' Sixth Christmas Record (Flexidisc, p/s, with 'Superpix' sales insert)	100
68	Lyntone LYN 1743/4	The Beatles' Sixth Christmas Record (Flexidisc, p/s, without "Superpix" sales insert)	100
69	Lyntone LYN 1970/1-IL	The Beatles' Seventh Christmas Record (Flexidisc, p/s, with 2 x foolscap fan club newsletters)	100
69	Lyntone LYN 1970/1-IL	The Beatles' Seventh Christmas Record (p/s)	50

(see also John Lennon, Paul McCartney/Wings, George Harrison, Ringo Starr, Pete Best Four, Quarry Men, Tony Sheridan, George Martin, Billy Preston, Yoko Ono)

BEATMEN

64	Pye 7N 15659	You Can't Sit Down/Come On Pretty Babe	20
65	Pye 7N 15792	Now The Sun Has Gone/Please Believe	40

MINT VALUE £

BEAT MERCHANTS
64	Columbia DB 7367	Pretty Face/Messin' With The Man	80
65	Columbia DB 7492	So Fine/She Said Yeah	70

BEATPUMP
80	Slow Lorries SLOW 1	THE FIVE MONTH PLAN EP (p/s)	25

BEAT SIX
64	Decca F 12011	Bernadine/The River And I	15

(see also Guys)

BEATSTALKERS
65	Decca F 12259	Ev'rybody's Talking 'Bout My Baby/Mr. Disappointed	80
66	Decca F 12352	Left Right Left/You'd Better Get A Better Hold On	60
66	Decca F 12460	A Love Like Yours/Base Line	60
67	CBS 2732	My One Chance To Make It/Ain't No Soul (Left In These Ole Shoes)	80
67	CBS 3105	Silver Treetop School For Boys/Sugar Coated Man	75
68	CBS 3557	Rain Coloured Roses/Everything Is For You	60
69	CBS 3936	Little Boy/When I'm Five	70

PAUL BEATTIE
57	Parlophone R 4385	I'm Comin' Home/Nothing So Strange	40
58	Parlophone R 4429	Me, Please Me/Wanderlust	10
58	Parlophone R 4468	A House, A Car, And A Wedding Ring/Banana	20
68	Parlophone R 4664	Slick Chick/The Big Bounce	30

E.C. BEATTY
59	Felsted AF 127	Ski King/I'm A Lucky Man	40

BEAU
69	Dandelion S 4403	1917 Revolution/Sleeping Town	10
69	Dandelion S 63751	BEAU (LP, black/red/silver label)	50
71	Dandelion DAN 8006	CREATION (LP, with The Way We Live)	40

(see also Way We Live)

BEAU BRUMMELS
65	Pye International 7N 25293	Laugh, Laugh/Still In Love With You Baby	6
65	Pye International 7N 25306	Just A Little/They'll Make You Cry	5
65	Pye International 7N 25318	You Tell Me Why/I Want You	8
65	Pye International 7N 25333	Don't Talk To Strangers/In Good Time	10
66	Pye International 7N 25342	Good Time Music/Sad Little Girl (unissued)	0
65	Pye International NPL 28062	INTRODUCING THE BEAU BRUMMELS (LP, mono only)	30

BEAU-MARKS
60	Top Rank JAR 377	Clap Your Hands/Daddy Said	30

(see also Del-Tones, Milton De Lugg Orchestra)

JIMMY BEAUMONT
66	London HLZ 10059	You Got Too Much Going For You/I Never Loved Her Anyway	100
66	London HLZ 10059	You Got Too Much Going For You/I Never Loved Her Anyway (DJ Copy)	200

BEAUTIFUL SOUTH
92	Go! Discs GOD 78	Bell Bottomed Tear/A Thousand Lies/They Used To Wear Black (p/s with postcards)	5
92	Go! Discs GOD 88	36D/Throw His Song Away/Trevor, You're Bizarre (p/s with postcards)	5
94	Go! Discs 828 507-1	MIAOW (LP, withdrawn HMV-style 'dog' sleeve with lyric inner)	30
94	Go! Discs 828 507-1	MIAOW (LP, 'cat' sleeve with lyric inner)	15
96	Go! Discs 828 845-1	BLUE IS THE COLOUR (LP, with lyric inner)	18
07	Mercury 175 252-3	SOUP ('deluxe Fan Edition', in sealed/stickered tin: CD, DVD, T-shirt and mug)	60

BEAVER & KRAUSE
72	Warner Bros K 46130	GANDHARVA (LP)	12
72	Warner Bros K 46184	ALL GOOD MEN (LP)	12

BEAVERS
58	Capitol CL 14909	Road To Happiness/Low As I Can Be	10

JACKIE BEAVERS
76	Jay Boy BOY 102	Trying To Get Back To You Girl/Trying To Get Back To You Girl (Version)	15

BEAZERS
64	Decca F 11827	Blue Beat/I Wanna Shout	45

(see also Chris Farlowe, Little Joe Cook)

BE-BOP DELUXE
73	Smile LAFS 001	Teenage Archangel/Jets At Dawn (mono, 1,000 only)	25
74	Harvest HAR 5081	Jet Silver (And The Dolls Of Venus)/Third Floor Heaven	6
75	Harvest HAR 5091	Between The Worlds/Lights (withdrawn)	50
75	Harvest HAR 5098	Maid In Heaven/Lights	5
76	Harvest HAR 5110	Kiss Of The Light/FUNKY PHASER & HIS UNEARTHLY MERCHANDISE: Shine	5
74	Harvest SHVL 813	AXE VICTIM (LP, gatefold sleeve)	18
75	Harvest SHSP 4045	FUTURAMA (LP)	12
76	Harvest SHVL 813	AXE VICTIM (LP, 2nd pressing gatefold sleeve)	12
76	Harvest SHSP 4053	SUNBURST FINISH (LP)	12
77	Harvest SHVL 816	LIVE! IN THE AIR AGE (LP, with bonus EP "Live! In The Air Age" [PSR 412])	20
78	Harvest SHSP 4091	DRASTIC PLASTIC (LP)	12
78	Harvest SHDW 410	THE BEST AND THE REST OF BE BOP DELUXE (LP)	15

(see also Bill Nelson, A-Austr, Axe Victim)

BE-BOP PRESERVATION SOCIETY
71	Dawn DNLS 3027	THE BE-BOP PRESERVATION SOCIETY (LP, gatefold sleeve, orange label with insert)	30

GILBERT BECAUD
59	HMV POP 574	The Day The Rains Came/Les Marches De Provence	5

BECAUSE
92	Haven HAVEN CD1	MAD, SCARED, DUMB & GORGEOUS (CD)	20

(see also Furniture)

SIDNEY BECHET

54	Vogue V 2391	Royal Garden Blues/Mon Homme	5
58	Vogue V 2394	Theme From The "Threepenny Opera"/Army Song	5
59	Vogue V 9141	Petit Fleur/Dans La Rue D'Antibes	8
59	Vogue V 9157	Le Marchand de Poissons/Si Tu Vois Ma Mere	5
60	Philips JAZ 110	My Woman's Blues/What A Dream (p/s)	5
55	Melodisc EPM 7-51	SIDNEY BECHET WITH HUMPHREY LYTTELTON'S BAND (EP)	10
56	Melodisc EPM 7-62	BECHET/SPANIER BIG FOUR (EP, with Mugsy Spanier)	10
56	Melodisc EPM 7-68	BECHET-SPANIER IN NEW YORK, BECHET-LYTTELTON IN LONDON (EP)	10
64	Melodisc MLP 12-148	REQUIEM A BECHET (LP)	12

(see also Humphrey Lyttelton, Mezz Mezzrow)

BECK

94	Geffen GFS 67	Loser/Alcohol/Fume (p/s)	8
94	Geffen GFSJB 67	Loser/Loser (jukebox issue, no p/s)	8
94	Geffen GFS 73	Pay No Mind (Snoozer)/Special People (withdrawn)	60
94	Geffen GFST 73	Pay No Mind (Snoozer)/Special People/Trouble All My Days/Super Golden (Sunchild) (12", p/s, withdrawn - at least 100 pressed up)	50
94	Geffen GFS 19235	Beercan/Spanking Room (p/s, 1500 copies)	30
96	Geffen GFS 22183	Devil's Haircut/Lloyd Price Express (Remix By John King) (p/s)	5
96	Geffen GFS 22205	The New Pollution/Electric Music And The Summer People (p/s)	5
97	Geffen GFS 22253	Sissyneck/Feather In Your Cap (p/s)	5
97	Select SELECT 12	Clock/The Little Drum Machine Boy/Totally Confused (with Select mag)	7
97	Geffen GFS 22276	Jack-Ass (Butch Vig Mix)/Strange Invitation/Devil Got My Woman/Jack-Ass(Lowrider Mix By Butch Vig) Burro Brother (Double 7" gatefold some have Butch Vig Mix with no Lowrider Mix)	6
99	Geffen 497182-7	Sexxlaws/Salt In The Wound (picture disc, stickered p/s)	5
00	Geffen 497312-7	Mixed Bizness/(Dirty Bixin Mizness Remix) (gatefold p/s - 1,500 copies)	5

BECK, BOGERT & APPICE

73	Epic S EPC 1251	Black Cat Moan/Livin' Alone	5
73	Epic EPC40 654 55 Beck	BOGERT & APPICE (LP)	12
75	CBS EQ 32140/Q 65455	BECK, BOGERT & APPICE (LP, quadrophonic)	18

(see also Jeff Beck, Vanilla Fudge, Cactus)

GORDON BECK (QUARTET)

68	Morgan MJ 1	GYROSCOPE (LP)	250
69	M. Minor MMLP/SMLP 21	EXPERIMENTS WITH POPS (LP, as Gordon Beck Quartet)	125
69	M. Minor MMLP/SMLP 22	HALF A JAZZ SIXPENCE (LP)	100
69	Major Minor SMLP 88	DR. DOOLITTLE LOVES JAZZ (LP)	50
72	Dire FO 341	BECK-MATTHEWSON-HUMAIR TRIO (LP)	30

(see also Seven Ages Of Man)

JEFF BECK

67	Columbia DB 8151	Hi-Ho Silver Lining/Beck's Bolero	10
67	Columbia DB 8227	Tallyman/Rock My Plimsoul	12
68	Columbia DB 8359	Love Is Blue (L'Amour Est Bleu)/I've Been Drinking	12
69	Columbia DB 8590	Plinth (Water Down The Drain)/Hangman's Knee (unissued)	0
72	Epic EPC 7720	Got The Feeling/Situation	8
75	Epic EPC 3334	She's A Woman/It Doesn't Really Matter	10
80	Epic EPC 8806	The Final Peace/Space Boogie	8
80	Epic EPCA 1009	The Final Peace/Scatter Brain/Too Much To Lose/Led Boots (12", p/s)	10
82	Rak RRP 3	Hi Ho Silver Lining/Beck's Bolero/Rock My Plimsoul (picture disc)	6
68	Columbia S(C)X 6293	TRUTH (LP, 1st pressing, blue/black labels, stereo with "sold in U.K." label text)	100
68	Columbia SX 6293	TRUTH (LP, 1st pressing, blue/black labels, mono with "sold in U.K." label text)	175
68	Columbia SX 6293	TRUTH (LP, 2nd pressing, silver/black labels, boxed Columbia logo, with "sold in U.K." label text mono)	70
69	Columbia SX 6351	BECK-OLA (LP, 1st pressing, blue/black labels, mono, existence unconfirmed)	70
69	Columbia S(C)X 6351	BECK-OLA (LP, 1st pressing, blue/black labels, stereo)	30
69	Columbia SCX 6293	TRUTH (LP, 3rd pressing, silver/black labels, stereo)	15
69	Columbia SCX 6351	BECK-OLA (LP, 2nd pressing, silver/black labels, mono/stereo)	15
72	Epic EPC 64619	ROUGH AND READY (LP, yellow label)	18
72	Epic EPC 64899	JEFF BECK GROUP (LP, yellow label)	12
72	Epic EQ 30973	ROUGH AND READY (LP, quadrophonic)	20
74	CBS EQ 31331	JEFF BECK GROUP (LP, quadrophonic)	20

(see also Yardbirds, Beck Bogert Appice, Donovan, Rod Stewart, Cozy Powell, Honeydrippers, Buddy Guy)

ROBIN BECK

79	Mercury BECK !2	Sweet Talk/Shake It Through The Night (12")	12

BECKETT

73	Raft RA 18506	Little Girl/My Lady	5
74	Raft RA 48502	BECKETT (LP, with lyric insert)	20

HAROLD BECKETT

71	Philips 6308 026	FLARE UP (LP)	120
72	RCA SF 8225	WARM SMILES (LP)	90
73	RCA SF 8264	THEME FOR FEGA (LP)	50
75	Cadillac SGC 1004	JOY UNLIMITED (LP)	20
76	Ogun OG 800	MEMORIES OF BACARES (LP, as Harry Beckett's Joy Unlimited)	15
70s	Ogun OG 020	GOT IT MADE (LP, as Harry Beckett's Joy Unlimited)	12

(see also Graham Collier, Galliard, Ninesense)

JENNY BECKETT

65	Parlophone R 5373	My Love And I/Lock Away Your Love	5

STUART BECKETT

60s	Sherwood SRS 1001	Kariline/Breakthrough	40

(KEE) LYN BECKFORD

68	Island WI 3144	Combination/Hey Little Girl	20
69	Jackpot JP 707	Kiss Me Quick/MRS. MILLER: Feel It	10
69	Big Shot BI 521	Suzie Wong (as K. Beckford)/SWINGING KINGS: Deebo	40
71	G.G. GG 4514	Groove Me/Groove Version (as Keeling Beckford)	10

MINT VALUE £

THEO(PHILUS) BECKFORD

61	Blue Beat BB 33	Jack And Jill Shuffle/Little Lady (as Theophilus Beckford & Clue J. & His Blues Blasters)	12
61	Blue Beat BB 50	Georgie And The Old Shoe/That's Me (as Theo Beckford & City Slickers)	12
62	Blue Beat BB 87	Walking Down King Street/The Clock (B-side actually by Sir D's Group)	12
62	Blue Beat BB 132	Bringing In The Sheep (song actually "Bringing In The Sheaves")/Run Away	12
62	Island WI 026	I Don't Want You (actually by King Edward's All Stars)/Seven Long Years	15
63	Island WI 106	Daphney/Boller Man	12
63	R & B JB 136	Bullo Man/Daphney	25
64	Blue Beat BB 250	She's Gone/Old Flame (as Cotheo Beckford, B-side act. by Frederick Hibbert)	15
64	Blue Beat BB 257	Don't Worry To Cry/Love Me Or Leave Me (as Theophilus Beckford, B-side actually by Lloyd Clarke)	12
64	Blue Beat BB 287	On Your Knees/Now You're Gone (with Yvonne Harrison)	15
65	Blue Beat BB 303	Dig The Dig (as Basil Gabbidon)/Don't Let Me Cry No More	15
65	Black Swan WI 452	Take Your Time/STRANGER COLE: Happy-Go-Lucky	20
65	Island WI 238	Trench Town People/PIONEERS: Sometime	25
65	Island WI 243	You Are The One Girl/Grudgeful People	20
65	Island WI 246	If Life Was A Thing/L. CLARKE: Parro Saw The Light (B-side actually "Pharaoh Saw The Light" by Lloyd Clarke)	12
65	Island WI 248	What A Whoe/Bajan Girl	20
68	Nu Beat NB 009	Easy Snappin'/ERIC MORRIS: My Lonely Days	15
69	Crab CRAB 25	Brother Ram Goat (as T. Beckford)/STARLIGHTS: What A Condition	20

(see also Eric Barnet[t], Maytals, Clue J & His Bluesblasters)

BOB BECKHAM

59	Brunswick 05808	Just As Much As Ever/Your Sweet Love	5
60	Brunswick 05822	Crazy Arms/Beloved	10
60	Brunswick LAT 8325	JUST AS MUCH AS EVER (LP)	12

GERRY BECKLES

61	Oriole CB 1606	No Love For Johnnie/Come Running Back	6

BEDASSE & CHIN'S CALYPSO QUINTET

55	Kalypso C 1003	Industrial Fair/Samson & Delilah	12
56	Kalypso C 1008	Big Boy & Teacher/Red Tomato	12
58	Kalypso XX 01	Walk & Talk/Night Food	12

BED BUGS

90	Snake Rattle 01	Haywire/No Safe Haven	15

DAVID BEDFORD

75	Virgin VDJ 10	An Extract From THE RIME OF THE ANCIENT MARINER - Part Two/An Extract From THE RIME OF THE ANCIENT MARINER - Part 2 (B&W girl and dragon logo)	25
70	Argo ZRG 638	MUSIC FOR ALBION MOONLIGHT (LP, 1 side by Elizabeth Lutyens)	25
72	Dandelion 2310 165	NURSE'S SONG WITH ELEPHANTS (LP, gatefold sleeve)	25
75	Virgin V2020	STAR'S END (LP, stickered)	15
77	Virgin V2090	INSTRUCTIONS FOR ANGELS (LP)	12

(see also Coxhill/Bedford Trio, Kevin Ayers & Whole World, Mike Oldfield, Roy Harper, Edgar Broughton Band)

BEDLAM

73	Chrysalis CFB 1	I Believe In You/Whiskey And Wine	8
73	Chrysalis CHR 1048	BEDLAM (LP)	20

(see also Cozy Powell, Ace Kefford Stand, Big Bertha, Youngblood)

BEDROCKS

68	Columbia DB 8516	Ob-La-Di-Ob-La-Da/Lucy	10

EDWIN BEE

68	Decca F 12781	I've Been Loving You/Call For My Baby	12

MOLLY BEE

57	London HLD 8400	Since I Met You, Baby/I'll Be Waiting For You	40
58	Capitol CL 14849	Going Steady (With A Dream)/Magic Mirror	5
58	Capitol CL 14880	Don't Look Back/Please Don't Talk About Me When I'm Gone	5
58	Capitol CL 14947	After You've Gone/Five Points Of A Star	5
64	Liberty LIB 55691	He Doesn't Want You/Our Secret	12
65	MGM MGM 1280	Single Girl Again/Keep It A Secret	5
58	Capitol T1097	YOUNG ROMANCE (LP)	20

BEE BEE CEE

77	Rel RE 48-S	You Gotta Know Girl/We Ain't Listening (p/s, 2,000 only)	70

JOHNNY BEECHER

63	Warner Bros WB89	Sax Fifth Avenue/Jack Sax The City	12

BEEFEATERS

64	Pye International 7N 25277	Please Let Me Love You/Don't Be Long	100
70	Elektra 2101 007	Please Let Me Love You/Don't Be Long (reissue)	15

(see also Byrds)

BEE GEES

67	Polydor 56727	Spicks And Specks/I Am The World	10
67	Polydor 56161	New York Mining Disaster 1941/I Can't See Nobody	6
67	Polydor 56178	To Love Somebody/Close Another Door	5
67	Polydor 56192	Massachusetts/Barker Of The U.F.O.	5
67	Polydor 56220	World/Sir Geoffrey Saved The World	5
68	Polydor 56229	Words/Sinking Ships	5
68	Polydor 56242	Jumbo/The Singer Sang His Song	5
68	Polydor 56273	I've Gotta Get A Message To You/Kitty Can	5
69	Polydor 56304	Odessa Parts 1 & 2 (unissued)	0
69	Polydor 56304	First Of May/Lamplight	5
69	Polydor 56331	Tomorrow Tomorrow/Sun In The Morning	5
69	Polydor 56343	Don't Forget To Remember/The Lord	5
70	Polydor 56377	I.O.I.O./Sweetheart	7
70	Polydor 2001 104	Lonely Days/Man For All Seasons	5
71	Polydor 2058 115	How Can You Mend A Broken Heart/Country Woman	5
81	RSO SNF 1	Night Fever (promo only 7" with p/s to coincide with ITV showing 'Saturday Night Fever' on Royal Wedding Day)	20

67	Polydor 582/583 012	BEE GEES FIRST (LP)...15
68	Polydor 582/583 020	HORIZONTAL (LP)..25
68	Polydor 236 221	RARE PRECIOUS AND BEAUTIFUL (LP)..15
68	Polydor 236 513	RARE PRECIOUS AND BEAUTIFUL VOL. 2 (LP)...15
68	Polydor 582/583 036	IDEA (LP)..15
69	Polydor 236 556	RARE PRECIOUS AND BEAUTIFUL VOL. 3 (LP)...15
69	Polydor 582 049/050	ODESSA (2-LP, felt cover, gatefold sleeve)...40
70	Polydor 2383 010	CUCUMBER CASTLE (LP)..15
70	Polydor 2310 069	TWO YEARS ON (LP)..15
71	Polydor 2383 052	TRAFALGAR (LP)...20
72	Polydor 2383 139	TO WHOM IT MAY CONCERN (LP)..12

(see also Barry Gibb, Robin Gibb, Maurice Gibb, Humpy Bong, Fut)

BEEKEEPERS
81	Rundown ACE 40	PLATFORM FIVE EP...10

MARK BEER
81	Rough Trade RT 070	Pretty/Per(version) (p/s)...5
81	My China TAO 001	DUST ON THE ROAD (LP)..15

BEES MAKE HONEY
73	EMI EMI 2078	Knee Trembler/Caldonia 5
73	EMI EMC 3013	MUSIC EVERY NIGHT (LP)..20

BEES (UK) (1)
67	Columbia Blue Beat DB 101	Jesse James Rides Again/The Girl In My Dreams 12
68	Columbia Blue Beat DB 111	The Prisoner From Alcatraz/The Ska's The Limit 10

BEES (UK) (2)
80	Paw THF 003	Leave Willie Alone/Mr Gaynor..20

BEES (UK) (3)
01	We Love You AMOUR 6LP	SUNSHINE HIT ME (LP, inner sleeve)...25

BILLY BEETHOVEN
75	DJM DJS 10377	Dreams (Out In The Forest)/We're Free...80

(see also Graham Bonnet)

BEEZ
79	Edible SNACK 001	Easy/Vagrant (gatefold p/s)...100
78	Edible SNACK 002	THE BEEZ EP: Do The Suicide (no p/s, stickered sleeve).........................100

B.E.F. (BRITISH ELECTRIC FOUNDATION)
91	Ten TEN 386	Free (Edit)/Secret Life Of Arabia (stickered/unstickered p/s, as B.E.F. Featuring Billy MacKenzie, unissued 200 copies only) 40
80	Virgin V 2888	MUSIC FOR STOWAWAYS (cassette)..12
82	Virgin VV 2219	MUSIC OF QUALITY & DISTINCTION VOL. 1 (5 x 7" box set & insert).........12

(see also Heaven 17, Billy MacKenzie)

SI BEGG MEETS NEIL LANDSTRUMM
01	Mosquito MSQ 017	TOKYO ASSASSIN (12" EP) 10

BEGGARS FARM
84	White Rabbit WR 1001	THE DEPTH OF A DREAM (LP)..25

BEGGARS HILL
76	Moonshine MS 60	BEGGARS HILL (LP, private pressing) 175

BEGGARS OPERA
70	Vertigo 6059 026	Sarabande/Think 20
72	Vertigo 6059 060	Hobo/Pathfinder..20
73	Vertigo 6059 088	Two Timing Woman/Lady Of Hell Fire 8
74	Vertigo 6059 105	Classical Gas/Sweet Blossom Woman 6
70	Vertigo 6360 018	ACT ONE (LP, large swirl label, gatefold sleeve) 80
71	Vertigo 6360 054	WATERS OF CHANGE (LP, small swirl label, gatefold sleeve)....................90
72	Vertigo 6360 073	PATHFINDER (LP, small swirl label, foldout poster cover)........................120
73	Vertigo 6360 090	GET YOUR DOG OFF ME! (LP, 'spaceship' label)......................................20

BEGINNING OF THE END
71	Atlantic 2091 097	Funky Nassau Parts 1 & 2 (initial pressing on red label).........................10
71	Atlantic 2091 097	Funky Nassau Parts 1 & 2...5
72	Atlantic 2091166	Monkey Tamarind/Hey Pretty Girl...15
76	Warner Bros. WEA K10021	Funky Nassau (Full Length Version)/Funky Nassau Parts 1 & 2 40
71	Atlantic K 40304	FUNKY NASSAU (LP)..30

DOMINIC BEHAN
59	Decca F 11147	The Bells Of Hell/The Captains And The Kings 5
60	Topic STOP 115	The Patriot Game/Erin Go Brath (p/s) 5
64	Piccadilly 7N 35172	Liverpool Lou/Love Is Where You Find It 5
65	Piccadilly 7N 35238	Arkle/Lonely Days...5
68	Major Minor MM 575	Wormwood Scrubs/Rifles Of The IRA 5
58	Collector JEL 3	SONGS OF THE STREETS (EP) 10
58	Collector JEL H	SINGS MRS. HOOLIGAN'S XMAS CAKE (EP)...10
69	Marble Arch MAL 1123	ARKLE (LP) 15

(see also Ewan MacColl)

BEIL TEECS
71	Bullet BU 491	So Far Away/BRUTE FORCE & IGNORANCE: So Far (Version).....................8

SVEINBJORN BEINTEINSSON
90	Durtro 005	EDDA (LP, with booklet) 20

HARRY BELAFONTE
54	HMV 7M 202	Hold 'Em Joe/Suzanne (Every Night When The Sun Goes Down)...............5
54	HMV 7M 224	I'm Just A Country Boy/Pretty As A Rainbow 5
55	Capitol CL 14312	Close Your Eyes/I Still Get A Thrill (Thinking Of You) 5
60	RCA 1247	There's a Hole In My Bucket (with ODETTA)/Chickens 5

(see also Lena Horne)

BELBORN
01	World Serpent WS7 005	Seelenruhe/Phoenix (picture disc)	5

BEL CANTOS
65	R&B MRB 5003	Feel Aw Right Parts 1 & 2	15

BELFAST GYPSIES
66	Island WI 3007	Gloria's Dream/Secret Police	75
77	Sonet SNTF 738	LEGENDARY MASTER RECORDINGS (LP)	25

(see also Them, Jackie McAuley, Freaks Of Nature)

ED 'TEX' BELIN
63	Starlite STEP 39	ED 'TEX' BELIN (EP)	10

ALEXANDER BELL
67	CBS 2977	Alexander Bell Believes/Hymn ... With Love	30

ARCHIE BELL & THE DRELLS
68	Atlantic 584 185	Tighten Up/Dog Eat Dog	15
68	Atlantic 584 217	I Can't Stop Dancing/You're Such A Beautiful Child	15
71	Atlantic 2091 156	Tighten Up/I Can't Stop Dancing/(There's Gonna Be A) Showdown	8
72	Atlantic K 10210	Here I Go Again/A World Without Music	8
73	Atlantic K 10263	There's Gonna Be A Showdown/Tighten Up	6
73	President PT 418	Girls Grow Up Faster Than Boys/Love's Gonna Rain On You	10
76	Portrait 7254	Don't Let Love Get You Down/Where Will You Go When The Party's Over/ The Soul City Walk	10
76	Portrait TA 7254	Don't Let Love Get You Down/Where Will You Go When The Party's Over/ The Soul City Walk (12")	8
76	Philly Int. 4803	Where Will You Go When The Party's Over?/I Swear You're Beautiful	15
86	Nightmare MARE 16	Look Back Over Your Shoulder/Look Back Over Your Shoulder (Dub Mix) (12")	25
68	Atlantic	TIGHTEN UP (LP)	20
72	Atlantic K 40454	HERE I GO AGAIN (LP)	20

BELINDA BELL
73	Columbia DB 8995	If Only You Believe/Stone Valley	5
73	Columbia SCXA 9255	STONE VALLEY (LP, gatefold sleeve)	15
73	One Up OU 2009	MUSIC OF W. GULGOWSKI (LP)	12

BENNY BELL & BLOCK BUSTERS
57	Parlophone R 4372	The Sack Dress/Dr. Jazz	10

CHARLES BELL & CONTEMPORARY JAZZ QUARTET
63	London HA-K/SH-K 8095	ANOTHER DIMENSION (LP)	30

EDDIE BELL
72	Injun 109	Johnny B. Goode In Hollywood/ROYCE PORTER: A Woman Can Make You Blue	15

ERIC BELL BAND
81	Hobo HOS 016	Lonely Man/Anyone Seen My Baby (p/s)	30

(see also Thin Lizzy, Noel Redding Band)

FREDDIE BELL & BELLBOYS
56	Mercury MT 122	Giddy-Up-A Ding Dong/I Said It And I'm Glad (78)	10
57	Mercury MT 141	Hucklebuck/Rompin' And Stompin' (78)	10
57	Mercury MT 146	Teach You To Rock/Take The First Train Out Of Town (78)	10
57	Mercury MT 149	Big Bad Wolf/Rockin' The Polonaise (78)	10
57	Mercury MT 159	Rockin' Is My Business/You're Gonna Be Sorry (78)	10
56	Mercury MEP 9508	ROCK WITH THE BELL BOYS (EP)	30
57	Mercury MEP 9512	ROCK WITH THE BELL BOYS VOL. 2 (EP)	45

FREDRICK BELL
68	Nu Beat NB 004	Rocksteady Cool/CARLTON ALPHONSO: I Have Changed	25

GARY BELL
67	CBS 202234	Is This What I Get For Loving You?/To Keep You	15
67	CBS 2646	Anyway That You Want Me/Leave It To Me	10

GRAHAM BELL
66	Polydor 56067	How Can I Say I Don't Love You/If You're Gonna Go	10
72	Charisma CB 201	Too Many People/Before You're A Man	5
73	Charisma CB 209	You Need A 60 Minute Man/The Whole Town Wants You Hung	5
75	Charisma CB 250	You Need A 60 Minute Man/That's The Way It Is	5
72	Charisma CAS 1061	GRAHAM BELL (LP, large 'mad hatter' label)	20

(see also Heavy Jelly, Griffin, Every Which Way, Skip Bifferty, Bell & Arc)

MADELINE BELL
63	HMV POP 1215	I Long For Your Love/Because You Didn't Care	15
64	Columbia DB 7257	You Don't Love Me No More/Don't Cross Over To My Side Of The Street	20
65	Columbia DB 7512	Daytime/Don't Cry My Heart	10
65	Philips BF 1448	What The World Needs Now Is Love/I Can't Wait To See My Baby's Face	20
66	Philips BF 1501	Don't Come Running To Me/I Got Carried Away	25
67	Philips BF 1611	Picture Me Gone/Go Ahead On	25
66	Philips BF 1526	One Step At A Time/You Won't See Me	15
68	Philips BF 1656	I'm Gonna Make You Love Me/I'm Gonna Leave You	15
68	Philips BF 1688	Thinkin'/Don't Give Your Love Away	7
68	Philips BF 1726	Hold It/What Am I Supposed To Do?	5
69	Philips BF 1799	We're So Much In Love/How Much Do I Love You	5
71	Philips 6006 082	If You Didn't Hear Me The First Time/You Walked Away	5
67	Philips (S)BL 7818	BELLS A POPPIN' (LP)	60
68	Philips SBL 7865	DOIN' THINGS (LP)	35
76	Pye NSPL 18483	THIS IS ONE GIRL (LP)	18

(see also Seven Ages Of Man, Underground, Ian Green [Revelation])

PADDIE BELL
65	Parlophone R5361	Everytime/The Rose And The Thorn	7

(see also Corries)

SIMON BELL
78	Pye 7N 46050	Givin' It Plenty/Love Like Lightning	8

MINT VALUE £

WILLIAM BELL

67	Atlantic 584 076	Never Like This Before/Soldier's Goodbye	12
69	Atlantic 584 259	Everyday Will Be Like A Holiday/Ain't Got No Girl	10
67	Stax 601 019	Eloise (Hang On In There)/One Plus One	5
68	Stax 601 038	A Tribute To A King/Every Man Oughta Have A Woman	5
69	Stax STAX 110	I Forgot To Be Your Lover/Bring The Curtain Down	8
69	Stax STAX 121	My Whole World Is Falling Down/All God's Children Got Soul	5
69	Stax STAX 128	Happy/Johnny I Love You	40
69	Atco 228 003	A TRIBUTE TO A KING (LP)	30
69	Stax SXATS 1016	BOUND TO HAPPEN (LP)	20
71	Stax 2362 009	WOW . . . WILLIAM BELL (LP)	20
72	Stax 2362 027	PHASES OF REALITY (LP)	25

(see also Judy Clay & William Bell)

BELLA & ME

| 67 | Columbia DB 8243 | Whatever Happened To The Seven Day Week/Help Me Break This Habit | 10 |

GEORGE BELLAMY

| 65 | Parlophone R 5282 | Where I'm Bound/How Could I Ever | 30 |
| 72 | Chapter One CH 167 | Maman/Come To The Party | 7 |

(see also Tornados)

PETER BELLAMY

68	Xtra XTRA 1010	PETER BELLAMY (LP)	25
68	Argo	MAINLY NORFOLK (LP)	40
69	Xtra XTRA 1075	FAIR ENGLAND'S SHORE (LP)	40
69	Topic 12T 200	THE FOX JUMPS OVER THE PARSON'S GATE (LP, blue label)	20
70	Argo ZFB 11	OAK, ASH AND THORN (LP)	20
72	Argo ZFB 37	WON'T YOU GO MY WAY (LP)	20
72	Argo ZFB 81	MERLIN'S ISLE OF GRAMARYE (LP)	20
74	Trailer LER 2089	TELL IT LIKE IT IS (LP)	15

(see also Young Tradition)

BELL & ARC

| 71 | Charisma CB 170 | She Belongs To Me/Dawn | 6 |
| 71 | Charisma CAS 1053 | BELL & ARC (LP, gatefold sleeve, pink scroll label) | 30 |

(see also Skip Bifferty, Arc, Every Which Way, Graham Bell)

BELL BROTHERS

| 68 | Action ACT 4510 | Tell Him No/Throw Away The Key | 20 |

BELLE STARS

| 83 | Stiff BUY 174 | Sweet Memory/Baseball Clothes (p/s) | 10 |
| 86 | Stiff PBUY 245 | World Domination (square picture disc) | 6 |

BELLE & SEBASTIAN

97	Jeepster JPR 7001	Dog On Wheels/The State I Am In (p/s, 1,000 only)	8
97	Jeepster JPR 12 001	Dog On Wheels/The State I Am In/String Bean Jim/Belle & Sebastian) (12")	15
97	Jeepster JPR 7002	Lazy Line Painter Jane/You Made Me Forget My Dreams (p/s, 1,000 only)	8
97	Jeepster JPR 12 002	Lazy Line Painter Jane/You Made Me Forget My Dreams/Photo Jenny/A Century Of Elvis (12")	15
98	Jeepster JPR 003	3 6 9 SECONDS OF LIGHT (12", EP)	8
00	Jeepster JPR12 018	Legal Man/Judy Is A Dick Slap (12" as Belle & Sebastian featuring the Maisonettes)	8
03	Rough Trade RTRADES 143	Final Day (12", 1-sided white label)	8
96	Elektric Honey EHRLP 5	TIGERMILK (LP, 1,000 only)	200
96	Jeepster JPRLP001	IF YOU'RE FEELING SINISTER (LP, gatefold)	20
96	Jeepster JPRLP007	TIGERMILK (LP, reissue)	18
98	Jeepster JPRLP003	THE BOY WITH THE ARAB STRAP (LP, gatefold)	18
00	Jeepster JPRLP010	FOLD YOUR HANDS CHILD, YOU WALK LIKE A PEASANT (LP, gatefold)	15
02	Jeepster JPRLP014	STORYTELLING (LP, gatefold)	15
03	My Own Work (No cat. no.)	THE CHRISTMAS ALBUM (CD)	25
06	Rough Trade RTRADELP 280	THE LIFE PURSUIT (2-LP)	18
10	Rough Trade RTRADELP 480	WRITE ABOUT LOVE (LP, with free 7")	15

(see also Amphetameanies)

BELLES

| 70 | President PT 311 | Don't Pretend/Words Can't Explain | 15 |

BELLFIELD

| 73 | Downtown DT 514 | Sugar Plum/Sugar Plum Dub | 6 |

BELL NOTES

59	Top Rank JAR 102	I've Had It/Be Mine	12
59	Top Rank JAR 102	I've Had It/Be Mine (78)	12
59	Top Rank JAR 147	Old Spanish Town/She Went That-A-Way	8
59	Top Rank JAR 147	Old Spanish Town/She Went That-A-Way (78)	15
59	Top Rank JAR 201	That's Right/Betty Dear	15

ERROL BELLOT

82	Jet Sounds JS 001	Don't Joke With Love/Wicked Them (with Militant Mikey, 12")	40
85	Jah Tubbys JT 012	New Kind Of Sound/Version (12", with the Offbeat Posse)	40
86	Jah Tubbys JT 019	Sound In Fury/Trouble Maker (12", with the Offbeat Posse)	40
00	Jah Tubbys JT 7002	Glory Hallalujah/DUB TEACHER: Glory Dub	15
00	Jah Tubbys JT 7004	Jah Creation/DISCIPLES RIDDIM SECTION: Creation Style	15
01	Jah Tubbys JT 7007	Roots Gone International/OFFBEAT POSSE: International Ridim	15
03	Jah Tubbys JT 014	It's War/Don't Judge (10", with the Offbeat Posse)	30
03	Jah Tubbys JT 10016	Praise H.I.M/New Life (10", with the Offbeat Posse)	30

ERROL BELLOT & DIXIE PEACH

| 03 | Jah Tubbys JT 10011 | The Warning/THE OFFBEAT POSSE: Dub Warning (10") | 30 |

(see also Dixie Peach)

BELLS

| 71 | Philips 6006116 | Stay Awhile/Simple Song Of Freedom | 6 |
| 72 | Polydor 2121-109 | Oh My Love/You, You. You | 8 |

MINT VALUE £

LOUIS BELLSON (ALL STARS/QUINTET/BAND/OCTET)

53	Capitol LC 6568	JUST JAZZ (LP)	15
57	Columbia Clef C 9040	DRUMORAMA (10" LP)	15
58	Columbia Clef CX 10142	AT THE FLAMINGO (LP)	15
59	HMV CLP 1343	THE BRILLIANT BELLSON SOUND (LP)	15
61	Columbia SCX 3418	AROUND THE WORLD IN PERCUSSION (LP)	15
66	HMV CLP/CSD 3558	THUNDERBIRD (LP)	15
67	Studio Two TWO 169	REPERCUSSION (LP, with Eric Delaney)	12
70	Pye NSPL 18349	LOUIE IN LONDON (LP, as Louie Bellson)	15
72	Parlophone PCS 7151	CONVERSATIONS (LP)	12

BELL SOUNDS
59	HMV POP 685	Marching Guitars/Chloe	5

BELL-TONES
62	Columbia DB 4845	Did You Ever See A Dream Walking?/Selina	5

TONY BELLUS
59	London HL 8933	Robbin' The Cradle/Valentine Girl	40
59	London HL 8933	Robbin' The Cradle/Valentine Girl (78)	20

BELMONTS
61	Pye International 7N 25094	Tell Me Why/Smoke From Your Cigarette	40
62	Stateside SS 128	Come On Little Angel/How About Me?	35

(see also Dion & Belmonts)

BELOVED
86	Flim Flam HARP 2	A Hundred Words (Radio Mix)/Slow Drowning (freebie)	5
86	Flim Flam HARP 3	This Means War/If Only (p/s)	5
86	Flim Flam HARP3T	This Means War/Let It Begin/Saints Preserve Us (12")	8
87	Flim Flam HARP 7	Forever Dancing/Surprise Me (p/s)	5
87	Flim Flam HARP 5T	HAPPY NOW: A Kiss Goodbye/If Pennies Came/Righteous Me (12", p/s)	8
87	Flim Flam HARP 7ET	Forever Dancing/Forever Dancing (Remix)/Surprise Me (12", p/s)	8
88	WEA YZ 311T	Loving Feeling (Feeling Lovely Mix)/Acid Love (Love & Ecstasy Mix) (12", p/s)	8

BELOVED ONES
68	CBS 3303	My Year Is A Day/She And I	15

BELT & BRACES ROADSHOW BAND
75	Belt & Braces Roadshow	BELT & BRACES ROADSHOW BAND (LP, with lyric sheet)	15

BELTANE FIRE
85	CBS A6285	Fortune Favours The Brave/(radio edit) (promo)	5

BELTONES
68	Trojan TR 628	No More Heartaches/I'll Follow You	20
69	Duke DU 17	Home Without You/Why Pretend	40
69	High Note HS 017	Mary Mary/Going Away	12
69	High Note HS 023	A Broken Heart/AFROTONES: All For One	15
72	Ackee ACK 150	Wrapped Up In Love/SOUND DIMENSION: Pasero	18

(see Bop & Beltones, Trevor Shield)

JOHN BELTRAN
96	Peacefrog PF 049	TEN DAYS OF BLUE (2-LP)	18

JESSE BELVIN
59	RCA RCA 1119	Guess Who/Funny	10
59	RCA RCA 1119	Guess Who/Funny (78)	10

BEN
71	Vertigo 6360 052	BEN (LP, gatefold sleeve, small swirl label)	1000

(see also Jonathan Kelly)

STEVE BENBOW
61	Parlophone R 4782	The Man Who Invented Beer/Rosybell	6
65	Columbia DB 7691	The Gallows Pole/I Can't Tell	5
68	L'gue Against Cruel Sports	Tattered Doll (mail-order only)	6
59	Collector JEB 2	STEVE BENBOW AND THE FOLK FOUR (EP)	10
62	HMV CLP 1603	STEVE BENBOW SINGS (LP)	15
63	HMV CLP 1687	I TRAVEL THE WORLD (LP)	15
67	Decca LK/SKL 4881	OF SITUATIONS AND PREDICAMENTS (LP)	12

BENDY DOG
72	Jam JAM 20	I Wanna Hear (Rock 'N' Roll Music)/Carry My Mind	10

BENGA
02	Big Apple BAM 002	Skank/Dose (12")	10
02	Big Apple BAM 002	Skank/Dose (12", blue vinyl)	25
03	Big Apple BAM 003	The Judgement (with Skream)/SKREAM: The Bug/BENGA: Amber (12")	30
03	Big Apple BAM 003	The Judgement (with Skream)/SKREAM: The Bug/BENGA: Amber (12", green vinyl)	30
04	Benga Beats BBV 01	BENGA BEATS VOLUME 1 EP (12")	20
04	Big Apple BAM 005	Hydro/Walkin' Bass/SKREAM: Elektro/Afrika (12")	20
04	Big Apple BAM 008	INVASION EP (2 x 12")	8

BENNY BENGIMAN
81	Negus Roots NERT 010	Health And Sorrow/Love A Dub Song	25

TONY BENJAMIN & THE SANE INMATES
82	Ariwa ARI 008	Treasures In The World/Psychological Pen (12")	30
83	Ariwa ARILP 009	AFRICAN REBEL (LP)	70

BENNY BENNETT
50s	Seeco LDS 024	BENNY BENNETT AND HIS ORCHESTRA (LP)	15

BOBBY BENNETT (U.K.)
67	CBS 202511	Just Say Goodbye/She Believes In Me	7
68	Columbia DB 8435	All My Life Is You/To Give (The Reason I Live)	7
69	Columbia DB 8532	Music Mother Made/You're Ready Now	50

BOBBY BENNETT (U.S.)
69	London HL 10274	Big New York/Baby, Try Me	15

BOYD BENNETT & HIS ROCKETS (WITH BIG MOE)
55	Parlophone MSP 6161	Everlovin'/Boogie At Midnight (with Big Moe)	350
55	Parlophone MSP 6161	Everlovin'/Boogie At Midnight (with Big Moe) (78)	30
55	Parlophone MSP 6180	Seventeen/Little Ole You-All (as Boyd Bennett & His Rockets)	250
55	Parlophone R 4063	Seventeen/Little Ole You-All (as Boyd Bennett & His Rockets) (78)	15
56	Parlophone MSP 6203	My Boy - Flat Top/Banjo Rock And Roll (with Big Moe)	250
56	Parlophone R 4121	My Boy - Flat Top/Banjo Rock And Roll (with Big Moe) (78)	20
56	Parlophone MSP 6233	Blue Suede Shoes/Oo-Oo-Oo (with Big Moe)	200
56	Parlophone MSP 6233	Blue Suede Shoes/Oo-Oo-Oo (with Big Moe) (78)	20
56	Parlophone R 4214	The Groovy Age/Hit That Jive, Jack (as Big Moe with Boyd Bennett & His Rockets)	300
56	Parlophone R 4214	The Groovy Age/Hit That Jive, Jack (as Big Moe with Boyd Bennett & His Rockets) (78)	30
56	Parlophone R 4252	The Most/Rockin' Up A Storm (as Big Moe with Boyd Bennett & His Rockets)	300
56	Parlophone R 4252	The Most/Rockin' Up A Storm (as Boyd Bennett & His Rockets) (78)	30
58	Parlophone R 4423	Click Clack/Move (as Boyd Bennett & His Rockets)	300
58	Parlophone R 4423	Click Clack/Move (as Boyd Bennett & His Rockets) (78)	30
59	Mercury AMT 1031	Tear It Up/Tight Tights (as Big Moe & His Orchestra)	60
59	Mercury AMT 1031	Tear It Up/Tight Tights (as Big Moe & His Orchestra) (78)	30

(see also Moon Mullican)

BRIAN BENNETT
67	Columbia DB 8294	Canvas/Slippery Jim De Grize	25
74	Fontana 6007 040	Chase Side Shoot-Up/Pegasus	20
76	DJM DJS 10714	Thunderbolt/Clearing Skies (promo in p/s)	12
76	DJM DJS 10714	Thunderbolt/Clearing Skies	5
77	DJM DJS 10756	Saturday Night Special/Farewell To A Friend (promo in p/s)	12
77	DJM DJS 10756	Saturday Night Special/Farewell To A Friend	5
77	DJM DJS 10791	The Girls Back Home/Jonty Jump (as the Brian Bennett Band)	12
78	DJM DJS 10843	Pendulum Force/Ocean Glide	5
82	DJM DJS 10981	Top Of The World/Soul Ice	8
67	Columbia S(C)X 6144	CHANGE OF DIRECTION (LP)	50
69	Col. Studio Two TWO 268	THE ILLUSTRATED LONDON NOISE (LP)	60
77	DJM DJF 20499	ROCK DREAMS (LP, with insert, as the Brian Bennett Band)	20
78	DJM DJF 20532	VOYAGE (LP)	20

(see also Shadows, Thunder Company, Wasp, Marty Wilde, Krewcats, Collage, Alan Skidmore, Big Jim Sullivan, Heat Exchange, Julian [Scott], Mean Machine)

BRUCE BENNETT
71	Big BG 311	If You Don't Mind/Lenore (both actually by Dobby Dobson)	7

CAROLE BENNETT
56	Capitol CL 14652	The Little Magician/I Was Your Only Love	5
57	Capitol CL 14692	Play The Music/Miser's Gold	10
57	Capitol CL 14725	Haunted Lover/Let The Chips Fall (Where They May)	25

CLIFF BENNETT & REBEL ROUSERS
61	Parlophone R 4793	You've Got What I Like/I'm In Love With You	30
61	Parlophone R 4836	That's What I Said/When I Get Paid	25
62	Parlophone R 4895	Poor Joe/Hurtin' Inside (Twist)	20
63	Parlophone R 5046	Everybody Loves A Lover/My Old Stand-By	18
63	Parlophone R 5080	You Really Got A Hold On Me/Alright	18
63	Parlophone DP 560	Poor Joe/Hurtin' Inside (Twist) (export issue, black label)	15
63	Parlophone DP 561	When I Get Paid/That's What I Said (export issue, black label)	20
64	Parlophone R 5119	Got My Mojo Working/Beautiful Dreamer	15
64	Parlophone R 5173	One Way Love/Slow Down	10
65	Parlophone R 5229	I'll Take You Home/Do You Love Him?	10
65	Parlophone R 5259	Three Rooms Of Running Water/If Only You'd Reply	15
65	Parlophone R 5317	I Have Cried My Last Tear/As Long As She Looks Like You	7
66	Parlophone R 5406	You Can't Love 'Em All/Need Your Loving Tonight	7
66	Parlophone R 5466	Eyes For You/Hold On I'm Coming	12
66	Parlophone R 5489	Got To Get You Into My Life/Baby Each Day	7
66	Parlophone R 5534	Never Knew Lovin' Could Be So Doggone Good/Don't Help Me Out	7
67	Parlophone R 5565	I'm Sorry/I'll Take Good Care Of You	10
67	Parlophone R 5598	I'll Be There/Use Me	6
69	Parlophone R 5792	Memphis Streets/But I'm Wrong	10
65	Parlophone GEP 8923	CLIFF BENNETT AND THE REBEL ROUSERS (EP)	35
65	Parlophone GEP 8936	TRY IT BABY (EP)	35
66	Parlophone GEP 8955	WE'RE GONNA MAKE IT (EP)	35
64	Parlophone PMC 1242	CLIFF BENNETT AND THE REBEL ROUSERS (LP, yellow/black label)	50
66	EMI Regal REG 1039	CLIFF BENNETT (LP, export issue)	20
67	Parlophone PMC/PCS 7017	GOT TO GET YOU INTO OUR LIFE (LP, yellow/black label)	35

CLIFF BENNETT BAND
68	Parlophone R 5666	Take Your Time/House Of A Thousand Dolls	5
68	Parlophone R 5691	You're Breaking Me Up (And I'm Wasting Away)/I Hear Her Voice	10
68	Parlophone R 5711	Lonely Weekends/Good Times	10
68	Parlophone R 5728	One More Heartache/Nobody Runs Forever	12
68	Parlophone R 5749	Back In The USSR/This Man	12
68	Parlophone PMC/PCS 7054	BRANCHES OUT (LP, yellow/black label, with "sold in the U.K." label text)	40

CLIFF BENNETT'S REBELLION
71	CBS 7231	Amos Moses/Movin' And Travelin' On	12
71	CBS 64487	CLIFF BENNETT'S REBELLION (LP)	18

(see also Charles Hodges, Rebel Rousers, Toefat, Screaming Lord Sutch & Savages)

DICKIE BENNETT
55	Decca F 10595	There, But For The Grace Of God Go I/Stars Shine In Your Eyes	5
56	Decca F 10697	Dungaree Doll/Can't We Be Partners (After The Dance)	10
56	Decca F 10782	You Don't Know Me/Cry Upon My Shoulder	5

DUSTER BENNETT
68	Blue Horizon 57-3141	It's A Man Down There/Things Are Changing	20

MINT VALUE £

Jo JO BENNETT

69	Blue Horizon 57-3148	Raining In My Heart/Jumpin' For Joy...20
69	Blue Horizon 57-3154	Bright Lights, Big City/Fresh Country Jam (with His House Band)...........................20
69	Blue Horizon 57-3164	I'm Gonna Wind Up Endin' Up Or I'm Gonna End Up Windin' Up With You/ Rock Of Ages, Cleft For Me...20
70	Blue Horizon 57-3173	I Chose To Sing The Blues/If You Could Hang Your Washing Like You Hang Your Lines 10
70	Blue Horizon 57-3179	Act Nice And Gentle/I Want You To Love Me 10
74	Rak RAK 177	Comin' Home/Pretty Little Thing 15
68	Blue Horizon 7-63208	SMILING LIKE I'M HAPPY (LP, with His House Band, i.e. Fleetwood Mac) 60
69	Blue Horizon 7-63221	BRIGHT LIGHTS... (LP, gatefold sleeve) 75
70	Blue Horizon 7-63868	12 DB's (LP, with lyric sheet)...40

(see also Fleetwood Mac)

JO JO BENNETT

67	Doctor Bird DB 1097	The Lecture/Cantelope Rock (with Fugitives) 40
67	Doctor Bird DB 1116	Rocksteady/Real Gone Loser (with Fugitives)..50
70	Explosion EX 2029	Groovy Jo Jo/Ten Steps To Soul (both actually with Mudie's All Stars)...........25
70	Trojan TR 7774	Leaving Rome/In The Nude (both with Mudie's All Stars) 8
71	Moodisc MU 3514	Snowbird/MUDIE'S ALLSTARS: Change The Tide...10
71	Moodisc HME 108	Poison Ivy/MUDIE'S ALLSTARS: Ivy Poison..8
70	Trojan TBL 133	GROOVY JO JO (LP, with Mudie's Allstars) 30

(see also Fugitives, I Roy)

JOE BENNETT & SPARKLETONES

57	HMV POP 399	Black Slacks/Boppin' Rock Boogie 150
57	HMV POP 399	Black Slacks/Boppin' Rock Boogie (78) 25
58	HMV POP 445	Rocket/Penny Loafers And Bobby Socks 150
58	HMV POP 445	Rocket/Penny Loafers And Bobby Socks (78) 25

KIM BENNETT

55	Decca F 10449	Softly Softly/ROLAND SHAW ORCHESTRA: Trumpeter's Lullaby 10
55	Decca F 10460	Melody Of Love/Ding Dong...10
55	Decca F 10599	The Kentuckian Song/Overnight 10
56	Decca F 10706	No, Not Much/You Can't Keep Running 7

(see also Roland Shaw)

LEE BENNETT & SUNLINERS

64	Decca F 12024	Poor Bachelor Boy/Fool, Fool, Fool 6

LORNA BENNETT

72	Blue Mountain BM 1013	Breakfast In Bed/Skank In Bed 10
75	Island WIP 6237	Breakfast In Bed/Skank In Bed (reissue) 6

NICK BENNETT

60	Columbia DB 4516	You Understand Me/Mr. Lonely 7

PETER E, BENNETT

71	RCA SF 8190	THE BALLAD OF GALDWAIN (LP, lyric insert, orange/white label)...................15

RAY BENNETT

62	Decca F 11550	Go Away Little Girl/Twistin' To The Blues 5
62	Decca DFE 8516	INTRODUCING RAY BENNETT (EP) 40

ROY BENNETT

68	Blue Cat BS 146	I Dangerous/DEE SET: I Know A Place 40

RUDI BENNETT

68	Decca F 12741	I'm So Proud/WHISTLING JACK SMITH: Havah Nagilah 5
68	Decca F12729	I'm So Proud/You're My Adee 20

TONY BENNETT

53	Columbia SCM 5048	Congratulations To Someone/Take Me 5
54	Columbia 39745	Here In My Heart/I'm Lost Again..5
57	Philips JK 1008	Whatever Lola Wants/Heart (jukebox issue) 8
59	Philips PB 1079	Till/Ask Anyone In Love...5

(see also Count Basie, John Barry)

VAL BENNETT

68	Island WI 3113	Jumping With Mr. Lee/ROY SHIRLEY: Keep Your Eyes On The Road 50
68	Island WI 3146	The Russians Are Coming (Take Five)/LESTER STERLING: Sir Lee's Whip 80
68	Trojan TR 611	Spanish Harlem/ROY SHIRLEY: If I Did Know...15
69	Trojan TR 640	Baby Baby/Barbara 20
69	Crab CRAB 6	Reggae City/CANNON KING: Mellow Trumpet (B-side actually by Carl 'King Cannon Ball' Bryan) 45
69	Camel CA 24	Midnight Spin/SOUL CATS: Money Money 15

(see also Roy Shirley, Max Romeo, Derrick Morgan, Clancy Eccles, Harry J Allstars, George A Penny, Lloyd Terrell,

JOHNNY BENNINGS & HIS RHYTHM & BLUES BAND

54	Esquire 10-376	Third Degree Blues/Timber (78) 10

MARC BENNO

71	A & M AMS850	Good Year/Second Story Window 8

JON BENNS

80	Aveda AVA 106	BENNS MEANS LAFFS (LP) 15

(see also The Enid)

BENNY & TINA

69	Mercury MF 1133	This Love Is Real/Over My Dead Body 10

BARRY BENSON

66	Parlophone R 5446	Stay A Little While/That's For Sure 35
66	Parlophone R 5484	Not A One Girl Guy/Sunshine Child 25
66	Parlophone R 5544	Always Waitin'/My Friend And I...8
67	Parlophone R 5578	Cousin Jane/Meet Jacqueline 20
67	Page One POF 034	I Can't Wait/Oh No 10

BOBBY BENSON & HIS COMBO

58	Philips PB 854	Taxi Driver, I Don't Care/Gentleman Bobby 6

GARY BENSON

66	Pye 7N 17032	This Man's Got No Luck/I'm So Tired	5
70	Penny Farthing PEN 727	Holly/Oak Tree	5
73	Birth RAB 1002	The Concert/To Kill Another Day	10
75	Penny Farthing PEN 895	The Reunion/The Joke	6
70	Penny Farthing PELS 506	THE REUNION (LP)	30
73	Birth RAB 5	THE CONCERT (LP, gatefold sleeve)	25

GEORGE BENSON (QUARTET)

66	CBS (S)BPG 62817	IT'S UPTOWN (LP, flipback sleeve, as George Benson Quartet)	25
67	CBS (S)BPG 62971	THE GEORGE BENSON COOKBOOK (LP)	18
73	CTI 6015	WHITE RABBIT (LP)	12

MARIE BENSON & THE LONDONAIRES

55	Decca F 10452	Mambo Italiano/Mobile	10

MICHAEL BENTINE

72	Polydor 2058294	Home Made Wine/The Olympic Showjumper	5

(see also Goons)

BRIAN BENTLEY & THE BACHELORS

60	Philips PB 1085	Wishing Well/Please Make Up Your Mind	25
60	Philips PB 1086	First Flight East/Sunday Break	5
62	Salvo SLO 1813	Caramba/Nellie Dean (99 copies only)	20

JAY BENTLEY & THE JET SET

64	Vocalion VN 9230	Watusi '64/I'll Get You	10

ACE BENTLEY

81	Traffic Light TL 181	Beat Boys/Sometimes In The Night (p/s)	10

BROOK BENTON

58	RCA RCA 1044	A Million Miles From Nowhere/Devoted	25
58	Mercury AMT 1014	It's Just A Matter Of Time/Hurtin' Inside	5
59	Mercury AMT 1043	Endlessly/So Close	7
59	Mercury AMT 1061	Thank You Pretty Baby/With All Of My Heart	5
59	Mercury AMT 1068	So Many Ways/I Want You Forever	5
60	Mercury AMT 1097	The Ties That Bind/Hither And Thither And Yon	5
60	Mercury AMT 1109	Kiddio/The Same One	10
60	Mercury AMT 1121	Fools Rush In/Somebody You'll Want Me To Want You	5
61	Mercury AMT 1134	For My Baby/Think Twice	5
61	Mercury AMT 1148	The Boll Weevil Song/Your Eyes	6
61	Mercury AMT 1157	Frankie And Johnny/It's Just A House Without You	7
61	Mercury AMT 1168	Revenge/Really Really	5
62	Mercury AMT 1172	Walk On The Wild Side/Somewhere In The Used To Be	8
62	Mercury AMT 1178	Hit Record/Thanks To The Fool	5
62	Mercury AMT 1194	Hotel Happiness/Still Waters Run Deep	5
63	Mercury AMT 1212	Two Tickets To Paradise/Don't Hate Me	10
63	Mercury AMT 1217	Baby You Got It Made/Stop Foolin' (with Damita Jo)	10
68	Atlantic 584 222	Do Your Own Thing/I Just Don't Know What To Do With Myself	6
69	Atlantic 584 266	Touch 'Em With Love/She Knows What To Do For Me	6
69	Atlantic 584 267	Nothing Can Take The Place Of You/Woman Wihout Love	6
70	Atlantic 584 315	Rainy Night In Georgia/Where Do I Go From Here	6
58	RCA RCX 169	BROOK BENTON (EP, tri centre)	20
58	Fontana TFE 17151	BROOK BENTON AT HIS BEST (EP)	10
60	Mercury SEZ 19009	WHEN I FALL IN LOVE (EP, stereo)	8
61	Mercury SEZ 19019	WHEN YOU'RE IN LOVE (EP, stereo)	8
61	Mercury SEZ 19024	SO WARM (EP, stereo)	8

BROOK BENTON & DINAH WASHINGTON

60	Mercury AMT 1083	Baby (You've Got What It Takes)/I Do	15
60	Mercury AMT 1099	A Rockin' Good Way/I Believe	15
69	Mercury MF 1100	A Rockin' Good Way/I Do	5
61	Mercury ZEP 10120	A ROCKING GOOD WAY (EP, mono)	15
61	Mercury SEZ 19022	A ROCKING GOOD WAY (EP, stereo)	15
64	Mercury 20069 MCL	THE TWO OF US (LP)	20

STEVE BERESFORD

75	Incus INCUS 15	TEATIME (LP)	50

BERETS

70	Avant Garde AVS 116	THE MASS FOR PEACE (LP, with insert)	20

BERKELEY KITES

68	Polydor 56742	Hang Up City/Mary-Go-Round	10
69	Polydor 56770	Alice In Wonderland/What Goes Up Must Come Down	10

BERLIN RITZ

80	Big Muff BM 001	Crazy Nights/You're Where I Belong (no p/s)	10

BERMUDAS

64	London HLN 9894	Donnie/Chu Sen Ling	15

BERNADETTE

67	Rim RIM 2	Come Kiss Me Love/Let Me Do The Talking	15
68	Philips 1725	Toys, Toys, Toys/Kiss And Run Away	6

JACKIE BERNARD

78	One Stop OSM 001	Keep Rowing/Version (12")	50

KENNY BERNARD (& WRANGLERS)

65	Pye 7N 15920	The Tracker/You Gotta Give (with Wranglers)	20
65	Pye 7N 15920	The Tracker/You Gotta Give (with Wranglers) (DJ Copy)	125
66	Pye 7N 17131	Nothing Can Change This Love/What Love Brings	70
66	Pye 7N 17131	Nothing Can Change This Love/What Love Brings (DJ Copy)	100
67	Pye 7N 17233	Ain't No Soul (Left In These Old Shoes)/Hey Woman	40
67	Pye 7N 17284	I Do/Isn't That A Good Idea	15
67	CBS 2936	Somebody/Pity My Feet	100

Rod BERNARD

| 67 | CBS 2936 | Somebody/Pity My Feet (DJ copy) | 150 |
| 68 | CBS 3860 | Victim Of Perfume And Lace/A Change Is Gonna Come | 25 |

(see also Kenny & Wranglers, Wranglers, Cat's Pyjamas)

ROD BERNARD
| 59 | London HLM 8849 | This Should Go On Forever/Pardon, Mr. Gordon | 25 |
| 59 | Mercury AMT 1070 | One More Chance/Shedding Teardrops Over You | 15 |

AGNES BERNELL
| 63 | HMV 7EG 8696 | THE LOST NOISES OFFICE (EP) | 20 |

BERNIE & BUZZ BAND
| 68 | Decca F 22829 | The House That Jack Built/PETE KELLY'S SOULUTION: Midnight Confessions (export issue) | 18 |
| 68 | Deram DM 181 | When Something's Wrong With My Baby/Don't Knock It | 35 |

(see also Pete Kelly's Soulution)

BERNIE & MYSTERIONS
| 81 | Chipping Norton CHIP 5 | Another Night/Front Seat Love (no p/s) | 8 |

ELMER BERNSTEIN
56	Brunswick 05544	Clark Street Parts 1 & 2 (gold print on label)	10
56	Brunswick 05544	Clark Street Parts 1 & 2 (silver print on label)	5
59	Capitol CL 15101	Staccato's Theme/The Jazz At Waldo's	5
63	MGM MGM 1238	Rat Race/Saints & Sinners	20
63	MGM MGM 1238	Rat Race/Saints & Sinners (DJ Copy)	40
66	United Artists UP 1163	The Magnificent Seven/Return Of The Seven	10
60	Capitol EAP1 1287	STACCATO (EP)	10
56	Brunswick LAT 8101	THE MAN WITH THE GOLDEN ARM (LP, soundtrack)	20
57	Brunswick LAT 8195	SWEET SMELL OF SUCCESS (LP, soundtrack)	20
57	London HA-P 2076	MEN IN WAR (LP, soundtrack)	15
58	London HA-D 2074/5	THE TEN COMMANDMENTS (2-LP, soundtrack)	15
58	London HA-D 2111	DESIRE UNDER THE ELMS (LP, soundtrack)	20
58	London HA-T 2125	GOD'S LITTLE ACRE (LP, soundtrack)	20
58	Capitol LCT 6165	KINGS GO FORTH (LP, soundtrack)	15
59	Capitol LCT 6180	SOME CAME RUNNING (LP, soundtrack)	15
62	MGM MGM-C 891	WALK ON THE WILD SIDE (LP, soundtrack)	15
63	MGM MGM-C 934	TO KILL A MOCKINGBIRD (LP, soundtrack)	20
63	United Artists ULP 1041	THE GREAT ESCAPE (LP, soundtrack, mono/stereo)	20
65	CBS (S)BPG 62558	THE SONS OF KATIE ELDER (LP, stereo, soundtrack, feat. Johnny Cash)	12
67	RCA Victor RD 7792	THE SILENCERS (LP, soundtrack, feat. Vikki Carr)	30
67	Fontana TL 5306	BABY, THE RAIN MUST FALL (LP, soundtrack)	15

ROCK BERNTSEN
| 84 | Forest Tracks FT 3017 | KELPERS AFTER ALL (LP, with insert) | 18 |

CHUCK BERRY
78s
56	London HLU 8275	Down Bound Train/No Money Down	70
57	London HLN 8375	You Can't Catch Me/Havana Moon	40
57	London HLU 8428	Roll Over Beethoven/Drifting Heart	40
57	Columbia DB 3951	School Day (Ring! Ring! Goes The Bell)/Deep Feeling	30
57	London HLM 8531	Rock And Roll Music/Blue Feeling	35
58	London HLM 8585	Sweet Little Sixteen/Reelin' And Rockin'	30
58	London HLM 8629	Johnny B. Goode/Around And Around	35
58	London HL 8677	Beautiful Delilah/Vacation Time	45
58	London HL 7055	Carol/Hey Pedro (export single)	50
58	London HL 8712	Carol/Hey Pedro	40
58	London HLM 8767	Sweet Little Rock And Roller/Jo Jo Gun	50
59	London HLM 8853	Almost Grown/Little Queenie	80
59	London HLM 8921	Back In The U.S.A./Memphis, Tennessee	80

SINGLES
56	London HLU 8275	No Money Down/Down Bound Train (silver lettering on label, triangular centre)	400
56	London HLU 8275	No Money Down/Down Bound Train (silver lettering on label, round centre)	250
57	London HLN 8375	You Can't Catch Me/Havana Moon (gold lettering on label)	375
57	London HLN 8375	You Can't Catch Me/Havana Moon (silver lettering on label)	150
57	London HLU 8428	Roll Over Beethoven/Drifting Heart	50
57	Columbia DB 3951	School Day (Ring! Ring! Goes The Bell)/Blue Feeling	60
57	London HLM 8531	Rock And Roll Music/Blue Feeling	50
58	London HLM 8585	Sweet Little Sixteen/Reelin' And Rockin'	50
58	London HLM 8629	Johnny B. Goode/Around And Around	25
58	London HL 8677	Beautiful Delilah/Vacation Time	30
58	London HL 8712	Carol/Hey Pedro	40
58	London HL 7055	Carol/Hey Pedro (export issue)	40
58	London HLM 8767	Sweet Little Rock And Roller/Jo Jo Gun	30
59	London HLM 8853	Almost Grown/Little Queenie	30
59	London HLM 8921	Back In The U.S.A./Memphis, Tennessee	25

(Originally issued with triangular centres; later silver top label/round centre pressings are worth half to two-thirds these values.)

60	London HLM 9069	Let It Rock/Too Pooped To Pop	25
60	London HLM 9159	Bye Bye Johnny/Mad Lad	25
61	Pye International 7N 25100	I'm Talkin' 'Bout You/Little Star (blue label)	30
61	Pye International 7N 25100	I'm Talkin' 'Bout You/Little Star (later red/yellow label)	10
63	Pye International 7N 25209	Go Go Go/Come On	12
63	Pye International 7N 25218	Memphis, Tennessee/Let It Rock	5
63	Pye International 7N 25228	Run Rudolph Run/Johnny B. Goode	10
64	Pye International 7N 25236	Nadine (Is It You?)/O Rangutang	10
64	Pye International 7N 25242	No Particular Place To Go/Liverpool Drive	5
64	Pye International 7N 25257	You Never Can Tell/Brenda Lee	12
64	Pye International 7N 25271	Little Marie/Go Bobby Soxer	12
65	Pye International 7N 25285	The Promised Land/The Things I Used To Do	10
65	Chess CRS 8006	I Got A Booking/Lonely School Days	10
65	Chess CRS 8012	Dear Dad/My Little Lovelight	10
65	Chess CRS 8022	It Wasn't Me/It's My Own Business	10
66	Chess CRS 8037	Ramona Say Yes/Lonely School Days	10

66	Mercury MF 958	Club Nitty Gritty/Laugh And Cry	12
67	Mercury MF 994	Back To Memphis/I Do Really Love You	10
68	Mercury MF 1057	St. Louis To Frisco/Ma Dear	10
69	Mercury MF 1102	Back To Memphis/Roll Over Beethoven	10
68	Chess CRS 8075	Johnny B. Goode/Sweet Little Sixteen	5
69	Chess CRS 8089	No Particular Place To Go/It Wasn't Me	5
72	Chess 6145 007	Rock And Roll Music/Johnny B. Goode/School Days	5
73	Chess 6145 020	Reelin' And Rockin' (Live)/I Will Not Let You Go	5
73	Chess 6145 027	South Of The Border (Live)/Bio	5
75	Chess 6145 038	Shake Rattle And Roll/I'm Just A Name	5
79	Atlantic K 11354	Oh What A Thrill/California	5

EPs

56	London REU 1053	RHYTHM AND BLUES WITH CHUCK BERRY (maroon/gold label, tri-centre)	150
56	London REU 1053	RHYTHM AND BLUES WITH CHUCK BERRY (later pressing, maroon/silver label, round centre)	60
60	London REM 1188	REELIN' AND ROCKIN' (maroon and gold label, tri centre)	250
60	London REM 1188	REELIN' AND ROCKIN' (round centre)	100
63	Pye Intl. NEP 44011	CHUCK BERRY	20
63	Pye Intl. NEP 44013	THIS IS CHUCK BERRY	20
64	Pye Intl. NEP 44018	THE BEST OF CHUCK BERRY	20
64	Pye Intl. NEP 44028	CHUCK BERRY HITS	20
64	Pye Intl. NEP 44033	BLUE MOOD	20
65	Chess CRE 6002	THE PROMISED LAND	20
65	Chess CRE 6005	COME ON	20
66	Chess CRE 6012	I GOT A BOOKING	25
66	Chess CRE 6016	YOU CAME A LONG WAY FROM ST. LOUIS	30

ALBUMS

58	London HA-M 2132	ONE DOZEN BERRYS	150
62	Pye Intl. NPL 28019	NEW JUKE BOX HITS	40
63	Pye Intl. NPL 28024	CHUCK BERRY	25
63	Pye Intl. NPL 28027	CHUCK BERRY ON STAGE	30
63	Pye Intl. NPL 28028	MORE CHUCK BERRY	25
64	Pye Intl. NPL 28031	THE LATEST AND THE GREATEST	25
64	Pye Intl. NPL 28039	YOU NEVER CAN TELL	30
65	Chess CRL 4005	CHUCK BERRY IN LONDON	30
65	Chess CRL 4506	FRESH BERRYS	30
66	Chess CRL 4548	CHUCK BERRY'S GREATEST HITS	15
67	Mercury 20110 (S)MCL	CHUCK BERRY IN MEMPHIS	20
67	Mercury 20112 (S)MCL	LIVE AT THE FILLMORE AUDITORIUM - SAN FRANCISCO	15
69	Mercury 20162 (S)MCL	CONCERTO IN B. GOODE	15
72	Chess 6310 113	BACK HOME	15
72	Chess 6310 115	SAN FRANCISCO DUES	15
72	Philips Int. 6619 008	ST. LOUIE TO FRISCO TO MEMPHIS (2-LP)	15

CHUCK BERRY/BO DIDDLEY

63	Pye Intl. NEP 44009	CHUCK AND BO (EP)	20
63	Pye Intl. NEP 44012	CHUCK AND BO, VOL. 2 (EP)	20
64	Pye Intl. NEP 44017	CHUCK AND BO, VOL. 3 (EP)	25
73	Chess 6145 012	BIG DADDIES (LP)	30
64	Pye Intl. NPL 28047	TWO GREAT GUITARS (LP, mono)	35

(see also Bo Diddley)

DAVE BERRY (& CRUISERS)

63	Decca F 11734	Memphis Tennessee/Tossin' & Turnin' (with Cruisers)	10
63	Decca F 11803	My Baby Left Me/Hoochie Coochie Man (B-side with Cruisers)	8
64	Decca F 11876	Baby It's You/Sweet And Lovely	7
64	Decca F 11937	The Crying Game/Don't Gimme No Lip Child	5
64	Decca F 12020	One Heart Between Two/You're Gonna Need Somebody	10
65	Decca F 12103	Little Things/I've Got A Tiger By The Tail	6
65	Decca F 12188	This Strange Effect/Now	6
65	Decca F 12258	I'm Gonna Take You There/Just Don't Know	8
66	Decca F 12337	If You Wait For Love/Hidden	10
66	Decca F 12435	Mama/Walk, Walk, Talk	5
66	Decca F 12513	Picture Me Gone/Ann	20
67	Decca F 12579	Stranger/Stick By The Book	7
67	Decca F 12651	Forever/And I Have Learned To Dream	10
68	Decca F 12739	Just As Much As Ever/I Got A Feeling	8
68	Decca F 12771	(Do I Figure) In Your Life/Latisha	15
69	Decca F 12905	Huma Lama Oh What A Life (by Dave Berry & Sponge)	7
70	Decca F 12999	Change Our Minds/Long Walk To D.C.	7
70	Decca F 13080	Chaplin House/Trees	8
72	CBS 7780	Movin' On (Turn Around)/Don't Bring Me Down	6
88	Flagstaff 002	Out Of Time/Serenade To Alice (p/s, 200 only)	8
64	Decca DFE 8601	DAVE BERRY (EP)	20
65	Decca DFE 8625	CAN I GET IT FROM YOU (EP)	25
64	Decca LK 4653	DAVE BERRY (LP)	35
66	Ace Of Clubs ACL 1218	ONE DOZEN BERRIES (LP, also stereo SCL 1218)	12
66	Decca LK 4823	THE SPECIAL SOUND OF DAVE BERRY (LP)	30
68	Decca LK/SKL 4932	DAVE BERRY '68 (LP)	25

(see also Cruisers)

LEN & BARBARA BERRY

| 60s | Greenwich Village GVR 229 | THE PORTWAY PEDDLERS (LP) | 50 |

MIKE BERRY (& THE OUTLAWS)

61	Decca F 11314	Will You Love Me Tomorrow/My Baby Doll (with The Outlaws)	30
61	HMV POP 912	Tribute To Buddy Holly/What's The Matter (with The Outlaws)	12
62	HMV POP 979	It's Just A Matter Of Time/Little Boy Blue (backing group miscredited as Admirals, actually The Outlaws)	10
62	HMV POP 1042	Every Little Kiss/How Many Times	15
62	HMV POP 1105	Don't You Think It's Time/Loneliness (with The Outlaws) (blue label)	10
62	HMV POP 1105	Don't You Think It's Time/Loneliness (with The Outlaws) (black label)	7

63	HMV POP 1142	My Little Baby/You'll Do It, You'll Fall In Love	10
63	HMV POP 1194	It Really Doesn't Matter/Try A Little Bit Harder	15
64	HMV POP 1257	This Little Girl/On My Mind	10
64	HMV POP 1284	Lovesick/Letter Of Love	12
64	HMV POP 1314	Who Will It Be/Talk (with Innocents)	10
64	HMV POP 1362	Two Lovers/Don't Try To Stand In My Way	10
65	HMV POP 1449	That's All I Ever Wanted From You/She Didn't Care	10
65	HMV POP 1494	It Comes And Goes/Gonna Fall In Love	10
66	HMV POP 1530	Warm Baby/Just Thought I'd 'Phone	12
67	Polydor 56182	Raining In My Heart/Eyes	10
72	York SYK 516	Going Down To Virginia/Love Her	10
72	York SYK 530	Drift Away/Keep Your Eyes On The Road	6
76	Polydor 2058 700	Tribute To Buddy Holly/Dial My Number	20
63	HMV 7EG 8793	IT'S TIME FOR MIKE BERRY (EP, with Outlaws)	25
63	HMV 7EG 8808	A TRIBUTE TO BUDDY HOLLY (EP)	30
72	York FYK 409	AMBUSH (LP)	15
72	York FYK409	DRIFT AWAY (LP)	15

(see also Outlaws, Le Roys, Shepperton Flames, Innocents [U.K], UK Jones)

RICHARD BERRY & PHARAOHS
64	Ember EMB EP 4527	RHYTHM AND BLUES VOL. 3 (EP)	200

CINDY LEE BERRYHILL
89	awareness AWP 001	Me, Steve, Kirk And Keith/Baby (Should I Have The Baby) (p/s)	6

BERRY STREET STATION
75	Crystal CR 7024	Chocolate Sugar/All I Want Is You	10

BERTY B AND DILLINJA
95	Lionheart BERT1	Lionheart/Art Of Control (12")	15

(see also Dillinja, Cybotron Featuring Dillinja)

BESHARA
84	Mass Media Music MM121004	Men Cry Too/Version (12", purple vinyl)	20

BESHERA
82	Home Supn HS 002	Glory Glory/Version (12")	80

ADAM BEST
70	Fontana SFL 13209	WALL OF SOUND (LP)	20

JON BEST
65	Decca F 12077	Young Boy Blues/Living Without Love	10

PETE BEST FOUR
64	Decca F 11929	I'm Gonna Knock On Your Door/Why Did I Fall In Love With You?	70

(see also Beatles, Lee Curtis & All Stars)

BEST EVER
75	Polydor 2001594	Rope A Dope/People's Choice (with Muhammad Ali)	20

RICHARD BESWICK & PHILIPP WACHSMANN
81	Bead Records BEAD 18	HELLO BRENDA! (LP)	25

BETA BAND
97	Regal REG 16	CHAMPION VERSIONS EP: Dry The Rain/I Know/B+A/Dog's Got A Bone (12", p/s, 1,000 only)	50
98	Regal REG 18	THE PATTY PATTY SOUND EP: Inner Meet Me/The House/The Monolith/ She's The One (2 x 12", p/s, 1,000 only)	30
99	Regal REG 30	THE BETA BAND (2-LP)	25
01	Regal REG 59	HOT SHOTS II (2-LP)	25
04	Regal REG 101	HEROS TO ZEROS (2-LP, gatefold sleeve)	20

(see also Aliens)

SIR JOHN BETJEMAN
74	Charisma CB 254	Licorice Fields Of Ponterfract/In The Public Gardens	8
74	Charisma CAS 1086	BANANA BLUSH (LP)	15
75	Charisma CAS 1096	LATE FLOWERING LOVE (LP, with Jim Parker)	15

BETTERDAYS
65	Polydor BM 56024	Don't Want That/Here 'Tis	175
96	Dig The Fuzz DIG 008	HOWLIN' (LP, with booklet)	15

HAROLD BETTERS
65	Sue WI 378	Do Anything You Wanna (Parts 1 & 2)	50

AL BETTS
73	Peer Int. PIL 9018	CONTRASTS IN JAZZ VOLUME 2 (LP)	15

BETWEEN PICTURES
81	A Side AS 002	Treat Me Like An Equal/Life On Your Own	15
81	Applause CLAP 3	Birthday Card/Down At The Factory (p/s)	6

JOHNNY BEV
62	Pye 7N 17030	Tell Her You Love Her/This Love I Lost	5
63	Pye 7N 15505	No Peace Of Mind/Summer Romance	5
63	Pye 7N 15523	Treat Her Right/For Always	5
63	Pye 7N 15576	What Am I To Do/Save All Your Kisses For Me	5
65	Columbia DB 7579	You Pass Me By/Leaving My Teardrops Behind	5
65	Columbia DB 7767	The World Goes Away/The House	5
67	CBS 3031	Soft As A Kiss/Welcome Stranger	5

BEVERLEY
66	Deram DM 101	Happy New Year/Where The Good Times Are	30
67	Deram DM 137	Museum/DENNY CORDELL TEA TIME ENSEMBLE: A Quick One For Sanity	35

(see also John & Beverley Martyn, Levee Breakers)

BEVERLEY SISTERS
55	Decca F 10539	I Remember Mama/I've Been Thinking	5
55	Decca F 10603	Humming Bird/Have You Ever Been Lonely?	5

55	Decca F 10641	My Heart Goes A-Sailing/Teddy Bear	7
56	Decca F 10705	Willie Can/I've Started Courtin'	5
56	Decca F 10729	Rickshaw Boy/You Ought To Have A Wife	5
56	Decca F 10770	Born To Be With You/It's Easy	5
56	Decca F 10813	Come Home To My Arms/Doodle-Doo-Doo	5
57	Decca F 10832	I Dreamed/Mama From The Train (A Kiss, A Kiss)	7
57	Decca F 10853	Greensleeves/I'll See You In My Dreams	5
57	Decca F 10893	Mr. Wonderful/Blow The Wind Southerly	8
57	Decca F 10909	Bye, Bye Love/It's Illegal, It's Immoral, Or It Makes You Fat	5
57	Decca F 10943	Riding Down From Bangor/The Young Cavaliero	5
58	Decca F 10971	Long Black Nylons/Without You	15

BEVERLEY'S ALLSTARS

65	Black Swan WI 449	Go Home/THEO BECKFORD: Ungrateful People	25
69	Trojan TR 683	Double Shot/Gimme Gimme Gal (B-side act. "Banana Water" by Mellotones)	35
70	Trojan TR 7729	Moon Dust/Fat Cat (both sides actually by Ansell Collins)	25

(see also Clarendonians, Gaylads, Ken Boothe, Glen Brown, Desmond Dekker, Bob Marley, Maytals, Melodians, Derrick Morgan, Pioneers, Rockstones, Bruce Ruffin, Delroy Wilson)

FRANK BEVERLY & BUTLERS

79	Inferno HEAT 4	If That's What You Wanted/Love (Your Pain Goes Deep) (with p/s)	10
79	Inferno HEAT 4	If That's What You Wanted/Love (Your Pain Goes Deep) (without p/s)	5

BEVERLY HILLS BLUES BAND

76	Warner Bros K 16752	Just Because/If I Can Just Get Through Tonight	15

(see also Four Seasons)

BEVIS FROND

88	Bucketfull/Brains BOB 21	High In A Flat/DREAM SYNDICATE: Blind Willie McTell (free with Bucketfull Of Brains issue 27, 33rpm, yellow die-cut sleeve)	12
88	Bucketfull/Brains BOB 21	High In A Flat/DREAM SYNDICATE: Blind Willie McTell (without Bucketfull Of Brains issue 27)	7
90	Clawfist PIS 1	Sexorcist/WALKINGSEEDS: Reflection In A Tall Mirror (p/s, mail-order only)	5
87	Woronzow WOO 3	MIASMA (LP, laminated cover, 500 copies only)	15
80s	Reckless RECKLP 13	MIASMA (LP, reissue, matt cover)	12
87	Woronzow WOO 4	INNER MARSHLAND (LP)	12
80s	Reckless RECKLP 14	INNER MARSHLAND (LP, reissue)	12
87	Woronzow WOO 5 1/2	BEVIS THROUGH THE LOOKING GLASS - THE GREAT MAGNET DISASTER (2-LP, 500 only, originals all signed, with booklet; counterfeits unsigned)	40
80s	Reckless RECKLP 9	BEVIS THROUGH THE LOOKING GLASS (LP, reissue)	12
88	Woronzow WOO 8	TRIPTYCH (LP)	12
80s	Reckless RECKLP 15	TRIPTYCH (LP, reissue)	15
90	Woronzow WOO 13	MAGIC EYE (LP, featuring Twink, 200 only)	12
91	Woronzow WOO 16	NEW RIVER HEAD (2-LP, 1st 500 with EP & insert)	18
92	Woronzow WOO 18	LONDON STONE (LP)	12
92	Woronzow WOO 26	SUPERSEEDER (2-LP)	15
93	Woronzow WOO 22	SPRAWL (2-LP, gatefold sleeve, with insert)	15
97	Woronzow WOO 406	NORTH CIRCULAR (3-LP, with insert, 750 only, signed & numbered)	25

(see also Von Trap Family, Room 13)

PAUL BEVOIR

85	Dance Network WORK 2	THE HAPPIEST DAYS OF YOUR LIFE (LP)	12

(see also Jetset)

RODNEY BEWES

69	Revolution REV 1003	Remember When/Dear Mother Love Albert	25
70	Revolution Pop REVP 1001	Dear Mother Love Albert/Meter Maid	30

(see also Highly Likely)

BEYOND THE IMPLODE

79	Diverse DIVE 101	LAST THOUGHTS EP (EP, 250 copies with hand-written labels, numbered, with 'Look Back' Fanzine)	150
80	Diverse DIVE 102	11th HOUR BREAKDOWN EP	70

BEYOND THE WIZARD'S SLEEVE

05	3rd Mynd 02	BEYOND THE WIZARD'S SLEEVE (LP)	15
06	3rd Mynd 03	SPRING (LP)	18
07	3rd Mynd 04	GEORGE (LP, red vinyl)	15
07	3rd Mynd 05	WEST (LP, clear vinyl)	15

BEYOND THE QUARRY

92	Flair (No Cat. No)	Comedown/Disappointment/One Way/Relegate (12", purple vinyl)	70

B-52'S

79	Island WIP 6527	6060-842/Hero Worship (p/s)	5
79	Island ILPS 9580	THE B-52's (LP, with bonus single "Rock Lobster"/"52 Girls" [PSR 438])	12
80	Island ILPS 9622	WILD PLANET (LP, in plastic bag with badge)	12

B FILM

80	Plastic Records BEE 001	Night Running/Danger Man	12

BG AND THE MOUSE

82	Maestro MR 003	Da Doo Ron Ron/Clever Boy (no p/s)	10

BG FROM BASS INC

88	Black Steel BS002	Rock The Boat (12")	12

MAURICIO BIANCHI

81	Sterile SR 2	SYMPATHY FOR A GENOCIDE (LP, 200 only)	200
83	Broken BV 3	THE PLAIN TRUTH (LP)	70

GENE BIANCO GROUP

60	Vogue V 9167	Alarm Clock Rock/Harp Rock Boogie	35

BIAS

02	Canteen CR 001	Delerious: Street Of Life/Sunrise	10

BIBBY

65	Blue Beat BB 289	Rub It Down/Wicked Man (actually by Harris Seaton)	20

(see also B.B. Seaton, Horace Seaton)

BIDDU

67	Regal Zonophone RZ 3002	Look Out Here I Come/Daughter Of Love	15
77	Epic EPC 5416	Soul Coaxing/Nirvana (12", p/s)	15
78	Epic EPCS 6230	Blacker Than Berry/James Bond Disco Theme (12", white label promo only)	15

BIFF BANG POW!

84	Creation CRE 003	Fifty Years Of Fun/Then When I Scream (foldaround sprayed p/s in poly bag)	30
84	Creation CRE 007	There Must Be A Better Life/The Chocolate Elephant Man (foldaway p/s in poly bag)	30
90	Caff CAFF 13	Sleep/TIMES: Extase (p/s, with insert)	20
89	Creation CRELP 046	THE ACID HOUSE ALBUM (LP, hand-sprayed sleeve)	12
91	Creation CRELP 099	L'AMOUR, DEMURE, STENHOUSEMUIR (LP)	20

(see also Laughing Apple, Times)

BIFFY CLYRO

99	Babi Yaga YAGA 001	Iname/All The Way Down (Chapter 2)/Travis Perkins (CD)	100
00	Electric Honey HER 013 CD	Thekidswhopoptodaywillrocktomorrow (CD, 1000 only)	80
01	Beggars Banquet BBQ 335	Justboy/Unsubtle/Being Gabriel (p/s)	20
01	Beggars Banquet BBQ 335CD	Justboy/Being Gabriel/Unsubtle (CD)	10
01	Beggars Banquet BBQ 352	27/Instructio4/Breatheher (CD)	12
01	Beggars Banquet BBQ 352	27/Breatheher/Instructio4 (p/s)	20
02	Beggars Banquet BBQ 358	57/Kill The Old, Torture Their Young (Evening Session Version) (p/s)	20
02	Beggars Banquet BBQ 358CD	57/Hope For An Angel/Time As An Imploding Unit/Waiting For Green (CD)	18
02	Beggars Banquet BBQ 361	Joy.Discovery. Invention/Toys Toys Toys Choke/Toys Toys Toys/ All The Way Down Chapter 2 (p/s)	12
02	Beggars Banquet BBQ 361CD	Toys, Toys, Toys, Choke, Toys, Toys, Toys/Joy. Discovery. Invention/ All The Way Down (Chapter 2) 2002 Version (CD)	18
03	Beggars Banquet BBQ 365	The Ideal Height/...And With The Scissorkick Is Victorious (p/s)	10
03	Beggars Banquet BBQ 374	Eradicate The Doubt/The Ideal Height (Live)/Justboy (Live) (p/s, numbered)	10
04	Beggars Banquet BB 377	Glitter And Trauma/There's No Such Thing As A Jaggy Snake (Peel Session) (p/s)	8
04	Beggars Banquet BBQ 379	My Recovery Injection/Diary Of Always (acoustic) (p/s)	5
07	14th Floor 14FLR21V1	Living Is A Problem Because Everything Dies/Loneliness (p/s, blue vinyl, poster)	5
07	14th Floor 14FLR21V2	Living Is A Problem Because Everything Dies/Kittens Cakes And Cuddles (p/s, red vinyl, poster)	5
07	14th Floor 14FR24V1	Folding Stars/Coward (stickered p/s, with poster, blue vinyl)	5
07	14th Floor 14FR24V2	Folding Stars/A Headline (stickered p/s, with poster, white vinyl)	5
07	14th Floor 14FLR27V1	Machines (Alternative Version)/Classical Machines (gatefold p/s, sky blue vinyl, poster, numbered)	8
02	Beggars Banquet BBQLP226	BLACKENED SKY (LP)	25
03	Beggars Banquet BBQLP233	THE VERTIGO OF BLISS (LP)	18
04	Beggars Banquet BBQLP238	INFINITY LAND (LP)	18
09	14th Floor 5051865629702	ONLY REVOLUTIONS (LP, 2-CD, DVD box set)	35

BIG AMONGST SHEEP

83	Rock Solid RSS 01	ASTROPOP (12" EP, p/s)	12
82	Rock Solid RSR 2001	TERMINAL VELOCITY (LP)	60

(see also Inner City Unit, Silverwing)

BIG AUDIO DYNAMITE

85	CBS CK 40220	THIS IS BIG AUDIO DYNAMITE (LP)	12

(see also The Clash)

BIG BARON

60	Top Rank JAR 404	Swinging Bells (Oberon Jump)/Romance	12

BIG BERTHA FEATURING ACE KEFFORD

69	Atlantic 584 298	This World's An Apple/Gravy Booby Jamm	35

(see also Cozy Powell, Ace Kefford Stand, Bedlam, Youngblood)

BIG BLACK

85	Homestead HMS 007	RACER-X (12" EP, with insert)	8
87	Blast First BFFP 14T	HEADACHE (12" p/s, 1,000 only, free 45, Heartbeat/"Things To Do Today"/"I Can't Believe")	12
87	Blast First BFFP 24	He's A Whore/The Model (p/s)	5
86	Homestead HMS 044	HAMMER PARTY (LP)	15
86	Blast First BFFP 11	ATOMIZER (LP)	15
87	Blast First BFFP 19	SONGS ABOUT FUCKING (LP, usually with sticker over 'Fucking')	18
87	NOT 2 (BUT 1)	SOUND OF IMPACT (LP, matt sleeve, numbered up to 1,000, with 8-page booklet)	30
87	NOT 2 (BUT 1)	SOUND OF IMPACT (LP, laminated sleeve, numbered from 1,001-1,500, with 8-page booklet)	20
92	Touch & Go TG 81	PIGPILE (LP, boxed set with video & T-shirt with insert)	30

(see also Rapeman)

BIG BOB

59	Top Rank JAR 185	Your Line Was Busy/What Am I	20

BIG BOPPER

58	Mercury AMT 1002	Chantilly Lace/The Purple People Eater Meets The Witch doctor	20
58	Mercury AMT 1002	Chantilly Lace/The Purple People Eater Meets The Witch doctor (78)	20
59	Mercury AMT 1017	Big Bopper's Wedding/Little Red Riding Hood	25
59	Mercury AMT 1017	Big Bopper's Wedding/Little Red Riding Hood (78)	20
59	Mercury AMT 1046	It's The Truth, Ruth/That's What I Am Talking About	30
59	Mercury ZEP 10004	THE BIG BOPPER (EP)	175
59	Mercury ZEP 10027	PINK PETTICOATS (EP)	175
58	Mercury MMC 14008	CHANTILLY LACE (LP)	200

BIG BOSS MAN

01	Blow Up BU017	Sea Groove/Sea Groove (Version)	20

BIG BOY BLUE

74	Penny Farthing PEN 844	Getting Hungry/Lonely	6

BIG BOY PETE

68	Camp 602 005	Cold Turkey/My Love Is Like A Spaceship	80
96	Tenth Planet TP 026	HOMAGE TO CATATONIA (LP)	18

(see also Miller, Pete Miller)

BIG BROTHER & HOLDING COMPANY

67	Fontana TF 881	Bye Bye Baby/All Is Loneliness	25
68	CBS 3683	Piece Of My Heart/Turtle Blues (p/s)	20
68	CBS 3683	Piece Of My Heart/Turtle Blues (without p/s)	7
68	London HLT 10226	Down On Me/Call On Me	10
67	Fontana TL 5457	BIG BROTHER & THE HOLDING COMPANY (LP, with Janis Joplin, mono)	50
67	Fontana (S)TL 5457	BIG BROTHER & THE HOLDING COMPANY (LP, with Janis Joplin, stereo)	35
68	CBS 63392	CHEAP THRILLS (LP, with Janis Joplin, laminated single sleeve, mono)	45
68	CBS (S)63392	CHEAP THRILLS (LP, with Janis Joplin, laminated single sleeve, stereo)	30
69	London HA-T/SH-T 8377	BIG BROTHER & THE HOLDING COMPANY (LP, reissue, mono/stereo)	20
71	CBS S 64118	BE A BROTHER (LP)	25

(see also Janis Joplin, Nick Gravenites)

BIG CARROT

73	EMI EMI 2047	Blackjack/Squint Eye Mangle	40
73	EMI EMI 2047	Blackjack/Squint Eye Mangle (Demo copy)	60

(see also Marc Bolan/T. Rex)

BIG CHARLIE

64	Blue Beat BB 241	Red Sea/You May Not Believe	20

BIG COUNTRY

84	Mercury COUNT 5-5	Wonderland/Giant//Lost Patrol (Live - parts 1 & 2) (2 x 7")	10
84	Mercury MERD 185	Where The Rose Is Sown/Belief In The Small Man//Wonderland (Live)/In A Big Country (Live)/Auld Lang Syne (Live) (2 x 7")	10
91	Vertigo 510230-1	NO PLACE LIKE HOME (LP)	15

(see also Skids)

BIG DADDY KANE

88	Cold Chillin'	Set It Off (Extended Mix)/Get Into It, Set It Off (12", p/s)	20

BIG DAISY

80	Elliejay 9428	Fever/Footprints (p/s)	250

(see also Wishbone Ash)

BIG DAVE (CAVANAUGH) & HIS ORCHESTRA

54	Capitol CL 14195	Loosely With Feeling/The Cat From Coos Bay (triangular centre)	10
55	Capitol CL 14245	Rock And Roll Party/Your Kind Of Love (triangular centre)	30

BIG DREAD

76	Nice One N002	I Got To Go Girl/Blood & Fire	12

BIG FLAME

84	Laughing Gun PLAQUE 001	Sink/The Illness/Sometimes (p/s, with insert)	10
85	Ron Johnson ZRON 3	Debra/Man Of few Syllables/Saragasso (7" EP p/s)	8
85	Ron Johnson ZRON 4	All The Irish Must Got To Heaven/Where's Our Carol/Cuba! (7" EP p/s)	8
86	Ron Johnson ZRON 7	Why Popstars Can't Dance/Chanel Samba/Breath Of A Nation (p/s)	8

BIG IN JAPAN

77	Eric's ERICS 0001	Big In Japan/CHUDDIE NUDDIES: Do The Chud (p/s)	15
78	Zoo CAGE 1	FROM Y TO Z AND NEVER AGAIN (EP, foldout p/s)	15

(see also Pink Industry/Military, Holly, Holly Johnson, Yachts, Bill Drummond, Creatures, Siouxsie & Banshees, Lightning Raiders)

BIG JOE (JOSEPH SPALDING)

73	Chanan Jah 1003	Natty Love/Musical Air Raid	8
73	Atra ATRA 005	Jah Guide/SWEET HARMONY: Student Dub	10
73	Atra ATRA 010	Down Santic Way/Santic Dub	12
74	Dip DL 5007	Selassie Skank/Version	12
74	Dip DL 5008	Weed Specialist/CHERRY & DUB MASTER: Rub A Daughter	12
74	Dip DL 5027	Hog In A Me Minty/Sweet Melody	12
75	Fab FAB 243	American Pum Pum/Tape White Wash	8
76	Bimbo Music BM 4	Zion Dread/D. MORGAN: What A Disturbance	12
76	Burning Sounds BS 008	Natty Dread Don't Bow/CHANNEL ONE: Natty Dubbing	10
77	ATA ATA 1001	Set Your Face At Ease/Version	20
77	Venture VEN7770	Natty Don't Make War/CHANNEL ONE FLYERS: War Dubbing	12
78	Attack ATT 8136	Tubby At The Controls/Dignity And Principle	10
79	Tribesman TM 013	Respect Jah Word (with Rodney)/The Profit Says (12")	20
77	Live & Love LAP001	KEEP ROCKING AND SWINGING (LP)	30
78	Trojan TRLS 152	AFRICAN PRINCESS (LP)	25

BIG JUMP BAND

73	Decca F 13411	All I Want/Utopia	10

BIG LUCKY, BIG AMOS & DONALD HINES

72	London SHU 8425	RIVER TOWN BLUES (LP)	25

BIG MAYBELLE

57	London HLC 8447	I Don't Want To Cry/All Of Me	55
57	London HLC 8447	I Don't Want To Cry/All Of Me (78)	20
59	London HLC 8854	Baby, Won't You Please Come Home/Say It Isn't So	30
59	London HLC 8854	Baby, Won't You Please Come Home/Say It Isn't So (78)	20
65	London HL 9941	Careless Love/My Mother's Eyes	20
67	CBS 2735	Turn The World Around The Other Way/I Can't Wait Any Longer	30
67	CBS 2926	Mama (He Treats Your Daughter Mean)/Keep That Man	35
68	Direction 58-3312	Quittin' Time/I Can't Wait Any Longer	25
68	Direction 58-3312	Quittin' Time/I Can't Wait Any Longer (DJ Copy)	40
67	CBS 62999	THE PURE SOUL OF BIG MAYBELLE (LP)	70

BIG MOOSE (WALKER)

68	Python PKM 01	Ramblin' Woman/Puppy Howl Blues	50

BIG PINK

08	House Anxiety HA 001	Too Young To Love/Crystal Visions	20

BIG ROY

76	Rockers 6	In The Desert/Natty Judge	6

BIG SLEEP
71	Pegasus PEG 4	BLUEBELL WOOD (LP, gatefold sleeve)	100

(see also Eyes Of Blue, Ancient Grease, Gentle Giant, Man, Ritchie Francis, Gary Pickford-Hopkins)

BIG SPENDERS
70	Gemini GMS 008	If It Feels Good, Do It/Why Don't Ya Tend To Your Business	12
70	Gemini GMS 010	Who's Making Love/Cum Ba Ye	15

BIG STAR
78	Stax STAX 504	September Gurls/Mod Lang	7
78	Aura AUS 103	Kizza Me/Dream Lover (p/s)	7
78	Aura AUS 107	Jesus Christ/Big Black Car	7
78	Stax SXSP 302	RADIO CITY/BIG STAR (2-LP)	25
78	Aura AUL 703	THIRD ALBUM (LP)	15
90	Big Beat WIK 53	NO. 1 RECORD (LP, reissue)	15
90	Big Beat WIK 54	RADIO CITY (LP, reissue)	15
09	Rhino 8122 73858-7	KEEP AN EYE ON THE SKY (4-CD box set)	40
11	Omnivore	BIG STAR III (replica test pressing in box, inserts, 2000 only)	40

(see also Alex Chilton, Box Tops)

BIG T
73	Avalanche AV 67324	Tea For Two/I Know A Place	25

BIG THREE (U.K.)
63	Decca F 11614	Some Other Guy/Let True Love Begin	15
63	Decca F 11689	By The Way/Cavern Stomp	10
63	Decca F 11752	I'm With You/Peanut Butter	10
64	Decca F 11927	If You Ever Change Your Mind/You've Got To Keep Her Under Hand	15
73	Polydor 2058 343	Some Other Guy/Let It Rock/If You Gotta Make A Fool Of Somebody	7
63	Decca DFE 8552	AT THE CAVERN (EP)	40
82	Decca DFE 8552	AT THE CAVERN (EP, reissue)	8
73	Polydor 2383 199	RESURRECTION (LP)	18
82	Edsel ED 111	CAVERN STOMP (LP, with insert)	15

(see also Escorts, Paddy Klaus & Gibson, Johnny Gustafson, Faron's Flamingos, Johnny & John)

BIG THREE (U.S.)
68	Roulette RCP 5002	THE BIG THREE FEATURING MAMA CASS (LP)	30

(see also Mama Cass [Elliot], Mamas & Papas)

BIG TROUBLE
72	Pye 7N45292	Cyclone Blues/You Said A Bad Word	15

BIG VERN & CHATTERBOX
93	Straight From The Bedroom	Volume 3 (12")	35

BIG WHEEL
73	Bell Bell 1310	Shake-A-Tail Part 1/Shake-A-Tail Part 2	8

BIG YOUTH
72	Blue Beat BB 424	Chi Chi Run/JOHN HOLT: OK Fred	25
73	Downtown DT 497	Dock Of The Bay/CRYSTALITES: Bass And Drums (Version)	20
73	Gayfeet CS 206	Medicine Doctor/Facts Of Life	20
73	Prince Buster PB 46	Chi Chi Run/Drums And Bass (Version)	12
73	Prince Buster PB 48	Leggo Beast/Leave Your Skeng	12
73	Prince Buster PB 50	Cain And Abel/Cain And Abel (Version)	20
73	Grape GR 3040	Foreman Versus Frazier/Foreman Versus Frazier Round Two	15
73	Grape GR 3044	JA To UK/JA To UK (Version)	12
73	Grape GR 3051	Opportunity Rock/Double Attack	20
73	Grape GR 3061	Concrete Jungle/Screaming Tonight	15
73	Green Door GD 4051	Cool Breeze/CRYSTALITES: Windstorm	25
73	Summit SUM 8542	A So We Say (with Dennis Brown)/WINSTON SCOTLAND: Scarface	8
74	Harry J. HJ 6682	Ride On Ride On/Wild Goose Chase (both with Dennis Brown)	8
75	Action ACT 101	Notty No Jester/Instrumental	8
75	Angem ANG 103	All Nations/ANSEL COLLINS : Stalag 17	12
75	Attack ATT 8096	House Of Dread Locks/GROOVEMASTER: Tangle Locks	8
75	Attack ATT 8104	Mammy Hot And Daddy Cold/GROOVEMASTERS: Some Like It Dread	8
75	Dip DL 5097	Big Youth Dread/Another Version	10
75	Lucky DL 5103	Natty Warning/Version	8
75	Klik KLP 9001	Dread Locks Dread	15
76	Lucky LY 6001	Get Up Stand Up/Version (with Dennis Brown)	8
77	Eji E 011	Strictly Rockers/AUGUSTUS PABLO : No Entry (12")	40
78	Wildflower WF 538	Jah Jah Love Them/Oven Baking	8
72	Fab MS 8	CHI CHI RUN (LP)	45
73	Trojan TRLS 61	SCREAMING TARGET (LP, orange & white label)	20
75	Klik KLP9001	DREAD LOCKS DREAD (LP)	15
76	Trojan TRLS 123	NATTY CULTURAL DREAD (LP)	12
76	Trojan TRLS 137	HIT THE ROAD JACK (LP)	12
77	Trojan BYD 1	REGGAE PHENOMENON (2-LP)	18
78	Virgin Front Line FL1011	ISIAH, FIRST PROPHET OF OLD (LP)	12
80	Trojan TRLS 189	EVERYDAY SKANK (LP)	12

(see also Upsetters, Keith Hudson)

BIG YOUTH & KEITH HUDSON
73	Pyramid PYR 7055	Can You Keep A Secret/HORACE ANDY & EARL FLUTE: Peter And Judas	25

(see also Keith Hudson)

BIGGA DREAD
02	Chariot Cha 001	Batty Dread/Closet Bwoy/Truck Inna Garage/Special Request (10")	30

BIGGLES
71	Philips 6006160	Gimme Gimme Some Lovin'/Can't Buy You	8

BARRY BIGGS
76	Dynamic DYLP 3005	MR. BIGGS (LP)	12

(see also Bob & Marcia)

EDWINA BIGLET AND THE MIDGETS
72   RCA RCA 2193   Thing/Vanessa's Luminous Coat 5

BIG OUTDOOR TYPE
84   Havasac SAC 01   Call You On Sundays/Seventeen (p/s) 50

BIJOUX TOO
86   Apex APE 002   Shadows In My Heart/Come On Back (oversized p/s, Welsh-only release).............30

BIKINIS
58   Columbia DB 4149   Bikini/Boogie Rock And Roll 25

BILBO BAGGINS
74   Polydor 2058 479   Saturday Night/Monday Morning Blues 12

(MR.) ACKER BILK (& HIS PARAMOUNT JAZZ BAND)
60   Melodisc 1547   Goodnight Sweet Prince/East Coast Trot 20
(see also Michael London)

BILL & BUSTER
70   A & M AMS 809   Bend Over Backwards/Going Back In Time 5

BILL THE MURDERER
78   SRT   I'd Find You/Spring Rain (no p/s) 100

BILLIE & EDDIE
59   Top Rank JAR 249   The King Is Coming Back/Come Back, Baby 25

BILLION DOLLAR BABIES
77   Polydor 2391 273   BATTLE AXE (LP) 12
(see also Alice Cooper)

TREVOR BILLMUSS
70   Charisma CB 130   Whoops Amour/Sunday Afternoon In Belgrave Square 15
71   B & C CB 158   English Pastures/Fishing Song 8
70   Charisma CAS 1017   FAMILY APOLOGY (LP) 25

BONNIE 'PRINCE' BILLY
01   Domino RUG 81CD   Just To See My Holly Home (CD promo) 12
07   No label or Cat. No.   BONNY (7" tour EP)..10
99   Domino WIGLP 59   I SEE A DARKNESS (LP) 20
01   Domino WIGLP 89   EASE DOWN THE ROAD (LP) 15
04   Domino WIGLP 140   SINGS GREATEST PALACE MUSIC (LP, 1-sided) 15
09   Domino WIGLP 233   BEWARE (LP) 15

BILLY & ESSENTIALS
63   London HLW 9657   Over The Weekend/Maybe You'll Be There 40

BILLY & LILLIE (& BILLY FORD & THUNDERBIRDS)
58   London HLU 8564   La Dee Dah/BILLY FORD'S THUNDERBIRDS: The Monster 30
58   London HLU 8564   La Dee Dah/BILLY FORD'S THUNDERBIRDS: The Monster (78) 10
58   London HLU 8630   Creepin', Crawlin', Cryin'/Happiness (with Billy Ford & Thunderbirds) 40
58   London HLU 8689   The Greasy Spoon/Hangin' On To You (with Billy Ford & Thunderbirds) (78)..........10
59   London HLU 8795   I Promise You/Lucky Ladybug 30
59   London HLU 8795   I Promise You/Lucky Ladybug (78) 10
59   Top Rank JAR 157   Bells, Bells, Bells/Honeymoonin' (as Billie & Lillie) 15
59   Top Rank JAR 157   Bells, Bells, Bells/Honeymoonin' (as Billie & Lillie) (78) 12

BIM & BAM
70   Crab CRAB 48   The Pill (with Clover)/TOMMY McCOOK: Spring Fever 15
70   Crab CRAB 49   Immigrant Plight (w/ Clover)/PETER AUSTIN & HORTENSE: Bang Shangalang.......15
73   Gayfeet GS 201   Fatty/Landlord 10

BIM, BAM & CLOVER
70   Trojan TR 7754   Party Time Parts 1 & 2 8

BINGO
79   Polydor 2066365   We Can't Get Enough/Mumblin' Man 40

SONNY BINNS (& RUDIES)
69   Downtown DT 420   The Untouchables/Lazy Boy 15
69   Downtown DT 424   Wheels/Night Train 12
70   Escort ES 818   Boss A Moon (as S. Binns)/BUNNY LEE ALLSTARS: Brotherly Love.......................40
(see also Rudies)

TONY BINNS
71   Explosion EX 2044   Love I Madly/Musical Shower 10
71   Explosion EX 2046   Humpty Dumpty/Got To Get A Message 8

BINTANGS
70   Decca F22995   Ridin' On The L And N/Down South Blues 18

BIONIC ECHO
86   Josiah KJ 003   Digital/Chatty Chatty Mouth (12") 80

BIOTA
85   Recommended DYS 12 & 13   RACKABONES (LP, with inserts) 30

JOHN BIRD
75   Transatlantic XTRA 1148   THE COLLECTED BROADCASTS OF IDI AMIN (LP) 12

KEV BIRD
91   Basement BRSS 003   Inside Your Mind (Full Length Mix)/En Bass (Original Mix)/En Bass (Crash Mix)
                                            (12", promo) 20
92   Basement BRSS 006   THE VISIT TO 14B EP (12", with The Wax Doctor)...15
92   Basement BRSS 012   This Is A Trip/Let's Turn It out/Eloquence (12") 10
94   Basement BRSS 031   Kano/Sub Zero (12") 10

BIRD LEGS & PAULINE
66   Sue WI 4014   Spring/In So Many Ways 40

STANLEY & JEFFREY BIRD
60   HMV POP 702   Johnny At The Crossheads/Betty, Betty (Go Steady With Me)................................10

BIRD TWINS
61	HMV POP 864	Momma - Poppa/Banned In Boston	6

BIRDS
64	Decca F 12031	You're On My Mind/You Don't Love Me (You Don't Care)	100
65	Decca F 12140	Leaving Here/Next In Line	90
65	Decca F 12257	No Good Without You Baby/How Can It Be	90
85	Demon WEST 901	THESE BIRDS ARE DANGEROUS (LP)	15

(see also Birds Birds, Ron Wood, Faces, Creation, Ashton Gardner & Dyke)

BIRDS BIRDS
66	Reaction 591 005	Say Those Magic Words/Daddy Daddy	500

(see also Birds, Gods)

BIRDS OF A FEATHER
69	Page One POF 156	Blacksmith Blues/Sing My Song And Pray	10
70	Page One POF 179	All God's Children Got Soul/Get It Together	6
72	Jam JAM 23	You Know Me Better/Summer Has Gone	5
72	DJM DJS 243	Thank You/Baby Don't You Bring Me Down	5
70	Page One POLS 027	BIRDS OF A FEATHER (LP)	150

(see also Chanters)

BIRDS & BRASS
70	Rediffusion ZS 57	SOUNDSATIONAL (LP)	15
74	Rediffusion 0100 171	... ARE BACK (LP)	15

JANE BIRKIN & SERGE GAINSBOURG
69	Fontana TF 1042	Je T'Aime, Moi Non Plus/Jane B (with p/s)	8
70	Major Minor MM 645	Je T'Aime Moi Non Plus/Jane B	5
72	Philips 6009 201	La Decadanse/Les Langues De Chat	5
74	Antic K 11511	Je T'Aime, Moi Non Plus/Jane B (3rd reissue, 'nude' p/s)	8
69	Fontana STL 5493	JANE BIRKIN AND SERGE GAINSBOURG (LP)	25

BIRMINGHAM
71	Grosvenor GRS 1011	BIRMINGHAM (LP)	80

(see also Dave Peace Quartet)

BIRTH CONTROL
71	Charisma CAS 1036	BIRTH CONTROL (LP, pink/white 'scroll' label)	125

BIRTHDAY PARTY
80	4AD AD 12	The Friend Catcher/Waving My Arms/Cat Man (p/s)	12
80	Missing Link ML-18	Mr. Clarinet/Happy Birthday	60
81	4AD AD 111	Release The Bats/Blast Off (p/s)	12
81	4AD AD 114	Mr. Clarinet/Happy Birthday (p/s)	10
81	(no cat. no.)	Mr. Clarinet/Missing Link (sold at gigs only)	50
82	4AD JAD 202	DRUNK ON THE POPE'S BLOOD/THE AGONY IS THE ECSTACY (12" EP, with Lydia Lunch)	18
87	Strange Fruit SFSP 020	PEEL SESSIONS 1 (12")	12
88	Strange Fruit SFSP 058	PEEL SESSIONS 2 (12")	12
81	4AD CAD 104	PRAYERS ON FIRE (LP, inner)	15
82	4AD CAD 207	JUNK YARD (LP, with inner)	20
92	4AD DAD 2016	HITS (2-LP)	25

(see also Nick Cave & Bad Seeds, Roland S. Howard & Lydia Lunch, These Immortal Souls)

BISH
80	Rainbow RS 2	Modern Women/He's So Foggy (p/s)	10

DICKIE BISHOP & SIDEKICKS
57	Decca F 10869	Cumberland Gap/No Other Baby	6
57	Decca F 10959	The Prisoner's Song/Please Remember Me	6
58	Decca F 10981	Skip To My Lou/No Other Baby	8
58	Decca F 11028	They Can't Take That Away From Me/Jumpin' Judy	6

(see also Chris Barber's Skiffle Group)

TOMMY BISHOP'S RICOCHETS
65	Decca F 12238	I Should Have Known/On The Other Hand	15

(see also Rock 'n' Roll Revival Show, Rush, Tinkerbell's Fairydust)

BITCH (1)
71	B & C CB 151	Laughing/House Where I Live	8
72	Warners K16235	Good Time Coming/At The Party	6

BITCH (2)
79	Hurricane FIRE 5	Big City/Wild Kids (p/s)	20

BITCH (3)
81	Rutland RX 101	First Bite/Maggie (with p/s & promo insert)	20
81	Rutland RX 101	First Bite/Maggie	15

BITCHES SIN
81	Neat NEAT 09	Always Ready For Love/Sign Of The Times (p/s)	8
83	Quiet QT 001	No More Chances/Overnight/Ice Angels (12", p/s)	25
83	Terminal TCAS 21	OUT OF MY MIND (EP, cassette, 6-track)	8
82	Heavy Metal HMRLP 4	PREDATOR (LP, textured sleeve)	20

BITCH MAGNET
91	Caff CAFF 14	Sadie/Ducks And Drakes (p/s, with insert)	10

BITCH SLAPS BITCH
98	Brighton Rock ROK 1	Ladyboy/Locked In a Limo (p/s, 200 only)	5

BITSTREAM
94	City Centre Offices	Crab Nebula (plain sleeve with inserts, 1000 only)	8

BITTER ALMOND
70	Warner Bros WB 8008	In The Morning/Silver	7
71	United Artists UP35197	Loving Each Other/We Need Someone	12

BITTER SUITE

73	Jam 43	Six O' Clock News/Here's Hoping	8
75	Bus Stop BUS 1028	How Married Are You Marianne/Love Is A Friend Of Mine	5

BITTER END SINGERS

67	Atlantic 584 075	A Taste Of Your Love/Everybody Knows My Name	10

BIZ

93	Warp WARP LP 9	ELECTRO SOMA (LP, orange vinyl)	15

BIZARRE INC

91	Vinyl Solution STORM 25	Playing With Knives (12")	10
91	Vinyl Solution STORM 25 RT	Playing With Knives (The Climax) (12")	10
91	Vinyl Solution STORM 32	Such A Feeling/Raise Me/Frenzy (12", white label promo)	8
91	Vinyl Solution STORM 32R	Such A Feeling (Love Decade Mix)/Raise Me (Eon's Ascension Mix) (12")	8
89	Blue Chip BLUE TEC. 1	TECHNOLOGICAL (LP)	15

BIZARRE UNIT

81	MRS MRS 004	Dancing/Away From The Screaming Car	20

(see also Paul Nova)

BJÖRK

93	One Little Indian 112TP7	Human Behavior : Underworld Mix/Close To Human Mix/Dom T Mix (12" p/s)	10
93	O. L. Indian 122TP7	Venus As A Boy : Edit/7" Dream Mix	6
96	O. L. Indian 193TP712TD	Possibly Maybe (Calcutta Cyber Café Mix)/I Miss You (Dobie's Rub Part One (12", 1,000 only)	12
96	O.L. Indian 193TP12DM	Enjoy (Beats Mix)/Possibly Maybe (Lucy Mix) (p/s, 1,000 only, numbered)	15
96	O.L. Indian 193TP12DM	Enjoy/Possibly Maybe (12", 1,000 only, numbered p/s)	18
96	O. L. Indian 193TP12TD	POSSIBLY MAYBE (12" EP, 1,000 only, numbered p/s)	12
97	O. L. Indian TPLP 81	JOGA (12" triple-pack, inner sleeves, p/s)	12
97	O. L. Indian 20 TP7 BOX	JOGA (CD box set, 3 x CD singles & 1-track video, 3,000 only)	30
97	O. L. Indian 20 TP7 BOX 212TP7BOX	BACHELORETTE (CD box set, 3 x CD singles & 1-track video, 3,000 only)	25
98	Fat Cat 12FAT 022	All Is Full Of Love (FunkstÖrung Remix)/The Shit (12", custom stamped sleeve)	12
98	One L. Indian 23TP7BOX	ALARM CALL (3 x CD singles & 1-track video)	25
98	One L. Indian 222TP7BOX	HUNTER (3 x CD singles & 1-track video)	25
99	One L. Indian 242TP7BOX	ALL IS FULL OF LOVE (2 x CD singles & 1-track video)	25
08	One L. Indian 805TP12	EARTH INTRUDERS (CD, DVD & 2 x 12")	20
08	One L. Indian 837TP12	DECLARE INDEPENDENCE (CD, DVD & 2 x 12")	20
08	One L. Indian 838TP12	INNOCENCE (CD, DVD & 2 x 12")	20
08	One L. Indian 853TP12	WANDERLUST (CD, DVD & 2 x 12")	20
93	O. L. Indian TPLP 31L	DEBUT (LP, 5,000 with 16-page lyric booklet)	25
93	O. L. Indian TPLP 31L	DEBUT (LP)	15
94	O. L. Indian 152TP 12	THE BEST MIXES FROM THE ALBUM "DEBUT" FOR THOSE PEOPLE WHO DON'T BUY WHITE LABELS (mini-LP)	20
95	One L. Indian TPLP 51L	POST (LP, pink vinyl, with inner sleeve)	25
95	One L. Indian TPLP 51CDL/X	POST (CD, digipak w/poster & lyric book, in PVC purse)	18
95	One L. Indian TPLP 51CDL/X	POST (CD, digipak w/poster & lyric book)	15
97	One L. Indian TPLP71	HOMOGENIC (LP)	25
00	One L. Indian TPLP151	SELMA SONGS (LP)	25
01	One L. Indian TPLP101	VESPERTINE (2 x LP, gatefold)	25
02	One L. Indian TPLP359	GREATEST HITS (2 x LP, gatefold)	20
02	One L. Indian TPLP365CD	GREATEST HITS & FAMILY TREE (CD x 6 boxed set)	25
03	One L. Indian TPLP355CDBOX	LIVEBOX (CD x 4, DVD)	25
04	One L. Indian TPLP358	MEDULLA (2 x LP)	25
06	One L. Indian TPLP101SACD	SURROUNDED (7 dualdisc box-set of all albums)	60
07	One L. Indian TPLP460H	VOLTA (2 x LP fold-out cover)	20

(see also Sugarcubes, Kukl)

BLACK

81	Rox ROX 17	Human Features/Electric Church (p/s)	20
82	Wonderful World WWW3	More Than The Sun/Jump (no p/s)	20

BILL BLACK'S COMBO

59	Felsted AF 129	Smokie Parts 1 & 2	15
59	Felsted AF 129	Smokie Parts 1 & 2 (78)	10
60	London HLU 9090	White Silver Sands/The Wheel	10
60	London HLU 9156	Josephine/Dry Bones	10
60	London HLU 9212	Don't Be Cruel/Rollin'	10
61	London HLU 9267	Blue Tango/Willie	6
61	London HLU 9306	Hearts Of Stone/Royal Blue	5
61	London HLU 9383	Ole Buttermilk Sky/Yogi	5
61	London HLU 9436	Movin'/Honky Train	6
61	London HLU 9479	Twist-Her/My Girl Josephine	10
62	London HLU 9594	So What/Blues For The Red Boy	10
62	London HLU 9645	Joey's Song/Hot Taco	7
63	London HLU 9721	Do It - Rat Now/Little Jasper	5
63	London HLU 9788	Monkey-Shine/Long Gone	5
64	London HLU 9855	Comin' On/Soft Winds	5
64	London HLU 9903	Tequila/Raunchy	5
64	London HLU 9925	Little Queenie/Boo-Ray	10
68	London HLU 10216	Turn On Your Love Light/Ribbon Of Darkness	5
60	London REU 1277	BILL BLACK'S COMBO (EP)	20
63	London REU 1369	THE UNTOUCHABLE SOUND OF BILL BLACK (EP)	20
62	London HA-U 2310	SOLID AND RAUNCHY (LP)	20
62	London HA-U 2427	LET'S TWIST (LP, mono)	20
62	London SAH-U 6222	LET'S TWIST (LP, stereo)	20
62	London HA-U 2433	MOVIN' (LP)	15
63	London HA-U 8080	THE UNTOUCHABLE SOUND OF BILL BLACK (LP)	15
63	London HA-U 8113	GREATEST HITS (LP)	15
64	London HA-U 8187	PLAYS CHUCK BERRY (LP)	15
68	London HA-U/SH-U 8367	BILL BLACK'S BEAT GOES ON (LP)	15
69	London HA-U/SH-U 8373	TURN ON YOUR LOVE LIGHT (LP)	15
69	London HA-U/SH-U 8389	SOULIN' THE BLUES (LP)	15

(see also Elvis Presley)

CILLA BLACK
63	Parlophone R 5065	Love Of The Loved/Shy Of Love..7
64	Parlophone GEP 8901	ANYONE WHO HAD A HEART (EP)..8
64	Parlophone GEP 8916	IT'S FOR YOU (EP)...12
67	Parlophone GEP 8967	TIME FOR CILLA (EP)..15
68	Parlophone PCS 7041	SHER-OO (LP, stereo, yellow/black label)...12

FRANK BLACK
| 93 | 4AD CADD 3004 | FRANK BLACK (LP, die-cut screen-printed sleeve, with lyric inner) ....15 |

(see also Pixies)

IKA BLACK & THE NATIONS CRK
| 81 | I One I IONE 001 | Human Life/Better Life (12")...30 |

JEANNE BLACK
| 60 | Capitol CL 15146 | Lisa/JEANNE & JANIE - Journey Of Love...5 |

(see also Janie, Jeanne & Janie)

LINCOLN BLACK
| 70 | Penny Farthing PEN 712 | Famous Last Words/You Built Me Up So High.....................................12 |

MARY BLACK
92	Grapevine GRALP 009	NO FRONTIERS (LP, with lyric inner sleeve).......................................25
92	Gravevine GRALP 005	NO FRONTIERS (LP, audiophile pressing, white sleeve)......................30
92	Grapevine GRALP 009	NO FRONTIERS (LP, audiophile pressing, red sleeve with different design and inner sleeve)..30
95	Grapevine GRALP 011	THE HOLY GROUND (LP, audiophile pressing) 20
95	Grapevine GRALP 014	CIRCUS (LP, audiophile pressing with lyric inner) 20

MATT BLACK & THE DOODLEBUGS
| 76 | Punk BCS 0005 | Punky Xmas/Nightmare (no p/s) ....8 |

BLACK ABBOTTS
70	Chapter One CH 123	She Looked Away/I Don't Mind..7
71	Evolution E 3001	How About Me/Everybody Needs A Little Sunshine 7
71	Evolution E 3004	Love Is Alive/The Painter..25

BLACK ACE
| 61 | XX MIN 701 | BLACK ACE (EP)..30 |
| 62 | Heritage HLP 1006 | BLACK ACE (LP, 99 copies only)...120 |

BLACK AND WHITE LOVERS
| 86 | Guillotine GR 001 | Best Years Of Our Lives/Boulevard Of Broken Dreams (p/s)...................8 |

BLACK ANGELS
| 84 | Gull GULP 1041 | KICKDOWN (LP) ....12 |

BLACK ARK PLAYERS
| 80 | Black Ark Intl. BALP 4000 | BLACK ARK IN DUB (LP) ....30 |

BLACK AXE
| 80 | Metal MELT 1 | Highway Rider/Red Lights (in p/s) ....15 |
| 80 | Metal MELT 1 | Highway Rider/Red Lights ....6 |

BLACKBEARD
| 80 | More Cut RDC 2002 | I WAH DUB (LP)..25 |

BLACK BEATLES
| 70 | Pama PM 804 | Reggae And Shout/LENOX BROWN: The Green Hornet.........................30 |

BLACKBIRDS
| 68 | Saga OPP 3 | No Destination/Space (either p/s or company sleeve, possibly promo only).............30 |
| 68 | Saga FID 2113 | NO DESTINATION (LP, black/silver label) ....40 |

BLACK BLOOD
| 76 | Bradleys 1002 | Rasteferai/Ewohe Dance..6 |

TONY BLACKBURN
65	Fontana TF 562	Don't Get Off That Train/Just To Be With You Again............................5
68	MGM 1375	So Much Love/In The Night..5
69	MGM 1467	It's Only Love/Janie..8

BLACKBYRDS
75	Fantasy FTC 114	Walking In Rhythm/The Baby..5
76	Fantasy FTC 122	Rock Creek Park/Flying High 5
78	Fantasy FTCT 194	Rock Creek Park/Don't Know What To Say (12")...............................20
85	Streetwave SWAVE 3	Rock Creek Park/Walking In Rhythm (12")..15
75	Fantasy FT 9444	BLACKBYRDS (LP)...20
75	Fantasy FT 522	FLYING START (LP)...15
76	Fantasy FTA 3003	CITY LIFE (LP) 12
77	Fantasy FT 534	ACTION (LP) 15
79	Fantasy FT 555	NIGHT GROOVES - THE BEST OF THE BLACKBYRDS (LP).................15

(see also Donald Byrd)

BLACK CAT BONES
68	Sceptre SALR 1216	COME ABOARD QE2 (LP, sold on liner, one track by Black Cat Bones) 25
70	Decca Nova DN 15	BARBED WIRE SANDWICH (LP, mono, blue/silver label) 300
70	Decca Nova SDN 15	BARBED WIRE SANDWICH (LP, stereo, blue/silver label)................500

(see also Leaf Hound, Brian Short, Free, Foghat)

BLACK CLAW
| 69 | Bell BLL 1089 | Across The Great Divide/Sally ....8 |

BLACK COCK
97	Black Cock Records BK 068	Cosmic/Give It Up (12") 35
97	Black Cock Records BK 076	Luna Party/Frog Scene (12") 50
95	Black Cock BCK 077	FREE RANGE EP (12") 40

(see also DH Harvey, Ersatz)

BLACK COUNTRY THREE
66	W.F.C. WS 100	BLACK COUNTRY SONGS (EP)	250
66	Transatlantic TRA 140	BLACK COUNTRY THREE (LP)	50

(see also Jon Raven)

BLACK CROWES
91	Def American 7-17580	HARD TO HANDLE (7 x 7" box set, with 2 bonus tracks)	20

BLACK DOG
91	GPR GENP(X) 2	PARALLEL EP (12", p/s)	30
92	Black Dog Prods BDP 001	VIRTUAL EP (12", p/s)	80
92	Black Dog Prods BDP 002	AGE OF SLACK (12", p/s)	100
92	Black Dog Prods BDP 003	BLACK DOG EP (12", p/s, 500 only)	125
92	GPR GENP(X) 3	VIR 2 L (12", custom sleeve)	100
92	GPR GENP (R) 03	VIR 2 L (12" remix)	70
92	GPR GENP(X) 9	VANTOOL EP (12", custom sleeve)	100
93	GPR GENP(X) 17	COST II (12", custom sleeve)	15
93	Rising High RSN 046	BLACK DOG PRODUCTIONS (12", 4-track, p/s)	20
91	GPR GPR 004	PARALLEL SQUELCH (LP)	30
92	GPR GPRLP 1	TEMPLE OF TRANSPARENT BALLS (2-LP, with poster)	45
92	GPR GPRLP 1	TEMPLE OF TRANSPARENT BALLS (2-LP, without poster)	30
93	GPR GPRCD 1	TEMPLE OF TRANSPARENT BALLS (CD)	20
95	GPR GPRLP 15	PARALLEL (2-LP)	35
95	GPR GPRCD 15	PARALLEL (CD)	30
95	Warp PUPLP 1	SPANNERS (2-LP)	40
95	Warp WAP LP 8LTD	BYTES (LP, bronze vinyl)	40

(see also Alter Ego, Plaid, Repeat, Unexplored Beats, Shiva)

BLACK DOG/SHIVA
92	GRP (no cat no)	VIR 2 L/Shout (12")	70

BLACK DYKE MILLS BAND
68	Apple APPLE 4	Thingumybob/Yellow Submarine	35

BLACK DYNAMITES
60	Top Rank JAR 319	Brush Those Tears/Lonely Cissy	20

BLACK EASTER
82	Illuminated KILL 13	READY TO ROT (EP, p/s)	10

BLACK-EDS
80	Acne ACNE 1	Isn't It Strange/Living Doll/Jimmy 2 Stroke (p/s)	20

BLACK FAITH
70	Phillips 6006065	Woman In My Life	10
70	Phillips 6007018	Song For A Dollar/Peace In The Family	10
74	Fresh Air 6121107	The Vow/Stop The World	15

BLACK FLAG
81	Alt. Tentacles VIRUS 9	Six Pack/I've Heard It All Before/American Waste (p/s)	12
84	SST SST 12001	Family Man/I Won't Stick Any Of You Unless And Until I Can Stick All Of You (12", p/s)	10

'FLIP' BLACK & BOYS UPSTAIRS
59	Capitol CL 15037	For You My Lover/Tell Her Mister Moon	10

J.D. BLACKFOOT
71	Mercury 6338 031	THE ULTIMATE PROPHECY (LP)	70

BLACKFOOT SUE
73	DJM DJS 296	Bye Bye Birmingham/Messiah	10
74	DJM DJS 326	You Need Love/Tobago Rose	12
73	Jam JAL 104	NOTHING TO HIDE (LP, gatefold sleeve with poster)	50
73	Jam JAL 104	NOTHING TO HIDE (LP, gatefold sleeve without poster)	20
75	DJM DJLPS 455	GUN RUNNING (LP, withdrawn)	65

BLACK GRAPE
95	Radioactive RAR 11224	IT'S GREAT WHEN YOU'RE STRAIGHT YEAH (LP)	15
97	Radioactive RAR 11716	STUPID STUPID STUPID (LP)	15

(see also Happy Mondays)

BLACK HARMONY
79	Burning Sounds BS 14	I'm Still Waiting/Love Marcus	8
79	Laser LAS 9	Don't Let It Go To Your Head/DEB PLAYERS : Don't Let It Go To Your Brain (12")	15

BLACKJACK
80	Polydor POSP 76	Without Your Love/Heart Of Mine (p/s)	18
79	Polydor 2391 411	BLACKJACK (LP)	18
80	Polydor	WORLDS APART (LP)	12

(see also Michael Bolotin, Michael Bolton)

BLACKJACKS
63	Pye 7N 15586	Woo Hoo/Red Dragon	20

(see also Pat Harris & Blackjacks)

BLACK KEYS
03	Fat Possum 111-7	Hard Row/Evil (p/s)	12
03	Fat Possum 1130-7	Have Love Will Travel/No Trust (live)/The Moan (live) (p/s, yellow vinyl)	10
04	Fat Possum 11747	10AM Automatic/Summertime Blues (p/s)	8
07	V2 VVR5048347	Just Got To Be/Black Door (p/s, no'd)	6
02	ALIVE 00441	THE BIG COME UP (LP)	12
06	VVR1042541	MAGIC POTION (LP)	15
09	VVR737199	BROTHERS (LP)	18

BLACK KNIGHTS
65	Columbia DB 7443	I Gotta Woman/Angel Of Love	25

BLACK LIPS
07	Vice VICE 001	Not A Problem/Dirty Hands (p/s)	6

MINT VALUE £

07	Vice VICE 004LP	GOOD BAD NOT EVIL (LP, gatefold)	20

BLACK MAMBAZO
58	Columbia DB 4135	Funny Night/Matsutshu	8

DON BLACKMAN
82	Arista RIST 30	Hearts Desire/Let Your Conscience Be Your Guide (12", EP)	15

HONOR BLACKMAN
68	CBS 3896	Before Today/I'll Always Be Loving You (in p/s)	30
68	CBS 3896	Before Today/I'll Always Be Loving You	10
64	Decca LK/SKL 4642	EVERYTHING I'VE GOT (LP, mono/stereo)	30
80	Deram 844057-1	KINKY BOOTS (LP)	20

(see also Patrick MacNee & Honor Blackman)

PAUL BLACKMAN
79	Daddy Kool DKR 123	Earth, Wind & Fire/A. Pablo: Ras-Menlik Congo (12")	20

RITCHIE BLACKMORE (ORCHESTRA)
65	Oriole CB 314	Getaway/Little Brown Jug (Spelt "Richie" on label)	500

(see also Outlaws, Neil Christian & Crusaders, Deep Purple, [Ritchie Blackmore's] Rainbow, Rally Rounders, Green Bullfrog, Rock Aid Armenia)

BLACK OAK ARKANSAS
75	Atlantic K 10621	Fancy Nancy/Keep On	7
71	Atlantic 2400 180	BLACK OAK ARKANSAS (LP)	15

BLACK PROPHETZ
91	GTI KICK8	Fax On Wax (EP)	12

BLACK RADICAL MK II
91	Mango 12 MNG 782DJ	Sign Of The Beast (12" - Grey Vinyl/Promo only)	8
93	Copastetic COPDIS8	THIS IS WAR (EP)	8
91	Mango MLPS1070	THE UNDILUTED TRUTH (LP)	12

BLACK RADICAL/SIR NOVA
88	Bass Inc B1001 500	B Boys Be Wise/We Outta Here (12")	30

BLACK REBEL MOTORCYCLE CLUB
02	Virgin VUSLP 224	BLACK REBEL MOTORCYCLE CLUB (LP)	15
03	Virgin VUSLP 245	TAKE THEM ON YOUR OWN (2-LP, gatefold, with inner sleeves)	18
05	Echo ECHLP 67	HOWL (2-LP, with inner sleeves)	30

BLACK RIDERS
85	Plastic Head GILP 555	CHOSEN FEW (LP)	15

BLACK ROOTS
84	Bullet BOL 9	Boys Will Be Boys/Liar (p/s, some with patch)	35
84	Nubian NR 001	Bristol Rock/Tribal War/The Father/The System (12")	20
85	Neat NEAT 4812	Nightmare/Need A Lot Of Lovin'/Rock Me Hard (12", p/s)	8
83	Bullet BOLT 3	BLACK ROSE (12" EP)	8
83	Bullet BOLT 6	WE'RE GONNA ROCK YOU (12" EP)	8
84	BBC REC 555	THE FRONT LINE (LP)	20
84	Bullet BULP 3	BOYS WILL BE BOYS (LP)	12
83	Kick KIC LP 02	BLACK ROOTS (LP)	25
84	BBC REC 5570	IN SESSION (LP)	20

BLACK ROSE
82	Teesbeat TB 5	Sucker For Your Love/No Point Runnin' (in p/s)	125
82	Teesbeat TB 5	Sucker For Your Love/No Point Runnin'	35

BLACK SABBATH
SINGLES
70	Fontana TF 1067	Evil Woman/Wicked World	100
70	Vertigo V2	Evil Woman/Wicked World (reissue, Vertigo 'swirl' sleeve)	30
70	Vertigo 6059 010	Paranoid/The Wizard (Vertigo 'swirl' sleeve)	20
72	Vertigo 6059 061	Tomorrow's Dream/Laguna Sunrise (Vertigo 'swirl' sleeve)	25
72	Phonogram DJ 005	Children Of The Grave/STATUS QUO: Roadhouse Blues (100 promo copies only)	400
73	WWA WWS 002	Sabbath Bloody Sabbath/Changes (company sleeve)	8
75	NEMS 6165 300	Am I Going Insane? (Radio)/Hole In The Sky (no p/s)	10
78	Vertigo SAB 001	Never Say Die/She's Gone (p/s)	8
78	Vertigo SAB 002	Hard Road/Symptom Of The Universe (purple or black vinyl)	6
80	Vertigo SAB 412	Die Young/Heaven And Hell (extended live) (12", p/s)	8
81	Vertigo SAB 512	Mob Rules/Die Young (live) (12", p/s)	10
82	Vertigo SABP 6	Turn Up The Night/Lonely Is The Word (picture disc)	6
82	Vertigo SABP 612	Turn Up The Night/Lonely Is The Word (12", picture disc)	8
86	Vertigo SABDJ 12	In For The Kill/Turn To Stone/Heart Like A Wheel (12", promo only)	15
87	Vertigo SABAF 1	4 SONGS FROM THE ETERNAL IDOL (12", p/s, promo only)	15
89	I.R.S. EIRS CB 107	Headless Cross (Edit)/Cloak And Dagger (signed label, stickered PVC sleeve)	6
89	I.R.S. EIRSPD 115	Devil And Daughter (1-sided picture disc)	5
89	I.R.S. EIRSB 115	Devil And Daughter (box set, 1-sided disc with stencil, insert & 2 postcards)	8
92	I.R.S. EIRSDJ 180	Master Of Insanity (edit)/Time Machine/Neon Knights (live)/TV Crimes (live)/ Die (live)/Children Of The Sea (live) (CD, no p/s, promo only)	12
10	Vertigo 00602527391199	Paranoid (Alternative Lyric Version)/METALLICA: Frantic (UNKLE Remix) (12", 1000 only)	20

ALBUMS
70	Vertigo VO 6	BLACK SABBATH (LP, 1st pressing, with black gatefold sleeve, no composers/publishers credits on cross; large swirl label with "A Philips record product" text on label)	400
70	Vertigo VO 6	BLACK SABBATH (LP, 2nd pressing, with white gatefold sleeve and Dunbar credit for 'Warning'; swirl label, with – allegedly – laminated sleeve)	200
70	Vertigo VO 6	BLACK SABBATH (LP, 2nd pressing, with white gatefold sleeve and Dunbar credit for 'Warning'; swirl label)	100
70	Vertigo 6360 011	PARANOID (LP, gatefold sleeve, 1st press large swirl label)	250
70	Vertigo 6360 011	PARANOID (LP, gatefold sleeve, 2nd press, small swirl label, laminated sleeve)	60
70	Vertigo 6360 011	PARANOID (LP, gatefold sleeve, 2nd press, small swirl label)	50
71	Vertigo 6360 050	MASTER OF REALITY (LP in box cover, swirl label, with poster)	400
71	Vertigo 6360 050	MASTER OF REALITY (LP in box cover, swirl label, without poster)	70
72	Vertigo 6360 071	BLACK SABBATH VOL. 4 (LP, 1st pressing, no "Made in England" beneath 1972 on top right hand side" gatefold sleeve with booklet attached, small swirl label)	100

72	Vertigo 6360 071	BLACK SABBATH VOL. 4 (LP, gatefold sleeve with booklet attached, 'spaceship' label) 125
73	Vertigo 6360 071	BLACK SABBATH VOL. 4 (LP, 2nd pressing, with "Made in England" beneath 1972 on top right hand side" gatefold sleeve with booklet attached, small swirl label) 35
73	WWA WWA 05	SABBATH BLOODY SABBATH (LP, 1st pressing, no ridge around rim, 1 Y 1/ 2 Y 1 matrix numbers, silver WWA logo, gatefold with "Manufactured and printed in England" (no "Howard's Printers" reference), inside image extends to edge of sleeve with no border, textured lyric inner) 50
75	NEMS 9119001	SABOTAGE (LP, 1st pressing with matrix numbers 1//Y2 S 1 3 5 & 2 Y2 S 1 1 4 with 'Sterling' stamped into dead wax on both sides, textured sleeve made by 'Robert Stace') 20
76	Vertigo 9102 750	TECHNICAL ECSTACY (LP) 12
76	NEMS NEL 6003	PARANOID (LP, reissue) 15
83	Vertigo SAB 10	LIVE EVIL (2-LP, orange Vertigo label) 15
85	Nems BSBLP 001	THE SABBATH COLLECTION (7-LP box set) 50
88	Castle BSBCD 001	THE BLACK SABBATH CD COLLECTION (6-CD box set with badge & book, numbered, 3,000 only) 40
89	IRS EIRSAPD 1002	HEADLESS CROSS (LP, picture disc with extra track) 15
90	IRS EIRSAPD 1038	TYR (LP, picture disc with 2 extra tracks) 12
94	IRS 07777132221 1	CROSS PURPOSES (LP) 35
97	Castle ORRLP 004	BLACK SABBATH (LP, reissue, 5000 only with free 7") 20
00	Raw Power RAWLP 145	THE BEST OF BLACK SABBATH (4-LP, gatefold sleeve, numbered and stickered) 30

(see also Ozzy Osborne, Dio, Elf, Cozy Powell, Quartz, Phenomena, Rock Aid Armenia, Brian May)

BLACK SLATE
76	King George KG 001	Mixed Up Man/Put Your Head On My Shoulder 8
78	Ted TCDD 006	Mind Your Motion/Version 30
78	Ted TCDD 008	Sticks Man (12") 30
78	Slate KG 008	Live Up To Love/Jah In The Ghetto (12") 10
81	TCD TCDLP 02	OGIMA (DUB SLATE) (LP) 40

BLACK STASH
| 76 | Seville 1004 | Mighty Love Man/Mighty Love Man Part 2 ......15 |

BLACK STONES
| 76 | Daddy Kool DK 003 | We Nah Go Suffer/Unity Dub ......6 |

BLACK SWAN
| 71 | Ember EMBS 303 | Echoes And Rainbows/Belong Belong (with p/s) ......15 |
| 71 | Ember EMBS 303 | Echoes And Rainbows/Belong Belong (without p/s) ......8 |

BLACK SYMBOL
| 80s | Black Symbol BS 001 | Non A Jah Jah Children Passing/Version ......35 |

BLACKTHORN
| 77 | WHM 1921 | BLACKTHORN (LP) ......60 |
| 78 | WHM 1923 | BLACKTHORN II (LP) ......100 |

BLACK UHURU
77	Carib Gems CG 015	Sun Is Shining/REVOLUTIONARIES : Version 15
77	Third World TWDIS 009	Natural Mystic/Sorry For The Man (12") 20
79	Warrior WAR 140	Bad Girl/African Love/PRINCE HAMMER - Yogi Bear (12") 20
79	DEB DEB 034	Rent Man/Rent Board/ALTON ELLIS - La La Means I Love You/Version (12") 15
79	DEB DEB 036	Wood For My Fire/EARL CUNNINGHAM/JAH THOMAS - Words Of The Father (12") 15
79	D Roy DDR 09	Plastic Smile/Guess Who's Coming To Dinner (12") 25
79	D-Roy DRDD 15	Shine Eye (featuring Keith Richards)/D-ROY BAND: Licking Stick (12") 25
80	Island 12WIP 6626	Sinsemilla (Discomix)/Guess Who's Coming To Dinner (Discomix) (12") 8
77	Third World TWS 925	LOVE CRISIS (LP, as Black Sounds Uhro) 40
79	D-Roy DRLP 1003	SHOWCASE (LP) 25
79	Virgon VX 1004	VITAL SELECTION (LP) 12
81	Greensleeves GREL 23	BLACK SOUNDS OF FREEDOM (LP) 20

(See also Don Carlos)

BLACK VELVET
69	Beacon BEA 129	African Velvet/Whatcha' Gonna Do 'Bout It 10
69	Beacon BEA 137	Peace And Love Is The message/Clown 12
70	Beacon BEA 151	Please Let Me In/Clown 20
70	Beacon BEA 162	What Am I To Do/Coal Mine 12
70	Beacon BEA 170	Thought I Had Me A Good Thing/Love Makes The World Go Round 10
71	Mams MAM 47	Make It Better/Tropicana 15
73	Pye 7N 45338	There Must Be A Way/Domestic Man 12
70	Beacon BEAS 16	THIS IS BLACK VELVET (LP) 25
73	Seven Sun SUNLP1	CAN YOU FEEL IT? (LP) 80
72	Pye NSPL 18392	PEOPLE OF THE WORLD (LP) 25

CHARLES BLACKWELL ORCHESTRA
61	HMV POP 977	Taboo/Midnight In Luxembourg 15
62	Columbia DB 4839	Supercar/Persian Theme 8
62	Columbia DB 4919	Freight Train/Death Valley 8
63	Columbia DB 4994	High Noon/For Me And My Gal 5
65	Columbia BD 7501	Meditation/La Bamba 7
67	United Artists UP 1157	Sailor From Gibraltar/Hoi 6
60	Triumph TRY 4000	THOSE PLUCKING STRINGS (LP, unreleased, test pressings only) 500

OTIS BLACKWELL
| 58 | London HLE 8616 | Make Ready For Love/When You're Around ......40 |
| 58 | London HLE 8616 | Make Ready For Love/When You're Around (78) ......25 |

RORY BLACKWELL & HIS BLACKJACKS
| 57 | Parlophone R 4326 | Bye Bye Love/Such A Shame ......20 |
| 57 | Parlophone R 4326 | Bye Bye Love/Such A Shame (78) ......10 |

SCRAPPER BLACKWELL
67	Collector JEN 7	SCRAPPER BLACKWELL (EP) 12
63	'77' LA 12/4	BLUES BEFORE SUNRISE (LP) 40
60s	Xtra XTRA 5011	MR SCRAPPER'S BLUES (LP) 25

BLACKWELLS (U.K.)
| 65 | Columbia DB 7442 | Why Don't You Love Me/All I Want Is Your Love ......30 |

BLACKWELLS (U.S.)

60	London HLW 9135	Unchained Melody/Mansion On The Hill	10
61	London HLW 9334	Love Or Money/Big Daddy And The Cat	6

BLACK WIDOW

70	CBS 5031	Come To The Sabbat/Way To Power	20
71	CBS 7596	Wish You Would/Accident	15
70	CBS 63948	SACRIFICE (LP, gatefold sleeve)	80
70	CBS 64133	BLACK WIDOW II (LP, gatefold sleeve)	80
72	CBS 64562	BLACK WIDOW III (LP, with inner)	80

(see also Pesky Gee, Agony Bag)

BLADE

88	Chart Moves 732-1532	Chart Moves (12", not officially released. Intended to be instructions to game of same name but never used in final version of game)	100
89	Raw Bass 1202	Lyrical Maniac/The Comin' Is Near/We're Going Independent (12")	20
89	691 Influential 1203	Lyrical Maniac/The Comin' Is Near/We're Going Independent (12")	12
89	691 Influential 1203	Mind Of An OrdinaryCitizen/ Forward (12")	18
91	691 Influential 1204	Rough It Up/Whatcha Waitin' For?/You Better Get Yours (12")	18
93	691 Influential 1206	Clear The Way/They Ain't Shit To Me (12", white vinyl, Blade gave this to fans who paid in advance for his THE LION GOES FROM STRENTH TO STRENGTH LP)	35
96	691 Influential SURV 1	Survival Of The Hardest Working (12")	20
97	Bomb 2006	Rhyme Bomb/The Way It Has To Be (12")	12
92	691 Influential 1205	SURVIVAL OF THE HARDEST WORKING (LP)	25
93	691 Influential 1202	THE LION GOES FROM STRENGTH TO STRENGTH (LP)	30
95	691 Influential 1208	PLANNED AND EXECUTED (LP)	15
95	691 Influential 1208	PLANNED AND EXECUTED (LP, limited edition on red vinyl)	30

ANDY BLADE

80	SMS SMS 001	Break The News/Girl With The Goods (p/s)	18

(see also Eater)

BLADE RUNNER

84	Ebony EBON 26	Back Street Lady/Too Far Too Late	6
84	Ebony EBON 21	HUNTED (LP)	15

BLADES

80	Energy NRG 3	Hot For You/The Reunion (p/s; Irish with paper labels)	20
80	Energy NRG 3	Hot For You/The Reunion (p/s; later UK pressing with plastic labels, in plastic sleeve)	15
81	Energy NRG 5	Ghost Of A Chance/Real Emotion (p/s; Irish with paper labels)	20
81	Energy NRG 5	Ghost Of A Chance/Real Emotion (p/s; later UK pressing with plastic labels, in plastic sleeve)	12
84	Reekus RKS 013	The Last Man In Europe/Sadlands (p/s)	12
85	Reekus RKS 15	Those Were The Days (p/s)	10
85	Reekus RKSY 15	Those Were The Days/Stand By Me Now (picture disc)	12
86	Reekus RKS 017	Downmarket/Truth Don't Hurt (as Blades with Paul Cleary)	10
84	Reekus RKLP 1	THE LAST MAN IN EUROPE (LP)	20
86	Reekus RKLP 3	RAY TOWN REVISITED (LP)	20

(see also Partisans)

BLADES OF GRASS

67	Stateside SS 2040	Happy/That's What A Boy Likes	15
68	Stateside SS 2101	Charlie And Fred/You Won't Find That Girl	10

BLAH BLAH BLAH

79	Absurd ABSURD 1	In The Army/Why Diddle? (p/s)	5
81	Some Bizzare	BLAH BLAH BLAH (LP, unreleased, stickered sleeve, white label test pressings only)	40

HAL BLAINE (& YOUNG COUGARS)

64	RCA RCA 1379	Gear Stripper/Challenger II (with Young Cougars)	30
64	RCA RD 7624	DEUCES, T'S, ROADSTERS AND DRUMS (LP, mono)	40
64	RCA SF 7624	DEUCES, T'S, ROADSTERS AND DRUMS (LP, stereo)	45

VIVIAN BLAINE

54	Parlophone MSP 6070	Changing Partners/Lonely	5

BLAIR

79	Miracle M4	Night Life/Virgo Princess	8
79	Miracle M4-12	Night Life/Virgo Princess (12")	40

ARNOLD BLAIR

76	Curtom NEET 1024	Trying To Get Next To You/I Won The Big Deal/House Party (12" with Fred Wesley)	15

BEVERLEY BLAIR

58	Mercury 7MT 209	With Love We Live/Tony	20

SALLY BLAIR

58	MGM MGM 1000	Whatever Lola Wants (Lola Gets)/Daddy	20

BARDI BLAISE

80	Din Disc DIN 8	Trans Siberian Express/Competition Side (p/s)	6

DAVID BLAKE

69	SNB 55-4178	We'll Meet Again/Now Is The Time	7

ERIC BLAKE

80	Carrere CAR 141	Sin City/Zero 6 (p/s)	10
81	Carrere CAR 179	Born To Be Special/80s Girl/Give Generously (p/s)	10

GARRY BLAKE

66	Columbia DB 7885	Strawberries And Cream/Look Out Now!	8
66	Columbia DB 7977	Wait Until Dark/Jungle Juice	8
66	Columbia DB 8074	The Danny Scipio Theme/Celebration Day	10
66	Studio 2 TWO 124	MORE SOUNDS LIKE SWINGING (LP)	12
67	Studio 2 TWO 174	THE IMPACT OF GARY BLAKE (LP)	12

KARL BLAKE

83	Glass GLASS 013	THE PREHENSILE TAPES (LP)	20
91	Tak Tak Tak TAK 07	MANDIBLES (cassette, 500 only)	15

(see also Lemon Kittens, Shock Headed Peters, Underneath, Gland Shrouds, Fur Fur, Sol Invictus)

KEITH BLAKE
68	Blue Cat BS 102	Musically/I'm Moving On	60

(see also Overtakers, Uniques)

SONNY BLAKE
64	Ember EMBS 195	Johnny Janvier/She's Mine	5

TIM BLAKE
78	Barclay Towers BAR 711	Generator Laserbeam/Woodland Voice (p/s)	8
78	Barclay Towers CLAY 7005	BLAKE'S NEW JERUSALEM (LP)	12

(see also Gong, Hawkwind)

WINSTON BLAKE & M-SQUAD
69	Crab 40	Big Thing/RUPIE EDWARDS : Exclusively Yours	20
71	Green Door GD 4003	Carrol Street/ANSELL COLLINS & M-SQUAD: Carol St. Version	12

ART BLAKEY JAZZ MESSENGERS
61	Fontana TFL 5116	OLYMPIA CONCERT (LP)	20
62	HMV CLP 1532	ART BLAKEY JAZZ MESSENGERS (LP, also stereo CSD 1423)	25
62	Fontana TFL 5184	DANGEROUS FRIENDSHIPS (LP, soundtrack)	18
63	United Artists (S)ULP 1017	THREE BLIND MICE (LP, mono/stereo)	20
64	Riverside RLP 438	CARAVAN (LP)	20
64	HMV CLP 1760	A JAZZ MESSAGE (LP)	20
64	Riverside RLP 464	UGETSU (LP)	30
65	Limelight (S)LML 4000	'S MAKE IT (LP)	20
66	Limelight (S)LML 4012	SOUL FINGER (LP)	20
66	Limelight (S)LML 4021	BUTTERCORN LADY (LP)	20
66	Fontana FJL 111	SOUL! (LP)	20
67	Limelight (S)LML 4023	HOLD ON, I'M COMIN' (LP)	20
67	Atlantic 590 009	BLUE MONK (LP, with Thelonious Monk)	20
68	Riverside 673013	KYOTO (LP)	20
69	Polydor 545101	DRUM THUNDER (LP)	15

(see also Annie Ross)

ART BLAKEY/MILES DAVIS
66	Fontana FJL 135	L'ASCENSEUR POUR L'ECHAFAUD/FEMME DISPARAISSANTE (LP, soundtrack, 1 side each)	30

(see also Thelonious Monk, Miles Davis)

ALAN BLAKLEY
75	DJM DJS 367	Sorry (Lyn's Song)/Windows Are Nice	8

BLAK TWANG
95	Sound Of Money SNM004	What's Going On?/Everyday News (12")	12
95	Sound Of Money SNM005	Queen's Head/Mr Jam Promota (12")	12
96	Sound Of Money SNM007	Real Estate (12")	10
96	Sound Of Money ANTI T3	Dettwork South East/Don't Let Dem Fool You (12")	10
98	Blak Jam BJAM 0003	19 LONG TIME (LP)	12
02	Bad Magic MAGIC LP 5	KIK OFF (2-LP)	15

MEL BLANC
58	Capitol CL 14950	I Taut I Taw A Puddy Cat/K-K-K-Katy	5
60	Warner Bros WB 26	Tweety's Twistmas Twouble/I Keep Hearing Those Bells	5

BURT BLANCA
60	Zodiac ZR 004	Texas Rider/Shamash	20

BLANCMANGE
80	Blaah Music MFT-1	IRENE AND MAVIS (EP, gatefold p/s)	40
82	London SHPD 8552	HAPPY FAMILIES (LP, picture disc)	12
84	London SHPD 8554	MANGE TOUT (LP, picture disc)	12

BILLY BLAND
60	London HL 9096	Let The Little Girl Dance/Sweet Thing	15
71	Atlantic 2091 130	Let The Little Girl Dance/Chicken Hop	5

BOBBY BLAND
61	Vogue V 9178	Cry Cry Cry/I've Been Wrong So Long	30
61	Vogue V 9182	Lead Me On/Hold Me Tenderly	30
61	Vogue V 9188	Don't Cry No More/St. James Infirmary	30
62	Vogue V 9190	You're The One (That I Need)/Turn On Your Love Light	30
62	Vogue V 9192	Blue Moon/Who Will The Next Fool Be?	30
64	Vocalion VP 9222	Ain't Nothing You Can Do/Honey Child	35
64	Vocalion VP 9229	After It's Too Late/Share Your Love With Me	30
65	Vocalion VP 9232	Yield Not To Temptation/How Does A Cheating Woman Feel?	40
65	Vocalion VP 9251	These Hands (Small But Mighty)/Today	40
66	Vocalion VP 9262	I'm Too Far Gone (To Turn Around)/ If You Could Read My Mind	25
66	Vocalion VP 9273	Good Time Charlie/Good Time Charlie (Working His Groove Bag)	35
68	Sue WI 4044	That Did It/A Touch Of The Blues	50
69	Action ACT 4524	Rockin' In The Same Old Boat/Wouldn't You Rather Have Me?	30
69	Action ACT 4538	Gotta Get To Know You/Baby I'm On My Way	30
69	Action ACT 4548	Share Your Love With Me/Honey Child	20
69	Action ACT 4553	Chains Of Love/Ask Me 'Bout Nothing But The Blues	20
74	ABC ABC 4014	Ain't No Love In The Heart Of The City/Twenty Four Blues	10
75	ABC ABC 4030	I Wouldn't Treat A Dog (The Way You Treat Me)/I Ain't Gonna Be The First To Cry	5
77	ABC ABC 4186	The Soul Of A Man/If I Weren't A Gambler	5
85	Kent Town 108	Shoes/Call On me/Getting Used To The Blues/Good Time Charlie (EP, p/s)	10
63	Vocalion VEP 170153	YIELD NOT INTO TEMPTATION (EP)	80
64	Vocalion VEP 170157	BOBBY BLAND (EP)	80
60	Vogue VA 160183	TWO STEPS FROM THE BLUES (LP)	150
61	Vocalion VA 160183	TWO STEPS FROM THE BLUES (LP)	70
61	Vogue VAP 8027	AIN'T NOTHING YOU CAN DO (LP)	75
64	Vocalion VAP 8027	AIN'T NOTHING YOU CAN DO (LP)	40
63	Vogue VAP 8034	CALL ON ME/ THAT'S THE WAY LOVE IS (LP)	75
64	Vocalion VAP 8034	CALL ON ME/ THAT'S THE WAY LOVE IS (LP)	40
66	Vocalion VAP 8041	HERE'S THE MAN (LP)	60

MINT VALUE £

68	Island ILP 974	A TOUCH OF THE BLUES (LP)	70
69	Action ACLP 6006	A PIECE OF GOLD (LP)	40
74	Polydor 2383 257	BLUES FOR MR. CRUMP (LP, with tracks by Junior Parker & Howlin' Wolf)	20

MARCIE BLANE
62	London HLU 9599	Bobby's Girl/A Time To Dream	25
63	London HLU 9673	What Does A Girl Do/How Can I Tell Him	25
63	London HLU 9744	Little Miss Fool/Ragtime Sound	25
63	London HLU 9787	You Gave My Number To Billy/Told You So	25
63	London REU 1393	MARCIE BLANE (EP)	150

BLANKS
79	Void SRTS/79/CUS/560	The Northern Ripper/Understand (p/s)	60

(see also Destructors)

BLANK STUDENTS
80	Dexter Discs	We Are Natives/I Want To Be Happy (500 only)	25

BLARNEY SISTERS
67	GO AJ11407	The Greatest Blessing/Golden Band	15

BLAST FURNACE AND THE HEATWAVES
78	HOT 1	BLUE WAVE (EP)	8

BLAZE
95	Nuphonic NUX 106	THE BLAZE TRACKS (EP)	8
99	Slip And Slide SLIP 99	Wishing You Were Here/(mixes) (2x12")	10

BLAZE X
80	Fixed Wheel FX 1	Some Hope/Rippy (Irish pressing, gatefold p/s)	100

BLAZER, BLAZER
78	Logo GO 362	Cecil B. Devine/Warsaw/Six O'Clock In The Morning (p/s)	10

BLAZERS
58	Fontana TFR 6010	ROCK AND ROLL (10" LP)	80

BLAZING SONS
83	Cool Ghoul COOL 002	Chant Down The National Front/N.F. Dub (no p/s)	10

(see also Phantom)

BLEACH BOYS
78	Tramp THF 002	Chloroform/You've Got Nothing (no p/s, 1,000 only)	60
85	Zombie International ZOMBO 103010	Stocking-Clad Nazi Death Squad Bitches/Death Before Disco/Gimme That Neutron Taste (12", p/s)	25

BLEAK HOUSE
80s	Buzzard BUZZ 1	Rainbow Warrior/Isandlhwana/Inquisition (in p/s)	100
80s	Buzzard BUZZ 1	Rainbow Warrior/Isandlhwana/Inquisition	30
82	Buzzard BUZZ 2	LIONS IN WINTER (Chase The Wind/No Reply/Down To Zero/ Flight Of The Salamander) (EP, p/s with insert)	90

BLEECHERS
69	Trojan TR 679	Ease Up/You're Gonna Feel It	15
69	Upsetter US 314	Come Into My Parlour/MELOTONES: Dry Up Your Tears	15
70	Col. Blue Beat DB 118	Send Me The Pillow (That You Dream On)/Adam And Eve	20
71	Duke DU 118	Put It Good/J.J. ALLSTARS: Good Good Version	10

(see also Busty Brown, Upsetters)

BLEEDING HEARTS
80	Crazy Plane SP 003	This Is The Way/OK	30

PETER BLEGVAD
77	Virgin V 2082	KEW RHONE (LP, with John Greaves)	15

(see also Slapp Happy)

BLENDELLS
64	Reprise RS 20291	La La La La La La/Huggies Bunnies	20
64	Reprise RS 20291	La La La La La La/Huggies Bunnies (DJ Copy)	40
64	Reprise RS 20340	Dance With Me/Get Your Baby	40
64	Reprise RS 20340	Dance With Me/Get Your Baby (DJ Copy)	50

CARLA BLEY
72	JCOA JT 4001	ESCALATOR OVER THE HILL (3xLP, with Paul Haines & Jack Bruce)	25
74	Watt WATT 1	TROPIC APPETITES (LP, gatefold sleeve)	15

(see also Jazz Composers Orchestra, Michael Mantler, Jack Bruce)

PAUL BLEY TRIO
69	Fontana SFJL 929	TOUCHING (LP)	60

(see also Bley-Peacock Synthesizer Show, Annette Peacock)

BLEY-PEACOCK SYNTHESIZER SHOW
72	Polydor 2425 043	REVENGE (LP)	200

(see also Annette Peacock, Paul Bley)

ARCHIE BLEYER & HIS ORCHESTRA
54	London HL 8035	Amber/Julie's Jump	30
54	London HL 8111	The Naughty Lady Of Shady Lane/While The Vesper Bells Were Ringing	30
55	London HLA 8176	Hernando's Hideaway/S'il Vous Plait	30
56	London HLA 8243	Nothin' To Do/JANET BLEYER: 'Cause You're My Lover	15
56	London HLA 8263	Bridge Of Happiness/You Tell Me Your Dream, I'll Tell You Mine (Gold Tri)	15
56	London REA 1036	PYJAMA GAME (EP)	10

B,L&G
71	Birds Nest BN 3	Live In The Mountains/Janie Slow Down	7

(see also Trevor Burton, Denny Laine, Steve Gibbons)

BLIND BLAKE
50	Tempo R 23	Hey Hey Daddy Blues/Brownskin Mama Blues (78)	15
50	Tempo R 40	Southern Rag/CC Pill Blues (78)	15
54	Jazz Collector L 97	Hot Potatoes/Southbound Rag (78)	15

58	Ristic LP 18	THE LEGENDARY BLIND BLAKE (10" LP)	50
59	Jazz Collector JLP 2001	THE LEGENDARY BLIND BLAKE (10" LP, reissue)	20
67	Riverside RLP 8804	BLUES IN CHICAGO (LP)	20

(see also Paramount Allstars)

BLIND BLAKE/CHARLIE JACKSON
| 50s | Heritage HLP 1011 | BLIND BLAKE AND CHARLIE JACKSON (LP, 99 only) | 70 |

BLIND BLAKE/RAMBLIN' THOMAS
| 59 | Jazz Collector JEL 4 | THE MALE BLUES VOLUME 3 (EP) | 10 |

BLIND FAITH
69	Island (no cat. no.)	Change Of Address From June 23rd 1969 (promo issue, 500 only)	300
69	Polydor 583 059	BLIND FAITH (LP, gatefold sleeve, first pressing with single paper on left gatefold stating distribution by Polydor and Island)	70
69	Polydor 583 059	BLIND FAITH (LP, gatefold sleeve, later issue without Polydor and Island distribution credit)	30

(see also Stevie Winwood, Ginger Baker, Eric Clapton)

BLIND FURY
| 85 | Roadrunner RR 9814 | OUT OF REACH (LP) | 12 |

BLINK 182
96	Grilled Cheese GRL 701	They Came To Conquer Uranus/Waggy (blue vinyl, p/s)	12
01	MCA MCS 40264	First Date/Don't Tell Me It's Over (picture disc, printed PVC sleeve)	10
04	Geffen MCS 40400	Always/I Miss You (Live In Minneapolis) (Picture disc)	5
05	MCA B000C5E791	Not Now/All The Small Things (live) (p/s, stickered)	5
05	MCA B000C5E78X	Not Now/Dammit (Live) (p/s. stickered)	5
97	Grilled Cheese LPGRL 4	DUDE RANCH (LP, gatefold sleeve)	20

BLINKERS
| 69 | Pye 7N 17752 | Original Sin/Dreams Secondhand | 50 |

BLINKY & EDWIN STARR
69	Tamla Motown TMG 720	Oh How Happy/Ooo Baby Baby (unissued, demos only)	375
70	Tamla Motown TMG 748	Oh How Happy/Ooo Baby Baby	10
70	T. Motown (S)TML 11131	JUST WE TWO (LP, as Edwin Starr & Blinky)	25

(see also Edwin Starr)

BLISS
| 69 | Chapter One CH 107 | Courtyards In Castile/Lifetime | 15 |

MELVIN BLISS
| 77 | Contempo CS 2013 | Reward/Synthetic Substitution | 40 |

BLITZ
81	No Future OI 1	ALL OUT ATTACK (EP, rubber-stamped labels, 500 only)	25
81	No Future OI 1	ALL OUT ATTACK (EP, reissue, initially with white labels)	15
81	No Future OI 1	ALL OUT ATTACK (EP, reissue, later printed labels)	10
82	No Future OI 6	Never Surrender/Razor In The Night (p/s)	12
82	No Future OI 16	Warriors/Youth (p/s)	12
82	No Future PUNK 1	VOICE OF A GENERATION (LP, with inner sleeve)	25

(see also Rose Of Victory)

BLITZ BOYS
| 80 | Told You So TYS 001 | Eddy's New Shoes/Eddie's Friend/She Told My Friends (foldover p/s) | 100 |

BLITZKRIEG (1)
81	Neat NEAT 10	Buried Alive/Blitzkrieg (p/s)	60
91	Roadrunner R 09302	10 YEARS OF BLITZKRIEG (EP)	10
85	Neat NEAT 1023	A TIME OF CHANGES (LP)	40

BLITZKRIEG (2)
| 82 | No future OI 8 | LEST WE FORGET (EP) | 10 |
| 83 | Sexual Phonograph SPH2 | Animals In Lipstick/Land Of Failure/No Compromise (p/s, SPH2 on cover but SPH3 on label) | 15 |

BLITZKRIEG BOP
77	Mortonsound MTN 3172/3	Let's Go/Nine Till Five/Bugger Off (p/s, 500 only)	100
77	Lightning GIL 504	Let's Go (re-recorded)/Life Is Just A So-So/Mental Case (p/s)	20
78	Lightning GIL 543	U.F.O./Bobby Joe (p/s)	20

BLIZZARD
| 71 | CBS CBS 7238 | Baby Blue/Mama, The Sparrow And The Tree | 8 |

BLOATED TOADS
| 79 | Shattered SHAT 4 | Why/Essential In Some Form/Happy Home/Yankee TV Victim (p/s, with insert) | 5 |

BLOC PARTY
04	Trash Aesthetics TA701	She's Hearing Voices/The Marshals Are Dead/The Answer (p/s clear vinyl, 500 only)	50
04	Moshi Moshi MOSHI10	Banquet/Staying Fat (p/s, 500 only)	20
04	Moshi Moshi MOSH110CD	Banquet/Staying Fat (CD, 2000 only)	15
04	Wichita WEBB067S	Little Thoughts/Storm And Stress (Blue vinyl, p/s)	10
05	Wichita WEBB088S	The Pioneers/The Pioneers (Bloc Party vs Mystery Jets) (numbered pic disc)	10
05	Wichita WEBB075LP	SILENT ALARM (LP)	30
05	Wichita WEBB075PD	SILENT ALARM (LP, picture disc)	30
05	Wichita WEBB090LP	SILENT ALARM REMIXED (2-LP)	15
07	Wichita WEBB 120 PD	A WEEKEND IN THE CITY (LP, picture disc)	15

BLOCKHEAD
| 04 | Ninja Tune ZEN 88 | MUSIC BY CAVELIGHT (2xLP) | 25 |

BLODWYN PIG
69	Island WIP 6059	Dear Jill/Sweet Caroline	12
69	Island WIP 6069	Walk On The Water/Summer Day	12
70	Chrysalis WIP 6078	Same Old Story/Slow Down	10
69	Island ILPS 9101	AHEAD RINGS OUT (LP, gatefold sleeve, pink label with black/orange circle logo)	60
69	Island ILPS 9101	AHEAD RINGS OUT (LP, gatefold sleeve, 'pink rim palm tree' label)	12
70	Chrysalis ILPS 9122	GETTING TO THIS (LP, gatefold sleeve, island logo and address in white on green label)	40

(see also Mick Abrahams, Jethro Tull)

BLOND

| 69 | Fontana TF 1040 | (I Will Bring You) Flowers In The Morning/I Wake Up And Call ....12 |
| 69 | Fontana STL 5515 | THE LILAC YEARS (LP, gatefold sleeve) ....125 |

(see also Tages)

BLONDE ON BLONDE

69	Pye 7N 17637	All Day All Night/Country Life 40
70	Ember EMB S 279	Castles In The Sky/Circles (in p/s) 20
70	Ember EMB S 279	Castles In The Sky/Circles (no p/s) 12
72	Ember EMB S 316	Sad Song For An Easy Lady/Happy Families (p/s) 15
79	Pye 7N 46189	Whole Lotta Love/Make Me Smile (p/s) 6
69	Pye NSPL 18288	CONTRASTS (LP, gatefold sleeve, blue/black label with logo/banner on top) 120
70	Ember NR 5049	RE-BIRTH (LP, gatefold sleeve) 80
71	Ember NR 5058	REFLECTIONS ON A LIFE (LP, gatefold sleeve) 80
70s	Ember LP 7005	BLONDE ON BLONDE (LP, unissued, test pressings only) 200

BLONDIE

77	Private Stock PVT 90	X Offender/In The Sun (unissued, promos or stock copies, no p/s) 2000
76	Private Stock PVT 105	In The Flesh/X Offender (no p/s) 20
77	Chrysalis CHS 2180	Rip Her To Shreds/In The Flesh/X Offender (p/s) 12
77	Chrysalis CHS 2180-12	Rip Her To Shreds/In The Flesh/X Offender (12", green labels, '75p' p/s) 8
78	Chrysalis CHS 2204	Denis (Denee)/Contact In Red Square (red/blue p/s) 5
78	Chrysalis CHS 2242	Picture This/Fade Away (And Radiate) (p/s, yellow vinyl) 8
78	Chrysalis CHE 2266	Hanging On The Telephone/Will Anything Happen (p/s, export issue) 6
78	Chrysalis CHE 2275	Heart Of Glass/Rifle Range (p/s, export issue with "pain in the ass" lyrics) 8
80	Flexi FLX 146 Lyntone LYN 10840/1	Speaking From The Studio (Blondie Fan Club flexidisc) Yuletown Throwdown (Rapture) (with Freddie)/ BRATTLES: The Christmas Song/SNUKY TATE: Santa's Agent (33rpm blue or orange vinyl flexi with Flexipop magazine issue 15) 15
89	Chrysalis CHSP 12 3342	Call Me (Remix)/Backfired (Remix)/Call Me (1989) (12", picture disc) 8
98	EMI 12 ATOM 150	ATOMIC 98 (Remixes) (12", p/s, withdrawn) 15
98	EMI CD ATOM 150	ATOMIC 98 (Remixes) (CD, withdrawn) 18
76	Private Stock PVLP 1017	BLONDIE (LP) 18
82	Chrysalis PCDL 1384	THE HUNTER (LP, picture disc) 15
89	Chrysalis CHR 1658	THE 12" MIXES (2-LP) 15
89	Chrysalis CCD 1658	THE 12" MIXES (CD) 8

(see also Debbie Harry, Wind In The Willows, Rodney & Brunettes)

BLOOBLO

76	Feelgood FLG 104	Please Mister Please/Chaka 12
76	Feelgood FG1	CHAKA (LP) 12
78	Mother & Son	IS THAT YOU (LP) 25

BLOOD

83	No Future OI 22	Megalomania/Calling The Shots/Parasite In Paradise (p/s) 20
83	Noise NOY 1	Stark Raving Normal/Mesrine (p/s) 15
82	Noise NOYZLP 1	FALSE GESTURES FOR A DEVIOUS PUBLIC (LP) 20
85	Conquest QUEST 3	SE PARARE NEX (LP) 15
89	Link Classics CLINK 5	FALSE GESTURES FOR A DEVIOUS PUBLIC (LP, reissue, red vinyl) 15

BARRY BLOOD

| 75 | Alaska ALA 24 | Poor Annie/On The Run ....50 |

BLOOD DIVINE

| 96 | Peaceville VILE 62 | AWAKEN (LP) ....18 |

(see also Cradle Of filth, Anathema)

BLOOD SHANTI

| 96 | Aba Shanti ABA 12003 | Tear Down Babylon/Verse 1/Verse 2/Verse 3 (12") ....20 |

BLOOD & ROSES

| 85 | Audiodrome ASSAULT | (Some) Like It Hot/Paradise ....5 |

BLOOD DONOR

79	Arista ARIRV 262	Rubber Revolution/Chemical Babies (P/S, red vinyl) 8
79	Arista ARIST 269	Rice Harvest/Something Happened (p/s) 10
81	Safari SAFE 29	Doctor/Soap Box Blues (p/s) 10

BLOOD RED SHOES

06	Jonson Family	Bless His Heart/Don't Always Say Yes/Victory For The Magpie (p/s, insert, 500 only) 40
06	Try Harder	Stitch Me Back/Meet Me At Eight (500 only) 40
07	V2 B000PHX186	It's Getting Boring By The Sea/Box Of Secrets (p/s) 5
10	V2 VVR736628	FIRE LIKE THIS (LP) 12

BLOODROCK

71	Capitol CL 15670	D.O.A./Children's Heritage 8
71	Capitol E-ST 491	BLOODROCK 2 (LP) 15
71	Capitol E-ST 765	BLOODROCK 3 (LP) 15

BLOOD SISTERS

| 79 | Sound City SCD 002 | Ring My Bell/Dub (12") ....20 |
| 79 | Sound City SCD 004 | What About Me/I'd Rather Go Blind (12") ....15 |

BLOOD, SWEAT & TEARS

68	CBS 3563	I Can't Quit Her/House In The Country 20
69	CBS 4116	You've Made Me So Very Happy/The Blues, Part 2 5
69	CBS 4220	Spinning Wheel/More And More 5
74	CBS 2462	Tell Me That I'm Wrong/Rock Reprise 20
68	CBS 63296	CHILD IS THE FATHER TO THE MAN (LP) 20

(see also Al Kooper, David Clayton-Thomas)

ROGER BLOOM'S HAMMER

| 67 | CBS 202654 | Out Of The Blue/Life's A Gamble ....12 |
| 67 | CBS 2848 | Polly Pan/Fifteen Degree Temperature Rise ....8 |

MIKE BLOOMFIELD

| 69 | CBS 63652 | IT'S NOT KILLING ME (LP) ....20 |

(see also Barry Goldberg Reunion, Stephen Stills, K.G.B.)

MIKE BLOOMFIELD & AL KOOPER
69	CBS 4094	The Weight/59th Street Bridge Song	10
69	CBS 66216	THE LIVE ADVENTURES OF MIKE BLOOMFIELD AND AL KOOPER (2-LP, mono)	50
69	CBS 66216	THE LIVE ADVENTURES OF MIKE BLOOMFIELD AND AL KOOPER (2-LP, stereo)	20

(see also Al Kooper, Paul Butterfield Blues Band, Electric Flag)

BLOOMFIELDS
| 72 | Pye 7N 45114 | The Loner/Homing In On The Next Trade Wind | 15 |

BLOSSOM TOES
67	Marmalade 598 002	What On Earth/Mrs Murphy's Budgerigar/Look At Me I'm You (in p/s)	70
67	Marmalade 598 002	What On Earth/Mrs Murphy's Budgerigar/Look At Me I'm You	30
68	Marmalade 598 009	I'll Be Your Baby Tonight/Love Is	30
68	Marmalade 598 012	Postcard/Everyone's Leaving Me Now	30
69	Marmalade 598 014	Peace Loving Man/Up Above My Hobby Horse's Head	30
69	Marmalade 598 022	New Day/Love Bomb (unissued, existence unconfirmed)	0
67	Marmalade 607 001	WE ARE EVER SO CLEAN (LP, mono)	500
67	Marmalade 608 001	WE ARE EVER SO CLEAN (LP, stereo)	600
69	Marmalade 608 010	IF ONLY FOR A MOMENT (LP)	600
88	Decal LIKD 43	COLLECTION (2-LP)	15

(see also B.B. Blunder, Stud, Kevin Westlake, Solid Gold Cadillac)

BLOSSOMS
58	Capitol CL 14833	Move On/He Promised Me	50
58	Capitol CL 14856	Little Louie/Have Faith In Me	40
58	Capitol CL 14947	No Other Love/Baby Daddy-O	40
68	MGM MGM 1435	Tweedle Dee/You Got Me Hummin'	20
71	Pama PM 814	Stand By/Soul And Inspiration	30

(see also Darlene Love, Allisons [U.S.])

MICHAEL BLOUNT
70	CBS 5248	Ryba Jyba/Acorn Street	15
70	CBS 7022	Sometimes/Angelina Baby	5
72	York SYK 519	Beautiful Morning/Feathered Cloud	5
72	York SYK 528	Tackle And Sack/Pretty Face	5
72	York SKY 535	Rosie/Trombone Man	5
71	CBS 64230	PATCHWORK (LP)	20
72	York FYK 401	SOUVENIRS (LP)	20
73	York FYK 414	FANTASIES (LP)	20

BLOWZABELLA
| 90 | Special Delivery SPD 1028 | VANILLA (LP) | 40 |
| 70s | Plant Life PLR 051 | IN COLOUR (LP) | 30 |

BLUE
73	RSO 2090 109	Red Light Song/Look Around	6
73	RSO 2090 114	Little Jody/The Way Things Are	6
73	RSO 2394 105	BLUE (LP)	15

(see also Poets, Thunderclap Newman)

BABBITY BLUE
| 65 | Decca F 12053 | Don't Make Me (Fall In Love With You)/I Remembered How To Cry | 10 |
| 65 | Decca F 12149 | Don't Hurt Me/Question | 12 |

BARRY BLUE
| 94 | Vinyl Solution STORM85 | Cancel Em All Out (12") | 8 |

BOBBY BLUE
| 70 | Duke DU 86 | Going In Circles (actually by Lloyd Charmers)/Doggone Right (actually by Bobby Davis) | 12 |

DAVID BLUE
69	Reprise RS20830	Beautiful Susan/You Don't Need A Thing	8
67	Elektra EKL 4003	DAVID BLUE (LP, red label)	40
72	Asylum SYL 9001	STORIES (LP)	18
73	Asylum SYL 9009	NICE BABY AND THE ANGEL (LP)	18
75	Asylum SYL 9025	COMIN' BACK FOR MORE (LP)	15
76	Asylum K 53056	CUPID'S ARROW (LP)	15

PAMELA BLUE
| 63 | Decca F 11761 | My Friend Bobby/Hey There Stranger | 80 |

BLUE RONDOS
| 64 | Pye 7N 15734 | Little Baby/Baby I Go For You | 40 |
| 65 | Pye 7N 15833 | Don't Want Your Lovin' No More/What Can I Do | 50 |

TIMOTHY BLUE
| 68 | Spark SRL 1014 | The Room At The Top Of The Stairs/She Won't See The Light | 20 |

BLUE ACES
64	Pye 7N 15672	Land Of Love/Love Song Of The Waterfall	15
64	Pye 7N 15713	I Beat You To It/I Just Can't Help Loving You	15
65	Pye 7N 15821	Ain't What You Say/You Don't Care	15
65	Columbia DB 7755	Tell Me What You're Gonna Do/All I Want	100
66	Columbia DB 7954	That's All Right/Talk About My Baby	170

(see also Riot Squad)

BLUE ANCHOR
| 79 | Workhouse WHR 6 | PLENTY LOVE & BACON (LP) | 15 |

BLUE & FERRIS
| 68 | Blue Cat BS 147 | You Stole My Money/Tell Me The Reason | 40 |

BLUE ANGEL
80	Polydor POSP 212	I'm Gonna Be Strong/Anna Blue (no p/s)	6
81	Polydor POSP 241	I Had A Love/Can't Blame Me	8
84	Polydor POSP 212	I'm Gonna Be Strong/Anna Blue (p/s, reissue)	8
80	Polydor 2391 486	BLUE ANGEL (LP)	25

(see also Cyndi Lauper)

MINT VALUE £

BLUE AQUARIUS
73   Akashic 998   The Ultimate Train/At The Feet Of The Master 25

BLUE ARSED FLY
95   Ferox FER 012   IN THE BAG EP (12") 15
96   Mosquito MSQ 04   BLUE ARSED FLY EP (12") 20
(see also Christian Vogel, Neil Landstrumm)

BLUE BEARD
71   Ember EMB S 302   Country Man/Sly Willy (in p/s) 30
71   Ember EMB S 302   Country Man/Sly Willy (no p/s) 20
71   Ember LT 7004   BLUE BEARD (LP, unreleased, test pressings only) 200

BLUEBEATERS
64   Piccadilly 7N 35181   Little David/Ain't Got A Care 10
64   Piccadilly 7N 35191   Early In The Morning/There I Go 8

BLUEBEATS
64   Ember EMB EP 4525   THE FABULOUS BLUEBEATS VOL. 1 (EP) 25
64   Ember EMB EP 4526   THE FABULOUS BLUEBEATS VOL. 2 (EP) 25

BLUE BEATS
60   Blue Beat 45/BB 20   Baby What You Done Me Wrong/Go Pretty Baby Go 15

BLUE-BELLES
62   HMV POP 1029   I Sold My Heart To The Junkman/Itty Bitty Twist 25
(see also Patti Labelle)

BLUE BELLS & JAH BERRY
78   Burning Rockers BRD 001   Teacher Teach, Teach The Youth/Golden Rule (12") 30

BLUEBERRIES
66   Mercury MF 894   It's Gonna Work Out Fine/Please Don't Let Me Know............................60

BLUE BLOOD
70   Sonet SNTF 615   BLUE BLOOD (LP) 25

BLUE BLUDD
87   Blud Donor no cat. No.   LIQUOR 'N' POKER (EP) 20

BLUEBOY
91   Sarah SARAH 55   Clearer/Alison (p/s, insert) 20
92   Sarah SARAH 65   Popkiss/Chelsea Guitar/Fearon (p/s, insert)...20
93   Sarah SARAH 74   Meet Johnny Rave/Elle/Air France (p/s)...15
93   Sarah SARAH 80   SOME GORGEOUS ACCIDENT EP (wraparound p/s in ply bay, insert) 15
93   Sarah SARAH 70   Cloud Babies (6" one-sided flexi with fanzine) 15
94   Sarah SARAH 88   River/Nimbus/Hit 15
95   Sarah SARAH 99   Dirty Mags/Loony Tunes/Toulouse (p/s) 20
96   Shinkansen SHINKANSEN 4   Love Yourself/Melancholia (p/s)...5
92   Sarah SARAH 612   IF WISHES WERE HORSES (LP) 40
94   Sarah SARAH 620   UNISEX (LP)...40

BLUE CATS
80   Charly CYS 1072   I'm Gonna Die/I'm Going Home (p/s) 8
81   Charly CYS 1075   Wild Night/Jump Cat Jump (p/s) 8
(see also G men, Beltane Fire)

BLUE CHEER
68   Philips BF 1646   Summertime Blues/Out Of Focus..25
68   Philips BF 1684   Just A Little Bit/Gypsy Ball 12
68   Philips BF 1711   Feathers From Your Tree/Sun Cycle 12
69   Philips BF 1778   West Coast Child Of Sunshine/When It All Gets Old 15
71   Philips 6051 010   Pilot/Babaji 15
68   Philips BL 7839   VINCEBUS ERUPTUM (LP, mono) 60
68   Philips (S)BL 7839   VINCEBUS ERUPTUM (LP, stereo) 30
68   Philips SBL 7860   OUTSIDEINSIDE (LP, gatefold sleeve) 45
69   Philips SBL 7896   NEW! IMPROVED! (LP) 40
69   Philips 6336 001   BLUE CHEER (LP) 40
71   Philips 6336 004   B.C. #5 THE ORIGINAL HUMAN BEING (LP) 45
(see also Leigh Stephens, Group B)

BLUE CHIPS
65   Pye 7N 15970   I'm On The Right Side/You're Good To Me...30
66   Pye 7N 17111   Some Kind Of Lovin'/I Know A Boy 45
66   Pye 7N 17155   Tell Her/Good Lovin' Never Hurt 30

BLUE DANUBE
80   EMI EMI 5070   You Are A Song (Du Bist Musik)/Let Me Hear That Song Again/Du Bist Musik....................10

BLUE DIAMONDS
60   Decca F 21292   Ramona/All Of Me...5

BLUE EPITAPH
74   Holyground HG 117   ODE (LP, 99 copies only) 400
91   Holyground HG 117   ODE (LP, reissue, folded gatefold sleeve) 25
(see also Magus)

BLUE EYES
91   Union Hall 001   Pick Up The Mic On A Soul Tip/The Law (12") 40
93   Buback BTT 028   Straight From The UK (12") 10

BLUE FEATHER
81   Mercury MERX 109   Lets Funk Tonight/Its Love (12") 8

BLUE FLAMES
63   R&B JB 114   J.A. Blues/Orange Street 60
63   R&B JB 126   Stop Right Here/Rik's Tune 60
(see also Georgie Fame & Blue Flames)

BLUE GOOSE
75	Anchor ANC 1015	Loretta/Call On Me	5
75	Anchor ANCL 2005	BLUE GOOSE (LP)	15

(see also Badfinger, Curtis Knight & Zeus, Motorhead)

BLUE HAZE
72	A&M AMS 891	Smoke Gets In Your Eyes/Anna Rosanna	5

BLUE HORIZON
71	Folk Heritage FHR 022S	BLUE HORIZON (LP)	350

BLUE JEANS
69	Columbia DB 8555	Hey Mrs. Housewife/Sandfly	50

(see also Swinging Blue Jeans, Ray Ennis & Blue Jeans)

BLUES MASTERS
63	Island WI 078	5 O'Clock Whistle/African Blood (both sides actually by Baba Brooks)	40

BLUE MAXI
70	Major Minor MM 705	Here Comes Summer/Famous Last Words	8

(see also Jean-Jacques Burnel & Dave Greenfield)

BLUE MEN
60	Triumph RGXST 5000	I HEAR A NEW WORLD (PART ONE) (EP)	300
60	Triumph RGXST 5001	I HEAR A NEW WORLD (PART TWO) (EP, only sleeves exist, this price is for sleeve)	25
60	Triumph TRX ST 9000	I HEAR A NEW WORLD (LP, unreleased, white label demos only)	800

(see also Joe Meek, Peter Jay & Blue Men, Rodd-Ken & Cavaliers)

BLUE MINK
70	Philips SBL 7926	MELTING POT (LP)	12
71	Philips 6308 024	OUR WORLD (LP)	12
73	EMI EMA 756	ONLY WHEN I LAUGH (LP, gatefold sleeve)	12
74	EMI EMC3021	FRUITY (LP)	15

BLUE MITCHELL
73	Mainstream MSL 1015	THE LAST TANGO = BLUES (LP)	18

BLUE MOVIES
79	ROK ROK 9	Mary Jane/THE NOISE: Criminal (company sleeve)	15

BLUE NILE
81	RSO RSO 84	I Love This Life/The Second Act (p/s)	25
84	Linn LKS 1	Stay/Saddle The Horses (white p/s)	8
84	Linn LKS 1-12	Stay/Saddle The Horses (12", white p/s)	8
84	Linn LKS 1	Stay (Remix)/Saddle The Horses (p/s)	5
84	Linn LKSD 1	Stay (Remix)/Saddle The Horses/Tinsel Town In The Rain/ Heatwave (Instrumental) (p/s, double pack)	8
84	Linn LKS 1-12	Stay (Extended Remix)/Saddle The Horses (12", p/s)	8
84	Linn LKS 2	Tinsel Town In The Rain/Heatwave (Instrumental) (p/s)	5
84	Linn LKS 2-12	Tinsel Town In The Rain (Extended)/Regret/Heatwave (Instrumental) (12", p/s)	8

BLUENOTES
60	Top Rank JAR 291	I Don't Know What It Is/You Can't Get Away From Love	10

BLUE NOTES
87	OGUN OG 532	BLUE NOTES FOR JOHNNY (LP)	20

BLUE ORCHIDS
81	Rough Trade RT 065	Disney Boys/The Flood (p/s)	5
81	Rough Trade RT 067	Work/The House That Faded Out (p/s)	5
82	Rough Trade RT 117T	AGENTS OF CHANGE (12" EP, in carrier bag)	8
84	Rough Trade ROUGH 36	GREATEST HITS (LP)	12

(see also Nosebleeds, Fall)

BLUE OX BABES
88	Go! Discs GOLP 14	APPLES AND ORANGES (LP, unissued, test pressings only)	50
88	Go! Discs ZGOLP 14	APPLES AND ORANGES (cassette, printed inlay, unreleased)	20

(see also Dexys midnight Runners)

BLUE ÖYSTER CULT
76	CBS 4483	(Don't Fear) The Reaper/R U Ready 2 Rock	5
76	CBS 4483	(Don't Fear) The Reaper/Tattoo Vampire (promo with different B-side)	10
78	CBS 5689	Going Through The Motions/Searching For The Celine	5
78	CBS 12-6333	(Don't Fear) The Reaper/R U Ready 2 Rock (12")	8
79	CBS 7763	Mirrors/Lonely Teardrops (clear vinyl, foil p/s)	5
81	CBS A 1453	Burnin' For You/Heavy Metal (p/s)	5
73	CBS 64904	BLUE ÖYSTER CULT (LP)	12

BLUE PHANTOM
72	Kaleidoscope KAL 101	DISTORTIONS (LP, laminated front cover, yellow label)	120

BLUE RIDGE RANGERS
73	Fantasy FTC 105	Hearts Of Stone/Somewhere Listening For My Name	6
73	Fantasy FTC 110	You Don't Own Me/Back In The Hills	6
73	Fantasy FT 511	BLUE RIDGE RANGERS (LP)	18

(see also John Fogerty, Creedence Clearwater Revival)

BLUES BAND
80	Blues Band BBBP 101	OFFICIAL BOOTLEG ALBUM (LP, numbered, with autographs, 3000 only)	18

(see also Paul Jones, McGuinness-Flint, Manfred Mann)

BLUES BENDERS
66	Rio R93	Girl Next Door/Leave Me Out	25

BLUES BUSTERS
59	Limbo XL101	Little Vilma/ Early One Morning	20
61	Starlite ST45 031	The Spiritual/ Lost My Baby	30
61	Blue Beat BB55	Donna/You're Driving Me Crazy	15
62	Blue Beat BB73	There's Always Sunshine/ You Had It Wrong	15
62	Starlite ST45 072	Your Love/ You Send Me Crazy	25

62	Island WI-023	Behold/ Oh Baby	20
62	Blue Beat BB102	Tell Me Why/ I've Done You Wrong	20
65	Island WI-214	How Sweet It Is/ I Had A Dream	40
65	Island WI-219	Wide Awake In A Dream (actually by Philip James solo)/ MAYTALS: Tell Me The Reason	75
65	Island WI-222	Wings Of A Dove/ BYRON LEE & DRAGONAIRES: Dan Is The Man	25
66	Doctor Bird DB1030	I've Been Trying/ Pretty Girls	40
67	Doctor Bird DB 1078	There's Always Sunshine/ Lovers' Reward	30
71	Dynamic DYN408	Each One Teach One/ Thinking Of You	5
71	Jay Boy BOY 44	I Can't Stop/Inspired To Love You	8
71	Trojan TR7819	Thinking Of You/ Version	5
65	Island ILP-923	BEHOLD!	60
67	Docto Bird DLM5008	BEST OF THE BLUES BUSTERS	50
78	Sarge LP1001	TRUTH	12
76	Dynamic DYLP 3007	PHILLIP & LLOYD (LP)	20

BLUES BY FIVE
64	Decca F 12029	Boom Boom/I Cried	120

BLUES COUNCIL
65	Parlophone R 5264	Baby Don't Look Down/What Will I Do	100

BLUES 5
64	Studio 36 (no cat. no.)	Hey Baby/When You're In Love	150

BLUES IMAGE
70	Atlantic 2091 009	Ride Captain Ride/Pay My Dues	5

BLUE SKIES
70	Fontana 6007026	Happy/Nightingale	12

BLUES MAGOOS
66	Mercury MF 954	(We Ain't Got) Nothin' Yet/Gotta Get Away	30
67	Fontana TF 848	One By One/Love Seems Doomed	15
71	Probe PRO 522	Can't Get Enough Of You/Sea Breeze Express	5
66	Fontana TL 5402	BLUES MAGOOS (LP, mono)	60
66	Fontana (S)TL 5402	BLUES MAGOOS (LP, stereo)	45
71	Probe SPB 1024	GULF COAST BOUND (LP)	20

BLUESOLOGY
65	Fontana TF 594	Come Back Baby/Time's Getting Tougher Than Tough	300
66	Fontana TF 668	Mister Frantic/Everyday (I Have The Blues)	300

(see also Stu Brown & Bluesology, Elton John, Long John Baldry, Elton Dean, Mark Charig)

BLUES PROJECT
67	Verve Forecast VS 1505	I Can't Keep From Crying/The Way My Baby Walks	35
67	Verve (S)VLP 6004	PROJECTIONS (LP)	40

(see also Al Kooper, Tommy Flanders, Seatrain)

BLUE STARS
65	Decca F 12303	Please Be A Little Kind/I Can Take It	200
94	Dig The Fuzz DIG 020	THE BLUE STARS (LP)	20

BLUE STEAM
78	Rip Off RIP 5	Lizard King/Cortina Cowboys (p/s)	10

BLUE SYSTEM
90	RCA PD 43734	Magic Symphony (7" Mix)/Magic Symphony (Fun Mix)/ Magic Symphony (Power Mix) (CD)	20

BLUETONES
95	Superior Quality TONE 001	Slight Return/The Fountainhead (blue vinyl, plain white sleeve in stickered polythene bag, 2,000 only sold by mail-order or at gigs, some numbered)	8
95	Superior Quality TONE 001	Slight Return/The Fountainhead (red vinyl, foldover p/s in poly bag, 1,000 only, export issue to Japan)	12
96	Superior Quality BLUE 003X	Slight Return/Don't Stand Me Down (red vinyl, export issue to Japan with Japanese text on rear of p/s)	10
96	Superior Quality BLUELP 004	EXPECTING TO FLY (LP)	20

BLUE TRAIN
87	Dreamworld DREAM 007T	LAND OF GOLD (12" EP)	40

BLUE U
72	York SYK 524	I've Been Looking For So Long/Melinda Marie	10

BLUE VELVET BAND
69	Warner Bros WS 1802	SWEET MOMENTS WITH THE BLUE VELVET BAND (LP, gatefold sleeve)	20

BLUEWATER FOLK
70	Folk Heritage FHJR 013S	BLUEWATER FOLK (LP)	80
70s	Moonraker MOO 1	BUGS, BLACK PUDDINGS AND CLOGS (LP, with insert)	12
70s	Moonraker MOO 2	A LANCASHIRE LIFE (LP, with insert)	12

BLUE YOGURT
70	Penny Farthing PEN 732	Lydia/Umbrella Man	15

BLUNDERBUSS
71	Penny Farthing PEN 762	New Day/Emma	12

COLIN BLUNSTONE
71	Epic EPC 7095	Mary, Won't You Warm My Bed/I Hope I Didn't Say Too Much Last Night	5
71	Epic EPC 7520	Caroline Goodbye/Though You Are Far Away	5
72	Epic EPC 7765	Say You Don't Mind/Let Me Come Closer (p/s)	5
72	Epic EPC 8434	I Don't Believe In Miracles/I've Always Had You	5
73	Epic EPC 1197	How Could We Dare To Be Wrong?/Time's Runnin' Out	5
73	Epic EPC 1775	Wonderful/Beginning	5
74	Epic EPC 2413	It's Magical/Summersong	5
71	Epic EPC 64557	ONE YEAR (LP, textured sleeve)	15
72	Epic EPC 65278	ENNISMORE (LP, textured sleeve)	15

(see also Zombies, Neil MacArthur, Mitchell-Coe Mysteries)

BLUNT INSTRUMENT

78	Diesel DCL 01	No Excuse/Interrogation (p/s)	8

BLUR

SINGLES

90	Food FOOD 26	She's So High (Edit)/I Know (7", p/s)	5
90	Food 12FOOD 26	She's So High (Definitive)/Sing/I Know (Extended) (12", p/s)	8
90	Food CDFOOD 26	She's So High/I Know (Extended)/Down (CD)	15
91	Food FOOD 29	There's No Other Way/Inertia (p/s)	5
91	Food 12 FOODX 29	There's No Other Way (The Blur Remix)/Won't Do It/ Day Upon Day (live) (12", p/s lists '12 FOODDX 29')	20
91	Food 12FOOD 29	There's No Other Way (Extended)/Inertia/Mr. Briggs/I'm All Over (12", p/s)	10
91	Food CDFOOD 29	There's No Other Way/Inertia/Mr. Briggs/I'm All Over (CD)	10
91	Food FOOD 31	Bang/Luminous (p/s)	5
91	Food CDFOOD 31	Bang/Explain/Luminous/Beserk (CD)	10
92	Food FOOD 37	Popscene/Mace (p/s)	15
92	Food 12FOOD 37	Popscene/I'm Fine/Mace/Garden Central (12", p/s)	20
92	Food CDFOOD 37	Popscene/Mace/Badgeman Brown (CD)	15
92	Food 12FOOD 40	For Tomorrow (Visit To Primrose Hill Extended)/Into Another/ Hanging Over/Peach (12", p/s)	10
93	Food FOODS 45	Chemical World/Maggie May (7" red vinyl, paper labels, p/s)	10
93	Food 12FOOD 45	Chemical World/Es Schmecht/Young And Lovely/My Ark (12", p/s with print)	8
91	Food 12BLUR 4	High Cool (Easy Listening Mix)/Bad Day (Leisurely Mix) (12", blue & gold company sleeve, promo, 1,000 only)	25
92	Food BLUR 6	The Wassailing Song (1-sided 7" gig freebie, as "Gold, Frankinscence and Blur" no p/s, 500 only)	175
93	Food FOODS 46	Sunday Sunday/Tell Me, Tell Me (B-side as "Blur featuring Seymour") (yellow vinyl 7", p/s)	12
93	Food 12FOODS 46	Sunday Sunday/Long Legged/Mixed Up (B-sides as 'Blur featuring Seymour') (12", p/s with print)	8
94	Food FOODS 47	Girls And Boys/Magpie/People In Europe (7" p/s, numbered)	12
94	Food CDFOOD 50	To The End/Girls And Boys (Pet Shop Boys 7" Remix)/Girls And Boys (Pet Shop Boys 12" Remix) (CD, slimline jewel case)	10
94	Food 56	End Of The Century/Red Necks (p/s, numbered)	6
96	Fan Club DEATH 1	Death Of A Party (demo) (CD, 1-track, card p/s, fan club issue, 3250 only)	12
96	FOOD 73	Stereotypes/The Man Who Left Himself/Tame (p/s, pink vinyl)	6
96	FOOD 77	Charmless Man/The Horrors (gatefold p/s, sealed with sticker)	6
97	Food FOOD 89	Beetlebum/Woodpigeon Song (p/s, red vinyl)	6
97	Food FOOD 93	Song 2/Get Out Of Cities (p/s. purple vinyl)	12
97	Food FOOD 98	On Your Own/Pop Scene (Live)/Song 2 (Live) (p/s, white vinyl)	7
97	Fan Club LOVE 001	I Love Her (CD, card p/s, fan club issue, 3,500 only)	12
98	Close 001	Close (fan club CD, card wallet)	12
98	Food FOODLH 117	Tender(Radio Edit)/Song 2 (jukebox copy, no centre)	5
99	Food 117	Tender/All We Want (p/s, blue vinyl, numbered)	6
99	Fan Club SING 001	Sing (To Me) as 'Blur featuring Seymour') (CD, card p/s, fan club issue)	12
99	Food BLURBOX 10	THE 10 YEAR ANNIVERSARY BOX SET (22xCD singles)	60
02	Fan Club WONT001	B-Sided Gig EP (I'm Fone/Bone Bag/No Monsters/Young & Lovely) (CD, card p/s fan club issue)	25
02	FCCD 06	Won't Do It/Come Together (Fan club CD, card wallet)	12
03	EMI R 6610	Crazy Beat/The Outsider (p/s, red vinyl 'Banksy' cover)	6
03	EMI R 6619	Good Song/Morricone (p/s, red vinyl)	7
03	Fan Club COLOURS 01	Colours (CD, card p/s, fan club issue)	25
05	Fan Club SGLAD 01	Some Glad Morning (CD, card wallet, fan club issue)	30
10	Parlophone LCO 3098	Fools Day (1-sided 7", jukebox centre, blue Parlophone sleeve, 1000 only)	35

ALBUMS : LPS

91	Food FOODLP 6	LEISURE (LP)	30
93	Food FOODLP 9	MODERN LIFE IS RUBBISH (LP, with inner)	30
94	Food FOODLP 10	PARKLIFE (LP, with inner)	40
95	Food FOODLP 14	THE GREAT ESCAPE (LP, with inner)	35
95	Food FOODLP 14	THE GREAT ESCAPE (LP, in 12" box with book and print. Produced by Vinyl Experience, 2000 only)	70
97	Food CFOODLP19	BLUR (2-LP)	30
99	Food FOODLP29	13 (2-LP, stickered, gategold, with inner sleeves)	40
00	Food FOODLPD 33	THE BEST OF (2-LP)	40
03	Parlophone 07243-582887-1-7	THINK TANK (2-LP)	25

PROMOS

90	no cat. no.	Bad Day/Bad Day (version) (white label)	25
92	Food 12BLUR5	Popscene (1-sided promo 12" in die cut company sleeve. 1000 only)	15
93	Food 12FOODDJ 40	For Tomorrow (Visit to Primrose Hill extended version/Into Another/Hanging Over (12" in company die cut sleeve)	15
94	Food CD5 BET BET BET	Girls and Boys/Jubilee/Trouble In The Message Centre/Lot 105 (Live CD promo produced for Mark Radcliffe show)	20
95	Food CDFOODDJ 59	This Is A Low (CD, promo only, plain card sleeve with set of 4 stamps)	15
97	Food 12BLURDJ 7	On Your Own (Crouch End Broadway Mix) (12", 1-sided, promo only)	10
97	Food CDIN 106	BLURB (CD, interview, promo only)	15
99	Food No Cat No	15ON13 (Interview CD, p/s)	10
00	Food 10FOODDJ 135	Music Is My Radar (12" one-sided w/10" cat. No., white die cut sleeve, stamped label)	10
03	Parlophone THINK1	THINK TANK (CD Promo in card wallet with unique Banksy artwork)	15
03	Parlophone THINK4	THINK TANK INTERVIEW CD (CD in promo p/s, track by track 52 min interview)	18
03	Parlophone THINK 3	Crazy Beat/Brothers And Sisters/Moroccan Peoples Revolutionary Bowls Club/Gene By Gene (12" sampler, white die-cut sleeve, stamped labels)	8
99	Food FOOD CDJX 29	13 (CD in duffelbag with folder, photos, ski-hat and biography, promo only)	50
99	Food 10FOODDJ 117	Tender (10" promo record plays inside to out, foil sealed)	20
02	The Bombo!	(red label, bearing Arabic writing which translates as "Don't bomb when you are the bomb"; large centre hole; 1,000 7" were pressed, but many were blown up)	50

(see also Graham Coxon, Gorillaz, Damon Albarn)

BLURT

80	Test Pressing TP 1	My Mother Was A Friend Of An Enemy Of The People/Get (p/s)	5
81	Armageddon AS 013	The Fish Needs A Bike/This Is My Royal Wedding Souvenir (p/s)	5

BLUSH

79	Venal Vinyl PMB 117	Everyday/Before We Came Together (no p/s, 200 only)	150

MINT VALUE £

JIMMY BLYTHE
54	London AL 3527	SOUTH SIDE BLUE PIANO (10" LP)	15
54	London AL 3529	SOUTH SIDE CHICAGO JAZZ (10" LP)	15

B-MOVIE
80	Dead Good DEAD 9	TAKE THREE (EP)	20
80	Dead Good BIG DEAD 12	NOWHERE GIRL (12" EP, with insert, 800 only)	20
81	Deram DM 443	Marilyn Dreams/Film Music (Part 1) (p/s)	5
81	Deram DMX 443	Marilyn Dreams/Film Music (Part 1) (12", p/s)	8
88	Wax 12 WAX 3	Nowhere Girl/Remembrance Day (12", p/s, 250 on orange vinyl, numbered)	10
88	Wax 12 WAX 3	Nowhere Girl/Remembrance Day (12", p/s, pink vinyl, numbered)	10
88	Wax 12 WAX 4	Polar Opposites/Taxi Driver (12", clear vinyl or picture disc)	8
88	Wax CD WAX 4	Polar Opposites/Taxi Driver (CD)	15
88	Wax WAXLP 1P	THE DEAD GOOD TAPES (LP, picture disc)	12
91	Dead Good GOOD 3	REMEMBRANCE DAYS (LP, with 7" "The Fool"/"Swinging Lights" [CHEAP 1])	12

BMX BANDITS
86	53rd & 3rd AGARR 3	Sad?/E102 (p/s, with comic)	10
87	53rd & 3rd AGARR 6	What A Wonderful World/The Day Before Tomorrow (p/s)	6
87	53rd & 3rd AGARR 612	What A Wonderful World/The Day Before Tomorrow/ Johnny Alucard/Sad?/Sandy's Wallet (12", p/s)	8

(see also Soup Dragons, Boy Hairdressers, Teenage Fanclub, Vaselines)

EDDIE BO
73	Action ACT 4609	Check Your Bucket Parts 1 & 2	20

BO & PEEP
64	Decca F 11968	Young Love/The Rise Of The Brighton Surf	50

(see also Andrew Oldham Orchestra)

HARRY BOARDMAN & DAVE HILLERY
71	Topic 12TS 215	TRANS PENNINE (LP)	15

BOARDS OF CANADA
94	Music 70 THS 012	HOOPER'S BAY (12" EP)	100
96	Skam SKA 008	Hi Scores/Turquoise Hexagon Sun/Nlagon/June 9th/ See Ya Later/Everything You Do Is A Balloon (12", p/s)	10
98	Skam KMAS 1	Aquarius/Chinook (p/s, with insert, 500 only)	60
98	Warp 10WARP LP 55P	Telephasic Workshop/Roygbiv (10" promo, 2000 only)	20
99	Warp WAP 114	THE PEEL SESSIONS (12", p/s)	15
05	Skam Ska 008	Hi Scores (12" reissue in brail embossed sleeve)	8
95	Music 70 BOARD 1	2ISM (LP, 100 copies only)	400
95	Music 70 BOARD 1	2ISM (Cassette, 100 copies only)	100
00	Warp Records WAP 144	In A Beautiful Place Out In The Country (12", EP)	40
98	Warp Records 10 WARP LP 55 P	MUSIC HAS THE RIGHT TO CHILDREN (10", Promo)	40
98	Warp Records, Skam WARP LP 55, SKALP001	MUSIC HAS THE RIGHT TO CHILDREN (2xLP)	65
02	Warp	GEOGADDI (LP, blue vinyl test pressing - etched - 10 only)	200
02	Warp/Music 70	GEOGADDI (3-LP)	60
02	Warp LP 70	TWOSIM (LP, reissue, die-cut sleeve)	20

BOARDWALKERS
60s	own label J.C. 1	A Miracle/Any Man's Girl	200

(see also Warren Davis)

TOOTER BOATMAN
72	Injun 108	Thunder & Lightning/The Will Of Love	15

BOATMEN
70s	Sweet Folk SFA 018	STRAIGHT FROM THE TUNNEL'S MOUTH (LP)	50

BOBALOUIS
81	WEA K18441	Not A Second Chance/City Boys	20

BOB & CAROL
67	CBS 2738	On My Life/Mary Jane	8

BOB (RELF) & EARL (NELSON)
65	Sue WI 374	Harlem Shuffle/I'll Keep Running Back	20
65	Sue WI 393	Baby I'm Satisfied/The Sissy	40
67	Sue WI 4030	Don't Ever Leave Me/Fancy Free	50
69	Island WIP 6053	Harlem Shuffle/I'll Keep Running Back (reissue)	6
69	B&C CB 102	Dancin' Everywhere/Baby It's Over	5
69	Warner Bros WB 6059	Everybody Jerk/He's A Playbrother	40
70	Uni UN 519	Pickin' Up Love's Vibrations/Uh, Uh, Naw Naw Naw	5
72	Jay Boy BOY 72	I Can't Get Away/I'll Keep Running Back	10
72	Jay Boy BOY 73	My Little Girl/His & Her Shuffle (as Bob & Earl Band)	10
73	Contempo C 4	Harlem Shuffle/Harlem Shuffle (Instrumental Version)	5
67	Sue ILP 951	HARLEM SHUFFLE (LP)	120
69	B & C BCB 1	BOB & EARL (LP)	15
69	Joy JOYS 199	TOGETHER (LP)	15

(see also Bob Relf, Jackie Lee, Earl Nelson, Hollywood Flames)

BOB & JERRY
58	Pye International 7N 25003	Ghost Satellite/Nothin'	20
58	Pye International 7N 25003	Ghost Satellite/Nothin' (78)	15
61	Philips PB 1205	Dreamy Eyes/We're The Guys (Who Drive Your Baby Wild)	10

BOB (ANDY) & MARCIA (GRIFFITHS)
70	Bamboo BAM 40	Always Together/BOB ANDY: Desperate Lover	20
70	Harry J. HJ 6605	Young, Gifted And Black/JAY BOYS: Young, Gifted & Black (Instrumental)	6
70	Escort ES 824	Young, Gifted And Black/BARRINGTON BIGGS: My Cheri Amour (Different version: no strings)	15
71	Trojan TR 7818	Pied Piper/Save Me	5
72	Trojan TR 7854	But I Do/I Don't Care	5
70	Trojan TBL 122	YOUNG, GIFTED & BLACK (LP)	30
72	Trojan TRLS 26	PIED PIPER (LP)	15

(see also Bob Andy, Marcia Griffiths)

BOB (ANDY) & TIE (TYRONE EVANS)
69   Coxsone CS 7086   I Don't Care/LASCELLES PERKINS: Little Green Apples 45

BOB(B)ETTES
57   London HLE 8477   Mr. Lee/Look At The Stars 60
57   London HLE 8477   Mr. Lee/Look At The Stars (78) 20
58   London HLE 8597   Come-A Come-A/Speedy 75
58   London HLE 8597   Come-A Come-A/Speedy (78) 20
60   London HLE 9173   I Shot Mr. Lee/Untrue Love 60
60   London HLE 9248   Have Mercy Baby/Dance With Me Georgie 40
60   Pye International 7N 25060   I Shot Mr. Lee/Billy (as Bobettes) 40
72   Action ACT 4603   That's A Bad Thing To Know/All In Your Mind 15
81   Revival 6008   Mr. Lee/I Shot Mr. Lee. 5

BOBBIE & VERA
69   Decca F 12897   I Know That He Knows/City Of Dreams 5

BOBBSEY TWINS
57   London HLA 8474   A Change Of Heart/Part-Time Gal 70

BOBBY & DAVE
71   Ackee ACK 116   Build My World Around You/LIZZY & TONY BOP: Sammy Version...................15
(see also Dave Barker, Lizzy & Dennis)

BOBBY & JIM
58   Capitol CL 14877   Carry My Books/A Lover Can Tell..10

BOBBY & LAURIE
66   Parlophone R 5480   Hitch Hiker/You'll Come 'Round 20

BOBBY & MIDNITES
84   CBS 26046   WHERE THE BEAT MEETS THE STREET (LP)..25
(see also Bob Weir, Grateful Dead)

BOBBY (ELLIS) & TOMMY (MCCOOK)
74   Attack ATLP 1004   GREEN MANGO (LP)...35

BOBCATS
67   Pye 7N 17242   Can't See For Looking/Let Me Get By 25

WILLIE BOBO
66   Verve VS 548   Sunshine Super Man/Sockit To Me 12
66   Verve SVLP9134   ELATION (LP) 20
71   A&M AMLS 68034   DO WHAT YOU WANT TO DO (LP)..25

FRIDA BOCCARA
69   Philips BF 1765   Through The Eyes Of A Child/So Fair 10

BOCKY & VISIONS
65   Atlantic AT 4049   I Go Crazy/Good Good Lovin' 45

BODAST
81   Cherry Red BRED 12   THE BODAST TAPES FEATURING STEVE HOWE (LP) 12
(see also Steve Howe, Tomorrow)

BODEAN
76   DJM DJS 10697   Saturday Woman/Flying High (promo, p/s) 7

BODGERS
82   SRTS/82/CUS/1484   Stutter/I Hate Phoning Girls (no p/s)..100

BODGER'S MATE
78   Cottage COT 521   BRIGHTER THAN USUAL (LP) 20

BODIES
79   Waldo's HS 007   Art Nouveau/Machinery (poster p/s, 5 different colours)..............................5

BODKIN
72   West CSA 104   BODKIN (LP, private pressing, red label 10-20 in silk screened cover)............1000
72   West CSA 104   BODKIN (LP, private pressing, red label, in posthumously designed sleeve) 700

BODY
81   Recession   THE BODY ALBUM (LP, private pressing with booklet) 50

BODY AND SOUL
70   Penny Farthing PEN 720   Here Comes That Feeling/Go Back To School..7

BODYSNATCHERS (1)
80   2-Tone CHS TT 9   Let's Do Rocksteady/Ruder Than You (paper label, company sleeve)................10
80   2-Tone CHS TT 12   Easy Life/Too Experienced (paper label, company sleeve) 10

BODYSNATCHERS (2)
97   Backbone (No Cat. No)   GENOCIDE (EP, 30 test copies) 400
(see also Icepick)

BOEING DUVEEN & BEAUTIFUL SOUP
68   Parlophone R 5696   Jabberwock/Which Dreamed It (demos with p/s)......................................200
68   Parlophone R 5696   Jabberwock/Which Dreamed It (demos without p/s)...................................100

BOFFALONGO
70   United Artists UP 35144   Dancing In The Moonlight/Endless Questions 7
71   United Artists UAG 29130   BEYOND YOUR HEAD (LP) 18

BOG UGLY AND THE WOOFTERS
78   Toadstool GOOD 2   Disco Veteran/I've Seen It Vomit (p/s) 25

BOGAZ
83   AGR 12 AGR 2   I've Got Love/I've Got Love (Instrumental) (12")..25

BOGDAN
81   Black Label GB 3   Oh Eddie/Reet Petite (p/s) 10
81   Brilliant HIT 1   Who Do You Think You Are?/Take Me Back (p/s).......................................10
(see also Whitesnake, Bernie Marsden)

BOGIES
| 64 | private press (no cat. no.) | THE BOGIES ON CAMPUS (LP) | 150 |
| 64 | private press (no cat. no.) | BYE BYE BOGIES (LP) | 150 |

ERIC BOGLE
77	Autogram ALLP 211	LIVE IN PERSON (LP)	35
81	Plant Life PLR 033	PLAIN AND SIMPLE (LP)	15
83	Plant Life PLR 046	SCRAPS OF PAPER (LP)	15
85	Topic 12TS 437	WHEN THE WIND BLOWS (LP)	15
88	Plant Life PLR 042	NOW I'M EASY (LP)	15

LEE BOGLE
| 71 | Black Swan BW 1406 | Tomorrow's Dreams/SWANS: Hot Pants Reggae | 8 |

BOGUS ORDER
| 90 | Ninja Tune ZEN 01 | ZEB BRAKES (LP) | 25 |

BUDDY BOHN
| 71 | Regal Zonophone RX 3040 | Piccalilli Lady/Summer Song | 8 |
| 71 | Purple TPSA 7503 | A DROP IN THE OCEAN (LP, gatefold sleeve) | 30 |

HOUSTON BOINES
| 66 | Blue Horizon 45 BH 1006 | Superintendent Blues/Monkey Motion (99 copies only, Ike Turner on piano) | 150 |

BOK BOK
| 80 | Bok Bok BOK 2 | Come Back To Me/Misfit (p/s) | 10 |

BOLA
95	Skam SKA 5	Forcasa 3/Krak Jakomo/Metalurg 2/Ballom (12", custom sleeve)	50
98	Skam KMAS002	KS (500 pressed)	30
01	Skam KMAS 007	Pae Paoe (1,000 pressed)	5
00	33 33Shapes	SHAPES (LP, 3x12")	35

MARC BOLAN
65	Decca F 12288	The Wizard/Beyond The Rising Sun (some as Marc Bölan)	500
65	Decca F 12288	The Wizard/Beyond The Rising Sun (demo copy)	350
66	Decca F 12413	The Third Degree/San Francisco Poet	500
66	Decca F 12413	The Third Degree/San Francisco Poet (demo copy)	350
66	Parlophone R 5539	Hippy Gumbo/Misfit	650
66	Parlophone R 5539	Hippy Gumbo/Misfit (demo copy)	400
72	Track 2094 013	Jasper C. Debussy/Hippy Gumbo/The Perfumed Garden Of Gulliver Smith (p/s, withdrawn)	50
72	Track 2094 013	Jasper C. Debussy/Hippy Gumbo/The Perfumed Garden Of Gulliver Smith (white label demo)	50
81	Rarn MBFS 001C	Sing Me A Song/Endless Sleep (Extended Version)/The Lilac Hand Of Menthol Dan (12", no p/s, clear vinyl, handwritten labels)	10
81	Rarn MBFS 001P	Sing Me A Song/Endless Sleep (Extended Version)/The Lilac Hand Of Menthol Dan (12", picture disc, misprinted with black rim)	15
81	Rarn MBFS 001P	Sing Me A Song/Endless Sleep (Extended Version)/The Lilac Hand Of Menthol Dan (12", picture disc, misprinted with white rim)	7
81	Rarn MBFS 001P	Sing Me A Song/Endless Sleep (Extended Version)/The Lilac Hand Of Menthol Dan (12", picture disc misprinted back-to-front)	15
81	Cherry Red CHERRY 29	You Scare Me To Death/The Perfumed Garden Of Gulliver Smith (initial copies with bronze label, glossy p/s & free flexidisc [Lyntone LYN 10086])	10
81	Cherry Red CHERRY 29	You Scare Me To Death/The Perfumed Garden Of Gulliver Smith (later pressing with silver label/matt p/s)	5
81	Cherry Red CHERRY 32	Cat Black/Jasper C. Debussy (p/s)	5
82	Cherry Red CHERRY 39	The Wizard/Beyond The Rising Sun/Rings Of Fortune (p/s)	5
72	Track 2406 101	HARD ON LOVE (LP, unreleased, white label test pressing, 2 copies only)	800
72	Track 2406 009	HARD ON LOVE (LP, unreleased, 2-sided EMIdisc acetate with "swearing intro")	2250
74	Track 2410 201	THE BEGINNING OF DOVES (LP, laminated sleeve, black/silver label)	35
81	Cherry Red PERED 20	YOU SCARE ME TO DEATH (LP, picture disc)	15
81	Cherry Red ERED 20	YOU SCARE ME TO DEATH (LP, gatefold sleeve; early copies with booklet stapled into sleeve; later copies with loose booklet)	12
89	Media Motion MEDIA 2	THE BEGINNING OF DOVES (LP, reissue, 750 only, withdrawn)	25
96	Edsel FBOOK 17	A WIZARD, A TRUE STAR (3-CD Box set)	25

(see also Marc Bolan/T. Rex, Marc Bolan & Gloria Jones, Toby Tyler, John's Children, Big Carrot, Dib Cochran & The Earwigs)

MARC BOLAN & GLORIA JONES
| 77 | EMI EMI 2572 | To Know You Is To Love You/City Port | 12 |

(see also Gloria Jones)

MARC BOLAN/T. REX
SINGLES
70	Octopus OCTO 1	Ride A White Swan/Summertime Blues/Jewel (unreleased, handwritten white label, 2/3 test pressings only)	2500
70	Fly BUG 1	Ride A White Swan/Is It Love/Summertime Blues (p/s, purple labels)	20
70	Fly BUG 1	Ride A White Swan/Is It Love/Summertime Blues (p/s, later pressing with mustard labels)	7
71	Fly	Hot Love/Woodland Rock/King Of The Mountain Cometh (IBC Sound Recordings Studios acetate)	280
71	Fly BUG 6	Hot Love/Woodland Rock/King Of The Mountain Cometh (mustard labels)	10
71	Fly BUG 6	Hot Love/Woodland Rock/King Of The Mountain Cometh (mustard labels, later pressing with 'fly' design)	5
71	Fly BUG 10	Get It On/There Was A Time/Raw Ramp (p/s, black label with silver 'fly' logo)	15
70s	Fly BUG 10	Get It On/There Was A Time/Raw Ramp (p/s, black label with white 'fly' or later silver 'fly' text)	6
71	Fly GRUB 1	Electric Warrior Preview Single: Jeepster/Life's A Gas (gig freebie, in pink envelope sleeve)	200
71	Fly GRUB 1	Electric Warrior Preview Single: Jeepster/Life's A Gas (gig freebie, originally in pink envelope sleeve, this price is for later standard paper sleeve)	145
71	Fly BUG 16	Jeepster/Life's A Gas (white 'fly' label)	5
71	Fly BUG 16	Jeepster/Life's A Gas (scarce issue w/out 'GRUB 1A' ref.)	6
72	EMI T REX 101	Telegram Sam/Cadillac/Baby Strange	6
72	Magni Fly ECHO 102	One Inch Rock/The Woodland Bop/The Throat Of Winter (unreleased, rejected 1-sided test pressing for B-side of "Deborah"/"One Inch Rock", stamped white label)	150
72	Magni Fly ECHO 102	Debora/One Inch Rock/The Woodland Bop/Seal Of Seasons (p/s)	6
72	EMI MARC X	Metal Guru (rejected 1-sided test pressing with Marc's annotation 'bad cut')	300

Year	Label/Cat	Description	Value
72	EMI MARC 1	Metal Guru/Thunderwing/Lady	6
72	EMI MARC 2	Children Of The Revolution/Jitterbug Love/Sunken Rags	6
72	EMI MARC 3	Solid Gold Easy Action/(5th Dimension track) (mispressing)	15
72	EMI MARC 3	Solid Gold Easy Action/(Partridge Family track) (mispressing)	15
72	EMI SPRS 346	Chariot Choogle/The Slider (promo only, 'T. Rex' picture label)	425
72	EMI SPRS 346	Chariot Choogle/The Slider (promo only, white label)	375
72	Lyntone	Christmas Time/Wanna Spend My Christmas With You/ Christmas/Everybody Knows It's Christmas (fan club flexi, with letter in brown envelope)	45
72	Lyntone	Christmas Time/Wanna Spend My Christmas With You/ Christmas/Everybody Knows It's Christmas (fan club flexi, without letter in brown envelope)	30
73	EMI MARC 5	The Groover/Midnight	6
73	EMI MARC 6	Truck On (Tyke)/Sitting Here	6
74	EMI MARC 7	Teenage Dream/Satisfaction Pony (credited to 'Marc Bolan & T. Rex')	6
74	EMI MARC 7	Teenage Dream/Satisfaction Pony (credited to 'Marc Bolan')	5
74	EMI MARC 8	Light Of Love/Explosive Mouth	6
74	EMI MARC 9	Zip Gun Boogie/Space Boss	6
75	EMI MARC 10	New York City/Chrome Sitar	6
75	EMI MARC 11	Dreamy Lady/Do You Wanna Dance?/Dock Of The Bay (as T. Rex Disco Party)	6
75	EMI MARC 12	Christmas Bop/Telegram Sam/Metal Guru (unreleased, A- & B-side paper labels exist, 2 sets only this price is for the labels)	1250
76	EMI MARC 13	London Boys/Solid Baby	6
76	Cube BUG 66	Hot Love/Get It On	6
76	EMI MARC 14	I Love To Boogie/Baby Boomerang	6
76	EMI MARC 15	Laser Love/Life's An Elevator	6
77	EMI MARC 16	The Soul Of My Suit/All Alone	8
77	EMI MARC 17	Dandy In The Underworld/Groove A Little/Tame My Tiger (p/s)	10
77	EMI MARC 18	Celebrate Summer/Ride My Wheels (p/s)	10
78	EMI MARC 19	Crimson Moon/Jason B. Sad (p/s)	10
77	Cube ANT 1	BOLAN'S BEST PLUS ONE (EP, p/s)	8
78	Cube ANT 2	Hot Love/Raw Ramp/Lean Woman Blues (p/s, misprinted Raw Amp, sleeve credits 'Bolan', label credits 'T.Rex')	8
79	Cube ANTS 001	Life's A Gas/Find A Little Wood/Once Upon The Seas Of Abyssinia/ Blessed Wild Apple Girl (12", p/s)	12
82	Marc ABOLAN 2	THE CHILDREN OF RARN (10" EP, p/s, 33rpm, gatefold sleeve with 12-page lyric book)	25
82	Marc SBOLAN 13	Mellow Love/Foxy Box/Lunacy's Back (p/s, blue vinyl, as Marc Bolan)	8
82	Rarn MBFS RAP 2	Deep Summer/Oh Baby/One Inch Rock (unreleased version) (12", p/s, blue vinyl)	10
83	Marc SBOLAN 12EP	CHRISTMAS BOP EP (12", p/s, OMBFS only, extra tracks: acoustic versions of "King Of The Rumbling Spires" & "Savage Beethoven")	10
83	Marc SBOLAN 14PD	Think Zinc/Till Dawn/Magical Moon (picture disc)	5
84	Marc On Wax SPS 1	Mister Motion (1-sided, from "Child Of The Revolution - 14 Greats" LP, p/s)	8
84	Cube BUG 99	Sailor Of The Highway/Do You Remember (7" in plain black sleeve)	15
84	Cube HBUG 99	RARE MAGIC (12" EP)	12
85	Cambra MAIN 1	(Whatever Happened To The) Teenage Dream (Ext.)/Solid Gold Segue (picture disc free with "Mainman" LP)	8
85	Marc PTANX 1	Megarex 1/Megarex 1 (shaped picture disc, with free plinth)	8
87	Marc MARCX 1	Children Of The Revolution (remix)/The Slider (remix)/Tear For The High Star (tribute by Dave Ash-B) (shaped picture disc)	8
87	Strange Fruit SFPS 031	PEEL SESSIONS (12")	15
94	Edsel MBPROMO 1	T. REX (CD, picture disc, 4-track sampler, tri-fold digipak, promo only)	20
97	Edsel MARC 20-50	20th Century Boy/Carsmile Smith & The Old One/ All My Love/Dandy In The Underworld (CD, gig freebie)	20
07	Edsel BOLAN 1	Metal Guru/The Slider (Acoustic Demo) (Blue vinyl, numbered, 1,000 only)	15
07	Edsel BOLAN 2	Children Of The Revolution/The Leopards (Electric Demo) (Red vinyl, numbered, 1,000 only)	15
07	Edsel BOLAN 3	20th Century Boy/Teenager In Love (Marc & Gloria acoustic duet) (White vinyl, numbered, 1,000 only)	12
07	Edsel TREXMAS 1	Christmas Bop/The Xmas Riff/Xmas Flexi message (7", promo)	60

ALBUMS

Year	Label/Cat	Description	Value
70	Fly HIFLY 2	T. REX (semi-gatefold sleeve, white label with 'Fly' logo)	40
71	Fly HIFLY 6	ELECTRIC WARRIOR (unreleased version with "Jeepster" on side 2, 1 test pressing copy only, with Marc's annotations on white sleeve)	700
71	Fly HIFLY 6	ELECTRIC WARRIOR (with poster & inner sleeve, stickered sleeve, white label with 'Fly' logo)	80
71	Fly HIFLY 6	ELECTRIC WARRIOR (with poster & inner sleeve, non-stickered sleeve, white label with 'Fly' logo)	40
72	Fly HIFLY 8	BOLAN BOOGIE (1-sided test pressing with "The Visit" instead of "Jewel")	375
72	Fly HIFLY 8	BOLAN BOOGIE	12
72	EMI BLN 5001	THE SLIDER (with lyric inner sleeve, sleeve with 'sniped' spine edges, flipbacks, blue/red T-Rex label)	30
73	EMI BLN 5002	TANX (with poster & inner sleeve)	20
73	EMI BLN 5003	GREAT HITS (with poster)	12
74	EMI BNLA 7751	ZINC ALLOY AND THE HIDDEN RIDERS OF TOMORROW (with 3-way numbered promo fold-out sleeve & inner, given as competition prize with letter from Pink or Mirabelle magazines, 1,000 only)	250
74	EMI BNLA 7751	ZINC ALLOY AND THE HIDDEN RIDERS OF TOMORROW (with 3-way promo fold-out sleeve & inner, without letter; numbered)	250
74	EMI BNLA 7751	ZINC ALLOY AND THE HIDDEN RIDERS OF TOMORROW (with 3-way promo fold-out sleeve & inner, without letter; unnumbered)	200
74	EMI BLNA 7751	ZINC ALLOY AND THE HIDDEN RIDERS OF TOMORROW (commercial gatefold sleeve with lyric inner sleeve)	18
75	EMI BNLA 7752	BOLAN'S ZIP GUN (diamond-cut laminated sleeve & inner sleeve, blue/red T-Rex label)	20
76	EMI BLNA 5004	FUTURISTIC DRAGON (with lyric inner sleeve)	22
77	EMI BLNA 5005	DANDY IN THE UNDERWORLD (with round-cut sleeve & lyric inner sleeve)	20
78	Cube HIFLD 1	MARC: THE WORDS AND MUSIC OF MARC BOLAN 1947-1977 (2-LP, gatefold sleeve, with free single [BINT 1])	18
81	Marc ABOLAN 1P	T. REX IN CONCERT (picture disc, 2 designs)	15
82	Cube/Dakota ICSX 1004	ACROSS THE AIRWAVES (picture disc)	12
82	Marc ABOLAN 3P	ELECTRIC WARRIOR (picture disc)	12
84	Marc ABOLAN 5	T. REXTASY (with 12" "Jam (live)"/ Elemental Child (live) [ABOLAN 5F], Official Fanclub only)	15
86	Marc On Wax WARRIOR 1/4	HISTORY OF T. REX (4-LP, numbered picture disc set, with free fanclub T-shirt)	45
86	Marc On Wax WARRIOR 1/4	HISTORY OF T. REX (4-LP, numbered picture disc set, without free fanclub T-shirt)	35

(see also Marc Bolan, Tyrannosaurus Rex, Dib Cochran & the Earwigs, John's Children, Big Carrot)

FRANCY BOLAND
75	Freedom FLP40176	PAPILLON NOIR (LP)	15

(see also Kenny Clarke with Francy Boland)

TOMMY BOLIN
76	Nemperor K 10730/NE 4	The Grind/Homeward Strut	10
75	Atlantic K 50208	TEASER (LP, stickered)	18
75	Atlantic K 50208	TEASER (LP, unstickered)	15
76	CBS S 81612	PRIVATE EYES (LP)	12

(see also James Gang, Deep Purple)

SIMON BOLIVAR ORCHESTRA
56	London HLG 8245	Meringue Holiday/Shy	5

BOLLARD
72	Satril SAT 1	I Need Your Love/Sunshine In The Morning	6

BOLLARDS
70s	Bumkin Records	BOLLARDS (LP)	15

BOLLWEEVIL
81	Ellie Jay EJSP 9715	Rock Solid/Sands Of Time (p/s)	75

MICHAEL BOLOTIN
75	RCA SF 8451	MICHAEL BOLOTIN (LP)	12

(see also Blackjack, Michael Bolton)

BOLSHOI
86	Beggars BEG 170TD	Books On The Bonfire/A Funny Thing/A Way (live) Billie Jean (live) (2x12", p/s)	8

BOLT THROWER
88	Vinyl Solution SOL 11	IN BATTLE THERE IS NO LAW (LP, with insert)	15
89	Earache MOSH 13	REALM OF CHAOS (LP, picture disc)	15
91	Strange Fruit SFRLP 116	PEEL SESSIONS 19880-90 (12")	20

BOMBADIL
72	Harvest HAR 5056	Breathless/When The City Sleeps (p/s)	15
75	Harvest HAR 5095	Breathless/When The City Sleeps (p/s, reissue)	8

(see also Barclay James Harvest)

BOMBAY DUCKS
80	Complete Control CON 1	Sympathy For The Devil/1-0-6-9 (p/s)	10
80s	United Dairies UD 05	DANCE MUSIC (LP)	15

BON JOVI
84	Vertigo VER 11	She Don't Know Me/Breakout (p/s)	20
84	Vertigo VERX 11	She Don't Know Me/Breakout (12", p/s)	30
84	Vertigo VER 14	Runaway/Breakout (live) (p/s)	20
84	Vertigo VERX 14	Runaway/Breakout (live)/Runaway (live) (12", p/s)	30
85	Vertigo VER 19	In And Out Of Love/Roulette (live) (p/s)	15
85	Vertigo VERP 19	In And Out Of Love/Roulette (live) (picture disc)	45
85	Vertigo VERX 19	In And Out Of Love/Roulette (live)/Shot Through The Heart (live) (12", p/s)	15
85	Vertigo VER 22	The Hardest Part Is The Night/Always Run To You (p/s)	10
85	Vertigo VERDP 22	The Hardest Part Is The Night/Always Run To You/Tokyo Road (live)/ Shot Through The Heart (live) (double pack, gatefold p/s)	15
85	Vertigo VERX 22	The Hardest Part Is The Night/Always Run To You/Tokyo Road (live) (12", p/s)	15
85	Vertigo VERXR 22	Red Hot And Two Parts Live: The Hardest Part Is The Night/ Tokyo Road (live)/In And Out Of Love (live) (12", p/s, red vinyl)	30
86	Vertigo VERP 26	You Give Love A Bad Name/Let It Rock (10", shaped picture disc)	20
86	Vertigo VERX 26	You Give Love A Bad Name/Let It Rock/Borderline (12", p/s with poster)	12
86	Vertigo VERXR 26	You Give Love A Bad Name/Let It Rock/ The Hardest Part Is The Night (live)/Burning For Love (live) (12", p/s, blue vinyl)	18
86	Vertigo VERPA 28	Livin' On A Prayer/Wild In The Streets (p/s, with patch, sealed)	20
86	Vertigo VERPA 28	Livin' On A Prayer/Wild In The Streets (p/s, with patch, unsealed)	10
86	Vertigo VERP 28	Livin' On A Prayer/Wild In The Streets (picture disc)	20
86	Vertigo VERXR 28	Livin' On A Prayer/Wild In The Streets/Edge Of A Broken Heart (12", green vinyl, p/s)	10
86	Vertigo VERXG 28	Livin' On A Prayer/Wild In The Streets/Only Lonely (live)/ Runaway (live) (12", gatefold p/s)	12
88	Mercury 080 042-2	Livin' On A Prayer/Borderline/Let It Rock/Wild In The Streets (CD Video)	15
87	Vertigo JOVS 1	Wanted Dead Or Alive/Shot Through The Heart (p/s, with metal stickers)	8
87	Vertigo JOVPB 112	Wanted Dead Or Alive/Shot Through The Heart/Social Disease (12", poster p/s)	15
87	Vertigo JOVR 112	Wanted Dead Or Alive/Shot Through The Heart/Social Disease/ Get Ready (live) (12", p/s, silver vinyl)	12
87	Vertigo JOVR 212	Never Say Goodbye/Raise Your Hands/Wanted Dead Or Alive (Acoustic Version) (12", yellow vinyl, PVC sleeve)	12
87	Vertigo	Never Say Goodbye (CD video)	20
87	Vertigo	Wanted Dead Or Alive (CD video)	20
87	Vertigo 080 042-2	Livin' On A Prayer/Borderline/Let It Rock/Wild In The Streets (CD video)	20
88	Vertigo JOVS 3	Bad Medicine/99 In The Shade (fold-out photofile p/s)	7
88	Vertigo JOVP 3	Bad Medicine/Lay Your Hands On Me/99 In The Shade (CD, card sleeve)	10
88	Vertigo JOVP 412	Born To Be My Baby/Love For Sale/Wanted Dead Or Alive (live) (12", picture disc)	10
88	Vertigo JOVCD 4	Born To Be My Baby/Love For Sale/Runaway/Livin' On A Prayer (CD)	10
89	Vertigo JOVCD 5	I'll Be There For You/Homebound Train/Borderline/Edge Of A Broken Heart (CD, card sleeve)	10
89	Vertigo JOVS 661	Lay Your Hands On Me/Bad Medicine (live) (red vinyl, stickered PVC sleeve)	5
89	Vertigo JOVS 662	Lay Your Hands On Me/Bad Medicine (live) (white vinyl, stickered PVC sleeve)	5
89	Vertigo JOVS 663	Lay Your Hands On Me/Bad Medicine (live) (blue vinyl, stickered PVC sleeve)	6
89	Vertigo JOVS 661-663	Lay Your Hands On Me/Bad Medicine (live) (3 x 7", red, blue or white vinyl, paper box set)	20
89	Vertigo JOVP 610	Lay Your Hands On Me/Bad Medicine (live)/Blood On Blood (10", picture disc with insert)	8
89	Vertigo JOVCD 6	Lay Your Hands On Me/You Give Love A Bad Name/Let It Rock (CD)	10
89	Vertigo JOVR 712	Living In Sin/Love Is War/The Boys Are Back In Town (12", white vinyl with stickered card insert)	10
89	Vertigo JOVCD 7	Living In Sin/Love Is War/Ride Cowboy Ride/Stick To Your Guns (CD, box set)	15
94	Vertigo JOVJB 14	Always (edit)/Always (jukebox issue, no p/s)	5
94	Vertigo JOVP 15	Someday I'll Be Saturday Night/Always (live) (picture disc with insert)	5
94	Vertigo JOVP 16	Please Come Home For Christmas/Back Door Santa (picture disc)	12

| 88 | Vertigo VERHP 38 | SLIPPERY WHEN WET (LP, picture disc with poster) ....15 |
| 88 | Vertigo VERHP 62 | NEW JERSEY (LP, picture disc, stickered PVC sleeve) ....15 |

JON BON JOVI
| 90 | Vertigo JBJ 212 | Miracle/Dyin' Ain't Much Of A Livin'/Interview With Jon Bon Jovi (12", p/s, with poster & numbered sticker) ....12 |
| 90 | Vertigo JBJP 212 | Miracle/Dyin' Ain't Much Of A Livin'/Going Back (live) (12", picture disc with insert) ....15 |

BONA DISH
82	In Phaze	BONA DISH ON C30 (cassette) 70
82	In Phase IP 010	EP (cassette) 40
82	In Phaze	CARDBOARD TUBE (cassette in cardboard tube packaging) 50

JOE BONAMASSA
| 06 | Provogue PRD71851 | YOU AND ME (LP, pressed in Netherlands) ....15 |

ELI BONAPARTE
| 70 | Decca F 13047 | Never An Everyday Thing/The Men From Birmingham ....5 |

BON-BONS
55	London HL 8139	That's The Way Love Goes/Make My Dreams Come True 70
55	London HL 8139	That's The Way Love Goes/Make My Dreams Come True (78 rpm) 10
56	London HLU 8262	Circle/Frog On A Log 50

BOBBY BOND
| 61 | Pye International 7N 25081 | You're A Livin' Doll/Sweet Love ....12 |
| 69 | Warner Bros WB 7292 | One More Mile, One More Town/If You're Leaving Me.................................5 |

BRIGITTE BOND
| 64 | Blue Beat BB 212 | Oh Yeah Baby/Blue Beat Baby...50 |

GRAHAM BOND (ORGANISATION)
64	Decca F 11909	Long Tall Shorty/Long Legged Baby (as Graham Bond Organization).......................50
65	Columbia DB 7471	Wade In The Water/Tammy (as Graham Bond Organisation).............................50
65	Columbia DB 7528	Tell Me (I'm Gonna Love Again)/Love Come Shining Through (as Graham Bond Organisation)...45
65	Columbia DB 7647	Lease On Love/My Heart's In Little Pieces (as Graham Bond Organisation)...........35
66	Columbia DB 7838	St James Infirmary/Soul Tango (as Graham Bond Organisation) 40
67	Page One POF 014	You've Gotta Have Love Babe/I Love You...55
70	Warner Bros WB 8004	Walking In The Park/Springtime In The City (solo)...................................15
71	Vertigo 6059 042	Twelve Gates To The City/Water Water (as Graham Bond with Magick) 30
65	Columbia 33SX 1711	THE SOUND OF '65 (LP, 1st pressing, with '33SX' on blue/black label and "sold in the U.K." label text) 400

(N.B, LP has '33SX' on the sleeve, but only the 1st pressings have '33SX' on the label)

65	Columbia 33SX 1750	THERE'S A BOND BETWEEN US (LP, 1st pressing, with '33SX' on blue/black label and "sold in the UK" label text) 400
66	Columbia SX 1711	THE SOUND OF '65 (LP, 2nd pressing, with 'SX' on blue/black label) 175
66	Columbia SX 1750	THERE'S A BOND BETWEEN US (LP, 2nd pressing, with 'SX' on blue/black label) ...125
69	Columbia SX 1711	THE SOUND OF '65 (LP, 3rd pressing, with boxed logo on silver/black label) 60
71	Warner Bros WS 3001	SOLID BOND (2-LP, gatefold sleeve, orange label)...................................50
71	Vertigo 6360 021	HOLY MAGICK (LP, gatefold sleeve, large swirl label, as Graham Bond & Magick) 120
71	Vertigo 6360 042	WE PUT OUR MAGICK ON YOU (LP, gatefold sleeve, swirl label, ...120
72	Philips 6382 010	BOND IN AMERICA (2-LP, solo [individual discs: 6499 200/1], unreleased) 30
72	Philips 6382 010	THIS IS GRAHAM BOND (LP, solo)...18

(see also Jack Bruce, Dick Heckstall-Smith, Ginger Baker, Duffy Power, Who, Don Rendell, Steve York's Camelo Pardalis)

GRAHAM BOND & PETE BROWN
| 71 | Greenwich GSS 104 | Lost Tribe/Macumbe/Milk Is Turning Sour In My Shoes (maxi-single)..............25 |
| 72 | Chapter One CHS-R 813 | TWO HEADS ARE BETTER THAN ONE (LP) ....200 |

(see also Pete Brown)

ISABEL BOND
68	Major Minor MM 565	Cry/When A Woman Loves A Man (in p/s) 20
68	Major Minor MM 565	Cry/When A Woman Loves A Man 5
69	Major Minor MM 627	Don't Forget About Me/You'll Never Get The Chance Again 10
68	Major Minor MMLP 28	THE HEART AND SOUL OF ISABEL BOND (LP) 40

JACKI BOND
65	Columbia DB 7719	My Sister's Boy/Now I Know 20
66	Strike JH 302	Tell Him To Go Away/Don't You Worry 25
66	Strike JH 320	He Say/Why Can't I Love Him 50

JANE BOND & UNDERCOVER MEN
| 86 | Dreamworld BIG DREAM 1 | POLITICALLY CORRECT (LP) ....12 |

JOHNNY BOND
60	London HLU 9189	Hot Rod Jalopy/Five-Minute Love Affair 30
60	London HL 7100	Hot Rod Lincoln/Five-Minute Love Affair (export issue)......................................20
65	London HLB 9957	Ten Little Bottles/Eleven More Months And Ten More Days (B-side with Cowboy Copas) 10
62	Stateside SL 10008	THAT WILD, WICKED BUT WONDERFUL WEST (LP) 20
63	London HA-B 8098	LIVE IT UP (LP, as Johnny Bond & His Friends On Stage) 20
65	London HA-B 8228	THE SONGS THAT MADE HIM FAMOUS (LP)..15
66	London HA-B 8272	FAMOUS HOT RODDERS I HAVE KNOWN (LP) 15
67	London HA-B 8316	THE BRANDED STOCK (LP) 12

JOYCE BOND
67	Airborne NBP 0011	It's Alright/Mrs. Soul..90
66	Island WI 3019	Tell Me What It's All About/Tell Me Right Now 50
67	Island WIP 6010	Do The Teasy/Sugar 15
67	Island WIP 6018	This Train/Not So With Me 15
68	Island WIP 6051	Ob-La-Di, Ob-La-Da/Robin Hood Rides Again (as Joyce Bond Review) 15
68	Pama PM 718	Back To School/They Wish 15
69	Pama PM 771	Mr. Pitiful/Let's Get Married (as Joyce Bond & Little John) 12
70	Upfront UPF 5	Wind Of Change/First In Line 7
71	Trojan TR 7837	Help Me Make It Through The Night/Reconsider Our Love 8
68	Island ILP 968	SOUL AND SKA (LP, mono only) 150
72	Windmill WMD 121	SOUL OF CHANGE (LP)...15

LOUIS BOND
| 74 | Cooltempo 2005 | Tell Me When/Instrumental | 8 |

MARGARET BOND
55	Decca F 10506	You'll Always Be My Lifetime Sweetheart/Where Is The One For Me	10
55	Decca F 10555	My Love's A Gentle Man/Mirror, Mirror	10
55	Decca F 10632	There's Always A First Time/Dancing In My Socks	10
57	Parlophone R 4283	Your Love Is My Love/Goodnight My Love, Pleasant Dreams	5
57	Parlophone R 4312	The Wind In The Willow/Young And In Love	5

OLIVER BOND
| 66 | Parlophone R 5476 | I Saw You All Alone/Let Me Love You | 15 |

(see also Oliver Bone)

PETER BOND
| 77 | Trailer LER 2108 | IT'S ALL RIGHT FOR SOME (LP, yellow label) | 15 |

RONNIE BOND (1)
| 69 | Page One POF 123 | Anything For You/Carolyn | 20 |

(see also Troggs)

RONNIE BOND (2)
| 80 | Clap CLAP 1 | Fly On The Wall/You Can't Expect Miracles To Happen Tonight (p/s) | 10 |

TONY BOND
| 66 | Decca SKL 4776 | PRESENTING TONY BOND (LP) | 20 |

(see also Kestrels)

GARY (U.S.) BONDS
60	Top Rank JAR 527	New Orleans/Please Forgive Me (as U.S. Bonds)	12
61	Top Rank JAR 566	Not Me/Give Me One More Chance (as U.S. Bonds)	10
61	Top Rank JAR 575	Quarter To Three/Time Ole Story (as U.S. Bonds)	10
61	Top Rank JAR 581	School Is Out/One Million Tears	10
61	Top Rank JAR 595	School Is In/Trip To The Moon	10
62	Top Rank JAR 602	Dear Lady Twist/Havin' So Much Fun	10
62	Top Rank JAR 615	Twist Twist Senora/Food Of Love	10
62	Stateside SS 111	Seven Day Weekend/Gettin' A Groove	15
62	Stateside SS 125	Copy Cat/I'll Change That Too	15
63	Stateside SS 144	Mixed Up Faculty/I Dig This Station	15
63	Stateside SS 179	Where Did That Naughty Little Girl Go?/Do The Limbo With Me	15
63	Stateside SS 219	What A Dream/I Don't Wanta Wait	15
64	Stateside SS 271	New Orleans/Quarter To Three	10
64	Stateside SS 308	My Sweet Baby Rose/Ella Is Yella	10
67	Stateside SS 2025	Send Her To Me/Workin' For My Baby	20
75	London HLA 10485	Grandma's Washboard Band/Believing You	5
61	Top Rank 35/114	DANCE 'TIL QUARTER TO THREE WITH U.S. BONDS (LP)	50
62	Stateside SL 10001	TWIST UP CALYPSO (LP)	20
63	Stateside SL 10037	THE GREATEST HITS OF GARY (U.S.) BONDS (LP)	15

OLIVER BONE & SOUNDS MAXIMUM
| 66 | Parlophone R 5527 | Knock On Wood/Jugger Tea | 30 |

(see also Oliver Bond)

MATTHEW BONES
| 71 | Pye 7N 45100 | I Am A Pixi/Two Sugars | 15 |

BONESHAKER
| 71 | London HLU 10332 | Sweetness/Badman Strikes Again | 40 |

LUIZ BONFA & MARIA TOLEDO
| 65 | Philips SBL 7703 | BRAZILIANA (LP) | 12 |
| 66 | Philips BL 7727 | THE BRAZILIAN SCENE (LP) | 12 |

BONGO HERMAN (DAVIS)
70	Songbird SB 1018	True Grit/True Grit Version 2 (both credited with Les Crystalites but actually with Les & Crystalites)	20
71	Songbird SB 1060	BONGO HERMAN & LES BUNNY: Know For I/CRYSTALITES: Version (B-side actually titled 'Know Fari')	15
71	Songbird SB 1066	BONGO HERMAN & LES BUNNY: Salaam (Peace)/CRYSTALITES: Scraper	12
72	Big BG 332	Eternal Drums/ERROL DUNKLEY: Darling Ooh Wee (both actually by Hugh Roy Junior)	15
72	Green Door GD 4049	African Breakfast/BONGO HERMAN & LES AND BUNNY: Chairman Of The Board	15
72	Songbird SB 1069	We Are Praying/CRYSTALITES: Version	10

BONGO LES & HERMAN
| 71 | Songbird SB 1050 | Home Sweet Home/Hail I | 12 |

(see also Heptones, Scotty, Meditators)

JUKE BOY BONNER
69	Blue Horizon 57-3163	Runnin' Shoes/Jackin' In My Plans	35
60s	Jan & Dil JR 451	MORE DOWN HOME BLUES (EP)	50
68	Flyright LP 3501	THE ONE MAN TRIO (LP)	45
69	Liberty LBS 83319	THINGS AIN'T RIGHT (LP)	40

GRAHAM BONNET
72	RCA RCA 2230	Rare Specimen/Whisper In The Night	25
73	RCA RCA 2380	Trying To Say Goodbye/Castles In The Air	15
74	DJM DJS 328	Back Row In The Stalls/Ghost Writer In My Eye	10
77	Ring O' 2017 105	It's All Over Now, Baby Blue/Heroes On My Picture Wall (company sleeve)	8
77	Ring O' 2017 106	Danny/Rock Island Line (promo p/s)	18
77	Ring O' 2017 106	Danny/Rock Island Line (company sleeve)	6
77	Ring O' 2017 110	Goodnight And Goodmorning/Wino Song (company sleeve)	6
78	Ring O' 2017 114/POSP 2	Warm Ride/10/12 Observation (company sleeve)	6
78	Ring O' POSP 002	Warm Ride/10/12 Observation (12", company sleeve)	6
81	Vertigo VER 4	That's The Way That It Is/Don't Tell Me To Go (p/s)	6
81	Vertigo VER 1	Night Games/Out On The Water (p/s)	5
81	Vertigo VER 2	Liar/Bad Days Are Gone (p/s)	6
77	Ring O' 2320 103	GRAHAM BONNET (LP, with inner sleeve)	18
81	Vertigo 6302 151	LINE UP (LP, with inner sleeve)	12

(see also Marbles, Rainbow, Cozy Powell, Forcefield, Fut, Michael Schenker Group, Jon Lord)

GRAHAM BONNEY
65	Columbia DB 7773	My Little World Is All Blue/Why Can't We Be Friends	12
66	Columbia DB 7843	Super Girl/Hill Of Lovin'	8
66	Columbia DB 7934	Baby's Gone/Later Tonight	15
66	Columbia DB 8005	No One Knows/Mixed Up Baby Girl	12
67	Columbia DB 8111	Thank You Baby/Briony	7
67	Columbia DB 8142	Happy Together/That Bad Day	7
67	Columbia DB 8283	Papa Joe/My Jenny	7
68	Columbia DB 8338	By The Way I Love You/Devil's Child	7
68	Columbia DB 8382	I'll Be Your Baby Tonight/Back From Baltimore	7
68	Columbia DB 8464	Frenzy/Something I've Got To Tell You	7
69	Columbia DB 8531	Get Ready/Fly Me High Lorelei	15
69	Columbia DB 8592	Leanda Angeline/Mixing The Wine	8
70	Columbia DB 8648	Sign On The Dotted Line/Words We Said	25
70	Columbia DB 8687	When Evelyn Was Mine/Sunny Has Gone	18
66	Columbia SX 6052	SUPER GIRL (LP)	30

(see also Riot Squad)

BONNIE
67	Ska Beat JB 270	Do You Get The Message/A Man Called Dan	15
69	Jolly JY 014	Loving You/Shoo Be Doo	10

BONNIE & SKITTO
63	Island WI 122	Get Ready (actually by Vikings [alias Maytals])/ DON DRUMMOND: The Rocket	30

BONNIE & TREASURES
65	London HLU 9998	Home Of The Brave/Our Song	40

BONO & GAVIN FRIDAY
94	Island CID 593	In The Name Of The Father (7" Edit)/(12" Remix)/(12" Beats Mix)/ (LP Instrumental) (CD)	15
94	Island 12IS593	In The Name Of The Father (7" Edit)/(12" Remix)/(12" Beats Mix)/ (LP Instrumental) (12" single)	10

(see also U2, Clannad & Bono, The Passengers, Virgin Prunes)

BONOBO
00	Tru Thoughts TRU 004	Terrapin (12")	15
01	Tru Thoughts TRU 013	THE SHARK EP (12")	8
00	Tru Thoughts TRU LP 007	ANIMAL MAGIC (2xLP)	30
01	Ninja Tune ZEN 63	ANIMAL MAGIC (2xLP)	30
02	Tru Thoughts TRU LP 031	ONE OFFS...REMIXES & B SIDES (2xLP)	30
03	Ninja Tune ZEN 80	DIAL M FOR MONKEY (2xLP)	30
06	Ninja Tune ZEN 119	DAYS TO COME (2xLP)	30

BONZO DOG (DOO-DAH) BAND
66	Parlophone R 5430	My Brother Makes The Noises For The Talkies/ I'm Gonna Bring A Watermelon To My Gal Tonight	30
66	Parlophone R 5499	Alley Oop/Button Up Your Overcoat	30
67	Liberty LBF 15040	Equestrian Statue/The Intro And The Outro	10
68	Liberty LBF 15144	Urban Spaceman/Canyons Of Your Mind (initially pressing with spoken intro to A-side)	10
68	Liberty LBF 15144	Urban Spaceman/Canyons Of Your Mind (later pressing without spoken intro to A-side)	5
69	Liberty LBF 15201	Mr. Apollo/Ready Mades	7
69	Liberty LBF 15273	I Want To Be With You/We Were Wrong	7
70	Liberty LBF 15314	You Done My Brain In/Mr. Slater's Parrot	7
73	United Artists UP 35602	The Intro And The Outro/Hello Mabel	7
74	United Artists UP 35662	Mr. Slater's Parrot/Noises For The Leg	7
92	China WOK 2021	No Matter Who You Vote For The Government Always Gets In/ NEIL INNES: Them (promo only)	15
67	Liberty LBL 83056	GORILLA (LP, mono with booklet)	60
67	Liberty LBS 83056	GORILLA (LP, stereo with booklet)	40
67	Liberty LBL/LBS 83056	GORILLA (LP, without booklet, blue label)	20
71	Liberty LBL/LBS 83158E	THE DOUGHNUT IN GRANNY'S GREENHOUSE (LP, gatefold sleeve, with booklet, blue label)	50
71	Liberty LBL/LBS 83158E	THE DOUGHNUT IN GRANNY'S GREENHOUSE (LP, gatefold sleeve, without booklet, blue label)	25
69	Liberty LBS 83257	TADPOLES (LP, die-cut sleeve, with insert, blue label)	40
69	Liberty LBS 83257	TADPOLES (LP, die-cut sleeve, without insert, blue label)	25
69	Liberty LBS 83290	KEYNSHAM (LP, gatefold sleeve, blue label)	35
72	United Artists UAS 29288	LET'S MAKE UP AND BE FRIENDLY (LP)	22
74	United Artists UAD 60071/2	THE HISTORY OF THE BONZOS (2-LP, gatefold sleeve with booklet)	25

(see also Vivian Stanshall, Neil Innes, Grimms, Roger Ruskin Spear, Topo D. Bill, New Vaudeville Band)

BETTY BOO
79	Grapevine GRP 125	Say It Isn't So/Say It Isn't So (Instrumental)	20

BOOGALOOS
69	President PT 253	Rule Britannia/Love Is Blind	12

JAMES BOOKER
61	Vogue V 9177	Cool Turkey/Gonzo	30
63	Vocalion VEP 170154	GONZO (EP)	50

BOOKER T (JAMAICA)
76	Ethnic Fight 2	Eleanor/Version	5

BOOKER T. & THE M.G.S
62	London HLK 9595	Green Onions/Behave Yourself	20
63	London HLK 9670	Jelly Bread/Aw' Mercy	15
63	London HLK 9784	Chinese Checkers/Plum Nellie	15
65	Atlantic AT 4033	Boot-Leg/Outrage	15
66	Atlantic AT 4063	Be My Lady/Red Beans And Rice	18
66	Atlantic 584 044	My Sweet Potato/Booker Loo	12
66	Atlantic 584 060	Jingle Bells/Winter Wonderland	15
67	Atlantic 584 088	Green Onions/Boot-Leg	12
67	Stax 601 009	Hip Hug Her/Summertime (initially dark blue label)	25
67	Stax 601 009	Hip Hug Her/Summertime (later pressing with light blue label)	18

67	Stax 601 018	Groovin'/Slim Jenkins' Place	10
67	Stax 601 026	Chinese Checkers/Plum Nellie (reissue)	10
68	Stax STAX 102	Soul Limbo/Heads Or Tails	5
69	Stax STAX 119	Time Is Tight/Hang 'Em High	5
69	Stax STAX 127	Soul Clap '69/Mrs. Robinson	6
69	Stax STAX 136	The Horse/Slum Baby	5
71	Stax 2025 026	Melting Pot/Kinda Easy Like	10
72	Stax 2025 074	Jamaica This Morning (as the MGs)/Fuquawi	6
63	London REK 1367	R&B WITH BOOKER T (EP)	20
64	Atlantic AET 6002	R&B WITH BOOKER T VOL. 2 (EP)	20
64	London HA-K 8182	GREEN ONIONS (LP, plum label)	60
65	Atlantic ATL 5027	SOUL DRESSING (LP, plum label, ist pressing with green & white sleeve)	50
66	Atlantic 587/588 033	GREEN ONIONS (LP, reissue, mono/stereo)	15
67	Atlantic 587 047	SOUL DRESSING (LP, reissue, with green & black sleeve)	20
67	Stax 589 002	AND NOW! (LP)	50
68	Stax 589 013	SOUL CHRISTMAS (LP)	18
68	Stax 230 002/231 002	DOIN' OUR THING (LP)	20
68	Stax (S)XATS 1001	SOUL LIMBO (LP)	18
69	Atco 228 004	GET READY (LP)	15
69	Stax (S)XATS 1005	UPTIGHT (LP, soundtrack, with Judy Clay)	15
69	Stax (S)XATS 1015	THE BOOKER T. SET (LP)	15
69	Atco 228 015	THE BEST OF BOOKER T. AND THE M.G.s (LP)	15
70	Stax SXATS 1031	McLEMORE AVENUE (LP)	15
71	Stax 2325 030	MELTING POT (LP)	15

(see also Mar-Keys, Steve Cropper, Albert King, Judy Clay)

BOOM
91	Music Of Life NOTE049	BOOM EP (12")	8
91	Music Of Life NOTE050	Delivering The Answer (12")	8

BOOMERANGS
64	Fontana TF 507	Rockin' Robin/Don't Let Her Be Your Baby	20
65	Fontana TF 555	Another Tear Falls/Fun Fun Fun	15

BOOMERANGS
66	Pye 7N 17049	Dream World/Upgraded	12

DANIEL BOONE
73	Penny Farthing PEN 800	Rock N Roll Bum/Sunday Morning Coming	5

PAT BOONE
SINGLES
55	London HLD 8172	Ain't That A Shame/Tennessee Saturday Night	40
55	London HLD 8197	At My Front Door/No Arms Can Ever Hold You	25
56	London HLD 8233	Gee Whittakers/Take The Time	20
56	London HLD 8253	I'll Be Home/Tutti Frutti	20
56	London HLD 8291	Long Tall Sally/Just As Long As I'm With You	30
56	London HLD 8303	I Almost Lost My Mind/I'm In Love With You	10
56	London HLD 8316	Two Hearts, Two Kisses/Rich In Love	12
56	London HLD 8346	Friendly Persuasion (Thee I Love)/Chains Of Love	10

(The above 45s were originally issued with gold lettering labels; later silver lettering copies are worth half these values.)

57	London HLD 8370	Don't Forbid Me/Anastasia	5
57	London HLD 8404	Why Baby Why/I'm Just Waiting For You	10
57	London HLD 8445	Love Letters In The Sand/Bernadine	5
57	London HLD 8512	Remember You're Mine/There's A Goldmine In The Sky	5
57	London HLD 8512	April Love/When The Swallows Come Back To Capistrano	5
59	London HLD 8824	There's Good Rockin' Tonight/With The Wind And The Rain In Your Hair	10
59	London HLD 8855	For A Penny/Wang Dang Taffy-Apple Tango	5
59	London HLD 8910	Rock Boll Weevil/Twixt Twelve And Twenty	5
59	London HLD 8974	A Fool's Hall Of Fame/Brightest Wishing Star	5

(The above 45s were originally issued with triangular centres; later round centre copies are worth two-thirds these values.)

64	Dot DS 16658	Beach Girl/Little Honda	10

EXPORT SINGLES
56	London HL 7007	I'll Be Home/Tutti Frutti	25
56	London HL 7010	Long Tall Sally/Just As Long As I'm With You	25
59	London HL 7070	With The Wind And The Rain In Your Hair/There's Good Rocking Tonight	5
59	London SLD 4002	For A Penny/Wang Dang Taffy-Apple Tango (both tracks stereo)	12

EPs
65	Dot DEP 20008	HEY BABY	8
65	Dot DEP 20012	MAKE THE WORLD GO AWAY	8
65	Dot DEP 20013	SWEET LITTLE SIXTEEN	8
65	DEP 20001	PAT BOONE HITS	10
56	London RE-D 1063	PAT BOONE SINGS THE HITS	10
57	London RE-D 1086	PAT BOONE SINGS THE HITS NO. 2	10
58	London RE-D 1112	PAT BOONE SINGS THE HITS NO. 3	8

ALBUMS
57	London HA-D 2024	PAT'S BIG HITS (LP)	15
57	London HA-D 2030	HOWDY! (LP)	15
57	London HA-D 2049	PAT! (LP)	20
63	London HA-D 8109	SINGS ... GUESS WHO? (LP, mono)	40
63	London SH-D 8109	SINGS ... GUESS WHO? (LP, stereo)	40
65	Dot (D)DLP 3594	BOSS BEAT (LP)	20

(see also Fontane Sisters)

BOONE FAMILY
74	Mowest MW 3022	Please Mr Postman/Friends	5

BOONES FARM
72	CBS 8212	If You Can't Be My Woman/Start Today	20

BOO RADLEYS
90	Actiion TAKE 4	ICHABOD & I (LP)	12

91	Rough Trade R3011	LEARNING TO WALK (LP)	15
92	Creation CFRELP 120	EVERYTHING'S ALRIGHT FOREVER (LP, first 1000 with free Sunfly 7")	15
93	Creation CRELP 149	GIANT STEPS (2-LP)	20

ANTHONY BOOTH
| 69 | Tangerine DP 0008 | Till Death Do Us Part/September Days | 7 |

BARRY BOOTH
| 68 | Pye NPL 18216 | DIVERSIONS! (LP, also stereo NSLP 18216)) | 12 |

(see also Monty Python)

BILL BOOTH REVIVAL MACHINE
| 75 | Private Press HEADSRTM/ CUS038 | FACE TO FACE (LP) | 18 |

KEN BOOTHE
66	Island WI 3020	The Train Is Coming/This Is Me	40
66	Island WI 3035	I Don't Want To See You Cry/Baby I Need You (B-side actually by Wailers)	90
66	Ska Beat JB 248	You're No Good/SOULETTES: Don't Care What The People Say	80
67	Doctor Bird DB 1110	Say You/LYN TAITT & JETS: Smokey Places	50
67	Coxsone CS 7006	Lonely Teardrops/Oowee Baby	70
67	Coxsone CS 7020	Home Home Home/SOUL BROTHERS: Windell	40
67	Caltone TONE 107	The One I Love/You Left The Water Running	75
67	Studio One SO 2000	Feel Good/Mustang Sally	35
67	Studio One SO 2012	Puppet On A String/ROLAND ALPHONSO: Look Away	20
67	Studio One SO 2014	Fatty Fatty (actually Heptones)/Mother Word (actually by Delroy Wilson)	20
67	Studio One SO 2026	Why Did You Leave (actually by Leroy Sibbles)/Don't Try To Reach Me (actually by Gaylads)	30
68	Studio One SO 2039	When I Fall In Love/HEPTONES: Christmas Time	35
68	Studio One SO 2041	The Girl I Left Behind/TERMITES: My Last Love	40
68	Studio One SO 2053	Tomorrow/Movin' Away	50
68	Fab FAB 63	I Remember Someone/Can't You See?	110
68	Coxsone CS 7041	Everybody Knows/GAYLADS: I'm Free	30
69	Coxsone CS 7094	Sherry/I've Got You	25
69	Studio One SO 2073	You're On My Mind/RICHARD ACE & SOUND DIMENSIONS: Love To Cherish	30
69	High Note HS 003	Lady With The Starlight/LESLIE BUTLER & COUNT OSSIE: Gay Drums	25
69	Bamboo BAM 4	Pleading/COUNT MATCHUKI & SOUND DIMENSION: Call 1143	40
69	Bamboo BAM 8	Be Yourself/SOUND DIMENSION: Rathid	45
70	Trojan TR 7716	Why, Baby Why/Keep My Love From Fading	7
70	Trojan TR 7756	Freedom Street/BEVERLEY'S ALLSTARS: Freedom Version	8
70	Trojan TR 7772	It's Gonna Take A Miracle/Now I Know	10
70	Trojan TR 7780	Drums Of Freedom/BEVERLEY'S ALLSTARS: Version	8
70	Gas GAS 169	Give To Me/Why	8
70	Jackpot JP 748	You Left The Water Running/PHIL PRATT ALL STARS: Cut Throat	20
70	Punch PH 30	Artibella/PRATT ALLSTARS: Version Of Artibella	25
70	Punch PH 33	Morning/Morning (Version)	8
71	Punch PH 70	Stop Your Crying/CONSCIOUS MINDS: Suffering Through The Nation	10
71	Banana BA 352	Original Six (Parts 1 & 2)	12
71	Summit SUM 8518	I Wish It Could Be Peaceful Again/BEVERLEY'S ALLSTARS: Peaceful Version	8
71	Summit SUM 8519	Your Feeling And Mine/BEVERLEY'S ALLSTARS: Your Feeling Version	8
71	Big Shot BI 590	So Nice/So Nice Version	8
71	Green Door GD 4002	Medley Version/Medley Version 2	8
71	Dynamic DYN 411	Hallelujah/Trying To Reach	8
72	Dynamic DYN 453	Tears From My Eyes/CONSCIOUS MINDS: Tears From My Eyes Version	8
72	Pama Supreme PS 369	Look What You've Done/LLOYD CHARMERS: Look What You've Done Version	10
72	Ashanti ASH 403	Make Me Feel Alright (with The Incrowd)/INCROWD: Down On The Corner	8
73	Trojan TR 7893	Is It Because I'm Black, Gold And Green	12
73	Green Door GD 4053	Silver Words/Rasta God Version	8
73	Mirto 100	Is It Because I'm Black?/Just Like A Shelter (as The Messengers)	5
74	Trojan TR 7920	Everything I Own/Drum Song	5
74	Trojan TR 7944	Crying Over You/Now You Can See Me Again	5
75	Fab FAB 270	Thinking/Moving Away	20
75	Torpedo TOR 35	Lady With The Starlight/Light Version	15
75	Torpedo TOR 54	Say You/You Version	8
79	Attack TACK 6	You're No Good/PRINCE JAMMY: Out Of Order Dub (12")	12
67	Studio One SOL 9001	MR. ROCK STEADY (LP)	150
73	Trojan TRLS 58	BLACK, GOLD AND GREEN (LP)	30
74	Trojan TRLS 83	LETS GET IT ON (LP)	20
79	Phil Pratt PP01LP	GOT TO GET AWAY (LP)	40

(see also Stranger & Ken, Keith Hudson, Gaylads, Richard Ace, Lloyd & Ken)

BOOTLES
| 64 | Vocalion VN 9216 | I'll Let You Hold My Hand/Never Till Now | 25 |

BOOTS
68	CBS 3550	Even The Bad Times Are Good/The Animal In Me	20
68	CBS 3833	Keep Your Lovelight Burning/Give Me One More Chance	25
70	Youngblood YB 1018	You Better Run/A To D	60

DAVE BOOTS
| 60s | Solent SM 013 | GREEN SATIN AND GOLD (LP) | 100 |

BOOTS FOR DANCING
80	Pop Aural POP 002	BOOTS FOR DANCING EP (12")	15
80	Pop Aural POP 006	Hesitate/Rain Song (p/s)	10
82	Repop X WAY 100	Ooh Bop Sh'bam/Money (p/s)	8

BOOTSY'S RUBBER BAND
77	Warner Bros K 16964T	Pinocchio Theory/Psychoticbumpschool/What's A Telephone (12")	8
78	Warner Bros K 17196T	Bootzilla/Hollywood Squares (12", p/s)	8
76	Warner Bros K 56200	STRETCHIN' OUT IN BOOTSY'S RUBBER BAND (LP)	15
77	Warner Bros K 56302	AHH... THE NAME IS BOOTSY, BABY! (LP, gatefold sleeve)	15
78	Warner Bros K 56424	BOOTSY? PLAYER OF THE YEAR (LP, gatefold sleeve)	12
79	Warner Bros K 56615	THE BOOT IS MADE FOR FONK-N (LP, with inner sleeve)	12
81	Warner Bros K 56998	THE ONE GIVETH, THE COUNT TAKETH AWAY (LP)	12

(see also Parliament, Funkadelic)

BOOVER BOYS
70	Torpedo TOR 22	A.G.G.R.O/Sha La La La Lee	100

CHARLIE BOP TRIO
77	Capitol CL 15940	Mr. Big Feet/MERRILL E MOORE: Boogie My Blues Away	6

BOP & BELTONES
67	Coxsone CS 7012	Treat Me Good/PETER TOUCH & WAILERS: Dancing Time (B-side actually by Bop & Beltones)	50

(see also Beltones, Soul Vendors, Jackie Mittoo)

RANNY BOP
70	Gas GAS 155	Pipe Dream/Suck Suck	10

BORDER
78	Pear PEAR 1	Song For J/Easy/Going Away (p/s, 500 only)	40

BORE-TOWN BOP
81	Vital VIS001	Try/Surf's Up (p/s)	15

BILLY BORLYNN
60	Philips PB 1031	Baby Listens/Liebelei	5
60	Philips PB 1057	Every Step Of The Way/It Takes Time	5

BORN B.C.
82	Xcentric Noise FIRST 1	THE POWER & THE PRIVILEGE (EP)	8

BOSCH
80	Trific TRIF 1	The Two Tree/Packing Jean (p/s)	25

BOSS
86	Power House (no cat. no.)	One Good Reason/Wake Up Children (p/s, with lyric sheet)	6

BOSS ATTACK
71	Fab FAB 187	Hell-El/TEARDROPS: Let Me Be Free	15

BOSS COMBO
62	Coral LVA 9205	GOLDEN ROCK AND ROLL INSTRUMENTALS (LP)	20

BOSS GUITARS
65	London HA-R/SH-R 8237	PLAY THE WINNERS (LP)	20

BOSS HOG
89	Amphetamie Reptile ARR6/68	DRINKIN', LECHIN' AND LYIN' (LP)	40
99	City Slang 20150	WHITEOUT (LP)	18

EARL BOSTIC (ORCHESTRA)
SINGLES
54	Parlophone MSP 6075	Off Shore/What! No Pearls	15
54	Parlophone MSP 6089	Deep Purple/Smoke Rings	15
54	Parlophone MSP 6105	Melancholy Serenade/Don't You Do It	15
54	Parlophone MSP 6110	Jungle Drums/Danube Waves	15
54	Parlophone MSP 6119	Mambolino/Blue Skies	15
54	Parlophone MSP 6131	These Foolish Things/Mambostic	15
54	Parlophone CMSP 8	Cherokee/The Song Is Ended (export issue)	15
55	Parlophone MSP 6162	Melody Of Love/Sweet Lorraine	15
56	Vogue V 2145	Flamingo/Sleep	18
56	Vogue V 2148	Moonglow/Ain't Misbehaving	18
56	Parlophone R 4208	The Bo-Do Rock (with Bill Doggett)/Mean To Me	20
56	Parlophone R 4232	For All We Know/Beyond The Blue Horizon	10
57	Parlophone R 4263	I Hear A Rhapsody/Harlem Nocturne	10
57	Parlophone R 4278	Bubbins Rock/Indiana (with Bill Doggett)	15
57	Parlophone R 4305	Avalon/Too Fine For Crying (B-side with Bill Jones)	10
57	Parlophone R 4370	Temptation/September Song	10
58	Parlophone R 4460	Over The Waves Rock/Twilight Time	10
59	Parlophone DP 553	Barcarolle/My Reverie (export single)	10
62	Ember JBS 708	Tuxedo Junction/Air Mail Special	10
66	Island WI 271	Honeymoon Night/PATSY COLE: Disappointed Bride	25

EPs
54	Parlophone GEP 8506	FLAMINGO	15
55	Parlophone GEP 8513	LINGER AWHILE	15
55	Parlophone GEP 8520	EARL BOSTIC AND HIS ALTO SAX	15
55	Vogue EPV 1010	EARL BOSTIC	15
56	Vogue EPV 1111	VELVET SUNSET	15
56	Parlophone GEP 8539	WRAP IT UP	12
58	Parlophone GEP 8701	BOSTIC BEAT	25
58	Parlophone GEP 8741	ROCKING WITH BOSTIC	25

ALBUMS
54	Vogue LDE 100	EARL BOSTIC AND HIS ORCHESTRA (10")	30
54	Parlophone PMD 1016	EARL BOSTIC AND HIS ALTO SAX (10" LP)	25
56	Parlophone PMD 1040	EARL BOSTIC AND HIS ALTO SAX No. 2	25
58	Parlophone PMD 1054	BOSTIC MEETS DOGGETT (10" LP, with Bill Doggett)	30
58	Parlophone PMD 1068	BOSTIC ROCKS (10" LP)	30
59	Parlophone PMD 1071	BOSTIC SHOWCASE OF SWINGING DANCE HITS (10" LP)	20
59	Parlophone PMD 1074	SWEET TUNES OF THE FANTASTIC FIFTIES	20
59	Parlophone PMD 1115	SWEET TUNES OF THE ROARIN' TWENTIES (10" LP)	15
59	Parlophone PMD 1117	SWEET TUNES OF THE SWINGIN' THIRTIES (10" LP)	15
59	Parlophone PMD 1119	SWEET TUNES OF THE SENTIMENTAL FORTIES (10" LP)	15
60	Parlophone PMC 1125	PLAYS THE HIT TUNES OF THE BIG BROADWAY SHOWS (12" LP)	15

(see also Bill Doggett, Sonny Carter)

BOSTON
76	Epic EPCH 81611	BOSTON (LP, audiophile pressing)	20
76	Epic EPC 81611	BOSTON (LP, picture disc)	12
78	Epic E 9945050	DON'T LOOK BACK (LP, picture disc)	12

| 86 | MCA MCGP 6017 | THIRD STAGE (LP, picture disc) | 15 |
| 94 | MCA MCGP 6017 | WALK ON (LP, picture disc) | 15 |

BOSTON BOPPERS
| 74 | Penny Farthing PEN 828 | Did You Get What You Wanted/Whirlwind Girl | 35 |

BOSTON CRABS
65	Columbia DB 7586	Down In Mexico/Who?	20
65	Columbia DB 7679	As Long As I Have You/Alley Oop	20
66	Columbia DB 7830	Gin House/You Didn't Have To Be So Nice	20

BOSTON DEXTERS
64	Contemporary CR 101	Matchbox/La Bamba	200
64	Contemporary CR 102	You've Been Talking About Me/Nothing's Gonna Change Me	150
64	Contemporary CR 103	What Kind Of Girl Are You/I've Got Troubles Of My Own	150
65	Columbia DB 7498	I Believe To My Soul/I've Got Something To Tell You	50
65	Columbia DB 7641	Try Hard/No More Tears	45

(see also Buzz, Tam White)

JACK ANGLIN BOSTON AND THE SOULITES
| 69 | Ackee ACK 103 | Starvation/Slave | 15 |

BO STREET RUNNERS
64	Decca F 11986	Bo Street Runner/Tell Me	40
65	Columbia DB 7488	Tell Me What You're Gonna Do/And I Do Just What I Want	60
65	Columbia DB 7640	Baby Never Say Goodbye/Get Out Of My Way	60
66	Columbia DB 7901	Drive My Car/So Very Woman (featuring Mike [Too Much] Patto)	60
64	Oak RGJ 131	BO STREET RUNNERS (EP, 49 copies only)	1000

(see also [Mike] Patto, Timebox, Chicago Line, Cheynes, Fleetwood Mac)

CONNIE BOSWELL
| 54 | Brunswick 05319 | T-E-N-N-E-S-S-E-E (Spells ...)/If I Give My Heart To You | 7 |
| 55 | Brunswick 05397 | How Important Can It Be?/Fill My Heart With Happiness | 7 |

EVE BOSWELL
53	Parlophone MSP 6006	Sugar Bush/Moon Above Malaya (China Nights)	10
55	Parlophone MSP 6158	Ready, Willing And Able/Pam-Poo-Dey	10
55	Parlophone MSP 6160	The Heart You Break (May Be Your Own)/Tika Tika Tok	10
56	Parlophone MSP 6208	Young And Foolish/Where You Are	10
56	Parlophone MSP 6220	It's Almost Tomorrow/Cookie	10
56	Parlophone MSP 6250	Saries Marias/Come Back My Love	10
56	Parlophone R 4230	True Love/Where In The World Is Billy?	10
57	Parlophone R 4275	Rock Bobbin' Boats/Tra La La	10
57	Parlophone R 4299	Chantez, Chantez/She Said (Aunt Magnolia)	5
57	Parlophone R 4328	With All My Heart/Sugar Candy	5
57	Parlophone R 4341	The Gypsy In My Soul/Stop Whistlin' Wolf	5
57	Parlophone R 4362	Swedish Polka (Chickadee)/Tell My Love	5
58	Parlophone R 4401	(I Love You) For Sentimental Reasons/Bobby	5
58	Parlophone R 4414	I Do/Love Me Again	5
58	Parlophone R 4455	Left Right Out Of Your Heart/Voom-Ba-Voom	5
58	Parlophone R 4479	More Than Ever (Come Prima)/I Know Why	8
58	Parlophone R 4492	Christmas Lullaby/The Christmas Tree	5
59	Parlophone R 4517	If I Had A Talking Picture Of You/Piccaninny	5
59	Parlophone R 4544	Wimoweh Cha Cha/Boegoeberg Se Dam	5
59	Parlophone R 4555	Once Again/You Are Never Far Away From Me	5
60	Parlophone R 4618	Misty/Turnabout Heart	5
69	Morgan MRS 19	This Is My Love/Lonely In A Crowd	5
76	EMI EMI 2517	Sugar Bush '76/This Time	5
57	Parlophone GEP 8601	THE ENCHANTING EVE (EP)	10
58	Parlophone GEP 8690	EVE BOSWELL'S SHOWCASE (EP)	8
58	Parlophone GEP 8717	EVE BOSWELL'S SHOWCASE NO. 2 (EP)	8
56	Parlophone PMD 1039	SUGAR AND SPICE (10" LP)	75
57	Parlophone PMC 1038	SENTIMENTAL EVE (LP)	200
59	Parlophone PMC 1105	FOLLOWING THE SUN AROUND (LP)	100

SIMON BOSWELL
| 75 | Transatlantic TRA 307 | MIND PARASITES (LP) | 15 |

(see also Advertising)

BOTHY BAND
75	Polydor 2383379	THE BOTHY BAND (LP)	18
76	Polydor 2383 417	OLD HAG YOU HAVE KILLED ME (LP)	12
77	Polydor 2383456	OUT OF THE WIND, INTO THE SUN (LP)	12

JUDY BOUCHER
| 86 | Orbitone OR 72 | Can't Be With You Tonight/Dreaming Of A Little Island (p/s) | 5 |

BOULEVARD
| 79 | Chopper CHOP 5D | MAGIC MAN (12", red vinyl, no p/s) | 15 |
| 81 | Boulevard VARD 1 | Dawn Raid/Take It Or Leave It (p/s) | 40 |

BOUNCING FLOWERS
| 81 | Rewind REWIND 8 | Fire/Expanding Cases (p/s) | 10 |

DENNIS BOVELL
78	Tempus TEMLP 001	STRICTLY DUBWISE (LP)	25
78	Ballistic LBR 1031	STRICTLY DUBWISE (LP)	12
81	Fontana 6381047	BRAIN DAMAGE (2-LP)	12

(see also Matumbi, Rama)

BOW BELLS
| 65 | Polydor 56030 | Not To Be Taken/I'll Try Not To Hold It Against You | 6 |
| 66 | Parlophone R 5520 | Belinda/When You're In | 6 |

(see also Nola York)

RICKY BOWDEN
| 63 | HMV POP 1162 | Alone To Cry/I'd Be Ashamed | 10 |

JIMMY BOWEN

57	Columbia DB 3915	I'm Stickin' With You/Ever Lovin' Fingers	60
57	Columbia DB 3915	I'm Stickin' With You/Ever Lovin' Fingers (78)	20
57	Columbia DB 3984	Warm Up To Me, Baby/I Trusted You	50
57	Columbia DB 3984	Warm Up To Me, Baby/I Trusted You (78)	15
57	Columbia DB 4027	Cross Over/It's Shameful	30
57	Columbia DB 4027	Cross Over/It's Shameful (78)	15
58	Columbia DB 4184	The Two Step/By The Light Of The Silvery Moon	25
58	Columbia DB 4184	The Two Step/By The Light Of The Silvery Moon/Spanish Cricket	10
65	Reprise RS 23043	The Eagle (demos & some issues list "The Golden Eagle")	20
67	Reprise RS 20592	Raunchy (with Chorus & Orchestra)/It's Such A Pretty World Today (wth Singers)	5
58	Columbia SEG 7757	MEET JIMMY BOWEN (EP)	70
58	Columbia SEG 7793	MEET JIMMY BOWEN NO. 2 (EP)	70

BEN BOWERS

55	Columbia SCM 5192	The Kentuckian Song/The Man From Laramie	10
56	Columbia SCM 5260	To You, My Love/I'm Still A King To You	5
57	Parlophone R 4317	Country Boy (with His Royal Jamaicans)/ Rum And Coconut Water (Rum And Coca-Cola)	5
57	Pye Jazz NJE 1001	BIG BEN BLUES (EP, with His Bluesicians)	8

DAVID BOWIE

SINGLES

66	Pye 7N 17020	Can't Help Thinking About Me/And I Say To Myself (with Lower Third)	300
66	Pye 7N 17079	Do Anything You Say/Good Morning Girl	400
66	Pye 7N 17157	I Dig Everything/I'm Not Losing Sleep	400
66	Deram DM 107	Rubber Band/The London Boys	450
67	Deram DM 123	The Laughing Gnome/The Gospel According To Tony Day (with inverted matrix number on label)	40
67	Deram DM 135	Love You Till Tuesday/Did You Ever Have A Dream	180
69	Philips BF 1801	Space Oddity/Wild Eyed Boy From Freecloud (mono, solid centre)	150
69	Philips BF 1801	Space Oddity/Wild Eyed Boy From Freecloud (mono, push-out centre)	20
69	Philips BF 1801	Space Oddity/Wild Eyed Boy From Freecloud (unreleased p/s, only 2 or 3 copies known to exist)	3000
69	Philips BF 1801	Space Oddity/Wild Eyed Boy From Freecloud (UK pressed stereo 45: unconfirmed)	0
		(is this really a UK pressing or a Dutch pressing as is generally acknowledged?)	
69	Philips BF 1801	Space Oddity/Wild Eyed Boy From Freecloud (mono, large centre)	15
70	Mercury MF 1135	The Prettiest Star/Conversation Piece	200
70	Mercury 6052 026	Memory Of A Free Festival Parts 1 & 2 (large centre)	200
70	Mercury 6052 026	Memory Of A Free Festival Parts 1 & 2 (push-out centre)	175
71	Mercury 6052 049	Holy Holy/Black Country Rock	150
72	RCA RCA 2160	Changes/Andy Warhol	25
72	RCA RCA 2199	Starman/Suffragette City (in p/s)	80
72	RCA 2199	Starman/Suffragette City (orange label)	5
72	RCA RCA 2302	The Jean Genie/Ziggy Stardust	5
72	RCA 2302	The Jean Genie/Ziggy Stardust (re-issue, black label)	5
72	Pye 7NX 8002	FOR THE COLLECTOR EP (Do Anything You Say/I Dig Everything//I Can't Help Thinking About Me/I'm Not Losing Sleep (re-issue, blue label with art sleeve)	20
72	Pye 7NX 8002	FOR THE COLLECTOR EP (Do Anything You Say/I Dig Everything//I Can't Help Thinking About Me/I'm Not Losing Sleep (re-issue, pink label with push-out centre)	20
72	Pye PRT 7NX 8002	FOR THE COLLECTOR EP (Do Anything You Say/I Dig Everything//I Can't Help Thinking About Me/I'm Not Losing Sleep (re-issue)	10
72	Pye 7NX 8002	FOR THE COLLECTOR EP (Do Anything You Say/I Dig Everything//I Can't Help Thinking About Me/I'm Not Losing Sleep (re-issue, pink label, solid centre)	6
72	Pye 7NX 8002	FOR THE COLLECTOR EP (Do Anything You Say/I Dig Everything//I Can't Help Thinking About Me/I'm Not Losing Sleep (re-issue, grey label)	6
72	RCA RCA 2263	John, I'm Only Dancing/Hang Onto Yourself (original pressing with slow 'acoustic guitar' version)	6
72	RCA RCA 2263	John, I'm Only Dancing/Hang Onto Yourself (Original version, orange label)	7
73	RCA RCA 2316	Life On Mars?/The Man Who Sold The World (in p/s)	20
73	RCA RCA 2316	Life On Mars?/The Man Who Sold The World	5
73	RCA RCA 2352	Drive-In Saturday/Round And Round	5
73	RCA 2263	John, I'm Only Dancing/Hang Onto Yourself (sax version, orange label)	7
73	Deram DM 123	The Laughing Gnome/The Gospel According To Tony Day (reissue, matrix number correct way up on label)	5
74	RCA RCA 2424	Sorrow/Amsterdam	5
74	RCA LPBO 5009	Rebel Rebel/Queen Bitch (label states "Bowie" not "David Bowie")	15
74	RCA LPBO 5009	Rebel Rebel/Queen Bitch (US import for UK market, as "David Bowie")	5
74	RCA LPBO 5021	Rock'N'Roll Suicide/Quicksand	7
74	RCA APBO 0293	Diamond Dogs/Holy Holy ("Bowie" not "David Bowie", solid centre)	25
74	RCA APBO 0293	Diamond Dogs/Holy Holy (as "Bowie" not "David Bowie", push-out centre)	10
74	RCA/Mainman	Bowie's Greatest Hits (excerpts from Knock On Wood/ Lyntone LYN 2929 Space Oddity/The Man Who Sold The World/Life On Mars?/Starman/Jean Genie/Sorrow/Diamond dogs) 33rpm 1-sided flexidisc with Record Mirror/Popswop magazines)	35
74	RCA RCA 2466	Knock On Wood/Panic In Detroit	5
75	RCA RCA 2523	Young Americans/Suffragette City	5
75	RCA RCA 2640	Golden Years/Can You Hear Me (as "Bowie" not "David Bowie")	5
75	Decca F 13579	The London Boys/Love You Till Tuesday (paper labels)	15
75	Decca F 13579	London Boys/Love You Till Tuesday (plastic moulded label)	8
75	RCA RCA 2579	Fame/Right	5
75	RCA RCA 2593	Space Oddity/Changes/Velvet Goldmine (p/s)	10
76	RCA RCA 2682	TVC15/We Are The Dead	5
76	RCA RCA 2726	Suffragette City/Stay (p/s)	15
76	RCA RCA 2726	Suffragette City/Stay (no p/s)	5
77	RCA PB 0905	Sound And Vision/A New Career In A New Town	5
77	RCA PB 0905	Sound And Vision/A New Career In A New Town (re-issue, black label)	7
77	RCA PB 1017	Be My Wife/Speed Of Life (solid centre)	20
77	RCA PB 1017	Be My Wife/Speed Of Life (push-out centre)	5
77	RCA PB 1121	Heroes/V-2 Schneider (Orange label, solid centre)	10
77	RCA PB 1121	Heroes/V-2 Schneider (Orange label, push-out centre)	5
77	RCA PB 1121	Heroes/V-2 Schneider (plastic moulded label in white sleve)	10
77	RCA PB 1121	Heroes/V-2 Schneider (plastic moulded label, no sleeve)	5
78	RCA BOW 1	Breaking Glass/Art Decade/Ziggy Stardust (p/s)	8

77	RCA PB 1190	Beauty And The Beast/Sense Of Doubt (sold centre centre with p/s) 20
78	RCA PB 1190	Beauty And The Beast/Sense Of Doubt (push-out centre with p/s) 8
79	RCA BOW 2	Boys Keep Swinging/Fantastic Voyage (p/s) 7
79	RCA BOW 3	DJ/Repetition (p/s) 7
79	RCA BOW 3	DJ/Repetition (p/s, green vinyl) 50
79	RCA LPBO 5009	Rebel Rebel/Queen Bitch (re-issue, black label) 7
79	RCA 2424	Sorrow/Amsterdam (re-issue) 7
79	RCA 2199	Starman/Suffragette City (re-issue, black label solid centre) 7
79	RCA 2199	Starman/Suffragette City (re-issue, black label/push-out centre) 5
79	RCA BOW 4	John, I'm Only Dancing (Again)(1975)/John, I'm Only Dancing (1972) (p/s) 7
79	RCA 2263	John, I'm Only Dancing/Hang Onto Yourself (re-issue, sax version, black label) 7
79	RCA BOW 12-4	John, I'm Only Dancing (Again) (Extended)/John, I'm Only Dancing (12", p/s) 8
79	RCA 2316	Life On Mars?/The Man Who Sold The World (re-issue, black label, solid centre) 15
79	RCA 2316	Life On Mars?/The Man Who Sold The World (re-issue, black label, push-out centre) 7
80	RCA 2263	John, I'm only Dancing/Hang Onto Yourself (re-issue, original version, black label) 7
80	RCA LPBO 5009	Rebel Rebel/Queen Bitch (re-issue, black label, B-side plays "Song For Bob Dylan")...........10
80	RCA BOW 5	Alabama Song/Space Oddity (pink vinyl, custom factory pressing, poster p/s) 500
80	RCA BOW 5	Alabama Song/Space Oddity (poster p/s) 10
80	RCA BOW 6	Ashes To Ashes/Move On (with 3 different p/s & 4 different sheets of 9 stamps) 12
80	RCA BOW 7	Fashion/Scream Like A Baby (p/s) 5
80	RCA BOW 8	Scary Monsters/Because You're Young (p/s) 5
80	RCA BOW 9	Up The Hill Backwards/Crystal Japan (orange label, solid centre, p/s) 8
80	RCA BOW 9	Up The Hill Backwards/Crystal Japan (black label, push-out centre, p/s) 5
81	RCA BOW 9	Up The Hill Backwards/Crystal Japan (orange label, push-out centre, p/s) 6
81	RCA BOW 10	Wild Is The Wind/Golden Years (push-out centre. with p/s) 7
81	RCA BOW 10	Wild Is The WInd/Golden Years (solid centre, p/s) 8
82	RCA BOW 11	IN BERTHOLT BRECHT'S "BAAL" (Baal's Hymn/Remembering Marie A//Ballad Of The Adventureres/The Drowned Girl/Dirty Song, EP, foldout p/s)...............................10
83	RCA BOW 511	Be My WIfe/Speed Of Life (Reissue, p/s) 5
82	RCA BOW 100	FASHIONS (10 x 7" picture discs in plastic wallet [BOWP 101-110], each £4) 50
83	EMI America EAP 157	China Girl/Shake It (picture disc) 7
83	EMI America 12 EA 158	Modern Love/Modern Love (Live) (12", p/s with poster) 8
83	RCA BOW 501	Drive-In Saturday/Round And Round (reissue, p/s) 5
83	RCA BOW 503	Rock 'n' Roll Suicide/Quicksand (reissue, p/s) 5
83	RCA BOW 502	Life On Mars?/The Man Who Sold The World (reissue, p/s) 5
83	RCA BOW 504	Diamond Dogs/Holy Holy (reissue, p/s) 5
83	RCA BOW 505	Knock On Wood/Panic In Detroit (Reissue) 5
83	RCA BOW 506	Young Americans/Suffragette City (Reissue) 5
83	RCA BOW 507	Fame/Right (Reissue, p/s) 5
83	RCA BOW 508	Golden Years/Can You Hear Me (Reissue) 5
83	RCA BOW 509	TVC15/We Are The Dead (Reissue, p/s) 5
83	RCA BOW 510	Sound And Vision/A New Career In A New Town (Reissue, p/s) 5
83	RCA BOW 512	Beauty And The Beast/Sense Of Doubt (Reissue, p/s) 5
83	RCA BOW 513	Heroes/V-2 Schneider (Reissue, p/s) 5
83	RCA BOW 514	Rebel Rebel/Queen Bitch (Reissue, p/s) 7
83	RCA BOW 514	Rebel Rebel/Queen Bitch (plays Song For Bob Dylan) (Reissue, p/s) 7
83	RCA BOW 515	The Jean Genie/Ziggy Stardust (Reissue, p/s) 5
83	RCA BOW 516	DJ/Repetition (Reissue, p/s) 5
83	RCA BOW 517	John I'm Only Dancing/Hang Onto Yourself (Reissue, p/s) 5
83	RCA BOW 518	Space Oddity/Changes/Velvet Goldmine (Reissue, p/s) 5
83	RCA BOW 519	Sorrow/Amsterdam (Reissue. p/s) 5
83	RCA BOW 520	Breaking Glass/Art Decade/Ziggy Stardust (Reissue, p/s) 5
84	EMI America EA 187	Tonight/Tumble And Twirl (poster p/s) 6
85	EMI America EAP 195	Loving The Alien (Remixed Version)/Don't Look Down (Remixed Version) (shaped picture disc) 10
85	EMI America 12EAP 195	Loving The Alien (Extended Dance Mix)/Don't Look Down (Extended Dance Mix)/Loving The Alien (Extended Dub Mix) (12" picture disc) 10
86	Virgin VSS 838	Absolute Beginners/Absolute Beginners (Dub Mix) (square picture disc) 6
86	EMI America EAP 216	Underground (Edited Version)/Underground (Instrumental) (shaped picture disc) 8
86	Virgin VSS 906	When The Wind Blows/When The Wind Blows (Instrumental) (shaped pic disc) 8
87	EMI America EAP 237	Time Will Crawl (Single Version)/Girls (Single Edit) (poster p/s) 8
87	EMI America EAP 239	Never Let Me Down/'87 And Cry (picture disc) 12
88	PRT PYX 6001	I'm Not Losing Sleep/I Dig Everything/Can't Help Thinking/Do Anything You Say (picture disc) 8
92	Warner Bros W 0127	Real Cool World/Real Cool World (Instrumental) (White label with "Made in the UK", art sleeve) 10
92	Warner Bros W 0127	Real Cool World/Real Cool World (Instrumental) (silver label, art sleeve) 10
93	BMG Arista 136977	Jump They Say (Radio Edit)/Pallas Athena (Don't Stop Praying Mix) (jukebox issue, no p/s) 6
93	Arista 74321 162267	Miracle Tonight/Looking For Lester (p/s) 7
93	Arista 74321 177057	The Buddah Of Suburbia/Dead Against It (p/s) 5
93	BMG Arista 74321 148687	Black Tie White Noise/You've Been Around (black moulded label, large centre) 15
93	BMG Arista 74321 148687	Black Tie White Noise/You've Been Around (silver moulded label, p/s) 7
95	RCA 329407	Strangers When We Meet (Edit)/The Man Who Sold The World (live) (green vinyl, stickered card p/s) 8
95	RCA 353847	Hallo Spaceboy (Remix)/The Heart's Filthy Lesson (Radio Edit) (pink vinyl, stickered card p/s) 10
95	RCA 74321 353847JB	Hallo Spaceboy (Remix)/The Heart's Filthy Lesson (Radio Edit) (juke box issue, moulded label) 10
97	RCA 307031	The Heart's Filthy Lesson (Alternative Mix)/(Bowie Mix)/(Rubber Mix)/ (Simple Text Mix)/(Filthy Mix) (12", picture disc) 8
97	RCA 7432 1475841	Dead Man Walking/Hous/Vigor Mortis/Paradox (plain sleeve, stickered) 6
97	RCA 512347	Seven Years In Tibet (Edit)/Seven Years In Tibet (Mandarin Version) (p/s, clear vinyl) 8
99	Parlophone QUEENPD 28	Under Pressure (Rah Mix) 6
99	Virgin VSP 1767	Survive/Seven (live) (picture disc) 8
99	Castle ESBO7 765	I DIG EVERYTHING: THE 1966 PYE SINGLES (box set) 20
02	Columbia COL 672744 7/6727447000	Slow Burn/Wood Jackson (orange vinyl, p/s) 15
09	Parlophone LCO 299	DAVID BOWIE : Heroes/TV ON THE RADIO : Heroes 40

SINGLES : DEMO SINGLES

66	Pye 7N 17020	Can't Help Thinking About Me/And I Say To Myself (Demo copy, push-out centre)...........1000
66	Pye 7N 17020	Can't Help Thinking About Me/And I Say To Myself (demo copy, solid centre)...................500

MINT VALUE £

Year	Cat No	Description	Value £
66	Pye 7N 17079	Do Anything You Say/Good Morning Girl (Demo copy, push-out centre)	1000
66	Pye 7N 17079	Do Anything You Say/Good Morning Girl (Demo copy, solid centre)	500
66	Pye 7N 17157	I Dig Everything/I'm Not Losing Sleep (Demo copy, push-out centre)	1000
66	Pye 7N 17157	I Dig Everything/I'm Not Losing sleep (Demo copy, solid centre)	500
66	Deram DM 107	Rubber Band/The London Boys (Demo copy)	300
67	Deram DM 123	The Laughing Gnome/The Gospel According To Tony Day (Demo copy)	200
67	Deram DM 135	Love You Till Tuesday/Did You Ever Have A Dream (Demo copy)	200
70	Mercury MF 1135	The Prettiest Star/Conversation Piece (Demo copy)	300
70	Mercury 6052 026	Memory Of A Free Festival Parts 1 & 2 (Demo copy, large centre)	300
70	Mercury 6052 026	Memory Of A Free Festival Parts 1 & 2 (Demo copy, push-out centre)	175
71	Mercury 6052 049	Holy Holy/Black Country Rock (Demo copy)	175
72	RCA 2160	Changes/Andy Warhol (Demo copy)	45
72	RCA 2160	Starman/Suffragette City (Demo copy in p/s)	75
72	RCA 2199	Starman/Suffragette City (Demo copy, not in p/s)	25
72	RCA 2302	The Jean Genie/Ziggy Stardust (Demo copy)	20
72	RCA 2263	John, I'm Only Dancing/Hang Onto Yourself (Demo copy)	25
73	RCA 2316	Life On Mars?/The Man Who Sold The World (Demo copy in p/s)	40
73	RCA 2316	Life On Mars?/The Man Who Sold The World (Demo copy without p/s)	15
73	RCA 2352	Drive-In Saturday/Round And Round (Demo copy)	30
73	RCA 2424	Sorrow/Amsterdam (Demo copy)	15
74	RCA LPBO 5009	Rebel Rebel/Queen Bitch (Demo copy, label states "Bowie" not "David Bowie")	25
74	RCA LPBO 5009	Rock'N'Roll Suicide/Quicksand (Demo copy)	20
74	RCA APBO 0293	Diamond Dogs/Holy Holy (Demo copy, as "Bowie" not "David Bowie", push-out centre)	25
74	RCA APBO 0293	Diamond Dogs/Holy Holy (as "Bowie" not "David Bowie", solid centre)	35
74	RCA 2466	Knock On Wood/Panic In Detroit (Demo copy)	15
75	RCA 2523	Young Americans (short version)/Young Americans (long version) (Demo copy)	25
75	RCA 2640	Golden Years/Can You Hear Me (Demo copy, solid centre, as "Bowie" not "David Bowie")	60
75	RCA 2640	Golden Years/Can You Hear Me (Demo copy, push-out centre, as "Bowie" not "David Bowie")	15
75	Decca F 13579	The London Boys/Love You Till Tuesday (Demo)	40
75	RCA 2579	Fame/Right (Demo copy)	15
75	RCA 2593	Space Oddity/Velvet Goldmine (Demo copy in p/s)	30
75	RCA 2593	Space Oddity/Velvet Goldmine (Demo copy, no p/s)	15
76	RCA 2682	TVC15/We Are The Dead (Demo copy)	15
76	RCA 2726	Suffragette City/Stay (Demo copy in p/s)	25
76	RCA 2726	Suffragette City/Stay (Demo copy, no p/s)	15
77	RCA PB 0905	Sound And Vision/A New Career In A New Town (Demo copy)	15
77	RCA PB 1017	Be My Wife/Speed Of Life (Demo copy in promo sleeve with titles on front)	500
77	RCA PB 1017	Be My Wife/Speed Of Life (Demo copy not in sleeve)	15
77	RCA PB 1121	Heroes/V-2 Schneider (Demo copy)	20
78	RCA BOW 1	Breaking Glass/Art Decade/Ziggy Stardust (Demo copy with p/s)	20
77	RCA PB 1190	Beauty And The Beast/Sense Of Doubt (Demo copy with p/s)	20
79	RCA BOW 2	Boys Keep Swinging/Fantastic Voyage (Demo copy)	15
79	RCA BOW 3	DJ/Repetition (Demo copy)	15
79	RCA BOW 4	John, I'm Only Dancing (Again)(1975)/John, I'm Only Dancing (1972) (Demo copy p/s)	15
80	RCA BOW 5	Alabama Song/Space Oddity (Demo copy, poster p/s)	20

SINGLES : IRISH PRESSINGS

Year	Cat No	Description	Value £
70	Mercury EMF 1135	The Prettiest Star/Conversation Piece (Irish pressing)	2000
73	RCA 2352	Drive-In Saturday/Round And Round (Irish pressing)	100
73	RCA 2424	Sorrow/Amsterdam (Irish pressing)	30
73	Deram DM(1) 123	The Laughing Gnome/The Gospel According To Tony Day (Irish pressing)	120
73	Deram DM(1) 123	The Laughing Gnome/The Gospel According To Tony Day (Irish pressing)	120
74	RCA LPBO 5009	Rebel Rebel/Queen Bitch (Irish pressing)	100
74	RCA LPBO 5021	Rock'N'Roll Suicide/Quicksand (Irish pressing)	100
75	RCA 2523	Young Americans/Sufragette City (Irish pressing)	100
79	RCA 2316	Life On Mars?/The Man Who Sold The World (Irish pressing)	100
82	RCA BOW 11	Wild Is The Wind/Golden Years (Irish pressing, p/s)	15
83	RCA BOW 503	Rock 'n' Roll Suicide/Quicksand (Irish pressing)	10
83	RCA BOW 502	Life On Mars?/The Man Who Sold The World (Irish pressing)	10
83	RCA BOW 504	Diamond Dogs/Holy Holy (Irish issue)	10
83	RCA BOW 501	Drive-In Saturday/Round And Round (Irish pressing, p/s)	10

ALBUMS

Year	Cat No	Description	Value £
67	Deram DML 1007	DAVID BOWIE (mono)	500
67	Deram SML 1007	DAVID BOWIE (stereo)	500
69	Philips SBL 7912	DAVID BOWIE (gatefold sleeve, black/silver label)	500
70	Decca PA 58	THE WORLD OF DAVID BOWIE (mono)	30
71	Mercury 6338 041	THE MAN WHO SOLD THE WORLD (LP, black/silver labels with 'dress' cover)	500
71	Mercury 6338 041	THE MAN WHO SOLD THE WORLD (cassette, with 'dress' cover)	50
71	RCA SF 8244	HUNKY DORY (orange label with lyric sheet, 1st pressing with laminated sleeve, no GEM logo on right hand top corner of rear cover and no Mainman reference on sleeve or labels)	350
71	RCA SF 8244	HUNKY DORY (orange label with lyric sheet)	25
72	RCA SF 8287	THE RISE AND FALL OF ZIGGY STARDUST AND THE SPIDERS FROM MARS (1st pressing, Stamped matrixes: BGBS 0864 1E/0865 1E (with A4S etched into dead wax on side 1, B2K etched into dead wax on side 2) with with 'Gem Productions' and no 'Mainman' logo on rear sleeve, "Victor" under RCA label not "International", glossy orange label with "Titanic/Chrysalis" credits on labels, lyric inner sleeve)	100
72	RCA LSP 4813	SPACE ODDITY (reissue of SBL 7912 in different sleeve, orange label with lyric inner sleeve & poster)	25
72	RCA LSP 4816	THE MAN WHO SOLD THE WORLD (orange label with inner sleeve & poster)	15
73	RCA RS 1001	ALADDIN SANE (gloss orange label with 'Victor' on right side, 'Shorewood' gatefold sleeve & lyric inner sleeve, with fan club membership folder. Matrix numbers: CPRY 4543-3T/4544-3T)	70
73	RCA RS 1001	ALADDIN SANE (orange label, gatefold sleeve & lyric inner sleeve)	25
73	RCA RS 1003	PIN UPS (LP, insert, orange label)	20
74	RCA APLI 0576	DIAMOND DOGS (LP, gatefold sleeve, orange label)	15
74	RCA APL 2-0771	DAVID LIVE (2-LP, 1st pressing, gatefold sleeve, orange label, photos on inners. 1st pressing has July 14th and 15th dates on inside cover, later pressings from 1974 have corrected dates of July 12nd and 13th)	20
76	RCA APL 1 1327	STATION TO STATION (LP, 1st pressing, 'Garrodprint Ltd' on sleeve with 'XX' in top right corner, matt orange label, lyric inner with cat no, Matrix numbers: two sets crossed out before APLI-1327-A-1E/B-1E)	40
76	RCA RS 1055	CHANGESONEBOWIE (with 'sax' version of "John I'm Only Dancing")	25

76	RCA APLI 1327	STATION TO STATION (with original colour proof sleeve)	500
77	RCA INTS 5065	LOW (red vinyl, semi-official 'factory custom pressing')	500
77	RCA PL12030	LOW (LP, insert, fan club flyer, stickered sleeve)	20
77	RCA PL12030	LOW (LP, insert, stickered sleeve)	12
77	RCA PL 12522	HEROES (LP, with insert)	20
78	RCA PL 02913	STAGE (2-LP, gatefold sleeve, yellow vinyl)	20
80	RCA BOW LP 2	SCARY MONSTERS (AND SUPER CREEPS) (purple vinyl, semi-official 'factory custom pressing')	600
80	RCA BOWLP2	SCARY MONSTERS AND SUPER CREEPS	20
80	K-Tel NE 1111	THE BEST OF BOWIE (with incorrect tracklisting)	12
81	RCA BL 43606	CHRISTIANE F. WIR KINDER VOM BAHNOF ZOO (soundtrack)	12
83	EMI America AMLP 3029	LET'S DANCE (picture disc)	12
84	RCA BOPIC 3	ZIGGY STARDUST (picture disc with numbered insert)	18
84	RCA BOPIC 5	DIAMOND DOGS (picture disc with numbered insert)	18
84	RCA BOPIC 4	PIN-UPS (picture disc with numbered insert)	18
84	RCA BOPIC 2	HUNKY DORY (picture disc with numbered insert)	18
84	RCA BOPIC 1	ALADDIN SANE (picture disc with numbered insert)	18
90	EMI EMC 3571	SPACE ODDITY (LP, 1990 reissue, gatefold with extra tracks)	25
90	EMI EMC 3577	ZIGGY STARDUST (LP, 1990 reissue, gatefold with unreleased tracks)	20
90	EMI EMC 3579	ALADDIN SANE (LP, 1990 reissue, gatefold)	12
94	MAINMAN GYLP 002	SANTA MONICA LIVE '72 (2xLP, clear vinyl)	40
95	RCA 307021	EXCERPTS FROM OUTSIDE (with 12" booklet & lyric sheet)	50
97	EMI TVC1	ZIGGY STARDUST (LP, 1997 reissue, EMI Centenary edition)	20
97	RCA 44949	EARTHLING (gatefold sleeve)	50
03	EMI 0724359451121	SOUND AND VISION (4-CD box set with booklet)	25

ALBUMS : CDS

84	Deram 800 087-2	DAVID BOWIE (withdrawn with white title)	60
85	RCA PD 84702	THE RISE AND FALL OF ZIGGY STARDUST AND THE SPIDERS FROM MARS (withdrawn)	20
84	RCA PD 84202	CHANGESTWOBOWIE (withdrawn)	30
84	RCA PD 89002	STAGE (2-CD, withdrawn)	40
84	RCA PD 94792	GOLDEN YEARS (withdrawn)	30
84	RCA PD 84234	LODGER (withdrawn)	20
84	RCA PD 84919	FAME AND FASHION (ALL TIME GREATEST HITS) (withdrawn)	50
84	RCA PD 83856	LOW (withdrawn)	20
84	RCA PD 83857	'HEROES' (withdrawn)	20
85	RCA PD 84813	SPACE ODDITY (withdrawn)	25
85	RCA PD 84654	THE MAN WHO SOLD THE WORLD (withdrawn)	25
85	RCA PD 84623	HUNKY DORY (withdrawn)	20
85	RCA PD 83890	ALADDIN SANE (withdrawn)	20
85	RCA PD 83889	DIAMOND DOGS (withdrawn)	25
85	RCA PD 84653	PIN-UPS (withdrawn)	20
85	RCA PD 80998	YOUNG AMERICANS (withdrawn)	20
85	RCA PD 81732	CHANGESONEBOWIE (withdrawn)	35
85	RCA PD 81327	STATION TO STATION (withdrawn)	25
85	RCA PD 83647	SCARY MONSTERS (AND SUPER CREEPS) (withdrawn)	25
86	RCA PD 82743	PETER AND THE WOLF (withdrawn)	20
93	Arista 17822-2	THE BUDDHA OF SUBURBIA (special edition in clear plastic case, with novel)	22

PROMOS

71	Gem BOWPROMO 1	BOWPROMO (LP, white label only, also known as HUNKY DORY SAMPLER Some with handwritten sleeve or Gem sticker on A-side, B-side features DANA GILLESPIE, 500 only)	1500
77	RCA BOW-1E	From The New Album 'Low' (1-sided promo, excerpts from Speed Of Life, Breaking Glass, What In The World, Sound And Vision)	1500
83	RCA LIFETIMES 1	LIFETIMES (LP, promo, numbered, with insert)	35
90	BMG BOW 908	SO FAR (CD, 8-track sampler for "Sound & Vision" box set)	50
91	Rykodisc VRCD 0142	BOWIE/ENO: IT'S TIME TO LISTEN (CD, 9-track sampler from Ryko reissues; includes "Sound + Vision", "Be My Wife", "Some Are", "Heroes", "Joe The Lion", Abdulmajid, DJ, Boys Keep Swinging, Look Back in Anger)	25
93	EMI BOWIE 1	SELECTIONS FROM THE SINGLES COLLECTION 10-track sampler,card p/s, promo only	18
93	BMG MEAT 1	Pallas Athena (12", white label, no p/s, includes two exclusive Meat Beat Manifesto remixes)	40
93	Back To Basics HOME 1	Night Flights/(B-side by Moodswings) (12")	18
93	BBC MMCD 0072	BBC SESSIONS 1969-1972 (CD, picture disc, promo-only, withdrawn)	75
95	RCA HALLO 2	Hallo Spaceboy (12" Remix) (12", 1-sided, no p/s)	18
95	BMG SOLO 1	EXCLUSIVE TOUR CD: Strangers When We Meet/MORRISSEY: The Boy Racer (Outside Tour CD)	90
95	RCA OUT 1	The Heart's Filthy Lesson (12", 1-sided promo)	10
96	RCA SPACE 2	Hallo Spaceboy (12" Remix) (1-sided 12", some copies listed as RCA HALLO 2, no p/s)	25
96	RCA SPACE 3	Hallo Spaceboy (Double Click Mix)/Hallo Spaceboy (Instrumental)/ Hallo Spaceboy (Lost In Space Mix) (12", no p/s)	50
99	Virgin CDVX 2900	'hours...' (hologram sleeve)	15
99	Virgin CDVDJ 2900	'hours...' (CD, card sleeve)	20
99	EMI QUEENWL 28	Under Pressure (Remixes) (with Queen) (12", white label, unreleased mix, promo only)	30
99	EMI CDLRL 015	ALBUM SAMPLER (CD, 17-track sampler, promo only)	20

(see also Davie Jones & King Bees, Davy Jones & Lower Third, Manish Boys, Arnold Corns, Spiders From Mars, Mick Ronson, Queen, Tao Jones Index, Bing Crosby)

DAVID BOWIE AND BING CROSBY

82	RCA BOW 12 (PRO)	Peace On Earth/Little Drummer Boy//Dialogue/Peace On Earth/LDB (Demo copy, p/s)	20
82	RCA BOW 12	Peace On Earth/Little Drummer Boy/Fantastic Voyage (push-out centre, p/s)	7
82	RCA BOW 12	Peace On Earth/Little Drummer Boy/Fantastic Voyage (solid centre, p/s)	8
82	RCA BOW 12	Peace On Earth/Little Drummer Boy/Fantastic Voyage (Irish pressing, p/s)	15

(see also David Bowie, Bing Crosby)

CANDY BOWMAN

81	RCA RCAT 148	Since I Found You/I Wanna Feel Your Love (12")	15

BOWMAN-HYDE PLAYERS

61	Ember EMB S 141	I Like A Little Honey/Teenage Kiss	8
61	Parlophone PMC 1155	SING ME A SOUVENIR (LP)	20

ALAN BOWN (SET)

65	Pye 7N 15934	Can't Let Her Go/I'm The One	25

Alan BOWN SET/JIMMY JAMES & VAGABONDS

66	Pye 7N 17084	Baby Don't Push Me/Everything's Gonna Be Alright	25
66	Pye 7N 17148	Headline News/Mister Pleasure	50
66	Pye 7N 17192	Emergency 999/Settle Down	60
67	Pye 7N 17256	Gonna Fix You Good (Everytime You're Bad)/I Really Really Care	50
67	Music Factory CUB 1	We Can Help You/Magic Handkerchief (as the Alan Bown!)	12
67	MGM MGM 1355	Toyland/Technicolour Dream	12
68	MGM MGM 1387	Story Book/Little Lesley	25
69	Deram DM 259	Still As Stone/Wrong Idea	10
69	Deram DM 278	Gypsy Girl/All I Can	6
70	Island WIP 6091	Pyramid/Crash Landing	5
75	CBS 3721	Rockford Files/I Don't Know	6
75	CBS 3366	Moanin'/Time To Change	6
68	Music Factory CUB LM/LS 1	OUTWARD BOWN (LP)	70
69	Deram DML/SML 1049	THE ALAN BOWN! (LP)	50
70	Island ILPS 9131	LISTEN (LP, with inner sleeve)	25
71	Island ILPS 9163	STRETCHING OUT (LP, gatefold sleeve)	25

(see also Robert Palmer, John Barry Seven, Bronco, Jonesy)

ALAN BOWN SET/JIMMY JAMES & VAGABONDS

68	Pye N(S)PL 18156	LONDON SWINGS - LIVE AT THE MARQUEE CLUB (LP, 1 side each)	30

(see also Jimmy James & Vagabonds)

ANDREW BOWN

70	Parlophone R 5856	Tarot (Theme From 'Ace Of Wands')/Lulli Rides Again	100

(see also Andy Bown)

ANDY BOWN

75	GM GMS 9039	Supersonic/Feeling Better	10
79	EMI EMI 2906	Another Shipwreck/Another Night With You	6
79	EMI EMI 2943	Good Advice/One More Chance	5
81	EMI EMI 5245	Say It Was Magic/One Forward Two Back Again (in p/s)	10
82	EMI EMI 5312	Marianne/One Forward Two Back Again	5
82	EMI EMI 5372	Help Me/Marianne (p/s)	5
72	Mercury 6310 002	GONE TO MY HEAD (LP)	20
73	GM GML 1001	SWEET WILLIAM (LP)	20

(see also Andrew Bown, Herd, Judas Jump, Status Quo, Rossi & Frost, Storyteller)

BOX CAR RACER

02	MCA MCS 40290	I Feel So/Cat Like Thief (picture disc)	12

(see also Blink 182)

DAVID BOX

64	London HLU 9874	If You Can't Say Something Nice/Sweet Sweet Day	20
64	London HLU 9924	Little Lonely Summer Girl/No One Will Ever Know	20

(see also Crickets)

BOXER

75	Virgin VDJ 12	All The Time In The World/Don't Wait (12", promo only)	15
75	Virgin V 2049	BELOW THE BELT (LP, gatefold sleeve with uncensored full-frontal back cover)	30
76	Virgin V2049	BELOW THE BELT (LP, censored sleeve)	15
76	Virgin V 2073	BLOODLETTING (LP, withdrawn)	100

(see also Patto, Timebox, Koobas, May Blitz)

BOX TOPS

67	Stateside SS 2044	The Letter/Happy Times	10
67	Stateside SS 2070	Neon Rainbow/She Knows How	12
68	Bell BLL 1001	Cry Like A Baby/The Door You Closed To Me	8
68	Bell BLL 1017	Choo Choo Train/Fields Of Clover	6
68	Bell BLL 1035	I Met Her In Church/People Gonna Talk	5
69	Bell BLL 1045	Sandman/Sweet Cream Ladies, Forward March	5
69	Bell BLL 1063	I Shall Be Released/I Must Be The Devil	5
69	Bell BLL 1068	Soul Deep/The Happy Song	6
69	Bell BLL 1084	Turn On A Dream/Together	5
70	Bell BLL 1097	You Keep Tightening Up On Me/Come On Honey	5
73	London HLU 10402	Sugar Creek Woman/It's All Over	5
68	Stateside (S)SL 10218	THE LETTER/NEON RAINBOW (LP)	20
68	Bell MBLL/SBLL 105	CRY LIKE A BABY (LP)	20
69	Bell MBLL/SBLL 108	NON-STOP (LP)	20
69	Bell SBLL 120	DIMENSIONS (LP)	20

(see also Big Star, Alex Chilton)

DENNY BOYCE & HIS ORCHESTRA/RHYTHM

58	Oriole CB 1458	Bad Boy/When Your Hair Has Turned To Silver	10

JUNIOR BOYCE (ACTUALLY JR. BYLES)

77	Observer OB 004	Natty Dreadlocks/Sick-More Tree/What Kind Of World/Sic Easy Stepping (12", with Ranking Buckers)	30

(see also Junior Byles)

TOMMY BOYCE

65	MGM MGM 1287	Pretty Thing/I Don't Have To Worry 'Bout You	10

TOMMY BOYCE & BOBBY HART

67	A&M AMS 705	Out And About/My Little Chickadee	5
67	A&M AMS 710	Sometimes She's A Little Girl/Love Every Day	5
68	A&M AMS 714	I Wonder What She's Doing Tonight?/Ambushers	5
68	A&M AMS 722	Goodbye Baby/Where Angels Go Trouble Follows	5
68	A&M AMS 729	Alice Long (You're Still My Favourite Girlfriend)/P.O. Box 9847	5
67	A&M AML 907	TEST PATTERNS (LP)	25

(see also Monkees, Tommy Boyce)

EDDIE BOYD

66	Blue Horizon 45 BH 1009	It's So Miserable To Be Alone/Empty Arms	150
67	Blue Horizon 57-3137	The Big Boat/Sent For You Yesterday (with Fleetwood Mac)	30
62	Esquire EP 247	BOYD'S BLUES (EP, as Eddie Boyd Blues Combo)	70
65	Fontana SFJL 905	FIVE LONG YEARS (LP)	60

67	Decca LK/SKL 4872	EDDIE BOYD AND HIS BLUES BAND FEATURING PETER GREEN (LP) 120
68	Blue Horizon 7-63202	7936 SOUTH RHODES (LP, with Fleetwood Mac)...70
68	Storyville SLP 4054	IN CONCERT (LP) 25

(see also Fleetwood Mac)

EDDIE BOYD/BUDDY GUY
66	Chess CRE 6009	WITH THE BLUES (EP, 2 tracks each) 25

(see also Buddy Guy)

JIMMY BOYD
53	Columbia SCM 5072	I Saw Mommy Kissing Santa Claus/Little Train A-Chuggin' In My Heart 10

CHARLES BOYER
65	London HL 10002	Where Does Love Go/PERRY BOTKIN JR: Theme From Where Love Goes............5
60	London HAT 8268	WHERE DOES LOVE GO (LP)..15

BOY FRIDAY
70	Downtown 470	Girl/Version Girl...12

BOY FRIDAY (& GROOVERS)
70	Downtown DT 470	Version Girl/Grumble Man 15
71	Downtown DT 471	Music So Good/Right Track (both with Groovers)...8
71	Downtown DT 472	Sounds I Remember/JOAN LONG: Reconsider Our Love 12
71	Downtown DT 473	Take A Message Ruby/Second Note 12
71	Downtown DT 476	There'll Always Be Sunshine/Sunshine Track 7
71	Downtown DT 477	Hot Pants Girl/Raunchy...12
71	Downtown DT 481	El Raunchy/Conversation (as Boy Friday & Collins) 6
71	J-Dan JDN 4416	I Don't Want No War/Third Note Swing 7
71	J-Dan JDN 4418	Situation Version/OUR BAND: Keep Tracking 7

(see also Dandy & Superboys)

BOYFRIENDS
78	United Artists UP 36424	I'm In Love Today/Saturday Night (p/s) 10
78	United Artists UP 36442	Jenny/Don't Ask Me To Explain (p/s) 10
78	United Artists UP 36478	Last Bus Home/Romance (p/s) 10

(see also Vibrators)

BOYFRIENDS
82	Plastic PRES 001	Boyfriend/Give A Little, Take A Little (p/s)..40

BOY GEORGE
88	Virgin BOY 105-12	Live My Life/Live My Life (Klub Mix)/Live My Life (12" Club Remix) (12", poster sleeve)..8
98	More Protein PROT 112	Sad (Mixes)/Butterfly (Mixes) 8
98	More Protein (no cat. no.)	Open House With Boy George & Family (CD-ROM, available at selected concerts) 20

(see also Culture Club, Jesus Loves You)

BOY HAIRDRESSERS
88	53rd & 3rd AGARR T12	Golden Showers/Tidalwave/The Assumption As An Elevator (12", p/s)............25

(see also Teenage Fanclub, BMX Bandits, Clouds)

BOY KRAZY
91	Polydor PZCD 158	That's What Love Can Do (Extended Version)/One Thing Leads To Another/ That's What Love Can Do (7" version) (CD, p/s) 10
91	Polydor 828 403-2	BOY KRAZY (CD) 20

BILLY BOYLE
62	Decca F 11503	My Baby's Crazy 'Bout Elvis/Held For Questioning..15
63	Decca F 11709	I'm Coming Home/Sunday's Child 5
63	Columbia DB 7111	Lovers Hill/She's New To You 5
63	Columbia DB 7127	Hootin' In The Kitchen/Lover's Hill 6
64	Columbia DB 7294	Walk, Walk, Walkin'/My Baby Tonight (with Le Roys)......................................7
70	UPC UPC112	Lookin' For Love/Pisces Man 20

(see also Le Roys)

A. BOYNE
70	Punch PH 36	Oh My Darling (actually Audley Rollins)/DENNIS SMITH: Ball Of Confusion 10

BILLY BOYO
82	Greensleeves GRELD 89	Righteousness/Itie Title Girl (12") 15

BOYRACER
92	Fluff HONEY 2	Railway/Reverse (p/s) 10
93	Sarah SARAH 76	B IS FOR BOYRACER EP (p/s, insert)..12
93	Sarah SARAH 85	FROM PURITY TO PURGATORY EP (p/s, insert) 12
94	Sarah SARAH 96	PURE HATED EP (p/s, insert)...12

BOYS IN DARKNESS
81	Bid For Freedom BID 1	Back To France/A Man An Island (no p/s) 15
81	Champagne BUBL-702	Back To France/A Man An Island (p/s)...10
81	Champagne BUBLY-702	Back To France/A Man An Island (12" p/s)...12

BOYS (JAMAICA)
69	Duke DU 19	Easy Sound/AFROTONES: Freedom Sound..20

(see also Harry J. Allstars)

BOYS BLUE
65	HMV POP 1427	You Got What I Want/Take A Heart 50

(see also Jeff Elroy & Boys Blue)

BOYS (U.K.) (1)
64	Pye 7M 15726	It Ain't Fair/I Want You 100
63	Parlophone R 5027	Polaris/Jumpin'...20

BOYS (U.K.) (2)
77	NEMS NES 102	I Don't Care/Soda Pressing (p/s) 15
77	NEMS NES 111	First Time/Whatcha Gonna Do/Turning Grey (p/s) 15
78	NEMS NES 116	Brickfield Nights/Teacher's Pet (p/s) 10
79	Safari SAFE 21	Kamikaze/Bad Days (p/s, with booklet)..6
80	Safari SAFE 23	Terminal Love/I Love Me (p/s) 5

80	Safari SAFE 27	You Better Move On/Schoolgirls (p/s) 5
80	Safari SAFE 31	Weekend/Cool (p/s) 5
80	Safari SAFE 33	Let It Rain/Lucy (p/s) 6
77	NEMS NES 6001	THE BOYS (LP) 15
78	NEMS NEL 6015	ALTERNATIVE CHARTBUSTERS (LP, with inner sleeve) 15
79	Safari 1-2 BOYS	TO HELL WITH THE BOYS (LP, with songbook & stickered sleeve) 20
80	Safari BOYS 4	BOYS ONLY (LP) 15
90	Receiver RRPL 135	LIVE AT THE ROXY APRIL '77 (LP) 12

(see also Yobs, Rowdies, Hollywood Brats)

BOYS (U.K.) (3)

88	Cleversounds BOYS 1	Happy Days/Standard Avenue/Learn How To Dance (p/s) 8

(see also Ocean Colour Scene)

BOZ

66	Columbia DB 7832	You're Just The Kind Of Girl I Want/Isn't That So 30
66	Columbia DB 7889	Meeting Time/No (Ah) Body Knows The Blues 30
66	Columbia DB 7941	Pinocchio/Stay As You Are 10
66	Columbia DB 7972	The Baby Song/Carry On Screaming 20
68	Columbia DB 8406	I Shall Be Released/Down In The Flood 20
68	Columbia DB 8468	Light My Fire/Back Against The Wall 15

(see also King Crimson, Bad Company, Alexis Korner)

BOZOS

78	Other BOZ 101	Weekend Girl/Fool Out Of Me 25

JANET BRACE

55	Brunswick 05272	Teach Me Tonight/My Old Familiar Heartache...6

BRACKEN

79	Look LKLP 6438	PRINCE OF THE NORTHLANDS (LP, private pressing, with insert) 60

KIM & KELLY BRADEN

67	Columbia DB 8312	Didn't I/You're Leaving, She's Crying, I'm Laughing..5
68	Columbia DB 8421	Happiness Is/Sing A Rainbow 5

BOBBY BRADFORD

73	Emanem 302	LOVE'S DREAM (LP) 30

BRADFORD SINGERS

62	Stateside SL 10026	BLACK NATIVITY (LP) 12
64	Stateside SL 10083	ANGEL ON VACATION (LP) 12

GEORGE BRADLEY & HIS BAND

65	HMV POP 1459	Breakout/Vendetta 10

JAN BRADLEY

63	Pye International 7N 25182	Mama Didn't Lie/Lovers Like Me 40

MARTIN BRADLEY

80	Greenwich Village GVR 205	TIME CAN'T STAND STILL (LP) 15

OWEN BRADLEY (ORCHESTRA/QUINTET)

56	Brunswick 05528	Theme From "The Threepenny Opera"/Lights Of Vienna (with Orchestra)...............................5
57	Brunswick 05700	White Silver Sands/Midnight Blues (as Owen Bradley Quintet) 5
58	Brunswick 05736	Big Guitar/Sentimental Dream (as Owen Bradley Quintet) 20
60	Brunswick LAT 8327	THE BIG GUITAR (LP) 30

BRADLEY STRYDER

92	Rephlex CAT 001	BRADLEY'S BEAT (12" EP, logo sleeve)..20
96	Rephlex CAT 020	BRADLEY'S ROBOT (12" EP, poster p/s) 10

BUDDY BRADSHAW

59	Capitol CL 15036	Nothing You Can Say/Tonight I Walk Alone 10

(see also Owen Gray)

SONNY BRADSHAW QUINTET

62	TOp TD 106	This Is Happiness/Island In The Sun 25

SONNY BRADSHAW (& YOUNG JAMAICA)

61	Duke DK 1003	Yellow Birds/Festival Jump Up 10
71	Big Shot BI 576	Wig Wam/Peace And Love (as Sonny Bradshaw & Young Jamaica) 10

TINY BRADSHAW & HIS ORCHESTRA

54	Parlophone CMSP 3	South Of The Orient/Later (export issue) 15
54	Parlophone MSP 6118	The Gypsy/Spider Web 15
55	Parlophone DP 418	Bradshaw Boogie/Walkin' The Chalk Line (78, export issue) 10
55	Parlophone MSP 6145	Overflow/Don't Worry 'Bout Me 15
54	Parlophone GEP 8507	TRAIN KEPT A ROLLING (EP) 50
56	Parlophone GEP 8552	POMPTON TURNPIKE (EP) 20
50s	Parlophone CGEP 2	TINY BRADSHAW (export EP) 25

TINY BRADSHAW ORCHESTRA/WYNONIE HARRIS

70	Polydor 623 273	KINGS OF RHYTHM AND BLUES (LP, 1 side each)...15

(see also Wynonie Harris)

DON BRADSHAW-LEATHER

72	Distance DIST 101	DISTANCE BETWEEN US (2-LP, gatefold sleeve, private pressing)...80

BOB BRADY & CONCHORDS

68	Bell BLL 1025	Everybody's Goin' To The Love-In/It's Been A Long Time Between Kisses 15
70	Bell BLL 1114	Everybody's Goin' To The Love-In/It's Been A Long Time Between Kisses (reissue) 5

JOE BRADY

63	Pye 7N 15569	The Great Train Robbery/Is THis Where We Say Goodbye?..6

MAJELLA BRADY

65	Rex R11015	Light In My Window/Girl 8

PHIL BRADY & THE RANCH SET

67	Go AJ 11406	Lonesome For You/Please Come Back 20

VICTOR BRADY
70	Polydor	BROWN RAIN (LP)	20

BRADY BUNCH
73	Paramount SPFL 284	MEET THE BRADY BUNCH (LP)	15

AL 'TNT' BRAGGS
66	Vocalion VP 9278	Earthquake/How Long (Do You Hold On)	20
66	Vocalion VP 9278	Earthquake/How Long (Do You Hold On) (DJ Copy)	60
68	Action ACT 4506	Earthquake/How Long (Do You Hold On) (reissue)	15
69	Action ACT 4526	I'm A Good Man/I Like What You Do To Me	15
65	Vocalion VEP 170163	AL 'TNT' BRAGGS (EP)	125

ERNEL BRAHAM
66	Rio R 79	Musical Fight/EDWARDS ALLSTARS: Pipeline	30

(see also Kent Walker)

ROY BRAHAM
64	R&B 166	Believe Me/Red Sea	30

BRAIN
67	Parlophone R 5595	Nightmares In Red/Kick The Donkey	160
87	Bam Caruso OPRA 63	Nightmares In Red/SRC: Black Sheep (jukebox edition, die-cut company sleeve)	10

(see also Giles Giles & Fripp, Trendsetters Ltd, League Of Gentlemen)

BRAIN DONOR
01	Impressario IMPODDLP001	LOVE PEACE AND FUCK (2-LP, green & white vinyl)	15
06	Invada INV031LP	DRAIN'D BONER (12" gatefold, picture disc)	10

BRAINBOX
69	Parlophone R 5775	Woman's Gone/Down Man	20
70	Parlophone R 5842	So Helpless/To You	15
70	Parlophone PCS 7094	BRAINBOX (LP, black/silver/white boxed Parlophone label)	200

(see also Jan Akkerman, Hunters, Focus)

BRAINCHILD
70	A&M AMS 805	Cage/Autobiography	10
70	A&M AMLS 979	HEALING OF THE LUNATIC OWL (LP, brown label)	70

BRAINIAC 5
80	Roach RR 5002	Working/Feel (p/s)	10
78	Roach RREP 5001	MUSHY DOUBT (EP, 33rpm, p/s)	10

BRAINKILLERS
93	VIbe Alive VALV 36	Crackhead/Dark Moon/Stupid/This Is Where It Takes Us (12", with Lewi Cifer)	25
93	VIbe Alive VALV 76	On A Different Mission/One Stype/Hurt Me/Girl U Look Good (12", stickered die-cut paper sleeve, with Lewi Cifer)	20
94	3rd Party, Kemet KM3RD#1	BORDER LINE EP (with FAMILY OF INTELLIGENCE) (12")	20
94	3rd Party 3RD 10	Screwface Part 2 (Hardcore Mix)/Screwface Part 3 (Mellow Mix) (12")	8

BRAINSTORM
79	Miracle M5	Lovin' Is Really My Game/Stormin' (12", red or black vinyl no p/s)	20

BRAINTAX
92	Low Life Low 2	FAT HEAD (EP 12" - 500 pressed)	45
97	Low Life Low 4	FUTURE YEARS (EP, 12")	30
99	Low Life Low 9	THE TRAVEL SHOW (EP, 12")	8
00	Low Life Low 11	Hardworking/Escuchame/First Joint (12", p/s)	8
06	Low Life Low 44	D90 Rules (Vocal)/D90 Rules (Instrumental)	5

BRAKES
80	Magnet MAGL	FOR WHY YOU KICKA MY DONKEY? (LP)	15

WILFRED BRAMBELL
63	Parlophone R 5058	Secondhand/Ragtime Ragabone Man	8

DELANEY BRAMLETT
64	Vocalion VP 9227	Heartbreak Hotel/You Never Looked Sweeter	15
65	Vocalion VP 9237	Liverpool Lou/You Have No Choice	30
65	Vocalion VP 9237	Liverpool Lou/You Have No Choice (DJ Copy)	50

(see also Delaney & Bonnie, King Curtis with Delaney & Friends)

BRAM STOKER
72	Windmill WMD 117	HEAVY ROCK SPECTACULAR (LP)	25

BILL BRAMWELL
58	Starlite ST45 004	My Old Man/Shoutin' In That Amen Corner	10
60	Decca F 11309	Candid Camera Theme/Frederika	5

BRAN
74	Gwawr GWA 104	BRAN EP	50
74	Sain 1038M	AIL DDECHRA (LP)	65
75	Sain 1038M	AIL-DDECHRA (LP)	300
76	Sain 1070M	HEDFAN (LP)	100
78	Sain 1120M	GWRACH Y NOS (LP)	40

BRAND
64	Piccadilly 7N 35216	I'm A Lover Not A Fighter/Zulu Stomp	100

BRAND NEW
03	Eat Sleep	Jude Law And A Semester Abroad/Am I Wrong (p/s)	30
03	Sore Point SORE 004S	The Quiet Things That No One Ever Knows/Jude Law And A Session Abroad (live in session) (die-cut sleeve, red vinyl)	15
04	Sore Point SORE 0145	The Quiet Things That No One Ever Knows/The No Seatbelt Song (live) (p/s, green vinyl)	8
04	Sore Point SORE 011S	Sic Transit Gloria...Glory Fades/Jaws Theme Swimming (Demo) (pink vinyl)	15

BRAND NEW HEAVIES
91	Acid Jazz JAZID 39P	Never Stop (12", company sleeve, withdrawn)	20

BILL BRANDON
73	Mercury 6052 186	I Am Free Of Your Love/(Take Another Little) Piece Of My Heart	8

JOHNNY BRANDON
56	Parlophone MSP 6238	Rock-A-Bye Baby/Lonely Lips	60
56	Parlophone R 4207	Shim Sham Shuffle/I Didn't Know	60
56	Decca F 10778	Glendora/Song For A Summer Night	20
57	Decca F 10858	Nothing Is Too Good For You/A Sort-Of-A-Feeling	10
59	Top Rank JAR 241	Santa Claus Jnr./I Heard A Bluebird Sing	5
55	Pye NEP 24003	JOHNNY BRANDON HITS (EP)	15

KIRK BRANDON & PACK OF LIES
87	SS SS1N2/SS2N1	KIRK BRANDON AND THE PACK OF LIES (EP)	8

(see also Theatre Of Hate, Spear Of Destiny, Senate, Pack)

TONY BRANDON
68	MGM MGM 1401	Candy Kisses/Get Going Baby	5
72	Chapter 1 SCH 178	Sleep Little Children/Juice	5

VERN BRANDON
62	Decca F 11472	Let Me Be The One/Gotta Know The Reason	20

BRAND X
79	Charisma CB 340-12	Soho/Dance Of The Illegal Aliens/Noddy Goes To Sweden/ Pool Room Blues (12", p/s)	8

(see also Phil Collins)

BRANDY BOYS
65	Columbia DB 7507	Gale Winds/Don't Come Knocking At My Door	10

BRANDY WINE BRIDGE
77	Cottage COT 311	THE GREY LADY (LP, as Brandywinebridge)	25
78	Cottage COT 321	AN ENGLISH MEADOW (LP, hand-drawn sleeve with insert)	25

BRANDY WINE SINGERS
68	President PT 204	Mandy/Two Little Boys	6

LINDA BRANNON
63	Columbia DB 7156	Funny Face/Will It Last	10

JOHNNY BRANTLEY'S ALL STARS
58	London HLU 8606	The Place/Pot Luck	20
58	London HLU 8606	The Place/Pot Luck (78 rpm)	10

BRASS ALLEY
73	Alaska ALA 11	You Better Run/Be My Friend	20

(see under Various Artists Eps)

BRASS CONSTRUCTION
75	United Artists UP 617	Movin'/Changin' (12")	10
82	United Artists UAS 29923	BRASS CONSTRUCTION (LP)	15

ANDRÉ BRASSEUR
65	Pye International 7N 25332	Early Bird Satellite/Special 230	10
67	CBS 202557	The Kid/Holiday	20
67	CBS 202557	The Kid/Holiday (DJ Copy)	50
71	CBS 2557	The Kid/Holiday (reissue)	8
66	CBS 62858	TASTY (LP)	15

BRASS INCORPORATED
70	Pye International 7N 25520	At The Sign Of The Swinging Cymbal/Just Like That	25

BRASS MONKEY
71	Philips 6303 025	BRASS MONKEY (LP)	30
71	Philips 6303 027	NO VISIBLE MEANS OF SUPPORT (LP)	30

BRASS TACKS
68	Big T BIG 110	I'll Keep On Holding On/Let The Sunshine In	35
68	Big T BIG 114	Maxwell Ferguson/Sunshine After The Rain	100

BRASS WYNDS
67	Pye 7N 17255	Music To Watch Girls By/Sugar's Sweet	5

BRATZ
80	A Famous Record AFR 1	The Bratz Are Coming/Coast To Coast/Everyone Wants To Be Elvis (p/s)	6

RICHARD BRAUTIGAN
69	Zapple ZAPPLE 03	LISTENING TO RICHARD BRAUTIGAN (LP, unreleased, acetates exist)	750

CEDRIC BRAVO
65	Ska Beat JB 229	Merry Christmas/Sugar Baby	15

LOS BRAVOS
66	Decca F 22419	Black Is Black/I Want A Name	5
66	Decca F 22484	I Don't Care/Don't Be Left Out In The Cold	5
66	Decca F 22529	Going Nowhere/Brand New Baby	20
67	Decca F 22615	I'm All Ears/You'll Never Get The Chances Again	8
67	Decca F 22682	Like Nobody Else/Wearing A Smile	5
68	Decca F 22765	Bring A Little Lovin'/Make It Last	12
69	Decca F 22853	Save Me, Save Me/Baby I Love You Because I Need You	5
70	Decca F 13064	People Talking Around/Every Dog Has His Night	5
66	Decca LK 4822	BLACK IS BLACK (LP)	18
68	Decca LK/SKL 4905	LOS BRAVOS (LP)	25

(see also Mike Kennedy)

ANTHONY BRAXTON
85	Leo 414/415/416	QUARTET (2-LP box set with insert)	35

ANTHONY BRAXTON & DEREK BAILEY
73	Emanem 601	DUO (2-LP)	30
84	Incus INCUS 43	ROYAL VOLUME 1 (LP)	20

(see also Derek Bailey)

PRISCILLA BRAZIER
| 74 | Dovetail DOVE 9 | PRISCILLA BRAZIER (LP) | 40 |
| 76 | Key KL 038 | SOMETHING BEAUTIFUL (LP) | 35 |

BREAD
| 69 | Elektra EKS 74044 | BREAD (LP) | 25 |

(see also David Gates, Pleasure Fair)

BREAD & BEER BAND
69	Decca F 12891	Dick Barton Theme (The Devil's Gallop)/Breakdown Blues	75
72	Decca F 13354	Dick Barton Theme (The Devil's Gallop)/Breakdown Blues (reissue)	40
69	Rubbish (no cat. no.)	THE BREAD AND BEER BAND (LP, 1 copy known to exist)	2000

(see also Elton John, Caleb)

BREAD, LOVE & DREAMS
69	Decca F 12958	Virgin Kiss/Switch Out The Sun	22
69	Decca LK/SKL 5008	BREAD, LOVE AND DREAMS (LP, unboxed large Decca on label)	200
70	Decca LK/SKL 5048	THE STRANGE TALE OF CAPTAIN SHANNON AND THE HUNCHBACK FROM GIGHA (LP, small boxed Decca label)	175
71	Decca SKL 5081	AMARYLLIS (LP, small boxed Decca label)	800

(see also Human Beast)

BREAKAWAYS
62	Pye 7N 15471	He's A Rebel/Wishing Star	18
63	Pye 7N 15585	That Boy Of Mine/Here She Comes	15
64	Pye 7N 15618	That's How It Goes/He Doesn't Love Me	15
65	Pye 7N 15973	Danny Boy/Your Kind Of Love	15
67	CBS 2833	Sacred Love/Don't Be A Baby	10
68	MCA MU 1018	Santo Domingo/So In Love Are We	10

(see also Vernons Girls, Burt Bacharach Orchestra, Mike Patto, Ken Cope, Sharades, De Laine Sisters)

BREAKDOWN
| 77 | MCP 001 | MEET ME ON THE HIGHWAY (LP, private pressing with insert) | 25 |

BREAKERS
| 81 | Riot RS 1001 | Radio Love/My Momma Told Me (p/s) | 20 |

BREAKING THE ILLUSION
| 92 | Lowlife LOW 1 | WHERE WILL IT END? (EP, 12" p/s, 1000 pressed) | 15 |
| 93 | Lowlife LOW 3 | LOSE YOUR ILLUSION (EP) | 12 |

BREAKOUT
| 81 | Guardian GRC 101 | Wall Of Solitude/Get Out Fight Back | 80 |

BREAKTHRU'
| 68 | Mercury MF 1066 | Ice Cream Tree/Julius Caesar | 25 |

BREAKWATER
| 86 | Arista ARIST 12674 | Say You Love Me Girl/Work It Out (12", p/s) | 15 |

BREATHING AGE
| 81 | Edge EDGE 13 | Here We Go/Camera Room (p/s) | 10 |

BREATHLESS
| 81 | Magnum Force MFEP 005 | SOCK HOP BOPPIN' (EP) | 20 |

PATRICIA BREDIN
| 59 | Top Rank JAR 257 | Till The Right Times Comes/I Live To Love You | 6 |

BREEDERS
90	4AD CAD 0006	POD (LP)	20
93	4AD CAD 3014	LAST SPLASH (LP, with free 7")	30
08	4AD CAD 2803	MOUNTAIN BATTLES (LP, inner sleeve and booklet)	15

JIMMY BREEDLOVE
57	London HLE 8490	Over Somebody Else's Shoulder/That's My Baby	100
57	London HLE 8490	Over Somebody Else's Shoulder/That's My Baby (78)	50
62	Pye International 7N 25121	You're Following Me/Fabulous	30
75	Pye Disco Demand DDS 110	I Can't Help Loving You/I Saw You	5

(see also Cues)

BOBBY BREEN
| 62 | Fontana 373 | When The Lights Go Out/Everybody Twist | 15 |

BUDDY BREGMAN & HIS ORCHESTRA
| 56 | HMV 7MC 40 | Theme From "Picnic"/Riviera (export issue) | 5 |

BRELLO CABAL
| 67 | CBS 3214 | Margarine Flavoured Pineapple Chunk/Follow That (as The Brello Cabal) | 10 |

(see also Anita Harris)

BEVERLEY BREMERS
72	Wand WN 18	Get Smart Girl/Don't Say You Don't Remember	15
72	Wand WN 28	We're Free/Colours Of Love	5
72	Wand WN 34	I'll Make You Music/I Made A Man Out Of You Jimmy	5

BRENDA & TABULATIONS
67	London HL 10127	Dry Your Eyes/The Wash	30
67	London HL 10174	When You're Gone/Hey Boy	25
68	Direction 58-3678	Baby You're So Right For Me/To The One I Love	10
69	Action ACT 4541	That's In The Past/I Can't Get Over Her	30
70	London HL 10325	A Child No One Wanted/'Scuse Uz Y'all	15
71	CBS 7279	Right On The Tip of My Tongue/Always And Forever	8
73	Epic EPC 1361	One Girl Too Late/The Magic Of Your Love	8
69	Action ACLP 6003	DRY YOUR EYES (LP)	50

BUDDY BRENNAN QUARTET
| 60 | London HLU 9049 | Big River/The Chase | 7 |

ROSE BRENNAN
| 55 | HMV 7M 299 | Ding Dong/Sincerely | 15 |

Walter BRENNAN

55	HMV 7M 328	Wake The Town And Tell The People/Ten Little Kisses	7
56	HMV 7M 360	You Are My Love/My Dublin Bay	7
56	HMV 7M 383	Band Of Gold/My Believing Heart	7
57	HMV POP 302	Without Love (There Is Nothing)/Tra La La	7
59	Top Rank JAR 152	Johnny Let Me Go/My Summer Diary	7
62	Philips BBE 12530	THE LUCK OF THE IRISH (EP)	8
63	Wing WL 1128	IRISH PUB FAVOURITES (EP)	8

WALTER BRENNAN

60	London HLD 9148	Dutchman's Gold/Back To The Farm	7
62	Liberty LIB 55436	Old Rivers/Epic Ride Of John H Glenn	5
62	Liberty LIB 55477	Houdini/The Old Kelly Place	5
63	Liberty LIB 55508	Mama Sang A Song/Who Will Take Gramma	5
64	Liberty LBY 1249	GUNFIGHT AT THE OK CORRAL (LP)	20

BRENT FORD & NYLONS

78	Brumbeat	19th Nervous Breakdown/Big Rock Candy Mountain (handmade foldout p/s)	50

TONY BRENT

56	Columbia DB 3844	Cindy Oh Cindy/Two Innocent Hearts	8
57	Columbia DB 3950	Dark Moon/The Game Of Love (A-One and A-Two)	7
57	Columbia DB 4043	Love By The Jukebox Light/We Belong Together	7
58	Columbia DB 4066	The Hours Will Soon Roll By/Don't Save Your Love For Me	6
58	Columbia DB 4177	Girl Of My Dreams/Don't Play That Melody	5
59	Columbia DB 4304	Why Should I Be Lonely/My Little Room	5
58	Columbia SEG 7824	TONY CALLS THE TUNE (EP)	10
58	Columbia SEG 7869	TIME FOR TONY (EP)	10
59	Columbia SEG 8019	OFF STAGE (EP)	10
59	Columbia SEG 8040	OFF STAGE NO. 2 (EP)	10
58	Columbia 33S 1125	OFF STAGE (10" LP)	20
60	Columbia SCX 3288	TONY TAKES FIVE (LP, stereo)	15
60	Columbia 33SX 1200	TONY TAKES FIVE (LP, mono)	15

(see also Coronets)

TONY BRENT & JULIE DAWN

53	Columbia SCM 5029	Ding Dong Boogie/When Are We Gonna Get Married?	15

(see also Julie Dawn)

BRENTWOOD ROAD ALLSTARS

70	Bamboo BAM 23	Love At First Sight/MAYTALS: Life Could Be A Dream	30
70	Bamboo BAM 25	Soul Shake/Moon Ride	30

GERRY BRERETON

53	Parlophone MSP 6056	From Here To Eternity/If You've Never Been In Love	7
54	Parlophone MSP 6081	The Book/Somewhere Someone (Is Saying A Prayer)	7
55	Columbia SCM 5195	A Million Helping Hands/Fair Sets The Wind For Love	7

(see also Eddie Calvert)

PAUL BRETT('S SAGE)

70	Pye 7N 17974	Three D Mona Lisa/Mediterranean Lazy Heat Wave	15
71	Dawn DNX 2508	Reason For Your Askin'/Everlasting Butterfly/Savannah Ladies/ To Everyman (Freedom) (p/s)	10
71	Dawn DNS 1010	Goodbye Forever/Good Old Fashioned Funky Kind Of Music	6
72	Dawn DNS 1021	Dahlia/Cottage Made For Two	6
73	Bradley's BRAD 301	Mr. Custer/Good Times, Hard Times	6
73	Bradley's BRAD 305	Summer Driftin'/Clocks (p/s)	7
70	Pye NSPL 18347	PAUL BRETT SAGE (LP, blue/black label with logo banner on top)	60
71	Dawn DNLS 3021	JUBILATION FOUNDRY (LP, gatefold sleeve, as Paul Brett's Sage, orange label)	40
72	Dawn DNLS 3032	SCHIZOPHRENIA (LP, foldout sleeve, as Paul Brett's Sage, lilac label)	40
73	Bradley's BRADL 1001	PAUL BRETT (LP, fully laminate envelope sleeve with inner)	30
73	Bradley's BRADL 1004	CLOCKS (LP)	15
75	PF private pressing PF 001	PHOENIX FUTURE (LP, 500 only, numbered on rear sleeve)	30
70s	private pressing	MUSIC MANIFOLD (LP, library issue)	25

(see also Elmer Gantry's Velvet Opera, Fire)

STEVE BRETT & MAVERICKS

65	Columbia DB 7470	Wishing/Anything That's Part Of You	85
65	Columbia DB 7581	Sad, Lonely And Blue/Candy	125
65	Columbia DB 7794	Sugar Shack/Chains On My Heart	100

(see also 'N Betweens, Slade)

TONY BREVETT

71	Supreme SUP 224	Don't Get Weary/BREVETT ALLSTARS: Version	15
71	Bullet BU 497	So Ashamed/GREGORY ISAACS: My Only Lover	10
74	Dip DL 5028	You Don't Love Me/Version	7
76	Stop Points SPR 001	Words Of Prophecy/Version	10

(see also Melodians, Glen Adams)

BREW

60s	Oak LONDON	Crossroads/Play Your Tune (acetate, unreleased, handwritten labels)	150

(see also Camel)

TERESA BREWER

SINGLES

54	Vogue Coral Q 2011	Skinny Minnie (Fishtail)/I Had Someone Else Before I Had You	12
54	Vogue Coral Q 2029	Au Revoir/Danger Signs	12
55	Vogue Coral Q 72043	Let Me Go, Lover (with Lancers)/Baby, Baby, Baby	10
55	Vogue Coral Q 72065	How Important Can It Be?/What More Is There To Say?	10
55	Vogue Coral Q 72066	Tweedlee Dee/Rock Love	20
55	Vogue Coral Q 72077	Pledging My Love/I Gotta Go Get My Baby	10
55	Vogue Coral Q 72083	You're Telling Our Secret/Time	8
55	Vogue Coral Q 72098	The Banjo's Back In Town/How To Be Very, Very Popular	6
56	Vogue Coral Q 72130	A Good Man Is Hard To Find/It's Siesta Time	6
56	Vogue Coral Q 72139	Rememb'ring/My Sweetie Went Away	6
56	Vogue Coral Q 72146	A Tear Fell/Bo Weevil	5

56	Vogue Coral Q 72172	A Sweet Old-Fashioned Girl/Goodbye, John	5
56	Vogue Coral Q 72199	Keep Your Cotton Pickin' Paddies Offa My Heart/ So Doggone Lonely	5
56	Vogue Coral Q 72213	Crazy With Love/The Moon Is On Fire	5
57	Vogue Coral Q 72224	Nora Malone/When I Leave The World Behind	5
57	Vogue Coral Q 72239	I'm Drowning My Sorrows/How Lonely Can One Be	5
57	Vogue Coral Q 72278	Lula Rock-A-Hula/Teardrops In My Heart	10
57	Vogue Coral Q 72292	You Send Me/Born To Love	10
58	Coral Q 72301	Careless Caresses/Mutual Admiration Society	5
58	Coral Q 72320	Saturday Dance/I Think The World Of You	5
58	Coral Q 72336	Pickle Up A Doodle/The Rain Falls On Ev'rybody	5
58	Coral Q 72340	The Hula Hoop Song/So Shy	5
58	Coral Q 72349	I Like Christmas/Jingle Bell Rock	5
58	Coral Q 72354	Satellite/The One Rose (That's Left In My Heart)	5
59	Coral Q 72364	Heavenly Lover/Fair Weather Sweetheart	7
59	Coral Q 72375	Bye Bye Baby Goodbye/Chain Of Friendship	6
59	Coral Q 72383	Bill Bailey, Won't You Please Come Home/Mexicali Rose	5
60	Coral Q 72405	Anymore/That Piano Man	5

EPs

50s	London BEP 6039	TERESA BREWER WITH THE ALL STARS (export issue)	10
50s	London BEP 6041	TERESA BREWER WITH JACK PLEIS AND THE ALL STARS (export issue)	10
59	Coral FEP 2013	HULA HOOP TIME WITH TERESA BREWER	10
59	Coral FEP 2036	WHEN YOUR LOVER HAS GONE PART 1	8
59	Coral FEP 2037	WHEN YOUR LOVER HAS GONE PART 2	8
59	Coral FEP 2038	WHEN YOUR LOVER HAS GONE PART 3	8
60	Coral FEP 2047	TERESA BREWER AND THE DIXIELAND BAND PART 1	8
60	Coral FEP 2048	TERESA BREWER AND THE DIXIELAND BAND PART 2	8
60	Coral FEP 2061	HOW DO YOU KNOW IT'S LOVE	10

ALBUMS

51	London H-APB 1006	SHOWCASE (10")	20
57	Vogue Coral LVA 9020	MUSIC! MUSIC! MUSIC!	30
58	Coral LVA 9075	FOR TEENAGERS IN LOVE	25
58	Coral LVA 9091	AT CHRISTMAS TIME	15
59	Coral LVA 9095	TIME FOR TERESA BREWER	15
59	Coral LVA 9100	WHEN YOUR LOVER HAS GONE (also stereo SVL 3003)	15
60	Coral LVA 9129	RIDIN' HIGH	15

(see also Snooky Lanson)

BREWER & SHIPLEY

70	Kama Sutra 2013 021	People Love Each Other/Tarkio Road	5
71	Kama Sutra 2013 015	One Toke Over The Line/People Love Each Other	5
70	Kama Sutra 2361 001	TARKIO ROAD (LP)	12
71	Kama Sutra 2361 005	WEEDS (LP)	12
72	Kama Sutra 2319 021	SHAKE OFF THE DEMON (LP)	12

BREWER'S DROOP

| 72 | RCA RCA 2216 | Sweet Thing/Heart Of Stone/It Ain't The Meat - It's The Motion (p/s) | 6 |
| 72 | RCA SF 8301 | OPENING TIME (LP, gatefold sleeve, orange label) | 25 |

(see also McGuinness Flint)

BRIAR

82	Happy Face MM 142	Rainbow (To The Skies)/Crying In The Rain (p/s)	12
87	PRT BRIART 1	Edge Of A Broken Heart/Don't Forget Me When You're On Your Own (shaped picture disc, with headband)	12
85	Heavy Metal HMRLP 41	TOO YOUNG (LP, with 7" & poster)	12
87	UK UKALP 002	CROWN OF THORNS (LP)	15

DICK BRICE

| 80s | Sylvan SYL 101R | A FEW ON 'IMS OWN (LP) | 50 |

BRIDGE

| 85 | Atlantic 9565(T) | Baby, Don't Hold Your Love Back/(Instrumental Version) (12") | 20 |

BOBBY BRIDGER

| 70 | Beacon BEA 149 | The World Is Turning On/Why Do I Love You | 10 |
| 70 | Beacon BEA 159 | Sugar Shaker/You're In Love | 12 |

(see also Errol Sobers)

MARC BRIERLEY

68	CBS 3857	Hold On, Hold On, The Garden Sure Looks Good Spread On The Floor/Autograph Of Time	15
69	CBS 4191	Stay A Little Longer Merry Ann/Flaxen Hair	10
69	CBS 4632	Lady Of The Light/Sunny Weather	10
70	CBS 5266	Be My Brother/If You Took The Bandage Off	8
60s	Transatlantic TRAEP 147	MARC BRIERLEY (EP)	50
68	CBS 63478	WELCOME TO THE CITADEL (LP, orange label with textured surface)	400
68	CBS 63835	HELLO (LP, gatefold sleeve, stickered sleeve, orange label)	100
69	CBS 63835	HELLO (LP, gatefold sleeve, no sticker, orange label)	90

(see also Tractor)

ANNE BRIGGS

63	Topic TOP 94	THE HAZARDS OF LOVE (EP, with leaflet)	160
71	Topic 12TS 207	ANNE BRIGGS (LP)	200
71	CBS 64612	THE TIME HAS COME (LP)	500

(see also A.L. Lloyd)

DUGGIE BRIGGS

| 78 | It IT 3 | Punk Rockin' Granny/I'm A Flasher (p/s) | 12 |
| 78 | It ITEP 5 | THE DUGGIE BRIGGS FLASHES ON IT AGAIN (EP) | 18 |

LILLIAN BRIGGS

| 60 | Coral Q 72408 | Not A Soul (Blanket Roll Blues)/Smile For The People | 5 |

ANNIE BRIGHT

| 70 | Columbia DB 8717 | Peaceful Mountain/Heartbreak House | 12 |
| 69 | Columbia DB 8587 | Concerning Love/Sneakin' Up On You | 15 |

GREG BRIGHT
| 69 | private pressing | ROOM BY GREG (LP) | 250 |

GREGORY BRIGHT
| 69 | Private Pressing | ROOM (LP) | 150 |

LEN BRIGHT COMBO
86	Empire LEN 1	Someone Must've Nailed Us Together/Mona (p/s)	18
86	Empire NICE 1	THE LEN BRIGHT COMBO (LP)	20
86	Ambassador AMBAS 1	COMBO TIME! (LP)	20

(see also Wreckless Eric, Milkshakes)

BRIGHTER
89	Sarah SARAH 019	Around The World In 80 Days (p/s, with inserts)	8
90	Sarah SARAH 27	Noah's ark/I Don't Think It Matters/Does Love Last Forever? (foldover p/s, postcard insert)	8
91	Sarah SARAH 56	Poppy Day/Half-Hearted/So You said (p/s, insert)	8
92	Sarah SARAH 69	DISNEY EP (10", p/s)	15
91	Sarah SARAH 404	LAUREL (LP, 10")	20

BRIGHT EYES
00	Wichita WEBB 005S	The Calendar Hung Itself/HER SPACE HOLIDAY :The Doctor And The DJ	8
01	Wichita WEBB 012S	3 NEW HIT SONGS FROM BRIGHT EYES EP (p/s)	8
04	Saddle Creek SCE 68	Lua/I Woke Up With This Song In My Head This Morning (p/s)	8
05	Saddle Creek SCE 79V	First Day Of My Life/When The President Talks To God (p/s)	10
10	Wichita WEBB 001 LPTEN	FEVERS AND MIRRORS (LP, reissue)	18

SARAH BRIGHTMAN
| 79 | Ariola Hansa AHAD 538 | The Adventures Of The Love Crusader (Long Version)/Lost In Space (The Nurgon Zone) (12", p/s, red vinyl as Sarah Brightman & Starship Troopers) | 10 |
| 90 | Polydor PZCD 74 | Something To Believe In/Brown Eyes/Love Changes Everything (CD single) | 30 |

IAN BRIGHTON
| 77 | Bead Records BEAD 3 | MARSH GAS (LP) | 50 |

BRIGHTON HORNS
| 66 | Stateside SS 526 | Surf Dell'amore/High Midnight | 10 |

BRIGHTWINTER
| 70s | Myrrh MYR 1030 | A BAND FOR ALL SEASONS (LP) | 25 |

BRILLIANT CORNERS
84	SS20 SS21	She's Got Fever/Black Water (red p/s)	15
84	SS20 SS21	She's Got Fever/Black Water (pink p/s)	30
84	SS20 SS22	Big Hip/Tangled Up In Blue (p/s)	10
88	McQueen MCQ2T	Why Do You Have To Go Out With Him?/Shangri La (12" p/s)	10
88	McQueen MCQLP	SOMEBODY UP THERE LIKES ME (LP, with inner)	15

JOHN BRIMACOMBE
| 72 | Pye 7N 45159 | Try A Little Harder/Four Sad Men | 8 |

BRIMSTONE
| 71 | Deram DM 322 | Keyhole Jake/The Monkey Song | 6 |
| 71 | Decca DF 13222 | If Ever You See Me/Work Out | 5 |

LOS BRINCOS
67	Page One POF 023	Lola/Passport (1st 5,000 in p/s)	35
67	Page One POF 023	Lola/Passport (no p/s)	10
67	Page One POF 031	Nobody Wants You Now/Train (as Brincos)	60

BRINDLEY BRAE
| 73 | Harmony DB 0002 | VILLAGE MUSIC (LP, 50 copies only, private pressing with insert) | 150 |

(see also Bev Pegg, Away From The Sand)

BRINSLEY SCHWARZ
70	United Artists UP 35118	Shining Brightly/What Do You Suggest	10
71	Liberty LBY 15419	Country Girl/Funk Angel	15
72	United Artists UP 35312	Country Girl/Funk Angel (reissue)	6
73	United Artists UP 35588	Speedo/I Worry	5
74	United Artists UP 35642	I've Cried My Last Tear/Bringdown	5
74	United Artists UP 35700	(What's So Funny 'Bout) Peace, Love And Understanding/ Ever Since You're Gone	6
75	United Artists UP 35768	Everybody/I Like You, I Don't Love You	6
75	United Artists UP 35812	There's A Cloud In My Heart/I Got The Real Thing	6
70	United Artists UAS 29111	BRINSLEY SCHWARZ (LP, gatefold sleeve, orange/pink label)	50
70	Liberty LBG 83427	DESPITE IT ALL (LP, gatefold sleeve)	35
72	United Artists UAS 29217	SILVER PISTOL (LP, with poster)	30
72	United Artists UAS 29374	NERVOUS ON THE ROAD (LP)	15
73	United Artists UAS 29489	PLEASE DON'T EVER CHANGE (LP)	20
74	United Artists UAS 29641	THE NEW FAVOURITES OF BRINSLEY SCHWARZ (LP)	12
98	Edsel EDCD 546	HEN'S TEETH (CD)	20

(see also Kippington Lodge, Hitters, Knees, Limelight, Nick Lowe, Ernie Graham, Rumour, Chilli Willi & Red Hot Peppers, Ducks Deluxe)

LLOYD BRISCO
| 64 | Rio R42 | Fabulous Eyes/What You See | 20 |
| 64 | Island WI 187 | Jonah The Master/Mr. Cleveland | 20 |

JOHNNY BRISTOL
75	MGM 2006 471	Memories Don't Leave Like People Do/It Don't Hurt No More	6
80	Ariola AHA 567	Love No Longer Has A Hold On Me/Till I See You Again	5
80	Ariola AHAD 567	Love No Longer Has A Hold On Me/Till I See You Again (12")	10

BRITANIA
| 73 | EMI EMI 2038 | Right Down The Line/Judy Brings Me Down | 8 |

BRITISH LIONS
78	Vertigo 6059 192	One More Chance To Run/Booster (p/s)	5
78	Vertigo 6059 201	International Heroes/Eat The Rich	5
78	Vertigo 9102 019	BRITISH LIONS (LP, with inner sleeve)	15

(see also Mott The Hoople, Medicine Head)

BRITISH SEA POWER
01	Golden Chariot BSP 01	Fear Of Drowning/A Wooden Horse (CD, 1000 only)	25
01	Rough Trade RTRADE S032	Remember Me/A Lovely Day Tomorrow (p/s, 1264 only)	5
02	Rough Trade RTRADE 048	The Lonely/Spirit Of St. Louis	10
02	Rough Trade RTRADES 069	Childhood Memories/Favours In The Beetroot Fields (p/s, 1000 only)	5
03	Rough Trade RTRADE S092	Carrion/Apologies To Insect Life (handdrawn, textured sleeve, 2003 only)	12
03	Rough Trade RTRADES 125	Remember Me/The Scottish Wildlife Experience (hand-drawn name on 2003 copies)	8
05	None	Thirteen Ways To Disappear (CD-R sent to first 13 buyers from BSP web shop)	20
05	Rough Trade RTRADS302	Remember Me/I Am A Cider Drinker (7" limited edition. 1,966 copies)	12

(see also The Wurzels)

BRITISH SHOES
79	NWJ SRTS/79/CUS 542	Running From Mummy/Where Would We Be Without Shoes (no p/s)	30

BRITISH WALKERS
65	Pye International 7N 25298	I Found You/Diddley Daddy	30

BRITT
66	Piccadilly 7N 35273	You Really Have Started Something/Leave My Baby Alone	30

(see also Britt Ekland)

MAY BRITT
59	Top Rank JAR 230	Falling In Love Again/Lola-Lola	6

TINA BRITT
65	London HLC 9974	The Real Thing/Teardrops Fell	60
65	London HLC 9974	The Real Thing/Teardrops Fell (DJ Copy)	100

BUDDY BRITTEN & REGENTS
62	Piccadilly 7N 35075	My Pride, My Joy/Long Gone Baby	15
62	Decca F 11435	Don't Spread It Around/The Beat Of My Heart	15
63	Oriole CB 1827	If You Gotta Make A Fool Of Somebody/Money	15
63	Oriole CB 1839	Hey There/I'll Cry No More	15
63	Oriole CB 1859	My Resistance Is Low/When I See You Smile	15
63	Oriole CB 1889	Money/Sorrow Tomorrow	20
64	Oriole CB 1911	I Guess I'm In The Way/Zip-A-Dee-Doo-Dah	15
65	Piccadilly 7N 35241	She's About A Mover/Since You've Gone	15
65	Piccadilly 7N 35257	Right Now/Jailer Bring Me Water	8

(see also Regents)

TERRY BRITTEN
69	Columbia DB8580	2000 Weeks/Bargain Day	100

CHRIS BRITTON
69	Page One POLS 022	AS I AM (LP, gatefold sleeve, blue/silver label)	400

(see also Troggs)

JEFF BRITTON & THE SPITFIRES
76	Decca F13643	Rub Out/Breakwood	30

MAGGIE BRITTON
80	Piccadilly 7P191	Goodship Earth/No Secrets	6

BRIXTON MARKET
69	Beacon BEA 138	Children Get Ready/Bangarang	15
69	Beacon SBEAB 8	BLACK FUNK (LP)	20

JO BROADBERY & THE STANDOUTS
80	Revenge REV-S-1	Out Of The Real/Breaking Down (no p/s)	10
80	Revenge REVLP-1	JO BROADBERRY AND THE STANDOUTS (LP)	20

BROADCAST
96	Wurlitzer Jukebox WJ 6	Accidentals/We've Got Time (p/s, with sticker)	40
96	Wurlitzer Jukebox WJ 6	Accidentals/We've Got Time (p/s, without sticker)	10
96	Duophonic DS 45-14	Living Room/Phantom (wraparound p/s, 1,500 only)	10
96	Duophonic DS 45-16	THE BOOK LOVERS EP (12", p/s, 2,000)	25
96	Duophonic DS 45-CD 16	THE BOOK LOVERS EP (CD, 2,500 only)	10
99	Warp 7WAP 125	Echo's Answer/Test Area	10
00	Warp 7WAP 132	Come On Let's Go/Distant Call (p/s)	8
00	Warp WAP 129	EXTENDED PLAY (12" EP)	10
00	Warp WAP 136	Drums On Fire/Come On Let's Go (Two Lone Swordsmen Mix) (12" black die-cut sleeve)	8
00	Warp WAP 141	EXTENDED PLAY TWO EP (12", p/s)	12
03	Warp WAP 162	Pendulum/Small Song IV/One Hour Empore/Still Feel Like Tears/Violent Playground/Minus Two (12" p/s)	15
03	Warp WAP 169 CD	MICROTRONICS VOLUME 01: STEREO RECORDED MUSIC FOR LINKS & BRIDGES (3" CD in miniature jewel case)	18
05	Warp 7WAP 193	America's Boy/Tender Buttons (p/s)	8
05	Warp WAP 199	MICROTRONICS VOLUME 02: STEREO RECORDED MUSIC FOR LINKS & BRIDGES (3" CD in miniature jewel case)	18
09	Warp WARPCD 189T	MOTHER IS THE MILKY WAY (CD, card slipcase, 750 only, tour issue)	20
10	Ghost Box GBX 704	GHOST BOX STUDY SERIES 04: FAMILIAR SHAPES & NOISES EP (p/s, with The Focus Group)	8
97	Warp WARPLP 52	WORK & NON WORK (LP)	25
00	Warp WARPLP 65	THE NOISE MADE BY PEOPLE (LP, gatefold sleeve, insert)	40
03	Warp WARPLP 106	HAHA SOUND (LP)	30
05	Warp WARPLP 136	TENDER BUTTONS (LP)	30
06	Warp WARPLP 146	THE FUTURE CRAYON (2-LP)	40
09	Warp WARPLP 189	INVESTIGATES WITCH CULTS OF THE RADIO AGE (LP, with the Focus Group)	30

BROADSIDE
71	Lincolnshire Ass. LA 4	THE GIPSY'S WEDDING DAY (10" LP)	50
73	Topic 12TS 228	THE MOON SHONE BRIGHT (As The Broadside From Grimsby) (LP, blue label)	40
75	Guildhall GHS 5	SONGS FROM THE STOCKS (LP)	80
75	Guildhall GHS 12	DRIVE THE DARK AWAY (LP)	50

BROADSIDE OUTCASTS
78	Profile GMOR 154	ABO EP	20

DAVE BROCK

83	Flicknife FLS 024	Social Alliance/Raping Robots In The Street (p/s)	5
83	Flicknife FLS 024P	Social Alliance/Raping Robots In The Street (picture disc)	8
84	Flicknife SHARP 018	EARTHED TO THE GROUND (LP)	12
88	Flicknife SHARP 042	AGENT OF CHAOS (LP)	12

(see also Dr. Technical & Machines, Hawkwind)

NORAH BROCKSTEDT

60	Top Rank JAR 353	Big Boy/Tell Me No Lies	10

PETER BROGGS

79	Hit Run HITDD 13	Higher Field Marshall (Feat. Prince Far I)/I And I A The Chosen One/PRINCE FAR I & BRIGADIER JAM DOWN : Loved By Everyone (12")	40
80	Cha Cha CHAD 25	Never Forget Jah/CORNWALL CAMPBELL : Rainbow (12")	30
80	Selena SO 006	Jah Golden Throne/DEXTER mcKINTYRE : 144.00 Saints	50

BROKEN BONES

84	Fall Out FALL 020	Decapitated/Problem/Liquidated Brains (p/s)	5
84	Fall Out FALL 025	Crucifix/Fight The Good Fight	5
85	Fall Out FALL 034P	Seeing Through My Eyes/The Point Of Agony/It's Like (picture disc)	5
85	Fall Out FALL 10034	Seeing Through My Eyes/The Point Of Agony/It's Like/Decapitated/Part 2/ Death Is Imminent (10", p/s)	7
83	Fall Out FALL LP 028	BROKEN BONES (LP)	15
84	Stoned Spliff 1	LIVE AT THE 100 CLUB (LP)	20

(see also Discharge)

BROKEN BOW

87	Sodium	Vagrant/Bite Back	25

BROKEN GLASS (1)

75	Capitol E-ST 11510	BROKEN GLASS (LP, with insert)	18

(see also Chicken Shack, Warhorse, Miller Anderson, Bronco)

BROKEN GLASS (2)

84	Streetwave MKHAN 17	Style Of The Street (12")	15

BROKEN ROSE

86	Exhibit 1 EXL 006	WAR TEARS (LP)	100

(see also Bizarre Unit, Paul Nova)

JOHN BROMLEY

68	Polydor 56224	What A Woman Does/My My	30
68	Polydor 56287	And The Feeling Goes/Sweet Little Princess	20
69	Polydor 56305	Melody Fayre/Sugar Love	40
69	Polydor 56340	Hold Me Woman/Weather Man	30
69	Atlantic 584 289	Kick A Tin Can/Wonderland Avenue U.S.A.	30
69	Polydor 583 048	SING (LP)	100

(see also Fleur De Lys, Three People)

BILLY BRIMSTONE

05	YNR YNR 021	Keep It Live (Vocal)/Keep It Live (Instrumental)	8

(see also Jehst)

BRONCO

70	Island WIP 6096	Lazy Now/A Matter Of Perspective	20
73	Polydor 2058 395	The Traveller/Steal That Gold	6
70	Island ILPS 9124	COUNTRY HOME (LP, gatefold sleeve, pink 'i' label)	40
70	Island ILPS 9124	COUNTRY HOME (LP, gatefold sleeve, 'pink rim palm tree' label)	15
71	Island ILPS 9161	ACE OF SUNLIGHT (LP, gatefold sleeve, 'pink rim palm tree' label)	25
73	Polydor 2383 215	SMOKIN' MIXTURE (LP, gatefold sleeve)	15

(see also Alan Bown Set)

BRONNT INDUSTRIES

05	Static Caravan	KAPITAL BROCKEN (EP) (8" lathe cut, clear vinyl, hand-stamped bag, 100 only)	25

BRONX CHEER

70	Parlophone R 5865	Drive My Car/Foxtrot	8
71	Dawn DNX 2512	Barrelhouse Player/Surprising Find/Whether Or Not/Party For One (p/s)	8
72	Dawn DNS 1019	Hold On To Me/Late Date	6
72	Dawn DNLS 3004	GREATEST HITS VOLUME 3 (LP, gatefold sleeve with insert, lilac label)	20

BRONZ

84	Bronze BRO 178	Send Down An Angel/Tiger (p/s)	5
84	Bronze BROX 178	Send Down An Angel/Tiger/Stranded (12", p/s)	8

DAVID BROOK

68	President PT 196	Witchfinder General/Janie	15

MICHAEL BROOK

92	4AD CAD 2007	COBALT BLUE (LP, featuring Brian Eno)	20
92	4AD TAD 2011	LIVE AT THE AQUARIUM (CD, digipak)	18

PATTI BROOK (& DIAMONDS)

60	Pye 7N 15300	Since You've Been Gone/That's The Way It's Gonna Be (as Patti Brook & Diamonds)	5
61	Pye 7N 15339	When The Red Red Robin/Look What You've Done To Me	5
61	Pye 7N 15378	Heaven Is Being With You/Your Love Came Into My Heart	5
62	Pye 7N 15422	I Love You, I Need You/Unloved, Unwanted	5

TONY BROOK & BREAKERS

64	Columbia DB 7279	Meanie Genie/Ooh Poo Pah Doo (in p/s)	200
64	Columbia DB 7279	Meanie Genie/Ooh Poo Pah Doo	100
65	Columbia DB 7444	Love Dances On/I Won't Hurt You	10

BROOK BROTHERS

60	Top Rank JAR 349	Green Fields/How Will It End?	10
60	Top Rank JAR 409	Please Help Me, I'm Falling/When Will I Be Loved	10
60	Pye 7N 15298	Say The Word/Everything But Love	7
61	Pye 7N 15333	Warpaint/Sometimes	5
61	Pye 7N 15352	Little Bitty Heart/Tell Her	5

61	Pye 7N 15369	Ain't Gonna Wash For A Week/One Last Kiss	5
61	Pye 7N 15387	Married/I Love Girls	5
62	Pye 7N 15409	He's Old Enough To Know Better/Win Or Lose	8
62	Pye 7N 15415	Too Scared/Tell Tale	5
62	Pye 7N 15441	Just Another Fool/Double Trouble	5
62	Pye 7N 15453	Welcome Home Baby/So Long	5
62	Pye 7N 15463	I Can't Make Up My Mind/Town Girl	5
63	Pye 7N 15498	Trouble Is My Middle Name/Let The Good Times Roll	5
63	Pye 7N 15527	I'm Not Jimmy/Side By Side (with RBQ)	7
63	Pye 7N 15570	Crosswords/Whistle To The Wind	7
61	Pye NEP 24140	BROOK BROTHERS HIT PARADE (EP)	15
61	Pye NEP 24148	BROOK BROTHERS HIT PARADE VOLUME 2 (EP)	15
62	Pye NEP 24155	BROOK BROTHERS (EP)	15
61	Pye NPL 18067	BROOK BROTHERS (LP)	25

(see also Brooks)

GARY BROOKER
81	Chrysalis CHS 2396	Leave The Candle/Chasing The Chop (Eric Clapton guest appearance)	100

BROOKLYN
80	Rondelet ROUND 3	I Wanna Be A Detective (p/s)	30
81	Rondelet ROUND 6	Hollywood/Late Again (p/s)	20
80	Rondelet ABOUT 3	YOU NEVER KNOW WHAT YOU'LL FIND (LP)	30

BROOKLYN BRIDGE
68	Pye International 7N 25473	From My Window I Can See/Little Red Boat By The River	8
69	Buddah 201 029	The Worst That Could Happen/Your Kite, My Kite	10
70	Buddah 2011 010	Free As The Wind/He's Not A Happy Man	6
70	Buddah 2011 034	Down By The River/Look Again	6

(see also Johnny Maestro, Crests)

BROOKS
64	Decca F 11868	Once In A While/Poor Poor Plan	8

(see also Brook Brothers)

BABA BROOKS
63	Island WI 078	5 O'Clock Whistle/African Blood (by Blues Masters)	40
63	Island WI 096	Bank To Bank (Parts 1 & 2)	30
63	Island WI 127	Three Blind Mice/BILLY & BOBBY: We Ain't Got Nothing	30
63	R&B JB 125	Water Melon Man/STRANGER COLE: Things Come To Those Who Wait	35
64	Black Swan WI 137	Portrait Of My Love/STRANGER COLE: Goodbye Peggy	20
64	Black Swan WI 412	Jelly Beans/ERIC MORRIS: Sampson	30
64	Black Swan WI 414	Key To The City/ERIC MORRIS: Solomon Grundie	40
64	Black Swan WI 434	Spider/Melody Jamboree	30
64	Black Swan WI 438	Cork Foot/HERSANG COMBO: B.B.C. Channel 2	30
65	Black Swan WI 442	Musical Workshop/DUKE WHITE: Be Wise	35
65	Black Swan WI 444	Bus Strike/DUKE WHITE: Sow Good Seeds	35
65	Black Swan WI 451	Ethiopia/ARCHIBALD TROTT: Promised Land	30
65	Black Swan WI 466	Baby Elephant Walk/DON DRUMMOND: Don's Special	35
65	Ska Beat JB 189	Dr. Decker/OWEN & LEON SILVERA : Woman	15
65	Ska Beat JB 220	One Eyed Giant (with His Band)/DYNAMITES: Walk Out On Me	40
65	Island WI 229	Guns Fever/DOTTY & BONNIE: Don't Do It	35
65	Island WI 233	Independent Ska/STRANGER & CLAUDETTE: Seven Days	30
65	Island WI 235	Duck Soup/ZODIACS: Renegade	150
65	Island WI 239	Vitamin A/ALTON ELLIS: Dance Crasher	50
65	Island WI 241	Teenage Ska/ALTON ELLIS: You Are Not To Blame	70
65	Rio R 061	Shenk I Sheck (& Band)/SHENLEY & HIACYNTH: Set Me Free	50
66	Doctor Bird DB 1042	The Clock (& Band)/LYN TAITT & COMETS & SILVERTONES: Raindrops	40
66	Doctor Bird DB 1046	Jam Session (with His Band)/CONQUERORS: What A Agony	40
67	Ska Beat JB 268	One Eyed Giant (with His Band)/DYNAMITES: Walk Out On Me (reissue)	20

*(see also Blues Masters, Eric Brooks, Stranger & Patsy, Riots, Joey Smith, Saints, Richard Brothers, Derrick Morgan, Lord Tanamo, Lord Brisco,
Hippy Boys, Roy Panton, Higgs & Wilson, Vinley Gayle, Joe White, Stranger & Patsy)*

CEDRIC 'IM' BROOKS
73	Tropical AL046	South African Reggae/Part 2	10
78	Water Lily ARCO LP 009	UNITED AFRICA (LP)	25

CHUCK BROOKS
69	Soul City SC 116	Black Sheep/I've Got To Get Myself Together	20
69	Soul City SC 116	Black Sheep/I've Got To Get Myself Together (DJ Copy)	75

D. BROOKS
70	Big BG 304	Oh Me Oh My (actually "Every Time" by Hi-Tals)/ANSEL COLLINS: Staccato (actually "Every Time Version" by Rupie Edwards Allstars)	12

DALE BROOKS
65	King KG 1025	Army Green/Reminds Me Of You	10
66	Stateside SS 553	I Wanna Be Your Girl/Like Other Girls Do	30

DONNIE BROOKS
60	London HLN 9168	Mission Bell/Do It For Me	5
60	London HLN 9253	Doll House/Round Robin	5
61	London HLN 9361	That's Why/Memphis	8
62	London HLN 9572	Oh, You Beautiful Doll/Just A Bystander	5
61	London HA-N 2391	THE HAPPIEST DONNIE BROOKS (LP)	25

ELKIE BROOKS
64	Decca F 11928	Something's Got A Hold On Me/Hello Stranger	35
64	Decca F 11983	Nothing Left To Do But Cry/Strange Though It Seems	35
65	Decca F 12061	The Way You Do The Things You Do/Blue Tonight	30
65	HMV POP 1431	He's Gotta Love Me/When You Appear	35
65	HMV POP 1431	He's Gotta Love Me/When You Appear (DJ Copy)	60
65	HMV POP 1480	All My Life/Can't Stop Thinking Of You	20
66	HMV POP 1512	Baby Let Me Love You/Stop The Music	25
69	NEMS 56-4136	Come September/If You Should Go	5
74	Island WIP 6187	Rescue Me/Sweet Nuthin's	5

74	Chrysalis CHS 2069	Sacrifice/ALICE COOPER: I'm Flash (p/s, unissued, promo only)	35
84	A & M SCREEN 1	SCREEN GEMS (CD, beware of copies!)	50

(see also Dada, Vinegar Joe, Steve York's Camelo Pardalis, Elki & Owen)

BROOKS & JERRY

68	Direction 58-3267	I Got What It Takes Parts 1 & 2	10
68	Direction 58-3267	I Got What It Takes Parts 1 & 2 (DJ Copy)	30

JOE BROOKS COLLECTIVE

71	CBS 7234	Messing Up The Mind Of A Young Girl/ Before The Sand Has Run Out Of The Hour Glass	12

JULIAN BROOKS

70	Pye 7N17996	Justine/Lazy Guy	25

MIKE BROOKS

79	Hit Run HIT DD 9	Love Is Like A Password/Feeling Of Reggae (12")	25
79	Hit Run HIT DD 23	Long Long Time/Dub In Time	30
76	Burning Sounds BSLP 1026	WHAT A GATHERING (LP)	15

NORMAN BROOKS & G-BOYS

54	London L 1166	Hello Sunshine/You're My Baby	30
54	London L 1202	Somebody Wonderful/You Shouldn't Have Kissed Me The First Time	30
54	London L 1228	A Sky-Blue Shirt And A Rainbow Tie/This Waltz With You	35
54	London HL 8015	I'm Kinda Crazy/I'd Like To Be In Your Shoes, Baby	30
54	London HL 8041	I Can't Give You Anything But Love (solo)/GO-BOYS: Johnny's Tune	30
54	London HL 8051	Candy Moon/My 3-D Sweetie	30
55	London HL 8115	Back In Circulation/Lou Lou Louisiana	30
54	London RE-P 1004	PRESENTING NORMAN BROOKS VOLUME 1 (EP)	40
55	London RE-P 1021	BABY MINE (EP)	40

PAM BROOKS

70	Big BG 307	Oh Me Oh My/ANSELL COLLINS: Staccato	18

RAY BROOKS

72	Polydor 2001334	Pictures/On My Own	10

WES BROOKS

77	ATA ATA 1003	Lay Down Your Arms/Version	70

MARK BROOM

95	Ferox FER 017	SHUFFLE THIS (12" EP)	8

BIG BILL BROONZY/CHICAGO BILL

51	Vogue V 2068	Back Water Blues/Lonesome Road Blues (78)	10
51	Vogue V 2073	In The Evenin'/Low Land Blues (78)	10
51	Vogue V 2074	John Henry/Blues In 1890 (78)	10
51	Vogue V 2075	Big Bill Blues/Hey Hey Baby (78)	10
51	Vogue V 2076	House Rent Stomp/The Moppin' Blues (78)	10
51	Vogue V 2077	Black, Brown And White/Feelin' Low Down (78)	10
52	Vogue V 2078	Make My Getaway/What I Used To Do (78)	10
52	Melodisc 1191	Keep Your Hands Off Her/Stump Blues (78, as Chicago Bill)	10
52	Melodisc 1203	Five Foot Seven/Plough Hand Blues (78, as Chicago Bill)	10
50s	private pressing	Keep Your Hand On Your Heart/T For Texas (78)	20
56	Pye Jazz NJ 2012	When Do I Get To Be Called A Man/Mindin' My Own Business (78)	10
57	Pye Jazz NJ 2016	Southbound Train/It Feels So Good (78)	10
58	Vogue V 2351	Guitar Shuffle/When Did You Leave Heaven	30
61	Storyville A 44053	Midnight Special/Black Brown And White	10
55	Vogue EPV 1024	HEY BUD BLUES (EP)	20
56	Vogue EPV 1074	SINGS THE BLUES (EP)	20
56	Vogue EPV 1107	GUITAR SHUFFLE (EP)	20
56	Pye Jazz NJE 1005	MISSISSIPPI BLUES VOLUME 1 (EP)	15
56	Pye Jazz NJE 1015	MISSISSIPPI BLUES VOLUME 2 (EP)	15
56	Melodisc EPM7 65	KEEP YOUR HANDS OFF (EP)	15
57	Pye Jazz NJE 1047	SOUTHERN SAGA (EP)	15
57	Columbia SEG 7674	BIG BILL BROONZY SINGS THE BLUES (EP)	15
57	Tempo EXA 61	BILL BAILEY WON'T YOU PLEASE COME HOME (EP)	15
58	Columbia SEG 7790	BIG BILL BROONZY SINGS THE BLUES NO. 2 (EP)	15
60	Mercury ZEP 10065	WALKIN' DOWN A LONESOME ROAD (EP)	15
60	Mercury ZEP 10093	HOLLERIN' BLUES (EP)	22
60s	Mercury/Emearcy MMB 12003	THE BLUES (LP)	20
62	Storyville SEP 383	BLUES ANTHOLOGY VOLUME 3 (EP)	12
64	Mercury 10003 MCE	BLUES-GOSPEL-SPIRITUAL (EP)	15
57	Vogue LAE 12009	BIG BILL BLUES (LP)	35
57	Philips BBL 7113	BIG BILL BROONZY (LP)	35
58	Vogue LAE 12063	THE BLUES (LP)	35
58	Pye Nixa Jazz NJL 16	TRIBUTE TO BIG BILL (LP)	35
59	Tempo TAP 23	AN EVENING WITH BIG BILL BROONZY (LP)	40
61	HMV CLP 1544	LAST SESSION PART 1 (LP)	25
62	HMV CLP 1551	LAST SESSION PART 2 (LP)	25
62	HMV CLP 1562	LAST SESSION PART 3 (LP)	25
65	Storyville SLP 143	AN EVENING WITH BROONZY (LP)	15
65	Fontana 688 206ZL	TROUBLE IN MIND (LP)	20
66	Mercury 20044 MCL	REMEMBERING BROONZY - THE GREATEST MINSTREL OF THE AUTHENTIC BLUES (LP)	30
66	Storyville SLP 188	BLUES IN EUROPE (LP)	18
67	Storyville 670 154	PORTRAITS IN BLUES VOLUME 2 (LP)	20
69	CBS Realm 52648	BIG BILL'S BLUES (LP)	15
69	Xtra XTRA 1093	SINGS COUNTRY BLUES (LP)	15

(see also Chicago Bill)

BIG BILL BROONZY & PETE SEEGER

64	Xtra XTRA 1006	IN CONCERT (LP)	20
66	Verve Folkways VLP 5006	IN CONCERT (LP, reissue, also stereo SVLP 506)	15

(see also Pete Seeger)

BIG BILL BROONZY/SONNY BOY WILLIAMSON [I]

65	RCA Victor RD 7685	BIG BILL AND SONNY BOY (LP)	30

(see also Sonny Boy Williamson [I])

BIG BILL BROONZY, SONNY TERRY & BROWNIE MCGHEE
64	Xtra XTRA 1004	BIG BILL BROONZY/SONNY TERRY/BROWNIE McGHEE (LP)	30

(see also Sonny Terry & Brownie McGhee, Washboard Sam)

BROTH
71	Mercury 6338 032	BROTH (LP)	50

BROTHER BARON
70s	Fab FAB 281	Your Love/Your Love Version	6

BROTHER BONES & HIS SHADOWS
60	Oriole CB 1030	Sweet Georgia Brown/Margie	6
60	Oriole EP 7031	BROTHER BONES AND HIS SIDEMEN (EP)	8

BROTHER BUNG
68	Avenue BEV 1054	BLUES CRUSADE (EP)	15

(see also Bob Pearce, Fresh)

BROTHER D & THE COLLECTIVE EFFORT
80	Island IPR 2005	How We Gonna Make The Black Nation Rise (12")	10

BROTHER DAN ALLSTARS
68	Trojan TR 601	Donkey Returns/Tribute To Sir K.B.	20
68	Trojan TR 602	Eastern Organ/JIVERS: Our Love Will Last	30
68	Trojan TR 603	Hold Pon Them/OWEN GRAY: Answer Me	18
68	Trojan TR 607	Read Up/Gallop	15
68	Trojan TR 608	Another Saturday Night/Bee's Knees	10
68	Trojan TBL 101	LET'S CATCH THE BEAT (LP)	45
69	Trojan TRL 1	FOLLOW THAT DONKEY (LP)	60

(see also Audrey, Pooch Jackson)

BROTHER SUSAN
74	EMI EMI 2117	See My Fingers Fly/Full Blooded Natural Man	12
74	EMI EMI 2174	Ride Ride Ride/Flash	12

BROTHER TREVOR & U BROWN
78	Matumbi Music	Skip Away/Selassi I (12")	20

(see also Matumbi)

BROTHER (1)
89	4th & Broadway 12BRW139	Beyond The 16th Parallel (12")	8
92	Tribal Bass TRIBE 10	Ghettogedden	8

BROTHER (2)
11	Chess Club CC 035	Darling Buds Of May/Homesick (Demo) (p/s, 500 only)	7

BROTHERHOOD (1)
69	Philips BF 1756	Paper Man/Give It To Me Now	15

BROTHERHOOD (2)
91	Bite It BITE 1	DESCENDANTS OF THE HOLOCAUST (EP)	25
91	Bite It BITE 2	Descendents Of The Holocaust (remix 12")	8
92	Bite It BITE 6	Way Of The Wise (12")	8
93	Bite It BITE 7	XXXIII (EP)	8
95	Bite It BHOODJ2	Alphabetical Response/One (12", promo)	8

BROTHERHOOD OF BREATH
74	Ogun OG 100	LIVE AT WILLISAU (LP, with Chris McGregor)	20

(see also Chris McGregor's Brotherhood Of Breath, Mark Charig)

BROTHERHOOD OF LIZARDS
89	Deltic DELT LP5	LIZARDLAND (LP)	20

(see also Gypp, Martin Newall, Cleaners From Venus)

BROTHERHOOD OF MAN
69	Deram DM 276	Love One Another/A Little Bit Of Heaven	6
70	Deram DM 317	This Boy/You Can Depend On Me	6
71	Deram DM 327	Reach Out Your Hand/Better Tomorrow	15
74	Dawn DNS 1055	When Love Catches Up With You/How Can You Love (p/s)	6

(see also Sue & Sunny, Sue & Sunshine, Stockingtops)

BROTHERLY LOVE
67	CBS 2978	Ocean Of Tears/Mr Average Man	15
73	CBS S CBS 1737	Public Enemy No.1/Here Stands A Better Man	5

BROTHERS
67	London HLU 10158	Love Story/The Girl's Alright	7

BROTHERS & SISTERS (U.K.)
68	private pressing	ARE WATCHING YOU (LP)	90

BROTHERS & SISTERS (U.S.)
69	CBS 4583	Mighty Quinn/Chimes Of Freedom	5
69	CBS 63746	DYLAN'S GOSPEL (LP)	20

BROTHERS GRIMM
65	Decca F 12224	Lost Love/Make It Or Break It	10
66	Ember EMB 222	A Man Needs Love/Looky Looky	50

(see also Barry & Tony)

BROTHERS KANE
66	Decca F 12448	Walking In The Sand/Won't You Stay Long	25

(see also Sarstedt Brothers, Peter Lincoln, Peter Sarstedt, Clive Sands, Wes Sands, Eden Kane)

BROTHERS TWO
68	Action ACT 4513	Here I Am, In Love Again/I'm Tired Of You Baby	15

BROTHERS WILLIAM
65	Parlophone R 5293	Linda Jane Blues/Honey Love	8

AYSHEA BROUGH

| 71 | RCA RCA 2105 | Master Jack/Both Sides Now | 7 |

(see also Ayshea)

EDGAR BROUGHTON BAND

69	Harvest HAR 5001	Evil/Death Of An Electric Citizen	15
70	Harvest HAR 5015	Out Demons Out/Momma's Reward	7
70	Harvest HAR 5021	Up Yours!/Officer Dan	8
70	Harvest HAR 5032	Apache Drop Out/Freedom	7
71	Harvest HAR 5040	Hotel Room/Call Me A Liar	8
72	Harvest HAR 5049	Gone Blue/Someone/Mr. Crosby	8
69	Harvest SHVL 757	WASA WASA (LP, gatefold sleeve, no EMI box on label with "the Gramophone Co" and "sold in U.K." label text)	170
69	Harvest SHVL 757	WASA WASA (LP, gatefold sleeve, later issue with EMI box on label)	50
70	Harvest SHVL 772	SING BROTHER SING (LP, gatefold sleeve, with lyric insert, no EMI on label)	60
71	Harvest SHVL 791	THE EDGAR BROUGHTON BAND (LP, 1st pressing, textured gatefold)	70
71	Harvest SHVL 791	THE EDGAR BROUGHTON BAND (LP, 2nd pressing with EMI boxed logo on side 1 only, textured gatefold)	30
72	Harvest SHTC 252	IN SIDE OUT (LP, multifold gatefold sleeve with lyric sheet, some copies come with Harvest "Letter of introduction".)	60
73	Harvest SHVL 810	OORA (LP, wraparound card sleeve in clear artwork plastic bag, inner sleeve)	60
75	Harvest SHSM 2001	A BUNCH OF 45s (LP)	15
76	Nems NEL 6006	BANDAGES (LP with lyric inner sleeve)	20

AL BROWN (JAMAICA)

71	Banana BA 360	No Soul Today/RUFFIANS: Where Did I Go Wrong (B-side actually "Bang Shang Alang" by Peter Austin & Hortense Ellis)	25
71	Fab FAB 186	Ain't Got No Soul/TEARDROPS: I Got A Feeling	20
76	Burning Sounds BS 001	Revival Festival/Version	5

AL BROWN'S TUNETOPPERS (U.S.)

| 60 | Top Rank JAR 374 | The Madison/Mo' Madison | 6 |

ARTHUR BROWN (CRAZY WORLD OF)

65	Lyntone LYN 770/1	You Don't Know (as Arthur Brown & Diamonds)/DIAMONDS: You'll Be Mine (Reading University Rag Week flexidisc)	60
67	Track 604 008	Devil's Grip/Give Him A Flower	12
68	Track 604 022	Fire!/Rest Cure (push-out centre)	6
68	Track 604 022	Fire!/Rest Cure (large centre)	5
68	Track 604 026	Nightmare/What's Happening (some copies list "Music Man" as B-side)	6
74	Gull GULS 4	Gypsies/Dance	5
75	Gull GULS 13	We Gotta Get Out Of This Place/Here I Am	5
77	Gull SIXPACK 4	SIX-PACK/SIX TRACK (EP, picture disc, die-cut sleeve with stand, 5,000 only)	6
68	Track 612 005	THE CRAZY WORLD OF ARTHUR BROWN (LP, mono, black/silver label)	80
68	Track 613 005	THE CRAZY WORLD OF ARTHUR BROWN (LP, stereo, black/silver labels)	70
74	Gull GULP 1008	DANCE (LP)	15
77	Gull GUD 2003/4	THE LOST EARS (2-LP, gatefold sleeve, as Arthur Brown's Kingdom Come)	22
82	Remote REA 101	REQUIEM (LP)	12
88	Reckless 2 RECK	STRANGELANDS (LP, unreleased)	0

(see also Kingdom Come, Nick Greenwood, Atomic Rooster, Crane/Farlowe)

BARRY BROWN

78	Tribesman TM 008	Unity Is Strength/DRUMMIE BENJI: Higher Region (12")	30
79	Justice JUDIS 126	Big Big Politician/No Wicked Shall Enter (12")	30
79	Sufferer's Heights SUFF 003	I Love Sweet Jah Jah/RANKING JOE : Youthman Promotion (12")	35
80	Daddy Kool DKR 124	Peace And Love (with Ranking Toyan) JAH THOMAS & ROOTS RADICS: Adapter Chapter (12")	50
80	Strong Like Sampson SLSD 07	Natty Dread Nah Run/ANTHONY JOHNSON: Life is not easy (12")	40
80	Strong Like... SLSD 010	Don't You Try/ANTHONY JOHNSON: Hey Mr Rich Man (12")	40
80	Attack TACK 17	Mr. CID/SCIENTIST AND ROOTS RADICAL BAND: King Tubby's Rockers (12")	30
80	Attack TACK 21	Separation/Scientist In A Fine Style (12")	40
80	Attack TACK 23	Living As A Brother/SCIENTIST: Second Hand Girl (12")	30
80	Justice JUDIS 135	We Can't Like This/From Creation I Man Free (12")	40
81	City Sounds CSD 003	Warmonger/ROOTS RADICS BAND: Radical Style (12", green vinyl)	50
81	Greensleeves GRED 68	Give Israel Another Try/Sweet Sixteen (12")	30
82	Selena SD004	Them Ha Fi Get A Beatin'/ROOTS RADICS BAND : Stop The Fighting (12")	40
82	Selena SD008	Physical Fitness/HEPTONES : Lovers Feeling (12", blue vinyl)	30
83	Downbeat DBD 004	Belly Full (with General Saint)/WAYNE WADE: Little Suzie (12")	40
84	Greensleeves GRED 150	Belly Move/Why The World Stay So (12")	20
80	Trojan TRLS 191	COOL PON YOUR CORNER (LP)	20
80	Third World TWS 937	SHOWCASE (LP)	40
84	Uptempo UT 003	ROOTS & CULTURE (LP)	25

BEN BROWN

| 67 | Polydor 56198 | Ask The Lonely/Sidewinder | 50 |

BOOTS BROWN & HIS BLOCKBUSTERS

58	RCA RCA 1078	Cerveza/Juicy	12
59	RCA RCA 1102	Jim Twangy/Trollin'	10
59	RCA RCA 1102	Jim Twangy/Trollin' (78)	10

(see also Shorty Rogers)

BUSTER BROWN

60	Melodisc 1559	Fannie Mae/Lost In A Dream	70
65	Sue WI 368	Fannie Mae/Lost In A Dream (reissue)	40
67	Island WI 3031	My Blue Heaven/Two Women	20
69	Blue Horizon 57-3147	Sugar Babe/I'm Going, But I'll Be Back	40
60s	XX MIN 713	B. AND BUSTER BROWN (EP, with B. Brown)	20
68	Doctor Bird DB 1158	Here Comes The Night/Don't Look Back	30
69	Upsetter US 304	What A Price/How Can I Forget?	12
69	Upsetter US 308	To Love Somebody/BLEECHERS: Farmer's In The Den	20
69	Punch PH 10	Broken Heart/Tribute To A King	12
70	Punch PH 38	Greatest Love/I Love You Madly	12
70	Escort ES 822	Fight For Your Right/MEDITATORS: Soul Fight (Busty Top A Pop) (B-side actually "Soul Fight" by Busty Brown)	25
70	Escort ES 845	Man Short (with Gaytones)/DAVE BARKER: She Want It	12

70	Gas GAS 154	I Love You Madly/Greatest Love	10
70	High Note HS 048	Man Short (with Gaytones)/GAYTONES: Another Version	12
71	Bullet BU 476	Never Love Another/Version	6
71	Punch PH 72	You Inspire Me/UPSETTERS: Version	6
71	Pama Supreme PS 356	Throw Away Your Gun/TWINKLE BROTHERS: Sad Song	20

CHARLES BROWN (BAND)

56	Vogue V 9061	I'll Always Be In Love With You/Soothe Me	350
56	Vogue V 9061	I'll Always Be In Love With You/Soothe Me (78)	60
57	Vogue V 9065	Confidential/Trouble Blues	500
57	Vogue V 9065	Confidential/Trouble Blues (78 rpm)	40
61	Parlophone R 4848	It's Christmas All Year Round/Christmas Question	10

(see also Brown Brothers)

CLARENCE 'GATEMOUTH' BROWN

65	Vocalion VE 170161	CLARENCE 'GATEMOUTH' BROWN (EP)	90
72	Python PLP 26	CLARENCE 'GATEMOUTH' BROWN VOL. 1: 1948-1953 (LP)	25
72	Python PLP 27	CLARENCE 'GATEMOUTH' BROWN VOL. 2: 1956-1965 (LP)	25

CLIFFORD BROWN (& HIS GROUP)

55	Vogue EPV 1027	GIGI GRYCE - CLIFFORD BROWN ORCHESTRA (EP)	10
55	Vogue EPV 1041	CONCEPTION (EP)	10
56	Vogue EPV 1119	CLIFFORD BROWN ENSEMBLE (EP)	10
54	Vogue LDE 042	CLIFFORD "BROWNIE" BROWN QUARTET (10" LP)	30
55	Vogue LDE 121	THE CLIFFORD BROWN SEXTET (10" LP)	30
58	Emarcy EJL 1278	STUDY IN BROWN (LP)	25

(see also Art Farmer, Sonny Rollins, Max Roach)

DENNIS BROWN

70	Bamboo BAM 56	Love Grows/SOUND DIMENSION: Less Problem	40
70	Banana BA 309	No Man Is An Island/SOUL SISTERS: Another Night	30
71	Banana BA 336	Never Fall In Love/Make It With You	30
71	Ocean OC 001	Little Green Apples/SOUND DIMENSION: Version	10
72	Duke DU 139	What About The Half/What About The Half Version	30
72	Explosion EX 2068	Black Magic Woman/PHILL PRATT ALL STARS: Black Magic Woman Pt 2	15
72	Pressure Beat PR 5513	Money In My Pocket/JOE GIBBS ALLSTARS: Money Love	15
72	Randy's RAN 526	Cheater/TOMMY McCOOK & IMPACT ALLSTARS: Harvest In The East	20
72	Randy's RAN 528	Meet Me On The Corner (actually unknown instrumental)/ IMPACT ALLSTARS: Version	10
72	Songbird SB 1074	Silhouettes/CRYSTALITES: Version	12
73	Ashanti ASH 402	It's Too Late/Song My Mother Used To Sing	12
73	Jackpot JP 813	He Can't Spell/CRYSTALITES: Acid Version	10
73	Smash SMA 2327	Concentration/Version	12
74	Sydna SYD 5027	No More Shall I Roam/Coming Home	10
76	Doctor DR 03	Out In The Rain/Version	8
76	Hawkeye HE 01	Whip Them Jah/Version	12
77	Observer OBS 999	Jah Is Watching/Hustling/Rock On/Murder Observer Style (12" with DILLINGER)	40
77	Observer OB 003	Tenement Yard/Kill Landlord/HORACE ANDY: Them Never Tell I/Teacher Gal (12", with Ranking Buckers)	25
77	DEB 0002	Half/Troubled World (12")	15
78	DEB DDDEB 010	Oh What A day/Man Next Door (12")	20
79	Observer OBS 902	Blessed Are The Men (The Pill)/ JUNIOR DELGADO : Cry Cry (12")	20
80	High Times HT 001	Blood City/FREDDIE McGREGOR : Natural Collie (12")	35
80	Pratt PP 30	Black Magic Woman/Version (12")	40
80	DEB DEB 039	I Don't Want To Be No General/General (Version) (12" with Ranking Dread)	12
84	Greensleeves GRED 167	It's Magic/PAD ANTHONY: Crazy Love (12")	25
86	Jakki JM 468	Rebel With A Cause/JACKIE MITTOO: Trade Mark (12")	25
73	Trojan TRLS 57	SUPER REGGAE & SOUL HITS (LP)	25
75	Trojan TRLS 107	JUST DENNIS (LP)	15
77	DEB DEBLP 01	WOLF AND LEOPARDS (LP)	25
78	Lightning LIP 7	VISIONS OF (LP)	25
78	Laser LASL 1	WORDS OF WISDOM (LP, stickered sleeve with free 12" Money In My Pocket)	25
78	Laser LASL 1	WORDS OF WISDOM (LP)	20
80	Laser LASL 6	JOSEPH'S COAT OF MANY COLOURS (LP)	18
86	Trojan TRSL 238	THE EXIT (LP)	15

(see also Big Youth & Dennis Brown, Hugh Roy, Big Youth, Sound Dimension)

DENNIS BROWN & ASWAD

80	Simba SM003	Promised Land/More Dub (12")	20

DUSTY BROWN

61	Starlite ST45 058	Please Don't Go/Well You Know	20

ERROL BROWN & CHOSEN FEW

72	Songbird SB 1082	People Make The World Go Round/People Make The World Go Round (Version)	8

(see also Hot Chocolate)

FAITH BROWN

70	CBS 4728	Lock Me In/The Game Of Love	5
71	Penny Farthing PEN 766	Any Way That You Want Me/City Wine	5
72	Regal Zonophone RZ 3063	Take Me With You/If We Only Have Love	5

(see also Carrolls)

FAY BROWN

55	Columbia SCM 5185	Unchained Melody/I Was Wrong	15

FUNKY BROWN

72	Sioux SI 018	African (Indian Reservation)/JUMBO STERLING: Elizabethan Reggae	6

GABRIEL BROWN

77	Policy Wheel PW 4592	GABRIEL BROWN AND HIS GUITAR (LP, withdrawn)	15

GEORGIA BROWN

55	Decca F 10489	My Crazy L'il Mixed Up Heart/Before We Know It	5
55	Decca F 10551	I Love To Dance With You/That's All I Need	5
55	Decca F 10616	I Went To The Village/Wrong Again	5
60	Decca F 11286	Blue Eyed Boy/Milord	5

MINT VALUE £

72	Bug 18	Turn Out The Light/I Scare Myself	5
63	Decca SKL 4586	SINGS GERSHWIN (LP)	12

GLEN BROWN

68	Blue Cat BS 131	Way Of Life (with Joe White & Trevor)/ KARL BRYAN & LYN TAITT: I'm So Proud	150
70	Summit SUM 8502	Collie And Wine/BEVERLEY'S ALLSTARS: Version	10
70	Songbird SB 1021	Love I/CRYSTALITES: Heavy Load	12
72	Songbird SB 1081	Smokey Eyes (with Crystalites)/Smokey Eyes (Version)	20
79	Kingley REX 4	Marcus Garvey Words/SLYFORD WALKER: Africa (12")	20
96	Blood & Fire BAFLP 015	TERMINATION DUB (LP, as Glen Brown & King Tubby)	15

GLENMORE BROWN & HOPETON LEWIS

68	Fab FAB 42	Girl You're Cold/Soul Man	100

(see also Hopeton Lewis & Glenmore Brown)

HENRY BROWN

61	'77' LA 12-5	HENRY BROWN BLUES (LP)	45

HUX BROWN & SCOTTY

71	High Note HS 056	Unbelievable Sounds/GAYTONES: Unbelievable Sounds Version	25

HYLO BROWN (& TIMBERLINERS)

59	Capitol CL 15075	You Can't Relive The Past/Thunder Clouds Of Love	5
60	Capitol CL 15139	I've Waited As Long As I Can/Just Any Old Love	5

IAN BROWN

98	Polydor 571 986-7	My Star/See The Dawn (7", p/s)	5
00	Polydor 561 908-1	Thriller/Billie Jean (12", p/s)	15
09	Fiction 2717752	Stellify/Crowning Of The Poor (red vinyl, 1000 only, numbered)	15
98	Polydor 539 916-1	UNFINISHED MONKEY BUSINESS (LP, gatefold, p/s)	15
99	Polydor 543 141-1	GOLDEN GREATS (LP, yellow vinyl, p/s)	20
01	Polydor 589 126-1	MUSIC OF THE SPHERES (LP)	25
02	Polydor SPHERE2	REMIXES OF THE SPHERES (2x12" Promo Sampler)	20
02	Polydor 065 927-1	REMIXES OF THE SPHERES (LP)	20
05	Fiction 987 287-3	THE GREATEST (2xCD Deluxe Book Edition)	20

(see also Stone Roses)

IRVING BROWN

70	Bamboo BAM 36	Today/SOUND DIMENSION: Young Gifted And Black Version	15
70	Bamboo BAM 58	I'm Still Around/Run Come	18
70	Bamboo BAM 61	Let's Make It Up (actually by Larry Marshall)/BURNING SPEAR: Free	35
71	Bamboo Now BN 1003	Now I'm Alone/Funky Night	18

(see also Larry Marshall)

JACKIE BROWN

72	High Note HS 057	One Night/GAYTONES: One Night Version	8
72	High Note HS 060	Last Dance/GAYTONES: Last Dance Version	8
75	Black Wax 10	Send Me The Pillow/MIGHTY TWO: Pillow With Strings	6

JAMES BROWN (& FAMOUS FLAMES)

SINGLES

60	Parlophone R 4667	Think/You've Got The Power (with Famous Flames)	40
60	Fontana H 273	This Old Heart/Wonder When You're Coming Home	30
62	Parlophone R 4922	Night Train/Why Does Everything Happen To Me (with Famous Flames)	40
62	Parlophone R 4952	Shout And Shimmy/Come Over Here (with Famous Flames)	30
63	London HL 9730	Prisoner Of Love/Choo-Choo (Locomotion) (with Famous Flames)	20
63	London HL 9775	These Foolish Things/(Can You) Feel It (Part 1) (with Famous Flames)	20
64	Philips BF 1368	Out Of Sight/Maybe The Last Time (& His Orchestra)	20
64	Sue WI 360	Night Train/Why Does Everything Happen To Me (with Famous Flames)	35
65	London HL 9945	Have Mercy Baby/Just Won't Do Right (with Famous Flames)	20
65	London HL 9990	Papa's Got A Brand New Bag Parts 1 & 2 (with Famous Flames)	18
65	Ember EMB S 216	Tell Me What You're Gonna Do/Lost Someone (p/s)	40
65	Ember EMB S 216	Tell Me What You're Gonna Do/Lost Someone	20
65	Philips BF 1458	Try Me/Papa's Got A Brand New Bag	20
66	Philips BF 1481	New Breed Parts 1 & 2	20
66	Pye International 7N 25350	I Got You (I Feel Good)/I Can't Help It (I Just Do-Do-Do) (with Famous Flames)	15
66	Pye International 7N 25367	Ain't That A Groove Parts 1 & 2 (with Famous Flames)	10
66	Pye International 7N 25371	It's A Man's Man's Man's World/Is It Yes Or Is It No? (with Famous Flames)	8
66	Pye International 7N 25379	Money Won't Change You Parts 1 & 2 (with Famous Flames)	15
66	Pye International 7N 25394	Don't Be A Drop-Out/Tell Me That You Love Me (with Famous Flames)	10
67	Pye International 7N 25411	Bring It Up/Nobody Knows (with Famous Flames)	10
67	Pye International 7N 25418	Kansas City/Stone Fox (with Famous Flames)	10
67	Pye International 7N 25423	Let Yourself Go/Good Rockin' Tonight (with Famous Flames)	10
67	Pye International 7N 25430	Cold Sweat Parts 1 & 2 (with Famous Flames)	10
67	Pye International 7N 25441	Get It Together Parts 1 & 2 (with Famous Flames)	15
68	Polydor 56740	I Can't Stand Myself/There Was A Time	15
68	Polydor 56743	I Got The Feelin'/If I Ruled The World	5
68	Polydor 56744	Licking Stick, Licking Stick Parts 1 & 2	5
68	Polydor 56752	Say It Loud, I'm Black And I'm Proud Parts 1 & 2	8
68	Polydor 56540	That's Life/Please, Please, Please (with Famous Flames)	15
69	Polydor 56776	Mother Popcorn Parts 1 & 2	6
69	Polydor 56780	The World Parts 1 & 2	6
69	Polydor 56783	Let A Man Come In And Do The Popcorn/Sometimes	10
69	Polydor 56787	There Was A Time/I Can't Stand Myself (When You Touch Me)	12
70	Polydor 56793	Ain't It Funky Now Parts 1 & 2	6
70	Polydor 2001 018	It's A New Day/Georgia On My Mind	6
70	Polydor 2001 071	Get Up, I Feel Like Being A Sex Machine Parts 1 & 2 (paper label)	6
70	Polydor 2001 071	Get Up, I Feel Like Being A Sex Machine Parts 1 & 2 (plastic label)	5
70	Polydor 2001 097	Call Me Super Bad Parts 1, 2 & 3	6
71	Polydor 2001 163	Soul Power Parts 1, 2 & 3	6
71	Polydor 2001 190	I Cried/Get Up, Get Into It, Get Involved	6
71	Polydor 2001 213	Hot Pants (She Got To Use What She Got To Get What She Wants) Parts 1, 2 & 3	6
71	Polydor 2001 223	Make It Funky Parts 1 & 2	6
71	Mojo 2093 006	Hey America!/Brother Rapp (Part 1)	6

Year	Label/Cat No.	Title	Value
71	Polydor 2066 153	I'm A Greedy Man Parts 1 & 2	6
72	Polydor 2066 185	King Heroin/Theme From King Heroin	20
72	Polydor 2066 210	There It Is Parts 1 & 2	7
72	Polydor 2066 216	Honky Tonk Parts 1 & 2	10
72	Polydor 2066 231	Get On The Good Foot Parts 1 & 2	7
72	Polydor 2066 283	What My Baby Needs Now Is A Little More Lovin'/ This Guy's In Love With You (with Lyn Collins)	15
73	Polydor 2066 285	I've Got A Bag Of My Own/I Know It's True	7
73	Polydor 2141 008	Papa's Got A Brand New Bag/Out Of Sight/It's A Man's Man's Man's World (p/s)	5
73	Polydor 2066 296	I Got Ants In My Pants Parts 1, 15 & 16	5
73	Polydor 2066 329	Think/Something	5
73	Polydor 2066 370	Woman Parts 1 & 2	5
74	Polydor 2066 411	Stone To The Bone/Sexy, Sexy, Sexy	5
74	Polydor 2066 485	My Thang/The Payback	5
74	Polydor 2066 513	It's Hell/Papa Don't Take No Mess	5
75	Polydor 2066 520	Funky President (People It's Bad)/Cold Blooded	5
76	Polydor 2066 642	Hot (I Need To Be Loved, Loved, Loved)/Superbad, Superslick (Part 1)	5
76	Polydor 2066 687	Get Up Offa That Thing/Release The Pressure	5
77	Polydor 2066 763	Bodyheat Part 1/Bodyheat Part 2	5
77	Polydor 2066 834	Honky Tonk/Brother Rapp	5
78	Polydor 2066 915	Eyesight/I Never, Never, Never Will Forget	5
78	Polydor 2066 984	Nature Parts 1 & 2	5
79	Polydor POSP 24	For Goodness Sakes, Look At Those Cakes/ Get Up, I Feel Like Being A Sex Machine (red label)	8
79	Polydor POSP 24	For Goodness Sakes, Look At Those Cakes/ Get Up, I Feel Like Being A Sex Machine (silver label)	5
79	Polydor POSPX 24	Get Up, I Feel Like Being A Sex Machine/For Goodness Sakes, Look At Those Cakes (12")	10
79	Polydor POSPX 68	It's Too Funky In Here/Are We Really Dancing? (12")	10
79	Polydor STEP 2	Star Generation/Let The Boogie Do The Rest	5
79	Polydor STEPX 2	Star Generation/Let The Boogie Do The Rest (12")	8
80	Polydor POSP 121	Regrets/Stone Cold Drag	5

EPs

Year	Label/Cat No.	Title	Value
64	London RE 1410	JAMES BROWN AND THE FAMOUS FLAMES	60
64	Ember EMB EP 4549	I DO JUST WHAT I WANT	40
66	Pye Intl. NEP 44059	I GOT YOU	40
66	Pye Intl. NEP 44068	I'LL GO CRAZY	40
67	Pye Intl. NEP 44072	PRISONER OF LOVE	40
67	Pye Intl. NEP 44076	HOW LONG DARLING	40
67	Pye Intl. NEP 44088	BRING IT UP	40
70	Polydor 580 701	TURN IT LOOSE	30

ALBUMS

Year	Label/Cat No.	Title	Value
64	London HA 8177	PURE DYNAMITE! (as James Brown & Famous Flames)	75
64	London HA 8184	LIVE AT THE APOLLO (as James Brown & Famous Flames)	60
64	Ember EMB 3357	TELL ME WHAT YOU'RE GONNA DO	40
64	Philips BL 7630	SHOWTIME	30
65	London HA 8203	UNBEATABLE 16 HITS	45
65	London HA 8231	PLEASE, PLEASE, PLEASE (as James Brown & Famous Flames)	80
65	Philips BL 7664	GRITS AND SOUL	50
65	London HA 8240	JAMES BROWN TOURS THE U.S.A. (with Famous Flames)	50
66	London HA 8262	PAPA'S GOT A BRAND NEW BAG (as James Brown & Famous Flames)	50
66	Philips BL 7697	JAMES BROWN PLAYS JAMES BROWN TODAY AND YESTERDAY	40
66	Pye Intl. NPL 28074	I GOT YOU (I FEEL GOOD)	50
66	Philips BL 7718	JAMES BROWN PLAYS NEW BREED	20
66	Pye Intl. NPL 28079	IT'S A MAN'S MAN'S WORLD	30
66	Pye Intl. NPL 28097	THE JAMES BROWN CHRISTMAS ALBUM	40
67	Pye Intl. NPL 28093	MIGHTY INSTRUMENTALS	30
67	Philips (S)BL 7761	HANDFUL OF SOUL	20
67	Pye Intl. NPL 28099	PAPA'S GOT A BRAND NEW BAG (reissue)	20
67	Pye Intl. NPL 28100	MR. EXCITEMENT	30
67	Polydor 582 703	THE JAMES BROWN SHOW (live)	20
67	Pye Intl. NPL 28103	SINGS RAW SOUL	20
67	Pye Intl. NPL 28104	LIVE AT THE GARDEN	35
68	Philips (S)BL 7823	JAMES BROWN PLAYS THE REAL THING	25
68	Polydor 623 032	MR. DYNAMITE	12
68	Polydor 184 100	MR. SOUL	12
68	Polydor 184 136	I CAN'T STAND MYSELF	20
69	Polydor 184 148	SOUL FIRE	15
69	Polydor 184 159	KING OF SOUL	12
60s	Polydor 2852 002	THE SOUL OF JAMES BROWN (reissue of "I Can't Stand Myself")	12
69	Mercury 20133 SMCL	JAMES BROWN SINGS OUT OF SIGHT	20
69	Polydor 583 729/30	LIVE AT THE APOLLO VOLUME TWO (2-LP)	18
69	Polydor 583 741	SAY IT LOUD - I'M BLACK AND I'M PROUD	20
69	Polydor 583 768	IT'S A MOTHER	20
69	Polydor 643 317	THIS IS ... JAMES BROWN	15
70	Polydor 583 742	GETTIN' DOWN TO IT	20
70	Polydor 184 319	THE POPCORN	20
70	Polydor 2343 010	AIN'T IT FUNKY	20
71	Polydor 2625 004	SEX MACHINE (2-LP)	20
71	Polydor 2310 022	SOUL ON TOP	20
71	Polydor 2310 029	IT'S A NEW DAY	20
71	Polydor 2310 089	SUPER BAD	20
72	Polydor 2659 011	REVOLUTION OF THE MIND: RECORDED LIVE AT THE APOLLO VOL. III (2-LP)	20
72	Polydor 2391 033	THERE IT IS	20
73	Polydor 2659 018	GET ON THE GOOD FOOT (2-LP)	20
73	Polydor 2391 057	SOUL CLASSICS (also issued as record club edition [ACB 00222])	12
73	Polydor 2490 117	BLACK CAESAR (soundtrack)	35
73	Polydor 2391 084	SLAUGHTER'S BIG RIP-OFF (soundtrack)	30
74	Polydor 2391 116	SOUL CLASSICS VOLUME TWO	12
74	Polydor 2659 030	THE PAYBACK (2-LP)	25
74	Polydor 2659 036	IT'S HELL (2-LP)	25

James BROWN (Jamaica)

75	Polydor 2391 164	REALITY	12
75	Polydor 2391 166	SOUL CLASSICS VOLUME THREE	12
75	Polydor 2391 175	SEX MACHINE TODAY	15
75	Polydor 2391 197	EVERYBODY'S DOIN' THE HUSTLE AND DEAD ON THE DOUBLE BUMP	15
77	Polydor 2391 300	MUTHA'S NATURE (by James Brown & the New J.B,'s)	15

(see also Lyn Collins, JBs, Maceo & All King's Men, Nat Kendrick & Swans)

JAMES BROWN (JAMAICA)

71	Punch PH 76	Don't Say/TRANS AM ALLSTARS: Don't Say Version	8
72	Ashanti ASH 408	Mama Don't Want To See You/Mama Don't Want To See You Version	7
75	Mango MAN 1001	Stop The War In Babylon/Dub In Peace	15

JANET BROWN

| 79 | Logo GO 366 | Iron Lady/The Coming Of The Leader | 6 |
| 79 | Logo MOGO 4006 | IRON LADY (LP) | 12 |

JERICHO BROWN

| 60 | Warner Bros WB 14 | Don'tcha Know (That I Love You)/Look For A Star | 10 |
| 64 | Warner Bros WB 141 | I'm Watching You/Wisdom Of A Fool | 6 |

JIM EDWARD BROWN

| 66 | RCA RCX 7179 | INTRODUCING JIM EDWARD BROWN (EP) | 15 |

(see also Browns)

JIM EDWARD (BROWN) & MAXINE BROWN

55	London HL 8123	Itsy Witsy Me/Why Am I Falling?	60
55	London HLU 8166	Your Love Is Wild As The West Wind/Draggin' Mainstreet	50
55	London HLU 8200	You Thought I Thought/Here Today And Gone Tomorrow (B-side with Bonnie)	45
55	London R-EP 1024	COUNTRY SONGS (EP)	20
55	London R-EU 1044	COUNTRY SONGS VOLUME 3 (EP)	20

JOE BROWN (& BRUVVERS)

59	Decca F 11185	People Gotta Talk/Comes The Day (solo, triangular centre)	15
60	Decca F 11207	Darktown Strutter's Ball/Swagger (solo)	5
60	Decca F 11246	Jellied Eels/Dinah	5
60	Pye 7N 15322	Shine/The Switch	5
61	Piccadilly 7N 35000	Crazy Mixed Up Kid/Stick Around	5
61	Piccadilly 7N 35005	Good Luck & Goodbye/I'm Henery The Eighth I Am	5
62	Piccadilly 7N 35024	What A Crazy World We're Living In/Popcorn	5
62	Decca F 11496	Comes The Day/People Gotta Talk (reissue)	5
64	Piccadilly 7N 35163	You Do Things To Me/Everybody Calls Me Joe	6
63	Piccadilly 7N 35138	Sally Ann/There's Only One You	6
69	Pye 7N 17339	With A Little Help From My Friends/(won't cha) Show Me Around	6
62	Decca DFE8500	A PICTURE OF JOE BROWN (EP)	10
62	Picadilly NEP 34025	JOE BROWN HIT PARADE (EP)	10
68	MCA MUP 247	JOE BROWN (LP)	12

(see also Vicki Brown, Browns Homebrew)

JOHNNY BROWN

| 61 | Philips PB 1119 | Walkin' Talkin' Kissin' Doll/Sundown | 10 |

KAY BROWN

| 56 | Brunswick 05595 | Me 'N' You 'N' The Moon/What Do You Think It Does To Me? | 5 |

KENT BROWN & RAINBOWS

| 68 | Fab FAB 53 | When You Going To Show Me How/Come Ya Come Ya | 10 |

(see also Kent & Jeannie, Sir D's Group)

LENNOX BROWN

| 72 | Green Door GD 4023 | High School Serenade/WINSTON SCOTLAND: On The Track (1st issue) | 7 |
| 72 | Bullet BU 501 | High School Serenade/WINSTON SCOTLAND: On The Track (2nd issue) | 7 |

(see also Jeff Barnes, Peter Tosh)

LEROY BROWN

| 78 | Revue REVD 10 | Blood A Go Run/Taxi (12") | 35 |

LES BROWN & HIS BAND OF RENOWN

54	Vogue Coral Q 2034	Ramona/Hot Point	5
54	Vogue Coral Q 2042	St. Louis Blues Mambo/Moon Song	5
55	Vogue Coral Q 72049	The Man That Got Away/Doodle-Doo-Doo	5
55	Capitol CL 14331	Frenesi/Perfidia	5
55	Capitol CL 14350	He Needs Me/Simplicity	5
55	Vogue Coral Q 72107	Lullaby Of Birdland/Bernie's Tune	5
56	Vogue Coral Q 72123	Hong Kong Blues (with Hoagy Carmichael & Band Of Renown)/ It's All Right With Me	10
56	Vogue Coral Q 72215	Flamingo/Midnight Sun	5
56	Capitol CL 14512	Sincerely Yours/Take Back Your Mink	5
56	Capitol CL 14611	That Certain Feeling/Hit The Road To Dreamland	5
56	Capitol CL 14631	Talk About A Party/Ancient History	5
57	Capitol CL 14675	Priscilla/The Best Years Of My Life	5
57	Capitol CL 14706	Original Joe/If I Had The Money	5
57	Vogue Coral Q 72242	Forty Cups Of Coffee/I'm Forever Blowing Bubbles	6

LES BROWN (JR)

| 60s | Vocalion VA 8011 | WILDREST DRUMS YET (LP) | 15 |

MAXINE BROWN

61	London HLU 9286	All In My Mind/Harry, Let's Marry	45
62	HMV POP 1102	Am I Falling In Love/Promise Me Anything	120
63	Stateside SS 188	Ask Me/Yesterday's Kisses	55
64	Pye International 7N 25272	Oh No Not My Baby/You Upset My Soul	30
65	Pye International 7N 25299	It's Gonna Be Alright/You Do Something To Me	30
65	Pye International 7N 25317	One Step At A Time/Anything For A Laugh	40
67	Pye International 7N 25410	I've Got A Lot Of Love Left In Me/Hold On (I'm Comin') (B-side with Chuck Jackson)	30
67	Pye International 7N 25434	Since I Found You/Gotta Find A Way	25
70	Major Minor MM 709	Reason To Believe/I Can't Get Along Without You	25
73	Avco 6105 022	Picked Up, Packed Up And Put Away/Bella Mia	10
75	Pye Disco Demand DDS 117	One In A Million/Let Me Give You My Lovin'	10

90s	Kent TOWN 110	It's Torture/I Got Love	12

(see also Chuck Jackson & Maxine Brown)

NAPPY BROWN (& HIS BAND)

55	London HL 8145	Don't Be Angry/It's Really You	400
55	London HL 8145	Don't Be Angry/It's Really You (78)	30
55	London HLC 8182	Pitter Patter/There'll Come A Day	350
55	London HLC 8182	Pitter Patter/There'll Come A Day (78)	30
57	London HLC 8384	Little By Little/I'm Getting Lonesome (& His Band) (gold lettering on label)	300
57	London HLC 8384	Little By Little/I'm Getting Lonesome (& His Band) (silver lettering on label)	150
57	London HLC 8384	Little By Little/I'm Getting Lonesome (& His Band) ((78 rpm)	15
58	London HLC 8760	It Don't Hurt No More/My Baby	75
58	London HLC 8760	It Don't Hurt No More/My Baby (78)	20

NOEL BROWN

50s	Parlophone MP 134	Take Me Back To Africa/Virgin Islands (Get Happy In A Hurry) (78, export)	5
68	Island WI 3149	Man's Temptation/Heartbreak Girl	60
69	Songbird SB 1012	By The Time I Get To Phoenix/Heartbreak Girl	5
70	Bullet BU 423	Phoenix (actually by "By The Time I Get To Phoenix")/Heartbreak Girl	6

(see also Bunny Brown)

OSCAR BROWN JNR

61	Philips PB 1097	But I Was Cool/Dat Dere	5
60	CBS 62229	SIN & SOUL (LP)	12

PAMELA BROWN

70	Joe JRS 8	People Are Running/CRITICS: School Days	15

PATRICK BROWN

82	Kufe EB 003	Fantasy/On The Right Track (12")	40

PETE BROWN(& PIBLOKTO)

69	Parlophone R 5767	The Week Looked Good On Paper/Morning Call (as Pete Brown & His Battered Ornaments, promo p/s)	65
69	Parlophone R 5767	The Week Looked Good On Paper/Morning Call (as Pete Brown & His Battered Ornaments)	22
69	Harvest HAR 5008	Living Life Backwards/High Flying Electric Bird (as Pete Brown & Piblokto!)	20
70	Harvest HAR 5023	Can't Get Off The Planet/Broken Magic (with His Battered Ornaments)	15
70	Harvest HAR 5028	Flying Hero Sandwich/My Last Band (as Pete Brown & Piblokto!)	25
69	Harvest SHVL 752	A MEAL YOU CAN SHAKE HANDS WITH IN THE DARK (LP, as Pete Brown & His Battered Ornaments, with "Sold in U.K" label text on 4 lines, stereo)	350
70	Harvest SHVL 768	THE ART SCHOOL DANCE GOES ON FOREVER (LP, as Pete Brown & Piblokto!, gatefold sleeve, no EMI on label)	300
70	Harvest SHVL 782	THOUSANDS ON A RAFT (LP, as Pete Brown & Piblokto!, gatefold sleeve, no EMI on label)	250
73	Deram SML 1103	THE NOT FORGOTTEN ASSOCIATION (LP, with Graham Bond)	100
77	Harvest SHSM 2017	MY LAST BAND (LP, as Pete Brown & Piblokto)	20
82	Discs Intl. INTLP 1	PARTY IN THE RAIN (LP, with Ian Lynn, private pressing)	15

(see also Battered Ornaments, Graham Bond & Pete Brown, Deke Leonard, Cream)

PINEY BROWN

54	Esquire 10-330	That's Right Little Girl/EDDIE CHAMBLEE: Blues For Eddie (78)	10

POLLY BROWN

72	Pye 7N 45197	I'll Cry My Heart Out For You/Teardrops WIll Fall	8
75	GTO GT 14	Dial L For Love/Love Lovin' You	6
76	GTO GT 61	Love Bug/Love Bug Buzzin'.	6
77	GTO GT 88	Beautiful Things For You/MY Heart Keeps Breaking Over You	6
73	Pye NSPL 18396	POLLY BROWN (LP)	20

ROY BROWN

57	London HLP 8398	I'm Sticking With You/Party Doll (gold label print)	500
57	London HLP 8398	I'm Sticking With You/Party Doll (later silver print pressing)	200
57	London HLP 8398	I'm Sticking With You/Party Doll (gold label print, later silver) (78)	50
57	London HLP 8448	Saturday Night/Everybody	500
57	London HLP 8448	Saturday Night/Everybody (78)	50

RUTH BROWN (& HER RHYTHMAKERS)

55	London HL 8153	Mambo Baby/Mama (He Treats Your Daughter Mean) (with Rhythmakers)	350
55	London HL 8153	Mambo Baby/Mama (He Treats Your Daughter Mean) (with Rhythmakers) (78)	30
55	London HLE 8210	As Long As I'm Moving/R.B. Blues (with Her Rhythmakers)	350
55	London HLE 8210	As Long As I'm Moving/R.B. Blues (with Her Rhythmakers) (78)	30
56	London HLE 8310	I Want To Do More/Sweet Baby Of Mine	200
56	London HLE 8310	I Want To Do More/Sweet Baby Of Mine (78)	30
57	London HLE 8401	Mom Oh Mom/I Want To Be Loved (But Only By You)	200
57	London HLE 8401	Mom Oh Mom/I Want To Be Loved (But Only By You) (78)	30
57	Columbia DB 3913	Lucky Lips/My Heart Is Breaking Over You	350
57	Columbia DB 3913	Lucky Lips/My Heart Is Breaking Over You (78)	40
57	London HLE 8483	When I Get You Baby/One More Time	100
57	London HLE 8483	When I Get You Baby/One More Time (78)	40
58	London HLE 8552	A New Love/Look Me Up	100
58	London HLE 8552	A New Love/Look Me Up (78)	30
58	London HLE 8645	Just Too Much/Book Of Lies	100
58	London HLE 8645	Just Too Much/Book Of Lies (78)	40
58	London HLE 8757	This Little Girl's Gone Rockin'/Why Me	80
58	London HLE 8757	This Little Girl's Gone Rockin'/Why Me (78)	40
58	London HL 7061	This Little Girl's Gone Rockin'/Why Me (export issue)	75
59	London HLE 8887	Jack O' Diamonds/I Can't Hear A Word You Say	40
59	London HLE 8887	Jack O' Diamonds/I Can't Hear A Word You Say (78)	20
59	London HLE 8946	I Don't Know/Papa Daddy	50
59	London HLE 8946	I Don't Know/Papa Daddy (78)	40
60	London HLK 9093	Don't Deceive Me/I Burned Your Letter	40
61	London HLK 9304	Sure 'Nuff/Here He Comes	30
64	Brunswick 05904	Yes Sir That's My Baby/What Happened To You	10
76	President PT 457	Sugar Babe/Stop Knocking	10
55	London REE 1038	THE QUEEN OF R&B (EP)	200
63	Philips BE 12537	GOSPEL TIME (EP)	50

MINT VALUE £

60	London Jazz LTZ-K 15187	LAST DATE WITH RUTH BROWN (LP)	60
62	Philips 652 012 BL	ALONG COMES RUTH (LP)	50
63	Philips 652 020 BL	GOSPEL TIME (LP)	40
64	Atlantic ATL 5007	THE BEST OF RUTH BROWN (LP, plum label)	100
76	President PTLS 1067	SUGAR BABE (LP)	20

RUTH BROWN/JOE TURNER
| 56 | London REE 1047 | THE KING AND QUEEN OF R&B (EP, 2 tracks each) | 200 |

SAMMI BROWN
| 68 | Fontana TF 947 | Daydream/Stop The Music | 7 |

SANDY BROWN('S JAZZ BAND)
58	Tempo A 124	African Queen/Special Delivery (as Sandy Brown's Jazz Band)	5
53	Esquire EP 28	SANDY BROWN'S JAZZ BAND (EP)	10
55	Tempo EXA 13	SANDY BROWN'S JAZZ BAND (EP)	10
55	Tempo EXA 33	SANDY BROWN'S JAZZ BAND (EP)	10
56	Tempo EXA 49	TRADITIONAL JAZZ SCENE '56 (EP)	10
57	Nixa NJE 1054	BLUE McJAZZ (EP)	10
57	Nixa NJE 1056	AFRO McJAZZ (EP)	10
53	Esquire 20-022	SANDY BROWN (10" LP, with Bobby Mickleburgh)	20
56	Tempo TAP 3	SANDY'S SIDEMEN PLAYING COMPOSITIONS BY AL FAIRWEATHER (LP)	25
57	Nixa Jazz Today NJL 9	McJAZZ (LP)	15
66	Fontana TE1 7473	SANDY BROWN ALL STARS (LP)	15
69	Fontana SFJL 921	HAIR AT ITS HAIRIEST (LP, as Sandy Brown & His Gentlemen Friends)	25
71	77 SEU 12/49	WITH THE BRIAN LEMON TRIO (LP)	12

(see also Wally Fawkes, Sandy & Teachers, Al Fairweather)

SHIRLEY BROWN
75	Stax STXS 2019	Woman To Woman/Yes Sir, Brother	6
75	Stax STXS 2032	I Can't Give You Up/It Ain't No Fun	20
77	Arista 102	Blessed Is The Woman (With A Man Like Mine)/Lowdown Dirty Good Lover	8
75	Stax STX 1031	WOMAN TO WOMAN (LP)	20

(see also Oliver Sain)

STU BROWN & BLUESOLOGY
| 67 | Polydor 56195 | Since I Found You Baby/Just A Little Bit | 300 |

(see also Bluesology, Elton John)

TEDDY BROWN
| 70 | Trojan TR 7793 | What Greater Love/Lady Love | 6 |
| 71 | Trojan TR 7827 | Walk The World Away/Senorita Rita | 6 |

TINY BROWN
| 50 | Capitol CL 13306 | No More Blues/Slow-Motion Baby (78) | 10 |

U BROWN
78	Cancer CAN 702	Starsky And Hutch/Version	6
77	Klik KLP 9018	SATTA DREAD (LP)	60
79	Virgin Frontline FL 1030	CAN'T KEEP A GOOD MAN DOWN (LP)	15

VIC BROWN COMBO
| 63 | Rio R 7 | Swanee River/Robert E. Lee | 15 |

VICKI BROWN
| 77 | Power Exchange PXL 012 | FROM THE INSIDE (LP) | 15 |

VINCENT BROWN
| 70 | Gas GAS 128 | Look What You're Going To Do/Hold On To What You Have Got | 8 |

WATSON T. BROWN (& EXPLOSIVE)
68	President PT 207	Some Lovin'/Home Is Where Your Heart Lies	6
68	President PT 221	Crying All Night/I Close My Eyes	10
70	Bell BLL 1109	Will You Still Love Me Tomorrow/Save The Last Dance For Me (solo)	6
71	MAM MAM 16	I'm On The Road Again/Feeling Bad	6

(see also Explosive)

WILLIAM BROWN
| 71 | Ackee ACK 128 | I'm Alone/BELTONES: Soul People | 10 |

BROWN BROTHERS
| 59 | Vogue V 9131 | Let The Good Times Roll/You're Right, I'm Left | 150 |
| 59 | Vogue V 9131 | Let The Good Times Roll/You're Right, I'm Left (78) | 40 |

(see also Charles Brown)

DUNCAN BROWNE
68	Immediate IM 070	On The Bombsite/Alfred Bell	25
70	Bell BLL 1119	Resurrection Joe/Final Asylum	12
73	Rak RAK 162	Send Me The Bill/My Only Son	6
78	Logo GO 329	Wild Places/Camino Real	6
68	Immediate IMSP 018	GIVE ME, TAKE YOU (LP, with insert, lilac label with "sold in U.K." label text)	400
73	RAK SRKA 6754	DUNCAN BROWNE (LP, gatefold sleeve)	50

FRIDAY BROWN(E)
66	Parlophone R 5396	Getting Nowhere/And (To Me He Meant Everything) (as Friday Browne)	25
66	Fontana TF 736	32nd Love Affair/Born A Woman	150
67	Fontana TF 851	Ask Any Woman/Outdoor Seminar	5
69	Fontana TF 996	Stand By Your Man/I Want To Rain	6
72	Philips 6006 239	Shake A Hand/Everything's Alright	5
73	Philips 6006 324	Groovy Kind Of Love/Salford	5
71	Philips 6308 074	FRIDAY BROWN (LP)	35

(see also Marianne & Mike, High Society, Manchester Mob, Graham Gouldman)

GEORGE BROWNE
54	Parlophone CMSP 6	Calypso Mambo/The Peanut Vendor (export issue)	10
54	Parlophone CMSP 17	Somebody Bad Stole De Wedding Bell (Who's Got De Ding Dong?)/ Matilda, Matilda! (export issue)	7
57	Columbia DB 3940	Sound Barrier/Te-Le-Le	7

(see also Humphrey Lyttleton)

JACKSON BROWNE

86	Elektra EKR 35P	For America (Edit)/Till I Go Down (Statue Of Liberty-shaped picture disc)	5
86	Elektra EKR 42P	In The Shape Of A Heart/Voice Of America (heart-shaped picture disc)	5
74	Asylum K2 43007	LATE FOR THE SKY (LP, quadrophonic)	15
85	Asylum K53070	RUNNING ON EMPTY (LP, Nimbus Supercut, mail order only via through Hi Fi Today)	50

SANDRA BROWNE (& BOYFRIENDS)

63	Columbia DB 4998	By Hook Or By Crook/Johnny Boy (as Sandra Browne & Boyfriends)	15
63	Columbia DB 7109	You'd Think He Didn't Know Me/Mama Never Told Me	15
65	Columbia DB 7465	Knock On Any Door/I Want Love	15

TEDDY BROWN(E)

59	Capitol CL 15059	A Corner In Paradise/The Everglades	5
61	Starlite ST45 033	Pretty Little Baby/Genevieve (as Teddy Brown)	8

THOMAS F. BROWNE

71	Vertigo 6325 250	WEDNESDAY'S CHILD (LP, gatefold sleeve, small swirl label)	175

(see also Gary Wright, The Gladiators)

TOBY BROWNE

64	Parlophone 5192	Play The Music, Keep On Dancing/Child	15

TOM BROWNE

80	Arista ARIST 12357	Funkin' For Jamaica (N.Y.)/Her Silent Smile (12")	10

DUKE BROWNER

79	Grapevine GRP 145	Crying Over You/Crying Over You (Instrumental)	20

(see also Kaddo Strings)

BROWNHILL'S STAMP DUTY

69	Columbia DB 8625	Maxwell's Silver Hammer/My Woman's Back	10

BILL BROWNING

80s	Roller Coaster RRC 2003	Wash Machine Boogie/Ramblin' Man (p/s)	8

BROWNS

59	RCA RCA 1140	The Three Bells/Heaven Fell Last Night (tri centre)	12
59	RCA RCA 1140	The Three Bells/Heaven Fell Last Night	5
59	RCA RCA 1140	The Three Bells/Heaven Fell Last Night (78)	20
59	RCA RCA 1157	Scarlet Ribbons (For Her Hair)/Blue Bells Ring (78)	10
60	RCA RCA 1176	Teen-Ex/The Old Lamplighter	8
60	RCA RCA 1193	Margo (The Ninth Of May)/Lonely Little Robin	8
60	RCA RCA 1218	Send Me The Pillow You Dream On/You're So Much A Part Of Me	5
60	RCA RCX 587	IN THE COUNTRY (EP, mono)	15
60	RCA SRC 7036	IN THE COUNTRY (EP, stereo)	20
59	RCA RD 27153	SWEET SOUNDS BY THE BROWNS (LP, mono)	15
59	RCA RD 27153/SF 5052	SWEET SOUNDS BY THE BROWNS (LP, stereo)	25

(see also Jim Edward & Maxine Brown)

BROWN'S FERRY FOUR

54	Parlophone CMSP 11	I Need The Prayers/Through The Pearly Gates (with Clyde Moody, export issue)	25

(see also Delmore Brothers, Grandpa Jones, Merle Travis)

GERRY BROWN'S JAZZMEN

61	Fontana TFL 5165	IT'S TRAD TIME! (LP)	12

BROWNS HOME BREW

72	Bell BELL 1211	Billy Come Down/Hit Me Across The Head With A Spoon	5
74	Vertigo 6360 114	TOGETHER (LP, spaceship label)	12

(see also Joe Brown)

BROWN SUGAR (1)

77	Lovers Rock CJ 613	I'm In Love With A Dreadlocks/Version	30
77	Lovers Rock CJ 614	Hello Stranger/Version	20
77	Lovers Rock CJ 619	Black Pride/Version	20
77	Lovers Rock CJ 624	Do You Really Love Me/Version	20

BROWN SUGAR (2)

80	Studio 16 WE 092	Dreaming Of Zion (12")	40
80	Studio 16 WE 106	Confession Hurts (12")	35
80	Studio 16 WE 113	Runaway Love (12")	40
80	African Drums AF 002	Hello Stranger/Black Is The Colour (12")	12
80	Black Roots BRLP 1000	NOT SO LUCKY (LP)	20

ANNETTE (REIS) & VICTOR BROX

65	Fontana TF 536	I've Got The World In A Jug/Wake Me And Shake Me	15
74	Sonet SNTF 663	ROLLIN' BACK (LP)	20

(see also Aynsley Dunbar Retaliation)

DAVE BRUBECK (QUARTET)

53	Vogue 45-2156	A Foggy Day/Lyons Busy	5
53	Vogue 45-2157	Mam'selle/Me And My Shadow	5
53	Vogue 45-2158	Frenesi/At A Perfume Counter	5
53	Vogue 45-2159	Body And Soul/Let's Fall In Love	5
53	Vogue 45-2160	I'll Remember April/Singin' In The Rain	5
53	Vogue 45-2161	Lullaby In Rhythm/You Stepped Out Of A Dream	5
54	Vogue V 2171	At A Perfume Counter/Me And My Shadow	5
54	Vogue V 2206	Frenesi/Mam'selle	5
60	Philips JAZ 106	I'm In A Dancing Mood/Lover (p/s)	5
54	Vogue LDE 090	DAVE BRUBECK TRIO (10" LP)	15
54	Vogue LDE 095	DAVE BRUBECK QUARTET (10" LP)	15
54	Vogue LDE 104	DAVE BRUBECK QUARTET VOL. 2 (10" LP)	15
55	Vogue LDE 114	DAVE BRUBECK QUARTET VOL. 3 (10" LP)	15
57	Fontana TFL 5017	DAVE DIGS DISNEY (LP)	15
59	Vogue LAE 12008	THE FABULOUS DAVE BRUBECK TRIO AND OCTET (LP)	15
59	Fontana TFL 5071	GONE WITH THE WIND (LP, also stereo STFL 501)	15
60	Vogue LAE 12114	DAVE BRUBECK QUARTET FEATURING PAUL DESMOND (LP)	15

(see also Jimmy Rushing, Carmen McRae)

MINT VALUE £

JACK BRUCE

65	Polydor BM 56036	I'm Getting Tired (Of Drinking And Gambling)/Rootin' Tootin'	80
71	Polydor 2058 153	The Consul At Sunset/Letter Of Thanks	15
74	RSO 2090 141	Keep It Down/Golden Days	5
69	Polydor 583 058	SONGS FOR A TAILOR (LP, laminated gatefold sleeve)	18
70	Polydor 2343 033	THINGS WE LIKE (LP)	18
71	Polydor 2310 070	THINGS WE LIKE (LP, reissue)	15
71	Polydor 2310 107	HARMONY ROW (LP, gatefold sleeve)	20
74	RSO 2394 143	OUT OF THE STORM (LP, with insert)	12

(see also Alexis Korner's Blues Incorporated, Cream, Manfred Mann, Graham Bond Organisation, John Mayall, West Bruce & Laing, Lifetime, Rocket 88, Carla Bley, Duffy Power, Cozy Powell)

TOMMY BRUCE (& BRUISERS)

60	Columbia DB 4453	Ain't Misbehavin'/Got The Water Boilin' (with Bruisers)	5
60	Columbia DB 4498	Broken Doll/I'm On Fire (with Bruisers)	10
60	Columbia DB 4532	On The Sunny Side Of The Street/My Little Girl (with Bruisers)	7
61	Columbia DB 4581	You Make Love So Well/I'm Crazy 'Bout My Baby (with Bruisers)	5
61	Columbia DB 4682	Love, Honour And Oh! Baby/I'm Gonna Sit Right Down And Write	10
62	Columbia DB 4776	Babette/Honey Girl, You're Lonely	8
62	Columbia DB 4850	Horror Movies/It's You	15
62	Columbia DB 4927	Buttons And Bows/London Boys	5
63	Columbia DB 7025	Let's Do It, Let's Fall In Love/Two Feet Left	5
63	Columbia DB 7132	Lavender Blue/Sixteen Years Ago Tonight	5
64	Columbia DB 7241	Let It Be Me/No More	5
64	Columbia DB 7387	Over Suzanne/It's Drivin' Me Wild	20
65	Polydor BM 56006	Boom Boom/Can Your Monkey Do The Dog (with Bruisers)	30
66	RCA RCA 1535	Monster Gonzales/I Hate Getting Up In The Morning	25
68	CBS CBS 3405	I've Been Around Too Long/Where The Colour Of The Soil Is Different	7
68	CBS CBS 3937	Heartbreak Melody/The Reason Why	7
61	Columbia SEG 8077	KNOCKOUT (EP)	70

CLAUDIA BRÜCKEN

90	Island 12ISX 471	Absolut[e] (Bastille Mix)/Absolut[e] (Shooting Star Mix) (12", remix, stickered title sleeve, promo only)	8

(see also Propaganda, Act, Glenn Gregory & Claudia Brucken)

HEIDI BRÜHL

60	Philips PB 1095	Ring Of Gold/I'll Belong To You Forever (in p/s)	10
60	Philips PB 1095	Ring Of Gold/I'll Belong To You Forever	5
63	Philips 345 579 BF	Marcel/Talk It Over With Someone	5
69	Philips BF 1768	The Drifter/Berlin	200
69	Philips BF 1768	The Drifter/Berlin (DJ Copy)	250

BRUISERS

63	Parlophone R 5042	Blue Girl/Don't Cry	15
63	Parlophone R 5092	Your Turn To Cry/Give It To Me	20

(see also [Peter] Lee Stirling & Bruisers)

BRUMBEATS

64	Decca F 11834	Cry Little Girl, Cry/I Don't Understand	25

BEAU BRUMMEL ESQUIRE

65	Columbia DB 7447	I Know Know Know/Shoppin' Around	8
65	Columbia DB 7538	The Next Kiss/Come And Get Me	12
65	Columbia DB 7675	A Better Man Than I/Teardrops	12
66	Columbia DB 7878	You Don't Know What You've Got/Take Me Like I Am	12

GEORGE BRUNIS

54	London AL 3536	NEW ORLEANS RHYTHM KINGS (LP)	20

BRUNNING (HALL) SUNFLOWER BLUES BAND

68	Saga FID 2118	BULLEN STREET BLUES (LP, as Brunning Sunflower Blues Band, with black/silver label)	30
69	Saga EROS 8132	TRACKSIDE BLUES (LP, black/silver labels)	45
70	Saga EROS 8150	I WISH YOU WOULD (LP, as Brunning Sunflower Blues Band, with black/silver labels)	75
71	Gemini GM 2010	THE BRUNNING/HALL SUNFLOWER BLUES BAND (LP, with white/red labels)	120

(see also Five's Company, Fleetwood Mac, Leaf Hound)

BRUNO

66	Parlophone R5450	Wonderboy/Window In My Room	25
66	Parlophone R5507	The English Girl/The Driver	25

TONY BRUNO

68	Capitol CL 15534	What's Yesterday/Small Town, Bring Down	50

BRUTE FORCE

69	Apple APPLE 8	King Of Fuh/Nobody Knows (unissued)	1200

BRUTUS

75	Purple PUR 126	Payroll/New Deal Princess	7

CARL BRYAN

69	Trojan TR 673	Red Ash/SILVERTONES: Bluebirds Flying Over	25
69	Duke DU 13	Soul Pipe/Overproof	15
69	Camel CA 22	Run For Your Life/TWO SPARKS: When We Were Young	12
69	Gas GAS 133	Stagger Back/The Creeper	45
69	Gas GAS 134	Walking The Dead/TREVOR & KEITH: Got What You Want	12

(see also Cannon Ball & Johnny Melody, King Cannon, Vincent Foster, Hugh Malcolm, King Cannonball, Glen Brown, Shenley Duffas, Alton Ellis, Kid Gungo, Jackie Mittoo, Johnny Moore, Joe White, Royals)

V. BRYAN ORCHESTRA

55	Kay CRS 028	Tan Tan - Calypso/CYRIL DIAS: Brass Crown (Vocal: Lord Superior) (78)	10

RAD BRYAN

71	Techniques TE 909	Jumping Jack/ANSELL COLLINS: Point Blank	12
71	Bullet BU 463	Shock Attack/Cuban Waltz	12
71	Big Shot BI 559	Just Do The Right Things/Corporal Jones	10
71	Big Shot BI 591	I'll Be Right There (actually by Techniques)/PLAYBOYS: Hot Pants Rock	12

71	Big Shot BI 592	My Best Girl/My Best Girl Version	20
71	Black Swan BW 1410	Girl You Rock My Soul/Version	15
72	Attack ATT 8040	Standing In The Rain (actually by Neville Grant)/Standing In The Rain Version	8
75	Love 1	Rock Children/Version	7

TIM BRYAN
| 71 | Phillips 6006026 | Mary Anne/It's So Easy | 8 |

WES BRYAN
58	London HLU 8607	Lonesome Love/Tiny Spaceman	40
58	London HLU 8607	Lonesome Love/Tiny Spaceman (78)	20
59	London HLU 8978	Honey Baby/So Blue Over You	50
59	London HLU 8978	Honey Baby/So Blue Over You (78)	30

BRYAN & BRUNELLES
| 65 | HMV POP 1394 | Jacqueline/Louie Louie | 50 |

FITZVAUGHN BRYAN'S ORCHESTRA
| 60 | Melodisc 45-1560 | Evening News/Hold Up Your Head And Smile (with Kenrick Patrick) | 10 |

ANITA BRYANT
59	London HLL 8983	Six Boys And Seven Girls/The Blessings Of Love	5
60	London HLL 9075	Little George (Got The Hiccoughs)/Love Look Away	5
60	London HLL 9247	Wonderland By Night/Pictures	5
61	London HLL 9281	Till There Was You/A Texan And A Girl From Mexico	5
61	London HLL 9353	Do-Re-Mi/An Angel Cried	5
61	Philips BF 1182	The Wedding/Seven Kinds Of Lonesome	5
62	CBS AAG 106	Free/One More Time With Billy	6
66	CBS 202026	Another Year, Another Love/My Mind's Playing Tricks On Me Again	60
62	CBS AAG 20005	KISSES SWEETER THAN WINE (EP)	10
61	London HA-L 2381	IN MY LITTLE CORNER OF THE WORLD (LP)	35

BOUDLEAUX BRYANT
| 60 | Polydor NH 66952 | Hot Spot/Touché (with Sparks) | 6 |
| *(see also Bood & Fileece Bryant)* | | | |

DON BRYANT
| 70 | London HA-U/SH-U 8409 | PRECIOUS SOUL (LP) | 50 |

JOHN BRYANT (1)
| 65 | Fontana H 625 | Tell Me What You See/Poor Unfortunate Me | 15 |
| 71 | Polydor 2383069 | JOHN BRYANT (LP, gatefold sleeve) | 20 |

JOHN BRYANT (2)
69	Decca 12894	She's In Need Of Love	25
68	MCA MU 1020	Columbine/I Bring The Sun	40
71	Polydor 2058-145	Back On The Road/I Won't Sleep Tonight/Ain't Got No Woman	6

LAURA K. BRYANT
| 58 | London HLU 8551 | Bobby/Angel Tears | 40 |
| 58 | London HLU 8551 | Bobby/Angel Tears (78) | 10 |

MARIE/MARGARET BRYANT
61	Kalypso XX 27	Water Melon/Tomato	6
61	Kalypso XX 28	Don't Touch Me Nylon/Little Boy	6
60s	Melodisc MLP 12 132	DON'T TOUCH ME NYLONS (LP, with sleeve)	25

RAY BRYANT TRIO/COMBO
60	Pye International 7N 25052	Little Susie Parts 2 & 4	5
60	Philips PB 1003	Little Susie Parts 1 & 3	5
60	Philips PB 1014	The Madison Time Parts 1 & 2	5

RUSTY BRYANT
| 57 | London HB-D 1066 | RUSTY BRYANT (10" LP) | 50 |
| 72 | Prestige PRST 10014 | FIRE EATER (LP) | 15 |

SANDRA BRYANT
| 67 | Major Minor MM 523 | Girl With Money/Golden Hours | 10 |
| 68 | Major Minor MM 553 | Out To Get You/There's No Lock Upon My Door | 30 |

GAVIN BRYARS
| 75 | Obscure 1 | THE SINKING OF THE TITANIC (LP) | 20 |
| *(see also Brian Eno)* | | | |

CALUM BRYCE
| 68 | Condor PS 1001 | Lovemaker/I'm Glad | 450 |

BERYL BRYDEN('S BACK-ROOM SKIFFLE)
56	Decca F 10823	Casey Jones/Kansas City Blues	40
56	Decca F 10823	Casey Jones/Kansas City Blues (78)	15
57	Decca (no cat. no.)	Rock Me/This Train (test pressing, with Alexis Korner & Cyril Davies)	150
63	Columbia DB 4860	I'm Movin' On/Moanin'	12
63	Columbia DB 7010	I'm Living With The Blues/Big Daddy	15
56	Melodisc EPM 7-69	BERYL BRYDEN WITH FATTY GEORGE'S JAZZ BAND (EP)	10
(see also Alexis Korner, Cyril Davies)			

BETSY BRYE
| 59 | Columbia DB 4350 | Sleep Walk/Daddy Daddy (Gotta Get A Phone In My Room) | 25 |

BRYGADA KRYZYS
| 82 | Fresh Records FRESH 13 | BRYGADA KRYZYS (LP) | 25 |

B SIDE
| 93 | B Promo B Side | Rip Piece Off/Can't Slow Me Down (12") | 30 |

B.T.B.
| 68 | Liberty LBF 15067 | Do It To 'Em/Sparrows And Daisies | 15 |

B.T.P. FOLDERS
| 80 | Future Earth FER 005 | Radio/All Of A Sudden (p/s) | 50 |

B12

93	Warp WAPLP 9LTD	ELECTRO - SOMA (2-LP, orange vinyl)	40
93	B12 09 CD	PRELUDE PT 1 (CD, 500 only)	25
93	B12 CD 1	REDCELL & STASIS (CD, 1500 only)	20
94	B12 15	B12 (12", 4-track promo only, 10 copies pressed)	40
07	B12 B1215	Practopia (12")	20

(see also Redcell, Musicology)

BUBA & SHOP ASSISTANTS

85	Villa 21 002	Something To Do/Dreaming Backwards (p/s, with insert in poly bag)	25

(see also Shop Assistants, Pastels)

BUBBLEGUM

68	Philips BF1677	Little Red Bucket/With The Sun In Your Hair	35

BUBBLEMEN

88	Beggars Banquet BUB1	The Bubblmen Are Coming/B Side (p/s, comic included)	8

(see also Bauhaus)

BUBBLES

63	Duke DK 1001	The Wasp/Bopping In The Barnyard (matrix: DK 1001A-1, plays Rocking Crickets by Hot Toddy's)	18
75	Decca F 13583	This Is Where The Hurdie Gurdie Heebie Geebie Greenie Meenie Man Came In/Zap N' Cat.	25
78	Rainbow RS 611	JAMIAS/Night Life	8
72	Bumble GE 117	Hazy Hazy Crazy Crazy/Audrey	8

BUBBLES & CO

65	Pye 7N 15875	Underneath My Pillow/Just One Girl	10

BUCCA

82	Plant Life PLR 039	THE HOLE IN THE HARPERS HEAD (LP)	20

BUCHANAN BROTHERS

69	Page One POF 139	Medicine Man Part 1/Part 2	8
69	Page One POF 154	Son Of A Lovin' Man/I'll Never Get Enough	5
70	Penny Farthing PEN 725	Rosianna/The Feeling That I Get When Your Near	6

GILLY BUCHANAN

80	Toe TOE 002	Me No Mix/PATRICK ANDY: Ain't No Me (12")	80

ROY BUCHANAN

72	Polydor 2066307	Sweet Dreams/John's Blues	5

LINDSEY BUCKINGHAM

81	Mercury MER 85	Trouble/That's How We Do It In L.A. (p/s)	5
82	Mercury MER 96	The Visitor (Bwana)/A Satisfied Mind (p/s)	5
82	Mercury MER 102	Mary Lee Jones/September Song (p/s)	6
83	Mercury MER 150	Holiday Road/Mary Lee Jones (p/s)	8
84	Mercury MER 168	Go Insane/Play In The Rain (p/s)	5
84	Mercury MER 176	Slow Dancing/D.W. Suite (p/s)	8
92	Mercury MER 371	Countdown/This Nearly Was Mine (p/s)	5
92	Mercury MER 380	Soul Drifter/Say You'll Meet Again (p/s)	5

(see also Fleetwood Mac)

BUCKINGHAM-NICKS

74	Polydor 2066 398	Don't Let Me Down Again/Races Are Run	15
76	Polydor 2066 700	Don't Let Me Down Again/Crystal	10
73	Polydor 2391 013	BUCKINGHAM-NICKS (LP, with insert, with stickered sleeve)	30
73	Polydor 2391 093	BUCKINGHAM-NICKS (LP, with insert, without stickered sleeve)	35
81	Polydor 2482 378	BUCKINGHAM-NICKS (LP, reissue with insert)	25

(see also Lindsay Buckingham, Stevie Nicks, Fleetwood Mac)

BUCKINGHAMS (U.K.)

65	Pye 7N 15848	I'll Never Hurt You No More/She Lied	5
65	Pye 7N 15921	To Be Or Not To Be/I Was Your First Guy	5

BUCKINGHAMS (U.S.)

67	Stateside SS 588	Kind Of A Drag/You Make Me Feel So Good	12
67	CBS 2859	Mercy Mercy Mercy/You Are Gone	12
67	CBS 2995	Hey Baby/And Our Love	15
68	CBS 2640	Don't You Care/Why Don't You Love Me	25
68	CBS 3559	Back In Love Again/You Misunderstand Me	6
69	CBS 3195	Susan/Foreign Policy	10

BOB BUCKLE

73	Ash ALP 107 S	COME LISTEN TO (LP)	50

JEFF BUCKLEY

93	Big Cat ABB 61XCD	LIVE AT SIN-E EP (Mojo Pin/Eternal Life/Je N'en Connais Pas La Fin/The Way Young Lovers Do (CD)	25
95	Columbia 662042 1	Last Goodbye (Edit)/Lover, You Should've Come Over (Live And Acoustic In Japan)/Tongue (Live) (10", p/s, 5000 only)	30
95	Columbia 661498	Last Goodbye/Last Goodbye (Full)/So Real (Live)/Dream Brother (Live) (12")	40
95	Columbia 88697098847	Hallelujah/I Know It's Over (Live 1995) (p/s, numbered sleeve, 2,700 only, blue/black vinyl)	10
94	Columbia 475928	GRACE (LP, with insert)	50
12	Columbia 4979721	MYSTERY WHITE BOY LIVE 95-96 (LP)	20

SEAN BUCKLEY & BREADCRUMBS

65	Stateside SS 421	It Hurts Me When I Cry/Everybody Knows	70

TIM BUCKLEY

67	Elektra EKSN 45008	Aren't You The Girl/Strange Street Affair Under Blue	12
67	Elektra EKSN 45018	Morning Glory/Knight-Errant	10
68	Elektra EKSN 45023	Once I Was/Phantasmagoria In Two	7
68	Elektra EKSN 45031	Wings/I Can't See You	7
68	Elektra EKSN 45041	Pleasant Street/Carnival Song	10
70	Straight S 4799	Happy Time/So Lonely	20

91	Strange Fruit SFPS082	THE PEEL SESSIONS: Morning Glory/Coming Home To You/ Sing A Song For You/Hallucinations/Troubadour/Once I Was (12", p/s) 10
66	Elektra EKL/EKS 4004	TIM BUCKLEY (LP, orange label)..60
67	Elektra EKL/EKS 318	GOODBYE AND HELLO (LP, orange label, gatefold sleeve) 55
68	Elektra EKS 74045	HAPPY SAD (LP, orange label) 50
69	Straight STS 1060	BLUE AFTERNOON (LP)..60
70	Elektra 2410 005	LORCA (LP)...40
71	Straight STS 1064	STARSAILOR (LP)..70
72	Warner Bros K 46176	GREETINGS FROM L.A. (LP, gatefold sleeve)..18
74	Discreet K 49201	SEFRONIA (LP)..20
74	Discreet K 59204	LOOK AT THE FOOL (LP)..18
90	Demon DFIEND 200	DREAM LETTER - LIVE IN LONDON 1968 (2-LP) 25

VERNON BUCKLEY

73	Grape GR 3057	Mr Softhand/G.G. ALLSTARS: Dub 6
73	Grape GR 3058	Ital Queen/G.G. ALLSTARS: Dub 6

MILT BUCKNER & HIS MUSIC

56	Capitol CL 14662	Night Mist/Good Time Express..5

SID BUCKNER PRODUCTIONS

76	Lyntone/Tropical Sounds DSR SB1008/1009	DUB SENSATION (LP, 50 copies, promo only in stamped white card sleeve) 150

TEDDY BUCKNER & HIS BAND

56	Vogue V 2369	Oh, Didn't He Ramble/Battle Hymn Of The Republic 5
56	Vogue V 2375	When The Saints Go Marching In/West End Blues 5
57	Vogue V 2414	Sweet Georgia Brown/That's My Home 5

BUCKY & STRINGS

62	Salvo SLO 1807	Lolita's On The Loose/Lonely Island (99 copies only) 20

BUD & HIS BUDDIES

58	Starlite ST45 006	June, July And August/Sing A Little Sweeter 5

BUD & TRAVIS

59	London HLU 8965	Bonsoir Dame/Truly Do...10
59	London HLU 8965	Bonsoir Dame/Truly Do (78)...10
60	London HLG 9211	The Ballad Of The Alamo/The Green Leaves Of Summer 10
61	London HA-G 2328	BUD AND TRAVIS IN CONCERT (LP, also stereo SAH-G 6128) 15

BILLY BUDD

69	Page One POF 138	Alice Long (You're Still My Favourite Girlfriend)/The Straight Life 20
70	Pye 7N 45010	You're Sailing Away/I'm Gonna Change It 12

ROY BUDD

65	Pye 7N 15807	Birth Of The Budd/M'Ghee M'Ghee 15
66	Parlophone R 5514	Summer Samba/Bahama Sound 5
67	Pye 7N 17279	Mr Rose/Summer Rain...10
68	Pye 7N 17652	Pavanne/Whizz Ball 5
69	Pye 7N 17773	Tijuana Piano/Lead On 5
70	Pye 7N 17987	Borsalino (Theme)/It Only Goes To Show 5
70	Pye 7N 45051	Carter (Theme)/Plaything (in p/s) 60
70	Pye 7N 45051	Carter (Theme)/Plaything 50
67	Pye N(S)PL 18177	PICK YOURSELF UP - THIS IS ROY BUDD (LP) 15
68	Pye NPL 18212	AT NEWPORT (LP) 18
71	Pye NSPL 18348	PLAYS SOLDIER BLUE AND OTHER THEMES (LP) 20
72	Polydor 2383 102	KIDNAPPED (Roy Budd/Mary Hopkin) 25
72	Pye NSPL 18389	CONCERTO FOR HARRY - SOMETHING TO HIDE (Roy Budd) 35
73	Pye NSPL 18398	FEAR IS THE KEY (LP, soundtrack) 50
76	Bradley's BRADS 8002	DIAMONDS (LP, soundtrack)...50
70s	Pye NSPL 19494	EVERYTHING'S COMING UP (LP)...15

BUDDY & SKETTO

62	Dice 45/CC 7	Little Schoolgirl/Hush Baby 12

(see also Father Sketto, Ruddy & Sketto, Sketto Rich)

BUDGIE

71	MCA MK 5072	Crash Course In Brain Surgery/Nude Disintegrating Parachutist Woman........15
72	MCA MK 5085	Whisky River/Guts 8
74	MCA MCA 133	Zoom Club (Edited Version)/Wondering What Everyone Knows 6
75	MCA MCA 175	I Ain't No Mountain/Honey..6
78	A&M AMS 7342	Smile Boy Smile/All At Sea 6
80	Active BUDGE	Wildfire/Wildfire (promo only) 10
80	Active BUDGE 1	IF SWALLOWED DO NOT INDUCE VOMITING (12" EP) 10
80	Active BUDGE 2	Crime Against The World/Hellbender (p/s) 8
81	RCA BUDGE 3	Keeping A Rendezvous/Apparatus (p/s) 5
81	RCA BUDGE 3	Keeping A Rendezvous/Apparatus (picture disc) 5
81	RCA BUDGE 4	I Turned To Stone (Part 1)/I Turned To Stone (Part 2) (orange vinyl).........5
82	RCA RCA 271	Bored With Russia/Don't Cry (poster p/s) 5
82	RCA RCAP 271	Bored With Russia/Don't Cry (picture disc) 5
71	MCA MKPS 2018	BUDGIE (LP, pink/red label, initial pressing with laminated sleeve and poster)........120
71	MCA MKPS 2018	BUDGIE (LP, pink/red label, with no poster) 50
71	MCA MKPS 2018	BUDGIE (LP, later pressing with blue/black label) 15
72	MCA MKPS 2023	SQUAWK (LP, 1st pressing, Matrix numbers: 7-LNMG-216-1l/262-1L, blue/black hexagon label, matt sleeve) 30
73	MCA MDKS 8010	NEVER TURN YOUR BACK ON A FRIEND (LP, blue/black label, g/fold sleeve) 25
74	MCA MCF 2546	IN FOR THE KILL (LP, rainbow label) 15
75	MCA MCF 2723	BANDOLIER (LP)..12
75	MCA MCF 2766	THE BEST OF BUDGIE (LP)...12
76	A&M AMLH 68377	IF I WAS BRITANNIA I'D WAIVE THE RULES (LP, silver/green label) 15
78	A&M AMLH 64675	IMPECKABLE (LP)..12
80	Active ACTLP 1	POWER SUPPLY (LP, with insert) 12
80	RCA RCALP 3046	POWER SUPPLY (LP, reissue, with different back sleeve) 20
81	RCA RCALP 6003	NIGHT FLIGHT (LP)..12
82	RCA RCALP 6054	DELIVER US FROM EVIL (LP) 12

(see also Tredegar, Phenomena, George Hatcher Band)

MINT VALUE £

DENNIS BUDLIMAR
67	Fontana TL 5307	THE CREEPER (LP)	20

BUENA VISTAS
66	Stateside SS 525	Hot Shot/T.N.T.	25

BUFFALO
81	Heavy Metal HEAVY 3	Battle Torn Heroes/Women Of The Night (p/s)	30
82	Heavy Metal HEAVY 15	Mean Machine/The Rumour (p/s)	25

BUFFALO SPRINGFIELD
67	Atlantic 584 077	For What It's Worth (Stop Hey What's That Sound)/ Do I Have To Come Right Out And Say It	25
67	Atlantic 584 145	Rock'n'Roll Woman/A Child's Claim To Fame	15
68	Atlantic 584 165	Expecting To Fly/Everydays	15
68	Atlantic 584 189	Uno-Mundo/Merry-Go-Round	12
69	Atco 226 006	Pretty Girl Why/Questions	10
72	Atlantic K 10237	Bluebird/Mr Soul/Rock'n'Roll Woman/Expecting To Fly (p/s)	5
67	Atlantic 587 070	BUFFALO SPRINGFIELD (LP, plum label, mispressing, lists "For What It's Worth" but plays "Baby Don't Scold Me"; matrix no. ends '1' mono)	70
67	Atlantic 588 070	BUFFALO SPRINGFIELD ((LP, plum label, mispressing, lists "For What It's Worth" but plays "Baby Don't Scold Me"; matrix no. ends '1' stereo)	50
67	Atlantic 587 070	BUFFALO SPRINGFIELD (LP, plum label, plays "For What It's Worth", mono)	40
67	Atlantic 588 070	BUFFALO SPRINGFIELD (LP, plum label, plays "For What It's Worth", stereo)	30
68	Atlantic 587 091	BUFFALO SPRINGFIELD AGAIN (LP, plum label, mono)	50
68	Atlantic 588 091	BUFFALO SPRINGFIELD AGAIN (LP, plum label, stereo)	40
69	Atco 228 024	LAST TIME AROUND (LP, plum label, gatefold sleeve)	25
69	Atco 228 012	RETROSPECTIVE (LP, plum label)	20
70	Atlantic 2464 012	EXPECTING TO FLY (LP, plum label)	20
72	Atlantic K 40014	BUFFALO SPRINGFIELD AGAIN (LP, reissue, green & orange label)	15
72	Atlantic K 40077	LAST TIME AROUND (LP, reissue, green & orange label, gatefold sleeve)	12
73	Atlantic K30028	ATLANTIC MASTERS (LP)	15

(see also Neil Young, Stephen Stills, Poco, Au-Go-Go Singers, Crosby Stills Nash & Young)

BUFFALO TOM
89	Caff CAFF 6	Enemy/Deep In The Ground (p/s)	25

BUFF MEDWAYS
00	Friends Of...FOBMFA 2	Fire/Manic Depression (die-cut sleeve)	8
01	Vinyl Japan PAD 74	Into Your Dreams/Highway Chile (p/s)	8
01	Hangman 004	Sally Sensation/Dawn Said What Have I Done	15
02	Transcopic TRAN 012	A Strange Kind Of Happyness/BILLY CHILDISH: Hound Dog (p/s, 500 only)	15
02	Transcopic TRAN 015	Troubled Mind/BILLY CHILDISH: Leave My Kitten Alone (p/s, 500 only)	12
02	Transcopic TRAN 017	Strood Lights/You Make Me Die (p/s)	12
03	Transcopic TRAN 025	Just 15/The Doo Rek (p/s)	8
03	Damaged Goods DAMGOOD 228	Merry Christmas Fritz/Stille Nacht (p/s, swirly white vinyl, 1000 only)	5
05	Damaged Goods DAMGOOD 238	(I'm A) Lie Detector/Dear Lorna (p/s)	5
01	Vinyl Japan ASKLP 132	THIS IS THIS (LP)	25
02	Transcopic TRANLP 016	STEADY THE BUFFS (LP)	20
03	Transcopic TRANLP 026	1914 (LP, as the Buffs)	20

(see also Billy Childish, Wild Billy Childish & Buff Medways, Nilkshakes, Thee Headcoats)

BUFFOONS
67	Columbia DB 8317	My World Fell Down/Tomorrow Is Another Day	18

BUG CENTRAL
99	Dole Office/DHSS 1	Gotta Get A Real Job/No Free Records (Unreleased, white label test pressings only)	35
00	BBP/Yellow Fever BBPV 5	MONEY & RIOTS EP (with inserts)	8
99	Helen Of Oi HOO 48	THE MEEK WILL INHERIT NOTHING (LP, with inserts)	15

THE BUGGER ALL STARS
81	Bead Records BEAD 19	THE BUGGER ALL STARS (LP)	20
83	Bead Records BEAD 21	BONZO BITES BACK (LP)	20

BUGGY
70	Parlophone R5832	The Rolly Pole Coaster/Harry The Keeper	15

SANDY BULL
69	Vanguard 19040	E PLURIBUS UNUM (LP)	25

BULLAMAKANKA
83	BBC REL 454	Dr Who Is Gonna Fix It/Harlequin	10

BULLDOG
72	MCA MU1166	No/Good Times Are Comin'	5

BULLDOG BREED
69	Deram DM 270	Portcullis Gate/Halo In My Hair	150
70	Deram Nova DN 5	MADE IN ENGLAND (LP, mono)	300
70	Deram Nova SDN 5	MADE IN ENGLAND (LP, stereo)	250

(see also Flies)

BULLDOGS
64	Mercury MF 808	John, Paul, George And Ringo/What Do I See	20

BULLET
71	Purple PUR 101	Hobo/Sinister Minister	20
75	Polydor 2058 548	Hanged Man/The Contract Man	10
75	Contour 2870 437	THE HANGED MAN (LP, TV soundtrack)	30

(see also Hard Stuff, Quatermass, Atomic Rooster)

BULLFROG
74	Cube BUG 44	Clancy/In The City	8

JOHN BULL BREED
66	Polydor BM 56065	Can't Chance A Breakup/I'm A Man	350

BULL MINSTRELS
73   Boston Sound/Guildhall GHS 9   HORNCASTLE FAYRE (LP) 20

BULLRING
70   CBS 4881   Birmingham Brass Band/Lady Of The Morning Sun 15

BULLSEYE
80   Kennet K1   No. 10,553/Why Don't You Let Me Know 8

BULLY BOYS BAND
70   Stateside SSL 5032   MOVIE SCENE - HEAVY SOUNDS FROM TODAY'S FILMS (LP)................................15

BULLY WEE (BAND)
75   Folksound   BULLYWEE (LP) 20
76   Red Rag RRR 007   THE ENCHANTED LADY (LP) 15
70s Red Rag RRR 017   SILVERMINES (LP, as Bullywee Band, with insert) 12
81   Jigsaw SAW 1   THE MADMAN OF GOTHAM (LP)..20

B. BUMBLE & STINGERS
61   Top Rank JAR 561   Bumble Boogie/School Day Blues 15
62   Top Rank JAR 611   Nut Rocker/Nautilus 5
62   Stateside SS 113   Apple Knocker/The Moon And The Sea 6
62   Stateside SS 131   Dawn Cracker/Scales 10
63   Stateside SS 192   Baby Mash/Night Time Madness 10
67   Mercury MF 977   Silent Movies/Twelfth Street Rag 10
72   Pye International 7N 25597   Down At Mother's Place/Manhattan Spiritual 10
62   Stateside SE 1001   THE PIANO STYLINGS OF B. BUMBLE (EP) 25
(see also Kim Fowley)

BUMBLE BEE SLIM
60s Fontana 688 138ZL   BEE'S BACK IN TOWN (LP) 25

BUMBLES
72   Purple PUR 107   Beep Beep/Buzz Off (promo only p/s) 25
72   Purple PUR 107   Beep Beep/Buzz Off 8
(see laos Hard Stuff, Atomic Rooster, Curtis Muldoon)

BUNCH
67   CBS 202506   We're Not What We Appear To Be/You Never Came Home 70
69   Beacon BEA 128   Red Rover, Red Rover/Happy Like This 7
72   Island WIP 6130   When Will I Be Loved/Willie And The Hand Jive 10
67   CBS 2740   Don't Come Back To Me/You Can't Do This...25
67   CBS 3060   Looking Glass Alice/Spare A Shilling 200
68   CBS 3692   Birthday/Still 30
68   CBS 3709   Birthday/Still (reissue) 15
72   Island ILPS 9189   ROCK ON (LP, with 1-sided flexi attached to die-cut sleeve: "Let There Be Drums" [WI 4002]) 70
72   Island ILPS 9189   ROCK ON (LP, without 1-sided flexi: "Let There Be Drums" [WI 4002])................20
(see also Peter & The Wolves, Sounds Around, John Pantry)

BUNCH OF FIVES
66   Parlophone R 5494   Go Home Baby/At The Station 70
(see also Viv Prince, Egg, Hullaballoos, Junior's Eyes, Outsiders [U.K.])

BUNDLE
70   Polydor 2058 029   Dirty La Rue/Progressive Underground 15

DAVE BUNDY
72   UK UK 10   Inside A Hole/Nicer Out 8

ROGER BUNN
70   Major Minor SMLP 70   PIECE OF MIND (LP, red/white/black label) 175
(see also Pete Browns Pitlokto, Roxy Music)

BUNNIES (OF LONDON)
68   Decca LK4951   CAUGHT LIVE AT THE PLAYBOY CLUB (LP) 20
69   Decca SKL5026   THE BUNNIES AGAIN SINGIN' AND SWINGIN' AT THE LONDON PLAYBOY CLUB (LP) 20

BUNNY & RICKY
75   Attack ATT 8107   Too Bad Bull (as Bunnie And Rickey)/UPSETTERS: Bad Cow 15
75   Attack ATT 8109   Bushwood Contrash/UPSETTERS: Callying Butt 15

BUNNY & RUDDY
68   Nu Beet NB 007   Rhythm & Soul/MONTY MORRIS: True Romance 25
68   Nu Beat NB 011   On The Town/MONTY MORRIS: Simple Simon 30

BINGY BUNNY
82   Cha Cha CHAD 46   Keep It In The Family (with MORWELLS)/SCIENTIST : Extended Dub/ Me & Jane (with MORWELLS)/SCIENTIST : Extended Dub (12") 40
82   Cha Cha CHAD 48   Street Lover (with MORWELLS)/NICODEMUS : How You Look Girl 'Pon The Street (12")......20
82   Cha Cha CHALP 015   ME & JANE (LP) 20

BINGY BUNNY & BONGO LES
73   Ackee ACK 506   International Scout/International Scout Version 12
(see also Bongo Les, Mediators)

BUNNY BROWN
72   Songbird SB 1073   Fat Boy/Fat Boy - Version 12
(see also Noel Brown, Winston Scotland)

BUNNY LION
79   Starlight SLP 900   RED (LP)...25

BUNNY WAILER
76   Island BUINNY 1   Blackheart Man/Amagideon (12") 20
77   Island IPR 2003   Get Up Stand Up/This Train (12") 20
78   Island IPR 2015   Love Fire/Love's Version (12")...15
78   Island IPR 2025   Roots, Radics, Rockers and Reggae/Fig Tree/Armagideon (12")....................20
79   Solomonic SM 001   Riding/Version (12") 30
81   Solomonic SM 01   Rise & Shine/Riding 20

81	Solomonic SM07	Rise & Shine/Solomonic Dub (12")	30
83	Solomonic SM 018	Boderation/THE SOLOMONIC PLAYERS - Badder ridim (12")	25

BOB BUNTING

68	Transatlantic TRA 166	YOU'VE GOT TO GO DOWN THIS WAY (LP)	45

VASHTI BUNYAN

70	Philips 6308 019	JUST ANOTHER DIAMOND DAY (LP)	1200

(see also Vashti, Fairport Convention, Dave Swarbrick, Robin Williamson)

BUOYS

70	Wand WN7	Timothy/It Feels Good	20
71	Wand MSW 8296	Give Up Your Guns/The Prince Of Thieves	15

ERIC BURDON (BAND)

75	United Artists UAS 29743	I'LL BE YOUR SUNSHINE (LP)	12
75	Capitol E-ST 11359	SUN SECRETS (LP, as Eric Burdon Band)	12
75	Capitol E-ST 11426	STOP (LP, as Eric Burdon Band)	15
78	Polydor 2302 078	SURVIVOR (LP, with 5 inserts with lyrics and drawings)	25
80	Polydor 2344 147	DARKNESS - DARKNESS (LP)	12

ERIC BURDON & THE ANIMALS

66	Decca F 12502	Mama Told Me Not To Come/See See Rider (unreleased)	0
66	Decca F 12502	Help Me Girl/See See Rider (amended issue with new A-side)	8
67	MGM MGM 1340	When I Was Young/A Girl Named Sandoz	8
67	MGM MGM 1344	Good Times/Ain't That So	8
67	MGM MGM 1359	San Franciscan Nights/Gratefully Dead	15
68	MGM MGM 1373	Sky Pilot (Parts 1 & 2)	12
68	MGM MGM 1412	Monterey/Anything	10
69	MGM MGM 1461	Ring Of Fire/I'm An Animal	10
69	MGM MGM 1481	River Deep Mountain High/Help Me Girl	10
67	MGM C(S) 8052	WINDS OF CHANGE (LP, yellow/black label with "sold in the U.K." label text)	70
68	MGM C(S) 8074	THE TWAIN SHALL MEET (LP, yellow black labels with "sold in the U.K." text)	70
68	MGM C(S) 8105	LOVE IS (LP, blue/gold labels with "sold in the U.K." text)	80
71	MGM 2619 002	LOVE IS (2-LP; individual LP nos.: 2354 006/7)	50

(see also Animals, Stud, Zoot Money's Big Roll Band, Family)

ERIC BURDON & WAR

70	Polydor 2001 072	Spill The Wine/Magic Mountain	10
71	Liberty LBF 15434	They Can't Take Away Our Music/Home Cookin'	5
71	United Artists UP 35217	Paint It Black/Spirit	5
70	Polydor 2310 041	ERIC BURDON DECLARES WAR (LP)	35
70	Liberty LDS 8400 3/4	BLACKMAN'S BURDON (2-LP, gatefold, with banned track "P.C. 3")	40
70	Liberty LDS 8400	BLACKMAN'S BURDON (2-LP, gatefold, without banned track "P.C. 3")	20
76	ABC ABCL 5207	LOVE IS ALL AROUND (LP)	12

(see also War)

ERIC BURDON & JIMMY WITHERSPOON

71	United Artists UP 35287	Soledad/Headin' For Home	6
71	United Artists UAG 29251	GUILTY! (LP, gatefold sleeve)	18

(see also Jimmy Witherspoon)

DAVE BURGESS (TRIO)

55	London HLB 8175	I Love Paris/Five Foot Two, Eyes Of Blue (Has Anybody Seen My Girl)	15
58	Oriole CB 1413	I'm Available/Who's Gonna Cry?	40
58	Oriole CB 1413	I'm Available/Who's Gonna Cry? (78)	10

SONNY BURGESS

60	London HLS 9064	Sadie's Back In Town/A Kiss Goodnight	250

JIM BURGETT

61	Philips PB 1133	Let's Investigate/The Living Dead	40

ELPEDO BURKE

75	Black Wax WAX 3	Madgie/MIGHTY CLOUD: Madgie Dub	6

KEVIN BURKE

78	Rockburgh ROC 105	IF THE CAP FITS (LP)	15

SOLOMON BURKE

61	London HLK 9454	Just Out Of Reach/Be Bop Grandma	50
62	London HLK 9512	Cry To Me/I Almost Lost My Mind	70
62	London HLK 9560	Down In The Valley/I'm Hanging Up My Heart For You	20
63	London HLK 9715	If You Need Me/You Can Make It If You Try	20
63	London HLK 9763	Can't Nobody Love You/Stupidity	20
64	London HLK 9849	He'll Have To Go/Rockin' Soul	20
64	London HLK 9887	Goodbye Baby (Baby Goodbye)/Someone To Love Me	20
64	Atlantic AT 4004	Everybody Needs Somebody To Love/Looking For My Baby	22
64	Atlantic AT 4014	The Price/More Rockin' Soul	15
65	Atlantic AT 4022	Got To Get You Off My Mind/Peepin'	20
65	Atlantic AT 4030	Maggie's Farm/Tonight's The Night	25
65	Atlantic AT 4044	Someone Is Watching/Dance, Dance, Dance	18
65	Atlantic AT 4061	Only Love (Can Save Me Now)/Little Girl That Loves Me	22
66	Atlantic AT 4073	Baby Come On Home/No, No, No, I Can't Stop Lovin' You Now	18
66	Atlantic 584 005	I Feel A Sin Comin' On/Mountain Of Pride	10
66	Atlantic 584 026	Keep Lookin'/Suddenly	10
67	Atlantic 584 100	Keep A Light In The Window Till I Come Home/Time Is A Thief	10
67	Atlantic 584 122	Take Me (Just As I Am)/I Stayed Away Too Long	10
68	Atlantic 584 191	I Wish I Knew (How It Would Feel To Be Free)/It's Just A Matter Of Time	10
68	Atlantic 584 204	Save It/Meet Me In Church	10
68	Bell BLL 1047	Uptight Good Woman/I Can't Stop (No No No)	10
69	Bell BLL 1062	Proud Mary/What Am I Living For	10
74	Anchor ABC 4002	Midnight And You/I Have A Dream	5
63	London REK 1379	TONIGHT MY HEART SHE IS CRYING (EP)	70
65	Atlantic AET 6008	ROCK'N'SOUL (EP)	60
63	London HA-K 8018	SOLOMON BURKE'S GREATEST (LP)	70
64	Atlantic ATL 5009	ROCK'N'SOUL (LP)	50

66	Atlantic 587/588 016	THE BEST OF SOLOMON BURKE (LP)	30
66	Atlantic 590 004	KING OF ROCK'N'SOUL (LP, reissue)	12
68	Atlantic 587 105	KING SOLOMON (LP)	35
68	Atlantic 587/588 117	I WISH I KNEW (LP)	30
69	Bell MBLL/SBLL 118	PROUD MARY (LP)	20
72	MGM 2315 048	THE ELECTRONIC MAGNETISM (LP)	15

(see also Soul Clan)

SONNY BURKE (U.K.)
62	Island WI 155	Let And Let Live/Our Love Is True	20
64	Black Swan WI 457	I Love You Still/It's Always A Pleasure	15
64	Black Swan WI 458	City In The Sky/Everyday I Love You More	15
65	Black Swan WI 469	Glad/Jeanie	15
65	Black Swan WI 470	Dance With Me/My Girl Can't Cook	15
65	Black Swan WI 471	Wicked People/Good Heaven Knows	15
66	Blue Beat BB 363	Blue Island/You Came And Left	12
67	Blue Beat BB 371	Look In Her Eyes/LLOYD CLARKE: Love Is Strange	30
67	Ska Beat JB272	Have Faith/Guinea Pig	18
68	Island ILP 972	THE SOUNDS OF SONNY BURKE (LP, mono only)	100

(see also Bob Andy, Gaylads, Ken Parker, Eddie Thornton Outfit, Glen Adams, Stranger Cole, Gaylads, Sonny & Yvonne)

SONNY BURKE OUTFIT
| 68 | Instant IN 003 | Baby Be My Girl/All You | 120 |

(see also Sonny Burke)

DAVE BURLAND
71	Trailer LER 2029	A DALESMAN'S LITANY (LP, red label)	25
72	Trailer LER 2082	DAVE BURLAND (LP)	20
75	Rubber RUB 012	SONGS AND BUTTERED HAYCOCKS (LP)	18
79	Rubber RUB 036	YOU CAN'T FOOL THE FAT MAN (LP)	15
80	Rubber RUB 012/036	DOUBLE TAKE (2-LP, reissue)	18

SASCHA BURLAND
| 61 | Philips PB 1152 | Gorilla Walk/Hole In My Soul | 7 |

BURLITZ
| 84 | Spartan SP 13 | Sleep Softly Mary/In The Dead Of The Night (p/s) | 8 |

PETER BURMAN
| 62 | Columbia 33SX 1452 | JAZZ TETE A TETE (LP) | 200 |

BURMOE BROTHERS
| 85 | Wild Blue Yonder WBY 121 | Skin/Leber Oder Lippenstift/Under The Blanket Of Love (12", p/s) | 15 |

(see also Marc Almond, Nick Cave)

BURN
| 00s | Virgin HUTCDP 146 | Facing The Music (1-sided, numbered gold-embossed p/s, 1000 only) | 20 |

CHRIS BURN & JOHN BUTCHER
| 85 | Bead Records BEAD 24 | FONETIKS (LP) | 20 |

JEAN-JACQUES BURNEL
| 79 | United Artists UP 36500 | Freddie Laker (Concorde And Eurobus)/Ozymandias (p/s) | 5 |
| 80 | United Artists BP 361 | Girl From The Snow Country/Ode To Joy (live)/ Do The European (live) (p/s, unissued) | 350 |

JEAN-JACQUES BURNEL & DAVE GREENFIELD
| 84 | Epic EPCA 4076 | Rain And Dole And Tea/Consequences (p/s) | 5 |

(see also, Blue Maxi, Stranglers)

BURNER
| 84 | High Roller 7HRR0132007 | Hammer Of The Gods/Time Is On My Side/Old Enough To Know Better (EP, p/s) | 10 |

JOHN BURNESS
| 69 | Columbia DB8536 | Theresa/I Don't Want You Anymore | 15 |

FRANCES BURNETT
59	Coral Q 72374	Please Remember Me/How I Miss You So (triangular centre)	70
59	Coral Q 72374	Please Remember Me/How I Miss You So (round centre)	40
59	Coral Q 72374	Please Remember Me/How I Miss You So (78)	15

KING BURNETT
| 75 | Dip DL 5056 | I Man Free/UPSETTERS: Version | 15 |
| 75 | Dip DL 5073 | Key Card/UPSETTERS: Domino Game | 15 |

REV. J.C. BURNETT/REV. GATES/REV. MOSELEY
| 60 | Fontana TFE 17265 | TREASURES OF NORTH AMERICAN NEGRO MUSIC VOLUME 6: PREACHERS AND CONGREGATIONS (EP) | 15 |

DORSEY BURNETTE
60	London HLN 9047	Juarez Town/(There Was A) Tall Oak Tree	10
60	London HLN 9160	Hey Little One/Big Rock Candy Mountain	15
61	London HLN 9365	(It's No) Sin/Hard Rock Mine	10
65	Tamla Motown TMG 534	Jimmy Brown/Everybody's Angel	225
65	Tamla Motown TMG 534	Jimmy Brown/Everybody's Angel (DJ copy)	250
69	Liberty LBF 15190	The Greatest Love/Thin Little, Simple Little, Plain Little Girl	5
63	London RE-D 1402	DORSEY BURNETTE SINGS (EP)	40
63	London HA-D 8050	DORSEY BURNETTE (LP)	60

(see also Johnny & Dorsey Burnette)

HANK C. BURNETTE
| 76 | Sonet SNTF 693 | DONT'T MESS WITH MY DUCKTAILS (LP) | 12 |
| 78 | Sonet SNTF 750 | ROCKABILLY GASSEROONIE (LP) | 12 |

JOHNNY BURNETTE (TRIO)
SINGLES
56	Vogue Coral Q 72177	Tear It Up/You're Undecided (as Johnny Burnette & Rock'N'Roll Trio)	500
56	Vogue Coral Q 72177	Tear It Up/You're Undecided (as Johnny Burnette & Rock'N'Roll Trio) (78)	150
57	Vogue Coral Q 72227	Honey Hush/Lonesome Train (as Johnny Burnette Trio)	500
57	Vogue Coral Q 72227	Honey Hush/Lonesome Train (as Johnny Burnette Trio) (78)	150

MINT VALUE £

57	Vogue Coral Q 72283	Touch Me/Eager Beaver Baby (as Johnny Burnette Trio)	200
57	Vogue Coral Q 72283	Touch Me/Eager Beaver Baby (as Johnny Burnette Trio) (78)	150
60	London HLG 9172	Dreamin'/Cincinnati Fireball	10
60	London HLG 9172	Dreamin'/Cincinnati Fireball (78)	350
60	London HLG 9254	You're Sixteen/I Beg Your Pardon	5
61	London HLG 9315	Little Boy Sad/Pledge Of Love	5
61	London HLG 9388	Girls/I've Got A Lot Of Things To Do	5
61	London HLG 9453	God Country And My Baby/Honestly I Do (withdrawn)	10
61	London HLG 9458	Settin' The Woods On Fire/I'm Still Dreaming	15
61	London HLG 9473	Big Big World/The Fool	10
62	Liberty LIB 55416	Clown Shoes/The Way I Am	8
62	Liberty LIB 55489	Damn The Defiant/Lonesome Waters	10
66	Liberty LIB 10235	Dreamin'/Little Boy Sad	6
62	Pye International 7N 25158	I Wanna Thank Your Folks/The Giant	10
63	Pye International 7N 25187	Remember Me/Time Is Not Enough	10
63	Capitol CL 15322	All Week Long/It Isn't There	25
64	Capitol CL 15347	Sweet Suzie/Walking Talking Doll	30
96	Cruisin' The 50s CASB 003	The Train Kept A Rollin'/Sweet Love On My Mind (300 copies only) (78)	30

EXPORT SINGLES

| 60 | London HLG 7104 | You're Sixteen/Settin' The Woods On Fire | 10 |
| 61 | London HL 7109 | Little Boy Sad/I Go Down To The River | 10 |

EPs

60	London RE-G 1263	DREAMING	30
61	London RE-G 1291	LITTLE BOY SAD	30
61	London RE-G 1309	BIG BIG WORLD	30
61	London RE-G 1327	GIRLS	30
63	Liberty LEP 2091	HIT AFTER HIT	20
64	Capitol EAP 20645	FOUR BY BURNETTE	150

ALBUMS

56	Coral LVC 10041	ROCK AND ROLL TRIO (10", as Johnny Burnette Trio)	800
61	London HA-G 2306	DREAMIN'	40
61	London HA-G 2349	YOU'RE SIXTEEN	40
61	London HA-G 2375	JOHNNY BURNETTE SINGS (mono)	40
61	London SAH-G 6175	JOHNNY BURNETTE SINGS (stereo)	50
62	Liberty LBY 1006	BURNETTE'S HITS AND OTHER FAVOURITES	40
64	Liberty LBY 1231	THE JOHNNY BURNETTE STORY	40
66	Ace Of Hearts AH 120	ROCK AND ROLL TRIO (reissue, as Johnny Burnette Trio)	40
68	Coral CP 10	TEAR IT UP (as Johnny Burnette Trio)	30

(see also Johnny & Dorsey Burnette)

JOHNNY & DORSEY BURNETTE

| 63 | Reprise R 20153 | Hey Sue/It Don't Matter Much | 70 |

(see also Johnny Burnette, Dorsey Burnette)

SMILEY BURNETTE

54	London HL 8071	Lazy Locomotive/That Long White Line	50
54	London HL 8071	Lazy Locomotive/That Long White Line (78)	10
54	London HL 8085	Chuggin' On Down "66"/Mucho Gusto	50
54	London HL 8085	Chuggin' On Down "66"/Mucho Gusto (78)	10

BURNIN' RED IVANHOE

| 70 | Warner Bros WS 3013 | BURNIN' RED IVANHOE (LP, green label) | 50 |
| 72 | Dandelion 2310 145 | W.W.W. (LP, gatefold sleeve) | 60 |

BURNING SPEAR

70	Bamboo 50	SOUND DIMENTION : Soul Food/BURNING SPEAR : Door Peeper	50
75	Fab FAB 240	Foggy Road/Version	20
78	Island Pre IPR 2027	Civilised Reggae/Social Living (12")	15
79	Burning Spear BS 001	Free The Whole Wide World/Jah Jah No Dead (12")	30
79	Tribesman TM 20	Free The Whole Wide World/Jah Jah No Dead (12")	30
82	Radic 12RIC114	Jah Is My Driver/Driver Dub/Distance/Forever	15
75	Island ILPS 9377	MARCUS GARVEY (LP, 1st pressing has stickered sleeve)	20
76	Island ILPS 9377	GARVEY'S GHOST (LP)	35
76	Island ILPS 9412	MAN IN THE HILLS (LP, gatefold)	15
77	Island MPLS 9431	DRY AND HEAVY (LP)	15
77	Island ILPS 9513	LIVE (LP)	12
82	Island SVLP 191	MARCUS GARVEY/GARVEY'S GHOST (2-LP, reissue)	20
04	Soul Jazz SJRLP 101	SOUNDS FROM BURNING SPEAR (2-LP)	20

(see also Irving Brown, King Cry Cry)

BURNING WITCH

| 98 | Trip 005 | CRIPPLED LUCIFER (CD, digipack) | 20 |

JAN BURNNETTE

62	Oriole CB 1716	I Could Have Loved You So Well/The Miracle Of Life	15
62	Oriole CB 1742	All At Once/Does My Heartache Show?	5
62	Oriole CB 1761	Teddy/Trust In Me	8
63	Oriole CB 1807	The Boy I Used To Know/Unimportant Things	8
63	Oriole CB 1841	Till I Hear The Truth From You/Fool In Love	8
64	Oriole CB 1905	Let Me Make You Smile Again/No Regrets	8
64	Oriole CB 1920	Too Young/The Four Winds And The Seven Seas	8
64	Oriole CB 1949	Love, Let Me Not Hunger/The One I Love (Belongs To Somebody Else)	5

EDDIE 'GUITAR' BURNS

| 72 | Action ACMP 100 | BOTTLE UP AND GO (LP) | 30 |
| 75 | Big Bear BEAR 7 | DETROIT BLACKBOTTOM (LP) | 20 |

GILLIAN BURNS

| 69 | Fontana TF 1044 | Hop Skip And Jump/Merry Go Round | 12 |

JACKIE BURNS & BELLES

| 63 | MGM MGM 1226 | He's My Guy/I Do The Best I Can | 90 |

JIMMY BURNS
79	Grapevine GRP 118	I Really Love You/I Love You Girl	25
79	Grapevine GRP 118	I Really Love You/I Love You Girl (DJ Copy)	30

LISA BURNS
78	MCA MCF 2849	LISA BURNS (LP)	15

RANDY BURNS
68	Fontana STL 5520	EVENING OF THE MAGICIAN (LP)	45

(see also Blue Cheer)

RAY BURNS
53	Columbia SCM 5077	Rags To Riches/Begorrah	10
54	Columbia SCM 5153	I Can't Tell A Waltz From A Tango/Lonely Nightingale	10
56	Columbia DB 3811	Condemned For Life (With A Rock And Roll Wife)/The Mare Piccola	35
57	Columbia DB 3966	Wonderful! Wonderful!/Bernadine	10
57	Columbia DB 3998	Dapper Dan/The Little Hut	10
58	Columbia DB 4107	Are You Sincere/The Best Dream Of All	10
55	Columbia SEG 7594	RAY BURNS (EP)	20

(see also Ruby Murray, Ronnie Harris, Diana Decker, Ray Martin)

BURNT OFFERING
94	Misanthropy 001	HVIS LYSET TAR OST (LP)	12
94	Misanthropy 002	DET SOMEGAG VAR (LP)	12

HAROLD BURRAGE
65	Sue WI 353	I'll Take One/A Long Ways Together	30
68	President PT 130	You Made Me So Happy/Take Me Now	10

KENNY BURRELL
61	Esquire 32-140	ALL NIGHT LONG (LP, as Kenny Burrell All Stars)	30
64	Verve VLP 9058	BLUE BLASH (LP, with Jimmy Smith)	20
65	Verve VLP 9099	GUITAR FORMS (LP)	20
67	Transatlantic PR 7315	SOUL CALL (LP)	15
66	Stateside SL 10163	CRASH! (LP, with Brother Jack McDuff)	15
68	Verve (S)VLP 9217	BLUES, THE COMMON GROUND (LP)	20
69	Verve SVLP 9246	NIGHT SONG (LP)	15

(see also Brother Jack McDuff, Jimmy Smith)

ROLAND BURRELL
84	C&E CEDI 105	Rip Off/Version (12")	80

WILLIAM S. BURROUGHS
80	Industrial IR 0016	NOTHING HERE NOW BUT THE RECORDINGS (LP)	80

TONY BURROWS
70	Bell BLL 1103	Melanie Makes Me Smile/I'll Get Along Somehow Girl	5
70	Bell BLL 1124	Every Little Move She Makes/I've Still Got My Heart, Joe	8

CHINA BURTON
79	Logo GO 354	You Don't Care (About Our Love)/(Instrumental Version)	20
79	Logo GO(T) 354	You Don't Care (About Our Love) (Long Version)/(Short Version)/(Instrumental Version) (12")	80

GARY BURTON (QUARTET)
68	RCA Victor SF 7923	LOFTY FAKE ANAGRAM (LP)	20
69	RCA SF 7980	IN CONCERT (LP)	15
69	RCA Victor SF 8015	GENUINE TONGUE FUNERAL (LP)	18
71	Atlantic 2400 107	GOOD VIBES (LP)	18
72	Atlantic K 40305	ALONE AT LAST (LP)	12
72	Atlantic K 40378	PARIS ENCOUNTER (LP, with Stefan Grappelli)	12

(see also Michael Gibbs)

HAL BURTON
58	Embassy WB 308	Move It/Susie Darling	10

JAMES BURTON
71	A&M AMLS 64293	THE GUITAR SOUNDS OF JAMES BURTON (LP)	50

(see also Jim & Joe, Shindogs)

JOHNNY BURTON
72	Philips 60006 238	Polevault Man/The Polythene Doll	35

TOMMY BURTON COMBO
64	Blue Beat BB 237	Lavender Blue/I'm Walking	20

TREVOR BURTON
71	Wizard WIZ 103	Fight For My Country/Janie Slow Down	30

(see also B,L&G; Uglys, Move, Balls, Denny Laine, Danny King's Mayfair Set, Magic Christians, Idle Race)

BURU
83	CSA CSALP 04	BURO (LP)	30

BURZUM
93	Misanthropy Amazon 001	HVIS LYSET TAR OSS (LP, marbled vinyl)	200
94	Misanthropy Amazon 002	DET SOM ENGANG VAR (LP, with stickered sleeve, inner sleeve and poster)	200
95	Misanthropy Amazon 003	BURZUM/ASKE (2-LP, gatefold sleeve)	100
96	Misanthropy Amazon 009	FILOSOFEM (3 - sided etched LP, stickered gatefold sleeve)	100
97	Misanthropy Amazon 013	DAUOI BALDRS (LP, with postcards and booklet, 1,000 only)	25
99	Misanthorpy Amazon 021	HILSSKJALF (LP, booket and insert, 1,000 only)	50
10	Back On Black BOBV 215LP	BELUS (LP, white vinyl)	50
10	Back On Black BOBV 215LP	BELUS (LP, black vinyl)	20
11	Back On Black BOBV 293LP	FALLEN (LP, clear vinyl)	20

LOU BUSCH & HIS ORCHESTRA
56	Capitol CL 14504	Zambesi/Rainbow's End	5

(see also Joe 'Fingers' Carr, Four Preps)

KATE BUSH
78	EMI EMI 2719	Wuthering Heights/Kite (p/s)	30

78	EMI EMI 2806	The Man With The Child In His Eyes/Moving (p/s)	15
79	EMI PSR 442/3	KATE BUSH ON STAGE (EP, double pack, gatefold sleeve, promo only)	60
81	EMI EMI 5201	Sat In Your Lap/Lord Of The Reedy River (p/s)	5
82	EMI EMI 5350	There Goes A Tenner/Ne T'Enfuis Pas (thick card, p/s)	5
84	EMI KBS 1	THE SINGLE FILE (13 x 7" box set with lyric booklet)	70
85	EMI KB 1	Running Up That Hill/Under The Ivy (gatefold p/s)	10
85	EMI 12 KB 2	Cloudbusting (Organon Mix)/Burning Bridges/My Lagan Love (12", p/s)	8
86	EMI KBP 4	The Big Sky (Single Mix)/Not This Time (picture disc)	8
89	EMI EMPD 119	This Woman's Work/Be Kind To My Mistakes (picture disc, with insert, PVC sl.)	5
90	EMI TRIB02	Rocket Man/Candle In The Wind (poster p/s)	8
93	EMI GIRL 1	Rubberband Girl (CD, 1-track "lyrical teaser", promo only)	15
93	EMI EM 280	Eat The Music/Big Stripey Lie (p/s, picture labels, release cancelled, 17 copies only)	1600
93	EMI 12EMPD 280	Eat The Music/Eat The Music (Madagascan Remix)/Big Stripey Lie (12", picture disc, unissued)	0
93	EMI CDEM 280	Eat The Music/(Madagascan Remix)/Big Stripey Lie (CD, unissued)	0
93	EMI MUSIC 1	Eat The Music (CD, 1-track promo for unissued single, no inlay, withdrawn)	150
93	EMI 12EMP 297	Moments Of Pleasure (Instrumental Version)/Home For Christmas (12" poster p/s)	8
94	EMI EMPD 355	And So Is Love/Rubberband Girl (USA Mix) (picture disc, PVC sleeve, with 60" x 40" poster, unnumbered or 5,000 numbered)	10
94	EMI EMPD 355	And So Is Love/Rubberband Girl (USA Mix) (picture disc, PVC sleeve, with 60" x 40" poster, unnumbered or 5,000 numbered)	6
05	EMI PROMO SAMPLER	KATE BUSH (CD in card sleeve, 9-track promotional back catalogue sampler Sent out prior to release of AERIAL album	20
05	EMI EM674	King Of The Mountain/Sexual Healing (picture disc)	5
78	EMI EMA 787	LIONHEART (LP, gatefold with gold embossed titles)	12
79	EMI EM CP 3223	THE KICK INSIDE (LP, picture disc, stickered sleeve)	50
79	EMI EM CP 3223	THE KICK INSIDE (LP, picture disc, stickered sleeve, second pressing with "manufactured in the U.K. by EMI Records Ltd" wording)	30
79	EMI EM CP 3223	THE KICK INSIDE (LP, picture disc, mispress with same picture both sides)	150
90	EMI KBBX 1	THIS WOMAN'S WORK (9-LP, box set)	120
90	EMI CDKBBX 1	THIS WOMAN'S WORK (CD, box set)	80
93	EMI 1047	THE RED SHOES (LP)	60
93	EMI (No Cat. No)	THE RED SHOES (CD, video, slide transparency, fountain pen, parchment discography & red ribbon box set, promo)	200
05	EMI 343960-1	AERIAL (2 x LP, gatefold)	50

(see also Peter Gabriel & Kate Bush, Lesley Duncan)

RAY BUSH & AVON CITIES' SKIFFLE

56	Tempo A 146	Hey Hey Daddy Blues/Green Corn	25
56	Tempo A 146	Hey Hey Daddy Blues/Green Corn (78)	10
56	Tempo A 149	Fisherman's Blues/This Little Light Of Mine	25
56	Tempo A 149	Fisherman's Blues/This Little Light Of Mine (78)	10
57	Tempo A 156	How Long, How Long, Blues/Julian Johnson	25
57	Tempo A 156	How Long, How Long, Blues/Julian Johnson (78)	10
57	Tempo A 157	Lonesome Day Blues/I Don't Know	25
57	Tempo A 157	Lonesome Day Blues/I Don't Know (78)	10
57	Tempo EXA 40	RAY BUSH & AVON CITIES' SKIFFLE (EP)	25
57	Tempo EXA 50	RAY BUSH & AVON CITIES' SKIFFLE NO. 2 (EP)	25

(see also Avon Cities Jazz Band)

BUSH BOYS

59	Capitol CL 15082	A Broken Vow/Never Before	5

BUSHKILLER

92	Danger 001	92 Salute/Bushkiller Draw (12")	25
94	Danger 002	TROUBLEMAKERS (EP)	45

BUSH TETRAS

81	Fetish FET 007	Things That Go Boom In The Night/Das Ah Riot (p/s)	10
82	Fetish FE 15	Can't Be Funky (unissued, stamped white label only, custom plain sleeve)	10
82	Fetish FET 16EP	RITUALS (12" EP)	15

BUSINESS

81	Secret SHH 123	Harry May/National Insurance Blacklist (p/s)	12
82	Secret SHH 132	SMASH THE DISCOS EP: Day-O (The Banana Boat Song)/Disco Girls/ Smash The Disco (p/s)	10
83	Secret SHH 150	OUT OF BUSINESS (12" EP, unissued, white label promo, 10 copies only)	100
85	Wonderful World Of... 121	Get Out Of My House/All Out Tonight/Foreign Girl/Outlaw (12", p/s)	25
85	Diamond DIA 001	Drinking N Driving/H-Bomb (live) (p/s)	15
85	Diamond DIA 001T	Drinking N Driving/H-Bomb (live)/Hurry Up Harry/Drinking 'N' Driving (original version) (12", p/s)	25
80s	Link LINK 1201	DO A RUNNER (12" EP)	12
83	Secret SEC 11	SUBURBAN REBELS (LP)	20
83	Syndicate SYNLP 2	1980-81 OFFICIAL BOOTLEGS (LP)	15
84	Syndicate SYNLP 6	LOUD, PROUD 'N' PUNK, LIVE (LP)	15
85	Harry May SE 13	SATURDAY HEROES (LP)	20
86	Dojo DOJO LP 35	SINGALONGABUSINESS (LP)	15
80s	Wonderful World WOWDLP 4	OFFICIAL BUSINESS 1980-81 (LP)	20
80s	Link LP 115	SATURDAY'S HEROES (LP)	12
80s	Wonderful World WOWDLP 5	SUBURBAN REBELS/SMASH THE DISCOS - BACK TO BACK VOL 2. (2xLP)	25
88	Link LINK LP 035	WELCOME TO THE REAL WORLD (LP)	12
90	Link LRMO 1	IN AND OUT OF BUSINESS (LP, mail-order, 550 only)	20

(see also UK)

BUSKERS

70	RCA 2023	If I Rules The World/Joey Friendship	5
73	Rubber RUB 007	LIFE OF A MAN (LP)	18
75	Hawk HALPX 142	THE BUSKERS (LP)	15

GEORGE HENRY BUSSEY/JIM BUNKLEY

71	Revival RVS 1003	GEORGE HENRY BUSSEY/JIM BUNKLEY (LP)	15

BUSTER

71	Parlophone R5881	Pasadena/Priscilla	10
73	Bradley BRAD 310	Motor Machine/Ring Around	15
74	Bradleys BRAD 7401	Superstar/Rainbows & Colours	15

BUSTER
77	RCA PL 25026	BUSTER (LP)	15

BUSTERS
63	Stateside SS 231	Bust Out/Astronauts	25

BUSTER('S) ALLSTARS
64	Blue Beat BB 244	Prince Royal/COSMO: One God	40
64	Blue Beat BB 269	The Tickler/COSMO: Rice And Badge	40
65	Blue Beat BB 294	Eye For Eye/South Virginia	35
65	Blue Beat BB 322	Happy Independence 65/STRANGER COLE: When The Party Is Over	25
65	Blue Beat BB 325	Congo Revolution/Little Darlin' - No One	120
65	Blue Beat BB 333	When The Party Is Over/Matilda (with Stranger Cole)	30
66	Blue Beat BB 342	Cincinnatti Kid/Sammy Dead	50
67	Blue Beat BB 372	Sounds And Pressure/My Darling (both actually by Hopeton Lewis)	45
67	Blue Beat BB 384	Take It Easy/Why Must I Cry (both actually by Hopeton Lewis)	25
69	Fab FAB 101	Pum Pum A Go Kill You/Oh Lady Oh	15
70	Fab FAB 124	The Rebel/The Preacher	15

(see also Prince Buster, Teddy King, Little Darling, Khandars, Higgs & Wilson, Owen Gray, Charmers, Fitzroy D Long, Maytals, Derrick Morgan, Eric Morris, Personalities, Roy & Millie, Zoot Simms, Spanish Boys, Spanish Town Skabeats)

BUSTER'S GROUP
61	Starlite ST45 052	Buster's Shack/ERIC MORRIS: Search The World	40
65	Blue Beat BB 395	This Gun For Hire/Yes Daddy	60

(see also Prince Buster, Rico, Owen Gray)

BUSTY & COOL
62	Blue Beat BB 144	Mr Policeman/What A World	20

TONY BUTALA
62	Salvo SLO 1801	Long Black Stockings/Rumors (99 copies only)	40

BUTCHER
82	Inept INEPT 002	On The Ground/Grow Up Don't Blow Up (p/s)	5
83	Inept INEPT 003	Stand And Fight (p/s, red vinyl)	5

(see also Intestines)

EDDIE BUTCHER
76	Free Reed FRR 003	I ONCE WAS A DAYSMAN (LP, with insert)	12

STAN BUTCHER
67	CBS 63072	SWING LIKE A BASTARD (LP)	45
66	CBS SS62838	HIS BIRDS AND BRASS (LP)	20

SAM BUTERA (& WITNESSES)
81	Capitol CL 16179	Bim Bam/Twinkie In Your Eyes (reissue)	10
58	HMV POP 476	Good Gracious Baby/It's Better Than Nothing At All	70
58	HMV POP 476	Good Gracious Baby/It's Better Than Nothing At All (78)	15
58	Capitol CL 14913	Bim Bam/Twinkle In Your Eye (as Sam Butera & Witnesses)	250
59	Capitol CL 14988	Handle With Care/French Poodle	20
64	Prima PR 1003	Skinnie Minnie/Little Liza Jane	18
56	HMV 7EG 8087	SAX SERENADE (EP)	40
60	London HA-D 2288	THE RAT RACE (LP, as Sam Butera & Witnesses)	30

(see also Louis Prima)

BILLY BUTLER (& ENCHANTERS)
69	Soul City SC 113	The Right Track/Boston Monkey	15
74	Epic S EPC 2508	The Right Track/Can't Live Without Her (Yellow label)	5
74	Epic S EPC 2508	The Right Track/Can't Live Without Her (Orange label)	8

CHAMP BUTLER
56	Vogue Coral Q 72163	The Joshua Tree/Down In Mexico	5

HAROLD BUTLER
77	Charmers 3	GOLD CONNECTION (LP)	50

JERRY BUTLER
58	London HL 8697	For Your Precious Love/Sweet Was The Wine (as Jerry Butler & the Impressions)	200
58	London HL 8697	For Your Precious Love/Sweet Was The Wine (as Jerry Butler & the Impressions) (78 rpm)	100
60	Top Rank JAR 389	I Found A Love/A Lonely Soldier	45
60	Top Rank JAR 531	He Will Break Your Heart/Thanks To You	55
61	Top Rank JAR 562	Find Another Girl/When Trouble Calls	35
61	Columbia DB 4743	Moon River/Aware Of Love	25
62	Stateside SS 121	Make It Easy On Yourself/It's Too Late	25
63	Stateside SS 158	You Can Run But You Can't Hide/I'm The One	30
63	Stateside SS 170	You Go Right Through Me/The Wishing Star	20
63	Stateside SS 195	Whatever You Want/You Won't Be Sorry	20
64	Stateside SS 252	Need To Belong/Give Me Your Love	25
64	Stateside SS 300	Giving Up On Love/I've Been Trying	20
65	Fontana TF 553	Good Times/I've Grown Accustomed To Her Face	20
65	Fontana TF 588	I Can't Stand To See You Cry/Nobody Needs Your Love	15
65	Mercury MF 932	Love (Oh, How Sweet It Is)/Loneliness	15
66	Sue WI 4003	I Stand Accused/I Don't Want To Hear Anymore	50
66	Sue WI 4009	Just For You/Believe In Me	50
67	Mercury MF 964	I Dig You Baby/Some Kinda Magic	8
67	Mercury MF 1005	Mr. Dream Merchant/'Cause I Love You So	8
68	Mercury MF 1035	Never Give You Up/Beside You	10
68	Mercury MF 1058	Hey Mr Western Union Man (Send A Telegram)/Just Can't Forget About You	10
69	Mercury MF 1078	Are You Happy/Strange I Still Love You	8
69	Mercury MF 1094	Only The Strong Survive/Just Because I Really Love You	10
69	Mercury MF 1122	Moody Woman/Go Away And Find Yourself	20
69	Mercury MF 1122	Moody Woman/Go Away And Find Yourself (DJ copy)	100
69	Mercury MF 1132	A Brand New Me/What's The Use Of Breaking Up	10
70	President PT 299	Make It Easy On Yourself/Moon River	8
72	Mercury 6052 036	One Night Affair/What's So Good About It (You're My Baby)	8
72	Mercury 6052 119	Moody Woman/A Brand New Me	15

MINT VALUE £

72	Mercury 6052 155	I Only Have Eyes For You/Ain't Understanding Mellow	5
72	Mercury 6052 168	One Night Affair/What's So Good About It (You're My Baby) (reissue)	5
63	Stateside SL 10032	HE WILL BREAK YOUR HEART (LP)	100
63	Stateside SL 10050	FOLK SONGS (LP)	40
68	Fontana (S)TL 5246	LOVE ME (LP)	45
68	Mercury 20118 (S)MCL	MR. DREAM MERCHANT (LP)	30
69	Mercury 20144 (S)MCL	SOUL GOES ON (LP)	35
69	Mercury 20154 (S)MCL	THE ICE MAN COMETH (LP)	30

(see also Betty Everett & Jerry Butler, Impressions, Gene & Jerry)

LESLIE BUTLER (& FUGITIVES)

67	Island WI 3069	Hornpipe Rock Steady/You Don't Have To Say You Love Me	35
67	Doctor Bird DB 1083	Winchester Rocksteady (with Fugitives)/ASTON CAMPBELL & CONQUERORS : Ramona	35
68	High Note HS 008	Top Cat/WEBBER SISTERS: Stars Above	25
68	High Note HS 009	Revival/GAYLADS: Over The Rainbow's End	12
75	Trojan TRLS 112	JA-GAN (LP)	30

(see also Ken Boothe, Fugitives, Gaylads)

BUTLIN'S REDCOAT REVUE

| 69 | Pama SECO 5 | BUTLINS'S REDCOAT REVIEW (LP) | 12 |

BUTTERCUPS

| 68 | Pama PM 742 | If I Love You/Loving You | 15 |
| 69 | Pama PM 760 | Come Put My Life In Order/If I Love You | 10 |

BILLY BUTTERFIELD & HIS ORCHESTRA

| 55 | London HLF 8181 | The Magnificent Matador/Sugar Blues Mambo | 35 |

BUTTERFIELD 8

| 88 | Go! Discs AGOLP 12 | BLOW (LP) | 12 |

(see also Madness, Terry Edwards)

PAUL BUTTERFIELD BLUES BAND,

66	London HLZ 10100	Come On In/I Got A Mind To Give Up Living	25
67	Elektra EKSN 45007	All These Blues/Never Say No	8
67	Elektra EKSN 45020	Run Out Of Time/One More Heartache	20
68	Elektra EKSN 45047	Get Yourself Together/Mine To Love	10
69	Elektra EKSN 45069	Where Did My Baby Go/In My Own Dream	10
70	Elektra 2101 012	Love March/Love Disease	6
65	Elektra EKL/EKS 294	PAUL BUTTERFIELD BLUES BAND (LP, with rare gold 'guitar player' label)	200
65	Elektra EKL/EKS 294	PAUL BUTTERFIELD BLUES BAND (LP, orange label)	50
66	Elektra EKL/EKS 315	EAST - WEST (LP, orange label)	50
67	Elek. EKL 4015/EKS 74015	THE RESURRECTION OF PIGBOY CRABSHAW (LP, orange label)	35
68	Elektra EKL 4025	IN MY OWN DREAM (LP, orange label, also stereo EKS 74025)	35
69	Elektra EKS 74053	KEEP ON MOVIN' (LP)	20
71	Elektra EKD 2001	LIVE (2-LP)	20
72	Elektra K 62011	GOLDEN BUTTER (LP, gatefold sleeve)	15

(see also John Mayall's Bluesbreakers, Mike Bloomfield)

BUTTERFLIES

| 68 | President PT 192 | Love Me Forever/He's Got Everything | 12 |

BUTTERFLYS

| 64 | Red Bird RB 10009 | Goodnight Baby/The Swim | 25 |

BUTTERSCOTCH

70	RCA 1937	Don't You Know (She Said Hello)/The Closer To You	7
70	RCA 1983	Surprise, Surprise/In This World Of Loving You	6
72	Jam 15	Can't You Hear A Song/All I Ever Wanna Do	7
70	RCA LSA 5000	BUTTERSCOTCH (LP, with insert and music book)	20

BUTTERSCOTCH CABOOSE

| 68 | Bell BLL 1023 | Melinda/Let A Little Sunshine In | 8 |

BUTTHOLE SURFERS

86	Red Rhino Europe RRELP 2	REMBRANDT PUSSYHORSE (LP)	12
85	Fundamental SAVE 5	PSYCHIC...POWERLESS...ANOTHER MAN'S SAC (LP)	15
85	Fundamental PRAY 69	CREAM CORN FROM THE SOCKET OF DAVIS EP (12" p/s)	8
83	Alternative Tentacles VIRUS 32	BROWN REASON TO LIVE EP (12", p/s)	8
87	Blast First BFFP 15	LOCUST ABORTION TECHNICIAN (LP)	12
89	Blast First BFF P41	WIDOWMAKER! (10" EP, with Reading Festival insert)	8
91	Rough Trade R 2081 2601	PIOUGHD (LP, with bonus 12")	12
93	Capitol EST 2285	ELECTRIC LARRYLAND (2-LP, one disc etched on one side, poster)	15
93	Capitol 0777 7 98798 1 6	INDEPENDENT WORM SALOON (LP)	25

BUTTONDOWN BRASS

68	Fontana TF 950	March Of The Little Brown Jugs/Frere Jacques	7
67	Fontana LPS 16255	HA HA HA (HEE-HEE-HEE) (LP)	15
76	DJM DJS 22046	FUNK IN HELL (LP)	40
76	DJM DJSLM2023	FIREDOG (LP)	15
77	DJM DJS 22076	COPS N'ROBBERS (LP)	15

(see also Ray Davies & Buttondown Brass)

BUTTS BAND

| 75 | ABC ABC4050 | Get Up, Stand Up/Mike's Blues | 12 |

SHEILA BUXTON

55	Columbia SCM 5193	Thank You For The Waltz/Just Between Friends	7
57	Columbia DB 3887	Perfect Love/I Love You Baby (My Baby Loves Me)	7
57	Columbia DB 4051	The In-Between Age/Charm	6
59	Top Rank JAR 144	The Valley Of Love/The Wonder Of You	6
59	Top Rank JAR 240	All I Do Is Dream Of You/Shakedown	5
60	Top Rank JAR 356	Sixteen Reasons/Goodnight, God I Love You	10

(see also Craig Douglas)

BUY OFF THE BAR

| 88 | Bi-Joopiter BIJOOP 023 | PARBOILED (LP, screen printed sleeve with insert) | 20 |

BUZZ & BUCKY
| 65 | Stateside SS 428 | Tiger A Go Go/Bay City | 50 |
(see also Ronny & The Daytonas)

BUZZ (1)
| 66 | Columbia DB 7887 | You're Holding Me Down/I've Gotta Buzz | 250 |
| 76 | Polydor2058 714 | Motorway Madness/Love Games | 10 |
(see also Boston Dexters, Tam White)

BUZZ (2)
| 79 | Redball RR 06 | Insanity/Him Not Me/Sick At Heart (p/s) | 30 |

BUZZARD
| 85 | PTO MSPT01 | Catch Me Alone/Raven Eyed Queen | 45 |

BUZZCOCKS
77	New Hormones ORG 1	SPIRAL SCRATCH (EP, plastic labels, p/s doesn't credit Howard Devoto)	60
77	United Artists UP 36316	Orgasm Addict/Whatever Happened To...? (p/s)	7
77	United Artists UP 36316B	Whatever Happened To? (1-sided test pressing)	50
78	United Artists UP36348	What Do I Get/Oh Shit	7
78	United Artists UP36348	What Do I Get?/Oh Shit (Mispress, plays Stranglers Peaches)	75
78	United Artists UP 36386	I Don't Mind/Autonomy	5
78	United Artists UP 36433	Love You More/Noise Annoys (p/s)	6
78	United Artists UP 36455	Ever Fallen In Love (With Someone You Shouldn't've?)/Just Lust	5
78	United Artists UP 36455	Ever Fallen In Love (With Someone You Shouldn't've?)/Just Lust (p/s mispressed with Gerry Rafferty track on B-side)	20
78	United Artists UP 36471	Promises/Lipstick (p/s)	7
78	New Hormones ORG 1	SPIRAL SCRATCH (EP, reissue, p/s credits Howard Devoto, paper label)	8
78	United Artists UALP 15	Moving Away From The Pulsebeat (12", 1-sided, die-cut co. sl., promo only)	20
79	United Artists UP 36499	Everybody's Happy Nowadays/Why Can't I Touch It? (p/s, available in 3 different colours)	5
79	United Artists UP 36541	Harmony In My Head/Something's Gone Wrong Again (p/s)	5
79	United Artists BP 316	You Say You Don't Love Me/Raison D'etre	5
80	United Artists BP 365	Why She's A Girl From The Chainstore/Are Everything (p/s)	5
80	United Artists BP 365 DJ	Why She's A Girl From The Chainstore/Are Everything (DJ promo)	20
80	United Artists BP371	Strange Thing/Airwaves Dream (p/s)	5
87	Strange Fruit SFPS044	PEEL SESSION EP (12")	8
89	EMI EM104	Ever Fallen In Love/Promises/Everybody's Happy Nowdays/Harmony in My Head (p/s)	8
91	New Hormones ORG 1	SPIRAL SCRATCH (EP, 2nd reissue, promo only 7")	10
91	New Hormones DV1T	SPIRAL SCRATCH (12" EP, reissue, numbered)	12
95	One Stop Music ONE 7001	Noise Annoys/Isolation (live) (p/s, 1,500 only)	5
95	United Artists ESP001	What Do I Get?/Mad Mad Judy/Raison D'Etre (Demo)	10
78	United Artists UAG 30159	ANOTHER MUSIC IN A DIFFERENT KITCHEN (LP, black inner sleeve, in printed carrier bag)	30
78	United Artists UAG 30159	ANOTHER MUSIC IN A DIFFERENT KITCHEN (LP)	12
78	United Artists UAG 30159	ANOTHER MUSIC IN A DIFFERENT KITCHEN (LP, mispressing without "I Need")	20
78	United Artists UAG 30197	LOVE BITES (LP, with embossed sleeve with insert)	12
79	United Artists UAG 30260	A DIFFERENT KIND OF TENSION (LP, with inner sleeve)	12
89	Strange Fruit SFRLP 104	PEEL SESSIONS (LP)	15
89	EMI LP PRODT 1	PRODUCT (5xLP boxed set with booklet)	40
89	Absolutely Free FREELP 02	LIVE AT THE ROXY (LP)	15
90	Receiver RRLP 131	LIVE AT THE ROXY (LP, reissue)	12
91	Document DLP 2	TIME'S UP (LP, mock bootleg, with bonus 33rpm interview single [FDLP 2])	20
00	Mute SCRATCH 2	TIMES UP (LP, reissue with poster)	12
(see also Pete Shelley, Things, Stevie's Buzz)

BUZZIN CUZZINS
| 94 | Azuli Records AZNY 024 | Let Me Show You Love (12") | 60 |

JAKI BYARD
67	Transatlantic PR 7419	LIVE! VOL 1 (LP, white purple label)	20
68	Transatlantic PR 7463	FREEDOM TOGETHER! (LP)	20
68	Transatlantic PR 7550	SUNSHINE OF MY SOUL (LP)	20

DON BYAS & HIS RHYTHM
| 56 | Vogue V 2390 | On The Way To Your Heart/The Portuguese Washerwomen | 10 |
| 64 | Realm RM 230 | ON 52ND STREET (LP) | 15 |

BYE LAWS
| 68 | Pye 7N 17481 | Then You Can Tell Me Goodbye/Come On Over To My Place | 8 |
| 69 | Pye 7N 17701 | Run Baby Run/To Sir With Love | 20 |

TREVOR BYFIELD
| 80 | Ethnic Fight EF 086 | Jah Guide/TREVOR & CLIVE: Sea Of Love (12") | 35 |

ANTHONY BYGRAVES
| 74 | Pye 7N 45429 | Painted Lady/Love Star Ship | 25 |

MAX BYGRAVES
| 53 | HMV 7M 112 | Cowpuncher's Cantata/True Loves And False Lovers | 10 |
| 53 | HMV 7M 113 | Little Sir Echo/Bygraves Boogie | 10 |
(see also Joan Regan)

JUNIOR BYLES
71	Bullet BU 499	Beat Down Babylon/UPSETTERS: Version	18
71	Upsetter US 365	Place Called Africa/UPSETTERS: Earthquake	20
72	Upsetter US 387	Festival Da Da/UPSETTERS: Version	18
72	Pama PM 857	Fever/GROOVERS: Soul Sister (B-side actually by Heptones)	35
72	Dynamic DYN 432	Pharaoh Hiding/UPSETTERS: Hail To Power	10
72	Randy's RAN 523	King Of Babylon/UPSETTERS: Nebuchadnezzer	18
72	Punch PH 109	Pharaoh Hiding/UPSETTERS: Hail To Power	18
73	Pama PM 878	Education Rock/KEN McKAY: Nobody Knows	10
73	Count Shelley CS 31	Break Up To Make Up/YOUTH MAN (DILLINGER): Plat Skank	8
74	Magnet MAG 27	Curly Locks/Now Generation	8
74	Dip DL 5035	Curly Locks/Now Generation	10
75	Dip DL 5074	Long Way/All The Way	12
75	Ethnic ETH 26	Mumbling And Grumbling/King Size Mumble	7

76	Jessus JI 006	Know Where You Are Going/JESSUS EXPERIENCE: Going To Zion	12
76	Ethnic Fight EF 042	Bury O Boy/ THE THING MUSIC CO: Version	8
76	Black Wax WAX 17	Pitchy Patchy/THE JA-MAN ALL STARS: 129 Beat Street	6
72	Trojan TRL 52	BEAT DOWN BABYLON (LP, beware of Canadian imports)	40

(see also King Chubby, Lloyd Terrell, Dennis Alpacone, Upsetters, Bob Marley, Lee & Junior)

JUNIOR BYLES & RUPERT REID
| 76 | Black Wax WAX 15 | Chant Down Babylon/THE JA-MAN ALL STARS: Version | 20 |

BOBBY BYRD
71	Mojo 2001 118	I Need Help Parts 1 & 2	8
71	Mojo 2027 003	I Know You Got Soul/If You Don't Work You Can't Eat	8
71	Mojo 2093 004	Hot Pants ... I'm Coming, I'm Coming, I'm Coming/Hang It Up	10
72	Mojo 2093 013	Keep On Doin' What You're Doin'/Let Me Know	8
72	Mojo 2093 017	If You Got A Love You'd Better Keep Hold Of It/ You've Got To Change Your Mind	8
72	Mojo 2093 020	Never Get Enough/My Concerto	8
73	Warner Bros K 16291	Try It Again/I'm On The Move	6
73	Mojo 2093 028	Saying It And Doing It Are Two Different Things/VICKI ANDERSON: Don't Throw Your Love In Garbage/In The Land Of Milk & Honey	10
87	Urban URB 8	I Know You Got Soul/Hot Pants	7
87	Urban URBX 8	I Know You Got Soul/Hot Pants ... I'm Coming, I'm Coming, I'm Coming/ I Know You Got Soul (Version) (12", die-cut company sleeve)	10

(see also JB's, James Brown, Anna King & Bobby Byrd, Vicki Anderson)

C. BYRD & SIR D.'S GROUP
| 60 | Blue Beat BB 49 | Baa Baa Black Sheep/LLOYD & CECIL: Come Over Here | 12 |

CHARLIE BYRD
| 62 | Riverside RLP 436 | BOSSA NOVA PELOS PASSAROS (LP) | 12 |
| 84 | Riverside RLP 9451 | THE GUITAR ARTISTRY OF CHARLIE BYRD (LP, Nimbus Supercut, mail oder only through Practical Hi Fi magazine) | 80 |

DONALD BYRD
65	Verve VS 532	Boom Boom/See See Rider	10
80	United Artists UP 622	Dominoes/Wind Parade	7
80	Blue Note 12 UP 622	Dominoes/Wind Parade (12")	30
81	Elektra K 12559	Love Has Come Around/Loving You (12")	8
55	Esquire 32-013	BYRD'S EYE VIEW (LP)	50
55	Esquire 32-019	BYRD JAZZ (THE MOTOR CITY SCENES) (LP, as Donald Byrd Sextet)	80
56	Esquire 32-032	JAZZ FOR THE CARRIAGE TRADE (LP)	50
60s	Esquire 32-039	INFORMAL JAZZ (LP)	25
70s	Blue Note BI 7243187515	KOFI (LP)	20
73	Blue Note BN-LA047	BLACKBYRD (LP)	15
75	Blue Note UAG 20001	PLACES AND SPACES (LP)	20

(see also Blackbyrds, Art Farmer)

RUSSELL BYRD
| 64 | Sue WI 305 | Hitch Hike Parts 1 & 2 | 50 |

ESTHER BYRDE
| 79 | Survival SUR 1 | Touch Me Take Me/Tracks Of Love | 50 |

BYRDS
SINGLES
65	CBS 201765	Mr. Tambourine Man/I Knew I'd Want You	8
65	CBS 201796	All I Really Want To Do/Feel A Whole Lot Better	8
65	CBS 202008	Turn! Turn! Turn! (To Everything There Is A Season)/ She Don't Care About Time	8
66	CBS 202037	Set You Free This Time/It Won't Be Wrong	12
66	CBS 202067	Eight Miles High/Why	12
66	CBS 202259	5D (Fifth Dimension)/Captain Soul	8
66	CBS 202295	Mr Spaceman/What's Happening?!?!	20
67	CBS 202559	So You Want To Be A Rock'n'Roll Star/Everybody's Been Burned	10
67	CBS 2648	My Back Pages/Renaissance Fair	10
67	CBS 2924	Lady Friend/Don't Make Waves	20
67	CBS 3093	Goin' Back/Change Is Now	12
68	CBS 3411	You Ain't Goin' Nowhere/Artificial Energy	8
68	CBS 3752	I Am A Pilgrim/Pretty Boy Floyd	8
69	CBS 4055	Bad Night At The Whiskey/Drug Store Truck Drivin' Man	12
69	CBS 4284	Lay Lady Lay/Old Blue (p/s)	12
69	CBS 4572	Wasn't Born To Follow/Child Of The Universe	8
70	CBS 4753	Jesus Is Just Alright/It's All Over Now Baby Blue	8
71	CBS 5322	Chestnut Mare/Just A Season	7
71	CBS 7253	I Trust/This Is My Destiny	10
72	CBS 7712	America's Great National Pastime/Farther Along (unreleased)	0
73	Asylum AYM 516	Things Will Be Better/For Free (promos in p/s)	12
73	Asylum AYM 516	Things Will Be Better/For Free (promos without p/s)	6
73	Asylum AYM 517	Full Circle/Long Live The King	6

EPs
66	CBS EP 6069	THE TIMES THEY ARE A' CHANGIN' (EP)	25
66	CBS EP 6077	EIGHT MILES HIGH (EP)	30
90	CBS 656544 5	FOUR DIMENSIONS EP (CD, picture disc)	8

ALBUMS
65	CBS BPG 62571	MR TAMBOURINE MAN (LP, mono)	45
65	CBS (S)BPG 62571	MR TAMBOURINE MAN (LP, stereo)	25
66	CBS BPG 62652	TURN! TURN! TURN! (LP, mono)	45
66	CBS (S)BPG 62652	TURN! TURN! TURN! (LP, stereo)	35
66	CBS BPG 62783	FIFTH DIMENSION (LP, mono)	40
66	CBS (S)BPG 62783	FIFTH DIMENSION (LP, stereo)	35
67	CBS BPG 62988	YOUNGER THAN YESTERDAY (LP, mono)	40
67	CBS (S)BPG 62988	YOUNGER THAN YESTERDAY (LP, stereo)	35
68	CBS BPG 63107	THE BYRDS' GREATEST HITS (LP, mono)	15
68	CBS BPG 63169	THE NOTORIOUS BYRD BROTHERS (LP, mono)	45
68	CBS (S)BPG 63169	THE NOTORIOUS BYRD BROTHERS (LP, stereo)	30

68	CBS 63353	SWEETHEART OF THE RODEO (LP, mono)	30
68	CBS 63353	SWEETHEART OF THE RODEO (LP, stereo)	35
69	CBS 63545	DR BYRDS & MR HYDE (LP, mono)	25

(Original copies of the above LPs were issued with rough-textured, plain orange labels & laminated sleeves; later copies are worth two-thirds these values.)

71	Bumble GEXP 8001	PRE-FLYTE (LP)	25
73	Asylum SYLA 8754	THE BYRDS (LP, gatefold sleeve)	12
75	CBS 63353	SWEETHEARTS OF THE RODEO (LP, reissue)	12

(see also Beefeaters, Roger McGuinn, David Crosby, Gene Clark, Gram Parsons, Gene Parsons, Skip Battin, Earl Scruggs, Flying Burrito Brothers, Evergreen Blueshoes, Dillard & Clark, Kentucky Colonels)

JERRY BYRNE
| 76 | Specialty SON 5011 | Lights Out/Honey Baby | 5 |

PACKIE BYRNE (& BONNIE SHALJEAN)
| 69 | EFDSS LP 1009 | PACKIE BYRNE (LP) | 20 |

EDD/EDWARD BYRNES
60	Warner Bros WB 5	Kookie, Kookie (Lend Me Your Comb) (with Connie Stevens)/You're The Top	5
60	Warner Bros WB 27	Lonely Christmas/Yulesville (as Edd Byrnes)	5
60	Warner Bros WEP 6010	KOOKIE (EP, mono)	10
60	Warner Bros WSEP 2010	KOOKIE (EP, stereo)	10
63	Warner Bros W(S)EP 6108	KOOKIE VOLUME 2 (EP)	10

(see also Connie Stevens)

MARTIN BYRNES
| 70 | Leader LEA 2004 | BYRNES (LP) | 15 |

DAVID BYRON
| 75 | Bronze ILPS 9342 | TAKE NO PRISONERS (LP, lyric inner sleeve) | 15 |

PAUL BYRON
| 60 | Decca F 11210 | Pale Moon/Year Ago Tonight | 5 |

SOL BYRON & IMPACTS
| 60s | Flamingo PR 5027 | Pride And Joy/Thou Shall Not Steal | 15 |

BYSTANDERS (1)
65	Pylot WD 501	That's The End/This Time	150
66	Piccadilly 7N 35330	(You're Gonna) Hurt Yourself/Have I Offended The Girl	25
66	Piccadilly 7N 35351	My Love - Come Home/If You Walk Away	30
67	Piccadilly 7N 35363	98.6/Stubborn Kind Of Fellow	20
67	Piccadilly 7N 35382	Royal Blue Summer Sunshine Day/Make Up Your Mind	30
67	Piccadilly 7N 35399	Pattern People/Green Grass	15
68	Pye 7N 17476	When Jezamine Goes/Cave Of Clear Light	50
68	Pye 7N 17540	This World Is My World/Painting The Time	15

(see also Man)

BYSTANDERS (2)
| 81 | Uncle Robert UR 001 | Nowhere To Hide/Sweet Fanny Adams/True Blue/I Wonder (EP) | 20 |

BYZANTIUM
73	A&M AMS 7064	What A Coincidence/My Seasons Changing With The Sun	7
72	private pressing	LIVE AND STUDIO ('BLACK AND WHITE') (LP, 100 only with insert)	300
72	A&M AMLH 68104	BYZANTIUM (LP, with poster, brown label)	100
72	A&M AMLH 68104	BYZANTIUM (LP, without poster)	40
73	A&M AMLH 68163	SEASONS CHANGING (LP, poster sleeve, brown labels)	100

(see also Ora)

B.Z.N.
| 73 | Birth RAB 1003 | Rolling Round The Band/Superman | 12 |

C

ANDY C
92	RAM RAMM 001	SOUR MASH EP (12")	50
93	RAM RAMM 003	BASS LOGIC EP (12")	30
93	RAM RAMM 006	Slip 'N' Slide/Bass Constructor (Sonz Of A Loop Da Loop Era Remix) (12")	25
95	RAM RAMM 12	Cool Down/Roll On (12")	15

(See also Randall and Andy C.)

ERROL C
| 76 | Concrete Jungle CJ 601 | Jah For I/4TH STREET ORCHESTRA: Version | 15 |

FANTASTIC JOHNNY C
67	London HL 10169	Boogaloo Down Broadway/Look What Love Can Make You Do	10
68	London HL 10212	Hitch It To The Horse/Cool Broadway	10
69	Action ACT 4543	Is There Anything Better Than Making Love/New Love	15
75	Island USA 8	Don't Depend On Me (Parts 1 & 2)	8
69	Action ACLP 6001	BOOGALOO DOWN BROADWAY (LP)	45

C & M CONNECTION
| 90 | Blue Chip BLUE c32 | Another Night (12") | 12 |

ROY C
66	Island WI 273	Shotgun Wedding/I'm Going To Make It	20
66	Island WI 273	Shotgun Wedding/High School Dropout (different B-side)	12
67	Ember EMB S 230	Twistin' Pneumonia/Tear Avenue	15
66	Ember NR 5055	THE SHOTGUN WEDDING MAN (LP)	30
75	Mercury 9100 017	SEX AND SOUL (LP)	15

MINT VALUE £

C. STAR
73	Jam JAM 56	Bad Boy/Alex	10

CABARET VOLTAIRE
78	Rough Trade RT 003	EXTENDED PLAY EP (paper p/s)	7
79	Rough Trade RT 018	Nag Nag Nag/Is That Me (p/s)	5
79	Rough Trade RT 035	Silent Command/Chance Versus Causality (p/s)	5
80	Rough Trade RT 060	Seconds Too Late/Control Addict (p/s)	5
79	Rough Trade ROUGH 4	MIX UP (LP)	12
80	Rough Trade ROUGH 7	LIVE AT THE Y.M.C.A 27.10.79 (LP)	12
80	Rough Trade ROUGH 11	VOICE OF AMERICA (LP)	12
81	Rough Trade ROUGH 27	RED MECCA (LP)	12
82	Rough Trade ROUGH 42	2 x 45 (2 x 12")	12

(see also Richard H. Kirk, Hafler Trio, Peter Hope & Richard H. Kirk, Stephen Mallinder, Pressure Co., Eric Random)

CABLES
68	Coxsone CS 7072	What Kind Of World?/My Broken Heart	40
68	Coxsone CS 7082	Soul Power/HEPTONES: Love Me Alway	125
68	Studio One SO 2060	Baby Why?/Be A Man	35
68	Studio One SO 2071	Love Is A Pleasure/Cheer Up	80
69	Studio One SO 2085	Got To Find Someone/ALEXANDER HENRY: Please Be True	30
69	Bamboo BAM 12	So Long/PRESSURE BOYS: More Love	25
70	Bamboo BAM 19	How Can I Trust You?/SOUND DIMENSIONS: How Can I Trust You? (Inst.)	15
70	Trojan TR 7792	Salt Of The Earth/Ring A Bell	10
70	Harry J. HJ 6614	Didn't I/JAY BOYS: Tilly	20
70	Harry J. HJ 6620	Feel Alright/Equal Rights	7
71	Big Shot BI 598	A Sometime Girl/IN CROWD BAND: A Sometime Girl Version	6
71	Duke DU 124	Mixing/IN CROWD BAND: In Orbit	8
72	Jackpot JP 787	Come On/Come On Version	6
73	Attack ATT 8053	Give Me A Chance/JAH FISH: King Of Zion	6

(see also K. Drummond, Dingle Brothers, Alton Ellis)

CABOOSE
70	Stax STAX 151	Black Hands, White Cotton/In My Hour Of Need	6

CACHE
81	Groove GP 111	Where Is My Sunshine/Jazzin' And Crusin'	6
81	Groove GP 111 T	Where Is My Sunshine/Jazzin' And Crusin' (12")	30

CACOPHONY
87	Roadrunner RR 349577	SPEED METAL SYMPHONY (LP)	12
88	Roadrunner RR 9577	GO OFF (LP, as Marty Friedman, Jason Becker & Cacophony)	12

(see also Marty Friedman, Megadeth)

CACTUS
70	Atco 2400 020	CACTUS (LP)	25
71	Atco 2400 114	ONE WAY ... OR ANOTHER (LP, reissue of above LP)	20
72	Atlantic K 40307	RESTRICTIONS (LP)	18
72	Atlantic K 50013	'OT AND SWEATY (LP)	18

(see also Vanilla Fudge, Leaf Hound, Beck Bogert Appice, Atomic Rooster)

CACTUS RAIN
90	Ten TEN 338	Till The Morning Comes/The Cani (p/s)	6

BILL CADDICK
79	Highway SHY 7006	REASONS BRIEFLY SET DOWN (LP)	15
76	Park SHP 102	Rough Music (LP)	15
77	Leader LER 2097	SUNNY MEMORIES (LP)	15

ALAN CADDY
64	HMV POP 1286	Tornado/Workout	40

(see also Tornados)

CADETS (U.K.)
63	Decca F 11677	Hello Trouble/Our First Quarrel	10
64	Pye 7N 15693	Chapel Of Love/I Gave My Wedding Dress Away	10
65	Pye 7N 15769	Are You Teasing Me?/My Heart Skips A Beat	5
65	Pye 7N 15852	Jealous Heart/Right Or Wrong	25
65	Pye 7N 15947	Baby Roo/Raining In My Heart	10
66	Pye 7N 17024	If I Had My Life To Live Over/Best Of All	5
66	Pye 7N 17167	At The Close Of A Long Long Day/True Love	5
69	Pye 7N 17762	Dying Ranger/Storeen Bawn	5
66	Marble Arch MAL 643	THE CADETS (LP)	12

CADETS (U.S.)
56	London HLU 8313	Stranded In The Jungle/I Want You (gold label lettering)	700
56	London HLU 8313	Stranded In The Jungle/I Want You (silver label lettering)	300
56	London HLU 8313	Stranded In The Jungle/I Want You (78)	40

CADILLAC
86	CBS A 7180	Valentino/Valentino (p/s)	8

EARL CADILLAC & HIS ORCHESTRA
59	Vogue V 9133	Zon, Zon, Zon/Il Suffit D'Une Melodie	10
59	Vogue V 9138	The Fish Seller/Tremendo Cha Cha Cha (Plegaria)	5

VINCE CADILLAC
78	Satril SAT 126	Memory Lane/Hello	5

CADILLACS
59	London HLJ 8786	Peek-A-Boo/Oh, Oh, Lolita	50
59	London HLJ 8786	Peek-A-Boo/Oh, Oh, Lolita (78)	20

BOBBY CADMAN
74	Regal Zonophone RZ3008	A Magic Spell/Own Up Time	30

CADO BELLE
76	Anchor 1033	Got To Love/Paper In The Rain	25

| 76 | Anchor 1038 | Stone Throw From Nowhere/Airport Shutdown | 8 |

SUSAN CADOGAN
74	Dip DL 5030	Hurt So Good/UPSETTERS: Loving Is Good	7
75	Lucky LY 5078	Feeling Right/Congratulations	7
75	Black Wax WAX 2	Love My Life/MR. VIBES: Love Vibes	8
76	Trojan TRLS 122	SUSAN CADOGAN (LP)	15

CAEDMON
| 78 | Private pressing | CAEDMON (LP, with insert, with bonus 7": Beyond The Second Mile/Give Me Jesus) | 175 |
| 78 | Private pressing | CAEDMON (LP, with insert, without bonus 7": Beyond The Second Mile/Give Me Jesus) | 100 |

CAERN
| 70s | Gem DES 1015 | A COLLECTION OF SCOTCH FOLK (LP) | 18 |

CAESAR & CLEO
65	Reprise R 20419	Love Is Strange/Let The Good Times Roll (in p/s)	25
65	Reprise R 20419	Love Is Strange/Let The Good Times Roll	15
65	Reprise R 30056	CAESAR AND CLEO (EP, 2 tracks each by Caesar & Cleo and Sonny & Cher)	20
(see also Sonny & Cher)			

CAESARS
| 65 | Decca F 12251 | On The Outside Looking In/Can You Blame Me? | 15 |
| 66 | Decca F 12462 | Five In The Morning/It's Superman | 10 |

CAFE SOCIETY
75	Konk KOS 5	Whitby Two-Step/Maybe It's Me	6
75	Konk KONK 102	CAFE SOCIETY (LP, with inner sleeve)	20
(see also Tom Robinson Band, Claire Hamill)			

BUTCH CAGE/MABEL LEE WILLIAMS
| 60s | Storyville SLP 129 | COUNTRY BLUES (LP) | 25 |

AUBREY CAGLE
| 62 | Starlite ST45 082 | Come Along Little Girl/Blue Lonely World | 150 |

CAGLIOSTRO
| 86 | él GPO 22 | Libera Me/Madmen And Lovers (p/s) | 8 |

JAMES CAGNEY
| 81 | United Artists UP 36385 | Yankee Doodle Dandy/Over There (B-side with Frances Langford) (p/s) | 8 |

JEREMY CAHILL
| 70s | Solent | September Blues/Yesterday | 15 |
| *(see also Shide & Acorn)* | | | |

PATRICIA CAHILL
70	Deram DM 320	Little Altar Boy/Rain	6
71	Deram DM 324	Colm Ban/Eighteen	6
70	Deram Nova SDN 22	SUMMER'S DAUGHTER (LP)	30
72	Rex RPS 104	IRELAND (LP)	15

CAIN
| 68 | Page One POF 054 | Her Emotion/Take Me Back One Time | 35 |
| 78 | SHP 103 | VISITOR 2035 (2-LP, fold-out lyric sheet) | 20 |

CAIN
| 80s | private pressing | CAIN (2-LP) | 30 |

TUBAL CAINE
| 70 | Attack ATT 8023 | I'm A Drifter Part 1/CIMARONS: I'm A Drifter Part 2 | 7 |

AL CAIOLA (ORCHESTRA)
56	London HLC 8285	Flamenco Love/From The Heart	15
61	London HLT 9294	The Magnificent Seven/The Lonely Rebel	10
61	London HLT 9325	Bonanza/Bounty Hunter	10
61	HMV POP 884	Bonanza/Bounty Hunter (as Al Caiola Orchestra, reissue)	5
61	HMV POP 889	The Magnificent Seven/The Lonely Rebel (as Al Caiola Orchestra)	10
62	Oriole CB 1732	Mambo Jambo/Twistin' At The Woodchoppers Mill	10
62	United Artists UP 1003	Big Guitar/Guns Of Navarone	10
66	United Artists UEP 1018	HIT T.V. THEMES (EP)	15
56	London HA-C 2017	DEEP IN A DREAM (LP)	12
57	London HA-C 2022	SERENADE IN BLUE (LP)	12
62	United Artists ULP 1003	SOLID GOLD GUITAR (LP)	12
66	United Artists (S)ULP 1115	SOUNDS FOR SPIES AND PRIVATE EYES (LP)	20
(see also Hugo Montenegro)			

CAIRN
| 70s | GES 1015 | A COLLECTION OF SCOTCH FOLK (LP) | 15 |

JOHN CAIRNEY
| 57 | HMV POP 424 | Two Strangers/A Certain Girl I Know (with Sammy San) | 5 |
| 68 | Waverley SLP 543 | Please/Deep Purple | 5 |

FORRIE CAIRNS
| 62 | Fontana 267240 TF | Salty Dog/Cockles And Mussels | 5 |

CAIRO
| 80 | Absurd ASK 15 | Movie Stars/Cuthbert's Birthday Treat (p/s) | 5 |

CAIR PARAVEL
| 76 | Koala KOA PO 16 | SOME OTHER MORNING (LP, insert) | 400 |

CAJUN MOON
76	Polydor 2058 801	No Honey No Love/Version	6
76	Chrysalis CHR 1116	CAJUN MOON (LP)	12
(see also Allan Taylor)			

CAKE
| 68 | MCA MUPS 303 | THE CAKE (LP) | 20 |
| 69 | MCA MUPS 390 | A SLICE OF CAKE (LP) | 20 |

MINT VALUE £

J.J. CALE

66	Liberty LIB 55881	Outside Lookin' In/In Our Time	18
72	A&M AMS 7018	Cajun Moon/Starbound	6
72	A&M AMS 7022	After Midnight/Crazy Mama	6
72	A&M AMLS 68105	NATURALLY (LP, tan label)	12
72	A&M AMLS 68157	REALLY (LP, tan label)	12
79	Shelter ISA 5018	FIVE (LP, with bonus single "Katy Cool"/"Juan And Maria Juarez Blues" [JJ-1])	15

(see also Leathercoated Minds)

JOHN CALE

74	Island WIP 6202	The Man Who Couldn't Afford To Orgy/Sylvia Said	10
77	Illegal IL 006	Jack The Ripper In The Moulin Rouge/Memphis (unissued, test pressings only)	25
81	A&M AMS 8130	Dead Or Alive/Honi Soit	5
83	Ze IS 113	Close Watch/I Keep A Close Watch (p/s)	5
84	Ze IS 157	Caribbean Sunset/(same) (unissued, promo only)	8
84	Ze IS 197	Ooh La La/Magazines (p/s)	5
77	Illegal IL 003	ANIMAL JUSTICE (12" EP)	10
71	CBS 64256	VINTAGE VIOLENCE (LP, orange label)	25
71	CBS 64259	CHURCH OF ANTHRAX (LP, with Terry Riley)	20
72	Reprise K 44212	ACADEMY IN PERIL (LP)	20
73	Reprise K 44239	PARIS 1919 (LP, with lyric insert)	20
74	Island ILPS 9301	FEAR (LP, pink rim)	15
75	Island ILPS 9317	SLOW DAZZLE (LP)	12
75	Island ILPS 9350	HELEN OF TROY (LP)	20
77	Island ILPS 9459	GUTS (LP)	12
07	EMI 37760	CIRCUS (3-LP with free 7", sealed)	20

(see also Velvet Underground, Nico, Terry Riley, Ayers Cale Nico & Eno, Judy Nylon)

CALEB (QUAYE)

67	Philips BF 1588	Baby Your Phrasing Is Bad/Woman Of Distinction (300-500 pressed)	950
00s	Philips BF1588	Baby Your Phrasing Is Bad/A Woman Of Distinction (limited edition reissue)	7

(see also Mirage, Hookfoot, Bread & Beer Band, Elton John)

CALEDONIANS

69	Fab FAB 103	Funny Way Of Laughing/Don't Please	15

(see also Clarendonians, Prince Buster)

CALENNIG

80	Greenwich Village GVR 214	SONGS AND TUNES FROM WALES (LP)	15

CALIFORNIA IN-CROWD

66	Fontana TF 779	Questions And Answers/Happiness In My Heart	50

CALIFORNIA MUSIC

74	RCA RCA 2488	Don't Worry Baby/Ten Years Harmony	12
76	RCA RCA 2661	Jamaica Farewell/California Farewell	12
78	RSO 014	I Can Hear Music/Love's Supposed To Be That Way (as California)	10

(see also Bruce Johnston, Beach Boys)

CALIFORNIA PINES

67	CBS 3074	Two Weeks In September Part 1/Part 2	7

CALIFORNIAN LICENSE

70	Philips 6006052	The Cage/Easter Song	12

CALIFORNIANS

67	CBS 2263	Golden Apples/Little Ship With A Red Sail	75
67	Decca F 12678	Follow Me/What Love Can Do	20
67	Decca F 12712	Sunday Will Never Be The Same/Can't Get You Out Of My Mind	10
68	Decca F 12758	Congratulations/What Is Happy, Baby?	10
68	Decca F 12802	Out In The Sun/The Sound	20
69	Fontana TF 991	Mandy, The Cooks Of Cake And Kindness	100
69	Fontana TF 1052	Sad Old Song/Weep No More	15
69	Chapter One CH 112	You've Got Your Troubles/Early Morning Sun	7

(see also Warren Zevon)

CALLAN & JOHN

69	CBS 4447	House Of Delight/Long Shadow Day	40

CALL GIRLS

88	53rd & 3rd AGAR 001	Primal World/VATICAN SHOTGUN SCARE: Thick Fat Heat Source (p/s)	8

CALLICOTT, (MISSISSIPPI) JOE

68	Blue Horizon 7-63227	PRESENTING THE COUNTRY BLUES (LP)	120
71	Revival RVS 1002	DEAL GONE DOWN (LP, as Joe Callicott)	22

TERRY CALLIER

90	Acid Jazz JAZID 27T	I Don't Want To See Myself (Without You)/(If I Could Make You) Change Your Mind (12")	15

CALLIES

71	Rubber RUB 002	ON YOUR SIDE (LP, gatefold sleeve)	15

CALLINAN-FLYNN

72	Mushroom 50 MR 17	We Are The People (The Road To Derry Town)/The Old Man And The Flower	30
72	Mushroom 150 MR 18	FREEDOM'S LAMENT (LP)	190

CALLIOPE

68	Buddah 203 016	STEAMED (LP)	15
69	Uni UN 514	Clear Mud/Wiser	15

JO CALLIS

81	Pop: Aural POP 12	Woah Yeah/Sinistrale/Dodo Boys (p/s)	5

(see also Rezillos, Shake, Human League)

CAB CALLOWAY

66	Stateside SS 509	History Repeats Itself/After Taxes	5
60	Fontana TFE 17216	CAB CALLOWAY (EP)	10

CALOOGIE
68	CBS 1095	Bleeker Street/Benedictus	10

GEORGE CALSTOCK
78	Hit Run DD2	The Ungodly (Feat. U Black)/DOCTOR PABLO: Righteous Melody (12")	35

EDDIE CALVERT
53	Columbia SCM 5003	My Yiddishe Momme/Hora Staccato	5
53	Columbia SCM 5004	Ave Maria/Just A-Wearyin' For You (as Eddie Calvert Orchestra)	5
54	Columbia SCM 5129	My Son, My Son/Sherpa Song	5
55	Columbia SCM 5168	Cherry Pink And Apple Blossom White/Roses Of Picardy	5
56	Columbia SCM 5237	The Man With The Golden Arm/Memories Of You	5

(see also Gerry Brereton)

ROBERT CALVERT
72	United Artists UP 35543	Ejection/Catch A Falling Starfighter (p/s)	25
79	Wake Up WUR 5	Cricket Star (p/s, 33rpm flexidisc, as Robert Calvert & 1st XI)	10
80	Flicknife FLS 204	Lord Of The Hornets/The Greenfly & The Rose (purple print p/s)	10
81	Flicknife FLS 204	Lord Of The Hornets/The Greenfly & The Rose (reissue, black print p/s)	5
74	United Artists UAS 29507	CAPTAIN LOCKHEED AND THE STARFIGHTERS (LP, embossed gatefold sleeve, with attached booklet and inner sleeve)	40
75	United Artists UAS 29852	LUCKY LIEF AND THE LONGSHIPS (LP, gatefold sleeve)	20
81	A-Side IF 0311	HYPE (SONGS OF TOM MAHLER) (LP)	15
84	Flicknife SHARP 021	FREQ (LP)	12
86	Demi Monde DMLP 1010	TEST TUBE CONCEIVED (LP)	12
88	Beat Goes On BGOLP 2	LUCKY LIEF AND THE LONGSHIPS (LP, gatefold sleeve, reissue)	20
88	Beat Goes On BGOLP 5	CAPTAIN LOCKHEED AND THE STARFIGHTERS (LP, gatefold sleeve with booklet, reissue)	12
89	Clear BLACK 1	ROBERT CALVERT AT THE QUEEN ELIZABETH HALL (LP, mail order only, with badge, poster & T-shirt, gatefold sleeve)	40

(see also Hawkwind, Imperial Pompadours, Catapilla, Adrian Wagner, John Stevens Away)

TABBY CALVIN & ROUNDERS
56	Capitol CL 14640	False Alarm/I Came Back To Say I'm Sorry	10

CAMALEONTI
68	CBS 3968	Applause/Applausi	15

CAMARQUE
83	Clubland SJP 848	Howl Of The Pack/Someone Just Like You (in p/s)	75
83	Clubland SJP 848	Howl Of The Pack/Someone Just Like You	30

CAMBERWELL NOW
86	Ink 19	GHOST TRADE (LP)	18

(see also This Heat)

CAMBODIANS
70	Duke DU 101	Coolie Man/J.J. ALLSTARS: Coolie Version	12

CAMBRIDGE BUSKERS
76	Polydor 2371984	DOUBLE CONCERTO (LP)	12
77	Polydor 2371766	ZWISCHEN PINTE UND PODIUM (LP)	12

CAMEL
73	MCA MUPS 1177	Never Let Go/Curiosity	6
80	Decca FR 13871	Your Love Is Stranger Than Mine/Neon Magic (p/s)	6
84	Decca CAMEL 1	Cloak And Dagger Man/Pressure Point (p/s)	5
73	MCA MUPS 473	CAMEL (LP, black/blue hexagon label)	120
74	Deram SML 1107	MIRAGE (LP, with insert, red/white label, small Deram logo)	25
73	MCA MUPS 473	CAMEL (LP, later rainbow label)	15
75	Decca SKL-R 5207	THE SNOW GOOSE (LP, laminated sleeve, insert)	20
76	Decca TXS-R 115	MOON MADNESS (LP, gatefold sleeve)	12
77	Decca TXS-R 124	RAIN DANCES (LP, with inner)	15
78	Decca TXS R 132	BREATHLESS (LP, insert)	15
78	Decca DBC-R 7/8	A LIVE RECORD (2-LP, gatefold)	15
79	Decca TXS R 137	I CAN SEE YOUR HOUSE FROM HERE (LP, insert)	15

(see also Pete Bardens, Gong/Camel, Caravan, Hatfield & The North)

CAMEL DRIVERS
68	Pye International 7N 25471	Sunday Morning 6 O'Clock/Give It A Try	15

CAMEOS
63	Columbia DB 7092	Powercut/High Low And Lonesomely	30
64	Columbia DB 7201	My Baby's Coming Home/Where E'er You Walk	30

CAMEOS
67	Toast TT 503	A Pretty Shade Of Blue/You Didn't Have To Be So Nice	8
68	Toast TT 508	On The Good Ship Lollipop/The Love Of A Boy	8

CAMERA OBSCURA (1)
80	Small Wonder SMALL 28	Destitution/Race In Athens (p/s)	6

CAMERA OBSCURA (2)
98	Andmoresounds AND 0945	Park And Ride/Swimming Pool	25
98	Andmoresounds AND 1145	Your Sound/Autumn Tides/Annawaltzerpose	20
06	Elefant ER-1123LP	LET'S GET OUT OF THIS COUNTRY (LP)	18
01	Andmoresounds AND 1733	BIGGEST BLUEST HI-FI (LP)	40

DION CAMERON & THREE TOPS
66	Rio R 111	Lord Have Mercy/Get Ready	12

(see also Dion & Three Tops)

G.C. CAMERON
76	Tamla Motown TMG 1033	Me And My Life/Act Like A Shotgun	10
80	Flamingo FM-11	Live For Love/If I love You	50

(see also Detroit Spinners)

ISLA CAMERON
64	Transatlantic TRAEP 109	LOST LOVE (EP)	25

(see also Ewan MacColl)

JOHN CAMERON (QUARTET)

67	Columbia DB 8120	You Owe Me/Walk Small (solo)	8
69	Deram DM 256	Troublemaker/Off Centre	60
67	Columbia SCX 6116	COVER LOVER (LP)	25
68	Columbia Studio Two TWO 197	WARM & GENTLE (LP)	20
69	Deram DML/SML 1044	OFF CENTRE (LP)	100

(see also Frog)

JOHNNY CAMERON

| 60 | Top Rank JAR 396 | I Double Dare You/Fantasy | 12 |

RAY CAMERON

| 67 | Island WIP 6003 | Doin' My Time/Getaway, Getaway Car | 12 |
| 75 | A&M AMS 7168 | Dynamite Party Part 1/Part 2 | 5 |

TONY CAMILLO

| 75 | A&M AMLH 63406 | BAZUKA (LP) | 12 |

AL CAMPBELL

79	Saferno SOF 004	Gone Down The Drain/One More Chance (12")	25
78	Chanan Jah TUFF 12	Sister Soul/Footstool	30
78	Deb DEB 018	Love The Way It Should Be/Version (12")	20
79	Nigara NADD 103	La-La Means I Love You (12")	40
80	Strong Like Sampson SLSD 14	Jah Shine On Me/SUGAR MINOTT: Halk Of Love (12")	35
80	JB JBD 019	You Jamming/You Jamming (Part 2) (12")	20
81	Greensleeves GRED 51	Unfaithful Children/WAILING SOULS: Who No Waan Come (12")	60
81	JB JBD 029	Feedback/Part 2 (12")	25
78	Terminal TMLP 1002	NO MORE RUNNING (LP)	80
78	ITAL IT001	LOVING MOODS OF (LP)	30
79	Burning Sounds BS 1036	DIAMONDS (LP)	20
79	Hawkeye HLD 03	RAINY DAYS (LP)	50
80	JB JBLP 002	LATE NIGHT BLUES (LP)	40
80	JB JBLP 005	WORKING MAN (LP)	50
81	Greensleeves GREL 30	OTHER SIDE OF LOVE (LP)	12

AL CAMPBELL & TRINITY

| 78 | Deb DEB 013 | Reggae Dance/Dragon Dance/AL CAMPBELL: Roots Man Style (12") | 20 |

ALEX CAMPBELL

65	Transatlantic TRASP 4	Been On The Road So Long/The Night Visiting Song (in p/s)	10
65	Transatlantic TRASP 4	Been On The Road So Long/The Night Visiting Song	6
68	Saga OPP 2	Victoria Dines Alone/Pack Up Your Sorrows	30
63	Society SOC 960	FOLK SESSION (LP)	12
64	Xtra XTRA 1014	ALEX CAMPBELL (LP, with Martin Carthy)	25
65	Polydor 623 035	IN COPENHAGEN (LP)	18
67	Saga ERO 8021	ALEX CAMPBELL AND HIS FRIENDS (LP, with Sandy Denny)	25
71	Ad-Rhythm/Tepee ARPS 1	THIS IS ALEX CAMPBELL VOL. 1 (LP)	30
71	Ad-Rhythm/Tepee ARPS 2	THIS IS ALEX CAMPBELL VOL. 2 (LP)	30
71	Boulevard 4007	16 BEST LOVED SONGS OF BONNIE SCOTLAND (LP)	15
72	Boulevard 4073	AT HIS BEST (LP)	20
76	Look LKLP 6043	NO REGRETS (LP)	12
79	Burlington BURL 002	ALEX CAMPBELL, ALAN ROBERTS AND DOUGIE MACLEAN (LP)	12
87	Sundown SDLP 2048	WITH THE GREATEST RESPECT (2-LP, reissue of "This Is..." Vols. 1 & 2)	18

(see also Sandy Denny)

AMBROSE CAMPBELL

| 66 | Columbia SX 6081 | HIGH LIFE TODAY (LP) | 60 |

BILL & PETE CAMPBELL

| 71 | Duke DU 123 | Come On Home Girl/You Are Mine | 7 |

CAT CAMPBELL & NICKY THOMAS

| 72 | Pressure Beat PB 5511 | Hammering/PETER TOSH: Medicine Man | 20 |

CHOKER CAMPBELL

65	Tamla Motown TMG 517	Mickey's Monkey/Pride And Joy (as Choker Campbell's Big Band)	140
65	Tamla Motown TMG 517	Mickey's Monkey/Pride And Joy (as Choker Campbell's Big Band) (DJ copy)	250
65	Tamla Motown TML 11011	HITS OF THE SIXTIES (LP, as Choker Campbell & His 16-Piece Band)	125

CHRISTINE CAMPBELL

| 62 | Parlophone GEP 8874 | WHEREVER I GO (LP) | 8 |

CORNELL CAMPBELL

63	Island WI 039	Rosabelle/Turndown Date (B-side actually "Under The Old Oak Tree")	30
63	Island WI 083	Each Lonely Night/ROLAND ALPHONSO: Steamline	20
64	Port-O-Jam PJ 4008	Jericho Road (with Dimple Hinds)/DON DRUMMOND & GROUP: Roll On Sweet Don	60
64	Rio R 38	Gloria/I'll Be True	25
72	Dynamic DYN 446	My Confession/AGGROVATORS: Version	12
72	Green Door GD 4042	Dearest Darling/Star Dust	15
72	Jackpot JP 801	Queen And The Minstrel/Put Yourself In My Place	15
72	Bullet BU 515	For Once In My Life/Didn't I?	15
73	Jackpot JP 809	Pity The Children/You're No Good	15
73	Jackpot JP 814	Harry Hippy/Just One Kiss	6
73	Green Door GD 4057	Give Me Love/Help Them O Lord	15
73	Duke DU 158	Shotgun Wedding/Girl Of My Dreams	10
73	Duke DU 159	The Very Best I Can/Heading For The Mountains	10
73	Ackee ACK 513	Give Me A Love/SHORTY PERRY: Message Of Love	6
75	Action ACT 102	Natty In A Greenwich Farm/Natty Version	10
75	Angen ANG 101	Talking Love/AGGROVATORS: Gorgon Dub	10
75	Angen ANG 105	The Gorgon Speaks/AGGROVATORS: Version	10
76	Angen ANG 122	A Tear Fell/My True Destination	6
76	Attack ATT 8125	I Will Never Change/Version	6
77	Third World TW57	The Investigator/Version	12
70s	Rocket VR 001	Many Rivers To Cross/Many Dub	8
76	Daddy Kool DK001	I Heart Is Clean/KING TUBBY AND THE OBSERVERS : Zinc Fence	10
77	Nationwide 1018	Let Me Go Girl/Version	7

77	Terminal TM 104	I Am A King/Watch And Peep	10
78	D-Roy 3	Listen Dread/Version	8
78	Third World 7529	Blessed Are They/New York City (With I ROY)	8
80	Cha Cha CHAD25	Rainbow/PETER BROGGS: Never Forget Jah (12")	30
80s	Live & Love LLDIS0022	Nothing Don't Come Easy/Version (12")	20
80	Papa D PD0167	Rasta Come From Jail (with SASSAFRASS/100 Pounds of Collie (with PAPA TULLO)	18
72	Trojan TBL 199	CORNELL CAMPBELL (LP)	50
75	Groundnation GROL 503	DANCE IN A GREENWICH FARM (LP)	40
76	Angen ANGL 03	GORGON (LP)	30
76	Third World TWS 301	STALOWATT (LP)	35
78	Justice JUSLP 09	ROPIN (LP)	25
79	Striker Lee TSL 104	NATTY DREAD IN A GREENWICH FARM (LP)	40
79	Burning Sounds BS 1034	SWEET BABY (LP)	18

(see also Eternals, Don Cornel & Eternals, Clarendonians, Charmers, Stranger & Patsy, GG Allstars)

DAVID CAMPBELL

67	Transatlantic TRA 141	DAVID CAMPBELL (LP)	25
72	Decca SKL 5139	SUN WHEEL (LP)	18

ERROL CAMPBELL

76	Shebazz SHE 001	Wolves/Follow	30

ETHNA CAMPBELL

64	Mercury MF 804	What's Easy For Two Is Hard For One/Again	20
64	Mercury MF 816	Girls Like Boys/Five Minutes More	10
71	Philips 6006475	The Old Rugged Cross/It Is No Secret	6
60s	Philips 6382138	FOR THE GOOD TIMES (LP)	15

GLEN CAMPBELL

61	Top Rank JAR 596	Turn Around, Look At Me/Brenda	7
62	Capitol CL 15268	Too Late To Worry, Too Blue To Cry/How Do I Tell My Heart Not To Break?	5
62	Capitol CL 15278	Here I Am/Long Black Limousine	5
63	Capitol CL 15295	Prima Donna/Oh My Darling	5
67	Speciality SPE 1002	Satisfied Mind/Can't You See I'm Trying	5
67	Ember EMB S 249	By The Time I Get To Phoenix/Burning Bridges/Gentle On My Mind (p/s)	5
68	Ember EMB S 252	I Wanna Live/Hey Little One	5
68	Ember EMB S 255	Dreams Of The Everyday Housewife/Combine	5
68	Ember EMB S 258	Straight Life/That's Not Home	5
69	Ember EMB S 261	Wichita Lineman/Back In The Race (p/s)	5
69	Ember EMB S 263	Galveston/Everytime I Itch I Wind Up Scratching You (p/s)	5
69	Capitol CL 15615	True Grit/Hava Nagila	5

(see also Sagittarius, Jimmy Slade)

IAN CAMPBELL (FOLK) GROUP

63	Topic STOP 102	The Sun Is Burning/The Crow On The Cradle (in title p/s)	15
63	Topic STOP 102	The Sun Is Burning/The Crow On The Cradle	7
64	Decca F 11802	Marilyn Monroe/The Bells Of Rhymney	7
65	Transatlantic TRASP 2	Kelly From Killane/Boys Of Wexford (with Boys From Wexford)	7
65	Transatlantic TRASP 5	The Times They Are A-Changin'/Across The Hills (in p/s)	20
65	Transatlantic TRASP 5	The Times They Are A-Changin'/Across The Hills	12
66	Transatlantic TRASP 6	Come Kiss Me/The First Time I Ever Saw Your Face (in p/s)	12
66	Transatlantic TRASP 6	Come Kiss Me/The First Time I Ever Saw Your Face	7
66	Transatlantic TRASP 7	Guantanamera/Mary Anne	6
66	Transatlantic TRASP 10	One Eyed Reilly/Snow Is Falling (solo)	6
67	Big T BIG 103	Lover Let Me In/Private Harold Harris (as Ian Campbell Four)	6
69	Major Minor MM 639	Break My Mind/Govan Cross Special (solo)	6
62	Topic TOP 82	SONGS OF PROTEST (EP)	15
64	Decca DFE 8592	IAN CAMPBELL FOLK GROUP (EP)	15
65	Transatlantic TRAEP 128	SAMPLER (EP)	12
63	Transatlantic TRA 110	THIS IS THE IAN CAMPBELL FOLK GROUP (LP)	40
64	Transatlantic TRA 118	ACROSS THE HILLS (LP)	30
67	Transatlantic TRA 151	NEW IMPRESSIONS (LP)	15
68	Transatlantic TRA 163	THE CIRCLE GAME (LP)	20
68	Xtra XTRA 1074	TAM O'SHANTER (LP, as Ian Campbell & John Dunkerley)	18
69	Transatlantic TRASAM 4	THE IAN CAMPBELL FOLK GROUP SAMPLER (LP)	12
69	Transatlantic TRASAM 12	SAMPLER 2 (LP, as Ian Campbell Folk Four)	12
69	Major Minor 602 204	CAMPBELL COUNTRY 'N' SOUL (LP)	12
69	MFP SMFP 1349	IAN CAMPBELL & FOLK GROUP WITH DAVE SWARBRICK (LP)	12
71	Acorn CF 233	HOPE IS A STAR (LP)	40
71	Argo ZFB 13	THE SUN IS BURNING (LP)	25
72	Pye PKL 5506	SOMETHING TO SING ABOUT (LP)	15

(see also Dave Swarbrick)

JIMMY CAMPBELL

69	Fontana TF 1009	On A Monday/Dear Marge (in p/s)	35
69	Fontana TF 1009	On A Monday/Dear Marge	25
70	Fontana TF 1076	Lyanna/Frankie Joe	6
70	Fontana 6007 025	Don't Leave Me Now/So Lonely Without You	6
69	Fontana STL 5508	SON OF ANASTASIA (LP, black/silver label)	100
70	Vertigo 6360 010	HALF BAKED (LP, gatefold sleeve, large swirl label)	125
72	Philips 6308 100	JIMMY CAMPBELL'S ALBUM (LP, black/silver label)	125

(see also Kirkbys, 23rd Turnoff, Rockin' Horse)

JO-ANN CAMPBELL

58	London HLU 8536	Wait A Minute/It's True	60
58	London HLU 8536	Wait A Minute/It's True (78)	20
60	HMV POP 776	Bobby, Bobby, Bobby/A Kookie Little Paradise	25
61	HMV POP 873	Motorcycle Michael/Puka Puka Pants	20
62	HMV POP 1003	You Made Me Love You/I Changed My Mind Jack	20
62	Columbia DB 4889	I'm The Girl From Wolverton Mountain/Sloppy Joe	10
62	Cameo Parkway CP 237	Mr Fix It Man/Let Me Do It My Way	15
63	Cameo Parkway CP 249	Mother Please/Waiting For Love	15
86	Charly CR 30248	MISS REET PETITE (LP)	12

MINT VALUE £

JUNIOR CAMPBELL
74	Deram SML 1106	SECOND TIME AROUND (LP)	15

(see also Marmalade, Clan, Dean Ford & Gaylords)

LLOYD CAMPBELL
76	Love LOV 2	FIGHTING DUB (LP, artist commonly listed as Skin, Flesh & Bone)	50

PAT CAMPBELL
70	Major Minor MCP 5051	JUST A QUIET CONVERSATION (LP)	15

ROY CAMPBELL (& JAZZBO JASPERS)
68	Giant GN 41	Another Saturday Night/Wonderful World (with Jazzbo Jaspers)	7
68	Jolly JY 003	Suzette/Engine Engine Number Nine	7

CAMPBELL FAMILY
65	Topic 12T 120	THE SINGING CAMPBELLS - TRADITIONS OF AN ABERDEEN FAMILY (LP, blue label)	15

PATRICK CAMPBELL-LYONS
73	Sovereign SOV 115	Everybody Should Fly A Kite/I Think I Want Him Too	15
73	Sovereign SOV 119	Out On The Road/Me And My Friend	15
77	Electric WOT 12	That's What My Guru Said Last Night/The Whistling Fiddler	5
73	Sovereign SVNA 7258	ME AND MY FRIEND (LP, gatefold sleeve)	300
81	Public PUBL 1	THE ELECTRIC PLOUGH (LP)	20

(see also Nirvana [U.K.], Pica, Hat & Tie, Aquila)

RAY CAMPI
78	Radar RAD 9	WILDCAT SHAKEOUT (LP)	12
74	Injun EP 200	ROCK 'N' ROLL (EP)	10

CAN
73	United Artists UP 35506	Spoon/I'm So Green	15
73	United Artists UP 35596	Moonshake/Future Days (Edit)	12
74	United Artists UP 35749	Dizzy Dizzy (Edit)/Splash (Edit)	10
76	Virgin VS 153	I Want More/... And More	7
76	Virgin VS 166	Silent Night/Cascade Waltz	5
77	Virgin VS 172	Don't Say No/Return	5
78	Lightning LIG 545	Can-Can/Can Can Disco	5
83	Cherry Red CHERRY 57	Moonshake/Turtles Have Short Legs/One More Night (12")	20
69	United Artists UAS 29094	MONSTER MOVIE (LP, burgundy label)	100
70	United Artists UAS 29283	SOUNDTRACKS (LP)	40
71	Utd. Artists UAD 60009/10	TAGO MAGO (2-LP, flip-top sleeve)	120
72	United Artists UAS 29414	EGE BAMYASI (LP, with inner sleeve)	45
73	United Artists UAS 29505	FUTURE DAYS (LP)	40
74	United Artists UAG 29673	SOON OVER BABALUMA (LP, original silver sleeve)	50
74	United Artists USP 103	LIMITED EDITION (LP)	50
75	Virgin V 2041	LANDED (LP)	18
76	Caroline CAD 3001	UNLIMITED EDITION (2-LP, gatefold sleeve)	40
76	Sunset SLS 50400	OPENER (LP)	18
76	Virgin V2071	FLOW MOTION (LP, some stickered stating "featuring the hit single I Want More")	18
77	Virgin V 2079	SAW DELIGHT (LP, with insert)	20
78	Lightning LIP 4	OUT OF REACH (LP)	15
78	United Artists UDM 105/6	CANNABALISM (2-LP, gatefold sleeve)	20
89	Mercury 838883	RITE TIME (LP)	18

CANAAN
73	Dovetail DOVE 3	CANAAN (LP)	25
76	Myrrh MYR 1042	OUT OF THE WILDERNESS (LP, with inner sleeve)	20

LOS CANARIOS
67	Major Minor MM 502	Three Two One Ah/What Can I Do For You	30
67	Major Minor MM 532	Get On Your Knees/Keep On The Right Side	30

CANCER
90	Vinyl Solution SOL 22	TO THE GORY END (LP)	25
91	Vinyl Solution SOL 28	DEATH SHALL RISE (LP)	20
93	Vinyl Solution SOL 35	THE SINS OF MANKIND (LP)	25

CANDIDO
57	HMV DLP 1182	THE VOLCANIC (10" LP)	20

CANDLE FACTORY
70s	CAVS	NIGHTSHIFT (LP, private pressing)	55

CANDLELIGHT
67	CBS 2002507	That's What I Want/The Happy Days Of Summer	20

CANDLEMASS
88	Active Records ACT LP7	ANCIENT DREAMS (LP, insert)	15
03	Powerline PRLP 010	DIAMONDS OF DOOM (2-LP, white vinyl, gatefold sleeve with iron-one transfer, 1000 only)	20

CANDLEWICK GREEN
73	Decca FR 13480	Who Do You Think You Are?/Fingers In Your Ears	7

PETER CANDOLI & HIS ORCHESTRA
56	Capitol CL 14615	St. Louis Blues - Boogie/The Big Top (Entry Of The Gladiators)	5
60	Warner Bros WB 2	Sunset Strip Cha-Cha/DON RALKE: 77 Sunset Strip	5

CANDY
69	Emerald MD 1119	Little Bit Of Soul/Signs Of Love	15
69	Grape GR 3017	Ace Of Hearts/BILLY JACK: Bet Yer Life I Do	20
70	Big Shot BI 599	Ace Of Hearts/BILLY JACK: Bet Your Life	10

CANDY CHOIR
66	Parlophone R 5472	Silence Is Golden/Shake Hands (And Come Out Crying)	15
67	CBS 3061	Children And Flowers/Marianne	10
68	CBS 3305	Alexander's Ragtime Band/No Grey Skies	10
70	Polydor 56369	Why Do You Cry My Love/Lucky Jim	5

(see also Summer Set, Barry Ryan)

CANDY DATES
65	Pye 7N 15944	A Day Just Like That/Well I Do	12

CANDY FLOSS
72	Polydor 2041360	Delta Queen/Looking Over My Shoulder	8

CANDY & KISSES
65	Cameo Parkway C 336	The 81/Two Happy People	100
65	Cameo Parkway C 336	The 81/Two Happy People (DJ copy)	150
85	Kent TOWN 104	Mr Creator/CHUCK JACKSON: Hand It Over (withdrawn)	40

CANDYLAND
91	Yes 1	Bitter Moon/I'm A Good Girl (p/s)	6

CANDYMEN
67	HMV POP 1612	Georgia Pines/Movies In My Mind	10

PENNY CANDY
60	Top Rank JAR 328	Come On Over/They Said	10

CANDY ROCK
75	Philips 6006 442	Captain Captain/Pocahontas	6

CANE
78	Lightning GIL 31	3 BY 3 EP (p/s)	15

CANIS MAJOR
80	Gem GEMLP 109	BUTTERFLY QUEEN (LP)	30

(see also Girlschool)

BOB CANN
70s	Topic 12TS 275	WEST COUNTRY MELODEON (LP)	18

CANNED HEAT
68	Liberty	Rollin' And Tumblin'/Bullfrog Blues (unreleased)	0
68	Liberty LBF 15090	On The Road Again/The World In A Jug	8
69	Liberty LBF 15169	Going Up The Country/One Kind Favour	6
69	Liberty LBF 15200	Time Was/Low Down	8
69	Liberty LBF 15255	Poor Moon/Sic 'Em Pigs	8
69	Liberty LBF 15302	Let's Work Together/I'm Her Man	6
70	Liberty LBF 15350	Sugar Bee/Shake It And Break It	8
70	Pye International 7N 25513	Spoonful/Big Road Blues	12
70	Liberty LBF 15395	Future Blues/Skat	6
70	Liberty LBF 15429	Christmas Blues/Do Not Enter	6
71	Liberty LBF 15439	Wooly Bully/My Time Ain't Long	6
72	United Artists UP 35348	Rockin' With The King (with Little Richard)/I Don't Care What You Tell Me	6
73	United Artists UP 35562	Keep It Clean/You Can Run But You Sure Can't Hide	6
67	Liberty LBL/LBS 83059E	CANNED HEAT (LP)	35
68	Liberty LBL/LBS 83103	BOOGIE WITH CANNED HEAT (LP)	30
69	Liberty LDS 84001E	LIVING THE BLUES (2-LP, gatefold sleeve)	30
69	Liberty LBS 83239	HALLELUJAH (LP, gatefold sleeve)	20
70	Pye Intl. NSPL 28129	VINTAGE HEAT (LP)	30
70	Liberty LBS 83303	CANNED HEAT COOKBOOK (LP)	15
70	Liberty LBS 83333	CANNED HEAT '70 CONCERT (RECORDED LIVE IN EUROPE) (LP, g/fold sleeve)	12
70	Liberty LBS 83364	FUTURE BLUES (LP, gatefold sleeve)	20
71	Liberty LPS 103/4	HOOKER'N'HEAT (2-LP, gatefold sleeve, with John Lee Hooker)	35
72	United Artists UAG 29304	HISTORICAL FIGURES AND ANCIENT HEADS (LP, gatefold sleeve)	15
73	United Artists UAS 29455	THE NEW AGE (LP)	15
76	United Artists REM 407	CANNED HEAT (EP)	10

(see also Harvey Mandel, John Lee Hooker)

CANNIBAL & HEADHUNTERS
65	Stateside SS 403	Land Of A Thousand Dances/I'll Show You How To Love Me	30
67	CBS 62942	LAND OF A 1000 DANCES (LP)	40

CANNIBALS
78	Big Cock F-UK 1	Good Guys/Nothing Takes The Place Of You (printed paper bag sleeve)	5
85	Hit Records REEBEE 2	Christmas Rock 'n' Roll/New Year's Eve Song (doublepack in stocking)	6

(see also Count Bishops)

PHIL CANNING
79	Woodbine St. WSR 002	Sell Out/Underground (p/s)	40

ACE CANNON
62	London HLU 9498	Tuff/Sittin'	8
62	London HLU 9546	Blues Stay Away From Me/Blues In My Heart	7
63	London HLU 9745	Cottonfields/Mildew	7
64	London HLU 9866	Searchin'/Love Letters In The Sand	7
67	London HLU 10105	Wonderland By Night/As Time Goes By	5
70	London HA-U/SH-U 8407	ACE OF SAX (LP)	20

FREDDY CANNON
59	Top Rank JAR 135	Tallahassee Lassie/You Know	20
59	Top Rank JAR 135	Tallahassee Lassie/You Know (78)	20
59	Top Rank JAR 207	Okefenokee/Kookie Hat	10
59	Top Rank JAR 247	Way Down Yonder In New Orleans/Fractured	5
60	Top Rank JAR 309	California, Here I Come/Indiana	5
60	Top Rank JAR 334	Chattanooga Shoeshine Boy/Boston (My Home Town)	5
60	Top Rank JAR 369	The Urge/Jump Over	5
60	Top Rank JAR 407	Happy Shades Of Blue/Guernavaca Choo Choo	6
60	Top Rank JAR 518	Humdinger/My Blue Heaven	10
61	Top Rank JAR 548	Muskrat Rumble/Two Thousand 88	5
61	Top Rank JAR 568	Buzz Buzz A Diddle It/Opportunity	20
61	Top Rank JAR 579	Transistor Sister/Walk To The Moon	5
61	Top Rank JAR 592	For Me And My Gal/Blue Plate Special	5
62	Top Rank JAR 609	Teen Queen Of The Week/Wild Guy	5
62	Stateside SS 101	Palisades Park/June July And August	8
62	Stateside SS 118	What's Gonna Happen When Summer's Done/Broadway	10

MINT VALUE £

62	Stateside SS 134	If You Were A Rock & Roll Record/The Truth Ruth	20
63	Stateside SS 155	Come On And Love Me/Four Letter Man	10
63	Stateside SS 183	The Ups And Downs Of Love/It's Been Nice	10
63	Stateside SS 201	Patty Baby/Betty Jean	20
63	Stateside SS 220	Everybody Monkey/Oh Gloria	7
64	Stateside SS 260	That's The Way Girls Are/Do What The Hippies Do	7
64	Warner Bros WB 123	Abigail Beecher/All American Girl	7
64	Stateside SS 298	Sweet Georgia Brown/What A Party	7
65	Warner Bros WB 5645	Action/Beechwood City	10
66	Warner Bros WB 5693	The Dedication Song/Come On Come On	8
69	London HLK 10252	Beautiful Downtown Burbank/If You Give Me A Title	7
79	Hot Rock 003	Hey Punk Rocker/At The Disco Down	7
60	Top Rank JKP 2058	THE EXPLOSIVE FREDDY (BOOM! BOOM!) CANNON (EP)	30
60	Top Rank JKP 2066	FOUR DIRECT HITS (EP)	20
61	Top Rank JKP 3010	ON TARGET (EP)	20
62	Stateside SE 1002	BLAST OFF WITH FREDDY CANNON (EP)	25
60	Top Rank 25/018	THE EXPLOSIVE FREDDY CANNON (LP)	30
61	Top Rank 35/106	FREDDY CANNON SINGS HAPPY SHADES OF BLUE (LP)	40
61	Top Rank 35/113	FREDDY CANNON FAVOURITES (LP)	40
63	Stateside SL 10013	BANG ON (LP)	40
64	Stateside SL 10062	STEPS OUT (LP)	40
64	Warner Bros WM/WS 8153	FREDDY CANNON (LP)	25

(see also Danny & Juniors)

JUDY CANNON
| 65 | Pye 7N 15900 | The Very First Day I Met You/Hello Heartache | 50 |

SEAN CANNON
| 77 | Cottage COT 411 | ROVING JOURNEYMAN (LP) | 30 |

CONROY CANNON
| 69 | Pama PM 769 | Oh Happy Day/Can't Get Along Without You | 8 |
| 69 | Atlantic 584 305 | My Bunny/Good Boy | 8 |

CANNON BALL & JOHNNY MELODY
| 69 | Big Shot BI 518 | Parapinto/Cool Hand Luke | 25 |

(see also Carl Bryan, King Cannon, Johnny Moore, Jackie Mittoo, Royals)

CANNONBALLS
| 61 | Coral Q 72428 | Cannonball Caboose/New Orleans Beat | 6 |
| 61 | Coral Q 72431 | Lullaby Of Birdland/Calliope Boogie | 6 |

CANNON BROTHERS
| 65 | Brit WI 1003 | Turn Your Eyes To Me/Don't Stop Now | 18 |

CANNONS
| 60 | Decca F 11269 | I Didn't Know The Gun Was Loaded/My Guy's Come Back | 12 |
| 61 | Columbia DB 4724 | Bush Fire/Juicy | 25 |

CANNY FETTLE
| 75 | Tradition TSR 023 | VARRY CANNY (LP) | 30 |
| 77 | Tradition TSR 027 | TRIP TO HARROGATE (LP) | 18 |

CANYON
| 75 | RCA RCA 2112 | Top Of The World/Boogie Down Broadway | 8 |

CAPABILITY BROWN
72	Charisma CB 193	Wake Up Little Sister/Windfall	6
73	Charisma CB 207	Midnight Cruiser/Silent Sounds	6
73	Charisma CB 217	Liar/Keep Death Off The Road (Drive On The Pavement)	6
70s	Charisma BCP 7	War (p/s)	6
72	Charisma CAS 1056	FROM SCRATCH (LP, lyric inner sleeve, pink 'scroll' label)	40
73	Charisma CAS 1068	VOICE (LP, gatefold sleeve, large 'Mad Hatter' label)	25

(see also Unit 4+2, Tony Rivers & Castaways, Fuzzy Duck)

JIM CAPALDI
74	Island WIP 6198	It's All Up To You/Whale Meat Again	5
72	Island ILPS 9187	OH HOW WE DANCED (LP, gatefold sleeve, pink rim label)	25
74	Island ILPS 9254	WHALE MEAT AGAIN (LP, pink rim label)	15
77	Island ILPS 9497	PLAY IT BY EAR (LP)	15

(see also Hellions, Traffic)

CAPE KENNEDY CONSTRUCTION CO.
| 69 | President PT 265 | The First Steps On The Moon/Armageddon | 100 |

CAPERCAILLIE
84	Etive/SRT 4KL 178	CASCADE (LP)	12
87	Grampian TV GPN 1001	THE BLOOD IS STRONG (LP, with insert)	12
87	Green Linnet SIF 1077	CROSSWINDS (LP, with insert)	12

(see also Etives)

CAPES & MASKS
| 65 | Fontana TL 5339 | COMIC BOOK HEROES (LP) | 50 |
| 65 | Nevis NEV R005 | COMIC BOOK HEROES (LP) | 18 |

CAPES OF GOOD HOPE
| 66 | Stateside SS 577 | Winter's Children/If My Monique Could Only Dance | 15 |

CAPITAL LETTERS
77	Greensleeves GRED 2	Smoking My Ganja/Natty Walk (12")	30
79	Greensleeves GRED 16	UK Skanking/Run Run Run (12")	30
79	Greensleeves GREL 7	HEADLINE NEWS (LP)	25

CAPITOL K
| 99 | Planet Mu ZIQ 015 | Postcard/JEGA: Untitled (100 in numbered p/s, those un-numbered =£4) | 10 |

CAPITOL SHOWBAND
| 67 | Marble Arch MAL 694 | THE CAPITOL SHOWBAND (LP) | 12 |

CAPITOLS (U.K.)
66	Pye 7N 17025	Honey And Wine/Boulavogue	12

CAPITOLS (U.S.)
66	Atlantic 584 004	Cool Jerk/Hello Stranger	22

(see also Three Caps)

CAPOEIRA TWINS
99	Blowpop Records BLOWP 001	4 x 3 (12")	15
00	FFRR FX 385	Four (4x3) (12")	8

ANDY CAPP
69	Treasure Isle TI 7052	Pop-A-Top/RICO: The Lion Speaks	15
70	Duke DU 69	The Law Parts 1 & 2	18
70	Duke DU 71	Poppy Show/Pop-A-Top (Part 2)	12

AL CAPPS
73	Stateside SS 2214	Shangri-La/Magician	10

DANNY CAPRI
55	Capitol CL 14265	Desirable/I Do, I Do	10
55	Capitol CL 14302	Don't Make A Liar Out Of Me/Angelica	10

CAPRICORN
70	MCA MK 5050	Liverpool Hello/How Did You Find Me	6

(see also Marty Wilde)

CAPRIS
61	Columbia DB 4605	There's A Moon Out Tonight/Indian Girl	100

CAPTAIN BEEFHEART & HIS MAGIC BAND
SINGLES
68	Pye International 7N 25443	Yellow Brick Road/Abba Zabba	35
68	A&M AMS 726	Moonchild/Who Do You Think You're Fooling	30
73	Reprise K 14233	Too Much Time/My Head Is My Only House Unless It Rains	12
74	Virgin VS 110	Upon The My-Oh-My/Magic Be	5
78	Buddah BDS 466	Sure 'Nuff 'N Yes I Do/Electricity	7
78	MCA MCA 366	Hard Workin' Man (Jack Nitzsche featuring Captain Beefheart)/ JACK NITZSCHE: Coke Machine	6
82	Virgin VS 534	Ice Cream For Crow/Light Reflected Off The Oceans Of The Moon	10

EPs
71	A&M AME 600	DIDDY WAH DIDDY (promo only)	250
79	Virgin SIXPACK 1	SIX-PACK/SIX TRACK (picture disc, die-cut p/s with stand, 5,000 only)	15
82	Virgin VS 534 12	LIGHT REFLECTED OFF THE OCEANS OF THE MOON (12" EP, p/s)	12
84	A&M AMY 226	THE LEGENDARY A&M SESSIONS (12" EP/mini-LP, Diddy Wah Diddy EP plus "Here I Am, I Always Am")	15
86	Edsel BLIMP 902	THE LEGENDARY A&M SESSIONS (12" EP, reissue)	15

ALBUMS
68	Pye Intl. NPL 28110	SAFE AS MILK (mono, flipback sleeve)	125
68	Liberty LBL 83172	STRICTLY PERSONAL (gatefold sleeve, mono)	80
68	Liberty LBS 83172	STRICTLY PERSONAL (gatefold sleeve, stereo)	50
69	Straight STS 1053	TROUT MASK REPLICA (2-LP, gatefold sleeve)	150
69	Buddah 623171	SAFE AS MILK (LP, reissue, stereo)	40
69	Pye/Marble Arch MAL 1117	SAFE AS MILK (LP, reissue, mono, 10 tracks not 12)	40
70	Straight STS 1063	LICK MY DECALS OFF, BABY	100
70	Buddah 2349 002	DROPOUT BOOGIE (stereo reissue of "Safe As Milk")	30
71	Buddah 2365 002	MIRROR MAN (gatefold die-cut sleeve)	40
71	Sunset SLS50208	STRICTLY PERSONAL (LP, reissue)	12
72	Reprise K 44162	THE SPOTLIGHT KID (tan 'riverboat' label, with lyric card insert)	35
72	Reprise K 44162	THE SPOTLIGHT KID (tan 'riverboat' label, without lyric card insert)	15
72	Reprise K 54007	CLEAR SPOT (PVC sleeve with card insert)	30
73	Reprise K 44244	LICK MY DECALS OFF, BABY	18
74	Virgin V 2015	UNCONDITIONALLY GUARANTEED ('two virgins' label)	20
74	Buddah BDLP 4004	MIRROR MAN	20
74	Virgin V 2023	BLUEJEANS & MOONBEAMS ('two virgins' label)	20
75	Reprise K 64026	TROUT MASK REPLICA (2-LP, gatefold sleeve, tan 'riverboat' label, matt sleeve)	40
76	Reprise K 84006	TWO ORIGINALS OF CAPTAIN BEEFHEART (2-LP, reissue of Lick My Decals Off, Baby & "The Spotlight Kid")	20
77	Pye FILD 008	THE FILE SERIES (2-LP, reissue of "Safe As Milk" & "Mirror Man", die-cut sleeve with inners)	18
79	Virgin V 2149	SHINY BEAST (BAT CHAIN PULLER)	20
80	Virgin V 2172	DOC AT THE RADAR STATION	25
70s	Reprise K 64026	TROUT MASK REPLICA (2-LP, gatefold sleeve, 2nd re-pressing, tan 'riverboat' label, soft laminated sleeve)	25
82	Virgin V 2237	ICE CREAM FOR CROW (with inner sleeve)	12
84	PRT NCP 1004	SAFE AS MILK (LP, reissue)	20
99	Buddah 91751	SAFE AS MILK (2-LP reissue)	20
08	Oz It Morpheus OZITLP 8006	DUST SUCKER (2-LP)	20

(see also Mu, Frank Zappa, Jack Nitzsche)

CAPTAIN BEYOND
72	Capricorn K 47503	CAPTAIN BEYOND (LP)	30

(see also Deep Purple, Iron Butterfly)

CAPTAIN LOCKHEED & THE STARFIGHTERS
73	United Artists UP 35543	Ejection/Catch A Falling Starfighter (p/s)	25
73	United Artists UP 35543	Ejection/Catch A Falling Starfighter (different mix of A-side, no p/s)	10

(see also Robert Calvert)

CAPTAIN MARRYAT
74	Thor THOR 1007 S	CAPTAIN MARRYAT (LP, 200 only)	2000

CAPTAIN ROCK & SKYRIDERS
72	Crystal CR 7028	Luppy Lu/Together	8

MINT VALUE £

CAPTAIN SINBAD
| 83 | Oak Sound OSLP 002 | AGAIN (LP) | 25 |
| 84 | Greensleeves GREL 34 | THE SEVEN VOYAGES OF SINBAD (LP) | 25 |

CAPTAIN ZERO
| 75 | Gull GULS 23 | Space Walk/I'm Only An Elf | 6 |

C.A. QUINTET
| 83 | Psycho PSYCHO 12 | TRIP THROUGH HELL (LP, reissue of U.S. 60s LP) | 15 |

CARAVAN
69	Verve VS 1518	A Place Of My Own/Ride	45
70	Decca F 13063	If I Could Do It All Over Again, I'd Do It All Over You/Hello, Hello	20
71	Decca F 23125	Love To Love You (And Tonight Pigs Will Fly)/Golf Girl	20
75	Decca FR 13599	Stuck In A Hole/Lover	5
76	BTM SBT 104	All The Way (With John Wayne's Single-Handed Liberation Of Paris)/ Chiefs And Indians (p/s)	6
77	Arista ARIST 110	Better By Far/Silver Strings	5
80	Kingdom KV 8009	Heartbreaker/It's Never Too Late (p/s)	6
68	Verve VLP 6011	CARAVAN (LP, 'pillar' sleeve, mono, brown/white label, with "sold in the U.K." text)	400
68	Verve SVLP 6011	CARAVAN (LP, 'pillar' sleeve, stereo)	300
70	Decca SKL 5052	IF I COULD DO IT ALL OVER AGAIN, I'D DO IT ALL OVER YOU (LP, boxed logo)	80
71	Deram SDL-R 1	IN THE LAND OF GREY AND PINK (LP, gatefold sleeve, 1st pressing with brown/white label)	100
71	Deram SDL-R 1	IN THE LAND OF GREY AND PINK (LP, gatefold sleeve, later pressing with red/white label)	40
72	Deram SDL 8	WATERLOO LILY (LP, gatefold sleeve, 1st pressing brown/white large Deram labels. SDL8 on sleeve and label)	125
72	Deram SDL 8	WATERLOO LILY (LP, gatefold sleeve later pressing with red/white labels and SDL-R 8 on labels and sleeves)	20
72	MGM 2353 058	CARAVAN (LP, reissue)	18
73	Deram SDL-R 12	FOR GIRLS WHO GROW PLUMP IN THE NIGHT (LP, gatefold sleeve, red/white label)	30
74	Deram SML-R 1110	CARAVAN AND THE NEW SYMPHONIA (LIVE AT DRURY LANE) (LP, red/white label)	20
75	Decca SKL-R 5210	CUNNING STUNTS (LP)	20
76	Decca DKL-R 8/1 & 8/2	CANTERBURY TALES (2-LP)	18
76	BTM BTM 1007	BLIND DOG AT ST. DUNSTAN'S (LP)	15
80	Kingdom KVL 9003	THE ALBUM (LP, laminated sleeve)	20

(see also Gringo, Matching Mole, Hatfield & The North, Spiro Gyra)

CARAVELLES
63	Decca F 11697	You Don't Have To Be A Baby To Cry/The Last One To Know	5
63	Decca F 11758	I Really Don't Want To Know/I Was Wrong	5
64	Decca F 11816	Have You Ever Been Lonely?/Gonna Get Along Without Ya Now	6
64	Fontana TF 466	You Are Here/How Can I Be Sure?	5
64	Fontana TF 509	I Don't Care If The Sun Don't Shine/I Like A Man	5
64	Polydor NH 59034	True Love Never Runs Smooth/Georgia Boy	7
66	Polydor 56137	Hey Mama You've Been On My Mind/New York	10
67	Polydor 56156	I Want To Love You Again/I Had To Walk Home Myself	5
68	Pye 7N 17654	The Other Side Of Love/I Hear A New Kind Of Music	5
63	Decca LK 4565	THE CARAVELLES (LP)	25

(see also Lois Lane)

CARAVELLI
| 69 | CBS 4275 | Theme From The Film Z/Isadora | 8 |

GUY CARAWAN
58	Pye Nixa 7N 15132	Old Man Atom (Talking Atomic Blues)/Michael Row The Boat Ashore	6
60	Collector JEA 4	SONGS FROM THE SOUTH (EP)	12
58	Topic 10T 24	MOUNTAIN SONGS AND BANJO TUNES (10" LP)	30
57	77 Records LP8	GUY CARAWAN, HIS BANJO AND GUITAR (10" LP)	50
67	Columbia SX 6065	A GUY CALLED CARAWAN (LP)	30

(see also Peggy Seeger & Guy Carawan)

CARCASS
88	Earache MOSH 06	REEK OF PUTREFACTION (LP)	30
89	Earache MOSH 18	SYMPHONIES OF SICKNESS (LP, picture disc)	30
91	Earache MOSH 42	NECROTICISM - DESCANTING THE INSALUBRIOUS (LP)	30

CARDBOARD ORCHESTRA
| 69 | CBS 4176 | Zebady Zak/Mary Tell Me Why | 8 |
| 69 | CBS 4633 | Nothing But A Sad Sad Show/Yes I Heard A Little Bird | 8 |

(see also Zior, Monument)

CARDIAC ARREST
| 79 | Another Record AN 1 | Running In The Street/T.V. Friends (p/s, 500 only) | 20 |
| 79 | Tortch TOR 002 | A BUS FOR A BUS ON A BUS (EP) | 20 |

CARDIACS
86	Alphabet ALPH 002	SEASIDE TREATS (12" EP, with poster & lyric insert)	20
87	Alphabet ALPH 006	THERE'S TOO MANY IRONS IN THE FIRE (12" EP, with poster)	10
88	Alphabet ALPH 008	Is This The Life/I'm Eating In Bed (p/s)	7
88	Alphabet ALPHT 008	Is This The Life/Loosefish Goosegash/I'm Eating In Bed (12", p/s)	12
88	Alphabet ALPH 009	Susannah's Still Alive/Blind In Safety And Leafy In Love (p/s)	6
91	Alphabet ALPH 015	DAY IS GONE (12" EP, with lyric sheet)	12
87	Alphabet ALPH 004	BIG SHIP (mini LP, with lyric insert)	18
87	Alphabet ALPH 005	RUDE BOOTLEG - LIVE AT READING '86 (LP, stamped sleeve with insert)	18
88	Torso CD 060	A LITTLE MAN AND A HOUSE AND THE WHOLE WORLD WINDOW (CD)	30
88	Alphabet ALPH 009T	Susannah's Still Alive/Blind In Safety And Leafy In Love/All His Geese Are Swans (12", p/s)	10
89	Alphabet ALPH 011	Baby Heart Dirt/I Hold My Love In My Arms (p/s)	7
88	Night Tracks SFNT 013	RADIO ONE EVENING SESSION: R.E.S./ Buds And Spawn/In A City Lining/ Is This The Life/Cameras (12" EP)	18
88	Alphabet ALPHLP 010	CARDIACS LIVE (LP)	18
88	Alphabet ALPH 012	ON LAND AND IN THE SEA (LP)	18
91	Alphabet ALPHLP 014	SONGS FOR SHIPS AND IRONS (LP)	15
92	Alphabet ALPHLP 017	HEAVEN BORN AND EVER BRIGHT (LP)	15

(see also Cardiac Arrest)

CARDIGAN BROTHERS
63	London HLU 9740	I Know Know Know/Let's Go To The Movies	5

CARDIGANS
95	Trampoline 523445-1	LIFE (LP)	25
96	Stockholm 53347-1	FIRST BAND ON THE MOON (LP)	25
00	Stockholm/Simply Vinyl SVLP 175	GRAN TURISMO (LP, with inner sleeve)	60
03	Stockholm 067 101-1	LONG GONE BEFORE DAYLIGHT (LP)	80

CARDINAL
94	Dedicated DEDLP 018	CARDINAL (LP)	18

CARDINALS
71	Nelmwood Audio NWA 1	SWEET & REFRESHING (LP)	30
72	Nelmwood Audio	ON TOP OF THE WORLD (LP)	22

JACK CARDWELL
54	Parlophone CMSP 24	Whiskey, Women And Loaded Dice/Slap-Ka-Dab (export issue)	30
54	Parlophone CMSP 27	Blue Love/Diddle Diddle Dumpling (export issue)	30
54	Parlophone DP 406	Blue Love/Diddle Diddle Dumpling (78, export issue)	5

CARE
83	Arista KBIRD 2	Flaming Sword/Misericorde (picture disc)	5
83	Arista KBIRD 122	Flaming Sword/Misericorde (12" p/s)	10

(see also Wild Swans, Lotus Eaters, Lightning Seeds)

CAREFREES
63	Oriole CB 1916	We Love You Beatles/Hot Blooded Lover	25
64	Oriole CB 1931	Aren't You Glad You're You/Paddy Wack	15

CARETAKER/ELLIS BAND
80s	Stonehouse 2	Majority Rules/Two Steps Forward	8

(see also Alton Ellis)

DAVE CAREY (JAZZ BAND)
53	Columbia SCM 5030	Broken Wings/Oh, Happy Day (as David Carey)	5
56	Tempo A 122	Kater Street Rag/Kansas City Kitty	10
56	Tempo A 133	I've Found A New Baby/Brown Skin Mama	10
56	Tempo A 138	Sunset Cafe Stomp/Sweet Georgia Brown	10
56	Tempo A 150	Ida, Sweet As Apple Cider/Button Up Your Overcoat	5
61	Philips PB 1158	Bingo (I'm In Love)/Paddlin' Madelin' Home (some in p/s)	5
56	Tempo EXA 38	DAVE CAREY JAZZ BAND (EP)	8
56	Tempo EXA 43	DAVE CAREY JAZZ BAND (EP)	8
56	Tempo EXA 51	DAVE CAREY JAZZ BAND (EP)	10
55	Tempo LAP 4	DAVE CAREY JAZZ BAND (LP)	12

CAREY & LLOYD
72	Attack ATT 8032	Do It Again (as Carey/Lloyd)/GARY RANGLIN: Watch It	6
72	Grape GR 3025	Come Down Part 1/DYNAMITES: Come Down Part 2	6

(see also Carey Johnson, Lloyd Young, Lloyd & Carey)

MARIAH CAREY
90	Columbia 655 932-2	Vision Of Love/Sent From Up Above/Medley (CD)	15
90	Columbia 656 364-2	Love Takes Time/Vanishing/You Need Me (CD)	15
90	Columbia 656 364-5	Love Takes Time/Vanishing/You Need Me/Vision Of Love (CD, picture disc)	25
91	Columbia 656 583-2	Someday (7" Jackswing Mix)/(12" Jackswing Mix)/(12" House Mix)(CD)	15
91	Columbia 656 583-5	Someday (7" Jackswing Mix)/Vision Of Love/Love Takes Time/ Alone In Love (CD, picture disc)	20
91	Columbia 656 931-2	There's Got To Be A Way (Album Version)/(12" Remix)/ (ALT Vocal Club Mix) (CD)	15
91	Columbia 656 931-5	There's Got To Be A Way (Album Version)/(7" Remix)/Someday (7" Jackswing Mix)/Vision Of Love (CD, picture disc)	15
92	Columbia 657 662-2	Can't Let Go (Edit)/To Be Around You/The Wind (CD, slimline jewel case)	12
92	Columbia 657 941-7	Make It Happen(radio edit)/Emotions (Special Motion Edit) (p/s)	5
92	Columbia 657 941-2	Make It Happen (Radio Edit)/(Ext. Version)/(Dub)/(C&C Classic Mix)/ (LP Version) (CD)	10
92	Columbia 658 137-9	I'll Be There (live)/Vision Of Love (live)/If It's Over/All In Your Mind (CD, picture disc)	5
92	Columbia 657 662-5	Can't Let Go (Edit)/I Don't Wanna Cry/All In Your Mind (CD)	12
94	Columbia 660 944-5	All I Want For Christmas Is You/Miss You Most (At Christmas Time) Silent Night (CD picture disc)	6
94	Columbia 661070 7	All I Want For Christmas Is You/Miss You Most (At Christmas Time) (jukebox issue)	30
98	Columbia MARIAH 1	12s (10x12" in box)	50

TONY CAREY
84	MCA MCA 873	Fine Fine Day/Say It's Over (p/s)	6
84	MCA MCFC 3212	SOME TOUGH CITY (LP, with inner sleeve)	12

(see also Rainbow)

HENSON CARGILL
68	Monument MON 1015	Skip A Rope/Very Well-Travelled Man	6
68	Monument SMO 5024	COMING ON STRONG (LP)	12

PATRICK CARGILL
73	Decca F13466	Father, Dear Father Christmas/If He Could Talk	6

CARGO
70	(No Label, LS 1674)	Killing Time/Love Will Turn You Round (Unissued, white labels only)	200

CARIBBEANS
69	Doctor Bird DB 1181	Let Me Walk By/AMBLINGS: Tell Me Why	20
69	Crab CR 14	Please Please/MATADORS: The Destroyer	15

CARIBBEATS
66	Ska Beat JB 246	The Bells Of St. Mary's/WINSTON RICHARDS: Loki	20
67	Double D DD 101	Highway 300/I Think Of You (actually by Merlene McKenzie)	40
67	Double D DD 103	I'll Try/If I Did Look	60
68	Double D DD 111	One Step/HAZEL WRIGHT: Please Help Me	60

(see also Bobby Aitken, Itals)

MINT VALUE £

CARIBBENN (THE)
65	Pye 7N 15961	Inside Out/Up My Street...10

CARIBOES
71	Bullet BU 479	Let It Be Me/All I Have To Do Is Dream..5

CARIBS
60	Starlite ST45 012	Taboo/Mathilda Cha Cha Cha!...15

CARIFTA ALLSTARS
72	Green Door GD 4040	The Harder They Come (actually by Charlie Ace)/Time Is Still Here......8

CARL & COMMANDERS
61	Columbia DB 4719	Farmer John/Cleanin' Up..20

DONOVAN CARLESS
71	Tropical ALO31	How Can I Tell Her About It/Be Thankful For What You Got...............15

CARLEW CHOIR
69	Spark SRL 1028	Huma-Lama/Give A Hand To This Clown..7

TOM CARLILE
67	CBS 3249	I Saw The Light/Nightingale...7

BELINDA CARLISLE
88	I.R.S. DIRM 118	Mad About You/I Never Wanted A Rich Man/Mad About You (Extended Mix) (3" CD) 20
87	Virgin VSCD 1036	Heaven Is A Place On Earth/We Can Change/Heaven Is A Place On Earth (Heavenly Version)/Heaven Is A Place On Earth (Acapella Version) (CD)......................15
88	Virgin VSTY 1074	Circle In The Sand/(Beach Party Mix)/(Seaside Groove Mix) (12", picture disc) 8
88	Virgin VSX 1114	World Without You (Remix)/Nobody Owns Me (box set, 2 cards & lyric sheet) 10
88	Virgin VSCD 1150	Love Never Dies... (Full Length Version)/I Feel Free (live)/Circle In The Sand (live)/Heaven Is A Place On Earth (live) (CD, with prints)...................10
89	Virgin VSCD 1230DJ	La Luna/Whatever It Takes (3" CD, picture disc, promo only)....................25

(see also Go-Go's, Smithereens)

BILL CARLISLE & CARLISLES
59	Mercury AMT 1063	Down Boy/Union Suit 40
64	Hickory 45-1254	Shanghai Rooster/Big John Henry's Girl 5

CARLISLE BROTHERS
59	Parlophone GEP 8799	FRESH FROM THE COUNTRY (EP)...30

DON CARLOS ORCHESTRA
54	HMV 7 MC 4	Delicado/Anything Can Happen (export issue) 5
56	HMV 7 MC 48	The Bandit/Mexicana (export issue)..5
60	Top Rank JAR 376	Mustapha/Josita..5
58	Pye Nlxa NPT 19028	CHA CHA CHA CARLOS (10" LP) 25
60	Columbia 33SX 1237	CRAZY LATIN (LP)..15

DON CARLOS
78	Dove 511	Plantation/Version..15
80	Pirate PIR 001	Nice Time/Get Up (12")..20
80	Negus Roots NERT003	I Love Jah/I Don't Care (12", as Don McCarlos)..............................35
81	Negus Roots NERT 004	Gimme Gimme Your Love/PAP TULLO: Gimme More Love (12") 30
82	Negus Roots NERT 015	Magic Man/Magic Dub (12")..12
82	Cha Cha CHAD 52	Can't Waste Time/PAPA BRUCE : No Time To Waste (10")...............20
83	Shuttle SH 008	Money & Women (with John Wayne)/CORNELL CAMPBELL/PURPLEMAN: Keep On Working (12")..............................20
83	Blacker Dread SCOM 003	From Creation/Versions (12") 30
83	Youth In Progress YP001	Jordan River/LITTLE JOHN: Reasons/LADY ANNE AND SANTANA; Love Life (12")..........20
85	Blacker Dread SCOM 020	Strictly Culture (Love We Culture Version)/MIKEY DREAD: Dubuling Mix (12") 25
80s	Rusty International RI 001	Isabel/BILLY BOYO: One Morning/CAPTAIN SINBAD & ROOTS RADICALS: Radication Dehbout (12")..............................20
81	Blue Moon BM 001	PROPHET (LP)..40
82	Negus Roots NERLP 001	SUFFERING (LP)...40
82	Negus Roots NERLP 005	HARVEST TIME (LP) 60
83	Burning sounds BRD 1053	SPREAD OUT INA DANCEHALL STYLE (LP) 20
84	Saxon International 5550	SAMMY DREAD MEETS DON CARLOS (LP, not released in sleeve) 25

(see also Black Uhuru)

WALTER CARLOS
69	CBS 4296	Brandenburg Concerto/Sinfonia To Cantata 5

DAVE CARLSEN
73	Spark SRLP 110	A PALE HORSE (LP, yellow/blue label)...40

RAY CARLSON
67	MGM MGM 1362	Speak No Sorrow/It's Getting Me Down Girl 6

CARL CARLTON (LITTLE)
68	Action ACT 4501	Competition Ain't Nothin'/Three Way Love.....................................40
68	Action ACT 4514	46 Drums 1 Guitar/Why Don't They Leave Us Alone 15
69	Action ACT 4537	Look At Mary Wonder/Bad For Each Other (as Carl Carlton) 10
75	ABC ABC 4040	Smokin' Room/Signed, Sealed, Delivered, I'm Yours (as Carl Carlton) 6
90s	Kent TOWN 105	Competition Ain't Nothin'/HESITATIONS: I'm Not Built That Way 10

EDDIE CARLTON
76	Cream CRM 5001	It Will Be Done (Parts 1 & 2)..10

CARLTON & HIS SHOES
68	Coxsone CS 7065	Love Me Forever/Happy Land 50
68	Studio One SO 2062	This Feeling/You And Me (Love Is A Treasure) 75
70s	Studio One PSOL 003	LOVE ME FOREVER (LP, laminated sleeve) 50

(see also Lee 'Scratch' Perry, Roy & Enid)

PAUL CARMAN
74	DJM DJS 317	In My World/School Love...6

CARMEN
74	Regal Zonophone RZ 3086	Flamenco Fever/Lonely House 10
74	Regal Zonophone RZ 3090	Bulerias/Stepping Stone 6

| 73 | R. Zonophone SRZA 8518 | FANDANGOS IN SPACE (LP, gatefold sleeve, red/silver label) | 30 |
| 75 | R. Zonophone SLRZ 1040 | DANCING ON A COLD WIND (LP, with inner sleeve, red/silver label) | 45 |

(see also Jethro Tull)

ROGER CARMEN, ROCK KEELING, MO THOMAS & ANN & STEVE MITCHELL

| 71 | Mosart Music MM 1 | FROST LAND (LP) | 25 |

HOAGY CARMICHAEL

55	Vogue Coral Q 72078	Crazy Otto Rag/Happy Hoagy's Medley	5
55	Vogue Coral Q 72095	Lazy River/I'm Just Wild About Mary	5
56	Vogue Coral Q 72123	Hong Kong Blues/LES BROWN: It's All Right With Me	10
56	Vogue Coral Q 72206	I Walk The Line/Flight To Hong Kong	5

JEAN CARN

| 79 | Philadelphoa Int. S PIR 13 8840 | Was That All It Was/Whats On Your Mind (12") | 10 |

CARNABY

| 65 | Piccadilly 7N 35272 | Jump And Dance/My Love Will Stay | 100 |

CARNABY STREET POP ORCHESTRA & CHOIR

| 69 | Carnaby CNLS 6003 | THE LONDON THEME (LP) | 50 |

CARNAGE

| 84 | Creative Reality REAL 07 | FACE THE FACTS (LP) | 12 |

CARNATIONS

| 65 | Blue Beat BB 285 | Mighty Man/What Are You Selling | 22 |

JUDY CARNE

| 61 | Decca F 11347 | Late Last Evening (with David Kernan)/A Plea For The Throne (with Betty Marsden & Pip Hinton) ('On The Brighter Side' cast) | 5 |
| 69 | Reprise RS 20680 | Right, Said Fred/Sock It To Me | 8 |

CARNEGY HALL

| 68 | Polydor 56224 | The Bells Of San Francisco/Slightly Cracked | 6 |

CARNIVAL

67	Columbia DB 8255	The Big Bright Green Pleasure Machine/Silver Dreams And Scarlet Memories	7
70	Liberty LBF 15252	Son Of A Preacher Man/Walk On By	6
70	Liberty LBS 83305	THE CARNIVAL (LP)	20

SASHA CARO

| 67 | Decca F 12687 | Grade 3 Section 2/Little Maid Song | 18 |
| 68 | Decca F12744 | Molotov Molotov/Never Play A B Side | 25 |

BOBBI CAROL

| 63 | Fontana 267 260TF | Will You Love Me Tomorrow/It Doesn't Matter | 5 |

CAROL & MEMORIES

| 66 | CBS 202086 | Tears On My Pillow/Crying My Eyes Out | 22 |

CAROLE & SHERRY

| 62 | Fontana 270 107 TF | I Ain't Ready Yet/Like I Gotta Get Away | 6 |

CAROLINA SLIM

| 72 | Flyright LP 4702 | CAROLINA BLUES AND BOOGIE (LP) | 20 |

CAROLINES

| 65 | Polydor BM 56027 | Love Made A Fool Of Me/Believe In Me | 20 |

CAROLLS

| 65 | Polydor BM 56046 | Give Me Time/Darling I Want You So Much | 20 |

(see also Carrols)

CAROLS

| 70 | Revolution REV 013 | Everyday I Have To Cry Some/FIRE SESSION: Sleeping Reggae | 10 |

(see also Carolls)

CAROUSELS

| 67 | Pye 7N 17353 | Holiday Romance/The Run Run | 15 |

BOB CARPENTER

| 76 | Celtic Music CM 027 | SILENT PASSAGE (LP) | 20 |

CARPENTER JOE

| 87 | Solo SOLO 2 | MAVERICK GENIUS (EP) | 20 |

(See also Doubt)

THELMA CARPENTER

| 61 | Coral Q 72422 | Yes, I'm Lonesome Tonight/Gimme A Little Kiss Will Ya, Huh? | 10 |
| 61 | Coral Q 72442 | Back Street/I Ought To Know | 10 |

CARPENTER'S APPRENTICE

| 72 | SRS 12107 | CHANGES (LP, with insert) | 100 |

CARPET BAGGERS

| 67 | Spin SP 2006 | Flea Teacher/On Sunday | 30 |

CARPETTES

77	Small Wonder SMALL 3	RADIO WUNDERBAR (EP)	15
78	Small Wonder SMALL 9	Small Wonder?/2 Ne 1 (p/s, 2,000 only)	30
79	Beggars Banquet BEG 27	I Don't Mean It/Easy Way Out (p/s)	10
80	Beggars Banquet BEG 32	Johnny Won't Hurt You/Frustration Paradise//Keys To Your Heart/Total Insecurity (double pack)	10
80	Beggars Banquet BEG 47	Nothing Ever Changes/You Never Realise/ Frustration Paradise (live) (p/s)	10
80	Beggars Banquet BEG 49	The Last Lone Ranger/Love So Strong/Fan Club (p/s)	10
79	Beggars Banquet BEGA 14	FRUSTRATION PARADISE (LP)	18
80	Beggars Banquet BEGA 21	FIGHT AMONGST YOURSELVES (LP)	20

CATHY CARR

56	London HLH 8274	Ivory Tower/Please, Please Believe Me	25
56	Vogue Coral Q 72175	Heartbroken/I'll Cry At Your Wedding	6
59	Columbia DB 4270	First Anniversary/With Love	6

59	Columbia DB 4317	I'm Gonna Change Him/The Little Things You Do	6
60	Columbia DB 4408	Little Sister/Dark River	6
63	Stateside SS 147	Sailor Boy/The Next Time The Band Plays A Waltz	12

JAMES CARR

66	Stateside SS 507	You've Got My Mind Messed Up/That's What I Want To Know	80
66	Stateside SS 507	You've Got My Mind Messed Up/That's What I Want To Know (DJ Copy)	140
66	Stateside SS 535	Love Attack/Coming Back To Me Baby	40
66	Stateside SS 535	Love Attack/Coming Back To Me Baby (DJ copy)	70
66	Stateside SS 545	You're Pouring Water On A Drowning Man/Forgetting You	20
67	Stateside SS 2001	The Dark End Of the Street/Loveable Girl	20
67	Stateside SS 2038	Let It Happen/A Losing Game	15
67	Stateside SS 2052	I'm A Fool For You/Gonna Send You Back To Georgia	25
68	Bell BLL 1004	A Man Needs A Woman/Stronger Than Love	12
69	B&C CB 101	Freedom Train/That's The Way Love Turned Out For Me	12
69	B&C CB 101	Freedom Train/That's The Way Love Turned Out For Me (DJ Copy)	50
72	Mojo 2092 053	Freedom Train/That's What I Want To Know	8
67	Stateside SL 10205	YOU GOT MY MIND MESSED UP (LP)	80
69	Bell MBLL/SBLL 113	A MAN NEEDS A WOMAN (LP)	20

JOE 'FINGERS' CARR

54	Capitol CL 14169	Piccadilly Rag/Fiddle-A-Delphia	6
55	Capitol CL 14359	The Barky-roll Stomp/Deep In The Heart Of Texas (with Carr-Hops)	6
55	Capitol CL 14372	Give Me A Band And My Baby/Zig-A-Zig (with Joy-Riders)	6
56	Capitol CL 14587	The Portuguese Washerwoman/Stumbling	6

(see also Lou Busch, Vicki Young)

JOHNNY CARR (& CADILLACS)

64	Decca F 11854	Remember That Night/Respectable	20
65	Fontana TF 600	Do You Love That Girl?/Give Him A Little Time	15
66	Fontana TF 681	Then So Do I/I'm Just A Little Bit Shy (solo)	10
67	Fontana TF 823	Things Get Better/You Got Me Baby (solo)	35

LEROY CARR

58	Fontana TFE 17051	TREASURES OF NORTH AMERICAN NEGRO MUSIC VOLUME 1 (EP)	12
64	RCA RCX 7168	R.C.A. VICTOR RACE SERIES VOL. 2 (EP)	12
63	CBS BPG 62206	BLUES BEFORE SUNRISE (LP)	50

LINDA CARR

67	Stateside SS 2058	Everytime/Trying To Be Good For You	40

LODY CARR

60	Top Rank 35-111	LADYBIRD (LP)	25

MIKE CARR

62	Decca F11448	That Certain Something/The Girl In THe Mountains	10
68	Columbia SCX 6248	UNDER PRESSURE (LP)	20
73	Ad-Rhythm ARPS 1020	MIKE CARR (LP)	18

PETER CARR

69	DJM DJS213	Angel And The Woman/Imagine Yourself	20

ROMEY CARR

70	Columbia DB 8710	These Things Will Keep Me Loving You/Stand Up And Fight	30
70	Columbia DB 8710	These Things Will Keep Me Loving You/Stand Up And Fight (DJ Copy)	50

VALERIE CARR

58	Columbia DB 4083	You're The Greatest/Over The Rainbow	5
58	Columbia DB 4131	When The Boys Talk About The Girls/Padre	6
58	Columbia DB 4225	Bad Girl/Look Forward	5
59	Columbia DB 4365	The Way To My Heart/I'm Only Asking	5
61	Columbia 33SCX 3307	EV'RY HOUR, EV'RY DAY OF MY LIFE (LP, stereo)	12

VIKKI CARR

67	Liberty LBF 15022	There I Go/One More Mountain	6
68	Liberty LBF 15166	With Pen In Hand/Can't Take My Eyes Off You	6
64	Liberty LBY 1208	DISCOVERY (LP)	15
65	Liberty LBY 1284	ANATOMY OF LOVE (lP)	10

WYNONA CARR

61	Reprise R 20033	I Gotta Stand Tall/My Faith	15

CARRAIG AONAIR

77	Gwerin	CARRAIG AONAIR (LP, insert)	40

JOE 'KING' CARRASCO & THE CROWNS

80	Stiff CROWN 1	Bueno/Tuff Enuff (vinyl 78, p/s)	10

CARRIAGE COMPANY

70	CBS 5209	In Your Room/Feel Right	30
71	CBS 7059	Paint The City Red/Jubilee	12

CARRICK FOLK FOUR

65	Thistle TM 90	Radio Scotland/Blue Nose	5

ANDREA CARROLL

63	London HLX 9772	It Hurts To Be Sixteen/Why Am I So Shy (some copies have Why Am I So Sorry as the B-side)	20

BARBARA CARROLL

59	London HLR 8981	North By Northwest/Far Away	8

BERNADETTE CARROLL

64	Stateside SS 311	Party Girl/I Don't Wanna Know	20

BOB CARROLL

55	MGM SP 1132	I Love You So Much It Hurts/My Dearest, My Darling, My Love	10
56	London HLU 8299	Red Confetti, Pink Balloons And Tambourines/Handwriting On The Wall	25
58	London HLT 8724	Hi Yo Silver/Tonto The Brave	15
58	London HLT 8724	Hi Yo Silver/Tonto The Brave (78)	10
59	London HLT 8888	I Can't Get You Out Of Your Heart/Since I'm Out Of Your Arms	10

CATHY CARROLL
62	Warner Bros WB 72	Poor Little Puppet/Love And Learn	10

DIAHANN CARROLL
59	London HLT 8788	The Big Country/Guiding Light	10
69	CBS 1725	Have I Changed/My Room	6

DON CARROLL
57	Capitol CL 14812	At Your Front Door/The Gods Were Angry With Me	10
58	Capitol CL 14823	In My Arms/The Things I Might Have Been	5

GINA CARROLL
65	Decca F 12297	Bye Bye Big Boy/Down The Street	20

JOHNNY CARROLL & HOT ROCKS
56	Brunswick 05580	Corrine Corrina/Wild Wild Women	800
56	Brunswick 05580	Corrine Corrina/Wild Wild Women (78)	100
56	Brunswick 05603	Crazy, Crazy Lovin'/Hot Rock	800
56	Brunswick 05603	Crazy, Crazy Lovin'/Hot Rock (78)	100
74	UK USA 1	Black Leather Rebel/Be-Bop-A-Lula (as Johnny Carroll & Blue Caps)	10

PAT CARROLL
72	Pye International 7N 25592	To The Sun/Out Of My Mind	7

RONNIE CARROLL
60	Philips PB 1004	Footsteps/Where My True Love Walks	5
62	Philips 326 550 BF	If Only Tomorrow/Think Of Her (p/s)	5
62	Philips 326 550 BF	If Only Tomorrow/Think Of Her	5
56	Philips BBE 12074	RONNIE CARROLL (EP)	8
63	Philips BL 7591	MR. & MRS. IS THE NAME (LP, with Millicent Martin)	12

(see also Millicent Martin)

TONI CARROLL
58	MGM MGM 987	Dreamsville/I've Never Felt This Way Before	10
58	MGM EP 689	THIS ONE IS TONI (EP)	20

CARROLLS
66	Polydor BM 56081	Surrender Your Love/The Folk I Love	25
66	Polydor BM 56081	Surrender Your Love/The Folk I Love (DJ Copy)	50
68	CBS 3710	Ever Since/Come On	5
68	CBS 3875	A Lemon Balloon And A Blue Sky/Make Me Belong To You	20
69	CBS 4401	We're In This Thing Together/We Know Better	15
67	CBS 3414	So Gently Falls The Rain/Nice To See You Darling	10

(see also Carols, Carolls, Faith Brown, Brotherly Love)

BEN CARRUTHERS & DEEP
65	Parlophone R 5295	Jack O' Diamonds/Right Behind You	60

CARS
78	Elektra K12301	My Best Friends Girl/Moving In Stereo (picture disc)	5

CHAD CARSON
63	HMV POP 1156	They Were Wrong/Stop Picking On Me	50

DEL CARSON
59	Decca F 11135	Jean/I Told Myself A Lie	5

JOE CARSON
63	Liberty LIB 55578	I Gotta Get Drunk (And I Shore Do Dread It)/Who Will Buy My Memories	25

JOHNNY CARSON
60	Fontana H 243	Fraulein/I Wish It Were You	6
60	Fontana H 259	The Train Of Love/First Proposal	6
60	Fontana H 277	You Talk Too Much/Now And Always	5
62	Ember EMB S 150	Teenage Batchelor/Are You Anyone's Girl?	5
63	Ember EMB S 161	The Tears Came Rolling Down/One Track Mind	8

KAY CARSON
56	Capitol CL 14565	Those Who Have Loved/The Fellow Over There	5
56	Capitol CL 14634	There's A Shadow Between Us/This Man	5

(see also Kit Carson)

KEN CARSON
55	London HLF 8213	Hawkeye/I've Been Working On The Railroad	40
55	London HLF 8213	Hawkeye/I've Been Working On The Railroad (78)	10
56	London HLF 8237	Let Her Go, Let Her Go/The Song Of Daniel Boone (The Daddy Of Them All)	12

KIT CARSON
56	Capitol CL 14524	Band Of Gold/Cast Your Bread Upon The Waters	10

(see also Kay Carson)

MINDY CARSON & GUY MITCHELL
53	Columbia SCM 5022	That's A Why/Train Of Love	20

(see also Guy Mitchell)

VINCE CARSON
55	HMV 7M 313	Sweetie, Sweet, Sweet Sue/My Possession	5

CARTE BLANCHE
79	Pye 7NL46193	Get Up On Your Feet/Do It Like You Like It (p/s)	15

ANITA CARTER
58	London HLA 8693	Blue Doll/Go Away Johnnie	10
60	London HLW 9102	Moon Girl/Mama Don't Cry At My Wedding	10

BENNY CARTER
54	HMV 7M 189	Blue Mountain/Sunday Afternoon	5
62	HMV CLP 1624/CSD1480	FURTHER DEFINITIONS (LP, mono/stereo)	20
66	HMV CLP/CSD 3576	FURTHER DEFINITIONS (LP, mono/stereo)	20

(see also Helen Humes)

BETTY CARTER
63   London HLK 9748   The Good Life/Nothing More To Look Forward To 7
(see also Ray Charles)

CAROLINE CARTER
65   Decca F 12239   The Ballad Of The Possibilities/We Want Love 15

CAROLYN CARTER
65   London HL 9959   It Hurts/I'm Thru...........40

CLARENCE CARTER
68	Atlantic 584 154	Thread The Needle/Don't Make My Baby Cry 18
68	Atlantic 584 176	Looking For A Fox/I Can't See Myself (Crying About You) 20
68	Atlantic 584 187	Funky Fever/Slip Away...........15
68	Atlantic 584 223	Too Weak To Fight/Let Me Comfort You 15
69	Atlantic 584 248	Snatchin' It Back/Making Love (At The Dark End Of The Street)...........15
69	Atlantic 584 272	The Feeling Is Right/You Can't Miss When You Can't Measure 10
70	Atlantic 584 309	Take It Off Him And Put It On Me/The Few Troubles I've Had 10
70	Atlantic 2091 030	Patches/I Can't Leave Your Love Alone 6
71	Atlantic 2091 045	It's All In Your Mind/Willie And Laura Mae Jones 6
71	Atlantic 2091 093	The Court Room/Getting The Bills (But No Merchandise) 6
71	Atlantic 2091 139	Slipped, Tripped And Fell In Love/I Hate To Love And Run 8
83	Certain ACENT 1	Messin' With My Mind/Messin' (Instrumental Version) 15
68	Atlantic 588 152	THIS IS CLARENCE CARTER (LP)...........20
69	Atlantic 588 172	THE DYNAMIC CLARENCE CARTER (LP) 20
69	Atlantic 588 191	TESTIFYIN' (LP) 20
70	Atlantic 2400 027	PATCHES (LP)...........20

HAL CARTER FIVE
62   Oriole CB 1709   Come On And Twist Me/Twistin' Time Is Here 10

HERBIE CARTER
68   Duke DU 4   Happy Time (actually by Keble Drummond)/BOYS: Smashville 50

JACK CARTER
70   Penny Farthing PEN 739   Morning/Fanny...........8

JEAN CARTER & CENTREPIECES
68   Stateside SS 2114   No Good Jim/And None 15
68   Stateside SS 2114   No Good Jim/And None (DJ Copy)...........25

JOHN CARTER & RUSS ALQUIST
68   Spark SRL 1017   The Laughing Man/Midsummer Dreaming 40
(see also Carter-Lewis & Southerners, Ivy League, Flowerpot Men)

JOHN CARTER
72   SPark SRL 1069   One More Mile To Freedom/The Saddest Word I Know 10

LYNDA CARTER
73   EMI 2005   It Might As Well Stay Monday/I Believe In Music 6
80   Motown TMG 1207   The Last Song/What's A Little Love Between Friends (p/s) 7
78   CBS EPC 83052   LYNDA CARTER (LP, as aka WONDER WOMAN)...........18

MARTIN CARTER
72   Tradition TSR 012   UPS & DOWNS (LP) 35
71   Tradition TSR 008   SOMEONE NEW (LP) 40

MEL CARTER
63	Pye International 7N 25212	When A Boy Falls In Love/So Wonderful 50
66	Liberty LIB 66113	Hold Me, Thrill Me, Kiss Me/Sweet Little Girl 20
65	Liberty LIB 66138	(All Of A Sudden) My Heart Sings/When I Hold The Hand Of The One I Love 10
66	Liberty LIB 66148	Love Is All We Need/I Wish I Didn't Love You So 10
66	Liberty LIB 66165	Band Of Gold/Detour...........10
66	Liberty LIB 66183	You You You/If You Lose Her...........10

MIKE CARTER (& DRAGONFLY)
84   Button BTN 117   My True Love/Talk To Me 6
See also Dragonfly

MOTHER MAYBELLE CARTER
64   London HA-R 8214   QUEEN OF THE AUTOHARP (LP)...........15

NEL CARTER
74   RCA 2503   Send Him Back To Me/Dreams 20

NICK CARTER
79   NC 001   ABSTRACTS & EXTRACTS (LP) 100

RON CARTER
76   CTI 6064   YELLOW AND GREEN (LP, gatefold) 12

SHEILA CARTER & EPISODE SIX
66   Pye 7N 17194   I Will Warm Your Heart/Incense...........30
(see also Episode, Episode Six)

SONNY CARTER WITH EARL BOSTIC & HIS ORCHESTRA
55   Parlophone MSP 6167   There Is No Greater Love/Oh Baby...........20
55   Parlophone MSP 6167   There Is No Greater Love/Oh Baby (78)...........10
(see also Earl Bostic)

CARTER STEPHENS CHORALE
68   Fontana TF 936   Peace! (Dream Of The Common Man)/The Promised Land...........15

SYDNEY CARTER
65   Eye Mark EMS 1002   When I Need A Neighbour/Judas And Mary (with Nadia Cattouse and Barry Beattie) 10
66   Elektra EPK 801   LORD OF THE DANCE (EP)...........15
(see also Nadia Cattouse)

ERROL CARTER
73   Cactus CT 71   Hold Up Your Head/SUCCESS ALL STARS: Tank Skank 30
76   Cactus CT 96   Ram Goat Malish Water/Ranking Dub...........60

CARTER-LEWIS & SOUTHERNERS

61	Piccadilly 7N 35004	So Much In Love/Back On The Scene	30
61	Ember EMB S 145	Two Timing Baby/Will It Happen To Me?	50
62	Piccadilly 7N 35085	Here's Hopin'/Poor Joe	30
62	Ember EMB S 165	Tell Me/My Broken Heart	50
63	Oriole CB 1835	Sweet And Tender Romance/Who Told You?	20
63	Oriole CB 1868	Your Momma's Out Of Town/Somebody Told My Girl	20
64	Oriole CB 1919	Skinny Minnie/Easy To Cry	40

(see also Ivy League, Flowerpot Men, White Plains, John Carter & Russ Alquist, Jimmy Page, Dawn Chorus)

MARTIN CARTHY

76	Topic STOP 7002	The Bonny Lass Of Anglesey/Palaces Of Gold	6
65	Fontana (S)TL 5269	MARTIN CARTHY (LP, black/silver label)	40
71	Philips 6308 049	LANDFALL (LP, black/silver label)	30
72	Peg PEG 12	SHEARWATER (LP, with insert, purple label)	25
72	Philips 6282 022	THIS IS MARTIN CARTHY (LP)	15
74	Deram SML 1111	SWEET WIVELSFIELD (LP, red/white label)	15

MARTIN CARTHY & DAVE SWARBRICK

67	Fontana TE 17490	NO SONGS (EP)	30
66	Fontana STL 5362	SECOND ALBUM (LP, black/silver label)	30
67	Fontana STL 5434	BYKER HILL (LP)	30
68	Fontana STL 5477	BUT TWO CAME BY (LP)	30
70	Fontana STL 5529	PRINCE HEATHEN (LP, black/silver label)	35
71	Pegasus PEG 6	SELECTIONS (LP, gatefold sleeve)	30

(see also Dave Swarbrick, Three City Four, Steeleye Span, Leon Rosselson, Alex Campbell, Nigel Denver)

CARTOONE

69	Atlantic 584 240	Knick Knack Man/A Penny For The Sun	12
69	Atlantic 588 174	CARTOONE (LP)	18

(see also Jimmy Page)

CARTOONS

84	Cage CAGE 2	Once The Victor/Instrumental Version (p/s)	10

FLIP CARTRIDGE

66	London HLU 10076	Dear Mrs Applebee/Don't Take The Lovers From The World	6

DAVE CARTWRIGHT

73	DJM DJS 10750	Band Of Hope/Queen Of The May (promo)	10
70	Harmony DB 0001	MIDDLE OF THE ROAD (LP, private pressing, 99 only, with insert)	200
72	Transatlantic TRA 255	A LITTLE BIT OF GLORY (LP, with inner sleeve)	20
73	Transatlantic TRA 267	BACK TO THE GARDEN (LP, with lyric inner sleeve)	20
75	Transatlantic TRA 284	DON'T LET YOUR FAMILY DOWN (LP, with lyric insert)	20

(see also Bev Pegg, Away From The Sand)

DICK CARUSO

60	MGM MGM 1077	Two Long Years/Yes Sir, That's My Baby	5
60	MGM MGM 1099	Pretty Little Dancin' Doll/We've Never Met	5

ALAN CARVELL

76	United Artists UP 36124	Georgia On My Mind/Never Give Your Love (To A New York Woman)	5

(see also Carvells, Five Sapphires, Telegrams)

CARVELLS

78	Rocket ROKN 540	Skateboard Queen/Skateboard Surfing	5
78	Rocket ROKN 544	Skateboard Riders/Skateboard King	5
78	Rocket ROLL 15	SKATEBOARD RAMPAGE (LP)	12

(see also Alan Carvell, Five Sapphires,Telegrams)

TRISTRAM CARY

70	Galliard GAL 4006	3 4 5 (LP, with booklet)	100
70	Galliard GAL 4007	NARCISSIS (Gatefold, with insert)	100
71	EMS (No Cat No)	TRIOS (2-LP, with booklet/instructions)	400
10	Trunk JBH035LP	IT'S TIME FOR TRISTRAM CARY (LP)	25

CASABLANCA

74	Rocket PIGL 7	CASABLANCA (LP, die-cut sleeve with inner lyric sleeve)	20

(see also Trees, Ginger Bakers Airforce)

CASANOVAS

00s	Singles Society 7STAS 3320	Nasty/Too Cool (numbered die-cut p/s, 500 only)	10

CASCADES

63	Warner Bros WB 88	Rhythm Of The Rain/Let Me Be	7
63	Warner Bros WB 98	Shy Girl/The Last Leaf	7
63	Warner Bros WB 103	I Wanna Be Your Lover/My First Day Alone	7
63	RCA Victor RCA 1358	Cinderella/A Little Like Loving	7
64	RCA Victor RCA 1378	Jeannie/For Your Sweet Love	5
65	Liberty LIB 55822	I Bet You Won't Stay/She'll Love Again	5
66	Stateside SS 515	Cheryl's Goin' Home/Truly Julie's Blues	12
69	Uni UN 508	Maybe The Rain Will Fall/Naggin' Cries	6
63	Warner Bros WEP 6106	RHYTHM OF THE RAIN (EP, mono)	30
63	Warner Bros WSE 6106	RHYTHM OF THE RAIN (EP, stereo)	35
63	Warner Bros WM 8127	RHYTHM OF THE RAIN (LP, mono)	30
63	Warner Bros WM 8127	RHYTHM OF THE RAIN (LP, stereo)	40

AL CASEY & K.C. ETTES

63	Pye International 7N 25215	Surfin' Hootenanny/Easy Picking	12

(see also Sanford Clark, Duane Eddy)

HOWIE CASEY & SENIORS

62	Fontana H 364	Double Twist/True Fine Mama	25
62	Fontana H 381	I Ain't Mad At You/Twist At The Top	20
63	Fontana TF 403	The Boll Weevil Song/Bony Moronie	20
62	Fontana TFL 5180	TWIST AT THE TOP (LP, mono)	80
62	Fontana STFL 592	TWIST AT THE TOP (LP, stereo)	100

Alvin CASH (& REGISTERS)

65	Wing WL 1022	LET'S TWIST (LP, reissue of "Twist At The Top")	25

(see also Freddie Starr)

ALVIN CASH (& REGISTERS)

65	Stateside SS 386	Twine Time/The Bump (as Alvin Cash & Crawlers)	30
65	Stateside SS 386	Twine Time/The Bump (as Alvin Cash & Crawlers) (DJ Copy)	60
66	Stateside SS 543	Philly Freeze/No Deposits, No Returns (as Alvin Cash & Registers)	25
66	Stateside SS 543	Philly Freeze/No Deposits, No Returns (as Alvin Cash & Registers) (DJ Copy)	40
68	President PT 115	Philly Freeze/No Deposits, No Returns (as Alvin Cash & Registers) (reissue)	5
68	President PT 119	Alvin's Boo-Ga-Loo/Let's Do Some Good Timing (as Alvin Cash & Registers)	10
68	President PT 129	Doin' The Ali Shuffle/Feel So Good	10
68	President PT 147	Charge/Diff'rent Strokes For Diff'rent Folks	10
71	President PT 351	Twine Time/Twine Awhile	8
72	President PT 383	Barracuda/Do It One More Time (as Alvin Cash & Crawlers)	8
67	President PTL 1000	THE PHILLY FREEZE (LP)	35

JOHNNY CASH (SOLO & WITH TENNESSEE TWO)

78s

57	London HL 8358	I Walk The Line/Get Rhythm	30
57	London HLS 8427	Train Of Love/There You Go	25
57	London HLS 8461	Next In Line/Don't Make Me Go	25
57	London HLS 8514	Home Of The Blues/Give My Love To Rose	25
58	London HLS 8586	Ballad Of A Teenage Queen/Big River (with Tennessee Two)	25
58	London HLS 8656	Guess Things Happen That Way/Come In, Stranger	20
58	London HLS 8709	The Ways Of A Woman In Love/You're The Nearest Thing To Heaven	30
59	Philips PB 874	All Over Again/What Do I Care	30
59	Philips PB 897	Don't Take Your Guns To Town/I Still Miss Someone	30
59	London HLS 8789	It's Just About Time/I Just Thought You'd Like To Know	30
59	London HLS 8847	Luther Played The Boogie/Thanks A Lot	40
59	Philips PB 928	Frankie's Man, Johnny/You Dreamer You	30
59	London HLS 8928	Katy Too/I Forgot To Remember To Forget	40
59	Philips PB 953	I Got Stripes/Five Feet High And Rising	25
59	London HLS 8979	You Tell Me/Goodbye, Little Darlin', Goodbye	40
59	Philips PB 979	The Little Drummer Boy/I'll Remember You	25

SINGLES

57	London HL 8358	I Walk The Line/Get Rhythm (gold label lettering)	150
57	London HL 8358	I Walk The Line/Get Rhythm (silver label lettering)	40
57	London HLS 8427	Train Of Love/There You Go	50
57	London HLS 8461	Next In Line/Don't Make Me Go	50
57	London HLS 8514	Home Of The Blues/Give My Love To Rose	40
58	London HLS 8586	Ballad Of A Teenage Queen/Big River (with Tennessee Two)	30
58	London HLS 8656	Guess Things Happen That Way/Come In, Stranger (with Tennessee Two)	20
58	London HLS 8709	The Ways Of A Woman In Love/You're The Nearest Thing To Heaven (with Tennessee Two)	20
59	Philips PB 874	All Over Again/What Do I Care	10
59	Philips PB 897	Don't Take Your Guns To Town/I Still Miss Someone	10
59	London HLS 8789	It's Just About Time/I Just Thought You'd Like To Know (with Tennessee Two)	20
59	London HLS 8847	Luther Played The Boogie/Thanks A Lot	30
59	Philips PB 928	Frankie's Man, Johnny/You Dreamer You	10
59	London HLS 8928	Katy Too/I Forgot To Remember To Forget	20
59	Philips PB 953	I Got Stripes/Five Feet High And Rising	10
59	London HLS 8979	You Tell Me/Goodbye, Little Darlin', Goodbye	10
59	Philips PB 979	The Little Drummer Boy/I'll Remember You	6
60	London HLS 9070	Straight A's In Love/I Love You Because	15
60	Philips PB 1017	Seasons Of My Heart/Smiling Bill McCall	15
60	London HLS 9182	Down The Street To 301/Story Of A Broken Heart	15
60	Philips PB 1075	Going To Memphis/Loading Coal	15
61	London HLS 9314	Oh Lonesome Me/Life Goes On	10
61	Philips PB 1148	Forty Shades Of Green/he Rebel - Johnny Yuma	5
61	Philips PB 1200	Tennessee Flat-Top Box/Tall Man	5
63	CBS AAG 159	Ring Of Fire/I'd Still Be There	5
63	CBS AAG 173	The Matador/Still In Town	5
63	CBS AAG 200	Understand Your Man/Dark As A Dungeon	5
65	CBS 201741	Orange Blossom Special/All God's Children Ain't Free	5
65	CBS 201760	It Ain't Me Babe/Time And Time Again	5
65	CBS 201809	Ring Of Fire/Streets Of Laredo	5
66	CBS 202046	The One On The Right Is On The Left/Cotton Pickin' Hands	5
66	CBS 202256	Everybody Loves A Nut/Austin Prison	5
67	CBS 202546	You Beat All I Ever Saw/Put The Sugar To Bed	5
67	CBS 3268	Rosanna's Going Wild/Long-Legged Guitar-Pickin' Man (with June Carter)	5
68	CBS 3438	Certain Kind Of Hurtin'/Another Song To Sing	5
68	CBS 3549	Folsom Prison Blues (live)/The Folk Singer	5
69	CBS 4638	Blistered/See Ruby Fall	5
76	CBS S 4287	One Piece At A Time/Go On Blues	5

EXPORT SINGLES

57	London HL 7020	Next In Line/Don't Make Me Go	35
57	London HL 7023	Home Of The Blues/Give My Love To Rose	35
58	London HL 7032	Ballad Of A Teenage Queen/Big River	25
58	London HL 7053	The Ways Of A Woman In Love/You're The Nearest Thing To Heaven	25
57	London HL 7131	Folsom Prison Blues/I Walk The Line	40

EPs

58	London RES 1120	JOHNNY CASH (triangular centre)	40
58	London RES 1120	JOHNNY CASH (round centre)	20
59	London RES 1193	JOHNNY CASH SINGS HANK WILLIAMS (triangular or centre)	40
59	London RES 1193	JOHNNY CASH SINGS HANK WILLIAMS (round centre)	20
59	London RES 1212	COUNTRY BOY (triangular centre)	40
59	London RES 1212	COUNTRY BOY (round centre)	20
59	London RES 1230	JOHNNY CASH NO. 2 (triangular centre)	40
59	London RES 1230	JOHNNY CASH NO. 2 (round centre)	20

60	Philips BBE 12377	THE TROUBADOR	20
60	Philips BBE 12318	GRANDFATHER'S CLOCK	15
60	Philips BBE 12395	SONGS OF OUR SOIL	15
61	Philips BBE 12494	STRICTLY CASH	15
64	CBS AGG 20050	FORTY SHADES OF GREEN	10
64	CBS EP 5576	FABULOUS JOHNNY CASH	10
64	CBS EP 5735	ORANGE BLOSSOM SPECIAL	10
64	CBS EP 5744	EVERYBODY LOVES A NUT	10
64	CBS EP 5964	RING OF FIRE	10
65	CBS EP 6061	IT AIN'T ME BABE	10
66	CBS EP 6073	MEAN AS HELL! - BALLADS FROM THE TRUE WEST (with Statler Brothers & Carter Family)	10
65	CBS EP 6109	SONGS OF KATIE ELDER	10
65	CBS EP 6147	HAPPINESS IS YOU	10
69	CBS EP 6601	FOLSOM PRISON BLUES	10
72	CBS EP 9155	LITTLE FAUSS AND BIG HALSY	10

ALBUMS

59	London HA-S 2157	SINGS THE SONGS THAT MADE HIM FAMOUS	40
59	London HA-S 2179	WITH HIS HOT AND BLUE GUITAR	40
59	Philips BBL 7298	THE FABULOUS JOHNNY CASH (mono)	20
59	Philips SBBL 554	THE FABULOUS JOHNNY CASH (stereo)	20
59	Philips BBL 7353	SONGS OF OUR SOIL	15
59	Philips BBL 7373	HYMNS BY JOHNNY CASH	15
60	Philips BBL 7358	NOW THERE WAS A SONG! (mono)	15
60	Philips SBBL 580	NOW THERE WAS A SONG! (stereo)	15
60	Philips BBL 7417	RIDE THIS TRAIN	15
61	CBS (S)BPG 62042	THE FABULOUS JOHNNY CASH (mono/stereo)	15
62	CBS (S)BPG 62015	HYMNS FROM THE HEART (mono/stereo)	15
62	CBS (S)BPG 62073	THE SOUND OF JOHNNY CASH (mono/stereo)	15
63	CBS BPG 62119	BLOOD SWEAT AND TEARS	15
63	CBS (S)BPG 62171	RING OF FIRE (mono/stereo)	15
63	CBS (S)BPG 62284	THE CHRISTMAS SPIRIT (mono/stereo)	15
64	CBS (S)BPG 62371	I WALK THE LINE (mono/stereo)	15
64	CBS (S)BPG 62463	BITTER TEARS (mono/stereo)	15
65	CBS (S)BPG 62501	ORANGE BLOSSOM SPECIAL (mono/stereo)	15
65	London HA-S 8220	THE ORIGINAL SUN SOUND OF JOHNNY CASH	15
66	London HA-S 8253	LONESOME ME	15
68	CBS LP 63308	LIVE AT FOLSOM PRISON (LP)	12
84	Charley SUN BOX-105	THE SUN YEARS (5-LP box set)	30
91	Mercury 848 051-1	THE MYSTERY OF LIFE (LP, features Bob Dylan on 1 track)	15
94	American 0731458679028	AMERICAN RECORDINGS (LP, inner)	30
96	American 51011 2793-1	UNCHAINED (LP, inner)	30
00	American 51011 279-14	AMERICAN III: SOLITARY MAN (LP)	25
06	American 0602517005099	AMERICAN V: A HUNDRED HIGHWAYS (LP)	25

CASH CREW
| 87 | Vinyl Lab VL 004 | Mission Impossible/Microphone Maniac (12" as Cash Crew (The Force) | 30 |

CASHMAN, PISTILLI & WEST
| 70 | Capitol CL 15633 | Goodbye Jo/She Never Looked Better | 6 |

CASH PUSSIES
| 79 | The Label TLR 010 | 99% Is Shit/Cash Flow (p/s) | 6 |
(see also Sex Pistols)

CASINO
| 81 | Ellie Jay EJSP 9609 | More Than Ever/Tonight (p/s) | 10 |

CASINO ROYALES
| 67 | London HLU 10122 | When I Tell You That I Love You/Love In The Open Air | 6 |

CASINOS
67	Ember EMB S 241	That's The Way/Too Good To Be True	40
67	President PT 123	Then You Can Tell Me Goodbye/I Still Love You	10
68	President PT 140	To Be Loved/Tailor Made	8
68	President PT 156	When I Stop Dreaming/Please Love Me	8
68	President PTL 1007	THEN YOU CAN TELL ME GOODBYE (LP)	25

TONY CASO
| 68 | London HL 10178 | Shadow On The Ground/I Don't Care Who Knows It | 7 |

CASPAR
| 79 | Rock Steady MICK 007 | Messin' Around/Make You Feel Like You're Mine (p/s) | 20 |
(see also 10cc)

PAUL CASS
| 75 | Rainbow Records RBW 2000 | Mini Marianne/Riverboat Rock | 30 |

CASSANDRA
79	D Roy DRDD 19	Sitting In The Park/D ROY BAND: Hyde Park Dub	30
80	D Roy DRDD 29	my Angel Baby/Thank You For The Many Things You've Done (12")	30
80	D Roy DRDD 31	I Must Be Dreaming/Trading Dub (12")	30

TOMMY CASSELL
| 70 | Injun 114 | Rockin' Rock A Rollin' Stone/Go Ahead On | 15 |

CASSETTE
| 79 | 1 track CAS 001 | THE FAST FORWARD EP: What's The Point/Product/All The Rage | 35 |

CASSETTES (1)
| 81 | Zip ZIP 101 | Reverberate/Don't Label Me (die-cut sleeve) | 50 |

CASSETTES (2)
| 82 | X-Ray X 001 | Call On Me/Fast Forward | 20 |

CASSIBER
| 84 | Recommended RE 0110 | BEAUTY AND THE BEAST (LP) | 15 |

MINT VALUE £

86	Recommended RE 0000	PERFECT WORLDS (LP)	12

DAVID CASSIDY

71	Bell BELL 1189	Cherish/All I Wanna Do Is Touch You	5

(see also Partridge Family)

STEVE CASSIDY

63	Ember EMB S 177	Ecstasy/I'm A Worrying	5

TED CASSIDY

65	Capitol CL 15423	The Lurch/Wesley	20

DITCH CASSIDY

71	Decca F13240	Pisces Apple Lady/Hamburger Midnight	20

CASTANARC

74	Peninsula PENCIL 10	JOURNEY TO THE EAST (LP, private pressing)	18

CASTAWAYS

65	London HL 10003	Liar Liar/Sam	40
65	London HL 10003	Liar Liar/Sam (DJ Copy)	70

CASTE

68	President PT 211	Don't Cast Aside/One Step Closer	6

JOEY CASTELL

57	Decca F 10966	I'm Left, You're Right, She's Gone/Tryin' To Get To You	250
57	Decca F 10966	I'm Left, You're Right, She's Gone/Tryin' To Get To You (78)	50

LACKSLEY CASTELL

79	Soundoff SOFD 003	My Collie tree/RISING SON : Stop Cheating	30
79	Sufferers Heights SUFF 01	What A great Day/PRINCE JAMMY: Slaughter House 5 (12")	50
79	Sound Off SOFD 003	My Collie Tree/RISING SUN: Stop Cheating (12")	50
80	Negus Roots NERT 001	African Queen/Queen In Dub (12")	25
80	Negus Roots NERT 003	I Love Jah/Version	40
81	Negus Roots NERT 005	Jah Is Watching You/PAPA TULLO: Sweet Reggae Music (12")	25
80	Black Joy DH 805	Jah Love Is Sweeter/ROCKERS BAND: Sweeter Rockers (12")	50
81	Negus Roots NERT 008	Government Man/P. TULLO: Straight To The Government (12" blue/black vinyl)	40
82	Negus Roots NERT 013	Speak Softly/Money A The Remedy (with PAPPA TULLO/ Take This Message To My Woman (12")	30
83	Negus Roots NERT 019	Johnny Brown/Mrs Brown (12")	20
83	Csa SPCSA 12006	Tug A War Game/EARL SIXTEEN: Rise In The Morning (12")	50
82	Negus Roots NERT LP 002	MORNING GLORY (LP)	60
83	Negus Roots NERT LP 008	AFRICAN LADY (LP)	40

CASTELLS

61	London HLN 9392	Sacred/I Get Dreamy	20
62	London HLN 9551	So This Is Love/On The Street Of Tears	25

CASTELLS

67	Masquerade MA 500	Two Lovers/Jerusalem	5

LEE CASTLE & BARONS

64	Parlophone R 5151	A Love She Can Count On/Foolin'	15

ROY CASTLE

65	CBS 201736	Doctor Terror's House Of Horrors/Voodoo Girl (with Tubby Hayes)	40
68	Olga OLE 12	Wonderful World/For All The World	5

CASTLE SISTERS (JAMAICA)

66	Ska Beat JB 257	Stop Your Lying/Don't Be A Fool	30

CASTLE SISTERS (USA)

59	Columbia DB 4335	Drifting And Dreaming/Lucky Girl	5

CAST OF THOUSANDS

66	Stateside SS 546	My Jenny Wears A Mini/Girl Do What You Gonna Do	45

CASTON & MAJORS

75	Tamla Motown TMG 938	Child Of Love/No One Will Know	15

(see also Radiants)

JIMMY CASTOR (BUNCH)

66	Philips BF 1543	Hey Leroy, Your Mama's Callin'/Ham Rock's Espanol	15
67	Philips BF 1590	Magic Saxophone/Just You Girl	20
71	Mercury 6052 110	Hey Leroy, Your Mama's Callin'/Ham Rock's Espanol (reissue)	8
73	RCA Victor APD1 0103	DIMENSION III (LP, quadrophonic)	18

FRANKIE CASTRO

56	Mercury MT 114	Goodbye, So Long, I'm Gone/Too Much (78)	10

CASUAL FOUR

70s	Specially Made For Us 102	I Can Tell/Love Potion No. 9	20

CASUALEERS

74	Pye Disco Demand DDS 103	Dance Dance Dance/Something About This Girl	6

CASUALS

65	Fontana TF 635	If You Walk Out/Please Don't Hide	10
68	Decca F 12737	Adios Amor (Goodbye My Love)/Don't Dream Of Yesterday	6
68	Decca F 22784	Jesamine/I've Got Something Too	7
68	Decca F 22852	Toy/Touched (p/s)	15
68	Decca F 22852	Toy/Touched	7
69	Decca F 22900	Fools Paradise/7 X 7	5
69	Decca F 22943	Sunflower Eyes/Never My Love	5
69	Decca F 22969	Caroline/Naughty Boy	8
70	Decca F 23027	My Name Is Love/I Can't Say	10
71	Decca F 23112	Someday Rock 'n' Roll Lady/A Letter Every Day	6
72	Parlophone R 5959	Tara Tiger Girl/Nature's Girl	15
74	Dawn DNS 1069	Witch/Good Times	20
69	Decca LK-R/SKL-R 5001	HOUR WORLD (LP, large unboxed logo on label)	35

(see also American Jam, Kansas Hook)

JOHNNY CASWELL
| 85 | Kent TOWN 106 | You Don't Love Me No More/STEINWAYS: You've Been Leading Me On | 20 |

CATAPILLA
| 71 | Vertigo 6360 029 | CATAPILLA (LP, gatefold sleeve, small swirl label) | 400 |
| 72 | Vertigo 6360 074L | CHANGES (LP, die-cut gatefold sleeve, small swirl label) | 1200 |

(see also Jon Stevens, Liar)

CATATONIA
94	Rough Trade 45rev33	Whale/You Can (p/s, 'Singles Club' release)	8
95	Nursery NYS 12L	Bleed/This Boy Can't Swim (red vinyl, numbered p/s, 1,000 only)	8
95	Blanco Y Negro SAM 1746	Blow The Millennium Blow/Beautiful Sailor (p/s, white vinyl Xmas 45, freebie)	5
98	Blanco Y Negro 20834-1	INTERNATIONAL VELVET (LP, 1,000 only, with free 12")	15

CATCH
| 77 | Logo GO 103 | Borderline/Black Blood (company sleeve) | 40 |

(see also Tourists, Eurythmics)

CATE BROTHERS
| 76 | Asylum 13062 | Where Can We Go/Instrumental | 20 |

CATFISH
| 70 | CBS 64006 | GET DOWN (LP, orange label) | 15 |
| 71 | Epic 64408 | LIVE CATFISH (LP) | 15 |

CATHEDRAL
92	Earache MOSH 40T	Soul Sacrifice/Autumn Twilight/Frozen Rapture/Golden Blood (Flooding)	12
95	Earache MOSH 152	HOPKINS (THE WITCHFINDER GENERAL) EP (12", p/s)	12
93	Earache MOSH 77C	THE ETHEREAL MIRROR (LP, blue vinyl)	30
94	Rise Above RISE 8	IN MEMORIAM (LP, purple vinyl)	25
95	Earache MOSH 130	THE CARNIVAL BIZARRE (2 x 10" LP, gatefold sleeve)	20

CATHERINE WHEEL
91	Wilde Club WILDE 4	SHE'S MY FRIEND (12", p/s, barcode on sleeve)	10
91	Wilde Club WILDE 5	PAINFUL THING EP (12", p/s)	10
91	Wilde Club WILDE 5CD	PAINFUL THING EP (CD single)	12
93	Fontana CW 512	Crank/Black Metallic/Painful Thing (12", picture disc)	8
92	Fontana 510903-1	FERMENT (LP, initially with free 12")	15
92	Fontana 510903-1	FERMENT (LP, without free 12")	12
93	Fontana 518 039-1	CHROME (LP with inner sleeve)	20

RAY CATHODE (BBC RADIOPHONICS)
| 62 | Parlophone R 4901 | Time Beat/Waltz In Orbit | 10 |

(see also BBC Radiophonic Workshop, George Martin)

CAT IRON
| 69 | Xtra XTRA 1087 | CAT IRON (LP) | 22 |

CAT MOTHER & ALL NIGHT NEWSBOYS
69	Polydor 56543	Good Old Rock'N'Roll/Bad News	8
70	Polydor 2066 026	I Must Be Dreaming/Last Go Round	6
69	Polydor 184 300	THE STREET GIVETH AND THE STREET TAKETH AWAY (LP)	20
70	Polydor 2425 021	ALBION DOO-WAH (LP, gatefold sleeve)	15
72	United Artists UAG 29313	CAT MOTHER & ALL NIGHT NEWS BOYS (LP, gatefold sleeve)	20
73	United Artists UAG 29381	LAST CHANCE DANCE (LP)	15

(see also Jimi Hendrix)

CATS 'N' JAMMER KIDS
| 77 | Ebony EYE 3 | Disco Drum/Disco Drum (Part 5) | 6 |
| 77 | EYEC 3 | DISCO DRUM | 0 |

CATS EYES
68	Deram DM 190	Smile Girl For Me/In A Fantasy World	10
68	Deram DM 209	I Thank You Marianne/Turn Around	10
69	Deram DM 251	Where Is She Now?/Tom Drum	25
70	MCA MK 5028	Loser/Circus	12
70	MCA MK 5043	Circus/Come Away Melinda	5
70	MCA MK 5056	The Wizard/Hey (Open Your Eyes)	20

CATS EYES (2)
| 11 | Polydor 2763913 | BROKEN GLASS EP (2 x 7") | 15 |

(see also Horrors)

CAT'S PYJAMAS
| 68 | Direction 58-3235 | Virginia Waters/Baby I Love You | 35 |
| 68 | Direction 58-3482 | Camera Man/House For Sale | 35 |

(see also Kenny Bernard)

CATS (1)
67	Parlophone R 5558	What A Crazy Life/Hopeless Try	7
68	Parlophone R 5663	What Is The World Coming To/How Could I Be So Blind?	10
69	Columbia DB 8524	I Gotta Know What's Going On/Lea	10
69	Columbia DB 8571	Why/Mandy, My Dear	5
70	Columbia DB 8655	Marian/Somewhere Up There	5
71	Columbia DB 8748	I Love You, I Do/Where Have I Been Wrong	5
71	Columbia DB 8816	One Way Mind/Country Woman	5
72	Columbia DB 8850	Dance, Dance, Dance/My Friend Joe	5
72	Columbia DB 8909	Let's Dance/I've Been In Love Before	5
71	Columbia SCX 6459	TAKE ME WITH YOU (LP)	12

CATS (2)
69	Baf BAF 1	Swan Lake/Swing Low	10
69	Baf BAF 2	My Girl/The Hog	8
69	Baf BAF 3	The Hig/Blues For Justice	8
69	Baf BAF 4	William Tell/Love Walk Right In	8
70	Crystal CR 7009	Sherman/What Can I Do	40

CLEM CATTINI ORK
65	Decca F 12135	No Time To Think/Impact	50

(see also Tornados, Aquarian Age, Rumplestiltskin, Spaghetti Head, Sounds Nice)

NADIA CATTOUSE
61	Parlophone R 4725	The Boy Without A Heart/Long Time, Boy	5
65	Parlophone R 5420	Port Mahon/A Little More Oil	7
66	Reality RE 503	Beautiful Barbados/Turn Around	5
60s	Church Miss. Soc. LIV/SP/81	The Larder/PAULINE FILBY: I'm Hungry	5
66	Reality RY 1001	NADIA CATTOUSE (LP)	40
70	RCA Victor SF 8070	EARTH MOTHER (LP, orange/white label)	30

(see also Sydney Carter)

THE CAUSE
82	Rising Sun RS 001	METRO POLICE EP (original copies with insert sleeve)	30
82	Rising Sun RS 001	METRO POLICE EP (without insert sleeve)	15

CAUSE N EFFECT
90	Foxadelic JTF1	Hype/That's What It Is	25
91	Foxadelic JTF2	Some Bite The Bullet (EP)	12

CAUSTIC WINDOW
92	Rephlex CAT 004	JOYREX J4 EP (12", 6-track)	40
92	Rephlex CAT 005	JOYREX J5 EP (12, 4-track, black vinyl)	50
92	Rephlex CAT 005	JOYREX J5 EP (12, 4-track, white vinyl)	40
93	Rephlex CAT 009 i	JOYREX J9 EP (10", picture disc, with bonus track "HMNA", 300 only)	80
93	Rephlex CAT 009 ii	JOYREX J9 EP (12" 4-track, initial batch in card mailer with bag of "space dust")	60
93	Rephlex CAT 009 ii	JOYREX J9 EP (12" 4-track)	50

(see also Aphex Twin)

CAVALIERS
86	él GPO 11	It's A Beautiful Game/The I.T. Man (p/s)	10
86	él ACME 4	A PERFECT ACTION (LP)	18

EDDIE CAVE & FYX
66	Pye 7N 17161	Fresh Out Of Tears/It's Almost Good	50

NICK CAVE (& BAD SEEDS)
84	Mute 7 MUTE 32	In The Ghetto/The Moon Is In The Gutter (p/s)	8
85	Mute 7 MUTE 38	Tupelo/The Six Strings That Drew Blood (p/s)	8
86	Lyntone LYN 18038	Scum (green vinyl flexidisc, with poster, concert freebie)	18
86	Lyntone LYN 18038	Scum (green vinyl flexidisc, without poster, concert freebie)	12
88	Mute MUTE 86	Oh Deanna/The Girl At The Bottom Of My Class (no p/s, DJ-only)	10
88	Mute 12MUTE86	Deanna/The Girl At The Bottom Of My Glass (12". with poster and postcard)	8
92	Mute LMUTE 140	Straight To You/Jack The Ripper (Acoustic Version) (limited issue, p/s)	8
92	Mute MUTE 148	I Had A Dream, Joe/The Good Son (live) (numbered p/s, 7,000 only)	8
94	Mute MUTE 160	Do You Love Me? (Single Version)/Cassiel's Song/Sail Away (silver vinyl, p/s, 1,000 copies)	10
94	Mute MUTE 169	Loverman (Single Version)/(I'll Love You) Till The End Of The World (picture disc, 2,000 only)	10
94	Mute MUTE 172	Red Right Hand/That's What Jazz Is To Me (red vinyl, p/s, with 2 different stickers & labels, 2,000 only)	10
85	Mute STUMM 21	THE FIRSTBORN IS DEAD (LP, with inner sleeve)	20
86	Mute STUMM 28	KICKING AGAINST THE PRICKS (LP)	20
86	Mute STUMM 34	YOUR FUNERAL...MY TRIAL (2-LP, gatefold sleeve, with inner sleeves)	20
88	Mute LSTUMM 52	TENDER PREY (LP, with bonus spoken word 12" And The Ass Saw The Angel [P STUMM 52]: "Autumn"/"Animal Static/Mah Sanctum/Lamentation, 5,000 only)	25
90	Mute LSTUMM 76	THE GOOD SON (LP, with bonus 7" "Acoustic Versions From Tender Prey" [P STUMM 76]: "The Mercy Seat"/"City Of Refuge"/"Deanna")	20
90	Mute STUMM 76	THE GOOD SON (LP, inner sleeve, without free 7")	12
90	Mute CDSTUMM 76	THE GOOD SON (CD, with bonus CD "Acoustic Versions From Tender Prey" [P STUMM 76]: "The Mercy Seat"/"City Of Refuge"/"Deanna")	18
92	Mute STUMM 92	HENRY'S DREAM (LP, with inner sleeve and art print)	20
94	Mute LSTUMM 123	LET LOVE IN (LP, with set of postcards or poster)	40
96	Mute STUMM 138	MURDER BALLADS (LP, with insert)	40
97	Mute STUMM 142	THE BOATMANS CALL (LP)	20
01	Mute STUMM 164	NO MORE SHALL WE PART (2-LP, with inner sleeves)	40
03	Mute STUMM 207	NOCTURAMA (2-LP, inners)	20
04	Mute STUMM 233	ABBATOIR BLUES (2-LP, inner sleeves and insert)	50
08	Mute STUMM 277	DIG LAZARUS DIG (LP, inners, booklet, and free 7")	25

(see also Birthday Party, Annie Hogan, Burmoe Brothers)

STUART & SANDY CAVE
77	Profile GMOR 143	DAWN ON SUNDAY (LP)	60

ANDY CAVELL
62	HMV POP 1024	Hey There Cruel Heart/Lonely Soldier Boy	40
62	HMV POP 1080	Always On Saturday/Hey There, Senorita	40
63	Pye 7N 15539	Andy/There Was A Boy	40
64	Pye 7N 15610	Shut Up/Tell The Truth	40

JIMMY CAVELLO & HIS HOUSE ROCKERS
57	Vogue Coral Q 72226	Rock, Rock, Rock/The Big Beat	250
57	Vogue Coral Q 72226	Rock, Rock, Rock/The Big Beat (78)	35
57	Vogue Coral Q 72240	Foot Stompin'/Ooh-Wee	250
57	Vogue Coral Q 72240	Foot Stompin'/Ooh-Wee (78)	35

(see also Alan Freed)

CAVEMAN
91	Profile PROFT 330DJ	I'm Ready/Pages & Pages/Back To Cause Mayhem (EP)	10
91	Profile FILER 406	POSITIVE REACTION (LP)	20

TERRY CAVENDISH ORCHESTRA
73	Pye NSPL 41023	ALL IN AN AFTERNOON'S WORK (LP)	15

CAVE OF THE LIVING STREAMS
74	Indigo Sound Studios UHC 1	SIXTEEN SONGS (LP, private pressing with booklet)	40

MONTE CAZAZZA

79	Industrial IR 0005	To Mom On Mother's Day/Candy Man (p/s, with outer polystyrene sleeve & insert, 2,500 only)	20
80	Industrial IR 0010	SOMETHING FOR NOBODY (EP)	20

(see also Psychic TV)

C.C.S. (COLLECTIVE CONSCIOUSNESS SOCIETY)

71	Rak 109	Walking/Salome	5
71	RAK 119	Tap Turns On The Water/Save The World	6
72	Rak 126	Brother/Mister What You Can't Have I Can Get	5
73	Rak RAK 154	The Band Played The Boogie/Hang It On Me	5
70	Rak SRAK 6751	C.C.S. (LP, gatefold sleeve)	20
72	Rak SRAK 503	C.C.S. (LP)	18
73	Rak SRAK 504	THE BEST BAND IN THE LAND (LP)	15

(see also Alexis Korner)

CEDARS

68	Decca F 22720	For Your Information/Hide If You Want To Hide	50
68	Decca F 22772	I Like The Way/I Don't Know Why	50

(see also Seaders)

CELEBRATION FEATURING MIKE LOVE

73	MCA 365	Almost Summer/Lookin' Good	8

(see also Beach Boys)

ADRIANO CELENTANO

72	Epic EPC 1886	Prisencohnensinaincusol/Disc Jockey	6

CELIA & THE MUTATIONS

77	United Artists UP 36262	Mony Mony/Mean To Me (p/s)	6
77	United Artists UP 36318	You Better Believe Me/Round And Around (p/s)	10

(see also Stranglers, Tonight)

CELTIC F.C.

67	Thistle	Celtic Celtic (p/s)	12
73	Polydor 2058332	Celtic Your Favourites In Green/Saturday	5

CELTIC FROST

84	Noise N 0017	MORBID TALES (mini LP, with poster)	40
84	Noise N 0017	MORBID TALES (mini LP, without poster)	25
86	Combat MX 8091	TO MEGA THERION (LP, gatefold, with inner sleeve)	25
87	NOISE NOISE 065	INTO THE PANDEMONIUM (LP, gatefold sleeve, with insert)	25
06	Century Media 9979951	MONOTHEIST (2-LP, gatefold, brown marbled vinyl, 100 only)	50

CENOTAPH CORNER

76	Cottage COT 501	UPS AND DOWNS (LP)	20
79	Cottage COT 031	EVERY DAY BUT WEDNESDAY (LP)	25

CENTIPEDE

71	RCA Neon NE 9	SEPTOBER ENERGY (2-LP, gatefold sleeve, black inner sleeve)	70
74	RCA DPS 2054	SEPTOBER ENERGY (2-LP, reissue, different cover)	20

(see also Mark Charig, Ian Carr, Elton Dean, Zoot Money, Alan Skidmore, Keith Tippett, Julie Tippetts, Mike Patto, Robert Wyatt)

CENTRY

80s	Conscious Sounds DPS 001	Stepping Time/Stepping Dub (12")	10

CENTURION

82	Centurion 0001	Two Wheels/Bitch (private pressing)	50
82	Centurion 0001	Two Wheels/Bitch (private pressing, mislabelled 'Nikki')	30

CENTURY 21 (GERRY ANDERSON TV SPIN-OFFS)

65	Century 21 MA 100	JOURNEY TO THE MOON (EP)	15
65	Century 21 MA 101	INTO ACTION WITH TROY TEMPEST (EP)	12
65	Century 21 MA 102	A TRIP TO MARINEVILLE (EP)	15
65	Century 21 MA 103	INTRODUCING THUNDERBIRDS (EP)	15
65	Century 21 MA 104	MARINA SPEAKS (EP)	15
65	Century 21 MA 105	TV CENTURY 21 THEMES (EP)	15
66	Century 21 MA 106	THE DALEKS (EP)	50
66	Century 21 MA 107	F.A.B. (EP)	18
66	Century 21 MA 108	THUNDERBIRD 1 (EP)	18
66	Century 21 MA 109	THUNDERBIRD 2 (EP)	18
66	Century 21 MA 110	THE STATELY HOME ROBBERIES (EP)	25
66	Century 21 MA 111	LADY PENELOPE & OTHER TV THEMES (EP)	25
66	Century 21 MA 112	THUNDERBIRD 3 (EP)	25
66	Century 21 MA 113	THUNDERBIRD 4 (EP)	25
66	Century 21 MA 114	THE PERILS OF PENELOPE (EP)	30
66	Century 21 MA 115	TOPO GIGIO IN LONDON (EP)	45
67	Century 21 MA 116	GREAT THEMES FROM GERRY ANDERSON'S THUNDERBIRDS (EP)	30
67	Century 21 MA 117	SPACE AGE NURSERY RHYMES (EP)	35
67	Century 21 MA 118	LADY PENELOPE AND PARKER (EP)	35
67	Century 21 MA 119	BRAINS AND TIN TIN (EP)	35
67	Century 21 MA 120	INTERNATIONAL RESCUE (EP)	35
67	Century 21 MA 121	THUNDERBIRDS (EP)	35
67	Century 21 MA 122	LADY PENELOPE (EP)	35
67	Century 21 MA 123	BRAINS (EP)	35
67	Century 21 MA 124	BRINK OF DISASTER (EP)	35
67	Century 21 MA 125	ATLANTIC INFERNO (EP)	35
67	Century 21 MA 126	RICOCHET (EP)	35
67	Century 21 MA 127	TINGHA & TUCKER & THE WOMBAVILLE BAND (EP)	35
67	Century 21 MA 128	ONE MOVE & YOU'RE DEAD (EP)	35
67	Century 21 MA 129	30 MINUTES AFTER NOON (EP)	35
67	Century 21 MA 130	TINGHA & TUCKER IN NURSERY RHYME TIME (EP)	35
67	Century 21 MA 131	INTRODUCING CAPTAIN SCARLET (EP)	30
67	Century 21 MA 132	CAPTAIN SCARLET AND THE MYSTERONS (EP)	30
67	Century 21 MA 133	CAPTAIN SCARLET IS INDESTRUCTIBLE (EP)	25
67	Century 21 MA 134	CAPTAIN SCARLET OF SPECTRUM (EP)	20

MINT VALUE £

67	Century 21 MA 135	CAPTAIN SCARLET VS. CAPTAIN BLACK (EP)	25
67	Century 21 MA 136	THEMES FROM GERRY ANDERSON'S CAPTAIN SCARLET (EP)	25
65	Century 21 LA 100	JOURNEY TO THE MOON (LP)	70
66	Century 21 LA 1	THE WORLD OF TOMORROW (LP)	50
66	Century 21 LA 2	LADY PENELOPE PRESENTS (LP)	50
66	Century 21 LA 3	JEFF TRACY INTRODUCES INTERNATIONAL RESCUE (LP)	50
66	Century 21 LA 4	LADY PENELOPE INVESTIGATES (LP)	50
66	Century 21 LA 5	THE TINGHA & TUCKER CLUB SONG BOOK (LP)	50
67	Century 21 LA 6	FAVOURITE TELEVISION THEMES (LP)	50
68	Marble Arch MAL 770	TV FAVOURITES VOL. 1 (LP)	20
68	Marble Arch MAL 771	TV FAVOURITES VOL. 2 (LP)	20

(see also Barry Gray, Dr. Who)

CEOLBEG
90	Ceolbeg Music CB 001	NOT THE BUNNY HOP (LP)	20

CERTAIN LIONS & TIGERS
70	Polydor 2344 002	SOUL CONDOR (LP)	40

CEYLEIB PEOPLE
68	Vocalion SAVL 8072	TANYET (LP)	200

FRANK CHACKSFIELD
54	Decca F10255	Song Of Canterbury/The Pied Piper	8
56	Decca F10639	In Old Lisbon/Memories Of You	8
56	Decca F 10743	The Donkey Cart/Two Banks Of The Seine	8

CHAD (STUART) & JEREMY (CLYDE)
64	Ember EMB S 180	Yesterday's Gone/Lemon Tree (as Chad Stuart & Jeremy Clyde)	6
64	Ember EMB S 186	Early In The Morning/Like I Love You Today (as Chad Stuart & Jeremy Clyde)	6
64	United Artists UP 1062	A Summer Song/No Tears For Johnnie (as Chad Stuart & Jeremy Clyde)	5
64	United Artists UP 1070	Willow Weep For Me/If She Was Mine	5
65	Ember EMB S 205	If I Loved You/No Tears For Johnnie	5
65	Ember EMB S 217	What Do You Want With Me?/Donna Donna	5
65	CBS 201769	Before And After/Evil-Hearted Me	5
65	CBS 201814	I Don't Want To Lose You/Pennies	5
66	CBS 202279	Distant Shores/Last Night	8
66	CBS b202397	You Are She/I Won't Cry	12
64	Ember EMB EP 4543	YESTERDAY'S GONE (EP)	12
65	United Artists UEP 1008	CHAD STUART AND JEREMY CLYDE (EP)	15

(see also John Barry, Jeremy Clyde)

ERNIE CHAFFIN
57	London HLS 8409	Feelin' Low/Lonesome For My Baby	150
57	London HLS 8409	Feelin' Low/Lonesome For My Baby (78)	40

CHAIN REACTION
77	Gull GULS 43	This Eternal Flame/Never Lose, Never Win	12
77	Gull GULS 53	Why Can't We Be Lovers/Hogtied	10
77	Gull GULS 77	Never Lose Never Win/Chase A Miracle	12

CHAINSAW
80	Square SQSP 2	Police And Politicians/Hole In The Road (p/s)	45
80	Pot Belly EJSP 9462	Lonely Without You/On The Highway	35
84	GMC CS 001	Long Legged Woman/Midnight Blue	30
84	Thunderbolt THBE 1006	MASSACRE (12" EP)	8

CHAIRMAN YOUTH
81	Last Ditch TRENCH 1	Uncertainty/Business Partners (p/s)	6

CHAIRMEN OF THE BOARD
70	Invictus INV 501	Give Me Just A Little More Time/Since The Days Of Pigtails	8
70	Invictus INV 501	Give Me Just A Little More Time/Since The Days Of Pigtails (DJ Copy)	20
70	Invictus INV 504	You've Got Me Dangling On A String/Patches	6
70	Invictus INV 504	You've Got Me Dangling On A String/Patches (DJ Copy)	20
71	Invictus INV 507	Everything's Tuesday/Bless You	6
71	Invictus INV 507	Everything's Tuesday/Bless You (DJ Copy)	15
71	Invictus INV 511	Pay To The Piper/When Will She Tell Me She Needs Me?	5
71	Invictus INV 511	Pay To The Piper/When Will She Tell Me She Needs Me? (DJ Copy)	15
71	Invictus INV 516	Chairman Of The Board/Hanging On To A Memory	5
71	Invictus INV 516	Chairman Of The Board/When Will She Tell Me She Needs Me? (different B-side)	5
72	Invictus INV 519	Working On A Building Of Love/Try On My Love For Size	5
72	Invictus INV 524	Elmo James/Bittersweet	5
72	Invictus INV 527	I'm On My Way To A Better Place/So Glad You're Mine	5
73	Invictus INV 530	Finders Keepers/Finders Keepers (Instrumental)	5
70	Invictus SVT 1002	CHAIRMEN OF THE BOARD (LP)	20
71	Invictus SVT 1003	IN SESSION (LP)	20
72	Invictus SVT 1006	BITTERSWEET (LP)	20
73	Invictus SVT 1009	GREATEST HITS (LP)	15
74	Invictus 65868	SKIN I'M IN (LP)	20

(see also Showmen, General Johnson, Norman Johnson)

CHAKA KHAN
80	Warner Bros. 17617T	Clouds/What You Did (12")	10
81	Warner Bros. LV 48	Wha'cha Gonna Do For Me/We Got The Love/I'm Every Woman (12", p/s)	12
78	Warner Bros SAM 254	I'm Every Woman/I'm Every Woman (12", promo only)	8

(see also Rufus & Chaka Khan)

CHAKACHAS
61	RCA RCA 1264	Twist Twist/Baila La Bamba	5
72	Polydor 2121 093	Jungle Fever/Chaka Cha	10
72	Polydor 2489 050	JUNGLE FEVER (LP)	20
73	Young Blood SYB 3003	CHAKACHAS (LP)	20

GEORGE CHAKIRIS
60	Triumph RGM 1010	Heart Of A Teenage Girl/I'm Always Chasing Rainbows	20

CHALAWA
78	Skynote SKYLP 14	EXODUS DUB (LP)	40

CHALICE
80	Galactic GALD 002	I'm Gonna Get You/Oi Nayga (12")	12

BRYAN CHALKER('S NEW FRONTIER)
70	Amity OTS 502	Ned Kelly/Four Girls From The Town Of Boston	6
72	Columbia DB 8883	Daddy Sang Bass/Lot 69	6
72	Chapter One SCH 179	Help Me Make It Through The Night/Eskimo Song	6
73	Chapter One SCH 185	Daisy A Day/Life Gets Tee-jus, Don't It	6
71	Avenue AVE 071	THE HANGING OF SAMUEL HALL (LP, textured sleeve, as Bryan Chalker's New Frontier)	15

CHALLENGER
81	CMC CM 0001	So Sure Of Yourself/Out To Kill	20

CHALLENGERS (U.K.)
61	Parlophone R 4773	Cry Of The Wild Goose/Deadline	15

CHALLENGERS (U.S.)
63	Stateside SS 177	Torquay/Bulldog	20
65	Vocalion V 9253	The Man From U.N.C.L.E./The Streets Of London	20
66	Vocalion V 9270	Walk With Me/How Could I	10
63	Stateside SL 10030	SURFBEAT (LP)	70
67	Vocalion VA-N 8069	WIPE OUT (LP, mono)	65
67	Vocalion SAV-N 8069	WIPE OUT (LP, stereo)	75

JUDITH CHALMERS & DAVID JACOBS
74	G&C	SOUNDS BEAUTIFUL (LP)	25

CHAMBER POP ENSEMBLE
68	Decca F 12789	Walk Away Renee/59th Street Bridge Song (Feeling Groovy)	6
68	Decca LK/SKL 4933	CHAMBER POP ENSEMBLE (LP)	20

CHAMBERPOT
76	Bead Records BEAD 2	CHAMBERPOT (LP)	50

JAMES CHAMBERS
71	Summit SUM 8523	Bongo Man/KEN BOOTHE: Now I Know	10

(see also Jimmy Cliff)

CHAMBERS BROTHERS
66	Vocalion VL 9267	Love Me Like The Rain/Pretty Girls Everywhere	20
66	Vocalion VL 9276	Call Me/Seventeen	20
67	CBS 202565	All Strung Out Over You/Falling In Love	10
68	Direction 58-3215	Up Town/Love Me Like The Rain	7
68	Direction 58-3671	Time Has Come Today/Dinah	12
68	Direction 58-3760	Time Has Come Today/Dinah (reissue)	8
68	Direction 58-3865	I Can't Turn You Loose/Do Your Thing	8
69	Direction 58-4098	Are You Ready/You Got The Power To Turn Me On	6
69	Direction 58-4318	People Get Ready/No, No, No, Don't Say Goodbye	6
69	Direction 58-4367	Wake Up/Everybody Needs Someone	10
70	Direction 58-4846	Love Peace And Happiness/If You Want Me To	7
70	Direction 58-5033	Let's Do It/To Love Somebody	7
71	CBS 5389	Funky/Love, Peace And Happiness	15
71	CBS 7689	By The Hair On My Chinny Chin Chin/Heaven	6
66	Vocalion VA-L/SAV-L 8058	PEOPLE GET READY (LP)	60
68	Liberty LBS 83272	SHOUT! (LP, blue label)	30
68	Direction 8-63407	THE TIME HAS COME (LP)	30
69	Direction 8-63451	A NEW TIME - A NEW DAY (LP)	30
70	Direction 8-66228	LOVE PEACE AND HAPPINESS (Live At Bill Graham's Fillmore West) (2-LP)	30
70	Liberty LBS 83276	FEELIN' THE BLUES (LP)	15
71	CBS 64156	A NEW GENERATION (LP)	15

CHAMELEON
71	CBS 5428	Who Am I/Coogans Keep	20

CHAMELEONS
82	Epic EPCA 2210	In Shreds/Less Than Human (p/s)	15
83	Statik STAT 30	As High As You Can Go/Pleasure And Pain (p/s)	6
83	Statik STAT 3012	As High As You Can Go/Pleasure And Pain/Paper Tigers (12", p/s)	10
83	Statik TAK 6	A Person Isn't Safe Anywhere These Days/Thursday's Child (p/s)	7
83	Statik TAK 6/12	A Person Isn't Safe Anywhere These Days/Thursday's Child/ Prisoners Of The Sun (12", p/s)	8
85	Statik TAK 29	In Shreds/Nostalgia (p/s)	6
85	Statik TAK 29/12	In Shreds/Less Than Human/Nostalgia (12", p/s)	10
85	Statik TAK 35/12	Singing Rule Britannia (While The Walls Close In)/Singing Rule Britannia (Radio 1 'Saturday Live' Session Version) (12", p/s)	8
86	Geffen GEF 4F/SAM 287	Tears/Paradiso//Swamp Thing/Inside Out (double pack, gatefold p/s)	7
90	Glass Pyramid EMC 1	TONY FLETCHER WALKED ON WATER (12" EP)	35
90	Glass Pyramid EMCD 1	TONY FLETCHER WALKED ON WATER (CD EP)	30
90	Glass Pyramid EMC 2	TRIPPING DOGS (LP)	30
85	Statik STATLP 17	SCRIPT OF THE BRIDGE (LP, picture disc)	20
85	Statik STATLP 22	WHAT DOES ANYTHING MEAN? BASICALLY (LP, gatefold sleeve, with insert)	12

(see also Sun & Moon, Reegs)

TEDDY CHAMES
68	Blue Cat BS 141	I Want It Girl/She Is Gone (actually by Teddy Charmes)	30

DES CHAMP ORCHESTRA
70	Page One POF 172	It Takes A Thief/My Own Thing	15

CHAMPIONS
63	Oriole CB 1854	Circlorama/Pinky	10

CHAMPIONS OF NATURE
00	White FOFF 1	The Fuck Off Song/An Undercurrent/360/Carpe Diem (EP)	30
00	White FOFF 2	Finalisation/Cold Dessert/Breakfast Of Champions (EP)	30
01	White SALSA001	Salsa Smurph/Jazzy Styles (12")	20

CHAMPS (JAMAICA)
64	Blue Beat BB 267	Walk Between Your Enemies/Do What I Say	20

CHAMPS (U.S.)
58	London HLU 8580	Tequila/Train To Nowhere	15
58	London HLU 8580	Tequila/Train To Nowhere (78)	10
58	London HL 8655	Midnighter/El Rancho Rock	15
58	London HL 8655	Midnighter/El Rancho Rock (78)	10
58	London HL 8715	Chariot Rock/Subway	15
58	London HL 8715	Chariot Rock/Subway (78)	10
59	London HLH 8811	Beatnik/Gone Train	12
59	London HLH 8811	Beatnik/Gone Train (78)	10
59	London HLH 8864	Caramba/Moonlight Bay	15
59	London HLH 8864	Caramba/Moonlight Bay (78)	10
60	London HLH 9052	Too Much Tequila/Twenty Thousand Leagues	10
61	London HLH 9430	Cantina/Panic Button	10
62	London HLH 9506	Tequila Twist/Limbo Rock	10
62	London HLH 9539	Experiment In Terror/La Cucaracha	10
62	London HLH 9604	Limbo Dance/Latin Limbo	10
59	London RE 1176	FOUR BY THE CHAMPS (EP)	25
59	London RE-H 1209	ANOTHER FOUR BY THE CHAMPS (EP)	25
59	London RE-H 1223	STILL MORE BY THE CHAMPS (EP)	25
61	London RE-H 1250	KNOCKOUTS! (EP)	30
58	London HA-H 2152	GO CHAMPS GO! (LP)	60
59	London HA-H 2184	EVERYBODY'S ROCKIN' WITH THE CHAMPS (LP)	60
62	London HA-H 2451	GREAT DANCE HITS (LP, early issue with flipback cover)	40
62	London HA-H 2451	GREAT DANCE HITS (LP)	15
77	London ZGH 141	THE BEST OF (LP)	12

ROB CHANCE & CHANCES-R
67	CBS 3130	At The End Of The Day/I've Got The Power	12

(see also Chances-R)

CHANCES ARE
67	Columbia DB 8144	Fragile Child/What Went Wrong	40

CHANCES-R
67	CBS 202614	Talking Out The Back Of My Head/I Aimed Too High	20
67	CBS 2940	Do It Yourself/Turn A New Leaf Over	12

(see also Rob Chance & Chances-R)

CHANCIS
64	Decca F 11860	Everybody's Laughing/Tell Me	15

CHANDELIERS
73	Penny Farthing PEN 809	Can't You Hear My Neartbrek/One Way Street	6

TIM CHANDELL
78	Orbitone 05	Keep Me/Let's Make Love	20

DANY CHANDELLE
65	Columbia DB 7540	Lying Awake/I Love You	30

BARBARA CHANDLER
63	London HLR 9823	Do You Really Love Me Too?/I Live To Love You	30
64	London HLR 9861	I'm Going Out With The Girls/Lonely New Year	30

GENE CHANDLER
62	Columbia DB 4793	Duke Of Earl/Kissing In The Kitchen	30
63	Stateside SS 185	Rainbow/You Threw A Lucky Punch	40
64	Stateside SS 331	Just Be True/A Song Called Soul	25
64	Stateside SS 364	Bless Our Love/London Town	25
65	Stateside SS 388	What Now/If You Can't Be True (Find A Part Time Love)	35
65	Stateside SS 401	You Can't Hurt Me No More/Everybody Let's Dance	25
65	Stateside SS 425	Nothing Can Stop Me/The Big Lie	60
65	Stateside SS 425	Nothing Can Stop Me/The Big Lie (DJ copy)	150
65	Stateside SS 458	Good Times/No One Can Love You (Like I Do)	35
66	Stateside SS 500	(I'm Just A) Fool For You/Buddy Ain't It A Shame	35
66	Chess CRS 8047	I Fooled You This Time/Such A Pretty Thing	40
66	Chess CRS 8047	I Fooled You This Time/Such A Pretty Thing (DJ copy)	80
67	Coral Q 72490	The Girl Don't Care/My Love	20
68	Soul City SC 102	Nothing Can Stop Me/The Big Lie (reissue)	15
69	Action ACT 4551	I Can't Save It/I Can Take Care Of Myself	60
69	President PT 234	Duke Of Earl/Stand By Me	8
70	Mercury 6052 033	Groovy Situation/Not The Marrying Kind	6
71	Mercury 6052 098	You're A Lady/Stone Cold Feeling	15
76	Brunswick BR 39	There Was A Time/ARTISTICS: I'm Gonna Miss You	10
65	Fontana TL 5247	DUKE OF EARL (LP)	100
67	Coral LVA 9236	THE GIRL DON'T CARE (LP)	60
69	MCA MUPS 367	THERE WAS A TIME (LP)	30
69	Action ACLP 6010	LIVE ON STAGE (LP)	50
71	Mercury 6338 037	SITUATION (LP)	20
74	Joy JOYS 136	A GENE CHANDLER ALBUM (LP)	15

GENE CHANDLER & BARBARA ACKLIN
74	Brunswick BR 30	From The Teacher To The Preacher/Little Green Apples	8

(see also Barbara Acklin, Gene & Jerry)

GEORGE CHANDLER
82	Polydor 436	This Could Be The Night/Can't Go Back No More	15

JEFF CHANDLER
54	Brunswick 05264	I Should Care/More Than Anyone	5
55	Brunswick 05380	Everything Happens To Me/Always	5
55	Brunswick 05417	My Prayer/When Spring Comes	5
55	Brunswick 05441	Foxfire/Shaner Maidel	5
55	Brunswick 05465	Only The Very Young/A Little Love Can Go A Long, Long Way	5

57	London HLU 8484	Half Of My Heart/Hold Me	5
57	London HLU 8484	Half Of My Heart/Hold Me (78)	10
58	London HA-U 2100	JEFF CHANDLER SINGS TO YOU (LP)	20

KAREN CHANDLER
55	Vogue Coral Q 72091	The Price You Pay For Love/The Man In The Raincoat	7
56	Brunswick 05570	Love Is The $64,000 Question/(I'm Just A) Beginner	10
56	Brunswick 05596	Tonight You Belong To Me/Crazy Arms (with Jimmy Wakely)	10
57	Brunswick 05662	Your Wild Heart/It's An International Language	7
62	Salvo SLO 1803	My Own True Love/You Made Me Love You (99 copies only)	10

(see also Jimmy Wakely)

KENNY CHANDLER
63	Stateside SS 166	Heart/Wait For Me	15
68	Stateside SS 2110	Beyond Love/Charity	60
68	Stateside SS 2110	Beyond Love/Charity (DJ Copy)	80

LEN CHANDLER
67	CBS 62931	TO BE A MAN (LP)	20

LORRAINE CHANDLER
75	Black Magic BM 105	Love You Baby/What Can I Do	8
77	Kent 6T 13	You Only Live Twice/METROS: My Imagination	30

CHANDONS
68	RCA RCA 1704	Timber/Never Been Loved Before	6

CHANGE
73	Orange OAS 222	Sunshine/Get Your Gun	25
74	Orange OAS 221	Lazy London Lady/Arkmaker	40
74	EMI EMI 2354	Wildcat/Hold On	10
73	Orange OAS 210	Yaketty Yak, Smacketty Smack/When The Morning Comes	8

CHANGIN' TIMES
65	Phillips BF 1442	Pied Piper/Thank You Babe	25
68	Bell BLL 1009	When The Good Sun Shines/Show Me The Way To Go Home	6

BRUCE CHANNEL
62	Mercury AMT 1171	Hey! Baby/Dream Girl	10
62	Mercury AMT 1177	Number One Man/If Only I Had Known	10
62	Pye International 7N 25137	Run Romance Run/Don't Leave Me	20
63	London HLU 9776	I Don't Wanna/Blue And Lonesome	20
64	London HLU 9841	Going Back To Louisiana/Forget Me Not	15
67	Stateside SS 2066	Mr. Bus Driver/It's Me	15
68	Bell BLL 1010	Keep On/Barbara Allen	5
68	Bell BLL 1030	Try Me/Water The Family Tree	5
72	UK USA 3	Kiss And Run/Don't Let Go	6
62	Mercury MMC 14104	HEY! BABY! (LP)	50
68	Bell MBLL/SBLL 110	KEEP ON (LP)	20

CHANNEL 4
79	Ripping RIP 1	Vampire/Channel 4 (numbered p/s with insert)	6

CHANNEL 3
82	No Future OI 11	I've Got A Gun/Manzanar/Mannequin (p/s)	10
82	No Future PUNK 2	I'VE GOT A GUN (LP)	12
83	No Future PUNK 7	AFTER THE LIGHTS GO OUT (LP)	12

SHALOM CHANOCH
72	DJM DJLPS 421	SHALOM (LP)	12

CHANTAYS
63	London HLD 9696	Pipeline/Move It	8
64	King KG 1018	Beyond/I'll Be Back Someday	20
66	Dot DS 26757	Pipeline/Move It (reissue)	5
63	London RED 1397	PIPELINE (EP)	40
63	London HA-D 8087	PIPELINE (LP, mono)	40
63	London SH-D 8087	PIPELINE (LP, stereo)	45
75	Contour 2870 389	PIPELINE (LP)	12

CHANTELLES
65	Parlophone R 5271	I Want That Boy/London My Home Town	25
65	Parlophone R 5303	The Secret Of My Success/Sticks And Stones	15
65	Parlophone R 5350	Gonna Get Burned/Gonna Give Him Some Love	15
66	Parlophone R 5431	I Think Of You/Please Don't Kiss Me	15
66	Polydor 56119	There's Something About You/Just Another Fool	20
67	CBS 2777	Blue Mood/The Man I Love	25

(see also Lana Sisters)

CHANTELS
58	London HLU 8561	Maybe/Come My Little Baby	300
58	London HLU 8561	Maybe/Come My Little Baby (78)	60
62	London HLL 9428	Look In My Eyes/Glad To Be Back	60
62	London HLL 9480	Well I Told You/Still	60
62	London HLL 9532	Here It Comes Again/Summertime	40
63	Capitol CL 15297	Swamp Water/Eternally	40
70	Roulette RO 514	Maybe/He's Gone	5

(see also Richard Barrett)

CHANTER
77	Expert ELP 1	SUBURBAN ETHNIA (LP, private pressing)	12

CHANTERS (1)
66	CBS 202454	Every Night (I Sit And Cry)/Where	30
67	CBS 202616	You Can't Fool Me/All Day Long	20
68	CBS 3400	What's Wrong With You/Right By Your Side	6
68	CBS 3668	My Love Is For You/Mississippi Paddleboat	8

(see also Birds Of A Feather)

MINT VALUE £

CHANTERS (2)
| 79 | Burning Rockers BRD 011 | Mash Down Babylon/I Told You So (12") | 25 |

CHANTS (U.K.)
63	Pye 7N 15557	I Don't Care/Come Go With Me	25
64	Pye 7N 15591	I Could Write A Book/A Thousand Stars	20
64	Pye 7N 15643	She's Mine/Then I'll Be Home	20
64	Pye 7N 15691	Sweet Was The Wine/One Star	20
66	Fontana TF 716	Come Back And Get This Loving Baby/Love Light	15
67	Decca F 12650	A Lover's Story/Wearing A Smile	20
67	Page One POF 016	Ain't Nobody Home/For You	15
68	RCA Victor RCA 1754	A Man Without A Face/Baby I Don't Need Your Love	100
68	RCA Victor RCA 1754	A Man Without A Face/Baby I Don't Need Your Love (DJ Copy)	130
69	RCA Victor RCA 1823	I Get The Sweetest Feeling/Candy	25
76	Chipping Norton CHIP 2	I've Been Trying/Lucky Old Me	30

(see also Real Thing)

CHANTS (U.S.)
| 58 | Capitol CL 14876 | Close Friends/Lost And Found | 25 |

CHAOS & JULIA SET
| 93 | Recoil RCL 001 | VOL. 1 ATMOSPHERE EP (12", plain sleeve) | 10 |
| 93 | Recoil RCL 002 | VOL. 2 - FEAR OF THE FUTURE (12", plain sleeve) | 12 |

(see also Global Communications)

CHAOS U.K.
| 79 | Chaotic Records VD 1 | Summer Of Hate/I Wanna To Be Left Alone (p/s, 500 only) | 150 |

CHAOS U.K. (BRISTOL)
82	Riot City RIOT 6	BURNING BRITAIN (EP)	8
82	Riot City RIOT 12	LOUD, POLITICAL AND UNCOMPROMISING (EP)	8
85	C.O.R. GURT 1	SHORT SHARP SHOCK (LP)	20
86	Manic Ears ACHE 1	RADIOACTIVE (LP, with inner, split with EXTREME NOISE TERROR)	20
89	Slap Up	THE CHIPPING SODBURY BONFIRE TAPES (LP)	12

CHAOTIC DISCHORD
81	Riot City 12 ROT 30	Don't Throw It Away (12")	15
83	Riot City RIOT RIOT 22	Never Trust A Friend/Are Students Safe? (p/s)	12
82	Riot City RIOT 10	FUCK THE WORLD (EP)	10
83	Riot City CITY 004	FUCK RELIGION, FUCK POLITICS, AND FUCK THE LOT OF YOU (LP)	15
84	Syndicate SYNLP 12	FUCK OFF YOU CUNT WHAT A LOAD OF BOLLOCKS (LP)	15
88	Not Very Nice GRR 3RV	VERY FUCKIN' BAD (LP)	12
86	Not Very Nice GRR 2	GOAT FUCKING VIRGIN KILERZ FROM HELL (LP)	12

CHAOTIC YOUTH
| 83 | Beat The System YOUTH 1 | SAD SOCIETY (EP) | 50 |

HARRY CHAPIN
73	Elektra 7E 1012	VERITIES & BALDERDASH (LP)	15
74	Elektra K 42155	SHORT STORIES (LP, gatefold sleeve)	15
78	Elektra K 52089	LIVING ROOM SUITE (LP)	15
79	Elektra K 62026	LEGENDS OF THE LOST & FOUND (LP)	18
79	Elektra ELK 62017	HARRY CHAPIN GREATEST STORIES LIVE (2xLP)	18
70s	Elektra FW 36872	IN SEQUEL (LP)	15
70s	Elektra K 42107	HEADS & TALES (LP)	15
70s	Elektra E1082	ON THE ROAD TO KINGDOM COME (LP)	15
70s	Elektra K 62021	DANCE BAND ON THE TITANIC (2xLP, gatefold sleeve)	20
70s	Ekektra 7E 1041	PORTRAIT GALLERY (LP, gatefold sleeve)	15

PAUL CHAPLAIN & HIS EMERALDS
| 60 | London HLU 9205 | Shortnin' Bread/Nicotine | 20 |

CHAPMAN AND WHITNEY
| 74 | Reprise K54017 | STREETWALKERS (LP, with inner) | 20 |

(see also Family, Streetwalkers)

COLIN CHAPMAN
| 60s | CCLP 1001 | FOLK SONGS VOL 1 (LP) | 15 |

GENE CHAPMAN
| 63 | Starlite ST45 102 | Oklahoma Blues/Don't Come Crying | 80 |

GRADY CHAPMAN
| 60 | Mercury AMT 1107 | Sweet Thing/I Know What I Want | 30 |

MICHAEL CHAPMAN
69	Harvest HAR 5002	It Didn't Work Out/Mozart Lives Upstairs	15
69	Harvest SHVL 755	RAINMAKER (LP, gatefold sleeve, with "Sold in U.K..." label text on 4 lines, No EMI on label)	100
69	Harvest SHVL 755	RAINMAKER (LP, gatefold sleeve, later pressing with with EMI on label)	40
70	Harvest SHVL 764	FULLY QUALIFIED SURVIVOR (LP, gatefold sleeve, 1st pressing with no EMI on label)	80
70	Harvest SHVL 764	FULLY QUALIFIED SURVIVOR (LP, gatefold sleeve, later pressing with with EMI on label)	20
70	Harvest SHVL 786	WINDOW (LP, gatefold sleeve, with no EMI on label)	70
70	Harvest SHVL 786	WINDOW (LP, gatefold sleeve, with EMI on label)	20
71	Harvest SHVL 798	WRECKED AGAIN (LP, gatefold sleeve, EMI on label)	50
73	Deram SML 1105	MILLSTONE GRIT (LP, red/white label)	18
74	Deram SML 1114	DEAL GONE DOWN (LP)	15
76	Decca SKL-R 5242	SAVAGE AMUSEMENT (LP, with lyric sheet, blue/silver label)	20
70s	Standard ESL 146	GUITARS (LP, library issue)	60

CHAPS
| 62 | Parlophone R 4979 | Poppin' Medley (Parts 1 & 2) | 25 |

(see also Outlaws)

CHAPTER FIVE
66	CBS 202395	Anything You Do Is Alright/You Can't Mean It	600
67	CBS 2696	One In A Million/Hey Hey (unissued, demos only)	250
90s	Goldmine/Soul Supply GS 009	You Can't Mean It/One In A Million	8

CHAPTER FOUR (U.K.)
| 60s | GSP 11009/10 | CHAPTER FOUR (EP, no p/s) | 90 |

CHAPTER FOUR (U.K.)
| 80 | Bridge BR 001 | HANGING AROUND STERLING (LP) | 35 |

CHAPTER FOUR (U.S.)
| 66 | United Artists UP 1143 | In My Life/In Each Other's Arms | 250 |

(see also Jay & Americans)

CHAPTER THREE (U.K.)
| 67 | CBS 2971 | Cold And Lonely Hours/Wrecking Crew | 7 |
| 67 | CBS BPG 63007 | RAMBLE AWAY (LP) | 18 |

CHAPTERHOUSE
| 91 | Dedicated STONE 003T | PEARL EP (12") | 8 |
| 91 | Dedicated DEDLP 001 | WHIRLPOOL (LP) | 20 |

(see also Slowdive)

CHAPTERS
| 65 | Pye 7N 15815 | Can't Stop Thinking About Her/Dance Little Lady | 50 |

CHARACTERS
| 86 | BEM BEM 101 | Love Talk/Where Has All The Love Gone (500 only) | 30 |

ERIC CHARDON
| 69 | Major Minor MM596 | One Love One Life/Sorrow Is My Name | 8 |

CHARGE (1)
| 73 | SRT private pressing | CHARGE (LP, 1 known copy) | 750 |
| 92 | Kissing Spell KSLP 9205 | CHARGE (LP, reissue, revised sleeve, 500 only) | 20 |

CHARGE (2)
| 70 | private pressing | Zeugma/Boring Song (art sleeve) | 20 |
| 81 | Test Pressing | You Deserve More Than A Maybe (p/s, 500 only, existence unconfirmed) | 20 |

CHARGE (3)
| 80 | YCAFO Records | You Get What You Deserve/Rather B Crazy/Angel Deceast (foldout p/s) | 60 |
| 82 | Test Pressing TP 3 | Kings Cross/Brave New World (p/s) | 12 |

CHARGERS
| 84 | Charge BCSK 01 | Desperaroes/Are You Out There (p/s) | 60 |

MARK CHARIG
| 77 | Ogun OG 710 | PIPEDREAM (LP) | 15 |

(see also Bluesology, B.B. Blunder, Reg King, Centipede, Keith Tippett, Julie Tippett, Brotherhood Of Breath, Elton Dean, Ninesense)

CHARIOT
84	Shades SHADE 2	ALL ALONE AGAIN (EP)	12
84	Shades SHADE 1	THE WARRIOR (LP)	15
86	Shades SHADE 4	BURNING AMBITION (LP)	15

CHARIOTS
| 62 | Piccadilly 7N 35061 | Problem Girl/Song Of A Broken Heart | 15 |

CHARLATANS (U.K.)
90	Dead Dead Good GOOD ONE TWELVE	Indian Rope/You Can Talk To Me/Who Wants To Know (12", 1st issue with barcode on p/s)	8
90	Dead Dead Good SIT 70T	The Only One I Know/Imperial 109 (Edit)/Everything Changed (12", p/s)	10
90	Dead Dead Good SIT 74T	Then/Taurus Moaner/Then (Alternate Take)/Taurus Moaner (Instrumental) (12", p/s)	10
91	Situation Two SIT 84T	Me In Time/Occupation/Monster (12" p/s)	8
90	Situation Two SIT 74T	Then/Taurus Moaner/Then (Alternate Take)/Taurus Moaner (Instrumental) (12", mispressing with vocal version of "Taurus Moaner" on both sides)	8
92	Situation Two SIT 88T	Weirdo/Theme From "The Wish"/Sproston Green (U.S. Version)/ Weirdo (Alternate Take) (12", with art print)	10
93	Dead Dead Good GOOD1CD	Indian Rope/You Can Talk To Me/Who Wants To Know (CD single)	10
93	Beggars Banquet CHAR 7	Subterranean (live) (CD, free with 109 fan club magazine)	12
94	Beggars Banquet CHAR 9	I Never Want An Easy Life/If Me And He Were Ever To Get There (12" 1-sided promo, die cut sleeve)	8
00	MCA MCS 40231	Impossible/You Got It. I Want It	8
90	Situation Two SITU 30L	SOME FRIENDLY (LP, 'some friendly edition' in white PVC sleeve with inner)	15
91	Live Live Good CB 2	ISOLATION 21.2.91 (LP, official live bootleg, sold via fan club, 1,000 only)	30
92	Situation Two SITU 37	BETWEEN 10TH AND 11TH (LP)	20
92	Situation Two SITU 37	BETWEEN 10TH AND 11TH (CD, box set with cassette & video, promo only)	20
94	Beggars Banquet BBCD 147	UP TO OUR HIPS (CD, box set with cassette & video, promo only)	25
95	Beggars Banquet BBQLP 174	THE CHARLATANS (2-LP)	25
97	Beggars Banquet BBQLP 190	TELLIN' STORIES (LP)	25
98	Beggars Banquet BBQLP 198	MELTING POT (2-LP)	25

(see also Electric Crayons, Makin' Time)

CHARLATANS (U.S.)
| 69 | Philips SBL 7903 | THE CHARLATANS (LP) | 90 |

(see also Mike Wilhelm, Tongue & Groove, Dan Hicks & His Hot Licks)

BOBBY CHARLES
| 56 | London HLU 8247 | See You Later, Alligator/On Bended Knee | 2500 |
| 56 | London HLU 8247 | See You Later, Alligator/On Bended Knee (78) | 300 |

BOBBY CHARLES
| 78 | Bearsville J 15508 | Small Town Talk/Grow Too Old | 10 |
| 72 | Bearsville K 45516 | BOBBY CHARLES (LP) | 15 |

DON CHARLES
62	Decca F 11424	Walk With Me My Angel/Crazy Man, Crazy	10
62	Decca F 11464	The Hermit Of Misty Mountain/Moonlight Rendezvous	10
62	Decca F 11528	It's My Way Of Loving You/Guess That's The Way It Goes	10
62	Decca F 11645	Angel Of Love/Lucky Star	10
63	Decca F 11645	Heart's Ice Cold/Daybreak	8
63	HMV POP 1271	Tower Tall/Look Before You Love	5
64	HMV POP 1307	If You Don't Know I Ain't Gonna Tell Ya/Voice On The Phone	5

64	HMV POP 1332	Big Talk From A Little Man/She's Mine	10
65	HMV POP 1382	Forgetting Me, Loving Him/A Long Time Ago	5
65	HMV POP 1420	Dream On Little Dreamer/We Only Live Once	5
65	HMV POP 1478	I Could Conquer The World/Time Will Tell	5
66	HMV POP 1542	Out Of This Cold/From The Beginning	5
67	Parlophone R 5564	So Let It Be/Bring Your Love To Me	5
67	Parlophone R 5596	Have I Told You Lately/Time Waits For Nobody	5
68	Parlophone R 5659	If I Had The Chance/(I've Got Everything) I've Got You	5
68	Parlophone R 5688	The Drifter/Great To Be Livin'	60
68	Parlophone R 5688	The Drifter/Great To Be Livin' (DJ Copy)	85
68	Parlophone R 5712	Your Name Is On My Heart/How Can I	5
63	Decca DFE 8530	DON CHARLES (EP)	70
67	Parlophone PMC/PCS 7021	HAVE I TOLD YOU LATELY (LP, mono/stereo)	20

GARY CHARLES

71	B & C CB 159	You've Been Away Too Long/Lovely Linda	6

JIMMY CHARLES

60	London HLU 9206	A Million To One/Hop Scotch Hop	25
63	Windsor WPS 120	Pitter Pitter Patter/How You Gonna Treat Me Now	10

JOHN CHARLES

60	Cetra SP 785	Sixteen Tons/Love In Portofino	5
60	Cetra SP 786	La Fine (The End)/Non Dimenticar	5

RAY CHARLES

78s

58	London HLE 8768	Rockhouse (Parts 1 & 2)	30
59	London HLE 8917	What'd I Say (Parts 1 & 2)	40
59	London HLE 9009	I'm Movin' On/I Believe To My Soul	40
60	HMV POP 792	Georgia On My Mind/Carry Me Back To Old Virginny	60

SINGLES

58	London HLE 8768	Rockhouse (Parts 1 & 2)	30
59	London HLE 8917	What'd I Say (Parts 1 & 2)	25
59	London HLE 9009	I'm Movin' On/I Believe To My Soul	20
60	London HLE 9058	Let The Good Times Roll/Don't Let The Sun Catch You Cryin'	20
60	HMV POP 774	Sticks And Stones/Worried Life Blues	15
60	London HLK 9181	Tell The Truth/You Be My Baby	15
60	HMV POP 792	Georgia On My Mind/Carry Me Back To Old Virginny	5
60	London HLK 9251	Come Rain Or Come Shine/Tell Me You'll Wait For Me	5
61	HMV POP 825	Ruby/Hard Hearted Hannah	5
61	HMV POP 838	Them That Got/I Wonder	25
61	London HLK 9364	Early In The Mornin'/A Bit Of Soul	15
61	HMV POP 862	One Mint Julep/Let's Go	15
61	HMV POP 935	Hit The Road Jack/The Danger Zone	10
61	London HLK 9435	I Wonder Who/Hard Times	10
62	HMV POP 969	Unchain My Heart/But On The Other Hand Baby	7
62	HMV POP 1017	Hide Nor Hair/At The Club	10
63	HMV POP 1133	Don't Set Me Free/The Brightest Smile In Town	5
63	HMV POP 1161	Take These Chains From My Heart/No Letter Today	5
63	HMV POP 1202	No One/Without Love (There Is Nothing)	5
63	HMV POP 1221	Busted/Making Believe	7
64	HMV POP 1251	That Lucky Old Sun/Mississippi Mud	5
64	HMV POP 1272	Baby Don't You Cry/My Heart Cries For You	5
64	HMV POP 1315	My Baby Don't Dig Me/Something's Wrong	10
64	HMV POP 1333	No One To Cry To/A Tear Fell	5
64	HMV POP 1350	Smack Dab In The Middle/I Wake Up Crying	5
65	HMV POP 1383	Makin' Whoopee/Move It On Over	5
65	HMV POP 1392	Cry/Teardrops From My Eye	5
65	HMV POP 1414	Light Out Of Darkness/Please Forgive And Forget	5
65	HMV POP 1437	I Gotta Woman/Without A Song	5
65	HMV POP 1457	Love's Gonna Live Here/I'm A Fool To Care	5
65	HMV POP 1484	The Cincinnati Kid/That's All I Am To You	5
66	HMV POP 1502	Crying Time/When My Dreamboat Comes Home	5
66	HMV POP 1519	Together Again/You're Just About To Lose Your Clown	20
66	HMV POP 1537	Let's Go Get Stoned/The Train	20
66	HMV POP 1551	I Chose To Sing The Blues/Hopelessly	25
66	HMV POP 1566	Please Say You're Fooling/I Don't Need No Doctor	50
66	HMV POP 1566	Please Say You're Fooling/I Don't Need No Doctor (DJ Copy)	80
67	Atlantic 584 093	What'd I Say/I Got A Woman	8
67	HMV POP 1589	You Win Again/Bye Bye Love	5
67	HMV POP 1595	Somebody Oughta Write A Book About It/Here We Go Again	5
67	HMV POP 1607	In The Heat Of The Night/Something's Got To Change	5
67	Stateside SS 2071	Yesterday/Never Had Enough Of Nothing Yet	5
68	Stateside SS 2120	Eleanor Rigby/Understanding	5
71	Tangerine 6121 001	Booty Butt/Zig Zag	5

EPs

59	London Jazz EZK 19043	THE GREAT RAY CHARLES	15
59	London Jazz EZK 19048	SOUL BROTHERS (with Milt Jackson)	15
61	London REK 1306	WHAT'D I SAY	20
61	London REK 1317	RAY CHARLES AT NEWPORT	15
62	HMV 7EG 8729	HIT THE ROAD JACK	15
62	HMV 7EG 8781	I CAN'T STOP LOVING YOU	15
63	HMV 7EG 8783	THE BALLAD STYLE OF RAY CHARLES	10
63	HMV 7EG 8801	THE SWINGING STYLE OF RAY CHARLES	10
63	HMV 7EG 8807	BABY IT'S COLD OUTSIDE (with Betty Carter)	10
63	HMV 7EG 8812	TAKE THESE CHAINS FROM MY HEART	10
63	London REB 1407	THE ORIGINAL RAY CHARLES VOLUME ONE	10
63	London REB 1408	THE ORIGINAL RAY CHARLES VOLUME TWO	10
63	London REB 1409	THE ORIGINAL RAY CHARLES VOLUME THREE	10
64	HMV 7EG 8841	BUSTED	10

64	HMV 7EG 8861	RAY CHARLES SINGS	10
64	Realm REP 4001	THE YOUNG RAY CHARLES	10
66	HMV 7EG 8932	RAY CHARLES LIVE IN CONCERT	10
66	HMV 7EG 8951	RAY CHARLES SINGS SONGS OF BUCK OWENS	10

ALBUMS

58	London Jazz LTZ-K 15134	THE GREAT RAY CHARLES	50
59	London Jazz LTZ-K 15146	SOUL BROTHERS (with Milt Jackson, mono)	25
59	London Jazz SAH-K 6030	SOUL BROTHERS (with Milt Jackson, stereo)	30
59	London Jazz LTZ-K 15149	RAY CHARLES AT NEWPORT (mono)	25
59	London Jazz SAH-K 6008	RAY CHARLES AT NEWPORT (stereo)	30
59	London HA-E 2168	YES INDEED	50
59	London HA-E 2226	WHAT'D I SAY	40
60	London Jazz LTZ-K 15190	THE GENIUS OF RAY CHARLES	40
60	HMV CLP 1387/CSD 1320	THE GENIUS HITS THE ROAD (mono)	18
60	HMV CLP 1387/CSD 1320	THE GENIUS HITS THE ROAD (stereo)	25
60	London HA-K 2284	RAY CHARLES IN PERSON	25
61	HMV CLP 1449/CSD 1362	DEDICATED TO YOU (mono)	15
61	HMV CLP 1449/CSD 1362	DEDICATED TO YOU (stereo)	18
61	HMV CLP 1475/CSD 1384	GENIUS + SOUL = JAZZ (mono)	15
61	HMV CLP 1475/CSD 1384	GENIUS + SOUL = JAZZ (stereo)	18
62	HMV CLP 1520/CSD 1414	RAY CHARLES AND BETTY CARTER (mono)	15
62	HMV CLP 1520/CSD 1414	RAY CHARLES AND BETTY CARTER (stereo)	18
62	London Jazz LJZ-K 15238	THE GENIUS SINGS THE BLUES	25
62	HMV CLP 1580/CSD 1451	MODERN SOUNDS IN COUNTRY & WESTERN (mono)	20
62	HMV CLP 1580/CSD 1451	MODERN SOUNDS IN COUNTRY & WESTERN (stereo)	25
63	HMV CLP 1613/CSD 1477	MODERN SOUNDS IN COUNTRY & WESTERN VOL. TWO (mono)	20
63	HMV CLP 1613/CSD 1477	MODERN SOUNDS IN COUNTRY & WESTERN VOL. TWO (stereo)	25
63	HMV CLP 8022	THE ORIGINAL RAY CHARLES	15
63	London HA-K 8023	THE RAY CHARLES STORY VOL. 1	15
63	London HA-K 8024	THE RAY CHARLES STORY VOL. 2	15
63	HMV CLP 1626/CSD 1482	GREATEST HITS (stereo)	12
63	London HA-K 8035	THE GENIUS AFTER HOURS	20
63	London HA-K/SH-K 8045	SOUL MEETING (with Milt Jackson)	25
63	HMV CLP 1678	INGREDIENTS IN A RECIPE FOR SOUL	15
64	HMV CLP 1728/CSD 1537	SWEET AND SOUR TEARS (mono)	12
64	HMV CLP 1728/CSD 1537	SWEET AND SOUR TEARS (stereo)	15
64	HMV CLP 1795/CSD 1566	HAVE A SMILE WITH ME (mono)	12
64	HMV CLP 1795/CSD 1566	HAVE A SMILE WITH ME (stereo)	12
65	HMV CLP 1872/CSD 1696	LIVE IN CONCERT (mono)	12
65	HMV CLP 1872/CSD 1696	LIVE IN CONCERT (stereo)	12
65	HMV CLP 1914/CSD 1630	C&W MEETS R&B mono)	12
65	HMV CLP 1914/CSD 1630	C&W MEETS R&B stereo)	12

(see also Raelets, Milt Jackson)

ROGER CHARLES
| 73 | Dawn DNS 1038 | Understand Each Other/Can't Forget | 6 |

SONNY CHARLES (& CHECKMATES LTD)
67	Ember EMB S 240	Mastered The Art Of Love/Please Don't Take My World Away	40
69	A&M AMS 752	Black Pearl/Lazy Susan	10
70	A&M AMS 787	It Takes A Little Longer/Welfare Man	6

(see also Checkmates Ltd)

TINA CHARLES
69	CBS 4015	Nothing In The World/Millions Of Hearts	15
69	CBS 4307	In The Middle Of The Day/Rich Girl	40
69	CBS 4658	Good To Be Alive/Same Old Story	50

CHILI CHARLES
| 74 | Virgin V2009 | BUSY CORNER (LP) | 12 |
| 75 | Virgin V 2028 | QUICKSTEP (LP) | 15 |

CHARLES, PAULETTE & GEE
| 71 | G.G. GG 4515 | Shock And Shake (Version 3)/WINSTON WRIGHT: Roll On (Version 2) (as Charlie, Paulette & Gee) | 10 |
| 71 | G.G. GG 4517 | Rock And Shake (Version 3) (actually "Lover's Affair" by Charlie Ace & Maytones)/Roll On (Version 2) (actually "My Love And I" by Winston Wright) | 10 |

(see also Charlie Ace)

DICK CHARLESWORTH (& HIS CITY GENTS)
| 61 | Top Rank 35-104 | MEET THE GENTS (LP) | 15 |
| 62 | HMV CLP 1495 | YES INDEED IT'S THE GENTS (LP) | 15 |

CHARLIE
| 72 | Bumble GE 111 | Dream Hero/Lament | 15 |
| 73 | Decca F 13451 | I Need Your Love/I'm So Happy | 20 |

CHARLIE BOY
| 71 | Trojan TR 7823 | Funky Strip/UPSETTERS: Mellow Mood | 25 |

(see also Lee Perry/Upsetters)

CHARLIE & FAY
| 72 | Pama 853 | Big 7/YOUTH PROFESSIONAL BAND : Version | 8 |

CHARLIE PARKAS
| 80 | Paranoid Plastics PPS 1 | The Ballad Of Robin Hood/Space Invaders (p/s) | 5 |

(see also Alberto Y Lost Trios Paranoias)

CHARLIES BROTHER
| 84 | Lost Moment LMO 100 | Wishing Tree/Further Adventures Of | 25 |

CHARLY & THE BOURBON FAMILY
| 71 | Decca F 23164 | Acapulco Gold/Boogachi | 15 |

CHARMAINES
| 98 | Kent 6T 18 | I Idolize You/M&M & THE PEANUTS: Can't Say No | 25 |

CHARMER

| 56 | Melodisc MEL 1353 | Back To Back, Belly To Belly/Is She Is Or Is She Ain't (78) | 10 |

CHARMERS (JAMAICA)

61	Blue Beat BB 42	Lonely Boy/I Am Going Back Home	20
62	Blue Beat BB 114	Crying Over You/Now You Want To Cry	20
63	Blue Beat BB 157	Time After Time/Done Me Wrong (with Prince Buster's Band)	15
60s	Blue Beat	How Could I Forget/Why Won't You Come Home? (with Prince Buster's Band) (white label only)	75
63	R&B JB 118	Angel Love/My Heart	20
63	R&B JB 121	Oh Why Baby/ROLAND ALPHONSO: Perhaps	30
64	R&B JB 151	What's The Use/I Am Through	20
64	R&B JB 156	In My Soul/Beware	20
64	Blue Beat BB 204	I'm Back/It's A Dream	20
64	Blue Beat BB 238	Waiting For You/You Are My Sunshine	20
64	Blue Beat BB 251	Dig Then Prince (actually Dip Them Prince)/Girl Of My Dreams (as The Charmer)	25
65	Blue Beat BB 279	Nobody Takes My Baby Away From Me/ BUSTER ALLSTARS: Mules Mules Mules	75
66	Blue Beat BB 345	Oh My Baby/STRANGER COLE: When The Party Is Over	20
66	Ska Beat JB 237	Best Friend/MAYTALS: My Darling	25
66	Rio R 78	You Don't Know/CORNELL CAMPBELL & ROY PANTON: Sweetest Girl	20
68	Coxsone CS 7043	Things Going Wrong/KEN BOOTHE: You Keep Me Hanging On	200
68	Treasure Isle TI 7036	Keep On Going (actually by Lloyd Charmers)/SILVERTONES: Don't Say No	20
70	Duke DU 87	Colour Him Father/Version	30
70	Trojan TR 7773	Sweeter She Is (actually by Lloyd Charmers, Dave Barker & Slim Smith)/ Fire Fire (actually by Lloyd Charmers)	12
70	Explosion EX 2026	Can I Get Next To You?/Big Five	7
70	Explosion EX 2035	Sweet Back/Music Talk (actually by Lloyd Charmers)	7
71	Bullet BU 473	Reggae In Wonderland/Wonder (Version)	6
71	Explosion EX 2045	Skinhead Train/TONY & CHARMERS: Everstrong (B-side with Tony Binns)	100
71	Explosion EX 2055	Reggae In Wonderland/Wonder - Version (both actually by Byron Lee & Dragonaires)	7
71	Supreme SUP 220	Just My Imagination/Gotta Get A Message To You (actually by Dave Barker)	25
71	Green Door GD 4000	Rasta Never Fails (actually by Lloyd Charmers & Ken Boothe)/ CHARMERS ALL STARS: Rasta Version	7
71	Green Door GD 4001	One Big Unhappy Family/CONSCIOUS MINDS: Africa Is Paradise	12
71	Pama Supreme PS 340	Red Head Duck/Jingle Jangle	6

(see also Spanishtown Skabeats, Lloyd & Ken, Lloydie & Lowbites, Lloyd Terrell)

LLOYD CHARMERS

67	Coxsone CS 7023	Time Is Getting Hard/TONY GREGORY: I Sit By The Shore	100
69	Duke DU 15	Cooyah/UNIQUES: Forever	20
69	Duke DU 16	Follow This Sound/Why Pretend	20
69	Duke DU 25	5 To 5/SOUL STIRRERS: Come See About Me	25
69	Duke DU 36	Safari (The Far East)/Last Laugh	15
69	Songbird SB 1001	Ling Ting Tong/LLOYD ROBINSON: Sweet Sweet	12
69	Songbird SB 1007	Duckey Luckey/In The Spirit	20
69	Camel CA 30	Confidential/TOMMY COWAN: House In Session	12
69	Explosion EX 2001	Death A Come/Zylon	25
70	Explosion EX 2032	Vengeance/Look A-Py-Py	35
70	Explosion EX 2034	Ready Talk/There Is Something About You	7
70	Trojan TR 7788	Oh Me Oh My/I Did It	12
70	Bullet BU 435	Dollars And Bonds/Sounds Familiar	40
70	Bullet BU 442	Reggae A Bye Bye/DAVE BARKER:Doctor Jekyll	15
70	Escort ES 820	Soul Of England/Shang I	18
70	Escort ES 836	Hi Shan/Soul At Large	15
70	Smash SMA 2302	Big Red Bum Ball/BUNNIE LEE ALLSTARS: Big Bum Ball Version	7
71	Black Swan BW 1405	Love You The Most/LOW BITES:Version	8
73	Green Door GD 4064	Save The People (as L. Charmers)/SCOTTY: Salvation Train	10
74	Harry J. HJ 6662	I'm Gonna Love You Just A Little Bit More/Have I Sinned	6
71	Pama Supreme PS 339	Shaft/Harry's Mood	10
71	Pama Supreme PS 346	Show Business/DEBBY & LLOYD: Gloria	8
72	Pama Supreme PS 355	Desiderata/Desiderata Music	8
70	Trojan TTL 25	REGGAE IS TIGHT (LP, orange/white label)	30
70	Trojan TTL 30	REGGAE CHARM (LP)	25
70	Pama SECO 25	HOUSE IN SESSION (LP, with Hippy Boys)	100

(see also Charmers, Lloyd Tyrell/Terrell, Ken Boothe, Hippy Boys, Wayne Howard, Martia Riley, Eric Donaldson)

CHARMERS (U.S.)

| 58 | Vogue V 9095 | He's Gone/Oh! Yes | 500 |
| 58 | Vogue V 9095 | He's Gone/Oh! Yes (78) | 45 |

CHARMETTES

| 63 | London HLR 9820 | Please Don't Kiss Me Again/What Is A Tear | 40 |

CHARMS (JAMAICA)

| 64 | Island WI 154 | Carry, Go, Bring Home (actually by Justin Hinds & Dominoes)/ Hill And Gully (actually by L. Reid's Group) | 15 |
| 66 | Rio R 98 | Everybody Say Yeah/This World Is Yours | 20 |

CHARMS (U.S.)

55	Parlophone MSP 6155	Hearts Of Stone/Ko Ko Mo (I Love You So)	500
55	Parlophone R3988	Hearts Of Stone/Ko Ko Mo (I Love You So) (78)	60
55	Parlophone DP 412	Hearts Of Stone/Bazoom, I Need Your Lovin' (78) (export issue)	50
55	Parlophone DP 423	Two Hearts/The First Time We Met (78) (export issue)	60

(see also Otis Williams & Charms, Tiny Topsy, Harmonizing Four)

CHARTBUSTERS

| 64 | London HLU 9906 | She's The One/Slippin' Thru Your Fingers | 15 |
| 64 | London HLU 9934 | Why/Stop The Music | 10 |

CHASE

| 71 | Epic EPC 7301 | Get It On In The Morning/River | 6 |

LINCOLN CHASE

| 57 | London HLU 8495 | Johnny Klingeringding/You're Driving Me Crazy (What Did I Do) | 30 |
| 61 | Philips PB 1103 | Miss Orangutang/Walking Slowly | 25 |

CHASERS
65	Decca F 12302	Hey Little Girl/That's What They Call Love	50
66	Parlophone R 5451	Inspiration/She's Gone Away	150
67	Philips BF 1546	The Ways Of A Man/Summer Girl	15

CHASERS
| 84 | SRT SRT4KS 304 | Raiders/Final Stand (300 only) | 60 |

CHASERS
| 01 | Changes One ChangesCD-002 | ONWARDS & UPWARDS EP (CD EP, 1,060 copies only, many signed) | 18 |

(see also Energetic Krusher, Wildhearts)

CHATEAUX
83	Ebony EBON 13	CHAINED AND DESPERATE (LP)	20
84	Ebony EBON 18	FIRE POWER (LP)	15
85	Ebony EBON 31	HIGHLY STRUNG (LP)	15

DEBABRATA CHAUDHURI
| 68 | MFP SMFP 2101 | SITAR MUSIC MEDITATIONS (LP) | 15 |

CHEAP BOOTS
| 70 | Fontana 6001 020 | Baby I Do Need You/Come And Stay With Me | 6 |

CHEAP TRICK
78	Epic S EPC 6199	So Good To See You/You're All Talk (withdrawn)	20
79	Epic S EPC 7144	Voices/Surrender (withdrawn)	5
79	Epic S EPC 7258	I Want You To Want Me (live)/I Want You To Want Me (studio) (DJ only)	6
79	Epic CT-1	Dream Police/Voice/I'll Be With You Tonight (sampler, promo only)	10

CHEATERS
| 80 | Parlophone R6041 | Nuthin' Ever Happens On Saturday/Hard Work/Stop Pushing (p/s) | 5 |
| 80 | Pre Fab Z 01 | I Wanna Be A Policeman/Baby What Do You Want Me To Do/From The Hip (foldout p/s) | 8 |

CHEATIN' HEARTS
| 66 | Columbia DB 8048 | Zip-Tease/The Bad Kind | 15 |

CHUBBY CHECKER
59	Top Rank JAR 154	The Class/Schooldays, Oh, Schooldays	30
59	Top Rank JAR 154	The Class/Schooldays, Oh, Schooldays (78)	15
60	Columbia DB 4503	The Twist/Toot	10
60	Columbia DB 4541	The Hucklebuck/Whole Lotta Shakin' Goin' On	15
61	Columbia DB 4591	Pony Time/Oh Susannah	10
61	Columbia DB 4652	Good Good Loving/Mess Around	15
61	Columbia DB 4691	Let's Twist Again/Everything's Gonna Be All Right	10
61	Columbia DB 4728	The Fly/That's The Way It Goes	10
62	Columbia DB 4808	Slow Twistin'/The Lose Your Inhibitions Twist	5
62	Columbia DB 4876	Dancin' Party/Gotta Get Myself Together	5
62	Pye International 7N 25160	Dancin' Party/Gotta Get Myself Together (reissue)	5
62	Cameo Parkway P 806	What Do You Say/Something To Shout About	6
62	Cameo Parkway P 824	Let's Twist Again/The Twist	5
62	Cameo Parkway P 849	Limbo Rock/Hitch Hiker	5
63	Cameo Parkway P 862	Let's Limbo Some More/Twenty Miles	5
63	Cameo Parkway P 873	Black Cloud/Birdland	5
63	Cameo Parkway P 879	Twist It Up/Surf Party	5
63	Cameo Parkway P 890	Loddy Lo/Hooka Tooka	8
64	Cameo Parkway P 907	Hey Bobba Needle/Spread Joy	10
64	Cameo Parkway P 920	Lazy Elsie Molly/Rosie	5
64	Cameo Parkway P 922	She Wants T'Swim/You Better Believe It Baby	15
65	Cameo Parkway P 936	Lovely, Lovely/The Weekend's Here	30
65	Cameo Parkway P 949	(At The) Discotheque/Do The Freddie	50
65	Cameo Parkway P 949	(At The) Discotheque/Do The Freddie (DJ copy)	150
65	Cameo Parkway P 959	Everything's Wrong/Cu Ma La Be Stay	40
65	Cameo Parkway P 959	Everything's Wrong/Cu Ma La Be Stay (DJ copy)	120
65	Cameo Parkway P 965	Two Hearts Make One Love/You Just Don't Know (What You Do To Me)	200
65	Cameo Parkway P 989	Hey You Little Boogaloo/Pussy Cat	30
65	Cameo Parkway P 989	Hey You Little Boogaloo/Pussy Cat (DJ Copy)	50
69	Buddah 201 045	Back In the U.S.S.R./Windy Cream	5
71	London HL 10331	Let's Go Down/Goodbye Victoria	5
73	Pye Int 25620	Gypsy/Reggae My Way	25
76	London HLU 10515	(At The) Discotheque/Slow Twistin'	5
78	London HLU 10557	You Just Don't Know (What You Do To Me)/ Two Hearts Make One Love (reissue)	10
78	London HLU 10557	You Just Don't Know (What You Do To Me)/ Two Hearts Make One Love (reissue) (DJ Copy)	20
93	Kent 6T 9	You Can't Lose Something You've Never Had/TEARDROPS: Here Comes The Lonliness	20
62	Columbia SEG 8155	KING OF THE TWIST (EP)	8
62	Cameo Parkway CPE 550	DANCIN' PARTY (EP)	12
61	Columbia 33SX 1315	TWIST WITH CHUBBY CHECKER (LP)	20
61	Columbia 33SX 1341	FOR TWISTERS ONLY (LP)	20
61	Columbia 33SX 1365	IT'S PONY TIME (LP)	20
62	Columbia 33SX 1445	TWIST ALONG WITH CHUBBY CHECKER (LP)	20
63	Cameo Parkway P 7036	CHUBBY CHECKER (LP)	15
71	London SHZ 8419	CHEQUERED (LP)	25

CHUBBY CHECKER & BOBBY RYDELL
62	Columbia DB 4802	Teach Me To Twist/Swingin' Together	10
62	Cameo Parkway C 205	Jingle Bell Rock/What Are You Doing New Year's Eve?	10
64	Cameo Parkway CPE 554	CHUBBY CHECKER AND BOBBY RYDELL IN LONDON (EP)	15
62	Columbia 33SX 1424	CHECKER AND RYDELL (LP)	15

CHUBBY CHECKER & DEE DEE SHARP
| 62 | Cameo Parkway C 1029 | DOWN TO EARTH (LP) | 30 |

(see also Dream Lovers, Bobby Rydell, Dee Dee Sharp)

CHECKERS
| 54 | Parlophone DP 403 | Over The Rainbow/CECIL YOUNG QUARTET: Oooh-Diga-Gow (78, export issue) | 25 |

CHECKMATES

61	Piccadilly 7N 35010	Rockin' Minstrel/Pompeii	10
63	Decca F 11603	You've Gotta Have A Gimmick Today/Westpoint	25
64	Decca F 11844	Sticks And Stones/Please Listen To Me	30
65	Decca F 12114	Around/I've Got To Know Now	15
65	Parlophone R 5337	Stop That Music/I've Been In Love Before	15
66	Parlophone R 5402	(You Got) The Gamma Goochie/It Ain't Right	20
66	Parlophone R 5495	Every Day Is Just The Same/I'll Be Keeping The Score	20
61	Pye NPL 18061	THE CHECKMATES (LP)	40

(see also Original Checkmates)

CHECKMATES LTD

67	Ember EMB S 235	Do The Walk (The Temptation Walk)/Glad For You	5

(see also Sonny Charles & Checkmates Ltd)

CHEE CHEE AND PEPPY

71	Buddah 2011 083	I Know I'm In Love/My Love Will Never Fade Away	5

CHEEKY

80	Woodbine St. WSR 005	Don't Mess Around/Get Outa My 'Ouse (no p/s)	40

CHEERS

54	Capitol CL 14189	Bazoom (I Need Your Lovin')/Arrivederci	30
55	Capitol CL 14248	Bernie's Tune/Whadaya Want?	20
55	Capitol CL 14280	Blueberries/Can't We Be More Than Friends	20
55	Capitol CL 14337	I Must Be Dreaming/Fancy Meeting You Here	20
55	Capitol CL 14377	Black Denim Trousers And Motorcycle Boots/Some Night In Alaska	40
55	Capitol CL 14377	Black Denim Trousers And Motorcycle Boots/Some Night In Alaska (78)	10
56	Capitol CL 14561	Chicken/Don't Do Anything	20
56	Capitol CL 14601	Que Pasa Muchacha/BERT CONVY: Heaven On Earth	10
56	Capitol EAP1 584	THE CHEERS (EP)	60

(see also Bert Convy [& Thunderbirds])

CHEETAHS

64	Philips BF 1362	Mecca/Goodnight Kiss	20
65	Philips BF 1383	Soldier Boy/Johnny	20
65	Philips BF 1412	Goodbye Baby (Baby Goodbye)/That's How It Goes	15
65	Philips BF 1453	Whole Lotta Love/The Party	15
66	Philips BF 1499	The Russian Boat Song/Gamble	15

(see also Carl Wayne & Cheetahs)

CHEFS

80	Attatrix RB 10	SWEETIE EP	15
81	Graduate GRAD 11	24 Hours/Thrush	12

CHELMSFORD COUNTY HIGH SCHOOL FOLK GROUP

70	Private Pressing	CHELMSFORD COUNTY HIGH SCHOOL FOLK GROUP (LP)	25

CHELSEA

77	Step Forward SF 2	Right To Work/The Loner (p/s, original pressing in card p/s)	15
77	Step Forward SF 2	Right To Work/The Loner (p/s)	8
77	Step Forward SF 5	High Rise Living/No Admission (p/s)	10
78	Step Forward SF 8	Urban Kids/No Flowers (p/s)	8
80	Step Forward SF 14	No One's Coming Outside/What Would You Do (p/s)	6
80	Step Forward SF 15	Look At the Outside/Don't Get Me Wrong (p/s)	6
80	Step Forward SF 16	No Escape/Decide (p/s)	6
82	Step Forward SF 22	Stand Out/Last Drink (p/s)	5
84	Chelsea CH 001	Give Me More/Sympathy For The Devil (p/s)	5
79	Step Forward SFLP 2	CHELSEA (LP, with inner sleeve)	25
81	Step Forward SFLP 5	ALTERNATIVE HITS (LP)	20
82	Step Forward SFLP 7	EVACUATE (LP)	15
84	Picasso PIK 003	LIVE AND WELL (LP)	12

CHELSEA SQUAD

72	Penny Farthing PEN 782	Blue Is The Colour/All Sing Together (Chelsea Football Team)	5
84	W&A YZ 23	Back On The Ball/(Club Mix) (blue vinyl, p/s)	5

CHEMICAL

92	Head Press SRT 92LS 3170	Distrurbance/Paranoia (12")	10
92	Head Press HP 002	THE VIRUS EP (12")	12
92	Basement BRSS 017	Hex/Sub Sector (12")	10

(see also Two Dark Troopers, DJ Chemistry Meets Jack Smooth)

CHEMICAL ALICE

81	Acidic GNOME 1	The Judge/Goodnight Vienna/Lands Of Home/Henry The King (12", p/s)	40

(see also Marillion)

CHEMICAL BROTHERS

91	Eastern Bloc	Sea Of Beats/Sea Of Beats (Justin Robertson Mix) (12", p/s, as Ariel)	80
91	Deconstruction PT 44888	Rollercoaster/Mustn't Grumble/Mustn't Grumble (God's Grumble Mix) (12", as Ariel)	30
93	Dust Brothers DB's 333	Song To The Siren (12", as Dust Brothers, no p/s, 500 only)	60
93	Junior Boys Own JBO 10	Song To The Siren/Song To The Siren (Sabres Of Paradise Mixes) (12", p/s)	30
94	Boys Own COLLECT 004	14TH CENTURY SKY EP (12", no p/s, as Dust Brothers)	20
94	Junior Boys Own JBO 20	MY MERCURY MOUTH EP (12", JBO sleeve, as Dust Brothers)	25
95	Junior Boys Own CHEMS TI	Leave Home/Leave Home (Sabres Of Paradise)/Let Me In Mate (12", p/s)	15
95	Junior Boys Own	Leave Home (Underworld Mix One)/Leave Home (Underworld Mix Two) (12", p/s)	15
95	Junior Boys Own XDUSTLP1	EXIT PLANET DUST (2-LP)	15
99	Freestyle Dust XDUST LP4	SURRENDER (2-LP, gatefold)	20
97	Freestyle Dust XDUST LP2	DIG YOUR OWN HOLE (2-LP, gatefold)	18
02	Virgin XDUST LP5	COME WITH US (2-LP)	18
04	Virgin XDUST LP7	PUSH THE BUTTON (2-LP)	18

CLIFTON CHENIER

69	Action ACT 4550	Black Gal/Frogs Legs	15
70	Specialty SNTF 5012	BAYOU BLUES (LP)	20
70	Harvest MHSP 4002	CLIFTON CHENIER'S VERY BEST (LP)	50

| 79 | Flyright FLY 539 | ZYDECO BLUES (LP, with other artists) ....20 |

CHEQUERED PAST

| 85 | Heavy Metal America | CHEQUERED PAST (LP, picture disc, 1,000 only) ....30 |

(see also Steve Jones)

CHER

65	Liberty LIB 66114	All I Really Want To Do/I'm Gonna Love You 5
66	Liberty LIB 66136	Where Do You Go/See See Rider 5
66	Liberty LIB 66160	Bang Bang (My Baby Shot Me Down)/Our Day Will Come 5
66	Liberty LIB 12034	I Feel Something In The Air/Come To Your Window 5
66	Liberty LIB 12038	Sunny/She's No Better Than Me 5
67	Liberty LIB 12046	Mama (When My Dollies Have Babies)/Behind The Door 5
67	Liberty LBF 15038	You Better Sit Down Kids/Elusive Butterfly 5
68	Atlantic 584 278	Walk On Gilded Splinters/Tonight I'll Be Staying Here With You 10
69	Atco 226 003	For What It's Worth/Hangin' On 5
71	MCA MU 1137	Classified 1A/Don't Put It On Me 5
72	MCA MU 1148	The Way Of Love/Fire And Rain 5
72	MCA MU 1158	Living In A House Divided/One Honest Man 5
72	MCA MU 1168	Don't Hide Your Love/First Time 5
75	Phil Spector Intl. 2010 006	A Love Like Yours (with Nilsson)/Hangin' On 20
76	Phil Spector Intl. 2010 013	A Woman's Story/Baby I Love You 15
66	Liberty LEP 4047	THE HITS OF CHER (EP) 15
65	Liberty LBY 3058	ALL I REALLY WANT TO DO (LP, mono) 20
65	Liberty (S)LBY 3058	ALL I REALLY WANT TO DO (LP, stereo) 20
66	Liberty LBY 3072	THE SONNY SIDE OF CHER (LP, mono) 15
66	Liberty (S)LBY 3072	THE SONNY SIDE OF CHER (LP, stereo) 15
66	Liberty LBY 3081	CHER (LP, mono) 20
66	Liberty (S)LBY 3081	CHER (LP, stereo) 20
68	Liberty LBL/LBS 83051	WITH LOVE, CHER (LP) 15
69	Atco 226 026/228 026	3614 JACKSON HIGHWAY (LP, gatefold sleeve, mono/stereo) 15

(see also Sonny & Cher, Caesar & Cleo, Nilsson)

VIVIENNE CHERING

| 66 | Decca F 12360 | I'll Do My Crying Tomorrow/Make My Dreams Come True ....10 |

(see also Flip & Dateliners)

CHEROKEE

| 71 | Probe PRO 550 | Girl, I've Got News For You/Write To You ....10 |

CHEROKEES (U.K.)

64	Decca F 11915	You've Done It Again Little Girl/Girl Girl Girl 10
64	Columbia DB 7341	Seven Daffodils/Are You Back In My World Now 15
65	Columbia DB 7473	Wondrous Place/Send Me All Your Love 10
65	Columbia DB 7704	I Will Never Turn My Back On You/Dig A Little Deeper 10
66	Columbia DB 7822	Land Of A 1000 Dances/Everybody's Needs 20

(see also Lee Diamond)

CHEROKEES (U.S.)

| 61 | Pye International 7N 25066 | Cherokee/Harlem Nocturne ....15 |

CHERRY

| 80s | Crashed Records CAR 91 | He's A Bum/He Rides With Me ....10 |

CHERRY BOYS

| 81 | Open Eye OE5 | Man To Man/So Much Confusion (p/s) ....6 |

DON CHERRY (1)

| 56 | Brunswick 05538 | Wanted Someone To Love/The Thrill Is Gone ....10 |
| 57 | Philips JK 1013 | The Last Dance/Don't You Worry (jukebox edition) ....15 |

DON CHERRY (2)

73	JCOA/Virgin J2001	RELATIVITY SUITE (LP) 25
74	Sonet SNTF 653	ETERNAL NOW (LP) 25
78	Sonet SNFF 669	LIVE IN ANKARA (LP) 25

CHERRY ORCHARD

88	Red Honey (No Cat. No)	So Blind (p/s, 1-sided flexi) 15
89	Red Honey ORCHARD 1	SING SISTER GLORY (12" EP) 18
90	Red Honey ORCHARD 3	For What It's Worth/For What It's Worth (Version) (12", no p/s, promo only) 18
90	Red Honey ORCHARD 2	HEALING FAITH LIKE FIRE (LP) 15

CHERRY PEOPLE

68	MGM MGM 1438	And Suddenly/Imagination 40
68	MGM MGM 1438	And Suddenly/Imagination (DJ copy) 60
69	MGM MGM 1472	Gotta Get Back/I'm The One Who Loves You 15
69	MGM MGM 1489	Light Of Love/On To Something New 8
69	MGM MGM 1489	Light Of Love/I'm The One Who Loves You 8
75	Black Magic BM 112	And Suddenly/Imagination (reissue) 8

CHERRY PIES

| 64 | Black Swan WI 448 | Do You Keep Dreaming/Sweeter Than Cherry Pie ....20 |

CHERRY SMASH

67	Track 604 017	Sing Songs Of Love/Movie Star 20
68	Decca F 12838	Goodtime Sunshine/Little Old Country Home Town 20
69	Decca F 12884	Fade Away Maureen/Green Plant 60

JIMMY CHERRY

| 76 | Gull GULS 36 | Capella/Slow Burning ....8 |

FRANKIE CHERVAL

| 62 | MGM MGM 1183 | How Come/Tag Along ....5 |

PETE CHESTER

| 60 | Pye 7N 15305 | Ten Swinging Bottles/Whole Lotta Shakin' On The Range (with Consulates) ....20 |
| 61 | Pye International 7N 25074 | Three Old Maids/Forest Fire (as Pete Chester & Group) ....20 |

(see also Five Chesternuts)

VIC CHESTER
57	Decca F 10882	Rock-A-Billy/First Date, First Kiss, First Love	15

CHESTERFIELDS
86	HOusehold Goods HOLD IT	Goodbye Goodbye/Better Smile/Last Train to Yeovil/Hopes for Lauren and Joseph (12")	8
86	Subway Org. SUBWAY 7	Completely & Utterly/Girl On A Boat (foldover p/s with insert in poly bag)	5
87	Subway Org. SUBORG 003	KETTLE (LP)	12
87	Subway Org. SUBORG 005	WESTWARD HO (LP)	12

MORRIS CHESTNUT
79	Grapevine GRP 128	Too Darn Soulful/You Don't Love Me Anymore (	20
79	Grapevine GRP 128	Too Darn Soulful/You Don't Love Me Anymore (DJ Copy)	30

CHEVIOT RANTERS
72	Topic 12T	THE SOUND OF THE CHEVIOTS (LP)	20
73	Topic 12TS 222	THE CHEVIOT HILLS (LP)	18
74	Topic 12TS 245	CHEVIOT BARN DANCE (LP)	18

CHEVLONS
66	Pye 7N 17145	Too Long Alone/It's My Problem	5

CHEVRONS (1)
60	Top Rank JAR 308	Lullaby/Day After Forever	8

CHEVRONS (2)
79	Shy Talk	Sindy's Got An Action Man/No More Tears (p/s)	25

CHEVY
80	Avatar AAA 104	Too Much Loving/See The Light (company sleeve)	20
80	Avatar AAA 107	The Taker/Life On The Run (p/s)	20
81	Avatar AAA 114	Just Another Day/Rock On	12
80	Avatar AALP 5001	THE TAKER (LP, with inner sleeve)	18

CHEYNES (1)
63	Columbia DB 7153	Respectable/It's Gonna Happen To You	100
64	Columbia DB 7368	Going To The River/Cheyne-Re-La	100
65	Columbia DB 7464	Down And Out/Stop Running Around	100

(see also Peter Bardens, Peter B's, Fleetwood Mac, Mark Leeman Five, Bo Street Runners)

CHEYNES (2)
71	Bell BLL 1144	April Fool/Gotta Get Back	6

CHIC
78	Atlantic K 11209	Le Freak/Savoir Faire (12")	10
79	Atlantic K 11310 (T)	Good Time /A Warm Summer Night (12")	8
79	Atlantic K11385T	My Forbidden Lover/What About Me? (12")	10

CHICAGO
69	CBS 4381	Questions 67 And 68/Listen	6
69	CBS 4503	I'm A Man (Parts 1 & 2) (withdrawn)	20
69	CBS 4715	I'm A Man/Does Anyone Really Know What Time It Is? (promo p/s)	25
69	CBS 66221	CHICAGO TRANSIT AUTHORITY (2-LP, orange label)	18
71	CBS 66405	IV (AT CARNEGIE HALL) (4-LP, orange label)	20
79	CBS 86093	STREET PLAYER (LP)	12

CHICAGO LINE
66	Philips BF 1488	Shimmy Shimmy Ko Ko Bop/Jump Back	200

(see also Mike Patto, Bo Street Runners, Viv Prince)

CHICAGO LOOP
66	Stateside SS 564	(When She Needs Good Lovin') She Comes To Me/This Must Be The Place	10

CHICANES
81	Dinosaur Discs DD 003	Cry A Little/Further Thoughts (p/s)	20
88	Bam Caruso NRIC 039	Cry A Little/Further Thoughts (p/s)	20

CHICK WITH TED CAMERON & D.J.'S
60	Pye 7N 15292	Early In The Morning/Cool Water	40

CHICKEN SHACK
67	Blue Horizon 57-3135	It's OK With Me Baby/When My Left Eye Jumps	15
68	Blue Horizon 57-3143	Worried About My Woman/Six Nights In Seven	15
68	Blue Horizon 57-3146	When The Train Comes Back/Hey Baby	15
69	Blue Horizon 57-3153	I'd Rather Go Blind/Night Life	15
69	Blue Horizon 57-3160	Tears In The Wind/The Things You Put Me Through	15
70	Blue Horizon 57-3168	Maudie/Andalucian Blues	10
70	Blue Horizon 57-3176	Sad Clown/Tired Eyes	15
73	Deram DM 381	Time Goes Passing By/Poor Boy	8
73	Deram DM 396	You Know You Could Be Right/The Loser	8
74	CBS 1832	I'd Rather Go Blind/Sad Clown	5
68	Blue Horizon 7-63203	FORTY BLUE FINGERS FRESHLY PACKED AND READY TO SERVE (LP, 1st pressing with 'stereo' sticker on sleeve)	80
69	Blue Horizon 7-63209	O.K. KEN? (LP, gatefold sleeve, 1st pressing with 'stereo' sticker on sleeve)	80
69	Blue Horizon 7-63218	100 TON CHICKEN (LP, gatefold, 1st pressing with 'stereo' sticker on sleeve)	80
70	Blue Horizon 7-63861	ACCEPT CHICKEN SHACK (LP, gatefold sleeve)	50
71	Deram SDL 5	IMAGINATION LADY (LP, gatefold sleeve, brown/white label with large Deram label)	50
72	Deram SDL 5	IMAGINATION LADY (LP, gatefold sleeve, later pressing with red/white label)	20
73	Deram SML 1100	UNLUCKY BOY (LP)	25

(see also Errol Dixon, Fleetwood Mac, Christine Perfect, Carmen Macrae, Broken Glass)

CHICKEN SHED
77	Colby AJ 370	ALICE (LP, hand-made sleeves)	90

CHICKS
63	Oriole CB 1828	What Are Boys Made Of?/Over The Mountain	20

CHICORY TIP
71	CBS 7118	My Girl Sunday/Doctor Man	20
71	CBS 7595	I Love Onions/Don't Hang Jack	20

CHIEF
81	Swamp WAM 114	Don't Touch The Receiver/Icebreaker (not released in p/s)	20

CHIEFS
58	London HLU 8624	Apache/Dee's Dream	20
58	London HLU 8624	Apache/Dee's Dream (78)	10
58	London HLU 8720	Enchiladas!/Moments To Remember	20
58	London HLU 8720	Enchiladas!/Moments To Remember (78)	10

CHIFFONS
63	Stateside SS 172	He's So Fine/Oh! My Lover	10
63	Stateside SS 202	One Fine Day/Why Am I So Shy	10
63	Stateside SS 230	A Love So Fine/Only My Friend	15
64	Stateside SS 254	I Have A Boyfriend/I'm Gonna Dry Your Eyes	15
64	Stateside SS 332	Sailor Boy/When Summer's Through	22
65	Stateside SS 437	Nobody Knows What's Going On (In My Mind But Me)/The Real Thing	30
66	Stateside SS 512	Sweet Talkin' Guy/Did You Ever Go Steady	10
66	Stateside SS 533	Out Of This World/Just A Boy	15
66	Stateside SS 559	Stop, Look And Listen/March	25
67	Stateside SS 578	My Boyfriend's Back/I Got Plenty Of Nuttin'	22
64	Stateside SE 1012	THEY'RE SO FINE (EP)	80
63	Stateside SL 10040	THE CHIFFONS - HE'S SO FINE (LP)	100
66	Stateside S(S)L 10190	SWEET TALKIN' GUY (LP)	100
72	London ZGP 125	SWEET TALKING GUY LP, Reissue)	15
84	Impact Act 002	DOO LANG DOO LANG (LP)	15
85	Impact ACT 007	FLIPS FLOPS & RARITIES (LP)	12

(see also Four Pennies)

CHILD
77	Pentagon PENT 1	Whats A Nice Girl Like You/Sad One Sided Love Affair	12

ANTHONY CHILD/ANDREW READ
99	Fat Cat 12FAT 031	Speedranch/Jansky Noise (12" EP, 'bullet hole' sleeve)	12

LORRAINE CHILD
64	Decca F 11969	You/Not This Time	10

ALAN CHILDE
76	Epic SEPC 4183	Rainmaker/Mind Blowing Love	6

SONNY CHILDE (& T.N.T.)
65	Decca F 12218	Giving Up On Love/Mighty Nice (Of You To Call)	150
66	Polydor 56108	Two Lovers/Ain't That Good News	15
66	Polydor 56141	Heartbreak/I Still Love You (as Sonny Childe & T.N.T.)	35
66	Polydor 582 003	TO BE CONTINUED (LP)	40

CHILD HAROLDS
68	Trident TRA 201	Diary Of My Mind/Loophole	30

BILLY CHILDISH
91	Hangman 37 UP	50 ALBUMS GREAT (LP)	30
93	Damaged Books DAMBOOK 1	TREMBLING OF LIFE (3 x 7" box set with book & 2 postcards)	20
87	Hangman HANG 9-UP	THE 1982 CASSETES (LP, blue & white sleeve, with poster)	50
87	Hangman HANG 9-UP	THE 1982 CASSETES (LP, blue & white sleeve, without poster)	30
88	Hangman HANG 16-UP	POEMS OF LAUGHTER & VIOLENCE (LP)	25
08	Aquarium AQU 000l-13	LIVE AT THE AQUARIUM (2-LP, 50 only, numbered and signed)	20

WILD BILLY CHILDISH & HIS FAMOUS HEADCOATS
94	Damaged Goods DAMGOODLP 30	LIVE AT THE WILD WESTERN ROOM (LP)	15
00	Buff Medway COCK 1-UP	I AM THE OBJECT OF YOUR DESIRE (LP)	20

BILLY CHILDISH & THE BLACKHANDS
93	Hangman 53 UP	LIVE IN THE NETHERLANDS (LP)	20

BILLY CHILDISH & THE NATURAL BORN LOVERS
89	Hangman 30 UP	LONG LEGGED BABY (LP)	30

BILLY CHILDISH & SEXTON MING
95	Hangman's Daughter KETCH 5 UP	Mussel Horse/Gaud Bless Old Mitchel (die-cut sleeve)	8
87	Hangman HANG 05 UP	WHICH DEAD DONKEY DADDY (LP)	12
87	Hangman HANG 10 UP	PLUMP PRIZES & LITTLE GEMS (LP)	15
87	Hangman HANG 12 UP	YPRES 1917 OVERTURE(LP)	30
98	Damaged Goods DAMGOOD 159LP	CHEEKY CHEESE (LP)	12

BILLY CHILDISH & THE SINGING LOINS
93	Hangmans Daughter SCRAG 1	AT THE BRIDGE (LP)	40

WILD BILLY CHILDISH
87	Hangman HANG 13 UP	I REMEMBER (LP)	25
87	Hangman HANG 2 UP	I'VE GOT EVERYTHING INDEED (LP)	35

WILD BILLY CHILDISH & THE BLACKHANDS
88	Hangman HANG-21 UP	PLAY CAPT'N CALYPSO'S HOODOO PARTY	20

(see also Milkshakes, Thee Mighty Caesars and Billy Childish & entries)

WILD BILLY CHILDISH & BIG RUSS WILKINS
87	Empire CPO 195	LAUGHING GRAVY (10" LP)	15

WILD BILLY CHILDISH & BUFF MEDWAYS
03	Aquarium (No Cat. No)	You Are All Phonys (p/s, 1-sided, white label other side etched, 100 numbered and signed by Childish)	40
03	Aquarium (No Cat. No)	You Are All Phonys (p/s, 1-sided, white label other side etched, 400 unsigned)	15
04	Aquarium (No Cat. No)	(I'm Not Going To Your Boring) Private View (p/s, 1-sided other side etched, 100 numbered and signed by Childish)	40
04	Aquarium (No Cat. No)	(I'm Not Going To Your Boring) Private View (p/s, 1-sided other side etched, 400 unsigned)	15
05	Damaged Goods DAMGOOD 239LP	MEDWAY WHEELERS (LP, 50 copies with numbered 'The Poundlands Poets' booklet	20

05	Damaged Goods DAMGOOD 239LP	MEDWAY WHEELERS (LP, without booklet)	15

(see also Buff Medways)

CHI-LITES

69	Beacon BEA 119	Pretty Girl/Love Bandit	70
71	MCA 1143DJ	What Do I Wish For (1-sided DJ copy)	15
70	MCA MUPS 397	GIVE IT AWAY (LP)	15
71	MCA MUPS 437	(FOR GOD'S SAKE) GIVE MORE POWER TO THE PEOPLE (LP)	15
72	MCA MUPS 457	A LONELY MAN (LP)	15

(see also Jackie Wilson)

CHILLIWACK

71	London HLU 10327	Everyday/Sundown	5
71	London SHU 8418	CHILLIWACK (LP)	15

(see also Collectors, Electric Prunes)

CHILLI WILLI & RED HOT PEPPERS

75	Mooncrest MOON 40	Breathe A Little/Friday Song	6
72	Revelation REV 002	KINGS OF THE ROBOT RHYTHM (LP, with lyric insert, inner sleeve and sticker)	60
72	Revelation REV 002	KINGS OF THE ROBOT RHYTHM (LP, with lyric insert, but without inner sleeve and sticker)	30
74	Mooncrest CREST 21	BONGOS OVER BALHAM (LP, with inner sleeve)	25

(see also Brinsley Schwarz, Jo-Ann Kelly, Mighty Baby, Savoy Brown, Hapshash And The Coloured Coat, Attractions, Action)

CHILLS

85	Normal 43	LOST EP (12")	15
84	Flying Nun Europe FNE 13	KALEIDOSCOPE WORLD (LP, with free 7")	30
84	Flying Nun Europe FNE 13	KALEIDOSCOPE WORLD (LP, without free 7")	20
90	Slash 828191	SUBMARINE BELLS (LP, with inner sleeve)	15
92	Slash 828322	SOFT BOMB (LP)	12

CHILLUM

71	Mushroom 100 MR 11	CHILLUM (LP, with photo insert)	90

(see also Secondhand)

ALEX CHILTON

80	Aura AUS 117	Hey! Little Child/No More The Moon Shines Lorena (p/s)	8

(see also Box Tops, Big Star)

CHIMES FEATURING DENISE (U.K.)

63	Decca F 11783	Say It Again/Can This Be Love?	5
64	Decca F 11885	I'll Be Waiting, I'll Be Here/Hello Heartache	5

(see also Little Frankie)

CHIMES (U.S.)

61	London HLU 9283	Once In A While/Summer Night	35

CHIMNEYS

80	Tagmemics 45-003	Do The Big Baby/Take Your Brain Out For A Walk (p/s, 500 only)	15

TSAI CHIN

59	Decca F 11192	The Ding Dong Song/The Second Spring	5
62	Decca F 11439	Chinese Charleston/How Shall I Do It	5
63	Decca F 11595	Buttons And Bows/Woa Yaw Nee	5
63	Decca F 11737	School In Cheltenham/Any Old Iron	5
64	Decca F 12039	Tokyo Melody/I Love A Man	5
62	Decca SKL/LK 4501	THE WORLD OF TSAI CHIN (LP)	15

CHINA DOLL

80	Wessex WEX 273	Oysters And Wine/Past Tense (p/s)	150

CHINA DOLLS

82	Speed FIRED 1	One Hit Wonder/Ain't Love Ain't Bad (p/s)	35

(see also Slade, Dummies)

CHINA DRUM

93	No label or Cat. No.	Simple/On My Way/Meaning (Acoustic) (p/s, 500 only gig freebie)	12
94	Fluffy Bunny FLUFF 06	Great Fire/Biscuit Barrel/Meaning/Down By The River (10")	20
94	Fluffy Bunny FLUFF 6CD	Great Fire/Biscuit Barrel/Meaning/Down By The River (CD, card wallet)	15
96	Mantra MNTLP1002	GOOSE FAIR (LP)	12
97	Mantra MNTLP1009	SELF MADE MANIAC (LP)	12

CHINA STREET

78	Criminal CRM 1	You're A Ruin/(I Wanna Be) Your M.P. (foldout lyric p/s in poly bag & badge)	10

CHINATOWN

81	Airship AP 138	Short And Sweet/How Many Times (p/s)	60
81	Airship AP 343	PLAY IT TO DEATH (LP)	85

CHINAWITE

83	Future Earth FER 014	Blood On The Streets/Ready To Satisfy (p/s)	30
85	Mausoleum SKULL 8351	RUN FOR COVER (LP)	12

CHRISTINE CHING

64	Decca 12027	Winter's Here Again/Jingle Bells	5

KES CHINS

62	Starlite ST45 089	Annie/Moody	8

CHIPS

75	Decca FR 13574	Love Matters/Gentle Teacher	5
75	Decca FR 13604	Twice A Week//Reelin In The Years	8

GEORGE CHISHOLM & BLUENOTES

56	Beltona BL 2671	Honky Tonk/D.R. Rock (with Bert Weedon)	10

(see also Bert Weedon)

CHITINIOUS ENSEMBLE

71	Deram SML 1093	CHITINOUS ENSEMBLE (LP)	300

CHOC
70	Decca F23106	Way Of Life/I Want You To Be My Girl	30

CHOC ICE
71	Polydor 2056189	Groovy Situation/Instrumental Version	15

CHOCOLATE BOYS
74	Decca F 13556	El Bimbo/Voltaire Pier	40
74	Decca F 13556	El Bimbo/Voltaire Pier (DJ Copy)	50

CHOCOLATE FROG
68	Atlantic 584 207	Butchers And Bakers/I Forgive You	40

(see also Fleur De Lys)

CHOCOLATE MILK
75	RCA RCA 2592	Action Speaks Louder Than Words/Ain't Nothing But A Thing	10
79	RCA RCAT 2592	I'm Your Radio/Actions Speak Louder Than Words (12")	15
77	RCA PL 11830	COMIN' (LP)	20

CHOCOLATE PIER
74	Decca FR 13556	El Bimbo/Voltaire Pier	10

CHOCOLATE WATCH BAND
67	Decca F 12649	The Sound Of The Summer/The Only One In Sight	45
67	Decca F 12704	Requiem/What's It To You	40
84	Big Beat WIK 25	44 (LP)	15

CHOCOLATS
76	Aquarius AQ 1	Voltaire Pier/Brasilia Carnival	50

(see also chocolate Boys)

CHOIR
68	Major Minor MM 537	It's Cold Outside/I'm Going Home	50
68	Major Minor MM 557	When You Were With Me/Changin' My Mind	40

CHOPPER
71	Decca F 13161	Singer Wihout A Song/Think I'm A Man	50

CHOPYN
75	Jet LPO 8	GRAND SLAM (LP)	20

(see also Ann Odell, Ray Russell, Simon Phillips, C.M.U)

CHORALE
85	Towerbell TVP 4	Mountain Men/Mountain Men (Remix) (p/s)	5

CHORALERNA
60s	Myrrh MYRRH 1047	LET THERE BE LIGHT (LP)	25
60s	Key KL 018	POWER (LP)	20

CHORDETTES
54	Columbia SCM 5158	Mr. Sandman/I Don't Wanna See You Cryin'	250
54	Columbia DB 3553	Mr. Sandman/I Don't Wanna See You Cryin' (78)	20
55	London HLA 8169	Humming Bird/Lonely Lips	50
55	London HLA 8169	Humming Bird/Lonely Lips (78)	10
56	London HLA 8217	Dudelsack Polka/I Told A Lie	40
56	London HLA 8264	Eddie My Love/Our Melody (triangular centre)	75
56	London HLA 8264	Eddie My Love/Our Melody (round centre)	30
56	London HLA 8302	Born To Be With You/Love Never Changes	30
56	London HA 7011	Born To Be With You/Love Never Changes (export issue)	30
56	London HLA 8323	Lay Down Your Arms/Teenage Goodnight	20
57	London HLA 8473	Echo Of Love/Just Between You And Me	20
57	London HLA 8497	Like A Baby/Soft Sands	20
58	London HLA 8566	Baby Of Mine/Photographs	20
58	London HLA 8584	Lollipop/Baby, Come-A-Back-A	20
58	London HLA 8654	Love Is A Two-Way Street/I Don't Know, I Don't Care	10
59	London HLA 8809	We Should Be Together/No Other Arms, No Other Lips	10
59	London HLA 8926	A Girl's Work Is Never Done/No Wheels (B-side with Jeff Crom & Jackie Ertel)	20
61	London HLA 9400	Never On Sunday/Faraway Star	5
62	London HLA 9519	The White Rose Of Athens/Adios (Goodbye My Love)	5
60	London RE-A 1228	THE CHORDETTES (EP)	45
58	London HA-A 2088	THE CHORDETTES (LP)	90
62	London HA-A 2441	THE CHORDETTES SING (LP)	40

CHORDS (U.K.)
79	Polydor 2059 141	Now It's Gone/Don't Go Back (p/s)	5
80	Polydor POSP 101	Maybe Tomorrow/I Don't Wanna Know/Hey Girl (p/s)	6
80	Polydor POSP 146	Something's Missing/This Is What They Want (p/s)	5
80	Polydor 2059 258	The British Way Of Life/The Way It's Got To Be (p/s)	6
80	Polydor POSP 185	In My Street/I'll Keep On Holding On (p/s)	6
81	Polydor POSP 270	One More Minute/Who's Killing Who (p/s)	6
81	Polydor POSP 288	Turn Away Again/Turn Away Again (Again) (p/s)	8
80	Polydor Super POLS 1019	SO FAR AWAY (LP, with stickered sleeve & 7" "Now It's Gone"/ Things We Said [KRODS 1])	20

(see also Rage)

CHORDS (U.S.)
54	Columbia SCM 5133	Sh-Boom (Life Could Be A Dream)/Little Maiden	2000
54	Columbia DB 3512	Sh-Boom (Life Could Be A Dream)/Little Maiden (78)	200

CHORDS FIVE
67	Island WI 3044	I'm Only Dreaming/Universal Vagrant	100
68	Polydor 56261	Same Old Fat Man/Hold On To Everythin' You've Got	40
69	Jay Boy BOY 6	Some People/Battersea Fair	80

(see also Smoke)

CHOSEN FEW (JAMAICA)
70	Songbird SB 1031	Time Is Hard/CRYSTALITES: Time Is Hard Part Two	12
70	Songbird SB 1032	Going Back Home/CRYSTALITES: Going Back Home Part Two	10

70	Songbird SB 1046	Why Can't I Touch You/INNER CIRCLE BAND: Touch You Version	15
71	Songbird SB 1061	Shaft/Shaft (Version)	12
71	Songbird SB 1067	Everybody Just A Stall/Everybody (Version)	10
72	Songbird SB 1070	Do Your Thing/Your Thing (Version)	18
72	Trojan TR 7864	Ebony Eyes/Ebony Eyes (Version)	6
72	Trojan TR 7882	Everybody Plays The Fool/You're A Big Girl Now	12
72	Grape	You're A Big Girl Now/Version	12
73	Trojan TR 7894	Am I Black Enough For You/Message From A Blackman	8
73	Duke DU 162	Children Of The Night/LLOYD CHARMERS: For The Good Times	7
73	Duke DU 163	Stoned In Love/MIKE CHUNG & NOW GENERATION: Stoned In Love (Version)	7
73	Duke DU 164	It's Too Late/MIKE CHUNG & NOW GENERATION: It's Too Late (Version)	7
73	Trojan TRLS 56	HIT AFTER HIT (LP)	25
75	Trojan TRLS 106	EVERYBODY PLAYS THE FOOL (LP)	30

CHOSEN FEW (U.K.) (1)

65	Pye 7N 15905	It Won't Be Around You Anymore/Big City	20
65	Pye 7N 15942	So Much To Look Forward To/Today, Tonight & Tomorrow	20

(see also Alan Hull, Lindisfarne, Skip Bifferty)

CHOSEN FEW (U.K.) (2)

74	Action ACT 4623	Funky Butter/Wondering	60
76	Polydor 2058 721	I Can Make Your Dreams Come True/Pretty Face	20
76	Miami MIA401	Night And Day/Funky Buttercup	60
78	Polydor 2058 975	You Mean Everything To Me/It Won't Be Long	30
77	Polydor 2058 752	Miracle Worker/Young And Foolish	25

CHOU PAHROT

79	Klub KEP 101	Buzgo Tram Chorus/Gwizgweela Gwamhnoo/Lemons (p/s)	10
79	Klub KLP 19	LIVE (LP, private pressing)	12

CHRIS AND FORBES

65	Philips BF 1451	Get Away From It All/I'm Running Away	8

CHRIS AND MAXINE

67	Philips BF 1587	Only A Thousand Times A Day/I've Made You My Mind	15

CHRIS & COSEY/CREATIVE TECHNOLOGY INSTITUTE

81	Rough Trade RT 078	October (Love Song)/Little Houses (p/s)	5
84	Intl. One CTI 002	Conspiracy International/The Gift Of Tongues/The Need (p/s)	7
84	C.T.I. CTI 1	HAMMER HOUSE EP (12")	10
84	C.T.I. CTI 2	GIFT OF TONGUES (12")	10
85	Rough Trade RTT 148	Sweet Surprise 1 (1984)/2 (1985) (12", p/s, with Annie Lennox & Dave Stewart)	8
91	World Serpent WS7 004	Passion (p/s, 1-sided, other side etched)	5
81	Rough Trade ROUGH 34	HEARTBEAT (LP, with insert)	20
81	Rough Trade COPY 008	HEARTBEAT (cassette with 2 bonus tracks)	15
82	Rough Trade ROUGH 44	TRANCE (LP)	15

(see also Throbbing Gristle, Chris Carter, Eurythmics, Cosey Fanni Tutti)

PETER CHRIS & OUTCASTS

66	Columbia DB 7923	Over The Hill/The Right Girl For Me	40

CHRIS & STUDENTS

61	Parlophone R 4806	Lass Of Richmond Hill/Ducks Away From My Fishin'	15

CHRIST CHILD

78	Barak BAR 5	Let Them Eat Rock/Five Finger Exercise	8

CHRISTIAN

71	Decca F 23137	Other Side Of Life/She	15

CHARLIE CHRISTIAN

50s	Philips BBL 7172	CHARLIE CHRISTIAN (LP)	20

FUD CHRISTIAN ALL STARS

71	Big Shot BI 571	Never Fall In Love (actually by Winston Heywood)/Never Fall In Love Version	8

HANS CHRISTIAN

68	Parlophone R 5676	All Of The Time/Never My Love	80
68	Parlophone R 5698	(The Autobiography Of) Mississippi Hobo/Sonata Of Love	110

(see also Jon Anderson, Yes)

JOHN CHRISTIAN DEE

68	Pye 7N 17566	Take Me Along/The World Can Pack Its Bags And Go Away	15
70	London HLH 10317	Come Forward The Man/Mr. & Mrs. Jones	5
69	Decca F12901	The World Can Pick Up Its Bags And Go Away/Stick To Your Guns	15

LIZ CHRISTIAN

67	CBS 202520	Suddenly You Find Love/Make It Work Out	80
67	CBS 202520	Suddenly You Find Love/Make It Work Out (DJ copy)	100
69	Spark SRL 1004	Call My Name/Think Of You Baby	8

(see also James Royal)

MARIA CHRISTIAN

85	MCA MCA 974	Wait Until The Weekend Comes/(Instrumental) (p/s)	15

NEIL CHRISTIAN (& CRUSADERS)

61	Private Pressing	Restless/Red Sails In The Sunset/Your Cheating Heart/Danny (1-sided 4 track 12" demo acetate, 6 made, Jimmy Page's first studio recording)	3000
62	Columbia DB 4938	The Road To Love/The Big Beat Drum	40
63	Columbia DB 7075	A Little Bit Of Someone Else/Get A Load Of This (with Crusaders)	20
66	Strike JH 301	That's Nice/She's Got The Action	10
66	Strike JH 313	Oops/She Said Yeah	10
66	Strike JH 319	Two At A Time/Wanna Lover	10
67	Pye 7N 17372	You're All Things Bright And Beautiful/I'm Gonna Love You Baby	15
73	Youngblood YB 1044	That's Nice/She's Got The Action	6
76	Satril SAT 106	She's Got The Power/Someone Following Me Around	20
66	Columbia SEG 8492	A LITTLE BIT OF SOMETHING ELSE (EP)	80

(see also Christian's Crusaders, Guy Hamilton, Jimmy Page, Ritchie Blackmore, Nicky Hopkins, Miki Dallon, Screaming Lord Sutch)

CHRISTIAN DEATH
83	Future FL 2	ONLY THEATRE OF PAIN (LP, with insert)	25
86	Jungle NOS 006	OFFICIAL ANTHOLOGY OF LIVE BOOTLEGS (LP, black & yellow sleeve)	12
86	Jungle NOS 006	OFFICIAL ANTHOLOGY OF LIVE BOOTLEGS (LP, pink vinyl)	12

CHRISTIAN'S CRUSADERS
64	Columbia DB 7289	Honey Hush/One For The Money	50

(see also Neil Christian & Crusaders)

CHRISTIE
71	CBS 9130	Everything's Gonna Be Alright/Freewheelin' Man/Magic Highway (p/s)	6
72	CBS S 8403	Fools Gold/Born To Lose	15
70	CBS 64108	CHRISTIE (LP)	15
71	CBS 64397	FOR ALL MANKIND (LP, gatefold sleeve, orange label)	20

(see also Acid Gallery, Epics, Outer Limits)

CHRISTIE BROTHERS STOMPERS
59	Parlophone GEP 8719	TOGETHER AGAIN (EP)	10
60	Esquire EP233	RUM & COCA COLA (EP)	10
60	Esquire EP243	STOMPIN' (EP)	10

DAVE CHRISTIE
68	Mercury MF1028	Love And The Brass Band/Penelope Breedlove	25

JOHN CHRISTIE
74	Polydor 2058 496	4th Of July (written by Paul McCartney)/Old Enough To Know Better (in p/s)	30
74	Polydor 2058 496	4th Of July (written by Paul McCartney)/Old Enough To Know Better	15
74	Polydor 2058 528	Everybody Knows/How Does It Feel (p/s)	6

KEITH CHRISTIE
54	Esquire 20-047	HOMAGE TO THE DUKE (LP)	15

LOU CHRISTIE
63	Columbia DB 4983	The Gypsy Cried/Red Sails In The Sunset	20
63	Columbia DB 7031	Two Faces Have I/All That Glitters Isn't Gold	20
63	Columbia DB 7096	How Many Teardrops/You And I (Have A Right To Cry)	15
66	MGM MGM 1297	Lightnin' Strikes/Cryin' In The Streets	10
66	MGM MGM 1297	Lightnin' Strikes/Cryin' In The Streets (DJ Copy)	40
66	MGM MGM 1308	Rhapsody In The Rain/Trapeze	8
66	MGM MGM 1317	Painter/Du Ronda	12
66	MGM MGM 1325	If My Car Could Only Talk/Song Of Lita	18
66	Colpix PX 735	Merry Go Round/Guitars And Bongos	10
67	King KG 1036	Outside The Gates Of Heaven/All That Glitters Isn't Gold	8
67	CBS 2718	Shake Hands And Walk Away Cryin'/Escape	15
67	CBS 2922	Gina/Back To The Days Of The Romans	10
69	Buddah 201 057	I'm Gonna Make You Mine/I'm Gonna Get Married	6
69	Buddah 201 073	She Sold Me Magic/Are You Gettin' Any Sunshine?	7
70	Buddah 201081	Love Is Over/Generation	5
70	Buddah 2011-052	Indian Lady/Glory River	6
71	Buddah 2011-074	Waco/Lighthouse	5
72	Buddah 2011-111	I'm A Song, Sing Me/Paper Song	5
72	Buddah 2011-127	Why Do Fools Fall In Love/I'm Gonna Get Married	5
72	Buddah 2011-148	Shuffle On Down To Pittsburgh/I'm Gonna Get Married	5
73	CTI Records CTS 4002	Beyond The Blue Horizon/Hey You Cajun	6
75	Elektra K 12188	Summer Days/The One And Only Original Sunshine Kid	5
76	Epic SEPC 4471	Riding In My Van/Summer In Malibu	5
76	Midland International MID 6	You're Gonna Make Love To Me/Fantasies	5
66	MGM MGM-C(S) 8008	LIGHTNIN' STRIKES (LP)	25
66	Colpix PXL 551	STRIKES AGAIN (LP)	25

SUSAN CHRISTIE
66	CBS 202261	I Love Onions/Take Me As You Find Me	15

TONY CHRISTIE (& TRACKERS)
66	CBS 202097	Life's Too Good To Waste/Just The Two Of Us	8
67	MGM MGM 1365	Turn Around/When Will I Ever Love Again?	8
68	MGM MGM 1386	I Don't Want To Hurt You Anymore/Say No More	8
68	MGM MGM 1440	My Prayer/I Need You	8

CHRISTIEN BROTHERS
69	Major Minor MM 628	I Reached For You/Answer Me	7

DEREK CHRISTIEN
70	Major Minor MM 676	When A Woman Has A Baby/Please Don't Go Away	30
70	Major Minor MM 713	Suddenly There's A Valley/I'll Be Coming Home	100

(see also Christien Brothers)

CHRISTINES'S CAT
89	Sarah SARAH 13	Your Love Is.... (5" flexi with two fanzines 'Lemonade: A Fanzine' and 'Cold: A Lie')	40

KEITH CHRISTMAS
69	RCA Victor SF 8059	STIMULUS (LP, with Mighty Baby, orange/white label)	150
70	B&C CAS 1015	FABLE OF THE WINGS (LP)	50
71	B&C CAS 1041	PIGMY (LP, gatefold sleeve)	40
74	Manticore K 53503	BRIGHTER DAY (LP, with inner sleeve)	15
76	Manticore K 53509	STORIES FROM THE HUMAN ZOO (LP, with insert)	15

(see also Mighty Baby, Magic Muscle)

CHRISTOPHER
70	Chapter One CH121	Sharkey/The Race	20

CHARA CHRISTOU
71	Somerville SVL 1	CELEBRATE HIS LOVE (LP)	25

JUNE CHRISTY
55	Capitol CL 14355	Pete Kelly's Blues/Kicks	10
56	Capitol T 725	JUNE CHRISTY (LP)	12

(see also Stan Kenton)

MINT VALUE £

CHROME

80	Red RS 12007	READ ONLY MEMORY (12" EP, with poster)	20
80	Red RS 12007	READ ONLY MEMORY (12" EP, without poster)	12
80	Beggars Banquet BEG 36	New Age/Information (p/s)	10
81	D. F. O. T. Mountain Y3	INWORLDS (12")	15
82	D. F. O. T. Mountain Z17	Firebomb/Shadows Of A Thousand Years (p/s)	10
80	Beggars Banquet BEGA 15	RED EXPOSURE (LP, with inner sleeve)	20
80	Beggars Banquet BEGA 18	HALF MACHINE LIP MOVES (LP, with poster insert)	20
80	Beggars Banquet BEGA 18	HALF MACHINE LIP MOVES (LP, without poster insert)	15
81	D. F. O. T. Mountain X6	BLOOD ON THE MOON (LP, with inner sleeve)	18
82	D. F. O. T. Mountain X18	3RD FROM THE SUN (LP, with insert)	15

CHEETAH CHROME

85	Children Of The Revolution GURT 3	I REFUSE IT! (Split LP with MOTHERFUCKERS)	35

CHROMING ROSE

90	EMI 5667 93774	LOUIS XIV (LP, some as picture disc)	12

CHRON GEN

81	Gargoyle GRGL 780	PUPPETS OF WAR (EP)	10
81	Step Forward SF 19	Reality/Subway Sadist (p/s)	5
82	Secret SEC 3	LIVING NEXT DOOR TO ALICE (EP, with Chronic Generation Oi magazine No. 1)	8
82	Secret SHH 129	Jet Boy Jet Girl/Abortions/Subway Sadist (p/s)	5
82	Secret SHH 139	Outlaw/Behind Closed Doors/Disco (p/s)	6
83	Secret SEC 3	CHRONIC GENERATION (LP, with free 7")	15
83	Secret SEC 3	CHRONIC GENERATION (LP, lyric insert)	12

CHRYSTAL BELLE SCRODD

86	United Dairies	BELLE DE JOUR (LP with insert)	25

(see also Nurse With Wound)

CHUBBY & HONEYSUCKERS

65	Venus VE 3	Come On Home/What Shall I Do?	12
66	Rio R 75	Emergency Ward/LEN & HONEYSUCKERS: One More River	12

CHUCK & BETTY

59	Brunswick 05815	Sissy Britches/Come Back Little Girl	30
59	Brunswick 05815	Sissy Britches/Come Back Little Girl (78)	15

CHUCK (JOSEPHS) & DOBBY (DOBSON)

60	Blue Beat BB 19	Til The End Of Time (as Chuck & Darby)/DUKE REID & HIS GROUP: What Makes Honey	20
60	Blue Beat BB 23	Cool School/DUKE REID & HIS GROUP: Joker	20
61	Starlite ST45 043	Sad Over You/Sweeter Than Honey	20
61	Starlite ST45 044	Lovey Dovey/Sitting Square	20
61	Blue Beat BB 39	Du Du Wap/I Love My Teacher (with Aubrey Adams & Du Droppers)	18
61	Blue Beat BB 59	Oh Fanny/Running Around	18
64	Blue Beat BB 246	Tell Me/I'm Going Home	15

CHUCK & GARY

58	HMV POP 466	Teenie Weenie Jeanie/Can't Make Up My Mind	60
58	HMV POP 466	Teenie Weenie Jeanie/Can't Make Up My Mind (78)	20

CHUCK & GIDEON

63	Parlophone R 5011	Cherry Berry Lips/The Tender Touch	5

CHUCKLES (1)

69	Bullet BU 416	Run Nigel Run/Come On Home	15

CHUCKLES (2)

72	Duke DU 144	Reggae Limbo/ZAP POW: Broken Contract	30

CHUCKS

63	Decca F 11569	Loo Be Loo/Anytime Is The Right Time	5
63	Decca F 11617	Mulberry Bush/That's All I Need	5
63	Decca F 11777	The Hitch Hiker/Humpity Dumpity	5
64	Decca DFE 8562	THE CHUCKS (EP)	20

CHUMBAWAMBA

85	Agit Prop AGIT 1	Revolution EP (booklet p/s)	8
88	Agit Prop AGIT 3	Smash Clause 28/Fight The Alton Bill (with booklet)	6
88	Agit Prop PROP 3	ENGLISH REBEL SONGS 1381-1914 (10" LP, with die-cut sleeve)	15
86	Agit Prop PROP 1	PICTURES OF STARVING CHILDREN SELL RECORDS (LP, with inner)	20
87	Agit Prop PROP 2	NEVER MIND THE BALLOTS... (LP, gatefold)	15
94	One Little Indian TPLP046CD	ANARCHY (CD)	20
95	One Little Indian TPLP056	SHOWBUSINESS (LP)	15

MIKIE CHUNG & NOW GENERATION

72	Green Door GD 4032	Breezing/NOW GENERATION: Breezing - Version	5
73	Duke DU 163	Stoned In Love/CHOSEN FEW: Stoned In Love	7
73	Duke DU 164	It's Too Late/CHOSEN FEW: It's Too Late	7

CHUNKY

73	Orange OAS 214	Albatross Baby/Road Runner Girl	30

CHURCH

82	Carrere CAR 212	Unguarded Moment/Busdriver (p/s)	5
82	Carrere CAR 247	Almost With You/Life Speeds Up (p/s)	5
82	Carrere CAR EP 257	Unguarded Moment/Interlude/Golden Dawn/Sisters (10", p/s)	8
83	Carrere CHURCH R5A	Different Man/I Am A Rock (no p/s)	7
83	Carrere CHURCH 5	SING SONGS (12" EP)	10
88	Arista 208895	STARFISH (LP, with bonus 5-track numbered 12")	15

EUGENE CHURCH

59	London HL 8940	Miami/I Ain't Goin' For That (round centre)	75
59	London HL 8940	Miami/I Ain't Goin' For That (round centre) (78)	30

CHICK CHURCHILL

73	Chrysalis CHR 1051	YOU AND ME (LP)	15

(see also Ten Years After, Cozy Powell, Jethro Tull, Bernie Marsden)

SAVANNAH CHURCHILL
53	Brunswick 05218	Shake A Hand/Shed A Tear (78)	10
60	London HLW 9273	I Want To Be/Time Out For Tears	5

CICCONE YOUTH
88	Blast First BFUS 28P	WHITEY ALBUM PROMO (EP, promo only)	12
86	Blast First BFFP 8T	Into The Groovey/Burnin' Up (12", p/s)	10

(see also Sonic Youth)

CIGARETTES
78	Dead Good KEVIN 1	THE CIGARETTES (EP, unreleased)	0
79	Company CIGCO 008	They're Back Again, Here They Come/I've Forgot My Number/ All We Want Is Your Money (gatefold p/s, initial pressing with red labels)	70
79	Company CIGCO 008	They're Back Again, Here They Come/I've Forgot My Number/All We Want Is Your Money (gatefold p/s, later pressing with black labels)	60
80	Dead Good DEAD 10	Can't Sleep At Night/It's The Only Way To Live (Die) (p/s)	40

CIM(M)AR(R)ONS
70	Hot Rod HR 105	Grandfather Clock/Kick Me Or I Kick You (as Cimarrons)	100
70	Reggae REG 3003	Bad Day At Black Rock (with Cimmaron Kid)/Fragile	50
71	Big Shot BI 562	Funky Fight/You Turned Me Down	10
71	Spinning Wheel SW 107	Soul For Sale/Bogus-ism	7
71	Downtown DT 486	Oh Mammy Blue/Oh Mammy Blue - Version	6
71	Downtown DT 487	Holy Christmas/Silent Night/White Christmas	6
71	Bullet BU 457	Call Me/Call Me (Part 2)	6
71	Bullet BU 458	Leave Me A Little Love/My Baby	6
74	Trojan TR7919	Over The Rainbow/We Are Not The Same	15
75	Vulcan VUL 1005	Tradition/Wicky Wacky	15
78	Cimarak CR002	Paul Bogle/Greedy Man (12")	20
82	IMP IMPS 50	With A Little Luck/Peggy Sue	5
82	Safari/MPL SAFE 49	Big Girls Don't Cry/How Can I Prove Myself To You?	5
83	MPL/Cimarons CIM 001	Love And Affection	12
83	MPL/Cimarons 12CIM 001	Love And Affection (12", less than 1000 pressed)	30
74	Trojan TRLS 77	IN TIME (LP)	12
78	Polydor 2383512	MAKA (LP, green vinyl)	12

(see also Reaction, Winston Groovy)

CINDERELLAS
59	Brunswick 05794	Mister Dee-Jay/Yum Yum Yum	25
59	Brunswick 05794	Mister Dee-Jay/Yum Yum Yum (78)	10
60	Philips PB 1012	The Trouble With Boys/Puppy Dog	25
64	Colpix PX 11026	Baby, Baby (I Still Love You)/Please Don't Wake Me	80

CINDERELLAS
64	Colpix PX 11026	Baby, Baby (I Still Love You)/Please Don't Wake Me (DJ Copy)	100

(see also Cookies)

CINDERS
63	Warner Bros WB 86	The Cinnamon Cinder/C'mon Wobble	20

(see also Darlene Love)

CINDY & LINDY
57	HMV POP 409	The Language Of Love/Tell Me Something Sweet	10
59	Coral Q 72368	Saturday Night In Tiajuana/The Wonder That Is You	10

CINEMA
82	Floppy FLOPPY 1	Donor Donor/Cinema Star (p/s)	8

CINEMATIC ORCHESTRA
99	Ninja Tune ZEN12 084	Channel 1 Suite/Ode To The Big Sea (12")	15
99	Ninja Tune ZEN 45	MOTION (2xLP)	30
00	Ninja Tune ZEN 50	REMIXES 98 - 2000 (2xLP)	20
02	Ninja Tune ZEN 59	EVERY DAY (2xLP)	35
03	Ninja Tune ZEN 78	MAN WITH A MOVIE CAMERA (2xLP)	40
07	Ninja Tune ZEN 122	MA FLEUR (2xLP)	25

CINEMATICS
80s	Pulsebeat CINE 001	FAREWELL TO THE PLAYGROUND (EP, foldover p/s)	25

(see also Razorcuts)

CINNAMON
69	Beacon BEA 111	You Won't See Me Leaving/Leaves Of Love	6
69	President PT 258	So Long Sam/Broken Hearted Me, Evil Hearted You	6

CINNAMON QUILL
69	Morgan MRS 17	Girl On A Swing/Take It Or Leave It	20
69	Morgan MRS 21	Candy/Hello, It's Me	45

GIGLIOLA CINQUETTI
74	CBS 2294	Go (Before You Break My Heart)/Si	5

CIRCLE (1)
60s	Circle GR 1	IN AID OF THE MILLFIELD BUILDING FUND (EP, private pressing)	150

CIRCLE (2)
02	Static Caravan/Resonance Staticresonance 6	PROSPEKT (2-LP, gatefold sleeve, black vinyl and green vinyl, 1000 only)	30

CIRCLES (1)
66	Island WI 279	Take Your Time/Don't You Love Me No More	100
99	Detour DRLP018	PRIVATE WORLD (LP)	12

(see also Plastic Penny, Savages, Tony Dangerfield & Thrills, Screaming Lord Sutch)

CIRCLES (2)
72	Sioux SIOUX 017	Mammy Blue/POOCH JACKSON & HARRY J. ALLSTARS: King Of The Road	7

(see also Bob Andy)

CIRCLES (3)
79	Graduate GRAD 4	Opening Up/Billy (p/s)	20
80	Vertigo ANGRY 1	Angry Voices/Summer Nights (p/s)	12
80	Chrysalis CHS 2418	Opening Up/Billy (p/s, reissue)	8
85	Graduate GRAD 17	Circles/Summer Nights (p/s)	25

CIRCUIT 7
84	Micro Rapp MIC 1 RAPP 023459	Video Boys/The Force (p/s red vinyl)	40
84	Rapp 023462	Modern Story/Eastern Dream (p/s, blue vinyl)	25

CIRCULUS
05	Rise Above RISE 7/064	Mirl It Is (Moog Up Mix)/WITCHCRAFT: Chylde Of Fire	10
05	Rise Above RISE 7/065	Swallow/My Body Is Made Of Sunlight	10
06	Rise Above RISE 7/094	Song Of Our Despair/Honeycomb (clear, purple or black vinyl)	8
05	Rise Above RISELP 63	THE LICK ON THE TIP OF MY ENVELOPE YET TO BE SENT (LP, brown vinyl gatefold sleeve, poster)	25
06	Rise Above RISELP 093	CLOCKS ARE LIKE PEOPLE (LP, white vinyl, free 1-sided 7", "Tapestry", 500 only)	25
06	Rise Above RISELP 093	CLOCKS ARE LIKE PEOPLE (LP, 700 on blue vinyl, 500 on black vinyl)	18

CIRCUS
67	Parlophone R 5633	Gone Are The Songs Of Yesterday/Sink Or Swim	20
68	Parlophone R 5672	Do You Dream/House Of Wood	45
69	Transatlantic TRA 207	CIRCUS (LP, gatefold sleeve, white/lilac label with 'T' logo)	90

(see also Philip Goodhand-Tait, King Crimson)

CIRCUS MAXIMUS
67	Vanguard VSD 79260	CIRCUS MAXIMUS (LP)	20
68	Vanguard VSD 79274	NEVERLAND REVISITED (LP)	20

MARTIN CIRCUS
79	Pye 12P 5001	Disco Circus/Ite Missa East (12", p/s)	10

CIRKUS
80	Guardian GRCA 4	Melissa/Amsterdam/Pick Up A Phone (EP)	20
73	RCB 1	CIRKUS ONE (LP, private pressing with gatefold sleeve, black/white label)	200
77	Shock SHOCK 1	FUTURE SHOCK (LP)	90

CITATIONS
63	Columbia DB 7068	Moon Race/Slippin' And Slidin'	30

CITY BOY
76	Vertigo 6360 126	CITY BOY (LP, spaceship label)	12
77	Vertigo 6360 151	YOUNG MEN GONE WEST (LP, spaceship label)	12

CITY GIANTS
87	Give It A Blast BLA 001	Little Next To Nothing/Where Love's Concerned/Have You Got Any Idea? (p/s)	15

CITY LIMITS
80s	Luggage RRP 1003	Morse Code Signals/If I Had Time/I Just Can't Say (EP)	100

CITY RAMBLERS SKIFFLE GROUP
57	Tempo A 158	Ella Speed/2.19 Blues	20
57	Tempo A 161	Mama Don't Allow/Tom Dooley	20
57	Tempo A 165	Delia's Gone/Boodle-Am Shake	20
57	Storyville SEP 327	I WANT A GIRL (EP)	40
57	Storyville SEP 345	I SHALL NOT BE MOVED (EP)	40
57	Tempo EXA 59	I WANT A GIRL (EP)	40
57	Tempo EXA 71	GOOD MORNING BLUES (EP)	40
57	Tempo EXA 77	DELIA'S GONE (EP)	40

(see also Henrik Johansen)

CITY SMOKE
66	Mercury MF 971	Sunday Morning/A Little Bit Of Love	7

CITY TALK
80	PAD PAD 001	Trick Of The Light/Nightmare	12

CITY WAITES
74	EMI EMI 2149	The Fox/One Of My Aunts	5
74	EMI EMC 3027	A GORGEOUS GALLERY OF GALLANT INVENTIONS (LP)	20
76	Decca SKL 5264	THE CITY WAITES (LP)	20
81	Hyperion A 66008	HOW THE WORLD WAGS (LP, gatefold sleeve, some with Hyperion insert)	40

CIVILIANS
79	Arista ARIST 318	MADE FOR TELEVISION EP	60

CIVILISED SOCIETY?
86	Manic Ears ACHE 2	SCRAP METAL (LP, with inner)	15
87	Manic Ears ACHE 6	VIOLENCE SUCKS (LP, with lyric inner)	15

C-JAM BLUES
66	Columbia DB 8064	Candy/Stay At Home Girl	35

CLAGGERS
71	DJM DJS 260	Some One/Umber Rag	15

CLAGUE
69	Dandelion S 4493	Mandy Lee/Bottle Up And Go (with Kevin Coyne)	12
69	Dandelion 4494	The Stride/I Wonder Where	12

(see also Coyne-Clague, Kevin Coyne, Claque, Siren)

CLAIM
89	Esurient Comms PACE 04	Wait & See/Business Boy/God, Cliffe & Me	12
90	Esurient Comms PACE 07	Losers Corner/Picking Up The Bitter Little Pieces	12
90	Caff CAFF 008	Birth Of A Teenager/Mike The Bike	20
91	Esurient Comms PACE 07	Sunday/Sporting Life	12
92	A Turntable Friend TURN 08	Say So/Plastic Grip/Waiting For Jesus	12
87	Trick Bag CU 0388	THIS PENCIL WAS OBVIOUSLY SHARPENED BY A LEFT-HANDED INDIAN KNIFE THROWER (EP)	18
85	Trick Bag TBR 001	ARMSTRONG'S REVENGE AND ELEVEN OTHER SHORT STORIES (LP)	30

| 88 | Esurient Comms PACE 003 | BOOMY TELLA (LP) | 30 |

CLAN OF XYMOX
| 85 | 4AD BAD 504 | A Day/Stranger (12") | 10 |

CLAN (1)
| 70 | Bullet BU 419 | Copycats/BUNNY LEE ALLSTARS: Hot Lead | 12 |

CLAN (2)
| 72 | Deram DM 356 | Pretty Belinda/Ode To Karen | 7 |

(see also Junior Campbell)

CLANCY'S ALLSTARS
| 68 | Pama PM 722 | C.N. Express Parts 1 & 2 (B-side actually "You Were Meant For Me" by Lee Perry) | 30 |

(see also Owen Gray)

CLANDESTINE
| 86 | Market Trader PITCH 1 | I'm All Over You (Like Jam On a Scone)/The Valley Of The Larne | 6 |

CLANNAD & BONO
| 89 | RCA PA42995A | In A Lifetime (7" picture disc) | 10 |

(see also U2, Bono & Gavin Friday, The Passengers)

JIMMY CLANTON
58	London HLS 8699	Just A Dream/You Aim To Please (as Jimmy Clanton & His Rockets)	25
58	London HLS 8699	Just A Dream/You Aim To Please (as Jimmy Clanton & His Rockets) (78)	15
58	London HL 7066	A Letter To An Angel/A Part Of Me (as Jimmy Clanton & Aces) (export issue)	25
59	London HLS 8779	A Letter To An Angel/A Part Of Me (as Jimmy Clanton & Aces)	25
59	London HLS 8779	A Letter To An Angel/A Part Of Me (as Jimmy Clanton & Aces) (78)	15
59	Top Rank JAR 189	My Own True Love/Little Boy In Love	20
59	Top Rank JAR 189	My Own True Love/Little Boy In Love (78)	10
60	Top Rank JAR 269	Go, Jimmy, Go/I Trusted You	20
60	Top Rank JAR 382	Another Sleepless Night/I'm Gonna Try	20
60	Top Rank JAR 509	Come Back (To Me)/Wait	10
61	Top Rank JAR 544	What Am I Gonna Do/If I	10
62	Stateside SS 120	Venus In Blue Jeans/Highway Bound	10
63	Stateside SS 159	Darkest Street In Town/Dreams Of A Fool	10
65	Stateside SS 410	Hurting Each Other/Don't Keep Your Friends Away	50
69	London HLP 10289	Curly/I'll Never Forget Your Love	5
59	London RES 1224	JUST A DREAM (EP)	100

CLAP
| 79 | SRTS SRTS/79/CUS | Hey Little Girl/20 Watts Of Power (p/s) | 20 |

CLAPHAM SOUTH ESCALATORS
| 81 | Upright UP YOUR 1 | Get Me To The World On Time/Leave Me Alone/Cardboard Cut Outs (p/s) | 12 |

(see also Meteors, Escalators, Tall Boys)

ERIC CLAPTON
66	Purdah 45-3502	Lonely Years/Bernard Jenkins (with John Mayall, 500 copies only)	400
70	Polydor 2001 096	I Am Yours (unissued)	0
70	Polydor 2001 096	After Midnight/Easy Now	10
74	RSO 2090 139	Willie And The Hand Jive/I Can't Hold Out Much Longer (p/s)	5
76	RSO 2090 208	Hello Old Friend/All Our Pastimes (p/s)	5
80	RSO JON 1	Wonderful Tonight (live)/Further On Up The Road (live) (promo only)	10
80	RSO JONX 1	Wonderful Tonight (live)/Further On Up The Road (live) (12", numbered p/s)	10
81	RSO RSO 75	Another Ticket/Rita Mae (p/s)	5
83	Duck W 9701P	The Shape You're In/Crosscut Saw (picture disc)	6
87	Duck W 8461F	Behind The Mask/Grand Illusion//Crossroads (live)/White Room (live) (double pack, gatefold p/s)	10
87	Duck W 8397F	It's In The Way That You Use It/Bad Influence//Behind The Mask/ Grand Illusion (double pack, shrinkwrapped with sticker)	8
88	Polydor PZCD 8	After Midnight (Extended Version)/I Can't Stand It/Whatcha Gonna Do/ Sunshine Of Your Love (CD, card sleeve)	15
89	BBC CD RSL 178	Edge Of Darkness/Shoot Out/Obituary/Escape From Northmoor/ Oxford Circus/Northmoor (with Michael Kamen, 3" CD with adaptor, 5" case)	15
89	Duck W 2644B	Bad Love/I Shot The Sheriff (live) (box set with family tree & 2 colour prints)	6
70	Polydor 2383 021	ERIC CLAPTON (LP, laminated sleeve, red label)	25
73	RSO 2479 702	CLAPTON (LP, withdrawn)	60
74	RSO QD 4801	461 OCEAN BOULEVARD (LP, quadrophonic)	18
82	RSO RSDX 3	TIME PIECES (2-LP, unissued)	0
84	Aston PD 20118	TOO MUCH MONKEY BUSINESS (LP, picture disc, with Yardbirds)	15

(see also Yardbirds, John Mayall, Cream, Blind Faith, Delaney & Bonnie, Derek & The Dominos, Viv Stanshall, King Curtis, Randy Crawford)

ALAN CLARE GROUP
62	Parlophone R 4938	Screwball/Love For Sale	5
65	Pye 7N 15764	Dog's Body/Mulligatawny	5
56	Decca DFE 6368	THE IMPROVISATIONS OF... (EP)	30
56	Decca DFE 6391	ALAN CLARE TRIO WITH BOB BURNS (EP)	30
58	Decca LK 4260	JAZZ AROUND THE CLOCK (LP)	30
68	Decca SKL 4965	YOUNG GIRL (LP)	15

KENNY CLARE & RONNIE STEPHENSON
67	Columbia SCX 6168	DRUM SPECTACULAR (LP, with Tubby Hayes, stereo)	40
67	Columbia SX 6168	DRUM SPECTACULAR (LP, with Tubby Hayes, mono)	30
72	Sounds Superb SPR90057	DRUM SPECTACULAR (LP, reissue with Tubby Hayes and Stan Tracey)	18

CLARENDONIANS
65	Ska Beat JB 219	Muy Bien (My Friend)/You Are A Fool	25
66	Ska Beat JB 261	Doing The Jerk/You Won't See Me	30
66	Island WI 284	Try Me One More Time/Can't Keep A Good Man Down	25
66	Island WI 3005	I'll Never Change/Rules Of Life	25
67	Island WI 3032	Shoo-Be-Doo-Be (I Love You)/Sweet Heart Of Beauty	25
67	Island WI 3041	You Can't Be Happy/Goodbye Forever	25
67	Studio One SO 2004	The Table's Going To Turn/I Can Go On	40
67	Studio One SO 2007	He Who Laughs Last/GAYLADS: Just A Kiss From You	45
67	Studio One SO 2017	Love Me With All Your Heart/Love Don't Mean Much To Me	40
67	Rio R 112	Rudie Bam Bam/Be Bop Boy	18

Alice CLARK

67	Rio R 115	Musical Train/Lowdown Girl	18
68	Caltone TONE 114	Baby Baby/Bye Bye Bye	80
69	Duke DU 97	Come Along/Try To Be Happy	10
69	Gas GAS 131	When I Am Gone/She Brings Me Joy	12
70	Trojan TR 7714	Lick It Back/BEVERLEY'S ALLSTARS: Busy Bee	8
70	Trojan TR 7719	Baby Don't Do It/BEVERLEY'S ALLSTARS: Touch Down	50
71	Green Door GD 4009	Seven In One (Medley) (both sides)	6
72	Attack ATT 8039	Bound In Chains/STUD ALLSTARS: Version	6
72	Pama PM 847	This Is My Story/VAL BENNETT: Caledonia	10
73	Pama PM 856	Good Hearted Woman/CORNELL CAMPBELL: What Happens	8
73	Techniques TE 925	Just One Look/Sinner Man	6
73	Dragon DRA 1006	Walking Up A One Way Street/DYNAMITES: Instrumental	30

(see also Lee & Clarendonians, Desmond Baker & Clarendonians, Four Aces, Prince Buster, Dennis Walks)

ALICE CLARK

| 69 | Action ACT 4520 | You Got A Deal/Say You'll Never | 20 |

CHRIS CLARK

67	Tamla Motown TMG 591	Love's Gone Bad/Put Yourself In My Place	150
67	Tamla Motown TMG 591	Love's Gone Bad/Put Yourself In My Place (DJ Copy)	200
67	Tamla Motown TMG 624	From Head To Toe/The Beginning Of The End	45
67	Tamla Motown TMG 624	From Head To Toe/The Beginning Of The End (DJ Copy)	80
68	Tamla Motown TMG 638	I Want To Go Back There Again/I Love You	30
68	Tamla Motown TMG 638	I Want To Go Back There Again/I Love You (DJ Copy)	60
68	T. Motown STML 11069	SOUL SOUNDS (LP, stereo)	90
68	T. Motown TML 11069	SOUL SOUNDS (LP, mono)	100

CLAUDINE CLARK

62	Pye International 7N 25157	Party Lights/Disappointed	20
63	Pye International 7N 25186	Walk Me Home From The Party/Who Will You Hurt?	20
67	Sue WI 4039	The Strength To Be Strong/Moon Madness	40

DAVE CLARK FIVE

62	Ember EMB S 156	Chaquita/In Your Heart (grey/pink labels)	40
62	Ember EMB S 156	Chaquita/In Your Heart (red/yellow labels)	30
62	Piccadilly 7N 35088	First Love/I Walk The Line	30
62	Piccadilly 7N 35500	That's What I Said/I Knew It All The Time	30
63	Columbia DB 7011	The Mulberry Bush/Chaquita	20
63	Columbia DB 7112	Do You Love Me/Doo-Dah	10
64	Columbia DB 7291	Can't You See That She's Mine/Because	6
64	Columbia DB 7335	Thinking Of You Baby/Whenever You're Around	6
64	Columbia DB 7377	Any Way You Want It/Crying Over You	6
65	Columbia DB 7453	Everybody Knows/Say You Want Me	10
65	Columbia DB 7503	Reelin' And Rockin'/Little Bitty Pretty One	6
65	Columbia DB 7580	Come Home/Mighty Good Loving (in p/s)	18
65	Columbia DB 7580	Come Home/Mighty Good Loving	7
65	Columbia DB 7625	Catch Us If You Can/Move On	7
65	Columbia DB 7744	Over And Over/I'll Be Yours	10
66	Columbia DB 7863	Try Too Hard/All Night Long	8
66	Columbia DB 7909	Look Before You Leap/Please Tell Me Why	8
66	Columbia DB 8028	Nineteen Days/I Need Love	6
67	Columbia DB 8152	You Got What It Takes/Sitting Here Baby	6
67	Columbia DB 8194	Tabatha Twitchit/Man In A Pin-Striped Suit (in export p/s)	20
67	Columbia DB 8194	Tabatha Twitchit/Man In A Pin-Striped Suit	5
67	Columbia DB 8286	Everybody Knows/Concentration Baby	5
68	Columbia DB 8342	No One Can Break A Heart Like You/You Don't Want My Lovin'	6
68	Columbia DB 8465	The Red Balloon/Maze Of Love	7
68	Columbia DB 8505	Live In The Sky/Children	5
69	Columbia DB 8545	The Mulberry Tree/Small Talk	5
69	Columbia DB 8591	Get It On Now/Maze Of Life (unreleased, acetates exist)	0
69	Columbia DB 8624	Put A Little Love In Your Heart/34-06	6
69	Columbia DB 8638	Good Old Rock'N'Roll Medley (Parts 1 & 2) (in p/s)	5
70	Columbia DB 8660	Everybody Get Together/Darling I Love You	5
70	Columbia DB 8681	Julia/Five By Five	10
70	Columbia DB 8689	Here Comes Summer/Break Down And Cry	6
70	Columbia DB 8724	Play More Good Old Rock'N'Roll Medley (Parts 1 & 2) (in p/s)	6
71	Columbia DB 8749	Southern Man/If You Wanna See Me Cry	5
71	Columbia DB 8791	Won't You Be My Lady/Into Your Life	8
72	Columbia DB 8963	All Time Greats Medley (Glad All Over/Do You Love Me/Bits & Pieces/Glad All Over)/Wild Weekend (in p/s)	15
64	Columbia SEG 8289	THE DAVE CLARK FIVE (EP)	15
65	Columbia SEG 8381	THE HITS OF THE DAVE CLARK FIVE (EP)	20
65	Columbia SEG 8447	WILD WEEKEND (EP)	25
64	Columbia 33SX 1598	SESSION WITH THE DAVE CLARK FIVE (LP, blue/black label, with "sold in the U.K..." label text)	35
64	Ember FA 2003	DAVE CLARK FIVE AND THE WASHINGTON D.C.'s (LP)	30
65	EMI Regal REG 2017	IN SESSION (LP, export issue)	35
65	Columbia SX 1756	CATCH US IF YOU CAN (LP, soundtrack, blue/black label)	45
67	Columbia SX 6105	THE DAVE CLARK FIVE'S GREATEST HITS (LP, blue/black label)	20
68	Columbia SX 6207	EVERYBODY KNOWS (LP, blue/black label)	20
69	Columbia SX 6309	5 BY 5 1964-69: 14 TITLES BY THE DAVE CLARK FIVE (LP, blue/black label)	30
70	Columbia SCX 6437	IF SOMEBODY LOVES YOU (LP)	30
72	Columbia SCX 6494	DAVE CLARK AND FRIENDS (LP, boxed logo on label)	20

(see also Dave Clark & Friends, Smith D'Abo, Mike Smith, Washington D.C.s)

DEE CLARK

59	London HL 8802	Nobody But You/When I Call On You	30
59	London HL 8802	Nobody But You/When I Call On You (78)	20
59	London HL 8915	Just Keep It Up (And See What Happens)/ Whispering Grass(Don't Tell The Trees)	20
59	London HL 8915	Just Keep It Up (And See What Happens)/ Whispering Grass(Don't Tell The Trees) (78)	20
59	Top Rank JAR 196	Hey, Little Girl/If It Wasn't For Love	15
59	Top Rank JAR 196	Hey, Little Girl/If It Wasn't For Love (78)	15
60	Top Rank JAR 284	How About That/Blues Get Off My Shoulder	10
60	Top Rank JAR 373	At My Front Door/Cling-A-Ling	25

60	Top Rank JAR 501	Gloria/You're Looking Good	10
61	Top Rank JAR 551	Your Friends/Because I Love You	12
61	Top Rank JAR 570	Raindrops/I Want To Love You	15
62	Columbia DB 4768	Don't Walk Away From Me/You're Telling Our Secrets	40
63	Stateside SS 180	I'm A Soldier Boy/Shook Up Over You	25
64	Stateside SS 355	Heartbreak/Warm Summer Breeze	15
65	Stateside SS 400	T.C.B./It's Impossible	20
70	Liberty LBF 15334	Where Did All The Good Times Go?/24 Hours Of Loneliness	10
60	Top Rank BUY 044	HOW ABOUT THAT! (LP)	30
70	Joy JOYS 130	YOU'RE LOOKING GOOD (LP)	12

DOTTY CLARK

61	London HLX 9418	It's Been A Long, Long Time/That's A Step In The Right Direction	10

GENE CLARK

67	CBS 202523	Echoes/I Found You	50
74	Asylum AYM 536	No Other/The True One	6
74	Asylum AYM 540	Life's Greatest Fool/From A Silver Phial	6
67	CBS 62934	GENE CLARK WITH THE GOSDIN BROTHERS (LP)	60
72	A&M AMLS 64297	WHITE LIGHT (LP)	25
74	Asylum SYL 9020	NO OTHER (LP)	20
77	RSO 2394 175	TWO SIDES TO EVERY STORY (LP)	12
84	Making Waves SPIN 122	FIREBYRD (LP)	12

(see also Byrds, Dillard & Clark)

GUY CLARK

75	RCA Victor APL1-1303	OLD NO. 1 (LP)	15
76	RCA Victor RS 1097	TEXAS COOKIN' (LP)	15

J. CLARK

80	Cha Cha CHAD 17	Babylon/One Man Live (12")	40

JIMMY 'SOUL' CLARK

76	Black Magic BM 115	Sweet Darlin'/Sweet Darlin' (Instrumental)	10

LARENA CLARK

66	Topic 12T 140	A CANADIAN GARLAND (LP)	15

MICHAEL CLARK

66	Liberty LIB 5893	None Of These Girls/Work Out	15

MICKY CLARK

65	HMV POP 1400	You Want My Love Again/Do You Ever Feel Lonely?	7

NOBBY CLARK

76	Epic S EPC 4381	Steady Love/Give Me The Heart	10
78	Mercury 6007164	Shake It Down/Lifes Long Highway	10

PAUL CLARK & FRIENDS

77	Myrrh MYR 1054	GOOD TO BE HOME (LP, with inner sleeve)	20
78	Myrrh MYR 1059	HAND TO THE PLOUGH (LP)	20

PETULA CLARK
SINGLES

57	Pye Nixa 7N 15096	With All My Heart/Gonna Find Me A Bluebird	8
57	Pye Nixa 7N 15112	Alone/Long Before I Knew You	5
58	Pye Nixa 7N 15126	Baby Lover/The Little Blue Man	5
58	Pye Nixa 7N 15135	Love Me Again/In A Little Moment	5
58	Pye Nixa 7N 15152	St. Tropez (Sur La Plage)/Devotion	5
58	Pye Nixa 7N 15168	I Wish I Knew/Fibbin'	5
59	Pye Nixa 7N 15182	Ever Been In Love/Lucky Day	8
59	Pye Nixa 7N 15191	Watch Your Heart/Suddenly	8
59	Pye Nixa 7N 15208	Where Do I Go From Here?/Mama's Talking Soft	5
59	Pye Nixa 7N 15220	Adonis/If I Had My Way	5
59	Pye Nixa 7N 15230	Dear Daddy/Through The Livelong Day (78)	6
59	Pye 7N 15244	I Love A Violin/Guitare Et Tambourin	12
60	Pye 7N 15281	Cinderella Jones/All Over Now	10
62	Pye 7N 15448	Ya Ya Twist/Si C'est Oui, C'est Oui	5
65	Pye 7N 15991	You're The One/Gotta Tell The World (in export p/s)	5
66	Pye 7N 17071	A Sign Of The Times/Time For Love	5

EPs

56	Pye Nixa NEP 24006	CHILDREN'S CHOICE	12
56	Pye Nixa NEP 24016	PETULA CLARK HIT PARADE	12
57	Pye Nixa NEP 24056	PETULA CLARK HIT PARADE NO. 2	10
57	Pye Nixa NEP 24060	YOU ARE MY LUCKY STAR PART 1	12
57	Pye Nixa NEP 24061	YOU ARE MY LUCKY STAR PART 2	12
57	Pye Nixa NEP 24062	YOU ARE MY LUCKY STAR PART 3	12
58	Pye Nixa NEP 24080	PETULA CLARK HIT PARADE NO. 3	10
58	Pye Nixa NEP 24089	PETULA CLARK SINGS IN FRENCH	10
58	Pye Nixa NEP 24094	A CHRISTMAS CAROL (mono)	10
58	Pye Nixa NSEP 85001	A CHRISTMAS CAROL (stereo)	12
65	Pye-Vogue VRE 5007	PETULA CLARK CHANTE EN ITALIEN	8

ALBUMS

56	Pye Nixa NPT 19002	PETULA CLARK SINGS (10")	60
56	Pye Nixa NPT 19014	A DATE WITH PET (10")	50
57	Pye Nixa NPL 18007	YOU ARE MY LUCKY STAR	50
59	Pye Nixa NPL 18039	PETULA CLARK IN HOLLYWOOD	40
62	Pye NPL 18070	IN OTHER WORDS - PETULA CLARK	15
63	Pye NPL 18098	PETULA	15
64	Pye-Vogue VRL 3001	LES JAMES DEAN	25
65	Pye-Vogue VRL 3010	PETULA '65 (in French)	25
66	Pye-Vogue VRL 3016	HELLO PARIS VOL. 1	20

ROBIN CLARK

61	Capitol CL 15230	It's Love/The Butterfly Tree	6

MINT VALUE £

ROY CLARK

59	HMV POP 581	Please Mr. Mayor/Puddin'	150
59	HMV POP 581	Please Mr. Mayor/Puddin' (78)	40
63	Capitol CL 15288	In The Mood/Texas Twist	15
63	Capitol CL 15317	Tips Of My Fingers/Spooky Movies	15
62	Capitol (S)T 1780	THE LIGHTNING FINGERS OF ROY CLARK (LP)	50

SANFORD CLARK

56	London HLD 8320	The Fool/Lonesome For A Letter (with Al Casey) (gold label print)	200
56	London HLD 8320	The Fool/Lonesome For A Letter (with Al Casey) (later silver print label)	100
56	London HLD 8320	The Fool/Lonesome For A Letter (with Al Casey) (78)	15
56	London HL 7014	The Fool/Lonesome For A Letter (with Al Casey) (export issue)	50
59	London HLW 8959	Run, Boy Run/New Kind Of Fool (triangular centre)	30
59	London HLW 8959	Run, Boy Run/New Kind Of Fool (round centre)	20
59	London HLW 8959	Run, Boy Run/New Kind Of Fool (78)	20
60	London HLW 9026	Son-Of-A-Gun/I Can't Help It (If I'm Still In Love With You)	20
60	London HLW 9095	Go On Home/Pledging My Love	20
68	Ember EMB S 250	Shades/Once Upon A Time	5
57	London RED 1105	PRESENTING SANFORD CLARK (EP)	100
60	London REW 1256	LOWDOWN BLUES (EP)	100
72	Ember CW 131	THEY CALL ME COUNTRY (LP)	15

(see also Al Casey)

TERRY CLARK

70	Myrrh MYR 1071	WELCOME (LP)	20

ALLAN CLARKE

72	RCA RCA 2244	You're Losing Me/A Coward By Name	10
75	EMI 2352	Born To Run/Why Don't You Call	5
72	RCA SF 8283	MY REAL NAME IS 'AROLD (LP, lyric insert, orange/white label)	20
73	EMI EMA 752	HEADROOM (LP, gatefold sleeve, lyric inner sleeve)	15
74	EMI EMC 3041	ALLAN CLARKE (LP)	12
76	EMI EMC 3130	I'VE GOT TIME (LP)	12

(see also Hollies)

ANNETTE CLARKE

73	Techniques TE 925	Just One Look/Sinner Man	10

BOB CLARKE

70	CBS 7435	Haunted/Run Colorado	30
72	CBS 17741	Sad/Some Ones Slipping Into My Mind	10

DAVE CLARKE

94	Bush 1012	Red 1 (of 3) (Protective Custody)/Zeno Xero (12", p/s, red vinyl)	15
94	Bush 1015	Red 2 (of 3) (Wisdom To The Wise)/Gonk (12", p/s, red vinyl)	12

ERIC CLARKE

78	Baal BAL 89004	LOVE THAT GROWS AND GROWS BAAL (LP)	60

JAMES CLARK(E) + SOUNDS

68	Fontana TF 918	A Man Of Our Times T.V. Series Theme/Spring Bossa	10
68	Fontana SFJL 966	A MAN OF OUR TIMES (LP)	50

JENNY CLARKE

64	Pye 7N 15661	Spring Will Be A Little Late This Year/Say You Love Me	5

JOHN COOPER CLARKE

79	Epic S EPC 12 7009	¡Gimmix!/I Married A Monster From Outer Space (Third Version) (p/s, triangular disc, orange vinyl)	6
79	Epic S EPC 7982	Splat/Twat/Sleepwalk (double-grooved A-side, p/s, with Epic inner sleeve)	5
78	CBS 83132	DISGUISE IN LOVE (LP)	20
80	Epic EPC 84083	SNAP, CRACKLE [&] BOP (LP, with 48-page book in sleeve pocket)	20
81	Epic EPC 84979	ME AND MY BIG MOUTH (LP)	15

JOHNNY CLARKE

74	Explosion EX 2089	None Shall Escape The Judgement/Every Rasta Is A Star	12
74	Pyramid PYR 7013	My Desire/Lemon Tree	12
74	Lord Koos KOOS42	Enter Into This Gate With Praise/KING TUBBY & THE AGGROVATORS : This Is The Hardest Version	12
74	Atra ATRA019	Everyday Wondering/Julie	7
74	Cactus CTEP32	Jump Back Baby	15
74	Harry J HJ6706	Move Out A Babylon/Move Out A Babylon (Instrumental)	10
74	Explosion EX2089	None Shall Escape The Judgement/Every Rasta Is A Star	12
75	Horse HOSS86	Move out Of Babylon/AGGROVATORS : Version	7
75	Horse HOSS100	Too Much War/AGGROVATORS : Version	8
75	Vulcan VUL 1001	I'm Gonna Put It On/KING TUBBY AND THE AGGROVATORS - Version	6
75	Attack ATT 8100	Rock With Me Baby/KING TUBBYS AND THE AGGROVATORS: A Crabit Version	6
75	Attack ATT 8118	Cold I Up/Cold I Up (Version)	6
76	Virgin VS159	Crazy Baldhead/Version	8
77	Virgin VS173	Roots, Natty Roots, Natty Congo/Version	8
77	Third World TW 70	Age is growing/Version	12
78	Star PTP1009	Every Knee Shall Bow/Version (With U Roy) (12")	25
78	Justice JUDIS 109	Pity Fool Fe Get Wise/Satisfaction (12")	50
78	Third World TW 92	Riding For A Fall/CLINT EASTWOOD AND THE AGROVATORS: Version	8
79	Greensleeves GRED20	Jah Love Is With I/Bad Days Are Going (12")	30
80	Cha Cha CHAD17	Babylon/One Man Live (as J. Clark) (12")	20
81	Chrysalis 122849	Babylon/Than You For The Many Things You've Done - Cassandra (12")	20
81	Art & Craft ACD 007	Can't Get Enough/Version (12')	20
81	Art & Craft ACD 014	Guide Us Jah/Version (12")	30
81	Art & Craft ACD 015	Rude Boy/Version (12")	20
82	Art & Craft ACD 018	You Better Try/Version (12")	20
82	Black Joy DH822	Stop Them Jah/Too Much War	12
82	Cha Cha CHAD 49	Give Me Love/Version (10")	15
83	Top Notch TOP005	Young Rebel/Version(10")	15
89	Jah Shaka SHAKA 876	Rosie/Rosie Dub (12")	12
75	Attack ATLP 1015	ENTER INTO HIS GATES WITH PRAISE (LP)	50

75	Vulcan VULP 001	PUT IT ON (LP)	30
76	Virgin V2076	AUTHORISED VERSION (LP, mono)	20
76	Attack ATLP101	ENTER INTO HIS GATES WITH PRAISE (LP, original first pressing)	25
76	Virgin V2058	ROCKERS TIME NOW (LP, mono credits on label)	30
77	Justice JUSLP 001	GIRL I LOVE YOU (LP)	40
77	Paradise PDLP 001	DON'T STAY OUT LATE (LP)	25
78	Third World TWS 932	KING IN A ARENA (LP, as Johnie Clark)	40
79	Paradise PDLP 008	SHOWCASE (LP)	30
82	Art and Craft ACDLP001	CAN'T GET ENOUGH (LP)	50
83	Ariwa ARI 007 LP	YARD STYLE (LP)	30
83	Vista VSLP 4016	MEETS CORNEL CAMPBELL (LP)	30

KENNY CLARKE

56	London LTZC 15004	KENNY CLARKE SEXTET (LP)	20
56	London LTZC 15008	KENNY CLARKE AND ERNIE WILKINS (LP)	20
57	London LTZC 15038	KENNY CLARKE (LP)	20
57	London LTZC 15047	KENNY CLARKE (LP)	20
57	Vogue LAE 12029	JAZZ INTERNATIONAL (LP)	25

KENNY CLARKE (WITH FRANCY BOLAND BIG BAND)

56	London LTZ C 15047	BOHEMIA AFTER DARK (LP)	15
57	Columbia SEG 7830	KENNY CLARKE QT. (EP)	10
63	London HA-K 8085	JAZZ IS UNIVERSAL (LP, with Francy Boland Big Band)	15
66	CBS SBPG 62567	NOW HEAR OUR MEANIN' (LP)	18
68	Polydor 583726	LATIN KALEIDOSCOPE (LP)	20
69	Polydor 583727	ALL SMILES (LP)	20
69	Polydor 583738	FELLINI 712 (LP)	20
69	Polydor 583054	LIVE AT RONNIE SCOTT'S - THE FIRST SET (LP)	20
69	Polydor 583055	LIVE AT RONNIE SCOTT'S - THE SECOND SET (LP)	20
70	Polydor 583739	FACES (LP)	15
70	Polydor 2310 147	OFF LIMITS (LP, reflective sleeve)	30
71	Polydor 2310 147	OFF LIMITS (LP)	12

(see also Francey Boland, Kenny Clarke)

LINDA CLARKE

67	Decca F 12709	Your Hurtin' Kinda Love/Send Me The Pillow You Dream On	10
68	Decca F 12787	Society's Child/Rain In My Heart	20

LLOYD CLARKE

62	Blue Beat BB 99	Good Morning/Now I Know A Reason (with Smithie's Sextet)	12
62	Blue Beat BB 104	Fool's Day/You're A Cheat (with Reco's All Stars)	12
62	Island WI 007	Love You The Most/LLOYD ROBINSON: You Said You Loved Me	15
62	Island WI 045	Japanese Girl/He's Coming	15
63	Rio R 16	Love Me/Half As Much	15
64	Rio R 23	Stop Your Talking/A Penny	15
64	Rio R 24	Fellow Jamaican/PATRICK & GEORGE: My Love	15
68	Island WI 3116	Summertime/VAL BENNETT: Soul Survivor	100
68	Blue Cat BS 136	Young Love/UNTOUCHABLES: Wall Flower	40
70	Escort ERT 849	Chicken Thief/STRANGER COLE: Tomorrow	7

(see also Derrick & Lloyd, Theo Beckford, Soulettes, Delroy Wilson, Laurel Aitken, Sonny Burke, Uniques)

MICKEY CLARKE

66	HMV 1483	Help Me/For Me	20

PAULA CLARKE

83	Oak Sound OSD 013	University/Didn't I Blow Your Mind (12")	40

RONA CLARKE

67	Westwood WRS 067	UTOPIAN DREAM (LP)	30

TERRY CLARKE

72	Polydor 2058191	Lady/Army Captains Daughter	10

TONY CLARKE

64	Pye International 7N 25251	Ain't Love Good, Ain't Love Proud/Coming Back Strong	22
65	Chess CRS 8011	The Entertainer/This Heart Of Mine	25
65	Chess CRS 8011	The Entertainer/This Heart Of Mine (DJ Copy)	50
69	Chess CRS 8091	The Entertainer/Ain't Love Good, Ain't Love Proud	8
74	Chess 6145 030	Landslide/The Entertainer	5

FREDDY CLARKE

78	Jungle Beat JBDC 805	Troubles/I Man (12" with I ROY)	80
81	Jungla Beat JBDC801	Fight I Down/VIN GORDON: Fire Horns (12", red vinyl)	45

CLARK-HUTCHINSON

68	Decca LK-R 5006	CLARK-HUTCHINSON (LP, one known copy, red Decca labels, no sleeve Matrix: ARL-8968.P-1A/1B	500
70	Decca Nova DN-R 2	A = MH2(LP, mono)	150
70	Decca Nova DN-R 2	A = MH2(LP, stereo)	75
70	Deram SML 1076	RETRIBUTION (LP)	60
71	Deram SML 1090	GESTALT (LP)	65

(see also Sam Gopal, Vamp, Upp)

CLARK SISTERS

59	London HLD 8791	Chicago/Opus 1	10
58	London RE-D 1198	SING, SING, SING (EP)	10
58	London HA-D 2128	SING, SING, SING (LP)	20
59	London HA-D 2177	THE CLARK SISTERS SWING AGAIN (LP, mono)	20
59	London SAH-D 2177	THE CLARK SISTERS SWING AGAIN (LP, stereo)	22

CLARO INTELECTO

02	Ai AI 003	PEACE OF MIND (12", first pressings in blue p/s)	15

CLASH

SINGLES

77	CBS S CBS 5058	White Riot/1977 (p/s, 'The Clash' or 'The CLASH' on label)	20
77	CBS CL 1	CAPITAL RADIO (EP, NME freebie, p/s)	50

MINT VALUE £

77	CBS S CBS 5293	Remote Control/London's Burning (live) (p/s)	10
77	CBS Promo S CBS 5293	Remote Control/London's Burning (Studio Version) ('A' Label Promo)	50
77	CBS S CBS 5664	Complete Control/The City Of The Dead (p/s)	10
78	CBS CBS 5834	Clash City Rockers/Jail Guitar Doors (p/s)	5
78	CBS S CBS 6383	(White Man) In Hammersmith Palais/The Prisoner (initially green, then pink, blue or yellow die-cut sleeve)	12
78	CBS S CBS 6788	Tommy Gun/1 - 2 Crush On You (p/s)	8
78	CBS S CBS 7082	English Civil War/Pressure Drop (p/s)	8
79	CBS S CBS 7324	I Fought The Law/Gates Of The West (2-track promo for COST OF LIVING EP)	30
79	CBS S CBS 7324	THE COST OF LIVING (EP, gatefold p/s & inner sleeve)	8
	(All the early Clash singles were re-pressed in 1979 with picture sleeves.)		
79	CBS S CBS 8087	London Calling/Armagideon Time (p/s, green or red shaded sleeve, white or yellow/orange label)	10
79	CBS 12 8087	London Calling/Armagidion Time/Armagidion Time (version)	15
80	CBS 8323	Bankrobber/Rockers Galore (p/s)	7
81	CBS A12 1133	The Magnificent Seven/The Magnificent Dance (12", p/s)	15
81	CBS S 2309	Know Your Rights/First Night Back In London (p/s, with free sticker)	10
82	CBS A 2479	Rock The Casbah/Long Time Jerk (p/s, with free stickers)	10
82	CBS A 11 2479	Rock The Casbah/Long Time Jerk (picture disc)	8
82	CBS A 13 2479	Rock The Casbah/Mustapha Dance	18
82	CBS A 2646	Should I Stay Or Should I Go/Straight To Hell (p/s)	10
82	CBS A 11 2646	Should I Stay Or Should I Go/Straight To Hell (picture disc)	8
82	CBS A 12 2646	Should I Stay Or Should I Go/Straight To Hell (12")	12
88	CBS CLASHB 2	London Calling/Brand New Cadillac/Rudie Don't Fail (box set)	12
11	Columbia 88697890297	The Magnificent Seven/The Cool Out (red vinyl, numbered, die-cut sleeve)	7

ALBUMS

77	CBS 82000	THE CLASH (LP, 10,000 only with sticker on inner sleeve for free NME Capital Radio EP freebie)	50
77	CBS 82000	THE CLASH (LP, 1st issue with orange/yellow labels)	20
78	CBS 82431	GIVE 'EM ENOUGH ROPE (LP, promo-only package with poster in folder)	200
78	CBS 82431	GIVE 'EM ENOUGH ROPE (LP)	15
79	CBS CLASH 3	LONDON CALLING (2-LP, stickered, with inner sleeves, 1st issue with black & white labels)	40
80	CBS FSLN	SANDINISTA (3-LP, stickered sleeve with 'Armagideon Times' insert)	35
82	CBS FMLN2	COMBAT ROCK (LP, inner sleeve and poster)	15
88	CBS 460244 1	THE STORY OF THE CLASH (2-LP)	20

(see also 101'ers, Janie Jones & Lash, Tymon Dogg, Ellen Foley, Futura 2000, Joe Strummer)

CLASS 50

77	Electric WOT 13	Freerider/Time Machine	12

CLASSICS IV

66	Capitol CL 15470	Pollyanna/Cry Baby (issued as if by the "Classics")	40
68	Liberty LBF 15051	Spooky/Poor People	8
69	Liberty LBF 15177	Stormy/Twenty Four Hours Of Loneliness	15
69	Liberty LBF 15196	Traces/Mary, Mary Row Your Boat	5
69	Liberty LBF 15231	Everyday With You Girl/Sentimental Lady	5

(see also Dennis Yost & Classics IV)

CLASSICS (JAMAICA)

69	Doctor Bird DB 1190	Worried Over Me/LAUREL AITKEN: Rice And Peas	40
70	New Beat NB 061	Same Old Feeling/So Much Love	8
70	New Beat NB 071	History Of Africa/Honeybee	8
70	Pama PM 830	Sex Education/POWER: Soul Flash	12
71	Punch PH 79	Cheerio Baby/Civilization	40

CLASSICS (U.S.)

61	Mercury AMT 1152	Life Is But A Dream/That's The Way	100
63	Stateside SS 215	Till Then/Enie Minie Mo	40

CLASSMATES

63	Decca F 11736	Let's Get Together Tonight/It's No Game	5
63	Decca F 11779	Go Tell It On The Mountain/Give Me A Girl	5
64	Decca F 11806	In Morocco/I Feel	5
64	Decca F 12047	Go Away/Pay Day	5

CLAUDETTE (& CORPORATION)

69	Jackpot JP 712	Let's Fall In Love/PROPHETS: Purple Moon	30
70	Grape GR 3020	Skinheads A Bash Them (with Corporation)/ CORPORATION: Walkin' Thru Jerusalem	200

(see also Corporation)

CASSIUS CLAY

64	CBS AAG 190	Stand By Me/I Am The Greatest	20
66	CBS 202190	Stand By Me/I Am The Greatest (reissue)	5
63	CBS BPG 62274	I AM THE GREATEST! (LP)	30

JUDY CLAY

67	Stax 601 022	You Can't Run Away From Your Heart/It Takes A Lotta Good Love	10

(see also Billy Vera & Judy Clay, Booker T. & M.G.'s)

JUDY CLAY & WILLIAM BELL

68	Stax STAX 101	Private Number/Love-Eye-Tis	5
69	Stax STAX 115	My Baby Specialises/Left Over Love	8

(see also William Bell, Billy Vera & Judy Clay)

OTIS CLAY

67	President PT 121	It's Easier Said Than Done/Flame In Your Heart	8
68	President PT 132	I'm Satisfied/I Testify	5
68	President PT 148	That's How It Is/Show Place	8
68	President PT 176	A Lasting Love/Got To Find A Way	5
69	Atlantic 584 282	Baby Jane/You Hurt Me For The Last Time	75
72	London HLU 10397	Trying To Live My Life Without You/Let Me Be The One	10
74	London HLU 10467	You Did Something To Me/It Was Jealousy	10
76	President PT 456	All I Need Is You/Special Kind Of Love	7
73	London SH-U 8446	TRYING TO LIVE MY LIFE WITHOUT YOU (LP)	30

TOM CLAY
72	Tamla Motown TMG 801	What The World Needs Now Is Love/The Victors	12

CLAY FAV
79	Own label	CONSIGNMENT STOCK (EP, 1,000, 200 with stamped "consignment Stock' sleeve, no p/s)	150
79	Own label	CONSIGNMENT STOCK (EP, 1,000, 800 without stamped "consignment Stock' sleeve, no p/s)	50

ALASDAIR CLAYRE
67	Elektra EUK 255	ALASDAIR CLAYRE (LP, some with mail order insert)	60
76	Acorn CF 252	ADAM AND THE BEASTS (LP)	25

ADAM CLAYTON & LARRY MULLEN
96	Mother MUM 75	Theme From Mission: Impossible/Theme From Mission: Impossible (Junior's Hard Mix Edit) (jukebox issue, no p/s, promo only)	5

(see also U2)

DOCTOR CLAYTON
65	RCA Victor RCX 7177	RCA RACE SERIES VOLUME 6 (EP)	10
70	RCA Intl. INTS 1176	PEARL HARBOUR BLUES (LP)	20

MERRY CLAYTON
70	A&M AMS 802	Gimme Shelter/Good Girls	20
73	Ode ODS 66301	Acid Queen/Underture (p/s)	15
70	A&M AMLS 995	GIMME SHELTER (LP)	30
72	A&M AMLS 67012	MERRY CLAYTON (LP)	30

(see also Raelets)

PAUL CLAYTON
61	London HLU 9285	Wings Of A Dove/So Long (It's Been Good To Know You)	15
61	London REU 1276	PAUL CLAYTON (EP)	130

STEVE CLAYTON
56	Vogue Coral Q 72200	Two Different Worlds/It Happened Again	5

VIKKI CLAYTON
88	Dambuster DAM 021	LOST LADY FOUND (LP)	20

(see also Fairport Convention)

CLAYTON SQUARES
65	Decca F 12250	Come And Get It/And Tears Fell	40
66	Decca F 12456	There She Is/Imagination	175

(see also Liverpool Scene, Andy Roberts, Mike Hart)

DAVID CLAYTON-THOMAS
72	CBS 64755	DAVID CLAYTON-THOMAS (LP, plain orange label)	12
72	CBS 65237	TEQUILA SUNRISE (LP, plain orange label)	12
73	RCA SF 8381	DAVID CLAYTON-THOMAS (LP, gatefold sleeve)	12

(see also Blood Sweat & Tears)

CLAYTOWN TROUPE
92	EMI 12 88007)	SKYBOUND (LP, withdrawn)	20

CLEAN
94	Dark Beloved Cloud DBC 020	Late Last Night/Psychedelic Clown (p/s)	8
86	Flying Nun FNE 29	COMPILATION (LP)	25
89	Flying Nun Europe FNE 29	IN-A-LIVE (Mini-LP)	20
90	Rough Trade ROUGH 143	VEHICLE (LP)	25

CLEANERS FROM VENUS
87	Ammunition JANGLE 1	Illya Kurayakin Looked At Me/Black And White And Blue All Over (p/s)	25
87	Ammunition JANGLE 1T	Illya Kurayakin Looked At Me/Albion's Daughter/Black And White And Blue All Over/Illya Kuryakin Looked At Me (Full Version) (12", p/s)	15
87	Ammunition JANGLE 2	Living With Victoria Grey/Sunday Afternoon (p/s)	20
87	Ammunition JANGLE 2T	Living With Victoria Grey/Sunday Afternoon/She's Checking You Out {12", p/s)	15
88	Ammunition JANGLE 3	Mercury Girl/Gamma Ray Blues	20
88	Ammunition JANGLE 3T	Mercury Girl/Gamma Ray Blues/The Iceberg Unicorn (12", p/s)	15
87	Ammunition CLEAN LP 1	GOING TO ENGLAND (LP)	30
88	Ammunition CLEAN LP 2	TOWN AND COUNTRY (LP)	30

(see also Gypp, Martin Newall, Brotherhood of Lizards)

CLEAR BLUE SKY
70	Vertigo 6360 013	CLEAR BLUE SKY (LP, gatefold sleeve, large swirl label)	400
90	Saturn SRLP 101	DESTINY (LP)	15

CLEAR LIGHT
67	Elektra EKSN 45019	Black Roses/She's Ready To Be Free	10
68	Elektra EKSN 45027	Night Sounds Loud/How Many Days Have Passed	20
67	Elektra EKL 4011	CLEAR LIGHT (LP, orange label, also stereo EKS 74011)	80
87	Edsel ED 245	BLACK ROSES (LP, reissue)	12

CLEARLIGHT
75	Virgin V 2029	SYMPHONY (LP, stickered sleeve)	20
75	Virgin V 2039	FOREVER BLOWING BUBBLES (LP)	20

(see also Gong, Steve Hillage)

CLEAR SPOT
98	Duophonic Super 45s	Psycho's Blues/Moonman Bop (33rpm, 300 copies on blue vinyl, p/s)	6

(see also Stereolab)

CLEARWAYS
64	Columbia DB 7333	I'll Be Here/I've Just Got A Letter	10

CLEFS
62	Salvo SLO 1810	Don't Cry/The Dream Train Special (99 copies only)	20

CLEFS OF LAVENDER HILL
66	CBS 202230	Stop, Get A Ticket/	20

CLEFTONES
56	Columbia DB 3801	You Baby, You/Little Girl Of Mine	500

MINT VALUE £

56	Columbia DB 3801	You Baby, You/Little Girl Of Mine (78)	60
61	Columbia DB 4678	Heart And Soul/How Do You Feel	150
61	Columbia DB 4720	(I Love You) For Sentimental Reasons/Deed I Do	100
63	Columbia DB 4988	Lover Come Back To Me/There She Goes	50

PAT CLEMENCE
64	HMV POP 1360	While I Live/Since I Don't Have You	5

JACK CLEMENT
58	London HLS 8691	Ten Years/Your Lover Boy	150
58	London HLS 8691	Ten Years/Your Lover Boy (78)	40

SOUL JOE CLEMENTS
69	Plexium PXM 10	Smoke And Ashes/Ever, Ever	150

CLEO
64	Decca F 11817	To Know Him Is To Love Him/ANDREW OLDHAM ORCHESTRA: There Are But Five Rolling Stones	25

(see also Andrew Oldham Orchestra, This 'N' That)

CLERKS
80	Rok ROK VIII/VII	No Good For Me/HAZARD: Gotta Change My Life (company sleeve)	12
84	Puddisc SRT8 KS 1538	Dancing With My Girl/On The Telephone/All I Want Is You (p/s)	5

CLEVELANDS
64	Philips BF 1315	Big Town/Lonely, Weary And Blue	5
64	Philips BF 1342	Little Girl In Calico/Everything Is Fine	5

CLICHE
80	Carrere CAR 133	I Know Your Name/Drawing The Line	100

CLIENTELE
98	Pointy POINT 001	What Goes Up/Five Day Morning (p/s)	15
99	Johnny Kane KANE 002	Reflections After Jane/An Hour Before The Light (p/s)	15
99	Pointy POINT 002	I Had To Say This/Monday's Rain (p/s)	15
02	Pointy POINT 008	Haunted Melody/Fear Of Falling (p/s)	5
00	Pointy POINT 004LP	SUBURBAN LIGHT (LP)	20
03	Pointy POINT 011LP	THE VIOLET HOUR (LP)	15

CLIENTELLE
79	Quest BRS 003	Can't Forget/Skyline (p/s)	125
81	Banana BANANA 505	DESTINATION UNKNOWN (LP, with insert)	120

JIMMY CLIFF
62	Blue Beat BB 78	I'm Sorry (with Cavaliers Combo)/BLUE BEATS: Roarin' (with Red Price)	30
62	Island WI 012	Hurricane Hatty/Dearest Beverley	18
62	Island WI 016	Miss Jamaica/Gold Digger	25
62	Island WI 025	Since Lately/I'm Free	25
63	Island WI 062	My Lucky Day/One-Eyed Jacks	25
63	Island WI 070	King Of Kings/SIR PERCY: Oh Yeah	30
63	Island WI 112	Miss Universe/The Prodigal	18
63	Black Swan WI 403	The Man (vocal version)/You Are Never Too Old	20
63	Black Swan WI 403	The Man (Instrumental version)/You Are Never Too Old	20
64	Stateside SS 342	One Eyed Jacks/King Of Kings	20
67	Island WIP 6004	Aim And Ambition/Give And Take	15
66	Fontana TF 641	Call On Me/Pride And Passion	15
67	Island WIP 6011	I Got A Feeling/Hard Road To Travel	15
67	Island WIP 6024	That's The Way Life Goes/Thank You	10
68	Island WIP 6039	Waterfall/Reward	35
69	Trojan TR 690	Wonderful World, Beautiful People/Hard Road To Travel (in p/s)	7
69	Trojan TR 690	Wonderful World, Beautiful People/Hard Road To Travel	5
70	Trojan TR 7722	Vietnam/She Does It Right	5
70	Trojan TR 7745	Suffering/Come Into My Life	5
70	Trojan TR 7745	Those Good Good Old Days/Pack Up Hang Ups	5
70	Trojan TR 7767	You Can Get It If You Really Want/Be Aware	5
70	Island WIP 6087	Wild World/Be Aware	5
70	Island WIP 6097	Synthetic World/I Go To Pieces	5
71	Island WIP 6103	Goodbye Yesterday/Breakdown	5
71	Island WIP 6110	Sitting In Limbo/The Bigger They Come	5
72	Island WIP 6132	Trapped/Struggling Man	5
68	Island ILP 962	HARD ROAD TO TRAVEL (LP)	60
69	Trojan TRLS 16	JIMMY CLIFF (LP)	20
71	Island ILPS 9159	ANOTHER CYCLE (LP)	18

(see also Jackie Edwards & Jimmy Cliff, James Chambers)

CLIFF DWELLERS
66	Polydor BM 56707	Hang On Stupid/I'm A Superman For You	15

CLIFFORD
73	Satril SAT 10	Drink Wine Susan/Looking Upon The Day	10

BUZZ CLIFFORD
61	Fontana H 297	Baby Sittin' Boogie/Driftwood	10
61	Fontana H 312	Three Little Fishes/Simply Because	10
62	Columbia DB 4903	More Dead Than Alive/Nobody Loves Me Like You	5
61	Fontana TFL 5147	BABY SITTIN' WITH BUZZ CLIFFORD (LP, mono)	20
61	Fontana STFL 567	BABY SITTIN' WITH BUZZ CLIFFORD (LP, stereo])	25

JOHN & JULIA CLIFFORD
77	Topic 12TS 311	THE HUMOURS OF LISHEEN (LP)	20

LINDA CLIFFORD
74	Paramount PARA 3051	After Loving You/Check Out Your Heart	75
78	Curtom K 17163T	If My Friends Could See Me Now/Runaway Love (12")	12

MIKE CLIFFORD
62	United Artists UP 1006	Close To Cathy/She's Just Another Girl	10

MATAYA CLIFFORD
76	Virgin V 2063	STAR FELL FROM HEAVEN (LP, red "mirror" girl label)	12

CLIFFTERS
62	Philips PB 1242	Django/Amapola (Pretty Little Poppy)	5

BILL CLIFTON
60	Melodisc 1554	You Don't Think About Me/Mail Carrier's Warning	5
63	Decca F 11793	Beatle Crazy/Little Girl Dressed In Blue	5

CLIMAX (CHICAGO) BLUES BAND
69	Parlophone R 5809	Like Uncle Charlie/Loving Machine	30
70	Harvest HAR 5029	Reap What I've Sowed/Spoonful	12
71	Harvest HAR 5041	Towards The Sun/Everyday (as Climax Chicago)	10
72	Harvest HAR 5065	Mole On The Dole/Like Uncle Charlie	12
69	Parlophone PMC/PCS 7069	CLIMAX CHICAGO BLUES BAND (LP, yellow/black label, with "sold in the UK.." text)	125
70	Parlophone PCS 7084	PLAYS ON (LP, yellow/black labels)	200
70	Parlophone PCS 7084	PLAYS ON (LP, later issue with boxed Parlophone logo)	50
70	Harvest SHSP 4009	A LOT OF BOTTLE (LP, no EMI logo on label, fully laminated sleeve)	45
71	Harvest SHSP 4015	TIGHTLY KNIT (LP, with EMI logo on label, flipback sleeve)	30
72	Harvest SHSP 4024	RICH MAN (LP)	18
74	Polydor 2383259	LIVE (LP)	15
75	Harvest SHSM 2003	1969 - 1972 (LP)	12

(see also Hipster Image)

CLIMAX INVASION
77	Top Secret TS1	The Advertiser (one-sided)	30

PATSY CLINE
57	Brunswick 05660	A Poor Man's Roses (Or A Rich Man's Gold)/Walkin' After Midnight	50
57	Brunswick 05660	A Poor Man's Roses (Or A Rich Man's Gold)/Walkin' After Midnight (78)	20
61	Brunswick 05855	I Fall To Pieces/Lovin' In Vain	15
61	Brunswick 05861	Crazy/Who Can I Count On	15
62	Brunswick 05866	She's Got You/Strange	5
62	Brunswick 05869	When I Get Through With You/Imagine That	5
62	Brunswick 05874	So Wrong/You're Stronger Than Me	5
62	Brunswick 05878	Heartaches/Why Can't He Be You	5
63	Brunswick 05883	Leavin' On Your Mind/Tra Le La La La Triangle	7
63	Brunswick 05888	Sweet Dreams/Back In My Baby's Arms	10
63	Decca 31262	Blue Moon Of Kentucky/Faded Love (export)	25
62	Brunswick OE 9490	SWEET DREAMS (EP)	30
62	Brunswick LAT 8394	SHOWCASE (LP)	20
62	Brunswick LAT 8510	SENTIMENTALLY YOURS (LP, mono)	20
62	Brunswick STA 8510	SENTIMENTALLY YOURS (LP, stereo)	20
63	Brunswick LAT 8549	A TRIBUTE TO PATSY CLINE (LP)	20
64	Brunswick LAT 8589	A PORTRAIT OF PATSY CLINE (LP, mono)	20
64	Brunswick STA 8589	A PORTRAIT OF PATSY CLINE (LP, stereo)	22
65	Ember CW 16	IN MEMORIAM (LP)	15
65	Fontana FJL 302	TODAY TOMORROW AND FOREVER (LP)	15
66	Fontana FJL 309	I CAN'T FORGET YOU (LP)	15

CLINIC
97	Aladdin's Cave Of Golf GOLF001	IPC Subeditors Dictate Our Youth/Porno/D.I.Y. (p/s, 500 copies only)	15
98	Aladdin's C.O.G. GOLF002	Monkey On Your Back/D.T. (p/s, 500 copies only)	6
98	Aladdin's C.O.G. GOLF003	Cement Mixer/Kimberley (p/s, 1,000 copies only)	8
00	Domino WIGLP 78	INTERNATIONAL WRANGLER (LP)	15
01	Domino WIGLP 261X	BUBBLEGUM (2-LP, pink vinyl, transfer, sticker, poster & badge)	18

BUDDY CLINTON
60	Top Rank JAR 287	Across The Street From Your House/How My Prayers Have Changed ...	20

DAVY CLINTON
68	NEMS 56-3855	Can I Bring Back Yesterday/The Girl With The Sun In Her Hair	35
68	President PT 290	House Of The Rising Sun/On A Rooftop In Memphis	6

GEORGE CLINTON
79	ABC ABC 4053	Please Don't Run From Me/Life And Breath	5
79	ABC ABC 4053	Please Don't Run From Me/Life And Breath (DJ Copy)	10

(do not see also Parliament, Funkadelic)

LARRY CLINTON
79	Grapevine GRP 120	She's Wanted In Three States/If I Knew	25
79	Grapevine GRP 120	She's Wanted In Three States/If I Knew (DJ Copy)	40

CLINTONES
73	Ackee ACK 515	Equal Rights/Version	6

CLIQUE (U.K.) (1)
65	Pye 7N 15786	She Ain't No Good/Time Time Time	100
65	Pye 7N 15853	We Didn't Kiss, Didn't Love, But Now We Do/You've Been Unfair	175
60s	private pressing	THE CLIQUE (EP, no p/s)	550
95	Dig The Fuzz DIG 003	THE COMPLETE RECORDINGS 1964/1965 (LP)	20

(see also Hammersmith Gorillas)

CLIQUE (U.K.) (2)
91	Guild GUIEP 001	INTRODUCING...THE CLIQUE (EP)	20
94	Detour DR 014	Reggie/She Doesn't Need You Anymore (p/s, red vinyl)	10
94	Detour DR 014	Reggie/She Doesn't Need You Anymore (pic disc, 200 only)	15
93	Detour DR 006	THE EARLY DAYS (EP)	15
03	Detour DRLP 021	VANBRUGH PARK (LP)	12

CLIQUE (U.S.)
69	London HLU 10286	Sugar On Sunday/Superman	20

JOHNNY CLIVE
62	Oriole CB 1793	Lazy Boy/Swiss Twistin' Baby	7
63	Oriole CB 1820	China Girl/Sue	5

MINT VALUE £

CLIVE & DOREEN
68	Treasure Isle TI 7033	What Can I Do/TOMMY MCCOOK: Black Power	30

CLIVE & GLORIA
63	R&B JB 113	Change Of Plan/Little Gloria	20
64	R&B JB 173	Money Money Money/Have I Told You Lately	20
64	King KG 1004	Do The Ska/You Made Me Cry	20

CLIVE & NAOMI
65	Ska Beat JB 181	You Are Mine/Open The Door	20

(see also Desmond Dekker)

CLOCK DVA
81	Fetish FET 008	Four Hours (Re-mixed)/Sensorium (p/s)	6
85	Fetish FET 008	FOUR HOURS EP (12", p/s)	8
81	Fetish FR 2002	THIRST (LP, with insert)	12
81	Industrial IRC 31	WHITE SOULS IN BLACK SUITS (cassette, with booklet)	20

CLOCKHOUSE
83	Picturesque PIC 1	Vanishing Point/Everyman (p/s)	7

CLOCKWORK CRIMINALS
82	Ace ACE 38	YOUNG AND BOLD (EP)	150

CLOCKWORK ORANGES
66	Ember EMB S 227	Ready Steady/After Tonight	25

CLOCKWORK SOLDIERS
84	Rot ASS 5	Wet Dreams/Suicide/In The Name Of Science (p/s)	15

BETTY CLOONEY
55	HMV 7M 311	I Love You A Mountain/Can't Do Without You	5

(see also Rosemary Clooney)

ROSEMARY CLOONEY
53	Columbia SCM 5019	Half As Much/Botch-A-Me (Ba-Ba-Baciami Piccina)	20
53	Columbia SCM 5027	If I Had A Penny/You're After My Own Heart	10
53	Columbia SCM 5028	On The First Warm Day/If Teardrops Were Pennies	10
53	Columbia SCM 5040	(Remember Me) I'm The One Who Loves You/Lover's Gold	10
53	Columbia SCM 5049	Blues In The Night/Who Kissed Me Last Night?	10
54	Columbia SCM 5093	I Still Feel The Same About You (with Betty Clooney)/Why Fight The Feeling	10
56	Philips JB 100	The Teddy Bear's Picnic/Kitty Kat's Party (78, picture label)	10
57	Philips JK 1010	Mangos/All The Pretty Little Horses (jukebox issue)	25
58	Philips PB 800	I Could Have Danced All Night/I've Grown Accustomed To Your Face	5
59	Philips PB 900	Tonight/Come Rain Or Come Shine	5
59	Coral Q 72357	Diga Me (Deega May-Tell Me)/A Touch Of The Blues	5
59	MGM MGM 1010	Love Eyes/Flattery (B-side with Jose Ferrer)	5
60	Coral Q 72388	Love, Love Away/I Wish I Were In Love Again	5
60	MGM MGM 1062	For You/I Wonder	5
60	RCA RCA 1203	Many A Wonderful Moment/Vaya, Vaya	5
54	Columbia SEG 7552	ROSEMARY CLOONEY AND HARRY JAMES (EP, company sleeve)	10
55	Philips BBE 12004	ROSEMARY CLOONEY (EP)	10
56	Philips BBE 12051	ROSEMARY CLOONEY (EP)	10
60	Coral FEP 2045	SWING AROUND ROSIE VOL. 1 (EP)	10
60	Coral FEP 2046	SWING AROUND ROSIE VOL. 2 (EP)	10
54	Philips BBR 8022	WHITE CHRISTMAS (10" LP)	15
55	Philips BBR 8047	ROSEMARY CLOONEY (10" LP)	12
56	Philips BBR 8073	AT THE LONDON PALLADIUM (10" LP)	12

(see also Bing Crosby)

ROSEMARY CLOONEY & MARLENE DIETRICH
53	Columbia SCM 5010	Too Old To Cut The Mustard/Good For Nothin'	15

(see also Marlene Dietrich, Betty Clooney, Bob Hope & Rosemary Clooney, Guy Mitchell)

CLOSE LOBSTERS
89	Caff CAFF 4	Just Too Bloody Stupid/All The Little Boys And Girls (p/s)	12

CLOSE SHAVE
99	Helen Of Oi! H 003	Attack/We Hate You (p/s, first pressing, 200 numbered copies)	8
88	Link LP 056	Oi! KINNOCK GIVE US BACK OUR ROSE (LP)	12

CLOUD
75	Kingsway DOVE 16	FREE TO FLY (LP)	20
77	Kingsway DOVE 44	WATERED GARDEN (LP, gatefold sleeve)	30
78	Dove 62	THE RESTING PLACE (LP)	20
85	Songs Of Fellow. SFR103	THE PROMISE (LP)	15

CLAUDE CLOUD
55	MGM MGM 820	Cloudburst/One Bone (78, as Claude Cloud & Thunderclaps)	20
57	MGM MGM 946	The Beat/Around The Horn (as Claude Cloud & His Orchestra)	15
55	MGM MGM-EP 517	LET'S GO CATSTATIC NO. 1 (EP, as Claude Cloud & Thunderclaps)	30
56	MGM MGM-D 142	ROCK 'N' ROLL (10" LP)	150

(see also Sonny Thompson, Sam 'The Man' Taylor)

CLOUD NINE
90s	Acid Jazz JAZID 87P	I Feel It (12", p/s, promo-only, withdrawn)	18
90s	Acid Jazz JAZID 78	MILLENNIUM (LP, withdrawn)	30

CLOUDS (1)
69	Island WIP 6055	Heritage/Make No Bones About It	20
69	Island WIP 6067	Scrapbook/Carpenter	20
69	Island ILPS 9100	THE CLOUDS SCRAPBOOK (LP, gatefold sleeve, first pressing with black/orange circle logo)	200
69	Island ILPS 9100	THE CLOUDS SCRAPBOOK (LP, second pressing, circle logo)	100
69	Island ILPS 9100	THE CLOUDS SCRAPBOOK (LP, later pressing 'pink rim palm tree')	25
71	Chrysalis ILPS 9151	WATERCOLOUR DAYS (LP, gatefold sleeve, 'green label with Island logo and Island address in white')	40

CLOUDS (2)
88	Subway Org. SUBWAY 12	Tranquil/Get Out Of My Dream (p/s)	5
88	Subway Org. SUBWAY 12T	Tranquil/Get Out Of My Dream/Village Green (12", p/s)	8

(see also Boy Hairdressers, Teenage Fanclub)

BRIAN CLOUGH
88	MCA MCA 658	You Can't Win 'Em All/It's Only A Game (p/s)	10

CLOUT
90	Mooncrest JWL 1000	We'll Bring The House Down/Jim Jam (p/s)	7

(see also Slade)

CLOVEN HOOF
82	Elemental EM 001	OPENING RITUAL (12" EP)	80
84	Neat NEAT 1013	CLOVEN HOOF (LP)	20
86	Trojan CH 002	FIGHTING BACK (LP, with poster)	25
86	Trojan CH 002	FIGHTING BACK (LP, without poster)	20

CLOVER
70	Liberty LBF 15341	Wade In The Water/Stealin'	10
69	Liberty LBS 83340	CLOVER (LP)	30
71	Liberty LBS 83487	FORTY-NINER (LP)	30

(see also Huey Lewis & News)

CLOVERLEAFS
56	MGM MGM 933	Step Right Up And Say Howdy/With Plenty Of Money And You (Gold Digger's Lullaby)	8

(see also Art Mooney)

CLOVERS
56	London HLE 8229	Nip Sip/If I Could Be Loved By You (gold label lettering)	800
56	London HLE 8229	Nip Sip/If I Could Be Loved By You (silver label lettering)	400
56	London HLE 8229	Nip Sip/If I Could Be Loved By You (78)	40
56	London HLE 8314	Love, Love, Love/Hey, Doll Baby	500
56	London HLE 8314	Love, Love, Love/Hey, Doll Baby (78)	50
56	London HLE 8334	From The Bottom Of My Heart/Your Tender Lips	500
56	London HLE 8334	From The Bottom Of My Heart/Your Tender Lips	50
58	London HL 7048	Wishing For Your Love/All About You (export issue)	250
58	London HL 7048	Wishing For Your Love/All About You (export issue) (78)	40
58	HMV POP 542	In The Good Old Summertime/Idaho	30
58	HMV POP 542	In The Good Old Summertime/Idaho (78)	20
59	London HLT 8949	Love Potion No. 9/Stay Awhile (triangular centre)	60
59	London HLT 8949	Love Potion No. 9/Stay Awhile (round centre)	40
59	London HLT 8949	Love Potion No. 9/Stay Awhile (78 rpm)	40
60	London HLT 9122	Lovey/One Mint Julep	30
60	London HLT 9154	Easy Lovin'/I'm Confessin' (That I Love You)	40
61	HMV POP 883	Honey Dripper/Have Gun	25
68	Atlantic 584 160	Your Cash Ain't Nothin' But Trash/I've Got My Eyes On You	15
69	Atlantic 587 162	LOVE BUG (LP)	60

CLOWN
72	CBS 7906	Lord Of The Ringside/Rumania	40

CLUES
81	Clues CLU 001	NO VACANCIES (EP)	10

CLUTCH
73	EMI 2010	Black Angel/The Frightners	8

CLUTHA (FOLK GROUP)
71	Argo ZFB 18	SCOTIA! (LP, as Clutha Folk Group)	15
74	Topic 12TS 242	SCOTS BALLADS, SONGS AND DANCE TUNES (LP, as Clutha)	12

CMETRIC
94	B12 B1210	Cmetric (12")	30

C.M.J.
68	Impression IMP 102	I Can't Do It All By Myself/Nothing At All	45
71	Mother MOT 3	La La La/Step Around It	50
65	Impression EPIM 501	THE C.M.J. TRIO (EP)	50
69	Impression IMPL 1001	C.M.J. LIVE AT THE BANKHOUSE (LP, private pressing)	80

C.M.U. (CONTEMPORARY MUSIC UNIT)
72	Transatlantic BIG 508	Heart Of The Sun/Doctor Am I Normal?	15
71	Transatlantic TRA 237	OPEN SPACES (LP, gatefold sleeve, clear plastic with foam inner, this price for mint record that has not reacted and been marked by plastic/foam inner)	150
71	Transatlantic TRA 237	OPEN SPACES (LP, gatefold sleeve, clear plastic with foam inner, this price for mint sleeve with record that has been marked by chemical reaction to the plastic/foam inner)	30
72	Transatlantic TRA 259	SPACE CABARET (LP, with lyric insert)	100

(see also Chopyn)

COACHMEN
59	Vogue V 9154	Those Brown Eyes/Bald Mountain	5

COACHMEN
66	Columbia DB 8057	Gabrielle/Seasons In The Sun	8

COACHOUSE RHYTHM SECTION
77	Ice ICE 3 12	Nobody Got Time/Time Warp (12")	25

(see also Eddy Grant)

COALESCE
95	Earache MOSH 140	002: 73-C/Grain Of Salt (p/s)	5

COASTERS
57	London HLE 8450	Searchin'/Young Blood	75
57	London HLE 8450	Searchin'/Young Blood (78)	10
57	London HL 7021	Searchin'/Young Blood (export issue)	30
58	London HLE 8665	Yakety Yak/Zing! Went The Strings Of My Heart	20

COASTERS (Jamaica)

58	London HLE 8665	Yakety Yak/Zing! Went The Strings Of My Heart (78)	20
58	London HLE 8729	The Shadow Knows/Sorry But I'm Gonna Have To Pass	50
58	London HLE 8729	The Shadow Knows/Sorry But I'm Gonna Have To Pass (78)	10
59	London HLE 8819	Charlie Brown/Three Cool Cats	10
59	London HL 7073	Charlie Brown/Three Cool Cats (export issue)	10
59	London HLE 8882	Along Came Jones/That Is Rock And Roll (silver top label)	15
59	London HLE 8882	Along Came Jones/That Is Rock And Roll (silver top label) (78)	10
59	London HLE 8938	Poison Ivy/I'm A Hog For You	15

(The above 45s were originally issued with triangular centres, later round centre copies are worth half to two-thirds these values.)

59	London HLE 8938	Poison Ivy/I'm A Hog For You (78)	15
60	London HLE 9020	What About Us/Run Red Run	20
60	London HLE 9020	What About Us/Run Red Run (78)	20
60	London HLK 9111	Besame Mucho (Parts 1 & 2)	50
60	London HLK 9111	Besame Mucho (Parts 1 & 2) (78)	80
60	London HLK 9151	Wake Me, Shake Me/Stewball	20
60	London HLK 9208	Shoppin' For Clothes/The Snake And The Bookworm	30
61	London HLK 9293	Wait A Minute/Thumbin' A Ride	15
61	London HLK 9349	Little Egypt/Keep On Rolling	15
61	London HLK 9413	Girls! Girls! Girls! (Parts 1 & 2)	15
62	London HLK 9493	(Ain't That) Just Like Me/Bad Blood	15
64	London HLK 9863	T'Ain't Nothin' To Me/Speedo's Back In Town	15
66	Atlantic 584 033	She's A Yum Yum/Saturday Night Fish Fry	12
67	Atlantic 584 087	Searchin'/Yakety Yak	10
67	CBS 2749	Soul Pad/Down Home Girl	15
68	Direction 58-3701	She Can/Everybody's Woman	10
71	Parlophone R 5931	Love Potion No. 9/D.W. Washburn	25
72	Stateside SS 2201	Cool Jerk/Talkin' 'Bout A Woman	30
72	London HLZ 10437	Love Potion No. 9/D. W. Washburn	5
59	London REE 1203	THE COASTERS (EP)	60
60	London HA-E 2237	GREATEST HITS (LP)	100
63	London HA-K 8033	COAST ALONG WITH THE COASTERS (LP)	100
66	Atlantic 588 134	COAST ALONG WITH THE COASTERS (LP, reissue)	25
67	Atlantic 590 015	ALL TIME GREATEST HITS (LP)	20
71	Joy JOYS 189	HUNGRY (LP)	20
74	London SHZ 8460	ON BROADWAY (LP)	15
76	DJM 22053	THE WORLD FAMOUS COASTERS (LP)	12

COASTERS (JAMAICA)

69	Doctor Bird DB 1182	Stoney Hill/RICK RODRIGUES & JOHNNY MOORE : Continental Shuffle	100

COAST ROAD DRIVE

74	Deram SML 1113	DELICIOUS AND REFRESHING (LP)	60

COAST TO COAST

82	Polydor POSP 451	The Bell/How Can I Be Sure	8

(see also Status Quo)

C.O.B. (CLIVE'S ORIGINAL BAND)

72	Polydor 2058 260	Blue Morning/Bones	15
71	CBS 69010	SPIRIT OF LOVE (LP, gatefold sleeve, orange label)	175
72	Polydor Folk Mill 2383 161	MOYSHE McSTIFF & THE TARTAN LANCERS OF THE SACRED HEART (LP, gatefold sleeve, red label)	400

(see also Famous Jug Band, Incredible String Band)

COBBLERS

70	Emblem JDR 314	WARM ARE THE SOUNDS (LP)	30

COBBLERS LAST

79	Banshee BAN 1012	BOOT IN THE DOOR (LP, with insert)	80

COBBS

69	Amalgamated AMG 845	Hot Buttered Corn/COUNT MACHUKI: It Is I	20
69	Amalgamated AMG 849	Space Doctor/LLOYD & DEVON: Baby Reggae	25

JUNIE COBB'S HOMETOWN BAND

59	Collector JDL 38	Chicago Buzz/East Coast Trot	10

BILLY COBHAM

73	Atlantic K40506	SPECTRUM (LP, gatefold)	20

COBRA (1)

78	Rip Off RIP 3	Graveyard Boogie/Looking For A Lady (p/s)	30

(see also Speed)

COBRA (2)

87	Ebony EBON 39	BACK FROM THE DEAD (LP)	18

COBWEB

71	Private Pressing SJP 762	You'll Go far/Broken Web	10

COCHISE

70	United Artists UP 35134	Watch This Space/59th St. Bridge Song	6
70	Liberty LBS 15425	Love's Made A Fool Of You/Words Of A Dying Man	6
71	Liberty LBF 15460	Why I Sing The Blues/Jed Colider	6
70	United Artists UAS 29117	COCHISE (LP, gatefold sleeve, orange/pink label)	30
70	Liberty LBS 83428	SWALLOW TALES (LP, black label)	20
72	United Artists UAS 29286	SO FAR (LP)	25

(see also B.J. Cole, Mick Grabham)

DIB COCHRAN & EARWIGS

70	Bell BLL 1121	Oh Baby/Universal Love	500

(see also Marc Bolan, Tyrannosaurus Rex, Tony Visconti, Rick Wakeman)

EDDIE COCHRAN

78s

57	London HLU 8386	20 Flight Rock/Dark Lonely Street	80
57	London HLU 8433	Sittin' In The Balcony/Completely Sweet	80

58	London HLU 8702	Summertime Blues/Love Again	100
59	London HLU 8792	C'mon Everybody/Don't Ever Let Me Go	150
59	London HLU 8880	Teenage Heaven/I Remember	300
59	London HLU 8944	Somethin' Else/Boll Weevil Song	300
60	London HLW 9022	Hallelujah, I Love Her So/Little Angel	400
60	London HLG 9115	Three Steps To Heaven/Cut Across Shorty	500
95	Cruisin' The 50s CASS 001	Three Steps To Heaven/Cut Across Shorty (reissue, 300 only)	30
96	Cruisin' The 50s CASB 004	Week-End/Cherished Memories (reissue, 400 only)	30

SINGLES

57	London HLU 8386	20 Flight Rock/Dark Lonely Street (triangular centre)	200
57	London HLU 8386	20 Flight Rock/Dark Lonely Street (silver-top label with triangular centre)	125
57	London HLU 8386	20 Flight Rock/Dark Lonely Street (round centre)	50
57	London HLU 8433	Sittin' In The Balcony/Completely Sweet	400
58	London HLU 8702	Summertime Blues/Love Again	25
59	London HLU 8792	C'mon Everybody/Don't Ever Let Me Go	25
59	London HLU 8880	Teenage Heaven/I Remember	35
59	London HL 7082	Teenage Heaven/Boll Weevil Song (export issue)	70
59	London HLU 8944	Somethin' Else/Boll Weevil Song	35
60	London HLW 9022	Hallelujah, I Love Her So/Little Angel (triangular centre)	40
	(The above 45s were originally issued with triangular centres, later round centre copies are worth half these values unless otherwise stated.)		
60	London HLW 9022	Hallelujah, I Love Her So/Little Angel (round centre)	25
60	London HLG 9115	Three Steps To Heaven/Cut Across Shorty	15
60	London HLG 9196	Sweetie Pie/Lonely	40
61	London HLG 9362	Weekend/Cherished Memories	20
61	London HLG 9460	Jeannie, Jeannie, Jeannie/Pocketful Of Hearts	30
61	London HLG 9464	Pretty Girl/Teresa	45
61	London HLG 9467	Undying Love/Stockin's 'n' Shoes	50
62	Liberty LIB 10049	Never/Think Of Me	20
63	Liberty LIB 10088	My Way/Rock And Roll Blues	15
63	Liberty LIB 10108	Drive-In Show/I Almost Lost My Mind	15
64	Liberty LIB 10151	Skinny Jim/Nervous Breakdown (black label)	60
66	Liberty LIB 10233	C'mon Everybody/Summertime Blues	15
66	Liberty LIB 10249	Three Stars/Somethin' Else	50
67	Liberty LIB 10276	Three Steps To Heaven/Eddie's Blues	35
68	Liberty LBF 15071	Summertime Blues/Let's Get Together	10
68	Liberty LBF 15109	Somethin' Else/Milk Cow Blues	10
70	Liberty LBF 15366	C'mon Everybody/Mean When I'm Mad	10

EPs

59	London REU 1214	C'MON EVERYBODY (orange sleeve, triangular centre)	100
59	London REU 1214	C'MON EVERYBODY (orange sleeve, round centre)	60
59	London REU 1214	C'MON EVERYBODY (yellow sleeve, silver-top label)	100
59	London REU 1214	C'MON EVERYBODY (yellow sleeve, round centre)	90
60	London REU 1239	SOMETHIN' ELSE (triangular centre)	110
60	London REU 1239	SOMETHIN' ELSE (round centre)	90
60	London REG 1262	EDDIE'S HITS	50
61	London REG 1301	CHERISHED MEMORIES OF EDDIE COCHRAN	50
62	Liberty LEP 2052	NEVER TO BE FORGOTTEN	40
63	Liberty LEP 2090	CHERISHED MEMORIES (VOL.1)	40
63	Liberty LEP 2111	C'MON EVERYBODY (reissue)	20
63	Liberty LEP 2122	SOMETHIN' ELSE (reissue)	20
63	Liberty LEP 2123	CHERISHED MEMORIES OF EDDIE COCHRAN (reissue)	30
63	Liberty LEP 2124	EDDIE'S HITS (reissue)	30
64	Liberty LEP 2165	C'MON AGAIN	35
64	Liberty LEP 2180	STOCKIN'S 'N' SHOES	35

ALBUMS

58	London HA-U 2093	SINGIN' TO MY BABY (initial pressing with laminated rear sleeve)	250
58	London HA-U 2093	SINGIN' TO MY BABY (without laminated rear sleeve)	200
60	London HA-G 2267	THE EDDIE COCHRAN MEMORIAL ALBUM	100
62	Liberty LBY 1109	CHERISHED MEMORIES	50
63	Liberty LBY 1127	THE EDDIE COCHRAN MEMORIAL ALBUM (reissue)	30
63	Liberty LBY 1158	SINGIN' TO MY BABY (reissue)	30
64	Liberty LBY 1205	MY WAY	70
88	Liberty ECB 1	THE EDDIE COCHRAN BOX SET (6-LP box set with booklet)	25

HANK COCHRAN

68	Monument LMO 5020	HEART OF HANK (LP)	15

JACKIE LEE COCHRAN

57	Brunswick 05669	Ruby Pearl (with Jimmy Pruett)/Mama Don't You Think I Know	2500
57	Brunswick 05669	Ruby Pearl (with Jimmy Pruett)/Mama Don't You Think I Know (78)	250

COCK & WOODPECKERS

71	Newbeat 93	Every Day And Every Night/I Fall In Love Everyday	15

BRUCE COCKBURN

71	True North WTN 003	HIGH WINDS WHITE SKY (LP)	15
71	True North TNX 7	SUNWHEEL DANCE (LP)	15

JARVIS COCKER

06	Rough Trade RTRADLP 340	THE JARVIS COCKER RECORD (LP, with bonus one-sided 7")	45

(see also Pulp)

JOE COCKER

64	Decca F 11974	I'll Cry Instead/Precious Words	100
68	Regal Zonophone RZ 3006	Marjorine/New Age Of The Lily	8
68	Regal Zonophone RZ 3013	With A Little Help From My Friends/Something's Coming On	5
69	Regal Zonophone RZ 3024	Delta Lady/She's So Good To Me	5
70	Regal Zonophone RZ 3027	The Letter/Space Captain	5
70	Fly BUG 3	Cry Me A River/Give Peace A Chance (p/s)	5
71	Fly BUG 9	High Time We Went/Black-Eyed Blues	5
72	Magni Fly ECHO 103	With A Little Help From My Friends/Delta Lady/The Letter (p/s)	5
72	Cube BUG 25	Woman To Woman/Midnight Rider (with Chris Stanton Band)	5

COCKERSDALE

83	Island WIP 6818	Ruby Lee/Talking Back To The Night (export issue)	7
60s	Oak	JOE COCKER (EP, existence unconfirmed)	500
67	Action ACT 002 EP	RAG GOES MAD AT THE MOJO (33rpm EP, 2 tracks by Joe Cocker's Blues Band, in conjunction with Sheffield University rag magazine Twikker)	50
69	Regal Zono. LRZ 1006	WITH A LITTLE HELP FROM MY FRIENDS (LP, mono, red/silver label with "sold in the U.K..." text)	90
69	Regal Zono. SLRZ 1006	WITH A LITTLE HELP FROM MY FRIENDS (LP, stereo, red/silver label with "sold in the U.K..." text)	60
69	Regal Zono. SLRZ 1011	JOE COCKER! (LP, red/silver label)	30
70	A&M AMLS 6002	MAD DOG & ENGLISHMEN (2-LP, multifold gatefold sleeve, brown label)	25
71	Fly HIFLY 3	COCKER HAPPY (LP, gatefold sleeve)	20

(see also Grease Band, Made In Sheffield)

COCKERSDALE
85	EFDSS ESLP 001	PROSPECT PROVIDENCE (LP)	20

COCKNEY REJECTS
79	Small Wonder SW 19	Flares'N'Slippers/Police Star/I Wanna Be A Star (p/s)	15
79	EMI EMI 5008	I'm Not A Fool/East End (p/s)	6
80	EMI EMI 5035	Bad Man!/The New Song (p/s)	6
80	Zonophone Z 2	The Greatest Cockney Rip-Off/Hate Of The City (p/s, yellow vinyl)	7
80	Zonophone Z 4	I'm Forever Blowing Bubbles/West Side Boys (p/s)	8
80	Zonophone Z 6	We Can Do Anything/15 Nights (p/s)	6
80	Zonophone Z 10	We Are The Firm/War On The Terraces (p/s)	8
81	Zonophone Z 20	Easy Life/Motorhead/Hang 'Em High (p/s)	6
80	Zonophone ZONO 101	GREATEST HITS VOLUME 1 (LP)	20
80	Zonophone ZONO 102	GREATEST HITS VOLUME 2 (LP, with inner sleeve & poster)	15
81	Zonophone ZEM 101	GREATEST HITS VOLUME 3 (LIVE AND LOUD) (LP)	15

COCKNEYS
64	Philips BF 1303	After Tomorrow/I'll Cry Each Night	15
64	Philips BF 1338	After Tomorrow/I'll Cry Each Night (reissue)	15
64	Philips BF 1360	I Know You're Gonna Be Mine/Oh No You Won't	15

COCK SPARRER
77	Decca FR 13710	Runnin' Riot/Sister Suzie (demos in p/s)	110
77	Decca FR 13710	Runnin' Riot/Sister Suzie (no p/s)	20
77	Decca FR 13732	We Love You/Chip On My Shoulder (no p/s)	20
77	Decca LFR 13732	We Love You/Chip On My Shoulder (12" p/s, with photo insert, 7,500 only)	25
82	Carrere CAR 255	England Belongs To Me/Argy Bargy (p/s, beware of bootlegs With "fuzzy" looking label logo on sleeve)	30
83	Razor RAZ 9	SHOCK TROOPS (LP)	25
84	Syndicate SYNLP 7	RUNNIN' RIOT IN 84	35
86	Razor RAZ 26	TRUE GRIT (LP)	15
87	Link LP 005	LIVE AND LOUD (LP)	12

(see also Little Roosters, Guttersnipes)

COCKTAIL CABINET
67	Page One POF 046	Puppet On A String/Breathalyser	25

COCOA TEA
88	Live And Love LLD 87	Lonesome Side/ADMIRAL TIBET: Reality Time (12")	30

COCONUT DOGS
80	Mongrel Music MM 001	Lipstick On The Glass/The Neighbours/Mannequin (no p/s, 1000 only)	50
81	Rialto TREB 136	Officers Mess/Germinate no p/s)	7

COCTEAU TWINS
82	4AD AD 303	LULLABIES EP (Feathers Oar Blades/Alas DIes Laughing/It's All But An Ark-Lark) (12")	8
83	4AD AD 303	PEPPERMINT PIG EP (Peppermint Pig (7" Version)/Laugh Lines/Hazel/Pepperment Pig (12" Extended Version) (12")	8
83	4AD AD 303	Peppermint Pig/Laugh Lines (p/s)	10
88	4AD CAD 807	BLUE BELL KNOLL (LP, tri-foldout sleeve)	12
90	4AD CAD 0012	HEAVEN OR LAS VEGAS (LP, with inner)	15
93	Fontana 518259-1	FOUR CALENDAR CAFE (LP)	40
96	Fontana 514-501-1	MILK AND KISSES (LP)	40
05	4AD CTBOX 2	LULLABIES TO VIOLAINE (4-CD box set, tactile cover)	40

(see also This Mortal Coil, Felt, Massive Attack, Harold Budd, Lonely Is An Eyesore, The Future Sound Of London)

CODE 071
92	Reinforced RIVET 1213	A London Sumtin' (12")	20
92	Reinforced RIVET 1230	A London Sumtin' (Remix) (12", with M.A.D)	8

CODEK
80	MCA MCA 550	Me Me Me/Demo (p/s)	6
80	MCA MCAT 550	Me Me Me (Full Length Version)/Demo (12", p/s)	25
82	Island 12WIP 6764	Tim Toum/Closer (12", p/s)	25

CODENAME JOHN
94	Prototype PRO 001	Deep Inside Of Me/(Inta) The Anthem (12")	12
94	Prototype PRO 002	Kindred/Dreams Of Heaven (Shorty/s Mix) (12", as John)	10

C.O.D.S
66	Stateside SS 489	Michael (The Lover)/Cry No More	25
66	Stateside SS 489	Michael (The Lover)/Cry No More (DJ copy)	60

CODY
71	Polydor 2058-100	I Belong With You/Wanna Make You Happy	6

JAMIE COE
59	Parlophone R 4600	Summertime Symphony/There's Gonna Be A Day	150
60	Parlophone R 4621	School Day Blues/I'll Go On Loving You	100
61	HMV POP 991	How Low Is Low/Little Dear Little Darling	20
63	London HLX 9713	The Fool/I've Got That Feeling Again	20

PETER & CHRIS COE
72	Trailer LER 2077	OPEN THE DOOR AND LET US IN (LP)	25
76	Trailer LER 2098	OUT OF SEASON, OUT OF RHYME (LP, yellow label)	20
79	Highway SHY 7007	GAME OF ALL FOURS (LP)	15

(see also Bandoggs)

TONY COE (QUINTET)

61	Philips B 10784L	SWINGIN' TILL THE GIRLS COME HOME (LP)	50
67	Columbia SCX 6170	TONY'S BASEMENT (LP)	70
78	Lee Lambert LAM100	COE-EXISTENCE (LP)	20

TONY COE & BRIAN LEMON TRIO

68	'77' SEU 12/41	TONY COE AND BRIAN LEMON TRIO (LP)	30

(see also Robert Farnon & Tony Coe)

JACK & CHARLIE COEN

77	Topic 12TS 337	THE BRANCH LINE (LP)	22

CARLTON COFFE

78	Justice JUS 110	Chant Away/Version (12")	35

COFFEE

80	Dee Lite DEX 1	I Wanna Be With You/Slip & Dip	8

COFFEE BAR SKIFFLERS

58	Embassy WEP 1008	SKIFFLE SESSION (EP)	10

(see also Chas McDevitt Skiffle Group)

COFFEE SET

69	Mercury MF 1113	Happy Birthday/Our Anniversary	6
69	Fontana LPS 16503	SAY IT WITH MUSIC (LP)	15

DENNIS COFFEY

72	A&M AMS 7010	Getting It On/Ride Sally Ride	5
71	A&M AMS 875	scorpio/Sad Song (with Detroit Guitar Band)	20
70	A&M AMLS 68035	EVOLUTION (LP)	15
71	A&M AMLS 68072	GOIN' FOR MYSELF (LP)	15
74	Sussex LPSX 9	INSTANT COFFEY (LP)	15

ALMA COGAN

53	HMV 7M 166	Over And Over Again/Isn't Life Wonderful (with Les Howerd)	30
53	HMV 7M 106	I Went To Your Wedding/You Belong To Me	30
53	HMV 7M 107	To Be Loved By You/The Homing Waltz (B-side with Larry Day)	30
54	HMV 7M 173	Ricochet (Rick-O-Shay)/The Moon Is Blue	30
54	HMV 7M 188	Bell Bottom Blues/Love Me Again	40
54	HMV 7M 196	Make Love To Me/Said The Little Moment	30
54	HMV 7M 219	The Little Shoemaker/Chiqui-Chaqui (Chick-ee Chock-ee)	30
54	HMV 7M 228	Little Things Mean A Lot/Canoodlin' Rag	30
54	HMV 7M 239	Skinnie Minnie (Fishtail)/What Am I Going To Do, Ma (The Doo-Ma Song)	45
54	HMV 7M 269	This Ole House/Skokiaan	30
54	HMV 7M 271	I Can't Tell A Waltz From A Tango/Christmas Cards	30
55	HMV 7M 286	Paper Kisses/Softly, Softly	25
55	HMV 7M 293	Chee-Chee-Oo-Chee (Sang The Little Bird)/Tika Tika Tok	25
55	HMV 7M 301	Tweedlee-Dee/More Than Ever Now	25
55	HMV 7M 316	Got'n Idea/Give A Fool A Chance	25
55	HMV 7M 337	Never Do A Tango With An Eskimo/Twenty Tiny Fingers	30
56	HMV 7M 367	Love And Marriage/Sycamore Tree	25
56	HMV 7M 415	Why Do Fools Fall In Love?/ (The Same Thing Happen With) The Birds And The Bees?	40
56	HMV POP 239	Mama Teach Me To Dance/I'm In Love Again	25
56	HMV POP 261	In The Middle Of The House/Two Innocent Hearts	25
57	HMV POP 284	You, Me And Us/Three Brothers	25
57	HMV POP 317	Whatever Lola Wants (Lola Gets)/Lucky Lips	30
57	HMV POP 336	Chantez, Chantez/Funny, Funny, Funny	20
57	HMV POP 367	Fabulous/Summer Love	30
57	HMV POP 392	That's Happiness/What You've Done To Me	20
57	HMV POP 415	Party Time/Please Mister Brown (Mister Jones, Mister Smith)	20
58	HMV POP 433	The Story Of My Life/Love Is	10
58	HMV POP 450	Sugartime/Gettin' Ready For Freddy	15
58	HMV POP 482	Stairway Of Love/Comes Love	15
58	HMV POP 500	Sorry, Sorry, Sorry/Fly Away Lovers	10
58	HMV POP 531	There's Never Been A Night/If This Isn't Love	15
59	HMV POP 573	Last Night On The Back Porch/Mama Says	15
59	HMV POP 608	Pink Shoelaces/The Universe	15
59	HMV POP 670	We Got Love/I Don't Mind Being All Alone	10
60	HMV POP 728	O Dio Mio/Dream Talk	10
60	HMV POP 760	The Train Of Love/The 'I Love You' Bit	10
60	HMV POP 815	Must Be Santa/Just Couldn't Resist Her With Her Pocket Transistor	5
61	Columbia DB 4607	Cowboy Jimmy Joe/Don't Read This Letter	6
61	Columbia DB 4679	With You In Mind/Ja-Da	5
61	Columbia DB 4749	All Alone/Keep Me In Your Heart	5
62	Columbia DB 4794	She's Got You/In The Shade Of The Old Apple Tree	8
62	Columbia DB 4912	Goodbye Joe/I Can't Give You Anything But Love	7
63	Columbia DB 4965	Tell Him/Fly Me To The Moon (Bossa Nova)	7
63	Columbia DB 7059	Hold Out Your Hand You Naughty Boy/Just Once More	7
64	Columbia DB 7233	The Tennessee Waltz/I Love You Too Much	5
64	Columbia DB 7390	It's You/I Knew Right Away	5
65	Columbia DB 7652	Snakes And Snails (And Puppy Dog Tails)/How Many Days, How Many Nights	35
65	Columbia DB 7786	Eight Days A Week/Help!	10
66	Columbia DB 8088	Now That I've Found You/More	10
55	HMV 7EG 8122	THE GIRL WITH A LAUGH IN HER VOICE (EP)	25
55	HMV 7EG 8151	THE GIRL WITH A LAUGH IN HER VOICE NO. 2 (EP)	25
56	HMV 7EG 8169	THE GIRL WITH A LAUGH IN HER VOICE NO. 3 (EP)	25
57	HMV 7EG 8437	SHE LOVES TO SING (EP)	25
58	HMV CLP 1152	I LOVE TO SING (LP)	50
61	Columbia 33SX 1345	ALMA SINGS WITH YOU IN MIND (LP, mono)	25
61	Columbia SCX 3391	ALMA SINGS WITH YOU IN MIND (LP)	40
62	Columbia 33SX 1469	HOW ABOUT LOVE! (LP, mono)	25
62	Columbia SCX 3459	HOW ABOUT LOVE! (LP, stereo)	40
67	Columbia SX 6130	ALMA (LP)	15

ALMA COGAN & RONNIE HILTON
(see also Ronnie Hilton, Angela & Fans)

| 57 | HMV 7EG 8352 | THE HITS FROM 'MY FAIR LADY' (EP, 1 side each) | 8 |

(see also Ronnie Hilton)

ALMA COGAN & FRANKIE VAUGHAN

| 54 | HMV 7M 226 | Do, Do, Do, Do, Do, Do, Do It Again/Jilted | 10 |

(see also Frankie Vaughan)

DON COGAN

| 58 | MGM MGM 984 | The Fountain Of Love/I'm Takin' Over | 25 |

SHAYE COGAN

| 58 | Columbia DB 4055 | Billy Be Sure/Doodle Doodle Doo | 15 |
| 60 | MGM MGM 1063 | Mean To Me/They Said It Couldn't Be Done | 50 |

(see also Buddy Morrow)

ALAN COHEN BAND

| 72 | Argo ZDA 159 | BLACK, BROWN AND BEIGE (LP) | 65 |

LEONARD COHEN

68	CBS 3337	Suzanne/So Long, Marianne	7
69	CBS 4245	Bird On The Wire/Seems So Long Ago, Nancy	7
71	CBS 7292	Joan Of Arc/Diamonds In The Mine	7
74	CBS 2494	Bird On The Wire (live)/Tonight Will Be Fine (live)	7
74	CBS 2699	Lover Lover Lover/Who By Fire	6
76	CBS 4306	Suzanne/Take This Longing	6
77	CBS 5882	Memories/Don't Go Home With Your Hard-On	6
78	CBS 6095	True Love Leaves No Traces/I Left A Woman Waiting	6
72	CBS EP 9162	McCABE AND MRS MILLER (EP, p/s)	8
68	CBS BPG 63241	SONGS OF LEONARD COHEN (LP, orange label, with stickered sleeve; mono)	20
68	CBS (S)BPG 63241	SONGS OF LEONARD COHEN (LP, orange label, with stickered sleeve; stereo)	18
68	CBS 63241	SONGS OF LEONARD COHEN (LP, orange label, re-pressing w/out prefix)	15

COIL (1)

| 79 | North'ton Wood H. HAV 1 | Motor Industry/Alcoholic Stork (p/s) | 15 |

COIL (2)

85	F & F/K.422 FFK 512	Panic/Tainted Love/Aqua Regis (12", red vinyl, 'hair'-textured p/s)	25
85	F & F/K.422 FFK 512	Panic/Tainted Love/Aqua Regis (12", black vinyl, 'hair'-textured p/s)	15
86	Force & Form/K.422	The Anal Staircase/Blood From The Air/Ravenous (12", p/s, on clear vinyl)	25
86	Force & Form/K.422 ROTA 121	The Anal Staircase/Blood From The Air/Ravenous (12", p/s)	15
87	Solar Lodge 001	HELLRAISER (10" EP, coloured vinyl [clear or pink, 500 each])	25
90	Shock SX 002	Wrong Eye/Scope (pink p/s, signed & lettered A-Z, 26 only)	45
90	Shock SX 002	Wrong Eye/Scope (974 with numbered white p/s)	15
90	Shock SX 002	Wrong Eye/Scope (1,000 with un-numbered yellow p/s)	10
90	Shock SX 002	Wrong Eye/Scope (green p/s, 300 only, some with gold/black sticker)	25
92	Clawfist 22	Airborne Bells/Is Suicide A Solution (p/s, 1,250 only)	25
94	Loci S1	Themes From Blue (p/s, 23 on yellow vinyl)	60
94	Loci S1	Themes From Blue (p/s, 1,000 on blue vinyl)	20
94	Eskaton 001	Nasa Arab/First Dark Ride (12", stickered plain black sleeve, 2,500 only)	15
95	Eskaton 003	PHILM (10" EP, with poster, 50 on clear vinyl in handmade p/s)	60
95	Eskaton 003	PHILM (10" EP, with poster, 2,000 only)	12
86	Threshold ROTA 1	HORSE ROTORVATOR (LP, with A5 card insert & stickers)	20
87	Threshold House LOCI 1	GOLD IS THE METAL (LP, red vinyl; with bonus 7": "The Wheel"/ The Wheal, unfinished proof sleeve without writing, 25 only)	200
87	Threshold House LOCI 1	GOLD IS THE METAL (LP, box set with 7", "The Wheel"/"The Wheal", poster & booklet in black linen folder, embossed sleeve, autographed)	300
87	Threshold House LOCI 1	GOLD IS THE METAL (LP, red vinyl [150 only] with inner sleeve; with bonus 7": "The Wheel"/"The Wheal")	70
87	Threshold House LOCI 1	GOLD IS THE METAL (LP, clear vinyl [500 only], with inner sleeve; with bonus 7": "The Wheel"/"The Wheal")	50
87	Threshold House LOCI CD1	GOLD IS THE METAL (CD, 1,000 only)	20
90	Normal NORMAL 77	GOLD IS THE METAL (LP, black vinyl re-pressing with 7": The Wheel/"Keel Hauler")	18
93	Loci CD 4b	STOLEN AND CONTAMINATED SONGS (CD, 1st edit with different artwork)	20
90s	Loci CD 6	ANGELIC CONVERSATION (CD, gold disc, 1,000 only)	20
95	Eskaton 007	WORSHIP THE GLITCH (2 x 10" LP, as Coil Vs. Elph, with insert, 50 with white optical plastic cover)	55
95	Eskaton 007	WORSHIP THE GLITCH (2 x 10" LP, as Coil Vs. Elph, with insert, 2,000 only)	25
95	Eskaton 006	WORSHIP THE GLITCH (CD, as Coil Vs. Elph, 500 only in black optical plastic)	20
99	Acme/Prescription DRUG8	ASTRAL DISASTER (LP, 99 copies signed and numbered by Balance And Christopherson, with insert, artwork in plastic bag)	100
99	Chalice GRAAL LP002	MUSICK TO PLAY IN THE DARK VOL 1 (LP, 500 only, white vinyl)	50
00	Threshold House LOC114	ASTRAL DISASTER (LP re-issue, 100 copies, grey vinyl signed lyric sheet and art	60
00	Chalice GRAAL LP004	MUSICK TO PLAY IN THE DARK VOL 2 (2 x LP, white vinyl, one side etched)	50
00	Chalice GRAAL LP004	MUSICK TO PLAY IN THE DARK VOL 2 (2 x LP, 100 copies with blue/green vinyl)	50
00	Chalice GRAAL LP004	MUSICK TO PLAY IN THE DARK VOL 2 (2 x LP, translucent purple, 4th side etched with picture of moon and has 'gold leaf' attached, art print on cover, 2 part print inserts – signed – 60 copies only)	300
00	Chalice GRAAL LP004	MUSICK VOL 2 (26 copy "trauma edition" lettered A-Z white sleeves smeared with Balance's blood.)	70
02	Eskaton 28	TIME MACHINES (Coil as Time Machines) (2 x LP, 1,000 55 clear, signed)	50
02	Eskaton 28	TIME MACHINES (Coil as Time Machines) (2 x LP, 1,000 only)	40

(see also Psychic TV, Throbbing Gristle, Current 93, Thighpaulsandra)

COINS

| 69 | Toast TT 513 | Love Power/You Can't Get Away From It | 6 |
| 69 | Toast TT 515 | Don't You Know It's Just A Game, Love? (actually by Miss White & Mr. Green)/ Crying Over You | 6 |

ALVADEAN COKER

| 55 | London HLU 8191 | Do Dee Oodle De Do I'm In Love/We're Gonna Bop | 750 |
| 55 | London HLU 8191 | Do Dee Oodle De Do I'm In Love/We're Gonna Bop (78) | 60 |

SANDY COKER & HIS BAND

| 54 | London HL 8109 | Meadowlark Melody/Toss Over | 70 |

COKI

05	DMZ DMZ 004	Officer/Mood Dub (12")	20
06	Tempa TEMPA 024	Tortured/Shattered (12")	8
07	Big Apple BAM 009	Red Eye/Beep/The SIgn/Hidden Treasure (12")	15
07	SMZ DMZ 013	Spongebob/The End (12")	15
08	DMZ DMZ 014	Triple Six/Road Rage (12")	8

RIC COLBECK QUARTET

70	Fontana 6383 001	THE SUN IS COMING UP (LP)	60

COLD BLOOD

70	Atlantic 584 319	You Got Me Hummin'/If You Will	10
70	Atlantic 588 218	COLD BLOOD (LP, plum/red label)	25
71	Atlantic 2400 102	SISYPHUS (LP, gatefold sleeve, plum/red label)	18
74	Warner Bros K 56047	LYDIA (LP)	15

COLDCUT

87	Ahead Of Our Time AHED 1201	Beats + Pieces/More Beats (12")	8
87	Ahead Of Our Time CCUT 8 TL	SAY KIDS EP (12", stickered die-cut black sleeve)	8
91	Ninja Tune ZEN12 004	Jade (12")	15
99	Ninja Tune ZEN12 012 R	Autumn Leaves (4 Remixes) (12")	8
94	Ninja Tune ZEN 12	PHILOSOPHY (2xLP, promo, different mixes to commercial release)	20
94	Ninja Tune ZEN 12	PHILOSOPHY (2xLP)	15

BEN COLDER

64	MGM MGM-EP 791	MAKE THE WORLD GO AWAY (EP)	10
82	BK BK 12	Tropicana/Instrumental	12

(see also Sheb Wooley)

COLD FISH

82	CBS A2779	Love Me Today/Strange Boy (p/s)	6

COLD FLY

73	Bus Stop BUS 1007	Caterpillar/Yesterday Started For Judy	8

COLD HAND BAND

82	BK BK 12	Tropicana/Instrumental	12

COLDPLAY

SINGLES

98	private pressing HGCD 633	SAFETY EP: Bigger, Stronger/No More Keeping My Feet On The Ground/ Such A Rush (CD, 500 only)	500
99	Fierce Panda NING 68	Brothers And Sisters/Easy To Please (wraparound p/s, 1000 only)	50
99	Fierce Panda NING 68CD	Brothers And Sisters/Easy To Please/Only Superstition	10
99	EMI EMI CDR 6528	THE BLUE ROOM EP (Bigger, Stronger/Don't Panic/See You Soon/High Speed/ Such A Rush (CD, digipak)	35
99	EMI EMI 12R 6528	THE BLUE ROOM EP (Bigger, Stronger/Don't Panic/See You Soon/High Speed/ Such A Rush) (12", numbered sleeve)	35
00	Parlophone R 6536	Shiver/For You/Careful Where You Stand (p/s)	10
00	Parlophone R 6536	Shiver/For You/Careful Where You Stand (CD, digipak)	10
00	Parlophone R 6538	Yellow/Help Is Around The Corner (7" ltd edn. Numbered single p/s)	15
00	Parlophone R 6549	Trouble/Brothers And Sisters (p/s, numbered, stickered poly outer)	10
01	COLDXMAS01	Mince Spies/Have Yourself A Merry Little Christmas/Yellow (Alpha Mix) (CD EP, 1000 only, given away with Coldplayground fanzine)	100
01	Parlophone 07243 879080-6-2	Don't Panic/You Only Live Twice (live)/Bigger Stronger (live) (12" p/s, withdrawn)	100
02	Parlophone R 6588	The Scientist/1:36/I Ran Away (p/s)	7
03	Parlophone R 6594	Clocks/Crest Of Waves (p/s)	7
03	Parlophone 12 R 6594	Clocks (Royksopp Trembling Heart Mix)/Royksopp Trembling Heart Instrumental Mix/God Put A Smile Upon Your Face (Def Inc. Remix feat. Mr. Thing) (12", die-cut sleeve, 1000 only)	12
05	Parlophone R6664	Speed Of Sound/Things I Don't Understand/Proof (10", clear vinyl)	8
07	Parlophone 3883247	THE SINGLES 1999 - 2006 (15 x 7" box set)	45

ALBUMS

00	Parlophone 5277831	PARACHUTES (LP)	18
02	Parlophone 540 5041	A RUSH OF BLOOD TO THE HEAD (LP, gatefold sleeve, with inner)	20
05	Parlophone 474 7861	X&Y (LP, gatefold sleeve with slip case and poster)	20
05	Parlophone 474 7862	X&Y (CD, with carrier bag, T shirt, key ring and wrist band)	30
11	EMI 087 5531	MYLO XYLOTO (LP with poster)	15

PROMOS

98	None	Ode To Deodorant/Brothers And Sisters (2-track cassette sent to concert promoters and radio DJ's. White label, attributed to The Coldplay with "contact Phil" and 0777 mobile no.)	300
99	Parlophone CDRDJ 6528	THE BLUE ROOM EP (Bigger, Stronger/Don't Panic/See You Soon/High Speed/ Such A Rush) (CD digipak)	35
99	Parlophone 12RDJ 6528	THE BLUE ROOM EP (Bigger, Stronger/Don't Panic/See You Soon/High Speed/ Such A Rush) (12")	30
00	EMI EMISAMP/13	You're Keeping Me Up All Night (EMI CD sampler with alternative version of Spies)	20
00	Parlophone 12RDJ 6538	Yellow/Help Is Round The Corner/No More Keeping My Feet On The Ground (12")	15
00	Parlophone 12RDJ 6549	Trouble/Brothers & Sisters/Shiver (12")	10
06	Parlophone (No cat no)	Talk (FK Dub Mix) 12" one-sided acetate 10 only DJ copies)	50
00	Parlophone CHUTE001	PARACHUTES (CD, blue card sleeve)	20
02	Parlophone COLDADJ001	A RUSH OF BLOOD TO THE HEAD (CD, numbered and sealed card sleeve)	20
02	Parlophone COLDINT001	A RUSH OF BLOOD TO THE HEAD (CD interview disc)	20
03	Parlophone CPLIVE	LIVE (2xCD)	35
05	Parlophone COLDINT2	X&Y (CD interview disc)	20
05	Parlophone (No cat. no)	X&Y (promo, numbered slipcase)	20
06	Parlophone (No cat. no)	Clocks (Royksopp remixes) (12" promo. die-cut sleeve)	15
09	Parlophone 50999 68407421	Strawberry Swing (Edit)/(Album Version)/Instrumental Version) (CD promo)	15

COLD TURKEY

72	Pye 7N 45142	Nobody's Fool/Sesame Street	15

COLD WAR

83	Namedrop NR 4	The Machinist/Illusion (p/s)	10

ANN COLE
84	Krazy Kat KK 782	GOT MY MOJO WORKING (LP)	15

B.J. COLE
73	United Artists UAS 29418	NEW HOVERING DOG (LP, laminated front sleeve)	30

(see also Cochise)

BOBBY COLE
68	CBS 3626	Mister Bo Jangles/Bus 22 To Jerusalem	5

CINDY COLE
65	Columbia DB 7519	A Love Like Yours/He's Sure The Boy I Love	25
66	Columbia DB 7973	Just Being Your Baby (Turns Me On)/Lonely City Blue Boy	35

(see also Jeannie & Big Guys)

CLAY COLE
62	London HLP 9499	Twist Around The Clock/Don't Twist (With Anyone Else But Me)	10

COZY COLE
58	London HL 8750	Topsy (Parts 1 & 2)	10
58	London HL 7065	Topsy (Parts 1 & 2) (export issue)	10
59	Mercury AMT 1015	St. Louis Blues/Father Co-operates	12
59	London HL 8843	Turvy (Parts 1 & 2)	10
59	London HL 8843	Turvy (Parts 1 & 2) (78)	10
62	Coral Q 72457	Big Noise From Winnetka (Parts 1 & 2)	10
57	MGM MGM-EP 622	COZY COLE ALL STARS (EP)	15

DON COLE & ALLEYNE
65	Fontana TF 522	Gotta Find My Baby/Something's Gotta Hold Of Me	5

JERRY COLE
65	Capitol CL 15397	Every Window In The City/Come On Over To My Place	12

KEITH COLE
71	Big BG 315	Musical Attack/RUPIE EDWARDS ALLSTARS: Shack Attack	8
71	Big BG 316	Music Alone Version 3/RUPIE EDWARDS ALLSTARS: Behold Another Version	8

LLOYD COLE & COMMOTIONS
84	Welcome To L. Vegas LC 1	Are You Ready To Be Heartbroken?/Down At The Mission (p/s, withdrawn)	30
85	Polydor COLET 5	Lost Weekend (extended)/Big World/Lost Weekend - (7" version) (10" p/s)	8
93	Phonogram 518318-1	BAD VIBES (LP, as Lloyd Cole)	20

NAT COLE1
70	Jackpot JP 717	Pack Of Cards/RITA & NAT COLE: Spread Joy	5
70	Jackpot JP 718	Love Making/SONNY BINNS & RITA: My Love	5
70	Jackpot JP 722	Sugar Sugar/SONNY BINNS & RITA: Sign Off	5
70	Explosion EX 2022	In The Summertime/Apollo Moon Walk	8
70	Creole CR 1002	Me And My Life/Instrumental	5

(see also Rita Alston)

NAT 'KING' COLE
SINGLES
54	Capitol CL 14149	Smile (Theme From 'Modern Times')/Make Her Mine	15
54	Capitol CL 14155	Unbelievable/Hajji Baba (Persian Lament)	10
54	Capitol CL 14172	I Am In Love/There Goes My Heart	10
54	Capitol CL 14203	If I Give My Heart To You/Hold My Hand	10
54	Capitol CL 14207	Papa Loves Mambo/Teach Me Tonight	10
55	Capitol CL 14215	Long Long Ago/Open Up The Doghouse (with Dean Martin)	10
55	Capitol CL 14235	A Blossom Fell/Alone Too Long	10
55	Capitol CL 14251	The Sand And The Sea/Darling, Je Vous Aime Beaucoup	10
55	Capitol CL 14295	If I May (with Four Knights)/I Envy	10
55	Capitol CL 14317	Annabelle/I'd Rather Have The Blues ('Kiss Me Deadly' Theme)	10
55	Capitol CL 14327	My One Sin/Don't Hurt The Girl	10
55	Capitol CL 14364	Love Is A Many-Splendored Thing/Autumn Leaves	10
55	Capitol CL 14378	Someone You Love/Forgive My Heart	10

ALBUMS
53	Capitol LC 6569	CAPITOL PRESENTS NAT KING COLE (10")	15
53	Capitol LC 6587	CAPITOL PRESENTS NAT KING COLE AND HIS TRIO VOLUME 1 (10")	15
53	Capitol LC 6593	CAPITOL PRESENTS NAT KING COLE AT THE PIANO (10")	15
53	Capitol LC 6594	CAPITOL PRESENTS NAT KING COLE AND HIS TRIO VOLUME 2 (10")	15
53	Capitol LC 6627	NAT KING COLE SINGS FOR TWO IN LOVE (10")	15
54	Capitol LCT 6003	NAT KING COLE TENTH ANNIVERSARY ALBUM	12
56	Capitol LC 6818	BALLADS OF THE DAY (10")	12
56	Capitol LC 6830	THE PIANO STYLE OF NAT KING COLE (10")	12
56	Brunswick LAT 8123	IN THE BEGINNING (as King Cole Trio)	15

PATSY COLE
66	Island WI 271	Disappointed Bride/EARL BOSTIC: Honeymoon Night	25

ROCKY COLE
61	Oriole CB 1635	Heaven And Earth/Huey's Song	5

STRANGER COLE
63	R&B JB 133	Out Of Many/Nothing Tried	25
63	Island WI 110	Stranger At The Door/Conqueror	25
63	Island WI 114	Last Love/STRANGER & KEN: Hush Baby	25
63	Island WI 126	We Are Rolling/Millie Maw	25
64	Island WI 137	Goodbye Peggy (actually plays "Goodbye Peggy Darling" by Roy Panton)/ BABA BROOKS: Portrait Of My Love	25
64	R&B JB 129	Morning Star/Beat Up Your Gum	18
64	Island WI 133	Til My Dying Days/STRANGER & PATSY: I Need You	25
64	Black Swan WI 413	Uno Dos Tres (act. with Ken Boothe)/Look (B-side actually by unknown artist)	20
64	Black Swan WI 415	Summer Day/Loving You Always (both actually by Dottie & Bonnie)	20
64	Black Swan WI 435	Little Boy Blue/ERIC MORRIS: Words Of Wisdom	20
65	Ska Beat JB 192	Pussy Cat/MAYTALS: Sweet Sweet Jenny	25
65	Island WI 169	Koo Koo Doo (with Owen & Leon)/GLORIA & DREAMLETTS: Stay Where You Are	20

65	Island WI 177	Run Joe (with Baba Brooks)/Make Believe	20
65	Blue Beat BB 322	When The Party Is Over/BUSTER'S ALLSTARS: Happy Independence '65	25
65	Blue Beat BB 333	Matilda (actually with Prince Buster)/BUSTER'S ALL STARS: When The Party Is Over	35
66	Doctor Bird DB 1025	We Shall Overcome/Do You Really Love Me (as Stranger Cole & Seraphines)	40
66	Doctor Bird DB 1040	Drop The Ratchet/Oh Yee Mahee (as Stranger Cole & Conquerors)	25
67	Doctor Bird DB 1066	You Took My Love (actually by Patsy Todd)/FUGITIVES: Living Soul	100
68	Island WI 3154	Jeboza Macoo/Now I Know (B-side actually with Gladdy Anderson)	45
68	Amalgamated AMG 801	Just Like A River (as Stranger Cole & Gladdy)/LEADERS: Hope Someday	20
69	Amalgamated AMG 838	What Mama Na Want She Get/We Two	18
69	Duke DU 27	Glad You're Living/Help Wanted	10
69	Unity UN 501	Last Flight To Reggae City (w/ Tommy McCook)/JUNIOR SMITH: Watch Dem Go	20
69	Unity UN 514	When I Get My Freedom/Life Can Be Beautiful	35
69	Escort ES 810	Pretty Cottage/To Me	10
69	Escort ES 811	Why Did You/Do You Remember	20
69	Escort ES 819	Leana Leana/Na Na Na	7
69	Escort ES 826	Loneliness/Remember	7
70	Escort ES 830	Little Things/Till The Well Runs Dry	6
70	Escort ES 831	Everything With You/Picture On The Wall	6
70	Escort ES 832	Pussy/Let Me In	6
70	Camel CA 54	Everyday Tomorrow/Let Your Head Up High	20
70	Pama PM 790	Come Dance With Me/Dance With Me	10
71	Bullet BU 488	Soul Sop/Stranger Cole Medley	15
71	Camel CA 72	Crying Every Night/DENNIS ALCAPONE & DELROY WILSON: It Must Come	10
71	Escort ERT 849	Tomorrow/SONNY BURKE: Chicken Thief	7
72	Tropical AL 0011	Mail Man (with Charlie Ace)/Mail Man (Version)	7
72	Jackpot JP 791	My Confession/LASCELS & HORTENSE: The Might Organ	6
72	Pama PM 848	The House Where Bombo Lives/Our High School Dance	5

(see also Stranger, Stranger & Gladys, Stranger & Patsy, Stranger & Ken, Rob Walker, Charmers, Lloyd Clarke, Don Drummond, Tommy McCook, Ernest Wilson, Delroy Wilson, Lester Sterling, Baba Brooks, Roland Alphonso)

BOBBY COLEMAN
| 66 | Pye International 7N 25365 | (Baby) You Don't Have To Tell Me/Pleasure Girl | 60 |
| 66 | Pye International 7N 25365 | (Baby) You Don't Have To Tell Me/Pleasure Girl (DJ Copy) | 90 |

FITZROY COLEMAN
| 61 | Starlite ST45 064 | Lucilla/Caribbean Sunset | 6 |

LONNIE COLEMAN & JESSE ROBERTSON
| 56 | London HLU 8335 | Dolores Diane/Oh Honey, Why Don'tcha | 70 |
| 56 | London HLU 8335 | Dolores Diane/Oh Honey, Why Don'tcha (78) | 10 |

ORNETTE COLEMAN
60	Contemporary LAC 12228	TOMORROW IS THE QUESTION (LP)	20
61	London Jazz LTZ-K 15199	CHANGE OF THE CENTURY (LP, mono)	25
61	London Jazz SAH-K 5099	CHANGE OF THE CENTURY (LP, stereo)	35
61	London Jazz LTZ-K 15228	THIS IS OUR MUSIC (LP, mono)	20
62	London Jazz LTZ-K 15241	THE ORNETTE COLEMAN QUARTET (LP, mono)	20
62	London Jazz SAH-K 6235	THE ORNETTE COLEMAN QUARTET (LP, stereo)	35
67	CBS 66023	CHAPPAQUA SUITE (2-LP)	25
68	Polydor 623 246/7	AN EVENING WITH ORNETTE COLEMAN (2-LP)	20
69	Impulse SIPL 518	ORNETTE AT 12 (LP)	20
72	Atlantic K 40278	TWINS (LP)	20
77	Blue Note BNS 40021	AT THE GOLDEN CIRCLE STOCKHOLM (LP, reissue)	12

ROGER COLEMAN
| 60 | Top Rank JAR 311 | Nobody's Fool/Endlessly | 8 |

COLENSO PARADE
| 86 | Fire BLAZE 11T | Fontana Eyes/Here Comes The Night/Anything/Our Man In Havana (12" p/s) | 8 |

(see also House Of Love)

COLETTE & BANDITS
| 65 | Stateside SS 416 | A Ladies Man/Lost Love | 20 |

COLEY
| 70s | Coley (Private Pressing) | GOODBYE BRAIN (LP) | 35 |

COLLAGE
| 73 | Studio Two TWO 410 | MISTY (LP) | 35 |

(see also Brian Bennett)

COLLECTIVE HORIZONTAL
| 79 | Dolmen DO 1 | COLLECTIVE HORIZONTAL EP (gatefold p/s, stickered white labels) | 12 |

COLLECTORS (CANADA)
| 70 | London HLU 10304 | I Must Have Been Blind/The Beginning | 6 |
| 69 | Warner Bros WS 1774 | GRASS AND WILD STRAWBERRIES (LP) | 22 |

(see also Chilliwack, Electric Prunes)

COLLECTORS (U.K.)
| 80 | Central Collection COL 1 | Different World/Talking Hands (p/s) | 6 |

COLLEGE BOYS (JAMAICA)
| 64 | Blue Beat BB 202 | Love Is A Treasure/Someone Will Be There | 25 |

COLLEGE BOYS (U.K.)
| 64 | Columbia DB 7306 | I Just Don't Understand/I'm Gonna Cry | 20 |
| 67 | Pye 7N 17294 | Good Times/San Antonio Rose | 10 |

KEITH COLLEY
| 63 | Stateside SS 234 | Enamorado/No Joke | 8 |

GRAHAM COLLIER SEXTET/SEPTET
67	Deram DML/SML 1005	DEEP DARK BLUE CENTRE (LP)	90
69	Fontana SFJL 922	DOWN ANOTHER ROAD (LP)	70
70	Fontana 6309 006	SONGS FOR MY FATHER (LP, as Graham Collier Music featuring Harry Beckett)	50
71	Philips 6308 051	MOSAICS (LP, live, as Graham Collier Music featuring Harry Beckett)	40
72	Saydisc SDL 244	PORTRAITS (LP)	20

| 75 | Cambridge Univ 521205638 | JAZZ LECTURE CONCERT (LP) | 35 |

(see also Harry Beckett)

MITTY COLLIER

| 64 | Pye International 7N 25275 | I Had A Talk With My Man/Free Girl | 20 |
| 64 | Pye International 7N 25275 | I Had A Talk With My Man/Free Girl (DJ Copy) | 40 |

ALBERT COLLINS

| 69 | Liberty LBS 83238 | LOVE CAN BE FOUND ANYWHERE (LP) | 40 |
| 73 | Tumbleweed TW 3501 | THERE'S GOTTA BE A CHANGE (LP) | 30 |

ANSEL(L) COLLINS

69	Trojan TR 699	Night Of Love/DERRICK MORGAN: Copy Cat	12
69	Trojan TR 7712	Cotton Dandy/CARL DAWKINS: Don't Get Weary	12
70	Trojan TR 7729	Moon Dust/Fat Cat	20
70	Trojan TR 7730	Monkey (Version I)/(Version II) (plays "High Voltage"/"High Voltage Version"; B-side actually by Beverley All Stars)	15
70	J-Dan JDN 4401	Cock Robin/KING DENNIS: Seven Zero	12
70	Techniques TE 907	Top Secret/Crazy Rhythm (both actually by Winston Wright)	15
71	Techniques TE 913	Nuclear Weapon/TECHNIQUES ALL STARS: La, La, La	15

(see also Dave & Ansell Collins, Conquerors, Lloyd Young, Prince Buster, Les Foster, Ethiopians, Eternals, Pam Brooks, Dennis Alcapone, Rad Bryan, Immortals)

CLANCY COLLINS ALL STARS (ACTUALLY, LLOYD CHALMERS)

| 71 | Smash SMA 2321 | Sir Collins Special/Conqueror (Actually, LENNOX BROWN : Heart of Knights) | 25 |

DAVE & ANSELL COLLINS

| 73 | Rhino RNO 111 | Hot Line/Sunshine Rock (label credits 'Dave Collins') | 15 |
| 71 | Trojan TBL 162 | DOUBLE BARREL (LP) | 25 |

DONIE COLLINS SHOWBAND

| 68 | Pye 7N 17682 | Get Down With It/I Can't Help Myself (Sugar Pie Honey Bunch) | 10 |

DOROTHY COLLINS

55	Vogue Coral Q 72111	My Boy - Flat Top/In Love	40
56	Vogue Coral Q 72116	Moments To Remember/Love And Marriage	5
56	Vogue Coral Q 72137	Seven Days/Manuello	15
56	Vogue Coral Q 72173	Treasure Of Love/He's Got Me, Hook, Line And Sinker	15
56	Vogue Coral Q 72193	Love Me As Though There Were No Tomorrow/Rock And Roll Train	40
56	Vogue Coral Q 72198	The Italian Theme/Cool It, Baby	40
56	Vogue Coral Q 72208	The Twelve Gifts Of Christmas/Mr. Santa	5
57	Vogue Coral Q 72232	Baby Can Rock/Would You Ever	25
57	Vogue Coral Q 72252	Mr. Wonderful/I Miss You Already	5
57	Vogue Coral Q 72262	Four Walls/Big Dreams	5
57	Vogue Coral Q 72287	Soft Sands/Sing It, Children, Sing It	5
59	Top Rank JAR 259	Baciare, Baciare/Everything I Have Is Yours	5
60	Top Rank JAR 401	Banjo Boy/Tintarella Di Luna	5
60	Top Rank JAR 523	Unlock Those Chains/I'll Be Yours, You'll be Mine	5
57	Coral LVA 9058	AT HOME WITH DOROTHY AND RAYMOND (LP)	35
55	London REP 1025	DOROTHY COLLINS SINGS (EP)	40

EDWYN COLLINS

87	Creation CRE 047T	Don't Shilly Shally/If Ever You're Ready (7" white label test pressing only)	40
87	Creation CRE 047T	Don't Shilly Shally/If Ever You're Ready (12", white label test pressing only)	35
87	Elevation ACIDB 6	My Beloved Girl/50 Shades Of Blue (Acoustic Version)/Clouds (Fogging Up My Mind)/What's The Big Idea? (box set with 3 postcards)	6
08	Heavenly HVN 180	Home Again/Searching For The Truth (7", 1500 copies in sealed brown envelope in PVC sleeve)	8
08	Heavenly HVN 180	Home Again/Searching For The Truth (7" one of 25 copies with hand decorated insert by 25 different people Including John Squire, Nicky Wire, Billy Childish and Jarvis Cocker)	50

(see also Orange Juice, Paul Quinn & Edwyn Collins)

GLENDA COLLINS

60	Decca F 11280	Take A Chance/Crazy Guy	15
61	Decca F 11321	Oh How I Miss You Tonight/Age For Love	15
61	Decca F 11417	Head Over Heels In Love/Find Another Fool	15
63	HMV POP 1163	I Lost My Heart In The Fairground/I Feel So Good	60
63	HMV POP 1233	If You Gotta Pick A Baby/In The First Place	80
64	HMV POP 1283	Baby It Hurts/Nice Wasn't It	65
64	HMV POP 1323	Lollipop/Everybody's Got To Fall In Love	50
65	HMV POP 1439	Johnny Loves Me/Paradise for Two	50
65	HMV POP 1475	Thou Shall Not Steal/Been Invited To A Party	70
66	Pye 7N 17044	Something I've Got To Tell You/My Heart Didn't Lie	75
66	Pye 7N 17150	It's Hard To Believe It/Don't Let It Rain On Sunday	75
90	Document CSAP LP 108	BEEN INVITED TO A PARTY (LP)	20

JOHNNY COLLINS

| 75 | Tradition TSR 020 | JOHNNY'S PRIVATE ARMY (LP) | 18 |

JOHNNY COLLINS & FRIENDS

| 73 | Tradition TSR 014 | THE TRAVELLER'S REST (LP, dark blue label, laminated sleeve) | 18 |

JUDY COLLINS

66	London HLZ 10029	I'll Keep It With Mine/Thirsty Boots	12
67	Elektra EKSN 45011	In My Life/Hard Lovin' Loser	5
67	Elektra EKSN 45043	Both Sides Now/Hey That's No Way To Say Goodbye	6
69	Elektra EKSN 45053	Some Day Soon/My Father	5
69	Elektra EKSN 45073	Chelsea Morning/Pretty Polly	5
69	Elektra EKSN 45077	Turn, Turn, Turn/Mr. Tambourine Man	5
65	Elektra EKL 209	MAID OF CONSTANT SORROW (LP)	20
65	Elektra EKS 7300	FIFTH ALBUM (LP, orange label)	12

LYN COLLINS

64	Sabre SA 0002	What Am I Gonna Do Without You?/When A Girl Meets A Bad, Bad Boy	20
74	Polydor 2066 490	Rock Me Again And Again And Again/Wide Awake In A Dream	15
74	Mojo 2093 029	Think (About It)/Me And My Baby Got Our Own Thing Going	10

88	Urban URBX 15	Yes It's You (by SWEET CHARLES)/Rock Me Again And Again And Again And Again/Think About It (12")	8
72	Polydor 2918 006	THINK (ABOUT IT) (LP)	40

(see also James Brown)

PETER COLLINS

70	Decca F 13048	Get In A Boat/Girl By The Sea	10
70	Decca Nova SDN 21	PETER COLLINS (LP, blue/silver label)	35

PHIL COLLINS

81	Virgin VSK 102	In The Air Tonight/The Roof Is Leaking (12-page cartoon booklet p/s)	5

(see also Genesis, Flaming Youth, Brand X, Peter Banks)

PHIL COLLINS & MARILYN MARTIN

85	Virgin VSSD 818	Separate Lives/Only You Know And I Know (2 interlocking picture discs)	5

(see also Brand X, Peter Banks, Genesis, Flaming Youth, Marilyn Martin)

RODGER COLLINS

67	Vocalion VF 9285	She's Looking Good/I'm Serving Time	25
67	Vocalion VF 9285	She's Looking Good/I'm Serving Time (DJ copy)	60

SHIRLEY COLLINS

60	Collector JEI 1508	SINGS IRISH (EP)	70
60	Collector JEB 3	THE FOGGY DEW (EP)	70
60	Collector JEB 5	ENGLISH SONGS (EP)	70
64	Collector JEB 9	ENGLISH SONGS VOL. 2 (EP, with Robin Hall)	70
63	Topic TOP 95	HEROES IN LOVE (EP)	70
59	Folkways FG 3564	FALSE TRUE LOVERS (LP)	130
60	Argo RG 150	SWEET ENGLAND (LP, blue/silver label)	150
64	Decca LK 4652	FOLK ROOTS, NEW ROUTES (LP, insert, with Davy Graham)	300
67	Topic 12T 170	THE SWEET PRIMROSES (LP, original pressing with blue label)	45
67	Topic 12T 170	THE SWEET PRIMROSES (LP)	25
68	Polydor 583 025	THE POWER OF THE TRUE LOVE KNOT (LP, with Incredible String Band)	250
71	Pegasus PEG 7	NO ROSES (LP, gatefold sleeve, with Albion Country Band)	50
74	Topic 12T 238	ADIEU TO OLD ENGLAND (LP, original pressing with blue label)	35
74	Topic 12T 238	ADIEU TO OLD ENGLAND (LP)	25
75	Deram SML 1117	A FAVOURITE GARLAND (LP)	50
76	Harvest SHSM 2008	AMARANTH (LP, textured sleeve)	30
78	Topic 12T 380	FOR AS MANY AS WILL (LP)	15
81	Righteous GDC 001	FOLK ROOTS, NEW ROUTES (LP, with Davy Graham)	20
83	Hannibal HNBL 1327	THE POWER OF THE TRUE LOVE KNOT (LP, reissue)	12
91	Mooncrest CREST 011	NO ROSES (LP, reissue)	15

SHIRLEY & DOLLY COLLINS

69	Harvest SHVL 754	ANTHEMS IN EDEN (LP, gatefold sleeve, with "Sold in U.K..." text on 4 lines)	150
69	Harvest SHVL 754	ANTHEMS IN EDEN (LP, gatefold sleeve, later issue with EMI logo on label)	100
70	Harvest SHVL 771	LOVE, DEATH AND THE LADY (LP, gatefold sleeve, no EMI logo on label)	120

(see also Davy Graham, Albion Country Band, Conundrum)

STEVE COLLINS

73	Big Shot BI 620	Ding A Ling Ting A Ling/Run Rhythm Run	15

TOMMY COLLINS

58	Capitol CL 14838	Think It Over Boys/All Of The Monkeys Ain't In The Zoo	10
58	Capitol CL 14894	Let Down/It Tickles	5
59	Capitol CL 15076	Little June/A Hundred Years From Now	5
60	Capitol CL 15118	Wreck Of The Old '97/You Belong In My Arms	5
57	Capitol T 776	WORDS AND MUSIC COUNTRY STYLE (LP)	15
59	Capitol T 1196	THIS IS TOMMY COLLINS (LP)	15

COLLINS BAND & BOB STACKIE

68	Collins Downbeat	Bob Stackie In Soho/LORD CHARLES & HIS BAND: Jamaican Bits And Pieces	45

(see also Sir Collins)

JOE COLMAN

90	Blast First FU10	INFERNAL MACHINE (LP, picture disc, 1,000 only)	18

COLONEL BAGSHOT

71	Parlophone R 5893	Georgia Fireball/Look In Her Eyes	15

COLONEL (1)

75	Ring O' 2017 104	Cokey Cokey/Away In A Manger (company sleeve)	10

COLONEL (2)

80	Virgin VS 380	Too Many Cooks (In The Kitchen)/I Need Protection (p/s)	6

(see also XTC, Mr. Partridge)

JERRY COLONNA

54	Brunswick 05243	Ebb Tide/The Velvet Glove	5
55	London HL 8143	Chicago Style/Baffi	10
56	HMV 7M 369	The Shifting, Whispering Sands/Waltz Me Around	5
55	Brunswick LA 8711	MUSIC FOR SCREAMING (10" LP)	12

COLORADOS

64	Oriole CB 1972	Lips Are Redder On You/Who You Gonna Hurt?	30

COLOR TAPES

79	Wavelength HURT 4	Cold Anger/Leaves Of China (p/s)	6

COLOSSEUM

69	Fontana TF 1029	Walking In The Park/Those About To Die	10
69	Fontana STL 5510	THOSE WHO ARE ABOUT TO DIE SALUTE YOU (LP, gatefold sleeve, black/silver labels)	80
69	Vertigo VO 1	VALENTYNE SUITE (LP, gatefold sleeve, large swirl label with Philips credit & inner bag)	120
70	Vertigo 6360 017	DAUGHTER OF TIME (LP, gatefold sleeve, with large swirl label & bag)	150
70	Vertigo 6360 017	DAUGHTER OF TIME (LP, gatefold sleeve, small swirl label)	25
71	Bronze ICD 1	COLOSSEUM LIVE (2-LP, gatefold, plastic inner)	40
72	Bronze BRNA 214	VALENTYNE SUITE (LP, reissue)	12

(see also Bakerloo, Dick Heckstall-Smith, Chris Farlowe, Greenslade, Humble Pie, John Mayall, Howard Riley Trio, Tempest, Mogul Thrash)

COLOURBOX

82	4AD AD 215	Breakdown/Tarantula (p/s)	6
82	4AD BAD 215	Breakdown/Tarantula (12", p/s)	8
83	4AD AD 304	Breakdown (Second Version)/Tarantula (Second Version) (different p/s)	5
86	4AD 605	The Official Colourbox World Cup Theme/Philip Glass (p/s)	5
85	4AD CAD 508	COLOURBOX (LP, stickered sleeve, 10,000 only, with bonus LP MAD 509)	18

(see also M/A/R/R/S)

COLOURED RAISINS

70	Trojan TR 7700	One Way Love/No More Heartaches	7

(see also Raisins)

COLOURFIELD

84	Chrysalis COLF D2	Thinking Of You/Wild Flames//Little Things/Thinking Of You (double pack)	5
85	Chrysalis COLF D4	Castles In The Air/Your Love Was Smashing//I Can't Get Enough Of You Baby/Castles In The Air (Instrumental Mix) (double pack, gatefold p/s)	5
87	Chrysalis CCD 1546	DECEPTION (CD)	20
89	Chrysalis CHR 1480	VIRGINS AND PHILISTINES (CD)	40

(see also Specials)

COLOURFUL SEASONS

68	MGM MGM 1433	Out Of The Blue/It's Gonna Break My Heart	6

COLO(U)RS OF LOVE

68	Page One POF 060	I'm A Train/Up On A Cotton Cloud	8
68	Page One POF 086	Just Another Fly/Twenty Ten	8
69	Page One POF 124	Mother Of Convention/Music Mother Made	8
75	DJM DJS 625	I Can Dream Can't I?/I'll Be Seeing You	6

COLOURS OUT OF TIME

81	Minsters In Orbit TVEYE 1	Dancing With Joy/Rock Section/Mambo Girls Mambo (hand-made pasted sleeve)	10

CHRISTOPHER COLT

68	Decca F 12726	Virgin Sunrise/Girl In The Mirror	40

TONY COLTON('S BIG BOSS BAND)

64	Decca F 11879	Lose My Mind/So Used To Loving You (solo)	30
65	Pye 7N 15886	I Stand Accused/Further On Down The Track (with Big Boss Band)	200
66	Pye 7N 17046	You're Wrong There Baby/Have You Lost Your Mind	40
66	Pye 7N 17117	I've Laid Some Down In My Time/Run Pony Rider	50
68	Columbia DB 8385	In The World Of Marnie Dreaming/Who Is She? (solo)	25

(see also Poet & One Man Band, Head Hands & Feet, Real McCoy, Peter B's)

JOHN COLTRANE

60	Esquire EP 229	SOUL OF 'TRANE (EP)	10
61	Esquire EP 239	BASS BLUES (EP)	10
64	Fontana 469 203TE	WHILE MY LADY SLEEPS (EP)	10
58	Esquire 32-079	THE FIRST TRANE (LP)	50
58	Esquire 32-089	SOUL TRANE (LP)	100
59	Esquire 32-091	TRANEING IN (LP)	25
60	Esquire 32-101	CATTIN' (LP)	25
60	London Jazz LTZ-K 15197	GIANT STEPS (LP)	40
61	Esquire 32-129	LUSH LIFE (LP)	25
61	London Jazz LTZ-K 15219	COLTRANE JAZZ (LP, also stereo SAH-K 6162)	20
62	London Jazz LTZ-K 15232	BAGS AND TRANE (LP, also stereo SAH-K 6192)	20
62	Columbia 33SX 1399	THE BIRDLAND STORY VOL. 1: ECHOES OF AN ERA (LP)	15
62	London Jazz LTZ-K 15239	OLE COLTRANE (LP, mono)	20
62	London Jazz SAH-K 6223	OLE COLTRANE (LP, stereo)	25
62	HMV CLP 1548	AFRICA/BRASS (LP, mono)	25
62	HMV SCD 1431	AFRICA/BRASS (LP, stereo)	40
62	HMV CLP 1590	LIVE AT THE VILLAGE VANGUARD (LP, mono)	20
62	HMV CSD 1456	LIVE AT THE VILLAGE VANGUARD (LP, stereo)	25
63	United Artists (S)ULP 1018	COLTRANE TIME (LP)	15
63	London HA-K/SH-K 8017	COLTRANE PLAYS THE BLUES (LP, as John Coltrane Group)	25
63	Esquire 32-179	STANDARD COLTRANE (LP)	25
63	HMV CLP 1629	COLTRANE (LP, also stereo CSD 1483)	25
63	HMV CLP 1647	BALLADS (LP, also stereo CSD 1496)	20
63	HMV CLP 1657	DUKE ELLINGTON & JOHN COLTRANE (LP, mono)	20
63	HMV CSD 1502	DUKE ELLINGTON & JOHN COLTRANE (LP, stereo)	25
64	HMV CLP 1695	IMPRESSIONS (LP, mono)	25
64	HMV CSD 1509	IMPRESSIONS (LP, stereo)	30
64	HMV CLP 1700	JOHN COLTRANE WITH JOHNNY HARTMAN (LP)	25
64	Realm RM 157	ON WEST 42ND STREET (LP)	20
64	Realm RM 181	TRANE RIDE (LP)	20
64	HMV CLP 1741	LIVE AT BIRDLAND (LP, also stereo CSD 1544)	20
65	HMV CLP 1799	CRESCENT (LP, mono)	25
65	HMV SCD 1567	CRESCENT (LP, stereo)	30
65	Stateside SL 10124	BLACK PEARLS (LP)	20
65	HMV CLP 1869	A LOVE SUPREME (LP, mono)	35
65	HMV CSD 1605	A LOVE SUPREME (LP, stereo)	50
65	Atlantic ATL/SAL 5022	MY FAVOURITE THINGS (LP)	20
65	Realm RM 52226	TANGANYIKA STRUT (LP)	20
65	HMV CLP 1897	COLTRANE PLAYS (LP, also stereo CSD 1619)	20
66	Stateside SL 10162	BAHIA (LP)	20
66	HMV CLP/CSD 3543	ASCENSION (LP, as John Coltrane Orchestra)	40
66	HMV CLP/CSD 3551	NEW THING AT NEWPORT (LP, with Archie Shepp)	35
66	Atlantic 587/588 004	THE AVANT-GARDE (LP, with Don Cherry)	35
66	HMV CLP 3575	MEDITATIONS (LP, mono)	20
66	HMV CSD 3575	MEDITATIONS (LP, flipback sleeve stereo)	30
67	Atlantic 587/588 039	COLTRANE'S SOUND (LP)	20
67	HMV CLP/CSD 3599	COLTRANE LIVE AT THE VILLAGE VANGUARD AGAIN! (LP)	25
67	HMV CLP/CSD 3617	OM (LP, withdrawn)	40
67	HMV CLP/CSD 3617	KULU SE MAMA (LP)	20
68	Transatlantic PR 7280	DAKAR (LP)	25

68	Transatlantic PR 7378	LAST TRANE (LP)	25
68	Impulse MIPL 502	EXPRESSION (LP, mono)	25
68	Impulse SIPL 502	EXPRESSION (LP, stereo)	18
69	Atlantic 588 139	THREE LITTLE WORDS (LP)	20
69	Impulse MIPL/SIPL 515	COSMIC MUSIC (LP, by Alice & John Coltrane)	30
70	Impulse SIPL 522	SELFLESSNESS (LP)	20
71	Probe SPB 1025	AFRO BLUE (LP)	15
72	Prestige PR 24003	JOHN COLTRANE (2-LP)	15
74	CBS PR 24037	BLACK PEARLS (2-LP)	18

(see also Miles Davis, Thelonious Monk, Cannonball Adderley, Don Cherry, Archie Shepp)

COLTS
65	Pye 7N 15955	San Miguel/Where Has Our Love Gone?	5

COLUMBIA BOYS
68	Pye 7N 17513	Baby Come Back/Born To Lose	8
69	Pye 7N 17763	That's My Pa/She Thinks I Still Care	7

COLUMBUS
70	Deram DM 294	Ev'rybody Loves The U.S. Marshall/Tired	10

RAY COLUMBUS INVADERS
60s	Zodiac AZ/1009	She's A Mod/INVADERS : Cruel Sea	20

COLWELL BROTHERS
56	Philips NBE 11047	COLWELL BROTHERS VOL. 1 (EP)	10
56	Philips NBE 11048	COLWELL BROTHERS VOL. 2 (EP)	10
60	Philips NBE 11117	AFRICA'S GOT THE ANSWER (EP)	10
60	Phillips NBE 1118	THERE'LL BE A NEW WORLD (EP)	10

STEVE COLYER
75	Polydor 2058 647	Hey Mary/I Found My Sunshine	6

KEN COLYER('S JAZZMEN)
55	Decca F 10504	Early Hours/Cataract Rag	5
55	Decca F 10519	If I Ever Cease To Love/The Entertainer	5
55	Decca F 10565	It Looks Like A Big Time Tonight/Red Wing	5
56	Tempo A 117	Just A Closer Walk With Thee/Sheik Of Araby	5
56	Tempo A 120	If I Ever Cease To Love You/Isle Of Capri	5
56	Tempo A 126	My Bucket's Got A Hole In It/Wabash Blues	5
56	Tempo A 136	Maryland, My Maryland/The World Is Waiting For The Sunrise	5
56	Decca FJ 10755	All The Girls Go Crazy About The Way I Walk/Dippermouth Blues	5
61	Columbia DB 4676	The Happy Wanderer/Maryland, My Maryland	5
55	Tempo EXA 26	KEN COLYER JAZZMEN (EP)	10
60	Decca DFE 6645	WALKING THE BLUES (EP, also stereo STO 143)	10
54	Decca LF 1152	NEW ORLEANS TO LONDON (10" LP)	20
54	Decca LF 1196	BACK TO THE DELTA (10" LP, as Ken Colyer's Jazzmen & Skiffle Group)	20
55	Vogue LDE 161	KEN COLYER IN NEW ORLEANS (10" LP)	20
56	Tempo LAP 11	KEN COLYER'S JAZZMEN (10" LP)	20
57	Decca LK 4178	CLUB SESSION (LP)	15
58	Decca LF 1301	MARCHING TO NEW ORLEANS (10" LP, as Ken Colyer & His Omega Brass Band)	15
59	Decca LF 1319	COLYER IN HAMBURG (10" LP)	15
59	Decca LK 4294	PLAYS STANDARDS (LP)	15
64	77 LEU 12/7	KEN COLYER AND THE ORIGINAL CRANE RIVER BAND (LP)	15
64	77 LEU 12/10	THE REAL KEN COLYER (LP)	15
65	K.C. KCS 1001	WANDERING (LP)	15
71	Joy JOYS 194	RAGTIME REVISITED (LP)	30

KEN COLYER'S SKIFFLE GROUP
55	Decca F 10631	Down By The Riverside/Take This Hammer	20
56	Decca FJ 10711	Streamline Train/Go Down Old Hannah	20
56	Decca FJ 10751	Down Bound Train/Mule Skinner	20
56	Decca FJ 10772	Old Riley/Stack O'Lee Blues	10
57	Decca FJ 10889	The Grey Goose/I Can't Sleep	10
57	Decca FJ 10926	Sporting Life/House Rent Stomp	10
57	Decca FJ 10972	Ella Speed/Go Down Sunshine	10
55	Decca DFE 6286	KEN COLYER'S SKIFFLE GROUP (EP, various coloured sleeves)	20
58	Decca DFE 6444	KEN COLYER'S SKIFFLE GROUP NO. 2 (EP)	15
60	Decca DFE 6563	KEN COLYER'S SKIFFLE GROUP IN HAMBURG (EP)	10

(see also Crane Skiffle Group)

VEE COMA
62	Pun PUN 001	Piccadilly/Independence Day	15

COMBAT 84
82	Victory VIC 1	ORDERS OF THE DAY (EP, wraparound p/s)	20
83	Victory VIC 2	Rapist/The Right To Choose/Barry Prudom (p/s)	20

PETER COMBE
78	Voyage VOY 001	Music Of The Day (Sing Birds Sing)/You Baby On My Mind	6

COMBINATIONS
72	Punch PH 99	1 2 3 A B C/Zee	6

COME
81	Come Org. WDC 883012	Come Sunday (cassette)	60
79	Come Org. WDC 88001	Come Sunday/Shaved Slits	30
79	Come Org. WDC 883001	COME PRESENT RAMPTON (cassette)	60
79	Come Org. WDC 88203	PRESENT RAMPTON (LP)	100
81	Come Org. WDC 881012	I'M JACK (LP, orange vinyl with insert)	80

(see also Whitehouse, New Order)

COMET GAIN
94	Soul Static SOUL 5	HOLLOWAY SWEETHEARTS EP	10
96	Wiiija WIJ 50V	SAY YES TO INTERNATIONAL SOCIALISM EP	8
97	Wiiija WIJ 66	Strength/A Film By Kenneth Anger/Letting Go (p/s)	7
98	Mei Mei MEI 001	Jack Nance Hair/We Are All Rotten/Record Prayer (p/s)	5

MINT VALUE £

| 01 | Fortuna Pop! FPOP 26 | You Can't Hide Your Love Forever/Beatnik (p/s) ....10 |

COMETS SHOWGROUP

| 70 | LRC SCG 1 | COMETS ON LOCATION (LP, private pressing, handmade sleeve) ....50 |

COMMANCHES

| 64 | Pye 7N 15609 | Tomorrow/Missed Your Loving ....10 |

(see also Bobby Allen)

COMMANDERS

55	Brunswick 05366	The Elephants' Tango/Commanders Overture 5
55	Brunswick 05433	The Cat From Coos Bay/Camptown Boogie 5
55	Brunswick 05467	The Monster/Cornball No. 1 5

(see also Louis Armstrong)

COMMENDABLES

| 80s | Lip CC 1 | London E1/Decaying House ....10 |

COMMERCIALS

| 81 | Fast Product COM 1 | Sixteen Again And Again/The Heroine Dies/Simon (p/s) ....8 |

COMMITTED

| 79 | Ace ACE 006 | Crash Victim/British Crimes/Fast Lane/Advertising (500 only)..................................100 |

COMMITTEE (1)

| 68 | Liberty LBF 15154 | Hard Way/Hey You...15 |

COMMITTEE (2)

| 69 | Pye 7N 17826 | Sleep Tight Honey/Memories Of Melinda ....6 |

COMMODORES (1)

55	London HLD 8209	Riding On A Train/Uranium 750
55	London HLD 8209	Riding On A Train/Uranium (78) 100
56	London HLD 8251	Speedo/Whole Lotta Shakin' Goin' On 750
56	London HLD 8251	Speedo/Whole Lotta Shakin' Goin' On (78) 100

COMMODORES (2)

| 69 | Atlantic 584 273 | Keep On Dancing/Rise Up ....25 |

COMMON ROUND

| 70s | Galliard GAL 4015 | FOUR PENCE A DAY (LP) ....15 |

COMMOTION UPSTAIRS

| 89 | Saucy SAUCY TT 17 | Lift Me Up/Not Like That/Too Bad/Fake (p/s)...100 |

COMMUTERS

| 79 | Long Corporation LONE 001 | Small Talk/Let's Talk About Girls/Angeline (p/s)...5 |

PERRY COMO

53	HMV 7M 102	The Ruby And The Pearl/My Love And Devotion 8
53	HMV 7M 110	Some Enchanted Evening/Bali Ha'i 8
53	HMV 7M 118	Don't Let The Stars Get In Your Eyes/To Know You (Is To Love You) (B-side with Fontane Sisters)...20
53	HMV 7M 124	Wild Horses/Please Believe Me 5
53	HMV 7M 138	My Lady Loves To Dance/A Bushel And A Peck (B-side with Betty Hutton)...5
53	HMV 7M 149	My One And Only Heart/Say You're Mine Again 5
53	HMV 7M 155	Hello, Young Lovers/We Kiss In A Shadow 5
53	HMV 7M 163	Pa-Paya Mama/Why Did You Leave Me? 5
54	HMV 7M 175	You Alone/Surprising 5
54	HMV 7M 200	Idle Gossip/Look Out The Window 5
54	HMV 7M 215	Wanted/Give Me Your Hand 5
54	HMV 7M 241	Hit And Run Affair/If You Were Only Mine 5
54	HMV 7M 263	There Never Was A Night So Beautiful/Papa Loves Mambo...5
54	HMV 7M 278	Frosty The Snowman/The Twelve Days Of Christmas 5
55	HMV 7M 296	Ko Ko Mo (I Love You So)/You'll Always Be My Lifetime Love...15
55	HMV 7M 305	Door Of Dreams/Nobody 5
55	HMV 7M 326	There's No Place Like Home For The Holidays/Tina Marie 5
56	HMV 7M 366	Fooled/The Rose Tattoo 5
56	HMV 7M 404	Hot Diggity (Dog Ziggity Boom)/My Funny Valentine...8
56	HMV 7MC 39	Hot Diggity (Dog Ziggity Boom)/Juke Box Baby (export issue) 10
56	HMV POP 240	Glendora/More...8
56	HMV 7MC 49	Glendora/More (export issue) 10
56	HMV POP 271	Moonlight Love/Chincherinchee 8
57	HMV POP 304	Somebody Up There Likes Me/Dream Along With Me (I'm On My Way To A star) 8
57	HMV 7MC 51	Somebody Up There Likes Me/Dream Along With Me (I'm On My Way To A Star) (export issue)...8
57	HMV POP 328	Round And Round/My House Is Your House...8
57	RCA RCA 1001	The Girl With The Golden Braids/My Little Baby 8
57	HMV POP 369	Silk Stockings/Childhood Is A Meadow 8
57	HMV POP 394	As Time Goes By/All At Once You Love Her 8

(see also Fontane Sisters, Betty Hutton)

LES COMPAGNONS DE LA CHANSON

| 53 | Columbia SCM 5005 | The Three Bells (The Jimmy Brown Song)/Ave Maria...8 |
| 53 | Columbia SCM 5056 | The Galley Slave/Dreams Never Grow Old ....8 |

COMPANY OF COWARDS

| 87 | Company Of Cowards COC 1 | 18 AGAIN EP (12")...70 |

COMPANY (1)

| 79 | United Artists BP 326 | We Wish You Well/Right Time For Love ....30 |

(see also Whitesnake)

COMPANY (2)

80	Incus INCUS 36	FABLES (LP) 50
80	Incus INCUS 38	FICTIONS (LP)...50
82	Incus INCUS 46	EPIPHANY (LP) 50
82	Incus INCUS 47	EPIPHANIES (LP)...50
83	Incus INCUS 51	TRIOS (LP)...50

COMPASS
74	MAM 115	No More Whiskey/Maybe She Will	7

COMPLETE CYCLE
70	Jay Boy BOY 23	I'm On The Road Again/Back On The Road Again	6

COMPLEX
70	CLPM 001	COMPLEX (LP, private pressing, 99 copies only)	750
71	Deroy	THE WAY WE FEEL (LP, private pressing, 99 copies only)	600
98	Tenth Planet TP 038	COMPLEX (LP, reissue, 1000, no'd)	30

(see also Monsoon, Misfits)

COMPLEXXION
79	UK Records INT 584	So Much In Love/Weekend (in p/s with bonus floppy gold disc)	8
79	UK Records INT 584	So Much In Love/Weekend	5

(see also wavelength)

COMPROMISE
66	CBS 202050	You Will Think Of Me/Love Minus Zero	7

COMSAT ANGELS
79	Junta JUNTA 1	Red Planet/I Get Excited/Specimen No. 2 (p/s)	6
79	Junta JUNTA 1	Red Planet/I Get Excited/Specimen No. 2 (p/s, later reissue on red vinyl)	8

BOBBY COMSTOCK (& COUNTS)
59	Top Rank JAR 223	The Tennessee Waltz/Sweet Talk (with Counts)	10
60	London HLE 9080	Jambalaya/Let's Talk It Over (as Bobby Comstock & Counts)	10
63	Stateside SS 163	Let's Stomp/I Want To Do It	15
63	Stateside SS 221	Susie Baby/Take A Walk	15
65	United Artists UP 1086	I'm A Man/I'll Make You Glad	10

COMUS
71	Dawn DNX 2506	Diana/In The Lost Queen's Eyes/Winter Is A Coloured Bird (p/s)	80
71	Dawn DNLS 3019	FIRST UTTERANCE (LP, gatefold sleeve with lyric sheet, orange label)	500
74	Virgin V 2018	TO KEEP FROM CRYING (LP, twin Virgin label)	40

(see also Gong, Henry Cow, Esperanto Rock Orchestra)

CON-CHORDS
65	Polydor BM 56059	You Can't Take It Away/Let Me Walk With You	25

CONCORDE
70	Attack ATT 8020	Let Me Out/I Belong To You	12

CONCORDS (1)
66	Emblem JDR 303	SOUL PURPOSE (LP)	30

CONCORDS (2)
69	Blue Cat BS 170	Buttoo/I Need Your Loving	40

CONCRETE SOX
87	Manic Ears ACHE 11	WHOOPS, SORRY VICAR! (LP)	12
88	C.O.R GURT 10	YOUR TURN NEXT (LP, with insert)	15

CONDEMNED 84
86	RFB SIN 2	Oi Ain't Dead!/Under Her Thumb/Follow The Leader/The Nutter (12", p/s, blue vinyl)	25
86	RFB SIN 2	Oi Ain't Dead!/Under Her Thumb/Follow The Leader/The Nutter (7", p/s, blue vinyl)	20
87	RFB SIN 3	IN SEARCH OF THE NEW BREED (12" EP)	25
88	Oi! OIR 003	BATTLE SCARRED (LP)	22
88	Grade 1	FACE THE AGGRESSION (LP)	22

JEFF CONDON
63	MGM MGM 1221	(Walkin' In) Freddy's Footsteps/Never You Mind	5

HOWIE G. CONDOR
65	Fontana TF 613	Big Noise From Winnetka/The Fix	10

CONEY ISLAND KIDS
55	London HLJ 8207	Baby, Baby You/Moonlight Beach	50

CONFLICT
83	Corp. Christi CHRIST IT'S 4	A Nation Of Animal Lovers/Liberate (poster p/s)	6
83	Mortarhate MORT EX001	The Serenade Is Dead (12" with insert)	8
85	Mortarhate MORT 15	The Battle Continues (both sides) (p/s, different colours, with insert)	5
86	Mortarhate MORT 20	THE UNGOVERNABLE FORCE (LP, inner)	12
88	FUND 1	FROM PROTEST TO RESISTANCE (LP, mail order, w/l, stickered plain sleeve)	12

CONGO ASHANTI ROY
82	On-U Sound DP 08	Hands & Feet/African Blood (10")	15

CONGOS
77	Black Swan BS 1	Congo Man/Congo Man Chant (12")	40
81	Go-Feet BEAT 2	HEART OF THE CONGOS (LP)	25
96	Blood & Fire BAFLP 009	HEART OF THE CONGOS (2-LP, reissue)	20

CONGREGATION
71	Columbia DB 8830	Softly Whispering I Love You/When Susie Takes The Plane	5

ARTHUR CONLEY
67	Atlantic 584 083	Sweet Soul Music/Let's Go Steady	10
67	Atlantic 584 121	Shake, Rattle And Roll/You Don't Have To See Me	5
67	Atlantic 584 143	Whole Lotta Woman/Love Comes And Goes	10
68	Atlantic 584 175	Funky Street/Put Our Love Together	10
68	Atlantic 584 197	People Sure Act Funny/Burning Fire	10
68	Atlantic 584 224	Aunt Dora's Love Soul Shack/Is That You Love	10
69	Atco 226 004	Star Revue/Love Sure Is A Powerful Thing	5
70	Atco 226 011	They Call The Wind Maria/Hurt	5
70	Atlantic 2091 025	All Day Singing/God Bless	5
71	Atlantic 2091 106	Sweet Soul Music/Shake, Rattle And Roll	8
71	Atlantic 2091 120	I'm Living Good/I'm So Glad You're Here	5
72	Capricorn K 17506	Rita/More Sweet Soul Music	5

MINT VALUE £

67	Atlantic 587 069	SWEET SOUL MUSIC (LP)	35
68	Atlantic 587 084	SHAKE, RATTLE AND ROLL (LP)	20
68	Atlantic 587/588 128	SOUL DIRECTION (LP)	20
69	Atco 228 019	MORE SWEET SOUL (LP)	15

(see also Soul Clan)

CONNARD
68	Spot JW 11	Amadhan/Desdemona	50

CONNECTION
92	Spare Beat SBRR 006	THE CONNECTION EP (12")	30
93	Spare Beat SBRR 008	THE CONNECTION EP VOL II (12")	30

BRIAN CONNELL & ROUND SOUND
66	Mercury MF 956	Just My Kind Of Loving/Something You've Got	10
66	Mercury MF 991	The Same Thing's Happened To Me/Mister Porter	10
68	Philips BF 1661	What Good Am I/Just Another Wedding Day	10
68	Philips BF 1718	I Know/Mister Travel Company	45

RAY CONNIFF & ROCKIN' RHYTHM BOYS
55	Vogue Coral QW 5001	Piggy Bank Boogie/Short Stuff	10

TERRY CONNOLLY & THE TRIXONS
67	Kinh KG 1069	You're Gonna Wonder About Me/Mama, I'm Not The Boy I Used To Be	20

BILLY CONNOLLY
72	Transatlantic TRA 258	LIVE! (LP)	12

(see also Humblebums; George Harrison, Ringo Starr & Eric Clapton appear on "Freedom")

BRIAN CONNOLLY
82	Carrere CAR 231	Hypnotised/Fade Away (p/s)	18

(see also Sweet)

CHRIS CONNOR
59	London HLE 8869	Hallelujah I Love Him So/I Won't Cry Anymore	6
60	London HLK 9124	I Only Want Some/That's My Desire	5
56	London EZ-N 19010	CHRIS CONNOR SINGS LULLABYS OF BIRDLAND (EP, with Ellis Larkin Trio)	10
57	London RE-N 1093	LONDON'S GIRL FRIENDS - NO. 2 (EP)	10
56	London HA-K 2030	PRESENTING CHRIS CONNOR (LP, also stereo SAH-K 6032)	12
56	London LZ-N 14007	SINGS LULLABYS FOR LOVERS (10" LP)	12
57	London HB-N 1074	CHRIS (10" LP)	12
57	London HA-K 2066	HE LOVES ME, HE LOVES ME NOT (LP)	12
60	London LZ-N 14036	THIS IS CHRIS (10" LP)	12
60	London LTZ-K 15142	A JAZZ DATE WITH (LP)	12

EDRIC CONNOR
57	Oriole CB 1362	Manchester United Calypso/Yorumba Highlife (78)	10
60	Argo EAF 9	9 SONGS FROM TRINIDAD (EP, with the Southlanders)	8
53	Argo RG 33	SONGS FROM JAMAICA (LP, with the Caribbeans)	15
55	Argo RG 57	SONGS FROM TRINIDAD (LP, with the Southlanders)	15
55	Argo RG 58	CALYPSO (LP)	15

KENNETH CONNOR
59	Top Rank JAR 138	Rail Road Rock/Ramona	12
61	Fontana H 321	Nearly A Nasty Accident/Smile	8

PAUL CONNOR
71	Polydor 2121045	Little Sparrow/I Don't Love You Any More	35
71	Polydor 2480072	EASY TO REMEMBER (LP)	40

TIM CONNOR
60	Decca F 11239	Rosemary/Love What Took So Long	20
62	HMV POP 1007	Lost Love/Down	15
62	HMV POP 1056	Without A Shoulder To Cry On/I've Fallen In Love	15
62	HMV POP 1096	Take This Message/Maybe	15

CAROL CONNORS
62	London HLN 9619	Big Big Love/Two Rivers	20

(see also Teddy Bears)

NORMAN CONNORS
74	Buddah BDS 5611	SLEWFOOT (LP)	20
77	Buddah BDLP 4043	AQUARIAN DREAM (LP)	40
77	Buddah BDLP 4043	YOU ARE MY STARSHIP (LP)	20

CONNY
61	HMV POP 867	Midi Midinette/CONNY & REX GILDO: Yes My Darling	15
61	Columbia DB 4714	No One Can Tell Me I'm Too Young/Lovable	20
62	Columbia DB 4845	Gino/Midi-Midinette	20

CONQUERORS
67	Doctor Bird DB 1119	Won't You Come Home Now?/Oh That Day	50
67	Treasure Isle TI 7035	Lonely Street/I Fell In Love	40
69	Amalgamated AMG 832	Secret Weapon (actually by Ansell Collins)/Jumpy Jumpy Girl	40
69	High Note HS 016	If You Can't Beat Them/Anywhere You Want To Go	12
69	High Note HS 025	National Dish/Mr D.J.	12
72	Fab FAB 22	You Hold The Handles/SOUL REBELS : Bongo Skank	150

(see also Stranger Cole & Conquerors, Baba Brooks)

BOB CONRAD
61	Warner Bros WB 54	Bye Bye Baby/Love You	10

JESS CONRAD
60	Decca F 11236	Cherry Pie/There's Gonna Be A Day	5
60	Decca F 11259	Unless You Meant It/Out Of Luck	5
61	Decca F 11315	Mystery Girl/The Big White House	5
61	Decca F 11348	This Pullover/Why Am I Living?	5
61	Decca F 11394	Walkaway/Every Breath I Take	5
61	Decca F 11412	Twist My Wrist/Hey Little Girl (p/s)	7

61	Decca F 11412	Twist My Wrist/Hey Little Girl (no p/s)	5
62	Decca F 11511	Pretty Jenny/You Can Do It If You Try	5
63	Decca F 11620	It's About Time/As You Like It	5
63	Columbia DB 4969	Take Your Time/I Know You	5
65	Pye 7N 15849	Hurt Me/It Can Happen To You	10
71	President PT 357	Here She Comes Again/My Idea	5
60	Decca DFE 6666	JESS CONRAD (EP)	10
62	Decca DFE 6702	TWIST MY WRIST (EP)	10
63	Decca DFE 8524	THE HUMAN JUNGLE (EP, with Rhet Stoller)	20
61	Decca LK 4390	JESS FOR YOU (LP)	40

(see also Guvners)

TONI CONRAD & FAUST
73	Caroline C 1501	OUTSIDE THE DREAM SYNDICATE (LP, as Tony Conrad)	45

(see also Faust)

CONSCIOUS MINDS
71	Big BG 318	Jamaican Boy/Brainwash	10
71	Ackee ACK 141	Paul, Marcus And Norman/Version	7
71	Punch PH 97	Paul, Marcus And Norman/Version (reissue)	6
71	Escort ERT 857	Peace Treaty/Brainwash	7

(see also Ken Boothe, Jamaicans, B.B.Seaton, Charmers)

CONSOLERS
67	President PT165	Someone Must Answer/No One	8

CONSORTIUM
68	Pye 7N 17635	All The Love In The World/Spending My Life Saying Goodbye	10
69	Pye 7N 17725	When The Day Breaks/Day The Train Never Came	30
69	Pye 7N 17797	Beggar Man/Cynthia Serenity	18
69	Pye 7N 17841	I Don't Want Her Anymore/The House Upon The Hill	7
70	Trend TNT 52	Melanie Cries Alone/Copper Coloured Years	7

CONSTRUCTION
90	White SDT17	Sudden Impact - In A State Of Experimentation	40
90	White SDT30	Transmission/Revenge Of The Dragon (12")	100
91	White SDT37	Change Your Attitude/Time To Get Raw (12")	75

CONSUMATES
68	Coxsone CS 7054	What Is It/ROLAND ALPHONSO: Musical Happiness	35

CONTINENTALS (1)
62	Oriole 1569	Bye Bye Blackbird/Everybody Loves My Baby	15
62	Island WI 010	Going Crazy/Give Me All Your Love	25

CONTINENTALS (2)
79	CBS S 7476	Fizz Pop (Modern Rock)/(I Lost My Love On A) 747	5

CONTINENTAL UPTIGHT BAND
71	Columbia SCX 6454	BEAUTIFUL FRIENDSHIP (LP, black/silver/white boxed Columbia label)	25

CONTINUUM
70	RCA Victor SF 8157	CONTINUUM (LP, gatefold, orange labels)	20
71	RCA Victor SF 8196	AUTUMN GRASS (LP, gatefold sleeve, orange label)	40

CONTOURS
62	Oriole CB 1763	Do You Love Me/Move Mister Man	30
63	Oriole CB 1799	Shake Sherry/You Better Get In Line	55
63	Oriole CB 1831	Don't Let Him Be Your Baby/It Must Be Love	75
64	Stateside SS 299	Can You Do It/I'll Stand By You	55
64	Stateside SS 299	Can You Do It/I'll Stand By You (DJ Copy)	90
65	Stateside SS 381	Can You Jerk Like Me/That Day She Needed Me	55
65	Stateside SS 381	Can You Jerk Like Me/That Day She Needed Me (DJ Copy)	90
65	Tamla Motown TMG 531	First I Look At The Purse/Searching For A Girl	55
65	Tamla Motown TMG 531	First I Look At The Purse/Searching For A Girl (DJ Copy)	120
66	Tamla Motown TMG 564	Determination/Just A Little Misunderstanding	55
66	Tamla Motown TMG 564	Determination/Just A Little Misunderstanding (DJ Copy)	130
67	Tamla Motown TMG 605	It's So Hard Being A Loser/Your Love Grows More Precious Every Day	35
67	Tamla Motown TMG 605	It's So Hard Being A Loser/Your Love Grows More Precious Every Day (DJ Copy)	70
70	Tamla Motown TMG 723	Just A Little Misunderstanding/First I Look At The Purse	8
70	Tamla Motown TMG 723	Just A Little Misunderstanding/First I Look At The Purse (DJ Copy)	40
65	Tamla Motown TME 2002	THE CONTOURS (EP)	110
63	Oriole PS 40043	DO YOU LOVE ME (LP)	250

CONTRABAND
74	Transatlantic BIG 518	Lady For Today/On The Road	6
74	Transatlantic TRA 278	CONTRABAND (LP, with lyric insert)	18

(see also Mae McKenna)

CONTRAST
69	Orange OAS 202	Hey That's No Way To Say Goodbye/We Can Make It If We Try	10

CONTRASTS FEATURING BOB MORRISON
64	Parlophone R 5095	I Can't Get You Out Of My Mind/Click When You're In Love	8
64	Parlophone R 5190	Call Me/Come On Let's Go	5
68	Monument MON 1018	What A Day/Lonely Child	10

(see also Bill Forbes)

CONTROLLED BLEEDING
86	Sterile SR 11	HEADCRACK (LP)	20

CONUNDRUM & RICHARD HARVEY
78	Streetsong No. 1	Black Birds Of Brittany/SHIRLEY COLLINS & ANNIE POWER: The Mariners Farewell (poster p/s)	18

(see also Bert Jansch, Shirley Collins)

CONVAIRS
66	HMV POP 1549	Tomorrow Is A Long Time/Midnight Mary	10

BERT CONVY & THUNDERBIRDS
55	London HLB 8190	C'mon Back/Hoo Bop De Bow	150
55	London HLB 8190	C'mon Back/Hoo Bop De Bow (78)	40
56	Capitol CL 14601	Heaven On Earth/CHEERS: Que Pasa Muchacha	10

(see also Cheers,Thunderbirds)

CONNIE CONWAY
| 60 | London HA-W 2214 | CONNIE CONWAY (LP) | 20 |

MIKE CONWAY
| 66 | Plexium PXM 1 | I'm Gonna Get Me A Woman/Reign Of King Sadness | 15 |

PAUL CONWAY
| 64 | Piccadilly 7N 35215 | Come A Little Bit Closer/Be Lonely Little Girl | 7 |

JIMMY CONWELL
| 72 | Jay Boy BOY 64 | Cigarette Ashes/Second Hand Happiness | 10 |
| 72 | Jay Boy BOY 64 | Cigarette Ashes/Second Hand Happiness (DJ Copy) | 25 |

COO-COO RACHAS
| 59 | Capitol CL 15024 | Chili Beans/Track Down | 15 |

RY COODER
71	Reprise RS 23497	How Can A Poor Man Stand Such Times And Live/Goin' To Brownsville	7
71	Reprise RSLP 6402	RY COODER (LP)	15
72	Reprise K 44142	INTO THE PURPLE VALLEY (LP, with lyric sheet)	12

(see also Captain Beefheart, Don Everly)

ENGLAND COOK
| 72 | Explosion EX 2063 | Samba Girl/NOW GENERATION: Samba (Version) | 5 |

LITTLE JOE COOK (U.K.)
| 65 | Sue WI 385 | Stormy Monday Blues (Parts 1 & 2) | 50 |

(see also Chris Farlowe, Beazers)

LITTLE JOE COOK (U.S.)
| 68 | Sonet SON 2002 | Don't You Have Feelings?/Hold On To Your Money | 20 |
| 74 | Sonet SON 2041 | Hold On To Your Money/Don't You Have Feelings? (reissue, sides reversed) | 8 |

PETER COOK (1)
| 65 | Pye 7N 15847 | Georgia/There And Bach Again | 20 |
| 65 | Decca F 12182 | The Ballad Of Spotty Muldoon/Lovely Lady Of The Roses | 12 |

(see also Peter London)

PETER COOK (2)
60s	Lyntone LYN 776	Watney's Pale Ale (Flexi, p/s)	10
61	Parlophone PMC 1145	BEYOND THE FRINGE (LP, with other artists)	20
63	Parlophone PMC 1190	BRIDGE ON THE RIVER WYE (LP, with other artists; mono)	20
63	Parlophone PCS 3036	BRIDGE ON THE RIVER WYE (LP, with other artists; stereo)	25
63	Parlophone PMC 1198	PETER COOK PRESENTS THE ESTABLISHMENT (LP, with other artists)	20
65	Decca LK 4722	PETER COOK PRESENTS MISTY MR. WISTY (LP)	25
65	Transatlantic TRA 131	PRIVATE EYE'S BLUE RECORD (LP, with other artists)	25

PETER COOK & DUDLEY MOORE
62	Parlophone R 4969	Excerpts From "Beyond The Fringe": Sitting On The Bench/The End Of The World (with Alan Bennett & Jonathan Miller)	10
65	Decca F 12158	Goodbyeee (& Dudley Moore Trio)/DUDLEY MOORE TRIO: Not Only But Also	10
66	Decca F 12380	Isn't She A Sweetie/Bo Dudley	10
67	Decca F 12551	The L.S. Bumble Bee/The Bee Side	12
67	Decca F 12710	Bedazzled/Love Me	60
65	Parlophone GEP 8940	PETER COOK AND DUDLEY MOORE (EP)	10
65	Decca DFE 8644	BY APPOINTMENT (EP)	10
65	Decca LK 4703	NOT ONLY PETER COOK BUT ALSO DUDLEY MOORE (LP)	15
66	Decca LK 4785	ONCE MOORE WITH COOK (LP)	15
68	Decca SKL 4923	BEDAZZLED (LP, stereo, soundtrack)	90
68	Decca LK 4981	GOODBYE AGAIN (LP, excerpts from TV series)	15

(see also Dudley Moore Trio)

COOK COUNTY
| 77 | Barak BAR 5 | Space Dancin'/Star Wars | 15 |

PAUL COOKE
| 71 | Ackee ACK 129 | That Girl Was Mine/No Harm | 5 |

ROGER (JAMES) COOKE
68	Columbia DB 8458	Skyline Pigeon/I'm Burning	7
69	Columbia DB 8510	Not That It Matters Anymore/Paper Chase	6
69	Columbia DB 8556	Stop/Someday	6
69	Columbia DB 8596	Smiling Through My Tears/Ain't That A Wonderful Thing (with Eve Graham)	8
70	Columbia DB 8729	Jubilation/Anticipation Grows	6
71	Columbia DB 8761	If You Would Stay/Mama Packed A Picnic Tea	6
71	Columbia DB 8806	People I Gotta Dream/Today I Killed A Man I Didn't Know	6
70	Regal Zonophone RZ 3005	We Will Get By/My Home City (as Roger Cook)	6
73	Regal Zonophone RZ 3074	She/Stay With Me (as Roger Cook)	6
70	Columbia SCX 6388	STUDY (LP, boxed logo on label)	20
72	Regal Zono. SRZA 8508	MEANWHILE ... BACK AT THE WORLD (LP, gatefold sleeve, red/silver label)	30
73	Regal Zono. SLRZ 1035	MINSTREL IN FLIGHT (LP)	20

(see also David & Jonathan)

SAM COOKE
57	London HLU 8506	You Send Me/Summertime	40
57	London HLU 8506	You Send Me/Summertime (78)	20
58	London HLU 8615	That's All I Need To Know/I Don't Want To Cry	40
58	London HLU 8615	That's All I Need To Know/I Don't Want To Cry (78)	20
58	HMV POP 568	Love You Most Of All/Win Your Love For Me	40
58	HMV POP 568	Love You Most Of All/Win Your Love For Me (78)	20
59	HMV POP 610	Everybody Likes To Cha Cha Cha/The Little Things You Do	40
59	HMV POP 610	Everybody Likes To Cha Cha Cha/The Little Things You Do (78)	20

59	HMV POP 642	Only Sixteen/Let's Go Steady Again	10
59	HMV POP 642	Only Sixteen/Let's Go Steady Again (78)	30
59	HMV POP 675	There, I've Said It Again/One Hour Ahead Of The Posse	30
60	London HLU 9046	Happy In Love/I Need You Now	25
60	RCA RCA 1184	Teenage Sonata/If You Were The Only Girl	20
60	HMV POP 754	Wonderful World/Along The Navajo Trail	10
60	RCA RCA 1202	Chain Gang/I Fall In Love Everyday	10
61	RCA RCA 1221	Sad Mood/Love Me	10
61	RCA RCA 1230	That's It, I Quit, I'm Movin' On/What Do You Say	15
61	RCA RCA 1242	Cupid/Farewell, My Darling	10
61	RCA RCA 1260	Feel It/It's Alright	10
62	RCA RCA 1277	Twisting The Night Away/One More Time	5
62	RCA RCA 1296	Bring It On Home To Me/Having A Party	8
62	RCA RCA 1310	Nothing Can Change This Love/Somebody Have Mercy	8
63	RCA RCA 1327	Send Me Some Loving/Baby Baby Baby	20
63	RCA RCA 1341	Another Saturday Night/Love Will Find A Way	5
63	RCA RCA 1361	Frankie And Johnny/Cool Train	10
63	RCA RCA 1367	Little Red Rooster/Shake Rattle And Roll	10
64	RCA RCA 1386	Good News/Basin Street Blues	6
64	RCA RCA 1405	Good Times/Tennessee Waltz	6
64	RCA RCA 1420	Cousin Of Mine/That's Where It's At	10
65	RCA RCA 1436	Shake/A Change Is Gonna Come	30
65	RCA RCA 1452	It's Got The Whole World Shakin'/Ease My Troublin' Mind	20
65	RCA RCA 1476	Sugar Dumpling/Bridge Of Tears	40
65	RCA RCA 1476	Sugar Dumpling/Bridge Of Tears (DJ Copy)	70
68	RCA RCA 1701	Another Saturday Night/DUANE EDDY: Dance With The Guitar Man (w/drawn)	15
63	RCA RCX 7117	HEART AND SOUL (EP)	20
64	RCA RCX 7128	SWING SWEETLY (EP)	25
58	HMV CLP 1261	SAM COOKE (LP, with Bumps Blackwell Orchestra)	100
59	HMV CLP 1273	ENCORE (LP)	80
61	RCA RD 27190	COOKE'S TOUR (LP, mono)	35
61	RCA SF 5076	COOKE'S TOUR (LP, stereo)	45
61	RCA RD 27215	HITS OF THE FIFTIES (LP, mono)	25
61	RCA RD SF 5098	HITS OF THE FIFTIES (LP, stereo)	40
61	RCA RD 27222	SWING LOW (LP)	35
62	RCA RD 27245	MY KIND OF BLUES (LP, mono)	30
62	RCA SF 5120	MY KIND OF BLUES (LP, stereo)	30
62	RCA RD 27263	TWISTIN' THE NIGHT AWAY (LP, mono)	30
62	RCA RD SF 5133	TWISTIN' THE NIGHT AWAY (LP, stereo)	40
63	RCA RDF 7539	MR. SOUL (LP, mono)	40
63	RCA SF 7539	MR. SOUL (LP, stereo)	45
63	RCA RD/SF 7583	NIGHT BEAT (LP)	40
63	RCA RD/SF 7583	NIGHT BEAT (LP)	45
64	RCA RD 7635	AIN'T THAT GOOD NEWS (LP, mono)	25
64	RCA SF 7635	AIN'T THAT GOOD NEWS (LP, stereo)	30
65	RCA RD 7674	AT THE COPA (LP, mono)	25
65	RCA SF 7674	AT THE COPA (LP, stereo)	30
65	RCA RD 7730	SHAKE (LP, mono)	40
65	RCA SF 7730	SHAKE (LP, stereo)	55
65	London HA-U 8232	THE SOUL STIRRERS FEATURING SAM COOKE (LP)	70
66	RCA RD/SF 7764	TRY A LITTLE LOVE (LP)	30
66	Immediate IMLP 002	THE WONDERFUL WORLD OF SAM COOKE (LP)	80
74	BBC	SAM COOKE AND OTHERS (LP, for radio use)	70

COOKIES

62	London HLU 9634	Chains/Stranger In My Arms	25
63	London HLU 9704	Don't Say Nothin' Bad About My Baby/Softly In The Night	25
63	Colpix PX 11012	Will Power/I Want A Boy For My Birthday	30
64	Colpix PX 11020	Girls Grow Up Faster Than Boys/Only To Other People	30

(see also Earl-Jean, Cinderellas, Dorothy Jones)

COOL

| 69 | DeWolfe DW/LP 3136 | POP SOUNDS (LP, music library only) | 35 |

(see also Elastic Band)

OLIVER COOL

| 60 | Columbia DB 4552 | Oliver Cool/I Like Girls | 10 |
| 61 | Columbia DB 4616 | Give Me The Summertime/I Said Yeah | 10 |

COOL BREEZE

71	Pathway PAT 103	People Ask What Love Is/There'll Be No More Sad Tomorrows	20
72	Decca F 13324	Summertime Sunshine/Sing Out Your Love	6
75	Bus Stop BUS 1023	Do It Some More/Citizen Jones	6
75	Bus Stop BUS 1027	You Gotta Love Me More/Turn On The Sun	6

COOL CATS

| 68 | Jolly JY 007 | What Kind Of Man/HEMSLEY MORRIS: Little Things | 60 |
| 69 | Jolly JY 009 | Hold Your Love/ALVA LEWIS: Hang My Head And Cry | 80 |

COOLERS

| 73 | Bread BR 1112 | The Youth Of Today/TYRONE TAYLOR: Close Observation | 6 |

EDDIE COOLEY & DIMPLES

| 57 | Columbia DB 3873 | Priscilla/Got A Little Woman | 150 |
| 57 | Columbia DB 3873 | Priscilla/Got A Little Woman (78) | 50 |

SPADE COOLEY & HIS FIDDLIN' FRIENDS

| 51 | Brunswick 04812 | Horse Hair Boogie/Down Yonder (78) | 10 |

COOL HAND FLEX

92	De Underground UG 08	Your Risk/Untitled/Untitled (12", white label)	12
92	Ruff Groove HN 05	Lock Me Up/I Don't Want No (12", stamped white label)	10
92	Ruff Groove UG 10	Welcome/Way Back Then/Woman (12")	10
92	In Touch INT 001	On The Strength/Your Risk/Go Insane (12")	25

MINT VALUE £

RITA COOLIDGE
83	A&M AM 007	All Time High/All Time High (Extended Instrumental) (p/s)	6
83	Scanlite BOND 1	All Time High/All Time High (Extended Instrumental) (p/s)	12

COOLIES
77	Electric WOT 14	Geisha Girl/Calling Out Your Name	25

JOE COOL & KILLERS
77	Ariola ARO 165	I Just Don't Care/My Way	6

(see also Killers)

COOL MEN
58	Parlophone GEP 8739	COOL FOR CATS NO. 1 (EP)	25
58	Parlophone GEP 8752	COOL FOR CATS NO. 2 (EP)	25

COOL NOTES
80	Jama JADC 0008	Billy The Kid/Kidnap My Baby (12")	12
80	Jama JADC 0024	My Tune (Re-Mix)/Version (12")	30
84	Sour Grapes SG 116	I Wanna Dance/Blowin It	25
84	Sour Grapes SGR 116	I Wanna Dance (Extended)/Blowin It (12")	80
84	Mass Media	Forgot How To Love/Why Can't We Be Friends (12")	30
85	Abstract Dance 12AD 001	You're Never Too Young/Sound Of Summer (12")	15
84	Mass Media MMLP 2	DOWN TO EARTH (LP)	60

COOL RUNNERS
82	MCA MCAT 760	Play The Game (So You Think It Funny)/Hawaiian Dream (12", p/s)	20
82	MCA MCAT 893	Checking Out/High On A Feeling (12", p/s)	40
84	Tai Wan TWD 1949	Checking Out/High On A Feeling (12", p/s, reissue as Nat King Cool & Cool Runners))	25

COOL SPOON (JEFF DIXON & ALTON ELLIS)
67	Coxsone CS 7031	Yakety Yak/SOUL VENDORS: Drum Song	25

COOL STICKY
68	Amalgamated AMG 825	Train To Soulsville/ERIC MONTY MORRIS: Cinderella (actually by Errol Dunkley)	50

CHRIS COOMBES
65	Holyground HG 110	WHERE IT'S AT (EP, 99 only)	35

NIGEL COOMBES & STEVE BERESFORD
80	Bead Records BEAD 16	IMPROVISED VIOLIN AND PIANO DUETS (LP)	25

ALICE COOPER
71	Straight W 7209	Eighteen/Body	90
71	Warner Bros K 16127	Under My Wheels/Desperado	6
72	Warner Bros K 16188	School's Out/Gutter Cat (p/s)	7
72	Warner Bros K 16214	Elected/Luney Tune (p/s)	8
73	Warner Bros/Lyntone LYN 2585/6	Slick Black Limousine/Extracts From: Unfinished Sweet/Elected/No More Mr Nice Guy/Billion Dollar Babies/I Love The Dead (33rpm flexi free with NME magazine)	5
73	Warner Brothers K16262	No More Mr. Nice Guy/Raped And Freezin' (possibly export only)	20
74	Warner Bros K 16409	School's Out/No More Mr. Nice Guy/Elected/Billion Dollar Babies (maxi-45)	5
74	Chrysalis CHS 2069	I'm Flash/ELKIE BROOKS: Sacrifice (p/s, promo only)	35
75	Anchor ANC 1012	Department Of Youth/Cold Ethyl (p/s)	6
75	Anchor ANE 12001	Welcome To My Nightmare/Department Of Youth/Black Widow/ Only Women Bleed (12" EP, p/s)	10
76	Warner Bros K 16792	I Never Cry/Got To Hell (p/s)	5
77	Warner Bros K 16935	(No More) Love At Your Convenience/It's Hot Tonight (p/s, gothic type on label)	5
80	Warner Bros K 17598	Clones (We're All)/Model Citizen (p/s)	8
86	MCA MCA 1090	He's Back (The Man Behind The Mask)/Billion Dollar Babies (poster p/s)	10
89	Epic ALICE 3	Bed Of Nails/I'm Your Gun (p/s, with poster)	8
89	Epic ALICEP 3	Bed Of Nails/I'm Your Gun/Go To Hell (live) (12", picture disc)	8
69	Straight STS 1051	PRETTIES FOR YOU (LP, purple label, gatefold sleeve)	80
69	Straight STS 1061	EASY ACTION (LP, purple label, gatefold sleeve)	70
71	Straight STS 1065	LOVE IT TO DEATH (LP, purple label, gatefold sleeve)	60
71	Warner Bros K 56005	KILLER (LP, olive green label, A1/B1 Matrix numbers, gatefold sleeve with perforated foldout calendar that must have '1972' in bottom left hand corner. Any with '1973' are repressings)	40
72	Warner Bros K 56007	SCHOOL'S OUT (LP, green label, 'desktop' gatefold sleeve, with 'paper panties' inner)	60
73	Warner Bros K 56013	BILLION DOLLAR BABIES (LP, 1st pressing, A1/B1 matrixes, 'Pil' etched into dead wax side 2, olive green label, gatefold embossed sleeve with round corners and K56013 in top right corner, 'WEA records printed in England' in bottom right on rear, attached perforated cards, with $ billion note & inner sleeve with large thumb notch)	25
73	Warner Bros K 46177	LOVE IT TO DEATH (LP, reissue, green label, gatefold sleeve)	15
73	Warner Bros K 66021	SCHOOL DAYS (2-LP, gatefold sleeve, reissue of STS 1051 & 1061)	18
74	Warner Bros K 56018	MUSCLE OF LOVE (LP, 'cardboard box' sleeve, with insert & inner sleeve)	15

(see also Billion Dollar Babies)

GARNELL COOPER & KINFOLKS
63	London HL 9757	Green Monkey/Long Distance	30

HENRY COOPER
76	DJM DJS 10734	Knock Me Down With A Feather/Knocked Out For Your Love (p/s)	12
76	DJM DJS 10734	Knock Me Down With A Feather/Knocked Out For Your Love	5

LES COOPER & SOUL ROCKERS
62	Stateside SS 142	Wiggle Wobble/Dig Yourself	20

MARTY COOPER CLAN
63	RCA Victor RD 7596	NEW SOUNDS - OLD GOODIES (LP)	15

MIKE COOPER
70	Dawn DNX 2501	Your Lovely Ways (Parts 1 & 2)/Watching You Fall (Parts 1 & 2) (p/s)	7
71	Dawn DNX 2511	Too Late Now/The Ballad Of Fulton Allen/Good Times (p/s)	7
72	Dawn DNS 1022	Time In Hand/Schwabisch Hall	6
60s	Saydisc SD 137	UP THE COUNTRY BLUES (EP)	80
68	Matchbox SDM 159	THE INVERTED WORLD (LP, with Ian A. Anderson)	70
69	Pye NSPL 18281	OH REALLY!? (LP, blue/black label with logo banner on top)	30
70	Dawn DNLS 3005	DO I KNOW YOU? (LP, gatefold sleeve, orange label)	30
70	Dawn DNLS 3011	TROUT STEEL (LP, with poster insert, gatefold sleeve, orange label)	35

71	Dawn DNLS 3026	PLACES I KNOW (LP, with insert, lilac label)	25
72	Dawn DNLS 3031	THE MACHINE GUN COMPANY (LP, lilac label)	25
74	Fresh Air 6370 500	LIFE AND DEATH IN PARADISE (LP)	20

(see also Ian A. Anderson, Heron)

BOB COOPER
56	Capitol EAP 1005	SHIFTING WINDS (EP)	8

COOPERETTES
75	Brunswick BR22	Shing A Ling/Don't Trust Him	15

COOPER TEMPLE CLAUSE
00s	private pressing	The Crayon Demos/Who Needs Enemies?/Let's Kill Music/Devil Walks In The Sand Demos (CD-R, in hand-crayoned sleeve, 120 only)	30
01	Morning MORNING 2	THE HARDWARE EP (Way Out West/Sister Soul/The Devil Walks In The Sand/ Solitude) (2 x 7", 1 black and 1 white vinyl, poly sleeves in box, 500 only)	30
01	Morning MORNING 6	THE WARFARE EP (Panzer Attack/ I'll Still Write/I'll Still Write [Acoustic]/Mansell) (2 x 7", 1 black and white 1 vinyl in box, 1000 only)	12
01	Morning MORNING 8	Let's Kill Music (Dirty Sanchez Mix)/Panzer Attack (Dirty Sanchez Mix) (12")	8
02	Morning MORNING 20	SEE THIS THROUGH AND LEAVE (6 x 7", limited, numbered box set)	12

JULIAN COPE
87	Antar 4503	Interview/Christmas Mourning/Transmitting (fan club box set, with card, biography, membership card, letter, photos & stickers)	30
91	Island JC 1	Safesurfer/If You Love Me At All (33rpm, sold at gigs, stickered white sleeve)	6
94	K.A.K. (no cat. no.)	Paranormal In The West Country (Original Version)/(String Quartet Version)/ (Acoustic Version)/(Krankenhausmusik Version)/(Acoustic Version)/(Krankenhausmusik Version) (Mail-order only via offer with "Queen Elizabeth" LP)	10
84	Mercury MERL 48	FRIED (LP, with poster & promo 12" [MADOX 5])	18
87	Island ILPS 9861	SAINT JULIAN (LP, with free 12" interview LP [JCCLP 1])	12
89	CopeCo JULP 89	SKELLINGTON (LP, mail order only)	25
89	CopeCo JUCD 89	SKELLINGTON (CD, mail order only)	20
90	Mofoco MOFOCO 90	DROOLIAN (LP, mail order only)	20
90	Mofoco MOFOCO CD 90	DROOLIAN (CD, mail order only)	18
91	Island ILPSD 9977	PEGGY SUICIDE (2-LP)	20
91	M-Gog MA-GOG 1	RITE (CD, with Donald Ross Skinner, mail order only)	20
92	Island ILPSD 9997	JEHOVAHKILL (2-LP, 4th side etched)	25
93	Ma-Gog MA-GOG 2	THE SKELLINGTON CHRONICLES (LP, mail order only)	18
93	Ma-Gog MA-GOG 2	THE SKELLINGTON CHRONICLES (CD, mail order only)	18
94	Echo ECHLP 1	AUTOGEDDON (LP, gatefold sleeve)	15
95	Echo ECHLP 5	20 MOTHERS (2-LP, black or purple vinyl)	25
96	Echo ECHLP 12	INTERPRETER (LP, with poster)	18
96	Echio ECHCD 12	INTERPRETER (CD in pizza-style cardboard box)	15
97	Ma-Gog MA-GOG 1	RITE (CD, mail order only)	15
99	Head Heritage HH6	ODIN (CD, mail oder ony, live)	20
99	Head Heritage HH7	YE SKELLINGTON CHRONICLES (CD, mail order only)	15
00	Head Heritage HH10	AN AUDIENCE WITH THE COPE (CD, with slipcase, mail order only)	15
01	Head Heritage HH12	DISCOVER ODIN (CD, mail order only, 10" x 5" package with booklet, signed & numbered, 1000 only)	40
02	Head Heritage HH13	RITE NOW (CD, mail order only)	15
03	Head Heritage HH14	ROME WASN'T BURNED IN A DAY (CD, mail order only)	15
03	Revell Discs 103	LIVE JAPAN '91 (CD, official bootleg, mail order only)	20
05	Southern Cross SC 113	CONCERT CLIMAX - LIVE IN THE HEARING OF THE MOTHERFUCKER (CD, oficial bootleg, mail order only)	20
05	Fuck Off & Di (No Cat. No.)	RITE BASTARD (CD, no cat no)	15
05	Head Heritage HH20	DARK ORGASM (2-CD, mail order only)	15

(see also Teardrop Explodes, Rabbi Joseph Gordan, Brain Donor, Elizabeth, L.A.M.F, Universal Panzies)

KEN COPE & BREAKAWAYS
63	Pye 7N 15524	Hands Off, Stop Muckin' About/Why Am I So Shy	7

(see also Breakaways)

SUZY COPE
61	HMV POP 941	Teenage Fool/Juvenile Delinquent	25
62	HMV POP 1047	Not Never Now/Kisses And Tears	25
63	HMV POP 1167	Biggity Big/Doing What You Know Is Wrong	25
65	CBS 201792	You Can't Say I Never Told You/And Now I Don't Want You	25

AL(L)AN COPELAND
57	Vogue Coral Q 72237	Feeling Happy/You Don't Know	15
57	Vogue Coral Q 72277	How Will I Know?/Will You Still Be Mine	7
59	Pye International 7N 25007	Flip Flop/Lots More Love (as Allan Copeland)	25
59	Pye International 7N 25007	Flip Flop/Lots More Love (as Allan Copeland) (78)	10

KEN COPELAND
57	London HLP 8423	Pledge Of Love/MINTS: Night Air	150
57	London HLP 8423	Pledge Of Love/MINTS: Night Air (78)	40

BOB & RON COPPER
63	EFDSS 1002	BOB & RON COPPER (LP)	35

COPPER FAMILY
71	Leader LED 2067	A SONG FOR EVERY SEASON (LP, sampler, tracks from 4-LP set)	40
71	Leader LEAB 404	A SONG FOR ALL SEASONS (4xLP)	70

COPPERFIELD
69	Instant IN 004	Any Old Time/I'm No Good For Her	15
69	Parlophone R 5818	I'll Hold Out My Hand/Far Away Love	6

(see also Quartz)

JOHNNY COPPIN
87	Rola RO 15	FOREST & VALE (LP)	20

COPS 'N ROBBERS
64	Decca F 12019	St. James Infirmary/There's Gotta Be A Reason	60
65	Pye 7N 15870	I Could Have Danced All Night/Just Keep Right On	25
65	Pye 7N 15928	It's All Over Now Baby Blue/I've Found Out	25

(see also Fairies)

COPY CATS
69 Bullet BU 419 Copy Cat (with Derrick Morgan)/BUNNY LEE ALL STARRS: Hot Lead.................12

CORAL
01 Deltasonic DLT 1 SHADOWS FALL EP (Shadows Fall/The Ballad Of Simon Diamond/A Sparrow's Song) (CD, 1000 only).................30
01 Deltasonic DLTCD 3 THE OLDEST PATH EP (The Oldest Path/God Knows/Short Balled/Flys (CD, 1000 only, picture disc)).................20
04 Deltasonic DLTLP014 MAGIC AND MEDICINE (2-LP, orange vinyl).................25

CORBAN
78 Acorn AC 002 A BREAK IN THE CLOUDS (LP, with insert).................18

HARRY H. CORBETT
67 Decca F 12714 Flower Power Fred/(I'm) Saving All My Love (with Unidentified Flower Objects).................25
(see also Wilfred Brambell, Wilfred Brambell & Harry H. Corbett, Faraway Folk)

MIKE CORBETT & JAY HIRSH
71 Atlantic 2091-126 Gypsy Child/Butterfly Day.................6
71 Atlantic 2400 141 MIKE CORBETT & JAY HIRSH (LP, gatefold sleeve).................20
(see also Mr. Flood's Party)

CORBY & CHAMPAGNE
66 Pye 7N 17203 Time Marches On/I'll Be Back.................5

JASON CORD
69 Chapter One CH 102 I've Got My Eyes On You/I Can't Take No More Of Your Lies.................6
69 Chapter One CH 110 Why Shouldn't I/Spring Never Came Twice.................6

FRANK CORDELL & HIS ORCHESTRA
56 HMV 7M 397 Port-Au-Prince/"Double Cross" TV Theme.................5
56 HMV 7M 419 Sadie's Shawl/Flamenco Love.................5
61 HMV POP 824 The Black Bear/Darling Charlie.................5
61 HMV POP 852 Theme From 'The Rebel'/Ou La La.................5

PHIL CORDELL
69 Warner Bros WB 8001 Pumping The Water/Red Lady.................35
(see also Thursday's Children)

CORDES
65 Cavern Sound IMSTL 1 Give Her Time/She's Leaving.................70

LOUISE CORDET
62 Decca F 11476 I'm Just A Baby/In A Matter Of Moments.................8
62 Decca F 11476 I'm Just A Baby/In A Matter Of Moments (export copy in p/s).................15
62 Decca F 11524 Sweet Enough/Someone Else's Fool.................8
62 Decca F 11524 Sweet Enough/Someone Else's Fool (export copy in p/s).................15
63 Decca F 11673 Around And Around/Which Way The Wind Blows.................15
64 Decca F 11824 Don't Let The Sun Catch You Crying/Loving Baby.................15
64 Decca F 11875 Don't Make Me Over/Two Lovers.................20
62 Decca DFE 8515 THE SWEET BEAT OF LOUISE CORDET (EP).................70

CORDUROYS
66 Planet PLF 122 Tick Tock/Too Much Of A Woman.................45

CHICK COREA (& RETURN TO FOREVER)
72 ECM ECM 1018/9 PARIS CONCERT FEBRUARY 1971 (2-LP, as Corea & Braxton & Holland).................15
74 Atlantic K 60081 INNER SPACE (2-LP).................15
74 People PLEO 9 SUNDANCE (LP).................15
(see also Return To Forever)

PADDY COREA
72 Explosion EX 2066 Soul And Inspiration/STAGS: You Must Be Trying My Faith.................6

CORKSCREW
79 Highway SHY 7005 FOR OPENERS (LP).................25

CORNBREAD & JERRY
61 London HLG 9352 L'il Ole Me/Loco Moto.................10

DON CORNEL & ETERNALS
70 Moodisc MU 3506 Christmas Joy/WINSTON & RUPERT: Musically Beat.................7

EDDIE CORNELIUS
80 GB Records GB 001 That's Love Making In Your Eyes/Hurry Up.................15

DON CORNELL
54 Vogue Coral Q 2013 Hold My Hand/I'm Blessed.................15
54 Vogue Coral Q 2037 S'Posin'/I Was Lucky.................10
55 Vogue Coral Q 72058 No Man Is An Island/All At Once.................8
55 Vogue Coral Q 72070 Give Me Your Love/When You Are In Love.................8
55 Vogue Coral Q 72071 Athena/Size 12.................8
55 Vogue Coral Q 72073 Stranger In Paradise/The Devil's In Your Eyes.................10
55 Vogue Coral Q 72080 Unchained Melody/Most Of All.................10
55 Vogue Coral Q 72104 Love Is A Many Splendored Thing/The Bible Tells Me So.................6
56 Vogue Coral Q 72132 There Once Was A Beautiful/Make A Wish.................6
56 Vogue Coral Q 72144 Teenage Meeting (Gonna Rock It Right)/I Still Have A Prayer.................30
56 Vogue Coral Q 72152 Rock Island Line/Na-Ne Na-Na.................10
56 Vogue Coral Q 72164 But Love Me (Love But Me)/Fort Knox.................7
56 Vogue Coral Q 72203 All Of You/Heaven Only Knows.................6
57 Vogue Coral Q 72218 See-Saw/From The Bottom Of My Heart.................15
57 Vogue Coral Q 72234 Let's Be Friends/Afternoon In Madrid.................6
57 Vogue Coral Q 72257 Sittin' In The Balcony/Let's Get Lost.................15
57 Vogue Coral Q 72276 Mama Guitar/A Face In The Crowd.................15
57 Vogue Coral Q 72291 There's Only You/Non Dimenticar.................6
58 Coral Q 72308 Before It's Time To Say Goodnight/Mailman, Bring Me No More Blues.................10
58 Coral Q 72313 I've Got Bells On My Heart/Keep God In The Home.................5
59 Pye International 7N 25041 Sempre Amore/Forever Couldn't Be Long Enough.................5
59 London HLD 8937 This Earth Of Mine/The Gang That Sang "Heart Of My Heart".................5

54	Vogue Coral LVC 10004	DON CORNELL FOR YOU (10" LP)	15
56	Coral LVA 9037	LET'S GET LOST (LP)	15

JERRY CORNELL
55	London HL 8157	Please Don't Talk About Me When I'm Gone/St. Louis Blues	25

LYN CORNELL
60	Decca F 11227	Like Love/Demon Lover	20
60	Decca F 11260	Teaser/What A Feeling	10
62	Decca F 11430	African Waltz/Moanin'	5
62	Decca F 11469	I Sold My Heart To The Junkman/Step Up And Rescue Me	25
63	Decca F 11750	Sally Go Round The Roses/You Can Kiss Me If You Like	10

CORNFLAKES
62	Fontana 267 227TF	Oh, Listen To The Band/Moonstruck	10

BARRY CORNISH
73	Jam 60	Questions/Stones From The Wishing Well	8

ARNOLD CORNS
71	B&C CB 149	Moonage Daydream/Hang Onto Yourself (Demo copy as 'The Arnold Corns')	75
71	B&C CB 149	Moonage Daydream/Hang Onto Yourself (as 'The Arnold Corns')	60
72	B&C CB 189	Hang Onto Yourself/Man In The Middle (Demo copy)	50
72	B&C CB 189	Hang Onto Yourself/Man In The Middle (reissue)	40
74	Mooncrest Moon 25	Hang Onto Yourself/Man In The Middle (Demo copy)	25
74	Mooncrest MOON 25	Hang Onto Yourself/Man In The Middle (reissue)	20

(see also David Bowie)

CORONADOS
64	London HL 9895	Love Me With All Your Heart/Querida	10
67	Stateside SS 2043	Johnny B. Goode/Shook Me Down	10

CORONETS
54	Columbia SCM 5117	Do, Do, Do, Do, Do, Do, Do It Again/I Ain't Gonna Do It No More	15
56	Columbia SCM 5235	Lizzie Borden/My Believing Heart	10
56	Columbia SCM 5261	There's No Song Like An Old Song/The Magic Touch	10
56	Columbia DB 3827	Someone To Love/The Rocking Horse Cowboy	10
56	Columbia SEG 7603	RHYTHM AND BLUES (EP, as Coronets with Eric Jupp Orchestra)	15

(see also Chris Sandford & Coronets, Tony Brent, Ronnie Harris, Benny Hill, Eric Jupp, Lee Lawrence)

CORONETS
68	Stresa BEV SP 1104/1105	I Wonder Why/You're Leaving Tomorrow	45

CORPORATION (JAMAICA)
70	Grape GR 3022	Sweet Musille/Walking Thru' Jerusalem	22

(see also Claudette & Corporation, Billy Jack)

CORPORATION (U.S.)
69	Capitol E-T/E-ST 175	THE CORPORATION (LP)	25

CORRIE FOLK TRIO/CORRIES
63	Waverley SLP 530	Love Is Teasing/O, Waly Waly (p/s)	8
63	Waverley ELP 129	CORRIE FOLK TRIO (EP)	12
63	Waverley ELP 131	YON FOLK SONGS IS FOR THE BURDS (EP)	12
63	Waverley ELP 132	MORE FOLK SONGS FOR THE BURDS (EP)	10
65	Parlophone GEP 8947	FROSTY WINDS (EP)	8
65	Waverley ZLP 2042	CORRIE FOLK TRIO WITH PADDIE BELL (LP, also stereo SZLP 2043)	15
65	Waverley ZLP 2050	THE PROMISE OF THE DAY (LP)	15

(see also Paddie Bell)

JAY C CORRY
76	Decca FR 13680	Love Me Or Leave Me/House Of Truth	12

CORSAIRS (JAMAICA)
70	Unity UN 558	Goodnight My Love/Lover Girl	8

CORSAIRS (U.K.)
67	CBS 202624	Pay You Back With Interest/I'm Going To Shut You Down	20

CORSAIRS (U.S.)
62	Pye International 7N 25142	I'll Take You Home/Sitting On Your Doorstep (with Jay 'Bird' Uzzel)	15

BOB CORT (SKIFFLE GROUP)
57	Decca FJ 10831	It Takes A Worried Man To Sing A Worried Blues/ Don't You Rock Me Daddy-O	20
57	Decca F 10892	Six-Five Special/Roll Jen Jenkins	20
57	Decca F 10899	Maggie May/Jessamine (with Liz Winters)	10
57	Decca F 10905	Schoolday (Ring! Ring! Goes The Bell)/Ain't It A Shame (To Sing Skiffle On Sunday)	20
57	Decca F 10951	'Bob Cort Skiffle Party' Medley (Parts 1 & 2)	5
58	Decca F 10989	The Ark (Noah Found Grace In The Eyes Of God)/Yes! Suh!	5
59	Decca F 11109	Foggy Foggy Dew/On Top Of Old Smokey (solo)	5
59	Decca F 11145	Waterloo/Battle Of New Orleans (solo)	5
59	Decca F 11160	Kissin' Time/I'm Gonna Get Married (solo)	5
59	William Timpson Ltd	The Shop In The Cellar (1-sided 78, 200 only)	15
60	Decca F 11256	Mule Skinner Blues/The Ballad Of Walter Williams (solo)	15
59	Decca DFE 6630	BARRACK ROOM BALLADS (EP)	10
61	Decca DFE 6686	BOB CORT'S GENTLEFOLK (EP, as Bob Cort's Gentlefolk)	10
57	Decca LK 4222	AIN'T IT A SHAME (LP)	20

(see also Liz Winters & Bob Cort)

DAVE 'BABY' CORTEZ
59	London HLU 8852	The Happy Organ/Love Me As I Love You	15
59	London HLU 8919	The Whistling Organ/I'm Happy	7
60	Columbia DB 4404	Piano Shuffle/Dave's Special	7
60	London HLU 9126	Deep In The Heart Of Texas/You're Just Right	15
62	Pye International 7N 25159	Rinky Dink/Getting Right	20
66	Roulette RK 7001	Countdown/Summertime (Cha Cha Cha)	10
60	London RE-U 1233	DAVE 'BABY' CORTEZ (EP)	40
64	London HA-U 8142	THE GOLDEN HITS OF DAVE 'BABY' CORTEZ (LP)	30

CORTINAS (1)

68	Polydor 56255	Phoebe's Flower Shop/Too Much In Love	15

CORTINAS (2)

77	Step Forward SF 1	Fascist Dictator/Television Families (p/s, first 1,000 in card sleeve)	20
77	Step Forward SF 1	Fascist Dictator/Television Families (p/s)	12
78	Step Forward SF 6	Defiant Pose/Independence (p/s)	12
78	Step Forward SF 6	Defiant Pose/Independence (12", pink die-cut sleeve)	12
78	CBS CBS 6759	Heartache/Ask Mr. Waverley (p/s)	8
78	CBS CBS 82831	TRUE ROMANCES (LP, with photo insert)	20

LEE CORVETTE

62	Decca	The Heart You Break (May Be Your Own)/Tender Love	10

CORVETTES

82	Bitchin BIT 100	Surf, Don't Walk/She'll Be Blonde (p/s)	15
84	Bitchin BIT 101	Girls Cars Girls Sun Girls Surf Girls Fun Girls/The Beach Is Not Enough (p/s)	18

LARRY CORYELL

69	Vanguard SVRL 19051	LADY CORYELL (LP)	12
69	Vanguard SVRL 19059	CORYELL (LP)	12
71	Vanguard 6359 005	SPACES (LP)	25
85	Nimbus/Novus AN 3024	STANDING OVATION (LP, Nimbus Supercut, mail order only sold via Practical Hi Fi magazine)	40

(see also Jazz Composers Orchestra)

BILL COSBY

67	Warner Bros WB 7072	Little Ole Man (Uptight! Everything's Alright)/Don'cha Know (in p/s)	35

COSMIC BABY/VANGELIS

94	East West SAM 1484	A TRIBUTE TO BLADERUNNER (12", double pack, promo only)	20

(see also Vangelis)

COSMIC EYE

72	Regal Zono. SLRZ 1030	DREAM SEQUENCE (LP)	200

COSMIC PSYCHOS

88	What Goes On GOES ON 23	COSMIC PSYCHOS (LP)	15

COSMO

63	Blue Beat BB 175	Gypsy Woman/Do Unto Others	10
64	Blue Beat BB 244	One God/BUSTER'S ALL STARS: Prince Royal (actually "Reincarnation")	50
64	Blue Beat BB 269	Rice And Badgee/BUSTER'S ALL STARS: The Tickler	50

(see also Cosmo & Dennis, Denzil Dennis)

COSMO & DENNIS (ALIAS DENZIL)

62	Blue Beat BB 145	Bed Of Roses/Tonight And Evermore (as Cosmo & Denzil)	10
65	Blue Beat BB 296	Sweet Rosemarie/Lollipop I'm In Love	12
65	Blue Beat BB 312	Come On Come On/I Don't Want You (As COSMO & DENZIL)	12

(see also Cosmo)

FRANK COSMO

63	Island WI 058	Revenge/Laughin' At You (B-side actually with Bobby Aitken)	15
63	Island WI 073	Dear Dreams/Go Go Go	15
63	Island WI 100	Merry Christmas/Greetings From Beverley's	20
63	R&B JB 119	I Love You/DON DRUMMOND: Close Of Play	22
64	Island WI 135	Better Get Right/Ameletia	20
64	Black Swan WI 446	Alone/Beautiful Book	20

(see also Two Kings)

COSMOTHEKA

70s	Shy SHY 7001	WINES & SPIRITS (LP)	35
85	Dambuster DAM 1	COSMOTHEKA (LP)	18

DON COSTA, HIS ORCHESTRA & CHORUS

55	London HLF 8186	Love Is A Many Splendoured Thing/Safe In The Harbour	20
59	London HLT 8992	I Walk The Line/Cat Walk	5

JACK COSTANZO

61	London HLG 9401	Theme From Route 66/Naked City Theme	5

JACK COSTANZO & TUBBY HAYES

62	Fontana TFL 5190	COSTANZO PLUS TUBBS - EQUATION IN RHYTHM (LP, mono)	40
62	Fontana STFL 598	COSTANZO PLUS TUBBS - EQUATION IN RHYTHM (LP, stereo)	30

(see also Tubby Hayes)

CELIA COSTELLO

75	Leader LEE 4054	CELIA COSTELLO (LP, with insert)	20

DANNY COSTELLO

57	Oriole CB 1393	Like A Brook Gets Lost In A River/That's Where I Shine	5

DAY COSTELLO

71	Spark SRL 1042	The Long And Winding Road/Free (Unlimited Horizons)	10

(see also Ross McManus)

ELVIS COSTELLO (& ATTRACTIONS)

77	Stiff BUY 11	Less Than Zero/Radio Sweetheart (p/s)	5
77	Stiff Buy 14	Alison/Welcome To The Working Week (p/s)	5
77	Stiff BUY 14	Alison/Welcome To The Working Week (p/s, A-side mispress on white vinyl)	300
77	Stiff BUY 15	(The Angels Wanna Wear My) Red Shoes/Mystery Dance	5
77	Stiff BUY 15	Red Shoes/Mystery Dance (p/s, mispress, plays "Dream Tobacco" by Max Wall)	8
77	Stiff BUY 20 DJ	Watching The Detectives (short version) /Blame It On Cain (live)/Mystery Dance (live) (promo copy)	40
77	Stiff BUY 20	Watching The Detectives/Blame It On Cain (live)/Mystery Dance (live) (phone book p/s)	8
78	Radar ADA 24	Radio Radio/Tiny Steps (12", promo-only, 500 pressed)	15
78	Radar RG 1	Talking In The Dark/Wednesday Week (p/s, gig freebie)	8
80	F-Beat XX 5P	New Amsterdam/Just A Memory/Dr Luther's Assistant/Ghost Train (picture disc)	6
80	2-Tone CHS TT 7	I Can't Stand Up For Falling Down/Girls Talk (unreleased, later a gig freebie, more common issue (see other price) has XX1 in run-off groove, 13,000 pressed)	50

80	2-Tone CHS TT 7	I Can't Stand Up For Falling Down/Girls Talk (unreleased, gig freebie, more common issue with XX1 in run-off groove, 13,000 pressed)	20
80	Stiff GRAB 3	STIFF SINGLES FOUR PACK (BUY 11, 14, 15 & 20 in clear plastic wallet)	20
81	F-Beat XX 17	A Good Year For The Roses/Your Angel Steps Out Of Heaven (withdrawn p/s)	10
93	Demon ECPROMO 1	TWO AND A HALF YEARS IN 31 MINUTES (CD, fold-out digipak, promo only)	10
78	Radar RAD 3	THIS YEAR'S MODEL (LP, with free 7" "Stranger In The House"/"Neat Neat Neat" (live) [die-cut company sleeve, SAM 83], 50,000 pressed; 1st 5,000 shrinkwrapped and stickered)	25
79	Radar RAD 15	ARMED FORCES (LP, foldout stickered sleeve with free EP Live At Hollywood High [p/s, SAM 90] & postcards)	20
79	Radar RAD 15	ARMED FORCES (LP, mispress, plays "[What's So Funny 'Bout] Peace, Love & Understanding" instead of "Two Little Hitlers"; sticker on insert)	25
86	IMP FIEND CD 21	ARMED FORCES (CD, with 'Peace, Love & Understanding")	18

(see also Nick Lowe, George Jones, Coward Brothers)

COTERIE
| 69 | Emerald GEM 1026 | A SWING TO FOLK (LP) | 40 |

BILLY COTTON
54	Decca F10299	Friends And Neighbours/The Kid's Last Fight	10
54	Decca F 10377	This Ole House/Somebody Goofed	10
55	Decca F 10630	The Dam Busters March/Bring Your Smile Along	10
56	Decca F 10702	Lizzie Berden/Little Child	8

(see also Alma Cogan)

JAMES COTTON (BLUES BAND)
| 78 | Buddah BDS 471 | Rock'n'Roll Music/Help Me | 5 |
| 68 | Vanguard SVRL 19035 | CUT YOU LOOSE! (LP, as James Cotton Blues Band) | 25 |

JIMMY COTTON
| 62 | Columbia SEG 8141 | CHRIS BARBER PRESENTS JIMMY COTTON (EP) | 30 |
| 62 | Columbia SEG 8189 | CHRIS BARBER PRESENTS JIMMY COTTON NO. 2 (EP) | 30 |

(see also James Cotton Blues Band, Alexis Korner)

JOSEPH COTTON
| 77 | Observer OB 001 | Fit And Ready/OBSERVER: Iron Fist (12") | 40 |

MIKE COTTON JAZZMEN
| 61 | Columbia DB 4697 | Senorita/The Colonel's Tune | 5 |
| 62 | Columbia DB 4821 | The Cobbler's Song/African Twist | 5 |

MIKE COTTON (SOUND)
62	Columbia DB 4910	The Tinker/Zulu Warrior (as the Mike Cotton Jazz Men)	10
63	Columbia DB 7029	Swing That Hammer/Heartaches (as Mike Cotton Jazzmen)	8
63	Columbia DB 7134	Midnite Flyer/One Mint Julep (as Mike Cotton Band)	10
64	Columbia DB 7267	I Don't Wanna Know/This Little Pig	60
64	Columbia DB 7382	Round And Round/Beau Dudley	50
65	Columbia DB 7623	Make Up Your Mind/I've Got My Eye On You	50
66	Polydor BM 56096	Harlem Shuffle/Like That	40
62	Columbia SEG 8144	COTTON PICKING (EP)	40
63	Columbia SEG 8190	THE WILD AND THE WILLING (EP)	40
64	Columbia 33SX 1647	MIKE COTTON SOUND (LP)	400

(see also Lucas & Mike Cotton Sound, Satisfaction)

COTTON CASINO
| 03 | Riot Season REPOSE 701 | Fly High/Open The Shine (white vinyl, p/s) | 8 |

(See also Acid Mothers Temple and the Melting Paraiso UFO)

JOHN(NY) COUGAR
| 78 | Riva RIVA 14 | I Need A Lover/Born Reckless (as Johnny Cougar, p/s) | 5 |
| 78 | Riva RIVA 16 | Factory/Alley Of The Angels (as Johnny Cougar, p/s) | 5 |

(see also John Cougar Mellencamp)

COUGARS
63	Parlophone R 4989	Saturday Night At The Duckpond/See You In Dreamland	12
63	Parlophone R 5038	Red Square/Fly-By-Nite	15
64	Parlophone R 5115	Caviare And Chips/While The City Sleeps	10
63	Parlophone GEP 8886	SATURDAY NIGHT WITH THE COUGARS (EP)	30

ROGER COULAM QUARTET
| 67 | CBS 52399 | ORGAN IN ORBIT (LP) | 20 |
| 70 | Fontana 16009 | BLOW HOT, BLOW COLD (LP) | 20 |

DENIS COULDRY (& SMILE)
| 68 | Decca F 12734 | James In The Basement (solo)/DENIS COULDRY & NEXT COLLECTION: I Am Nearly There | 40 |
| 68 | Decca F 12786 | Penny For The Wind/Tea And Toast, Mr. Watson? (as Denis Couldry & Smile) | 20 |

(see also Felius Andromeda)

COULSON, DEAN, MCGUINNESS, FLINT
| 72 | DJM DJS 267 | Lay Down Your Weary Tune/Tiny Montgomery/I Wanna Be Your lover | 6 |
| 72 | DJM DJLPS 424 | LO AND BEHOLD (LP, gatefold sleeve) | 18 |

(see also Manfred Mann, McGuinness Flint, Dennis Coulson, Lyle McGuinness Band)

DENNIS COULSON
| 73 | Elektra K 42148 | DENNIS COULSON (LP, gatefold sleeve) | 15 |

PHIL COULTER ORCHESTRA
| 68 | Pye 7N 17511 | Congratulations/Gold Rush | 25 |

COUNT BISHOPS
74	Purple PUR 122	Gazaroody/The So, So Song	10
75	Chiswick SW 1	SPEEDBALL (EP, 1st 1,000 in glossy p/s, promos £10)	8
77	Chiswick S12	Baby You're Wrong/Stay Free (p/s)	8
78	Chiswick NS 35	Mr Jones/Human Bean/Route 66/Too Much Too Soon (unissued, test pressings only, as Bishops)	18
77	Chiswick WIK 1	THE COUNT BISHOPS (LP)	12
78	Chiswick CH 7	LIVE AT THE ROUNDHOUSE (10" mini-LP)	12

(see also Cannibals)

MINT VALUE £

COUNT BUSTY & RUDIES
68	Melody MRC 003	You Like It/The Reggay	10

COUNT DOWNE & ZEROS
64	Ember EMB S 189	Hello My Angel/Don't Shed A Tear	35

(see also Peter & Headlines)

COUNT FIVE
66	Pye International 7N 25393	Psychotic Reaction/They're Gonna Get You	60
87	Edsel ED 225	PSYCHOTIC REACTION (LP)	12

COUNT HALA
69	Rude Boy RBH 005	Cut Price Pussy/THE ATTACKERS : Police In Z Cars Blues	50
70	Rude Boy RBH 006	Gems Of Christies/Cut Price Meow	25

COUNT HOUSE FOLK MUSIC CLUB
65	own label MSCH 2	MORE SINGING AT THE COUNT HOUSE (LP, private pressing)	250

COUNT LASHER
59	Caribou 106	Caribou Calabash/Dalvey Girl	20

COUNT MACHUKI
10	Randys THB 7002	Pepper Pot/WINSTON SAMUELS: Lick It Back	10

COUNT OSSIE & HIS MYSTIC REVELATION
71	Ashanti ASH 404	Rasta Reggae/Samia	12
71	Moodisc MU 3515	Whispering Drums/SLIM SMITH & UNIQUES: Give Me Some More Loving	15
71	Moodisc HM 105	Whispering Drums/SLIM SMITH & UNIQUES: Give Me Some More Loving	15
74	Ashanti NTI 1301	GROUNATION (3-LP, with Mystic Revelation Of Rastafari)	50

(see also Jackie Estick, Gaylads, Soul Defenders)

COUNT OSSIE & THE REVOLUTIONARIES
78	Charmers CH 0012	Hog Head/TRINITY: Dog Meat (12")	40

COUNT STICKY
68	Amalgamated AMG 825	Train To Soulsville/ERIC MORRIS : Cinderella	40

COUNT SUCKLE
70	Q 2200	Lavender Blues/Humpty Dumpty	10
70	Q 2201	Please Don't Go/FREDDIE & THE NOTES: Bread On The Table	12

COUNT VICTORS
62	Coral Q 72456	Peepin' 'N' Hidin'/Don't Laugh At Me ('Cos I'm A Fool)	15
63	Coral Q 72462	Road Runner/Lorie	15

COUNTDOWNS
63	United Artists UP 1024	Mouse On The Moon/The Big Safari	10

(see also John Barry)

COUNTING CROWS
94	Geffen GFS 69	Mr Jones/Raining In Baltimore/Mr Jones (live) (p/s)	10
93	Geffen GEF 24528	AUGUST AND EVERYTHING AFTER (LP)	50

COUNTRY BOY
64	Blue Beat BB 236	I'm A Lonely Boy (actually by Shenley Duffas)/EDWARD'S ALL STARS: He's Gone Ska	30

COUNTRY EXPRESS
70	Lucky LU 104	Watching Trains Go By/Blue Against Grey	8

COUNTRY FEVER
69	Bell BLL 1052	Too Much Of nothingTears Of Rage	8
71	Lucky LU 106	Mental Revenge/My World Has Ended	10

COUNTRY FOLK
70s	Thule SLP 101	THE COUNTRY FOLK (LP, private pressing)	180

COUNTRY FUNK
70	Polydor 248 2018	COUNTRY FUNK (LP)	18

COUNTRY GAZETTE
72	United Artists UAG 29404	TRAITOR IN OUR MIDST (LP)	15
73	United Artists UAS 29491	DON'T GIVE UP YOUR DAY JOB (LP)	12

(see also Flying Burrito Brothers)

COUNTRY GENTLEMEN
63	Decca F 11766	Greensleeves/Baby Jean	10

(see also High Society, Peter Cowap)

COUNTRY HAMS
74	EMI EMI 2220	Walking In The Park With Eloise/Bridge On The River Suite (p/s, red & brown label)	60
82	EMI EMI 2220	Walking In The Park With Eloise/Bridge On The River Suite (p/s, reissue, beige label)	15

(see also Paul McCartney/Wings, Chet Atkins, Floyd Cramer)

COUNTRY JOE & THE FISH
67	Fontana TF 882	Not So Sweet Martha Lorraine/Love	12
69	Vanguard VA 3	Here I Go Again/It's So Nice To Have Love	7
70	Vanguard 6076 250	I-Feel-Like-I'm-Fixin'-To-Die Rag/Maria	8
67	Fontana TFL 6081	ELECTRIC MUSIC FOR THE MIND AND BODY (LP, flipback sleeve, also Stereo STFL 6087)	40
68	Fontana TFL 6086	I-FEEL-LIKE-I'M-FIXIN'-TO-DIE (LP, flipback sleeve)	40
68	Vanguard SVRL 19006	TOGETHER (LP)	20
69	Vanguard SVRL 19026	ELECTRIC MUSIC FOR THE MIND AND BODY (LP, reissue)	20
69	Vanguard SVRL 19029	I-FEEL-LIKE-I'M-FIXIN'-TO-DIE (LP, reissue)	15
69	Vanguard SVRL 19048	HERE WE ARE AGAIN (LP)	20
70	Vanguard SVRL 19058	THE BEST OF COUNTRY JOE AND THE FISH (LP)	12
70	Vanguard 6359 002	C.J. FISH (LP)	18
73	Vanguard VSD 27/28	THE LIFE AND TIMES OF (2-LP, gatefold sleeve, quadrophonic)	20
75	Vanguard VSD 79244	ELECTRIC MUSIC FOR THE MIND AND BODY (LP, reissue)	15
73	Vanguard VSD 27/28	THE LIFE AND TIMES OF (2-LP, gatefold sleeve, stereo)	15
80	Piccadilly PIC 3009	THE EARLY YEARS (LP, private pressing, withdrawn)	40
87	Decal LIK 8	THE FIRST THREE EPS (LP, as Country Joe McDonald, The Mostly Fish Recordings)	12

(see also Country Joe McDonald)
COUNTRY JUG
72	Decca F 13270	I'm Sorry/Do You Wanna?/Flying	8

(see also Ray Dorset)
COUNTRYMEN
69	Jayboy BOY 3	After All/White Rose Of Athens	5

WAYNE/JAYNE COUNTY (& ELECTRIC CHAIRS)
77	Illegal IL 002	Stuck On You/Paranoia Paradise/The Last Time (p/s)	10
77	Sweet F.A. WC 1	Fuck Off/On The Crest (p/s)	12
78	Safari SAFE 1	Eddie And Sheena/Rock And Roll Cleopatra (p/s, with cartoon insert)	15
78	Safari SAFE 1	Eddie And Sheena/Rock And Roll Cleopatra (p/s, without cartoon insert)	10
78	Safari SAFE 6	I Had Too Much To Dream Last Night/Fuck Off (unissued)	0
78	Safari WC 2	BLATANTLY OFFENZIVE (EP, gold vinyl)	10
78	Safari SAFE 9	Trying To Get On The Radio/Evil Minded Momma (p/s)	5
78	Safari SAFELS 13	Berlin (Long Version)/Waiting For The Marines/Midnight Pal (12", p/s, pink vinyl)	8
79	Illegal IL 005	Thunder When She Walks/What You Got (p/s)	6
83	Safari WCP 3	Fuck Off/Toilet Love (picture disc)	6
78	Safari LONG 1	ELECTRIC CHAIRS (LP)	20
78	Safari GOOD 1	STORM THE GATES OF HEAVEN (LP, multicoloured or grey marbled vinyl)	18
79	Safari GOOD 2	THINGS YOUR MOTHER NEVER TOLD YOU (LP)	18

(see also Mystere Five's)
DIANA COUPLAND
60	HMV POP 690	Love Him/I Am Loved	5

COURIERS
66	Ember EMB S 218	Take Away/Done Me Wrong (with p/s)	80
66	Ember EMB S 218	Take Away/Done Me Wrong	25

(see also William E. Kimber)
COURIERS
69	Ash ALP 201	PACK UP YOUR SORROWS (LP)	30

COURTEENERS
07	Loog LOOG 022	Cavorting/No You Didn't, No You Don't (p/s, 750 only)	20
07	Loog LOOG 023	Cavorting/No You Didn't, No You Don't (CD single)	18

COURT MARTIAL
82	Riot City RIOT 11	NO SOLUTION (EP)	12

DEAN COURTNEY
96	Kent 6T 12	Today Is My Day/SHARON SCOTT: (Putting My Heart) Under Lock And Key	35

COURTYARD MUSIC GROUP
74	Deroy	JUST OUR WAY OF SAYING HELLO (LP, private pressing)	250

COUSIN EMMY & HER KINFOLK
56	Brunswick OE 9258	KENTUCKY MOUNTAIN BALLADS VOL. 1 (EP)	10
56	Brunswick OE 9259	KENTUCKY MOUNTAIN BALLADS VOL. 2 (EP)	10

COUSINS (U.K.)
64	Decca F 11924	Yes Sir That's My Baby/Two Lovely Black Eyes	5

DAVE COUSINS
72	A&M AMS 7032	Going Home/Ways And Means	6
72	A&M AMLS 68118	TWO WEEKS LAST SUMMER (LP, brown label)	45
79	Old School SLURP 1	OLD SCHOOL SONGS (LP, private pressing with Brian Willoughby)	35
80	Passport PVC 8901	OLD SCHOOL SONGS (LP, reissue with different sleeve)	12

(see also The Strawbs)
DON COVAY (& GOODTIMERS)
61	Pye International 7N 25075	Pony Time/Love Boat	30
61	Philips PB 1140	Shake Wid The Shake/Every Which Way	30
62	Cameo Parkway C 239	The Popeye Waddle/One Little Boy Had Money	30
64	Atlantic AT 4006	Mercy, Mercy/Can't Stay Away	12
65	Atlantic AT 4016	Take This Hurt Off Me/Please Don't Let Me Know	12
65	Atlantic AT 4056	See Saw/I Never Get Enough Of Your Love	10
66	Atlantic AT 4078	Sookie Sookie/Watching The Late Late Show	12
66	Atlantic 584 025	You Put Something In Me/Iron Out The Rough Spots	12
66	Atlantic 584 059	See Saw/Somebody's Got To Love You	12
67	Atlantic 584 082	Shingaling '67/I Was There	10
67	Atlantic 584 094	Sookie Sookie/Mercy Mercy	10
67	Atlantic 584 114	40 Days - 40 Nights/The Usual Place	10
70	Atlantic 2091 018	Everything I Do Goin' Be Funky/Key To The Highway	5
65	Atlantic ATL 5025	MERCY! (LP, plum label)	80
67	Atlantic 587 062	SEE-SAW (LP)	30
69	Atlantic K 50225	HOUSE OF BLUE LIGHT (LP)	25
75	Mercury 9100010	HOT BLOOD (LP)	12

(see also Soul Clan)
DAVID COVERDALE
77	Purple PUR 133	Hole In The Sky/Blindman	8
78	Purple PUR 136	Breakdown/Only My Soul	8
90	Epic 656 292 7	Last Note Of Freedom/HANS ZIMMER: Car Building (poster p/s)	8
90	Epic 656 292 6	Last Note Of Freedom/HANS ZIMMER: Car Building (12", p/s)	8
77	Purple TPS 3509	DAVID COVERDALE'S WHITESNAKE (LP, with inner)	15
77	Purple TPS 3509TC	DAVID COVERDALE'S WHITESNAKE (LP, white label promo, plain sleeve, with insert)	25
78	Purple TPS 3513	NORTHWINDS (LP, with inner sleeve)	15

(see also Coverdale-Page, Whitesnake, Deep Purple, Wizard's Convention, Roger Glover, Jimmy Page)
COVERS
79	Decca FR 13880	Modern Girls/Head Out On The Road	30
81	Polydor POSP 233	Too Hot To Handle/Tinted Windows (p/s)	6

JULIEN COVEY & MACHINE
67	Island WIP 6009	A Little Bit Hurt/Sweet Bacon	50

Julie COVINGTON

78	Island WIP 6442	A Little Bit Hurt/Sweet Bacon (reissue)	15
87	Sunset	A Little Bit Hurt/Sweet Bacon (reissue)	12

JULIE COVINGTON
70	Columbia DB 8649	The Magic Wasn't There/The Way Things Ought To Be	15
70	Columbia DB 8705	Tonight Your Love Is Over/If I Had My Time Again	15
72	RCA RCA 2181	Day By Day/With Me It Goes Deeper	6
71	Columbia SCX 6466	THE BEAUTIFUL CHANGES (LP)	150

(see also Rock Follies)

COWBOY
71	Atlantic 2466 022	REACH FOR THE SKY (LP)	15
72	Atlantic K 40312	5'LL GETCHA TEN (LP, with insert)	15

COWBOY COPAS
54	Parlophone CMSP 10	I Can't Go On/A Wreath On The Door Of My Heart (export issue)	30
54	Parlophone MSP 6079	Tennessee Senorita/If You Will Let Me Be Your Love	30
54	Parlophone MSP 6109	A Heartbreak Ago/The Blue Waltz	30
55	Parlophone MSP 6164	I'll Waltz With You In My Dreams/Return To Sender	30
60	Melodisc M 1566	Alabam/I Can	20
55	Parlophone GEP 8527	FAVOURITE COWBOY SONGS (EP)	15
56	Parlophone GEP 8575	WESTERN STYLE (EP)	15
50s	Parlophone CGEP 3	COWBOY COPAS (EP, export issue)	15
62	Top Rank JKP 3014	COUNTRY MUSIC (EP)	15
63	Stateside SE 1003	COUNTRY HITS (EP)	15
61	Melodisc MLP 12-119	COWBOY COPAS (LP)	20

(see also Johnny Bond)

COWBOYS INTERNATIONAL
79	Virgin VS 253	Aftermath/Pt. 2 (orange vinyl, p/s)	10

(see also Public Image Ltd.)

STANLEY COWELL
72	Freedom FLP40104	BRILLIANT CIRCLES (LP)	25

COWSILLS
67	MGM MGM 1353	The Rain, The Park And Other Things/River Blue	30
68	MGM MGM 1383	We Can Fly/A Time For Remembrance	18
68	MGM MGM 1400	In Need Of A Friend/Mr. Flynn	8
68	MGM MGM 1424	Indian Lake/Newspaper Blanket	6
68	MGM MGM 1441	Poor Baby/Meet Me At The Wishing Well	6
69	MGM MGM 1469	Hair/What Is Happy	6
69	MGM MGM 1484	The Prophecy Of Daniel And John The Divine/Gotta Get Away From It All	6
69	MGM MGM 1490	Love American Style/Silver Threads And Golden Needles	6
71	London HLU 10329	On My Side/There Is A Child	6
67	MGM C/CS 8059	THE COWSILLS (LP)	30
68	MGM CS 8077	WE CAN FLY (LP)	25
68	MGM CS 8095	CAPTAIN SAD AND HIS SHIP OF FOOLS (LP)	20
68	MGM C8111	IN CONCERT (LP)	15

BILLY COX
71	Pye Intl. NSPL 25158	NITRO FUNCTION (LP, blue/black label with logo-banner on left)	80

(see also Jimi Hendrix)

HARRY COX
65	EFDSS LP 1004	ENGLISH FOLK SINGER (LP)	15
65	DTS Records LFX 4	ENGLISH FOLK SINGER (LP)	15

IDA COX
59	Fontana TFE 17136	IDA COX (EP)	10
54	London AL 3517	SINGS THE BLUES (10" LP)	50
60s	Riverside RLP 374	BLUES FOR RAMPART STREET (LP)	12
75	Gannet GEN 5371-5376	PARAMOUNT RECORDINGS (6-LP box set)	20

(see also Ma Rainey)

IDA COX/ETHEL WATERS
50s	Poydras 104	IDA COX AND ETHEL WATERS (EP)	25

MICHAEL COX
59	Decca F 11166	Boy Meets Girl/Teenage Love	20
59	Decca F 11166	Boy Meets Girl/Teenage Love (78)	10
59	Decca F 11182	Too Hot To Handle/Serious	20
59	Decca F 11182	Too Hot To Handle/Serious (78)	10
60	Triumph RGM 1011	Angela Jones/Don't Want To Know	10
60	Ember EMB S 103	Angela Jones/Don't Want To Know (export issue)	40
61	HMV POP 789	Along Came Caroline/Lonely Road	15
61	HMV POP 830	Teenage Love/Linda	10
61	HMV POP 905	Sweet Little Sixteen/Cover Girl	25
62	HMV POP 972	Young Only Once/Honey Cause I Love You	8
62	HMV POP 1065	Stand Up/In April	10
63	HMV POP 1137	Don't You Break My Heart/Hark Is That A Cannon I Hear	10
63	HMV POP 1220	Gee What A Party/See That Again	10
64	HMV POP 1293	Rave On/Just Say Hello	20
65	HMV POP 1417	Gypsy/It Ain't Right	10
66	Parlophone R 5436	I Hate Getting Up In The Morning/Love 'Em And Leave 'Em	5
67	Parlophone R 5580	I'll Always Love You/You Never Can Tell (Till You Try)	8

SONNY COX
70	Pama PM 815	Choking Kind/Chocolate Candy	12

WALLY COX
61	Vogue V 9175	I Can't Help It/The Heebie Jeebees	15
74	Pye Disco Demand DDS 105	This Man/I've Had Enough	8
74	Pye Disco Demand DDS 105	This Man/I've Had Enough (DJ Copy)	15
89	Kent 6T 5	This Man Wants You/SIX TEASERS: Doing The Hundred	15

LOL COXHILL

78	Chiltern Sound CS 100	MURDER IN THE AIR (12" EP)	35
71	Dandelion DSD 8008	EAR OF THE BEHOLDER (2-LP, gatefold sleeve)	90
71	Dandelion DSD 69001	EAR OF THE BEHOLDER (2-LP, gatefold sleeve)	50
72	Mushroom 150 MR 23	TOVERBAL SWEET (LP)	80
73	Caroline C 1503	COXHILL MILLER (LP, with Stephen Miller)	20
74	Caroline C 1507	THE STORY SO FAR ... OH REALLY? (LP, with Stephen Miller)	25
75	Caroline C 1514	LOL COXHILL & WELFARE STATE (LP)	18
75	Caroline C 1515	FLEAS IN THE CUSTARD (LP)	18
76	Ogun OG 510	DIVERSE (LP)	15
78	Ogun OG 525	THE JOY OF PARANOIA (LP)	15
78	Ictus 0008	MOOT (LP)	25
80	Pipe PIPE 1	SLOW MUSIC (LP)	30

(see also Stephen Miller & Lol Coxhill, Kevin Ayers, Steve York's Camelo Pardalis)

COXHILL BEDFORD DUO

71	Polydor 2001 253	Pretty Little Girl (Parts 1 & 2)	25
72	Dandelion 2058 214	Mood/WILL DANDY & DANDYLETTES: Sonny Boy/Oh Mein Papa	20

(see also David Bedford, Lol Coxhill)

GRAHAM COXON

00	Transcopic 10 RDJ 6541	Oochy Woochy/That's When I Reach For My Revolver (10" promo p/s)	6
06	Parlophone R 6721	What Ya Gonna Do Now?/Bloody Annoying	6
04	EMI R 6632	Freakin' Out/Feel Right (numbered p/s)	5
07	Regal SCO16	This Old Town (with Paul Weller)/Each New Morning/ Black River (7" die-cut sleeve)	5
98	Transcopic TRANLP 005	THE SKY IS TOO HIGH (LP, inner sleeve, 4 postcards)	20
01	Transcopic TRANLP 010	CROW SIT ON BLOOD TREE (2-LP, with inners & print, signed, 1,000 only)	30
01	Transcopic TRANLP 010	CROW SIT ON BLOOD TREE (2-LP, with inners & print, 1,000 only)	20
02	Transcopic TRANLP 018	THE KISS OF MORNING (2xLP, 10" x 10" picture book)	18
04	EMI 5775191	HAPPINESS IN MAGAZINES (LP)	15
06	Live Here Now (No cat no)	BURNT TO BLITZ : AT THE ASTORIA (2xCD sold at 25/10/06 only)	20
06	Parlophone 350 5191	LOVE TRAVELS AT ILLEGAL SPEEDS (2-LP)	15
09	Transcopic TRANS 102X	THE SPINNING TOP (2-LP)	15

(see also Blur)

KEVIN COYNE

72	Dandelion 2001 357	Cheat Me/Flowering Cherry	7
80	Virgin VGD 3504	SANITY STOMP (EP, double pack)	8
72	Dandelion 2310 228	CASE HISTORY (LP)	120
73	Virgin VD 251/2	MARJORY RAZORBLADE (2-LP, gatefold sleeve with "130 Notting Hill Gate" credit, black/white label)	25
73	Virgin VD 2501	MARJORY RAZORBLADE (2-LP, gatefold sleeve, later pressing without "130 Notting Hill Gate" credit)	15
74	Virgin V 2012	BLAME IT ON THE NIGHT (LP, lyric insert, coloured 'twin Virgin' label)	25
75	Virgin V 2033	MATCHING HEAD AND FEET (LP, laminated sleeve, lyric poster, coloured "twin-Virgin" label)	15
76	Virgin V 2047	HEARTBURN (LP, "mirror" girl green/white rim)	12
78	Virgin V 2096	DYNAMITE DAZE (LP)	12
79	Virgin V 2110	MILLIONAIRES AND TEDDY BEARS (LP)	12
80	Dandelion BUTBOX 1	DANDELION YEARS (3-LP, re-issue of Siren LP's Siren, Strange Locomotion and Coynes Case History)	25
90	Strange Fruit SRFLP 112	PEEL SESSIONS (LP)	12

(see also Clague, Coyne-Clague, Siren, Gordon Smith)

COYNE-CLAGUE

69	Dandelion S 4494	The Stride/I Wonder Where	8

CRABBY APPLETON

70	Elektra 2101 006	Go Back/Try	12
70	Elektra EKS 74067	CRABBY APPLETON (LP)	20
71	Elektra EKS 74106	ROTTEN TO THE CORE (LP)	20

CRACK (1)

80	JSO EAT 4	Making The Effort/Easy Street	8

CRACK (2)

82	RCA RCA 214	Don't You Ever Let Me Down/I Can't Take It (die-cut 'Battle of the Bands' sleeve)	25
82	RCA RCA 255	Going Out/The Troops Have Landed (p/s)	15
83	RCA CRACK 1	All Or Nothing/I Caught You Out (p/s)	30
83	Link LP073	IN SEARCH OF THE CRACK (LP)	20

CRACKED MIRROR

83	CMLP 001	CRACKED MIRROR (LP, private pressing, 200 only)	80

CRACKERS

69	Fontana TF 995	Honey Do/It Happens All The Time	15

(see also Merseys)

SARAH CRACKNELL

87	3 Bears TED 001	Love Is All You Need/Coastal Town (p/s)	10
97	Gut CDGUT 7	Goldie (Radio Edit)/(Original Version)/Empire State High/ Aussie Soap Girl (CD, slimline jewel case, withdrawn)	10

(see also St. Etienne, 50 Year Void, Lovecut D.B.)

CRACK THE SKY

76	Lifesong ELS 45016	We Want Mine/Invaders From Mars	8
76	Lifesong LSLP 6005	ANIMAL NOTES (LP, with inner sleeve)	15

(BILLY) 'CRASH' CRADDOCK

59	Philips PB 966	Boom Boom Baby/Don't Destroy Me (as 'Crash' Craddock) (78 rpm = £20)	30
59	Philips PB 966	Boom Boom Baby/Don't Destroy Me (as 'Crash' Craddock) (78)	15
60	Philips PB 1006	Since She Turned Seventeen/I Want That (as 'Crash' Craddock)	30
60	Philips PB 1092	Good Time Billy (Is A Happiness Fool)/Heavenly Love	15
61	Mercury AMT 1146	How Lonely He Must Be/Truly True	10

CRADLE OF FILTH

94	Cacophonous NIHIL1	THE PRINCIPLE OF EVIL MADE FLESH (LP)	20

CARL CRAIG

94	Open OPENT-001	Throw/Remake Uno (as CARL CRAIG PRESENTS PAPERCLIP PEOPLE) (12")	15
94	Open OPENT-004	Throw (The Remixes) (as CARL CRAIG PRESENTS PAPERCLIP PEOPLE) (12")	12
95	Blanco Y Negro EG 80T	Science Fiction (12")	8
04	Carl Craig (White) CCR002	Volume Two (2x12")	25
95	Blanco Y Negro 509-99865-1	LANDCRUISING (2xLP)	15
01	Obsessive EVSLP20	ABSTRACT FUNK THEORY (as CARL CRAIG PRESENTS...) (2xLP)	15

PAUL CRAIG

| 66 | CBS 202406 | Midnight Girl/Autumn | 10 |

CRAIG (1)

| 65 | King KG 1022 | Ain't That A Shame/International Blues | 18 |
| 66 | Fontana TF 715 | I Must Be Mad/Suspense | 300 |

CRAIG (2)

| 66 | Fontana TF 665 | A Little Bit Of Soap/Ready Steady Let's Go | 80 |

(see also Galliard)

DON CRAINE'S NEW DOWNLINERS SECT

| 67 | Pye 7N 17261 | I Can't Get Away From You/Roses | 250 |

(see also Downliners Sect)

FLOYD CRAMER

54	London HL 8012	Fancy Pants/Five Foot Two Eyes Of Blue	40
54	London HL 8012	Fancy Pants/Five Foot Two Eyes Of Blue (78)	10
54	London HL 8062	Jolly Cholly/Oh! Suzanna	40
54	London HL 8062	Jolly Cholly/Oh! Suzanna (78)	10
55	London HLU 8195	Rag-A-Tag/Aunt Dinah's Quiltin' Party	30
55	London HLU 8195	Rag-A-Tag/Aunt Dinah's Quiltin' Party (78)	10
58	RCA RCA 1050	Flip Flop And Bop/Sophisticated Swing	40
58	RCA RCA 1050	Flip Flop And Bop/Sophisticated Swing (78)	20
60	RCA RCA 1211	Last Date/Sweetie Baby	5
61	RCA 1231	On The Rebound/Mood Indigo	5
61	RCA 1259	Hang On/Your Last Goodbye	6
62	RCA 1301	Hot Pepper/For Those That Cry	5
62	RCA 1275	Chattanooga Choo Choo/Let's Go	7
62	RCA 1284	Lovesick Blues/The First Hurt	6
62	RCA 1311	Losers Weeper/Swing Low	6
62	RCA 1325	Java/Melissa	7
55	London REP 1023	PIANO HAYRIDE (EP, with Louisiana Hayride Band)	30

(see also Country Hams)

FLOYD CRAMER/HOUSTON ROBERTS

| 65 | Fontana FJL 308 | FLOYD CRAMER/HOUSTON ROBERTS (LP, one side each) | 12 |

CRAMP

| 78 | Rip Off RIP 7 | She Doesn't Love Me/Suzy Lie Down (p/s) | 10 |

CRAMPS

79	Illegal ILS 12013	GRAVEST HITS (12" EP, blue vinyl)	30
79	Illegal ILS 12013	GRAVEST HITS (12" EP, black vinyl)	15
80	Illegal ILS 0017	Fever/Garbage Man (withdrawn 1st 'full band' p/s)	20
80	Illegal ILS 0017	Fever/Garbage Man (p/s; re-pressing in different p/s with 4 separate shots)	15
80	Illegal ILS 0017	Garbage Man/Mystery Plane (Unreleased test pressing)	150
80	Illegal ILS 021	Drug Train/Love Me/I Can't Hardly Stand It (p/s)	15
81	IRS PFS 1003	Goo Goo Muck/She Said (p/s, yellow vinyl)	15
81	IRS PFSX 1008	The Crusher/Save It/New Kind Of Kick (12", p/s)	15
85	Big Beat NS 110	Can Your Pussy Do The Dog?/Blue Moon Baby (p/s, orange see-through vinyl)	8
86	Big Beat NS 115	What's Inside A Girl/Give Me A Woman (p/s, purple vinyl)	10
86	Big Beat NS 115	What's Inside A Girl/Get Off The Road/Give Me A Woman (12", p/s, white vinyl)	12
89	Enigma ENVPD 17	Bikini Girls With Machine Guns/Jackyard Backoff (picture disc)	8
89	Enigma ENV 19	All Women Are Bad/King Of The Drapes/Teenage Rage/High School Hellcats (12", pic disc)	8
90	Enigma 12ENV22	Creature From The Black Leather Lagoon/Jailhouse Rock/Beat Out My Love	15

(shrinkwrapped inner with sticker)

80	Illegal ILP 005	SONGS THE LORD TAUGHT US (LP, white label with "Drug Train" in place of "T.V. Set")	175
80	Illegal ILP 005	SONGS THE LORD TAUGHT US (LP, with "T.V. Set")	25
81	IRS SP 70016	PSYCHEDELIC JUNGLE (LP)	20
83	Illegal ILP 012	OFF THE BONE (LP, white label, with different mix of "Drug Train", around 50 copies pressed, unreleased)	100
83	Illegal ILP 012	OFF THE BONE (LP, with 3-D sleeve & glasses)	40
83	Illegal ILP 012	OFF THE BONE (LP, picture disc with extra track)	15
84	Big Beat NED 6	SMELL OF FEMALE (LP, red see-through vinyl)	20
84	Big Beat BEDP 6	SMELL OF FEMALE (LP, picture disc)	20
84	Big Beat NED 6	SMELL OF FEMALE (LP, 2nd issue, black vinyl)	15
86	Big Beat WIKA 46	A DATE WITH ELVIS (LP, with poster)	12
86	Big Beat WIKA 46	A DATE WITH ELVIS (LP, blue vinyl)	25
90	Enigma ENVLP 1001	STAY SICK (LP)	12
91	Big Beat WIKDP 101	LOOK MOM NO HEAD (LP)	15
91	Big Beat WIKPD 101	LOOK MOM NO HEAD (LP, picture disc)	15
90	Illigal ILP 5	SONGS THE LORD TAUGHT US (LP, reissue)	15
91	Windsong WINDSONG 4	LUX (3 x 12" box set, with poster, T-shirt & book, numbered, withdrawn)	50

(see also Beast)

CRANBERRIES

94	Island IS 559	Linger/Pretty (p/s, 2nd issue with b/w picture)	6
91	Xeric XER 014	Uncertain/Nothing Left At All (p/s)	15
91	Xeric XER 014T	Uncertain/Nothing Left At All/Pathetic Senses/Them (12", p/s)	20
91	Xeric XER 014CD	Uncertain/Nothing Left At All/Pathetic Senses/Them (CD)	40
94	Island ILPS 8029	NO NEED TO ARGUE (LP)	25
99	Mercury/Island 524 644 1	BURY THE HATCHET (2-LP)	40

CRANE/FARLOWE

| 73 | Dawn DNS 1034 | Can't Find A Reason/Moods | 7 |

(see also Atomic Rooster, Crazy World Of Arthur Brown, Chris Farlowe, Katmandu)

LES CRANE
71	Warner Bros K16119	Desiderata/A Different Drummer	7

TONY CRANE
65	Polydor BM 56008	Ideal Love/Little You	15
66	CBS 202022	Even The Bravest/I Still Remember	20
67	Pye 7N 17337	Anonymous Mr Brown/In This World	15
68	Pye 7N 17517	Scratchin' Ma Head/Patterns In The Sky	20

(see also Bob Miller, Merseys/Merseybeats)

CRANE RIVER JAZZ BAND
53	Parlophone MSP 6008	Lily Of The Valley/Till We Meet Again	5
57	77 LP/4	ORIGINAL CRANE RIVER JAZZ BAND (LP)	20
57	77 LP/5	ORIGINAL CRANE RIVER JAZZ BAND (LP)	20
57	77 LP/17	ORIGINAL CRANE RIVER JAZZ BAND (LP)	20
57	77 LP/18	ORIGINAL CRANE RIVER JAZZ BAND (LP)	20

(see also Ken Colyer)

CRANIUM PIE
11	Regal Crabmophone WINKLE 002	MECHANISMS (PART 1) LP, red vinyl card inserts)	30

CRANNOG
76	Crannog CR 1	CRANNOG (LP)	25

CRASH
82	Crash EJSP 9819	FIGHT FOR YOUR LIFE (EP, no p/s)	30

CRASHERS
69	Amalgamated AMG 834	Hurry Come Up/Off Track	100

CRASS
78	Small Wonder WEENY 2	THE FEEDING OF THE 5000 (12" EP, with 4-page insert & poster)	15
78	Crass 621984	THE FEEDING OF THE 5000 (12" EP, reissue with "Reality Asylum")	8
79	Crass 521984/1	Reality Asylum/Shaved Women (brown cardboard gatefold p/s)	20
79	Crass 521984/1	Reality Asylum/Shaved Women (later pressing in white newspaper foldout sleeve)	6
80	Crass/Xntrix 421984/1	Bloody Revolutions/POISON GIRLS: Persons Unknown (foldout p/s)	8
80	Crass 421984/5	Nagasaki Nightmare/Big A Little A (foldout p/s, with patch)	20
80	Crass 421984/5	Nagasaki Nightmare/Big A Little A (foldout p/s, without patch)	6
81	Crass 421984/6	Rival Tribal Rebel Revel/Bully Boys Out Fighting (flexidisc with Toxic Graffiti fanzine)	20
81	Crass 421984/6	Rival Tribal Rebel Revel/Bully Boys Out Fighting (hard vinyl promo, p/s)	40
81	Crass COLD TURKEY 1	Merry Crassmass/Merry Crassmass - Have Fun (p/s)	6
81	Crass 321984/IF flexi	Our Wedding (free flexi sent to readers of Loving -'for the price of a Stamp'. By Creative Recording And Sound Services – CRASS' with mailer envelope)	300
82	Crass 221984/6	How Does It Feel (To Be The Mother Of 1000 Dead?)/The Immortal Death/ Don't Tell Me You Care (foldout p/s)	8
83	Crass 121984/3	Sheep Farming In The Falklands/Gotcha! (live) (foldout p/s with lyric insert)	8
83	(no label)	Gotcha! (clear flexidisc)	10
83	Crass 121984/4	Who Dunnit? (Parts 1 & 2) (p/s, brown vinyl)	6
84	Crass 1984	YOU'RE ALREADY DEAD EP	7
79	Crass 521984	STATIONS OF THE CRASS (2-LP, fold-out sleeve, black and white inners, original issue with "Pay no more than £3.00" on sleeve)	15
81	Crass 321984	PENIS ENVY (LP, original pressing with "pay no more than £2.25 on sleeve)	15
82	Crass BOLLOX 2U2	CHRIST THE ALBUM (2-LP, box set with booklet)	20
83	Crass 121984	YES SIR, I WILL (LP, fold-out sleeve, original issue with "Pay no more than £2.75" on sleeve)	15

(see also Anne Anxiety, Joy De Vivre, Eve Libertine, Poison Girls)

CRATOR
79	Recordiau Lloer SEL 0001	Blas Da/Fy Mreuddwyd I/Gelyn Yr Awyr (EP, 1000 only, no p/s)	20

CRAVATS
78	The Cravats CH 004	Gordon/Situations (p/s)	25
79	Small Wonder SMALL 15	The End/Burning Bridges/I Hate The Universe (p/s)	8
80	Small Wonder SMALL 25	You're Driving Me Mad/I Am The Dregs (p/s)	10
81	Small Wonder SMALL 26	Off The Beach/And The Sun Shone On (p/s)	8
82	Crass 221984/2	RUB ME OUT (EP, 21" x 14" poster p/s)	12
85	Reflex 12 RE 10	THE LAND OF THE GIANTS (12" EP)	12
80	Small Wonder CRAVAT 1	THE CRAVATS IN TOYTOWN (LP, with inner sleeve)	25

(see also Very Things)

CAROLYN CRAWFORD
65	Stateside SS 384	When Someone's Good To You/My Heart	150
65	Stateside SS 384	When Someone's Good To You/My Heart (DJ copy)	220

HANK CRAWFORD
63	London HAK 8103	SOUL OF THE BALLAD (LP)	18

JAMES 'SUGARBOY' CRAWFORD
73	Chess 6145 024	Jock-o-mo (Iko Iko)/BOBBY CHARLES: See You Later, Alligator	6

JIMMY CRAWFORD
60	Columbia DB 4525	Long Stringy Baby/Unkind	50
61	Columbia DB 4633	Love Or Money/Does My Heartache Show	10
61	Columbia DB 4717	I Love How You Love Me/Our Last Embrace	6
62	Columbia DB 4895	Thank You/There'll Be No Goodbyes	10
63	Columbia DB 4975	Another Of Your Toys/Young And Afraid	15
63	Columbia DB 7175	Don't Worry About Bobby/Take This Rose	12
69	CBS 4429	Love Wonderful Love/Strange Song	6
70	CBS 4891	I Can Make It With You/I'm Gonna Change The Plans You Made	6

JOHNNY CRAWFORD
62	Pye International 7N 25145	Cindy's Birthday/Patti Ann	10
62	London HL 9605	Your Nose Is Gonna Grow/Something Special	5
62	London HL 9638	Rumors/No One Really Loves A Clown	5
63	London HL 9669	Proud/Lonesome Town	7

64	London HL 9836	Judy Loves Me/Living In The Past	7
62	London RE 1343	JOHNNY CRAWFORD (EP)	30
64	London RE 1416	WHEN I FALL IN LOVE (EP)	30
63	London HA 8060	RUMORS (LP)	40
64	London HA 8197	JOHNNY CRAWFORD - HIS GREATEST HITS (LP)	40

CRAWFORD BROTHERS
57	Vogue V 9077	Midnight Mover Groover/Midnight Happenings	250
57	Vogue V 9077	Midnight Mover Groover/Midnight Happenings (78)	50
59	Vogue V 9140	It Feels Good/I Ain't Guilty (triangular or round centre)	250
59	Vogue V 9140	It Feels Good/I Ain't Guilty (triangular or round centre) (78)	50

CRAWLING CHAOS
| 80 | Factory FAC 17 | Sex Machine/Berlin (p/s) | 20 |

PEE WEE CRAYTON
| 71 | Vanguard VSD 6566 | THINGS I USED TO DO (LP) | 15 |

CRAZE
79	Cobra COB 3	Motions/Spartans (p/s)	5
80	Harvest HAR 5200	Motions/Spartans (reissue in different p/s)	5
80	Harvest HAR 5205	Lucy/Stop Living In The Past (p/s)	6

(see also Skunks, Hard Corps)

CRAZY CAVAN AND THE RHYTHM ROCKERS
| 73 | Crazy Rhythm CR 01 | Teddy Boy Boogie/Bop Little Baby | 8 |
| 74 | Crazy Rhythm CR 02 | Teddy Boy Rock'N'Roll/Rockabilly Star/Wildest Cat In Town/Little Teddy Girl | 10 |

CRAZY ELEPHANT
69	Major Minor MM 609	Gimme Gimme Good Lovin'/Dark Part Of My Mind	6
69	Major Minor MM 623	Sunshine Red Wine/Pam	5
70	Major Minor MM 672	There's A Better Day Coming/Space Buggy	5
69	Major Minor SMLP 62	CRAZY ELEPHANT (LP, red/white/black label)	40

CRAZY FEELINGS
| 67 | Polydor NH 56723 | Please Lie/Time Is Running Out | 6 |

CRAZY HORSE
| 72 | Reprise RSLP 6438 | CRAZY HORSE (LP) | 22 |
| 72 | Reprise K 44171 | LOOSE (LP, gatefold sleeve) | 15 |

(see also Neil Young, Nils Lofgren, Jack Nitzsche)

CRAZY HOUSE
| 82 | T.W. PROP 2 | THEY DANCE LIKE THIS FROM AS FAR OFF AS THE CRAZY HOUSE (LP, insert) | 15 |

CRAZY PAVING
| 70 | MCA KM55057 | Anytime Sunshine/Sweet Brandy | 12 |

CRAZY ROCKERS
| 64 | King KG 1001 | Third Man Theme/Mama Papa | 5 |

PAPA JOHN CREACH
| 71 | Grunt FTR 1003 | PAPA JOHN CREACH (LP) | 12 |
| 73 | Grunt FTR 1009 | FILTHY (LP) | 12 |

(see also Jefferson Airplane)

CREAM
66	Reaction 591 007	Wrapping Paper/Cat's Squirrel	20
66	Reaction 591 011	I Feel Free/N.S.U.	12
67	Reaction 591 015	Strange Brew/Tales Of Brave Ulysses	15
68	Polydor 56258	Anyone For Tennis (The Savage Seven Theme)/Pressed Rat And Warthog	10
68	Polydor 56286	Sunshine Of Your Love/SWLABR	8
68	Polydor 56300	White Room/Those Were The Days	8
69	Polydor 56315	Strange Brew/Wrapping Paper (unissued)	0
69	Polydor 56315	Badge/What A Bringdown	7
71	Polydor 2058 120	I Feel Free/Wrapping Paper	6
72	Polydor 2058 285	Badge/What A Bringdown (reissue)	6
66	Reaction 593 001	FRESH CREAM (LP, mono)	100
66	Reaction 594 001	FRESH CREAM (LP, stereo)	70
67	Reaction 593 003	DISRAELI GEARS (LP, 1st pressing, with label miscredits to 'Windfall Music' and 'Apple Publishing', '1967' on side 2 label, A1/B1 matrix, sleeve laminated on front & back, mono)	250
67	Reaction 593 003	DISRAELI GEARS (LP, 2nd pressing, with label credits of 'Immediate Music' and 'Copyright Control', sleeve laminated on front & back, mono)	100
67	Reaction 594 003	DISRAELI GEARS (LP, sleeve laminated on front & back, stereo)	90
68	Reaction 593 003	DISRAELI GEARS (LP, sleeve laminated on front only, mono)	40
68	Reaction 594 003	DISRAELI GEARS (LP, sleeve laminated on front only, stereo)	30
68	Polydor 582 031/2	WHEELS OF FIRE (2-LP, gatefold sleeve, mono; set no. 2612 001)	70
68	Polydor 583 031/2	WHEELS OF FIRE (2-LP, gatefold sleeve, stereo; set no. 2612 001)	50
68	Polydor 582/583 033	WHEELS OF FIRE - IN THE STUDIO (LP, mono)	40
68	Polydor 583 033	WHEELS OF FIRE - IN THE STUDIO (LP, stereo)	30
68	Polydor 582/583 040	WHEELS OF FIRE - LIVE AT THE FILLMORE (LP, mono)	40
68	Polydor 582/583 040	WHEELS OF FIRE - LIVE AT THE FILLMORE (LP, stereo)	30
69	Polydor 583 053	GOODBYE (LP, gatefold sleeve)	18
69	Polydor 583 060	THE BEST OF CREAM (LP)	12
70	Polydor 2383 016	LIVE CREAM (LP)	15
71	Polydor 2855 002	CREAM ON TOP (LP, mail-order compilation)	35
72	Polydor 2383 119	LIVE CREAM VOL. 2 (LP)	12
80	RSO 2658 142	CREAM (7-LP set including "Fresh Cream", "Disraeli Gears", "Wheels Of Fire", Goodbye, "Live Cream" & "Live Cream Vol. 2")	40
92	UFO CR 1	CREAM IN GEAR (96-page book packaged with "Disraeli Gears" CD)	20

(see also Eric Clapton, Jack Bruce, Ginger Baker, Blind Faith)

CREAMERS
| 89 | Fierce FRIGHT 045 | Sunday Head/Think I'm Gonna Be Sick (p/s) | 10 |

JOAN CREARY
| 71 | Fab FAB 181 | Your Best Friend/Version | 7 |

CREATION (U.K.)

66	Planet PLF 116	Making Time/Try And Stop Me (with Planet sleeve)	50
66	Planet PLF 116	Making Time/Try And Stop Me (without Planet sleeve)	35
66	Planet PLF 119	Painter Man/Biff Bang Pow (with Planet sleeve)	45
66	Planet PLF 119	Painter Man/Biff Bang Pow (without Planet sleeve)	35
67	Polydor 56177	If I Stay Too Long/Nightmares	50
67	Polydor 56207	Life Is Just Beginning/Through My Eyes	100
68	Polydor 56230	How Does It Feel To Feel/Tom Tom	75
68	Polydor 56246	Midway Down/The Girls Are Naked	50
73	Charisma CB 213	Making Time/Painter Man	8
77	Raw RAW 4	Making Time/Painter Man (reissue, p/s)	10
84	Edsel E 5006	Making Time/Uncle Bert (p/s)	10
73	Charisma Perspective CS 8	THE CREATION '66-67 (LP)	45
82	Edsel ED 106	HOW DOES IT FEEL TO FEEL (LP, with foldout insert)	15
82	Line OLLP 5242	RE-CREATION - THE REST OF THE CREATION (LP)	12

(see also Mark Four, Birds, Ashton Gardner & Dyke, Kennedy Express, Eddy Phillips, Smiley, Spectrum)

CREATION (U.S.)

72	Stateside SS 2205	I Got The Fever/Soul Control	12

(see also Prophets)

CREATION REBEL

79	Hit Run HIT DD8	Beware/Natty Conscience Free (12")	40
81	On-U Sound DP3	Independent Man Dub/CREATION REBEL : Dub	30
78	Hit Run APLP 9001	DUB FROM CREATION (LP)	70
79	Hit Run APLP 9004	REBEL VIBRATIONS (LP)	70
81	4D Rhythms 4DLP1	STARSHIP AFRICA (LP)	40
81	Static STATLP 04	PSYCHOTIC JONKANOO	30
82	On-U Sound ON-U LP08	STARSHIP AFRICA (LP)	30
82	Cherry Red BRED 21	THREAT TO CREATION (LP)(With the New Age Steppers)	15

CREATIONS

67	Rio R 133	Meet Me At Eight/Searching	18
68	Amalgamated AMG 818	Holding Out/Get On Up	30
69	Punch PH 2	Mix Up Girl/Qua Kue Shut	90

(see also Little Roys)

CREATION STEPPER

79	Tribesman TM 22	What You Are Not Supposed To Do/Children Obey Your Parents (12")	15
80	Nationwide NWD 015	Homeward Bound/version (12")	80
81	Moa Anbassa MA005	Treat Me Unkind/Unkind Dub (12")	15
04	Jah Tuibbys JT 10019	King Nebuchadnezzar (with the Disciples Riddim Section)/The Nebuchadnezzar Skarock (with the Dread-UK Crew) (12")	30

(see also Fred Locks)

CREATIVE SOURCE

75	Polydor 2066680	Don't Be Afraid (Take My Love)/Pass The Feelin' On	12
73	Sussex LPSX6	CREATIVE SOURCE (LP)	15

CREATIVE THIEVES

91	Stress Records 12 STR 02	Nasty Rhythm (12")	8

CREATOR & NORMA

63	Island WI 105	We Will Be Lovers/Come On Pretty Baby	10

CREATORS

96	Blind Side BS002	HAVE A MASTER PLAN (EP)	8

CREATURES

66	CBS 202048	Turn Out The Light/It Must Be Love	12
66	CBS 202350	String Along/Night Is Warm	12
67	CBS 2666	Looking At Tomorrow/Someone Needs You	12

CREEDENCE CLEARWATER REVIVAL

69	Liberty LBF 15223	Proud Mary/I Put A Spell On You (withdrawn)	20
69	Liberty LBF 15223	Proud Mary/Born On The Bayou	6
69	Liberty LBF 15230	Bad Moon Rising/Lodi	7
69	Liberty LBF 15250	Green River/Commotion	6
70	Liberty LBF 15283	Down On The Corner/Fortunate Son	7
70	Liberty LBF 15310	Travellin' Band/Who'll Stop The Rain	8
70	Liberty LBF 15354	Up Around The Bend/Run Through The Jungle (in p/s)	10
70	Liberty LBF 15354	Up Around The Bend/Run Through The Jungle	5
70	Liberty LBF 15384	Long As I Can See The Light/Lookin' Out My Back Door (in p/s)	10
70	Liberty LBF 15384	Long As I Can See The Light/Lookin' Out My Back Door	5
71	Liberty LBF 15440	Have You Ever Seen The Rain/Hey Tonight	5
71	United Artists UP 35261	Sweet Hitch-Hiker/Door To Door	6
72	Fantasy F 676	Someday Never Comes/Tearin' Up The Country	5
72	Fantasy FTC 101	Born On The Bayou/I Put A Spell On You	5
73	Fantasy FTC 104	It Came Out Of The Sky/Side O' The Road	5
69	Liberty LBS 83259	CREEDENCE CLEARWATER REVIVAL (LP, blue label)	50
69	Liberty LBS 83261	BAYOU COUNTRY (LP, blue label)	40
69	Liberty LBS 83273	GREEN RIVER (LP, blue label)	40
70	Liberty LBS 83338	WILLY AND THE POORBOYS (LP, blue label)	40
70	Liberty LBS 83388	COSMO'S FACTORY (LP)	30
71	Liberty LBG 83400	PENDULUM (LP, gatefold sleeve)	15

(see also Golliwogs, John Fogerty, Tom Fogerty, Blue Ridge Rangers)

CREEPERS

66	Blue Beat BB 366	Beat Of My Soul/LLOYD ADAMS: I Wish Your Picture Was You	20

CREME CARAMEL

69	Pye International 7N 25495	My Idea/Excursion	6

CRESCENDOS

58	London HLU 8563	Oh Julie/My Little Girl	100
58	London HLU 8563	Oh Julie/My Little Girl (78)	20

MINT VALUE £

CRESCENTS (1)
| 58 | Columbia DB 4093 | Wrong/Baby, Baby, Baby | 100 |
| 58 | Columbia DB 4093 | Wrong/Baby, Baby, Baby (78) | 20 |

CRESCENTS (2)
| 64 | London HLN 9851 | Pink Dominos/Breakout | 25 |

CRESSIDA
70	Vertigo VO 7	CRESSIDA (LP, gatefold sleeve, large swirl label)	500
71	Vertigo 6360 025	ASYLUM (LP, gatefold sleeve, large swirl label)	700
11	Record Collector RCLP 002	TRAPPED IN TIME - THE LOST TAPES (LP)	30

(see also Uriah Heep, Black Widow)

CRESTAS
| 65 | Fontana TF 551 | To Be Loved/When I Fall In Love | 25 |

CRESTERS
| 64 | HMV POP 1249 | I Just Don't Understand/I Want You | 10 |
| 64 | HMV POP 1296 | Put Your Arms Around Me/Do It With Me | 5 |

(see also Mike Sagar & Cresters, Richard Harding)

CRESTS
59	London HL 8794	Sixteen Candles/Beside You	60
59	London HL 8794	Sixteen Candles/Beside You (78)	20
59	Top Rank JAR 150	Flower Of Love/Molly Mae	25
59	Top Rank JAR 150	Flower Of Love/Molly Mae (78)	15
59	Top Rank JAR 168	Six Nights A Week/I Do	25
59	Top Rank JAR 168	Six Nights A Week/I Do (78)	25
59	London HL 8954	The Angels Listened In/I Thank The Moon	60
59	London HL 8954	The Angels Listened In/I Thank The Moon (78)	25
60	Top Rank JAR 302	A Year Ago Tonight/Paper Crown	25
60	Top Rank JAR 372	Step By Step/Gee (But I'd Give The World)	25
60	HMV POP 768	Always You/Trouble In Paradise	25
60	HMV POP 808	Isn't It Amazing/Molly Mae	25
61	HMV POP 848	Model Girl/We've Got To Tell Them	20
62	HMV POP 976	Little Miracles/Baby I Gotta Know	25
63	London HLU 9671	Guilty/Number One With Me	25

(see also Johnny Maestro)

CREW
| 69 | Plexium PXM 12 | Marty/Danger Signs | 10 |
| 70 | Decca F 13000 | Cecilia/1970 | 7 |

CREW-CUTS
53	Mercury MB 3135	Crazy 'Bout Baby/Angela Mia	10
54	Mercury MB 3159	Oop-Shoop/Do Me Good, Baby (78)	10
56	Mercury 7MT 2	Angels In The Sky/Seven Days (export issue)	30
57	Mercury MT 161	Susie-Q/Such A Shame	15
57	Mercury MT 178	I Sit In My Window/Hey, You Face (78)	18
58	RCA RCA 1075	Hey, Stella!/Forever, My Darling	30
58	RCA RCA 1075	Hey, Stella!/Forever, My Darling (78)	20
56	Mercury MEP 9002	PRESENTING THE CREW-CUTS (EP)	60
56	Mercury MPT 7501	THE CREW-CUTS ON PARADE (10" LP)	80

BOB CREWE (GENERATION)
60	London HLI 9077	Water Boy/Voglio Cantare (solo)	5
64	Stateside SS 356	Maggie Maggie May/We Almost Made It	6
67	Stateside SS 582	Music To Watch Girls By/Girls On The Rocks	8
67	Stateside SS 2032	You Only Live Twice/A Lover's Concerto	10
67	Philips BL 7788	PLAY THE FOUR SEASONS HITS (LP, as Bob Crewe Orch.)	25
67	Stateside SL 10210	MUSIC TO WATCH GIRLS BY (LP)	35
68	Stateside S(S)L 10260	BARBARELLA (LP, soundtrack)	75

THE CRIBS
03	Squirrel No 5	Baby Don't Sweat/You and I (other 2 tracks by JEN SCHANDE)	30
03	Wichita WEBB 051S	Baby Don't Sweat/Another Number (p/s, yellow vinyl)	10
04	Wichita WEBB 059S	You Were Always The One/Song From Practice 1 (p/s)	10
04	B-Unique KAISER	Plays Kaiser Chiefs (gig only 7" given away free, stickered sleeve)	10
04	Wichita WEBB 061S	What About Me/Feelin' It (yellow vinyl, p/s)	12
05	Wichita WEBB 074 s	Hey Scenesters!/North Of England (p/s, clear vinyl)	7
05	Wichita WEBB 074 SX	Hey Scenesters!/You're Gonna Loose Us (p/s, clear vinyl)	7
05	Wichita WEBB 097S	You're Gonna Lose Us/The Wrong Way To Be (Live At Reading) (in box)	8
05	Wichita WEBB 097SX	You're Gonna Lose Us/I Was Her Man But I Done Her Wrong (p/s)	6
05	Wichita WEBB 097S	COLLECTORS BOX SET (8x7" box set, coloured vinyl)	50
09	Wichita WEBB 220LP	IGNORE THE IGNORANT (LP)	15

(see also The Smiths, Wrinkle)

CRICKETS FEATURING BUDDY HOLLY
78s
57	Vogue Coral Q 72279	That'll Be The Day/I'm Lookin' For Someone To Love	20
57	Coral Q 72298	Oh Boy!/Not Fade Away	15
58	Coral Q 72279	That'll Be The Day/I'm Lookin' For Someone To Love	20
58	Coral Q 72307	Maybe Baby/Tell Me How	20
58	Coral Q 72329	Think It Over/Fool's Paradise	25
58	Coral Q 72343	It's So Easy/Lonesome Tears	25

SINGLES
57	Vogue Coral Q 72279	That'll Be The Day/I'm Lookin' For Someone To Love	25
57	Coral Q 72298	Oh Boy!/Not Fade Away	20
58	Coral Q 72279	That'll Be The Day/I'm Lookin' For Someone To Love (2nd issue)	20
58	Coral Q 72307	Maybe Baby/Tell Me How	20
58	Coral Q 72329	Think It Over/Fool's Paradise	20
58	Coral Q 72343	It's So Easy/Lonesome Tears	20

(Originally issued with triangular centres; later round centre copies are worth around half these values.)
| 68 | Decca AD 1012 | Oh, Boy/That'll Be The Day (export issue) | 75 |

EPs

58	Coral FEP 2003	THE SOUND OF THE CRICKETS (triangular or round centre)	30
59	Coral FEP 2014	IT'S SO EASY (triangular or round centre)	30
60	Coral FEP 2060	FOUR MORE BY THE CRICKETS	30
60	Coral FEP 2062	THAT'LL BE THE DAY	30

ALBUMS

73	Philips 6308 149	BUBBLEGUM, BOP, BALLADS & BOOGIES (LP)	15
58	Vogue Coral LVA 9081	THE CHIRPING CRICKETS (Vogue-Coral labels & Coral sleeve)	150
58	Coral LVA 9081	THE CHIRPING CRICKETS (re-pressing with Coral labels & sleeve)	100

(see also Buddy Holly)

CRICKETS

78s

59	Coral Q 72365	Love's Made A Fool Of You/Someone, Someone	40
59	Coral Q 72382	When You Ask About Love/Deborah	60

SINGLES

59	Coral Q 72365	Love's Made A Fool Of You/Someone, Someone	15
59	Coral Q 72382	When You Ask About Love/Deborah	15
60	Coral Q 72395	More Than I Can Say/Baby My Heart	15
61	Coral Q 72417	Peggy Sue Got Married/Don'tcha Know	15
61	Coral Q 72440	I Fought The Law/A Sweet Love	15
61	London HLG 9486	He's Old Enough To Know Better/I'm Feeling Better	15
62	Liberty LIB 55441	Don't Ever Change/I Am Not A Bad Guy	5
62	Liberty LIB 55495	Little Hollywood Girl/Parisian Girl	6
63	Liberty LIB 10067	My Little Girl/Teardrops Fall Like Rain	5
63	Liberty LIB 10092	Don't Try To Change Me/Lost And Alone	5
63	Liberty LIB 10113	Right Or Wrong/You Can't Be In Between	5
64	Liberty LIB 10145	Lonely Avenue/Playboy	5
64	Liberty LIB 55696	(They Call Her) La Bamba/All Over You	5
64	Liberty LIB 10174	I Think I've Caught The Blues/We Gotta Get Together	6
66	Liberty LIB 55603	April Avenue/Don't Say You Love Me	5
68	Liberty LBF 15089	My Little Girl/Lonely Avenue	5
72	United Artists UP 35457	Don't Ever Change/Playboy	5
73	Philips 6006 269	My Rockin' Days/Lovesick Blues	5
73	Philips 6006 294	Hayride/Wasn't It Nice In New York City (in p/s)	10
73	Philips 6006 294	Hayride/Wasn't It Nice In New York City	5
74	Mercury 6008 006	Ooh Las Vegas/Rhyme And Time	5
79	Rollercoaster RRC 2001	Cruise In It/Rock Around With Ollie Vee (1st 2,000 with 'single photo' p/s)	5
79	Rollercoaster RRC 2001	Cruise In It/Rock Around With Ollie Vee (p/s)	5
87	Rollercoaster RRC 2007	Forever In Mind/The Weekend/Your M-M-Memory/Three-Piece (tri-centre in overprinted p/s)	5
88	MPL/CBS TSH 1	T-Shirt/Hollywould (p/s)	5

EPs

60	Coral FEP 2053	THE CRICKETS (initial trangular centre)	40
60	Coral FEP 2053	THE CRICKETS (later round centre)	20
61	Coral FEP 2064	THE CRICKETS DON'T EVER CHANGE	20
63	Liberty (S)LEP 2094	STRAIGHT NO STRINGS (mono/stereo)	20
64	Liberty LEP 2173	COME ON	20

ALBUMS

61	Coral LVA 9142	IN STYLE WITH THE CRICKETS	30
62	Liberty LBY 1120	SOMETHING OLD, SOMETHING NEW, SOMETHING BLUE, SOMETHING ELSE! (mono)	20
62	Liberty (S)LBY 1120	SOMETHING OLD, SOMETHING NEW, SOMETHING BLUE, SOMETHING ELSE! (stereo)	25
65	Liberty LBY 1258	THE CRICKETS - A COLLECTION	20
71	CBS 64301	ROCKIN' 50's ROCK 'N' ROLL (LP)	15

(see also Buddy Holly, Jerry Allison & Crickets, Ivan, Sonny Curtis, Earl Sinks, Sinx Mitchell, David Box)

CRICKETS & BOBBY VEE

63	Liberty LEP 2084	JUST FOR FUN (EP)	15
63	Liberty LEP 2116	BOBBY VEE MEETS THE CRICKETS (EP, mono)	10
63	Liberty (S)LEP 2116	BOBBY VEE MEETS THE CRICKETS (EP, stereo)	10
63	Liberty LEP 2149	BOBBY VEE MEETS THE CRICKETS VOL. 2 (EP)	10
62	Liberty LBY 1086	BOBBY VEE MEETS THE CRICKETS (LP, mono)	12
62	Liberty (S)LBY 1086	BOBBY VEE MEETS THE CRICKETS (LP, stereo)	12

(see also Bobby Vee)

JIMMY CRIKIT

70	MCA MK 5047	Isabella/Love Is A See Saw	8

CRIME

80	Punk Products PP 1	Johnny Come Home/Generation Gap (p/s, beware of bootlegs)	100

CRIME (U.S.)

90	Solar Lodge DOOMED 2	SAN FRANCISCO'S DOOMED (LP)	15

THE CRIMEWATCH PROJECT

92	Strategic Dance Initiative SDI 004	Boomzabang/Kis My Neck/Friday Night Style (white label 12", stickered paper sleeve)	80

CRIMINAL CLASS

82	Inferno HELL 7	Fighting The System/Soldier (p/s)	15

CRIMINAL JUSTICE

85	Endangered Music EDR 2	HIERARCHY OF HELL (EP)	12

THE CRIMINAL MINDS

90	TCM SRT90L2748	GUILTY AS CHARGED (EP)	150
91	TCM EP002	TALES FROM THE WASTELAND (EP)	120

CRIMSON BRIDGE

72	Myrrh Ms 6224	FILL YOUR HEAD WITH (LP)	25

GEOFF CRIPPS & LOUISA RUGG

85	Steam Pie SPR 1003S	ICARUS (LP)	12

CRISIS (1)
79	Peckham Action NOTH 1	No Town Hall (Southwark)/Holocaust/P.C. One Nine Eight Four (p/s)	20
79	Ardkor CRI 002	UK '79/White Youth (p/s)	15
80	Ardkor CRI 003	HYMNS OF FAITH (12" EP)	20
81	Ardkor CRI 004	Alienation/Brückwood/Hospital (p/s, with insert)	18
82	Crisis NOTH 1/CRI 002	HOLOCAUST UK (12" EP)	15

(see also Death In June, Current 93, Theatre Of Hate)

CRISIS (2)
70s	private pressing	ANOTHER FINE MESS (LP)	35

CRISP
73	EMI 2050	Sally And Jake/Dimbledale (A Land Not Far Away)	5

MARILYN CRISPELL
83	Leo LR 118	RHYTHMS HUNG IN UNDRAWN SKY (LP)	15
85	Leo LR 126	AND YOUR IVORY VOICE SINGS (LP)	15

CRISPY AMBULANCE
79	Aural Assault AAR 001	From The Cradle To The Grave/4 Minutes From The Frontline (glossy p/s)	15
79	Aural Assault AAR 001	From The Cradle To The Grave/4 Minutes From The Frontline (matt p/s)	8
81	Factory FAC 32	Unsightly And Serene: Not What I Expected/Deaf (10", p/s)	12
89	Temps Moderne LTMV:X	FIN (LP)	12

(see also Ram Ram Kino)

GARY CRISS
62	Stateside SS 104	Our Favourite Melodies/Welcome Home To My Heart	15
62	Stateside SS 123	My Little Heavenly Angel/The Girl That I Told You About	8
63	Stateside SS 164	Long Lonely Nights/I Still Miss You So	8
63	Stateside SS 265	Sweet, Warm And Soft/Little Joe	8
65	Stateside SS 427	Hands Off Buddy/If This Is Goodbye	5

PETER CRISS
79	Casablanca CAN 139	You Matter To Me/Hooked On Rock And Roll (p/s, green vinyl with mask)	20
79	Casablanca CAN 139	You Matter To Me/Hooked On Rock And Roll (p/s, black vinyl)	8
80	Mercury 6302 065	OUT OF CONTROL (LP)	12

(see also Kiss)

LINDA CRISTAL
59	Coral Q 72350	Strictly For Pleasure (A Perfect Romance)/It's Better In Spanish	5

CRISTINA
80	Ze 12WIP 6560	Is That All There Is/Jungle Love	15

BOBBY CRISTO & REBELS
64	Decca F 11913	The Other Side Of The Track/I've Got You Out Of My Mind	45

MARY CRISTY
76	Polydor 2056 513	Thank You For Rushing Into My Life/We Can't Hide This Time	10

CRITICS
81	Moody Music 80C1	Town Girl/Without You/Plastic Valentine (foldout p/s)	15

CRITICS & NYAH SHUFFLE
70	Joe JRS 1	Behold/SEXY FRANKIE: Tea, Patty, Sex And Ganja	25

CRITICS GROUP
66	Argo ZDA 46	A MERRY PROGRESS TO LONDON (LP, with insert)	25
68	Argo ZDA 82	THE FEMALE FROLIC (LP, with insert)	20
68	Argo DA 86	WATERLOO PETERLOO (LP, yellow label with insert)	20
71	Argo ZDA 138	YE MARINERS ALL (LP)	15

CRITTERS
66	London HLR 10047	Younger Girl/Gone For Awhile	15
66	London HLR 10071	Mr. Dieingly Sad/It Just Won't Be That Way	15
66	London HLR 10101	Bad Misunderstanding/Forever Or No More	15
67	London HLR 10119	Marryin' Kind Of Love/New York Bound	25
67	London HLR 10149	Don't Let The Rain Fall Down On Me/Walk Like A Man Again	15
67	London HA-R 8302	THE CRITTERS (LP)	45

JIM CROCE
72	Vertigo 6073 251	Operator/Rapid Roy	6
72	Vertigo 6360 700	YOU DON'T MESS AROUND WITH JIM (LP, gatefold sleeve, swirl label)	40
74	Vertigo 6360 702	I GOT A NAME (LP)	12
73	Vertigo 6360 701	LIFE & TIMES (LP, with spiral label)	200
70s	Life Song 135004	LIFE & TIMES (LP)	15
70s	Life Song 135004	GREATEST CHARATOR (LP)	15

CROCHETED DOUGHNUT RING
67	Polydor 56204	Two Little Ladies (Azalea And Rhododendron)/Nice	30
67	Deram DM 169	Havana Anna/Happy Castle	40
68	Deram DM 180	Maxine's Parlour/Get Out Your Rock And Roll Shoes	25

(see also Force Five, Doughnut Ring, Fingers, Daddy Lindberg)

BARRY CROCKER
71	Pye 7N 25567	Love Is A Beautiful Song/Sarah's Coming Home	6

TONY CROCKET
82	Alternative ALT 010	Queen Of Hearts/Plane Jane (12", p/s)	50

CROFT
71	Maple MP 1	The Dream/Henry And His Friends	200

CROFTERS
69	Say Disc SD 113	PILL FERRY (EP)	10
69	Saydisc SD 129	DRINK UP THEE CIDER (EP)	8
69	Beltona SBE 103	CROFTERS (LP)	15

NICOLE CROISILLE
77	Decca F13708	The Loving Song/Tell Me What I Want To Hear/Telephone Moi	6

TONY CROMBIE

54	Decca F 10424	Stop It All/All Of Me (& His Orchestra) 5
55	Decca F 10454	Perdido/Love You Madly (& His Orchestra) 5
55	Decca F 10547	Early One Morning/Flying Home (& His Orchestra) 5
55	Decca F 10592	Flying Hickory/String Of Pearls (& His Orchestra) 5
55	Decca F 10637	I Want You To Be My Baby (with Annie Ross)/Three Little Words 5
56	Columbia DB 3822	Teach You To Rock/Short'nin' Bread Rock (as Tony Crombie & Rockets).........................50
56	Columbia DB 3822	Teach You To Rock/Short'nin' Bread Rock (as Tony Crombie & Rockets) (78) 10
56	Columbia DB 3859	Sham Rock/Let's You And I Rock (as Tony Crombie & Rockets)....................................40
57	Columbia DB 3880	Rock, Rock, Rock/The Big Beat (as Tony Crombie & Rockets) (78) 20
57	Columbia DB 3881	Lonesome Train (On A Lonesome Track)/We're Gonna Rock Tonight (78, as Tony Crombie & Rockets)...20
57	Columbia DB 3921	London Rock/Brighton Rock (as Tony Crombie & Rockets)..30
57	Columbia DB 3921	London Rock/Brighton Rock (as Tony Crombie & Rockets) (78) 15
57	Columbia DB 4000	Sweet Beat/Sweet Georgia Brown (as Tony Crombie & His Sweet Beat) 10
57	Columbia DB 4000	Sweet Beat/Sweet Georgia Brown (as Tony Crombie & His Sweet Beat)(78) 10
58	Columbia DB 4076	Dumplin's/Tw'on Special 10
58	Columbia DB 4076	Dumplin's/Tw'on Special (78) 10
58	Columbia DB 4145	Unguaua/Piakukaungchung (as Tony Crombie Men) 5
58	Columbia DB 4189	Rock-Cha-Cha/The Gigglin' Gurgleburp (as Tony Crombie Men)..................................5
58	Columbia DB 4189	Rock-Cha-Cha/The Gigglin' Gurgleburp (as Tony Crombie Men) (78) 10
59	Columbia DB 4253	Champagne Cha Cha/Shepherd's Cha Cha (as Tony Crombie Men) 5
59	Top Rank JAR 182	Man From Interpol Theme/Interpol Cha Cha Cha & Chase (as Tony Crombie Orchestra)......10
59	Top Rank JAR 182	Man From Interpol Theme/Interpol Cha Cha Cha & Chase (as Tony Crombie Orchestra) (78)..10
62	Ember JBS 706	Gutbucket/Just Like Old Times 7
56	Decca DFE 6247	PRESENTING TONY CROMBIE NO. 1 (EP) 10
56	Decca DFE 6281	PRESENTING TONY CROMBIE NO. 2 (EP) 10
57	Columbia SEG 7676	ROCK ROCK ROCK (EP) 80
57	Columbia SEG 7686	LET'S YOU AND I ROCK (EP) 80
61	Decca DFE 6670	FOUR FAVOURITE FILM THEMES (EP) 10
59	Columbia SEG 7882	SWINGIN' DANCE BEAT NO. 1 (EP) 10
59	Columbia SEG 7896	SWINGIN' DANCE BEAT NO. 2 (EP) 10
59	Columbia SEG 7918	ATMOSPHERE (EP, as Tony Crombie & His Men) 10
56	Columbia 33S 1117	TONY CROMBIE & HIS SWEETBEAT (10" LP) 40
57	Columbia 33S 1108	ROCKIN' WITH TONY CROMBIE & ROCKETS (10" LP) 150
58	Columbia SCX 3262	ATMOSPHERE (LP)...50
59	Top Rank 35/043	MAN FROM INTERPOL (LP, TV series music, by Tony Crombie & Band) 20
61	Tempo TAP 30	JAZZ INC. (LP) 150
60	Top Rank BUY 027	DRUMS! DRUMS! DRUMS! (LP, as Tony Crombie & His Band) 30
61	Decca SKL 4114	SWEET WIDE AND BLUE (LP) 30
61	Decca LK 4385	TWELVE FAVOURITE FILM THEMES (LP, also stereo SKL 4127) 15
61	Ember EMB 3336	WHOLE LOTTA TONY (LP) 40

(see also Annie Ross, Ray Ellington, London Jazz Quartet)

BILL CROMPTON

58	Fontana H 152	A Hoot An' A Holler/The Popocatepetl Beetle 10
59	Fontana H 178	Out Of Sight, Out Of Mind/My Lover 10

CROMWELL

75	Cromwell WELL 006	First Day 20
75	Cromwell WELL 005	AT THE GALLOP (LP, private pressing) 120

(see also Establishment)

LINK CROMWELL (LENNY KAYE)

66	London HLB 10040	Crazy Like A Fox/Shock Me 25

(see also Patti Smith Group)

ANDREW CRONSHAW

77	Trailer LREP 1	CLOUD VALLEY (EP) 10
74	Xtra XTRA 1139	A IS FOR ANDREW, Z IS FOR ZITHER (LP) 15
77	Trailer LER 2104	EARTHED IN CLOUD VALLEY (LP)..15

CROOKED OAK

76	Folkland FL 0102	FROM LITTLE ACORNS GROW (LP, 500 only) 60
79	Eron ERON 019	THE FOOT O'WOR STAIRS (LP) 25

CROOKS

79	Blue Print BLU 2002	Modern Boys/The Beat Goes On (die-cut p/s) 6
80	Blue Print BLU 2006	All The Time In The World/Bangin' My Head (p/s) 10
80	Blue Print BLUP 5002	JUST RELEASED (LP)..12

DAVID CROOKS

70	Jackpot JP 759	I Won't Hold It Against You (actually by Dave Barker)/ BOBBY JAMES: King Of Hearts 7

(see also Dave Barker)

STEVE CROPPER

70	Stax STAX 147	Funky Broadway/Crop Dustin'...10
69	Stax SXATS 1008	WITH A LITTLE HELP FROM MY FRIENDS (LP)...............................30

STEVE CROPPER & ALBERT KING

69	Stax SXATS 1020	JAMMED TOGETHER (LP, with Pops Staples)..............................20

(see also Booker T. & M.G.'s, Albert King)

BING CROSBY

54	Brunswick 03384	White Christmas/Let's Start The New Year Right 8
54	Brunswick 05224	What A Little Moonlight Can Do/Down By The Riverside (with Gary Crosby)...............5

(see also Gary Crosby, Louis Armstrong, Bob Hope, Fred Astaire, Peggy Lee)

BOB CROSBY & HIS BOBCATS

59	London HLD 8828	Petite Fleur/Such A Long Night 5

(see also Modernaires)

DAVID CROSBY

71	Atlantic 2401 005	IF I COULD ONLY REMEMBER MY NAME (LP, gatefold sleeve, red/plum label) 30

(see also Byrds, Crosby [Stills] Nash [& Young])

MINT VALUE £

GARY CROSBY

58	HMV POP 550	Judy, Judy/Cheatin' On Me	60
58	HMV POP 550	Judy, Judy/Cheatin' On Me (78)	10
59	HMV POP 648	The Happy Bachelor/This Little Girl Of Mine	5
57	Vogue VA 160118	GARY CROSBY (LP)	15

(see also Bing Crosby, Louis Armstrong)

CROSBY & NASH

| 72 | Atlantic K 10192 | Southbound Train/Whole Cloth | 7 |
| 72 | Atlantic K 50011 | GRAHAM NASH & DAVID CROSBY (LP, foldout sleeve) | 20 |

PHIL CROSBY

| 63 | Reprise R 20220 | Where The Blue Of The Night (Meets The Gold Of The Day)/Little By Little | 8 |

CROSBY, STILLS & NASH

69	Atlantic 584 283	Marrakesh Express/Helplessly Hoping	10
69	Atlantic 584 304	Suite: Judy Blue Eyes/Long Time Gone	10
69	Atlantic 588 189	CROSBY, STILLS & NASH (LP, gatefold sleeve, with lyric sheet)	22

CROSBY, STILLS, NASH & YOUNG

70	Atlantic 2091 002	Teach Your Children/Country Girl	7
70	Atlantic 2091 010	Woodstock/Helpless	8
70	Atlantic 2091 023	Ohio/Find The Cost Of Freedom	7
70	Atlantic 2091 039	Our House/Deja Vu	10
88	Atlantic A 9003TX	American Dream/Compass/Soldiers Of Peace/Ohio (12", p/s)	8
70	Atlantic 2401 001	DÉJA VU (LP, gatefold sleeve, pasted-on photo on front, plum/red label)	25
71	Atlantic 2657 004	FOUR WAY STREET (2-LP, gatefold sleeve with lyric sheet)	25

(see also David Crosby, Stephen Stills [Manassas], Graham Nash, Neil Young)

CROSS

87	Virgin VST 1007	Cowboys And Indians (Full Length Version 5.53)/Love Lies Bleeding (She's A Wicked Wily Waitress) (12", p/s)	10
87	Virgin CDEP 10	Cowboys And Indians (4.20)/Cowboys And Indians (Full Length Version 6.12)/ Love Lies Bleeding (She's A Wicked Wily Waitress) (CD, promo only)	35
88	Virgin VST 1026	Shove It! (Extended Mix)/Shove It! (Metropolix)/Rough Justice (12", p/s)	8
88	Virgin VST 1062	Heaven For Everyone/Love On A Tightrope (Like An Animal)/Contact (12", p/s)	8
88	Virgin VS 1100	Manipulator/Stand Up For Love (p/s)	5
88	Virgin VST 1100	Manipulator (Extended)/Stand Up For Love/Manipulator (7" Version) (12", p/s)	8
80	Parlophone 6251	Power To Love/Passion For Trash (p/s)	5
90	Parlophone 12R 6251	Power To Love (Extended Version)/Passion For Trash/ Power To Love (7" Version) (12", p/s)	10
90	Parlophone PCS 7342	MAD, BAD AND DANGEROUS TO KNOW (LP)	15
90	Parlophone CDPCS 7342	MAD, BAD AND DANGEROUS TO KNOW (CD)	40

(see also Roger Taylor, Queen)

JIMMIE CROSS

66	Red Bird RB 10042	Super Duper Man/Hey Little Girl	30
71	Decca F 13224	Can You Believe It?/Blind Willie Johnson	7
72	Decca F 13316	Peace In The End/Prophets Guiders	7

(see also T2)

CROSS & ROSS

| 72 | Decca EPS 1 | CROSS & ROSS (EP) | 75 |
| 72 | Decca SKL 5129 | BORED CIVILIANS (LP, blue/silver labels) | 300 |

CROSSBEATS

65	Pilgrim PSR 7002	I Know/He Waits (p/s)	5
67	Pilgrim PSR 7003	Step Aside/Forgive Me (p/s or art sleeve)	8
60s	Pilgrim PSR 7004	Busy Man/Change (p/s)	6
60s	Pilgrim KLP 12	CRAZY MIXED UP GENERATION (LP)	20

CROSS COUNTRY

| 72 | Atlantic K 10353 | In The Midnight Hour/A Smile Song | 6 |

(see also Tokens)

ANDRAE CROUCH (& DISCIPLES)

70s	Light LS 7014	JUST ANDRAE (LP)	30
70s	Light LS 7018	DISCIPLES LIVE AT CARNEGIE HALL (LP)	30
70s	Light LS 7019	KEEP ON SINGING (LP)	30
70s	Light LS 7025	TAKE ME BACK (LP)	30
70s	Myrrh MYR 1188	NO TIME TO LOSE (LP)	30
70s	Light LS 7052	I'LL BE THINKING OF YOU (LP)	25
78	Light LSD 7048	LIVE IN LONDON (LP)	20
70s	Light LSD 7034	BEST OF (2xLP)	40

CROW

70	Stateside SS 2159	Evil Woman, Don't Play Your Games With Me/Gonna Leave A Mark	6
70	Stateside SS 2171	Slow Down/Cottage Cheese	10
70	Stateside SS 2180	Don't Try To Lay No Boogie Woogie On The King Of Rock And Roll/Satisfied	6
75	Right On R101	Your Autumn Of Tomorrow/Uncle Funk	15
70	Stateside SSL 10301	CROW MUSIC (LP)	18
70	Stateside SSL 10310	CROW BY CROW (LP)	15

SHERYL CROW

93	A&M 580 380-7	Run, Baby, Run/All By Myself (p/s)	5
93	A&M 580 381-2	Run, Baby, Run/All By Myself/The Na-Na Song/Reach Around Jerk (CD)	10
94	A&M 580 462-7	What Can I Do For You (Radio Edit)/Volvo Cowgirl 99 (p/s)	5
94	A&M 580 568-7	Run, Baby, Run/Leaving Las Vegas (Acoustic Version) (p/s)	5
94	A&M 580 569-2	Run, Baby, Run/Leaving Las Vegas (Acoustic Version)/ All By Myself/Reach Around Jerk (CD)	10
94	A&M 581 147-2	Run, Baby, Run/Can't Cry Anymore/Reach Around Jerk/I Shall Believe (CD, 'The Nashville Sessions', box set with poster & numbered 'obi')	15
94	A&M 580 644-7	Leaving Las Vegas/Leaving Las Vegas (Live In Nashville) (p/s, with postcard)	5
96	A&M 581 902-7	If It Makes You Happy (Edit)/All I Wanna Do (jukebox issue, no p/s)	6
96	A&M 580 918-7	Strong Enough/No One Said It Would Be Easy (p/s)	5
95	A&M 540 368-2/	TUESDAY NIGHT MUSIC CLUB (CD, 2nd issue, with patchwork/montage cover and bonus 6-track CD "Sheryl Crow Live" [540 367-2])	25

CROWBAR
84	Skinhead SKIN 1	Hippie Punks/White Riot (p/s)	45

CROWD
79	SRT SRTS/79/CUS 377	Ronnie (Is A Headbanger)/A Little Of What I Fancy/Let's Fly Together (p/s)	6

CROWDED HOUSE
87	Capitol CDCL 416	World Where You Live (Extended Version)/Something So Strong/ Don't Dream It's Over/That's What I Call Love (CD, card sleeve)	10
88	Capitol CDCL 498	Better Be Home Soon/Kill Eye/Don't Dream It's Over (live)/ Better Be Home Soon (CD)	15
88	Capitol CDCL 509	Sister Madly/Mansion In The Slums/Something So Strong (live) (CD)	18
91	Capotol CDCD (S) 661	It's Only Natural/It's Only Natural (Live)/Hole In The River (live)/The Burgular's Song (Medley)/It's Only Natural/Sister Madly (live)/There Goes God (live)/Chocolate Cake (live) (2xCD single, gatefold wallet sleeve)	12
92	Capitol CDCL 655	Four Seasons In One Day (LP)/Dr. Livingstone/Recurring Dream/ Anyone Can Tell (CD, in collector's box)	10
92	Capitol CH 1/2	LIVE AT THE TOWN AND COUNTRY CLUB, LONDON, NOVEMBER 9 1991 (2-CD, in PVC gatefold wallet & inserts, promo only, autographed)	60
92	Capitol CH 1/2	LIVE AT THE TOWN AND COUNTRY CLUB, LONDON, NOVEMBER 9 1991 (2-CD, in PVC gatefold wallet & inserts, promo only)	40

(see also Split Enz, Tim Finn)

CROWFOOT
70	Paramount PARA 3008	California Rock 'N' Roll/Maybe I Can Learn To Live	5
70	Paramount SPFL 265	CROWFOOT (LP)	12

DON CROWN & HIS BUSKING BUDGIES
70	Orange OA 5507	Budgerigar Man/Piper Call A Tune	15
71	President PT 340	Mrs Wilson's Budgie/Flying Machines	10

JUDITH CROWNE
73	Dart ART 2034	Steamhammer/I Will Need Your Love	10

CROWNS
68	Pama PM 725	I Know, It's Alright/I Surrender	25
68	Pama PM 736	Jerking The Dog/Keep Me Going	30
68	Pama PM 745	She Ain't Gonna Do Right/I Need Your Loving	25
68	Pama PM 759	Since You Been Gone/Call Me	25
68	Pama PMLP 6	MADE OF GOLD (LP)	45

CROWS
54	Columbia SCM 5119	Gee/I Love You So	2000
54	Columbia DB 3478)	Gee/I Love You So (78)	150

TREVOR CROZIER'S BROKEN CONSORT
72	Argo AFB 60	PARCEL OF OLD CRAMS (LP)	35

CRUCIFIX
83	Corpus Christi CHRIST ITS 11	DEHUMANISATION (LP)	18

CRUCIFIXION
80	Miramar MIR 4	The Fox/Death Sentence (no p/s)	80
82	Neat NEAT 19	Take It Or Leave It/On The Run (p/s)	10
84	Neat NEAT 37	Green Eyes/Moon Rising/Jailbait (p/s)	10
84	Neat NEAT 3712	Green Eyes/Jailbait/Moon Rising (12", p/s, purple or green vinyl)	20
84	Neat NEAT 3712	Green Eyes/Jailbait/Moon Rising (12", p/s)	8

ARTHUR 'BIG BOY' CRUDUP
64	RCA RCA 1401	My Baby Left Me/I Don't Know It	40
64	RCA RCX 7161	RHYTHM AND BLUES VOL. 4 (EP)	25
69	Blue Horizon 7-63855	MEAN OLE FRISCO (LP)	80
70	Delmark DS 614	LOOK ON YONDERS WALL (LP)	25
71	Delmark DS 621	CRUDUP'S MOOD (LP)	25
72	RCA RD 8224	THE FATHER OF ROCK 'N' ROLL (LP)	30
74	United Artists UAS 29092	ROEBUCK MAN (LP)	35

CRUELLA DE VILLE
83	EMI 5412	Gypsy Girl/Blue Blue Blues (p/s)	5
83	EMI 12 EMI 5412	Gypsy Girl/Blue Blue Blues/Gyspy Girl (Edit) (12")	10
84	EMI CDLP 1984	I'll Do The Talking/Hollywood Hong Kong Swing/Oceans (p/s)	5

CRUISERS (1)
65	Decca F 12098	It Ain't Me Babe/Baby What You Want Me To Do	30

(see also Dave Berry, Godley & Creme)

CRUISERS (2)
73	EMI 2202	Schoolgirls/College Collage	6

SIMON CRUM
58	Capitol CL 14965	Stand Up, Sit Down, Shut Your Mouth/Country Music Is Here To Stay	20
59	Capitol CL 15077	I Fell Out Of Love With Love/Morgan Poisoned The Water Hole	10
61	Capitol CL 15183	Enormity In Motion/Cuzz Yore So Sweet	10

(see also Ferlin Husky)

RAY CRUMLEY
77	Magnet MAG 103	It's Uncanny/All The Way In Love With You	10

CRUNCH
72	Youngblood YB 1064	Let's Do It Again/Not Tonight Josephine	7

CRUSADERS
71	Rare Earth SRE 3001	OLD SOCKS NEW SHOES (LP)	15
72	Blue Thumb ILPS 9218	CRUSADERS (2-LP)	15
73	Mowest MWS 7004	HOLLYWOOD (LP)	20
75	ABC ABCD 607	SOUTHERN COMFORT (2-LP)	15

(see also Jazz Crusaders)

BETTYE CRUTCHER
74	Stax STX 1035	LONG AS YOU LOVE ME (LP)	18

CRUX/CRASH
82	No Future OI 18	KEEP ON RUNNING (12" EP)	12

CRY (1)
80	Sayonara S-3221083	Looking To The Future/Alone (p/s)	30

CRY (2)
87	Crazy Flowerpot CFP 001	Party After Dark (with p/s)	80
87	Crazy Flowerpot CFP 001	Party After Dark	15
87	Crazy Flowerpot CFP 002	Give Her An Ice Cream (no p/s)	20

CRYER
80	Happy Face MM 124	The Single/Hesitate (p/s, with 2 inserts)	65

BARRY CRYER
58	Fontana H 139	The Purple People Eater/Hey! Eula	8
58	Fontana H 151	Nothin' Shakin'/Seven Daughters	8
59	Fontana H 177	Angelina/Kissin'	8

CRYIN' SHAMES
66	Decca F 12340	Please Stay/What's News Pussycat	20
66	Decca F 12425	Nobody Waved Goodbye/You	30

(see also Paul & Ritchie & Cryin' Shames, Gary Walker & Rain)

CRYING SHAMES
80	Logo GO 385	That's Rock'n'Roll/Too Late (p/s)	12

CRY OF THE INNOCENT
82	Pagan CUS 1436	THe Haunting/Still Forever (p/s)	20

CRYSBAS
79	Sain	Draenog Marw/Y Nhw (p/s)	25
79	Sain 72E	Mae'di Bwrw/Blws Ty Golchi//Mor Gryg wr Morgrug/Amser (p/s)	25

CRYSTAL CASTLES
07	Merok ME 002	Alice Practice/Air War/Love And Caring (p/s)	40
07	Trouble TROUBLE 1	XxzxcuZx Me/HEALTH: Crimewave (200 only, green vinyl white label promo)	30
07	Trouble TROUBLE 1	XxzxcuZx Me/HEALTH: Crimewave (500 only, gig freebie, die-cut stamped sleeve)	12
07	Trouble TROUBLE 001	XxzxcuZx Me/HEALTH: Crimewave (1000 only, p/s)	8
07	Trouble DUDE 003	Air War/Air War (David Wolf Remix) (7" p/s)	7
07	Rough Trade	Pre Untrust/S&MSMS (demo)/Fuck Nicole/And Prolapse (7" given away as 'ticket' to Rough Trade In-Store appearance, 500 only)	20
08	Play It Again Sam PIAS 451 1092 140 DIFB 1092	Courtship Dating/Trash Hologram (Demo) (p/s)	7
10	Polydor/Fiction LC06444/ 2735606	Doe Deer/Mother Knows Best/Insectica/Seed (12" EP, 500 only, p/s)	30
08	Different DIFB 1200PLP	CRYSTAL CASTLES (2-LP)	20

CRYSTAL MANSION
70	Polydor 2058-070	Carolina in My Mind/If I Live	6

CRYSTALITES
69	Big Shot BI 510	Biafra/Drop Pan	40
69	Nu Beat NB 036	Splash Down/Finders Keepers	100
69	Songbird SB 1015	Musical Madness Parts 1 & 2	12
69	Songbird SB 1016	The Bad Parts 1 & 2	12
69	Explosion EX 2002	Doctor Who (Parts 1 & 2)	12
69	Explosion EX 2003	Barefoot Brigade/Slippery	12
69	Explosion EX 2005	Bombshell/Bag-A-Wire (B-side actually by Bobby Ellis & Crystalites)	12
69	Explosion EX 2006	A Fistful Of Dollars/The Emperor (B-side actually by Bobby Ellis & Crystalites)	45
70	Explosion EX 2010	The Bad/The Bad Version	12
70	Bullet BU 424	A Fistful Of Dollars/BOBBY ELLIS: Crystal	12
70	Songbird SB 1017	The Undertaker/Stop That Man (B-side actually "Easy Ride" by Ike Bennett & Crystalites)	15
70	Songbird SB 1020	Lady Madonna/Ghost Rider	12
70	Songbird SB 1024	Isies/Isies (Version 2)	12
70	Songbird SB 1025	Stranger In Town/Stranger In Town (Version 2)	12
70	Songbird SB 1030	Sic Him Rover/Drop Pon	25
70	Songbird SB 1035	Overtaker (Version I)/Overtaker (Version II)	10
70	Songbird SB 1035	Undertaker's Burial/Ghost Rider	12
70	Songbird SB 1036	Short Story/No Baptism (Version 2)	45
71	Songbird SB 1057	Earthly Sounds/Version	12
73	Grape GR 3050	Blacula/Version	25

(see also Chosen Few, Scotty, Ramon & Crystalites, Kingstonians, Bongo Herman, Denzil Laing, Derrick Harriot, Ethiopians, Dennis Brown, Glen Brown, Big Youth)

CRYSTALS
62	Parlophone R 4867	There's No Other Like My Baby/Oh Yeah Maybe Baby	150
62	London HLU 9611	He's A Rebel/I Love You Eddie	15
63	London HLU 9661	He's Sure The Boy I Love/Walking Along (La-La-La)	15
63	London HLU 9732	Da Doo Ron Ron/Git It	10
63	London HLU 9773	Then He Kissed Me/Brother Julius	10
64	London HLU 9837	Little Boy/Uptown (withdrawn)	150
64	London HLU 9852	I Wonder/Little Boy	50
64	London HLU 9909	All Grown Up/PHIL SPECTOR GROUP: Irving (Jaggered Sixteenths)	15
65	United Artists UP 1110	My Place/You Can't Tie A Girl Down	50
69	London HLU 10239	Da Doo Ron Ron/He's A Rebel	5
74	Warners/Spector K 19010	Da Doo Ron Ron/Then Kissed Me (blue vinyl)	6
76	Phil Spector Intl. 2010 020	All Grown Up/The Twist	7
63	London RE-U 1381	DA DOO RON RON (EP)	75
63	London HA-U 8120	HE'S A REBEL (LP)	125
76	Phil Spector 2307006	SING THEIR GREATEST HITS (LP)	15

(see also Darlene Love, Bob B. Soxx & Blue Jeans, Phil Spector)

CRYTUFF & THE ORIGINALS
79	Hit Run APLP 9006	DUB TO AFRICA (LP) (Pre-release)	45

C.S.A.
96	Squariel Records SQ003	Don't/'Till I Waltz Again With You (p/s)	6

CSA
78	Goat GOAT 001	STOCKADE (LP)	40

JOE CUBA SEXTET
66	Pye International 7N 25401	Bang! Bang!/Push, Push, Push	35

CUBAN HEELS
78	Housewives' Choice JY 1/2	Downtown/Do The Smoke Walk (p/s)	30

CUBY & BLIZZARDS
68	Philips BF 1638	Distant Smile/Don't Know Which Way To Go	15
68	Philips BF 1719	Windows Of My Eyes/Checkin' Up On My Baby	10
69	Philips BF 1827	Apple Knocker's Flophouse/Go Down Sunshine	25
69	Philips (S)BL 7874	DESOLATION (LP, black/silver labels)	80
69	Philips SBL 7918	APPLE KNOCKERS FLOPHOUSE (LP)	45

'CUDDLY' DUDLEY (HESLOP)
59	HMV POP 586	Lots More Love/Later	20
59	HMV POP 586	Lots More Love/Later (78)	10
60	HMV POP 725	Too Pooped To Pop/Miss In-Between	25
61	Ember EMB S 136	Sitting On A Train/One Thing I Like	10
62	Piccadilly 7N 35090	Monkey Party/The Ferryboat Ride (as Cudley Dudley)	6
64	Oriole International ICB 9	Blarney Blues/Peace On Earth	6
64	Oriole International ICB 10	Way Of Life/When Will You Say You'll Be Mine	15

CUDDLY TOYS
80	Fresh FRESH 010	Madman/Join The Girls (p/s)	12
81	Parole PURLE 9	Astral Joe/Slowdown (p/s)	12
81	Fresh FRESH 10	Mothman/Jo In The Girls (p/s, with 5 stickers)	12
81	Fresh FRESH 20	Astral Joe/Slowdown (p/s, reissue)	12
81	Fresh FRESH 25	Someone's Crying/Bring On The Ravers (p/s)	8

(see also Raped)

CUES
56	Capitol CL 14501	Burn That Candle/O My Darlin'	250
56	Capitol CL 14501	Burn That Candle/O My Darlin' (78)	20
56	Capitol CL 14651	Crackerjack/The Girl I Love (featuring Jimmy Breedlove)	200
56	Capitol CL 14651	Crackerjack/The Girl I Love (featuring Jimmy Breedlove) (78)	20
57	Capitol CL 14682	Prince Or Pauper/Why	150
57	Capitol CL 14682	Prince Or Pauper/Why (78)	15

(see also Jimmy Breedlove)

CUFF-LINKS
69	MCA MU 1101	Tracy/Where Do You Go?	5
70	MCA MU 1112	when Julie Comes Around/Sally Ann (You're Such A Pretty Girl)	6
70	MCA MU 1128	Robin's World/Lay A Little Love On Me	6
70	MCA MUP(S) 398	TRACY (LP)	20

XAVIER CUGAT
63	Mercury AMT 1202	Watermelon Man/Swinging Shepherd Blues	10

CLIVE CULBERTSON
79	Rip Off RIP 9	Time To Kill/Busy Signal (initially came in brown paper bag sleeve)	75
85	Mint Chew 101	I Can't Fight It/You Don't Have A Dream	20

CHRIS CULLEN
82	Zim Zam Z1	Coincidence/I'll See You Later (p/s)	15

JAMIE CULLUM TRIO
99	Own label	HEARD IT ALL BEFORE (CD, private pressing, 700 only)	50

CULPEPPER'S ORCHARD
72	Polydor 2480 123	SECOND SIGHT (LP)	130

CULT
80s	Beggars Banquet 235H	Sun King/Edie (Ciao Baby)/She Sells Sanctuary (12", holographic plastic sleeve.)	12
84	B. Banquet BEGA 57P	DREAMTIME (LP, picture disc)	12
84	B. Banquet BEGA 57	DREAMTIME (white label test pressing, with unique version of "Go West")	30
80s	Beggars Banquet	ELECTRIC (LP, gatefold sleeve gold vinyl, 5,000 only)	25
91	Beggars Banquet CBOX 1	SINGLES COLLECTION (10-CD box set, picture discs with booklet)	30
93	Beggars Banquet BEGA 1230B	PURE CULT (4-LP box set)	35
94	Beggars Banquet BBQLP 164	THE CULT (2-LP)	40

(see also Death Cult, Southern Death Cult, Lonesome No More, Theatre Of Hate, Studio Sweethearts)

CULT FIGURES
79	Rather GEAR 4/RT 020	Zip Nolan (Highway Patrolman)/P.W.T. (Playing With Toys)/ Zip Dub (gatefold p/s)	8

(see also Swell Maps)

CULT HERO
79	Fiction FICS 006	I'm A Cult Hero/I Dig You (p/s, 2,000 only)	50

(see also Cure)

CULT MANIAX
82	Elephant Rock ROCK 001	Blitz/Lucy Looe (p/s)	6
82	Elephant Rock ROCK 002	American Drea/Elephant Rock	15
82	Next Wave NXT 2/BAK 1	Frenzie/The Russians Are Coming/Black Horse/Death March (p/s, withdrawn most have band-inflicted scratch through Black Horse)	45
84	Xcentric SIXTH 1	FULL OF SPUNK! (EP, fold-over p/s in polythene bag)	6
84	Xcentric EIGTH 1	THE AMAZING ADVENTURES OF JOHNNY THE DUCK AND THE BATH TIME BLUES (EP)	6
84	Xcentric Noise EIGHT 1T	THE AMAZING ADVENTURES OF JOHNNY THE DUCK AND THE BATH TIME BLUES (12", EP, lyric insert)	8
85	Xcentric Noise TENTH 1	WHERE DO WE ALL GO (12" EP)	8

CULTURE
77	Sky Note DD 003	The Cultures Trod On/THE REVOLUTIONARIES, CULTURE AND RANKING TREVOR: Trod On In Dub (A-side as "The Cultures") (12" white pasted sleeve)	25

MINT VALUE £

78	Lightning LIG 515	Jah Pretty Face/Natty Dread Taking Over	5
78	Sky Note SKY LP 016	IN DUB (LP)	45
78	Lightning LIP 1	TWO SEVENS CLASH (LP)	25
78	Virgin FL 1016	HARDER THAN THE REST (LP)	15

CULTURE CLUB

82	Virgin VSY 558	Time (Clock Of The Heart)/White Boys Can't Control It (picture disc)	5
84	Virgin VSY 694	The War Song/La Cancion De Guerra (picture disc, withdrawn)	65
86	Virgin VSY 861	God Thank You Woman/From Luxury To Heartache (picture disc)	8
82	Virgin VP 2232	KISSING TO BE CLEVER (LP, picture disc, with insert)	12
83	Virgin VP 2285	COLOUR BY NUMBERS (LP, picture disc)	12
84	Virgin VP 2330	WAKING UP WITH THE HOUSE ON FIRE (LP, picture disc, with insert)	12

(see also Boy George, Jesus Loves You, The Edge)

CULTURE PAUL

80s	Music House MH 2	Mini Van Man (12")	40

CULTURE SHOCK

87	Bluurg FISH 19	GO WILD (LP)	12

CULVER STREET PLAYGROUND

68	President PT 145	Alley Pond Park/A Decent Sort Of Guy	12

ANDREW CULVERWELL

71	Polydor 2343 035	WHERE IS THE LOVE? (LP)	15

CUMBERLAND THREE

60	Columbia DB 4460	Johnny Reb/Come Along Julie	5
64	Parlophone R 5113	The Cumberland Crew/Chilly Winds	5
61	Columbia 33SX 1302	FOLK SCENE, U.S.A. (LP, also stereo SCX 3364)	12
61	Columbia 33 SX 1325	CIVIL WAR ALABAMA VOL 2 (LP)	15
64	Parlophone PMC 1223	INTRODUCING (LP)	15

(see also John Stewart)

DAVID CUMMING

67	Philips BF 1545	Rubber Rabbit/The Parrots Of Simple Street	6

BARBARA CUMMINGS

67	London HLU 10110	She's The Woman/There's Something Funny Going On	7

JON CUNDO

72	Bamboo BAM 69	Love Is Strange/When We Were Children	8

(see also Joncuno)

DAVID CUNNINGHAM

80	Piano PIANO 001	GREY SCALE (LP)	35

EARL CUNNINGHAM

70s	One Top OSM 002	Got To Know That Place/Gates Are Wide Open (12")	100
80	Freedom Sounds FS 0017	Never Give Up/Follow Fashion (12")	25
84	Time TRLP 002	JOHN TOM (LP)	20

H. CUNNINGHAM

71	Tropical AL 004	Ethiopian Son/TROPICAL ALLSTARS: Version 2	5

RUPERT CUNNINGHAM

70	Duke DU 98	Funky/Sugar Cane	5

CUPIDS

58	Vogue V 9102	Now You Tell Me/Lillie Mae	900
58	Vogue V 9102	Now You Tell Me/Lillie Mae (78)	150

CUPID'S INSPIRATION

68	NEMS 56-3500	Yesterday Has Gone/Dream	15
68	NEMS 56-3702	My World/Everything Is Meant To Be	7
69	Bell BLL 1069	The Sad Thing/Look At Me	7
69	CBS 4509	Boat Trip/Time Only Knows	20
70	CBS 4722	Without Your Love/Different Guy	8
70	CBS 4994	Are You Growing Tired Of My Love/Sunshine	8
74	DJM DJS 300	Yesterday Has Gone/My World	6
69	NEMS 6-63553	YESTERDAY HAS GONE (LP, gatefold, as Cupid's Inspiration Featuring T. Rice-Milton)	20

(see also Gordon Haskell, Paper Blitz Tissue)

CUPOL

80	4AD BAD 9	Like This For Ages/Kluba Cupol (12", p/s, 45/33rpm)	12

(see also Wire)

CUPPA T

67	Deram DM 144	Miss Pinkerton/Brand New World	25
68	Deram DM 185	Streatham Hippodrome/One Man Band	20

(see also Overlanders)

CUPS

68	Polydor 56777	Good As Gold/Life And Times	40

(see also Gallagher & Lyle)

MIKE CURB CONGREGATION

70	Polydor 2058 075	Burning Bridges/Sweet Gingerbread Man	5

CURE

SINGLES

78	Small Wonder SMALL 11	Killing An Arab/10.15 Saturday Night (p/s, 15,000 only, beware of counterfeits)	25
79	Fiction FICS 001	Killing An Arab/10.15 Saturday Night (p/s, reissue)	20
79	Fiction FICS 002	Boys Don't Cry/Plastic Passion ('soldier' p/s, typed matrix, 'but Bill does' on A side runout and 'land of 1000 motorhomes' on B)	20
79	Fiction FICS 005	Jumping Someone Else's Train/I'm Cold (p/s, typed matrix)	25
80	Fiction FICS 010	A Forest/Another Journey By Train (p/s)	15
80	Fiction FICS 10	A Forest/Another Journey By Train (2nd pressing, "radiophonic" sleeve)	8
80	Fiction FICS 010	A Forest/Another Journey By Train ('radiophonic' die-cut sleeve)	10
80	Fiction FICSX 010	A Forest (Extended Version)/Another Journey By Train (12", p/s)	30

81	Fiction FICS 012	Primary/Descent (p/s) 15
81	Fiction FICSX 012	Primary (Extended)/Descent (12", p/s) 25
81	Fiction FICS 014	Charlotte Sometimes/Splintered In Her Head (p/s) 15
81	Fiction FICSX 014	Charlotte Sometimes/Splintered In Her Head/Faith (live) (12", p/s) 18
82	Fiction FICS 015	The Hanging Garden/Killing An Arab (live) (p/s) 10
82	Fiction FICG 015	The Hanging Garden/100 Years//A Forest/Killing An Arab (double pack, gatefold p/s, 5,000 only) 15
82	Lyntone LYN 12011	Lament (1-sided flexidisc, red vinyl) 40
82	Lyntone LYN 12011	Lament (1-sided flexidisc, green vinyl) 15
82	Lyntone LYN 12011	Lament (1-sided flexidisc, red vinyl with Flexipop issue 22) 50
82	Lyntone LYN 12011	Lament (1-sided flexidisc, green vinyl, with Flexipop issue 22) 18
82	Fiction FICS 17	Let's Go To Bed/Just One Kiss (p/s) 8
82	Fiction FICSX 017	Let's Go To Bed (Extended)/Just One Kiss (Extended) (12", p/s) 12
83	Fiction FICS 018	The Walk/The Dream (paper labels, poster p/s) 20
83	Fiction FICSP 018	The Walk/The Dream (picture disc) 35
83	Fiction FICSX 018	Upstairs Room/The Dream/The Walk/Lament//Let's Go To Bed (Extended)/ Just One Kiss (Extended) (12" double pack, shrinkwrapped with sticker)............30
83	Fiction FICS 19	Lovecats/Speak My Language (p/s) 8
83	Fiction FICSP 019	The Lovecats/Speak My Language (picture disc, PVC sleeve) 35
84	Fiction FIXSP 020	The Caterpillar/Happy The Man (picture disc, printed PVC sleeve) 30
85	Fiction 080182-2	In Between Days/The Exploding Boy/A Few Hours After This/ Six Different Ways (live)/Push (live) (CD Video) 45
85	Fiction FICSG 23	Close To Me (Remix)/A Man Inside My Mouth (poster p/s; some copies with blue & white 'Head On The Door' sticker) 15
85	Fiction FICST 23	HALF AN OCTOPUS: Close To Me (Remix)/A Man Inside My Mouth/New Day/ Stop Dead (10" EP, p/s)...18
85	Fiction 080180-2	Close To Me (12" Remix)/A Man Inside My Mouth/Stop Dead/ New Day (CD Video)..........45
87	Fiction FICSG 25	Why Can't I Be You?/A Japanese Dream//Six Different Ways (live)/ Push (live) (numbered double pack, gatefold p/s) 12
87	Fiction FICS 26	Catch/Breathe (p/s, in carrier bag) 8
87	Fiction FICSP 26	Catch/Breathe (clear vinyl, printed PVC sleeve) 18
87	Fiction 080186-2	Catch/Breathe/A Chain Of Flowers/Icing Sugar (Remix) (CD Video) 45
87	Fiction FICS 27	Just Like Heaven/Snow In Summer (p/s, numbered, white vinyl) 8
87	Fiction FICS 27	Just Like Heaven/Snow In Summer (p/s, mispress, A-side plays both sides)....20
87	Fiction FICSP 27	Just Like Heaven/Snow In Summer (picture disc in custom PVC sleeve) 20
87	Fiction FIXCD 27	Just Like Heaven (Remix)/Snow In Summer/Sugar Girl (CD, card sleeve) 25
87	Strange Fruit SFPS 050	PEEL SESSIONS EP (12") 12
88	Fiction FIXCD 28	Hot Hot Hot!!! (Extended Remix)/Hot Hot Hot!!! (Remix)/Hey You!!! (Extended Remix) (CD, card sleeve with insert for 10 Imaginary Years book) 20
89	Fiction FICSG 29	Lullaby (Remix)/Babble (gatefold p/s, numbered with sticker) 8
89	Fiction FICSP 29	Lullaby (Remix)/Babble (clear vinyl, numbered printed 'spider web' PVC sleeve) ...18
89	Fiction FICVX 29	Lullaby (Remix)/Babble/Out Of Mind (12", pink vinyl, numbered with stickers) 18
89	Fiction FICCD 29	Lullaby (Remix)/Babble/Out Of Mind/Lullaby (Extended Remix) (3" CD, gatefold p/s)....18
89	Fiction FICSG 30	Lovesong/2 Late ('The Love Box' set with linen print) 12
89	Fiction FICCD 30	Lovesong (7" Mix)/2 Late/Fear Of Ghosts/Lovesong (Extended Mix) (CD) 10
90	Fiction FICPA 34	Pictures Of You (Remix)/Last Dance (live) (p/s, green vinyl, no'd sticker) 6
90	Fiction FICPA 34	Pictures Of You (Remix)/Last Dance (live) (p/s, green vinyl, mispress, plays "Last Dance" both sides) 30
90	Fiction FICPB 34	Pictures Of You (Remix)/Prayers For Rain (p/s, purple vinyl, numbered sticker)....10
90	Fiction FICXA 34	Pictures Of You (Extended Remix)/Last Dance (live)/Fascination Street (Live) (12") 18
90	Fiction FICCDA 34	Pictures Of You (Remix)/Last Dance (live)/Fascination Street (live) (CD) 10
90	Fiction FICCDB 34	Pictures Of You (Strange Mix)/Prayers For Rain (live)/Disintegration (live) (CD)....10
90	Fiction FICDP 35	Never Enough (Big Mix)/Harold & Joe/Let's Go To Bed (Milk Mix) (CD, with window sticker, numbered slimline jewel case) 10
90	Fiction 080184-2	Why Can't I Be You? (12" Remix)/A Japanese Dream (5.40 Remix)/Hey You!!! (CD Video) ...45
91	Fiction FICDR 36	Close To Me (Closer Mix)/Just Like Heaven (Dizzy Mix)/Why Can't I Be You (12" remix) (CD, with poster, shrinkwrapped with card insert and numbered sticker) 8
92	Fiction FICS 42	Friday I'm In Love/Halo (p/s) 5
92	Fiction FICCD 42	Friday I'm In Love/Halo/Scared Of You/Friday I'm In Love (Strangelove Mix) (12", p/s, different coloured or marbled vinyl) 25
92	Fiction FICS 46	A Letter To Elise/The Big Hand (p/s) 5

ALBUMS

79	Fiction FIX 1	THREE IMAGINARY BOYS (with inner sleeve, postcard & badge) 50
79	Fiction FIX 1	THREE IMAGINARY BOYS (LP, with inner sleeve and "Limited edition special price" stamped in gold on cover) 20
80	Fiction FIXD 004	SEVENTEEN SECONDS (LP) 12
82	Fiction FIX D7	PORNOGRAPHY (LP, with inner sleeve) 12
84	Fiction FIXS 9	THE TOP (with badge & poster, green inner sleeve) 20
84	Fiction FIXS 9	THE TOP (with promo plastic snake & top) 35
86	Fiction 815 011-2	BOYS DON'T CRY (CD, original non-picture disc, with "Object" & "World War" & without "So What") 30
86	Fiction FIXH 12	STANDING ON A BEACH - THE SINGLES (LP, gatefold with inner sleeve)........12
87	Fiction FIXH 13/FIXHA 13	KISS ME, KISS ME, KISS ME (with bonus orange vinyl 6-track 12" [FIXHA 13], in custom PVC sleeve) 50
89	Fiction FIXH 14	DISINTERGRATION (LP, with inner sleeve) 15
89	Fiction FIXHP 14	DISINTEGRATION (picture disc, printed PVC sleeve) 30
90	Fiction FIXCD 17	ENTREAT (CD, exclusive to HMV, card p/s, yellow photo) 25
92	Fiction 513 600-0	LIMITED EDITION CD BOX (15 x CD hinged box set, 2,500 only) 200
97	Fiction FIXLP 30	GALORE (2-LP, inners) 30
04	Fiction 981463	JOIN THE DOTS: B-SIDES AND RARITIES 1978-2001 (4-CD box set) 20

PROMOS

79	Fiction	Boys Don't Cry 45
79	Fiction CUR 1	Grinding Halt/Meat Hook (12", stickered sleeve) 70
81	Fiction FICS 12	Primary (1-sided, no p/s) 25
82	Fiction CURE 1	One Hundred Years/The Hanging Garden (12", p/s, promo/gig freebie) 70
82	Lyntone LYN 12011	Lament (hard vinyl test pressing, no p/s) 400
84	Fiction KAREN 1	THE TOP (12", 1-sided, 3-track sampler) 55
88	Fiction FICSDJ 28	Hot Hot Hot!!! (Remix)/Hey You!!! (Remix) (die-cut title p/s) 15
89	Fiction DISIN 1	DISINTEGRATION (CD, 4-track sampler) 20
89	Fiction CIFCD 3	STRANGER THAN FICTION (CD, 6-track sampler, 1000 only) 100
90	Fiction CUREPROCD 3	THE CURE - AN INTERVIEW (CD) 25
90	Fiction CUREPROCD 1	MIXED UP (CD, 4-track sampler) 15
80s	Fiction FICS DJ 42	Friday I'm In Love (Promo in die-cut Fiction sleeve) 20

MINT VALUE £

92	Fiction CURE 1	CLASSIC CURE: Love Cats/Close To Me (Closer Mix)/Lovesong/ Charlotte Sometimes/Lullaby/Why Can't I Be You/A Forest (CD, sampler, inlay)	25
93	Fiction SHOWPRO 1	SHOWPRO: Just Like Heaven/Doing The Unstuck (CD, 2-track sampler)	20
93	Fiction PARISPRO 01	PARISPRO: Catch/Play For Today (CD, 2-track sampler)	20
96	Fiction FICSTX 53	Gone! (Ultraliving Mix) (12", same track both sides, with 'DJ' insert)	12
97	Fiction FICSX 54	Wrong Number (Single Mix)/(ISDN Mix)/(Digital Exchange Mix)/ (Dub Analogue Exchange Mix)/(Crossed Line Mix)/(Engaged Mix)/(P2P Mix) (12", double pack, p/s promo only)	25
97	Fixtion FIXCD.COM 1	FIVE SWING LIVE (CD, 5-track sampler, available via the internet, 5,000 only)	30
04	Fiction CUREBOX1	JOIN THE DOTS (CD, sampler in card sleeve)	10

(see also Cult Hero, Siouxsie & Banshees, Glove, Fools Dance, Tim Pope, Lockjaw, Obtainers)

MARTIN CURE & PEEPS
67	Philips BF 1605	It's All Over Now/I Can Make The Rain Fall Up	40

(see also Peeps, Rainbows)

CURIOSITY SHOPPE
68	Deram DM 220	Baby I Need You/So Sad	100

JOHNNY CURIOUS & STRANGERS
78	Illegal IL 009	In Tune/Road To Cheltenham/Pissheadsville/Jennifer (p/s)	10
79	Bugle BLAST 2	Someone Else's Home/Backwards In The Night (p/s)	12

CURLEY MOORE
71	Pye 25570	Funky Yeah/Shelly's Rubber Band	35

CURLY
75	EPIC EPC 3145	High Flying Bird/Breakout	6
71	Pye 25570	Funky Yeah/Shelly's Rubber Band	12

CURRANT KRAZE
70	Deram DM 292	Lady Pearl/Breaking The Heart Of A Good Man	6

CURRENT 93
83	L.A.Y.L.A.H. L.A.Y. 1	Lashtal/Salt/Caresse (12", white p/s)	22
83	L.A.Y.L.A.H. L.A.Y. 1	Lashtal/Salt/Caresse (12", white p/s [reissue from in 1988 with dark p/s and "1988" on label])	18
85	L.A.Y.L.A.H. L.A.Y. 14	NIGHTMARE CULTURE (12" EP, with Sickness Of Snakes [i.e. Coil feat. Boyd Rice]; matt black & red sleeve)	22
87	L.A.Y.L.A.H. L.A.Y. 18	HAPPY BIRTHDAY PIGFACE CHRISTUS (12" EP)	22
87	Maldoror MAL 108	Crowleymass/Christmassacre/Crowleymass (Mix Mix Mix) (12", p/s)	28
88	Yangki 002	FAITH'S FAVOURITES EP (Ballad Of The Pale Girl/NURSE WITH WOUND: Swamp Rat) (12", laminated p/s)	28
88	Maldoror MAL 088	The Red Face Of God/The Breath And The Pain Of God (12", p/s, with insert, 666 only)	40
89	Yangki 003	DEATH OF THE CORN (12" EP, with Sol Invictus; 'art' sleeve)	18
90	Harbinger 001	No Hiding From The Blackbird/NURSE WITH WOUND: Burial Of The Stoned Sardine (p/s, remixed reissue of giveaway 7")	12
90	Shock SX 003	She Is Dead And All Fall Down/God Has Three Faces And Wood Has No Name (folded sleeve in bag, 1,000 only, this price for 26 copies that were signed/lettered)	45
90	Shock SX 003	She Is Dead And All Fall Down/God Has Three Faces And Wood Has No Name (folded sleeve in bag, 1,000 only)	22
90	Cerne 004	This Ain't The Summer Of Love (live) (with Sol Invictus, gig freebie, printed labels, this price for 93 copies with ticket)	30
90	Cerne 004	This Ain't The Summer Of Love (live) (with Sol Invictus, gig freebie, printed labels)	20
92	Durtro DURTRO 004	LOONEY RUNES (12", live EP, 2,000 only, with poster)	20
94	Ptolemaic Terrascope POT6	Broken Birds Fly/RANDY CALIFORNIA: The American Society/The Whale Song (free with Ptolemaic Terrascope mag)	10
94	Ptolemaic Terrascope POT6	Broken Birds Fly/RANDY CALIFORNIA: The American Society/The Whale Song (without Ptolemaic Terrascope mag)	8
94	Durtro DURTRO 022	THE FIRE OF THE MIND (CD EP, free with book 'Simply Being')	55
95	Durtro DURTRO 025	Tamlin/How The Great Satanic Glory Faded (12", numbered with insert, 2,000 only)	28
95	Durtro DURTRO 025	Tamlin/How The Great Satanic Glory Faded (CD, numbered, 3,000 only)	18
95	Durtro DURTRO 028	Where The Long Shadows Fall (12", 1-sided clear vinyl with insert, 2,000 only)	18
96	Durtro DURTRO 033	The Seven Seals/(various artists) (CD, mail order)	18
84	L.A.Y.L.A.H. LAY 008	DOGS BLOOD RISING (LP)	25
86	Maldoror UDO 22M	IN MENSTRUAL NIGHT (LP, 25 with handmade inserts & cover)	100
86	Maldoror UDO 22M	IN MENSTRUAL NIGHT (LP)	20
86	United Dairies UD 022	IN MENSTRUAL NIGHT (LP, picture disc)	20
87	L.A.Y.L.A.H. LAY 20	SWASTIKAS FOR NODDY (LP, with insert)	25
88	Maldoror MAL 666	CHRIST AND THE PALE QUEENS MIGHTY IN SORROW (3-sided LP, with inserts, 93 copies only)	100
88	Maldoror MAL 777	IMPERIUM (LP, black label, with insert)	28
88	Maldoror MAL 777	IMPERIUM (LP, later pressing with white label)	18
89	Maldoror MAL 093	DAWN (LP)	60
89	Durtro DURTRO 001	LIVE AT BAR MALDOROR (LP, white label, 1,000 only)	55
80s	Maldoror MAL 123	NATURE UNVEILED (LP, with insert & free 7": "No Hiding From The Blackbird/NURSE WITH WOUND: Burial Of The Sardine")	30
80s	Maldoror MAL 123	NATURE UNVEILED (LP, with insert)	20
90	United Dairies UD 029	EARTH COVERS EARTH (mini-LP)	35
90	Cerne 00123	THE CERNE BOX SET (3-LP set, includes "Horse"; other LPs by Sol Invictus & Nurse With Wound, 2,000 only)	70
90	United Dairies UD 033CD	CROOKED CROSSES FOR THE NODDING DOG (CD)	18
90	NER BADVC 693	1888 (LP, split with Death In June, 500 each on clear & red vinyl)	35
90	NER BADVC 693	1888 (LP, split with Death In June, black vinyl)	25
92	Durtro DURTRO 006	ISLAND (LP, with insert, 2,000 only)	20
92	Durtro DURTRO 011	THUNDER PERFECT MIND (2-LP, with insert)	20
94	Durtro DURTRO 018	OF RUINE, OR SOME BLAZING STARRE (LP, blue vinyl w/insert, 2,000 only)	18
94	Durtrohoho 019	LUCIFER OVER LONDON (LP, red vinyl with insert, 2,000 only)	20
96	Durtro DURTRO 026	ALL THE PRETTY LITTLE HORSES (LP, clear vinyl with insert, 2,000 only)	12
96	United Dairies UDOR 4	WHEN THE MAY RAIN COMES (CD, mail order, free with 'Ultrasonic Seraphim' [2-CD by SAND])	15
01	United Durtro UDOR 8	BRIGHT YELLOW MOON (CD, with Nurse With Wound, first 1,000 with bonus CD)	25

(see also Nurse With Wound, 23 Skidoo, Psychic TV, Crisis, Death In June, Sol Invictus, Steven Stapleton & David Tibet, Tibet & Stapleton)

DAVID CURRIE
71	Philips 6006165	I Don't Want To Talk About It/The Question	10

CLIFFORD CURRY
69	Action ACT 4549	She Shot A Hole In My Soul/We're Gonna Hate Ourselves In The Morning	10

| 69 | Pama PM 793 | You Turn Out The Light/Good Humour Man | 10 |
| 69 | Pama PM 797 | I Can't Get A Hold Of Myself/Ain't No Danger | 50 |

TIM CURRY
| 74 | Ode ODE 66103 | Sweet Transvestite/Time Warp (in p/s) | 8 |
| 74 | Ode ODE 66103 | Sweet Transvestite/Time Warp | 5 |

TED CURSON QUARTET
| 64 | Fontana 688310 ZL | TEARS FOR DOLPHY (LP) | 35 |

CURTAINS
| 95 | Detour DR 025 | In My Street/Family Affair (p/s, blue vinyl, 100 only) | 7 |

DAN CURTIN
94	Peacefrog PF 018X	PARALLEL EP (12", sampler, plain sleeve)	10
95	Peacefrog PF 023	PURVEYORS OF FINE FUNK - HEIGHTS TRAX VOL 1 EP (12", plain sleeve)	15
95	Peacefrog PF 024	DREAMS NOT OF TODAY EP (12", plain sleeve)	10
95	Peacefrog PF 032	PURVEYORS OF FINE FUNK - HEIGHTS TRAX VOL 2 EP (12", plain sleeve)	10
96	Peacefrog PF 058	PURVEYORS OF FINE FUNK VOL 3 EP (12", plain sleeve)	10
97	Peacefrog PF 064	PURVEYORS OF FINE FUNK VOL 4 EP (12", plain sleeve)	8
94	Peacefrog PF 018	THE SILICON DAWN (2-LP)	18
94	Peacefrog PF 018CD	THE SILICON DAWN CD (CD)	15
95	Peacefrog PF 038	WEB OF LIFE (2-LP)	18

ALLEN CURTIS
| 64 | Hickory 45-1226 | Fireball Mail/The Hole He Said He'd Dig For Me | 5 |

CHRIS CURTIS
| 66 | Pye 7N 17132 | Aggravation/Have I Done Something Wrong | 40 |
| (see also Searchers) | | | |

CLEM CURTIS & FOUNDATIONS
72	Pye 7N 45150	I've Never Found A Girl (To Love Me Like You)/Point Of No Return	30
75	Riverdale RS 105	Sweet Happiness/Lady Luck	30
(See also the Foundations)			

DENNY CURTIS
| 68 | Plexium PXM 2 | Crying Over You/You Don't Love Me No More | 6 |
| 69 | Plexium PXM 6 | Message/You Gotta Be Mine | 6 |

EDDIE CURTIS
| 63 | Oriole CB 1852 | Leavin Town/Faithful Kind (with Hellions) | 10 |

JOE CURTIS
| 72 | Spiral DIT 4 | Black Is Beautiful/This Is Love | 8 |

JOHNNY CURTIS
66	Parlophone R 5529	Our Love's Disintegrating/(I'd Be) A Legend In My Time	70
67	Parlophone R 5582	Jack And The Beanstalk/Go On Back	30
68	Major Minor MM 564	Pickin' Up Pebbles/Gentle On My Mind	7

LEE CURTIS (& ALL STARS)
63	Decca F 11622	Little Girl/Just One More Dance (solo)	20
63	Decca F 11690	Let's Stomp/Poor Unlucky Me	25
64	Decca F 11830	What About Me/I've Got My Eyes On You	20
64	Philips BF 1385	Ecstasy/A Shot Of Rhythm And Blues	20
(see also Pete Best Four)			

LYNNE CURTIS
| 64 | Decca F11869 | House For Sale/My Little Boy | 8 |

MAC CURTIS
57	Parlophone R 4279	The Low Road/You Ain't Treatin' Me Right	2500
57	Parlophone R 4279	The Low Road/You Ain't Treatin' Me Right (78)	275
74	Polydor 2310 293	ROCKABILLY KINGS (LP, with Charlie Feathers)	25

SONNY CURTIS
60	Coral Q 72400	The Red Headed Stranger/Talk About My Baby	40
64	Colpix PX 11024	A Beatle I Want To Be/So Used To Loving You	15
64	Liberty LIB 55710	I Pledged My Love To You/Bo Diddley Bach	20
85	Songworks S1	I Think I'm In Love/A Whole Lot Less To Me Than Meets The Eye	5
85	Songworks S2	Heart Of Gold/Why Did You Say 'I Do' To Me	5
90	Ritz 217	I'm No Stranger To The Rain/Rock Around With Ollie Vee	5
(see also Crickets)			

DAVE CURTISS & TREMORS
63	Philips BF 1257	You Don't Love Me/Sweet Girl Of Mine	10
63	Philips BF 1285	What Kind Of Girl Are You?/Dreamer's Funfair	10
64	Philips BF 1330	Summertime Blues/I'm A Hog For You Baby	10

CURTISS MALDOON
71	Regal Zonophone 3038	You Make Me Happy (And You Make Me Sad)/Amber Man	5
72	Purple PUR 106	One Way Ticket/Next Time	7
71	Purple TPS 3501	CURTISS MALDOON (LP)	30
73	Purple TPS 3502	MALDOON (LP)	15

ROCKY CURTISS & HARMONY FLAMES
| 59 | Fontana TFE 17172 | U.S.A. HIT PARADE (EP) | 40 |

BOBBY CURTOLA (& MARTELLS)
61	Columbia DB 4672	Don't You Sweetheart Me/My Heart's Tongue-Tied (solo)	20
62	London HL 9577	Fortune Teller/Johnny Take Your Time (solo)	20
62	London HL 9639	Aladdin/I Don't Want To Go On Without You (solo)	20
63	Decca F 11670	Gypsy Heart/I'm Sorry	20
63	Decca F 11725	Three Rows Over/Indian Giver	20

CURVE
91	Anxious ANXP 27	Blindfold/Ten Little Girls (picture disc)	8
93	Anxious	FALLING FREE - APHEX TWIN REMIX (12", 1-sided promo only, 500 only)	20
93	Anxious ANXCDS 42	BLACKERTHREETRACKERTWO EP (CD, with Future Sound Of London mix)	10

MINT VALUE £

CURVED AIR

71	Warner Bros WB 8023	It Happened Today/What Happens When You Blow Yourself Up	7
72	Warner Bros K 16164	Sarah's Concern/Phantasmagoria	6
71	Warner Brothers K 16092	Backstreet Luv/Everdance	5
84	Pearl Key PK 07350	Renegade/We're Only Human (p/s)	15
70	Warner Bros K 56004	AIR CONDITIONING (LP, picture disc, with booklet, 10,000 only)	50
70	Warner Bros K 56004	AIR CONDITIONING (LP, picture disc)	50
70	Warner Bros WSX 3012	AIR CONDITIONING (LP, green label, laminated sleeve)	30
70	Warner Bros K 56004	AIR CONDITIONING (LP, green label)	12
71	Warner Bros K 46092	SECOND ALBUM (LP, die-cut 'leaves' fold-out sleeve, green label)	30
72	Warner Bros K 46158	PHANTASMAGORIA (LP, green label, with inner lyric card)	18
73	Warner Bros K 46224	AIR CUT (LP, green label, gatefold sleeve)	18
75	Deram SML 1119	LIVE (LP, red/white label)	20

(see also Kirby, Sonja Kristina, [Darryl Way's] Wolf, Trace, Legs, Stretch, Police)

PETER CUSACK

77	Bead Records BEAD 5	AFTER BEING IN HOLLAND FOR TWO YEARS (LP)	40
84	Bead Records BEAD 22	BIRD JUMPS INTO WOOD (LP, with Clive Bell)	20

CUSTERS TRACK

70	Major Minor MM698	On The Run/Hello Heaven	12

IVOR CUTLER TRIO

67	Parlophone R 5624	I Had A Little Boat/A Great Grey Grasshopper	12
59	Fontana TFE 17144	OF Y'HUP (EP)	20
61	Decca DFE 6677	GET AWAY FROM THE WALL (EP)	20
61	Decca LK 4405	WHO TORE YOUR TROUSERS? (LP)	60
67	Parlophone PCS 7040	LUDO (LP)	70
74	Virgin V2021	DANDRUFF (LP, as Ivor Cutler)	30
75	Virgin V2037	VELVET DONKEY (LP)	20
76	Virgin V2056	JAMMY SMEARS (LP)	20
78	Harvest SHSP4084	LIFE IN A SCOTCH SITTING ROOM VOL 2 (LP)	20
85	Virgin OVED 12	JAMMY SMEARS (LP, reissue)	15

T. TOMMY CUTRER (& GINNY WRIGHT)

54	London HL 8093	Mexico Gal/Wonderful World (B-side with Ginny Wright)	60
54	London HL 8093	Mexico Gal/Wonderful World (B-side with Ginny Wright) (78)	10

(see also Ginny Wright)

CUTTERS

59	Decca F 11110	I've Had It/Rockaroo	15

(see also Neville Taylor & Cutters)

CYAN THREE

66	Decca F 12371	Since I Lost My Baby/Face Of A Loser	20

CYANIDE

78	Pye 7N 46048	I'm A Boy/Do It (p/s)	25
78	Pye 7N 46094	Mac The Flash/Hate The State (demo copies in p/s)	60
78	Pye 7N 46094	Mac The Flash/Hate The State (demo copies in p/s)	15
79	Pinnacle PIN 23	Fireball/Your Old Man (p/s)	40
78	Pye NSPL 18554	CYANIDE (LP)	40

CYBERMEN

78	Rockaway AERE 101	THE CYBERMEN (EP, available in 2 different sleeves with info sheet)	100
78	Rockaway AERE 101	THE CYBERMEN (EP, available in 2 different sleeves without info sheet)	40
79	Rockaway LUV 002	You're To Blame/It's You I Want (with inserts)	40

CYBERNETIC SERENDIPITY GROUP

68	ICA ICA 1/2	CYBERNETIC SERENDIPITY MUSIC (LP, private pressing)	100

CYBOTRON FEATURING DILLINJA

96	Prototype PRO004	Threshold/Hot To (12")	10
98	Prototype PRO 010	Light Years/Revelations (12")	10
00	Valve CYBX 001	NASTY WAYZ (EP)	15

(see also Dillinja)

CYCLONE

79	Magnet MAG 159	Palisades Park/Crazy Haze (p/s)	8

(see also Matchbox)

CYCLONES (1)

64	Oriole CB 1898	Nobody/Little Egypt	60

CYCLONES (2)

71	Banana BA 338	My Sweet Lord/DENNIS BROWN: Silky (B-side actually by Monty Alexander & Cyclones)	12

CYCLOP'S EYE

72	Phoenix PHO12	Rolling Thunder/Kentucky Freeway	12

CYLOB

95	Rephlex CAT 015	INDUSTRIAL FOLKSONGS (12", initially in polystyrene sleeve)	12

CYMANDE

73	Alaska ALA 4	The Message/Zion I	8
73	Alaska ALA 10	Bra/Ras Tafarian Folk Song	8
74	Contempo CS 2019	Brothers On The Slide/Pon De Dungle	25
73	Alaska ALKA 100	CYMANDE (LP)	20
74	Contempo CLP 508	PROMISED HEIGHT (LP)	20

JOHNNY CYMBAL

60	MGM MGM 1106	It'll Be Me/Always, Always	25
63	London HLR 9682	Mr Bass Man/Sacred Lovers Vow	10
63	London HLR 9731	Teenage Heaven/Cinderella Baby	20
63	London HLR 9762	Dum Dum Dee Dum/Surfing At Tijuana	20
64	London HLR 9911	Mitsou/Robinson Crusoe On Mars	15
65	United Artists UP 1093	Go V.W. Go/Sorrow And Pain	15
63	London RER 1375	MISTER BASS MAN (EP)	40

64	London RER 1406	CYMBAL SMASHES (EP)	40

(see also Derek)

CYMBALINE
65	Pye 7N 15916	Please Little Girl/Coming Home Baby	35
65	Mercury MF 918	Top Girl/Can You Hear Me?	25
66	Mercury MF 961	I Don't Want It/Where Did Love Go Wrong	8
66	Mercury MF 975	Peanuts And Chewy Macs/Found My Girl	10
67	Philips BF 1624	Matrimonial Fears/You Will Never Love Me	70
68	Philips BF 1681	Down By The Seaside/Fire	25
69	Philips BF 1749	Turn Around/Come Back Baby	5

CYMERONS
64	Decca F 11976	I'll Be There/Making Love To Another	15
66	Polydor 56098	Everyday (Will Change)/I Can See You	7

CYNIC
83	Cynic CYN 1	Suicide/No Time At All (no p/s)	75

CYNICS
85	Sounds Cynical CYNIC 1	Don't Give In (Fight to Win)/Breaking Out/One Way Out (foldout p/s)	8

CYNTHIA & ARCHIE
64	R&B JB 168	Every Beat/DELROY WILSON: Sammy Dead	25

CYRKLE
66	CBS 202064	Red Rubber Ball/How Can I Leave Her	8
66	CBS 202246	Turn Down Day/Big Little Woman	8
67	CBS 202516	Bony Maronie/Please Don't Ever Leave Me	8
67	CBS 202577	I Wish You Could Be There/The Visit (She Was Here)	8
67	CBS 2790	We Had A Good Thing Goin'/Two Rooms	8
67	CBS 2917	Penny Arcade/Words	8
67	CBS 62977	NEON (LP)	35

CZAR
70	Philips 6006 071	Oh Lord I'm Getting Heavy/Why Don't We Be A Rock'n'Roll Band	35
70	Fontana 6309 009	CZAR (LP, black/silver label, laminated sleeve)	1000

(see also Hungry Wolf)

HOLGER CZUKAY
79	EMI EMC 3319	MOVIES (LP)	15

(see under Jah Wobble, Can)

D

ROB D
95	Mo' Wax MW 037	Clubbed To Death/(Mixes) (12", p/s)	25

TONY D & SHAKEOUTS
64	Piccadilly 7N 35168	Is It True/Never Let Her Go	25

DA BAND
78	Rip Off RIP 2	I Like It/Pirate's Lullaby (p/s)	20

DA BIZ
80	Small Operations SO 002	On The Beach/This Is No Audition (p/s)	10
80	Sire SIR 4045	On The Beach/This Is No Audition (p/s, reissue)	6

DAB HAND
85	Celtic Music CM 025	HIGH ROCK AND LOWATER (LP)	18

MIKE D'ABO
69	Immediate IM 075	See The Little People — Gulliver's Travels/Anthology Of Gulliver's Travels Part 2 (withdrawn)	30
70	Uni UNS 525	Let It Roar/California Line	7
70	Bell BLL 1134	Miss Me In The Morning/Arabella, Cinderella	6
72	A&M AMS 7016	Belinda/Little Miss Understood	6
74	A&M AMS 7121	Fuel To Burn/Hold On Darlin'	6
70	Uni UNLS 114	D'ABO (LP, gatefold sleeve)	40
72	A&M AMLH 68097	DOWN AT RACHEL'S PLACE (LP, with lyric insert)	15
74	A&M AMLH 63634	BROKEN RAINBOWS (LP)	15

(see also Manfred Mann, Band Of Angels, Gulliver's Travels, Smith & D'Abo)

KAREN D'ACHE
89	SRT KDA 2	Spin And Cry/Divide And Rule	6

RITA DACOSTA
75	Contempo CS 2060	Don't Bring Me Down/No! No! No!	8

DADA
71	Atco 2400 030	DADA (LP, mustard/blue label)	60

(see also Robert Palmer, Elkie Brooks, Paul Korda, Vinegar Joe)

DADDY COLONEL
85	Bubblers UKMC7	Take A Tip From Me/Lyric Banton (12")	20

DADDY DEWDROP
71	Stateside SS2192	Foxhunting On The Weekend/March Of The White Corpuscles	15

DADDY LONGLEGS
70	Warner Bros WB 8012	High Again/To The Rescue (Wet Putso)	5
70	Warner Bros WS 3004	DADDY LONGLEGS (LP)	30
71	Vertigo 6360 038	OAKDOWN FARM (LP, gatefold sleeve, swirl label)	200
72	Polydor 2371 261	THREE MUSICIANS (LP)	15

MINT VALUE £

73	Polydor 2371 323	SHIFTING SANDS (LP)	25

(see also Daylight)

DADDY MAXFIELD
73	Pye 7N 45266	Rave 'N' Rock/Smilin' Again	50

DADDY-O'S
58	Oriole CB 1454	Got A Match?/Have A Cigar	15

DADDY'S ACT
67	Columbia DB 8242	Eight Days A Week/Gonna Get You	18

DAD'S ARMY PLATOON
71	Columbia DB 8766	Dad's Army March/What Did You Do In The War?	6
72	Columbia DB 8952	We Stood Alone/Down Our Way (AS DAD'S ARMY CHOIR)	6

D.A.F. (DEUTSCHE AMERIKANISCHE FREUNDSCHAFT)
80	Mute MUTE 011	Der Rauber Und Der Prinz/Tanz Mit Mir (p/s)	6
81	Mute MUTE005	Kebabtraume/Gewalt (p/s)	6
81	Virgin VS 418	Der Mussolini/Der Räuber Und Der Prinz (co. sleeve)	8
81	Virgin VS 418-12	Der Mussolini/Der Räuber Und Der Prinz (12", p/s, original issue)	10

CALVIN DAFOS
66	Blue Beat BB 347	Brown Sugar/I'm Gone	22
69	Doctor Bird DB 1174	Lash Them/CDs: Medicine Master	20

DAFT PUNK
94	Soma 014	Alive/The New Wave (12" EP, company sleeve)	12
95	Soma 025	Da Funk/Rollin' And Scratchin' (12" EP, company sleeve)	10
96	VIRGIN V 2821	HOMEWORK (2-LP)	20
01	Virgin V 2940	DISCOVERY (2-LP)	15
01	Virgin V 2952	ALIVE 1997 (LP)	15

DAGABAND
80	Rutland RX 100	Test Flight/Images (p/s)	5
83	MHM A-M 094	Second Time Around/Reds Under The Beds/I Can See For Miles (p/s)	25

DAGGERMEN
86	Empire UPW 258J	INTRODUCING THE DAGGERMEN (EP, die-cut company sleeve)	10
86	Own Up DAG 001	DAGGERS IN MY MIND (LP)	12

(see also James Taylor Quartet)

DAGGERS (1)
74	Scotty SC 003	Live Your Life Alone/Circles Of Dust	60

DAGGERS (2)
07	Fandango/Galagos 18	Money/Magazine (die cut sleeve)	12

(see also Hurts)

DAILY FLASH
84	Psycho PSYCHO 32	I FLASH DAILY (LP)	20

TONY DAINES
63	Fontana TF 433	Chapel In The Moonlight/Echo Of Footsteps	7
64	Fontana TF 472	Too Late/I Told You So	5

BILLY DAINTY
62	Decca F11499	Cry Upon My Shoulder/If I'd Known You	6

DAISY CHAINSAW
91	Jeva JVA 001	Get Real Pleasure/Love Your Money (p/s)	10

DAISY CLAN
70	Pye Intl. 7N 25532	Love Needs Love/Glory Be	30
71	Decca F23169	San Francisco China Town/Ridin' A Rainbow	20

DAISY PLANET
60s	Oak (no cat. no.)	DAISY PLANET (EP, no p/s)	60

DAKOTA JIM
66	Blue Beat BB 358	Only Soul Can Tell (actually by Slim Smith)/DAKOTA'S ALLSTARS: Call Me Master (actually by Prince Buster All Stars)	150

(see also Slim Smith)

DAKOTAS
63	Parlophone R 5044	The Cruel Sea/The Millionaire	10
63	Parlophone R 5064	Magic Carpet/Humdinger	12
64	Parlophone R 5203	Oyeh/My Girl Josephine	30
67	Page One POF 018	I'm 'N 'Ardworkin' Barrow Boy/Seven Pounds Of Potatoes	35
68	Philips BF 1645	I Can't Break The News To Myself/The Spider And The Fly	100
63	Parlophone GEP 8888	MEET THE DAKOTAS (EP)	35

(see also Billy J. Kramer & Dakotas)

MICHAEL D'ALBUQUERQUE
74	RCA SF 8383	WE MAY BE CATTLE BUT WE ALL HAVE NAMES (LP, with lyric sheet)	20
76	Warner Bros K 56276	STALKING THE SLEEPER (LP)	12

(see also E.L.O., Michael Albuquerque)

ALAN DALE
55	Vogue Coral Q 72072	Cherry Pink And Apple Blossom White/I'm Sincere	6
55	Vogue Coral Q 72089	Sweet And Gentle/You Still Mean The Same To Me	6
55	Vogue Coral Q 72105	Rockin' The Cha-Cha/Wham! (There I Go In Love Again)	20
56	Vogue Coral Q 72121	Robin Hood/Lisbon Antigua	6
56	Vogue Coral Q 72156	Dance On/Mr. Moon	6
56	Vogue Coral Q 72166	The Birds And The Bees/I Promise	6
56	Vogue Coral Q 72191	Be My Guest/Pardners (with Buddy Hackett)	8
56	Vogue Coral Q 72194	The Test Of Time/I Cry More	6
57	Vogue Coral Q 72225	Don't Knock The Rock/Your Love Is My Love	30
57	Vogue Coral Q 72231	The Girl Can't Help It/Lonesome Road	30
58	MGM MGM 986	Volare/Weeping Willow In The Wind	6

(see also Johnny Desmond)

DICK DALE & HIS DELTONES
63	Capitol CL 15296	Peppermint Man/Surf Beat	20
63	Capitol CL 15320	The Scavenger/Wild Ideas	20
88	Pulch Wave PSC 666	Pick And Play/The Wedge (p/s)	6
63	Capitol T 1886	SURFERS' CHOICE (LP)	60
63	Capitol T/ST 1930	KING OF THE SURF GUITAR (LP, mono/stereo)	60

GLEN DALE
66	Decca F 12475	Good Day Sunshine/Make Me Belong To You	8
68	Page One POF 059	I've Got You On My Mind/Now I See You	10
68	Page One POF 105	I've Got Something Too/Something's Gotten Hold Of My Heart	5

(see also Fortunes)

DALE & GRACE
63	London HL 9807	I'm Leaving It Up To You/That's What I Like About You	15
64	London HL 9857	Stop And Think It Over/Bad Luck	15
69	London HL 10249	I'm Leaving It Up To You/Love Is Strange	10
64	London RE 1428	DALE AND GRACE NO. 1 (EP)	40
64	London RE 1429	DALE AND GRACE NO. 2 (EP)	40
64	London RE 1430	DALE AND GRACE NO. 3 (EP)	45

JACKIE DALE
78	Freedom Sounds FSD 020	Stop And Think Me Over/Bucket Bottom (12", with Prince Allah)	20

JIM DALE
57	Parlophone R 4329	Piccadilly Line/I Didn't Mean It	12
57	Parlophone R 4343	Be My Girl/You Shouldn't Do That	8
57	Parlophone R 4356	All Shook Up/Wandering Eyes (with Vipers & King Brothers)	15
57	Parlophone R 4376	Just Born (To Be Your Baby)/Crazy Dream	10
58	Parlophone R 4402	Sugartime/Don't Let Go	10
58	Parlophone R 4424	Tread Softly Stranger/Jane Belinda	6
59	Parlophone R 4522	Gotta Find A Girl/The Legend Of Nellie D.	6
60	Academy AD 001	Somewhere There's A Someone/If You Come Back	6
62	Piccadilly 7N 35039	One Boy, One Girl/My Resistance is Low	5
63	Piccadilly 7N 35100	Start All Over Again/It's For Them	5
65	Columbia DB 7449	Forget Tomorrow/Is It OK?	5
57	Parlophone GEP 8656	JIM DALE (EP)	30
58	Parlophone PMD 1055	JIM (10" LP)	60
69	Pye NSPL 18289	MEET JIM DALE (LP)	15

PAUL DALE BAND
82	KA KA 6/PAUL 1	Alright On The Night/Hold On (p/s, clear vinyl)	12
82	KA KA 6/PAUL 1	Alright On The Night/Hold On (p/s)	6

(see also Marseille)

SYD DALE ORCHESTRA
65	Decca F 22300	C'mon In/Disc A Go Go	10

DALEK I LOVE YOU
79	Vertigo DALEK 1	Freedom Fighters/Two Chameleons (p/s, as Dalek I)	6
83	Korova KOW 31	Horrorscope/These Walls We Build	7

DALEKS
80	Exterminated Products EXPS 1	Rejected/Man Of The World/This Life (fold-out, p/s)	15

(see under Century 21)

DALES
75	Deroy 953	LUCKY THIRTEEN (LP)	30

DALE SISTERS
60	HMV POP 781	The Kiss/Billy Boy, Billy Boy	10
61	Ember EMB S 140	My Sunday Baby/All My Life	20
62	Ember EMB S 151	Secrets/Road To Love	10

DÄLEX
81	Dodgy DODGY 1	Juvenile/Action Man Touched (p/s)	20

BASIL DALEY
68	Studio One SO 2054	Hold Me Baby/HEPTONES: I Got A Feeling	25

JIMMY DALEY & DING-A-LINGS
57	Brunswick 05648	Rock, Pretty Baby/Can I Steal A Little Love	130
57	Brunswick 05648	Rock, Pretty Baby/Can I Steal A Little Love (78)	20

GRAHAM DALLEY
66	Hollick & Taylor HT/LP 1068	GRAHAM DALLEY AT THE BARN (LP)	15

SALVADOR DALI
62	Decca SET 230	DALI IN VENICE (LP, gatefold sleeve with booklet. Dali does not sing or talk - he just did the cover)	50

DALIDA
60	HMV POP 793	Never On A Sunday/MILKO PAPAYAKI: Parle Doucement	7
57	Felsted ESD 3043	DALIDA IS HER NAME (EP)	20
59	Felstead ESD 3077	PARDON MY ENGLISH (EP)	25
57	Felsted SDL 86053	THE GLAMOUROUS DALIDA (10" LP)	40
66	Fontana TL 5348	DALIDA (LP)	15

DALLAS BOYS
67	Major Minor MM 534	He Won't Love You (Like I Do)/What Do You Know About Losin'	5

(see also Five Dallas Boys)

TONI DALLI
58	Columbia SEG 7397	SONGS FROM THE SHOWS (EP)	8
64	Decca LK 4641	THE VOICE OF (LP)	12

DALLIONS
62	Oriole CB 1794	Teardrops In The Rain/Loop De Loop	15

MIKI DALLON
65	RCA RCA 1438	Do You Call That Love?/Apple Pie	20
65	RCA RCA 1478	I Care About You/I'll Give You Love	40
66	Strike JH 306	Cheat And Lie/(I'm Gonna Find A) Cave	40
66	Strike JH 318	What Will Your Mama Say Now?/Two At A Time	8

(see also Neil Christian & Crusaders)

DAVID & MARIANNE DALMOUR
| 65 | Columbia 33SX 1715 | INTRODUCING (LP) | 20 |
| 66 | Columbia SCX 6005 | STRANGE ENCHANTMENT (LP) | 25 |

KAREN DALTON
| 71 | Paramount SPFL 271 | IN MY OWN TIME (LP) | 50 |

DALTONS
| 67 | Fab FAB 30 | Never Kiss You Again/RIGHTEOUS FLAMES: When A Girl Loves A Boy | 40 |

(see also Prince Buster)

ROGER DALTREY
73	Track 2094 014	Thinking/There Is Love	6
75	A&M AMS 7206	Orpheus Song/Love's Dream	6
75	Lyntone LYN 3176/7	Wagner's Dream/Love's Theme/RICK WAKEMAN: Count Your Blessings (flexidisc with 19 magazine)	10
77	Polydor 2058 896	One Of The Boys/You Better Put Something Inside Me (p/s)	6
77	Polydor 2058 948	Say It Ain't So Joe/Satin And Lace (withdrawn, existence unconfirmed)	20
77	Polydor 2121 319	Written On The Wind/Dear John	8
78	Polydor 2058 986	Say It Ain't So Joe/The Prisoner	8
73	Track 2406 107	DALTREY (LP, gatefold sleeve)	20
75	Polydor 2442 135	RIDE A ROCK HORSE (LP, with inner sleeve)	15
80	Polydor POLD 5034	McVICAR (LP, soundtrack, clear vinyl)	18
80	Polydor POLD 5034	McVICAR (LP, soundtrack)	12

(see also Who, High Numbers, McEnroe & Cash)

GLEN DALY
| 61 | Piccadilly 7N 35017 | The Celtic Song/If Only We Had Old Ireland Over Here | 7 |

TONI DALY
| 66 | Columbia DB 8043 | Like The Big Man Said/You Can't Get No Water | 7 |

(see also Antoinette)

DALYS
65	Fontana TF 546	Me Japanese Boy/Never Kind Of Love	5
65	Fontana TF 637	She's My Girl/When Love Has Gone	5
66	Strike JH 317	Don't Go Breaking My Heart/Little Stranger	6
67	Fontana TF 809	Sweet Maria/Leaving Time	5
67	Fontana TF 841	A Fistful Of Dollars/Man With No Name	6
68	Fontana TF 907	Let Me Go Lover/A Place In The Sun	5
69	Fontana TF 988	Early Morning Rain/Chanson D'Amour	5

DAMARIS
| 83 | CBS 4172 | What About My Love/Hooray For Love (12") | 30 |

DAMASCUS
| 80s | Private pressing | OPEN YOUR EYES (12" EP, with insert) | 100 |
| 80s | Private pressing | OPEN YOUR EYES (12" EP, later with different back sleeve, with insert) | 75 |

(see also Thin End Of The Wedge)

DAMBALA
78	Isis ISIS 001	Rebel/MILITANT BARRY : Version	20
78	Music Hive MH001	Zimbabwe/GUS ANYIA : Visins Of War	40
79	Radic RIC 107	Babylon/No Go (As Dambala featuring Gus Anyia)	40
81	Blank IS 1002	Rally Round/Version (12" p/s)	40

DAMITA JO
54	HMV 7MC 2	I'd Do It Again/Do I, Do I, Do I (B-side with Steve Gibson)(export issue)	20
60	Mercury AMT 1085	Widow Walk/Dearest Darling	5
60	Mercury AMT 1116	I'll Save The Last Dance For You/Forgive	7
60	Mercury AMT 1133	Keep Your Hands Off Him/Hush, Somebody's Calling My Name	5
61	Mercury AMT 1141	Do What You Want/Sweet Georgia Brown	5
61	Mercury AMT 1155	I'll Be There/Love Laid Its Hands On Me	5
61	Mercury ZEP 10118	I'LL SAVE THE LAST DANCE FOR YOU (EP)	15
61	Mercury MMC 14089	I'LL SAVE THE LAST DANCE FOR YOU (LP, mono)	20
61	Mercury CMS 18059	I'LL SAVE THE LAST DANCE FOR YOU (LP, stereo)	25
62	Mercury MMC 14105	LIVE AT THE DIPLOMAT (LP)	12

DAMNED (1)
| 74 | Youngblood YB 1067 | Morning Bird/Theta | 40 |

(see also Motordamn)

DAMNED (2)
SINGLES
76	Stiff BUY 6	New Rose/Help! (first pressing with push-out centre, 'Street music co' credit on label, 'is this a record' & 'a bilbo boppa' on A side run out, 'Damned Beatles & 'Bilbo master room' on B. 'Delga' credit on p/s)	25
76	Stiff BUY 6	New Rose/Help! (p/s, later issues)	5
77	Stiff BUY 10	Neat Neat Neat/Stab Yor Back/Singalongascabies (glossy p/s, first pressing solid centre)	25
77	Stiff BUY 10	Neat Neat Neat/Stab Yor Back/Singalongascabies (glossy p/s, second pressing push-out centre)	20
77	Stiff DAMMED 1	Stretcher Case Baby/Sick Of Being Sick (p/s, NME competition & gig freebie)	100
77	Stiff BUY 18	Problem Child/You Take My Money (p/s, originally with press-out centre)	10
77	Stiff BUY 18	Problem Child/You Take My Money (p/s)	5
77	Stiff BUY 24	Don't Cry Wolf/One Way Love (promo grey label with small "A")	30
77	Stiff BUY 24	Don't Cry Wolf/One Way Love (20,000 on pink vinyl, no p/s)	12
77	Stiff BUY 24	Don't Cry Wolf/One Way Love (black vinyl)	5
78	Dodgy Demo Co. SGS 105	Love Song/Burglar (mail order issue/gig freebie, plain sleeve, stickered labels)	25
79	Chiswick CHIS 112	Love Song/Noise Noise Noise/Suicide (red vinyl, 4 different sleeves)	8

79	Chiswick CHIS 112	Love Song/Noise Noise Noise/Suicide (4 different sleeves)	5
79	Chiswick CHIS 116	Smash It Up/Burglar (p/s)	5
79	Chiswick CHIS 120 ADJ-1	I Just Can't Be Happy Today/Ballroom Blitz ('A' Label DJ promo copy)	200
79	Chiswick CHIS 120	I Just Can't Be Happy Today/Ballroom Blitz/The Turkey Song (p/s)	5
80	Chiswick CHIS 130	White Rabbit/Rabid (Over You)/Seagulls (unissued in U.K., Europe-only, 2 x 1-sided white-label test pressings exist, hand-written labels)	400
80	Chiswick CHIS 135	The History Of The World Part 1/I Believe The Impossible/Sugar And Spite (p/s)	5
80	Chiswick CHIS 12 135	The History Of The World Part 1/I Believe The Impossible/ Sugar And Spite (12", p/s)	8
80	Chiswick CHIS 139 DJ	There Ain't No Sanity Clause/Hit Or Miss (double A side demo)	30
80	Chiswick CHIS 139	There Ain't No Sanity Clause/Hit Or Miss/Looking At You (live) (p/s)	5
81	Stiff GRAB 2	Four Pack (4 x 7" [BUY 6, 10, 18 & 24], in a plastic wallet)	50
82	Big Beat NS 75	Love Song/Noise Noise Noise/Suicide (3 different sleeves, blue vinyl)	6
82	Big Beat NS 76	Smash It Up/Burglar (p/s, red vinyl)	6
82	Big Beat NS 77	Wait For The Blackout/CAPTAIN SENSIBLE & SOFTIES: Jet Boy, Jet Girl (p/s, red/black 'Damned' labels)	5
82	Big Beat NSP 77	Wait For The Blackout/CAPTAIN SENSIBLE & SOFTIES: Jet Boy, Jet Girl (picture disc)	5
82	Big Beat NS 80	Lively Arts/Teenage Dream (p/s, green vinyl)	10
82	Bronze BRO 149	Lovely Money/Lovely Money (Disco Mix)/I Think I'm Wonderful (p/s)	6
82	Bronze BROP 149	Lovely Money/Lovely Money (Disco Mix)/I Think I'm Wonderful (picture disc)	7
82	Bronze BRO 156	Dozen Girls/Take That/Mine's A Large One, Landlord/Torture Me (p/s)	6
82	Bronze BRO 159	Generals/Disguise/Citadel Zombies (p/s)	8
83	Big Beat NS 85	White Rabbit/Rabid (Over You)/Seagulls (p/s)	8
84	Plus One DAMNED 1P	Thanks For The Night/Nasty (picture disc)	6
84	Plus One DAMNED 1	Thanks For The Night/Nasty (p/s, 1,000 each on red, white & blue vinyl)	10
84	Plus One DAMNED 1T	Thanks For The Night/Nasty/Do The Blitz (12", no'd p/s, multicoloured vinyl)	15
84	Plus One DAMNED 1T	Thanks For The Night/Nasty ('woman'-shaped pic disc w/ plinth, 1,000 only)	25
85	MCA GRIM 1	Grimly Fiendish/Edward The Bear (autographed gatefold p/s, 1,000 only)	8
85	MCA GRIMP 1	Grimly Fiendish/Edward The Bear (picture disc)	5
85	MCA GRIMT 1	Grimly Fiendish (Spic'n'Span Mix)/Edward The Bear (12", autographed p/s)	10
85	MCA GRIM 2/GRIMY 2	Edition Premier: The Shadow Of Love/Nightshift/Let There Be Rats/ Wiped Out (double pack)	5
85	MCA GRIM 3	Is It A Dream (Wild West End Mix)/Street Of Dreams (live) (p/s, with 5 badges)	5
85	Stiff BUY DJ 238	New Rose/Help!/I'm So Bored (promo reissue)	20
86	Stiff BUY 6/BUY DJ 6A	New Rose/Help!/I'm So Bored (1-sided) (double pack, stickered PVC sleeve with insert, 1st disc on white vinyl, 2nd disc actually plays "I Fall" [live])	20
86	MCA GRIMT 4	Eloise/Temptation/Beat Girl (12", p/s, 2,000 on blue vinyl)	8
86	Stiff BUY 6	New Rose/Help! (reissue, red vinyl, PVC sleeve, with card insert)	8
90s	Sugar & Spite SS 01	History Of The World Part 1 (Psychedelic Mix) (1-sided flexi credited to 'The Dimmed' wraparound p/s free with Sugar & Spite fanzine.	12
91	Deltic DELT 7T	Fun Factory/CAPTAIN SENSIBLE: Freedom/Pasties/A Riot On Eastbourne Pier (12" p/s, blue vinyl, mail-order only, 2000 only)	8
02	Stiff FBUPC 004	New Rose/Help! (reissue with free CD single)	15

ALBUMS

77	Stiff SEEZ 1	DAMNED DAMNED DAMNED (LP)	20
77	Stiff SEEZ 1	DAMNED DAMNED DAMNED (LP, 2,000 with Eddie & Hot Rods photograph on rear sleeve; shrinkwrapped with title sticker)	250
77	Stiff SEEZ 1	DAMNED DAMNED DAMNED (LP, 2,000 with Eddie & Hot Rods photograph on rear sleeve; not shrinkwrapped with title sticker)	100
77	Stiff SEEZ 2	MUSIC FOR PLEASURE (LP)	25
79	Chiswick CWK 3011	MACHINE GUN ETIQUETTE (LP, with inner sleeve)	15
81	Ace DAM 1	THE BEST OF THE DAMNED (LP, red or blue vinyl)	12
82	Ace DAM 3	THE BLACK ALBUM (LP, single reissue, 12,000 with lyrics & poster)	12
82	Ace DAM 2	MACHINE GUN ETIQUETTE (LP, reissue, blue or white/clear vinyl with inner)	12
83	Stiff MAIL 2	DAMNED, DAMNED, DAMNED/MUSIC FOR PLEASURE (2-LP, reissue, yellow vinyl, 4000 by mail-order only)	25
83	Stiff MAIL 2	DAMNED DAMNED DAMNED/MUSIC FOR PLEASURE (2-LP, reissue, gatefold sleeve, mail-order, 5000 only)	25
83	Damned PDAMU 2	LIVE IN NEWCASTLE (LP, 5,000 by mail-order only)	15
83	Damned PDAMU 2	LIVE IN NEWCASTLE (LP, picture disc, 5,000 only)	15
84	Big Beat NED 1	LIVE SHEPPERTON 1980 (LP, with 'Collectors Catalogue', 5,000 only)	12
85	MCA MCFW 3275	PHANTASMAGORIA (LP, white vinyl, with inner)	15
86	Dojo DOJOPD 46	STRAWBERRIES (LP, reissue picture disc)	12
86	Stiff GET 4	THE CAPTAIN'S BIRTHDAY PARTY — LIVE AT THE ROUNDHOUSE (mini-LP, 45rpm, blue vinyl, stickered plain white sleeve)	12
87	Demon PFIEND 91	DAMNED DAMNED DAMNED (LP, reissue picture disc)	12
87	Demon FIEND 108	MUSIC FOR PLEASURE (LP, reissue, orange vinyl)	12
89	Essential ESCLP 008	FINAL DAMNATION (LP, green vinyl, with poster)	12
92	Reviever RRLP 159	LIVE AT THE LYCEUM (LP, clear vinyl)	12

(see also Bartok, Captain Sensible, Rat Scabies, Rat & Whale, Edge, Magic Michael, Maxim's Thrash, Naz Nomad & Nightmares, Auntiepus, Disco Brothers, Phantom Chords, Tank, Eddie & Hot Rods, U.F.O., Tanz Der Youth)

KENNY DAMON

65	Mercury MF 907	While I Live/Fountain In Capri	8
66	Mercury MF 936	World Of No Return/Are You Everything That's Beautiful	5
67	Mercury MF 959	Only Your Love/Sold To The Man With The Broken Heart	5
68	Mercury MF 1014	Turn Her Away/Till Then My Love	5

(see also Kenny Roberts)

RUSS DAMON

64	Stateside SS 258	Hip Huggers/Heaven Sent	12

STUART DAMON

70	Reflection REF L7	STUART 'CHAMPION' DAMON (LP)	20

DAMON & NAOMI

97	Earworm WORM 3	The Navigator/Awake In A Muddle (p/s)	8

(see also Galaxie 500)

VIC DAMONE

57	MGM MGM 949	And This Is My Beloved (with Howard Keel)/Night Of My Nights	5
57	MGM MGM 950	Stranger In Paradise (with Ann Blyth)/ANN BLYTH:Baubles, Bangles And Pearls	5
58	Philips PB 819	On The Street Where You Live/Arrivederci Roma	5
58	Philips PB 837	The Only Man On The Island/When My Love Smiles	5
68	Ember EMB 268	Don't Let Me Go/For Once In My Life (p/s)	5

MINT VALUE £

DAN

57	Mercury MPT 7514	ALL-TIME SONG HITS (10" LP)	12
57	Philips BBL 7144	THAT TOWERING FEELING! (LP)	12
57	Philips BBL 7234	ANGELA MIA (LP)	12
58	Philips BBL 7259	CLOSER THAN A KISS (LP)	12

(see also Howard Keel, Easy Riders)

DAN

87	All The Madmen MAD LP 09	AN ATTITUDE HITS (mini-LP)	12
87	Meantime COX 002b	WHERE HAVE ALL THE CHILDREN GONE (LP)	12
88	Workers Playtime PLAY LP 4	MOTHER WITH CHILD AND BUNNY (LP)	12
89	Meantime COX 013c	KICKING ASS AT TJ'S (LP, with flexi)	15

RUPIE DAN

| 82 | Flag FLG 101 | My Black Race/Black Race Dub (12") | 40 |

JONAH DAN

| 89 | Conscious Sounds JKPD 001 | MEETS THE BUSH CHEMISTS AT CONSCIOUS SOUNDS (LP) | 25 |

VIC DANA

62	Liberty LIB 51	I Will/Proud	10
62	Liberty LIB 64	A Very Good Year For The Girls/Looking For Me	6
64	Liberty LIB 92	Warm And Tender/Shangri-La	5
65	Liberty LIB 309	Moonlight And Roses/What'll I Do	5
65	Liberty LIB 313	Crystal Chandelier/What Now My Love (Et Maintenant)	5
66	Liberty LIB 319	I Love You Drops/Sunny Skies	5
66	Liberty LIB 322	Million And One/My Baby Wouldn't Leave Me	5
63	Liberty LBY 1193	MORE (LP)	15

DANCE CHAPTER

80	4AD AD 18	Anonymity/New Dance (p/s, with card insert)	8
80	4AD AD 18	Anonymity/New Dance (p/s)	6
81	4AD BAD 115	CHAPTER II (12" EP, most with mismatched A&B-side labels)	10

DANCELAND ROCK GROUP

| 62 | Danceland Y 2032 | Anytime/Because They're Young | 15 |
| 63 | Danceland Y 2043 | William Tell/Last Night Was Made For Love | 15 |

DANCER

| 75 | Dawn DNS 1118 | Hate Generator/Love Seeds | 10 |

DANCER, PRANCER & NERVOUS

| 59 | Capitol CL 15097 | The Happy Reindeer/Dancer's Waltz (p/s) | 12 |
| 59 | Capitol CL 15097 | The Happy Reindeer/Dancer's Waltz | 6 |

(see also Singing Reindeer)

DANCING DID

79	Fruit & Veg F&V 1	Dancing Did/Lorry Pirates (p/s)	18
80	Fruit & Veg F&V 2	The Haunted Tearooms/Squashed Things On The Road (p/s)	10
82	Stiff BUY 136	The Lost Platoon/The Human Chicken (withdrawn 'cavalry' p/s)	15
82	Stiff BUY 136	The Lost Platoon/The Human Chicken (sunset p/s)	5
82	Kamera Records KAM 009	AND DID THOSE FEET (LP, with insert)	25

DANDO SHAFT

70	Youngblood YB 1012	Cold Wind/Cat Song	15
72	RCA RCA 2246	Sun Clog Dance/This Gift	10
70	Youngblood SSYB 6	AN EVENING WITH DANDO SHAFT (LP, white/red label)	100
71	RCA Neon NE 5	DANDO SHAFT (LP, gatefold sleeve, black inner sleeve)	150
72	RCA Victor SF 8256	LANTALOON (LP, with poster, orange label)	150
72	RCA Victor SF 8256	LANTALOON (LP, without poster, orange label)	60
77	Rubber RUB 034	KINGDOM (LP)	40

(see also Hedgehog Pie)

DANDY (& SUPERBOYS)

64	Dice CC 21	Rudie Don't Go/It's Just Got To Be	15
65	Dice CC 24	You Got To Pray/I Got To Have You (as Dandy & Barbara)	15
65	Blue Beat BB 308	To Love You/I'm Looking For Love	15
65	Blue Beat BB 319	Hey Boy Hey Girl/So Long Baby (as Dandy & Del)	15
65	Blue Beat BB 327	My Baby/I'm Gonna Stop Loving You	15
65	Blue Beat BB 336	I Found Love/You've Got Something Nice	15
66	Dice CC 29	The Operation/A Little More Ska	15
66	Ska Beat JB 247	The Fight/Do You Know	15
67	Ska Beat JB 269	One Scotch One Bourbon One Beer/Maximum Pressure	20
67	Ska Beat JB 273	Rudie A Message To You/Til Death Do Us Part	10
67	Ska Beat JB 279	You're No Hustler/No No	15
67	Giant GN 3	My Time Now/East Of Suez (with Superboys)	25
67	Giant GN 5	Puppet On A String/Have Your Fun (with Superboys)	10
67	Giant GN 7	We Are Still Rude/Let's Do Rocksteady (with Superboys)	15
67	Giant GN 10	Somewhere My Love/My Kind Of Love (with Superboys)	10
67	Giant GN 15	There Is A Mountain/This Music Got Soul (with Superboys)	12
68	Giant GN 20	Charlie Brown/Groovin' At The Cue	10
68	Giant GN 23	Propagandist/Giant March	20
68	Giant GN 27	Sweet Ride/Up The Hill (with Superboys)	10
68	Giant GN 30	Tears On My Pillow/Mad Them (with Superboys)	10
68	Giant GN 36	I'm Back With A Bang Bang/Jungle Walk (with Superboys)	10
68	Trojan TR 618	The Toast/Kicks Out	12
69	Columbia Blue Beat DB 112	Play It Cool/Rude With Me	8
68	Downtown DT 401	Move Your Mule/Reggae Me This	18
69	Downtown DT 402	Come Back Girl/Shake Me Wake Me	15
69	Downtown DT 404	Tell Me Darling/Cool Hand Luke	15
69	Downtown DT 406	Doctor Sure Shot/Put On Your Dancing Shoes	7
69	Downtown DT 410	Reggae In Your Jeggae/DREAMERS: Reggae Shuffle	5
69	Downtown DT 411	You Don't Care/Tryer (both sides with Audrey)	5
69	Downtown DT 415	Rocksteady Gone/Walking Down	7
69	Downtown DT 416	I'm Your Puppet/Water Boy	7
69	Downtown DT 421	Games People Play/AUDREY: One Fine Day	7
69	Downtown DT 429	People Get Ready/RUDIES: Near East	35

69	Downtown DT 434	Be Natural, Be Proud/Who Do You Want To Run To	7
69	Downtown DT 437	Come On Home/Love Is All You Need	7
69	Downtown DT 442	Everybody Loves A Winner/Try Me One More Time	7
69	Downtown DT 445	Let's Come Together (with Israelites)/JAKE WADE: Music Fever	7
69	Downtown DT 453	Won't You Come Home/Baby Make It Soon	7
70	Downtown DT 456	Raining In My Heart/First Note	7
70	Downtown DT 457	Build Your Love (On Solid Foundation)/Let's Talk It Over (p/s)	7
70	Downtown DT 458	Build Your Love (On Solid Foundation)/Let's Talk It Over	5
70	Downtown DT 462	Morning Side Of The Mountain (as Dandy & Audrey)/AUDREY: Show Me Baby	7
70	Downtown DT 468	How Glad I Am/I'm So Glad (as Dandy & Audrey)	7
70	Trojan TR 7800	Take A Letter Maria/You're Coming Back	6
71	Downtown DT 483	Could It Be True/Your Eyes Are Dreaming (as Dandy & Jackie)	6
71	Downtown DT 484	Daddy's Home/Everyman	6
71	Trojan TR 7816	Same Old Fashioned Way/Out Of Many, One People	6
72	Trojan TR 7857	What Do You Want To Make Those Eyes At Me For/Talking About Sally	6
67	Giant GNL 1000	ROCKSTEADY WITH DANDY (LP)	50
68	Trojan TRL 2	DANDY RETURNS (LP)	45
69	Trojan TRL 17	I NEED YOU (LP, with Audrey)	25
70	Trojan TTL 26	YOUR MUSICAL DOCTOR (LP)	20
70	Trojan TBL 118	MORNINGSIDE OF THE MOUNTAIN (LP, with Audrey)	25

(see also Bobby Thompson, Sugar & Dandy, Rub A Dubs, Don Martin, Boy Friday, Audrey, Little Sal with Dandy & Superboys)

BARBARA DANE
66	Delyce/Envoy EIS 8876	AMERICAN FOLK SONGS ANTHOLOGY (LP)	15

CHRIS DANE
55	London HLA 8165	Cynthia's In Love/My Ideal	40
55	London HLA 8165	Cynthia's In Love/My Ideal (78)	10

JERRY DANE
60	Decca F 11234	You're My Only Girl/Nothing But The Truth	5
60	Decca F 11284	Let's/Awhile In Love	5
63	Windsor WPS 127	Everybody Go Wild/Watcha Want (p/s)	15
63	Windsor WPS 127	Everybody Go Wild/Watcha Want	10

PATRICK DANE
65	Columbia DB 7466	In My Baby's Eyes/The Only One (with Quiet Five)	6
65	Columbia DB 7749	Go Out And Get Somebody/Go On Your Way (with Club '69)	8
68	MGM MGM 1403	When You Lose The One You Love/Home (as Patrick Dane & Mark 7)	6

(see also Quiet Five)

CAL DANGER
62	Fontana 267 225 TF	Restless/Teenage Girlie Blues	70

(see also Tony Dangerfield)

A.P. DANGERFIELD
68	Fontana TF 935	Conversations (In A Station Light Refreshment Bar)/Further Conversations	30

KEITH DANGERFIELD
68	Plexium P 1237	No Life Child/She's A Witch	200

TONY DANGERFIELD & THRILLS
64	Pye 7N 15695	I've Seen Such Things/She's Too Way Out	70

(see also Savages, Circles, Cal Danger)

DANGEROUS GIRLS
78	Happy Face MM 115	Dangerous Girls/I Don't Want To Eat (With The Family) (p/s)	10
79	Happy Face MM 116	TAAGA EP (orange/red, pink and B&W picture sleeves)	8
80	Human HUM 1	Man In The Glass/MO75 (p/s)	6
81	Human HUM 6	Step Out/Sidekick Phenomenon/Men In Suits (p/s)	6

DANI
74	Pye International 7N 25667	La Vie A 25 Ans/Pour Que Ça Dure (p/s)	6
74	Pye International 7N 25667	That Old Familiar Feeling/Pour Que Ça Dure	12

ERROLL DANIEL
69	Paradox PAR 45902	No Excuses/Go Back	20

DANIEL IN THE LION'S DEN
70	Trojan TR 7797	Dancing In The Sun/LION'S DEN: Chick A Bow	6

DANIELLE
66	Philips BF 1532	I'm Gonna Marry The Boy/Magic Carpet Of Love	8
67	Philips BF 1574	Oh Mama/Come A Little Closer	7

BILLY DANIELS
56	Vogue V 2386	I Live For You/Medley: Easy To Love, etc.	5
56	Oriole CB 1087	I Get A Kick Out Of You/Too Marvelous For Words	5
56	Oriole CB 1095	That Old Black Magic/I Concentrate On You	5
60	Vogue V 9172	That Old Black Magic/My Yiddishe Mamma	6
56	Mercury MEP 9001	BILLY DANIELS (EP)	8
60	Mercury ZEP 10066	THAT OLD BLACK MAGIC (EP)	8
53	Oriole/Mercury MG 10003	TORCH HOUR (10" LP, Oriole label with stickered U.S. Mercury sleeve)	12
54	Mercury MG 25103	TORCH HOUR (10" LP, reissue)	12
54	Mercury MG 25163	SONGS AT MIDNIGHT (10" LP)	15
56	Mercury MPT 7505	SONGS AT MIDNIGHT (10" LP, reissue)	12

JULIUS DANIELS
65	RCA RCX 7175	R.C.A. VICTOR RACE SERIES VOL. 4 (EP)	15

MAXINE DANIELS
57	Oriole CB 1366	Coffee-Bar Calypso/Cha-Cha Calypso	12
58	Oriole CB 1402	I Never Realised/Moonlight Serenade	6
58	Oriole CB 1440	You Brought A New Kind Of Love To Me/Somebody Else Is Taking My Place	6
58	Oriole CB 1449	When It's Springtime In The Rockies/My Summer Heart	6
58	Oriole CB 1462	Passionate Summer/Lola's Heart	8

MIKE DANIELS & HIS BAND
57	Parlophone R 4285	Hiyawatha/Don't You Think I Love You	8

MINT VALUE £

| 57 | Columbia 33SX 1256 | MIKE ON MIKE (LP) | 40 |

ROLY "YO YO" DANIELS
60s	Stardisc SD 101	Yo Yo Boy/The Teacher (p/s)	15
61	Parlophone R 4759	Late Last Evening/Bella Bella Marie	5
62	Decca F 11501	Yo Yo Boy/The Teacher (reissue)	10

SAM DANIELS
| 63 | Sway SW 003 | Tell Me Baby/ERNIE FAULKENER: Beautiful Girl (both with Planets) | 12 |

REV R.A. DANIELS
| 51 | Capitol CL 13530 | He's The Lily Of The Valley/I Shall Wear A Crown (78) | 25 |

JOHNNY DANKWORTH ORCHESTRA
53	Parlophone MSP 6026	Honeysuckle Rose (with Cleo Laine)/Swingin'	10
53	Parlophone MSP 6032	Moon Flowers/Two Ticks	10
53	Parlophone MSP 6037	I Get A Kick Out Of You (with Frank Holder)/Easy Living (with Cleo Laine)	10
54	Parlophone MSP 6067	S' Wonderful/Younger Every Day	10
54	Parlophone MSP 6077	The Slider/It's The Talk Of The Town	10
54	Parlophone MSP 6083	The Jerky Thing/My Buddy	10
54	Parlophone MSP 6092	Runnin' Wild/Oo-Be-Doop	10
54	Parlophone MSP 6113	Perdido/Four Of A Kind	10
54	Parlophone MSP 6139	Bugle Call Rag/You Go To My Head	10
55	Capitol CL 14285	Singin' In The Rain/Non-Stop London	10
56	Parlophone MSP 6255	Experiments With Mice/Applecake	15
57	Parlophone R 4274	All Clare/Melbourne Marathon	5
57	Parlophone R 4294	Duke's Joke/Coquette	5
57	Parlophone R 4321	Big Jazz Story/Firth Of Fourths	5
58	Parlophone R 4456	The Colonel's Tune/Jim And Andy's	5
59	Top Rank JAR 209	We Are The Lambeth Boys/Duet For 16	5
59	Top Rank JAR 209	We Are The Lambeth Boys/Duet For 16 (78)	10
61	Columbia DB 4695	The Avengers/Chano	15
61	Columbia DB 4751	String Of Camels/Winter Wail	5
62	No label 19517	Music For The New Prestige Film (1-sided white label)	15
62	Columbia DB 4852	Cannonball/S.O. Blues	5
62	Fontana TF 396	Hoe Down/Sing Sing Sing	6
63	Fontana TF 422	The Avengers/Off The Cuff	15
64	Fontana TF 512	Beefeaters/Down A Tone	35
65	Fontana TF 643	Sands Of The Kalahari/Night Thoughts	6
66	Fontana TF 675	Return From The Ashes/Piano Theme	5
66	Fontana TF 700	Modesty Blaise Theme/The Frost Report	10
67	Fontana TF 805	(Ain't That) Just Like A Woman/Accident	10
73	Philips 6006 337	Tomorrows World/Bitter Lemons	10
78	BBC RESL 63	Telford's Change/Serenade For Sylvia (p/s)	8
61	Columbia SEG 8137	AFRICAN WALTZ (EP)	12
58	Parlophone GEP 8653	DANKWORTH WORKSHOP NO. 1 (EP)	20
58	Parlophone GEP 8697	DANKWORTH WORKSHOP NO. 2 — EXPERIMENTS WITH DANKWORTH (EP)	15
60	Columbia SEG 8037	THE CRIMINALS (EP, soundtrack; also stereo ESG 7825)	15
56	Parlophone PMD 1042	JOURNEY INTO JAZZ (10" LP)	20
58	Parlophone PMC 1076	THE VINTAGE YEARS (LP)	20
59	Parlophone PMC 1043	FIVE STEPS TO DANKWORTH (LP)	20
60	Top Rank 30/019	LONDON TO NEWPORT (LP)	40
61	Columbia 33SX 1280	JAZZ ROUTES (LP, also stereo SCX 3347)	30
62	Columbia	COLLABORATION! (LP, with London Philharmonic)	15
63	Columbia 33SX 1572	CURTAIN UP (LP)	15
64	Fontana TL/STL 5203	WHAT THE DICKENS! (LP)	20
64	Encore ENC 165	FROM 7 ON (LP)	20
65	Fontana TL 5229	THE ZODIAC VARIATIONS (LP, mono)	25
65	Fontana STL 5229	THE ZODIAC VARIATIONS (LP, stereo)	30
67	Stateside S(S)L 10213	FATHOM (LP, soundtrack)	40
68	Fontana TL 5445	THE $1,000,000 COLLECTION (LP)	20
69	Fontana LPS 16261	OFF DUTY (LP)	18
72	Philips 6308 122	FULL CIRCLE (LP)	15
73	Philips 6308 169	LIFELINE (LP)	15
83	Sepia RSR 2011	ZODIAC VARIATIONS (LP, reissue)	12

(see also Cleo Laine, Philip Green, Tony Mansell, Kenny Wheeler & Johnny Dankworth)

DANLEERS
| 58 | Mercury AMT 1003 | One Summer Night/Wheelin' And A-Dealin' | 200 |
| 58 | Mercury AMT 1003 | One Summer Night/Wheelin' And A-Dealin' (78) | 40 |

DANNY & NOGOODNIKS
| 82 | Chrysalis CHS 2667 | Bike/Spaghetti (p/s) | 10 |

(see also Adam Ant, Adam & The Ants)

DANNY BOYS
| 89 | Ugly Man UG 1 | Days Of The Week (12" EP) | 15 |

DANNY & THE JUNIORS
58	HMV POP 436	At The Hop/Sometimes (When I'm All Alone)	15
58	HMV POP 467	Rock And Roll Is Here To Stay/School Boy Romance	40
58	HMV POP 467	Rock And Roll Is Here To Stay/School Boy Romance (78)	18
58	HMV POP 504	Dottie/In The Meantime	30
58	HMV POP 504	Dottie/In The Meantime (78)	25
60	Top Rank JAR 510	Twistin' U.S.A./Thousand Miles Away	15
61	Top Rank JAR 552	Pony Express/Daydreamer	15
61	Top Rank JAR 587	Back To The Hop/The Charleston Fish	15
62	Top Rank JAR 604	Twistin' All Night Long/Twistin' England (with Freddy Cannon)	15
63	London HL 9666	Oo-La-La-Limbo/Now And Then	12
68	Stateside SS 2117	At The Hop/LLOYD PRICE: (You've Got) Personality	5

C. DANOVAN (ACTUALLY DON CARLOS)
| 73 | Randy's RAN 529 | Sweet Caroline/IMPACT ALL STARS: Caroline (Version) | 5 |

DANSE MACABRE
| 88 | Wild West/Alchemy 1 | THINK ABOUT DEATH EP | 20 |

DANSE SOCIETY

81	Society SOC 3-81	The Clock/Continent (brown, black & white foldout p/s)	15
81	Society SOC 3-81	The Clock/Continent (re-pressing, black & white foldout p/s)	5
81	Pax PAX 2	There Is No Shame In Death/Dolphins/These Frayed Edges (12", p/s, blue vinyl)	20
82	Pax SOC 5	Woman's Own/We're So Happy (p/s)	8
82	Pax PAX 5	Woman's Own/Continent/We're So Happy/Belief (12", with spined p/s)	10
84	Society SOC V 127	2,000 Light Years From Home (12" blue vinyl, 50-150 pressed)	60

DANSETTE DAMAGE

78	Shoestring LACE 001	New Musical Express/The Only Sound (p/s, Robert Plant on backing vocals)	150
79	Pinnacle PIN 30	20013/4 Approximately/Must Be Love (p/s)	8
94	Shoestring BLOO 2LP	SOLD AS SEEN (LP, gatefold sleeve, 500 only)	30

DANTA

72	Epic EPC 7776	Freeway/Mau Mau	30
73	Epic SEPC 1466	Crossfire/Daddy's Gone	20

DANTALIAN'S CHARIOT

67	Columbia DB 8260	The Madman Running Through The Fields/The Sun Came Bursting Through My Cloud	120
95	Tenth Planet TP 015	CHARIOT RISING (LP, numbered, 1,000 only)	25

(see also Zoot Money's Big Roll Band)

DANTE (1)

61	Brunswick 05857	Bye Bye Baby/That's Why	12

DANTE (2)

71	CBS 7382	Queen Of Sheba/Feelin' The Heat	15

RON DANTE

68	MCA MK5003	It's About Time/Behold	8
70	RCA 1992	Let Me Bring You Up/How Do You Know	8

RONNIE DANTE

64	Stateside SS 351	Don't Stand Up In A Canoe/If You Love Me Laurie	5

TROY DANTE (& INFERNOS)

63	Decca F 11639	The Face/Give Me Some More	8
63	Decca F 11746	It's Alright/Tell Me (as Troy Dante & Infernos)	8
64	Fontana TF 445	Tell Me When/It Had To Be (as Troy Dante & Infernos)	8
64	Fontana TF 477	This Little Girl/Loving Eyes (as Troy Dante & Infernos)	12
64	Fontana TF 498	Baby/Tell Me Now	8
65	Fontana TF 541	I Wish I Knew/Sad Tears	8
66	Polydor NH 56110	I'll Never Know/Security	7
68	Columbia DB 8381	My Friend The Scarecrow/Emma May Kingston	7
69	MCA MK 5003	It's About Time/Behold	8
69	MCA MU 1056	Little Star/These Are Not My People	6

DANTE & EVERGREENS

60	Top Rank JAR 402	Alley-Oop/The Right Time	12

DAN THE BANJO MAN

73	Rare Earth RES 110	Dan The Banjo Man/Everything Will Rhyme	6

DAPHINE

79	My Records MY 12	The World Is Moving On/Just Another Flirt (P/S)	8

JOE DARENSBOURG & HIS DIXIE FLYERS

58	Vogue V 2409	Yellow Dog Blues/Careless Love	5

DARIEN SPIRIT

73	Charisma CAS 1065	ELEGY TO MARILYN (LP, large "Mad Hatter" label, with lip intact!)	30

BOBBY DARIN

78s

56	Brunswick 05561	Rock Island Line/Timber (as Bobby Darin & Jaybirds)	30
58	London HLE 8666	Splish Splash/Judy Don't Be Moody	20
58	London HLE 8679	Early In The Morning/Now We're One	20
58	London HLE 8737	Queen Of The Hop/Lost Love	40
59	London HLE 8793	Mighty Mighty Man/You're Mine (as Bobby Darin with Rinky Dinks)	40
59	London HLE 8815	Plain Jane/While I'm Gone	40
59	London HLE 8867	Dream Lover/Bullmoose	20
59	London HLK 8939	Mack The Knife/Was There A Call For Me	40
60	London HLK 9034	La Mer (Beyond The Sea)/That's The Way Love Is	50
60	London HLK 9086	Clementine/Down With Love	50
60	London HLK 9142	Bill Bailey Won't You Please Come Home/Tall Story	60

SINGLES

56	Brunswick 05561	Rock Island Line/Timber (as Bobby Darin & Jaybirds)	150
58	London HLE 8666	Splish Splash/Judy Don't Be Moody	25
58	London HLE 8679	Early In The Morning/Now We're One (as Rinky-Dinks featuring Bobby Darin)	30
58	London HLE 8737	Queen Of The Hop/Lost Love	30
58	London HL 7060	Queen Of The Hop/Lost Love (export issue)	20
59	London HLE 8793	Mighty Mighty Man/You're Mine (as Bobby Darin with Rinky Dinks)	30
59	London HLE 8815	Plain Jane/While I'm Gone	30
59	London HL 7078	Plain Jane/Dream Lover (export issue)	25
59	London HLE 8867	Dream Lover/Bullmoose	5
58	London HLK 8939	Mack The Knife/Was There A Call For Me	5
60	London HLK 9034	La Mer (Beyond The Sea)/That's The Way Love Is	5

(The above 45s were originally issued with triangular centres, later round centre pressings are worth around two thirds these values.)

60	London HLK 9086	Clementine/Down With Love	5
60	London HLK 9142	Bill Bailey Won't You Please Come Home/Tall Story	5
60	Brunswick 05831	Hear Them Bells/The Greatest Builder	6
60	London HLK 9197	Beachcomber/Autumn Blues (credited to 'Bobby Darin At The Piano')	6
60	Lonson HLK 9215	Somebody To Love/I'll Be There	5
61	London HLK 9303	Lazy River/Oo-Ee-Train	5
61	London HLK 9375	Nature Boy/Look For My True Love	5
61	London HLK 9407	Theme From "Come September"/Walk Bach To Me (with Orchestra)	6

61	London HLK 9429	You Must Have Been A Beautiful Baby/Sorrow Tomorrow	5
61	London HLK 9474	Multiplication (From "Come September")/Irresistible You	5
62	London HLK 9540	What'd I Say/Ain't That Love	5
62	London HLK 9575	Things/Jailer Bring Me Water	5
62	Atlantic HLK 9575	Things/Jailer Bring Me Water	20
62	Capitol CL 15272	If A Man Answers/A True, True Love	5
62	London HLK 9624	Baby Face/You Know How	5
63	London HLK 9663	I've Found A New Baby/Keep A-Walkin'	5
63	Capitol CL 15286	You're The Reason I'm Living/Now You're Gone	5
63	Capitol CL 15306	Eighteen Yellow Roses/Not For Me	10
63	Capitol CL 15328	Be Mad Little Girl/Since You've Been Gone	6
64	Capitol CL 15338	I Wonder Who's Kissing Her Now/As Long As I'm Singing	5
64	Atlantic AT 4002	Milord/Golden Earrings	6
64	Capitol CL 15360	The Things In This House/Wait By The Water	5
65	Capitol CL 15401	When I Get Home/Lonely Road	5
65	Capitol CL 15414	Gyp The Cat/That Funny Feeling	5
65	Atlantic AT 4046	We Didn't Ask To Be Brought Here/Funny What Love Can Do	10
66	Atlantic 584 014	Mame/Walking In The Shadow Of Love	6
66	Atlantic 584 051	If I Were A Carpenter/Rainin'	6
67	Atlantic 584 063	The Girl That Stood Beside Me/Reason To Believe	6
67	Atlantic 584 079	Lovin' You/Amy	5
67	Atlantic 584 105	The Lady Came From Baltimore/I Am	6
67	Atlantic 584 147	At The Crossroads/She Knows	5
68	Bell BLL 1040	Change/Long Line Rider	5
69	Bell BLL 1090	Sugar-Man/Jive	5
70	Major Minor MM 697	Maybe We Can Get It Together/RX-Pyro (Prescription: Fire) (as Bob Darin)	5
74	Mowest MW 3014	Blue Monday/Moritat: Mack The Knife	5

EPs

59	London REE 1173	BOBBY DARIN (tri centre)	60
59	London REE 1173	BOBBY DARIN (round centre)	30
59	London REE 1225	BOBBY DARIN NO. 2 (tri centre)	60
59	London REE 1225	BOBBY DARIN NO. 2 (round centre)	30
60	London REK 1243	THAT'S ALL	15
61	London REK 1286	FOR TEENAGERS ONLY	30
61	London REK 1290	UP A LAZY RIVER	15
61	London REK 1310	TWO OF A KIND (with Johnny Mercer)	15
61	London REK 1321	THE 25TH DAY OF DECEMBER	15
61	London REK 1334	LOVE SWINGS	15
62	London REK 1338	TWIST WITH BOBBY DARIN	20
62	London REK 1342	THINGS!	15
65	Atlantic AET 6013	MILORD	10

ALBUMS

58	London HA-E 2140	BOBBY DARIN	50
59	London HA-E 2172	THAT'S ALL	20
59	London HA-K 2235	THIS IS DARIN (mono)	25
59	London SAH-K 6067	THIS IS DARIN (stereo)	25
60	London HA-K 2291	DARIN AT THE COPA (mono)	20
60	London SAH-K 6103	DARIN AT THE COPA (stereo)	20
60	London HA-K 2311	FOR TEENAGERS ONLY	50
61	London HA-K 2363	TWO OF A KIND (with Johnny Mercer; mono)	20
61	London SAH-K 6164	TWO OF A KIND (with Johnny Mercer; stereo)	25
61	London HA-K 2372	THE BOBBY DARIN STORY	20
61	London HA-K 2394	LOVE SWINGS (mono)	20
61	London SAH-K 6194	LOVE SWINGS (stereo)	25
62	London HA-K 2456	DARIN SINGS RAY CHARLES (mono)	25
62	London SAH-K 6243	DARIN SINGS RAY CHARLES (stereo)	35
62	Capitol T 1791	OH! LOOK AT ME NOW	15
62	London HA-K 8030	THINGS AND OTHER THINGS	20
63	London HA-K 8102	IT'S YOU OR NO-ONE (mono)	25
63	London SH-K 8102	IT'S YOU OR NO-ONE (stereo)	30
63	Capitol T 1826	EARTHY	15
63	Capitol T 1866	YOU'RE THE REASON I'M LIVING	15
63	Capitol T 1942	EIGHTEEN YELLOW ROSES & 11 OTHER HITS (mono)	20
63	Capitol (S)T 1942	EIGHTEEN YELLOW ROSES & 11 OTHER HITS (stereo)	25
64	Capitol T 2007	GOLDEN FOLK HITS (mono)	20
64	Capitol (S)T 2007	GOLDEN FOLK HITS (stereo)	20
65	Capitol T 2194	FROM HELLO DOLLY TO GOODBYE CHARLIE	12
65	Atlantic ATL 5014	BOBBY DARIN WINNERS	12
65	Capitol T 2322	I WANNA BE AROUND	12
66	Capitol T 2571	THE BEST OF BOBBY DARIN	12
66	Atlantic 587/588 014	SINGS THE SHADOW OF YOUR SMILE	12
66	Atlantic 587/588 020	IN A BROADWAY BAG (MAME)	12
66	Atlantic 587/588 051	IF I WERE A CARPENTER	12
67	Atlantic 587 065	THE BOBBY DARIN STORY	12
67	Atlantic 587 073	SOMETHING SPECIAL	30
67	Atlantic 587 076	INSIDE OUT	12

(see also Rinky Dinks)

DARK (1)

72	SIS 0102	DARK ROUND THE EDGES (LP, private pressing, 12 copies with colour gatefold sleeve & booklet)	4000
72	SIS 0102	DARK ROUND THE EDGES (LP, private pressing, 8 copies with black & white gatefold sleeve)	3000
72	SIS 0102	DARK ROUND THE EDGES (LP, private pressing, 40 copies with single black & white sleeve)	2000
90	Swank/Darkside 001	DARK ROUND THE EDGES (LP, reissue, U.K. pressing marketed in U.S.)	30
91	Swank/Darkside 001	DARK ROUND THE EDGES (LP, as above, with different insert, 225 only)	20
92	Kissing Spell KSCD 9204	DARK ROUND THE EDGES (CD, with 8-page booklet, 1,500 only)	25
95	Acme AC 8009LP	ARTEFACTS FROM THE BLACK MUSEUM (LP, 500 only, with insert)	15

DARK (2)
79	Fresh FRESH 2	My Friends/John Wayne (p/s)	6

DARK ANGEL
86	Under One Flag FLAG 6	DARKNESS DESCENDS (LP)	15
89	Under One Flag FLAG 30	LEAVE SCARS (LP)	12
90	Under One Flag M FLAG 42	LIVE SCARS (Mini-LP)	12
91	Under One Flag FLAG 54 DM	TIME DOES NOT HEAL (2-LP)	20
08	Back On Black BOBV 060 LP	DARKNESS DESCENDS (LP, reissue, purple vinyl, gatefold sleeve)	12
10	Back On Black BOBV 261 LP	TIME DOES NOT HEAL (2-LP, reissue, gatefold sleeve)	15

DARKER SHADE OF BLACK
71	Jackpot JP 758	War/JEFF BARNES: People's Version	8

DARKNESS
02	Must Destroy DUSTY 001CD	I Believe In A Thing Called Love/Love On The Rocks With No Ice/Love Is Only A Feeling (CD)	40
03	Must Destroy DESTROYER 6	Get Your Hands Off My Woman (Clean Version)/(Dirty Version)/Best Of Me (p/s, 2000 only)	10
03	Must Destroy DARK 02	Christmas Time (Don't Let The Bells End)/I Love You 5 Times (promo-only box set, in giftwrap, with card)	15

DARKSIDE
90	Situation 2 SITU 29P	ALL THAT NOISE (LP, picture disc, die-cut sleeve)	12

(see also Spacemen 3)

DARK STAR
81	Avatar AAA 105	Lady Of Mars/Rock 'N' Romancin' (company sleeve)	12
81	Steel Strike no cat. no.	Lady Of Mars/Rock 'N' Romancin' (12", 250 pressed)	90
81	Avatar AALP 5003	DARK STAR (LP, with patch)	20
81	Avatar AALP 5003	DARK STAR (LP)	15
87	FM WKFMLP 97	REAL TO REEL (LP)	15

DARKTHRONE
91	Peaceville VILE 22	SOULSIDE JOURNEY (LP, picture disc)	50
92	Peaceville VILE 28	A BLAZE IN THE NORTHERN SKY (LP)	50
93	Peaceville VILE 35	UNDER A FUNERAL MOON (LP)	50
94	Peaceville VILE 43	TRANSILVANIAN HUNGER (LP)	80

DARLETTES
70	President PT 317	Lost/Sweet Kind Of Loneliness	15

DARLING BUDS
87	Darling Buds DAR 1	If I Said/Just To Be Seen (p/s, with insert, 2,000 only)	12
87	Darling Buds DAR 1	If I Said/Just To Be Seen (p/s, without insert, 2,000 only)	6
90	Native NTV 54	Shame On You/Valentine//It's All Up To You/Spin/Think Of Me/ That's The Reason (triple-pack in envelope sleeve)	6

DARLINGS
67	CBS 2932	Saturday Town/Wish You Were Here	20

BILL DARNEL
55	London HLU 8204	My Little Mother/Bring Me A Bluebird (with Frank Weir & His Orchestra)	40
56	London HLU 8234	The Last Frontier/Rock-A-Boogie Baby	50
56	London HLU 8267	Guilty Lips/Ain't Misbehavin'	30
56	London HLU 8292	Tell Me More/Satin Doll	30

(see also Frank Weir & His Orchestra)

GUY DARRELL (& MIDNIGHTERS)
63	Oriole CB 1932	Go Home Girl/You Won't Come Home (as Guy Darrell & Midnighters)	15
64	Oriole CB 1964	Sorry/Sweet Dreams (as Guy Darrell & Midnighters)	15
65	CBS 201806	Stupidity/One Of These Days	10
66	CBS 202033	Somewhere They Can't Find Me/It Takes A Lot To Laugh	10
66	CBS 202082	I've Been Hurt/Blessed	25
66	CBS 202082	I've Been Hurt/Blessed (demo)	40
66	CBS 202296	Big Louie/My Way Of Thinking	6
67	CBS 202510	Hard Lovin'/I've Never Had A Love Like That	12
67	CBS 202642	Crystal Ball/Didn't I	6
67	Piccadilly 7N 35406	Evil Woman/What You Do About That	20
67	Pye 7N 17435	Cupid/What's Happened To Our Love	5
68	Pye 7N 17586	Skyline Pigeon/Everything	5
69	Page One POF 120	Turn To Me/What's Her Name	6
69	Page One POF 141	Birds Of A Feather/Keep The Rain From My Door	6
69	Page One POF 155	How Are You/Turtle Turquoise And The Hare (as Guy Darrell Syndicate)	6
73	Santa Ponsa PNS4	I've Been Hurt/Blessed (reissue)	5
74	Santa Ponsa PNS 19	You're Ready Now/Turn To Me	6
74	Santa Ponsa PNS 10	Hard Road/We've Thrown It All Away	6
72	CBS 53364	GUY DARRELL (LP)	20
73	Santa Ponsa PNL 502	I'VE BEEN HURT (LP)	15

JAMES DARREN
59	Pye International 7N 25019	Gidget/There's No Such Thing (as Jimmy Darren)	10
59	Pye International 7N 25034	Angel Face/I Don't Wanna Lose You (as Jimmy Darren)	15
60	Pye International 7N 25059	Because They're Young/Let There Be Love	8
61	Pye International 7N 25116	Goodbye Cruel World/Valerie	7
62	Pye International 7N 25125	Her Royal Majesty/If I Could Only Tell You	6
62	Pye International 7N 25138	Conscience/Dream Big	7
62	Pye International 7N 25155	Mary's Little Lamb/The Life Of The Party	8
62	Pye International 7N 25168	Hail To The Conquering Hero/Too Young To Go Steady	8
63	Pye International 7N 25170	Pin A Medal On Joey/I'll Be Loving You	8
63	Colpix PX 708	Backstage/Gegetta	10
65	Warner Bros WB 5648	Because You're Mine/Millions Of Roses	6
66	Warner Bros WB 5689	Tom Hawk/I Want To Be Lonely	6
67	Warner Bros WB 5874	All/Misty Morning Eyes	6
59	Pye Intl. NEP 44004	P.S. I LOVE YOU (EP)	25
62	Pye Intl. NEP 44008	JAMES DARREN HIT PARADE (EP)	20
63	Pye Intl. NPL 28021	LOVE AMONG THE YOUNG (LP)	30

JEANNIE DARREN & SECOND CITY SOUND

MINT VALUE £

69	Major Minor MM 611	River Deep, Mountain High/Julie	7

MAXINE DARREN
65	Pye 7N 15796	How Can I Hide It From My Heart/Don't You Know	10

CHRIS DARROW
73	United Artists UAG 29453	CHRIS DARROW (LP)	15
74	United Artists UAG 29634	UNDER MY OWN DISGUISE (LP)	15

(see also Kaleidoscope, Nitty Gritty Dirt Band)

DARTELLS
63	London HLD 9719	Hot Pastrami/Dartell Stomp	20

BARRY DARVELL
60	London HL 9191	Geronimo Stomp/How Will It End?	80

DARWIN'S THEORY
67	Major Minor MM 503	Daytime/Hosanna	40

NITAE DASGUPTA
72	Mushroom 100 MR 22	SONGS OF INDIA (LP)	35

DAS KABINETTE
83	Klosette PL0026	The Cabinet/Fudge It (p/s, 500 only)	100

DAS SCHNITZ
79	Ellie Jay EJSP 9249	4 AM (EP, custom sleeve)	70

DATE WITH SOUL
67	Stateside SS 2062	Yes Sir, That's My Baby/PRISCILLA: He Noticed Me	50

(see also Jack Nitzsche, Brian Wilson, Sonny & Cher, Darlene Love/Blossoms, Jackie De Shannon, the Paris Sisters)

DAT POLITICS
04	Chicks On Speed COSR 15	GO PET GO (LP)	15

DAUGHTERS OF ALBION
69	Fontana STL 5486	DAUGHTERS OF ALBION (LP)	30

DAUGHTERS OF THE CROSS
69	Chapter One CHL 802	GO TELL IT ON THE MOUNTAIN (LP)	20

DAVANI & RYAN
72	Philips 6308 132	FUNKY COUNTRY (LP)	20

DAVE DAVANI & D MEN
63	Columbia DB 7125	Don't Fool Around/She's The Best For Me	15
64	Decca F 11896	Midnight Special/Sho' Know A Lot About Love	20

(see also Davani & Ryan)

DAVE DAVANI (FOUR)
65	Parlophone R 5329	Top Of The Pops/Workin' Out	40
66	Parlophone R 5490	Tossin' And Turnin'/Jupe	50
66	Parlophone R 5525	One Track Mind/On The Cooler Side	35
72	Philips 6006 195	King Kong Blues/Come Back Baby (solo)	12
65	Parlophone PMC 1258	FUSED (LP)	90

(see also Davani & Ryan)

DAVE & DIAMONDS
65	Columbia DB 7692	I Walk The Lonely Night/You Do Love (p/s)	35
65	Columbia DB 7692	I Walk The Lonely Night/You Do Love	15

(see also Dave Russell)

DAVE & DON
67	Polydor 56212	What A Feeling/That's My Way	6

BOB DAVENPORT (& RAKES)
60	Collector JEB 4	GEORDIE SONGS (EP)	15
62	Topic TOP 83	WOR GEORDIE (EP, with Rakes)	15
66	Columbia SX 1786	BOB DAVENPORT AND THE RAKES (LP, with Rakes)	40
71	Trailer LER 3008	BOB DAVENPORT& THE MARSDEN RATTLERS (LP, red label)	22
73	Trailer LER 2088	PAL OF MY CRADLE DAYS (LP, red label)	18
77	Topic 12TS 318	POSTCARDS HOME (LP, with lyric sheet)	15

D.A.V.E. THE DRUMMER
90s	Yolk YOLK 05	Steamliner/Jaws (12", with Jerome Hill)	40
00	Smitten SMT 38	Proper/What You Need (12")	8
00	Smitten SMT 46	DIG YOUR OWN GRAVE EP (2x12", p/s)	10
00	Smitten SMTLTD 02	Effective Therapy (1-sided 12", green vinyl)	15

ALAN DAVEY
87	Hawkfan HWFB 3/4	THE ELF EP (double pack, 2 x 7" with insert in wraparound p/s in poly bag)	20

(see also Hawkwind)

(SHAUN) DAVEY & (JAMES) MORRIS
73	York FYK 417	DAVEY AND MORRIS (LP, with insert)	110

(see also Strawbs)

DAVID
69	Philips BF 1776	Light Of Your Mind/Please Mister Policeman	200
69	President PT286	The Who The Why/President	6
70	Fontana TF 1081	I'm Going Back/Selppin	60

ALAN DAVID
64	Decca F 11956	I Want So Much To Know You/I Can't Go Wrong	10
65	Decca F 12084	Hurt/I Found Out Too Late	50
65	Decca F 12130	Crazy 'Bout My Baby/A Thousand Years Too Late	10
67	Polydor BM 56201	Flower Power/Completely Free	30
69	Page One POF116	Oh What A Naughty Man/I've Got To Know	10
65	Decca LK 4674	ALAN DAVID (LP)	40

DAVID & DAVID
70	Columbia DB8678	In The City/Good Morning Morning	20

DAVID & EMBERS
63	Decca F 11717	What Is This/Teddy Bear Special	7

(see also Embers)

DAVID & GIANTS
68	Capitol CL 15915	Ten Miles High/Super Love	10

DAVID & GOLIATH
71	Concord CON 025	Why Do You Pretend/I Wonder Where	8

DAVID & JONATHAN
66	Columbia DB 7950	Lovers Of The World Unite/Oh My World	5
67	Columbia DB 8208	She's Leaving Home/One Born Every Minute	6
67	Columbia S(C)X 6031	DAVID AND JONATHAN (LP)	25

(see also Roger Cook, Edison Lighthouse, White Plains)

DAVID & ROZAA
70	Philips 6006 040	Time Of Our Life/We Can Reach An Understanding	20
71	Philips 6006 094	The Spark That Lights The Flame/Two Can Share	20

(see also David Essex, Rozaa & Wine)

DIANNE DAVIDSON
72	Janus 6146 019	Sympathy/All I Wanted	8
72	Janus 6146 021	Ain't Gonna Be Treated This Way/All I Wanted (All The Time)	5
72	Janus 6310 209	BACKWOODS WOMAN (LP)	12

FRANKIE DAVIDSON & HI MARKS
61	Starlite ST45 5037	You're Driving Me Crazy/I Care For You (B-side with Unicords)	10
61	London HL 9309	Detour/Just For Today	8
63	HMV POP 1220	Broken Wings/Have You Ever Been To London Town	6
64	HMV POP 1256	Lickin' And A-Stickin'/I Love To Shake	10
68	Decca F 22780	Hector The Trash Collector/Somebody Come And Take My Wife	5

TOMMY DAVIDSON
56	London HLU 8219	Half Past Kissing Time/I Don't Know Yet But I'm Learning	90
56	London HLU 8219	Half Past Kissing Time/I Don't Know Yet But I'm Learning (78)	20

HUTCH DAVIE
58	London HLE 8667	At The Woodchopper's Ball/Honky Tonk Train Blues (& Honky Tonkers)	10
60	London HLE 9076	Sweet Georgia Brown/Heartaches	5
62	Pye International 7N 25149	But I Do/Time Was (& Orchestra)	5
60	London HA-E 2216	MUCH HUTCH (LP)	20

ALUN DAVIES
65	Parlophone R 5384	Girls Were Made To Love And Kiss/Rose Marie	6
68	Mercury MF 1043	One Day Soon/Pretend You Don't See Her	6
72	CBS 58302	Waste Of Time/Portobello Road	6
72	CBS 65108	DAYDO (LP, gatefold sleeve)	25

(see also Cat Stevens, Sweet Thursday)

BARRY DAVIES
70	Beacon BEA 114	I Wish It Would Rain/Strange Days	30

BAZ DAVIES
80	BAT EJSP 9397	Back In 1969/Easy On My Mind	8

BOB DAVIES
63	London HLU 9767	Rock'N'Roll Show/With You Tonight	25

CYRIL DAVIES (R&B ALLSTARS)
63	Pye International 7N 25194	Country Line Special/Chicago Calling	25
63	Pye International 7N 25221	Preachin' The Blues/Sweet Mary	40
69	Pye 7N 17663	Country Line Special/Sweet Mary	15
64	Pye Intl. NEP 44025	THE SOUND OF CYRIL DAVIES (EP)	75
57	'77' LP 2	THE LEGENDARY CYRIL DAVIES (10" LP, 99 only, with Alexis Korner)	300
70	Folklore F-LEAT 9	THE LEGENDARY CYRIL DAVIES (LP, reissue)	75

(see also Alexis Korner, Beryl Bryden)

DAVE DAVIES
67	Pye 7N 17356	Death Of A Clown/Love Me Till The Sun Shines	8
67	Pye 7N 17429	Susannah's Still Alive/Funny Face	10
68	Pye 7N 17514	Lincoln County/There's No Life Without Love	20
69	Pye 7N 17678	Hold My Hand/Creeping Jean	20
68	Pye NEP 24289	DAVE DAVIES HITS (EP)	300

(see also Kinks)

IRVING DAVIES & METHOD MEN
62	Decca F 11456	The Method/ABC The Method	6

JACKIE DAVIES & HIS QUARTET
57	Pye Nixa N 15115	Land Of Make Believe/Over The Rainbow (78)	50

(see also Chico Arnez)

MARION DAVIES
69	Columbia DB 8589	Walk Out Of My Mind/This Is My Lonely Life	7

(see also Ladybirds)

MIAR DAVIES
64	Decca F 11805	Ten Good Reasons/I Won't Remember You	10
64	Decca F 11894	I Hear You Knocking/Navy Blue	10

NICOLA DAVIES
68	SNB 55-3627	Infatuation/My Boy	10

RAY DAVIES & BUTTONDOWN BRASS
73	Pye NSPL 41021	I BELIEVE IN MUSIC (LP)	15
74	Philips 6382 103	THEMES FROM THE EXORCIST, FRENCH CONNECTION AND OTHER GREAT FILMS (LP)	15

Ray DAVIES

75	Philips 6382 111	FLASHPOINT (LP)	15

(see also Buttondown Brass; this is not Ray Davies of the Kinks)

RAY DAVIES
86	Virgin VS 865-12	Quiet Life/Voices In The Dark/GIL EVANS: Va Va Voom (12", p/s)	8
86	Virgin VS 865	Quiet Life/Voices In The Dark (p/s)	5

(see also Kinks)

RON DAVIES
70	A & M AMS 799	It Ain't Easy/Silent Song Through The Land	6
70	A&M AMLS 993	SILENT SONG THROUGH THE LAND (LP, green label)	30

RUPERT DAVIES
63	Parlophone R5067	December Dreams/Smoking My Pipe (La Pipa)	7

TYRONE DAVIES
77	D-Roy FORCE 2012	Mind Blowing Decisions/Trenchtown Skank	20

BARRINGTON DAVIS
72	Montague MONS 2	TRACKS OF MIND (LP, with lyric inner sleeve)	60

BETTE DAVIS (& DEBBIE BURTON)
63	London HLU 9711	Whatever Happened To Baby Jane?/ DEBBIE BURTON:I've Written A Letter To Daddy	12
76	EMI 2415	Mother Of The Bride/It Can't Be Wrong (as Miss Bette Davis)	8
76	EMI EMA 778	MISS BETTE DAVIS (LP)	30

BETTY DAVIS
75	Island USA 2011	Shut Off The Light/He Was A Big Freak	6
75	Island ILPS 9329	NASTY GAL (LP)	25

BILLIE DAVIS
63	Decca F 11572	Tell Him/I'm Thankful	10
63	Decca F 11572	Tell Him/I'm Thankful (export copies with p/s)	15
63	Decca F 11658	He's The One/V.I.P.	10
63	Decca F 11658	He's The One/V.I.P. (export copies with p/s)	15
63	Columbia DB 7115	Bedtime Stories/You And I	15
64	Columbia DB 7195	That Boy John/Say Nothin' Don't Tell	15
64	Columbia DB 7246	School Is Over/Give Me Love	15
64	Columbia DB 7346	Whatcha Gonna Do/Everybody Knows (as Billie Davis & Le Roys)	35
65	Piccadilly 7N 35227	Last One To Be Loved/You Don't Know	10
65	Piccadilly 7N 35266	No Other Baby/Hands Off	18
66	Piccadilly 7N 35308	Heart And Soul/Don't Take All Night	10
66	Piccadilly 7N 35350	Just Walk In My Shoes/Ev'ry Day	100
67	Decca F 12620	Wasn't It You?/Until It's Time For You To Go	10
67	Decca F 12696	Angel Of The Morning/Darling Be Home Soon	10
68	Decca F 12823	I Want You To Be My Baby/Suffer	10
69	Decca F 12870	Make The Feeling Go Away/I'll Come Home	10
69	Decca F 12923	I Can Remember/Nobody's Home To Go Home To	20
69	Decca F 12977	Nights In White Satin/It's Over	18
70	Decca F 13049	Venid Con Migo/Love (Spanish export issue)	7
70	Decca F 13085	There Must Be A Reason/Love	20
72	Regal Zonophone RZ 3050	I Tried/Touch My Love	5
76	United Artists UP 36117	Any Way That You Want Me/Somewhere Along The Line	5
76	United Artists UP 46066	I've Been Loving Someone Else/Beyond The Pale	5
78	Magnet MAG 124	Run Joey Run/East Come Easy Go	5
70	Decca LK 5029	BILLIE DAVIS (LP, mono)	55
70	Decca SKL 5029	BILLIE DAVIS (LP, stereo)	50

(see also Keith & Billie, Le Roys, Mike Sarne)

BLIND GARY DAVIS/REVEREND GARY DAVIS
63	'77' LA 12-14	PURE RELIGION AND BAD COMPANY (LP)	30
60s	Fontana 688 303 ZL	HARLEM STREET SINGER (LP)	45
64	Xtra XTRA 1009	REV. GARY DAVIS/SHORT STUFF MACON (LP, 1 side each)	22
66	Xtra XTRA 5014	SAY NO TO THE DEVIL (LP)	25
67	Xtra XTRA 5042	A LITTLE MORE FAITH (LP)	25
69	Fontana SFJL 914	BRING YOUR MONEY HONEY (LP)	25
71	Transatlantic TRA 244	RAGTIME GUITAR (LP)	15
72	Transatlantic TRA 249	CHILDREN OF ZION (LP)	15
77	Kicking Mule SNKF 103	LET US GET TOGETHER (LP)	18

BOBBY DAVIS (JAMAICA)
71	Banana BA 342	Got To Get Away/We'll Cry Together (with BARBARA DUNKLEY)	12
71	Banana BA 344	Return Your Love/RILEY'S ALLSTARS: Version	10
71	Beacon 114	Strange Days/I Wish It would Rain	12

(see also Barbara Dunkley)

BOBBY DAVIS (U.S.)
61	Starlite ST45 056	I Was Wrong/Hype You Into Selling Your Head	50

BONNIE DAVIS
55	Brunswick 05507	Pepper-Hot Baby/For Always, Darling	40

CLIFFORD DAVIS
69	Reprise RS 27003	Before The Beginning/Man Of The World	10
70	Reprise RS 27008	Come On Down And Follow Me/Homework	15
71	Reprise K 14282	Before The Beginning/Man Of The World (reissue)	7

DANNY DAVIS ORCHESTRA (U.S.)
58	London HL 8766	Trumpet Cha-Cha-Cha/Lonesome Trumpet	7
65	MGM MGM 1277	Main Theme From "The Saint"/Little Bandits Of Juarez	10
64	London HAR 8204	THEY'RE PLAYING OUR SONG (LP, with Ruby & Romantics)	40

(see also Ruby & Romantics, Byron Lee)

DANNY DAVIS & BYRON LEE
64	MGM 1256	Night Train From Jamaica/Ska Dee Dah	18

DANNY DAVIS (U.K.)
60	Parlophone R 4657	Love Me/You're My Only Girl	20

60	Parlophone R 4796	Talking In My Sleep/Lullaby Of Love	15
61	Pye 7N 15391	Tell All The World/Rumours	10
62	Pye 7N 15427	Rome Wasn't Built In A Day/Tell Me	5
62	Pye 7N 15470	Patches/September In The Rain	5

(see also Marauders)

DEL DAVIS

| 71 | Bread BR-1105 | Baby Don't Wake Me/Wishing And Hoping | 150 |
| 72 | Trojan 7870 | Baby Don't Wake Me/Sugarloaf Hill | 100 |

EDDIE ('LOCKJAW') DAVIS

56	Parlophone GEP 8587	EDDIE 'LOCKJAW' DAVIS TRIO (EP)	10
57	Parlophone GEP 8678	LOCKJAW (EP)	10
58	Parlophone GEP 8685	EDDIE 'LOCKJAW' DAVIS TRIO (EP)	10
59	Esquire EP 217	EDDIE 'LOCKJAW' DAVIS (EP)	10
61	Esquire EP 237	EDDIE 'LOCKJAW' DAVIS QUARTET (EP)	10
60	Esquire 32-104	THE EDDIE 'LOCKJAW' DAVIS COOK BOOK (LP)	20
60	Esquire 32-117	VERY SAXY, with Coleman Hawkins, Arnett Cobb & Bobby Tate (LP)	20
61	Esquire 32-128	JAWS IN ORBIT (LP)	25
64	Stateside SL 10102	THE FIRST SET — LIVE AT MINTONS (LP, with Johnny Griffin)	20

(see also Coleman Hawkins, Johnny Griffin)

EDWARD H. DAVIS

| 74 | Sain SAIN 1016M | HEN FFORDD GYMREIG O FYW (LP) | 20 |
| 76 | Sain SAIN 1053M | SNEB YN BECSO DAM (LP) | 15 |

JACKIE DAVIS

| 59 | Capitol CL 15005 | Frenesi/Gonna Get A Girl | 6 |
| 60 | Capitol ST 1419 | TIGER ON THE HAMMOND (LP) | 12 |

JESSE (ED) DAVIS

71	Atlantic 2091 076	Every Night Is Saturday Night/Washita Love Child (as Jesse Davis)	6
71	Atco 2400 106	JESSE 'ED' DAVIS (LP)	18
72	Atlantic K 40329	ULULU (LP)	15

JIMMY DAVIS

| 66 | Bounty BY 6009 | MAXWELL STREET (LP) | 25 |

KIM DAVIS

66	Decca F 12387	Don't Take Your Lovin' Away/Feelin' Blue	20
67	CBS 202568	Tell It Like It Is/Losing Kind	12
68	CBS 3260	Until It's Time For You To Go/I Hold No Grudge	7
69	CBS 4210	Are You Ready For Love/Taste Of Excitement	7

(see also Kim D, Kim & Kinetics)

LARRY DAVIS/FENTON ROBINSON

| 72 | Python PLP 24 | LARRY DAVIS AND FENTON ROBINSON (LP, 99 copies only) | 70 |

MAXWELL DAVIS

| 66 | Ember FA 2040 | BATMAN THEME AND OTHER BAT SONGS (LP) | 30 |

MELVIN DAVIS

| 69 | Action ACT 4531 | Save It/This Love Was Meant To Be | 35 |

MILES DAVIS

53	Esquire 20-017	MILES DAVIS PLAYS (10")	35
53	Esquire 20-021	MILES DAVIS ALL STARS (10")	35
53	Vogue LDE 028	MILES DAVIS ALL STARS (10")	30
54	Esquire 20-052	MILES DAVIS ALL STARS (A HIFI MODERN JAZZ JAM SESSION) (10")	35
54	Vogue LDE 064	MILES DAVIS AND HIS ORCHESTRA (10")	30
54	Esquire 20-056	MILES DAVIS ALL STARS (A SECOND HIFI MODERN JAZZ JAM SESSION) (10")	35
54	Capitol LC 6683	CLASSICS IN JAZZ (10")	30
55	Esquire 20-041	MILES DAVIS QUINTET (10")	35
55	Esquire 20-062	DIG (10")	50
55	Esquire 20-072	MILES DAVIS QUINTET (10")	30
56	Esquire 32-012	THE MUSINGS OF MILES	30
55	Esquire 32-021	HIS NEW QUINTET (10")	75
56	Philips BBL 7140	'ROUND ABOUT MIDNIGHT	20
57	Esquire 32-028	CHANGES	20
57	Esquire 32-030	BIRTH OF THE COOL	20
57	Vogue LDE 191	NATURE BOY	30
57	Fontana TFL 5007	MILES AHEAD	25
58	Fontana TFL 5035	MILESTONES	25
58	Esquire 32-048	COOKIN'	30
58	Esquire 32-068	RELAXIN' WITH THE MILES DAVIS QUARTET	50
59	Esquire 32-090	BAGS' GROOVE	30
59	Fontana TFL 5056	PORGY AND BESS (mono)	20
59	Fontana STFL 507	PORGY AND BESS (stereo)	25
60	Fontana TFL 5081	JAZZ TRACK — "L'ANSCENSEUR POUR L'ECHAFAUD"	20
60	Fontana TFL 5089	THE MOST OF MILES	15
60	Fontana TFL 5072	KIND OF BLUE (mono)	40
60	Fontana STFL 513	KIND OF BLUE (stereo)	40
60	CBS SBPG 62066	KIND OF BLUE (stereo)	40
60	CBS BPG 62066	KIND OF BLUE (mono)	40
60	Esquire 32-088	BLUE HAZE	20
60	Esquire 32-098	WALKIN'	25
60	Esquire 32-100	MILES DAVIS AND THE MODERN JAZZ GIANTS VOL. 2	25
60	Esquire 32-108	WORKIN' WITH THE MILES DAVIS QUINTET	20
61	Font. TFL 5100/STFL 531	SKETCHES OF SPAIN	20
61	Esquire 32-118	EARLY MILES	20
61	Esquire 32-138	STEAMIN' WITH THE MILES DAVIS QUINTET	40
61	Fontana TFL 5163	FRIDAY NIGHT AT THE BLACKHAWK, SAN FRANCISCO (VOL. 1) (with Cannonball Adderley & John Coltrane; also stereo STFL 580)	15
61	Fontana TFL 5164	SATURDAY NIGHT AT THE BLACKHAWK, SAN FRANCISCO (VOL. 2) (with Cannonball Adderley & John Coltrane; also stereo STFL 581)	15
62	Fontana TFL 5172	SOMEDAY MY PRINCE WILL COME (also stereo STFL 587)	15

62	Transatlantic PR 7254	THE ORIGINAL QUINTET...20
63	CBS BPG 62389	MILES AND MONK AT NEWPORT (with Thelonious Monk, also stereo SBPG 62389) ...18
64	Vocalion LAEF 584	BLUE MOODS...20
65	Stateside SL 10111	MILES DAVIS AND JOHN COLTRANE...15
66	CBS 62577	E.S.P....20
66	Stateside SL 10168	MILES DAVIS PLAYS FOR LOVERS...15
66	Fontana FJL 135	BACK TO BACK...18
67	CBS 63248	NEFERTITI...20
69	CBS 63551	FILLES DE KILIMANJARO (stereo)...20
69	CBS 63630	IN A SILENT WAY...25
70	CBS 64010	BITCHES BREW (2-LP)...25
70	CBS 70089	A TRIBUTE TO JACK JOHNSON...25
71	CBS 66257	MILES DAVIS AT FILLMORE (2-LP)...20
72	CBS 64575	LIVE-EVIL (2-LP, gatefold)...30
72	CBS 65246	ON THE CORNER...25
72	Prestige PR 24001	MILES DAVIS (2-LP)...15
72	Prestige PR 24012	TALLEST TREES (2-LP)...15
73	CBS CQ 30997/Q 66236	BITCHES BREW (2-LP, quadrophonic)...30
73	CBS GQ 30954/Q 67219	LIVE-EVIL (2-LP, quadrophonic)...30
74	Columbia 88024	BIG FUN (LP, gatefold)...20
85	CBS 62066	KIND OF BLUE (LP, Nimbus Supercut, mail order from Practical Hi Fi magazine) ...80
98	Sony C4K 65570	COMPLETE BITCHES BREW SESSIONS (5-CD box set)...50
07	Legacy 88697062392	COMPLETE ON THE CORNER SESSIONS (6-CD, Metal box sleeve) ...60

MILES DAVIS/ART BLAKEY

66	Fontana FJL 135	L'ASCENSEUR POUR L'ECHAFAUD/LA FEMME DISPARAISSANTE (LP, soundtrack, 1 side each)...30

(see also Art Blakey, Thelonius Monk, Dizzy Gillespie, Milt Jackson, Cannonball Adderley, Charlie Parker)

PAT DAVIS

75	Black Wax WAX 8	I'm Just A Girl/SKIN, FLESH & BONES: Girl Version...5

PAUL DAVIS

74	London HLM 10473	Ride'Em Cowboy/I'm The Only Sinner (In Salt Lake City) ...5

RONNIE DAVIS

75	Angen ANG 104	The Good News/AGGROVATORS: Version...8
75	Angen ANG 110	Maga Lion/AGGROVATORS: Version ...8
75	Attack ATT 8088	I Lost My Lover/MATADOR ALL STARS: Bula Dub ...8
75	Attack ATT 8116	Tradition/Tradition (Version) ...8
77	Third World TWDIS 005	Anywhere Don't Watch Your Woman (with Dillinger)/ BARRY BROWN : Mr Money Man (12")...25
77	Hawkeye HE 011	Used To Be My Girl/HAWKEYE IN SESSION - My Dub ...10
76	Dip DLP 5028	BEAUTIFUL PEOPLE FROM JAMAICA (LP)...40

SAMMY DAVIS (JNR.)

54	Brunswick 05326	Because Of You (Parts 1 & 2)...5
55	Brunswick 05383	The Birth Of The Blues/Love (Your Magic Spell Is Everywhere)...5
55	Brunswick 05389	Six Bridges To Cross/Glad To Be Unhappy...5
55	Brunswick 05409	And This Is My Beloved/The Red Grapes ...5
55	Brunswick 05428	Love Me Or Leave Me/Something's Gotta Give ...6
55	Brunswick 05450	That Old Black Magic/Give A Fool A Chance ...6
55	Brunswick 05469	Hey There/My Funny Valentine...6
55	Brunswick 05478	Backtrack/It's Bigger Than You And Me ...5
56	Brunswick 05518	In A Persian Market/The Man With The Golden Arm ...6
56	Capitol CL 14562	Azure/Dedicated To You ...5
56	Brunswick 05583	Adelaide/I'll Know ...5
56	Brunswick 05594	Earthbound/Five...5
56	Brunswick 05611	Frankie And Johnny/Circus...5
56	Brunswick 05617	You're Sensational/Don't Let Her Go ...5
56	Brunswick 05629	All Of You/Just One Of Those Things ...8
57	Brunswick 05637	The Golden Key/All About Love ...5
57	Brunswick 05647	Dangerous/The World Is Mine Tonight...5
57	Brunswick 05668	Too Close For Comfort/Jacques D'Iraque ...8
57	Brunswick 05694	Goodbye, So Long, I'm Gone/French Fried Potatoes And Ketchup ...8
57	Brunswick 05717	Mad Ball/The Nearness Of You ...5
57	Brunswick 05724	Long Before I Knew You/Never Like This...5
58	Brunswick 05732	I'm Comin' Home/Hallelujah, I Love Her...5
60	Brunswick 05830	Happy To Make Your Acquaintance/Baby, It's Cold Outside (with Carmen McRae) ...8
62	Reprise R 20048	What Kind Of Fool Am I/Gonna Build A Mountain...6
63	Reprise R 20227	The Shelter Of Your Arms/Falling In Love With You ...25
64	Reprise R 20289	Not For Me/Bang Bang ...15
69	MCA MK 1072	Rhythm Of Life/Pompeii Club/Rich Man's Frug ...30
72	MGM 2006 095	The Candy Man/I Want To Be Happy ...8
76	20th Century BTC 2292	Baretta's Theme/I Heard A Song ...10
50	Brunswick OE 9445	BOY MEETS GIRL (EP, with Carmen McRae) ...8
56	Capitol EAP1 555	SAMMY DAVIS JNR. (EP)...8
63	Reprise 30028	SAMMY (EP)...20
70	Tamla Motown STML 11160	SOMETHING FOR EVERYONE (LP) ...30

(see also Dean Martin)

SILKIE DAVIS

70	Torpedo TOR 2	Conversations/TWIZZLE & HOT ROD ALL-STARS: Peace & Tranquility...5
70	Torpedo TOR 12	When I Was A Little Girl/I'm So Lonely ...5

SKEETER DAVIS

60	RCA Victor RCA 1201	No Never/(I Can't Help You) I'm Falling Too ...5
61	RCA Victor RCA 1222	My Last Date With You/Someone I'd Like To Forget...5
63	RCA Victor RCA 1328	The End Of The World/Somebody Loves You...5
63	RCA Victor RCA 1345	I'm Saving My Love/Somebody Else On Your Mind...5
63	RCA Victor RCA 1363	I Can't Stay Mad At You/It Was Only My Heart ...5
64	RCA Victor RCA 1384	He Says The Same Things To Me/How Much Can A Lonely Heart Stand ...5
64	RCA Victor RCA 1398	Now You're Gone/Gonna Get Along Without You Now ...5
65	RCA Victor RCA 1474	Sun Glasses/He Loved Me Too Little ...10
64	RCA Victor RCX 7153	SILVER THREADS AND GOLDEN NEEDLES (EP)...15

63	RCA Victor SF 7563	THE END OF THE WORLD (LP, mono) 15
63	RCA Victor SF 7563	THE END OF THE WORLD (LP, stereo) 15
63	RCA Victor RD 7604	CLOUDY, WITH OCCASIONAL TEARS (LP, mono) 12
63	RCA Victor RD 7604	CLOUDY, WITH OCCASIONAL TEARS (LP, stereo) 15
64	RCA Victor RD 7676	LET ME GET CLOSE TO YOU (LP) 15

SKEETER DAVIS & BOBBY BARE
| 65 | RCA RD 7711 | TUNES FOR TWO (LP) .... 20 |

(see also Bobby Bare)

SMILEY DAVIS
| 53 | London L 1189 | Big Mamou/Play Girl (78, actually by Smiley Lewis) .... 130 |

SPENCER DAVIS (GROUP)
64	Fontana TF 471	Dimples/Sittin' And Thinkin' 30
64	Fontana TF 499	I Can't Stand It/Midnight Train 25
65	Fontana TF 530	Every Little Bit Hurts/It Hurts Me So 15
65	Fontana TF 571	Strong Love/This Hammer 20
65	Fontana TF 632	Keep On Running/High Time Baby 7
66	Fontana TF 679	Somebody Help Me/Stevie's Blues 7
66	Fontana TF 739	When I Come Home/Trampoline 10
66	Fontana TF 762	Gimme Some Loving/Blues In F 7
67	Fontana TF 785	I'm A Man/I Can't Get Enough Of It 12
67	Fontana TF 854	Time Seller/Don't Want You No More 15
67	United Artists UP 1203	Mr. Second Class/Sanity Inspector 8
68	United Artists UP 2213	After Tea/Moonshine 8
68	United Artists UP 2226	Short Change/Picture Of Heaven 8
73	Vertigo 6059 076	Catch You On the Rebop/The Edge 8
73	Vertigo 6059 087	Livin' In A Back Street/Sure Need A Helping Hand 6
65	Fontana TE 17444	YOU PUT THE HURT ON ME (EP) 25
65	Fontana TE 17450	EVERY LITTLE BIT HURTS (EP) 30
66	Fontana TE 17463	SITTIN' AND THINKIN' (EP) 35
65	Fontana TL 5242	THEIR FIRST LP (LP, laminated front, black/silver label) 70
66	Fontana TL 5295	THE SECOND ALBUM (LP, laminated front cover, flipbacks, island) label on rear) 80
66	Fontana TL 5359	AUTUMN '66 (LP, laminated front sleeve, flipbacks. black/silver label) 50
67	United Artists ULP 1186	HERE WE GO ROUND THE MULBERRY BUSH (LP, soundtrack, with Traffic, mono) 40
67	United Artists (S)ULP 1186	HERE WE GO ROUND THE MULBERRY BUSH (LP, soundtrack, with Traffic, stereo) 35
68	United Artists ULP 1192	WITH THEIR NEW FACE ON (LP, mono, blue/silver label) 50
68	United Artists (S)ULP 1192	WITH THEIR NEW FACE ON (LP, stereo) 25
68	Wing WL 1165	EVERY LITTLE BIT HURTS (LP, reissue of "Their First LP") 15
68	Island ILP 970 9070	THE BEST OF THE SPENCER DAVIS GROUP FEATURING STEVIE WINWOOD (LP, plain pink label, flipback sleeve; sleeve lists "Please Do Something" but plays "Together Till The End Of Time", mono) 30
68	Island ILPS 9070	THE BEST OF THE SPENCER DAVIS GROUP FEATURING STEVIE WINWOOD (LP, plain pink label, flipback sleeve; sleeve lists "Please Do Something" but plays "Together Till The End Of Time", stereo) 15
69	CBS 63842	LETTERS FROM EDITH (LP, unissued, 50 white label test pressings only) 400
71	United Artists UAS 29177	IT'S BEEN SO LONG (LP, solo with Peter Jameson, 'envelope' cover) 15
72	United Artists UAS 29361	MOUSETRAP (LP, solo) 15
73	Vertigo 6360 088	GLUGGO (LP, die cut, gatefold sleeve, 'spaceship' label) 20
74	Vertigo 6360 105	LIVIN' IN A BACK STREET (LP) 12

(see also Stevie Winwood, Traffic, Anglos, Blind Faith, Ray Fenwick, Pete York, Hardin & York, Murgatroyd Band, Mirage, Portobello Explosion, Shotgun Express)

STEVE DAVIS
| 68 | Fontana TF 922 | Takes Time To Know Her/She Said Yeah .... 75 |

TYRONE DAVIS
68	Stateside SS 2092	What If A Man/Bet You Win 45
69	Atlantic 584 253	Can I Change My Mind/A Woman Needs To Be Loved 12
69	Atlantic 584 265	Is It Something You've Got?/Undying Love 12
69	Atlantic 584 288	All The Waiting Is Not In Vain/Need Your Lovin' Everyday 12
70	Atlantic 2091 003	Turn Back The Hands Of Time/I Keep Coming Back 15
71	Atlantic 2091 078	Could I Forget You/Just My Way Of Loving You 10
71	Atlantic 2091 131	One Way Ticket/We Got A Love 10
72	Atlantic K 10207	Can I Change My Mind/Turn Back The Hands Of Time/One Way Ticket 8
73	Brunswick BR 4	Without You In My Life/How Could I Forget You 10
73	Brunswick BR 6	There It Is/You Wouldn't Believe 10
74	Brunswick BR 10	I Wish It Was Me/You Don't Have To Beg To Stay 10
76	Brunswick BR 31	Turning Point/Don't Let It Be Too Late 10
77	Brunswick BR 40	Ever Lovin' Girl/Forever 10
70	Atlantic 588 209	CAN I CHANGE MY MIND (LP) 30
71	Atlantic 2465 021	TURN BACK THE HANDS OF TIME (LP) 30
73	Brunswick BRLS 3002	I HAD IT ALL THE TIME (LP) 35
73	Brunswick BRLS 3005	GREATEST HITS (LP) 18

WALTER DAVIS
| 64 | RCA RCX 7169 | R.C.A. VICTOR RACE SERIES VOL. 3 (EP) .... 15 |
| 70 | RCA Intl. INTS 1085 | THINK YOU NEED A SHOT (LP) .... 15 |

WARREN DAVIS MONDAY BAND
| 67 | Columbia DB 8190 | Wait For Me/I Don't Wanna Hurt You .... 30 |
| 67 | Columbia DB 8270 | Love Is A Hurtin' Thing/Without Fear .... 20 |

(see also Boardwalkers)

BRIAN DAVISON
| 70 | Charisma CAS 1021 | BRIAN DAVISON'S EVERY WHICH WAY (LP, pink 'scroll' label) .... 40 |

(see also Habits, Nice, Every Which Way, Refuge)

DAVISON BROTHERS
| 60 | Philips PB 1053 | Journey Of Love/Seven Days A Week .... 60 |

WILD BILL DAVISON
| 55 | Melodisc MLP 501 | WILD BILL DAVISON (LP) .... 15 |

TIM DAWE
| 69 | Straight ST(S) 1058 | PENROD (LP) .... 45 |

CARL DAWKINS

67	Rio R 136	All Of A Sudden/Running Shoes	18
67	Rio R 137	Baby I Love You/Hard Time	18
68	Blue Cat BS 114	I Love The Way You Are/DERMOTT LYNCH: I Can't Stand It	20
68	Duke DU 3	I'll Make It Up/J.J. ALL STARS: One Dollar Of Music	30
69	Nu Beat NB 030	Rodney's History/DYNAMITES: Tribute To Drumbano	35
70	Duke DU 93	Get Together/FAMILY MAN: Instalment Plan	8
70	Duke DU 95	This Land/J.J. ALL STARS: Land Version	12
70	Trojan TR 7765	Satisfaction/Things A Get Bad To Worse	7
71	Big Shot BI 570	Perseverence/J.J. ALL STARS: Perseverence (Version)	12
71	Explosion EX 2051	I Feel Good/J.J. ALL STARS: I Feel Good Version Two	10
71	Explosion EX 2059	Make It Great/STONE: What A Day	6
71	New Beat NB 086	Walk A Little Prouder/YOUTH PROFESSIONALS: Walk (Version)	6
72	Duke DU 133	My Whole World/Men A Broken Heart	6

(see also Rass Dawkins, Untouchables, Winston Wright, Ansell Collins, Roland Alphonso, West Indians)

HORRELL DAWKINS
66	Ska Beat JB 240	Cling To Me/Butterfly	25

JIMMY DAWKINS
73	Mojo 2027 011	The Things I Used To Do/Put It On The Hawg	8
71	Delmark DS 623	FAST FINGERS (LP)	22
78	Sonet SNTF 758	TRANSATLANTIC 770 (LP)	15

RASS DAWKINS (& WAILERS)
71	Upsetter US 368	Picture On The Wall/UPSETTERS: Picture Version	25

(see also Bob Marley/Wailers, Carl Dawkins)

DAWN AND CHRISTINE
78	Burning Rockers BRD 002	We Love Collie Weed (with Clint Eastwood)/LAWES ROCKERS: Collie Weed Version (12")	30

JULIE DAWN
53	Columbia SCM 5035	Wild Horses/A Whistling Kettle And A Dancing Cat	10

(see also Tony Brent & Julie Dawn, Cyril Stapleton)

DAWN TRADER
80	AFE 1980	NO ONE GONNA BETTER ME (EP, private pressing)	40

DAWNBREAKERS
65	Decca F 12110	Let's Live/Lovin' For You	15

DAWN CHORUS (1)
69	MCA MK 5004	A Night To Be Remembered/Crying All Night	15

(see also Carter-Lewis)

DAWN CHORUS (2)
85	Dawn DAWN 1	Teenage Kicks/Dream Lover (p/s)	18

DAWN & DEEJAYS
65	RCA RCA 1470	These Are The Things About You/I Will Think Of You	18

DAWNWATCHER
80	Dawnwatcher DWS 001	Spellbound/Hall Of Mirrors	75
82	Dawnwatcher DWS 002	Backlash (p/s)	20

DAWNWIND
76	Amron ARN 5003	LOOKING BACK ON THE FUTURE (LP, private pressing)	80

DONNA DAWSON
73	Trojan TR 7892	You Can't Buy Me Love/First Cut Is The Deepest	6

LES DAWSON
69	Chapter One CH 106	Send Her Roses/I'm Just Another Sweetheart	6

LESLEY DAWSON
66	Mercury MF 924	Pastel Shades Of Love/The Time Has Come	5
67	Mercury MF 946	Just Say Goodbye/Just A Passing Phase	8
67	Mercury MF 965	Run For Shelter/I'll Climb On A Rainbow	35

DANIELLE DAX
83	Initial IRC 009	POP-EYES (LP, with 'Meat Harvest' cover & lyric sheet)	40

(see also Lemon Kittens)

DAY
94	Detour DR 019	Another Country/Gospel (p/s, 100 on green vinyl)	7

BING DAY
59	Mercury AMT 1047	I Can't Help It/Mama's Place	60

BOBBY DAY (& SATELLITES)
57	HMV POP 425	Little Bitty Pretty One/When The Swallows Come Back To Capistrano (as Bobby Day & Satellites)	150
57	HMV POP 425	Little Bitty Pretty One/When The Swallows Come Back To Capistrano (as Bobby Day & Satellites) (78)	25
58	London HL 8726	Rockin' Robin/Over And Over	20
58	London HL 8726	Rockin' Robin/Over And Over (78)	15
59	London HL 8800	The Bluebird, The Buzzard And The Oriole/Alone Too Long	40
59	London HL 8800	The Bluebird, The Buzzard And The Oriole/Alone Too Long (78)	28
59	London HL 8964	Love Is A One Time Affair/Ain't Gonna Cry No More	15
59	London HL 8964	Love Is A One Time Affair/Ain't Gonna Cry No More (78)	20
60	London HLY 9044	My Blue Heaven/I Don't Want To	25
61	Top Rank JAR 538	Over And Over/Gee Whiz	20
65	Sue WI 388	Rockin' Robin/Over And Over (reissue)	15

DORIS DAY
SINGLES
53	Columbia SCM 5038	April In Paris/Your Mother And Mine (with Four Lads)	10
53	Columbia SCM 5039	That's What Makes Paris Paree/I Know A Place	10
53	Columbia SCM 5044	A Bushel And A Peck/If I Were A Bell	10
53	Columbia SCM 5045	The Second Star To The Right (with Four Lads) I'm Gonna Ring The Bell Tonight	10

53	Columbia SCM 5059	The Cherries/Papa, Won't You Dance With Me?	10
53	Columbia SCM 5062	Mister Tap-Toe/Why Should We Both Be Lonely?	10
53	Columbia SCM 5067	We Kiss In A Shadow/Something Wonderful	10
53	Columbia SCM 5075	That's The Way He Does It/Cuddle Up A Little Closer	10
54	Columbia SCM 5087	A Load Of Hay/It Had To Be You	10
55	Columbia SCM 5171	Just One Of Those Things/Sometimes I'm Happy	10
57	Philips JK 1020	Twelve O'Clock Tonight/Today Will Be Yesterday Tomorrow! (jukebox issue)	10
57	Philips JK 1031	The Party's Over/Rickety-Rackety Rendezvous (jukebox issue)	10
64	CBS AAG 219	Oowee Baby/The Rainbow's End	15

EPs

| 59 | Philips SBBE 9006 | LET'S FLY AWAY (stereo) | 8 |

ALBUMS

54	Columbia 33S 1038	LULLABY OF BROADWAY (10", 2 different sleeve designs)	20
54	Philips BBR 8026	THE VOICE OF YOUR CHOICE (10")	15
55	Philips BBR 8040	YOUNG AT HEART (10", with Frank Sinatra)	15
55	Philips BBL 7047	LOVE ME OR LEAVE ME	15
56	Philips BBR 8094	DORIS DAY FAVOURITES (10")	15
56	Philips BBR 8104	CALAMITY JANE (10", with Howard Keel)	15
57	Philips BBL 7120	DAY DREAMS	15
57	Philips BBL 7137	DORIS AND FRANK (6 tracks each by Doris Day & Frank Sinatra)	15
57	Philips BBL 7142	DAY BY DAY	15
58	Philips BBL 7175	DAY IN HOLLYWOOD	15
58	Philips BBL 7211	DAY BY NIGHT	15

(see also Four Lads, Frank Sinatra, Frankie Laine, Howard Keel)

DORIS DAY & JOHNNIE RAY

| 53 | Columbia SCM 5033 | Ma Says, Pa Says/A Full Time Job | 20 |

(see also Johnnie Ray)

JACKIE DAY

| 67 | Sue WI 4040 | Before It's Too Late/Without A Love | 250 |
| 09 | Kent 6T 25 | Get To Steppin/LARRY BANKS: My Life Is No Better | 20 |

JILL DAY

55	Parlophone MSP 6169	Sincerely/Chee-Chee-Oo Chee (Sang The Little Bird)	10
55	Parlophone MSP 6177	Promises/Whistlin' Willie	10
56	HMV 7M 362	I Hear You Knocking/Far Away From Everybody	10
56	HMV 7M 391	A Tear Fell/Holiday Affair	10
56	HMV POP 254	Happiness Street (Corner Sunshine Square)/Somewhere In The Great Beyond	6
57	HMV POP 288	I Dreamed/Give Her My Love When You See Her	6
57	HMV POP 320	Mangos/Cinco Robles (Five Oaks)	10
70	B&C CB117	I'll Think About You/The Way Of Love	5

JOHNNY DAY

| 69 | Stax STAX 111 | Stay Baby Stay/I Love Love (listed as Johnny Daye on demos) | 20 |

KENNY DAY

60	Top Rank JAR 339	Teenage Sonata/My Love Doesn't Love Me At All (p/s)	10
60	Top Rank JAR 339	Teenage Sonata/My Love Doesn't Love Me At All	5
61	Top Rank JAR 400	Why Don't We Do This More Often/The Sheik Of Morocco (p/s)	10
61	Top Rank JAR 400	Why Don't We Do This More Often/The Sheik Of Morocco	5

MURIEL DAY

66	Pye 7N 17197	A Petal From A Faded Rose/I Wear His Heart	10
69	CBS 4115	The Wages Of Love/Thinking Of You	15
69	Page One POF 151	Optimistic Fool/Nine Times Out Of Ten	60
69	Page One POF 151	Optimistic Fool/Nine Times Out Of Ten (DJ copy)	100

SYLVIA DAY

| 68 | SNB 55-3859 | You Don't Understand/Show A Little Love | 10 |

TANYA DAY & NU-NOTES

| 64 | Polydor NH 52331 | His Lips Get In The Way/I Get So Lonely | 8 |

TERRY DAY

| 62 | CBS AAG 104 | That's All I Want/I Waited Too Long | 20 |

(see also Rip-Chords, Rogues)

DAYBREAKERS

| 67 | John Hassell 814/5 | DAYBREAKERS (LP) | 40 |
| 67 | John Hassell HAS LP 1126 | VOL 2 (LP) | 40 |

DAY BROTHERS

| 60 | Oriole CB 1575 | Angel/Just One More Kiss | 20 |

JOEL DAYDE

| 71 | Barclay BAR 7 | Mammy Blue/You've Got Freedom | 25 |

JENNIFER DAYE

| 80 | Arawak ARK DD 018 | Together/Version (12") | 10 |

DAYLIGHT

| 71 | RCA RCA 2106 | Lady Of St. Clare/Wednesday People | 10 |
| 71 | RCA SF 8194 | DAYLIGHT (LP, gatefold sleeve, orange label) | 60 |

(see also Daddy Longlegs)

DAYLIGHTERS

| 64 | Sue WI 343 | Oh Mom! (Teach Me How To Uncle Willie)/Hard-Headed Girl | 45 |

DAY N NIGHT

| 70 | DJM DJS 220 | I Just Need Somebody/Such A Lot To Talk About | 12 |

DAY OF THE PHOENIX

| 70 | Greenwich GSLP 1002 | WIDE OPEN N-WAY (LP) | 80 |
| 72 | Chapter One CHS-R 812 | THE NEIGHBOUR'S SON (LP, red/silver label) | 50 |

DAYS OF GRACE

| 82 | DJM DJS 10988 | My Life Is A Video/21st Century (P/S) | 6 |

DAYSHIFT
| 80 | Wot WOT 1 | Living In The UK/Cedric Wazza Superstar/Yeah Eh Oh Yeah (p/s) | 20 |

DAYTRIPPERS
| 71 | Trojan TR 7839 | The Birds And The Bees/My Family | 5 |

DAZZLE
| 75 | DJM DJS 384 | Jim'll Fix It/Leave It Up To Jim | 10 |

DAZZLERS
78	Charisma CB 325	Phonies/Kick Out (5,000 copies in fold-out p/s with poly bag)	8
79	Charisma CB 330	Lovely Crash/Feeling In Your Heart (p/s)	7
79	Charisma CB 338	Feeling Free/No One Ever Knows (p/s)	10

DBX
93	Peacefrog PF 015	Alien EP (12", plain sleeve)	12
94	Peacefrog PF 022	Losing Control/Beat Phreak/Live Wire/Spock's Brain (12", plain sleeve)	22
95	Peacefrog PR 025	Losing Control Remixes (12", plain sleeve)	20

D.C. 10'S
| 80 | Certain Euphoria ACE 451 | Bermuda/I Can See Through Walls | 10 |

DDR
| 90s | Smitten SMTLTD 05 | The Gift (12", 1-sided yellow vinyl, 500 only) | 60 |

SIMON DE LACY
| 68 | Spark 1001 | Baby Come Back To Me/Goodbye Love | 25 |

BOBBY DEACON
| 60 | Pye 7N 15270 | A Fool Was I/Where's My Love? | 10 |
| 60 | Pye 7N 15299 | I Love You So/Your Kisses Are Fine | 5 |

GEORGE DEACON & MARION ROSS
| 73 | Xtra XTRA 1130 | SWEET WILLIAM'S GHOST (LP, with lyric insert) | 50 |

DEAD FLOWERS
87	Lout 001	TV/Fallout	10
91	Mystic Stones RUNE 2	SMELL THE FRAGRANCE, FREE YOUR MIND (LP)	15
92	Mystic Stones RUNE 12	MOONTAN (LP)	15
94	Delerium DELEC LP 022	ALTERED STATE CIRCUS (LP)	15

DEAD MANS SHADOW
81	Pig Records HOG 1	Neighbours/Morons With Power/Poxy Politics/War Ploys (p/s and sticker)	20
81	Subversive Anarcho 1	HEATHROW TOUCHDOWN (Shared EP with ACTION PACT)	20
82	Rondelet ROUND 16	Bomb Scare/Another Hiroshima/Fighting For Reality (p/s)	10
83	Expulsion OUT 4	Toleration Street/In My Dream (p/s)	5

DEADBEATS
| 80 | Red Rhino RED 3 | Choose You/Julie's New Boyfriend (p/s) | 10 |

DEAD BOYS
77	Sire SRE 1004	Sonic Reducer/Down In Flames (no p/s)	25
77	Sire 6078 609	Sonic Reducer/Little Girl/Down In Flames (12", p/s)	15
78	Sire SRE 1029	Tell Me/Not Anymore/Ain't Nothin' To Do (p/s)	25
77	Sire 9103 329	YOUNG, LOUD & SNOTTY (LP)	25
78	Sire SRK 6054	WE HAVE COME FOR YOUR CHILDREN (LP)	20
87	Line LILP 400200	NIGHT OF THE LIVING DEAD BOYS (LP)	15
99	Rude LP00010	3RD GENERATION NATION (LP, clear vinyl, mail order only)	15

(see also Stiv Bators, Lords Of The New Church, Wanderers)

DEAD CAN DANCE
84	4AD BAD 408	GARDEN OF THE ARCANE DELIGHTS EP (12", p/s)	8
96	4AD DCD 2	Nierika/Dedicace Outo/The Snake And The Moon (12", promo red vinyl, PVC sleeve)	12
84	4AD CAD 404	DEAD CAN DANCE (LP)	15
85	4AD CAD 512	SPLEEN AND IDEAL (LP)	15
87	4AD CAD 705	WITHIN THE REALM OF A DYING SUN (LP)	15
88	4AD CAD 808	THE SERPENT'S EGG (LP)	15
90	4AD CAD 0007	AION (LP)	20
93	4AD DAD 3013	INTO THE LABYRINTH (2-LP)	30
94	4AD DAD 4015	TOWARDS THE WITHIN (2-LP)	25
96	4AD DAD 608	SPIRITCHASER (2-LP)	30

DEAD FINGERS TALK
| 79 | Pye 46156 | This Crazy World/The Boyfriend (p/s) | 20 |

DEAD KENNEDYS
80	Fast Products FAST 12	California Uber Alles/Man With The Dogs (p/s, moulded or paper labels)	6
81	Statik STAT EP 2	IN GOD WE TRUST (12" EP, with insert)	10
81	Cherry Red CHERRY 13	Holiday In Cambodia/Police Truck ('digger' p/s)	5
81	Cherry Red CHERRY 13	Holiday In Cambodia/Police Truck ('burning man' p/s, with lyric sheet)	6
81	Cherry Red CHERRY T13	Holiday In Cambodia/Police Truck (12")	10
81	Cherry CHERRY 16	Kill The Poor/In-Sight (p/s)	8
81	Cherry CHERRY 24	Too Drunk To Fuck/The Prey (p/s, with lyric sheet)	5
82	Statik STAT 24	Nazi Punks Fuck Off/Moral Majority (p/s)	5
82	Statik STAT 22	Bleed for Me/Life Sentence (p/s)	7
82	Statik STAT 27	Halloween/Saturday Night Holocaust (p/s)	7
81	Cherry Red B RED 10	FRESH FRUIT FOR ROTTING VEGETABLES (LP, with insert & 'Heads' pic on rear)	25
80	Cherry Red B RED 10	FRESH FRUIT FOR ROTTING VEGETABLES (LP, with insert & without 'Heads' pic on rear)	20
85	Statik/Alternative Tentacles VIRUS 45	FRANKENCHRIST (LP, with poster)	18
86	Statik/Alternative Tentacles VIRUS 50	BEDTIME FOR DEMOCRACY (LP)	12
87	Alternative Tent. VIRUS 57	GIVE ME CONVENIENCE... (LP, with booklet and "Buzzbomb From Pasadena" flexidisc)	15
82	Statik/Alternative Tent. VIRUS 27	PLASTIC SURGERY DISASTERS (LP, with booklet)	12

(see also East Bay Ray, Lard)

DEADLY HEADLEY
| 82 | On U Sound ONULP 14 | 35 YEARS FROM ALPHA (LP) | 35 |

DEADLY TOYS

79	Bonhard/Hunt DT 1	Nice Weather/Roll On Doomsday/I'm Logical/Deadly Mess Around (EP, in hand-made gatefold sleeve)	50
79	Bonhard/Hunt DT 1	Nice Weather/Roll On Doomsday/I'm Logical/Deadly Mess Around (EP)	20

DEAD OR ALIVE

80	Inevitable INEV 005	I'm Falling/Flowers (foldout p/s)	12
81	Inevitable INEV 008	Number Eleven/Name Game (live) (p/s)	8
82	Black Eyes BE 1	It's Been Hours Now/Whirlpool/Nowhere To Nowhere/ It's Been Hours Now (Alternative Mix) (12", p/s)	20
82	Black Eyes BE 2	The Stranger/Some Of That (p/s)	8
83	Epic A 3399	Misty Circles/Misty Circles (Instrumental) (p/s)	8
83	Epic TA 3399	Misty Circles (Dance Mix)/Misty Circles (Dub Mix)/Selfish Side (12", p/s)	10
83	Epic A 3676	What I Want/The Stranger (Remix) (white 'floppy hat' p/s, withdrawn)	35
83	Epic TA 3676	What I Want (Dance Mix)/The Stranger (12", p/s, with poster)	18
83	Epic QA 3676	What I Want (Dance Mix)/The Stranger (12", p/s, without poster)	8
84	Epic A 4069	I'd Do Anything/Anything (Dub) (p/s)	5
84	Epic QA 4069	I'd Do Anything/Anything (Dub)/Give It To Me (10", p/s)	10
84	Epic TA 4069	I'd Do Anything/Misty Circles/What I Want/Give It To Me (12", p/s)	8
84	Epic WA 4271	That's The Way (I Like It)/Keep That Body Strong (That's The Way) (picture disc)	6
84	Epic A 4510	What I Want (Remix)/The Stranger (poster p/s)	15
84	Epic A 4510	What I Want (Remix)/The Stranger (2nd issue, 'dreadlock' p/s)	8
84	Epic TA 4510	What I Want (Dance Mix)/The Stranger (12", p/s)	10
84	Epic XPR 1257	MIGHTY MIX: Wish You Were Here/What I Want/Do It/Misty Circles/ Absolutely Nothing/Sit On It/You Make You Wanna/That's The Way (I Like It) (12", white label, promo only)	20
84	Epic A4861ADJ	You Spin Me Round (Big Ben Mix) (1-sided, stickered p/s, promo only)	15
84	Epic TX 4861/TA 4510	You Spin Me Round (Like A Record) (Murder Mix)/Misty Circles (Extended Mix)/What I Want (Dance Mix)/The Stranger (12", p/s, double pack, gatefold p/s)	15
85	Epic A 6086	Lover Come Back To Me/Far Too Hard (blue p/s, withdrawn)	150
85	Epic WA 6086	Lover Come Back To Me/Far Too Hard (fan-shaped picture disc with plinth)	10
85	Epic QTA 6086	Lover Come Back To Me (Extended Remix)/Far Too Hard (12", p/s)	10
85	Epic GA6360	In Too Deep/I'd Do Anything (gatefold p/s)	5
87	Epic BURNSD1	Something In My House (7" double pack, stickered shrinkwrapped sleeve)	8
87	Epic BURNSG1	Something In My House/DJ Hit That Button (gatefold 'pop up' p/s)	6
87	Epic XPR 1328	CLEAN AND DIRTY: Something In My House (Mortevicar Mix)/Something In My House (Naughty XXX Mix) (12", white label, plain white sleeve)	40
88	Epic BURNSQ 4	Turn Around And Count 2 Ten (I Had A Disco Dream Mix)/Something In My House (Instru-Mental)/Then There Was You/Come Inside (12", p/s autographed)	25
88	Epic BURNSQ 4	Turn Around And Count 2 Ten (I Had A Disco Dream Mix)/Something In My House (Instru-Mental)/Then There Was You/Come Inside (12", p/s)	20
88	Epic BURNSC 4	Turn Around And Count 2 Ten/Something In My House (Instru-Mental)/ Turn Around And Count 2 Ten (I Love BPM Mix)/(Instru-Mental (CD, picture disc)	20
88	Epic BURNSP4	Turn Around And Count 2 Ten/Something In My House (instrumental) (fold-out poster p/s)	8

(see also Nightmares In Wax, Sisters Of Mercy, Pauline Murray & Invisible Girls, International Chrysis, Mission)

DEAD SEA FRUIT

67	Camp 602 001	Kensington High Street/Put Another Record On	15
68	Camp 602 004	Love At The Hippiedrome/My Naughty Bluebell	15
67	Camp 603 001	DEAD SEA FRUIT (LP)	70

DEAD WEATHER

09	Third Man TMR 001	Hang You From The Heavens/Are Friends Electric? (luminous vinyl, 'Halloween' cover, 100-only)	120

(see also The Kills/White Stripes/Raconteurs)

DEADWOOD

71	Decca F13109	The Turning Of Them All/They Don't Help Me None	45
71	Decca F13179	Me And My Friends/Little Joe	12

DEAD WRETCHED

82	Inferno HELL 5	Convicted/Infiltrator (p/s)	5
82	Tempest HELL 2	NO HOPE FOR ANYONE EP	20

DEAF AIDS

80	Conspiracy CONS1	Heroes/Bored Christine (p/s)	15

BILL DEAL & RHONDELLS

69	MGM MGM 1466	May I/Day By Day My Love Grows Stronger	6
69	MGM MGM 1479	I've Been Hurt/I've Got My Needs	15
69	MGM MGM 1488	What Kind Of Fool Do You Think I Am/Are You Ready For This	10

DEALER

83	Windrush WR 1030	Better Things To Do/Suspected Foul Play (p/s)	100
86	Ebony EBON 42	FIRST STRIKE (LP)	12

DEALERS

76	Private Stock PVT 73	Midnight Dog/Higher Than God's Hat	6

ALAN DEAN

55	MGM SP 1116	The Song From "Desiree"/Tonight, My Love	5
55	MGM SP 1139	Remember Me, Wherever You Go/Love Is All That Matters	5
56	MGM SP 1173	Without You/Take A Bow	5
57	Columbia DB 3932	Rock 'n' Roll Tarantella/Life Is But A Dream	20

ALAN DEAN & HIS PROBLEMS

64	Decca F 11947	The Time It Takes/Dizzy Heights	40
65	Pye 7N 15749	Thunder And Rain/As Time Goes By	60

LITTLE BILLY DEAN

67	Strike JH 325	That's Always Like You/Tic Toc	20

BOBBY DEAN

65	Parlophone R 5254	More And More/Saint James' Infirmary	5

DEREK DEAN & FRESHMEN

66	Pye 7N 17037	So This Is Love/King Cole Yenka	5

(see also Derek & Freshmen)

ELTON DEAN

71	CBS 64539	ELTON DEAN (LP)	45
77	Ogun OG 610	THE CHEQUE IS IN THE MAIL (LP, with Joe Gallivan & Kenny Wheeler)	15
78	Ogun OG 530	THE BOLOGNA TAPE (LP)	20

(see also Bluesology, Soft Machine, Centipede, Ninesense, Julie Tippetts, Hugh Hopper, Mike Hugg, Reg King, Keith Tippett)

EMIL DEAN

| 67 | CBS 3106 | Ave Maria/Now You're Gone | 6 |
| 68 | Island WIP 6033 | This Is Our Anniversary/Lonely Boy | 12 |

(see also Nirvana [UK])

HAZELL DEAN

75	Decca F 13613	Our Day Will Come/Instrumental	6
76	Decca F 13668	Got You Where I Want You/You Were There	6
77	Decca F 13683	Look What I've Found At The End Of A Rainbow/Where Are We Going	6
77	Decca F 13736	No One's Ever Gonna Love You (The Way That I Love You)/ Just One More Time	6
77	Decca F 13751	Who Was That Lady (I Saw You With)/One Bad Mistake	6
81	Carlin Music Corp. CMC 1004	THE SOUND OF BACHARACH & DAVID (LP, promo only)	25

JIMMY DEAN

59	Philips PB 940	Weekend Blues/Sing Along	5
60	Philips PB 984	There's Still Time, Brother/Thanks For The Dream	6
61	Philips PB 1187	Big Bad John/I Won't Go Hunting With You Jake	5
61	Philips PB 1210	To A Sleeping Beauty/The Cajun Queen	5
62	Philips PB 1223	Smoke Smoke (Smoke) That Cigarette/Dear Ivan	5
62	CBS AAG 107	Steel Men/Little Bitty Big John	5
62	CBS AAG 122	Little Black Book/Please Pass The Biscuits	5
61	Philips BBE 12501	JIMMY DEAN (EP)	10
66	CBS EP 6075	THE BEST OF JIMMY DEAN (EP)	10
61	Philips BBL 7537	BIG BAND JOHN AND OTHER FABULOUS SONGS AND TALES (LP)	20

NORA DEAN

69	Upsetter US 322	The Same Thing You Gave To Daddy/UPSETTER PILGRIMS: A Testimony	50
70	Trojan TR 7735	Barbwire/BRONS: Calypso Mama	20
71	Randy's RAN 508	Want Man/RANDY'S ALL STARS: Man	20
71	High Note HS 050	I Must Get A Man/The Valet	10
71	Bullet BU 472	Peace Begins Within/SLICKERS: Go Back Home	80
71	Gas GAS 165	Greedy Boy/KEITH: Please Stay (B-side actually by Slim Smith)	10
72	Big Shot BI 611	Night Food Reggae/PROPHETS: Jaco	8
73	Bread BR 1117	Mama/Man A Walk And Talk	6
76	Attack ATT 8126	Scorpion/Version	6
79	Nationwide NWLP 007	PLAY ME A LOVE SONG (LP)	30

(see also Hugh Roy)

PAUL DEAN (& SOUL SAVAGES)

| 65 | Decca F 12136 | You Don't Own Me/Hole In The Head (as Paul Dean & Thoughts) | 18 |
| 66 | Reaction 591 002 | She Can Build A Mountain/A Day Gone By (as Paul Dean & Soul Savages) | 15 |

(see also Oscar, Thoughts)

PAULA DEAN & NYAH SHUFFLE

| 70 | Joe's JRS 2 | Since I Met You Baby/Jug Head | 15 |

ROGER DEAN'S LYSIS

| 77 | Mosaic GCM 762 | LYSIS LIVE (LP) | 15 |
| 77 | Mosaic GCM 774 | CYCLE (LP) | 15 |

TERRI DEAN

| 59 | Top Rank JAR 141 | I'm Confessin' (That I Love You)/I Blew Out The Flame | 10 |
| 59 | Top Rank JAR 179 | Adonis/You Treat Me Like A Boy | 10 |

TRACEY DEAN

| 74 | Decca FR 13497 | Moonshiner/Boy On The Ball | 10 |

DEAN & JEAN

64	Stateside SS 249	Tra La La La Suzy/I Love The Summertime	20
64	Stateside SS 283	Hey Jean Hey Dean/Please Don't Tell Me How	20
64	Stateside SS 313	Thread Your Needle/I Wanna Be Loved	20

(see also Brenda Lee Jones)

DEAN & MARK

64	Hickory 45-1227	With Tears In My Eyes/Kissin' Games	10
64	Hickory 45-1249	When I Stop Dreaming/There Oughta Be A Law	10
65	Hickory 45-1294	Just A Step Away/Fallen Star	10

(see also Newbeats, Larry Henley)

JASON DEANE

| 66 | King KG 1049 | Make Believe/Don't Ever Want To See You No More | 30 |
| 67 | King KG 1060 | Down In The Street/Ain't Got No Love | 40 |

(see also Jason Dene)

DEANO

65	Columbia DB 7728	Just A Child In This World/Little Miss With-It	10
66	Columbia DB 7898	Starlight, Starbright/I'm So Happy	10
66	Columbia DB 7965	Please Don't Talk To The Lifeguard/When You Wish Upon A Star	15
67	Columbia DB 8233	What's The Matter With The Matador?/Baby, Let Me Be Your Baby	10
65	Columbia SEG 8470	DEANO (EP)	40

BLOSSOM DEARIE

66	Fontana TF 719	I'm Hip/Wallflower Lonely, Cornflower Blue	8
67	Fontana TF 788	Sweet Georgie Fame/One Note Samba	8
67	Fontana TF 886	Once I Loved/Sunny	8
67	Fontana TF 934	The Music Played/Discover Who I Am	8
68	Fontana TF 986	Hey John/59th Street Bridge Song	8
67	Fontana TL 5399	SWEET BLOSSOM DEARIE (LP)	40
67	Fontana TL 5352	BLOSSOM TIME AT RONNIE'S (LP)	50
67	Fontana STL 5454	SOON IT'S GONNA RAIN (LP)	35
70	Fontana 6309 015	THAT'S THE WAY I WANT IT TO BE (LP)	75

DEAR MR. TIME

70	Square SQ 3	Prayer For Her/Light Up A Light	50
71	Square SQA 101	GRANDFATHER (LP, black/white label)	200

DEATH

87	Under One Flag FLAG 12	SCREAM BLOODY GORE (LP, with inner sleeve)	12
88	Under One Flag FLAG 24	LEPROSY (LP, inner)	20
90	Under One Flag FLAG 38	SPIRITUAL HEALING (LP)	20
90	Under One Flag FLAG 38	SPIRITUAL HEALING (LP, picture disc)	20
92	Under One Flag M FLAG 71	FATE (LP)	15
07	Back On Black BOBV 059	INDIVIDUAL THOUGHT PATTERNS (LP, reissue, red splatter vinyl)	15
07	Back On Black BOBV 059	INDIVIDUAL THOUGHT PATTERNS (LP, reissue,clear vinyl)	15
07	Back On Black BOBV 058	HUMAN (LP, reissue, red splatter vinyl)	15
07	Back On Black BOBV 055	SCREAM BLOODY GORE (2-LP, reissue, orange vinyl, 500 only)	20
07	Back On Black BOBV 055	SCREAM BLOODY GORE (2-LP, red splatter vinyl, 1000 only)	15
07	Back On Black BOBV 056	LEPROSY (LP, reissue, red and white splatter vinyl, gatefold p/s)	15
08	Back On Black BOBV 071	THE SOUND OF PERSEVERANCE (2-LP, reissue, red splatter vinyl, gatefold)	15
09	Black Sleeves BLACK 113	LIVE IN L.A. (DEATH & RAW) (2-LP reissue)	15

DEATH ADDICT

83	Stench STN 1	Killing Time/Dead And Buried (p/s)	12

DEATH ANGEL

87	Under One Flag FLAG 14	THE ULTRA-VIOLENCE (LP)	15

DEATH CAB FOR CUTIE

02	Fierce Panda NING 126	We Laugh Indoors (New Mix)/Debate Exposed Doubt (Acoustic SBN Session Track) (p/s)	10
02	Fierce Panda NING 116	I Was A Kaleidoscope/405 (Acoustic) (p/s)	10
03	Fierce Panda NING 149	The New Year/TV Trays (p/s)	8
04	Fierce Panda NING 158	The Sound Of Settling/This Charming Man (p/s)	8
05	Atlantic AT 0217	Soul Meets Body (Radio Edit)/Jealousy Rides With Me (p/s)	5
06	Atlantic AT 0232X	Crooked Teeth/Talking Like Turnstiles (p/s)	5
06	Atlantic AT 0232	Crooked Teeth (Album Version)/World Shut Your Mouth (red vinyl, fold-out sleeve in stickered PVC sleeve)	5
06	Atlantic AT 0246X	I Will Follow You Into The Dark/Brothers On A Hotel Bed (Rolling Stone Originals Session) (Orange vinyl, poster p/s)	5
06	Atlantic AT 0246	I Will Follow You Into The Dark/Photobooth (Rolling Stone Originals Session) blue vinyl, poster p/s)	5
11	Atlantic 7567 88268-4	In Living Stereo (1-sided, white die-cut sleeve, Record Store Day release, 300 only)	8

DEATH CULT

83	Situation 2 SIT 29	God's Zoo/God's Zoo (These Times) (p/s)	5
83	Situation 2 SIT 29 T	God's Zoo/God's Zoo (These Times) (12", p/s)	8

(see also Cult, Southern Death Cult)

DEATH IN JUNE

84	New European SA 29634	Heaven Street/We Drive East/In The Night Time (12", 2,000 with brown/gold embossed/textured sleeve)	60
84	New European SA 29634	Heaven Street/We Drive East/In The Night Time (12", later pressing of 2,000 with blue/white sleeve)	50
84	New European SA 30634	State Laughter/Holy Water (p/s)	40
84	New European 12BADVC 6	She Said Destroy/The Calling (p/s)	25
84	New European 12BADVC 6	The Calling/She Said Destroy/Doubt To Nothing (12", p/s with insert)	35
85	New European BADVC 69	Born Again/The Calling (Mk II)/Carousel (Bolt Mix) (12", p/s)	25
85	New European BADVC 73	...And Murder Love/A.M.L. (Instrumental) (p/s)	25
85	New European 12BADVC73	Come Before Christ And Murder Love/Torture By Roses (12", p/s)	25
87	New European BADVC 10	To Drown A Rose/Zimmerit/Europa/The Gates Of Heaven (10", p/s)	20
88	Cenaz CENAZ 09	Born Again/The Calling (Mk II)/Carousel (Remix) (12" picture disc, 1st pressing with silver print & rim, 970 only)	25
88	Cenaz CENAZ 09	Born Again/The Calling (Mk II)/Carousel (Remix) (12" picture disc, 2nd pressing bronze print & rim)	20
94	Twilight Command NERO I	SUNDOGS (Rose Clouds Of Holocaust/13 Years Of Carrion) (p/s with sticker)	7
92	New European BADVC 8	CATHEDRAL OF TEARS (12" EP, picture disc with sticker)	25
93	New European BADVC 63	PARADISE RISING (12" EP)	18
96	Twilight. Command NERO XIII	Kapo!/Occidental Martyr (p/s)	18
85	New European BADVC 3	THE GUILTY HAVE NO PRIDE (LP)	25
92	Leprosy UBADVC 4	BURIAL (LP, standard sleeve, green vinyl)	35
80s	Leprosy UBADVC 4	BURIAL (LP, 'quilted' sleeve, brown, pink, white & other coloured vinyl)	35
90s	Leprosy UBADVC 4	BURIAL (LP, textured sleeve, various coloured vinyl)	35
85	New European BADVC 13	NADA (LP, blue sleeve)	40
85	New European BADVC 13	NADA (LP, brown sleeve)	25
85	New European BADVC 13	NADA (LP, picture sleeve)	15
86	New European BADVC 726	LESSON ONE: MISANTHROPY (LP, embossed sleeve with insert)	25
87	New European BADVC 11	BROWN BOOK (LP, textured sleeve with inner & insert; export copies with extra inserts & postcards)	35
87	New European BADVC 11	BROWN BOOK (LP, textured sleeve with inner & insert)	25
88	New European BADVC 9	THE WORLD THAT SUMMER (2-LP, gatefold textured sleeve)	30
88	New European BADVC 88	WALL OF SACRIFICE (LP, red sleeve)	70
88	New European BADVC 88	WALL OF SACRIFICE (LP, green/yellow sleeve)	40
89	New European BADVC 93	93 DEAD SUN WHEELS (mini-LP, with Current 93)	20
92	Leprosy LEPER 2	NIGHT AND FOG (LP, red vinyl, 1,000 only)	30
93	New European BADVC 36	BUT WHAT ENDS WHEN THE SYMBOLS SHATTER (LP, with inner & insert, 500 on purple vinyl)	40
93	New European BADVC 36	BUT WHAT ENDS WHEN THE SYMBOLS SHATTER (LP, with inner & insert, 3,000 on black vinyl)	20
93	New European BADVCCD 36	BUT WHAT ENDS WHEN THE SYMBOLS SHATTER (CD, gold disc digipak, 5,000 only)	20
93	New European BADVCCD 96	SOMETHING IS COMING (2-CD, digipak, 5,000 only)	25
94	New European BADVC 38	ROSE CLOUDS OF HOLOCAUST (LP, with insert & inner)	12
94	New European BADVCCD 38	ROSE CLOUDS OF HOLOCAUST (CD, digipak, 5,000 only)	20
95	New European BADVC 39	BLACK WHOLE OF LOVE (box set with 12", 10", 7" & CDs with inserts)	30
96	New European BADVC 96	SOMETHING IS COMING (2-LP, textured sleeve with insert)	15

(see also Crisis, Current 93, Boyd Rice & Friends, Sol Invictus)

DEATH IN VEGAS

02	Concrete HARD 5112	Leather Girls (Original Mix)/Natja (LAMF Mix)/Natja (Zoo Station) (12", double pack, p/s)	8

MINT VALUE £

03	Concrete	So You Say You've Lost Your Baby (7", pink vinyl, white labels featuring Paul Weller) 15
97	Concrete HARD 22 LP 12	DEAD ELVIS (2-LP) 20
99	Concrete HARD 41 LP	CONTINO SESSIONS (2-LP)..20
02	Concrete HARD 5312	SCORPIO RISING (2-LP, gatefold sleeve with inners)................................20

(see also Dead Elvis)

DEATH SENTENCE
| 82 | Beat The System DEATH 1 | DEATH & PURE DESTRUCTION (EP) ....10 |

DEATH FROM ABOVE
| 05 | 679 LO78X | Blood On Our Hands/Better Off Dead (p/s, red vinyl) ....5 |

DEB MUSIC PLAYERS
| 78 | Deb DEB LP 003 | UMOJA - LOVE AND UNITY (LP) ....40 |

DEBONAIRES (U.K.)
| 66 | Pye 7N 17151 | A Love Of Our Own/The Night Meets The Dawn ....5 |
| 66 | Pye 7N 17204 | Crying Behind Your Smile/Forever More ....5 |

DEBONAIRES (U.S.)
| 70 | Track 604 035 | I'm In Love Again/Headache In My Heart ....50 |

DEBONAIRS
| 63 | Parlophone R 5054 | That's Right/When True Love Comes Your Way ....5 |

DEBS
| 65 | Mercury MF 888 | Sloopy's Gonna Hang On/Under A Street Light......................................10 |

DEB-TONES
| 59 | RCA RCA 1137 | Knock, Knock — Who's There?/I'm In Love Again..................................25 |
| 59 | RCA RCA 1137 | Knock, Knock — Who's There?/I'm In Love Again (78).............................15 |

DEBUTANTES
| 80 | Rok ROK XVII/XVIII | Man In The Street/INNOCENT BYSTANDERS: Where Is Johnny (company sleeve)..................6 |

DECAMERON
73	Vertigo 6360 097	SAY HELLO TO THE BAND (LP) 15
73	Mooncrest CREST 19	MAMMOTH SPECIAL (LP, lyric insert) 25
75	Transatlantic TRA 304	THIRD LIGHT (LP) 15
76	Transatlantic TRA 325	TOMORROWS'S PANTOMIME (LP)..20

YVONNE DE CARLO
| 55 | Capitol CL 14380 | Take It Or Leave It/Three Little Stars...8 |

PAULO DE CARVALHO
| 74 | Pye International 7N 25647 | (And Then) After Love/E Depois Do Adeus (p/s) ....10 |

DE CASTRO SISTERS
54	London HL 8104	Teach Me Tonight/It's Love 30
55	London HL 8137	Boom Boom Boomerang/Let Your Love Walk In 25
55	London HL 8158	I'm Bewildered/To Say You're Mine...25
55	London HLU 8189	If I Ever Fall In Love/Cuckoo In The Clock..30
55	London HLU 8212	Christmas Is A-Comin'/Snowbound For Christmas 25
56	London HLU 8228	Give Me Time/Too Late Now 25
56	London HLU 8296	No One To Blame But You/Cowboys Don't Cry 25
58	HMV POP 527	Who Are They To Say?/When You Look At Me..5
59	HMV POP 583	Teach Me Tonight Cha Cha/The Things I Tell My Pillow 5

DECEMBER
| 96 | Elfenblut SAG 44 | River Of Blood/Venus In Chains (red vinyl, p/s, 1000 only) ....10 |

DECISION
| 68 | MCA MU 1027 | In The Shade Of Your Love/Constable Jones ....7 |

DIANA DECKER
54	Columbia SCM 5083	Oh, My Papa/Crystal Ball 10
54	Columbia SCM 5096	The Happy Wanderer/Till We Two Are One...10
54	Columbia SCM 5120	Jilted/The Man With The Banjo..10
54	Columbia SCM 5123	Kitty In The Basket/Never Never Land 10
54	Columbia SCM 5130	Mama Mia/Percy The Penguin 10
54	Columbia SCM 5145	Sisters/Abracadabra 25
55	Columbia SCM 5166	Open The Window Of Your Heart/The Violin Song 8
55	Columbia SCM 5173	Apples, Peaches And Cherries/Paper Valentine 8
56	Columbia SCM 5246	Rock-A-Boogie Baby/Willie Can..30

(see also Ray Burns, Ruby Murray)

DECLINO
| 85 | Children Of the Revolution GURT 7 | MUCCHIO SELVAGGIO (split LP with NEGAZIONE)..................................75 |

DECORATORS
| 81 | New Hormones ORG 5 | Twilight View/Reflections (p/s) ....5 |

NINA DECOSTA
| 80 | Rokel ROK 12 | Don't Want To Lose You/Instrumental Version (12").............................50 |

DECOYS
| 64 | Studio 36 KEP 108 | DECOYS (EP, 500 only) ....30 |

DE DANAAN
82	Cara CARA 1	Hey Jude/St. Jude's Hornpipe/Trip To Taum Reel/Teetotaller 5
75	Polydor 2904 005	DE DANAAN (LP) 15
77	Decca SKL-R 5287	DE DANAAN — SELECTED JIGS AND REELS (LP) 18
80	Decca SKL 5318	BANKS OF THE NILE (LP)..12

DEDICATED MEN'S JUG BAND
| 65 | Piccadilly 7N 35245 | Boodle-Am-Shake/Come On Boys ....5 |
| 66 | Piccadilly 7N 35283 | Don't Come Knocking/One Time Blues...5 |

DEDRINGER
| 80 | DinDisc DIN 10 | Sunday Drivers/We Don't Mind (p/s) ....5 |
| 80 | DinDisc DIN 11 | Innocent 'Till Proven Guilty/Maxine//Took A Long Time/ We Don't Mind (double pack) ......8 |

81	DinDisc DIN 12	Direct Line/She's Not Ready (p/s)	5
82	Neat NEAT 18	Hot Lady/Hot Licks And Rock'N'Roll (p/s)	5
81	DinDisc DID 7	DIRECT LINE (LP)	12
83	Neat NEAT 1009	SECOND RISING (LP, with inner sleeve)	12

BRIAN DEE
| 75 | Atlantic 2460 255 | HAMMOND EXCITEMENT (LP) | 12 |

DAVE DEE
70	Fontana TF 1074	My Woman's Man/Gotta Make You Part Of Me	5
70	Fontana 6007 021	Annabella/Kelly	5
70	Philips 6006 061	Everything About Her/If I Believed In Tomorrow	5
71	Philips 6006 100	Wedding Bells/Sweden	5
71	Philips 6006 154	Hold On/Mary Morning, Mary Evening	5
71	Philips 6006 180	Swingy/Don't You Ever Change Your Mind	5

(see also Dave Dee, Dozy, Beaky, Mick & Tich)

DAVE DEE, DOZY, BEAKY, MICK & TICH
65	Fontana TF 531	No Time/Is It Love	25
65	Fontana TF 586	All I Want/It Seems A Pity	25
65	Fontana TF 630	You Make It Move/I Can't Stop	10
67	Fontana TF 798	Touch Me Touch Me/Marina	6
68	Fontana TF 903	The Legend Of Xanadu/Please	5
74	Antic K 11510	She's My Lady/Babeigh	6
67	Fontana TE 17488	LOOS OF ENGLAND (EP)	12
66	Fontana TL 5350	DAVE DEE, DOZY, BEAKY, MICK & TICH (LP)	20
66	Fontana TL 5388	IF MUSIC BE THE FOOD OF LOVE PREPARE FOR INDIGESTION (LP, mono)	25
66	Fontana STL 5388	IF MUSIC BE THE FOOD OF LOVE PREPARE FOR INDIGESTION (LP, stereo)	35
67	Fontana (S)TL 5441	GOLDEN HITS OF DAVE DEE, DOZY, BEAKY, MICK & TICH (LP)	15
68	Fontana (S)TL 5471	IF NO-ONE SANG (LP)	20
69	Fontana SFL 13002	DDDBM&T (LP)	12
70	Fontana SFL 13173	TOGETHER (LP)	12

(see also Dozy Beaky Mick & Tich [D,B,M & T], Dave Dee)

JAY DEE
| 74 | Warner Bros. 7798 | Strange Games And Funky Things/Intrumental | 7 |

JEANNIE DEE
| 69 | Beacon BEA 115 | Come Into My Arms/Sun Shine On Me | 7 |
| 69 | Beacon BEA 142 | Don't Go Home My Little Darling/Come See About Me | 15 |

JOEY DEE & STARLI(GH)TERS
61	Columbia DB 4758	Peppermint Twist (Parts 1 & 2)	8
62	Columbia DB 4803	Hey, Let's Twist/Roly Poly	10
62	Columbia DB 4842	Shout (Parts 1 & 2)	10
62	Columbia DB 4862	Ya Ya/Fanny Mae	10
62	Columbia DB 4905	What Kind Of Love Is This?/Wing Ding	10
63	Columbia DB 4955	I Lost My Baby/Keep Your Mind On What You're Doin'	10
63	Columbia DB 7005	Baby You're Driving Me Crazy/Help Me Pick Up The Pieces	10
63	Columbia DB 7055	Hot Pastrami With Mashed Potatoes (Parts 1 & 2)	10
63	Columbia DB 7102	Dance, Dance, Dance/Let's Have A Party (features Ronettes uncredited)	10
63	Columbia DB 7277	Down By The Riverside/Getting Nearer (features Ronettes uncredited)	10
61	Columbia 33SX 1406	DOIN' THE TWIST LIVE AT THE PEPPERMINT LOUNGE (LP)	20
62	Columbia 33SX 1461	BACK AT THE PEPPERMINT LOUNGE (LP)	20
62	Columbia 33SX 1502	ALL THE WORLD IS TWISTIN' (LP)	25
63	Columbia 33SX 1532	JOEY DEE (LP)	25
63	Columbia 33SX 1607	DANCE DANCE DANCE (LP, with Starlighters, also with Ronettes uncredited)	25

(see also Young Rascals)

JOHNNIE DEE
| 65 | Columbia DB 7612 | Frankie's Angel/Everything's Upside Down | 7 |

JOHNNY DEE
| 57 | Oriole CB 1367 | Sittin' In The Balcony/A-Plus Love | 150 |
| 57 | Oriole CB 1367 | Sittin' In The Balcony/A-Plus Love (78) | 20 |

(see also John D. Loudermilk)

KIKI DEE
63	Fontana TF 394	Early Night/Lucky High Heels	20
63	Fontana TF 414	Don't Put Your Heart In His Hand/I Was Only Kidding	12
64	Fontana TF 443	Miracles/That's Right, Walk On By	18
64	Fontana TF 490	(You Don't Know) How Glad I Am/Baby I Don't Care	12
65	Fontana TF 596	Runnin' Out Of Fools/There He Goes	10
66	Fontana TF 669	Why Don't I Run Away From You?/Small Town	20
67	Fontana TF 792	I'm Going Out (The Same Way I Came In)/We've Got Everything Going For Us	15
67	Fontana TF 833	I/Stop And Think	10
67	Fontana TF 870	Excuse Me/Patterns	10
68	Fontana TF 926	Can't Take My Eyes Off You/Hungry Heart	10
68	Fontana TF 983	Now The Flowers Cry/On A Magic Carpet Ride	200
70	Tamla Motown TMG 739	The Day Will Come Between Sunday And Monday/My Whole World Ended (The Moment You Left Me)	25
72	Philips 6006 352	Excuse Me/Patterns	8
73	Rocket PIG 2	Lonnie And Josie/The Last Good Man In My Life	7
65	Fontana TE 17443	KIKI DEE (EP)	40
66	Fontana TE 17470	KIKI DEE IN CLOVER (EP)	30
68	Fontana (S)TL 5455	I'M KIKI DEE (LP)	45
70	Tamla Motown STML 11158	GREAT EXPECTATIONS (LP)	45

(see also Elton John)

LENNY DEE
| 55 | Brunswick 05440 | Plantation Boogie/Birth Of The Blues | 7 |

RICKY DEE & EMBERS
| 62 | Stateside SS 136 | Workout/JOHN MOBLEY: Tunnel Of Love | 15 |

MINT VALUE £

SANDRA DEE
61	Brunswick 05858	Tammy Tell Me True/Let's Fall In Love	10

SIMON DEE
69	Chapter one CH 105	Julie/Whatever Happened To Us	7

TAMMI DEE
71	Downtown DT 479	Val/MUSIC DOCTORS: Bank Raid	12

TOMMY DEE
59	Melodisc 1516	Three Stars/TEEN JONES (TONES): I'll Never Change (tri centre)	40
59	Melodisc 1516	Three Stars/TEEN JONES (TONES): I'll Never Change (round centre)	15
59	Melodisc 1516	Three Stars/TEEN JONES (TONES): I'll Never Change (78)	10

DEE & DYNAMITES
60	Philips PB 1081	Blaze Away/South Bound Gasser	5

DEE AND THE QUOTIUM
69	Jay Boy Boy 8	Someday You'll Need Someone/Send Some Flowers To Jule	45

MAURICE DEEBANK
84	Cherry Red MRED 61	INNER THOUGHT ZONE (LP)	12

(see also Felt)

DEEE LITE
90	Elektra EKR 114T	Groove Is In The Heart/(Peanut Butter Mix)/What Is Love? (Holographic Goatee Mix)/(Rainbow Beard Mix) (12" original pressing with "EW" in centre of label)	10

DEEJAY FRIENDLY
96	Deejay Friendly PK 01	Piano Me Softly (12" promo)	8

DEEJAYS
65	Polydor BM 56034	Dimples/Coming On Strong	60
65	Polydor BM 56501	Blackeyed Woman/I Just Can't Go To Sleep	110

ANTHONY DEELEY
68	Pama PM 728	Anytime Man/Don't Change Your Mind About Me	10

ANGELA DEEN
64	Fontana TF 491	There's So Much About My Baby That I Love/Gotta Hand It To The Boy	8

CAROL DEENE
61	HMV POP 922	Sad Movies (Make Me Cry)/Don't Forget	10
62	HMV POP 973	Norman/On The Outside Looking In	6
62	HMV POP 1027	Johnny Get Angry/Somebody's Smiling	10
62	HMV POP 1058	Some People/Kissin'	5
62	HMV POP 1086	James/It Happened Last Night	8
63	HMV POP 1123	Let Me Do It My Way/Growin' Up	5
63	HMV POP 1200	Oh Oh Oh Willie/I Want To Stay Here	5
64	HMV POP 1275	Who's Been Sleeping In My Bed?/Love Is Wonderful	5
64	HMV POP 1337	Very First Kiss/Hard To Say Goodnight	5
65	HMV POP 1405	Most People Do/I Can't Forget Someone Like You	5
65	Columbia DB 7743	He Just Don't Know/Up In The Penthouse	5
66	Columbia DB 7890	Dancing In Your Eyes/Please Don't Be Unfaithful Again	10
67	Columbia DB 8107	Love Not Have I/Time	10
68	CBS 3206	When He Wants A Woman/I'm Not Crying	5
69	Conquest CXT 102	One More Chance/Invisible Tears	5
79	RIM 003	Ready For The Times To Get Better/It's So Easy	5
70	World Records ST 1031	A LOVE AFFAIR (LP)	15

DEEP END
78	Private pressing	BEGGED AND BORROWED (LP, listed as CPLP 016)	15

DEEP FEELING
69	Page One POF 160	Oh Darlin'/Feelin'	40
70	DJM DJS 231	Do You Wanna Dance/The Day My Lady Cried	6
70	Page One POF 165	Do You Love Me/Move On	6
70	Page One POF 177	Skyline Pigeon/We've Thrown It All Away	6
71	DJM DJS 237	Sweet Dust And Red Wine/Turn Around	6
74	Santa Ponsa PN 512	Lets Spend The Night Together/Avalon	8
71	DJM DJLPS 419	DEEP FEELING (LP)	150

(see also Raw Material)

DEEP FREEZE
70s	Guardian GRL 43	Keeping You In Furs/Don't Look Back	5

DEEP FREEZE MICE
86	Cordelia ERICAT 002	Zoology/These Floors Are Smooth (500 copies, no sleeve)	15
86	Cordelia ERICAT 016	NEURON MUSIC (12" EP, also featuring Mr. Concept, Yung Analysts and Rimarimba)	20
93	Farce 042	Slow Shiny Bricks/George Bailey Lassoes A Refrigerator (Remix) (300 numbered copies)	10
79	Mole Embalming MOLE 1	MY GERANIUMS ARE BULLETPROOF (LP, 1st 250 copies with paste-on sleeve, 8-page booklet & various A4 inserts)	120
79	Mole Embalming MOLE 1	MY GERANIUMS ARE BULLETPROOF (LP, printed sleeve, 1500 only)	70
81	Mole Embalming MOLE 2	TEENAGE HEAD IN MY REFRIGERATOR (LP, 400 copies with red cover)	45
81	Mole Embalming MOLE 2	TEENAGE HEAD IN MY REFRIGERATOR (LP, 800 printed)	50
81	Inedible MOLE 3	GATES OF LUNCH (LP, 1,000 pressed, various inserts)	40
82	Mole Embalming MOLE C1	TEENAGE HEAD IN MY REFRIGERATOR/LED ZEPPELIN 2 (cassette, around 30 copies)	50
83	Mole Embalming MOLE 4	SAW A RANCH BURNING LAST NIGHT (LP, 120 in wraparound sleeve)	40
83	Mole Embalming MOLE 4	SAW A RANCH BURNING LAST NIGHT (LP, 1000 copies)	40
84	Inedible MOLE 3	GATES OF LUNCH (LP, 1,000 pressed, these 150 copies with wraparound poster sleeve with insert)	55
84	Cordelia ERICAT 001	I LOVE YOU LITTLE BOBO WITH YOUR DELICATE GOLDEN LIONS (2 x LP)	60
84	Cordelia ERICAT 004	HANG ON CONSTANCE, LET ME HEAR THE NEWS (LP, 120 wraparound poster sleeve with insert)	40
84	Cordelia ERICAT 004	HANG ON CONSTANCE, LET ME HEAR THE NEWS (LP, 1000 copies)	20
84	Mole Embalming MOLE C2	MY GERANIUMS ARE BULLETPROOF (cassette, 30 copies only)	50
84	Mole Embalming MOLE C3	TEENAGE HEAD IN MY REFRIGERATOR (cassette, around 30 copies)	50
86	Cordelia/Unlikely CERICAT 001	I LOVE YOU LITTLE BOBO WITH YOUR DELICATE GOLDEN LIONS (double cassette, around 25 copies)	25

87	Cordelia ERICAT 013	RAIN IS WHEN THE EARTH IS TELEVISION (LP, 1000 copies only)	20
87	Cordelia ERICAT 024	WAR, FAMINE, DEATH, PESTILENCE & MISS TIMBERLAKE (LP, 1000 copies)	20
88	Cordelia ERICAT 027	THE TENDER YELLOW PONIES OF INSOMNIA (LP, 1000 copies)	20
89	Logical Fish 1	I LIVE IN SWITZERLAND (LP, 500 copies)	15

DEEP PURPLE

SINGLES

68	Parlophone R 5708	Hush/One More Rainy Day (in promo-only p/s)	350
68	Parlophone R 5708	Hush/One More Rainy Day	35
68	Parlophone R 5745	Kentucky Woman/Wring That Neck (withdrawn)	60
69	Parlophone R 5763	Emmaretta/Wring That Neck	35
69	Harvest HAR 5006	Hallelujah (I Am The Preacher)/April Part 1 (in promo-only p/s)	250
69	Harvest HAR 5006	Hallelujah (I Am The Preacher)/April Part 1	30
70	Harvest PSR 325	Concerto, 1st Movement (edit)/Concerto, 2nd Movement (edit) (promo, possibly some commercial)	35
70	Harvest HAR 5020	Black Night/Speed King	6
71	Harvest HAR 5033	Strange Kind Of Woman/I'm Alone	6
71	Harvest HAR 5045	Fireball/Demon's Eye	6
72	Purple PUR 102	Never Before/When A Blind Man Cries	6
74	Purple PUR 117	Might Just Take Your Life/Coronarias Redig	8
76	Purple PUR 130	You Keep On Moving/Love Child	8
77	Purple PUR 132	Smoke On The Water/Woman From Tokyo/Child In Time (10,000 with p/s)	7
85	Polydor POSPP 719	Perfect Strangers (edit)/Son Of Alerik (edit) (picture disc)	7
87	Polydor POSPP 843	Call Of The Wild/Strange Ways (12", picture disc)	10
88	Polydor POC 4	Hush ('88 Re-recording)/Dead Or Alive (Live) (black vinyl, p/s)	7
88	Polydor POC 4	Hush ('88 Re-recording)/Dead Or Alive (Live) (blue vinyl, p/s)	5
88	Polydor RX 4	Hush ('88 Re-recording)/Dead Or Alive (Live)/Bad Attitude (12", gatefold p/s)	8
88	Polydor 080 088-2	Bad Attitude/Black And White/Unwritten Law/Strangeways (CD Video)	15
90	RCA PT 49224	Love Conquers All (Edit)/Truth Hurts (die-cut picture disc, with insert)	7
93	BMG DP 001	Anya/Excerpts of: Time To Kill/The Battle Rages On/Talk About Love (CD single, promo)	20
95	EMI 7243 8 82214 67	Black Night (Remix)/Black Night (Original Mix)/Speed King (12", purple vinyl, numbered limited edition)	8

EPs

77	Purple PUR 135	NEW LIVE AND RARE VOL. 1 (EP, 15,000 on purple vinyl)	8
78	Purple PUR 137	NEW LIVE AND RARE VOL. 2 (EP)	8
80	Harvest SHEP 101	NEW LIVE AND RARE VOL. 3 (EP)	8

ALBUMS : PARLOPHONE

68	Parlophone PMC 7055	SHADES OF DEEP PURPLE (LP, yellow/black label, mono, with "sold in U.K..." text)	500
68	Parlophone PCS 7055	SHADES OF DEEP PURPLE (LP, yellow/black label, stereo, with "sold in U.K..." text)	300
69	Parlophone PCS 7055	SHADES OF DEEP PURPLE (LP, stereo repressing, laminated sleeve, white/black label)	30

ALBUMS : HARVEST

69	Harvest SHVL 751	THE BOOK OF TALIESYN (LP, laminated gatefold sleeve, first pressing with "sold in U.K." text spread over 4 lines, no EMI on label)	150
69	Harvest SHVL 751	THE BOOK OF TALIESYN (LP, laminated sleeve, second pressing with "sold in U.K." text spread over 5 lines)	70
69	Harvest SHVL 751	THE BOOK OF TALIESYN (LP, laminated sleeve, third pressing without "sold in U.K." text)	40
69	Harvest SHVL 759	DEEP PURPLE (LP, laminated gatefold sleeve, no EMI logo on label)	100
69	Harvest SHVL 759	DEEP PURPLE (LP, laminated gatefold sleeve, later pressing with EMI logo on label)	20
70	Harvest SHVL 767	CONCERTO FOR GROUP AND ORCHESTRA (LP, laminated gatefold sleeve, no EMI logo on label)	40
70	Harvest SHVL 767	CONCERTO FOR GROUP AND ORCHESTRA (LP, laminated gatefold sleeve, later pressing with EMI logo on label)	20
70	Harvest SHVL 777	IN ROCK (LP, laminated gatefold sleeve with "file under popular: pop groups", "Printed and Made by Garrod & Lofthouse Ltd." A2, B1 matrix, "The Gramophone Co" text around label rim not "EMI Records" no EMI logo on label, advertising inner sleeve with "Patent no's 1,125,555 & 1,072,844" at bottom)	80
70	Harvest SHVL 777	IN ROCK (LP, laminated gatefold sleeve, later pressing with EMI logo on label)	20
71	Harvest SHVL 759	DEEP PURPLE (LP, laminated gatefold sleeve, non EMI pressing with indented circular groove around spindle hole)	20
71	Harvest SHVL 793	FIREBALL (LP, textured gatefold sleeve, with lyric insert)	80
71	Harvest SHVL 751	THE BOOK OF TALIESYN (LP, laminated gatefold sleeve with 'Ernest J. Day' printing credit, fourth pressing with EMI logo on label)	40
75	Harvest SHVL 751	THE BOOK OF TALIESYN (LP, laminated gatefold sleeve, fifth pressing with EMI logo)	15
76	Harvest SHVL 751	THE BOOK OF TALIESYN (LP, laminated gatefold sleeve with 'Garrod & Lofthouse Ltd' printing credit, sixth pressing with EMI logo on slightly more yellow label)	15
77	Harvest SHSM 2016	SHADES OF DEEP PURPLE (LP, reissue)	12
78	Harvest SHSM 2026	THE SINGLES A's AND B's (LP, purple vinyl)	15
80	Harvest SHSM 2016	SHADES OF DEEP PURPLE (LP, 'dismembered doll-limb' sleeve, withdrawn)	150
80	Harvest SHDW 412	IN CONCERT (2-LP)	12
82	Harvest SHSP 4124	LIVE IN LONDON (LP)	12
99	Harvest 7243 4 99469 10	BOOK OF TALIESYN (LP, 180gm vinyl, gatefold sleeve in stickered PVC outer)	20

ALBUMS : PURPLE

72	Purple TPSP 3511/12	MADE IN JAPAN 2-LP, First pressing, "Gramophone Co" on label rim, MATRIX TPS 3511 A-1U/B-1U/TPS 3512 A-1U/B1-U, "Porky" (side 1), "Delta Pork" (side 2), "Pecko" (side 3), "Peckie" (Side 4) etched into dead wax, double gatefold sleeve, many originals with £3.25 price sticker)	40
72	Purple TSPS 3511/12	MADE IN JAPAN 2-LP, Contract pressing, no mother or stamper details at 3 and 9 'o' clock, (just number "3" at 9 "o" clock. Ridge around inside of label half an inch from the rim, no "Made in Gt. Britain" at foot of label, no brackets on "Made In Japan" on labels, double gatefold sleeve)	40
72	Purple TPSA 7504	MACHINE HEAD (LP, laminated gatefold sleeve, with lyric insert)	25
73	Purple TPSA 7508	WHO DO WE THINK WE ARE (LP, 1st pressing with 'The Gramophone Co' on rim of label, -1U matrix numbers on both sides, laminated gatefold sleeve with 'File under popular: pop groups', with lyric insert)	20
74	Purple Q4TPS 7504	MACHINE HEAD (LP, laminated gatefold sleeve, quadrophonic)	45
74	Purple TPS 3505	BURN (LP, First Pressing: "The Gramophone Co" on rim, MATRIX TPS 3505 A-1U/B-1U, "Porky & Mel * Trish" etched into dead wax side 1/"Pecko" etched into dead wax on side 2. Spine wording on top edge as well as spine)	30
74	Purple TPS 3505	BURN (LP, Second Pressing: "EMI Records" on rim, -1U Matrixes)	15
74	Purple TPS 3505	BURN (LP, hybrid pressing with: "The Gramophone Co" on one label and "EMI Records" on the other)	20
74	Purple TPS 3505	BURN (LP, later pressings with "EMI Records" on both labels)	12

MINT VALUE £

74	Purple TPS 3508	STORMBRINGER (LP, 1st pressing, matrixes TPS3508 A-1U/B-1U, 'Kendun' stamped in dead wax, "EMI Records Ltd" on label rim, spine wording on top edge and spine, "7411 Garrod & Lofthouse Ltd" on bottom right corner of sleeve) 20
75	Purple TPSA 7515	COME TASTE THE BAND (LP, laminated gatefold sleeve with inner) 15
79	Purple TPS 3514	THE MARK 2 PURPLE SINGLES (LP, purple vinyl) 15

ALBUMS : OTHER LPS

84	Polydor POLHP 16	PERFECT STRANGERS (LP, picture disc, with extra track & die-cut sleeve) 15
84	Polydor DEEP 1A	DEEP PURPLE INTERVIEW (LP, 1-sided, promo-only, stickered white sleeve) 18
85	EMI EJ 26 0343 0	IN ROCK (LP, picture disc with poster) 20
85	EMI EJ 34 0344 0	FIREBALL (LP, picture disc with poster) 20
85	EMI EG 26 0345 0	MACHINE HEAD (LP, picture disc with poster) 20
85	EMI PUR 1/E 2606131	DEEP PURPLE — ANTHOLOGY (2-LP, blue vinyl) 25
86	Polydor DEEP 2A	HOUSE OF BLUE LIGHT (interview LP, promo-only, plays same both sides, stickered black sleeve) 15
87	Polydor 831 318-2	HOUSE OF BLUE LIGHT (CD) 20
88	Connoisseur VSOP 125	SCANDINAVIAN NIGHTS (2-LP, gatefold sleeve, with booklet) 18
91	Connoisseur DPVSOPLP 163	IN THE ABSENCE OF PINK – KNEBWORTH 85 (2xLP gatefold) 15
91	EMI 96129	ANTHOLOGY (3-LP) 20
93	BMG 74321 15420-1	THE BATTLE RAGES ON (LP, with inner sleeve) 20
95	EMI 7243 8 34019 18	DEEP PURPLE IN ROCK (2-LP, purple vinyl, gatefold sleeve with inners) 35
97	EMI DEEPP 3	MACHINE HEAD (2-LP, 'EMI 100' remixed anniversary edition, purple vinyl, gatefold sleeve, with insert) 35
97	EMI LPCENT 25	SHADES OF DEEP PURPLE (LP, 'EMI 100', 180gm vinyl edition, yellow/black label) 30
97	EMI DEEPP 2	FIREBALL (2-LP, gatefold sleeve with inners & limited edition print) 30
98	EMI PP 074	VERY BEST OF (2-LP, purple vinyl) 30
98	EMI 7243 8 57864 19	MADE IN JAPAN (2-LP, numbered, purple vinyl, gatefold sleeve with inners) 30

(see also Ritchie Blackmore, Rainbow, Gillan, [David Coverdale's] Whitesnake, Tommy Bolin, [Sheila Carter &] Episode Six, Jon Lord, Roger Glover, Green Bullfrog, Wizard's Convention, Elf, Maze, M.I. Five, Warhorse, Captain Beyond, John Lawton, Hell Preachers Inc., Glen Hughes, Trapeze, Leading Figures, Paice Ashton & Lord, Silverhead, Pete York Percussion Band)

DEEP RIVER BOYS

54	HMV 7M 174	Sweet Mama Tree Top Tall/A Kiss And Cuddle Polka 20
54	HMV 7M 280	Shake, Rattle And Roll/St. Louis Blues 40
56	HMV 7M 361	Rock-A-Beatin' Boogie/Just A Little Bit More! 40
56	HMV POP 263	That's Right/Honey Honey 20
57	HMV POP 395	Whole Lotta Shakin' Goin' On/There's A Goldmine In The Sky 30
58	HMV POP 449	Not Too Old To Rock And Roll/Slow Train To Nowhere 25
58	HMV POP 537	Itchy Twitchy Feeling/I Shall Not Be Moved 10
59	Top Rank JAR 172	Nola/Kissin' 5
59	Top Rank JAR 174	I Don't Know Why (I Just Do)/Timbers Gotta Roll (with Harry Douglass) 10
60	Top Rank JAR 352	Go Galloway, Go/Dum Dum De Dum (with Harry Douglass) 7
62	HMV POP 1081	Settle Down/Ashes Of Roses 5

(see also Fats Waller, Harry Douglass & Deep River Boys)

DEEP SET

68	Pye 7N 17594	That's The Way Life Goes/Hello Amy 60
69	Major Minor MM 607	I Started A Joke/Spicks And Specks 8
70	Target 7N 45018	Cinnamon Girl/You'll Never Know 100

DEEP SIX

| 66 | Liberty LIB 55882 | Counting/When Morning Breaks .... 8 |

DEEP SWITCH

| 86 | SWITCH 1 | NINE INCHES OF GOD (LP, private pressing) .... 40 |

DEEP TIMBRE

| 72 | Westwood WR 5006 | DEEP TIMBRE (LP) .... 40 |

DEEP WATER

| 70 | Pye 7N 17946 | Take A Look Around/Poor Little Me .... 6 |

DEEP THROATS

| 78 | Limp LMP 1 | Rock N Roll Discharge/Miami Connection .... 15 |

DEERHUNTER

| 07 | 4AD CAD 2822 | MICROCASTLE/WEIRD ERA CONT. (LP) .... 15 |

(see also Atlas Sound)

SAM DEES

69	Major Minor MM 655	If It's All Wrong (It's All Right)/Don't Keep Me Hangin' On 30
75	Atlantic K 10676	Fragile, Handle With Care/Save The Love At Any Cost 100
89	RCA PB 43129	After All/Always Something (p/s) 15
75	Atlantic K 50142	THE SHOW MUST GO ON (LP) 30
97	Soul Supply GS0002	Lonely For You Baby/SAM FLETCHER: I'd Think It Over (promos [GS 0002X] £12) 10

SAM DEES & BETTYE SWANN

| 76 | Atlantic K 10719 | Storybook Children/Just As Sure .... 15 |

(see also Bettye Swann)

DEE SET

| 68 | Blue Cat BS 146 | I Know A Place/ROY BENNETT: I Dangerous .... 40 |

DEF J

| 92 | Kold Sweat KS122 | Just Save It (12") .... 15 |

(see also Encona Coarse)

DEF LEPPARD

79	Bludgeon Riffola SRT/CUS/232	THE DEF LEPPARD EP: Ride Into The Sun/Getcha Rocks Off/The Overture (red label, p/s with lyric insert, 150 only) 350
79	Bludgeon Riffola SRT/CUS/232	THE DEF LEPPARD EP: Ride Into The Sun/Getcha Rocks Off/The Overture (red label, with p/s, 850 only) 250
79	Bludgeon Riffola SRT/CUS/232	THE DEF LEPPARD EP: Ride Into The Sun/Getcha Rocks Off/The Overture (red label, /without p/s, 850 only) 60
79	Bludgeon Riffola MSB 001	Ride Into The Sun/Getcha Rocks Off/The Overture (reissue, yellow label, 15,000 pressed, no p/s) 18
79	Phonogram 6059 240	Getcha Rocks Off/Ride Into The Sun/The Overture (2nd reissue, no p/s) 10
79	Phonogram 6059 240	Getcha Rocks Off/Ride Into The Sun/The Overture (mispressing, both sides play "The Overture") 40

79	Phonogram 6059 247	Wasted/Hello America (p/s)	12
80	Phonogram LEPP 1	Hello America/Good Morning Freedom (p/s)	12
81	Phonogram LEPP 2	Let It Go/Switch 625 (p/s, 10,000 shrinkwrapped with patch)	15
81	Phonogram LEPP 2	Let It Go/Switch 625 (p/s)	12
82	Phonogram LEPP 3	Bringin' On The Heartbreak/Me And My Wine (p/s)	35
82	Phonogram LEPP 312	Bringin' On The Heartbreak/Me And My Wine/You Got Me Runnin' (12", p/s)	18
83	Phonogram VER 5	Photograph/Bringin' On The Heartbreak	10
83	Phonogram VERP 5	Photograph/Bringin' On The Heartbreak (camera-shaped fold-out/pop-up sleeve, 500 only)	25
83	Phonogram VERX 5	Photograph/Bringin' On The Heartbreak/Mirror, Mirror (12", p/s)	20
83	Phonogram VER 6	Rock Of Ages/Action! Not Words (p/s)	7
83	Phonogram VERP 6	Rock Of Ages/Action! Not Words (guitar-shaped picture disc)	35
83	Phonogram VERQ 6	Rock Of Ages/Action! Not Words (foldout 'rock box' cube sleeve, 500 only)	40
83	Phonogram VERX 6	Rock Of Ages/Action! Not Words (12", p/s)	18
83	Phonogram VERDJ 8	Too Late/Foolin' (p/s, DJ-only promo with rear band photo in football kit)	150
83	Phonogram VER 8	Too Late For Love/Foolin' (p/s)	12
83	Phonogram VERX 8	Too Late For Love/Foolin'/High And Dry (12", p/s)	20
84	Phonogram VER 9	Photograph/Bringin' On The Heartbreak (reissue, 'wallet' p/s)	10
84	Phonogram VERG 9	Photograph/Bringin' On The Heartbreak ('wallet' p/s, 500 only)	35
84	Phonogram VERX 9	Photograph/Bringin' On The Heartbreak/Mirror, Mirror (12", p/s)	15
87	Phonogram LEPC 1	Animal/Animal (Extended Mix)/Tear It Down (12", p/s, red vinyl)	15
87	Phonogram LEPCD 1	Animal/Women/Animal (Extended Mix)/Tear It Down (CD, no'd, 1,000 only)	25
87	Phonogram LEPS 2	Pour Some Sugar On Me/I Wanna Be Your Hero (tri-shaped picture disc in silver 12" foldout p/s with tour dates)	15
87	Phonogram LEPPX 2	Pour Some Sugar On Me (Extended Version)/Pour Some Sugar On Me (Extended)/I Wanna Be Your Hero (12", picture disc, unissued)	0
87	Phonogram LEPS 3	Hysteria/Ride Into The Sun (1987 Version) (p/s, shrinkwrapped with patch)	10
87	Phonogram LEPX 313	Hysteria/Ride Into The Sun (1987 Version)/Love And Affection (live) (12", envelope box sleeve with poster & international discography, 5,000 only)	15
87	Phonogram LEPCD 3	Hysteria/Ride Into The Sun (1987 Version)/Love And Affection (live)/ I Wanna Be Your Hero (CD, 5,000 only with titles in red, numbered)	15
88	Phonogram LEPP 4	Armageddon It! (The Atomic Mix)/Ring Of Fire (poster p/s)	7
88	Phonogram LEPXB 4	Armageddon It!/Armageddon It! (The Atomic Mix)/Ring Of Fire (12", numbered box set with poster, enamel badge & 5 postcards, 5,000 only)	18
88	Phonogram LEPCD 4	Armageddon It! (The Atomic Mix)/Ring Of Fire/Animal/ Pour Some Sugar On Me (CD, picture disc)	15
88	Phonogram LEPG 5	Love Bites/Billy's Got A Gun (live) (no'd gatefold p/s with 8-page lyric book)	8
88	Phonogram LEPXB 5	Love Bites/Billy's Got A Gun (live)/Excitable (Orgasmic Mix) (12", box set with 4 cardboard inserts, 5,000 only)	18
88	Phonogram LEPCD 5	Love Bites/Rocket (The Lunar Mix)/Billy's Got A Gun (live) (CD, card sleeve)	12
89	Phonogram LEPC 6	Rocket/Release Me (foldout 'Brit' pack, envelope sleeve with 3 inserts)	8
89	Phonogram LEPXP 6	Rocket (The Lunar Mix)/(Radio Edit)/Release Me (12", picture disc, numbered)	15
89	Phonogram LEPXP 6	Rocket (The Lunar Mix)/(Radio Edit)/Release Me (12", picture disc, un-numbered)	10
89	Phonogram LEPXC 6	Rocket (The Lunar Mix)/Release Me/Rock Of Ages (live) (12", calendar pack)	15
89	Phonogram LEPCD 6	Rocket (The Lunar Mix)/Rock Of Ages (live)/Release Me (CD)	12
92	Phonogram DEFXP 7	Let's Get Rocked/Only After Dark/Too Late For Love (live) (12", picture disc, with insert)	10
92	Phonogram DEFCD 7	Let's Get Rocked/Only After Dark/Women (live) (CD, picture disc, in box with space for 4 CDs)	10
88	Bludgeon Riffola 080 458-2	Love Bites/Rocket (Lunar Mix)/Billy's Got A Gun (live)/ Love Bites (Video) (CD Video)	20
89	Bludgeon Riffola 080 034-2	Rock Of Ages/Stagefright/Billy's Got A Gun/Too Late For Love/ Rock Of Ages (Video) (CD Video)	20
89	Bludgeon Riffola 080 626-2	Animal (Extended Version)/Animal/Tear It Down/Animal (Video) (CD Video)	20
90	Bludgeon Riffola 080 990-2	Rocket (Radio Edit)/Release Me/Rock Of Ages/Rocket (Video) (CD Video)	20
87	Phonogram HYSPD 1	HYSTERIA (LP, picture disc)	15
89	Phonogram 836 606-2	THE FOUR ALBUMS (4-CD box set, with booklet)	50
92	Phonogram 510 978-1	ADRENALIZE (LP, picture disc, 5,000 only, numbered, die-cut sleeve)	15
94	Phonogram (no cat. no.)	ADRENALIZE — MAHOGANY BOX SET (CD, picture disc, with interview picture CD, 3 booklets, signed/no'd certificate, signed photo & plectrum, 1,000 only)	200
95	Mercury DLINT 3	1980-1995 VAULT — AN INTERVIEW WITH JOE ELLIOT & RICK SAVAGE (CD, promo only)	20

(see also Lucy, Gogmagog)

DEF TEX

91	Sound Clash SCR003	MASTER BLASTER (EP)	60
92	Sound Clash SCR 001	TUTORIAL SESSIONS (EP)	15
94	Sound Clash CLASH003	HERBS & VERBS (EP)	8
95	Sound Clash SCR007	MOON MEDITATION (EP)	8
99	Son SON008	Poetic Speech Techniques (12")	12
00	Son SON013	Synchronise (12")	8
01	Monkey Face MF01	Sing Sad Songs (7")	10
01	Son SONCD018	SERENE BUG (LP)	15

DEFECTS

81	Casualty CR 001	Dance 'Til You Drop/Guilty Conscience/Brutality (p/s)	15
82	WXYZ ABCD-3	Survival/Brutality (p/s)	5
85	WXYZ LMNOP2	DEFECTIVE BREAKDOWN (LP, with insert)	15

DEFENDANTS

80s	Edible EAT 001	Headmaster/Such A Spiv (stickered insert cover & stickered labels)	12

DEFENDERS

68	Doctor Bird DB 1104	Set Them Free/Don't Blame The Children (actually by Lee Perry & Sensations)	30

(see also Lee Perry)

DEFIANT POSE

81	Groucho Marxist WH 4	Someone Else's War/After The Bang (p/s)	8

ZION DE GALLIER

68	Parlophone R 5686	Me/Winter Will Be Cold	25
68	Parlophone R 5710	Dream Dream Dream/Geraldine	20

(see also Mark Wirtz)

GLORIA DE HAVEN

55	Brunswick 05369	So This Is Paris/The Two Of Us	5
55	Brunswick 05457	Red Hot Pepper Pot/Won't You Save Me?	15

59	Oriole CB 1524	Dearly Beloved/Life 5

DE-HEMS

72	President PT 388	Don't Cross That Line/Lover Let Me Go 20

DEIGHTON TASK FORCE

89	White REACT1	Neighbourhood (12") 100

(see also Unique 3)

JACK DE JOHNETTE

70	CBS 64076	COMPLEX (LP) 20

DE JOHN SISTERS

57	Mercury MT 174	What Am I/Where Would I Be..5
60	London HLT 9127	Yes Indeed/Be Anything (But Be Mine) 5

DEK & JERRY

66	Philips BF 1494	What's The Matter With Me?/Don't Waste Your Time..........8

DESMOND DEKKER (& ACES)

63	Island WI 054	Honour Your Mother And Father (as Desmond Decker & Beverley's Allstars)/ Madgie ('63) (with Beverley's Allstars) 20
63	Island WI 111	Parents/Labour For Learning (solo) 30
64	Island WI 158	Jeserine/King Of Ska (as Desmond Dekkar & His Cherry Pies) ...30
64	Black Swan WI 455	Dracula (as Desmond Dekkar)/DON DRUMMOND: Spitfire 50
65	Island WI 181	Get Up Adine (as Desmond Dekkar, actually with Four Aces)/Be Mine Forever (as Patsy & Desmond; song is act. "Down Down Down" by Clive & Naomi).....35
65	Island WI 202	This Woman (as Desmond Dekker & Four Aces)/ LEE PERRY & UPSETTERS: Si Senora (B-side actually by Ossie & Upsetters) 25
67	Pyramid PYR 6003	Wise Man/ROLAND ALPHONSO: Middle East 30
67	Pyramid PYR 6004	007 (Shanty Town)/ROLAND ALPHONSO: El Torro 15
67	Pyramid PYR 6006	It's A Shame/ROLAND ALPHONSO: On The Move 25
67	Pyramid PYR 6008	Rudy Got Soul/ROLAND ALPHONSO: The Cat 30
67	Pyramid PYR 6011	Rude Boy Train/ROLAND ALPHONSO: Nothing For Nothing ...20
67	Pyramid PYR 6012	Mother's Young Girl/SOUL BROTHERS: Confucius 35
67	Pyramid PYR 6017	Unity/Sweet Music 20
67	Pyramid PYR 6020	Sabotage/Pretty Africa 15
67	Pyramid PYR 6020	Sabotage/It Pays 15
67	Pyramid PYR 6026	It Pays/Young Generation 15
68	Pyramid PYR 6031	Beautiful And Dangerous/I've Got The Blues 20
68	Pyramid PYR 6035	Bongo Gal/Shing A Ling 15
68	Pyramid PYR 6037	To Sir, With Love/Fu Manchu 150
68	Pyramid PYR 6044	Mother Pepper/Don't Blame Me 15
68	Pyramid PYR 6045	Try Me/I'm Leaving 15
68	Pyramid PYR 6047	Hey Grandma/Young Generation 15
68	Pyramid PYR 6051	Music Like Dirt (Intensified)/Coconut Water 15
68	Pyramid PYR 6054	It Mek/Writing On The Wall 8
68	Pyramid PYR 6058	Israelites/BEVERLEY'S ALLSTARS: The Man 7
68	Pyramid PYR 6059	Christmas Day/I've Got The Blues 10
69	Pyramid PYR 6068	It Miek/Problems 5
69	J.J. PYR 6058	Israelites/BEVERLEY'S ALLSTARS: The Man (reissue, mis-labelled copy) 5
70	Trojan TR 7777	You Can Get It If You Really Want/Perseverance 5
70	Trojan TR 7802	The Song We Used To Sing/Get Up Little Suzie 5
71	Trojan TR 7847	Lightning Stick/Troubles And Miseries 5
72	Trojan TR 7876	It Gotta Be So/The First Time For A Long Time 5
73	Rhino RNO 115	Sing A Little Song/I'm A Busted Lad 5
80	Stiff BUY 70	Israelite/Why Fight? 6
10	Trojan THB 7001	Sugar & Spice/Sentimental Reasons 10
10	Trojan THB 7005	Dancing Time/Beverley's Special 10
67	Doctor Bird DLM 5007	007 SHANTY TOWN (LP) 100
69	Doctor Bird DLM 5013	THE ISRAELITES (LP, solo) 120
69	Trojan TTL 4	THIS IS DESMOND DEKKAR (LP, label credits Dekker) 25
70	Trojan TBL 146	YOU CAN GET IT IF YOU REALLY WANT (LP) 18

(see also Al Barry, Skatalites, Maytals)

GEORGE DEKKER

71	Trojan TR 7879	Time Hard/SYDNEY, GEORGE & JACKIE: Fall In Love 6

HOWARD DEKKER

74	A Rover AR 01	Me Throw Me Corn/On The Fire 12

DELACARDOS

61	HMV POP 890	Hold Back The Tears/Mister Dillon 60

DE LAINE SISTERS

62	Piccadilly 7N 35070	It Might As Well Rain Until September/Puppet On A String 10

(see also Ladybirds, Breakaways)

DEL AMITRI

83	No Strings NOSP 1	Sense Sickness/The Difference Is (p/s) 30
85	Chrysalis CHS 12 2925	Hammering Heart/Lines Running North/Brown Eyed Girl (12", p/s) ...12
89	A&M AM 527	Stone Cold Sober/The Return Of Maggie Brown/Talk It To Death (p/s) ...10
89	A&M CDEE 515	Kiss This Thing Goodbye/No Holding On/Slowly, It's Coming Back (3" CD, card sleeve) 12
90	A&M AMX 589	Spit In The Rain/Scared To Love/The Return Of Maggie Brown/ Talk It To Death (10", in box with lyric insert) 12

DELANEY & BONNIE (& FRIENDS)

69	Elektra EKSN 45066	Get Ourselves Together/Soldiers Of The Cross (withdrawn)....20
69	Atlantic 584 308	Comin' Home/Groupie (Superstar) 8
69	Apple SAPCOR 7	THE ORIGINAL DELANEY & BONNIE (LP, unreleased, no sleeve) ...1500
69	Elektra EKS 74039	THE ORIGINAL DELANEY & BONNIE — ACCEPT NO SUBSTITUTE (LP, commercial release of above LP) 18
69	Stax SXATS 1029	HOME (LP) 15
70	Atlantic 2400 013	ON TOUR WITH ERIC CLAPTON (LP) 20
71	Atco 2400 029	TO BONNIE FROM DELANEY (LP) 15
72	CBS 64959	TOGETHER (LP) 12

(see also Eric Clapton, Delaney Bramlett, King Curtis with Delaney & Friends, Shindogs)

ERIC DELANEY BAND

60	Parlophone R 4646	Bass Drum Boogie/Let's Get Organised	5
62	Parlophone R 4925	Manhattan Spiritual/Down Home	5
57	Pye Nixa NEP 24066	AT THE BBC FESTIVAL (EP)	10
59	Pye NIXA NEP 24115	THESE SWINGIN' JINGLES (EP)	8
56	Pye NIAX NP 19018	HI-FI DELANEY (10" LP)	20
60	Parlophone PMC 1120	SWINGIN' TO THE SHOWS (LP)	12

ERIC DELANEY'S BIG BEAT SIX

65	Pye 7N 15782	The Big Beat/Big Noise From Winnetka	6

DEL-CAPRIS

79	Grapevine GRP 112	Hey Little Way Out Girl (actually by Construction)/EULA COOPER: Beggars Can't Be Choosey (p/s)	10

DELEGATION

77	State 25	The Promise Of Love/It Only Happens	25

DELFONICS

68	Bell BLL 1005	La La Means I Love You/Can't Get Over Losing You	5
68	Bell BLL 1016	Together We Can Make Such Sweet Music/Bad Bad Weather	5
68	Bell BLL 1042	Ready Or Not Here I Come/Somebody Loves You	5
69	Bell BLL 1066	You Can't Be Loving Him/Let It Be Me	8
69	Bell BLL 1073	Funny Feeling/You Got Yours	5
70	Bell BLL 1099	Didn't I (Blow Your Mind This Time)/Down is Up, Up Is Down	5
70	Bell BLL 1467	With These Hands/Let It Be Me	20
68	Bell SBLL 106	LA-LA MEANS I LOVE YOU (LP)	25
69	Bell SBLL 121	THE SOUND OF SEXY SOUL (LP)	20
71	Bell SBLL 137	THE DELFONICS (LP)	15
72	Bell SBLL 217	TELL ME THIS IS A DREAM	20
74	Bell BELLS 245	ALIVE AND KICKING (LP)	15

TERESA DEL FUEGO

81	Satril HH 155	Don't Hang Up/Wonder Wonder (no p/s)	8

DELGADOS

95	Radar SCAN 07	THE LAZARWALKER EP (p/s)	10
96	Chemikal Underground CHEM 004	Cinecentre/Thirteen Gliding Prices/Mule Emulator (p/s)	5
96	Boa HISS 4	Liquidation Girl/VAN IMPE: Piranha (hand-painted brown paper bag p/s, 500 only)	15

DELICATES

59	London HLT 8953	Ronnie Is My Lover/Black And White Thunderbird	100
59	London HLT 8953	Ronnie Is My Lover/Black And White Thunderbird (78)	30
60	London HLT 9176	Too Young To Date/The Kiss	60

DELICATESSAN

67	Vocalion VN 9286	The Red Baron's Revenge/The Dog Fight (Der Hundtkampf)	10

DE LITE

89	Circa YRTPRX 35	Wild Times (12")	30

DELITES

80	Grapevine GRP 127	Lover/Tell Me Why	25

JOHNNY DE LITTLE

61	Columbia DB 4578	Not Guilty/They	10
62	Columbia DB 4907	Lover/You Made Me Love You	10
63	Columbia DB 7023	Days Of Wine And Roses/Ride On	8
63	Columbia DB 7044	The Wind And The Rain/Unchained Melody	8
65	CBS 201790	The Knack/What To Do With Laurie	8

(see also John Barry)

DELIVERANCE

92	European Rhyme ERR001	Serious Public Disorder/Do Not Disturb (12")	25
94	Nut Cracker NUT001	Dead Funny/Up And Down The Country (12")	35
95	Nut Cracker NUT002	INJECT INTELLECT (EP)	15
96	Nut Cracker NUT003	Twisted Mystics/Sedating Your Aims (12")	12
87	Metalworks VOV 664	DEVIL'S MEAT (LP)	15
89	Metalworks VOV 673	EVIL FRIENDSHIP (LP, lyric inner)	15
90	Metalworks VOV 679	THE BOOK OF LIES (LP)	15

DELKOM

91	Wau! Mr Modo MWS 034R	Superjack — Orbital Infusion 2000/Neutron 9000 Mix (12", 500 only)	12

DENNIS D'ELL

67	CBS 202605	It Breaks My Heart In Two/Better Use Your Head (withdrawn)	400
67	CBS 202605	It Breaks My Heart In Two/Better Use Your Head (withdrawn: DJ copy)	300
67	Decca F 12647	A Woman Called Sorrow/The Night Has A Thousand Eyes (as Denny D'ell)	15
76	Polydor 2058 715	Home Is Home/Morning Without You (as Denis D'ell)	7

(see also Honeycombs)

JIMMY DELL

58	RCA RCA 1066	Teeny Weeny/BARRY DE VORZON: Barbara Jean	65
58	RCA RCA 1066	Teeny Weeny/BARRY DE VORZON: Barbara Jean (78)	40

DELL-VIKINGS

57	London HLD 8405	Come Go With Me/How Can I Find A True Love (gold label lettering)	150
57	London HLD 8405	Come Go With Me/How Can I Find A True Love (silver label lettering)	50
57	London HLD 8405	Come Go With Me/How Can I Find A True Love (78)	20
57	London HLD 8464	Whispering Bells/Little Billy Boy	40
57	Mercury MT 169	Cool Shake/Jitterbug Mary (78)	40
58	Mercury 7MT 199	The Voodoo Man/Can't Wait	40
58	Mercury 7MT 199	The Voodoo Man/Can't Wait (78)	20
59	Mercury AMT 1027	Flat Tyre/How Could You	60
59	Mercury AMT 1027	Flat Tyre/How Could You (78)	20
62	HMV POP 1072	Kilimanjaro/Confession Of Love	20
63	HMV POP 1145	An Angel Up In Heaven/The Fishing Chant	10

(see also Chuck Jackson)
DELLINGER
77	Carib Gems GG 004	Melting Pot/Version	7

(see also Dillinger)
PETE DELLO & FRIENDS
71	Nepentha 6437 001	INTO YOUR EARS (LP, gatefold sleeve)	500

(see also Honeybus, Lace, Red Herring, Leah, John Killigrew, Magic Valley, Grant Tracy & Sunsets, Sunsets)
DELLS
63	Pye International 7N 25178	The (Bossa Nova) Bird/Eternally	25
67	Chess CRS 8066	O-O I Love You/There Is	15
68	Chess CRS 8071	Wear It On Our Face/Please Don't Change Me Now	20
68	Chess CRS 8079	Stay In My Corner/Love Is So Simple	8
68	President PT 223	It's Not Unusual/Stay In My Corner	15
68	Chess CRS 8084	Always Together/I Want My Momma	8
69	Chess CRS 8099	I Can Sing A Rainbow/Love Is Blue-Hallelujah Baby	6
69	Chess CRS 8102	Oh What A Night/Believe Me	7
69	President PT 270	Oh What A Night/Moving On	7
69	Chess CRS 8105	On The Dock Of The Bay/When I'm In Your Arms	7
71	Chess 6145 001	The Love We Had Stays On My Mind/Freedom Means	7
72	Chess 6145 008	It's All Up To You/Oh, My Dear	6
73	Chess 6145 022	Give Your Baby A Standing Ovation/Run For Cover	30
68	Chess CRLS 4554	GREATEST HITS (LP)	25
69	Chess CRLS 4555	LOVE IS BLUE/OH, WHAT A NIGHT (LP)	30
71	Joy JOYS 186	OH WHAT A NIGHT (LP)	15

ELAINE DELMAR
59	Fontana H 227	I Loves You Porgy/Porgy	8
67	CBS 3191	What Love Can Do/Too Much Loneliness	5
68	CBS 63511	Sneakin' Up On You	40
68	CBS 3876	Shadow Of The Evening/When I Learn To Love Again	5
69	CBS 4408	The World Is Ours/The Rhythm Of Life	5
69	CBS 4017	Why Can't I Go To Him/Those Were The Days	5
70	CBS 5329	Hurt So Bad/The Train	5
60	Columbia SEG 8060	A SWINGING CHICK (EP)	25
68	EMI SX6222	LA BELLE ELAINE (LP)	35
68	CBS 63511	SNEAKIN' UP ON YOU (LP)	35

DEL MONAS
85	Empire JLM 14	Sally Sue Brown/Dangerous Charms (7" die cut sleeve)	15
84	Big Beat SW 101	COMIN' HOME BABY - VOLUME ONE (7" EP)	12
84	Big Beat SW 102	HELLOW WE LOVE YOU - VOLUME TWO (7" EP)	12
85	Big Beat WIK 35	DANGEROUS CHARMS (LP)	20
85	Empire SYF 95	5 (LP)	25
88	Hangman HANG 20 UP	5 (LP, reissue)	15
89	Hangman HANG 28 UP	DEL MONAS (LP)	18
99	Vinyl Japan ASKLP 107	DANGEROUS CHARMS (LP, reissue)	15

DANNY DELMONTE
63	Oriole CB 1894	John Kennedy/Come Summer	7
64	Oriole CB 1958	Worry/Till I'm Back With You Darlin' Again	6

DELMONTES
80s	Rational RATE 3	Don't Cry Your Tears/So It's Not To Be (yellow or blue p/s)	8

DELMONTS
71	Spiral DIT 1	A Ra Chicera/Sorry For My Jealousy	6
72	Spiral DIT 2	Gimmie Gimmie Your Loving/Now Is The Time For Love	8

DELMORE BROTHERS
58	Parlophone GEP 8728	COUNTRY AND WESTERN (EP)	20

(see also Brown's Ferry Four, Grandpa Jones, Merle Travis)
AL DE LORY
65	London HLU 9999	Yesterday/Traffic Jam	20
70	Capitol CL 15644	Song From MASH/Feeling Of Love	5

DELROY & SPORTY
71	Banana BA 322	Lovers Version/DUDLEY SIBLEY: Having A Party	15

DELROY & TENNORS
71	Camel CA 62	Donkey Shank/MURPHY'S ALL STARS: Donkey Track	10

DELTA 5
79	Rough Trade RT 31	Mind Your Own Business/Now That You've Gone (p/s)	10
80	Rough Trade RT 41	Anticipation/You (p/s)	7
81	Rough Trade RT 61	Try/Colour (p/s)	7

DELTA CATS
69	Bamboo BAM 3	I Can't Re-Live (song actually "I Can't Believe")/I've Been Hurt	40

(see also Thrillers)
DELTA KINGS
61	London RE-R 1318	AT SUNDOWN (EP)	10
61	London Jazz LTZ-R 15204	AT SUNDOWN (LP, mono)	15
61	London Jazz SAH-R 6118	AT SUNDOWN (LP, stereo)	20

DELTA RHYTHM BOYS
54	Brunswick 05353	Mood Indigo/Have A Hope, Have A Wish, Have A Prayer	10
52	Esquire 15-001	DELTA RHYTHM BOYS WITH THE METRONOME ALLSTARS (10" LP)	15

DELTAS
64	Blue Beat BB 265	Georgia/The Party	20
65	Blue Beat BB 275	The Visitor/SKATALITES: Hanging The Beam	40

DELTA SKIFFLE GROUP
58	Esquire EP 162	DELTA SKIFFLE GROUP (EP)	50

DELTONES (JAMAICA)
71	Green Door GD 4010	Chopsticks/DES BRYAN: Belmont Street	8
72	Trojan TRM 9001	Chopsticks/I Got It/Put It On	6

DELTONES (U.K.)
70	Columbia DB 8719	Gimme Some Lovin'/Have A Little Talk With Myself	20

DEL-TONES (U.S.)
59	Top Rank JAR 171	Moonlight Party/Rockin' Blues	100
59	Top Rank JAR 171	Moonlight Party/Rockin' Blues (78	35

(see also Beau-Marks)

DELTRON 3030
00	Ark ARK 75	DELTRON 3030 (2xLP)	20

(see also Gorillaz, Blur, Damon Albarn)

MILTON DE LUGG ORCHESTRA
65	Columbia DB 7474	The Addams Family Theme/The Alfred Hitchcock Theme	15
66	Columbia DB 7762	The Munsters Theme/The Addams Family Theme	15

(see also Beau-Marks)

DELUSION
79	Wizzo WIZZO 2	Pessimists Paradise/Desert Island (gatefold p/s)	8

LEO DE LYON
54	MGM SP 1087	The Band Played On/Say It Isn't So	7
60	Oriole CB 1561	Rich In Love/The Blue Train	7
60	Oriole MG 20053	LEO DE LYON (LP)	20

ARIN DEMAIN
90s	Goldmine/Soul Supply GS 028	Silent Treatment/PARIS: Sleepless Nights	8

RALPH DE MARCO
59	London HLL 9010	Old Shep/More Than Riches	7
59	London HLL 9010	Old Shep/More Than Riches (78)	15

DEMENSIONS
60	Top Rank JAR 505	Over The Rainbow/Nursery Rhyme Rock	60
61	Coral Q 72437	Count Your Blessings Instead Of Sheep/Again	20

(see also Wheels, James Brothers, Fox)

DEMENTED ARE GO
93	Fury FEP 705	MARIJUANA EP	8
86	ID NOSE 9	IN SICKNESS AND IN HEALTH (LP)	20
88	ID NOSE 21	KICKED OUT OF HELL (LP)	20
89	Link MLP 084	THE DAY THE EARTH SPAT BLOOD (LP, as the Demon Teds)	15
90	Link LRM 05	GO GO DEMENTED (LP, blue vinyl)	15
91	Fury F 3016	ORGASMIC NIGHTMARE (LP, blue vinyl)	15
93	Fury DAGLP 1	TANGENTAL MADNESS ON A PLEASANT SIDE OF HELL (LP, white vinyl)	15

(ROD) DEMICK & (HERBIE) ARMSTRONG
70	Decca F 13056	We're On The Right Track/Dreaming (as Demick-Armstrong)	6
71	Mam MAM 10	If I Ever Get To You/Girl	5
71	Mam MAM-AS 1001	LITTLE WILLY RAMBLE (LP, black/silver labels)	25
72	A&M AMLH 68908	LOOKIN' THROUGH (LP, inner sleeve, brown label)	50

DEMOB
81	Round Ear ROUND 1	Anti Police/Teenage Adolescence (foldout p/s)	15
81	Round Ear ROUND 1	Anti Police/Teenage Adolescence (later standard p/s)	10
81	Round Ear EAR 3	No Room For You/Think Straight/New Breed (p/s)	15

DEMOLITION
81	Demolition Rock ZEL SPS 296	Hooker Hater/Axeman (p/s)	250

DEMON
81	Clay CLAY 4	Liar/Wild Woman (p/s, red vinyl)	8
82	Carrere CAR 226	One Helluva Night/Into The Nightmare (picture disc)	6
83	Clay CLAY 25	The Plague/The Only Sane Man (p/s)	6
84	Clay CLAY 41	Wonderland/Blackheath (p/s)	6
84	Clay 12CLAY 41	Wonderland/Blackheath/Nowhere To Run (12", p/s)	8
88	Clay CLAY 48D	Tonight (The Hero Is Back)/Hurricane/Night Of The Demon/ Don't Break The Circle (double pack)	5
81	Carrere CA 651	NIGHT OF THE DEMON (LP, pressed in France)	20
82	Carrere CAL 139	THE UNEXPECTED GUEST (LP)	12
83	Clay CLAYLP 6	THE PLAGUE (LP, gatefold sleeve, with insert)	15
83	Clay CLAYLP 6P	THE PLAGUE (LP, picture disc)	20
84	Clay CLAYLP 15	BRITISH STANDARD APPROVED (LP)	12
90	Sonic SONICLP 1	NIGHT OF THE DEMON (LP)	15
90	Flametrader LP 1	ONE HELLUVA NIGHT (2-LP)	18

DEMON BOYZ
88	Music Of Life NOTE 013	Northside/Rougher Than An Animal	12
88	Music Of Life NOTE 022	Vibez (12")	8
89	Music Of Life NOTE 26	Recognition/Lyrical Culture (12")	8
90	Mango 12 MNS 738	International Karate (12")	5
92	Tribal Bass Tribe4	DETT (12")	10
92	Tribal Bass Tribe9	Glimity Glamity/Junglist (12")	20
89	Music Of Life DEMON1	RECOGNITION (LP)	12
92	Tribal Bass Tribe11	ORIGINAL GUIDANCE – THE SECOND CHAPTER (LP)	60

DEMON D
95	Voyager VOD 94	Let The Jazz Take You/Together (12")	8

DEMON FUZZ
70	Dawn DNX 2504	I Put A Spell On You/Message To Mankind/Fuzz Oriental Blues (p/s)	50
70	Dawn DNX 2504	I Put A Spell On You/Message To Mankind/Fuzz Oriental Blues	10
70	Dawn DNLS 3013	AFREAKA! (LP, gatefold sleeve, orange label)	130

DEMON PACT
81	Slime PACT 1	Eaten Alive/Raiders (p/s)	50
81	Slime PACT 2	Escape/Demon Pact (unreleased, labels only)	0

DEMON PREACHER
78	Illegal SRTS/CUS/78110	Royal Northern (N7)/Laughing At Me/ Steal Your Love/Dead End Kidz (numbered p/s)	100
78	Small Wonder SMALL TEN	Little Miss Perfect/Perfect Dub (p/s)	15

(see also Demons, Alien Sex Fiend, Fenzyx)

DEMON ROCKA
82	Unity UN 001	Iron Lady/Stick Together	12

DEMONS (JAMAICA)
69	Big Shot BI 523	You Belong To My Heart/Bless You	10

DEMONS (U.K.)
80	Crypt Music DEM 1	Action By Example/I Wish I Was A Dog (p/s)	12

(see also Alien Sex Fiend, Demon Preacher)

DEMONSTRATORS
64	Warner Bros WB 132	Sweet Violets/Ultra Violet	12

JASON DENE
66	Parlophone R 5485	Opportunity/It's Me	8

(see also Jason Deane)

TERRY DENE
57	Decca F 10895	A White Sport Coat/The Man In The Phone Booth	20
57	Decca F 10914	Start Movin'/Green Corn	15
57	Decca F 10938	Come And Get It/Teenage Dream	15
57	Decca F 10964	Lucky Lucky Bobby/Baby, She's Gone	15
58	Decca F 10977	The Golden Age/C'Min And Be Loved	10
58	Decca F 11016	Stairway Of Love/Lover, Lover!	6
58	Decca F 11037	Seven Steps To Love/Can I Walk You Home	10
58	Decca F 11076	Who Baby Who/Pretty Little Pearly	10
59	Decca F 11100	I've Got A Good Thing Going/Bimbombey	8
59	Decca F 11136	There's No Fool Like A Young Fool/I've Come Of Age	10
59	Decca F 11154	Thank You Pretty Baby/A Boy Without A Girl	8
59	Decca F 11154	Thank You Pretty Baby/A Boy Without A Girl (78)	12
60	Oriole CB 1562	Geraldine/Love Me Or Leave Me	20
61	Oriole CB 1594	Like A Baby/Next Stop Paradise	15
63	Aral PS 107	The Feminine Look/Fever (all in p/s)	15
82	Logo GO 412	Paralysed/Lorna (The Girl In The Long Black Dress)	10
88	Charm C 45001	Jingle Bear Rock/Peace In The Valley	5
57	Decca DFE 6459	TERRY DENE NO. 1 (EP)	30
57	Decca DFE 6507	THE GOLDEN DISC (EP)	35
66	Herald ELR 107	TERRY DENE NOW (EP)	20
74	Decca SPA 368	I THOUGHT TERRY DENE WAS DEAD (LP)	15

DENE BOYS
57	HMV POP 374	Bye Bye Love/Love Is The Thing	20
58	HMV POP 455	Skylark/I Walk Down The Street	8

DENE FOUR
59	HMV POP 666	Hush-a-bye/Something New	25

(see also Dene Boys)

DENIGH
80	Ace ACE 16	No Way/Running (no p/s)	50

DENIM
92	Boys Own BOIX 12	Middle Of The Road/Ape Hangers/Robin's Nest/The Great Grape Ape Hangers (12")	10
97	EMI RADIODJ 1	Summer Smash (promo, withdrawn)	20
92	Boys Own 82849	BACK IN DENIM (LP)	40
96	Echo ECH LP8	DENIM ON ICE (LP)	25
97	EMI ADISC 001	NOVELTY ROCK (LP)	15
97	EMI ADISCCD 001	NOVELTY ROCK (CD)	18

(see also Felt, Go-Kart Mozarts)

DENIMS
65	CBS 201807	I'm Your Man/Ya Ya	75

ROGER DENISON
66	Parlophone R 5545	I'm On An Island/I'm Running Out Of Time	12
67	Parlophone R 5566	It Just Doesn't Seem To Be My Day/She Wanders Through My Mind	50

DENIZENS
79	Big SOLD 5	People Of The Night/Ammonia Subway (p/s)	10
80	Citizen	IN THE CROWD EP (with 16-page booklet)	12

CLAUDE DENJEAN
71	Decca PFS 4212	MOOG! (LP)	12

SUE DENNING
65	Columbia DB 7486	Kiss Me Once Again/Goodtime Johnny	20

WADE DENNING & PORT WASHINGTONS
67	MGM MGM 1339	Tarzan's March/Batman	15

D.D. (DENZIL) DENNIS
70	Crab CRAB 53	Rain Is Ginna Fall/This Game Ain't Free	15
70	Crab CRAB 60	Having A Party/Man With Ambition	10
70	Pama Supreme PS 301	My Way/Happy Days	10
71	Punch PH 93	Christmas Message/Cool It Girl	10
71	Pama Supreme PS 330	I'm A Believer/I'll Make The Way Easy	10
74	Pama Supreme PS 391	Women And Money/UPSETTERS: Ten Cent Skank	12

(see also Denzil Dennis)

D D DENNIS - BROTHER LLOYD'S ALL STARS

68	Mercury MF 1064	Save The Last Dance For Me/Will You Still Love Me Tomorrow	15

DENZIL DENNIS

63	Blue Beat BB 181	Seven Nights In Rome/Love Is For Fools (as DENZIL)	15
68	Trojan TR 614	Donkey Train/Down By The Riverside	12
68	Trojan TR 615	Me Nah Worry/Hush Don't You Cry	12
68	Jolly JY 011	Oh Carol/Where Has My Little Girl Gone	8
70	Mary Lyn ML 100	I Guess I'd Better Start Believing/When Will You Ever Learn	10
70	Pama Supreme PS 304	Painful Situation/Nothing Has Changed	5
71	Pama Supreme PS 350	South Of The Border/GRAHAM: Long Island	12
72	Pama Supreme PS 375	Mama We're All Crazy Now/ROY SHIRLEY: A Lady's A Man's Best Friend	7
72	Duke DU 142	I Forgot To Be Your Lover/I've Got To Settle Down	5
73	Grape GR 3059	People Got To Be Friends/Ups And Downs (actually by Pat Rhoden)	5
74	Arrow AR 003	If/How Can I Touch You	8

(see also D.D. Dennis, Cosmo & Dennis, Denzil & Pat, Denzil & Jennifer, Les & Silkie)

JACKIE DENNIS

58	Decca F 10992	La Dee Dah/You're The Greatest	8
58	Decca F 11011	Miss Valerie/My Dream	6
58	Decca F 11033	The Purple People Eater/You-Oo	7
58	Decca F 11060	More Than Ever (Come Prima)/Linton Addie	7
58	Decca F 11090	Gingerbread/Lucky Ladybug	7
59	Top Rank JAR 129	Summer Snow/Night Bird	5
58	Decca DFE 6513	JACKIE DENNIS NO. 1 (EP)	35

DENNIS & LIZZY

70	Camel CA 56	Everybody Bawlin'/Mr Brown	10
73	Pyramid PYR 7002	Ba-Ba-Ri-Ba-Shank/TOMMY McCOOK ALL STARS: Buck And The Preacher	12

(see also Dennis Alcapone, Lizzy & Dennis)

DENNISONS

63	Decca F 11691	(Come On) Be My Girl/Little Latin Lupe Lu	20
64	Decca F 11880	Walkin' The Dog/You Don't Know What Love Is	25
64	Decca F 11990	Nobody Like My Babe/Lucy (You Sure Did It This Time)	35

MARTIN DENNY (& HIS ORCHESTRA)

59	London HLU 8860	Quiet Village/Llama Serenade	6
58	London HB-U 1079	EXOTICA (10" LP, mono only)	12
58	London SAH-U 6004	FORBIDDEN ISLAND (LP, stereo only)	12
59	London HA-U 2196	AFRO-DESIA (LP, also stereo SAH-U 6048)	12
60	London HA-U 2208	QUIET VILLAGE (LP, also stereo SAH-U 6055)	12

SANDY DENNY

72	Island WIP 6141	Here In Silence/Man Of Iron (theme from Pass Of Arms film, in p/s)	40
72	Island WIP 6141	Here In Silence/Man Of Iron (theme from Pass Of Arms film)	25
72	Island WIP 6142	Listen Listen/Tomorrow Is A Long Time	8
73	Island WIP 6176	Whispering Grass/Friends (p/s)	8
73	Island WIP 6176	Whispering Grass/Friends	5
74	Island WIP 6195	Like An Old Fashioned Waltz (unissued)	0
76	Mooncrest MOON 54	Make Me A Pallet On Your Floor/This Train	6
77	Island WIP 6391	Candle In The Wind/Still Waters Run Deep (unissued, promo only)	30
11	Island 276-797-3	I'm A Dreamer (Second Demo)/Who knows Where The Time Goes? (First Demo)	8
67	Saga EROS 8041	SANDY AND JOHNNY (LP, with Johnny Silvo, black/silver label)	40
70	Saga EROS 8153	SANDY DENNY (LP)	30
71	Island ILPS 9165	THE NORTH STAR GRASSMAN AND THE RAVENS (LP, gatefold sleeve, 'pink rim palm tree' label)	45
72	Island ILPS 9207	SANDY (LP, gatefold sleeve, original pressing with 'pink rim palm tree' label)	40
72	Island ILPS 9207	SANDY (LP, gatefold sleeve)	12
73	Island ILPS 9258	LIKE AN OLD FASHIONED WALTZ (LP, gatefold sleeve, 'pink rim palm tree' label)	40
73	Hallmark SHM 813	ALL OUR OWN WORK (LP, with Strawbs)	15
77	Island ILPS 9433	RENDEZVOUS (LP, with lyric inner sleeve)	25
78	Mooncrest CREST 28	THE ORIGINAL SANDY DENNY (LP)	25
97	Strange Fruit SFRSCD 006	THE BBC SESSIONS 1971-73 (CD, limited edition, withdrawn – beware of bootlegs)	30
85	Island SDSP 100	WHO KNOWS WHERE THE TIME GOES (4-LP, box set with booklet)	50

(see also Fairport Convention, Bunch, Strawbs, Fotheringay, Alex Campbell, Trevor Lucas, Richard Thompson)

SUSAN DENNY

65	Melodisc MEL 1596	Don't Touch Me/Johnny	35

DENNY & WILSON

72	Hillcrest HCT 6	Hey Hey Girl/CARLTON ALPHONSO: Girl I Love You	6

DENTISTS

85	Spruck SP 003	Strawberries Are Growing In My Garden (And It's Wintertime)/ Burning The Thoughts From My Skin/Doreen (p/s)	12
85	Spruck SP 004	YOU AND YOUR BLOODY ORANGES (12" EP, p/s)	10
86	Tambourine SP 006	DOWN AND OUT IN PARIS AND CHATHAM (12" EP, brown/white or group p/s)	10
87	Tambourine URINE 3	Writhing On The Shagpile/Just Like Oliver Reed/A Strange Way To Go About Things/Calm You Down/The Turquoise Castle (12", p/s)	10
85	Spruck SPR 001	SOME PEOPLE ARE ON THE PITCH THEY THINK IT'S ALL OVER IT IS NOW (LP)	15

MICKEY DENTON

61	London HLX 9398	The Steady Kind/Now You Can't Give Them Away	8

KARL DENVER

64	Decca F 11903	Love Me With All Your Heart/Am I That Easy To Forget	5
65	Mercury MF 878	Cry A Little Sometimes/Today Will Be Yesterday Tomorrow	5
65	Mercury MF 904	Marta/I'll Never Forget To Remember	5
65	Mercury MF 926	The Tips Of My Fingers/I'm Alone Because I Love You	5
68	Page One POF 063	You've Still Got A Place In My Heart/I Still Miss Someone (as Karl Denver Trio)	5
74	Emerald MD 1181	Sonny Boy/Careless Love	5

NIGEL DENVER

64	Decca DFE 8580	FOLK SINGER (EP)	15
66	Decca LK 4728	MOVIN' ON (LP, featuring Martin Carthy)	40
67	Decca LK 4844	REBELLION (LP)	20

67	Major Minor MMLP 1	SCOTTISH REPUBLICAN SONGS (LP)	20
68	Decca SKL 4943	FOLK OLD AND NEW (LP)	20

DENZIL & JENNIFER
70	Escort ES 824	Young, Gifted And Black/OWEN GRAY: I Am Satisfied	7

DENZIL (DENNIS) & PAT (RHODEN)
69	Downtown DT 403	Dream/Sincerely	12

WILBUR DE PARIS' NEW ORLEANS BAND
59	London HLE 8816	Petite Fleur/Over And Over Again	5

LYNSEY DE PAUL
73	MAM SS 504	SURPRISE (LP)	15
73	MAM MAME 3002	LYNSEY SINGS (LP)	15
74	Jet LP 07	TASTE ME - DON'T WASTE ME (LP, with insert)	15
75	Jet LP 14	LOVE BOMB (LP, with insert)	15

DEPECHE MODE
SINGLES
81	Lyntone LYN 10209	Sometimes I Wish I Was Dead/FAD GADGET: King Of The Flies (test pressing)	150
81	Lyntone LYN 10209	Sometimes I Wish I Was Dead/FAD GADGET: King Of The Flies (red flexidisc free with Flexipop magazine, issue 11)	25
81	Mute MUTE 013	Dreaming Of Me/Ice Machine (p/s)	5
83	Mute L12BONG 2	Get The Balance Right/My Secret Garden (live)/See You (live)/ Satellite (live) (12", numbered p/s)	8
83	Mute L12BONG 3	Everything Counts/Boys Say Go (live)/New Life (live)/Nothing To Fear (live)/The Meaning Of Love (live) (12", numbered p/s)	8
83	Mute L12BONG 4	Love In Itself (2)/Just Can't Get Enough (live)/Photograph Of You (live)/Shout (live)/Photographic (live) (12", numbered p/s)	8
85	Mute D12BONG 9	It's Called A Heart (Mixes)/Fly On The Windscreen (Mixes) (12", p/s, dbl-pack)	8
87	Mute L12BONG 14	Never Let Me Down Again (Tsangarides Mix)/Pleasure Little Treasure (Join Mix)/To Have And To Hold (Spanish Taster) (12", p/s)	8
87	Mute CDBONG 14	Never Let Me Down Again (Split Mix)/Pleasure Little Treasure (Join Mix)/ To Have And To Hold (Spanish Taster)/Never Let Me Down Again (Aggro Mix) (CD in pouch)	8
87	Mute P12 BONG 14	Never Let Me Down Again (7" Mix)/Pleasure Little Treasure (7" Mix)/Never Let Me Down Again (12" Split Mix) (12")	50
89	Mute 10BONG 16	Everything Counts (Absolute Mix)/(1983 12" Mix)/Nothing (US 7" Mix) (10", envelope p/s, with 2 postcards & window sticker)	10
89	Mute LCDBONG 16	Everything Counts (Tim Simenon & M. Saunders Remix)/Nothing (Justin Strauss Remix)/Strangelove (Tim Simenon & M. Saunders Remix) (3" CD 'filofax' page-p/s)	15
89	Mute L12BONG 17	Personal Jesus (Mixes)/Dangerous (Hazchemix) (12", p/s)	15
89	Mute LCDBONG 17	Personal Jesus (Pump Mix)/Personal Jesus (Telephone Stomp Mix)/ Dangerous (Hazchemix) (3" CD)	15
90	Mute XL12BONG 18	Enjoy The Silence (The Quad: Final Mix) (12", 1-side etched, p/s)	8
90	Mute L12BONG 20	World In My Eyes (Dub In My Eyes)/(Mode To Joy)/Happiest Girl (The Pulsating Orbital Mix) (12", p/s with inner, in sealed blue PVC pack)	8
90	Mute LCDBONG 20	World In My Eyes (Dub In My Eyes)/World In My Eyes (Mode To Joy)/ Happiest Girl (The Pulsating Orbital Vocal Mix)/Sea Of Sin (Sensoria)/World In My Eyes (Mayhem Mode)/Happiest Girl (Jack Mix) CD	15
91	Mute DMBX 1	1 (6-CD single box set, with booklet)	15
91	Mute DMBX 2	2 (6-CD single box set, with booklet)	15
91	Mute DMBX 3	3 (6-CD single box set, with booklet)	15
02	Mute MUTE 12BONG 33	Goodnight Lovers (ISAN Falling Leaf Mix)/When The Body Speaks (Acoustic Version)/The Dead Of Night (Electronicat Remix) (12", red vinyl, p/s)	8
06	Mute BONG 38	John The Revelator (UNKLE Dub)/Lilian (Robag Wruhme Slomoschen Killer) (Picture disc in sealed PVC band, stickered)	6

ALBUMS
87	Mute STUMM 47	MUSIC FOR THE MASSES (LP, clear vinyl)	50
87	Mute STUMM 47	MUSIC FOR THE MASSES (LP, with bonus 12" "Strangelove (Maximix)"/"Never Let Me Down Again (Split Mix)" [HMV1])	40
89	Mute STUMM 101	101 (2-LP, stickered gatefold sleeve, inner sleeves and booklet)	20
97	Mute STUMM 148	ULTRA (LP, inner sleeve with transfer)	25
98	Mute P12MUTEL5	REMIXES 86-98 (3-LP)	40
98	Mute MUTEL 5	THE SINGLES 86-98 (3-lp, box set with booklet, numbered)	40
04	Mute MUTEL 8	MUTE REMIXES 81-04 (6 x LP box set, numbered)	50
09	Mute STUMM 300	SOUNDS OF THE UNIVERSE (2-LP)	20
09	Mute BXSTUMM300	SOUNDS OF THE UNIVERSE (4-CD/DVD set)	40

PROMOS
86	Mute RR BONG 10	Breathing In Fumes/Stripped (Highland Mix) (12", white labels, some stamped)	80
86	Mute 7BONG 12	A Question Of Time (Edited)/Black Celebration (Live) (white label)	40
86	Mute L12 BONG 12	A Question Of Time (New Town Mix)/A Question Of Time (Live) / Black Celebration (Black Tulip Mix)/More Than A Party (Live) (12", printed labels with stamped number, plain black die-cut sleeve)	30
87	Mute BONG 14R	Never Let Me Down Again/Pleasure Little Treasure	40
87	Mute R BONG 13	Strangelove (Radio Edit)/Strangelove (p/s)	80
87	Mute DANCE BONG 13	Strangelove (Blind Mix)/(Fresh Ground Mix) (12", promo-only remix some on blue vinyl)	80
87	Mute CLUB BONG 13	Strangelove (12 Inch Maxi Mix)/Strangelove (Pain Mix) (12", promo)	80
87	Mute 12BONG 14	Never Let Me Down Again (Split Mix)/Pleasure Little Treasure (Glitter Mix)/ Never Let Me Down Again (Aggro Mix) (12")	40
87	Mute DJBONG 15	Behind The Wheel (DJ Remix)/Behind The Wheel (LP Mix)	120
87	Mute D BONG 15	Behind The Wheel (Shep Mix)/Behind The Wheel (LP Mix)/Route 66 (7" Mix) (12")	30
89	Mute PP12BONG 16	Strangelove (Hijack Mix)/Nothing (12")	18
89	Mute BONG 16R	Everything Counts (Live – Radio Edit)/Nothing (Live Mix) (stickered p/s)	20
89	Mute P12 BONG 16	Everything Counts (Tim Simenon/Mark Saunders Remix)/(Alan Moulder Remix) (12", black die-cut sleeve)	15
89	Mute P12 BONG 17	Personal Jesus (Pump Mix)/Dangerous (Hazchemix) (12", black die-cut sleeve)	15
89	Mute BONG 17	Personal Jesus/Dangerous (censored black rear p/s)	40
87	Mute (no cat. no.)	THE B-SIDES (4-LP test pressings in title box)	800
87	Mute (no cat. no.)	THE B-SIDES (4-cassette set)	200
90	Mute BONG 18	Enjoy The Silence/Memphisto ('A' label)	25
90	Mute RCDBONG 18	Enjoy The Silence (7")/Memphisto (7") (CD)	20
90	Mute P12 BONG 18	Enjoy The Silence (Bass Line)/(Ricki Tik Tik Mix)/(7" Mix) (12", die-cut Mute sleeve)	20
90	Mute BONG 19R	Policy Of Truth (7" Version)/Kaleid (Remix) (CD)	20

90	Mute R7 BONG 19	Policy Of Truth (Radio Edit)/Kaleid (p/s) 20
90	Mute P12 BONG 19	Policy Of Truth (Capitol Mix)/(Pavlov's Dub)/(Trancentral)/Kaleid (Remix) (12", die-cut Mute sleeve) 15
90	Mute 12BONG 20	World In My Eyes (Oil Tank Mix)/Happiest Girl (Kiss-A-Mix)/Sea Of Sin (Sensoria) (12", white label, numbered, stickered sleeve) 30
90	Mute BONG 20R	World In My Eyes (7" Version)/Happiest Girl (Jack Mix)/Sea Of Sin (Tonal Mix) (p/s, 33rpm) 20
90	Mute P12 BONG 20	World In My Eyes (Mayhem Mode Mix)/Happiest Girl (The Pulsating Orbital Mix) (12", die-cut Mute sleeve) 20
90	Mute XLCDBONG 18	Enjoy The Silence (The Quad: Final Mix) (3" CD, 1-track) 15
90	Mute PSTUMM 64	VIOLATOR (12" EP, 4-track sampler) 30
93	Mute P12 BONG 21	I Feel You (Throb Mix)/(Seven Inch Mix)/(Babylon Mix)/One Caress (12", die-cut Mute sleeve) 20
93	Mute BONG 22	Walking In My Shoes/My Joy (large centre hole) 30
90	Mute (no cat. no.)	VIOLATOR (LP, CD & cassette in 12" x 12" picture box with insert) 100
93	Mute BONG 23	Condemnation (Paris Mix)/Death's Door (Jazz Mix) (large centre hole) 30
93	Mute PL12BONG 23	Rush (Spiritual Guidance Mix)/Rush (Amylnitrate Mix)/Rush (Wild Planet Vocal Mix) (12") 40
93	Mute P12 BONG 22	Walking In My Shoes (Grungy Gonads Mix)/(Seven Inch Mix)/My Joy (Seven Inch Mix)/(Slow Slide Mix) (12", die-cut Mute sleeve) 20
93	Mute P 12 BONG 23	Condemnation (Paris Mix)/Death's Door (Jazz Mix)/Rush (Spiritual Guidance Mix) (12". die-cut Mute sleeve) 30
93	Mute VERBONG 1	SONGS OF FAITH & DEVOTION (interview CD) 50
93	Mute (no cat. no.)	SONGS OF FAITH & DEVOTION (4-CD box set) 300
94	Mute P12 BONG 24	In Your Room (The Jeep Rock Mix)/Higher Love (Adrenaline Mix)/In Your Room (Extended Zephyr Mix) (12", die-cut Mute sleeve) 25
94	Mute DEPRO 1	DEPRO 1 (13-track compilation CD) 50
97	Mute PL 12 BONG 25	Barrel Of A Gun (One Inch Punch Mix [Version 2])/Painkiller (Original Mix)/Barrel Of A Gun (3 Phase Mix)/Barrel Of A Gun (Original Mix) (12", p/s) 8
97	Mute BONG 26	It's No Good (Club 69 Future Mix)/It's No Good (Club 69 Future Dub)/It's No Good (Club 69 Funk Dub) (12") 35
97	Mute PL12BONG 26	It's No Good (Club 69 mixes) (12") 40
97	Mute P12BONG26	It's No Good (Hardfloor Mix)/(Speedy J Mix)/(Motor Bass Mix)/(Andrea Parker Mix)/(Dom T Mix) (12") 8
97	Mute XLCDBONG 26	It's No Good (Live) (CD) 70
97	Mute P12 BONG 27	Home (Jedi Knights Remix [Drowning In Time])/(Air "Around The Golf" Remix)/(Meant To Be)/(Grantby Mix) (12", 33rpm, die-cut p/s) 12
97	Mute P12BONG 28	Useless (CJ Bolland Funky Sub Mix)/Useless (the Kruder & Dorfmeister Session™) (12", die-cut p/s) 20
97	Mute BXSTUMM 148	ULTRA (box set, with CD, T-shirt, stickers & EPK video, soap box pack) 80
98	Mute P12BONG 29	Only When I Lose Myself (Dan The Automator Mix)/Only When I Lose Myself (Subsonic Legacy Mix)/Painkiller (Kill The Pain — DJ Shadow Vs Depeche Mode)/Headstar (12", die-cut p/s) 8
98	Mute (no cat. no.)	THE SINGLES 86>98 (15" x 6" box set, with 3 CDs, video tape & cards) 120
01	Mute PL12BONG 30	Dream On (Dave Clarke Club Mix)/Dream On (Bushwacka Blunt Mix) (12", p/s) 8
01	Mute PL12BONG 30	Dream On (Octagon Man Mix)/(Octagon Man Dub)/(Dave Clarke Acoustic Mix)/(Kid 606 Mix) 12" p/s) 12
01	Mute PL12BONG 32	Freelove (Deep Dish Freedom Mix)/Freelove (Josh Wink Vocal Interpretation)/Freelove (Deep Dish Freedom Dub)/Freelove (Power Productions Remix) (12", doublepack, p/s) 10
01	Mute PXL 12 BONG 31	I Feel Loved (Umek Mix)/(Thomas Brinkman Remix)/(Chamber's Remix) (12", p/s) 10
01	Mute IPKSTUMM 190	EXCITER (interview CD with bonus multimedia disc) 30
01	Mute BCDSTUMM 190	EXCITER (interview CD with bonus multimedia disc, in long box) 60
04	Mute P12BONG 34	REMIXES 81 – 04 SAMPLER : Enjoy The Silence (Richard X Extended Mix)/(Ewan Pearson Extended Instrumental)/Timo Maas Extended Remix)/Ewan Pearson Extended Remix) (2 x 12") 20
04	Mute ACD MUTEL8	REMIXES 81 – 04 (3 x CD, insert & press release) 30
06	Mute PXL12 BONG 39	Just Can't Get Enough – (Dirty South Mix)/Personal Jesus (Timo Maas Remix) 5
06	Mute DMINT06CD	THE BEST OF VOLUME 1 - Interview Disc CD (p/s) 25
06	Mute PLCDBONG39	REMIXES – THE BEST OF VOLUME 1 1 CD (p/s) 20

DEPRAVED

| 86 | Children Of Rev. GURT 6 | COME ON DOWN (LP, with lyric inner) ....12 |
| 86 | Children Of the Revolution GURT 14 | STUPIDITY MAKETH THE MAN (LP, insert) ....12 |

DEPRESSIONS

77	Barn 2014 112	Living On Dreams/Family Planning (p/s) 10
78	Barn 2014 119	Messing With Your Heart/Street Kid (p/s) 10
78	Barn 2014 122	Get Out Of This Town/Basement Daze (p/s) 10
78	Barn 2314 105	THE DEPRESSIONS (LP) 25

DEPUTIES

| 66 | Strike JH 305 | Given Half A Chance/Where Do People Go ....12 |

DEPUTY DAWG

| 96 | Peacefrog P F053 | GUN SLINGER EP (12", plain sleeve) ....10 |

(see also Luke Slater)

DEREK

| 68 | London HLZ 10230 | Cinnamon/This Is My Story ....12 |

(see also Johnny Cymbal)

DEREK & THE DOMINOES

70	Polydor 2058 057	Tell The Truth/Roll It Over (withdrawn) 80
70	Polydor 2058 130	Layla/Bell Bottom Blues (original, red paper label) 6
74	RSO 2090 104	Why Does Love Got To Be Sad?/Presence Of The Lord 5
82	RSO RSO 87	Layla/ERIC CLAPTON: Wonderful Tonight (p/s) 5
82	RSO RSOX 87	Layla/ERIC CLAPTON: Wonderful Tonight (live) (12", p/s) 8
71	Polydor 2625 005	LAYLA AND OTHER ASSORTED LOVE SONGS (2-LP, gatefold sleeve) 30
73	RSO 2659 020	IN CONCERT (2-LP, gatefold sleeve) 15

(see also Eric Clapton, Bobby Whitlock)

DEREK & FRESHMEN

| 65 | Oriole CB 305 | Gone Away/I Stand Alone ....15 |

(see also Derek Dean & Freshmen)

MINT VALUE £

FRANK DE ROSA & HIS ORCHESTRA
58	London HLD 8576	Big Guitar/Irish Rock	20

DERRICK (MORGAN) & JENNIFER
70	Crab CRAB 47	Need To Belong/Let's Have Some Fun	10
70	Crab CRAB 54	Rocking Good Way/Wipe These Tears	5

(see also Derrick Morgan)

DERRICK (MORGAN) & LLOYDS (CLARKE)
62	Blue Beat BB 135	Love And Leave Me (actually by Lloyd Clarke)/Merry Twist (actually "Whistle Stop Tour" by Roy Richards)	15

(see also Derrick Morgan, Lloyd Clarke)

DERRICK (MORGAN) & NAOMI (CAMPBELL)
65	Island WI 193	Two Of A Kind/I Want A Lover (credited to Derrick Morgan)	25
65	Ska Beat JB 185	Heart Of Stone/DERRICK MORGAN: Let Me Go	18
65	Ska Beat JB 188	I Wish I Were An Apple/DERRICK MORGAN: Around The Corner	18

(see also Derrick Morgan, Naomi, Don Drummond)

DERRICK (MORGAN) & PATSY (TODD)
61	Blue Beat BB 57	Feel So Fine/ROLAND ALPHONSO & GROUP: Mean To Me	18
61	Blue Beat BB 65	Baby Please Don't Leave Me/Let The Good Times Roll	20
62	Blue Beat BB 97	Love Not To Brag/DRUMBAGO'S ALL STARS: Duck Soup	20
62	Blue Beat BB 100	In My Heart (actually by Derrick Morgan)/BELL'S GROUP: Kingston 13	15
62	Blue Beat BB 106	Oh Shirley/BASIL GABIDON'S GROUP: Sam The Fisherman (B-side actually by Roland Alphonso)	18
62	Blue Beat BB 121	Crying In The Chapel/Come Back My Love	15
62	Blue Beat BB 123	Oh My Love/Let's Go To The Party	15
62	Island WI 018	Housewife's Choice/Gypsy Woman	18
63	Blue Beat BB 152	Little Brown Jug/Mow Sen Wa (with Lloyd Clarke)	15
63	Blue Beat BB 160	Trying To Make You Mine (actually "Baby Please Don't Leave Me" by Derrick Morgan)/Hold Me	15
63	Island WI 055	Sea Wave/Look Before You Leap	20
64	Blue Beat BB 207	Lover Boy/The Moon	15
64	Blue Beat BB 224	Steal Away/Money	15
64	Blue Beat BB 247	Troubles/Right (B-side actually "Baby Face")	15
65	Blue Beat BB 291	You I Love/Let Me Hold Your hand (song actually "Steal Away")	15
65	Blue Beat BB 318	Eternity/Want My Baby	15
65	Island WI 224	The National Dance/DESMOND DEKKER & FOUR ACES: Mount Zion	25
66	Island WI 288	I Found A Queen/It's True My Darling	18
68	Nu Beat NB 008	Hey Boy, Hey Girl/Music Is The Food Of Life	12

(see also Derrick Morgan, Patsy Todd)

DERRICK (MORGAN) & PAULETT
69	Nu Beat NB 027	I'll Do It/Give You My Love	12

(see also Derrick Morgan, Paulette)

DERRICK (MORGAN) & PAULINE (MORGAN)
68	Pyramid PYR 6027	You Never Miss Your Water/DERRICK MORGAN: Got You On My Mind	12
68	Pyramid/J.J. PYR 6063	Don't Say/DERRICK MORGAN: Johnny Pram Pram	15

(see also Derrick Morgan, Patsy Todd, Basil Gabbidon)

DERRICK & SOUNDS
68	Pye 7N 17601	Power Of Love/I'll Take You Home	5
69	Pye 7N 17709	My Sly Sadie/I Can't Lose That Girl	5
69	Pye 7N 17801	Morning Papers And Margarine/Winter Of Your Love	12

DERRINGERS
61	Capitol CL 15189	(If You Cry) True Love, True Love/Sheree	15

GLEN DERRY ORCHESTRA
61	Oriole CB 1609	Blue Sax/Beatnik	10

DES (BRYAN) ALLSTARS
70	Grape GR 3014	Night Food Reggae/Walk With Des	50
70	Grape GR 3015	If I Had A Hammer/Hammer Reggae	20
70	Grape GR 3016	Henry The Great/Black Scorcher	25

DES & DAVE
64	Columbia DB 7414	Christmas Dream/Lonely City	7
66	Columbia DB 7957	That's Us/Gotta Little Gal	7

HENRI DES
70	United Artists UP 35109	Return/Retour	18

SUGAR PIE DE SANTO
64	Pye International 7N 25249	Soulful Dress/Use What You Got	25
64	Pye International 7N 25267	I Don't Wanna Fuss/I Love You So Much	30
66	Chess CRS 8034	There's Gonna Be Trouble/In The Basement (B-side with Etta James)	30
69	Chess CRS 8093	Soulful Dress/There's Gonna Be Trouble	20

(see also Etta James & Sugar Pie De Santo)

MICHAEL DES BARRES
74	Purple PUR 123	Leon/New Moon Tonight	8

(see also Silverhead, Detective, Phoenix)

DESCENDANTS
67	CBS 202545	Garden Of Eden/Lela	50

DESECTORS
70	GAS GAS 137	King Kong/Please Stay	6

DESERT SESSIONS (JOSH HOLME)
03	Island IS 835	Crawl Home/The Whores Hustle And The Hustlers Whore (p/s)	20

(see also P J Harvey)

DESERT WOLVES
87	Ugly Man UGLY 6	Love Scattered Lives/Stopped In My Tracks (p/s)	20
87	Ugly Man UGLY 6T	Love Shattered Lives/Stopped In My Tracks/Desolation/ Sunday Morning (12", p/s)	25

88	Ugly Man UGLY 9	Speak To Me Rochelle/Besotted (p/s)	15
88	Ugly Man UGLY 9T	Speak To Me Rochelle/Mexico/Besotted/La Petite Rochelle (12", p/s)	20

JACKIE DE SHANNON

62	Liberty LIB 55497	You Won't Forget Me/I Don't Think So Much	20
63	Liberty LIB 55563	Needles And Pins/Did He Call Today Mama?	20
64	Liberty LIB 55645	When You Walk In The Room/Till You Say You'll Be Mine	20
64	Liberty LIB 10165	Dancing Silhouettes/Hold Your Head High	15
64	Liberty LIB 10175	Don't Turn Your Back On Me/Be Good Baby	18
65	Liberty LIB 10192	She Don't Understand Him Like I Do/The Prince	12
65	Liberty LIB 10202	What The World Needs Now Is Love/It's Love Baby	7
65	Liberty LIB 12019	A Lifetime Of Loneliness/I Remember The Boy	10
66	Liberty LIB 66171	Come And Get Me/Splendour In The Grass	5
66	Liberty LIB 66202	I Can Make It With You/To Be Myself	5
66	Liberty LIB 66224	Come On Down/Find Me Love	20
68	Liberty LBF 15133	The Weight/Effervescent Blue	6
69	Liberty LBF 15238	Put A Little Love In Your Heart/Always Together	6
70	Liberty LBF 15281	Love Will Find A Way/I Let Go Completely	7
70	Liberty LBF 15324	What The World Needs Now/Keep Me In Mind	5
72	Atlantic K 10184	Vanilla Olay/I Wanna Roo You	5
75	CBS 3669	Let The Sailors Dance/Dreamin' As One	5
72	Atlantic K 10241	Only Love Can Break Your Heart/Would You Like To Learn To Dance	5
65	Liberty LEP 2233	JACKIE (EP)	40
64	Liberty LBY 1182 (S)	THIS IS JACKIE DE SHANNON (LP)	25
65	Liberty LBY 1245	DON'T TURN YOUR BACK ON ME (LP)	25
65	Liberty LBY 3063	THIS IS JACKIE DE SHANNON (LP)	20
66	Liberty (S)BLY 3085	ARE YOU READY FOR THIS? (LP)	25
68	Liberty LBS 83117E	GREAT PERFORMANCES (LP)	20
69	Liberty LBS 83148E	ME ABOUT YOU (LP)	20
70	Liberty LBS 83304	PUT A LITTLE LOVE IN YOUR HEART (LP)	20
72	Atlantic K 40396	JACKIE (LP)	15

(see also Date With Soul)

DESIGN (1)

70	CBS 5112	Willow Stream/Coloured Mile	7
71	Epic EPC 7119	Jet Song/Minstrel's Theme	15
72	Regal Zonophone RZ 3044	Colour All The World/Lazy Song	7
72	Regal Zonophone RZ 3060	Mayday/Yellow Bird (Have You No Home)	6
73	Regal Zonophone RZ 3082	One Sunny Day/End Of The Party	6
71	Epic EPC 64322	DESIGN (LP)	15
71	Epic EPC64653	TOMORROW IS SO FAR AWAY (LP, with lyric insert, stickered sleeve)	20
73	Regal Zono. SLRZ 1037	DAY OF THE FOX (LP, textured sleeve, red/silver label)	15

DESIGN (2)

86	Dental 12DENT001	I Want You I Need You/Never Gonna Give You Up (12")	40

DESIRELESS

88	CBS 565 902-9	FRANCOIS (CD)	15

DESI ROOTS

79	Hawkeye HD 018	Hung-Up/Up-Town Rebel (12")	20
80	Hawkeye HD 025	Weed Fields/Hawkeye All Stars – Burning (12")	40
80	Hawkeye HD 033	Go Deh Right/Revolutionaries Go Right Deh (12")	30
80	Hawkeye HLP 007	DO IT RIGHT (LP)	35

ANDY DESMOND

74	Konk KOS2	So It Goes/She Can Move Mountains	5
75	Konk KOS4	Beware/Only Child	5

(see also Gothic Horizon)

JOHNNY DESMOND

55	Vogue Coral Q 72099	Yellow Rose Of Texas/You're In Love With Someone	10
56	Vogue Coral Q 72115	Sixteen Tons/Ballo Italiano	10
57	Vogue Coral Q 72261	A White Sports Coat (And A Pink Carnation)/Just Lookin'	10
57	Vogue Coral Q 72269	Shenandoah Rose/Consideration	5
58	Philips PB 890	Willingly/Apple (when Ya Gonna Fall From The Trees?)	5
58	MGM MGM 994	Hot Cha Cha/I'll Close My Eyes	5
60	Coral Q 72398	The Most Happy Fella/LANCERS: Joey, Joey, Joey	5
60	Philips PB 1044	Hawk/Playing The Field	25
62	Top Rank JAR 612	Twistin' Rose Of Texas/ Hello Honey	10
66	Polydor BM 56703	My Melancholy Baby/The Common Touch	5
67	Stateside SS 373	Rio Conchos/Fate In The Hunter	7
56	Vogue Coral LVA 9035	SOUVENIR D'ITALIE (LP)	12

LORRAE DESMOND (& REBELS)

54	Decca F 10375	Hold My Hand/On The Waterfront	10
54	Decca F 10398	Far Away (My Love Is Far Away)/No One But You	10
54	Decca F 10404	I Can't Tell A Waltz From A Tango/For Better, For Worse (with Johnston Brothers)	10
55	Decca F 10461	A Boy On Saturday Night/Why — Oh Why?	10
55	Decca F 10510	Don't/Where Will The Baby's Dimple Be?	10
55	Decca F 10533	Stowaway/Heartbroken (B-side with Johnston Brothers)	10
55	Decca F 10612	You Should Know/Wake The Town And Tell The People	6
56	Parlophone R 4239	Written On The Wind/A House With Love In It	6
57	Parlophone R 4287	You Won't Be Around/Play The Music (as Lorrae Desmond & Rebels)	8
57	Parlophone R 4320	Kansas City Special/Preacher, Preacher (as Lorrae Desmond & Rebels)	6
57	Parlophone R 4361	Ding-Dong Rock-a-billy Weddin'/Cabin Boy (as Lorrae Desmond & Rebels)	10
58	Parlophone R 4400	Two Ships/Little David	8
58	Parlophone R 4430	Down By The River/The Secret Of Happiness	6
58	Parlophone R 4463	Soda Pop Hop/Blue, Blue Day	20
59	Parlophone R 4534	Tall Paul/Wait For It	10
60	Parlophone R 4670	Tell Me Again/Get Your Daddie's Car Tonight	10

MIKE DESMOND

57	Columbia DB 3954	Young And In Love/Two Loves (as Michael Desmond)	6
57	Columbia DB 4018	Chances Are/If You're Not Completely Satisfied (as Michael Desmond)	6

MINT VALUE £

PAUL DESMOND
60	RCA 1373	Take Ten/Embarcadero	6
65	RCA RS 7701	BOSSA ANTIGUA (LP, label with red spot)	15

(see also Gerry Mulligan, Dave Brubeck)

DESOLATION ANGELS
84	AM AM 266	Valhalla/Boadicea (p/s)	40
85	Thameside TRR 111	DESOLATION ANGELS (LP)	50

DESPERATE BICYCLES
77	Refill RR 1	Smokescreen/Handlebars (p/s, same tracks both sides)	25
77	Refill RR 2	The Medium Was Tedium/Don't Back The Front (p/s, same tracks both sides)	25
78	Refill RR 3	NEW CROSS NEW CROSS (EP)	25
78	Refill RR 4	Occupied Territory/Skill (p/s)	20
78	Refill RR 7	Grief Is Very Private/Obstructive/Conundrum	20
80	Refill RR 6	REMORSE CODE (LP)	35

DESSIE & JOHN
69	Downtown DT 440	Boss Sound/Everything Is Alright	10

DESSUS
81	Ellie Jay EJSP 9710	Ghetto Children/Dessus Jammin' (with p/s)	25
81	Ellie Jay EJSP 9710	Ghetto Children/Dessus Jammin' (without p/s)	12

DESTROY ALL MONSTERS
79	Cherry Red CHERRY 3	Bored/You're Gonna Die (p/s, red vinyl)	5
79	Cherry Red CHERRY 7	Meet The Creeper/November 22nd 1963 (p/s)	5
79	Cherry Red CHERRY 9	Nobody Knows/What Do I Get? (p/s)	5

(see also MC5)

DESTROYER
81	Clean Kill SJP 829	Evil Place/Stand And Deliver (no p/s)	50

DESTROYERS
70	Amalgamated AMG 856	Niney Special/Danger Zone	18
70	Pressure Beat PR 5505	Pressure Tonic/Machuki's Cooking (B-side actually with Count Machuki)	35

(see also Soul Brothers, Nicky Thomas)

DESTRUCTORS
82	KILL 3	Electronic Church/Khymer Rouge Boogie (rubber-stamped white label, 500 only given away with copies of Trees And Flowers punkzine)	50
82	Carnage BOOK 2	Meaningless Names/AK 47/Police State/Dachau/Death Squad (p/s)	5
82	Carnage Benelux KILL 2	Religion/Soldier Boy/Agent Orange/Corpse Gas (p/s)	5
82	Illuminated ILL 14	Jailbait/Kalgsnocov/Sewage Worker/Image (p/s)	10
82	Carnage Records BOOK 2	SENSELESS VIOLENCE (EP)	10
82	Illuminated JAMS 55	EXORCISE THE DEMONS OF YOUTH (EP, with insert)	8
82	Death DEATH 1	MERRY XMAS & FUCK OFF (LP)	20
83	Radical Change RCLP 2	ARMAGEDDON IN ACTION (LP)	20

(see also Blanks)

DETAILS
80	Energy NRG 2	Keep On Running/Run'ins (p/s)	5
80	Energy NRG 002	Keep On Running/Run'ins (12", stickered plain sleeve, promo only)	8

FRANK DETAILS
80	Buzz Bomb BB 1	False Pretences/Stranger On A Train (p/s)	10

DETECTIVE
77	Swansong SS K59405	DETECTIVE (LP, with inner)	12
78	Swansong SS 8504	IT TAKES ONE TO KNOW ONE (LP, with inner sleeve)	12

(see also Michael Des Barres)

DETERGENTS
65	Columbia DB 7513	Leader Of The Laundromat/Ulcers	10
65	Columbia DB 7591	I Don't Know/The Blue Kangaroo	6

DETONATORS (1)
78	Local LR 1	Need Love Tonight/Great Big Ghetto/Shoob Shooby Do/Give Me A Helping Hand (p/s)	6

DETONATORS (2)
79	Burning Rockers BR 1008	GANGSTER (LP)	30

DETOURS (1)
68	CBS 3213	Run To Me Baby/Hangin' On	40
68	CBS 3401	Whole Lotta Lovin'/Pieces Of You	175

(see also Gene Latter)

DETOURS (2)
76	MCA 249	Try To Hold On/Love To	5

DETRIUS
90	Under One Flag FLAG 55	PERPETUAL DEFIANCE (LP, with inner sleeve)	15

DETROIT WITH MITCH RYDER
72	Paramount PARA 3022	It Ain't Easy/Long Neck Goose	5
72	Paramount SPFL 277	DETROIT (LP)	20

(see also Mitch Ryder)

DETROIT EMERALDS
71	Pye International 7N 25544	Do Me Right/Just Now And Then	6
71	Janus 6146 004	Wear This Ring/I Bet You Get The One	5
72	Janus 6146 007	You Want It, You Got It/Till You Decide To Come Home	5
72	Janus 6146 015	Do Me Right/Baby Let Me Take You In My Arms	5
72	Janus 6146 020	Feel The Need In Me/And I Love Her	5
73	Westbound 6146108	You're Getting A Little Too Smart/Lee	5

DETROIT ESCALATOR CO.
96	Ferox FERLP 2	SOUNDTRACK (313) (LP)	20

DETROIT SPINNERS

65	Tamla Motown TMG 514	Sweet Thing/How Can I? (demo credited to 'Spinners')	425
65	Tamla Motown TMG 514	Sweet Thing/How Can I? (demo credited to 'Detroit Spinners')	250
65	Tamla Motown TMG 514	Sweet Thing/How Can I? (stock copies credited to 'Spinners')	425
65	Tamla Motown TMG 523	I'll Always Love You/Tomorrow May Never Come (as 'Spinners')	110
65	Tamla Motown TMG 523	I'll Always Love You/Tomorrow May Never Come (as 'Detroit Spinners')	75
65	Tamla Motown TMG 523	I'll Always Love You/Tomorrow May Never Come (as 'Spinners' or 'Detroit Spinners' DJ Copy)	250
67	Tamla Motown TMG 627	For All We Know/I'll Always Love You (1st pressing with tall, narrow print)	25
67	Tamla Motown TMG 627	For All We Know/I'll Always Love You (2nd pressing)	18
70	Tamla Motown TMG 755	It's A Shame/Together We Can Make Such Sweet Music (unissued)	0
70	Tamla Motown TMG 755	It's A Shame/Sweet Thing (as Motown Spinners)	7
71	Tamla Motown TMG 766	Together We Can Make Such Sweet Music/Truly Yours (as Motown Spinners)	7
74	Tamla Motown TMG 871	Together We Can Make Such Sweet Music/Bad Bad Weather	5
80	Atlantic K 11558	Split Decision/Now That You're Mine Again	5
80	Atlantic K 11558	Split Decision/Now That You're Mine Again (12")	12
68	T. Motown TML 11060	THE DETROIT SPINNERS (LP, mono)	50
68	T. Motown STML 11060	THE DETROIT SPINNERS (LP, stereo)	60
71	T. Motown STML 11182	SECOND TIME AROUND (LP, as Motown Spinners)	20

(see also Spinners, G.C. Cameron)

DETROITS

70	Fontana 6438 006	'TIS US OURSELVES (LP)	12

DEUCE

86	1986 Powermetal VB004	Backs To The Ball/Queen Of The Night/Jealousy	10

DEUCE COUP

67	Mercury MF 1013	A Clown In One Town/Angela (in p/s)	12
67	Mercury MF 1013	A Clown In One Town/Angela (no p/s)	6

DEUCE OF HEARTS

66	CBS 202345	Closer Together/The Times They Are A Changin'	10

JIMMY DEUCHAR

54	Esquire EP 53	JIMMY DEUCHAR (EP)	40
55	Tempo EXA 18	JIMMY DEUCHAR ENSEMBLE (EP)	40
56	Esquire EP 93	JIMMY DEUCHAR QUARTET (EP)	40
56	Esquire EP 103	JIMMY DEUCHAR QUARTET (EP)	40
58	Tempo EXA 79	OPUS DE FUNK (EP, as Jimmy Deuchar Sextet)	40
58	Tempo EXA 81	SWINGIN' IN STUDIO TWO (EP)	40
59	Tempo EXA 88	WAIL (EP, with Victor Feldman Quintet)	40
54	Esquire 20-059	DIG DEUCHAR, DON'T DANCE (LP)	80
55	Tempo LAP 2	JIMMY DEUCHAR ENSEMBLE (10" LP)	250
56	Tempo TAP 4	TOP TRUMPETS (LP)	250
56	Vogue LDE	SHOWCASE (LP)	60
58	Tempo TAP 20	PAL JIMMY (LP)	700

(see also Victor Feldman)

BIG PETE DEUCHAR/DUKER

63	Fontana 267 278 TF	Google Eye/There's A Hand Leading Me (as Big Pete Deuchar)	10
63	Fontana TF 423	It Comes And Goes/Married By The Bible	10
65	Columbia DB 7763	Goin' In Training/I Saw Your Face In The Moon (as Big Pete Duker)	8

DEUS

94	Island 155981854 018-7	Suds & Soda/Secret Hell (limited edition, numbered)	40
94	Island 1215598854-019-1	Suds And Soda (Extended Version)/Texan Coffee/Secret Hell/Furniture In The Far West (12")	18
94	Island 15599/854 150 7	Via/Violins And Happy Endings	8
94	Island 1215599/854 131-1	Via/Violins And Happy Endings/Great American Nude/Strip Mix (12")	8
95	Island 15603/854 188-7	Hotel Lounge (Be The Death Of Me)/Jigsaw You (Live) (limited edition, die-cut sleeve)	8
96	Island 630/854 682-7	Theme From Turnpike/Overflow/My Little Contessa (7" picture disc)	10
96	Island 1015630/854 682-0	Theme From Turnpike/Overflow/My Little Contessa (10", gatefold sleeve)	10
96	Island IS 643/854 718	Little Arithmetics/My Wife Jan (picture disc)	8
96	Island IS 663	Little Arithmetics/Fell Off The Floor, Man (Dust Brothers Edit) (picture disc)	10
96	Island 15645/845726-7	Roses/I Suffer Rock (7" picture disc)	8
99	Island 15750/562-109-7	Sister Dew (Album Version)/Thirteen (Live) (with poster)	8
99	Island IS 714	Instant Street/Dream Sequence 1 (Demo) (p/s)	8
94	Island ILPS8028/524-0451	WORST CASE SCENARIO (LP, limited edition with postcard and CD booklet)	80
96	Island ILPS 8052/52429-1	IN A BAR UNDER THE SEA (LP, with inner sleeve)	80
99	Island ILPS 8082/524 643-1	THE IDEAL CRASH (LP)	40
05	V2 VVR 1034711	POCKET REVOLUTION (2-LP)	25

DEVASTATION

84	Creative Reality REAL 8	DRAG YOU DOWN EP	20

DEVIANTS

68	Stable STA 5601	You Got To Hold On/Let's Loot The Supermarket	20
67	Underground Imp. IMP 1	PTOOFF! (LP, foldout sleeve, private pressing via IT magazine)	350
68	Stable SLP 007	DISPOSABLE (LP, gatefold sleeve, red/black label)	250
69	Transatlantic TRA 204	THE DEVIANTS (LP, with booklet, white/lilac label with 't' logo)	250
69	Transatlantic TRA-R 204	THE DEVIANTS (LP, without booklet, white/lilac label with 't' logo)	100
69	Decca LK-R/SKL-R 4993	PTOOFF! (LP, reissue, large unboxed logo on label)	90
84	Psycho PSYCHO 25	HUMAN GARBAGE (LIVE AT DINGWALLS '84) (LP)	15

(see also Mick Farren, Pink Fairies, Larry Wallis)

DEVIATED INSTINCT

86	Peaceville WARP 2	WELCOME TO THE ORGY EP	15
88	Peaceville VILE 3	ROCK 'N' ROLL CONFORMITY (LP, inner)	25
90	Prophecy PRO 004	NAILED EP (12", p/s)	20
90	Peaceville VILE 16	GUTTURAL BREATH (LP)	20

DEVIL'S HOLE GANG

70s	Slow Burning Fuse SSSS 1	Free The People/Isn't It/Something To Look Forward To (p/s, with insert)	12

JOHNNY DEVLIN (& DETOURS)

64	Pye 7N 15598	Sometimes/If You Want Someone (as Johnny Devlin & Detours)	10

66	CBS 202085	Hung On You/Prove It	8
66	CBS 202339	My Strength; Heart Of Soul/I Can't Get You Off My Mind	7
67	CBS 202452	Tender Lovin' Care/Five O'Clock World	7
67	CBS 2751	Hurtin'/You Gotta Tell Me	7

DEVO

78	Stiff DEV 1	Jocko Homo/Mongoloid (foldout p/s)	5
78	Stiff DEV 2/BOY 1	(I Can't Get No) Satisfaction/Sloppy (I Saw My Baby Getting) (p/s)	5
78	Stiff BOY 2	Be Stiff/Social Fools (clear vinyl)	5
79	Elevator NICE 1	Mechanical Man/Blockhead/Blackout/Auto-Modern (official bootleg, red/yellow stamped sleeves)	8
85	Warner Bros W9119	Shout/C'mon (p/s)	5
78	Virgin V 2106	Q: ARE WE NOT MEN? (LP, various coloured vinyl)	15
78	Virgin VP 2106	Q: ARE WE NOT MEN? (LP, picture disc, with 'Flimsy Wrap' 33rpm 1-sided flexidisc [VDJ 27/Lyntone LYN 6260])	15
80	Virgin V 2162	FREEDOM OF CHOICE (LP, stickered sleeve with poster)	12

DEVON (RUSSELL) & SEDRIC (MYTON)

| 69 | Blue Cat BS 158 | What A Sin Thing/Short Up Dress | 30 |

DEVON (RUSSELL) & TARTANS

| 68 | Nu Beat NB 021 | Let's Have Some Fun/Making Love | 18 |

(see also Tartans)

DEVONNES

| 06 | Kent 6T 21 | Doin'/The Gittin' Up/MAYBERRY MOVEMENT: I See Him Making Love To You | 20 |

BARRY DE VORZON

58	RCA RCA 1066	Barbara Jean/JIMMY DELL: Teeny Weeny	65
58	RCA RCA 1066	Barbara Jean/JIMMY DELL: Teeny Weeny (78)	40
60	Philips PB 993	Betty Betty (Go Steady With Me)/Across The Street	25

(see also Barry & Tamerlanes, Jimmy Dell)

DEVOTED

| 68 | Page One POF 076 | I Love George Best/United (p/s) | 25 |
| 68 | Page One POF 076 | I Love George Best/United | 15 |

DEVOTIONS

| 64 | Columbia DB 7256 | Rip Van Winkle/I Love You For Sentimental Reasons | 100 |

JANINE DE WAYLENE & HER MARTENOT

| 60 | Top Rank JAR 363 | Faces In The Dark(Martenot Theme)/Farewell Christina | 5 |
| 60 | Oriole CB 1576 | Faces In The Dark(Martenot Theme)/Farewell Christina | 6 |

DEWDROPS

| 67 | Blue Beat BB 381 | Somebody's Knocking/By And By | 18 |

BRIAN DEWHURST

| 75 | Folk Heritage FHR 075 | THE HUNTER & THE HUNTED (LP, black label and laminated sleeve) | 20 |

KEITH DEWHURST & ALBION BAND

| 80 | Charisma CDS 4020 | LARK RISE TO CANDLEFORD (A COUNTRY TAPESTRY) (LP, soundtrack) | 12 |

(see also Albion Band)

HARRY DE WIT

| 79 | Bead Records BEAD 11 | APRIL '79 (LP) | 25 |
| 79 | Bead Records BEAD 12 | FOR HARM (LP, with Philipp Wachsmann) | 25 |

DANNY DEXTER

| 63 | London HLU 9690 | Sweet Mama/Go On | 19 |

EDDIE DEXTER & HIS BAND

| 55 | Capitol CL 14371 | Moonlight/The Verse Of Stardust | 8 |

RAY DEXTER & LAYABOUTS

| 62 | Decca F 11538 | The Coalman's Lament/Lonely Weekend | 30 |

DEXYS MIDNIGHT RUNNERS

85	Mercury DEXYS 13	An Extract From 'This Is What She's Like'/'This Is What She's Like' Finale (p/s)	5
85	Mercury DEXYSD 13	An Extract From 'This Is What She's Like'/'This Is What She's Like' Finale// Marguerita Time/Reminisce Part One (double pack, gatefold p/s)	8
85	Mercury DEXYS 1310	This Is What She's Like/Marguerita Time (10", p/s)	8
85	Mercury MERH 56	DON'T STAND ME DOWN (LP)	15

(see also Killjoys, Kevin Rowland)

TRACEY DEY

| 64 | Stateside SS 287 | Go Away/Gonna Get Along Without You Now | 18 |

DEZIGN

| 84 | EN AY DZ 256 | Love Myth/Let's Go (no p/s) | 10 |

BOBBY D'FANO

| 62 | Palette PG 9038 | Message Of Love/The Kiss That Broke My Heart | 10 |

DHARMA BLUES BAND

| 69 | Major Minor SMCP 5017 | DHARMA BLUES (LP, yellow/white/black label) | 75 |

(see also Hawkwind)

ALI BEN DHOWN

| 67 | Piccadilly 7N 35395 | Musapha/Turkish Delight | 30 |

DIAGONAL

| 10 | Rise Above 127 FREE | Stop/ASTRA: Empty Spaces (300 only, gig freebie) | 12 |

DIAGRAM BROTHERS

80	Construct CON 1	We Are All Animals/There Is No Shower/Would I Like To Live In Prison	15
81	New Hormones ORG 9	Bricks/Postal Bargains (p/s)	8
82	New Hormones ORG 21	DISCORDO EP	8

DIALS (JAMAICA)

| 69 | Duke DU 48 | Bye Bye Love/It's Love | 7 |
| 69 | Duke DU 49 | Love Is A Treasure/DIAMONDS: I Want To Be | 7 |

DIALS (U.K.)

79	Wessex WEX 266	Maxine/Hey Denise (p/s)	7
79	Scene ACT1	All I Hear/Running (p/s)	10

BRIAN DIAMOND & THE CUTTERS

63	Decca F 11724	Jealousy Will Get You Nowhere/Brady Brady	15
64	Fontana TF 452	Shake, Shout And Go/Wotcha Gonna Do Now Pretty Baby	18
65	Pye 7N 15779	Big Bad Wolf/See If I Care	15
65	Pye 7N 15952	Bone Idol/Sands Of Time	15

GREGG DIAMOND'S BIONIC BOOGIE

79	Urban URBX 16	Hot Butterfly/Mess Up The Boogie/When The Shit Hits The Fan (12", p/s)	10
79	Polydor PB 50	Chains/Hot Butterfly	5
79	Polydor POSPX 50	Chains/Hot Butterfly (12")	15
79	Polydor 2391 322	BIONIC BOOGIE (LP)	12

JERRY DIAMOND

57	London HLE 8496	Sunburned Lips/Don't Trust Love	40
57	London HLE 8496	Sunburned Lips/Don't Trust Love (78)	20

LEE DIAMOND (& CHEROKEES)

61	Fontana H 310	I'll Step Down/Josephine (as Lee Diamond & Cherokees)	18
61	Fontana H 345	Stop Your Crying/You'll Want Me	18

(see also Cherokees)

NEIL DIAMOND

66	London HLZ 10049	Solitary Man/Do It	12
66	London HLZ 10072	Cherry, Cherry/I'll Come Running	10
66	London HLZ 10092	I Got The Feelin' (Oh No No)/The Boat That I Row	10
67	London HLZ 10111	You Got To Me/Someday Baby	10
67	London HLZ 10126	Girl, You'll Be A Woman Soon/You'll Forget	8
67	London HLZ 10151	Thank The Lord For The Night Time/The Long Way Home	8
67	London HLZ 10161	Kentucky Woman/The Time Is Now	8
68	London HLZ 10177	New Orleans/Hanky Panky	10
68	London HLZ 10187	Red Red Wine/Red Rubber Ball	7
68	Uni UN 503	Brooklyn Roads/Holiday Inn Blues	5
71	President PT 335	Kentucky Woman/Cherry, Cherry/I Thank The Lord For The Night Time (p/s)	5
66	London HA-Z 8307	THE FEEL OF NEIL DIAMOND (LP)	40

DIAMOND BOYS

62	Parlophone GIB 102	Fool In Love/New Orleans (export issue)	25
63	RCA RCA 1351	Hey Little Girl/What'd I Say	15

(see also Albert Ammons)

DIAMOND HEAD

80	Happy Face MMDH 120	Shoot Out The Lights/Helpless (p/s)	15
80	Media SCREEN 1	Sweet And Innocent/Streets Of Gold (p/s)	15
81	DHM DHM 004	Waited Too Long/Play It Loud (p/s)	7
81	DHM DHM 005	DIAMOND LIGHTS EP (Diamond Lights/ We Won't Be Back/I Don't Got/It's Electric) (12", p/s)	20
82	MCA DHMT 101	FOUR CUTS (12" EP, with insert)	12
83	MCA DHMT 103	Makin' Music/(Andy Peebles Interview) (p/s)	8
83	MCA DHMT 103	Makin' Music/(Andy Peebles Interview) (12", p/s)	15
83	MCA DHMT 104	Out Of Phase/The Kingmaker (p/s)	5
83	MCA DHMP 104	Out Of Phase/The Kingmaker (picture disc)	6
83	MCA DHMT 104	Out Of Phase/The Kingmaker/Sucking My Love (live) (12", p/s)	25
92	Bronze	Wild In The Streets (12", p/s, 1 side etched)	8
80	DHM MMDHLP 105	LIGHTNING TO THE NATIONS (LP, plain or printed white labels, plain white sleeve, sold at gigs, signed in blue ink & available via Sounds)	65
80	DHM MMDHLP 105	LIGHTNING TO THE NATIONS (LP, plain or printed white labels, plain white sleeve, sold at gigs)	50
81	MCA DH 1001	LIVING ON BORROWED TIME (LP, gatefold sleeve with inner sleeve, with poster & fan club insert)	25
81	MCA DH 1001	LIVING ON BORROWED TIME (LP, gatefold sleeve with inner sleeve)	15
83	MCA DH 1002	CANTERBURY (LP, with lyric and tour dates sheet, first pressing faulty and jumps)	15
86	Metal Masters METALP 110	BEHOLD THE BEGINNING (LP, remixed reissue of 1st LP)	20
87	FM WKFMLP 92	AM I EVIL (LP, with inner sleeve)	20
93	Bronze/Essential ESSLP 192	DEATH AND PROGRESS (LP)	12

DIAMONDS (JAMAICA)

72	Songbird SB 1079	Mash Up/DYNAMITES: Mash Up (Version)	6
75	Attack ATT 8108	Jah Jah Bless Your Dreadlocks/Version	10
75	Attack ATT 8113	Just Can't Figure Out/Just Can't Figure Out (Version)	8
75	Black Wax WAX 5	Country Living/A Living Version	8
78	Virgin V2102	PLANET EARTH (LP)	20

(see also Dymonds, Sir Collins Band)

DIAMONDS (U.K.)

63	Philips BF 1264	The Lost City/Chasey Chasey (John Peel)	10

DIAMONDS (U.S.)

55	Vogue Coral Q 72109	Black Denim Trousers And Motorcycle Boots/Nip Sip	40
55	Vogue Coral Q 72109	Black Denim Trousers And Motorcycle Boots/Nip Sip (78)	10
58	Mercury 7MT 187	Silhouettes/Honey Bird	30
58	Mercury 7MT 195	The Stroll/Land Of Beauty	25
58	Mercury 7MT 207	Don't Let Me Down/High Sign	25
58	Mercury 7MT 208	Straight Skirts/Patsy	50
58	Mercury 7MT 233	Where Mary Go?/Kathy-O	8
58	Mercury AMT 1004	Eternal Lovers/Walking Along	8
59	Mercury AMT 1024	She Say (Oom Dooby Doom)/From The Bottom Of My Heart	10
59	Mercury AMT 1024	She Say (Oom Dooby Doom)/From The Bottom Of My Heart (78)	15
60	Mercury AMT 1086	Tell The Truth/Real True Love	30
61	Mercury AMT 1156	One Summer Night/It's A Doggone Shame	15
57	Mercury MEP 9515	PRESENTING THE DIAMONDS (EP)	40
57	Mercury MEP 9523	THE DIAMONDS VOL. 1 (EP)	40
58	Mercury MEP 9527	THE DIAMONDS VOL. 2 (EP)	40

MINT VALUE £

58	Mercury MEP 9530	THE DIAMONDS VOL. 3 (EP)	40
59	Mercury ZEP 10003	DIG THE DIAMONDS (EP)	40
59	Mercury ZEP 10020	THE DIAMONDS MEET PETE RUGOLO (EP)	20
59	Mercury ZEP 10026	DIAMONDS ARE TRUMPS (EP)	40
60	Mercury ZEP 10053	STAR STUDDED DIAMONDS (EP)	40
61	Mercury ZEP 10097	PETE RUGOLO LEADS THE DIAMONDS (EP, mono)	25
61	Mercury SEZ 10912	PETE RUGOLO LEADS THE DIAMONDS (EP, stereo)	30
57	Mercury MPT 7526	THE DIAMONDS (10" LP)	60
60	Mercury MMC 14039	SONGS FROM THE OLD WEST (LP)	15

(see also Pete Rugolo)

DIAMOND TWINS
| 66 | HMV POP 1508 | Crying The Night Away/Start The World Spinning Again | 6 |

(see also Sonia Kent)

ALENA DIANE
| 06 | Names NAMES 25 | SONGS WHISTLED THROUGH WHITE TEETH (EP, 10", 500 only) | 12 |

DIANE & JAVELINS
| 66 | Columbia DB 7819 | Heart And Soul/Who's The Girl | 55 |

(PAUL) DI'ANNO
84	FM VHF 1	Heart User/Road Rat (p/s)	8
84	FM WKFM LP1	DI'ANNO (LP, blue vinyl, stickered sleeve)	15
84	FM WKFM PD1	DI'ANNO (LP, picture disc)	18
87	Powerstation AMP 13	CHILDREN OF MADNESS (LP, as Paul DI'ANNO's BATTLEZONE)	12

(see also Gogmagog, Iron Maiden)

DIATONES
| 61 | Starlite ST45 057 | Ruby Has Gone/Oh Baby Come Dance With Me | 100 |

DANNY DIAZ & THE CHECKMATES
| 69 | Pye 7N 17690 | Solomon Grundy/Goodbye Baby | 15 |

MANU DIBANGO
73	London HL 10423	Soul Makossa/Lily	10
73	London SH 8451	O BOSO (LP)	20
75	Creole CRLP 503	MAKOSSA MUSIC (LP)	15
78	Decca SKL-R 5296	AFROVISION (LP)	12
79	Decca SKL-R 5303	MANU '76 (LP)	12

BILLY DICE & SHENLEY DUFFUS
| 73 | Pama 874 | Women Smarter/Standing On The Hill | 8 |

DICE THE BOSS
69	Joe DU 50	Brixton Cat Big And Fat/JOPES ALL STARS : Solitude	65
69	Duke/Joe DU 51	Gun The Man Down/JOE MANSANO: The Thief	30
69	Duke/Joe DU 52	But Officer/JOE'S ALL STARS: Reggae On The Shore	50
70	Duke/Joe DU 57	Your Boss D.J./TITO SIMON: Read The News	40
70	Joe's JRS 17	The Informer/Cool It	40
70	Explosion EX 2017	Funky Monkey/JOE'S ALL STARS: Funky Monkey Version	15
70	Explosion EX 2020	Funky Duck/Dunkier Than Duck	15

(see also Pama Dice, Joe The Boss, Ray Martel)

LLOYD DICE
| 70 | Joe JRS 5 | Trial Of Pama Dice/JOE: Jughead Returns | 25 |

(see also Trevor Lloyd)

PAMA DICE
70	Reggae 3002	Brixton Pum Pum Wrecker/JOE ALLSTARS: Version (White label, possibly unreleased)	100
69	Jackpot JP 715	Honky Tonk Popcorn/Bongo Man	12
69	Jackpot JP 716	Sin, Sun And Sex/Reggae Popcorn	12
70	Reggae REG 3001	Brixton Fight/OPENING: Tea House	150

(see also Dice The Boss, Joe The Boss)

DICEMEN
| 83 | Random MCPS RR1 | Number 19/A Year Without You/Sunrise/Today | 15 |

DICK & DEE DEE
61	London HLG 9408	The Mountain's High/I Want Someone	10
62	London HLG 9483	Goodbye To Love/Swing Low	12
62	Liberty LIB 55412	Tell Me/Will You Always Love Me	5
63	Warner Bros WB 96	Young And In Love/Say To Me	5
63	Warner Bros WB 111	Where Did The Good Times Go/Guess Our Love Must Show	5
63	Warner Bros WB 119	Turn Around/Don't Leave Me	5
64	Warner Bros WB 126	All My Trails/Don't Twice, It's All Right	5
64	Warner Bros WB 138	Remember When/You Were Mine	5
64	Warner Bros WB 145	Thou Shalt Not Steal/Just 'Round The River Bend	5
65	Warner Bros WB 156	Be My Baby/Room 404	15
65	Warner Bros WB 5671	Use What You've Got/P.S. 1402	8
63	Warner Bros WM 8132	YOUNG AND IN LOVE (LP, mono)	25
63	Warner Bros WS 8132	YOUNG AND IN LOVE (LP, stereo)	30
63	Warner Bros WM 8150	TURN AROUND (LP, mono)	25
63	Warner Bros WS 8150	TURN AROUND (LP, /stereo)	30

DICKENS
| 80 | Hawkmoon ROCK 101 | STANDING OUT (LP, private pressing) | 12 |

(see also Ice)

CHARLES DICKENS
65	Pye 7N 15887	That's The Way Love Goes/In The City	25
65	Pye 7N 15938	I Stand Alone/Hey Little Girl	10
66	Immediate IM 025	So Much In Love/Our Soul Brothers	40

(see also Habits)

DOLES DICKEN'S BAND
| 58 | London HLD 8639 | Piakukaungchung (Pie-ah-coo-ka-ung-chung)/Our Melody | 10 |

LITTLE JIMMY DICKENS

| 54 | Columbia DC 670 | Then I Had To Turn Around/Hot Diggity Dog (78, export issue) ....8 |
| 66 | CBS BPG 62404 | MAY THE BIRD OF PARADISE FLY UP YOUR NOSE (LP) ....12 |

DICKIES

78	A&M AMS 7351	Give It Back/You Drive Me Ape (white vinyl, p/s) 5
78	A&M AMS 7368	Paranoid/I'm OK, You're OK (p/s, milky vinyl) 5
78	A&M AMS 7403	Silent Night/The Sounds Of Silence (p/s, white vinyl) 6
79	A&M AMS 7431	Banana Splits/Hideous/Got It At The Store (yellow vinyl, p/s) 5
79	A&M AMS 7491	Manny, Moe And Jack/She Loves Me Not (p/s, black vinyl only) 8
80	A&M AMS 7504	Fan Mail/Tricia Toyota (I'm Stuck In A Pagoda) (opaque or translucent red vinyl, poster p/s) 6
80	A&M AMS 7544	Gigantor/Bowling With Bedrock Barney (yellow vinyl, p/s with full colour or b&w reverse) 8
90	Overground OVER 12	Just Say Yes/Ayatollah You So (p/s with lyric sheet, mauve, blue or white vinyl, 2,000 of each colour) 7
95	Plastic Head HOLE 008	Make It So/Oh Baby (p/s, black vinyl, 1,000 only) 5
79	A&M AMLE 64742	THE INCREDIBLE SHRINKING DICKIES (LP, black or yellow vinyl) 12
79	A&M AMLE 64742	THE INCREDIBLE SHRINKING DICKIES (LP, blue vinyl, with black or red-and-black on sleeve) 12
79	A&M AMLE 64742	THE INCREDIBLE SHRINKING DICKIES (LP, orange vinyl, with black or red-and-black on sleeve) 15
79	A&M AMLH 68510	DAWN OF THE DICKIES (LP, blue vinyl) 15
79	A&M AMLH 68510	DAWN OF THE DICKIES (LP, black vinyl) 12

(see also Chuck Wagon)

BRUCE DICKINSON

90	EMI EM 138	Tattooed Millionaire/Ballad Of Mutt (paper label, glossy p/s) 5
90	EMI EMPD 138	Tattooed Millionaire/Ballad Of Mutt (shaped picture disc) 10
90	EMI EMPD 138	Tattooed Millionaire/Ballad Of Mutt (uncut shaped picture disc) 30
90	EMI EMPD 142	All The Young Dudes/Darkness Be My Friend (shaped picture disc with plinth) 10
90	EMI EMPD 142	All The Young Dudes/Darkness Be My Friend (uncut shaped picture disc) 25
90	EMI EMPD 151	Dive! Dive! Dive!/Riding With The Angels (live)/Sin City (live)/ Black Night (live) (12", picture disc) 10
94	EMI EM 341	Shoot All The Clowns/Over And Out (p/s, clear vinyl with insert) 5

(see also Iron Maiden, Samson, Xero, Rock Aid Armenia)

BARBARA DICKSON

74	RSO 2090 144	Here Comes The Sun/The Long And Winding Road 5
70	Decca SKL 5041	THRO' RECENT YEARS (LP, with Archie Fisher) 40
71	Decca SKL 5058	DO RIGHT WOMAN (LP) 40
72	Decca SKL 5116	FROM THE BEGGAR'S MANTLE FRINGED WITH GOLD (LP) 35
74	RSO 2394 141	JOHN, PAUL, GEORGE, RINGO AND BERT (LP, with London cast) 30

DICK TURPIN

| 70 | Evolution E 2446 | If You've Got The Time/Madeline ....150 |

DICTATORS WITH TONY & HOWARD

| 63 | Oriole CB 1934 | So Long Little Girl/Say Little Girl ....20 |

(see also Tony & Howard)

DICTATORS

77	Asylum K 13091	Search And Destroy/Sleepin' With The TV On 5
77	Asylum K 13091	Search And Destroy/Sleepin' With The TV On (12" p/s) 8
75	Epic S EPC 80767	GO GIRL CRAZY (LP) 20
77	Asylum K 53061	MANIFEST DESTINY (LP, lyric inner) 15
78	Asylum K53083	BLOOD BROTHERS LP, inner) 15

BO DIDDLEY

59	London HLM 8913	The Great Grandfather/Crackin' Up 60
59	London HLM 8913	The Great Grandfather/Crackin' Up (78) 40
59	London HLM 8975	Say Man/The Clock Strikes Twelve 60
59	London HLM 8975	Say Man/The Clock Strikes Twelve (78) 40
60	London HLM 9035	Say Man, Back Again/She's Alright 75
60	London HLM 9112	Road Runner/My Story 50
62	Pye Intl. 7N 25165	You Can't Judge A Book By The Cover/I Can Tell 30
63	Pye Intl. 7N 25193	Who Do You Love?/The Twister 20
63	Pye Intl. 7N 25210	Bo Diddley/Detour 20
63	Pye Intl. 7N 25216	You Can't Judge A Book By The Cover/I Can Tell (reissue) 10
63	Pye Intl. 7N 25217	Pretty Thing/Road Runner 15
63	Pye Intl. 7N 25227	Bo Diddley Is A Lover/Doin' The Jaguar 15
64	Pye Intl. 7N 25235	Memphis/Monkey Diddle 15
64	Pye Intl. 7N 25243	Mona/Gimme Gimme 18
64	Pye Intl. 7N 25258	Mama Keep Your Big Mouth Shut/Jo-Ann 15
65	Chess CRS 8000	Hey Good Lookin'/You Ain't Bad (As You Claim To Be) 15
65	Chess CRS 8014	Somebody Beat Me/Mush Mouth Millie 18
65	Chess CRS 8021	Let The Kids Dance/Let Me Pass 15
66	Chess CRS 8026	500% More Man/Stop My Monkey 15
66	Chess CRS 8036	We're Gonna Get Married/Easy 15
67	Chess CRS 8053	Ooh Baby/Back To School 15
67	Chess CRS 8057	Wrecking My Love Life/Boo-Ga-Loo Before You Go 20
68	Chess CRS 8078	Another Sugar Daddy/I'm High Again 10
69	Chess CRS 8088	Bo Diddley 1969/Soul Train 12
72	Chess 6145 002	I Said Shut Up Woman/I Love You More Than You'll Ever Know 5
56	London RE-U 1054	RHYTHM AND BLUES WITH BO DIDDLEY (EP, gold label lettering) 200
63	Pye Intl. NEP 44014	HEY! BO DIDDLEY (EP) 25
64	Pye Intl. NEP 44019	THE STORY OF BO DIDDLEY (EP) 25
64	Pye Intl. NEP 44031	BO DIDDLEY IS A LUMBERJACK (EP) 25
64	Pye Intl. NEP 44036	DIDDLING (EP) 25
65	Chess CRE 6008	I'M A MAN (EP) 25
66	Chess CRE 6023	ROOSTER STEW (EP) 25
59	London HA-M 2230	GO BO DIDDLEY (LP) 400
62	Pye Jazz NJL 33	BO DIDDLEY IS A GUNSLINGER (LP) 40
63	Pye Intl. NPL 28025	HEY! BO DIDDLEY (LP) 30
63	Pye Intl. NPL 28026	BO DIDDLEY (LP) 30

MINT VALUE £

63	Pye Intl. NPL 28029	BO DIDDLEY RIDES AGAIN (LP)	30
63	Pye Intl. NPL 28032	BO DIDDLEY'S BEACH PARTY (LP)	30
64	Pye Intl. NPL 28034	BO DIDDLEY IN THE SPOTLIGHT (LP)	30
64	Pye Intl. NPL 28049	16 ALL-TIME HITS (LP)	20
64	Chess CRL 4002	HEY GOOD LOOKIN' (LP)	20
65	Chess CRL 4507	LET ME PASS (LP)	25
67	Chess CRL 4525	THE ORIGINATOR (LP)	25
67	Marble Arch MAL 751	SURFIN' WITH BO DIDDLEY (LP)	15
68	Chess CRL 4529	SUPER BLUES (LP, with Muddy Waters & Little Walter)	40
68	Chess CRL 4537	THE SUPER SUPER BLUES BAND (LP, with Muddy Waters & Howlin' Wolf)	40
71	Chess 6310107	ANOTHER DIMENSION (LP)	20
73	Chess 6499 476	THE LONDON SESSIONS (LP)	12

(see also Chuck Berry & Bo Diddley)

DIDDY MEN
| 65 | Columbia DB 7782 | The Song Of The Diddy Men/Hello Doddy (Hello Dolly) | 5 |

DIDJITS
| 95 | Touch & Go RCRPA 11 | Pigs (1-sided white label) | 5 |

DIE ELECTRIC EELS
| 78 | Rough Trade RT 008 | Agitated/Cyclotron (p/s) | 15 |

DIE LAUGHING
| 80 | Ocean OC 003 | Hard Living Man/You Got The Power (p/s) | 50 |

DIESEL M
| 94 | Choci's Chewns CCB 001 | M for multiple (12", blue vinyl, 666 only) | 25 |
| 95 | Choci's Chewns DDL 001 | M For Mangoes (12", red vinyl, 666 only) | 25 |

(see also Mμ-Ziq)

MARLENE DIETRICH
52	Columbia SCM 5010	Too Old To Cut The Mustard/Good For Nothing (with Rosemary Clooney)	15
57	London HLD 8492	Near You/Another Spring, Another Love	12
65	HMV POP 1379	Where Have All The Flowers Gone?/Blowin' In The Wind	5
57	HMV 7EG 8257	MARLENE DIETRICH IN 'THE BLUE ANGEL' (EP)	15
58	London RED 1146	MARLENE DIETRICH (EP)	10
53	Brunswick LA 8591	SOUVENIR ALBUM (10" LP)	20
54	Philips BBR 8006	AT THE CAFÉ DE PARIS (10" LP, introduced by Noel Coward)	20
59	Philips BBL 7322	LILI MARLENE (LP)	15
60	Philips BBL 7386	DIETRICH IN RIO (LP, also stereo SBBL 571)	15
63	HMV CLP 1659	RETURNS TO GERMANY (LP)	15

(see also Rosemary Clooney)

DIF JUZ
81	4AD BAD 109	HU/RE/MI/CS (12" EP)	10
81	4AD BAD 116	VIBRATING AIR: Heset/Diselt/Gunet/Soarn (12" EP)	15
83	Red Flame RFM 24	WHO SAYS SO (LP)	12

DIGA RHYTHM BAND
| 76 | United Artists UAG 29975 | DIGA RHYTHM BAND (LP) | 25 |

(see also Grateful Dead, Mickey Hart, Jerry Garcia)

RICHARD DIGANCE & FRIENDS
| 78 | Chrysalis CHR 1187 | AT THE Q.E.H. (LP) | 12 |

STEVE DIGGLE
| 80 | Faulty Products FEP 7000 | Fifty Years Of Comparative Wealth/Shut Out The Light/ Here Comes The Fire Brigade (unreleased) | 0 |

(see also Buzzcocks, Flag Of Convenience)

DIGITAL MYSTIKS & LEOFAH
| 04 | DMZ DMZ 001 | Twisup/B/Chainba (with Loefah) (12" white labels) | 45 |
| 04 | DMZ DMZ 002 | Lost City/Jah Fire/Horror Show/Dread Commands (EP) | 25 |

DIGITAL MYSTIKZ
04	Big Apple BAM 004	Pathways/Ugly/Mawo Dub/Da Wrath (12")	20
05	DMZ DMZ 005	Neverland/Struck (12")	25
06	DMZ DMZ 005	Haunted/Anti War Dub (12")	60
06	DMZ DMZ 008	Ancient Memories/Ancient Memories (Skream Remix) (12")	25
10	DMZ DMZLP 001	RETURN II SPACE (3-LP)	18
10	DMZ DMZLP 001	RETURN II SPACE (3-LP, picture discs, 200 only but no indication on sleeve if you get picture discs or black vinyl!)	40

DIGITAL PRINCESS
| 02 | Mosquito MSQ 019 | LISTEN TO ME TENDER (12" EP) | 8 |

DILLARD & CLARK
69	A&M AMS 764	Radio Song/Why Not Your Baby	40
69	A&M AMLS 939	THE FANTASTIC EXPEDITION OF DILLARD & CLARK (LP)	18
69	A&M AMLS 966	THROUGH THE MORNING, THROUGHTHENIGHT (LP)	18

(see also Gene Clark, Byrds, Dillards)

MOSES & JOSHUA (DILLARD)
67	Stateside SS 2059	My Elusive Dreams/What's Better Than Love (as Moses & Joshua Dillard)	25
67	Stateside SS 2059	My Elusive Dreams/What's Better Than Love (as Moses & Joshua Dillard) (DJ Copy)	40
68	Bell BELL 1018	Get Out Of My Heart/They Don't Want Us Together (as Moses & Joshua)	20
72	Mojo 2092 054	My Elusive Dreams/Get Out Of My Heart	15

DILLARDS
65	Capitol CL 15420	Nobody Knows/Ebo Walker	8
69	Elektra EKSN 45048	Reason To Believe/Nobody Knows	6
69	Elektra EKSN 45062	She Sang Hymns Out Of Tune/Single Saddle	5
69	Elektra EKSN 45081	Rainmaker/West Montana Hanna	5
66	Bounty BY 6019	BACK PORCH BLUEGRASS (LP)	20
68	Elektra EKS 7265	LIVE!!! ALMOST!!! (LP)	15
68	Elektra EKS 74035	WHEATSHEAF SUITE (LP)	12
70	Elektra EKS 74054	COPPERFIELDS (LP)	12

(see also Dillard & Clark)

DILLINGER

73	Duke DU 149	Headquarters (as Dellenger)/CHENLEY DUFFAS: Black Girl In My Bed	10
73	Downtown DT 512	Tighten Up Skank/Middle East Rock	20
76	Black Swan WIP 6355	Bionic Dread/Eastman Skank	10
79	Island ISL 976	Cokane In My Brain/Power	5
77	Black Swan WIP 6380	Natty BSc/Buckingham Palace	10
77	Black Swan WIP 6416	Cocaine In My Brain/Buckingham Palave/Ragnampiza	10
77	Black Swan BS 7	Cocaine In My Brain/Buckingham Palace/Ragnampiza (12")	20
79	Jamaica Sound JSD 921	Dread Call Fred/Lamb's Bread (let go the dread) (12", with Sugar Minott)	8
76	Black Swan ILPS 9455	BIONIC DREAD (LP)	50
76	Black SwanILPS9385	CB200 (LP)	15
77	Magnum DEAD 1001	TALKIN' BLUES (LP)	50
77	Magnum BB27	TALKIN' BLUES (LP, reissue)	20
77	Third World TWS 919	TOP RANKING (LP)	20

(see also David Isaacs)

DILLINGER V TRINITY

78	Burning Sounds BSLP 1003	CLASH (LP)	35

TODD DILLINGHAM

95	Woronzow WOO 25	SGT. KIPPER (2-LP)	15

DILLINJA

93	Cybotron DILL 01	Steal The Way/Forever Fierce (1-sided 12")	20
93	Cybotron DILL 03	From Beyond/Ride It Hard (1-sided 12")	20
93	Cybotron DILL 04	Sine/Dark Science (1-sided 12")	30
93	Tough Toonz TT 02	DILLINJA EP (12", promo only, four untitled tracks)	20
93	Wave Form DIL 08	TEST [2] EP (12", as Dillinger)	15
94	Deadly Vinyl D2	Deadly Ceremonies/Sovergin Melody (12")	30
94	Deadly Vinyl D3	Deadly Deep Subs/Calculus Beats (12")	30
94	Logic Productions DM 003	You Don't Know (Remix)/Heavenly Bass (12")	15
94	Deadly Vinyl DIL 06	MAJESTIC B-LINE EP (12")	12
94	IQ IQ 001	3.01 In The Morning/Catch The Vibe (12", as Dillinja And Mr E)	10
94	Logic Productions DM 001	Moods/Deep Love (Remix) (12", as Dillinja And Mystery)	12
94	Logic Productions DM 002	You Don't Know/Warrior (12")	10
94	Heavyweight HW 003	VOL 3 (10", two untitled tracks, as Dillinja And Ruffkut)	12
94	JA 1	South Side (Riffin Mix)/Stompers Delight (12")	8
95	Deadly Vinyl D4	Deadly Deep Subs (Remix)/Perfect Match (12")	12
95	Philly Blunt PB 005	Muthaf*cka/Sky (12")	12
95	Metalheadz MET 006	The Angel Fell/Ja Know Ya Big/Brutal Bass (12")	8

(See also Cybotron featuring Dillinja)

PHYLLIS DILLON

66	Doctor Bird DB 1061	Don't Stay Away (as Phillis Dillon)/TOMMY McCOOK & SUPERSONICS: What Now	60
67	Trojan TR 006	This Is A Lovely Way/Thing Of The Past (as Phyllis Dellon)	60
67	Treasure Isle TI 7003	This Is A Lovely Way/Thing Of The Past	25
67	Treasure Isle TI 7015	Perfidia/It's Rocking Time	40
68	Treasure Isle TI 7041	I Wear This Ring/Don't Touch Me Tomato	15
69	Trojan TR 651	Love Is All I Had/Boys And Girls Reggae (as Phillis Dylon)	50
69	Trojan TR 671	The Right Track/TOMMY McCOOK & SUPERSONICS: Moonshot	15
69	Trojan TR 686	Lipstick On Your Collar (as Phillis Dillon)/TOMMY McCOOK & SUPERSONICS: Tribute To Rameses	12
70	Duke Reid DR 2508	This Is Me/Skabuvie (act. "If Your Name Is Andy"/"Ska Vovi" by Dorothy Reid)	12
70	Duke DU 76	Walk Through This World/The Rooster	8
71	Treasure Isle TI 7058	One Life To Live, One Love To Give/TOMMY McCOOK: My Best Dress	15
71	Treasure Isle TI 7070	Midnight Confession/TOMMY McCOOK & SOUL SYNDICATE: Version	15
72	Sioux SI 009	In The Ghetto/NYAH EARTH: Knight Of The Long Knives	20
72	Trojan TRL 41	ONE LIFE TO GIVE (LP)	45

DIMENSIONALS

53	London L 1217	Sleepy Time Gal/DON BAKER/DIMENSIONALS: Drinkin' Pop-Sodee Odee (78)	15

DIMENSIONS

65	Parlophone R 5294	Tears On My Pillow/You Don't Have To Whisper	35

DIMPLES

66	Decca F 12537	The Love Of A Lifetime/My Heart Is Tied To You	40

(see also Gospel Garden, Amazing Blondel)

DIMPLES & EDDIE WITH RICO'S COMBO

62	Planetone RC 3	Fleet Street/Good Bye World	20

D INFLUENCE

90s	Acid Jazz JAZID 30T	I'm The One (12", p/s)	15

DINGER

85	Face Value FVRA 221	Air Of Mystery/I Love To Love (no p/s)	35

(see also Erasure)

DINGLE BROTHERS

71	Dynamic DYN 418	You Don't Know/CABLES: Rich Man, Poor Man	6

MARK DINNING

60	MGM MGM 1053	Teen Angel/Bye Now Baby	10
60	MGM MGM 1069	You Win Again/A Star Is Born (A Love Is Dead)	6
60	MGM MGM 1101	The Lovin' Touch/Come Back To Me (My Love)	6
61	MGM MGM 1125	Top Forty, News, Weather And Sport/Suddenly	15
62	MGM MGM 1148	In A Matter Of Moments/What Will My Mary Say	5
62	MGM MGM 1155	All Of This For Sally/The Pickup	7
65	Hickory 45-1293	Dial Al 1-4883/I'm Glad We Fell In Love	5

DINNING SISTERS

55	London HLF 8179	Drifting And Dreaming/Truly	20
56	London HLF 8218	Hold Me Tight/Uncle Joe	20

(see also Tennessee Ernie Ford)

DINO
65	RCA 1494	Now I Know/Te Lo Hegli Occhi	6

DINO, DESI & BILLY
65	Reprise R 20367	I'm A Fool/So Many Ways	12
66	Reprise R 23047	Not The Loving Kind/Chimes Of Freedom	12

KENNY DINO
61	HMV POP 960	Your Ma Said You Cried In Your Sleep Last Night/Dream A Girl	15

DINOSAUR JR
88	Blast First BFFP 30	Freak Scene (censored)/Keep The Glove (plain white labels, no p/s, promo only)	5
89	Blast First BFFP 47CD	Just Like Heaven/Throw Down/Chunks (A Last Rites Tune)/Freak Scene (Uncensored Version)/Keep The Glove (CD, picture disc)	10
97	Trade 2 TRDSC 009	I'm Insane (2000 copies pressed)	5
06	Blast first PIL 0713	Been There All The Time/Back To Your Heart	6
89	Blast first BFFP 31	BUG (LP)	15
91	Blanco Y Negro BYN 24	GREEN MIND (LP)	15
93	Blanco Y Negro BYN 28	WHERE YOU BEEN (LP)	15
94	Blanco Y Negro 4509 96933-1	WITHOUT A SOUND (LP)	15

DINOSAUR L
86	City Beat CBE 1205	Go Bang! 5/Clean On YOur Bean 1 (12", p/s)	10
88	City Beat CBX 1205	Dinosaur L Bangs Again/Go Bang (Original Version) (12")	8

DIO
75	Purple PUR 128	Sitting In A Dream (as Ronnie Dio featuring Roger Glover & Guests)/ JOHN LAWTON: Little Chalk Blue	15
83	Vertigo DIOP 2	Rainbow In The Dark/Stand Up And Shout (live) (picture disc)	7
84	Vertigo DIOP 4	Mystery/Eat Your Heart Out (live) (picture disc)	6
85	Vertigo DIOD 5	Rock'n'Roll Children/Sacred Heart (gatefold p/s)	5
85	Vertigo DIOW 512	Rock'n'Roll Children/We Rock (live)/The Last In Line (live) (12", white vinyl, stickered PVC sleeve)	8
85	Vertigo DIOFP 6	Hungry For Heaven/King Of Rock And Roll (p/s, with poster & sticker)	5
85	Vertigo DIOP 6	Hungry For Heaven/King Of Rock And Roll (dragon-shaped picture disc)	8
85	Vertigo DIOW 612	Hungry For Heaven/The Message (12", white vinyl)	8
86	Vertigo DIOP 710	THE DIO EP (10", shaped picture disc)	8
86	Vertigo DIO 712	THE DIO EP (12", p/s with family tree)	8
86	Vertigo DIO 712	THE DIO EP (2x7" gatefold sleeve)	8
87	Vertigo DIOP 912	Hey Angel/Why Are They Watching Me?/Rock'n'Roll Children/Mystery (12", picture disc with insert)	8
86	Vertigo VERB 40	INTERMISSION (mini-LP with postcards & discography, stickered sleeve)	12
93	Vertigo 518486-1	STRANGE HIGHWAYS (LP, on 'swirl' label, with inner sleeve)	15

(see also Elf, Rainbow, Roger Glover, Black Sabbath, John Lawton)

DION (& BELMONTS)
78s
58	London HL 8646	I Wonder Why/Teen Angel (as Dion & Belmonts)	40
58	London HL 8718	I Can't Go On (Rosalie)/No One Knows (as Dion & Belmonts)	30
59	London HL 8799	Don't Pity Me/Just You (as Dion & Belmonts)	30
59	London HLU 8874	A Teenager In Love/I've Cried Before (as Dion & Belmonts)	30
59	Pye International 7N 25038	A Lover's Prayer/Every Little Thing I Do (as Dion & Belmonts)	50
60	London HLU 9030	Where Or When/That's My Desire (as Dion & Belmonts)	70

SINGLES
58	London HL 8646	I Wonder Why/Teen Angel (as Dion & Belmonts)	60
58	London HL 8718	I Can't Go On (Rosalie)/No One Knows (as Dion & Belmonts)	50
59	London HL 8799	Don't Pity Me/Just You (as Dion & Belmonts)	50
59	London HL 8874	A Teenager In Love/I've Cried Before (mispressing as Dion & Delmonts)	40
59	London HLU 8874	A Teenager In Love/I've Cried Before (as Dion & Belmonts)	30

(The above 45s were originally issued with triangular centres, round-centre re-pressings are worth half to two-thirds of these values.)

59	Pye International 7N 25038	A Lover's Prayer/Every Little Thing I Do (as Dion & Belmonts)	50
60	London HLU 9030	Where Or When/That's My Desire (as Dion & Belmonts)	50
60	Top Rank JAR 368	When You Wish Upon A Star/My Private Joy (as Dion & Belmonts)	20
60	Top Rank JAR 503	In The Still Of The Night/Swinging On A Star (as Dion & Belmonts)	20
60	Top Rank JAR 521	Lonely Teenager/Little Miss Blue	20
61	Top Rank JAR 545	Havin' Fun/North-East End Of The Corner	15
61	Top Rank JAR 586	Runaround Sue/Runaway Girl	15
62	HMV POP 971	The Wanderer/The Majestic	10
62	HMV POP 1020	Lovers Who Wander/(I Was) Born To Cry	10
62	Stateside SS 115	Little Diane/Lost For Sure	10
62	Stateside SS 139	Love Came To Me/Little Girl	10
63	CBS AAG 133	Ruby Baby/He'll Only Hurt You	12
63	Stateside SS 161	Sandy/Faith	20
63	CBS AAG 145	This Little Girl/The Loneliest Man In The World	8
63	CBS AAG 209	Come Go With Me/King Without A Queen	15
63	CBS AAG 161	Be Careful Of Stones That You Throw/I Can't Believe (That You Don't Love Me Anymore)	7
63	CBS AAG 169	Donna, The Prima Donna/You're Mine	7
63	CBS AAG 177	Drip Drop/No One's Waiting For Me	7
64	CBS AAG 188	I'm Your Hoochie Coochie Man/The Road I'm On (Gloria)	10
64	CBS AAG 224	Johnnie B. Goode/Chicago Blues	10
65	CBS 201728	Sweet, Sweet Baby/Unloved, Unwanted Me (as Dion Di Mucci)	10
65	CBS 201780	Spoonful/Kickin' Child	5
66	HMV POP 1565	Berimbau (as Dion & Belmonts)/My Girl The Month Of May	15
67	HMV POP 1586	Movin' Man/For Bobbie (as Dion & Belmonts)	10
68	London HLP 10229	Abraham, Martin And John/Daddy Rollin'	5
69	London HLP 10277	Both Sides Now/You Better Watch Yourself (Sonny Boy)	5
70	Warner Bros WB 7356	If We Only Have Love/Natural Man	5
70	Warner Bros WB 7401	Your Own Back Yard/Sit Down, Old Friend	5
71	Warner Bros WB 6120	Close To It All/Windows	5
71	Warner Bros K 16100	Peaceful Place/Sunniland	5
72	Warner Bros K 16132	Sanctuary/Brand New Morning	5
75	Phil Spector Intl. 2101 005	Make The Woman Love Me/Running Close Behind You	6
75	Phil Spector Intl. 2010 012	Born To Be With You/Good Lovin' Man	8

EPs

62	HMV 7EG 8745	SWINGALONG WITH DION	70
63	Stateside SE 1006	DION'S HITS	40

ALBUMS

59	London HA-U 2194	PRESENTING DION AND THE BELMONTS (as Dion & Belmonts)	300
60	Top Rank 25-027	THE TOPPERMOST — VOL. 1 (as Dion & Belmonts, with others)	75
61	HMV CLP 1539	RUNAROUND SUE	100
63	Stateside SL 10034	LOVERS WHO WANDER	80
63	CBS (S) BPG 62137	RUBY BABY (mono/stereo)	25
64	CBS (S) BPG 62203	DONNA THE PRIMA DONNA (mono/stereo)	25
67	HMV CLP 3618	TOGETHER AGAIN (as Dion & Belmonts, also stereo CSD 3618)	30
73	Warner Brothers K 46208	REUNION — LIVE AT MADISON SQUARE GARDEN, 1972 (with Belmonts)	12
75	Phil Spector Intl. 2307 002	BORN TO BE WITH YOU	12

(see also Belmonts)

DION (CAMERON) & THREE TOPS

67	Doctor Bird DB 1101	Miserable Friday/This World Has A Feeling	30
72	Big BG 331	Three Tops Time/UNDERGROUND PEOPLE: Tops (Version)	10

(see also Three Tops)

CELINE DION

93	Columbia 474743	COLOUR OF MY LOVE (LP)	25

DIOS MALOS

06	Full Time Hobby FTH 012S	I Want It All/Asshole (p/s, 500 only)	8

DIPLOMATS

67	Caltone TONE 108	Meet Me At The Corner/Do It To Me Baby (by Lloyd & Groovers)	25
68	Caltone TONE 109	Going Alone/My Heart My Soul (by Lloyd & Groovers)	30
68	Caltone TONE 112	Strong Man/Listen To The Music (by Lloyd & Groovers)	30
68	Direction 58-3899	I Can Give You Love/I'm So Glad I Found You	20
98	Kent 6T 19	I Really Love You/DEBRA JOHNSON: To Get Love	30

DIPLOMATS

82	Exchange EX 1	Memories Of You/I'll Keep Holding On (p/s)	7

(see also Scene)

DIRECT CURRENT MCS

90	Underground Recordz TUBE1	Keep In Step/Gangland Rap (12")	45

DIRECT HITS

82	Whaam! WHAAM 007	Modesty Blaise/Sunny Honey Girl (p/s)	60
85	Direct POP 001	Christopher Cooper/She Really Didn't Care (p/s)	7
80	Bootleg BOOT 004	COLLISIONS AT TEEN JUNCTION (LP, white card sleeve with home made printed front and back, lyric insert)	30
84	Whaam! BIG 7	BLOW UP (LP)	30
90s	Tangerine TANG 9	THE MAGIC ATTIC (CD)	12

(see also Exits)

DIRECTION

93	Detour DR 003	Yesterday/The Kids Wanna New Direction (p/s, 1,000 only)	6

DIRECTIONS

79	Tortch TOR 004	Three Bands Tonite/On The Train (p/s, with badge)	80
79	Tortch TOR 004	Three Bands Tonite/On The Train (p/s)	75

(see also Big Sound Authority)

DIRECTIONS IN JAZZ UNIT

64	Philips BL 7625	DIRECTIONS IN JAZZ (LP)	100

DIRE STRAITS

80	Vertigo MOVIE 1	Romeo And Juliet/Solid Rock	5
85	Vertigo DSPIC 10	Money For Nothing/Love Over Gold (live) (shaped picture disc with plinth)	12
85	Vertigo DSPIC 11	Brothers In Arms/Going Home — Theme From 'Local Hero' (Live Version) (oblong picture disc in stickered PVC sleeve)	10
85	Vertigo 884 285-2	Brothers In Arms (short)/Going Home (live)/Brothers In Arms (long)/ Why Worry (CD, promo only)	30
88	Vertigo 080 130-2	Money For Nothing (Full Length Version)/One World/So Far Away (CD Video)	15
88	Vertigo 080 134-2	Walk Of Life/Why Worry (LP Version)/Ride Across The River (CD Video)	15
89	Vertigo 080 128-2	Sultans Of Swing/Wild West End/Down The Waterline (CD Video)	15
89	Vertigo 080 132-2	Brothers In Arms (Full Length Version)/Your Latest Trick/ Ride Across The River (CD Video)	15
89	Vertigo 080 136-2	Twisting By The Pool/Two Young Lovers/If I Had You/ Twisting By The Pool (live) (CD Video)	15
82	Vertigo HS 6359 034	MAKING MOVIES (LP, half-speed master recording)	15
82	Vertigo HS 9102 021	DIRE STRAITS (LP, half-speed master recording)	15

(see also Mark Knopfler, Notting Hillbillies)

DIRK & STIG

78	Ring O' 2017 109/DIB 1	Ging Gang Goolie/Mr. Sheene (unissued)	0
79	EMI EMI 2852	Ging Gang Goolie/Mr. Sheene (p/s, khaki vinyl)	18
79	EMI EMI 2852	Ging Gang Goolie/Mr. Sheene (p/s, black vinyl)	10

(see also Rutles, Neil Innes)

DIRT

82	Crass 321984/6	OBJECT REFUSE REJECT ABUSE EP	8
82	Crass 221984/7	NEVER MIND THE DIRT HERE'S THE BOLLOCKS (LP)	18

DIRTY BLUES BAND

68	Stateside S(S)L 10234	DIRTY BLUES BAND (LP)	40
69	Stateside S(S)L 10268	STONE DIRT (LP)	35

(see also Bacon Fat and Juicy Lucy)

DIRTY DOG

78	Lightning GIL 511	Let Go Of My Hand/Shouldn't Do It/Gonna Quit/Guitar In My Hand (p/s)	25

DIRTY HARRY

73	Unity UN 573	Big Haire/YOUNG DOUG: Skank In Skank	5

| 76 | Treble C CCC 015 | Djamballa (with Bobby Ellis)/BIG JOE: Rock Up A Zion ....8 |

DIRTY PRETTY THINGS
| 06 | Mercury 9856418 | WATERLOO (LP, with free 7") ....15 |

(see also Libertines)

DIRTY STRANGERS
| 89 | Thrill TH 3 | Bathing Belles/Oh Yeah/Hands Up (p/s, featuring Keith Richards)..................................8 |

(see also Rolling Stones)

DIRTY TRICKS
| 75 | Polydor 2383351 | DIRTY TRICKS (LP, red label) ....30 |

DIRTY BEACHES
| 10 | Italian Beach Babes IBB 006 | Golden Desert Sun/Night Drive (p/s, 300 only) ....15 |
| 10 | Italian Beach Babes IBB 010 | No Fun/No Where Fast (p/s, 500 only) ....7 |

DIRTY PROJECTORS
| 11 | Domino RUG 418T | MOUNT WITTENBERG (LP, with Bjork, 3D sleeve, insert, first 500 hand-numbered with signed print) ....25 |

DISASTER
| 91 | Tone Deaf TONE DEAF 1 | WAR CRY (LP) ....50 |

DISCHARGE
80	Clay CLAY 1	Realities Of War/They Declare It/But After The Gig/Society's Victim (p/s) 10
80	Clay CLAY 3	Fight Back/War's No Fairy Tale/Always Restrictions/You Take Part In Creating This System/Religion Instigates (p/s)...10
80	Clay CLAY 5	Decontrol/It's No TV Sketch/Tomorrow Belongs To Us (p/s) 10
81	Clay CLAY 6	Never Again/Death Dealers/Two Monstrous Nuclear Stock-Piles (p/s) 9
81	Clay PLATE 2	WHY (12" EP) 10
82	Clay CLAY 14	State Violence, State Control/Doomsday (p/s) 10
83	Clay CLAY 29	Price Of Silence/Born To Die In The Gutter (p/s) 7
84	Caly CLAY 34	The More I See/Protest And Survive (p/s) 8
85	Clay CLAY 45	Ignorance/No Compromise (p/s) 6
82	Clay CLAYLP 3	HEAR NOTHING, SEE NOTHING, SAY NOTHING (LP, original issue has "Pay no more than £3.99" on top right of sleeve)..20
84	Clay CLAYLP 12	NEVER AGAIN (LP, red vinyl) 18
87	Clay CLAY LP 24	1980-1986 (LP) 12

(see also Broken Bones)

DISCIPLE
| 95 | Boom Shaka Lacka BSL 004 | Chant Of Freedom/Unhackled (Version) 10" ....30 |
| 69 | Parlophone R 5760 | Cherie Alamayonaika/Caucasoid Junkie ....35 |

DISCIPLES OF BELIAL
| 95 | Praxis PRAXIS 17 | GOAT OF MENDES EP (12") ....40 |
| 97 | Praxis PRAXIS 7 | Lucifer We Praise Thee/Sell Your Soul To The Devil/One God (p/s) ....50 |

DISCIPLES RIDDIM SECTION
| 03 | Jah Tubbys JT 10018 | Roots Workout/Mission Of Dub (10") ....25 |

DISCO DUB BAND
| 76 | Movers MO 1 | For the Love Of Money/For The Love Of Money Part 2 ....30 |

DISCO 2000
| 87 | KLF Comms. D 2001 | I Gotta CD (7" Edit) (unissued, white labels only) ....18 |
| 87 | KLF Comms. D 2000 | I Gotta CD/I Love Disco 2000 (12", p/s) ....12 |

(see also J.A.M.s, KLF, Timelords, Bill Drummond, Space)

DISCO DREAD
| 93 | Dub Jockey DJ 023 | Ancient Vibrations/Modern Dub ....10 |

DISCO DREAM AND ANDROIDS
| 79 | Wake UP WUR 2 | DISCO DREAM AND THE ANDROIDS (LP) ....25 |

DISCO INFERNO
| 91 | Che CHE 2 | OPEN DOORS (LP) ....15 |
| 94 | Rough Trade R 3071 | D.I. GO POP (LP)..35 |

DISCORDS
| 91 | Hangman 41 UP | SECOND TO NO-ONE (LP) ....15 |

DISCO STUDENTS
| 79 | Yeah Yeah Yeah UHHUH 1 | South Africa House/Kafkaesque (no p/s)..15 |
| 80 | Yeah Yeah Yeah UHHUH 2 | A Boy With A Penchant For Open-Necked Shirts/Pink Triangles/Credit (no p/s) ....15 |

DISCO VOLANTE
| 84 | Catalyst Box CBR 001 | No motion/Click Punishment Tank Live! (p/s) ....60 |

DISCO ZOMBIES
79	South Circular SGS 106	Drums Over London/Heartbeats Love (black, white & pink or black, white & green handmade wraparound p/s)...40
79	Uptown/Wizzo WIZZO 1	THE INVISIBLE (EP) 25
81	Dining Out TUX 2	Here Come The Buts/Mary Millington (p/s) 15

(see also Steppes, Fifty Fantastics)

DISCS
| 65 | Columbia DB 7477 | Not Meant To Be/Come Back To Me ....10 |

BABA DISE
| 69 | Gas GAS 118 | Wanted/SENSATIONS: I'll Always Love You..30 |

DISGUISE
| 78 | Chiswick CHIS 107 | Hey Baby/Juvenile Delinquent ....12 |

DISORDER (1)
80	Ace ACE 12	Air Raid/Law And Disorder (1st 100 in custom 'War Book' p/s).....................................200
80	Ace ACE 12	Air Raid/Law and Disorder...70
80	Durham Book Centre BOOK 1	Reality Crisis/1984 (over sized p/s) 30

DISORDER (2)
| 81 | Disorder ORDER 1 | Complete Disorder/Insane Youth/Today's World/Violent Crime (p/s)..............................8 |

81	Disorder ORDER 2	Distortion To Deafness/More Than Fights/Daily Life/ You've Got To Be Someone (p/s) 8
82	Disorder 12ORDER 3	PERDITION (12" EP) 8
83	Disorder ORDER 4	MENTAL DISORDER (EP) 8
84	Disorder AARGH! 1	UNDER THE SCALPEL BLADE (LP, with poster) 15
84	Disorder 12 ORDER 5	THE SINGLES COLLECTION (12" EP) 10
85	Disorder AARGH 2	GI FAEN I NASJONALITENTEN DIN (LP) 15
86	Disorder AARGH 3	ONE DAY SON ALL THIS WILL BE YOURZ (split LP with KAFKA PROCESS)........15

DISRUPTERS

81	Radical Change RC 1	Young Offender/U.K. Solider/No Place For You (p/s) 8
82	Radical Change RC 2	Shelters For The Rich/Animal Farm/Self Rule (p/s) 10
83	Radical Change RC 6	Bomb Heaven/Die With Mother (p/s) 8
85	Radical Change 12 RC 8	ALIVE IN THE ELECTRIC CHAIR (12" EP, with insert) 20
83	Radical Change RCLP1	UNREHEARSED WRONGS (LP) 30
84	Radical Change RCLP3	PLAYING WITH FIRE (LP) 20

TOM DISSIVELT

| 62 | Philips 430 736 PE | ELECTRONIC MOVEMENTS (EP) ....20 |
| 65 | Philips BL 7681 | FANTASY IN ORBIT (LP) ....50 |

DISTANT COUSINS

| 66 | CBS 202352 | She Ain't Loving You/Here Today, Gone Tomorrow ....18 |
| 67 | CBS 2800 | Mister Sebastian/Empty House ....10 |

SACHA DISTEL

| 60 | Philips PB 1040 | Sacha's Tune/Love Is Like A Violin ....5 |

DISTRACTIONS

79	TJM TJM 2	YOU'RE NOT GOING OUT DRESSED LIKE THAT (12" EP) 12
79	Factory FAC 12	Time Goes By So Slow/Pillow Fight (p/s) 15
80	Island WIP 6533	It Doesn't Bother Me/One Way Love 10
80	Island WIP 6568	Boys Cry (Where No One Can See Them)/Paracetamol Paralysis (p/s) 6
80	Island ILPS 9604	NOBODY'S PERFECT (LP, sleeve designed by Peter Saville) 15

DISTRAINERS

| 79 | DJ Records BECK 885 | Say Goodbye/Spies In Your Eyes (no p/s, 300 only).....................125 |

DISTRIBUTORS

| 80 | Tap TAP 1 | TV Me/Wireless (various foldover p/s) ....8 |
| 81 | Red Rhino RED 9 | Hold/Get Rid Of These Things/Wages For Lovers (12", p/s) ....8 |

DISTURBED

| 79 | Parole PURL: 3 | I Don't Believe/Betrayed (p/s).......................................10 |

DIVERSIONS

| 76 | Gull GULS 28 | But Is It Funky/To Make Us Happy.....................................5 |

DIVINE

| 84 | Proto ENAT 118 | You Think You're A Man/You Think You're A Man (Remix)/Give It Up (12", p/s)........8 |

DIVINE COMEDY

91	Setanta SET 008	Timewatch/Jerusalem/The Rise And Fall (12", p/s) 10
92	Setanta SET 011	Europop: New Wave/Intifada/Monitor/Timewatch/Jerusalem/ The Rise And Fall (12", p/s)........10
92	Setanta SET 011CD	Europop: New Wave/Intifada/Monitor/Timewatch/Jerusalem/ The Rise And Fall (CD) 15
93	Setanta CAO 008	Lucy/The Pop Singer's Fear Of The Pollen Count/I Was Born Yesterday (mail order, p/s)........8
93	Setanta DC 001	Indulgence No. 1: Hate My Way/Untitled Melody/Europe By Train (picture disc) 8
94	Setanta DC 002	Indulgence No. 2: A Drinking Song/When The Lights Go Out All Over Europe/Tonight We Fly (handfinished wraparound p/s, stamped labels) 15
90	Setanta SETLPM 002	FANFARE FOR THE COMIC MUSE (LP, with inner sleeve) 40
90	Setanta SETCD 002	FANFARE FOR THE COMIC MUSE (CD, beware of counterfeits)............30
94	Setanta SETCD 013	Promenade (CD, with bonus 4-track live CD) 30
93	Setanta SET LP 11	LIBERATION (LP) 30
94	Setanta SETLP13	PROMENADE (LP) 30
96	Setanta SETLP 25	CASSANOVA (LP) 30
97	Setanta SETCDL 036	A SHORT ALBUM ABOUT LOVE (numbered boxed digipak, with 3 postcards)........15
98	Setanta SETLP 57	FIN DE SIECLE (LP) 20

DIXIE BELLES

63	London HLU 9797	(Down At)Papa Joe's/Rock, Rock, Rock................................10
64	London HLU 9842	Southtown, U.S.A./Why Don't You Set Me Free?........................10
64	London REU 1434	THE DIXIE BELLES (EP) 25
64	London HA-U/SH-U 8152	DOWN AT PAPA JOE'S (LP, with Cornbread & Jerry) 20

DIXIE CUPS

64	Pye International 7N 25245	Chapel Of Love/Ain't That Nice 15
64	Red Bird RB 10006	People Say/Girls Can Tell (some copies on Pye label) 10
64	Red Bird RB 10012	You Should Have Seen The Way He Looked At Me/No True Love 15
64	Red Bird RB 10017	Little Bell/Another Boy Like Mine 15
65	Red Bird RB 10024	Iko Iko/Gee Baby Gee 12
65	Red Bird RB 10032	Gee The Moon Is Shining Bright/I'm Gonna Get You Yet...............20
65	HMV POP 1453	Two Way Poc A Way/That's Where It's At.............................15
66	HMV POP 1524	What Kind Of Fool/Danny Boy 25
66	HMV POP 1557	Love Ain't So Bad (After All)/Daddy Said No 30
71	Buddah 2011 079	Chapel Of Love/People Say 5
65	Red Bird RB 20100	CHAPEL OF LOVE (LP) 60
66	HMV CLP 1916	RIDING HIGH (LP) 50
79	Charly CRM 2004	TEEN ANGUISH (LP)..15

DIXIE DRIFTER

| 65 | Columbia DB 7710 | Soul Heaven/Three Chairs Theme ....12 |

DIXIE FOUR

| 60s | Rarities RA 3 | THE DIXIE FOUR (EP) ....25 |

DIXIE HUMMINGBIRDS

| 64 | Vogue V 2422 | Have A Talk With Jesus/In The Morning ....10 |
| 64 | Vogue LAE-P 588 | PRAYER FOR PEACE (LP) ....20 |

DIXIELANDERS
63	Vocalion V 9209	Cyclone/Mardyke	35

DIXIELAND JUG BLOWERS
54	HMV 7M 223	Memphis Shake/Boodle-Am-Shake	12
54	HMV 7M 233	Hen Party Blues/Carpet Alley Breakdown	12

(see also Johnny Dodds)

DIXIE PEACH
85	Jah Tubby JT 005	Just Worries/Pure Worries (12")	60
85	Jah Tubbys JT 014	Spin Spin/Spin Style (12", with the Offbeat Posse)	40
86	Jah Tubby JT 018	Slaughter/Slaughter Mix (12")	60
86	Y&D YDD 0102	Raggamuffin And Rambo/Ragamuffin Style (12")	40
87	Y&D YDD 0106	Get Up And Skank/LONG MAN AND THE OFFBEAT POSSE: Skank With Me/OFFBEAT POSSE: The Skank (12")	40
87	Y&D YDD 0112	Hold Onto Your Man/Tonight Is The Night (12")	30
88	Y&D YDD 0119	Running Around/Run Come Follow Me Now (12")	30
00	Jah Tubbys JT 7003	Every Step/DISCIPLES RIDDIM SECTION: Step Dub	20
01	Jah Tubbys JT 7008	I Heard Them Bawling/OFFBEAT POSSE: Bawling For Riddim	20
03	Jah Tubbys JT 10013	Sufferers Time/What Am I to Do? (10", with the Offbeat Posse)	30
03	Jah Tubbys JT 10017	Jah Jah Army/Who's Gonna Stop Us? (10", with the Offbeat Posse)	30
06	Jah Tubbys JT 10027	Roots Vibration (with the Roots Squad)/Got To Be Humble (with WD Production)	20

THE DIXIES
64	Parlophone R 5223	Love Made A Fool/Valley Of Tears	15

ERROL DIXON
60	Blue Beat BB 27	Midnight Track/Anytime Anywhere	15
61	Blue Beat BB 46	Mama Shut Your Door/Too Much Whisky	15
62	Blue Beat BB 86	Bad Bad Woman/Early This Morning	15
62	Island WI 017	Morning Train/Lonely Heart	20
63	Island WI 069	I Love You/Tell Me More	20
63	Carnival CV 7001	Oo Wee Baby/Twisting And Shaking	10
63	Carnival CV 7004	Mean And Evil Woman/Tutti Frutti	10
64	Oriole CB 1945	Rocks In My Pillow/Give Me More Time (as Errol Dixon & Bluebeaters)	70
66	Blue Beat BB 337	Gloria/Heavy Shuffle	12
66	Blue Beat BB 344	You're No Good/Midnight Bus	12
66	Rainbow RAI 104	I Need Someone To Love/I Want (as Errol Dixon & Goodtime Band)	30
66	Fab EP 1	I Need Someone To Love/I Want (reissue)	20
67	Ska Beat JB 271	Midnight Party/It Makes No Difference	20
67	Direct DS 5002	I Don't Want/The Hoop	60
67	Decca F 12613	Six Questions/Not Again	15
67	Decca F 12717	True Love Never Runs Smooth/What Ya Gonna Do (B-side with Judy Kay)	8
68	Decca F 12826	Back To The Chicken Shack (as Big City Blues Of Errol Dixon)/ I Done Found Out	8
69	Doctor Bird DB 1197	Why Hurt Yourself/She Started To Scream	18
60s	Carnival CU 7002	Crazy Baby/Our First Love (with Maynell Wilson)	10
70	Gas GAS 148	Something On Your Mind/I Need Love	8
72	Transatlantic BIG 503	Let The Love Shine into Your Heart/In A Moment Of Weakness	10
65	Decca DFE 8626	SINGS FATS (EP, with Honeydrippers)	60
68	Decca LK/SKL 4962	BLUES IN THE POT (LP, with Chicken Shack)	100
70	Transatlantic TRA 225	THAT'S HOW YOU GOT KILLED BEFORE (LP)	25

(see also Chicken Shack)

HUGH DIXON
64	London HA-U 8188	FRANTIC GUITARS (LP)	15

JEFF DIXON
67	Coxsone CS 7015	The Rock/HAMBOYS: Harder On The Rock	35
68	Studio One SO 2051	Tickle Me/ENFORCERS: Forgive Me	50

WILLIE DIXON & ALLSTARS
56	London HLU 8297	Walking The Blues/Crazy For My Baby	1500
56	London HLU 8297	Walking The Blues/Crazy For My Baby (78)	150
64	Pye International 7N 25270	Crazy For My Baby/Walkin' The Blues (reissue)	25

TEX DIXSON
70	Ackee ACK 111	Funky Trombone/Crying Horn	10
70	Ackee ACK 112	My Ring/Here I Am	10

DIXXY SISTERS
54	Columbia SCM 5105	Spin The Bottle Polka/The Game Of Broken Hearts	10

DIZZY MANS BAND
70	Warner Bros WB 8015	Tickatoo/My Love	5

DJ B AND EZM.
92	Industrial Noize DE 001	Can't Beat Ruff Beats/Shockin' To The Break Of Dawn (12", stamped white label)	35

DJ CHEMISTRY MEETS JACK SMOOTH
94	Homegrown HG 015	Alchemy/Freefall (12")	12

(see also Chemistry, Jack Smooth)

DJ CRYSTL
92	Lucky Spin LSR 001	Suicidal/Drop XTC (12")	20
93	Dee Jay Recordings DJX 008	Crystalize/Deep Space (12")	15
93	Dee Jay Recordings DJX 010	Meditation/Warpdrive (12")	20
93	Force Ten FTR 001	The Dark Cryst/Inna Year 3000 (12")	10
94	Dee Jay Recordings DJX 016	Your Destiny/Sweet Dreamz (12")	8
94	Dee Jay Recordings DJX 020	Let It Roll/Paradise (12")	12
94	Lucky Spin STU 01	Untitled (1-sided, white label 12")	8

DJ CRYSTL & SLIPMASTER J
92	Lucky Spin LSR 004	Frantic Situation/Drop XTC (12")	25

DJ CYCLONE
96	Acid Fever MDMA 9612	909 TRAX EP: Trak 101/Trak 3/4/Trak 303/Trak 23 (12")	20
96	Acid Fever MDMA 9613	Innersense (Halfcore Remix)/Innersense (Original Hardcore Mix)/ Mushroom Of Fire/Non-sense (12")	20

96	Acid Fever MDMA 9614 303	Joy Ride/Cycloid Spiral Motion/Circular Motion/Cycloid Spiral Slow Motion (12")	20
97	Acid Fever MDMA 9703	STATE OF THE PLANET EP (12" two tracks, other two tracks by OCTODRED)	15

DJ DADO
96	Steppin' Out IAN 045T	Face It (Club Mix)/(Radio Edit)/(Alternative Mix)/(Status Mix) (12")	15

DJ EXCEL
91	(No company) EDUC 2	Just When You Thought It Was Safe/Breakbeat 1/Breakbeat 2/Breakbeat 3 /Breakbeat 4 (12")	30

DJ FOOD
00	Ninja Tune ZEN12 015/021	Classic House Tracks From The Vaults (12")	10
90	Ninja Tune ZEN 02	JAZZ BRAKES VOL. 1 (LP)	15
91	Ninja Tune ZEN 03	JAZZ BRAKES VOL. 2 (LP)	25
92	Ninja Tune ZEN 04	JAZZ BRAKES VOL. 2 (2xLP)	15
92	Ninja Tune ZEN 5	JAZZ BRAKES VOL. 3 (2-LP)	15
93	Ninja Tune ZEN 06	JAZZ BRAKES VOL. 4 (2xLP)	15
94	Ninja Tune ZEN 10	JAZZ BRAKES VOL. 5 (2-LP)	15

DJ FORCE & EVOLUTION
93	Knifeforce KF 003	Fall Down On Me/The Force Will Be With You/Escape The Feeling/Mine All Mine (12")	30
93	Knifeforce KF 003	Fall Down On Me/The Force Will Be With You/Escape The Feeling/Mine All Mine (12", red vinyl, 200 only)	35
93	Knifeforce KF 011	Twelve Midnight/Lost It (12")	20
93	Knifeforce KF 16	Poltergeist/Perfect Dreams (10", some on clear vinyl)	20
93	Knifeforce KF 019	Perfect Dreams (Citadel Of Kaos Remix)/Perfect Dreams (Original Mix)/Fall Down On Me (Remix) (12")	10
94	Knifeforce KF 028	Perfect Dreams (Vices & Wishdokta Remix/TIMESPAN: Music (Ramos & Supreme Remix) (12", p/s)	8

DJ GOLLUM
96	UK 44 UK44 07	Pleasant Experience/Mystic Fusion (12")	30
98	UK44 UK44 15	The Energy (Trance Mix)/The Energy (Rave Mix)/The Energy (Mix Mix) (12", p/s)	10

(see also Gollum & Gary D, M-Zone & DJ Gollum)

DJ HARVEY
96	Noid Recordings NOID 0066	I Am A Man/MONSIEUR D: HOt Love (12")	20
98	Black Cock Records BK 016	LOVE HOTEL EP (12")	12
00	Black Cock Records BK 017	LOVE HOTEL EP 2 (12")	8
00	Weekend Inc WKD 069	Done Turn Me/Protect And Survive (Fuck Loop) (12")	20

(see also Black Cock, Ersatz)

DJ JINX
92	Music Madness MM 003	Devotion/Paradise Project/Paradise Project (Bounty Remix) (12")	40

DJ KRUSH
95	Mo' Wax MW 033	A Whim/89.9 Megamix by DJ SHADOW (12", stickered p/s, Promo 12" 033)	8
95	Mo' Wax MW 033	A Whim/89.9 Megamix by DJ SHADOW (12", DJ Copy)	10
93	Mo' Wax MWLP 001	JAZZ HIP JAP (LP)	25
94	Mo' Wax MWLP 025	STRICTLY TURNTABLIZED (2-LP)	15
97	Mo' Wax MW 077 LP	MILIGHT (2-LP)	15
98	Mo' Wax MW 088 LP	HOLONIC (LP)	20
99	Columbia 492893 1	KAKUSEI (2-LP)	15

(see also DJ Shadow)

DJ MAXI JAZZ
91	Tam Tam TT047	Through The Mirror (12", promo)	8
92	Namu NAMU1	EP (EP)	12
92	Namu NAMU2	More Of What You Need (12")	8
92	Namu NAMU3	Moving Up (EP)	10

(see also Faithless)

DJ MAYHEM
92	Basement BRSS 008	Damage/Metrix: The Remix/Signal Generator (12")	15
92	Basement BRSS 016	Storm Trooper/Cold Acid (12")	15

(see also Two Dark Troopers)

DJ MINK FEAT. 2WICE THE TROUBLE
89	FON T18	Hey Hey Can You Relate (4 mixes) (12")	25
90	Warp WAR4	Hey Hey Can U Relate (3 mixes) (12")	12

DJ NUT NUT
93	Virtual Motion VM 001	Forbidden Planet/Set My Mind Free (12")	12
94	Production House PNT 058 R	The Rumble (Remixes) (12")	25
94	Production House PNT 058	The Rumble/Virtual Reality (10" with PURE SCIENCE)	8
94	Babylon BR 001	Press UP (VIP Mix)/Press Up (Dub Mix) (12", stamped white labels)	15
94	Hard Step HRD 001	Special Dedication (Ladies Mix)/Bloodclart Hour (12")	20
96	London Some 'ting LS 006	Special Dedication (DJ Ron Remix)/Special Dedication (The Dream Team Remix) (12")	10

DJ PESHAY
93	Reinforced RIVET 1248	PROTÉGÉ EP (12")	20

DJ SHADOW
93	Mo' Wax MW 014	In/ Flux/Hindsight (12", plain sleeve, with obi sticker, with the Groove Robbers)	15
93	Mo' Wax MW 014	In/ Flux/Hindsight (12" picture disc, plastic sleeve, with the Groove Robbers)	20
94	Mo' Wax MW 024	Lost And Found/DJ KRUSH: Kemuri (12", p/s)	8
94	Mo' Wax MW 027	What Does Your Soul Look Like (parts 1, 3 & 4) (12" p/s)	8
96	Mo' Wax MW 058	Stem/Red Bus Needs To Leave (p/s)	5
97	Mo' Wax MW 063s	High Noon/Organ Donor (Extended Overhaul) (p/s)	10
97	Mo' Wax MW 063	High Noon/Devil's Advocate/Organ Donor (Extended Overhaul) (p/s)	8
97	Mo Wax MW 084	Q-BERT MIX: Camel Bobsled Race/(Mixes) (12")	8
06	Gabacradabra CT 010	Gabacradabra (7", 500 only hand-stamped white label given away At door of London Indig02 gig 2007)	30
10	New Futility TNF2	Def Surrounds Us/Def Surrounds US (Neil Landstrumm Remix) (12" promo, 100 only, hand-made sleeve stamped on rear, green vinyl)	30
11	Island ROKK 12	I Gotta Rokk (Irn Mnky Swagger Mix)/Def Surrounds Us (Rockwell Mix) (12" promo, white vinyl)	10
98	Mo' Wax MW 059	ENDTRODUCING (2-LP, gatefold, spine opening sleeve)	15
96	Mo Wax MW059LP	ENDTRODUCING (2-LP, gatefold, centre opening sleeve)	20

02	Island ILPSD8118586981-1	THE PRIVATE PRESS (2-LP)	20

(see also Q-Bert, U.N.K.L.E.)

DJ SIDE PHONE/DJ CYDER CLONE
97	Acid Fever MDMA 9705	ACID FLUFF EP (12", three tracks each)	20

DJ TOKEN PACE & TOXIC KEV
92	Face The Bass FBR 001	Losing You/Dreamers Revenge (12")	40

DJ TOOLZ
93	Ninja Tune TOOL 1	BREAK BEATS 'N' GROOVES VOL. 1 (LP)	12
93	Ninja Tune TOOL 2	BREAK BEATS 'N' GROOVES VOL. 2 (LP)	12
93	Ninja Tune TOOL 3	BREAK BEATS 'N' GROOVES VOL. 3 (LP)	12
95	Ninja Tune TOOL 4	BREAK BEATS 'N' GROOVES VOL. 4 (LP)	12

DJ TRACE
91	Orbital 12 ORBIT 11	Inception/Ain't Gonna Wait No More/Love Dove Sound (12")	20
92	(No company, no number)	Rudeboy Hardcore/Untitled/Untitled (white label 12" with 'DJ Trace' and phone number stamped on labels. A-side samples 'Orinoco flow')	10
92	Orbital 12OUT 997	Teach Me To Fly/Inception (After Dark Remix) (12")	18
93	Lucky Spin LSR 003	Lost Entity (London side)/Lost entity (New York side) (12")	10
93	Dee Jay Recordings DJX 007	Never Felt This Way (One Step Ahead)/Never Felt This Way (Intel Mix)	8

DJ TRACE & ED RUSH
93	Lucky Spin LSR 008	Don Bad Man/Clean Gun (12")	10

DJ TREMA & THE AVENGER
93	DBS 22	Untitled/Untitled (12", white label, "DBS 22" etched in run-out groove)	45

DJ VADIM
95	Jazz Fudge JFR 001	ABSTRACT HALLUCINATING GASES (EP)	12
95	Jazz Fudge JFR 002	HEDZ AIN'T READY (EP)	10
96	Ninja Tune ZEN 1245	AURAL PROSTITUTION (EP)	8
97	Ninja Tune ZEN1251	CONQUEST OF THE IRRATIONAL (EP)	12
98	Ninja Tune ZEN 31/2	U.S.S.R. RECONSTRUCTION (2 x 12")	15

D'JURANN JURANN
74	Dawn DNS 1068	Streakin'/Oh! Janine	10

(see also Paul King, King Earl Boogie Band, Mungo Jerry)

JED(RZEZ) DMOCHOWSKI
83	Whaam! WHAAM 009	Sha-La-La-La (Dance With Me)/Ruined City (with 'Jed' on p/s)	8
83	Whaam! WHAAM 009	Sha-La-La-La (Dance With Me)/Ruined City (without 'Jed' on p/s)	10
82	Whaam! WHAAM 84	STALLIONS OF MY HEART (LP)	12

(see also V.I.P.'s)

DMS
91	Production House PNT 032	Exterminate (12")	15
92	Production House PNT 039	Vengeance/Love Overdose (Remix) (12")	15

DNA
81	Rough Trade RTO 86	A TASTE OF DNA (12" EP, p/s)	15

DNV
79	New Pleasures Z2	Mafia/Death In Venice/Goodbye 70s (foldout p/s)	20

(see also Another Pretty Face, Funhouse, Waterboys, TV21)

D.O.A.
93	Alt. Tentacles VIRUS 120	It's Not Unusual/Dead Men Tell No Tales (yellow vinyl)	5
83	Alt. Tentacles VIRUS 31	BLOODIED BUT UNBOWED — THE DAMAGE TO DATE 1978-84 (12" EP)	8
84	Alt. Tentacles VIRUS 24	WAR ON 45 (12" EP)	8
85	Alt. Tentacles VIRUS 42	DON'T TURN YOUR BACK (ON DESPERATE TIMES) (LP)	12
85	Alt. Tentacles VIRUS 44	LET'S WRECK THE PARTY (LP, with insert & small 'spy' logo)	12

CARL DOBKINS JNR.
59	Brunswick 05804	My Heart Is An Open Book/My Pledge To You	15
59	Brunswick 05811	If You Don't Want My Lovin'/Love Is Everything	15
60	Brunswick 05817	Lucky Devil/(There's A Little Song A-Singing) In My Heart	10
60	Brunswick 05832	Exclusively Yours/One Little Girl	10
60	Brunswick LAT 8329	CARL DOBKINS JNR. (LP)	50

BOBBY DOBSON
69	Punch PH 4	Strange/Your New Love	10

(see also Dobby Dobson)

BONNIE DOBSON
69	RCA RCA 1901	I'm Your Woman/I Got Stung	8
70	RCA SF 8079	BONNIE DOBSON (LP)	35
72	Argo ZFB 79	BONNIE DOBSON (LP)	30
76	Polydor 2383 400	MORNING DEW (LP)	15

DOBBY DOBSON (& DELTAS)
65	King KG 1008	Cry A Little Cry/Diamonds And Pearls (as Dobby Dobson & Deltas)	15
67	Trojan TR 011	Loving Pauper/TOMMY McCOOK & SUPERSONICS: Sir Don	20
68	Studio One SO 2068	Walking In The Footsteps/SOUL VENDORS: Studio Rock	50
68	Coxsone CS 7058	Seems To Me I'm Losing You/GAYLADS: Red Rose	35
69	Blue Cat BS 171	Strange/Your New Love	25
69	Punch PH 12	The Masquerade Is Over/Love For Ambition	10
70	Success RE 906	Crazy/RUPIE EDWARDS ALL STARS: Your New Love	6
70	Big BG 303	That Wonderful Sound/I Wasn't Born Yesterday	6
70	Big BG 310	Halfway To Paradise/Utopia	5
71	Dynamic DYN 426	Carry That Weight/More Weight	5
69	Pama SECO 33	STRANGE (LP)	65
70	Trojan TBL 145	THAT WONDERFUL SOUND (LP)	35

(see also Bobby Dobson, Chuck & Dobby, Bruce Bennett, Ernest Wilson & Freddy)

LYN DOBSON
74	Fresh Air 6370 501	JAM SANDWICH (LP)	30

(see also Manfred Mann, Soft Machine, Miller Anderson)

DOC SCOTT

91	Absolute 2 ABS 001DJR	Surgery (Remix) (12")	8
92	Absolute 2 ABS 006DJ	The N.H.S. EP Vol 2 - The Second Chapter EP (12")	10
92	Absolute 2 ABS 006DJR	The N.H.S. EP Vol 2 - The Second Chapter (Remix) EP (12")	60
92	Absolute 2 ABS 006DJRR	The N.H.S. EP Vol 2 - The Second Chapter (Remix) (12")	8
94	Metalheadz MET 004	Far Away (Fourteen Flavors Of Funk)/It's Yours (12")	20
95	Metalheadz METH 015	Drumz '95 (Nasty Habits Remix)/Blue Skies (12")	15
94	Reinforced RIVET 1256	Last Action Hero EP (12")	15
94	Metalheadz MH 001	Doc Scott/GOLDIE : Unreleased Metal (12")	20

ROY DOCKER

68	Domain D3	Mellow Moonlight/MUSIC THROUGH SIX: Riff Raff	30
69	Pama PM 750	When/Go	15
69	Pama PM 756	Everyday Will Be Like A Holiday/I'm An Outcast	8

DR. ATOMIC

93	Guerilla GRRR42	Schudelfloss (12")	20

DOCTOR BROWN

95	Magic Gnome	ANOTHER REALM (LP, 500 only)	15

DR. CALCULUS

86	10 DIXCD 45	DESIGNER BEATNIK (CD)	25

(see also Stephen "Tin Tin Duffy)

DOCTOR DARK

76	Target TGT 102	Red Hot Passion/Instrumental (no p/s)	7

(see also Snivelling Shits)

DOCTOR FATHER

70	Pye 7N 17977	Umbopo/Roll On	10

(see also 10cc, Godley & Creme, Hotlegs)

DR. FEELGOOD & THE INTERNS (U.S.)

62	Columbia DB 4838	Dr. Feelgood/Mister Moonlight	25
64	Columbia DB 7228	Blang Dong/The Doctor's Doogie	25
66	CBS 202099	Don't Tell Me No Dirty/Where Did You Go	20
68	Capitol CL 15569	Sugar Bee/You're So Used To It	20
64	Columbia SEG 8310	DR. FEELGOOD AND THE INTERNS (EP)	75

(see also Piano Red)

DR. FEELGOOD (U.K.)

74	United Artists UP 35760	Roxette/(Get Your Kicks On) Route 66 (no p/s)	5
75	United Artists UP 35815	She Does It Right/I Don't Mind (no p/s)	5
75	United Artists UP 35857	Back In The Night/I'm A Man	5
77	United Artists UP 36304	She's A Windup/Hi-Rise (p/s)	5
77	United Artists 12UP 36304	She's A Windup/Hi-Rise/Homework (12", die-cut sleeve)	8
77	United Artists UP 36332	Baby Jane/Looking Back (p/s)	6
77	United Artists 12UP 36332	Baby Jane/Looking Back/You Upset Me Baby (live) (12", p/s)	8
79	United Artists	As Long As The Price Is Right/Down At The (Other) Doctors (p/s, either black, blue, brown or violet vinyl, 3 different p/s designs)	5
86	Stiff BUY 253	Don't Wait Up/Something Good (shrink-wrapped with bonus 45: "Back In The Night"/"Milk And Alcohol" [FBUY 56]) (p/s)	5
75	United Artists UAS 29727	DOWN BY THE JETTY (LP, mono only)	12
75	United Artists UAS 29880	MALPRACTICE (LP)	12
76	United Artists UAS 29990	STUPIDITY (LP, with stickered covers & bonus 7": "Riot In Cell Block No. 9"/"Johnny B. Goode" [FEEL 1])	15
79	United Artists UAK 30239	AS IT HAPPENS (LP, with inner sleeve & bonus 7" "Encore EP": "Riot In Cell Block No. 9"/"The Blues Had A Baby And They Named It Rock'N'Roll"/"Lights Out"/"Great Balls Of Fire" [p/s, FEEL 2], with inner sleeve)	15

(see also Wilko Johnson, Lew Lewis, Oil City Sheiks)

DR. HOOK

73	CBS 1037	The Cover Of "Radio Times" (1-sided, promo only, by Dr. Hook & Friends)	20
78	Capitol CL 15992	The Radio/Only Sixteen/I'm A Lamb (p/s)	5
78	Capitol PSLP 314	FOR YOU FROM DR. HOOK (EP, promo only)	15
71	CBS 64754	DR. HOOK AND THE MEDICINE SHOW (LP, plain orange label)	15
71	CBS 65132	SLOPPY SECONDS (LP, plain orange label)	15

DR. JOHN (THE NIGHT TRIPPER)

70	Atco 2091 019	Wash Mama Wash/Mama Roux	12
72	Atlantic K 10158	Iko Iko/Huey Smith Medley	6
72	Atlantic K 10214	Wang Dang Doodle/Big Chief	5
73	Atlantic K 10291	Right Place, Wrong Time/I Been Hoodooed	10
73	Atlantic K 10329	Such A Night/Life	6
68	Atco 587/588 147	GRIS GRIS (LP, plum label, mono/stereo)	35
69	Atco 228 018	BABYLON (LP, plum label)	22
70	Atco 2400 015	REMEDIES (LP, plum label)	20
71	Atlantic 2400 161	THE SUN, MOON AND HERBS (LP, plum label, gatefold sleeve with insert)	25
72	Atlantic K 40384	GUMBO (LP, green & orange label, gatefold sleeve)	15
72	Atlantic K 40168	GRIS GRIS (LP, reissue, green & orange label)	15
72	Atlantic K 40250	THE SUN, MOON AND HERBS (LP, reissue, green & orange label, gatefold sleeve with insert)	15
73	Atco K 50017	IN THE RIGHT PLACE (LP, U.K. disc in U.S. stickered 3-way gatefold sleeve)	20
73	CBS 65659	TRIUMVIRATE (LP, with John Hammond & Mike Bloomfield)	15
74	Atlantic K 50035	DESITIVELY BONNAROO (LP)	15
75	DJM DJSLM 2019	CUT ME WHILE I'M HOT (LP)	20
75	United Artists UAG 29902	HOLLYWOOD BE THY NAME (LP, with inner sleeve)	15

DR. K'S BLUES BAND

68	Spark SRLP 101	DR. K'S BLUES BAND (LP, red/silver label)	120

DR. MARIGOLD'S PRESCRIPTION

68	Pye 7N 17493	My Old Man's A Groovy Old Man/People Get Ready	6
69	Pye 7N 17832	You've Got To Build Your Love/My Picture Of Love	6
70	Bell BLL 1096	Breaking The Heart Of A Good Man/Night Hurries On By	6
70	Bell BLL 1126	Sing Along, Sing Along, Sing Along/Father Jim	6

MINT VALUE £

71	Bell BLL 1149	Muddy Water/Come With Me	6

DR. MIX & THE REMIX
79	Rough Trade ROUGH 6	Wall Of Noise (12")	20

DR. OCTAGON
96	Mo Wax MW 046LP	ECOLOGYST (3-LP)	20
96	Mo' Wax MWLP 046	OCTAGONECOLOGYST (3-LP)	20
96	Mo' Wax MW064LP	INSTRUMENTALYST (OCTAGON BEATS) (LP)	20

DOCTOR PABLO
84	On U Sound ON U 30	NORTH OF THE RIVER THAMES (LP)	20

DOCTOR ROCKIT
96	Clear CLR 411	Ready To Rockit EP (2 x 10", p/s)	8
96	Clear CLR 416	D For Doktor EP (12", p/s)	12

DR. STRANGELY STRANGE
69	Island ILPS 9106	KIP OF THE SERENES (LP, pink label, with black/orange circle logo)	300
69	Island ILPS 9106	KIP OF THE SERENES (LP, later 'palm-tree' label with remix)	100
70	Vertigo 6360 009	HEAVY PETTING (LP, gatefold sleeve, large swirl label; original pressing has machine etched matrix in the run out grooves, beware of counterfeits)	300

(see also Sweeney's Men, Gary Moore)

DR. TECHNICAL & MACHINES
83	Hawkfan HWFB 1	Zones/Processed (1-sided with insert, mail-order issue, no p/s)	25

(see also Dave Brock, Hawkwind)

DR. WEST'S MEDICINE SHOW & JUNK BAND
67	CBS 202492	The Eggplant That Ate Chicago/You Can't Fight City Hall Blues	10
67	CBS 202658	Gondoliers, Shakespeares, Overseers/Daddy I Know	8
68	Page One POF 061	Bullets La Verne/Jigsaw	50
70	Page One POF 176	Gondoliers, Shakespeares, Overseers/Daddy I Know (reissue)	6
69	Page One POLS 017	THE EGGPLANT THAT ATE CHICAGO (LP)	25

(see also Norman Greenbaum)

DR. WHO
76	Argo ZSW 564	DR. WHO AND THE PESCATONS (LP, spoken word, read by Tom Baker & Elizabeth Sladen)	18
79	BBC REC 364	GENESIS OF THE DALEKS (LP, spoken word)	15
81	RNIB	TALKING BOOK (reel-to-reel tape, read by Gabriel Wolf)	20
82	BBC 2LP-22001	DOCTOR WHO COLLECTOR'S EDITION (2-LP, includes "Genesis Of The Daleks" [BBC 22364], "Sound Effects" [BBC 22316], & bonus 7" "Doctor Who"/"The Astronauts" [RESL 451], with poster)	30

(see also BBC Radiophonic Workshop, Century 21, Jon Pertwee)

DR. Z
70	Fontana 6007 023	Lady Ladybird/People In The Street	100
71	Vertigo 6360 048	THREE PARTS TO MY SOUL (LP, gatefold sleeve, small swirl label)	1500

(see also Gorilla Grip)

DOCTORS OF MADNESS
77	Polydor 2058 921	Bulletin/Waiting (p/s)	6

PAT DODD
59	Pye International 7N 25030	Stag Party/Odds'n'Dodds	7

DODD'S ALLSTARS
69	Coxsone CS 7096	Mother Aitken (actually by Lord Power)/What A Love (actually by Denzil Laing)	25

JOHNNY DODDS
53	London AL 3505	JOHNNY DODDS VOLUME 1 (10" LP)	15
54	London AL 3513	JOHNNY DODDS VOLUME 2 (10" LP)	15
55	Vogue Coral LRA 10025	JOHNNY DODDS VOL. 1 (10" LP)	15
55	HMV DLP 1073	JOHNNY DODDS WASHBOARD STOMP (10" LP)	15
56	London AL 3555	JOHNNY DODDS VOLUME 3 (10" LP)	15
57	London AL 3560	JOHNNY DODDS VOLUME 4 (10" LP)	15

(see also Dixieland Jugblowers)

NELLA DODDS
65	Pye 7N 25281	Come See About Me/You Don't Love Me Anymore	50
65	Pye 7N 25281	Come See About Me/You Don't Love Me Anymore (DJ Copy)	75
65	Pye 7N 25291	Finders Keepers, Losers Weepers/A Girl's Life	35
65	Pye 7N 25291	Finders Keepers, Losers Weepers/A Girl's Life (DJ Copy)	50

DODGERS (1)
60	Downbeat CHA 2	Let's Make A Whole Lot Of Love/You Make Me Happy	25

DODGERS (2)
70	S & S SC 002	True Love/TONY SEXTON: Baby I Will Be Yours	12

DODO'S
67	Polydor BM 56153	I Made Up My Mind/Can't Make It Out	30

ERNIE K-DOE
62	London HLP 9487	I Cried My Last Tear/A Certain Girl	25

(see under 'K')

DOES IT OFFEND YOU, YEAH?
07	Private Pressing	LIVE AT THE FEZ CLUB (12" white label)	20

DOGFEET
71	Reflection HRS 7	Sad Story/On The Road	15
71	Reflection HRS 12	Since I Went Away/Evil Woman	35
70	Reflection REFL 8	DOGFEET (LP, white/brown label)	1000
94	Kissing Spell CA 36001	DOGFEET (LP, reissue)	25

TYMON DOGG
81	Ghost Dance GHO 1	Lose This Skin (featuring the Clash)/Indestructible (p/s)	10

(see also Timon, Clash)

DOGGEREL BANK

73	Charisma CAS 1079	SILVER FACES (LP, gatefold sleeve, large "Mad Hatter" label)	20
75	Charisma CAS 1102	MISTER SKILLCORN DANCES (LP, small "Mad Hatter" label)	25

BILL DOGGETT

55	Parlophone DP 411	Gumbo/Tara's Theme (78, export issue)	10
55	Parlophone DP 432	Christmas Song/Winter Wonderland (78, export issue)	10
56	Parlophone CMSP 39	Honky Tonk (Parts 1 & 2) (gold label lettering, export issue)	25
56	Parlophone R 4231	Honky Tonk (Parts 1 & 2) (gold label lettering, later silver)	20
57	Parlophone R 4265	Slow Walk/Peacock Alley	10
57	Parlophone R 4306	Ram-Bunk-Shush/Blue Largo	10
57	Parlophone R 4379	Hot Ginger/Soft	10
58	Parlophone R 4413	Leaps And Bounds (Parts 1 & 2)	10
60	Parlophone R 4629	Smokie/Evening Dreams	10
61	Warner Bros WB 32	The Hully Gully Twist/Jackrabbit	10
61	Warner Bros WB 46	You Can't Sit Down (Parts 1 & 2)	15
57	Parlophone GEP 8644	HONKY TONK (EP)	30
57	Parlophone GEP 8674	PLAYS DUKE ELLINGTON (EP)	10
58	Parlophone GEP 8711	BILL DOGGETT (EP)	10
58	Parlophone GEP 8727	RAINBOW RIOT (EP)	10
59	Parlophone GEP 8771	A JOLLY CHRISTMAS (EP)	10
58	Parlophone PMD 1067	DAME DREAMING (10" LP)	20
59	Parlophone PMD 1073	DANCE AWHILE WITH DOGGETT (10" LP)	30
60	Parlophone PMC 1118	DOGGETT'S BIG CITY DANCE PARTY (LP)	25
60	Parlophone PMC 1124	ON TOUR (LP)	20
61	Warner Bros WM 402	3046 PEOPLE DANCED 'TIL 4 A.M. (LP, live, as Bill Doggett & His Combo)	15
62	Parlophone PMC 1165	BACK WITH MORE BILL DOGGETT (LP)	15
62	Warner Bros WM 4056	THE BAND WITH THE BEAT (LP, with His Combo)	15
65	HMV CLP 1884	WOW (LP)	18

(see also Ella Fitzgerald, Earl Bostic)

DOGGS

71	Chapter 1 CH156	Billy's Gotta Run/Why Do I Lie	5

DOGMATIC ELEMENT

82	Cattle Company CC001/562CUS 1412	Strange Passion/Just Friends (p/s, 1000 only)	15
84	Cattle Company CC002/ SRT4KS128	False Emotions/Not Now (p/s, 1000 only)	10

DOGROSE

72	Satril SAT 2	Paradise Row/Sunday Morning	15
73	Satril SAT 6	All For The Love Of City Lights/All Of The Love Of Each Other	15
72	Satril SATL 4002	ALL FOR THE LOVE OF DOGROSE (LP)	22

DOGS

05	Fallout IS874/986	London Bridge/End Of An Era (Custom printed parcel tape label)	5

DOGS D'AMOUR

88	China WOL 7	THE (UN)AUTHORISED BOOTLEG (LP)	30

DOG SOLDIER

75	United Artists UA 29769	DOG SOLDIER (LP)	20

(see also Miller Anderson, Keef Hartley)

THE DOG THAT BIT PEOPLE

71	Parlophone R 5880	Lovely Lady/Merry-Go-Round	45
71	Parlophone PCS 7125	THE DOG THAT BIT PEOPLE (LP, black/silver label with boxed logo)	500
95	Shoestring BL003	THE DOG THAT BIT PEOPLE (CD, reissue)	25

(see also Norman Haines, Locomotive)

DOGWATCH

79	Bridgehouse BHLP 002	PENFRIEND (LP, with insert)	20

NED DOHENY

81	CBS 9481	To Prove My Love/On The Swing Shift (p/s)	8
81	CBS 13-9481	To Prove My Love/On The Swing Shift (12", p/s)	10

JIM DOHERTY TRIO

65	Decca LK 4684	EXECUTIVE SUITE (LP)	50

DOKKEN

82	Carrere CAR 229	We're Illegal/Paris Is Burning (p/s)	5
82	Carrere CAL 136	BREAKIN' THE CHAINS (LP)	12

JOE DOLAN

67	Piccadilly 7N 35368	House With The Whitewashed Gable/Work Day Blues	6
67	Pye 7N 17354	Tar And Cement/Time Of My Life	6
69	Pye 7N 17738	Make Me An Island/If You Care A Little Bit About Me	5
69	Pye 7N 17833	Teresa/My First Love	6
70	Pye 7N 17891	You're Such A Good Looking Woman/Something Happens	5
76	Pye 7N 45702	I Need You/Caterina Ballerina	5
65	Pye 7N 15902	Don't Ever Let That Little Chance Go By/My Own Peculiar Way	5

DAVE DOLBY

73	Bell 1418	Shine A Light/Your Weight Is Your Mind	6

DOLE

78	Ultimate ULT 402	New Wave Love/Hungry Men No Longer Steal Sheep But Are There Hanging Judges? (die-cut p/s)	30

MICKY DOLENZ

67	London HLH 10117	Don't Do It/FINDERS KEEPERS: (We Wear) Lavender Blue	12
67	London HLH 10152	Huff Puff/OBVIOUS: Fate	12
73	MGM 2006 265	Daybreak/Love War	8
74	MGM 2006 392	Ooh She's Young/Love War	8
79	Chrysalis CHS 2297	Love Light/Alicia	6

(see also Monkees)

DOLL
78	Beggars Banquet BEG 4	Don't Tango On My Heart/Trash	5

ANDY DOLL
62	Starlite ST45 068	Wild Desire/Wyat	15
63	Starlite STLP II	ON STAGE (LP, by Andy Doll Band & Guests)	15

LINDA DOLL & SUNDOWNERS
64	Piccadilly 7N 35166	Bonie Maronie/He Don't Want Your Love Anymore	15

DOLLIES
65	CBS 201788	You Touch Me Baby/I Can't Go On	10

DOLLY MIXTURE
80	Chrysalis CHS 2459	Baby It's You/New Look Baby (p/s)	25
81	Respond RESP 1	Been Teen/Honky Honda/Ernie Ball (p/s)	25
82	Respond RESP 4	Everything And More/You And Me On The Sea Shore (p/s)	15
83	Dead Good Dolly Platters DMS 1	Remember This/Listening Pleasure/Borinda's Lament (p/s)	18
84	Cordelia ERICAT 017	FIRESIDE EP (12" p/s)	30
84	DM 1	DEMONSTRATION TAPES (2-LP, rubber stamped, hand-numbered signed sleeves with insert)	70

DOLPHIN
76	Private Stock PVT 52	Then I Kissed Her/The Glyders	6
76	Private Stock PVT 67	Goin' Back/Think Ahead	10
77	Private Stock PVT 91	Only Seventeen/Take Care Of The Ocean	5
77	Private Stock PVT 122	Imagination Dancing/The Actress	6
78	Private Stock PVT 154	Carry Me Away/Linda Lovelace	6
80	Gale 5	Hey Joe/Dubby Dubby	5
77	Private Stock PVLP 1055	GOODBYE (LP)	12
80	Gale GALELP 02	MOLECULES (LP)	12

DOLPHINS
65	Stateside SS 375	Hey Da Da Dow/I Don't Want To Go On Without You	15

ERIC DOLPHY
60	Esquire 21-123	OUTWARD BOUND (LP)	90
61	Esquire 32-153	OUT THERE (LP)	60
61	Esquire 32-173	AT THE 5 SPOT VOL. 1.(LP)	60
64	Fontana TL5284	LAST DATE (LP)	60
65	Fontana 688521XL	MEMORIAL ALBUM (LP)	30
69	Transatlantic PR 7311	OUTWARD BOUND (LP)	15
67	Xtra 5039	SCREAMING THE BLUES (LP, with Oliver Nelson Sextet)	20

ERIC DOLPHY & BOOKER LITTLE
66	Stateside SL 10160	ERIC DOLPHY AND BOOKER LITTLE MEMORIAL ALBUM (LP)	15

BILLY DOLTON
61	Parlophone R 4733	Winkie Doll/Girls	15

DOME
80	4AD CAD 16	3R4 (12")	8
80	Dome DOME 1	DOME (LP)	20
80	Dome DOME 2	DOME 2 (LP)	20
81	Dome DOME 3	DOME 3 (LP)	20

(see also Wire, Gilbert & Lewis)

DOMINANT FORCE
91	Gangster GAGR001	Criminals/Raptivity (12")	20
92	Ital Juice DOMF 12 002	We're Ready/When We Flex (12")	8

ANNA DOMINO
86	Factory FAC 158	Summer (p/s)	12

FATS DOMINO

78s
54	London HL 8007	Rose Mary/You Said You Love Me	40
54	London HL 8063	Little School Girl/You Done Me Wrong	40
54	London HL 8096	Don't Leave Me This Way/Something's Wrong	30
55	London HL 8124	Love Me/Don't You Hear Me Calling You	30
55	London HL 8133	Thinking Of You/I Know	25
55	London HLU 8173	Ain't That A Shame/La La	10
56	London HLU 8256	Bo Weevil/Don't Blame It On Me	10
56	London HLU 8309	When My Dream Boat Comes Home/So Long	10
56	London HLU 8330	Blueberry Hill/I Can't Go On (Rosalie)	10
57	London HLU 8356	Honey Chile/Don't You Know	10
57	London HLP 8377	Blue Monday/What's The Reason I'm Not Pleasing You	10
57	London HLP 8407	I'm Walkin'/I'm In The Mood For Love	12
57	London HLP 8449	The Valley Of Tears/It's You I Love	10
57	London HLP 8471	What Will I Tell My Heart/When I See You	10
57	London HLP 8519	Wait And See/I Still Love You	10
58	London HLP 8575	The Big Beat (from the film)/I Want You To Know	12
58	London HLP 8628	Sick And Tired/No, No	10
58	London HLP 8663	Little Mary/The Prisoner's Song	10
58	London HLP 8727	Young School Girl/It Must Be Love	15
58	London HLP 8759	Whole Lotta Loving/Coquette	10
59	London HLP 8822	When The Saints Go Marching In/Telling Lies	20
59	London HLP 8865	Margie/I'm Ready	20
59	London HLP 8942	I Want To Walk You Home/I'm Gonna Be A Wheel Some Day (tri centre)	20
59	London HLP 9005	Be My Guest/I've Been Around	40
60	London HLP 9073	Country Boy/If You Need Me	40
60	London HLP 9163	Walking To New Orleans/Don't Come Knockin'	60

SINGLES
55	London HL 8124	Love Me/Don't You Hear Me Calling You	200
55	London HL 8133	Thinking Of You/I Know	150

55	London HLU 8173	Ain't That A Shame/La La	90
56	London HLU 8256	Bo Weevil/Don't Blame It On Me	100
56	London HLU 8280	I'm In Love Again/My Blue Heaven	100
56	London HLU 8309	When My Dream Boat Comes Home/So Long	50
56	London HLU 8330	Blueberry Hill/I Can't Go On (Rosalie)	50
57	London HLU 8356	Honey Chile/Don't You Know	100
57	London HLP 8377	Blue Monday/What's The Reason I'm Not Pleasing You	50

(Originally issued with triangular centres & gold lettering labels; later silver-label re-pressings are worth around half these values.)

57	London HLP 8407	I'm Walkin'/I'm In The Mood For Love	20
57	London HLP 8449	The Valley Of Tears/It's You I Love	20
57	London HLP 8471	What Will I Tell My Heart/When I See You	20
57	London HLP 8519	Wait And See/I Still Love You	20
58	London HLP 8575	The Big Beat (From The Film)/I Want You To Know	20
58	London HLP 8628	Sick And Tired/No, No	20
58	London HLP 8663	Little Mary/The Prisoner's Song	20
58	London HLP 8727	Young School Girl/It Must Be Love	30
58	London HLP 8759	Whole Lotta Loving/Coquette	20
59	London HLP 8822	When The Saints Go Marching In/Telling Lies	10

(HLP 8407 through to 8822 45s were issued with triangular centres & silver lettering on all-black labels; later copies are worth around half these values.)

59	London HLP 8865	Margie/I'm Ready (triangular centre & silver-top)	10
59	London HLP 8865	Margie/I'm Ready (later round centre)	5
59	London HLP 8942	I Want To Walk You Home/I'm Gonna Be A Wheel Some Day (round)	10
59	London HLP 9005	Be My Guest/I've Been Around (triangular centre)	20
59	London HLP 9005	Be My Guest/I've Been Around (round centre)	5

(All subsequent London 45s for Fats Domino after London HLP 9005 were issued with round centres & silver-top labels.)

60	London HLP 9073	Country Boy/If You Need Me	10
60	London HLP 9133	Tell Me That You Love Me/Before I Grow Too Old	10
60	London HLP 9163	Walking To New Orleans/Don't Come Knockin'	10
60	London HLP 9198	Three Nights A Week/Put Your Arms Around Me, Honey	10
60	London HLP 9244	My Girl Josephine/Natural Born Lover	10
61	London HLP 9301	What A Price/Ain't That Just Like A Woman	10
61	London HLP 9327	Fell In Love On Monday/Shu-Rah	10
61	London HLP 9374	It Keeps Rainin'/I Just Cry	30
61	London HLP 9415	Let The Four Winds Blow/Good Hearted Man	10
61	London HLP 9456	What A Party/Rockin' Bicycle	10
62	London HLP 9520	Jambalaya/You Win Again	8
62	London HLP 9557	My Real Name/My Heart Is Bleeding	10
62	London HLP 9590	Dance With Mr. Domino/Nothing New (Same Old Thing)	10
62	London HLP 9616	Did You Ever See A Dream Walking/Stop The Clock	10
63	London HLP 9738	You Always Hurt The One You Love/Trouble Blues	10
63	HMV POP 1164	There Goes My Heart Again/Can't Go On Without You	10
63	HMV POP 1197	When I'm Walkin'/I've Got A Right To Cry	8
63	HMV POP 1219	Red Sails In The Sunset/Song For Rosemary	8
63	HMV POP 1265	Just A Lonely Man/Who Cares	8
64	HMV POP 1281	I Don't Want To Set The World On Fire/Lazy Lady	7
64	HMV POP 1303	If You Don't Know What Love Is/Something You Got Baby	40
64	HMV POP 1324	Mary Oh Mary/Packin' Up	8
64	HMV POP 1370	Kansas City/Heartbreak Hill	8
65	Mercury MF 869	(I Left My Heart) In San Francisco/I Done Got Over It	5
65	Mercury MF 873	What's That You Got?/It's Never Too Late	5
65	HMV POP 1421	Why Don't You Do Right?/Wigs	5
67	HMV POP 1582	I'm Livin' Right/I Don't Want To Set The World On Fire	5
67	Liberty LBF 12055	It Keeps Rainin'/Blue Monday	15
67	Liberty LBF 12055	It Keeps Rainin'/Blue Monday (DJ Copy)	30
68	Liberty LBF 15098	Walking To New Orleans/Blueberry Hill	5
68	Reprise RS 20696	Honest Mamas Love Their Papas Better/One For The Highway	30
68	Reprise RS 20763	Lady Madonna/One For The Highway	10
69	Reprise RS 20810	Everybody's Got Something To Hide Except Me And My Monkey/ So Swell When You're Well	5
69	Liberty LBF 15274	I'm Ready/The Fat Man	5
69	Mercury MF 1104	What's That You Got?/Jambalaya (On The Bayou)	5
78	Sonet SON 2168	Sleeping On The Job/After Hours	5

EXPORT SINGLES

57	London HL 7028	Wait And See/I Still Love You	30
58	London HL 7040	Sick And Tired/No, No	30
58	London HL 7054	The Big Beat (From The Film)/Little Mary	30

EPs

55	London RE-P 1022	BLUES FOR LOVE (1st pressing with gold lettering label)	30
55	London RE-P 1022	BLUES FOR LOVE (2nd pressing with silver lettering label)	20
56	London RE-U 1062	BLUES FOR LOVE VOL. 2 (1st pressing with gold label)	30
56	London RE-U 1062	BLUES FOR LOVE VOL. 2 (2nd pressing with silver label)	20
57	London RE-U 1073	FATS (export issue, plain sleeve)	100
57	London RE-P 1079	HERE COMES FATS VOL. 1	30
58	London RE-P 1080	HERE COMES FATS VOL. 2	30
58	London RE-P 1115	CARRY ON ROCKIN' PART 1	70
58	London RE-P 1116	CARRY ON ROCKIN' PART 2	70
58	London RE-P 1117	BLUES FOR LOVE VOL. 3	30
58	London RE-P 1121	BLUES FOR LOVE VOL. 4	30
58	London RE-P 1138	HERE COMES FATS VOL. 3	30
59	London RE-P 1206	THE ROCKIN' MR. D VOL. 1	30
59	London RE-P 1207	THE ROCKIN' MR. D VOL. 2	30

(The above EPs were originally issued with triangular centres; round-centre re-pressings are worth two-thirds these values.)

60	London RE-P 1261	BE MY GUEST	30
60	London RE-P 1265	THE ROCKIN' MR. D VOL. 3	30
62	London RE-P 1340	WHAT A PARTY	30
64	HMV 7EG 8862	RED SAILS IN THE SUNSET	20
65	Liberty LEP 4026	MY BLUE HEAVEN	20
66	Liberty LEP 4045	ROLLIN'	20

ALBUMS

56	London HA-U 2028	FATS' ROCK AND ROLLIN'..	100
56	London HA-P 2041	CARRY ON ROCKIN'..	150
57	London HA-P 2052	HERE STANDS FATS DOMINO..	100
56	London HA-P 2073	THIS IS FATS DOMINO..	70
58	London HA-P 2087	THIS IS FATS..	70
58	London HA-P 2135	THE FABULOUS "MR. D"...	60
59	London HA-P 2223	LET'S PLAY FATS DOMINO..	60
60	London HA-P 2312	A LOT OF DOMINOES!...	50
61	London HA-P 2364	I MISS YOU SO..	50
61	London HA-P 2420	LET THE FOUR WINDS BLOW..	50
61	London HA-P 2426	WHAT A PARTY...	50
62	London HA-P 2447	TWISTIN' THE STOMP..	50
63	London HA-P 8039	JUST DOMINO..	50
63	London HA-P 8084	WALKING TO NEW ORLEANS..	50
63	HMV CLP 1690	HERE COMES FATS DOMINO (also stereo CSD 1520)..........	30
63	HMV CLP 1740	FATS ON FIRE (also stereo CSD 1543)...............................	30
65	Liberty LBY 3033	MILLION SELLERS BY FATS VOL. 1......................................	15
65	Liberty LBY 3046	MILLION SELLERS BY FATS VOL. 2......................................	15
65	HMV CLP 1821	GETAWAY WITH FATS DOMINO (also stereo CSD 1580)......	20
65	Mercury (S)MCL 20070	DOMINO '65 (mono/stereo)..	15
68	Stateside (S)SL 10240	FANTASTIC FATS..	15

DOMINOES (JAMAICA)

68	Melody MRC 001	Tears In Your Eyes/Johnny Darling...................................	10
68	Melody MRC 002	A Tribute (actually by Ann Reid)/Hooray (actually by Uniques)........	10

DOMINOES (U.K.)

58	Reading Rag LYN 545	Bye Bye Johnny/Yakety Yak..	15

DOMINOES (U.S.)

51	Vogue V 9012	Sixty Minute Man/I Can't Escape From You (78).................	50
52	Vogue V 2135	Have Mercy, Baby/That's What You're Doing To Me (78).....	40
67	Vogue V 212	Sixty Minute Man/I Can't Escape From You......................	30
56	Vogue EPV 1113	RHYTHM AND BLUES (EP, 2 tracks by Swallows)................	300

(see also Billy Ward & Dominoes, Clyde McPhatter, Jackie Wilson)

DON DAVID AND DEAN

64	United Artists UP 1064)	No Need to Cry/Fairy Tales...	10

DON, DICK & JIMMY

54	Columbia SCM 5110	Brand Me With Your Kisses/Angela Mia.............................	15
55	London HL 8117	You Can't Have Your Cake And Eat It Too/That's What I Like....	30
55	London HL 8144	Make Yourself Comfortable/(Whatever Happened To The) Piano Players (That Played Like This)....	15
56	HMV POP 280	That's The Way I Feel/Two Voices In The Night..................	10
55	London RE-U 1043	DON, DICK AND JIMMY (EP)...	30

SAM DONAHUE & HIS ORCHESTRA

55	Capitol CL 14349	Saxaboogie/September In The Rain..................................	10

TROY DONAHUE

63	Warner Bros WB 111	Live Young/Somebody Loves Me.......................................	5

MIKE DONALD & BOB SIDDALL

74	Tradition Century TSC 2	A BUG'S EYE VIEW (LP, 100 copies only)...........................	30

(see also Mike Donald)

MIKE DONALD

71	Folk Heritage FHR 021	YORKSHIRE SONGS OF THE BROAD ACRES (LP, first pressing, textured sleeve with black and white photo)....	30
71	Folk Heritage FHR 021	YORKSHIRE SONGS OF THE BROAD ACRES (LP, second pressing, laminated sleeve with colour photo)....	20
72	Galliard GAL 4020	NORTH BY NORTH EAST (LP)..	20
82	Tradition PRS PR 001	THROUGH PEAKS AND DALES (LP, Peak Railway Society Production)...	15

ERIC DONALDSON

71	Dynamic DYN 420	Cherry Oh Baby/LLOYD CHARMERS: Sir Charmers Special....	5
71	Dynamic DYN 423	Love Of The Common People/DRAGONAIRES: The Dragon's Net....	5
71	Dynamic DYN 425	Just Can't (Happen This Way)/Just Can't (Happen This Way) Version....	5
72	Dynamic DYN 431	I'm Indebted/I'm Indebted (Version)................................	5
72	Dynamic DYN 439	Miserable Woman/The Lion Sleeps...................................	5
72	Dynamic DYN 445	Blue Boot/Blue Boot (Version)...	5
72	Dynamic DYN 452	Little Did You Know/Little Did You Know (Version).............	5
73	Dragon DRA 1017	What A Festival/I ROY & ERIC: Festival Version..................	5
73	Dragon DRA 1018	The Way You Do The Things You Do/Version.......................	5
73	Dragon DRA 1020	Watch What You're Doing To Me/You Must Believe Me........	5
73	Dragon DRA 1027	A Weh We A Go Go/SOUL DEFENDERS: Version..................	5
72	Trojan TRL 42	ERIC DONALDSON (LP)...	15
70s	Dynamic DYLP 3003	KEEP ON RIDING (LP)..	12

(see also Prunes, Satchmo)

DON & DENNY

60s	Loop LOO 504	(Ain't That)Just Like Me/Feeling Groovy...........................	40

DON & DEWEY

64	London HL 9897	Get Your Hat/Annie Lee..	30
66	Cameo Parkway CP 750	Soul Motion/Stretchin' Out...	40
67	Sue WI 4032	Soul Motion/Stretchin' Out (reissue)................................	30
71	Specialty SNTF 5006	DON AND DEWEY (LP)...	15

(see also Dewey Terry)

DON & GOODTIMES

67	Columbia DB 8199	I Could Be So Good To You/And It's So Good.....................	12
67	Columbia DB 8266	Happy And Me/If You Love Her, Cherish Her And Such........	8

DON & JUAN
62	London HLX 9529	What's Your Name?/Chicken Necks 25

DON & PETE
66	Columbia DB 7881	And I'm Crying Again/Time Will Tell 5

DONAYS
62	Oriole CBA 1770	Devil In His Heart/Bad Boy 150

LONNIE DONEGAN
78s
56	Oriole CB 1329	The Passing Stranger/TOMMY REILLY: The Intimate Stranger 10
56	Columbia DB 3850	On A Christmas Day/Take My Hand, Precious Lord 10
59	Pye N 15237	San Miguel/Talking Guitar Blues 15
60	Pye N 15256	My Old Man's A Dustman/The Golden Vanity 10
60	Pye N 15267	I Wanna Go Home (The Wreck Of The John B)/Jimmy Brown The Newsboy 10
60	Pye N 15327	Lorelei/In All My Wildest Dreams 20

SINGLES
55	Decca F 10647	Rock Island Line/John Henry (as Lonnie Donegan Skiffle Group) (tri-centre) 25
56	Decca FJ 10695	Diggin' My Potatoes/Bury My Body (as Lonnie Donegan Skiffle Group) (tri-centre) 25
56	Columbia DB 3850	On A Christmas Day/Take My Hand, Precious Lord (as Lonnie Donegan with Chris Barber's Jazz Band) 25
57	Pye Nixa 7N 15116	Jack O' Diamonds/Ham 'N' Eggs 10
58	Pye Nixa 7N 15129	The Grand Coolie Dam/Nobody Loves Like An Irishman 10
58	Pye Jazz 7NJ 2006	Midnight Special/When The Sun Goes Down 25
58	Pye Nixa 7N 15148	Sally, Don't You Grieve/Betty, Betty, Betty 10
62	Pye 7N 3109	The Comancheros/Medley (export, p/s) 20
62	Pye 7N 15455	Pick A Bale Of Cotton/Steal Away (some in p/s) 6
66	Pye 7N 15493	The Market Song/Tit-Bits (with MAX MILLER) 5
66	Pye 7N 15993	World Cup Willie/Where In This World Are We Going (in p/s) 10
66	Pye 7N 15993	World Cup Willie/Where In This World Are We Going 5
68	Columbia DB 8371	Toys/Relax Your Mind 5
72	Pye 7N 45184	Speak To The Sky/Get Out Of My Life 5
76	Decca F 13669	I've Lost My Little Willie/Censored 5

EPs
56	Decca DFE 6345	THE LONNIE DONEGAN SKIFFLE GROUP (tri-centre) 15
56	Jazz Today JTE 107	BACKSTAIRS SESSION 15
56	Pye Nixa Jazz NJE 1014	BACKSTAIRS SESSION (reissue) 10
56	Pye Nixa Jazz NJE 1017	SKIFFLE SESSION 15
57	Pye Nixa NEP 24031	HIT PARADE 8
57	Pye Nixa NEP 24040	HIT PARADE VOL. 2 8
58	Pye Nixa NEP 24067	HIT PARADE VOL. 3 8
58	Pye Nixa NEP 24081	HIT PARADE VOL. 4 8
59	Pye Nixa NEP 24104	HIT PARADE VOL. 5 8
59	Pye Nixa NEP 24114	HIT PARADE VOL. 6 8

ALBUMS
56	Pye Nixa NPT 19012	LONNIE DONEGAN SHOWCASE (10") 25
57	Pye Nixa NPTs19027	LONNIE (10" LP, stereo) 45
58	Pye Nixa NPT 19027	LONNIE (10" LP) 30
59	Pye NPL 18063	MORE TOPS WITH LONNIE (LP) 15
62	Pye NPL 18073	SING HALLELUJAH (LP) 25
65	Pye NPL 18126	THE LONNIE DONEGAN FOLK ALBUM 25
70	Decca SKL 5068	LONNIEPOPS (LP) 12

(see also Monty Sunshine, Chris Barber, Max Miller)

DONKEYS
80	Rhesus GO APE 102	What I Want/Four Letters (yellow or orange label, p/s) 12
80	Rhesus GO APE 3	No Way/You Jane (p/s) 10
80	Rhesus GO APE 105	Don't Go/Living Legends (p/s) 10
80	Back Door DOOR 006	No Way/You Jane (reissue, p/s) 7
80	Deram DM-R 431	What I Want/Four Letters (reissue, p/s) 5
81	MCA MCA 721	Let's Float/Watched By Everyone (p/s) 10
81	MCA MCA 737	Listen To Your Radio/Watched By Everyone (as Donkees) (p/s) 10

JIMMY DONLEY
57	Brunswick 05715	South Of The Border/The Trail Of The Lonesome Pine 20
59	Brunswick 05807	The Shape You Left Me In/What Must I Do 100
59	Brunswick 05807	The Shape You Left Me In/What Must I Do (78) 20

DONNA & FREEDOM SINGERS
70	Bamboo BAM 53	Oh Me Oh My (actually by Jerry Jones)/JACKIE MITTOO: Gold Mine 20

PAUL DONNER
78	Wildfire WRP 22	Yesterday's Roses - No More Baby/Carolina Feel It Burning (P/S) 6

RAL DONNER
61	Parlophone R 4820	You Don't Know What You've Got/So Close To Heaven 12
61	Parlophone R 4859	Please Don't Go/I Didn't Figure On Him 25
62	Parlophone R 4889	I Don't Need You/She's Everything (I Wanted You To Be) 25
62	Stateside SS 109	Bells Of Love/Loveless Life 25
63	Reprise R 20141	I Got Burned/A Tear In My Eye 35
78	Thunder TD 7801	The Day The beat Stopped/I Got Burned/Run Little Linda (coloured vinyl) 8
79	Pye NSPL 28269	YOU DON'T KNOW WHAT YOU'VE GOT (LP) 20

DONNIE & DREAMERS
61	Top Rank JAR 571	Count Every Star/Dorothy 50

DONOVAN
65	Pye 7N 15801	Catch The Wind/Why Do You Treat Me Like You Do 5
65	Pye 7N 15866	Colours/To Sing For You 5
65	Pye 7N 15984	Turquoise/Hey Gyp (Dig The Slowness) 8
66	Pye 7N 17067	Josie/Little Tin Soldier 10
66	Pye 7N 17088	Remember The Alamo/The Ballad Of A Crystal Man 15

MINT VALUE £

66	Pye 7N 17241	Sunshine Superman/The Trip	7
67	Pye 7N 17267	Mellow Yellow/Preachin' Love	6
67	Pye 7N 17403	There Is A Mountain/Sand And Foam	6
68	Pye 7N 17457	Jennifer Juniper/Poor Cow	6
68	Pye 7N 17537	Hurdy Gurdy Man/Teen Angel	10
68	Pye 7N 17660	To Susan On The West Coast Waiting/Atlantis (unreleased)	0
68	Pye 7N 17660	Atlantis/I Love My Shirt	6
69	Pye 7N 17778	Goo Goo Barabajagal (Love Is Hot)/Bed With Me (with Jeff Beck Group)	12
69	Pye 7N 17778	Barabajagal/Trudi (shortened A-side title & retitled B-side)	10
70	Dawn DNS 1006	Ricki Ticki Tavi/Roots Of Oak (as Donovan with Open Road)	6
70	Dawn DNS 1006	Riki Tiki Tavi (shortened spelling of A-side)/Roots Of Oak (with Open Road)	5
70	Dawn DNS 1007	Celia Of The Seals (with Danny Thompson)/Mr. Wind	6
72	private pressing	The Music Makers (one-sided, paper sleeve, 50 only)	50
73	Epic EPC 1471	I Like You/Earth Sign Man	6
73	Epic EPC 1644	Maria Magenta/Intergalactic Laxative (p/s)	6
73	Epic EPC 1960	Sailing Homeward/Lazy Daze (p/s)	6
74	Epic EPC 1960	Sailing Homeward/Yellow Star (p/s, reissue with different B-side; some copies list both Donovan & Andrew Oldham as producers)	6
75	Epic EPC 2661	Rock'n'Roll With Me/Divine Daze Of Deathless Delight (in p/s)	20
75	Epic EPC 2661	Rock'n'Roll With Me/Divine Daze Of Deathless Delight	6
75	Epic EPC 3037	Rock And Roll Souijer/Love Of My Life	5
77	Rak RAK 265	The Light/The International Man (p/s)	8
77	Rak RAK 265	The Light/The International Man	5
81	Luggage LUG 03	Lay Down Lassie/Love Is Only A Feeling (p/s)	7
92	Silhouette MDCDKR 3	Newest Bath Guide/Moira MacCavendish/Brother Sun, Sister Moon (CD)	18
65	Pye NEP 24219	THE UNIVERSAL SOLDIER (EP, incorrectly lists 'Summer 1955' instead of 'Summer 1965' as date on rear sleeve)	8
65	Pye NEP 24219	THE UNIVERSAL SOLDIER (EP)	8
65	Pye NEP 24229	COLOURS (EP)	15
66	Pye NEP 24239	DONOVAN VOL. 1 (EP)	15
68	Pye NEP 24287	CATCH THE WIND (EP)	15
68	Pye NEP 24299	HURDY GURDY DONOVAN (EP)	20
65	Pye NPL 18117	WHAT'S BIN DID AND WHAT'S BIN HID (LP, some with misprinted Side 2 label)	25
65	Pye NPL 18128	FAIRYTALE (LP, some copies with blank rear sleeve)	35
66	World Records ST 951	DONOVAN (LP)	18
67	Pye NPL 18181	SUNSHINE SUPERMAN (LP)	35
68	Pye NPL 20000	A GIFT FROM A FLOWER TO A GARDEN (2-LP, black or navy blue box set, separate halves with or without taped hinge; with 12 inserts in folder, mono)	100
68	Pye N(S)PL 20000	A GIFT FROM A FLOWER TO A GARDEN (2-LP, black or navy blue box set, separate halves with or without taped hinge; with 12 inserts in folder, stereo)	80
68	Pye NPL 18237	DONOVAN IN CONCERT (LP, mono)	20
68	Pye N(S)PL 18237	DONOVAN IN CONCERT (LP, stereo)	18
69	Pye NPL 18283	DONOVAN'S GREATEST HITS (LP, gatefold sleeve with booklet, mono)	12
70	Dawn DNLS 3009	OPEN ROAD (LP, gatefold sleeve)	30
71	Dawn DNLD 4001	H.M.S. DONOVAN (2-LP, First pressing, orange label, MATRIX: DNLP 4001 A-1 *T/B-1 *T/C-1*T/D-1*T :gatefold sleeve, with foldout poster)	150
72	Dawn DNLD 4001	H.M.S. DONOVAN (2-LP, Second pressing, lilac label, gatefold sleeve, with foldout poster)	60
72	Dawn DNLD 4001	H.M.S. DONOVAN (2-LP, Second pressing, lilac label, gatefold sleeve, without foldout poster)	20
73	Dawn DNLD 4001	H.M.S. DONOVAN (2-LP, Third pressing, white label with pink and blue sunrise, gatefold sleeve)	40
71	Dawn DNLD 4001	H.M.S. DONOVAN (2-LP, gatefold sleeve, without foldout poster)	25
73	Pye 11PP 102	FOUR SHADES ("H.M.S. Donovan"/"Greatest Hits"/"Open Road") (4-LP box set)	50
73	Epic EPC 69050	ESSENCE TO ESSENCE (LP, gatefold sleeve, lyric insert, with sticker)	15
90	Permanent PERMLP 2	DONOVAN RISING (LP, 500 only)	12

(see also Jeff Beck, Open Road)

DONTELLS
| 65 | Fontana TF 566 | In Your Heart/Nothing But Nothing | 50 |
| 74 | President PT 373 | In Your Heart/Nothing But Nothing (reissue) | 10 |

DICKY DOO & DON'TS
58	London HLU 8589	Click Click/Did You Cry	30
58	London HLU 8589	Click Click/Did You Cry (78)	20
58	London HLU 8754	Leave Me Alone/Wild, Wild Party (with Orchestra)	30
58	London HLU 8754	Leave Me Alone/Wild, Wild Party (with Orchestra) (78)	30
60	Top Rank JAR 318	Wabash Cannonball/WEST TEXAS MARCHING BAND: The Drums Of Richard A Doo	15

DOOF
| 80 | Namedrop NR1 | EXIST (10" mini-LP, with booklet) | 15 |

(see also Exhibit A)

DOOKIE SQUAD
| 94 | Dookie DS 001 | 6FT Under/Mad Shit (12") | 25 |

DOOLEY SISTERS
| 55 | London HL 8128 | Ko Ko Mo (I Love You So)/Heart Throb | 30 |

DOOM
89	Discard DISC 001	POLICE BASTARD EP	15
89	Strange Fruit SFPMA 203	DOUBLE PEEL SESSIONS (LP, with insert)	12
88	Peaceville VILE 4	WAR CRIMES INHUMAN BEINGS (LP, white vinyl)	18
89	Peaceville VILE 11	BURY THE DEBT NOT THE DEAD (split LP with NO SECURITY)	18
92	VInyl Japan DISCLP5	DOOMED FROM THE START - THE DEMOS ALBUM (LP)	12

JOHN DOONAN
| 72 | Leader LEA 2043 | FLUTE FOR THE FEIS (LP) | 15 |

DOONICANS
| 87 | Probe Plus PP 23T | THE FISHERMAN'S WAY (12" EP) | 10 |

DOOR & THE WINDOW
79	NR NR 1	Subculture/Fashion Slaves/Nostradamus/Don't Kill Colin/Wurst Ban	25
79	NB Records NB 3	He Feels Like A Doris/I Like Sound/Innocent/Dig/Production Line (white label with stickers & insert p/s in poly bag)	5
80	NB Records NB 5	DETAILED TWANG (LP, blank labels)	12

(see also Alternative TV)

DOORS
SINGLES

67	Elektra EKSN 45009	Break On Through (To The Other Side)/End Of The Night	50
67	Elektra EKSN 45012	Alabama Song (Whisky Bar)/Take It As It Comes	25
67	Elektra EKSN 45014	Light My Fire/The Crystal Ship	20
67	Elektra EKSN 45017	People Are Strange/Unhappy Girl	20
67	Elektra EKSN 45022	Love Me Two Times/Moonlight Drive	15
68	Elektra EKSN 45030	We Could Be So Good Together/The Unknown Soldier	15
68	Elektra EKSN 45037	Hello, I Love You, Won't You Tell Me Your Name/Love Street	10
69	Elektra EKSN 45050	Touch Me/Wild Child	10
69	Elektra EKSN 45059	Wishful Sinful/Who Scared You?	10
69	Elektra EKSN 45065	Tell All The People/Easy Ride	10
70	Elektra 2101 004	You Make Me Real/The Spy	10
70	Elektra 2101 008	Roadhouse Blues/Blue Sunday	10
71	Elektra EK 45726	Love Her Madly/(You Need Meat) Don't Go No Further	6
71	Elektra K 12021	Riders On The Storm/The Changeling	6
72	Elektra K 12036	Tightrope Ride/Variety Is The Spice Of Life	5
72	Elektra K 12048	Ship W/ Sails/In The Eye Of The Sun	5
72	Elektra K 12059	Get Up And Dance/Tree Trunks	5
79	Elektra K 12215/SAM 94	Love Me Two Times/Hello, I Love You// Ghost Song/Roadhouse Blues (double pack)	8
83	Elektra E 9974T	Gloria/Love Me Two Times (12", p/s with poster)	10
91	Elektra EKR 125TW	Light My Fire/People Are Strange/Soul Kitchen (12", p/s, with poster)	8
92	Final Vinyl FV 1/2	INTERVIEW TAPES (2 x 7" box set, with 7 inserts, numbered, 500 only)	10

ALBUMS

67	Elektra EKL 4007	THE DOORS (orange label, mono)	150
67	Elektra EKS 4007	THE DOORS (orange label, stereo)	80
68	Elektra EKL 4014	STRANGE DAYS (textured orange label, inner sleeve, mono)	150
68	Elektra EKS 4014	STRANGE DAYS (textured orange label, inner sleeve, stereo)	90
68	Elektra EKL 4024	WAITING FOR THE SUN (orange label, gatefold sleeve with insert, mono)	150
68	Elektra EKS 4024	WAITING FOR THE SUN (orange label, gatefold sleeve with insert, stereo)	90
69	Elektra EKS 75005	THE SOFT PARADE (orange label, gatefold sleeve, with lyric sheet)	100
70	Elektra EKS 75007	MORRISON HOTEL (orange label, gatefold sleeve)	70
70	Elektra 2665 002	ABSOLUTELY LIVE (2-LP, red label, gatefold sleeve)	25
71	Elektra K 74079	13 ('butterfly' label, compilation)	15
71	Elektra K 42090	L.A. WOMAN ('butterfly' label, round-cornered, die-cut PVC 'window' sleeve & yellow inner sleeve)	30
71	Elektra K 42104	OTHER VOICES ('butterfly' label, gatefold sleeve)	15
72	Elektra K 62009	WEIRD SCENES INSIDE THE GOLDMINE (2-LP, 'butterfly' label, gatefold sleeve)	20
72	Elektra K 62116	FULL CIRCLE ('butterfly' label, gatefold sleeve)	15
78	Elektra K 52111	AN AMERICAN PRAYER ('butterfly' label, gatefold sleeve, with 8-page booklet)	20
88	HMV C 8816	L.A. WOMAN (CD, HMV box set, 2,500 only, numbered with booklet)	18

(see also Ray Manzarek)

DOORS OF PERCEPTION

91	Lizard Nation LN 002	ACID DREAMS (12" EP, includes Jim Morrison sample, withdrawn)	8
91	Lizard Nation LN 001	SO JOIN MR. DREAMS (LP, with inner sleeve and booklet)	15
91	Lizard Nation LN 001	SO JOIN MR. DREAMS (LP, with inner sleeve)	12

D.O.P.E.

92	Spare Beat SBRR 002	When I Was Young (Original Mix)/RIchard's First Trip (12")	12
93	Rugged Vinyl RUGGED 1	THE DOPE ON PLASTIC EP (12")	10
93	Rugged Vinyl RUGGED 3	THE DOPE ON PLASTIC PT. II (12")	8
94	Rugged Vinyl RUGGED 8	Dope On Plastic Pt. III/Dope On Plastic (Original Rugged Mix) (10" picture disc)	8

DOPE ON PLASTIC

94	Wave DJC 001	Wave Dub/Out Of Time/East A Bit/It's A Dream (12")	100

MIKE DORANE & CIMARONS

71	Ackee ACK 144	Penguin Funk/Ad-Lib	12

DOREEN (CAMPBELL) & ALL STARS

67	Rainbow RAI 114	Rude Girls/Please Stay	15

DOREEN (SHAFFER) & JACKIE (OPEL)

65	Ska Beat JB 208	Welcome Home/You And I	35

(see also Jackie & Doreen)

KENNY DORHAM & SONNY ROLLINS

58	London LTZU 15133	JAZZ CONTRASTS (LP)	15

DORIAN

70	Ember EMB S 285	Psychedelic Lipstick/Help For My Waiting	6

DORIS

81	ABCD ABCD 1	Sitting Here Waiting (no p/s)	5
82	ABCD ABCD 3	GYPSY LADY (LP, actually credited to A Band Called Doris)	250
98	EMI/Mr. Bongo MRBLP 010	DID YOU GIVE THE WORLD SOME LOVE TODAY, BABY? (LP, reissue of Swedish 60s LP)	15

HAROLD DORMAN

60	Top Rank JAR 357	Mountain Of Love/To Be With You	20
61	London HLS 9386	There They Go/I'll Stick By You	25

STACY DORNING

74	Scratchy CHR 1070	STACY DORNING (LP, with Duncan Browne)	12

DOROTHY

80	Industrial IR 0014	I Confess/Softness (p/s)	8

RALPH DORPER

83	Operation Twilight OPT 18	THE ERASERHEAD EP (12")	20

(see also Propaganda)

CHRIS DORS

61	Fontana H 329	That's When Your Heartaches Begin/They Called It Love	10

DIANA DORS

53	HMV B 10613	I Feel So Mmm.../A Kiss And A Cuddle (78)	25
60	Pye 7N 15242	April Heart/Point Of No Return	10
60	Pye N 15242	April Heart/Point Of No Return (78)	20
64	Fontana TF 506	So Little Time/It's Too Late	50
66	Polydor BM 56111	Security/Gary	10
77	EMI EMI 2705	Passing By/It's A Small World	5
82	Nomis NOM 1	Where Did They Go/It's You Again (with Gary Dors)	5
60	Pye NPL 18044	SWINGIN' DORS (LP, foldout sleeve, red vinyl)	100

RAY DORSET (WITH MUNGO JERRY)

72	Dawn DNS 1018	Cold Blue Excursion/I Need It (solo)	5
79	Satellite RAY 001	Forgotten Land/New Way Of Life (solo, unreleased; 100 promos only)	6
72	Dawn DNLS 3033	COLD BLUE EXCURSION (LP, solo; gatefold sleeve with lyric inner, lilac label)	30

(see also Mungo Jerry, Good Earth, County Jug, Macon Jug, Katmandu, Insiders, Panache, Made In England)

DORSETS

65	Sue WI 391	Pork Chops/Cool It	40

GERRY DORSEY

59	Decca F 11108	Mister Music Man/Crazy Bells	15
59	Decca F 11108	Mister Music Man/Crazy Bells (78)	15
59	Parlophone R 4595	I'll Never Fall In Love Again/Every Day Is A Wonderful Day	10
61	Parlophone R 4739	Big Wheel/The Sentimental Joker	10
64	Pye 7N 15622	Baby I Do/Take Your Time	10
65	Hickory 45-1337	Baby Turn Around/Things I Wanna Do	35

JACK DORSEY ORCHESTRA

64	Pye 7N 15730	Ringo's Dog/March Of The Gonks (as BIG BAND)	10
65	Polydor 56020	Dance Of The Daleks/Likely Lads	18
66	Polydor 56090	Alfie's Theme/Alfie's Theme Too	30
68	Pye 7N 17501	Soul Coaxing/Elizabeth's Waltz	10

LEE DORSEY

62	Top Rank JAR 606	Do-Re-Mi/People Gonna Talk	25
65	Sue WI 367	Do-Re-Mi/Ya Ya	40
65	Stateside SS 441	Ride Your Pony/The Kitty Cat Song	12
65	Stateside SS 465	Work Work Work/Can You Hear Me	12
66	Sue WI 399	Messed Around/When I Meet My Baby	40
66	Stateside SS 485	Get Out Of My Life, Woman/So Long	10
66	Stateside SS 506	Confusion/Neighbour's Daughter	8
66	Stateside SS 528	Working In A Coalmine/Mexico	10
66	Stateside SS 528	Working In A Coalmine/Mexico (yellow vinyl)	50
66	Stateside SS 552	Holy Cow/Operation Heartache	7
67	Stateside SS 593	Rain Rain Go Away/Gotta Find A Job	5
67	Stateside SS 2017	My Old Car/Why Wait Until Tomorrow	6
67	Stateside SS 2055	Go-Go Girl/I Can Hear You Callin'	10
68	President PT 226	Ya Ya/Give Me You	5
68	Bell BLL 1006	Can You Hear Me/Cynthia	5
69	Bell BLL 1051	I'm Gonna Sit Right Down And Write Myself A Letter/Little Baby	5
69	Bell BLL 1060	Ride Your Pony/Get Out Of My Life, Woman	5
69	Bell BLL 1074	Everything I Do Gonh Be Funky/There Should Be A Book	12
71	Mojo 2066 063	Occapella/Yes We Can Part 1	5
72	Mojo 2093 009	Freedom For The Stallion/If She Won't (Find Someone Who Will)	5
66	Stateside SE 1038	RIDE YOUR PONY (EP)	30
66	Stateside SE 1043	YOU'RE BREAKING ME UP (EP)	30
65	Sue ILP 924	THE BEST OF LEE DORSEY (LP)	60
66	Stateside S(S)L 10177	LEE DORSEY — RIDE YOUR PONY (LP)	30
66	Stateside S(S)L 10192	THE NEW LEE DORSEY (LP)	25
71	Polydor 2489 006	YES WE CAN (LP)	25

LEE DORSEY & BETTY HARRIS

69	Buffalo BFS 1002	Love Lots Of Lovin'/Take Care Of Your Love	20

(see also Betty Harris)

D.O.S.E.

95	Colosseum TOGA 001TJX	Plug Myself In (with Mark E. Smith) (p/s, numbered, 1-sided, 500 only)	10

(see also Fall)

JOHNNY DOT & DASHERS

62	Salvo SLO 1805	I Love An Angel/Just For You (99 copies only)	50

DOTTY & BONNIE

64	Rio R 43	I'm So Glad/DOUGLAS BROTHERS: Got You On My Mind	12
64	Island WI 143	Your Kisses/Why Worry	18
64	Island WI 148	Dearest/Tears Are Falling	15
65	Ska Beat JB 183	Foul Play/ROLAND ALPHONSO & GROUP: Yard Broom	35
67	Ska Beat JB 274	I'll Know/Love Is Great	15

(see also Bonnie Frankson, Eric Morris, Don Drummond, Skatalites, Baba Brooks)

DOUBLE FEATURE

67	Deram DM 115	Baby Get Your Head Screwed On/Come On Baby	70
67	Deram DM 165	Handbags And Gladrags/Just Another Lonely Night	10

DOUBLES WITH GAY BLADES

59	HMV POP 613	Hey Girl!/Little Joe	150

DOUBT

80	Solo SOLO 1	Fringes/Lookaway/Contrast Disorder/Time Out (EP, with no p/s but insert)	20

(See also Carpenter Joe)

SUZANNE DOUCET

68	Liberty LBF 15150	Swan Song/Cry My Heart	12

DOUGHNUT RING

68	Deram DM 215	Dance Around Julie/The Bandit	30

(see also Crocheted Doughnut Ring)

JOHNNY DOUGHTY
77	Topic 12TS 324	ROUND RYE BAY FOR MORE (LP, with insert)	15

CARL DOUGLAS (& BIG STAMPEDE)
66	Go AJ 11401	Crazy Feeling/PETER PERRY SOUL BAND: Keep It To Myself	35
67	Go AJ 11408	Let The Birds Sing/Something For Nothing	50
67	United Artists UP 1206	Nobody Cries/Serving A Sentence Of Life	175
67	United Artists UP 1206	Nobody Cries/Serving A Sentence Of Life (DJ Copy)	200
68	United Artists UP 2227	Sell My Soul To The Devil/Good Hard Worker	30
68	Pye 7N 45551	Witchfinder General/Crazy Feeling	20
71	CBS 7101	Do You Need My Love/Lean On Me	60
72	Blue Mountain BM 1007	Somebody Stop This Madness/Ain't No Use (as Karl Douglas)	10
79	Pye 7N 46155	Choose Between Two Lovers/Shame (red vinyl)	6

CHIC DOUGLAS
58	Fontana H 121	I'm Not Afraid Anymore/Jo-Ann	10

CRAIG DOUGLAS
58	Decca F 11055	Nothin' Shakin'/Sitting In A Tree House	25
58	Decca F 11075	Go Chase A Moonbeam/Are You Really Mine	12
59	Top Rank TR 5004	Battle Of New Orleans/Dream Lover/SHEILA BUXTON: Personality/ Where Were You On Our Wedding Day/BERT WEEDON: I Need Your Love Tonight ('King-Size' 7", special sleeve)	10
61	Top Rank JAR 555	A Hundred Pounds Of Clay/Hello Spring	5
61	Top Rank JAR 556	A Hundred Pounds Of Clay (censored version)/Hello Spring (p/s)	15
61	Top Rank JAR 556	A Hundred Pounds Of Clay (censored version)/Hello Spring	7
62	Top Rank JAR 603	Another You/A Change Of Heart	10
62	Top Rank JAR 610	When My Little Girl Is Smiling/Ring A Ding	5
62	Columbia DB 4854	Our Favourite Melodies/Rainbows	5
63	Decca F 11575	Town Crier/I'd Be Smiling Now	5
63	Decca F 11665	Danke Shoen/Teenage Mona Lisa	5
63	Decca F 11722	I'm So Glad I Found Her/Love Her While She's Young	5
63	Decca F 11763	Counting Up The Kisses/From Russia With Love	5
64	Fontana TF 458	Silly Boy/Love Leave Me Alone	5
64	Fontana TF 475	Come Closer/She's Smiling At Me (as Craig Douglas & Tridents)	8
65	Fontana TF 525	Across The Street/Party Girl	5
65	Fontana TF 580	Around The Corner/Find The Girl	5
69	Pye 7N 17746	How Do You Feel About That/Then	12
69	Pye 7N 17863	Raindrops Keep Falling On My Head/Don't Mind If I Cry	7
71	Crystal CR 7011	All Kinds Of People/Evenin' Rain	7
76	Cube BUG 72	Who's Sorry Now/From Both Sides Now	8
77	Cube BUG 76	Turn Away/Baby Blue	8
59	Top Rank JKR 8033	CRAIG SINGS FOR 'ROXY' (EP)	15
60	Decca DFE 6633	CRAIG (EP)	15
62	Decca DFE 8509	CUDDLE UP WITH CRAIG (EP)	10
63	Columbia SEG 8219	CRAIG MOVIE SONGS (EP)	25
60	Top Rank BUY 049	CRAIG DOUGLAS (LP)	25
61	Top Rank 35-103	BANDWAGON BALL (LP)	20
62	Columbia 33SX 1468	OUR FAVOURITE MELODIES (LP)	40

(see also Bert Weedon)

DEV DOUGLAS
66	Parlophone R5462	What Am I Doing Here/I've Got Lovin'	12

DONNA DOUGLAS
58	Fontana H 158	The Shepherd/I'm Dancing With Tears In My Eyes	5
59	Fontana H 223	Six Boys And Seven Girls/Into Each Life Some Rain Must Fall	5
61	Piccadilly 7N 35014	Tammy Tell Me True/Memory Lane	5
62	Piccadilly 7N 35031	The Message In A Bottle/If This Is Love	7
62	Piccadilly 7N 35042	Matelot/All The Other Girls	6
63	Piccadilly 7N 35111	It's A Pity To Say Goodnight/Do I Know	5
63	Piccadilly 7N 35135	He's So Near/Turn Around	5
64	Pye 7N 15654	Blue Star/Java Jones	5

JACK DOUGLAS
68	Columbia DB 8393	Swanee River/Call Alf (Why Does Love Pass Me By)	8

JAN DOUGLAS
64	Vocalion V 9226	More And More/Walkin' In The Rain	10

JOHNNY DOUGLAS (& HIS ORCHESTRA/COMBO)
54	Decca F 10276	Ballet Of The Bells/Solfeggio (as Johnny Douglas & His Orchestra)	5
63	Speyside SK 1501	Ski Jump/Clementine (as Johnny Douglas Combo)	5
65	RCA 1444	Crack In The World/Time	10

KIRK DOUGLAS & MELLOMEN
55	Brunswick 05408	A Whale Of A Tale/And The Moon Grew Brighter And Brighter	5

LEW DOUGLAS & HIS ORCHESTRA
54	MGM SP 1093	Caesar's Boogie/Turn Around Boy	15

MARK DOUGLAS
62	Ember EMB S 166	It Matters Not/Upside Down	75

NORMA DOUGLAS
57	London HLZ 8475	Be It Resolved/Joe He Gone	25

BOBB & DEAN DOUGLAS
67	Deram DM 132	I Can Make It With You/Phone Me	50

DOUGLAS BROTHERS
66	Rio R 57	Valley Of Tears/CHARMERS: Where Do I Turn	15
66	Rio R 63	Down And Out/RONALD WILSON: Lonely Man	125

(see also Dotty & Bonnie)

HARRY DOUGLASS & DEEP RIVER BOYS
60	Top Rank JAR 352	Dum Dum De Dum/Go Galloway, Go	7

(see also Deep River Boys)

RONNIE DOVE

64	Stateside SS 314	Sweeter Than Sugar/I Believed In You	6
64	Stateside SS 346	Say You/Let Me Stay Today	6
64	Stateside SS 366	Right Or Wrong/Baby, Put Your Arms Around Me	6
65	Stateside SS 392	Hello Pretty Girl/Keep It A Secret	6
65	Stateside SS 412	One Kiss For Old Times' Sake/Bluebird	7
65	Stateside SS 436	A Little Bit Of Heaven/If I Live To Be A Hundred	7
65	Stateside SS 462	I'll Make All Your Dreams Come True/I Had To Lose You	6
65	Stateside SS 480	Kiss Away/Where In The World	6
66	Stateside SS 492	When Liking Turns To Loving/I'm Learning How To Smile Again	6
66	Stateside SS 510	Let's Start All Over Again/That Empty Feeling	6
66	Stateside SS 524	Happy Summer Days/Long After	6
66	Stateside SS 542	I Really Don't Want To Know/Years Of Tears	6
66	Stateside SS 571	Cry/Autumn Rhapsody	6
70	Stateside SS 2003	One More Mountain To Climb/All	6
70	Stateside SS 2018	My Babe/Put My Mind At Ease	6
70	Stateside SS 2047	I Want To Love You For What You Are/I Thank You For Your Love	6
70	Stateside SS 2086	Dancin' Out Of My Heart/Back From Baltimore	6
68	Stateside SS 2119	Mountain Of Love/Never Gonna Cry (The Way I'll Cry Tonight)	10
65	Stateside SL 10149	RONNIE DOVE (LP)	30

DOVELLS

61	Columbia DB 4718	The Bristol Stomp/Out In The Cold Again	20
62	Columbia DB 4810	Do The New Continental/Mopitty Mope Stomp	20
62	Columbia DB 4877	Bristol Twistin' Annie/The Actor	20
62	Cameo Parkway P 845	Hully Gully Baby/Your Last Chance	10
63	Cameo Parkway P 861	You Can't Run Away From Yourself/Save Me Baby	10
63	Cameo Parkway P 867	You Can't Sit Down/Stompin' Everywhere	25
63	Cameo Parkway P 882	Betty In Bermudas/Dance The Froog	10
63	Cameo Parkway P 901	Be My Girl/Dragster On The Prowl	25
79	London HAU 8515	CAMEO PARKWAY SESSIONS (LP)	15

(see also Len Barry)

DOVES

98	Manchester MANC 9	Seven Day Smile (with Jane Weaver)/ANDY VOTEL & JANE WEAVER: Gutter Girl (p/s)	12
98	Manchester MANCCD 9	Seven Day Smile (with Jane Weaver)/ANDY VOTEL & JANE WEAVER: Gutter Girl/JANE WEAVER: You're Not The Only Person That I Used To Know (CD)	15
99	Casino CHIP 003	Here It Comes/Meet Me At The Pier/(Acoustic Version) (10", p/s)	15
98	Casino CHIP 001	CEDAR EP: Cedar Room/Rise/Zither (10", wraparound p/s)	50
99	Casino CHIP 002	SEA EP (10", p/s)	30
99	Casino CHIP 002CD	SEA EP (CD, gatefold card sleeve)	30
00	Heavenly HVN9610	Catch The Sun/Valley/Down To Sea (10")	15
02	Heavenly HVN115-10	Pounding/Satellites (Soulsavers Remix)/M62 (Four Tet Remix) (10")	15
05	Heavenly HVNLP50	SOME CITIES (2-LP)	20
00	Heavenly HVNLP 26	LOST SOULS (2-LP)	20
02	Heavenly HVNLP 35	THE LAST BROADCAST (2-LP)	20
09	Heavenly HVNLP67	KINGDOM OF RUST (2-LP)	15

(see also Badly Drawn Boy, Sub Sub, Jane Weaver v Doves)

NICK DOW

79	Dingles DIN 306	BURD MARGARET (LP)	15

BRENT DOWE

71	Summit SUM 8521	Knock Three Times/GAYLADS: This Time I Won't Hurt You	6
71	Summit SUM 8525	Put Your Hand In The Hand/Miracle (B-side actually "It Took A Miracle Version" by Beverley's All Stars)	6
71	Summit SUM 8530	Freedom Train/BEVERLEY'S ALL STARS: Freedom Train (Version)	6
73	Green Door GD 4061	Reggae Makossa/No Nola (B-side actually by Melodians)	8
76	Student STU 1006	It was Love/Version	8

(see also Melodians)

JOE DOWELL

61	Mercury AMT 1161	The Bridge Of Love/Just Love Me	5
62	Mercury AMT 1180	Little Red Rented Rowboat/The One I Left For You	5
60s	Wing	WOODEN HEART (LP)	12

JOHN DOWIE

81	Factory FAC 19	It's Hard To Be An Egg/Mind Sketch (white vinyl, clear sleeve, with white feather)	15

DOWLANDS

62	Oriole CB 1748	Little Sue/Julie (as Dowlands & Soundtracks)	50
62	Oriole CB 1781	Big Big Fella/Don't Ever Change	100
63	Oriole CB 1815	Break Ups/A Love Like Ours	50
63	Oriole CB 1892	Lonely Johnny (song actually titled "Lucky Johnny")/Do You Have To Have Me Blue?	800
64	Oriole CB 1897	All My Loving/Hey Sally (as Dowlands & Soundtracks)	15
64	Oriole CB 1926	I Walk The Line/Happy Endings	40
64	Oriole CB 1947	Wishing And Hoping/You Will Regret It	80
65	Columbia DB 7547	Don't Make Me Over/Someone Must Be Feeling Sad	40

DOWNBEATS

61	Starlite ST45 051	Thinkin' Of You/Midnight Love	200

BRUCE DOWNER

71	Summit SUM 8524	Free The People (actually by Bruce Ruffin)/BEVERLEY'S ALL STARS: Free The People (Version)	6

ROLAND DOWNER & COUNT OSSIE

68	Doctor Bird DB 1130	Ethiopian Kingdom/A Ju Ju Wah	90

BOB DOWNES

70	Vertigo 6059 011	No Time Like The Present/Keep Off The Grass	35
70	Philips SBL 7922	BOB DOWNES' OPEN MUSIC (LP)	150
70	Vertigo 6360 005	ELECTRIC CITY (LP, gatefold sleeve, large swirl label)	200
70	Music For Pleasure MFP 1412	DEEP DOWN HEAVY (LP, red/silver label)	20
73	Ophenian BDOM 001	DIVERSIONS (LP)	25
74	Ophenian BDOM 002	EPISODES AT 4AM (LP, with insert)	22

| 75 | Ophenian BDOM 003 | HELLS ANGELS (LP) | 30 |

(see also Rock Workshop)

DEIRDRE DOWNES & BROADSIDERS
| 69 | Pye 7N 17781 | Lady Mary/Did He Mention My Name | 5 |

DOWNHILL
| 79 | Bead Records BEAD 8 | DOWNHILL (LP) | 30 |

DOWN HOME
| 86 | Lismor Folk LIFL 7011 | DOWN HOME FIDDLE MUSIC VOLUME ONE (LP) | 15 |

BIG AL DOWNING
| 64 | Sue WI 341 | Yes I'm Loving You/Please Come Home | 45 |

DON DOWNING
| 73 | People PEO 102 | Lonely Days Lonely Nights/I'm So Proud Of You | 6 |

DOWNLINERS SECT
64	Columbia DB 7300	Baby What's Wrong/Be A Sect Maniac	30
64	Columbia DB 7347	Little Egypt/Sect Appeal	15
64	Columbia DB 7415	Find Out What's Happening/Insecticide	30
65	Columbia DB 7509	Wreck Of The Old '97/Leader Of The Sect	30
65	Columbia DB 7597	I Got Mine/Waiting In Heaven Somewhere	30
65	Columbia DB 7712	Bad Storm Coming/Lonely And Blue	30
66	Columbia DB 7817	All Night Worker/He Was A Square	30
66	Columbia DB 7939	Glendora/I'll Find Out	70
66	Columbia DB 8008	The Cost Of Living/Everything I've Got To Give	25
64	Contrast Sound RBCSP 1	NITE IN GREAT NEWPORT STREET (EP)	300
65	Columbia SEG 8438	THE SECT SING SICK SONGS (EP)	100
64	Columbia 33SX 1658	THE SECT (LP)	200
65	Columbia 33SX 1745	THE COUNTRY SECT (LP)	120
66	Columbia SX 6028	THE ROCK SECT'S IN (LP, mono, black/blue label with "sold in the U.K..." text)	150
66	Columbia S(C)X 6028	THE ROCK SECT'S IN (LP, stereo, blue/black label with "sold in the U.K..." text)	200
93	Hangman HANG 42 UP	BIRTH OF SUAVE (LP)	15

(see also Don Crane's Downliners Sect)

DOWN TO EARTH
| 71 | Downtown DT 485 | Under The Boardwalk/Under The Boardwalk (Version) (B-side actually "Double Barrel Version") | 7 |

DOWNTOWN ALL STARS
| 69 | Downtown DT 426 | Everybody Feel Good/RUDIES: Downtown Jump | 8 |

GENE DOZIER & UNITED FRONT
| 74 | Mercury 6167 007 | Give The Women What They Want/The Best Girl I Ever Had | 20 |

LAMONT DOZIER
74	Probe PRO 618	Trying To Hold On To My Woman/We Don't Want Nobody To Come	5
74	Anchor ABC 4003	Fish Ain't Bitin'/Breaking Out All Over	5
75	Anchor ABC 4056	All Cried Out/Rose	5
77	Warner Bros K 16942	Going Back To My Roots/Going Back To My Roots (Version)	8
81	CBS A 1235	To Cool Me Out/Starting Over	10
74	ABC ABCL 5042	OUT HERE ON MY OWN (LP)	15
75	ABC ABCL 5096	BLACK BACH (LP)	12

(see also Holland & Dozier)

DOZY, BEAKY, MICK & TICH (D.B.M.&T.)
69	Fontana TF 1061	Tonight Today/Bad News	5
70	Fontana 6007 022	Mr. President/Frisco Annie (as D.B.M.&T)	6
70	Fontana 6006 066	Festival/Leader Of A Rock 'N' Roll Band	6
70	Philips 6308 029	FRESH EAR (LP, gatefold sleeve, credited to D.B.M.&T)	25

(see also Dave Dee Dozy Beaky Mick & Tich)

DP'S
| 78 | Barn 2314107 | IF YOU KNOW WHAT I MEAN (LP) | 15 |

(see also The Depressions)

DRAGON
| 76 | Acorn CF 268 | DRAGON (LP, gatefold sleeve) | 60 |

DRAGONFLY
74	Retreat RTS 257	Gondola/Almost Abandoned (demo)	15
75	Retreat RTS 261	Driving Around The World/Since I Left My Home	8
74	Retreat RTL 6002	ALMOST ABANDONED (LP)	25
80s	Dragonfly DF 001	SILENT NIGHTS EP (p/s, private pressing)	150

DRAGONS
| 69 | Page One | Heart Transplantation/Hello I Love Maria | 40 |

DRAGONSFIRE
| 82 | Belltree BTR 001 | RISING PHOENIX (LP, with insert) | 20 |

(see also Spinning Wheel)

DRAGONSLAYER
| 83 | Cavalier CAV 017 | Broken Hearts/Satan Is Free/I Want Your Life (Early copies with band name as 'Slayer'. NO STICKER) | 120 |
| 83 | Cavalier CAV 017 | Broken Hearts/Satan Is Free/I Want Your Life (Early copies had band name as 'Slayer', these later copies have sticker with new name – Dragonslayer – covering it) | 80 |

DRAG SET
| 66 | Go AJ 11405 | Get Out Of My Way/Day And Night | 250 |

(see also Open Mind)

DRAGSTER
| 81 | Heavy Metal HEAVY 4 | Ambition/Won't Bring You Back (p/s) | 30 |

CHARLIE DRAKE
| 58 | Parlophone R 4461 | Splish Splash/Hello, My Darlings | 5 |
| 58 | Parlophone R 4478 | Volare/Itchy Twitchy Feeling | 5 |

MINT VALUE £

58	Parlophone R 4496	Tom Thumb's Tune/Goggle Eye Ghee	5
59	Parlophone R 4552	Sea Cruise/Starkle, Starkle Little Twink	5
60	Parlophone R 4675	Naughty/Old Mr. Shadow	5
60	Parlophone R 4701	Mr. Custer/Glow Worm	5
61	Parlophone R 4824	My Boomerang Won't Come Back/She's My Girl	5
62	Parlophone R 4875	Tanglefoot/Drake's Progress	5
62	Parlophone R 4918	I Bent My Assigai/Sweet Freddy Green	5
63	Parlophone R 5057	I've Lost The End Of My Yodel/I Can Can't I	6
64	Parlophone R 5143	I'm Too Heavy For The Light Brigade/The Reluctant Tight-Rope Walker	7
64	Parlophone R 5209	Charles Drake 007/Bumpanology (Bump Head Blues)	8
67	Pye 7N 17269	Who Is Sylvia/I Wanna Be In A Group	6
71	Columbia DB 8829	Puckwudgie/Toffee And Tears	5
73	EMI 2079	Someone Opened Watergate And They All Got Wet/'Ello Erf	6
75	Charisma CB 270	You Never Know/I'm Big Enough For Me (produced by Peter Gabriel)	8
76	Sol Doon SDRO 24S	Super Punk/Someone	8
58	Parlophone GEP 8720	HELLO MY DARLINGS (EP)	10
60	Parlophone GEP 8812	NAUGHTY CHARLIE DRAKE (EP)	12
64	Parlophone GEP 8903	HITS FROM THE MAN IN THE MOON (EP)	10
60s	Music For Pleasure MFP 1310	HELLO MY DARLINGS (LP)	12

NICK DRAKE

79	Island RSS 7	Introduction/Hazy Jane II/Time Has Told Me/Fruit Tree/Rider On The Wheel ("Fruit Tree" sampler, 1-sided promo only)	200
69	Island ILPS 9105	FIVE LEAVES LEFT (LP, 1st pressing, pink label, black 'circle' logo, g/fold sleeve)	800
69	Island ILPS 9105	FIVE LEAVES LEFT (LP, gatefold sleeve, 2nd pressing, 'pink rim label, 'palm tree' logo)	150
70	Island ILPS 9134	BRYTER LAYTER (LP, 'pink rim label, 'palm tree' logo)	400
71	Longman (no cat. No.)	INTERPLAY ONE (2xLP, educational recording for schools, Drake plays guitar on three tracks, 2 booklets and 'teachers' notes)	400
72	Island ILPS 9184	PINK MOON (LP, 'pink rim label, 'palm tree' logo, gatefold sleeve)	400
79	Island NDSP 100	FRUIT TREE (3-LP, box set with booklet)	70
85	Island ILPS 9826	HEAVEN IN A WILD FLOWER (THE BEST OF NICK DRAKE) (LP)	20
86	Hannibal HNBX 5302	FRUIT TREE (4-LP, expanded reissue with booklet)	75
86	Hannibal HNBL 1318	TIME OF NO REPLY (LP)	20
89	Island ILPS 9105	FIVE LEAVES LEFT (LP, reissue, 'blue with white palm tree' label)	12
89	Island ILPS 9134	BRYTER LAYTER (LP, reissue, 'blue with white palm tree' label)	12
89	Island ILPS 9184	PINK MOON (LP, reissue, 'blue with white palm tree' label)	12
91	Hannibal HNCD 5402	FRUIT TREE (4-CD, with booklet in 12" x 12" box)	70
00	Simply Vinyl SVLP 163	FIVE LEAVES LEFT (LP, 180gm Simply vinyl repressing)	15
04	Island ILPS 8141	MADE TO LOVE MAGIC (LP, gatefold with inner sleeve)	25
07	Island FRUITCD 1	THE PICK OF THE FRUIT TREE (CD, sampler featuring River Man, Way To Blue, Cello Song, Fruit Tree, Northern Sky, Pink Moon, From The Morning)	15
07	Sunbeam SBR2LP 5041	FAMILY TREE (2-LP)	20

PETE DRAKE

| 63 | Philips BF 1332 | Forever/Sleep Walk | 8 |

DRAMATICS

72	Stax 2025 053	Whatcha See Is Whatcha Get/Thankful For Your Love	8
72	Stax 2025 101	In The Rain/Get Up And Get Down	6
73	Stax 2025 117	Toast To A Fool/Your Love Was Strange	12
73	Stax 2025 181	Hey You, Get Off My Mountain/Devil Is Dope	6
76	ABC ABC 4101	You're Fooling You/I'll Make It So Good	6
72	Stax 2362 025	WHATCHA SEE IS WHATCHA GET (LP)	15
74	Stax STX 1021	A DRAMATIC EXPERIENCE (LP)	15
75	ABC ABCL 5121	DRAMATIC JACKPOT (LP, gatefold sleeve)	12
75	ABC ABCL 5150	DRAMA V (LP, gatefold sleeve)	12

BARRY DRANSFIELD

| 72 | Polydor Folk Mill 2383 160 | BARRY DRANSFIELD (LP, red label) | 250 |
| 78 | Topic 12TS 5386 | BOWIN' AND SCRAPIN' (LP) | 25 |

(see also Robin & Barry Dransfield, Dransfields)

ROBIN DRANSFIELD

| 80 | Topic 12TS 414 | TIDEWAVE (LP) | 15 |

(see also Robin & Barry Dransfield, Dransfields)

ROBIN & BARRY DRANSFIELD

70	Trailer LER 2011	THE ROUT OF THE BLUES (LP, first pressing, white Trailer 'test' label)	40
70	Trailer LER 2011	THE ROUT OF THE BLUES (LP, second pressing, dark red label/silver logo and text)	30
71	Trailer LER 2026	LORD OF ALL I BEHOLD (LP)	30
75	Trailer LER 2011	THE ROUT OF THE BLUES (LP, 70s repressing, red and black or yellow labels)	20
82	Highway	THE ROUT OF THE BLUES (LP, 80s repressing, black and white 'Highwayman' labels)	12
82	Highway/Trailer LER 2011	THE ROUT OF THE BLUES (LP, Trailer labels and sleeves with 'Highway Records' stickers over 'Trailer' logo on sleeve)	15

(see also Robin Dransfield, Barry Dransfield, Dransfields)

DRANSFIELDS

76	Transatlantic TRA 322	THE FIDDLER'S DREAM (LP)	20
77	Free Reed 018	POPULAR TO CONTRARY BELIEF (LP, credited to Robin and Barry Dransfield)	12
78	Transatlantic TRA 386	BOWIN' AND SCRAPIN' (LP)	12

(see also Robin & Barry Dransfield, Robin Dransfield, Barry Dransfield)

RUSTY DRAPER

56	Mercury MT 101	Are You Satisfied?/Wabash Cannonball (78)	10
56	Mercury MT 113	Rock And Roll Ruby/House Of Cards (78)	10
56	Mercury MT 128	In The Middle Of The House/Pink Cadillac (78)	10
58	Mercury MT 194	Buzz Buzz Buzz/I Get The Blues When It Rains (78)	10
58	Mercury 7MT 211	Gamblin' Gal/That's My Doll	10
58	Mercury 7MT 229	Chicken-Pickin' Hawk/June, July And August	15
58	Mercury MT 229	Chicken-Pickin' Hawk/June, July And August (78)	10
59	Mercury AMT 1019	Shoppin' Around/With This Ring	30
59	Mercury MT 1019	Shoppin' Around/With This Ring (78)	10
59	Mercury AMT 1034	The Sun Will Always Shine/Hey Li Lee Li Lee Li	5
60	Mercury AMT 1101	Mule Skinner Blues/Please Help Me, I'm Falling	10

61	Mercury AMT 1127	Jealous Heart/Ten Thousand Years Ago	10
63	London HLU 9786	Night Life/That's Why I Love You Like I Do	7
65	London HLU 9989	Folsom Prison Blues/You Can't Be True, Dear	7
56	Mercury MEP 9506	PRESENTING RUSTY DRAPER (EP)	40
59	Mercury ZEP 10016	RUSTY DRAPER (EP)	20
60	Mercury ZEP 10059	RUSTY IN GAMBLING MOOD (EP)	20
60	Mercury ZEP 10095	MULE SKINNER BLUES (EP)	25
64	London RE-U 1431	RUSTY DRAPER NO. 1 (EP)	20
64	London RE-U 1432	RUSTY DRAPER NO. 2 (EP)	20
60	Mercury MMC 14040	HITS THAT SOLD A MILLION (LP)	15

MIKEY DREAD (AKA MICKEY CAMPBELL

79	Do It DUNE 24	Heavyweight Style/Rub A Dub (12")	20
79	Warrior WAR 125	Barber Saloon/CARLTON PATTERSON: Wash Wash (12")	20
81	Dread At The Controls DATC 003	Warrior Stylee/Israel Stylee (12")	25
82	Dread At The Controls DATCD 008	Roots & Culture/Jungle Dread (12")	25
77	Hawkeye HALP 001	DUB (LP)	15
79	Dread At The Controls DTCLP 002	AFRICAN ANTHEM – THE MIKEY DREAD SHOW DUBWISE (LP)	30
80	Dread At The Controls DTCLP 006	WORLD WAR III (LP)	15
80	Dread At The Controls DTLP 001	MASTER SHOWCASE (LP)	30
82	Dread At The Controls DATCLP 008	JUNGLE SIGNAL (LP)	30
83	Dread At The Controls DTLP 009	DUB MERCHANT (LP)	25

DREADZONE

93	Creation CRELP 162	360 DEGREES (LP)	20
94	Totem TTPLP 002	PERFORMANCE (LP)	15
95	Virgin V 2778	SECOND LIGHT (2-LP)	18

DREAMBOYS

| 80 | St Vitus SV1 | Bela Lugosi's Birthday/Outer Limits/Shall We Dance | 25 |

DREAMERS

| 68 | Columbia DB 8340 | The Maybe Song/The Long Road | 10 |

(see also Freddie & Dreamers)

DREAMERS

| 69 | Downtown DT 407 | Sweet Chariot/Let's Go Downtown | 10 |
| 69 | Downtown DT 408 | I Second That Emotion/Dear Love | 10 |

DREAMLETS

| 65 | Ska Beat JB 182 | Really Now/SKATALITES: Street Corner | 50 |

DREAMLOVERS

| 61 | Columbia DB 4711 | When We Get Married/Just Because | 200 |

(see also Chubby Checker)

DREAM MERCHANTS

| 67 | Decca F 12617 | Rattler/I'll Be With You In Apple Blossom Time | 10 |

DREAM POLICE

70	Decca F 12998	I'll Be Home (In A Day Or So)/Living Is Easy	10
70	Decca F 13078	Our Song/Much Too Much	8
70	Decca F 13105	I've Got No Choice/What's The Cure For Happiness?	8

(see also Average White Band)

DREAMS

68	United Artists UP 2249	I Will See You There/A Boy Needs A Girl	35
69	CBS 4247	Baby I'm Your Man/Softly, Softly	25
69	Dolphin 4432	Casatschok/Don't You Ask Me	7
70	CBS 64203	DREAMS (LP)	20
72	CBS 64597	IMAGINE MY SURPRISE (LP)	20

DREAM THEATER

94	East West A 5835	Lie/Space-Dye Vest/To Live Forever/Another Day (live) (p/s)	8
94	East West A 5835 T	Lie/Take The Time (Demo)/Space-Dye Vest (12", p/s)	10
89	MCA MCF 3445	WHEN DREAM AND DAY UNITE (LP)	12
92	Atco 7567 92148 1	IMAGES AND WORDS (LP)	15

DREAMTIMERS

| 61 | London HLU 9368 | The Dancin' Lady/An Invitation | 25 |

DREAM WEAVERS

56	Brunswick 05515	It's Almost Tomorrow/You've Got Me Wondering (gold label lettering)	20
56	Brunswick 05515	It's Almost Tomorrow/You've Got Me Wondering (silver label lettering)	10
56	Brunswick 05568	A Little Love Can Go A Long, Long Way/Into The Night (featuring Wade Buff)	15
56	Brunswick 05607	You're Mine/Is There Somebody Else? (featuring Wade Buff)	10

MIKE DRED

| 90 | Machine Codes DH VOL 1 | THE MIGHTY DRED EP (12") | 12 |
| 93 | Machine Codes CODE A | FU-CHIN-RA EP (12") | 10 |

DRED & FRED

| 92 | Ironworks D&F 001 | Down Too Long/CREATIVE STEPPERS: Creative Version (12") | 30 |

DREGS

| 79 | Disturbing DRO 1 | THE DREGS EP (p/s, numbered, stamped sleeve, 500 only) | 50 |

LEN DRESSLAR

| 56 | Mercury 7MT 3 | Chain Gang/These Hands (export issue) | 15 |

JOHN DREVAR('S EXPRESSION)

67	MGM MGM 1367	The Closer She Gets/When I Come Home	200
67	MGM MGM 1367	The Closer She Gets/When I Come Home (DJ Copy)	300
68	Polydor BM 56290	What Greater Love/I've Decided (solo)	10

MINT VALUE £

ALAN DREW
63	Columbia DB 7090	Here Comes The Rain/Always The Lonely One	5

PATTI DREW
68	Capitol CL 15557	Workin' On A Groovy Thing/Without A Doubt	15
68	Capitol CL 15575	Hard To Handle/Just Can't Forget About You	8

DREXCIYA
93	Rephlex Cat 017	3 - MOLECULAR ENHANCEMENT EP (12", 4-track)	25
95	Warp WAP 57	THE JOURNEY HOME EP (12", company sleeve)	25

DRIFTERS (U.K.)
59	Columbia DB 4263	Feelin' Fine/Don't Be A Fool (With Love)	50
59	Columbia DB 4263	Feelin' Fine/Don't Be A Fool (With Love) (78)	50
59	Columbia DB 4325	Driftin'/Jet Black	45

(see also Shadows, Cliff Richard, Jet Harris, Tony Meehan)

DRIFTERS (U.S.)
78s
56	London HLE 8344	Soldier Of Fortune/I Gotta Get Myself A Woman	50
58	London HLE 8686	Moonlight Bay/Drip-Drop	40
59	London HLE 8892	There Goes My Baby/Oh, My Love	60
59	London HLE 8988	Dance With Me/True Love, True Love	60
60	London HLE 9081	This Magic Moment/Baltimore	80

SINGLES
56	London HLE 8344	Soldier Of Fortune/I Gotta Get Myself A Woman	1000
58	London HLE 8686	Moonlight Bay/Drip-Drop	200
59	London HLE 8892	There Goes My Baby/Oh, My Love	30
59	London HLE 8988	Dance With Me/True Love, True Love	15
60	London HLE 9081	This Magic Moment/Baltimore	18
60	London HLK 9145	Lonely Winds/Hey Senorita	18
60	London HLK 9201	Save The Last Dance For Me/Nobody But Me	5
61	London HLK 7114	Save The Last Dance For Me/This Magic Moment (export issue)	10
61	London HLK 7115	I Count The Tears/Dance With Me (export issue)	20
61	London HLK 9287	I Count The Tears/Sadie My Lady	25
61	London HLK 9326	Some Kind Of Wonderful/Honey Bee	15
61	London HLK 9382	Please Stay/No Sweet Lovin'	15
61	London HLK 9427	Sweets For My Sweet/Loneliness Or Happiness	10
62	London HLK 9500	Room Full Of Tears/Somebody New Dancin' With You	10
62	London HLK 9522	When My Little Girl Is Smiling/Mexican Divorce	10
62	London HLK 9554	Stranger On The Shore/What To Do	8
62	London HLK 9626	Up On The Roof/Another Night With The Boys	10
63	London HLK 9699	On Broadway/Let The Music Play	15
63	London HLK 9750	Rat Race/If You Don't Come Back	15
63	London HLK 9785	I'll Take You Home/I Feel Good All Over	8
64	London HLK 9848	Vaya Con Dios/In The Land Of Make Believe	8
64	London HLK 9886	One Way Love/Didn't It	10
64	Atlantic AT 4001	Under The Boardwalk/I Don't Want To Go On Without You	12
64	Atlantic AT 4008	I've Got Sand In My Shoes/He's Just A Playboy	15
64	Atlantic AT 4012	Saturday Night At The Movies/Spanish Lace	12
65	Atlantic AT 4019	At The Club/Answer The Phone	12
65	Atlantic AT 4023	Come On Over To My Place/Chains Of Love	12
65	Atlantic AT 4034	Follow Me/The Outside World	15
65	Atlantic AT 4040	I'll Take You Where The Music's Playing/Far From The Maddening Crowd	12
66	Atlantic AT 4062	We Gotta Sing/Nylon Stockings	15
66	Atlantic AT 4084	Memories Are Made Of This/My Island In The Sun	12
66	Atlantic 584 020	Up In The Streets Of Harlem/You Can't Love 'Em All	12
67	Atlantic 584 065	Baby What I Mean/Aretha	22
68	Atlantic 584 152	I'll Take You Where The Music's Playing/On Broadway	6
68	Atlantic 584 195	Still Burning In My Heart/I Need You Now	10
69	Atlantic 584 246	Saturday Night At The Movies/Under The Boardwalk	10
71	Atlantic 2091 064	A Rose By Any Other Name/Be My Lady	7
77	Arista 94	I'll Know When True Love Really Passes By/A Good Song Never Dies	30
76	Atlantic K 10700	You Gotta Pay Your Dues/Black Silk	15
78	Arista 202	Closely Guarded Secret/I Can't Believe It's Over	20
79	Epic EPC 7806	Pour Your Little Heart Out Parts 1 & 2	70

EPs
61	London RE-K 1282	THE DRIFTERS' GREATEST HITS	30
63	London RE-K 1355	THE DRIFTERS	30
63	London RE-K 1385	DRIFTIN'.	30
64	Atlantic AET 6003	DRIFTIN' VOL. 2.	30
65	Atlantic AET 6012	TONIGHT.	30

ALBUMS
60	London HA-K 2318	THE DRIFTERS' GREATEST HITS	60
62	London HA-K 2450	SAVE THE LAST DANCE FOR ME	50
65	Atlantic ATL 5015	OUR BIGGEST HITS	40
65	Atlantic ATL/STL 5023	THE GOOD LIFE WITH THE DRIFTERS (mono/stereo)	40
66	Atlantic ATL/STL 5039	I'LL TAKE YOU WHERE THE MUSIC'S PLAYING (mono/stereo)	40
67	Atlantic 587 038	BIGGEST HITS	20
67	Atlantic 587 061	I'LL TAKE YOU WHERE THE MUSIC'S PLAYING (reissue)	12
67	Atlantic 590 010	SOUVENIRS	20
67	Atlantic 587 063	SAVE THE LAST DANCE FOR ME (reissue)	20
68	Atlantic 587 123	ROCKIN' AND DRIFTIN'.	40
68	Atlantic 587 144	GOOD GRAVY (as Clyde McPhatter & Drifters)	50
69	Atlantic 587/588 160	UP ON THE ROOF	20

(see also Clyde McPhatter, Ben E. King, Bobby Hendricks)

DRIFTING SLIM
66	Blue Horizon 45-1005	Good Morning Baby/My Sweet Woman (99 copies only)	120

DRIFTWOOD

70	Decca F 13084	Shylock Bay/The Wind Cries Above You	6
71	Decca F 13139	Say The Right Things/Still I'll Stay With You	6
70	Decca SKL 5069	DRIFTWOOD (LP, blue/silver label with boxed logo)	70

(see also Neil Harrison)

DRINKING ELECTRICITY

80	Pop Aural POP 004	Shaking All Over China (p/s)	5
80	Pop Aural POP 005	Shake Some Action/Shake Some Action (Cheap Version)	6
80	Pop Aural POP 008	Cruising Missiles/Shaking All Over (Dub) (p/s)	8

JULIE DRISCOLL

63	Columbia DB 7118	Take Me By The Hand/Stay Away From Me	35
65	Parlophone R 5296	Don't Do It No More/I Know You	35
66	Parlophone R 5444	I Didn't Want To Have To Do It/Don't Do It No More	20
67	Parlophone R 5588	I Know You Love Me Not/If You Should Ever Leave Me	20
67	Marmalade 598 005	Save Me Pts 1 & 2	35
71	Polydor 2383077	JULIE DRISCOLL — 1969 (LP)	50

JULIE DRISCOLL, BRIAN AUGER & TRINITY

68	Marmalade 598 006	This Wheel's On Fire/A Kind Of Love In (3-print push out or large centre, Marmalade sleeve)	8
68	Marmalade 598 011	Road To Cairo/Shadows Of You	8
69	Marmalade 598 018	Take Me To The Water/Indian Rope Man	60
67	Marmalade 607002	OPEN (mono, first pressing, with 1-sided insert and non laminated cover produced by "Upton Printing")	150
67	Marmalade 607 002	OPEN (LP, mono)	100
67	Marmalade 608 002	OPEN (LP, stereo)	80
68	M. For Pleasure MFP 1265	JOOLS/BRIAN (LP, tracks shared by Julie Driscoll & Brian Auger)	18
69	Marmalade 608 005/6	STREET NOISE (2-LP, gatefold sleeve)	250
69	Marmalade 608 014	STREET NOISE PART 1 (LP)	35
69	Marmalade 608 015	STREET NOISE PART 2 (LP)	35
70	Polydor 2334004	BEST OF (LP, 99p series)	20

(see also Brian Auger & Trinity, Working Week, Julie Tippetts, B.B. Blunder)

DRIVE

78	NRG NE 467	Jerkin'/Push'N'Shove (no p/s)	50

DRIVER

79	Rods ROD 1	Like A Mirror/Here I Am (p/s)	20
79	Rods ROD 2	I'm Not Dreaming/So They Say	15
80	Rods HOT 1	YOU BETTER TAKE IT (LP, 300 only)	60

DRIVERS

83	Greyhound GRK 701	Talk All Night/Sister (p/s)	6
84	Nouveau NMS 5	Things/Stolen Treasure (p/s)	6
83	Greyhound GRK 3301	SHORT CUTS (LP)	12

(see also Nick Van Eede)

DRIVESHAFT

80	Undercover DC 02	Cold As Ice/I Know What You Are After (features Noel Redding who also produced the single)	50
82	Undercover DC 03	Heartbreaker/Now That It's Over (p/s)	25

DRIZABONE

94	4th & Broadway 12 BRW 264	Pressure (Roger's Soul Sensation Mix)/Pressure (album version)/Pressure (Bonus Beats Mix)/Pressure (Bone Idol Remix)/Pressure (Nu Solution Mix)/Pressure (Underground Network Mix) (12", p/s)	15

D-ROK

91	Warhammer DROK 08722	Get Out Of My Way (D-Mix)/Renegade/Get Out Of My Way (Airnix) (12", p/s)	10
91	Warhammer DROK 08710	OBLIVION (LP)	12

(see also Brian May)

DROME

94	Ninja Tune ZEN 11	THE FINAL CORPORATE COLONIZATION OF THE UNCONSCIOUS (2 x LP)	15

FRANK D'RONE

59	Mercury ART 1040	Fascinating Rhythm/Yesterdays	5
60	Mercury AMT 1123	Strawberry Blonde (The Band Rocked On)/Time Hurries By	5
59	Mercury ZEP 10033	FRANK D'RONE SINGS (EP)	8
59	Mercury ZEP 10116	THE BAND ROCKED ON (EP)	12
60	Mercury MMC 14053	AFTER THE BALL (LP)	12

DRONES

77	Valer VRS 1	Bone Idle/I Just Wanna Be Myself (gatefold p/s, made in France)	12
77	Valer VRS 1	Bone Idle/I Just Wanna Be Myself (gatefold p/s, made in England)	6
77	Valer VRSP 1	Be My Baby/Lift Off The Bans (12", white label, unreleased)	50
77	Valer	Be My Baby (Take Two)/The Clique (white label, unrel., many autographed)	20
77	Ohms GOOD MIX 1	TEMPTATIONS OF A WHITE COLLAR WORKER (EP, different coloured sleeves, some with writing on inner sleeve)	15
80	Fabulous JC 4	Can't See/Fooled Today (p/s)	7
77	Valer VRLP 1	FURTHER TEMPTATIONS (LP)	35

DRONGOS FOR EUROPE

81	Kite DFE 001	ADVERSE CHORUS EP	40

DROWNING CRAZE

81	Situation 2 SIT 3	Storage Case/Damp Bones (p/s)	8
81	Situation 2 SIT 13	Trance/I Love The Fjords (p/s)	8
82	Situation 2 SIT 16	Heat/Replays (p/s)	8

DRUDGE

90	Deaf DEAF 01	SUPPOSE IT WAS YOU (split LP with Agathocles)	20

DRUG ADDIX

78	Chiswick SW 39	MAKE A RECORD (EP)	12

(see also Kirsty MacColl)

DRUID

76	EMI SPSR 395	Barnaby- Kestrel/Nothing But Morning	12
75	EMI EMC 3081	TOWARDS THE SUN (LP, with inner sleeve)	20
76	EMI EMC 3128	FLUID DRUID (LP, with inner sleeve)	20

DRUID CHASE

67	CBS 3053	Take Me In Your Garden/I Wanna Get My Hands On You	30

DRUIDS (1)

63	Parlophone R 5097	Long Tall Texan/Love So Blue	20
64	Parlophone R 5134	It's Just A Little Bit Too Late/See What You've Done	20

DRUIDS (2)

71	Argo ZFB 22	BURNT OFFERING (LP)	81
73	Argo ZFB 39	PASTIME WITH GOOD COMPANY (LP)	45

(see also Giles Farnaby's Dream Band)

DRUM CLUB

93	Butterfly BFLT10A	Sound System Volume 1 (12")	10
93	Big Life DC PROMO 2	Big Life (2 x 12" promo)	15

DRUMBAGO

63	Island WI 085	I Am Drunk (actually by Raymond Harper & Drumbago's Group)/Sea Breeze (actually by Sammy & Drumbago's Group)	20
68	Blue Cat BS 145	Reggae Jeggae (with Blenders)/TYRONE TAYLOR: Delilah	60
69	Trojan TR 638	Dulcemania (with Dynamites)/CLANCY ECCLES: China Man	20

(see also Derrick Patsy, Dennis Walks)

BILL DRUMMOND

87	Creation CRE 039T	King Of Joy/The Manager (12", p/s)	25

(see also Big In Japan, Lori & Chameleons, J.A.M.s, KLF, Disco 2000, Timelords)

DON DRUMMOND

62	Island WI 021	Schooling The Duke/Bitter Rose (as Don Drummond Orchestra; B-side is actually by Shenley Duffus)	30
63	Black Swan WI 406	Scrap Iron/DRAGONAIRE: Prevention	25
63	Blue Beat BB 179	Reload/Far East	30
63	Island WI 094	Scandal/My Ideal (B-side actually by W. Sparks)	25
63	R&B JB 103	Royal Flush/MAYTALS: Matthew Mark	30
63	R&B JB 105	The Shock/TONETTES: Tell Me You're Mine	25
64	Ska Beat JB 178	Silver Dollar/TOMMY McCOOK: My Business	30
64	Island WI 149	Eastern Standard Time/DOTTY & BONNIE: Sun Rises	25
64	Island WI 153	Musical Storeroom/STRANGER COLE: He Who Feels	25
64	Island WI 162	Garden Of Love/STRANGER COLE: Cherry May	40
65	Island WI 192	Stampede (with Drumbago)/JUSTIN HINDS & DOMINOES: Come Bail Me	25
65	Island WI 204	Coolie Baby/LORD ANTICS: You May Stray	25
65	Island WI 208	Man In The Street/RITA & BENNY: You Are My Only Love	40
65	Island WI 242	University Goes Ska/DERRICK & NAOMI: Pain In My Heart	40
69	Studio One SO 2078	Heavenless/GLEN BROWN & DAVE BARKER: Lady Lovelight	45
69	Trojan TR 678	Memory Of Don/JOHN HOLT: Darling I Love You	15
69	Coxsone CSL 8021	IN MEMORY OF DON DRUMMOND (LP)	80
69	Studio One SO 9008	THE BEST OF DON DRUMMOND (LP)	120
69	Trojan TTL 23	MEMORIAL ALBUM (LP)	25

(see also Joe White, Rhythm Aces, Roy & Millie, Movers, Desmond Dekker, Shenley Duffas, Hi-Tones, Duke Reid, Soul Brothers, Baba Brooks, Bonnie & Skitto, Eric Morris, Pioneers, Stranger & Patsy, Techniques, Winston Wright)

DON DRUMMOND JUNIOR

67	Caltone TONE 104	Sir Pratt Special/HEMSLEY MORRIS: Love Is Strange	90
68	Caltone TONE 124	Dirty Dozen/PHIL PRATT: Reach Out	90
70	Jackpot JP 710	Memory Of Don Drummond/TOBIES: Resting	20

(see also Vincent Gordon)

JOHN DRUMMOND

68	Page One POF 084	Break My Mind/Molly Bye Bye	7

K. DRUMMOND

73	Jackpot JP 810	Your Pretty Face/Your Pretty Face (Version)	5

(see also Cables)

LEE DRUMMOND

66	Fontana TF 728	Messrs Lindsay, Parker & Flynn/Sitting And Drinking Alone	8

PETE DRUMMOND & THE VHF BAND

72	Warner Bros K 16232	Rocking At The BBC/Goodbye (vinyl 78)	25

DRUNKEN MASTER

93	Kold Sweat KSEP209	DEVIL IN DISGUISE (EP)	8

(see also SLR/Dashy D & Cue Tips)

ROY DRUSKY

59	Brunswick 05785	Wait 'N' See/Just About That Time	10
69	Mercury SMCL 20180	MY GRASS IS GREEN (LP)	12

REGINA DRUTTON

68	CBS 5684	A Hard Man Is Good To Hold Onto/Tell Me Lies Again	5

DRY ICE

69	B&C CB 115	Running To The Convent/Nowhere To Go	25

(see also Pluto)

DRY RIB

79	Clockwork COR 001	THE DRY SEASON (EP, 33rpm, photocopied foldover p/s, screen-printed labels)	30

(see also Television Personalities, Times, L'Orange Mechanik)

DRY WATERS

72	Denby DEN 003	Crystal Ball/The Magic Valley	120

AMANCIO D'SILVA

69	Columbia S(C)X 6322	INTEGRATION (LP)	300

71	Columbia SCX 6465	REFLECTIONS (LP)	30

(see also Cosmic Eye)

D.S.K.F.

92	WG 001	NEW SCIENCE EP (12", stickered white label)	70

D.S.P.

92	FX FXUKT 10	Obsession/Revenge Attack/Intravenus/Kebab (12")	20

D TO THE K

88	BPM BP12004	Hard But Live/Ease Up Your Mind (12")	20

DUALS

61	London HL 9450	Stick Shift/Cruising	25

DUBBING IN THE U.K.

81	Star Light SDLP 902	DUBBING IN THE U.K.(LP)	30

DUBS

57	London HLU 8526	Could This Be Magic/Such Lovin'	250
57	London HLU 8526	Could This Be Magic/Such Lovin' (78)	40
58	London HL 8684	Gonna Make A Change/Beside My Love	300
58	London HL 8684	Gonna Make A Change/Beside My Love (78)	30

DUB SYNDICATE

84	On-U Sound ON-U LP 18	POUNDING SYSTEM (LP)	18
86	On-U Sound ON-U LP 38	TUNES FROM THE MISSING CHANNEL (LP)	20
89	On-U Sound ON-U LP4	STRIKE THE BALANCE (LP)	15
91	On-U Sound ON-U LP5	STONED IMMACULATE (LP)	15

DIANE DUCANE

79	Contact WN 2	Better Late Than Never/One Day	30

JOHN DU CANN

77	Arista ARIST 128	Throw Him In Jail/Street Stutter	5
77	Arista ARIST 145	Where's The Show/Hang Around	5
79	Vertigo 6059 241	Don't Be A Dummy/If I'm Makin' (p/s)	5

(see also Attack, Andromeda, Five Day Week Straw People, Atomic Rooster, Hard Stuff, Status Quo)

DUCHESS OF BEDFORD

56	HMV POP 361	Luck's In Love With You/MRS GERALD LEGGE: I'm In Love	8

DUCKS DELUXE

73	RCA RCA 2438	Coast To Coast/Bring Back That Packard Car	6
75	RCA RCA 2531	I Fought The Law/Cherry Pie	6
74	RCA LPL1 5008	DUCKS DELUXE (LP)	15
74	RCA SF 8402	TAXI TO THE TERMINAL ZONE (LP)	12
79	Blue Moon BMLP 001	LAST NIGHT OF A PUB ROCK BAND (2-LP)	15

(see also Motors, Tyla Gang, Brinsley Schwarz)

DUDLEY

60	Vogue V 9171	Lone Prairie Rock/El Pizza	20

DAVE DUDLEY

63	United Artists UP 1029	Six Days On The Road/I Feel A Cry Coming On	10
67	Mercury MF 1003	Trucker's Prayer/Don't Come Cryin' To Me	5
68	Mercury MF 1037	There Ain't No Easy Run/Why Can't I Be With You? (It's A Shame)	5

ROBERTA DUDLEY

50	Tempo R 22	Krooked Blues/When You're Alone (78)	15
51	Poydras 3	Krooked Blues/When You're Alone (shellac 45)	8

(see also Kid Ory)

DU-ETTES

72	President PT 382	Every Beat Of My Heart/Sugar Daddy	8
72	President PT 398	Please Forgive Me/Lonely Days	8

JACK DUFF BAND

68	Avenue AVE 077	THE ENCHANTED ISLE (LP)	15

D DUFFUS

79	Jay Dee JD 009	Is It Just A Dream/Cheaters (12")	50

SHENLEY DUFFAS

62	Island WI 036	Give To Get/What You Gonna Do (as S. Duffas; B-side actually with Millie Small)	20
63	Island WI 063	Fret Man Fret/Doreen	20
63	Island WI 093	What A Disaster/I Am Rich	20
63	Island WI 115	Know The Lord/TOMMY McCOOK: Ska Ba	45
63	Island WI 125	Easy Squeal/Things Ain't Going Right	20
63	R&B JB 134	No More Wedding Bells/Let Them Fret	15
64	R&B JB 146	Big Mouth/FRANKIE ANDERSON: Peanut Vendor	20
64	R&B JB 152	Christopher Columbus/CARL BRYAN ORCHESTRA: Barber Chair	18
64	R&B JB 154	Mother-In-Law/DON DRUMMOND & GROUP: Festival	18
64	Black Swan WI 440	Digging A Ditch/He's Coming Down	18
64	Black Swan WI 443	Gather Them In/Crucifixion	20
64	Rio R 41	I Will Be Glad/Heariso (as Shandly Duffus)	18
65	Island WI 182	La La La/UPCOMING WILLOWS: Jonestown Special	40
65	Island WI 184	You Are Mine/UPCOMING WILLOWS: Red China	30
65	Island WI 186	Rukumbine/One Morning	25
72	Upsetter US 380	Bet You Don't Know/UPSETTERS: Ring Of Fire	18
72	Dynamic DYN 451	Peace (with Soul Avengers)/UPSETTERS: Peace — Version	7
72	Grape GR 3031	Sincerely/Sincerely — Version (with Upsetters)	8

(see also Chenley Duffus, Billy Dyce)

CHRIS DUFFIN

76	Deroy ADM LP 864	HEY SANDY (LP)	250

DUFFO

79	Beggars Banquet BEG 15	Give Me Back My Brain/Duff Record	5

MINT VALUE £

CHENLEY DUFFUS
72	Upsetter US-386	To Be A Lover/Baby Lose Burning	10
72	Pama PM 859	At The End/Good Night My Love	8

(see also Shenley Duffas)

DUFFY (1)
73	Chapter One SCHR 184	The Joker/Running Away	18
70	Chapter One CHS-R 814	SCRUFFY DUFFY (LP, red/silver label)	200

DUFFY (2)
07	A&M 175 410-6	Rockferry/Oh Boy (p/s, 1,500 only)	10
04	Awen REG150 CD	Dim Dealltwriaeth/Hedfan Angel/Cariad Dwi'n Unig (CD single as Aimee Duffy)	25

CHRIS DUFFY
68	SNB 55-3681	Mr Jones Mr Brown Mr Smith And Not Forgetting Charlie Green/Something For Now	10

STEPHEN 'TIN TIN' DUFFY
85	10	She Loves Me/She Loves It (p/s, withdrawn)	40
85	10	Baby Impossible (p/s, withdrawn)	40

(see also Hawks, Tin Tin, Dr. Calculus, Lilac Time)

DUFFY'S NUCLEUS
67	Decca F 22547	Hound Dog/Mary Open The Door	50

(see also Duffy Power, Pentangle, John McLaughlin)

DON DUGGAN
68	Pye 7N 17633	Let Her Dance/Westmeath Bachelor (with Savoys)	6

BILLY DUKE
62	Ember EMB S 153	Walking Cane/Amen	5
62	Ember EMB S 160	Ain't She Pretty/Timbuctu	5
64	London HLU 9907	While The Bloom Is On The Rose/I'm The Lonesomest Guy In Town	5
65	London HLU 9960	Sugar'N'Spice/Prisoner Of Love	5

DENVER DUKE & JEFFREY NULL BLUEGRASS BOYS
63	Starlite STEP 33	DENVER DUKE & JEFFREY NULL BLUEGRASS BOYS (EP)	15

DORIS DUKE
71	Mojo 2092 005	To The Other Woman/I Don't Care Anymore	8
71	Mojo 2092 017	If She's Your Wife Who Am I?/It Sure Was Fun	15
73	Mainstream MSS 302	Business Deal/Nobody But You	8
74	Contempo 7703	Grasshopper/Please Come Back	8
76	Contempo CX15	Woman Of The Ghetto/TAMIKO JONES: Let It Flow	5
71	Mojo 2916 001	I'M A LOSER (LP)	20
71	Mojo 2916 006	A LEGEND IN HER OWN TIME (LP)	20
75	Contempo CRM 111	A LEGEND IN HER OWN TIME (LP, reissue)	15
75	Contempo CLP 519	WOMAN (LP)	20

PATTY DUKE
65	United Artists UP 1103	Don't Just Stand There/Everything But Love	10
65	United Artists UP 1116	Say Something Funny/Funny Little Butterflies	8
65	United Artists (S)ULP 1123	DON'T JUST STAND THERE (LP, mono/stereo)	40
66	United Artists UP 1131	Whenever She Holds You/Nothing But You	15

JAMES DUKE
86	Creole CRT 93	Hold On/Zyzafon (12", p/s)	250

DUKE ALL STARS
68	Blue Cat BS 111	Letter To Mummy And Daddy (Parts 1 & 2)	20

DUKE & DUCHESS
55	London HLU 8206	Borrowed Sunshine/Get Ready For Love (with Sir Hubert Pimm)	40

(see also Sir Hubert Pimm)

DUKE OF BURLINGTON
71	Decca F23120	Flash/Slot Machine	15

AGGIE DUKES
57	Vogue V 9090	John John/Well Of Loneliness	400
57	Vogue V 9090	John John/Well Of Loneliness (78)	60

DUKES NOBLEMEN
69	Philips BF 1691	City Of Windows/Thank You For Your Loving	25

DUKES OF ILLYRIA
70	IAMBIG 0001	Food Of Love/Come Away Death	20

DUKES OF STRATOSPHEAR
87	Virgin VSY 982	You're A Good Man Albert Brown/Vanishing Girl (p/s, 5,000 on multi-coloured vinyl)	8
85	Virgin WOW 1	25 O'CLOCK (LP)	18
87	Virgin VP 2440	PSONIC PSUNSPOT (LP, gatefold sleeve, 5,000 on multi-coloured vinyl)	30

(see also XTC, Mr. Partridge)

DULCIMER
71	Nepentha 6437 003	AND I TURNED AS I HAD TURNED AS A BOY (LP, gatefold sleeve)	200
80	Happy Face MMLP 1021	A LAND FIT FOR HEROES (LP, private pressing)	15

LIZA DULITTLE
68	Pye 7N 17590	I've Got To Get A Grip Of Myself/Did You Hear A Heart Break Last Night?	8

(see also Margo & Marvettes)

DUM
74	RAK RAK 179	In The Mood/Watching The Clock	5

(see also Mud)

DUM DUM
72	Phillips 6414-318	Peter Gunn/Cosa Nostra	15

JOHNNY DUMAR
68	CBS 3545	Illusion/You Went Away	5

DUMB ANGELS

88	Fierce FRIGHT 033	Love And Mercy/Love And Mercy (p/s, numbered)	55

(see also Pooh Sticks)

DUMBELLES

80	Polydor POSP 209/EGO 3	Giddy Up/A Christmas Dream (no p/s)	10

(see also Roxy Music)

JOHN DUMMER (BLUES BAND)

68	Mercury MF 1040	Travelling Man/40 Days (as John Dummer Blues Band)	20
69	Mercury MF 1119	Try Me One More Time/Riding At Midnight (as John Dummer Blues Band)	15
70	Fontana 6007 027	Happy/Nightingale (unissued in U.K.; France-only)	0
70	Philips 6006 111	Nine By Nine/Going In The Out (credited to either Famous Music Band or John Dummer Band)	15
71	Philips 6006 176	Medicine Weasel/The Endgame (with Nick Pickett)	5
73	Vertigo 6059 074	Ooblee-Dooblee Jubilee/The Monkey Speaks His Mind (as John Dummer Oobleedooblee Band)	5
69	Mercury SMCL 20136	CABAL (LP, black/silver label)	200
69	Mercury SMCL 20167	JOHN DUMMER BAND (LP, black/silver label)	200
70	Philips 6309 008	FAMOUS MUSIC BAND (LP, gatefold sleeve, black/silver labels)	150
72	Philips 6382 039	THIS IS THE JOHN DUMMER BLUES BAND (LP)	20
73	Philips 6382 040	VOLUME II — TRY ME ONE MORE TIME (LP)	20
72	Vertigo 6360 056	BLUE (LP, gatefold sleeve, small swirl label)	400
73	Vertigo 6360 083	OOBLEEDOOBLEE JUBILEE (LP, as John Dummer Oobleedooblee Band, small swirl label)	100

(see also Darts, Nick Pickett, Dave Kelly, Famous Music Band, Tony McPhee)

DUMMIES

79	Cheapskate FWL 001	When The Lights Are Out/She's The Only Woman (no p/s)	8
80	Pye 7P 163	When The Lights Are Out/She's The Only Woman (no p/s, reissue)	5
80	Cheapskate CHEAP 003	Didn't You Used To Use To Be You?/Miles Out To Sea (p/s)	8
81	Cheapskate CHEAP 014	Maybe Tonite/When I'm Dancin' I Ain't Fightin' (p/s)	10

(see also China Dolls, Slade)

DUMMY RUN

97	Hot Air BSE LP 002	ICE CREAM HEADACHE (LP)	12

(see also Stock, Hausen & Walkman)

DUNAMIS

79	Daybreak DB 2602	I CAN FLY (LP, signed)	60
79	Daybreak DB 2602	I CAN FLY (LP, un-signed)	15

AYNSLEY DUNBAR (RETALIATION)

67	Blue Horizon 3109	Warning/Cobwebs (in p/s)	60
67	Blue Horizon 3109	Warning/Cobwebs	25
68	Liberty LBF 15132	Watch 'N' Chain/Roamin' And Ramblin'	15
68	Liberty LBL/LBS 83154	AYNSLEY DUNBAR RETALIATION (LP, mono/stereo)	45
68	Liberty LBL/LBS 83177	DR. DUNBAR'S PRESCRIPTION (LP, mono/stereo)	60
69	Liberty LBS 83223	TO MUM FROM AYNSLEY AND THE BOYS (LP)	60
70	Liberty LBS 83316	REMAINS TO BE HEARD (LP)	60
71	Warner Bros WS 3010	BLUE WHALE (LP, green label)	40

(see also John Mayall & Bluesbreakers, Heavy Jelly, Annette & Victor Brox, Excheckers)

SCOTT DUNBAR

71	Ahura Mazda AMS SDS 1	FROM LAKE MARY (LP)	30

JOHNNY DUNCAN (& BLUE GRASS BOYS)

57	Columbia DB 3925	Kaw-Liga/Ella Speed (gold label lettering)	20
57	Columbia DB 3925	Kaw-Liga/Ella Speed (silver label lettering)	10
57	Columbia DB 3959	Last Train To San Fernando/Rock-A-Billy Baby (gold label lettering)	20
57	Columbia DB 3959	Last Train To San Fernando/Rock-A-Billy Baby (silver label lettering)	10
57	Columbia DB 3996	Blue, Blue Heartache/Jig Along Home	8
57	Columbia DB 4029	Footprints In The Snow/Get Along Home, Cindy	8
58	Columbia DB 4074	Goodnight Irene/If You Love Me Baby	10
58	Columbia DB 4118	Itching For My Baby/I Heard The Bluebirds Sing	8
58	Columbia DB 4167	All Of The Monkeys Ain't In The Zoo/More And More	8
58	Columbia DB 4179	My Lucky Love/Geisha Girl	8
59	Columbia DB 4282	Rosalie/This Train	7
59	Columbia DB 4311	Kansas City/That's All Right Darlin'	5
60	Columbia DB 4415	Any Time/Yellow, Yellow Moon (solo)	6
61	Pye 7N 15358	Tobacco Road/Sleepy-Eyed John (solo)	5
61	Pye 7N 15380	The Legend Of Gunga Din/Hannah (solo)	5
62	Pye 7N 15420	A Long Time Gone/Waitin' For The Sandman (solo)	5
63	Columbia DB 7164	The Ballad Of Jed Clampett/Will You Be Mine? (as Johnny Duncan & Kingpins)	5
64	Columbia DB 7334	Dang Me/Which Way Did He Go? (solo)	5
66	Columbia DB 7833	My Little Baby/I Thank My Lucky Stars (solo)	5
57	Columbia SEG 7708	Johnny Duncan And His Blue Grass Boys (EP)	15
57	Columbia SEG 7733	Johnny Duncan And His Blue Grass Boys NO. 2 (EP)	15
58	Columbia SEG 7753	Footprints In The Snow (EP)	15
58	Columbia SEG 7850	Tennessee Sing Song (EP)	15
57	Columbia 33S 1122	TENNESSEE SONG BAG (10" LP)	30
58	Columbia 33S 1129	JOHNNY DUNCAN SALUTES HANK WILLIAMS (10" LP)	30
61	Columbia 33SX 1328	BEYOND THE SUNSET (LP)	20
70	Lucky LUS 3012	BACK IN TOWN (LP)	15

(see also Chris Barber's Skiffle Group)

LESLEY DUNCAN (& JOKERS)

63	Parlophone R 5034	I Want A Steady Guy/Movin' Away (as Lesley Duncan & Jokers)	15
64	Parlophone R 5106	Tell Me/You Kissed Me Boy	15
64	Mercury MF 830	When My Baby Cries/Did It Hurt?	10
65	Mercury MF 847	Just For The Boy/See That Guy	20
65	Mercury MF 876	Run To Love/Only The Lonely And Me	20
65	Mercury MF 939	Hey Boy/I Go To Sleep	10
68	RCA 1746	Lullaby/I Love You, I Love You	6
69	CBS 4585	Sing Children Sing/Exactly Who Are You	7
79	CBS 8061	Sing Children Sing/Rainbow Games (p/s, with Kate Bush)	10

MINT VALUE £

| 71 | CBS 64202 | SING CHILDREN SING (LP, gatefold sleeve, orange labels) | 20 |
| 72 | CBS 64807 | EARTH MOTHER (LP, gatefold sleeve, orange labels) | 15 |

(see also Mitchell/Coe Mysteries, Pete Townshend, Phil Lynott, Madeline Bell, Joe Brown & Vicki Brown)

TOMMY DUNCAN
| 66 | Sue WI 4002 | Dance, Dance, Dance/Let's Try It Over Again | 40 |

TOMMY DUNCAN & HIS WESTERN ALL STARS
| 50 | Capitol CL 13261 | Gamblin' Polka Dot Blues/Chattanooga Shoe Shine Boy (78) | 10 |

DIANE DUNCANE
| 79 | Contact 2 | Better Late Than Never/One Day | 15 |

DUNCANS
| 81 | Impact IMP 3 | Too Damn Hot/Communication (12") | 12 |

BARBARA DUNKLEY
| 71 | Banana BA 342 | We'll Cry Together/BOBBY DAVIS: Got To Get Away | 7 |

DELROY DUNKLEY
| 70 | Hot Rod HR 109 | I Wish You Well/TONY & DELROY: Impossible Love | 10 |

ERROL(L) DUNKLEY
67	Rio R 109	Love Me Forever/VIETNAM ALLSTARS: The Toughest	100
67	Rio R 131	You're Gonna Need Me/Seek And You'll Find	35
68	Island WI 3150	Once More/I'm Not Your Man	35
68	Amalgamated AMG 800	Please Stop Your Lying/Feel So Fine (B-side actually by Tommy McCook & Band)	35
68	Amalgamated AMG 805	I'm Going Home/I'm Not Your Man	30
68	Amalgamated AMG 807	The Scorcher/Do It Right Tonight	50
68	Amalgamated AMG 820	Love Brother/I Spy	20
69	Fab FAB 117	I'll Take You In My Arms/KING CANNON: Daphney Reggae	10
70	Unity UN 554	My Special Prayer/Never Hurt The One You Love	7
70	Banana BA 302	Satisfaction/CECIL LOCKE: Sing Out Loud	15
71	Big BG 324	Deep Meditation/RUPIE EDWARDS ALL STARS: Meditation Version	20
71	Big BG 327	Three In One/RUPIE EDWARDS ALL STARS: One In Three	6
71	Nu Beat NB 091	Three In One/RUPIE EDWARDS ALL STARS: One In Three	8
71	Explosion EX 2053	O Lord/KEITH with IMPACT ALL STARS: Raindrops (B-side actually "My Baby" by Lloyd Charmers)	6
72	Camel CA 87	Black Cinderella/PHIL PRATT ALLSTARS: Our Anniversary (B-side actually Tropic Shadows)	12
73	Grape GR 3039	Why Did You Do It/One Love	8
73	Count Shelley CS 3039	Girl You Cried/Where Must I Go	6
73	Ackee 507	Keep The Pressure Down/Version	30
76	Daddy Kool DK 002	Eunoch Power/INTIMIDATORS: Straight To Him Chest	6
77	Aries ARI 001	Hard Luck Story/To Hell And Forward (p/s both with Jah Steach, actually Jah Stitch)	80
78	Arawak ARK DD 002	Little Way Different/Differentiah (with Dreadful Julio) (12")	25
82	Success SRLD 014	If You Say So/AFRICAN BROTHERS: Mystery Or Nature	10
70s	Attack AT 1003	YOU NEVER KNOW (LP)	30
73	Attack ATLP 1003	DARLING OOH! (LP)	30
79	Black Joy DH 802	DISCO SHOWCASE (LP)	30
76	Third World TWLP 101	SIT AND CRY OVER YOU (LP)	40
79	Trojan TR 179	DARLING OOH! (LP, reissue)	15

(see also Errol & His Group, Gaynor & Erroll], Mister Versatile, Don Lee, Ken Parker, Bongo Herman)

GEORGE DUNN
| 73 | Leader LEE 4042 | GEORGE DUNN (LP, with insert) | 18 |

TONY DUNNING (& TREMELOS)
60	Palette PG 9006	Seventeen Tomorrow/Be My Girl	10
61	Palette PG 9018	Pretend/Don't Bother To Call	12
61	Palette PG 9027	Under Moscow Skies/Sixteen Candles	10

DUNNO
| 71 | M&M FFMS 100013 | Sunday Girl/Magic Beat | 20 |

BLIND WILLIE DUNN'S GIN BOTTLE FOUR WITH KING OLIVER
| 54 | Columbia SCM 5100 | Jet Black Blues/Blue Blood Blues | 25 |
| 54 | Columbia DB3440 | Jet Black Blues/Blue Blood Blues (78) | 20 |

(see also Eddie Lang & Lonnie Johnson)

PETE DUNTON
| 73 | Rockfield ROC3 | Taking Time/Still Confused | 12 |

DUPARS
| 76 | Contempo 2104 | Love Cookin'/Instrumental | 30 |

CHAMPION JACK DUPREE
51	Jazz Parade B 16	Fisherman's Blues/County Jail Special (78)	30
62	Storyville A 45051	Whiskey Head Woman/Shirley May	20
67	Decca F 12611	Barrelhouse Woman/Under Your Hood	20
67	Blue Horizon 45-1007	Get Your Head Happy/Easy Is The Way (with T.S. McPhee)	120
68	Blue Horizon 57-3140	I Haven't Done No-One No Harm/How Am I Doing It (with Stan Webb)	20
69	Blue Horizon 57-3152	Ba'la Fouche/Kansas City	20
69	Blue Horizon 57-3158	I Want To Be A Hippy/Goin' Back To Louisiana	25
61	Storyville SEP 381	BLUES ANTHOLOGY VOL. 1 (EP)	15
64	RCA RCX 7137	RHYTHM AND BLUES VOL. 1 (EP)	15
64	Decca DFE 8586	LONDON SPECIAL (EP, with Keith Smith Climax Band)	60
65	Ember EMB 4564	JACK DUPREE (EP)	25
59	London Jazz LTZ-K 15171	BLUES FROM THE GUTTER (LP)	60
61	London Jazz LTZ-K 15217	CHAMPION JACK'S NATURAL AND SOULFUL BLUES LP, mono)	60
61	London Jazz SAH-K 6150	CHAMPION JACK'S NATURAL AND SOULFUL BLUES LP, stereo)	70
65	Storyville SLP 145	TROUBLE TROUBLE (LP)	20
65	Xtra XTRA 1028	CABBAGE GREENS (LP)	20
65	Storyville SLP 161	PORTRAITS IN BLUES (LP)	35
66	Decca LK/SKL 4747	FROM NEW ORLEANS TO CHICAGO (LP)	120
67	Storyville 670 194	CHAMPION JACK DUPREE (LP)	20
67	Decca SKL 4871	CHAMPION JACK DUPREE AND HIS BIG BLUES BAND (LP)	120
68	Blue Horizon 7-63206	WHEN YOU FEEL THE FEELING YOU WAS FEELING (LP)	100

69	Blue Horizon 7-63214	SCOOBYDOOBYDOO (LP) 100

(see also T.S. McPhee)

CHAMPION JACK DUPREE/JIMMY RUSHING
64	Ember CJS 800	TWO SHADES OF BLUE (LP) 18

(see also Jimmy Rushing)

SIMON DUPREE & BIG SOUND
66	Parlophone R 5542	I See The Light/It Is Finished 10
67	Parlophone R 5574	Reservations/You Need A Man...15
67	Parlophone R 5594	Day Time, Night Time/I've Seen It All Before 10
67	Parlophone R 5646	Kites/Like The Sun Like The FIre (with Jacqui Chan).....................................6
68	Parlophone R 5670	For Whom The Bell Tolls/Sleep..7
68	Parlophone R 5697	Part Of My Past/This Story Never Ends 8
68	Parlophone R 5727	Thinking About My Life/Velvet And Lace 8
69	Parlophone R 5757	Broken Hearted Pirates/She Gave Me The Sun 10
69	Parlophone R 5816	The Eagle Flies Tonight/Give It All Back 10
67	Parlophone PMC/PCS 7029	WITHOUT RESERVATIONS (LP, yellow & black label, with "sold in the U.K..." text, laminated sleeve) 80

(see also Moles, Gentle Giant, Jacqui Chan, Shape Of The Rain)

DUPREES
62	HMV POP 1073	You Belong To Me/Take Me As I Am 40
62	Stateside SS 143	My Own True Love/Ginny 15
63	London HLU 9678	I'd Rather Be Here In Your Arms/I Wish I Could Believe You 20
63	London HLU 9709	Gone With The Wind/Let's Make Love Again 20
63	London HLU 9774	Why Don't You Believe Me?/My Dearest One 20
63	London HLU 9813	Have You Heard?/Love Eyes 20
64	London HLU 9843	It's No Sin/The Sand And The Sea 20
65	CBS 201803	Around The Corner/They Said It Couldn't Be Done 20
66	CBS 202028	She Waits For Him/Norma Jean 15
68	MGM MGM 460	My Special Angel/Ring Of Love 10
70	Polydor 2058 077	Check Yourself/The Sky's The Limit 35

DURAN DURAN
81	EMI 12EMI 5137	Planet Earth (Night Version)/Planet Earth/Late Bar (12", p/s) 8
81	EMI 12EMI 5168	Careless Memories/Fame/Khanada (12", p/s) 8
81	EMI 12EMI 5206	Girls On Film (Night Version)/Girls On Film/Faster Than Light (12", p/s) 8
81	EMI 12EMI 5254	My Own Way (Night Version)/Like An Angel/My Own Way (Short Version)(12", p/s) 8
82	EMI 12EMI 5327	Save A Prayer/Hold Back The Rain (12" remix) (12", p/s) 8
82	EMI 12EMI 5346	Rio (Part 1)/Rio (Part 2)/My Own Way (12", p/s) 8
84	EMI DURANP 2	The Reflex/Make Me Smile (poster p/s) 5
84	EMI 12 DURANP 2	The Reflex (Dance Mix)/Make Me Smile/The Reflex (12", picture disc) 8
88	Parlophone CDDD 11	All She Wants Is (45 Mix)/Skin Trade (Parisian Mix)/I Believe — All I Need To Know (Medley) (3" CD) 10
89	Parlophone CDDD 12	Do You Believe In Shame?/The Krush Brothers LSD Edit/Notorious (live)/ God (London)/This Is How A Road Gets Made (3" CD) 15
89	Parlophone CDDD 13	Burning The Ground/Decadance/Decadance (Extended Mix) (CD, 2,000 only)...................20
93	Parlophone CDDDS 16	Ordinary World (Single Version)/Save A Prayer/Skin Trade/ My Antarctica (CD, fold-out pack) 15
95	Parlophone 72438518981	THANK YOU (LP, with poster) 35

(see also Arcadia, Power Station)

JIMMY DURANTE
69	Paramount PARA 3002	Monte Carlo Or Bust/They're Playing Chester's Song..................................6

(see also Ethel Merman, Groucho Marx)

ALLISON DURBIN
69	Decca LK-R/SKL-R 4996	I HAVE LOVED ME A MAN (LP)..40

JUDITH DURHAM
67	Columbia DB 8207	The Olive Tree/The Non Performing Lion Quickstep 5
67	Columbia DB 8290	Again And Again/Memories 8

(see also Seekers, Keith Potger)

JUDITH DURHAM
71	A&M AMS 823	Climb Ev'ry Mountain/What Could Be A Better Way......................................5
74	Pye 7N 45312	I Wanna Dance To Your Music/Mama's Got The Blues 6
74	Pye NSLP 18431	THE HOTTEST BAND IN TOWN (LP) 15

KENNY DURHAM
58	London LTZU 15133	JAZZ CONTRASTS (LP, with Sonny Rollins) 18

TERRY DURHAM
69	Deram DML/SML 1042	CRYSTAL TELEPHONE (LP, with insert, red/white label with large logo) 30

(see also Storyteller)

DURUTTI COLUMN
82	Factory FAC 64	I Get Along Without You Very Well/Prayer (p/s) 7
80	Factory FACT 14	THE RETURN OF THE DURUTTI COLUMN (LP, with sandpaper sleeve, with Martin Hannett's "Testcard" flexidisc [FACT 14C]) 200
80	Factory FACT 14	THE RETURN OF THE DURUTTI COLUMN (LP, with sandpaper sleeve, without Martin Hannett's "Testcard" flexidisc [FACT 14C]) 70
79	Factory FACT 14	THE RETURN OF THE DURUTTI COLUMN (reissue, different sleeve) 20
82	Factory FACT 44	LC (LP, with inner) 20
83	Factory FACT 74	ANOTHER SETTING (LP, with perfumed cut-out insert) 20
83	VU VINI 1	LIVE AT THE VENUE LONDON (LP)...25
86	Factory FACT 164c	VALUABLE PASSAGES (cassette in box with insert) 35
86	Factory FACT 14C	THE RETURN OF THE DURUTTI COLUMN (reissue, cassette in box with insert)...................35
86	Factory FACT 44c	LC (reissue, cassette in box with insert) 35
86	Factory FACT 74c	ANOTHER SETTING (reissue, cassette in box with insert) 35
86	Factory FACT 84c	WITHOUT MERCY (reissue, cassette in box with insert) 35
88	Factory FACT 244	VINI REILLY (LP, with free p/s 7" "I Know Very Well How I Got My Note Wrong" [FAC 244++] by Vincent Gerard & Steven Patrick) 45
88	Factory FACD 244	VINI REILLY (CD, with 3" CD "I Know Very Well How I Got My Note Wrong" [FAC CD 244++] by Vincent Gerard & Steven Patrick) 40

(see also Nosebleeds, Gammer & His Familiars, Morrissey)

IAN DURY (& THE BLOCKHEADS)

77	Stiff BUY 23	Sweet Gene Vincent/You're More Than Fair (promo pressing small "A" on label)	10
80	Stiff BUY 90	I Want To Be Straight/That's Not All (Band photo p/s)	7
77	Stiff BUY 17	Sex & Drugs & Rock & Roll/Razzle In My Pocket (p/s)	5
77	Stiff BUY 23	Sweet Gene Vincent/You're More Than Fair (p/s)	5
78	Stiff BUY 2712	What A Waste/Wake Up (12", plain white sleeve, 100 only)	100
78	Stiff BUY 38	Hit Me With Your Rhythm Stick/There Ain't Half Been Some Clever Bastards (red vinyl, p/s, one copy known)	300
78	Stiff FREEBIE 1	Sex And Drugs And Rock And Roll/England's Glory/Two Steep Hills (p/s, free at NME party/competition)	8
77	Stiff SEEZ 4	NEW BOOTS AND PANTIES!! (LP, with bonus track 'Sex And Drugs And Rock And Roll')	20
77	Stiff SEEZ 4	NEW BOOTS AND PANTIES!! (LP, limited edition gold vinyl)	25

(see also Kilburn & The High Roads, Greatest Show On Earth, Loving Awareness)

ANDREW DURYER

75	Real RR 2003	BALLADS OF A WANDERER (LP)	25

JEAN DUSHON

65	Chess CRL 4000	MAKE WAY FOR JEAN DUSHON (LP)	40

DUSK

71	Bell BLL 1167	I Hear Those Church Bells Ringing/I Cannot See To See You	12

PAT DUSKY AND MARINES

67	Stardust STP 1	I Fall To Pieces/This Can Be The Night	6

LA DÜSSELDORF

78	Radar ADA 5	La Düsseldorf/Silver Cloud (unissued, white label promo only)	25
80	Teldec	Dampfrieman/Individuellos (12", p/s)	10
81	Albion ION 1025	Tintarella Di (some might have p/s)	10
78	Radar RAD 7	DUSSELDORF (LP)	20
78	Radar RAD 10	VIVA (LP, with lyric inner)	15
80	Albion ALB 107	INDIVIDUELLOS (LP)	20

(see also Neu!)

DUST

75	20th Century BTC 1009	Rebound/Pieces	7

DUST BROTHERS

93	Dust Brothers DBS 333	Song To The Siren (12" single sided)	100
93	Dust Brothers DB's 333	Song To The Siren (12", no p/s, 500 only)	120
93	Junior Boys Own JBO 10	Song To The Siren/Song To The Siren (Sabres Of Paradise Mixes) (12", p/s)	25
94	Dust Up Beats NS 1	Loops Of Fury (12")	25
94	Boys Own COLLECT 004	14TH CENTURY SKY EP (12", no p/s)	15
94	Junior Boys Own JBO 20	MY MERCURY MOUTH EP (12", JBO sleeve)	15

(see also Chemical Brothers)

SLIM DUSTY

57	Columbia DB 4212	A Pub With No Beer/Once When I Was Mustering (with His Country Rockers)	5
59	Columbia DB 4294	The Answer To A Pub With No Beer/Winter Winds (with His Bushlanders)	5
60	Columbia SEG 8009	SLIM DUSTY AND HIS COUNTRY ROCKERS (EP)	10

DUTCH

68	Phillips	What Is Soul/Down Here	12

DUTCH SWING COLLEGE BAND

51	Saturn EGX 106	Alexander's Ragtime Band/Birthday Blues (78 picture disc)	20

DUTCHESS

81	B'kreig Waxworks EJSP 9580	Your Love/Dead And Gone	150

JACQUES DUTRONC

66	Vogue VRS 7015	Et Moi, Et Moi, Et Moi/Mini-Mini-Mini	15
66	Vogue VRS 7021	Les Cactus/L'Espace D'Une Fille	12
66	Vogue VRS 7024	J'Aime Les Filles/L'Idole	12
67	Vogue VRS 7027	Le Plus Difficile/Les Rois De La Reforme	12
67	Vogue VRL 3029	JACQUES DUTRONC (LP)	60

JOSE DUVAL

57	London HLR 8458	Message Of Love/That's What You Mean To Me	25

D & V

83	Crass 121984/1	THE NEAREST DOOR (EP)	10
85	Crass CAT NO 1	INSPIRATION GAVE THEM MOTIVATION (LP)	18

MARK DWAYNE

62	Oriole CB 1712	Remember Me Huh/Poorest Boy In Town	8
62	Oriole CB 1744	Today's Teardrops/Little Bitty Heart	8

JUDY DYBLE

06	Fungus 006	SONGS FROM THE SPINDLE AND THE WHORL (LP, hand-made sleeves, 250 only, numbered)	30

BILLY DYCE

72	G.G. GG 4532	Be My Guest/HUGH ROY: Way Down South	10
72	G.G. GG 4534	Take Warning/TYPHOON ALL STARS: Warning (Version)	8
72	G.G. GG 4537	Time Is Still Here/G.G. ALL STARS: Time — Version	7
72	Pama PM 835	Be My Guest/HUGH ROY: Way Down South	10
73	Pama PM 874	Woman Smarter/SHENLEY DUFFAS: Standing On The Hill	6
73	Bread BR 1115	You Need Love (with Millions)/G.G. ALL STARS: Love — Dub	6

DYKE & BLAZERS

67	Pye International 7N 25413	Funky Broadway (Parts 1 & 2)	20

MICHAEL DYKE

70s	Attack ATT 8112	Saturday Night Special/CHINNA : Saturday Night Version	20

BOB DYLAN

SINGLES

65	CBS 201751	The Times They Are A-Changin'/Honey, Just Allow Me One More Chance	8
65	CBS 201753	Subterranean Homesick Blues/She Belongs To Me	8
65	CBS 201781	Maggie's Farm/On The Road Again	8
65	CBS 201811	Like A Rolling Stone/Gates Of Eden	8
65	CBS 201824	Positively 4th Street/From A Buick 6	10
66	CBS 201900	Can You Please Crawl Out Your Window/Highway 61 Revisited	15
66	CBS 202053	One Of Us Must Know (Sooner Or Later)/Queen Jane Approximately	20
66	CBS 202307	Rainy Day Women Nos. 12 & 35/Pledging My Time	10
66	CBS 202258	I Want You/Just Like Tom Thumb's Blues (live)	12
66	CBS 2700	Leopard-Skin Pill-Box Hat/Most Likely You Go Your Way And I'll Go Mine (p/s)	45
66	CBS 2700	Leopard-Skin Pill-Box Hat/Most Likely You Go Your Way And I'll Go Mine	10
67	CBS 2476	Mixed Up Confusion/Corrine Corrina (unissued in U.K.)	0
69	CBS 4219	I Threw It All Away/The Drifter's Escape	6
70	CBS 5122	Wigwam/Copper Kettle (The Pale Moonlight)	5
71	CBS 7329	Watching The River Flow/Spanish Is The Loving Tongue	5
71	CBS 7688	George Jackson (Acoustic)/George Jackson (Big Band Version)	8
73	CBS 1158	Just Like A Woman/I Want You (p/s, 'Hall Of Fame Hits' series)	6
74	CBS 2006	A Fool Such As I/Lily Of The West	6
74	Island WIP 6168	On A Night Like This/Forever Young	6
75	CBS 3160	Tangled Up In Blue/If You See Her, Say Hello	6
75	CBS 3665	Million Dollar Bash/Tears Of Rage	6
76	CBS SCBS 3878	Hurricane (Part 1)/(Full Version) (some list 'Pt 1'/'Pt 2'; with p/s)	8
76	CBS SCBS 3878	Hurricane (Part 1)/(Full Version) (some list 'Pt 1'/'Pt 2'; without p/s)	5
76	CBS 3945	Lay Lady Lay/I Threw It All Away (p/s)	5
76	CBS 4859	Stuck Inside Of Mobile With The Memphis Blues Again/Rita May (p/s; demos have "Rita May" as A-side)	12
76	CBS 4859	Rita May/Stuck Inside Of Mobile With The Memphis Blues Again (demos with "Rita May" as A-side)	8
78	CBS 12-6499	Baby Stop Crying/New Pony (12", p/s)	8
78	CBS 12-6718	Is Your Love In Vain?/We Better Talk This Over (12", p/s)	8
78	CBS 6935	Changing Of The Guard/Sènor	5
81	CBS A 1406	Heart Of Mine/Let It Be Me	5
83	CBS A 3916	Union Sundown/Angels Flying Too Close To The Ground (p/s)	5
84	CBS A 4055	Jokerman/Licence To Kill (p/s, embossed or standard label)	5
84	CBS A 4055	Jokerman (Special Faded Radio Version)/Licence To Kill (p/s, promo only)	15
85	CBS GA 5020	Highway 61 Revisited (live)/It Ain't Me Babe (live) (gatefold p/s)	8
85	CBA TA 6469	When The Night Comes Falling Down (Full Length Version)/Dark Eyes (12", p/s)	8
86	MCA 23633	Band Of The Hand/M. RUBINI: Theme From Joe's Death (12", p/s)	8
87	CBS 651 148-6	The Usual/Got My Mind Made Up/They Killed Him (12", p/s; mispricing, 3rd track plays either "Drifting Too Far From Shore" or "Precious Memories")	8
88	CBS 6514066	Silvio/When Did You Leave Heaven? (p/s)	6
89	CBS 6553588	Everything Is Broken/Dead Man, Dead Man/I Want You (Live) (12" with limited edition album sleeve print)	20
89	CBS 6553587	Everything Is Broken/Death Is Not The End (p/s)	6
90	CBS 6556436	Political World/Ring Them Bells/Silvio/ All Along The Watchtower (Live) (12" p/s)	6
90	CBS 6563047	Unbelievable/10,000 Men (p/s grey shaded not laminated/brown shaded laminated)	6
00	Columbia 6693797	Things Have Changed/Blind Willy McTell (numbered p/s)	6

EPs

64	CBS 6051	DYLAN (Bob Dylan below song titles, solid/push-out centre, designer credits in bottom right corner, p/s)	40
64	CBS 6051	DYLAN (Bob Dylan vertically on left; 'EXTENDED PLAY' on 1 line above 'EP 6051', push out centre – no designer credits, p/s)	45
65	CBS 6051	DYLAN (Bob Dylan vertically on left; 'EXTENDED PLAY' on 2 lines above 'EP 6051', solid centre, no designer credits, p/s)	45
66	CBS 6070	ONE TOO MANY MORNINGS (Only EP in Europe with five songs, p/s)	50
66	CBS 6070	MR. TAMBOURINE MAN (length of EP on both sides: 27mm 'EXTENDED PLAY' on 1 line, 'Blossom Music LTD' on both sides. Solid/push-out centre, p/s)	50
66	CBS 6078	MR. TAMBOURINE MAN (length of EP divided over 2 lines, 'EXTENDED PLAY' divided over 2 lines, 'Blossom Music' (side 1) 'Bossom Music Ltd' (Side 2)	50
65	Fontana TFE 18009	WITH GOD ON OUR SIDE (Joan Baez and Bob Dylan title track)/PETE SEEGER: The Bells of Rhymney/JOAN BAEZ: Waggoner's Lad, p/s)	75
65	Fontana TFE 18010	BLOWIN' IN THE WIND (BOB DYLAN: Blowin' In The Wind/JOAN BAEZ: Oh Freedom/ PETE SEEGER: Careless Love, p/s)	75
65	Fontana TFE 18011	YE PLAYBOYS AND PLAYGIRLS (Bob Dylan and Pete Seeger title track/JOAN BAEZ: Te Ador, Te Manha/PETE SEEGER: This Land Is Mine, p/s)	75

ALBUMS

62	CBS BPG 62022	BOB DYLAN (mono)	50
62	CBS SBPG 62022	BOB DYLAN (stereo)	40
63	CBS BPG 62193	THE FREEWHEELIN' BOB DYLAN (mono)	50
63	CBS SBPG 62193	THE FREEWHEELIN' BOB DYLAN (stereo)	40
63	CBS BPG 62251	THE TIMES THEY ARE A-CHANGIN' (mono)	50
63	CBS SBPG 62251	THE TIMES THEY ARE A-CHANGIN' (stereo)	40
64	CBS BPG 62429	ANOTHER SIDE OF BOB DYLAN (mono)	50
64	CBS SBPG 62429	ANOTHER SIDE OF BOB DYLAN (stereo)	40
65	CBS BPG 62515	BRINGING IT ALL BACK HOME (mono)	50
65	CBS SBPG 62515	BRINGING IT ALL BACK HOME (stereo)	40
65	CBS BPG 62572	HIGHWAY 61 REVISITED (mono)	50
65	CBS SBGP 62572	HIGHWAY 61 REVISITED (stereo)	40
66	CBS BPG 66012	BLONDE ON BLONDE (2-LP, 8 or 9 photos on inside gatefold sleeve, mono)	60
66	CBS (S)BPG 66012	BLONDE ON BLONDE (2-LP, 8 or 9 photos on inside gatefold sleeve, stereo)	40
67	CBS BPG 62847	BOB DYLAN'S GREATEST HITS (mono)	18
68	CBS BGP 63252	JOHN WESLEY HARDING (mono)	30

(The above LPs were originally issued with rough textured labels & flipback sleeves, without 'CBS Records' credit on rear sleeve & with inner sleeves advertising other CBS LPs.)

68	CBS (S)BGP 63252	JOHN WESLEY HARDING (stereo)	15
69	CBS (M) 63601	NASHVILLE SKYLINE (mono)	30
69	CBS (S) 63601	NASHVILLE SKYLINE (mono/stereo)	15
70	CBS S 64085/6	SELF PORTRAIT	15
71	CBS S 67239	MORE BOB DYLAN GREATEST HITS	15
73	CBS S 69049	DYLAN	15
74	Island ILPS 9261	PLANET WAVES ('pink rim palm tree' label, with inner sleeve)	15

MINT VALUE £

74	Island IDBD-1	BEFORE THE FLOOD	15
75	CBS 69097	BLOOD ON THE TRACKS (orange label, red inner with painting on rear sleeve)	20
75	CBS 69097	BLOOD ON THE TRACKS (orange label, red inner with liner notes on rear sleeve)	25
75	CBS S 88147	THE BASEMENT TAPES	20
76	CBS S 86003	DESIRE	15
76	CBS CBS 86016	HARD RAIN	15
78	CBS CBS 86067	STREET LEGAL	20
79	CBS CBS 96004	AT BUDOKAN (with poster and 16 page booklet)	25
98	CBS CK265759-1	LIVE 1966 (2-LP)	40

(see also Dick Farina, Band, George Harrison, Traveling Wilburys, Doug Sahm, Earl Scruggs)

DYMONDS
| 71 | Big BG 326 | Girl You Are Too Young/RUPIE EDWARDS ALL STARS: Version | 6 |

DYNAMETRIX
| 91 | Kold Sweat KS118 | Keep The Crowd Dancing (12") | 8 |
| 94 | Kold Sweat KSLP 08 | A MEASURE OF FORCE (LP) | 12 |

DYNAMIC CONCEPT
| 74 | Power Exchange PX 103 | California Part 1/California Part 2 | 5 |

DYNAMIC CORVETTES
| 75 | Contempo CS 2059 | Funky Music Is The Thing (Parts 1 & 2) | 5 |

DYNAMIC GANG (BOB ANDY & MARCIA GRIFFITHS)
| 71 | Moodisc MU 3511 | I'll Never Believe In You/LLOYD WILLIS: Black Attack | 12 |

DYNAMIC MCS
| 87 | Tuff GrooveTUFF002 | I Feel Dynamic (12") | 100 |

DYNAMICS (JAMAICA)
| 68 | Blue Cat BS 104 | My Friends/NEVILLE IRONS: Soul Glide | 45 |
| 69 | Punch PH 1 | The Burner/Juckie Juckie (B-side actually by Tommy McCook & Carl Bryan) | 20 |

DYNAMICS (U.S.)
63	London HLX 9809	Misery/I'm The Man	50
64	King KG 1007	So In Love With Me/Say You Will	25
69	Atlantic 584 270	Ice Cream Song/The Love That I Need	20

DYNAMITES
69	Duke DU 30	John Public/CLANCY ECCLES: Fire Corner (B-side actually by King Stitt)	10
69	Duke DU 31	I Don't Care (actually by Dingle Brothers)/CLANCY ECCLES: Shoo-Be-Do	20
69	Clandisc CLA 200	Mr. Midnight (Skokiaan)/KING STITT: Who Yeah	15
70	Clandisc CLA 212	Black Beret/BARRY & AFFECTIONS: Love Me Tender	12
70	Clandisc CLA 219	Sha La La La/Pop It Up	8
71	Clandisc CLA 237	Hello Mother/FABULOUS FLAMES: Hi-De-Ho	5
69	Trojan/Clandisc TTL 21	FIRE CORNER (LP, with King Stitt)	20

(see also Clancy Eccles & Dynamites, Baba Brooks, Dennis Alcapone, Diamonds, Joe Higgs, Silvertones, Carl Dawkins, Chris Leon, Hopeton Lewis, Melodians, Cynthia Richards, Soul Twins, Stranger & Gladys, Carey & Lloyd)

DYNASTY
| 72 | Top Nix 134 | Tutankhamen/Let's Boogie | 15 |

DYNATONES
59	Top Rank JAR 149	Steel Guitar Rag/The Girl I'm Searching For	10
59	Top Rank JAR 149	Steel Guitar Rag/The Girl I'm Searching For (78)	20
66	Pye International 7N 25389	The Fife Piper/And I Always Will	50

ALAN DYSON
| 68 | Pye NPL 18218 | THE STILL SMALL VOICE OF...(LP) | 20 |

RONNIE DYSON
| 71 | CBS 7449 | When You Get Right Down To It/Sleeping Sun | 6 |
| 74 | CBS 2430 | We Can Make It Last Forever/Just A Little Love From Me | 5 |

E, THE
| 88 | SUN 57 | Kites/Kites (Instrumental) p/s | 5 |

VINCE EAGER (& THE VAGABONDS)
58	Decca F 11023	Tread Softly Stranger & Yea Yea (as Vince Eager & The Vagabonds; unissued, 2 x 1-sided demos only)	30
58	Parlophone R 4482	Five Days, Five Days/No More	30
58	Parlophone R 4482	Five Days, Five Days/No More (78)	10
59	Parlophone R 4531	When's Your Birthday, Baby?/The Railroad Song	15
59	Parlophone R 4531	When's Your Birthday, Baby?/The Railroad Song (78)	15
59	Parlophone R 4550	This Should Go On Forever/No Other Arms, No Other Lips	15
59	Top Rank JAR 191	Makin' Love/Primrose Lane	5
59	Top Rank JAR 191	Makin' Love/Primrose Lane (78)	15
60	Top Rank JAR 275	Why/El Paso	5
60	Top Rank JAR 307	Lonely Blue Boy/No Love Have I	10
61	Top Rank JAR 539	(I Wanna) Love My Life Away/I Know What I Want	5
61	Top Rank JAR 593	The World's Loneliest Man/Created In A Dream	5
63	Piccadilly 7N 35110	Any Time Is The Right Time/Heavenly	5
63	Piccadilly 7N 35157	I Shall Not Be Moved/It's Only Make Believe	5
58	Decca DFE 6504	VINCE EAGER AND THE VAGABONDS NO. 1 (EP)	100

EAGLE
| 70 | Pye International 7N 25530 | Kickin' It Back To You/Come In, It's All For Free | 15 |
| 69 | Pye Intl. NSPL 28138 | COME UNDER NANCY'S TENT (LP) | 40 |

EAGLES (JAMAICA)

69	Songbird SB 1006	Rudam Bam/Prodigal Boy (B-side actually "Any Little Bit" by Crystals)	8
72	Duke Reid DR 2522	Your Enemies Can't Hurt You/Version	7
73	Techniques TE 927	Rub It Down/TOMMY McCOOK ALL STARS: Rub It Down — Version	6

(see also Jamaican Eagles, Roy Richards)

EAGLES (U.K.)

62	Pye 7N 15451	Bristol Express/Johnny's Tune	10
62	Pye 7N 15473	Exodus: The Main Theme/March Of The Eagles	12
62	Pye 7N 15503	The Desperados/Special Agent	10
63	Pye 7N 15550	Come On Baby (To The Floral Dance)/Theme From Station Six Sahara	10
63	Pye 7N 15571	Eagles Nest/Poinciana (unreleased)	0
64	Pye 7N 15613	Andorra/Moonstruck	10
64	Pye 7N 15650	Write Me A Letter/Wishin' And Hopin'	10
62	Pye NEP 24166	NEW SOUND T.V. Themes (EP)	20
63	Pye NPL 18084	SMASH HITS (LP)	45

(see also Valerie Mountain)

EAGLES (U.S.)

72	Asylum AYM 505	Take It Easy/Get You In The Mood (promo only p/s)	8
75	Asylum K 53003	DESPERADO (LP, audiophile pressing, mail-order via Hi-Fi Today mag)	80

SNOOKS EAGLIN

60s	Storyville A 45056	Country Boy/Alberta (some with p/s)	15
60s	Storyville SEP 386	BLUES ANTHOLOGY VOL. 6 (EP)	20
61	Heritage HLP 1002	SNOOKS EAGLIN (LP, 99 only)	100
63	Storyville SLP 119	NEW ORLEANS STREET SINGER (LP)	25
64	Storyville SLP 140	VOL. 2 — BLUES FROM NEW ORLEANS (LP)	15
70s	Storyville 670 146	PORTRAITS IN BLUES VOLUME 1 (LP)	18

JIM EANES

59	Melodisc 1530	Christmas Doll/It Won't Seem Like Christmas	10

EARCANDY

93	Poor Person Prod. PPPR 1	SPACE IS JUST A PLACE (LP, handmade sleeve, 500 only)	20
94	Poor Person Prod. PPPR 2	TIME IS JUST A STATE OF MIND (LP, handmade sleeve)	20
95	Poor Person Prod. PPPR 5	SOUND IS JUST THE WAY YOU EAR IT (LP, handmade sleeve with insert, numbered, 600 only)	20
95	Poor Person Prod. PPPR 8	TASTING 1,2,3, TASTING (LP, handmade sleeve & insert, numbered, 500 only)	20

EARGASM

81	Venture EAR 26	This Is Lovers Rock/Name That Tune (as Eargasm, P Pop & Beagle)	20
80	Venture CUT 007	LOVERS DUB (LP)	40

ROBERT EARL

60	Philips BBL 7394	SHOWCASE (LP)	12

CHARLES EARLAND

78	Mercury 9199831	Let The Music Play/Broken Heart (12")	15

EARL & DEAN

66	Strike JH 323	Slowly Goin' Out Of My Head/Little Buddy	7

KENNETH EARLE

60	Decca F 11205	The New Frankie And Johnny/40-30-40	10
60	Decca F 11224	Standing On The Corner/Put Your Arms Around Me, Honey	5

EARL-JEAN

64	Colpix PX 729	I'm Into Somethin' Good/We Love And Learn	30
64	Colpix PX 748	Randy/They're Jealous Of Me	30

(see also Cookies)

JOSEPH EARLOCKS

80s	Freedom Sounds FSD014	Free Up The Blackman/JAMAICANS & I DAUGHTER : Country Life (12")	20

EARLS

63	Stateside SS 153	Remember Then/Let's Waddle	40
63	London HL 9702	Never/I Keep-A Tellin' You	50
71	Atlantic 2091 129	Remember Then/I Believe	10

EARLY B

82	Black Solidarity BSI 001	Imitator/Mi Huh Know (with Papa San)	40

EARTH

69	CBS 4671	Resurrection City/Comical Man	40
69	Decca F 22908	Stranger Of Fortune/Everybody Sing The Song	15

EARTH & FIRE

73	Polydor 2001-435	Maybe Tomorrow, Maybe Tonight/Theme From Atlantis	8
70	Penny Farthing PEN 741	Mechanical Lover/Ruby Is The One	5
70	Polydor 56790	Seasons/Paradise	15
71	Nepentha 6129 001	Invitation/Wild And Exciting	15
72	Polydor 2001 356	Memories/From The End To The Beginning	8
71	Nepentha 6437 004	EARTH AND FIRE (LP, gatefold sleeve)	600
73	Polydor 2310 262	ATLANTIS (LP, laminated sleeve)	20

EARTH & STONE

79	Cha Cha CHAD 09	Sweet Africa/Dance With Me (12")	30
79	Cha Cha CHAD 013	False Ruler/Don't Let Them Fool You (12")	50
79	Cha Cha CHAD 015	Slave Driver/Magic Woman (12")	30
79	Cha Cha CHADLP 007	KOOL ROOTS (LP)	60
77	Different DIFF 105	BACK TO AFRICA (LP)	50

EARTHBOUND

79	Archway AR 17945	Liberated Lady/Song For South Kensington/Robot (12" p/s)	20

EARTH BOYS

59	Capitol CL 14979	Barbara Ann/Space Girl	25

MINT VALUE £

EARTH LEAKAGE TRIP

91	Moving Shadow SHADOW 1	PSYCHOTRONIC EP (12", p/s)..15
92	Rising High RSN 17	THE VIRTUALITY EP (12")..8
92	Rising High RSN 30	NEOPOLITAN EP (12")..8

EARTHLINGS

| 65 | Parlophone R 5242 | Landing Of The Daleks/March Of The Robots..50 |

EARTH OPERA

68	Elektra EKSN 45035	Close Your Eyes And Shut The Door/Dreamless..8
69	Elektra EKSN 45049	American Eagle Tragedy/When You Were Full Of Wonder..7
69	Elektra EKSN 45061	Alfie Finney/Home To You..7
68	Elektra EKS 74016	EARTH OPERA (LP, gatefold sleeve)..35
69	Elektra EKS 74038	GREAT AMERICAN EAGLE TRAGEDY (LP)..25

(see also Rowan Brothers)

EARTHQUAKE

| 74 | Cloud One HIT 4 | Friday On My Mind/Madness (p/s)..10 |

EARTHQUAKERS

| 67 | Stateside SS 2050 | Whistling In The Sunshine/Dreaming In The Moonlight..10 |

EARTHQUAKES

| 69 | Duke DU 54 | Pair Of Wings/I Can't Stop Loving You..12 |
| 69 | Duke DU 56 | Earthquake/Simmering..20 |

(see also Sir Collins & Earthquakes)

TIM EASLEY

| 68 | Bell BLL 1036 | Susie Q (Parts 1 & 2)..10 |

EAST RIVER PIPE

93	Sarah SARAH 75	Helmet On/Happytown/Axl Or Iggy (foldover p/s, insert)..12
93	Sarah SARAH 78	She's A Real Good Time/My Life Is Wrong/Times Square Go-Go Boy (foldover p/s in poly bag, insert)..12
93	Sarah SARAH 405	GOODBYE CALIFORNIA (10" LP)..20
94	Sarah SARAH 621	POOR FRICKY (LP)..25
95	Sarah SARAH 407	EVEN THE SUN WAS AFRAID (10" LP)..30

EAST BAY RAY

| 84 | Alt. Tentacles VIRUS 34 | Trouble In Town/Poisonheart (p/s)..5 |

(see also Dead Kennedys)

EASTER MONDAY

| 89 | SRT TTWW001 | EASTER MONDAY EP (numbered foldover p/s, 500 only)..15 |

EAST MAIN ST. EXPLOSION

| 69 | Fontana TF 1039 | Hop, Skip And Jump/Little Jackie Horner..6 |

EAST OF EDEN

70	Deram SML 1050	SNAFU (LP, mono, red/white label with small logo - existence unconfirmed)..0
68	Atlantic 584 198	King Of Siam/Ballad Of Harvey Kaye..100
69	Deram DM 242	Northern Hemisphere/Communion..10
70	Deram DM 297	Jig-A-Jig/Marcus Junior..8
71	Deram DM 338	Ramadhan/In The Snow For A Blow/Better Git It In Your Soul/ Have To Whack It Up A Bit ..10
72	Harvest HAR 5055	Boogie Woogie 'Flu/Last Dance Of The Clown (p/s)..8
73	United Artists UP 35567	Sin City Girls/All Our Yesterdays..5
69	Deram DML 1038	MERCATOR PROJECTED (LP, mono, red/white label with large logo)..80
69	Deram SML 1038	MERCATOR PROJECTED (LP, stereo, red/white label with large logo)..60
70	Deram SML 1050	SNAFU (LP, stereo, red/white label with small logo)..40
71	Decca SPA 157	WORLD OF EAST OF EDEN (LP, credited on sleeve and blue/silver label as a Deram release)..12
71	Harvest SHVL 792	EAST OF EDEN (LP, gatefold sleeve, early copies with EMI box on side 1 label but no EMI box on side 2)..50
71	Harvest SHVL 792	EAST OF EDEN (LP, gatefold sleeve)..30
72	Harvest SHVL 792	EAST OF EDEN (LP, gatefold sleeve, non EMI 2nd pressing with indented centre perimeter)..35
71	Harvest SHVL 796	NEW LEAF (LP, gatefold sleeve, with EMI on label)..40

EASTWOOD

70	SRT SRTS7332	Little Miss Lucy/Living To Learn..200
71	CBS 7076	I Am Free/Gypsy..45
72	CBS 7325	Orphan/Another Day In My Life..25

ALAN JAMES EASTWOOD

68	President PT 209	Blackbird Charlie/My Sun (as Bugsy Eastwood)..6
71	President PT 320	Seeds/Boston..6
72	President PT 379	Closer To The Truth/Strange News..20
71	President PTLS 1037	SEEDS (LP)..40

CLINT EASTWOOD (1)

62	Cameo Parkway C 240	Rowdy/Cowboy Wedding Song (in p/s)..10
62	Cameo Parkway C 240	Rowdy/Cowboy Wedding Song..5
62	Cameo SC 1056	COWBOY FAVOURITES... (LP)..30

CLINT EASTWOOD (2)

79	Greensleeves GRED 25	True True Love/Me Go Deh Already (12")..15
77	Jamaica Sounds JSLP 0010	JAH LIGHTS SHINING (LP)..15
78	Cha Cha CHALP003	DEATH IN THE ARENA (LP)..45
78	Third World TWS933	AFRICAN YOUTH (LP)..35
79	Burning Vibrations BV 1001 LOVE AND HAPPINESS (LP)	LOVE AND HAPPINESS (LP)..20
80	Greensleeves GREL 17	SEX EDUCATION (LP)..15

EASTWOOD & POWELL

| 71 | President PT 352 | Beautiful/Opal Blue Sunday..8 |

ALAN EASTWOOD

| 73 | President PT 403 | Moonchild/Red Shoe Truckin'..8 |

EASYBEATS

66	United Artists UP 1144	Come And See Her/Make You Feel Alright (Women)	20
66	United Artists UP 1157	Friday On My Mind/Made My Bed, Gonna Lie In It	8
66	United Artists UP 1175	Who'll Be The One?/Saturday Night	12
67	United Artists UP 1183	Heaven And Hell/Pretty Girl	12
67	United Artists UP 1201	The Music Goes Round My Head/Come In, You'll Get Pneumonia	12
68	United Artists UP 2209	Hello, How Are You?/Falling Off The Edge Of The World	8
68	United Artists UP 2219	The Land Of Make-Believe/We All Live Happily	8
68	United Artists UP 2243	Good Times/Lay Me Down And Die	8
69	Polydor 56335	St. Louis/Can't Find Love	8
70	Polydor 2001 028	(Who Are My) Friends?/Rock'n'Roll Boogie	6
67	United Artists (S)ULP 1167	GOOD FRIDAY (LP)	120
68	United Artists (S)ULP 1193	VIGIL (LP)	70
70	Polydor Special 2482 010	FRIENDS (LP)	60

(see also Paintbox, Haffy's Whisky Sour, Harry Vanda, Grapefruit)

EASY RIDERS

58	Philips PB 823	Salute To Windjammer/Kari Waits For Me	6
60	London HLR 9204	Young In Love/Saturday's Child	6
60	London HA-R 2323	REMEMBER THE ALAMO (LP, mono)	12
60	London SAH-R 6126	REMEMBER THE ALAMO (LP, stereo)	15

(see also Terry Gilkyson & Easy Riders, Vic Damone, Frankie Laine)

EASY STREET

76	Polydor 2058807	Feels Like Heaven/Shadows On The Wall (no p/s)	10
70s	Muscle Music AP 591	Person To Person/Easy Come Easy Go	30
77	Polydor 2058873	Flying/Blame The Love	12
77	Polydor 2383 444	UNDER THE GLASS (LP)	12

EAT

90	Yes YES 3	Psycho Couch/Alien Detector (p/s)	10

EATER

77	The Label TLR 001	Outside View/You (p/s)	10
77	The Label TLR 003	Thinkin' Of The USA/Space Dreamin'/Michael's Monetary System (p/s)	10
77	The Label TLR 004	Lock It Up/Jeepster (p/s)	10
77	The Label TLR 004/12	Lock It Up/Jeepster (12", p/s)	8
78	The Label TLR 007	GET YOUR YO-YO'S OUT (EP, white vinyl; blue, green or red p/s)	8
78	The Label TLR 007	GET YOUR YO-YO'S OUT (12" EP, white vinyl; (blue, green or red p/s)	10
78	The Label TLR 009	What She Wants She Needs/Reaching For The Sky (p/s)	6
78	The Label TLRLP 001	THE ALBUM (LP, with inner sleeve)	30
85	De Lorean EAT 1	THE HISTORY OF EATER (LP, 1,000 each on red, white & blue vinyl, with bonus 7" [EAT FREEBIE 1])	12
85	De Lorean EAT 1	THE HISTORY OF EATER (LP, green vinyl)	12

(see also Andy Blade)

EATHOPIANS

69	Nu Beat NB 038	Buss Your Mouth (actually "Contention" by Ethiopians)/REGGAE BOYS: Rough Way Ahead (B-side actually by Keith Blake & Hi-Tals)	45
68	Crab 4	Reggie Hit The Town/Ding Dong Bell	36

(see also Ethiopians)

KOOKIE EATON

68	Condor PS 1002	Cream Machine/Joke B Side	15

EAZIE RYDER

78	Graduate GRAD 1	Motorbikin'/City Lights (p/s)	15

EBONIES

68	Philips BF 1648	Never Gonna Break Your Heart Again/Shoeshine Boy	10

EBONY

84	Touched TOUCH 1	Dream Girl/We'll Fight Back (p/s)	6

EBONY DUBSTERS

03	Ebony EBR 028	EBONY DUBS VOL. 2 (12", p/s one side etched)	20

EBONY SISTERS

69	Bullet BU 401	Let Me Tell You Boy/RHYTHM RULERS: Mannix	12
70	Bullet BU 420	Each Time/BUNNY LEE ALLSTARS: Boss Walk	20

(see also Sister)

BUDDY EBSEN

65	Valiant VS 128	HOWDY HILLBILLIES (LP)	15

KATJA EBSTEIN

70	Liberty LBF 15317	No More Love For Me/Without Love	30

ECCENTRICS

65	Pye 7N 15850	What You Got/Fe Fi Fo Fum	45

CLANCY ECCLES (& DYNAMITES)

61	Blue Beat BB 34	River Jordan/I Live And I Love (with Hersan & His City Slickers)	15
61	Blue Beat BB 67	Freedom/More Proof	25
63	Island WI 044	Judgement/Baby Please (B-side actually with Paulette)	25
63	Island WI 098	Glory Hallelujah/Hot Rod (B-side actually by Roland Alphonso)	25
65	Ska Beat JB 194	Sammy No Dead/Roam Jerusalem	20
65	Ska Beat JB 198	Miss Ida/KING ROCKY: What Is Katty	20
67	Doctor Bird DB 1156	Feel The Rhythm/Easy Snapping (B-side actually by Theo Beckford)	30
67	Pama PM 701	What Will Your Mama Say/Darling Don't Do That	25
67	Pama PMB 703	Western Organ/Mother's Advice (actually by The Clancy Set)	20
68	Pama PM 712	The Fight/Great	20
68	Nu Beat NB 006	Festival '68/I Really Love You	25
69	Trojan TR 639	Sweet Africa/Let Us Be Lovers	30
69	Trojan TR 647	Bangarang Crash/DYNAMITES: Rahthid	50
69	Trojan TR 648	Constantinople/Deacon Sun	30
69	Trojan TR 649	Demonstration/VAL BENNETT: My Girl	30
69	Trojan TR 658	Fattie Fattie/SILVERSTARS: Last Call	30

Jimmy ECHO

MINT VALUE £

69	Duke DU 9	Auntie Lulu/SLICKERS: Bag A Boo	55
69	Duke DU 31	Shoo-Be-Do/DYNAMITES: I Don't Care (B-side actually by Dingle Brothers)	20
69	Clandisc CLA 201	The World Needs Loving/DYNAMITES: Dollar Train (B-side actually by Clancy Eccles)	20
69	Clandisc CLA 206	Dance Beat/KING STITT: The Ugly One	25
70	Clandisc CLA 209	Open Up/HIGGS & WILSON: Agane (B-side actually "Again")	10
70	Clandisc CLA 211	Promises/Real Sweet (both sides with Dynamites)	8
70	Clandisc CLA 212	Black Beret (with Dynamites)/BARRY & AFFECTIONS: Love Me Tender	12
70	Clandisc CLA 213	Phantom/Skank Me (both sides with Dynamites) (B-side actually by Barry & Affections)	12
70	Clandisc CLA 214	Africa/Africa Part Two (both sides with Dynamites)	6
70	Clandisc CLA 221	Unite Tonight/Uncle Joe	6
70	Clandisc CLA 227	Credit Squeeze/DYNAMITES: Credit Squeeze	6
71	Clandisc CLA 231	Sweet Jamaica/DYNAMITES: Going Up West	6
71	Clandisc CLA 232	Rod Of Correction/Rod Of Correction Version	6
71	Clandisc CLA 235	John Crow Skank/KING STITT: Merry Rhythm	10
71	Clandisc CLA 236	Power For The People/DYNAMITES: Power For The People — Version	8
71	Pama Supreme PS 332	What Will Your Mama Say/TIGER: United We Stand	10
72	Clandisc CLA 239	Hallelujah, Free At Last/DYNAMITES: Sha-La-La	8
72	Attack ATT 8037	Ganja Free/DYNAMITES: Ganja (Version)	12
69	Clandisc TTL 22	FREEDOM (LP)	30
69	Trojan TTL 22	FREEDOM (LP)	40
70	Clandisc TBL 124	HERBSMAN REGGAE (LP)	50
73	Big Shot BILP 101	TOP OF THE LADDER (LP)	20

(see also Dynamites, Drumbago, Marlene Webber, Westmorelites)

JIMMY ECHO
65	Columbia DB 7629	After Tonight/Practise What You Preach	6

ECHO & BUNNYMEN
79	Zoo CAGE 004	Pictures On My Wall/Read It In Books (p/s, 4000 only)	8
83	Korova KOW 26	The Cutter/Way Out And Up We Go/Zimbo (12", with bonus Peel Session [KOW 26C])	8
84	Korova KOW 35F/	Seven Seas/All You Need Is Love//The Killing Moon/Stars Are Stars/ Villiers Terrace (numbered double pack, gatefold p/s)	8
88	Korova KOW 43P	Bring On The Dancing Horses/Over Your Shoulder ('cow'-shaped picture disc in stickered PVC sleeve)	6
81	Korova KODE 1	CROCODILES (LP, with bonus 7", "Do It Clean"/"Read It In Books" [SAM 128] & inner sleeve)	12
83	Korova KODE 6	PORCUPINE (LP, with bonus Peel Session [KOW 26C])	12
85	Korova KODE 13	SONGS TO LEARN AND SING (LP, with lyric booklet & 7", "The Pictures On My Wall"/"Read It In Books" [p/s, yellow/blue labels, CAGE 004], no "Voodoo Billy" run-off groove message; signed)	25

(see also Ian McCulloch, Will Sergeant)

ECHO BASE
84	DEP International DEP 14	Out Of My Reach/Splash Down (p/s)	12
85	DEP International DEP 19	Puppet At The Go Go/Genius + Soul = Jazz (p/s)	12
85	DEP International LPDEP 9	BUY ME (LP)	15

(see also Ocean Colour Scene)

ECHOES (U.K.)
62	Fontana 267254 TF	Cloak And Dagger/Sounds Like Winter	10
62	Fontana TF 392	The Happy Whistler/Sticks And Stones	8
63	Fontana TF 415	The Jog/Marching Thru'	10
64	Fontana TF 439	My Little Girl/More	10
64	Philips BF 1370	Don't You Believe Them/I'll Get Over You	10
66	Philips BF 1480	Got To Run/Thanks A Lot	10
68	Philips BF 1687	Searchin' For You Baby/Listen To Me Baby	15

ECHOES (U.S.)
60	Top Rank JAR 399	Born To Be With You/My Guiding Light	25
61	Top Rank JAR 553	Baby Blue/Boomerang	22

ECHOES & CELESTIALS (JAMAICA)
61	Hornet H 1004	Are You Mine/I'll Love You Forever	18
62	Blue Beat BB 89	Are You Mine/I'll Love You Forever (reissue)	10

BILLY ECKSTINE
53	MGM SP 1011	Kiss Of Fire/I Apologise	6
53	MGM SP 1020	Come To The Mardi Gras/Be Fair	5
53	MGM SP 1040	Coquette/A Fool In Love	5
53	MGM SP 1055	I've Never Been In Love Before/I'll Know	5
53	MGM SP 1060	St. Louis Blues (Parts 1 & 2) (as Billy Eckstine & Metronome All Stars)	5
54	MGM SP 1082	Tenderly/Fortune Telling Cards	5
54	MGM SP 1084	Rendezvous/Don't Get Around Much Anymore	5
54	MGM SP 1095	Seabreeze/Sophisticated Lady	5
54	MGM SP 1101	No One But You/I Let A Song Go Out Of My Heart	20
54	MGM SP 1107	Beloved/Olay Olay (The Bullfighter's Song)	5
55	MGM SP 1117	Mood Indigo/Do Nothin' Till You Hear From Me	5
55	MGM SP 1124	What More Is There To Say?/Prelude To A Kiss	5
55	MGM SP 1136	Love Me Or Leave Me/The Life Of The Party	5
55	MGM SP 1140	More Than You Know/La De Do De Do (Honey Bug Song)	5
56	MGM SP 1153	Farewell To Romance/Lost In Loveliness	5
56	MGM SP 1167	Good-bye/You've Got Me Crying Again	5
56	MGM SP 1170	The Show Must Go On/You'll Get Yours	5
56	MGM MGM 925	Solitude/I Got It Bad (And That Ain't Good)	5
57	MGM MGM 948	A Man Doesn't Know/My Fickle Heart	5
57	HMV POP 341	Pretty, Pretty/Blue Illusion	5
57	MGM MGM 970	Bring Back The Thrill/Over The Rainbow	5
65	Tamla Motown TMG 533	Had You Been Around/Down To Earth	90
65	Tamla Motown TMG 533	Had You Been Around/Down To Earth (DJ copy)	150
57	Parlophone GEP 8672	A DATE WITH RHYTHM (EP, with His All Star Band)	10
54	MGM MGM-D 126	TENDERLY (10" LP)	12
56	MGM MGM-D 138	THAT OLD FEELING (10" LP)	12
58	MGM MGM-D 151	A WEAVER OF DREAMS (10" LP)	12
66	T. Motown TML 11025	THE PRIME OF MY LIFE (LP, mono)	55

66	T. Motown STML 11025	THE PRIME OF MY LIFE (LP, stereo)	65
67	T. Motown TML 11046	MY WAY (LP, mono)	50
67	T. Motown STML 11046	MY WAY (LP, stereo)	60
69	T. Motown (S)TML 11101	GENTLE ON MY MIND (LP, mono/stereo)	45

(see also Sarah Vaughan & Billy Eckstine)

ECLECTION
68	Elektra EKSN 45033	Nevertheless/Mark Time	12
68	Elektra EKSN 45040	Another Time, Another Place/Betty Brown	12
68	Elektra EKSN 45042	Please/Saint George And The Dragon	12
68	Elektra EKSN 45046	Please (Mark II)/In The Early Days	10
76	Elektra K 12196	Nevertheless/Please	5
68	Elektra EKL 4023	ECLECTION (LP, gatefold sleeve, also stereo EKS 74023)	50

(see also Fotheringay, Dorris Henderson, Trevor Lucas, Mogul Thrash)

ECOLOGY
92	Vicious Pumpin'	THE COMMUNAL MIND EP (12", stamped white label)	20
92	Vicious Pumpin' OBS 004	ECOLOGY EP (12", stamped white label)	30
92	Vicious Pumpin' VIC 002	THE SMOKIN' JAM EP (12", stamped white label)	20
93	Vicious Pumpin' VIC 010	Vicious House/Take Me Higher (12", stamped white label)	15

ECSTASY CLUB
88	Swordfish DROP 1	JESUS LOVES THE ACID (EP, 12")	15
88	Flim Flam FFR1207	JESUS LOVES THE ACID (EP, 12")	20
88	Flim Flam FFR1207	JESUS LOVES THE ACID (EP, 12" picture disc)	20
89	LD Records	JESUS LOVES THE ACID (EP, 12")	20

ECSTASY, PASSION & PAIN
74	Pye International 7N 25641	Don't Burn Your Bridges Behind You/I Wouldn't Give You Up	5
74	Pye International 7N 25660	Good Things Don't Last Forever/Born To Lose You	8
74	Pye International 7N 25669	Ask Me/I'll Take The Blame	5

ECTOMORPH
90s	Woronzow WOO 15	THE FURIOUS SLEEPER (LP, with poster & inserts, 500 only)	20

EDDIE & THE CRAZY JETS
64	King KG 1000	Come On Let's Slop/Down By The Riverside	6

EDDIE & THE HOT RODS
76	Island WIP 6270DJ	Writing On The Wall/Cruisin' (In The Lincoln) (promos in generic title p/s)	25
76	Island WIP 6270	Writing On The Wall/Cruisin' (In The Lincoln) (in black & white p/s)	15
76	Island WIP 6270	Writing On The Wall/Cruisin' (In The Lincoln)	5
76	Island WIP 6306	Wooly Bully/Horseplay (Weary Of The Schmaltz) (p/s)	8
76	Island WIP 6354	Teenage Depression/Shake (p/s)	10
77	Island WIP 6388	I Might Be Lying/Ignore Them (p/s)	10
77	Island 12WIP 6401	Do Anything You Wanna Do/Schoolgirl Love (12", white stickered sleeve)	8
77	Island IEP 5	AT THE SPEED OF SOUND (12", plain sleeve)	8
77	Island WIP 6411	Quit This Town/Distortion May Be Expected (p/s)	5
77	Island 12WIP 6438	Life On The Line/Do Anything You Wanna Do (live)/(I Don't Know) What's Really Going On (live)/Why Can't It Be (live) (12", p/s)	10
76	Island ILPS 9457	TEENAGE DEPRESSION (LP, with poster)	25
76	Island ILPS 9457	TEENAGE DEPRESSION (LP, without poster)	15

(see also Rods, Rob Tyner & Hot Rods, Lew Lewis)

JASON EDDIE & THE CENTREMEN
65	Parlophone R 5388	Whatcha Gonna Do Baby/Come On Baby (as Jason Eddie & the Centremen)	175
66	Parlophone R 5473	Singing The Blues/True To You (as Jason Eddie & the Centremen)	175
69	Tangerine DP 0010	Heart And Soul/Playing The Clown (solo)	50

EDDIE & JERRY
72	Hillcrest HCT 4	Hail Rasta Man Hail/UPSETTERS: Scorcher	8

EDDIE'S CROWD
66	CBS 202078	Baby Don't Look Down/Take It Easy Baby	90

DUANE EDDY (& THE REBELS)
78s
58	London HL 8669	Rebel-Rouser/Stalkin'	15
58	London HL 8723	Ramrod/The Walker (as Duane Eddy & Rebels, actually by Al Casey)	15
58	London HL 8764	Cannonball/Mason-Dixon Lion (as Duane Eddy & Rebels)	15
59	London HLW 8821	The Lonely One/Detour	20
59	London HLW 8879	Peter Gunn/Yep!	40
59	London HLW 8929	Forty Miles Of Bad Road/The Quiet Three	30
59	London HLW 9007	Some Kind-A Earthquake/First Love, First Tears	30
60	London HLW 9050	Bonnie Came Back/Movin' 'N' Groovin'	40
60	London HLW 9104	Shazam!/The Secret Seven	40
60	London HLW 9162	Because They're Young/Rebel Walk	60

SINGLES
58	London HL 8669	Rebel-Rouser/Stalkin' (initially with triangular centre)	15
58	London HL 8669	Rebel-Rouser/Stalkin' (later round centre)	6
58	London HL 8723	Ramrod/The Walker (as Duane Eddy & Rebels, actually by Al Casey tri-centre centre)	15
58	London HL 8723	Ramrod/The Walker (as Duane Eddy & Rebels, actually by Al Casey round centre)	8
58	London HL 8764	Cannonball/Mason-Dixon Lion (as Duane Eddy & Rebels, tri centre)	15
58	London HL 8764	Cannonball/Mason-Dixon Lion (as Duane Eddy & Rebels, round centre)	8
59	London HLW 8821	The Lonely One/Detour (triangular centre)	15
60	London HLW 9050	Bonnie Came Back/Movin' 'N' Groovin' (tri centre)	15
59	London HLW 8821	The Lonely One/Detour (round centre)	8
59	London HLW 8879	Peter Gunn/Yep! (triangular or round centre)	12
59	London HLW 8929	Forty Miles Of Bad Road/The Quiet Three (triangular centre)	10
59	London HLW 8929	Forty Miles Of Bad Road/The Quiet Three (round centre)	6
59	London HLW 9007	Some Kind-A Earthquake/First Love, First Tears (tri centre)	15
59	London HLW 9007	Some Kind-A Earthquake/First Love, First Tears (round centre)	6
60	London HLW 9050	Bonnie Came Back/Movin' 'N' Groovin'	5
60	London HLW 9104	Shazam!/The Secret Seven	5

60	London HLW 9162	Because They're Young/Rebel Walk	5
60	London HLW 9225	Kommotion/Theme For Moon Children	5
61	London HLW 9257	Pepe/Lost Friend	6
61	London HLW 9324	Theme From Dixie/The Battle	5
61	London HLW 9370	Ring Of Fire/Gidget Goes Hawaiian	6
61	London HLW 9406	Drivin' Home/My Blue Heaven	6
61	London HLW 9477	The Avenger/Londonderry Air	6
61	Parlophone R 4826	Caravan (Parts 1 & 2) (actually by Al Casey)	8
62	RCA RCA 1288	Deep In The Heart Of Texas/Saints And Sinners	6
62	RCA RCA 1300	The Ballad Of Paladin/Wild Westerner	5
62	RCA RCA 1316	(Dance With The) Guitar Man/Stretchin' Out (with Rebelettes)	5
63	RCA RCA 1329	Boss Guitar/Desert Rat (with Rebelettes)	6
63	RCA RCA 1344	Lonely Boy, Lonely Guitar/Joshin'	6
63	RCA RCA 1357	You're Baby's Gone Surfin'/Shuckin'	10
63	RCA RCA 1369	My Baby Plays The Same Old Song On His Guitar All Night Long/ Guitar'd And Feather'd	8
64	RCA RCA 1389	The Son Of Rebel Rouser/The Story Of Three Loves	8
64	RCA RCA 1425	Guitar Star/The Iguana	15
65	Colpix PX 779	Trash/South Phoenix	15
65	Colpix PX 788	The House Of The Rising Sun/Don't Think Twice, It's All Right	15
66	Reprise RS 20504	Daydream/This Guitar Was Made For Twangin'	15
67	Reprise RS 20557	Monsoon/Roarin'	15
68	Reprise RS 20690	Niki Hoeky/Velvet Nights (Theme From "Elvira Madigan")	15
68	RCA RCA 1701	Dance With The Guitar Man/SAM COOKE: Another Saturday Night (withdrawn)	15
68	London HLW 10191	Peter Gunn/Rebel-Rouser	5
69	CBS 3962	Break My Mind/Loving Bird	15
75	Target 101	Love Confusion/Love Is A Warm Emotion	5

EXPORT SINGLES

58	London HL 7057	Ramrod/The Walker (as Duane Eddy & Rebels)	20
59	London HL 7072	The Lonely One/Detour	20
59	London HL 7076	Yep!/Three-30-Blues	30
59	London SLW 4001	Peter Gunn/Yep! (stereo)	90
59	London HL 7080	Forty Miles Of Bad Road/The Quiet Three	15
60	London HL 7090	Bonnie Come Back/Lost Island	15
60	London HL 7096	Because They're Young/Rebel Walk	15

EPs

58	London RE 1175	REBEL ROUSER (as Douane Eddy)	20
59	London RE-W 1216	THE LONELY ONE	20
59	London RE-W 1217	YEP!	15
60	London RE-W 1252	BECAUSE THEY'RE YOUNG	10
60	London RE-W 1257	TWANGY	15
61	London RE-W 1287	PEPE	15
61	London RE-W 1303	DUANE EDDY PLAYS MOVIE THEMES	20
61	London RE-W 1341	TWANGY NO. 2	20
63	RCA RCX 7115	A COUNTRY TWANG	25
63	RCA RCX 7129	MR. TWANG	25
64	RCA RCX 7146	TWANGIN' UP A SMALL STORM	30
65	Colpix PXE 304	COTTONMOUTH	50

ALBUMS

58	London HA-W 2160	HAVE 'TWANGY' GUITAR, WILL TRAVEL	45
59	London HA-W 2191	ESPECIALLY FOR YOU (mono)	20
59	London SAH-W 6045	ESPECIALLY FOR YOU (stereo with different version of "Tuxedo Junction")	20
60	London HA-W 2236	THE "TWANG'S" THE "THANG!" (mono)	20
60	London SAH-W 6068	THE "TWANG'S" THE "THANG!" (stereo)	30
60	London HA-W 2285	SONGS OF OUR HERITAGE (gatefold sleeve, mono)	20
60	London SAH-W 6119	SONGS OF OUR HERITAGE (gatefold sleeve, stereo)	22
61	London HA-W 2325	A MILLION DOLLARS' WORTH OF TWANG	25
61	London HA-W 2373	GIRLS, GIRLS, GIRLS (mono)	25
61	London SAH-W 6173	GIRLS, GIRLS, GIRLS (stereo)	30
62	London HA-W 2435	A MILLION DOLLARS' WORTH OF TWANG VOL. 2	25
62	RCA RD 27264/SF 5134	TWISTIN' AND TWANGIN' (mono/stereo)	25
62	RCA RD/SF 7510	TWANGY GUITAR — SILKY STRINGS (mono)	15
62	RCA SF 7510	TWANGY GUITAR — SILKY STRINGS (stereo)	25
63	RCA RD/SF 7545	DANCE WITH THE GUITAR MAN (mono)	20
63	RCA SF 7545	DANCE WITH THE GUITAR MAN (stereo)	25
63	RCA RD/SF 7560	TWANG A COUNTRY SONG (mono)	20
63	RCA SF 7560	TWANG A COUNTRY SONG (stereo)	25
63	RCA RD/SF 7568	TWANGIN' UP A STORM (mono)	20
63	RCA SF 7568	TWANGIN' UP A STORM (stereo)	25
64	RCA RD/SF 7621	LONELY GUITAR (mono)	20
64	RCA SF 7621	LONELY GUITAR (stereo)	22
64	RCA RD/SF 7656	WATER SKIING (mono)	25
64	RCA SF 7656	WATER SKIING (stereo)	30
65	RCA RD/SF 7689	TWANGIN' THE GOLDEN HITS (mono)	15
65	RCA SF 7689	TWANGIN' THE GOLDEN HITS (stereo)	25
65	RCA RD/SF 7754	TWANGSVILLE (mono)	20
65	RCA SF 7754	TWANGSVILLE (stereo)	25
65	Colpix PXL 490	DUANE A-GO-GO-GO	25
66	Colpix PXL 494	DUANE EDDY DOES BOB DYLAN	25
67	Reprise R(S)LP 6218	THE BIGGEST TWANG OF THEM ALL (mono)	15
67	Reprise R(S)LP 6218	THE BIGGEST TWANG OF THEM ALL (stereo)	18
67	Reprise RLP 6240	THE ROARIN' TWANGIES (mono only)	30

(see also Lee Hazlewood)

PEARL EDDY

54	HMV 7M 262	Devil Lips/That's What A Heart Is For	12

EDDY & TEDDY

61	London HLU 9367	Bye Bye Butterfly/Star Crossed Lovers	15

EDDYSONS
68	Olga OLE 010	Ups And Downs/Sweet Memories	7

DAVID EDE BAND
60	Pye 7N 15280	Easy Go/The Blue Bird (as David Ede & Rabin Rock)	15
61	Pye 7N 15329	Obsession/Bootnik	12
61	Pye 7N 15370	Last Night/Ding Dong John (as David Ede & Go Man Go Men)	20
61	Pye 7N 15394	Twelfth Street Rag/No Hats On Ilkley	6
62	Pye 7N 15417	Twistin' Those Meeces To Pieces/Twistin' The Trad (as David Ede & Rabin Band)	15

(see also Oscar Rabin)

EDEN STREET SKIFFLE GROUP
57	Headquarter & General Stores	SKIFFLE ALBUM NO. 1 (10 x 7" 78rpm clear flexidiscs in p/s)	70

TONI EDEN
60	Columbia DB 4409	Teen Street/No One Understands (My Johnny)	25
60	Columbia DB 4458	Grown Up Dreams/Whad'ya Gonna Do	20
60	Columbia DB 4527	Will I Ever/The Waitin' Game	15
61	Decca F 11342	Send Me/Interesting Facts	12

EDEN'S CHILDREN
68	Stateside (S)SL 10235	EDEN'S CHILDREN (LP)	70

EDGE
78	Albion ION 4	Macho Man/I'm Cold (p/s)	8
79	Hurricane FIRE 3	Downhill/American Excess (p/s, white vinyl)	8
96	Volume VOL 19	Little Girl Blue/The Hopeless Dreams Of Neville Been (p/s)	8
79	Chiltern Sound CSLP	UNEASY PEACE (LP)	15
80	Hurricane FLAK 102	SQUARE 1 (LP)	15

(see also Damned, Culture Club)

THE EDGE WITH SINÉAD O'CONNOR
86	Virgin VS 897	Heroine (Theme From "Captive")/Heroine (Mix II) (p/s)	5
86	Virgin VS 897-12	Heroine (Theme From "Captive")/Heroine (Mix II) (12", p/s)	8
86	Virgin V 2401	CAPTIVE (LP, soundtrack)	12

(see also U2, Jah Wobble)

HARRY 'SWEETS' EDISON SEXTET
60	HMV POP 720	Hollering At The Watkins/K.M. Blues	6
56	Vogue LDE 118	HARRY EDISON QUARTET (10" LP)	12

EDISON LIGHTHOUSE
71	Bell BLL 1136	It's Up To You Petula/Let's Make It Up	5
71	Bell BLL 1153	What's Happening/Take A Little Time	6
72	Bell BLL 1206	Find Mr. Zebedee?/Reconsider, My Belinda	6
81	Greenstone GRS 3441	Endearing Young Charms/Livin' On A Roller	6

(see also Flowerpot Men, White Plains, David & Jonathan, First Class)

EDITORS
04	Kitchenware SKCD77	Bullets/You Are Fading/Dust In The Sunlight (CD, 500 only)	40
04	Kitchenware SKX77	You Are Fading/Dust In The Sunlight (500 only)	40
05	Kitchenware SKX78	Munich/Disappear, p/s)	10
07	Kitchenware (no cat no)	Escape The Nest (Demo)/When Anger Shows (Demo) (Fan club 7", 1,000 only)	20
05	Kitchenware KWX 34	THE BACK ROOM (LP, gatefold sleeve)	15
09	Kitchenware KWX43	IN THIS LIGHT AND ON THIS EVENING (LP)	12

LADA EDMUND JR
75	MCA MU 172	The Larue/Soul Au Go-Go	10
75	MCA MU 172	The Larue/Soul Au Go-Go (DJ Copy)	20

DAVE EDMUNDS (& ROCKPILE)
71	Regal Zonophone RZ 3032	I'm-A Comin' Home/Country Roll	10
71	Regal Zonophone RZ 3037	Blue Monday/I'll Get Along	10
72	Regal Zonophone RZ 3059	Down, Down, Down/It Ain't Easy	10
77	Swan Song SSK 19411	I Knew The Bride/Back To Schooldays	6
90	Capitol 10CL 568	King Of Love/Stay With Me Tonight (45rpm)/King Of Love (78 rpm) (10", p/s)	30
90	Capitol 12CL 568	King Of Love/Stay With Me Tonight/Every Time I See Her (12", p/s)	10
71	Regal Zono. SRZA 8503	ROCKPILE COLLECTION (LP, unreleased)	0
72	Regal Zono. SLRZ 1026	ROCKPILE (LP)	35
75	Rockfield RRL 101	SUBTLE AS A FLYING MALLET (LP)	20
80	Harvest SHSM 2032	SINGLES A'S & B'S (LP, as Dave Edmunds & Love Sculpture)	12
82	Arista SPART 1184	DE 7TH (LP, with bonus EP "Live At The Venue" [JUKE 1])	12

(see also Image, Human Beans, Love Sculpture, Rockpile, Andy Fairweather-Low)

EDOUARD
66	CBS 202200	My Name Is Edouard/N'aie Pas Peur Antoinette (p/s)	8

EDSELS
61	Pye International 7N 25086	Rama Lama Ding Dong/Bells	120

EDWARD & HARDING
71	Stateside SS 2196	Mr. Sunlight/Blackbird	10

ADINA EDWARDS
72	Dynamic DYN 454	Talk About Love/Don't Forget To Remember	6
60s	Tabernacle TLP 1005	JESUS IS MINE (LP)	15

(see also Coxsone Dodd)

BOBBY EDWARDS
61	Top Rank JAR 584	You're The Reason/I'm A Fool Loving You	15

BRENT EDWARDS
63	Pye International 7N 25197	Pride/Over The Weekend	12

C EDWARDS & SYMBOLIC
80	Symbolic BS 02	Loving Jah/Loving One & All (12")	80

CHUCK EDWARDS
68	Soul City SC 104	Downtown Soulville/I Need You	20

MINT VALUE £

68	Soul City SC 104	Downtown Soulville/I Need You (DJ Copy)	100

DEVON EDWARDS

82	CF 12	Bad Boy Lay Down Flat/JAH RUBAL : Burst Shot	35

GARY EDWARDS (COMBO)

62	Oriole CB 1700	Twist Or Bust/The Franz Liszt Twist (as Gary Edwards Combo)	10
62	Oriole CB 1717	The Method/Twistful Thinkin'	12
62	Oriole CB 1733	Africa/One Fifteen A.M.	10
62	Oriole CB 1759	Hopscotch/Theme For A Broken Dream	10

IDIATER EDWARDS

85	Pressure HAVE 2	Loving Sweet Devotion/Version	70

(WILFRED) JACKIE EDWARDS

60	Starlite ST45 016	We're Gonna Love/Your Eyes Are Dreaming (as Wilfred Edwards & Caribs)	25
60	Starlite ST45 026	I Know/Tell Me Darling (as Wilfred Edwards)	25
61	Starlite ST45 046	Whenever There's Moonlight/Heaven Just Knows (as Wilfred Edwards)	25
61	Starlite ST45 062	More Than Words Can Say/I Love You No More (as Wilfred Edwards)	25
62	Starlite ST45 076	Little Bitty Girl/Never Go Away (as Wilfred Edwards)	25
62	Island WI 008	All My Days/Hear Me Cry (as Wilfred Jackie Edwards)	18
62	Island WI 019	One More Week/Tears Like Rain (as Wilfred Edwards)	18
62	Decca F 11547	Lonely Game/Suddenly	15
63	Black Swan WI 404	Why Make Believe/Do You Want Me (as Wilfred Jackie Edwards & Velvetts)	15
64	Black Swan WI 416	The Things You Do/Little Smile (as Wilfred Jackie Edwards)	15
64	Black Swan WI 426	Why Make Believe/Do You Want Me Again	22
64	Fontana TF 465	Sea Cruise/Little Princess	15
64	Sue WI 329	Stagger Lee/Pretty Girl	40
65	Aladdin WI 601	He'll Have To Go/Gotta Learn To Love Again	12
65	Aladdin WI 605	Hush/I Am In Love With You No More (p/s)	12
65	Aladdin WI 611	The Same One/I Don't Know	15
65	Island WI 255	White Christmas/My Love And I	20
66	Island WI 270	Sometimes/Come On Home	20
66	Island WI 274	L-O-V-E/What's Your Name	40
66	Island WI 287	Think Twice/Oh Mary	20
66	Island WI 3006	I Feel So Bad/I Don't Want To Be Made A Fool Of	250
66	Island WI 3018	Royal Telephone/It's No Secret	15
67	Island WI 3030	Only A Fool Breaks His Own Heart/The End	15
67	Island WIP 6008	Come Back Girl/Tell Him You Lied	25
68	Island WIP 6026	Julie On My Mind/If This Is Heaven	15
68	Island WI 3157	You're My Girl/Heaven Only Knows	15
69	Direction 58-4096	Why Must I Be Alone/I'm Gonna Make You Cry	6
69	Direction 58-4402	Too Experienced/Someone To Love	6
69	Direction 58-4630	Oh Manio/Here We Go Again	6
70	CBS 5147	Tell Me Why Say Goodbye/Walter Walter	6
71	Horse HOSS 1	I Must Go Back/Baby I Want To Be Near You (in p/s)	20
71	Horse HOSS 1	I Must Go Back/Baby I Want To Be Near You	15
71	Bread BR 1107	Johnny Gunman/JACKIE'S BOYS: Johnny Gunman Version	10
72	Bread BR 1108	I Do Love You/Who Told You So?	8
76	Island WIP 6285	I Feel So Bad/Come On Home (reissue)	20
66	St. Mary's IEP 701	SACRED HYMNS VOL. 1 (EP, in p/s)	40
66	St. Mary's IEP 701	SACRED HYMNS VOL. 1 (EP)	15
66	St. Mary's IEP 702	SACRED HYMNS VOL. 2 (EP, with St. Mary's label, in p/s)	40
66	St. Mary's IEP 702	SACRED HYMNS VOL. 2 (EP, with St. Mary's label)	15
66	St. Mary's IEP 702	SACRED HYMNS VOL. 2 (EP, with red-and-white Island label; in p/s)	40
66	St. Mary's IEP 702	SACRED HYMNS VOL. 2 (EP, with red-and-white Island label)	15
66	Island IEP 708	HUSH! (EP)	45
64	Island ILP 906	THE MOST OF WILFRED JACKIE EDWARDS (LP)	50
64	Island ILP 912	STAND UP FOR JESUS (LP)	50
66	Island ILP 931	COME ON HOME (LP)	50
66	Island ILP 936	THE BEST OF JACKIE EDWARDS (LP)	50
66	Island ILP 940	BY DEMAND (LP)	50
67	Island ILP(S) 960	PREMATURE GOLDEN SANDS (LP)	40
69	Island IWPS 4	PUT YOUR TEARS AWAY (LP)	40
69	Direction 8-63977	LET IT BE ME (LP)	25
70	Trojan TTL 40	THE MOST OF WILFRED JACKIE EDWARDS (LP, as Wilfred Jackie Edwards)	25
70	Trojan TTL 45	COME ON HOME (LP)	25
70	Trojan TTL 46	BY DEMAND (LP)	25
70	Trojan TTL 57	PREMATURE GOLDEN SANDS (LP, reissue)	25
72	Trojan TRLS 47	I DO LOVE YOU (LP)	20
82	Black Music BMLP 801	KING OF THE GHETTO (LP)	60

(see also Wilfred & Millicent, Wilfred & Millie, Jackie & Millie, Jackie's Boys)

JACKIE EDWARDS & JIMMY CLIFF

68	Island WIP 6036	Set Me Free/Here I Come	10
68	Island WIP 6042	You're My Girl/Heaven Only Knows	10

(see also Jackie & Millie, Millie, Jimmy Cliff, Wilfred & Millie, Jackie's Boys)

JIMMY EDWARDS (& PROFILE)

79	Warner Bros K 17415	Nora's Diary/Call Me A Fraud (features Sham 69) (p/s)	20
79	Warner Bros K 17464	Twentieth Century Time/Seven Hail Marys (features Pretenders) (p/s)	6
80	Polydor 2059 240	Toys/Hard Heart (p/s)	5
80	Polydor 2059 256	Cabaret/Drag It Back (p/s, solo)	5
81	Polydor POSP 240	In The City/Five Minute Girl (p/s, solo)	5

(see also Time U.K., Pretenders, Sham 69)

JIMMY EDWARDS (U.S.)

58	Mercury 7MT 193	Love Bug Crawl/Honey Lovin'	500
58	Mercury MT 193	Love Bug Crawl/Honey Lovin' (78)	50

JONATHAN & DARLENE EDWARDS

60	Philips BBL 7412	JONATHAN & DARLENE EDWARDS IN PARIS (LP, also stereo SBBL 590)	12

(see also Gordon MacRae, Jo Stafford)

MILL EDWARDS
73	Action ACT 4617	I Found Myself/Don't Forget About Me	20

NOKIE EDWARDS
77	Cream CR 9006	NOKIE (LP)	15

(see also Ventures)

O.G. EDWARDS
88	Dance Yard YARDT 4	Only You (Know What I Like)/Only You (Know What I Like) (Extended Version) (12")	40

PAUL EDWARDS
76	Cottage COT 301	LONGSTONE FARM (LP)	18

R. EDWARDS & SOCIAL EAGLES
73	Dip DL 5014	One Sunday Morning/Version Sunday Morning (with Allstars)	6
73	Dip DL 5014	One Sunday Morning/AFRICAN BROTHERS: Mysterious Nature (2nd issue, different B-side)	10

RUPIE EDWARDS (ALL STARS)
62	Blue Beat BB 90	Guilty Convict/Just Because (as Rupert Edwards & Smithie's Sextet)	25
68	Doctor Bird DB 1163	I Can't Forget/I'm Writing Again	25
69	Crab CRAB 35	Long Lost Love/Uncertain Love	20
70	Crab CRAB 41	Sharp Pan Ya Machete/Redemption	12
70	Explosion EX 2030	Full Moon/Baby	20
70	Explosion EX 2031	Love At First Sight/I Need Your Care	8
70	Success RE 902	Grandfather Clock/Promoter's Grouse	25
70	Success RE 905	Handicap/If You Can't Beat Them	15
70	Success RE 909	Pop Hi (as Rupie Edwards All Stars)/VAL BENNETT AND BUNNY LEE ALL STARS: High Tide	15
71	Bullet BU 494	I'm Gonna Live Some Life/RUPIE EDWARDS ALLSTARS: Rock 'In'	6
71	Nu Beat NB 082	Black Man/Tell The People	10
71	Nu Beat NB 091	One In Three/ERROLL DUNKLEY: Three In One	8
71	Big BG 320	Soulful Stew/Soulful Stew — Version Two (as Rupie Edwards Allstars)	10
71	Big BG 324	Deep Meditation (version)/ERROLL DUNKLEY: Deep Meditation	20
71	Big BG 327	One In Three/ERROLL DUNKLEY: Three In One	6
71	Bullet BU 462	My Love (actually by Gaylads)/Stronger Love (both as Rupie Edwards All Stars)	8
72	Big BG 333	Press Along/Press Along — Version (as Rupie Edwards Allstars)	6
72	Big BG 335	Jimmy As Job Card (actually titled "Jimmy Has A Job Card")/ Riot (as Rupie Edwards Allstars)	15
72	Big BG 337	Christmas Parade (actually by Rupie Edwards Allstars)/ UNDERGROUND PEOPLE: Santa	5
78	Success SLD 016	Oh Black People/NOEL TEMPO : It's Time To Be Free (12")	30
75	Cactus CTLP 106	IRE FEELING (LP)	25
75	Cactus CTLP 107	DUB BASKET (LP)	80
76	Cactus CTLP 117	DUB BASKET CHAPTER 2 (LP)	40
76	Cactus CTLP 120	JAMAICA SERENADE (LP)	30
77	Success SUCLP	101 DUB CLASSICS (LP)	60

(see also R. Edwards & Social Eagles, Gaylads, Heptones, Ethiopians, Dymonds, Dobby Dobson, Keith Cole, Country Boy, Keith Cole, Laurel Aitken, Dennis Alcapone, Gregory Isaacs, Itals, Hugh Roy, Kingstonians, Little George, Mediators, Max Romeo, I Roy, B

SAMUEL EDWARDS
69	Blue Cat BS 159	Want It Want It/SPARKERS: Israel	35

TOM EDWARDS
57	Vogue Coral Q 72236	What Is A Teen Age Girl?/What Is A Teen Age Boy?	6

TOMMY EDWARDS
53	MGM SP 1030	(Now And Then, There's) A Fool Such As I/Take These Chains From My Heart	10
56	MGM SP 1168	Baby, Let Me Take You Dreaming/MARION SISTERS: Life Could Not Be Better	10
58	MGM 989	It's All In The Game/Please Love Me Forever	6
59	MGM MGM-C 774	IT'S ALL IN THE GAME (LP)	20
59	MGM MGM-C 791	FOR YOUNG LOVERS (LP)	20
60	MGM MGM-C 824	YOU STARTED ME DREAMING (LP)	20

VINCE EDWARDS (U.K.)
67	United Artists UP 1179	I Can't Turn Back Time/The Lively One	20
68	United Artists UP 2230	County Durham Dream/It's The Same Old Song	6
68	United Artists UP 2236	Aquarius/Hair	5

VINCE EDWARDS (U.S.)
58	Capitol CL 14825	Wilget/Lollipop	10
62	Brunswick 05872	Don't Worry About Me/And Now	8
64	Colpix PX 771	No Not Much/See That Girl (p/s)	10

WEBLEY EDWARDS
60	Capitol ST1033	FIRE GODDESS (LP)	20

JOHN EDWARDS
95	Kent 6T 11	Ain't That Good Enough/LOLEATTA HOLLOWAY: This Man's Arms	25

EDWARDS HAND
71	RCA SF 8154	STRANDED (LP, orange label)	20
73	Regal Zono. SRZA 8513	RAINSHINE (LP, unissued, demos only)	100

(see also Picadilly Line)

WINSTON EDWARS
75	Fay FLP 2004	NATTY LOCKS DUB (LP)	200

EDWICK RUMBOLD
66	CBS 202393	Specially When/Come Back	120
67	Parlophone R 5622	Shades Of Grey/Boggle Woggle	250

EEK A MOUSE
81	Love Linch LL019	No Wicked/Trying To Be Free (12")	50
82	Greensleeves GRED 88	Do You Remember/TOYAN : Strictly The Dread (12")	15
81	Greensleeves GREL 31	WA-DO-DEM (LP)	12
82	Greensleeves GREL 41	SKIDIP! (LP)	15
83	Greensleeves GREL 86	ASSASSINATOR (LP)	15
84	Greensleeves GRED 65	MOUSEKETEER (LP)	15

EELS

96	Dreamworks DRMS 22174	Novocaine For The Soul/Fucker (p/s)	5
97	Dreamworks DRMS 22277	Your Lucky Day In Hell/Altar Boy (p/s)	5
97	Dreamworks DRMS 22238	Susan's House/Stepmother (p/s)	5
98	Dreamworks DRMS 22346	Last Stop: This Town/Funeral Parlour (p/s)	6
98	Dreamworks DRMS 22373	Cancer For The Cure/Everything's Gonna Be Cool This Christmas (p/s)	5
00	Dreamworks 450 978-7	Mr E's Beautiful Blues/Birdgirl On A Cell Phone (Picture disc, stickered PVC sleeve)	8
00	Dreamworks 450945-7	Flyswatter/Vice President Fruitley (Picture disc, stickered PVC sleeve)	12
01	Dreamworks 450 893-1	Souljacker Part 1/I Write The B-Sides (picture disc, insert in stickered PVC sleeve)	10
05	Vagrant 988-188-0	Hey Man (Now You're Really Living)/After The Operation (yellow vinyl, stickered p/s)	5
96	Dreamworks DRLP 50001	BEAUTIFUL FREAK (LP)	100
01	Dreamworks 450 335-1	SOULJACKER (LP)	40

E.F. BAND

80	Rok ROK XI/XII	Another Day Gone/SYNCHROMESH: October Friday (die-cut co. sleeve)	30
80	Aerco/EF Band EF 1	Night Angel/Another Day Gone (p/s)	30
80	Aerco/EF Band EF 1	Night Angel/Another Day Gone	15
80	Redball RR 026	Self Made Suicide/Sister Syne (with wraparound p/s)	30
80	Redball RR 026	Self Made Suicide/Sister Syne	7
80	Redball RR 036	The Devil's Eye/Comprende (with wraparound p/s)	25
80	Redball RR 036	The Devil's Eye/Comprende	7
82	Bullet CULP 2	DEEP CUT (LP)	15

WILLIE EGANS

70s	Flyright LP 6000	ROCKS, BOOGIES AND ROLLS (LP)	15

JULIE EGE

71	CBS 5431	Love/In One Of Your Weaker Moments	6

JOSEPH EGER

70	Charisma CAS 1008	CLASSICAL HEADS (LP, gatefold sleeve, "pink scroll" label)	25

EGG

69	Deram DM 269	Seven Is A Jolly Good Time/You Are All Princes	35
70	Deram Nova (S)DN 14	EGG (LP, red/silver labels, with sticker on rear sleeve correcting credits)	120
70	Deram Nova (S)DN 14	EGG (LP, red/silver labels)	70
71	Deram SML 1074	THE POLITE FORCE (LP, red/white label with small logo)	75
74	Caroline C 1510	THE CIVIL SURFACE (LP, red/white/red "twin" label)	50

(see also Hatfield & The North, Arzachel, Bunch Of Fives, Khan)

EGGY

69	Spark SRL 1024	Hookey/You're Still Mine	45

EGYPT

88	HTD 7HTD 1	Crazy Horses /Got No Fear (p/s)	10
88	HTD HTD LP 1	EGYPT (LP, with inner)	15

(see also Paul Samson)

EGYPTIAN EMPIRE

91	Fokus FKFR 1	The Horn Track (Original Mix)/The Horn Track (Mickey Finn Fog Horn Mix) (12")	20
92	FFRR TABX 115	The Horn Track (Original Mix)/The Horn Track (Foghorn Mix)/The Horn Track (Toxic 2 Mix) (12")	15

EIFFEL TOWER

69	Chappell LPC 1032	THE EIFFEL TOWER (LP, library edition)	15

8-EYED SPY

82	Fetish FE 19	Diddy Wah Diddy/Dead You Me B Side (p/s)	12
81	Fetish FR 2003	8-EYED SPY (LP, with inner sleeve)	20

(see also Lydia Lunch)

808 STATE

88	Creed STATE 003	Let Yourself Go (303 Mix)/Let Yourself Go (D50 Mix)/Deepville (12", plain stickered sleeve)	8
89	ZTT ZANG 1TX	Pacific — 909 (Mellow Birds Mega Edit)/Bonus Bird Beats/Cobra Bora (12", plain stickered sleeve)	8
89	ZTT ZANG 2CD	THE EXTENDED PLEASURES OF DANCE EP (CD, withdrawn)	30
93	ZTT SAM 933	10 X 10 (Vox Mix)/10 X 10 (Beats Version) (12", promo only)	8
88	Creed STATE 002	NEWBUILD (LP)	12

(see also Hit Squad)

EIGHTH WONDER

88	CBS SCARE Y1	I'm Not Scared/I'm Not Scared (Disco Mix)/J'ai Pas Peur (10", p/s, with Pet Shop Boys)	15
88	CBS SCAREC 1	I'm Not Scared (Disco Mix)/I'm Not Scared/J'ai Pas Peur (CD, with Pet Shop Boys)	15

(see also Pet Shop Boys, Rock Aid Armenia)

EIGHTIES LADIES

86	Music Of Life MOLIF 6	Turned On To You/Sing Me/And I Knew That Love 12", p/s)	20

(see also Roy Ayers)

EINSTÜRZENDE NEUBAUTEN

85	Some Bizzare BART 12	Yü-Gung/Seelebrennt/Sand (12", p/s)	10
83	Mute STUMM 14	STRATEGIES AGAINST ARCHITECTURE (LP)	12
87	Some Bizarre BART 332	FUENF AUF NACH OBEN OFFEN RICHTERSKALA (LP)	12
89	Some Bizarre BART 333	HAUS DER LUEGE (LP)	15

EIRE APPARENT

67	Track 604 019	Follow Me/Here I Go Again	20
69	Buddah 201 039	Rock'N'Roll Band/Yes I Need Someone	20
72	Buddah 2011 117	Rock'N'Roll Band/Yes I Need Someone (reissue)	10
69	Buddah 203 021	SUN RISE (LP, featuring Jimi Hendrix, black/silver labels)	150

(see also Ernie Graham, Henry McCulloch)

EJECTED

82	Riot City RIOT 14	HAVE YOU GOT 10p? (EP)	10
82	Riot City RIOT 19	NOISE FOR THE BOYS (EP)	10
83	Riot City RIOT 28	PRESS THE BUTTON (EP)	8

| 82 | Riot City CITY 003 | A TOUCH OF CLASS (LP) | 25 |
| 83 | Riot City CITY 007 | THE SPIRIT OF REBELLION (LP) | 25 |

BRITT EKLAND
| 79 | Jet JETP 161 | Do It To Me (Once More With Feeling)/Private Party (picture disc) | 5 |

(see also Britt)

EKSEN TRICK BRICK BAND
| 78 | Aerco AERL 17 | SKY STORY (LP, with insert) | 30 |

EKSEPTION
70	Philips 318 992 BF	Air/Dharma For One	5
72	Philips 6012 219	Ava Maria/Dharma For One	5
69	Philips 6314 001	BEGGAR JULIAN'S TIME TRIP (LP)	15
70	Philips 6314 005	EKSEPTION (LP)	18
71	Philips 6423 005	EKSEPTION III (LP, laminated sleeve)	15
72	Philips 6423 019	00.04 (LP)	15
72	Philips 6423 042	V (LP, gatefold sleeve)	15
74	Philips 6423 079	CLASSICS IN POP (LP)	12

EL PAS(S)O
| 71 | Big Shot BI 572 | Out De Light, Baby/Mosquito I (both actually by Dennis Alcapone) | 15 |
| 71 | Punch PH 61 | Mosquito One/Out De Light (reissue) | 12 |

(see also Dennis Alcapone)

MARGARET ELAINA
| 73 | Bullet BU 522 | Ben/RICHIE & NOW GENERATION: Laughing Stock Version | 5 |

ELAINE
| 63 | Columbia DB 7091 | I Never Wonder Where My Baby Goes/Look But Don't Touch | 12 |

ELAINE & DEREK
63	Piccadilly 7N 35105	Hey Paula/Goodbye Twelve-Hallo Teens	5
64	Decca F 11914	All The Sheep In The World/The Boy I'm Gonna Marry	5
65	Decca F 12054	Invisible Tears/Come On Now	5

ELASTICA
93	Deceptive BLUFF 003	Stutter/Pussycat (numbered die-cut sleeve, 1,500 only)	15
93	Deceptive BLUFF 003	Stutter/Pussycat (White label test pressing)	15
94	Deceptive BLUFF 004	Line Up/Vaseline (numbered die-cut sleeve, 1,500 only)	10
94	Deceptive BLUFF 010	Connection/See That Animal (numbered die-cut sleeve, 3,000 only)	5
00	Deceptive BLUFF 077	Mad Dog / Suicide (numbered brown printed sleeve)	5
95	Deceptive BLUFF 014LP	ELASTICA (LP, with flexidisc & booklet, no'd & stickered sleeve, 5,000 only)	35
95	Deceptive BLUFF 014LP	ELASTICA (LP, with flexidisc & booklet, no'd & stickered sleeve, 5,000 only, mispressed labels)	40
95	Deceptive BLUFF 014LP	ELASTICA (LP)	15

(see also Suede)

ELASTIC BAND
68	Decca F 12763	Think Of You Baby/It's Been A Long Time Baby	45
68	Decca F 12815	Do Unto Others (From "Mr. Rose" T.V. Series)/8½ Hours Of Paradise	60
69	Decca Nova (S)DN 6	EXPANSIONS ON LIFE (LP, mono)	200
69	Decca Nova (S)DN 6	EXPANSIONS ON LIFE (LP, stereo)	150

(see also Mayfield's Mule, Sweet, Andy Scott, Love Affair, Northwind)

ELASTICK BAND
| 67 | Stateside SS 2056 | Spazz/Papier Mache (unissued, demos only) | 300 |

DONNIE ELBERT
58	Parlophone R 4403	Let's Do The Stroll/Wild Child	100
58	Parlophone R 4403	Let's Do The Stroll/Wild Child (78)	40
65	Sue WI 377	A Little Piece Of Leather/Do Wat'cha Wanna	35
65	Sue WI 396	You Can Push It (Or Pull It)/Lily Lou	30
67	CBS 2807	Get Ready/Along Came Pride	20
68	Polydor BM 56234	In Between The Heartaches/Too Far Gone	20
68	Polydor BM 56265	This Old Heart Of Mine (Is Weak For You)/Run Little Girl	10
68	New Wave NW 001	Baby Please Come Home/Without You	8
69	Deram DM 235	Without You/Baby Please Come Home (reissue)	8
69	R&B UP 2000	Without You/(different B-side) (white label test pressing only)	8
72	Epic EPC 7943	Get Ready/Alone Came Pride	5
72	Mojo 2092 040	This Old Heart Of Mine (Is Weak For You)/Good To Me	5
72	Jay Boy BOY 70	Half As Old/Baby Let Me Love You Tonite	5
73	London HLU 10370	A Little Piece Of Leather/If I Can't Have You	6
79	Echo EC 7001	Are You Ready (Willing And Able)/You Keep Me Crying (With Your Lying)	8
97	Joe Boy JBV 1	So Soon/Can't Get Over Losing You (p/s with numbered certificate, 300 only)	20
69	Polydor 236 560	TRIBUTE TO A KING (LP)	50
73	Ember EMB 3421	THE ROOTS OF DONNIE ELBERT (LP)	20

ELBOW
98	Soft Records Softrec001	NOISEBOX EP: Powder Blue/Red/George Lassoes The Moon (Original version)/Theme From Munroe Kelly/Can't Stop (CD, 200 copies – 150 numbered)	200
98	Soft Records Softrec001	NOISEBOX EP: Powder Blue/Red/George Lassoes The Moon (Original version)/Theme From Munroe Kelly/Can't Stop (CD, 200 copies – 50 un-numbered)	100
00	Uglyman UGLY 20 CD	NEWBORN EP (CD, jewel case)	20
01	Uglyman UGLY 25	ANY DAY NOW EP (10", p/s)	10
05	V2 VVR 5032547	Forgot Myself/McGregor (mis-press A side plays Madness' 'Shame and Scandal')	10
01	V2 VVR 1015881	ASLEEP IN THE BACK (2-LP)	50
03	V2 VVR 102181-1	CAST OF THOUSANDS (LP)	45
05	V2 VVR 103255-1	LEADERS OF THE FREE WORLD (LP)	35

ELCORT
| 66 | Parlophone R 5447 | Tammy/Searchin' | 20 |

ERIC ELDER
| 70 | Philips 6006 081 | San Tokay/Sunflower | 5 |

ELDORADOS (JAMAICA)
| 70 | Bullet BU 428 | Savage Colt/The Clea Hog | 25 |

MINT VALUE £

ELDORADOS (RHODESIA)
63	Decca DFE 8543	THE ELDORADOS (EP)	100

ELDORADOS (U.S.)
72	Mojo 2092 050	Loose Booty (Parts 1 & 2)	10

ROY ELDRIDGE QUINTET
55	Columbia/Clef 33C 9005	ROY ELDRIDGE QUINTET (LP)	15

ROY ELDRIDGE & CLAUDE BOLLING
56	Vogue V 2373	Wild Man Blues/Fireworks	10

ELECAMPANE
75	Dame Jane ODJ 1	WHEN GOD'S ON THE WATER (LP, private pressing with insert)	50
78	Dame Jane ODJ 2	FURTHER ADVENTURES OF MR PUNCH (LP, private pressing with booklet)	20

ELECKTROIDS
95	Warp WARPLP 35	ELEKTROWORLD (2-LP)	100

ELECTRIC EXPRESS
71	Atlantic 2091 165	It's The Real Thing Part 1/Part 2	8

ELECTRIC BANANA
67	De Wolfe DW/LP 3040	ELECTRIC BANANA (LP, 10", original issue, tricolour label)	100
67	De Wolfe DWLP 3040	ELECTRIC BANANA (LP, second issue, with other artists)	30
68	De Wolfe DWLP 3069	MORE ELECTRIC BANANA (LP)	100
69	De Wolfe DWLP 3123	EVEN MORE ELECTRIC BANANA (LP)	40
73	De Wolfe DWLP 3284	HOT LICKS (LP)	40
76	De Wolfe DWLP 3381	THE RETURN OF THE ELECTRIC BANANA (LP)	25
79	Butt NOTT 001	THE SEVENTIES (LP)	18
80	Butt NOTT 003	THE SIXTIES (LP)	18
97	Tenth Planet TP 031	THE ELECTRIC BANANA BLOWS YOUR MIND (LP, numbered, 1,000 only)	15

(see also Pretty Things, Zac Zolar & Electric Banana)

ELECTRIC CIRCUS
90	White Label Only	Rhythm & Rhyme/Time	10

ELECTRIC CRAYONS
89	Emergency MIV 3	Hip Shake Junkie/Happy To Be Hated (p/s)	20

(see also Charlatans)

ELECTRIC FLAG
68	CBS 3584	Groovin' Is Easy/Over-Lovin' You	10
69	CBS 4066	Sunny/Soul Searchin'	7
68	CBS 62394	A LONG TIME COMIN' (LP)	20
69	CBS 63462	THE ELECTRIC FLAG — AN AMERICAN MUSIC BAND (LP)	15
71	CBS 64337	THE BEST OF ELECTRIC FLAG (LP)	12

(see also Mike Bloomfield, Buddy Miles, Barry Goldberg)

ELECTRIC FRANKENSTEIN
98	One Louder LOUDER 24	ACTION HIGH (LP)	12

ELECTRICIANS
67	Columbia DB 8228	Champion House Theme/DON HARPER & ELECTRICIANS: Shin Bone	7

(see also Don Harper)

ELECTRIC INDIAN
69	United Artists UP 35039	Keem-O-Sabe/Broad Street	5

(see also Len Barry)

ELECTRIC JOHNNY
61	London HLU 9384	Black-Eyes Rock/Johnny On His Strings	40

ELECTRIC LIGHT ORCHESTRA (E.L.O.)
72	Harvest HAR 5053	10538 Overture/1st Movement (Jumping Biz)	6
72	Harvest HAR 5063	Roll Over Beethoven/Manhattan Rumble (49th Street Massacre) (with withdrawn B-side)	10
72	Harvest HAR 5063	Roll Over Beethoven/Queen Of The Hours	5
73	Harvest HAR 5077	Showdown/In Old England Town (Boogie 2) (Instrumental)	8
81	Jet ELO 2	Mr Blue Sky/Across The Border/Telephone Line/Don't Bring Me Down (withdrawn, in p/s)	8
81	Jet ELO 2	Mr Blue Sky/Across The Border/Telephone Line/Don't Bring Me Down (withdrawn)	5
81	Jet JETP 12018	Ticket To The Moon/Here Is The News (12" picture disc)	12
71	Harvest SHVL 797	ELECTRIC LIGHT ORCHESTRA (gatefold sleeve, with inner sleeve & lyric insert)	50
72	Harvest SHVL 806	ELO 2 (LP, gatefold sleeve with EMI box on label)	15
73	Harvest Q4SHVL 797	ELECTRIC LIGHT ORCHESTRA (quadrophonic, promo only)	80
74	Harvest SHSP 4037	SHOWDOWN (LP)	15
76	Jet JETLP 19	OLE ELO (LP)	15
77	Jet UAG 30091	ON THE THIRD DAY (new mix, new sleeve & inner sleeve)	15
78	Jet JETBX 1	THREE LIGHT YEARS (3-LP, boxed set of "On The Third Day", "Eldorado" & "Face The Music", with booklet & inserts)	18
78	Jet JETLP 200	A NEW WORLD RECORD (red vinyl, with inner sleeve)	15
78	Jet JETLP 201	FACE THE MUSIC (green vinyl, with inner sleeve)	15
78	Jet JETLP 202	ON THE THIRD DAY (clear vinyl, with inner sleeve)	15
78	Jet JETLP 203	ELDORADO (yellow vinyl, with inner sleeve)	15
78	Jet JETDP 400	OUT OF THE BLUE (2-LP, clear or dark blue vinyl, with inner sleeves, with cut-out spaceship, poster & insert)	25

(see also Idle Race, Jeff Lynne, Move, Roy Wood, Michael D'Albuquerque, Wilson Gale & Co., Tandy-Morgan)

ELECTRIC PRUNES
66	Reprise RS 20532	I Had Too Much To Dream (Last Night)/Luvin'	30
67	Reprise RS 20564	Get Me To The World On Time/Are You Lovin' Me More (But Enjoying It Less)	30
67	Reprise RS 20607	The Great Banana Hoax/Wind-Up Toys	20
67	Reprise RS 23212	A Long Day's Flight/The King Is In His Counting House	18
68	Reprise RS 20652	Everybody Knows You're Not In Love/You Never Had It Better	30
73	Elektra K 12102	I Had Too Much To Dream (Last Night)/KNICKERBOCKERS: Lies	7
79	Radar ADA 16	I Had Too Much To Dream (Last Night)/Luvin' (p/s)	8
67	Reprise R(S)LP 6248	THE ELECTRIC PRUNES (LP, mono/stereo)	125
68	Reprise R(S)LP 6275	MASS IN F MINOR (LP, mono/stereo)	90
68	Reprise RSLP 6316	RELEASE OF AN OATH (LP)	90

73	Reprise K 34003	MASS IN F MINOR (LP, reissue)	12
86	Edsel ED 179	LONG DAY'S FLIGHT (LP)	15
97	Heartbeat HB 67	STOCKHOLM '67 (LP, gatefold sleeve with booklet)	20

ELECTRIC TOILET
83	Psycho PSYCHO 8	IN THE HANDS OF KARMA (LP, reissue of U.S. LP)	15

ELECTRIC WIZARD
95	Rise Above RISE 11	Demon Lung/OUR HAUNTED KINGDOM: Aquatic Fanatic (blue vinyl, p/s)	20
98	Bad Acid TRIP 1	Supercoven/Burnout (12", p/s)	20
08	Rise Above RISE 12/116	The Processean (Procession) (1-sided 12", 500 only sold at Rise Above 20th Anniversary Gig, ULU London 13th December 2008)	60
08	Rise Above RISE 12/116	The House On The Border/REVEREND BIZARRE: The Gates Of Nanna (12", 500 clear, 500 purple, 500 silver and 500 black vinyl, censored p/s)	20
08	Rise Above RISE 12/116	The House On The Border/REVEREND BIZARRE: The Gates Of Nanna (12", 350 red vinyl, uncensored p/s, poster)	50
95	Rise Above RISE 009	ELECTRIC WIZARD (LP, green vinyl)	50
04	Rise Above RISELP 48	WE LIVE (2-LP, purple vinyl)	50
04	Rise Above RISELP 52	DOPETHRONE (2-LP, white vinyl, reissue, first issued on CD in 2000)	70
06	Rise Above RISELP 48	WE LIVE (2-LP, gatefold sleeve, reissue with 1-sided 7" "The Living Dead At Manchester Morgue")	50
07	Rise Above RISELP 74	LET US PREY (2-LP, 100 clear vinyl, reissue first issued on CD in 2002)	60
07	Rise Above RISELP 74	LET US PREY (2-LP, 500 dark red, 500 black vinyl, reissue first issued on CD in 2002)	40
07	Rise Above RISELP 100	WITCHCULT TODAY (2-LP, 200 green vinyl, foil gatefold sleeve, poster, patch)	50
07	Rise Above RISELP 100	WITCHCULT TODAY (2-LP, 500 silver vinyl, foil gatefold sleeve, poster, patch)	40
10	RISELP 130	BLACK MASSES (2-LP, gatefold p/s, poster, comic, embroidered patch in box, 400 only)	40

ELECTRO HIPPIES
87	Strange Fruit SFPS 042	PEEL SESSIONS (12", metallic finish with insert)	8
88	Peaceville VILE 02	THE ONLY GOOD PUNK... IS A DEAD ONE (LP)	12
89	Peaceville VILE 13	LIVE (LP, clear vinyl)	12
89	Necrosis NECR 0001	PLAY FAST OR DIE (LP)	15

ELECTRONIC
89	Factory FAC 257	Getting Away With It (Full Length Version)/Getting Away With It (Inst.) (12", p/s)	8
93	Parlophone 10RD 6311	Disappointed (7" Mix)/Disappointed (12" Remix) (10", promo only)	8
99	Parlophone 12R651	Late At Night/Make It Happen (Original Version)/Make It Happen (Darren Price Mix) (12" withdrawn)	12
91	Factory FACT 290	ELECTRONIC (LP)	12

(see also New Order, Smiths, Pet Shop Boys)

ELECTRONIC EXPERIENCED
93	Basement BRSS 025	V-10 Overload/No. 303 (12")	25
94	Basement BRSS 032	I.Q./I.Q. More (12")	25

ELECTROSCOPE
97	Wurlitzer Jukebox WJ 19	THE VANISHING PLANET PULSAR EP (p/s)	8
97	Wurlitzer Jukebox WJ 23	SOMMERSON EP (p/s)	8

ELECTROTUNES
80	Cobra COS 5	If This Ain't Love/Bodywork (p/s)	5

ELEGANTS
58	HMV POP 520	Little Star/Getting Dizzy	20
58	HMV POP 520	Little Star/Getting Dizzy (78)	20
58	HMV POP 551	Please Believe Me/Goodnight	60
58	HMV POP 551	Please Believe Me/Goodnight (78)	30

ELEGY
94	ART ART 6	APPLIED RHYTHM TECHNOLOGY (12" EP)	8

ELEKTRAS
63	United Artists UP 1027	All I Want To Do Is Run/It Ain't Easy	30

ELEKTRIC MUSIC
93	East West YZ 755	TV/Television (p/s)	8
93	East West YZ 755T	TV/Television (12", p/s)	8
93	East West SAM 1252	Lifestyle (Edit-Style Mix)/(Club-Style Mix)/(Phoneme-Style Mix) (10", promo)	20

(see also Kraftwerk)

ELENA
65	Columbia DB 7598	Evening Time/Road Of Love	20

ELEPHANT BAND
72	Mojo 2092 036	Stone Penguin/Groovin' At The Apollo	45

ELEPHANT NOISE
91	Own Label	This song Is Our Friend/Halloween Day/Remember The Big Time/Cactus Talk (12" EP)	100

ELEPHANT'S MEMORY
69	Buddah 201055	Crossroads Of The Stepping Stones/Yoghurt Song	6
69	Buddah 201067	Old Man Willow/Jungle Gym At The Zoo	25
70	CBS 5207	Mongoose/I Couldn't Dream	25
72	Apple APPLE 45	Power Boogie/Liberation Special	20
69	Buddah 203 022	ELEPHANT'S MEMORY (LP)	25
72	Apple SAPCOR 22	ELEPHANT'S MEMORY (LP, gatefold sleeve with inner sleeve)	30

(see also John Lennon, Yoko Ono)

ELERI, JANET & DIANE
70s	Fanfare FR 2196	THE ANSWER (LP)	100

ELEVATORS
80	Koala KOA 401	Your I's Are Too Close Together/That's My Baby	60

11.59
74	Dovetail DOVE 4	THIS IS OUR SACRIFICE OF PRAISE (LP, with insert)	40

ELF
74	Purple PUR 118	L.A. 59/Ain't It All Amusing	10
74	Purple TPS 3506	CAROLINA COUNTRY BALL (LP)	30

(see also Roger Glover, Dio, Rainbow, Deep Purple, Black Sabbath)

ELFLAND ENSEMBLE

ELFLAND ENSEMBLE
| 77 | Chrysalis CHS 2151 | Too Much Magic (feat. Derek Brimstone)/Lizarel (featuring Mary Hopkin) (p/s) | 6 |
| 77 | Chrysalis CHS 2193 | Beyond The Fields We Know/Alveric's Journey | 6 |

(see also Mary Hopkin)

STEVE ELGIN
| 74 | Dawn DNS 1093 | Don't Leave Your Lover Lying Around (Dear)/Seductress | 10 |

ELGINS
66	Tamla Motown TMG 551	Put Yourself In My Place/Darling Baby	130
66	Tamla Motown TMG 551	Put Yourself In My Place/Darling Baby (DJ Copy)	150
66	Tamla Motown TMG 583	Heaven Must Have Sent You/Stay In My Lonely Arms	80
66	Tamla Motown TMG 583	Heaven Must Have Sent You/Stay In My Lonely Arms (DJ Copy)	120
67	Tamla Motown TMG 615	It's Been A Long Long Time/I Understand My Man	35
67	Tamla Motown TMG 615	It's Been A Long Long Time/I Understand My Man (DJ Copy)	50
68	Tamla Motown TMG 642	Put Yourself In My Place/Darling Baby (reissue)	25
71	Tamla Motown TMG 771	Heaven Must Have Sent You/Stay In My Lonely Arms (reissue)	7
71	Tamla Motown TMG 787	Put Yourself In My Place/It's Gonna Be Hard Times	7
68	T. Motown (S)TML 11081	DARLING BABY (LP, mono/stereo)	100

ELIAS HULK
| 70 | Youngblood SSYB 8 | UNCHAINED (LP, laminated front cover, red/white label) | 900 |

(see also Babe Ruth)

ELIGIBLES
59	Capitol CL 15067	Faker, Faker/24 Hours (Till My Date With You)	10
59	Capitol CL 15098	The Little Engine/My First Christmas With You	10
60	Capitol CL 15203	Young Is My Lover/East Of West Berlin	8
60	Capitol (S)T 1310	ALONG THE TRAIL (LP)	20
61	Capitol (S)T 1411	LOVE IS A GAMBLE (LP)	20

ELIJAH
| 71 | Ackee ACK 121 | Selassie High/Mount Zion | 6 |

ELIMINATORS
| 66 | Pye NPL 18160 | GUITARS AND PERCUSSION (LP, pink black label) | 25 |

ELIXIR
85	Elixir ELIXIR 1	Treachery (Ride Like The Wind)/Winds Of Time (folded p/s with insert)	80
86	Elixir ELIXIR 2	THE SON OF ODIN (LP, private pressing with insert)	60
90	Sonic SONICLP 9	LETHAL POTION (LP, features Clive Burr)	15

(see also Iron Maiden)

ELIZABETH (1)
| 73 | Paramount PARA 3032 | Stop Killing Me With Kindness/Oh Bird | 6 |
| 68 | Vanguard SVRL 19010 | ELIZABETH (LP) | 100 |

ELIZABETH (2)
| 77 | Creole CR 139 | God Save The Sex Pistols/Silver Story | 15 |

ELIZABETH (3)
94	Echo Special Prods ESPLP2	QUEEN ELIZABETH (LP, mail order only, with inner sleeve)	18
97	Head Heritage HH2	QUEEN ELIZABETH 2 - ELIZABETH VAGINA (2-CD mail order, 1000 only)	30
02	Head Heritage HH100	QUEEN ELIZABETH 2 - ELIZABETH VAGINA (2-CD reissue, mail order, different artwork)	25

(see also Julian Cope)

ELKI & OWEN & RIM RAM BAND
| 69 | Revolution REV 004 | Groovie Kinda Love | 8 |

(see also Elkie Brooks, Owen Gray)

JIMMY ELLEDGE
62	RCA RCA 1274	Swanee River Rocket/Funny How Time Slips Away	15
65	Hickory 45-1363	Pink Dally Rue/(I'd Be) A Legend In My Time	10
64	RCA RCX 7132	FUNNY HOW TIME SLIPS AWAY (EP)	20

ELLI
| 99 | Dig The Fuzz DIG 038 | ELLI (LP, 500 only) | 18 |
| 67 | Parlophone R 5575 | Never Mind/I'll Be Looking Out For You | 20 |

YVONNE ELLIMAN
71	MCA MK 5063	I Don't Know How To Love Him/Jesus Christ Superstar Overture	5
73	Purple PUR 114	I Can't Explain/Hawaii	25
73	Purple TPS 3504	FOOD OF LOVE (LP)	15

DUKE ELLINGTON & HIS (FAMOUS) ORCHESTRA
33	Levy's/Oriole	Souvenir Of Duke Ellington's First Visit To England (1-sided 78)	70
53	HMV 7M 156	Otto Make That Riff Staccato/Time's A-Wastin'	10
54	HMV 7MC 1	Flamingo/Jump For Joy (export issue)	10
54	HMV 7MC 9	In A Sentimental Mood/I Let A Song Go Out Of My Heart (export issue)	6
54	HMV 7M 170	The Flaming Sword/BARNEY BIGARD ORCHESTRA: A Lull At Dawn	6
54	Capitol CL 14186	Smile/If I Give My Heart To You	6
55	Capitol CL 14229	Twelfth Street Rag (Mambo)/Chile Bowl	6
55	Capitol CL 14260	Tyrolean Tango/All Day Long	6
55	Columbia SCM 5182	Brown Betty/Ting-A-Ling	6
59	Philips PB 946	Anatomy Of A Murder/Flirtibird	8
59	Philips PB 243	Skin Deep (Parts 1 & 2) (with Louis Bellson)	10
53	HMV DLP 1007	ELLINGTON'S GREATEST (10")	12
53	Columbia 33SX 1022	MASTERPIECES	12
53	Vogue LDE 035	DUKE ELLINGTON AND THE CORONETS (10")	12
53	Capitol LC 6616	PREMIERED BY ELLINGTON (10")	12
54	Capitol LC 6670	THE DUKE PLAYS ELLINGTON (10")	12
54	HMV DLP 1025	GREAT ELLINGTON SOLOISTS (10")	12
54	HMV DLP 1034	ELLINGTON HIGHLIGHTS, 1940 (10")	12
54	Columbia 33S 1044	JAZZ COCKTAIL (10")	25
60	Philips SBBL 514	ANATOMY OF A MURDER (soundtrack)	25

MARC ELLINGTON
| 68 | Philips BF 1665 | I Shall Be Released/Mrs. Whittle | 8 |

69	Philips BF 1742	Did You Give The World Some Love Today Baby/Bless The Executioner	8
69	Philips BF 1779	Four In The Morning/Peggy Day	8
71	Charisma CB 161	Alligator Man/Song For A Friend	8
69	Philips (S)BL 7883	MARC ELLINGTON (LP, black/silver labels)	100
71	Charisma CAS 1033	RAINS, REINS OF CHANGES (LP, envelope cover with lyric insert)	50
72	Philips 6308 120	A QUESTION OF ROADS (LP, gatefold sleeve, black/silver label)	100
72	Xtra XTRA 1154	MARC TIME (LP, with Fairport Convention)	40
73	Philips 6308 143	RESTORATION (LP, blue/silver label)	100

(see also Fairport Convention, Matthews Southern Comfort)

RAY ELLINGTON QUARTET

53	Columbia SCM 5050	The Little Red Monkey/Kaw-Liga	20
54	Columbia SCM 5088	All's Going Well (My Lady Montmorency) (with Marion Ryan)/Ol' Man River	20
54	Columbia SCM 5104	Rub-A-Dub-Dub/The Owl Song	15
54	Columbia SCM 5147	A.B.C. Boogie/Christmas Cards	30
55	Columbia SCM 5177	Ko Ko Mo (I Love You So)/Woodpecker	30
55	Columbia SCM 5187	Play It Boy, Play/The Irish Were Egyptians Long Ago	20
55	Columbia SCM 5199	Cloudburst/Pet	15
56	Columbia SCM 5250	Hold Him Tight/Who's Got The Money?	10
56	Columbia SCM 5274	Keep The Coffee Hot/Lucky 13	10
56	Columbia DB 3821	Stranded In The Jungle/Left Hand Boogie	30
56	Columbia DB 3838	Giddy-Up-A Ding Dong/The Green Door	30
57	Columbia DB 3905	Marianne/That Rock 'N' Rollin' Man	30
57	Columbia DB 4013	Don't Burn Me Up/Swaller-Tail Coat	10
58	Columbia DB 4057	Living Doll/Long Black Nylons (solo)	20
58	Pye Nixa 7N 15159	The Sultan Of Bezaaz/You Gotta Love Somebody	6
59	Pye Nixa 7N 15189	Chip Off The Old Block/Charlie Brown	15
59	Oriole CB 1512	Carina/I Was A Little Too Lonely	10
60	Ember EMB S 102	The Madison/Jump Over (with Tony Crombie Orchestra) (p/s with insert)	15
60	Ember EMB S 114	Très Jolie/Dracula's Three Daughters	10
63	Ember EMB S 172	Too Old To Cut The Mustard/She Lied	10
64	Ember EMB S 188	Rhythm Of The World/If You Can't Say Something Nice	10
59	Pye Nixa NPL 83011	THAT'S NICE (LP, with Judd Proctor, mono)	20
59	Pye Nixa NSPL 83011	THAT'S NICE (LP, with Judd Proctor, stereo)	25

(see also Tony Crombie, Marion Ryan)

ELLINGTONS

79	Grapevine GRP 114	(I'm Not) Destined To Become A Loser/MILLIONAIRES: You've Got To Love Your Baby	10
79	Grapevine GRP 114	(I'm Not) Destined To Become A Loser/MILLIONAIRES: You've Got To Love Your Baby (DJ Copy)	20

BILL ELLIOT & ELASTIC OZ BAND

71	Apple APPLE 36	God Save Us/Do The Oz (initially with p/s)	50
71	Apple APPLE 36	God Save Us/Do The Oz	20

(see also Splinter, John Lennon/Yoko Ono)

DEREK & DOROTHY ELLIOT

72	Trailer LER 2023	DEREK & DOROTHY ELLIOT (LP)	15
76	Tradition TSR 025	YORKSHIRE RELISH (LP)	15

MAMA CASS (ELLIOT)

68	RCA Victor RCA 1726	Dream A Little Dream Of Me/Midnight Voyage (as Mama Cass)	6
68	Stateside SS 8002	California Earthquake/Talkin' To Your Toothbrush	6
69	Stateside SS 8014	I Can Dream Can't I?/Move A Little Closer Baby	5
69	Stateside SS 8021	It's Getting Better/Who's To Blame? (as Mama Cass)	5
69	Stateside SS 8031	Make Your Own Kind Of Music/Lady Love	5
70	Stateside SS 8039	New World Coming/Blow Me A Kiss	5
70	Stateside SS 8057	A Song That Never Comes/I Can Dream, Can't I?	5
71	Probe PRO 512	Good Times Are Comin'/Welcome To The World	6
71	Probe PRO 519	Easy Come, Easy Go/Ain't Nobody Else Like You	6
68	Stateside S(S)L 5004	DREAM A LITTLE DREAM (LP)	20
69	Stateside S(S)L 5014	BUBBLEGUM, LEMONADE AND SOMETHING FOR MAMA (LP)	18
72	RCA SF 8306	THE ROAD IS NO PLACE FOR A LADY (LP)	15

(see also Mamas & Papas, Big Three, Dave Mason & Cass Elliot, Mugwumps)

ELLIOT MANSIONS

71	President PT 323	Float On Up/Shades And Shadows	12
72	President PT 361	Don't Want To Live Inside Myself/Three Score And Ten	6

BERN ELLIOTT (& FENMEN)

63	Decca F 11770	Money/Nobody But Me	10
64	Decca F 11852	New Orleans/Everybody Needs A Little Love	10
64	Decca F 11970	Good Times/What Do You Want With My Baby (as Bern Elliott & Klan)	10
65	Decca F 12051	Guess Who/Make It Easy On Yourself (solo)	12
65	Decca F 12171	Lipstick Traces/Voodoo Woman (solo)	20
64	Decca DFE 8561	BERN ELLIOTT AND THE FENMEN (EP)	30

(see also Fenmen)

DAVID ELLIOTT

72	Atlantic K40374	DAVID ELLIOTT (LP, with lyric insert)	20

JACK ELLIOTT

69	Leader LEA 4001	JACK ELLIOTT OF BIRTLEY (LP, with booklet)	20

(see also Elliotts Of Birtley)

(RAMBLIN') JACK ELLIOTT

56	Topic TRC 98	Talking Miner Blues/Pretty Boy Floyd (78)	25
57	Topic TRC 103	Old Blue/Rambling Blues (78)	25
57	Topic TRC 104	Streets Of Laredo/Boll Weevil (78)	25
65	Fontana TF 575	More Pretty Girls/Roll On Buddy (as Jack Elliott)	5
65	Columbia DB 7593	Rusty Jigs And Sandy Sam/Rocky Mountain Belle (as Ramblin' Jack Elliott)	6
58	77 Records EP/1	JACK ELLIOTT SINGS Vol 1. (EP)	100
58	77 Records EP/2	JACK ELLIOTT SINGS Vol. 2. (EP)	100
60	Columbia SEG 8046	KID STUFF (EP)	10
61	Collector JEA 5	RAMBLING JACK ELLIOTT (EP)	20

64	Collector JEA 6	BLUES AND COUNTRY (EP) 20
55	Topic T 5	WOODY GUTHRIE'S BLUES (8" mini-LP) 40
57	Topic 10T 15	JACK TAKES THE FLOOR (10" LP) 40
59	Columbia 33SX 1166	RAMBLIN' JACK ELLIOT IN LONDON (LP) 20
62	Encore ENC 194	IN LONDON (LP, reissue of Columbia 33SX 1166) 20
60	Columbia 33SX 1291	RAMBLIN' JACK ELLIOT SINGS WOODY GUTHRIE & JIMMIE RODGERS (LP) 40
61	77 LP 1	JACK ELLIOT SINGS (10" LP, spelt 'Elliot' on sleeve) 175
65	Fontana TFL 6044	JACK ELLIOTT (LP) 20
65	Stateside SL 10143	JACK ELLIOT COUNTRY STYLE (LP) 20
66	Stateside SL 10167	SINGS THE SONGS OF WOODY GUTHRIE (LP) 20
68	Reprise RSLP 6284	YOUNG BRIGHAM (LP) 15
70	Reprise RSLP 6387	BILL DURHAM SACKS AND RAILROAD SACKS (LP) 15
57	Topic 10T 14	THE RAMBLING BOYS (10" LP, stickered Topic sleeve, insert) 60
63	Topic 12T 105	THE RAMBLING BOYS (LP, reissue of above with 2 extra tracks) 50
64	Topic 12T 106	MULESKINNERS (LP) 30
67	Bounty BY 6036	ROLL ON BUDDY - THE JACK ELLIOTT AND DERROLL ADAMS STORY VOL. 1 (LP) 55

MARI ELLIOTT

| 76 | GTO GT 58 | Silly Billy/Half Past One ....10 |

(see also Poly Styrene, X Ray Spex)

MIKE ELLIOTT

| 72 | Ackee ACK 151 | Milk And Honey/Burst A Shirt ....7 |

PETER ELLIOTT

57	Parlophone R 4355	To The Aisle/All At Once (You Love Her) 5
58	Parlophone R 4457	Devotion/No Fool Like An Old Fool 5
59	Parlophone R 4514	Call Me/Flamingo 5
59	Parlophone R 4529	The Young Have No Time/Over And Over 5
61	Top Rank JAR 390	Waiting For Robert E. Lee/Toot Toot Tootsie 5
61	Fontana 325	Three Little Peggies/The Devil's Workshop 5
66	Strike JH 311	Thinking/Song Is Love 5

SHAWN ELLIOTT

62	Stateside SS 124	Goodbye My Lover/Ain't That A Shame 5
63	Stateside SS 174	Sincerely And Tenderly/Why Don't You Love Me Anymore 8
64	Rio R 51	Shame And Scandal In The Family/My Girl 8
64	Columbia DB 7418	My Girl/Shame And Scandal In The Family (reissue) 8
71	London HLK 10347	Child Is Father To The Man/Any Dream Will Do 12

SIDNEY ELLIOTT

| 69 | Spark SRL 1021 | Who Dat Girl/Strawberry Blonde ....12 |
| 71 | CBS 7683 | Desperation/Came To See Me Yesterday ....8 |

ELLIOTTS OF BIRTLEY

| 69 | Xtra XTRA 1091 | A MUSICAL PORTRAIT OF A DURHAM MINING FAMILY (LP) ....15 |

(see also Jack Elliott)

ELLIOTT'S SUNSHINE

| 68 | Philips BF 1649 | Is It Too Late/'Cos I'm Lonely ....10 |

ELLIS

| 72 | Epic SEPC 1052 | El Doomo/Your Game ....6 |
| 73 | Epic SEPC 1627 | Open Road/Leaving In The Morning ....6 |

(see also Steve Ellis)

ALTON ELLIS (& FLAMES)

65	Island WI 239	Dance Crasher (with Flames)/BABA BROOKS: Vitamin A 50
65	Island WI 241	You Are Not To Blame/BABA BROOKS: Teenage Ska 70
66	Doctor Bird DB 1044	Blessings Of Love/Nothing Sweeter (as Alton & Flames) 60
66	Doctor Bird DB 1049	The Preacher (as Alton & Flames)/LYNN TAITT & COMETS: Tender Loving Care 40
66	Doctor Bird DB 1055	Shake It (with Flames)/SILVERTONES: Whoo Baby 45
66	Doctor Bird DB 1059	Girl I've Got A Date (with Flames)/LYN TAITT & TOMMY McCOOK: The Yellow Basket 40
67	Island WI 3046	Cry Tough (with Flames)/TOMMY McCOOK & SUPERSONICS: Mr Solo 50
67	Treasure Isle TI 7004	Rocksteady (with Flames)/TOMMY McCOOK & SUPERSONICS: Wall Street Shuffle...........40
67	Treasure Isle TI 7010	Duke Of Earl/All My Tears (with Flames) 35
67	Treasure Isle TI 7016	Ain't That Loving You/TOMMY McCOOK/SUPERSONICS: Tommy's Rocksteady 25
67	Treasure Isle TI 7030	Oowee Baby/How Can I (with Flames) 25
67	Treasure Isle TI 7044	Willow Tree/I Can't Stop Now 25
67	Trojan TR 004	Ain't That Loving You (with Flames)/TOMMY McCOOK & SUPERSONICS: Comet Rocksteady 25
67	Trojan TR 009	Wise Birds Follow Spring/TOMMY McCOOK & SUPERSONICS: Soul Rock...........25
67	Studio One SO 2028	I Am Just A Guy/SOUL VENDORS: Just A Little Bit Of Soul 40
67	Studio One SO 2033	Only Sixteen/Baby (both actually by Heptones) 20
68	Studio One SO 2037	Live And Learn/HEPTONES: Cry Baby Cry 35
68	Trojan TR 630	I Can't Stand It/Trying To Reach My Goal 25
68	Trojan TR 642	Breaking Up/Party Time 18
68	Nu Beat NB 010	I Can't Stand It/Tonight 45
68	Nu Beat NB 013	Bye Bye Love/MONTY MORRIS: My Lonely Days 12
68	Nu Beat NB 014	La La Means I Love You/Give Me Your Love 15
68	Pama PM 707	The Message/Some Talk 18
68	Pama PM 717	My Time Is The Right Time/JOHNNY MOORE: Tribute To Sir Alex 25
68	Coxsone CS 7071	A Fool/SOUL VENDORS: West Of The Sun 50
69	Studio One SO 2084	Change Of Plans/CABLES: He'll Break Your Heart (B-side act. by Mad Lads) 40
69	Gas GAS 105	Diana/Some Talk 10
69	Bamboo BAM 2	Better Example/DUKE MORGAN: Lick It Back 70
69	Duke DU 14	Diana/Personality 25
70	Duke DU 72	Remember That Sunday/TOMMY McCOOK & SUPERSONICS: Last Lick 40
70	Gas GAS 151	Suzie/Life Is Down In Denver (some copies credit Alton Ellis & Flames) 12
70	Gas GAS 161	Deliver Us/NEVILLE HINDS: Originator 10
70	Duke Reid DR 2501	What Does It Take To Win Your Love/TOMMY McCOOK: Reggae Meringue 12
70	Duke Reid DR 2512	You Made Me So Very Happy/TOMMY McCOOK & SUPERSONICS: Continental 25
70	Bamboo BAM 29	Tumbling Tears/SOUND DIMENSION: Today Version 18
70	Techniques TE 903	It's Your Thing/TECHNIQUES ALL STARS: Get Left 15
70	Techniques TE 905	I'll Be Waiting/TECHNIQUES ALL STARS: I'll Be Waiting Version............................15

71	Banana BA 318	Sunday Coming/CARL BRYAN: Sunday Version	12
71	Banana BA 330	Bam Bye/Keep On Yearning	18
71	Banana BA 347	Hey World/Harder And Harder	20
71	Gas GAS 164	Back To Africa/NEVILLE HINDS: Originator	10
71	Fab FAB 165	Good Good Loving/Since I Fell For You	40
71	Bullet BU 466	Black Man's Pride/LEROY PALMER: Groove With It	18
71	Bullet BU 485	Don't Care/True Born African	18
71	Smash SMA 2319	A Little Loving/DELROY WILSON & ALTON ELLIS: Loving Version	7
71	Smash SMA 2320	I'll Be There/ITALS: Rude Boy Train	7
71	Big Shot BI 589	Be True/Be True — Version	5
72	Big Shot BI 602	I'm Trying/Luna's Mood	15
72	Spur SP 3	All That We Need Is Love/KEITH HUDSON: Better Love	30
72	Grape GR 3029	Big Bad Boy/HUDSON'S ALLSTARS: Big Bad Version	7
72	Ackee ACK 145	Oppression/Oppression Version (both with Zoot Simms)	45
72	Ackee ACK 148	Let's Stay Together/Version	30
72	Ackee ACK 502	Too Late To Turn Back Now/IMPACT ALLSTARS: Version	12
72	Jackpot JP 796	Play It Cool/AGGROVATORS: King Of The Zozas	10
72	Camel CA 94	Wonderful World/FAB DIMENSION: Wonderful Version	6
72	Pama PM 840	Girl I've Got A Date/Eat Bread	5
72	Pama Supreme PS 347	Moon River/I Can't Find Out	7
72	Pama Supreme PS 361	Working On A Groovy Thing/HARLESDEN SKANKERS: Version	8
73	Ackee ACK 511	Alton's Official Daughter/Aquarius Dub (both with Herman)	15
73	Harry J. HJ 6653	Deliver Us To Africa/Nyah Medley	5
73	Pyramid PYR 7003	Truly/LLOYD COXSONE SIX: Cruising	5
73	A&M AMS 7093	Shoo BeDoo Be Doo/I Love You True	12
77	Venture VEN7709	Confusion/Version	10
79	Cha Cha	Children Are Crying/Mr. Ska Beana	15
83	Fashion FAD 013	Too Late To Turn Back Now/Party Mix (12")	12
67	Coxsone CSL 8008	SINGS ROCK AND SOUL (LP)	90
69	Coxsone CSL 8019	THE BEST OF ALTON ELLIS (LP)	60
71	Bamboo BDLPS 214	SUNDAY COMING (LP)	40
80	Cha Cha	MR. SKABEANA (LP)	20
77	Trojan HRLP 708	STILL IN LOVE (LP)	25
73	Count Shelly SSLO 02	ALTON ELLIS'S GREATEST HITS (LP)	40

(see also Alton & Eddy, Hortense Ellis, Hortense & Alton, Flames [Jamaica], Righteous Flames,Tony Gordon)

ALTON ELLIS & THE HEPTONES

80	Cha Cha CHAD 21	Mr. Ska Beana/ALTON ELLIS: Ain't No Music (12")	25

BOBBY ELLIS

68	Island WI 3136	Dollar A Head (with Crystalites)/RUDY MILLS: I'm Trapped	25
74	Dragon DRA 1033	Up Park Camp/Verse 4	6

(see also Jerry Lewis, Derrick Harriot, Rudy Mills, Crystalites, Keith & Tex, Eric Morris, Roy Richards, Soul Vendors)

DAVE ELLIS

72	Sonet SNTF 646	ALBUM (LP)	25

ELLIS DEE PROJECT

92	Ellis Dee Project LSD 001	Do You Want Me/Rock To The Max (12")	20
92	Ellis Dee Project LSD 003	Dance Factor (1-sided 12")	20
92	Ellis Dee Project LSD 004	Dance Factor (Rennie P Remix)/Don't Stop Rocking (12")	10
92	Ellis Dee Project LSD 005	Desire/Renegade (12")	10

DON ELLIS (ORCHESTRA)

69	CBS 4518	Eli's Comin'/House In The Country	5
68	Liberty LBL 8306OE	LIVE IN THREE QUARTER TIME (LP)	20
68	CBS 63230	ELECTRIC BATH (LP)	25
68	CBS 63356	SHOCK TREATMENT (LP)	15
69	CBS 63680	THE NEW DON ELLIS BAND GOES UNDERGROUND (LP)	15
71	CBS 66261	DON ELLIS AT FILLMORE (2-LP)	15

HERB ELLIS-JIMMY GIUFFRE ALL STARS

60	HMV POP 721	Goose Grease/My Old Flame	6

HORTENSE ELLIS

63	R&B JB 101	I'll Come Softly/I'm In Love (with Alton Ellis)	20
65	Blue Beat BB 295	I've Been A Fool/Hold Me Tenderly	25
67	Fab FAB 20	Somebody Help Me (with Buster's All Stars)/ PRINCE BUSTER & ALL STARS: Rock & Shake	60
70	Bullet BU 427	Last Date/PAT SATCHMO: Cherry Pink	45
70	Gas GAS 160	To The Other Man/MUSIC BLENDERS: Raindrops	7
70	Techniques TE 908	To The Other Man/TECHNIQUES ALL STARS: To The Other Man Version	7
71	Gas 166	I Shall Sing/Stand By Your Man	15
72	Green Door GD 4035	Bringing In The Sheaves (with Stranger Cole)/Version	6
73	Tropical AL020	Woman in The Ghetto/Instrumental Version	20
78	Kawk Eye HE 007	Unexpected Places/Lovers Places	10
76	Third World TWS 918	JAMAICA'S FIRST LADY OF SONG (LP)	20

(see also Hortense & Alton, Hortense & Delroy, Hortense & Jackie, Alton Ellis, Duke Reid, Three Tops, Jackie Opal)

JAMES ELLIS

62	Philips PB 1230	Johnny Todd/Trottin' To The Fair	5

JO-JO ELLIS

72	Fury FY 302	The Fly/Perdona Mia	30

LARRY ELLIS

58	Felsted AF 110	Buzz Goes The Bee/Nothing You Can Do	15

MATTHEW ELLIS

71	Regal Zonophone RZ 3033	Avalon/You Are	15
71	Regal Zonophone RZ 3039	Birthday Song/Salvation	10
72	Regal Zonophone RZ 3045	Palace Of Plenty/Two By Two	12
71	Regal Zono. SRZA 8501	MATTHEW ELLIS (LP, gatefold sleeve, red/silver labels)	40
72	Regal Zono. SRZA 8505	AM I...? (LP, gatefold sleeve, red/silver labels)	50

(see also Procol Harum, Chris Spedding)

MINT VALUE £

SHIRLEY ELLIS

63	London HLR 9824	The Nitty Gritty/Give Me A List	10
65	London HLR 9946	The Name Game/Whisper To Me Wind	8
65	London HLR 9961	The Clapping Song/This Is Beautiful	8
65	London HLR 9973	The Puzzle Song/I See It, I Like It, I Want It	8
66	London HLR 10021	Ever See A Diver Kiss His Wife While The Bubbles Bounce About Above The Water?/Stardust	8
67	CBS 202606	Soul Time/Waitin'	40
67	CBS 202606	Soul Time/Waitin' (DJ copy)	60
67	CBS 2817	Sugar Let's Shing-A-Ling/How Lonely Is Lonely	15
71	CBS 7463	Soul Time/Waitin' (reissue)	15
77	CBS 4901	Soul Time/Waitin' (2nd reissue, blue coloured vinyl)	10
67	CBS (S)BPG 63044	SOUL TIME WITH SHIRLEY ELLIS (LP)	60

(see also Love Affair, Widowmaker, Zoot Money, Peter Bardens)

(STEVE) ELLIS

70	CBS 4992	Loot/More More More	90
70	CBS 5199	Evie/Fat Crow	5
71	CBS 7037	Take Your Love/Jingle Jangle Jasmine	5
71	CBS 7411	Hold On/Goody Goody Dancing Shoes	5
72	Ariola ARO 107	Rag And Bone/Save All Your Encores	5
72	Epic EPC 64878	RIDING ON THE CREST OF A SLUMP (LP, as Ellis)	20
73	Epic EPC 65650	WHY NOT? (LP, as Ellis)	20

(see also Ellis)

ANDY ELLISON

68	Track 604 018	It's Been A Long Time/JOHN'S CHILDREN: Arthur Green	70
68	CBS 3357	Fool From Upper Eden/Another Lucky Lie	45
68	S.N.B. 55-3308	You Can't Do That/Casbah	75
68	S.N.B. 55-3308	You Can't Do That/Cornflake Zoo (second issue, different B-side)	85

(see also John's Children, Jet, Radio Stars)

LORRAINE ELLISON

66	Warner Bros WB 5850	Stay With Me/I Got My Baby Back	12
66	Warner Bros WB 5850	Stay With Me/I Got My Baby Back (1969 re-pressing)	5
68	Warner Bros WB 2094	Try (Just A Little Bit Harder)/In My Tomorrow	5
70	Warner Bros WB 7394	You've Really Got A Hold On Me/You Don't Know Anything About Love	10
71	Mercury 6052 073	Call Me Anytime You Need Some Lovin'/Please Don't Teach Me To Love You	30
70	Warner Bros WS 1821	STAY WITH ME (LP)	40

ELMER HOCKETT'S HURDY GURDY

68	Parlophone R 5716	Fantastic Fair/MOOD MOSAIC: The Yellow Spotted Capricorn	15

(see also Mood Mosaic, Mark Wirtz)

IAN ELMS

82	Squid Marks SMT 013	GOOD NIGHT (LP, with insert)	180

ELOY

83	Heavy Metal HMINT 1	Fools/Heartbeat (p/s)	5
83	Heavy Metal HMPD 1	Fools/Heartbeat (picture disc)	6
83	Heavy Metal HMPD 1	Fools/Heartbeat (clear vinyl)	6
82	Heavy Metal HMILP 1	PLANETS (LP, clear vinyl with inner sleeve)	15
82	Heavy Metal HMIPD 1	PLANETS (LP, picture disc)	18
82	Heavy Metal HMILP 3	TIME TO TURN (LP, clear vinyl with inner sleeve)	12
82	Heavy Metal HMIPD 3	TIME TO TURN (LP, picture disc)	18
83	Heavy Metal HMIPD 12	PERFORMANCE (LP, picture disc)	15
84	Heavy Metal HMIPD 21	METROMANIA (LP, picture disc)	18
89	FM Revolver REV PD120	RA (LP, picture disc)	15

JEFF ELROY & BOYS BLUE

66	Philips BF 1533	Honey Machine/Three Woman	30

(see also Boys Blue)

ELTI-FITS

80	Worthing Street WSEF 1	GOING STRAIGHT (EP, various foldover picture sleeves)	10

ELVES

70	MCA MU 1114	Amber Velvet/West Virginia	7

CAROL ELVIN

63	Columbia DB 7095	'Cos I Know/C'mon Over	10
65	Parlophone R 5228	Don't Leave Me/'Cos I Love You	10

LEE & JAY ELVIN

59	Fontana H 191	So The Story Goes/When You See Her	20
59	Fontana H 191	So The Story Goes/When You See Her (78)	15

(see also Jerry Lordan)

ELVIS HITLER

90	GWR GWLP 37	DISGRACELAND (LP)	20

EMANON

77	Clubland SJP 777	Raging Pain/Rip A Bough (stamped sleeve)	30

BOBBIE EMBER

65	Polydor BM 56062	Why Can't You Bring Me Home/When Love Isn't There	10

EMBERS

63	Decca F 11625	Chelsea Boots/Samantha	20

(see also David & Embers, Three's A Crowd)

EMBRACE

96	Fierce Panda NING 29	All You Good Good People/My Weakness Is None Of Your Business (p/s, 1,300 only, not numbered)	5
96	Fierce Panda NING 29	All You Good Good People/My Weakness Is None Of Your Business (p/s, 1,300 only, numbered)	15
98	BBC BOX SET	EMBRACE EP'S (6 x 12"s in black box, numbered, 100 only)	80
99	Hut HUTDX 103/CD 109	ABBEY ROAD SESSIONS (2xCD gatefold, one CD mail-order from fanclub)	30

EMBRYO
80	Rampant RAM 001	I'm Different/You Know He Did (p/s)	15

(see also Jump Squad)

EMCEE 5
62	Columbia SEG 8153	LET'S TAKE FIVE (EP)	175
62	Alpha International DB 92	VOLUME ONE (EP)	150

EMERALDS (U.K.)
65	Decca F 12096	Don't Listen To Your Friends/Say You're Mine	7
65	Decca F 12304	King Lonely The Blue/Someone Else's Fool	40

EMERALDS (U.S.)
64	London HL 9839	Donkey Kick Back/Sittin' Bull	10

KEITH EMERSON
76	Manticore K 13513	Honky Tonk Train Blues/Barrel House Shake Down (p/s)	6
80	Atlantic K 11612	Taxi Ride (Rome)/Mater Tenebrarum (p/s)	6
81	MCA MCA 697	I'm A Man/Nighthawks Main Title Theme (p/s)	7

(see also Emerson Lake & Palmer, Nice, V.I.P.'s, Rock Aid Armenia)

EMERSON, LAKE & PALMER
73	Lyntone/Manticore LYN 2762	Brain Salad Surgery/(excerpts from "Brain Salad Surgery" LP) (flexidisc in gatefold p/s free with NME)	15
74	Manticore K 13503	Jerusalem/When The Apple Blossoms Bloom In The Windmills Of Your Mind, I'll Be Your Valentine (with p/s)	10
77	Atlantic K 10946	Fanfare For The Common Man/Brain Salad Surgery (p/s)	5
77	Atlantic K 10946T	Fanfare For The Common Man (Album Version)/Brain Salad Surgery (12", p/s)	12
70	Island ILPS 9132	EMERSON, LAKE AND PALMER (LP, pink label)	90
70	Island ILPS 9123	EMERSON, LAKE AND PALMER (LP, pink label, later 'pink rim palm tree')	15
71	Island ILPS 9155	TARKUS (LP, gatefold sleeve, 'pink rim palm tree' label)	20
71	Island HELP 1	PICTURES AT AN EXHIBITION (LP, gatefold sleeve)	15
72	Island ILPS 9186	TRILOGY (LP, gatefold sleeve. pink rim label)	15
73	Manticore K 53501	BRAIN SALAD SURGERY (LP, fold-out die cut sleeve with poster)	25

(see also Emerson Lake & Powell, Nice, Keith Emerson, Greg Lake, Shame, Asia, King Crimson, Stray Dog, Atomic Rooster)

EMERSON, LAKE & POWELL
86	Polydor POSP 804	Touch And Go/Learning To Fly (p/s)	5
86	Polydor POSPX 804	Touch And Go/Learning To Fly/The Locomotion (12", p/s)	8

(see also Emerson Lake & Palmer, Cozy Powell)

KATHLEEN EMERY
97	Jazzman JM001	Sometimes I Feel Like A Motherless Child/Evil Ways (hand numbered sticker on paper sleeve, 500 only)	20

ÉMIGRÉ
79	Chrysalis CHS 2291	Poison/Trouble Shooter	6

EMJAYS
59	Top Rank JAR 145	All My Love All My Life/Cross My Heart	50
59	Top Rank JAR 145	All My Love All My Life/Cross My Heart (78)	20

ENDAF EMLYN
71	Parlophone R 5929	Paper Chains/Madryn	5
72	Parlophone R 5954	Goodbye Cherry Lill/All Of My Life	10

DAVID EMMANUEL
83	White Lodge WLT 1	Giving It Up For Love/Stir It Around (12")	50

ROBERT EMMANUEL
84	Black Roots BR 181262	Leave Natty Business/BARRINGTON LEVY & DARBAZ: Jah Black (12")	20
85	CF CMF 02	Fashion Dread/No Beggy Beggy (12")	50

EMMET SPICELAND
68	Page One POF 089	Lowlands Low/Bunclody	7
69	Page One POF 143	So Long Marianne/In Search Of Franklin	7
68	Page One POLS 011	THE FIRST (LP, with stickered sleeve, blue/silver labels)	60
68	Page ONe POLS 011	THE FIRST (LP, without sticker on sleeve, blue/silver labels)	50
77	Hawk HALP 166	THE EMMET SPICELAND ALBUM (LP, reissue of above LP)	35

EMMETT
65	Columbia DB 7582	Baby Ain't No Lie/Hard Travelling	5
65	Columbia DB 7695	Nancy/Kilkenny Mountains	5

FRED EMNEY
58	Decca TRI DFE 6554	FRED EMNEY (EP)	20

E-MOTIONS
90s	Slammin 1	E-MOTIONS (EP)	20

EMOTIONS
69	Downtown DT 446	Give Me Love/HORACE FAITH: Daddy's Home	10

EMOTIONS (JAMAICA)
66	Ska Beat JB 263	Rude Boy Confession/Heartbreaking Gypsy	35
67	Caltone TONE 100	A Rainbow/TONY & DOREEN: Just You And I	40
68	Caltone TONE 118	Soulful Music/No Use To Cry	30
68	Caltone TONE 129	Careless Hands/TOMMY McCOOK & SUPERSONICS: Caltone Special	50
69	High Note HS 018	The Storm/Easy Squeeze	10
69	High Note HS 026	Rum Bay/PATSY: Find Someone	8
70	Supreme SUP 209	Halleluiah/MATADOR ALLSTARS: Boat Of Joy	6
71	Prince Buster PB 22	Walking Along/Sometimes	15

(see also Romeo & Emotions, Horace Faith)

EMOTIONS (U.K.)
62	London HLR 9640	Echo/Come Dance Baby	50
63	London HLR 9701	L-O-V-E/A Million Reasons	60
63	Stateside SS 237	A Story Untold/One Life One Love One You	40
65	Polydor BM 56025	Lonely Man/Line Shooter	5

EMOTIONS (U.S.)

69	Stax STAX 123	So I Can Love You/Got To Be The Man	7
69	Stax STAX 134	I Like It/Best Part Of A Love Affair	8
69	Deep Soul DS 9104	Somebody New/Brushfire	30
75	Stax STXS 2020	Baby I'm Through/I Wanna Come Back	6
70	Stax SXATS 1030	SO I CAN LOVE YOU (LP)	20

EMPEROR (NORWAY)

93	Candlelight 002	EMPEROR (LP)	20
95	Candlelight 008	IN THE NIGHTSIDE ECLIPSE (LP)	20
98	Candlelight 023	ANTHEMS TO THE WELKIN AT DUSK (LP, gatefold sleeve)	20
99	Candlelight 035	IX :EQUILIBRIUM (LP, gatefold sleeve)	20
01	Candlelight 052	EMPERIAL VINYL PRESENTATION (Numbered box set with 5 picture disc LPs and booklet. 3000 only)	60

EMPERORS

| 66 | Stateside SS 565 | Karate/I've Got To Have Her | 30 |
| 68 | Pama 786 | I've Got To Have Her/Karate | 25 |

EMPIRE

| 81 | Dinosaur DE 004 | Hot Seat/All These Things (p/s) | 10 |
| 80 | White Line DE 001 | EXPENSIVE SOUND (LP) | 12 |

(see also Generation X)

EMSKI

| 11 | Diggers With Gratitude DWG 011 | THE COMPLEX ENGINEER (EP) | 12 |

EMU

| 72 | Columbia DB 8903 | A Friend Like Me/Emu | 8 |

EN ROUTE

| 79 | Barn BARN 006 | Break Down Your Defences/Rusty Capri | 30 |

ENCHANTED FOREST

| 68 | Stateside SS 2080 | You're Never Gonna Get My Lovin'/Suzanne | 25 |

ENCHANTERS

| 67 | Warner Bros WB 2054 | We Got Love/I've Lost All Communications | 25 |

ENCONA COURSE (FEATURING DEF J)

| 91 | Edutainment EDUT001 | Rhyme Grenade/Taste Of The Future/Hit Men (EP) | 45 |
| 92 | White (No Cat. No.) | VIA COARSEVILLE (EP) | 30 |

THE END

65	Philips BF 1444	I Can't Get Any Joy/Hey Little Girl	30
68	Decca F 22750	Shades Of Orange/Loving, Sacred Loving	40
69	Decca LK-R/SKL-R 5015	INTROSPECTION (LP, large unboxed logo on label)	450
96	Tenth Planet TP 025	IN THE BEGINNING ... THE END (LP, gatefold sleeve, numbered, 1,000 only)	15
97	Tenth Planet TP 033	RETROSPECTION (LP, numbered, 1,000 only)	15

(see also Tucky Buzzard, Bill Wyman, Innocents, Bobby Angelo, Tuxedo)

ENDEVERS

68	Decca F 12817	Remember When We Were Young/Taking Care Of Myself	30
68	Decca F 12859	She's My Girl/She's That Kind Of Girl	30
69	Decca F 12939	Sunny And Me/I Really Hope You Do	10

ENDGAMES

| 93 | Virgin VS 640 | Miracle In My Heart/Miracle In My Heart (Instrumental) | 6 |
| 83 | Virgin VS 640 | Miracle In My Heart/Ecstacy (Centurion MIx) (12") | 20 |

END PHENOMENA

| 70 | Hollick And Taylor | END PHENOMENA (LP) | 50 |

SERGIO ENDRIGO

| 68 | Pye International 7N 25502 | Marianne/Il Dolce Paese | 10 |

ENDVRA

| 97 | Elfenblut SAG V | GREAT GOD PAN (CD box with 11 tarot cards) | 18 |

MELVIN ENDSLEY

57	RCA RCA 1004	I Like Your Kind Of Love/Is It True?	40
57	RCA RCA 1004	I Like Your Kind Of Love/Is It True? (78)	15
58	RCA RCA 1051	I Got A Feelin'/There's Bound To Be	40
58	RCA RCA 1051	I Got A Feelin'/There's Bound To Be (78)	20

ENEMY (1)

81	Tin Tin NM 1	50,000 Dead/Society's Fool/Neutral Ground (p/s)	8
82	Fallout FALL 001	Fallen Hero/Tomorrow's Warning/Prisoner Of War (p/s, with inner)	7
82	Fallout FALL 004	Punks Alive/Piccadilly Sidetracks/Twist And Turn (p/s, orange vinyl)	7
83	Fallout FALL 014	Last Rites/Why Not (p/s)	5
84	Rot ASS 9	Last But Not Least/Images (live) (p/s)	6
83	Fallout FALL LP 015	THE GATEWAY TO HELL (LP)	18

ENEMY (2)

| 06 | Stiff BUY 265 | 40 Days And 40 Nights/Dancin' All Night (numbered sticker on die-cut Stiff sleeve, with free sticker, 1000 only) | 10 |

ENERGETIC KRUSHER

| 89 | Vinyl Solution SOL 17 | PATH TO OBLIVION (LP, with insert, features Danny McCormack) | 20 |

(see also Chasers, Wildhearts)

ENERGY

81	GRN 1	CONQUER THE WORLD: Conquer The World/Make It/Law Breaker (EP, no p/s)	75
80	BIPS BECK 927	ENERGISED (EP)	50
83	Aros AROS 11233	Nowhere To Hide/Fight For Your Freedom (no p/s)	50

SCOTT ENGEL

58	Vogue V 9125	Blue Bell/Paper Doll	400
58	Vogue V 9125	Blue Bell/Paper Doll (78)	80
59	Vogue V 9145	The Livin' End/Good For Nothin' (with Count Dracula & Boys)	400

59	Vogue V 9145		The Livin' End/Good For Nothin' (with Count Dracula & Boys) (78)................100
59	Vogue V 9150		Charlie Bop/All I Do Is Dream Of You..300
59	Vogue V 9150		Charlie Bop/All I Do Is Dream Of You (78)..75
66	Liberty LEP 2261		SCOTT ENGEL (EP) 50

(see also Scott Walker, Walker Brothers)

SCOTT ENGEL & JOHN STEWART
| 66 | Capitol CL 15440 | | I Only Came To Dance With You/Greens ....40 |

(see also Scott Walker, Walker Brothers)

ENGINE
| 87 | Beak BEAK 1 | | Getting Away From It All (p/s) ....5 |
| 88 | BH SIXFIFTY 1 | | WELL OILED (LP)...12 |

ENGLAND (1)
| 76 | Deroy DER 1356 | | ENGLAND (LP, private pressing)..350 |

ENGLAND (2)
77	Arista ARIST 88		Pariffinalea/Nanagram...6
77	Arista ARTY 153		GARDEN SHED (LP, allegedly with booklet)..60
77	Arista ARTY 153		GARDEN SHED (LP, allegedly some with booklet) 40

ENGLAND FOOTBALL SQUAD
70	Pye 7N 17920		Back Home/Cinnamon Stick...7
70	Pye 7N 17920		Back Home/Cinnamon Stick (some with 'football centre).................................15
70	Pye 7N 17920		Back Home/Cinnamon Stick (with 'football centre and p/s) 25
70	Pye 7N 17920		Back Home/Cinnamon Stick (in promo 'BOAC' sleeve) 100
70	Pye NSPL 18337		THE WORLD BEATERS SING THE WORLD BEATERS (LP, round fold-out sleeve)........30
82	Event EV 002		ENGLAND IN THE WORLD CUP 1982 (LP, gatefold sleeve) 12

ENGLAND'S GLORY
| 73 | Venus VEN 105 | | ENGLAND'S GLORY (LP, private pressing, pink label, 25 copies only, Venus VEN 105 in run-out groove; beware of white label counterfeits) ....1000 |
| 87 | Five Hours Back TOCK 4 | | ENGLAND'S GLORY (LP, stickered sleeve) ....12 |

(see also Only Ones)

ENGLAND SISTERS
| 60 | HMV POP 710 | | Heartbeat/Little Child ....50 |

ENGLISH
| 81 | Albion ION 1008 | | Hooray For The English/When You Fly (p/s) ....10 |

ENGLISH COUNTRY BLUES BAND
| 83 | Rogue FMSL 2004 | | HOME AND DERANGED (LP)..15 |

ENGLISH DOGS
83	Clay PLATE 6		MAD PUNX AND ENGLISH DOGS (12")...15
84	Ros ASS 17		TO THE ENDS OF THE EARTH (12" EP, p/s)..20
86	Under One Flag 12 FLAG 101		METALMORPHOSIS (12" EP, p/s) 10
83	Clay LP 10		INVASION OF THE PORKY MEN (LP, inner)..20
85	Rot ASS 20		FORWARD INTO BATTLE (LP)..15
86	Under One Flag FLAG 4		WHERE LEGEND BEGAN (LP)...15

ERROL(L) ENGLISH
70	Big Shot BI 547		I Don't Want To Love You/Love Is Pure 6
70	Big Shot BI 548		Once In My Life/Rabbit In A Cottage 6
70	Torpedo TOR 8		Open The Door To Your Heart/That Will Do...6
70	Torpedo TOR 9		Where You Lead Me/Hitchin' A Ride 6
70	Torpedo TOR 16		Sad Girl/Welcome Me Back Home 6
70	Torpedo TOR 22		Sha La La La Lee/BOVVER BOYS: A.G.G.R.O...50
71	Duke DU 99		Sometimes (with Champions)/Sugar Cane 6

(see also Junior English, Errol & Champions)

MR JOE ENGLISH
| 69 | Fontana TF 3034 | | Lay Lady Lay/Two Minute Silence..15 |

JUNIOR ENGLISH
69	Camel CA 35		Nobody Knows (with Tony Sexton)/Somewhere..6
71	Pama PM 828		Jesamine/SYDNEY ALL STARS: The Flash 8
72	Pama PM 841		Miss Playgirl/Once In My Life...8
72	Pama PM 866		I Don't Want To Die/Land Of Sea And Sand 8
72	Pama PM 869		Daniel/Perfidia..8
72	Banana BA 368		Anniversary/Girls Like You 8
73	Pama Supreme PS 381		Garden Party/Version 8
79	Burning Rockers BRD 004		Love And Key/Key Down (12", red vinyl) 20
79	Burning Rockers BRD 009		Natural High/In Loving You (12")..12
74	Cactus CTLP 102		THE DYNAMIC (LP) 30
75	Horse HRLP 707		THE GREAT (LP) 15
80	Burning Rockers BR 1010		LOVERS KEY (LP)...25

(see also Errol English)

ENGLISH ROSE
| 70 | Polydor 2058 040 | | Yesterday's Hero/To Jackie ....10 |

(see also Neat Change, Love Affair)

ENGLISH SUBTITLES
79	Small Wonder SMALL 22		Time Tunnel/Sweat/Reconstruction (p/s) 5
82	Glass 007/10 SEC 21		Tannoy/Cars On Fire (folded p/s in bag with insert).......................................6
82	Glass GLASS LP 013		ORIGINAL DIALOGUE (LP, with inner sleeve) 12

ENGLISH McCOY
| 88 | Nowyertalkin' 7TALK 2 | | Give Me Something To Believe In/Breaking Down (p/s) ....100 |
| 88 | Nowyertalkin' 12TALK 2 | | GIVE ME SOMETHING TO BELIEVE IN (12" EP) ....200 |

ENID
76	Buk BUK 3002		The Lovers/In The Region Of The Summer Stars 8
77	EMI International INT 540		Golden Earrings/Omega (p/s) 6
79	Pye 7P 106		Dambusters March — Land Of Hope And Glory/The Skye Boat Song (p/s, blue vinyl)...........6
80	Pye 7P 187		Fool/Tito (p/s) 6

MINT VALUE £

80	EMI EMI 5109	Golden Earrings/665 The Great Bean (p/s)	6
81	Bronze BRO 127	When You Wish Upon A Star/Jessica (p/s)	6
81	Bronze BRO 134	Heigh Ho/Twinkle Twinkle Little Star (p/s)	6
82	Rak RAK 349	And Then There Were None/Letter From America (p/s)	5
76	Buk BULP 2014	IN THE REGION OF THE SUMMER STARS (LP, 1st issue, white label, with insert, without mention of "Enid" on front cover; distributed by Decca)	20
77	Buk BULP 2014	IN THE REGION OF THE SUMMER STARS (2nd issue, black label, with "Enid" on front cover)	12
84	The Stand LE 1	"THE LIVERPOOL ALBUM" (untitled mini-album, sold at gigs, 800 only)	20
84	The Stand THE STAND 1	THE STAND (fan club issue, 5,000 only, autographed)	25
84	The Stand THE STAND 1	THE STAND (fan club issue, 5,000 only, some autographed)	15
85	The Stand THE STAND 2	THE STAND 1985-1986 (fan club issue, 2,000 only, autographed)	12
85	The Stand THE STAND 2	THE STAND 1985-1986 (fan club issue, 2,000 only)	15

(see also Robert John Godfrey, Godfrey & Stewart, William Arkle, Glen Baker, Kim Wilde)

ETHEL ENNIS
| 64 | RCA SF 7654 | ONCE AGAIN (LP) | 15 |

RAY ENNIS & BLUE JEANS
| 68 | Columbia DB 8431 | What Have They Done To Hazel?/Now That You've Got Me (You Don't Seem To Want Me) | 25 |

(see also Swinging Blue Jeans, Blue Jeans)

SEAMUS ENNIS
| 68 | Ember FA 2054 | THE BONNY BUNCH OF ROSES (LP, reissue) | 12 |
| 70 | Leader LEA 2003 | SEAMUS ENNIS (LP) | 12 |

BRIAN ENO
74	Island WIP 6178	Seven Deadly Finns/Later On	10
75	Island WIP 6233	The Lion Sleeps Tonight (Wimoweh)/I'll Come Running	6
78	Polydor 2001 762	The King's Lead Hat/R.A.F. (B-side with Snatch)	6
83	EG EGO 12	Silver Morning/Deep Blue Day (with Daniel Lanois & Roger Eno) with wraparound promo p/s with Eno notes on back)	8
73	Island ILPS 9268	HERE COME THE WARM JETS (LP)	25
74	Island ILPS 9309	TAKING TIGER MOUNTAIN (BY STRATEGY) (LP, gatefold sleeve)	20
75	Island ILPS 9351	ANOTHER GREEN WORLD (LP)	20
75	Island HELP 22	EVENING STAR (LP, as Fripp & Eno)	20
75	Obscure OBS 3	DISCREET MUSIC (LP)	20
76	Editions EG EGM 1	MUSIC FOR FILMS (LP, private pressing)	100
77	Polydor 2302 071	BEFORE AND AFTER SCIENCE (LP, with 4 Peter Schmidt prints)	30
77	Polydor 2683082	HERE COME THE WARM JETS/BEFORE & AFTER SCIENCE (2-LP reissue)	25
78	Polydor 2310623	MUSIC FOR FILMS (LP)	25
78	EG AMB 001	AMBIENT 1 - MUSIC FOR AIRPORTS (LP, inner)	15
82	EG EGED 20	AMBIENT 4 (LP)	15
83	EG EGBS 002	WORKING BACKWARDS 1983-1973 (9-LP box set with "Music For Films, Vol. 2" LP & "Rarities" 12")	150
90s	SML ESL 003CD	TEXTURES (CD)	30

(see also Ayers Cale Nico & Eno, Roxy Music, Passengers, Robert Fripp, Lady June, David Toop, Gavin Bryars, Toto)

BRIAN ENO & DAVID BYRNE
| 81 | EG EGO 1 | The Jezebel Spirit/Regiment (p/s) | 10 |
| 81 | EG EGLP 48 | MY LIFE IN THE BUSH OF GHOSTS (LP) | 15 |

(see also David Byrne, Talking Heads)

ENORMOUS ROOM
| 86 | Sharp CAL 5 | 100 Different Words/Sylvia's Children/Melanie And Martin/ You Wrote A Book (12", p/s) | 8 |

ENOS & SHEILA
| 68 | Blue Cat BS 138 | Tonight You're Mine/UNTOUCHABLES: Your Love | 30 |

(see also Enos McLeod)

ENOUGH'S ENOUGH
| 68 | Tattoo TT 101 | Please Remember/Look Around You Baby | 700 |

ENSEMBLE
| 82 | Stiff WIN 1 | Viva Scotland, England, Ireland/Viva Scotland, England, Ireland ("A" label promo) | 15 |

ENSLAVED
| 90s | Candlelight 001MLP | HORDANES LAND (EP) | 60 |

ENTICERS
| 72 | Atlantic 2091 136 | Calling For Your Love/Storyteller | 35 |

JIMI ENTLEY SOUND
| 02 | Espionage Disk ESP 001 | Apache/Charlie's Theme | 25 |

(see also Portishead)

ENTOMBED
91	Earache 7 MOSH 38	Crawl/Forsaken (p/s)	10
91	Earache MOSH 38T	Crawl/Forsaken/Bitter Loss (12" p/s)	12
92	Earache MOSH 52 T	Stranger Eons/Dusk/Shreds Of Flesh (12", p/s)	10
93	Earache 7 MOSH 114	Out Of Hand/God Of Thunder/Black Breath (p/s)	12
93	Earache MOSH 114 T	Out Of Hand/God Of Thunder/Black Breath (12", p/s)	12
93	Earache 7 MOSH 94 T	HOLLOWMAN EP (6 track 12", p/s)	15
95	Earache 7 MOSH 132	Night Of The Vampire/NEW BOMB TURKS: I Hate People (p/s)	6
89	Earache MOSH 21P	LEFT HAND PATH (LP, picture disc)	20
90	Earache MOSH 21	LEFT HAND PATH (LP, insert)	25
91	Earache MOSH 21	LEFT HAND PATH (LP, white vinyl, stickered sleeve, 2000 only)	30
91	Earache MOSH 37	CLANDESTINE LP, embossed sleeve, insert)	20
93	Earache MOSH 82	WOLVERINE BLUES (LP, lyric insert)	30
97	Music For Nations MFN 216	TO RIDE, SHOOT STRAIGHT AND SPEAK THE TRUTH (LP, with "Family Favourites" 12")	50
98	Music For Nations MFN 244	SAME DIFFERENCE (LP)	40
07	Back On Black BOBV 067 LP	SERPENT SAINTS/THE TEN AMENDMENTS (LP, red vinyl)	15

JOHN ENTWISTLE('S OX)
71	Track 2094 008	I Believe In Everything/My Size	10
75	Decca FR 13567	Mad Dog/Cell No.7 (as John Entwistle's Ox)	8
81	WEA K 79249P	Too Late The Hero/I'm Coming Back (picture disc, some autographed)	10
81	WEA K 79249P	Too Late The Hero/I'm Coming Back (picture disc, some autographed)	6

71	Track 2406 005	SMASH YOUR HEAD AGAINST THE WALL (LP, gatefold, black/silver label)	30
72	Track 2406 104	WHISTLE RYMES (LP, gatefold sleeve, black/silver labels)	25
75	Decca TXS 114	MAD DOG (LP, as John Entwistle's Ox, with poster, lyric insert)	25
75	Decca TXS 114	MAD DOG (LP, as John Entwistle's Ox, without poster, lyric insert)	15

(see also Who, Rigor Mortis)

ENYA

87	BBC RESL 201	I Want Tomorrow/The Celts Theme (p/s)	7
87	BBC CDRSL 201	I Want Tomorrow/The Celts Theme/To Go Beyond I/To Go Beyond II (3" CD)	25
88	WEA YZ 312 CD	Orinoco Flow/Smaotin.../Out Of The Blue (3" CD)	12
88	WEA YZ 356 CD	Evening Falls/Oiche Chiun (Silent Night)/Morning Glory (3" CD)	15
89	WEA YZ 368 CD	Storms In Africa (Part II)/Storms In Africa (Part I) (3" CD, card sleeve)	15
89	WEA YZ 368 CDX	Storms In Africa (Part II)/The Celts/Aldebaran/Storms In Africa (Part I) (5" CD, picture disc)	15
91	WEA YZ 604 CDX	Caribbean Blue/Orinoco Flow/As Baile/Oriel Window (CD, digipak)	10
91	WEA YZ 635 T	How Can I Keep From Singing/O'che Chi'n (Silent Night) (12", metallic p/s)	10
92	WEA YZ 640 CDX	Book Of Days/Watermark/On Your Shore/Exile (CD, box set with 4 prints)	12
87	BBC REB 605	ENYA (LP)	15
87	BBC BBCCD 605	ENYA (CD)	25

JAY EPAE

61	Mercury AMT 1132	Putti Putti/Hawaiian Melody	6

EPICS (JAMAICA)

70	Bamboo BAM 37	Your Love/Driving Me Crazy	15

EPICS (U.K.)

65	Pye 7N 15829	There's Just No Pleasing You/My Little Girl	10
66	Pye 7N 17053	Just How Wrong Can You Be/Blue Turns To Grey	10
68	CBS 3564	Travelling Circus/Henry Long	20

(see also Acid Gallery, Christie, T. Rex)

EPIDEMIC

89	Metalcore CORE 4	THE TRUTH OF WHAT WILL BE (LP)	20

EPILEPTICS

80	Stortbeat/Mirror BEAT 8	1970'S EP (black & white p/s, stencilled white labels)	20
81	Spiderleg SDL 1	1970'S EP (re-recorded, printed labels, folded different printed b&w p/s)	15
81	Spiderleg SDL 2	LAST BUS TO DEBDEN (EP, hand-written labels & photocopied p/s)	12

(see also Licks, Flux Of Pink Indians)

EPISODE

68	MGM MGM 1409	Little One/Wide Smiles	30

(see also Episode Six)

EPISODE FOUR

86	Lenin & McCarthy LENM 001T	STRIKE UP MATCHES EP (p/s with insert, 500 only, many destroyed)	150

(see also East Village)

EPISODE SIX

66	Pye 7N 17018	Put Yourself In My Place/That's All I Want	25
66	Pye 7N 17110	I Hear Trumpets Blow/True Love Is Funny That Way	20
66	Pye 7N 17147	Here, There And Everywhere/Mighty Morris Ten	20
67	Pye 7N 17244	Love, Hate, Revenge/Baby Baby Baby	40
67	Pye 7N 17330	Morning Dew/Sunshine Girl	25
67	Pye 7N 17376	I Can See Through You/When I Fall In Love	40
68	Chapter One CH 103	Lucky Sunday/Mr. Universe	20
69	Chapter One CH 104	Mozart Versus The Rest/Jak D'Or	20
87	PRT PYL 6026	PUT YOURSELF IN MY PLACE (LP)	15
97	RPM RPM 178	THE RADIO ONE CLUB SESSIONS LIVE 1968/69 (CD)	25

(see also Episode, Sheila Carter & Episode Six, Neo Maya, Roger Glover, Jon Lord, Gillan, Deep Purple, Quatermass)

MINNIE EPPERSON

68	Action ACT 4503	Grab Your Clothes (And Get On Out)/No Love At All	60

PRESTON EPPS

59	Top Rank JAR 140	Bongo Rock/Bongo Party	20
59	Top Rank JAR 180	Bongos In Pastel/Doin' The Cha Cha Cha	10
60	Top Rank JAR 345	Bongo Boogie/Flamenco Boogie	15
60	Top Rank JAR 413	Bongo Bongo Bongo/Hully Gully Bongo	12
60	Top Rank JAR 522	Bongola/Blue Bongo	8
70	President PT 294	Bongo Rock/SANDY NELSON: Teen Beat	6
60	Top Rank JKP 2060	RUSHING FOR PERCUSSION (EP, with Sandy Nelson)	20

(see also Sandy Nelson)

EQUA

83	MR FOX FOX 1	In The Red/City Dub	20
83	Mr Fox FOX 1	In The Red/City Dub (12")	60

EQUALS

67	President PT 117	I Won't Be There/Fire	8
67	President PT 135	Baby, Come Back/Hold Me Closer	6
67	President ZAM 2	I'm A Poor Man/Can't Find A Girl To Love Me (Export only)	30
67	President PT 158	Give Love A Try/Another Sad And Lonely Night	7
68	President PT 180	I Get So Excited/The Skies Above	6
68	President PT 200	Laurel And Hardy/The Guy Who Made Her A Star	6
68	President PT 222	Softly Softly/Lonely Rita	6
69	President PT 260	Viva Bobby Joe/I Can't Let You Go	6
69	President PT 275	Rub A Dub Dub/After The Lights Go Down Low	6
70	President PT 288	Soul Brother Clifford/Happy Birthday Girl	6
70	President PT 303	I Can See But You Don't Know/Gigolo Sam	40
70	President PT 325	Black Skin Blue Eyed Boys/Ain't Got Nothing To Give You	5
70	President PT 345	Help Me Simone/Love Potion	6
70	Presiden ZAM 1	Let's Go To The Moon/Watching The Girls (export)	25
72	CBS 7874	Stand Up And Be Counted/What Would You Do To Survive	6
73	President PT 405	Honey Bee/Put Some Rock & Roll In Your Soul	6
73	President PT 414	Diversion/Here Today Gone Tomorrow	15

74	President PT 422	Hang Up My Rock & Roll Shoes/She Lives For Today	6
75	President PT 436	Georgetown Girl/We've Got It All Worked Out	6
76	Mercury 6007 104	Kaiwana Sunshine Girl/Soul Mother	6
76	Mercury 6007 106	Funky Like A Train/If You Didn't Miss Me	15
76	Mercury 6007 107	Funky Like A Train/If You Didn't Miss Me (12")	12
77	Mercury 6007 139	Irma La Douce/Ar'e Harry	6
77	President PT 464	Beautiful Clown/Daily Love	6
78	Ice GUY 5	Red Dog/Something Beautiful	6
88	Club JAB 58	Funky Like A Train/Born Ya!/Funky Like A Train (extended) (reissue)	7
88	Club JABX 58	Funky Like A Train/Born Ya!/Funky Like A Train (extended) (12", reissue)	20
68	President PTE 1	BABY COME BACK (EP)	20
68	President PTE 2	THE EQUALS (EP)	25
67	President PTL 1006	UNEQUALLED EQUALS (LP)	22
68	President PTL 1015	EQUALS EXPLOSION (LP)	20
68	President PTL(S) 1020	SENSATIONAL EQUALS (LP)	20
68	President PTL(S) 1025	SUPREME (LP)	18
69	President PTLS 1030	THE EQUALS STRIKE AGAIN (LP)	18
69	President PTLS 1050	BEST OF THE EQUALS (LP)	18
70	President PTLS 1038	AT THE TOP (LP, gatefold, poster)	18
76	Mercury 9109 601	BORN YA! (LP)	25
78	Ice ICEL 1002	MYSTIC SISTER (LP)	25

(see also Little Grants & Eddie, Pyramids, Hickory, Little Brother Grant, Zappata Schmitt, Seven Letters/Syramip, Thirty-Second Turn-Off)

EQUATIONS

69	Fontana TF 1035	Waiting On The Shores Of Nowhere/You Stood Beside Me	10

EQUINOX

73	Boulevard BLVD 4118	HARD ROCK (LP, black/silver labels)	25

EQUIPE 84

67	Major Minor MM 517	Auschwitz/Twenty Ninth Of September	20

ERASMUS CHORUM

72	Chapter 1 SCM 173	Oh Lord, The Holy House On Sunday/Mary Jane	15
73	Alaska 19	I Don't Want Our Loving To Die/That Is Why	10
73	Alaska ALA 13	Jungle/That Is Why	25

ERASURE

SINGLES

85	Mute L12MUTE 40	Who Needs Love (Like That) (Mexican Mix)/Push Me Shove Me (Tacos Mix) (12", p/s)	20
85	Mute L12MUTE 42	Heavenly Action (Yellow Brick Mix)/Don't Say No (Ruby Red Mix) (12", p/s, L12 cat. no. must be listed on sleeve & label)	40
85	Mute DMUTE 42	Heavenly Action/Don't Say No (Ruby Red Mix)//Who Needs Love (Like That) (Mexican Mix)/Push Me Shove Me (Tacos Mix) (12" shrinkwrapped double pack)	20
86	Mute 12MUTE 45	Oh L'Amour/March On Down The Line/Gimme! Gimme! Gimme! (12", 'Thomas The Tank Engine' p/s, withdrawn)	15
87	Mute CDMUTE 56	It Doesn't Have To Be/Sometimes/Oh L'Amour/Heavenly Action/Who Needs Love (Like That)/Gimme! Gimme! Gimme!/In The Hall Of The Mountain King (CD, 7" sized 'tray' p/s)	10
88	Mute LCDMUTE 93	Crackers International II: Stop! (Mark Saunders Remix)/Knocking On Your Door (Mark Saunders Remix)/God Rest Ye Merry Gentlemen (3" CD, Xmas pack with card and gift label 6" x 3" sleeve)	20
90	Mute XL12MUTE 99	Supernature (Mark Saunders Remix)/You Surround Me (Gareth Jones Remix)/Supernature (Daniel Miller & Phil Legg Remix) (12", envelope p/s)	10
90	Mute XL12MUTE 109	Blue Savannah (Der Deutsche Mix II)/Blue Savannah (Der Deutsche Mix I) (12", 1-sided, numbered envelope p/s)	10
94	Mute MUTE 166	I Love Saturday/Dodo/Because You're So Sweet (unreleased, p/s only)	30

ALBUMS

99	Mute EBX 1	ERASURE 1 (5-CD box set)	30
99	Mute EBX 2	ERASURE 2 (5-CD box set)	30
95	Mute STUMM 115	I SAY I SAY I SAY (LP, with booklet)	30
97	STUMM 155	COWBOY (LP)	20

PROMOS

86	Mute P12MUTE 45	Oh L'Amour/March On Down The Line/Gimme! Gimme! Gimme! (12", plain white sleeve, dark blue vinyl)	20
89	Mute (no cat. no.)	WILD (CD, promo-only box set, with LP, 12", , stickers, postcard, photo & info sheet)	100
90	Mute ERAS 1	Push Me Shove Me (Moonbeam Mix)/(Catatonic Mix)/Senseless (Avalon Mix) (12", p/s)	20
90	Mute ERAS 2	ERAS 2: Who Needs Love Like That (Winnie Cooper Mix)/ Ship Of Fools (Orbital South Seas Isles Of Holy Beats Mix) (12" die-cut title sleeve)	18
90	Mute ERAS 3	Sometimes (Danny Rampling Mix) (12", die-cut title sleeve)	20
90s	Mute P12MUTE 195	Don't Say Your Love Is Killing Me (Tall Paul Mix)/(John Pleased Wimmin Flashback Vox)/Oh L'Amour (Tin Tin Out Remix)/(Matt Darey Mix) (12", white label test pressing with press release & release sheet, 10 copies only)	70
91	Mute CDSTUMM 95	CHORUS (promo CD, with and booklet)	60
92	Mute (no cat. no.)	POP! THE FIRST 20 HITS (CD, promo-only box set, with T-shirt, info sheets, 2-LP, video tape, &)	100
94	Mute PL12 MUTE 166	Ghost (12", 1-sided)	15
97	Mute PL12 MUTE 208	Rain (Blue Amazon Twisted Circles Mix)/In My Arms (Dekkard Dub)/ Sometimes (John "00" Flemings Full Vocal Club Mix)/Sometimes (John "00" Flemings Give It Some Welly Dub Mix) (12" p/s)	6
97	Mute PL12 MUTE 208	Rain (John Of The Pleased Wimmin Vocal Mix)/(John Of The Pleased Wimmin Dub)/Sometimes (John "00" Flemings Full Vocal Club Mix)/In My Arms (BBE Mix) (12" p/s)	6
92	Mute ERAS 5 EARS5CD	POP (CD, 19-track compilation, without "Take A Chance On Me" & "Who Needs Love Like That [Hamburg Mix]", numbered, promo only)	30
92	Mute CRERASINT 1	POP (CD, interview disc)	20
96	Mute ERAS SAY 1	I SAY I SAY I SAY (CD, interview disc)	20
96	Mute ERAS SAY 2	ERASURE (CD, interview disc)	20
96	Mute ERAS SAY 3	COWBOY (CD, interview disc)	20

(see also Depeche Mode, Dinger)

ERAZERHEAD

81	Test Pressing TP 4	Ape Man/Wipeout/Rock And Roll Zombie (p/s)	5
82	Flicknife FLS 208	Shell Shock/She Can Dance (p/s)	5
82	Flicknife FLS 210	Teenager In Love/All For Me (p/s)	5

| 84 | Flicknife SHARP 025 | SHELL SHOCKED - BEST OF (LP) | 12 |

EREHWON

| 81 | Harvest HAR 5213 | Tiny Goddess/The Hero (p/s) | 5 |

(see also Patrick Campbell-Lyons)

ERIC (SYKES) & HATTIE (JACQUES)

| 63 | Decca LK 4507 | ERIC, HATTIE AND THINGS (LP) | 12 |

(see also Eric Sykes & Hattie Jacques)

ERIC HYSTERIC & ESOTERICS

| 80 | Wasted Vinyl WASTE 1 | Tropical Vision/Dance And Sing (p/s) | 5 |

ERIC & THE VIKINGS

| 86 | Kool Kat 5 | Hurting/My Baby Ain't No Play Thing (red vinyl) | 25 |

ROKY ERICKSON (& THE ALIENS)

77	Virgin VS 180	Bermuda/The Interpreter (p/s)	10
80	CBS 8888	Creature With The Atom Brain/The Wind And More (with The Aliens)	8
80	CBS 9055	Mine Mine Mind/Bloody Hammer (Acoustic Version) (p/s, with The Aliens)	8
80	CBS SCBS 84463	ROKY ERICKSON & THE ALIENS (LP)	15
86	Demon FIEND 66	GREMLINS HAVE PICTURES (LP)	15
87	5 Hours Back TOCK 007	CASTING THE RUNES (LP)	15
87	Five Hours Back TOCK 7P	CASTING THE RUNES (LP, picture disc)	25
92	Swordfish SFMD LP2	LOVE TO SEE YOU BLEED (LP)	25
92	Swordfish SFMD LP 1	MAD DOG (LP)	25

(see also 13th Floor Elevators)

ERIK

| 93 | PWL PWLT 270 | The Devil & The Deep Blue Sea (mixes) (12", p/s, withdrawn) | 8 |
| 93 | PWL PWCD 270 | The Devil & The Deep Blue Sea (mixes) (CD, withdrawn) | 12 |

ERNIE & ED

| 72 | Jay Boy BOY 58 | Beautiful World/Indication | 50 |

ERROL (ENGLISH) & CHAMPIONS

| 70 | Jackpot JP 732 | Lonely Boy/Da Boo | 7 |
| 70 | Jackpot JP 738 | Lonely Boy/TONY & CHAMPIONS: All Of My Life | 8 |

(see also Errol English)

ERROL (DUNKLEY) & HIS GROUP

| 65 | Blue Beat BB 284 | Gypsy/Miss May (actually by Errol Dunkley & Roy Shirley) | 25 |

(see also Errol Dunkley)

ERROL (DUNKLEY) & U ROY

| 72 | Punch PH 105 | Darling Ooh Wee/GOD SONS: Merry Up Version | 12 |

E.R. & THE ROUGH RIDERS

| 69 | Polydor 56361 | Heya/I'm Alive | 15 |

ERSATZ

| 81 | Raw RAW 35 | Motorbody Love/One Good Reason/Gimme A Chance (poster p/s) | 6 |
| 81 | Leisure Sounds SRS 32 | Smile In Shadow/House Of Cards (p/s) | 6 |

(see also DJ Harvey)

BOOKER ERVIN

| 61 | Parlophone PMC 1170 | THE BOOK (LP) | 40 |

DEE ERVIN

| 72 | Signpost SG 4356 | DEE ERVIN SINGS (LP) | 20 |

BLUEGRASS ERWIN

| 59 | Top Rank JAR 252 | I Won't Cry Alone/I Can't Love You | 5 |

ESCALATORS

83	Big Beat NS 86	Something's Missing/The Edge (p/s)	8
83	Big Beat NS 87	The Munsters Theme/Monday (p/s)	8
83	Big Beat WIKM15	MOVING STAIRCASES (LP)	18

(see also Clapham South Escalators, The Meteors)

ESCORTS (JAMAICA)

| 70 | Big Shot BI 535 | I'm So Afraid/Mother Nature | 40 |
| 74 | Fab FAB 245 | Sixpense/Loving Feeling | 15 |

(see also Sensations)

ESCORTS (U.K.)

64	Fontana TF 453	Dizzy Miss Lizzy/All I Want Is You	25
64	Fontana TF 474	The One To Cry/Tell Me Baby	30
64	Fontana TF 516	I Don't Want To Go On Without You/Don't Forget To Write	20
65	Fontana TF 570	C'Mon Home Baby/You'll Get No Lovin' That Way	25
66	Fontana TF 651	Let It Be Me/Mad Mad World	25
66	Columbia DB 8061	From Head To Toe/Night Time	35

(see also Big Three, Paddy Klaus & Gibson, Swinging Blue Jeans, Terry Sylvester)

ESCORTS (U.S.)

| 63 | Coral Q 72458 | Submarine Race Watching/Somewhere | 25 |

ESCORTS & KAY JUSTICE

| 54 | Columbia SCM 5132 | If You Took Your Love From Me/Yes, Indeed | 15 |

ESCOURTS

| 76 | Alaska ALA 1014 | Disrespect Can Wreck/Bam A Lam A Boogie | 8 |

ESG

| 81 | Factory FAC 34 | You're No Good/UFO (p/s) | 30 |

ESKIMOS & EGYPT

| 81 | Village VILS 102 | The Cold/A Year/Screams And Whispers (EP, p/s) | 60 |

ESOTERIC/ESOTERIK

| 96 | Club Craft OR 100 | Dancing With The Devil/Esoteric Vs. Hybrid (12") | 50 |

96	Club Craft OR 200	Ultimate Straightness/Playing With Voices (12")..40
96	Club Craft OR 300	Elegant Panning/3 After That One (12")..30
96	Club Craft OR 400	Odd Sins/Odd Sins (12")...80
96	Crowd Control CROWD 005T	Desert Planet/Mayhem (12", as Esoterik)..80
96	Utmostfear UTMOST 1301	Falling, Floating, Flying/Ultimate Straightness (12")......................................40
96	Utmostfear UTMOST 1302	Curley And Ramon/Mad Strings (12")..40
97	Crowd Control CROWD 006	Mayhem/Purdey's Effect/In The Hills (12", as Esoterik)...................................80
98	Utmostfear UTMOST 1303	Untitled/Untitled (12", label bears legend "Curley Truly Unique 1973-1998") 40

(See also Spiral Tribe)

ESOTERIC (2)
| 11 | Aesthetic Death ADLP 003 | EPISTEMOLOGICAL DESPONDENCY (2-LP, reissue of 1994 CD release, numbered gatefold sleeve, insert, 350 only) ....25 |

ESP
| 89 | Radical DJ INT 14 | It's You (12")..80 |

ESPERANTO ROCK ORCHESTRA
73	A&M AMLH 68175	ESPERANTO ROCK ORCHESTRA (LP, gatefold sleeve, brown label)...........................25
74	A&M AMLH 63624	DANSE MACABRE (LP, as Esperanto, silver/gold labels).......................................20
75	A&M AMLS 68294	LAST TANGO (LP, as Esperanto, silver/brown labels)..30

(see also Keith Christmas, Comus)

ESPERS
| 03 | Wichita WEBB084LP | ESPERS (LP)...50 |

ESPRIT DE CORPS
73	Jam JAM 24	If (Would It Turn Out Wrong)/Picture On The Wall 15
81	Come 0001	Anxiety/The Tea Cup Song (hand-made silk-screened sleeve)...........................30
73	Jam JAM 32	Lonely/Do You Remember Me (Like I Remember You)....................................10

(see also David Ballantyne, Just Plain Smith, Just Plain Jones)

ESQUERITA
| 58 | Capitol CL 14938 | Rockin' The Joint/Esquerita And The Voola ....100 |
| 72 | Specialty SPE 6603 | WILDCAT SHAKEOUT (LP)..30 |

ESQUIRES
67	Stateside SS 2048	Get On Up/Listen To Me..20
68	Stateside SS 2077	And Get Away/Everybody's Laughing 20
73	Action ACT 4618	My Sweet Baby/Henry Ralph 45
68	London HA-Q/SH-Q 8356	GET ON UP AND GET AWAY (LP)..40

ESQUIVEL
| 63 | Reprise R 6046 | MORE OF OTHER WORLDS, OTHER SOUNDS (LP)...15 |

ESSENTIAL LOGIC
78	Cells SELL ONE	Aerosol Burns/World Friction (p/s) 8
79	Rough Trade RT29	Popcorn Boy/Flora Force (p/s) 12
80	Rough Trade RT50	Eugene (p/s) 10
81	Rough Trade RT74	Fanfare In The Garden/The Captain (p/s) 7

(see also X-Ray Spex)

ESSEX
63	Columbia DB 7077	Easier Said Than Done/Are You Going My Way..15
63	Columbia DB 7122	A Walkin' Miracle/What I Don't Know Won't Hurt Me (with Anita Humes) 20
63	Columbia DB 7178	She's Got Everything/Out Of Sight, Out Of Mind 20
63	Columbia 33SX 1593	EASIER SAID THAN DONE (LP)...60
64	Columbia 33SX 1613	A WALKIN' MIRACLE (LP)..60

DAVID ESSEX
65	Fontana TF 559	And The Tears Came Tumbling Down/You Can't Stop Me Loving You 50
65	Fontana TF 620	Can't Nobody Love You/Baby I Don't Mind...45
66	Fontana TF 680	This Little Girl Of Mine/Brokenhearted 45
66	Fontana TF 733	Thigh High/De Boom Lay Boom...40
68	Uni UN 502	Love Story/Higher Than High 20
68	Pye 7N 17621	Just For Tonight/Goodbye 20
69	Decca F 12935	That Takes Me Back/Lost Without Linda 40
69	Decca F 12967	The Day The Earth Stood Still/Is It So Strange? 30
79	Vertigo 6059 233	M.O.D./M.O.D. (2) (as M.O.D., songwriting credited to D. Cook, p/s, allegedly mispressed on 2-Tone label)..75
79	Vertigo 6059 233	M.O.D./M.O.D. (2) (as M.O.D., songwriting credited to D. Cook, p/s) 7

(see also David & Rozaa, Us)

ESSJAY
| 71 | DJM DJS 254 | Twins Of Evil/Fastback ....35 |

ASTON ESSON
| 80 | Studio 16 STD 01 | Woman Of My Dreams/Version (12")...30 |

NEVILLE ESSON
| 61 | Blue Beat BB 37 | Lover's Jive/Wicked And Dreadful (with Clue J. & His Blues Busters) ....18 |

ESTABLISHMENT
| 81 | Foetain | BAD CATHOLICS (LP)..30 |

(see also Cromwell)

'SLEEPY' JOHN ESTES
66	Delmark DJB 3	SLEEPY JOHN'S GOT THE BLUES (EP)...40
63	Esquire 32-195	THE LEGEND OF SLEEPY JOHN ESTES (LP)..60
63	'77' LA 12-27	TENNESSEE JUG BUSTERS — BROKE AND HUNGRY (LP)....................................40
65	Storyville SLP 172	PORTRAITS IN BLUES VOLUME 10 (LP)..22
72	Delmark DS 619	ELECTRIC SLEEP (LP)..20
71	Delmark DS 613	BROWNSVILLE BLUES (LP)...25

JOHN ESTES/FURRY LEWIS/WILL SHADE
| 71 | Revival RVS 1008 | OLD ORIGINAL TENNESSEE BLUES (LP)...20 |

JACKIE ESTREK
| 61 | Blue Beat BB 64 | Boss Girl/COUNT OSSIE & GROUP: Cassavubu...30 |

| 63 | Island WI 042 | Since You've Been Gone/Daisy I Love You | 15 |
| 66 | Ska Beat JB 256 | The Ska/Daisy I Love You | 18 |

DEON ESTUS
| 89 | Mika MIKCD 2 | Heaven Help Me/It's A Party/Love Can't Wait/Me Or The Rumours (Instrumental) (CD, card p/s) | 12 |

(see also George Michael)

ETCETERAS
| 64 | Oriole CB 1950 | Where Is My Love/Bengawan Solo | 15 |
| 64 | Oriole CB 1973 | Little Lady/Now I Know | 20 |

ETERNAL
| 90 | Sarah SARAH 031 | Sleep/Breathe/Take Me Down (p/s) | 8 |

ETERNALS (JAMAICA)
69	Coxsone CS 7091	Queen Of The Minstrels/Stars	40
70	Moodisc MU 3506	Christmas Joy/WINSTON & RUPERT: Musically Beat	7
71	Moodisc MU 3507	Push Me In The Corner/MUDIE'S ALL STARS: Mudie's Madness (B-side actually by Ansell Collins)	12
71	Moodisc MU 3508	Keep On Dancing/HAZEL WRIGHT: My Jealous Eyes	10

(see also Don Cornel & Eternals)

ETERNALS (U.S.)
59	London HL 8995	Rockin' In The Jungle/Rock 'N' Roll Cha-Cha (triangular centre)	150
59	London HL 8995	Rockin' In The Jungle/Rock 'N' Roll Cha-Cha (round centre)	50
59	London HL 8995	Rockin' In The Jungle/Rock 'N' Roll Cha-Cha (78)	35

ETERNAL SCREAM
| 81 | Eternal 01 | Hypocrite/Action In My Life (p/s) | 15 |
| 81 | Eternal 02 | How I Wish/Child (p/s) | 20 |

ETERNAL TRIANGLE
| 69 | Decca F 12979 | I Guess The Lord Must Be In New York City/Perfumed Candle | 6 |
| 69 | Decca F 12954 | Turn To Me/Window | 7 |

ETERNITY'S CHILDREN
| 68 | Capitol CL 15558 | Mrs Bluebird/Little Boy | 25 |

ETHEL THE FROG
80	Best SRTSFMR 014	Eleanor Rigby/Fight Back	60
80	EMI EMI 5041	Eleanor Rigby/Fight Back (reissue)	10
80	EMI EMC 3329	ETHEL THE FROG (LP, with Terry Hopkinson & Doug Sheppard)	18

ETHIOPIAN IRATION BLOOD RELATIVE & IDREN
| 79 | Greensleeves GRED 21 | This Foundation/Elders and Deacons/How Can A Man/Jah Children Come (12") | 40 |

ETHIOPIANS
66	Ska Beat JB 260	Live Good (credited to the Etheopians)/SOUL BROTHERS: Soho	50
66	Island WI 3015	I Am Free/SOUL BROTHERS: Shanty Town	70
67	Rio R 110	Owe Me No Pay Me/SHARKS: I Wouldn't Baby	20
67	Rio R 114	I'm Gonna Take Over Now/JACKIE MITTOO: Home Made	35
67	Rio R 123	What To Do/JACKIE MITTOO: Got My Bugaloo	120
67	Rio R 126	Dun Dead A'Ready/BOB ANDY: Stay In My Lonely Arms	25
67	Rio R 130	Train To Skaville/You Are The Girl (B-side actually by Gladiators)	25
67	Doctor Bird DB 1092	I Need You/Do It Sweet	35
67	Doctor Bird DB 1096	The Whip/Cool It, Amigo	25
67	Doctor Bird DB 1103	Stay Loose, Mama/The World Goes Ska	50
68	Doctor Bird DB 1141	Come On Now/Sh'Boom	45
68	Doctor Bird DB 1147	Engine 54/Give Me Your Love	150
68	Doctor Bird DB 1148	Train To Glory/You Got The Dough	55
68	Doctor Bird DB 1169	Everything Crash/I'm Not Losing You	40
68	Crab CRAB 2	Fire A Muss Tail/Blacker Black (B-side actually by Count Ossie)	40
68	Crab CRAB 5	Reggie Hit The Town/Ding Dong Bell	35
69	Crab CRAB 7	I Am A King/What A Big Surprise	30
69	Doctor Bird DB 1172	Not Me/Cut Down	40
69	J J Records DB 1185	Hong Kong Flu/Clap Your Hands	18
69	J J Records DB 1186	What A Fire/You	20
69	Doctor Bird DB 1199	Everyday Talking/Sharing You	20
69	Trojan TR 666	Woman Capture Man/One	12
69	Trojan TR 697	Well Red/J.J. ALLSTARS: R.F.K.	12
69	Nu Beat NB 031	My Testimony/J.J. ALL STARS: One Dollar Of Soul	20
69	Nu Beat NB 038	Buss Your Mouth/GLEN ADAMS (Actually REGGAE BOYS) Rough Way Ahead	45
69	Duke DU 35	My Girl/ANSELL COLLINS: Bigger Boss	40
70	Duke DU 61	Mek You Go On So/WINSTON WRIGHT & J.J. ALL STARS: Neck Tie	25
70	Duke Reid DR 2507	Mother's Tender Care/TOMMY McCOOK: Soldier Man	5
70	Bamboo BAM 26	Walkie Talkie/SOUND DIMENSION: Moan And Groan	20
70	Bamboo BAM 38	You'll Want To Come Back/JACKIE MITTOO: Baby Why (Instrumental) (B-side actually by Sound Dimension)	30
70	J.J. JJ 3302	Wreck It Up/Don't Go	8
70	J.J. JJ 3303	Hong Kong Flu/Everything Crash	20
70	Gas GAS 142	Satan Girl/MATADORS: The Pum	6
70	High Note HS 042	Praise For I (actually "Praise Fari")/GAYTONES: Charrie Part II	12
70	Songbird SB 1040	No Baptism/CRYSTALITES: No Baptism (Version Two)	15
70	Songbird SB 1047	Good Ambition/CRYSTALITES: Ambition Version	6
71	Randy's RAN 509	Mi Want Girl/RANDY'S ALL STARS: Girl — Version	7
71	Randy's RAN 510	True Man, Free Man/RANDY'S ALL STARS: Truthful — Version	7
71	Randy's RAN 512	Mr. Tom/Sad News	7
71	Fab FAB 180	Monkey Money/Version	8
71	Treasure Isle TI 7067	Pirate/TOMMY McCOOK & SOUL SYNDICATE: Depth Charge	8
71	Songbird SB 1059	What A Pain/CRYSTALITES: Pain Version	6
71	Songbird SB 1062	Lot's Wife/DERRICK HARRIOTT: Slave	6
71	Songbird SB 1064	Best Of Five (Parts 1 & 2)	6
71	Big Shot BI 569	He's Not A Rebel/J.J. ALL STARS: He's Not A Rebel — Version	15
71	Big Shot BI 574	The Selah/Don't Let Me Go	10
71	Duke DU 102	Drop Him/J.J. ALL STARS: Drop Him Version	6
71	Duke DU 108	Rim Bim Bam/RANDY'S ALL STARS: Rim Bim Bam Version	7

Year	Label/Cat	Title	Value
71	Explosion EX 2050	Starvation/TROJAN ALL STARS: Starvation Version	6
71	G.G. GG 4519	Love Bug/Sound Of Our Forefathers	7
71	Supreme SUP 221	Love Bug/Sound Of Our Forefathers	8
71	Supreme SUP 226	Starvation/MAXIE & GLEN: Jordan River	8
71	Big BG 330	Solid As A Rock/RUPIE EDWARDS ALL STARS: Solid As A Rock Version	6
71	Punch PH 96	Solid As A Rock/RUPIE EDWARDS ALL STARS: Solid As A Rock Version	6
71	G.G. GG 4533	Israel Want To be Free/TYPHOON ALL STARS: Israel (Version)	12
72	Prince Buster PB 38	You Are For Me/Playboy	8
72	Techniques TE 919	Promises/TIVOLIS: Promises — Version	6
73	Harry J. HJ 6646	The Word Is Love/The Word Is Love — Version	5
74	Harry J. HJ 6663	Buy You A Ring/Pray Muma	5
74	Cactus CT 37	Better Man/Skanking Man	6
74	Cactus CT 46	Conquering Lion/Lion Head	8
75	Dragon DRA 1032	Knowledge Is Power/Power Version	5
75	Tropical ALO54	Another Moses/Moses	10
76	Attack ATT 8131	Another Moses/SYLFORD WALKER: I Can't Understand	10
78	Sensation SSD015	Hail Rasta/Version (12")	15
68	Doctor Bird DLM 5011	THE ETHIOPIANS GO ROCK STEADY/ENGINE 54 (LP, this is a UK pressing in a Jamaican sleeve)	400
69	Trojan TTL 10	REGGAE POWER (LP)	40
70	Trojan TBL 112	WOMAN CAPTURE MAN (LP)	45
77	Third World TWS 15	SLAVE CALL (LP)	30

(see Eathopians, Soul Brothers, Soul Vendors, Hamliins)

ETHNIC FIGHT BAND

Year	Label/Cat	Title	Value
75	Ethnic Fight EF 4416	OUT OF ONE MAN COMES MANY DUBS (LP)	80
77	Ethnic Fight EF 4444	MUSIC EXPLOSION DUB (LP)	90

ETIVES

Year	Label/Cat	Title	Value
81	Ayrespin AYRC 106	A BREATH OF FRESH AIR ()	20
84	Ayrespin AYRC 015	AN GAOL A THUG MI OG (MY LOVE OF EARLY DAYS) (LP)	20

(see also Capercaillie)

TONY ETORIA

Year	Label/Cat	Title	Value
77	GTO GT 89	I Can Prove It/Angel For Lovers To Be	10

ETTA (JAMES) & HARVEY (FUQUA)

Year	Label/Cat	Title	Value
60	London HLM 9180	If I Can't Have You/My Heart Cries	50

(see also Etta James, Moonglows, Harvey & Moonglows)

JACK EUBANK'S ORCHESTRA

Year	Label/Cat	Title	Value
61	London HLU 9312	What'd I Say/Chiricahua	10
62	London HLU 9501	Searchin'/Take A Message To Mary	5

EUGENE & BURST

Year	Label/Cat	Title	Value
71	Supreme SUP 225	Let It Fall/DENZIL & BURST: Can't Change	6

EUGENIUS

Year	Label/Cat	Title	Value
94	August Rust 008	MARY QUEEN OF SCOTS (LP)	15

(see also Teenage Fanclub)

EUPHOREAL

Year	Label/Cat	Title	Value
91	Ninja Tune ZEN 12 005	THE JUNGLE TEKNO EP (12")	8

EUROPEANS

Year	Label/Cat	Title	Value
79	Heartbeat PULSE 2	Europeans/Voices (p/s)	5

EUROPEANS

Year	Label/Cat	Title	Value
83	A&M AMLX 68558	VOCABULARY (LP)	12
84	A&M SCOT 1	LIVE (LP)	12
84	A&M AMA 5034	RECURRING DREAMS (LP)	12

(see also Marillion)

EUROPEAN TOYS

Year	Label/Cat	Title	Value
83	SUBVERSIVE SUB 008	I Am The Creator/Keep It All/So Look At Me Now (p/s)	10

EURYTHMICS

Year	Label/Cat	Title	Value
81	RCA RCA 68	Never Gonna Cry Again/Le Sinistre (p/s)	8
81	RCA RCAT 68	Never Gonna Cry Again (Extended)/Le Sinistre (Extended) (12", p/s)	25
81	RCA RCA 115	Belinda/Heartbeat, Heartbeat (p/s)	15
82	RCA RCA 199	This Is The House/Home Is Where The Heart Is (p/s)	15
82	RCA RCAT 199	This Is The House/Your Time Will Come (live)/Never Gonna Cry Again/ 4/4 In Leather (live)/Take Me To Your Heart (live) (12", p/s)	35
82	RCA RCA 230	The Walk/Step On The Beast/The Walk (Part 2) (p/s)	12
82	RCA RCAT 230	The Walk/Invisible Hands/Dr Trash/The Walk (Part 2) (12", printed die-cut sleeve)	35
82	RCA DAP 1	Love Is A Stranger/Monkey, Monkey (picture disc)	5
82	RCA DAT 1	Love Is A Stranger/Let's Just Close Our Eyes/Monkey, Monkey (12", blue p/s)	5
83	RCA DAP 2	Sweet Dreams (Are Made Of This)/I Could Give You (A Mirror) (picture disc)	6
83	RCA DAT 2	Sweet Dreams (Are Made Of This)/I Could Give You (A Mirror)/ Baby's Gone Blue (12", p/s)	8
83	RCA DAP 3	Who's That Girl?/You Take Some Lentils ... And You Take Some Rice (picture disc)	7
83	RCA DAT 3	Who's That Girl?/You Take Some Lentils ... And You Take Some Rice/ ABC (Freeform) (12", p/s)	8
83	RCA DA 4/EUC 001	Right By Your Side/Right By Your Side (Party Mix) (stickered p/s with free shrinkwrapped (RCA EUC 001)	25
83	RCA DAP 4	Right By Your Side/Right By Your Side (Party Mix) (picture disc)	6
83	RCA DAT 4	Right By Your Side/Right By Your Side (Special Mix)/ Pluse Something Else (12", p/s)	8
84	RCA DAP 5	Here Comes The Rain Again/Paint A Rumour (picture disc)	5
84	RCA DAT 5	Here Comes The Rain Again/This City Never Sleeps (live)/ Paint A Rumour (Long Version) (12", p/s)	8
84	Virgin VSY 728-12	Sexcrime (1984) (Extended Mix)/Sexcrime (1984) (Single Version)/ I Did It Just The Same (12" picture disc)	10
85	Virgin VSY 734	Julia/Ministry Of Love (picture disc in pop-up p/s)	8
85	RCA PB 40375	It's Alright (Baby's Coming Back)/Conditioned Soul ('video still' p/s)	5
85	RCA PB 40375/PB 40101	It's Alright (Baby's Coming Back)/Conditioned Soul//Would I Lie To You?/ Here Comes That Sinking Feeling (double pack, with free coloured vinyl 7")	12
85	RCA PB 40376/PB 40102	It's Alright (Baby's Coming Back)/Conditioned Soul/Tous Les Garçons Et Les Filles//Would I Lie To You? (E.T. Mix)/Would I Lie To You? (Extended	

		Remix)/Here Comes That Sinking Feeling (12", double pack, gatefold PVC sleeve; 2nd on yellow, red or blue viny 10
85	RCA BYTI 100	I Love You Like A Ball And Chain (mono)/I Love You Like A Ball And Chain (stereo) (promo only) 8
86	RCA DA 8	Thorn In My Side/In This Town (p/s, with shrinkwrapped enamel badge) 10
86	RCA DA 9P	The Miracle Of Love/When Tomorrow Comes (live) (shaped picture disc) 8
87	RCA DAT 14P	Shame (Dance Mix)/I've Got A Lover (Back In Japan)/Shame (12", p/s & print) 8
88	RCA DA 15X	I Need A Man/I Need You/There Must Be An Angel (Playing With My Heart) (live)/ Missionary Man (live) (10", p/s) 8
88	RCA DA 15CD	I Need A Man/Missionary Man (Live Version)/I Need You/I Need A Man (Macho Mix) (CD, picture disc in numbered metal tin) 8
89	Flexi FLX 880	DAVE AND ANNIE'S CHRISTMAS MESSAGE '89 (fan club flexidisc, foldout p/s) 10
90	Flexi FLX 1000	DAVE AND ANNIE'S CHRISTMAS MESSAGE '90 (fan club flexidisc, foldout p/s) 10
83	RCA RCALP 6063	SWEET DREAMS (LP, picture disc) 12
84	RCA PLP 70109	TOUCH (LP, picture disc) 30

(see also David A. Stewart, ACatch, Tourists, Chris & Cosey, Stewart & Harrison)

JOHN EVAN BAND
90	A New Day NRS/CD 1	THE JOHN EVAN BAND LIVE '66 (CD, 500 only) 30

(see also Jethro Tull)

BARBARA EVANS
59	RCA RCA 1122	Souvenirs/Pray For Me, Mother (triangular centre) 25
59	RCA RCA 1122	Souvenirs/Pray For Me, Mother (78) 12
61	Mercury AMT 1151	Charlie Wasn't There/Nothing You Can Do 5

BILL EVANS
59	Fontana FJL 104	DIG IT (LP) 15
59	Riverside 12-315	PORTRAIT IN JAZZ (LP) 80
63	Verve VLP 9054	CONVERSATIONS WITH MYSELF (LP) 20
67	Verve VLP 9161	A SIMPLE MATTER OF CONVICTION (LP) 20

BRIAN EVANS
71	CBS 5392	We're Going Wrong/Paradise Lost 50
71	CBS 7293	This Is My Woman/If You Still Want Me (as Bryan Evans) 10

BRYAN EVANS
72	Columbia DB 8911	Turnaround Sunday/Re-United 8

CHRISTINE EVANS
65	Philips BF 1406	Growing Pains/Someone In Love 5
66	Philips BF 1496	Somewhere There's Love/Right Or Wrong 6
67	Melodisc MEL 1620	I'm Gonna Tell Tony/Someone In Love 10

DAVE EVANS
71	Village Thing VTS 6	THE WORDS IN BETWEEN (LP) 40
72	Village Thing VTS 14	ELEPHANTASIA (LP) 45
74	Kicking Mule SNKF 107	SAD PIG DANCE (LP, with booklet) 20
74	Kicking Mule SNKF 122	TAKE A BITE OUT OF LIFE (LP) 18

GIL EVANS ORCHESTRA
60	Vogue LAE 12234	GREAT JAZZ STANDARDS (LP) 20
61	HMV CLP 1456	OUT OF THE COOL (LP) 20

JOHN EVANS
62	Palette PG 9040	Melodie Pour Madame/Cry Me A River 10

LARRY EVANS
56	London HLU 8269	Crazy 'Bout My Baby/Henpecked 750
56	London HLU 8269	Crazy 'Bout My Baby/Henpecked (78) 75

MAUREEN EVANS
58	Embassy WB 300	Carolina Moon/Stupid Cupid 10
58	Embassy WB 303	Fever/Born Too Late 10
58	Embassy WB 309	The Hula Hoop Song/Hoopa Hoola 6
58	Embassy WB 313	I'll Get By/Someday (You'll Want Me To Want You) 6
58	Embassy WB 316	The Day The Rains Came/You Always Hurt The One You Love 6
58	Embassy WB 319	To Know Him Is To Love Him/Kiss Me, Honey Honey, Kiss Me 10
59	Embassy WB 344	Goodbye Jimmy, Goodbye/May You Always 6
59	Embassy WB 348	Lipstick On Your Collar/What A Diff'rence A Day Made 10
59	Embassy WB 356	Broken-Hearted Melody/Plenty Good Lovin' 6
59	Embassy WB 371	Among My Souvenirs/Happy Anniversary 10
59	Oriole CB 1517	Don't Want The Moonlight/The Years Between 6
60	Oriole CB 1533	The Big Hurt/I Can't Begin To Tell You 10
60	Oriole CB 1533	The Big Hurt/I Can't Begin To Tell You (78) 15
60	Oriole CB 1540	Love, Kisses And Heartaches/We Just Couldn't Say Goodbye 10
60	Oriole CB 1550	Paper Roses/Please Understand 10
60	Oriole CB 1550	Paper Roses/Please Understand (78) 15
61	Oriole CB 1563	Mama Wouldn't Like It/My Little Corner Of The World 6
61	Oriole CB 1578	As Long As He Needs Me/Where Is Love? 6
61	Oriole CB 1581	Till/Why Don't You Believe Me 7
61	Oriole CB 1613	My Foolish Heart/Oh Gypsy Oh Gypsy 7
62	Oriole CB 1743	Never In A Million Years/We Had Words 7
62	Oriole CB 1760	Like I Do/Starlight Starbright 5
63	Oriole CB 1804	Pick The Petals/Melancholy Me 6
63	Oriole CB 1806	Tomorrow Is Another Day/Acapulco Mexico 10
63	Oriole CB 1851	What A Difference A Day Made/Oh What A Guy 7
63	Oriole CB 1875	Like You Used To Do/As You Love Her 7
64	Oriole CB 1906	I Love How You Love Me/John John 6
64	Oriole CB 1939	He Knows I Love Him Too Much/Don't Believe Him 6
64	Oriole CB 1969	Get Away/I've Often Wondered 10
65	CBS 201733	All The Angels Sing/Speak Sugar Speak 8
65	CBS 201752	Never Let Him Go/Poco Sole 12
67	CBS 202621	Somewhere There's Love/It Takes A Little Time 8
68	CBS 3222	I Almost Called Your Name/Searching For Home 8
63	Oriole EP 7076	MELANCHOLY ME (EP) 30
63	Oriole PS 40046	LIKE I DO (LP) 30

(see also Matt Bryant & Linda Joyce)

MILL EVANS
01	Kent 6T 17	Ain't You Glad/MILLIONAIRES: I'm The One Who Loves You	20

PAUL EVANS (& CURLS)
59	London HLL 8968	Seven Little Girls Sitting In The Back Seat/Worshipping An Idol (with Curls)	10
59	London HLL 8968	Seven Little Girls Sitting In The Back Seat/Worshipping An Idol (78)	15
60	London HLL 9045	Midnite Special/Since I Met You, Baby	30
60	London HLL 9129	Happy-Go-Lucky Me/Fish In The Ocean	6
60	London HLL 9183	Brigade Of Broken Hearts/Twins	6
60	London HLL 9239	Hushabye Little Guitar/Blind Boy	20
62	London HLR 9636	The Bell That Couldn't Jingle/Gilding The Lily	6
63	London HLR 9770	Even Tan/Ten Thousand Years	6
63	London RE-R 1349	PAUL EVANS (EP)	40
60	London HA-L 2248	PAUL EVANS SINGS THE FABULOUS TEENS (LP)	100

ROGER EVANS & SWANSEA CITY FOOTBALL CLUB
79	Rotor Pro 001	Swansea City/The Ballad Of Swansea Jack	8

RUSSELL EVANS & NITEHAWKS
66	Atlantic 584 010	Send Me Some Cornbread/The Bold	30

TOMMY EVANS
00	YNR YNR003	THE TIME CAPSULE (12", EP, stickered white sleeve)	8
01	YNR YNR005	THE 4 ELEMENTS (12", EP, stickered black die-cut sleeve)	8
02	YNR YNR007	The 4 Horsemen/Not Nice (12", stickered black die-cut sleeve)	8

TONY EVANS BAND
71	Polydor 2058 101	Hot Pants/Beach Bird	15

GUY EVANS
93	Voiceprint VP 112 CD	LONG HELLO VOLUME 4 (CD)	18

(see also Van Der Graaf Generator)

EVEN AS WE SPEAK
90	Sarah SARAH 37	Nothing Ever Happens/Blue Suburban Skies/Bizarre Love Triangle/ Goes So Slow/A Stranger Calls (p/s, insert)	10
91	Sarah SARAH 49	One Step Forward/Must Be Something Else/Best Kept Secret (p/s, insert)	6
91	Sarah SARAH 59	Beautiful Day/Nothing Much At All (p/s, insert)	6
93	Sarah SARAH 79	(All You Find Is) Air/Getting Faster/Blue Eyes Deceiving Me (p/s, insert)	6
93	Sarah SARAH 614	FERAL POP FRENZY (LP)	25

EVEN DOZEN JUG BAND
66	Bounty BY 6023	THE EVEN DOZEN JUG BAND (LP)	25

(see also Lovin' Spoonful, John Sebastian)

EVENING OUTS
80	Refill RR5	Channel/Stammer (no p/s, hand stamped labels)	100

EVENSONG
73	Philips 6006 276	I Was Her Cowboy/Gypsy	15

EVER RED
88	Supertone STR 007	Dem No Ruff Like We/Hot Number (12")	40

BETTY EVERETT
64	Stateside SS 259	You're No Good/Chained To Your Love	20
64	Stateside SS 280	It's In His Kiss (The Shoop Shoop Song)/Hands Off	20
64	Stateside SS 321	I Can't Hear You/Can I Get To Know You	22
64	Fontana TF 520	Getting Mighty Crowded/Chained To A Memory	20
64	King KG 1002	Happy I Long To Be/Your Loving Arms	20
65	Sue WI 352	I've Got A Claim On You/Your Love Is Important To Me	60
68	President PT 215	It's In His Kiss (The Shoop Shoop Song)/Getting Mighty Crowded	8
69	President PT 251	You're No Good/Hands Off	8
69	MCA Soul Bag BAG 3	I Can't Say No To You/Better Tomorrow Than Today	10
69	MCA MU 1055	There'll Come A Time/Take Me	8
70	Uni UN 517	Sugar/Hold On	8
71	Liberty LBF 15428	I Got To Tell Somebody/Why Are You Leaving Me	15
72	President PT 372	Trouble Over The Weekend/The Shoe Doesn't Fit	10
65	Fontana TL 5236	IT'S IN HIS KISS (LP)	60
68	Joy JOYS 106	IT'S IN HIS KISS (LP, reissue)	15
69	Uni UNLS 109	THERE'LL COME A TIME (LP)	25

BETTY EVERETT & JERRY BUTLER
64	Stateside SS 339	Let It Be Me/Ain't That Lovin' You Baby	10
65	Fontana TF 528	Smile/Love Is Strange	8
68	President PT 214	Let It Be Me/Smile	8
69	President PT 252	Our Day Will Come/Just Be True	6
65	Fontana TL 5237	DELICIOUS TOGETHER (LP)	50
68	Joy JOYS 123	DELICIOUS TOGETHER (LP, reissue)	12

(see also Jerry Butler)

KENNY EVERETT
68	MGM 1421	It's Been So Long/Without Her	10
69	Deram DM 245	And Now For A Little Train Number/Nice Time	8
77	DJM DJS 10810	Captain Kremmen (Retribution)/Retribution	5

ROY EVERETT
70	Parlophone R 5857	Turn On You Own Heat/Look At That Old Bird	10

VINCE EVERETT
65	Fontana TF 606	Bless You/'Til I Lost You	10
67	Fontana TF 818	Endlessly/Who's That Girl?	10
68	Fontana TF 915	Every Now And Then/Barbarella	10

EVERGREEN BLUES
67	Mercury MF 1012	Midnight Confessions/(Yes) That's My Baby	10
68	Mercury MF 1025	Laura (Keep Hangin' On)/Yesterday's Coming	6
68	Mercury 20122 SMCL	7 DO ELEVEN (LP)	20

EVERGREEN BLUESHOES

69	London HA-U/SH-U 8399	THE BALLAD OF THE EVERGREEN BLUESHOES (LP)	20

(see also Skip Battin, Byrds)

EVERLY BROTHERS

78s

57	London HLA 8440	Bye Bye, Love/I Wonder If I Care As Much	10
57	London HLA 8498	Wake Up Little Susie/Maybe Tomorrow	10
58	London HLA 8554	Should We Tell Him/This Little Girl Of Mine	15
58	London HLA 8618	All I Have To Do Is Dream/Claudette	10
58	London HLA 8685	Bird Dog/Devoted To You	12
58	London HLA 8781	Problems/Love Of My Life	15
59	London HLA 8863	Poor Jenny/Take A Message To Mary	20
59	London HLA 8934	('Til) I Kissed You/Oh, What A Feeling	30
60	London HLA 9039	Let It Be Me/Since You Broke My Heart	60
60	Warner Bros WB 1	Cathy's Clown/Always It's You	100
60	London HLA 9157	When Will I Be Loved/Be-Bop-A-Lula	60
60	Warner Bros WB 19	Lucille/So Sad (To Watch Good Love Go Bad)	200

SINGLES

57	London HLA 8440	Bye Bye, Love/I Wonder If I Care As Much (triangular centre)	15
57	London HLA 8440	Bye Bye, Love/I Wonder If I Care As Much (round centre)	6
57	London HLA 8498	Wake Up Little Susie/Maybe Tomorrow (triangular centre)	15
57	London HLA 8498	Wake Up Little Susie/Maybe Tomorrow (round centre)	10
58	London HLA 8554	Should We Tell Him/This Little Girl Of Mine (triangular centre)	20
58	London HLA 8554	Should We Tell Him/This Little Girl Of Mine (round centre)	8
58	London HLA 8618	All I Have To Do Is Dream/Claudette (triangular centre)	7
58	London HLA 8685	Bird Dog/Devoted To You (triangular centre)	7
58	London HLA 8781	Problems/Love Of My Life (triangular centre)	7
59	London HLA 8863	Poor Jenny/Take A Message To Mary (triangular centre)	7
59	London HLA 8934	('Til) I Kissed You/Oh, What A Feeling (triangular centre)	7
60	London HLA 9039	Let It Be Me/Since You Broke My Heart (triangular centre)	18
60	Warner Bros WB 1	Cathy's Clown/Always It's You	6
60	London HLA 9157	When Will I Be Loved/Be-Bop-A-Lula	8
60	Warner Bros WB 19	Lucille/So Sad (To Watch Good Love Go Bad)	5
60	London HLA 9250	Like Strangers/Leave My Woman Alone	5
61	Warner Bros WB 33	Walk Right Back/Ebony Eyes	5
61	Warner Bros WB 42	Temptation/Stick With Me Baby	5
61	Warner Bros WB 50	Muskrat/Don't Blame Me	6
62	Warner Bros WB 56	Crying In The Rain/I'm Not Angry	5
62	Warner Bros WB 67	How Can I Meet Her?/That's Old Fashioned	5
62	Warner Bros WB 79	No One Can Make My Sunshine Smile/Don't Ask Me To Be Friends	5
63	Warner Bros WB 94	So It Will Always Be/Nancy's Minuet	7
63	Warner Bros WB 99	It's Been Nice/I'm Afraid	8
63	Warner Bros WB 109	The Girl Sang The Blues/Love Her	10
64	Warner Bros WB 129	Ain't That Lovin' You Baby/Hello Amy	10
64	Warner Bros WB 135	The Ferris Wheel/Don't Forget To Cry	10
64	Warner Bros WB 143	You're The One I Love/Ring Around My Rosie (withdrawn)	20
64	Warner Bros WB 146	Gone, Gone, Gone/Torture	10
65	Warner Bros WB 154	You're My Girl/Don't Let The Whole World Know	10
65	Warner Bros WB 158	That'll Be The Day/Give Me A Sweetheart	10
65	Warner Bros WB 161	The Price Of Love/It Only Costs A Dime	5
65	Warner Bros WB 5628	The Price Of Love/It Only Costs A Dime (reissue)	7
65	Warner Bros WB 5639	I'll Never Get Over You/Follow Me	7
65	Warner Bros WB 5649	Love Is Strange/Man With Money	10
66	Warner Bros WB 5682	It's All Over/I Used To Love You (unissued)	0
66	Warner Bros WB 5743	(You Got) The Power Of Love/Leave My Girl Alone	10
66	Warner Bros WB 5754	I've Been Wrong Before/Hard Hard Year	10
67	Warner Bros WB 7520	Bowling Green/I Don't Want To Love You	10
67	Warner Bros WB 7062	Mary Jane/Talking To The Flowers	10
67	Warner Bros WB 7088	Love Of The Common People/A Voice Within	10
68	Warner Bros WB 7192	It's My Time/Empty Boxes	10
68	Warner Bros WB 7226	Milk Train/Lord Of The Manor	10
69	Warner Bros WB 6056	Cathy's Clown/Walk Right Back	5
70	Warner Bros WB 6074	Good Golly, Miss Molly/Oh, Boy!	8
70	Warner Bros WB 7425	Yves/Human Race	10
72	RCA Victor RCA 2232	Ridin' High/Stories We Could Tell	10
73	RCA Victor RCA 2286	Not Fade Away/Lay It Down	7
77	Warner Bros K 17004	Silent Treatment/Dancing On My Feet	5
80	Old Gold SET 1	THE EVERLY BROTHERS SINGLES SET (15 x p/s 7", box set with book)	20

EPs

58	London RE-A 1113	THE EVERLY BROTHERS	25
58	London RE-A 1148	THE EVERLY BROTHERS — NO. 2	25
58	London RE-A 1149	THE EVERLY BROTHERS — NO. 3	20
59	London RE-A 1174	THE EVERLY BROTHERS — NO. 4	20
59	London RE-A 1195	SONGS OUR DADDY TAUGHT US PART 1	25
59	London RE-A 1196	SONGS OUR DADDY TAUGHT US PART 2	25
59	London RE-A 1197	SONGS OUR DADDY TAUGHT US PART 3	25
60	London RE-A 1229	THE EVERLY BROTHERS — NO. 5	30

(The above EPs were originally issued with triangular centres, later round-centre editions are worth half to two-thirds of these values.)

61	Warners WEP 6034	ESPECIALLY FOR YOU (mono)	25
61	Warners W(S)EP 6034	ESPECIALLY FOR YOU (stereo)	30
61	London RE-A 1311	THE EVERLY BROTHERS — NO. 6	30
62	Warners WEP 6049	FOREVERLY YOURS (mono)	25
62	Warners W(S)EP 6049	FOREVERLY YOURS (stereo)	30
62	Warners WEP 6056	IT'S EVERLY TIME (mono)	25
62	Warners W(S)EP 6056	IT'S EVERLY TIME (stereo)	30
63	Warners WEP 6107	A DATE WITH THE EVERLY BROTHERS VOL. 1 (mono)	25
63	Warners W(S)EP 6107	A DATE WITH THE EVERLY BROTHERS VOL. 1 (stereo)	30
63	Warners WEP 6109	A DATE WITH THE EVERLY BROTHERS VOL. 2 (mono)	25

63	Warners W(S)EP 6109	A DATE WITH THE EVERLY BROTHERS VOL. 2 (stereo)	30
63	Warners WEP 6111	INSTANT PARTY VOL. 1 (mono)	25
63	Warners W(S)EP 6111	INSTANT PARTY VOL. 1 (stereo)	30
63	Warners WEP 6113	INSTANT PARTY VOL. 2 (mono)	25
63	Warners W(S)EP 6113	INSTANT PARTY VOL. 2 (stereo)	30
63	Warners WEP 6115	BOTH SIDES OF AN EVENING — FOR DANCING VOL. 1 (mono)	25
63	Warners W(S)EP 6115	BOTH SIDES OF AN EVENING — FOR DANCING VOL. 1 (stereo)	30
64	Warners WEP 6117	BOTH SIDES OF AN EVENING — FOR DREAMING VOL. 2 (mono)	25
64	Warners W(S)EP 6117	BOTH SIDES OF AN EVENING — FOR DREAMING VOL. 2 (stereo)	30
64	Warners WEP 6128	THE EVERLY BROTHERS SING GREAT COUNTRY HITS VOL. 1	25
64	Warners WEP 6131	THE EVERLY BROTHERS SING GREAT COUNTRY HITS VOL. 2	25
64	Warners WEP 6132	THE EVERLY BROTHERS SING GREAT COUNTRY HITS VOL. 3	25
65	Warner Bros WEP 6138	BOTH SIDES OF AN EVENING — FOR FUN VOL. 3	20
65	Warner Bros WEP 604	THE PRICE OF LOVE	25
65	Warner Bros WEP 608	ROCK'N'SOUL VOL. 1	25
65	Warner Bros WEP 609	ROCK'N'SOUL VOL. 2	25
66	Warner Bros WEP 610	LOVE IS STRANGE	25
66	Warner Bros WEP 612	PEOPLE GET READY	25
66	Warner Bros WEP 618	WHAT AM I LIVING FOR?	25
67	Warner Bros WEP 622	LEAVE MY GIRL ALONE	25
67	Warner Bros WEP 623	SOMEBODY HELP ME	25
72	Warner Bros K 16209	CRYING IN THE RAIN	8
74	Warner Bros K 16407	WAKE UP LITTLE SUSIE	8

ALBUMS

58	London HA-A 2081	THE EVERLY BROTHERS	40
58	London HA-A 2150	SONGS OUR DADDY TAUGHT US	40
60	Warner Bros WM 4012	IT'S EVERLY TIME (also stereo WS 8012)	30
60	Warner Bros WM 4012	IT'S EVERLY TIME (also stereo WS 8012)	35
60	London HA-A 2266	THE FABULOUS STYLE OF THE EVERLY BROTHERS	30
60	Warner Bros WM 4028	A DATE WITH THE EVERLY BROTHERS (mono)	30
60	Warner Bros WS 8028	A DATE WITH THE EVERLY BROTHERS (stereo)	35
61	Warner Bros WM 4052	BOTH SIDES OF AN EVENING (also stereo WS 8052)	30
61	Warner Bros WM 4052	BOTH SIDES OF AN EVENING (also stereo WS 8052)	35
62	Warner Bros WM 4061	INSTANT PARTY (also stereo WS 8061)	30
62	Warner Bros WM 4061	INSTANT PARTY (also stereo WS 8061)	35
62	Warner Bros WS 8108	THE GOLDEN HITS OF THE EVERLY BROTHERS (stereo)	12
62	Warner Bros WM 8116	CHRISTMAS WITH THE EVERLY BROTHERS AND THE BOYS TOWN CHOIR (mono)	35
62	Warner Bros WS 8116	CHRISTMAS WITH THE EVERLY BROTHERS AND THE BOYS TOWN CHOIR (stereo)	45
63	Warner Bros WM 8138	SING GREAT COUNTRY HITS (mono)	30
63	Warner Bros WS 8138	SING GREAT COUNTRY HITS (stereo)	40
65	Warner Bros WM 8169	GONE GONE GONE (mono)	30
65	Warner Bros WS 8169	GONE GONE GONE (stereo)	30
65	Warner Bros WM 8171	ROCK 'N' SOUL (mono)	25
65	Warner Bros WS 8171	ROCK 'N' SOUL (stereo)	30
65	Warner Bros WS 1578	ROCK 'N' SOUL (reissue, stereo)	15
65	Warner Bros W(S) 1605	BEAT 'N' SOUL	25
65	Warner Bros W 1620	IN OUR IMAGE (mono)	25
65	Warner Bros W(S) 1620	IN OUR IMAGE (stereo)	30
67	Warner Bros W 1646	TWO YANKS IN ENGLAND (mono)	25
67	Warner Bros W (S)1646	TWO YANKS IN ENGLAND (stereo)	30
67	Warner Bros W1676	THE HIT SOUND OF THE EVERLY BROTHERS (mono)	25
67	Warner Bros W (S) 1676	THE HIT SOUND OF THE EVERLY BROTHERS (stereo)	30
67	Warner Bros W 1708	THE EVERLY BROTHERS SING (mono)	25
67	Warner Bros W(S) 1708	THE EVERLY BROTHERS SING (stereo)	30
70	Warner Bros WS 1858	THE EVERLY BROTHERS SHOW (2-LP)	15

(see also Don Everly, Phil Everly)

DON EVERLY

74	Ode ODS 66046	Warmin' Up The Band/Evelyn Swing	5

PHIL EVERLY

73	RCA RCA 2409	The Air That I Breathe/God Bless Older Ladies	5
74	Pye 7N 45398	Invisible Man/It's True	5
74	Pye 7N 45415	Sweet Music/Goodbye Line	5

(see also Cliff Richard)

EVERREADY'S

80	Taaga TAG 3	Don't Do It Again/Martian Girl (gatefold p/s)	15

LENNY EVERSONG

57	Vogue Coral Q 72255	Jezebel/Jealousy	6

EVERYBODY

70	Page One POF 163	The Shape Of Things To Come/Do Like The Little Children Do	12

EVERYBODY'S CHILDREN

70	Fontana TF 1070	The Time Is Now/Abide With Me	5

EVERY MOTHER'S SON

67	MGM MGM 1341	Come And Take A Ride In My Boat/I Believe In You	25
67	MGM MGM 1350	Put Your Mind At Ease/Proper Four Leaf Clover	25
67	MGM MGM 1372	Pony With The Golden Mane/Dolls In The Clock	10
67	MGM C(S) 8044	EVERY MOTHER'S SON (LP)	40
68	MGM C(S) 8061	EVERY MOTHER'S SON'S BACK (LP)	35

EVERYONE

71	Charisma CB 146	Trouble At The Mill/Radio Lady	5
71	B&C CAS 1028	EVERYONE (LP, gatefold sleeve, attached envelope with booklet)	40

(see also Andy Roberts)

EVERYONE ELSE

79	Woodbine St WSR 001	Schooldays/Brainwashed/Out Of My Mind/Don't Call Us (p/s)	100

EVERYONE INVOLVED

72	Arcturus ARC 3	The Circus Keeps On Turning/Motor Car Madness	30

| 72 | Arcturus ARC 4 | EITHER OR (LP, private pressing, embossed plain white sleeve with inserts) | 200 |

EVERYTHING BUT THE GIRL

| 82 | Cherry Red CHERRY 37 | Night And Day/Feeling Dizzy/On My Mind (yellow p/s) | 5 |
| 83 | Cherry Red 12CHERRY 37 | Night And Day/Feeling Dizzy/On My Mind (12", p/s) | 8 |

(see also Ben Watt, Marine Girls, Tracey Thorn)

EVERYTHING IS EVERYTHING

| 69 | Vanguard VA 1 | Witchi Tai To/Oooh Baby | 15 |
| 68 | Vanguard SVRL 19036 | EVERYTHING IS EVERYTHING (LP) | 25 |

EVERY WHICH WAY

| 70 | Charisma BD 1 | Go Placidly/The Light | 12 |

(see also Brian Davison, Griffin, Heavy Jelly, Skip Bifferty, Graham Bell, Bell & Arc)

EVIL ED

| 01 | YNR YNR4 | THE TOURNAMENT ROUND 1 (12", EP stickered black die-cut sleeve) | 10 |
| 02 | Hidden Identity HID1 | THE TOURNAMENT ROUND 2 (12" EP) | 10 |

EVOLUTION

| 90 | Positive Vinyl PV 001 | Came Outa Nowhere (12") | 20 |
| 91 | Positive Vinyl PV 002 | Metropolis (12") | 20 |

EWAN (MCDERMOTT) & DENVER

| 67 | Giant GN 17 | I Want You So Bad/ERIC McDERMOTT: I'm Gonna Love You | 10 |

EWAN (MCDERMOTT) & JERRY (MCCARTHY)

67	Blue Beat BB 385	Oh Babe/Dance With Me (with Carib Beats)	18
67	Giant GN 5	The Right Track/We Got To Be One	10
67	Giant GN 10	Rock Steady Train/My Baby Is Gone	10
67	Giant GN 14	Tennessee Waltz/You've Got Something	15

TERRY EWERS

| 68 | Polydor 583028 | ANOTHER WANTED MAN (LP) | 12 |

EX

| 86 | Ron Johnson ZRON 11 | '1936' THE SPANISH REVOLUTION (double pack with book) | 20 |

EX/ALERTA

| 84 | CNT CNT 017 | THE RED DANCE PACKAGE (12", split EP) | 15 |

EXCALIBUR

88	Clay PLATE 1	HOT FOR LOVE (Hot For Love/Early In The Morning/Come On And Rock/ Death's Door (12" EP)	15
90	Active 12ATV 101	Carole Ann/Early In The Morning/Sick & Tired (12", p/s)	8
85	Conquest QUEST 5	THE BITTER END (mini-LP)	18

EXCEL

| 79 | ARSS XL1 | If It Rains/Rolling Home/She's One Of The Boys/Rock Show (EP, p/s) | 100 |
| 80 | Polydor POSP 110 | What Went Wrong?/Junita (p/s) | 8 |

EXCELS

| 67 | Atlantic 584 133 | California On My Mind/The Arrival Of Mary | 25 |

EXCELSIOR SPRING

| 69 | Instant IN 002 | Happy Miranda/It | 35 |

EXCEPTIONS

| 65 | Decca F 12100 | What More Do You Want?/Soldier Boy | 25 |

(see also Orchids)

EXCEPTION(S)

67	CBS 202632	The Eagle Flies On Friday/Girl Trouble	70
67	CBS 2830	Gaberdine Saturday Night Street Walker/Sunday Night At The Prince Rupert	30
68	President PT 181	Rub It Down/It's Snowing In The Desert	6
68	President PT 205	Helicopter/Back Room	6
68	President PT 218	Tailor Made Babe/Turn Over The Soil	6
69	President PT 236	Jack Rabbit/Keep The Motor Running	8
69	President PT 271	Pendulum/Don't Torture Your Mind	12
69	President PTLS 1026	THE EXCEPTIONAL EXCEPTION (LP, yellow/black labels)	40

(see also Bugsy Eastwood, Fotheringay, Fairport Convention)

EXCHANGE MART

| 72 | President PT 385 | Yeah My Friend/I Know That I'm Dreaming | 15 |

EXCHECKERS

| 64 | Decca F 11871 | All The World Is Mine/It's All Over | 25 |

(see also Aynsley Dunbar Retaliation)

EXCITER

| 85 | Music For Nations MFN 47 | LONG LIVE THE LOUD (LP, inner) | 12 |
| 86 | Music For Nations MFN 61 | UNVEILING THE WICKED (LP, with inner) | 12 |

EXCITERS

63	United Artists UP 1011	Tell Him/Hard Way To Go	10
63	United Artists UP 1017	He's Got The Power/Drama Of Love	10
63	United Artists UP 1026	Get Him/It's So Exciting	20
64	United Artists UP 1041	Do-Wah-Diddy/If Love Came Your Way	25
65	Columbia DB 7479	I Want You To Be My Boy/Tonight, Tonight	25
65	Columbia DB 7544	Just Not Ready/Are You Satisfied	20
65	Columbia DB 7606	Run Mascara/My Father	20
66	London HLZ 10018	A Little Bit Of Soap/I'm Gonna Get Him Someday	20
66	London HLZ 10038	You Better Come Home/Weddings Make Me Cry	40
69	United Artists UP 2274	Do Wah Diddy Diddy/Hard Way To Go	10
71	Jay Boy BOY 38	Soul Motion/You Know It Ain't Right	20
74	Contempo CS 2033	Blowing Up My Mind (Vocal)/Blowing UP My Mind (Instrumental)	5
65	United Artists UEP 1005	DO WAH DIDDY DIDDY (EP)	80
64	United Artists ULP 1032	THE EXCITERS (LP)	100

EXCURSION

| 69 | Gemini GMX 5029 | NIGHT TRAIN (LP) | 18 |

(see also Jerry Allen)

EXECUTIVE(S) (1)
64	Columbia DB 7323	March Of The Mods/Why, Why, Why	10
64	Columbia DB 7393	Strictly For The Beat/No Room For Squares	10
65	Columbia DB 7573	It's Been So Long/You're For Me (as Executives)	10
65	Columbia DB 7770	Return Of The Mods/How Sad	10
66	Columbia DB 7919	Lock Your Door/In My Arms (as Executives)	8

EXECUTIVE(S) (2)
67	CBS 202652	Smokey Atmosphere/Sensation	30
67	CBS 3067	Ginza Strip/I'll Always Love You	25
68	CBS 3431	Tracy Took A Trip/Gardena Dreamer (as Executive, with promo only p/s)	40
68	CBS 3431	Tracy Took A Trip/Gardena Dreamer (as Executive)	30
69	CBS 4013	I Ain't Got Nobody/To Kingdom Come (as Executive)	30

EXECUTIVES (3)
80	Attrix RB 05	Shy Little Girl/Never Go Home/JOHNNIE & LUBES: I Got Rabies/ Terror In The Parking Lot (p/s)	7

EXECUTIVE SUITE
74	Cloud One HIT 1	When The Fuel Runs Out/When The Fuel Runs Out	5
74	Polydor 2310400	EXECUTIVE SUITE 1 (LP)	30

EXHIBIT A
80	Irrelevant Wombat DAMP 1	NO ELEPHANTS THIS SIDE OF THE WATFORD GAP (EP, with insert)	25
80	Irrelevant Wombat DAMP 2	DISTANCE (EP)	15

(see also Doof)

EXILE
77	Boring BO 1	DON'T TAX ME (EP, 1,000 only p/s)	30
78	Charly CYS 1033	The Real People/Tomorrow Today/Disaster Movie (p/s)	15

EXILES
66	Topic 12T 143	FREEDOM, COME ALL YE (LP)	15
67	Topic 12T 164	THE HALE AND THE HANGED (LP)	15

EXIT 13
82	Artlos Music LOS 001	CELIA'S LAST WEDNESDAY (LP)	25

EXITS (1)
78	Way Out WOO 1	YODELLING (EP, numbered, gatefold p/s, hand-stamped labels)	60

EXITS (2)
78	Red Lightning GIL 519	The Fashion Plague/Cheam (p/s, labels on wrong sides)	100

(see also Direct Hits)

EXIT STANCE (1)
84	Morterace MORT 11	WHILE BACKS ARE TURNED (LP, with insert)	20
84	Fight Back FIGHT 4	CRIME AGAINST HUMANITY (EP)	15

EXIT STANCE (2)
84	Exit stance ES 002	Esthetics/Conspiracy Of Silence	30

EXOCET
86	Exocet EXO 1PS12	STALEMATE (EP)	50

EXODUS
85	Music For Nations MFN 44	BONDED BY BLOOD (LP)	12
87	Music For Nations MFN 38	PLEASURES OF THE FLESH (LP, inner)	12

EXODUS (JAMAICA)
71	Duke DU 103	Pharaoh's Walk/Little Caesar	12
72	Sioux SI 001	Pharaoh's Walk No. 9/SAMMY JONES: Worried Over You	6
72	Sioux SI 010	Julia Sees Me/LLOYD THE MATADOR: The Train (Engine 54)	12

EXORDIUM
70s	Face To Face FTF 1001	TROUBLE WITH ADAM (LP, private pressing)	20

EXOTIC GUITARS
69	London SHD 8382	THOSE WERE THE DAYS (LP)	12

EXOTICS (1)
64	Decca F 11850	Cross My Heart/Ooh La La	10
68	Columbia DB 8418	Don't Lead Me On/You Can Try	25

EXOTICS (2)
70	Pye 7N 17925	I Don't Want Nobody (To Lead Me On)/Driftaway	6

EXPELAIRES
79	Zoo CAGE 007	To See You/Frequency (p/s)	5

(see also Mission)

EXPELLED
82	Riot City RIOT 8	Dreaming/No Life, No Future/What Justice (p/s)	6
82	Riot City RIOT 17	Government Policy/Make It Alone (p/s)	6
84	Riot City 12RIOT 33	THE SINGLES (12" EP)	8

EXPERIMENTS WITH ICE
81	United Dairies EX 001	EXPERIMENTS WITH ICE (LP)	25

EX PISTOLS
84	Cherry Red/Virgina Pistol 76p	Land Of Hope And Glory/The Flowers of Romansk (Picture disc)	10

EXPLICIT CORPSE
81	Gistol	That Day Before.../I Gotta Gistol (stickered white labels, plastic gatefold p/s)	5

EXPLOITED
81	Exploited EXP 001	Army Life/Fuck The Mods/Crashed Out (p/s)	8
81	Exploited EXP 002	Exploited Barmy Army/I Believe In Anarchy/What You Gonna Do? (p/s)	8
81	Secret SHH 110	Dogs Of War/Blown To Bits (live) (p/s)	5
81	Secret SHH 112	Army Life/Fuck The Mods/Crashed Out (p/s, reissue)	5
81	Secret SHH 120	Dead Cities/Hitler's In The Charts Again/Class War (p/s)	5

83	Blurg/Pax PAX 15	Rival Leaders/Army Style/Singalongabushell (p/s)	6
81	Exploited EXP 1001	PUNK'S NOT DEAD (LP)	12
81	Exploited EXP 1002	ON STAGE (LP, some on yellow vinyl)	12
83	Pax PAX 18	LET'S START A WAR (LP)	12
87	Rough Justice JUST 6	DEATH BEFORE DISHONOUR (LP, inner)	12

EXPLORER
84	Rock Shop RSR 006	EXPLODING (LP)	40

EXPLOSIVE
68	President PT 221	Crying All Night/I Close My Eyes	6
69	President PT 244	Cities Make The Country Colder/Step Out Of Line	20
69	President PT 262	Who Planted Thorns In Miss Alice's Garden?/I Get My Kicks From Living	15
70	President PT 286	I'm Gonna Use What I Got To Get What I Need/Am I A Fool? (with Del Taylor)	6
70	President PT 302	This Ain't The Road To Freedom/Today Is Today	6
71	Plexium PXM 20	Hey Presto, Magic Man/Get It Together	60
71	Plexium PXM 24	Love Doesn't Come Easy/See You In The Morning	6

(see also Watson T. Browne & Explosive)

EXPORT
79	Atlantic K 11344	Julie Bitch/Nice To Know You	15
80	His Master's Vice VICE 2	You've Got To Rock/Wheeler Dealer (title sleeve)	18
80	His Master's Vice VICE 1	EXPORT (LP)	18

EXPOSURE
80	Angular Music ACUTE 1	Style & Fashion/Video Eyes (p/s)	10

EXPOZER
80	Hit Hard HARD 1	Rock Japan/On My Knees (p/s)	12
80	Hit Hard	EXPOSED AT LAST (LP)	12

EXPRESSION
82	A&M AM 149	With Closed Eyes/Nothing Changes (p/s)	6

EXTERNAL MENACE
82	Beat The System!! MENACE 1	YOUTH OF TODAY (EP)	15
83	Beat The System!! MENACE 2	NO VIEWS (EP)	15

EXTREEM
66	Strike JH 326	On The Beach/Don't You Ignore Me	20

EXTREME NOISE TERROR
88	Head Eruption HURT 1	A HOLOCAUST IN YOUR HEAD (LP, with inner)	20

EXTREME NOISE TERROR/CHAOS U.K.
86	Manic Ears ACHE 01	EAR SLAUGHTER — RADIOACTIVE (LP)	15
87	Strange Fruit SFPS 048	PEEL SESSIONS (12", metallic finish with insert)	8

EXUMA
71	Mercury 6052 080	Damn Fool/You Don't Know What's Going On	6
72	Kama Sutra 2013 053	Monkberry Moon Delight/Obeah Man Come Back	8
70	Mercury 6338 018	EXUMA (LP)	12

EYE FULL TOWER
67	Polydor BM 56734	How About Me?/Carol Cartoon	7

EYEHATEGOD
00	People Like You 772521	SOUTHERN DISCOMFORT (LP, white vinyl with inner)	20

EYELESS IN GAZA
80	Ambivalent Scale ASR 2	Kodak Ghosts Run Amok/China Blue Vision/The Feeling's Mutual (wraparound p/s)	15
81	Cherry Red CHERRY 20	Invisibility/Three Kittens/Plague Of Years (p/s, with insert)	5
81	Cherry Red CHERRY 31	Others/Jane Dancing/Ever Present/Avenue With Trees (p/s)	5
82	Cherry Red CHERRY 47	Veil Like Calm/Taking Steps (p/s)	8
81	Cherry Red BRED 18	CAUGHT IN THE FLUX (LP, with bonus 12" EP [12 BRED 18], with inner)	12
82	Cherry Red BRED 36	DRUMMING THE BEATING HEART (LP)	12

(see also Martyn Bates)

EYES
65	Mercury MF 881	When The Night Falls/I'm Rowed Out	200
66	Mercury MF 897	The Immediate Pleasure/My Degeneration	150
66	Mercury MF 910	Man With Money/You're Too Much	175
65	Mercury MF 934	Good Day Sunshine/Please Don't Cry	100
78	RAW 29	Once In A Lifetime/Hello I Love You	5
66	Mercury 10035 MCE	THE ARRIVAL OF THE EYES (EP)	350
84	Bam Caruso KIRI 028	BLINK (LP, 2 different sleeves)	18
87	Bam Caruso MARI 038	SCENE BUT NOT HEARD (mini-LP)	15

(see also Pupils)

EYES OF BLUE
66	Deram DM 106	Heart Trouble/Up And Down	60
67	Deram DM 114	Supermarket Full Of Cans/Don't Ask Me To Mend Your Broken Heart	50
68	Mercury MF 1049	Largo/Yesterday	15
69	Mercury SMCL 20134	THE CROSSROADS OF TIME (LP, black/silver labels with 'Mercury' logo)	150
69	Mercury SMCL 20164	IN FIELDS OF ARDATH (LP, black/silver label with Mercury logo)	150

(see also Ancient Grease, Big Sleep, Man, Ritchie Francis, Gary Pickford-Hopkins, Gentle Giant)

EYNESBURY GIANT
78	Ultimate URL 602	FROM THE CASK (LP, with insert)	20

WILL EZELL
54	London AL 3539	GIN MILL JAZZ (10" LP)	25

(see also Paramount Allstars)

EZY MEAT
84	Electric Storm ES 0001	NOT FOR WIMPS (LP, with insert, Irish only)	50
86	Electric Storm ES 0002	ROCK YOUR BRAINS OUT (LP, with insert, Irish only)	40

EZY RIDER
82	English Steel	POWER (LP)	150

FABIAN
59	HMV POP 587	I'm A Man/Hypnotized	30
59	HMV POP 587	I'm A Man/Hypnotized (78)	25
59	HMV POP 612	Turn Me Loose/Stop Thief!	30
59	HMV POP 643	Tiger/Mighty Cold (To A Warm, Warm Heart)	15
59	HMV POP 659	Got The Feeling/Come On And Get Me	15
60	HMV POP 695	Hound Dog Man/This Friendly World	12
60	HMV POP 724	String Along/About This Thing Called Love	10
60	HMV POP 778	I'm Gonna Sit Right Down And Write Myself A Letter/Strollin' In The Springtime	10
60	HMV POP 800	Tomorrow/King Of Love	10
60	HMV POP 810	Kissin' And Twistin'/Long Before	10
61	HMV POP 829	You Know You Belong To Somebody Else/Hold On	10
61	HMV POP 869	Grapevine/David And Goliath	10
61	HMV POP 934	You're Only Young Once/The Love That I'm Giving To You	10
82	Revival 6017	Tiger/Turn Me Loose	5
59	HMV CLP 1301	HOLD THAT TIGER (LP)	60
60	HMV CLP 1345	THE FABULOUS FABIAN (LP)	50
61	HMV CLP 1433	YOUNG AND WONDERFUL (LP, mono)	40
61	HMV CSD 1352	YOUNG AND WONDERFUL (LP, stereo)	50

FABIAN (JAMAICA)
77	Tribesman TM 004	Prophecy/Prophecy Dub	30
78	Tribesman TM 08	Prophecy/JIMMY LINDSAY : Easy (12")	40
78	Island 12 WIP 6431	Prophecy/JIMMY LINDSAY: Easy (12")	25

FABIONS
| 69 | Bullet BU 410 | V. Rocket/Smile (B-side actually "My Baby" by Tennors) | 180 |

FABLE
70	Penny Farthing PEN 725	Minstrel Song/She Said Yes	5
71	Penny Farthing PEN 751	With A Boy Like You/She Said Yes	5
73	Magnet MAG 5002	FABLE (LP, gatefold sleeve, white/red labels)	15

(see also Trapeze, Uriah Heep)

BENT FABRIC
| 61 | Columbia DB 4753 | The Alleycat/Markin' Time | 6 |

GREGORY FABULOUS
| 03 | Jah Tubbys JT 10015 | Get Up/Moving To Zion (10", with the Offbeat Posse) | 20 |
| 04 | Jah Tubbys JT 10022 | Love Jah/Tra-La-La (10", with Prof. Natty) | 20 |

FABULOUS COUNTS
| 71 | Mojo 2092 021 | Get Down People/Lunar Funk | 8 |

FABULOUS DIALS
| 63 | Pye International 7N 25200 | Bossa Nova Stomp/Forget Me Not | 25 |

FABULOUS FIVE INC.
| 73 | Ahanti SHAN 104 | FABULOUS FIVE INC. (LP) | 25 |

FABULOUS FLAMES
| 70 | Clandisc CLA 224 | Holly Holy/LORD CREATOR: Kingston Town | 12 |
| 71 | Trojan TR 7822 | Growing Up/Lovitis | 6 |

(see also Dynamites)

FABULOUS IMPACT
| 90 | Kent 6T 6 | Baby Baby, I Want You/HAMPTONS: No No No No No No No Not My Girl (100 Club 6T's All-nighter anniversary disc) | 30 |

FABULOUS SHADES
| 71 | Tropical AL 005 | Lonely Man/Version 2 | 8 |

FABULOUS SWINGTONES
| 58 | HMV POP 471 | Geraldine/You Know Baby | 350 |
| 58 | HMV POP 471 | Geraldine/You Know Baby (78) | 50 |

FABULOUS TALBOT BROTHERS
| 50s | Melodisc M 1507 | Bloodshot Eyes/She's Got Freckles | 20 |
| 50s | Melodisc M 1507 | Bloodshot Eyes/She's Got Freckles (78) | 10 |

FACES
70	Warner Bros WB 8005	Flying/Three-Button Hand-Me-Down	10
70	Warner Bros WB 8014	Wicked Messenger/Nobody Knows (unissued)	0
70	Warner Bros WB 8018	Had Me A Real Good Time/Rear Wheel Skid	8
73	Warner Bros K 16247	Cindy Incidentally/Skewiff (Mend The Fuse) (with lyric insert, no p/s)	8
73	Warner Bros K 16281	Borstal Boys (withdrawn, any pressed?)	0
73	NME SF1 139	Dishevelment Blues/Ooh La La Preview (flexidisc free with NME)	10
74	Warner Bros K 16494	You Can Make Me Dance, Sing Or Anything/As Long As You Tell Him (credited to Rod Stewart and the Faces, p/s)	8
77	Riva RIVA 8	THE FACES (EP, p/s)	8
70	Warner Bros WS 3000	FIRST STEP (LP, orange label, gatefold sleeve)	80
71	Warner Bros WS 3011	LONG PLAYER (LP, blue & silver label, stitched die-cut '78rpm' style sleeve)	40
71	Warner Bros K 46053	FIRST STEP (LP, reissue, green label, gatefold sleeve)	20
71	Warner Bros K 56006	A NOD IS AS GOOD AS A WINK ... TO A BLIND HORSE (LP, green label, with poster)	35
71	Warner Bros K 56006	A NOD IS AS GOOD AS A WINK ... TO A BLIND HORSE (LP, green label, without poster)	12
72	Warner Bros K 46064	LONG PLAYER (LP, reissue, blue & silver label, stitched die-cut '78rpm'-style sleeve)	20
73	Warner Bros K 56011	OOH-LA-LA (LP, green label, 'Faces' sleeve with lyric poster)	25
74	Warner Bros K 46053	FIRST STEP (LP, 2nd reissue, 'Burbank' label, gatefold sleeve)	12

74	Warner Bros K 56011	OOH-LA-LA (LP, 'Burbank' label, 'Faces' sleeve, with lyric poster)	20
74	Warner Bros K 56011	OOH-LA-LA (LP, 'Burbank' label, 'Faces' sleeve, without lyric poster)	12
74	Warner Bros K 56006	A NOD IS AS GOOD AS A WINK ... TO A BLIND HORSE (LP, reissue, 'Burbank' label)	15
75	Warner Bros K 66027	TWO ORIGINALS OF . . . (2-LP, reissue of "First Steps" & "Long Player", gatefold sleeve)	20

(see also Small Faces, Rod Stewart, Ronnie Lane & Slim Chance, Ron Wood, Jeff Beck Group, Kenney Jones)

FACE TO FACE
| 72 | Face To Face FTF 002 | FACE TO FACE (LP) | 40 |

FACTION
| 83 | Bluurg FISH 7 | YOU'VE GOT THE FIRE EP (fold-out p/s) | 5 |

FACTORY
68	MGM MGM 1444	Path Through The Forest/Gone	1000
69	CBS 4540	Try A Little Sunshine/Red Chalk Hill	1400
70	OAK RGJ718	Time Machine/Castle On The Hill (99 copies only)	400

(see also Peter & Wolves, Norman Conquest, John Pantry, Velvet Hush)

FACTORY
| 82 | Future Earth FER 011 | You Are The Music/History Of The World (silver die-cut sleeve) | 20 |

FACTORY FLOOR
08	Outside OUT 0015	Bipolar/You Were Always Wrong (p/s, orange vinyl, 500 only)	15
08	One Of One ON 01	PLANNING APPLICATION EP (12" p/s, 500 only)	20
10	Blast First Petite PTYT 035 V	Lying/16-16-9-2--1-14-9-7/A Wooden Box/Solid Sound (10" clear vinyl with DVD, 2000 only)	10
10	Blast First Petite PTVT 048	Lying (Stephen Morris Mix)/Lying (Original)/Lying (Chris Carter Mix)/A Wooden Box (Original) (2x12" in plastic sleeve, 200 only)	15

FACTOTUMS
65	Immediate IM 009	In My Lonely Room/Run In The Green And Tangerine Flaked Forest	40
65	Immediate IM 022	You're So Good To Me/Can't Go Home Anymore My Love	30
66	Piccadilly 7N 35333	Here Today/In My Room	22
66	Piccadilly 7N 35355	I Can't Give You Anything But Love/Absolutely Sweet Marie	20
67	Pye 7N 17402	Cloudy/Easy Said, Easy Done	15
69	CBS 4140	Mr And Mrs Regards/Driftwood	20

FADELA
| 88 | Factory FAC 197 | N'sel Fik/Ateni Bniti (12") | 10 |

FADERS
| 79 | Rip Off RIP 8 | Cheatin'/Library Book (in bag p/s) | 50 |

FAD GADGET
| 81 | Lyntone LYN 10209 | King Of The Flies/DEPECHE MODE: Sometimes I Wish I Was Dead (red vinyl flexidisc free with Flexipop magazine, issue 11) | 25 |

FADING COLOURS
| 66 | Ember EMB S 229 | (Just Like) Romeo And Juliet/Billy Christian | 20 |
| 67 | Ember EMB S 237 | Be With Me/You're No Use | 10 |

(see also Orange Seaweed)

FAERIE SYMPHONY
| 77 | Decca F13735 | Dance Of The Enashee (Da Oine Sidhe)/The Unseelie Court | 8 |

DONALD FAGAN
| 82 | Warners W3696 | THE NIGHTFLY (LP) | 12 |

BRIAN FAHEY (& HIS ORCHESTRA)
59	Parlophone R 4655	Street Of A Thousand Bongos/Waltz For Beatniks	8
60	Parlophone R 4686	At The Sign Of The Swingin' Cymbal/The Clanger	20
62	Parlophone R 4909	At The Sign Of The Swingin' Cymbal/The Clanger (reissue, as Brian Faye & His Orchestra)	12
65	Parlophone R 5262	Gidian's Way/Love Theme From "In Harm's Way"	10
65	United Artists UP 1115	Twang/You Can't Catch Me	10
67	Parlophone R 5615	The Plank/Stay On the Island	8
68	Columbia DB 8447	Late Night Extra/Oh The Pity Of It All	8
69	Major Minor MM 656	Open House/Countdown	25
67	Studio Two TWO 175	TIME FOR TV (LP)	15

JOHN FAHEY
67	Transatlantic TRA 173	THE TRANSFIGURATION OF BLIND JOE DEATH (LP, with booklet)	40
67	Transatlantic TRA 173	THE TRANSFIGURATION OF BLIND JOE DEATH (LP, without booklet)	20
68	Vanguard SVRL 19033	YELLOW PRINCESS (LP)	25
68	Vanguard SVRL 19055	REQUIA (LP)	30
69	Takoma SNTF 607	BLIND JOE DEATH (LP)	20
69	Takoma SNTF 608	DEATH CHANTS, WALTZES & MILITARY BREAKDOWNS) (LP)	20
72	Sonet SNTF 628	AMERICA (LP)	25
72	Reprise K 44213	OF RIVERS AND RELIGION (LP)	20
73	Reprise K 44246	AFTER THE BALL (LP)	20
74	Takoma SNTF 675	JOHN FAHEY, PETER LANG AND LEO KOTTKE (LP)	15
77	Transatlantic TRA 173	THE TRANSFIGURATION OF BLIND JOE DEATH (LP, reissue, picture label)	25

(see also Leo Kottke)

JAD FAIR
| 80 | Armageddon AEP 003 | THE ZOMBIES OF MORA-TAU (EP, die-cut p/s with insert) | 15 |

(see also Half Japanese)

JAD FAIR & PASTELS
| 91 | Paperhouse PAPER 013T | THIS COULD BE THE NIGHT EP (12", p/s) | 15 |
| 92 | Paperhouse PAPER 018CD | HE CHOSE HIS COLOURS WELL (CD EP) | 10 |

(see also Pastels)

YVONNE FAIR
| 75 | Tamla Motown TMG 1013 | It Should Have Been Me/You Can't Judge A Book By It's Cover | 5 |
| 75 | Tamla Motown STML 12008 | THE BITCH IS BLACK (LP) | 12 |

WERLY FAIRBURN & DELTA BOYS
| 56 | London HLC 8349 | I'm A Fool About Your Love/All The Time | 1000 |

MINT VALUE £

| 56 | London HLC 8349 | I'm A Fool About Your Love/All The Time (78) | 150 |

JOHNNY FAIRE
| 58 | London HLU 8569 | Bertha Lou/Till The Law Says Stop | 600 |
| 58 | London HLU 8569 | Bertha Lou/Till The Law Says Stop (78) | 150 |

FAIRFIELD PARLOUR
70	Vertigo 6059 003	Bordeaux Rosé/Chalk On The Wall	20
70	Vertigo 6059 008	Just Another Day/Caraminda/I Am All The Animals/Song For You	40
76	Prism PRI 1	Bordeaux Rosé/Baby Stay For Tonight (as Fairfield Parlor)	10
70	Vertigo 6360 001	FROM HOME TO HOME (LP, gatefold sleeve, large swirl label)	350
91	UFO BFTP 003	FROM HOME TO HOME (LP, reissue)	30
03	Circle CPWL 104	PLEASE LISTEN TO THE PICTURES (2-LP, BBC sessions, split release with Kaleidoscope)	20

(see also Kaleidoscope [U.K.], I Luv Wight)

FAIRIES
64	Decca F 11943	Don't Think Twice, It's Alright/Anytime At All	125
65	HMV POP 1404	Get Yourself Home/I'll Dance	200
65	HMV POP 1445	Don't Mind/Baby Don't	125

(see also Twink, Cops 'N Robbers)

FAIRPORT CONVENTION
SINGLES
67	Track 604 020	If I Had A Ribbon Bow/If (Stomp)	75
68	Island WIP 6047	Meet On The Ledge/Throwaway Street Puzzle (pink label)	20
69	Island WIP 6064	Si Tu Dois Partir/Genesis Hall	8
70	Island WIP 6089	Now Be Thankful/Sir B. McKenzie's Daughter's Lament	10
70	Polydor 2058 014	If (Stomp)/Chelsea Morning	12
71	Island WIP 6128	John Lee/The Time Is Near (in p/s)	12
71	Island WIP 6128	John Lee/The Time Is Near	6
73	Island WIP 6155	Rosie/Knights Of The Road	6
75	Island WIP 6241	White Dress/Tears (in p/s)	12
75	Island WIP 6241	White Dress/Tears	6
78	Hawk HASP 423	Jam's O'Donnell's Jig/The Last Waltz (Irish-only)	15
79	Simons PMW 1	Rubber Band/The Bonny Black Hare	12
86	Sunrise Bong 1	Quazi B Goode/MIKE SILVER: Where Would You Rather Be Tonight	10
87	Island 12IF 324	Meet On The Ledge (Re-recorded)/John Barleycorn (live)/ Sigh Bheg Sigh Mhor (live) (12", p/s, with poster)	10
87	Island 12IF 324	Meet On The Ledge (Re-recorded)/John Barleycorn (live)/ Sigh Bheg Sigh Mhor (live) (12", p/s, without poster)	8

ALBUMS : POLYDOR ALBUMS
68	Polydor 582 035	FAIRPORT CONVENTION (mono, laminated sleeve)	250
68	Polydor 582/583 035	FAIRPORT CONVENTION (stereo, laminated sleeve)	200
76	Polydor Special 2384 047	FAIRPORT CONVENTION (LP, reissue)	15

ALBUMS : ISLAND ALBUMS
69	Island ILPS 9092	WHAT WE DID ON OUR HOLIDAYS (1st pressing, laminated front cover, pink label with orange/black 'circle')	200
69	Island ILPS 9092	WHAT WE DID ON OUR HOLIDAYS (2nd pressing, pink label with black 'block' logo)	60
69	Island ILPS 9092	WHAT WE DID ON OUR HOLIDAYS (3rd pressing, pink label with 'i' logo)	50
70	Island ILPS 9092	WHAT WE DID ON OUR HOLIDAYS (4th pressing, pink rim label with 'palm tree' logo)	20
69	Island ILPS 9102	UNHALFBRICKING (1st pressing, pink label with black 'block' logo)	200
69	Island ILPS 9102	UNHALFBRICKING (2nd pressing, pink label with 'i' logo)	60
70	Island ILPS 9102	UNHALFBRICKING (3rd pressing, pink rim label with 'palm tree' logo)	40
69	Island ILPS 9115	LIEGE AND LIEF (gatefold sleeve, 1st pressing, pink label with 'i' logo)	150
70	Island ILPS 9115	LIEGE AND LIEF (gatefold sleeve, 2nd pressing, pink rim label with 'palm tree' logo)	20
70	Island ILPS 9130	FULL HOUSE (white label test pressing, with "Poor Will & The Jolly Hangman")	250
70	Island ILPS 9130	FULL HOUSE (1st pressing, pink 'i' label, gatefold sleeve lists "Poor Will & The Jolly Hangman")	50
70	Island ILPS 9130	FULL HOUSE (2nd pressing, with pink 'i' label, gatefold sleeve without reference to "Poor Will & The Jolly Hangman")	30
70	Island ILPS 9130	FULL HOUSE (gatefold sleeve, 3rd pressing, pink rim label with 'palm tree' logo)	15
71	Island ILPS 9162	ANGEL DELIGHT (gatefold sleeve with 'stuck-on' photos, pink rim label)	20
71	Island ILPS 9176	BABBACOMBE LEE (gatefold sleeve, with innersleeve and booklet, with sticker, pink rim label)	35
71	Island ILPS 9176	BABBACOMBE LEE (gatefold sleeve, with innersleeve and booklet, without sticker)	18
72	Island ICD 4	THE HISTORY OF FAIRPORT CONVENTION (2-LP, with 12-page booklet & blue ribbons)	20
72	Island ICD 4	THE HISTORY OF FAIRPORT CONVENTION (2-LP, later pressing with book & green, red or light blue ribbons)	18
73	Island ILPS 9208	ROSIE	15
73	Island ILPS 9246	FAIRPORT NINE (gatefold sleeve)	18
74	Island ILPS 9285	LIVE CONVENTION (with insert)	15
75	Island ILPS 9313	RISING FOR THE MOON (with insert, 'palm tree' label)	15
75	Island ISS 2	FAIRPORT TOUR SAMPLER (free in NME competition, 500 only)	120
76	Island ILPS 9389	GOTTLE O' GEER	18
76	Island HELP 28	LIVE AT THE L.A. TROUBADOR 1974	30

ALBUMS : OTHER ALBUMS
77	Vertigo 9102 015	BONNY BUNCH OF ROSES (gatefold sleeve)	18
78	Vertigo 9102 022	TIPPLER'S TALES (with lyric insert)	15
79	Woodworm BEAR 22	FAREWELL FAREWELL (gatefold sleeve)	20
79	Simons GAMA 1	FAREWELL FAREWELL (reissue, gatefold sleeve)	18
82	Woodworm WR 001	MOAT ON THE LEDGE — LIVE 1981	12
83	Woodworm WRC 1	AT 2 (AIRING CUPBOARD TAPES 2) ()	15
84	Woodworm (no cat. no.)	THE BOOT (2- cassette in video box, 1,000 only)	20
87	Hannibal HNBL	HEYDAY - LIVE AT THE BBC (LP, 2 different issues with alternative versions of 'Reno Nevada')	12
87	Woodworm (no cat. no.)	THE OTHER BOOT (2-cassette in video box, 1,000 only)	20
88	Woodworm (no cat. no.)	THE THIRD LEG (2-cassette in video box, 1,000 only)	20
89	BGO BGOCD 72	TIPPLER'S TALES (CD)	20
92	Vertigo 512882	BONNY BUNCH OF ROSES/TIPPLERS TALES (CD)	25

(see also Richard Thompson, Ian Matthews, Dave Swarbrick, Sandy Denny, Ashley Hutchings, Trevor Lucas, Albion Band. Bunch, Fotheringay. Vashti Bunyan, Trader Horne, Thieves, Allan Taylor, Krysia, Marc Ellington, Brian Maxine, Steeleye Span, Vikki clayton)

FAIRUZ

57	Parlophone LPVD 1	FAIRUZ SINGS (10" LP, Export)	50
58	Parlophone LPVD 4	FAIRUZ SINGS AGAIN (10" LP, Export)	60
66	Parlophone LPVDX 106	DAMASCUS FESTIVAL (LP)	30

FAIR WARNING

87	Areba ERA 2	Rocking At The Speed Of Light EP (12", p/s)	30

FAIRWAYS (FEATURING GARY STREET)

69	Mercury MF 1116	Yoko Ono/I Don't Care	12

FAIR WEATHER

70	RCA RCA 1977	Natural Sinner/Haven't I Tried (To Be A Good Man)	6
70	RCA RCA 2040	Road To Freedom/Tutti Frutti	8
71	RCA Neon NE 1000	Lay It On Me/Looking For The Red Label Pt 2	15
71	RCA Neon NE 1	BEGINNING FROM AN END (LP, gatefold sleeve, black inner sleeve)	50

(see also Andy Fairweather-Low, Amen Corner, Wynder K. Frog)

AL FAIRWEATHER

57	Columbia SEG 7653	AL FAIRWEATHER'S JAZZ BAND (EP)	8
58	Tempo EXA 63	AL FAIRWEATHER'S JAZZMEN (EP, with Henrick Johansen)	10
58	Nixa NJT 511	FAIRWEATHER FRIENDS (LP)	15
60	Columbia 33SX 1159	AL AND SANDY (LP)	15
60	Columbia 33SX 1221	AL'S PALS (LP)	15
61	Columbia 33SX 1306	DOCTOR McJAZZ (LP, also stereo SCX 3367, with Sandy Brown)	20
63	Columbia 33SX 1509	THE INCREDIBLE McJAZZ (LP, with Sandy Brown's All Stars)	20

(see also Sandy Brown, Henrik Johansen, Albert Nicholas)

ANDY FAIRWEATHER-LOW

86	Stiff BUY 252	Bossa Nova/House Of Blue Light (p/s)	5

(see also Amen Corner, Fair Weather, Gary Pickford-Hopkins & Friends, Dave Edmunds & Rockpile)

FAIRY'S MOKE

75	Deroy 1175	FAIRY'S MOKE (LP, private pressing, actually various artists LP)	80

(see also Baby Sunshine)

FAIRYTALE

67	Decca F 12644	Guess I Was Dreaming/Run And Hide	110
67	Decca F 12665	Lovely People/Listen To Mary Cry	60

ADAM FAITH (& ROULETTES)

SINGLES

58	HMV POP 438	(Got A) Heartsick Feeling/Brother Heartache And Sister Tears	150
58	HMV POP 438	(Got A) Heartsick Feeling/Brother Heartache And Sister Tears (78)	50
58	HMV POP 557	High School Confidential/Country Music Holiday	150
58	HMV POP 557	High School Confidential/Country Music Holiday (78)	50
59	Top Rank JAR 126	Ah, Poor Little Baby!/Runk Bunk (blue label)	30
59	Top Rank JAR 126	Ah, Poor Little Baby!/Runk Bunk (blue label) (78)	50
59	Parlophone R 4591	What Do You Want?/From Now Until Forever	5
59	Parlophone R 4591	What Do You Want?/From Now Until Forever (78)	30
60	Parlophone R 4623	Poor Me/The Reason (78)	40
60	Parlophone R 4665	Made You/When Johnny Comes Marching Home	5
60	Parlophone R 4665	Made You/When Johnny Comes Marching Home (78)	25
65	Parlophone R 5289	Someone's Taken Maria Away/I Can't Think Of Anyone Else (with Roulettes)	5
65	Parlophone R 5349	I Don't Need That Kind Of Lovin'/I'm Used To Losing You	5
66	Parlophone R 5398	Idle Gossip/If You Ever Need Me	5
66	Parlophone R 5412	To Make A Big Man Cry/Here's Another Day	5
66	Parlophone R 5516	Cheryl's Goin' Home/Funny Kind Of Love	5
67	Parlophone R 5556	What More Can Anyone Do/You've Got A Way With Me	5
67	Parlophone R 5635	Cowman Milk Your Cow/Daddy, What'll Happen To Me	10
67	Parlophone R 5649	To Hell With Love/Close The Door	5
68	Parlophone R 5673	You Make My Life Worth While/Hey Little Lovin' Girl	5
74	Warner Bros. K 16431	I Believe In Love/RAB NOAKES: Sitting In The Corner Blue	8

EPs

60	Parlophone GEP 8811	ADAM'S HIT PARADE	8
60	Parlophone SGE 2014	ADAM NO. 1 (stereo)	8
60	Parlophone SGE 2015	ADAM NO. 2 (stereo)	8
60	Parlophone SGE 2018	ADAM NO. 3 (stereo)	8
61	Parlophone GEP 8841	ADAM'S HIT PARADE VOL. 2	8
62	Parlophone GEP 8851	ADAM FAITH NO. 1	8
62	Parlophone GEP 8852	ADAM FAITH NO. 2	8
62	Parlophone GEP 8854	ADAM FAITH NO. 3 (with John Barry)	8
62	Columbia SEG 8138	BEAT GIRL (2 Faith tracks, with John Barry Orchestra)	20
62	Parlophone GEP 8862	ADAM'S HIT PARADE VOL. 3	8
63	Parlophone GEP 8877	ADAM'S LATEST HITS	8
64	Parlophone GEP 8893	TOP OF THE POPS (with Roulettes)	12
64	Parlophone GEP 8904	FOR YOU — ADAM	12
65	Parlophone GEP 8929	A MESSAGE TO MARTHA — FROM ADAM	12
65	Parlophone GEP 8939	SONGS AND THINGS	12

ALBUMS

60	Columbia 33SX 1225	BEAT GIRL (soundtrack, with John Barry Orchestra)	50
60	Parlophone PMC 1128	ADAM (mono)	18
60	Parlophone PCS 3010	ADAM (stereo)	18
60	EMI Regal (S)REG 1033	ADAM (mono/stereo export issue in different sleeve)	15
61	Parlophone PMC 1162	ADAM FAITH (mono)	15
61	Parlophone PCS 3025	ADAM FAITH (stereo)	18
62	Parlophone PMC 1192	FROM ADAM WITH LOVE (mono)	12
62	Parlophone PCS 3038	FROM ADAM WITH LOVE (stereo)	18
63	Parlophone PMC 1213	FOR YOU — ADAM (mono)	15
63	Parlophone PMC 1213	FOR YOU — ADAM (stereo)	18

MINT VALUE £

| 64 | Parlophone PMC 1228 | ON THE MOVE (with Roulettes) | 40 |
| 65 | Parlophone PMC 1249 | FAITH ALIVE! (with Roulettes) | 40 |

(see also Roulettes, John Barry)

AUSTIN FAITH
| 71 | Dynamic DYN 407 | 634 5789/DYNAMIC BOYS: Warm And Tender Love | 7 |

(see also Austin Faithful)

FAITH BROTHERS
| 67 | Tabernacle TS 1002 | I Am Saved Now/Too Near My Heavenly Home | 20 |

GEORGE FAITH
77	Island IPR 2034	Diana/To Be A Lover (12")	15
77	Black Swan BS 2	To Be A Lover/UPSETTERS: Rastaman Shuffle (12")	20
77	Black Swan BS 3	I've Got The Groove/Diana (12")	20
77	Black Swan BS 4	Midnight Hour/Turn Back The Hands Of Time (12")	20
77	Black Swan BS 5	All The Love I've Got/So Fine (12")	20
79	Warrior WAR 134	Don't Be Afraid/BUNNY SCOTT : What's The Use/Never Had It So Good (act. Jimmy Riley) (12")	12
77	Black Swan ILPS 9504	TO BE A LOVER (LP)	30

HORACE FAITH
69	B&C CB 104	Spinning Wheel/Like I Used To Do	10
69	Downtown DT 446	Daddy's Home/EMOTIONS: Give Me A Love	10
70	Trojan TR 7766	Susie Is Sorrow/DERRICK PEPPER: Don't Go	8
70	Trojan TR 7790	Black Pearl/Help Me Help Myself	7
70	A&M AMS 817	Shame And Scandal In The Family/REGGAE STRINGS: Reggae Strings	6
76	DJM DJS 10687	I Can't Understand It/Gimme Good Lovin'	30

AUSTIN FAITHFUL
68	Blue Cat BS 140	Uncle Joe/Can't Understand	150
68	Pyramid PYR 6016	I'm In A Rocking Mood/ROLAND ALPHONSO: Stream Of Life	80
69	Pyramid PYR 6028	Eternal Love/ROLAND ALPHONSO: Goodnight My Love	80
69	Pyramid PYR 6042	Ain't That Peculiar?/Miss Anti-Social	40

(see also Austin Faith)

FAITHFUL DAWN
| 94 | Dawn 001 | The Sequel (Original mix)/Dark Beat Mix (12", white label – 300 only) | 20 |

MARIANNE FAITHFULL
64	Decca F 11923	As Tears Go By/Greensleeves	7
64	Decca F 12007	Blowin' In The Wind/The House Of The Rising Sun	10
65	Decca F 12075	Come And Stay With Me/What Have I Done Wrong?	8
65	Decca F 12162	This Little Bird/Morning Sun	6
65	Decca F 12193	Summer Nights/The Sha La La Song	7
65	Decca F 12268	Yesterday/Oh Look Around You	7
66	Decca F 12408	Tomorrow's Calling/That's Right Baby	10
66	Decca F 22524	Counting/I'd Like To Dial Your Number	18
66	Decca F 12443	Is This What I Get For Loving You?/Tomorrow's Calling	15
69	Decca F 12889	Something Better/Sister Morphine (withdrawn)	55
75	NEMS NES 004	Dreamin' My Dreams/Lady Madalaine	10
76	NEMS NES 013	All I Wanna Do In Life/Wrong Road Again	10
77	NEMS NES 014	Wrong Road Again/The Way You Want Me To Be	10
78	NEMS NES 117	The Way You Want Me To Be/That Was The Day (Nashville)	10
79	Island WIP 6491	The Ballad Of Lucy Jordan/Brain Drain (p/s)	7
80	Island 12WIP 6542	Broken English/Why D'Ya Do It? (12", p/s)	10
80	Decca F 13890	As Tears Go By/Come And Stay With Me/This Little Bird/Summer Nights (p/s)	6
65	Decca DFE 8624	GO AWAY FROM MY WORLD (EP)	40
65	Decca LK 4688	COME MY WAY (LP)	65
65	Decca LK 4689	MARIANNE FAITHFULL (LP)	65
66	Decca LK 4778	NORTH COUNTRY MAID (LP)	75
67	Decca LK/SKL 4854	LOVEINAMIST (LP)	100
69	Decca (S)PA 17	THE WORLD OF MARIANNE FAITHFULL (LP)	15
76	NEMS NEL 6007	DREAMIN' MY DREAMS (LP)	15
78	NEMS NEL 6012	FAITHLESS (LP)	12
92	Island ILPM 9570	BROKEN ENGLISH (LP)	12

FAITH NO MORE
88	Slash LASH 17	We Care A Lot/Spirit (p/s)	12
88	Slash LASHX 17	We Care A Lot/Spirit/Chinese Arithmetic (Radio Mix) (12", p/s)	12
88	Slash LASH 18	Annie's Song (Remix)/Greed (p/s)	12
88	Slash LASHP 18	Annie's Song (Remix)/Greed (picture disc)	12
88	Slash LASHX 18	Anne's Song (Remix)/Greed (12", p/s)	15
89	Kerrang! FIEND 3	Sweet Emotion/(Balaam & The Angel track) (flexidisc with Kerrang! Mag)	15
90	Slash LASPD 21	Epic/War Pigs (live) (shaped picture disc)	12
90	Slash LASCD 21	Epic/War Pigs (live)/Surprise You're Dead (live)/Chinese Arithmetic (live) (CD, card sleeve)	15
90	Slash LASPD 26	Epic/Falling To Pieces (live) (shaped picture disc, 12" insert in PVC sleeve)	8
90	Slash LASPD 26	Epic/Falling To Pieces (live)/Epic (live)/As The Worm Turns (live) (CD)	10
92	London LASH 44	I'm Easy/Be Aggressive (red vinyl, p/s)	8
90	London/Slash 850 228	KING FOR A DAY, FOOL FOR A LIFETIME (7 x 7" box set)	35
89	Slash 828154	THE REAL THING (LP)	12
89	Slash 828 217-1	THE REAL THING (LP, picture disc)	25

FAKES
| 79 | Deep Cuts DEEP TWO | Production/Look-Out (p/s) | 5 |

EDDIE FALCON
| 60 | Columbia DB 4420 | The Young Have No Time To Lose/My Thanks To You | 8 |
| 61 | Columbia DB 4646 | Linda Rose/If Ever I Should Fall In Love | 8 |

FALCONS (U.K.)
| 64 | Philips BF 1297 | Stampede/Kazutzka | 20 |

FALCONS (U.S.)
| 59 | London HLT 8876 | You're So Fine/Goddess Of Angels | 120 |
| 59 | London HLT 8876 | You're So Fine/Goddess Of Angels (78) | 80 |

| 62 | London HLK 9565 | I Found A Love/Swim (some labels credit B-side as "Swin") | 50 |

(see also Wilson Pickett, Eddie Floyd)

FALL OUT BOY

| 04 | Sorepoint SORE 010S | Dead On Arrival/Dead On Arrival (acoustic) blue vinyl, die-cut sleeve | 6 |
| 05 | Sorepoint SORE 038S | Grand Theft Autumn/Where Is Your Boy/MY AWESOME COMPILATION: As Always (yellow vinyl, die-cut sleeve) | 6 |

THE FALL

SINGLES

78	Step Forward SF 7	Bingo-Masters' Breakout! (EP)	20
78	Step Forward SF 9	It's The New Thing/Various Times (p/s)	15
79	Step Forward SF 11	Rowche Rumble/In My Area (p/s)	15
80	Step Forward SF 13	Fiery Jack/Second Dark Age/Psykick Dancehall 2 (black-and-white p/s)	15
80	Step Forward SF 13	Fiery Jack/Second Dark Age/Psykick Dancehall 2 (yellow p/s)	10
80	Rough Trade RT 048	How I Wrote Elastic Man/City Hobgoblins (p/s)	10
80	Rough Trade RT 056	Totally Wired/Putta Block (p/s)	10
81	Rough Trade RT 071	SLATES (10" EP, 33rpm)	18
81	Kamera ERA 001	Lie Dream Of A Casino Soul/Fantastic Life (p/s)	12
82	Kamera ERA 004	Look, Know/I'm Into C.B. (p/s)	10
82	Rough Trade RT 133	The Man Whose Head Expanded/Ludd Gang (p/s)	10
82	Kamera ERA 014	Marquis Cha Cha/Papal Visit (p/s, B-side plays "Room To Live", withdrawn)	60
83	Rough Trade RT 143	Kicker Conspiracy/Wings/Container Drivers/New Puritan (g/fold double pack)	12
84	Beggars Banquet BEG 116	C.R.E.E.P./Pat-Trip Dispenser (p/s)	6
84	Beggars Banquet BEG 116T	C.R.E.E.P./(Extended Version)/Pat-Trip Dispenser (12", p/s, green vinyl)	8
84	Beggars Banquet BEG 116TP	C.R.E.E.P./(Extended Version)/Pat-Trip Dispenser (12", p/s, with art print)	8
84	Beggars Banquet BEG 120E	CALL FOR ESCAPE ROUTE (7"/12" double pack EP)	8
85	Beggars Banquet BEG 150	Cruiser's Creek (p/s)	6
85	Beggars Banquet BEG 150T	Cruiser's Creek (12", p/s)	8
87	Beggars Banquet BEG 187H	There's A Ghost In My House/Haf Found Bormann (hologram p/s)	5
87	Beggars Banquet BEG 200P	Hit The North (Parts 1 & 2) (picture disc, printed PVC sleeve)	5
87	Beggars Banquet BEG 200T	Hit The North (Parts 1 & 2) (12", gatefold sleeve)	8
87	Beggars Banquet BEG 206B	Victoria/Tuff Life Boogie (box set with inserts & badge)	5
88	Beggars Banquet FALL 2B	Jerusalem (Remix)/Acid Priest 2088 (Remix)//Big New Prinz (Remix)/Wrong Place Right Time No. 2 (Remix) (double pack box set, with postcard)	5
89	Beggars Banquet BEG 226	Cab It Up/Dead Beat Descendant (p/s)	6
90	Cog Sinister SINR 5	Popcorn Double Feature/Zandra (p/s)	6
91	Cog Sinister FALL !	So What About It/Edinburgh Man (promo only)	15
92	Cig Sinister SINS 8	Free Range/Everything Hurtz (p/s)	6
94	Permanent 10SPERM 14	15 Ways (10", p/s)	8
96	Jet JET 500	The Chiselers/Chilinist (p/s)	8
01	Flitwick MK45 1FG	I Wake Up In The City/Rude (All The Time) (500 only)	70

ALBUMS

79	Step Forward SFLP 1	LIVE AT THE WITCH TRIALS (LP)	20
79	Step Forward SFLP 4	DRAGNET (LP, with insert)	20
80	Rough Trade ROUGH 10	TOTALE'S TURNS (IT'S NOW OR NEVER) (LP)	20
80	Rough Trade ROUGH 18	GROTESQUE (AFTER THE GRAMME) (LP)	20
81	Step Forward SFLP 6	THE EARLY YEARS 1977-79 (LP)	20
82	Kamera KAM 005	HEX EDUCATION HOUR (LP)	20
83	Rough Trade 062	PERVERTED BY LANGUAGE (LP)	15
84	Beggars Banquet BEGA 58	WONDERFUL AND FRIGHTENING WORLD OF (LP)	12
85	Beggars Banquet BEGA 67	THIS NATIONS SAVING GRACE (LP, gatefold with inner sleeve)	15
85	Situation 2 SITU 13	HIP PRIEST AND KAMERADAS (LP)	12
86	Beggars Banquet BEGA 75	BEND SINISTER (LP)	12
88	Beggars Banquet BEGA 96	I AM A KURIOUS ORANGE (LP, gatefold)	12
90	Cog Sinister 842204	EXTRICATE (LP)	12
91	Cog Sinister 848594	SHIFT-WORK (LP)	12
93	Permanent PERMLP 12	THE INFOTAINMENT SCAM (LP)	12
95	Cog Sinister PERMLP 36	TWENTY SEVEN POINTS (2-LP, gatefold)	25
97	Artful ARTFUL LP 9	LEVITATE (LP)	70
99	Artful ARTFULP 17	THE MARSHALL SUITE (2-LP)	80
05	BBC CMXBX982	COMPLETE PEEL SESSIONS (6-CD box set)	30
08	Sanctuary 1766796	IMPERIAL WAX SOLVENT (LP)	60

(see also D.O.S.E.)

FALLEN ANGELS (U.S.)

| 67 | London HL 10166 | I Don't Want To Fall/Most Children Do | 10 |
| 68 | London HA-Z/SH-Z 8359 | THE FALLEN ANGELS (LP) | 50 |

JOHNNY FALLIN

| 59 | Capitol CL 15043 | Party Kiss/The Creation Of Love | 60 |
| 59 | Capitol CL 15091 | Wild Streak/If I Could Write A Love Song | 50 |

FALLING LEAVES

| 65 | Parlophone R 5233 | She Loves To Be Loved/Not Guilty | 70 |
| 66 | Decca F 12420 | Beggar's Parade/Tomorrow Night | 40 |

FALLOUT (1)

81	No label or Cat. No.)	Conscription/Democracy?/Nuclear Power/Them & Us/Laughable Attack/Sign Away (fold-out sleeve)	5
84	I FLP 2	BUTCHERY (10" EP, with lyric inner)	8
83	Own Label F3 LP 1	HOME COOKED MEAT (LP, with 2 inserts)	12

FALLOUT (2)

| 90 | Azuli AZ001 | The Morning After (12") | 20 |

FALLOUT CLUB

| 79 | Secret SHH104 | The Falling Years/The Beat Boys (p/s) | 15 |
| 81 | Happy Birthday UR3 | Dream Soldiers/Pedestrian Walk Way (p/s) | 15 |

FALSE IDOLS

| 78 | Old Knew Wave BOG 005 | Broken Judy/Marbled Hands/H-Brain (tri-fold p/s) | 10 |
| 78 | Old Knew Wave BOG 007 | Ego Wino/Good Night (p/s, pink vinyl) | 5 |

MINT VALUE £

AGNETHA FALTSKOG

82	Epic EPC A 2824	Never Again/Just For The Fun (p/s, with Tomas Ledin)	12
83	Epic EPC A 3436	The Heat Is On/Man (p/s)	6
83	Epic EPC WA 3436	The Heat Is On/Man (picture disc)	30
83	Epic EPC A 3622	Wrap Your Arms Around Me/Take Good Care Of The Children (p/s)	6
83	Epic EPC TA 3622	Wrap Your Arms Around Me/The Heat Is On/ Take Good Care Of The Children (Extended) (12", p/s)	12
83	Epic EPC A 3812	Can't Shake Loose/To Love (p/s)	6
83	Epic EPC A 3812	Can't Shake Loose/To Love (poster p/s)	15
83	Epic EPC WA 3812	Can't Shake Loose/To Love (picture disc)	25
85	Epic EPC A 6133	I Won't Let You Go/You're There (p/s)	6
85	Epic EPC TA 6133	I Won't Let You Go (Extended)/You're There (12", p/s)	12
86	Sonet SON 2317	The Way You Are/Fly Like The Eagle (p/s, with Ola Hanansson)	10
88	WEA YZ 170	The Last Time/Are You Gonna Throw It All Away (p/s)	6
88	WEA YZ 170T	The Last Time (Extended Remix)/The Last Time/ Are You Gonna Throw It All Away (12", p/s)	12
88	WEA YZ 177	I Wasn't The One (Who Said Goodbye)/If You Need Somebody Tonight (p/s, with Peter Cetera)	6
88	WEA YZ 177T	I Wasn't The One (Who Said Goodbye) (Extended Version)/(Yo No Fui [Quien Dijo Adios])/If You Need Somebody Tonight (12", p/s, with Peter Cetera)	12
88	WEA YZ 300	Let It Shine/Maybe It Was Magic (p/s)	8
88	WEA YZ 300T	Let It Shine (Extended)/('Bright' Mix)/Maybe It Was Magic (12", p/s)	12
98	Polydor POLPROCD 2	The Queen Of Hearts (Nar Du Tar Mej I Din Fam) (CD, promo only)	30
74	Embassy EMB 31094	AGNETHA (LP)	40

(see also Abba)

GEORGIE FAME (& THE BLUE FLAMES)
SINGLES

64	Columbia DB 7193	Do The Dog/Shop Around	25
64	Columbia DB 7255	Green Onions/Do-Re-Mi	18
64	Columbia DB 7328	Bend A Little/I'm In Love With You (solo)	20
64	Columbia DB 7428	Yeh Yeh/Preach And Teach (some copies list "Yeah, Yeah" on label)	6
64	Columbia DB 7428	Yeh Yeh/Preach And Teach (99 promo copies only with p/s)	75
65	Columbia DB 7494	In The Meantime/Telegram	10
65	Columbia DB 7633	Like We Used To Be/It Ain't Right	10
65	Columbia DB 7727	Something/Outrage	10
66	Columbia DB 7946	Getaway/El Bandido	10

(The above 45s were credited to Georgie Fame & Blue Flames)

66	Columbia DB 8015	Sunny/Don't Make Promises	10
66	Columbia DB 8096	Sitting In The Park/Many Happy Returns	10
67	CBS 202587	Because I Love You/Bidin' My Time (p/s)	7
67	CBS 2945	Try My World/No Thanks (p/s)	7
67	CBS 3124	The Ballad Of Bonnie And Clyde/Beware Of The Dog (p/s)	5
68	CBS 3526	By The Time I Get To Phoenix/For Your Pleasure	5
69	CBS 4295	Peaceful/Hideaway (with John Barry)	6
69	CBS 4659	Seventh Son/Fully Booked	8
70	CBS 5035	Entertaining Mr. Sloane/Somebody Stole My Thunder (DJ Copy)	150
70	CBS 5035	Entertaining Mr. Sloane/Somebody Stole My Thunder	100
70	CBS 5131	Fire And Rain/Someday Man	5
77	Island WIP 6384	Daylight/Three Legged Mule	40
77	Island WIP 6384	Daylight/Three Legged Mule (12")	30

EPs

64	Columbia SEG 8334	RHYTHM AND BLUEBEAT	50
64	Columbia SEG 8382	RHYTHM AND BLUES AT THE FLAMINGO	40
64	Columbia SEG 8393	FAME AT LAST	30
65	Columbia SEG 8406	FATS FOR FAME	30
65	Columbia SEG 8454	MOVE IT ON OVER	30
66	Columbia SEG 8518	GETAWAY	30
67	CBS EP 6363	KNOCK ON WOOD	30
80	RSO 2252 136	BLUE BEAT	10

ALBUMS

64	Columbia 33SX 1599	RHYTHM AND BLUES AT THE FLAMINGO	80
64	Columbia 33SX 1638	FAME AT LAST	35
66	Columbia SX 6043	SWEET THINGS	25
66	Columbia SX 6076	SOUND VENTURE	40
67	Columbia SX 6120	HALL OF FAME	20
67	CBS (S)BPG 63018	TWO FACES OF FAME	20
68	CBS (S) 63293	THE THIRD FACE OF FAME (mono/stereo)	15
69	CBS S 63786	SEVENTH SON	15
69	Regal Starline SRS5002	GEORGIE FAME AND THE BLUE FLAMES	15
71	CBS S 64350	GOING HOME	15
72	Reprise K 44183	ALL ME OWN WORK (LP, gatefold sleeve)	20
74	Island ILPS 9293	GEORGIE FAME	20

(see also Blue Flames, Jimmy Nicol, Perry Ford & Sapphires, Annie Ross)

GEORGIE FAME & ANNIE ROSS

81	Bald Eagle	Drip Drop/One Morning In May (12" p/s 50 copies only)	40

FAMILY

67	Liberty LBF 15031	Scene Thru The Eye Of A Lens/Gypsy Woman (mispress, B-side plays "Let Me Be Good To You" by Otis Redding)	150
67	Liberty LBF 15031	Scene Thru The Eye Of A Lens/Gypsy Woman	200
68	Reprise RS 23270	Me My Friend/Hey Mr. Policeman	20
68	Reprise RS 23315	Second Generation Woman/Home Town	15
69	Reprise RS 27001	No Mule's Fool/Good Friend Of Mine (p/s)	15
69	Reprise RS 27001	No Mule's Fool/Good Friend Of Mine	5
70	Reprise RS 27005	Today/Song For Lots (p/s)	15
70	Reprise RS 27005	Today/Song For Lots	5
70	Reprise RS 27009	The Weaver's Answer/Strange Band/Hung Up Down (in p/s)	5
71	Reprise K 14090	In My Own Time/Seasons (in p/s)	5
71	Reprise SAM 1	Larf And Sing/Children (promo only)	15

73	Raft RA 18501	Boom Bang/Stop This Car 7
73	Raft RA 18503	Sweet Desiree/Drink To You 7
68	Reprise RLP 6312	MUSIC IN A DOLL'S HOUSE (LP, 1st pressing with 'Steamboat' label, insert, mono)............200
68	Reprise R(S)LP 6312	MUSIC IN A DOLL'S HOUSE (LP, 1st pressing, with 'Steamboat' label, insert, stereo) 100
69	Reprise RLP 6340	FAMILY ENTERTAINMENT (LP, 1st pressing, with 'Steamboat' label mono, with poster) 100
69	Reprise RSLP 6340	FAMILY ENTERTAINMENT (LP, 1st pressing with 'Steamboat' label, stereo, with poster).......60
70	Reprise RSLP 9001	A SONG FOR ME (LP, 1st pressing with 'Steamboat' label, with lyric sheet)........................60
70	Reprise RSX 9005	ANYWAY (LP, custom polythene sleeve) 35
71	Reprise RMP 9007	OLD SONGS NEW SONGS (LP)..25
71	Reprise K 54003	FEARLESS (LP, multi gatefold sleeve, lyric insert) 30
72	Reprise K 54006	BANDSTAND (LP, 'window' die-cut sleeve, lyric inner) 30
73	Raft RA58501	IT'S ONLY A MOVIE (LP, lyric inner and 'banger' insert) 40
73	Raft RA 58501	IT'S ONLY A MOVIE (LP, lyric inner and no 'banger' insert) 15
73	Raft RA 58501	IT'S ONLY A MOVIE (LP, no lyric inner and no 'banger' insert) 12

(see also Farinas, Stud, Mogul Thrash, Hellions, Ashton Gardner & Dyke, Revolution, Streetwalkers)

FAMILY AFFAIR
68	Saga STFID 2124	THE FAMILY AFFAIR (LP) 15

FAMILY CAT
78	Union UN 005	Used To Be My Girl/Long Time 10
91	Bad Girl BGRLT 009T	Color Me Grey/I Must Have Been Blind/Great Ugly Place (12", p/s) 8

(see also P.J. Harvey)

FAMILY CIRCLE
69	Attack AT 8001	Phoenix Reggae/BIG L: Music Box 8
69	Attack AT 8002	Reggae Krishna/Official...40
69	JJ DB 1300	Give Peace A Chance/GEORGE LEE: Reggae Groove 8

FAMILY DOGG
67	MGM MGM 1360	The Storm/Family Dogg 20
68	Fontana TF 921	I Wear A Silly Grin/Couldn't Help It 15
68	Fontana TF 968	Brown-Eyed Girl/Let It Rain...7
69	Bell BLL 1055	A Way Of Life/Throw It Away 7
69	Bell BLL 1077	Arizona/The House In The Heather 6
72	Buddah 2011-143	Sweet America/Rikers Island 10
70	Bell BLL 1100	When Tomorrow Comes Tomorrow/This Unhappy Heart Of Mine 6
69	Bell SBLL 122	A WAY OF LIFE (LP, with members of Led Zeppelin, gatefold) 25
72	Buddah 2318 061	THE VIEW FROM ROWLAND'S HEAD (LP, gatefold, lyric insert) 20

(see also Steve Rowland, Christine Holmes, Albert Hammond)

FAMILY FODDER
80	Fresh FRESH 15	Debbie Harry/Version (p/s) 7
80	Fresh FRESH 22	Savoir Faire/Carnal Knowledge (p/s) 6
79	Parole/Fresh PURL 4	Playing Golf/My Baby Takes Valium (p/s) 5
79	Fresh Records FRESH 9	SUNDAY GIRLS (12")...15
82	Fresh 42	The Big Dig/Plant Life (p/s) 10

FAMILY MAN (ASTON BARRETT)
70	Escort ERT 834	Midnight Sunshine/GREGORY & STICKY: You Are My Sunshine.................................8
72	Downtown DT 491	Herb Tree/STUDIO SOUND: Holy Poly (reissue) 8

(see also Hippy Boys, Upsetters, Bob Marley & Wailers, Carl Dawkins)

FAMILY ON HOLIDAY
81	Fabidoo S81CUS 1140	Who's A Pretty Boy Then/You're As Cute As A Dead Gerbil (p/s) 15

FAMILY PRIDE
73	Rex RPS 108	FAMILY PRIDE (LP)...20

FAMILY QUEST
84	Jungle Rhythm SWE-T2	Outerspace 84 Rap...25
86	Streetwave MKHAN74	Sleepwalking (12")..12

FAMOUS ECCLES & MISS FREDA THING
56	Parlophone R 4251	My September Love/COUNT JIM MORIARTY & GRAVELEY STEPHENS: You Gotta Go Oww! (with The Alberts)..12

(see also Spike Milligan, Goons)

FAMOUS JUG BAND
69	Liberty LBF 15224	The Only Friend I Own/A Leaf Must Fall 10
69	Liberty LBS 83263	SUNSHINE POSSIBILITIES (LP, blue labels) 70
70	Liberty LBS 83355	CHAMELEON (LP, textured sleeve, blue labels) 80

(see also Incredible String Band, C.O.B.)

FAMOUS MUSIC BAND
69	Philips 6006 111	Nine By Nine/Going In The Out (with John Dummer) 8

(see also John Dummer)

FAMOUS PLAYERS
80	Page 45 AH 1001	Who's Kissing You (p/s) 70

FANATICS
89	Chapter 22 12 CHAP 38	SUBURBAN LOVE SONGS (12" EP) 18

(see also Ocean Colour Scene)

FAN-CLUB
78	M&S SJP 791B	Avenue/Night Caller (p/s, photocopied insert)..15

(see also Transvision Vamp)

FANCY
73	Sticky STY 3	Starlord/Brother John 25
74	Antic K11514	Touch Me/I Don't Need Your Love 8
75	Arista ARISTA 3	She's Riding The Rock Machine Part 1/Part 2 8
76	Arista ARIST 32	Music Maker/Bluebird 8

(see also Ray Fenwick, Judas Priest)

FANDANGO
73	York SYK 562	High Class Girl/Sha La La 12

(see Nic Simper's Fandango, under 'S')

COSEY FANNI TUTTI
83	Flowmotion	TIME TO TELL (cassette with booklet)	50
93	Conspiracy Int. CTI 93004 SE	TIME TO TELL (CD with fold-out booklet and cards)	25

(see also Throbbing Gristle, Chris & Cosey)

FANNY
70	Reprise RSLP 6416	FANNY (LP)	12
72	Reprise K 44144	CHARITY BALL (LP, lyric insert)	12

FANS
79	Fried Egg EGG 3	Giving Me That Look in Your Eyes/Stay The Night/He'll Have To Go (p/s)	50
79	Albion ION 0004	True (dayglo inner, inc bonus 7" & lyric sheet)	20
80	Albion FAN 01	Cars And Explosions/Dangerous Goodbyes (p/s)	20
81	Fried Egg EGG 10	You Don't Live Here Anymore/Following You (p/s)	60

DAVID FANSHAWE
75	Philips 6558 001	AFRICAN SANCTUS (LP)	12

FANTASIA
67	Stateside SS 2031	Gotta Get Away/She Needs My Love	15

FANTASTIC BAGGYS
76	United Artists UP 36142	Summer Means Fun/JAN & DEAN: Surf City/Sidewalk Surfin'	15

(see also Jan & Dean, Bruce Johnston)

FANTASTIC FOUR
68	Tamla Motown TMG 678	I Love You Madly/I Love You Madly (Instrumental)	22
68	T. Motown TML 11105	THE FANTASTIC FOUR (LP, mono)	60
69	T. Motown STML 11105	THE FANTASTIC FOUR (LP, stereo)	50

FANTASTIC PUZZLES
76	Right On 106	Come Back/Come Back Part 2	20

FANTASTIC SOMETHING
84	Cherry Red CHERRY 61	If She Doesn't Smile (It'll Rain)/The Thousand Guitars Of St. Dominiques (p/s)	12

FANTASTICS
68	MGM MGM 1434	Baby Make Your Own Sweet Music/Who Could Be Lovin' You	20
68	MGM MGM 1434DJ	Baby Make Your Own Sweet Music/ Who Could Be Lovin' You (DJ promo)	30
69	Deram DM 264	Face To Face With Heartache/This Must Be My Rainy Day	6
70	Deram DM 283	Waiting Round For Heartaches/Ask The Lonely	20
71	Deram DM 334	For Old Times Sake/Exodus Main Theme	6
71	Mojo 2027 004	Baby Make Your Own Sweet Music/Who Could Be Lovin' You? (reissue)	5

(see also Velours)

FANTASY
73	Polydor 2058 405	Politely Insane/I Was Once Aware	30
73	Polydor 2383 246	PAINT A PICTURE (LP, gatefold sleeve, red label)	450

FANTOMS
83	Ear To Ear GRIN 1	Hearts Of Stone (Break Hearts OF Glass)/Really Mystified (p/s)	10

BARRY FANTONI
66	Fontana TF 707	Little Man In A Little Box/Fat Man	35
67	Columbia DB 8238	Nothing Today/The Spanish Lady Tango	8

FAPARDOKLY
83	Psycho PSYCHO 5	FAPARDOKLY (LP, 300 only)	20

(see also Mu)

FARAWAY FOLK
70s	Tabitha TAB 3	Shadow Of A Pie/Folsom Prison Blues/Rent A Man/Soulful Shade Of Blue	12
70s	RA EP 7001	INTRODUCING THE FARAWAY FOLK (EP)	25
70s	RA LP 6006ST	LIVE AT THE BOLTON (LP)	30
72	RA LP 6012ST	TIME AND TIDE (LP)	30
73	RA LP 6019	ON THE RADIO (LP)	30
74	RA LP 6022	ONLY AUTHORISED EMPLOYEES TO BREAK BOTTLES (LP, with Harry H. Corbett)	22
75	RA LP 6029	SEASONAL MAN (LP, gatefold sleeve with insert)	60
80s	RA	BATTLE OF THE DRAGONS ()	15

(see also Harry H. Corbett)

FAR CRY
69	Vanguard SVRL 19041	THE FAR CRY (LP)	30

DON FARDON
67	Pye International 7N 25437	(The Lament Of The Cherokee) Indian Reservation/Dreamin' Room	10
68	Pye International 7N 25475	(The Lament Of The Cherokee) Indian Reservation/Dreamin' Room (reissue)	5
69	Pye International 7N 25483	We Can Make It Together/Coming On Strong	25
69	Pye International 7N 25486	Good Lovin'/Ruby's Pictures On My Wall	8
69	Youngblood YB 1003	I'm Alive/Keep On Loving Me	40
69	Young Blood YB 1007	It's Been Nice Loving You/Let The Love Live	7
70	Young Blood YB 1010	Belfast Boy/Echoes Of The Cheers	30
70	Young Blood YB 1013	Delta Queen/Hometown Baby	5
70	Young Blood YB 1015	Indian Reservation/Hudson Bay	10
71	Young Blood YB 1021	Girl/Sandiago	6
71	Young Blood YB 1027	Follow Your Drum/Get Away John	6
70	Young Blood SSYB 4	I'VE PAID MY DUES! (LP)	20
70	Young Blood SSYB 13	RELEASED (LP)	18

(see also Sorrows)

FAR EAST FAMILY BAND
75	Vertigo 6370 850	NIPPONJIN (LP)	40

DICK FARINA & ERIC VON SCHMIDT
63	Folklore F-LEUT/7	DICK FARINA & ERIC VON SCHMIDT (LP, featuring 'Blind Boy Grunt')	80

(see also Bob Dylan, Richard & Mimi Farina, Four For Fun)

RICHARD & MIMI FARINA
65	Fontana STFL 6060	CELEBRATIONS FOR A GREY DAY (LP)	35
65	Fontana STFL 6075	REFLECTIONS IN A CRYSTAL WIND (LP)	35
73	Vanguard VSD 21/22	THE BEST OF RICHARD & MIMI FARINA (2-LP)	15

(see also Dick Farina & Eric Von Schmidt)

FARINAS
64	Victor Buckland Sound Studio	Bye Bye Johnny/All You Gotta Do/Twist And Shout (as James King & Farinas)	500
64	Fontana TF 493	You'd Better Stop/I Like It Like That	80

(see also Family)

ALEXANDER FARIS ORCHESTRA
76	BBC RESL 37	Wings/The Sussex Lad (p/s)	6

CHRIS FARLOWE (& THUNDERBIRDS)
62	Decca F 11536	Air Travel/Why Did You Break My Heart?	60
63	Columbia DB 7120	I Remember/Push Push (as Chris Farlowe & Thunderbirds)	40
64	Columbia DB 7237	Girl Trouble/Itty Bitty Pieces (as Chris Farlowe & Thunderbirds)	40
64	Columbia DB 7311	Just A Dream/What You Gonna Do? (as Chris Farlow & Thunderbirds)	40
64	Columbia DB 7379	Hey, Hey, Hey, Hey/Hound Dog (as Chris Farlow & Thunderbirds)	25
65	Columbia DB 7614	Buzz With The Fuzz/You're The One (withdrawn, as Chris Farlow & Thunderbirds, demos more common £100)	200
65	Immediate IM 016	The Fool/Treat Her Good	15
66	Immediate IM 023	Think/Don't Just Look At Me	25
66	Immediate IM 035	Out Of Time/Baby Make It Soon (3.13 version, CBS pressing, matrix 1F//1)	7
66	Immediate IM 035	Out Of Time/Baby Make It Soon (3.28 version, Philips pressing, matrix 1F V2)	7
66	Columbia DB 7983	Just A Dream/Hey, Hey, Hey, Hey	15
66	Immediate IM 038	Ride On Baby/Headlines	12
67	Immediate IM 041	My Way Of Giving/You're So Good To Me	15
67	Immediate IM 049	Yesterday's Papers/Life Is But Nothing	8
67	Immediate IM 056	Moanin'/What Have I Been Doin'?	8
67	Immediate IM 065	Handbags And Gladrags/Everyone Makes A Mistake	10
68	Immediate IM 066	The Last Goodbye/Paperman Fly In The Sky (B-side with Thunderbirds)	15
68	Immediate IM 071	Paint It Black/I Just Need Your Lovin'	12
69	Immediate IM 074	Dawn/April Was The Month	15
70	Polydor 2066 017	Black Sheep Of The Family/Fifty Years (as Chris Farlowe with The Hill)	6
70	Polydor 2066 046	Put Out The Light/Questions (as Chris Farlowe & Hill)	10
75	Polydor 2066 650	We Can Work It Out/Only Women Bleed	5
78	Beeb BEEB 022	Gangsters (as Chris Farlowe & Dave Greenslade)/DAVE GREENSLADE'S GANGSTERS: Sarah Gant Theme	6
80	VIRGIN SV102	OUT OF TIME - THE IMMEDIATE CATALOGUE (2 x 7")	8
65	Decca DFE 8665	CHRIS FARLOWE (EP)	100
65	Immediate IMEP 001	FARLOWE IN THE MIDNIGHT HOUR (EP)	50
66	Immediate IMEP 004	CHRIS FARLOWE HITS (EP)	40
66	Island IEP 709	STORMY MONDAY (EP)	120
66	Columbia SX 6034	CHRIS FARLOWE AND THE THUNDERBIRDS (LP, black/blue labels with "sold in the U.K..." text)	150
66	Music For Pleasure MFP 1186	STORMY MONDAY (LP, reissue of Chris Farlowe & Thunderbirds LP)	30
66	Immediate IMLP 005	14 THINGS TO THINK ABOUT (LP, lilac label)	60
66	Immediate IMLP 006	THE ART OF CHRIS FARLOWE (LP, mono, lilac label)	70
66	Immediate IMSP 006	THE ART OF CHRIS FARLOWE (LP, stereo, lilac label)	100
67	EMI Regal REG 2025	CHRIS FARLOWE (LP, export issue)	35
68	Immediate IMCP 010	THE BEST OF CHRIS FARLOWE VOLUME ONE (LP, lilac label)	30
69	Immediate IMLP 021	THE LAST GOODBYE (LP, pink label with "sold in U.K..." text)	100
70	Polydor 2425 029	FROM HERE TO MAMA ROSA (LP, as Chris Farlowe & Hill, gatefold sleeve, insert)	60
75	Polydor 2469 259	THE CHRIS FARLOWE BAND LIVE (LP)	12
86	Unicorn PHZA 60	BORN AGAIN (LP)	12

(see also Thunderbirds, Beazers, Little Joe Cook, Crane/Farlowe, Atomic Rooster, Colosseum, Dave Greenslade, Spectrum)

FARM
74	Spark SRL1105	Fat Judy/Gysy Mountain Woman	15

ART FARMER
54	Esquire 20-033	ART FARMER SEXTET — WORK OF ART (10" LP)	40
55	Esquire 32-037	MUSIC FOR THAT WILD PARTY (LP)	30
56	Esquire 32-072	TWO TRUMPETS (LP, with Donald Byrd)	35
56	Esquire 32-137	FARMERS MARKET (LP)	30
57	Esquire 32-037	WILD PARTY LP with Gigi Gryce)	40
59	London SAH-T 6028	MODERN ART (LP)	25
60	London Jazz LTZ-T 15184	BRASS SHOUT (LP)	20
60	London Jazz LTZ-T 15198	THE AZTEC SUITE (LP)	20
60	Pye Jazz NJL 45	MEET THE JAZZTET (with Benny Golson)	25
61	Esquire 32-120	EARTHY (LP)	30
64	London HA-K/SH-K 8135	INTERACTION (LP, as Art Farmer Quartet featuring Jim Hall)	20

(see also Clifford Brown, Benny Golson, Donald Byrd)

JULES FARMER
59	London HLP 8967	Love Me Now/Part Of Me (Is Still With You)	15
59	London HLP 8967	Love Me Now/Part Of Me (Is Still With You) (78)	10

MYLENE FARMER
89	Polydor 080 360-2	Ainsi Soit Je. . . (Maxi Remix)/Ainsi Soit Je. . . (Lamentations)/ Ainsi Soit Je. . . (Classic Bonus Beats) (CD Video, export only)	45
91	Polydor 873 738 7	Desenchantee (Edited Version)/Desenchantee (Chaos Mix) (Promo only)	20

FARMLIFE
82	Dining Out TUX 19	Susie's Party/Simple Men	6
83	Whaam! WHAAM 13	Big Country 1 & 2 (unreleased; Echantillan test pressings only)	40

GILES FARNABY'S DREAM BAND
73	Argo AFW 112	Newcastle Brown/29th Of May	12
73	Argo ZDA 158	GILES FARNABY'S DREAM BAND (LP)	45

(see also Druids)

FARNBOROUGH FIREWORK FACTORY
72	Decca F13290	Too Many People/She's Against The Law	8

ROBERT FARNON ORCHESTRA

56	Decca F 10818	Westminister Waltz/Poodle Parade	8
72	MCA MCA 117	Colditz March/That Italian Summer	6
58	Decca DFE 6470	JOURNEY INTO MELODY (EP)	8
55	Decca LK 4119	CANADIAN IMPRESSIONS (LP)	20
56	Vogue Coral LVA 9003	GENTLEMEN MARRY BRUNETTES (LP, soundtrack)	30
60	Delyse ECB 3157/DS 6057	CAPTAIN HORATIO HORNBLOWER (LP, soundtrack, mono)	40
60	Delyse DS 6057	CAPTAIN HORATIO HORNBLOWER (LP, soundtrack, stereo)	50
68	Philips SBL 7867	SHALAKO (LP, soundtrack)	15

(see also Jack Saunders)

ROBERT FARNON & TONY COE

70	Chapter One CHS 804	POP MAKES PROGRESS (LP)	30

(see also Tony Coe)

FARON'S FLAMINGOS

79	Raw RAW 28	Bring It On Home/C'mon Everybody	12
63	Oriole CB 1834	Do You Love Me?/See If She Cares	25
63	Oriole CB 1867	Shake Sherry/Give Me Time	30

(see also Big Three, Mojos)

WAYNE FARO'S SCHMALTZ BAND

69	Deram DM 222	There's Still Time/Give It Time	40

FARQUAHAR

71	Elektra EK45713	Hanging On By A Thread/Start Living	6
71	Elektra EKS 74088	FARQUAHAR (LP)	12

GARY FARR (& THE T-BONES)

65	Columbia DB 7608	Give All She's Got/Don't Stop And Stare (as Gary Farr & T-Bones)	50
68	Marmalade 598 007	Everyday/Green (with Kevin Westlake)	25
69	Marmalade 598 017	Hey Daddy/The Vicar And The Pope	25
71	CBS 5430	Revolution Of The Seasons/Old Man Boulder	12
65	Columbia SEG 8414	DEM BONES, DEM BONES, DEM T-BONES (EP)	100
69	Marmalade 608 013	TAKE SOMETHING WITH YOU (LP)	250
71	CBS 64138	STRANGE FRUIT (LP, with Richard Thompson & Mighty Baby)	100

(see also T-Bones, Richard Thompson, Mighty Baby, Meic Stevens, Kevin Westlake & Gary Farr)

MARY ANN FARRAR & SATIN SOUL

76	Brunswick BR 38	Stoned Out Of My Mind/Living In The Footsteps Of Another Girl	10

BILLY FARRELL

58	Philips PB 828	Yeah Yeah/Someday (You'll Want Me To Want You)	22

DO & DENA FARRELL

57	HMV POP 427	Young Magic/New Love Tonight	15

MICK FARREN

78	Logo GO 321	Half Price Drinks/I Don't Want To Go This Way (thick card p/s, black and yellow on front)	6
78	Stiff LAST 4	ALL SCREWED UP (EP, as Mick Farren & Deviants)	8
70	Transatlantic TRA 212	MONA (THE CARNIVOROUS CIRCUS) (LP, lilac label with "t" logo)	100
78	Logo LOGO 2010	VAMPIRES STOLE MY LUNCH MONEY (LP, with lyric insert)	25
84	Psycho PSYCHO 20	MONA (THE CARNIVOROUS CIRCUS) (LP, reissue)	20

(see also Deviants, Twink)

FARRIERS

69	Broadside BRO 112	FARRIERS (LP)	20
76	Broadside BRO 119	KEMPION BRUMMAGEM BALLADS (LP, featuring Dick Brice)	50

MIA FARROW

68	Dot DOT 116	Lullaby From Rosemary's Baby (Parts 1 & 2)	8

FARTZ

82	Alt. Tentacles VIRUS 17	WORLD FULL OF HATE (12" EP with poster)	25

FASCINATIONS

67	Stateside SS 594	Girls Are Out To Get You/You'll Be Sorry	75
67	Stateside SS 594	Girls Are Out To Get You/You'll Be Sorry (DJ copy)	150
68	Sue WI 4049	Girls Are Out To Get You/You'll Be Sorry (reissue)	40
71	Mojo 2092 004	Girls Are Out To Get You/You'll Be Sorry (2nd reissue)	8
71	Mojo 2092 018	I'm So Lucky He Loves Me/Say It Isn't So	8

FASCINATORS

58	Capitol CL 14942	Chapel Bells/I Wonder Who	350
59	Capitol CL 15062	Oh, Rose Marie/Fried Chicken And Macaroni	150

FASCINATORS

81	Penthouse PENT 9	Blue Movies/Monochrome Moon (p/s)	70

FASHION

79	Fashion FM 001	Steady Eddie Steady/Killing Time (p/s)	5
79	Fashion FM 002	Citinite/Wastelife (p/s)	5
80	Fashion FM 003	Silver Blades/Silver Blades (A Deeper Cut) (p/s)	5
81	Arista 12440	Move On/Mutant Dance Move (p/s)	10
79	Fashion FML001	PRODUCT PERFECT (LP)	15

FASHIONS

68	Stateside SS 2115	I.O.U. (A Lifetime Of Love)/When Love Slips Away	10
69	Evolution E 2444	I.O.U. (A Lifetime Of Love)/He Gives Me Love (La La La)	5

FAST

76	CBS SCBS 6236	Boys Will Be Boys/Wow Pow Bash Crash	6

FAST BREEDERS & RADIO ACTORS

78	Nuke NUKE 235	Nuclear Waste/Digital Love (in p/s, with insert)	18
78	Nuke NUKE 235	Nuclear Waste/Digital Love	10

(see also Radio Actors)

FAST CARS
79	Streets Ahead SA 3	The Kids Just Wanna Dance/You're So Funny (1,000 only, p/s)..250

FAST EDDIE (1)
82	Well Suspect BLAM 001	My Babe/Help Me/Sweet Sensations (p/s) 8

FAST EDDIE (2)
88	Westside DJINT 04	Acid Thunder (12")...25
88	Westside PROMO 18	My Melody/Halloween House (12") (with Slick Master Rick)..20

FAST SET
80	Axis AXIS 1	Junction One/Children Of The Revolution (p/s)..20

FASTBACKS
89	Subway SUBWAY 26	Wrong Wrong Wrong/In America (p/s) 6

FAT
71	RCA LSA 3009	FAT (LP)..30

FATAL CHARM
87	Native 7N TV 20	Lucille/To Master A Plan (p/s)..6
79	Company CR 005	Paris/Glitterbit/Out Of My Head 8

FATAL MICROBES
79	Small Wonder SMALL 20	Violence Grows/Beautiful Pictures/Cry Baby (p/s) 8

(see also Pete Fender)

FATAL MICROBES/POISON GIRLS
79	Small Wonder WEENY 3	FATAL MICROBES MEET THE POISON GIRLS (12" EP, with insert)...8

(see also Poison Girls)

FATHEAD
83	Greensleeves GRED 118	Champion/Stop All The Fight (12")..20

FATHER'S ANGELS
68	MGM MGM 1459	Don't Knock It/Bok To Bach...250
68	MGM MGM 1459	Don't Knock It/Bok To Bach (DJ Copy) 300
75	Black Magic BM 103	Back To Bach/Disco Trucking 6

FATHER'S BROWN
70	Decca F23059	Maybe/The Yellow Moon Is High 20

FATMAN VERSUS JAH SHAKA
80	Live & Love LAP12	DUB CONFRONTATION (LP) 15

FAT MATTRESS
69	Polydor 56352	Naturally/Iridescent Butterfly 10
69	Polydor 56367	Magic Forest/Bright New Way 15
70	Polydor 2058 053	Highway/Black Sheep Of The Family 15
69	Polydor 582/583 056	FAT MATTRESS (LP, open-out sleeve, red label)..50
70	Polydor 2383 025	FAT MATTRESS II (LP, red label)...50

(see also Noel Redding Band, Jimi Hendrix Experience, Flowerpot Men, Juicy Lucy)

FATS & CHESSMEN
62	Pye International 7N 25122	Big Ben Twist/Old Macdonald Had A Twist...6

ERIC FATTER
69	Camel CA 20	Since You've Been Gone (actually Eric Fratter)/WINSTON HINES: Cool Down (B-side actually by Winston Hinds) 12

(see also Eric Fratter, Afrotones)

FAT TULIPS
90	Heaven HV 01	Where's Clare Grogan Now?/To Put It Bluntly (p/s)..6
90	Heaven HV 02	FOUR SONGS FOR SIMON EP..6
90	Heaven HV 04	FERENSWAY EP (hand-painted sleeve)...6
91	Marineville MARINE 1	Passionate Friend/Treason/Reward (p/s, 'The Tulip Explodes' artwork) 6
88	Sweet William BILLY 001	You Opened My Eyes/ROSEHIPS: Ask Johnny Dee (33rpm flexi, p/s w/insert)....................15

ERNIE FAULKNER
63	Sway SW 003	Beautiful Girl/SAM DANIELS: Tell Me Baby (both with The Planets).....................................10

NEWTON FAULKNER
07	Brightside 8869722312	HAND BUILT BY ROBOTS (LP)..12

FAUST
72	Faust/Polydor 2001-299	It's A Bit Of A Pain/So Far 25
79	Recommended RR 2.5	It's A Bit Of A Pain/So Far (p/s, reissue)..8
96	Die Stadt 011	Right Between Yr Eyes (p/s, Uberschall Festival single,with Stereolab and Foetus) 20
90	Chemical Imbalance CI 08	Live In Hamburg (issued free with Chemical Imbalance magazine) 25
97	CRDC 11	Mikrowaves, Magic Brew And R Be Yr Ey (10", p/s) 8
79	Recommended RR 1.5	EXTRACTS FROM FAUST PARTY 3: Extract 1/Extract 4 (EP) 12
80	Recommended RR 6.5	EXTRACTS FROM FAUST PARTY 3: Extract 2/Extract 6 (EP) 12
71	Polydor 2310 142	FAUST (LP, initial pressing on clear vinyl, with clear sleeve & clear insert)......................120
71	Polydor 2310 142	FAUST (LP, insert)..50
72	Polydor 2310 196	SO FAR (LP, with 9 prints in wallet) 120
73	Virgin VC 501	THE FAUST TAPES (LP)..25
73	Virgin V 2004	FAUST IV (LP) 25
79	Recommended R.R. 2	SO FAR (LP, reissue, with 10 insert prints, numbered, 600 only)..40
80	Recommended RR 6	THE FAUST TAPES (LP, plastic bag cover) 20
90	Table Of The Elements 26	CONCERTS 1: LIVE IN HAMBURG (CD)..30
94	Table Of The Elements 27	CONCERTS 2: LIVE IN LONDON (CD)...30

(see also Toni Conrad & Faust)

FAVOURITES
80	4 Play FOUR 002	S.O.S./Favourite Shoes (p/s) 25
80	4 Play FOUR 003	Angelica/Cold (p/s) 20

FAVOURITE SONS
65	Mercury MF 911	That Driving Beat/Walkin' Walkin' Walkin' 150

MINT VALUE £

WALLY FAWKES (& HIS TROGLODYTES)

57	Decca FJ 10855	Petite Fleur/Baby Brown (with Sandy Brown Quintet)	8
57	Decca FJ 10936	Sent For You Yesterday And Here You Came Today/Why Can't You Behave	10
58	Decca F 11002	The Pilot Fish And The Whale/Pale Blues	10
57	Decca DEF 6407	AND HIS TROGLODYTES (EP)	12
60	Decca DFE 6600	FLOOK DIGS JAZZ (EP)	12
61	Decca STO 136	A NIGHT AT THE SIX BELLS (EP)	20
56	Decca LF 1214	TAKIN' IT EASY (LP, with Bruce Turner)	20
58	Decca LF 312	FAWKES ON HOLIDAY (LP)	30

(see also Sandy Brown)

CHARLIE FAWN

| 80 | Warner Bros K 17566 | Always Something There To Remind Me/Poet For A Generation | 8 |

BILL FAY

67	Deram DM 143	Some Good Advice/Screams In The Ears	60
70	Deram Nova SDN 12	BILL FAY (LP, stereo)	300
70	Deram Nova DN 12	BILL FAY (LP, mono)	350
71	Deram SML 1079	TIME OF THE LAST PERSECUTION (LP, red/white label)	1000

FAY & BITTER SWEET

| 74 | A Rover AR 02 | You're A Pirate Lover/Message To You | 6 |

ALMA FAYE

| 78 | Flamingo FM 6 | I Believed/Instrumental | 30 |

FRANCIS FAYE

61	Vogue V 9186	I Wish I Could Shimmy Like My Sister Kate/Night And Day	10
61	Verve VLP 9007	SWINGING ALL THE WAY (LP)	12
65	Stateside SL 10129	YOU GOTTA GO! GO! GO! (LP)	20

LITTLE RITA FAYE

| 53 | MGM MGM 671 | Rock City Boogie/Wait A Little Longer (78) | 10 |

FAZE ACTION

95	Nuphonic NUX 102	Full Motion (12")	8
00	Nuphonic NUX 150	Samba (12")	8
99	Nuphonic NUX 139	MOVING CITIES (2xLP)	15

FAZED IDJUTS

| 00 | U Star USR 002 | Dust Of Life (12") | 20 |

F.B.I. (FOLK BLUES INC.)

73	A&M AMS 7050	I Wonder What She's Doing Tonight/Boogaloo Boo-Boo	10
76	Good Earth GD 6	F.B.I./The Time Is Right To Leave The City	25
77	Good Earth GDS 802	F.B.I. (LP)	50
66	Eyemark EMS 1006	Don't Hide/When The Ship Comes In	25

FEAR OF FLYING (1)

| 81 | Fear Of Flying 001 | Tired/This Thing | 8 |

FEAR OF FLYING (2)

| 06 | Young And Lost YALC 0011 | Three's A Crowd/Forget-Me-Nots (p/s) | 7 |

FEARN'S BRASS FOUNDRY

| 68 | Decca F 12721 | Don't Change It/John White | 50 |
| 68 | Decca F 12835 | Now I Taste The Tears/Love, Sink And Drown | 25 |

FEAR OF FALLING

| 83 | Excellent XL 7 | Like A Lion/You My Prodigal Son (p/s) | 20 |

CHARLIE FEATHERS

| 76 | Red Neck R 100 | Tongue Tied Jill/Gone Gone Gone | 7 |
| 76 | Charley CEP 116 | CHARLIE FEATHERS (EP) | 8 |

CHARLIE FEATHERS/MAC CURTIS

| 74 | Polydor 2310 293 | ROCKABILLY KINGS (LP, withdrawn) | 20 |

(see also Mac Curtis)

FEATURES (1)

| 77 | Progress PR 01 | Drab City/Job Satisfaction | 50 |

FEATURES (2)

80	Double D DDEE 3	Go Now/Make Me Wanna	10
80	ASM HIT 06	She Makes Me Blue/Don't Let Them Know	20
81	AFM PET 01	Monday-Friday/Cue The Next Army	20

FEDERALMEN

| 70 | London HLU 10303 | Soul Serenade/Scorcher | 8 |

FEDERALS (JAMAICA)

67	Island WI 3126	Penny For Your Song/I've Passed This Way Before	30
68	Island WI 3152	Shocking Love/By The River	25
69	High Note HS 024	Wailing Festival/Me And My Baby (B-side actually "By The River")	15
70	Camel CA 40	In This World/You Better Call On Me (B-side actually "Shocking Love")	10

FEDERALS (U.K.)

63	Parlophone R 4988	Brazil/In A Persian Market	15
63	Parlophone R 5013	Boot Hill/Keep On Dancing With Me	15
64	Parlophone R 5100	The Climb/Dance With A Dolly	15
64	Parlophone R 5139	Marlena/Please Believe Me	15
64	Parlophone R 5193	Twilight Time/Lost And Alone	15
65	Parlophone R 5320	Bucket Full Of Love/Leah	25

(see also Winston's Fumbs, Yes)

FEEDER

96	Echo ECS 13	TWO COLOURS: Pictures Of Rain/Chicken On A Bone (p/s, clear vinyl)	50
96	Echo ECSCD 13	TWO COLOURS: Pictures Of Rain/Chicken On A Bone (CD, 1,000 only)	50
96	Echo ECS 27	Stereo World/My Perfect Day (p/s)	30
97	Echo ECS 32	Tangerine/Rhubarb (die-cut p/s)	15

97	Echo ECS 36	Cement/Pictures Of Pain (red vinyl, p/s)	6
97	Echo ECS 42	Crash/Here In The Bubble (clear vinyl, numbered p/s)	6
97	Echo ECS 44	High/Wishing For The Sun (sky blue vinyl, p/s)	5
98	Echo ECS 052	Suffocate/Eclipse (purple vinyl, p/s)	5
99	Echo ECS 75	Day In Day Out/Dance To Disco/Honeyfuzz (white vinyl, p/s)	5
01	Echo ECS 106	Buck Rogers/Sex Type Drug (orange vinyl. p/s)	5
01	Echo ECS 107	Seven Days In The Sun/Just A Day (p/s)	5
01	Echo ECS 116	Turn/Come Back Around (purple vinyl, p/s)	5
01	Echo ECS 121	Just A Day/Early (orange vinyl, p/s)	5
01	Echo	Turn/Bad Hair Day (6-12 white label promo competition prizes. 7" die-cut sleeve)	20
04	Echo ECS157A/B -1	Tumble and Fall/Victoria (12" white label promos auctioned for Warchild charity)	20
96	Echo ECHLP 9	SWIM (LP)	25
97	Echo ECHLP15	POLYPHENE (LP, vinyl re-issue of original CD album, with free High 7")	25
99	Echo ECHLP 28	YESTERDAY WENT TOO SOON (LP)	25
01	Echo ECHLP 34	ECHO PARK (LP, gatefold)	30
04	Echo ECHLP52	PICTURE OF PERFECT YOUTH (3xLP)	35
04	Echo ECHCD52	PICTURE OF PERFECT YOUTH (CD, internet only release - deleted)	25

FEELIES

79	Stiff (no cat. no.)	Fa Ce La/The Boy With Perpetual Nervousness/ Everybody's Got Something To Hide (Except Me And My Monkey) (flexidisc, promo only, free with Be Stiff fanzine issue 6, 5,000 only)	6
79	Rough Trade RT 24	Fa Ce La/Raised Eyebrows (p/s)	10
80	Stiff BUY 65	Everybody's Got Something To Hide/Original Love (p/s)	7
80	Stiff SEEZ 20	CRAZY RHYTHMS (LP)	25
86	Rough Trade ROUGH 104	THE GOOD EARTH (LP)	18

FELDER'S ORIOLES

65	Piccadilly 7N 35247	Down Home Girl/Misty	40
65	Piccadilly 7N 35269	Sweet Tasting Wine/Turn On Your Lovelight	20
66	Piccadilly 7N 35311	I Know You Don't Love Me No More/Only Three Can Play	20
66	Piccadilly 7N 35332	Back Street/Something You Got	25

(see also V.I.P.s, Mike Patto)

VICTOR FELDMAN BIG BAND/QUARTET

56	Tempo A 142	Big Top/Cabaletto	10
57	Tempo A 154	Jackpot/You Are My Heart's Desire	10
62	Fontana 267233	A Taste Of Honey/Valerie	10
55	Tempo EXA 29	BIG BAND (EP)	50
57	Tempo EXA 57	VICTOR FELDMAN IN LONDON -- THE QUARTET VOLUME 1 (EP)	60
57	Tempo EXA 67	VICTOR FELDMAN IN LONDON VOLUME 2 (EP)	60
58	Tempo EXA 85	MUTUAL ADMIRATION (EP, with Dizzy Reece)	60
53	Esquire EP 43	MODERN JAZZ QUARTET (EP)	40
53	Esquire EP 54	MODERN JAZZ QUARTET (EP)	20
53	Esquire EP 64	MODERN JAZZ QUINTET/SEXTET (EP)	25
53	Esquire EP 84	MODERN JAZZ QUARTET/SEXTET (EP)	20
54	Esquire EP 104	MODERN JAZZ QUARTET (EP)	40
54	Esquire EP 114	VIC FELDMAN ENCORE (EP)	15
54	Esquire 20 - 046	MULTIPLE TALENTS (LP)	60
55	Esquire 20 - 064	EXPERIMENT IN TIME (LP)	50
55	Tempo LAP 5	VICTOR FELDMAN'S SEXTET (10" LP)	200
56	Tempo LAP 6	VICTOR FELDMAN MODERN JAZZ QUARTET (10" LP)	170
57	Tempo TAP 8	VICTOR FELDMAN IN LONDON VOL. 1 (LP)	150
57	Tempo TAP 12	VICTOR FELDMAN IN LONDON VOL. 2 (LP)	140
58	Tempo TAP 19	TRANSATLANTIC ALLIANCE (LP)	300
59	Contemporary LAC 12172	THE ARRIVAL OF VICTOR FELDMAN (LP)	20
80s	Jasmine JASM 2002	TRANSATLANTIC ALLIANCE (LP, reissue)	12
80s	Jasmine JASM 2023	IN LONDON VOL. 1 (LP, reissue)	12
80s	Jasmine JASM	IN LONDON VOL. 2 (LP, reissue)	12

(see also Dizzy Reece, Tubby Hayes)

VICTOR FELDMAN, TERRY GIBBS & LARRY BUNKER

| 60 | Top Rank 30/007 | VIBES TO THE POWER OF THREE (LP) | 20 |

JOSE FELICIANO

67	RCA RCA 1608	My Foolish Heart/Only Once	10
68	RCA RCA 1715	Light My Fire/California Dreamin'	6
68	RCA RCA 1769	Hi Heel Sneakers/Hitchcock Railway	5
69	RCA RCA 1871	And The Sun Will Shine/Rain	5
70	RCA RCA 1998	Destiny/Susie-Q	5
71	RCA 2071	Shake A Hand/There's No One About	6
74	RCA RCA PB10094	Golden Lady/Virgo	10

FELIUS ANDROMEDA

| 72 | Cactus CT 2 | After The Storm/Rainbow Chasing (as Andromeda) | 15 |
| 67 | Decca F 12694 | Meditations/Cheadle Heath Delusions | 50 |

(see also Denis Couldry)

FELIX & HIS GUITAR

| 59 | London HLU 8875 | Chili Beans/Puerto Rican Riot | 10 |

LENNIE FELIX, BRIAN LEMON, KEITH INGHAM, RALPH SUTTON

| 75 | 77 77S 58 | PIANO SUMMIT (LP) | 20 |

JULIE FELIX

65	Decca F 12246	Someday Soon/I've Got Nothing But Time	6
66	Fontana TF 734	I Can't Touch The Sun/Rainy Day	6
67	Fontana TF 875	The Magic Of The Playground/Somewhere There's Gotta Be Me	6
68	Fontana TF 969	That's No Way To Say Goodbye/The World Goes Round And Round	6
70	RAK 101	If I Could/Alone	5
71	RAK 106	Snakeskin/Watching Waiting	40
72	RAK 14	Clothos Web/Windy Morning	25
65	Decca DFE 8613	SINGS BOB DYLAN & WOODY GUTHRIE (EP)	10
66	Fontana TE 17474	SONGS FROM THE FROST REPORT (EP)	10
64	Decca LK 4626	JULIE FELIX (LP)	18

MINT VALUE £

65	Decca LK 4683	SINGS DYLAN AND GUTHRIE (LP)	18
65	Decca LK 4724	SECOND ALBUM (LP)	12
66	Decca LK 4820	THE THIRD ALBUM (LP)	12
67	Fontana (S) TL 5437	FLOWERS (LP)	12
77	Monte Rosa CTC 5007	HOTA CHOCOLATA (LP)	12

MIKE FELIX
| 66 | Pye 7N 17058 | You Belong To Me/Booga Dee | 25 |
| 67 | Decca F 12701 | Blueberry Hill/I Don't Think You Want Me Anymore | 8 |

(see also Migel 5)

RORY FELLOWES
| 68 | S n B 55-3877 | Nina/Endlessly Friendlessly Blue | 20 |

GRAHAM FELLOWS
| 85 | Wicked Frog FROG 01 | LOVE AT THE HACIENDA (LP) | 40 |

(see also Jilted John)

FELT
79	Shanghai S79/CUS 321	Index/Break It (p/s, early copies have poem on rear sleeve, yellow labels)	100
79	Shanghai S79/CUS 321	Index/Break It (p/s, no notes on rear sleeve)	60
81	Cherry Red CHERRY 26	Something Sends Me To Sleep/Red Indians/Something Sends Me To Sleep (Version)/Red Indians (p/s)	18
82	Cherry Red CHERRY 45	My Face Is On Fire/Trails Of Colour Dissolve (p/s)	18
83	Cherry Red CHERRY 59	Penelope Tree/A Preacher In New England (p/s)	12
83	Cherry Red 12CHERRY 59	Penelope Tree/A Preacher In New England/ Now Summer's Spread Its Wings Again (12", p/s)	15
84	Cherry Red CHERRY 78	Mexican Bandits/The World Is As Soft As Lace (p/s)	12
84	Cherry Red CHERRY 81	Sunlight Bathed The Golden Glow/Fortune (p/s)	15
84	Cherry Red 12CHERRY 81	Sunlight Bathed The Golden Glow/Fortune/Sunlight Strings (12", p/s)	12
85	Cherry Red 12CHERRY 89	Primitive Painters/Cathedral (12", p/s, with Liz Frazer)	10
86	Creation CRE 027	Ballad Of The Band/I Didn't Mean To Hurt You (p/s)	12
86	Creation CRE 027T	Ballad Of The Band/I Didn't Mean To Hurt You/Candles In A Church/Ferdinand (12", p/s)	15
86	Creation CRE 032	Rain Of Crystal Spires/I Will Die With My Head In Flames (p/s)	12
86	Creation CRE 032T	Rain Of Crystal Spires/Gather Up Your Wings And Fly/I Will Die With My Head In Flames/Sandman's On The Rise Again (12", p/s)	12
87	Creation CRE 048T	The Final Resting Of The Ark/Autumn/Fore Circle/There's No Such Thing As Victory/Buried Wild Blind (12", p/s)	12
88	Cherry Red CDCHERRY 89	Primitive Painters/Cathedral (reissue, picture CD)	10
88	Creation CRE 060	Space Blues/Tuesday's Secret (ltd. ed. die-cut company sleeve)	12
88	Creation CRE 060T	Space Blues/Be Still/Female Star/Tuesday's Secret (12")	25
89	el GPO F44	Get Out Of My Mirror (1-side flexi, in-store freebie)	12
82	Cherry Red MRED 25	CRUMBLING THE ANTISEPTIC BEAUTY (LP)	20
84	Cherry Red MRED 57	THE SPLENDOUR OF FEAR (LP)	25
84	Cherry Red BRED 63	STRANGE IDOLS PATTERN (LP)	20
85	Cherry Red B-RED 65	IGNITE THE SEVEN CANNONS AND SET SAIL FOR THE SUN (LP, textured sleeve with lyric insert)	18
86	Creation CRELP 009	LET THE SNAKES CRINKLE THEIR HEADS TO DEATH (LP)	20
86	Creation CRELP 011	FOREVER BREATHES THE LONELY WORD (LP, with inner sleeve)	40
87	Creation CRELP 017	POEM OF THE RIVER (LP)	25
87	Cherry Red BRED 79	GOLD MINE TRASH (LP, with inner)	15
88	Creation CRELP 030	PICTORIAL JACKSON REVIEW (LP)	20
88	Creation CRELP 033	TRAIN ABOVE THE CITY (LP)	20
89	el ACME 24	ME AND A MONKEY ON THE MOON (LP)	20
90	Creation CRELP 069	BUBBLEGUM PERFUME (LP)	25

(see also Denim, Versatile Newts, Maurice Deebank, Cocteau Twins)

NARVEL FELTS
| 75 | ABC 4062 | Reconsider Me/Foggy Mountain Morning | 6 |

FEMININE TOUCH FEATURING DUKE DURRELL
| 76 | Paladin PAL 11 | You Make Me Come Alive/You Make Me Come Alive (Instrumental) | 5 |

FENCE
| 80 | BFD BFD 2 | Thinking That I Shouldn't/Thru With You/Hey Girl (p/s) | 15 |

JAYMES FENDA & VULCANS
| 64 | Parlophone R 5210 | Mistletoe Love/The Only Girl | 12 |

FREDDY FENDER
| 74 | ABC 4045 | Before The Next Teardrop Falls/Waiting For Your Love | 5 |

JAN FENDER
71	Prince Buster PB 5	Sea Of Love/PRINCE BUSTER: Heaven Help Us All	15
71	Fab FAB 164	Sweet P/CLIFF & ORGANIZERS: Mr Brown	25
71	Fab FAB 166	Holly Holy Version/Old Kentrone Version (as Jal Fender)	12

PETE FENDER
| 81 | Xntrix 2002 | FOUR FORMULAS (EP, in 8" silk-screened book p/s) | 30 |
| 81 | Xntrix 2002 | FOUR FORMULAS (EP, p/s) | 8 |

(see also Fatal Microbes, Omega Tribe)

FENDER BENDERS
| 79 | Sticky SL 001 | Big Green Thing/Hillman Hunter Paranoia (textured p/s, various colours) | 6 |

FENDERMEN
| 60 | Top Rank JAR 395 | Mule Skinner Blues/Torture | 12 |
| 60 | Top Rank JAR 513 | Don't You Just Know It/Beach Party | 20 |

FENMEN
64	Decca F 11955	Rag Doll/Be My Girl	20
65	Decca F 12269	I've Got Everthing You Need Babe/Every Little Day Now	15
66	CBS 202075	California Dreamin'/Is This Your Way?	12
66	CBS 202236	Rejected/Girl Don't Bring Me Down	25

(see also Bern Elliott & Fenmen, Pretty Things, Zac Zolar & Electric Banana)

PETER FENTON
| 66 | Fontana TF 748 | Marble Breaks, Iron Bends/Small Town | 15 |
| 67 | Fontana TF 789 | I Was Lord Kitcheners Valet/Walking In Circles | 15 |

SHANE FENTON (& FENTONES)

61	Parlophone R 4827	I'm A Moody Guy/Five Foot Two, Eyes Of Blue	10
62	Parlophone R 4866	Walk Away/Fallen Leaves On The Ground	10
62	Parlophone R 4883	It's All Over Now/Why Little Girl	10
62	Parlophone R 4921	Cindy's Birthday/It's Gonna Take Magic	10
62	Parlophone R 4951	Too Young For Sad Memories/You're Telling Me	10
63	Parlophone R 4982	I Ain't Got Nobody/Hey Miss Ruby	10
63	Parlophone R 5020	A Fool's Paradise/You Need Love (solo)	10
63	Parlophone R 5047	Don't Do That/I'll Know (solo)	10
64	Parlophone R 5131	Hey, Lulu/I Do, Do You?	15
72	Fury FY 305	Eastern Seaboard/Blind Fool	20
77	EMI NUT 2696	SHANE FENTON & THE FENTONES (EP)	10
74	Contour 2870 409	GOOD ROCKIN' TONIGHT (LP)	12

(see also Fentones)

FENTONES

62	Parlophone R 4899	The Mexican/Lover's Guitar	10
62	Parlophone R 4937	The Breeze And I/Just For Jerry	20

(see also Shane Fenton)

FENWAYS

65	Liberty LIB 66082	Walk/Whip And Jerk	25

RAY FENWICK

78	Mercury 6007 176	Queen Of The Night/I Wanna Boogie	6
71	Decca SKL 5090	KEEP AMERICA BEAUTIFUL, GET A HAIRCUT (LP, blue/silver label with small logo)	60

(see also Spencer Davis Group, After Tea, Fancy, Ian Gillan Band, Wizard's Convention, Murgatroyd Band, Marlon, Forcefield, Syndicats, South Coast Ska Kings, Rupert's People)

FENWYCK

68	ERA ERA 100	State Of Mind/Away	50

FERDIA

78	Polydor 2904 012	A SIGH FOR OLD TIMES (LP)	15

FERDINAND & DILL

70	Pama PM 805	Take Back Your Nicklet/Blueberry Hill	8

WINSTON FERGUS

79	Burning Rockers BRD 016	Corner Girl/Corner Dub (12")	25
82	Burning Rockers BRD 037	Pay To Live/Earth In Dub (12")	40
82	Fergie Music FM 002	In Ting Sound/My Own Way Heart (12")	150
78	Arawak ARK DD 001	Fly Natty Dread/Loving Pauper (12")	40

H-BOMB FERGUSON

54	Esquire 10-372	Feel Like I Do/My Love (78)	25

HELENA FERGUSON

67	London HLZ 10164	Where Is The Party?/My Terms	50

JESSIE LEE FERGUSON & OUTER LIMITS

69	Pye International 7N 25492	New Shoes/Puttin' It On, Puttin' It Off	12

JOHNNY FERGUSON

60	MGM MGM 1059	Angela Jones/Blue Serge And White Lace	12
61	MGM MGM 1119	No One Can Love You/The Valley Of Love	7

MAYNARD FERGUSON ORCHESTRA

58	Emarcy EJL 1270	JAM SESSION (LP)	15
58	Emarcy EJL 1275	AROUND THE HORN (LP)	20
58	Emarcy EJL 1287	DIMENSIONS (LP)	20
59	Columbia 33SX 1146	MESSAGE FROM NEWPORT (LP)	20
60	Mercury MMC 14050	THE BOY WITH LOTS OF BRASS (LP, also stereo CMS 18034)	20
60	Columbia 33SX 1210	MESSAGE FROM BIRDLAND (LP, also stereo SCX 3245)	18
60	Columbia 33SX 1270	JAZZ FOR DANCING (LP, also stereo SCX 3338)	20
61	Columbia 33SX 1301	NEWPORT SUITE (LP, also stereo SCX 3368)	20
62	Columbia 33SX 1439	MAYNARD 62 (LP)	20
66	Fontana TL 5274	BLUES ROAR (LP)	20
66	Fontana TL 5293	COLOR HIM WILD (LP)	20
67	Fontana TL 5310	SEXTET (LP)	20
68	Atlantic 2464008	FREAKY (LP)	20
69	CBS 63514	BALLAD STLYE OF MAYNARD FERGUSON (LP)	40
70	CBS 64101	WORLD OF (M.F. HORN) (LP)	12
71	CBS 64432	ALIVE AND WELL IN LONDON (LP)	20
72	CBS 65027	M.F. HORN 2 (LP, gatefold)	15
73	CBS 65589	M.F. HORN 3 (LP)	20
73	CBS 65952	M.F. HORN 4 (LIVE AT JIMMYS) (LP)	20

ALEX FERGUSSON

92	Private Pressing AF 001	ALEX FERGUSSON (LP, white label, 500 copies, no sleeve)	25

(see also Alternative TV, Psychic TV)

FERKO STRING BAND

55	London HL 8140	Alabama Jubilee/Sing A Little Melody	25
55	London HLF 8183	Ma (She's Making Eyes At Me)/You Are My Sunshine	25
55	London HLF 8215	Happy Days Are Here Again/Deep In The Heart Of Texas	25
58	London HL 7052	Happy Days Are Here Again/Alabama Jubilee (export issue)	18
56	London RE-F 1041	PHILADELPHIA MUMMERS PARADE VOL. 1 (EP)	10
56	London RE-F 1052	PHILADELPHIA MUMMERS PARADE VOL. 2 (EP)	10
57	London HB-C 1064	THE FERKO STRING BAND VOL. 1 (10" LP)	15

FERMENA

71	Pama PM 839	Come What May/Version (B-side with Ranny)	8
73	Pama PM 879	Wonderful Dreams/Version	8

PHIL FERNANDO

58	Pye Nixa 7N 15142	Blonde Bombshell/Make Ready for Love	15
62	Palette PG 9029	(Come On And) Do The High Life/High Life Girl	10

MINT VALUE £

ANDY FERNBACH
69	Liberty LBL/LBS 83233	IF YOU MISS YOUR CONNEXION (LP, blue label)	150

(see also Groundhogs)

MAJA FERNICK
72	Philips 6006 196	Give Me Your Love Again/Flowers In The City	30

DIANE FERRAZ & NICKY SCOTT
66	Columbia DB 7824	Me And You/Don't Pretend	8
66	Columbia DB 7897	You've Got To Learn/Like You As You Are	5
66	Columbia DB 7963	Sh-Boom, Sh-Boom/Allah Mobish	5

(see also Nicky Scott, Ferris Wheel)

JOE FERRER & HIS DEVILS BOYS
61	Oriole CB 1629	Rockin' Crickets/Blue Guitar	20

FERRET
74	Deram DM 412	Hudson Bay/Henry's Song	7

EUGENE FERRIS
66	Planet PLF 112	There Was A Smile In Your Eyes/Soft Moonlight (without p/s)	15
66	Planet PLF 112	There Was A Smile In Your Eyes/Soft Moonlight (with p/s)	30

GEORGE FERRIS
71	Ackee ACK 117	With Every Dream/Diana	6

FERRIS WHEEL
67	Pye 7N 17387	I Can't Break The Habit/Number One Guy	25
68	Pye 7N 17538	Let It Be Me/You Look At Me	8
68	Pye 7N 17631	The Na Na Song/Three Cats	8
69	Polydor 56366	Can't Stop Now/I Know You Well	6
67	Pye NPL 18203	CAN'T BREAK THE HABIT (LP)	40
70	Polydor 583 066	FERRIS WHEEL (LP, lyric insert, red label)	25

(see also Linda Lewis, West Five)

BRYAN FERRY
73	Island IDJ 1	These Foolish Things/Sympathy For The Devil/Baby I Don't Care/ Loving You Is Sweeter Than Ever (promo)	30
74	Island WIP 6196	The 'In' Crowd/Chance Meeting (in p/s)	8
75	Island WIP 6234	You Go To My Head/Re-Make, Re-Model (DJ copies in generic promo p/s)	20
78	Polydor PPSP 10	Hold On I'm Coming/Take Me To The River (12", unissued, promo only, numbered stamped p/s)	20
73	Island ILPS 9239	THESE FOOLISH THINGS (LP, unissued gatefold sleeve)	400
76	Island ILPS 9367	LET'S STICK TOGETHER (LP, original issue)	15
78	Polydor POLD 5003	THE BRIDE STRIPPED BARE (LP, original with A//3 P matrix, includes 'Broken Wings', white label test pressings only)	200
94	Virgin V2751	MAMOUNA (LP)	40

(see also Roxy Music)

CATHERINE FERRY
76	Barclay BAR 42	One, Two, Three/1, 2, 3	12

MANFREDO FEST
79	Bluebird BRT 1	Jungle Kitten (5.30)/Jungle Kitten (3.36)/Send In The Clowns (12")	10

FESTIVAL
78	Nevis NEV 107	Something In Your Smile/Let's Make Love	45

FEVER
71	Decca F23156	The Moth And The Flame/It's So Peaceful	10

FEVER TREE
68	MCA MU 1043	San Francisco Girls/Come With Me	10
68	Uni UNLS 102	FEVER TREE (LP)	80
68	MCA MUPS 347	ANOTHER TIME, ANOTHER PLACE (LP)	50

FIAT LUX
83	Polydor FIAT 1	Photography/Aqua Vitae (p/s)	5

FICKLE FINGER
69	Page One POF 150	Fickle Lizzie-Anne/Cellophane Mary Jane	10

(see also Matchmakers, Mark Wirtz)

FICKLE PICKLE
70	Fontana TF 1069	Millionaire/Sam And Sadie	15
70	Philips 6006 038	Maybe I'm Amazed/Sitting On A Goldmine	6
72	B & C CB 178	California Calling/Doctor Octopus	12

FIDD
69	Polydor 56320	Guai Guai (From the film 'Baby Love')/Happy Walk	25

FI-DELS
72	Jay Boy BOY 69	Try A Little Harder/You Never Do Right (	15
72	Jay Boy BOY 69	Try A Little Harder/You Never Do Right (DJ Copy)	30
70s	DJM DJS 689	Try A Little Harder/KEYMAN STRINGS: Instrumental Version (DJ copy p/s £20)	10

KEITH FIELD
68	Polydor 56278	The Day That War Broke Out/Stop Thief	45

ALAN FIELDING
61	Decca F 11404	Scatter Brain/I've Got To Learn To Forget	8
62	Decca F11518	Too Late To Worry, Too Blue To Cry/You Reap Just What You Sow	6

FENELLA FIELDING
66	Columbia DB 8086	Big Bad Mouse/Later	7

JERRY FIELDING & HIS ORCHESTRA
54	London HL 8017	When I Grow Too Old To Dream/Button Up Your Overcoat	30
55	London HL 7001	Faintly Reminiscent/Blues Serenade (export issue)	15
55	London HL 7002	Pea-nut Vendor/Can't Help Lovin' Dat Man (export issue)	15
55	London HL 7003	Tea For Two/Here In My Arms (export issue)	15

55	London HL 7004	I'm In Love/Blue Prelude (export issue)	15
55	Brunswick 05399	The Gypsy In My Soul/The Glory Of Love	10
55	London RE-P 1026	DANCE DATE VOL. 1 (EP)	15
54	London H-APB 1022	FAINTLY REMINISCENT (10" LP)	15
54	London H-APB 1027	PLAYS A DANCE CONCERT (10" LP)	15
58	Brunswick LAT 8244	FIELDINGS ESRMULA (LP)	15

FIELD MICE

88	Sarah SARAH 012	Emma's House/When You Sleep/Fabulous Friend/The Last Letter (p/s)	15
88	Sarah SARAH 18	Sensitive/When Morning Comes To Town/Penguins (foldout p/s, with poster)	18
89	Caff CAFF 2	I Can See Myself Alone Forever/Everything About You (foldaround p/s in poly bag with insert)	25
90	Sarah SARAH 024	Autumn Store Pt. 1/If You Need Someone/World In Me (p/s)	15
90	Sarah SARAH 025	Autumn Store Pt. 2/Anyone Else Isn't You/Bleak (p/s)	12
91	Sarah SARAH 44	September's Not So Far Away/Hello And Goodbye (p/s, with insert)	20
91	Sarah SARAH 57	Missing The Moon/A Wrong Turn And Raindrops/An Earlier Autumn (12", p/s)	10
90	Sarah SARAH 38	SO SAID KAY EP 10", p/s)	18
90	Sarah SARAH 402	SNOWBALL (10" LP)	20
90	Sarah SARAH 601	SKYWRITING (LP)	20
90	Sarah SARAH 606	COASTAL (LP)	45
91	Sarah SR607	FOR KEEPS (LP)	30

FIELDS

69	Uni UNLS 104	FIELDS (LP)	60
71	CBS 7555	A Friends Of Mine/Three Minstrels	15
71	CBS 69009	FIELDS (LP, with poster)	70
71	CBS 69009	FIELDS (LP, without poster)	30

(see also Rare Bird, Greenslade)

BILLY FIELDS

| 55 | MGM SP 1126 | Sincerely/Thrilled | 6 |
| 59 | Mercury AMT 1067 | The Greatest Love In The World/No Other Love | 10 |

ERNIE FIELDS & HIS ORCHESTRA

59	London HL 8985	In The Mood/Christopher Columbus (with tri-centre)	8
59	London HL 8985	In The Mood/Christopher Columbus (78)	15
60	London HL 9100	Chattanooga Choo Choo/Workin' Out	18
60	London HL 9227	Raunchy/My Prayer	10
60	London RE 1260	SAXY (EP)	40
60	London HA 2263	IN THE MOOD (LP)	40

IRVING FIELDS TRIO & ORCHESTRA

| 54 | Parlophone CMSP 9 | Mr. Piano Player/Cuban Carnival (export issue) | 10 |

KANSAS FIELDS & MILTON SEALEY

| 56 | Ducretet DEP 95017 | KANSAS FIELDS & MILTON SEALEY (EP) | 10 |

FIELDS OF THE NEPHILIM

84	Tower N1	BURNING THE FIELDS (12" EP, red/black p/s)	30
85	Tower N1/Jung. JUNG 28T	BURNING THE FIELDS (12" EP, green p/s with insert & band photo label)	8
85	Tower N1/Jung. JUNG 28T	BURNING THE FIELDS (12" EP, green & other coloured vinyl export issue)	8
86	Situation 2 SIT 42	Power/Secrets (7", white label promos only, stickered plain sleeve)	15
87	Situation 2 SIT 46	Preacher Man/Laura II (p/s, swith Beggars Banquet sticker)	35
87	Situation 2 SIT 46	Preacher Man/Laura II (p/s)	25
87	SITUATION 2 SIT 48T	Blue Water (1 track 12" promo)	20
87	Situation 2 SIT 48	Blue Water/In Every Dream Home A Heartache (p/s)	10
87	Situation 2 SIT 48T	Blue Water (Electrostatic)/In Every Dream Home A Heartache (live)/Blue Water (Hot Wire) (12", p/s, with poster)	15
87	Situation 2 SIT 48T	Blue Water (Electrostatic)/In Every Dream Home A Heartache (live)/Blue Water (Hot Wire) (12", p/s, without poster)	8
87	House Of Dolls HOD 15	Dawnrazor (on free EP with House Of Dolls magazine, issue 15)	8
89	Situation 2 SIT 57	Psychonaut/Celebrate (Second Seal) (blue/green p/s)	5
90	Beggars Banquet BEG 250	Sumerland/Phobia (live) (no p/s)	5
88	Situation 2 SITU 22	THE NEPHILIM (LP, gatefold sleeve, with inner)	12
88	Situation 2 SITU 22L	THE NEPHILIM (LP, 2 x 45rpm 12", gatefold sleeve, numbered)	20

FIEND

| 84 | Endangered EDR 1 | STAND ALONE EP | 18 |

FIESTAS

59	London HL 8870	So Fine/Last Night I Dreamed	45
59	London HL 8870	So Fine/Last Night I Dreamed (78)	35
71	Atlantic 2091 121	So Fine/Broken Heart	8

FIFE REIVERS

| 69 | Columbia SCX 6371 | FIFE REIVERS (LP) | 12 |

15 16 17

| 77 | Morpheus DEB 06 | Black Skin Boy/Version | 15 |
| 78 | Deb DEB 003 | Emotion/Castro Black (with Dennis Bovell) | 15 |

FIFTH AVENUE

| 65 | Immediate IM 002 | The Bells Of Rhymney/Just Like Anyone Would Do (in blue/white Immediate sleeve) | 40 |
| 65 | Immediate IM 002 | The Bells Of Rhymney/Just Like Anyone Would Do (in black/white Immediate sleeve) | 30 |

(see also Denny Gerrard, Warm Sounds)

FIFTH AVENUE BAND

| 69 | Reprise RSPL 6369 | FIFTH AVENUE BAND (LP) | 35 |

FIFTH COLUMN

| 66 | Columbia DB 8068 | Benjamin Day/There's Nobody There | 35 |

(see also Gerry Rafferty)

5TH DIMENSION

67	Liberty LIB 12051	Go Where You Wanna Go/Too Poor To Die	35
67	Liberty LIB 12051	Go Where You Wanna Go/Too Poor To Die (DJ Copy)	45
67	Liberty LIB 15037	Paper Cup/Poor Side Of Town	20
67	Liberty LBF 15014	Up Up And Away/Pattern People	6
67	Liberty LIB 12056	Another Day, Another Heartache/Rosecrans Blvd.	8

FIFTH ESTATE

68	Liberty LBF 15052	Carpet Man/Magic Garden	15
68	Liberty LBF 15072	Stoned Soul Picnic/Sailboat Song	10
68	Liberty LBF 15081	Ticket To Ride/Orange Air	6
68	Liberty LBF 15130	California Soul/It'll Never Be The Same	12
68	Liberty LBF 15143	Sweet Blindness/Good News	5
69	Liberty LBF 15180	California Soul/I'll Never Be The Same Again	5
69	Liberty LBF 15193	Aquarius — Let The Sun Shine In/Don'tcha Hear Me Callin' To Ya	5
69	Liberty LBF 15288	Wedding Bell Blues/Let It Be Me	5
69	Liberty LBF 15243	Sunshine Of Your Love/Working On A Groovy Thing	6
69	Liberty LBF 15308	Blowing Away/Skinny Man	6
70	Liberty LBF 15356	I'll Be Lovin' You Forever/Train Keep On Movin'	25
68	Liberty LBL/LBS 83098E	MAGIC GARDEN (LP)	15
67	Liberty LBL/LBS 83038	UP UP AND AWAY (LP)	15
68	Liberty LBL/LBS 83155E	STONED SOUL PICNIC (LP)	15
69	Liberty LBS 83205	AGE OF AQUARIUS (LP)	12
70	Liberty LBS 83228	THE FANTASTIC 5th DIMENSION (LP)	12

FIFTH ESTATE

67	Stateside SS 2034	Ding Dong The Witch Is Dead/Rub A Dub	10
67	Stateside SS 2068	Heigh Ho/It's Waiting There For You	10
68	Stateside SS 2105	Do Drop In/That's Love	7
69	Stateside SS 2125	Coney Island Sally/Tomorrow Is My Turn	10

FIFTY FANTASTICS

79	South Circular SGS 108	God's Got Religion/STEPPES: The Beat Drill (white label)	10
80	Dining Out TUX 5	God's Got Religion/The Beat Drill (reissue, foldout p/s, hand made labels)	10

(see also Steppes, Disco Zombies)

FIFTY FIVE DEGREES

79	No label or cat number	There's Gonna Be A Showdown/There's Gonna Be A Showdown (p/s)	20

FIFTY FOOT HOSE

69	Mercury SLML 4030	CAULDRON (LP)	140

50 YEAR VOID

92	BLADE 1	Blade's Love Machine (1-sided 12", white label promo, 100 only)	30

(see also St. Etienne, Sarah Cracknell)

FIGGY DUFF

80	Dingles DIN 326	FIGGY DUFF (LP)	40
85	Celtic CM 023	AFTER THE TEMPEST (LP, with insert)	30

NESTOR FIGUERAS, DAVID TOOP & PAUL BURWELL

77	Bead Records BEAD 6	NESTOR FIGUERAS, DAVID TOOP & PAUL BURWELL (LP)	40

PAULINE FILBY

60s	Church Miss. Soc. LIV/SP/81	I'm Hungry/NADIA CATTOUSE: The Larder	8
68	Herald ELR 1081	MY WORLD BY PAULINE FILBY (EP)	20
69	Herald LLR 567	SHOW ME A RAINBOW (LP)	90

(see also Narnia, Accolade, Gordon Giltrap)

PHILIP JOHN FILBY

71	Dart ART2007	David McKenzie/Close My Eyes And Stick With Me	8

FILE UNDER POP

79	Rough Trade RT 011	Heathrow/Corrugate/Heathrow SLB (p/s)	6

(see also AK Process)

FILMCAST

84	True Friends Music TF004	The Distant Heart/World Of Light	25

FILTHY RICH

87	JM TR 102	She's 17/Love Ain't A Fool (p/s)	20

(see also Trident)

FINAL CONFLICT

86	Futuresound FS 001	EP (EP)	10
86	Futuresound FS 002	THE TIME HAS ARRIVED (EP, with 22-page booklet)	10
89	Futuresound VFS 001	My England/Across The Room (stickered white sleeve)	20

FINAL TOUCH

70s	Myrrh MYR 1188	LOVE SONG (LP)	25

FINCH

78	Rockburgh ROC 103	GALLEONS OF PASSION (LP)	18

FINDERS KEEPERS (U.K.)

66	CBS 202249	Light/Power Of Love (withdrawn, promos may exist)	65
66	CBS 202249	Light/Come On Now	20
67	Fontana TF 892	Friday Kind Of Monday/On The Beach	40
68	Fontana TF 938	Sadie (The Cleaning Lady)/Without Her	20

(see also Trapeze, Glenn Hughes, News)

FINDERS KEEPERS (U.S.)

67	London HLH 10117	Lavender Blue/MICKEY DOLENZ: Don't Do It	12

JEM FINER

00s	no cat. no.	LONGPLAYER (LP, with book)	15

FINGERS (1)

66	Columbia DB 8026	I'll Take You Where The Music's Playing/My Way Of Thinking	20
67	Columbia DB 8112	All Kinds Of People/Circus With A Female Clown	45

(see also Crocheted Doughnut Ring, Legend)

FINGERS (2)

79	Ratchet RAT 102	Saints Alive/We're Alright	40

FINGERS INC.

87	Jack Trax 12 J TRAX 8	Distant Planet Club Mix/Distant Planet Dub Mix (12", stickered die-cut company sleeve)	45

88	Desire WANTX 6	Can You Feel It/My House (Acapella) (12", die-cut p/s)	30
88	Jack Trax JTX 20	Can You Feel It (4 Mixes) (12", p/s)	25
88	Jack Trax JTX 8	Distant Planet (Remix, 4 Mixes) (12")	60
89	Jack Trax JTX 2	Never No More Lonely/Music Takes Me Up/Distant Planet (Club MIx) (12")	30
88	Jack Trax FING 1	ANOTHER SIDE (2-LP, gatefold sleeve)	30

FINI TRIBE (101)

84	Finiflex LT 1001	CURLING & STRETCHING EP (12", p/s, original issue)	10
88	Finiflex FT 002	DESTIMONY EP (12", p/s)	10
91	Finiflex/One Little Indian	101: Sonic Shuffle (Edit)/101: 303 (3D Bass Edit) (promo only, plain stickered sleeve)	5

FINK BROTHERS

| 85 | Zarjazz JAZZ S2 | Mutants IN Mega-City One/Mutant Blues (shaped picture disc) | 10 |
| 85 | Zarjazz JAZZ2-12 | Mutants IN Mega-City One/Mutant Blues (12", p/s with poster) | 12 |

(see also Madness)

LEE FINN & RHYTHM MEN

| 63 | Starlite ST45 103 | High Class Feelin'/Pour Me A Glass Of Wine | 100 |

FINN MACCUILL

| 77 | private pressing | SINK YE SWIM YE (LP) | 80 |

SIMON FINN

| 70 | Mushroom 100 MR 2 | PASS THE DISTANCE (LP, with lyric insert, white/brown labels) | 300 |

TIM FINN

| 83 | Epic A 3932 | Fraction Too Much Friction/Below The Belt (p/s) | 5 |
| 94 | Capitol | LIVE AT THE BORDERLINE (CD, promo only) | 15 |

(see also Split Enz, Crowded House)

LARRY FINNEGAN

62	HMV POP 1022	Dear One/Candy Lips	15
62	London HLU 9613	Pretty Suzy Sunshine/It's Walkin' Talkin' Time	20
65	Ember EMB S 207	The Other Ringo (A Tribute To Ringo Starr)/When My Love Passes By (p/s)	20
65	Ember EMB S 207	The Other Ringo (A Tribute To Ringo Starr)/When My Love Passes By	10

MIKE FINNIGAN

| 78 | CBS 6656 | Just One Minute More/Blood Is Thicker Than Water | 10 |

FIRE

68	Decca F 12753	Father's Name Is Dad/Treacle Toffee World	500
68	Decca F 12856	Round The Gum Tree/Toothie Ruthie	50
70	Pye NSPL 18343	THE MAGIC SHOEMAKER (LP, blue/black labels with logo banner at top)	500
97	Tenth Planet TP 029	UNDERGROUND AND OVERHEAD: THE ALTERNATE FIRE (LP, gatefold sleeve, numbered, 1,000 only)	18

(see also Strawbs, Paul Brett's Sage)

FIREBALLS

59	Top Rank JAR 218	Torquay/Cry Baby	20
60	Top Rank JAR 276	Bulldog/Nearly Sunrise	15
60	Top Rank JAR 354	Foot-Patter/Kissin'	15
60	Top Rank JAR 507	Vaquero (Cowboy)/Chief Whoopin'-Koff	15
61	Pye International 7N 25092	Quite A Party/Gunshot	12
62	Stateside SS 106	Rik-A-Tik/Yacky Doo	10
63	Stateside SS 151	Carioca/Find Me A Golden Street	10
65	Stateside SS 417	Baby What's Wrong/Yummie Yama Papa	10
67	Stateside SS 2095	Bottle Of Wine/Ain't That Rain	5
68	Stateside SS 2106	Goin' Away/Groovy Motions	15
69	Stateside SS 2134	Come On, React!/Woman Help Me	5
69	London HLZ 10260	Long Green/Light In The Window	5
61	Top Rank 35/105	VAQUERO (LP)	70
68	Stateside S(S)L 10237	BOTTLE OF WINE (LP)	15
69	London HA/SH 8396	COME ON, REACT! (LP)	20

(see also Jimmy Gilmer, Buddy Holly)

FIREBIRD (1)

| 74 | Bell Bell 1370 | Two Wheels/Side Tracking | 5 |

FIREBIRD (2)

| 79 | Rat SRTS79/CUS576 | Change/Nightride | 40 |

FIREBRAND

| 85 | What WR 71 | Never Felt This Way Before/I'm Leaving (p/s) | 50 |

FIRECLOWN

| 83 | Fireclown FC 1001 | INVASION EP (Magic/Poor Man/Invasion) (10", no p/s) | 12 |

FIRE ENGINES

80	Codex Comms. CDX 01	Get Up And Use Me/Everything's Roses (p/s)	15
81	Pop:Aural POP 010	Candy Skin/Meat Whiplash (foldout p/s in poly bag)	12
81	Pop:Aural POP 013	Big Gold Dream/Sympathetic Anaesthetic (p/s)	6
81	Pop:Aural POP 01312	Big Gold Dream/Sympathetic Anaesthetic/New Thing In Cartons (12", non-gatefold p/s; gatefold p/s £5)	10
81	Accessory ACC 001	LUBRICATE YOUR LIVING ROOM (LP, in plastic bag)	20

FIRE EXIT

| 79 | Time Bomb Explosion 1 | Timewall/Talkin' About Myself (p/s, stamped labels) | 10 |

FIREFLIES

59	Top Rank JAR 198	You Were Mine/Stella Got A Fella	20
59	Top Rank JAR 198	You Were Mine/Stella Got A Fella (78)	20
60	London HLU 9057	I Can't Say Goodbye/What Did I Do Wrong	50

FIREFLY

| 71 | Decca F131192 | My Friend/Younger Days | 8 |

FIRE KINGS

| 77 | Terminal TM 107 | Poor Man Cry/Version | 8 |

MINT VALUE £

FIREMAN

98	Hydra HYPRO 12 007	Rushes: Bison/Fluid/Appletree Cinnabar Amber (12" with massive fold-out poster)	100
98	Hydra HYPRO 12 007	Rushes: Bison/Fluid/Appletree Cinnabar Amber (12" without massive fold-out poster)	20
99	Hydra HYPRO 12 008	Fluid (12", p/s, promo only)	35
99	Hydra HYPRO CD 008	Fluid (CD, promo only)	20
93	Parlophone FIRE 1	STRAWBERRIES OCEANS SHIPS FOREST (2-LP, clear vinyl, numbered white sleeve, with inners, promo only)	100
93	Parlophone PCSD 145	STRAWBERRIES OCEANS SHIPS FOREST (2-LP, clear vinyl, red sleeve, with inners)	100
98	HYPRO CD007	RUSHES (CD 3-track album promo)	20
98	Hydra 4970551	RUSHES (LP)	100

(see also Paul McCartney, Youth)

FIRE SESSION

70	Revolution REV 10	Souvenir/Bad Girl	10
70	Revolution REV 13	Sleeping Reggae/CAROLS: Everyday I Have To Cry Some	10
70	Revolution REV 14	Death Of The Ugly One/Big Feet	20

FIRESIGN THEATRE

68	CBS 65129	WAITING FOR THE ELECTRICIAN OR SOMEONE LIKE HIM (LP)	12
68	CBS 65130	HOW TO BE IN TWO PLACES AT ONCE WHEN YOU'RE NOT ANYWHERE AT ALL? (LP)	12
72	CBS CQ 30737	FIRESIGN THEATRE (LP, quadrophonic)	15

FIRESTONES

62	Decca F 11436	Party Twist (Medley) (Parts 1 & 2)	6

FIRING SQUAD (1)

64	Parlophone R 5152	A Little Bit More/Bull Moose	40

FIRING SQUAD (2)

80	Shattered SHAT 5	Big Red Car/Night Manoeuvres (p/s)	6

FIRKIN THE FOX

84	Woodworm WR 005	BEHIND BARS (LP)	25

FIRM

85	Atlantic A 9586P	Radioactive/Together (shaped picture disc)	8
85	Atlantic 781 239-2	THE FIRM (CD)	15
86	Atlantic 781 628-2	THE FIRM MEAN BUSINESS (CD)	15

(see also Jimmy Page, Rock Aid Armenia)

FIRST AID

77	Decca TXS 117	NOSTRADAMUS (LP)	40

FIRST CHOICE

73	Pye International 7N 25613	This Is The House Where Love Died/One Step Away (unissued, demos may exist, this price for acetate)	400
74	Bell BLL 1376	The Player (Parts 1 & 2)	8
73	Bell BELLS 229	ARMED AND EXTREMELY DANGEROUS (LP)	18

FIRST CLASS

74	Sunny EON 102	Beach Baby/Surfer Queen	6
74	UK UKAL 1008	THE FIRST CLASS (LP)	18
76	UK UKAL 1022	S.S.T. (LP)	18

(see also White Plains, Edison Lighthouse, Brotherhood Of Man, Carter-Lewis & Southerners, Ivy League)

FIRST DOWN

90	Cobden Capers FD1	Jaw Warfare/From Now On/Dedication	70
93	Ill Gotten Gains FD002	LET THE BATTLE BEGIN (EP)	40
94	Blitz Vinyl EFA61008	MAD DOGS AND ENGLISHMAN (EP)	12
94	Blitz Vinyl EFA61009	WORLD SERVICE (LP)	20

FIRST EDITION

68	Reprise RS 20655	Just Dropped In (To See What Condition My Condition Was In)/ Shadow In The Corner Of Your Mind	40
68	Reprise RS 20693	Charlie The Fer'de Lance/Look Around I'll Be There	8
69	Reprise RS 20799	But You Know I Love You/Homemade Lies	5
68	Reprise RSLP 6276	THE FIRST EDITION (LP)	15

(see also Kenny Rogers)

FIRST GEAR

64	Pye 7N 15703	A Certain Girl/Leave My Kitten Alone	200
65	Pye 7N 15763	The 'In' Crowd/Gotta Make Their Future Bright	70

FIRST IMPRESSION

67	Saga SOC 1045	BEAT CLUB (LP)	12

FIRST IMPRESSION/GOOD EARTH

68	Saga FID 2117	SWINGING LONDON (LP)	25

(see also Good Earth, Mungo Jerry)

FIRST IMPRESSIONS

65	Pye 7N 15797	I'm Coming Home/Looking For Her	25

(see also Legends)

FIRST LIGHT

82	Oval FLIGHT 22/12	Don't Be Mistaken/Horse With No Name (12" p/s)	8

FIRST NATIONAL NOTHING (FEATURING J MARKS)

70	CBS 5120	Purple Song/I Got The Answer (purple vinyl)	8

FIRST OFFENCE

90	Blip Blip3T	Tell Em What You Like (12")	8
91	Corona CRNT4	Round And Round/Three Steps (12")	8
91	Blip Blip 5T	Just Try Me (12")	8
88	Metal Other OTH 11	FIRST OFFENCE (LP, with insert)	30
88	Metal Other OTH 11	FIRST OFFENCE (LP, without insert)	25

1ST OFFENCE

82	Chaos	NIGHT THE PUNKS TURNED UGLY EP (fold put sleeve)	15

FIRST STEPS
80	English Rose ER I	The Beat Is Back/She Ain't In Love/Let's Go Cuboids (p/s, with insert)	25
81	English Rose ER III	Anywhere Else But Here/Airplay/I Got The News (p/s)	20

CLARE FISCHER
62	Fontana 688124 ZL	FIRST TIME OUT (LP)	15

WILD MAN FISCHER
69	Reprise RSLP 6332	AN EVENING WITH WILD MAN FISCHER (gatefold sleeve)	60

(see also Frank Zappa)

FISCHERMAN'S FRIEND
91	EG OP 51	Money (12", with "Orb Clubmix", 500 only)	12

FISH
89	EMI 12EMPD 109	State Of Mind/The Voyeur (I Like To Watch)/State Of Mind (Presidential Mix) (12", picture disc)	8

(see also Marillion)

F F & Z (FISHBAUGH FISHBAUGH & ZORN)
72	CBS 8163	Everybody Got Out Of Bed/Spaced On Happy	20

ARCHIE FISHER
68	Xtra XTRA 1070	ARCHIE FISHER (LP)	25
70	Decca SKL 5057	ORFEO (LP)	50
82	Celtic Music CM 007	ARCHIE FISHER (LP, reissue)	20

(see also Barbara Dickson)

ARCHIE FISHER, BARBARA DICKSON & JOHN MACKINNON
69	Trailer LER 3002	THE FATE O' CHARLIE: SONGS OF THE JACOBITE REBELLIONS (LP, first pressing, white label)	60
69	Trailer LER 3002	THE FATE O' CHARLIE: SONGS OF THE JACOBITE REBELLIONS (LP, second pressing, red label)	30

CHIP FISHER
59	Parlophone R 4604	Poor Me/No One	15
59	RCA RCX 143	AT THE SUGAR BOWL (EP)	100

CILLA FISHER & ARTIE TREZISE
76	Trailer LER 2100	BALCANQUHAL (LP, yellow label)	15
79	Kettle KAC 1	FOR FOUL DAY AND FAIR (LP)	15

EDDIE FISHER
53	HMV 7M 101	I'm Yours/That's The Chance You Take	10
53	HMV 7M 115	Everything I Have Is Yours/You'll Never Know	10
53	HMV 7M 116	Trust In Me/Forgive Me	10
53	HMV 7M 117	Outside Of Heaven/Lady Of Spain	12
53	HMV 7M 125	Even Now/If It Were Up To Me	10
53	HMV 7M 126	Downhearted/Am I Wasting My Time On You	10
53	HMV 7M 133	I'm Walking Behind You (with Sally Sweetland)/Hold Me	10
53	HMV 7M 146	Just Another Polka/When I Was Young (Yes, Very Young)	8
53	HMV 7M 159	Wish You Were Here/A Fool Was I	10
53	HMV 7M 168	Many Times/With These Hands	10
54	HMV 7M 172	Oh My Papa/(I Never Missed You) Until You Said "Goodbye"	10
54	HMV 7M 185	How Deep Is The Ocean?/That Old Feeling	6
54	HMV 7M 201	April Showers/Just To Be With You	6
54	HMV 7M 212	I'm In The Mood For Love/A Girl, A Girl	6
54	HMV 7M 235	May I Sing To You?/My Friend	6
54	HMV 7M 242	How Do You Speak To An Angel?/My Arms, My Heart, My Love	6
54	HMV 7M 251	I Need You Now/Heaven Was Never Like This	6
54	HMV 7M 257	They Say It's Wonderful/Green Years	6
54	HMV 7M 266	Count Your Blessings Instead Of Sheep/White Christmas	6
55	HMV 7M 294	(I'm Always Hearing) Wedding Bells/A Man Chases A Girl	10
56	HMV 7M 374	Dungaree Doll/If It Hadn't Been For You	10
56	HMV POP 273	Cindy, Oh Cindy/Fanny	12

FAYE FISHER
65	Columbia DB 7575	Our Love/I Just Don't Know What To Say	7
65	Columbia DB 7732	Oh Heartache You're Bothering Me/It's You	7

MATTHEW FISHER
73	RCA SF8380	JOURNEY'S END (LP)	15
74	RCA APL 1	I'LL BE THERE (LP)	12

(see also Procol Harum, Green Bullfrog)

RAY FISHER
72	Trailer LER 2038	THE BONNY BIRD (LP, red label)	25
72	Trailer LER 2038	THE BONNY BIRD (LP, later yellow label)	12

SONNY FISHER
77	Ace NST 59	Rockin' Daddy/I Can't Lose (78)	20

TONI FISHER
60	Top Rank JAR 261	The Big Hurt/Memphis Belle	8
60	Top Rank JAR 341	How Deep Is The Ocean/Blue, Blue, Blue	7
62	London HLX 9564	West Of The Wall/What Did I Do	7

FISHER BROTHERS
64	London HLN 9928	Big Round Wheel/By The Time You Read This Letter	10

FISHER FAMILY
60s	Topic TOP 67	FAR OVER THE FORTH (EP)	8
66	Topic 12T 137	THE FISHER FAMILY (LP)	15

FISHERFOLK
78	Celebration CR 1007	WORSHIP WITH THE FISHERFOLK (LP)	12
80	Celebration CR 1025	THE SUN'S GONNA SHINE (LP)	12
82	Celebration CR 1028	JOY IN THE MORNING (LP)	12
82	Celebration CR 1030	WILLING TO ROW (LP)	12

FISH TURNED HUMAN
79	Sequel PART 1	TURKEYS IN CHINA (EP)	15

FIST
80	Neat NEAT 04	Name Rank And Serial Number/You'll Never Get Me In One Of Those (p/s, with poster insert)	10
80	Neat NEAT 04	Name Rank And Serial Number/You'll Never Get Me In One Of Those (p/s)	8
80	MCA MCA 615	Name Rank And Serial Number/You'll Never Get Me (In One Of Those) (p/s, reissue, with poster insert)	30
80	MCA MCA 615	Name Rank And Serial Number/You'll Never Get Me (In One Of Those) (p/s, reissue, without poster insert)	20
80	MCA MCA 640	Forever Amber/Brain Damage (p/s)	12
81	MCA MCA 663	Collision Course/Law Of The Jungle (p/s)	100
81	MCA MCA 663	Collision Course/Law Of The Jungle	30
82	Neat NEAT 021	The Wanderer/Too Hot (p/s)	10
80	MCA MCF 3082	TURN THE HELL ON (LP)	15
85	Neat NEAT 1003	BACK WITH A VENGEANCE (LP, yellow vinyl)	30
85	Neat NEAT 1003	BACK WITH A VENGEANCE (LP)	15

JOHN FITCH & ASSOCIATES
71	Beacon BEA 117	Romantic Altitude/Stoned Out Of It	90

FITS
82	Rondelet ROUND 13	Think For Yourself: Burial/Straps (p/s)	5
83	Corpus Christi ITS 9	Tears Of A Nation/Bravado/Breaking Point (p/s)	6
84	Trapper FIT 1	Action/Achilles Heel (p/s)	7
85	Trapper FIT 2	Fact Or Fiction/Give Away (p/s)	5
81	Beat The System FIT 1	YOU SAID WE'D NEVER MAKE IT (EP, wraparound p/s)	10
82	Rondelet ABOUT 6	NOTHING AND NOWHERE (LP)	12
82	Rondelet ABOUT 6	YOU'RE NOTHING, YOU'RE NOWHERE (LP)	15

FITZ & COOLERS
68	Nu Beat NB 003	Cover Me/Darling	12

ELLA FITZGERALD
SINGLES
54	Brunswick 05324	Who's Afraid (Not I, Not I, Not I)/I Wished On The Moon (with Gordon Jenkins)	8
55	Brunswick 05392	Lullaby Of Birdland/Later	8
55	Brunswick 05427	Moanin' Low/Take A Chance On Love	6
55	Brunswick 05468	Lover, Come Back To Me/Old Devil Moon	7
55	Brunswick 05473	Pete Kelly's Blues/Hard Hearted Hannah	6
55	Brunswick 05477	Soldier Boy/Air Mail Special (with Bill Doggett)	6
56	Brunswick 05514	My One And Only Love/(Love Is) The Tender Trap	6
56	Brunswick 05539	Ella's Contribution To The Blues/Early Autumn	7
56	Brunswick 05584	You'll Never Know/But Not Like Mine	5
56	HMV POP 266	The Silent Treatment/The Sun Forgot To Shine This Morning	5
57	HMV POP 290	A Beautiful Friendship/Too Young For The Blues	7
57	HMV POP 316	Hotta Chocolatta/Stay There	6
57	HMV POP 348	Johnny One Note/To Keep My Love Alive	5
57	HMV POP 373	Ev'ry Time We Say Goodbye/Manhattan	5
57	HMV POP 380	Goody Goody/A Tisket, A Tasket	5
58	HMV POP 486	The Swingin' Shepherd Blues/Midnight Sun	6
58	HMV POP 499	Beale Street Blues/St. Louis Blues	5
58	HMV POP 518	Your Red Wagon/Trav'lin Light	5
59	Brunswick 05783	My Happiness/A Satisfied Mind	5
59	HMV POP 657	But Not For Me/You Make Me Feel So Young	6
59	HMV POP 686	The Christmas Song/You Make Me Feel So Young	5
60	HMV POP 701	Like Young/Beat Me Daddy Eight To The Bar	5
60	HMV POP 719	It's All Right With Me/Don'cha Go Way Mad (with Oscar Peterson)	5
60	HMV POP 736	Mack The Knife/Lorelei	6
60	HMV POP 782	How High The Moon (Parts 1 & 2)	10
60	HMV POP 809	Good Morning Blues/Jingle Blues	5
60	HMV POP 817	We Three Kings Of Orient Are/White Christmas	5
61	HMV POP 849	The Lady Is A Tramp/Misty	5
62	Verve VS 502	Desafinado/Stardust	5
65	Verve VS 519	Can't Buy Me Love/Sweetest Sound	6
65	Verve VS 524	Why Was I Born/All The Things You Are	5
66	Stateside SS 569	These Boots Were Made For Walkin'/Stardust (DJ Copy)	50
66	Stateside SS 569	These Boots Were Made for Walkin'/Stardust	5
69	Reprise RS 20850	Get Ready/Open Your Window	25
69	Polydor 56767	Hey Jude/Sunshine Of Your Love	10
71	Reprise RS 23507	I Heard It Through The Grapevine/Days Of Wine & Roses	6

ALBUMS
53	Brunswick LA 8581	SOUVENIR ALBUM (10")	20
54	Brunswick LA 8648	ELLA SINGS GERSHWIN (10")	20
55	Brunswick LAT 8056	ELLA — SONGS IN A MELLOW MOOD	15
56	Brunswick LAT 8091	SWEET AND HOT	15
56	Brunswick LAT 8115	LULLABIES OF BIRDLAND	15
58	Columbia 33CX 10126	AT THE OPERA HOUSE (LP)	15
68	Polydor 583737	SUNSHINE OF YOUR LOVE (LP)	20

(see also Oscar Peterson, Count Basie, Ink Spots)

ELLA FITZGERALD & LOUIS ARMSTRONG
56	HMV CLP 1098	ELLA AND LOUIS (LP)	20

ELLA FITZGERALD/BILLIE HOLIDAY
58	Columbia Clef 33CX 10100	AT NEWPORT (LP)	15

G.F. FITZGERALD
70	Uni UNLS 115	MOUSEPROOF (LP, gatefold sleeve, with insert, yellow swirl label)	150

(see also Sam Gopal)

PATRIK FITZGERALD
78	Small Wonder SMALL 6	Buy Me, Sell Me/The Little Dippers/Trendy/The Backstreet Boys (p/s)	8

79	Polydor 2059 091	All Sewn Up/Hammersmith Odeons (p/s)	8
79	Polydor 2059 135	Improve Myself/The Bingo Crowd/My New Family (p/s, as Patrik Fitzgerald)	8
78	Small Wonder WEENY ONE	THE PARANOID WARD/THE BEDROOM TAPES (12" EP)	10
81	Ellie Jay AHPF 001	Without Sex/Pop Star, Pop Star	5
82	Red Flame RF 708	Personal Loss/Straight Boy	5
79	Polydor 2383 533	GRUBBY STORIES (LP)	12
80s	Final Solution FSEP 001	TONIGHT (EP)	8

MAGGIE FITZGIBBON

59	Pye Int. 7N 25047	Kooka Burra/The Right Kind Of Man	7
68	Page One PDF 057	I'll Walk Alone/Girls Are Made Loving (p/s)	8
70	CBS 5166	Please Don't Look Back/Broken Up	6
68	Page One POL 006	A NEWCOMER, ME? (LP)	12

FITZROY (STERLING) & HARRY

| 70 | Bullet BU 439 | Reggae Sounds Are Boss/Goodbye My Love | 15 |
| 70 | Escort ERT 827 | Pop A Top Train/Doing The Moonwalk | 15 |

FIVE AMERICANS

66	Pye International 7N 25354	I See The Light/The Outcasts	25
66	Pye International 7N 25373	Evol — Not Love/Don't Blame Me	20
67	Stateside SS 2012	Western Union/Now That It's All Over	10
68	Stateside SS 2036	Sound Of Love/Sympathy	7

5 A.M. EVENT

| 66 | Pye 7N 17154 | Hungry/I Wash My Hands (In Muddy Water) | 300 |

FIVE & A PENNY

| 68 | Polydor 56282 | You Don't Know Where Your Interest Lies/Mary Go Round | 40 |
| 68 | Polydor 56282 | You Don't Know Where Your Interest Lies/Mary Go Round (2nd pressing injection moulded) | 5 |

FIVE BLIND BOYS

| 64 | Vocalion EPVP 1276 | NEGRO SPIRITUALS (EP, 2 tracks by Spirits Of Memphis) | 20 |
| 64 | Vocalion EPVP 1282 | FIVE BLIND BOYS (EP) | 10 |

FIVE BLOBS

| 58 | Philips PB 881 | The Blob/Saturday Night In Tijuana | 20 |
| 58 | Philips PB 881 | The Blob/Saturday Night In Tijuana (78) | 12 |

FIVE BY FIVE

| 68 | Pye International 7N 25477 | Fire/Hang Up | 50 |

FIVE CARD STUD

| 67 | Philips BF 1567 | Beg Me/Once | 15 |

FIVE CHESTERNUTS

| 58 | Columbia DB 4165 | Jean Dorothy/Teenage Love | 250 |
| 58 | Columbia DB 4165 | Jean Dorothy/Teenage Love (78) | 100 |

(see also Shadows, Pete Chester)

FIVE COUNTS

| 62 | Oriole CBA 1769 | Watermelon Walk/Spanish Nights | 30 |

FIVE CRESTAS

| 66 | Excel ES SP 288/289 | How Sweet It Is (To Be Loved By You)/You Used To Love Me (private pressing) | 100 |

FIVE DALLAS BOYS

57	Columbia DB 4005	Shangri-La/By The Fireside	5
57	Columbia DB 4041	I Never Had The Blues/All The Way	5
58	Columbia DB 4102	26 Miles (Santa Catalina)/Sail Along, Silv'ry Moon	6
58	Columbia DB 4154	Big Man/Lonesome Traveller	8
58	Columbia DB 4231	Fatty Patty/Do You Wanna Jump Children?	8
59	Columbia DB 4313	Morning Papers/I'm Aware	7
60	Columbia DB 4445	Boston Tea Party/Ramona	6
61	Columbia DB 4599	One Finger One Thumb Keep Movin'/Nice To Know You Care	6
60	Columbia SEG 8035	THE FIVE DALLAS BOYS (EP)	15

(see also Dallas Boys)

FIVE DAY RAIN

| 70 | Private pressing | FIVE DAY RAIN (LP, no sleeve, 20-30 copies only) | 800 |
| 93 | Private pressing | FIVE DAY RAIN (LP re-pressing in signed, numbered sleeve, signed note in run-out groove & letter of authenticity, 25 only) | 80 |

(see also Scots Of St. James, Hopscotch, One Way Ticket, Glencoe)

FIVE DAY WEEK STRAW PEOPLE

| 68 | Saga FID 2123 | FIVE DAY WEEK STRAW PEOPLE (LP, black/silver labels) | 200 |

(see also Attack, Andromeda, John Du Cann)

FIVE DE MARCO SISTERS

53	MGM SP 1043	Bouillabasse/I'm Never Satisfied	5
54	Brunswick 05349	Love Me/Just A Girl That Men Forget	5
55	Brunswick 05425	Dreamboat/Two Hearts, Two Kisses (Make One Love)	6
55	Brunswick 05474	The Hot Barcarolle/Sailor Boys Have Talk To Me In English	5
56	Brunswick 05526	Romance Me/This Love Of Mine	5

FIVE DU-TONES

| 63 | Stateside SS 206 | Shake A Tail Feather/Divorce Court | 20 |
| 68 | President PT 134 | Shake A Tail Feather/Divorce Court (reissue) | 8 |

FIVE EMPREES

| 65 | Stateside SS 470 | Little Miss Sad/Hey Lover | 15 |

FIVE FINGER DEATH PUNCH

| 09 | Park/Spinefarm SPI360LP.272045 | WAR IS THE ANSWER (2-LP, red vinyl) | 20 |

FIVE FLEETS

| 58 | Felsted AF 103 | Oh What A Feeling/I Been Cryin' | 200 |
| 58 | Felsted AF 103 | Oh What A Feeling/I Been Cryin' (78) | 70 |

FIVE FLIGHTS UP
70	Bell BLL 1123	Do What You Wanna Do/Black Cat	6

FIVE GO DOWN TO THE SEA
84	Abstract 12 ABS 027	THE GLEE CLUB (12" EP)	8
85	Creation CRE 021T	Singing In Braille/Aunt Nelly/Silk Brain Worm/Women (12", p/s)	8

FIVE HAND REEL
76	Rubber RUB 019	FIVE HAND REEL (LP, with lyric insert)	12
78	RCA PL 25150	EARL O'MORAY (LP)	12

FIVE KEYS
54	Capitol CL 14184	Ling, Ting, Tong/I'm Alone	500
54	Capitol CL 14184	Ling, Ting, Tong/I'm Alone (78)	50
55	Capitol CL 14313	The Verdict/Make Me Um Pow Pow (triangular centre)	500
55	Capitol CL 14313	The Verdict/Make Me Um Pow Pow (78)	50
55	Capitol CL 14325	(Close Your Eyes) Take A Deep Breath/Doggone It, You Did It(tri centre)	450
55	Capitol CL 14325	(Close Your Eyes) Take A Deep Breath/Doggone It, You Did It (78)	40
56	Capitol CL 14545	Gee Whittakers!/'Cause You're My Lover	300
56	Capitol CL 14545	Gee Whittakers!/'Cause You're My Lover (78)	25
56	Capitol CL 14582	She's The Most/I Dreamt I Dwelt In Heaven	250
56	Capitol CRE 14582	She's The Most/I Dreamt I Dwelt In Heaven (78)	25
56	Capitol CL 14639	That's Right/Out Of Sight, Out Of Mind	150
56	Capitol CL 14639	That's Right/Out Of Sight, Out Of Mind (78)	20
57	Capitol CL 14686	The Wisdom Of A Fool/Now Don't That Prove I Love You?	150
57	Capitol CL 14686	The Wisdom Of A Fool/Now Don't That Prove I Love You? (78)	25
57	Capitol CL 14736	Four Walls/Let There Be You	100
57	Capitol CL 14736	Four Walls/Let There Be You (78	30
57	Capitol CL 14756	The Blues Don't Care/This I Promise You	150
57	Capitol CL 14756	The Blues Don't Care/This I Promise You (78)	40
58	Capitol CL 14829	From Me To You/Whippety Whirl	150
58	Capitol CL 14829	From Me To You/Whippety Whirl (78)	45
58	Capitol CL 14967	One Great Love/Really-O Truly-O	150
57	Capitol T 828	THE FIVE KEYS ON STAGE! (LP)	180

FIVE MILES OUT
73	Action ACT 4614	Super Sweet Girl Of Mine/Set Your Mind Free	25

FIVE NITES
64	Decca F 11963	With A Loving Kiss/Let's Try Again	15

FIVE OF DIAMONDS
65	Oak RGJ 150 FD	FIVE OF DIAMONDS (EP)	400

FIVE OR SIX
81	Cherry Red CHERRY 19	Another Reason/The Trial (p/s)	5
81	Cherry Red 12CHERRY 23	Polar Exposure (12" EP)	8
82	Cherry Red 12CHERRY 43	FOUR FROM FIVE OR SIX (12" EP)	8
82	Cherry Red FRIZBEE 2	A THRIVING AND HAPPY LAND (LP)	12

FIVE ROYALES
60	Ember EMB S 124	Dedicated To The One I Love/Miracle Of Love	150

FIVE SAPPHIRES
78	Rocket ROKN 539	Love Music/Where Did All The Good Times Go	7
79	Warner Bros K 17307	Duke of Earl/Oh My Darlin'	5
79	Warner Bros K 17360	Once In A While/Falling in Love	5

(see also Alan Carvell, Carvells, Telegrams)

FIVE SATINS
57	London HL 8501	To The Aisle/Wish I Had My Baby	750
57	London HL 8501	To The Aisle/Wish I Had My Baby (78)	150
59	Top Rank JAR 199	Wonderful Girl/Weeping Willow	50
59	Top Rank JAR 239	Shadows/Toni My Love	50
60	MGM MGM 1087	Your Memory/I Didn't Know	60

FIVE SMITH BROTHERS
54	Decca F 10403	A.B.C. Boogie/Veni-Vidi-Vici (with Dennis Wilson Quartet)	20
55	Decca F 10507	Paper Valentine/You're As Sweet Today (As Yesterday)	7
55	Decca F 10527	Don't Worry/I'm In Favour Of Friendship	7
56	Decca F 10698	You Took My Heart (My Only Heart)/The Grass Is Green	5
55	Parlophone GEP 8667	UP NORTH WITH THE FIVE SMITH BROTHERS (EP)	10

FIVE STAIRSTEPS (& CUBIE)
68	Pye International 7N 25448	A Million To One/Something's Missing (with Cubie)	10
69	Buddah 201 026	Stay Close To Me/I Made A Mistake (with Cubie)	10
69	Buddah 201 070	We Must Be In Love/Little Young Lovers (with Cubie)	10
70	Buddah 201 083	Dear Prudence/O-o-h Child	15
70	Buddah 2011 036	O-o-h Child/Who Do You Belong To?	8

(see also Stairsteps)

FIVE STEPS BEYOND
67	CBS 202490	Not So Young Today/Meanwhile Back In My Heart	25
95	Tenth Planet TP 019	FAINT HEARTS AND FAIR MAIDS (LP, 600 only)	15
96	Tenth Planet TP 021	SMILE (LP, with A4 booklet, 600 only)	15

FIVE THIRTY/5.30
87	Other 12 OTH 2	THE CATCHER IN THE RYE EP (12", p/s)	20

FIVE TOWNS
67	Direction 58-3115	It Isn't What You've Got/Advice	10

FIVEPENNY PIECE
72	Columbia SCX 6488	FIVEPENNY PIECE (LP)	12
73	Columbia SCX 6536	MAKIN' TRACKS (LP)	12
75	EMI EMC 3077	WISH YOU WERE HERE (LP)	12
76	EMI EMC 3234	BOTH SIDES OF (LP)	12
77	One Up OU 2050	ON STAGE (LP)	15

FIVER
| 70s | EMI 2401 | When Love Walks Out The Door/I Don't Wanna Be Alone Tonight...................6 |

FIVE'S COMPANY
66	Pye 7N 17118	Sunday For Seven Days/The Big Kill...............12
66	Pye 7N 17162	Some Girls/Big Deal................6
66	Pye 7N 17199	Session Man/Dejection................18
69	Saga FID 2151	THE BALLAD OF FRED THE PIXIE (LP)................18

(see also Brunning Hall Sunflower Blues Band)

FIXED PENALTY
92	FPT 001	Man Of Action/All Of Us (12").................12
92	FPT 002	To You/Bubble Up (12").................10
92	FPT 004	Party Rocker (12".................10

FIXER
| 78 | Rainbow RSL 116 | Bright And Rosy (no p/s).................40 |

FIXIT
| 79 | Ellie Jay SJSP9246 | Eighteen Plus/April Fool.................50 |

FIZZARUM
| 99 | City Centre Offices BLOCK 2 | Phut Of Plex (clear vinyl, plain black sleeve, with inserts; 650 copies only).................8 |

FIZZBOMBS
| 87 | Narodnik NRK 003 | Sign On The Line/The Lines That (p/s).................10 |
| 88 | Calculus KIT 002T | THE SURFIN' WINTER EP (12", p/s).................8 |

FIZZLER
| 79 | Aerco AERS 105 | Brill Plus (You Know Us)/Margy's SOng (no p/s, 500 only).................10 |

ROBERTA FLACK
| 69 | Atlantic 584 294 | Compared To What/Hey, That's No Way To Say Goodbye.................6 |

(see also Donny Hathaway)

FLACK OFF
| 80 | Sofa | FLACK OFF EP: COCKTAILS AT SIX.................20 |

FLAG OF CONVENIENCE
| 82 | Sire SIR 4057 | Life On The Telephone/The Other Man's Sin (no p/s).................6 |

(see also Steve Diggle, Buzzcocks)

FLAIRS
| 57 | Oriole CB 1392 | Swing Pretty Mama/I'd Climb The Hills And Mountains.................500 |
| 57 | Oriole CB 1392 | Swing Pretty Mama/I'd Climb The Hills And Mountains (78).................100 |

LES FLAMBEAUX
| 71 | Mushroom 100 MR 13 | LES FLAMBEAUX (LP, 2 different sleeve designs).................30 |

FLAME
| 70 | Stateside SS 2183 | See The Light/Get Your Mind Made Up.................18 |
| 71 | Stateside SSL 10312 | THE FLAME (LP).................30 |

(see also Flames [South Africa], Beach Boys)

FLAME
| 77 | RCA PC 12160 | QUEEN OF THE NEIGHBOURHOOD (LP).................12 |

(see also Aerosmith)

FLAME 'N' KING & BOLD ONES
| 79 | Grapevine GRP 123 | Ho Happy Day/Ain't Nobody Jivin'.................20 |

FLAMES (SOUTH AFRICA)
| 68 | Flame FAN 101/1 | Streamliner/Follow The Sun (p/s).................20 |
| 68 | Page One FOR(S) 009 | BURNING SOUL (LP).................50 |

(see also Flame, Beach Boys)

FLAMES (1)
64	Island WI 130	He's The Greatest/Someone Going To Bawl (both actually by the Maytals).................40
64	Island WI 136	Little Flea/Good Idea (both actually by the Maytals).................40
64	Island WI 138	When I Get Home/Neither Silver Nor Gold (both actually by the Maytals).................40
64	Island WI 139	Broadway Jungle/Beat Lied (both actually by the Maytals).................70
64	Blue Beat BB 205	Helena Darling/My Darling (both actually by Plamers).................20

(see also Maytals, Vikings)

FLAMES (2)
68	Nu Beat NB 020	Mini Really Fit Dem/Soul Train (both actually by Alton Ellis & Flames).................10
69	Nu Beat NB 028	You've Lost Your Date/Little Girl.................20
73	Ackee ACK 528	Feeling Good/Zig Zag.................6

(see also Alton Ellis & Flames, Righteous Flames, Larry Marshall)

FLAMING STARS
95	Vinyl Japan PAD 23	HOSPITAL, HEAVEN OR HELL (EP).................10
95	Vinyl Japan PAD 28	The Face On The Bar Room Floor/Get Carter (p/s).................5
95	Vinyl Japan PAD 30	MONEY TO BURN (EP).................10
96	Vinyl Japan PAD 31	DOWNHILL WITHOUT BRAKES (EP).................10
96	Vinyl Japan PAD 34	Ten Feet Tall/Spaghetti Junction (p/s).................5
97	Vinyl Japan PAD 35	Bury My Heart At Pier 13/Down To You (Live In London) (p/s).................5
97	Vinyl Japan PAD 37	New Hope For The Dead/Are You Being Served (p/s).................5
98	Vinyl Japan PAD 59	Sweet Smell Of Success/The Day The Earth Caught Fire (p/s, numbered, 2000 only).................6
00	Vinyl Japan PAD 71	You Don't Always Want What You Get/Saturday Night Special (p/s).................6
01	Vinyl Japan PAD 73	Some Things You Don't Forget/Only Tonight (p/s).................6
02	Vinyl Japan PAD 79	A Little Bit Like you/The Man Who Would Be King (p/s).................6
04	Vinyl Japan PAD 84	Spilled Your Pint/Sixty Nine (p/s).................5
05	Vinyl Japan PAD 85	Stranger On The Fifth Floor/New Hope For The dead (Live In Germany) (p/s).................5
96	Vinyl Japan ASKLP 62	SONGS FROM THE BAR ROOM FLOOR (LP).................25
99	Vinyl Japan ASKLP 83	PATHWAY (LP).................20
00	Vinyl Japan ASKLP 121	A WALK ON THE WIRED SIDE (LP).................20
02	Vinyl Japan ASKLP 139	SUNSET & VOID (LP).................20
04	Vinyl Japan ASKLP 146	NAMED AND SHAMED (LP).................20

FLAMING LIPS

89	Glitterhouse EFA 40153	Drug Machine In Heaven/Strychnine/What's So Funny (About Peace, Love And Understanding) (p/s)	20
91	City Slang 04063-05	Unconsciously Screamin'/Ma, I Didn't Notice/Let Me Be It/Lucifer Rising (clear vinyl, hologram sleeve)	8
92	Warners PRO S 5452	Ballrooms Of Mars/MR BUNGLE: Sudden Death (promo, grey vinyl, no p/s)	15
94	Warners SAM 1431	She Don't Use Jelly/Translucent Egg/Turn It On (Bluegrass Version)/The Process (12" promo)	15
95	Warners W 0322CDX	Bad Days (Edit)/Ice Drummer (Suicide Tribute Album Contribution)/When You Smiled (I Lost My Only Idea)/Put The Waterbug In The Policeman's Ear (Ghetto Blaster Recording At The Art School, September 1993) (CD 'squidgy pack')	10
96	Warners WO 370CD	Brainville/Evil Will Prevail (Recorded On 'Brave New World', KCRW, Santa Monica)/Waterbug (Recorded On 'Brave New World', KCRW, Santa Monica)	6
98	Warners PRO CD 9295	The Big Ol' Bug Is The New Baby Now (Stereo Mix) (enhanced CD-Rom, stickered cardboard sleeve)	10
86	Enigma 2173-1	HEAR IT IS (LP with poster)	15
89	Enigma ENVLP523	TELEPATHIC SURGERY (LP)	18
90	City Slang SLANG 005	IN A PRIEST DRIVEN AMBULANCE (2-LP)	18
03	Warner Brothers 9362481411	YOSHIMI BATTLES THE PINK ROBOTS (LP, inner sleeve, pink vinyl)	20
06	Warner Bros. WEA 9362 49966-1	AT WAR WITH THE MYSTICS (2-LP, one orange & one turquoise LP)	20
10	Warner Bros/ 520857-1	EMBRYONIC (2-LP, blue/yellow vinyl)	20
10	Warner Bros. 523541-1	DOING THE DARK SIDE OF THE MOON (LP, green vinyl, CD, insert, 500 only)	20

JOHNNY FLAMINGO

57	Vogue V 9089	My Teen-Age Girl/When I Lost You	120
57	Vogue V 9089	My Teen-Age Girl/When I Lost You (78)	40
58	Vogue V 9100	So Long/Make Me A Present Of You	75
58	Vogue V 9100	So Long/Make Me A Present Of You (78)	50

FLAMINGOS

57	London HLN 8373	Would I Be Crying?/Just For A Kick	600
57	London HLN 8373	Would I Be Crying?/Just For A Kick (78)	100
57	Brunswick 05696	The Ladder Of Love/Let's Make Up	500
57	Brunswick 05696	The Ladder Of Love/Let's Make Up (78)	80
59	Top Rank JAR 213	Love Walked In/Yours	50
60	Top Rank JAR 263	I Only Have Eyes For You/I Was Such A Fool	80
60	Top Rank JAR 367	Nobody Loves Me Like You/You, Me And The Sea	40
60	Top Rank JAR 519	Mio Amore/At Night	35
66	Philips BF 1483	Boogaloo Party/Nearness Of You	25
69	Philips BF 1786	Boogaloo Party/Nearness Of You (reissue, in p/s)	10
69	Philips BF 1786	Boogaloo Party/Nearness Of You (reissue)	8
70	Polydor 2066-007	Buffalo Soldier/Fontaineous Combustion	10
69	Philips SBL 7906	HITS NOW AND THEN (LP)	45

FLAMIN' GROOVIES

71	Kama Sutra 2013 031	Teenage Head/Evil-Hearted Ada	12
72	Kama Sutra 2013 042	Gonna Rock Tonite/Keep A-Knockin'/SHA NA NA: Rock'n'Roll Is Here To Stay/At The Hop/Duke Of Earl	8
72	United Artists UP 35392	Slow Death/Talahassie Lassie (in promo only p/s)	25
72	United Artists UP 35392	Slow Death/Talahassie Lassie	7
72	United Artists UP 35464	Married Woman/Get A Shot Of Rhythm And Blues	10
76	Sire 6198 086	Don't Lie To Me/She Said Yeah/Shake Some Action (p/s)	7
76	Sire 6078 602	Shake Some Action/Teenage Confidential (p/s, 2 different versions of A-side)	6
76	Kama Sutra KSS 707	Teenage Head/Headin' For The Texas Border	5
78	Sire 6078 619	Feel A Whole Lot Better/Paint It Black/Shake Some Action (p/s)	5
78	Sire 6078 619	Feel A Whole Lot Better/Paint It Black/Shake Some Action (12", p/s)	8
76	United Artists REM 406	SLOW DEATH (EP)	10
71	Kama Sutra 2683 003	FLAMIN' GROOVIES (2-LP)	20
77	Sire 9103 251	SHAKE SOME ACTION (LP)	20
78	Sire 9103 333	THE FLAMIN' GROOVIES NOW! (LP)	15

(see also Mike Wilhelm)

FLAMING YOUTH

69	Fontana TF 1057	Guide Me Orion/From Now On (Immortal Invisible)	20
70	Fontana 6001 002	Every Man, Woman And Child/Drifting	18
70	Fontana 6001 003	From Now On/Space Child	18
69	Fontana STL 5533	ARK II (LP, with laminated multifold plastic window sleeve)	120
69	Fontana STL 5533	ARK II (LP, later sleeve pressing with unlaminated multifold plastic window sleeve)	60
69	Fontana STL 5533	ARK II (LP, gatefold sleeve, white front, black/silver labels)	50

(see also Genesis, Phil Collins, Jackson Heights)

FLAMMA-SHERMAN

68	SNB 55-3488	No Need To Explain/Bassa Love	20
68	SNB 55-3769	Love Is In The Air/Super Day	18
69	SNB 55-4142	Move Me/Where Is He	18
69	SNB 55-4142	Move Me/Where Is He (DJ copy)	50

FLANAGAN & ALLEN

| 57 | Columbia SEG 7709 | TOGETHER AGAIN (EP) | 8 |
| 55 | Columbia 33S 1010 | SUCCESSES (10" LP) | 12 |

BUD FLANAGAN

| 69 | Pye 7N 17854 | Who Do You Think You're Kidding Mr. Hitler?/BERNARD BEDFORD CHORUS: It Ain't Gonna Rain No mo'! | 10 |

TOMMY FLANAGAN

| 59 | Esquire 32-156 | THE CATS (LP) | 50 |

FLANAGAN BROTHERS

| 58 | Vogue Coral Q 72342 | Salton City/Early One Evening | 20 |
| 58 | Vogue Coral Q 72342 | Salton City/Early One Evening (78) | 10 |

TOMMY FLANDERS

| 69 | Verve SVLP 6020 | MOONSTONE (LP) | 20 |

(see also Blues Project)

FLARES

61	London HLU 9441	Foot Stompin'/Hotcha Cha-Cha Brown	25
63	London HA-U 8034	FOOT STOMPIN' HITS (LP)	75

FLASH

72	Sovereign SOV 105	Small Beginnings/Morning Haze	7
73	Sovereign SOV 116	Watch Your Step/Lifetime	7
72	Sovereign SVNA 7251	FLASH (LP, laminated outer gatefold sleeve)	25
72	Sovereign SVNA 7255	FLASH IN THE CAN (LP, in unissued 'band in studio' proof sleeve)	25
72	Sovereign SVNA 7255	FLASH IN THE CAN (LP, gatefold sleeve)	20
73	Sovereign SVNA 7260	OUT OF OUR HANDS (LP, gatefold sleeve)	30

(see also Peter Banks, Yes)

FLASH & BOARD OF DIRECTORS

68	Bell BLL 1007	Busy Signal/Love Ain't Easy	10

FLASH CADILLAC & THE CONTINENTAL KIDS

75	Private Stock PVT 29	Hot Summer Girls/Time Will Tell	6
77	Private Stock PVT 92	See My Baby Jive/Brown Water (Apocalypse Blues)	6
75	Private Stock PVLP 1002	SONS OF THE BEACHES (LP)	15

FLASHPOINT

87	Private pressing FP 01	NO POINT OF REFERENCE (LP)	40

FLAT EARTH SOCIETY

83	Psycho PSYCHO 17	WALEECO (LP)	20

FLATMATES

86	Subway Organisation SUBWAY 6	I Could Be In Heaven/Tell Me Why/So In Love With You (foldaround p/s with insert in poly bag)	6
88	Subway Org. SUBWAY 17T	Shimmer/On My Mind/If Not For You/Bad (12", p/s, with 'flat sharing guide')	8

(LESTER) FLATT & (EARL) SCRUGGS

61	Mercury ZEP 10106	C & W TRAIL BLAZERS NO. 4 (EP)	10
64	Mercury 10010 MCE	COUNTRY AND WESTERN ACES (EP)	10

LINDA FLAVELL

66	Decca F 12312	And The Trouble With Me Is You/Over And Over	12

FLAVOUR

68	Direction 58-3597	Sally Had A Party/Shop Around	15

LOS FLECHAZOS

94	Detour Records DRO 13	Try It/You Drove Me Crazy (p/s, 100 red vinyl)	7

FLEETWOOD MAC

SINGLES

67	Blue Horizon 57-3051	I Believe My Time Ain't Long/Rambling Pony (as Peter Green's Fleetwood Mac, with p/s)	100
67	Blue Horizon 57-3051	I Believe My Time Ain't Long/Rambling Pony (as Peter Green's Fleetwood Mac)	20
68	Blue Horizon 57-3138	Black Magic Woman/The Sun Is Shining	10
68	Blue Horizon 57-3139	Need Your Love So Bad/Stop Messin' Around	10
68	Blue Horizon 57-3145	Albatross/Jigsaw Puzzle Blues	6
69	Immediate IM 080	Man Of The World/EARL VINCE & VALIANTS: Somebody's Gonna Get Their Head Kicked In Tonight	10
69	Blue Horizon 57-3157	Need Your Love So Bad/Black Magic Woman (unissued)	0
69	Blue Horizon 57-3157	Black Magic Woman/No Place To Go (unissued)	0
69	Blue Horizon 57-3157	Need Your Love So Bad/No Place To Go	6
69	CBS 3051	I Believe My Time Ain't Long/Rambling Pony (reissue)	6
69	Reprise RS 27000	Oh Well (Parts 1 & 2)	6
70	Reprise RS 27007	The Green Manalishi (With The Two-Prong Crown)/ World In Harmony (initially with p/s)	30
70	Reprise RS 27007	The Green Manalishi (With The Two-Prong Crown)/ World In Harmony	8
71	Reprise RS 27010	Dragonfly/The Purple Dancer	5
71	CBS/Blue Horizon 3145	Albatross/Jigsaw Puzzle Blues (reissue)	5
72	Reprise K 14194	Spare Me A Little Of Your Love/Sunny Side Of Heaven	6
73	Reprise K 14280	Did You Ever Love Me?/The Derelict	5
73	CBS 1722	Black Magic Woman/Stop Messin' Around	5
73	CBS 8306	Albatross/Need Your Love So Bad (p/s, 'Hall Of Fame Hits' reissue)	5
74	Reprise K 14315	For Your Love/Hypnotised	5
75	Reprise K 14388	Heroes Are Hard To Find/Born Enchanter	5
75	DJM DJS 10620	Man Of The World/DANNY KIRWAN: Second Chapter	5
75	Reprise K 14403	Warm Ways/Blue Letter (with p/s)	6
76	Reprise K 14413	Over My Head (Edit)/I'm So Afraid	5
76	Reprise K 14430	Rhiannon/Sugar Daddy (with p/s)	6

ALBUMS

68	Blue Horizon 7-63200	PETER GREEN'S FLEETWOOD MAC (mono, laminated front cover)	70
68	Blue Horizon 7-63200	PETER GREEN'S FLEETWOOD MAC (stereo, with stereo sticker, laminated front)	60
68	Blue Horizon 7-63205	MR. WONDERFUL (gatefold sleeve)	60
69	Blue Horizon 7-63215	THE PIOUS BIRD OF GOOD OMEN	35
69	Reprise RSLP 9000	THEN PLAY ON (gatefold sleeve, 'steamboat' label)	30
70	Reprise RSLP 9004	KILN HOUSE (gatefold sleeve, with insert)	35
70	Reprise RSLP 9004	KILN HOUSE (gatefold sleeve, without insert)	20
71	CBS Blue Horizon 63875	THE ORIGINAL FLEETWOOD MAC	30
72	Reprise K 44181	BARE TREES	20
77	Reprise K 54043	FLEETWOOD MAC (white vinyl with lyric sheet)	18
77	Warner Bros K 56344	RUMOURS (white vinyl with lyric sheet)	18

(see also Mick Fleetwood's Zoo, Peter Green, Stevie Nicks, Buckingham-Nicks, Jeremy Spencer, Christine Perfect, Danny Kirwan, John Mayall, Otis Spann, Eddie Boyd, Duster Bennett, Chicken Shack, Shotgun Express, Bo Street Runners, Cheynes, Tramp, Brunning Hall Sunflower Blues Band)

FLEETWOODS

59	London HLU 8841	Come Softly To Me/I Care So Much	10
59	London HLU 8841	Come Softly To Me/I Care So Much (78)	25
59	London HLU 4003	Come Softly To Me/I Care So Much (stereo export issue)	25
59	London HLU 8895	Graduation's Here/Oh Lord Let It Be Me	20
59	London HLU 8895	Graduation's Here/Oh Lord Let It Be Me (78)	35
59	Top Rank JAR 202	Mr. Blue/You Mean Everything To Me	15

59	Top Rank JAR 202	Mr. Blue/You Mean Everything To Me (78)	40
60	Top Rank JAR 294	Outside My Window/Magic Star (in p/s)	20
60	Top Rank JAR 294	Outside My Window/Magic Star	10
60	Top Rank JAR 383	Runaround/Truly Do	10
61	London HLG 9341	Tragedy/Little Miss Sad One	15
61	London HLG 9426	He's The Great Imposter/Poor Little Girl	15
62	Liberty LIB 62	They Tell Me It's Summer/Lovers By Night Strangers By Day	12
63	Liberty LIB 75	Goodnight My Love Pleasant Dreams/Jimmy Beware	12
64	Liberty LIB 93	Ruby Red Baby Blue/Lonesome Town	12
65	Liberty LIB 10191	Almost There/Before And After (Losing You)	12
60	Top Rank BUY 028	MR BLUE (LP, with 3 tracks by Little Bill & Bluetones, Frantics and Bonnie Guitar)	30
61	London HA-G 2388	SOFTLY (LP, mono)	50
61	London SAH-G 6188	SOFTLY (LP, stereo))	60
61	London HA-G 2419	DEEP IN A DREAM (LP)	50

HELEN FLEMING
| 66 | Blue Beat BB 341 | Eve's Ten Commandments/Don't Take Your Love Away | 15 |

JOY FLEMING
| 75 | Antic K 11518 | A Bridge Of Love/Divorcee | 10 |
| 76 | Private Stock PVT 54 | Are You Ready For Love/Alabama Standby | 10 |

RAY FLEMING
| 63 | MGM MGM 1196 | I'm Glad I Have You/Humpty Dumpty | 10 |

WADE FLEMONS
59	Top Rank JAR 206	Slow Motion/Walking By The River	15
60	Top Rank JAR 327	What's Happening?/Goodnight, It's Time To Go	15
60	Top Rank JAR 371	Easy Lovin'/Woops Now	15

FLESH FOR LULU
| 86 | Dojo DOJOLP39 | FRESH FLESH (LP) | 12 |

FLESHEATERS
| 81 | Initial IRC 007 | A MINUTE TO PRAY, A SECOND TO DIE (LP) | 18 |

FLESH VOLCANO
| 87 | Some Bizzare SLUT 1 | Slut/The Universal Cesspool/Bruisin' Chain (12", p/s) | 10 |
(see also Marc Almond, Foetus)

AMELIA FLETCHER
| 91 | Fierce FRIGHT 052 | Can You Keep A Secret/Wrap My Arms Around Him (p/s) | 8 |

DARROW FLETCHER
| 66 | London HLU 10024 | The Pain Gets A Little Deeper/My Judgement Day | 75 |
| 66 | London HLU 10024 | The Pain Gets A Little Deeper/My Judgement Day (DJ copy) | 150 |

DON FLETCHER
| 66 | Vocalion VP 9271 | Two Wrongs Don't Make A Right/I'm So Glad | 25 |

GUY FLETCHER
| 69 | Pye 7N 17765 | Magic Woman/All Fall Down | 6 |
| 71 | Philips 6303013 | GUY FLETCHER (LP, gatefold sleeve, black/silver lables) | 20 |

SAM FLETCHER
| 59 | MGM MGM 1024 | Time Has A Way/No Such Luck | 6 |
| 60 | RCA RCA 1255 | Tall Hope/You're So Far Away From Home | 6 |

FLEUR-DE-LYS
65	Immediate IM 020	Moondreams/Wait For Me	250
66	Immediate IM 032	Circles/So Come On	800
66	Polydor 56124	Mud In Your Eye/I've Been Trying	800
67	Polydor 56200	I Can See A Light/Prodigal Son	80
68	Polydor 56251	The Gong With The Luminous Nose/Hammer Head	300
68	Atlantic 584 193	Stop Crossing The Bridge/Brick By Brick (Stone By Stone)	65
69	Atlantic 584 243	Liar/One Girl City	200
(see also John Bromley, Terry Durham, Tony & Tandy, Sharon Tandy, Rupert's People, Shyster, Quotations, Bryn Haworth, Chocolate Frog, Gordon Haskell, Waygood Ellis)

FLEURITY
| 94 | Aesthetic Death ADEP 001 | A DARKER SHADE OF EVIL EP (p/s) | 20 |
| 08 | Aesthetic Death ADLP 001 | MIN TID SKAL KOMME (2-LP, numbered sleeve, insert, 600 only) | 18 |

FLEVANS
| 04 | Tru Thoughts TRU 069 | MAKE NEW FRIENDS EP (12") | 8 |

VIC FLICK SOUND
| 70 | Chapter One CH 136 | Hang On/Wonderful World | 15 |
| 71 | Chapter One CH 155 | Quest For Love/Clarice | 6 |

FLIES
66	Decca F 12533	I'm Not Your Stepping Stone/Talk To Me	175
67	Decca F 12594	House Of Love/It Had To Be You	80
68	RCA RCA 1757	The Magic Train/Gently As You Feel	60
(see also Bulldog Breed, T2)

MICK FLINN BAND
| 78 | EMI EMI 2805 | Doin' It Right/Do What You Wanna Do | 20 |
(see also Mixtures)

FLINT
| 03 | Cool Kills 989009-3 | ASTEROIDS (1-track 10", neon pink vinyl with inner sleeve) | 10 |

SHELBY FLINT
| 61 | Warner Bros WB 30 | Angel On My Shoulder/Somebody | 12 |
| 66 | London HLT 10068 | Cast Your Fate To The Wind/The Lilly | 20 |

FLINTLOCK
| 76 | Pinnacle P 8438 | Russian Roulette/Saddle My Horse | 6 |

FLINTLOCKS
66	Decca F 12412	What Goes On?/I Walked Right Into A Heaven	10

FLINTSTONES
64	HMV POP 1266	Safari/Work Out	20

BUNNY FLIP
72	Pressure Beat PB 5510	Shanky Dog (actually "Skanky Dog" by Winston Scotland)/JOE GIBBS & NOW GENERATION: Boney Dog	10

(see also Winston Scotland)

FLIP & DATELINERS
64	HMV POP 1359	My Johnny Doesn't Come Around Anymore/Please Listen To Me	70

(see also Vivienne Chering)

FLIPPER
81	Alt. Tentacles VIRUS 8	Ha Ha Ha/Love Canal (p/s, with insert)	15
82	Subterranean SUB UK1	ALBUM GENERIC FLIPPER (LP)	35

FLIPS
62	London HLU 9490	Rockin' Twist/Oh, You Beautiful Doll — Twist	15

FLIRTATIONS
68	Deram DM 195	Someone Out There/How Can You Tell Me?	10
68	Deram DM 216	Nothing But A Heartache/Christmas Time Is Here Again	25
69	Deram DM 252	What's Good About Goodbye My Love?/Once I Had A Love	8
70	Deram DM 281	Keep On Searchin'/Moma I'm Coming Home	8
70	Deram DM 295	Can't Stop Loving You/Everybody Needs Somebody	8
71	Deram DM 329	Give Me Love/This Must Be The End Of The Line	8
72	Deram DM 351	Need Your Lovin'/I Wanna Be There	8
71	Polydor 2058 167	Little Darlin'/Take Me In Your Arms And Love Me	20
73	Mojo 2092 058	Why Didn't I Think Of That?/Oh Mia Bamba	6
72	Polydor 2058 249	Love A Little Longer/Hold On To Me Babe	8
74	Polydor 2058 295	Dirty Work/No Such Thing As A Miracle	6
98	London Traffic TRAF 1	Nothing But A Heartache (1-sided, reissue promo, 500 only)	10
69	Deram DML/SML 1046	SOUNDS LIKE THE FLIRTATIONS (LP)	40
72	Deram SPA 218	THE WORLD OF THE FLIRTATIONS (LP)	12
75	RCA SF8448	LOVE MAKES THE WORLD GO ROUND (LP)	15

(see also Pearly Gates, Gypsies)

FLO & EDDIE
73	Reprise K 14261	Afterglow/Carlos And De Bull	5
72	Reprise K 44201	THE PHLORESCENT LEECH AND EDDIE (LP)	15
73	Reprise K 44234	FLO AND EDDIE (LP)	15

(see also Turtles, Frank Zappa/Mothers Of Invention)

FLOATING BRIDGE
69	Liberty LBS 83271	FLOATING BRIDGE (LP)	80

FLOCK
70	CBS 4932	Tired Of Waiting For You/Store Bought — Store Thought	8
69	CBS 63733	THE FLOCK (LP, orange label)	15
70	CBS 64055	DINOSAUR SWAMPS (LP, orange label, gatefold sleeve)	20

(see also Mahavishnu Orchestra)

THE FLOOD
84	Midnight Music DING 7	Cold Cold World/2 Shots Of Jealousy	10

DICK FLOOD
59	Felsted AF 125	The Three Bells/Far Away	5

FLORENCE AND THE MACHINE
09	Moshi Moshi 2726062	You've Got The Love/You've Got The Love (Jamie XX Re-Write) (p/s)	6
08	Moshi Moshi 171	Dog Days Are Over/You've Got The Love (p/s)	8
08	Moshi Moshi MOMO15	Kiss With A Fist/Hospital Beds (p/s)	8
09	Moshi Moshi 2710003	Rabbit Heart (Raise It Up)/Are You Hurting The One You Love? (p/s	5

FLORIBUNDA ROSE
67	Piccadilly 7N 35408	One Way Street/Linda Loves Linda	50

(see also Scrugg, John T. Kongos)

FLOWCHART
90s	Enraptured RAPT 4527	NO. 7 IN THE STRESS FREE SERIES: Gip Part One/Gip Part 2 (in box)	6

FLOWERPOT MEN
67	Deram DM 142	Let's Go To San Francisco (Parts 1 & 2)	5
68	Page One POF 065	Mighty Quinn/Voices From The Sky	10
67	Deram DM 160	A Walk In The Sky/Am I Losing You?	8
68	Deram DM 183	A Man Without A Woman/You Can Never Be Wrong	8
69	Deram DM 248	In A Moment Of Madness/Young Birds Fly	10
88	C5 C5-526	LET'S GO TO SAN FRANCISCO (LP)	12

(see also Ivy League, Friends, Carter-Lewis & Southerners, Edison Lighthouse, Fat Mattress, Gordon Haskell, Kestrels, One & One)

FLOWERS & FROLICS
77	Free Reed FRR 016	BEES ON HORSEBACK (LP, featuring June Tabor & Bob Davenport)	35

FLOWERS IN THE DUSTBIN
84	All The Madmen MAD 7	FREAKS RUN WILD IN THE DISCO (12" EP)	15
85	Mortarhate MORT 16	Nails Of The Heart/All Fools Day/The Reason Why	12
86	Cold Harbour COLD 1002	Lick My Crazy Colours!/The Continuing Tragedy Of Mr. Smith/Stranger In A strange Land	12

LLOYD FLOWERS & RECO'S RHYTHM GROUP
62	Blue Beat BB 88	I'm Going Home/Lover's Town	15

(LLOYD) FLOWERS & ALVIN (RANGLIN)
72	Explosion EX 2067	Howdy And Tenky/SHORTY PERRY: Sprinkle Some Water	7
72	Grape GR 3028	In De Pum Pum/MAYTONES: If Loving You Was Wrong	6
72	Bullet BU 512	Howdy And Tenky/SHORTY PERRY: Sprinkle Some Water	7
73	Duke DU 150	Rastaman Going Back Home/LITTLE YOUTH: Barble Dove Skank	6

MINT VALUE £

PHIL FLOWER(S)
69	A&M AMS 766	Like A Rolling Stone/Keep On Sockin' It Children	20

FLOWER SERMON
92	Rough Trade 45REV 13	Sugar Lullaby (p/s with insert)	8

FLOWER SHOPPE
72	Polydor 2066 096	You've Come A Long Way/Kill The Monster	10

FLOWER TRAVELLING BAND
71	Atlantic 2091 128	Satori (Enlightment) (Parts 1 & 2)	20

BOBBY FLOYD
72	Pama PM 860	Sound Doctor/YOUNG DILLINGER: Doctor Skank	20

EDDIE FLOYD
66	Atlantic 584 041	Knock On Wood/Got To Make A Comeback	10
67	Stax 601 001	Raise Your Hand/I've Just Been Feeling Bad (dark blue label)	10
67	Stax 601 001	Raise Your Hand/I've Just Been Feeling Bad (light blue label)	8
67	London HL 10129	Set My Soul On Fire/Will I Be The One?	8
67	Speciality SPE 1001	Never Get Enough Of Your Love/Bye Bye Baby	8
67	Stax 601 016	Things Get Better/Good Love, Bad Love	12
67	Stax 601 024	On A Saturday Night/Under My Nose	12
68	Stax 601 035	Big Bird/Holding On With Both Hands	12
68	Stax STAX 104	I've Never Found A Girl (To Love Me Like You Do)/I'm Just The Kind Of Fool	12
69	Stax STAX 108	Bring It On Home To Me/Sweet Things You Do	7
69	Stax STAX 116	I've Got To Have Your Love/Girl I Love You	5
69	Stax STAX 125	Don't Tell Your Mama/Consider Me	5
70	Stax STAX 153	My Girl/Laurie	5
72	Polydor 2025 098	Yum Yum Yum/I Want Some/Tears Of Joy	5
74	Stax STXS 2005	Soul Street/The Highway Man	5
81	I-Spy SEE 9	The Beat Song/London ('I-Spy' sleeve)	5
67	Stax 589 006	KNOCK ON WOOD (LP)	35
68	Stax (S)XATS 1003	I'VE NEVER FOUND A GIRL (LP)	25
69	Stax SXATS 1023	YOU'VE GOT TO HAVE EDDIE (LP)	20
70	Stax SXATS 1036	CALIFORNIA GIRL (LP)	20

(see also Falcons, Primettes/Eddie Floyd)

FLUEGAL KNIGHTS
67	CBS 2951	Everybody Loves My Baby/Two Different Worlds	5
68	CBS 3677	Desert/Mrs Robinson	5

FLUFF
70	DJM DJS 215	Make Believe/Love Machine	12

FLUTTERS
	STEW 101	Haunted Staircase/Something For The Children (P/S)	10

FLUX (OF PINK INDIANS)
81	Crass 321984/2	NEU SMELL (EP, foldout poster sleeve)	8
85	Spiderleg SDL 16	TAKING A LIBERTY (EP, as Flux, with booklet sleeve)	8
83	Spiderleg SDL 8	STRIVE TO SURVIVE CAUSING THE LEAST SUFFERING POSSIBLE (LP, with booklet)	15
84	Spiderleg SDL 13	THE FUCKING CUNTS TREAT US LIKE PRICKS (2-LP)	18
87	Overground OVER 87	LIVE STATEMENT (LP, 1,000 only)	12

(see also Epileptics, Licks)

FLY ON THE WALL
79	Next Wave NEXT 1	DEVON DUMB (EP, numbered)	25

FLYING BRIX
80	Modello MHMS 194	BLACK COLOURS EP (p/s, with booket, 500 only)	20

FLYING BURRITO BROTHERS
69	A&M AMS 756	The Train Song/Hot Burrito No. 1	8
70	A&M AMS 794	Older Guys/Down In The Churchyard	5
70	A&M AMS 816	Tried So Hard/Lazy Days	5
72	A&M AMS 871	White Line Fever/Colorado	5
69	A&M AML(S) 931	THE GILDED PALACE OF SIN (LP)	25
70	A&M AMLS 983	BURRITO DELUXE (LP)	18
71	A&M AMLS 64295	THE FLYING BURRITO BROTHERS (LP)	15
72	A&M AMLS 64343	LAST OF THE RED-HOT BURRITOS (LP)	15

(see also Byrds, Gram Parsons, Gene Parsons, Stephen Stills & Manassas, Rick Roberts, Country Gazette, Skip Battin)

FLYING CIRCUS
71	Harvest SHSP 4010	PREPARED IN PEACE (LP, no EMI box on label)	40

FLYING COLOURS
81	No Records NO 1	Abstract Art/Ape Notes (p/s)	25

FLYING LIZARDS
81	Virgin V2190	FOURTH WALL (LP)	18
80	Virgin 2473791	FLYING LIZARDS (LP)	20

FLYING LOTUS
07	Warp WAP 228	Reset (12")	15
10	Warp WAP 195	COSMOGRAMMA (2-LP, plastic sleeves and grease proof sleeve, MP3 download)	18

FLYING MACHINE
69	Pye 7N 17722	Smile A Little Smile For Me/Maybe We've Been Loving Too Long	7
69	Pye 7N 17722	Baby Make It Soon/Smile A Little Smile For Me	6
69	Pye 7N 17811	Send My Baby Home Again/Look At Me, Look At Me	7
70	Pye 7N 17914	Hanging On The Edge Of Sadness/Flying Machine	7
70	Pye 7N 45001	The Devil Has Possession Of Your Mind/Hey Little Girl	25
70	Pye 7N 45093	Yes I Understand/Pages Of Your Life	6
70	Pye NSPL 18328	DOWN TO EARTH WITH THE FLYING MACHINE (LP, blue/black label with logo-banner on top)	30

(see also Pinkertons, Pinkerton's Assorted Colours, Tony Newman)

FLYING SAUCER ATTACK

92	Heartbeat FSA 6	Soaring High/Standing Stone (p/s, 500 only, 1st few with autographed postcards)	25
92	Heartbeat FSA 6	Soaring High/Standing Stone (p/s, 500 only, with various different designs)	20
93	Heartbeat FSA 61	Wish/Oceans (p/s, 700 only)	20
94	Domino RUG 23	Land Beyond The Sun/Everywhere Was Everything (p/s, hand-painted rear sleeve, 500 only)	6
95	Domino RUG 41	Outdoor Miner/Psychic Driving (p/s)	5
95	Planet PUNK 008	Beach Red Lullaby/Second Hour (p/s, 1,300 only)	6
96	Enraptured RAPT 4505	At Night/JESSAMINE: From Hereto And Now Otherwise (500 on clear vinyl)	12
96	Enraptured RAPT 4505	At Night/JESSAMINE: From Hereto And Now Otherwise (2500 on black vinyl)	8
98	Earworm WORMSC 1	Land Beyond The Sun (2 -Track Version)/Instrumental For Silence (green vinyl, 500 only)	6
94	Heartbeat FSA 62	FLYING SAUCER ATTACK (LP, 1,000 only)	30
94	Domino WIGLP 12	DISTANCE (LP)	15
94	Domino WIGLP 20	FURTHER (LP, gatefold sleeve, insert)	20
95	Domino WIGLP 22	CHORUS (LP, inert)	15

FLYING SAUCERS

75	Harbour HRB 12	Beer, Bourbon and Wine/Teenage Boogie	5
76	Alaska ALA2001	Fabulous/Fish On The Line	6
76	Alaska ALA 2003	Keep On Comming/Shadow Walk	6
76	Alaska ALA 2014	Texas Calls You Home/Pretty Baby (p/s)	8
78	Alaska ALA 2014	Texas Calls You Home/Pretty Baby	6
76	Nevis NEV LP 114	PLANET OF THE DRAPES (LP)	12
91	Rawking Music	THE ROCKING SANDY FORD (LP)	25

FLYING SQUAD

78	Epic S EPC 6375	Drive On/Baltimore Baby	5
78	Epic S EPC 6542	Backroom Boys (Night After Night)/Tell Me What To Do	5
78	Epic EPC 82875	FLYING SQUAD (LP)	12

(see also Status Quo)

STEVE FLYNN

67	Parlophone R 5625	Mr Rainbow/Let's Live For Tomorrow	45
68	Parlophone R 5689	Your Life And My Life/Come Tomorrow	10

(see also Mark Wirtz)

FLYS

78	EMI EMI 2747	Love And A Molotov Cocktail/Can I Crash Here?/Civilisation (p/s)	12
78	EMI EMI 2795	Fun City/E.C. 4 (p/s)	10
78	EMI EMIY 2867	Waikiki Beach Refugees/We Don't Mind The Rave (p/s, yellow vinyl)	10
79	EMI EMI 2907	Beverley/Don't Moonlight On Me (p/s)	6
79	EMI EMI 2936	Name Dropping/Fly V Fly (p/s, some on green vinyl)	15
79	EMI EMI 2979	We Are The Lucky Ones/Living In The Sticks (p/s)	8
79	Parlophone R 6030	16 Down/Night Creatures/Lois Lane/Today Belongs To Me (p/s)	5
77	Zama ZA 10 EP	BUNCH OF FIVE (33rpm EP, die-cut p/s)	50
78	EMI EMC 3249	WAIKIKI BEACH REFUGEES (LP)	15
80	Parlophone R 6063	FOUR FROM THE SQUARE (demo copies)	20

FLYTE REACTION

91	Woronzow W0014	SONGS IN A CIRCLE (LP)	20

FOALS

06	Try Harder	Try This On Your Piano/Look At My Furrows Of Worry (700 only, hand-numbered)	25
07	Transgressive TRANS049	FOALS LIVE (12" promo, 1000 only p/s)	25
07	Transgressive TRANS 050	Hummer/Astronauts And All (p/s, 1000 only)	20
07	Transgressive TRANS 053	Mathletics/Big Big Love (1,500 only)	20
08	Transgressive TRANS 069	Cassius/The Chronic (p/s)	6
08	Transgressive TRANS 069X	Cassius/A Song For You (p/s)	6
08	Transgressive TRANS 089.5	Super Inuit/HOLY FUCK: Balloons (die cut sleeve decorated by band, 250 only)	15

FOCAL POINT

68	Deram DM 186	Love You Forever/Sycamore Sid	50

FO'C'SLE

72	Tradition TSC 1	FROM THE FOREST (LP, 100 copies only)	25

FOCUS

71	Polydor 2001 134	House Of The King/Black Beauty	5
71	Blue Horizon 2094 006	Hocus Pocus/Janis	15
72	Blue Horizon 2096 008	Tommy/Focus II	15
71	Polydor 2344 003	IN AND OUT OF FOCUS (LP, gatefold sleeve)	15
71	Blue Horizon 2096 2931	MOVING WAVES (LP, 1st pressing, white/blue labels, Matrixes: Side 1, 2931002 A etched (with 2431011 crossed out) A//1 V 420 1 1 2, Side 2 2931002 B etched (243101 stamped not crossed out) B//1 V 420 11 4, Blue Horizon logo on rear of E.J. Group sleeve)	25
72	Polydor 2659 016	FOCUS III (2-LP, gatefold sleeve)	15
76	SHSP 4069	SHIP OF MEMORIES (LP)	15
73	Polydor 2442 118	AT THE RAINBOW (multifold sleeve)	15

(see also Jan Akkerman, Brainbox, Robin Lent)

FOCUS THREE

67	Columbia DB 8279	10,000 Years Behind My Mind/The Sunkeeper	70

FOETUS ÜBER FRISCO

82	Self Immolation WOMB 125/ SUSC 12	Custom Built For Capitalism/1.0.4.5./Birthday (12", p/s)	8
85	Self Immolation. WOMB UNC 7.12	Finely Honed Machine/Sick Minutes (12")	8

FOETUS UNDER GLASS

85	Self Immolation. WOMB S201	Spite Your Face/OKFM (p/s)	15

(see also You've Got Foetus On Your Breath, Philip & His Foetus Vibrations, Scraping Foetus Off The Wheel,

FOGCUTTERS

64	Liberty LIB 55793	Cry Cry Cry/You Say	15

DAN FOGELBIRD

77	Full Moon S EPC 5483	Nether Lands/Loose Ends	6

JOHN FOGERTY

74	Fantasy FTC 111	Comin' Down The Road/Ricochet	5
75	Fantasy FTC 119	Rockin' All Over The World/The Wall	5
75	Fantasy FTC 120	Almost Saturday Night/Sea Cruise	5
76	Fantasy FTC 133	You Got The Magic/Evil Thing	5
75	Fantasy FT 526	JOHN FOGERTY (LP)	12

(see also Creedence Clearwater Revival, Blue Ridge Rangers)

TOM FOGERTY

71	United Artists UP 35264	Goodbye Media Man (Parts 1 & 2)	5
72	Fantasy F 680	Cast The First Stone/Lady Of Fatima	5
73	Fantasy FTC 109	Joyful Resurrection/Heartbeat	5
72	Fantasy FAN 9407	TOM FOGERTY (LP)	12

(see also Creedence Clearwater Revival, Ruby)

FOGG

| 74 | EMI EMI 2182 | Water In My Wine/Just Like Me | 8 |

FOGGY

72	York SYK 534	How Come The Sun/Take Your Time	10
73	York SYK 542	Kitty Starr/She's Far Away (p/s)	15
73	York SYK 542	Kitty Star/She's far Away (no p/s)	10
72	York FYK 411	SIMPLE GIFTS (LP, with insert, featuring Strawbs)	30
75	Canon CNN 5759	PATCHWORK (LP)	20

(see also Strawbs, Foggy Dew-O)

FOGGY DEW-O

68	Decca F 12776	Reflections/Grandfather's Clock	8
71	York SYK 503	Me And Bobby McGee/Feelin' Groovy	6
68	Decca LK/SKL 4940	THE FOGGY DEW-O (LP, blue/silver labels with large unboxed logo)	25
70	Decca LK/SKL 5035	BORN TO TAKE THE HIGHWAY (LP, blue/silver label with small boxed logo)	15

(see also Strawbs, Foggy)

FOGHAT

72	Bearsville K15501	What A Shame / Hole To Hide In	6
74	Bearsville K15511	Long Way To Go / Ride Ride Ride	6
74	Bearsville K15517	Step Outside (edit) /Mabellene	5
76	Bearsville K15522	Slow Ride (edit) / Save Your Loving	5
77	Bearsville K15537	I Just Want To Make Love To You (live edit) / Fool For The City (live edit)	5
79	Bearsville WIP6582	Third Time Lucky / Somebody's Been Sleeping In My Bed	5
72	Bearsville K45503	FOGHAT (LP)	20
73	Bearsville K45514	FOGHAT — ROCK'N'ROLL (LP)	12

(see also Black Cat Bones, Savoy Brown, Warren Philips & The Rockets)

ELLEN FOLEY (& CLASH)

81	Epic EPC A 9522	The Shuttered Palace/Beautiful Waste Of Time (p/s)	6
81	Epic EPC A 1160	Torchlight/Game Of A Man (p/s)	6
81	Epic SEPC 84809	SPIRIT OF ST. LOUIS (LP, with inner sleeve)	15

(see also Clash)

RED FOLEY

54	Brunswick 05307	Pin Ball Boogie/Jilted (78)	10
54	Brunswick 05321	Skinnie Minnie (Fishtail)/Thank You For Calling	15
55	Brunswick 05508	Croce Di Oro (Cross Of Gold) (with Betty Foley)/The Night Watch	10
55	Brunswick 05363	Hearts Of Stone/RED FOLEY & BETTY FOLEY: Never	20
60	Brunswick STA 3034	SING ALONG WITH RED FOLEY (LP, stereo)	12

(see also Roberta Lee)

RED FOLEY & ERNEST TUBB

| 55 | Brunswick OE 9148 | COUNTRY DOUBLE DATE (EP, with Minnie Pearl) | 20 |
| 57 | Brunswick LAT 8206 | RED AND ERNIE (LP) | 15 |

(see also Ernest Tubb)

SIMON FOLEY

| 77 | Look LKLP 6324 | TO STRIVE WITH PRINCES (LP, with booklet) | 20 |

FOLKAL POINT

| 72 | Midas MR 003 | FOLKAL POINT (LP) | 1500 |

FOLK DEVILS

| 84 | Ganges RAY 1 | Hank Turns Blue/Chewin' The Fat (with p/s) | 15 |
| 84 | Ganges RAY 1 | Hank Turns Blue/Chewin' The Fat | 8 |

CALVIN FOLKES

63	Rio R 5	Someone/Kentucky Home	10
63	Rio R 8	You'll Never Know/Is It Time?	10
64	Port-O-Jam PJ 4117	My Bonnie/What A Day	12
64	Port-O-Jam PJ 4118	Hello Everybody/IRVING SIX: King's Boogie	12

FOLKLANDERS

| 60s | Urban PB 001 | TWO LITTLE FISHES (EP) | 10 |

FOLK(S) BROTHERS

61	Blue Beat BB 30	Carolina/I Met A Man (original, blue label, as Folks Brothers)	18
60s	Fab BB 30	Carolina (as Folks Brothers)/ERIC 'HUMPTY DUMPTY' MORRIS: Humpty Dumpty	7
70s	Blue Beat BB 30	Carolina/I Met A Man (reissue, white label, as Folk Brothers)	6

FOLK SONG CLUB

| 65 | white label (no cat. no.) | IMPERIAL COLLEGE (LP, private pressing) | 100 |

FOLKWAYS

| 72 | Folk Heritage | NO OTHER NAME (LP) | 12 |

EDDIE FONTAINE

55	HMV 7M 304	Rock Love/All My Love Belongs To You (with Neal Hefti & Excels)	250
55	HMV B 10852	Rock Love/All My Love Belongs To You (with Neal Hefti & Excels) (78)	40
56	Brunswick 05624	Cool It, Baby/Into Each Life Some Rain Must Fall	200
56	Brunswick 05624	Cool It, Baby/Into Each Life Some Rain Must Fall (78)	40

58	London HLM 8711	Nothin' Shakin' (But The Leaves On The Trees)/Don't Ya Know	50
58	London HLM 8711	Nothin' Shakin' (But The Leaves On The Trees)/Don't Ya Know (78)	20

FONTAINES
87	51st Parallel FONT 1	I Want Everything/Bernadette (p/s)	30

ARLENE FONTANA
59	Pye International 7N 25010	I'm In Love/Easy	10

WAYNE FONTANA & THE MINDBENDERS
63	Fontana TF 404	Hello! Josephine/Road Runner	25
63	Fontana TF 418	For You, For You/Love Potion No.9	15
64	Fontana TF 436	Little Darlin'/Come Dance With Me	20
64	Fontana TF 451	Stop Look And Listen/Duke Of Earl	10
64	Fontana TF 497	Um, Um, Um, Um, Um, Um/First Taste Of Love	5
65	Fontana TF 535	The Game Of Love/Since You've Been Gone	6
65	Fontana TF 579	It's Just A Little Bit Too Late/Long Time Comin'	10
65	Fontana TF 611	She Needs Love/Like I Did	8
69	Fontana H 1022	Um, Um, Um, Um, Um, Um/The Game Of Love (p/s)	8
64	Fontana TE 17421	ROAD RUNNER (EP)	50
64	Fontana TE 17435	UM, UM, UM, UM, UM, UM (EP)	20
65	Fontana TE 17449	THE GAME OF LOVE (EP)	18
65	Fontana TE 17453	WALKING ON AIR (EP)	40
64	Fontana TL 5230	WAYNE FONTANA AND THE MINDBENDERS (LP)	60
65	Fontana TL 5257	ERIC, RICK, WAYNE, BOB — IT'S WAYNE FONTANA AND THE MINDBENDERS (LP)	65
67	Wing WL 1166	WAYNE FONTANA AND THE MINDBENDERS (LP, reissue)	15

(see also Wayne Fontana, Mindbenders)

WAYNE FONTANA
65	Fontana TF 642	It Was Easier To Hurt Her/You Made Me What I Am Today	10
66	Fontana TF 684	Come On Home/My Eyes Break Out In Tears	5
66	Fontana TF 737	Goodbye Bluebird/The Sun's So Hot Today	6
66	Fontana TF 770	Pamela Pamela/Something Keeps Calling Me Back	6
67	Fontana TF 827	24 Sycamore/From A Boy To A Man	6
67	Fontana TF 866	The Impossible Years/In My World	12
67	Fontana TF 889	Gina/We All Love The Human Race	6
68	Fontana TF 911	Storybook Children/I Need To Love You	6
68	Fontana TF 933	The Words Of Bartholomew/Mind Excursion	6
68	Fontana TF 976	Never An Everyday Thing/Waiting For A Break In The Clouds	40
69	Fontana TF 1008	Dayton Ohio 1903/Say Goodbye To Yesterday	7
69	Fontana TF 1054	Charlie Cass/Linda (withdrawn issue)	25
69	Fontana TF 1054	We're Building A Love/Charlie Cass	10
69	Fontana TF 1027	Come On Home/Pamela Pamela (p/s)	10
70	Philips 6006 035	Give Me Just A Little More Time/I'm In Love (withdrawn)	150
70	Philips 6006 035	Give Me Just A Little More Time/I'm In Love (withdrawn) (DJ Copy)	100
73	Warner Bros K 16269	Together/One Man Woman	6
66	Fontana (S)TL 5351	WAYNE ONE (LP, black/silver labels)	25
69	Fontana SFL 13144	WAYNE ONE (LP, reissue)	12

(see also Mindbenders)

FONTANE SISTERS
54	London HL 8099	Happy Days And Lonely Nights/If I Didn't Have You	70
54	London HL 8099	Happy Days And Lonely Nights/If I Didn't Have You (78)	12
55	London HL 8113	Hearts Of Stone/Bless Your Heart	70
55	London HL 8126	Rock Love/You're Mine	70
55	London HLD 8177	Seventeen/If I Could Be With You	100
55	London HLD 8211	Rolling Stone/Daddy-O	50
55	London HLD 8211	Rolling Stone/Daddy-O (78)	10
56	London HLD 8225	Adorable/Playmates	40
56	London HLD 8225	Adorable/Playmates (78)	10
56	London HLD 8265	Eddie My Love/Yum Yum	50
56	London HL 7009	Eddie My Love/Yum Yum (export issue)	40
56	London HLD 8289	I'm In Love Again/You Always Hurt The One You Love (gold lettering label)	40
56	London HLD 8289	I'm In Love Again/You Always Hurt The One You Love (later silver lettering label)	15
56	London HLD 8289	I'm In Love Again/You Always Hurt The One You Love (78)	12
56	London HLD 8318	Voices (with narration by Pat Boone)/Willow Weep For Me (gold lettering label)	20
56	London HLD 8318	Voices (with narration by Pat Boone)/Willow Weep For Me (later silver lettering label)	10
56	London HLD 8343	Silver Bells/Nuttin' For Christmas	15
57	London HLD 8378	The Banana Boat Song/Lonesome Lover Blues (gold lettering)	15
57	London HLD 8378	The Banana Boat Song/Lonesome Lover Blues (silver lettering)	10
57	London HLD 8415	Please Don't Leave Me/Still	10
57	London HLD 8488	Fool Around/Which Way To Your Heart?	10
58	London HLD 8621	Chanson D'Amour (Song Of Love)/Cocoanut Grove	10
59	London HLD 8861	Billy Boy/Encore D'Amour	10
60	London HLD 9037	Listen To Your Heart/Please Be Kind	5
60	London HLD 9078	Theme From "A Summer Place"/Darling, It's Wonderful	5
55	London RE-D 1029	FONTANE SISTERS NO. 1 (EP)	40
55	London RE-D 1037	FONTANE SISTERS NO. 2 (EP)	40
57	London HA-D 2053	THE FONTANES SING (LP)	60

(see also Pat Boone, Perry Como)

SAM FONTEYN
66	Parlophone R 5519	Lost In Space/BERNARD SHARPE: Jorrocks	10

BILLY FONTEYNE
63	Oriole CB 1917	Little Child/Look Before You Leap	15

FOO FIGHTERS
95	Roswell CL 753	This Is A Call/Winnebago (p/s)	6
95	Roswell 12CL 753	This Is A Call/Winnebago/Podunk (12", luminous vinyl)	20
95	Roswell CL 757	I'll Stick Around/How I Miss You (red vinyl, p/s)	8
95	Roswell 12CL 757	I'll Stick Around/How I Miss You (12" p/s)	15
95	Roswell CL 762	For All The Cows/Watershed (blue vinyl, p/s)	8
95	Roswell CDCL 762	For All The Cows/(live version)/Watershed (live) (CD)	10

FOOL

95	Roswell CL 768	Big Me/Floaty/Gas Chamber (white vinyl, p/s)	10
97	Roswell CL 788	Monkey Wrench/Up In Arms (red vinyl, p/s)	10
97	Roswell CL 792	Everlong/Drive Me Wild (blue vinyl, p/s)	25
97	Roswell CL 796	My Hero/Dear Lover (red vinyl, stickered poly sleeve, with insert)	10
00	RCA 74321 79012-7	Breakout/Stacked Actors (live) (p/s)	5
00	RCA 74321 80926-7	Next Year/Big Me (live) (p/s)	6
02	RCA 74321 97315-7	All My Life/Sister Europe (numbered p/s)	6
03	RCA 74321 98955-7	Times Like These/Lack Of Illision (numbered p/s)	6
03	RCA 82876 56370-7	Have It All/Darling Nikki (p/s)	5
03	BMG 82876-52256-7	Low/Never Talking To You Again (Live Version) (numbered p/s, 3,000 only)	10
05	RCA 82876 72279-7	D.O.A./Razor (Acoustic) (p/s, yellow vinyl)	6
05	RCA 82876 74965-7	Resolve/World (Demo) (p/s)	5
05	RCA 82876 70121-7	Best Of You/Spill (p/s)	5
07	RCA 88697 13999-7	The Pretender/Bangin' (clear vinyl, p/s)	5
07	RCA 88697 19036-7	Long Road To Ruin/Holiday In Cambodia (p/s)	5
95	Roswell EST 2266	FOO FIGHTERS (LP)	30
97	Roswell EST 2295	THE COLOUR AND THE SHAPE (LP)	60
99	RCA 07863678921	THERE IS NOTHING LEFT TO LOSE (LP)	35
02	RCA 74321973481	ONE BY ONE (LP, gatefold sleeve with inner)	35
05	BMG 82876680381	IN YOUR HONOUR (4-LP)	40

FOOL

69	Mercury MF 1111	We Are One/Shining Light	10
69	Mercury SMCL 20138	THE FOOL (LP, gatefold sleeve. black/silver labels)	75

FOOLS DANCE

87	L. T. T. Slaughter LTS 22	They'll Never Know/Empty Hours (p/s)	10
87	L. T. T. Slaughter LTS 22T	They'll Never Know/The Collector/Empty Hours/The Ring (12", p/s)	15
85	Top Hole Turn TURN 19	FOOLS DANCE (mini-LP)	20
86	Top Hat TH 22	FOOLS DANCE (mini-LP, reissue)	12

(see also Cure, Stranglers)

FOOT IN COLD WATER

73	Island WIP 6162	(Isn't Love Unkind) In My Life/Deep Freeze	7
74	Elektra K12164	I Know What You Need/Para – Dice	8
74	Elektra K 52011	OR ALL AROUND US (LP)	20

CHUCK FOOTE

62	London HLU 9495	You're Running Out Of Kisses/Come On Back	10

FORBES

77	Power Exchange PX 253	The Beatles/Sweet Kiss Of Fire	7

BILL FORBES

58	Columbia DB 4232	My Cherie/God's Little Acre	6
59	Columbia DB 4269	Once More/Believe In Me	8
59	Columbia DB 4386	Too Young/It's Not The End Of The World	6
61	Columbia DB 4566	You're Sixteen, You're Beautiful/Backward Child	15
61	Columbia DB 4619	That's It, I Quit, I'm Moving On/Big City Boy	15
61	Columbia DB 4747	Goodbye Cruel World/Next Time	12
62	Columbia DB 4855	Laughter Or Tears/Like A Good Girl Should	6
62	Columbia DB 4945	Poker Face/Marianne	6

(see also Contrasts)

SMOKY FORBES

71	Beacon BEA 176	My Kind Of Music/Loves Goes	6

FORCEFIELD

87	President PT 551	Smoke On The Water/Shine It On Me (p/s)	5
88	President PT 578	Heartache/I Lose Again (Instrumental Version) (p/s)	5

(see also Cozy Powell, Graham Bonnet, Ray Fenwick, Whitesnake)

FORCE FIVE

64	United Artists UP 1051	Don't Make My Baby Blue/Shaking Postman	30
65	United Artists UP 1089	Yeah, I'm Waiting/I Don't Want To See You Again	35
65	United Artists UP 1102	Baby Don't Care/Come Down To Earth	35
65	United Artists UP 1118	I Want You Babe/Gee Too Tiger	50
66	United Artists UP 1141	Don't Know Which Way To Turn/Baby Let Your Hair Down	45

(see also Crocheted Doughnut Ring)

FORCE WEST

65	Decca F 12223	I Can't Give What I Haven't Got/Why Won't She Stay	12
66	Columbia DB 7908	Gotta Find Another Baby/Talkin' About Our Love	15
66	Columbia DB 7963	When The Sun Comes Out (Weatherman)/Gotta Tell Somebody	12
67	Columbia DB 8174	All The Children Sleep/Desolation	15
68	CBS 3632	I'll Walk In The Rain/What's It To Be?	8
68	CBS 3798	I'll Be Moving On/Like The Tide, Like The Ocean	8
69	CBS 4385	Sherry/Mister Blue	8

FORD & THE COALITION

94	Shot In The Dark COAL 2616	The Coalition (12")	15

BICK FORD

63	Parlophone R 5018	Cheat Cheat/Sweet And Tender Romance	8

CLINTON FORD

60	Oriole EP 7027	GOES TRADITIONAL (EP)	8
62	Oriole EP 7069	CLINT (EP)	8
62	Oriole EP 7071	CLINT ALL OVER AGAIN (EP)	8
63	Columbia 33SX 1560	THE MELODY MAN (LP) (also stereo SCX 3496)	12
65	Columbia SCX 3529	LISTEN WITH US (LP) (stereo)	12

(see also Hallelujah Skiffle Group)

DEAN FORD (& GAYLORDS)

64	Columbia DB 7264	Twenty Miles/What's The Matter With Me?	25
64	Columbia DB 7402	Mr Heartbreak's Here Instead/I Won't	25
65	Columbia DB 7610	The Name Game/That Lonely Feeling	25

| 76 | EMI 2717 | The Fever/You Are The One | 6 |
| 75 | EMI EMC 3079 | DEAN FORD (LP) | 15 |

(see also Gaylords, Marmalade, Junior Campbell)

DEE DEE FORD

| 60 | London HLU 9245 | Good-Morning Blues/I Just Can't Believe | 40 |

(see also Don Gardner & Dee Dee Ford)

EDDIE/EDDY FORD

| 72 | Pressure Beat PB 5512 | You Wrong Fe Trouble Joshua/KENNETH POWER: Joshua Row Us Home | 7 |
| 73 | Duke Reid DR 2523 | Guess I This Riddle/Riddle Version (as Eddie Ford) | 5 |

EMILE FORD (& THE CHECKMATES)

59	Pye Nixa 7N 15225	What Do You Want To Make Those Eyes At Me For?/Don't Tell Me Your Troubles	5
59	Pye Nixa 7N 15225	What Do You Want To Make Those Eyes At Me For?/ Don't Tell Me Your Troubles (78)	12
60	Pye 7N 15245	On A Slow Boat To China/That Lucky Old Sun	5
60	Pye 7N 15268	You'll Never Know What You're Missin' 'Til You Try/Still	10
60	Pye 7N 15279	Red Sails In The Sunset/Afraid	5
60	Pye 7N 15282	Them There Eyes (solo)/Question	5
60	Pye 7N 15314	Counting Teardrops/White Christmas	5
61	Pye 7N 15331	What Am I Gonna Do/A Kiss To Build A Dream On	7
61	Piccadilly 7N 35003	Half Of My Heart/Gypsy Love (solo)	10
61	Piccadilly 7N 35007	After You've Gone/Hush, Somebody's Calling My Name	10
61	Piccadilly 7N 35019	The Alphabet Song/Keep A-Lovin' Me (solo)	8
62	Piccadilly 7N 35033	I Wonder Who's Kissing Her Now/Doin' The Twist (solo)	8
62	Piccadilly 7N 35078	Your Nose Is Gonna Grow/Rains Come	8
63	Piccadilly 7N 35116	Hold Me Thrill Me Kiss Me/Doin' What You Do To Me	8
69	Decca F 12959	Set Me Free/Don't Remind Me (export issue)	12
79	Transdics TR7	Dance With Me/How Can I Live Without You	6
59	Pye NEP 24119	EMILE (EP)	15
60	Pye NEP 24124	EMILE FORD HIT PARADE (EP)	12
60	Pye NEP 24133	EMILE FORD HIT PARADE VOL. 2 (EP)	15
60	Pye NPL 18049	NEW TRACKS WITH EMILE (LP)	20
61	Piccadilly NPL 38001	EMILE (LP)	25

'TENNESSEE' ERNIE FORD

54	Capitol CL 14005	Give Me Your Word/River Of No Return	20
54	Capitol CL 14006	Catfish Boogie/Kiss Me Big	25
55	Capitol CL 14261	His Hands/I Am A Pilgrim	10
55	Capitol CL 14273	Losing You/There Is Beauty In Everything	10
56	Capitol CL 14500	Sixteen Tons/You Don't Have To Be A Baby To Cry	25
56	Capitol CL 14506	The Ballad Of Davy Crockett/Farewell	15
56	Capitol CL 14557	That's All/Bright Lights And Blonde-Haired Women	10
61	Capitol CL 15210	Little Red Rockin' Hood/I Gotta Have My Baby Back	20
77	Capitol CL 15923	Shot Gun Boogie/Smoky Mountain Boogie	5
56	Capitol EAP 1014	SIXTEEN TONS (EP)	10
61	Capitol EAP1 20067	ANTICIPATION BLUES (EP)	15
52	Capitol LC 6573	CAPITOL PRESENTS (10" LP)	25
56	Capitol LC 6825	THIS LUSTY LAND (10" LP)	12
58	Capitol T 888	OL' ROCKIN' ERN (LP)	25
60	Capitol T 1380	SIXTEEN TONS (LP)	15

(see also Dinning Sisters)

'TENNESSEE' ERNIE FORD & BETTY HUTTON

| 54 | Capitol CL 14133 | This Must Be The Place/The Honeymoon's Over (green label) | 18 |

FRANKIE FORD

59	London HL 8850	Sea Cruise/Roberta (with Huey 'Piano' Smith & Clowns) (black triangular centre)	60
59	London HL 8850	Sea Cruise/Roberta (with Huey 'Piano' Smith & Clowns) (later silver-top triangular centre)	30
59	London HL 8850	Sea Cruise/Roberta (with Huey 'Piano' Smith & Clowns) (78 rpm)	40
59	Top Rank JAR 186	Alimony/Can't Tell My Heart (What To Do) (with Huey 'Piano' Smith & Clowns)	12
59	Top Rank JAR 186	Alimony/Can't Tell My Heart (What To Do) (78)	40
60	Top Rank JAR 282	Cheatin' Woman/HUEY 'PIANO' SMITH & CLOWNS: Don't You Just Know Kokomo	20
60	Top Rank JAR 299	Time After Time/I Want To Be Your Man	10
60	London HLP 9222	You Talk Too Much/If You've Got Troubles	20
65	Sue WI 366	Sea Cruise/Roberta (with Huey 'Piano' Smith & Clowns) (reissue)	25
65	Sue WI 369	What's Going On?/Watchdog	30

(see also Huey Piano Smith)

JASON FORD & THE BULLDOGS

| 62 | Piccadilly 7N 35193 | Nobody Knows/Am I The One | 10 |

JOHN FORD

| 73 | UK UKR31 | It's Alright Bill/Captain Of Your Ship | 8 |

JON FORD

68	Philips BF 1690	Two's Company, Three's A Crowd/Place In Your Heart	7
69	Philips BF 1791	I Know It's Love/Look Before You Leap	6
69	Philips BF 1817	Ice Cream Man/This Was The Time	6
70	Philips BF 1833	Yesterday When I Was Young/Running Around	6
70	Philips 6006 030	You've Got Me Where You Want Me/You're All Alone Tonight	100
70	Philips 6006 030	You've Got Me Where You Want Me/You're All Alone Tonight (DJ Copy)	150

LITA FORD & OZZY OSBOURNE

| 89 | Dreamland A 49396 | Close My Eyes Forever (Remix)/Under The Gun (p/s) | 5 |
| 89 | Dreamland PA 49396 | Close My Eyes Forever (Remix)/Under The Gun/Blueberry (12", picture disc) | 8 |

(see also Ozzy Osbourne, Runaways)

MIKE FORD & THE CONSULS

| 63 | Piccadilly 7N 35127 | Jumping Jeremiah/The Greenman | 15 |

PERRY FORD (& SAPPHIRES)

59	Parlophone R 4573	Bye, Bye Baby, Goodbye/She Came As A Stranger	15
60	Parlophone R 4633	Crazy Over You/Garden Of Happiness	15
60	Parlophone R 4683	Don't Weep (Little Lady)/Little Grown-Up	15

Ricky FORD (& TENNESSEANS)

62	Decca F 11497	Baby, Baby (Don't You Worry)/Prince Of Fools (with Sapphires & Blue Flames) 15

(see also Ivy League, Georgie Fame)

RICKY FORD (& TENNESSEANS)
63	Parlophone R 5018	Sweet And Tender Romance/Cheat Cheat 10
64	Parlophone R 5230	You Are My Love/Long Way From Home (with Tennesseans)...................................7

SIR TED FORD
79	Ardent ADS 9001	Disco Music/I've Got A Goal...65
77	Barak BAR 3	I Wanna Be Near You/Ridin' Too High..10

JOHN FORDE
77	EMI EMI 2656	Stardance/Flight Of The Jumping Bean (12", p/s, some on blue vinyl) 50
77	Sidewalk 12 YSID 107	Woman/Stardance/Don't You Know Who Did It (12", p/s) 50

EDDIE 'BUSTER' FOREHAND
69	Action ACT 4519	Young Boy Blues/You Were Meant For Me 20

FOREHEADS IN A FISHTANK
80	Stuff Records FAB 4	She Loves You, Yeah/Baby Love (p/s) 8

FOREIGN LEGION
86	Rent-A-Racket RRR0001	TRENCHLINE (EP) 12
89	Schlawiner SO5	SURF CITY (EP, 350 copies only, black/green vinyl)..10
90	Venture VR/FL 100	WELCOME TO FORT ZINDERNEUF (LP) 15

FOREIGN PRESS
80	Streets Ahead SA 1	Downpour/Crossfire/Behind The Glass 12

JOHN FOREMAN
66	Reality RY 1004	THE 'OUSES IN BETWEEN (LP) 15

FORERUNNERS
64	Solar SRP 100	Bony Maronie/Pride 60

FORERUNNERS
60s	Key KL 008	THE FORERUNNERS (LP) 18
60s	Key KL 004	RUNNING BACK (LP) 18

FOREST SWORDS
10	No Pain In Pop NPIP 013	Rattling Cage/Hjurt (p/s) 8

FOREST (1)
69	Harvest HAR 5007	Searching For Shadows/Mirror Of Life..20
69	Harvest SHVL 760	FOREST (LP, gatefold sleeve, no EMI logo on label) 300
70	Harvest SHVL 784	FULL CIRCLE (LP, gatefold sleeve, no EMI logo on label) 500
88	Zap! ZAP 3	FULL CIRCLE (LP, reissue) 25

FOREST (2)
76	Midland International MID 1	Do Ya (Do Ya Want My Love)/I'll Stay With You 8

SHARON FORESTER
73	Ashanti ASH 403	Silly Wasn't I?/NOW-GEN: Silly Wasn't I? — Version 6
74	Ashanti SHAN 105	SHARON (LP)...20

FOREVER AMBER
69	Advance (no cat. no.)	THE LOVE CYCLE (LP, private pressing, 99 copies only) 2000

FOREVER MORE
70	RCA RCA 2024	Put Your Money On A Pony/Yours 6
70	RCA SF 8016	YOURS FOREVER MORE (LP, gatefold sleeve, orange label) 40
71	RCA LSA 3015	WORDS ON BLACK PLASTIC (LP, laminated front sleeve)...................................30

(see also Scots Of St. James, Hopscotch)

FOREVER PEOPLE
92	Sarah SARAH 54	Invisible/Sometimes (p/s, insert) 10

FORK IN THE ROAD
70	Ember EMB 311	I Can't Turn Around/Skeleton In My Closet (test pressing)...............................150
70	Ember EMB S 311	I Can't Turn Around/Skeleton In My Closet...100

FORMAT
69	CBS 4600	Maxwell's Silver Hammer/Music Man...10

(see also Fourmost)

FORMATIONS
68	MGM MGM 1399	At The Top Of The Stairs/Magic Melody 120
68	MGM MGM 1399	At The Top Of The Stairs/Magic Melody (DJ Copy) 220
71	Mojo 2027 001	At The Top Of The Stairs/Magic Melody (reissue) 5

FORMERLY FAT HARRY
71	Harvest SHSP 4016	FORMERLY FAT HARRY (LP, with EMI logo on label) 70

(see also Country Joe and the Fish)

FORMINX
65	Vocalion V 9235	Jenka Beat/Geronimo Jenka 30

(see also Aphrodite's Child, Vangelis)

FORMULA
65	HMV POP 1438	Close To Me/If Ever 10

FORMULA 1
65	Warner Bros WB 155	I Just Can't Go To Sleep/Sure Know A Lot About Love..30

FORMULA TWO
72	CBS SCBS 8285	Easy Times/Girl Who Lives Next Door 6

ANDY FORRAY
68	Parlophone R 5715	Sarah Jane/Don't Care Anymore 10
68	Parlophone R 5729	The Proud One/Messin' Round With Me 15
68	Decca F 12733	Epitaph To You/Dream With Me 80
69	Fontana TF 999	Let The Sunshine In/Baby Is Coming..10

HELEN FORREST

56	Capitol CL 14594	Taking A Chance On Love/I Love You Much Too Much	10
56	Capitol LC 6834	VOICE OF THE NAME BANDS (10" LP)	15

JANE FORREST

56	Columbia SCM 5213	Sincerely Yours/A Girl Can't Say	10

FOR(R)ESTERS

65	Polydor 56038	Broken Hearted Clown/Lonely Boy	10
65	Polydor 56057	How Can I Tell Her/So Shy	10
66	Polydor 56104	Early Morning Hours/World Is Mine	8
66	Columbia DB 8040	Sometimes When You're Lonely/Today Or Tomorrow (as Forresters)	7
66	Columbia DB 8086	Mr. Smith/Ship On The Sea (as Foresters)	10
67	Columbia DB 8176	Comin' Home In The Evening/Sunshine's On Its Way (as Foresters)	6

THOMAS FORSTNER

89	Ariola 112 298	Song Of Love/Nur Ein Lied (p/s, withdrawn)	5
89	Ariola 662 298	Song Of Love (12" Version)/Nur Ein Lied/Song Of Love (7") (CD, withdrawn)	8

BRUCE FORSYTH

59	Parlophone R4535	I'm In Charge/So Far So Good	5
68	Pye 7N 17460	I'm Backing Britain/There's Not Enough Love In The World (p/s)	6
60	Parlophone GEP 8807	I'M IN CHARGE (EP)	10
60	Parlophone PMC 1132	MR ENTERTAINMENT (LP, also stereo PCS 3031)	15

FORTES MENTUM

68	Parlophone R 5684	Saga Of A Wrinkled Man/Mr. Partridge Passed Away Today	50
68	Parlophone R 5726	I Can't Go On Loving You/Humdiggle We Love You	12
69	Parlophone R 5768	Gotta Go/Marrakesh	12

(see also Angel Pavement, Pussy)

LANCE FORTUNE

60	Pye 7N 15240	Be Mine/Action (with Johnny Prendy, alias John Barry)	5
60	Pye 7N 15260	This Love I Have For You/All On My Own	8
60	Pye 7N 15297	I Wonder/Will You Still Be My Girl?	8
61	Pye 7N 15347	Who's Gonna Tell Me?/Love Is The Sweetest Thing	12

FORTUNES

63	Decca F 11718	Summertime Summertime/I Love Her Still (as Fortunes & Cliftones) (in p/s)	30
63	Decca F 11718	Summertime Summertime/I Love Her Still (as Fortunes & Cliftones)	15
64	Decca F 11809	Caroline/If You Don't Want Me Now	30
64	Decca F 11912	Come On Girl/I Like The Look Of You (curved logo)	15
64	Decca F 11985	Look Homeward Angel/I'll Have My Tears To Remind Me	15
66	Decca F 12321	This Golden Ring/Someone To Care	6
66	Decca F 12429	You Gave Me Somebody To Love/Silent Street	6
66	Decca F 12485	Is It Really Worth Your While?/Am I Losing My Touch	6
67	Decca F 12612	Our Love Has Gone/Truly Yours	6
67	United Artists UP 1188	The Idol/His Smile Was A Lie	10
68	United Artists UP 2218	Loving Cup/Hour At The Movies	6
68	United Artists UP 2239	Seasons In The Sun/Louise	6
69	United Artists UP 35027	Ballad Of The Alamo/Save A Little Dream	6
69	United Artists UP 35054	Lifetime Of Love/Sad Sad Sad (withdrawn, existence unconfirmed)	0
69	United Artists UP 35054	Books And Films/Sad Sad Sad	7
71	Capitol CL 15671	Here Comes That Rainy Day Feeling Again/Bad Side Of Town	5
65	Decca LK 4736	THE FORTUNES (LP, mono)	35
65	Decca SKL 4736	THE FORTUNES (LP, stereo)	60
72	Capitol ST 21891	THE FORTUNES (LP)	15

(see also Glen Dale)

48 CHAIRS

79	Absurd Absurd 3	Snap It Around/Psycle Sluts (p/s)	5

45'S

79	Chopper CHEAP 5	Couldn't Believe A Word/Lonesome Lane (no p/s)	7
79	Stiff BUY 52	Couldn't Believe A Word/Lonesome Lane (no p/s, reissue)	5
81	45's Records ONE 45	Secrets And Whispers/Driving/Little Honda (p/s)	8

49 AMERICANS

80	Choo Choo Train CHUG 2	TOO YOUNG TO BE IDEAL (12" EP)	10
80	Choo Choo Train CHUG 1	EL PLURIBUS UNUM (LP)	12

FORUM

67	London HLM 10120	The River Is Wide/I Fall In Love (All Over Again)	15
70	B&C CB 119	The River Is Wide/I Fall In Love (All Over Again) (reissue)	5

FORWARD INTENSE

92	Harm HARM1	Stated/Imply The Calm (12")	50

SHIRLEY FORWOOD

57	London HLD 8402	Two Hearts (With An Arrow Between)/Juke Box Lovers	30

FOSSIL

74	Pennine PSS14	Black Night/For Your Love/Smile On Me/Wishing Well	35

BOBBY FOSTER

70	Bread BR 1101	Tell Me Why You Say Goodbye/YOUTH: I'll Make Him Believe In You	6

FRANK FOSTER

60s	Esquire 32 033	WAIL FRANK WAIL (LP)	18

JACKIE FOSTER

63	Sway SWAY 001	Dry Up Your Tears/Try To Understand	20
63	Planetone RC 13	Oh Leona/I Fell In Love	15

JOHN FOSTER

66	Island ILP 939	JOHN FOSTER SINGS (LP)	40

LARRY FOSTER & SOUL EXPLOSION

70	Fab FAB 130	Boom Biddy Boom/Next To Me (actually by Sugar Simone)	10

(see also Sugar Simone)

LES FOSTER

69	Wolf WM 02	You And Your Love/Turning Point (actually by D Dennis)	12
70	Torpedo TOR 7	Run Like A Thief/Nobody's Fool	8

LES FOSTER & ANSELL COLLINS

73	Camel CA 102	The Man In Your Life/Version	5

(see also Dave & Ansell Collins, Sugar Simone, Lance Hannibal)

LESLIE FOSTER

69	Jolly JY 022	Muriel/Nowhere To Hide	7

VINCENT FOSTER

69	Escort ES 803	Shine Eye Gal/Who Nest (B-side actually "Who Next" by Carl Bryan)	6

FOTHERINGAY

70	Island WIP 6085	Peace In The End/Winter Winds	15
70	Island ILPS 9125	FOTHERINGAY (LP, pink label/'i' logo, gatefold sleeve)	120
70	Island ILPS 9125	FOTHERINGAY (LP, later issue, pink rim label/'palm tree' logo, gatefold sleeve)	25

(see also Sandy Denny, Trevor Lucas, Eclection, Exception[s], Fairport Convention, Mick Greenwood)

FOUL PLAY

92	Oblivion OR 001	VOLUME 1 EP: The Alchemist/Ragatere/Ricochet/Feel The Vibe (12")	25
92	Oblivion OR 002	VOLUME 2 EP: Survival/Dubbing You/Ricochet (No Stopping The Remix)/Feel The Vibe (Again) (12")	25
93	Section 5 SECTION 04	Finest Illusion/Screwface (12" white label)	60
93	Section 5 SECTION 4	Finest Illusion/Screwface (12" printed labels)	50
93	Section 5 SECTION 4	Finest Illusion/Screwface (12", 2nd pressing, black labels, actually no labels at all!)	50
93	Moving Shadow SHADOW 29	VOLUME III EP: Open your mind/Murder most foul/Survival (remix)/ Dub in U (12", p/s)	8
93	Moving Shadow SHAD 29R	VOLUME III REMIXES: Open your mind (Tango remix)/Open your mind (Foul Play remix)(10", p/s)	8
93	Moving Shadow SHAD 29R2	VOLUME III REMIXES PART 2: Open Your Mind (Nookie Remix)/Finest Illusion (Legal Mix)(10", p/s)	10

FOUNDATIONS

67	Pye 7N 17366	Baby, Now That I've Found You/Come On Back To Me	6
68	Pye 7N 17417	Back On My Feet Again/I Can Take Or Leave Your Loving	6
68	Pye 7N 17503	Any Old Time (You're Lonely And Sad)/We Are Happy People	6
68	Pye 7N 17636	Build Me Up Buttercup/New Direction	6
69	Pye 7N 17702	In The Bad Bad Old Days/Give Me Love	5
69	Pye 7N 17809	Born To Live, Born To Die/Why Did You Cry	12
69	Pye 7N 1784	Baby I Couldn'tSee/Penny Sir	10
70	Pye 7N 17904	Take A Girl Like You/I'm Gonna Be A Rich Man	10
70	Pye 7N 17956	I'm Gonna Be A Rich Man/Who Am I	10
71	MCA MCA 5075	Stoney Ground/I'll Give You Love	20
77	Summit SU 100	Where Were You When I Needed Your Love/Love Me Nice 'n Easy	6
78	Psycho P 2603	Closer To Loving You/Change My Life	250
68	Pye NEP 24297	IT'S ALL RIGHT (EP)	25
67	Pye NPL 18206	FROM THE FOUNDATIONS (LP)	20
68	Pye NPL 18227	ROCKING THE FOUNDATIONS (LP)	20
69	Pye N(S)PL 18290	DIGGING THE FOUNDATIONS (LP, gatefold sleeve)	20

(see also Pluto)

FOUNDED

82	Heroes ER 02	Looking For Love/Run To Hell	60

JAMES FOUNTAIN

76	Cream CRM 5002	Seven Day Lover/Malnutrition	5

PETE FOUNTAIN

60	Coral Q 72404	Columbus Stockade Blues/Sentimental Journey (78)	15

(see also Brenda Lee)

THE 4

64	Decca F 11999	It's Alright/There's Nothing Like It	20

FOUR GUNS

85	Gun 001	Sign Of The Crimes/Spirit Of The Thing (no'd p/s, 500 only)	20

FOUR IDLE HANDS

90	Good Vibrations GOT 21	99 Streets/Friday Man	12

FOUR PLUGS

80	Disposable THROWAY ONE	Wrong Treatment/Biking Girl (p/s)	20

FOUR ACES (JAMAICA)

65	Island WI 178	Hoochy-Koochy-Kai-Po/River Bank Coberly Again	25
65	Island WI 178	Hoochy-Koochy-Kai-Po/SKATALITES: Sucu Sucu (different B-side)	25
65	Island WI 179	Sweet Chariot/Peace And Love	15
65	Island WI 180	Little Girl/CLARENDONIANS: Day Will Come	18

(see also Desmond Dekker)

FOUR ACES (U.K.)

60s	Anton/E.R.S. EAG 178/179	Why Do You/Fortune Teller (private pressing)	250

FOUR ACES (U.S.)

54	Brunswick 05256	The Gang That Sang "Heart Of My Heart"/Heaven Can Wait	10
54	Brunswick 05308	Three Coins In The Fountain/Wedding Bells (Are Breaking Up This Gang Of Mine)	15
54	Brunswick 05322	It Shall Come To Pass/Dream	10
54	Brunswick 05348	It's A Woman's World/The Cuckoo Bird In The Pickle Tree	6
54	Brunswick 05355	Mister Sandman/((I'll Be With You) In Apple Blossom Time	25
55	Brunswick 05379	Melody Of Love/There Is A Tavern In The Town	6
55	Brunswick 05401	There Goes My Heart/Take Me In Your Arms	5
55	Brunswick 05418	Stranger In Paradise/You'll Always Be The One	20
55	Brunswick 05429	Sluefoot/I'm In The Mood For Love	5
55	Brunswick 05480	Love Is A Many Splendored Thing/Shine On Harvest Moon	20
55	Brunswick 05504	Jingle Bells/The Christmas Song (Merry Christmas To You)	7

56	Brunswick 05562	To Love Again/Charlie Was A Boxer	5
56	Brunswick 05566	The Gal With The Yaller Shoes/Of This I'm Sure	5
56	Brunswick 05573	If You Can Dream/It's The Talk Of The Town	5
56	Brunswick 05589	A Woman In Love/I Only Know I Love You	8
56	Brunswick 05601	Dreamer/Let's Fall In Love	5
56	Brunswick 05613	You Can't Run Away From It/Written On The Wind	5
56	Brunswick 05623	Friendly Persuasion (Thee I Love)/Someone To Love	8
58	Brunswick 05767	The World Outside/The Christmas Tree (78)	12
59	Brunswick 05773	The World Outside/The Inn Of The Sixth Happiness	6
59	Brunswick 05773	The World Outside/The Inn Of The Sixth Happiness (78)	12
50s	Decca A 73010	I'm Yours/I Understand (export issue)	10
54	Brunswick OE 9090	PRESENTING THE FOUR ACES (EP)	10
57	Brunswick OE 9324	ACES SING FILM TITLES (EP)	10
53	Brunswick LA 8614	JUST SQUEEZE ME (10" LP)	20
59	Brunswick STA 3014	THE SWINGIN' ACES (LP, stereo)	15

(see also Al Alberts)

4 DEGREES
65	Oak RGJ 187	4 DEGREES (LP, 1-sided, no sleeve)	425

FOUR DOLLS
57	Capitol CL 14778	Three On A Date/Proud Of You	15
58	Capitol CL 14845	Whoop-A-Lala/I'm Following You	15

FOUR ESCORTS
54	HMV 7M 277	Loop De Loop Mambo/Love Me	15

FOUR ESQUIRES
55	London HL 8152	The Sphinx Won't Tell/Three Things (A Man Must Do)	30
56	London HLA 8224	Adorable/Thunderbolt	20
57	London HL 8376	Look Homeward Angel/Santo Domingo (78) (unreleased on both 78 and 45)	0
58	London HLO 8533	Love Me Forever/I Ain't Been Right Since You Left	10
58	London HLO 8579	Always And Forever/I Walk Down The Street	12
58	London HL 8746	Hideaway/Repeat After Me	10
58	London HL 8746	Hideaway/Repeat After Me (78)	10
59	Pye Intl. 7N 25012	Non E Cosi/Land Of You And Me	5
59	Pye Intl. 7N 25027	Act Your Age/So Ends The Night	5
60	Pye Intl. 7N 25049	Wouldn't It Be Wonderful/Wonderful One	5

FOUR EVERS
66	CBS 202549	A Lovely Way To Say Goodnight/The Girl I Wanna Bring Home	45

FOUR FOR FUN
63	Waverley ELP 113	FOUR FOR FUN (EP)	60

(see also Dick Farina, Carolyn Hester)

FOUR FRESHMEN
54	Capitol CL 14196	Love Turns Winter To Spring/Mood Indigo	7
55	Capitol CL 14338	Day By Day/How Can I Tell Her	7
56	Capitol CL 14610	Graduation Day/Lonely Night In Paris	6
56	Capitol CL 14633	You're So Far Above Me/He Who Loves And Runs Away	7
62	Capitol CL 15244	Teach Me Tonight/Shangri La	7
54	Capitol LC 6685	VOICES IN MODERN (10" LP)	12

FOUR FULLER BROTHERS
69	MCA MU 1068	Groupie/Bitter Honey	10

FOUR GEES
67	President PT 160	Ethiopia/Rough Rider	7

FOUR GIBSON GIRLS
58	Oriole CB 1447	No School Tomorrow/June, July And August	20
58	Oriole CB 1453	Safety Sue/VARIOUS ARTISTS: Safety Sue	15

FOUR GUYS
55	Vogue Coral Q 72054	Half Hearted Kisses/Mine	12

(see also Modernaires)

4 HERO
98	Reinforced/Talking Loud	TWO PAGES (4x12")	25
95	Reinforced LP 004	PARALLEL UNIVERSE (2-LP)	40

FOUR INSTANTS
66	Society	DISCOTHEQUE (LP)	40

FOUR JACKS
58	Decca F 10984	Hey! Baby/The Prayer Of Love	25
58	Decca DFE 6460	HEY! BABY (EP)	70

FOUR JACKS & A JILL
68	RCA Victor RCA 1669	Master Jack/I Looked Back	7

FOUR JONES BOYS
55	Decca F 10568	A Real Romance/When I Let You Go	6
55	Decca F 10671	Moments To Remember/Sing-ing-ing-ing	6
56	Decca F 10717	Tutti Frutti/Are You Satisfied?	20
56	Decca F 10789	Happiness Street (Corner Of Sunshine Square)/Someone To Love	6
56	Decca F 10829	Priscilla/It Isn't Right	10

(see also Jones Boys, Annette Klooger)

FOUR JUST MEN
64	Parlophone R 5186	That's My Baby/Things Will Never Be The Same	80

(see also Just Four Men, Wimple Winch)

FOUR KENTS
68	RCA RCA 1705	The Moving Finger Writes/Searchin'	20

FOUR KESTRELS
61	Decca F 11333	Sound Off/Can't Say I Do	6

FOUR KINSMEN

| 67 | Decca F 22671 | It Looks Like The Daybreak/Forget About Him | 15 |

(see also Kinsmen)

FOUR KNIGHTS

54	Capitol CL 14076	I Get So Lonely/Till Then	25
54	Capitol CL 14154	Easy Street/In The Chapel In The Moonlight	20
54	Capitol CL 14204	I Don't Wanna See You Cryin'/Saw Your Eyes	20
55	Capitol CL 14244	Honey Bunch/Write Me, Baby	30
55	Capitol CL 14290	Inside Out/Foolishly Yours	15
56	Capitol CL 14516	Guilty/You	15
59	Coral Q 72355	Foolish Tears/O' Falling Star	15
59	Coral Q 72355	Foolish Tears/O' Falling Star (78)	10
55	Capitol EAP1 506	THE FOUR KNIGHTS (EP)	30
53	Capitol LC 6604	SPOTLIGHT SONGS (10" LP)	40

(see also Nat 'King' Cole)

FOUR LADS

| 57 | Philips JK 1021 | Golly/I Just Don't Know (jukebox issue) | 10 |
| 60 | Philips PB 1000 | Standing On The Corner/Sunday | 5 |

(see also Johnnie Ray, Frankie Laine, Doris Day)

FOUR LEAVED CLOVER

| 65 | Oak RGJ 207 | Alright Girl/Why | 500 |

FOUR MACS

| 64 | Parlophone R 5204 | Come Back Silly Girl/Darlin' | 8 |

(see also Sands Of Time)

FOUR MATADORS

| 66 | Columbia DB 7806 | A Man's Gotta Stand Tall/Fast Cars And Money | 70 |

FOURMOST

63	Parlophone R 5056	Hello Little Girl/Just In Case	6
63	Parlophone R 5078	I'm In Love/Respectable	6
64	Parlophone R 5128	A Little Loving/Waiting For You	6
64	Parlophone R 5157	How Can I Tell Her/You Got That Way	6
64	Parlophone R 5194	Baby I Need Your Loving/That's Only What They Say	5
65	Parlophone R 5304	Everything In The Garden/He Could Never	6
65	Parlophone R 5379	Girls Girls Girls/Why Do Fools Fall In Love?	5
66	Parlophone R 5491	Here, There And Everywhere/You've Changed	10
66	Parlophone R 5528	Auntie Maggie's Remedy/Turn The Lights Down	10
68	CBS 3814	Apples, Peaches, Pumpkin Pie/He Could Never	12
69	CBS 4041	Rosetta/Just Like Before	40
69	CBS 4461	Easy Squeezy/Do I Love You?	20
72	Phoenix SNIX 126	Goodnight Sweet Dreams/Memphis	8
64	Parlophone GEP 8892	THE SOUND OF THE FOURMOST (EP)	50
64	Parlophone GEP 8917	THE FOURMOST (EP)	50
65	Parlophone PMC 1259	FIRST AND FOURMOST (LP)	130
75	Fourmost SOF 001	THE FOURMOST (LP)	15

(see also Format)

FOURMYULA

| 69 | Columbia DB 8549 | Honey Chile/Come With Me | 20 |

FOUR PALMS

| 58 | Vogue V 9116 | Jeanie, Joanie, Shirley, Toni/Consideration | 600 |
| 58 | Vogue V 9116 | Jeanie, Joanie, Shirley, Toni/Consideration (78) | 150 |

FOUR PENNIES (U.K.)

63	Philips BF 1296	Do You Want Me To/Miss Bad Daddy	12
64	Philips BF 1322	Tell Me Girl/Juliet	5
64	Philips BF 1322	Juliet/Tell Me Girl (A- & B-sides supposedly flipped after original release)	5
64	Philips BF 1349	I Found Out The Hard Way/Don't Tell Me You Love Me	5
64	Philips BF 1366	Black Girl/You Went Away	5
65	Philips BF 1398	The Way Of Love/A Place Where No-One Goes	6
65	Philips BF 1435	Until It's Time For You To Go/Till Another Day	7
66	Philips BF 1469	Trouble Is My Middle Name/Way Out Love	5
66	Philips BF 1491	Keep The Freeway Open/Square Peg	5
66	Philips BF 1519	No Sad Songs For Me/Cats	10
64	Philips BBE 12561	THE FOUR PENNIES (EP)	15
64	Philips BBE 12562	SPIN WITH THE PENNIES (EP)	15
64	Philips BBE 12570	THE SWINGING SIDE OF THE FOUR PENNIES (EP)	12
64	Philips BBE 12571	THE SMOOTH SIDE OF THE FOUR PENNIES (EP)	12
64	Philips BL 7642	TWO SIDES OF THE FOUR PENNIES (LP)	35
66	Philips BL 7734	MIXED BAG (LP)	70
67	Wing WL 1146	JULIET (LP)	18

(see also Lionel Morton, Fritz Mike & Mo)

FOUR PENNIES (U.S.)

63	Stateside SS 198	My Block/Dry Your Eyes	40
63	Stateside SS 244	When The Boy's Happy (The Girl's Happy Too)/Hockaday Part 1	30
79	Ensign ENY 23	When The Boy's Happy/CARLO: Little Orphan Girl	5

(see also Chiffons)

FOUR + ONE

| 65 | Parlophone R 5221 | Time Is On My Side/Don't Lie To Me | 100 |

(see also In Crowd, Tomorrow, Keith West)

FOUR PREPS

57	Capitol CL 14727	Falling Star/Where Wuz You	5
57	Capitol CL 14747	I Cried A Million Tears/Moonstruck In Madrid	5
57	Capitol CL 14768	Again 'n' Again 'n' Again/Promise Me Baby	5
57	Capitol CL 14783	Band Of Angels/How About That?	5
58	Capitol CL 14815	26 Miles (Santa Catalina)/Fools Will Be Fools	5
58	Capitol CL 14873	Big Man/Stop, Baby	5

60	Capitol CL 15128	Got A Girl/(Wait Till You) Hear It From Me	6
61	Capitol CL 15217	More Money For You And Me (Medley)/Swing Down Chariot	5
57	Capitol EAP1 862	DREAMY EYES (EP)	8
58	Capitol EAP1 1015	TWENTY SIX MILES (EP)	8
59	Capitol EAP1 1064	BIG MAN (EP)	8

4 SAXOPHONES IN 12 TONES
| 56 | Vogue V 2355 | Fantastic/Frankly Speaking | 7 |

FOUR SEASONS
SINGLES
62	Stateside SS 122	Sherry/I've Cried Before	6
63	Stateside SS 145	Big Girls Don't Cry/Connie-O	6
63	Stateside SS 169	Walk Like A Man/Lucky Ladybug	6
63	Stateside SS 194	Ain't That A Shame/Soon (I'll Be Home Again)	8
63	Stateside SS 216	Candy Girl/Marlena	10
63	Stateside SS 241	Santa Claus Is Coming To Town/Christmas Tears	15
64	Stateside SS 262	Peanuts/Silhouettes	15
64	Philips BF 1317	Dawn (Go Away)/No Surfin' Today	8
64	Philips BF 1334	Ronnie/Born To Wander	8
64	Stateside SS 315	Alone/Long Lonely Nights	10
64	Philips BF 1347	Rag Doll/Silence Is Golden	6
64	Stateside SS 343	Since I Don't Have You/Sincerely	15
65	Philips BF 1364	Save It For Me/Funny Face	8
65	Philips BF 1372	Big Man In Town/Little Angel	7
65	Philips BF 1395	Bye Bye Baby (Baby Goodbye)/Searching Wind	7
65	Philips BF 1411	Toy Soldier/Betrayed	8
65	Philips BF 1420	Girl Come Running/Cry Myself To Sleep	10
65	Philips BF 1439	Let's Hang On!/On Broadway Tonight	7
66	Philips BF 1474	Working My Way Back To You/Too Many Memories	5
66	Philips BF 1493	Opus 17 (Don't Worry 'Bout Me)/Beggar's Parade	10
66	Philips BF 1511	I've Got You Under My Skin/Huggin' My Pillow	8
67	Philips BF 1538	Tell It To The Rain/Show Girl	12
67	Philips BF 1556	Beggin'/Dody (as the 4 Seasons)	15
67	Philips BF 1584	C'mon Marianne/Let's Ride Again	7
67	Philips BF 1600	Around And Around/WONDER WHO: Lonesome Road	10
67	Philips BF 1621	Watch The Flowers Grow/Raven	12
68	Philips BF 1651	Will You Love Me Tomorrow?/Silhouettes	10
68	Philips BF 1685	Saturday's Father/Goodbye Girl	10
69	Philips BF 1743	Electric Stories/Pity	10
69	Philips BF 1763	Rag Doll/Working My Way Back To You (p/s)	7
71	Philips 6051 018	Rag Doll/Let's Hang On/I've Got You Under My Skin (maxi-single)	5
71	Warner Bros K 16107	Whatever You Say/Sleeping Man (withdrawn, 300 only) As Frankie Valli and the...)	45
64	Stateside SE 1011	THE FOUR SEASONS SING (EP)	60

ALBUMS
63	Stateside SL 10033	SHERRY AND 11 OTHERS	40
63	Stateside SL 10042	AIN'T THAT A SHAME	50
63	Stateside SL 10051	THE FOUR SEASONS' GREETINGS	35
64	Philips BL 7611	BORN TO WANDER	20
64	Philips BL 7621	DAWN (GO AWAY) AND 11 OTHER GREAT SONGS	20
64	Philips BL 7643	RAG DOLL	18
65	Philips BL 7663	ENTERTAIN YOU	20
65	Philips (S)BL 7687	SING BIG HITS BY BURT BACHARACH ... HAL DAVID ... BOB DYLAN	18
65	Philips BL 7699	WORKING MY WAY BACK TO YOU	18
66	Philips (S)BL 7719	GOLD VAULT OF HITS	12
67	Philips (S)BL 7751	SECOND VAULT OF GOLDEN HITS	12
67	Philips (S)BL 7752	LOOKIN' BACK	15
67	Philips (S)BL 7753	CHRISTMAS ALBUM	25
69	Philips (S)BL 7880	THE GENUINE IMITATION LIFE GAZETTE	25

(see also Beverly Hills Blues Band, Frankie Valli, Wonder Who)

FOUR SENSATIONS
| 52 | London L 1137 | Heaven Knows Why/Believing In You (78) | 25 |
| 52 | Melodisc P 216 | Raindrops/When Honeymoon Lane Becomes Memory Lane (78) | 10 |

FOUR SIGHTS
| 64 | Columbia DB 7227 | But I Can Tell/And I Cry | 15 |

4-SKINS
81	Clockwork Fun CF 101	One Law For Them/Brave New World (p/s)	15
81	Secret SHH 125	Yesterday's Heroes/Justice/Get Out Of My Life (p/s)	10
82	Secret SHH 141	Lowlife/Bread Or Blood (p/s)	10
82	Secret SEC 4	THE GOOD, THE BAD AND THE 4-SKINS (LP, with photo inner)	18
83	Syndicate SYN 1	A FISTFUL OF ... 4-SKINS (LP)	18
84	Syndicate SYN LP 5	FROM CHAOS TO 1984 (LP)	20

(see also Plastic Gangsters)

FOUR SPICES
| 57 | MGM MGM 944 | Armen's Theme (Yesterday And You)/Fire Engine Boogie | 150 |
| 57 | MGM MGM 944 | Armen's Theme (Yesterday And You)/Fire Engine Boogie (78) | 20 |

FOUR SQUARES
| 64 | Hollick & Taylor HT 1009 | FOUR SQUARES (EP) | 100 |

(see also Pink People)

FOURTEEN (14)
68	Olga OLE 002	Through My Door/Meet Mr. Edgar	20
68	Olga OLE 006	Umbrella/Drizzle (Rain)	20
68	Olga OLE 006	Umbrella/Drizzle (Rain) (Demo)	45
68	Olga S 051	Easy To Fool/Frosty Stars On A Window Pane	15

14 ICED BEARS
| 86 | Frank COPPOLA 101 | Inside/Blue Suit/Cut (hand-printed paper bag sleeve) | 25 |
| 87 | Frank CAPRA 202 | Like A Dolphin/Balloon Song/Train Song/Lie To Choose (12", p/s) | 10 |

MINT VALUE £

88	Sarah SARAH 005	Come Get Me/Unhappy Days/Sure To See (poster p/s)	40
89	Thunderball 7TBL 2	Mother Sleep (7", unreleased, Mayking test pressings only)	25
90s	Thunderball Surfacer 002	Falling Backwards/World I Love/CROCODILE RIDE: Ex-Hipster/Satellite (Speed Mix) (numbered & stickered mailer, 1,000 only)	8

FOUR TET

98	Output OPR 14	THIRTYSIXTWENTYFIVE EP (2 one-sided 12", p/s)	18
02	Domino RUG 139	I'm On Fire (Part 1)/I'm On Fire (part 2) (p/s)	5
09	Text TEXT 006	Wolf Cub (12", black label, plain black sleeve)	15
99	Output OPR21	DIALOGUE (LP)	30
01	Domino WIGLP94	PAUSE (LP)	18
02	Domino WIGLP126	ROUNDS (2xLP)	18
05	Domino WIGLP 154	EVERYTHING ECSTATIC (2xLP, one sided etched, with bonus CD)	18
10	Domino WIGLP 254	THERE IS LOVE IN YOU (2-LP)	15

(see also Fridge, Thom Yorke)

FOUR TONES

58	Decca F 11074	Voom Ba Voom/Rickshaw Boy	15

FOUR TOPHATTERS

55	London HLA 8163	Leave-a My Gal Alone/Go Baby Go	300
55	London HLA 8163	Leave-a My Gal Alone/Go Baby Go (78)	35
55	London HLA 8198	Forty Five Men In A Telephone Booth/Wild Rosie	300
55	London HLA 8198	Forty Five Men In A Telephone Booth/Wild Rosie (78)	35

FOUR TOPS
SINGLES

64	Stateside SS 336	Baby I Need Your Lovin'/Call On Me	50
64	Stateside SS 336	Baby I Need Your Lovin'/Call On Me (DJ Copy)	60
65	Stateside SS 371	Without The One You Love (Life's Not Worthwhile)/Love Has Gone	60
65	Stateside SS 371	Without The One You Love (Life's Not Worthwhile)/Love Has Gone (DJ Copy)	130
65	Tamla Motown TMG 507	Ask The Lonely/Where Did You Go?	90
65	Tamla Motown TMG 507	Ask The Lonely/Where Did You Go? (DJ copy)	150
65	Tamla Motown TMG 515	I Can't Help Myself/Sad Souvenirs	25
65	Tamla Motown TMG 515	I Can't Help Myself/Sad Souvenirs (DJ copy)	100
65	Tamla Motown TMG 528	It's The Same Old Song/Your Love Is Amazing	25
65	Tamla Motown TMG 528	It's The Same Old Song/Your Love Is Amazing (DJ copy)	100
65	Tamla Motown TMG 542	Something About You/Darling I Hum Our Song	30
65	Tamla Motown TMG 542	Something About You/Darling I Hum Our Song (DJ copy = £100)	100
66	Tamla Motown TMG 553	Shake Me, Wake Me (When It's Over)/Just As Long As You Need Me	35
66	Tamla Motown TMG 553	Shake Me, Wake Me (When It's Over)/Just As Long As You Need Me (DJ copy)	100
66	Tamla Motown TMG 568	Loving You Is Sweeter Than Ever/I Like Everything About You	30
66	Tamla Motown TMG 568	Loving You Is Sweeter Than Ever/I Like Everything About You (DJ copy £100)	100
66	Tamla Motown TMG 579	Reach Out, I'll Be There/Until You Love Someone (small print, later large print = £15)	18
66	Tamla Motown TMG 579	Reach Out, I'll Be There/Until You Love Someone (DJ copy)	100
67	Tamla Motown TMG 589	Standing In The Shadows Of Love/Since You've Been Gone (small print))	15
67	Tamla Motown TMG 589	Standing In The Shadows Of Love/Since You've Been Gone (later large print)	8
67	Tamla Motown TMG 589	Standing In The Shadows Of Love/Since You've Been Gone (DJ copy)	100
67	Tamla Motown TMG 601	Bernadette/I Got A Feeling	15
67	Tamla Motown TMG 601	Bernadette/I Got A Feeling (DJ copy)	100
67	Tamla Motown TMG 612	Seven Rooms Of Gloom/I'll Turn To Stone	15
67	Tamla Motown TMG 612	Seven Rooms Of Gloom/I'll Turn To Stone (DJ copy)	65
67	Tamla Motown TMG 623	You Keep Running Away/If You Don't Want My Love	12
67	Tamla Motown TMG 623	You Keep Running Away/If You Don't Want My Love (DJ copy)	65
67	Tamla Motown TMG 634	Walk Away Renee/Mame	12
67	Tamla Motown TMG 634	Walk Away Renee/Mame (DJ copy)	60
68	Tamla Motown TMG 647	If I Were A Carpenter/Your Love Is Wonderful	12
68	Tamla Motown TMG 647	If I Were A Carpenter/Your Love Is Wonderful (DJ copy)	60
68	Tamla Motown TMG 665	Yesterday's Dreams/For Once In My Life	15
68	Tamla Motown TMG 665	Yesterday's Dreams/For Once In My Life (DJ copy)	60
68	Tamla Motown TMG 675	I'm In A Different World/Remember When	15
68	Tamla Motown TMG 675	I'm In A Different World/Remember When (DJ copy)	60
69	Tamla Motown TMG 698	What Is A Man?/Don't Bring Back Memories	12
69	Tamla Motown TMG 698	What Is A Man?/Don't Bring Back Memories (DJ copy)	70
69	Tamla Motown TMG 710	Do What You Gotta Do/Can't Seem To Get You Out Of My Mind	18
69	Tamla Motown TMG 710	Do What You Gotta Do/Can't Seem To Get You Out Of My Mind (DJ copy)	70
70	Tamla Motown TMG 736	It's All In The Game/Love (Is The Answer)	7
70	Tamla Motown TMG 736	It's All In The Game/Love (Is The Answer) (DJ copy)	40
70	Tamla Motown TMG 752	Still Water (Love)/Still Water (Peace)	7
70	Tamla Motown TMG 752	Still Water (Love)/Still Water (Peace) (DJ copy)	40
71	Tamla Motown TMG 770	Just Seven Numbers (Can Straighten Out My Life)/I Wish I Were Your Mirror	7
71	Tamla Motown TMG 770	Just Seven Numbers (Can Straighten Out My Life)/I Wish I Were Your Mirror (DJ copy)	30
71	Tamla Motown TMG 785	Simple Game/You Stole My Love	7
71	Tamla Motown TMG 785	Simple Game/You Stole My Love (DJ copy)	30
72	Tamla Motown TMG 803	Bernadette/I Got A Feeling/It's The Same Old Song	7
72	Tamla Motown TMG 803	Bernadette/I Got A Feeling/It's The Same Old Song (DJ copy)	30
72	Tamla Motown TMG 829	I'll Turn To Stone/Love Feels Like Fire	10
72	Tamla Motown TMG 829	I'll Turn To Stone/Love Feels Like Fire (DJ copy)	30
72	Probe PRO 575	Keeper Of The Castle/Jubilee With Soul	5
73	Probe PRO 596	Are You Man Enough/Peace Of Mind	5
74	Probe PRO 612	I Just Can't Get You Out Of My Mind/Am I My Brother's Keeper	15
75	ABC ABC 4057	Seven Lonely Nights/I Can't Hold On Much Longer	5
83	Tamla Motown TMG 1320	Medley/TEMPTATIONS: Papa Was A Rolling Stone	35

EPs

66	Tamla Motown TME 2012	THE FOUR TOPS (EP, flipback sleeve)	30
67	Tamla Motown TME 2018	FOUR TOP HITS	35

ALBUMS

65	Tamla Motown TML 11010	THE FOUR TOPS	80
66	Tamla Motown TML 11021	SECOND ALBUM (mono)	40
66	Tamla Motown STML 11021	SECOND ALBUM (stereo)	50

66	Tamla Motown TML 11037	FOUR TOPS ON TOP (mono)	35
66	Tamla Motown STML 11037	FOUR TOPS ON TOP (stereo)	45
67	Tamla Motown TML 11041	FOUR TOPS LIVE! (mono)	25
67	Tamla Motown (S)TML 11041	FOUR TOPS LIVE! (stereo)	30
67	Tamla Motown STML 11056	REACH OUT (stereo)	25
68	Tamla Motown STML 11061	FOUR TOPS GREATEST HITS (stereo)	25
68	Tamla Motown TML 11061	FOUR TOPS GREATEST HITS (mono)	20
69	Tamla Motown (S)TML 11087	YESTERDAY'S DREAMS (mono/stereo)	25
69	Tamla Motown TML 11113	FOUR TOPS NOW (mono)	25
70	Tamla Motown TML 11138	SOUL SPIN (mono)	25
70	Tamla Motown STML 11138	SOUL SPIN (stereo)	20
70	Tamla Motown STML 11149	STILL WATERS RUN DEEP	20
71	Tamla Motown STML 11173	CHANGING TIMES	20
71	Tamla Motown STML 11195	GREATEST HITS VOL. 2	12
72	Tamla Motown STML 11206	NATURE PLANNED IT	12
73	Probe SPB 1064	KEEPER OF THE CASTLE	15
73	Probe SPB 1077	SHAFT IN AFRICA (soundtrack, with Johnny Pate)	25
73	Probe SPBA 6277	MAIN STREET PEOPLE	12
74	Probe SPBA 6283	MEETING OF THE MINDS	20
74	ABC ABCL 5035	SHAFT IN AFRICA (soundtrack, reissue)	15
67	Tamla Motown TML 11056	REACH OUT (mono)	25
69	Tamla Motown STML 11113	FOUR TOPS NOW (stereo)	20

(see also Supremes & Four Tops)

FOUR TUNES

54	London L 1231	I Gambled With Love/Marie (78)	40
54	London HL 8050	Do, Do, Do, Do, Do Do It Again/My Wild Irish Rose (78)	20
55	London HL 8151	I Sold My Heart To A Junkman/The Greatest Feeling In The World	120
55	London HL 8151	I Sold My Heart To A Junkman/The Greatest Feeling In The World (78)	35
55	London HLJ 8164	Tired Of Waitin'/L'Amour, Toujours L'Amour (Love Everlasting)	50
55	London HLJ 8164	Tired Of Waitin'/L'Amour, Toujours L'Amour (Love Everlasting) (78)	30

FOURUM

78	Sirius SP 519	FOURUM (LP)	20
81	Guardian GRC 95	SINGING THE DALES (LP)	20

FOUR VOICES

58	Philips PB 864	Tell Me You're Mine/Tight Spot	5

FOUR WINDS

58	London HLU 8556	Short Shorts/Five Minutes More	35

HARRY FOWLER

61	HMV POP 891	Buddies (with Mario Fabrizl)/Flower Flogger	8

KIM FOWLEY

66	Parlophone R 5521	Lights/Something New And Different	25
66	CBS 202243	They're Coming To Take Me Away Ha-Haaa!!/You Get More For Your Money On The Flip Side Of This Record Talking Blues	15
66	CBS 202338	Lights (The Blind Can See)/Something New And Different (reissue)	15
66	Island WI 278	The Trip/Beautiful People	15
72	Action ACT 4606	Born To Make You Cry/Thunder Road	7
73	Capitol CL 15743	International Heroes/E.S.P. Reader	5
77	Island WIP 278	The Trip/Beautiful People (p/s, reissue)	10
78	Mercury 6005 009	Control/Rubber Rainbow	5
79	Illegal ILS 012	Rubber Rainbow/In My Garage (p/s)	5
80	Island WIP 6555	1989: Waiting For The Next Ten Years/1987: Lost Like A Lizard In Snow	5
73	Capitol E-ST 11159	INTERNATIONAL HEROES (LP)	25

(see also Freaks Of Nature, Hollywood Argyles, Napoleon XIV, B. Bumble & Stingers)

(THE) FOX

68	CBS 3381	Mister Carpenter/Seek And You Find	250

FOX (1)

70	Fontana 6007 016	Second Hand Love/Butterfly	25
70	Fontana 6309 007	FOR FOX SAKE (LP, laminated sleeve, black/silver labels)	300

FOX (2)

75	GTO GTLP 006	TAILS OF ILLUSION (LP, textured sleeve, lyric inner)	12

(see also Wooden Horse, Demick & Armstrong)

BOB FOX & STU LUCKLEY

78	Rubber RUB 028	NOWT SO GOOD'LL PASS (LP)	15

DON FOX

57	Decca F 10927	Be My Girl/You'll Never Go To Heaven	10
57	Decca F 10955	The Majesty Of Love/Party Time	10
58	Decca F 10983	Pretend You Don't See Her/Wasteland	10
58	Decca F 11057	She Was Only Seventeen/When You're A Long, Long Way Away	10
60	Triumph RGM 1022	T'ain't What You Do/Out There	40
61	Oriole CB 1643	Don't Fool With Love/If You Go	5
60s	Honey Hit TB 125	Three Swinging Clicks/I Found The Girl I Love In My Home Town (in p/s)	15
60s	Honey Hit TB 125	Three Swinging Clicks/I Found The Girl I Love In My Home Town	5
69	B & C CB 110	Once In A While/You Belong To My Heart	5

PAUL FOX

90	Sound Business SB 1	Writing On The Wall/Version/LIBERATION TRIBE: African Mask (12")	40

UFFA FOX

60	Parlophone PMC 1112	UFFA SINGS (LP)	15

FOX IN SOCKS

81	Jest 001	Sound Patterns/Lonely House (p/s)	25

FOXTROT

74	RCA APBO 0169	Cave Man Billy/These Passing Days	5

FOXX

71	MCA MUPS 419	REVOLT OF EMILY YOUNG (LP)	15

INEZ FOXX

63	Sue WI 301	Mockingbird/He's The One You Love (actually by Inez & Charlie Foxx)	25
64	Sue WI 304	Jaybirds/Broken-Hearted Fool (actually by Inez & Charlie Foxx)	25
64	Sue WI 314	Ask Me/Hi Diddle Diddle (actually by Inez & Charlie Foxx)	25
64	Sue WI 323	Hurt By Love/Confusion (actually by Inez & Charlie Foxx)	25
71	Pye International 7N 25546	You Shouldn't Have Set My Soul On Fire/Live For Today	10
73	Stax 2025 151	You Hurt Me For The Last Time/Watch The Dog (That Brings The Bone)	8

INEZ & CHARLIE FOXX

64	Sue WI 307	Competition/Here We Go Round The Mulberry Bush (as Charlie & Inez Foxx)	30
64	Sue WI 356	La De Da I Love You/Yankee Doodle Dandy	30
65	London HLC 9971	My Momma Told Me/I Feel Alright	10
65	London HLC 10009	Hummingbird/If I Need Anyone (Let It Be You)	10
66	Stateside SS 556	Come By Here/No Stranger To Love	30
67	Stateside SS 586	Tightrope/My Special Prayer	30
67	Stateside SS 586	Tightrope/My Special Prayer (DJ copy)	75
67	Direction 58-2712	I Ain't Goin' For That/Undecided	10
67	Direction 58-3192	(1, 2, 3, 4, 5, 6, 7) Count The Days/A Stranger I Don't Know	10
68	Direction 58-3816	Come On In/Baby Drop Your Dime	10
69	Direction 58-4042	Baby Give It To Me/You Fixed My Heartache	40
69	London HLC 10250	Mockingbird/Hummingbird (unissued)	0
69	United Artists UP 2269	Mockingbird/Hurt By Love	8
69	United Artists UP 35013	La De Da I Love You/Don't Do It No More	8
71	Pye International 7N 25561	Tightrope/Baby Take It All	10
83	Sue ENS 2	Mockingbird (EP)	15
64	Sue ILP 911	MOCKINGBIRD (LP)	100
65	London HA-C 8241	INEZ AND CHARLIE FOXX (LP, plum label)	70
65	London HA-C 8241	INEZ AND CHARLIE FOXX (LP, later black label)	40
68	Direction 8-63085	COME BY HERE (LP)	30
68	Direction 8-63281	GREATEST HITS (LP)	20
69	United Artists UA(S) 29025	MOCKINGBIRD (LP)	15
71	Pye PKL 4406	GREATEST HITS (LP)	12

JOHN FOXX

80	Virgin VS 338	No-One Driving (2.53 DJ Version)/Glimmer//This City/Mr. No (double pack, stickered gatefold p/s, matrix no. VS 338 A5DJ)	15
80	Virgin VS 360	Burning Car/20th Century (picture disc)	5
82	Virgin VS 543	Endlessly/Ghosts On Water//Dance With Me/A Kind Of Wave (double pack)	5
84	Virgin VS 615	Your Dress/Woman On A Stairway//Lifting Sky/Annexe (double pack)	5
84	Virgin VSP 645	Like A Miracle/Wings And A Wind (shaped picture disc)	6
85	Virgin VS 771	The Stars On Fire/What Kind Of Girl (p/s, with bonus single)	5
80	Virgin V 2146	METAMATIC (LP)	12
81	Virgin V 2194	THE GARDEN (LP)	12

(see also Ultravox)

FRABJOY & RUNCIBLE SPOON

69	Marmalade 598 019	I'm Beside Myself/Animal Song	30

(see also Godley & Creme, Doctor Father, Hotlegs, Mockingbirds, 10cc)

FRAGILE FRIENDS

83	KC KCT1	NOVELTY WEARS OFF (12" EP)	25
84	KC KC 001	Paper Doll/What I Call Beautiful	35

FRAGMENTS

80	Shattered SHAT 2	Some Other Guy/Intro Mental (p/s)	10

FRAME

66	RCA RCA 1556	My Feet Don't Fit In His Shoes/She	18
67	RCA RCA 1571	Doctor Doctor/I Can't Go On	65
70	Pye 7N 45213	Rockin' Machine/One More Time	10
74	Seven Sun SSUN 12	Billy The Dreamer/Rocking Machine	20

FRAMED

82	Thunderbay TBR 021	Into My Life/Wonderland	20

(see also Girlschool)

FRAMES

79	Brain Booster BBC 2	False Accusations/69 (no p/s)	6

FRAN & ALAN

66	Mercury MF 95	Seein' The Right Love Go Wrong/There's A place	5
68	MGM MGM 1428	Such A Pity/Mrs Robinson	8

PETER FRANC

73	Dawn DNS 1033	I'll Move Along/Song For Every Season	6
73	Dawn DNS 1039	Ballad Of the Superstar/Strange Kind Of Woman	6
74	Dawn DNS 1088	Flag Of Convenience/At Home With You	6
73	Dawn DNLS 3043	PROFILE (LP)	12
73	Dawn DNLS 3051	EN ROUTE (LP)	12

FRANCIS

67	Blue Beat BB 379	Warn The People (actually by Willie Francis)/SWINGERS: Simpleton (actually by Peter Tosh & Crackers)	40
72	Fab FAB 182	Rocking Machine/SOUL CLANS: Flying Rhythm	25
73	Fab FAB 251	Locks/Version	12

B. FRANCIS

65	Ska Beat JB 193	Judy Crowned/Who Crunch	15

BOBBY FRANCIS

67	Doctor Bird DB 1153	Chain Gang/Venus	150

(see also Winston Francis)

CLAIRE FRANCIS

66	Polydor 56079	I've Got My Own Thing Going/Here I Go Again	7
67	Polydor 56142	But I Don't Care/If You Don't Know	7

CONNIE FRANCIS

SINGLES

56	MGM SP 1169	My First Real Love (with Jaybirds)/Believe In Me (Crede Mi)	200
56	MGM SP 1169	My First Real Love (with Jaybirds)/Believe In Me (Crede Mi) (78)	40
56	MGM MGM 932	My Sailor Boy/Everyone Needs Someone	70
56	MGM MGM 932	My Sailor Boy/Everyone Needs Someone (78)	20
57	MGM MGM 945	Little Blue Wren/I Never Had A Sweetheart	50
57	MGM MGM 945	Little Blue Wren/I Never Had A Sweetheart (78)	30
57	MGM MGM 962	Eighteen/Faded Orchid	50
57	MGM MGM 962	Eighteen/Faded Orchid (78)	25
58	MGM MGM 975	Who's Sorry Now?/You Were Only Fooling (While I Was Falling In Love)	6
58	MGM MGM 982	I'm Sorry I Made You Cry/Lock Up Your Heart	6
58	MGM MGM 985	Carolina Moon/Stupid Cupid	5
58	MGM MGM 993	I'll Get By/Fallin'	10
58	MGM MGM 998	You Always Hurt The One You Love/In The Valley Of Love	6
59	MGM MGM 1001	My Happiness/Happy Days And Lonely Nights	5
59	MGM MGM 1001	My Happiness/Happy Days And Lonely Nights (78)	15
59	MGM MGM 1012	If I Didn't Care/Toward The End Of The Day	5
59	MGM MGM 1012	If I Didn't Care/Toward The End Of The Day (78)	20
59	MGM MGM 1018	Lipstick On Your Collar/Frankie	5
59	MGM MGM 1018	Lipstick On Your Collar/Frankie (78)	20
59	MGM MGM 1036	Plenty Good Lovin'/You're Gonna Miss Me	8
59	MGM MGM 1036	Plenty Good Lovin'/You're Gonna Miss Me (78)	20
59	MGM MGM 1046	Among My Souvenirs/Do You Love Me Like You Kiss Me?	5
59	MGM MGM 1046	Among My Souvenirs/Do You Love Me Like You Kiss Me? (78)	30
60	MGM MGM 1060	Valentino/It Would Be Worth It	5
60	MGM MGM 1070	Mama/Teddy (withdrawn; demos more common, £40)	40
60	MGM MGM 1070	Mama/Teddy (withdrawn; demo copy)	30
61	MGM MGM 1121	Where The Boys Are/Baby Roo	5
62	MGM MGM 1151	Don't Cry On My Shoulder/Mr. Twister	6
62	MGM MGM 1165	Vacation/It's Gonna Take Me Some Time	10
62	MGM MGM 1171	Playin' Games/I Was Such A Fool	8
62	MGM MGM 1185	I'm Gonna Be Warm This Winter/Pretty Little Baby	10
62	MGM MGM 1193	Follow The Boys/Tonight's My Night	6
63	MGM MGM 1202	If My Pillow Could Talk/Lollipop Lips	8
63	MGM MGM 1207	Drownin' My Sorrows/Look At Him	8
63	MGM MGM 1212	Your Other Love/Whatever Happened To Rosemary	8
63	MGM MGM 1220	The Summer Of His Years/My Buddy	8
63	MGM MGM 1224	Blue Winter/Souvenirs	7
63	MGM MGM 1236	Be Anything (But Be Mine)/Tommy	8
64	MGM MGM 1253	Don't Ever Leave Me/Waiting For You	6
65	MGM MGM 1265	Forget Domani/I Don't Want To Be No Better Off	6
65	MGM MGM 1271	My Child/No One Ever Sends Me Roses	10
65	MGM MGM 1282	Roundabout/Love Is Me, Love Is You	8
66	MGM MGM 1293	Jealous Heart/Can I Rely On You?	8
66	MGM MGM 1295	The Phoenix Love Theme — Senza Fine/Bossa Nova Hand Dance	6
66	MGM MGM 1305	Love Is Me, Love Is You/I'd Let You Break My Heart All Over Again	7
66	MGM MGM 1320	Somewhere My Love (Lara's Theme)/Letter From A Soldier (Dear Mama)	7
66	MGM MGM 1327	Spanish Nights And You/Games That Lovers Play	6
67	MGM MGM 1334	Another Page/Souvenir D'Italie	5
67	MGM MGM 1336	Time Alone Will Tell/Born Free	10
67	MGM MGM 1347	My Heart Cries For You/If My Friends Could See Me Now (Medley)	8
68	MGM MGM 1381	My World Is Slipping Away/Till We're Together	6
68	MGM MGM 1407	Why Say Goodbye?/Addio Mi Amore	7
68	MGM MGM 1446	Somebody Else Is Taking My Place/Brother Can You Spare A Dime?	7
69	MGM MGM 1471	The Wedding Cake/Overhill Underground	8
69	MGM MGM 1493	Mr. Love/Zingara	10

EPs

56	MGM MGM-EP 658	A GIRL IN LOVE	20
58	MGM MGM-EP 677	HEARTACHES	20
58	MGM MGM-EP 686	CONNIE FRANCIS	20
59	MGM MGM-EP 697	IF I DIDN'T CARE	20
60	MGM MGM-EP 711	YOU'RE MY EVERYTHING	20
60	MGM MGM-EP 717	ROCK AND ROLL MILLION SELLERS NO. 1	20
60	MGM MGM-EP 720	ROCK AND ROLL MILLION SELLERS NO. 2	20
60	MGM MGM-EP 731	ROCK AND ROLL MILLION SELLERS NO. 3	20
60	MGM MGM-EP 742	FIRST LADY OF RECORD (laminated or matt rear sleeve)	20
61	MGM MGM-EP 756	WHERE THE BOYS ARE	20
61	MGM MGM-EP 759	CONNIE FRANCIS FAVOURITES	20
61	MGM MGM-EP 760	SINGS ITALIAN FAVOURITES	20
63	MGM MGM-EP 769	CONNIE'S AMERICAN HITS	20
63	MGM MGM-EP 773	HEY RING-A-DING	40
63	MGM MGM-EP 775	WHAT KIND OF FOOL AM I?	20
63	MGM MGM-EP 780	MALA FEMMENA	12
63	MGM MGM-EP 783	FROM ITALY ... WITH LOVE	12
65	MGM MGM-EP 789	SINGS FOR MAMA	8

ALBUMS

58	MGM MGM-D 153	WHO'S SORRY NOW? (10")	30
59	MGM MGM-C 782	MY THANKS TO YOU	20
59	MGM MGM-C 786	THE EXCITING CONNIE FRANCIS	20
59	MGM MGM-C 797	CHRISTMAS WITH CONNIE	20
60	MGM MGM-C 804	ROCK AND ROLL MILLION SELLERS NO. 1	50
60	MGM MGM-C 812	COUNTRY AND WESTERN GOLDEN HITS	20
60	MGM MGM-C 819	FUN SONGS FOR CHILDREN	20
60	MGM MGM-C 821	SINGS ITALIAN FAVOURITES (mono)	12
60	MGM MGM-CS 6002	SINGS ITALIAN FAVOURITES (stereo)	15
60	MGM MGM-C 831	CONNIE'S GREATEST HITS	15
60	MGM MGM-C 836	SPANISH AND LATIN AMERICAN FAVOURITES (mono)	12
60	MGM MGM-CS 6012	SPANISH AND LATIN AMERICAN FAVOURITES (stereo)	15
61	MGM MGM-C 879	DO THE TWIST	40

MINT VALUE £

62	MGM MGM-C 916	COUNTRY MUSIC CONNIE STYLE (mono)	12
62	MGM MGM-CS 6062	COUNTRY MUSIC CONNIE STYLE (stereo)	15
63	MGM MGM-CS 6068	FOLLOW THE BOYS (stereo))	15
78	United Artists ULP 30182	WHO'S HAPPY NOW? (withdrawn sleeve with different lettering)	40

CONNIE FRANCIS & MARVIN RAINWATER
58	MGM MGM 969	The Majesty Of Love/You My Darling You	35
58	MGM MGM 969	The Majesty Of Love/You My Darling You (78)	20

(see also Marvin Rainwater)

(KING) JOE FRANCIS
65	Blue Beat BB 323	Wicked Woman/King Joe's Ska (as King Joe Francis)	15
65	Ska Beat JB 184	Waggling Tails/I Don't Want You No More	20
66	Ska Beat JB 262	Scarborough Ska/I Got A Scar (as Joe Francis & Ricky Logan & Snowballs)	20
66	Rio R 90	Have My Body (song actually "Have Mercy Baby")/Everybody's Got To Know (as King Joe Francis & Hijackers)	15
66	Rio R 94	Days Are Lonely/My Baby	25
67	Rainbow RAI 114	My Granny/Pull It Out (as J. Francis & Rico's Boys)	15

JOHNNIE FRANCIS
55	Decca F 10440	Funny Thing/Give Me The Right	5

LEE FRANCIS (1)
65	Decca F 12148	Ciao/If He Wants Me	5

(see also Vernons Girls)

LEE FRANCIS (2)
79	Lee & Roy L 2	A Lonely I & I/Paradise (12")	15
79	Lee & Roy L 3	Shadows Of My Youth/Deception Of Consciousness (12")	15

NAT FRANCIS
66	Blue Beat BB 346	Mama Kiss Him Goodnight/Tra La La (with Prince Buster Junior & Sunsets)	20
66	Blue Beat BB 361	Just To Keep You (credited to B. Junior)/You Only Want My Money	18
67	Blue Beat BB 376	Seven Nights Of Love/Feeling Blue	20

PAT FRANCIS
77	Western Kingston WK 506	Rasta Protest/Part 2	8

RITCHIE FRANCIS
72	Pegasus PEG 11	SONGBIRD (LP, gatefold textured sleeve)	25

(see also Eyes Of Blue, Big Sleep)

STEVE FRANCIS
64	King KG 1012	Watch Your Step/Lovey Dovey	8

WILBERT FRANCIS & VIBRATORS
66	Ska Beat JB 267	Memories Of You/CHUCK JACQUES: Now That You're Gone	25

(see also Little Willie, Vibrators [Jamaica])

WILLIE FRANCIS
69	Bullet BU 415	Motherless Children/I Am Not Afraid	25
71	Escort ERT 848	Burn Them/Poor Boy	10
71	Bullet BU 489	Willie's Rouster/Rouster Version	15
71	Pama PM 829	Oh What A Mini/Version	10
74	Magnet MA 38	Quick March/Africa Melody (actually by Charlie Organaire)	10

(see also Martin Riley)

WINSTON FRANCIS
69	Coxsone CS 7089	Reggae And Cry/FREEDOM SINGERS: Easy Come Easy Go (B-side actually by Righteous Flames)	35
69	Studio One SO 2086	The Games People Play/ALBERT GRIFFITHS: The Kicks	35
69	Punch PH 5	Too Experienced/JACKIE MINTO: Mule Jerk (B-side actually by Jackie Mittoo)	15
69	Bamboo BAM 10	The Same Old Song/SOUND DIMENSION: Rattle On	45
70	Bamboo BAM 46	Turn Back The Hands Of Time/Soul Bowl	25
70	Bamboo BAM 48	California Dreaming/JACKIE MITTOO & SOUND DIMENSION: Soul Stew	35
72	Camel CA 99	Ten Times Sweeter Than You/Fat Boy	20
72	Rhino RNO 102	A Little Today A Little Tomorrow/Love Thy Neighbour	7
73	Fab FAB 271	Mr Fix It/Version	8
74	Ashanti ASH 415	California Dreaming/SOUND DIMENSION: Soul Food (reissue)	8
70	Bamboo BDLP 207	MR FIX IT (LP)	50
71	Bamboo BDLPS 216	CALIFORNIA DREAMING (LP)	60

(see also Bobby Francis, Jerry & Freedom Singers, Zimm & Dee Dee)

CLAUDE FRANCOIS
66	Fontana TF 725	In My Memory/Gone From My Mind	40
67	Fontana TF 799	Bench Number 3 Waterloo Station/Run To Daddy	100
77	EMI EMC 3189	HIS HITS IN ENGLISH (LP)	30

FRANCO-LONDON ORCHESTRA
66	Philips BF 1562	Theme From Robinson Crusoe/Adrift	10

JACKSON C. FRANK
78	B&C BCS 0012	Blues Run The Game/Milk & Honey	20
65	Columbia DB 7795	Blues Run The Game/Can't Get Away From My Love	100
65	Columbia 33SX 1788	JACKSON C. FRANK (LP)	300
78	B&C BCLP 4	AGAIN (LP, reissue of above LP)	40

STANLEY FRANK
77	Power Exchange PX 247	S'cool Days/On A Line (p/s)	5

FRANK & BARBARIANS
62	Oriole CB 1758	The Bouncer/Concerto In The Stars	15

FRANKIE & CLASSICALS
67	Philips BF 1586	I Only Have Eyes For You/What Shall I Do?	200
74	Pye Intl. DDS 101	What Shall I Do?/Goodbye Love, Hello Sadness	5

FRANKIE GOES TO HOLLYWOOD

SINGLES

83	ZTT P ZTAS 1	Relax (Move)/One September Monday (picture disc)	5
83	ZTT 12 ZTAS 1	Relax (Original Mix)/Ferry Across The Mersey/Relax Bonus (Again) (12", ZTT sleeve or standard p/s, some copies play at 33rpm but list 45rpm)	10
83	ZTT 12 ZTAS 1 (matrix no.: 1A 2U)	Relax (Sex Mix [alias 8.20 "New York Mix"])/Ferry Across The Mersey Relax Bonus (Again) (12", p/s, 45rpm)	12
83	ZTT 12 ZTAS 1 (matrix no.: 1A 5U)	Relax (Sex Mix)/Ferry Across The Mersey/Relax Bonus (Again) (12", p/s, 45rpm, different 'U.S. chequered' p/s)	8
83	ZTT 12P ZTAS 1	Relax (Sex Mix)/Ferry Across The Mersey/Relax Bonus (Again) (12", picture disc)	5
84	ZTT P ZTAS 3	Two Tribes (Carnage)/One February Friday (Only Bullets Can Stop Them Now)/War (hidden) (picture disc)	6
84	ZTT P ZTAS 5	The Power Of Love/The World Is My Oyster (picture disc)	5
84	ZTT 12X ZTAS 5	The Power Of Love/The World Is My Oyster/Welcome To The Pleasuredome (Pleasurefix)/The Only Star In Heaven (Starfix) (12", g/fold p/s with 5 photos)	8
84	ZTT CTIS 105	The Power Of Love (Extended Version)/Trapped And Scrapped/Holier Than Thou (, picture 'envelope' box)	8
85	ZTT ZTAS 7	Welcome To The Pleasure Dome (Altered Reel) (actually plays "Video Mix 5.05")/Happy Hi Get It On (p/s, blue label)	5
85	ZTT P ZTAS 7	Welcome To The Pleasure Dome (Alternative Reel ["Fruitiness Mix"])/ Happy Hi/Get It On (apple-shaped picture disc)	8
86	ZTT ZTD 22	Rage Hard/(Don't Lose What's Left) Of Your Little Mind ('pop-up fists' p/s)	5
86	ZTT 12 ZTAX B 22	Rage Hard (++ Mix)/Roadhouse Blues/(Don't Lose What's Left) Of Your Little Mind (extended) (12", in 'action series 22' box)	8
83	ZTT ZTAS 1DJ	Relax " The Last Seven Inches/One September Monday (white label, stamped label, no p/s)	5
84	ZTT XZTAS 3DJ	Two Tribes (Carnage)/Relax (U.S. Mix) (12", ZTT sleeve)	10
84	ZTT XZIP 1	Two Tribes (Hibakusha)/War (Hide Yourself)/Two Tribes/ One February Friday (12", ZTT sleeve)	15
84	ZTT ZTAS 5 DJ-A	The Power Of Love (5.28)/The World Is My Oyster (12")	10
86	ZTT 12 ZTAK 25	Warriors (The Attack Mix) (12", white label, featuring Gary Moore)	10
93	ZTT SAM 1231	Relax (Ollie J. Remix) (6.38)/(Trip-Ship Edit) (6.12)/(Ollie J.'s Seven Inches)/ (Jam & Spoon Hi-N-R-G Mix) (7.55)/(C Jam & Spoon Trip-O-Matic Fairy Tale Space mix) &7.52)/(MCMXCIII) (3.45) (12", double pack, gatefold sleeve)	6
94	ZTT (no cat. No.)	Two Tribes (808 State Remix) (10" 1-sided red or blue vinyl)	8

(see also Spitfire Boys)

FRANKIE & JOHNNY

66	Decca F 22376	Never Gonna Leave You/I'll Hold You	250
66	Decca F 22376	Never Gonna Leave You/I'll Hold You (DJ Copy)	250
66	Parlophone R 5518	Climb Ev'ry Mountain/I Wanna Make You Understand	25
78	Inferno HEAT 8	I'll Hold You/Never Gonna Leave You (reissue)	10

(see also Maggie Bell)

FRANKIE & LARRY

60	Capitol CL 15153	Not Yet/A Fool For You	12

FRANKIE & THE PHANTOMS

74	RCA LPBO 5013	Rock 'N' Roll Band/Jamburger	6

FRANKIE & TIMEBREAKERS

68	Philips BF 1696	I'll Be Home/Is There Anybody	7

ARETHA FRANKLIN

SINGLES

67	Atlantic 584 157	(I Can't Get No) Satisfaction/Chain Of Fools	8
61	Fontana H 271	Love Is The Only Thing/Today I Sing The Blues (with Ray Bryant Combo)	15
61	Fontana H 343	Rock-A-Bye Your Baby With A Dixie Melody/Operation Heartbreak	10
65	CBS 201732	Can't You Just See Me/You Little Miss Raggedy Anne	20
67	CBS 202468	Cry Like A Baby/Swanee	6
67	CBS 3059	Take A Look/Lee Cross	6
67	Atlantic 584 084	I Never Loved A Man (The Way I Love You)/Do Right Woman – Do Right Man	8
67	Atlantic 584 115	Respect/Save Me	8
67	Atlantic 584 127	Baby I Love You/Going Down Slow	10
67	Atlantic 584 141	(You Make Me Feel Like A) Natural Woman/Never Let Me Go	8
67	Atlantic 584 157	(I Can't Get No) Satisfaction/Night Life (withdrawn B-side)	12
67	Atlantic 584 157	Chain Of Fools/(I Can't Get No) Satisfaction	8
68	Atlantic 584 172	Since You've Been Gone/Ain't No Way	10
68	Atlantic 584 186	Think/You Send Me	8
68	Atlantic 584 206	I Say A Little Prayer/See-Saw	10
69	Atlantic 584 239	Don't Let Me Lose This Dream/The House That Jack Built	8
69	Atlantic 584 252	The Weight/The Tracks Of My Tears	8
69	Atlantic 584 285	Share Your Love With Me/Pledging My Love/The Clock	8
69	Atlantic 584 306	Eleanor Rigby/It Ain't Fair	8
70	Atlantic 584 322	Call Me/Son Of A Preacher Man	8
70	Atlantic 2091 027	Don't Play That Song/The Thrill Is Gone	5
70	Atlantic 2091 042	Border Song (Holy Moses)/You And Me (unissued)	0
70	Atlantic 2091 044	Oh No, Not My Baby/You And Me	5
71	Atlantic 2091 063	You're All I Need To Get By/The Border Song	5
71	Atlantic 2091 111	I Say A Little Prayer/(I Can't Get No) Satisfaction	5
71	Atlantic 2091 127	A Brand New Me/Spirit In The Dark	10
71	Atlantic 2091 168	Rock Steady/Oh Me, Oh My	10
72	Atlantic K 10154	Daydreaming / I've Been Loving You Too Long	8
72	Atlantic K 10224	Rock Steady/All The King's Horses	8

EPs

62	Fontana TE 467217	TODAY I SING THE BLUES	50

ALBUMS

61	Fontana TFL 5173	ARETHA	70
65	CBS (S)BPG 62566	YEAH!!! — IN PERSON	40
65	CBS (S)BPG 62744	SOUL SISTER	40
67	Atlantic 587/588 066	I NEVER LOVED A MAN	15
67	CBS (S)BPG 62969	TAKE IT LIKE YOU GIVE IT	20
67	CBS 63160	LEE CROSS	15
67	Atlantic 587/588 085	ARETHA ARRIVES	12
67	CBS 64536	GREATEST HITS	12

Carolyn FRANKLIN

68	Atlantic 587/588 099	LADY SOUL	12
68	CBS 63269	TAKE A LOOK AT ARETHA FRANKLIN	12
68	Atlantic 587/588 114	ARETHA NOW	15
68	CBS 63064	GREATEST HITS VOL. 2	12
68	Atlantic 587/588 149	ARETHA IN PARIS — LIVE AT THE OLYMPIA	15
69	Atlantic 588 169	SOUL '69	12
69	Chess (S)CRL 54550	SONGS OF FAITH	12
70	Atlantic 2400 004	THIS GIRL'S IN LOVE WITH YOU	12
70	Atlantic 2464 007	I SAY A LITTLE PRAYER	12
70	Atlantic 2400 021	DON'T PLAY THAT SONG	12
71	Atlantic 2400 136	LIVE AT THE FILLMORE WEST (gatefold sleeve)	12

CAROLYN FRANKLIN

69	RCA Victor RCA 1851	Boxer/I Don't Want To Lose You	8
70	RCA Victor RCA 2009	All I Want To Be Is Your Woman/You Really Didn't Mean It	5
69	RCA RD/SF 8035	BABY DYNAMITE! (LP)	20

ERMA FRANKLIN

67	London HLZ 10170	Piece Of My Heart/Big Boss Man	15
68	London HLZ 10201	Open Up Your Soul/I Just Ain't Ready For Love	10
68	London HLZ 10220	The Right To Cry/Don't Catch The Dog's Bone	10
69	Soul City SC 118	Don't Wait Too Long/Time After Time	25
69	MCA MU 1073	Gotta Find Me A Lover (24 Hours A Day)/Change My Thoughts From You	15
71	Jay Boy BOY 36	I Just Ain't Ready For Love/The Right To Cry	10
71	Jay Boy BOY 41	Piece Of My Heart/Big Boss Man (reissue)	10
70	MCA MUP MUPS 394	SOUL SISTER (LP)	25

MARIE FRANKLIN

| 68 | MGM MGM 1455 | You Ain't Changed/Don'tcha Bet No Money | 10 |

GORDON FRANKS

60	Oriole CB 1541	Inn For Trouble/Twinkle Toes	6
62	Parlophone R 4910	Rag Trade Rag/Sid's Tune	6
62	Parlophone R 4929	Outbreak Of Murder/Johnny's Tune	7
60	Oriole EP 7030	SONGS FROM FOLLOW THAT GIRL (EP)	8
67	Deram SML 701	ORCHESTRAL IN THE NIGHT (LP)	12
67	Deram (S)DML 706	STRINGS IN THE NIGHT (LP)	12

JOHNNY FRANKS

55	Melodisc P 230	Tweedle Dee/Shake, Rattle And Roll (78)	25
56	Melodisc 1355	Rock Candy Baby/Sing-ing-ing (78)	12
58	Melodisc 1459	Good Old Country Music/Cheatin' On Me	7
58	Melodisc 1459	Good Old Country Music/Cheatin' On Me (78)	20

BONNIE (BLUE) FRANKSON

68	Jolly JY 014	Loving You/Shoo Be Do (both with Joe Nolan Band)	12
69	Jolly JY 021	London City/Dearest (both with Joe Nolan & Dynamic Heatwave)	12
69	Columbia Blue Beat DB 114	Dearest/London City	15
70	Ackee ACK 110	I'm So Glad/Lonely Road (both with Dotty)	8
73	Ackee ACK 512	Getting Things Together/Version	6

(see also Dotty & Bonnie)

FRANTIC ELEVATORS

79	TJM TJM 5	Voice In The Dark/Passion/Every Day I Die (p/s)	40
80	TJM TJM 6	Hunchback Of Notre Dame/See Nothing And Everything/Don't Judge Me (unreleased; demos only)	150
80	Eric's ERIC'S 6	You Know What You Told Me/Production Prevention (p/s)	50
81	Crackin' Up CRAK 1	Searching For The Only One/Hunchback Of Notre Dame (p/s)	20
82	No Waiting WAIT 1	Holding Back The Years/Pistols In My Brain (p/s)	20
87	TJM TJM 101	THE EARLY YEARS (mini-LP)	20
88	Receiver KNOB 2	THE EARLY YEARS (mini-LP, reissue with new sleeve & interview disc, as Mick Hucknall & Frantic Elevators)	15

(see also Simply Red)

FRANZ FERDINAND

03	Domino RUG164T	Darts Of Pleasure/Van Tango/Shopping For Blood (12", p/s 500 only)	10
04	Domino RUG172	Take Me Out/Truck Stop (3,000 only, p/s)	5
04	Domino PRINCIPP01	Take Me Out (Naum Gabo Remix) (7" white label promo)	5
05	Domino RUG211TP	Do You Want To (Erol Alkan's Glam Racket Mix/Original Version (12" white label)	8
05	New! NEW001	Get Up and Use Me (Franz Ferdinand)/Jacqueline (The Fire Engines) (7" single)	8
06	Domino DC 001	Swallow Smile/Take Me Out (Acoustic) (fan club release)	20
03	Chateau CHAT001	LIVE 2003 (LP, 10-track official bootleg/promo 500 copies)	20
09	Domino WIG 205X	TONIGHT: FRANZ FERDINAND (6 x 7", 2 x CD & DVD box set)	30

(see also The Karelia, The Ampheta Meanies)

ANDY FRASER BAND

| 75 | CBS 80731 | THE ANDY FRASER BAND (LP) | 20 |
| 75 | CBS 81027 | IN YOUR EYES (LP) | 12 |

(see also Free, Sharks)

JOHN FRASER

58	Pye 7N 15118	Trolley Stop/Don't Take Your Love From Me	5
59	Pye 7N 15212	Bye Bye, Baby, Goodbye/Golden Cage	7
58	Pye NEP 24068	PRESENTING JOHN FRASER (EP)	15

PHILLIP FRASER

| 78 | White Rum/Red Stripe 102 | Need To Be Loved/Loving Version | 6 |

TERRY FRASER

| 69 | Rude Boy RBH 001 | Beng Beng Chitty/Soul Food | 25 |

FRATELLIS

| 06 | Island IS 924 | THE FRATELLIS EP: Creeping Up The Backstairs/Stacie Anne/The Gutterati? (pink vinyl) | 10 |
| 06 | No Label | Cigarillo/Got Ma Nuts From A Hippy (Demo) (gig freebie, 500 only) | 15 |

FRATERNITY BROTHERS

| 59 | HMV POP 582 | Passion Flower/A Nobody Like Me (B-side with Gil Fields) | 6 |

FRATERNITY OF MAN
70	Stateside SS 2166	Don't Bogart Me/Wispy Paisley Skies 12

ERIC FRATTER
69	Trojan TR 655	Since You've Been Gone/AFROTONES: Things I Love 8

(see also Eric Fatter)

FRAYS
65	Decca F 12153	Keep Me Covered/Walk On 150
65	Decca F 12229	My Girl Sloopy/For Your Precious Love 50

(see also Mike Patto)

NORMA FRAZER
65	Ska Beat JB 223	Heartaches/Everybody Loves A Lover 120
67	Coxsone CS 7017	The First Cut Is The Deepest/BUMPS OAKLEY: Rag Doll 30
67	Studio One SO 2024	Come By Here/WAILERS: I Stand Predominate 250
68	Coxsone CS 7060	Respect/Time 60

(see also Sound Dimension, Righteous Homes, Viceroys, Tommy McCook)

PHILIP FRAZER
76	Student STU 1003	Blue Bird/Dub 8

DALLAS FRAZIER
66	Capitol CL 15445	Elvira/That Ain't No Stuff 6
66	Capitol CL 15457	Just A Little Bit Of You/Walkin' Wonder 5
59	Capitol EAP 1035	DALLAS FRAZIER (EP) 20

FRAZIER CHORUS
87	Virgin VSCD 1192	Sloppy Heart/Anarchy In The UK/String/Typical (3" CD in heart-shaped box) 12
91	Virgin CDV 2654	RAY (CD, with bonus remix CD) 20

FREAKS OF NATURE
66	Island WI 3017	People! Let's Freak Out/The Shadow Chasers 90

(see also Kim Fowley, Belfast Gypsies, Jackie McAuley)

STAN FREBERG
54	Capitol CL 14187	Sh-Boom (Life Could Be A Dream) (with The Toads)/C'est Ci Bon 30
55	Capitol CL 14316	The Lone Psychiatrist/The Honey-Earthers (with Daws Butler) 25
56	Capitol CL 14509	The Yellow Rose Of Texas/Rock Around Stephen Foster 20
56	Capitol CL 14571	The Great Pretender/The Quest For Bridey Hammerschlaugen (B-side with June Foray) 20
56	Capitol CL 14608	Heartbreak Hotel/Rock Island Line 22
57	Capitol CL 14712	Banana Boat (Day-O)/Tele-vee-shun 20
58	Capitol CL 14966	Green Chritma (with Daws Butler)/The Meaning Of Christmas (with Jud Conlon Chorale) 10
60	Capitol CL 15122	The Old Payola Roll Blues (with Jesse White)/ Sh-Boom (Life Could Be A Dream) 15
55	Capitol EAP1 496	ANY REQUESTS (EP) 12
56	Capitol EAP1 628	THE REAL SAINT GEORGE (EP) 12
61	Capitol EAP1 1101	OMAHA (EP) 12
61	Capitol EAP1 20050	THE GREAT PRETENDER (EP) 12
61	Capitol EAP1 20115	FREBERG AGAIN (EP, with Daws Butler) 12
57	Capitol T 777	A CHILD'S GARDEN OF FREBERG (LP) 20
58	Capitol LCT 6170	THE BEST OF THE STAN FREBERG SHOWS (LP) 20
58	Capitol LCT 6171	THE BEST OF THE STAN FREBERG SHOWS VOL. 2 (LP) 20
61	Capitol W 1573	PRESENTS THE UNITED STATES OF AMERICA (LP) 20

FRED BANANA COMBO
78	Warm AWMR 2004	No Destination Blues/Jerk Off All Nite Long (p/s) 5

FRED BLOGGS BAND
76	Firebrand DMO 12	Mr Sun/Seaside/Moonrock/The Tribe 8

JOHN FRED & HIS PLAYBOY BAND
67	Pye International 7N 25442	Judy In Disguise (With Glasses)/When The Lights Go Out 6
68	Pye International 7N 25453	Hey Hey Bunny/No Letter Today 20
68	Pye International 7N 25462	We Played Games/Lonely Are The Lonely 7
68	Pye International 7N 25470	Little Dum Dum/Tissue Paper 7
68	CBS 3475	Shirley/High Heel Sneakers 10
69	MCA MU 1088	Silly Sarah Carter/Back In The USSR 6
67	Pye Intl. NPL 28111	AGNES ENGLISH (LP) 20

FRED LOCKS
78	Tribesman TM 20	Love & Only Love/Stricker Ishion 15
78	Revelations FRW 375	Love & Harmony/Joy & Harmony (featuring Brigadier Jerry) (p/s) 25
78	Lloyd Coxsone LC 001	Voice Of The Poor/LEVI ROOTS: Poor Man's Story 25
78	Form 1091	LOVE & HARMONY (LP) 30
80	Rev 001 LP	NEBUCHADNEZZER KING OF BABYLON (FRED LOCKS MEETS CREATORS) (LP) 60
82	Regal RLP 002	LOVE AND ONLY LOVE (LP, with CREATION STEPPERS) 45
83	Vulcan VULA 502	BLACK STAR LINER (LP, with poster) 20

FREDDIE & THE DREAMERS
63	Columbia DB 7032	If You Gotta Make A Fool Of Somebody/Feel So Blue 6
64	Columbia DB 7322	Just For You/Don't Do That To Me 5
65	Columbia DB 7526	A Little You/Things I'd Like To Say 6
65	Columbia DC 763	A Windmill In Old Amsterdam/A Love Like You (export issue) 15
66	Columbia DB 7857	If You've Gotta Minute Baby/When I'm Home With You 6
66	Columbia DB 7929	Playboy/Some Day 15
66	Columbia DB 8033	Turn Around/Funny Over You 8
67	Columbia DB 8137	Hello, Hello/All I Ever Want Is You 7
67	Columbia DB 8200	Brown And Porter's (Meat Exporters) Lorry/Little Brown Eyes 10
68	Columbia DB 8496	Little Big Time/FREDDIE GARRITY: You Belong To Me 10
68	Columbia DB 8517	It's Great/Gaberdine Mac 8
69	Columbia DB 8606	Get Around Downtown Girl/What To Do 8
71	Philips 6006 098	Susan's Tuba/You Hurt Me Girl 10
78	Polydor 2059 041	Here We Go/I Saw Ya 10
63	Columbia SEG 8275	IF YOU GOTTA MAKE A FOOL OF SOMEBODY (EP) 10
63	Columbia SEG 8287	SONGS FROM THE FILM "WHAT A CRAZY WORLD" (EP) 12
64	Columbia SEG 8302	YOU WERE MADE FOR ME (EP) 10

MINT VALUE £

64	Columbia SEG 8323	OVER YOU (EP)..10
64	Columbia SEG 8349	FREDDIE SINGS JUST FOR YOU (EP)..10
65	Columbia SEG 8403	READY, FREDDIE, GO! (EP)..10
65	Columbia SEG 8457	FREDDIE AND THE DREAMERS (EP)..10
67	EMI Regal	SEE YOU LATER ALLIGATOR (Export issue)....................................35
63	Columbia 33SX 1577	FREDDIE AND THE DREAMERS (LP)..15
64	Columbia 33SX 1663	YOU WERE MAD FOR ME (LP)...15
66	Columbia SX 6069	IN DISNEYLAND (LP, mono)...15
66	Columbia S(C)X 6069	IN DISNEYLAND (LP, stereo)..18
67	Columbia SX 6177	KING FREDDIE AND THE DREAMING KNIGHTS (LP).....................20

(see also Freddie Garrity, Dreamers)

FREDDIE & THE DREAMERS/PETER & GORDON

64	Columbia SEG 8337	JUST FOR YOU (EP, 2 tracks each) 20

(see also Peter & Gordon)

FREDDIE & FITZY

60s	Dr Bird 1033	Do Good/SOUL BROTHERS: On The Town 30

DOTTY FREDERICK

59	Top Rank JAR 106	Ricky/Just Wait 50
59	Top Rank JAR 106	Ricky/Just Wait (78) 12

TOMMY FREDERICK & HI-NOTES

58	London HLU 8555	Prince Of Players/I'm Not Pretending.......................................50
58	London HLU 8555	Prince Of Players/I'm Not Pretending (78) 20

BILL FREDERICKS

76	Polydor 2058 946	Lose Someone Like You/Love With You 15
76	Polydor	Lose Someone Like You/What 30
77	Polydor 2058 895	Lovers/It's Just A Matter Of Time 5
78	Polydor 2059 035	Almost/Wind Of Change 5

DOLORES FREDERICKS

56	Brunswick 05540	Cha Cha Joe/Whole Lotta Shakin' Goin' On 30

MARC FREDERICKS

56	London HLD 8281	Mystic Midnight/Symphony To Anne 20

FREE (HOLLAND)

69	Philips BF 1738	Soul Party/Down To The Bone..15
69	Philips BF 1754	Keep In Touch/Taking It Away 40

FREE (U.K.)

69	Island WIP 6054	Broad Daylight/The Worm..60
69	Island WIP 6062	I'll Be Creepin'/Sugar For Mr Morrison......................................60
70	Island WIP 6082	All Right Now/Mouthful Of Grass (pink label)............................8
70	Island WIP 6093	The Stealer/Lying In The Sunshine 5
71	Island WIP 6100	My Brother Jake/Only My Soul..5
72	Island WIP 6129	Little Bit Of Love/Sail On 5
72	Island WIP 6146	Wishing Well/Let Me Show You 5
73	Island WIP 6082	All Right Now/Mouthful Of Grass (reissue pink rim, palm tree label) 8
73	Island WIP 6160	Travellin' In Style/Easy On My Soul 5
76	Island WIP 6082	All Right Now/Mouthful Of Grass (reissue, orange palm tree label).....20
76	Island WIP 6351	The Hunter/Worry 5
78	Island IEPJB 6	All Right Now/Wishing Well (jukebox copy, short version) 25
82	Island PIEP 6	THE FREE EP (12", picture disc)...10
69	Island ILPS 9089	TONS OF SOBS (LP, gatefold sleeve, 1st pressing, pink label/ black & orange 'circle' logo) 200
69	Island ILPS 9089	TONS OF SOBS (LP, gatefold sleeve, 2nd pressing, pink label/black 'block' logo) ...70
70	Island ILPS 9089	TONS OF SOBS (LP, gatefold sleeve, 3rd pressing, pink label/'i' logo) 30
71	Island ILPS 9089	TONS OF SOBS (LP, gatefold sleeve, 4th pressing, pink rim label/ 'palm tree' logo)...15
69	Island ILPS 9104	FREE (LP, gatefold sleeve, 1st pressing, pink label/'i' logo) 150
70	Island ILPS 9104	FREE (LP, gatefold sleeve, 2nd pressing, pink rim label/'palm tree' logo) ..15
70	Island ILPS 9120	FIRE AND WATER (LP, 1st pressing, pink label/'i' logo) 100
70	Island ILPS 9120	FIRE AND WATER (LP, 2nd pressing, pink rim label/'palm tree' logo)........15
70	Island ILPS 9138	HIGHWAY (LP, pink rim, palm tree label) 20
71	Island ILPS 9160	LIVE (LP, in envelope sleeve with inner, pink rim, palm tree label).........30
72	Island ILPS 9192	FREE AT LAST (LP)..25
72	Island ILPS 9217	HEARTBREAKER (LP, lyric inner sleeve, pink rim, palm tree label) 20
74	Island ISLD 4	THE FREE STORY (2-LP, gatefold, with 4-page booklet, numbered)........25

(see also Paul Kossoff, Rabbit, Kossoff Kirke Tetsu & Rabbit, Sharks, Andy Fraser Band, Black Cat Bones, Rock Aid Armenia)

FREE WINDS

66	MJB REV LP 397	FROM A NEW DIRECTION (LP) 20

FREE AGENTS

80	Groovy STP 1	FREE AGENTS (LP, 1000 only, hand-made sleeve)........................20

(see also Pete Shelley, Eric Random)

ALAN FREED & HIS ROCK'N'ROLL BAND

57	Vogue Coral Q 72219	Teen Rock/Right Now, Right Now (with Alan Freed's Rock'n'Rollers) 100
57	Vogue Coral Q 72219	Teen Rock/Right Now, Right Now (with Alan Freed's Rock'n'Rollers)(78) ...20
57	Vogue Coral Q 72230	Rock'n'Roll Boogie/Teener's Canteen (with Alan Freed's Rock'n'Rollers) ..100
57	Vogue Coral Q 72230	Rock'n'Roll Boogie/Teener's Canteen (with Alan Freed's Rock'n'Rollers)(78) ..20
56	Vogue Coral LVA 9033	ROCK'N'ROLL DANCE PARTY VOL. 1 (LP, featuring Modernaires) 60
57	Vogue Coral LVA 9066	ROCK'N'ROLL DANCE PARTY VOL. 2 (LP, with Jimmy Cavello) 90

(see also Jimmy Cavello)

FREE DESIGN

69	Project 3	HEAVEN/EARTH (LP) 30

BOB FREEDMAN ORCHESTRA

63	Island ILP 101	MUSIC TO STRIP BY (LP, with free G string)................................40
63	Island ILP 101	MUSIC TO STRIP BY (LP, without G string).................................12

J.A. FREEDMAN

| 69 | Decca F12963 | When You Walked Out Of My Life/Love's Got A Minf Of It's Own | 25 |
| 69 | Decca LK 5021 | MY NAME IS J.A. FREEDMAN, I ALSO SING (LP) | 50 |

FREEDOM

68	Mercury MF 1033	Where Will You Be Tonight/Trying To Get A Glimpse Of You (in p/s)	45
68	Mercury MF 1033	Where Will You Be Tonight/Trying To Get A Glimpse Of You	30
69	Plexium PXM 3	Escape While You Can/Kandy Kay	10
70	Probe PRO 504	Frustrated Woman/Man Made Laws	20
71	Vertigo 6059 051	Thanks/Miss Little Louise	30
70	Probe SPBA 6252	FREEDOM (LP, gatefold sleeve, pink label)	100
71	Vertigo 6360 050	THROUGH THE YEARS (LP, gatefold sleeve, small swirl label)	200
72	Vertigo 6360 072	FREEDOM IS MORE THAN A WORD (LP, die cut gatefold sleeve, small swirl label)	300

(see also Mick Abrahams, Procol Harum, Snafu)

FREEDOM GROUP

| 72 | Randy's RAN 525 | Sing A Song Of Freedom (actually by Max Romeo)/IMPACT ALLSTARS: Song Of Freedom (Version) | 7 |

FREEDOM OF CHOICE

| 70 | Wand | Doctor Tom/Rat Man | 20 |

FREEDOM SINGERS (JAMAICA)

| 67 | Studio One SO 2010 | Have Faith/Work Crazy | 40 |
| 70 | Bamboo BAM 21 | Give Peace A Chance/SOUND DIMENSION: In Cold Blood | 30 |

(see also Winston Francis)

FREEDOM SINGERS (U.K.)

| 70 | New Beat NB 059 | Election (with Live Stocks)/FLECE & LIVE SHOCKS: Tomorrow's World | 10 |
| 71 | New Beat NB 074 | Your Testimony/Train Coming | 8 |

FREED UNIT

99	Out-There OTT 06	MASONIC YOUTH (9" EP, triangular clear vinyl, 100 only)	50
01	Out-There OTT 09	SIX SIDED (9" EP, clear vinyl, 100 only)	25
98	Out-There OTTLP 04	FIELD REPORTS FROM OUT-THERE (LP, clear vinyl)	18
98	Enraptured RAPTLP 19	THINGS ARE LOOKING UP... (LP, orange vinyl)	15

FREE FERRY

| 69 | CBS 4456 | Mary, What Have You Become?/Friend | 8 |
| 70 | CBS 4647 | Haverjack Drive/Flying | 20 |

FREEFORM

| 95 | Skam SKA 3 | Fane/Recut/Rail/Siamese Telebox/The Brink/Many/Freeform Dub (12") | 25 |
| 95 | Skam SKA 4 | FREE EP (12") | 25 |

ALAN FREEMAN AND THE TALMY STONE BAND

| 62 | Decca F 11543 | Madison Time/Madison Time | 10 |

ART FREEMAN

| 66 | Atlantic 584 053 | Slippin' Around/Can't Get You Out Of My Mind | 175 |

BOBBY FREEMAN

58	London HLJ 8644	Do You Want To Dance?/Big Fat Woman	40
58	London HLJ 8644	Do You Want To Dance?/Big Fat Woman (78)	25
58	London HLJ 8721	Betty Lou Got A New Pair Of Shoes/Starlight	50
58	London HLJ 8721	Betty Lou Got A New Pair Of Shoes/Starlight (78)	35
59	London HLJ 8782	Shame On You Miss Johnson/Need Your Love	50
59	London HLJ 8782	Shame On You Miss Johnson/Need Your Love (78)	40
59	London HLJ 8898	Mary Ann Thomas/Love Me	40
59	London HLJ 8898	Mary Ann Thomas/Love Me (78)	40
60	London HLJ 9031	Sinbad/Ebb Tide (The Sea)	15
60	Parlophone R 4684	(I Do The) Shimmy Shimmy/You Don't Understand Me	20
64	Pye International 7N 25260	C'mon And Swim (Parts 1 & 2)	20
64	Pye International 7N 25280	S-W-I-M/That Little Old Heartbreaker Me	25
66	Pye International 7N 25347	The Duck/Cross My Heart	30
66	Pye International 7N 25347	The Duck/The Devil (2nd issue with different B-side)	10

BUD FREEMAN

66	Fontana TL 5370	BUD FREEMAN ESQ. (LP)	20
68	Fontana TL 5414	FREEMAN & CO (LP)	20
73	Philips 6308 254	SONG OF THE TENOR (LP)	20

CAROL FREEMAN

| 67 | CBS 202579 | The Rolling Sea/Leaving You Now | 15 |

ERNIE FREEMAN

57	London HLP 8523	Raunchy/Puddin'	20
57	London HL 7029	Dumplin's/Beautiful Weekend (export issue)	15
58	London HLP 8558	Dumplin's/Beautiful Weekend	15
58	London HLP 8660	Indian Love Call/Summer Serenade	10
60	London HLP 9041	Big River/Night Sounds	7
65	London HLP 9944	Raunchy '65/Jivin' Around	10
56	London RE-U 1059	ERNIE FREEMAN AND HIS RHYTHM GUITAR (EP)	30
59	London RE-P 1210	ERNIE FREEMAN VOL. 2 (EP)	30

EVELYN FREEMAN EXCITING VOICES

| 69 | London HLU 10287 | I Heard The Voice/I Dreamed Last Night | 5 |

GEORGE FREEMAN

| 71 | Jay Boy BOY 54 | I'm Like A Fish/Why Are You Doing This To Me | 25 |

MARGARET FREEMAN

| 61 | Starlite ST45 040 | Forbidden Fruit/Mister Ting A Ling | 15 |

PAUL FREEMAN

| 71 | Punch PH 82 | Don't Give Up/UPSETTERS: Give Up (Version) | 12 |

RUSS FREEMAN & CHET BAKER QUARTET

| 60 | Vogue EPV 1255 | RUSS FREEMAN & CHET BAKER QUARTET (EP) | 12 |

(see also Chet Baker)

FREE MOVEMENT
72	CBS 7768	The Harder I Try/Comin' Home	30

FREE 'N EASY
68	Oak RGJ 628	FREE 'N EASY (LP, private pressing [Warren Coley W.C.P. 001])	100

FREE SOULS
64	Blue Beat BB 264	I Want To Be Free/Angel	20

FREESTYLE ORCHESTRA
89	SBK 12SBKDJ 7011	Keep On Pumping It Up (12", promo only)	15

FREEWAY
79	Decca F 13824	I Love The Music/Sarah Girl (p/s)	8
79	Decca F 13843	That Was The Greatest Song/Lost In A Dream (p/s)	8
79	Decca TXS 131	FREEWAY (LP)	18

(see also Terry Melcher)

FREEWHEELERS
65	HMV POP 1406	Why Do You Treat Me Like A Fool?/Ad Lib Blues	8

FREEZE
79	A1.A.1.1.A.1	IN COLOUR (EP, p/s)	15
80	A1 A.1.1.S.1	Celebration/Cross-Over	8

ACE FREHLEY
78	Casablanca CAN 135	New York Groove/Snow Blind (p/s, blue vinyl with mask)	30
78	Casablanca CAN 135	New York Groove/Snow Blind (no p/s, black vinyl)	5

(see also Kiss)

DON FRENCH
59	London HLW 8884	Lonely Saturday Night/Goldilocks	60
59	London HLW 8884	Lonely Saturday Night/Goldilocks (78)	30
59	London HLW 8989	Little Blonde Girl/I Look Into My Heart	150
59	London HLW 8989	Little Blonde Girl/I Look Into My Heart (78)	50

RAY FRENCH
66	Pye 7N 17215	Since I Lost My Baby/Gun Me Down	5

FRENCH REVOLUTION
69	Decca F 22898	Nine Till Five/Why?	80

ROBERT FRENCH
85	Uptemp UTO 10	Something On My Mind/Help Yourself (12")	40

FRENCH IMPRESSIONISTS
82	Operation Twilight OPT 020	Santa Baby/THICK PIGEON: Jingle Bell Rock/MONKS IN THE SNOW: A Theme For This Special Evening (P/s, last track uncredited)	20
82	Operation Twilight 12OPT 20	Santa Baby/Jingle Bell Rock (12", p/s)	10

(see also Aztec Camera)

FRENZ
70	Sugar SU 101	Mee Lei Moi/I Hear Music	12
71	Sugar ESS 103	It's A Secret/Dusty Shoes	10

FRENZY (1)
76	DJM DJS 633	Poser/Things You Do (To Me)	15

FRENZY (2)
81	Frenzy FRENZY 1	This Is The Last Time/Gypsy Dancer (no p/s)	50
81	Frenzy FRENZY 2	Blackburn Rovers/Up The Rovers	35
81	Frenzy FRENZY 3	Without You/Thanks For Nothing (no p/s)	50
84	Nervous NEP 002	Robot Riot/All Alone (p/s)	6
84	Nervous 12 NEP 002	Robot Riot/All Alone/Cry Or Die/Torment (12", p/s, 1st 500 on blue vinyl)	10
84	Nervous 12 NEP 002	Robot Riot/All Alone/Cry Or Die/Torment (12", p/s)	8
86	ABC EYE T7	I See Red/Whose Life (p/s)	10
86	ABC EYE T7	I See Red/Who's Life/Don't Give Up (12", p/s)	8
85	Nervous NERD 016	HALL OF MIRRORS (LP, orange vinyl)	12
86	I.D. NOSE 8	CLOCKWORK TOY (LP)	15
87	I.D. NOSE 19	SALLY'S PINK BEDROOM (LP)	15

FRESH
70	RCA RCA 2003	Stoned In Saigon/Just A Note	7
70	RCA SF 8122	FRESH OUT OF BORSTAL (LP)	20
71	RCA LSA 3027	FRESH TODAY (LP)	18

(see also Paul Korda, Brother Bung, Fruit Machine)

FRESH
92	Magnet MAG 1008CD	Did I Say "Ti Amo" (mixes) (CD)	12

FRESH AIR
69	Pye 7N 17736	Running Wild/Stop, Look, Listen	200
72	Philips 6006 187	It Takes Too Long/Here Comes Summer	6
72	Columbia DB 8872	Bye Bye Jane/It's All Over	6
71	Philips 6006 163	In The Sun/Too Many Reasons	7

FRESH MAGGOTS
71	RCA RCA 2150	Car Song/What Would You Do	30
71	RCA SF 8205	FRESH MAGGOTS (LP, orange label)	500

FRESH MEAT
73	Deram DMR 384	Never Mind The Money/Candy Eyes	7
73	Raft RA 18504	Hobo/If You Can't Live (You're Dead)	12

FRESH SKI & MO ROCK
88	Tuff Groove TUFF003	Talking Pays/Pick Up On This (12")	80
91	Conscious CON003	THE LONG AWAITED PAROXYSM (EP)	20
11	Diggers With Gratitude DWG 010	THE COARSE SELECTORS (EP)	15

FRESH WINDOWS
67	Fontana TF 839	Fashion Conscious/Summer Sun Shines	160

FRESHIES
78	Razz RAZZXEP 1	BAISER (EP, with Chris Sievey solo tracks, 33rpm, no'd, handwritten labels)	20
79	Razz RAZZXEP 2	STRAIGHT IN AT NO. 2 (EP, handwritten labels with inserts, 1,000 only, numbered, green or orange p/s)	12
79	Razz RAZZ 3	THE MEN FROM BANANA ISLAND WHOSE STUPID IDEAS NEVER CAUGHT ON IN THE WESTERN WORLD AS WE KNOW IT (EP, black & white photocopied p/s or numbered blue p/s)	8
79	Razz RAZZ 5	We're Like You/CHRIS SIEVEY: Hey (p/s)	6
80	Absurd A9	Octopus/Sheet Music	6
80	Razz RAZZ 6	Yellow Spot/If It's News (p/s)	6
80	Razz RAZZ 7	No Money/Oh Girl (p/s)	6
80	Razz RAZZ 8	RED INDIAN MUSIC (EP, with Chris Sievey)	8
80	Razz RAZZ 11	I'm In Love With The Girl On The Virgin Manchester Megastore Checkout Desk/Singalong Version (p/s, with free lyric book)	12
80	Razz RAZZ 12	I'm In Love With The Girl On The Manchester Checkout Desk (Radio Version)/Singalong Version ('bleeped') (white label radio issue, 200 only)	10
80	Razz RAZZ 13	One To One/House Beautiful (unreleased)	0
81	MCA MCA 693	Wrap Up The Rockets And It's Gonna Get Better/Tell Her I'm Ill	6
81	CV CVS 1	If You Really Love ... Buy Me A Shirt/I Am A Walrus (p/s)	6
80	Razz CS-4	ROUGH AND READY (12-track cassette album , 1,000 only)	12
81	Razz CS-5	LONDON PLAYS (cassette, live & radio sessions, 1,000 only)	12
85	ETS 1	JOHNNY RADAR STORY (20-track , with bonus Frank Sidebottom 8-track: "Firm Favourites")	12

(see also Chris Sievey, Going Red?)

FRESHMEN
67	Pye 7N 17432	Papa Oom Mow Mow/Let's Dance	12
68	Pye 7N 17592	Go Granny Go/Look At The Sunshine	18
69	Pye 7N 17689	Just To See You Smile/Indian Lake	8
69	Pye 7N 17757	She Sang Hymns Out Of Tune/Mr. Beverly's Heavy Days	8
70	CBS 4842	Halfway To Where/Time Hasn't Changed Her	6
70	CBS 5168	Banquet For The World/Time Hasn't Changed Her	6
71	CBS 7241	One Bad Thing/Everywhere There Is Love	6
72	CBS 7694	Swanee River/Take The Time It Takes	10
68	Pye N(S)PL 18263	MOVIN' ON (LP)	70
70	CBS 64099	PEACE ON EARTH (LP)	30

STEPHEN FRETWELL
03	Tape Recordings TAPE 001	Something's Got To Give/Whenforever/Honey	20

FRIDA
82	Epic EPC A 2603	I Know There's Something Going On/Threnody (p/s)	10
82	Epic EPC A 2863	To Turn To Stone/I Got Something (p/s)	10
82	Epic EPC A 2863	To Turn To Stone/I Got Something (p/s, clear vinyl)	10
83	Epic EPC A 3435	Here We'll Stay/Strangers (p/s)	10
83	Epic EPC A 3983	Time/I Am A Seeker (p/s, with B.A. Robertson)	8
84	Epic EPC A 4717	Shine/That's Tough (p/s)	8
84	Epic EPC TA 4717	Shine (6.27 Version)/That's Tough (12", p/s)	12
84	Epic EPC A 4886	Heart Of The Country/Slowly (p/s)	15
84	Epic EPC TA 4886	Heart Of The Country/Slowly/I Know There's Something Going On (Extended) (12", p/s)	20

(see also Abba)

CAROL FRIDAY
65	Parlophone R 5297	Gone Tomorrow/Show Me The Way	10
65	Parlophone R 5369	Everybody I Know/Wasted Days	30
67	Parlophone R 5567	Big Sister/I Look Around Me	10

FRIDAY CLUB
85	2 Tone CHSTT28	Window Shopping/Window Shopping (instrumental) (p/s)	40
85	2 Tone CHSTT1228	Window Shopping (extended version)/Window Shopping (instrumental) 12" (p/s)	45

FRIDAY KNIGHTS
60	Oriole CB 1579	Poor Man's Roses/Don't Open That Door	10

FRIDGES
80	Ink-Ink II 01	Lynn Freeze/Shower Of B's/That's Why I Took Up The Harmonica/ No Room! (p/s, with insert)	5

MARTY FRIEDMAN
86	Shrapnel RR 95291	DRAGON'S KISS (LP)	12

(see also Megadeth, Cacophony)

BRIAN JOSEPH FRIEL
74	Dawn DNLS 3054	BRIAN JOSEPH FRIEL (LP, gatefold sleeve with insert, pink 'sun' label)	20
75	Dawn DNLS 3064	ARRIVERDERCI ARDROSSAN (LP, punk 'sun' label)	12

FRIEND & LOVER
68	Verve VS 1515	Reach Out Of The Darkness/Time Is On Your Side	15

TERRY FRIEND & FRIENDS
77	Tramp (no cat. no.)	COME THE DAY (LP, private pressing, 100 only)	40

(see also Stonefield Tramp)

FRIENDLY FIRES
07	Moshi Moshi MOMO 11	Paris/Ex-Lover	10
08	XL XLS 387	Jump In The Pool (one-sided hand-numbered and stencilled sleeve, white labels, 250 only)	15
10	XL XLS 414	Skeleton Boy (1-sided 7" other side etched)	8
10	XL XLT 486	Hold On (Instrumental)/HOY GHOST :On Board/On Board (Instrumental) (12")	6

FRIENDLY HOPEFULS
81	Abstract ABS 004	Tribute To The Punks Of '76/Tribute To The Punks Of '76 (Disco Dub Mix) (p/s, coloured vinyl)	5

FRIENDS (1)
68	Deram DM 198	Piccolo Man/Mythological Sunday	30

(see also Flowerpot Men, Ivy League)

FRIENDS (2)
70   United Artists UP 35146   Futz/Costa Del Sol 7

FRIENDS (3)
74   Merlin HF 4   FRIENDS (LP, white label test pressing, 1 copy only!) 1500

(see also Ithaca, Alice Through The Looking Glass, Agincourt, Tomorrow Come Someday, BBC Radiophonic Workshop)

FRIENDS (4)
75   Caroline C1511   FRIENDS (LP, stickered with £1.49 price tag and quote from Jazz Forum) 20

FRIENDS (5)
83   Rock Shop RSR 002   Night Walker/Wasted Time (no p/s) 25

FRIENDS AGAIN
83   Moonboot MOON 1   Honey At The Core/Lucky Star (p/s) 6
84   Mercury FAEP 1   THE FRIENDS AGAIN EP: Lullaby No. 2 Love On Board/Wand You Wave/ Thank You For Being An Angel/Sunkissed (New Version)/State Of Art (Remix) (double pack, stickered gatefold p/s) 8

FRIENDS O' MINE
72   Westwood WRS 021   FRIENDS O' MINE (LP, 250 copies only) 80

(see also Mark Kjeldsen)

FRIENDS OF DISTINCTION
69   RCA 1838   Grazing In The Grass/I Really Hope You Do 10
69   RCA SF 8032   GRAZIN' (LP) 15

FRIENDS OF ST. FRANCIS
74   Charisma CB 229   The Man Who Turned On The World/How Is The World Today 6

FRIENDSHIP
70   B&C CB 133   The World Is Going To Be A Better Place/Million Hearts 5

FRIGHTY
88   Y & D YDD 0132   Feel So Good (with the Offbeat Posse)/Life (with Colonel Mite) (12") 8
01   Jah Tubbys JT 7009   Call On jah Name/OFFBEAT POSSE: Call On Dub 15
03   Jah Tubbys JT 10012   Jah Jah Is Coming/Fright Jah Jah Is Coming Version/Dub Is Coming (10", with the Offbeat Posse) 20

FRIJID PINK
70   Deram DM-R 288   The House Of The Rising Sun/Drivin' Blues 6
70   Deram DM 309   Sing A Song Of Freedom/End Of The Line 6
70   Deram DM 321   Heartbreak Hotel/Bye Bye Blues 6
71   Deram DM 332   Music For The People/Sloony 6
71   Deram DM 336   We're Gonna Be There (When Johnny Comes Marching Home)/Shortly Kline 7
71   Deram DM 347   Lost Son/I Love Her 7
70   Deram SML 1062   FRIJID PINK (LP) 50
70   Deram SML 1077   DEFROSTED (LP) 50

(ROBERT) FRIPP & (BRIAN) ENO
73   Island HELP 16   NO PUSSYFOOTING (LP, gatefold sleeve, black label with pink 'i' logo) 25
75   Island HELP 22   EVENING STAR (LP, black label with pink 'i' logo) 20

(see also Giles Giles & Fripp, King Crimson, Brian Eno, Roxy Music)

JACKIE FRISCO
63   Decca F 11566   You Can't Catch Me/Sugar Baby 15
63   Decca F 11692   When You Ask About Love/He's So Near 10

VONNIE FRITCHIE
55   London HLU 8178   Sugar Booger Avenue/There I Stood (To Throw Old Shoes And Rice) 50

FRED FRITH
74   Caroline C 1508   GUITAR SOLOS (LP) 20
76   Caroline C 1518   GUITAR SOLOS 2 (LP) 25

(see also Henry Cow)

FRITZ, MIKE & MO
65   Philips BF 1427   Somebody Stole The Sun/Let Me Hear Your Voice 10
65   Philips BF 1441   What Colour Is A Man?/So Now You're Gone 8

(see also Four Pennies)

LEFTY FRIZZELL
63   CBS BPG 62188   THE ONE AND ONLY LEFTY FRIZZELL (LP) 15
66   CBS BPG 62595   THE SAD SIDE OF LOVE (LP) 15

CONNY FROBOESS & REX GILDO
62   HMV HMV 1671   GERMANY'S TEENAGE STARS (LP) 35

FROCK
78   Frock Music FM 7848   SILKIE (LP, 250 only) 40

EDGAR FROESE
74   Virgin V 2016   AQUA (LP) 15
75   Virgin V 2040   EPSILON IN MALAYSIAN PALE (LP beige "mirror" girl label) 15

(see also Tangerine Dream)

FROG
73   Jam JAM 39   Witch Hunt (Theme From Psychomania)/Living Dead (die-cut company sleeve) 150

(see also John Cameron)

RAYMOND FROGGATT
68   Polydor 56249   Callow-La-Vita/Lost Autumn 6
68   Polydor 56274   Just A Little Bit Of Love/ABC Gold Fish 5
68   Polydor 56284   The Red Balloon/Lost Autumn 6
71   Bell BLL 1156   The Singer/Church Fete 6
68   Polydor 583 044   THE VOICE AND WRITING OF RAYMOND FROGGATT (LP, gatefold) 18
72   Bell BELLS 207   BLEACH (LP) 18
74   Reprise K 44257   ROGUES AND THIEVES (LP) 12
84   Happy Face MMLP 1032   WHY (LP, gatefold) 12

(see also Monopoly)

FROGMEN
61	Oriole CB 1617	Underwater/Mad Rush (withdrawn)	100

FROGMORTON
76	Philips 6308 261	AT LAST (LP, blue/silver labels)	20

JANE FROMAN
55	Capitol CL 14208	The Song From "Desiree" (We Meet Again)/Mine	5
55	Capitol CL 14209	The Finger Of Suspicion Points At You/My Shining Hour	5
55	Capitol CL 14254	I Wonder/I'll Never Be The Same	5
56	Capitol CL 14658	You'll Never Walk Alone/One Little Candle	5
56	Capitol EAP1 600	JANE FROMAN (EP)	8
56	Capitol EAP1 889	SONGS AT SUNSET (EP)	8
56	Capitol EAP2 889	SONGS AT SUNSET (EP)	8
56	Capitol EAP3 889	SONGS AT SUNSET (EP)	8
52	Capitol LC 6554	WITH A SONG IN MY HEART (10" LP)	12
53	Capitol LC 6605	YOURS ALONE (10" LP)	12

FROM WEST TO EAST
72	Zella JHPS 128	FROM WEST TO EAST (LP)	20

FRONT
77	The Label TLR 005	System/Queen's Mafia (p/s)	8

DOM FRONTIERE & HIS ORCHESTRA
57	London HLU 8385	Jet Rink Ballad/Uno Mas	15
57	London HLU 8385	Jet Rink Ballad/Uno Mas (78)	12

FRONT LINE
65	Atlantic AT 4057	I Don't Care/Got Love	40

FRONTLINE ORCHESTRA
81	Ice ICET 50	Don't Turn You Back On Me/No Entry (12")	40

FROST
69	Vanguard SVRL 19056	ROCK AND ROLL MUSIC (LP)	18
69	Vanguard SVRL 19052	FROST MUSIC (LP)	18

(see also Alice Cooper)

BERNIE FROST
74	Vertigo 6059 108	The House/What Do You Want To Hear Today	50

(see also Status Quo, Rossi & Frost, Boz Frost)

BOZ FROST
73	Vertigo 6059 083	Foreign Lady/Big White Seagull	25

(see also Status Quo, Rossi & Frost, Bernie Frost)

FROST LANE
71	Cutty Wren MM 1	FROST LANE (LP, actually various artists LP)	45

MAX FROST & TROOPERS
68	Capitol CL 15565	Shape Of Things To Come/Free Lovin'	25

(see also Millicent Martin)

FROZEN TEAR
69	Ra RA 5001	The Hunter/You Know What Has To Be (99 copies only)	300

FRUGAL SOUND
66	Pye 7N 17062	Norwegian Wood/Cruel To Be Kind	15
66	Pye 7N 17129	Just Outside The Door/I'm On Your Side	6
67	RCA Victor RCA 1556	Backstreet Girl/Reason To Believe	6
67	RCA Victor RCA 1595	Abilene/Love Is A New Face	5
68	RCA Victor RCA 1659	All Strung Out/Miss Mary	5

FRUIT EATING BEARS
78	DJM DJS 857	Door In My Face/Going Through The Motions (company sleeve)	45
78	Raw RAW 9	Chevy Heavy (p/s)	25
78	Lightning GIL 509	Chevy Heavy/Fifties Cowboy (p/s)	40

FRUIT GUMS
70	Fab FAB 138	Sweet Pork/Crying All Night	6

FRUIT MACHINE
69	Spark SRL 1003	Follow Me/Cuddly Toy	80
69	Spark SRL 1027	I'm Alone Today/Sunshine Of Your Love (in title p/s)	130
69	Spark SRL 1027	I'm Alone Today/Sunshine Of Your Love	80

(see also Rare Bird)

FRUMPY
71	Philips 6003 133	Life Without Pain/Morning	20
71	Philips 6305 067	ALL WILL BE CHANGED (LP, black/silver labels)	90
72	Philips 6305 098	FRUMP 2 (LP, black & blue vinyl)	60

(see also Atlantis)

FRUUPP
74	Dawn DNS 1087	Prince Of Heaven/Jaunting Car	10
73	Dawn DNLS 3053	FUTURE LEGENDS (LP, gatefold sleeve)	50
74	Dawn DNLS 3058	SEVEN SECRETS (LP, with lyric insert)	40
74	Dawn DNLH 2	THE PRINCE OF HEAVEN'S EYES (LP, gatefold sleeve, with book)	50
74	Dawn DNLH 2	THE PRINCE OF HEAVEN'S EYES (LP, gatefold sleeve, without book)	20
75	Dawn DNLS 3070	MODERN MASQUERADES (LP, gatefold sleeve, with lyric insert)	30

MARK FRY
06	Sunbeam SBRLPS 028	DREAMING WITH ALICE (LP, 180 gram vinyl reissue of original 1972 Italian pressing)	20

FUCHSIA
71	Pegasus PEG 8	FUCHSIA (LP)	250

FUCKED UP
11	Fucked Up FU 010	The Other Shoe/The Truest Road (p/s, lyric sheet, original U.K. tour 7")	15

FUD (CHRISTIAN) & DEL
73	Duke DU 165	Beef Sticker/PRINCE HERON: Ten Commandments	6
73	Songbird SB 1086	Dr. Fud/FUD CHRISTIAN ALLSTARS: La-Fud-Del Skank	6

FUD CHRISTIAN ALLSTARS
71	Big Shot BI 571	Never Fall In Love (actually by Winston Heywood)/Never Fall In Love Version	8

(see also Linkers, Ansel Linkers)

FUDGE TUNNEL
91	Earach MOSH 36	HATE SONGS IN E MINOR (LP, with free 7")	15
94	Earache MOSH 119LP	THE COMPLICATED FUTILITY OF IGNORANCE (LP)	18

FUGAZI
88	Dischord 30	FUGAZI (LP)	12
89	Dischord DIS 44	REPEATER (LP)	12
91	Dischord DIS 60V	STEADY DIET OF NOTHING (LP, inner)	12
93	Dischord DIS 60V	IN ON THE KILL TAKER (LP)	15
95	Dischord DIS 90V	RED MEDICINE (LP)	15

FUGI
71	Blue Horizon 2096 005	Red Moon (Parts 1 & 2)	25

FUGITIVE
81	Private pressing FMR 050	Need My Freedom	20

FUGITIVES (JAMAICA)
67	Doctor Bird DB 1082	Musical Pressure/LESLIE BUTLER & FUGITIVES: Winchester Rocksteady	30
67	Doctor Bird 1097	Lecture/Canteloupe Rock	40

(see also Jo Jo Bennett & Fugitives, Two Kings, Jo Jo Bennett, Stranger Cole)

FUGITIVES (U.S.)
61	Vogue V 9176	Freeway/Fugitive	30

FUGS
68	Big T BIG 115	Crystal Liaison/When The Mode Of The Music Changes	12
68	Transatlantic TRA 180	TENDERNESS JUNCTION (LP, with poster)	50
68	Transatlantic TRA 180	TENDERNESS JUNCTION (LP, without poster)	20
68	Transatlantic TRA 181	IT CRAWLED INTO MY HAND, HONEST (LP)	35
69	Fontana (S)TL 5501	VIRGIN FUGS (LP)	25
69	Fontana (S)TL 5513	THE FUGS ... FIRST ALBUM (LP)	35
69	Fontana (S)TL 5524	FUGS II (LP)	30
69	Reprise RSLP 6359	THE BELLE OF AVENUE A (LP)	30
70	Reprise 6396	GOLDEN FILTH - LIVE AT THE FILLIMORE EAST (LP)	30

FULHAM FURIES
78	GM GMS 9050	These Boots Are Made For Walking/Under Pressure (no p/s)	35

(see also Lurkers)

BLIND BOY FULLER
57	Philips BBL 7512	BLIND BOY FULLER 1935-40 (LP)	25
68	Matchbox SDR 143	BLIND BOY FULLER ON DOWN VOLUME 1 (LP)	15
69	Matchbox SDR 168	BLIND BOY FULLER ON DOWN VOLUME 2 (LP)	15
60s	Flyright LP 105	CAROLINA BLUES (LP)	15

BOBBY FULLER FOUR
66	London HLU 10030	I Fought The Law/Little Annie Lou	30
66	London HLU 10041	Love's Made A Fool Of You/Don't You Ever Let Me Know	15
73	President PT 394	Another Sad And Lonely Night/Only When I Dream	10
67	President PTL 1003	MEMORIAL ALBUM (LP)	40

(see also Randy Fuller)

CURTIS FULLER/TOMMY FLANAGAN
58	Pye PYE28009	IT'S MAGIC (LP)	30

GIL FULLER & DIZZY GILLESPIE
66	Fontana 688 147 ZL	MAN FROM MONTEREY (LP)	15

(see also Dizzy Gillespie)

JERRY FULLER
59	London HLH 8982	The Tennessee Waltz/Charlene	5
59	London HLH 8982	The Tennessee Waltz/Charlene (78)	22
61	London HLN 9439	Guilty Of Loving You/First Love Never Dies	8
62	Salvo SLO 1802	Lipstick And Rouge/Mother Goose At The Bandstand (99 copies only)	150

JESSE FULLER
65	Good Time Jazz GV 2426	San Francisco Bay Blues/New Midnight Special	10
67	Good Time Jazz GV 2427	Runnin' Wild/The Monkey And The Engineer	10
67	Fontana TF 821	Going Back To My Old Used To Be/Bye And Bye	10
58	Good Time Jazz LAG 12159	JESSE FULLER (LP)	25
60	Good Time Jazz LAG 12279	LONE CAT (LP)	25
60	Topic 10T 59	WORKING ON THE RAILROAD (10" LP)	35
63	Good Time Jazz LAG 574	SAN FRANCISCO BAY BLUES (LP)	20
65	Stateside SL 10154	JESSE FULLER'S FAVOURITES (LP)	20
66	Fontana TL 5313	SESSION WITH JESSE FULLER (LP)	25
66	Topic 12T 134	MOVE ON DOWN THE LINE (LP)	35
66	Stateside SL 10166	SAN FRANCISCAN BAY BLUES (LP, reissue)	18
60s	Vocalion VRLP 574	SAN FRANCISCO BAY BLUES (LP)	20
60s	Evolution Z 1004	LIVE IN LONDON (LP)	30

JOHNNY FULLER
73	Speciality SON 5017	Haunted House/Swinging At The Creek	5

RANDY FULLER
67	President PT 111	It's Love, Come What May/The Things You Do	10

(see also Bobby Fuller Four)

FULL MOON
87	Luna SRT 7K51283	The Eternal Now/Nemesis	25
92	Demi Monde DMLP 1031	EUPHORIA (LP)	20

FULL TIME MEN
86	Shigaku SHIG 1T	I Got Wheels/One More Time/Way Down South (12", p/s)	8

(see also R.E.M.)

LOWELL FULSON/FULSOM
53	London L 1199	I Love My Baby/The Blues Came Rollin' In (78)	30
65	Sue WI 375	Too Many Drivers/Key To Your Heart	40
66	Sue WI 4023	Talking Woman/Blues Around Midnight	40
66	Outasite 45-502	Stop And Think/Baby (with Leon Blue)	70
66	Polydor 56515	Black Nights/Little Angel	20
67	Fontana TF 795	Tramp/Pico	20
76	Jet JET 770	Do You Love Me?/Monday Morning	5
69	Fontana SFJL 920	SAN FRANCISCO BLUES (LP)	30
69	Polydor 2384 038	IN A HEAVY BAG (LP, as Lowell Fulsom)	20

FUMBLE
72	Sovereign SOV 110	Hullo Mary Lou/Hanging On	5
73	Sovereign SOV 118	Million Seller/Get Up	5
73	Sovereign SOV 121	Alexandra Park (Palisades Park)/Mama I Can't Tell You	6
72	Sovereign SVNA 7254	FUMBLE (LP, gatefold sleeve)	12

FUN AND GAMES
69	MCA MU 1083	We Got To Sayu Goodbye	8

FUNBOY FIVE
80s	Cool Cat Daddy-O PHUN 1	Life After Death/Compulsive Eater (foldover p/s)	18

FUNERAL FOR A FRIEND
02	Mighty Atom MTY 338	Between Order And Model/Juno/Red Is The New Black (CD)	25
03	Infectious EW 269	Juneau/Getaway Plan (white vinyl, p/s)	15
03	Warner EW 274	She Drove Me To Daytime TV/Bullet Theory (blue vinyl, p/s)	15
03	Infectious INFEC 126S	Four Ways — This Year's Most Open Heartbreak/She Drove Me To Daytime Television//Kiss And Make Up (All Bets Are Off)/Escape Artists Never Die (2 x 7" red vinyl, gatefold p/s)	20
03	Infectious INFEC 12CDS	Four Ways — This Year's Most Open Heartbreak/She Drove Me To Daytime Television/Kiss And Make Up (All Bets Are Off)/Escape Artists Never Die (CD 2000 only)	15

FUN FOUR
80	NMC NMC 010	Singing In The Showers/By Products/Elevator Crush (p/s)	25

(see also Orange Juice)

FUN 4
80	NMC 1	Singing In the Shower/Elevator Crash	40

FUNGUS
73	Fungus FUN 1	Premonitions Parts 1 & 2 (LP, private pressing)	100

(see also Secondhand, Seventh Wave)

FUNHOUSE
82	Ensign ENY 222	Out Of Control/This Could Be Hell (p/s)	6
82	Ensign ENYT 222	Out Of Control (Full Version)/This Could Be Hell (12", p/s)	10

(see also Another Pretty Face, DNV, Waterboys)

FUNKADELIC
70	Pye International 7N 25519	I Got A Thing, You Got A Thing, Everybody's Got A Thing/Fish, Chips & Sweat	10
71	Pye International 7N 25548	You & Your Folks, Me & Mine/Funky Dollar Bill	10
71	Janus 6146 001	Can You Get To That/Back In Our Minds	10
70	Pye Intl. NSPL 28137	FUNKADELIC (LP)	100
71	Pye Intl. NSPL 28144	FREE YOUR MIND AND YOUR ASS WILL FOLLOW (LP)	80
71	Janus 6310 201	MAGGOT BRAIN (LP)	50
75	20th Century W 215	LET'S TAKE IT TO THE STAGE (LP)	20
78	Warner Bros K 56299	HARDCORE JOLLIES (LP)	15
78	Warner Bros K 56539	ONE NATION UNDER A GROOVE (LP, with free 12" "One Nation Under A Groove")	15

(see also Parliament, Parlet, Bootsy's Rubber Band, Dolby's Cube, P-Funk Allstars)

FUNKALOO
79	Rough RMS 122	ROBOT DANCER (LP)	50

FUNK BAND INC.
76	Beeb 12	Get It Off/Part 2	10

FUNKGUS
76	Baal BAL 89002	II (LP)	25

FUNKMASTERS
84	Master Funk MF4	It's Over/(Versions) (12")	10

FUNKY BOTTOM CONGREGATION
69	Beacon BEA 122	Hare-Krishna/Things About Yourself	20

FUNKY BROWN & INNER CIRCLE
74	Rhino 128	I See You/Song Of The Swallow	10

FINBAR & EDDIE FUREY
68	Transatlantic TRA 168	FINBAR AND EDDIE FUREY (LP, laminated front sleeve, white/lilac labels)	20
69	Xtra XTRA 1077	TRADITIONAL IRISH PIPE MUSIC (LP)	18
69	Transatlantic TRA 191	THE LONESOME BOATMAN (LP)	20
72	Dawn DNLS 3037	THE DAWNING OF THE DAY (LP, with lyric insert, lilac label)	20

FINBAR FUREY & BOB STEWART
76	Crescent ARS 110	TOMORROW WE PART (LP)	12

FUR FUR
80s	Daark Inc. D.I. 7	FUR FUR ()	12

(see also Karl Blake, Danielle Dax, Lemon Kittens, Gland Shrouds)

MINT VALUE £

FURNITURE

80	Para 1	Shaking Story/Take A Walk Down Town (p/s)	30
80	Survival SUR 023	Dancing The Hard Bargain/Robert Nightmans Story	7
84	Survival SUR 12023	Dancing The Hard Bargain (Extended)/Robert Nightmans Story (12", p/s)	12
84	Premonition PREM 12002	Love Your Shoes/Escape Into My Arms/Throw Away The Script (Inst) (12", p/s)	12
85	PREM 3	I Can't Crack/Switch Off/Pause/I Can't Crack (Broken Mix) (12", p/s)	12
86	Stiff BUY 251	Brilliant Mind/To Gus	6
86	Stiff BUYIT 251	Brilliant Mind (Extended)/Brilliant Mind (7" Mix)/To Gus (12", p/s)	10
86	Stiff BUY 254	Love Your Shoes/Turnupspeed	7
86	Stiff BUYIT 254	Love Your Shoes (Extended)/Love Your Shoes (7" Mix)/Turnupspeed/Me And You And The Name (12", p/s)	10
90	Arista 12844	One Step Behind You/It Continues (P/S)	6
91	Survival SURT 53	Brilliant Mind (Extended)/Brilliant Mind (7" Version)/On A Bus With Peter Nero/Brilliant Strings (12", p/s)	12
83	Premonition PREM 4CA	WHEN THE BOOM WAS ON (Mini-LP)	25
86	Premonition PREM 6	THE LOVEMONGERS (LP)	25
86	Stiff SEEZ 64	THE WRONG PEOPLE (LP)	15
91	Survival SURCD 13	SHE GETS OUT THE SCRAPBOOK (CD)	18

(see also Because)

FURRY DICE

80	White Line WHLS 001	Rudi Don't Take Your Love To Town/K.G.B. (p/s)	6

FURRY PHREAKS (FEATURING TERRA DEVA)

98	FSUK FSUKT3P	SOOTHE (2 x 12" promo)	10

TOMMY FURTADO

57	London HLA 8418	Sun Tan Sam/Isabella	40
57	London HLA 8418	Sun Tan Sam/Isabella (78)	10

FURY

77	Arista 150	Miss Demeanor/Stay On Your feet	6

BILLY FURY

78s

59	Decca F 11102	Maybe Tomorrow/Gonna Type A Letter	150
59	Decca F 11128	Margo/Don't Knock Upon My Door	200
59	Decca F 11158	Angel Face/Time Has Come	250
59	Decca F 11189	My Christmas Prayer/Last Kiss	300

SINGLES

59	Decca F 11102	Maybe Tomorrow/Gonna Type A Letter (triangular centre)	25
59	Decca F 11102	Maybe Tomorrow/Gonna Type A Letter (later pressing with round centre)	15
59	Decca F 11128	Margo/Don't Knock Upon My Door (triangular centre)	30
59	Decca F 11128	Margo/Don't Knock Upon My Door (later pressing with round centre)	20
59	Decca F 11158	Angel Face/Time Has Come (triangular centre)	30
59	Decca F 11158	Angel Face/Time Has Come (later pressing with round centre)	20
59	Decca F 11189	My Christmas Prayer/Last Kiss (triangular centre)	50
59	Decca F 11189	My Christmas Prayer/Last Kiss (later pressing with round centre)	25
60	Decca F 11200	Colette/Baby How I Cried (triangular centre)	40
60	Decca F 11200	Colette/Baby How I Cried (later pressing with round centre)	15
60	Decca F 11237	That's Love/You Don't Know (as Billy Fury & Four Jays)	25
60	Decca F 11267	Wondrous Place/Alright, Goodbye	25
60	Decca F 11311	A Thousand Stars/Push Push	15
61	Decca F 11334	Don't Worry/Talkin' In My Sleep (with Four Kestrels)	15
61	Decca F 11349	Halfway To Paradise/Cross My Heart	5
61	Decca F 11384	Jealousy/Open Your Arms	5
61	Decca F 11409	I'd Never Find Another You/Sleepless Nights	5
62	Decca F 11437	Letter Full Of Tears/Magic Eyes	15
62	Decca F 11458	Last Night Was Made For Love/King For Tonight	6
62	Decca F 11485	Once Upon A Dream/If I Lose You	6
62	Decca F 11508	Because Of Love/Running Around	10
63	Decca F 11582	Like I've Never Been Gone/What Do You Think You're Doing Of?	10
63	Decca F 11655	When Will You Say I Love You?/All I Wanna Do Is Cry	5
63	Decca F 11701	In Summer/I'll Never Fall In Love Again	5
63	Decca F 11744	Somebody Else's Girl/Go Ahead And Ask Her	15
63	Decca F 11792	Do You Really Love Me Too?/What Am I Gonna Do?	10
64	Decca F 11888	I Will/Nothin' Shakin' (But The Leaves On The Trees) (some B-sides list "Nothin' Shakin' ")	15
64	Decca F 11939	It's Only Make Believe/Baby What Do You Want Me To Do?	10
64	Decca F 40719	Hippy Hippy Shake/Glad All Over (export-only, with p/s)	80
64	Decca F 40719	Hippy Hippy Shake/Glad All Over (export-only)	50
65	Decca F 12048	I'm Lost Without You/You Better Believe It, Baby	10
65	Decca F 12178	In Thoughts Of You/Away From You	8
65	Decca F 12230	Run To My Lovin' Arms/Where Do You Run?	10
66	Decca F 12325	I'll Never Quite Get Over You/I Belong To The Wind	12
66	Decca F 12409	Don't Let A Little Pride Stand In Your Way/Didn't See The Real Thing Come Along	12
66	Decca F 12459	Give Me Your Word/She's So Far Out She's In	15
67	Parlophone R 5560	Hurtin' Is Loving/Things Are Changing	30
67	Parlophone R 5605	Loving You/I'll Go Along With It Now	20
67	Parlophone R 5634	Suzanne In The Mirror/It Just Don't Matter Now	40
67	Parlophone R 5658	Beyond The Shadow Of A Doubt/Baby Do You Love Me?	40
68	Parlophone R 5681	Silly Boy Blue/One Minute Woman	40
68	Parlophone R 5723	Phone Box/Any Morning Now	40
68	Parlophone R 5747	Lady/Certain Things	40
69	Parlophone R 5788	I Call For My Rose/Bye Bye	50
69	Parlophone R 5819	All The Way To The U.S.A./Do My Best For You	50
70	Parlophone R 5845	Why Are You Leaving?/Old Sweet Roll (Hi-De-Ho)	50
70	Parlophone R 5874	Paradise Alley/Well ... All Right	50
72	Fury FY 301	Will The Real Man Please Stand Up/At This Stage	40
74	Warner Bros WB 16402	I'll Be Your Sweetheart/Fascinating Candle Flame	30
76	NEMS NES 018	Halfway To Paradise/Turn My Back On You	10
81	Polydor POSP 355	Be Mine Tonight/No Trespassers (p/s)	5

82	Polydor POSP 488	Love Or Money/Love Sweet Love (p/s)......5
82	Polydor POSP 528	Devil Or Angel/Don't Tell Me Lies ('guitar' p/s)......5
82	Polydor POSP 528	Devil Or Angel/Don't Tell Me Lies ('microphone' p/s)......6
83	Polydor POSP 558	Forget Him/Your Words (p/s)......5
83	Polydor POSP 558	Let Me Go Lover/Your Words (same p/s as above but diff. A-side, 500 only)......20
83	Lyntone LYN 13078/BF 1	Devil Or Angel/Lost Without You (flexi free within memorial concert booklet)......20
83	Private pressing	BILLY FURY IN INTERVIEW WITH STUART COLEMAN (10", 500 white label copies only, 1st 200 numbered)......30
83	Private pressing	BILLY FURY IN INTERVIEW WITH STUART COLEMAN (10", 500 white label copies only, un-numbered) 20

EPs

59	Decca DFE 6597	MAYBE TOMORROW (triangular centre, orange/red p/s)......80
59	Decca DFE 6597	MAYBE TOMORROW (round centre, orange/red p/s)......60
59	Decca DFE 6597	MAYBE TOMORROW (round centre, yellow p/s)......120
61	Decca DFE 6694	BILLY FURY......60
62	Decca DFE 6699	BILLY FURY NO. 2......70
62	Decca DFE 6708	PLAY IT COOL......25
62	Decca DFE 6708	PLAY IT COOL (export issue, blue/green 'crouching' cover)......100
62	Decca DFE 8505	BILLY FURY HITS......30
63	Decca DFE 8525	BILLY FURY AND THE TORNADOS......40
63	Decca DFE 8558	AM I BLUE......50
65	Decca DFE 8641	BILLY FURY AND THE GAMBLERS......125
73	Ronco MR EP 001	LONG LIVE ROCK (with others, no p/s)......25
83	Decca DFE 8686	MY CHRISTMAS PRAYER......15

ALBUMS

60	Decca LF 1329	THE SOUND OF FURY (10")......200
60	Ace Of Clubs ACL 1047	BILLY FURY......30
61	Ace Of Clubs ACL 1083	HALFWAY TO PARADISE......30
63	Decca LK 4533	BILLY......40
63	Decca LK 4548	WE WANT BILLY! (with Tornados, mono)......40
63	Decca SKL 4548	WE WANT BILLY! (with Tornados, stereo)......45
65	Decca LK 4677	I'VE GOTTA HORSE (soundtrack)......40
67	Ace Of Clubs ACL 1229	THE BEST OF BILLY FURY......25
76	Decca DPA 3033/4	THE BILLY FURY STORY (2-LP)......15
81	Decca LFT 1329	THE SOUND OF FURY (10", reissue)......15
83	Red Bus BUSLP 1003	THE MISSING YEARS......20
84	Magnum Force MFLP 1027	LOVING YOU (LP)......15

(see also Tornados, Gamblers)

FURYS

63	Stateside SS 182	Never More/Zing! Went The Strings Of My Heart......12
72	Jay Boy BOY 61	What Is Soul?/I Lost My Baby......8
72	Jay Boy BOY 68	I'm Satisfied With You/Just A Little Mixed Up......15
72	Jay Boy BOY 68	I'm Satisfied With You/Just A Little Mixed Up (DJ Copy) 30

FURY'S TORNADOES

74	Warner Bros K 16442	Telstar '74/I Would Give You Anything 8

(see also Billy Fury)

F.U.S.E.

93	Warp WAP38	Train Tracs (12", some white vinyl, p/s)......10
93	Warp LP12LTD	Dimension Intrusion (2-LP, white vinyl)......15

FUSION ORCHESTRA

73	EMI EMI 2056	When My Mama's Not At Home/Nuthouse Rock 8
73	EMI EMA 758	A SKELETON IN ARMOUR (LP, gatefold sleeve)......60

FUSION (1)

79	Plastic Fantastic PFUL 1104	COLD OUTSIDE EP (12")......8
80	Telephone TEL 101	TILL I HEAR FROM YOU (LP, blue vinyl) 20

FUSION (2)

95	Ferox FER 015	FREESTYLE EP (12")......8
96	Ferox FER 021	GALAXY OF FUTURE VISIONS (12" EP) 10

FUT

70	Beacon BEA 160	Have You Heard The Word/Futting Around 30

(see also Graham Bonnet, Bee Gees, Marbles, Maurice Gibb, Steve & Stevie; this record has NO Beatles involvement)

FUTURE BEAT ALLIANCE

99	Ferox FER 035	ABACO (12" EP)......10

FUTURE BODIES

80	No label or cat no	Terrorist/Science Of Romance (p/s, lyric insert, rubber stamped labels)......45

FUTURE DAYZE

82	Polydor POSP 455	House On The Hill/Silent Room (p/s)......8

FUTURE PAST

91	B12 03	Our Paths Meet/Harmony Park/Your Hand In My Mind/Dance Intellect/ TV People (12", black vinyl)......50

FUTURE SOUND OF LONDON

91	Jumpin' & Pumpin' TOT 17	Papua New Guinea/Papua New Guinea (Andrew Weatherall Mix) (p/s)......6
91	Jumpin' & Pumpin' 12TOT 11	PULSE: Bring On The Pulse/In The Mind Of A Child/ Hardhead/Pulse State (first 2 tracks credited to Indo Tribe which is FSOL under an assumed name) 12
91	Jumpin' & Pumpin' 12TOT 16	PULSE 3: Tingler/Owl/Bite The Bullet/Calcium 12
91	Jumpin' & Pumpin' 12TOT 17	Papua New Guinea (Dali Mix)/(Dumb Child Of Q Mix)/ (Qube Mix) (p/s) 12
92	Jumpin' & Pumpin' 12TOT 17R	Papua New Guinea (Andrew Weatherall Mix)/(Dub Mix)/(Journey To Pyramid)/ (Monsoon Mix)/(Graham Massey Mix)/(Dumb Child Of Q Mix) (p/s)......8
94	Virgin promo 500	Slider/Snake Hips/You're Creeping Me Out/Herd Killing/Live In New York (2 x 12" p/s, promo only, 500 copies, FSOL under different names)......15
94	Virgin VST 1540P	Far Out Son Of Lung And The Ramblings Of A Madman/ Snake Hips/Smokin' Japanese Babe/Amoeba (white vinyl, promo only)......20
95	Virgin SEMTEX DJ 1	Semtex (Part 1)/Semtex (Part 2)/We Have Explosive/Semtex (stamped sleeve, promo only, 500 copies)......15

FUTUREHEADS

92	Jumpin' & Pumpin' CDSTOT 17	Papua New Guinea/(Andrew Weatherall Mix)/(Dub Mix)/ (Journey To Pyramid)/(Graham Mix)/(Journey To The Pyramid)/(Graham Mix)/(Dumb Child Of Q)/Hamish McDonald Mix)	8
93	Virgin VSCDT 1478	Cascade (Part 1)/(Part 2)/(Part 3)/(Part 4)/(Part 5)/Short Form	8
92	Jumpin'/Pumpin' LPTOT 2	ACCELERATOR (2-LP)	15
94	Virgin V 2722	LIFEFORMS (2-LP, stickered gatefold sleeve with inner sleeves)	20
94	Virgin V 2755	ISDN (LP, embossed, fold-out black sleeve with insert)	20
96	Virgin V 2814	DEAD CITIES (2-LP, gatefold sleeve with inners)	20
97	Virgin isdnshow 1	ISDN Show (CD, promo only, no inlay)	20

(see also Amorphous Androgynous, Art Science Technology, Humanoid,

FUTUREHEADS

01	Private Pressing	The first Demo (4-track CD, handwritten sticker)	30
02	Private Pressing	1-2-3 Nul Demo (5-track CD)	30
02	Project C'naut PCOS 001	Nul Book Standard — Park Inn/Robot/My Rules/Stupid And Shallow (p/s)	15
03	Fantastic Plastic FP7035	1-2-3-NUL! EP: Carnival Kids/Ticket/Cabaret/A Picture Of Dorian Gray (p/s, with sticker and badge)	15
03	Fantastic Plastic FPS035	1-2-3-NUL! EP: Carnival Kids/Ticket/Cabaret/A Picture Of Dorian Gray (CD, p/s)	10
03	Fantastic Plastic FP 7036	First Day/Balsch/Piece Of Crap (red or clear vinyl, p/s, 500 only)	5
03	Private Pressing	Hounds Of Love (1-track white label: gig/fanclub 7")	10
04	Private Pressing	Meantime/Decent Days & Nights Remixes (1000, white label gig/fanclub 7")	6
04	679 579 L07T	FUTUREHEADS (2-LP)	18

FUZZ

71	Mojo 2916 010	FUZZ (LP)	20

FUZZ FACE

68	Page One POF 065	Mighty Quinn/Voices From The Sky	5

FUZZBIRD

95	Fuzzbird FR3	Can't Believe A Word/A Man Named Fly (p/s)	8

FUZZTONES

85	ABC S 006	She's Wicked/Epitaph For A Head (p/s)	6

FUZZY DUCK

71	MAM MAM 37	Double Time Woman/Just Look Around You	15
71	MAM MAM 51	Big Brass Band/One More Hour	15
90	Reflection MM50	Double Time Woman/One More Hour	8
71	MAM AS 1005	FUZZY DUCK (LP, laminated front sleeve, black/silver labels)	500
90	Reflection MM 05	FUZZY DUCK (LP, reissue with booklet & single "Double Time Woman"/ "One More Hour" [MMS 01])	25

(see also Andromeda, Greatest Show On Earth, Alvin Lee, Capability Brown, Cockney Rebel))

FUZZY LOGIC

92	Guerilla GRRR29	Obsession (12")	8

FX

79	Southern Rock SR 4501	THE SOUTH'S GONNA RISE AGAIN (EP, oversized folding p/s)	100

FYNN MCCOOL

70	RCA RCA 1956	U.S. Thumbstyle/Diamond Lil	8
70	RCA SF 8112	FYNN McCOOL (LP, gatefold sleeve)	150

(see also Shakespears, Grapefruit, Sleepy)

G

WINSTON G (& WICKED)

65	Parlophone R 5266	Please Don't Say/Like A Baby	35
66	Parlophone R 5330	Until You Were Gone/That Way Too (as Winston G. & Wicked)	18
66	Decca F 12444	Cloud Nine/I'll Make You Cry Tomorrow	18
67	Decca F 12559	Mother Ferguson's Love Dust/Judge And Jury	75
67	Decca F 12623	Riding With The Milkman/Bye Bye Baby	20

B(ASIL) GABBIDON

61	Blue Beat BB 069-A	Warpaint Baby (miscredited to B. Cabbidon & Buster's Group)/ I Was Wrong (miscredited to Chuck & Dobbie with Buster's Group)	20
62	Blue Beat BB 111-A	Ivoree/Lover Man	20
62	Blue Beat BB 124	Independence Blues/For My Love (as B. Gabbidon)	20
62	Blue Beat BB 129-A	Our Melody/Going Back To Ja (with Randy's All Stars)	20
62	Island WI 033	I Found My Baby (actually by Roy Braham)/No Fault Of Mine	30
63	Island WI 076	I Bet You Don't Know/3 x 7	30
63	Island WI 089	St. Louis Woman/Get On The Ball	40
63	Blue Beat BB 155-A	Eana Mena/Since You Are Gone (with Prince Buster All Stars)	20
63	Blue Beat BB 161	I'll Find Love (with Prince Buster All Stars)/ MELLOW LARKS: What You Gonna Do?	20
65	Blue Beat BB 288	Tick Tock (actually by Theo Beckford)/The Streets Of Glory (actually by Theo Beckford & Yvonne Harrison)	20

(see also Derrick Patsy & Basil, Mellow Larks, Derrick Morgan)

PETER GABRIEL

77	Charisma CB 301	Solsbury Hill/Moribund The Burgermeister (p/s)	6
77	Charisma CB 302	Modern Love/Slowburn (no p/s, 'nude' picture label, withdrawn)	30
78	Charisma CB 311	D.I.Y./Perspective (p/s, purple label, Irish-only sleeve)	8
78	Charisma CB 311	D.I.Y./Perspective (p/s, silver label, possibly Irish-only sleeve)	8
78	Charisma CB 319	D.I.Y. (Remix)/Mother Of Violence/Teddy Bear (no p/s, withdrawn)	20
82	Charisma SHOCK 1	Shock The Monkey/Soft Dog (Instrumental) (p/s)	5
82	Charisma SHOCK 1	Shock The Monkey/Soft Dog (Instrumental) (same p/s as above)	10
82	Charisma SHOCK 122	Shock The Monkey/Soft Dog (Instrumental) (picture disc)	8
82	Charisma SHOCK 350	Shock The Monkey/Shock The Monkey (Instrumental) (12", same p/s as [SHOCK 12])	15
82	Charisma CB 405	I Have The Touch/Across The River (p/s)	5

83	Charisma GAB 12	I Don't Remember (live)/Solsbury Hill (live)/Kiss Of Life (live) (12", shrinkwrapped stickered double pack, with 12" white label [GAB 122], "Games Without Frontiers"/Schnappschuss (Ein Familienfoto)", no p/s)	8
92	Virgin PGS 7	Digging In The Dirt/Bashi-Bazouk (black label, jukebox issue)	5
92	Virgin PGSDG 712	Digging In The Dirt/Digging In The Dirt (Instrumental)/Quiet Steam/ Bashi-Bazouk (12", p/s, withdrawn)	8
92	Virgin PGSDX 8	Steam/Games Without Frontiers (Massive DB Mix)/Steam (Oh, Oh, Let Off Steam Mix)/Games Without Frontiers (live) (CD in fold-out house-shaped box)	8
80	Reformation RSR 113	CHROMEDOME (LP)	20

(see also Genesis, Youssou 'Ndour & Peter Gabriel, Colin Scot, Charlie Drake)

PETER GABRIEL & KATE BUSH
86	Charisma/Virgin PGSP 2	Don't Give Up/In Your Eyes (Special Mix) (poster p/s in stickered PVC sleeve)	6

(see also Kate Bush)

RUSS GABRIEL
93	Ferox FER 002	PEACE EP (12", plain sleeve)	18
94	Ferox FER 006	DARWINIAN EP (12", plain sleeve)	8
95	Input Neuron INMD(X)1	FUTURE FUNK VOL. 1 (12", double pack, p/s)	10

(see also Fusion, Too Funk)

RUSS GABRIEL & AFFIE YUSUF
94	Ferox FER 005	Sian's Tune/Deep Space (12")	18

GABRIEL & ANGELS
63	Stateside SS 150	That's Life (That's Tough)/Don't Wanna Twist No More	20

GABRIELLI BRASS
65	Polydor 56031	Angel Cake/Cat Walk	10
65	Polydor 56047	Ride Your Pony/Anyone Who Had A Heart	10
68	Polydor 56252	'Canterbury Tales' Theme/Working My Way Back To You	15

GABY & CABLES
72	Duke DU 129	Only Love Can Make You Smile/Only Love Version	10

(see also Gaby & Wilton)

GABY & WILTON
72	Camel CA 92	Only Love/CHARLEY ACE: The Ten Commandments Of Joshua	10

(see also Gaby & Cables)

PABLO GAD
77	Caribbean CBN 318	International Dread/International Dub	10
77	Caribbean CBM 320	Kunte Kinte/Jah Jah Say (with The Equators)	10
78	Burning Sounds BDS 009	Bloodsuckers/Jail House Pressure (12", red vinyl)	20
79	Burning Rockers BRD 007	Visions Of Pablo/Tru I De A Jail (12")	20
79	Burning Rockers BRD 008	Natty Loving/Trodding On Home (12")	20
79	Burning Rockers BRD 020	Riddle I Dis/Iration (12")	20
79	Burning Sounds BS 042	Blood Suckers/Blood Suckers Dub	6
79	Burning Sounds BSD 015	Throw Your Dreams/What Makes A Natty Dread Cry (12", red vinyl)	20
79	Burning Rockers BRD 014	Trafalgar Square/Chereene (12", red vinyl)	20
80	Burning Rockers BRD 043	Hard Time/Lighter Shade Of Black (12")	15
80	Burning Rockers BRD 044	Black Before Creation/Reggae Music (12")	15
80	Greensleeves GRED 33	Fly Away Home/Well Insane (12")	20
80	Jis Majesty HMD 012	Oh Jah/Little Young Girl (12")	35
80	FORM D001	Gun Fever/Fever Dub (12")	15
80	FORM D003	Nursery Rhyme/Bubbling Angelo (12", purple vinyl)	8
81	FORM D005	P.G. In Love/RANKING SIMEON: Ranking Love (12")	20
81	FORM D017	Beggarman's Child/Poor Man Versus Rich Man Dub (12")	10
86	Jah Shaka SHAKA 853	King Of Kings/Lord Of Lords (12")	10
96	Reggae On Top ROT 013	Sha Sha Mane/Dub (12")	10
80	Burning sounds BS 1038	TRAFALGAR SQUARE (LP)	15
80	Federation Or Reggae FORM LP 1099	HARD TIMES (LP, red vinyl)	30

GADGETS
79	Final Solution FSLP 001	GADGETREE (LP, with insert, blue or beige picture on sleeve)	20
80	Final Solution FSLP 002	LOVE, CURIOSITY, FRECKLES & DOUBT (LP)	20
83	Glass GLALP 006	THE BLUE ALBUM (LP, with inner sleeve)	12

(see also The The, Matt Johnson, Colin Lloyd Tucker)

MEL GADSON
60	London HLX 9105	Comin' Down With Love/I'm Gettin' Sentimental Over You	20

GAGALACTYCA
90	Holyground HG 1135/ Magic Mixture MM 3	GAGALACTYCA (LP, with booklet, actually by Lightyears Away & Thundermother, 425 only)	40

(see also Bill Nelson, David John & Mood)

MAJOR YURI GAGARIN
61	Britone MK 100	CONQUEST OF SPACE (EP)	20

GAGS
79	Look LKLP 6312	DEATH IN BUZZARD'S GULCH (LP)	30

LITTLE SAMMY GAHA
73	Decca FR 13436	Rock 'N' Roll Is Back Again/Come 'N' On Strong	10

DAVID GAHAN
08	Mute STUMM 288	HOURGLASS (2-LP, gatefold with CD)	15
08	Mute LSTUMM 288	HOURGLASS REMIXES (2-LP & CD of remixes)	18

(see also Depeche Mode)

BASIL GAIL
70	Bullet BU 454	I Wish/Black Is Black	8

SLIM GAILLARD (QUARTET/TRIO)
48	MGM MGM 107	Tip Light/Arabian Boogie (78, as Slim Gaillard and his Trio)	40
50	MGM MGM 265	Communications/Serenade To A Poodle (78)	30
50	MGM MGM 281	Organ-Oreenie/to (78, as Slim Gaillard Sextet)	30
50	Parlophone R 3291	Jam Man/JOHNNY OTIS: Harlem Nocturne (78)	20

56	Parlophone GEP 8595	SLIM GAILLARD NO. 1 (EP)	15
56	Columbia Clef SEB 10046	MUSICAL AGGREGATIONS (EP)	15
60	London RED 1251	SLIM GAILLARD RIDES AGAIN (EP)	25

(see also Meade 'Lux' Lewis & Slim Gaillard)

DONNA GAINES
71	MCA MK 5060	Sally Go Round The Roses/So Said The Man	60

(see also Donna Summer)

PEGGY GAINES
98	Kent 6T 14	When The Boy That You Love/SAN FRANCISCO TKOS: Make Up Your Mind	25

GAINORS
58	London HLU 8734	The Secret/Gonna Rock Tonite	100
58	London HLU 8734	The Secret/Gonna Rock Tonite (78)	25

CHARLOTTE GAINSBOURGH
09	Because BEC5772607	IRM (2-LP)	15

G.A.K.
94	Warp WAP 48	GAK EP (12")	40
94	Warp WAP 48CD	GAK (CD)	40

(see also Aphex Twin)

GALACTIC FEDERATION
66	Polydor BM 56093	The March Of The Sky People/Moon Shot	25

GALACTIC SYMPOSIUM
80	Vague VOG 2	Money/In The Navy (gatefold p/s)	6

GALAHAD (1)
73	BellBLL 1273	Rocket Summer/Elephant Stomp	20
72	Polydor 2058 215	Let's Dance/Jellyroll	10

GALAHAD (2)
87	Private pressing G 1001	Dreaming From The Inside/The Opiate (p/s, 500 only)	12

DIAMANDA GALAS
86	Mute STUMM 33	SAINT OF THE PIT (12" EP, p/s with inner)	8
82	Y Y 18	LITANIES DU SATAN (LP)	30

GALAXIE 500
89	Chemical Imbalance C 1005	Oblivious/tracks by other artists (free with issue 8 of Chemical Imbalance magazine)	7
90	Rough Trade ROUGH TRADE T246	Blue Thunder/Victory Garden/Ceremony/Cold Night (12" EP)	10
90	Caff CAFF 9	Rain/Don't Let Your Youth Go To Waste (p/s, with insert in bag)	25
89	Shimmy Disc Europe SDE 8908 LP	TODAY (LP)	20
89	Schemer 8905 CD	TODAY (CD, with 2 extra tracks)	15
89	Rough Trade ROUGH 146	ON FIRE (LP)	30
90	Rough Trade ROUGH 156	THIS IS OUR MUSIC (LP, with sticker and 3 postcards)	25
91	Rough Trade ROUGH 146L	ON FIRE (LP, reissue with shrinkwrapped CD single)	20
96	Rykodisc RCD 10355	GALAXIE 500 (4-CD box set with booklet)	30

(see also Damon & Naomi)

GALAXIES
60	Capitol CL 15158	The Big Triangle/Until The Next Time	15

EDDIE GALE
69	Blue Note BST 84294	GHETTO MUSIC (LP)	15

SANDRA GALE
63	Ember EMB S 162	Hello Heartbreak/If She's Right For You	10

SUNNY GALE
53	HMV 7M 147	Teardrops On My Pillow/Send My Baby Back To Me	10
54	HMV 7M 243	Goodnight, Well It's Time To Go/Close To Me	10
55	HMV 7M 344	C'est La Vie/Looking Glass	10
57	Brunswick 05659	Two Hearts (With An Arrow Between)/Maybe You'll Be There	10
57	Brunswick 05661	Come Go With Me/Please Go	10
58	Brunswick 05753	A Certain Smile/Just Friends	10
61	London HLU 9322	Please Love Me Forever/Sunny	10

GALE BROTHERS
66	Parlophone R 5535	Every Day Of My Life/All Strung Out	6

GALENS
63	London HLH 9804	Baby I Do Love You/Love Bells	35

FRANCE GALL
65	Philips BF 1408	Poupée De Cire, Poupeé De Son/Le Coeur Qui Jazze	12
88	WEA YZ 316 CD	Ella Elle L'a (CD, slimline jewel case)	15

HUGHIE GALLAGHER
67	Outlet TOL 101	THE FLAGS ARE OUT FOR CELTIC (LP)	15

RORY GALLAGHER
71	Polydor 2383 044	RORY GALLAGHER (LP)	30
71	Polydor 2383 076	DEUCE (LP)	25
72	Polydor 2383 112	LIVE! IN EUROPE (LP, gatefold sleeve)	20
73	Polydor 2383 189	BLUEPRINT (LP)	18
73	Polydor 2383 230	TATTOO (LP)	20
74	Polydor 2659 031	IRISH TOUR '74 (2-LP)	15
87	Capo/Demon XFIEND 98	DEFENDER (LP, with bonus 7", "Seems To Me"/"No Peace For The Wicked")	12

(see also Taste, Killing Floor, Joe O'Donnell)

GALLAGHER-LYLE
67	Polydor BM 56170	Trees/In The Crowd	18
72	Capitol ST 21906	GALLAGHER AND LYLE (LP)	20
73	A&M AMLH 68148	WILLIE AND THE LAPDOG (LP)	18
73	A&M AMLS 8207	SEEDS (LP)	12

(see also James Galt, McGuinness Flint, Cups)

GALLAHADS
55   Capitol CL 14282   Ooh-Ah/Careless..15

RONNIE GALLANT
62   Warner Bros WB 61   In The Night/The Hole In The Wall 30

GALLANTS
64   Capitol CL 15366   Happy Beat/Rhino 10
65   Capitol CL 15408   Man From U.N.C.L.E. Theme/Vagabond 15

GALLERY
69   Midas   THE WIND THAT SHAKES THE BARLEY (LP)................700
78   Look LK LP 6029   EACH DAY THROUGH (LP) 100

GALLIARD
70   Deram DM 306   I Wrapped Her In Ribbons/The Hermit And The Knight 10
70   Deram Nova (S)DN 4   STRANGE PLEASURE (LP, red/silver labels) 200
70   Deram SML 1075   NEW DAWN (LP, white/red labels with small logo) 350
(see also Craig)

GALLIARDS
60   Topic STOP 101   Black And White/Bahnuah..7

BOB GALLION
59   MGM MGM 1028   Out Of A Honky Tonk/You Take The Table And I'll Take The Chairs ...10
60   MGM MGM 1057   Froggy Went A Courtin'/Hey! Joe 10
65   Hickory 45-1300   I Don't Have The Right (To Disagree)/Thank The Devil For Hideaways ...5

GALLON DRUNK
93   Clawfist XPIG 21   Known, Not Wanted/TINDERSTICKS: We Have All The Time In The World ('singles club' release, p/s, 1,400 only)................15
02   Sweet Nothing SNLP 012   FIRE MUSIC (2-LP) 18

GALLOW GLASS CEILI BAND
60   Top Rank RX 30314   COME TO THE CEILI (LP) 12

GALLOWS
07   Holy Roar HRR 006V   Just Because You Sleep Next To Me Doesn't Mean You're Safe/Abandon Ship/Will Someone Shoot That Fucking Snake/Swarm Over Death (white vinyl, 500 only)................25
07   Warner Bros. WEA425X   In The Belly Of A Shark/Sick Of Feeling Sick (live) (p/s, blue vinyl) 7
07   Thirty Days Of Night TDON 015   Sick Of Feeling Sick/If Credits What Matters I'll Take Credit/NOVEMBER COMING FIRE: Return Of The Black Dog/Bear Away (split 7", p/s, various coloured vinyl) 10

JAMES GALT
65   Pye 7N 15936   Comes The Dawn/My Own Way....................................12
65   Pye 7N 17021   With My Baby/A Most Unusual Feeling..........................75
65   Pye 7N 17021   With My Baby/A Most Unusual Feeling (DJ Copy) 100
(see also Gallagher-Lyle)

GAMA BOMB
09   MOSH382LP   TALES FROM THE GRAVE IN SPACE (LP, 300 on green vinyl, 700 on black vinyl = £10)................12

GAMBIT OF SHAME
82   Dead Hedgehog DHE 7009   No Bounds/18 Out Of 20 (p/s) 15

GAMBLERS
63   Decca F 11780   You've Really Got A Hold On Me/Can I See You Tonight? 15
64   Decca F 11872   Nobody But Me (Kissin' Time)It's So Nice 15
65   Decca F 12060   Now I'm All Alone/Find Out What's Happening................30
66   Decca F 12399   Doctor Goldfoot (And His Bikini Machine)/It Seems So Long 20
67   Parlophone R 5557   Cry Me A River/Who Will Buy 30
(see also Billy Fury)

FREDDIE GAMBRELL
59   Vogue LAE 12205   FREDDIE GAMBRELL (LP) 20

GAME
65   Pye 7N 15889   But I Do/Gotta Keep On Moving Baby 80
66   Decca F 12469   Gonna Get Me Someone/Gotta Wait 200
67   Parlophone R 5553   The Addicted Man/Help Me Mummy's Gone (withdrawn) 1000
67   Parlophone R 5553   The Addicted Man/Help Me Mummy's Gone (withdrawn) (demo copy) 600
67   Parlophone R 5569   It's Shocking What They Call Me/Help Me Mummy's Gone 500

GAMMA
80   Elektra K12480   Something In The Air/Mayday 10

GAMMER
77   Pennine (EP) PSS 147   Market Place - Your Alone/San Diego (P/S) 12

GAMMER & HIS FAMILIARS
84   Gammer GAMMER 5   Will The New Baby/All Above (12", p/s) 8
(see also Durutti Column)

GANDALF THE GREY
80s   Heyoka   THE GREY WIZARD AM I (LP, reissue of U.S. LP) 25

RON GANDERTON
82   Centridge CENT 2   Giggle Amongst The Tears/Smothered In Love (p/s) 8

LITTLE JIMMY GANDY
69   Roulette RO 510   Cool Thirteen/I'm Not Like The Others (Existence unconfirmed)........20

GANELIN TRIO
80   Leo LR 102   CATALOGUE, LIVE IN EAST GERMANY (LP) 15
83   Leo LR 112   NEW WINE...(LP) 30

GANG STARR
90   CBS 656377-7   Jazz Thing (Video Mix)/Jazz Thing (Movie Mix) (p/s) 10

GANGBUSTERS
63   Fontana TF 419   The Memory Of Your Face/When We Met................5

GANG OF FOUR

80	Fast Product FAST 5	DAMAGED GOODS (EP, original with b&w labels, with sticker)	20
86	Strange Fruit SFPS 008	PEEL SESSIONS (12")	15
79	EMI EMC 3313	ENTERTAINMENT (LP, with inner sleeve)	20
82	EMI EMC 3412	SONGS OF THE FREE (LP, with inner sleeve)	12
81	EMI EMC 3364	SOLID GOLD (LP, with insert)	15

GANGSTERS (1)

79	Stortbeat A45/B45	Harlow Town/Record Company	20
79	Stortbeat BEAT 3	Best Friend/Best Friend Dub (p/s)	10
79	Stortbeat BEAT 2	GANGSTERS (LP)	20

GANGSTERS (2)

80	Big Bear BB 25	Rudi The Red Nose Reindeer/White Christmas	5
80	Big Bear BB 28	Wooly Bully/We Are The Gangsters	5

GANIM'S ASIA MINORS

58	London HLE 8637	Daddy Lolo/Halvah	12

ALAN GANLEY QUARTET

58	Pye Nixa NJE 1046	GONE GANLEY (EP)	150

CECIL GANT

74	Flyright LP 4710	ROCK LITTLE BABY (LP)	15
75	Flyright LP 4714	CECIL'S BOOGIE (LP)	15
79	Magpie 1816	KILLER DILLER BOOGIE (LP)	15

CLENTT GANT

60	Starlite ST45 023	I'm Just A Lucky So-And-So/I Need You So	5

DON GANT

65	Hickory 45-1297	Early In The Morning/Don't Ya Even Cry	5

ELMER GANTRY'S VELVET OPERA

67	Direction 58-3083	Flames/Salisbury Plain	20
68	Direction 58-3481	Mary Jane/Dreamy	20
69	Direction 58-3924	Volcano/A Quick 'B'	20
68	Direction 8-63300	ELMER GANTRY'S VELVET OPERA (LP, laminated front sleeve, yellow/black labels)	125

(see also Velvet Opera, Stretch, Strawbs, Hudson-Ford, Paul Brett's Sage)

GANTS

65	Liberty LIB 55829	Road Runner/My Baby Don't Care	35
67	Liberty LIB 55940	I Wonder/Greener Days	15
88	Bam Caruso KIRI 067	I WONDER (LP)	12

GARBAGE

95	Discordant CORD 001	Vow/Torn Apart (embossed metal 'G' logo sleeve, with insert, 3,000 pressed [934 issued], stickered, sealed)	20
95	Discordant CORD 001	Vow/Torn Apart (embossed metal 'G' logo sleeve, with insert, 3,000 pressed [934 issued], stickered, unsealed)	20
95	Discordant CORD 001	Vow/Torn Apart (plain black embossed 'G' logo sleeve, with insert in poly bag, 500 only, sealed)	12
95	Discordant CORD 001	Vow/Torn Apart (plain black embossed 'G' logo sleeve, with insert in poly bag, 500 only, unsealed)	15
95	Mushroom SX 1138	Subhuman/1 Crush (embossed rubber 'G' logo sleeve, with SX 1138 insert, some in white 'G' logo carrier bag, 3,000 only; with incorrect insert [S1138])	20
95	Mushroom S 1138	Subhuman/1 Crush (embossed card 'G' logo sleeve, with insert, 2,000 pressed [1,000 issued])	10
95	Mushroom D 1138	Subhuman/1 Crush/Vow (CD, embossed inlay, stickered case, 3,000 only)	10
95	Mushroom SX 1199	Only Happy When It Rains/Girl Can't Come/Sleep (double-grooved B-side, stickered 'hologram prismaboard' 'G' logo sleeve, with inner sleeve & insert; some in blue 'G' logo carrier bag, 5000 only)	5
96	Mushroom SX 1271	Stupid Girl/Dog New Tricks (The Pal Mix) (10,000 only, stickered blue 'Tak-Tile' cloth 'G' logo sleeve, with stickered shrinkwrap)	5
01	Mushroom TRASH 27	Androgyny/Androgyny (Neptunes Remix) (12")	15
95	Mushroom L 31450	GARBAGE (LP) (as 2 x 45rpm 12", with inner sleeves)	15
95	Mushroom LX 31450	GARBAGE (LP) (as 6 x 7" singles in box set with 3 inserts [now import only], sealed)	20
95	Mushroom LX 31450	GARBAGE (LP) (as 6 x 7" singles in box set with 3 inserts [now import only], unsealed)	15

(see also Goodbye Mr. MacKenzine)

GARBO

82	Rarn RARN 201	Dancing Strange/Why Don't You Call Me?/Everyday Hallucinations (with p/s)	200
82	Rarn RARN 201	Dancing Strange/Why Don't You Call Me?/Everyday Hallucinations (without p/s)	50

GARBO'S CELLULOID HEROES

78	Big Bear BB 13	Only Death Is Fatal/Won't You Come to my Funeral (p/s)	10

VIN GARBUTT

72	Trailer LER 2078	THE VALLEY OF TEES (LP, red label)	15
75	Trailer LER 2081	THE YOUNG TIN WHISTLE PEST (LP, yellow label)	15
76	Trailer LER 2102	KING GOODEN (LP, yellow label)	15

JERRY GARCIA

71	Douglas DGL 69013	HOOTEROLL? (LP, with Howard Wales)	20
72	Warner Bros K 46139	GARCIA (LP)	15
74	Round RX 59301	GARCIA (LP)	12
76	United Artists UAG 29921	REFLECTIONS (LP)	12

(see also Grateful Dead, Diga Rhythm Band, Old & In The Way)

RUSS GARCIA ORCHESTRA

58	London HAU 2141	FANTASTICA! (LP)	30

GARDEN ODYSSEY (ENTERPRISE)

69	Deram DM 267	Sad And Lonely/Sky Pilot (8/M/1) (as Garden Odyssey Enterprise)	80
72	RCA RCA 2159	Joker/Have You Ever Been To Georgia (as Garden Odyssey)	8

(see also Graham Gouldman)

BORIS GARD(I)NER (& LOVE PEOPLE)

69	High Note HS 010	Lucky Is The Boy/Bobby Sox To Stockings	100
69	Doctor Bird DB 1205	Elizabethan Reggae/Hooked On A Feeling	25

69	Duke DU 21	Never My Love/The Bold One	20
69	Duke 39	Elizabethan Reggae/BYRON LEE : Soul Serenade	15
70	Treasure Isle TI 7056	Hooked On A Feeling/MESSAGE: Turn Around Twice	10
70	Big Shot BI 537	Sweet Soul Special/Memories Of Love (with Love People)	10
70	Big Shot BI 538	Darkness/Watch This Music (B-side actually "Keep Out") (with Love People)	12
70	Big Shot BI 539	Hot Shot/Watch This Music (with Love People)	40
70	Dynamic DYN 404	Commanding Wife/Band Of Gold (as Boris Gardner & Happening)	6
70	Trojan TR 7753	Dynamic Pressure/Reggae Me Dis, Reggae Me Dat	7
70	Trojan TBL 121	REGGAE HAPPENING (LP)	30

PAUL GARDINER
81	Beggars Banquet BEG 61	Stormtrooper In Drag/Night Talk (p/s)	5
81	Beggars Banquet BEG 61T	Stormtrooper In Drag/Night Talk (12", unreleased, white label promos only)	700
84	Numa NU 1	Venus In Furs/No Sense (p/s)	5
84	Numa NUM 1	Venus In Furs (Extended Mix)/No Sense/Venus In Furs (7" Mix) (12", p/s)	10

(see also Tubeway Army, Gary Numan)

AVA GARDNER
| 53 | MGM SP 1005 | Can't Help Lovin' Dat Man/Bill | 10 |

DAVE GARDNER
| 58 | Brunswick 05740 | Hop Along Rock/All By Myself (B-side with Anita Kerr Singers) | 30 |
| 58 | Brunswick 05740 | Hop Along Rock/All By Myself (B-side with Anita Kerr Singers) (78) | 10 |

DON GARDNER & DEE DEE FORD
62	Stateside SS 114	I Need Your Loving/Tell Me	20
62	Stateside SS 130	Don't You Worry/I'm Coming Home To Stay	20
68	Soul City SC 101	Don't You Worry/I'm Coming Home To Stay (reissue)	10

(see also Baby Washington & Don Gardner, Dee Dee Ford)

JOANNE GARDNER
| 70s | Polydor | JOANNE GARDNER (LP) | 15 |

JOHNNY GARFIELD
| 65 | Pye 7N 15758 | Stranger In Paradise/Anyone Can Lose A Heart | 45 |

(see also Simon & Garfunkel, Tom & Jerry)

ART GARFUNKEL
| 74 | CBS CQ 31474/Q 69021 | ANGEL CLARE (LP, quadrophonic) | 12 |

FRANK GARI
| 60 | London HLU 9277 | I Ain't Got A Girl/Utopia | 10 |
| 61 | London HL 9371 | Lullaby Of Love/Tonight Is Our Last Night | 7 |

JUDY GARLAND
53	MGM SP 1001	A Couple Of Swells/Medley: I Love A Piano/Snooky Ookums/When The Midnight Choo Choo Leaves (with Fred Astaire)	12
56	Brunswick 02886	Over The Rainbow/The Jitterbug (78)	18
56	MGM SP 1157	Look For The Silver Lining/Who?	10
57	Capitol CL 14789	Rock-a-bye Your Baby With A Dixie Melody/After You've Gone	6
57	Capitol CL 14790	I Feel A Song Coming On/Just Imagine	6
57	Capitol CL 14791	By Myself/It's Lovely To Be Back In London	6
57	Capitol CL 17691	It's Lovely To Be Back In London (1-sided 7" given to audience at Gala Premiere of extended engagement at Dominion Theatre (p/s with insert)	15
55	Philips BBE 12012	BORN IN A TRUNK - SELECTIONS FROM A STAR IS BORN (EP)	10
56	MGM MGM-EP 568	IF YOU FEEL LIKE SINGING (EP)	10
56	MGM MGM-EP 672	WORDS AND MUSIC - SOUNDTRACK EXCERPTS (EP, 1 track with June Allyson & Mickey Rooney)	10
55	Brunswick LA 8725	JUDY AT THE PALACE (10" LP)	12
55	MGM MGM-D 134	BORN TO SING (10" LP)	12
59	Capitol (S)T 1188	THE LETTER (LP, with paste-on letter intact)	25
59	Capitol (S)T 1188	THE LETTER (LP, without paste-on letter intact)	12

(see also Fred Astaire)

RED GARLAND
60	Esquire 32- 096	MANTECA (LP)	15
60	Esquire 32-099	ALL MORNING LONG (LP)	75
61	Esquire 32-116	RED IN BLUES VILLE (LP)	25
61	Esquire 32-126	AT THE PRELUDE (LP)	20
61	Esquire 32-136	SOUL JUNCTION (LP)	30
62	Esquire 32-146	ROJO (LP)	20
62	Esquire 32-166	HIGH PRESSURE (LP)	20

BILLY GARNER
| 00 | BGPS 006 | Brand New Girl/JACQUELINE JONES : Can't Stop The Show | 15 |

ERROL GARNER
53	Vogue LDE 034	ERROL GARNER TRIO VOLUME ONE (10" LP)	12
54	Felsted EDL 87002	MARGIE (10" LP)	12
54	Philips BBR 8002	PLAYS FOR DANCING (10" LP)	12
55	Philips BBR 8045	SOLO FLIGHT (10" LP)	12
55	Columbia 33S 1050	PIANO MOODS (10" LP)	12
55	Columbia 33S 1059	PIANO GEMS (10" LP)	12
55	Oriole MG 26042	GONE WITH GARNER (10" LP)	12
55	Felsted EDL 87015	PASSPORT TO FAME (10" LP)	12

KAY GARNER
| 64 | Oriole CB 1951 | I Still Get Jealous/Squeeze Me | 10 |

REGGIE GARNER
| 76 | Capitol CL 15874 | Hot Line/Blessed Be The Name Of My Baby | 5 |

BLIND LEROY GARNET
| 52 | Jazz Collector L 74 | Chain 'Em Down/Louisiana Glide (78) | 15 |

COL GARNET
| 66 | Page One POF 002 | With A Girl Like You/Monday Monday | 12 |

ALF GARNETT (& FAMILY)
68	Pye NPL 18192	SEX AND OTHER THOUGHTS (LP)	18

GALE GARNETT
64	RCA RCA 1418	We'll Sing In The Sunshine/Prism Song	10
65	RCA RCA 1451	I'll Cry Alone/Where Do You Go To Go Away?	60
65	RCA RCA 1451	I'll Cry Alone/Where Do You Go To Go Away? (DJ Copy)	85
65	RCA RD 7726	MY KIND OF FOLK SONGS (LP)	30
66	RCA RD 7750	LOVIN' PLACE (LP)	20

LAURENT GARNIER
93	Warp WAP 36	A BOUT DE SOUFFLE (12", company sleeve)	8

RACHELLE GARNIEZ
09	Third Man TMR 004	My House Of Peace (1-sided, 100 only, luminous vinyl)	40

VERNON GARRETT
67	Stateside SS 2006	If I Could Turn Back The Hands Of Time/You And Me Together	40
67	Stateside SS 2006	If I Could Turn Back The Hands Of Time/You And Me Together (DJ copy)	80
67	Stateside SS 2026	Shine It On/Things Are Lookin' Better	40
67	Stateside SS 2026	Shine It On/Things Are Lookin' Better (DJ copy)	75
68	Action ACT 4508	Shine It On/Things Are Lookin' Better (reissue)	30

DAVID GARRICK
65	Piccadilly 7N 35231	Go/When The World Was Our Own	7
65	Piccadilly 7N 35263	One Little Smile/We Must Be In Love	7
66	Piccadilly 7N 35317	Lady Jane/Let's Go Somewhere	6
66	Piccadilly 7N 35335	Dear Mrs Applebee/You're What I'm Living For	7
67	Piccadilly 7N 35371	I've Found A Love/(You Can't Hide) A Broken Heart	5
67	Piccadilly 7N 35377	A Certain Misunderstanding/I'm Looking Straight At You	5
67	Piccadilly 7N 35402	Don't Go Out In The Rain (You're Gonna Melt, Sugar)/ Theme For A Wishing Heart	7
67	Pye 7N 17409	Ave Maria/Please Stay	5
67	Pye 7N 17409	Ave Maria/You Don't Know (different B-side)	5
68	Pye 7N 17509	Rainbow/I'll Be Home	6
68	Pye 7N 17610	A Little Bit Of This (And A Little Bit Of That)/Flutterby Butterfly	6
69	Pye 7N 17685	Maypole Mews/Like To Get To Know You Better	5
69	Pye 7N 17820	Poor Little Me/Molly With The Hair Like Silver	5
69	Columbia DB 8680	Bake Me A Woman/House In The Heather	7
71	Columbia DB 8784	Mary In The Morning/Beautiful People	7
67	Piccadilly NEP 34056	DAVID (EP)	30
66	Piccadilly NPL 38024	A BOY CALLED DAVID (LP, mono)	20
66	Piccadilly N(S)PL 38024	A BOY CALLED DAVID (LP, stereo)	22
67	Piccadilly N(S)PL 38035	DON'T GO OUT INTO THE RAIN, SUGAR (LP)	20
68	Pye NSPL 18223	LIVE! (LP, blue/black label)	30

MICHAEL GARRICK
65	Argo EAF/ZFA 92	ANTHEM - MICHAEL GARRICK QUINTET (EP, mono/stereo)	60
66	Argo EAF 115	BEFORE NIGHT/DAY (EP)	60
63	Airborne	CASE OF JAZZ (EP, with Shake Keane)	200
64	Airborne	MOONSCAPE (LP)	1250
64	Argo ZDA 26/27	POETRY AND JAZZ IN CONCERT (2-LP, with Norma Winstone)	60
65	Argo (Z)DA 33	OCTOBER WOMAN (LP, as Michael Garrick Quintet, with Joe Harriott)	100
65	Argo (Z)DA 36	PROMISES (LP, as Michael Garrick Sextet, with Ian Carr)	120
68	Argo (Z)DA 88	BLACK MARIGOLDS (LP, as Michael Garrick Septet)	120
68	Airborne NBP 0021	JAZZ PRAISES AT ST. PAULS (LP)	45
69	Argo ZPR 264/5	POETRY AND JAZZ IN CONCERT 250 (2-LP, as Michael Garrick Quintet)	80
69	Erase EO 2545	JAZZ CANTATA (LP, 'Farnham Festival' release)	150
70	Argo ZDA 135	HEART IS A LOTUS (LP, as Michael Garrick Sextet with Norma Winstone)	100
72	Argo ZDA 153	COLD MOUNTAIN (LP, as Michael Garrick Trio)	150
72	Argo ZDA 154	HOME STRETCH BLUES (LP, as Michael Garrick Band with Norma Winstone)	120
73	Impulse AS 49	ILLUMINATION (LP, as Michael Garrick Sextet)	40
74	Argo ZDA 163	TROPPO (LP)	80
81	Hep Records HEP2011	YOU'VE CHANGED (LP)	20
07	Trunk JBH 022 LP	MOONSCAPE (LP, reissue 500 only)	30

(see also Ian Carr, Norma Winstone, Joe Harriott, Garrick's Fairground)

GARRICK'S FAIRGROUND
71	Argo AFW 105	Epiphany/Blessed Are The Peacemakers	20
72	Argo ZAGF 1	MR. SMITH'S APOCALYPSE (LP)	70

(see also Michael Garrick)

FREDDIE GARRITY
68	Columbia DB 8348	Little Red Donkey/So Many Different Ways	6
74	Bus Stop BUS 1017	Hello Kids/It's Good For You	7
74	Bus Stop BUS 1022	The Chicken Song/Pooh Pooh Pooh	7
70	Starline SRS 5019	OLIVER IN THE OVERWORLD (LP, soundtrack)	12

(see also Freddie & Dreamers)

ROBIN GARSIDE & PAUL GOUGH
77	Northern Sound NSR 01	SEA SONGS (LP)	15

MORT GARSON
69	A & M AMLS 960	ELECTRIC HAIRPEICES (LP)	20

ROBIN GARTON & HIS BAND
58	Martello MC 100	Topsy/Jump For Me	5

GARUDA
77	EMI EMC 3174	GARUDA (LP)	40

REX GARVIN & MIGHTY CRAVERS
66	Atlantic 584 028	Sock It To 'Em J.B. (Parts 1 & 2)	18
67	Atlantic 584 097	I Gotta Go Now (Up On The Floor)/Believe It Or Not	25

JOHN GARY
59	Top Rank JAR 177	Let Them Talk/Tell My Love	7
60	Top Rank JAR 392	Little Things Mean A Lot/Ever Since I Met Lucy	7

GARY & ARIELS
64	Fontana TF 476	Say You Love Me/Town Girl	15

(see also Garry Mills)

GARY & STU
72	Carnaby 6151 003	Sweet White Dove/Good Lady Fair	8
72	Carnaby 6302 012	HARLAN FARE (LP, white label with 'crab' logo)	80

(see also Koobas, March Hare)

GAS
80	Polydor POSP 192	It Shows In Your Face/Tomorrow (p/s)	35
81	Polydor POSP 264	Ignore Me/Do It, Don't Tell Me (p/s)	20
81	Polydor POSP 296	Treatment/That's It (12", p/s)	30
81	Polydor POSP 344	The Finger/Knock It Down (p/s)	18
82	Polydor POSP 411	Breathless/Heartache/Hostage (p/s)	7
81	Polydor POLE 1052	EMOTIONAL WARFARE (LP)	15

GASKIN
81	Rondelet ROUND 7	I'm No Fool/Sweet Dream Maker (p/s)	25
82	Rondelet ROUND 21	Mony Mony/Queen Of Hams (p/s)	18
81	Rondelet ABOUT 4	END OF THE WORLD (LP, gatefold sleeve)	25
82	Rondelet ABOUT 8	NO WAY OUT (LP, with inner)	20

GASLIGHT
69	Jay Boy BOY 17	Move/And So To Sleep	18
70	SDE 32732	GASLIGHT (2-LP, private pressing, gatefold sleeve with inserts, 2nd disc by Gaslight Choir)	40

GASLIGHT ANTHEM
09	Side One Dummy SD 13827	Great Expectations/Miles Davis & The Cool (Acoustic) (p/s)	8

GASOLIN
71	CBS 64685	GASOLIN (LP, gatefold sleeve, orange/black label)	40
72	CBS 65229	2 (LP, gatefold sleeve, orange/black label)	30
73	CBS 65798	3 (LP, orange label)	20
75	Epic SEPC 81436	WHAT A LEMON (LP, yellow/black label)	30

GASOLINE BAND
72	Cube HIFLY 9	GASOLINE BAND (LP, cube label)	200

GASPAR NETSCHER ENSEMBLE
68	Pye 7N 17556	Get Out Of My Bed Darling/Until You're Here Beside Me	8

GASS
65	Parlophone R 5344	One Of These Days/I Don't Know Why	30
66	Parlophone R 5456	The New Breed/In The City	60
67	CBS 202647	Dream Baby (How Long Must I Dream?)/Jitterbug Sid	30
71	Polydor 2058 147	Something's Got To Change Your Ways/Mr Banana	10
70	Polydor 2383 022	JUJU (LP, featuring Peter Green)	100
70	Polydor 2383 022	JUJU (LP, featuring Peter Green, alternative sleeve, black/gold with Gass logo on front and drawing on rear, record has same matrix as other issue and red Polydor labels)	200
71	Polydor 2383 035	CATCH MY SOUL - THE ROCK-OTHELLO (LP, cast recording featuring Gass)	20

(see also Hummingbird, Humble Pie, Streetwalkers, Peter Green)

GASS COMPANY
68	President PT 170	Everybody Needs Love/Nightmare	60

(see also Wake)

GAS WORKS
73	Regal Zonophone RZ 3075	Standing Stiff/Keep On Rolling	6
73	Regal Zonophone RZ 3080	God's Great Spaceship/Cider With Rosie	6
73	Regal Zono. SRLZ 1036	GAS WORKS (LP)	15

DAVID GATES
60	Top Rank JAR 504	The Happiest Man Alive/The Road That Leads To Love	30

(see also Bread)

PEARLY GATES
74	Polydor 2058 443	Johnny And The Juke-Box/They Were Good Times	5
70	MCA MU 1109	Free/Carole's Epic Song	12

(see also Flirtations, Gypsies)

RAY GATES
66	Decca F 12502	It's Such A Shame/Have You Ever Had The Blues	40

GATES OF EDEN
66	Pye 7N 17195	Too Much On My Mind/I'm Warning You	25
67	Pye 7N 17252	In Your Love/Snoopy Versus The Red Baron	12
67	Pye 7N 17278	1 To 7/Hey Now	30

GATEWAY SINGERS
57	Brunswick LAT 8176	PUTTIN' ON THE STYLE (LP)	18

GATHERERS
73	Duke DU 153	Words Of My Mouth/UPSETTERS: Version	70

LUCHO GATICA
54	Parlophone CMSP 16	Besame Mucho/Las Muchachas De La Plaza De Espana (export issue)	8

GATOR CREEK
71	Mercury 6052 058	Danny's Song/Take A Look	15
71	Mercury 6338 035	GATOR CREEK (LP)	15

DICK GAUGHAN
72	Trailer LER 2072	NO MORE FOREVER (LP, red label)	25
76	Rubber RUB 019	FIVE HAND REEL (LP)	20
78	Topic 12TS384	GAUGHAN (LP, tan label)	15
81	Topic 12TS419	HANDFUL OF EARTH (LP)	15

GEORGES GAVARENTZ

69	Philips SBL 7898	THEY CAME TO ROB LAS VEGAS (LP, soundtrack)	60

JIMMY GAVIN

57	London HLU 8478	I Sit In My Window/Lonely Chair	80
57	London HLU 8478	I Sit In My Window/Lonely Chair (78)	15

JOHNNY GAVOTTE

60	Parlophone R 4631	It's Not Too Late/Can't Forget	10

ELAINE GAY

54	Parlophone MSP 6140	Love/Instantly	12
55	Parlophone R 3997	Rock Love/Ebony Eyes (78)	10

MAC GAYDEN

73	EMI EMA 760	McGAVOCK GAYDEN (LP)	20

(see also Area Code 615)

MARVIN GAYE

63	Oriole CBA 1803	Stubborn Kind Of Fellow/It Hurt Me Too	90
63	Oriole CBA 1803	Stubborn Kind Of Fellow/It Hurt Me Too (DJ Copy)	200
63	Oriole CBA 1846	Pride And Joy/One Of These Days	90
63	Oriole CBA 1846	Pride And Joy/One Of These Days (DJ Copy)	200
63	Stateside SS 243	Can I Get A Witness?/I'm Crazy 'Bout My Baby	50
63	Stateside SS 243	Can I Get A Witness?/I'm Crazy 'Bout My Baby (DJ Copy)	90
64	Stateside SS 284	You're A Wonderful One/When I'm Alone I Cry	50
64	Stateside SS 284	You're A Wonderful One/When I'm Alone I Cry (DJ Copy)	90
64	Stateside SS 326	Try It Baby/If My Heart Could Sing	40
64	Stateside SS 326	Try It Baby/If My Heart Could Sing (DJ Copy)	70
64	Stateside SS 360	How Sweet It Is (To Be Loved By You)/Forever	30
64	Stateside SS 360	How Sweet It Is (To Be Loved By You)/Forever (DJ Copy)	50
65	Tamla Motown TMG 510	I'll Be Doggone/You've Been A Long Time Coming	40
65	Tamla Motown TMG 510	I'll Be Doggone/You've Been A Long Time Coming (DJ Copy)	120
65	Tamla Motown TMG 524	Pretty Little Baby/Now That You've Won Me	40
65	Tamla Motown TMG 524	Pretty Little Baby/Now That You've Won Me (DJ Copy)	80
65	Tamla Motown TMG 539	Ain't That Peculiar?/She's Got To Be Real	30
65	Tamla Motown TMG 539	Ain't That Peculiar?/She's Got To Be Real (DJ Copy)	90
66	Tamla Motown TMG 552	One More Heartache/When I Had Your Love	30
66	Tamla Motown TMG 552	One More Heartache/When I Had Your Love (DJ Copy)	80
66	Tamla Motown TMG 563	Take This Heart Of Mine/Need Your Lovin' (Want You Back)	35
66	Tamla Motown TMG 563	Take This Heart Of Mine/Need Your Lovin' (Want You Back) (DJ Copy)	80
66	Tamla Motown TMG 574	Little Darlin' (I Need You)/Hey Diddle Diddle	35
66	Tamla Motown TMG 574	Little Darlin' (I Need You)/Hey Diddle Diddle (DJ Copy)	120
67	Tamla Motown TMG 618	Your Unchanging Love/I'll Take Care Of You	20
67	Tamla Motown TMG 618	Your Unchanging Love/I'll Take Care Of You (DJ Copy)	50
68	Tamla Motown TMG 640	You/Change What You Can	20
68	Tamla Motown TMG 640	You/Change What You Can (DJ Copy)	40
68	Tamla Motown TMG 676	Chained/At Last (I Found A Love)	18
69	Tamla Motown TMG 686	I Heard It Through The Grapevine/Need Somebody	7
69	Tamla Motown TMG 705	Too Busy Thinking 'Bout My Baby/Wherever I Lay My Hat	7
69	Tamla Motown TMG 718	That's The Way Love Is/Gonna Keep On Tryin' Till I Win Your Love	8
70	Tamla Motown TMG 734	Abraham, Martin And John/How Can I Forget?	7
71	Tamla Motown TMG 775	What's Going On?/God Is Love	8
71	Tamla Motown TMG 796	Save The Children/Little Darling (I Need You)	8
72	Tamla Motown TMG 802	Mercy Mercy Me (The Ecology)/Sad Tomorrows	6
72	Tamla Motown TMG 817	Inner City Blues/Wholly Holy	10
73	Tamla Motown TMG 846	Trouble Man/Don't Mess With Mister 'T'	12
74	Tamla Motown TMG 882	Come Get To This/Distant Lover	15
66	Tamla Motown TME 2016	MARVIN GAYE (EP)	55
67	Tamla Motown TME 2019	ORIGINALS FROM MARVIN GAYE (EP)	44
64	Stateside SL 10100	MARVIN GAYE (LP)	200
65	Tamla Motown TML 11004	HOW SWEET IT IS TO BE LOVED BY YOU (LP)	60
65	Tamla Motown TML 11015	HELLO BROADWAY (LP)	80
66	T. Motown TML 11022	A TRIBUTE TO THE GREAT NAT KING COLE (LP, mono)	65
66	T. Motown STML 11022	A TRIBUTE TO THE GREAT NAT KING COLE (LP, stereo)	80
66	T. Motown TML 11033	MOODS OF MARVIN GAYE (LP, mono)	50
66	T. Motown STML 11033	MOODS OF MARVIN GAYE (LP, stereo)	60
68	T. Motown TML 11065	MARVIN GAYE'S GREATEST HITS (LP, mono)	20
68	T. Motown STML 11065	MARVIN GAYE'S GREATEST HITS (LP, stereo)	20
69	T. Motown (S)TML 11091	IN THE GROOVE (LP, mono/stereo)	30
69	T. Motown (S)TML 11119	M.P.G. (LP, mono/stereo)	25
69	T. Motown TML 11123	MARVIN GAYE AND HIS GIRLS (LP, mono, with T. Terrell, M. Wells & K. Weston)	25
70	T. Motown STML 11123	MARVIN GAYE AND HIS GIRLS (LP, stereo, with T. Terrell, M. Wells & K. Weston)	22
70	T. Motown TML 11136	THAT'S THE WAY LOVE IS (LP, mono)	30
70	T. Motown STML 11136	THAT'S THE WAY LOVE IS (LP, stereo)	20
71	Tamla Motown STML 11190	WHAT'S GOING ON? (LP, with lyric sheet)	20
72	Tamla Motown STML 11201	THE HITS OF MARVIN GAYE (LP)	12
73	Tamla Motown STML 11225	TROUBLE MAN (LP, soundtrack)	20
76	Tamla Motown STML 12025	I WANT YOU (LP)	12
78	Tamla Motown TMSP 6008	HERE, MY DEAR (2-LP)	25

MARVIN GAYE & TAMMI TERRELL

67	Tamla Motown TMG 611	Ain't No Mountain High Enough/Give A Little Love	30
67	Tamla Motown TMG 611	Ain't No Mountain High Enough/Give A Little Love (DJ Copy)	80
67	Tamla Motown TMG 625	Your Precious Love/Hold Me Oh My Darling	25
67	Tamla Motown TMG 625	Your Precious Love/Hold Me Oh My Darling (DJ Copy)	50
67	Tamla Motown TMG 635	If I Could Build My Whole World Around You/If This World Were Mine	15
67	Tamla Motown TMG 635	If I Could Build My Whole World Around You/If This World Were Mine (DJ Copy)	30
68	Tamla Motown TMG 655	Ain't Nothin' Like The Real Thing/Little Ole Boy, Little Ole Girl	12
68	Tamla Motown TMG 655	Ain't Nothin' Like The Real Thing/Little Ole Boy, Little Ole Girl (DJ Copy)	30
68	Tamla Motown TMG 668	You're All I Need To Get By/Two Can Have A Party	8
69	Tamla Motown TMG 681	You Ain't Livin' Till You're Lovin'/Oh How I'd Miss You	12
69	Tamla Motown TMG 697	Good Lovin' Ain't Easy To Come By/Satisfied Feelin'	8

69	Tamla Motown TMG 715	The Onion Song/I Can't Believe You Love Me	6
69	Tamla Motown TMG 715	The Onion Song/I Can't Believe You Love Me (demo in p/s)	50
68	T. Motown TML 11062	UNITED (LP, mono)	40
68	T. Motown STML 11062	UNITED (LP, stereo)	45
68	T. Motown (S)TML 11084	YOU'RE ALL I NEED (LP, mono/stereo)	40
70	T. Motown TML 11132	EASY (LP, mono)	20
70	T. Motown STML 11132	EASY (LP, stereo)	18
70	T. Motown (S)TML 11153	GREATEST HITS (LP)	15

MARVIN GAYE & MARY WELLS

64	Stateside SS 316	Once Upon A Time/What's The Matter With You, Baby?	35
64	Stateside SS 316	Once Upon A Time/What's The Matter With You, Baby? (DJ Copy)	80
64	Stateside SL 10097	TOGETHER (LP)	75

MARVIN GAYE & KIM WESTON

64	Stateside SS 363	What Good Am I Without You?/I Want You Around	40
64	Stateside SS 363	What Good Am I Without You?/I Want You Around (DJ Copy)	80
67	Tamla Motown TMG 590	It Takes Two/It's Got To Be A Miracle (This Thing Called Love)	12
67	Tamla Motown TMG 590	It Takes Two/It's Got To Be A Miracle (This Thing Called Love) (DJ Copy)	70
67	T. Motown TML 11049	TAKE TWO (LP, mono)	40
67	T. Motown STML 11049	TAKE TWO (LP, stereo)	45

(see also Diana Ross, Tammi Terrell, Mary Wells, Kim Weston)

GAYLADS

64	R&B JB 159	There'll Come A Day/BILLY COOKE: Iron Bar	50
64	R&B JB 165	What Is Wrong With Me?/Whap Whap	60
66	Island WI 281	Goodbye Daddy/Your Eyes	30
66	Island WI 291	You Never Leave Him/Message To My Girl	30
66	Island WI 3002	Stop Making Love/They Call Her Dawn	50
66	Doctor Bird DB 1014	Lady With The Red Dress/Dinner For Two	15
66	Doctor Bird DB 1031	You Should Never Do That/WINSTON STEWART: I Don't Know Why I Love You	25
66	Rymska RA 104	You Should Never Do That/TECHNIQUES: So Many Times	35
67	Island WI 3022	Don't Say No/SONNY BURKE: You Rule My Heart	40
67	Island WI 3025	You No Good Girl/Yes Girl	30
67	Studio One SO 2002	Tears From My Eyes/Never Let Your Country Down	100
67	Studio One SO 2009	Won't You Come Home/PETER & HORTENSE : I've Been Lonely	50
67	Studio One SO 2013	I Am Going To Cool It (actually by Little Roy)/ MELODIANS: Let's Join Together	60
67	Studio One SO 2017	Love Me With All Your Heart/I Don't Care	40
67	Studio One SO 2021	IF You Knew/Festival Day	80
67	Rio R 125	Put On Your Style/SOUL BROTHERS: Soul Serenade	50
68	Blue Cat BS 110	Go Away/SOUL VENDORS: Julie On My Mind	30
68	Doctor Bird DB 1124	It's Hard To Confess/I Need Your Loving	40
68	Doctor Bird DB 1145	She Want It/Joy In The Morning	40
68	Fab FAB 62	Looking For A Girl/Aren't You The Guy	100
68	Hi Note HS 001	A B C Rocksteady/LESLIE BUTLER & COUNT OSSIE: Soul Drums	35
69	Trojan TR 688	You Had Your Chance/Wha' She Do Now	12
69	Upsetter US 323	The Same Things/I Wear My Slanders	20
70	Trojan TR 7703	There's A Fire/Last Time	8
70	Trojan TR 7738	That's What Love Will Do/This Time I Won't Hurt You	10
70	Trojan TR 7743	Young, Gifted And Black/BEVERLEY'S ALLSTARS: Moon Glow	10
70	Trojan TR 7763	Tell The Children The Truth/Something Is Wrong Somewhere	8
70	Trojan TR 7771	Soul Sister/BEVERLEY'S ALLSTARS: Soul Version	12
70	Trojan TR 7782	It's All In The Game/BEVERLEY'S ALLSTARS: Version II	8
70	Trojan TR 7799	Fire And Rain/Cold And Lonely Night	6
71	Ackee AC 141	Accept My Apologies (actually by B.B. Seaton & Ken Boothe)/ My Version (actually by Conscious Minds)	6
71	Big BG 319	Can't Hide The Feeling/RUPIE EDWARDS ALLSTARS: Version	6
71	Camel CA 79	Seven In One Medley (Parts 1 & 2)	6
71	Summit SUM 8514	My Jamaican Girl/BEVERLEY'S ALLSTARS: Version	6
71	Bullet BU 462	My Love/Stranger Love	7
74	Dip DL 5009	You Made A Mistake/Shower Of Blessings	6
67	Coxsone CSL 8005	ROCKSTEADY (LP)	125
67	Coxsone CSL 8006	SUNSHINE IS GOLDEN (LP)	75

(see also Gaylords, Rockstones, Delano Stewart, Ken Boothe, B.B. Seaton, Brent Dowe, Dobby Dobson, Jackie Mittoo, Heptones, Clarendonians, Soul Vendors)

VINLEY GAYLE

| 64 | Black Swan WI 453 | Go-Go/BABA BROOKS: Take Five | 30 |

GAYLET(T)S

68	Island WI 3129	Silent River Runs Deep/You're My Kind Of Man	40
68	Island WI 3141	I Like Your World/Lonely Feeling	25
68	Big Shot BI 502	If You Can't Be Good/Something About My Man	12
69	Big Shot BI 516	Son-Of-A-Preacher-Man/That's How Strong My Love Is	12
70	London HLJ 10302	Son-Of-A-Preacher-Man/I Like Your World	7

(see also Bob Andy)

GAYLORDS (JAMAICA)

| 66 | Island WI 269 | Chipmunk Ska/What Is Wrong? (both actually by Gaylads) | 25 |

(see also Gaylads)

GAYLORDS (U.K.)

| 66 | Columbia DB 7805 | He's A Good Face But He's Down And Out/You Know It Too | 15 |

(see also Dean Ford & Gaylords, Marmalade)

GAYLORDS (U.S.)

| 60 | Mercury MMC 14032 | THAT'S AMORE (LP) | 12 |

WILTON 'BOGEY' GAYNAIR QUARTET

61	Tempo EXA 103	BLUE BOGEY VOLUME ONE (EP)	60
59	Tempo TAP 25	BLUE BOGEY (LP)	400

GAYNOR (JUNIOR ENGLISH) & ERROL (DUNKLEY)

| 65 | Blue Beat BB 286 | My Queen/ROLAND ALPHONSO: Roland Plays Prince (B-side actually "Hanging The Beam" by Skatalites) | 60 |

(see also Errol Dunkley)

GLORIA GAYNOR
| 78 | Polydor 2066922 | For The First Time In My Life/This Love Affair | 6 |

MEL GAYNOR
55	Decca F 10497	Just A Man/How Important Can It Be?	5
55	Decca F 10542	With You Beside Me/Oh, My Love	5
55	Decca F 10618	Bella Notte/Sweet Kentucky Rose	5

(see also Oscar Rabin)

MITZI GAYNOR
59	Top Rank JAR 258	Happy Anniversary/Play For Keeps	5
60	Top Rank JAR 289	I Don't Regret A Thing/The Touch Of Time	5
58	HMV 7EG 8460	MITZI (EP)	10

ROSEMARY GAYNOR
| 55 | Columbia SCM 5196 | Ain't That A Shame/A Happy Song | 15 |

PAUL GAYTEN
57	London HL 8503	Yo, Yo, Walk/TUNE WEAVERS: Happy Happy Birthday Baby	200
57	London HL 8503	Yo, Yo, Walk/TUNE WEAVERS: Happy Happy Birthday Baby (78 rpm)	40
59	London HLM 8998	The Hunch/Hot Cross Buns	90
59	London HLM 8998	The Hunch/Hot Cross Buns (78 rpm)	50

GAYTONES (JAMAICA)
70	High Note HS 037	Target (actually "Musical Fight" by Crashers)/PATSY: Find Someone (song actually "True Love")	30
70	High Note HS 048	Ten To One/Another Version	12
71	High Note HS 055	Heart Of The Knights/One Toke Over The Line (B-side actually by Stranger & Gladdy)	15
71	Green Door GD 4016	Jamaican Hilite (Parts 1 & 2)	8
73	Smash SMA 2330	Blackman Kingdom Come/Swing And Dine (B-side actually by Melodians)	8
73	Action ACT 4610	Soul Makossa/Soul Makossa Part 2	8

(see also Righteous Flames, Max Romeo, Ethiopians, Jackie Brown, Jean & Gaytones, Huxbrown & Scotty, Charlie Ace, Delano Stewart, Teddy & Conquerors)

GAYTONES (U.S.)
| 73 | Action ACT 4610 | Soul Makossa/Soul Makossa (Version) | 15 |

GBH
82	Clay CLAY 8	No Survivors/Self Destruct/Big Women (p/s)	8
82	Clay CLAY 11	Sick Boy/Slit Your Own Throat/Am I Dead Yet? (p/s)	8
82	Clay CLAY 16	Give Me Fire/Mantrap (p/s)	8
82	Clay CLAY 16P	Give Me Fire/Mantrap (picture disc)	8
83	Clay CLAY 22	Catch 23/Hellhole (p/s)	8
84	Clay CLAY 36	Do What You Do/Four Men (p/s)	8
82	Clay CLAYLP 4	CITY BABY ATTACKED BY RATS (LP)	20
81	Clay PLATE 3	LEATHER, BRISTLES, STUDS AND ACNE (LP)	15

G-CLEFS
56	Columbia DB 3851	Ka-Ding Dong/Darla, My Darlin'	750
56	Columbia DB 3851	Ka-Ding Dong/Darla, My Darlin' (78 rpm)	35
61	London HLU 9433	I Understand/Little Girl I Love You	5
62	London HLU 9530	A Girl Has To Know/(There Never Was A Dog Like) Dad	10
62	London HLU 9563	Make Up Your Mind/Call Me Away	15

GEDDES AXE
80	ACS ACS 1	Return Of The Gods/Wildfire/Aftermath (p/s, with insert)	20
81	Steel City AXE 1	Sharpen Your Wits/Rock 'N' Roll (p/s)	50
82	Bullet BOLT 4	Escape From New York/Day The Wells Ran Dry/Six Six Six (12", p/s)	8

MICKEY GEE
| 77 | Sonet SON 2124 | Dr Livingstone/Jodi | 6 |

RON GEESIN
65	RRG 319/320	RON GEESIN (EP, handmade p/s, 100 only)	100
67	Transatlantic (S)TRA 161	A RAISE OF EYEBROWS (LP)	50
72	KPM KPM 1102	ELECTROSOUND (LP, library issue, 1,000 only)	50
73	Ron Geesin RON 28	AS HE STANDS (LP)	20
75	KPM KPM 1154	ELECTROSOUND VOL. 2 (LP, library issue, 1,000 only)	45
75	Ron Geesin RON 31	PATRUNS (LP)	15
77	Ron Geesin RON 323	RIGHT THROUGH (LP)	18
77	KPM KPM 1201	ATMOSPHERES (LP, library issue, 1,000 only)	30

(see also Bridget St. John, Pink Floyd, Original Downtown Syncopators, Amory Kane)

RON GEESIN & ROGER WATERS
| 70 | Harvest SHSP 4008 | MUSIC FROM THE BODY (LP, soundtrack; green labels with Waters/Geesin photos) | 50 |

(see also Roger Waters, Pink Floyd)

MAX GELDRAY
| 59 | Parlophone GEP 8764 | GOON WITH THE WIND (EP) | 10 |

HERB GELLER QUARTET
| 56 | London RE-U 1067 | SENSATIONAL SAX OF HERB GELLER (EP) | 15 |

HERB GELLER
| 75 | Atlantic SD 1681 | RHYME & REASON (LP) | 25 |

GEMAGE
| 80 | Private pressing BGA 1 | Story So Far/Bring Me Death (no p/s) | 50 |

GEMINI (PORTUGAL)
| 78 | Philips 6031 070 | Dal-Li-Dou (Falling In Love)/Dal-Li-Dou | 12 |

GEMINI (U.K.) (1)
| 65 | Columbia DB 7638 | Space Walk/Goodbye Joe (demos may credit the 'Original Tornados') | 50 |
| 69 | President PT 257 | Something Special/Never Say Die | 8 |

(see also Tornados)

GEMINI (U.K.) (2)
| 69 | President PT 257 | Never Say Die/Something Special | 6 |

GEMINI (U.K.) (3)
| 81 | Airship AP 345 | COUNTER BALANCE (LP) | 60 |

GENE
| 94 | Costermonger COST 1 | For The Dead/Child's Body (p/s, 1,994 numbered copies only) | 10 |
| 96 | Costermonger GENE 2LP | TO SEE THE LIGHTS (2-LP) | 15 |

GENE & GARY
| 09 | Kent 6T 26 | Baby Without You/PARAMOUNT FOUR: Sorry Ain't The Word | 20 |

GENE & DEBBE
67	London HLE 10165	Go With Me/Torch I Carry	8
68	London HLE 10179	Playboy/I'll Come Running	12
68	London HLE 10203	Lovin' Season/Love Will Give Us Wings	8

GENE & EUNICE
56	Vogue V 9062	I Gotta Go Home/Have You Changed Your Mind?	200
56	Vogue V 9062	I Gotta Go Home/Have You Changed Your Mind? (78)	40
57	Vogue V 9066	Move It Over, Baby/This Is My Story	150
57	Vogue V 9066	Move It Over, Baby/This Is My Story (78)	40
57	Vogue V 9071	Let's Get Together/I'm So In Love With You	150
57	Vogue V 9071	Let's Get Together/I'm So In Love With You (78)	30
57	Vogue V 9083	Doodle Doodle Doo/Don't Treat Me This Way	150
57	Vogue V 9083	Doodle Doodle Doo/Don't Treat Me This Way (78)	30
58	Vogue V 9106	I Mean Love/The Angels Gave You To Me	150
58	Vogue V 9106	I Mean Love/The Angels Gave You To Me (78)	30
58	Vogue V 9126	Strange World/The Vow	50

(The above 45s were originally issued with triangular centres; later issues with round centres are worth about half the values listed.)

58	Vogue V 9126	Strange World/The Vow (78)	40
59	Vogue V 9136	Bom Bom Lulu/Hi Diddle Diddle	100
59	Vogue V 9136	Bom Bom Lulu/Hi Diddle Diddle (78)	40
59	London HL 8956	Poco-Loco/Go-On Kokomo	50
59	London HL 8956	Poco-Loco/Go-On Kokomo (78)	60

GENE & GENTS
| 68 | Pye 7N 17532 | C'mon Everybody/Hound Dog | 10 |

GENE & JERRY
71	Mercury 6052 050	You Just Can't Win/Sho' Is Groovin'	10
71	Mercury 6052 087	Everybody Is Waiting/Ten And Two	8
71	Mercury 6338 051	ONE AND ONE (LP)	25

(see also Gene Chandler, Jerry Butler)

GENE LOVES JEZEBEL
| 82 | Situation 2 SIT 18T | Shavin' My Neck/Sun & Insanity/Machismo/Glad To Be Alive (12", p/s) | 8 |
| 82 | Situation 2 SIT 20 | Screaming (For Emaline)/So Young (Heave Hard, Heave Ho) (p/s) | 8 |

GENERAL LEVY
90	Musik Street MS 005	You Can't Hurry Love (with Junior Dunn)/JAZWAD: You Can't Hurry Dub (12", red or blue labels)	80
93	Ffrr/Fashion F214	Monkey Man (Fashion Radio Edit)/Mad Them (p/s)	20
93	Ffrr/Fashion FX 214	WICKEDER GENERAL EP (12", p/s)	25
92	Fashion FADLP 024	THE WICKEDER GENERAL (LP)	40

GENERAL STRIKE
| 79 | Canal CANAL 01 | Part 1: My Body/Part 2: (Parts Of) My Body (p/s) | 5 |

GENERATION GAP
| 69 | Pye 7N 17845 | She's Coming Home/Reach The Top | 8 |
| 70 | Pye 7N 17979 | Any Old Time You're Lonely And Sad/Rainbows 'N' Sorrows | 8 |

GENERATION X
77	Generation X GX 101	Your Generation/Listen! (white label test pressing, official bootleg sold at gigs, no p/s)	50
77	Chrysalis CHS 2165	Your Generation/Day By Day (p/s, original copies with 'A' on label with band credits on front)	6
77	Chrysalis CHS 2165	Your Generation/Day By Day (p/s)	5
77	Chrysalis CHS 2165	Your Generation/Day By Day (sleeve only, unissued, featuring 'pre-peroxide' Billy Idol; 1 copy known to exist)	500
77	Chrysalis CHS 2189	Wild Youth/Wild Dub (Version) (p/s)	5
77	Chrysalis CHS 2189	Wild Youth/Wild Dub (Version) (p/s, mispressing, plays "No No No", B-side matrix: CHS 2189 B/1)	40
78	Chrysalis CHS 2207	Ready Steady Go/No No No (p/s)	5
79	Chrysalis CHS(A) 2261	King Rocker/Gimme Some Truth (pink vinyl, Tony James p/s)	5
79	Chrysalis CHS(B) 2261	King Rocker/Gimme Some Truth (red vinyl, Billy Idol p/s)	5
79	Chrysalis CHS(C) 2261	King Rocker/Gimme Some Truth (yellow vinyl, Mark Laff p/s)	7
79	Chrysalis CHS(D) 2261	King Rocker/Gimme Some Truth (orange vinyl, Bob Andrews p/s)	6
79	Chrysalis CHS 2261	King Rocker/Gimme Some Truth (black vinyl, Bob Andrews p/s)	5
79	Chrysalis CHS 2330	Friday's Angels/Trying For Kicks/This Heat (p/s, black vinyl)	15
81	Chrysalis CHS 2488	Dancing With Myself/Untouchables/King Rocker/Rock On (as Gen X, p/s, on clear vinyl)	8
78	Chrysalis CHR 1169	GENERATION X (LP, with 'T-shirt offer' wraparound)	25

(see also Billy Idol, Sigue Sigue Sputnik, Empire, Westworld)

GENERATOR (FEATURING GARY NUMAN)
| 94 | JVO JVOT 001 | Are 'Friends' Electric? (Eccentric Mix)/Bring Back The Love/ Going Home (12", p/s) | 8 |

(see also Gary Numan)

GENESIS
SINGLES
68	Decca F 12735	The Silent Sun/That's Me	400
68	Decca F 12735	The Silent Sun/That's Me (promo copy)	325
68	Decca F 12775	A Winter's Tale/One Eyed Hound	375
68	Decca F 12775	A Winter's Tale/One Eyed Hound (promo copy)	350
68	London F12775	A Winter's Tale/One Eyed Hound (export promo single)	500
69	Decca F 12949	Where The Sour Turns To Sweet/In Hiding	400

MINT VALUE £

69	Decca F 12949	Where The Sour Turns To Sweet/In Hiding (promo copy)	375
70	Charisma GS 1/2	Looking For Someone/Visions Of Angels (promo only)	600
71	Charisma CB 152	The Knife (Parts 1 & 2) (in p/s)	450
71	Charisma CB 152	The Knife (Parts 1 & 2)	100
72	Charisma CB 181	Happy The Man/Seven Stones (some belated copies in p/s; beware counterfeits)	450
72	Charisma CB 181	Happy The Man/Seven Stones	100
72	Charisma CB 181	Happy The Man/Seven Stones (promo copy)	150
73	Charisma (no cat. no.)	Twilight Alehouse (1-sided flexidisc free with Zig Zag)	35
73	Charisma (no cat. no.)	Twilight Alehouse (1-sided flexidisc free with Zig Zag & later via fan club, without magazine)	20
73	Charisma (no cat. no.)	Twilight Alehouse (black vinyl, white label test pressings)	70
73	Charisma (no cat. no.)	Twilight Alehouse (1-sided flexidisc free via fan club, with letter, sticker, poster and Genesis "revolver")	80
74	Charisma CB 224	I Know What I Like (In Your Wardrobe)/Twilight Alehouse	8
74	Charisma CB 224	I Know What I Like (In Your Wardrobe)/Twilight Alehouse (promos with press release)	100
74	Charisma CB 238	Counting Out Time/Riding The Scree	10
74	Charisma CB 238	Counting Out Time/Counting Out Time (promo)	60
75	Charisma CB 251	The Carpet Crawlers/The Waiting Room (Evil Jam)	25
75	Charisma CB 251	The Carpet Crawlers/The Waiting Room (Evil Jam) (promos copies)	65
76	Charisma CB 277	A Trick Of The Tail/Ripples (purple label)	8
77	Charisma CB 300	Your Own Special Way/It's Yourself	5
78	Charisma CB 309	Follow You, Follow Me/Ballad Of Big (p/s)	5
78	Charisma CB 315	Many Too Many/The Day The Light Went Out/Vancouver (p/s)	5
80	Charisma CB 369	Misunderstanding/Evidence Of Autumn (p/s)	5
81	Charisma CB 391	Keep It Dark/Naminanu (p/s)	5
82	Charisma CB 393	Man On The Corner/Submarine (blue label, with p/s)	5
82	Charisma CB 393	Man On The Corner/Submarine (blue label, without p/s)	5
82	Lyntone LYN 11806	The Lady Lies (live) (green flexidisc free with Flexipop mag, issue 21)	10
83	Lyntone LYN 13143	Firth Of Fifth (live edit) (flexidisc, with numbered gatefold p/s)	15
83	Charisma/Virgin TATA Y-1	That's All/Taking It All Too Hard (shaped picture disc)	12
84	Charisma/Virgin ALS 1	Illegal Alien/Turn It On Again (live) (shaped picture disc)	12
84	Charisma/Virgin CB 300	Your Own Special Way/It's Yourself (blue label reissue, no p/s)	6
84	Charisma/Virgin CB 356	Turn It On Again/Behind The Lines Part 2 (blue label reissue, no p/s)	6
84	Charisma/Virgin CB 369	Misunderstanding/Evidence Of Autumn (blue label reissue, no p/s)	6
86	Charisma/Virgin	In Too Deep (Unedited)/Do The Neurotic (Unedited) (12" picture disc in stickered sleeve)	8
86	Virgin SNEG 3-12	Land Of Confusion/Land Of Confusion (Extended)/Feeding The Fire/ Do The Neurotic (CD, gatefold p/s)	10
87	Virgin CDEP 1	Tonight, Tonight, Tonight (Edit)/In The Glow Of The Night/ Invisible Touch (12" Remix)/Tonight, Tonight, Tonight (CD, gatefold p/s)	40
88	Charisma/Virgin CDT 40	SPOT THE PIGEON EP (Match Of The Day/Pigeons/Inside And Out) (3" CD, card sleeve)	15
88	Charisma/Virgin CDF 40	SPOT THE PIGEON EP (Match Of The Day/Pigeons/Inside And Out) (5" export CD, card sleeve)	15
89	Virgin VVD 359	Domino: (Part 1) In The Glow Of The Night/(Part 2) The Last Domino (3" CD free with "Invisible Touch Tour" video)	15
92	Virgin GENS 10	Invisible Touch (live)/Abacab (live) (no'd gatefold p/s)	8
98	Virgin SOLO2	Live Rehearsal: Mama (live)/Calling All Stations (live)/Invisible Touch (live)/ Follow You, Follow Me (live)/Turn It On Again (live) (CD 5-track promo)	40

ALBUMS

69	Decca LK 4990	FROM GENESIS TO REVELATION (mono, with 'mono' peephole, with red/pink lyric sheet, red/silver unboxed logo)	1000
69	Decca SKL 4990	FROM GENESIS TO REVELATION (stereo, with stereo 'peephole', with lyric sheet, unboxed logo)	400
70	Decca SKL 4990	FROM GENESIS TO REVELATION (stereo, with lyric sheet, blue/silver boxed logo)	70
70	Decca KSKC 4990	FROM GENESIS TO REVELATION (tape, boxed logo)	35
70	Charisma CAS 1020	TRESPASS (original pink scroll label & gatefold sleeve with lyric sheet)	80
71	Charisma CAS 1052	NURSERY CRYME (LP, textured sleeve, original pink scroll label, gatefold sleeve)	80
72	Charisma CAS 1058	FOXTROT (LP, gatefold sleeve, large 'Mad Hatter' logo and B&C credit on label)	30
73	Charisma CAS 1074	SELLING ENGLAND BY THE POUND (LP, insert, large 'Mad Hatter' logo)	25
73	Charisma CLASS 1	LIVE (LP, non laminated sleeve, large 'Mad Hatter' logo, with 'Charisma Live Giants - £1.99' sticker on front cover)	30
73	Charisma CLASS 1	LIVE (LP, non laminated sleeve, large 'Mad Hatter' logo)	25
74	Charisma CGS 101	THE LAMB LIES DOWN ON BROADWAY (2-LP, small 'Mad Hatter' label, original pressing with "Marketed by B&C..." label text on both LPs and "Printed and Made by Bruin B.V. Zaandam/Holland" credit on sleeve, some with Gold Chase contest insert)	75
74	Decca SKL 4990	IN THE BEGINNING (reissue of 1st LP, 'snake' sleeve with lyric insert)	20
75	Charisma CGS 102	GENESIS COLLECTION VOLUME ONE (2-LP, boxed set of Trespass & "Nursery Cryme" in original sleeves, with poster)	95
75	Charisma CGS 103	GENESIS COLLECTION VOLUME TWO (2-LP, boxed set of Foxtrot & "Selling England By The Pound", with poster)	95
91	Virgin Edits 1	WE CAN'T DANCE (CD, 6 track promo - tour edition marketed by Volkswagon)	50
91	Virgin GEN CD	WE CAN'T DANCE (CD & tape, housed in custom promo box With three hand numbered watercolours)	90
93	Virgin GENBOX1	LIVE: THE WAY WE WALK (2xCD in wooden box with certificate & badge (1000 only)	120
97	Virgin GENLP6	CALLING ALL STATIONS (2xLP fourth sided etched with band picture)	60
98	Virgin CDBOX6	GENESIS ARCHIVE 1967 – 1975 (4 CD Box Set)	30
98	Virgin CDBOX98	GENESIS ARCHIVE 1967 - 1975 (CD 12-track promo digipack)	30
98	Virgin VCDJBOX98	GENESIS ARCHIVE 1967 - 1975 The Interviews (2xCD promo, p/s)	65
99	Virgin VGP 000270	TURN IT ON AGAIN - THE HITS (CD, in store promo p/s - each song played for 1 min)	50
00	Virgin CDBOX7	GENESIS ARCHIVE 2: 1976 - 1992 (3xCD Box Set)	50
07	EMI CDBOX12	GENESIS 1976 - 1882 (2007 UK 12 disc set comprising of 6 Hybrid SA CD's)	70
07	EMI CDBOX13	GENESIS 1983 - 1998 (2007 UK 10 disc set comprising of 5 Hybrid SA CD's)	60
08	Virgin LPBOX 14	1970 - 1975 (6-LP box set, inners & inserts)	80

(see also Flaming Youth, Phil Collins, Mike Rutherford, Peter Gabriel, Steve Hackett, Anthony Phillips, Brand X, Quiet World)

GENEVA

80	Valiant ROUND1	2.30/Geneva Street (p/s)	10

GENEVEVE

66	CBS 202061	Once/Just A Whisper (in p/s)	20
66	CBS 202061	Once/Just A Whisper	25
66	CBS 202096	Nothing In The World/Summer Days	9
67	CBS 202524	That Can't Be Bad/I Love Him, I Need Him	9

GENGHIS KHAN (GERMANY)
| 79 | CBS 12-7317 | Genghis Khan/Desert Land (12", clear vinyl with p/s insert) | 8 |

GENGHIS KHAN (U.K.)
| 83 | Genghis Khan GK 1 | DOUBLE DEALIN' (If Heaven Is Hell/Highway Passion//Midnight Rendezvous Mean Streak) (EP, double pack) | 80 |
| 83 | Wabbit WAB 61/63 | Love You/Lady Lady/Mongol Nation/Gone For A Drive (double pack) | 40 |

GENOCIDE
| 79 | Safari SAP 2 | IMAGES OF DELUSION (EP) | 10 |

GENOCIDE EXIT
| 80 | Slam SEM 016 | FUTURE VIBES (EP) | 10 |

GENOCIDES
| 82 | Action TAKE 1 | IS THAT ALRIGHT? - tracks are Come Again (You Make Me Wanna)/Born To Lose (p/s) | 5 |

GENTILES (JAMAICA)
| 70 | High Note HS 046 | Your Destiny/Lock Love Away (actually by Melodians) | 10 |

(see also Melodians)

GENTILES (U.K.)
| 68 | Pye 7N 17530 | Goodbye Baby/Marlena | 8 |

GENTLE DESPITE
| 90 | Sarah SARAH 26 | THE DARKEST BLUE EP (p/s, insert) | 8 |
| 91 | Sarah SARAH 45 | Torment To Me/Bittersweet Kiss/Shadow Of A Girl (p/s, insert) | 8 |

JOHNNY GENTLE
59	Philips PB 908	Wendy/Boys And Girls (Were Meant For Each Other)	10
59	Philips PB 945	Milk From The Coconut/I Like The Way	5
60	Philips PB 988	Darlin' Won't You Wait/This Friendly World	5
60	Philips PB 1069	After My Laughter Came Tears/Sonja	5
61	Philips PB 1142	Pick A Star/Darlin'	5
59	Philips BBE 12345	THE GENTLE TOUCH (EP)	35

(see also Darren Young)

TIM GENTLE & HIS GENTLEMEN
| 65 | Oriole CB 1988 | Without You/Someone's In The Kitchen With Dinah | 15 |

GENTLE GIANT
73	WWA WWP 1001	In A Glass House/An Inmate's Lullaby	12
74	WWA WWS 017	The Power And The Glory/Playing The Game	12
77	Chrysalis CHS 2160	I'm Turning Around/Just The Same (live)	6
70	Vertigo 6360 020	GENTLE GIANT (LP, 1st pressing, gatefold sleeve, large swirl label)	250
71	Vertigo 6360 020	GENTLE GIANT (LP, 2nd pressing, gatefold sleeve, small swirl label)	70
71	Vertigo 6360 041	ACQUIRING THE TASTE (LP, gatefold sleeve, small swirl label)	175
72	Vertigo 6360 070	THREE FRIENDS (LP, 1st pressing, no "made in England" under 1972 on top right hand side of label, gatefold sleeve, small swirl label)	120
72	Vertigo 6360 070	THREE FRIENDS (LP, 2nd pressing, "made in England" under 1972 on top right hand side of label, gatefold sleeve, small swirl label)	40
72	Vertigo 6360 080	OCTOPUS (LP, gatefold sleeve, small swirl label)	150
73	WWA WWA 002	IN A GLASS HOUSE (LP, silk-screen cover, with photo insert & lyric inner)	50
74	WWA WWA 010	THE POWER AND THE GLORY (LP, with insert, sleeve has 2 rounded corners)	40
75	Vertigo 6360 020	GENTLE GIANT (LP, reissue, gatefold sleeve, spaceship label)	15
75	Vertigo 6641 334	GIANT STEPS - (THE FIRST FIVE YEARS) 1970-1975 (2-LP, gatefold sleeve, spaceship label)	15
75	Chrysalis CHR 1093	FREE HAND (LP, lyric insert, green label)	15
76	Chrysalis CHR 1115	INTERVIEW (LP, green label, with lyric inner sleeve)	12
77	Vertigo 9286 946	PRETENTIOUS (2-LP, gatefold sleeve)	15
77	Chrysalis CTY 1133	LIVE (PLAYING THE FOOL) (2-LP, with 12-page booklet)	20
77	Chrysalis CHR 1152	THE MISSING PIECE (LP, with inner sleeve)	15
78	Chrysalis CHR 1186	GIANT FOR A DAY (LP, with mask insert & lyric inner sleeve)	15
80	Chrysalis CHR 1285	CIVILIAN (LP, with lyric inner sleeve)	15

(see also Simon Dupree & Big Sound, Moles)

GENTLE INFLUENCE
| 69 | Pye 7N 17666 | Never Trust In Tomorrow/Easy To Love | 15 |
| 69 | Pye 7N 17743 | Always Be A Part Of My Living/Captain Reale | 22 |

GENTLE PEOPLE (1)
| 67 | Columbia DB 8276 | It's Too Late/Sea Of Heartbreak | 12 |

GENTLE PEOPLE (2)
95	Rephlex CAT 040R	JOURNEY (12", Aphex Twin Remix)	8
97	Rephlex CAT 045 LP	SOUNDTRACKS FOR LIVING (2-LP)	15
99	Rephlex CAT 088 LP	SIMPLY FABOO (2-LP)	15

GENTLE POWER OF SONG
| 67 | Polydor 56211 | Constant Penelope/A Court Garden Party, Circa 1580 | 8 |
| 67 | Polydor 2310 285 | CIRCUS (LP) | 25 |

GENTLE RAIN
| 73 | Polydor 2310 285 | MOODY (LP) | 175 |

GENTLE RESPITE
| 90 | Sarah SARAH 026 | DARKEST BLUE EP: Summer In Me/Darkest Blue/If I Touch (wraparound p/s, with insert) | 15 |

BILL GENTLES
69	Gas GAS 104	Long Life/SCHOOLBOYS: O Tell Me	10
70	Pama PM 801	What A Woman/Sleepy Cat	8
70	Punch PH 54	Fight The Good Fight/Fight Beat	8
71	Escort ERT 853	Bachelor Boy/SCORPIONS: Colour Rites	8
72	Bullet BU 506	Pure In Heart/Clean Hands	6

(see also Bill Jentles, Bill Jenties)

GENTLE TOUCH
| 65 | London HLR 10175 | Among The First To Know/Merry Go Round | 7 |
| 83 | Tristar TRI3 | Dreams Of You/Dreams Of You (Instrumental) | 6 |

GENTRY
70	Dolphin DO571	Long Road/Sing Me A Sad Song/Attempt Contact (EP, Irish pressing)	250

ART GENTRY
72	Mojo 2092 048	Breakthrough/Wonderful Dream	15

BO GENTRY & RITCHIE CORDELL
69	CBS 4299	Stone Go-Getter/Hung Up	5

BOBBIE GENTRY
67	Capitol CL 15511	Ode To Billie Joe/Mississippi Delta	5
67	Capitol (S)T 2830	ODE TO BILLIE JOE (LP)	12
68	Capitol ST2964	LOCAL GENTRY (LP)	12
68	Capitol (S)T 2842	THE DELTA SWEETE (LP)	12
69	Capitol E-(S)T 155	TOUCH 'EM WITH LOVE (LP)	12
70	Capitol ST21609	I'LL NEVER FALL IN LOVE AGAIN (LP)	12
71	Capitol E-ST494	PATCHWORK (LP)	12

GENTRY ICE
88	Jack Trax JTX 15	Do You Wanna Jack/Lost In The Sound (with Adonis) (12")	20

GENTRYS
65	MGM MGM 1284	Keep On Dancing/Make Up Your Mind	20
66	MGM MGM 1296	Brown Paper Sack/Spread It On Thick	25
66	MGM MGM 1312	Everyday I Have To Cry/Don't Let It Be	15
68	Bell BLL 1012	I Can't Go Back To Denver/You Better Come Home	8

GENTS
81	Posh POSH 001	The Faker/The Pink Panther	20
82	Kosmic KOS 6886	Schooldays/True Stories (p/s)	8
83	Posh POSH 007	Revenge/Girl (p/s)	5
85	Posh no cat. no.	Lambs To The Slaughter/Friday On My Mind	5
85	Lambs To The Slaughter GN7	Shout/The Faker (p/s)	5
80s	Posh MEGA 1	Revenge/Over Me/The Gent (p/s)	5
77	GG no cat. no.	HOW IT ALL BEGAN (LP)	12

GEOFFREY
78	Music Bank BECK 694	ABH (Who Wants To Listen To Punk Rock?)/Colt 45 Rock (p/s)	15

GEORDIE
72	Regal Zonophone RZ 3067	Don't Do That/Francis Was A Rocker	5
82	EMI EMI 2031	Can You Do It/Red Eyed Lady	20
73	EMI EMC 3001	HOPE YOU LIKE IT (LP)	30
74	EMI EMA 764	DON'T BE FOOLED BY THE NAME (LP)	40
76	EMI EMC 3134	SAVE THE WORLD (LP)	20
83	Neat NEAT 1008	NO SWEAT (LP)	20

(see also Influence, AC/DC)

BARBARA GEORGE
62	London HL 9513	I Know (You Don't Love Me No More)/Love (Is Just A Chance You Take)	25
64	Sue WI 316	Send For Me/Bless You	50

EARL GEORGE
73	Count Shelly CS 025	Gonna Give Her All The Love/PRINCE JAZZBO: Wise Shepherd	6
76	Terminal TM 103	Love Depression/Love Is Something	8
76	Terminal TM 106	So Many Ways/Part 2	8

GEORGE GOLDEN
64	R&B JB145	Fire In My Feet/ One More Chance	15
64	R&B JB157	Don't You Know/ Nancy Tell Me	15

LLOYD GEORGE
62	London HLP 9562	Lucy Lee/Sing Real Loud	75

GEORGETTES
58	London HL 8548	Love Like A Fool/Oh Tonight	50
58	London HL 8548	Love Like A Fool/Oh Tonight (78)	30
60	Pye International 7N 25058	Down By The River/A Pair Of Eyes	10

GEORGIA SLIM/WALTER ROLAND
59	Jazz Collector JEL 2	THE MALE BLUES VOL. 1 (EP)	10

GEORGIA TOM
60s	Riverside RLP 8803	GEORGIA TOM AND FRIENDS (LP)	20

(see also Paramount Allstars)

GEORGIE'S VARSITY 5
61	Vogue Pop V 9189	When My Sugar Walks Down The Street/Five Foot Two, Eyes Of Blue	10

GERALDINE
71	Beltona Sword SBE 128	GERALDINE (LP)	130

GERALDO 1969
69	Morgan MRS 22	QE2/Hello Again	8

WESLEY GERMS
72	Upsetter US 390	Whiplash/UPSETTERS: Whiplash Version	12

GERONIMO BLACK
72	Uni UNLS 126	GERONIMO BLACK (LP)	40

(see also Frank Zappa/Mothers Of Invention)

DENNY GERRARD
70	Deram Nova DN 10	SINISTER MORNING (LP, mono, with High Tide)	150
70	Deram Nova SDN 10	SINISTER MORNING (LP, stereo, with High Tide)	100

(see also Warm Sounds, High Tide, Open Road, Fifth Avenue)

GERRY & THE HOLOGRAMS
79	Absurd ABSURD 4	Gerry And The Holograms/Increased Resistance (p/s)	15
79	Absurd ABSURD 5	The Emperor's New Music (unplayable record, glued into p/s)	8

GERRY & THE PACEMAKERS

63	Columbia DB 4987	How Do You Do It?/Away From You	5
63	Columbia DB 7041	I Like It/It's Happened To Me	5
63	Columbia DB 7126	You'll Never Walk Alone/It's All Right	5
64	Columbia DB 7189	I'm The One/You've Got What I Like	5
64	Columbia DB 7268	Don't Let The Sun Catch You Crying/Show Me That You Care	6
64	Columbia DB 7353	It's Gonna Be Alright/It's Just Because	7
64	Columbia DB 7437	Ferry Cross The Mersey/You You You	5
65	Columbia DB 7504	I'll Be There/Baby, You're So Good To Me	5
65	Columbia DB 7738	Walk Hand In Hand/Dreams	5
66	Columbia DB 7835	La La La/Without You	8
66	Columbia DB 8044	Girl On A Swing/A Fool To Myself	8
74	DJM DJS 298	Remember (The Days Of Rock And Roll)/There's Still Time	10
63	Columbia SEG 8257	HOW DO YOU DO IT? (EP)	12
64	Columbia SEG 8295	YOU'LL NEVER WALK ALONE (EP, in misprinted sleeve listing "It's All Right" instead of "Jambalaya" on front)	25
64	Columbia SEG 8295	YOU'LL NEVER WALK ALONE (EP)	15
64	Columbia SEG 8311	I'M THE ONE (EP)	15
64	Columbia SEG 8346	DON'T LET THE SUN CATCH YOU CRYING (EP)	15
64	Columbia SEG 8367	IT'S GONNA BE ALRIGHT (EP)	20
65	Columbia SEG 8388	GERRY IN CALIFORNIA (EP)	30
65	Columbia SEG 8397	HITS FROM 'FERRY CROSS THE MERSEY' (EP)	30
65	Columbia SEG 8426	RIP IT UP (EP)	35
63	Columbia 33SX 1546	HOW DO YOU LIKE IT? (LP, mono)	20
63	Columbia 33SCX 1546	HOW DO YOU LIKE IT? (LP, stereo)	30
65	Columbia 33SX 1693	FERRY CROSS THE MERSEY (LP, soundtrack, with Cilla Black & Fourmost, mono)	25
65	Columbia 33SCX 1693	FERRY CROSS THE MERSEY (LP, soundtrack, with Cilla Black & Fourmost, stereo)	35
65	EMI Regal REG 2018	YOU'LL NEVER WALK ALONE (LP, export issue)	25

(see also Gerry Marsden)

GERVASE

68	Decca F12822	Pepper Grinder/Visions	20

GESCOM

94	Skam SKA 2	Dan One/Five/Cicada/Sciew Spo (12", card folder p/s)	35
95	Skam SKA 3	Snackwitch/Mag (12", bubblewrap sleeve with insert)	40
95	Skam SKA 3	Snackwitch/Mag (12", second issue, black sleeve)	20
95	Clear CLR 408	THE SOUNDS OF MACHINES OUR PARENTS USED (12", p/s)	35
96	Skam SKA 7	KEY NELL 1/2/3/4 (12", bubblewrap sleeve)	15
98	Skam SKA010 THAT	THAT (EP) (12", p/s 2 inserts)	15
98	Sakm SKA010 THIS	THIS (EP) (12", p/s)	15
96	Warp WAP 88	Keynell/Keynell (12", p/s, remixes by Autechre)	10

(see also Autechre, Ad Vance Vs Gescom)

GESTURES

65	Stateside SS 379	Run Run Run/It Seems To Me	25

STAN GETZ (QUARTET/QUINTET)

62	HMV POP 1061	Disafinado/Jazz Theme From Dr. Kildare	5
64	Verve VS 520	The Girl From Ipanema (with JOAO GILBERTO)/Blowin' In The Wind	5
54	Vogue EPV 1016	STAN GETZ QUARTET (EP)	10
53	Esquire 20-007	STAN GETZ PLAYS (LP, 10")	25
54	Vogue LDE 089	AT STORYVILLE (LP, 10")	25
55	Vogue LDE 147	STAN GETZ QUARTET (LP, 10")	25
55	Columbia Clef 33CX 10000	AT THE SHRINE NO. 1 (LP, as Stan Getz Quintet)	18
55	Columbia Clef 33CX 10001	AT THE SHRINE NO. 2 (LP, as Stan Getz Quintet)	18
62	HMV CLP 1577	FOCUS (LP, also stereo CSD 1448)	15
63	Verve VLP 9013	JAZZ SAMBA (LP, with Charlie Byrd, mono)	12
63	Verve (S)VLP 9013	JAZZ SAMBA (LP, with Charlie Byrd, stereo)	15
63	Verve VLP 9024	BIG BAND BOSSA NOVA (LP)	12
63	Verve VLP 9038	JAZZ SAMBA ENCORE! (LP, with Luiz Bonfa, mono)	12
63	Verve (S)VLP 9038	JAZZ SAMBA ENCORE! (LP, with Luiz Bonfa, stereo)	15
64	Verve VLP 9065	GETZ-GILBERTO (LP)	12
65	MGM MGM-C 8001	MICKEY ONE (LP, soundtrack, mono, with booklet)	20
65	MGM MGM-C(S) 8001	MICKEY ONE (LP, soundtrack, stereo, with booklet)	25

(see also Dizzy Gillespie, Gil Fuller & Dizzy Gillespie, Astrud Gilberto, Joao Gilberto, Johnny Smith)

G-FORCE

80	Jet JET 183	Hot Gossip/Because Of Your Love (p/s)	20
80	Jet JET 194	You/Trust Your Lovin' (no p/s)	12
80	Jet JET 7005	White Knuckles/Rockin' And Rollin'/I Look At You (p/s)	15
80	Jet JETLP 229	G-FORCE (LP, with inner sleeve and patch)	20
80	Jet JETPD 229	G-FORCE (LP, picture disc)	18

(see also Gary Moore)

G.G. ALLSTARS

70	Explosion EX 2012	Champion/MAYTONES: Funny Man	10
70	Explosion EX 2014	Barabus/This Kind Of Life	10
70	Explosion EX 2023	Man From Carolina/Gold On Your Dress (B-side actually by Slickers)	10
70	Explosion EX 2024	African Melody/Serious Love (B-side actually by Maytones)	8
70	Explosion EX 2025	Ganja Plane/Deep River	8
70	Gas GAS 153	So Alive/Mercy Mr D.J.	8
70	Escort ERT 835	African Melody/Man From Carolina	7
70	G.G. GG 4501	Music Keep On Playing (actually by Cornell Campbell)/ Music Keep On Playing Version	7
71	G.G. GG 4508	Cleanliness Version 2/MAYTONES: Cleanliness	7
71	G.G. GG 4510	Rocking On The G.G. Beat (actually by Maytones)/WINSTON WRIGHT: Rocking On The G.G. Beat Version II	8
71	G.G. GG 4511	Lonely Nights (actually by Eric Donaldson & West Indians)/ MAYTONES: Let The Version Play	8
71	G.G. GG 4513	All One Nation (actually by Maytones)/VAL BENNETT: Judgement Warrant	8
71	G.G. GG 4526	Rod Of Righteousness (actually "Stretch Forth His Hand" by Jah Huntly)/ DENNIS ALCAPONE: King Of Kings (B-side actually "King Of Glory")	20
72	G.G. GG 4530	Donkey Face Version/MAYTONES: Donkey Face	8
72	Pama PM 846	I'm Feeling Lonely Version/MAYTONES: I'm Feeling Lonely	6

73	Bullet BU 528	People Get Funny Version/MAYTONES: People Get Funny	6
70	Trojan TBL 129	MAN FROM CAROLINA (LP)	30

(see also Paulette & Gee, Billy Dyce, Maytones, Charlie Ace, Monty Morris, Starlights, Lloyd & Carey, Gladdy & Stranger, Heptones, Shorty Perry, Barbara Jones)

G.G.F.H.
94	Peaceville CC8	Welcome To The Process/Too Much Punch/Dread (green vinyl, p/s)	15

G.G. RHYTHM SECTION
69	Blue Cat BS 165	T.N.T./MAYTONES: Botheration	30

AMOS GHERKIN QUARTET
70	Parlophone R 5872	Blakey And Me/Theme From An Unmade Silent Movie	8

GHETTO CHILDREN
73	CBS 1450	I Just Gotta Find Somebody To Love Me/Rat-A-Tat-Tat	10

GHETTO TEARS
84	Ghetto Tears GT 001	Ghetto Children/Ghetto Prayers (12" p/s)	80

WESS & DORI GHEZZI
74	Bradleys BRAD 7404	Let It Be Free/Turn Around	7
75	Bradleys BRAD 7515	Fallin'/Era	8

GHOST
69	Gemini GMS 007	When You're Dead/Indian Maid	20
70	Gemini GMS 014	I've Got To Get To Know You/For One Second	30
70	Gemini GME 1004	WHEN YOU'RE DEAD - ONE SECOND (LP, laminated front cover, with extra track, "I've Got To Get To Know Her")	450
70	Gemini GME 1004	WHEN YOU'RE DEAD - ONE SECOND (LP, laminated front cover, without extra track, "I've Got To Get To Know Her")	350
87	Bam Caruso KIRI 077	FOR ONE SECOND (LP, reissue of "When You're Dead" with extra track)	12

(see also Velvett Fogg, Shirley Kent, Virginia Tree, Wizzard)

GHOST DANCE
86	Karbon KAR 604	The Grip Of Love/Where Spirits Fly (p/s)	8
88	Karbon KAR XL 303	GATHERING DUST (LP)	15

(see also Skeletal Family, All About Eve, Sisters Of Mercy)

GHOSTS
80	Arista ARIST 347	My Town/I'm Your Man (no p/s)	8

BILL GIANT
61	MGM MGM 1135	Better Let Her Go/When I Grow Too Old To Dream	12

BILLY GIANT
65	Pye 25337	Leave My Girl Alone/Nice Girls	20

GIANT CRAB
68	Uni UN 509	Hot Line Conversation/E.S.P.	35

GIANT HAYSTACKS
83	BSB BSB 01	Baby I Need You/Baby I Need You (Instrumental) (p/s)	7

GIANTS
60s	Polydor LPHM 46426	IN GERMANY (LP, mono)	25
60s	Polydor SLPHM 237626	IN GERMANY (LP, stereo)	30

GIANT SIZE C
91	Afrocentric AFRO 1	Perspective (12")	35
93	Afrocentric AFRO 3	Hate (12")	12

GIANT SUNFLOWER
67	CBS 2805	February Sunshine/Big Apple	20
67	CBS 3033	Mark Twain/What's So Good About Goodbye?	10

BARRY GIBB
70	Polydor 2058 030	I'll Kiss Your Memory/This Time	8

(see also Bee Gees)

MAURICE GIBB
70	Polydor 2058 013	Railroad/I've Come Back	8

(see also Bee Gees, Fut)

ROBIN GIBB
69	Polydor 56337	Saved By The Bell/Alexandria Good Time (withdrawn)	20
69	Polydor 56368	One Million Years/Weekend	8
70	Polydor 56371	August October/Give Me A Smile	7
69	Polydor 583 085	ROBIN'S REIGN (LP)	25

(see also Bee Gees)

DOUG GIBBONS
65	Decca F 12122	I Got My Tears To Remind Me/I Found Out	6

STEVE GIBBONS (BAND)
71	Wizard WIZ 102	Alright Now/Lay Some Lovin' Down	10
77	Polydor 2058 889	Tulane/Now You Know Me	7
82	RCA RCA 174	Loving Me, Loving You/That Makes It Tough/No Money Down (picture disc)	5
71	Wizard SWZA 5501	SHORT STORIES (LP, gatefold sleeve, lyric insert, yellow vinyl)	80
71	Wizard SWZA 5501	SHORT STORIES (LP, gatefold sleeve, lyric insert, black vinyl)	30

(see also Uglys, Magic Christians, B,L&G)

CALY GIBBS
71	Amalgamated AMG 870	Seeing Is Believing/JOE GIBBS ALLSTARS: Ghost Capturer	30

(see also Carlton Gibbs)

CARLTON GIBBS
70	Amalgamated AMG 872	Ghost Walk/Joy Stick	30

GEORGIA GIBBS
55	Vogue Coral Q 72088	Ballin' The Jack/I Still Feel The Same About You	10
56	Vogue Coral Q 72182	If I Were A Bell/I'll Know	10

57	RCA RCA 1011	Sugar Candy/I'm Walking The Floor Over You	10
58	RCA RCA 1029	Great Balls Of Fire/I Miss You	35
58	Mercury 7MT 210	Arriverderci Roma/24 Hours A Day	10
58	Columbia DB 4201	The Hula Hoop Song/Keep In Touch	8
59	Columbia DB 4259	The Hucklebuck/Better Loved You'll Never Be	8
60	London HLP 9098	The Stroll That Stole My Heart/Seven Lonely Days	8
65	Stateside SS 423	Let Me Cry On Your Shoulder/Venice Blues	8
55	Mercury EP-1-3265	THE MAN THAT GOT AWAY (EP)	10
56	Mercury MEP 9505	SWEET GEORGIA GIBBS (EP)	10
57	Mercury MEP 9516	SWEET GEORGIA GIBBS VOL. 2 (EP)	10
56	Mercury MPT 7500	SINGS THE OLDIES (10" LP)	20
57	Mercury MPT 7511	HER NIBS MISS GIBBS (10" LP)	20
57	Mercury MPL 6508	SWINGING WITH HER NIBS (LP)	20

JOE GIBBS (& DESTROYERS)

68	Amslgamated AMG 822	People Grudgeful (as Sir Joe)/Pan-Ya Machete (actually the Pioneers)	50
70	Amalgamated AMG 855	Nevada Joe (act. by Johnny Lover)/Straight To The Head (act. by Destroyers)	50
70	Amalgamated AMG 858	Franco Nero (actually by Count Machuki & Destroyers)/ Version Two (actually by Destroyers)	25
70	Amalgamated AMG 859	Rock The Clock/Version Two	50
70	Amalgamated AMG 860	Let It Be/Turn Back The Hands Of Time (both actually by Nicky Thomas)	18
70	Amalgamated AMG 861	La La/Reggae Fever (as Joe Gibbs All Stars)	40
70	Amalgamated AMG 865	Hijacked/Life Is Down In Denver	50
70	Amalgamated AMG 867	Movements/Caesar	40
70	Amalgamated AMG 869	Perfect Born Yah/Red Red Wine (as Jo Gibs All Stars)	20
70	Amalgamated AMG 868	Gift Of God (actually by Lizzy)/The Rapper	12
70	Pressure Beat PR 5504	News Flash/Version Two	12
72	Pressure Beat DB5513	Money In My Pocket/Money Love	25
73	Jackpot JP 811	Ration/Version (as Joe Gibbs All Stars)	8
78	Lightning LIP 10	AFRICAN DUB ALMIGHTY (LP, with The Professionals)	20

(see also Lizzy, Reggae Boys, Bunny Flip, Destroyers, Dennis Brown, Caly Gibbs, Nicky Thomas)

MICHAEL GIBBS

70	Deram DML/SML 1063	MICHAEL GIBBS (LP)	50
71	Deram SML 1087	TANGLEWOOD '63 (LP)	50
72	Polydor 2683 011	JUST AHEAD (2-LP)	35
74	Polydor 2383 252	IN THE PUBLIC INTEREST (LP, with Gary Burton)	35
70s	Bronze ILPS 9353	ONLY CHROME ... WATERFALL (LP)	15

(see also Neil Ardley, Gary Burton)

TERRY GIBBS SEXTET

| 56 | Vogue Coral LVA 9013 | TERRY (LP) | 20 |
| 56 | Vogue Coral LVA 9009 | JAZZTIME USA (LP, as Terry Gibbs Quartet & Sextet) | 20 |

(see also Terry Gibbs Big Band)

TERRY GIBBS BIG BAND

59	Mercury CMS 18016	LAUNCHING A NEW BAND (LP)	15
61	HMV/Verve CLP 1560	THE EXCITING TERRY GIBBS BIG BAND (LP, mono)	12
61	HMV/Verve CSD 1439	THE EXCITING TERRY GIBBS BIG BAND (LP, stereo)	15

NICK GIBLER

| 76 | Chrysalis CHS 2104 | Roxy Roller/Prophet's Tale | 6 |

DON GIBSON

56	MGM SP 1177	Sweet Dreams/The Road Of Life Alone	150
56	MGM SP 909	Sweet Dreams/The Road Of Life Alone (78)	30
58	RCA RCA 1056	Oh Lonesome Me/I Can't Stop Lovin' You	15
58	RCA RCA 1056	Oh Lonesome Me/I Can't Stop Lovin' You (78)	15
58	RCA RCA 1073	Blue Blue Day/Too Soon	20
58	RCA RCA 1073	Blue Blue Day/Too Soon (78)	10
58	RCA RCA 1098	Give Myself A Party/Look Who's Blue	20
58	RCA RCA 1098	Give Myself A Party/Look Who's Blue (78)	10
59	RCA RCA 1110	A Stranger To Me/Who Cares?	20
59	RCA RCA 1110	A Stranger To Me/Who Cares? (78)	20
59	RCA RCA 1150	Don't Tell Me Your Troubles/Heartbreak Avenue	18
59	RCA RCA 1150	Don't Tell Me Your Troubles/Heartbreak Avenue (78)	15
59	RCA RCA 1158	Big Hearted Me/I'm Movin' On	15

(Originally issued with triangular centres; later round-centre copies are worth half these values.)

59	RCA RCA 1158	Big Hearted Me/I'm Movin' On (78)	15
60	RCA RCA 1183	Just One Time/I May Never Get To Heaven	12
60	RCA RCA 1200	Far Far Away/A Legend In My Time	10
60	RCA RCA 1217	Sweet Dreams/The Same Street	10
61	RCA RCA 1243	Sea Of Heartbreak/I Think It's Best (To Forget Me)	10
66	RCA RCA 1524	(Yes) I'm Hurting/My Whole World Is Hurt	5
60	RCA RCX 1050	BLUE AND LONESOME (EP)	20
62	RCA RCX 213	LOOK WHO'S BLUE (EP)	20
62	RCA RCX 214	THAT GIBSON BOY (EP)	20
63	RCA RCX 7122	MAY YOU NEVER BE ALONE (EP)	15
60	RCA RD 27158	THE GIBSON BOY (LP)	100
62	RCA Victor RD/SF 7506	SOME FAVOURITES OF MINE (LP)	12
63	RCA Victor RD/SF 7576	I WROTE A SONG (LP)	12
64	RCA Victor RD 7641	GOD WALKS THESE HILLS (LP)	12

GINNY GIBSON

| 55 | MGM SP 1121 | Like Ma-a-d/Once There Was A Little Girl | 15 |
| 58 | MGM MGM 953 | Whatever Lola Wants (Lola Gets)/If Anything Should Happen | 15 |

JODY GIBSON & MULESKINNERS

| 59 | Parlophone R 4579 | Kissin' Time/Man On My Trail | 15 |
| 60 | Parlophone R 4645 | If You Don't Know/So You Think You've Got Troubles | 20 |

LORNE GIBSON TRIO

62	Decca F 11519	Little Black Book/What Kind Of Love Is This?	5
63	Decca F 11684	Some Do, Some Don't (Some Will, Some Won't)/Heaven's Above	5
64	Decca F 11814	Hang Up The Phone/I Think It's Best To Forget Me	5

64	Decca F 12005	The Girl I Loved/Don't Go Near The Indians	5
65	Decca F 12102	Red Roses For A Blue Lady/Talking To Your Picture	5
66	Decca F12450	Roses From A Stranger/Jingle Jangle	20
69	RCA 1917	Eva Magdalena/A Thing Called Love	7

STEVE GIBSON & RED CAPS

57	HMV POP 417	Silhouettes/Flamingo	200
57	HMV POP 417	Silhouettes/Flamingo (78)	30

WAYNE GIBSON (& DYNAMIC SOUNDS)

63	Decca F 11713	Linda Lu/Beachcomber	20
64	Decca F 11800	Come On Let's Go/DYNAMIC SOUNDS : Pop The Whip	20
64	Pye 7N 15680	Kelly/See You Later Alligator	20
65	Pye 7N 15798	Portland Town/Please Baby Please	10
65	Parlophone R 5357	Ding Dong The Witch Is Dead/In The Night	8
65	Columbia DB 7683	One Little Smile/Baby, Baby, Baby Pity Me	30
66	Columbia DB 7911	Under My Thumb/It Always Happens (Icey) (solo)	20
66	Columbia DB 7911	Under My Thumb/It Always Happens (Icey) (solo) (DJ copy)	100
66	Columbia DB 7998	For No One/He's Got The Whole World In his Hands (solo)	10
74	Pye DDS 2001	Under My Thumb/The Game	6

GIBSONS

65	CBS 202015	Any Time That You're Lonely/Born To Be Free	7
66	CBS 202063	Come Summertime/Summer Affair	7
66	Deram DM 103	Two Kinds Of Lovers/Hey Girl	6
67	Deram DM 119	The Magic Book/You Know I Need Your Lovin'	12
67	Major Minor MM 524	Night And Day/City Life	20
67	Major Minor MM 538	Lazy Summer Day/She's Not Like Any Girl	15
67	Major Minor MM 547	Only When You're Lonely/Ode To A Dolls House	7

GIDEANS LEAGUE

72	Parlophone R 5933	Hey! Did You Know You've Got Your Face on Upside Down /You've Got A Mind Of Your Own	6

GIDIAN (& UNIVERSALS)

66	Columbia DB 7826	Try Me Out/There Isn't Anything	20
66	Columbia DB 7916	Fight For Your Love/See If She Cares	8
66	Columbia DB 8041	Feeling/Don't Be Sentimental (as Gidian & Universals)	10
70	UPC UPC 107	That's Love/We Are The Happiest	6

(see also Universals, Chris Lamb & Universals)

COLIN GIFFIN

69	CBS 4030	Changes In Our Time/When I Was So Young	40

GIFT BOX

85	Steed Stted 01	Steiner's Lament/Worm Purple	5

GIFT (1)

81	Venus ORBIT 1	Crashing Down/It'll End In Tears (p/s)	20

GIFT (2)

88	Red Communications RED 001	You Don't Feel For Me/Torn Apart (p/s)	20

GIFTED CHILDREN

81	Whaam! WHAAM 001	Painting By Numbers/Lichtenstein Girl (p/s)	60

(see also Television Personalities)

GIGGETTY

78	Pye 7N 46136	Black Country Christmas/Motorway Mess	6
75	GE 100	DAWN TO DUSK IN THE BLACK COUNTRY (LP, with insert, credited to Giggetty and Jim Wm. Jones)	40
77	Bridge GE 101	TAMBOURINE (LP)	30
80	Bridge GE 103	BLACK COUNTRY TIME (LP, also listed as Revolver REV LP1)	30

GIGGLES

74	EMI 2212	Maria (The Enchildas Song)/Your Mother Wouldn't Like It	6
75	EMI EMI 2288	Glad To Be Alive/High School Girls	6
76	EMI EMI 2512	Just Another Saturday Night In The City/Bazooka (p/s)	6
77	EMI EMI 2640	Reaching Out/Street Dancer	6

GILBERTO GIL

71	Famous SFM 1001	GILBERTO GIL (LP)	40

GILBERT

67	CBS 3089	Disappear/You	15
68	CBS 3399	What Can I Do?/You	15
69	Major Minor MM 613	Mister Moody's Garden/I Wish I Could Cry	20

(see also Gilbert O'Sullivan)

GEORGE GILBERT

74	Mime LPMS 7041	MEDWAY FLOWS SOFTLY (LP, with insert)	15

HERSCHEL BURKE GILBERT

63	London HLD 9655	Dick Powell Theme/Nervous Teaser Theme	5

GILBERT & LEWIS

81	4AD AD 106	Ends With The Sea/Hung Up To Dry Whilst Building An Arch (p/s)	6
82	Cherry Red BRED 27	MZUI (LP, PVC cover, insert sleeve)	12

(see also Wire, Dome, Cupol)

ASTRUD GILBERTO

64	Verve VS 520	Girl From Ipanema (with Stan Getz)/STAN GETZ & JOAO GILBERTO: Blowin' In The Wind	5
65	Verve VLP 9107	THE SHADOW OF YOUR SMILE (LP)	15
66	Verve (S)VLP 9163	A CERTAIN SMILE AND A CERTAIN SADNESS (LP)	15
67	Verve SVLP 9137	BEACH SAMBA (LP)	15
68	Verve 2317 021	WINDY (LP)	15
69	Verve (S)VLP 9242	I HAVEN'T GOT ANYTHING BETTER TO DO (LP)	15
72	C.T.I. CTL 1	GILBERTO WITH TURRENTINE (LP, with Stanley Turrentine)	15

(see also Stan Getz, Stanley Turrentine)

JOAO GILBERTO
61	Parlophone PMC 1248	BOSSA-FINADO (LP)	15

(see also Stan Getz)

GILCHRIST
75	Route RT 03	Guardian In The Sky/Heading For The Grave	7

GILDED CAGE
69	Tepee TPR 1003	Long Long Road (For The Broken Heart)/Baby Grumpling	40

(see also She Trinity)

COSMO GILE
60	Top Rank JAR 410	Bambina D'Amsterdam/Tintarella Di Luna	6

GILES, GILES & FRIPP
68	Deram DM 188	One In A Million/Newly-Weds	90
68	Deram DM 210	Thursday Morning/Elephant Song	80
68	Deram DML 1022	THE CHEERFUL INSANITY OF GILES, GILES AND FRIPP (LP, mono)	100
68	Deram SML 1022	THE CHEERFUL INSANITY OF GILES, GILES AND FRIPP (LP, stereo)	130
70	Deram SPA 423	THE CHEERFUL INSANITY OF GILES, GILES AND FRIPP (LP, stereo reissue)	25

(see also Brain, Trendsetters Ltd, League Of Gentlemen, King Crimson, Fripp & Eno, McDonald & Giles)

TOM GILFELLON
72	Trailer LER 2079	LOVING MAD TOM (LP, red label)	15
76	Topic 12TS 282	IN THE MIDDLE OF THE TUNE (LP, blue label)	15

GILGAMESH
75	Caroline CA 2007	GILGAMESH (LP)	30

(see also Hugh Hopper, Colosseum, Whitesnake)

TERRY GILKYSON & EASY RIDERS
58	Philips JK 1007	Marianne/Goodbye Chaquita (jukebox issue)	18
60	Fontana TFE 17326	STROLLING BLUES (EP)	12
60	Fontana TFE 17327	LONESOME RIDER (EP)	10
61	London RER 1333	ROLLIN' (EP)	12
53	Brunswick LA 8618	GOLDEN MINUTES OF FOLK MUSIC (10" LP)	25
61	London HA-R 2301	ROLLIN' (LP, also stereo SAH-R 6111)	15
61	London HA-R 2301	ROLLIN' (LP, also stereo SAH-R 6111)	18
61	London HA-R 2323	REMEMBER THE ALAMO (LP, as Easyriders Including Terry Gilkyson)	15

(see also Easy Riders)

JONATHAN GILL
73	Pye 7N 45206	I've Got To Please You/Isandulu Road	15

(IAN) GILLAN (BAND)
78	Island R 553-B	Twin Exhausted (live)/Smoke On The Water (live)/ILLUSION: Madonna Blue/Revolutionary (12", promo only, as Ian Gillan Band)	20
78	Island WIP 6423	Mad Elaine/Mercury High (as Ian Gillan Band, company sleeve)	8
79	Acrobat BAT 1212	She Tears Me Down/Puget Sound/Vengeance/Mr. Universe (12", stickered card sleeve, promo only)	20
79	Acrobat BAT 12	Vengeance/Smoke On The Water	7
80	Virgin VS 355	Sleeping On The Job/Higher And Higher (p/s, with free patch)	6
80	Virgin SS 362	No Easy Way/Handles On Her Hips/Might As Well Go Home (p/s)	5
80	Virgin VS 377	Trouble/Your Sister's On My List/Mr. Universe (live)/Vengeance (live)/Smoke On The Water (live) (7" double pack, gatefold)	10
81	Lyntone LYN 10599	Higher And Higher/Spanish Guitar (same tracks both sides, hard vinyl test pressing, handwritten white labels)	35
81	Virgin VSK 103	Mutually Assured Destruction/The Maelstron (gatefold, with booket)	6
82	Virgin VSY 519	Living For The City/Purple Sky (picture disc, mispressed, B-side plays Breaking Chains, some with explanatory sticker)	8
82	Virgin VSY 519	Living For The City/Purple Skies (picture disc)	8
88	Virgin TVS 1088	South Africa (extended mix)/South Africa/John (12", p/s, as Ian Gillan)	8
90	Teldec SAM 678	Talking To You/Moonshine/Gut Reaction/No Good Luck (12", clear vinyl promo, in PVC wallet with insert & postcard)	10
91	East West SAM 906	Toolbox/Hang Me Out To Dry/Dirty Dog/Pictures Of Hell (12" promo, die-cut sleeve)	10
76	Polydor/Oyster 2490 136	CHILD IN TIME (LP, gatefold sleeve, as Ian Gillan Band)	15
77	Island ILPS 9511DJ	IAN GILLAN BAND SAMPLER (LP, 1-sided promo for "Scarabus", company sleeve)	20
78	Island ILPS 9545	LIVE AT THE BUDO-KAN (LP, unissued)	0
80	Virgin V 2171	GLORY ROAD (LP, with bonus LP "For Gillan Fans Only" [VDJ 32], stickered, embossed sleeve & inner sleeves)	15
82	Virgin VP 2236	MAGIC (LP, picture disc)	12

(see also Episode Six, Deep Purple, Ray Fenwick, Split Knee Loons, John McCoy, Johnny Gustafson, Bernie TormÃ©, Thunderstick, Jerusalem, Quatermass, Colin Towns, White Spirit, Zzebra, Rock Aid Armenia)

DANA GILLESPIE
65	Pye 7N 15872	Donna Donna/It's No Use Saying If	15
65	Pye 7N 15962	Thank You Boy/You're A Heartbreak Man	15
67	Pye 7N 17280	Pay You Back With Interest/Adam Can You Beat That	8
68	Decca F 12847	You Just Gotta Know My Mind/He Loves Me, He Loves Me Not	60
74	RCA RCA 0211	Weren't Born A Man/All Gone	5
74	RCA RCA 2466	Andy Warhol/Dizzy Heights	5
75	RCA RCA 2489	Really Love That Man/Hold Me Gently	5
69	Decca LK 5012	BOX OF SURPRISES (LP, mono)	100
69	Decca SLK 5012	BOX OF SURPRISES (LP, stereo)	150
73	RCA APL1 0354	WEREN'T BORN A MAN (LP)	25
74	RCA APL1 0682	AIN'T GONNA PLAY NO SECOND FIDDLE (LP, gatefold sleeve)	15

(see also David Bowie)

DIZZY GILLESPIE (QUINTET)
55	Vogue EPV 1022	DIZZY GILLESPIE (EP)	8
55	Vogue EPV 1049	DIZZY GILLESPIE WITH STRINGS (EP)	8
52	Esquire 20-003	OPERATIC STRINGS (10" LP)	15
53	Vogue LDE 017	DIZZY GILLESPIE PLAYS (10" LP)	15
53	Vogue LDE 033	DIZZY GILLESPIE PLAYS - JOHNNY RICHARDS CONDUCTS (10" LP)	15
54	Vogue LDE 039	PARIS CONCERT (10" LP)	15
54	Vogue LDE 076	DIZZY GILLESPIE AND ORCHESTRA (10" LP)	15
54	HMV DLP 1047	DIZZY GILLESPIE AND HIS ORCHESTRA (10" LP)	15

54	Felsted EDL 87006	DIZZY GILLESPIE'S OPERATIC STRINGS - JEALOUSY (10" LP)	15
55	Vogue LDE 135	DIZZY GILLESPIE AND HIS ORCHESTRA (10" LP)	15
55	Columbia Clef 33CX 10002	DIZZY GILLESPIE AND HIS ORCHESTRA (LP)	15
58	Columbia Clef 33CX 10144	DIZZY IN GREECE (LP)	15
62	HMV CLP 1484	GILLESPIANA (LP, also stereo CSD 1392)	15
71	Pye PKL 4403	SOULED OUT (LP)	15

(see also Miles Davis, Lalo Schifrin)

DIZZY GILLESPIE & STAN GETZ

| 55 | Columbia Clef 33C 9009 | DIZZY GILLESPIE - STAN GETZ SEXTET (LP) | 15 |
| 55 | Columbia 33C 9027 | MORE OF (10" LP) | 15 |

(see also Stan Getz)

DIZZY GILLESPIE & CHARLIE PARKER

| 61 | Vogue LAE 12252 | DIZ 'N BIRD IN CONCERT (LP) | 15 |

(see also Charlie Parker)

DOBIE GILLIS

| 68 | United Artists UP 2212 | How Peculiar/I Wish I Was Harry | 8 |

JIMMY GILMER & FIREBALLS

62	London HLD 9632	I'm Gonna Go Walkin'/Born To Be With You (as Chimmy Gilmer)	15
63	London HLD 9789	Sugar Shack/My Heart Is Free	10
64	London HLD 9827	Daisy Petal Pickin'/When My Tears Have Dried	10
64	London HLD 9872	Ain't Gonna Tell Nobody/Young Am I	10
64	London HLD 9898	Look At Me/I'll Send For You	10
65	Stateside SS 418	Thunder 'N' Lightnin'/What Do You Do	10
65	Stateside SS 472	She Belongs To Me/Rambler's Blues	10
68	London HL 10232	Three Squares/Baby	6
64	London HA-D/SH-D 8150	SUGAR SHACK (LP)	25
65	Dot DLP 3577	BUDDY'S BUDDY - BUDDY HOLLY SONGS BY JIMMY GILMER (LP)	40

(see also Fireballs, Jim & Monica)

DAVID GILMOUR

78	Harvest HAR 5167	There's No Way Out Of Here/Deafinitely (no p/s)	7
84	Harvest 12HAR 5226	Blue Light (LP Version)/Cruise (12", p/s)	10
84	Harvest HAR 5229	Love On The Air/Let's Get Metaphysical (p/s)	5
84	Harvest HARP 5229	Love On The Air/Let's Get Metaphysical (shaped picture disc)	12
84	Harvest 12HAR 5229	Love On The Air/Let's Get Metaphysical (12", p/s)	8
06	EMI 696	Smile/Island Jam (clear vinyl)	5
06	EMI EMIDJ 733	Take a Breath (1-sided clear vinyl promo)	80
06	EMI EM 717. 0946 384878 7 6	Arnold Layne (vocal by David Bowie)/Arnold Layne (vocal by Richard Wright)//Dark Globe (p/s)	6
78	Harvest SHVL 817	DAVID GILMOUR (LP)	15

(see also Pink Floyd, Joker's Wild, Rock Aid Armenia, Unicorn)

BILL GILONIS & TIM HODGKINSON

| 79 | Woof WOOF 001 | I DO I DO I DON'T I DON'T (EP, silkscreened sleeve) | 12 |

JAMES GILREATH

| 63 | Pye International 7N 25190 | Little Band Of Gold/I'll Walk With You | 10 |
| 63 | Pye International 7N 25213 | Lollipops, Lace And Lipstick/Mean Ole River | 12 |

GORDON GILTRAP (BAND)

77	Electric WOT 11	Lucifer's Cage/The Echoing Green (demos only)	10
78	Electric WOT 19	Heartsong/The Deserter (demos only)	10
78	Electric WOT 29	Fear Of The Dark/Catwalks Blues/Inner Dream (12" picture disc)	8
95	Munchkin MRC 1	THE BROTHERHOOD SUITE (cassette, 300 only)	30
73	Philips 6006 344	No Way Of Knowing/I See A Road	15
68	Transatlantic TRA 175	GORDON GILTRAP (LP, lilac label with 't' logo)	50
69	Transatlantic TRA 202	PORTRAIT (LP)	45
71	MCA MKPS 2020	A TESTAMENT OF TIME (LP, red/pink 'dogbone' label)	40
73	Philips 6308 175	GILTRAP (LP, with lyric insert, blue/silver label)	20

(see also Accolade, Pauline Filby, Catherine Andrews)

GIMMICKS

| 70 | Decca Eclipse ECS-R 2054 | BRAZILIAN SAMBA (LP) | 30 |

GIMMIX

| 79 | Elektra K 12377 | Too Much/Testing Testing 1 2 3 | 15 |

GINGER JUG BAND

| 70s | GJB 001 | GINGER JUG BAND (LP, private pressing) | 25 |

GINGER SNAPS

| 65 | RCA RCA 1483 | The Sh Down Down Song/I've Got Faith In Him | 20 |

GINGER ALE

| 70 | Famous FAM 102 | In The Sand/Get Off My Life Woman | 8 |

GINGERBREAD (1)

| 69 | B&C CB 113 | How Are You/Easy Girl | 6 |

GINGERBREAD (2)

| 71 | Pye 7N 45054 | Pollution/Moody Trudy | 8 |

GINGRINI

| 73 | Harry J. HJ 6647 | Zion 'Iah/Zion 'Iah (Version) | 6 |

GINHOUSE

| 71 | Charisma CAS 1031 | GINHOUSE (LP, gatefold sleeve) | 150 |

(see also Kestrel. Mouse, Sammy)

GINO & GINA

| 58 | Mercury 7MT 230 | Pretty Baby/Love's A Carousel | 30 |
| 58 | Mercury MT 230 | Pretty Baby/Love's A Carousel (78 rpm) | 20 |

ALLEN GINSBERG

| 60s | Cape Goliard | Wales: A Visitation (single issued with book of same title) | 15 |
| 65 | Better Books (no cat. no.) | ALLEN GINSBERG READING AT BETTER BOOKS (LP) | 20 |

65	Love Books Ltd. LB 0001	ALLEN GINSBERG, LAURENCE FERLINGHETTI, GREGORY CORSO & ANDREI VOZNESENSKY READING AT THE ARCHITECTURAL ASSOCIATION (LP)	20
68	Transatlantic TRA 192	GINSBERG'S THING (LP)	15

(see also Ginsbergs)

GINSBERGS
67	Saga Psyche PSY 3002	THE GINSBERGS AT THE ICA (LP)	15

(see also Allen Ginsberg)

GINSENG SPARTA
83	Guardian GRC 210	Forbidden Fruit/Lazy Hazy Day	25

GINTY
80	Wild Dog DOG 25	I Am The Walrus/A Little Understanding/Say You Don't Mind	10

MARCELLO GIOMBINI
70	United Artists UP 35110	Sabata - Main Title/Banjo Arrives	10

GIORGIO
66	Page One POF 003	Full Stop/Believe Me	6
67	Page One POF 028	How Much Longer Must I Wait/Bla Bla Diddly	12
69	MCA MCA 1094	Happy Birthday/Looky Looky	5

(see also Giorgio Moroder, Giorgio & Marco's Men)

GIORGIO & MARCO'S MEN
66	Polydor 56101	Run Run/Girl Without A Heart	7
68	Electratone EP 1003	Baby I Need You/Maureen	70

GIPSY LOVE
72	BASF BAP 5026	GIPSY LOVE (LP)	20

CHUCK GIRARD
75	Myrrh MYR 1025	CHUCK GIRARD (LP)	15
70s	Myrrh MYR 1065	WRITTEN ON THE WIND (LP)	15
70s	myrrh MYR 1089	THE STAND (LP)	15

MARTINE GIRAULD
92	Opaz OP 001SRH	REVIVAL (12" EP, p/s)	8

GIRGIO
69	MCA 5023	Stop/Believe Me	20

GIRL TALK (U.S.)
04	Apostles 12AP03	STOP CLEVELAND HATE EP (12")	12

GIRL
79	Jet JET 159	My Number/My Number (Version) (clear vinyl, PVC sleeve, with 2 stickers)	5

(see also Def Leppard, Bernie Torme)

GIRL GUIDED MISSILES
79	Seandee CND 01	Desperate Men/Fully Qualified Robot (p/s, 1000 only)	60

GIRL OF MY BEST FRIEND
89	Ambition AMB 003	Warm Around You/Seasons (p/s)	8

GIRLFRIENDS
63	Colpix PX 712	Jimmy Boy/For My Sake	60

GIRLIE
69	Treasure Isle TI 7053	Boss Cocky/LOVE SHOCKS: Musical True	35
69	Bullet BU 400	Madame Straggae/LAUREL AITKEN: Stupid Married Man	20
69	Duke DU 42	African Meeting (as Girlie & Junior)/JOSH: Higher And Higher	10
70	Joe JRS 7	Small Change/Mind Your Business (as Girlie & Joe [Mansano])	12
70	Ackee ACK 124	Decimilization/Decimilization Version (as Girlie & Paul)	6

(see also Laurel Aitken & Girlie)

GIRLS
09	Fantasy Trashcan FANTASY 001	Laura/Oh Boy (p/s, 500 only)	5
09	Fantasy Trashcan FANTASY 002	Lust For Life/Life In San Francisco (p/s, 500 only)	7
09	Fantasy Trashcan FANTASY 004	Hellhole Ratrace/Solitude (10" p/s)	10

GIRLS ALOUD
03	Polydor JUMP 2	Jump (Almighty Vocal Mix)/Jump/Girls Allowed (Almighty Vocal Mix)/Jump (Almighty Dub Mix) (12" pink glitter promo)	20
03	Polydor NGA 2	No Good Advice - Doublefunk Vocal Mix/Doublefunk Dub Mix/Dreadzone Vocal/Clean Version (12" promo, p/s)	12
04	Universal 9867985	Love Machine/Love Machine - Tony Lamenza Mix (7" picture disc, numbered, stickered sleeve)	8
05	Polydor 9870427	Wake Me Up/Loving Is Easy/Wake Me Up - Gravitas Club Mix (7" picture disc, numbered, stickered)	8
05	Polydor 9874045	Long Hot Summer/Long Hot Summer - Tony Lamezma Rides Again/Jump - Almighty Vocal Mix) (12", p/s)	15
08	Fascination/Polydor 1788935	The Promise/Girl Overboard (7" picture disc, numbered)	10
09	Fascination/Polydor 1794887	Loving Kind/Memory Of You (7" picture disc, numbered, stickered)	8
09	Polydor 2704480	Untouchable (Radio Mix)/Love Is The Key - Thriller Jill Mix (7" picture disc, numbered, stickered)	8
04	Polydor WHATGA 3	WHAT WILL THE NEIGHBOURS SAY? (LP, promo, pink vinyl)	20

GIRLS AT OUR BEST
80	Records RR 001	Getting Nowhere Fast/Warm Girls (p/s)	10
81	Record Records RR 002	Politics/It's Fashion (p/s)	5
81	Happy Birthday UR 4	Go For Gold/I'm Beautiful Now (p/s)	8
81	Happy Birthday UR 6	Fast Boyfriends/This Train (p/s)	8
81	Happy Birthday RULP 1	PLEASURE (LP, with lyric insert, 1st 10,000 with free 'pleasure bag' with 2 postcards, sticker & stencil)	12

GIRLSCHOOL
79	City NIK 6	Take It All Away/It Could Be Better (p/s, red vinyl, pink p/s, b&w front photo)	7
79	City NIK 6	Take It All Away/It Could Be Better (p/s, black vinyl, orange p/s)	5
79	Mulligan LUNS 723	Take It All Away/It Could Be Better (Irish version, no p/s, red vinyl)	8
84	Bronze BROX176	Burning In The Heat/Surrender (12", p/s + booklet)	8
88	GWR GWR14	Head Over Heals/Action (unissued)	10

MINT VALUE £

81	Bronze BRON 534	HIT AND RUN (LP, red vinyl)	15

(see also Motorhead, Killjoys, Framed)

GIRL TALK (U.K.)
84	Innervision IVST 4	Can The Rhythm (mixes) (12", p/s)	12

GIST
81	Rough Trade RT 58	This Is Love/Yanks (p/s)	8
81	Rough Trade RT 85	Love At First Sight/Light Aircraft (p/s)	7
83	Rough Trade RT 125	Fool For A Valentine/Fool For A Version (p/s)	7

GITS
89	Stig STIG 0019	Too Many People/Happy Song (p/s)	40

GITTE
64	Columbia DB 7440	The Heart That You Break (May Be Your Own)/Seems Just Like Old Times	10

JIMMY GIUFFRE
55	Capitol LC 6699	JIMMY GIUFFRE (10" LP)	20
57	London Jazz LTZK 15059	THE JIMMY GIUFFRE CLARINET (LP)	15
58	London Jazz LTZK 15130	JIMMY GIUFFRE (LP)	15
58	London Jazz LTZK 15137	TRAV'LIN' LIGHT (LP)	15
58	London LTZ-K 15130	JIMMY GIUFFRE 3 (LP)	15

(see also Shelly Manne)

GIZMO
75	President PT 443	Just Like Velvet/Jesus Help Me Sleep	8

GLADDY (ANDERSON) & FOLLOWERS
69	Blue Cat BS 172	Judas/The World Come To An End	22

(see also Stranger & Glady)

GLADDY (ANDERSON) & STRANGER (COLE)
73	Pama PM 872	Dedicated To Illiteracy/G.G. ALLSTARS: Dub	8

(see also Gladstone Anderson, Stranger Cole, Stranger & Glady)

GLADIATORS (1)
63	HMV POP 1134	Bleak House/Tovaritch	25

(see also Nero & Gladiators)

GLADIATORS (2)
68	Direction 58-3854	Girl Don't Make Me Wait/Can't Get Away From Heartbreak	18
69	Direction 58-4308	Waiting On The Shores Of Nowhere/I'll Always Love You	18
69	Direction 58-4507	As Long As I Live/Everything	10
69	Direction 58-4660	Twelfth Of Never/Lovin' My Baby Back Home	8
82	Nighthawk NIGHTHAWK	SYMBOL OF REALITY (LP)	20

GLADIATORS (JAMAICA)
69	Studio One SO 2072	Hello Carol/RICHARD ACE: More Reggae	35
69	Studio One SO 2086	Kicks/Games People Play	45
69	Doctor Bird DB 1114	The Train Is Coming/So Fine	30
70	Rock Steady Rev. REVR 12	Unusual Reggae/Andue	20
69	Bamboo BAM 7	Anywhere/SOUND DIMENSION: Baby Face	30
70	Duke DU 58	My Girl (actually by Glen Adams)/You Were To Be	20
72	Ackee ACK 149	Sonia/SOUND DIMENSION: Solas	20
76	Virgin V2062	TRENCHTOWN MIX UP (LP)	20
78	Virgin Frontline FL 1002	PROVERBIAL REGGAE (LP)	18
78	Virgin Frontline FL 1035	NATURALITY (LP)	18
79	Virgin Frontline FL 1048	SWEET SO TILL (LP)	18
81	Virgin VX 1003	VITAL SELECTION (LP)	15
82	Nighthawk NIGHTHAWK	SYMBOL OF REALITY (LP)	20

GLADIOLAS
57	London HLO 8435	Little Darlin'/Sweetheart, Please Don't Go	250
57	London HLO 8435	Little Darlin'/Sweetheart, Please Don't Go (78 rpm)	75

(see also Maurice Williams & Zodiacs)

GLASGOW
84	Neat NEAT 40	Stranded/Heat Of The Night (p/s)	15
84	Clydebank CLY 001	GLASGOW'S MILES BETTER (12" EP)	12

LUD GLASKIN
62	UPC 3428	To My Good Friend Jack Cotton, the 'Allo Twist (1-sided private pressing)	25

GLASS
82	Glass GLASS1	New Colours/Sweet Entropy (p/s)	22

GLASS MUSEUM
80	Fflang NAFF 1	Free Kings/Alternative Take	8
82	RGM RGM 001	Going Towards Pleasure/You're Changing	5

PHILIP GLASS
70s	Chatham Square LP 1001/2	MUSIC WITH CHANGING PARTS (2-LP)	25
70s	Chatham Square LP 1003	MUSIC IN FIFTHS/MUSIC IN A SIMILAR MOTION (LP)	20
70s	Folkways FTS 33902	TWO PAGES (LP)	20
76	Caroline CA 2010	MUSIC IN 12 (PARTS 1 & 2) (LP, 1st pressing in matt textured sleeve)	18
78	Shandar SHAN 83515	SOLO MUSIC (LP)	15
82	CBS 73640	GLASSWORKS (LP)	12
85	CBS 13M39672	SATYAGRAHA (3-LP box set, booklet)	20
86	CBS M342457	AKHNATEN (3-LP box set, booklet)	20

(see also Ray Manzarek)

GLASS HARP
72	MCA MUPS 431	GLASS HARP (LP)	25
72	MCA MUPS 449	SYNERGY (LP)	22

GLASS HOUSE
70	Invictus INV 506	Stealing Moments From Another Woman's Life/If It Ain't Love, It Don't Matter	8
71	Invictus INV 510	I Can't Be You/He's In My Life	8

GLASS MENAGERIE
68	Pye 7N 17518	She's A Rainbow/But That's When I Start To Love Her	12
68	Pye 7N 17568	You Didn't Have To Be So Nice/Let's All Run To The Sun	10
68	Pye 7N 17615	Frederick Jordan/I Said Goodbye To Me	240
69	Polydor 56318	Have You Forgotten Who You Are/Do You Ever Think?	10
69	Polydor 56341	Do My Thing Myself/Watching The World Pass By	25

(see also Paladin, Toe-Fat)

GLASS OPENING
68	Plexium P 1236	Silver Bells And Cockle Shells/Does It Really Matter	300

GLASVEGAS
04	Rebelstance J 21091979	I'm Gonna Get Stabbed/Ina Lvs Rab (CD-R, self release with lyric inner)	100
06	Waks WAKS 0035	Go Square Go/Legs 'N' Show (400 only, with lyric insert)	60
07	Sane Man SAN 001	Daddy's Gone/Flowers And Football Tops (p/s, 1,000 only, numbered)	25
08	Sane Man SAN 02	It's My Own Cheating Heart That Makes Me Cry/Be My Baby (2,000 only)	7
08	Columbia GOWOW012	GLASVEGAS (LP)	15

GLAXO BABIES
79	Heartbeat PULSE5	Christine Keeler/Nova Bossanova (p/s)	10
79	Heartbeat PULSE 3	THIS IS YOUR LIFE (12" EP)	12
80	Cherry Red PULSE 8	Shake (The Foundations)/She Went To Pieces (Live 28-03-79)	7
80	Rough Trade Y6	LIMITED ENTERTAINMENT EP	6
80	Heartbeat HBM 3	PUT ME ON THE GUEST LIST (LP)	25
80	Heartbeat HB 2	NINE MONTHS TO THE DISCO (LP)	20

CAPTAIN GLEASON'S GARDEN BAND
55	Capitol CL 14323	In The Good Old Summertime/The Band Played On	5

GLEN (BROWN) & LLOYD (ROBINSON)
66	Ska Beat JB 250	Live And Let Others Live/Too Late	45
67	Doctor Bird DB 1099	Feel Good Now/What You've Got (credited as Lloyd Glen)	45

GLENCOE
72	Epic EPC 8383	Look Me In The Eye/Telephonia	6
72	Epic EPC 65207	GLENCOE (LP)	20
73	Epic EPC 65717	SPIRIT OF GLENCOE (LP)	15

(see also Hopscotch, Five Day Rain, Greatest Show On Earth, Loving Awareness)

DARRELL GLENN
54	HMV 7MC 23	In The Chapel In The Moonlight/Once And Only Once (export issue)	8

GLIDE
95	Ochre OCH 003	EXCERPTS FROM A SPACE AGE FREAK OUT (Part 1) (orange vinyl, p/s)	5
97	Enraptured RAPT 4512	Glide (Yosum Remix)/Grind Theme 3 (wraparound p/s)	5

(see also Echo & Bunnymen)

GLITTERHOUSE
68	Stateside SS 2129	Barbarella/BOB CREWE: An Angel Is Love	20
68	Stateside SS 2129	Barbarella/Love Drags Me Down (different B-side)	18

GLOBAL COMMUNICATIONS
93	Evolution EVO 04	KEONGAKU EP (12", 4-track, plain sleeve)	25
94	Dedicated DEDLP 014L	76: 14 (2-LP, gatefold sleeve with bonus 12" [DEDLP 0145])	30
94	Dedicated DEDLP 014	76: 14 (2-LP, gatefold sleeve)	25
94	Dedicated DEDCD 014L	76: 14 (CD, gatefold, wraparound sleeve)	10
94	Dedicated SESLP 014 DJ	9 25 (1-sided 12")	8
96	Dedicated DED 21LP	REMOTION - THE GLOBAL COMMUNICATIONS REMIX ALBUM (2-LP)	20

(see also Mystic Institute, Link, Reload, Reload & E621, Chaos & Julia Set, Jedi Knights)

GLOBAL METHOD
92	Not On Label GM1	VIBE TRIBE (EP)	110

GLOBAL VILLAGE TRUCKING COMPANY
76	Caroline C 1516	GLOBAL VILLAGE TRUCKING COMPANY (LP, with lyric insert, b/s & red label, twins logo)	20

(see also Byzantium, Man)

GLOBE SHOW
69	Page One POF 128	Yes Or No/Gettin' On Back	30

(see also Chris Shakespeare Globe Show)

GLOBE TROTTERS
54	Parlophone CMSP 18	At Sundown/My Gal Sal (export issue)	15
54	Parlophone GEP 8528	SATURDAY NIGHT HOP (EP)	18

GLOBETROTTERS
70	RCA RCA 2017	Gravy/Cheer Me Up	10
71	RCA SF 8158	THE GLOBETROTTERS (LP)	15

GLOOMYS
68	Columbia DB 8391	Daybreak/Queen And King	15
71	DJM DJS 240	I'm A Bum/Let Me Dream	10

GLORIA
69	Columbia DB 8568	The Last Seven Days/Merry Dance	15

GLORIA MUNDI
78	RCA PB 5068	Fight Back/Do It (p/s)	5
78	RCA PB 5118	Glory To The World/Nothing To Say (p/s)	8
78	RCA PL2 5157	I INDIVIDUAL (LP, with inner sleeve)	12
79	RCA PL2 5244	THE WORD IS OUT (LP, with lyric inner)	12

GLORIES
67	CBS 2786	I Stand Accused (Of Loving You)/Wish They Could Write A Song	25
67	CBS 2786	I Stand Accused (Of Loving You)/Wish They Could Write A Song (DJ Copy)	40
67	Direction 58-3084	(I Love You Babe But) Give Me My Freedom/Security	20
68	Direction 58-3300	Sing Me A Love Song/Oh Baby That's Love	15
68	Direction 58-3646	My Sweet Sweet Baby/Stand By (I'm Comin' Home)	10

GLORY HUNTER
79	Rock Hard CPS 027	Thoughts Of Destiny/At The Crossroads (no p/s)	800

GLORY LANDERS
69	IBA SECC 1203	VOLUME 1 (LP)	15

GLOVE
83	Wonderland SHE 3	Like An Animal/Mouth To Mouth (p/s, some sleeves with centre holes)	5
83	Wonderland SHEX 3	Like An Animal (Club, What Club? Mix)/Like Animal/Mouth To Mouth (12", p/s, some sleeves with centre hole)	8
83	Wonderland SHE 5	Punish Me With Kisses/The Tightrope (p/s)	8
83	Wonderland SHELP 2	BLUE SUNSHINE (LP, mispressing with double-printed sleeve)	20

(see also Cure, Siouxsie & Banshees, Creatures)

ROGER GLOVER (& GUESTS)
74	Purple PUR 125	Love Is All/Old Blind Mole/Magician Moth	10
84	Safari SAF EP 1	Love Is All/Sitting In A dream/Little Chalk Blue/Homeward	5
84	Polydor POSP 678	The Mask/So Remote (p/s, solo)	8
74	Purple TPSA 7514	THE BUTTERFLY BALL (AND THE GRASSHOPPER'S FEAST) (LP, g/fold sleeve)	15
78	Polydor 2391 306	ELEMENTS (LP, solo)	12
84	Polydor POLD 5139	THE MASK (LP, solo, with insert)	15

(see also [Sheila Carter &] Episode [Six], Deep Purple, Elf, Eddie Hardin, Whitesnake, Rainbow, Glenn Hughes, John Lawton, Wizard's Convention, Marlon, Green Bullfrog, David Coverdale, Dio)

JEREMY GLUCK
86	Flicknife SHARP 037	I KNEW BUFFALO BILL (LP)	15

(see also Barracudas)

G MEN
82	Cro Magnon	G-MEN (EP, 1000 only)	15

(see also Blue Cats, Beltane fire)

GMP
93	Kold Sweat KSEP 212	HARDCORE WINS AGAIN (EP)	8

GMT
91	Mausoleum BONE 12-83102	One By One (12", p/s)	10

GNAC
98	Earworm WORM 29	The Moustache/Armchair Thriller (p/s, black vinyl)	6

GNANK
99	Gnank GNANK 01	Gnank Gnank/Oi, Gnank (p/s)	8

GNASHER
74	Purple PUR 119	Medina Road/Easy Meat	10

GNIDROLOG
72	RCA SF 8261	IN SPITE OF HARRY'S TOE-NAIL (LP, gatefoldsleeve, orange label)	100
72	RCA SF 8322	LADY LAKE (LP, with lyric insert)	250
72	RCA SF 8322	LADY LAKE (LP, without lyric insert)	100

(see also Pork Dukes, Steeleye Span)

GNOMES OF ZURICH
66	Planet PLF 121	Please Mr Sun/I'm Coming Down With The Blues (with custom 'Planet' sleeve)	50
66	Planet PLF 121	Please Mr Sun/I'm Coming Down With The Blues (without custom 'Planet' sleeve)	30
67	CBS 202556	Hang On Baby/Blues For My Baby	30
67	CBS 2694	High Hopes/Pretender	30
67	RCA Victor RCA 1606	Second Fiddle/Publicity Girl	60

G-NOTES
58	Oriole CB 1456	Ronnie (How I Wish He'd Notice Me)/I Would	20

PETER GOALBY
75	Magnet MAG 45	You Are Day You Are Night/Captain's Log	5

GOAT
82	Real Kavoom ARK 1	REAL KAVOOM (12" EP)	8

GOBBLEDEGOOKS
64	Decca F 12023	Now And Again/Where Have You Been	15

GOBBLINZ
79	Pinnacle P 8454	London/Women In Love (p/s)	80
80s	Bacon SLICE 01	Love Me Too/All Of This And More (no p/s)	80

GO-BETWEENS
80	Postcard 80-4	I Need Two Heads/Stop Before You Say It (brown label & brown co. sleeve)	25
80	Postcard 80-4	I Need Two Heads/Stop Before You Say It (yellow label & cream co. sleeve)	18
80	Postcard 81-9	Your Turn My Turn/World Weary (company sleeve)	12
82	Rough Trade RT 108	Hammer The Hammer/By Chance (p/s)	10
83	Rough Trade RT 124	Cattle And Cane/Heaven Says (p/s)	10
83	Rough Trade RT 114	Man O'Sand To Girl O'See/This Girl Black Girl (p/s)	6
86	Beggars Banquet BEG 155	Spring Rain/The Life At Hand/Little Joe (p/s)	5
86	Situation 2 SIT 44T	ABLE LABEL SINGLES (12" EP)	8
87	Beggars Banquet BEG 183D	Right Here/When People Are Dead/A Little Romance//Don't Call Me Gone/ A Little Romance (live) (double pack)	6
88	Beggars Banquet BEG 218B	Streets Of Your Town/Wait Until June (box set)	8
89	Strange Fruit SFPS 074	PEEL SESSIONS (12" EP)	8
81	Rough Trade ROUGH 45	SEND ME A LULLABY (LP)	15
82	Rough Trade ROUGH 54	BEFORE HOLLYWOOD (LP)	15
86	Beggars Banquet BEGA 72	LIBERTY BELLE AND THE BLACK DIAMOND EXPRESS (LP)	12
90	Beggars Banquet BEGA 104	1978 - 1990 (2-LP)	15

GOBLIN
79	EMI EMC 3222	SUSPIRIA (LP, soundtrack)	35

GOD MACHINE
92	Fiction FICSX 44	Ego/Temptation (The Experimental Zen Mix)/Piano Song (12", p/s)	8
93	Fiction FICSX 47	Home/All My Colours/Train/Fever (12", p/s)	20

92	Fiction FICSX 44	Desert Song/Prostitute/Commitment/Pictures Of A Bleeding Boy (12", p/s)	20
93	Fiction FIXH 23	SCENES FROM THE SECOND STOREY (2-LP)	35
94	Fiction FIXH 27	ONE LAST LAUGH IN A PLACE OF DYING (LP)	80

VIC GODARD (& SUBWAY SECT)

80	Oddball/MCA 585	Split Up The Money/Out Of Touch (p/s, with Subway Sect)	5
81	Rough Trade RT 068	Stop That Girl/Instrumentally Scared/Vertical Integration (p/s, w/Subway Sect)	5
81	Club Left CLUB 1	Stamp Of A Vamp/Hey Now (I'm In Love) (p/s, with Subway Sect)	5
85	El Benelux EL 4	Holiday Hymn/Nice On The Ice (p/s)	5
85	El Benelux EL 4T	Holiday Hymn/Nice On The Ice/Stop That Girl/Ice On The Volcano/ T.R.O.U.B.L.E. (12", p/s)	10
93	Postcard DUBH 937	Won't Turn Back/Won't Turn Back (Version) (p/s, 1,000 only)	5
80	Oddball/MCA MCF 3070	WHAT'S THE MATTER BOY? (LP, with Subway Sect)	20
82	London SH 8549	SONGS FOR SALE (LP, with Subway Sect)	18
85	Rough Trade ROUGH 56	A RETROSPECTIVE (LP, inner sleeve, with Subway Sect)	20
85	MCA/EI 01	HOLIDAY HYMN (LP, 10 test pressings only; abandoned issue of "T.R.O.U.B.L.E.")	30
86	Rough Trade ROUGH 86	T.R.O.U.B.L.E. (LP)	12
93	Postcard DUBH 936	END OF THE SURREY PEOPLE (LP)	12

(see also Subway Sect, Spirit Of The Sect)

KEITH & DONNA GODCHAUX

| 75 | Round RX 104 | KEITH & DONNA GODCHAUX (LP) | 18 |

(see also Grateful Dead)

GEOFF GODDARD

61	HMV POP 938	Girl Bride/For Eternity	50
62	HMV POP 1068	My Little Girl's Come Home/Try Once More	50
63	HMV POP 1160	Saturday Dance/Come Back To Me	40
63	HMV POP 1213	Sky Men/Walk With Me My Angel	100

GODFATHER DON

07	Diggers With Gratitude DWG 002	SLAVE OF NEW YORK (EP, 150 only)	100
09	Diggers With Gratitude DWG 005	BILLY BATHGATE (12", 20 only, green vinyl)	150
09	Diggers With Gratitude DWG 005	BILLY BATHGATE (12", 280 only, black vinyl)	30

GODFLESH

91	Earache MOSH 30 T	SLAVESTATE (12", p/s)	12
91	Earache MOSH 30 T (R)	SLAVESTATE REMIXS EP (12", p/s)	8
91	Earach MOSH 47 T	Slateman/Wound'91 (12", p/s)	8
91	Earache MOSH 47 T	Slateman/Wound'91 (p/s)	6
91	Earache MOSH 56T	Cold World/Nihil/Nihil (Total Belief Mix)/Nihil (No Belief Mix) (12", p/s)	15
94	Earache MOSH 116 LP	Merciless/Blind/Unworthy/Flowers (12", p/s)	8
95	Earache MOSH 127 T	Crush My Soul/Crush My Soul (Ultramix)/Xnoybis (Psychofuckdub) (12", p/s)	8
94	Earache MOSH 116	Merciless/Blind/Unworthy/Flowers (2 x 7", white vinyl, gatefold p/s)	15
88	Swordfish FLESH LP 1	GODFLESH (LP, textured sleeve, inner)	15
89	Earache MOSH 15	STREETCLEANER (LP)	15
92	Earache MOSH 32	PURE (LP, poster, insert)	18
94	Earache MOSH 85	SELFLESS (LP, insert)	20

HUGH GODFREY

67	Coxsone CS 7001	A Dey Pon Dem/SOUL BROTHERS: Take Ten	80
67	Studio One SO 2008	My Time/MARCIA GRIFFITHS: Hound Dog	60
67	Studio One SO 2015	Go Tell Him/MARCIA GRIFFITHS: After Laughter	60

(see also Soul Brothers)

RAY GODFREY

| 78 | Grapevine GRP 111 | Come And Get These Memories/I'm The Other Half Of You | 5 |

ROBERT JOHN GODFREY

| 74 | Charisma CAS 1084 | FALL OF HYPERION (LP) | 40 |

(see also Enid, Godfrey & Stewart, Don Bradshaw)

GODFREY & STEWART

88	The Enid ENID 11	THE SEED AND THE SOWER (LP)	15
80s	The Stand HEARTLP	JOINED BY THE HEART (LP, fan club issue, 2,000 only)	20
80s	The Stand HEARTC	JOINED BY THE HEART (, fan club issue)	12

(see also Robert John Godfrey, Enid)

GODIEGO

| 78 | Satril SATL 4009 | THE WATER MARGIN (LP, TV soundtrack) | 12 |

GODLEY & CREME

| 68 | Blinkers 1215 | Goodnight Blinkers/Hello Blinkers (die-cut sleeve) | 250 |
| 79 | Mercury SAMP 017 | 5 O'Clock/The Flood//Lost Weekend/Honolulu (double pack sampler, promo) | 10 |

(see also Mockingbirds, Hotlegs, 10cc, Dave Berry, Frabjoy & Runcible Spoon, Cruisers, Whirlwinds, Doctor Father)

GODS

67	Polydor 56168	Come On Down To My Boat Baby/Garage Man	180
68	Columbia DB 8486	Baby's Rich/Somewhere In The Street	60
69	Columbia DB 8544	Hey! Bulldog/Real Love Guaranteed	40
69	Columbia DB 8572	Maria/Long Time, Sad Time, Bad Time	40
68	Columbia SX 6286	GENESIS (LP, mono, blue/black label with "sold in U.K..." text)	300
70	SCX 6286	GENESIS (LP, stereo, silver/black label)	120
70	Columbia SCX 6372	TO SAMUEL A SON (LP, black/silver labels with boxed logo)	300
76	Harvest SHSM 2011	GODS (LP)	30

(see also Uriah Heep, Shame, Toe-Fat, Birds Birds, Carmen, Jethro Tull)

GOD'S GIFT

| 79 | Newmarket no cat. no. | THESE DAYS (EP) | 10 |
| 81 | New Hormones ORG 14 | Soldiers/Anthony Perkins/No God/The Hunger Of Millions (12", p/s) | 8 |

GOD SONS

| 72 | Green Door GD 4024 | Merry Up/Merry Up - Version | 10 |
| 71 | Philips 6006155 | All Dressed In White/We've Not Made It | 15 |

(see also Errol & U Roy, Carl Masters)

GODSPEED! YOU BLACK EMPEROR
99	Constellation CST 006	SLOW RIOT FOR NEW ZERO KANADA (12" EP)	15

GODZ
67	Fontana STL 5500	CONTACT WITH THE GODZ (LP)	25
69	Fontana STL 5512	GODZ II (LP)	25

GOGMAGOG
85	F. For Thought YUMT 109	I Will Be There/Living In A Timewarp/It's Illegal, It's Immoral, It's Unhealthy But It's Fun (12", p/s & insert)	35

(see also Iron Maiden, Di'Anno, Def Leppard, Whitesnake, Gillan, White Spirit)

GO GO THUNDER
75	RCA RCA 2494	The Race/Mrs. Mann	20

GO-GO'S (U.K.)
64	Oriole CB 1982	I'm Gonna Spend My Christmas With A Dalek/Big Boss Man (in p/s)	50
64	Oriole CB 1982	I'm Gonna Spend My Christmas With A Dalek/Big Boss Man	30

GO-GO'S (U.S.)
80	Stiff BUY 78	We Got The Beat/How Much More (p/s)	6
81	I.R.S. PFP 1007	Our Lips Are Sealed/Surfing And Spying (p/s, pink vinyl)	6
81	I.R.S. GOGO 101	Automatic/Tonite (picture disc)	5
90	A&M AMP 712	Cool Jerk/We Got The Beat (picture disc)	5

(see also Belinda Carlisle, Jane Wiedlin)

GOING RED?
81	Razz CLEAN 1	Some Boys/Tune Kevin's Strings (p/s)	8
81	MCA MCA 673	Some Boys/Tune Kevin's Strings (reissue, p/s)	5

(see also Freshies, Chris Sievey, Jilted John)

HERBIE GOINS & NIGHT-TIMERS
66	Parlophone R 5478	No. 1 In Your Heart/Cruisin'	125
66	Parlophone R 5478	No. 1 In Your Heart/Cruisin' ('DJ Copy')	175
66	Parlophone R 5533	The Incredible Miss Brown/Comin' Home To You	120
67	Parlophone PMC 7026	NUMBER ONE IN YOUR HEART (LP)	150

(see also Night-Timers, Alexis Korner's Blues Incorporated)

GO-KART MOZART
99	West Midlands Records BRUM 1	INSTANT WIGWAM AND IGLOO MIXTURE (LP, 1,000 only, with poster and small sealing sticker over opening)	25

(see also Felt)

DAVID GOLD
97	Fat Cat 10FAT 001	Respect City Police (10")	40

HARRY GOLD WITH NORRIE PARAMOR ORCHESTRA
54	Columbia SCM 5144	Be Good To Me/Frou Frou	5

(see also Norrie Paramor)

MARTY GOLD
70	Avco Embassy 6466 001	MOOG PLAYS THE BEATLES (LP)	12

BARRY GOLDBERG (REUNION)
68	Pye International 7N 25465	Another Day/Capricorn Blues (as Barry Goldberg Reunion)	7
68	Pye Intl. NSPL 28116	BARRY GOLDBERG REUNION (LP)	20
69	Buddah 203 020	TWO JEWS BLUES (LP, with Mike Bloomfield)	15
71	Buddah 2318 038	BLASTS FROM MY PAST (LP)	12

(see also Electric Flag, Mike Bloomfield)

GOLDEBRIARS
64	Columbia DB 7384	Sea Of Tears/I've Got To Love Somebody	15

GOLDEN APPLES OF THE SUN
65	Decca F 12194	Monkey Time/Chocolate Rolls, Tea And Monopoly (unissued, test pressings only)	80
65	Immediate IM 010	Monkey Time/Chocolate Rolls, Tea And Monopoly	70

GOLDEN CRUSADERS
64	Columbia DB 7232	I'm In Love With You/Always On My Mind	10
64	Columbia DB 7357	Hey Good Lookin'/Come On, Come On	10
65	Columbia DB 7485	I Don't Care/That Broken Heart Is Mine	10

GOLDEN DAWN
88	Sarah SARAH 009	My Secret World/Spring-Heeled Jack/The Railway Track (p/s, with poster)	12
89	Sarah SARAH 017	George Hamilton's Dead/The Sweetest Touch/Let's Build A Dyonsphere (p/s, with poster)	12

GOLDEN EARRING(S)
68	Capitol CL 15552	I've Just Lost Somebody/The Truth About Arthur (as Golden Earrings)	25
68	Capitol CL 15567	Dong Dong Di Ki Di Gi Dong/Wake Up - Breakfast (as Golden Earrings)	15
69	Major Minor MM 601	Just A Little Peace In My Heart/Remember My Friend (as Golden Earrings)	20
69	Major Minor MM 633	It's Alright But It Could Be Better/Where Will I Be (as Golden Earrings)	12
70	Major Minor MM 679	Another Forty-Five Miles/I Can't Get Hold Of Her	25
70	Polydor BM 56514	That Day/Words I Need	20
70	Polydor 2001 073	Back Home/This Is The Time Of Year	8
72	Polydor 2001 346	Buddy Joe/Avalanche	5
73	Track 2094 116	Radar Love/Just Like Vince Taylor	6
74	Track 2094 121	Instant Poetry/From Heaven, From Hell	5
74	Track 2094 126	Candy's Going Bad/She Flies On Strange Wings	5
75	Track 2094 130	Ce Soir/Lucky Number	5
69	Major Minor SMLP 65	EIGHT MILES HIGH (LP)	100
70	Polydor 2310049	GOLDEN EARRING (LP, gatefold sleeve)	50
71	Polydor 2310 135	SEVEN TEARS (LP)	30
72	Polydor 2310 210	TOGETHER (LP)	18
73	Polydor 2482 329	GOLDEN EARRING (LP)	12
73	Track 2406 109	HEARING EARRING (LP, braille sleeve)	18
73	Track 2406 112	MOONTAN (LP, gatefold sleeve with insert)	18
75	Polydor 2480 330	TO THE HILT (LP)	12

GOLDEN FLEECE
67	Decca F 12669	Athens 6 a.m./Girl From Syracuse	6

GOLDEN GATE QUARTET
53	Columbia SCM 5054	Moses Smote The Waters/Bones, Bones, Bones	7
56	Columbia SEG 7700	SINGS GREAT SPIRITUALS (EP)	8
58	Fontana TFR 6009	THAT GOLDEN CHARIOT (10" LP)	20
59	Columbia 33SX 1172	SHOUT FOR JOY! (LP)	15

GOLDEN GATE STRINGS
65	Columbia DB 7634	Mr. Tambourine Man/With God On Our Side	30

GOLDEN HORDE
80s	Hot Wire HWS 855	Young And Happy/Little UFO/Fiona (p/s)	5
85	Hot Wire/I.D. NOSE 7	THE CHOCOLATE BISCUIT CONSPIRACY (LP)	12

GOLDFRAPP
00	Mute P STUMM 188	FELT MOUNTAIN ALBUM SAMPLER (12" promo, p/s)	10
00	Mute 12MUTE 247	Lovely Head/(Stare Mesto Mix)/(Miss World Mix) (12", p/s)	8
00	Mute STUMM 188	FELT MOUNTAIN (LP, with inner)	50
03	Mute STUMM 196	BLACK CHERRY (LP)	25
05	Mute STUMM 250	SUPERNATURE (LP)	20
08	Mute STUMM 280	SEVENTH TREE (LP, with poster)	15

GOLDIE
95	FFRR 828 614-1	TIMELESS (2-LP, gatefold)	18

GOLDIE (& GINGERBREADS)
65	Decca F 12070	Can't You Hear My Heartbeat/Little Boy	15
65	Decca F 12126	That's Why I Love You/Skip	15
65	Decca F 12199	Sailor Boy/Please Please	15
66	Immediate IM 026	Goin' Back/Headlines (solo)	30
66	Fontana TF 693	I Do/Think About The Good Times (solo)	25
69	Decca F 12931	Can't You Hear My Heartbeat/That's Why I Love You	5
	(see also Ten Wheel Drive)		

GOLDIE LOOKIN' CHAIN
04	Gold Dust	THE MANIFESTO (CD, sold at gigs)	15

JOHN GOLDING
74	Cottage 101S	DISCARDED VERSE (LP, 2,000 only)	20

GOLD LEAF
73	Penbrook PEN 1	After The Rain/The Sun	150

VIVIEN GOLDMAN
81	Window WIN 1	Launderette/Private Armies (gatefold p/s, with PiL)	20
81	Window 12WIN 1	Launderette/Private Armies (12", different p/s, with PiL)	30
	(see also Public Image Ltd)		

ANNA GOLDRICK
60s	Polydor 2384030	IT'S HERSELF (LP)	25

GOLDRUSH
73	Decca F13380	For A Few Dollars More/No More - No Less	6

BOBBY GOLDSBORO
63	Stateside SS 193	The Runaround/The Letter	20
63	United Artists UP 1046	See The Funny Little Clown/Hello Loser	10
64	United Artists UP 1054	Whenever He Holds You/If She Was Mine	10
65	United Artists UP 1079	Little Things/I Just Can't Go On Pretending	15
65	United Artists UP 1091	Voodoo Woman/It Breaks My Heart	12
65	United Artists UP 1104	If You Wait For Love/If You've Got A Heart	10
66	United Artists UP 1120	Broomstick Cowboy/Ain't Got Time For Happy	10
66	United Artists UP 1128	It's Too Late/I'm Goin' Home	15
66	United Artists UP 1128	It's Too Late/I'm Goin' Home (DJ copy)	45
66	United Artists UP 1135	I Know You Better Than That/When Your Love Has Gone	7
66	United Artists UP 1146	Take Your Love/Longer Than Forever	25
67	United Artists UP 1156	It Hurts Me/Pity The Fool	10
67	United Artists UP 1166	No Fun At The Fair/Hold On	35
67	United Artists UP 1177	Too Many People/Goodbye To All You Women	50
67	United Artists UP 1177	Too Many People/Goodbye To All You Women (DJ copy)	85
68	United Artists UP 2223	Autumn Of My Life/She Chased Me	10
69	United Artists UP 2264	Love Arrester/Dissatisfied Man	15
69	United Artists UP 35034	Muddy Mississippi Line/Richer Man Than I	8
69	United Artists UP 35053	Letter To Emily/Tomorrow Is Forgotten	5
73	United Artists UP 35558	Summer (The First Time)/Childhood - 1949	5
65	United Artists UEP 1006	LITTLE THINGS (EP)	45
66	United Artists UEP 1016	THE TALENTED BOBBY GOLDSBORO (EP)	45
65	United Artists ULP 1118	I CAN'T STOP LOVING YOU (LP)	35
66	United Artists (S)ULP 1135	IT'S TOO LATE (LP)	35
67	United Artists (S)ULP 1163	SOLID GOLDSBORO - GREATEST HITS (LP)	22
68	United Artists (S)ULP 1195	HONEY (LP, black label)	20
68	United Artists (S)ULP 1206	WORD PICTURES (LP)	20
69	United Artists UAS 29008	TODAY (LP)	18

GOLDSMITH
83	Bedlam BLM 001	Life Is Killing Me/Music Man (p/s)	50

GOLDTOP
88	Gee Street GOLD 001	My Introduction (12")	8

GOL GAPPAS
86	él GPO 21	West 14/Roman (p/s)	12

GOLGOTHA
84	Golgotha GOTH 002	DANGEROUS GAMES (Dangerous Games/Old England's Green/Air/ The Great Divide (EP, no p/s)	90
90	Communique CMGLP 003	UNMAKER OF WORLDS (EP, p/s)	15

GOLIARD
76	Broadside BRO 127	FORTUNE MY FOE (LP, with booklet)	18

GOLIATH
70	CBS 5312	Port And Lemon Lady/I Heard About A Friend	10
70	CBS 64229	GOLIATH (LP)	150

GOLLIWOGS
66	Vocalion VF 9266	Brown-Eyed Girl/You Better Be Careful	50
67	Vocalion VF 9283	Fragile Child/Fight Fire	50
72	Fantasy FAN 5996	GOLLIWOGS (LP, pressed in U.S. for U.K. distribution)	15

(see also Creedence Clearwater Revival)

GOLLUM & GARY D
97	UK 44 RMX 3	Black Arrows (Lord Of The Rings Mix)/Black Arrows (Poisoned Tip Mix)/Black Arrows (Original E.D.M. Mix) (12", p/s)	10

(see also DJ Gollum)

BENNY GOLSON
59	Esquire 32-125	GONE WITH GOLSON (LP)	30
60	Esquire 32-105	GROOVIN' WITH GOLSON (LP)	30

BENNY GOLSON & ART FARMER
62	Pye International 7N 25120	Blues March/Serenata	5
65	Stateside SL 10150	STOCKHOLM SOJOURN (LP)	12

(see also Art Farmer)

GOMEZ
98	Hut HUTDLP 49	BRING IT ON (2-LP)	30
99	Hut HUTDLP 54	LIQUID SKIN (2-LP, gatefold, inner)	30
02	Hut HUTDLP 72	IN OUR GUN (2-LP, gatefold)	30

IAN GOMM
78	Albion ION 5	24 Hour Service/Black And White	6

GONADS
82	Secret SHH 134	PEACE ARTISTS (EP)	8
82	Secret SHH 131	PURE PUNK FOR NOW PEOPLE (EP)	8

GONDOLIERS
58	Starlite ST45 001	Fly, Seagull, Fly/God's Green Acres	6

RON GONELLA
60s	Lismor LILP 5017	FIDDLER'S FANCY (LP)	12

GONG
71	Philips 6332 033	CONTINENTAL CIRCUS (LP, soundtrack)	20
71	Caroline C1520	CAMEMBERT ELECTRIQUE (LP, 'twin' label)	15
73	Virgin V 2002	RADIO GNOME INVISIBLE PART 1 - THE FLYING TEAPOT (LP, gatefold sleeve, 1st pressing original with black & white label design)	30
73	Virgin V 2002	RADIO GNOME INVISIBLE PART 1 - THE FLYING TEAPOT (LP, gatefold sleeve, 2nd pressing with colour girl and dragon label design)	15
73	Virgin V 2007	RADIO GNOME INVISIBLE PART 2 - ANGEL'S EGG (LP, 1st pressing, stickered gatefold sleeve, initially with b&w label; with booklet)	40
73	Virgin V 2007	RADIO GNOME INVISIBLE PART 2 - ANGEL'S EGG (LP, 1st pressing, gatefold sleeve, initially with b&w label; without booklet)	30
74	Virgin V2007	RADIO GNOME INVISIBLE PART 2 - ANGEL'S EGG (LP, 2nd pressing, coloured "girl/dragon label")	15
74	Caroline C 1505	CAMEMBERT ELECTRIQUE (LP, unissued, released as Virgin VC 502 with 1505 matrix struck through and 502 added as well as a V in front of the C)	0
74	Virgin VC 502	CAMEMBERT ELECTRIQUE (LP)	12
74	Virgin V 2019	YOU (LP, 1st pressing, with lyric insert, coloured 'twin' label)	15
75	Virgin V 2046	SHAMAL (LP, gatefold)	15
77	Virgin V 2074	GAZEUSE (LP, green "mirror" girl label, with poster)	12
78	Virgin V 2099	EXPRESSO II (LP)	12

(see also Mother Gong, Gilli Smyth & Mother Gong, Daevid Allen, Steve Hillage, Clearlight, Radio Actors, Sphynx, Tim Blake, Comus)

GONG/CAMEL/HENRY COW/GLOBAL TRUCKING COMPANY
73	Greasy Truckers GT 4997	GREASY TRUCKERS (2-LP, 1 side each; with insert)	18

(see also Camel, Henry Cow, Global Trucking Company)

GONKS
64	Decca F 11984	The Gonk Song/That's All Right, Mamma	30

(see also Twinkle)

RON GONNELLA
70s	LISMOR LILP 5017	FIDDLERS FANCY (LP)	12

PAUL GONSALVES
64	Vocalion LAE 587	BOOM JACKIE BOOM CHICK (LP)	1000
70	Deram SML 1064	HUMMINGBIRD (LP)	80

(see also Tubby Hayes & Paul Gonsalves)

GONZALEZ
74	EMI EMC 3046	GONZALEZ (LP)	50
75	EMI EMC 3100	OUR ONLY WEAPON IS OUR MUSIC (LP)	18

BELLE GONZALEZ
72	Columbia DB 8852	Bottles/I Hate Sunday	18
65	Jupiter JEPOC 37	POETS SET IN JAZZ (EP, as Belle Gonzalez & Sextet)	18
66	Jupiter JEPOC 39	CONTEMPORARY POETS SET IN JAZZ (EP)	18
72	Columbia SCX 6484	BELLE (LP)	80

(see also Mark Wirtz)

GOO.Q
80	Rising Star PCD 1	I'm A Computer/Love Outa Hate (paper p/s)	5

DOUGLAS GOOD & GINNY PLENTY
68	Stateside SS 2104	Sunny And Me/Living In A World Of Make Believe	5

JACK GOOD'S FAT NOISE
60	Decca F 11233	The Fat Washerwoman/The Fat Noise	10

ELMER GOODBODY
76	Charisma CB 279	Do Ya/Mad About You	8

GOODBYE MR. MACKENZIE
84	Scruples YTS 1	Death Of A Salesman/LINDY BERGMAN: Locked Inside Your Prison (no p/s, 500 only)	25
86	Precious Org. JEWEL 2	The Rattler/Candlestick Park (p/s)	6
86	Precious Org. JEWEL 2T	The Rattler/Candlestick Park/The End (12", p/s)	10
87	Clandestiny MACK 1	Face To Face/Secrets/Good Deeds (12", p/s, 1,000 only)	10
90	Parlophone PCS 7345	HAMMER AND TONGS (LP, unreleased, white label test pressings only)	40

(see also Garbage)o

GOOD EARTH
68	Saga FID 2112	IT'S HARD ROCK AND ALL THAT (LP)	15
70	Saga FID 8157	IN THE SUMMERTIME (LP, with tracks by Macon Jug)	12

(see also First Impression/Good Earth, Mungo Jerry, Ray Dorset)

GOOD GUYS
70	Duke DU 82	Death Rides/Destruction	10
70	Duke DU 83	Wreck It Up/Dynamic Groove	10
70	Duke DU 84	Happiness/Latissimo	8

(see also Byron Lee & Dragonaires)

PHILIP GOODHAND-TAIT (& STORMSVILLE SHAKERS)
66	Parlophone R 5448	I'm Gonna Put Some Hurt On You/It's A Lie (with Stormsville Shakers)	20
66	Parlophone R 5498	No Problem/What More Do You Want (with Stormsville Shakers)	25
66	Parlophone R 5547	You Can't Take Love/J.C. Greaseburger (solo)	20
70	DJM DJLPS 411	REHEARSAL (LP)	15
71	DJM DJLPS 416	I THINK I'LL WRITE A SONG (LP, gatefold)	15
72	DJM DJLPS 425	SONGFALL (LP, gatefold)	20
76	Chrysalis CHR 1113	OCEANS AWAY (LP)	12
77	Chrysalis CHR 1146	TEACHING AN OLD DOG NEW TRICKS (LP, with insert)	12

(see also Circus, Larry Williams, Love Affair)

JOHNNY GOODISON
70	Deram DM 319	A Little Understanding/One Mistake	20

(see also Quotations, Johnny B. Great)

LEMME B GOOD
65	Mercury MF 874	I Can't Stop Myself/Mother May I	8

GOODLETTSVILLE FIVE
64	London HLW 9854	Eef/Bailey's Gone Eefing	8

JOHN GOODLUCK
74	Tradition TSR 015	SUFFOLK MIRACLE (LP, with insert)	25
75	Sweet Folk & Country SFA 047	SPEED THE PLOUGH: TRADITIONAL SONGS OF SUFFOLK (LP)	25
88	Big Ben FE 065	THE MAN WHO PUT THE ENGINE IN THE CHIP SHOP: MORE RAILWAY SONGS OF DAVE GOULDER (LP)	12

DAVE GOODMAN & FRIENDS
78	The Label TLR 008	Justifiable Homicide/Take Down Your Fences (p/s, 1st 15,000 on red vinyl)	8

GOOD MISSIONARIES
80	Kif KIF'S 1	Good Missionary (Parts 1 & 2) (p/s)	5
79	Deptford Fun City DLP 04	FIRE FROM HEAVEN (LP)	15

(see also Mark Perry, Alternative TV)

GOOD RATS
69	London HLR 10237	The Hobo/The Truth Is Gone	20

GOOD SHIP LOLLIPOP
69	Ember EMB S 276	Maxwell's Silver Hammer/How Does It Feel (in p/s)	12
69	Ember EMB S 276	Maxwell's Silver Hammer/How Does It Feel	6

GOOD TIME LOSERS
67	Fontana TF 791	Trafalgar Square/Where Did My Heart Go	6

GOODTIMERS
62	Fontana H 360	It's Twistin' Time/Twisting Train	10

GOOD VIBRATIONS
70	Ember EMB S 270	Call Me Lightning/Nantucket Ferry	6

ROD GOODWAY
90	Woronzow WOO 12	ETHEREAL COUNTERBALANCE (LP)	18

RON GOODWIN CONCERT ORCHESTRA
53	Parlophone MSP 6035	Limelight/The Song From Moulin Rouge	18
53	Parlophone MSP 6055	Tropical Mirage/The Man Between	12
54	Parlophone MSP 6064	Grand Waltz Of The Flowers And Dragonflies/The Lobster Quadrille	10
54	Parlophone MSP 6103	The Sons Of The High Seas/Guadalcanal March	12
54	Parlophone MSP 6115	Cara Mia/Three Coins In The Fountain	12
54	Parlophone MSP 6136	Midnight Blue/On The Waterfront	12
55	Parlophone MSP 6159	Under The Linded Tree/Last Love	10
56	Parlophone MSP 6221	Concetta/Handyman	10
56	Parlophone 45 R-4235	War And Peace/The Christmas Tree	10
57	Parlophone R 4297	Skiffling Strings (Swinging Sweetheart)/I'll Find You	15
57	Parlophone R 4349	Swedish Polka/Lingering Lovers	12
58	Parlophone R 4391	Colonel Bogey And The River Kwai March/Laughing Sailor	8
58	Parlophone R 4508	Latin Lovers/Blue Grotto	10
58	Parlophone R 4608	Lolita/All Strung Up	10
59	Parlophone R 4537	The Whirlpool Theme/Herman's Theme From Whirlpool	12
60	Parlophone R 4632	Tracey's Theme/My Girl	10
60	Parlophone R 4663	Love Theme From Ben Hur/Theme From The Unforgiven	10
60	Parlophone R 4687	Walkin' Down To Washington/Sunshine Cruise	10
61	Parlophone R 4821	Murder She Says/Double Scotch	25

63	Parlophone R 5053	Moonstrike/Midsummer Madness	12
64	Parlophone R 5146	633 Squadron/Love Them From 633 Squadron	10
65	Parlophone R 5239	The Fat Man/Colonel Schmendrick	10
65	Parlophone R 5394	Theme From The Early Birds/Theme From The Alphabet Murders	12
69	United Artists UP 35040	Battle Of Britain Theme/Luftwaffe March	10
54	Parlophone PMD 1014	FILM FAVOURITES (10" LP)	15
56	Parlophone PMD 1038	MUSIC TO SET YOU DREAMING (10" LP)	15
58	Parlophone PCS 3002	MUSIC FOR AN ARABIAN NIGHT (LP)	15
58	Parlophone PCS 3006	OUT OF THIS WORLD! (LP)	20
64	United Artists ULP 1071	633 SQUADRON (LP, soundtrack)	20
65	Stateside SL 10136	THOSE MAGNIFICENT MEN IN THEIR FLYING MACHINES (LP, soundtrack)	20
66	Polydor 582 004	THE TRAP (LP, soundtrack)	40
68	Stateside (S)SL 10259	DECLINE AND FALL ... OF A BIRDWATCHER (LP, soundtrack)	80
69	Paramount SPFL 255	MONTE CARLO OR BUST! (LP, soundtrack)	40
76	EMI EMC 3148	ESCAPE FROM THE DARK (LP, soundtrack)	15

(see also 20th Century Fox Orchestra, Parlophone Pops Orchestra)

GOOFERS

55	Vogue Coral Q 72051	Hearts Of Stone/You're The One	50
55	Vogue Coral Q 72051	Hearts Of Stone/You're The One (78)	20
55	Vogue Coral Q 72074	Flip, Flop And Fly/My Babe	50
55	Vogue Coral Q 72074	Flip, Flop And Fly/My Babe (78)	20
55	Vogue Coral Q 72094	Goofy Drybones/Nare	30
55	Vogue Coral Q 72094	Goofy Drybones/Nare (78)	15
56	Vogue Coral Q 72124	Sick! Sick! Sick!/Twenty One	25
56	Vogue Coral Q 72124	Sick! Sick! Sick!/Twenty One (78)	15
56	Vogue Coral Q 72171	Tear Drop Motel/Tennessee Rock And Roll	40
56	Vogue Coral Q 72171	Tear Drop Motel/Tennessee Rock And Roll (78)	25
57	Vogue Coral Q 72267	Wow!/Push, Push, Push Cart	25
57	Vogue Coral Q 72267	Wow!/Push, Push, Push Cart (78)	25
57	Vogue Coral Q 72289	The Dipsy Doodle/Take This Heart	25
57	Vogue Coral Q 72289	The Dipsy Doodle/Take This Heart (78)	15

GOOM

72	Pye 7N 25587	Massai Part 1/Massai Part 2	15

DEREK GOOM

80	BBCRESL 84	Julient Bravo/Madelena (p/s)	6

GOONS

56	Parlophone R 4251	My September Love/You Gotta Go Oww (with Eric Sykes)	10
56	Decca F 10756	I'm Walking Backwards For Christmas/Bluebottle Blues	10
56	Decca F 10780	The Ying Tong Song/Bloodnok's Rock 'N' Roll Call	10
57	Decca F 10885	Eeh! Ah! Oh! Ooh!/I Love You	10
64	Decca LF 1332	UNCHAINED MELODIES (10" LP)	15

(see also Peter Sellers, Spike Milligan, Michael Bentine, Famous Eccles, Eric Sykes)

SAM GOPAL

69	Stable STA 5602	Horse/Back Door Man (unissued, existence unconfirmed)	0
69	Stable SLE 8001	Escalator/Angry Faces/Cold Embrace/The Sky is Burning (LP sampler)	70
69	Stable SLE 8001	ESCALATOR (LP, gatefold sleeve, black/silver label)	300
68	Stable SLE 8001	ESCALATOR (LP, gatefold sleeve, label stating "DJ Copy not for resale")	400

(see also Hawkwind, Motorhead, Vamp, Isaac Guillory, Clark-Hutchinson, G. F. Fitzgerald)

PETE(R) GORDENO

61	Fontana H 319	Be My Girl/Haven't Got Time (as Pete Gordeno)	8
62	Parlophone R 4862	I Got Eyes/You're Following Me	8
76	Zoot 1001	WITH FEELING (LP)	12

ANITA GORDON

55	Brunswick 05456	Lonesome Like Nobody Knows/His Hands	10

BARRY GORDON

56	MGM MGM 928	I Can't Whistle/The Milkman's Polka	10
56	MGM MGM 935	Rock Around Mother Goose/Nuttin' For Christmas	20

CHANCE GORDON

63	Pye 7N 15475	Instant Love/You Don't Want My Love	20

CHRIS GORDON

68	Derpy ADMLP 390	IN THE EARLY MORNING RAIN (LP)	200

CURTIS GORDON

57	Mercury MT 163	Sixteen/Cry, Cry (78)	20

DEXTER GORDON

60s	Fontana Jazz FJL 907	MASTER SWINGERS (LP, with Wardell Gray)	15

(see also Wardell Gray)

JOE GORDON (FOLK FOUR)

59	HMV POP 600	Gotta Travel On/Ho Ro My Nutbrown Maid	5
59	HMV POP 634	Dream Lover/Dance To Your Daddy	10
60	HMV POP 737	Football Crazy/By The Bright Shining Light Of The Moon	6
59	HMV 7EG 8454	JOE GORDON FOLK HOUR (EP)	15
60	HMV CLP 1379	THE GAY GORDON (LP)	12

PETER GORDON

62	Parlophone R 4931	Down By The Riverside/The Boys Kept Hanging Around	10
65	Decca F 12088	Have You Looked Into Your Heart?/Don't Come To Me	8
68	MCA MU 1009	Born To Be Wanted/Shout It From The Hilltop	5
68	MCA MU 1058	My Girl Maria/I Appreciate So Much	5

PHIL GORDON

55	Brunswick 05481	Get A Load Of That Crazy Walk/Strip Polka	10
56	Brunswick 05545	Down The Road Apiece/I'm Gonna Move To The Outskirts Of Town	40

ROBERT GORDON WITH LINK WRAY

77	Private Stock PVTS 127	Endless Sleep & The Fool/The Fool (12", B-side plays at 78rpm)	10

| 77 | Private Stock PVLP 1027 | ROBERT GORDON WITH LINK WRAY (LP) | 15 |
| 79 | RCA PL 13294 | ROCKBILLY BOOGIE (LP, solo) | 12 |

(see also Link Wray)

RONNIE GORDON
| 63 | R&B JB 127 | Shake Some Time/Comin' Home | 40 |

ROSCO(E) GORDON
60	Top Rank JAR 332	Just A Little Bit/Goin' Home (as Rosco Gordon)	25
63	Stateside SS 204	Just A Little Bit/What I Wouldn't Do	25
65	Vocalion V-P 9245	Keep On Doggin'/Bad Dream	30
65	Island WI 256	Surely I Love You/What You Do To Me	25
66	Island WI 272	No More Doggin'/Goin' Home	30

TONY GORDON
| 73 | Grape GR 3056 | Be True (actually by Alton Ellis)/Navajo Trail | 6 |

(see also Alton Ellis)

VINCENT GORDON
69	Coxsone CS 7085	Soul Trombone/LARRY & ALVIN: Your Cheating Heart	50
69	Duke DU 37	Everybody Bawlin'/SILVERTONES: Come Look Here	15
69	Crab CRAB 16	Walking By/VICEROYS: Promises Promises	25
74	Big Shot BI 630	Come Go With Me/SKIN, FLESH & BONES: Dub Ali Dub	7
75	DIP DLP 5001	MUSICAL BONES (LP, plain sleeve, white label)	300
79	Attack TACK 10	Liquid Horns (as Vin Gordon & Corner Shots)/ JUNIOR & CORNER SHOTS: Liquidator (12")	18
70s	Trojan TRO 9058	Liquid Horns/JUNIOR: Liquidator	10

(see also Don Drummond Junior)

TREV GORDON
| 66 | Pye 7N 17168 | Floating/Everyone Knows (possibly demo only) | 15 |

CHARLIE GORE
54	Parlophone CMSP 19	I'll Find Somebody/Heaven Sent You To Me (export issue)	25
54	Parlophone DP 379	I'll Find Somebody/Heaven Sent You To Me (78)	10
54	Parlophone CMSP 26	Two Of A Kind/It's A Long Walk Back To Town (export issue)	20
54	Parlophone DP 397	Two Of A Kind/It's A Long Walk Back To Town (78)	10
54	Parlophone CMSP 30	I Didn't Know/Oh! Mis'rable Love (export issue)	20

(see also Hawkshaw Hawkins, Ruby Wright)

LESLEY GORE
63	Mercury AMT 1205	It's My Party/Danny	10
63	Mercury AMT 1210	Judy's Turn To Cry/Just Let Me Cry	10
63	Mercury AMT 1213	She's A Fool/The Old Crowd	10
64	Mercury MF 803	You Don't Own Me/Run Bobby Run	12
64	Mercury MF 810	That's The Way Boys Are/That's The Way The Ball Bounces	12
64	Mercury MF 821	I Don't Wanna Be A Loser/It's Gotta Be You	10
64	Mercury MF 829	Maybe I Know/Wonder Boy	8
65	Mercury MF 846	The Look Of Love/Little Girl Go Home	15
65	Mercury MF 862	Sunshine Lollipops And Rainbows/You've Come Back	12
65	Mercury MF 872	My Town, My Guy And Me/Girl In Love	15
65	Mercury MF 889	I Won't Love You Anymore (Sorry)/No Matter What You Do	15
66	Mercury MF 902	Young Love/I Just Don't Know If I Can	10
66	Mercury MF 963	California Nights/I'm Going Out (The Same Way I Came In)	10
66	Mercury MF 984	I'm Fallin' Down/Summer And Sandy	18
68	Mercury MF 1017	Magic Colours/It's A Happening World	10
75	A&M AMS 7184	Immortality/Give It To Me, Sweet Thing	5
64	Mercury 10017 MCE	LESLEY GORE (EP)	35
63	Mercury MMC 14127	I'LL CRY IF I WANT TO (LP)	40
63	Mercury 20001 MCL	SINGS OF MIXED-UP HEARTS (LP)	30
64	Mercury 20020 MCL	BOYS BOYS BOYS (LP)	30
64	Mercury 20033 MCL	GIRL TALK (LP)	30
65	Mercury 20071 MCL	MY TOWN, MY GUY & ME (LP)	30
65	Mercury 20076 MCL	ALL ABOUT LOVE (LP)	30
67	Wing WL 1183	GIRL TALK (LP, reissue)	15

GORGONI, MARTIN & TAYLOR
71	Buddah 2011 102	Sweet Dream Woman/Got The feeling Everything Got Away	6
72	Buddah 2011-137	Toly Toly Guyluesha/I Can Make You Cry	7
72	Buddah 2318 067	GORGONI, MARTIN AND TAYLOR (LP)	15

GORILLA GRIP
| 78 | Birnback KOM 019 | King Of The Pipes/Birnback Island (500 only no p/s) | 20 |

(see also DR Z)

GORILLAS
75	Chiswick NS 4	She's My Gal/Why Wait 'Til Tomorrow	6
78	Chiswick NS 8	Gatecrasher/Gorilla Got Me	15
78	Raw RAW 14	It's My Life/My Son's Alive	6
81	Chiswick CHIS 151	Move It/A Song For Rita	6
78	Raw RWLP 103	MESSAGE TO THE WORLD (LP, with insert)	20

(see also Hammersmith Gorillas, Jesse Hector)

GORILLAZ
01	7RDJ 6552	Clint Eastwood/Dracula (33 rpm dinked 7" - cartoon die-cut stickered sleeve)	12
01	Parlophone (no Cat no)	Tomorrow Comes Today/Tomorrow Dub (7" white label, stamped promo)	8
02	EMI SMVG 004	L'IL DUB CHEFIN (10" 4-track sampler)	8
05	Parlophone R 6663	Feel Good Inc./68 State (picture disc in die-cut card sleeve)	8
05	Parlophone 07243 474873 2 3	WE ARE THE DURY (interview CD, p/s, promo)	30
06	Parlophone R 6685	Kids With Guns/El Manana (p/s, red vinyl, poster)	7
10	Parlophone 10R 6802	White Flag/Pirate's Progress (10", p/s, 1000 only, Record Store Day release)	8
01	Parlophone 7243 5 311 38 10	GORILLAZ (2-LP)	20
05	Parlophone 07243 873838 1 4	DEMON DAYS (2-LP)	40
05	Parlophone 07243 873838	DEMON DAYS INSTRUMENTALS (2-LP, promo die-cut stickered sleeve)	50
10	Parlophone 5099962616614	PLASTIC BEACH (2-LP)	18

(see also Blur, Damon Albarn)

GORKY'S ZYGOTIC MYNCI

93	Ankst ANKST/GZM 040	PATIO (10" EP)	15
94	Ankst ANKST 048	Merched Yn Neud Gwallt Eu Gilydd/Bocs Angelica/ When You Laugh At Your Own Garden In A Blazer (p/s)	8
94	Ankst ANKST 053	Game Of Eyes/Pentref Wrth Y Mor (p/s)	6
95	Ankst ANKST 053	Pentref Wrth Y Môr/The Game Of Eyes (p/s)	15
95	Ankst ANKST 058	Gewn Ni Gorffen/12 Impressionistic Soundscapes (clear vinyl, die-cut p/s, mail order only, 1,000 copies)	10
98	Mercury ANKST GZM 5	Let's Get Together (In Our Minds)/Billy And The Sugarloaf Mountain/Hwiangerdd Mar (numbered p/s)	7
95	Ankst ANKST 059	BWYD TIME (LP, gatefold sleeve)	20
97	Fontana 534 769	BARAFUNDLE (LP)	25
98	Fontana 558 822-1	GORKY 5 (LP)	12
99	Mantra MNTPL 1015	SPANISH DANCE TROUPE (LP)	18
00	Mantra MNTLPM 1023	THE BLUE TREES (LP)	18
01	Mantra MNTLP 1025	HOW I LONG TO FEEL THAT SUMMER IN MY HEART (LP)	20

JOHN GORMAN

73	Island WIP 6151	WPC Hodges/I Remember	5
77	DJM DJF 20491	GO MAN GORMAN (LP)	15

(see also Scaffold, Grimms)

EYDIE GORMÉ

54	Vogue Coral Q 2014	Frenesi/Climb Up The Wall	10
54	Vogue Coral Q 2027	Tea For Two/Sure	10
55	Vogue Coral Q 72092	Give A Fool A Chance/A Girl Can't Say	10
55	Vogue Coral Q 72103	Soldier Boy/What Is The Secret Of Your Success?	10
56	London HL 8227	Sincerely Yours/Come Home	15
57	HMV POP 400	Kiss In Your Eyes/Your Kisses Kill Me	7
58	HMV POP 432	Love Me Forever/Until They Sail	10
58	HMV POP 493	You Need Hands/The Gentleman Is A Dope	6
58	HMV POP 513	Gotta Have Rain/To You, From Me	6
58	HMV POP 529	Dormi, Dormi, Dormi/Be Careful, It's My Heart	7
59	HMV POP 577	Separate Tables/The Voice Of My Heart	8
59	HMV POP 616	I'm Yours/Don't Take Your Love From Me	6
60	HMV POP 767	The Dance Is Over/Too Young To Know	10
62	CBS AAG 105	Yes, My Darling Daughter/Sonny Boy	8
63	CBS AAG 131	Blame It On The Bossa Nova/Guess I Should Have Loved Him More	7
63	CBS AAG 149	Don't Try To Fight It Baby/Theme From Light Fantastic	10
63	CBS AAG 163	I Want To Stay Here/Ain't Love (as STEVE & EYDIE)	6
63	CBS AAG 170	Everybody Go Home/The Message	10
63	CBS AAG 178	I Can't Stop Talking About You/To The Movies We Go (AS STEVE & EYDIE)	7
67	CBS 202470	Everybody Go Home/The Message (reissue)	5

(see also Steve Lawrence)

FRANK GORSHIN

66	Pye International 7N 25402	The Riddler/Never Let Her Go (in p/s)	75
66	Pye International 7N 25402	The Riddler/Never Let Her Go	35

PETER GOSLING

70	Sonet SON 2010	Values/Peace	10

GOSPEL CLASSICS

68	Chess CRS 8080	More Love, That's What We Need/You Need Faith	75
68	Chess CRS 8080	More Love, That's What We Need/You Need Faith (DJ copy)	150

GOSPELFOLK

69	Emblem 7DR 324	PRODIGAL (LP)	200

GOSPEL GARDEN

68	Camp 602 006	Finders Keepers/Just A Tear	40

(see also Dimples, Amazing Blondel)

GOSPEL OAK

70	Uni UNS 527	Recollections Of Jessica/Brown Haired Girl	6
70	Uni UNLS 113	GOSPEL OAK (LP)	70

GOSPEL PEARLS

63	Liberty LBY 1191	THE GOSPEL PEARLS (LP)	25

GOTAN PROJECT

01	XL XLLP 148	LA REVANCHA DEL TANGO (2-LP)	25

GOTHIC GIRLS

83	Backs NCH 007	Outrage/Devil (p/s)	10

GOTHIC HORIZON

70	Argo AFW 102	The Jason Lodge Poetry Book/Wilhelmina Before Sunrise	12
71	Argo AFW 104	Marjorie/Song	10
72	Argo AFW 107	If You Can Smile/Thoughts	8
72	Argo AFW 108	Girl With Guitar/Can't Bear To Think About You	8
71	Argo ZFB 26	THE JASON LODGE POETRY BOOK (LP)	65
72	Argo ZDA 150	TOMORROW IS ANOTHER DAY (LP)	60

GOTH TRAD

07	Deep Medi Musik MEDI 05	Cut End/Flags (12")	20
07	Skud SKUD 001	Back To Chill/Swamp/The Gate (12")	10
08	Deep Medi Musik MEDI 09	Law/The Clown (12")	8
08	Skud SKU 002	Far East Assassin/Far East Assassin (DJ Distance Remix) (12")	10

KEVIN GOULD

70s	Myrrh MYR 1028	TRUE STORIES BY (LP)	12

MORTON GOULD

60	RCA Victor RD 27028	JUNGLE DRUMS (LP)	20

TERRY GOULD

69	Sing SING 1001	SEVERAL KINDS OF LOVING (LP)	12

DALE GOULDER & LIZ DYER
70	Argo ZFB 10	JANUARY MAN (LP)	40
71	Argo ZFB 30	RAVEN & CROW (LP)	40

DAVE GOULDER
73	Big Ben BB 0004	REQUIEM FOR STEAM: THE RAILWAY SONGS OF DAVE GOULDER (LP)	15

GRAHAM GOULDMAN
66	Decca F 12334	Stop! Stop! Stop! (Or Honey I'll Be Gone...)/Better To Have Loved And Lost	150
68	RCA Victor RCA 1667	Upstairs, Downstairs/Chestnut	40
69	Spark SRL 1026	Windmills Of Your Mind/Harvey's Theme (as Graham Gouldman Orchestra)	15
72	CBS 7739	Nowhere To Go/Growing Older	7

(see also 10cc, Whirlwinds, Mockingbirds, High Society, Frabjoy & Runcible Spoon, Manchester Mob, Garden Odyssey Enterprise, Friday Browne, Doctor Father)

GOVE
69	London HLE 10295	Sunday Morning Early/Death Letter Blues	12
72	UNI UNs547	Carry On (Till The Band Adjourns)/I've Been Thinking Of You Lately	8

JOHN GRAAS SEPTET
54	London RE-P 1003	FRENCH HORN VOL. 1 (EP)	10

GRAB GRAB THE HADDOCK
84	Cherry Red 12CHERRY 83	THREE SONGS BY GRAB GRAB THE HADDOCK (12" EP)	8

(see also Marine Girls, Tracey Thorne)

MICK GRABHAM
72	United Artists UP 35391	On Fire For You Baby/Sweet Blossom Woman	5
72	United Artists UAS 29341	MICK THE LAD (LP, laminated front cove sleeve)	20

(see also Plastic Penny, Cochise, Procol Harum)

GRACE
77	Zipp ZB 003	Old Stories/Rule Britannia (in p/s)	60
77	Zipp ZB 003	Old Stories/Rule Britannia (no p/s)	20
80	MCA MCA 628	Fire Of London/Beatnik (p/s)	5
81	MCA MCA 667	Billy Boy/Ad Mad (p/s)	15

GRAME GRACE
75	RCA SF 8418	HAIL ME (LP, with insert)	15
76	RCA RCA 2633	Flambouyant Streak/Don't Hang Around Like That	6

CHARLIE GRACIE
57	Parlophone R 4290	Butterfly/Ninety-Nine Ways (initially gold lettering on label)	50
57	Parlophone R 4290	Butterfly/Ninety-Nine Ways (later pressing with silver lettering on label)	25
57	Parlophone R 4313	Fabulous/Just Lookin' (initially gold lettering on label)	50
57	Parlophone R 4313	Fabulous/Just Lookin' (later pressing with silver lettering on label)	25
57	London HL 8467	Wandering Eyes/I Love You So Much It Hurts (tri-centre)	40
57	London HLU 8521	Cool Baby/You Got A Heart Like A Rock (tri-centre)	30
57	London HLU 8521	Cool Baby/You Got A Heart Like A Rock (78)	10
58	London HLU 8596	Crazy Girl/Dressin' Up (tri-centre)	30
58	London HLU 8596	Crazy Girl/Dressin' Up (78)	10
59	Coral Q 72362	Doodlebug/Hurry Up, Buttercup (tri-centre)	30
59	Coral Q 72362	Doodlebug/Hurry Up, Buttercup (78)	30
59	Coral Q 72373	Angel Of Love/I'm A Fool, That's Why (tri-centre)	15
59	Coral Q 72373	Angel Of Love/I'm A Fool, That's Why (later round centre)	10
59	Coral Q 72373	Angel Of Love/I'm A Fool, That's Why (78)	20
59	Coral Q 72381	Oh-Well-A/Because I Love You So	15
59	Coral Q 72381	Oh-Well-A/Because I Love You So (78)	25
60	Columbia DB 4477	The Race/I Looked For You	10
62	London HLU 9603	Pretty Baby/Night And Day, U.S.A.	20
65	Stateside SS 402	He'll Never Love You Like I Do/Keep My Love Next To Your Heart	75
65	Stateside SS 402	He'll Never Love You Like I Do/Keep My Love Next To Your Heart (DJ copy)	150
78	London HLU 10563	Fabulous/Makin' Whoopie/Wow...w (tri centre)	10
57	Parlophone GEP 8630	THE FABULOUS CHARLIE GRACIE (EP)	50

GRACIOUS!
68	Polydor 56333	Beautiful/What A Lovely Rain	35
70	Vertigo 6059 009	Once On A Windy Day/Fugue In D Minor	30
70	Vertigo 6360 002	GRACIOUS! (LP, gatefold sleeve, large swirl label)	450
72	Philips Intl. 6382 004	THIS IS ... GRACIOUS!! (LP, black/silver labels)	200

GRADUATE
80	Precision PAR 100	Elvis Should Play Ska/Julie Julie (p/s)	5
80	Precision PAR 104	Ever Met A Day/Shut Up (p/s, 1980 issue PAR 117 with no p/s = £3)	6
80	Precision PAR 111	Ambition/Bad Dreams (p/s)	5
81	Precision PAR 117	Shut Up/Ever Met A Day (reissue, no p/s)	5
80s	Blue Hat 5 BHR	Mad One/Somebody Put Out The Fire	10
80	Precision PART 001	ACTING MY AGE (LP)	12

(see also Tears For Fears)

GRADUATES
79	Graduate GRAD 1	If You Want It/Hey Young Girl (p/s)	6

GRAFFIA
81	Magic 102	Stop It Stop/Cymer Di (die-cut company sleeve)	10

GRAFITTI
76	Beeb 19	Dear Prudence/Come Together	20

BILLY GRAHAM & ESCALATORS
67	Atlantic 584 073	Ooh Poo Pah Doo/East 24th Avenue	15

BOB GRAHAM EXPERIENCE
78	Anchor ANC 1055	Blast Off (Percussion In Space)/Malfunction	6

BOBBY/BOBBIE GRAHAM
65	Fontana TF 521	Skin Deep/Zoom Widge And Wag (as Bobbie Graham)	28
66	Fontana TF 667	Teensville/Grotty Drums (as Bobby Graham)	15

(see also Outlaws, Jimmy Page)

CHICK GRAHAM & COASTERS
64	Decca F 11859	Education/I Know	12
64	Decca F 11932	A Little You/Dance Baby Dance	12

DAV(E)Y GRAHAM
68	Decca F 12841	Both Sides Now/Tristano	12
62	Golden Guinea GGL 0224	THE GUITAR PLAYER (LP)	50
64	Decca LK 4649	FOLK, BLUES AND BEYOND (LP)	175
66	Decca LK 4780	MIDNIGHT MAN (LP)	90
68	Decca LK/SKL 4969	LARGE AS LIFE AND TWICE AS NATURAL (LP)	120
69	Decca LK/SKL 5011	HAT (LP)	100
70	Decca SKL 5056	HOLLY KALEIDOSCOPE (LP, as Davy Graham & Holly)	120
70	Decca LK 4649	FOLK, BLUES AND BEYOND (LP, second issue with boxed Decca logo and laminated front cover)	80
70	President PTLS 1039	GODINGTON BOUNDARY (LP, with Holly)	40
76	Eron ERON 007	ALL THAT MOODY (LP, private pressing)	200

DAVY GRAHAM/THAMESIDERS
63	Decca DFE 8538	FROM A LONDON HOOTENANNY (EP, 2 tracks each)	18

DAVY GRAHAM & ALEXIS KORNER
62	Topic TOP 70	3/4 A.D. (EP, first pressing in mauve sleeve with cream label)	90
62	Topic TOP 70	3/4 A.D. (EP, later pressings with lilac sleeve and blue label)	60
62	Topic TOP 70	3/4 A.D. (EP, later pressings with bronze sleeve and blue label)	30

(see also Alexis Korner)

ERNIE GRAHAM
78	Stiff OFF 2	Romeo And The Lonely Girl/Only Time Will Tell (p/s)	7
71	Liberty LBS 83485	ERNIE GRAHAM (LP, textured sleeve, black label)	200

(see also Clancy, Eire Apparent, Brinsley Schwarz, Help Yourself, Nick Lowe)

KENNY GRAHAM'S AFRO-CUBISTS
60	Starlite ST45 013	Bongo Chant/Beguine	10
57	Pye Jazz NJE 1053	PRESENTING KENNY GRAHAM PART 1 (EP)	20
57	Esquire EP 34	CARIBBEAN SUITE (EP)	20
57	Esquire EP 68	KENNY GRAHAM'S AFRO CUBISTS (EP)	20
57	Esquire EP 83	KENNY GRAHAM'S AFRO CUBISTS (EP)	25
56	MGM MGM-C 764	MOONDOG AND SUNCAT SUITES (LP, as Kenny Graham & His Satellites)	100
57	Nixa NJL 12	PRESENTING KENNY GRAHAM (LP)	100
57	Esquire 20-012	KENNY GRAHAM AFRO CUBISTS (LP)	80
57	Esquire 20-023	CARIBBEAN SUITE (LP)	100

(see also Yolanda)

LEN GRAHAM
77	Topic 12TS 334	WIND AND WATER (LP)	12

LEO GRAHAM
73	Upsetter US 399	News Flash/UPSETTERS: Flashing Echo	15
73	Summit SUM 8539	Three Blind Mice/UPSETTERS: Mice Skank	12

LOU GRAHAM
58	Coral Q 72322	Wee Willie Brown/You Were Mean Baby	500
58	Coral Q 72322	Wee Willie Brown/You Were Mean Baby (78)	150

LYNDA GRAHAM
62	Philips 326 552BF	As Long As The River Flows/When I'm Sixteen	8
63	Philips BF 1249	Without Your Love/Wait And See	8
64	Philips BF 1308	You'd Better Believe It/That's The Last Thing I'd Do	10

GRAHAM CENTRAL STATION
74	Warner Bros K 46206	GRAHAM CENTRAL STATION (LP)	15

(see also Sly & Family Stone)

RON GRAINER ORCHESTRA
64	HMV POP 1366	Not So Much A Programme, More A Way Of Life/Ascot Gavotte	10
67	Pye 7N 17383	A Man In A Suitcase/Andorra (pink label, later blue)	12
67	RCA Victor RCA 1635	The Prisoner/Happening Sunday	75
69	RCA Victor RCA 1898	The Paul Temple Theme/The Jazz Age	10
79	RK 1021	Tales Of The Unexpected/Malice Aforethought (p/s)	7
79	Six Of One 6 OF 1	THE PRISONER ARRIVAL (EP, fan club issue)	30
69	RCA Intl. INTS 1020	THEMES LIKE... (LP)	15
78	RK LB 003	TALES OF THE UNEXPECTED (LP)	15

ROSS GRAINER
79	Music Factory MF102	Cardiff Roses/Wind And The Trees	12

COLIN GRAINGER & THE FRANK CORDELL ORCHESTRA
58	HMV POP 484	This I Know/Are You?	7
59	HMV POP 639	Love Only Me/Plain And Simple Girl	7

GLENDA GRAINGER
60s	Audio Fidelity AFSP 007	Mr. Kiss Kiss Bang Bang/Who	12

BILLY GRAMMER
58	London HLU 8752	Gotta Travel On/Chasing A Dream	12
59	Felsted AF 121	Bonaparte's Retreat/The Kissing Tree	8
59	Felsted AF 128	Willy, Quit Your Playing/It Takes You	8
61	Brunswick 05851	Rainbow Round My Shoulder/Columbus Stockade Blues	8
59	Felsted GEP 1005	BILLY GRAMMER HITS (EP)	30

GERRY GRANAHAN
58	London HL 8668	No Chemise, Please/Girl Of My Dreams	20
58	London HL 8668	No Chemise, Please/Girl Of My Dreams (78)	20
60	Top Rank JAR 262	It Hurts/RICHIE ROBIN: Strange Dream	15

ROCCO GRANATA
59	Oriole CB 1525	Marina/Manuela	5

| 59 | Oriole CB 1525 | Marina/Manuela (78) | 15 |
| 61 | Oriole CB 1564 | Julia/Rocco Cha Cha | 5 |

GRANDADDY

| 03 | V2 VVR1012251 | SUMDAY (2-LP, with inner sleeves) | 20 |

GRAND FUNK RAILROAD

70	Capitol CL 15632	Heartbreaker/Please Don't Worry	8
70	Capitol CL 15661	Closer To Home/Aimless Lady	5
71	Capitol CL 15668	Inside Looking Out/Paranoid (33rpm)	8
71	Capitol CL 15689	I Can Feel Him In The Morning/Are You Ready/Mean Mistreater (33rpm maxi-single)	12
71	Capitol CL 15705	People, Let's Stop The War/Save The Land	5
72	Capitol CL 15738	Rock And Roll Soul/Flight Of Phoenix	5
69	Capitol E-ST 307	ON TIME (LP)	50
70	Capitol E-ST 406	GRAND FUNK (LP)	40
70	Capitol E-ST 471	CLOSER THAN HOME (LP)	40
71	Capitol E-SW 764	SURVIVAL (LP)	25
72	Capitol E-AS 853	E PLURIBUS FUNK (LP, circular 'silver coin' sleeve)	25
73	Capitol E-AST 11099	PHOENIX (LP, gatefold sleeve)	18

GRANDISONS

| 63 | RCA RCA 1339 | All Right/True Romance | 12 |

GRANDMASTER RICHIE RICH

| 85 | Spin Offs 12off1 | Check It Out/Scratch It Out (12") | 12 |
| 85 | Spin Offs 12off2 | Don't Be Flash/Flash Scratch (12") | 12 |

GRAND PRIX

80	RCA RCA 7	Thinking Of You/Feels Good (p/s)	15
83	Chrysalis PRIX 2	Shout/Keep On Believing (p/s, with patch)	8
83	Chrysalis PRIXP 2	Shout/Keep On Believing (picture disc)	6
83	Chrysalis PRIXX 2	Shout (12", p/s)	12

(see also McAuley Schenker Group, Praying Mantis, Stratus, Uriah Heep)

GRAND UNION

| 68 | CBS 3956 | Slowly But Surely/She Said | 40 |

(see also Enough's Enough)

GERRI GRANGER

| 63 | London HLX 9759 | Just Tell Him Jane Said Hello/What's Wrong With Me | 15 |

GRANNIE

| 71 | SRT SRT 71138 | GRANNIE (LP, private pressing of 99 copies only, homemade sleeve) | 1000 |

GRANNY

| 73 | DJM DJS. 291 | Lady/Weirdie Deirdre's Dilemma | 18 |

GRANNY'S INTENTIONS

67	Deram DM 158	The Story Of David/Sandy's On The Phone Again	25
68	Deram DM 184	Julie Don't Love Me Anymore/One Time Lovers	18
68	Deram DM 214	Never An Everyday Thing/Hilda The Bilda	25
70	Deram DM 293	Take Me Back/Maybe	20
70	Deram SML 1060	HONEST INJUN (LP, white/red label with small logo)	100

(see also Gary Moore)

AMY GRANT

| 82 | Myrrh MYR 1124 | AGE TO AGE (LP, with lyric insert) | 15 |

CLINTON GRANT

| 75 | Circle 5 | I've Been Trying/Second Attempt | 10 |

CY GRANT

| 62 | Melodisc 45-1433 | Heavy Weather/Lucky Oyster (tri centre) | 10 |

DOMINIC GRANT

| 68 | Mercury MF 1032 | I've Been There/Don't Stop Girl | 50 |

EARL GRANT

58	Brunswick 05762	The End/Hunky Dunky Doo	7
60	Brunswick 05824	House Of Bamboo/Two Loves Have I	10
62	Brunswick 05870	Swingin' Gently/Evening Rain	7

EDDY GRANT

| 74 | Torpedo TOR 30 | My Queen Tonight/Hello Africa | 5 |
| 75 | Torpedo TOR 53 | Nobody's Got Time (Part 1)/Nobody's Got Time (Part 2) | 10 |

(see also Equals, Coach House Rhythm Section)

ERKEY GRANT & EARWIGS

| 63 | Pye 7N 15521 | I'm A Hog For You/I Can't Get Enough Of You | 30 |

GOGI GRANT

55	London HLB 8192	Suddenly There's A Valley/Love Is	15
56	London HLB 8257	Who Are We/We Believe In Love	20
56	London HLB 8282	Wayward Wind/No More Than Forever	20
57	London HLB 8364	You're In Love/When The Tide Is High	15
58	London HLB 8550	The Golden Ladder/All Of Me	10
58	RCA RCA 1038	It's A Wonderful Thing To Be Loved/What A Beautiful Combination	5
58	RCA RCA 1047	Bonjour Tristesse/Johnny's Dream	6
59	RCA RCA 1101	Say A Prayer For Me Tonight/TONY MARTIN: She Is Not Thinking Of Me	5
59	RCA RCA 1105	Kiss Me Honey Honey Kiss Me/Two Dreams	6
60	London HLG 9185	Goin' Home/I'm Going To Live The Life	6
56	London REB 1057	GOGI GRANT (EP, export issue)	15
57	London HA-B 2032	SUDDENLY THERE'S GOGI GRANT (LP)	30
58	RCA RD 27054	BOTH ENDS OF THE CANDLE (LP, soundtrack)	15
59	RCA RD 27097	GIGI (LP, with Tony Martin)	15
60	London HA-G 2242	IF YOU WANT TO GET TO HEAVEN - SHOUT! (LP, mono)	15
60	London SAH-G 6072	IF YOU WANT TO GET TO HEAVEN - SHOUT! (LP, stereo)	25

(see also Tony Martin)

MINT VALUE £

JANIE GRANT
61	Pye International 7N 25093	Triangle/She's Going Steady With You	18
62	Pye International 7N 25148	That Greasy Kid Stuff/Trying To Forget You	18

JULIE GRANT
62	Pye 7N 15430	Somebody Tell Him/Ev'ry Letter You Write	10
62	Pye 7N 15447	So Many Ways/Unimportant Things	10
62	Pye 7N 15461	When You're Smiling/Lonely Sixteen	10
62	Pye 7N 15483	Up On The Roof/When You Ask About Love	5
63	Pye 7N 15508	Count On Me/Then, Only Then	5
63	Pye 7N 15526	That's How Heartaches Are Made/Cruel World	10
63	Pye 7N 15545	Don't Ever Let Me Down/Somebody Cares	10
63	Pye 7N 15590	Hello Love/It's Alright	12
64	Pye 7N 15684	Come To Me/Can't Get You Out Of My Mind	10
64	Pye 7N 15615	Every Day I Have To Cry/Watch What You Do With My Baby	10
64	Pye 7N 15652	You Are Nobody 'Til Somebody Loves You/I Only Care About You	10
65	Pye 7N 15756	Baby Baby (I Still Love You)/My World Is Empty Without You	10
65	Pye 7N 15812	Giving Up/Cause I Believe In You	10
65	Pye 7N 15884	Lonely Without You/As Long As I Know He's Mine	10
65	Pye 7N 15937	Stop/When The Lovin' Ends	15
62	Pye NEP 24171	THIS IS JULIE GRANT (EP)	20

LEE GRANT (& CAPITOLS)
66	Parlophone R 5531	Breaking Point/Don't Cry Baby (with Capitols)	20
70	Decca F 13029	A Little Love And Understanding/I Got To Get You Out Of My Mind (solo)	7

LITTLE BROTHER (GRANT)
70	Torpedo TOR 27	Baby Don't Let Me Down/Brother Strong Man (as Little Brother)	7
70	Torpedo TOR 28	Let's Do It Together/Hey Man, Why (as Little Brother Grant & Zapatta Schmidt)	7

(see also Equals)

NEVILLE GRANT
73	Downtown DT 509	Sick And Tired/PRINCE DJANGO: Hot Tip	80

NORMAN GRANT ORCHESTRA
61	Starlite ST45 060	Jive Medley/Speak Low	7

TOP GRANT
62	Island WI 034	Searching/David & Goliath	15
62	Island WI 052	Suzie/Jenny	15
63	Island WI 072	Riverbank Coberley (as Top-Grant)/Nancy	15
63	Island WI 074	Money Money Money/Have Mercy On Me	18
63	Island WI 077	War In Africa/The Birds	15

(see also Rhythm Aces)

GRAPE
92	Pencil Toast PENT 001	Baby In A Plastic Bag/Listen To Your Heart (p/s)	25

(see also P.J. Harvey)

GRAPEFRUIT
68	RCA Victor RCA 1656	Dear Delilah/The Dead Boot	8
68	RCA Victor RCA 1677	Elevator/Yes	25
68	RCA Victor RCA 1716	C'mon Marianne/Ain't It Good	6
68	Stateside-Dunhill SS 8005	Someday Soon/Theme For Twiggy	7
69	Stateside-Dunhill SS 8011	Round Going Round/This Little Man	7
69	RCA Victor RCA 1855	Deep Water/Come Down To The Station	7
70	RCA Victor RCA 1907	Lady Godiva/Thunder And Lightning	6
71	Deram DM 343	Universal Party/Sha Sha	6
69	Stateside-Dunhill S(S)L 5008	AROUND GRAPEFRUIT (LP, black/white/red label with "sold in the U.K..." text)	80
69	RCA Victor SF 8030	DEEP WATER (LP)	60

(see also Tony Rivers & Castaways, Easybeats, Fynn McCool, Sleepy)

GRAPEVINE
68	Liberty LBF 15063	Things Ain't What They Used To Be Anymore/Ace In The Hole	8

GRAPHITE
72	Beacon BEA 109	Gimme Your number/Chestnut Loke (possibly promo only)	15

GRASSROOTS
66	RCA Victor RCA 1532	Where Were You When I Needed You/These Are Bad Times	10
67	Pye International 7N 25422	Let's Live For Today/Depressed Feeling	10
67	Pye International 7N 25431	Things I Should Have Said/Tip Of My Tongue	6
68	RCA Victor RCA 1682	Melody For You/Hey Friend	5
68	RCA Victor RCA 1737	Midnight Confessions/Who Will You Be Tomorrow	12
69	Stateside-Dunhill SS 8006	Bella Linda/Hot Bright Lights	5
69	Stateside-Dunhill SS 8012	All Good Things Come To An End/Melody For You	5
69	Stateside-Dunhill SS 8018	The River Is Wide/(You Gotta) Live For Love	5
69	Stateside-Dunhill SS 8023	Who Will You Be Tomorrow/Midnight Confessions	8
69	Stateside-Dunhill SS 8029	I'd Wait A Million Years/Fly Me To Havana	12
71	Probe PRO 515	Temptation Eyes/Keepin' Me Down	8
69	Stateside S(S)L 5005	GOLDEN GRASS (LP)	25
70	Stateside SSL 5012	LEAVING IT ALL BEHIND (LP)	25

(see also P.F. Sloan)

GRASS-SHOW
96	Food FOOD 94	Freak Show/Sympathetic Television (picture disc, poster sleeve)	5

GRATEFUL DEAD
67	Warner Bros WB 7186	Born Cross-Eyed/Dark Star	50
70	Warner Bros WB 7410	Uncle John's Band/New Speedway Boogie	12
71	Warner Bros.	Truckin'/Johnny B. Goode (unissued)	0
72	Warner Bros K 16167	One More Saturday Night (as Grateful Dead with Bobby Ace)/Bertha	7
73	Atlantic K 19301	Let Me Sing Your Blues Away/Here Comes Sunshine	7
74	United Artists UP 36030	U.S. Blues/Loose Lucy	6
77	Warner Bros SAM 79	Dark Star/Born Cross-Eyed (p/s, mail-order issue with Dark Star magazine)	40
79	Arista ARIST 236	Good Lovin'/Stagger Lee	6

87	Arista RIS 35	Touch Of Grey/My Brother Esau (grey vinyl, p/s)	6
67	Warner Bros W 1689	THE GRATEFUL DEAD (LP, mono)	100
67	Warner Bros W(S) 1689	THE GRATEFUL DEAD (LP, stereo)	60
68	Warner Bros W 1749	ANTHEM OF THE SUN (LP, mono)	75
68	Warner Bros WS 1749	ANTHEM OF THE SUN (LP, stereo)	50
69	Warner Bros WS 1790	AOXOMOXOA (LP)	65
70	Warner Bros WS 1830	LIVE/DEAD (2-LP)	40
70	Warner Bros WS 1869	WORKINGMAN'S DEAD (LP, matt sleeve)	35
71	Warner Bros WS 1893	AMERICAN BEAUTY (LP)	25
71	Warner Bros K 66009	LIVE DEAD (SKULL AND ROSES) (2-LP)	25
71	Warner Bros. K66002	LIVE DEAD (LP, reissue)	18
72	Polydor 2310 171	HISTORIC DEAD (LP)	25
72	Polydor 2310 172	VINTAGE DEAD (LP)	25
72	Warner Bros K 66019	EUROPE '72 (3-LP, triple fold-out sleeve)	25
73	Warner Bros K 46246	HISTORY OF GRATEFUL DEAD (BEAR'S CHOICE) (LP)	12
73	Warner Bros K 49301	WAKE OF THE FLOOD (LP)	15
74	Warner Bros K 56024	SKELETONS FROM THE CLOSET: THE BEST OF GRATEFUL DEAD (LP)	12
74	Warner Bros K 59302	FROM THE MARS HOTEL (LP)	12
75	United Artists UA 29895	BLUES FOR ALLAH (LP)	12
76	United Artists UAD 60131/2	STEAL YOUR FACE (2-LP, gatefold sleeve, with sampler LP For Dead Heads Only [FREE 2] in inner sleeve)	20

(see also Jerry Garcia, Mickey Hart, Kingfish, Robert Hunter, Bob Weir, Keith & Donna Godchaux, Silver [U.S.], Diga Rhythm Band)

GRAVE
03	Century Media	MORBID WAYS TO DIE (Numbered box set with 6 picture disc LPs and booklet, 2000 only)	60

GRAVEDIGGAZ
94	Gee Street GEEA 14	NIGGAMORTIS (LP, with inner sleeve)	20

NICK GRAVENITES
69	CBS 63818	MY LABORS (LP)	22

(see also Big Brother & Holding Company)

BILLY GRAVES
59	Felsted AF 119	The Shag (Is Totally Cool)/Uncertain (export issue)	70

CARL GRAVES
75	A&M AM 7151	Baby Hang Up The Phone/Walk Softly	5

GRAVY TRAIN
71	Vertigo 6059049	Alone In Georgia/Can Anybody Hear Me	30
73	Dawn DNS 1036	Strength Of A Dream/Tolpuddle Episode	8
74	Dawn DNS 1058	Starbright Starlight/Good Time Thing	8
75	Dawn DNS 1115	Climb Aboard The Gravy Train/Sanctuary	8
70	Vertigo 6360 022	GRAVY TRAIN (LP, gatefold sleeve, large swirl label)	150
71	Vertigo 6360 051	BALLAD OF A PEACEFUL MAN (LP, gatefold sleeve, small swirl label)	600
73	Dawn DNLS 3046	SECOND BIRTH (LP)	70
74	Dawn DNLH 1	STAIRCASE TO THE DAY (LP, gatefold sleeve, pink 'sun' label)	70

(see also Mandalaband)

BARRY GRAY (ORCHESTRA)
62	Lyntone LYN 249/250	Sabotage/Supercar Song/Supercar Twist (flexi, with p/s may exist)	30
62	Lyntone LYN 249/250	Sabotage/Supercar Song/Supercar Twist (flexi)	15
64	Melodisc MEL 1591	Fireball/Zero G (by Barry Gray & His Spacemakers; in p/s)	55
64	Melodisc MEL 1591	Fireball/Zero G (by Barry Gray & His Spacemakers)	20
65	Pye 7N 17016	Thunderbirds/Parker - Well Done (in p/s)	35
65	Pye 7N 17016	Thunderbirds/Parker - Well Done	15
67	Pye 7N 17391	Captain Scarlet/The Mysterons Theme (in p/s)	35
67	Pye 7N 17391	Captain Scarlet/The Mysterons Theme	15
68	Pye 7N 17625	Joe 90 - Title Theme/Joe 90 - Hijacked (in p/s)	50
68	Pye 7N 17625	Joe 90 - Title Theme/Joe 90 - Hijacked	25
62	Golden Guinea GGL 0106	SUPERCAR - FLIGHT OF FANCY (LP, with Edwin Astley)	50
67	United Artists ULP 1159	THUNDERBIRDS ARE GO! (LP, soundtrack, mono)	100
67	United Artists (S)ULP 1159	THUNDERBIRDS ARE GO! (LP, soundtrack, stereo)	120
87	Fanderson MAF 1	MUSIC FROM THE 21st CENTURY (7" mail order only mini-album, 33prm)	10
98	Fanderson FANSP 7	SPACE 1999: YEAR ONE (2-CD, mail order only)	25
98	Fanderson FANSF6	SUPERCAR & FIREBALL XL5 (CD, mail order only)	30

(see also Century 21, Mary Jane with Barry Gray, Richard Harvey)

BARRY GRAY
04	Trunk JBH 010	UFO: THE ORIGINAL TELEVISION SERIES SOUNDTRACK (LP, 500 only, 250 on clear vinyl)	40
04	Trunk JBH 010	UFO: THE ORIGINAL TELEVISION SERIES SOUNDTRACK (LP, 500 only, 250 on black vinyl)	40

DOBIE GRAY
65	London HL 9953	The "In" Crowd/Be A Man	10
65	London HL 9953	The "In" Crowd/Be A Man (DJ Copy)	40
65	Pye International 7N 25307	See You At The Go Go/Walk With Love	25
65	Pye International 7N 25307	See You At The Go Go/Walk With Love (DJ Copy)	50
69	London HL 10268	The "In" Crowd/Be A Man (reissue)	7
73	MCA MU 1184	Drift Away/City Stars	5
73	MCA MU 1221	Now That I'm Without You/Loving Arms	6
75	Black Magic BM 107	Out On The Floor/Be A Man	5
74	Sydna SYD 5028	Good Old Days/Never Ending Love	8

DOLORES GRAY
55	Brunswick 05382	Heat Wave/After You Get What You Want, You Don't Want It	15
55	Brunswick 05407	Rock Love/One	30
55	Brunswick 05407	Rock Love/One (78)	10
57	Capitol CL 14732	There'll Be Some Changes Made/Fool's Errand	7
57	Capitol CL 14770	I'm Innocent/My Mama Likes You	5
63	Philips 326 582BF	Mornin' Train/Our Day Will Come	5

DORIAN GRAY
67	Parlophone R 5612	Behind The Tear/Walking Down A Back Street	5
68	Parlophone R 5667	I've Got You On My Mind/Move On	12
68	Parlophone R 5705	Love Is All That It Should Be/Let Me Go Home	5

68	Parlophone R 5732	Jingle Down A Hill/Get Goin' Baby	8

HERBIE GRAY

68	Giant GN 38	We're Staying Here/Life Ska	18

(see also Gene Rondo, Owen & Dandy, Tony Tribe)

JERRY GRAY & HIS ORCHESTRA

54	Brunswick 05351	The Ooh And Ah Mambo/Kettle Drum Hop	5

JIMMIE GRAY

82	JKO 12JKO 100	The Kool People (Vocal)/The Kool People (Instrumental) (12")	40

JOHNNIE 'THE GASH' GRAY

58	Fontana H 123	Big Guitar/Tequila	20
58	Fontana H 134	Apache/Zach's Tune	20

LES GRAY

77	Warner Bros K 16883	A Groovy Kind Of Love/U.S. Style (p/s)	5
77	Warner Bros K 17004	What Do You Want To Make Those Eyes At Me For/Stand Still Stella	5
79	Warner Bros. K 17316	I Think Of You/I Think I'll Go That Way	5

(see also Mud)

LORRAINE GRAY

64	Fontana TF 435	Are You Getting Tired Of Your Little Toy?/ The Boy That I Want Doesn't Want Me	10
64	Fontana TF 484	The Little Girl That Cries/Talk To Him	6

MAUREEN GRAY

61	HMV POP 944	I Don't Want To Cry/Come On And Dance	10

OWEN GRAY

60	Starlite ST45 015	Far Love/Please Let Me Go	35
60	Starlite ST45 019	Jenny Lee/The Plea	40
60	Blue Beat BB 8	Cutest Little Woman/Running Around (with Ken Richards Band)	20
61	Blue Beat BB 43	Sinners Weep/Get Drunk (with Hersan & His City Slickers)	20
61	Starlite ST45 032	Mash It (Parts 1 & 2)	40
62	Starlite ST45 078	I Feel Good/Someone To Help Me	40
62	Starlite ST45 088	Let Me Go Free/In My Dreams	40
62	Blue Beat BB 75	Rockin' In My Feet/Nobody Else (with Jets)	20
62	Blue Beat BB 91	Millie Girl (with Buster's Group)/DERRICK MORGAN: Headache	25
62	Blue Beat BB 103	Lonely Days/No Good Woman (with Sonny Bradshaw Quartet)	18
62	Blue Beat BB 108	Keep It In Mind/Do You Want To Jump (with Les Dawson Combo)	18
62	Blue Beat BB 113	Best Twist/Grandma-Grandpa (B-side with Hersan & His City Slickers)	18
62	Blue Beat BB 127	Pretty Girl/Twist So Fine	18
62	Blue Beat BB 136	They Got To Move/I Love Her	18
62	Blue Beat BB 139	Tree In The Meadow/Lizebella (with Buster's Group)	18
62	Island WI 002	Patricia/Twist Baby	20
62	Island WI 020	Audrey/Dolly Baby (with Ernest Rauglin [sic] Orchestra)	20
62	Island WI 030	Midnight Trail/Time Will Tell	20
62	Island WI 048	I'm Still Waiting/Last Night	10
62	Chek TD 101	Come On Baby/My One Desire	15
62	Dice CC 3	On The Beach/Young Lover	15
63	Blue Beat BB 147	Big Mabel/Don't Come Knocking (with Edwards' Groupe)	15
63	Blue Beat BB 188	Call Me My Pet/Give Me Your Love	15
63	Blue Beat BB 201	Snow Falling/Oowee Baby (as Owen Gray & His Big Brother)	15
64	Blue Beat BB 217	Draw Me Nearer/Daddy's Girl	15
65	Blue Beat BB 290	Daddy's Gone/BUSTER'S ALLSTARS: Johnny Dark	30
65	Aladdin WI 603	Gonna Work Out Fine/Dolly Baby	12
65	Aladdin WI 607	Can I Get A Witness/Linda Lu	12
65	Island WI 252	Shook Shimmy And Shake/I'm Going Back	20
65	Island WI 258	You Don't Know Like I Do/Take Me Serious (with Sound System)	15
65	Venus VE 2	Too Many Heartaches/Baby It's True	10
66	Island WI 252	Shook, Shimmy And Shake/Gonna Work Out Fine	30
66	Island WI 267	Paradise/Bye Bye Love	10
66	Blue Beat BB 365	I'm Gonna Say So Long/The Days I'm Living	12
67	Island WIP 6000	Help Me/Incense	25
67	Collins Downbeat CR 003	Collins Greetings/Rock It Down (with Sir Collins & Band)	60
67	Collins Downbeat CR 004	I'm So Lonely (with Sir Collins & Band)/EL RECO, SIR COLLINS & J. SATCH: Shock Steady	80
68	Collins Downbeat CR 007	Am Satisfy (with Sir Collins & Band)/BOB STACKIE & SIR COLLINS & BAND: Sweet Music	120
68	Collins Downbeat CR 009	Grab It, Hold It, Feel It (with Bob Stackie)/DAN SIMMONS: Way Out Sound	65
68	Collins Downbeat CR 010	I'm Gonna Take You Back (with Bob Stackie)/GLEN ADAMS: King Sized	75
68	Coxsone CS 7047	Give Me A Little Sign/Ain't Nobody Home	200
68	Coxsone CS 7053	Give It To Me/Isn't It So	80
68	Blue Cat BS 123	These Foolish Things/This I Promise	30
68	Blue Cat BS 156	I Can't Stop Loving You/Tell Me Darling	30
68	Trojan TR 632	Lovey Dovey/Grooving	15
68	Revolution REV 001	Sitting In The Park/You've Got It	12
69	Fab FAB 90	Three Coins In The Fountain/Tennessee Waltz	10
69	Fab FAB 120	Understand My Love/Apollo 12	10
69	Fab FAB 96	Ay Ay Ay/Let It Be Me (with Rudies)	15
69	Fab FAB 126	Swing Low/Release Me	10
69	Trojan TR 650	I Can't Stop Loving You/Tell Me Darling	8
69	Trojan TR 670	Too Experienced/I Really Loved You Baby	12
69	Duke DU 12	Reggae Dance/I Know	10
69	Duke DU 33	Seven Lonely Days/He Don't Love You Like I Do	8
69	Downtown DT 423	Groovin'/HERBIE GRAY & RUDIES: These Memories	7
69	Downtown DT 428	Lovey Dovey (with Dandy)/HERBIE GRAY & RUDIES: Kitty Wait	5
69	Camel CA 25	Girl What You Doing To Me/Woman A Grumble	15
69	Camel CA 34	Don't Take Your Love Away/Two Lovers	5
69	Camel CA 37	Every Beat Of My Heart/Don't Cry	5
70	Camel CA 50	Don't Sign The Paper/Packing Up Loneliness	5
70	Camel CA 51	Bring Back Your Love/Got To Come Back	5
70	Upfront UPF 3	Dream Lover/Mudda-Granma-Reggae (with Maximum Breed)	7
70	Bamboo BAM 47	I Can Feel It/I Don't Want (To Lose Your Love)	12

70	Crab CRAB 52	Just A Little Loving/DERRICK MORGAN: Take A Letter Maria	5
70	Pama PM 810	Sugar Dumpling/I Don't Know Why	8
70	Pama Supreme PS 299	I Am In Love Again/RANDY WILLIAMS: Version	6
70	Pama Supreme PS 302	Candida/When Will I Find My Way	6
70	Pama Supreme PS 310	You Gonna Miss Me/I Hear You Knocking	6
70	Supreme SUP 206	Surfin'/All The Love	6
70	Ackee ACK 102	No More/Don't Leave Me (both as Owen Gray & Omen)	15
71	Ackee ACK 123	Whispering Bells/CLANCY'S ALLSTARS: Whiplash (B-side actually "Jacket" by Dave Barker)	10
71	Camel CA 60	Groove Me/No Other One	15
71	Camel CA 73	Nothing Can Separate Us/Girl I Want You To Understand	6
71	Punch PH 87	Sincerely/Hold On I'm Coming	6
71	Pama Supreme PS 325	Summer Sand/Something To Remind Me	6
71	Pama Supreme PS 332	Greatest Hits (Parts 1 & 2)	6
72	Pama Supreme PS 351	Time/GRAHAM: Harlesden High Street	8
72	Pama Supreme PS 358	Hail The Man/I'll Follow You	6
72	Pama Supreme PS 360	Amazing Grace (with Graham Hawk)/SKETTO RICH: Don't Stay Out Late	6
70s	Rock Steady Rev. REV 004	Groovy Kind Of Love (with Elki & Rim Ram Band)/RIM RAM BAND: The Whistler	5
76	Angen ANG 121	Blazing Fire/Version	6
61	Starlite STLP 5	OWEN GRAY SINGS (LP)	120
63	Melodisc MLP 12-153	CUPID (LP)	45
69	Trojan TTL 24	REGGAE WITH SOUL (LP)	30
77	Trojan TRLS 139	FIRE AND BULLETS (LP)	20
78	Trojan TRLS 150	DREAMS OF OWEN GRAY (LP)	15

(see also Laurel & Owen, Gray Brothers, Elki & Owen, Owen & Milie, Owen & Dandy, Dennis Lowe, Survivors, Denzil & Jennifer, Brother Dan, Glen Adam)

SHANE GRAY
68	Page One POF 102	Sing Out Loud/Come Back To My Heart Again	10

VERA GRAY
66	HMV CLP3531	LISTEN, MOVE & DANCE 4 (LP)	25

WARDELL GRAY
54	Brunswick LA 8646	THE CHASE (LP, with Dexter Gordon)	25
65	Stateside SL 10144	WARDELL GRAY MEMORIAL ALBUM (VOL. 1) (LP)	15
65	Stateside SL 10145	WARDELL GRAY MEMORIAL ALBUM (VOL. 2) (LP)	15

GRAY BROTHERS
68	Blue Cat BS 124	Always/Big Man	30

(see also Owen Gray)

KATHRYN GRAYSON
53	MGM SP 1002	(All Of A Sudden) My Heart Sings/Jealousy	5
53	MGM SP 1014	Smoke Gets In Your Eyes/The Touch Of Your Hand (B-side with Howard Keel)	5
54	MGM SP 1078	I Hate Men/ANN MILLER & TOMMY RALL: Always True To You In My Way	5
54	MGM SP 1076	So In Love/ANN MILLER: Too Darn Hot	5

LARRY GRAYSON
72	York MYK 602	WHAT A GAY DAY (LP)	15

MILTON GRAYSON
60	London HLU 9068	Forget You/The Puppet	8

RUDY GRAYZELL
54	London HL 8094	Looking At The Moon And Wishing On A Star/The Heart That Once Was Mine	300
54	London HL 8094	Looking At The Moon And Wishing On A Star/The Heart That Once Was Mine (78)	50

GRAZINA
62	HMV POP 1094	Lover Please Believe Me/So What	15
63	HMV POP 1149	Don't Be Shy/Another Like You	15
63	HMV POP 1212	Be My Baby/I Ain't Gonna Knock On Your Door	20
64	Giv-A-Disc LYN 568	Stay Awhile/Let Me Go Lover (with magazine)	10

(see also Lady Murray, Mr & Mrs Murray, Le Roys, Cliff Richard)

GREASE BAND
72	Harvest HAR 5052	Laughed At The Judge/All I Want To Do/Jesse James	6
75	Goodear EAR 602	New Morning/Pontardawe Hop	5
71	Harvest SHVL 790	THE GREASE BAND (LP, textured sleeve first pressing)	50
72	Harvest SHVL 790	THE GREASE BAND (LP, second pressing with EMI boxed logo)	20
75	Goodear EAR 2902	AMAZING GREASE (LP)	15

(see also Joe Cocker, Wynder K. Frog, Made In Sheffield, Henry McCullough)

JOHNNY B. GREAT (& GOODMEN)
63	Decca F 11740	School Is In/She's A Much Better Lover Than You (with Goodmen)	10
64	Decca F 11804	Acapulco 1922/You'll Never Leave Him (solo)	8

(see also Quotations, Johnny Goodison)

GREAT ACES
72	Fab FAB 191	Gold And Silver/Liberty Rock	7
72	Fab FAB 200	Liberty Rock/Rock My Soul	7
72	Fab FAB 201	I Didn't Mean It/Boots And Shoes	6
72	Fab FAB 202	Baby Girl/Version	6
73	Fab FAB 203	Banana/My Sweet Lord	6

GREAT AWAKENING
69	London HLU 10284	Amazing Grace/Silver Waterfall	6

GREAT BRITISH HEROES (AKA GBH)
78	Lightning Records GIL 534	Eric Miller/Don't Give A Damn (unreleased, 1 known only)	1000

GREATEST SHOW ON EARTH
70	Harvest HAR 5012	Real Cool World/Again And Again	20
70	Harvest HAR 5026	Tell The Story/Mountain Song	6
77	Harvest HAR 5129	Magic Touch Woman/Again And Again	8
70	Harvest SHVL 769	HORIZONS (LP, gatefold sleeve, no EMI on label)	90
70	Harvest SHVL 783	THE GOING'S EASY (LP, gatefold sleeve, no EMI logo on label)	80
75	Harvest SHSM 2004	THE GREATEST SHOW ON EARTH (LP)	15

MINT VALUE £

(see also Living Daylights, Ian Dury & Blockheads, Fuzzy Duck, Glencoe, Naturals)

GREAT EXPECTATIONS
72	Polydor 2058241	I'm So Glad I Gotcha/Time And Place	8
73	Polydor 2058348	Devils Gun/Bigger And Better	8
81	Phillips (no cat no)	Midnight Man/Pt. 2	15

GREAT METROPOLITAN STEAM BAND
69	MCA MNP/S 403	THE GREAT METROPLITAN STEAM BAND (LP)	35

GREAT SATURDAY NIGHT SWINDLE
77	CBS 82044	GREAT SATURDAY NIGHT SWINDLE (LP, Irish-only issue)	12

(see also Rosemary Taylor)

GREAT SOCIETY
68	CBS 63476	CONSPICUOUS ONLY IN ITS ABSENCE (LP)	35

(see also Jefferson Airplane)

GREAT UNCLE FRED
67	Strike JH 324	I'm In Love With An Ex-Beauty Queen/Singalong Version	20

JOE GRECH
71	Electro ES 152	Marija L-Maltija/In-Nassab (export issue)	6

BUDDY GRECO
57	London HLR 8452	With All My Heart/Game Of Love (with B-G Skiffle Band)	10
58	London HLR 8613	I've Grown Accustomed To Her Face/On The Street Where You Live (as Buddy Greco & His Quartet)	5
60	Fontana H 255	The Lady Is A Tramp/Like Young	6
62	Columbia DB 4924	Mr. Lonely/Sentimental Fool	5
65	Columbia DB 7790	Mr. Kiss Kiss Bang Bang/Passing Pastels	5
56	Vogue Coral LVA 9021	AT MISTER KELLY'S (LP)	15

(see also Johnny Desmond)

GREEDIES
80	Vertigo GREED 1	A Merry Jingle/A Merry Jangle (p/s)	6

(see also Professionals, Thin Lizzy, Sex Pistols)

AL GREEN(E)
68	Stateside SS 2079	Back Up Train/Don't Leave Me (as Al Greene & Soul Mates)	20
68	Stateside SS 2079	Back Up Train/Don't Leave Me (as Al Greene & Soul Mates) (DJ copy)	40
69	Action ACT 4540	Don't Hurt Me No More/Get Yourself Together (by Al Greene)	10
70	London HLU 10300	You Say It/Gotta Find A New World	7
71	London HLU 10324	I Can't Get Next To You/Ride Sally Ride	7
71	Bell BLL 1188	Back Up Train/Don't Leave Me (as Al Green & Soul Mates, reissue)	12
71	London HLU 10337	Tired Of Being Alone / Right Now, Right Now	5
71	London HLU 10348	Let's Stay Together/Tomorrow's Dream	5
72	London HLU 10369	Look What You've Done For Me/I've Never Found A Girl	5
72	London HLU 10382	I'm Still In Love With You/Old Time Relovin'	5
72	London HLU 10393	You Ought To Be With Me/What Is This Feeling	5
73	London HLU 10406	Call Me/What A Wonderful Thing Love Is	5
73	London HLU 10419	Love And Happiness/So You're Leaving	5
73	London HLU 10426	Here I Am/I'm Glad You're Mine	5
74	London HLU 10443	Living For You/It Ain't No Fun To Me	5
74	London HLU 10452	Let's Get Married/So Good To Be Here	5
74	London HLU 10470	Sha La La (Make Me Happy)/School Days	5
75	London HLU 10482	L.O.V.E./I Wish You Were Here With Me	5
75	London HLU 10493	Oh Me Oh My/Strong As Death	5
75	London HLU 10511	Full Of Fire/Could I Be The One	5
76	London HLU 10527	Let It Shine/There's No Way	5
76	London HLU 10542	Keep Me Crying/There Is Love	5
69	Action ACLP 6008	BACK UP TRAIN (LP)	60
71	London SHU 8424	AL GREEN GETS NEXT TO YOU (LP)	20
72	London SHU 8430	LET'S STAY TOGETHER (LP)	20
72	London SHU 8443	I'M STILL IN LOVE WITH YOU (LP)	15
73	London SHU 8457	CALL ME (LP)	15
74	London SHU 8464	LIVIN' FOR YOU (LP)	15
74	London SHU 8479	EXPLORES YOUR MIND (LP)	15
77	London STO U 8685	I TRIED TO TELL MYSELF (EP)	10

BARRY GREEN
63	Ember JBS 713	Together/Collective Marriage	20
72	Decca F 13282	Papa Do/Boomerang	9

BRIAN GREEN
68	Fontana SFJL 912	BRIAN GREEN DISPLAY (LP)	40

GARLAND GREEN
69	MCA Soul Bag BAG 9	Jealous Kinda Fella/I Can't Believe You Quit Me	10
98	Kent 6T 16	Come Through Me/JUNIOR MCCANTS: Try Me For Your New Love	30

GRANT GREEN
65	Verve VLP 9111	HIS MAJESTY KING FUNK (LP)	25

IAN GREEN (REVELATION)
67	Polydor 56194	Last Pink Rose/Green Blues (solo)	30
69	CBS 3997	When You Love A Man/Santa Maria	6
69	CBS 4623	Revelation/Groover's Grave	6
70	CBS 63840	REVELATION (LP)	30

(see also Madeline Bell, Rosetta Hightower)

JIMMY GREEN
73	Duke DU 155	Suspicion/LLOYD'S ALL STARS: Suspicion - Version	7
73	Green Door GD 4062	I'll Be Standing By/LLOYD'S ALL STARS: I'll Be Standing By "Version"	6

(see also Jimmy London)

KATHE GREEN
69	Deram DM 279	If I Thought You'd Ever Change Your Mind/Primrose Hill	7

69	Deram SML 1039	RUN THE LENGTH OF YOUR WILDNESS (LP, white/red label)	35

KEITH GREEN

60s	Bird 118	NO COMPROMISE (LP)	30

LLOYD GREEN

75	Monument S MNT 81245	STEEL RIDES (LP)	20

PETER GREEN

71	Reprise RS 27012	Heavy Heart/No Way Out	15
72	Reprise K 14141	Beast Of Burden/Uganda Woman (with Nigel Watson)	15
78	PVK PV 16	Apostle/Tribal Dance	8
79	PVK PV 24	In The Skies/Proud Pinto (p/s)	5
80	PVK PV 36	Walking In The Road/Woman Don't	5
80	PVK PV 41	Loser Two Times/Momma Doncha Cry	5
81	PVK PV 103	Give Me Back My Freedom/Lost My Love	5
81	PVK PV 112	Promised Land/Bizzy Lizzy	5
70	Reprise RSLP 9006	THE END OF THE GAME (LP, with Nigel Watson)	40
80	PVK PVLS 102	LITTLE DREAMER (LP, with inner sleeve)	12

(see also Fleetwood Mac, Peter B's, Shotgun Express, John Mayall & Bluesbreakers, Gass, Peter Bardens, Katmandu, Gass)

PHILIP GREEN & PINEWOOD STUDIO ORCHESTRA

60	Top Rank JAR 355	League Of Gentlemen March/"Golden Fleece" Theme	10

SALLY GREEN

62	Philips PB 1243	It Hurts Too Much To Laugh/When's He Gonna Kiss Me	15

TEDDY GREEN

63	Piccadilly 7N 35131	Can I Take You Out Tonight/Talk	8
63	Piccadilly 7N 35146	Gee What A Party/Dream Chaser	10

TOM GREEN

74	Action ACT 4621	Rock Springs Railroad Station/Endless Confusion	100

GREEN ANGELS

65	Parlophone R 5390	Rockin' Red Wing/Let It Happen	15
66	Parlophone R 5512	An Exile's Dream/Hannigan's Hooley	6

NORMAN GREENBAUM

70	Reprise RS 20885	Spirit In The Sky/Milk Cow	5
70	Reprise RS 20846	Jubilee/Skyline	8
70	Reprise RS 20919	Canned Ham/Junior Cadillac	8
71	Reprise RS 21008	California Earthquake/Rhode Island Red	8
70	Reprise RSLP 6365	SPIRIT IN THE SKY (LP)	20
70	Page One POLS 017	WITH DR. WEST'S MEDICINE SHOW & JUNK BAND (LP)	22

(see also Dr. West's Medicine Show & Junk Band)

GREEN BEAN

69	Regal Zonophone RZ 3017	The Garden's Lovely/Sittin' In The Sunshine	7

GREENBEATS

64	Pye 7N 15718	If This World Were Mine/You Must Be The One	5
65	Pye 7N 15843	So Sad/I'm On Fire	5
67	Spin SP 2007	Pretty Woman/Thing	15

GREEN BULLFROG

72	MCA MKPS 2021	GREEN BULLFROG (LP, black/blue 'hexagon' label)	150

(see also Deep Purple, Ritchie Blackmore, Roger Glover, Tony Ashton, Matthew Fisher)

GREEN DAY

94	Reprise W 0247	Longview/On The Wagon (p/s)	8
94	Reprise W 0247 T	Longview/Going To Pasalacqua (Infatuation)/FOD (Live)/ Christy Road (Live) (10", green vinyl, stickered PVC sleeve)	25
94	Reprise W 0257	Basket Case/Tired Of Waiting For You (Green vinyl, numbered p/s)	10
94	Reprise W 0257 CD2	Basket Case/On The Wagon/Tired Of Waiting For You/ 409 In Your Coffee Maker (CD, green jewel case, numbered sleeve)	10
94	Reprise W 0269 T	Welcome To Paradise/Chump (Live)/Emenius Sleepus (green vinyl 12", stickered PVC sleeve)	12
95	Reprise W 0279 X	Basket Case/2,000 Light Years Away (Live) (numbered poster p/s, green vinyl)	12
95	Reprise W 0287X	Longview/Welcome To Paradise (live) (2nd issue with sticker sheet, p/s)	10
95	Reprise W 0294X	When I Come Around/She (live) (Ltd edn picture disc with insert)	8
95	Reprise W 0320 X	Geek Stink Breath/I Want To Be On TV (p/s, red vinyl)	6
95	Reprise W 0327	Stuck With Me/When I Come Around (Live) (p/s)	8
98	Reprise W 0438	Redundant/The Grouch (live) (p/s)	10
94	Reprise 9362 45529 1	DOOKIE (LP, with crowd photo on back cover, green vinyl, numbered sticker)	30
95	Reprise 9362 46046 1	INSOMNIAC (LP, with inner)	30
97	Reprise 9362 46794 1	NIMROD (LP, with inner)	40
04	Reprise 9362-41777-1	AMERICAN IDIOT (2-LP)	20

CLAUDE 'FATS' GREENE & ORCHESTRA

66	Island WI 290	Fats Shake 'Em Up Parts 1 & 2 (actually with Al Thomas)	15

JACK GREENE

66	Brunswick 05969	There Goes My Everything/The Hardest Easy Thing	6
68	Decca AD 1005	What Locks The Door/My Elusive Dreams (export issue)	8

JEANIE GREENE

69	Atlantic 584 226	Sure As Sin/I've Been A Long Time Loving You	10

KELLIE GREENE

64	Stateside SS 303	Madrigal/Foggy Day	12

LAURA GREENE

79	Grapevine GRP 135	Can't Help Loving Dat Man/It's A Good Day For A Parade	5

(see also Diane Renay)

GREENFIELD

71	Philips 6113002	Sweet America/Dorothys Daughter	15

GREENFIELD & COOK

72	Polydor 2121-105	Only Lies/You Return	8

MINT VALUE £

GREENGAGE
78	RCA PB 5069	Rosie/River	8

GREEN GINGER THREE
65	Decca DFE 8623	FROM THE LAND OF GREEN GINGER (EP)	15

GREEN JELLY
72	Z 74321 15142-7	Three Little Pigs/Joey The Cowboy (p/s)	6

LEE GREENLEE
59	Top Rank JAR 226	Cherry, I'm In Love With You/Starlight	7

GREEN MAN
75	Private pressing	WHAT AILS THEE? (LP)	100

GREEN RIVER
90	Tupelo TUP CD17	DRY AS A BONE EP (CD)	20
85	Homestead HMS 031	COME ON DOWN (LP, with insert)	20

(see also Mudhoney)

ARTHUR GREENSLADE (& GEE MEN)
61	Decca F 11363	Rockin' Susannah/Eclipse (with Gee Men)	10
66	Columbia DB 7865	Watermelon Man/Serenade To A Broken Jaw	10

ARTHUR GREENSLADE
72	Deram DM 349	Flirt (Pour Un Flirt)/Rainy Day Love	5

DAVE GREENSLADE
73	Warner Bros K 16264	Temple Song/An English Western	5
73	Warner Bros K 46207	GREENSLADE (LP, gatefold sleeve, green label)	25
73	Warner Bros K 46259	BEDSIDE MANNERS ARE EXTRA (LP, gatefold sleeve 'Burbank' label)	20
74	Warner Bros K 56055	SPYGLASS GUEST (LP, gatefold sleeve)	15
75	Warner Bros K 56126	TIME AND TIDE (LP, gatefold sleeve)	12
76	Warner Bros K 56306	CACTUS CHOIR (LP, lyric insert)	15
80	EMI EMSP 332	THE PENTATEUCH OF THE COSMOGONY (2-LP, with 47-page book, as Dave Greenslade)	40

(see also Wes Minster Five, Alan Price Set, Geno Washington & Ram Jam Band, Chris Farlowe, Colosseum, Samurai, Web, King Crimson, Stackridge)

SIDNEY GREENSTREET
55	Brunswick OE 9171	THE CASK OF AMONTILLADO (EP)	12

GREEN TELESCOPE
86	Imaginary MIRAGE 001	Two By Two/Make Me Stay/Thinkin' About Toady (p/s, various designs)	8
86	Wump BIF 4811	Face In The Crowd/Thoughts Of A Madman (p/s)	5

GREEN VELVET
95	Open OPENP 017	Flash (The Relief Remixes) (12")	15

ELLIE GREENWICH
67	United Artists UP 1180	I Want You To Be My Baby/Goodnight, Goodnight	25
68	United Artists UP 2214	Sunshine After The Rain/A Long Time Comin'	10
70	Bell BLL 1105	I Don't Wanna Be Left Outside/Ain't That Peculiar	10
73	MGM 2006 306	Maybe I Know/Goodnight Baby/Baby I Love You	8
73	MGM 2315 243	LET IT BE WRITTEN, LET IT BE SUNG (LP)	30

(see also Popsicles, Raindrops [U.S.])

GREEN WILLOW
80	Cotswold Music SFA 115	COTSWOLD MUSIC (LP)	30

GREEN WINDOWS
73	Decca F 13427	Twenty Years/Story Of A Man	8

JONNY GREENWOOD
03	Parlopone 5951471	BODYSONG (LP)	20

(see also Radiohead)

MICHAEL GREENWOOD
64	Oriole CB 1943	Buy Your Kid A Guitar/The Bellringer's Nightmare	5

MICK GREENWOOD
71	MCA MDKS 8003	THE LIVING GAME (LP, gatefold sleeve, pink/orange 'dogbone' label)	20
72	MCA MKPS 2026	TO FRIENDS (LP, black/blue 'hexagon' label)	20

(see also Fotheringay)o

NICHOLAS GREENWOOD
72	Kingdom KVLP 9002	COLD CUTS (LP)	900

(see also Crazy World Of Arthur Brown, Khan, Bryn Howarth)

GREENWOOD SINGERS/GREENWOODS
66	London hLR 10048	Please Don't Sell My Daddy No More Wine/Southbound	5

STOCKER GREENWOOD & FRIENDS
79	Changes	BILLY + NINE (LP)	20

BIG JOHN GREER
51	HMV JO 360	Woman Is A Five Letter Word/Got You On My Mind (78, export issue)	15

GINNY GREER
57	Brunswick 05673	Five Oranges, Four Apples/Kiss Me Hello (But Never Goodbye)	6

GREGER
66	Polydor 249 1103	IN THE NIGHT (LP)	25

MAX GREGER
70	Polydor 241 8022	SUNSHINE STARSHINE (LP)	12

BOBBY GREGG & FRIENDS
62	Columbia DB 4825	The Jam (Parts 1 & 2)	15

GREGORY
66	Pye 7N 17128	Walk With Faith In Your Heart/More Than Yesterday	5

BRIAN GREGORY
65	HMV POP 1412	Give Me Your Word/The Ballad Of Dick Turpin	5

GLENN GREGORY & CLAUDIA BRÜCKEN
85	ZTT P ZTAS 15	When Your Heart Runs Out Of Time/(Drumless) (book-shaped picture disc)	5

(see also Heaven 17, Propaganda, Act)

IA(I)N GREGORY
60	Pye 7N 15295	Time Will Tell/The Night You Told A Lie (as Ian Gregory)	30
61	Pye 7N 15397	Can't You Hear The Beat Of A Broken Heart/Because	25
62	Pye 7N 15435	Mr. Lovebug/Pocketful Of Dreams	35
63	Columbia DB 7085	Yellow Teddy Bear/How Many Times	12

JOHNNY GREGORY & HIS ORCHESTRA
61	Fontana H 341	Route 66/M Squad	7
61	Fontana TFE 17325	MAVERICK! (EP)	8
61	Fontana TFE 17331	BONANZA (EP)	8
62	Fontana TFE 17389	THE T.V. THRILLERS (EP)	10
72	Philips 6308 111	SPIES AND DOLLS (LP)	20
74	United Artists UAG 29546	A MAN FOR ALL SEASONS (LP)	40
74	United Artists QUAG 29546	A MAN FOR ALL SEASONS (LP, quadrophonic)	75

(see also Chaquito)

TONY GREGORY
66	Doctor Bird DB 1007	Baby Come On Home/Marie Elena	25
66	Doctor Bird DB 1016	Give Me One More Chance/I've Lost My Love	25
67	Island WI 3029	Get Out Of My Life/SOUL BROTHERS: Sugar Cane	30
67	Coxsone CS 7013	Only A Fool (Breaks His Own Heart)/Pure Soul	30
71	Horse HOSS 3	Bouncing All Over The World/Tell Me	6
67	Coxsone CSL 8011	TONY GREGORY SINGS (LP)	50

(see also Lloyd Charmers)

GREHAN SISTERS
66	Rex EPR 5005	THE GREHAN SISTERS (EP)	10
67	Transatlantic TRA 160	ON GALTYMORE MOUNTAINS (LP)	15

STAN GREIG'S JAZZ BAND
59	Tempo EXA 90	STAN GREIG'S JAZZ BAND (EP)	25
80s	Calligraph CLGLP 004	BLUES EVERY TIME (LP)	20

GREMLINS
66	Mercury MF 981	The Coming Generation/That's What I Want	18
67	Mercury MF 1004	You Gotta Believe It/I Can't Say	18

JOYCE GRENFELL
65	HMV POP 1407	Nursery School Flowers/I'm Going To See You Today	6

JOYCE GRENFELL & STANLEY HOLLOWAY
59	Caedmon TC 1104	BAB BALLADS & CAUTIONARY TALES (LP)	12

(see also Stanley Holloway)

JOEL GREY
54	MGM SPC 1	Last Night In The Back Porch/Two-Faced (export issue)	18
57	Capitol CL 14779	Everytime I Ask My Heart/Moonlight Swim	7
58	Capitol CL 14832	Be My Next/Shoppin' Around	20
61	London HLX 9442	Brigitte Bardot/BURT AND THE BACKBEATS: Felicidade	6

RONNIE GREY & JETS
55	Capitol CL 14329	Run, Manny, Run/Sweet Baby	20

SARAH GREY & ELLIE ELLIS
86	Greenwich Village GVR 231	YOU GAVE ME A SONG (LP, with insert)	15

GREYHOUND
71	Trojan TR 7820	Black And White/Sand In Your Shoes	5
71	Trojan TR 7834	Follow The Leader/Funky Jamaica	5
71	Trojan TR 7848	Moon River/I've Been Trying/Pressure Is Coming On	5
72	Trojan TRLS 27	BLACK AND WHITE (LP)	15

(see also Tillermen)

GRID
93	Virgin VSTX 1442	CRYSTAL CLEAR (Orb Mixes) (12", 4-track, clear vinyl)	8

(see also Timothy Leary Meets The Grid)o

ANDREW GRIDLEY
83	ADG 001	Lost In Time/Reflections/Taking A Chance On Love/I'm A Fool In Love	10

GRIDS
80	Kings Head	NEW ANTHEMS (EP)	20

ROOSEVELT GRIER
68	Action ACT 4515	People Make The World/Hard To Forget	22
69	Pama PM 774	Who's Got The Ball	15
69	Pama PM 784	C'mon Cupid/High Society Woman	20

GRANT GRIEVES
70	Injun 106	Four On The Floor/M1 Automatic	10

GRIFFIN
69	Bell BLL 1075	I Am The Noise In Your Head/Don't You Know	30
72	MGM 2006 088	What Happens In The Darkness/Calling You	10

(see also Heavy Jelly, Skip Bifferty, Every Which Way, Bell & Arc, Happy Magazine, Ginger Baker's Airforce)

GRIFFIN BROTHERS' ORCHESTRA
52	Vogue V 2139	Weepin' And Cryin' (with Tommy Brown)/The Teaser Boogie (78)	10

JOHNNY GRIFFIN
69	Polydor 583734	THE MAN I LOVE (LP)	35
70	Youngblood SSYB 11	FOOT PATTING (LP)	40

MINT VALUE £

JOHNNY GRIFFIN BIG SOUL BAND

| 61 | Riverside REP 3203 | THE BIG SOUL BAND (EP, with Clark Terry & Bobby Timmons) | 10 |
| 61 | Riverside RLP 12-3331 | THE BIG SOUL BAND (LP, also stereo [RLP 9331] | 20 |

(see also Eddie 'Lockjaw' Davis)

MERV GRIFFIN

| 61 | London HLL 9339 | The Charanga/Along Came Joe | 10 |

SYLVIA GRIFFIN

| 88 | Rocket BLAST 7 | Love's A State Of Mind/Forgive The Girl (p/s, features George Harrison) | 8 |
| 88 | Rocket BLAST 712 | Love's A State Of Mind/Forgive The Girl/Lonely Heart (12", p/s, features George Harrison) | 12 |

VINCENT GRIFFIN

| 77 | Topic 12TS 338 | TRADITIONAL FIDDLE MUSIC FROM COUNTY CLARE (LP) | 12 |

VIRGIL GRIFFIN

| 71 | Jay Boy BOY 43 | La Da Da Da Da/Climbing | 6 |

ANDY GRIFFITH

55	Capitol CL 14263	Ko Ko Mo (I Love You So)/Make Yourself Comfortable	25
56	Capitol CL 14619	No Time For Sergeants/Make Yourself Comfortable	6
57	Capitol CL 14766	Mama Guitar/A Face In The Crowd	25
57	Capitol CL 14766	Mama Guitar/A Face In The Crowd (78)	15
58	Capitol CL 14936	Midnight Special/She's Bad, Bad Business (with Dixie Seven)	15
56	Capitol EAP1 630	ANDY GRIFFITH (EP)	15
60	Capitol ST 1105	SHOUTS THE BLUES AND OLD TIMEY SONGS (LP, mono)	12
60	Capitol ST 1105	SHOUTS THE BLUES AND OLD TIMEY SONGS (LP, stereo)	15

JOE GRIFFITHS

| 69 | Philips SBL 7902 | OUT OF THE HEAD OF...(LP, black/silver labels) | 20 |

MARCIA GRIFFITHS

66	Island WI 285	Funny/KING SPARROW: Beggars Have No Choice (B-side actually by Leonard Dillon & Wailers; some copies credit Marcia Griffiths on both sides)	50
67	Studio One SO 2008	Hound Dog (actually by Norma Fraser)/HUGH GODFREY: My Time	60
67	Studio One SO 2015	After Laughter/HUGH GODFREY: Go Tell Him	60
68	Coxsone CS 7035	Mojo Girl (actually Nora Dean)/HAMLINS: Tell Me That You Love Me	150
68	Coxsone CS 7055	Feel Like Jumping/HORACE TAYLOR: Thundering Vibrations	50
68	Coxsone CS 7062	Hold Me Tight/BASIES: Home Sweet Home (B-side actually by Basses)	150
68	Studio One SO 2047	Words (as Marcia Griffiths & Jeff Dixon)/SHARKS: How Could I Live	30
68	Studio One SO 2059	Truly/SIMMS & ROBINSON: Drought	40
69	Gas GAS 111	Tell Me Now/STAN HOPE: The Weight	70
69	High Note HS 029	Talk (Parts 1 & 2) (correct title is actually "Toil")	15
69	Escort ES 808	Don't Let Me Down/REGGAEITES: Romper Room (B-side actually by Peter Tosh)	100
69	Trojan TR 693	Put A Little Love In Your Heart/J BOYS: Jay Fever	8
70	Harry J. HJ 6613	Put A Little Love In Your Heart/JAY BOYS: Bah Oop Ah	7
70	Harry J. HJ 6623	Band Of Gold/JAY BOYS: Cowboy (Version II)	7
70	Bamboo BAM 59	Shimmering Star/SOUND DIMENSION: Mun-Dun-Gu (B-side actually Im & David)	50
75	Torpedo TOR 47	Survival/Version	40
83	Island 1215112	Electric Boogie/Electric Boogies (12")	8
70	Trojan TRLS 94	SWEET BITTER LOVE (LP)	25
79	Sky Note SKYLP 09	NATURALLY (LP)	18
74	Trojan TRLS94	SWEET BITTER LOVE (LP, orange/white label)	25

(see also Bob & Marcia, Peter Touch/Tosh, Roy Richards, Soul Vendor, Bob Andy, Della Humphrey, Mr. Foundation, Bob Marley)

VICTOR GRIFFITHS

| 70 | Punch PH 29 | I Am Proud Of You/KING VICTOR ALL STARS: Version | 10 |

JOHNNY GRIGGS

| 83 | Hit HLS 3 | When You Go Away/Eldorado Theme (p/s) | 5 |

FERRE GRIGNARD

| 68 | Atlantic 584 158 | Yellow You Yellow Me/La Si Do | 7 |
| 70 | Major Minor SMLP 72 | CAPTAIN DISASTER (LP) | 15 |

CAROL GRIMES (& DELIVERY)

70	B&C CB 129	Harry Lucky/Homemade Ruin (with Delivery)	12
74	Virgin VS 109	You're The Only One/Southern Boogie	7
76	Decca FR 13674	I Betcha Didn't Know/Dynamite	6
70	Charisma CAS 1023	FOOLS MEETING (LP, with Delivery, gatefold sleeve)	200
74	Caroline CA 2001	WARM BLOOD (LP, black/white/red 'twins' labels)	25
75	Decca SKL-R 5268	CAROL GRIMES (LP, blue/silver labels)	20

(see also Uncle Dog, Babylon)

GRIMMS

73	Island HELP 11	GRIMMS (LP, black/silver label with pink 'i' logo)	12
73	Island ILPS 9248	ROCKIN' DUCK (LP, die cut 'duck' sleeve outside single sleeve, pink rim, palm tree logo)	20
76	DJM DJLPS 470	SLEEPERS (LP)	15

(see also Neil Innes, Liverpool Scene, Scaffold, Mike McGear, McGough & McGear, John Gorman, Zoot Money, Patto, Viv Stanshall, Andy Roberts, Bashers)

GRIM REAPER

| 83 | Ebony EBON 16 | SEE YOU IN HELL (LP) | 20 |
| 85 | Ebony EBON 32 | FEAR NO EVIL (LP) | 20 |

GRIN

71	CBS 5239	We All Sung Together/See What A Love Can Do	5
71	CBS 7405	Everybody's Missin' The Sun/18 Faced Lover	5
76	CBS 4339	Soft Fun/Slippery Fingers	5
71	Epic EPC 64272	GRIN (LP)	12
72	CBS 64652	1 + 1 (LP)	12
73	Epic EPC 65166	ALL OUT (LP)	12

(see also Nils Lofgren)

GRINDERMAN

| 07 | MUTE 370 | Get It On (1-sided 7" other side etched, p/s) | 18 |

07	Mute MUTE 373	No Pussy Blues (edit)/Chain Of Flowers (numbered, stickered p/s, poster)	8
07	Mute MUTE 381	(I Don't Need You To) Set Me Free (embossed p/s, one-sided etched disc)	15
10	Mute 12 MUTE 441	Heathen Child/Star Charmer/Super Heathen Child (12", red vinyl, poster, first pressing with black sticker)	10
07	STUMM 272	GRINDERMAN (LP)	12

(see also Nick Cave)

GRINDERSWITCH
76	Capricorn 2089 030	Picking The Blues/The Best I Can	7

JANNY GRINE
70s	Sparrow BIRD 104	FREE INDEED (LP)	25

GRINGO
71	MCA MKS 5067	I'm Another Man/Soft Mud	6
71	MCA MKPS 2107	GRINGO (LP, red/pink 'dogbone' label)	60

(see also Caravan)

JOE GRINNE
69	Coxsone CS 7098	Mr Editor/How I Feel (both sides actually by Melodians)	40

GRISBY DYKE
69	Deram DM 232	The Adventures Of Miss Rosemary La Page/Mary Anne She	30

GRIZZARDS
98	Baban GRIZ 5	Grizzling/The Green Griz (p/s)	8

GROBBERT & DUFF
72	Sunlamp GRA 101	I Am I Think/The Man From Naz	100

PIERRE GROCOLAS
79	Decca FR13852	Flying Love/You're Gonna Dance	12

DEWEY GROOM
62	Starlite ST45 085	Butane Blues/That's All I Want Out Of Life	30
63	Starlite ST45 095	You're Tearing My Heart Out Of Me/Walking Papers	10
63	Starlite ST45 105	Heartaches For Sale/Sometimes If I'm Lucky	8

GROOP
68	CBS 3204	Woman You're Breaking Me/Mad Over You	30
68	CBS 3351	Lovin' Tree/Night Life	20
69	Bell BLL 1070	A Famous Myth/Tears And Joys	15
69	Bell BLL 1080	The Jet Song (When The Weekend's Over)/Nobody At All	18

GROOVE
69	Parlophone R 5783	The Wind/Play The Song	35

GROOVE
80	Trendy WHIP 1	Heart Complaint/I Wanna Be Your Pygmy	15

GROOVE FARM
87	Raving Pop Blast RPBGF 1	SORE HEADS AND HAPPY HEARTS (EP, with insert & handwritten labels)	8
87	Raving Pop Blast RPBGF 2	ONLY THE MOST IGNORANT GUTLESS SHEEP-BRAINED POLTROON CAN DENY THEM NOW (EP)	8
87	Subway Org. SUBWAY 15T	GOING BANANAS WITH THE GROOVE FARM (12" EP)	8
88	Subway Organisation	The Big Plastic Explosion! (It's Alright, It's Alright) (Dance Mix)/Nancy Sinatra/ Baby Blue Marine/Riot On Sunset Strip/Red Dress (p/s)	6
88	Subway Organisation	Driving In Your New Car (Mini Mix)/Expanding Reindeer/I Can't Dance With You/Epistle To Duppy (12", white label promos only, with press release)	10

GROOVE TUNNEL
95	Detour DR 023	Rainy Day/How Do You Feel (p/s, white vinyl)	7

GROOVERS
71	Camel CA 83	Put Me Down Easy/I Want To Go Back Home	6
71	Escort ERT 863	Bend Down Low/The Burning Feeling	6

(see also Lloyd & Groovers, Alva Lewis, Junior Byles, Dennis Walks)

WINSTON GROOV(E)Y
69	Grape GR 3005	Leaving Me Standing/Little Girl	12
69	Grape GR 3008	Merry X-mas/I Am Lonely	8
69	Nu Beat NB 041	Island In The Sun/Work It Up	10
69	Nu Beat NB 042	Josephine/Champagne And Wine	8
70	New Beat NB 053	Standing At The Corner/You Send Me	8
70	New Beat NB 055	Yellow Bird/For Your Love	6
70	New Beat NB 058	Here Is My Heart/Birds And Flowers	6
70	New Beat NB 066	Groovin'/Sugar Mama	6
70	New Beat NB 073	Tennessee Waltz/Old Man Trouble	6
70	Attack ATT 8018	I Can't Go On/Only You	10
70	Attack ATT 8019	You Can't Turn Your Back On Me/PAMA DICE: The Worm	10
70	Jackpot JP 708	Funky Chicken/CIMARRONS: Part 2 (B-side actually unknown instrumental)	10
70	Jackpot JP 709	Funny/CIMARRONS: Funny Version Two	10
70	Torpedo TOR 11	Please Don't Make Me Cry/Motion On The Ocean	12
70	Crab CRAB 63	I Like The Way/Tell Me Why	8
71	Crab CRAB 64	I've Got The Find A Way To Win Mary Back/Wanna Be There	8
71	Bullet BU 471	I Wanna Be Loved/Get Back Together	8
71	Pama PM 827	Don't Break My Heart/How Long Will This Go On	10
71	Pama Supreme PS 323	Free The People/Not Now	8
72	Pama Supreme PS 349	What You Gonna Do/Why Did You Leave	8
72	Pama Supreme PS 364	Sylvia's Mother/Here Is My Heart	8
73	Explosion EX 2086	Nose For Trouble/RHYTHM RULERS: Version	8
74	Explosion EX 2088	Please Don't Make Me Cry/So Easy	8
69	Pama PMP 2011	FREE THE PEOPLE (LP)	40

(see also King Horror, Upsetters)

WALTER GROSS
54	MGM SP 1070	Blue Moon/Tenderly	5
54	MGM SP 1071	You Won't Forget Me (with India Adams)/Follow Me	5

G.G. GROSSETT

69	Crab CRAB 10	Run Girl Run/DENNIS WALKS: The Drifter	80
69	Crab CRAB 33	Greater Sounds/Live The Life I Love	12

STEFAN GROSSMAN

70	Big T BIG 133	Pretty Little Tune/Little Sally Walker	7
71	Big T BIG 140	'Joe Hill' - Themes	7
68	Fontana (S)TL 5463	AUNT MOLLY'S MURRAY FARM (LP)	25
69	Fontana STL 5485	THE GRAMERCY PARK SHEIK (LP)	20
70	Transatlantic TRA 217	YAZOO BASIN BOOGIE (LP)	15
71	Transatlantic TRA 246	THOSE PLEASANT DAYS (LP, with lyric insert)	15
72	Transatlantic TRA 257	HOT DOGS (LP)	12
73	Transatlantic TRA 264	LIVE! (2-LP, gatefold sleeve)	15
73	Transatlantic TRA 274	GUITAR INSTRUMENTALS (LP)	12

(see also John Renbourn)

LUTHER GROSVENOR

71	Island WIP 6109	Here Comes The Queen/Heavy Day	6
72	Island WIP 6124	All The People/Waiting	6
71	Island ILPS 9168	UNDER OPEN SKIES (LP, gatefold sleeve pink rim palm tree logo)	40

(see also Hellions, Revolution, Art, Spooky Tooth, Mott The Hoople, Widowmaker)

CARL GROSZMANN

70	Decca F 13065	Thunderbird/Missouri Woman	6
75	Ring O' 2017 103	I've Had It/C'mon And Roll	15
77	Ring O' 2017 107	Face Of A Permanent Stranger/Your Own Affair (promo p/s)	15
77	Ring O' 2017 107	Face Of A Permanent Stranger/Your Own Affair (company sleeve)	10
75	Ring O' 2320 102	CARL GROSZMANN (LP, unreleased)	0

GROUND ATTACK

81	Ground Attack GAR 001	THE RED LION EP (Red Lion/Every Mother's Son) (gatefold p/s)	100
81	Ground Attack GAR 001	THE RED LION EP (Red Lion/Every Mother's Son) (later pressing with no p/s)	20

GROUNDHOGS

68	Liberty LBF 15174	You Don't Love Me/Still A Fool	30
69	Liberty LBF 15263	B.D.D./TONY McPHEE: Gasoline	35
70	Liberty LBF 15346	Eccentric Man/Status People	20
73	W. Wide Artists WWS 006	Sad Go Round/Over Blue	6
74	W. Wide Artists WWS 012	Plea Sing, Plea Sing/TONY McPHEE: Dog Me Bitch	6
76	United Artists UP 36095	Live A Little Lady/Boogie Withus	6
76	United Artists UP 36177	Pastoral Future/Live Right (as Tony McPhee & Groundhogs)	6
68	Liberty LBL 83199E	SCRATCHING THE SURFACE (LP, mono, blue label)	100
68	Liberty LBS 83199E	SCRATCHING THE SURFACE (LP, stereo, blue label)	50
69	Liberty LBS 83253	BLUES OBITUARY (LP, blue label)	65
70	Liberty LBS 83295	THANK CHRIST FOR THE BOMB (LP, gatefold sleeve, 1st pressing blue label)	70
70	Liberty LBS 83295	THANK CHRIST FOR THE BOMB (LP, gatefold sleeve, 2nd pressing black label)	30
71	Liberty LBG 83401	SPLIT (LP, gatefold sleeve, black label)	30
72	United Artists UAG 29347	WHO WILL SAVE THE WORLD... (LP, gatefold sleeve)	30
72	United Artists UAG 29419	HOGWASH (LP, tri-fold sleeve)	25
73	United Artists UDF 31	GROUNDHOGS' BEST 1969-1972 (2-LP, red HK/DA/73 inside sleeve))	15
74	W. Wide Artists WWA 004	SOLID (LP, with lyric insert)	15
76	United Artists UAS 29917	CROSSCUT SAW (LP)	15
76	United Artists UAS 29994	BLACK DIAMOND (LP)	12
84	Psycho PSYCHO 24	HOGGIN' THE STAGE (2-LP, with EP, stickered gatefold sleeve)	18
85	Landslide LANDLP 102	RAZORS EDGE (LP)	12
87	Demi Monde DMLP 1014	BACK AGAINST THE WALL (LP)	12
89	HTD Records HTDLP 2	NO SURRENDER (LP)	12

(see also John Lee's Groundhogs, Tony McPhee, Herbal Mixture, Home, Andy Fernbach, John Lee Hooker)

GROUP

72	Charisma CB 197	Bovver Boys/Piraeus Football Club/An Open Letter To George Best	6

(see also Neil Innes)

GROUP B

67	Vocalion VF 9284	I Know Your Name Girl/I Never Really Know	25

(see also Blue Cheer)

GROUP 1850

69	Philips SBL 7884	AGEMO'S TRIP TO MOTHER EARTH (LP, gatefold sleeve)	300

GROUP IMAGE

69	Stable SLE 8005	A MOUTH IN THE CLOUDS (LP)	80

GROUP ONE

58	HMV POP 463	She's Neat/Made For Each Other	30
58	HMV POP 492	Chanson D'Amour/Londonderry Air	5

GROUP SIX

59	Oriole CB 1488	Rock-A-Boogie/Rockin' The Blues	25
59	Oriole CB 1488	Rock-A-Boogie/Rockin' The Blues (78)	20

GROUP THERAPY

69	Philips BF 1744	River Deep Mountain High/Remember What You Said	6
69	Philips BF 1792	Can't Stop Lovin' You Baby/I Must Do	6
69	Philips SBL 7883	YOU'RE IN NEED OF GROUP THERAPY (LP)	20

GROUP TWO

68	Columbia DB 8374	It's Raining Outside/Western Man, Eastern Lady	7

GROUP X

63	Fontana 267 274 TF	There Are 8 Million Cossack Melodies - And This Is One Of Them/ Teneriffe (in p/s)	15
63	Fontana 267 274 TF	There Are 8 Million Cossack Melodies - And This Is One Of Them/ Teneriffe	8
63	Fontana TF 417	Roti Calliope/Cross Beat	20

GROUT

79	Urinating Vicar	DO IT YOURSELF (EP) (100 only, sound quality very poor)	400

GROW UP

80	Object Music OM12	JOANNA EP	10
79	Object OM 05	GROW UP (EP)	12
79	Object Music OBJ 5	THE BEST THING (LP)	20
81	UP Records GROWL 1	WITHOUT WINDS (LP)	15

GRUDGE

73	Black Label BL 002	When Christine Comes Around/I'm Gonna Smash Your Face In	50

GRUMBLE

73	RCA Victor RCA 2384	Da Doo Ron Ron/Pig Bin An' Gone	5

(see also 10cc)

GRUMBLEWEEDS

71	Phillips 78434	Never Before/Fiona McLaughlin	15
72	Phillips 6006208	String Of Beads (Good Old Leeds)/Simple Little Things	12
73	Decca F 13416	Trees/I Am A Grumbleweed	6
74	Decca F13513	(Hey Babe) Follow Me/Won't Say No Again	20

GRUNT FUTTOCK

72	Regal Zonophone RZ 3042	Rock 'N' Roll Christian/Free Sole	40

(see also Move, Roy Wood)

DAVE GRUSIN

85	Arista GRP 5610	MOUNTAIN DANCE (LP, Nimbus Supercut, mail order only through Practical Hi Fi magazine)	40

GRUVY BEATS

70	Nu Beat NB 048	Share Your Popcorn/LAUREL AITKEN: Mr. Popcorn	15
70	Nu Beat NB 049	Blue Mink/LAUREL AITKEN: I've Got Your Love	15

GIGI GRYCE

60	Esquire 32-151	SAYIN' SOMETHIN' (LP)	20
60	Esquire	RAT RACE BLUES (LP)	30

GRYPHON

77	Harvest HAR 5125	Spring Song/Fall Of The Leaf	6
73	Transatlantic TRA 262	GRYPHON (LP, gatefold sleeve)	25
74	Transatlantic TRA 282	MIDNIGHT MUSHRUMPS (LP)	12
74	Transatlantic TRA 287	RED QUEEN TO GRYPHON THREE (LP)	15
75	Transatlantic TRA 302	RAINDANCE (LP)	12
77	Harvest SHSP 4063	TREASON (LP, with lyric inner sleeve)	20

(see also Richard Harvey, The Banned)

G.T.O.'S

67	Polydor 56721	She Rides With Me/Rudy Vadoo	75

(see also Joey & Continentals)

G.T.O.'S (GIRLS TOGETHER OUTRAGEOUSLY)

70	Straight STS 1059	PERMANENT DAMAGE (LP)	120

(see also Jeff Beck, Frank Zappa)

G.T.R.

86	Arista GTR 1	When The Heart Rules The Mind/Reach Out (poster sleeve)	6
86	Arista GTRSD 1	When The Heart Rules The Mind/Reach Out (picture disc)	8

(see also Steve Hackett)

GUANA BATZ

84	Big Beat SW 89	You're So Fine/Rockin' In My Coffin/Jungle Rumble/Guana Rock (p/s)	6
84	Big Beat NS 96	The Cave/Werewolf Blues (p/s)	5
85	I.D. NOSE 4	HELD DOWN ... AT LAST (LP)	12

GUARDIANS OF THE RAINBOW

68	President PT 186	What Do You Do When You've Lost Your Love/Cry Alone	6

JOSE GUARDIOLA & ROSE MARY

63	HMV POP 1147	Algo Prodigioso/Di Papa	7

GUERNICA

87	Idol 12 ID 2	ORANGE AND RED EP (12")	30

LENNIS GUESS

75	Route RT 11	Just Ask Me/Workin' For My Baby	5

GUESS WHO

65	Pye International 7N 25305	Shakin' All Over/Till We Kissed	25
66	King KG 1044	His Girl/It's My Pride	30
67	Fontana TF 831	This Time Long Ago/There's No Getting Away From You	15
67	Fontana TF 861	Miss Felicity Grey/Flying On The Ground Is Wrong	10
70	RCA 1870	Laughing/Undu	5
70	RCA 1943	American Woman/No Sugar Tonight	6
69	RCA SF 8037	WHEATFIELD SOUL (LP)	15
70	RCA SF 8107	AMERICAN WOMAN (LP)	15

EARL GUEST

62	Columbia DB 4707	Honky Tonk Train Blues/Winkle Picker Stomp	10
62	Columbia DB 4926	The Girl From The Fair Isle/Twistin' John	5
64	Columbia DB 7212	Begin The Beguine/Foxy	15

GUEST & EDWARDS

72	Phillips 6006231	All Alone/Sing You A Picture	20

REG GUEST SYNDICATE

65	Mercury MF 927	Underworld/Guys, Guns, Dolls And Danger	100
66	Mercury 20089MCL	UNDERWORLD (LP)	40

GUGGENHEIM

72	Indigo GOLP 7001	GUGGENHEIM (LP, private pressing)	50

GUIDED BY VOICES

99	Creation CRE 325	Teenage FBI/Flying Into Ashes/Tropical Robots (p/s)	10

GUILLEMOTS
05	Fantastic Plastic FPS050	I SAW SUCH THINGS IN MY SLEEP EP (CD, p/s)	15
05	Fantastic Plastic FPS050	I SAW SUCH THINGS IN MY SLEEP EP (10", 300 only p/s)	40
05	Fantastic Plastic FPTEN055	Trains To Brazil/My Chosen One/Go Away (10", 1,000 only, p/s)	8
06	Polydor IC00309	THROUGH THE WINDOWPANE (2-LP, gatefold sleeve, inner sleeves & booklet)	20

ISAAC GUILLORY
74	Atlantic K 40521	ISAAC GUILLORY (LP)	18

(see also Shames, Sam Gopal)

GUILLOTEENS
65	Pye International 7N 25324	I Don't Believe/Hey You	60

BONNIE GUITAR
58	London HLD 8591	A Very Precious Love/Johnny Vagabond	25
59	Top Rank JAR 260	Candy Apple Red/Come To Me, I Love You	10
58	London HA-D 2122	MOONLIGHT AND SHADOWS (LP)	30

GUITAR CRUSHER WITH JIMMY SPURRILL
69	Blue Horizon 57-3149	Since My Baby Hit The Numbers/Hambone Blues	30

(see also Wild Jimmy Spurrill)

GUITAR RED
63	Pye International 7N 25219	Just You And I/Old Fashioned Love	40

GUITAR SHORTY
72	Flyright LP 500	CAROLINA SLIDE GUITAR (LP)	15

GULLIVER
70	Elektra 2101 011	Every Day's A Lovely Day/Angelina	6
70	Elektra 2101 017	Angelina/Christine	5
70	Elektra 2410 006	GULLIVER (LP)	18

GULLIVER'S PEOPLE
66	Parlophone R 5435	Splendor In The Grass/Took This Land	20
66	Parlophone R 5464	Fi Fo Fum/Over The Hills	10
68	Parlophone R 5709	On A Day Like This/My Life	10
69	Columbia DB 8588	Somehow, Somewhere/I Found Love	10

GULLIVER'S TRAVELS
69	Instant INLP 003	GULLIVER'S TRAVELS (LP, withdrawn, front laminated sleeve, flipbacks)	120

(see also Mike D'Abo, Andrew Oldham)

GUMBAE CULTURE
85	Leyson LR 0105	Take It Easy/Ghetto Youth (12")	15

GUN
68	CBS 3764	Race With The Devil/Sunshine	5
68	CBS 3764	Race With The Devil/3-4 In The Middle (different B-side)	10
69	CBS 4052	Drives You Mad/Rupert's Travels	7
69	CBS 4443	Hobo/Don't Look Back	7
69	CBS 4443	Hobo/Long Hair Wild Man (different B-side)	10
70	CBS 4952	Runnin' Wild/Drown Yourself In The River	6
69	CBS M63552	GUN (LP, mono, laminated front sleeve, orange label)	150
69	CBS 63552	GUN (LP, stereo, laminated front sleeve, orange label)	50
69	CBS 63683	GUNSIGHT (LP)	45

(see also Baker-Gurvitz Army, Parrish & Gurvitz, Rupert's People, Three Man Army, Knack)o

GUN CLUB
82	Animal/Chrysalis CHCAT 2635	The Fire Of Love/Walking With The Beast (p/s)	6
82	Beggars Banquet BEG 80	Ghost On The Highway/Sex Beat (p/s)	20
83	Animal/Chrysalis GUN 1	Death Party/House On Highland Avenue/The Lie (p/s)	8
83	Animal/Chrysalis GUN 12	Death Party/House On Highland Avenue/The Lie/Light Of The World/ Come Back Jim (12", p/s)	10
88	Red Rhino RED 89	The Breaking Hands/Crabdance (p/s)	8
88	Red Rhino RED 89 12	The Breaking Hands/Crabdance/Nobody's City (12", p/s)	10
90	Fire BLAZE 47T	The Great Divide/Crabdance/St. John's Divine Part 2 (p/s)	12
81	Beggars Banquet BEGA 37	THE FIRE OF LOVE (LP)	25
82	Animal CHR 1398	MIAMI (LP)	18
83	ABC ABC LP 1	THE BIRTH THE DEATH THE GHOST (LP)	18
84	Animal CHR 1398	LAS VEGAS STORY (LP)	15
08	Retro Delux RDBX 004	THE LIFE AND TIMES OF JEFFREY LEE PIERCE AND THE GUN CLUB (4-CD box set)	30

(see also Jeffrey Lee Pierce, Kid Congo Powers)

JON GUNN
67	Deram DM 133	I Just Made Up My Mind/Now It's My Turn	15
67	Deram DM 166	If You Wish It/I Don't Want To Get Hung Up On You Babe	15

JIM GUNNER
60	Decca F 11276	Hoolee Jump/Footloose (as Jim Gunner & Echoes)	15
61	Fontana H 313	Desperado/Baghdad (as Jim Gunner & His Sidekicks)	20

TONY GUNNER
62	London HLU 9492	Rough Road/You Gotta Get Home	20

SARAH OGAN GUNNING
67	Topic 12T 171	A GIRL OF CONSTANT SORROW (LP, mono, blue label)	20

GUNS FOR HIRE
80	Korova KOW 6	My Girlfriend's Boyfriend/I'm Famous Now (p/s)	10

(see also Main T. Possee)

GUNSHOT
90	Vinyl Solution STORM18	Battle Creek Brawl (12")	8
93	Vinyl Solution FART6	To Those Who Deserve It (7")	12
94	Vinyl Solution STEAM 92	SINGLES CONNECTION (LP, red vinyl)	15

GUNS N' ROSES
87	Geffen GEF 22	It's So Easy/Mr Brownstone (p/s)	10

87	Geffen GEF 22T	It's So Easy/Mr Brownstone/Shadow Of Your Love/Move To The City (12", p/s)	12
87	Geffen GEF 22TP	It's So Easy/Mr Brownstone/Shadow Of Your Love/ Move To The City (12", picture disc with stickered PVC sleeve)	40
87	Geffen GEF 30	Welcome To The Jungle/Whole Lotta Rosie (live) (red p/s)	8
87	Geffen GEF 30T	Welcome To The Jungle/Whole Lotta Rosie (live)/It's So Easy (live)/Knockin' On Heaven's Door (live) (12", red p/s)	20
87	Geffen GEF 30TW	Welcome To The Jungle/Whole Lotta Rosie (live)/It's So Easy (live)/Knockin' On Heaven's Door (live) (12", poster p/s)	10
87	Geffen GEF 30P	Welcome To The Jungle/Whole Lotta Rosie (live)/It's So Easy (live)/Knockin' On Heaven's Door (live) (12", picture disc)	40
88	Geffen GEF 43	Sweet Child O' Mine/Out Ta Get Me (p/s, with wraparound sticker)	5
88	Geffen GEF 43TE	Sweet Child O' Mine/Out Ta Get Me/Rocket Queen (10", revolving p/s)	15
88	Geffen GEF 43TV	Sweet Child O' Mine/Out Ta Get Me/Rocket Queen (12", metallic p/s)	10
88	Geffen GEF 47	Welcome To The Jungle/Nightrain (p/s)	5
88	Geffen GEF 47TV	Welcome To The Jungle/Nightrain/You're Crazy (Acoustic Version) (12", p/s, with patch)	8
88	Geffen GEF 47TP	Welcome To The Jungle/Nightrain/You're Crazy (Acoustic Version) (12", picture disc)	10
88	Geffen GEF 47CD	Welcome To The Jungle/Nightrain/You're Crazy (Acoustic Version) (3" CD with adaptor, 5" case)	12
89	Geffen GEF 50P	Paradise City/I Used To Love Her (gun-shaped clear picture disc)	12
89	Geffen GEF 50P	Paradise City/I Used To Love Her (gun-shaped white picture disc)	15
89	Geffen GEF 50X	Paradise City/I Used To Love Her (p/s, slotted in holster p/s)	7
89	Geffen GEF 55W	Sweet Child O' Mine (Remix)/Out Ta Get Me (with tattoo)	10
89	Geffen GEF 55 X	Sweet Child O' Mine/Out Ta Get Me (Limited edition sticker pack)	10
89	Geffen GEF 55P	Sweet Child O' Mine/Out Ta Get Me/Rocket Queen (shaped pic disc & sticker)	12
89	Geffen GEF 55P	Sweet Child O' Mine/Out Ta Get Me/Rocket Queen (12" uncut shaped pic disc)	100
89	Geffen GEF 55T	Sweet Child O' Mine (Remix)/Move To The City/Whole Lotta Rosie (live)/ It's So Easy (live) (12", p/s)	10
89	Geffen GEF 55CD	Sweet Child O' Mine (Remix)/Move To The City/Whole Lotta Rosie (live)/ It's So Easy (live) (3" CD)	10
89	Geffen GEF 56T	Patience/Rocket Queen/W. Axl Rose Interview (12", p/s)	8
89	Geffen GEF 56CD	Patience/Rocket Queen/W. Axl Rose Interview (3" CD, gatefold card sleeve)	12
89	Geffen GEF 60X	Nightrain/Reckless Life (live) (p/s, with patch)	7
89	Geffen GEF 60P	Nightrain/Reckless Life (live) (case-shaped picture disc, stickered PVC sleeve)	12
89	Geffen GEF 60CD	Nightrain/Knockin' On Heaven's Door (live)/Reckless Life (live) (3" CD, gatefold card sleeve)	10
91	Geffen GFSTP 6	You Could Be Mine/Civil War (12", clear vinyl with insert in PVC sleeve)	8
91	Geffen GFST 9	Don't Cry/Don't Cry (Alternate Lyrics)/Don't Cry (Demo) (12", hologram p/s)	8
91	Geffen GFS 18	November Rain (LP version)/Sweet Child O' Mine (LP version) (p/s)	5
91	Geffen GFSX 17	Live And Let Die (LP Version)/Live And Let Die (live) (12", yellow/orange vinyl, die-cut p/s)	8
92	Geffen GFST 18	November Rain/Sweet Child O' Mine (live)/Patience (live) (12", p/s, 1 side etched)	8
93	Geffen GFS 70	Since I Don't Have You/You Can't Put Your Arms Around A Memory (p/s, orange vinyl)	6
08	Geffen 0602517906075	Chinese Democracy/Shackler's Revenge (p/s, promo)	10
87	Geffen 9240 148	APPETITE FOR DESTRUCTION (LP, withdrawn 'robot' sleeve)	25
91	Geffen GEF 24415	USE YOUR ILLUSION I (2 x LP)	25
91	Geffen GEF 24420	USE YOUR ILLUSION II (2 x LP)	25

ARTHUR GUNTER

72	Blue Horizon 2431 012	BLUES AFTER HOURS (LP)	140
70s	Contempo COLP 119	BLACK AND BLUES (LP)	25

HARDROCK GUNTER

| 55 | Brunswick OE 9167 | MOUNTAIN MUSIC (EP) | 25 |

(see also Red Foley, Roberta Lee)

GURU GURU

73	Atlantic K 50022	DON'T CALL US WE'LL CALL YOU (LP)	15
74	Atlantic K 50044	DANCE OF THE FLAMES (LP)	18

GURU GURU/ULI TREPTE

| 80s | United Dairies UDT 07 | LIVE 72 & 73 (LP, 1 side each) | 18 |

GURU JOSH

| 90 | Deconstruction PT 44140 | Freaky Dreamer (12") | 15 |

GURUS

| 66 | United Artists UP 1160 | Blue Snow Night/Come Girl | 30 |

JOHNNY GUSTAFSON

65	Polydor 56022	Just To Be With You/Sweet Day	20
65	Polydor 56043	Take Me For A Little While/Make Me Your Number One	40

(see also Big Three, Merseybeats, Quotations, Hard Stuff, Johnny & John, Ian Gillan Band, G-Force)

CARL GUSTAV & 84'S

| 81 | Convulsive CN 001 | I Want To Kill Russians/Through Birds, Through Fire, But Not Through Glass (p/s) | 10 |

ARLO GUTHRIE

67	Reprise RS 20644	Motorcycle Song/Now And Then	8
70	Reprise RS 20877	Alice's Rock'N'Roll Restaurant/Coming In To Los Angeles	5
70	Reprise RS 20951	Valley To Pray/Gabriel's Mother's Hiway Ballad No. 16 Blues (demo-only)	7
67	Reprise RSLP 6267	ALICE'S RESTAURANT (LP, mono)	20
67	Reprise RLP 6267	ALICE'S RESTAURANT (LP, stereo)	20
68	Reprise RSLP 6269	ARLO (LP)	20
69	Reprise RSLP 6346	RUNNING DOWN THE ROAD (LP)	15
70	Reprise RSLP 6411	WASHINGTON COUNTY (LP)	15

GWEN GUTHRIE

| 86 | 4th + Broadway BRW 1252 | Seventh Heaven/It Should Have Been You/Getting Hot (12", p/s) | 12 |

SHEILA GUTHRIE

| 63 | Fontana TF 399 | Mirror Mirror/It Doesn't Mean A Thing | 8 |

WOODY GUTHRIE

51	Melodisc 1141	Ramblin' Blues/Talkin' Columbia Blues (78)	15
55	Melodisc EPM7 84	HARD AIN'T IT HARD (EP)	20
55	Melodisc EPM7 85	WORRIED MAN BLUES (EP)	20
55	Melodisc EPM7 91	HEY LOLLY LOLLY (EP)	20
55	Melodisc MLP 12-106	MORE SONGS BY GUTHRIE (LP)	40

58	Topic 12T 31	BOUND FOR GLORY (LP)	35
64	RCA RD 7642	DUST BOWL BALLADS (LP)	25
65	Xtra XTRA 1012	WOODY GUTHRIE (LP)	12
66	Xtra XTRA 1064	WOODY GUTHRIE (LP)	12

GUTTERSNIPES

| 88 | Razor GUTT 1 | Addicted To Love/Love's Young Dream (p/s) | 8 |
| 88 | Razor RAZ 42 | THE POOR DRESS UP (LP) | 12 |

(see also Cocksparrer)

GUTTERSNYPES

94	Liberty Grooves LIB 004	TRIALS OF LIFE (Radio Edits) (12" EP)	18
94	Liberty Grooves LIB 005	TRIALS OF LIFE (12" EP)	8
94	Liberty Grooves LIB 006	TRIALS OF LIFE EP (Instrumentals)	18
94	Liberty Grooves LIB004	The Trials Of Life (Green vinyl radio edit) (12")	15
94	Liberty Grooves LIB005	The Trials Of Life (Blue, Red) (12")	10
94	Liberty Grooves LIB005	The Trials Of Life (White vinyl, promo version, limited edition, personalised by band) (12")	40
94	Liberty Grooves LIB006	The Trials Of Life (Clear vinyl instrumentals) (12")	20

GUV'NERS

| 63 | Piccadilly 7N 35117 | Let's Make A Habit Of This/The Kissing Had To Stop | 10 |

(see also Jess Conrad, Dickie Pride, Nelson Keene)

BARRY GUY

| 76 | Incus INCUS 22 | STATEMENTS V-XI FOR DOUBLE BASS AND VIOLONE (LP) | 50 |

(see also Derek Bailey Barry Guy & Paul Rutherford)

BUDDY GUY

65	Chess CRS 8004	Let Me Love You Baby/Ten Years Ago	20
68	Fontana TF 951	Mary Had A Little Lamb/Sweet Little Angel	18
72	Atlantic K 10195	Honey Dripper/Man Of Many Words	6
91	Silvertone ORE 30	Mustang Sally/Trouble Don't Last (with Jeff Beck, p/s)	5
65	Chess CRE 6004	CRAZY MUSIC (EP)	40
68	Vanguard SVRL 19001	COMING AT YOU (LP)	45
68	Vanguard SVRL 19002	MAN AND HIS BLUES (LP)	45
68	Vanguard SVRL 19004	BLUES TODAY (LP)	30
69	Vanguard SVRL 19008	THIS IS BUDDY GUY! (LP)	30
69	Vanguard SVRL 79290	HOT AND COOL (LP)	30
69	Chess CRL(S) 4546	I LEFT MY BLUES IN SAN FRANCISCO (LP)	35
69	Python KM 2	FIRST TIME I MET THE BLUES (LP)	70
70	Harvest SHSP 4006	BUDDY AND THE JUNIORS (LP, with Junior Mance & Junior Wells)	65
70	Red Lightnin' RL 001	IN THE BEGINNING (LP)	15
72	Atlantic K 40240	PLAY THE BLUES (LP, with Junior Wells)	18
73	Vanguard VSD 79323	HOLD THAT PLANE (LP)	18

(see also Junior Wells, Eddie Boyd/Buddy Guy)

GUYS

| 69 | Tepee TPR SP 1001 | You Go Your Way/Little Girl | 20 |

(see also Beat Six)

GEORGE GUZMAN

| 68 | London SH 8384 | INTRODUCING GEORGE GUZMAN (LP) | 30 |

GYGAFO

| 89 | Holyground HG 1155 | LEGEND OF THE KINGFISHER (LP, 160 copies only, posthumously designed semi-gatefold sleeve with insert) | 60 |

GYMSLIPS

82	Abstract ABS 011 48	Crash/Miss Nunsweeta (p/s)	5
83	Abstract ABS 014	Big Sister/Yo Yo/Pie And Mash (p/s)	5
83	Abstract ABS 016F	Robot Man/Multi-Coloured Sugar/Take Away (p/s)	5
85	Abstract 12 ABS 033	Evil Eye/In Wonderland/Don't Lead Me On (12", p/s)	8
83	Abstract ABT 006	ROCKING WITH THE RENEES (LP, with insert)	20

GYNAECOLOGISTS

| 81 | Teesbeat TB 2 | The Red Pullover/The Offence (hand made p/s, 500 only) | 12 |

GYPP

| 79 | Shy Talk AC 1065 | YAAH EP: Marigoldz/Titania/Sister Darling (p/s) | 20 |

(see also Martin Newell, Cleaners From Venus, Brotherhood Of Lizards)

GYPPO

| 79 | United Artists | High Rise Love/Free Enterprise (possibly, only promo copies exist) | 100 |

GYPSIES

| 67 | CBS 201785 | Jerk It/Diamonds, Rubies, Gold And Fame | 40 |

(see also Flirtations, Pearly Gates)

GYPSY

71	United Artists UP 35202	What Makes A Man A Man/I Want To Be Beside You	6
71	United Artists UAG 29155	GYPSY (LP)	15
72	United Artists UAS 29420	BRENDA AND THE RATTLESNAKE (LP)	15

(see also Legay)

GYPSY

| 84 | Private Pressing | We Came To Be Free/Get It Right | 50 |

H

HABIBIYYA

| 72 | Island HELP 7 | IF MAN BUT KNEW (LP, with inner sleeve, black/silver label, pink 'i' logo) | 25 |

(see also Mighty Baby)

HABITS
66	Decca F 12348	Elbow Baby/Need You	40

(see also Charles Dickens, Nice, Brian Davison)

HACKENSACK
72	Island WIP 6149	Moving On/River Boat	12
71	Polydor 2383 263	UP THE HARD WAY (LP, with inner sleeve)	80
74	Zel UZ 003	HERE COMES THE JUDGE (LP, private pressing, as Hack & Sack)	100

(see also Megaton, Tiger [U.K.], Nicky Moore Band, Samson)

STEVE HACKETT
78	Charisma CB 312	How Can I?/Kim (with Ritchie Havens)	10
78	Charisma CB 318	Narnia (Remix)/Please Don't Touch	7
79	Charisma CB 334	Every Day/Lost Time In Cordoba	5
79	Charisma CB 341	Clocks - The Angel Of Mons/Acoustic Set	5
79	Charisma CB 341-12	Clocks - The Angel Of Mons /Acoustic Set/Tigermoth (12", p/s)	8
80	Charisma CB 357	The Show/Hercules Unchained (p/s)	5
80	Charisma CB 368	Sentimental Institution/The Toast (p/s)	5
83	Charisma CELL 12	Cell 151/Air Conditioned Nightmare/Time Lapse At Milton Keynes (12", p/s; with bonus white label 12" "Clocks - The Angel Of Mons"/"Acoustic Set"/"Tigermoth" [CELL 13], 2000 only)	8
01	Camino CAMCD 23	LIVE ARCHIVE (4-CD box set)	25
01	Camino CAMCD 23	LIVE ARCHIVE (5-CD box set, limited edition with extra CD)	25

(see also Peter Banks, Genesis, GTR, Quiet World)

VERNON HADDOCK'S JUBILEE LOVELIES
65	Columbia SX 6011	VERNON HADDOCK'S JUBILEE LOVELIES (LP)	125

HADOUKEN!
07	Surface Noise SN 0102)	That Boy That Girl/Tuning In (mail order only, 500 pressed p/s)	20

HAFFY'S WHISKY SOUR
71	Deram DM 345	Shot In The Head/Bye Bye Bluebird	10

(see also Easybeats, Paintbox)

HAFLER TRIO
84	Doublevision DVR 4	BANG! - AN OPEN LETTER (LP, with insert)	25
86	Charrm 3	THREE WAYS OF SAYING TWO - THE NETHERLANDS LECTURES (LP, stickered sleeve with booklet)	25
86	Touch T 05	THE SEA ORG (10", 'audio/visual' package with booklet)	20

(see also Cabaret Voltaire)

HAGALAZ RUNEDANCE
97	Elfenblut SAG III	When The Trees Were Silenced/A Tale Of Fate (Folkswang Awaits) (p/s, insert)	10

SAMMY HAGAR
77	Capitol E-ST 11599	SAMMY HAGAR (LP, red vinyl)	12
79	Capitol E-ST 11983	STREET MACHINE (LP, with free single)	12

(see also Van Halen, Madonna, Montrose)

HAGAR THE WOMB
84	Abstract Sounds 12ABS 029	FUNNERY IN THE NUNNERY (12" EP)	15
84	Mortarhate MORT 2	WORD OF THE WOMB (12" EP)	15

EARLE HAGEN
64	Colpix PX 740	Nancy's Theme/New Interns Watusi	5

MERLE HAGGARD & STRANGERS
68	Capitol CL 15540	The Legend Of Bonnie And Clyde/I Started Loving You Again	5
87	Premier PMP 1003	TO ALL THE GIRLS I'VE LOVED BEFORE (LP, withdrawn)	15

MEL HAGUE
60s	LK/LP 6558	MERRY-GO-ROUND (LP, signed)	18
60s	LK/LP 6558	MERRY-GO-ROUND (LP)	12

JOYCE HAHN
57	London HLA 8453	Gonna Find Me A Bluebird/I Saw You, I Saw You	20
57	London HLA 8453	Gonna Find Me A Bluebird/I Saw You, I Saw You (78)	10

PAUL HAIG
82	Operation Twilight OPT 03	Running Away/Time (p/s)	5
84	Island ISX 198	The Only Truth (U.S. Remix)/Instrumental/Ghost Rider (12", p/s)	8
89	Circa YRT 25	Something Good (Extended Version)/Over You/Free To Go (Technology)/Something Good (Radio Edit) (12")	10
89	Circa YRTX 25	Something Good (Remix)/The Last Kiss/Free To Go (Public)/Over You (12")	8
98	Syntactic NICE 49	Listen To Me (Looking/Irresponsible) (handmade p/s, with Billy McKenzie)	20
81	Rational no cat. no.	DRAMA (cassette mini-LP)	15
84	Island ILPS 9742	RHYTHM OF LIFE (LP)	12
85	Operation Afterglow OPA 3	THE WARP OF PURE FUN (LP, inner sleeve)	12

(see also Josef K, Rhythm Of Life, Juggernauts, Billy McKenzie)

ROBERT HAIGH
85	Laylah LAY 09	JULIET OF THE SPIRITS EP (12")	25
86	Laylah LAY 21	MUSIC FROM THE ANTE CHAMBER EP (12")	25
87	United Dairies UDT 034	THE BEST OF ROBERT HAIGH (cassette)	20
88	United Dairies UD 026	VALENTINE OUT OF SEASON (LP)	40
89	Le Rey LR 103	A WALTZ IN PLAIN C (CD)	100

(see also SEMA)

NORMAN HAINES (BAND)
70	Parlophone R 5871	Daffodil/Autumn Mobile (as Norman Haines Band)	20
71	Parlophone SPSR 338	Den Of Iniquity/Everything You See (Mr. Armageddon) (promo only)	45
72	Parlophone R 5960	Give It To You Girl/Elaine (as Norman Haines)	20
71	Parlophone PCS 7130	DEN OF INIQUITY (LP, black/silver label with boxed logo)	900
94	Shoestring BL001	DEN OF INIQUITY (LP, reissue)	30
94	Shoestring BL001	DEN OF INIQUITY (CD)	18

(see also Avalanche, Brumbeats, The Dog That Bit People, Locomotive)

HAIR (1)

69	Pye NSPL 18314	RAVE UP (LIVE FROM THE SHAFTESBURY THEATRE) (LP)	70

(see also Alex Harvey, Hairband)

HAIR (2)

70	Columbia SCX 6452	HAIRPIECE (LP, black/silver labels with boxed logo)	250

HAIRBAND

69	Bell BLL 1076	Big Louis/Travelling Song	18
69	Bell SBLL 69	BAND ON THE WAGON (LP, blue/silver/black label with "solin on the U.K..." text)	60

(see also Alex Harvey, Hair)

HAIRCUT 100

83	Arista CLIP 5	Whistle Down The Wind (withdrawn)	10
82	Arista HCC 101	BLUE HAT FOR A BLUE DAY (LP, withdrawn, test pressings only)	20

HAIRPOWER

70	CBS 4961	Royal International Love-in/Be There, Be Hair	5

HAL

05	Heavenly HVN 147	Keep Love As Your Golden Rule/THE MAGIC NUMBERS: Animla Sola (Double A side tour single - 500 only p/s)	10

HAL HOPPERS

54	London HL 8107	More Love/Do Nothin' Blues	40
55	London HL 8129	Mother Of Pearl/Baby I've Had It	40

I. HALCIDEONS AND I. JARZIF

78	Greensleeves GRED 7	Rise Ethiopians/Signs Of The Messiah (12")	40

DENNIS HALE

55	Parlophone MSP 6153	The Butterscotch Mop/S'posin'	10

(see also Jack Parnell)

TERENCE HOLDERWAY HALE

60	Fontana H 285	Beauty And The Beast/My New Year's Eve	7

BILL HALEY (& HIS COMETS)

78s

53	London L 1190	Crazy Man, Crazy/Whatcha Gonna Do (as Bill Haley with Haley's Comets) (gold label lettering)	30
53	London L 1216	Pat-A-Cake/Fractured (as Bill Haley with Haley's Comets, gold label)	30
54	London HL 1190	Crazy Man, Crazy/Whatcha Gonna Do (as Bill Haley with Haley's Comets) (reissue, silver label lettering)	20
54	London HL 1216	Pat-A-Cake/Fractured (reissue, silver label lettering, as Bill Haley with Haley's Comets)	20
54	Brunswick 05338	Shake, Rattle And Roll/A.B.C. Boogie (gold lettering)	10
55	London HL 8142	Green Tree Boogie/Sundown Boogie	20
55	London HLF 8161	Farewell, So Long, Goodbye/I'll Be True	18
55	London HLF 8194	Ten Little Indians/Rocking Chair On The Moon	20
56	Melodisc 1376	I'm Gonna Dry Ev'ry Tear With A Kiss/Why Do I Cry Over You	60
57	London HLF 8371	Rock The Joint/Yes Indeed!	15
57	Brunswick 05658	Forty Cups Of Coffee/Choo Choo Ch'Boogie	12
57	Brunswick 05688	(You Hit The Wrong Note) Billy Goat/Rockin' Rollin' Rover	12
57	Brunswick 05719	Miss You/The Dipsy Doodle	15
58	Brunswick 05735	Mary, Mary Lou/It's A Sin	15
58	Brunswick 05742	Skinny Minnie/How Many	15
58	Brunswick 05752	Lean Jean/Don't Nobody Move	15
58	Brunswick 05766	Whoa Mabell/Chiquita Linda	25
59	Brunswick 05788	I Got A Woman/Charmaine	30
59	Brunswick 05805	Shaky/Caldonia	30
59	Brunswick 05810	Joey's Song/Ooh! Look-A There, Ain't She Pretty	40

SINGLES

54	Brunswick 05317	(We're Gonna) Rock Around The Clock/Thirteen Women (gold lettering on label)	60
54	Brunswick 05317	(We're Gonna) Rock Around The Clock/Thirteen Women (silver lettering on label)	25
54	Brunswick 05338	Shake, Rattle And Roll/A.B.C. Boogie (gold lettering on label)	40
54	Brunswick 05338	Shake, Rattle And Roll/A.B.C. Boogie (silver lettering on label)	20
55	Brunswick 05373	Happy Baby/Dim, Dim The Lights (I Want Some Atmosphere) (gold lettering on label)	40
55	Brunswick 05373	Happy Baby/Dim, Dim The Lights (I Want Some Atmosphere) (silver lettering on label)	20
55	Brunswick 05405	Birth Of The Boogie/Mambo Rock (gold lettering on label)	40
55	Brunswick 05405	Birth Of The Boogie/Mambo Rock (silver lettering on label)	20
55	London HL 8142	Green Tree Boogie/Sundown Boogie (gold lettering on label)	150
55	London HL 8142	Green Tree Boogie/Sundown Boogie (silver lettering on label)	50
55	Brunswick 05453	Two Hound Dogs/Razzle Dazzle (gold lettering on label)	40
55	Brunswick 05453	Two Hound Dogs/Razzle Dazzle (silver lettering on label)	20
55	London HLF 8161	Farewell, So Long, Goodbye/I'll Be True (gold lettering on label)	100
55	London HLF 8161	Farewell, So Long, Goodbye/I'll Be True (silver lettering on label)	50
55	London HLF 8194	Ten Little Indians/Rocking Chair On The Moon (gold lettering on label)	120
55	London HLF 8194	Ten Little Indians/Rocking Chair On The Moon (silver lettering on label)	60
55	Brunswick 05509	Rock-A-Beatin' Boogie/Burn That Candle (gold lettering on label)	40
55	Brunswick 05509	Rock-A-Beatin' Boogie/Burn That Candle (silver lettering on label)	20
56	Brunswick 05530	See You Later, Alligator/The Paper Boy (On Main Street, USA) (gold lettering on label)	40
56	Brunswick 05530	See You Later, Alligator/The Paper Boy (On Main Street, USA) (silver lettering on label)	20
56	Brunswick 05565	The Saints Rock 'N' Roll/R-O-C-K	15
56	Brunswick 05582	Rockin' Through The Rye/Hot Dog Buddy Buddy	15
56	Brunswick 05615	Rip It Up/Teenager's Mother	15
56	Brunswick 05616	Rudy's Rock/Blue Comet Blues	15
57	Brunswick 05640	Don't Knock The Rock/Calling All Comets	15
57	Brunswick 05641	Hook, Line And Sinker/Goofin' Around	15
57	London HLF 8371	Rock The Joint/Yes Indeed! (gold label)	150
57	London HLF 8371	Rock The Joint/Yes Indeed! (silver label)	75
57	Brunswick 05658	Forty Cups Of Coffee/Choo Choo Ch'Boogie	15
57	Brunswick 05688	(You Hit The Wrong Note) Billy Goat/Rockin' Rollin' Rover	15

57	Brunswick 05719	Miss You/The Dipsy Doodle	15
58	Brunswick 05735	Mary, Mary Lou/It's A Sin	15
58	Brunswick 05742	Skinny Minnie/How Many	20
58	Brunswick 05752	Lean Jean/Don't Nobody Move	15
58	Brunswick 05766	Whoa Mabel!/Chiquita Linda	15
59	Brunswick 05788	I Got A Woman/Charmaine	15
59	Brunswick 05805	Shaky/Caldonia	15
59	Brunswick 05810	Joey's Song/Ooh! Look-A There, Ain't She Pretty	15

(The above 45s were originally issued with triangular centres; later round centres are worth two-thirds of these values.)

60	Brunswick 05818	Puerto Rican Peddler/Skokiaan	10
60	Warner Bros WB 6	Candy Kisses/Tamiami	10
61	London HLU 9471	Spanish Twist/My Kind Of Woman	10
63	Stateside SS 196	Tenor Man/Up Goes My Love	10
64	Warner Bros WB 133	Rock Around The Clock/Love Letters In The Sand	10
64	Brunswick 05910	Happy Baby/Birth Of The Boogie	15
64	Brunswick 05917	The Green Door/Yeah! She's Evil	15
68	MCA MU 1013	(We're Gonna) Rock Around The Clock/Shake, Rattle And Roll	5
68	Pye International 7N 25455	Crazy Man, Crazy/Dance With A Dolly (With A Hole In Her Stocking)	15
73	Sonet SON 2016	Me And Bobby McGee/I Wouldn't Have Missed It For The World	5
74	Sonet SON 2043	Crazy Man, Crazy/Lawdy Miss Clawdy	5
79	Sonet SON 2202	God Bless Rock And Roll/So Right Tonight	5

EXPORT SINGLES

54	Decca BM 05317	(We're Gonna) Rock Around The Clock/Thirteen Women	70
55	Decca BM 05405	Birth Of The Boogie/Mambo Rock	50
55	Decca BM 05509	Rock-A-Beatin' Boogie/Burn That Candle	50
56	Decca BM 05530	See You Later Alligator/The Paper Boy (On Main Street, USA)	50
56	Decca BM 31163	The Saints Rock 'N' Roll/R-O-C-K	40
56	Decca BM 31164	Rockin' Through The Rye/Hot Dog Buddy Buddy	40
56	Decca BM 31171	Rip It Up/Teenager's Mother	40
57	Decca BM 31174	Don't Knock The Rock/Choo Choo Ch'Boogie	40
68	Decca AD 1010	(We're Gonna) Rock Around The Clock/Shake, Rattle And Roll	20

EPs

55	Brunswick OE 9129	DIM, DIM THE LIGHTS (gold lettering label, 'stage' p/s, various colours)	40
55	Brunswick OE 9129	DIM, DIM THE LIGHTS (silver lettering label, 'stage' or 'cameo' p/s)	25
55	London REF 1031	ROCK AND ROLL	50
56	London REF 1049	LIVE IT UP PART 1	35
56	London REF 1050	LIVE IT UP PART 2	35
56	Brunswick OE 9214	ROCK AND ROLL WITH BILL HALEY	25
56	Brunswick OE 9250	ROCK AROUND THE CLOCK	20
56	Brunswick OE 9250	ROCK AROUND THE CLOCK (round centre, different sleeve, same design as "Bill Haley" [OE 9459])	35
56	London REF 1058	LIVE IT UP PART 3	35
56	Brunswick OE 9278	ROCK'N'ROLL STAGE SHOW PART 1	20
56	Brunswick OE 9279	ROCK'N'ROLL STAGE SHOW PART 2	20
56	Brunswick OE 9280	ROCK'N'ROLL STAGE SHOW PART 3	20
58	Brunswick OE 9349	ROCKIN' THE OLDIES PART 1	25
58	Brunswick OE 9350	ROCKIN' THE OLDIES PART 2	25
58	Brunswick OE 9351	ROCKIN' THE OLDIES PART 3	30

(Originally issued with triangular centres, later round-centre copies are worth two-thirds this value.)

59	Brunswick OE 9446	ROCKIN' AROUND THE WORLD	60
59	Brunswick OE 9459	BILL HALEY	50

(The above EPs were originally issued with triangular centres, later round-centre copies are worth half to two-thirds these values.)

60	Warners WEP 6001	BILL HALEY AND HIS COMETS	40
61	Warners WEP 6025	BILL HALEY'S JUKE BOX (mono)	40
61	Warners WSEP 6025	BILL HALEY'S JUKE BOX (stereo)	50
64	Warners WEP 6133	BILL HALEY VOLUME 1	40
64	Warners WEP 6136	BILL HALEY VOLUME 2	40

ALBUMS

55	London H-APB 1042	LIVE IT UP (10", gold lettering on label)	100
55	London H-APB 1042	LIVE IT UP (10", silver lettering on label)	60
56	Brunswick LAT 8117	ROCK AROUND THE CLOCK	30
56	Brunswick LAT 8139	ROCK AND ROLL STAGE SHOW	30
57	London HA-F 2037	ROCK THE JOINT	80
57	Brunswick LAT 8219	ROCKIN' THE OLDIES	60
57	Brunswick LAT 8268	ROCKIN' THE JOINT	60
59	Brunswick LAT 8295	BILL HALEY'S CHICKS (mono)	65
59	Brunswick STA 3011	BILL HALEY'S CHICKS (stereo)	85
60	Brunswick LAT 8326	STRICTLY INSTRUMENTAL	60
62	Columbia 33SX 1460	TWISTIN' KNIGHTS AT THE ROUNDTABLE (LIVE!)	30
62	Ace Of Hearts AH 35	ROCKIN' THE OLDIES	15
64	Ace Of Hearts AH 66	BILL HALEY'S CHICKS	15
65	Xtra XTRA 1027	BILL HALEY & THE COMETS	30
65	Warner Bros W 1391	BILL HALEY'S JUKE BOX	50

(see also Kingsmen, Jodimars, Nick Nantos & His Fireballs)

HALF JAPANESE

81	Armageddon AS 009	Spy/I Know How It Feels ... Bad/My Knowledge Was Wrong (p/s)	5
81	Armageddon ABOX 1	1/2 GENTLEMEN NOT BEASTS (3-LP box set with poster, booklet & lyric insert)	80
81	Armageddon ARM 7	LOUD (LP)	12

(see also Jad Fair)

HALFBREED

75	United Artists UAG 29877	HALFBREED (LP, fold out sleeve)	20

HALF PINT

85	Greensleeves GRED 178	Freedom Fighter/Hold On (12")	25

ADELAIDE HALL

60	Oriole CB 1556	Common Sense/Blue Bird On My Shoulder	10

MINT VALUE £

BARBARA HALL
75	EMI INT 514	You Brought It On Yourself/Drop My heart Off At The Door	10

BOB HALL & ALEXIS KORNER
78	Logo GO 331	Pinetop's Boogie Woogie/All I Got Is You	12

(see also Brunning Hall Sunflower Blues Band, Alexis Korner)

CAROLINE HALL
70	Major Minor MM 689	Dream Boy/Julie	5
71	Decca F 13146	Hold My Hand/Put A Light In The Window	6

DARYL HALL & SOUNDS OF BLACKNESS
94	Mercury MERMC 404	Gloryland/(mixes) (picture disc, in poster sleeve)	10

DEREK HALL & MIKE COOPER
60s	Kennet KRS 766	OUT OF THE SHADES (EP)	35

DOLORES HALL
72	Jay Boy BOY 77	Good Lovin' Man/W-O-M-E-N	8

(see also Jackie Lee & Dolores Hall)

DORA HALL
64	King KG 1003	Hello Faithless/You've Got Me Cryin' Again	5

JIMMY GRAY HALL
74	Epic EPC 2312	Be That Way/Possessed By The Moon	20

JUANITA HALL
62	Storyville SEP 382	STORYVILLE BLUES ANTHOLOGY VOL. 2 (EP)	10

LANI HALL
83	A&M AM 159	Never Say Never Again/MICHAEL LEGRAND: Un Chanson D'Amour (p/s)	8
74	A&M AMLS 64359	SUNDOWN LADY (LP)	15

LARRY HALL
60	Parlophone R 4625	Sandy/Lovin' Tree	15
62	Salvo SLO 1811	Ladder Of Love/The One You Left Behind (99 copies only)	20

RENE HALL'S ORCHESTRA
58	London HLU 8581	Twitchy/Flippin'	50

ROBIN HALL (& JIMMY MACGREGOR)
60	Collector JDS 3	Football Crazy/Rosin The Beau (with p/s)	15
60	Collector JDS 3	Football Crazy/Rosin The Beau	10
60	Decca F 11266	Football Crazy/Rosin The Beau (reissue, p/s)	10

(see also Galliards)

RONNIE HALL
61	Piccadilly 7N 35001	The Code Of Love/Who Cares	5
61	Piccadilly 7N 35015	She's Mine/My Heart Is The Lover	5
62	Piccadilly 7N 35040	My Very First Love/The Day After Forever	5
65	Fontana TF 569	I'll Stand Aside/I'm Getting Nowhere	5

ROY HALL
56	Brunswick 05531	See You Later, Alligator/Don't Stop Now (gold label lettering)	500
56	Brunswick 05531	See You Later, Alligator/Don't Stop Now (78)	100
56	Brunswick 05555	Blue Suede Shoes/Luscious	400
56	Brunswick 05555	Blue Suede Shoes/Luscious (78)	100
56	Brunswick 05627	Diggin' The Boogie/Three Alley Cats	550
56	Brunswick 05627	Diggin' The Boogie/Three Alley Cats (78)	100
70	Injun 105	One Monkey Don't Stop The Shop/Flood Of love	12

TONY HALL
77	Free Reed FRR 012	FIELDVOLE MUSIC (LP, with insert)	20

CHANCE HALLADAY
62	Vogue V 9203	John Henry/Thirteen Women	25

HALLELUJAH SKIFFLE GROUP
58	Oriole CB 1429	I Saw The Light/A Closer Walk With Thee (with Clinton Ford)	20

(see also Clinton Ford)

HALLIARD
67	Saga SOC 1058	IT'S THE IRISH IN ME (LP)	30
68	Broadside BRO 106	THE HALLIARD AND JON RAVEN (LP)	50

(see also Jon Raven, Nic Jones)

DICK HALLMAN
56	Brunswick 05608	Two Different Worlds/Love Me As Though There Were No Tomorrow	5
60	Vogue V 9162	Born To Be Loved/Just Squeeze Me But Don't Teeze Me	6

GERRY HALLOM
84	Fellside FE 036	A RUN A MINUTE (LP)	15

HALLUCINOGEN
95	Dragonfly BFLLP 15	TWISTED (2xLP, yellow vinyl or one green and one pink or black vinyl)	15

JOHNNY HALLYDAY
62	Philips BF 1238	Shake The Hand Of A Fool/Hold Back The Sun	6
63	Philips 373 012BF	Hey Little Girl/Caravan Of Lonely Men	6
65	Philips BF 1449	Pour Moi Tu Es La Seule/They Call Him A Man	8
61	Philips BBL 7556	SINGS AMERICA'S ROCKIN' HITS (LP)	150
62	Philips 432 813BE	ROCKING (EP)	100
66	Vogue VRE 5013	JOHNNY HALLYDAY (EP)	100

HALOS
61	London HLU 9424	Nag/Copycat	40

STUART HAMBLEN
54	HMV 7MC 20	This Ole House/When My Lord Picks Up The 'Phone (export issue)	25
55	HMV 7MC 30	Go On By/Just A Man (export issue)	10
56	HMV 7M 394	Hell Train/A Few Things To Remember	15

BILLY HAMBRIC
79	Grapevine GRP 139	She Said Goodbye/I Found True Love	10

CLAIRE HAMILL
72	Island WIP 6122	When I Was A Child/Alice In The Streets Of Darlington	6
72	Island WIP 6133	Baseball Blues/Smile Your Blues Away	6
81	WEA K 18440	First Night In New York/Ultraviolet Light (B-side with Gary Numan) (p/s)	7
72	Island ILPS 9182	ONE HOUSE LEFT STANDING (LP, lyric inner sleeve)	40
73	Island ILPS 9225	OCTOBER (LP, gatefold sleeve, pink rim palm tree label)	20
74	Konk KONK 101	STAGE DOOR JOHNNIES (LP, gatefold sleeve, blue label)	15
75	Konk KONK 104	ABRACADABRA (LP, featuring Cafe Society, with lyric insert, blue label)	15

(see also Cafe Society, Gary Numan, Wishbone Ash)

HAMILTON
79	Muscle SJP 806/MUS 001	Jet Set Girl/Methodone And Coconuts (500 only, no p/s)	100

BILLY HAMILTON & STRANDSMEN
67	Philips BF 1622	Try To Remember/Don't You Believe It	7

(see also Strandsmen)

CHICO HAMILTON QUINTET
65	HMV POP 1451	Carol's Walk/Chic Chic Chico	5
58	Vogue LAE 12045	CHICO HAMILTON QUINTET IN HIFI (LP)	20
64	HMV CLP 1807	MAN FROM TWO WORLDS (LP)	20
66	Impulse MIPL/SIPL 503	THE FURTHER ADVENTURES OF EL CHICO (LP)	15
68	Solid State USS 7010	THE GAMUT (LP)	12

DAVID HAMILTON
70s	Spectre SP 501	A Special Goodnight To You/Just For The Weekend	8

EDWARD HAMILTON & ARABIANS
80	Grapevine GRP 134	Baby Don't You Weep/I'm Gonna Love You	10

GARY HAMILTON
67	Decca F 12697	Let The Music Play/Don't Ask	12
69	CBS 4674	Easy Rider/Hare Krishna	6

(see also Hamilton & [Hamilton] Movement)

GAVIN HAMILTON
67	King KG 1067	It Won't Be The Same/Turn The Key Softly	150

GEORGE HAMILTON IV
57	London HL 8361	A Rose And A Candy Bar/If You Don't Know (gold label print)	150
57	London HL 8361	A Rose And A Candy Bar/If You Don't Know (later silver label print)	40
57	London HL 8361	A Rose And A Candy Bar/If You Don't Know (78)	20
57	HMV POP 429	Why Don't They Understand/Even Tho'	6
58	HMV POP 474	Now And For Always/One Heart	10
58	HMV POP 505	I Know Where I'm Goin'/Who's Taking You To The Prom?	5
58	HMV POP 534	Your Cheatin' Heart/When Will I Know?	10
60	HMV POP 813	Before This Day Ends/Loneliness Is All Around Us	5
72	Uni UNS 480	Evel Knievel/Boy From The Country	5
58	HMV CLP 1202	ON CAMPUS (LP)	18
59	HMV CLP 1263	SING ME A SAD SONG - A TRIBUTE TO HANK WILLIAMS (LP)	20

GUY HAMILTON
65	HMV POP 1418	A Lifetime Of Loneliness/Give The Game Away	15

(see also Neil Christian)

(KINGSIZE) HAMILTON & PLATTERMEN
66	Emerald MD 1048	Shake/I Got To Know	25

M. HAMILTON
67	Ska Beat JB 265	Something Gotta Ring/DENNIS LYNWARD & HIS GROUP: Jazz Session	20

MILTON HAMILTON
73	Explosion EX 2069	Long Long Road/Version	8
77	Wolf WM 005	Children Are You Ready/Part 2	8

ROY HAMILTON (1)
58	Fontana H 113	Don't Let Go/The Right To Love	25
58	Fontana H 113	Don't Let Go/The Right To Love (78)	10
58	Fontana H 143	Crazy Feelin'/In A Dream	15
58	Fontana H 143	Crazy Feelin'/In A Dream (78)	10
59	Fontana H 180	Pledging My Love/My One And Only Love	15
59	Fontana H 180	Pledging My Love/My One And Only Love (78)	10
59	Fontana H 193	I Need Your Loving/Somewhere Along The Way	15
59	Fontana H 193	I Need Your Loving/Somewhere Along The Way (78)	10
61	Fontana H 298	You Can Have Her/Abide With Me	15
61	Fontana H 320	You're Gonna Need Magic/To The One I Love	15
63	MGM MGM 1210	Theme From "The VIPs"/The Sinner	15
64	MGM MGM 1251	There She Is/The Panic Is On	300
64	MGM MGM 1251	There She Is/The Panic Is On (DJ copy)	550
65	MGM MGM 1268	A Thousand Tears Ago/Sweet Violet	15
66	RCA RCA 1500	And I Love Her/Tore Up Over You	15
69	Deep Soul DS 9106	Dark End Of The Street/100 Years Ago	40
59	Fontana TFE 17160	WHY FIGHT THE FEELING (EP)	20
60	Fontana TFE 17163	THE MOOD MOVES (EP)	20
61	Fontana TFE 17170	COME OUT SWINGING (EP)	20
63	Columbia 33SX 1473	GREATEST HITS (LP)	40
64	MGM MGM-C 960	WARM SOUL (LP)	60

ROY HAMILTON (2)
83	HBS K CAP 1	Turn Up The Music/Instrumental Version (12", with Capiche)	20

RUSS HAMILTON
58	Oriole EP 7005	RUSS HAMILTON (EP)	15
58	Oriole MG 20031	WE WILL MAKE LOVE (LP)	30

MINT VALUE £

SCOTT HAMILTON
65	Parlophone R5341	When Things Go Wrong/I Wonder	6
66	Parlophone R 5492	Good Day Sunshine/For No One	10

HAMILTON & MOVEMENT
65	Polydor BM 56026	Really Saying Something/I Won't See You Tonight	80
67	CBS 202573	I'm Not The Marrying Kind/My Love Belongs To You	40

(see also Gary Hamilton, Paul Stewart Movement)

HAMLET
67	Decca F12571	She Won't See The Light/Go Play In Your Own Yard	20

HAMLETT
72	Pye 7N45171	Where'd The Day Go/Vampire Man	15

HAMLINS
67	Coxsone CS 7021	Trying To Keep A Good Man Down/BOB MARLEY/MARCIA GRIFFITHS : Oh My Darling	90
67	Coxsone CS 7022	Soul And Inspiration/ETHIOPIANS: Let's Get Together	35
68	Coxsone CS 7048	Sentimental Reasons/SOUL VENDORS: Last Waltz	150
68	Blue Cat BS 115	Sugar And Spice/SOUL VENDORS: Mercy Mercy Mercy	150

(see also Minstrels)

JACK HAMMER
61	Oriole CB 1634	Young Only Once/Juliette	15
62	Oriole CB 1645	Kissin' Twist/Melancholy Boy	10
62	Oriole CB 1728	Crazy Twist/Twist Talk	10
62	Oriole CB 1753	Don't Let Baby Know/Number 2539	15
66	Polydor 56091	Thanks/Love Ladder	20
67	Polydor 56158	Joe Poor Loves Daphne Rich/Ode To A Discotheque	50
69	United Artists UP 35029	What Greater Love/The Mason Dixon Line	30
60s	Youngblood B 1023	Swim/Colour Combination	60
63	Oriole PS 40020	HAMMER + BEAT = TWIST (LP)	80
66	Polydor 582001	BRAVE NEW WORLD (LP)	100

HAMMER (1)
73	Vertigo 6059084	Rock Off/Rock And Roll Band	5

HAMMER (2)
85	Ebony EBON 29	CONTRACT WITH HELL (LP)	15

(see also Holland)

HAMMERHEAD
81	Linden Sounds LS 009	Time Will Tell/Lonely Man (p/s)	60

HAMMERS
69	President PT 247	Baby And Me/Little Butterfly	5
69	President PT 276	Sugar Baby/Power Of Love	5

HAMMERS (JAMAICA)
70	Gas GAS 162	Hotter Than Scorcher/Someday Could See You	10

(see also Joan Ross)

HAMMERSMITH GORILLAS
74	Penny Farthing PEN 849	You Really Got Me/Leavin' 'Ome (p/s)	15
77	Raw RAW 2	You Really Got Me/Leavin' 'Ome (reissue, company sleeve)	15

(see also Gorillas, Helter Skelter, Jesse Hector)

HAMMERSMITH WELSH MALE VOICE CHOIR
69	Pama SECO 1	WE'LL KEEP A WELCOME (LP, souvenir at the investiture of HRH Prince Charles at the Prince Of Wales)	12

PETER HAMMILL
75	Charisma CB 245	Birthday Special/Shingle Song	8
78	Charisma CB 339	The Polaroid (credited to Ricky Nadir)/The Old School Tie	10
78	Charisma PH 001	Crying Wolf/This Side Of The Looking Glass (promo only)	30
81	Virgin VS 424	My Experience/Glue (p/s)	5
82	Naive NAV 3	Paradox Drive/Now More Than Ever (p/s)	6
83	Naive NAV 8	Film Noir/Seven Wonders	6
84	Charisma CB 414	Just Good Friends/Just Good Friends (Instrumental) (p/s)	5
86	Foundry FOUND 3	Painting By Numbers/You Hit Me Where I Live (p/s)	5
86	Foundry FOUND 312	Painting By Numbers (Extended)/You Hit Me Where I Live/Shell (12", p/s)	8
71	Charisma CAS 1037	FOOL'S MATE (LP, gatefold sleeve, pink 'scroll' label)	50
73	Charisma CAS 1067	CHAMELEON IN THE SHADOW OF THE NIGHT (LP, gatefold sleeve, large 'Mad Hatter' label))	30
74	Charisma CAS 1083	THE SILENT CORNER AND THE EMPTY STAGE (LP, gatefold sleeve., with lyric inner, large 'Mad Hatter' label)	20
74	Charisma CAS 1089	IN CAMERA (LP, with inner sleeve, small 'Mad Hatter' label)	20
75	Charisma CAS 1099	NADIR'S BIG CHANCE (LP, laminated sleeve, with inner sleeve small 'Mad Hatter' label)	15
77	Charisma CAS 1125	OVER (LP, with inner lyric sleeve, small 'Mad Hatter' label)	15
78	Charisma CAS 1137	THE FUTURE NOW (LP, with insert)	15

(see also Van Der Graaf Generator, Le Orme, Rikki Nadir, Colin Scot)

ALBERT HAMMOND
73	Mums SMUM 1759	The Peacemaker/Who's For Lunch Today	7

CLAY HAMMOND
72	Jay Boy BOY 78	Dance Little Girl/Twin Brother	5

JOHN HAMMOND
65	Fontana TF 560	Baby Won't You Tell Me/I Love The Life I Live	15
68	Atlantic 584 190	Brown Eyed Handsome Man/Crosscut Saw	18
64	Fontana TFL 6046	BIG CITY BLUES (LP)	60
65	Fontana TFL 6059	SO MANY ROADS (LP)	50
71	CBS 64365	SOURCE POINT (LP)	25
72	CBS 65051	I'M SATISFIED (LP)	25
72	Vanguard VSD 11/12	THE BEST OF JOHN HAMMOND - SOUTHERN FRIED (2-LP)	20

CURLEY HAMNER & COOPER BROTHERS
59	Felsted SD 80061	Twistin' And Turnin'/King And Queen	10

BILLY HAMON

78	Bronze BRO 58	Butch Things/Amusement Arcade (p/s)	20

SUSAN HAMPSHIRE

65	Decca F 12185	When Love Is True/When The World Was Our Own	15

LIONEL HAMPTON (& HIS HAMP-TONES)

57	Vogue V 2405	Flying Home/Perdido (with Just Jazz All Stars)	10
57	Vogue V 2406	Hamp's Boogie Woogie/The Blues (with Just Jazz All Stars)	10
56	MGM MGM-EP 552	LIONEL HAMPTON & HIS ORCHESTRA (EP)	8
51	Brunswick LA 8527	HAMP'S BOOGIE WOOGIE (10" LP)	12
52	Brunswick LA 8551	MOONGLOW (10" LP)	12
53	Vogue LDE 043	LIONEL HAMPTON'S "JAZZ TIME PARIS" VOLUME 1 (10" LP)	12
54	Vogue LDE 051	NEW SOUNDS FROM EUROPE VOLUME 2 - FRANCE (10" LP)	12
54	Vogue LDE 063	LIONEL HAMPTON VOLUME 3 (10" LP)	12
54	Felsted EDL 87007	THE HAMP IN PARIS IN PARIS VOLUME 1 (10" LP)	12
54	Felsted EDL 87008	THE HAMP IN PARIS IN PARIS VOLUME 2 (10" LP)	12
55	Felsted PDL 85002	LIONEL HAMPTON AND HIS NEW FRENCH SOUND VOLUME 1 (10" LP)	12
55	HMV CLP 1023	HOT MALLETS (LP)	15
55	Columbia Clef 33C 9011	LIONEL HAMPTON QUARTET (10" LP)	12
55	Philips BBL 7015	APOLLO HALL CONCERT 1954 (LP)	12

(see also Sonny Parker)

PAUL HAMPTON

58	Philips PB 787	Play It Cool/Classy Babe (78)	18

SLIDE HAMPTON & HIS BAND

62	London HA-K/SH-K 8008	JAZZ WITH A TWIST (LP)	18
62	London LZT-K 15225	LONDON JAZZ (LP, as Slide Hampton Octet)	18

HERBIE HANCOCK

63	Blue Note 45-1887	Blind Man, Blind Man (Parts 1 & 2)	20
70	Warner Bros WB 7358	Fat Mama/Wiggle-Waggle	15
74	CBS 2329	Chameleon/Vein Melter	6
75	CBS 3059	Palm Grease/Butterfly	6
83	CBS TA 3577	Rockit (extended)/You Bet Your Love/I Thought It Was You (12")	8
71	Warner Bros WS 1834	FAT ALBERT ROTUNDA (LP)	20
71	Warner Bros K 46077	MWANDISHI (LP)	20
72	Warner Bros K 46164	CROSSINGS (LP)	15
74	Warner Bros K 46039	FAT ALBERT ROTUNDA (LP, reissue)	15
74	CBS 60193	THRUST (LP)	20
74	CBS 80546	DEATH WISH (LP, soundtrack)	15
74	CBS 65582	SEXTANT (LP)	12
74	CBS 65928	HEADHUNTERS (LP)	15
75	CBS 69185	MAN CHILD (LP)	12

(see also Headhunters)

TONY HANCOCK

63	Pye 7N 15575	Wing Commander Hancock - Test Pilot/The Threatening Letters (with Kenneth Williams)	6
63	Piccadilly FTF 38500	FACE TO FACE (LP, interview disc)	40

(see also Sidney James, Kenneth Williams)

OWEN HAND

61	Transatlantic TRA 127	SOMETHING NEW (LP)	120
66	Transatlantic TRA	I LOVED A LASS (LP)	100

JOHNNY HANDLE

61	Topic TOP 78	STOTTIN' DOON THE WAAL (EP)	10
75	Topic 12TS 270	THE COLLIER LAD (LP)	15

(see also Louise Killen & Johnny Handle, High Level Ranters)

HANDLEY FAMILY

73	GL 100	Wam Bam/Rum Dum And Baccy	8

HANDSLIPS

81	Victoria Park VICKY 1	Too Young To Date (But Not To Masturbate)/Art School Is For Wankers	6

HANDSOME BEASTS

81	Heavy Metal HEAVY 1	All Riot Now/Mark Of The Beast (p/s)	25
81	Heavy Metal HEAVY 2	Breaker/One In A Crowd/Crazy (wraparound p/s)	8
82	Heavy Metal HEAVY 11	Sweeties/You're One Your Own (p/s, with card sheet)	8
82	Heavy Metal HMRLP 2	BEASTIALITY (LP)	20

WAYNE HANDY

58	London HL 8547	Say Yeah/Could It Be (B-side with King Sisters)	200
58	London HL 8547	Say Yeah/Could It Be (B-side with King Sisters) (78)	50

PAUL HANFORD

60	Parlophone R 4680	Itsy Bitsy Teenie Weenie Little Polka Dot Bikini/Why Have You Changed Your Mind	10
60	Parlophone R 4694	If You Ain't Got Love/Ev'ry Little Girl	10
61	Parlophone R 4745	Everything/Cigarettes And Coffee Blues	10
61	Parlophone R 4813	Memphis Address/Flutter Flutter	10
62	Oriole CB 1779	Don't Be/Habit Of Loving You	10
63	Oriole CB 1830	Just When I Need You Most/Judy	10
63	Oriole CB 1866	The Minute You're Gone/High School Dance	10

HANGMAN'S BEAUTIFUL DAUGHTERS

87	Dreamworld DREAM 11	Love Is Blue/Popular Trend (p/s)	7

HANNA BARBERA (CARTOON SOUNDTRACK EPS)

66	Hanna Barbera HBE 1	FLINTSTONES - HANSEL AND GRETEL (EP)	10
66	Hanna Barbera HBE 2	UNCLE REMUS - BRER RABBIT AND THE TAR BABY (EP)	10
66	Hanna Barbera HBE 3	FLINTSTONES - GOLDILOCKS, BEAROSAURUS (EP)	10
66	Hanna Barbera HBE 4	SNAGGLEPUSS TALES - WIZARD OF OZ (EP)	15
66	Hanna Barbera HBE 5	YOGI BEAR AND BOO BOO TELL JACK AND THE BEANSTALK (EP)	10
66	Hanna Barbera HBE 6	FRED FLINTSTONE & BARNEY RUBBLE - SONG FROM MARY POPPINS (EP)	15
67	Hanna Barbera HBE 7	TOP CAT - ROBIN HOOD (EP)	15

MINT VALUE £

67	Hanna Barbera HBE 8	YOGI BEAR AND BOO BOO - LITTLE RED RIDING HOOD (EP).....................10
67	Hanna Barbera HBE 9	FLINTSTONES - THREE LITTLE PIGS (EP)...................................10
67	Hanna Barbera HBE 10	AUGIE DOGGY AND DOGGY DADDY - SONGS FROM PINOCCHIO (EP) 10
67	Hanna Barbera HBE 11	PEBBLES AND BAMM BAMM - WE WISH YOU A MERRY CHRISTMAS (EP).......10
68	Hanna Barbera HBE 12	MERRY CHRISTMAS - ORGAN AND CHIMES (EP) 8
68	Hanna Barbera HBE 13	MAGILLA GORILLA AND OGEE - ALICE IN WONDERLAND (EP) 8
68	Hanna Barbera HBE 14	PEBBLES AND BAMM BAMM - SONGS FROM THE GOOD SHIP LOLLIPOP (EP).....10

BOBBY HANNA

67	Decca F 12604	Thanks To You/Here I Stand 5
67	Decca F 12695	Blame It On Me/Goin' Where The Lovin' Is 7
68	Decca F 12738	Too Much Love/What Do I Want For Tomorrow 5
68	Decca F 12783	Written On The Wind/Everybody Needs Love 15
68	Decca F 12833	To Wait For Love (Is To Waste Your Life Away)/Is It Wrong...................6
69	Decca F 22917	Winter Love (E' L'Amore)/Time 6

GEORGE HANNA & SARAH ANNE O'NEILL

78	Topic 12TS 372	ON THE SHORES OF LOUGH NEAGH (LP) 12

JOSH HANNA

65	Parlophone R 5385	When I Love You/Love Me, Love Me 6
66	Decca F 12532	Shut Your Mouth/Sweet To My Soul 20

PAUL HANNAH

94	Ferox FER 007	CONTROL EP (12", plain sleeve) 12
95	Ferox FER 010	ADVENTURES IN TECHNO SOUL (12" EP) 8

ROSS HANNAMAN

67	Columbia DB 8217	Down Thru' Summer/I'll Give All My Love To Southend.......................5
67	Columbia DB 8288	1969/Probably On A Thursday (with p/s) 50
67	Columbia DB 8288	1969/Probably On A Thursday 40
74	Bellwood BW1	A NIGHT AT FACTOTUM (LP, 100 only, as John and Rosalind) 20

HANNIBAL

74	B&C HB 1	Winds Of Change/Winter 6
70	B&C CAS 1022	HANNIBAL (LP, gatefold sleeve) 120
(see also Wizzard)		

LANCE HANNIBAL

69	Blue Cat BS 148	Read The News/RECO & RHYTHM ACES: Return Of The Bullet.................20
(see also Sugar Simone, Les Foster)		

HANOI ROCKS

83	Lick LIX 1	Malibu Beach/Rebel On The Run (p/s) 5
83	Lick LIXPD 1	Malibu Beach/Rebel On The Run (picture disc) 8
84	CBS A 4513	Up Around The Bend/Until I Get You (p/s, with free transfer) 8
84	CBS DA 4513	Up Around The Bend/Until I Get You//Under My Wheels/I Feel Alright/ Train Kept A Rollin' (double pack)..8
84	CBS TA 4513	Up Around The Bend/Back To The Mystery City/Until I Get You/ Mental 84 Beat (12", p/s, with free transfer) 8
84	CBS WA 4732	Underwater World/Shakes/Magic Carpet Ride (12", picture disc) 8
84	CBS WA 4685	Don't You Ever Leave Me/Oil And Gasoline/Malibu Beach (Calypso) (12", 3-D picture disc)...8
82	Lick LICLPPD4	SELF DISTRUCTION BLUES (LP, picture disc) 15
83	Lick LICLP 1	BACK TO THE MYSTERY CITY (LP, white vinyl) 12
(see also Fallen Angels, Dark, Idle Flowers, Urban Dogs, Suicide Twins)		

JERRY HANSEN & RAMBLERS DANCE BAND

67	Decca WAP 24	DANCE WITH THE RAMBLERS (LP) 20

ANNETTE HANSHAW

65	VJM VEP 31	THAT'S ALL (EP) 10

HANSON

73	Manticore K43507	NOW HEAR THIS (LP, gatefold sleeve) 20

HANSON & KARLSSON

67	Polydor 184 196	SWEDISH UNDERGROUND (LP) 15
69	Polydor 462 60	MONUMENT (LP) 60
69	Polydor 583 564	MAN AT THE MOON (LP) 60
(see also Bo Hansson)		

BO HANSSON

72	Charisma CAS 1059	LORD OF THE RINGS (LP, insert, large 'Mad Hatter' label) 20
78	Charisma CAS 1059	LORD OF THE RINGS (LP, 1978 reissue with different sleeve, same cat no) 12
73	Charisma CAS 1073	MAGICIANS'S HAT (LP, large 'Mad Hatter' label) 15

HAPPENINGS

66	Fontana TF 735	See You In September/He Thinks He's A Hero 10
66	Fontana TF 766	Go Away Little Girl/Tea Time 8
67	Pye International 7N 25501	My Mammy/I Believe In Nothing 7
67	Stateside SS 587	Goodnight My Love/Lillies By Monet 8
67	Stateside SS 2013	I Got Rhythm/You're In A Bad Way 8
67	BT Puppy BTS 45532	Why Do Fools Fall In Love/When The Summer Is Through 7
67	BT Puppy BTS 45530	My Mammy/I Believe In Nothing 5
68	BT Puppy BTS 45538	Music Music Music/When I Lock My Door 6
68	BT Puppy BTS 45540	Randy/Love Song Of Mummy And Dad 8
68	BT Puppy BTS 45543	Breaking Up Is Hard To Do/Anyway 6
68	BT Puppy BTS 45545	Crazy Rhythm/Love Song Of Mummy And Dad............................5
69	BT Puppy BTS 45546	Where Do I Go, Go-Be-In (Hare Krishna)/New Day Comin' 5
67	Fontana TL 5383	BYE BYE, SO LONG, FAREWELL ... SEE YOU IN SEPTEMBER (LP)................35
67	BT Puppy BTLP 1003	PSYCLE (LP) 40
68	BT Puppy BTLPS 1004	GOLDEN HITS (LP) 20

HAPPY CONFUSION

69	Penny Farthing PEN 706	Yes Sir/Hereditary Impediment 15

HAPPY FAMILY

82	4AD AD 204	Puritans/Innermost Thoughts/The Mistake (p/s) 15

(see also Josef K, Momus)

HAPPY MAGAZINE
68	Polydor 56233	Satisfied Street/Do Right Woman Do Right Man	20
69	Polydor 56307	Who Belongs To You (Ooby Dooby Doo)/Beautiful Land	10

(see also Griffin)

HAPPY MONDAYS
85	Factory FAC 129	Delightful/This Feeling/Oasis (12" p/s)	40
86	Factory FAC 142	Freaky Dancing (Live)/The Egg (p/s)	12
87	Factory FAC 176	Tart Tart/Little Matchstick Owen's Rap (12", p/s)	8
87	Factory FACT 170	SQUIRREL & G-MAN TWENTY FOUR HOUR PARTY PEOPLE PLASTIC FACE CARNT SMILE (WHITE OUT) (LP, with "Desmond", 5,000 in plastic sleeve)	25
87	Factory FACT 170	SQUIRREL & G-MAN TWENTY FOUR HOUR PARTY PEOPLE PLASTIC FACE CARNT SMILE (WHITE OUT) (LP, with "Desmond")	15
87	Factory FACT 170c	SQUIRREL & G-MAN TWENTY FOUR HOUR PARTY PEOPLE PLASTIC FACE CARNT SMILE (WHITE OUT) (cassette)	30
87	Factory FACT 170c	SQUIRREL & G-MAN TWENTY FOUR HOUR PARTY PEOPLE PLASTIC FACE CARNT SMILE (WHITE OUT) (cassette, in box with insert)	25
90	Factory FACT 320	PILLS 'N' THRILLS & BELLYACHES (LP, withdrawn 'sweet wrapper' sleeve)	20
90	Factory FACT 320	PILLS 'N' THRILLS & BELLYACHES (LP)	12
92	Factory FACT 420	...YES PLEASE (LP)	12
07	Sequel SEQLP 012	UNCLE DYSFUNKTIONAL (LP)	12

HAPPY REFUGEES
82	Gymnasium REF no 1	Warehouse Sound/Enshrined In A Memory (p/s)	8
84	Gymnasium HREF 002	LAST CHANGE SALOON (LP)	15

HAPSHASH & THE COLOURED COAT
69	Liberty LBF 15188	Colinda/The Wall	25
67	Minit MLS 40001E	FEATURING THE HUMAN HOST AND THE HEAVY METAL KIDS (LP, with Art, red vinyl (MLL 40001) with insert)	175
67	Minit MLS 40001E	FEATURING THE HUMAN HOST AND THE HEAVY METAL KIDS (LP, with Art, later pressing on black vinyl)	40
69	Liberty LBL/LBS 83212R	THE WESTERN FLYER (LP, with Mike Batt, blue label)	70

(see also Tony McPhee, Warm Sounds, Marc Bolan/T. Rex, Art, Mike Batt)

HARBOUR LITES
65	HMV POP 1426	Come Back Silly Girl/Revenge	10
65	HMV POP 1465	I Would Give All/They Call The Wind Maria	10
66	Fontana TF 682	Run For Your Life/Lonely Journey	12

HARDBACK
86	Streetwave 7 BOSS 3	The Champ/Bust The Champ	6

HARD CORPS
84	Hard Corps HC 01	Dirty/To Breathe (12", hand-written white labels, numbered)	25
84	Survival SUR 026	Dirty/Respirer (To Breathe) (white or printed labels, stickered plain black sleeve)	10
84	Survival SUR 12 026	Dirty/Respirer (To Breathe) (12", with sticker in plain black sleeve)	12
85	Immaculate 12 IMMAC 2	Je Suis Passée (Extended French Version)/(Extended Club Dub Mix) (12", p/s)	12
85	Polydor HARDX 1	Je Suis Passée (Extended)/(Instrumental Mix)/(Dub Mix) (12", p/s)	8
85	Polydor HARDA 1	Je Suis Passée (Hard Mix)/(French Mix)/(Dub Mix) (12", gatefold PVC sleeve, various colours, with poster)	25
85	Polydor HARD 2	To Breathe/Metal And Flesh (unreleased)	30
85	Polydor HARDX 2	To Breathe/Metal And Flesh/To Breathe (Instrumental) (12", unreleased)	40
87	Rhythm King TYPE 3T	Lucky Charm/Porte-Bonheur/Lucky Charm (The Music) (12", p/s)	8
90	Concrete P. CPPRODLP 011	METAL AND FLESH (LP, clear vinyl)	15
90	Concrete P. CPPRODCD 011	METAL AND FLESH (CD)	25

(see also Craze, Skunks, T.U.F.F.)

HARDFLOOR
92	Harthouse HARTUK 1	HARDTRANCE ACPERIENCE EP (12", 4-track)	10

HARD HORSE
71	Dart ART 2001	Let It Ride/Hang old Freddy	15
72	Dart ART 2012	(Get It) Up Down/So Long I'm Moving On	30

(EDDIE) HARDIN & (PETE) YORK
69	Bell BLL 1064	Tomorrow Today/Candlelight (as Hardin-York)	30
69	Bell SBLL 125	TOMORROW TODAY (LP, gatefold sleeve, blue/silver/black label, with "Sold in the U.K..." text)	30
70	Bell SBLL 136	HARDIN & YORK (THE WORLD'S SMALLEST BIG BAND) (LP, gatefold)	30
71	Bell SBLL 141	FOR THE WORLD (LP, existence unconfirmed)	20
71	Decca SKL 5095	FOR THE WORLD (LP, reissue, blue/silver label with boxed logo)	15

(see also Eddie Hardin, Pete York, Spencer Davis Group)

EDDIE HARDIN
72	Decca F 13307	Why Does Everybody Put Me Down/Spend Your Money Honey	5
72	Decca TXS 106	HOME IS WHERE YOU FIND IT (LP, gatefold sleeve, green/silver label)	25

(see also Hardin-York, Spencer Davis Group, Roger Glover, Wizards Convention)

RICHARD HARDIN
61	HMV POP 887	Jezebel/Temptation	25

(see also Cresters, Mike Sagar & Cresters)

TIM HARDIN
66	Verve VS 1504	Hang On To A Dream/A Reason To Believe	12
67	Verve VS 1511	The Lady Came From Baltimore/Black Sheep Boy	10
68	Verve VS 1516	Don't Make Promises/Smugglin' Man	7
69	CBS 4441	A Simple Song Of Freedom/Question Of Birth	5
71	Verve 2009 006	If I Were A Carpenter/Hang On To A Dream	8
66	Verve (S)VLP 5018	TIM HARDIN 1 (LP)	40
67	Verve (S)VLP 6002	TIM HARDIN 2 (LP)	35
67	Atlantic 587/588 082	THIS IS TIM HARDIN (LP, plum label)	25
68	Verve (S)VLP 6010	LIVE IN CONCERT (LP)	30
69	Verve (S)VLP 6016	TIM HARDIN 4 (LP)	25
69	Verve (S)VLP 6019	THE BEST OF (LP)	20
69	CBS (S/M) 63571	SUITE FOR SUSAN MOORE AND DAMIAN (LP, gatefold sleeve, mono/stereo)	18
70	CBS 64335	BIRD ON A WIRE (LP)	15

Mike HARDING

72	CBS 65209	PAINTED HEAD (LP)	18
74	Verve 2683 048	TIM HARDIN 1/2 (2-LP, gatefold reissue)	20

(see also Eddie Hardin, Pete York, Spencer Davis Group)

MIKE HARDING
86	Moonraker M 003	BOMBERS MOON (LP)	20

ROSEMARY HARDMAN (& BOB AXFORD)
69	Folk Heritage no cat. no.	QUEEN OF HEARTS (LP)	125
71	Trailer LER 2075	FIREBIRD (LP)	25
71	Trailer LER 3018	SECOND SEASON CAME (LP, by Rosemary Hardman & Bob Axford)	25
75	Alida Star Cottage	JERSEY BURGER (LP)	120
78	Plant Life PLR 014	EAGLE OVER BLUE MOUNTAIN (LP, with insert)	12
80	Plant Life PLR 023	ROSIE HARDMAN (LP)	12
83	Plant Life PLR 053	THE WEAKNESS OF EVE (LP, with lyric insert)	12

HARD MEAT
69	Island WIP 6066	Rain/Burning Up Years	15
70	Warner Bros WB 8010	Ballad Of Marmalade Emma And Teddy Grimes/Yesterday, Today, Tomorrow	6
70	Warner Bros WS 1852	HARD MEAT (LP, gatefold sleeve with photo insert)	50
70	Warner Bros WS 1879	THROUGH A WINDOW (LP, green label)	70

HARDNOISE
89	White HNX001	Untitled (different recording to Music Of Life version - 300 pressed) (12")	50
90	Music Of Life NOTE40	Untitled (12")	10
91	Music Of Life NOTE48	Serve Tea, Then Murder/Mice In The Presence Of The Lion(12")	8

HARD RAIN
88	London LON 185	Diamonds/Monkey House (p/s)	12
88	London LONX 185	Diamonds/Monkey House/Diamonds (7" Version) (12", p/s)	15

HARD ROAD
79	Goodstuff LP 1002	NO PROBLEM (LP, private pressing)	15

HARD ROCK SOUL MOVEMENT
85	Elite 43	Do It Any Way You Wanna (12")	8
86	Elite DAZZ56	The Beat Is Mine/Double Def Fresh (12")	8
86	Elite Elite 46	Double Def Fresh/Def Hypnosis (12")	8

HARDSHIP POST
95	Sub Pop SP 295	Watching You/Your Sunshine (red vinyl)	5

HARD SKIN
96	Helen Of Oi H0031LP	HARD NUTS AND HARD CUNTS (LP, green vinyl)	15
07	No Future OI 28	New Age/FUCKED UP: Toronto FC (250 copies with fold-out sleeve, 50 with hard cover)	15

HARD STUFF
72	Purple PUR 103	Jay Time/The Orchestrator	30
73	Purple PUR 116	Inside Your Life/(It's) How Do You Do It!	10
72	Purple TPSA 7505	BULLETPROOF (LP, gatefold sleeve)	60
73	Purple TPSA 7507	BOLEX DEMENTIA (LP, textured gatefold sleeve)	75

(see also Andromeda, Atomic Rooster, John Du Cann, Five Day Week Straw People, Johnny Gustafson, Bullet, Quatermass)

HARD TRAVELLIN'
71	Flams Ltd PR 1065	HARD TRAVELLIN' (LP, private pressing)	100

HARDWARE
79	Narc NARC 001	Speed Unit/Wall To Wall/Walking/Fire (folded p/s)	8
79	Narc NARC 002	Rubberface/Face The Flag/The Seven Minutes (p/s)	5

HARDWARE
85	Reset 7REST 7	Dance/Hey (p/s)	8
85	Reset 12REST 7	Dance/Hey (12", p/s)	15

HARDY
71	Ackee ACK 131	Glorious Morning/Hearing's Not Seeing	6

DAVE HARDY
76	Red Rag RRR 008	LEAVING THE DALES (LP)	12

FRANCOISE HARDY
64	Pye 7N 15612	Catch A Falling Star/Only Friends	8
64	Pye 7N 15653	Tous Les Garcons Et Les Filles/L'Amour S'en Va	6
64	Pye 7N 15696	Pourtant Tu M'Aimes/Jaloux	8
64	Pye 7N 15740	Et Meme/Le Temps De L'Amour	8
65	Pye 7N 15802	All Over The World/Another Place	7
66	Vogue VRS 7001	Just Call And I'll Be There/You Just Have To Say The Word	7
66	Vogue VRS 7004	So Many Friends/However Much	10
66	Vogue VRS 7010	This Little Heart/The Rose	7
66	Vogue VRS 7011	La Maison Ou J'ai Grandi/Je Ne Suis La Pour Personne	7
66	Vogue VRS 7014	Autumn Rendezvous/It's My Heart	7
66	Vogue VRS 7020	Si C'est Ca/Je Serai La Pour Toi	7
66	Vogue VRS 7025	Voila/Qui Peut Dire	7
67	Vogue VRS 7026	On Se Quitte Toujours/Les Petits Garcons	8
68	United Artists UP 1208	Now You Want To Be Loved/Tell Him You're Mine	10
68	United Artists UP 2253	Will You Love Me Tomorrow/Loving You	10
69	United Artists UP 35011	Comment Te Dire Adieu/La Mer, Les Etoiles Et Le Vent	10
70	United Artists UP 35070	All Because Of You/Time Passing By	10
70	United Artists UP 35105	Soon Is Slipping Away/The Bells Of Avignon	10
64	Pye NEP 24188	C'EST FAB (EP)	10
64	Pye NEP 24192	FRANCOISE SINGS IN ENGLISH (EP)	10
64	Pye NEP 24193	C'EST FRANCOISE (EP)	10
65	Vogue VRE 5000	FRANCOISE (EP)	10
65	Vogue VRE 5001	FRANCOISE HARDY (EP)	10
65	Vogue VRE 5003	DIS LUI NON (EP)	10
66	Vogue VRE 5008	LE TEMPS DES SOUVENIRS (EP)	10
66	Vogue VRE 5012	CHANTE EN ALLEMAND (EP)	12
66	Vogue VRE 5015	L'AMITIE (EP)	12

66	Vogue VRE 5017	MON AMIE LA ROSE (EP)	12
67	Vogue VRE 5018	AUTUMN RENDEZVOUS (EP)	12
64	Pye NPL 18094	FRANCOISE HARDY (LP)	15
64	Pye NPL 18099	IN VOGUE (LP)	12
65	Vogue VRL 3000	FRANCOISE HARDY (LP)	18
66	Vogue VRL 3021	FRANCOISE HARDY (LP)	18
66	Vogue VRL 3023	LE MEILLEUR DE FRANCOISE HARDY (LP)	15
66	Vogue VRL 3025	SINGS IN ENGLISH (LP)	15
67	Vogue VRL 3028	FRANCOISE (LP)	15
67	Vogue VRL 3031	VOILA! FRANCOISE HARDY (LP)	15
68	United Artists SULP 1191	IL N'Y A PAS D'AMOUR HEUREUX (LP)	20
68	United Artists ULP 1207	EN ANGLAIS (LP)	25
70	United Artists UAS 29046	ONE-NINE-SEVEN-ZERO (LP)	40

LAVELL HARDY

| 68 | Direction 58-3261 | Don't Lose Your Groove/Women Of The World | 15 |

COLIN HARE

70	Penny Farthing PEN 736	Grannie, Grannie/For Where Have You Been	12
71	Penny Farthing PEN 750	Underground Girl/Fighting For Peace	10
72	Warner Bros K 16203	Didn't I Tell You/Seek Not In The Wide World	10
71	Penny Farthing PELS 516	MARCH HARE (LP)	300

(see also Honeybus)

WINSTON HAREWOOD

| 71 | Camel CA 64 | I Will Never Fall In Love Again (actually by Winston Heywood)/ LA-FUD-DIL ALL-STARS: La-Fud-Dil (actually "La-Fud-Del") | 8 |

(see also Winston Heywood)

RON HARGRAVE

| 58 | MGM MGM 956 | Latch On/Only A Daydream | 3000 |
| 58 | MGM MGM 956 | Latch On/Only A Daydream (78) | 400 |

HARLAN COUNTY

| 70 | Nashville 6076 002 | Dr. Handy's Dandy Candy/Big Heat | 8 |
| 70 | Nashville 6336 002 | HARLAN COUNTY (LP, red/black label) | 25 |

HARLEM SPEAKEASY

| 68 | Polydor 56270 | Aretha/Sight Of Pegasus | 15 |

HARLESDEN MONKS

| 72 | Pama Supreme PS 352 | Time/Harlesden High Street | 7 |
| 72 | Pama Supreme PS 352 | Rock Me Mister Ping Wing/Breakdown Rock | 30 |

STEVE HARLEY (& COCKNEY REBEL)

73	EMI EMI 2051	Sebastian/Rock And Roll Parade	5
74	EMI EMI 2191	Psychomodo/Such A Dream (unreleased)	0
74	EMI EMI 2191	Mr Soft/Such A Dream (with 'Orchestrated by Alan Powell' credit)	5
74	EMI EMI 2233	Big Big Deal/Bed In The Corner	5
77	EMI EMI 2922	Someone's Coming/Riding The Waves (For Virginia Woolf)	5
95	Windsong WINCD 073	LIVE AT THE BBC (CD)	15

(see also Anderson Harley & Batt)

HARLOW

| 79 | Pepper UP 36452 | Harry De Mazzio/Nothing To You | 100 |

LEE HARMER'S POPCORN

| 68 | Page One POF 053 | Love Is Coming/Hello Sunshine | 20 |

HARMONIANS

| 70 | Junior JR 112 | Music Street/Version | 15 |
| 70 | Ackee ACK 107 | Music Street/Group Of Girls | 10 |

(see also Tony & Hippy Boys, Winston Shan)

HARMONICA FATS

| 63 | Stateside SS 184 | Tore Up/I Get So Tired | 40 |
| 68 | Action ACT 4507 | Tore Up/I Get So Tired (reissue) | 20 |

HARMONISERS

| 69 | Duke DU 32 | Mother Hen/WINSTON SINCLAIR: Chastise Them | 15 |

HARMONIZING FOUR

| 66 | Rymska RA 102 | Who Knows/Heart Of Stone (actually by Charms) | 20 |

(see also Charms)

HARMONY BEACH

| 83 | Surf King SK 1 | HARMONY BEACH (EP, private pressing) | 18 |

HARMONY GRASS

68	RCA RCA 1772	Move In A Little Bit Closer Baby/Happiness Is Toy Shaped	8
69	RCA RCA 1828	First Time Loving/What A Groovy Day	7
69	RCA RCA 1885	I Remember/Summer Dreaming	7
70	RCA RCA 1928	Mrs. Richie/Teach Me How (withdrawn)	10
70	RCA RCA 1928	Cecilia/Mrs. Richie	7
70	RCA RCA 2011	Stand On Your Own Two Feet/Sing In The Sunshine	7
70	RCA SF 8034	THIS IS US (LP)	30

(see also Capability Brown, Tony Rivers & Castaways)

HARMONY TRIO

| 69 | Emblem 7DR 323 | LET'S FACE IT (LP) | 12 |

JOE HARNELL

| 62 | London HLR 9637 | Fly Me To The Moon - Bossa Nova/Harlem Nocturne | 6 |
| 78 | MCA MCA 397 | The Incredible Hulk Theme/Love Theme | 5 |

BILLY HARNER

| 71 | Kama Sutra 2013 029 | What About The Music/Please Spare Me This Time | 20 |
| 71 | Kama Sutra 2013 029 | What About The Music(instrumental)/Please Spare Me This Time | 900 |

MINT VALUE £

BUD HARPER
65	Vocalion VP 9252	Mr. Soul/Let Me Love You	50
65	Vocalion VP 9252	Mr. Soul/Let Me Love You (DJ copy)	80

CHARLIE HARPER
80	Gem GEMS 35	Barmy London Army/Talk Is Cheap (p/s, green or yellow vinyl)	5
81	Ramkup CAC 005	Freaked/Jo (p/s)	5

(see also U.K. Subs, Long Tall Shorty, Urban Dogs)

DON HARPER ORCHESTRA
68	Columbia DB 8519	World Of Sport March/England 88	15
73	Columbia DB 9023	World Of Sport/"Dr. Who" Theme (as Don Harper's Homo Electronicus)	25
74	Columbia SCX 6559	HOMO ELECTRONICUS (LP)	40

(see also Electricians)

HERBIE HARPER
56	London LZ N14031	PLEASE, NO MORE SHAGGY DOG STORIES (LP)	20

JANICE HARPER
57	HMV POP 376	Bon Voyage/Tell Me That You Love Me Tonight	8
58	Capitol CL 14899	Devotion/In Time	10
59	Capitol CL 14977	I Was Hoping You'd Ask Me/I'm Making Love To You	8
59	Capitol CL 15026	Let Me Call You Sweetheart/Just Whistle (	5
60	Capitol CL 15159	Only Once/Love Me Now, Love Me Never	5
59	Capitol T 1195	WITH FEELING (LP)	20

JESSIE HARPER
92	Kissing Spell KSLP 9203	GUITAR ABSOLUTION IN THE SHADE OF A MIDNIGHT SUN (LP, reissue of acetate-only album)	20

(see also Human Instinct)

JOE 'HARMONICA' HARPER
58	MGM MGM 983	Lazy Train/Her Lips Were Like Velvet	8

MIKE HARPER
70	Concord CON 026	You've Got Too Much Going For You/This Time	10

ROY HARPER
SINGLES
66	Strike JH 304	Take Me Into Your Eyes/Pretty Baby (in wraparound p/s)	50
66	Strike JH 304	Take Me Into Your Eyes/Pretty Baby	25
67	CBS 203001	Midspring Dithering/Zengem	20
68	CBS 3371	Life Goes By/Nobody's Got Any Money In The Summer	22
72	Harvest HAR 5059	Bank Of The Dead (Valerie's Song)/Little Lady (in p/s)	10
72	Harvest HAR 5059	Bank Of The Dead (Valerie's Song)/Little Lady	6
74	Harvest HAR 5080	(Don't You Think We're) Forever/Male Chauvinist Pig Blues	6
74	Harvest HAR 5089	Home (live)/Home (studio)	6
75	Harvest HAR 5096	When An Old Cricketer Leaves The Crease/Hallucinating Light (Acoustic Version) (p/s)	6
75	Harvest HAR 5102	Grown-Ups Are Just Silly Children/Referendum (Legend)	5
75	EMI PSR 407	Referendum/Another Day (live)/Tom Tiddler's Ground (live) (promo only)	8
77	Harvest HAR 5120	One Of Those Days In England/Watford Gap (p/s)	5
77	Harvest HAR 5140	Sail Away/Cherishing The Lonesome (as Roy Harper's Black Sheep)	7
78	Harvest HAR 5160	When An Old Cricketer Leaves The Crease/Home (studio) (p/s)	5
80	Harvest HAR 5203	Playing Games/First Thing In The Morning (p/s)	6
80	Harvest HAR 5207	Short And Sweet/Water Sports (live)/Unknown Soldier (live) (p/s)	6
82	Public PUBS 1001	No One Gets Out Here Alive/Casualty (live) (p/s)	5
83	Public PUBS 1002	I Still Care/Goodbye Ladybird (p/s)	6
85	B. Banquet BEG 131	Elizabeth (Short Version)/Advertisement (Short Version) (p/s)	5
88	Regal Zonophone HR 1	Laughing Inside/Laughing Inside (p/s, promo only; as Harry Rope)	10
88	EMI EM 46	Laughing Inside/Laughing Inside (Acoustic Version) (p/s)	5

ALBUMS : ORIGINAL LPS
66	Strike JHL 105	SOPHISTICATED BEGGAR	400
67	CBS BPG 63184	COME OUT FIGHTING GHENGIS SMITH (mono, orange label)	80
67	CBS SBPG 63184	COME OUT FIGHTING GHENGIS SMITH (stereo, orange label)	90
69	Liberty LBL 83231	FOLKJOKEOPUS (mono, blue label)	90
69	Liberty LBS 83231	FOLKJOKEOPUS (stereo, blue label)	70
69	Harvest SHVL 766	FLAT, BAROQUE AND BERSERK (gatefold sleeve; first pressing with "H. Ash" label credit)	70
71	Harvest SHVL 789	STORMCOCK (gatefold sleeve with lyric insert, no EMI logo on label)	40
73	Harvest SHVL 808	LIFEMASK (foldout 'door' sleeve, with insert)	30
74	Harvest SHSP 4027	VALENTINE (1st pressing, with 'Made in GT. Britain' on bottom of label, initially with lyric booklet)	30
74	Harvest SHSP 4027	VALENTINE (1st pressing with 'Made in GT. Britain' at bottom of label, without lyric booklet)	15
74	Harvest SHDW 405	FLASHES FROM THE ARCHIVES OF OBLIVION (2-LP, gatefold sleeve)	35
75	Harvest SHSP 4046	HQ (with lyric inner sleeve, EMI logo on label)	15
77	Harvest SHSP 4060	BULLINAMINGVASE (with inner sleeve & "Watford Gap"; some with 7" single, Referendum/"Another Day" (live)/"Tom Tiddler's Ground" [PSR 407])	15
77	Harvest SHSP 4060	BULLINAMINGVASE (2nd pressing with "Breakfast With You")	12
77	Harvest SHSP 4077	COMMERCIAL BREAK (unreleased; test pressing with proof sleeve)	300
78	Harvest SHSM 2025	HARPER 1970-1975	12
78	Harvest	HARPER 1970-1975 (6-LP box set)	100
80	Harvest SHVL 820	THE UNKNOWN SOLDIER (with inner sleeve)	12
82	Public TC PUBLP 5001	WORK OF HEART (on 'real time' high quality tape, different sleeve, 250 only)	12
84	Hard Up PUB 5002	BORN IN CAPTIVITY (880 only)	30
92	Hard Up HU 2	BORN IN CAPTIVITY II (LIVE) (cassette)	15

ALBUMS : REISSUE ALBUMS
71	Harvest SHVL 766	FLAT, BAROQUE AND BERSERK (gatefold sleeve; second pressing with "H. Ash" label credit and boxed EMI logo)	25
70	Young Blood SSYB 7	RETURN OF THE SOPHISTICATED BEGGAR (LP, with "Hup Hup Spiral" closed run-out groove, different sleeve)	20
71	Harvest SHVL 789	STORMCOCK (gatefold sleeve with lyric inner, with EMI logo on label)	20
73	Birth RAB 3	RETURN OF THE SOPHISTICATED BEGGAR (LP, 2nd reissue, with "Hup Hup Spiral" closed run-out groove, different sleeve)	15

74	Harvest SHSP 4027	VALENTINE (2nd pressing without 'Made in GT. Britain' at bottom of label, without lyric booklet)	15
75	Sunset SLS 50373	FOLKJOKEOPUS (LP)	15
77	Big Ben BBX 502	THE SOPHISTICATED BEGGAR (LP, different rear sleeve)	12
77	CBS Embassy EMB 31544	THE EARLY YEARS (LP, reissue of "Come Out Fighting Ghengis Smith", different sleeve)	12
86	Awareness AWL 1002	WORK OF HEART (LP, different sleeve with inner; later pressing with only "No One Gets Out Of Here Alive"/"Casualty (live) [PUBS 1001])	12
86	Awareness AWL 1002	WORK OF HEART (LP, different sleeve with inner; 1st 1,000 with 2 x 7" "No One Gets Out Of Here Alive"/"Casualty (live) [PUBS 1001]) & "Still Care"/"Goodbye Ladybird" [PUBS2])	15
86	Awareness AWL 1002	WORK OF HEART (, different sleeve, 250 only on 'real time' quality tape)	12
93	Hard Up HUCD 003	FLAT, BAROQUE & BERSERK (CD, in box with 40-page booklet & poster, signed)	20

(see also Rory Phare, Per Yarroh, Pink Floyd)

TIM HARPER
95	Peacefrog PF 047	I Feel A Groove (12", plain sleeve)	8

HARPER'S BIZARRE
67	Warner Bros WB 5890	59th Street Bridge Song (Feelin' Groovy)/Lost My Love Today	8
67	Warner Bros WB 7528	Come To The Sunshine/The Debutante's Ball	5
67	Warner Bros WB 7063	Anything Goes/Malibu U	7
67	Warner Bros WB 7090	Chattanooga Choo Choo/Hey You In The Crowd	5
68	Warner Bros WB 7172	Cotton Candy Sandman (Sandman's Coming)/Virginia City	5
68	Warner Bros WB 7223	Battle Of New Orleans/Green Apple Tree	5
69	Warner Bros WB 7238	I Love You, Alice B. Toklas!/Look To The Rainbow	5
70	Warner Bros WB 7388	Anything Goes/Virginia City	5
67	Warner Bros W 1693	FEELIN' GROOVY (LP)	20
67	Warner Bros W 1716	ANYTHING GOES (LP)	25
68	Warner Bros W(S) 1739	THE SECRET LIFE OF HARPER'S BIZARRE (LP)	15

SLIM HARPO
61	Pye International 7N 25098	Rainin' In My Heart/Don't Start Cryin' Now	25
63	Pye International 7N 25220	Don't Start Cryin' Now/Rainin' In My Heart	25
66	Stateside SS 491	Baby Scratch My Back/I'm Gonna Miss You (Like The Devil)	30
66	Stateside SS 527	Shake Your Hips/Midnight Blues	40
66	Stateside SS 557	I'm A King Bee/I Got Love If You Want It	45
67	Stateside SS 581	I'm Your Breadmaker Baby/Loving You (The Way I Do)	30
67	President PT 164	I'm Gonna Keep What I've Got/I've Got To Be With You Tonight	10
68	Liberty LBF 15176	Something Inside Me/PAPPA LIGHTFOOT: Wine Whisky And Women	20
68	President PT 187	Tip On In (Parts 1 & 2)	15
70	Blue Horizon 57-3175	Folsom Prison Blues/Mutual Friend	30
65	Stateside SL 10135	A LONG DRINK OF THE BLUES (LP, with Lightnin' Slim)	80
68	President PTL 1017	TIP ON IN (LP)	50
70	Blue Horizon 7-63854	HE KNEW THE BLUES (LP)	150
72	Blue Horizon 2431 013	TRIGGER FINGER (LP)	135
76	Flyright LP 520	BLUES HANGOVER (LP)	18
78	Sonet SNTF 769	HE KNEW THE BLUES (LP)	25
80	Flyright FLY 558	GOT LOVE IF YOU WANT IT (LP)	18

(see also Lightnin' Slim)

GEORGE HARRASSMENT & HOMOSEXUALS
80s	Black Noise 12 NO 6	MASAI SLEEP WALKING (LP)	12

(see also Homosexuals)

HARRIER
84	Black Horse HARR 1T	OUT ON THE STREET EP (Out On The Street/Nickels And Dimes/Shine On) (12", p/s)	15

DERRICK HARRIOT(T) (& CRYSTALITES)
62	Blue Beat BB 131	I Care/Have Faith In Me (as Derrick Harriott & Vagabonds)	15
63	Blue Beat BB 178	Be True/I Won't Cry	15
64	Island WI 157	What Can I Do (The Wedding)/Leona	12
65	Island WI 170	I Am Only Human (as Derak Harriott)/OWEN AND LEON SILVERA: I Want My Cock (probably withdrawn)	50
65	Island WI 170	I Am Only Human (as Derak Harriott)/ROY PANTON: Good Man	30
65	Island WI 237	My Three Loves/The Jerk	30
65	Island WI 245	Together/Mama Didn't Lie	30
65	Ska Beat JB 199	Monkey Ska/Derrick!	30
66	Doctor Bird DB 1002	Jon Tom/AUDREY WILLIAMS: Solas Market	20
67	Island WI 3063	The Loser/Bless You	80
67	Island WI 3064	Happy Times/You My Everything	35
67	Island WI 3077	Walk The Streets/BOBBY ELLIS: Step Softly (B-side with Desmond Miles Seven)	80
67	Island WI 3089	Solomon/BOBBY ELLIS: The Emperor (B-side with Desmond Miles Seven)	45
68	Island WI 3135	Do I Worry?/BOBBY ELLIS & CRYSTALITES: Shuntin'	80
68	Island WI 3147	Born To Love You/IKE & CRYSTALITES: Alfred Hitchcock	40
68	Island WI 3153	Tang Tang Festival Song/CRYSTALITES: James Ray	40
69	Big Shot BI 505	Standing In/Bumble Bee	50
69	Big Shot BI 511	Another Lonely Night/Been So Long	15
70	Songbird SB 1013	Riding For A Fall/I'm Not Begging	10
70	Songbird SB 1014	Sitting On Top/You Were Meant For Me	10
70	Songbird SB 1022	Go Bye Bye/Laugh It Off	12
70	Songbird SB 1028	Message From A Black Man/(Version II)	10
70	Songbird SB 1029	Psychedelic Train (w/ Chosen Few)/Psychedelic Train (Pt. 2) (with Crystalites)	12
70	Songbird SB 1033	No Man Is An Island/CRYSTALITES: No Man Is An Island Part 2	10
70	Songbird SB 1042	Groovy Situation/CRYSTALITES: The Crystal Groove	10
70	Songbird SB 1043	Psychedelic Train Chapter Three/CRYSTALITES: Groovy Situation Version II	7
71	Songbird SB 1052	Candy/CRYSTALITES: Candy Version	15
71	Songbird SB 1055	Lollipop Girl/CRYSTALITES: Lollipop Version	7
71	Songbird SB 1063	Medley In 5 (Parts 1 & 2)	7
72	Songbird SB 1065	Have You Seen Her/CRYSTALITES: Have You Seen Her - Version	7
72	Songbird SB 1068	Over The River/River (Version)	7
72	Songbird SB 1071	Since I Lost My Baby/Baby (Version)	7
72	Songbird SB 1078	Being In Love/Love (Version)	6
72	Songbird SB 1084	Don't Rock The Boat/Rock (Version)	7
73	Attack ATT 8056	Brown Baby/CRYSTALITES: Brown Baby Version	6
73	Explosion EX 2071	Let Me Down Easy/Let Me Down Easy - Version	7

MINT VALUE £

74	Harry J. HJ 6675	Some Guys Have All The Luck/Some Guys Have All The Luck - Version	6
65	Island ILP 928	THE BEST OF DERRICK HARRIOTT (LP)	120
67	Island ILP 955	DERRICK HARRIOTT'S ROCKSTEADY PARTY (LP, actually v/a LP)	300
68	Island ILP 983	THE BEST OF VOLUME TWO (LP, as Derrick Harriott & Crystalites)	150
69	Pama SECO 13	SINGS JAMAICA REGGAE (LP)	150
70	Trojan TTL 43	THE BEST OF DERRICK HARRIOTT (LP)	40
70	Trojan TTL 54	ROCKSTEADY PARTY (LP)	55
70	Trojan TBL 114	THE UNDERTAKER (LP, as Derrick Harriott & Crystalites)	25
70	Trojan TBL 141	PSYCHEDELIC TRAIN (LP, as Derrick Harriott & Crystalites)	30
81	Trojan TRTS 198	SONGS FOR MIDNIGHT LOVERS (LP)	12

JOE HARRIOTT

56	Jazz Today JTE 106	WITH STRINGS (EP)	20
56	Pye Jazz NJE 1003	NO STRINGS (EP)	50
50s	Melodisc EPM7 117	COOL JAZZ WITH JOE (EP)	40
57	Columbia SEG 7665	JOE HARRIOTT QUARTET (EP)	75
59	Columbia SEG 7939	BLUE HARRIOTT (EP)	35
61	Columbia SEG 8070	A GUY CALLED JOE (EP)	25
60	Jazzland JLP 49	FREE FORM (LP)	120
62	Columbia 33SX 1477	ABSTRACT (LP)	250
63	Columbia 33SX 1627	MOVEMENT (LP)	400
64	Columbia 33SX 1692	HIGH SPIRITS (LP)	400
66	Columbia S(C)X 6025	DOUBLE QUINTET (LP, with John Mayer)	45
67	Melodisc SLP 12150	SWINGS HIGH (LP)	75
67	Columbia S(C) 6122	INDO-JAZZ FUSIONS (LP, with John Mayer)	35
68	Columbia S(C)X 6215	INDO-JAZZ FUSIONS II (LP, with John Mayer)	45
68	Columbia S(C)X 6249	PERSONAL PORTRAIT (LP)	50
69	Columbia SCX 6354	HUM-DONO (LP, with Amancio D'Silva)	700
73	One Up OU 2011	MEMORIAL 1973 (LP)	25

(see also Tony Kinsey Trio & Joe Harriott, John Mayer, Michael Garrick)

JOE HARRIOTT/DON RENDELL QUARTET

57	MGM MGM-EP 615	JAZZ BRITANNIA (EP, 2 tracks each)	40

(see also Don Rendell)

ANITA HARRIS

61	Parlophone R 4830	I Haven't Got You/Mr One And Only	7
64	Vocalion V 9223	Lies/Don't Think About Love	7
65	Decca F 12082	Willingly/At Last Love	6
65	Pye 7N 15868	Trains And Boats And Planes/Upside Down	7
65	Pye 7N 15894	I Don't Know Anymore/When I Look At You	8
65	Pye 7N 15971	London Life/I Run To Hide	7
66	Pye 7N 17069	Something Must Be Done/Funny Kind Of Feeling	10
66	CBS 2724	Just Loving You/Butterfly With Coloured Wings	5
67	CBS 2991	The Playground/B.A.D. For Me	10
68	CBS 3765	Le Blon/Dusty Road	5
67	Pye NEP 24288	ANITA HARRIS (EP)	15
68	CBS EP 6401	DREAM A LITTLE DREAM OF ME (EP)	10
66	CBS BGP/SBPG 62894	SOMEBODY'S IN MY ORCHARD (LP)	15
67	CBS 63182	JUST LOVING YOU (LP)	12
69	CBS 63927	CUDDLY TOY (LP)	12
70	CBS S 64258	ANITA IN JUMBLELAND (LP)	12

(see also Brello Cabal)

ARTIE HARRIS & HIS BOYS

63	Oriole CB 1816	Go Go Gaudeamus/Mexicana	8

BETTY HARRIS

63	London HL 9796	Cry To Me/I'll Be A Liar	20
65	Stateside SS 475	What A Sad Feeling/I'm Evil Tonight	20
67	Stateside SS 2045	Nearer To You/12 Red Roses	20
69	Action ACT 4535	Ride Your Pony/Trouble With My Lover	15
69	Action ACLP 6007	SOUL PERFECTION (LP)	80

(see also Betty Harris & Lee Dorsey)

BRENDA JO HARRIS

69	Roulette RO 503	I Can Remember/Play With Fire	8

EDDIE HARRIS

69	Atlantic 584 218	Listen Here/Theme - In Search Of A Movie	10
69	Atlantic 584 232	It's Crazy/Live Right Now (unissued)	0
74	Atlantic K 10513	Is It In?/Funkarama	7
75	Atlantic K 10561	I Need Some Money/Don't Want Nobody	7
76	Atlantic K 10741	Get On Up And Dance/Why Must We Part	5
62	Stateside SL 10009	BREAKFAST AT TIFFANY'S (LP)	12
63	Stateside SL 10018	MIGHTY LIKE A ROSE (LP)	12
63	Stateside SL 10049	GOES TO THE MOVIES (LP)	12
65	Atlantic SAL 5045	THE IN SOUND (LP)	12
69	Atlantic 588 177	SILVER CYCLES (LP)	12
73	Atlantic K 40220	THE ELECTRIFYING EDDIE HARRIS (LP)	12

HAL HARRIS

78	Ace NS 47	Jitterbop Baby/I Don't Know When	5

JET HARRIS

62	Decca F 11466	Besame Mucho/Chills And Fever	8
62	Decca F 11488	Main Title Theme (from The Man With The Golden Arm)/Some People	8
64	Decca F 11841	Big Bad Bass/Rifka	10
67	Fontana TF 849	My Lady/You Don't Live Twice	25
75	SRT SRT 75355	Theme For A Fallen Idol/This Sportin' Life (initial pressing)	10
75	SRT SRT 75355	Theme/This Sportin' Life (later pressing with shortened A-side title)	5
78	SRT SRT 77389	Guitar Man/Theme	8
62	Decca DFE 8502	JET HARRIS (EP)	20
78	Ellie Jay EJSP 8622	INSIDE JET HARRIS - THE LAST CONCERT (LP, 2,500 only)	20
70s	Q LPMM 1038	ANNIVERSARY ALBUM (LP)	20

(see also Shadows, Jet Harris & Tony Meehan, Keith Meehan, Peter Rawes)

JET HARRIS & TONY MEEHAN
63	Decca F 11563	Diamonds/Footstomp	5
63	Decca F 11644	Scarlett O'Hara/(Doing The) Hully Gully	5
63	Decca F 11710	Applejack/The Tall Texan	6
80	Decca F 13892	Diamonds/Scarlett O'Hara/Applejack/Man With The Golden Arm (p/s)	5
63	Decca DFE 8528	JET AND TONY (EP)	20
76	Decca REM 1	REMEMBERING (LP)	12

(see also Shadows, Jet Harris, Tony Meehan, Vipers Skiffle Group)

JOHNNY HARRIS
65	Mercury MF 942	Mynah Hop/Here Comes The Boot	15
69	Warner Bros WB 8000	Footprints On The Moon/Lulu's Theme	10
70	Warner Bros WB 8016	Fragment Of Fear/Stepping Stones	25
70	Warner Bros WS 3002	MOVEMENTS (LP, 1st pressing with orange labels)	50
72	Warner Bros K 46054	MOVEMENTS (LP, reissue)	20
73	Warner Bros K 46187	ALL TO BRING YOU MORNING (LP)	15

JUNE HARRIS
65	CBS 201774	Over And Over Again/Stand Back	12

MAX HARRIS
69	Pye 7N 17730	Theme From The Film 'Baby Love'/Roberts Theme From 'Baby Love'	6

OSCAR HARRIS
70	Upfront UPF 6	T.O.P/I Don't Wanna Listen	10

PAT HARRIS & BLACKJACKS
63	Pye 7N 15567	The Hippy Hippy Shake/You Gotta See Your Mama Ev'ry Night	25

(see also Blackjacks)

PHIL HARRIS
54	HMV 7M 199	I Know An Old Lady/Take Your Girlie To The Movies	8
54	HMV 7M 231	I Guess I'll Have To Change My Plan/The Persian Kitten	8
55	HMV 7M 289	I Wouldn't Touch You With A Ten-Foot Pole/There's A Lot More	8
70	Buena Vista DF 478	Thomas O'Malley Cat/SCATMAN CROTHERS: Everybody Wants To Be A Cat	5

RICHARD HARRIS
68	RCA RCA 1699	MacArthur Park/Paper Chase	6
68	Stateside SS 8001	The Yard Went On Forever/Lucky Me	5
70	Stateside SS 8054	Ballad Of 'A Man Called Horse'/The Morning Of The Mourning Of Another Kennedy	5
71	Probe PRO 540	My Boy/Why Did You Leave Me	5
68	RCA Victor RD/SF 7947	A TRAMP SHINING (LP)	15
68	Stateside (S)SL 5001	THE YARD WENT ON FOREVER (LP)	15

(see also Jim Webb)

ROLF HARRIS
64	Columbia DB 7349	Ringo For President/Headhunter	7
66	Columbia SEG 8516	JAKE THE PEG (EP)	8
63	SCX 1507	SUN ARISE (LP, stereo)	20

RONNIE HARRIS (& CORONETS)
54	Columbia SCM 5138	Hold My Hand/No One Can Change Destiny	6
54	Columbia SCM 5139	I Love Paris/I Still Believe	6
55	Columbia SCM 5159	Don't Go To Strangers/Surprisingly (as Ronnie Harris & Coronets)	6
55	Columbia SCM 5176	Stranger In Paradise/I Wonder	6
56	Columbia SCM 5242	I've Changed My Mind A Thousand Times/Come To Me (with Coronets)	6
56	Columbia DB 3836	That's Right/A House With Love In It	10
57	Columbia DB 3877	Armen's Theme (Yesterday And You)/Dancing Chandelier	5
57	Columbia DB 3934	Dear To Me/It's Not For Me To Say (B-side with Russ Conway)	5

(see also Coronets, Ruby Murray, Ray Burns, Russ Conway)

ROY HARRIS
72	Topic 12TS 217	THE BITTER AND THE SWEET (LP, blue label)	15
75	Topic 12TS 256	CHAMPIONS OF FOLLY (LP)	12

SCOTT HARRIS
68	Morgan MR7S	Barry Johnson's Sad Eyes Inn/Morning Sun	30

SHAKEY JAKE HARRIS
69	Liberty LBS 83217	FURTHER ON UP THE ROAD (LP)	40
73	Polydor 2391 015	THE DEVIL'S HARMONICA (LP)	28

HARRIS SISTERS
55	Capitol CL 14232	Kissin' Bug/We've Been Walkin' All Night	20

SUZANNE HARRIS
70	R.F.S. Records RFS 8270	Here Come The Beautiful People/We're Using Up The World (p/s)	20

THURSTON HARRIS (& SHARPS)
57	Vogue V 9092	Little Bitty Pretty One/I Hope You Won't Hold It Against Me (with Sharps)	200
57	Vogue V 9092	Little Bitty Pretty One/I Hope You Won't Hold It Against Me (with Sharps) (78)	35
58	Vogue V 9098	Do What You Did/I'm Asking Forgiveness (as Thurston Harris & Sharps) (78)	40
58	Vogue V 9098	Do What You Did/I'm Asking Forgiveness (as Thurston Harris & Sharps)	250
58	Vogue V 9108	Be Baba Leba/I'm Out To Getcha	250
58	Vogue V 9108	Be Baba Leba/I'm Out To Getcha (78)	40
58	Vogue V 9122	Smokey Joe's/Only One Love Is Blessed	150
58	Vogue V 9122	Smokey Joe's/Only One Love Is Blessed (78)	40
58	Vogue V 9127	Tears From My Heart/Over Somebody Else's Shoulder	100
58	Vogue V 9127	Tears From My Heart/Over Somebody Else's Shoulder (78)	60
59	Vogue V 9139	Purple Stew (as Thurston Harris & Masters)/I Hear A Rhapsody	150
59	Vogue V 9139	Purple Stew (as Thurston Harris & Masters)/I Hear A Rhapsody (78)	50
59	Vogue V 9144	You Don't Know How Much I Love You/In The Bottom Of My Heart	100
59	Vogue V 9144	You Don't Know How Much I Love You/In The Bottom Of My Heart (78)	50
59	Vogue V 9146	Hey Little Girl/My Love Will Last	150
59	Vogue V 9146	Hey Little Girl/My Love Will Last (78)	50
59	Vogue V 9149	Runk Bunk/Bless Your Heart	200

MINT VALUE £

59	Vogue V 9149	Runk Bunk/Bless Your Heart (78)	50
59	Vogue V 9151	Slip-Slop/Paradise Hill	200
59	Vogue V 9151	Slip-Slop/Paradise Hill (78)	60
66	Sue WI 4016	Little Bitty Pretty One/I Hope You Won't Hold It Against Me (reissue)	30

(see also Sharps)

WEE WILLIE HARRIS

57	Decca F 10970	Rockin' At The Two 'I's/Back To School Again	40
57	Decca F 10970	Rockin' At The Two 'I's/Back To School Again (78)	30
58	Decca F 10980	Love Bug Crawl/Rosie Lee	40
58	Decca F 10980	Love Bug Crawl/Rosie Lee (78)	30
58	Decca F 11044	Got A Match/No Chemise, Please!	30
58	Decca F 11044	Got A Match/No Chemise, Please! (78)	20
60	Decca F 11217	Wild One/Little Bitty Girl	20
63	HMV POP 1198	You Must Be Joking/Better To Have Loved	10
66	Parlophone R 5504	Someone's In The Kitchen With Diana/Walk With Peter And Paul (some A-sides list 'Dina')	10
66	Polydor 56140	Listen To The River Roll Along/Try Moving Baby (writing in black or white)	30
74	Decca F 13516	Together/Rock'n'Roll Jamboree	5
58	Decca DFE 6465	ROCKING WITH WEE WILLIE (EP)	150

WYNONIE 'MR BLUES' HARRIS

51	Vogue V 2006	All She Wants To Do Is Rock/Drinkin' Wine Spo-Dee-O-Dee (78)	30
52	Vogue V 2111	Luscious Woman/Lovin' Machine (78)	25
52	Vogue V 2127	Bloodshot Eyes/Lollipop Mama (78)	15
52	Vogue V 2128	Just Like Two Drops Of Water/Good Mornin' Judge (78)	15
52	Vogue V 2133	Night Train/Do It Again Please (78)	30
52	Vogue V 2134	Rock, Mr. Blues/Put It Back (78)	30
52	Vogue V 2144	Teardrops From My Eyes/Keep On Churnin' (Till The Butter Comes) (78)	30
52	Vogue V 2166	I Like My Baby's Pudding/Adam Come And Get Your Rib (78)	35
56	Vogue V 2127	Bloodshot Eyes/Lollipop Mama (triangular centre)	125
56	Vogue V 2127	Bloodshot Eyes/Lollipop Mama (round centre)	75
56	Vogue EPV 1103	WYNONIE 'MISTER BLUES' HARRIS (EP)	120
61	Blue Beat BBEP 301	BATTLE OF THE BLUES (EP)	80

WYNONIE HARRIS/EDDIE 'CLEANHEAD' VINSON

| 72 | Polydor 2343 048 | JUMP BLUES (LP) | 22 |

(see also Tiny Bradshaw/Wynonie Harris, Eddie 'Cleanhead' Vinson)

HARRISON

| 84 | Skipping Rope SKIP 1 | There Is No Refrain/Simply This (p/s) | 40 |

DANNY HARRISON

62	Starlite ST45 77	No One To Love Me/All The World is Lonely	6
62	Starlite ST45 91	Broken Love Affair/Have I Wasted My Life	6
63	Starlite ST45 108	Have You Ever Been Lonely/Mary Ann I'm Lonesome	6
65	Coral Q 72479	Speak Of The Devil/I'm A Rollin' Stone	15
62	Starlite STEP 23	INTRODUCING DANNY HARRISON (EP)	20

EARL HARRISON

| 67 | London HL 10121 | Humphrey Stomp/Can You Forgive Me | 50 |
| 67 | London HL 10121 | Humphrey Stomp/Can You Forgive Me (DJ Copy) | 100 |

GEORGE HARRISON

SINGLES

71	Apple R 5884	My Sweet Lord/What Is Life (in colour 'head' p/s)	12
71	Apple R 5912	Bangla-Desh/Deep Blue (with rare p/s [beware of new-looking counterfeits!])	80
71	Apple R 5912	Bangla-Desh/Deep Blue	5
73	apple R 5988	Give Me Love (Give Me Peace On Earth)/Miss O'Dell	5
74	Apple R 6001	Dark Horse/I Don't Care Anymore (unissued)	0
74	Apple R 6002	Ding Dong, Ding Dong/I Don't Care Anymore (no p/s)	5
75	Apple R 6001	Dark Horse/Hari's On Tour (Express) (p/s)	10
75	Apple R 6007	You/World Of Stone (p/s)	8
76	Apple R 6012	This Guitar (Can't Keep From Crying)/Maya Love (no p/s)	35
76	Apple R 5884	My Sweet Lord/What Is Life (reissue, black & white 'gnome' p/s)	10
76	Dark Horse K 16856	This Song/Learning How To Love You (issued with U.S. p/s)	10
77	Dark Horse K 16896	True Love/Pure Smokey (no p/s)	6
77	Dark Horse K 16967	It's What You Value/Woman Don't You Cry For Me (no p/s)	15
79	Dark Horse K 17327	Blow Away/Soft Touch (p/s)	5
79	Dark Horse K 17284	Love Comes To Everyone/Soft Hearted Hana	15
79	Dark Horse K 17423	Faster/Your Love Is Forever (with charity stickered plain white die-cut sleeve)	15
79	Dark Horse K 17423	Faster/Your Love Is Forever (picture disc, stickered PVC sleeve with insert)	35
81	Dark Horse K 17807	All Those Years Ago/Writing On The Wall (p/s)	5
81	Dark Horse K 17837DJ	Teardrops (Edited Version)/Save The World (DJ promo only, no p/s)	25
81	Dark Horse K 17837	Teardrops/Save The World (p/s)	10
82	Dark Horse 929 864-7	Wake Up My Love/Greece (p/s)	8
86	Ganga Publishing B.V.	Shanghai Surprise (with Vicki Brown) (unreleased, 1-sided promo only; no catalogue number, matrix: SHANGHAI 1)	700
87	Dark Horse W 8178	Got My Mind Set On You/Lay His Head (p/s, green label)	8
87	Dark Horse W 8178B	Got My Mind Set On You/Lay His Head (box set with 2 postcards)	20
87	Dark Horse W 8178T	Got My Mind Set On You (Extended Version)/Got My Mind Set On You (Single Version)/Lay His Head (12", p/s with poster)	15
87	Dark Horse W 8178TP	Got My Mind Set On You (Extended Version)/Got My Mind Set On You (Single Version)/Lay His Head (12", picture disc)	20
88	Dark Horse W 8131B	When We Was Fab/Zig Zag (box set with fold-out poster & cut-out)	10
88	Dark Horse W 8131	When We Was Fab (Unextended Version)/Zig Zag/That's The Way It Goes (Remix)/When We Was Fab (Reverse End) (12", p/s)	10
88	Dark Horse W 8131TP	When We Was Fab (Unextended Version)/Zig Zag/That's The Way It Goes (Remix)/When We Was Fab (Reverse End) (12", picture disc)	20
88	Dark Horse W 8131CD	When We Was Fab (Unextended Version)/Zig Zag/That's The Way It Goes (Remix)/When We Was Fab (Reverse End) (3" CD with 5" adaptor, 5" case)	12
88	Dark Horse W 7913	This Is Love/Breath Away From Heaven (p/s)	8
88	Dark Horse W 7913T	This Is Love/Breath Away From Heaven/All Those Years Ago (12", p/s)	15
88	Dark Horse W 7913CD	This Is Love/Breath Away From Heaven/All Those Years Ago/Hong Kong Blues (3" CD with adaptor, 5" case)	12

89	Dark Horse W 2696	Cheer Down/That's What It Takes (p/s) 8
89	Dark Horse W 2696T	Cheer Down/That's What It Takes/Crackerbox Palace (12", p/s) 15
89	Dark Horse W 2696CD	Cheer Down/That's What It Takes/Crackerbox Palace (3" CD, gatefold card sleeve) 20
88	Genesis SGH 777	SONGS BY GEORGE HARRISON (Limited Edition) (EP, 33rpm, issued with limited edition book Songs By George Harrison) 900
88	Genesis SGHCD 777	SONGS BY GEORGE HARRISON (CD EP, issued with limited edition book) 800
92	Genesis SGH 778	SONGS BY GEORGE HARRISON VOL. 2 (EP, with limited edition book Songs By George Harrison Vol. 2) 400
92	Genesis SGHCD 778	SONGS BY GEORGE HARRISON VOL. 2 (CD EP, with limited edition book) 600
03	Parlophone R 6601	Any Road/Marwa Blues (p/s) 7

ALBUMS

68	Apple APCOR 1	WONDERWALL MUSIC (soundtrack; with insert, black inner sleeve, mono) ...250
68	Apple SAPCOR 1	WONDERWALL MUSIC (soundtrack; with insert, black inner sleeve, stereo) ...90
69	Zapple ZAPPLE 02	ELECTRONIC SOUND (with inner sleeve) 175
71	Apple STCH 639	ALL THINGS MUST PASS (3-LP box set with poster & lyric inner sleeves; initial batch in U.K. Box) 90
71	Apple STCH 639	ALL THINGS MUST PASS (3-LP box set with poster & lyric inner sleeves; later batch in U.S. box) 40
72	Apple STCX 3385	THE CONCERT FOR BANGLA DESH (3-LP box set, orange inside with BMI/ASCAP label credits, with booklet, featuring Bob Dylan) 70
73	Apple PAS 10006	LIVING IN THE MATERIAL WORLD (gatefold sleeve with inner) 18
74	Apple PAS 10008	DARK HORSE (LP, gatefold sleeve, inner sleeve, lyric insert) 20
75	Apple PAS 100009	EXTRA TENURE (LP with inner) 20
76	Dark Horse K56319	THIRTY THREE AND A THIRD (LP, gatefold with inner) 15
82	Dark Horse 923734-1	GONE TROPPO (LP, with inner) 15
87	Dark Horse 925643-1	CLOUD NINE (LP, with inner) 15
91	EPIC EPC 468835 1	THE CONCERT FOR BANGLA DESH (3-LP set in single sleeve) 25
92	Dark Horse 759926964-1	LIVE IN JAPAN (2xLP in single sleeve) 35
92	Apple SAPCOR 1	WONDERWALL MUSIC (reissue, gatefold sleeve with inner sleeve) 20
96	Zapple ZAPPLE 02	ELECTRONIC SOUND (reissue, with inner sleeve) 30
01	Parlophone 5304741	ALL THINGS MUST PASS (3-LP, reissue) 20
02	Dark Horse 5419691	BRAINWASHED (Gatefold LP with sticker on cover) 20

ALBUMS : CDS

87	Dark Horse WX 123	CLOUD NINE 20
87	Parlophone CDS 7466888	ALL THINGS MUST PASS (2-CD, with Apple logo) 15
87	Parlophone CDS 7466888	ALL THINGS MUST PASS (2-CD, without Apple logo) 20
89	Dark Horse K 9257262	THE BEST OF DARK HORSE 1976-1989 40
92	Dark Horse 7599269642	LIVE IN JAPAN (2-CD) 30
02	Dark Horse 580 3450	BRAINWASHED (CD box set) 25

(see also Beatles, Traveling Wilburys, Billy Connolly & Chris Tummings, Sylvia Griffin)

KATHLEEN HARRISON

| 66 | Columbia DB 7871 | Mrs. Thursday/Call Round Any Old Time ....5 |

MIKE HARRISON

71	Island ILPS 9170	MIKE HARRISON (LP, gatefold sleeve, pink rim, palm tree label) 25
72	Island ILPS 9209	SMOKESTACK LIGHTNING (LP, laminated sleeve, pink rim, palm tree label) ...20
75	Good Ear EAR 7002	RAINBOW RIDER (LP) 15

(see also Art, Spirit, Spooky Tooth)

NEIL HARRISON

| 74 | Decca F13520 | Sad Eyes/Bicycle Driver ....10 |
| 74 | Deram SML 1115 | ALL DRESSED UP AND NOWHERE TO GO (LP, white/red label with small logo) ...12 |

(see also Driftwood)

NOEL HARRISON

65	Decca F 12001	Trees/To Ramona 6
66	Decca F 12314	A Young Girl Of Sixteen/Tomorrow Is My Turn 6
66	Decca F 12345	It's All Over Now Baby Blue/Much As I Love You 6
67	Reprise RS 20615	Suzanne/Life Is A Dream 6
68	Reprise RS 20758	Windmills Of Your Mind/Leitch On The Beach 5
69	Reprise RS23395	Sparrow/California Weekend 10
69	Decca F 12918	Love Minus Zero/Just Can't Wait 6
57	HMV 7EG 8383	NOEL HARRISON (EP) 15
65	Decca DFE 8616	NOEL HARRISON (EP) 10
65	Decca DFE 8639	TO RAMONA (EP) 12
60	Philips BBL 7399	AT THE BLUE ANGEL (LP) 12
69	Reprise RSLP 6321	THE GREAT ELECTRIC EXPERIMENT IS OVER (LP) 15

REGGIE HARRISON

| 63 | Cameo Parkway P 863 | A Lonely Piano/HIPPIES: Memory Lane ....20 |

WILBERT HARRISON

59	Top Rank JAR 132	Kansas City/Listen My Darling 20
59	Top Rank JAR 132	Kansas City/Listen My Darling (78) 30
62	Island WI 031	I'm Broke/Off To School 20
65	Sue WI 363	Let's Stick Together/Kansas City Twist 20
70	London HL 10307	Let's Work Together/Stagger Lee 15
73	Action ACT 4613	Get It While You Can/Amen 8
70	London HA/SH 8415	LET'S WORK TOGETHER (LP) 40

WILBERT HARRISON/BABY WASHINGTON

| 71 | Joy JOYS 191 | BATTLE OF THE GIANTS (LP, 1 side each) ....18 |

(see also Baby Washington)

YVONNE HARRISON

| 67 | Caltone TONE 102 | The Chase/Take My Hand ....100 |
| 75 | Camel CA 2003 | Knotty Screw Face/UNDERGROUND PEOPLE: Face Dub ....12 |

DEBBIE/DEBORAH HARRY

| 93 | Chrysalis TC-CHS 4900 | I Can See Clearly/Standing In My Way (B-side with Joey Ramone) ....7 |

(see also Wind In The Willows, Blondie, New York Blondes)

HARRY J. ALL STARS

| 69 | Harry J. TR 675 | Liquidator/GLEN & DAVE: La La Always Stay (green label) ....8 |

MINT VALUE £

69	Harry J. TR 675	Liquidator/GLEN & DAVE: La La Always Stay (white label) 5
70	Harry J. HJ 6601	The Big Three/Lavender (B-side actually "Lavender Blue" by Lloyd Robinson) 6
70	Harry J. HJ 6608	Reach For The Sky/Interrogator 6
70	Harry J. HJ 6621	Return Of The Liquidator (actually "Tons Of Gold" by Val Bennett)/All Day 12
72	Harry J. HJ 6641	Down Side Up/Down Side Up - Version 8
73	Explosion EX 2073	Chirpy Chirpy Cheep Cheep/Chirpy Chirpy (Instrumental) 5
73	Blue Mountain BM 1028	U.F.O./Reggae With The Birds 5
70	Trojan TBL 104	THE LIQUIDATOR (LP) 20

(see also Jay Boys, Bob Andy, John Holt, Lizzy)

HARRY & RADCLIFFE
| 69 | Camel CA 26 | History/Just Be Alone ....20 |
| 69 | Punch PH 8 | History/Just Be Alone ....6 |

WARREN HARRY
| 76 | Sonet SON-2088 | I don't Care/Backwards Forwards ....15 |
| 78 | HAH 1/EJSP-8632 | 1965/Radio Show (500 only, no p/s) ....30 |

HARSH REALITY
68	Philips PB 1710	Tobacco Ash Sunday/How Do You Feel 18
69	Philips PB 1769	Heaven And Hell/Praying For Reprieve 18
69	Philips (S)BL 7891	HEAVEN AND HELL (LP, gatefold sleeve, blue/silver labels) 300

(see also Matthews Southern Comfort)

CAJUN HART
| 69 | Warner Bros WB 7258 | Got To Find A Way/Lover's Prayer ....200 |
| 69 | Warner Bros WB 7258 | Got To Find A Way/Lover's Prayer (DJ Copy) ....300 |

DERRY HART & HARTBEATS
| 59 | Decca F 11138 | Come On Baby/Nowhere In This World ....25 |
| 59 | Decca F 11138 | Come On Baby/Nowhere In This World (78) ....18 |

MICKEY HART
| 73 | Warner Bros. K 46182 | ROLLING THUNDER (LP) ....15 |

(see also Grateful Dead, Diga Rhythm Band)

MIKE HART
70	Dandelion S 4781	Yawney Morning Song/Almost Liverpool 8 7
74	Deram DM 409	Son Son/Bad News Man 6
70	Dandelion 63756	MIKE HART BLEEDS (LP, black/red/silver labels) 50
72	Dandelion 2310 211	BASHER, CHALKY, PONGO AND ME (LP, as Mike Hart & Comrades) 50

(see also Clayton Squares, Liverpool Scene)

STEVE HART
| 68 | CBS 3732 | The master Of Man/Without You ....5 |

TIM HART
| 79 | Chrysalis CHR 2335 | Overseas/Hillman Avenger (p/s) ....7 |
| 79 | Chrysalis CHR 1218 | TIM HART (LP) ....12 |

(see also Steeleye Span)

TIM HART & MADDY PRIOR
68	Tepee TPRM 104	FOLK SONGS OF OLDE ENGLAND VOL. 1 (LP, gatefold sleeve) 70
69	Tepee TPRM 105	FOLK SONGS OF OLDE ENGLAND VOL. 2 (LP, gatefold sleeve) 70
69	Ad-Rhythm ARPS 3	FOLK SONGS OF OLDE ENGLAND VOL. 1 (LP, reissue) 25
69	Ad-Rhythm ARPS 4	FOLK SONGS OF OLDE ENGLAND VOL. 2 (LP, reissue) 25
71	B& C CAS 1035	SUMMER SOLSTICE (LP, gatefold sleeve) 30

(see also Steeleye Span, Maddy Prior, Silly Sisters)

CIARAN HARTE
| 80 | Glass 003 | Love Is Strange/Shimahero (p/s) ....20 |

JOHN HARTFORD
| 69 | RCA SF 8039 | JOHN HARTFORD (LP) ....12 |

HARTLEPOOL FC
| 72 | United Artists UP 35358 | Who Put The Sugar In My Tea/Never Say Die ....10 |

KEEF HARTLEY (BAND)
69	Deram DM 250	Leave It 'Till The Morning/Just To Cry 12
69	Deram DM 273	Waiting Around/Not Foolish, Not Wise 12
70	Deram DM 316	Roundabout (Parts 1 & 2) 12
73	Deram DM 380	Dance To The Music/You And Me 8
69	Deram DML 1037	HALFBREED (LP, mono, gatefold sleeve, 1st pressing has 'mono/stereo' holes on rear sleeve, white/red label) 80
69	Deram SML 1037	HALFBREED (LP, stereo, gatefold sleeve, 1st pressing has 'mono/stereo' holes on rear sleeve, white/red label) 60
69	Deram DML 1054	THE BATTLE OF N.W.6 (LP, mono, gatefold sleeve, 1st pressing with 'mono/stereo' holes on rear sleeve, white/red labels) 60
69	Deram SML 1054	THE BATTLE OF N.W.6 (LP, stereo, gatefold sleeve, 1st pressing with 'mono/stereo' holes on rear sleeve, white/red labels) 45
70	Deram SML 1071	THE TIME IS NEAR (LP, with booklet, white/red labels with small logo) 40
70	Deram SML 1071	THE TIME IS NEAR (LP, without booklet, white/red labels with small logo) 20
71	Deram SDL 2	OVERDOG (LP, gatefold sleeve, white/brown labels with small logo) 30
71	Deram SDL 4	LITTLE BIG BAND (LP, white/brown label, gatefold sleeve) 30
72	Deram SDL 9	SEVENTY SECOND BRAVE (LP, gatefold sleeve) 25
73	Deram SDL 13	LANCASHIRE HUSTLER (LP, gatefold sleeve, as Keeg Hartley) 22
74	Deram DPA 3011/2	THE BEST OF (2-LP, gatefold sleeve) 20
70s	Deram SDN 30251/2	THE BATTLE OF N.W.6/THE TIME IS NEAR (2-LP, gatefold sleeve) 20

(see also Rory Storm & Hurricanes, Artwoods, John Mayall's Bluesbreakers, Miller Anderson, Dog Soldier, Henry Lowther, Wynder K. Frog)

TREVOR HARTLEY
| 80 | Matumbi MA 006 | Skip Away/Selassi (12") ....25 |

HARVEST
| 80 | Secular Records SEC 001 | Fashion Parade/Will You Be The One ....70 |

HARVEST MINISTERS
| 92 | Sarah SARAH 64 | You Do My World The World Of Good/Petticoats (p/s, insert) ....12 |

92	Sarah SARAH 68	Six O'Clock Is Rosary/The First Star (p/s, insert)	15
93	Sarah SARAH 84	If It Kills Me And It Will/Can Go It Alone (p/s, insert)	12
93	Sarah SARAH 616	LITTLE DARK MANSIONS (LP)	20

HARVESTERS

| 72 | Westwood WRS 015 | THE HARVESTERS (LP) | 25 |

ALEX HARVEY

64	Polydor NH 52264	I Just Wanna Make Love To You/Let The Good Times Roll	40
64	Polydor NH 52907	Got My Mojo Working/I Ain't Worried Baby (as Alex Harvey & His Soul Band)	55
65	Polydor BM 56017	Ain't That Just Too Bad/My Kind Of Love (as Alex Harvey & His Soul Band)	45
65	Fontana TF 610	Agent 00 Soul/Go Away Baby	35
66	Fontana TF 764	Work Song/I Can Do Without Your Love	25
67	Decca F 12640	The Sunday Song/Horizon's	50
67	Decca F 12660	Maybe Some Day/Curtains For My Baby	60
69	Fontana TF 1063	Midnight Moses/Roman Wall Blues	80
72	Vertigo 6059 070	There's No Lights On The Christmas Tree Mother, (They're Burning Big Louie Tonight)/Harp	40
75	Vertigo ALEX 001	Delilah (live)/Soul In Chains (p/s)	5
75	Vertigo ALEX 002	Gamblin' Bar Room Blues/Shake That Thing (p/s)	5
76	Mountain PSLP 183	Amos Moses/$25 For A Massage (promo only 12")	12
77	Mountain TOP 32	Mrs Blackhouse/Engine Room Boogie (p/s)	6
64	Polydor LPHM 46424	ALEX HARVEY AND HIS SOUL BAND (LP)	200
64	Polydor LPHM 46441	THE BLUES (LP)	175
69	Fontana (S)TL 5534	ROMAN WALL BLUES (LP)	300
73	Vertigo 6360 081	FRAMED (LP, as The Sensational Alex Harvey Band, gatefold sleeve, small swirl label)	200
72	Vertigo 6360 081	FRAMED (LP, as The Sensational Alex Harvey Band, gatefold sleeve, later spaceship label)	30
73	Vertigo 6360 103	NEXT (LP, as The Sensational Alex Harvey Band, spaceship label, 1st pressing, side 1 Matrix 1Y//1 1 6 3)	20
74	Vertigo 6360 112	THE IMPOSSIBLE DREAM (LP, gatefold sleeve, spaceship label)	15
75	Vertigo 9102 003	TOMORROW BELONGS TO ME (LP, gatefold sleeve, spaceship label)	15
75	Vertigo 6360 122	THE SENSATIONAL ALEX HARVEY BAND 'LIVE' (LP, spaceship label)	12
77	K-Tel NE 984	ALEX HARVEY PRESENTS THE LOCH NESS MONSTER (LP, withdrawn, gatefold stickered sleeve, with 16-page 'descriptive diary')	40
78	Mountain TOPS 114	ROCK DRILL (with 'No Complaints Department'.)	35
78	Mountain TOPS 114	ROCK DRILL (Later copies with revised Track listing stickered on sleeve)	12
79	RCA PL 25257	THE MAFIA STOLE MY GUITAR (LP, as Alex Harvey - The New Band)	12
83	Power Supply AMP 2	THE SOLDIER ON THE WALL (LP, solo)	20
84	Samurai SAH 117PD	S.A.H.B. LIVE (LP, reissue, picture disc)	12

(see also Tear Gas, Hairband, Rock Workshop, Nazareth, Michael Schenker Group, Tandoori)

CARL HARVEY MEETS THE DUB MASTER

| 78 | Cancer CANLP 003 | ECSTACY OF MANKIND (LP) | 40 |

JANCIS HARVEY

73	Pilgrim King KLPS 47	DISTANCE OF DOORS (LP)	45
73	Westwood WRS 029	WORDS YOU LEFT BEHIND (LP)	55
74	Westwood WRS 038	JANCIS HARVEY (LP)	55
75	Westwood WRS 054	TIME WAS NOW (LP)	55
76	Westwood WRS 107	A PORTRAIT OF JANCIS HARVEY (LP)	45
79	Westwood WRS 144	FROM THE DARKNESS CAME LIGHT (LP)	40

JANE HARVEY

| 60 | Pye International 7N 25046 | I'm Gonna Go Fishin'/Hundred Dreams From Now | 6 |

LANCE HARVEY & KINGPINS

| 64 | Pye 7N 15647 | He's Telling You Lies/How Do You Fix A Broken Heart | 10 |
| 64 | Lyntone LYN 509 | SINCE YOU WALKED OUT ON ME (Keele Rag flexidisc EP, with The Escorts) | 15 |

HARVEY (FUQUA) & MOONGLOWS

| 58 | London HLM 8730 | Ten Commandments Of Love/Mean Old Blues | 300 |
| 58 | London HLM 8730 | Ten Commandments Of Love/Mean Old Blues (78) | 85 |

(see also Moonglows, Etta & Harvey)

PETER HARVEY

62	Columbia DB 4873	Rainin' In My Heart/Please Don't Tell Joe	7
63	Columbia DB 7030	Wishing You The Best Of Luck My Friend/Lovin' Can Be Lonesome	5
64	Columbia DB 7192	Heart Of Ice/Trace Of A Heartache	5
64	Columbia DB 7331	Big Man In A Big House/Date With A Heartache	5

P.J. HARVEY

90	Private Pressing	P. J. Harvey (3-track demo , 'wooden' p/s includes pictures of P. J. and lyrics to Dress)	70
91	Too Pure PURE 5	Dress/Water (demo)/Dry (demo) (12")	20
92	Too Pure PURECD 5	Dress/Water (demo)/Dry (demo) (CD)	20
92	Too Pure PURES 8	Sheela-Na-Gig/Joe (p/s, 400 only)	45
92	Too Pure PURE 8	Sheela-Na-Gig/Hair (demo)/Joe (demo) (12", p/s)	20
92	Too Pure PURECD 8	Sheela-Na-Gig/Hair (demo)/Joe (demo) (CD)	20
93	Island 12IS 538	50 Ft Queenie/Mansize (demo)/Hook (demo)/Reeling (12", p/s)	12
93	Island 12IS 569	Mansize/Wang Dang Doodle/Daddy (12", p/s)	20
93	Island CID 569	Mansize/Wang Dang Doodle/Daddy (CD)	20
95	Island IS 607	Down By The Water/Lying In The Sun/Somebody's Down Somebody's Name (p/s)	8
95	Island CID 607	Down By The Water/Living In The Sun/Somebody's Down Somebody's Name (CD)	10
95	Island 12IS 614	C'Mon Billy/Darling Be There/Maniac (12", p/s)	10
95	Island IS 610	Send His Love To Me/Long Time Coming (Evening Session) (7" picture disc in 12" poster p/s)	12
95	Island CIDD J610	Send His Love To Me (Promo-only CD, exclusive 'rose dress' sleeve)	30
01	Island IS 785	This Is Love/Angline (live) (p/s)	8
04	Island CIDDJ866	Who The Fuck? (CD, unreleased single, promo only)	10
04	Island IS 873	Shame/97 (p/s)	8
04	Island IS 861	The Letter/Bows And Arrows (p/s)	8
04	Island CIDV 873	Shame/The Letter (video)/You Come Through (video) (DVD)	10
06	Island PJCD6	Tracks from 'Please Leave Quietly' (CD, promo only)	15
07	Island 1747513	When Under Ether/Wait (p/s)	8
07	Island 1753491	The Piano/Heaven (p/s)	8

Richard HARVEY

92	Too Pure PURE(D) 10	DRY (LP, 1st 5,000 with bonus LP, "Demonstrations", inner sleeve and no'd sticker) 60
92	Too Pure PURE 10	DRY (LP with inner but without "Demonstrations")..30
92	Too Pure PUREDCD 10	DRY (CD, 1st 5,000 with additional "Demonstrations" LP tracks) 60
93	Island 5146961	RID OF ME (LP)..45
90s	Island ILPM 2079	4 TRACK DEMOS (LP, with inner) 25
95	Island 524-178 2	THE B-SIDES CD (picture disc CD, 2,000 only, digipak, beware of bootleg copies)..........15
95	Island CIDZ 8035	TO BRING YOU MY LOVE & THE B-SIDES CD (2-CD) 30
95	Island PJCD1	INTERVIEW (CD promo)...20
95	Island ILPS 8035	TO BRING YOU MY LOVE (LP, with inner) 45
98	Island ILPS 8076	IS THIS DESIRE? (LP, with inner) 50
99	Island DESIRE CD1	IS THIS DESIRE? (CD, interview disc, slimline case, promo only) 20
00	Island ILPS 8099	STORIES FROM THE CITY, STORIES FROM THE SEA (LP, with inner) 20
04	Island ILPS 8143	UH HUH HER (LP, with inner) 40

(see also Automatic Dlamini, Family Cat, Grape, John Parish & Polly Jean Harvey)

RICHARD HARVEY
83	Anderburr HX 1010	Theme From Terrahawks (3.00)/Variations On The Theme (3.17) (p/.s) 10
83	Anderburr HX 1010	Theme From Terrahawks (4.50)/Variations On The Theme (7.25) (12", p/s with poster) 12
75	Transatlantic TRA 292	DIVISIONS ON A GROUND (LP) 15

(see also Gryphon, Barry Gray, The Banned)

TINA HARVEY
| 73 | UK UK 24 | Nowhere To Run/Tina's Second Song ....15 |
| 73 | UK UKAL 1002 | TINA HARVEY (LP, bule/silver labels) ....25 |

HARVEY BOYS
| 57 | London HLA 8397 | Nothing Is Too Good For You/Marina Girl ....50 |
| 57 | London HLM 8730 | Nothing Is Too Good For You/Marina Girl (78) ....15 |

HARVEY'S PEOPLE
| 69 | Galliard GAL 4001 | LOVING AND LIVING (LP)..15 |

CHRISTINE HARWOOD
| 70 | Birth RAB 1 | NICE TO MEET MISS CHRISTINE (LP, white 'rabbit' child' label)............................120 |

GORDON HASKELL
69	CBS 4509	Boat Trip/Time Only Knows 8
70	CBS 4795	Oo-La-Di-Doo-Da-Day/Born To Be Together 8
90	Wilderness WLD 700	Hambledon Hill/Mystical Illusion (p/s) 6
69	CBS 63741	SAILIN' MY BOAT (LP) 100
72	Atlantic K 40311	IT IS AND IT ISN'T (LP, with lyric insert) 30
73	RCA	SERVE AT ROOM TEMPERATURE (LP, unissued) 200

(see also Fleur-De-Lys, Cupid's Inspiration, Flowerpot Men, King Crimson)

JACK HASKELL (& HONEY-DREAMERS)
| 57 | London HL 8426 | Around The World/Away Out West...25 |
| 58 | Oriole CB 1442 | The Night Of The Senior Prom/Hungry For Love (with Honey-Dreamers).......................7 |

MICHAEL HASLAM
| 65 | Parlophone R 5267 | There Goes (The Forgotten Man)/My Heart Won't Say Goodbye ....6 |

JOE HASSELVANDER
| 85 | Pentagram DEVIL 3 | LADY KILLER (LP) ....15 |

HASSLES
| 67 | United Artists UP 1199 | You Got Me Hummin'/I'm Thinkin'..20 |

(see also Billy Joel)

HASTINGS OF MALAWI
| 81 | Papal 003 | VIBRANT STAPLER OBSCURES CHARACTERISTIC GROWTH (LP, red vinyl)........................12 |

(see also Nurse With Wound)

HAT & TIE
| 66 | President PT 105 | Chance For Romance/California Jazz Club U.S.A. ....15 |
| 67 | President PT 122 | Bread To Spend/Finding It Rough (demos credit A-side as "Bread").........................150 |

(see also Patrick Campbell-Lyons, Nirvana [U.K.])

TONY HATCH ORCHESTRA
59	Top Rank JAR 107	Chick/Side Saddle 5
59	Top Rank JAR 165	Rhoom Ba-Cha/Stetson 6
61	Pye International 7N 25085	Rocking Waltz/Devil's Herd 8
61	Pye International 7N 25068	Tim Frazer's Theme/Girls Of Copenhagen 6
61	Pye International 7N 25109	La Paloma/Theme From Rosemary 6
61	Pye 7N 15316	Two-Some/Last Summer 6
61	Pye 7N 15408	The Ghost Squad/What's All That About 7
62	Pye 7N 15434	Ben Casey Theme/Perry Mason Theme 6
62	Pye 7N 15440	Theme From 'The Naked City'/In Party Mood 6
62	Pye 7N 15460	Out Of This World Theme/Cyril's Tune (in p/s) 10
62	Pye 7N 15460	Out Of This World Theme/Cyril's Tune 5
62	Pye 7N 15494	Theme From The Dick Powell Show/Sharon 6
63	Pye 7N 15537	The Wonderful World Of The Brothers Grimm/Spanish Main Theme 6
63	Pye 7N 15583	Mondo Cane Theme/Girls Of Copenhagen 6
65	Pye 7N 15754	Crossroads Theme/The Marie Celeste (in p/s) 10
65	Pye 7N15754	Crossroads Theme/The Marie Celeste 5
65	Pye 7N15972	Man Alive/Crosstown Commuter 8
65	Pye 7N 15930	Maori/Sugar And Spice 6
66	Pye 7N 17169	Crossroads Theme/Round Every Corner (in p/s) 10
66	Pye 7N 17169	Crossroads Theme/Round Every Corner 5
67	Pye 7N 17263	Comedy Tonight/You're Lovely 10
69	Pye 7N 17814	Theme From Who-Dun-It/The Champions 30
69	Pye 7N 17864	The Doctors - Theme/Love Song 6
73	Pye 7N 45210	Memories Of Summer/Best In Football 6
74	Pye 7N 45326	The World At War/Sportsnight 5
78	EMI EMI 2780	Sweeney 2/Regan's Key 12
83	Tube TUBE 003	Airline/The HI-FA 6
65	Pye NPL/NSPL 18124	THE TONY HATCH SOUND (LP) 12
66	Pye NPL 18164	A LATIN HAPPENING (LP) 15

(see also Jackie Trent)
GEORGE HATCHER BAND
77 United Artists UP 36233 Black Moon Rising/Find A New Lover (p/s) 7

(see also Budgie)
HATE
70 Famous SFMA 5752 HATE KILLS (LP, gatefold sleeve, orange labels) 80

BOBBY HATFIELD
68 Verve VS 570 Hang-Ups/Soul Cafe 10
68 Verve VS 576 Only You/The Wonder Of You 10
72 Warner Bros K 16163 Oo-Wee-Baby, I Love You/Rock'n'Roll Woman 12

(see also Righteous Brothers, Ringo Starr)
HATFIELD & THE NORTH
74 Virgin VS 116 Let's Eat (Real Soon)/Fitter Stoke Has A Bath 8
74 Virgin V 2008 HATFIELD AND THE NORTH (LP, gatefold sleeve, red 'twin' label) 35
76 Virgin V 2008 HATFIELD AND THE NORTH (LP, gatefold sleeve, repressing on "red mirror girl" label) 20
75 Virgin V 2030 THE ROTTER'S CLUB (LP, red Virgin inner, coloured 'twin' label) 25
79 Virgin VR 5 AFTERS (LP, withdrawn) 30

(see also Matching Mole, Egg, Khan, Camel, National Health, Caravan)
DONNY HATHAWAY
70 Atco 226 010 The Ghetto (Parts 1 & 2) 10
72 Atlantic K 10193 The Ghetto (Parts 1 & 2)/Little Ghetto Boy 8
73 Atlantic K 10354 Love Love Love/Someday We'll Be Free 8
71 Atco 2465 019 EVERYTHING IS EVERYTHING (LP) 18
71 Atlantic 2400 143 DONNY HATHAWAY (LP) 15
72 Atlantic K 40369 LIVE (LP) 15
73 Atlantic K 40487 EXTENSION OF A MAN (LP) 15

(see also Roberta Flack)
HAVANA LETS GO
81 Polydor POSP 364 Spanish Cabaret/Continental Shelf (in p/s) 18
81 Polydor POSP 364 Spanish Cabaret/Continental Shelf (no p/s) 8

ALAN HAVEN
62 Fontana 267253 My Mothers's Eyes/Lean Baby 10
64 United Artists UP 1057 Theme From "A Jolly Bad Fellow"/Jee B'ees (with John Barry) 12
65 Fontana TF 542 Image/Romance On The North Sea 12
65 Fontana TF 590 The Knack/Satin Doll (with John Barry) 12
66 Fontana TF 658 Flamingo/Shangri-La 6
67 Fontana TF 835 Image/Romance Of The North Sea (reissue) 10
65 Fontana TL 5232 LENNON & MCCARTNEY (LP) 15
71 CBS S 63900 ST. ELMO'S FIRE (LP) 12

JIM HAVEN
75 Penny Farthing PEN 868 Do It In Slow Motion/Do It In Slow Motion (Part 2) 10

RICHIE HAVENS
69 Big T BIG 119 Oxford Town/My Own Way 5
69 Verve VS 1512 Three Day Eternity/No Opportunity Necessary No Experience Needed 5
69 Verve VS 1519 Lady Madonna/Indian Rope Man 15
68 Verve (S)VLP 6005 SOMETHIN' ELSE AGAIN (LP) 20
68 Verve (S)VLP 6008 MIXED BAG (LP) 20
69 Verve (S)VLP 6014 1983 (LP) 20
69 Verve (S)VLP 6021 STONEHENGE (LP) 15
69 Transatlantic TRA 187 ELECTRIC HAVENS (LP) 15
69 Transatlantic TRA 199 THE RICHIE HAVENS RECORD (LP) 15

HAVENSTREET
76 Rissole (no cat. no.) THE END OF THE LINE (LP, private pressing with booklet) 50

CYRIL HAVERMANS
73 MGM 2315 261 CYRIL (LP, gatefold sleeve, blue/gold 'lion' label) 20
74 MGM 2315 311 MIND WAVE (LP, blue/gold 'lion' label) 15

PAT HAWES WITH DAVE CAREY'S RHYTHM
56 Tempo A 141 Snowy Morning Blues/Sheik Of Araby 5
56 Tempo LAP 9 PAT HAWES (10" LP) 20

HAWK & CO.
81 Epic EPC A 1735 Nite Life/Nite Life (Version) 5
82 Epic EPC A 2223 Livin' For The Good Times/Sweet Talker 5

(see also Shadows)
GRAHAM HAWK & OWEN GRAY
72 Pama Supreme PS 360 Amazing Grace/SKETTO RICH: Don't Stay Out Late 5

JACKSON HAWKE
76 CBS 5034 Into The Mystic/Fortune 6

TOMMY HAWKE
60 Top Rank JAR 348 Good Gravy (I'm In Love Again)/Umpteen Years (And A Million Tears) 10

HAWKEYES
57 Capitol CL 14764 Someone Someday/Who Is He? 20

BUDDY BOY HAWKINS/WILLIAM MOORE
50s Heritage RE 102 BUDDY BOY HAWKINS/WILLIAM MOORE (EP) 60

(see also Blind Lemon Jefferson)
CAROL HAWKINS
73 Polydor 2058 387 Listen/All For One 8

COLEMAN HAWKINS
53 Capitol LC 6580 CLASSICS IN JAZZ (10" LP) 20
53 Capitol LC 6650 CAPITOL PRESENTS COLEMAN HAWKINS AND SONNY GREER (10" LP) 15
54 HMV DLP 1055 TEN COLEMAN HAWKINS' SPECIALS (10" LP) 15

MINT VALUE £

Coleman HAWKINS GROUP

59	HMC CLP 1293	GENIUS OF COLEMAN HAWKINS (LP)	15
59	Felsted FJA 7005	THE HIGH AND MIGHTY HAWK (LP, also stereo SJA 2005)	15
61	Esquire 32-095	SOUL (LP)	25
61	Esquire 32-102	HAWK EYES (LP)	22
61	Moodsville MV 7	COLEMAN HAWKINS (LP)	18
62	Swingsville SVLP 2001	COLEMAN HAWKINS WITH THE RED GARLAND TRIO (LP)	15
62	Swingsville SVLP 2005	THE COLEMAN HAWKINS ALL STARS (LP)	15
62	Swingsville SVLP 2013	STASCH (LP)	15
63	HMV CLP 1630	DESAFINADO (LP, also stereo CSD 1484)	15
64	Verve VLP 9044	ALIVE! AT THE VILLAGE GATE (LP)	20
64	HMV CLP 1689	TODAY AND NOW (LP)	20
64	CBS BPG 62157	BACK IN BEAN'S BAG (LP, with Clark Terry)	15
64	Fontana FJL 102	SWING' (LP)	15
65	Fontana TL 5273	MEDITATION (LP)	15
66	Fontana SJL 131	CATTIN' (LP)	15

(see also Hines & Eldridge, Milt Jackson & Coleman Hawkins, Eddie 'Lockjaw' Davis, Sir Charles Thompson)

COLEMAN HAWKINS GROUP

58	London LTZC 15048	COLEMAN HAWKINS GROUP (LP)	18

(see also Coleman Hawkins)

COLEMAN HAWKINS & LESTER YOUNG

65	Stateside SL 10117	CLASSIC TENORS (LP)	12

DALE HAWKINS

57	London HL 8482	Susie-Q/Don't Treat Me That Way	500
57	London HL 8482	Susie-Q/Don't Treat Me That Way (78)	100
58	London HLM 8728	La-Do-Dada/Cross Ties	50
58	London HLM 8728	La-Do-Dada/Cross Ties (78)	40
59	London HLM 8842	Yea-Yea/Lonely Nights	50
59	London HLM 8842	Yea-Yea/Lonely Nights (78)	40
59	London HLM 9016	Liza Jane/Back To School Blues	50
59	London HLM 9016	Liza Jane/Back To School Blues (78)	40
60	London HLM 9060	Hot Dog/Our Turn	50
69	Bell SBLL 127	L.A., MEMPHIS AND TYLER, TEXAS (LP)	18
73	Checker 6467 301	OH! SUSIE Q (LP)	15

ERSKINE HAWKINS QUINTET

60	Brunswick LAT 8374	THE HAWK BLOWS AT MIDNIGHT (LP, also stereo STA 3042)	15

HAWKSHAW HAWKINS

51	Vogue V 9003	Doghouse Boogie/Yesterday's Kisses (78)	15
51	Vogue V 9027	Slow Coach/Two Roads (78)	12
54	Parlophone CMSP 1	Betty Lorraine/CHARLIE GORE & LOUIS INNIS: Mexican Joe (export issue)	30
50s	Parlophone DP 336	I Hope You're Crying Too/I'm A Lone Wolf (export 78)	10
63	London HL 9737	Lonesome 7-7203/Everything Has Changed	10
58	Parlophone GEP 8742	COUNTRY AND WESTERN (EP)	40
58	Vogue VE 170117	HAWKSHAW HAWKINS - COUNTRY AND WESTERN (EP)	40
64	London HA 8181	THE ALL NEW HAWKSHAW HAWKINS (LP)	20

(see also Charlie Gore, Louis Innis)

JUNE HAWKINS

55	Brunswick 05370	Beat Out Dat Rhythm On A Drum/MURIEL SMITH & CARMEN JONES CHORUS: Dat's Love	8

RONNIE HAWKINS (& HAWKS)

59	Columbia DB 4319	Forty Days (To Come Back Home)/One Of These Days	50
59	Columbia DB 4345	Mary Lou/Need Your Lovin' (Oh So Bad)	50
60	Columbia DB 4412	Southern Love (Whatcha-Gonna' Do)/Love Me Like You Can	20
60	Columbia DB 4442	Clara/Lonely Hours	30
63	Columbia DB 7036	Bo Diddley/Who Do You Love?	30
70	Roulette RO 512	Who Do You Love?/Bo Diddley	5
70	Atlantic 584 320	Down In The Alley/Matchbox	7
70	Atlantic 2091 007	Bitter Green/Forty Days	5
72	Monument MNT 8292	Cora Mae/Ain't That A Shame	5
60	Columbia SEG 7983	ROCKIN' WITH RONNIE (EP, mono)	100
60	Columbia ESG 7792	ROCKIN' WITH RONNIE (EP, stereo)	110
60	Columbia SEG 7988	ROCKIN' WITH RONNIE (EP, mono)	100
60	Columbia ESG 7795	ROCKIN' WITH RONNIE (EP, stereo)	110
60	Columbia 33SX 1238	MR. DYNAMO (LP, mono)	100
60	Columbia SCX 3315	MR. DYNAMO (LP, stereo)	110
60	Columbia 33SX 1295	THE FOLK BALLADS OF RONNIE HAWKINS (LP, mono)	50
60	Columbia SCX 3358	THE FOLK BALLADS OF RONNIE HAWKINS (LP, stereo)	60
70	Roulette RCP 1003	ARKANSAS ROCK PILE (LP, with The Band)	20
70	Atlantic 2400 009	RONNIE HAWKINS (LP)	15
72	Monument MNT 65122	ROCK & ROLL RESURRECTION (LP)	15

(see also Band, Levon & Hawks)

SCREAMIN' JAY HAWKINS

58	Fontana H 107	I Put A Spell On You/Little Demon (78)	100
65	Columbia DB 7460	The Whammy/Strange	40
65	Sue WI 379	I Hear Voices/Just Don't Care	40
66	Sue WI 4008	I Put A Spell On You/Little Demon (unissued)	0
69	Direction 58-4097	I Put A Spell On You/Little Demon	20
80	Polydor POSP 183	I Put A Spell On You/Armpit 6 (with Keith Richards)	10
66	Planet PLL 1001	THE NIGHT AND DAY OF SCREAMIN' JAY HAWKINS (LP)	125
69	Direction (S) 8-63481	I PUT A SPELL ON YOU (LP, mono or stereo)	60
69	Mercury SMCL 20178	WHAT THAT IS (LP)	40

(see also Keith Richards)

HAWKLORDS

78	Charisma HL 1	PSI Power/Death Trap (no p/s, promo only)	12
78	Charisma CB 323	PSI Power/Death Trap (no p/s)	8
79	Charisma CB 332	25 Years/(Only) The Dead Dreams Of A Cold War Kid (no p/s)	6
79	Charisma CB 332 12	25 Years/(Only) The Dead Dreams Of A Cold War Kid/PXR 5 (12", grey vinyl)	10

79	Charisma CB 332 12	25 Years/(Only) The Dead Dreams Of A Cold War Kid/PXR 5 (12", mispressed on black vinyl) 12
82	Flicknife FLS 209	Who's Gonna Win The War?/Time Of (p/s) 6
78	Charisma CDS 4014	25 YEARS ON (LP, with inner sleeve, sold with separate tour book) 20
78	Charisma CDS 4014	25 YEARS ON (LP, with inner sleeve) 15

(see also Hawkwind)

HAWKS
| 69 | Stateside SS 2147 | The Grissle/SHEEP: Hide And Seek ....12 |

HAWKS
| 81 | Five Believers FB 001 | Words Of Hope/Sense Of Ending (p/s) ....12 |

(see also Lilac Time, Stephen 'Tin Tin' Duffy)

ALAN HAWKSHAW
70	Tangerine DP 0005	Puppet On A String/Everybody Knows 5
79	BBC RESL 64	Grange Hill/Stoned (as Hawkshaw) 20
72	Studio Two TWO 391	27 TOP TV THEMES AND COMMERCIALS (LP) 30
72	KPM 1080	FLUTE FOR MODERNS (with Alan Parker and Joe Hailer) (LP) 35

(see also Shadows)

JOHNNY HAWKSWORTH (ORCHESTRA)
65	Pye 7N 15969	Lunar Walk/It's Murder (as Johnny Hawksworth Orchestra) 15
66	Columbia DB 8059	Goal - World Cup 1966" Theme (as Sounds Of Johnny Hawksworth) 6
67	Columbia DB 8129	Wack Wack/On The Tiles 8

(see also Johnny's Jazz)

HAWKSWORTH-VERRELL JAZZ GROUP
| 56 | Decca FJ 10726 | Ring Dem Bells/Always ....6 |

HAWKWIND

SINGLES
70	Liberty LBF 15382	Hurry On Sundown/Mirror Of Illusion 250
72	United Artists UP 35381	Silver Machine/Seven By Seven ('machine' art p/s) 15
73	United Artists (WD 3637)	Sonic Attack (1-sided promo in cloth sleeve) 250
73	United Artists UP 35566	Urban Guerilla/Brainbox Pollution 15
73	United Artists USEP 1	HURRY ON HAWKWIND (EP) 40
74	United Artists UP 35715	The Psychedelic Warlords (Disappear In Smoke)/It's So Easy 8
75	United Artists UP 35808	Kings Of Speed/Motorhead (in p/s) 40
75	United Artists UP 35808	Kings Of Speed/Motorhead 6
76	Charisma CB 289	Kerb Crawler/Honky Dorky 5
77	Charisma CB 299	Back On The Streets/The Dream Of Isis (p/s) 6
77	Charisma CB 305	Quark, Strangeness & Charm/Forge Of Vulcan 7
78	United Artists UP 35381	Silver Machine/Seven By Seven (reissue, black-on-white p/s) 5
78	United Artists 12UP 35381	Silver Machine/Seven By Seven (12", silver p/s) 10
80	Bronze BRO 98	Shot Down In The Night/Urban Guerilla 5
80	Bronze BRO 98	Shot Down In The Night/Urban Guerilla (1-sided gold vinyl flexidisc) 30
80	Bronze BRO 109	Who's Gonna Win The War?/Nuclear Toy (p/s, cream labels) 12
80	Bronze BRO 109	Who's Gonna Win The War?/Nuclear Toy (p/s, green labels) 5
81	RCA RCA 137	Angels Of Death/Trans-Dimensional Man (p/s) 5
82	RCA Active RCA 267	Silver Machine/Silver Machine (Full Version)/Psychedelic Warlords (p/s) 5
82	RCA Active RCAP 267	Silver Machine/(Full Version)/Psychedelic Warlords (picture disc) 10
82	Flicknife FLS 005	Motorhead/Valium Ten (p/s) 5
82	Flicknife FLST 005	Motorhead/Valium Ten (extended) (12", p/s) 5
83	United Artists UP 35381	Silver Machine/Seven By Seven (reissue, white-on-black p/s) 5
83	Liberty UPP 35381	Silver Machine/Seven By Seven (picture disc) 5
83	Liberty UPP 35381	Silver Machine/Seven By Seven (mispressed picture disc, plays Beatles' "Ask Me Why") 15
83	Flicknife FLS 025	Motorway City/Master Of The Universe (p/s) 5
83	Flicknife FLS 214	Hawkwind And Co: Your Last Chance (p/s, sampler with Robert Calvert & Michael Moorcock) 6
84	Flicknife FLEP 104	THE EARTH RITUAL PREVIEW (12" EP) 8
85	Flicknife FLS 032	Needle Gun/Arioch (p/s) 5
85	Flicknife FLST 032	Needle Gun (extended)/Arioch (p/s) 8
86	Flicknife FLS 033	Zarozinia/Assault And Battery (live) (p/s) 5
86	Samurai HW 001	Silver Machine/Magnu (motorcycle-shaped picture disc) 15
86	Flicknife FLS 034-A	Motorhead/Hurry On Sundown (p/s with insert) 5
90	Receiver REPLAY 3014	THE EARLY YEARS LIVE (12", p/s, blue vinyl) 12
93	4 Real 4R 1	SPIRIT OF THE AGE (SOLSTICE REMIXES) (12" EP) 12
93	4 Real 4R 2	DECIDE YOUR FUTURE (12" EP) 10
93	4 Real 4R2T	DECIDE YOUR FUTURE EP (12") 8
94	Emerg. Broadcast EBS 110	QUARK, STRANGENESS & CHARM (12" EP, clear vinyl, 200 only) 15

ALBUMS
70	Liberty LBS 83348	HAWKWIND (LP, gatefold sleeve; blue label) 300
70	Liberty LBS 83348	HAWKWIND (LP, gatefold sleeve; black label) 45
71	United Artists UAG 29202	IN SEARCH OF SPACE (LP in foldout 'door' sleeve, with 'log book') 70
71	United Artists UAG 29202	IN SEARCH OF SPACE (LP in foldout 'door' sleeve, without 'log book') 25
72	United Artists UAG 29364	DOREMI-FASOL-LATIDO (LP, with inner sleeve, with poster) 70
72	United Artists UAG 29364	DOREMI-FASOL-LATIDO (LP, with inner sleeve, without poster) 20
73	Utd. Artists UAD 60037/8	SPACE RITUAL ALIVE (2-LP, foldout sleeve with inners) 40
74	United Artists UAG 29672	HALL OF THE MOUNTAIN GRILL (LP, with inner sleeve) 20
75	United Artists UAG 29766	WARRIOR ON THE EDGE OF TIME (LP, foldout pop-up sleeve with inner) 45
76	United Artists UAK 29919	ROADHAWKS (LP, gatefold sleeve with poster & sticker) 15
76	United Artists UAK 29919	ROADHAWKS (LP, gatefold sleeve) 12
76	Mushroom	THE XENON CODEX (LP, with inner, gatefold sleeve) 12
77	Charisma CDS 4008	QUARK STRANGENESS AND CHARM (LP) 20
79	Charisma CDS 4016	P.X.R.5 (LP, with family tree poster, with picture of incorrectly wired plug on rear) 30
79	Charisma CDS 4016	P.X.R.5 (LP, without family tree poster, but with uncensored wired plug on rear) 15
80	Bronze BRON 530	LEVITATION (LP, blue vinyl) 12
81	RCA Active RCALP 6004	SONIC ATTACK (LP, with insert) 12
82	RCA Active RCALP 9004	CHURCH OF HAWKWIND (LP, with lyric booklet) 15
82	RCA Active RCALP 6055	CHOOSE YOUR MASQUES (LP) 12
84	Liberty SLP 1972921	HAWKWIND (LP, reissue, picture disc, die-cut) 15
84	Flicknife PSHARP 014	ZONES (LP, picture disc reissue) 12

84	Flicknife SHARP 022	STONHENGE: THIS IS HAWKWIND DO NOT PANIC (LP, with 12", gatefold sleeve or single sleeve with poster)	15
85	Flicknife SHARP 033	CHRONICLE OF THE BLACK SWORD (LP, with inner sleeve)	12
85	Flicknife SHARP 033CD	CHRONICLE OF THE BLACK SWORD (CD, with 3 extra tracks)	18
86	Hawkfan HWFB 2	HAWKFAN 12 (LP, with poster, sticker insert & carrier bag, 600 only)	70
86	RCA NL 71150	ANGELS OF DEATH (LP)	12
86	Samurai SMR 046	APPROVED HISTORY OF HAWKWIND 1967-1982 (3-LP, pic discs & booklet)	40
87	Flicknife HWBOX 01	OFFICIAL PICTURE LOG BOOK (4-LP box set, [3 picture discs & interview disc] with badge & insert)	35
92	Essential ESSLP 181	ELECTRIC TEPEE (2-LP, 5,000 only, numbered)	35
94	Emerg. Broadcast EBS 111	THE BUSINESS TRIP (2-LP, clear vinyl, 1,500 only)	20
95	Dojo DOJO CD 244	ELECTRIC TEPEE (CD, picture disc, unreleased)	20
95	Emergency Broadcast System EBSLP 118	ALIEN 4 (2-LP, gatefold sleeve)	15
96	Emergency Broadcast System EBSLP 120	LOVE IN SPACE (2-LP, gatefold)	25
96	Emergency Broadcast System EBSCD20	LOVE IN SPACE (CD)	30
99	HAWK VP999	HAWKWIND 1997 (CD, mail-order only to "Hawkwind Passport" holders)	25

(see also Hawklords, Robert Calvert, Michael Moorcock, Inner City Unit, Sphynx, Dave Brock, Steve Swindells, Tim Blake, Huw Lloyd Langton Group, Alan Davey, Motorhead, Sonic Assassins, Dr. Technical & Machines, Sam Gopal, Magic Muscle, Opal Butterfly, Nik Turner, Widowmaker, Adrian Shaw)

DEANE HAWLEY
61	Liberty LIB 55359	Pocketful Of Rainbows/That Dream Could Never Be	10

RICHARD HAWLEY
05	Mute STUMM 251	COLES CORNER (LP)	15

GOLDIE HAWN
72	Reprise K 14211	Carey/I'll Be Your Baby Tonight	6

BRYN HAWORTH
74	Island ILPS 9287	LET THE DAYS GO BY (LP, with inner sleeve)	12
75	Island ILPS 9332	SUNNY SIDE OF THE STREET (LP, pink rim)	12

(see also Fleur De Lys, Nicholas Greenwood)

HAYDEN HOUSE
69	NEMS 56-4499	House Beside The Mine/Lady Wants More	25

HAYDEN WOOD
70	NEMS 4803	Sixty Years On/The Last One To Know	25
73	Jam JAM 46	I Don't Want To Lose You/Hand Me Down	6

HAYDOCK'S ROCKHOUSE
66	Columbia DB 8050	Cupid/She Thinks	70
67	Columbia DB 8135	Lovin' You/Mix A Fix	100

(see also Hollies)

BILL HAYES
53	MGM SP 1036	The Donkey Song/My Ever-Lovin'	15
55	London HL 8149	The Berry Tree/Blue Black Hair	30
56	London HLA 8220	Ballad Of Davy Crockett/Farewell	30
56	London HLA 8239	Kwela Kwela/The White Buffalo	20
56	London HLA 8300	Das Ist Musik/I Know An Old Lady	20
56	London HLA 8325	The Legend Of Wyatt Earp/That Do Make It Nice	20
57	London HL 8430	Wringle Wrangle/Westward Ho The Wagons	20
59	London HLR 8833	Wimoweh/Goin' Down The Road Feelin' Bad (with Buckle Busters)	8
56	London RE-A 1051	GREAT PIONEERS OF THE WEST (EP)	25

ISAAC HAYES
69	Stax STAX 133	Walk On By/By The Time I Get To Phoenix	5
70	Stax STAX 154	I Stand Accused/I Just Don't Know What To Do With Myself	5
71	Stax 2025 020	You've Lost That Lovin' Feelin'/Our Day Will Come	5
71	Stax 2025 029	Never Can Say Goodbye/I Can't Help It (If I'm Still In Love With You)	5
72	Stax 2025 069	Theme From "Shaft"/Cafe Regio's	5
72	Stax 2025 089	Let's Stay Together/Ain't That Loving You (For More Reasons Than One) (with David Porter)	5
72	Stax 2025 146	Theme From The Men/Type Thang	5
74	Stax STXS 2004	Title Theme From Tough Guys/Hung Up On My Baby	5
69	Stax SXATS 1028	HOT BUTTERED SOUL (LP)	15
70	Stax SXATS 1032	THE ISAAC HAYES MOVEMENT (LP)	18
70	Stax 2465 016	BLUE HAYES (LP)	18
71	Stax 2325 026	TO BE CONTINUED (LP)	18
71	Stax 2325 014	THE ISAAC HAYES MOVEMENT (LP, reissue)	12
71	Stax 2659 007	SHAFT - ORIGINAL SOUNDTRACK (2-LP, soundtrack, gatefold sleeve)	15
72	MGM 2315 115	SHAFT'S BIG SCORE! (LP, soundtrack)	20
72	Atlantic K 40327	IN THE BEGINNING (LP)	12
72	Stax 2628 004	BLACK MOSES (2-LP, cruciform sleeve)	30
74	Stax 2325 111	JOY (LP)	12
74	Stax STXD 4001/2	TRUCK TURNER (2-LP, soundtrack)	15

LINDA HAYES
55	Parlophone MSP 6174	Please Have Mercy (with Platters)/Oochi Pachi (with Tony Williams)	300
55	Parlophone R 4038	Please Have Mercy (with Platters)/Oochi Pachi (with Tony Williams) (78)	50

(see also Platters)

PETER LIND HAYES
60	Brunswick 05821	Life Gets Tee-jus Don't It/Sing Me A Happy Song	12

(see also Peter & Mary)

TUBBY HAYES
56	Tempo A 148	Ode To Ernie/No, I Woodyn't	10
62	Fontana H 397	Sally/I Believe In You (as Tubby Hayes Quintet)	25
55	Tempo EXA 14	THE LITTLE GIANT (EP)	75
55	Tempo EXA 17	TUBBY HAYES AND HIS ORCHESTRA (EP)	30
55	Tempo EXA 27	THE SWINGING GIANT NO. 1 (EP, as Tubby Hayes Quartet)	50

56	Tempo EXA 28	THE SWINGING GIANT NO. 2 (EP, as Tubby Hayes Quartet)	50
56	Tempo EXA 36	MODERN JAZZ SCENE (EP, as Tubby Hayes & His Orchestra)	50
57	Tempo EXA 55	AFTER LIGHTS OUT (EP, as Tubby Hayes Quintet)	60
57	Tempo EXA 75	TUBBY HAYES AND THE JAZZ COURIERS (EP)	60
58	Tempo EXA 82	THE EIGHTH WONDER (EP, solo)	60
09	Trunk TTT005	VOODOO SESSION (EP, 666 copies only)	25
57	Tempo TAP 6	AFTER LIGHTS OUT (LP, as Tubby Hayes Quintet)	400
57	Tempo TAP 15	JAZZ COURIERS (LP)	300
60	Tempo TAP 29	TUBBY'S GROOVE (LP, as Tubby Hayes Quartet)	400
61	Fontana TFL 5142	TUBBS (LP, also stereo STFL 562)	150
61	Ember EMB 3337	AN EVENING WITH MR. PERCUSSION (LP, with Tony Kinsey)	70
61	Fontana TFL 5183	TUBBS IN NEW YORK (LP, also stereo STFL 595)	120
63	Fontana 680 998 TL	DOWN IN THE VILLAGE (LP, mono)	300
63	Fontana 886 163TY	DOWN IN THE VILLAGE (LP, stereo)	200
64	Fontana (S)TL 5195	RETURN VISIT! (LP)	140
64	Fontana TL 5200	LATE SPOT AT SCOTT'S (LP)	250
66	Fontana (S)TL 5221	TUBBS' TOURS (LP, with Orchestra)	70
66	Fontana (S)TL 5410	100% PROOF (LP)	70
67	Wing WL 1162	TUBBS IN NEW YORK (LP, reissue)	15
69	Fontana SFJL 911	MEXICAN GREEN (LP)	100
71	Fontana 6309 002	THE TUBBY HAYES ORCHESTRA (LP)	30
72	Philips 6382 041	THIS IS JAZZ - 100% PROOF (LP)	15
82	Jasmine JASM 2015	AFTER LIGHTS OUT (LP, reissue)	20
90	CBS Masterpeices CBS 466363-1	TUBBY HAYES WITH CLARK TERRY THE NEW YORK SESSIONS (LP, reissue)	25
09	Gearbox GB 1502	BBC JAZZ FOR MODERNS (LP)	30

(see also Jack Constanzo & Tubby Hayes, Jazz Couriers, London Jazz Quartet, Dave Lee, Ronnie Scott, Roy Castle)

TUBBY HAYES & CLEO LAINE

| 61 | Fontana TFL 5151 | PALLADIUM JAZZ DATE (LP, also stereo STFL 570) | 40 |

(see also Cleo Laine)

TUBBY HAYES & PAUL GONSALVES ALLSTARS

| 67 | Columbia SX 6003 | JUST FRIENDS (LP) | 110 |
| 60s | World Record Club T 631 | CHANGE OF SETTING (LP) | 120 |

(see also Paul Gonsalves)

TUBBY HAYES ORCHESTRA

| 81 | Mole MOLE 2 | MEXICAN GREEN (LP, reissue) | 20 |
| 81 | Mole MOLE 4 | TUBBS' TOURS (LP, reissue) | 15 |

TUBBY HAYES QUARTET

| 90 | MMO 79 | 67 LIVE - FOR MEMBERS ONLY (LP) | 20 |

LOU HAYLES

| 77 | Myrrh MYR 1055 | DON'T HIDE AWAY (LP) | 22 |

ROY HAYNES QUARTET

| 62 | HMV CLP 1628 | OUT OF THE AFTERNOON (LP) | 25 |

ROY HAYNES, PHINEAS NEWBORN, PAUL CHAMBERS TRIO

| 61 | Esquire 32-103 | WE THREE (LP) | 25 |

STEVE HAYNES BAND

| 78 | Black Bear BLA 2005 | Back In My Arms Again/Walk On By (p/s) | 20 |
| 78 | Black Bear BLA 2008 | Save Me Save Me/Strong Good Lovin' (p/s) | 15 |

HAYSTACK

| 69 | United Artists UP 35024 | Letter To Josephine/Love You're Making A Fool Of Me | 6 |
| 69 | United Artists UP 35035 | Tahiti Farewell/Pantomime People | 6 |

HAYSTACKS BALBOA

| 70 | Polydor | Spoiler/Bruce's Twist | 25 |
| 70 | Polydor 2489 002 | HAYSTACKS BALBOA (LP) | 100 |

JUSTIN HAYWARD

65	Pye 7N 17041	London Is Behind Me/Day Must Come	150
66	Parlophone R 5496	I Can't Face The World Without You/I'll Be Here Tomorrow	200
77	Deram DM 428	One Lonely Room/Songwriter (Part 2)	7
80	CBS 11-7731	The Eve Of The War/Horsell (12" picture disc)	15

(see also Wilde Three, Moody Blues)

RICK HAYWARD

| 71 | Blue Horizon 2431 006 | RICK HAYWARD (LP) | 175 |

(see also Accent, Christine Perfect)

SUSAN HAYWARD

| 56 | MGM MGM-EP 555 | I'LL CRY TOMORROW - SOUNDTRACK SELECTION (EP) | 15 |
| 62 | Fontana 267224 | You Bet I Would/I Won't Give My Lips To Anyone | 10 |

JOE HAYWOOD

| 65 | Island WI 218 | Warm And Tender Love/I Would If I Could | 22 |

LEON HAYWOOD

66	Vocalion VL 9280	Ain't No Use/Hey, Hey, Hey	30
66	Vocalion VL 9280	Ain't No Use/Hey, Hey, Hey (DJ copy)	50
67	Vocalion VL 9288	Ever Since You Were Sweet Sixteen/Skate Awhile	25
69	MCA Soul Bag BAG 5	Mellow Moonlight/Tennessee Waltz	10
70	Capitol CL 15634	I Wanna Thank You/I Was Sent To Love You	15
73	Pye International 7N 25611	La La Song/There Ain't Enough Hate Around To Make Me Turn Around	5
75	20th Century BTC 2191	Come On And Get Yourself Some/BMF (Beautiful)	5
75	20th Century BTC 2228	I Wanta Do Something Freaky To You/I Know What Love Is	6
78	Fantasy FTC 151	Baby Reconsider/Would I	15
67	Vocalion VAL 8064	SOUL CARGO (LP)	75
69	MCA MUPS 369	IT'S GOT TO BE MELLOW (LP)	20
73	Pye Intl. NSPL 28177	BACK TO STAY (LP)	25
75	20th Century BT 476	COME AND GET YOURSELF SOME (LP)	15

HAZE (1)
74	Haze HAZE 00174	HAZE (LP, 100 only)	100

HAZE (2)
81	Mushroom MUSH 1	The Night/Dig Them Mushrooms	20
85	Gabadon GABS 003	THE EMBER (12" EP)	8
84	Gabadon GABL 001	C'EST LA VIE (LP)	25

HAZEL
93	Sub Pop SP74 241	Jilted (blue vinyl)	5

HAZEL & JOLLY BOYS
67	Doctor Bird DB 1063	Stop Them/Deep Down	20

RONNIE HAZELHURST
78	Polydor 2384 107	SIXTEEN SMALL SCREEN GREATS (LP)	12

HAMMOND HAZLEWOOD
67	Pye 7N 17273	I Can Make The Rain Fall Up/The Hawkmoth And The Flame	12
69	Columbia DB 8579	Hey Love, Let Me In/Let The Sunshine In	10

LEE HAZLEWOOD
60	London HLW 9223	Words Mean Nothing/The Girl On Death Row (with Duane Eddy)	35
66	MGM MGM 1310	Sand/My Autumn's Done Come	10
67	MGM MGM 1348	My Baby Cried All Night Long/These Boots Are Made For Walkin'	12
67	Reprise RS 20613	Ode To Billie Joe/Charlie Bill Nelson	10
68	Reprise RS 20667	Rainbow Woman/I Am, You Are	10
72	RCA RCA 2185	Big Red Balloon/Down From Dover (with Nancy Sinatra)	10
73	Stateside SS 2225	Poet/Come Spend The Morning	10
66	MGM MGM-CS 8014	THE VERY SPECIAL WORLD OF LEE HAZLEWOOD (LP)	30
68	Reprise RSLP 6297	LOVE AND OTHER CRIMES (LP)	25
69	London HA-N/SH-N 8398	TROUBLE IS A LONESOME TOWN (LP)	40
72	Reprise K 44161	REQUIEM FOR AN ALMOST LADY (LP)	30
74	Stateside SSL 10315	POET, FOOL OR BUM (LP)	30

(see also Nancy Sinatra & Lee Hazlewood, Duane Eddy)

OSTERWALK HAZY
72	Jam JAM 22	Oumbalo Oumbalo/Tai Weh	15

HAZZARD
81	Rammy EJSP9600	Snake In The Grass/Kicked To The Ground (p/s)	100

TONY HAZZARD
66	Columbia DB 7927	You'll Never Put Shackles On Me/Calling You Home	20
68	CBS 3452	Sound Of The Candyman's Trumpet/Everything's Gone Wrong	5
69	CBS 63608	TONY HARRARD SINGS (LP, orange label)	60
71	Bronze ILPS 9174	LOUDWATER HOUSE (LP, gatefold sleeve, lyric inner sleeve)	20
73	Bronze ILPS 9222	WAS THAT ALRIGHT THEN? (LP, gatefold sleeve, lyric inner sleeve)	20

MICHAEL HEAD & STRANDS
95	Megaphone Music MEGA 01	THE MAGICAL WORLD OF THE STRANDS (LP, gatefold sleeve)	60

(see also Pale Saints, Shack)

ROY HEAD (& TRAITS)
65	Pye International 7N 25340	Just A Little Bit/Treat Me Right	15
65	Vocalion VP 9248	Treat Her Right/So Long, My Love	20
66	Vocalion VP 9254	Apple Of My Eye/I Pass The Day	15
66	Vocalion VP 9269	My Babe/Pain	20
66	Vocalion VP 9274	Wigglin' And Gigglin'/Driving Wheel	20
66	London HLZ 10097	To Make A Big Man Cry/Don't Cry No More	15
70	Stateside SS 8050	Mama Mama/I'm Not A Fool Anymore	7
75	London HLD 10487	The Most Wanted Woman In Town/Gingers Breadman	8
66	Pye Intl. NEP 44053	JUST A LITTLE BIT OF ROY HEAD (EP)	50
70	Stateside SSL 5033	SAME PEOPLE (LP)	25

(see also Traits)

HEAD (1)
75	Canon CNN 5970	RED DWARF (LP)	40

HEAD (2)
79	Ellie Jay MB1	Nothing To Do In A Town Like Leatherhead/University '79	60
96	Headhunter HH 7 01	Gnu/Demonizer 48/48 (p/s, 1000 only)	15

HEADACHE
77	Lout 001	Can't Stand Still/No Reason For Your Call (p/s)	20

HEAD ARSE FUSION BAND
00	U-Star US 009	UNTITLED EP (12")	50

HEADCOATEES (THEE)
91	Damaged Goods DAMGOOD 12	Santa Claus/Evil Things (picture disc)	5
91	Hangman HANG 38 UP	GIRLSVILLE (LP)	20

(see also Milkshakes, Headcoatees)

HEADCOATS (THEE)
90	Sub Pop SP71	Time Will Tell/Davey Crockett (Gabba Hey) (p/s)	8
92	Sub Pop SP151	Ballad Of Hollis Brown/Grizzly Bear (p/s, blue vinyl)	8
89	Hangman HANG 29 UP	HEADCOATS DOWN (LP)	20
90	Hangman HANG 23 UP	THE KIDS ARE ALL SQUARE (LP)	20
91	Hangman HANG 40 UP	W.O.A.H. (LP)	20
01	Hangman HANG 54 UP	LIVE AT THE DIRTY WATER CLUB (LP)	20

(see also Milkshakes, Thee Headcoats)

HEADHUNTERS
76	Arista ARTY 116	SURVIVAL OF THE FITTEST (LP)	25
77	Arista SPART 1046	STRAIGHT FROM THE GATE (LP)	12

(see also Herbie Hancock)

HEADLESS CHICKENS
89	Hometown Atrocities 1	THE HOMETOWN ATROCITIES EP (wraparound p/s with 3 inserts, 'kylie')	80
89	Hometown Atrocities 1	THE HOMETOWN ATROCITIES EP (wraparound p/s, 'glossy')	60
89	Maelstrom Storm 1	THE HOMETOWN ATROCITIES EP (repress of above)	30

(see also Radiohead)

HEADLINERS
59	Parlophone R 4593	The Bubble Car Song/Andy's Theme	10

HEADLINERS
65	Decca F 12209	That's The Way I Must Go/Four Seasons	8
65	Decca F 12279	What Became Of Love/Even Though	7

HEAD MACHINE
70	Major Minor SMLP 79	ORGASM (LP, laminated front sleeve, red/white/black labels)	300

(see also Uriah Heep)

MURRAY HEAD
65	Columbia DB 7635	Alberta/He Was A Friend Of Mine	8
65	Columbia DB 7771	The Bells Of Rhymney/Don't Sing No Sad Songs For Me	10
67	Columbia DB 8102	Someday Soon/You Bore Me	8
67	Immediate IM 053	She Was Perfection/Secondhand Monday	70
69	MCA MK 5019	Superstar/John 1941 (p/s, with Trinidad Singers)	7
71	MCA MKS 5019	Superstar/John 1941 (p/s, reissue)	6
73	CBS 65503	NIGEL LIVED (LP, gatefold sleeve and booklet)	30
75	Island ILPS 9347	SAY IT AIN'T SO (LP, gatefold sleeve, blue rim palm tree label)	12

HEAD OF DAVID
89	Blast First WANT 001	WHITE ELEPHANT (LP, mail-order only)	12

HEADS
94	Rooster ROOSTER 1	Quad/Woke Up/Looking At You (p/s, 500 only, with "Rizla" papers)	45
94	Rooster ROOSTER 1	Quad/Woke Up/Looking At You (p/s, 500 only, without "Rizla" papers)	30
95	Headhunter HED 718	Television/Steamroller '95/Jellystoned Park (8.47 Edit) (p/s)	20
95	Rooster ROOSTER 2	Coogan's Bluff/J Walking/Theme (p/s 1000 only)	20
97	Buchers Hook HOOK 003	Dirty Water/MAGIC DIRT: Goofy Dumb (p/s, 1000 only)	10
98	Rocket LAUNCH 1	You Can Lean Back/LILLYDAMWHITE: Master F (p/s, 550 only, insert)	10
00	Rocket LAUNCH 008	Spilff Riff (Conga'd Out)/75 (All Of It) (p/s, 4 inserts, First press 100 yellow vinyl)	20
00	Rocket LAUNCH 008	Spilff Riff (Conga'd Out)/75 (All Of It) (p/s, 4 inserts, First press 400 black vinyl)	15
00	Rocket LAUNCH 008	Spilff Riff (Conga'd Out)/75 (All Of It) (p/s, 4 inserts, Second press, 300 purple vinyl)	10
95	Headhunter HUK 001	RELAXING WITH... (LP)	40
00	Sweet Nothing SNLP 007	EVERYBODY KNOWS WE GOT NOWHERE (2-LP)	35
02	Rocket LAUNCH 015	SESSIONS 02 (LP, limited edition of 100, blue vinyl with free 7", 10 inserts)	100
02	Rocket LAUNCH 015	SESSIONS 02 (LP, 900 copies, black vinyl)	35
02	Sweet Nothing SNLP 011	UNDER SIDED (2-LP)	30
03	Rocket LAUNCH 018	AT LAST (LP)	35
05	Invada INV 015	33 (LP, blue or black vinyl)	20
05	Invada INV 017	DEAD IN THE WATER (2-LP, pink marbled vinyl)	30
06	Rocket/Invada LAUNCH 26/ INVLP 24	UNDER THE STRESS OF A HEADLONG DIVE (2-LP)	20
09	Rocket LAUNCH 033LP	COLLISIONS V.1 (LP, one side Heads one side WHITE HILLS, 150 orange vinyl with poster)	30
09	Rocket LAUNCH 033LP	COLLISIONS V.1 (LP, one side Heads one side WHITE HILLS, 150 orange vinyl without poster)	20
09	Rocket LAUNCH 033LP	COLLISIONS V.1 (LP, one side Heads one side WHITE HILLS, 700 black vinyl)	12

HEADS, HANDS & FEET
71	Island WIP 6115	Warming Up The Band/Silver Mine	5
71	Island ILPS 9149	HEADS, HANDS AND FEET (LP, gatefold, pink rim palm tree label)	25
72	Island ILPS 9185	TRACKS (LP, gatefold, pink rim palm tree label)	22
73	Atlantic K40465	OLD SOLIDERS NEVER DIE (LP, gatefold sleeve, lyric insert)	15
90s	See For Miles	HOME FROM HOME (THE MISSING ALBUM) (CD)	15
90s	See For Miles	HEADS HANDS AND FEET (CD)	15

(see also Don Everly, Tony Colton, Poet & One Man Band)

HEADSTONE
74	EMI EMA 766	BAD HABITS (LP, gatefold sleeve)	20
75	EMI EMC 3673	HEADSTONE (LP)	20

HEALEY SISTERS
64	HMV POP 1313	Give Me Back My Heart/After The Party	8

HEART BEATS
80	Red Shadow REDS 2	Talk To Me/Don't Want Romance (p/s)	5
81	Nothing Shaking SHAD 1	Go/One Of The People (p/s, blue vinyl)	15

HEART BOUND
74	Decca F 13510	Baby Ruth/Sailor Man	8

HEART (1)
76	Arista Arista 86	Crazy On You/Soul Of The Sea	6
77	Arista ARISTA 140	Heartless/Here Song (withdrawn)	8
86	Capitol CLP 406	Nothin' At All (Extended Remix)/The Wolf (heart-shaped picture disc)	6
87	Capitol CLP 457	Who Will You Run To?/Nobody Home (picture disc)	10
77	Arista SPART 1024	MAGAZINE (LP, withdrawn)	15
77	Arista SPART 1024	MAGAZINE (LP, picture disc)	15
90	Capitol HGIFT 1	HEART BOX SET (3-LP: "Heart", "Bad Animals" & "Brigade" + 24pp booklet)	18

HEART (2)
78	On U Sound LP 20	NOAH HOUSE OF DREAD (LP)	30

HEARTBREAKERS
77	Track 2094 135	Chinese Rocks/Born To Lose (p/s)	10
77	Track 2094 135T	Chinese Rocks/Born To Lose (12", p/s)	15
77	Track 2094 137	One Track Mind/Can't Keep My Eyes On You (live)/Do You Love Me (p/s)	10

77	Track 2094 142	It's Not Enough/Let Go (p/s, withdrawn)	250
79	Beggars Banquet BEG 21	Get Off The Phone (live)/I Wanna Be Loved (live) (p/s)	5
88	Jungle JUNG 38 T	SHE WANTS TO MAMBO (12" EP)	8
77	Track 2409 218	L.A.M.F. (LP)	30
79	Beggars Banquet BEGA 9	LIVE AT MAX'S KANSAS CITY (LP, with inner bag)	15
81	Jungle FREUD 1	D.T.K. - LIVE AT THE SPEAKEASY (LP, white or pink vinyl)	18
84	Jungle FREUD 4	L.A.M.F. REVISITED (LP, picture disc)	18
84	Jungle FEEUD 4	L.A.M.F. REVISITED (white label with withdrawn test proof sleeve)	150
88	Jungle FREUDP 1	D.T.K. - LIVE AT THE SPEAKEASY (LP, reissue, picture disc)	18

(see also New York Dolls, Johnny Thunders)

HEARTS (U.K.)
64	Parlophone R 5147	Young Woman/Black Eyes	20

HEARTS (U.S.)
64	Stateside SS 268	Dear Abby/Dear Abby (Instrumental)	22

HEARTS & FLOWERS
67	Capitol CL 15492	Rock'N'Roll Gypsies/Road To Nowhere	12
68	Capitol CL 15549	She Sang Hymns Out Of Tune/Tin Angel	8

HEARTS OF SOUL
70	Columbia DB 8670	Waterman/Fat Jack	20

HEAT EXCHANGE
79	EMI EMI 2988	Shake Down/You're Gonna Love This (p/s)	5
79	EMI 12EMI 2988	Shake Down/You're Gonna Love This (12", p/s)	8
79	EMI EMC 3306	ONE STEP AHEAD (LP)	12

(see also Brian Bennett)

HEATERS
70	Upsetter US 329	Melting Pot/UPSETTERS: Kinky Mood	12

JIMMY HEATH
60	Riverside RLP 333	REALLY BIG (LP)	15

TED HEATH ORCHESTRA
53	Confectioners' benevolent Fund (Dickie Valentine) (78, promo)	Candy Queen Waltz (with Dennis Lotis)/The Girl On The Candy Box (with Dickie Valentine) (78, promo)	10
54	Decca F 10246	Skin Deep/Walking Shoes	15
56	Decca F 10746	The Faithful Hussar/Siboney	5
58	Decca F 11000	Swingin' Shepherd Blues/Raunchy	5
58	Decca F 11003	Tequila/Little Serenade	5
58	Decca F 11025	Tom Hark/Cha Cha Baby	5
62	Decca PFM 24004	BIG BAND PERCUSSION (also stereo PFS 34004)	15

(see also Joan Regan, Bobbie Britton, Johnston Brothers, Annette Klooger)

HEATHCLIFFE
68	Tangerine DP 0001	Holly Bush And Mistletoe/My World	8

HEATHER
65	King KG 1027	I'll Come Softly/No One In The Whole Wide World	7

HEATWAVE
70	Penny Farthing PEN 738	Sister Simon (Funny Man)/Rastus Ravel	30

HEAVEN
71	CBS 66293	BRASS ROCK 1 (2-LP, ornate fold-out sleeve)	90

HEAVEN & EARTH
73	London SHO 8448	REFUGE (LP)	50

HEAVENLY
89	Sarah SARAH 30	I Fell In Love Last Night/Over And Over (p/s)	15
91	Sarah SARAH 41	Our Love Is Heavenly/Wrap My Arms Around Him (p/s, insert)	10
91	Sarah SARAH 51	So Little Deserve/I'm Not Scared Of You (p/s, insert)	10
93	Sarah SARAH 81	P.U.N.K. Girl/Hearts And Crosses (p/s, insert)	10
93	Sarah SARAH 82	Atta Girl/Dig Your Own Grave/So? (p/s, insert)	10
96	Wiiija WIJ 58	Space Manatee/You Tore Me Down/Art School (p/s)	10
92	Sarah SARAH 610	LE JARDIN DE HEAVENLY (LP)	25
94	Sarah SARAH 623	THE DECLINE AND FALL OF HEAVENLY (LP)	20
96	Wiiija WIJLP 1053	OPERATION HEAVENLY (LP)	15

HEAVEN 17
82	Virgin VS 483	Height Of The Fighting (He-La-Hu)/Honeymoon In New York (unissued, no p/s)	15

(see also B.E.F., Human League, Glenn Gregory & Claudia Brucken)

HEAVY COCHRAN
78	Psycho P 2611	I've Got Big Balls/Well, Fairly Big	5
79	Psycho P 2619	I've Got A Little Prick/It's 12 Inches Long, But I Don't Use It As A Rule	6

(see also Lieutenant Pigeon)

HEAVY DUTY BREAKS
85	Illuminated ILL 5512	Heavy Duty Breaks (Radio Version)/Bonus Beats (12", p/s)	8
85	Illuminated JAMS 49	HEAVY DUTY BREAKS (LP, remixes of other artists)	12

(see also Youth, Killing Joke)

HEAVY FEATHER
71	Penny Farthing	Beautiful And Black/Ceilings	10

HEAVY JEFF
74	Harry J HJ 6689	Black Pepper/Pepper Rock	8

HEAVY JELLY
69	Head HDS 4001	Time Out Chewn In/The Long Wait	20
69	Island WIP 6049	I Keep Singing The Same Old Song/Blue	30
70	Island HELP	HEAVY JELLY (LP, promo only)	180
84	Psycho PSYCHO 30	TAKE ME DOWN TO THE WATER (LP, reissue of "Heavy Jelly")	12

(see also Jackie Lomax, Aynsley Dunbar Retaliation, Skip Bifferty, Griffin, Graham Bell, Arc)

HEAVY METAL KIDS
74	Atlantic K 50047	HEAVY METAL KIDS (LP, with poster)	15
77	Rak SRAK 523	KITSCH (LP)	15

(see also Gary Holton, Kids)

HEAVY PETTIN'
82	Neat NEAT 17	Roll The Dice/Love Times Love (p/s)	10
83	Polydor HEPP 3	Love Times Love/Shout It Out (shaped picture disc)	8

HEAVY PUKE
80	(No label or cat no)	Spunk Bunny/Ozymandias (p/s, handwritten white labels)	30

HEAVYWEIGHT
91	One After D ODE3	The Way Of The Future (12")	45

HEAVYWEIGHTS
69	Spark SRL 1033	Utterly Funky/Shambala	30

BOBBY HEBB
66	Philips BF 1503	Sunny/Bread	5
66	Philips BF 1522	A Satisfied Mind/Love Love Love	40
67	Philips BF 1541	Love Me/Baby I'm Crazy	10
67	Philips BF 1570	I Love Everything About You/Some Kinda Magic	10
67	Philips BF 1610	Everything Is Coming Up Roses/Bound By Love	8
68	Philips BF 1702	You Want To Change Me/Dreamy	50
72	Philips 6051 023	Love Love Love/Sunny	10
72	Philips 6051 025	Some Kind Of Magic/Good Lovin'	6
66	Philips BL 7740	SUNNY (LP)	40

HEBREW CHILDREN & INNER CIRCLE
73	Ackee ACK 508	Dog And Bone/Version	6

DICK HECKSTALL-SMITH (QUINTET)
57	Pye Jazz NJE 1037	VERY SPECIAL OLD JAZZ (EP, as Dick Heckstall-Smith Quintet)	30
72	Bronze ILPS 9196	DUST IN THE AIR SUSPENDED MARKS THE PLACE ... WHERE A STORY ENDED (LP, gatefold sleeve with lyric inner sleeve)	40

(see also Graham Bond Organisation, John Mayall & Bluesbreakers, Alexis Korner, Colosseum, Rocket 88)

HECTOR
73	DJM DJS 289	Wired Up/Ain't Got Time	30
74	DJM DJS 303	Bye Bye Bad Days/Lady	30

JESSE HECTOR
99	No Hit NO HIT EP 1961	Fast Train To Memphis/My Bucket's Got A Hole In It/All By Myself/ Nightmares (p/s)	6

(see also Hammersmith Gorillas, Gorillas, Helter Skelter)

HEDGEHOG AFFAIR
92	Purple Heart PH 002	RUSH TILL DAWN PRESENTS THE HEDGEHOG AFFAIR EP (12")	12
92	Basement BRSS 005	RUSH TILL DAWN PRESENTS THE HEDGEHOG AFFAIR PT. 2 EP (12")	12
92	Basement BRSS 010	RUSH TILL DAWN PRESENTS THE HEDGEHOG AFFAIR PT. 3 EP (12")	12
93	Sound Entity SENT 1203	RUSH TILL DAWN PRESENTS THE HEDGEHOG AFFAIR PT. 4 EP (12")	12
94	Sound Entity SENT 1206	RUSH TILL DAWN PRESENTS THE HEDGEHOG AFFAIR PT. 5 EP (12")	20

HEDGEHOG PIE
76	Rubber ADUB 8	Well I Know/Go With The Flow	6
71	Rubber RUB 004	HIS ROUND (LP, with Tony Capstick, first pressing with black label on side 1 and white label on side 2)	20
75	Rubber RUB 009	HEDGEHOG PIE (LP)	25
75	Rubber RUB 014	GREEN LADY (LP)	60
78	Rubber RUB 024	JUST ACT NORMAL (LP, with lyric insert)	20

(see also Dando Shaft)

HEDGEHOPPERS ANONYMOUS
65	Decca F 12298	Don't Push Me/Please Don't Hurt Your Heart For Me	6
66	Decca F 12400	Baby (You're My Everything)/Remember	10
66	Decca F 12479	Daytime/That's The Time	10
66	Decca F 12530	Stop Press/Little Memories	8

(see also Alan Avon & Toy Shop, Jonathan King, Mick Tinsley)

HEFNER
97	Boogie Wonderland BWL 023	Lee Remick/Schoolgirls Knees (p/s)	15
98	Sticky STICKY 23	A Hymn For The Alcohol/My Art College Days Are Over (p/s, 500 only)	15
99	Too Pure PURE 93 S	The Hymn For The Cigarettes/Grandmother Dies (7")	6
99	Too Pure PURE98S	I Took Her Love For Granted/A Belly Full Of Babies (7")	6
97	Boogie Wonderland BWL020	A BETTER FRIEND EP (7" p/s with two inserts)	20
98	Too Pure PURE 64	THE HEFNER SOUL: Flowers/A Hymn For The Coffee/Broadmare/The Girl From The Coast/More Christian Girls (10" EP)	10
02	Too Pure PURE 125X	THE HEFNER BRAIN: When The Angels Play Their Drum Machines/Dark Hearted Discos/The Baggage Reclaim Song/Can't Help Losing You/All I'll Ever Need (10" p/s)	8
98	Too Pure PURE 83LP	BREAKING GOD'S HEART (LP)	20
99	Too Pure PURE92LP	THE FIDELITY WARS (LP)	20
00	Too Pure PURE 106 LP	WE LOVE THE CITY (LP)	15
00	Too Pure PURE 99LP	BOXING HEFNER (LP)	18
01	Too Pure PURE 105LP	DEAD MEDIA (LP)	15

NEAL HEFTI & ORCHESTRA
66	RCA Victor RCA 1521	The Batman Theme/Batman Chase	30
89	RCA PB 49571PD	The Batman Theme (1966 Version)/Batman Chase (picture disc)	8
54	Vogue/Coral LVC 10005	SWINGIN' ON A CORAL REEF (10" LP)	15
65	Warner Bros W 1599	HARLOW (LP, soundtrack)	25
65	United Artists (S)ULP 1098	HOW TO MURDER YOUR WIFE (LP, soundtrack)	25
66	RCA Victor RD 7795	BOEING BOEING (LP, soundtrack)	20
66	United Artists (S)ULP 1141	DUEL AT DIABLO (LP, soundtrack)	18
67	London HA-D 8337	BAREFOOT IN THE PARK (LP, soundtrack)	30
68	Dot (S)LPD 514	THE ODD COUPLE (LP, soundtrack)	30

LUCILLE HEGAMIN
| 73 | VJM VLP 50 | BLUE FLAME (LP) | 15 |

DONALD HEIGHT
66	London HLZ 10062	Talk Of The Grapevine/There'll Be No Tomorrow	130
66	London HLZ 10062	Talk Of The Grapevine/There'll Be No Tomorrow (DJ copy)	150
67	London HLZ 10116	Three Hundred & Sixty Five Days/I'm Willing To Wait	100
67	London HLZ 10116	Three Hundred & Sixty Five Days/I'm Willing To Wait (DJ copy)	140
71	Avco Embassy 6105 005	Dancin' To The Music Of Love/Rags To Riches To Rags	75
71	Jay Boy BOY 32	Talk Of The Grapevine/There'll Be No Tomorrow (reissue)	15
72	Jay Boy BOY 51	Three Hundred & Sixty Five Days/I'm Willing To Wait (reissue)	10
72	Jay Boy BOY 60	We Gotta Make Up/I Can't Get Enough	10

RONNIE HEIGHT
| 60 | London HLN 9144 | The One Finger Symphony/Mem'ries & Habits | 5 |

HEINZ (& WILD BOYS)
63	Decca F 11652	Dreams Do Come True/Been Invited To A Party	25
63	Decca F 11693	Just Like Eddie/Don't You Knock At My Door	7
63	Decca F 11768	Country Boy/Long Tall Jack	8
64	Decca F 11831	You Were There/No Matter What They Say	10
64	Decca F 11920	Please Little Girl/For Loving Me This Way	20
64	Columbia DB 7374	Questions I Can't Answer/The Beating Of My Heart	20
65	Columbia DB 7482	Diggin' My Potatoes/She Ain't Comin' Back (with Wild Boys)	40
65	Columbia DB 7559	Don't Think Twice, It's All Right/Big Fat Spider	30
65	Columbia DB 7656	End Of The World/You Make Me Feel So Good	40
65	Columbia DB 7779	Heart Full Of Sorrow/Don't Worry Baby	40
66	Columbia DB 7942	Movin' In/I'm Not A Bad Guy	45
70s	Cargo CPS 010	Country Boy/Just Like Eddie	10
63	Decca DFE 8545	HEINZ (EP)	60
63	Decca DFE 8559	LIVE IT UP (EP)	40
64	Decca LK 4599	TRIBUTE TO EDDIE (LP)	80
76	Decca REM 7	REMEMBERING (LP)	15

(see also Tornados, Saints)

HEISENBERG
| 89 | Uncertain HEI 5001 | No More Dreams/Rain (p/s) | 20 |

HELDEN
| 83 | Zica ZICA 01 | Holding On/Once Upon A Time In The ... (p/s) | 5 |
| 83 | Zica 12 ZICA 01 | Holding On/Once Upon A Time In The ... (12", p/s) | 15 |

(see also Ultravox)

HELICOPTER
| 72 | Maple Annie MA 102 | I Belong To Yesterday/Lonely Tonight | 25 |

(see also Galliard)

HELL
| 83 | Deadly Weapons DWS 666 | Save Us From Those Who Would Save Us/Death Squad | 75 |

RICHARD HELL (& VOIDOIDS)
76	Stiff BUY 7	(I Could Live With You In) Another World/(I Belong To The) Blank Generation/ You Gotta Lose (with p/s, numbered, 5,000 only with 4 point press-out centre)	12
76	Stiff BUY 7	(I Could Live With You In) Another World/(I Belong To The) Blank Generation/ You Gotta Lose (repressing for THE STIFF BOX SET & numbered 001)	6
77	Sire 6078 608	Blank Generation/Liar's Beware/Who Says? (no p/s)	8
77	Sire 6078 608	Blank Generation/Liars Beware/Who Says? (12", p/s)	10
79	Radar ADA 30	The Kid With The Replaceable Head/I'm Your Man (p/s)	7
94	Overground OVER 36	Another World/Blank Generation/Love Comes In Spurts (p/s, reissue, 2,000 only)	5
96	Codex CODE 3X	GO NOW (10", p/s, 1,000 only, etched yellow vinyl)	8
77	Sire 9103 327	BLANK GENERATION (LP, with inner sleeve)	20
77	Sire 9103 327	BLANK GENERATION (LP, without inner sleeve)	12
83	I.D. NOSE 2	DESTINY STREET (LP)	12

(see also Neon Boys)

HELLACOPTERS
99	Butcher's Hook HOOK 004	A House Is Not A Motel/POWDER MONKEYS: Destination X (p/s)	5
01	Polar 158 801 2	FLIGHT CASE (enhanced CD EP, box set with patch & insert)	12
01	Sweet Nothing 12SN007	HIGH ENERGY ROCK 'N' ROLL (mini-LP)	20
04	Sweet Nothing SNLP 040	STRIKES LIKE LIGHTNING (3 x 7" box set, cards, badge & pendant)	30

(see also Super$hit666)

HELLANBACH
| 84 | Neat NEAT 1006 | NOW HEAR THIS (LP, with inner sleeve) | 15 |
| 84 | Neat NEAT 1019 | THE BIG ... H (LP, with insert) | 15 |

HELLHAMMER
| 84 | Noise N 008 | APOCALYPTIC RAIDS (12" EP, 45/33rpm) | 50 |
| 08 | Century Media 9977392 | DEMON ENTRAILS (3-LP, 180gm vinyl with booklet and poster) | 80 |

DAVE HELLING
| 65 | Stateside SS 409 | It Ain't Me Babe/If You're Gonna Leave Me | 10 |
| 66 | Planet PLF 101 | Christine/The Bells | 40 |

HELLIONS
65	Piccadilly 7N 35213	Daydreaming Of You/Shades Of Blue	25
65	Piccadilly 7N 35232	Tomorrow Never Comes/Dream Child	25
65	Piccadilly 7N 35265	A Little Lovin'/Think It Over	25

(see also Revolution, Traffic, Roaring Sixties, Jim Capaldi, Dave Mason, Luther Grosvenor, Family, Spooky Tooth)

HELL IS FOR HEROES
| 00s | Chrysalis CHS 5143 | I Can Climb Mountains/Get Low (blue vinyl, p/s) | 7 |
| 00s | EMI 5515397 | Night Vision/Can't You Hear It (clear vinyl, p/s) | 6 |

HELLO
72	Bell BELL 1238	You Move Me/Ask Your Mama	15
72	Bell BELL 1265	C'mon/Wench	5
73	Bell BELL 1333	Another School Day/C'mon Get Together (p/s)	6

76	Bell BELL 1479	Teenage Revolution/Keeps Us Off The Streets (demo copies only)	100
76	Bell BELLS 263	KEEP US OFF THE STREETS (LP)	15

HELLO PEOPLE
74	ABC 4034	Future Shock/Destiny	6

HELL PREACHERS INC.
69	Marble Arch MALS 1169	SUPREME PSYCHEDELIC UNDERGROUND (LP)	50

BOBBY HELMS
57	Brunswick 05711	Fraulein/(Got A) Heartsick Feeling	12
57	Brunswick 05721	My Special Angel/Standing At The End of My World	12
58	Brunswick 05730	No Other Baby/The Magic Song	20
58	Brunswick 05741	Love My Lady/Just A Little Lonesome	20
58	Brunswick 05748	Jacqueline/Living In The Shadow Of The Past	15
58	Brunswick 05754	Schoolboy Crush/Borrowed Dreams	15
58	Brunswick 05765	Jingle Bell Rock/Captain Santa Claus	20
59	Brunswick 05786	Miss Memory/New River Train	10
59	Brunswick 05801	Soon It Can Be Told/I Guess I'll Miss The Prom	10
59	Brunswick 05813	My Lucky Day/Hurry Baby	12
59	Brunswick 05813	My Lucky Day/Hurry Baby (78)	20
61	Brunswick 05852	Sad Eyed Baby/You're The One	8
60	Brunswick OE 9461	BOBBY HELMS (EP)	40
57	Brunswick LAT 8250	SINGS TO MY SPECIAL ANGEL (LP)	75

JIMMY HELMS
63	Pye 7N 45440	Ragtime Girl/Romeo & Juliet	100
73	Capitol CL 15762	My Little Devil/Magnificent Sanctuary Band	6
73	Fly BUG 27	Gonna Make You An Offer You Can't Refuse/Words And Music	6

HELP
71	MCA MWPS 4039	SECOND COMING (LP)	80

HELP YOURSELF
71	Liberty LBF 15459	Running Down Deep/Paper Leaves	8
72	United Artists UP 35355	Heaven Row/Brown Lady	8
72	United Artists UP 35466	Mommy Won't Be Home For Christmas/Johnny B. Goode	6
71	Liberty LBS 83484	HELP YOURSELF (LP)	70
72	United Artists UAS 29287	STRANGE AFFAIR (LP, with inner sleeve)	45
72	United Artists UAS 29413	BEWARE OF THE SHADOW (LP)	35
73	United Artists UDG 4001 [UAS 29487/FREE 1]	THE RETURN OF KEN WHALEY/HAPPY DAYS (2-LP set in envelope sleeve with LPs in individual sleeves)	50
73	United Artists UAS 29487	THE RETURN OF KEN WHALEY (LP)	20

(see also Man, Deke Leonard, Tyla Gang, Wreckless Eric)

HELPLESS HUW
78	US US 001	Still Love You (In My Heart)	5
80	US US 002	Sid Vicious Was Innocent/Going Through The Motions/ Baby We're Not In Love/When You're Weary (p/s in bag)	15

HELTER SKELTER
77	Sticky STY 102	I Need You/Goodbye Baby	30

(see also Gorillas, Hammersmith Gorillas, Jesse Hector)

HEMLOCK
73	Deram DM 379	Mr Horizontal/Beggar Man	12
73	Deram SML 1102	HEMLOCK (LP, white/red label with small logo)	90

(see also Miller Anderson, Keef Hartley Band, Dog Soldier)

BERTHA HENDERSON/ROSA HENDERSON
60	Jazz Collector JEL 14	THE FEMALE BLUES VOL. 2 (EP)	10

BILL HENDERSON
60	Top Rank JAR 412	Sweet Pumpkin/Joey, Joey, Joey	8

DORRIS HENDERSON
65	Columbia DB 7567	The Hangman/Leaves That Are Green	15
67	Fontana TF 811	Message To Pretty/Watch The Stars	10
65	Columbia SX 6001	THERE YOU GO (LP, with John Renbourn)	140
67	Fontana (S)TL 5385	WATCH THE STARS (LP, with John Renbourn)	175

(see also Eclection, John Renbourn)

EDMONIA HENDERSON
51	Tempo R 43	Mama Don't Want A Sweet Man Any More/Hateful Blues (78)	10

FINIS HENDERSON
83	Motown TMGT 1304	Skip To My Lou/I'd Rather Be Gone/Vina Del Mar (12")	20

FLETCHER HENDERSON
50s	Audubon AAF-AAK	FLETCHER HENDERSON (6 x 10" LP set)	25

(see also Clara Smith & Fletcher Henderson)

JOE HENDERSON
62	London HLU 9553	Snap Your Fingers/If You See Me Cry	12
63	London REU 1376	JOE HENDERSON (EP)	30

LORNA HENDERSON
60	Oriole CB 1549	Lollipops To Lipstick/Steady Eddie	25
60	Oriole CB 1549	Lollipops To Lipstick/Steady Eddie (78)	18
60	Oriole CB 1590	A Thousand Stars/Murray, What's Your Hurry?	10

MARIAN HENDERSON
70	MCA MK 5046	Antique Annies Magic Lantern Show/Lady Of Carlisle	8

BOBBY HENDRICKS
58	London HL 8714	Itchy Twitchy Feeling/A Thousand Dreams	60
58	London HL 8714	Itchy Twitchy Feeling/A Thousand Dreams (78)	30
59	Top Rank JAR 193	Little John Green/Sincerely, Your Lover	20
61	Mercury AMT 1163	I'm Coming Home/Every Other Night	10
64	Sue WI 315	Itchy Twitchy Feeling/Thousand Dreams (reissue, as Bobby Henricks)	20

(see also Drifters)

HUGH HENDRICKS & UPSETTERS

70	Spinning Wheel SW 103	Land Of Kinks/O'NEIL HALL: This Man	15

JON HENDRICKS

56	Brunswick 05521	Four Brothers/Cloudburst (with Dave Lambert Singers)	6
68	Verve VS 572	No More/Rainbow's End	5
71	Philips 6006 088	I Got Soul/Slow Train	5
61	Vogue EPV 1268	A GOOD GIT-TOGETHER (EP)	8
60	Vogue LAE 12231	A GOOD GIT-TOGETHER (LP)	12

(see also Dave Lambert)

JIMI HENDRIX (EXPERIENCE)

SINGLES

66	Polydor 56139	Hey Joe/Stone Free	15
67	Track 604 001	Purple Haze (1-sided promo, white label with black text)	250
67	Track 604 001	Purple Haze/51st Anniversary (white label)	20
67	Track 604 001	Purple Haze/51st Anniversary (black label)	15
67	Track 604 001	Purple Haze/51st Anniversary (black label, alternative mix, but no way of telling from either label or matrix number))	25
67	Track 604 004	The Wind Cries Mary/Highway Chile	12
67	Track 604 007	The Burning Of The Midnight Lamp/The Stars That Play With Laughing Sam's Dice	10
67	Decca F 22652	How Would You Feel/You Don't Want Me (with Curtis Knight, test pressing, unreleased)	500
67	Track 604 009	How Would You Feel/You Don't Want Me (with Curtis Knight)	12
67	London HL 10160	Hush Now/Flashing (with Curtis Knight; in export p/s)	30
67	London HL 10160	Hush Now/Flashing (with Curtis Knight)	10
68	Track 604 025	All Along The Watchtower/Long Hot Summer Night	12
69	Track 604 029	Crosstown Traffic/Gypsy Eyes	12
69	Track 604 033	Let Me Light Your Fire/The Burning Of The Midnight Lamp	10
70	London HLZ 10321	Ballad Of Jimi/Gloomy Monday (with Curtis Knight)	8
70	London HL 7126	Ballad Of Jimi/Gloomy Monday (with Curtis Knight, export issue)	30
70	Track 2095 001	Voodoo Chile/Hey Joe/All Along The Watchtower (p/s; later copies have white border on sleeve)	15
70	Track 2095 001	Voodoo Chile/Hey Joe/All Along The Watchtower (p/s; later copies with white border on sleeve)	8
70	Track 2095 001	Voodoo Chile/Hey Joe/All Along The Watchtower	6
71	RCA RCA 2033	No Such Animal (Parts 1 & 2) (initially in p/s, with Curtis Knight uncredited)	25
71	RCA RCA 2033	No Such Animal (Parts 1 & 2) (with Curtis Knight uncredited)	6
71	Track 2094 007	Angel/Night Bird Flying	7
71	Track 2094 010	Gypsy Eyes/Remember/Purple Haze/Stone Free (in p/s)	25
71	Track 2094 010	Gypsy Eyes/Remember/Purple Haze/Stone Free	8
72	Polydor 2001 277	Johnny B. Goode/Little Wing	6
73	Reprise K 14286	Hear My Train A-Comin/Rock Me Baby	6
73	Polydor/Sound For Industry SFI 1572	Red House/Spanish Castle Magic (1-sided flexidisc with Rolling Stone)	15
80	Polydor 2608 001	6 SINGLES PACK (6 plain sleeve singles [2141 275-280], open-out card p/s)	20
82	CBS CBS A 2749	Fire/Are You Experienced? (p/s)	6
89	Castle Comms. HENPD 01	Hey Joe/Purple Haze/Radio One Theme (12", picture disc)	8
89	Polydor PO 33	Purple Haze/51st Anniversary (p/s, reissue)	5
90	Polydor PO 71	Crosstown Traffic/Voodoo Chile (p/s)	5
90	Polydor PO 100	All Along The Watchtower/Voodoo Chile/Hey Joe (p/s)	5

ALBUMS : TRACK LPS

67	Track 612 001	ARE YOU EXPERIENCED (mono, laminated (front and back) sleeve)	500
67	Track 612 001	ARE YOU EXPERIENCED (mono, matt sleeve)	250
67	Track 612 003	AXIS: BOLD AS LOVE (laminated gatefold sleeve, with gatefold insert mono)	500
67	Track 612 003	AXIS: BOLD AS LOVE (laminated gatefold sleeve, without gatefold insert, mono)	150
67	Track 613 003	AXIS: BOLD AS LOVE (laminated gatefold sleeve, with gatefold insert, stereo)	300
67	Track 613 003	AXIS: BOLD AS LOVE (laminated gatefold sleeve, without gatefold insert, stereo)	120
68	Track 612 004	SMASH HITS (mono)	60
68	Track 613 004	SMASH HITS (stereo)	25
68	Track 612 008/009	ELECTRIC LADYLAND (2-LP, plain white non-gatefold sleeve, labels marked "Test Pressing", mono)	1000
68	Track 613 008/009	ELECTRIC LADYLAND (2-LP, laminated gatefold sleeve, stereo, blue text inside sleeve)	400
68	Track 613 008/009	ELECTRIC LADYLAND (2-LP, laminated gatefold sleeve, stereo, white text inside sleeve)	200
68	Track 613 010	ELECTRIC LADYLAND PART 1 (stereo only)	30
68	Track 613 017	ELECTRIC LADYLAND PART 2 (stereo only)	30
70	Track Super 2406 002	BAND OF GYPSYS (original 'puppet' sleeve, beware of 'fake' copies on eBay)	150
70	Track Super 2406 002	BAND OF GYPSYS (repressing, gatefold 'Isle Of Wight' sleeve)	40
70	Track Super 2406 002	BAND OF GYPSYS (2nd repressing, single sleeve)	20
70	Track 2407 010	BACKTRACK 10: ARE YOU EXPERIENCED? (budget reissue, mono, some state mono but play stereo)	20
70	Track 2407 010	BACKTRACK 10: ARE YOU EXPERIENCED? (budget reissue, stereo, but in Mono sleeve)	50
70	Track 2407 011	BACKTRACK 11: AXIS: BOLD AS LOVE (budget reissue, stereo)	20
71	Track 2856 002	ELECTRIC JIMI HENDRIX (mail-order only Record Club release)	800
71	Track 2408 101	THE CRY OF LOVE (gatefold sleeve)	30
71	Track 2408 101	THE CRY OF LOVE (red vinyl, factory custom pressing, 3 copies only)	2000
74	Track 603003	ARE YOU EXPERIENCED (LP, stereo with POLYDOR INT. GmbH on label, this is NOT the 1967 Stereo issue of ARE YOU EXPERIENCED)	40
88	Track/HMV C 881-16	ARE YOU EXPERIENCED (LP, box set, ltd. ed. of 2,500, no'd, with certificate)	30

ALBUMS : POLYDOR LPS

71	Polydor 2302 016	ISLE OF WIGHT	15
71	Polydor 2302 018	HENDRIX IN THE WEST (gatefold sleeve)	15
72	Polydor 2302 020	WAR HEROES	15
72	Polydor 2302 023	THE CRY OF LOVE (gatefold sleeve, reissue)	12
73	Polydor 2302 268	SMASH HITS (stereo reissue)	12
73	Polydor 2480 005	BAND OF GYPSYS (reissue, different sleeve)	12
73	Polydor ACB 00219 Super	SMASH HITS (LP, Audio Club Of Great Britain issue)	15
73	Polydor 2657 012	ELECTRIC LADYLAND (2-LP, laminated gatefold sleeve, reissue)	25
73	Polydor 2310 271	ELECTRIC LADYLAND PART 1 (reissue)	15
73	Polydor 2310 272	ELECTRIC LADYLAND PART 2 (reissue)	15
74	Polydor 2310 301	LOOSE ENDS	15

75	Polydor 2310 398	CRASH LANDING	12
75	Polydor 2310 415	MIDNIGHT LIGHTNING	12
78	Polydor 2612 034	THE ESSENTIAL JIMI HENDRIX (2-LP, with bonus 1-sided 33rpm 7" Gloria [JIMI 1] in special bag)	18
78	St. Michael 2102/0102	JIMI HENDRIX (cat. no. also listed as Polydor 2891 139)	50
78	St. Michael/Poly. 2891 139	JIMI HENDRIX (cassette)	20
80	Polydor 2625 040	JIMI HENDRIX (13-LP box set [11 x LP + 1 x 2-LP])	75
80	Polydor POLS 1023	NINE TO THE UNIVERSE	15
84	Polydor SPDLP 3	ELECTRIC LADYLAND (2-LP, non-laminate gatefold sleeve, 2nd reissue)	25
87	Polydor 833 004-1	LIVE AT WINTERLAND (2-LP, with poster)	18
88	Polydor/HMV C88 LP 1-16	ARE YOU EXPERIENCED? (box set sold via HMV stores, 1,500 only)	12
90	Polydor 847 2311	CORNERSTONES: JIMI HENDRIX 1967-1970	12

ALBUMS : OTHER LPS

68	London HA/SH 8349	GET THAT FEELING (with Curtis Knight)	30
68	London HA/SH 8369	STRANGE THINGS (with Curtis Knight)	30
71	Ember NR 5057	EXPERIENCE - THE ORIGINAL SOUNDTRACK (gatefold sleeve)	12
71	Reprise K 40430	LIVE AT THE MONTEREY INTERNATIONAL POP FESTIVAL (shared with Otis Redding)	35
71	Reprise K 44159	RAINBOW BRIDGE (matt gatefold sleeve, 'steamboat' label, soundtrack)	20
72	Ember NR 5061	MORE EXPERIENCE (soundtrack)	12
73	Reprise K 64017	SOUNDTRACK RECORDINGS FROM THE FILM JIMI HENDRIX (2-LP)	18
73	Ember NR 5068	IN THE BEGINNING (textured gatefold sleeve)	15
74	Ember EMB 3428	LOOKING BACK WITH JIMI HENDRIX	15
75	DJM DJLMD 8011	FOR REAL (2-LP, gatefold sleeve)	18
89	Castle Comms. HBLP 100	LIVE AND UNRELEASED - THE RADIO SHOW (5-LP)	30

ALBUMS : CDS

84	Track 821 993 2	BAND OF GYPSYS	35
88	Polydor/HMV C88 LP 1-11	ARE YOU EXPERIENCED? (box set via HMV stores, 1,500 only)	18
89	Castle Comms. HBCD 100	LIVE AND UNRELEASED - THE RADIO SHOW (3-CD, box set)	18
89	Polydor 831 312-2	HENDRIX IN THE WEST	18
89	Polydor 837 574-2	LOOSE ENDS	18

(see also Eire Apparent, Jayne Mansfield, McGough & McGear, Noel Redding Band, Fat Mattress, Curtis Knight, Billy Cox, Buddy Miles, Riot Squad)

MARGIE HENDRIX

66	Mercury MF 976	I Call You Lover But You Ain't Nothin' But A Tramp/The Question	25
67	Mercury MF 1001	Restless/On The Right Track	30

TONY HENDRIX

69	Pye Int. 7n 25485	The Grooviest Girl In The World/Majestic World	8

LARRY HENLEY

64	Hickory 45-1272	My Reasons For Living/Stickin' Up For My Baby	12

(see also Newbeats, Dean & Mark)

CHRISTIE HENNESSY

73	Westwood	CHRISTIE HENNESSY (LP)	35

HENNESSYS

69	Cambrian CLP 593	THE ROADS AND THE MILES (LP)	80
60s	Music Factory MF 106	KARDIFF AFTER DARK (LP)	90

ADRIAN HENRI

60s	Charivari	ADRIAN HENRI (LP)	45
60s	Argo PLP 1194	ADRIAN HENRI AND HUGO WILLIAMS (LP)	40

(see also Liverpool Scene, McGough & McGear)

ANN HENRY

60	Top Rank JAR 292	Like Young/Sugar Blues	10

BOB HENRY

65	Philips BF 1450	I Need Someone/Built Like A Man	18

(see also Robert Henry)

CLARENCE ('FROGMAN') HENRY

57	London HLN 8389	Ain't Got No Home/Troubles Troubles (as Clarence Henry) (gold lettering on label)	150
57	London HLN 8389	Ain't Got No Home/Troubles Troubles (as Clarence Henry) (silver lettering on label)	120
57	London HLN 8389	Ain't Got No Home/Troubles Troubles (as Clarence Henry) (78)	60
61	Pye International 7N 25078	But I Do/Just My Baby And Me	10
61	Pye International 7N 25089	You Always Hurt The One You Love/Little Suzy	10
61	Pye International 7N 25108	Lonely Street/Why Can't You	10
61	Pye International 7N 25115	Standing In The Need Of Love/On Bended Knees	10
62	Pye International 7N 25123	A Little Too Much/I Wish I Could Say The Same	10
62	Pye International 7N 25141	Dream Myself A Sweetheart/Lost Without You	10
62	Pye International 7N 25169	The Jealous Kind/Come On And Dance	15
64	London HLU 9936	Little Green Frog/Have You Ever Been Lonely?	10
66	London HLU 10025	Ain't Got No Home/Baby, Ain't That Love?	10
61	Pye Intl. NEP 44007	CLARENCE 'FROGMAN' HENRY HIT PARADE (EP)	50
61	Pye Intl. NPL 28017	YOU ALWAYS HURT THE ONE YOU LOVE (LP)	60

MILTON HENRY

76	Cactus CT85	Gypsy Woman/Dub	25

PIERRE HENRY

66	Philips 4FE 8000	LE VOYAGE FROM THE TIBETAN BOOK OF THE DEAD (LP)	20
66	Philips 4FE 8504	VARIATIONS FOR A DOOR AND A SIGH (LP, UK record in French sleeve)	20
68	Philips 4FE 8004	MASS FOR THE PRESENT TIME (LP)	40

RICHARD HENRY

68	Regal Zonophone RZ 3014	Oh Girl/Lay Your Head Upon My Shoulder	6

ROBERT HENRY

66	Philips BF 1476	Walk Away Like A Winner/That's All I Want	70

(see also Bob Henry)

HENRY III

67	Island WI 3078	Thank You Girl/Take Me Back	22
67	Island WI 3081	I'll Reach The End/Won't Go Away (B-side actually Lee's Special by Don Tony Lee)	40

MINT VALUE £

| 67 | RCA RCA 1568 | So Much Love/Sitting In The Park | 20 |
| 70 | Dynamic DYN 402 | Out Of Time/VICEROYS: Love For Everyone (both with Hubcap & Wheels) | 8 |

(see also Uniques)

DANNY HENRY
| 81 | Three Kings TK50 | Sharon My Love/Version/African Gold (12") | 40 |

HENRY & LIZA
| 73 | Dragon DRA 1004 | Hole Under Cratches/TIVOLIS: Hole Under Cratches (Instrumental) (actually "Hole Under Crutches") | 6 |

(see also Max Romeo)

HENRY & LOUIS
| 80s | 2 Kings 2K7001 | Jah Jah Never Fail/Dub Never Fail I | 15 |

HENRY COW
73	Virgin V 2005	THE LEGEND (LP)	50
74	Virgin V 2011	UNREST (LP, gatefold sleeve, black/white 'twin' label)	30
75	Virgin V 2027	IN PRAISE OF LEARNING (LP)	25
76	Caroline CAD 3002	CONCERTS (LP)	30
79	Broadcast BC 1	WESTERN CULTURE (LP)	15

(see also Slapp Happy, Art Bears, Fred Frith, Gong/Henry Cow/Global Trucking Company)

HENRY ESSENCE
| 79 | Ellie Jay Records EJSP9392 | Margarita/14 Year Old Lover (500 only, p/s) | 150 |

JUDY HENSKE
| 66 | Reprise RS 20485 | Road To Nowhere/Sing A Rainbow | 15 |
| 65 | Reprise RS 6203 | DEATH DEFYING (LP) | 30 |

JUDY HENSKE & JERRY YESTER
| 69 | Straight STS 1052 | FAREWELL ALDEBARAN (LP) | 40 |

KEN HENSLEY
| 73 | Bronze ILPS 9223 | PROUD WORDS ON A DUSTY SHELF (LP, gatefold sleeve, lyric inner, Isalnd credit on label) | 25 |
| 75 | Bronze ILPS 9307 | EAGER TO PLEASE (LP, lyric inner, Island credit on label) | 18 |

ROBERT HENRY HENSLEY
| 68 | Polydor 56295 | You're Gonna See Me Cry/Montage | 8 |

NICKY HENSON
| 63 | Parlophone R 4976 | Till I See You Cry/What Does It Mean? | 20 |

DAVID HENTSCHEL
| 75 | Ring O' 2017 101 | Oh My My/Devil Woman | 8 |

NAT HEPBURN
| 60s | Jump Up JU 516 | River/Political Girl | 6 |

HEPBURNS
87	Cherry Red 12CHERRY 98	GOALMOUTH INCIDENT (12" EP)	8
89	Let's Zine! (No Cat. No.)	Where You Belong/WALTONES: She Looks Right Through Me (Demo Version) (1-sided flexi, with Zine fanzine issue 10)	15
90	Magic MAGIC 01T	Electrified (From Countryside To City)/London Welshman/Dive (12", p/s)	25
88	Cherry Red BRED 83	THE MAGIC OF THE HEPBURNS (LP)	15

HEP STARS
66	Decca F 22446	Sunny Girl/No Response	45
67	Olga OLE 001	Wedding/Consolation	25
68	Olga OLE 013	Let It Be Me/Groovy Summertime (withdrawn, supposedly reissued 1969)	45
68	Olga OLE 014	Malaika/It's Nice To Be Back (in export p/s)	55
68	Olga OLE 014	Malaika/It's Nice To Be Back	25

(see also Abba)

HEPTONES
66	Rio R 104	Gunmen Coming To Town/TOMMY McCOOK & SUPERSONICS: Riverton City	70
67	Ska Beat JB 266	We've Got Love/I Am Lonely	80
67	Caltone TONE 105	Schoolgirls/Ain't That Bad?	60
67	Studio One SO 2005	A Change Is Gonna Come/Nobody Knows	60
67	Studio One SO 2014	Fat Girl/DELROY WILSON: Mother Word	30
67	Studio One SO 2021	If I Knew/Festival Day	50
67	Studio One SO 2026	Why Did You Leave?/GAYLADS: Don't Try To Reach Me	30
67	Studio One SO 2030	Why Must I?/SLIM SMITH: Try Again	30
67	Studio One SO 2031	Take Me (actually by The Soul Vendors)/DELROY WILSON: I'm Not A King	50
67	Studio One SO 2033	Only Sixteen/Baby	20
68	Studio One SO 2040	Tripe Girl/DELROY WILSON: Mr. D.J.	30
68	Studio One SO 2049	Cry, Baby, Cry/Mama	30
68	Studio One SO 2052	Dock Of The Bay/KING ROCKY (ELLIS): The Ruler	125
68	Studio One SO 2055	Party Time/Oil In Your Lamp	30
68	Coxsone CS 7052	Love Won't Come Easy/Gee Wee	30
68	Coxsone CS 7068	Equal Rights/Ting-A-Ling	35
68	Coxsone CS 7082	Soul Power/Love Me Always	125
69	Coxsone CS 7092	Sweet Talking/Ob-La-Di	30
69	Studio One SO 2083	I Shall Be Released/Love Me Always	20
69	Bamboo BAM 11	I Shall Be Released/Love Me Always (Power) (reissue)	20
70	Bamboo BAM 28	Young, Gifted and Black/SOUND DIMENSION: Joyland	20
70	Bamboo BAM 39	Young Generation/You Turned Away	20
70	Bamboo BAM 43	Message From A Blackman/SOUND DIMENSION: Jamaica Underground	25
70	Upsetter US 339	Hurry Up/Thanks We Get	20
70	Banana BA 311	Be A Man/U ROY: Shock Attack	12
71	Banana BA 325	Suspicious Minds/Haven't You Any Fight Left?	10
71	Banana BA 349	Freedom Line/SOUND DIMENSION: Version	15
72	Green Door GD 4020	Hypocrite/JOHNNY LOVER: Straight To The Head	12
72	Prince Buster PB 37	Our Day Will Come/PRINCE BUSTER: Protection	12
72	Ashanti ASH 411	I'm In The Mood For Love/TOMMY McCOOK & NOW GENERATION: Eight Years After	8
72	Duke DU 143	Save The Last Dance For Me/Be The One	6
72	Pama PM 843	You've Lost That Lovin' Feelin'/RUPIE EDWARDS ALLSTARS: Feeling Version	8

72	Pama Supreme PS 367	Save The Last Dance For Me/Save The Last Dance Version	7
72	Ackee ACK 407	I Miss You (Parts 1 & 2)	5
73	Ackee ACK 414	Let Me Hold Your Hand/Version	5
73	Jaguar JAG 103	Drifting Away/BONGO LES: Zion Drum	10
73	Grape GR 3053	Old Time/G.G. ALLSTARS: Dub	7
73	Smash SMA 2328	Soul Sister/IMPACT ALLSTARS: Soul Sister (Version)	7
73	Count Shelley CS 017	Now I Know/AUGUSTUS PABLO: Version	12
74	Pama Supreme PS 390	Thanks We Get/Oppression (both actually by Delroy Butler)	10
75	Faith FA 012	Party Time/Version	5
76	Cancer CAN 003	Cool Rasta/Rasta Dub	12
76	Trojan Horse HOSS 124	Cool Rasta/Dreadlock	12
67	Studio One SOL 9002	THE HEPTONES (LP)	150
68	Studio One SOL 9010	ON TOP (LP)	200
72	Trojan TBL 183	THE HEPTONES AND THEIR FRIENDS MEET THE NOW GENERATION (LP)	35
75	Island ILPS 9297	BOOK OF RULES (LP)	20
76	Island ILPS 9456	PARTY TIME (LP)	20
76	Island ILPS 9381	NIGHT FOOD (LP)	20
76	Trojan TRLS 128	COOL RASTA (LP)	12
78	Third World TDWD1	BETTER DAYS (LP)	20

(see also Barry Llewellyn, Soul Vendors, Ronald & Lloyd, Ed Nangle, Love Generation, Alton Ellis, Basil Daley, Ken Boothe, Jackie Mittoo)

HERB & KAY
54	Parlophone MSP 6127	This Ole House/Angels In The Sky	30
54	Parlophone CMSP 23	This Ole House/Angels In The Sky (export issue)	30
55	Parlophone CMSP 31	Coffee Blues/Juke Box Jig (export issue)	30

HERBAL MIXTURE
| 66 | Columbia DB 8021 | A Love That's Died/Tailor Made | 175 |
| 66 | Columbia DB 8083 | Machines/Please Leave My Mind | 225 |

(see also Tony McPhee, Groundhogs)

HERBALISER
| 97 | Ninja Tune ZEN 28 | BLOW YOUR HEADPHONES (LP) | 18 |

HERBIE & ROYALISTS
| 68 | Saga FID 2121 | SOUL OF THE MATTER (LP) | 20 |

HERBIE'S PEOPLE
65	CBS 202005	Sweet And Tender Romance/You Thrill Me To Pieces	25
66	CBS 202058	One Little Smile/You Never Know	20
67	CBS 202584	Residential Area/Humming Bird	12

HERD
65	Parlophone R 5284	Goodbye Baby, Goodbye/Here Comes The Fool	50
65	Parlophone R 5353	She Was Really Saying Something/It's Been A Long Time Baby	50
66	Parlophone R 5413	So Much In Love/This Boy's Always Been True	60
67	Fontana TF 819	I Can Fly/Diary Of A Narcissist	12
67	Fontana TF 856	From The Underworld/Sweet William	7
67	Fontana TF 887	Paradise Lost/Come On - Believe Me (in p/s)	20
67	Fontana TF 887	Paradise Lost/Come On - Believe Me	7
68	Fontana TF 925	I Don't Want Our Loving To Die/Our Fairy Tale	6
68	Fontana TF 975	Sunshine Cottage/Miss Jones	8
69	Fontana TF 1011	The Game/Beauty Queen	8
71	B&C CB 154	You've Got Me Hangin' From Your Lovin' Tree/I Don't Wanna Go To Sleep Again	6
72	Bumble GEX 1	From The Underworld/Paradise Lost/On My Way Home (maxi-single)	5
73	Bumble GE 120	I Don't Want Our Loving To Die/The Game	5
68	Fontana (S)TL 5458	PARADISE LOST (LP, flipback sleeve, black/silver labels)	35
72	Bumble GEMP 5001	NOSTALGIA (LP)	25

(see also Peter Frampton, Humble Pie, Judas Jump, Andy Bown, Preachers)

HERE & NOW
78	Charly CYS 1055	End Of The Beginning/Choke A Koala (p/s)	5
79	Charly CEP 122	A Dog In Hell/Floating Anarchy Radio (p/s)	5
80	Charly NOW 1	Give And Take	5
78	Deptford Fun City DLP 02	WHAT YOU SEE ... IS WHAT YOU ARE (LP, 1 side by Alternative TV)	12
83	Chick CHRL 003	FANTASY SHIFT (LP)	25

(see also Daevid Allen)

HERESY
85	Earache EAR 01	NEVER HEALED EP Flexii	20
89	In Your Face FACE 4	WHOSE GENERATION? EP (gatefold p/s)	8
87	Earache MOSH 2	HERESY/CONCRETE SOX (split LP)	15
88	In Your Face FACE 01	FACE UP TO IT! (LP)	15
89	In Your Face FACE 07	13 ROCKING ANTHEMS (LP)	15

HERESY/CONCRETE SOX
| 87 | Manic Ears MOSH 2 | HERESY/CONCRETE SOX (LP, 1 side each) | 15 |

HERETIC
| 84 | Thunderbolt THBE 1004 | BURNT AT THE STAKE EP (Water Of Vice/Keep On Telling Those Lies/ Fever Of Love/Watch Me Grow (12", p/s) | 25 |

HERITAGE
81	Rondelet ROUND 8	Strange Place To Be/Misunderstood (p/s)	20
82	Rondelet ABOUT 12	REMORSE CODE (LP, with lyric insert)	35
82	Plant Life PLR 040	LIVING BY THE AIR (LP)	15

HERMAN (CHIN-LOY)
71	Big Shot BI 573	El Fishy/HERMAN'S ALLSTARS: Nightmare (B-side actually "In The Spirit" by Lloyd Charmers)	12
71	Big Shot BI 577	Tar Baby (actually "Crazy Baby" by U. Roy Jr.)/TOMMY McCOOK: Archie	7
71	Big Shot BI 578	New Love/AUGUSTUS PABLO: The Mood	7
71	Big Shot BI 579	East Of The River Nile Version/AUGUSTO PABLO: East Of The River Nile	40
71	Duke DU 107	To The Fields/HERMAN'S VERSION MEN: Fields Version	18
71	Ackee ACK 133	Dunce Cap/AQUARIANS: Version Cap	8
71	Ackee ACK 140	Youth Man/AQUARIANS: Version	8
71	Explosion EX 2049	Love Brother/Uganda	6

MINT VALUE £

71	Escort ERT 854	Love Brother/Love Brother Version (B-side actually by Tommy McCook)......7
71	Punch PH 55	Hold The Ghost/AQUARIUS SOUL BAND: Duppy Dance......15
71	Punch PH 58	Listen To The Beat/AQUARIANS: Sounds Only......7

(see also Jimbilin)

PRIEST HERMAN
| 64 | Blue Beat BB 266 | We Are Praying/BUSTER'S ALLSTARS: Dallas, Texas......40 |

WOODY HERMAN
54	London HL 8013	Wooftie/Moten Stomp (as Woody Herman & New Third Herd)......20
54	London HL 8031	Fancy Woman/Eight Babies To Mind (as Woody Herman's Woodchoppers)......20
54	Capitol CL 14183	Muskrat Ramble/Woodchopper's Mambo (Woody Herman & His Orchestra)......12
55	London HL 8122	Sorry 'Bout The Whole Darned Thing/Love's A Dog (with New Third Herd)......15
66	CBS 202522	Sidewinder/Greasy Sack Blues......30
69	Chess CRS 8095	Hush/Light My Fire......10

(see also David Rose Orchestra)

HERMAN'S HERMITS
64	Columbia DB 7338	I'm Into Something Good/Your Hand In Mine......5
64	Columbia DB 7408	Show Me Girl/I Know Why......5
65	Columbia DB 7475	Silhouettes/Can't You Hear My Heartbeat?......5
65	Columbia DB 7546	Wonderful World/Dream On......5
65	Columbia DB 7670	Just A Little Bit Better/Take Love, Give Love......5
65	Columbia DB 7791	A Must To Avoid/The Man With The Cigar......5
66	Columbia DB 7861	You Won't Be Leaving/Listen People......7
66	Columbia DB 7947	This Door Swings Both Ways/For Love......7
66	Columbia DB 8012	No Milk Today/My Reservation's Been Confirmed......6
66	Columbia DB 8076	East-West/What Is Wrong, What Is Right?......8
67	Columbia DB 8123	There's A Kind Of Hush (All Over The World)/Gaslite Street......5
67	Columbia DB 8235	Museum/Moonshine Man......6
68	Columbia DB 8327	I Can Take Or Leave Your Loving/Marcel's......5
68	Columbia DB 8404	Sleepy Joe/Just One Girl......5
68	Columbia DB 8446	Sunshine Girl/Nobody Needs To Know......5
68	Columbia DB 8504	Something's Happening/The Most Beautiful Thing In My Life......5
69	Columbia DB 8563	My Sentimental Friend/My Lady......5
68	EMI SLES 15	No Milk Today/There's A Kind Of Hush (promo only, white label)......10
68	EMI SLES 16	London Look (promo only, white label)......8
69	Columbia DB 8626	Here Comes The Star/It's Alright Now......8
70	Columbia DB 8656	Years May Come, Years May Go/Smile Please......5
71	RCA RCA 2135	She's A Lady/Gold Mandala (Listed as HERMITS on 7")......6
72	RCA RCA 2265	The Man/Effen Curly......6
74	Buddah BDS 700	Train/Ride On The Water (withdrawn)......30
65	Columbia SEG 8380	HERMANIA (EP)......15
65	Columbia SEG 8440	MRS BROWN YOU'VE GOT A LOVELY DAUGHTER (EP)......12
65	Columbia SEG 8442	HERMAN'S HERMITS HITS (EP)......10
66	Columbia SEG 8477	A MUST TO AVOID (EP)......12
66	Columbia SEG 8503	MUSIC FROM THE SOUNDTRACK "HOLD ON" (EP)......15
67	Columbia SEG 8520	DANDY (EP)......15
65	Columbia 33SX 1727	HERMAN'S HERMITS (LP)......25
65	Columbia SX 6303	MRS BROWN YOU'VE GOT A LOVELY DAUGHTER (LP, soundtrack, mono, with manuscript).12
65	Columbia S(C)X 6303	MRS BROWN YOU'VE GOT A LOVELY DAUGHTER (LP, soundtrack, stereo, with manuscript).15
66	Columbia SX 6084	BOTH SIDES OF HERMAN'S HERMITS (LP)......20
67	Columbia S(C)X 6174	THERE'S A KIND OF HUSH ALL OVER THE WORLD (LP)......20
60s	Regal SREG 1117	HERMAN'S HERMITS (LP, export issue)......20
60s	Columbia SCXC 27	THE BEST OF HERMAN'S HERMITS (LP, export issue)......20
60s	Columbia SCXC 32	THE BEST OF HERMAN'S HERMITS VOL. 2 (LP, export issue)......20
60s	Columbia SCXC 34	THERE'S A KIND OF HUSH ALL OVER THE WORLD (LP, export issue)......25
60s	Columbia SCXC 35	BLAZE (LP, export issue)......25

(see also Peter Noone)

HERMITS
| 71 | RCA 2135 | She's A Lady (Say What You Want To Say)/Gold Mandela......6 |
| 75 | Private Stock PVT 19 | Ginny Go Softly/Long Haired Blue Eyed Boy......5 |

HEROES
| 75 | United Artists UP 36016 | Growing Up/Losing You......8 |

(see also Motors)

TED HEROLD
| 60 | Polydor NH 66817 | I Don't Know Why/Moonlight......15 |

HERON
70	Dawn DNS 1015	Take Me Back Home/Minstrel And A King......15
71	Dawn DNX 2509	Bye And Bye/Through Time/Only A Hobo/I'm Ready To Leave (p/s)......25
71	Dawn DNLS 3010	HERON (LP, with insert, some with "this album was recorded live in a field" sticker)......200
72	Dawn DNLS 3025	TWICE AS NICE & HALF THE PRICE (2-LP, with postcard)......200
72	Dawn DNLS 3025	TWICE AS NICE & HALF THE PRICE (2-LP, without postcard)......80

(see also Mike Cooper)

MIKE HERON('S REPUTATION)
71	Island WIP 6101	Call Me Diamond/Lady Wonder (p/s)......5
75	Neighbourhood NBH 3109	Evie/Down On My Knees After Memphis (as Mike Heron's Reputation)......5
78	Zoom ZUM 5	Sold On Your Love/Portland Rose (p/s)......5
71	Island ILPS 9146	SMILING MEN WITH BAD REPUTATIONS (LP, gatefold sleeve, pink rim, palm tree label)......30
75	Neighborhood 80637	MIKE HERON'S REPUTATION (LP)......15

(see also Incredible String Band)

BERNARD HERRMAN
69	Phase 4 Stereo PFS 4173	THE GREAT MOVIE THRILLERS (LP)......18
75	Phase 4 Stereo PFS 4309	THE FANTASY FILM WORLD OF BERNARD HERRMANN (LP)......18
76	Phase 4 Stereo PFS 4337	THE MYSTERIOUS FILM WORLD OF BERNARD HERRMANN (LP)......18

KRISTIN HERSH
| 94 | 4AD CADD 4002CD | HIPS & MAKERS (CD, digipak with postcards)......12 |

(see also Throwing Muses)

EVERIT HERTER
60	Capitol CL 15142	Don't Get Serious/Boys Were Made For Girls	10

PAT HERVEY & TIARAS & ART SNIDER
63	RCA 1332	Tears Of Misery/Brother, Can You Spare A Dime (as Pat Hervey)	7
67	President PT 110	Can't Get You Out Of My Mind/Givin' In	7

HERZFELD
93	Duophonic DS45 07	Two Mothers/Who The Scroungers Are (p/s, mail order only)	6

HESITATIONS
68	London HLR 10198	The Impossible Dream (The Quest)/Nobody Knows You When You're Down And Out	8
69	London HLR 10180	Born Free/Push A Little Bit Harder	20
68	London HA-R/SH-R 8360	THE NEW BORN FREE (LP)	20

CAROLYN HESTER
65	Dot DS 16750	Ain't That Rain?/Ten Thousand Candles	5
65	Dot DS 16751	Playboys And Playgirls/High Flyin' Bird	8
65	Dot DS 26750	Come On Back/Three Young Men	5
65	Dot DS 26751	What Does It Get You?/Now He's Gone	10
66	CBS 202409	A Reason To Believe/Early Morning Rain	5
65	Dot DLP 3604	THAT'S MY SONG (LP)	15
66	Dot DLP 3638	AT TOWN HALL (LP)	15
66	CBS (S)BPG 62033	CAROLYN HESTER (LP)	30
69	Pye Intl. NSPL 28121	THE CAROLYN HESTER COALITION (LP)	20
71	Ember CW 138	THURSDAY'S CHILD HAS FAR TO GO (LP)	12

(see also Four For Fun)

JOHN HETHERINGTON
70	RCA 1965	It's Only Me/Dreamboat Avenue	8

HEWETT SISTERS
59	HMV POP 567	Baby-O/Jerri-Lee (I Love Him So)	25
59	HMV POP 567	Baby-O/Jerri-Lee (I Love Him So) (78)	10

BEN HEWITT
59	Mercury AMT 1041	You Break Me Up/I Ain't Givin' Up Nothin'	50
59	Mercury AMT 1055	For Quite A While/Patricia June	35
59	Mercury AMT 1084	I Want A New Girl Now/My Search	50
60	Mercury ZEP 10035	BREAK IT UP WITH BEN HEWITT (EP)	200
84	Bear Family BFX 15150	THEY WOULD CALL ME ELVIS (LP, gatefold)	15

GARTH HEWITT
70s	Myrrh MYR 1051	LOVE SONGS FOR THE EARTH (LP)	30
70s	Myrrh MYR 1078	I'M GRATEFUL (LP)	30

RICHARD HEWSON ORCHESTRA
76	Splash CPLP 1002	LOVE IS (LP)	30

PETER HEWSON
83	Reset RES 2	Take My Hand/Her (p/s)	40
83	Reset REST 2	Take My Hand/Her (12", p/s)	60

HEX
93	Ninja Tune ZEN 05	SOUNDTRACK TO GLOBAL CHAOS (LP)	20
93	Ninja Tune ZEN 07	DIGITAL LOVE (LP)	20

HEXSTATIC
03	Ninja Tune ZEN 10 133	Telemetron (10", clear vinyl, promo)	15

EDDIE HEYWOOD
58	Mercury 7MT 131	Heywood's Bounce/Soft Summer Breeze	8
64	Stateside SS 264	Theme From The Film "The Prize"/Li'l Darlin'	6

(see also Hugo Winterhalter)

WINSTON HEYWOOD (& HOMBRES)
71	Dynamic DYN 424	Bam-Sa-Bo/Version	8
72	Dynamic DYN 441	Stop The War/Version	6
72	Dynamic DYN 457	Seek And You'll Find/Version	6
73	Attack ATT 8046	Da Doo Ron Ron/Version	6

(see also Winston Harewood, Fud Christian All Stars)

HI-LO'S
62	Reprise RS 20095	A Taste Of Honey/My Baby Just Cares For Me	5
57	London HA-U 2026	UNDER GLASS (LP)	15
58	Philips BBL 7154	SUDDENLY IT'S THE HI-LO'S (LP)	12
59	Philips BBL 7288	AND ALL THAT JAZZ (LP)	12

HI-NUMBERS
65	Decca F 12233	Heart Of Stone/Dancing In The Street	70

LENNIE HIBBERT & COUNT OSSIE BAND
69	Doctor Bird DB 1113	Pure Sole/PATSY: A Man Is Two Faced	120

(see also Sound Dimension)

AL HIBBLER
55	Brunswick 05420	Unchained Melody/Daybreak (gold label)	25
55	Brunswick 05420	Unchained Melody/Daybreak (silver label)	15
55	Brunswick 05454	They Say You're Laughing At Me/I Can't Put My Arms Around A Memory	8
55	London HL 8184	Now I Lay Me Down To Dream/Danny Boy	35
55	Brunswick 05492	He/Breeze (Blow My Baby Back To Me)	5
56	Brunswick 05523	The Eleventh Hour Melody/Let's Try Again	5
56	Brunswick 05552	After The Lights Go Down Low/Stella By Starlight	5
57	HMV 7EG 8326	AL HIBBLER SINGS LOVE SONGS (EP)	8

EDDIE HICKEY
59	Decca F 11153	Lady May/Cap And Gown	10
60	Decca F 11204	Who Could Be Bluer?/Plain Jane	10
60	Decca F 11241	Another Sleepless Night/Barbara	10

MINT VALUE £

ERSEL HICKEY
| 59 | Fontana H 198 | You Threw A Dart/Don't Be Afraid Of Love | 70 |
| 59 | Fontana H 198 | You Threw A Dart/Don't Be Afraid Of Love (78) | 20 |

DWAYNE HICKMAN
| 60 | Capitol CL 15164 | I'm A Lover, Not A Fighter/I Pass Your House | 10 |

HICKORY
| 68 | Lyntone 1928 | Scottish Magic (Promo flexi for Tartan Ale, p/s) | 20 |
| 69 | CBS 3963 | Green Light/Key | 30 |

(see also Equals)

HICKORY SIX
| 64 | Oak RGJ 149 | Feelin Blue/Hello My Darling | 80 |

COLIN HICKS (& CABIN BOYS)
57	Pye 7N 15114	Wild Eyes And Tender Lips/Empty Arms Blues (with Cabin Boys)	20
57	Pye 7N 15114	Wild Eyes And Tender Lips/Empty Arms Blues (with Cabin Boys) (78)	10
57	Pye 7N 15125	La Dee Dah/Wasteland	15
57	Pye 7N 15125	La Dee Dah/Wasteland (78)	10
58	Pye 7N 15163	Little Boy Blue/Jambalaya	15
58	Pye 7N 15163	Little Boy Blue/Jambalaya (78)	20

DAN HICKS & HIS HOT LICKS
| 72 | Blue Thumb ILPS 9204 | STRIKING IT RICH (LP) | 18 |

(see also Charlatans (U.S.)

JIMMY HICKS
| 72 | London HLU 10396 | I'm Mr. Big Stuff/Tell Her That I Love You | 15 |

HIDDEN CAMERAS
| 04 | Rough Trade RTRADST 117 | PLAY THE BBC SESSIONS EP (10", 2,000 only) | 8 |

HIDDEN IDENTITY
| 94 | Pure RudenessHIDBBB1 | Blunted Bumpkin Buskers (EP) | 35 |

(see also Evil Ed)

HIDDEN STRENGTH
| 76 | United Artists UAS 29949 | HIDDEN STRENGTH (LP) | 15 |

HIDEAWAYS
| 69 | Action ACT 4544 | Hide Out/Jolly Joe | 18 |
| 71 | Jay Boy BOY 29 | Hide Out/Jolly Joe (reissue) | 6 |

HI-FI
| 84 | Butt MGLS 003 | Louie Louie/Summertime | 8 |

(see also Ian Matthews)

HI-FI FOUR
| 56 | Parlophone MSP 6210 | Band Of Gold/Davy, You Upset My Life | 175 |
| 56 | Parlophone MSP 6210 | Band Of Gold/Davy, You Upset My Life (78) | 10 |

HI FI'S
63	Piccadilly 7N 35130	Take Me Or Leave Me/I'm Struck	8
64	Pye 7N 15635	Will Yer Won't Yer/She's The One	10
64	Pye 7N 15710	I Keep Forgettin'/Why Can't I Stop Loving You?	35
65	Pye 7N 15788	Baby's In Black/Kiss And Run	6
66	Alp 595 010	It's Gonna Be Morning/I Wanna Hear You Say Yeah	70

ALEX 'HURRICANE' HIGGINS
| 82 | Solid STOP 003 | One-Four-Seven/Life's In The Pocket (p/s) | 8 |

LIZZIE HIGGINS
| 75 | Topic 12TS 260 | UP AND AWA WI THE LAVEROCK (LP, gatefold sleeve) | 12 |

JOE HIGGS
67	Coxsone CS 7004	Neighbour Neighbour/MELODIANS: I Should Have Made It Up	80
67	Island WI 3026	I Am The Song/Worry No More	50
68	Island WI 3131	You Hurt My Soul/LYNN TAITT: Why Am I Treated So Bad?	100
70	Clandisc CLA 208	Mademoiselle/DYNAMITES: Lion	12
71	Big BG 312	Burning Fire/RUPIE EDWARDS ALL STARS: Version	6
71	New Beat NB 087	Mother Radio/DAWN SHARON: Little Deeds	6
71	Supreme SUP 215	Burning Fire/RUPIE EDWARDS ALL STARS: Push And Pull	6
72	Sioux SI 005	The World Is Spinning Around/THE REACTION: Hallelujah	6
72	Sioux SI 014	The Wave Of War/JUMBO STERLING: Shaft	6
72	Sioux SI 021	Lay A Foundation/JACKIE ROWLAND: Lay A Foundation (Version)	5
76	Ethnic Fight EF 038	Creation/AUGUSTUS PABLO & SUPER 8 CORPORATION: Creative Version	15
75	Grounation GROL 508	LIFE OF CONTRADICTION (LP)	45
78	1 STOP STOP 1002	UNITY IS POWER (LP)	15

(see also Higgs & Wilson, Bob Marley/Wailers, Soul Vendors)

(JOE) HIGGS & (ROY) WILSON
60	Blue Beat (B)B 3	Manny Oh/When You Tell Me Baby (yellow label/blue writing [B3] or blue label/silver writing [BB 3]) (with Ken Richards & His Comets)	20
61	Starlite ST45 035	Pretty Baby/I Long For The Day	20
61	Starlite ST45 036	Lover's Song/It Is A Day	20
61	Starlite ST45 042	Come On Home/The Robe	20
61	Starlite ST45 053	Sha Ba Ba/Change Of Mind	20
62	Blue Beat BB 95	How Can I Be Sure/Mighty Man	25
63	R&B JB 109	Let Me Know/Bye And Bye	15
63	Blue Beat BB 190	If You Want Pardon/BABA BROOKS BAND: Musical Communion	20
63	Island WI 081	Last Saturday Morning/Praise The Lord	20
64	Rio R 29	Love Is Not For Me/Gone Is Yesterday	15
65	Blue Beat BB 277	Pain In My Heart/BUSTER ALL STARS: Going West	25
70	Clandisc CLA 218	Don't Mind Me/GLEN AND ROY: Angel	8

(see also Clancy Eccles)

HIGH
| 69 | CBS 4164 | Long Live The High/Beggar Man Dan | 30 |

HIGH & MIGHTY
66	HMV POP 1548	Tryin' To Stop Cryin'/Escape From Cuba	35

HIGH AUTHORITY
91	Optimisim OPT 12005	I'm The Man (12")	15

HIGH BROOM
70	Island WI 6088	Dancing In The Moonlight/Percy's On The Run	15
73	Columbia DB 8969	Dancing In The Moonlight/Percy's On The Run (reissue)	7

(see also Leviathan, Mike Stuart Span, Jason Crest, Holy Mackerel)

HIGHBURY MARCHERS
72	Columbia DB 8930	The Official Arsenal March/Arsenal Boogie	8

HIGH KEYS
63	London HLK 9768	Que Sera Sera/Daddy, Ooh Long Legs	40

HIGH LEVEL RANTERS
68	Topic 12TS 186	NORTHUMBERLAND FOR EVER (LP, blue label, 2 different sleeves)	18
69	Leader/Trailer LER 2007	THE LADS OF NORTHUMBERLAND (LP)	18
70	Trailer LER 2020	KEEP YOUR FEET STILL GEORDIE HINNIE (LP)	12
71	Trailer LER 2030	HIGH LEVEL (LP)	12
75	Topic 2-12TS 271/2	THE BONNY PIT LADDIE (2-LP, blue label)	18
77	Broadside BRO 128	ENGLISH SPORTING BALLADS (LP, 1-side Martin Wyndham-Read, 2,000 only)	25
79	Topic 12TS 388	FOUR IN A BAR (LP)	12

HIGHLY LIKELY
74	BBC RESL 10	Whatever Happened To You? (Likely Lads Theme)/God Bless Everyone	10

(see also Mike Hugg, Rodney Bewes)

HIGH NUMBERS
64	Fontana TF 480	Zoot Suit/I'm The Face (textured labels with "Mono" on labels)	900
80	Back Door DOOR 4	I'm The Face/Zoot Suit (reissue, picture sleeve, silver plastic labels))	20
92	Fontana TF 480	I'm The Face/Zoot Suit (reissue, smooth labels with "stereo" on labels, die-cut sleeve from Fontana Box)	20

(see also Who)

HIGH SOCIETY (1)
66	Fontana TF 771	People Passing By/Star Of Eastern Street	22

(see also Friday Browne, Graham Gouldman, Country Gentlemen, Manchester Mob)

HIGH SOCIETY (2)
70	CBS 4746	Only You Only You/Tell Me Now	15

HIGH STREET EAST
69	Rubber RUBBER ONE	Newcastle Brown/Everybody Knows (p/s)	70
69	Rubber RUBBER ONE	Newcastle Brown/Everybody Knows (no p/s)	45

HIGH TIDE (1)
69	Liberty LBS 83264	SEA SHANTIES (LP, gatefold sleeve, blue label)	180
70	Liberty LBS 83294	HIGH TIDE (LP, blue label)	120

(see also Hawkwind, Misunderstood, Denny Gerrard, Magic Muscle, Third Ear Band)

HIGH TIDE (2)
81	Sunday Morning (No Cat. No.)	Baby Dancing/Letter From A Coward (mail-order only)	8

DEAN HIGHTOWER
60	HMV CLP 1360	TWANGY - WITH A BEAT (LP)	50

DONNA HIGHTOWER
60	Capitol ST 1273	GEE BABY (LP)	15

ROSETTA HIGHTOWER
68	Toast TT 506	Pretty Red Balloons/How Can You Mistreat (The One You Love)?	25
68	Toast TT 509	I Can't Give Back The Love I Feel For You/Big Bird	80
69	CBS 4584	One Heart For Sale/What Do I Do?	10
70	CBS 4758	April Fools/I'll Hold Out My Hand	6
70	CBS 4988	Persuader/Come Together	6
71	CBS 7068	Go Pray For Tomorrow/Give Me Just A Little More Line	6
73	Philips 6006 291	The Walls Fell Down/Captain's Army	6
71	CBS 64201	HIGHTOWER (LP)	40
71	Rediffusion ZS 88	ROSETTA HIGHTOWER (LP)	15

(see also Orlons, Ian Green [Revelation])

HIGH TREASON
80	Burlington BURLS 001	Saturday Night Special/Waste My Love (p/s)	140
80	Burlington BURLS 001	Saturday Night Special/Waste My Love (no p/s)	80

HIGHWAY
74	EMI EMC 3019	HIGHWAY (LP)	15
75	EMI EMA 770	SMOKING AT THE EDGE (LP, gatefold sleeve)	18

HIGHWAYMEN
62	United Artists UP 1001	Birdman (with narration from Burt Lancaster)/Cindy Oh Cindy	5
64	United Artists ULP 1083	HOMECOMING (LP)	12

HIGH WINDOWS
68	CBS 3208	Maybe Someday/Your Eyes	10
68	CBS 3437	Anybody Need A Lover/El El Israel	8

HIGSONS
82	Two Tone CHSTT21	Tear The Whole Thing Down/Ylang Ylang (p/s, paper labels)	10
82	Two Tone CHSTT121	Tear The Whole Thing Down/Ylang Ylang (12", p/s)	12
83	Two Tone CHSTT24	Run Me Down/Put The Punk Back Into Funk (p/s, paper labels)	10
83	Two Tone CHSTT 1224	Run Me Down (extended)/Instrumental/Put The Punk Back Into Funk (1 & 2) (12", p/s)	12
82	Two Tone CHS TT 1	The Whole Thing Down/Ylang Ylang (12" promo shared with Apollinaires)	35
81	Waap 1 WAAPLP	ATTACK OF THE CANNIBAL ZOMBIE B MEN (LP)	12

(see also New York New York, Serious Drinking)

HIJACK
88	Music Of Life NOTE016	Style Wars (12")	10
88	Syndicate 655517 6	The Badman is Robbin'/Hold No Hostage/Doomsday (12" EP)	8
88	Music Of Life NOTE021	Hold No Hostage/Doomsday Of Rap (12")	8
89	Music Of Life NOTE016R	Style Wars Revenge (12")	8
91	Rhyme Syndicate 6555176	HORNS OF JERICHO (LP)	35
96	Reservoir RES 18	THE ORIGINAL HORNS OF JERICHO (LP)	80

HILARY HILARY
| 80 | Modern STP 2 | How Come You're So Dumb/Rich Kid Blues (p/s) | 60 |

(see also Roger Taylor, Queen)

RAY HILDEBRAND
| 70s | Myrrh MST 6508 | SPECIAL KIND OF MAN (LP) | 20 |

DIANE HILDEBRANDE
| 69 | Elektra EKSN 45055 | Jan's Blues/Early Morning Blues And Greens | 10 |
| 69 | Elektra EKL 4031 | EARLY MORNING BLUES AND GREENS (LP) | 20 |

HI-LITERS
| 58 | Mercury AMT 1011 | Dance Me To Death/Cha Cha Rock | 150 |
| 58 | Mercury AMT 1011 | Dance Me To Death/Cha Cha Rock (78) | 75 |

HI LITES
| 65 | London HL 9967 | Hey Baby/Groovey | 20 |

ALEX HILL
| 53 | Vocalion V 1027 | Stompin' 'Em Down/Track Head Blues (78) | 18 |

(see also Paramount Allstars)

BENNY HILL
55	Decca F 10442	I Can't Tell A Waltz From A Tango/Teach Me Tonight	10
56	Columbia SCM 5238	Memories Are Made Of This/Who Done It? (as Benny Hill & Coronets)	10
61	Pye 7N 15327	Gather In The Mushrooms/Pepys' Diary	6
61	Pye 7N 15359	Transistor Radio/Gypsy Rock	6
62	Pye 7N 15520	Harvest Of Love/bamba 3688	5
65	Pye 7N 15974	What A World/I'll Never Know	6
66	Pye 7N 17026	My Garden Of Love/The Andalucian Gypsies	5
92	EMI ERNPD 1	Ernie/Ting A Ling A Loo (shaped picture disc)	5

(see also Coronets)

BUNKER HILL & RAYMEN
| 62 | Stateside SS 135 | Hide & Go Seek Parts 1 & 2 | 25 |

CHIPPIE HILL/HOCIEL THOMAS
| 72 | Collectors Edition 1001 | CHIPPIE HILL AND HOCIEL THOMAS (LP) | 12 |

DAVID HILL
57	Vogue V 9076	All Shook Up/Melody For Lovers (with Ray Ellis Orchestra, probably unreleased)	200
57	Vogue V 9076	All Shook Up/Melody For Lovers (78, with Ray Ellis Orchestra)	70
58	RCA RCA 1041	That's Love/Keep Me In Mind (with Joe Relsman's Orchestra & Chorus)	175
58	RCA RCA 1041	That's Love/Keep Me In Mind (78, with Joe Relsman's Orchestra & Chorus)	70

JESSIE HILL
| 60 | London HLU 9117 | Ooh Poo Pah Doo Parts 1 & 2 | 25 |

MICHAEL HILL
60	Parlophone R 4700	Joey's Song/Juke's Jingle	5
60	Parlophone R 4700	Beatnik Boogie/Mike's Tune	5
61	Parlophone R 4727	Glory Rock/Blue On Blue	5

RONNI HILL
| 77 | Creole CR 138 | You Keep Me Hanging On/I Wouldn't Give You Up (as Roni Hill) | 10 |

VINCE HILL
62	Piccadilly 7N 35043	The Rivers Run Dry/Not Any More	8
62	Piccadilly 7N 35068	There You Go/Just As Long As (You Belong To Me)	5
63	Piccadilly 7N 35108	A Day At The Seaside/Tricks Of The Trade	8
63	Piccadilly 7N 35118	As It Was Written/Is There Anyone At Home	5
63	Piccadilly 7N 35148	Blue Velvet/Like Anything	5
64	Piccadilly 7N 35161	If You Knew/Fools & Lovers	5
64	Piccadilly 7N 35192	It's Only Make Believe/Let The Wind Blow	5
65	Columbia DB 7781	Take Me To Your Heart Again/Push Push	6
66	Columbia SEG 8509	FOUR SIDES OF VINCE HILL (EP)	10

(see also [Jackie &] Raindrops, Elmer Bernstein)

Z.Z. HILL
65	R&B MRB 5005	Someone To Love Me/Have Mercy Someone	30
69	Action ACT 4532	Make Me Yours/What Am I Living For?	75
71	Mojo 2092 019	Faithful And True/I Think I'd Do It	8
75	United Artists UP 35727	I Keep On Loving You/Whoever's Thrilling You	8
77	CBS 5553	Love Is So Good When You're Stealin' It/Need You By My Side	8
66	Sue IEP 711	GIMME GIMME (EP, 2 tracks each by Z.Z. Hill & Intentions; in p/s)	300
66	Sue IEP 711	GIMME GIMME (EP, 2 tracks each by Z.Z. Hill & Intentions)	100
69	Action ACLP 6004	WHOLE LOT OF SOUL (LP)	60
72	Mojo 2916 013	THE BRAND NEW Z.Z. HILL (LP)	20
75	Contempo CLP 515	THE BRAND NEW Z.Z. HILL (LP, reissue)	15

(see also Intentions)

STEVE HILLAGE
76	Virgin VS 161	It's All Too Much/Shimmer	10
77	Virgin VS 171	Hurdy Gurdy Man/Om Nama Shivaya	5
77	Virgin VS 197	Not Fade Away/Saucer Surfing	5
77	Virgin VDJ 23	Leylines To Glassdome/GLEN PHILLIPS: Lies (p/s, gig freebie)	6
78	Virgin VS 212	Getting Better/Palm Trees (Love Guitar) (in p/s)	8
78	Virgin VS 212	Getting Better/Palm Trees (Love Guitar)	5
78	Virgin VDJ 25	Getting Better/Palm Trees (Love Guitar) (12", p/s)	12
79	Virgin SIXPACK 2	SIX PACK/SIX TRACK (EP, picture disc, 5,000 only, die-cut p/s with stand)	10

79	Virgin VS 313	Don't Dither, Do It/Getting In Tune (p/s) 6
82	Virgin VS 551	Alone (p/s)...6
82	Virgin VS 574	Kamikaze Eyes (p/s) 10
75	Virgin V 2031	FISH RISING (LP, lyric insert, coloured 'twin' label) 20
77	Virgin VGD 3501	LIVE HERALD (2-LP, with limited edition mail order lyric sheet in English, French or German)..30
78	Virgin V 2098	GREEN (LP, green vinyl, with insert)..15
79	Virgin VR1	RAINBOW DOME MUSIC (LP, clear vinyl, stickered sleeve)..............................15
83	Virgin V 2244	FOR TO NEXT (LP, stickered, with bonus instrumental LP "And Not Or" OVED 8)............12

(see also Gong, Khan, Arzachel, Clearlight, Radio Actors, System 7)

HILLER BROTHERS

60s	Honey Hit TB 124	Little Darlin'/Changin' My Mind (with p/s) 10
60s	Honey Hit TB 124	Little Darlin'/Changin' My Mind 6

JANE HILLERY

66	Columbia DB 7918	You've Got That Hold On Me/Take Me Away 40

(see also Magistrates)

MABLE HILLERY

69	Xtra XTRA 1063	IT'S SO HARD TO BE A NIGGER (LP)...30

GILLIAN HILLS

65	Vogue VRS 7005	Tomorrow Is Another Day/Look At Them 10

HILLTOPPERS

52	Vogue V 9045	Trying/You Made Up My Mind (featuring Jimmy Sacca) (78) 10
53	London L 1204	P.S. I Love You/I'd Rather Die Young (78) 10
54	London HL 8003	Love Walked In/To Be Alone (78) 15
54	London HL 8026	From The Vine Came The Grape/Time Will Tell..40
54	London HL 8070	Poor Butterfly/Wrapped Up In A Dream...40
54	London HL 8081	Will You Remember?/The Old Cabaret..40
54	London HL 8092	If I Didn't Care/Bettina...40
55	London HL 8116	Time Waits For No One/You Try Somebody Else..40
55	London HLD 8168	The Kentuckian Song/I Must Be Dreaming 30
55	London HLD 8208	Searching/All I Need Is You 50
56	London HLD 8221	Only You (And You Alone)/(It Will Have To Do) Until The Real Thing Comes Along (gold label lettering)...40
56	London HLD 8221	Only You (And You Alone)/(It Will Have To Do) Until The Real Thing Comes Along (silver label lettering)..20
56	London HLD 8255	My Treasure/Last Word In Love...50
56	London HLD 8278	Do The Bop/When You're Alone...100
56	London HLD 8278	Do The Bop/When You're Alone (78)..30
56	London HLD 8298	Tryin'/D-A-R-L-I-N' 30
56	London HLD 8333	So Tired/Faded Rose 30
57	London HLD 8381	Marianne/You're Wasting Your Time 20
57	London HLD 8441	I'm Serious/I Love My Girl 25
57	London HLD 8455	A Fallen Star/Footsteps...25
57	London HLD 8528	The Joker/Chicken, Chicken...40
58	London HLD 8603	You Sure Look Good To Me/Starry Eyes...20
60	London HLD 9038	Alone/The Prisoner's Song 15
55	London RE-P 1012	PRESENTING THE HILLTOPPERS 30
55	London RE-D 1030	THE HILLTOPPERS VOL. 2 30
57	London RE-D 1099	THE HILLTOPPERS VOL. 3 30
57	London HA-D 2029	THE TOWERING HILLTOPPERS..50
57	London HA-D 2071	TOPS IN POPS 40

(see also Sacca, Billy Vaughn)

NICKY HILTON

65	Decca F 12099	Give Us Your Blessing/Always In My Heart 6

RONNIE HILTON

55	HMV 7M 285	Prize Of Gold/A Blossom Fell..15
55	HMV 7M 303	Just Say You Love Her/My Loving Hands...10
56	HMV 7M 336	Bella Notte/He..10
56	HMV 7M 358	Young And Foolish/Moments To Remember 10
56	HMV 7M 382	The Last Frontier/Here Comes My Love..6
56	HMV 7M 390	No Other Love/It's All Been Done Before (B-side with Alma Cogan)..................15
56	HMV 7M 413	Who Are We/Give Me My Ranch 6
56	HMV POP 248	A Woman In Love/I Just Found Out About Love..6
56	HMV POP 274	Two Different Worlds/Constant And True...6
57	HMV POP 291	The Wisdom Of A Fool/Amore 6
57	HMV POP 307	For Your Love/Once 6
67	HMV POP 1600	If I Were A Rich Man/Laughing Gnome (Bowie penned B-side).........................40
55	HMV DLP 1109	BY THE FIRESIDE (10" LP)..15
59	HMV CLP 1295	I'M BEGINNING TO SEE THE LIGHT (LP)...15

(see also Alma Cogan)

HILTONAIRES

67	Coxsone CSL 8004	THE BEST OF THE HILTONAIRES (LP)..70

HIM & THE OTHERS

66	Parlophone R 5510	I Mean It/She's Got Eyes That Tell Lies 850

JUSTIN HINDS/HINES (& DOMINOES)

64	Ska Beat JB 176	King Samuel/River Jordan 25
65	Ska Beat JB 187	Mother Banner/DON DRUMMOND & HIS GROUP: Apanga 55
65	Island WI 171	Botheration/Satan (as Justin Hines & Dominoes) 30
65	Island WI 174	Jump Out Of The Frying Pan/Holy Dove (as Justin Hines & Dominoes) 30
65	Island WI 194	Rub Up, Push Up/The Ark 25
65	Island WI 232	Turn Them Back/TOMMY McCOOK: Rocket Ship 60
65	Island WI 236	Peace And Love/Skalarama (B-side actually by Lyn Taitt & Comets) 40
66	Doctor Bird DB 1048	The Higher The Monkey Climbs/Fight For Your Right 30
67	Island WI 3048	On A Saturday Night/Save A Bread 22
67	Treasure Isle TI 7002	Here I Stand/No Good Rudie 20
67	Treasure Isle TI 7005	Carry Go Bring Come/Fight Too Much 30

MINT VALUE £

67	Treasure Isle TI 7014	On A Saturday Night/Save A Bread 20
67	Treasure Isle TI 7017	Once A Man/TOMMY McCOOK & SUPERSONICS: Persian Cat....................20
68	Treasure Isle TI 7063	Botheration/VINCENT HINDS: Mouth Trombone 15
68	Treasure Isle TI 7068	Mighty Redeemer (Parts 1 & 2) 15
69	Trojan TR 652	You Should've Known Better/TOMMY McCOOK & SUPERSONICS: Third Figure...............12
70	Duke Reid DR 2511	Say Me Say/I Want It 8
70	Duke DU 67	Drink Milk/Everywhere I Go (as Justin Hines & Dominoes) 8
72	Treasure Isle TI 7068	Mighty Redeemer/DUKE REID'S ALL STARS: Version 12
75	Pama PM 4001	Sinners Where You Going To Hide?/If It's Love You Need 8
76	Island ILPS 9416	JEZEBEL (LP) 30

(see also Lyn Taitt, Skatalites, Don Drummond)

NEVILLE HINDS
70	Duke Reid DR 2503	Sunday Gravy (as Neville Hines)/JOHN HOLT: Write Her A Letter 20
70	Camel CA 44	London Bridge/SCORCHERS: Things And Time (B-side act. by Wailing Souls) 20
70	Gas GAS 126	I Who Have Nothing/You Send Me 8
71	Explosion EX 2043	Delivered/Specially For You (B-side actually by Blake Boy) 6
72	Upsetter US 384	Blackman's Time/UPSETTERS: Version 10
73	Harry J HJ 6657	Musical Splendour/JOHN CROW GENERATION: Musical Drum & Bass 6

(see also Neville Irons & Byron Lee & The Dragonaires, Lloyd Robinson, Marvels, Alton Ellis)

RUPERT HINE
72	Purple PUR 105	Hamburgers/A Varlet Lad T'was Samuel Green (Historical Moments - Part 7) 6
76	Electric WOT 8	Snakes Don't Dance Fast/Hopi Smile 6
71	Purple TPSA 7502	PICK UP A BONE (LP, with David MacIver, textured gatefold sleeve) 35
73	Purple TPSA 7509	UNFINISHED PICTURE (LP, gatefold sleeve) 60

(see also Jon Pertwee, Quantum Jump)

EARL 'FATHA' HINES
54	Mercury MG 25018	EARL HINES AND HIS ALL STARS (10" LP) 12
55	Vogue Coral LRA 10031	FATS WALLER SONGS (10" LP) 12
55	Columbia 33S 1063	PIANO MOODS (10" LP) 12
56	HMV DLP 1132	GRAND TERRACE SWING (10" LP) 12

(see also Louis Armstrong)

FRAZER HINES
| 68 | Major Minor MM 579 | Who's Dr. Who?/Punch And Judy Man ....60 |

HINES, HINES & DAD
| 68 | CBS 3667 | Something Extra/Hambone ....5 |

SONNY HINES
| 65 | King KG 1009 | Anytime, Any Day, Anywhere/Nothing Like Your Love ....15 |

HINES & ELDRIDGE
| 69 | Mercury SMWL 21041 | HINES AND ELDRIDGE WITH COLEMAN HAWKINS VOLUME 2 (LP) ....12 |

(see also Coleman Hawkins, Earl Hines, Roy Eldridge)

HINGE
| 68 | RCA RCA 1721 | The Village Postman/You'd Better Go Home ....10 |

CLIVE HINTON
| 68 | President PT231 | HOW COULD I EVER LEAVE (EP) ....12 |

JOE HINTON
64	Vocalion VP 9224	Funny How Time Slips Away/You Gotta Have Love 30
66	Vocalion VP 9258	Just A Kid Named Joe/Pledging My Love 15
66	Vocalion VA-P 8043	FUNNY HOW TIME SLIPS AWAY (LP) 120

HIPPIES
| 63 | Cameo Parkway P 863 | Memory Lane/REGGIE HARRISON: A Lonely Piano ....20 |

HIPPOLYTES
| 77 | Top Deck TD 003 | Don;t Make The Promises/I Love Sue ....7 |

HIPPY BOYS
69	Trojan TR 668	Love/The Whole Family 15
69	Trojan TR 669	Michael Row The Boat Ashore/Who Is Coming To Dinner 20
69	Bullet BU 412	Hog In A Me Minte/Lorna Run 25
69	Bullet BU 413	What's Your Excuse?/Tell Me Tell 15
69	Camel CA 29	Cat Nip/Cooyah (both as Hippie Boys) 20
69	High Note HS 021	Doctor No Go/Sailing (B-side actually "Faberge" by Baba Brooks & Band)............18
69	High Note HS 030	Chicken Lickin'/BABA BROOKS: Old Man Flint 12
69	High Note HS 035	Reggae Pressure/SOUL RHYTHMS: It Hurts (B-side actually Soul Rhythms)..........15
69	Unity UN 528	Dreams To Remember/Peace Maker 50
70	High Note HS 038	Piccadilly Hop/Nigeria 40
70	Duke DU 92	Cloud Burst/LLOYD CHARMERS: Message From A Black Man 30
70	Explosion EX 2032	Vengeance/Look-Ea-Py-Py 30
71	Big Shot 580	Voodoo/LITTLE ROY: Hard Fighter 10
69	Big Shot BSLP 5005	REGGAE WITH THE HIPPY BOYS (LP, actually on High Note label)................60
11	Sunspot LP 003	REGGAE WITH THE HIPPY BOYS, (LP reissue, 350 only, signed insert)............30

(see also Upsetters, Family Man, Danny Williams, Tony, Hippy Boys, Cynthia Richards, Pioneers)

HIPSTER IMAGE
| 65 | Decca F 12137 | Can't Let Her Go/Make Her Mine ....500 |

(see also Climax Chicago Blues Band)

HIRSCHE NICHT AUFS SOFA
| 86 | United Dairies UD 018 | MELCHIOR (LP, with Insert) ....30 |

AL HIRT
| 63 | RCA 1380 | Java/I Can't Get Started ....6 |
| 67 | RCA RCA 1590 | Theme From "The Monkees"/Tarzan March ....5 |

(see also Ann-Margret)

HI-SPOTS
| 58 | Melodisc 1457 | Lend Me Your Comb/I Don't Hurt Anymore ....22 |
| 58 | Melodisc 1473 | Secretly/I Got ....22 |

58	Melodisc 1473	Secretly/I Got (78)	10

ALFRED HITCHCOCK

58	London HA-P 2130	MUSIC TO BE MURDERED BY (LP, music by Jeff Alexander Orchestra, mono)	40
58	London SH-P 6012	MUSIC TO BE MURDERED BY (LP, music by Jeff Alexander Orchestra, stereo)	50
60	Wonderland LP 89	ALFRED HITCHCOCK PRESENTS GHOST STORIES FOR YOUNG PEOPLE (LP, read by Peter Allen)	30

(see Jeff Alexander)

ROBYN HITCHCOCK (& THE EGYPTIANS)

81	Armageddon AS 008	The Man Who Invented Himself/Dancing On God's Thumb (p/s, some with flexidisc "It's A Mystic Trip"/"Grooving On An Inner Plane" [4 SPURT 1])	8
81	Armageddon AS 008	The Man Who Invented Himself/Dancing On God's Thumb (p/s, some without flexidisc "It's A Mystic Trip"/"Grooving On An Inner Plane" [4 SPURT 1])	6
82	Albion ION 103	America/It Was The Night/How Do You Work This Thing? (p/s)	8
82	Midnight Music DING 2	Eaten By Her Own Dinner/Listening To The Higsons/Dr. Sticky (p/s)	7
82	Midnight Music DONG 2	Eaten By Her Own Dinner/Grooving On An Inner Plane/Messages Of The Dark The Abandoned Brain/Happy The Golden Prince (12", p/s)	10
84	Midnight Music DONG 8	The Bells Of Rhymney/Falling Leaves/Winter Love/ The Bones In The Ground (12", p/s)	8
85	Midnight Music DONG 12	Heaven/Dwarfbeat/Some Body (12", p/s)	8
85	Midnight Music DONG 17	Brenda's Iron Sledge (live)/Only The Stones Remain/The Pit Of Souls (Part I-IV) (12", p/s)	8
83	Albion 12 ION 1036	Nightride To Trinidad (Long Version)/Kingdom Of Love/Midnight Fish (12", p/s)	10
86	Glass Fish OOZE 1	If You Were A Priest/The Crawling (p/s)	5
84	Bucketfull/Brains BOB 8	Happy The Golden Prince (hard vinyl white label test pressing, 20 only)	30
81	Armageddon ARM 4	BLACK SNAKE DIAMOND RôLE (LP)	12

(see also Soft Boys, Knox)

HI-TENSION

77	Island IPR 2007	Hi-Tension/Girl I Bet Cha (12")	8
79	Island WIP 6493	There's A Reason/If It Moves You	5
79	Island 12 WIP 6493	There's A Reason/If It Moves You (12")	20
78	Island ILPS 9564	HI-TENSION (LP, with poster)	15

HI-TONES

62	Island WI 029	Going Steady/Darlin' Elaine	25
62	Wasp W 004	I'm In Love With You/Singing A Song	30
63	Island WI 086	Ten Virgins (actually by Angelic Brothers)/Too Young To Love (actually by Larry Marshall)	25
63	R&B JB 123	You Hold The Key/DON DRUMMOND: Rock Away	50

HIT PACK

65	Tamla Motown TMG 513	Never Say No To Your Baby/Let's Dance	140
65	Tamla Motown TMG 513	Never Say No To Your Baby/Let's Dance (DJ copy)	175

HIT PARADE (1)

84	JSH JSH 1	Forever/Stop (die-cut p/s)	10
84	JSH JSH 2	My Favourite Girl/It Rained On Monday Morning (die-cut p/s)	10
85	JSH JSH 3	The Sun Shines In Gerrards Cross/You Hurt Me Too (die-cut p/s)	10
85	JSH JSH 4	You Don't Love Me Then/Huevo's Mexicana (die-cut p/s with card)	10
86	JSH JSH 5	See You In Havana/Wipe Away The Tears (die-cut p/s)	10
87	JSH JSH 6	I Get So Sentimental/Sue (die-cut p/s)	10
90	Sarah SARAH 90	Autobiography/The Dispossessed/Now The Holiday's Over (p/s, insert)	20
91	Sarah SARAH 58	In Gunnersbury Park/Harvey (ps, insert)	12

HIT PARADE (2)

82	Crass 221984/12	BAD NEWS (EP)	25
84	Crass 1984/2	PLASTIC CULTURE : Product of The Troubles/Media Son (12")	18
86	Crass No 9	NICK NACK PADDY WHACK (LP, with lyric inner)	25

HIT SQUAD

88	Eastern Bloc EASTERN 01	Wax On The Melt/SPM MC Tunes/Shure.4 (12", white label promo only, plain stickered sleeve)	30

(see also 808 State)

HITTERS

73	United Artists UP 35530	Hypocrite/The Version	22

(see also Brinsley Schwarz)

HMC

93	New Electronica ELEC 03P	Science Funktion (12", promo)	30

HOAX

80	Hologram HOAX 1	ONLY THE BLIND CAN SEE IN THE DARK (EP, 2000 only)	30
81	Hologramme HOAX 6	BLIND PANIC EP (p/s, 2000 only)	15
81	Hologram HOAX 3	SO WHAT (12" EP, p/s, blue vinyl, 2000 only)	15
82	Hologram HOAX 4	QUIET IN THE SIXPENNY'S (p/s, 2000 only)	15

HOBBIES OF TODAY

85	Rune CAST 02/LYN 16721/2	In My Minds Eye/You (Company sleeve)	15

HOBBIT

72	Satril SAT 7	Only Friends/Everything's Turning Out Fine	10
71	Deroy	FIRST AND LAST (LP, private pressing)	80

HOBBITS

68	Decca AD 1004	Daffodil Days (The Affection Song)/Sunny Day Girl (export issue)	20
68	MCA MU 1002	Daffodil Days (The Affection Song)/Sunny Day Girl	8
67	MCA MUP 301	DOWN TO MIDDLE EARTH (LP)	35

HOBBS

78	Big SOLD 4	Bop Around The Shop/(You've Got Me In A) Whirl Girl (gatefold p/s & insert)	6

HOBBY HORSE

72	Bell BELL 1248	Summertime, Summertime/Sweet And Low	12

(see also Mary Hopkin)

HOBBY SHOP

68	Columbia DB 8395	Why Must It Be This Way?/Talk To Me	10

(see also Danny Storm)

MINT VALUE £

LES HOBEAUX
57	HMV POP 377	Oh, Mary Don't You Weep/Toll The Bell Easy	10
57	HMV POP 377	Oh, Mary Don't You Weep/Toll The Bell Easy (78)	10
57	HMV POP 403	Mama Don't Allow/Hey, Hey, Daddy Blues	15
57	HMV POP 403	Mama Don't Allow/Hey, Hey, Daddy Blues (78)	10
58	HMV POP 444	Dynamo/Two Ships	15
58	HMV POP 444	Dynamo/Two Ships (78)	15
57	HMV 7EG 8297	SOHO SKIFFLE (EP)	50

HOBNAIL
72	Bell Bell 1250	She's Just A Friend Of Mine/Boy Scout Jambouree	12

HOBO
76	United Artists UAS 29809	HOBO (LP)	15

HOBOKEN
73	Oak	HOBOKEN (LP, 6 copies only)	450

TREVOR HOCKEY
70s	Beau Brummie TET 120ST	Happy 'Cos I'm Blue/THE BLUES PLAYERS: Keep Right On To The End Of The Road (p/s)	40

EDMUND HOCKRIDGE
53	Parlophone MSP 6027	Luck Be A Lady/I'll Know	5
53	Parlophone MSP 6028	I've Never Been In Love Before/My Time Of Day	5

(see also Joan Regan)

CHRIS HODGE
72	Apple APPLE 43	We're On Our Way/Supersoul (in p/s)	30
72	Apple APPLE 43	We're On Our Way/Supersoul	20
74	RCA LPBO 5007	Beautiful Love/Sweet Lady From The Sky	6
74	DJM DJS 10337	I Love You/Old James Dean	5

MARVA HODGE
70	Polydor 56792	The Ghetto/Sometimes	8

CHARLES HODGES
69	Major Minor MM 654	Try A Little Love/Someone To Love	20

(see also Outlaws, Cliff Bennett's Rebellion)

EDDIE HODGES
61	London HLA 9369	I'm Gonna Knock On Your Door/Ain't Gonna Wash For A Week	12
62	London HLA 9505	Bandit Of My Dreams/Mugmates	15
62	London HLA 9576	(Girls, Girls, Girls) Made To Love/I Make Believe It's You	10
63	MGM MGM 1232	Just A Kid In Love/Avalanche	10
65	Stateside SS 442	New Orleans/Hard Times For Young Lovers	10
65	Stateside SS 469	Love Minus Zero - No Limit/The Water Is Over My Head	10
62	London REA 1353	EDDIE HODGES (EP)	40

(see also Hayley Mills & Eddie Hodges)

JOHNNY HODGES & HIS ORCHESTRA
52	Vogue LD 011	JOHNNY HODGES (10" LP)	15
56	Columbia/Clef C 9051	IN A TENDER MOOD (10"LP)	12
57	Columbia EC CLEF 10098	ELLINGTON ALL STARS (LP)	12

INGFRIED HOFFMAN
67	Polydor 583 015	SOUL BOND (LP)	15

HOFFNER BROTHERS
72	Bullet BU 513	The King Man Is Back/SHALIMAR ALL STARS: Version	5
72	Green Door GD 4039	The King Man Is Back/SHALIMAR ALL STARS: Version (reissue)	5
73	Ackee ACK 521	Open Up The Gates/Version	5
73	Grape GR 3042	Let Me Dream (Parts 1 & 2)	5

GERARD HOFFNUNG
60	Decca LF 1330	AT THE OXFORD UNION (10" LP)	12

ANNIE HOGAN
85	Doublevision DVR 9	PLAYS KICKABYE (12" EP)	15

(see also Marc Almond, Nick Cave, Soft Cell)

CLAIRE HOGAN
59	Top Rank JAR 161	Sing A Smiling Song/I Wonder	10

(see also Teresa Brewer)

SILAS HOGAN
71	Blue Horizon 2431 008	TROUBLE AT HOME (LP)	110
70s	Flyright FLY 595	I'M A FREE-HEARTED MAN (LP)	15

HOGARTH
68	Liberty LBF 15156	Suzie's Getting Married/I've Been Dreaming	10

JAMES HOGG
72	Regal Zonophone RZ 3054	Lovely Lady Rock/Happy Sad	15
72	Regal Zonophone RZ 3068	California Blues/Everybody Smile	10

JAMES HOGG BAND
73	Regal Zonophone 3078	Gotta Be A Winner/Everybody Smile	10

SMOKEY HOGG
64	Realm RM 197	I'M SO LONELY (LP)	25
72	Ember EMB 3405	SINGS THE BLUES (LP)	20
70s	Specialty SNTF 5018	U BETTER WATCH THAT JIVE (LP)	15

(see also John Lee Hooker/Lightnin' Hopkins/Smokey Hogg)

HOGGS
80	Now 2001	See It Now/Time On The Line (p/s)	20

HOGS
69	Jay Boy BOY 5	It's All Coming To Me Now/Motor Cycle Rider	15

SUZI JANE HOKUM
66	MGM MGM 1323	Need All The Help I Can Get/Home	60

HOKUS POKE
72	Vertigo 6360 064	EARTH HARMONY (LP, die-cut gatefold sleeve, small swirl label)	300

RON HOLDEN
60	London HLU 9116	My Babe/Love You So	70

MARK HOLDER & THE POSITIVES
73	Atlantic K10280	Whatever's Fair/Why Dear Lord	25

RAM HOLDER BROTHERS
66	Parlophone R 5471	Just Across The River/Ram Blues	30

(see also Ram Jam Band, Ram John Holder)

RAM JOHN HOLDER
67	Columbia DB 8157	I Need Somebody/She's Alright	12
67	Columbia DB 8262	My Friend Jones/It Won't Be Long Before I Love You	25
68	Beacon BEA 108	I Just Came To Get My Baby/Yes I Do	10
69	Upfront UPF 2	Goodwill To All Mankind/BLACK VELVET: Goodwill Sermon	8
70	United Artists UP 35117	Where Do The Dreams Go?/Miracle Happens Every Day	6
63	Melodisc MLP 12-133	RAM BLUES GOSPEL AND SOUL (LP)	60
69	Beacon BEAS 2	BLACK LONDON BLUES (LP, white/black label with "Sold in U.K..." text)	60
70	Beacon BEAS 17	BOOTLEG BLUES (LP, gatefold sleeve with lyric poster, white/black labels)	80
70	Beacon BEAS 17	BOOTLEG BLUES (LP, gatefold sleeve without lyric poster, white/black labels)	30

(see also Ram Jam Band, Ram Holder Brothers, Geno Washington)

HOLE
91	City Slang EFA 04070-45/	Teenage Whore/Drown Soda (p/s, lilac, clear or green vinyl, 500 of each)	20
91	City Slang EFA 04070	Teenage Whore/Drown Soda (12")	8
93	City Slang EFA 04916-45	Beautiful Son/Old Age/20 Years In The Dakota (purple vinyl)	5
94	City Slang EFA 04936-7	Miss World/Rock Star (Alternate Mix) (pink vinyl)	6
95	Geffen GFS P94	Violet/Old Age (purple vinyl)//Violet/He Hit Me (And It Felt Like A Kiss) 7" double pack)	10
96	Mirromax 573 164-7	Gold Dust Woman/N.Y. LOOSE: Spit (gatefold p/s, 2 x 1-sided 7"s, with etched B-sides, 5,000 numbered)	8
98	Geffen GFS22345	Celebrity Skin/Best Sunday Dress (p/s)	5
91	City Slang SLANG 012	PRETTY ON THE INSIDE (LP, blue vinyl)	25
94	City Slang EFA 04935-1	LIVE THROUGH THIS (LP, 3000 on white vinyl)	40
94	City Slang EFA 04935-1	LIVE THROUGH THIS (LP, black vinyl)	20
98	Geffen GEF 25164	CELEBRITY SKIN (LP)	20

BILLIE HOLIDAY
56	Vogue V 2408	Detour Ahead/Blue, Turning Grey Over You	20
59	MGM MGM 1033	Don't Worry About Me/Just One More Chance	10
54	Columbia 33S 1034	BILLIE HOLIDAY (10" LP)	35
54	Brunswick LA 8676	LOVER MAN (10" LP)	35
55	Philips BBR 8032	FAVOURITES (10" LP)	35
56	Columbia Clef 33C 9023	AT JAZZ AT THE PHILHARMONIC (10" LP)	20
56	Columbia Clef 33CX 10019	MUSIC FOR TORCHING (LP)	35
57	Columbia Clef 33CX 10064	VELVET MOOD (LP)	40
57	Columbia Clef 33CX 10076	SOLITUDE (LP)	30
57	Columbia Clef 33CX 10092	LADY SINGS THE BLUES (LP)	30
59	Columbia Clef 33CX 10145	SONGS FOR DISTINGUÉ LOVERS (LP)	30
59	MGM MGM-C 792	BILLIE HOLIDAY (LP)	15
59	Fontana TFL 5032	LADY IN SATIN (LP)	15
60	Fontana TFL 5106	A BILLIE HOLIDAY MEMORIAL (LP)	15
61	HMV CLP 1414	THE UNFORGETTABLE LADY DAY (LP)	15
62	Stateside SL 10007	BILLIE HOLIDAY (LP)	15
66	Island ILP 929	LAST LIVE RECORDING (LP)	30

CHICO HOLIDAY
59	RCA RCA 1117	Young Ideas/Cuckoo Girl	35
59	RCA RCA 1117	Young Ideas/Cuckoo Girl (78)	12
61	Coral Q 72443	God, Country And My Baby/Fools (withdrawn)	30
59	RCA RCX 171	CHICO HOLIDAY (EP)	80

JIMMY HOLIDAY
63	Vocalion POP V 9206	How Can I Forget/Janet	30
64	London HLY 9868	I Lied/Alison	20
66	Liberty LIB 12040	Baby I Love You/You Won't Get Away	20
67	Liberty LIB 12048	Give Me Your Love/The Turning Point	20
67	Liberty LIB 12053	Everybody Needs Help/I'm Gonna Move To The City	20
68	Minit MLF 11008	Give Me Your Love/The Beauty Of A Girl In Love	15
69	Minit MLL/MLS 40010	SPREAD YOUR LOVE (LP)	60

JIMMY HOLIDAY & CLYDIE KING
67	Liberty LIB 12058	Ready, Willing And Able/We Got A Good Thing Goin'	30
67	Liberty LIB 12058	Ready, Willing And Able/We Got A Good Thing Goin' (DJ copy)	50
72	United Artists UP 35371	Ready, Willing And Able/JIMMY HOLIDAY: Give Me Your Love	10

(see also Clydie King)

JOHNNY HOLIDAY
59	London RE 1226	SENTIMENTAL HOLIDAY (EP)	10
59	London RE 1227	HOLIDAY FOR ROMANCE (EP)	10

HOLIDAYMAKERS
89	Woosh WOOSH 4	Cincinnati/Seventh Valley Girl (p/s)	10
89	Maker 00IT	Gay Cowboy (12", p/s)	8

HOLIDAYS
66	Polydor 56720	I'll Love You Forever/Makin' Up Time	125

(see also Edwin Starr)

HOLLAND
84	Ebony EBON 17	EARLY WARNING (LP)	12

Brian HOLLAND

(see also Black Rose, Hammer)

BRIAN HOLLAND

74	Invictus INV 2553	I'm So Glad/I'm So Glad (Version)	20

(BRIAN) HOLLAND & (LAMONT) DOZIER

72	Invictus INV 525	Why Can't We Be Lovers/Don't Leave Me	5
73	Invictus INV 528	Don't Leave Me Starvin' For Your Love (Parts 1 & 2)	5

(see also Lamont Dozier, Brian Holland)

EDDIE HOLLAND

62	Fontana H 387	Jamie/Take A Chance On Me	400
63	Oriole CBA 1808	If It's Love (It's All Right)/It's Not Too Late	500

LYNN HOLLAND

64	Ember EMB S 198	And The Angels Sing/I Can't Read Your Writing (For My Tears) (in p/s)	12
64	Ember EMB S 198	And The Angels Sing/I Can't Read Your Writing (For My Tears)	6
65	Polydor BM 56035	Oh Darling How I Miss You/Before	5
67	Polydor 56166	One Man In My Life/Wand'rin Boy	20
67	Polydor 56187	Come And Love/May God Help You And Protect You	25
66	Polydor 56129	All You Love In The World/Loneliness	6
71	Pye 7N 45041	The Last Time/In A Railway Carriage	8
67	Polydor 236217	OH DARLING HOW I MISS YOU (LP)	25

(see also Holly)

MALCOLM HOLLAND

70	Fontana TF 1075	Dawning Of the Day/Wndy	10

TONY HOLLAND

63	HMV POP 1135	Sidewalk/Time Goes By	50

MICHAEL HOLLIDAY

56	Columbia SCM 5221	Sixteen Tons/The Rose Tattoo	20
56	Columbia SCM 5252	Nothin' To Do/Perfume, Candy And Flowers	10
56	Columbia SCM 5273	Hot Diggity (Dog Ziggity)/The Gal With The Yaller Shoes	20
56	Columbia DB 3813	The Runaway Train/Ten Thousand Miles	20
57	Columbia DB 3871	Yaller Yaller Gold/I Saw Esau	8
57	Columbia DB 3919	Love Is Strange/My House Is Your House	8
57	Columbia DB 3948	Four Walls/Wringle Wrangle	8
57	Columbia DB 3973	All Of You/It's The Good Things We Remember	7
57	Columbia DB 3992	Old Cape Cod/Love You Darlin'.	7
58	Columbia DB 4058	The Story Of My Life/Keep Your Heart	7
58	Columbia DB 4087	In Love/Rooney	5
58	Columbia DB 4121	Stairway Of Love/May I?	5
58	Columbia DB 4155	I'll Always Be In Love With You/I'll Be Lovin' You, Too	5
58	Columbia DB 4188	She Was Only Seventeen/The Gay Vagabond	5
58	Columbia DB 4216	My Heart Is An Open Book/Careless Hands	5
60	Columbia DB 4378	Starry Eyed/The Steady Game	5
60	Columbia DB 4437	Skylark/Dream Talk	5
60	Columbia DB 4475	Little Boy Lost/The One Finger Symphony	5

EPs

60	Columbia SEG 7986	FOUR FEATHER FALLS (mono)	12
60	Columbia ESG 7793	FOUR FEATHER FALLS (stereo)	18

ALBUMS

58	Columbia 33S 1114	HI! (10")	15

(see also Edna Savage)

SU(SAN) HOLLIDAY

64	Columbia DB 7363	Dark Despair/The Other Side (demos list A-side as "[Street Of] Dark Despair")	15
64	Columbia DB 7403	Any Day Now/Don't Come Knocking At My Door	15
65	Columbia DB 7616	Sometimes/Long Haired Boy	12
65	Columbia DB 7709	Nevertheless (I'm In Love With You)/Moonglow	12
66	Columbia SX 6067	I WANNA SAY HELLO (LP, as Su Holliday)	75

(see also Susan Singer)

TIM HOLLIER

70	Fontana TF 1080	In This Room/Love Song	6
71	Philips 6006 130	Circle Is Small/In A Corner Of My Life/Time Stood Still	6
68	United Artists (S)ULP 1211	MESSAGE TO A HARLEQUIN (LP, laminated front sleeve, blue/silver labels)	60
70	Fontana 6309 003	TIM HOLLIER (LP, laminated sleve, black/silver labels)	200
71	Philips 6308 044	SKY SAIL (LP, laminated sleeve, black/silver labels)	35

(see also Amory Kane)

HOLLIES

SINGLES

63	Parlophone R 5030	(Ain't That) Just Like Me/Hey, What's Wrong With Me	15
63	Parlophone R 5052	Searchin'/Whole World Over	10
63	Parlophone R 5077	Stay/Now's The Time	8
64	Parlophone R 5104	Just One Look/Keep Off That Friend Of Mine	7
64	Parlophone R 5137	Here I Go Again/Baby That's All	7
64	Parlophone R 5178	We're Through/Come On Back	6
65	Parlophone R 5232	Yes I Will/Nobody	6
65	Parlophone R 5287	I'm Alive/You Know He Did	6
65	Parlophone R 5322	Look Through Any Window/So Lonely	7
65	Parlophone R 5392	If I Needed Someone/I've Got A Way Of My Own	8
66	Parlophone R 5409	I Can't Let Go/Running Through The Night	7
66	Parlophone R 5469	Bus Stop/Don't Run And Hide	7
66	United Artists UP 1152	After The Fox (with Peter Sellers)/BURT BACHARACH: The Fox-Trot	35
66	Parlophone R 5508	Stop! Stop! Stop!/It's You	8
67	Parlophone R 5562	On A Carousel/All The World Is Love	6
67	Parlophone R 5602	Carrie Anne/Signs That Will Never Change	6
67	Parlophone R 5637	King Midas In Reverse/Everything Is Sunshine	10
68	Parlophone R 5680	Jennifer Eccles/Open Up Your Eyes	6

68	Parlophone R 5733	Listen To Me/Do The Best You Can	7
69	Parlophone R 5765	Sorry Suzanne/Not That Way At All	7
69	Parlophone R 5806	He Ain't Heavy, He's My Brother/'Cos You Like To Love Me	6
70	Parlophone R 5837	I Can't Tell The Bottom From The Top/Mad Professor Blyth	5
70	Parlophone R 5862	Gasoline Alley Bred/Dandelion Wine	5
71	Parlophone R 5905	Hey Willy/Row The Boat Together	5
72	Polydor 2058 199	The Baby/Oh Granny	5
72	Parlophone R 5939	Long Cool Woman (In A Black Dress)/Cable Car	6
72	Polydor 2058 289	Magic Woman Touch/Indian Girl	5
73	Polydor 2058 403	The Day That Curly Billy Shot Down Crazy Sam McGee/Born A Man	5
74	Polydor 2058 435	The Air That I Breathe/No More Riders	5
74	Polydor 2058 476	Son Of A Rotten Gambler/Layin' To The Music	5
74	Polydor 2058 533	I'm Down/Hello Lady Goodbye	5
75	Polydor 2058 595	Sandy (Fourth Of July, Asbury Park)/Second-Hand Hangups	5
75	EMI EMI 2353	Long Cool Woman In A Black Dress/Carrie Anne	5
76	Polydor 2058 694	Boulder To Birmingham/Crocodile Woman (She Bites)	6
76	Polydor 2058 719	Star/Love Is The Thing	6
76	Polydor 2058 779	Daddy Don't Mind/C'mon	6
76	Polydor 2058 799	Wiggle That Wotsit/Corrine	6
76	Polydor 2058 880	Hello To Romance/48 Hour Parole	6
77	Polydor 2058 906	Amnesty/Crossfire	6
78	EMI EMI 2813	Look Through Any Window/I'm Alive/Just One Look (p/s)	6
79	Polydor POSP 35	Something To Live For/Song Of The Sun	6
79	Polydor POSPX 35	Something To Live For/Song Of The Sun/The Air That I Breathe (12", p/s)	12
80	Polydor 2059 246	Soldier's Song/Draggin' My Heels	10
80	Polydor POSP 175	Heartbeat/Take Your Time	8
87	Columbia 12DB 9146	This Is It/You Gave Me Strength/You're All Woman (12", p/s)	10
87	Columbia DB 9151	Reunion Of The Heart/Too Many Hearts Get Broken (p/s)	5
90	SRT 90LS 2407	Purple Rain/Naomi/Two Shadows (12", p/s, available only at gigs)	8

EPs

64	Parlophone GEP 8909	THE HOLLIES	40
64	Parlophone GEP 8911	JUST ONE LOOK	35
64	Parlophone GEP 8915	HERE I GO AGAIN	35
64	Parlophone GEP 8927	WE'RE THROUGH	35
65	Parlophone GEP 8934	IN THE HOLLIES STYLE	50
65	Parlophone GEP 8942	I'M ALIVE	35
66	Parlophone GEP 8951	I CAN'T LET GO	35

ALBUMS

64	Parlophone PMC 1220	STAY WITH THE HOLLIES (mono)	90
64	Parlophone PCA 3054	STAY WITH THE HOLLIES (stereo, large 'stereo' on sleeve)	150
65	Parlophone PMC 1235	IN THE HOLLIES STYLE (mid-sized mono on front sleeve, "Sold in U.K..." text)	100
65	Parlophone PMC 1261	THE HOLLIES (small mono on front sleeve, "Sold in U.K..." text)	100
66	Parlophone PMC 7008	WOULD YOU BELIEVE? (mono, with "Sold in U.K..." text)	70
66	Parlophone PCS 7008	WOULD YOU BELIEVE? (stereo, "Sold in U.K..." text)	120
66	Parlophone PMC 7011	FOR CERTAIN BECAUSE (gatefold sleeve, mono, with "Sold in U.K..." text)	35
66	Parlophone PCS 7011	FOR CERTAIN BECAUSE (gatefold sleeve, stereo, with "Sold in U.K..." text)	60
67	Parlophone PMC 7022	EVOLUTION (mono, with "Sold in U.K..." text)	50
67	Parlophone PCS 7022	EVOLUTION (stereo, with "Sold in U.K..." text)	70
67	Parlophone PMC 7039	BUTTERFLY (mono, with "Sold in U.K..." text)	40
67	Parlophone PCS 7039	BUTTERFLY (stereo, with "sold in U.K..." text)	80
67	EMI Regal SREG 2024	THE HOLLIES (export compilation)	20
67	World Records ST 979	THE VINTAGE HOLLIES (stereo reissue of "In The Hollies Style")	30
68	World Records ST 1035	STAY WITH THE HOLLIES (record club reissue)	25
68	Parlophone PMC/PCS 7057	THE HOLLIES' GREATEST	15
69	Parlophone PMC 7078	THE HOLLIES SING DYLAN (mono, with "Solid in U.K..." text)	30
69	Parlophone PCS 7078	THE HOLLIES SING DYLAN (stereo, with "Sold in U.K..." text)	25
69	Parlophone PCS 7092	HOLLIES SING HOLLIES (gatefold sleeve)	18

(All Parlophone LPs listed above were originally issued with yellow/black labels; 1970s pressings with silver & black labels are worth £8)

70	Parlophone PCS 7116	CONFESSIONS OF THE MIND (with colour insert)	18
71	Parlophone PAS 10005	DISTANT LIGHT (gatefold sleeve)	15
71	Regal Starline SRS 5013	STOP! STOP! STOP! (reissue of "For Certain Because")	12
72	Parlophone PCS 7148	THE HOLLIES' GREATEST HITS VOL. 2	12
72	Polydor 2383 144	ROMANY (gatefold sleeve)	12
74	Polydor 2383 262	HOLLIES (with lyric insert)	12
75	Polydor 2442 128	ANOTHER NIGHT (gatefold sleeve)	12
76	Polydor 2442 141	WRITE ON (with lyric inner)	12
76	Polydor 2383 421	RUSSIAN ROULETTE (with lyric inner)	12
78	Polydor 2383 474	A CRAZY STEAL (with lyric inner)	12
78	Parlophone PMC 7174	THE BEST OF THE HOLLIES' EPs	12
78	Parlophone PMC 7176	THE OTHER SIDE OF THE HOLLIES	15
79	Polydor 2442 160	FIVE THREE ONE - DOUBLE SEVEN O FOUR (with lyric insert)	12
79	St. Michael 2102/0101	UP FRONT (sold through Marks & Spencer in conjunction with Polydor)	18

(see also Allan Clarke, Graham Nash, Terry Sylvester, Haydock's Rockhouse, Peter Sellers & Sophia Loren)o

HOLLINGWORTH

| 71 | Columbia DB 8808 | Jump On My Wagon/This Town | 18 |

MARK HOLLIS

| 03 | Polydor 537 688-1 | MARK HOLLIS (LP, reissue of 1997 CD-only album, 180gm pressing with inner) | 70 |

(see also Talk Talk)

BRENDA HOLLOWAY

64	Stateside SS 307	Every Little Bit Hurts/Land Of A Thousand Boys	50
64	Stateside SS 307	Every Little Bit Hurts/Land Of A Thousand Boys (DJ Copy)	130
65	Tamla Motown TMG 508	When I'm Gone/I've Been Good To You	80
65	Tamla Motown TMG 508	When I'm Gone/I've Been Good To You (DJ copy)	200
65	Tamla Motown TMG 519	Operator/I'll Be Available	75
65	Tamla Motown TMG 519	Operator/I'll Be Available (DJ copy)	150
66	Tamla Motown TMG 556	Together Till The End Of Time/Sad Song	120
66	Tamla Motown TMG 556	Together Till The End Of Time/Sad Song (DJ copy)	150
66	Tamla Motown TMG 581	Hurt A Little Everyday/Where Were You (demos credit Brenda Holiday)	90

MINT VALUE £

66	Tamla Motown TMG 581	Hurt A Little Everyday/Where Were You (demos credit Brenda Holiday) (DJ copy)............100
67	Tamla Motown TMG 608	Just Look What You've Done/Starting The Hurt All Over Again 60
67	Tamla Motown TMG 608	Just Look What You've Done/Starting The Hurt All Over Again (DJ copy) 100
67	Tamla Motown TMG 622	You've Made Me So Very Happy/I've Got To Find It 45
69	Tamla Motown TMG 700	Just Look What You've Done/You've Made Me So Very Happy 18
68	T. Motown (S)TML 11083	THE ARTISTRY OF BRENDA HOLLOWAY (LP, mono/stereo) 100

LOLEATTA HOLLOWAY

71	United Artists UP 35273	Bring It On Up/Rainbow '71' 8
96	Kent 6T 11	This Mans Arms/JOHN EDWARDS: Ain't That Good Enough 25

PATRICE HOLLOWAY

66	Capitol CL 15484	Love And Desire/Ecstasy 150
66	Capitol CL 15484	Love And Desire/Ecstasy (DJ Copy) 250

HOLLOW GROUND

80	Guardian GR/HG C57	FLYING HIGH EP (Flying High/Warlord/Rock On/Don't Chase The Dragon) (in p/s)............150
80	Guardian GR/HG C57	FLYING HIGH EP (Flying High/Warlord/Rock On/Don't Chase The Dragon)...................45

BUDDY HOLLY

78s

56	Brunswick 05581	Blue Days - Black Nights/Love Me 350
57	Vogue Coral Q 72293	Peggy Sue/Everyday 150
58	Coral Q 72293	Peggy Sue/Everyday 15
58	Coral Q 72288	Listen To Me/I'm Gonna Love You Too 25
58	Coral Q 72325	Rave On/Take Your Time 30
58	Coral Q 72333	Early In The Morning/Now We're One 35
58	Coral Q 72346	Heartbeat/Well ... All Right 50
59	Coral Q 72360	It Doesn't Matter Anymore/Raining In My Heart 30
59	Brunswick 05800	Rock Around With Ollie Vee/Midnight Shift 200
59	Coral Q 72376	Peggy Sue Got Married/Crying, Waiting, Hoping 200
60	Coral Q 72392	Heartbeat/Everyday 400

SINGLES

56	Brunswick 05581	Blue Days - Black Nights/Love Me 800
57	Vogue Coral Q 72293	Peggy Sue/Everyday 50
58	Coral Q 72293	Peggy Sue/Everyday 20
58	Coral Q 72288	Listen To Me/I'm Gonna Love You Too 25
58	Coral Q 72325	Rave On/Take Your Time 25
58	Coral Q 72333	Early In The Morning/Now We're One 25
58	Coral Q 72346	Heartbeat/Well ... All Right 25
58	Coral Q 72360	It Doesn't Matter Anymore/Raining In My Heart 10
59	Brunswick 05800	Rock Around With Ollie Vee/Midnight Shift 40
59	Coral Q 72376	Peggy Sue Got Married/Crying, Waiting, Hoping 25

(The above 45s were originally issued with triangular centres; reissues with round centres are worth two-thirds these values.)

60	Coral Q 72392	Heartbeat/Everyday 20
60	Coral Q 72397	True Love Ways/Moondreams 10
60	Coral Q 72411	Learning The Game/That Makes It Tough 10
61	Coral Q 72419	What To Do/That's What They Say 10
61	Coral Q 72432	Baby I Don't Care/Valley Of Tears 10
61	Coral Q 72445	Look At Me/Mailman, Bring Me No More Blues 15
62	Coral Q 72449	Listen To Me/Words Of Love 15
62	Coral Q 72455	Reminiscing/Wait Till The Sun Shines, Nellie 10
63	Coral Q 72459	Brown-Eyed Handsome Man/Slippin' And Slidin' 10
63	Coral Q 72463	Bo Diddley/It's Not My Fault 10
63	Coral Q 72466	Wishing/Because I Love You 10
63	Coral Q 72469	What To Do/Umm Oh Yeah 12
64	Coral Q 72472	You've Got Love/An Empty Cup (as Buddy Holly & The Crickets) 25
64	Coral Q 72475	Love's Made A Fool Of You/You're The One 20
66	Coral Q 72483	Maybe Baby/That's My Desire 40
68	Decca AD 1009	Rave On/Peggy Sue (p/s, export reissue)..75
68	MCA MU 1012	Peggy Sue/Rave On (reissue)..5
69	MCA MU 1059	Love Is Strange/You're The One...10
69	MCA MU 1081	It Doesn't Matter Anymore/Maybe Baby (reissue) 5
70	MCA MU 1116	Rave On/Umm Oh Yeah (Dearest) 5
73	MCA MMU 1198	That'll Be The Day/Well All Right/Every Day...5
74	MCA MCA 119	It Doesn't Matter Anymore/True Love Ways/Brown Eyed Handsome Man 5
75	MCA MCA 207	Oh Boy!/Every Day (as Buddy Holly & Crickets)...5
76	MCA MCA 252	True Love Ways/It Doesn't Matter Anymore/Raining In My Heart/Moondreams (p/s) 5
76	MCA MCA 253	Peggy Sue/Rave On/Rock Around With Ollie Vee/Midnight Shift (p/s) 5
76	MCA MCA 254	Maybe Baby/Think It Over/That'll Be The Day/It's So Easy (p/s, as Buddy Holly & Crickets)..5
78	MCA MCA 344	Wishing/Love's Made A Fool Of You (p/s)...5
83	MCA HR 001	That'll Be The Day/True Love Ways (as Buddy Holly & Crickets) (with/without The History Of Rock issue 1; "Made in France" on label) 7
83	MCA HR 001	That'll Be The Day/True Love Ways (as Buddy Holly & Crickets) (with/without The History Of Rock issue 1; "Made In Gt. Britain" on label)...........................5
84	MCA BHB 1	THAT'LL BE THE DAY (10 x 7" box set, comprising BH1-10 in p/s)........................40
89	MCA MCAV 1368	Oh Boy!/Well ... All Right/Mailman Bring Me No More Blues/Everyday (10", p/s)................8

EPs

58	Coral FEP 2002	LISTEN TO ME (brown cover, sleeve shows Holly without glasses; disc credits title as "Buddy Holly") 400
58	Coral FEP 2002	LISTEN TO ME (re-pressing, various shades of green/brown p/s, shows Holly with glasses; disc credits title as "Buddy Holly") 40
58	Coral FEP 2005	RAVE ON (various shades of green/brown p/s)..40
59	Coral FEP 2014	IT'S SO EASY..40
59	Coral FEP 2015	HEARTBEAT...40
59	Coral FEP 2032	BUDDY HOLLY...40
59	Brunswick OE 9456	BUDDY HOLLY NO. 1...75
59	Brunswick OE 9457	BUDDY HOLLY NO. 2...75

(The above EPs were originally issued with triangular centres; later pressings with round-centres are worth between half and two thirds of these values.)

60	Coral FEP 2044	THE LATE GREAT BUDDY HOLLY (tri centre) 60

60	Coral FEP 2044	THE LATE GREAT BUDDY HOLLY (round centre)	25
64	Coral FEP 2065	BUDDY - BY REQUEST	45
64	Coral FEP 2066	THAT TEX-MEX SOUND	60
64	Coral FEP 2067	WISHING	55
64	Coral FEP 2068	SHOWCASE VOLUME 1	45
64	Coral FEP 2069	SHOWCASE VOLUME 2	45
65	Coral FEP 2070	BUDDY HOLLY SINGS	45

ALBUMS

58	Vogue Coral LVA 9085	BUDDY HOLLY (Vogue-Coral labels & Coral sleeve)	120
58	Coral LVA 9085	BUDDY HOLLY	50
59	Coral LVA 9105	THE BUDDY HOLLY STORY('High Fidelity Coral' logo on sleeve)	30
60s	Coral LVA 9105	THE BUDDY HOLLY STORY (reissue, different 'roll-neck sweater' sleeve with small 'Coral' logo)	50
60	Coral LVA 9127	THE BUDDY HOLLY STORY VOL. II.	25
61	Ace Of Hearts AH 3	THAT'LL BE THE DAY	20
63	Coral LVA 9212	REMINISCING	30
64	Coral LVA 9222	SHOWCASE	30
65	Coral LVA 9227	HOLLY IN THE HILLS (with Bob Montgomery, withdrawn mispressing, sleeve & label list "Wishing", plays "Reminiscing"; matrix no's end with 1B both sides)	50
65	Coral LVA 9227	HOLLY IN THE HILLS (corrected edition, with Bob Montgomery, plays "Wishing", matrix numbers end with 1B on one side & 2B on other)	70
68	MCA MUP 320	WISHING (mono only, reissue of "Holly In The Hills")	20
69	MCA MUPS 371	GIANT	20

(Originally issued with yellow labels; later variations exist with various twin-toned designs.)

75	World Records SM 301/5	THE BUDDY HOLLY STORY (5-LP box set)	20
79	MCA Coral CDMSP 807	THE COMPLETE BUDDY HOLLY (6-LP box set with sepia-tinted book)	30
80	Marks & Spencer IMP 114	HEARTBEAT	30
83	MCA MCM 1002	FOR THE FIRST TIME ANYWHERE	12
86	Rollercoaster ROLL 2013	SOMETHING SPECIAL FROM BUDDY HOLLY	12

(see also Crickets, Fireballs)

STEVIE HOLLY
| 66 | Planet PLF 107 | A Strange World/Little Man | 30 |

HOLLY (1)
| 65 | Fontana TF 980 | On With The Game/Paradise Lost | 8 |

(see also Lynn Holland)

HOLLY (2)
| 79 | Eric's ERIC'S 003 | Yankee Rose/Treasure Island/Desperate Dan (p/s) | 25 |
| 79 | Eric's ERIC'S 007 | Hobo Joe/Stars Of The Bars (p/s) | 20 |

(see also Frankie Goes To Hollywood, Big In Japan)

HOLLY & JOEY
| 82 | Virgin VS 478 | I Got You Babe/HOLLY & THE ITALIANS: One More Dance (p/s) | 12 |

(see also Ramones, Deborah Harry)

HOLLY & THE ITALIANS
80	Oval OVAL 1016	Tell That Girl To Shut Up/Chapel Of Love (p/s)	5
81	Virgin VS 411	I Wanna Go Home/Fanzine (p/s)	15
81	Virgin VS 429	Just For Tonight/Baby Gets It All (p/s)	7
81	Virgin V 2186	THE RIGHT TO BE ITALIAN (LP, with lyric insert)	15

HOLLYRIDGE STRINGS
| 61 | Capitol CL 15233 | The Guns Of Navarone/Moon River | 6 |
| 61 | Capitol CL 15237 | The Comancheros/A Thunder Of Drums | 6 |

HOLLYWOOD ARGYLES
60	London HLU 9146	Alley Oop/Sho' Know A Lot About Love	10
60	London HLU 9146	Alley Oop/Sho' Know A Lot About Love (78)	12
60	Top Rank JAR 530	Gun Totin' Critter Called Jack/GARY PAXTON: Bug-Eye	20

(see also Kim Fowley, Skip & Flip, Gary Paxton)

HOLLYWOOD BRATS
| 80 | Cherry Red A RED 6 | HOLLYWOOD BRATS (LP) | 12 |

HOLLYWOOD FLAMES
57	London HL 7030	Buzz Buzz Buzz/Crazy (export issue)	50
58	London HL 8545	Buzz Buzz Buzz/Crazy	75
58	London HL 8545	Buzz Buzz Buzz/Crazy (78)	20
59	London HLW 8955	Much Too Much/In The Dark	75
59	London HLW 8955	Much Too Much/In The Dark (78)	50
60	London HLE 9071	If I Thought You Needed Me/Every Day Every Way	50

HOLLYWOOD FREEWAY
| 72 | Deram DM 359 | I've Been Moved/Cool Calamares | 6 |
| 73 | Pye 7N 45273 | You're The Song (That I Can't Stop Singing)/This Feeling Called Love | 8 |

(see also Tony Rivers)

HOLLYWOOD HURRICANES
| 64 | Prima PR 1009 | Beavershot/Have Love Will Travel | 6 |

KENNY HOLLYWOOD
| 62 | Decca F 11546 | Magic Star/The Wonderful Story Of Love | 25 |

HOLLYWOOD KILLERS
| 78 | Rollerball | Goodbye Suicide/Tramp | 50 |

HOLLYWOOD VINES
| 61 | Capitol CL 15191 | When Johnny Comes Slidin' Home/Cruisin' | 25 |

MIKE HOLM
| 70 | Major Minor MM 659 | Mendocino/Cutey Girl | 6 |

PETER HOLM
| 67 | Major Minor MM504 | This Is Not The Way/You Will Be Mine | 10 |

BILL HOLMAN OCTET
54	Capitol KC 65000	Cousin Jack/Plain Folks	8

EDDIE HOLMAN
65	Cameo Parkway P 960	This Can't Be True/A Free Country	50
69	Action ACT 4547	I Love You/I Surrender	70
70	Stateside SS 2160	(Hey There) Lonely Girl/It's All In The Game	10
70	Stateside SS 2170	Since I Don't Have You/Don't Stop Now	8
77	Salsoul SZ 2026	This Will Be A Night To Remember/Time Will Tell	6

CHRISTINE HOLMES
64	Mercury MF 813	This Is My Prayer/My Dream	10
64	Mercury MF 819	Play Me A Sad Song (Mr DJ)/Doesn't He Know	10
64	Mercury MF 831	Goodbye Boys Goodbye/Is It Love	10
65	Mercury MF 851	Many Things From Your Window/You'd Better Believe It	7
65	Mercury MF 887	Goin' Where The Lovin' Is/Where There's Some Smoke There's Fire	7

(see also Family Dogg)

DAVID HOLMES
97	Go Beat GOB 6	Don't Die Just Yet (Mogwai Mix)/Holiday Girl (Arab Strap Mix) (p/s, 500 only)	8
02	13 Amp APM 001LP	COME GET IT I GOT IT (2xLP)	20

(see also Mogwai)

ELDRIDGE HOLMES
68	Pama PM 746	Beverley/Wait For Me Baby	18

IVAN HOLMES
67	Columbia DB 8119	The Light, The Love And The Life/Cocaine	7

JAKE HOLMES
69	Polydor 56547	How Are You (Parts 1 & 2)	5
70	Ember EMB S 269	Saturday Night/Diner Song (p/s)	20
70	Polydor 2066 040	So Close/Django And Friend	5
70	Polydor 583 579	JAKE HOLMES (LP)	25
70	Polydor 2425 036	SO CLOSE SO VERY FAR TO GO (LP)	22
72	CBS 64905	HOW MUCH TIME (LP)	20

JOE HOLMES & LEN GRAHAM
79	Topic 12TS 401	AFTER DAWNING (LP)	12

LEROY HOLMES & ORCHESTRA
59	MGM 1044	Sweet Leicani/Alice Blue Gown	6
59	MGM 1058	Theme From A Summer Place/Indiscreet	6
68	United Artists UP 2222	The Good, The Bad And The Ugly/Live For Life	5

RICHARD 'GROOVES' HOLMES
66	CBS 202240	Misty/Groove's Groove	7
67	Transatlantic PR 7435	SOUL MESSAGE (LP)	25
68	Transatlantic PR 7493	RICHARD 'GROOVES' HOLMES (LP)	18

HOLOCAUST (1)
80	Phoenix PSP 1	Heavy Metal Mania/Only As Young As You Feel (p/s)	20
80	Phoenix 12 PSP 1	Heavy Metal Mania/Love's Power/Only As Young As You Feel (12", p/s)	30
80	Phoenix 12 PSP 2	Smokin' Valves/Friend Or Foe (p/s)	10
80	Phoenix 12 PSP 2	Smokin' Valves/Friend Or Foe/Out My Book (12", p/s)	30
81	Phoenix PSP 3P	HOLOCAUST LIVE (EP)	25
82	Phoenix 12 PSP 4	Comin' Through/Don't Wanna Be A Loser/Good Thing Going (12", p/s)	30
81	Phoenix PSLP 1	THE NIGHTCOMERS (LP)	40
83	Phoenix PSPLP 4	LIVE (HOT CURRY AND WINE) (LP)	25
84	Phoenix PSPLP 5	NO MAN'S LAND (LP)	20

HOLOCAUST (2)
79	Pile Driver HOL 201	Slay That Dragon/Take Me To Your Lawyer/So Called Civilised Way (12", no p/s)	800

HOLOGRAM
82	Phoenix PSPLP 2	STEAL THE STARS (LP)	12

HOLOSADE
88	Powerstation AMP 16	HELL HOUSE (LP)	12

ERROL HOLT
79	Hit Run HIT DD16	Yes Yes Yes/ROD TAYLOR: No One Can Tell I About Jah (12")	60
77	Lior ROAR 111	Come Rock Me/Congo Dread (12")	20
78	Star Time EHLF 427	I Am Not A King (with PRINCE FAR I)/Version (12")	40
79	Hit Run HIT DD25	Sweet Reggae Music/PRINCE FAR I: Hairdressing Salon	90
70s	Dread DDLP 102	VISION OF AFRICA (LP)	30

JOHN HOLT
63	Island WI 041	I Cried A Tear/I'll Stay	30
68	Trojan TR 643	Tonight/Oh How It Hurts (B-side actually by Paragons)	25
69	Trojan TR 661	Ali Baba/I'm Your Man	35
69	Trojan TR 674	What You Gonna Do Now/Have You Ever Been To Heaven	12
69	Trojan TR 694	Have Sympathy/HARRY J ALLSTARS: Spyrone	15
69	Trojan TR 7702	Wooden Heart/All My Life	10
70	Duke Reid DR 2506	Come Out Of My Bed/WINSTON WRIGHT: Hide And Seek	12
70	Duke DU 73	Stealing, Stealing/WINSTON WRIGHT: Stealing, Stealing (Volume 2)	12
70	Duke DU 77	The Working Kind/Open Jaw	15
70	Jackpot JP 735	A Little Tear/JEFF BARNS: Get In The Groove	12
70	Bamboo BAM 44	A Love I Can Feel/JOHNNY LAST: Long Liver Man (B-side act. by Hugh Black)	12
70	Bamboo BAM 55	A Stranger In Love/WAILERS: Jailhouse (Good Rudy)	40
70	Bamboo BAM 62	Holly Holy/Do You Love Me?	12
70	Banana BA 314	Why Can't I Touch You/SOUND DIMENSION: Touching Version	10
70	Smash SMA 2303	My Heart Is Gone/PHIL PRATT ALL STARS: Version	6
70	Smash SMA 2305	I Had A Talk With My Woman/MAXINE: Life Is Not The Same Anymore	6
70	Supreme SUP 212	Share My Rest/AL BROWN: Always	40
70	Unity UN 548	Sometimes/BUNNY LEE ALL STARS: Lash-La-Rue	30
70	Unity UN 549	Sea Cruise/LEE'S ALL STARS: Niney's Hop	8
70	Unity UN 552	Walking Along/LEE'S ALL STARS: Warefare	45

70	Unity UN 556	Give Her All The Love/BUSTY BROWN: Nobody But You	6
70	Success RE 903	Fat Girl, Sexy Girl/Man And Woman	20
71	Banana BA 340	O.K. Fred/Fancy Make-Up	12
71	Banana BA 345	Build Our Dreams/LEROY SIBBLES: Love In Our Nation	15
71	Treasure Isle TI 7061	Let's Build Our Dreams/TOMMY McCOOK & SUPERSONICS: Testify Version	20
71	Treasure Isle TI 7065	Sister Big Stuff/TOMMY McCOOK & SUPERSONICS: Black River	20
71	Treasure Isle TI 7066	Paragons Medley/TOMMY McCOOK & SUPERSONICS: Medley Version	18
71	Ashanti ASH 401	Again/MUDIES ALL STARS: Ten Steps To Soul Version	10
71	Camel CA 78	Linger A While/Version	7
71	Escort ERT 847	Knock On Your Door/URIEL ALDRIDGE: Set Me Free	6
71	Jackpot JP 772	Stick By Me/It's A Pleasure	6
71	Jackpot JP 774	It's A Jam In The Streets/A Man Needs A Woman	6
71	Jackpot JP 784	Anymore/Lost Love	6
71	Moodisc MU 3513	It May Sound Silly/MUDIE ALL STARS: Instrumental	6
71	Moodisc HM 105	It May Sound Silly/MUDIE ALL STARS: Instrumental (reissue)	10
71	Punch PH 60	Strange Things/WINSTON WRIGHT: Want Money (B-side act. G.G. All Stars)	12
71	Smash SMA 2324	Mother And Father Love/AGGROVATORS: Mother Love Version	6
71	Prince Buster PB 26	All I Want From You/Version	12
72	Blue Beat BB 424	O.K. Fred/BIG YOUTH: Chi Chi Run	20
72	Prince Buster PB 40	Close To Me/Version	7
72	Prince Buster PB 41	Get Ready/Version	7
72	Prince Buster PB 42	Rain From The Skies/Version	7
72	Prince Buster PB 43	The First Time/Version	7
72	Prince Buster PB 49	For Your Love/Version	7
72	G.G. GG 4529	Keep It Up/A Love Like Yours	6
72	Fab FAB 188	A Little Happiness/DELROY WILSON: Diamond Rings	10
72	Jackpot JP 790	Don't You Know/Riding For A Fall	6
72	Jackpot JP 807	Looking Back/I'll Be There	6
72	Pama PM 845	I'll Always Love You/SLIM SMITH: 3 x 7 Rock And Roll	10
72	Pama PM 852	Pledging My Love/I Will Know What To Do	10
73	Fab FAB 224	Let's Go Dancing/Version	10
73	Fab FAB 244	Let's Go Dancing/Version (reissue)	10
73	Attack ATT 8045	Time And The River/Version	5
73	Smash SMA 2329	Don't Break Your Promise/I've Been Admiring You	12
73	Ackee ACK 513	Ecstacy/Version	6
83	Greensleeves GRED 120	Police In Helicopter/Youth Pon The Corner (12")	20
70	Bamboo BDLP 210	A LOVE I CAN FEEL (LP)	60
70s	Melodisc MLP 12170	GREATEST HITS (LP)	40
70s	Melodisc MLP 12180	OK FRED (LP)	45
70s	Melodisc MLP 12191	JOHN HOLT & FRIENDS (LP)	45
71	Trojan TRL(S) 37	STILL IN CHAINS (LP)	15
72	Trojan TRL(S) 43	HOLT (LP)	12
73	Trojan TRLS 55	THE FURTHER YOU LOOK (LP)	12
72	Trojan TBL 184	PLEDGING MY LOVE (LP)	12
74	Attack ATLP 1010	A LOVE I CAN FEEL (LP)	15
83	Arrival ALP 008	POLICE IN HELICOPTER (LP)	25

(see also Jay & Joya, Little John, Neville Hinds, Jeff Barnes, Danny Simpson, Hugh Roy, U Roy Junior, Don Drummond, Interns)

GARY HOLTON

84	Magnet GARY 2	Catch A Falling Star/Angel (star-shaped picture disc)	8

(see also Heavy Metal Kids, Kids, Slade)

ROOSEVELT HOLTS

68	Blue Horizon 7-63201	PRESENTING THE COUNTRY BLUES (LP)	85

HOLY FUCK

10	YTO48S	Red Lights/Dr Dr E	5

HOLY MACKEREL

72	CBS 8447	Rock-A-Bye/New Black Shoes	6
72	CBS 65297	HOLY MACKEREL (LP)	20
93	Tenth Planet TP 005	CLOSER TO HEAVEN (LP, numbered, 500 only)	15

(see also Jason Crest, High Broom)

HOLY MODAL ROUNDERS

68	Elektra EKL 4026	THE MORAY EELS EAT THE HOLY MODALS (LP, mono)	35
68	Elektra EKS 74026	THE MORAY EELS EAT THE HOLY MODALS (LP, stereo)	35
70	Transatlantic TRA 7451	HOLY MODAL ROUNDERS (LP)	35
70	Transatlantic TRA	HOLY MODAL ROUNDERS 2 (LP)	30

HOM BRU

82	Celtic Music CM 009	OBADEEA: MUSIC FROM SHETLAND AND BEYOND (LP)	12

HOMBRES

67	Verve VS 1510	Let It Out (Let It All Hang Out)/Go Girl Go	15

HOME

72	CBS 7809	Fancy Lady, Hollywood Child/Shady Lady	6
72	(No Cat No)	You'll Get A Helping Hand At Barclays/Dreamer (p/s)	15
71	CBS 64356	PAUSE FOR A HOARSE HORSE (LP, gatefold sleeve)	35
72	CBS 64752	HOME (LP)	20
73	CBS 65550	THE ALCHEMIST (LP)	25

(see also Groundhogs, AC/DC, WIshbone Ash, Blue Rondos)

HOMER & JETHRO

54	HMV 7M 211	Swappin' Partners/Crazy Mix-Up Song	12
54	Parlophone CMSP 2	Don't Let Your Sweet Love Die/When It's Long Handle Time In Tennessee (export issue)	10
59	RCA RCA 1148	Waterloo/The Battle Of Kookamonga	6
59	Parlophone GEP 8791	WANTED FOR MURDER OF THE STANDARDS (EP)	10
70	RCA LSA 3172	COUNTRY COMEDY (LP)	12

HOMERS KNODS

69	Pye 7N 17731	All She Said Was Goodbye/Mr Rainbow	20

HOME SERVICE

84	Coda NAT 001	THE MYSTERIES (LP)	15

HOMESICK JAMES

| 64 | Sue WI 319 | Crossroads/My Baby's Sweet | 60 |
| 65 | Sue WI 330 | Set A Date/Can't Afford To Do It | 40 |

HOMESICK JAMES/SNOOKY PRYOR

| 74 | Caroline C 1502 | HOMESICK JAMES AND SNOOKY PRYOR (LP) | 20 |

HOMESTEAD

| 68 | Road R3946 | She/Will You Leave | 15 |

HOMOSEXUALS

78	L'Orelei PF 151	Hearts In Exile/South South Africans (p/s, with insert)	15
79	Black Noise F12 No. 2	Divorce Proceedings/Mecho Madness (12", plain sleeve with sticker)	10
81	Black Noise BN 1	BIGGER THAN THE NUMBER YET MISSING THE DOT (EP, clear vinyl, fold-around hand-painted sleeve)	15
84	Recommended RR 18	THE HOMOSEXUALS RECORD (LP, with inserts)	20

(see also George Harrassment & Homosexuals, Ice La Bas, Amos & Sara, Nancy Sesay & Melodaires, L-Voag, Sir Alick & Phraser)

MINAKO HONDA

| 87 | Columbia DB 9153 | Golden Days (English Version)/Crazy Nights (English Version) (p/s, features Brian May) | 35 |

HONDELLS

64	Mercury MF 834	Little Honda/Hot Rod High	25
65	Mercury MF 925	Younger Girl/All American Girl	25
66	Mercury MF 967	Cheryl's Goin' Home/Show Me Girl	25

HONEST MEN

| 69 | Tamla Motown TMG 706 | Cherie/Baby | 50 |
| 69 | Tamla Motown TMG 706 | Cherie/Baby (DJ Copy) | 60 |

HONEYBOY

71	Trojan TR 7835	Jamaica/ITALS: Sea Wave	7
72	Banana BA 375	Homeward Bound/Peace In The Land	100
75	B & C BC 002	Darlin' Coming Home/SIR COLLINS: We A Come Dread	25
74	Cactus CTLP 101	IMPOSSIBLE LOVE (LP)	25

HONEYBUS

67	Deram DM 131	Delighted To See You/The Breaking Up Scene	12
67	Deram DM 152	Do I Figure In Your Life?/Throw My Love Away	12
68	Deram DM 182	I Can't Let Maggie Go/Tender Are The Ashes	5
68	Deram DM 207	Girl Of Independent Means/How Long	12
69	Deram DM 254	She Sold Blackpool Rock/Would You Believe	25
70	Deram DM 289	Story/The Right To Choose	7
72	Bell BLL 1205	She Is The Female To My Soul/For Where Have You Been	6
73	Warner Bros K 16250	For You/Little Lovely One	8
76	Decca F 13631	I Can't Let Maggie Go/Julie In My Heart	5
70	Deram DML/SML 1056	STORY (LP)	120
73	Warner Bros K 46248	RECITAL (LP, withdrawn, test pressings only)	300
79	See For Miles SEE 264	AT THEIR BEST (LP)	15

(see also Pete Dello, Colin Hare, Lace, Magic Valley, Red Herring)

HONEYCOMBAK

| 69 | Carousel CAR 1 | Sex Change Sadie/It's My Life | 50 |

HONEYCOMBS

64	Pye 7N 15664	Have I The Right/Please Don't Pretend Again	5
64	Pye 7N 15705	Is It Because/I'll Cry Tomorrow	8
64	Pye 7N 15736	Eyes/If You've Got To Pick A Baby	12
65	Pye 7N 15781	Don't Love You No More/I'll See You Tomorrow (withdrawn, promo only)	120
65	Pye 7N 15827	Something Better Beginning/I'll See You Tomorrow	10
65	Pye 7N 15890	That's The Way/Can't Get Through To You	6
65	Pye 7N 15979	This Year, Next Year/Not Sleeping Too Well Lately	10
66	Pye 7N 17089	Who Is Sylvia?/How Will I Know	15
66	Pye 7N 17138	It's So Hard/I Fell In Love	15
66	Pye 7N 17173	That Loving Feeling/Should A Man Cry	18
69	Pye 7N 17741	Have I The Right/Please Don't Pretend Again (stereo reissue)	6
65	Pye NEP 24230	THAT'S THE WAY (EP)	45
64	Pye NPL 18097	THE HONEYCOMBS (LP)	60
65	Pye NPL 18132	ALL SYSTEMS GO! (LP)	80
66	Golden Guinea GGL 0350	THE HONEYCOMBS (LP, reissue in different sleeve)	20

(see also Lemmings, Dennis D'Ell, Martin Murray)

HONEYCONE

70	Hot Wax HWX 103	While You're Out Looking For Sugar/The Feeling's Gone	8
71	Hot Wax HWX 105	Girls It Ain't Easy/Take Me With You	6
71	Hot Wax HWX 107	Want Ads/We Belong Together	10
72	Hot Wax HWX 111	One Monkey Don't Stop No Show/Stick Up	6
72	Hot Wax HWX 112	The Day I Found Myself/When Will It End	6
72	Hot Wax HWX 116	Sittin' On A Time Bomb/It's Better To Have Loved And Lost	10
71	Hot Wax SHW 5002	HONEYCONE (LP)	20
71	Hot Wax SHW 5004	SWEET REPLIES (LP)	15
72	Hot Wax SHW 5005	SOULFUL TAPESTRY (LP)	15
73	Hot Wax SHW 5010	LOVE, PEACE AND SOUL (LP)	18

HONEYCRACK

95	PPP1	King Of Misery/5 Minutes (numbered p/s, 1500 only sold at gigs)	5
95	PPPCD1	King Of Misery/5 Minutes (numbered card p/s, 1500 only sold at gigs)	5
96	Epic 484230 0	PROZAIC (LP, with inner sleeve, white vinyl, 2000 only)	12

(see also Jellys, Wildhearts)

HONEYDEW

| 70 | Argo AFW 101 | Part Of This Game/To Make You Mine | 20 |
| 70 | Argo ZFB 15 | HONEYDEW (LP) | 125 |

HONEYDRIPPERS

| 84 | Es Paranza SAM 220 | Sea Of Love/Rickin' At Midnight (7" radio promo) | 10 |

84	Es Paranza 790 220-1	THE HONEYDRIPPERS VOL. ONE (10" LP)	8

(see also Robert Plant)

HONEYEND
72	Spark SRL 1072	Heartbreaker/Beautiful Downtown	20

HONEYS
63	Capitol CL 15299	Surfin' Down The Swanee River/Shoot The Curl	50

(see also American Spring, Beach Boys)

HONEYTONES
58	London HLX 8671	Don't Look Now, But.../I Know, I Know	60
58	London HLX 8671	Don't Look Now, But.../I Know, I Know (78)	35

HONEYTREE
70s	Myrrh MYR 1039	EVERGREEN (LP)	20

HONG GANG
72	Sioux SI 004	Reggae Mento/MONTEGO MELON: Swan Lake	5
73	Sioux SI 025	Smoking Wild/ROOSEVELT SINGERS: Heavy Reggae	5

(see also Bob Andy)

HOOD
92	Fluff HONEY 4	Sirens/Fault/Your Sixth Sense (p/s, 500 only)	12
93	Fluff HONEY 6	I Didn't Think You Were Going To Hit Me In The Face/In The Trap Of Doing/Choosing A Grimace (wraparound p/s, 500 only)	10
95	Orgasm ORGASM 08	A Harbour Of Thoughts/Disappointed/Uneven Conversation Should Point To Cause/Forced By The Reasoning Hand/John Clyde-Evans/Silo Crash (p/s)	7
95	555 Recordings 555 01	LEE FAUST'S MILLION PIECE ORCHESTRA: Biochemistry Revision Can Wait/England's Fine Fields/Rocck? I Can't Even Spell The Word/Stricken office Worker (EP, 1,000 copies only)	8
96	Earworm WORM 1	SECRETS NOW KNOWN TO OTHERS: Forhead/Crow Blown West/Beware! Falling Ox/I'm Turning Into A Cart/Further Woodland/20X/Visions Of Old Machinery/Sometimes Doomed/You Should Never Feel Alone In This World/Crushed By Life (EP, 1,000 only)	8
96	Love Train PUBE 11	I've Forgotten How To Live/The Weather Side Of The Stone Mill Tower/ Dimensions TBA	8
98	Rocket Racer ROCKET 04	The Year Of Occasional Lull/Fog Projections (1000 only, numbered, 20 with red artwork)	10
98	Rocket Racer ROCKET 04	The Year Of Occasional Lull/Fog Projections (1000 only, numbered, 980 with black artwork)	5
98	Happy Go Lucky HGL 12	Filmed Initiative/As Evening Changed The Day (different photo on each p/s)	12
98	555 Recordings 555 13	(The) Weight/Fallen Farmer/We Are Not Promote/Impossible Calm/Feel The Rush (Coming In From The Avant Garde)/I Know What To Squander/Mast-On-Hill/Collapsing Climate Soul (p/s)	6
00	Jonathon Whiskey 04	I Can't Find My Brittle Youth/Song Of The Sea/STEWARD: Silver Soda Pop/I'm A Woman NOt Just A Toy/Flatter Me With Concern For Prejudice (envelope sleeve, 250 only)	20
94	Fluff ARC 01	CABLED LINEAR TRACTION (LP, 200 only)	40
98	Domino WIGLP 42	RUSTIC HOUSES FORLORN VALLEYS (LP)	30
99	Domino WIGL 61	THE CYCLE OF DAYS AND REASONS (LP)	25
01	Domino WIGLP 102	COLD HOUSE (LP)	20

ROBBIN HOOD
56	MGM SP 1178	The Rock-A-Bye Blues/Beautiful, Beautiful Love	15

HOODOO RHYTHM DEVILS
78	Fantasy FTC 147	Gotta Lot Of Love In My Soul/MDR Of Love	15

HOOK
68	Uni UN 507	In The Beginning/Show You The Way	10

MARCUS HOOK ROLL BAND
72	Regal Zonophone RZ 3061	Natural Man/Boogalooing Is For Wooing	15
73	Regal zonophone RZ 3072	Louisina Lady/Ghoochie Coochie Har Kau	8

EARL HOOKER
69	Blue Horizon 57-3166	Boogie Don't Blot/Funky Blues	30
70	Blue Horizon 7-63850	SWEET BLACK ANGEL (LP)	100
70	Stateside SSL 10298	DON'T HAVE TO WORRY (LP)	60

(see also John Lee Hooker)

JOHN LEE HOOKER
78s
52	Vogue V 2102	Hoogie Boogie/Whistlin' And Moanin' Blues	50
54	London HL 8037	Need Somebody/Too Much Boogie	50

SINGLES
63	Stateside SS 203	Boom Boom/Frisco Blues	22
64	Stateside SS 297	Dimples/I'm Leaving	20
64	Stateside SS 341	I Love You Honey/Send Me Your Pillow	20
64	Pye International 7N 25255	High Priced Woman/Sugar Mama	20
64	Polydor NH 52930	Shake It Baby/Let's Make It Baby	20
65	Sue WI 361	I'm In The Mood/Boogie Chillun	40
66	Chess CRS 8039	Let's Go Out Tonight/In The Mood	20
66	Planet PLF 114	Mai Lee/Don't Be Messing With My Bread (with Groundhogs)	50
70	President PT 295	Dimples/Boom Boom	8

EPs
60	Riverside REP 3202	WEDNESDAY EVENING	25
60	Riverside REP 3207	DEMOCRAT MAN	25
64	Stateside SE 1019	THE BLUES OF JOHN LEE HOOKER	30
64	Stateside SE 1023	I'M JOHN LEE HOOKER	30
64	Ember EP 4561	THINKING BLUES	40
65	Pye Intl. NEP 44034	LOVE BLUES	35
65	Chess CRE 6000	DOWN AT THE LANDING	35
65	Atlantic AET 6010	JOHN LEE HOOKER	35
66	Chess CRE 6007	WALKING THE BOOGIE	30
66	Chess CRE 6014	THE JOURNEY	30
66	Chess CRE 6021	REAL FOLK BLUES VOL. 3	30

MINT VALUE £

| 73 | Impulse 9103 | SERVES YOU RIGHT TO SUFFER | 15 |

ALBUMS

60	Advent LP 2801	JOHN LEE HOOKER AND HIS GUITAR	80
62	Riverside RLP 12-838	THE FOLK BLUES OF JOHN LEE HOOKER	45
62	Stateside SL 10014	THE FOLK LORE OF JOHN LEE HOOKER	50
63	London HA-K 8097	DON'T TURN ME FROM YOUR DOOR	80
64	Stateside SL 10053	THE BIG SOUL OF JOHN LEE HOOKER	70
64	Stateside SL 10074	I WANT TO SHOUT THE BLUES	60
64	Pye Intl. NPL 28042	HOUSE OF THE BLUES	60
64	Fontana 688 700 ZL	THE FOLK-BLUES OF HOOKER	45
65	Fontana FJL 119	BLUE!	70
65	Ember EMB 3356	SINGS THE BLUES	35
65	Riverside RLP 008	BURNING HELL	35
65	Chess CRL 4500	JOHN LEE HOOKER PLAYS AND SINGS THE BLUES	60
66	HMV CLP 5032	IT SERVES YOU RIGHT TO SUFFER (mono)	45
66	HMV CSD 3542	IT SERVES YOU RIGHT TO SUFFER (stereo)	50
66	Ember (ST)EMB 3371	DRIFTIN' THROUGH THE BLUES	25
67	Chess CRL 4527	THE REAL FOLK BLUES	40
67	HMV CLP/CSD 3612	LIVE AT THE CAFE A GO GO	40
67	Atlantic Special 590 003	DRIFTIN' BLUES	18
68	Joy JOY(S) 101	I'M JOHN LEE HOOKER	15
68	Joy JOY(S) 124	BURNIN'	15
68	Stateside (S)SL 10246	URBAN BLUES	40
69	Joy JOYS 129	TRAVELIN'	12
69	Stateside (S)SL 10280	SIMPLY THE TRUTH	50
69	Joy JOYS 133	THE FOLKLORE OF JOHN LEE HOOKER	15
69	Joy JOYS 142	CONCERT AT NEWPORT	15
69	Joy JOYS 147	THE BIG SOUL OF JOHN LEE HOOKER	15
69	Storyville 673 005	YOU'RE LEAVIN' ME BABY	15
69	Joy JOYS 152	IN PERSON	15
70	Storyville 673 020	TUPELO BLUES	30
70	Stax SXATS 1025	THAT'S WHERE IT'S AT	20
71	Probe SPB 1016	IF YOU MISS 'IM . . . I GOT 'IM (with Earl Hooker)	30
71	Probe SPB 1034	ENDLESS BOOGIE	15
71	Stax 2362 017	THAT'S WHERE IT'S AT!	20
71	Xtra XTRA 1114	JOHN LEE HOOKER	40
71	United Artists UAS 29235	COAST TO COAST BLUES BAND	22
72	Probe SPB 1057	NEVER GET OUT OF THESE BLUES ALIVE	18
73	Green Bottle GN 4002	JOHNNY LEE	18
75	ABC ABCL 5059	FREE BEER AND CHICKEN	15
85	Virgin VPBLP 22	CHILL OUT (LP)	25

(see also Canned Heat, Carlos Santana & Buddy Miles, John Lee's Groundhogs)

JOHN LEE HOOKER/LIGHTNIN' HOPKINS/SMOKEY HOGG

| 73 | Specialty SNTF 5013 | HOOKER HOPKINS HOGG (LP) | 20 |

(see also Lightnin' Hopkins, Smokey Hogg)

STEVE HOOKER & HEAT

| 77 | Takeaway TAKE 1/ EJR 577 | If You Don't Do The Business/Rock & Roll Doctor/I'm Hooked/ Marionette (stamped white sleeve with insert) | 8 |

HOOKFOOT

69	Page One POF 144	Way Of The Musician/Hookfoot	6
72	DJM DJS 265	Sweet Sweet Funky Music/The Opener	8
73	DJM DJS 293	So You Want To Be A Rock And Roll Star/Mr. Money	8
71	DJM DJLPS 413	HOOKFOOT (LP, gatefold sleeve)	30
72	DJM DJLPS 422	GOOD TIMES A' COMIN' (LP, gatefold sleeve)	25
73	DJM DJLPS 428	COMMUNICATION (LP, gatefold sleeve)	20
73	DJM DJLPS 435	ROARING (LP)	12
75	DJM DJLMD 8013	HEADLINES (2XLP)	18

(see also Elton John, Loot, Caleb, Soul Agents)

MARSHALL HOOKS & CO.

| 71 | Blue Horizon 2096 002 | I Want The Same Thing Tomorrow/Hookin' It | 20 |
| 71 | Blue Horizon 2431 003 | MARSHALL HOOKS & CO. (LP) | 100 |

HOOKY

| 72 | RCA Victor SF 8247 | THE COLLECTED TALES OF HOOKY NO.1 (LP, gatefold sleeve) | 20 |

HOOTEN(ANNY) SINGERS

| 64 | United Artists UP 1082 | Gabrielle/Darling (most copies list artist as Hooten Singers) | 35 |

(see also Abba, Hep Stars, Northern Lights)

BOB HOPE

| 58 | London HLU 8593 | Paris Holiday/Nothing In Common (with Bing Crosby) | 10 |

(see also Bing Crosby, Rosemary Clooney)

LYN(N) HOPE

57	Vogue V 9081	Blue Moon/Blues For Anna Bacca	20
57	Vogue V 9081	Blue Moon/Blues For Anna Bacca (78)	10
57	Vogue V 9082	Eleven Till Two/Blues For Mary	20
58	Vogue V 9115	Temptation/The Scrunch (78)	10
60	Blue Beat BB 21	Shockin'/Blue And Sentimental	20
57	Vogue VE 170103	LYNN HOPE AND HIS TENOR SAX (EP)	40
60	Vogue VE 170146	LYNN HOPE AND HIS TENOR SAX (EP)	60

PETER HOPE & RICHARD H. KIRK

| 85 | Doublevision DVR 15 | Leather Hands (Master Mix)/(Radio Mix)/(Crash Mix) (12", p/s) | 8 |

(see also Cabaret Voltaire, Richard H. Kirk)

HOPE STREET

| 71 | Parlophone R5982 | Wait Until Tomorrow/Ladies At The Bottom Of the Garden | 12 |

HOPE & KEEN

| 71 | Excello XLO2 | Crazy House/You Can Go My Way | 12 |

HOPE OF THE STATES

00s	Seeker SEEK 001	Black Dollar Bills/Everything For Everyone (Demo)/Sts'Ikel (Demo) (CD, numbered & signed, 1000 only)	25

HOPETOWN (LEWIS) & GLENMORE (BROWN)

68	Fab FAB 43	Skinny Leg Girl/Live Like A King	45

MARY HOPKIN

68	Apple APPLE 2	Those Were The Days/Turn Turn Turn (later pressing crediting Mary Hopkins)	8
68	Apple APPLE 2	Those Were The Days/Turn Turn Turn (First pressing)	10
68	Apple APPLE 2	Those Were The Days/Turn Turn Turn (blank Apple label on A-side)	12
69	Apple APPLE 7	Lontana Dagli Occhi/Game (Europe-only, unreleased in U.K.)	0
69	Apple APPLE 9	Prince En Avignon/The Game (France-only, unreleased in U.K.)	0
69	Apple APPLE 10	Goodbye/Sparrow	6
69	Apple APPLE 16	Que Sera Sera/Fields Of St. Etienne (unreleased)	0
69	Cambrian CSP 703	Aderyn Llwyd/Y Blodyn Gwyn (p/s)	18
70	Cambrian CSP 712	Pleserau Serch/Tyrd Yn Ôl (p/s)	18
70	Apple APPLE 22	Temma Harbour/Lontano Dagli Occhi (black or green lettering on p/s)	6
70	Apple APPLE 26	Knock, Knock Who's There?/I'm Going To Fall In Love Again (p/s)	6
70	Apple APPLE 27	Que Sera Sera/Fields Of St. Etienne (unreleased in U.K., acetates only)	0
70	Apple APPLE 30	Think About Your Children/Heritage (p/s)	6
71	Apple APPLE 34	Let My Name Be Sorrow/Kew Gardens (p/s)	15
71	Apple APPLE 39	Water, Paper And Clay/Jefferson (p/s)	20
72	Regal Zonophone RZ 3070	Mary Had A Baby/Cherry Tree Carol	6
76	Good Earth GD 2	If You Love Me (I Won't Care): (some copies list "If You Love Me")/Tell Me Now	6
77	Good Earth GD 11	Wrap Me In Your Arms/Just A Dreamer (p/s)	10
68	Cambrian CEP 414	LLAIS SWYNOL MARY HOPKIN (EP)	15
69	Cambrian CEP 420	MARY AC EDWARD (EP, with Edward Morris Jones)	15
69	Apple APCOR 5	POST CARD (LP, laminated sleeve, with black or white inner sleeve, mono)	20
69	Apple (S)APCOR 5	POST CARD (LP, laminated sleeve, with black or white inner sleeve, stereo)	15
71	Apple SAPCOR 21	EARTH SONG - OCEAN SONG (LP, gatefold sleeve, 'Apple' inner sleeve)	30
72	Apple SAPCOR 23	THOSE WERE THE DAYS (LP, with 'Apple' inner sleeve)	70
77	Decca SPA 546	THE WELSH WORLD OF MARY HOPKIN (LP)	25
89	Trax Modem 1045	SPIRIT (LP)	20
91	Apple SAPCOR 5	POST CARD (LP, reissue, gatefold sleeve with bonus 12" [SAPCOR 52])	30
92	Apple SAPCOR 21	EARTH SONG/OCEAN SONG (LP, reissue, gatefold sleeve with inner)	30

(see also Hobby Horse, Sundance, Oasis, Elfland Ensemble, Bob Johnson & Pete Knight, Roy Budd, Elmer Bernstein)

ANTHONY HOPKINS

86	Juice AA 5	Distant Star/Ordinary Man (p/s)	5

JOEL & LIGHTNIN' HOPKINS

60	Heritage H 1000	BLUES FROM EAST TEXAS (LP, 99 copies only)	120

(see also Lightnin' Hopkins)

LIGHTNIN' HOPKINS

61	Bluesville BVLP 1019	LIGHTNIN' HOPKINS (LP)	80
62	'77' LA 12/1	SAM LIGHTNIN' HOPKINS - THE ROOSTER CROWED IN ENGLAND (LP 99 copies only)	150
63	Stateside SL 10031	LIGHTNIN' STRIKES (LP)	70
63	Realm RM 128	LIGHTNIN' HOPKINS SINGS THE BLUES (LP)	30
63	Realm RM 171	DIRTY HOUSE BLUES (LP)	30
64	Stateside SL 10076	BLUES HOOT (LP, some tracks by Sonny Terry & Brownie McGhee)	40
65	Stateside SL 10110	HOOTIN' THE BLUES (LP)	40
65	Stateside SL 10155	DOWN HOME BLUES (LP)	40
65	Fontana AH 183	THE BLUES (LP)	35
65	Fontana 688 301 ZL	LAST NIGHT BLUES (LP)	35
66	Fontana 688 801 ZL	BURNIN' IN L.A. (LP)	35
66	Fontana 688 803 ZL	BLUE BIRD BLUES (LP)	35
66	Fontana 688 807 ZL	BLUES PARTY (LP)	35
66	Ember EMB 3389	A TIME FOR BLUES (LP)	25
66	Ember EMB 3416	LIVE AT THE BIRD LOUNGE (LP)	25
67	Ember EMB 3423	I'VE BEEN BUKED AND SCORNED (LP)	25
66	Verve (S)VLP 5003	ROOTS OF HOPKINS (LP)	25
66	Verve (S)VLP 5014	LIGHTNIN' STRIKES (LP, reissue)	18
66	Saga ERO 8001	LIGHTNIN' HOPKINS (LP)	15
67	Xtra XTRA 5036	BLUES IN MY BOTTLE (LP)	18
68	Xtra XTRA 5044	GOT TO MOVE YOUR BABY (LP, reissue of Fontana 688 301 ZL)	20
68	Minit MLL/MLS 40006	EARTH BLUES (LP)	40
69	Liberty LBL 83254	KING OF DOWLING STREET (LP)	30
69	Joy JOY(S) 115	LIGHTNIN' STRIKES (LP, 2nd reissue)	15
69	Polydor 545 019	THAT'S MY STORY (LP)	25
70	Ace Of Hearts (Z)AHT 183	THE BLUES (LP)	15
70	Poppy PYS 11000	LIGHTNIN'! VOLUME 1 (LP)	20
70	Poppy PYS 11002	LIGHTNIN'! VOLUME 2 (LP)	20
71	Liberty LBS 83293	THE CALIFORNIA MUDSLIDE (AND EARTHQUAKE) (LP)	30
71	Mayfair AMLB 4000 1/2	LIGHTNIN' STRIKES (2-LP)	18
71	Blue Horizon 2431 005	LET'S WORK AWHILE (LP)	120
71	Xtra XTRA 1127	THE ROOTS OF LIGHTNIN' HOPKINS (LP)	18
71	Boulevard BLVD 4001	LIGHTNIN' HOPKINS (LP)	12
72	Carnival 2941 005	LONESOME LIGHTNIN' (LP)	18

(see also Sonny Terry & Brownie McGhee, Joel & Lightnin' Hopkins, Lightnin' Hopkins & John Lee Hooker, Big Joe Williams)

LIGHTNIN' HOPKINS & JOHN LEE HOOKER

69	Storyville 616 001	THERE'S GOOD ROCKIN' TONIGHT! (LP)	35
72	Storyville SLP 174	LIGHTNIN' HOPKINS AND JOHN LEE HOOKER (LP)	35

(see also John Lee Hooker/Lightnin' Hopkins/Smokey Hogg)

LINDA HOPKINS

61	Coral Q 72423	I Diddle Dum Dum/All In My Mind	20
62	Coral Q 72448	Mama's Doin' The Twist/My Mother's Eyes	20

LINDA HOPKINS & JACKIE WILSON

63	Coral Q 72464	Shake A Hand/Say I Do	15
65	Coral Q 72480	Yes Indeed/When The Saints Go Marching In	15

(see also Jackie Wilson)

NICKY HOPKINS

66	CBS 202055	Mr Big/Jenni	18
67	Polydor 56175	Mister Pleasant/Nothing As Yet	18
68	MGM MGM 1419	Top Pops No. 1 (Medley)/(Part 2)	8
68	Fontana TF 906	High On A Hill/Trumpet Serenade (actually by Nigel Hopkins)	6
73	CBS CBS 1328	Speed On/Sundown In Mexico	5
66	CBS (S)BPG 62679	THE REVOLUTIONARY PIANO OF NICKY HOPKINS (LP)	60
73	CBS 65416	THE TIN MAN WAS A DREAMER (LP, gatefold sleeve)	40

(see also Aquarian Age, Neil Christian & Crusaders, Cyril Davies R&B All-Stars, Poet & One Man Band, Quicksilver Messenger Service, Sweet Thursday)

WASH HOPKINS SINGERS

69	Action ACT 4546	He's Got Blessing/Rock In A Weary Land	20

HOPKIRK AND LEE

98	Gallery Records GAL001CD	Beneath The Apple Tree (CD, EP, 1000 copies)	10
98	Rough Trade/For Us 001	Beneath The Apple Tree (7" 1,000 copies)	15

HUGH HOPPER

73	CBS 65466	1984 (LP)	30
76	Compendium FIDARDO 4	CRUEL BUT FAIR (LP)	15
77	Compendium FIDARDO 7	HOPPERTUNITY BOX (LP)	15
78	Ogun OG 527	ROGUE ELEMENT (LP, as Hopper, Dean, Gowen, Sheen - 'Soft Heap')	20

(see also Caravan, Elton Dean, Gilgamesh, Isotope, Matching Mole, Ninesense, Soft Machine)

HOPSCOTCH

69	United Artists UP 2231	Look At The Lights Go Up/Same Old Fat Man	140
69	United Artists UP 35022	Long Black Veil/Easy To Find	10

(see also Scots Of St. James, Five Day Rain, Forever More, Glencoe)o

HORACE & IMPERIALS

68	Nu Beat NB 012	Young Love/Days Like These	15

HORATIO

70	Penny Farthing PEN 729	I've Gotta Have You/A Sad Song With A Happy Soul	5

HORDEN RAIKES

73	Folk Heritage FHR 042	KING COTTON (LP)	15
72	Folk Heritage FHR 026	HORDEN RAIKES (LP)	20

HORIZON

81	SRT SRTS 81432	Stage Struck/Remember The Bad Boys	10

HORIZON

83	Orbit TRIP 4	Sunshine Reggae/Nightlife	6

(see also Mungo Jerry)

PAUL HORN

68	Liberty LBL 83084E	COSMIC CONSCIOUSNESS (LP)	18

KENNETH HORNE

69	Pye NPL 18291	ROUND THE HORNE (LP)	15

LENA HORNE

55	HMV 7M 309	Love Me Or Leave Me/I Love To Love	5
55	HMV 7M 319	It's All Right With Me/It's Love	5
56	HMV 7M 423	If You Can Dream/What's Right For You (Is Right For Me)	5
56	MGM MGM 917	Can't Help Lovin' Dat Man/The Man I Love	5
59	RCA RCA 1120	A New Fangled Tango/Honeysuckle Rose	5
65	United Artists UP 1101	The Sand And The Sea/It Had Better Be Tonight	25
71	Buddah 2011 078	Maybe I'm Amazed/Feels So Good	5

(see also Harry Belafonte)

HANK HORNSBY

57	MGM MGM 955	Pots And Pans/Cotton	6
58	MGM MGM 972	The Legend Of The Birds And Bees/Girls Girls Girls	6

HORNSEY AT WAR

70s	War WAR 001	DEAD BEAT REVIVAL (EP, numbered p/s)	40

HORRORCOMIC

77	Lightning/B&C BVZ 0007	I'm All Hung Up On Pierrepoint/The Exorcist/Sex In The Afternoon (p/s)	40
78	Lightning GIL 512	I Don't Mind/England 77 (p/s)	90
79	B&C BCS 18	Jesus Crisis/Cut Your Throat (p/s)	400

HORRORS

06	Loog LOOG 18-7X	Count In Fives/A Knife In Their Eye (p/s, inner p/s, stickered PVC sleeve)	10
06	Loog LOOG 18-7	Count In Fives/Who Says (black sleeve, barcode sticker, with sticker inside)	10
06	Loog LOOG 015	Sheena Is A Parasite/Jack The Ripper (p/s, insert, 500 only)	50
06	Loog LOOG 016	Death At The Chapel/Crawdaddy Simone (p/s, 500 only with sticker)	15
07	Loog 1725544	Gloves/Kicking Kay (p/s)	8
07	Loog 1725539	Gloves/Death At The Chapel (p/s)	8
07	Loog 1735625	She Is The New Thing/Draw Japan (Dandi Wind Remix) p/s)	8
07	Loog 1735628	She Is The New Thing/Sister Leonella (p/s)	8
09	XL XLS 417	Who Can Say/You Never Could Tell (p/s)	8
09	XL XLS 468	Whole New Way/Primary Colours (p/s)	8
07	Polydor 172 419-9	STRANGE HOUSE (LP, stickered gatefold sleeve, inner)	45
09	XL XLLP 418	PRIMARY COLOURS (2-LP, poster)	20
11	XL XLLP 539	SKYING (2-LP with 5 prints)	15

FRANK HORROX

60	Embassy WEP 1038	JAZZ SESSION (EP, featuring Don Rendell)	15

HORSE

70	RCA Victor SF 8109	HORSE (LP)	250

(see also Saturnalia, Atomic Rooster)

HORSEPOWER
| 79 | Square SQS 2 | Outrageous/Highway Robbery | 10 |

HORSLIPS
73	Oats OAT 1	High Reel/Furniture	5
73	Oats OAT 2	Dearg Doom/The Shamrock Shore	5
73	Oats MOO 3	HAPPY TO MEET ... SORRY TO PART (LP, booklet octagonal sleeve)	45
73	Oats MOO 5	THE TAIN (LP, gatefold sleeve, lyric inner sleeve)	20
76	DJM DJF 20498	THE BOOK OF INVASION - A CELTIC SYMPHONY (LP, with lyric inner sleeve)	12
75	RCA Victor SF 8432	THE UNFORTUNATE CUP OF TEA (LP, orange label)	15

HORTENSE (ELLIS) & ALTON (ELLIS)
| 65 | Island WI 230 | Don't Gamble With Love/Something You Got (B-side actually by Alton Ellis & Flames) | 25 |

(see also Hortense Ellis, Alton Ellis, Mr. Foundation)

HORTENSE (ELLIS) & DELROY (WILSON)
| 66 | Rio R 119 | We're Gonna Make It/SOUL BROTHERS: Ska Shuffle | 25 |

(see also Hortense Ellis, Delroy Wilson)

HORTENSE (ELLIS) & JACKIE (OPEL)
| 64 | R&B JB 138 | Stand By Me/JACKIE OPEL: Solid Rock | 50 |

(see also Hortense Ellis, Jackie Opel)

JOHNNY HORTON
59	Philips PB 932	The Battle Of New Orleans/All For The Love Of A Girl	5
59	Philips PB 932	The Battle Of New Orleans/All For The Love Of A Girl (78)	25
59	Philips PB 951	Sal's Got A Sugar Lip/Johnny Reb	8
59	Philips PB 951	Sal's Got A Sugar Lip/Johnny Reb (78)	15
59	Philips PB 976	Take Me Like I Am/I'm Ready If You're Willing	5
60	Philips PB 995	Sink The Bismarck!/The Same Old Tale The Crow Told Me	10
60	Philips PB 1062	North To Alaska/The Mansion You Stole	5
61	Philips PB 1130	When It's Springtime In Alaska/Mr. Moonlight	5
61	Philips PB 1132	Sleepy Eyed John/They'll Never Take Her Love From Me	5
61	Philips PB 1170	Miss Marcy/Ole Slew Foot	7
62	Philips PB 1226	Words/Honky Tonk Man	10
63	CBS AAG 132	All Grown Up/I'm A One Woman Man	8
60	Mercury ZEP 10074	THE FANTASTIC JOHNNY HORTON (EP)	40
64	Mercury 10008 MCE	COUNTRY AND WESTERN ACES (EP)	20
60	Philips BBL 7464	THE SPECTACULAR JOHNNY HORTON (LP)	20
61	Philips BBL 7536	HONKY TONK MAN (LP)	25
63	London HA-U 8096	DONE ROVIN' (LP)	20

ROBERT HORTON
60	Pye 7N 15285	(Roll Along) Wagon Train/Sail Ho!	6
61	Pye 7N 15357	The Girl That I Marry/Time After Time	5
66	Pye 7N 17031	Shenadoah/Maria	6

WALTER 'SHAKEY' HORTON
70	London HAK/SHK 8405	SOUTHERN COMFORT (LP, as Shakey Horton)	120
74	Xtra XTRA 1135	WALTER 'SHAKEY' HORTON WITH HOT COTTAGE (LP)	30
74	Sonet SNTF 677	BIG WALTER HORTON (LP, with Carey Bell)	22

LA/THE HOST
| 85 | Quiet QU 1 | The Big Sleep/Just Breaking Away (p/s) | 8 |

HOT BUTTER
| 73 | Pye International NSPL 28169 | POPCORN (LP) | 15 |
| 73 | Pye International NSPL 28181 | MORE HOT BUTTER (LP) | 15 |

HOT CHIP
00	Victory Garden VG14	MEXICO EP (CD)	20
04	Moshi Moshi HOTCHIP7	Hittin Skittles/Back To The Future (300 only, hand-made sleeve)	10
05	No label or cat no	ALL FILLER NO KILLER! (tour only CD-R 7 track)	30
06	No label	MIXTURE (CD-R mix, animal p/s, 17 tracks)	30
07	EMI CHIPS 01	Rehab (AMY WINEHOUSE: Hot Chip Remix)/In The Morning (JUNIOR BOYS: Hot Chip Remix) (12")	8
04	Moshi Moshi MOSHILP 06	COMING ON STRONG (LP, 500 only)	15
06	EMI 094634741811	THE WARNING (2-LP with free 7", Won't Wash/Bally)	20
08	EMI 5099952057717	MADE IN THE DARK (LP)	15
10	Vinyl Factory VF 012	ONE LIFE STAND (LP with free 7" Bubble/Do Not Wait, no'd gatefold sleeve, 1000 only)	25
10	Live Here Now/EMI CDLHN 78	LIVE 10th NOVEMBER LONDON ALEXANDRA PALACE (2-CD-R, silkscreened sleeve)	18

HOT CHOCOLATE (BAND)
69	Apple APPLE 18	Give Peace A Chance/Living Without Tomorrow (as Hot Chocolate Band)	60
70	Rak RAK 103	Love Is Life/Pretty Girls (with promo p/s)	5
73	Rak RAK 139	You Could Have Been A Friend/Go Go Girl	15
79	Rak 12RAK 29	Mindless Boogie/Don't Turn It Off (12" p/s)	8

(see also Errol Brown & Chosen Few, Tony Wilson)

HOT CITY
| 71 | London HLU 10344 | Leaving/I Believe In Life | 15 |

HOT CLUB
| 82 | RAK 346 | The Dirt That She Walks On Is Sacred Ground To Me/Heat (p/s) | 12 |
| 82 | RAK 346 | The Dirt That She Walks On Is Sacred Ground To Me/Heat (12", p/s) | 10 |

(see also Rich Kids, Spectres)

HOTFOOT GALE
| 78 | Charly SYS 1044 | Washin' Machine Boogie/Everybody's Feelin' Allright | 6 |

HOTLEGS
70	Fontana 6007 019	Neanderthal Man/You Didn't Like It Because You Didn't Think Of It	5
71	Philips 6006 140	Lady Sadie/The Loser	8
71	Philips 6308 047	THINKS: SCHOOL STINKS (LP, gatefold sleeve, black/silver label)	40
71	Philips 6308 080	SONG (LP, gatefold sleeve, black/silver label)	50

(see also 10cc, Mindbenders, Godley & Creme, Tristar Airbus, Ramases)

HOT POTATO
| 73 | PMTB 1 | HOT POTATO (LP, private pressing) | 25 |

HOT RAIN
| 90 | Pine Tree TWIG 002 | STAY TRUE (12", EP) | 25 |

HOT RATS
| 09 | No label or cat no | Damaged Goods/Fight For Your Right To Party (tour 7", 150-only, die-cut sleeve, signed) | 12 |

(see also Supergrass)

HOT ROCKS
| 73 | Bell Bell 1326 | Chopper/Roly Poly | 6 |

HOT ROCKS & JAH LOXLEY
| 80s | Gemini GSM 025 | Jah Jah No Parcial/Badda Badda | 20 |

HOT ROD
| 69 | Joe's DU 41 | The Judge/RON: Soul Of Soul Of Joel | 12 |
| 73 | President PT 397 | I Want You (All Night Long)/Love Is All Right (Hey) | 10 |

HOT ROD ALLSTARS
69	Duke DU 59	Lick A Pop/Treasure	40
70	Duke DU 65	Paint Your Wagon/Organ Man	140
70	Duke DU 66	Return Of The Bad Man/Caysoe Reggae	20
70	Trojan TR 7732	Strong Man/Sentimental	20
70	Trojan TR 7733	Virgin Soldier/Brixton Reggae Festival	50
70	Torpedo TOR 1	Pussy Got Nine Life/BOSS SOUNDS: Lick It Back	60
70	Torpedo TOR 5	Skinheads Don't Fear/Ten Commandments From The Devil	100
70	Torpedo TOR 10	Moonhop In London/Skinhead Moondust	150
70	Torpedo TOR 14	Control Your Doggy/Follow The Stars	30
70	Hot Rod HR 104	Skinhead Speaks His Mind/CARL LEVEY: Carnaby Street	150
70	Hot Rod HR 107	Strictly Invitation/PATSY & PEGGY: Dog Your Woman	100
70	Hot Rod HR 108	Beautiful World/Shocks Of A Drugs Man	15

(see also Setters, Betty Sinclair)

HOTRODS
| 65 | Columbia DB 7693 | I Don't Love You No More/Ain't Coming Back No More | 50 |

HOT SPRINGS
| 66 | Columbia DB 7821 | It's All Right/All I Know About Love | 20 |

HOT THUMBS O'RILEY
| 73 | Charisma CAS 1071 | HOT THUMBS O'RILEY (LP, gatefold sleeve, large 'Mad Hatter' label) | 30 |

HOT-TODDYS
| 59 | Pye International 7N 25020 | Rockin' Crickets/Shakin' And Stompin' | 30 |
| 59 | Pye International 7N 25020 | Rockin' Crickets/Shakin' And Stompin' (78) | 35 |

(see also Rockin' Rebels)

HOT TUNA
72	Grunt 65-0502	Keep On Truckin'/Water Song	5
76	Grunt RCG 1002	It's So Easy/I Can't Be Satisfied	5
70	RCA SF 8125	HOT TUNA (LP)	20
71	RCA LSP 4550	ELECTRIC LIVE (FIRST PULL UP, THEN PULL DOWN) (LP)	12
72	Grunt FTR 1004	BURGERS (LP, with purple inner sleeve)	12

(see also Jefferson Airplane)

HOT VULTURES
| 77 | Red Rag RRR 015 | THE EAST STREET SHAKES (LP) | 20 |
| 79 | Plant Life PLR 018 | UP THE LINE (LP) | 20 |

(see also Ian (A) Anderson)

HOT WATER
| 78 | Duff | Different Morning/Premium Bondage | 8 |
| 79 | Duff DWR 101 | Get Lost!/Bird's Eye View (p/s) | 7 |

HOUGHTON WEAVERS
78	Folk Heritage FHR 106	SIT THI DOWN (LP)	15
79	Folk Heritage FHR 111	CLATTER O' CLOGS (LP)	15
80	EMI HW 1001	UP YOUR WAY (LP)	15
80	EMI HW 1002	ALIVE & KICKING (LP)	15
83	EMI HW 1003	IN THE RARE OLD TIMES (LP)	15
85	Folk Heritage FHR 128	KEEP FOLK SMILING (LP)	12
86	Folk Heritage FHR 129	IT'S GOOD TO SEE YOU (LP)	12

HOUNDHEAD HENRY/FRANKIE JAXON
| 60 | Jazz Collector JEL 10 | THE MALE BLUES VOLUME 6 (EP) | 18 |

HOUR GLASS
| 68 | Liberty LBL/LBS 83219E | THE HOUR GLASS (LP) | 30 |
| 74 | United Artists USD 303/4 | THE HOUR GLASS (2-LP) | 18 |

(see also Allman Brothers)

HOUSE CREW
91	Production House PNT 029	Keep The Fire Burning/Get On Up (12")	12
91	Production House PNT 029R	Keep The Fires Burning (Remixes) (12")	20
92	Production House PNT 035	We Are Hardcore/Maniac (Hypermix) (12")	15
92	Production House PNT 035R	We Are Hardcore/Maniac (Remixes) (12")	15
93	Production House PNT 047	The Theme/Euphoria (12")	25
93	Production House PNT 047R	The Theme/Euphoria (Remixes) (12")	25
94	Production House PNT 060	Superhero (My Knight) (12")	15
94	Production House PNT 060R	Superhero (Remixes) (12")	15
94	Production House PNT 060RX	Superhero (Remixes II) (12")	15

HOUSEHOLD
| 67 | United Artists UP 1190 | I Guess I'll Learn How To Fly/Nothing You Can Do But Cry | 6 |
| 68 | United Artists UP 2210 | Twenty First Summer/Winter's Coming On | 6 |

HOUSEHOLD NAMES

| 81 | Blue Chip BC 104 | White Light/Much Too Young To Love ....7 |

HOUSEMARTINS

85	Go! Discs GOD 7	Flag Day/Stand At Ease (p/s) 5
85	Go! Discs GOD 7/GOD 9	Flag Day/Stand At Ease/Sheep/Drop Down Dead (shrinkwrapped double pack)................6
85	Go! Discs GODX 7	Flag Day/Stand At Ease/Coal Train To Hatfield Main (12", p/s) 8
86	Go! Discs GODP 9	Sheep/I'll Be Your Shelter/Drop Down Dead (picture disc) 5
86	Go! Discs GODP 11	Happy Hour/The Mighty Ship (shaped picture disc) 5
86	Go! Discs GODP 13	Think For A Minute/Who Needs The Limelight (shaped picture disc)........................5
86	Go! Discs GODP 16	Caravan Of Love/When I First Met Jesus (rectangular picture disc)......................5
86	Go! Discs GODB 16	THE HOUSEMARTINS' CHRISTMAS BOX SET (4 singles in foldout sleeve, signed)........25
07	Mercury 175 252-3	SOUP ('deluxe Fan Edition', in sealed/stickered tin: CD, DVD, T-shirt and mug)..........60

(see also Beautiful South)

HOUSEMASTER BALDWIN

| 88 | Koolkat KOOLT 21 | DELTA HOUSE (12", p/s) ....10 |
| 88 | Koolkat KOOLT 22 | DON'T LEAD ME (12", p/s) ....10 |

HOUSE OF LORDS

| 69 | B&C CB 112 | In The Land Of Dreams/Ain't Gonna Wait Forever......................................25 |

HOUSE OF LOVE

87	Creation CRE 043T	Shine On/Love/Flow (12", p/s, 4,000 only)..20
87	Creation CRE 044T	Real Animal/Plastic/Nothing To Me (12", p/s, 4,000 only) 20
88	Creation CRE 053	Christine/Loneliness Is A Gun (die-cut '99p' sleeve)....................................5
88	Creation CRE 057	Destroy The Heart/Blind (p/s) 5
88	Creation CRE 057T	Destroy The Heart/Blind/Mr Jo (12", p/s) 10
89	Fontana HOLR212	I Don't Know Why I Love You/Clothes/Secrets/The Spy (12")..............................5
89	Fontana HOLG4	The Beatles & The Stones/Love IV (fold-out flower p/s, numbered & poster) 5
92	Love 1	ROYAL ALBERT HALL EP (10" gig freebie, stickered) 25
88	Creation CRELP 034	HOUSE OF LOVE (LP, with free 7", "Shine On/Christine", matt sleeve)...................20

HOUSESHAKERS

| 72 | Contour 2870160 | DEMOLITION ROCK (LP) ....12 |

BOBBI HOUSTON

| 74 | Action ACT 4622 | I Want To Make It With You (Parts 1 & 2)..8 |

CISCO HOUSTON

60	Top Rank 30/028	THE CISCO SPECIAL (LP) 50
62	Fontana TFL 6007	CISCO SPECIAL! (LP) 25
62	Fontana TFL 6014	SINGS SONGS OF WOODY GUTHRIE (LP)...20
68	Fontana FJL 412	I AIN'T GOT NO HOME (LP)..15
69	Ember CW 135	CISCO HOUSTON AND WOODY GUTHRIE (LP) 15

CISSY HOUSTON

70	Major Minor MM 700	He/I Believe/I'll Be There 5
70	Major Minor MM 716	The Long And Winding Road/Be My Baby 5
70	Pye International 7N 25537	I Just Don't Know What To Do With Myself/This Empty Place 40
71	Pye International 7N 25545	The Long And Winding Road/Be My Baby (reissue) 5
71	Janus 6146 003	Darling Take Me Back/Hang On To A Dream 5
72	Janus 6146 027	Midnight Train To Georgia/I'm So Glad I Can Love Again 5
70	Major Minor SMLP 80	PRESENTING CISSY HOUSTON (LP)..30

(see also Sweet Inspirations)

DAVID HOUSTON

55	London HL 8147	Blue Prelude/I'm Sorry I Made You Cry 50
55	London HL 8147	Blue Prelude/I'm Sorry I Made You Cry (78) 10
63	Columbia DB 7159	Mountain Of Love/Poor Little Angeline 7
66	Columbia DB 7997	Almost Persuaded/We Got Love 7

DAVID HOUSTON & TAMMY WYNETTE

| 67 | Columbia DB 8246 | My Elusive Dreams/Marriage On The Rocks ....8 |

SAM HOUSTON

| 65 | Island WI 172 | My Mother's Eyes/Danny Boy ....12 |

THELMA HOUSTON

69	Stateside SS 8026	Jumpin' Jack Flash/Sunshower...5
72	Tamla Motown TMG 799	I Want To Go Back There Again/Pick Of The Week 12
72	Mowest MW 3001	No One's Gonna Be A Fool Forever/What If 7
73	Mowest MW 3004	Black California/I'm Letting Go (withdrawn)..60
69	Stateside (S)SL 5010	SUNSHOWER (LP)..12
73	Mowest MWS 7003	THELMA HOUSTON (LP) 12

ROWAND S. HOWARD & NIKKI SUDDEN

| 87 | Creation CRE 040T | Wedding Hotel/Hello Wolf/Girl Without A Name/Wedding Hotel (Original Mix) (12", p/s) .10 |

(see also Swell Maps, Last Bandits, Jeremy Gluck)

BRIAN HOWARD & SILHOUETTES

62	Columbia DB 4914	Somebody Help Me/Young And Evil 25
63	Columbia DB 7067	The Worryin' Kind/Come To Me 25
64	Fontana TF 464	Back In The U.S.A./Hooked 20

JAN HOWARD

| 60 | London HL 7088 | The One You Slip Around With/I Wish I Could Fall In Love Again (export issue) ....25 |

JOHN HOWARD

| 75 | CBS 80473 | KID IN A BIG WORLD (LP, with insert) ....25 |

JOHNNY HOWARD BAND

60	Decca F 11298	Up The Wall/Orbit 5
62	Decca F 11423	Mind Reader/Spanish Gipsy Dance 8
64	Decca F 11925	Rinky Dink/Java 8
65	Decca F 12065	El Pussy Cat/A Tune Called Harry 5
65	Decca LK 4735	THE EASY BEAT SOUND (LP)..20
67	Deram DML/SML 1001	THE VELVET TOUCH OF JOHNNY HOWARD (LP)..12

| 67 | Deram SHL 1012 | LOVE IS THE SWEETEST THING (LP) ....12 |

KEITH HOWARD

| 80 | Rods HOT 2 | LOOKING FOR YOU (LP, some sleeves contain Driver artwork on opposite sides of sleeve) ..35 |

(see also Victory)

LES HOWARD

| 53 | HMV 7M 127 | Love Evermore/I Lived When I Met You ....10 |
| 53 | HMV 7M 171 | Rags To Riches/From Here To Eternity ....10 |

NOAH HOWARD

| 69 | Polydor Super 2383093 | THE BLACK ARK (LP) ....40 |

ROLAND S. HOWARD & LYDIA LUNCH

| 86 | 4AD BAD 210 | Some Velvet Morning/I Fell In Love With A Ghost (12", p/s, with postcard) ....12 |

(see also Lydia Lunch, Birthday Party)

WAYNE HOWARD

| 70 | Explosion EX 2042 | All Kinds Of Everything/Cool And Easy (B-side actually by Lloyd Charmers) ....7 |

JACK HOWARTH

| 71 | Fontana 6438042 | OW DO (LP) ....12 |

HOWDY BOYS

| 80 | Spectacle SP 1 | Spectacle/Dancing In The Depression (p/s) ....15 |

CATHERINE HOWE

71	Reflection HRS 11	Nothing More Than Strangers/It Comes With The Breezes 20
71	Reflection REFL 11	WHAT A BEAUTIFUL PLACE (LP, laminated front sleeve 'correction' sticker on rear sleeve) 800
75	RCA Victor SF 8407	HARRY (LP) 20
79	Ariola ARL 5013	DRAGONFLY DAYS (LP) 12

STEVE HOWE

| 75 | Atlantic K50151 | BEGINNINGS (LP, gatefold sleeve) ....15 |

(see also Yes)

EDDIE HOWELL

| 76 | Warner Bros K 16701 | Man From Manhattan/Waiting In The Wings (features members of Queen) ....18 |
| 77 | Warner Bros K 16866 | Sweet On You/Miss Amerika (features Gary Moore) ....10 |

(see also Queen, Gary Moore, Brian May, Freddie Mercury)

EDDY HOWELL

| 69 | Parlophone R5756 | Easy Street/Judy's Good ....45 |

FRANKIE HOWERD

54	Decca F 10420	(Don't Let The) Kiddy Geddin/Abracadabra 10
58	Columbia DB 4230	It's All Right With Me/Song And Dance Man 10
64	Decca F 12028	Last Word On The Election/Last Word On The Election (Part 2) 7
70	Pye 7N 45061	Up Je T'Aime/All Through The Night 5
71	Columbia DB 8757	Up Pompeii/Salute! 5
63	Decca LK 4556	AT THE ESTABLISHMENT (LP) 15
63	HMV CLP 1685	A FUNNY THING HAPPENED ON THE WAY TO THE FORUM (LP)........15

CHRIS HOWLAND

| 58 | Columbia DB 4114 | Mama (Ma, He's Making Eyes At Me)/Fraulein ....7 |
| 59 | Columbia DB 4194 | Susie Darlin'/The Rain Falls On Ev'rybody ....10 |

HOWLIN' WOLF

61	Pye International 7N 25101	Little Baby/Down In The Bottom 25
63	Pye International 7N 25192	Just Like I Treat You/I Ain't Superstitious 25
64	Pye International 7N 25244	Smokestack Lightnin'/Going Down Slow ('Slow' on B-side label) 25
64	Pye International 7N 25244	Smokestack Lightnin'/Going Down Slow ("South' on B-side label) 20
64	Pye International 7N 25269	Little Girl/Tail Dragger 22
64	Pye International 7N 25283	Love Me Darling/My Country Sugar Mama 22
65	Chess CRS 8010	Killing Floor/Louise 15
65	Chess CRS 8016	Ooh Baby/Tell Me What I've Done 15
69	Chess CRS 8097	Evil/Tail Dragger 15
56	London REU 1072	RHYTHM AND BLUES WITH HOWLIN' WOLF (EP) 250
63	Pye Intl. NEP 44015	SMOKESTACK LIGHTNIN' (EP) 40
64	Pye Intl. NEP 44032	TELL ME (EP) 30
66	Chess CRE 6017	REAL FOLK BLUES (EP) 30
64	Chess CRL 4006	MOANIN' IN THE MOONLIGHT (LP) 100
65	Chess CRL 4508	POOR BOY (LP) 45
66	Ember EMB 3370	BIG CITY BLUES (LP) 25
69	Chess CRLS 4543	THE HOWLIN' WOLF ALBUM (LP) 25
71	Syndicate Chapter SC 003	GOING BACK HOME (LP) 20
71	Chess 6310 108	MESSAGE TO THE YOUNG (LP) 22
71	Rolling Stones COC 49101	THE LONDON SESSIONS (LP) 20
71	Python PLP 13	HOWLIN' WOLF (LP) 60

(see also Hubert Sumlin)

HOWLIN' WOLF/JUNIOR PARKER/BOBBY BLAND

| 74 | Polydor 2383 257 | BLUES FOR MR. CRUMP (LP) ....30 |

HOWLIN' WOLF, MUDDY WATERS & BO DIDDLEY

| 68 | Chess CRL 4537 | THE SUPER SUPER BLUES BAND (LP) ....45 |

(see also Muddy Waters, Bo Diddley)

LINDA HOYLE

| 70 | Vertigo 6059 018 | Eli's Coming/United States Of Mind (as Linda Hoyle & Affinity) ....40 |
| 71 | Vertigo 6360 060 | PIECES OF ME (LP, gatefold sleeve, small swirl label) ....900 |

(see also Affinity, Nucleus)

H.P. LOVECRAFT

67	Philips BF 1620	Wayfarin' Stranger/The Time Machine 7
68	Philips BF 1639	The White Ship (Parts 1 & 2) (unissued) 0
68	Philips BF 1639	The White Ship/I've Been Wrong Before 15
67	Philips (S)BL 7830	H.P. LOVECRAFT (LP) 70

68	Philips SBL 7872	H.P. LOVECRAFT II (LP, without watermark at start of each side)	45
68	Philips SBL 7872	H.P. LOVECRAFT II (LP, with watermark at start of each side)	15
72	Philips 6336 210	THIS IS H.P. LOVECRAFT (LP)	25
72	Philips 6336 213	H.P. LOVECRAFT VOL. 2 (LP)	20

HQ SQUAD
89	Music Of Life NOTE33	Burial Proceedings In The Course Of Three Knights/Onslaught (12")	15

HRATCH
70	Decca F13007	Beautiful Bare Back Rider/Ain't It Tough	10
74	EMI 2170	You/Just In Case	6
77	DJM DJS 10765	Another Way Of Going Home/Life (promo only in p/s)	8

HT
66	Polydor 56127	You & Me/Love Can Wait	10

FREDDIE HUBBARD
70	CTI 6001	RED CLAY (LP)	25
74	MSP/BASF BAP 5036	THE HUB OF HUBBARD (LP)	20

HUBCAP & WHEELS
70	Dynamic DYN 403	One Pound Weight/VICEROYS: Come Dance	6

(see also Byron Lee & Dragonaires)

WENDY HUBER
65	Philips BF 1446	Come Away Melinda/I Belong To The Wind	10

ROY HUDD
66	Polydor 56136	The Day We Won The Cup/Ramsey's Men	8

HUDDERSFIELD TRANSIT AUTHORITY
72	Polydor 2001284	Runaway/Bayou Farm	15
72	Polydor 2001344	A Different Drum/One Of The Old Time Greats	6

HUDSON BROTHERS
75	Rocket PIG 18	Rendezvous/Medley: These Things We Do/Home And Four Others	6

JACK HUDSON
72	Folk Heritage FHR 041	SUMMER DAYS AND YOU (LP)	20

JOHNNY HUDSON & TEENBEATS
63	Decca F 11679	Charms/Makin' Up Is So Much Fun	10

KEITH HUDSON (& CHUCKLES)
69	Big Shot BI 528	Tambourine Man/Old Fashioned Way (both actually by Ken Boothe)	20
70	Smash SMA 2311	Don't Get Me Confused/D. SMITH: Ball of Confusion (B-side actually by Dennis Alcapone)	20
71	Smash SMA 2526	Light Of Day/I Thought You Knew	20
72	Spur SP 1	Darkest Night On A Wet Looking Road/Version	50
72	Duke DU 145	Satan Side (with Chuckles)/DON T. JUNIOR: Evil Spirit	35
72	Downtown DT 492	True To My Heart/BIG YOUTH: Ace 90 Skank	15
73	Summit SUM 8541	Melody Maker/Uncover Me	25
75	Atra AT28	Lost All Sense Of Direction/Jah Jah	8
75	Faith FA 025	Blackbelt Jones/Version	20
77	Tunde TR 1000	I Wanna Be Where You Are/Still Water (12")	25
78	Greensleeves GRED 8	Bloody Eyes/Dub	20
79	Greensleeves GRED 26	Nuh Skin Up/Felt We Felt The Strain (12")	25
75	Magnet MGT 007	ENTER THE DRAGON (LP)	200
75	Mamba KH1	FLESH OF MY SKIN, BLOOD OF MY BLOOD (LP)	150
75	Mamba MAM 002	TORCH OF FREEDOM (LP)	40
75	Atra LP1001	TORCH OF FREEDOM (LP, same as Mamba issue)	50
75	ATRA ATLP 1002	PICK A DUB (LP)	80
76	Third World TWL 106	REBEL DUB (LP, produced by Keith Hudson)	70
76	Virgin V2056	TOO EXPENSIVE (LP)	25
77	BRD 001	BRAND (LP)	50
79	Greensleeves GREL 5	RASTA COMMUNICATION (LP)	25
88	Atra LP 1004	FLESH OF MY SKIN (LP)	20
94	Blood & Fire LP 003	PICK A DUB (LP, reissue)	15
01	Simply Vinyl SVLP 283	PICK A DUB (LP, reissue)	15

(see also Big Youth, Alton Ellis, Hugh Roy, Delroy Wilson)

KEITH HUDSON & FAMILY MAN
70s	Mamba MAM 003	PICK A DUB (LP)	50

KEITH HUDSON & I ROY
73	Randy's RAN 534	Silver Platter/Jean You Change Everything	20

(see also I Roy)

ROCK HUDSON
59	Brunswick 05816	Pillow Talk/Roly Poly	7
70	Warner Bros WB 8006	Gone With The Cowboys/Meantime	6

KEITH HUDSON
75	Mamba MAM 101	Wild Fire/Version	12

HUDSON-FORD
73	A&M AMS 7116	Floating In The Wind/Revelations	8
73	A&M AMS 7078	Pick Up The Pieces/This Is Not The Way (To End A War Or Die)	5
74	A&M AMS 7096	Burn Baby Burn/Angels (p/s)	5
73	A&M AMLH 68208	NICKELODEON (LP, lyric insert, brown label)	15
77	Arnakata ARN 5001	REPERTOIRE (LP, for publishers' use)	20

(see also Strawbs, Monks, Elmer Gantry's Velvet Opera)

HUDSON PEOPLE
78	Hithouse HIT 1	Trip To Your Mind/Power To The Hour (12")	60
79	Ensign ENY 2712	Trip To Your Mind/Power To The Hour (12", different mix)	40

HUEYS
69	London HLU 10264	Coo-Coo Over You/You Ain't No Hippie	12

HUG
75	Polydor 2058 553	Keep Pushing On/City	6
75	Polydor 2383 330	NEON DREAM (LP)	20

(see also Mike Hugg)

MIKE HUGG
72	Polydor 2058 265	Blue Suede Shoes Again/Fool No More	5
73	Polydor 2058 359	Stress And Strain/Tonight	5
72	Polydor 2383 140	SOMEWHERE (LP, gatefold sleeve)	20
73	Polydor 2383 213	STRESS AND STRAIN (LP)	20

(see also Manfred Mann, Hug, Highly Likely, Elton Dean)

HUGGY BEAR
92	Wiija WIJ 16V	RUBBING THE IMPOSSIBLE TO BURST EP (2000 only)	8

BOBBY HUGHES EXPERIENCE
99	Ultimate Diler UDRLP 008	FUSA RIOT (2xLP)	20

CAROL HUGHES
58	Columbia DB 4094	Lend Me Your Comb/First Date	15

DANNY HUGHES
69	Pye 7N 17750	Hi Ho Silver Lining/I Washed My Hands In Muddy Water	15

(see also Orange Machine)

DAVID HUGHES
59	Top Rank JAR 205	Teach Me (How To Love Him)/You Would Have Done The Same	5
55	Philips BBE 12020	DAVID HUGHES (EP)	8
55	Delyse EDP 205	CHRISTMAS WITH DAVID HUGHES (EP)	8

FRED HUGHES
65	Fontana TF 583	Oo Wee Baby I Love You/Love Me Baby	25
76	Brunswick BR 37	Baby Boy/JOHNNY JONES & KING CASUALS: Purple Haze	10
76	DJM DJS 10717	Oo Wee Baby I Love You/My Cries Oh	6

GLENN HUGHES
79	Safari SAFE 14	I Found A Woman/L.A. Cut Off (p/s)	5
77	Safari LONG 2	PLAY ME OUT (LP, with inner sleeve)	15

(see also Deep Purple, News, Finders Keepers, Trapeze, Roger Glover, Hughes-Thrall)

JIMMY HUGHES
63	London HL 9680	I'm Qualified/My Loving Time	30
64	Pye International 7N 25254	Steal Away/Lollipops, Lace And Lipstick	25
66	Sue WI 4006	Goodbye My Love/It Was Nice	40
66	Atlantic 584 017	Neighbour, Neighbour/It's A Good Thing	22
67	Atlantic 584 135	Hi-Heel Sneakers/Time Will Bring You Back	15
69	Stax STAX 117	Sweet Things You Do/Let 'Em Down Baby	8
69	Stax STAX 126	I'm Not Ashamed To Beg Or Plead/Chains Of Love	12
67	Atlantic 587 068	WHY NOT TONIGHT? (LP)	75
69	Stax SXATS 1010	SOMETHING SPECIAL (LP)	30

NIA HUGHES
70	Penny Farthing PEN 724	Turn On The Sun/The Wind	8

RHETTA HUGHES
11	Shotgun 107	Cry Myself To Sleep/Giving Up My Heartaches	10
70s	Polydor 184 223	RELIGHT MY FIRE (LP)	80

HUGHES-THRALL
82	Epic EPC 25052	HUGHES-THRALL (LP, with inner sleeve)	15

(see also Glenn Hughes)

HUGO & LUIGI
57	Columbia DB 3978	Rockabilly Party/Shenandoah Rose	15

ALAN HULL
70	Big T BIG 129	We Can Swing Together/Obadiah's Grave	10
75	Warner Brothers K16599	One More Bottle Of Wine/Squire	6
73	Charisma CAS 1069	PIPEDREAM (LP, gatefold sleeve, booklet, large 'Mad Hatter' label)	20
75	Warner Bros K56121	SQUIRE (LP, 'Burbank' label)	15

(see also Lindisfarne, Chosen Few, Radiator)

HULLABALLOOS
64	Columbia DB 7392	I'm Gonna Love You Too/Why Do Fools Fall In Love	10
65	Columbia DB 7558	I'll Show You How To Love/Did You Ever	10
65	Columbia DB 7626	Don't Stop/I Won't Turn Away Now	10

(see also Bunch Of Fives)

GEORGE HULTGREEN
70	Warner Bros WB 8017	Say Hello/Before You Say Goodbye	6

HUMAN BEANS
67	Columbia DB 8230	Morning Dew (Take Me For A Walk)/It's A Wonder	65

(see also Love Sculpture, Dave Edmunds)

HUMAN BEAST
70	Decca LK/SKL 5053	VOLUME ONE (LP)	500

(see also Bread Love & Dreams)

HUMAN BEINGS
80	Airship AP 159	Amnesia/New Song/Mrs Marshall (p/s and sticker)	12

HUMAN BEINZ
67	Capitol CL 15529	Nobody But Me/Sueno	60
67	Capitol CL 15529	Nobody But Me/Sueno (DJ Copy)	100
68	Capitol CL 15542	Turn On Your Lovelight/It's Fun To Be Clean	25

HUMAN CONDITION
81	THC 1	THE HUMAN CONDITION (Live at Collegiate Theatre 13th September 1981) (cassette, black inlay, white writing)	25

81	THC 1	THE HUMAN CONDITION (Live in Europe November 1981) (cassette, white inlay, black writing)	25

(see also Jah Wobble, PiL)

HUMAN INSTINCT

65	Mercury MF 951	Can't Stop Around/I Want To Be Loved By You My Friend	40
66	Mercury MF 972	The Rich Man/Illusions	70
67	Mercury MF 990	Go-Go/I Can't Live Without You	40
68	Deram DM 167	A Day In My Mind's Mind/Death Of The Seaside	125
68	Deram DM 177	Renaissance Fair/Pink Dawn	80

(see also Jessie Harper)

HUMAN LEAGUE

78	Fast Product FAST 4	Being Boiled/Circus Of Death (p/s, original issue with b&w picture labels)	15
79	Fast Product FAST 10	THE DIGNITY OF LABOUR (12" EP, with spoken-word flexidisc [F10x/VF 1])	15
79	Virgin VS 294	Empire State Human/Introducing (p/s)	5
80	Virgin SV 105	HOLIDAY '80 (EP, double pack, purple & blue labels, 10,000 only)	8
80	Virgin VS 351	Empire State Human/Introducing//Only After Dark/Toyota City (Long Version) (double pack, p/s, shrinkwrapped)	20
80	Virgin VS 351	Only After Dark/Toyota City (Long Version) (p/s)	6
80	Virgin VS 351	Empire State Human/Introducing (p/s, reissue)	5
80	Virgin VS 351-12	Empire State Human/Introducing (12", p/s)	8
81	Virgin VS 395	Boys And Girls/Tom Baker (gatefold or non-gatefold p/s)	5
81	Virgin SV 105-12	HOLIDAY '80 (12", 5-track EP, withdrawn)	20
79	Virgin VS 2133	REPRODUCTION (LP)	12
80	Virgin V 2160	TRAVELOGUE (LP)	12

(see also Heaven 17, Men, Respect, Jo Callis)

HUMANOID

88	Westside WSR 7	Stakker Humanoid (Part 1)/Stakker Humanoid (Part 2) (p/s)	8
88	Westside Human 1989	GLOBAL (LP)	12

(see also Future Sound Of London, Art Science Technology)

HUMANTE & RABBIT IN THE MOON

95	Rising High RSN 106	East (The Remixes) (12")	15

HUMBLEBUMS

69	Big T BIG 122	Saturday Roundabout Sunday/Bed Of Mossy Green	6
69	Big T BIG 127	Coconut Tree/Her Father Didn't Like Me Anyway	6
70	Big T BIG 130	Shoeshine Boy/My Apartment	6
69	Transatlantic TRA 186	THE FIRST COLLECTION OF MERRY MELODIES (LP)	12
69	Transatlantic TRA 201	THE NEW HUMBLEBUMS (LP, lilac/white label with 't' logo)	20
70	Transatlantic TRA 218	OPEN UP THE DOOR (LP, laminated sleeve)	15
74	Transatlantic TRA 288	THE COMPLETE HUMBLEBUMS (3-LP, box set of above albums)	20

(see also Gerry Rafferty, Billy Connolly)

HUMBLE PIE

69	Immediate IM 082	Natural Born Bugie/Wrist Job	6
69	Immediate IM 082	Natural Born Bugie/Wrist Job (later pressing in p/s)	10
70	A&M AMS 807	Big Black Dog/Strange Days	7
71	A&M AMS 862	I Don't Need No Doctor/A Sonig For Jennie	7
72	A&M AMS 7003	Hot'n'Nasty/You're So Good For Me	7
73	A&M AMS 7052	Black Coffee/Say No More	7
73	A&M AMS 7070	Get Down To It/Honky Tonk Woman	7
73	A&M AMS 7090	Oh La De Da/Outcrowd	7
75	A&M AMS 7185	Rock'n'Roll Music/Scored Out	7
80	Jet JET 180	Fool For A Pretty Face/You Soppy Pratt (p/s)	7
69	Immediate IMSP 025	AS SAFE AS YESTERDAY IS (LP, lyric inner sleeve, pink label)	60
69	Immediate IMSP 027	TOWN AND COUNTRY (LP, lyric inner sleeve, pink label)	60
70	A&M AMLS 986	HUMBLE PIE (LP, textured gatefold sleeve, brown label)	60
71	A&M AMLS 2013	ROCK ON (LP)	20
71	A&M AMLH 63506	PERFORMANCE - ROCKIN' THE FILLMORE (2-LP)	20
72	A&M AMLS 64342	SMOKIN' (LP)	20
73	A&M AMLD 6004	EAT IT (2-LP, gatefold sleeve, booklet, brown label)	25
74	A&M AMLH 63611	THUNDERBOX (LP)	15
75	A&M AMLS 68282	STREET RATS (LP)	15
79	Jet LP231	ON TO VICTORY (LP)	20
80	Atco SD 38 131	GO FOR THE THROAT (LP)	20

(see also Steve Marriott, Small Faces, Peter Frampton, Herd, Natural Gas)

HUMBUG

70	CBS 4811	Groovin' With Mr Bloe/Marianna	5
70	CBS 5208	I Got A Feeling (Vocal)/I Got A Feeling (Instrumental)	20

HELEN HUMES

53	Brunswick 05193	I Cried For You/Mean Way Of Loving (78)	10
56	Vogue V 2048	Million Dollar Secret/If I Could Be With You One Hour Of The Day	10
56	Vogue V 2048	Million Dollar Secret/If I Could Be With You One Hour Of The Day (78)	10
59	Contemporary CV 2415	When The Saints Come Marching In/Bill Bailey, Won't You Please Come Home (with Benny Carter's All-Stars)	5
59	Contemporary CV 2415	When The Saints Come Marching In/Bill Bailey, Won't You Please Come Home (with Benny Carter's All-Stars) (78)	10
61	Contemporary LAC 12245	HELEN HUMES AND THE BENNY CARTER ALL STARS (LP)	15

(see also Benny Carter, Jimmy Witherspoon/Helen Humes)

BOBBI HUMPHREY

75	Blue Note UAG 20003	FANCY DANCER (LP)	12

DELLA HUMPHREY

69	Action ACT 4525	Don't Make The Good Girls Go Bad/Your Love Is All I Need	25
72	Fab FAB 183	Dreamland (actually by Marcia Griffiths)/Version	35

LES HUMPHRIES SINGERS

75	Antic K11519	She's Really Something Else/Mexico	8
76	Atlantic K11527	Indian War/Little Sparrow	8

HUMPY BONG
70	Parlophone R 5859	Don't You Be Too Long/We're Alright 'Till Then	15

(see also Bee Gees, Jonathan Kelly, Morgan)

HUNGER
84	Psycho PSYCHO 14	STRICTLY FROM HUNGER (LP, reissue of U.S. LP)	15

HUNGRY TOUCH
88	Firehorse HT 188	Shake The System/She's Got The Hungry Touch/Riding High (12" p/s)	50

HUNGRY WOLF
70	Philips 6308 009	HUNGRY WOLF (LP, laminated sleeve, black/silver labels)	200

(see also Czar, Alan Parker, Ugly Custard)

GERALDINE HUNT
69	Roulette RO 515	Never Never Leave Me/Push Sweep	20
75	EMI EMI 2275	You/It's All For You	6

MARSHA HUNT
69	Track 604 030	Walk On Gilded Splinters/Hot Rod Poppa	15
69	Track 604 034	Desdemona/Hippy Gumbo	20
70	Track 604 037	Keep The Customer Satisfied/Lonesome Holy Roller	10
73	Vertigo 6059 080	Beast Day/Somebody To Love (as Marsha Hunt's 22)	20
73	Vertigo 6059093	Medusa/Bop City (as Marsha Hunt's 22)	20
76	Electric WATT 1	C'est La Vie/Do You Really Believe In Voodoo	10
71	Track 2410 101	WOMAN CHILD (LP)	80

TOMMY HUNT
62	Top Rank JAR 605	The Door Is Open/I'm Wondering	20
68	Direction 58-3216	I Need A Woman Of My Own/Searchin' For My Baby Looking Everywhere	30
72	Polydor 2058 236	Mind, Body & Soul/One More Mountain To Climb	5
74	Pye 7N 45325	Sleep Tight Honey/Time Alone Will Tell	5
75	Spark SRL 1132	Crackin' Up/Get Out	5
76	Spark SRL 1146	Loving On The Losing Side/Sunshine Girl	5
76	Spark SRL 1148	One Fine Morning/Sign On The Dotted Line/Loving You Is	5
85	Kent TOWN 103	The Work Song/IVORYS: Please Stay	10

(see also Ivorys)

WILLIE AMOS HUNT
67	Camp 602 003	Would You Believe/My Baby Wants To Dance	60

HUNT & TURNER
72	Village Thing VTS 11	MAGIC LANDSCAPE (LP)	60

CAROL HUNTER
73	Purple PUR 115	Look Out Cleveland/5/4 March	7
73	Purple TPS 3503	THE NEXT VOICE YOU HEAR (LP)	15

DANNY HUNTER (& GIANTS)
60	HMV POP 722	Make It Up/Little Girl (as Danny Hunter & Giants)	20
60	HMV POP 775	Who's Gonna Walk Ya Home?/Lonely And Blue	20
61	Fontana H 300	Lost Weekend/Age For Love	15

DAVE HUNTER
65	Oriole CB 1985	Evergreen/ Tree/Too Late	15
68	RCA RCA 1766	Love Me A Lifetime/She's A Heartbreaker	35
69	RCA RCA 1841	Don't Throw Your Love To The Wind/Hitchcock Railway	12

GREG HUNTER
66	Parlophone R 5483	Five O'Clock World/Away From Happiness	10

IAN HUNTER
75	CBS 3486	Who Do You Love/Boy	5
76	CBS 4268	All American Alien Boy (Version)/Rape	5
76	CBS 4479	You Nearly Did Me In/A Letter From Britannia To The Union Jack	15
77	CBS 5229	Justice Of The Peace/The Ballad Of Little Star (as Ian Hunter's Overnight Angels)	8
77	CBS 5497	England Rocks/Wild 'N' Free (as Ian Hunter's Overnight Angels)	5
79	Chrysalis CHS 2324	When The Daylight Comes/Life After Death (p/s, white vinyl with mask)	5
79	Chrysalis CHS 2346	Ships/Wild East (p/s)	5
79	Chrysalis CHS 2390	Cleveland Rocks/Bastard (p/s)	5
80	Chrysalis CHS 2434	We Gotta Get Out/Medley: Once Bitten Twice Shy/Bastard/Cleveland Rocks/ Sons And Daughters/One Of The Boys (live double pack, stickered gatefold p/s)	5
81	Chrysalis CHS 2542	Lisa Likes Rock 'n' Roll/Noises (p/s, clear vinyl)	5
83	CBS A 3541	All Of The Good Ones Are Taken/Death 'N' Glory Boys (p/s)	5
83	CBS TA 3541	All Of The Good Ones Are Taken/Death 'N' Glory Boys/Traitor (12", p/s)	8
83	CBS A 3855	Somethin's Goin' On/All Of The Good Ones Are Taken (Slow Version) (p/s)	5
83	CBS A 3855	Somethin's Goin' On (Radio Edit)/All Of The Good Ones Are Taken (Slow Version) (promo only, no p/s)	5
77	CBS	YOU'RE NEVER ALONE WITH A SCHIZOPHRENIC (LP, unissued; later issued on Chrysalis CHR 1214)	12
77	CBS 81993	OVERNIGHT ANGELS (LP, gatefold sleeve)	12

(see also Mott The Hoople, At Last The 1958 Rock & Roll Show, Apex Rhythm & Blues All Stars, Mick Ronson, Roger Taylor)

IVORY JOE HUNTER
50	MGM MGM 271	I Almost Lost My Mind/S.P. Blues (78, with Orchestra)	20
56	London HLE 8261	A Tear Fell/I Need You By My Side	300
56	London HLE 8261	A Tear Fell/I Need You By My Side (78)	20
57	Columbia DB 3872	Since I Met You, Baby/You Can't Stop This Rockin' And Rollin'	250
57	Columbia DB 3872	Since I Met You, Baby/You Can't Stop This Rockin' And Rollin' (78)	20
57	London HLE 8486	Love's A Hurting Game/Empty Arms	150
57	London HLE 8486	Love's A Hurting Game/Empty Arms (78)	20
61	Capitol CL 15220	I'm Hooked/Because I Love You	30
61	Capitol CL 15226	You Better Believe It, Baby/May The Man Win	30

ROBERT HUNTER
74	Round RX 101	TALES OF THE GREAT RUM RUNNERS (LP)	15
75	Round RX 105	TIGER ROSE (LP)	12
80	Dark Star DSLP 8001	JACK O'ROSES (LP)	15

(see also Grateful Dead)

SUSAN HUNTER
55	Brunswick 05458	Not Yet/Was That The Right Thing To Do?	8

TAB HUNTER
57	London HLD 8380	Young Love/Red Sails In The Sunset (gold label)	20
57	London HLD 8380	Young Love/Red Sails In The Sunset (silver label)	5
57	London HLD 8410	Ninety-Nine Ways/I Don't Get Around Much Anymore	5
58	London HLD 8535	Don't Let It Get Around/I'm Alone Because I Love You	10
60	Warner Bros WB 8	(What Can I Give) My Only Love/(I'll Be With You) In Apple Blossom Time	5
60	Warner Bros WB 20	Waitin' For The Fall/Our Love	5
61	London HLD 9381	The Wild Side Of Life/My Devotion	5
62	London HLD 9559	Born To Lose/I Can't Stop Lovin' You	5
58	London RE-D 1134	TAB HUNTER (EP)	10
61	Warner Bros WEP 6023	TAB HUNTER (EP, mono)	15
61	Warner Bros WSEP 2023	TAB HUNTER (EP, stereo)	15
60	Warner Bros WS 4008	TAB HUNTER (LP, mono)	20
60	Warner Bros WS 8008	TAB HUNTER (LP, stereo)	20
61	London HA-D 2401	YOUNG LOVE (LP, mono)	20
61	London SAH-G 6201	YOUNG LOVE (LP, stereo)	20

HUNTER MUSKETT
73	Bradleys BRAD 303	John Blair/Silver Coin (p/s)	6
70	Decca Nova SDN 20	EVERY TIME YOU MOVE (LP, blue/silver labels)	300
73	Bradleys BRADL 1003	HUNTER MUSKETT (LP, lyric inner sleeve)	35

HUNTERS (HOLLAND)
66	RCA RCA 1541	Russian Spy And I/Spring	20

(see also Jan Akkerman, Brainbox)

HUNTERS (U.K.)
60	Fontana H 276	Teen Scene/Santa Monica Flyer	25
61	Fontana H 303	Golden Ear-rings/Tally Ho	15
61	Fontana H 323	The Storm/How's M'Chicks?	20
64	Fontana TF 514	Teen Scene/Someone Else's Baby	15
61	Fontana TFL 5140	TEEN SCENE: THE HUNTERS PLAY THE BIG HITS (LP, mono)	30
61	Fontana STFL 561	TEEN SCENE: THE HUNTERS PLAY THE BIG HITS (LP, stereo)	50
62	Fontana TFL 5175	HITS FROM THE HUNTERS (LP, mono)	50
62	Fontana STFL 572	HITS FROM THE HUNTERS (LP, stereo)	50

(see also Dave Sampson & Hunters, Maisie McDaniel)

HUNTING LODGE
85	Sterile SER 04	NOMAD SOULS (LP)	20

HUNTSMEN
64	London HA-U 8175	PRESENTING THE HUNTSMEN (LP)	12

HURDY GURDY
72	CBS 64781	HURDY GURDY (LP, gatefold sleeve)	200

ARTHUR HURLEY & GOTTLIEB
73	CBS 1779	Sunshine Ship/Bobbys Song	6

RED HURLEY
77	EMI 2575	Listen To The Children/Just A Little Love	6

RED VINCENT HURLEY
76	Pye 7N 45583	When/Just A Little Love (p/s)	7

HURRICANE STRINGS
63	Columbia DB 7027	Venus/In The Carrick	15

HURRICANES
71	Upsetter US 363	Got To Be Mine/UPSETTERS: Version	12

(see also Dave Barker)

MIKE HURST (& METHOD)
64	Philips BF 1353	Half Heaven Half Heartache/Look In Your Eyes	5
65	Philips BF 1389	The Last Time You'll Walk Out On Me/Something Told Me	6
65	Philips BF 1424	Show Me Around/I'm Running Away	7
71	Capitol CL 15681	Show Me The Way To Georgia/Over Again	6

(see also Springfields, Remo Four, Ashton Gardner & Dyke, Sundance)

MISSISSIPPI JOHN HURT
65	Vanguard SVRL 19005	THE IMMORTAL MISSISSIPPI JOHN HURT (LP)	35
66	Vanguard SVRL 19032	MISSISSIPPI JOHN HURT (LP)	35
67	Fontana TFL 6079	MISSISSIPPI JOHN HURT (LP)	35
71	Spokane SPL 1001	THE ORIGINAL 1928 RECORDINGS (LP)	50
71	Vanguard VSD 19/20	THE BEST OF MISSISSIPPI JOHN HURT (2-LP)	18
73	Vanguard VSD 79327	LAST SESSIONS (LP)	20
72	Vanguard VSD 79220	TODAY (LP)	20

HURTS
10	Sony 88697741857	Better Than Love/Mother Nature (white label, p/s, 500 only)	12
10	Major MAJRE 017	Wonderful Life/(Mantronix Remix) (p/s, no'd)	8

(see also Daggers (2))

HUSH
68	Fontana TF 944	Elephant Rider/Grey	500

HÜSKER DÜ
84	SST SST 025	Eight Miles High/Masochism World (live) (p/s)	12
85	SST 051	Makes No Sense At All/Love Is All Around (p/s)	5
86	Warner Bros W 8612	Sorry Somehow/All This I've Done For You (p/s)	5
86	Warner Bros W 8612	Sorry Somehow/All This I've Done For You//Celebrated Summer (Acoustic)/ Flexible Flyer (double pack, gatefold sleeve)	8
86	Warner Bros W 8612T	Sorry Somehow/All This I've Done For You/Celebrated Summer (Acoustic)/ Flexible Flyer/Fattie (12", p/s)	8
86	Warner Bros W 8746	Don't Want To Know If You're Lonely/All Work And No Play (p/s)	5

MINT VALUE £

86	Warner Bros W 8746T	Don't Want To Know If You're Lonely/All Work And No Play/ Helter Skelter (live) (12", p/s)	10
87	Warner Bros W 8456	Could You Be The One/Everytime (p/s)	10
87	Warner Bros W 8456T	Could You Be The One/Everytime/Charity, Chastity, Prudence, Hope (12", p/s)	10
87	Warner Bros W 8276	Ice Cold Ice/Gotta Lotta (p/s)	5
87	Warner Bros W 8276T	Ice Cold Ice/Gotta Lotta/Medley (12", p/s)	10
81	Alternative Tentacles VIRUS 25	LAND SPEED RECORD (LP)	18
82	Bespoke BES 03 LP	EVERYTHING FALLS APART (LP)	20
83	SST SST 020	METAL CIRCUS (LP)	20
84	SST SST 020	ZEN ARCADE (2-LP)	20
86	Warner Bros WX40	CANDY APPLE GREY (LP)	15
87	Warner Bros WB 925544	WAREHOUSE SONGS & STORIES (2-LP)	18
09	Rhino 8122798853	CANDY APPLE GREY (LP, reissue, 180gm vinyl)	12

HUSKY

75	Anchor ANC 1026	Give It Up/Silence Of Dreams	6
76	Anchor ANC 1030	Pretty Little Linda/Make It Turn Out Right	6

FERLIN HUSKY (& HIS HUSH PUPPIES)

57	Capitol CL 14702	Gone/Missing Persons (as Ferlin Husky & His Hush Puppies)	10
57	Capitol CL 14753	A Fallen Star/Prize Possession	12
57	Capitol CL 14785	This Moment Of Love/Make Me Live Again	5
57	Capitol CL 14785	This Moment Of Love/Make Me Live Again (78)	10
58	Capitol CL 14824	Wang Dang Doo/What'cha Doin' After School	20
58	Capitol CL 14824	Wang Dang Doo/What'cha Doin' After School (78)	10
58	Capitol CL 14883	Slow Down Brother/The Drunken Driver (& His Hush Puppies)	10
58	Capitol CL 14916	I Feel That Old Heartache Again/I Saw God	8
58	Capitol CL 14922	The Kingdom Of Love/Terrific Together	7
58	Capitol CL 14954	I Will/All Of The Time	5
60	Capitol CL 15160	Wings Of A Dove/Next TO Jimmy	5
57	Capitol EAP1 718	SONGS OF THE HOME AND HEART (EP)	10
57	Capitol EAP1 837	FERLIN HUSKY HITS (EP)	10
57	Capitol EAP1 921	COUNTRY MUSIC HOLIDAY (EP)	10
59	Parlophone GEP 8795	COUNTRY ROUND UP (EP)	10
60	Capitol EAP1 1280	FERLIN'S FAVOURITES (EP)	10
60	Capitol EAP2 1280	FERLIN'S FAVOURITES (EP)	10
60	Capitol EAP3 1280	FERLIN'S FAVOURITES (EP)	10
58	Capitol T 880	BOULEVARD OF BROKEN DREAMS (LP)	20

(see also Simon Crum)

JACQUES HUSTIN

74	EMI EMI 2143	Fleur De Liberté/Freedom For The Man	15

HUSTLER

74	Firefly AMS501	Get Outa My 'Ouse/Happy Days	5
74	A&M AMLS 68276	HIGH STREET (LP)	12
75	A&M AMLH 33001	PLAY LOUD (LP)	12

HUSTLERS

63	Philips BF 1275	Gimme What I Want/Not Much	7
64	Mercury MF 807	Be True To You/You Can't Sit Down	7
64	Mercury MF 817	Sick Of Giving/Easy To Find	20

WILLIE HUTCH

73	Tamla Motown TMG 862	Brother's Gonna Work It Out/I Choose You	15
73	Tamla Motown STMA 8003	THE MACK (LP, soundtrack)	15
73	Tamla Motown STML 11247	FULLY EXPOSED (LP)	15
74	Tamla Motown STML 11269	FOXY BROWN (LP, soundtrack)	15
74	Tamla Motown STML 11280	THE MARK OF THE BEAST (LP)	20
75	Tamla Motown STML 12015	ODE TO MY LADY (LP)	20
76	Tamla Motown STML 12023	CONCERT IN BLUES (LP)	15

ASHLEY HUTCHINGS

72	Island HELP 5	MORRIS ON (LP, actually by various folk artists)	18
76	Island HELP 24	RATTLEBONE AND ROUGHJACK (LP)	25
76	Harvest SHSM 2012	SON OF MORRIS ON (LP, actually by various folk artists)	18
77	Harvest SHSP 4073	KICKIN' UP THE SAWDUST (LP)	12

(see also Albion Band, Fairport Convention, Steeleye Span, Bunch)

HUTCH HUTCHINS

77	Goodwood GM 12324	FEELS LIKE RAIN (LP)	35

SAM HUTCHINS

69	Bell BLL 1044	Dang Me/I'm Tired Of Pretending	10

LEROY HUTSON

75	Warner Bros K 16536	All Because Of You Parts 1 & 2	10
74	Buddah BDLP 4013	THE MAN (LP)	20
75	Warner Bros K 56139	HUTSON (LP)	50

J.B. HUTTO & HIS HAWKS

73	Delmark DS 617	HAWK SQUAT (LP)	30

BETTY HUTTON

53	HMV 7M 103	Somebody Loves Me/Jealous (B-side with Pat Morgan)	10
56	Capitol CL 14568	Sleepy Head/Hit The Road To Dreamland	8
54	Capitol LC 6639	CAPITOL PRESENTS BETTY HUTTON (10" LP)	15

(see also Hutton Sisters, Perry Como, 'Tennessee' Ernie Ford)

DANNY HUTTON

66	MGM MGM 1314	Funny How Love Can Be/Dreamin' Isn't Good For You	15
65	Pye International 7N 25325	Roses And Rainbows/Monster Shindig	5

(see also Three Dog Night)

HUTTON SISTERS (BETTY & MARION)

55	Capitol CL 14250	Ko Ko Mo (I Love You So)/Heart Throb	25

(see also Betty Hutton)

HYACINTH GIRLS
88	REd RED 002	HAPPY NOW? 40

CHARLIE HYATT
65	Island IEP 707	RASS! (EP, as Bam & Charlie Hyatt)..30
66	Island ILP 932	KISS ME NECK (LP) 35

LEON HYATT
76	Nationwide NW 1014	40 Days And Nights/Third World Affairs 15

TANYA HYDE
79	Waldo's DS 008	Herr Wunderbar/Auf Der Anderen Seite (p/s) 15

HYDRA
74	Capricorn 2089 008	Glitter Queen/It's So Hard...5
74	Capricorn 2429 120	HYDRA (LP) 12

HYGRADES
65	Columbia DB 7734	She Cared/We're Through 15

BRIAN HYLAND
60	London HLR 9161	Itsy Bitsy Teeny Weeny Yellow Polka Dot Bikini/Don't Dilly Dally, Sally (78) 100
60	London HLR 9113	Rosemary/Library Love Affair...20
60	London HLR 9161	Itsy Bitsy Teeny Weeny Yellow Polka Dot Bikini/Don't Dilly Dally, Sally.........6
60	London HLR 9203	Four Little Heels/That's How Much 6
61	London HLR 9262	Lop Sided, Over Loaded/I Gotta Go ('Cause I Love You) 6
61	HMV POP 915	Let Me Belong To You/Let It Die 7
61	HMV POP 955	The Night I Cried/I'll Never Stop Wanting You 6
62	HMV POP 1013	Ginny Come Lately/I Should Be Gettin' Better 8
62	HMV POP 1051	Sealed With A Kiss/Summer Job 8
62	HMV POP 1079	Warmed Over Kisses/Walk A Lonely Mile.....................................5
63	HMV POP 1113	I May Not Live To See Tomorrow/It Ain't That Way At All 5
63	HMV POP 1143	If Mary's There/Remember Me..5
63	HMV POP 1169	Somewhere In The Night/I Wish Today Was Yesterday 5
63	HMV POP 1188	I'm Afraid To Go Home/Save Your Heart For Me 5
63	HMV POP 1237	Let Us Make Our Own Mistakes/Nothing Matters But You 5
64	Philips BF 1326	Here's To Our Love/Two Kinds Of Girls 5
65	Philips BF 1429	Stay Away From Her/I Can't Keep A Secret 5
65	Philips BF 1486	3,000 Miles/Sometimes They Do..5
66	Philips BF 1508	The Joker Went Wild/I Can Hear The Rain 20
66	Philips BF 1528	Run Run Look And See/Why Did You Do It 7
66	Philips BF 1555	Hung Up In Your Eyes/Why Mine 5
67	Philips BF 1569	Holiday For Clowns/Yesterday I Had A Girl 5
69	Dot 124	A Million To One/It Could All Begin Again (in You) 7
67	Philips BF 1601	Get The Message/Kinda Groovy 5
70	Uni UN 530	Gypsy Woman/You And Me 5
72	Uni UN 540	I Love Every Little Thing About You/With My Eyes Wide Open ...5
62	HMV 7EG 8780	SEALED WITH A KISS (EP) 20
61	London HA-R 2289	THE BASHFUL BLONDE (LP) 100
62	HMV CLP 1553	LET ME BELONG TO YOU (LP)...50
63	HMV CLP 1759	COUNTRY MEETS FOLK (LP) 40
66	Philips BL 7762	THE JOKER WENT WILD (LP) 25
68	Fontana SFL 13008	HERE'S TO OUR LOVE (LP) 20

C. HYMAN
65	Ska Beat JB 200	The Ska Rhythm/The Ska Is Moving On 18

DICK HYMAN TRIO
56	MGM SP 1164	Theme From The Threepenny Opera/Baubles, Bangles And Beads 6
67	Command SCMD 105	BRAZILIAN IMPRESSIONS (LP) 15
69	Command SCMD 508	MOOG - THE ELECTRIC ECLECTICS OF DICK HYMAN (LP)............20
70	Command SCMD 946	THE AGE OF ELECTRONICUS (LP)..30

PHYLLIS HYMAN
79	Arista ARIST 323	You Know How To Love Me/Give A Little More (12", p/s) 10

HYPA KONCEPT
91	No Label L8 001	Party People (Come Together) (3 Mixes) (12", hand written labels) 20
92	Club State CSR 12001	Love Addict (4 Mixes) (12", stamped white label)......................40

HYPER ON EXPERIENCE
93	Moving Shadow SHADOW 40	THE FAMILY WE NEVER HAD EP (12", p/s, as Hyper-On Experience)..........15
93	Moving Shadow SHADOW 30	DEAF IN THE FAMILY EP (12", white label stamped with cat. no. only as Hyper On exp.)......60
93	Moving Shadow SHADOW 30	DEAF IN THE FAMILY EP (12", p/s as Hyper-On Experience) 40
94	Moving Shadow SHADOW 40	THE FAMILY WE NEVER HAD (12" picture disc) 50

JANIS IAN
67	Verve Folkways VS 1503	Society's Child (Baby I've Been Thinking)/Letter To Jon 20
67	Verve Folkways VS 1506	Society's Child (Baby I've Been Thinking)/Letter To Jon (reissue) 5
68	Verve Folkways VS 1513	Sunflakes Fall, Snowrays Call/Insanity Comes Quietly To The Structured Mind 10
67	Verve F'ways (S)VLP 6001	JANIS IAN (LP) 30
67	Verve Forecast (S)VLP 6003	FOR ALL THE SEASONS OF YOUR MIND (LP) 30
68	Verve Forecast (S)VLP 6009	THE SECRET LIFE OF J. EDDY FINK (LP) 20
70	Verve Folkways SVLP 6023	WHO REALLY CARES? (LP)...25
71	Capitol E-ST 683	PRESENT COMPANY (LP) 20
85	CBS 60636	BETWEEN THE LINES (LP, Nimbus Supercut, mail order only through Practical Hi Fi magazine) 40

MINT VALUE £

IAN (EDWARD) & ZODIACS

63	Oriole CB 1849	Beechwood 4-5789/You Can Think Again	45
65	Fontana TF 548	Just The Little Things/This Won't Happen To Me (as Ian Edward with Zodiacs)	30
66	Fontana TF 708	No Money, No Honey/Where Were You?	50
66	Fontana TF 753	Wade In The Water/Come On Along, Girl	65
65	Wing WL 1074	GEAR AGAIN - 12 HITS (LP)	30

(see also Koppykats, Wellington Wade)

IAN (MEESON) & BELINDA (GILLET)

89	Odeon ODO 112	Who Wants To Live Forever?/Who Wants To Live Forever? (Instrumental) (p/s, feat. Brian May, handful signed by Brian May for Blood Transfusion staff)	40
89	Odeon ODO 112	Who Wants To Live Forever?/Who Wants To Live Forever? (Instrumental) (p/s, feat. Brian May)	7
89	Odeon 12ODO 112	Who Wants To Live Forever?/Who Wants To Live Forever? (Instrumental)/ Who Wants To Live Forever? (Original Demo) (12", p/s, feat. Brian May)	10

(see also Brian May)

IAN & SYLVIA

63	Fontana TF 426	Four Strong Winds/Long Lonesome Road	7
65	Fontana TFL 6053	EARLY MORNING RAIN (LP)	30
68	Vanguard SVRL 19004	THE BEST OF IAN & SYLVIA (LP)	12

I BENJAHMAN

83	Lion Kingdom LKLP 01	INTRODUCING A FRACTION OF JAH ACTION (LP)	35

IBM 7090 COMPUTER & DIGITAL TO SOUND TRANSCUDER

62	Brunswick STA 8523	MUSIC FOR MATHEMATICS (LP)	40

RAS IBUNA

85	Studio Now SNT 01	Diverse Doctrine/Version/COOL BREEZE: Wi Nuh Want Nun A Dat (12")	12

ICARUS

69	Spark SRL 1012	The Devil Rides Out/You're In Life	175
72	Pye Int. NSPL 28161	THE MARVEL WORLD OF ICARUS (LP, laminated sleeve, blue/black labels)	150

(see also Soft Machine)

ICE CREAM

74	Fontana 6007 039	Shout It Out/Hold Yourself Tight	25

ICE FACTORY

83	No Label	JERUSALEM EP	35

ICE (1)

67	Decca F 12680	Anniversary (Of Love)/So Many Times	80
68	Decca F 12749	Ice Man/Whisper Her Name (Maria Laine)	120

(see also Affinity)

ICE (2)

79	Storm SR 3307	SAGA OF THE ICE KING (LP, private pressing with booklet)	80

(see also Dickens)

ICED EARTH

02	Century Media	DARK GENESIS (5-CD box set, initial issues with mispressed labels)	25

ICEPICK

97	Backbone BR971AA	Phenomenal Criminal/Brixtonites Pt 1(12")	15
98	Backbone ICEEP1 BB002	ICEPICK (EP)	10

(see also Bodysnatchers)

ICICLE WORKS

82	Troll Kitchen WORKS 1	Nirvana/Love Hunt/Scirocco (p/s)	5

(see also Ian McNabb, Melting Bear)

ICI LA BAS

79	Black Noise NO 4	ICI LA BAS (12" EP, with booklet)	20

ICON AD

82	Radical Change RC 3	DON'T FEED US SHOT!! (Fight For Peace/Face The Facts/What's Your Name (fold out p/s)	10
83	Radical Change RC 4	LET THE VUTURES FLY : Say No/Medals/For The Dead/Trident 1 And 2	10

ICONS OF FILTH

83	Corpus Christi CHRIST ITS 7	USED, ABUSED, UNAMUED EP (fold-out p/s)	10
84	Mortarhate MORT 10	BRAIN DEATH EP (p/s with insert)	10
85	Mortarhate MORT 18	THE FILTH AND THE FURY EP (Fold-out p/s)	10
97	BBP/Yellow Fever BBPV3/YF1	SHOW US YOU CARE EP (12 test pressings with red fold-out p/s and inserts)	25
97	BBP/Yellow Fever BBPV3/YF1	SHOW US YOU CARE EP (fold-out p/s, inserts)	6
84	Mortarhate MORT 5	ONWARD CHRISTIAN SOLDIERS (LP)	20

IDEALS

61	Pye International 7N 25103	Knee Socks/Mary's Lamb	40

DAVID IDEMA

72	Buddah 2011 130	House On Holy Road/Dream Weaver	6

IDES OF MARCH

66	London HLU 10058	You Wouldn't Listen/I'll Keep Searching (as I'des Of March)	12
68	London HLU 10183	Hole In My Soul/Girls Don't Grow On Trees	12
70	Warner Bros WB 7378	Vehicle/Lead Me Home, Gently	6
70	Warner Bros WB 7403	Superman/Home	6
70	Warner Bros WS 1863	THE IDES OF MARCH (LP)	20

(see also Survivors)

IDIOTS

80s	Blue Angle BLI 2	Operation Julie/(Why Does Politics Turn Men Into) Toads (p/s)	5

(see also Tone Deaf & Idiots)

IDJUT BOYS

94	U Star US 001	IDJUT BOY EP (12")	50
94	U Star US 003	PHANTOM SLASHER EP (12")	40
96	Noid NOID ONE	Girth Soup/Crouton Bonus/DJ HARVEY: Keep On Trying/Drums in 6 Twelve (12")	15

| 98 | Noid NOIDLP 001 | NOID LONG PLAYER (2xLP) ....50 |

IDJUT BOYS & DJ HARVEY
| 96 | Noid NOID ONE | Untitled (12")...25 |

IDJUT BOYS & LAJ
95	U Star US 004	Not Reggae (12") 40
95	U Star US 006	Foolin' (12")..20
95	U star US 007	BEARD LAW (EP) 15

ERIC IDLE & NEIL INNES
| 76 | BBC REB 233 | THE RUTLAND WEEKEND SONGBOOK (LP) ....12 |

IDLE FLOWERS
| 84 | Miles Ahead AHEAD 1 | All I Want Is You/Fizz Music (p/s) ....8 |

(see also Hanoi Rocks)

IDLE RACE
67	Liberty LBF 15026	The Imposters Of Life's Magazine/Sitting In My Tree 70
68	Liberty LBF 15054	The Skeleton And The Roundabout/Knocking Nails Into My House 25
68	Liberty LBF 15101	The End Of The Road/The Morning Sunshine 15
68	Liberty LBF 15129	I Like My Toys/The Birthday (unissued) 0
69	Liberty LBF 15218	Days Of Broken Arrows/Warm Red Carpet (B-side act. "Worn Red Carpet") 20
69	Liberty LBF 15242	Come With Me/Reminds Me Of You 22
71	Regal Zonophone RZ 3036	Dancing Flower/Bitter Green 12
76	United Artists UP 36060	The Skeleton And The Roundabout/Morning Sunshine 5
68	Liberty LBL 83132	THE BIRTHDAY PARTY (LP, mono) 100
68	Liberty LBS 83132	THE BIRTHDAY PARTY (LP, stereo) 70
69	Liberty LBS 83221	THE IDLE RACE (LP) 80
71	Regal Zono. SLRZ 1017	TIME IS (LP) 170
73	Sunset SLS 50354	ON WITH THE SHOW (LP) 15
76	Sunset SLS 50381	THE BIRTHDAY PARTY (LP, reissue)...15

(see also Mike Sheridan & Nightriders, Nightriders, Mike Sheridan's Lot, Lemon Tree, Jeff Lynne, Move, E.L.O., Trevor Burton, Steve Gibbons Band, Wizzard)

IDLEWILD
97	Human Condition HC 0017	Queen Of The Troubled Teens/Faster/Self Healer (p/s, 1,000 only) 50
97	Fierce Panda NING 42	Chandelier/I Want To Be A Writer (p/s)..12
97	Deceptive BLUFF 057	Satan Polaroid/House Alone (die-cut p/s, numbered, 1,500 only) 10
98	Food FOOD 28	HOPE IS IMPORTANT (LP) 15
00	Food FOODLP 32	100 BROKEN WINDOWS (LP) 15
02	Parlophone 5402431	THE REMOTE PART (LP, with inner sleeve) 15
09	Diverse DIV 020LP	POST ELECTRIC BLUES (LP) 12

BILLY IDOL
82	Chrysalis CHS 12 2543	Mony Mony/Baby Talk/Untouchables/Dancing With Myself (12", p/s) 8
82	Chrysalis CHSP 2625	Hot In The City/Dead On Arrival (picture disc)..5
93	Chrysalis CHR 6000	CYBERPUNK (LP, inner)..15

(see also Generation X)

IDOLS (1)
| 65 | Mercury MF 840 | Don't Walk Away/You Don't Care ....20 |

(see also Mike Sax & Idols)

IDOLS (2)
| 79 | Ork NYC 2 | You/Girl That I Love (p/s) ....8 |

(see also New York Dolls)

I. E. M. (INCREDIBLE EXPANDING MINDFUCK)
| 96 | Chromatic CHR 001 | I.E.M. (LP) ....30 |
| 03 | Gates Of Dawn GOD 007 | HAVE COME FOR YOUR CHILDREN (LP, 2 x 12" no sleeve with 2 postcard inserts, 90 only, includes track not on CD version)..35 |

(see also Porcupine Tree)

IF
70	Island WIP 6083	Raise The Level Of Your Conscious Mind/I'm Reaching Out On All Sides 10
71	United Artists UP 35263	Far Beyond/Forgotten Roads...6
72	United Artists UP 35356	You In Your Small Corner/Waterfall 6
70	Island ILPS 9129	IF (LP, 1st pressing, pink label/'i' logo) 50
71	Island ILPS 9129	IF (LP, 2nd pressing, pink rim label/'palm tree' logo) 25
71	Island ILPS 9137	IF2 (LP, pink label, pink rim label/'palm tree' logo) 30
71	United Artists UAG 29158	IF3 (LP, gatefold sleeve) 30
72	United Artists UAG 29315	IF IV (LP, gatefold sleeve with inner) 30
75	Gull GULP 1007	TEA BREAK OVER - BACK ON YOUR 'EADS (LP) 15
74	Gull GULP 1004	NOT JUST ANOTHER BUNCH OF PRETTY FACES (LP, with inner sleeve) 15

(see also Ferris Wheel, Terry Smith)

TECWYN IFAN
| 76 | Sain Sain 1071 | DREF WEN (LP, with insert) ....80 |

KRIS IFE
67	MGM MGM 1369	Hush/The Spectator 50
68	MGM MGM 1390	This Woman's Love/I Gotta Feeling 12
68	Music Factory CUB 3	Give And Take/Sands Of Time 20
68	Parlophone R 5741	Imagination/I'm Coming 'Round 20
69	Parlophone R 5770	Haven't We Had A Good Time?/Will I Ever Fall In Love Again? 10
73	Bumlade GE122	Wherever You Are/The Sun, The Sea, The Sand And The Wine 25

(see also Quiet Five, Judd)

I GAD
| 92 | Nuff Tuff TUF 006 | Brutality/ENHANCERS: Brutal Dub/Wicked Man/MANDINKA: Rootsman Corner/ ENHANCERS: Wicked Dub (12")..50 |

'IGGINBOTTOM
| 69 | Deram DML/SML 1051 | 'IGGINBOTTOM'S WRENCH (LP) ....200 |

(see also Soft Machine)

IGNERANTS
| 79 | Rundown ACE 008 | Radio Interference/Wrong Place, Wrong Time (p/s) | 30 |

IGUANA
| 72 | Polydor 2383 108 | IGUANA (LP, gatefold sleeve) | 25 |

IGUANAS
| 65 | RCA RCA 1484 | This Is What I Was Made For/Don't Come Runnin' To Me | 40 |

I HAICIDEONS & I JARZIF
| 78 | Greensleeves GRED 7 | Rise Ethiopians/Signs Of The Messiah (12") | 40 |

I JAH MAN (LEVI)
76	Lucky LY 6016	Jah Heavy Load/Heavy Dub	80
76	Concrete CJ 756	I Am Levi/Part 2	100
77	Ghetto Rocker PRE 1	Africa/Afrodub (handwritten labels)	40
78	Island WIP 6458	Heavy Load/I'm A Levi	20
85	Jahmani JM1 501	Moulding/Jah Is Coming Again (12")	40

I-JOG & TRACKSUITS
| 78 | Tyger TYG 1 | Red Box/Worrying Man (p/s) | 6 |

IKE (B) & CRYSTALITES
| 68 | Island WI 3134 | Illya Kuryakin/Anne Marie (B-side miscredited to Bobby Ellis & Crystalites) | 60 |
| 68 | Island WI 3151 | Try A Little Merriness/Patricia (as Ike B & Crystalites) | 20 |

IKETTES
62	London HLU 9508	I'm Blue/Find My Baby	25
65	Stateside SS 407	Peaches'N'Cream/The Biggest Players	35
65	Stateside SS 434	(He's Gonna Be) Fine Fine Fine/How Come	25
65	Sue WI 389	Prisoner In Love/Those Words	40
66	Polydor 56506	I'm So Thankful/Don't Feel Sorry For Me	20
66	Polydor 56516	(Never More) Lonely For You/Sally Go Round The Roses	20
66	London HLU 10081	What'cha Gonna Do?/Down, Down	80
67	Polydor 56533	I'm So Thankful/Don't Feel Sorry For Me (reissue)	8
73	Mojo 2092 063	Peaches'N'Cream/Sally Go Round The Roses	8
85	Kent 6T1	MARY LOVE: Hey Stoney Face/IKETTES: It's Been So Long/ETTA JAMES: Wallflower	20
65	Stateside SE 1033	FINE FINE FINE (EP)	125

(see also Ike & Tina Turner, P.P. Arnold)

ILANIT
| 77 | Pye International 7N 25739 | I'm No One (If You Leave Me)/I Can't Say I Love You (p/s) | 10 |

I LIFE
| 64 | R&B JB 140 | Kiss You Gave Me/No More | 18 |

ILLUSION
69	Dot DOT 122	Did You See Her Eyes?/Falling In Love	8
70	Dot DOT 133	Together/Don't Push It	5
70	Dot DOT 137	Let's Make Each Other Happy/Beside You (unissued)	0
70	Paramount PARA 3007	Let's Make Each Other Happy/Beside You	5
69	Dot (S)LPD 531	ILLUSION (LP)	25
70	Dot SLPD 537	TOGETHER (AS A WAY OF LIFE) (LP)	22
70	Paramount SPFL 264	IF IT'S SO (LP, originally planned for Dot SLPD 539)	15

ILLUSIONS
| 83 | Zella ZEL LPS 405 | ILLUSIONS (LP, 100 only, with insert) | 50 |

ILLUSIVE DREAM
| 69 | RCA Victor RCA 1791 | Electric Garden/Back Again | 30 |

(see also Christine Perfect)

ILLUSTRATION
| 69 | Pye Int. NSPL 28140 | ILLUSTRATION (LP) | 25 |

SOLOMON ILORY
| 63 | Blue Note 45-1899 | Yabe E (Farewell) (Parts 1 & 2) | 12 |

ERIK ILOTT, SHANTYMAN
| 73 | Folk'sle Records FOR 7 | SHIPSHAPE & BRISTOL FASHION (LP, card foldout sleeve, pasted on photo & 25 page booklet) | 40 |

I LUDICRIOUS
| 87 | Kaleidoscope KSLP 004 | IT'S LIKE EVERYTHING ELSE (LP) | 12 |

I LUV WIGHT
| 70 | Philips 6006 043 | Let The World Wash In/Mediaeval Masquerade (in p/s) | 75 |
| 70 | Philips 6006 043 | Let The World Wash In/Mediaeval Masquerade | 35 |

(see also Kaleidoscope, Fairfield Parlour)

IMAGE
65	Parlophone R 5281	Come To The Party/Never Let Me Go	40
65	Parlophone R 5352	Home Is Anywhere/I Hear Your Voice Again	40
66	Parlophone R 5442	I Can't Stop Myself/Let's Make The Scene	40

(see also Dave Edmunds)

IMAGES
| 65 | Polydor 56011 | I Only Have Myself To Blame/Head Over Heels | 30 |

IMAGINATION
| 82 | R & B RBS 208 | Just An Illusion/Just An Illusion (Instrumental) (12") | 8 |

IM & COUNT OSSIE
| 71 | Banana CA 357 | So Long Rastafari Calling/Give Me Back My Language & Culture | 40 |

IM (CEDRIC BROOKS) & DAVID
| 70 | Bamboo BAM 57 | Candid Eye/SOUND DIMENSION: Federated Backdrop | 40 |

NATALIE IMBRUGLIA
| 98 | RCA 74321 52799-2 | Torn/Contradictions/Diving In The Deep End (CD, withdrawn) | 12 |

IMITATIONS
71 Crystal CR 7013   Walking Up A One Way Street/One Way Street - Version 6

IMMEDIATE
05 Fierce Panda NING161   Never Seen/Say This (p/s) 7

IMMORTALS (1)
69 Amalgamated AMG 851   Bongo Jah/ANSELL COLLINS: My Last Waltz.................................40

IMMORTALS (2)
86 MCA MCA 1057   No Turning Back/No Turning Back (The Chocks-Away Mix) (p/s)..........30
86 MCA MCAT 1057   No Turning Back (Joy Stick Mix)/No Turning Back/No Turning Back (The Chocks-Away Mix) (12", p/s) 35

(see also Queen)

IMPAC
66 CBS 202402   Too Far Out/Rat Tat Ta Tat 100

IMPACT
83 Cyanide   PUNK CHRISTMAS EP 20

IMPACT ALL STARS
71 Bullet BU 483   Dandy Shandy Version 4/Go Back Version 3 7
71 Randy's RAN 519   Go Back Version 4/Version 3 7
71 Supreme SUP 223   Go Back/Version 8
(see also Randy's All Stars, Alton Ellis, Gregory Issacs, Errol Dunkley, C. Danovan, Heptones, Dennis Brown, Horace Andy)

IMPALAS
59 MGM MGM 1015   Sorry (I Ran All The Way Home)/Fool, Fool, Fool 20
59 MGM MGM 1015   Sorry (I Ran All The Way Home)/Fool, Fool, Fool (78) 25
59 MGM MGM 1031   Oh, What A Fool/Sandy Went Away 30
60 MGM MGM 1068   Peggy Darling/'Bye Everybody 30
59 MGM MGM-EP 696   SORRY (I RAN ALL THE WAY HOME) (EP)..400

IMPALERS
79 Decca F 13862   Gimme Some Lovin'/Wild About It...10

IMPERIAL POMPADOURS
80 Pompadour POMP 001   ERSATZ (LP, actually Inner City Unit with Robert Calvert & Barney Bubbles) 40
(see also Inner City Unit, Robert Calvert)

IMPERIALS
68 Nu Beat NB 012   Young Love/Days Like These 25

IMPERIALS
72 Key KL 012   TIME TO GET IT TOGETHER (LP)...18
74 Key KL 025   FOLLOW THE MAN WITH THE MUSIC (LP)..15

IMPERIALS (JAMAICA)
69 Bullet BU 417   Black Is Soul/Always With You 12

IMPERSONATORS
69 Big Shot BI 524   Make It Easy On Yourself/I've Tried Before......................................12
(see also Moffat Allstars)

IMPOSSIBLE DREAMERS
80 Merciful Release MR 1   Books Books Books/Not A Love Song/Waiting For The Girl/ What Can You Do When You See Someone As Beautiful As You? 8

IMPOSSIBLE YEARS
85 Dreamworld DREAM 1   SCENES WE'D LIKE TO SEE (12" EP) 12

IMPOSTERS
69 Mercury MF 1080   Apache '69/Q Three...20

IMPRESSIONS
58 London HL 8697   For Your Precious Love/Sweet Was The Wine (as Jerry Butler & Impressions) 220
58 London HL 8697   For Your Precious Love/Sweet Was The Wine (78, as Jerry Butler & Impressions)......80
61 HMV POP 961   Gypsy Woman/As Long As You Love Me...40
63 HMV POP 1129   I'm The One Who Loves You/I Need Your Love....................................40
63 HMV POP 1226   It's Alright/You'll Want Me Back...25
64 HMV POP 1262   Talkin' About My Baby/Never Too Much Love....................................20
64 HMV POP 1295   I'm So Proud/I Made A Mistake 18
64 HMV POP 1317   Keep On Pushing/I Love You (Yeah) 20
64 HMV POP 1343   You Must Believe Me/See The Real Me 18
65 HMV POP 1408   People Get Ready/I've Been Trying 18
65 HMV POP 1429   Woman's Got Soul/Get Up And Move 18
65 HMV POP 1446   A Meeting Over Yonder/I Found That I've Lost 18
65 HMV POP 1472   I Need You/Never Could You Be 18
65 HMV POP 1492   Amen/Long Long Winter 12
66 HMV POP 1498   You've Been Cheatin'/Just One Kiss From You 30
66 HMV POP 1498   You've Been Cheatin'/Just One Kiss From You (DJ Copy).........................75
66 HMV POP 1516   Since I Lost The One I Love/Falling In Love With You 15
66 HMV POP 1526   Too Slow/No One Else...15
66 HMV POP 1545   Can't Satisfy/This Must End 40
66 HMV POP 1545   Can't Satisfy/This Must End (DJ Copy)..75
67 HMV POP 1581   You Always Hurt Me/Little Girl..22
68 Stateside SS 2083   We're A Winner/You've Got Me Runnin'..18
68 Buddah 201 021   Fool For You/I'm Loving Nothing 10
69 Stateside SS 2139   Can't Satisfy/You've Been Cheatin' 20
69 Buddah 201 062   Choice Of Colors/Mighty Mighty Spade And Whitey 15
70 Buddah 2011 030   Check Out Your Mind/Can't You See?...10
70 Buddah 2011 045   (Baby) Turn On To Me/Soulful Love 6
71 Buddah 2011 068   Ain't Got Time/I'm So Proud 6
71 Buddah 2011 087   Love Me/Do You Want Me To Win 6
71 Buddah 2011 099   Inner City Blues/Amen/Keep On Pushin' 6
72 Buddah 2011 124   Our Love Goes On And On/This Love's For Real 6
73 Probe PRO 584   People Get Ready/We're Rolling On 8
65 HMV 7EG 8896   IT'S ALL RIGHT (EP)...70

MINT VALUE £

66	HMV 7EG 8954	SOULFULLY (EP)	70
64	HMV CLP 1743	THE NEVER ENDING IMPRESSIONS (LP)	80
65	HMV CLP 1935	BIG SIXTEEN (LP, mono)	40
65	HMV CSD 1642	BIG SIXTEEN (LP, stereo)	50
66	HMV CLP/CSD 3548	RIDIN' HIGH (LP)	50
67	HMV CLP/CSD 3631	THE FABULOUS IMPRESSIONS (LP)	50
68	Stateside (S)SL 10239	WE'RE A WINNER (LP)	30
68	Joy JOYS 104	FOR YOUR PRECIOUS LOVE (LP, with Jerry Butler)	15
69	Buddah 203 012	THIS IS MY COUNTRY (LP)	20
69	Stateside (S)SL 10279	BIG SIXTEEN (VOL. 2) (LP)	20
70	Buddah 2359 003	THE YOUNG MOD'S FORGOTTEN STORY (LP)	30
70	Buddah 2359 009	AMEN (LP)	18
71	Buddah 2318 017	CHECK OUT YOUR MIND (LP)	18
72	Buddah 2318 059	TIMES HAVE CHANGED (LP)	18
75	ABC ABCL 5104	BIG SIXTEEN (LP, reissue)	15

(see also Curtis Mayfield, Jerry Butler)

IMPROVING SILENCE

77	Perky Pat CS LP 145/6	IMPROVING SILENCE EP (1,000, p/s with 8 page book insert)	40

IMPS

58	Parlophone R 4398	Dim Dumb Blonde/Let Me Lie	20
58	Parlophone R 4398	Dim Dumb Blonde/Let Me Lie (78)	15

IN CROWD (JAMAICA)

71	Spinning Wheel SW 105	Bush Jacket/Soul Face	20
78	Savannah SVN 12-1	Riding High/Version (12")	12
78	Cactus CT 111	Back A Yard/Yard (12")	15
78	Cactus CTLP 125	HIS MAJESTY IS COMING (LP)	25

IN CROWD (U.K.)

65	Parlophone R 5276	That's How Strong My Love Is/Things She Says	80
65	Parlophone R 5328	Stop! Wait A Minute/You're On Your Own	65
65	Parlophone R 5364	Why Must They Criticize?/I Don't Mind	60

(see also Tomorrow, Keith West, Steve Howe, Four + One)

INCROWD (U.K.)

69	Deram DM 272	Where In The World/I Can Make Love To You	15

IN EMBRACE

82	Glass GLASS 024	Sun Brings Smiles/Play In Light (p/s)	8

IN FLAMES

72	Pama PM 842	Rocket Man/I'm All Broke Up	6

INADEQUATES

59	Capitol CL 15051	Pretty Face/Audie	25

INCAS

65	Lyntone LYN 765/6	KEELE RAG RECORD (EP, flexidisc, with 3 other bands)	40
66	Parlophone R 5551	One Night Stand/I'll Keep Holding On	60

INCOGNITO

80	Ensign ENY 4412	Parisienne Girls/Summers Ended (12")	12
81	Ensign ENVY 504	JAZZ FUNK (LP)	12

INCREDIBLE BONGO BAND

73	MGM 2006 161	Bongo Rock/Bongolia	12
72	MGM 2315 255	BONGO ROCK (LP)	30
76	DJM DJS 20452	BONGO ROCK (LP, reissue)	15

INCREDIBLE HOG

73	Dart ART 2026	Lame/Tadpole	12
73	Dart 65372	VOLUME 1 (LP, laminated sleeve, pink/white/black label)	200

INCREDIBLE KIDDA BAND

78	Psycho P 2608	Everybody Knows/No Nerve (in p/s)	50
78	Psycho P 2608	Everybody Knows/No Nerve (no p/s)	30
79	Carrere CAR 119	Fighting My Way Back/Saturday Night Fever (as KIDDA BAND)	130

INCREDIBLES

67	Stateside SS 2053	There's Nothing Else To Say/Heart And Soul	150
67	Stateside SS 2053	There's Nothing Else To Say/Heart And Soul (DJ copy)	200
74	Contempo CS 9008	There's Nothing Else To Say/Another Dirty Deal	10
74	Contempo CLP 512	HEART AND SOUL (LP)	25

INCREDIBLE STRING BAND

SINGLES

67	Elektra EKSN 45013	Way Back In The 1960s/Chinese White (white-label promo)	50
68	Elektra EKSN 45028	Painting Box/No Sleep Blues	10
69	Elektra EKSN 45074	Big Ted/All Writ Down	10
70	Elektra 2101 003	This Moment/Black Jack Davy	6
72	Island WIP 6145	Black Jack David/Moon Hang Low	5
73	Island WIP 6158	At The Lighthouse Dance/Jigs	5

ALBUMS : ORIGINAL ALBUMS

66	Elektra EUK 254	THE INCREDIBLE STRING BAND (1st pressing, white label, green logo, black lettering)	200
67	Elektra EUK 257	THE 5000 SPIRITS OR THE LAYERS OF THE ONION (mono, orange label)	120
67	Elektra EUKS 7257	THE 5000 SPIRITS OR THE LAYERS OF THE ONION (LP, stereo, orange label, laminated sleeve)	80
68	Elektra EUKS 7258	THE HANGMAN'S BEAUTIFUL DAUGHTER (mono, orange label, with lyric insert)	45
68	Elektra EUKS 7258	THE HANGMAN'S BEAUTIFUL DAUGHTER (stereo, orange label, with lyric insert)	60
68	Elektra EKL 4036/7	WEE TAM/THE BIG HUGE (2-LP, red label, laminated gatefold sleeve, with insert; also stereo EKS 74036/7)	45
69	Elektra EKS 74057	CHANGING HORSES (red/white label, gatefold sleeve)	40
70	Elektra 2469 002	I LOOKED UP (red/white label)	30
70	Elektra 2665 001	U (2-LP, red/white label, gatefold sleeve, with foldover lyric insert)	30
70	Elektra 2665 001	U (2-LP, red label, gatefold sleeve, without foldover lyric insert)	25

70	Island ILPS 9140	BE GLAD FOR THE SONG HAS NO ENDING (pink rim label/'palm tree' logo) 18
71	Island ILPS 9172	LIQUID ACROBAT AS REGARDS THE AIR (gatefold sleeve, with inner, pink rim label/'palm tree' logo) 18
72	Island ILPS 9211	EARTHSPAN (with lyric inner sleeve, pink rim label/'palm tree' logo) 15
73	Island ILPS 9229	NO RUINOUS FEUD (with inner sleeve, pink rim label/'palm tree' logo) 15
74	Island ILPS 9270	HARD ROPE AND SILKEN TWINE (with inner sleeve, pink rim label/'palm tree' logo) 15
76	Island ISLD 9	SEASONS THEY CHANGE (2-LP, gatefold sleeve) 25

ALBUMS : REISSUE ALBUMS

68	Elektra EUK 257	THE 5000 SPIRITS OR THE LAYERS OF THE ONION (LP, mono, red label) 25
66	Elektra EUK 254	THE INCREDIBLE STRING BAND (2nd pressing, orange label) 50
68	Elektra EKL 254	THE INCREDIBLE STRING BAND (3rd pressing, red label) 20
68	Elektra EKS 7257	THE 5000 SPIRITS OR THE LAYERS OF THE ONION (LP, stereo, red label) 40
68	Elektra EKL 4036	WEE TAM (red label, also stereo EKS 74036) 15
68	Elektra EKL 4037	THE BIG HUGE (red label, also stereo EKS 74037) 15
72	Elektra K 62002	U (2-LP, 'butterfly' label, gatefold sleeve, with foldover lyric insert) 15

INCUBUS
| 84 | Guardian GRC 2165 | TO THE DEVIL A DAUGHTER (LP) ....18 |

PETER IND
61	Esquire 32 159	LOOKING OUT (LP) 100
68	Wave LP 3	IMPROVISATION (LP) 30
69	Wave LP 4	TIME FOR IMPROVISATION (LP) 30
69	Wave LP 5	JAZZ AT THE RICHMOND FESTIVAL (LP, with Charlie Burchell, Bernie Cash & Derek Phillips) 30
70	Wave LP 20	COTRA-BACH (LP, with Bernard Cash) 30
74	Wave LP 29	NO KIDDING (LP, with Chas Burchell, Tox Drohar & Dave Cliff) 30

INDECENT EXPOSURE
| 84 | Index IS A1 | Riots (Single Version)/A Matter Of Time (no p/s) ....7 |

INDEX
| 78 | Index INDY 001 | Jetlag/Total Bland (1st pressing, 500 only, push out centre, die cut stickered sleeve) ....30 |
| 78 | Index INDY 001 | Jetlag/Total Bland (2nd pressing, 500 only, solid centre, die cut sleeve) ....15 |

INDIAN SUMMER
| 71 | RCA Neon NE 3 | INDIAN SUMMER (LP, gatefold sleeve) ....175 |
(see also Badfinger, Ross)

INDO-BRITISH ENSEMBLE
| 69 | MFP 1307 | CURRIED JAZZ (LP) ....25 |

INDO JAZZMEN
| 68 | Saga FID 2145 | RAGAS AND REFLECTIONS (LP) ....15 |

INERTIA
| 80s | Inertial ERT 1 | The Screen/4 Submarine (p/s) ....5 |

INFANTES JUBILATE
| 68 | Music Factory CUB 5 | Exploding Galaxy/Take It Now ....60 |

INFA RIOT
81	Secret SHH 117	Kids Of The 80s/Still Out Of Order (p/s) 10
82	Secret SHH 133	The Winner/School's Out (p/s) 6
82	Secret SEC 7	STILL OUT OF ORDER (LP) 15
(see also Infas)

INFAS
| 84 | Panache PAN 101 | Sound And Fury/Triffic Spiff Ya O.K. (p/s) ....8 |
| 84 | Panache PANLP 501 | SOUND AND FURY (LP) ....12 |
(see also Infa Riot)

INFERNAL BLUES MACHINE
| 76 | London SHU 8496 | ADIOS AMIGOS (LP) ....15 |

INFINITY PROJECT
89	Fabulous FABU 004	HYPERACTIVE (12" EP, sponged cover) 10
90	Fabulous FABU 005	UPHOLD THE LAW (12" EP) 10
90	Fabulous FABU 016	TRIBADELIC MELTDOWN (12" EP) 8

INFLUENCE
| 69 | Orange OAS 201 | I Want To Live/Driving Me Wild ....25 |
(see also John Miles, Geordie, Smokestack Crumble)

INFORMATION
| 69 | Beacon BEA 121 | Orphan/Oh Strange Man ....30 |
| 70 | Evolution E 2461S | Lovely To See You/Face To The Sun ....20 |

NICK INGHAM
| 75 | EMI EMI 2452 | American Pie/Brass Knuckles/Terminator ....12 |
| 75 | Studio Two TWOX 1045 | TERMINATOR (LP) ....25 |

RED INGLE
| 59 | Capitol EAP 20052 | CIGAREETS, WHUSKY AND WILD WILD WOMEN (EP) ....12 |

JORGEN INGMANN
61	Fontana H 311	Cherokee/Anna 5
61	Fontana H 353	Hear My Song - Violetta/Pinetop's Boogie Woogie 5
62	Fontana 267 237 TF	Africa/Johnny's Tune 5
63	Columbia DB 7013	I Loved You (Dansevise)/Little Boy (as Grethe & Jorgen Ingmann) 5

INGRAM
83	Streetwave WAVE 3	DJ's Delight/Smoothin Groovin (12") 12
83	Streetwave WAVLP 001	WOULD YOU LIKE TO FLY (LP, with bonus 12") 30
83	Streetwave WAVLP 001	WOULD YOU LIKE TO FLY (LP, without bonus 12") 20

LUTHER INGRAM
| 70 | Stax STAX 142 | My Honey And Me/Puttin' Game Down ....8 |
| 70 | Stax STAX 148 | Home Don't Seem Like A Home/Ain't That Lovin' You? ....8 |

I 'N' I ONENESS MEETS UK PLAYERS

72	Koko KOS 2202	IF LOVING YOU IS WRONG I DON'T WANT TO BE RIGHT (LP, photo insert)	20

I 'N' I ONENESS MEETS UK PLAYERS
97	Jah Works JW 018S	Further/Further Into Dub (12")	20

INITIALS
64	London HLR 9860	School Day/Song Is Number One	18

INK SPOTS
54	Parlophone MSP 6063	Here In My Lonely Room/Flowers, Mister Florist, Please	15
54	Parlophone MSP 6074	Ebb Tide/If You Should Say Goodbye	15
54	Parlophone MSP 6126	Planting Rice/Yesterdays	10
55	Parlophone MSP 6152	Melody Of Love/Am I Too Late?	10
55	Brunswick OE 9158	SWING HIGH SWING LOW VOL. 1 (EP)	10
50s	Britone LP 1003	THE INK SPOTS (10" LP)	15

(see also Ella Fitzgerald)

AUTREY INMAN
63	Decca DFE 8571	AMERICAN COUNTRY JUBILEE NO. 1 (EP)	15

INMATES
79	Soho SH 7	Dirty Water/Danger Zone (gatefold p/s)	8
79	Radar ADA 47	The Walk/Talkin' Woman (p/s)	5
81	Radar ADA 63	(I Thought I Heard A) Heartbeat/Tallahassie Lassie (p/s)	5

INNER CITY EXPRESS
78	Ebony EYE 5	Fat On Funk/Sho' Dig Dancin' (12")	20

INNER CITY UNIT
79	Riddle RID 001/ICU 45	Solitary Ashtray/So Try As Id (Dub Version) (plain sleeve with colour insert)	8
79	Riddle RID 003	Paradise Beach/Amyl Nitrate (company die-cut sleeve)	8
81	Avatar AAA 113	Beer, Baccy, Bingo And Benidorm/In The Mood (Nude) (red vinyl, no p/s)	5
82	Avatar AAA 119	Bones Of Elvis/Sid's Song (no p/s)	5
85	Jettisoundz JZ 5	BLOOD AND BONE (12" EP, p/s)	8
79	Riddle RID 002	PASS OUT (THE 360° PSYCHO DELERIA SOUND) (LP)	15
81	Avatar AALP 5004	THE MAXIMUM EFFECT (LP, with insert)	12

(see also Hawkwind, Sphynx, Radio Actors, Imperial Pompadours, Catherine Andrews, Big Amongst Sheep, Nik Turner)

INNER MINDS
70	New Beat NB 067	Witchcraft Man/Night In Cairo	7
70	New Beat NB 069	Pum Pum Girl/Freedom	7
71	Bullet BU 465	Arawak Version/Cuffy Cuffy	7
71	Shades SHA 11	Dreams Of Yesterday/Never Over The Land	8
72	Shades SHA 12	Jesse James Hits Back/Let Me In	10

NEIL INNES
72	United Artists UP 35358	Slush/Rawlinson's End (this is a different version from that on the Vivian Stanshall LP)	30
73	United Artists UP 35495	How Sweet To Be An Idiot/The Age Of Desperation	10
73	United Artists UP 35639	Momma B/Immortal Invisible	7
74	United Artists UP 35676	Re-cycled Vinyl Blues/Fluff On The Needle	7
74	United Artists UP 35745	Lie Down And Be Counted/Bandwagon	7
75	United Artists UP 35772	What Noise Annoys An Oyster/Oo-Chuck-A-Mao-Mao	7
77	Arista ARISTA 106	Lady Mine/Crystal Balls	6
77	Arista ARISTA 123	Silver Jubilee (A Tribute)/Drama On A Saturday Night	6
78	Warner Bros K 17182	Protest Song/The Hard-To-Get	6
79	Polydor 2059 247	Kenny And Liza/Human Race	6
82	MMC MMC 100	Them/Rock Of Ages	6
82	MMC MMC 103	Mr. Eurovision/Ungawa	6
73	United Artists UAG 29492	HOW SWEET TO BE AN IDIOT (LP)	30
82	MMC MMC 001	OFF THE RECORD (2-LP)	30

(see also Grimms, Bonzo Dog [Doo Dah] Band, Rutles, World, Dirk & Stig, Group)

INN KEEPERS
71	Banana BA 328	Duppy Serenade/Sunshine Version (actually by Dennis Alcapone)	18

(see also Winston Matthews)

INNOCENCE
66	Kama Sutra KAS 203	There's Got To Be A Word!/I Don't Wanna Be Around You	10
66	Kama Sutra KAS 206	Mairzy Doats And Dozy Doats/Lifetime Of Lovin' You	10

INNOCENT BYSTANDERS
80	Rok ROK XVII/XVIII	Where Is Johnny?/DEBUTANTES: The Man In The Street (company sleeve)	6

INNOCENT VICARS
80	No Brain INV 001	She's Here/Antimatter (p/s, hand-stamped labels)	60

INNOCENTS (U.K.)
63	Columbia DB 7098	Stepping Stones/Grazina	15
63	Columbia DB 7173	A Fine, Fine Bird/Spanish Holiday	15
64	Columbia DB 7314	Stick With Me Baby/Not More Than Everything	10

(see also Mike Berry, Innocents & Leroys)

INNOCENTS (U.K.)
80	Kingdom KV 8010	One Way Love/Every Wednesday Night At Eight (p/s)	10

(see also Woodentops, Advertising, Secret Affair)

INNOCENTS (U.S.)
60	Top Rank JAR 508	Honest I Do/My Baby Hully Gullys	30
61	Top Rank JAR 541	Gee Whiz/Please Mr Sun	40

(see also Kathy Young)

INNOCENTS & LEROYS
64	Regal Zonophone RZ 502	HOT SIX: Don't Throw Your Love Away/My Girl Lollipop/I Love You Because; Not Fade Away/Tell Me When/I Believe (maxi-single, plain sleeve)	10

(see also Innocents [U.K.], Le-Roys)

INQUISITIVE PEOPLE
67	Decca F 12699	Big White Chief/Rhapsody Of Spring	10

INSANE

82	Insane INSANE 1	Why Die?/War And Violence (p/s)	15
82	Riot City RIOT 3	Politics/Dead And Gone/Last Day (p/s)	10
82	No Future OI 10	El Salvador/Nuclear War/Chinese Rock (p/s, with Rising Free Fanzine)	25

INSANE CLOWN POSSE

98	Island ISP 705	Hokus Pokus/Prom Queen (picture disc)	15

INSANE MACBETH

00	Insane LP1	THE RETARDATION PROJECT (LP, 100 only)	60
01	Insane 1203	True Heart (12")	12

(see also Kinetic Effect)

INSECT TRUST

69	Capitol E-(S)T 109	THE INSECT TRUST (LP)	80

INSEX

79	Dining Out TUX 3	Inner Sanction/Fractured (p/s)	12

INSIDE OF A ROUGH TRADE SHOP

98	For Us/Out-There FU 005/ OV 003	CARNAGE: LIVE EP (CD, 50 only, numbered, with full-colour back tray art)	30
98	For Us/Out-There FU 005/ OV 003	CARNAGE: LIVE EP (CD, 50 only, numbered, without full-colour back tray art)	20

INSIDE OV A BUTCHER'S SHOP

98	Out-There OTT CD 2	Banking On Death - Carnage (CD, 50 only, numbered hand-made sleeve with fake dollar bill)	20

INSIDE OV A COFFIN

98	Out-There OTT 1	Banking On Death (7", existence unconfirmed)	0
98	Out-There OTT CD 1	Banking On Death (CD, 50 only, in hand-made sleeve with fake dollar bill)	20

(see also Freed Unit)

INSIDERS

80	Satellite SATS 1002	Rollin' & Strollin'/She Had To Go (features Ray Dorset)	10

(see also Ray Dorset)

INSPIRAL CARPETS

80s	Own label	SONGS OF SHALLOW INTENSITY (p/s, demo)	20
80s	Own label	WAITING FOR OURS (p/s, demo)	20
80s	Own label	COW (p/s, demo)	20
88	Playtime AMUSE 2	Keep The Circle Around/Theme From Cow (p/s)	15
88	Playtime AMUSE 4	Butterfly/You Can't Take The Truth (unreleased, white label promos only)	12
88	Playtime AMUSE 4T	TRAIN SURFING (12" EP, unreleased, white label test pressings only)	15
88	Playtime AMUSE 2T	PLANE CRASH EP	30
87	Debris DEB 6	Garage Full Of Flowers/METRO TRINITY (flexi, 4000 pressed, free with Debris magazine)	15
89	Dung 4	DUNG 4 (cassette LP)	20
94	Mute LDUNG 25	DEVIL HOPPING (LP, with free red vinyl 10" EP)	12

INSPIRATIONS (JAMAICA)

69	Camel CA 11	Down In The Park/Love Oh Love	25
69	Camel CA 21	Wonder Of Love/Cinderella	30
70	Amalgamated AMG 857	Take Back Your Duck/Nothing For Nothing	12
70	Amalgamated AMG 861	La La/Reggae Fever	15
70	Amalgamated AMG 862	The Train Is Coming/Man Oh Man	10
71	Upsetter US 355	Confusion/THE UPSETTERS: Confusion version	25
70	Trojan TTL 27	REGGAE FEVER (LP)	40

(see also Untouchables, Niney)

INSPIRATIONS (U.S.)

67	Polydor 56730	Touch Me, Kiss Me, Hold Me/What Am I Gonna Do With You?	200

INSTANT AGONY

83	Flicknife FLS 022	No Sign Of Life/Taste Of Power (p/s)	5
83	Flicknife FLS 028	Nicely Does It/We Don't Need You (p/s)	5

INSTANT AUTOMATONS

80	Deleted DEP 001	PETER PAINTS HIS FENCE EP (2x7", numbered, fold-out sleeve with inserts and stickers)	25

INSTANT FUNK

79	Salsoul SSLP 1511	I GOT MY MIND MADE UP (LP)	15

INSTANT SUNSHINE

68	Page One POF 085	Here We Go Again/Methylated	7
68	Page One POL 007	LIVE AT TIDDY DOLS (LP, blue/silver labels)	15

INSTITUTE OF FORMAL RESEARCH

97	Bubblehead BH 005	VOLUME ONE: FILE UNDER SUBCONSCIOUS (CD, features Zoot Horn Rollo)	20

(see also Mick Taylor, Chris Spedding)

INSTITUTION

79	Industrial Accident SGS 112	Jane and John/Stephanie (500 only, hand stamped labels)	30

(see also Jazz Butcher)

INSYNC VS MYSTERON

95	Peacefrog PF 033	AUDIBLE ILLUSION EP (12", plain sleeve)	10
97	Fat Cat 12FAT 004	TALES FROM THE CRYPT (12", custom sleeve)	15

INTELLIGENT COMMUNICATIONS

91	Jumpin' & Pumpin' 12TOT 15	PRINCIPLES OF MOTION EP (12", p/s)	10

(see also Future Sound Of London)

INTENSE DEGREE

88	Strange Fruits SFPS 053	THE PEEL SESSIONS EP (12", p/s)	10
88	Earache MOSH 9	WAR IN MY HEAD (LP, with inner)	15

INTENSITY

73	Eden EDEN LP 68	TURN ABOUT INSIDE OUT PLASTIC COATED HUMANS (LP)	150

INTENSIVE CARE
84	Punishment Block CELL 1	COWARDS EP (p/s)	8
87	Back To Back BTB 001	REBELS, ROCKETS AND RUBBERMEN (12", p/s)	12

INTENTIONS (U.K.)
72	Pye 7N 45123	There's Nobody I'd Sooner Love/Hurry On Home	5

INTENTIONS (U.S.)/Z.Z. HILL
66	Sue IEP 711	GIMME GIMME (EP, 2 tracks each by Intentions & Z.Z. Hill; 2 tracks mistakenly credited to Jackie Day on sleeve; in p/s)	300
66	Sue IEP 711	GIMME GIMME (EP, 2 tracks each by Intentions & Z.Z. Hill; 2 tracks mistakenly credited to Jackie Day on sleeve; no p/s)	100

INTERGALACTIC TOURING BAND
77	Charisma CB 306	Lone Station/Space Command	6

INTERNATIONAL CHRYSIS
94	PWL PWLT 303	Rebel Rebel (The Hole Mix)/Rebel Rebel (Extended Mix) (12", promo only)	15

(see also Dead Or Alive)

INTERNATIONAL PENPALS
03	Radical Wallpaper RADWAL 001	Day They Ate Ronald Reagan (p/s)	12

INTERNS (JAMAICA)
70	Jackpot JP 729	See You At Sunrise/LITTLE WONDER: Out Of Reach (B-side actually "Just Out Of Reach" by John Holt)	8
79	Burning Rockers BR 1003	DETOUR (LP)	30

(see also Viceroys, Bob Marley & Wailers)

INTERNS (U.K.)
64	Philips BF 1320	Don't You Dare/Here There Everywhere	15
64	Philips BF 1345	Cry To Me/There's Love For You	15
66	Parlophone R 5479	Is It Really What You Want?/Just Like Me	50
67	Parlophone R 5586	Ray Of Sunshine/Please Say Something Nice	10

(see also Shadows)

INTERPOL
00	CHEM047CD	fukd i.d #3 PDA/Precipitate/Roland/5 (CD, stickered card sleeve, 1,000 only)	60
02	Matador OLE 546-7	PDA/Specialist (p/s)	50
02	Matador OLE 546-2	PDA/NYC/Specialist (CD, digipak, with slipcase)	10
00s	Matador OLE 5827	Say Hello To The Angels/NYC (p/s)	8
07	Capitol/Parlophone CL 894	The Heinrich Maneuver/Concert Introduction (p/s)	8
07	Capitol/Parlophone CLS 894	The Heinrich Maneuver/Wrecking Ball (p/s)	8
03	Black Sessions 1803	LIVE - BLACK SESSIONS (LP, red splatter vinyl)	30
04	Matador OLE 616-1	ANTICS (LP)	15
04	Matador (no. Cat. No)	ANTICS (5 x 7" box set, only from Interpol Space Art Gallery, London)	50
05	Matador OLE 675	ANTICS - REMIXES (LP)	30
07	Capitol/Parlophone 0946 3 96248 1	OUR LOVE TO ADMIRE (2-LP)	20

INTERSTATE ROAD SHOW
69	President PT 249	Grindy Grind/All I Want To Do Is To Love You	8

INTESTINES
81	Alternative Capitalists AC51	Life In A Cardboard Box/New Recruit (p/s)	25

IN THE NURSERY
84	Paragon VIRTUE 5	Witness To A Scream/1984 (p/s)	15
85	New European BADVC 55	Sonority - A Strength (12" EP)	10
83	Paragon VIRTUE 2	WHEN CHERISHED DREAMS COME TRUE (mini-LP, silk-screened g/fold p/s)	25

IN THE WOODS...
96	Misanthropy OVL 69	White Rabbit/Mourning The Death Of Aase (p/s)	10
98	Misanthropy OVL 68	Let There Be More Light/Child Of Universal Tongue (p/s)	10
95	Misanthropy AMAZON 004	HEART OF THE AGES (LP, with booklet)	70
97	Misanthropy AMAZON 11	OMNIO (2-LP, gatefold sleeve, 1-sided etched disc)	50

INTIMATE STRANGERS
75	Alaska ALA 1005	Love Sounds/The Track	50

INTRA VEIN
79	Bum FP 001	Speed Of The City/Sick (printed PVC sleeve)	40
79	Bum FP 001	Speed Of The City/Sick (stamped plain sleeve)	30

(see also Veins)

INTRIGUE
82	Pressure PRESS D 1003	I Like It (Vocal)/I Like It (Instrumental) (12")	60
84	Music Power MPR(T) 1	No Turning Back/Call Of The Heart (12")	25
86	Intrigue INT 12-001	One Touch/Touch Down (12")	15

INTRIGUES
69	London HL 10293	In A Moment/Scotchman Rock	15

INTROZE
82	Monarch MON 037	Doin' The Lambeth Walk/Kids In Uniform	50

INTRUDERS (1)
59	Top Rank JAR 158	Frankfurters And Sauerkraut/Creepin'	10

INTRUDERS (2)
66	London HL 10069	Up And Down The Ladder/United	40
69	Action ACT 4523	Slow Drag/So Glad I'm Yours	15
69	Ember EMB S 254	Cowboys To Girls/Turn Back The Hands Of Time	15
72	Ember EMB S 325	Cowboys To Girls/GOOD VIBRATIONS: Shake A Hand	7

INVADERS (JAMAICA)
67	Columbia Bluebeat DB 105	Limbo Girl/Soul Of The Jungle	10
68	Columbia Bluebeat DB 109	Stop Teasing/Invaders At The Carnival	10
68	Studio One SO 2044	Soulful Music/SOUL VENDORS: Happy Organ	70
71	G.G. GG 4527	Got To Go Home/PAULETTE & GEE: How Long Will You Stay?	7

INVADERS (U.K.)
70s	Jovian ZIT 2	Launderama/Plastic Nose	5

INVICTAS
64	United Artists UP 1013	Green Bow Tie/Touch Of Orchid	7

INVISIBLE MAN
92	Timeless DJ 005	On A Mission/Twisted/Intro (Think About It)/ The End (Drug Induced Psychosis Mix)/Bonus Turbo Cut (12")	30
93	Timeless DJ 006	The Beginning/The End (12")	20
93	Timeless DJ 007	Skyliner/Power (12")	20
93	Timeless DJ 008	Skyliner (Remix)/MYSTERON: U Don't Know (12")	20
95	Timeless DJ 010	Skyliner (Top Buzz's 95 VIP Mix)/The Beginning (Innerspace Remix) (12")	10

INVITATIONS (JAMAICA)
71	Crab CRAB 66	Birmingham Cat/Now You're On Your Own	8

INVITATIONS (U.S.)
65	Stateside SS 453	Hallelujah/Written On The Wall	75
65	Stateside SS 478	What's Wrong With My Baby?/Why Did My Baby Turn Bad?	150
65	Stateside SS 478	What's Wrong With My Baby?/Why Did My Baby Turn Bad? (DJ copy)	300
70	Jay Boy BOY 24	How'd We Ever Get This Way?/Picking Up	35
72	Mojo 2092 055	What's Wrong With My Baby?/Why Did My Baby Turn Bad? (reissue)	8
74	Polydor 2066 366	Let's Love And Find Together/Love Has To Grow	10

INXS
81	RCA RCA 89	Just Keep Walking/Scratch	10
83	Mercury INXS 1	Don't Change/You Never Used To Cry (p/s)	8
83	Mercury INXS 121	Don't Change/You Never Used To Cry/Golden Playpen (12", p/s)	12
83	Mercury INXS 2	The One Thing/The Sax Thing (p/s)	8
83	Mercury INXS 212	The One Thing (6.10)/Black And White (12", p/s)	12
84	Mercury INXS 3	Original Sin/Jan's Song (live)/To Look At You (live) (p/s)	5
84	Mercury INXS 312	Original Sin/Original Sin (Extended Version)/Jan's Song (live)/ To Look At You (live) (12", p/s)	8
84	Philips PH 2	I Send A Message/Mechanical (p/s, in envelope pack with postcard & biography)	15
84	Philips PH 2	I Send A Message/Mechanical (p/s)	5
84	Philips PH 212	I Send A Message (Long Distance)/Mechanical/I Send A Message (Local Call) (12", p/s)	15

IONA
78	Silver Scales	CUCKOO (LP)	35
70s	Celtic Music CM 001	IONA (LP)	35

I.O.W. CHEROKEES
66	69 69EP 001	I.O.W. CHEROKEES (EP, private pressing)	40

I.P.O.H
73	Pye 7N 45215	Caveman Billy/Doggy	8
75	CBS 3408	In Pursuit Of Happiness/Spearhead	7

DON IPPOLITO ORCHESTRA
55	Parlophone MSP 6187	Camptown Racer Mambo/Can't Do It Mambo	5

IPSISSIMUS
69	Parlophone R 5774	Hold On/Lazy Woman	60

IQ
84	Jim White/IQ PROMO 101	Awake And Nervous/Through The Corridors (12", no p/s, 500 only)	30
84	IQFREEB 1	Hollow Afternoon (1-sided, Marquee gig freebie)	30
86	STAL Other Boxer 1	Nomzamo (Demo) (1-sided fan club single)	18
86	Sahara IQSD 1	It All Stops Here/Intelligence Quotient (shaped picture disc)	18
87	RLOG Another Boxer 1	Fascination/The Bold Grenadier Pt. 1 (fan club single)	18
88	RLOG One More Boxer 1	A Different Magic Roundabout (Honest!)/The Big Balls Of Bert Christ (fan club single)	12
92	MIMP 00000001	BLUBA NEENY NOO: Last Human Gateway (Acoustic Middle Section)/ A Bit Of Love Lost (CD, fan club single, 361 copies only)	18
85	STAL BOXER 1	NINE IN A POND IS HERE (2-LP, 1,000 copies only)	20

(see also Niadem's Ghost)

IQ PROCEDURE (ROOTS MANUVA)
94	Bluntly Speaking PHAT2	Run Tings/Can U Get With This/Big Up (12")	8

IQ ZERO
79	Object Music OM 9	(Everybody Kills) Insects/Electromotion/Quirky Pop Music (p/s)	20
79	Logo GO 374	She's So Rare/Crazy Dolls (p/s)	15

IRATION STEPPAS
94	Iration Steppa BS 159	Scud Missile/High Rise Vibrations (12")	30
03	Tandori Space TS 012	Too Much War/Stop The War Dub/What's Wrong/What's Wrong Dub (10")	25

IRATION STEPPAS & TENA STELIN
01	Tandori Space TSR 001	War Inna Babylon/Dub Version	20
01	Tandori Space TSR 002	Jungle Jungle/Dub Version	20

(see also Tena Stelin)

IRISH MIST
75	SRT/Custom 012	ROSIN THE BOW (LP)	15

IRISH ROVERS
67	Brunswick STA 8679	FIRST OF THE IRISH ROVERS (LP)	12
68	MCA MUPS 310	THE UNICORN (LP)	12
69	MCA MUPS 353	LIVERPOOL LOU (LP)	12

IRISH TRADITION
79	Green Linnet SIF 1016	THE CORNER HOUSE (LP)	15

IRONBELLY
70	Parlophone R5864	Woha! Buck/Wild About My Loving	10

IRON BUTTERFLY
68	Atlantic 584 188	Possession/Unconscious Power	15
69	Atlantic 584 254	Soul Experience/In The Crowds	12
70	Atlantic 2091 024	In-A-Gadda-Da-Vida/Termination	10

MINT VALUE £

68	Atco 2465 015	HEAVY (LP)	25
68	Atlantic 587/588 116	IN-A-GADDA-DA-VIDA (LP)	30
69	Atco 228 011	BALL (LP, gatefold sleeve)	25
70	Atlantic 2400 014	LIVE (LP)	18
71	Atlantic 2401 003	METAMORPHOSIS (LP)	20

(see also Ramatam, Captain Beyond)

IRON CROSS

72	Spark 1079	Little Bit Of Soul/Sunshine	6
74	Spark 1112	Everybody Rock On/All The Time	10

IRON HORSE

71	Bell BLL1148	The Obeah Man/Magic Love	20

IRON MAIDEN (1)

70	Gemini GMS 006	Falling/Ned Kelly	45

IRON MAIDEN (2)
SINGLES

80	EMI EMI 5032	Running Free/Burning Ambition (p/s)	25
80	EMI EMI 5065	Sanctuary/Drifter (live)/I've Got The Fire (live) (uncensored p/s)	35
80	EMI EMI 5065	Sanctuary/Drifter (live)/I've Got The Fire (live) (censored p/s)	15
80	EMI EMI 5105	Women In Uniform/Invasion (p/s)	15
80	EMI 12EMI 5105	Women In Uniform/Phantom Of The Opera (live)/Invasion (12", p/s)	15
81	EMI EMI 5145	Twilight Zone/Wrathchild (p/s)	15
81	EMI EMI 5145	Twilight Zone/Wrathchild (p/s, clear vinyl)	25
81	EMI EMI 5145	Twilight Zone/Wrathchild (p/s, red vinyl)	30
81	EMI EMI 5145	Twilight Zone/Wrathchild (p/s, brown vinyl mispressing)	800
81	EMI TCEMI 5145	Twilight Zone/Wrathchild	8
81	EMI EMI 5184	Purgatory/Genghis Khan (p/s)	30
82	EMI EMI 5263	Run To The Hills/Total Eclipse (p/s)	6
82	EMI EMIP 5263	Run To The Hills/Total Eclipse (picture disc, mispressed with b-side picture on both sides)	30
82	EMI EMIP 5263	Run To The Hills/Total Eclipse (picture disc)	20
82	EMI EMI 5287	The Number Of The Beast/Remember Tomorrow (live) (p/s)	5
82	EMI EMI 5287	The Number Of The Beast/Remember Tomorrow (live) (p/s, red vinyl)	12
83	EMI EMI 5378	Flight Of Icarus/I've Got The Fire (p/s)	5
83	EMI 12EMIP 5378	Flight Of Icarus/I've Got The Fire (12", picture disc)	20
83	EMI EMI 5397	The Trooper/Cross-Eyed Mary (p/s)	5
83	EMI EMIP 5397	The Trooper/Cross-Eyed Mary (soldier-shaped picture disc)	25
83	EMI EMIP 5397	The Trooper/Cross-Eyed Mary (uncut shaped picture disc)	200
84	EMI EMI 5489	2 Minutes To Midnight/Rainbow's Gold (p/s)	5
84	EMI 12EMI 5489	2 Minutes To Midnight/Rainbow's Gold/Mission From 'Arry (12", picture disc)	15
84	EMI EMI 5502	Aces High/King Of Twilight (p/s)	8
84	EMI EMI 5502	Aces High/King Of Twilight (mispress, A side label on both sides)	10
84	EMI 12EMIP 5502	Aces High/King Of Twilight/The Number Of The Beast (live) (12", picture disc)	20
85	EMI EMI 5532	Running Free (live)/Sanctuary (live) (poster p/s)	7
85	EMI 12EMIP 5532	Running Free (live)/Sanctuary (live)/Murders In The Rue Morgue (live) (12", picture disc)	20
85	EMI EMI 5542	Run To The Hills (live)/Phantom Of The Opera (live) (with Xmas card)	8
85	EMI 12EMIP 5542	Run To The Hills (live)/Phantom Of The Opera (live)/ Losfer Words (The Big 'Orra) (live) (12", picture disc)	20
86	EMI EMIP 5583	Wasted Years/Reach Out (computer-shaped picture disc)	15
86	EMI EMI 5589	Stranger In A Strange Land/That Girl (foldout poster p/s)	6
86	EMI 12EMIP 5589	Stranger In A Strange Land/That Girl/Juanita (12", picture disc)	18
88	EMI EMS 49	Can I Play With Madness/Black Bart Blues (p/s, with sticker & transfer)	5
88	EMI EMP 49	Can I Play With Madness/Black Bart Blues (shaped picture disc)	18
88	EMI EMP 49	Can I Play With Madness/Black Bart Blues (uncut shaped picture disc)	100
88	EMI CDEM 49	Can I Play With Madness/Black Bart Blues/Massacre (CD)	12
88	EMI EMS 64	The Evil That Men Do/Prowler '88 (gatefold p/s)	5
88	EMI EMP 64	The Evil That Men Do/Prowler '88 (shaped picture disc)	10
88	EMI EMP 64	The Evil That Men Do/Prowler '88 (uncut shaped picture disc)	80
88	EMI 12EMS 64	The Evil That Men Do/Prowler '88/Charlotte The Harlot '88 (12", poster p/s)	8
88	EMI CDEM 64	The Evil That Men Do/Prowler '88/Charlotte The Harlot '88 (CD, picture disc)	10
88	EMI EMS 79	The Clairvoyant (live)/The Prisoner (live) (clear vinyl, poster p/s)	6
88	EMI EMP 79	The Clairvoyant (live)/The Prisoner (live) (shaped picture disc)	15
88	EMI EMP 79	The Clairvoyant (live)/The Prisoner (live) (uncut shaped picture disc)	80
88	EMI CDEM 79	The Clairvoyant (live)/The Prisoner (live)/Heaven Can Wait (live) (CD, picture disc)	8
89	EMI EM 117	Infinite Dreams (live)/Killers (live) (with free patch)	5
89	EMI EMPD 117	Infinite Dreams (live)/Killers (live) (shaped picture disc with insert)	7
89	EMI EMPD 117	Infinite Dreams (live)/Killers (live) (uncut shaped picture disc)	80
89	EMI 12EM 117	Infinite Dreams (live)/Killers (live)/Still Life (live) (12", poster p/s)	8
90	EMI 12EMPD153	Holy Smoke/All In Your Mind/Kill Me Ce Soir (12" picture disc with insert)	12
90	EMI EM 171	Bring Your Daughter ... To The Slaughter/I'm A Mover (1-sided etched, p/s)	6
90	EMI EMPD 171	Bring Your Daughter ... To The Slaughter/I'm A Mover (picture disc 'brain' pack)	8
90	EMI 12EMP 171	Bring Your Daughter ... To The Slaughter/I'm A Mover (12", calendar pack)	10
90	EMI 12EMPD 171	Bring Your Daughter ... To The Slaughter/I'm A Mover/ Communication Breakdown (12", picture disc, die-cut sleeve)	12
90	EMI CDEM 171	Bring Your Daughter...To The Slaughter/I'm A Mover (UK pressed CD single)	100
92	EMI 12EMP 229	Be Quick ...Or Be Dead/Nodding Donkey Blues/Space station No.5 (12" picture disc, with insert)	10
92	EMI EMPD 240	From Here To Eternity/I Can't See My Feeling (shaped picture disc with insert)	10
92	EMI EMPD 240	From Here To Eternity/I Can't See My Feeling (uncut shaped picture disc)	60
92	EMI EMPD 263	Fear Of The Dark (live)/Hooks In You (live) (shaped picture disc, with insert)	10
92	EMI EMP 263	Fear Of The Dark (live)/Tailgunner (live) (poster p/s)	5
92	EMI EMPD 263	Fear Of The Dark (live)/Hooks In You (live) (uncut shaped picture disc)	60
92	EMI EMPD 263	Fear Of The Dark (live)/Hooks In You (live) (shaped picture disc, with mispressed B-side "Tailgunner" [live])	18
95	EMI CDEMS 398	Man On The Edge/The Edge of Darkness/Judgement Day/Blaze Bailey interview (CD)	25
95	EMI 12EM 398	Man On The Edge/I Live My Way (12", picture disc, with poster, die-cut sleeve)	15
95	EMI CDMAN 2	Man On The Edge/The Edge Of Darkness/Sign Of The Cross (CD)	50
98	EMI EM 507	The Angel And The Gambler/Blood On The World's Hands (Live) (picture disc)	12
98	EMI 8860690	Futureal/ The Evil That Men Do(live)/ The Angel And The Gambler (video) (CD digi-pack Fan Club only issue with poster)	50

00	EMI CDEMDJ 568	The Wicker Man (CD, 1-track promo in slim jewel case)	10
00	EMI EM 576	Out Of The Silent Planet/Aces High (live) (red vinyl, p/s insert)	6
02	EMI EM 612	Run To The Hills/Total Eclipse (live) (red vinyl, p/s)	6
02	EMI CDEMDJ 612	Run To The Hills/Run To The Hills Live (CD, custom card sleeve)	10
03	EMI EM 627	Wildren Dreams/Pass The Jam (green vinyl, stickered p/s)	6
03	EMI EM 633	Rainmaker/Dance Of Death (Orchestral version) (blue vinyl, stickered p/s)	6
04	EMI CDEM 636	No More Lies/ Paschendale/Journeyman/No More Lies video (Tour CD box set)	15
05	EMI EM 662	The Trooper (live)/Another Life (live) (p/s, poster, blue vinyl)	6
05	EMI 12EM 662	The Trooper (live)/The Trooper/Murders In The Rue MOrgue (live) (12", picture disc)	12
05	EMI 666A	The Number Of The Beast/The Number Of The Beast (live at Brixton) (red vinyl, p/s, poster)	6
06	EMI 3738012	A Matter Of Life And Death (CD, 4-track in custom sleeve slim jewel case)	15
06	EMI EM 714	Different World/Fear Of The Dark (Live 2006) (Picture disc, insert in stickered PVC sleeve)	6

SINGLES : PROMOS

80	EMI EMI 5032 DJ	Running Free (One-sided 7" DJ copy)	50
80	EMI EMI 5065	Sanctuary/Drifter (live)/I've Got The Fire (live) (DJ copy, censored p/s)	50
90	EMI EMDJ 153	Holy Smoke (1-sided 7" DJ copy)	50
90	EMI 12EMP 153	Holy Smoke/All In Your Mind/Kill Me Ce Soir (12", gold vinyl test pressing, promo only)	150
90	EMI EM 171	Bring Your Daughter ... To The Slaughter/I'm A Mover (Clear or white vinyl Test pressing for 12" picture disc)	100
90	EMI (no cat. no.)	NO PRAYER FOR THE DYING (CD, with interview , photos & bio, promo only)	100
92	EMI (no cat. No.)	FEAR OF THE DARK (CD, interview , EPK video, colour booklet, A4 poster in luminous flip top box)	150
95	EMI CDMAN 1	Man On The Edge (CD 1-track promo, slim jewel case)	12
96	EMI CDMDJ 443	Virus (CD, 1-track single edit, jewel case)	12
96	EMI BEST 001	BEST OF THE BEAST (CD, Steve Harris interview disc, commercial CD, video, in 40cm x 30cm, flip-up 3D presentation box with 60-page book, 2 photographs, biography, promo only)	200
97	EMI CDINPROF 001	In Profile (CD, 31 track edit band history picture disc custom sleeve)	35
98	EMI CDONPROF 001	IN PROFILE (CD)	30
98	EMI VIRTCDXI 002	The Angel And The Gambler (CD, 1-track edit version in custom card sleeve)	15
98	EMI VIRTCDXI 003	Futureal (CD, 1-track in custom card sleeve)	25
98	EMI VIRTCDXI 004	Futureal (CD, 1-track in custom card sleeve)	15
98	EMI HELLROM001	Maiden Hell promotional CD-Rom in full colour custom sleeve	25
98	EMI CDPP 044	Virtual XI Advance Listening CD custom sleeve jewel case	15
98	EMI VIRTCDXI 001	An Introduction To Virtual XI (CD, 3-track Futureal/ The Angel And The Gambler/ Lightning Strikes Twice custom card sleeve)	20
99	EMI EDHUNTER 666	ED HUNTER DEMO (CD-Rom, card p/s with booklet, press info and photo)	40
00	EMI CDEMDJ 576	Out Of The Silent Planet (CD, 3 tracks in slim jewel case)	12
00	EMI no cat. no.	Tommy Vance Previews: The Wicker Man/Ghost Of The Navigator/ Brave New World/Dream Of Mirrors/The Nomad (CD-R with Thomas The Vance intros)	50
00	EMI CDBWDJ001	BRAVE NEW WORLD (5-track sampler CD)	20
00	EMI CDIN 130	BRAVE NEW WORLD (promo interview CD)	25
02	EMI EDDIE 001	EDWARD THE GREAT (5-track promo sampler CD)	15
02	EMI IMRIODJ001	ROCK IN RIO (5-track 'Regal Sampler' sampler CD)	15
02	EMI RIOINTCD 001	ROCK IN RIO (Promo interview CD, with colour booklet)	50
02	EMI CDSP255	EDDIE'S ARCHIVE (CD, 8 track sampler in card sleeve)	50
03	EMI DODUKDJ001	DANCE OF DEATH (5-track sampler CD, card sleeve)	18
03	EMI CDEMDJ633	Rainmaker (CD, 1-track promo in custom card sleeve)	10
03	EMI DODRAD001	Dance Of Death (CD, promo interview, slim jewel case)	20
03	EMI CDEMDJ627	Wildest Dreams (CD, 1-track promo in custom card sleeve)	10
04	EMI CDEMDJ636	No More Lies (CD, 1-track promo in custom card sleeve)	15
04	EMI CDEMDJ 653	The Number Of The Beast/The Number Of The Beast (Priceless edit) (CD)	12
04	BMG PUB049	Int Iron Maiden 10 track promo CD in custom sleeve	50
05	EMI CDEMDJ662	The Trooper/The Trooper (live) (Promo CD, gatefold card sleeve)	12
06	EMI 3749682	A Matter Of Life And Death (CD promo interview in custom sleeve slim jewel case)	20
06	EMI CDEMDJ703	The Reincarnation Of Benjamin Breeg (CD, 2-track in custom card sleeve)	10
06	EMI CDEMDJ714	Different World/ Different World video (CD/DVD, custom gatefold sleeve)	10

EPs

79	EMI EMCP 3400	THE SOUNDHOUSE TAPES (EP mispressing with labels on wrong sides, Matrix numbers ROK-1A SA LYN 7627-1T/ROK-1B EG SA LYN 7628-1T, p/s)	600
79	Rock Hard ROK 1	THE SOUNDHOUSE TAPES (EP, p/s; Matrix ROK-1A EG SA LYN 7627-1T/ ROK-1B EG SA LYN 7628-1T. counterfeits have slightly glossier sleeves. Any with different p/s and coloured vinyl are also counterfeit)	200
81	EMI 12EMI 5219	MAIDEN JAPAN EP (12" EP, p/s)	15
93	EMI 12EMP 288	HALLOWED BE THY NAME EP (12", picture disc)	12

ALBUMS

80	EMI EMC 3330	IRON MAIDEN (LP, with poster)	35
80	EMI EMC 3330	IRON MAIDEN (LP, without poster)	15
82	EMI EMC 3400	NUMBER OF THE BEAST (LP, inner)	12
82	EMI EMCP 3400	THE NUMBER OF THE BEAST (LP, picture disc, with inner)	40
83	EMI EMA 800	PIECE OF MIND (LP, black card inner)	12
84	EMI EJ 2402001	POWERSLAVE (LP, textured sleeve, inner)	12
84	EMI POWERP 1	POWERSLAVE (LP, picture disc)	40
85	EMI ES 24 0426 3	LIVE AFTER DEATH (2-LP)	18
86	EMI EMC 3512	SOMEWHERE IN TIME (LP, inner)	12
88	EMI EMD 1006	SEVENTH SON OF A SEVENTH SON (LP, inner)	12
88	EMI EMDP 1006	SEVENTH SON OF A SEVENTH SON (LP, picture disc, with banner)	35
90	EMI EMD 1017	NO PRAYER FOR THE DYING (LP, inner)	12
90	EMI EMPD 1017	NO PRAYER FOR THE DYING (LP, picture disc, die cut sleeve)	20
90	EMI (no cat. no.)	THE FIRST TEN YEARS - UP THE IRONS (10 x 12" double packs, box set available by mail order with tokens from records)	175
90	EMI (no cat. no.)	THE FIRST TEN YEARS - UP THE IRONS (10 x CD, box set available by mail order with tokens from CDs)	100
93	EMI DON 1	LIVE AT DONINGTON (3-LP, numbered)	60
93	EMI EMD 1042	A REAL LIVE ONE (LP, gatefold sleeve with inner sleeve)	20
93	EMI EMD 1048	A REAL DEAD ONE (LP, gatefold sleeve and inner sleeve)	20
95	EMI 724383581917	THE X FACTOR (2-LP, clear vinyl, gatefold with inner)	60
96	EMI (no cat. No.)	THE STORY SO FAR PART 1 (5xCD box set, 1000 copies only)	300
96	EMI (no cat. no.)	THE STORY SO FAR PART 2 (5xCD box set, 1000 copies only)	300

IRON VIRGIN

			MINT VALUE £
96	EMI EMDX 1097	BEST OF THE BEAST (4-LP box set, with inners, book and bonus tracks)	100
97	EMI LPCENT 7	THE NUMBER OF THE BEAST (LP, reissue, 180gm vinyl)	30
98	EMI LPCENT 35	IRON MAIDEN (LP, reissue, 180gm vinyl)	30
98	EMI 4979990	EDDIE'S HEAD (13 CD boxset, plastic skull with flashing eyes)	175
98	EMI 4939151	VIRTUAL XI (2-LP gatefold, with inner sleeves)	60
00	EMI 526 6051	BRAVE NEW WORLD (2-LP, picture disc, gatefold, inner sleeves)	25
02	EMI 538 6431	ROCK IN RIO (3-LP, picture discs, trifold sleeve)	40
02	EMI 544 2772	EDDIE'S ARCHIVE (6-CD, tin box with insert, shot glass, pewter ring and Parchment. 1st issue blue lining)	100
02	EMI 544 2772	EDDIE'S ARCHIVE (6-CD, tin box with insert, shot glass, pewter ring and Parchment. 2nd issue red lining)	80
03	EMI 592 3401	DANCE OF DEATH (2xLP, picture disc, gatefold sleeve and inner sleeves)	30
05	EMI 336 4371	DEATH ON THE ROAD (2xLP, picture disc gatefold)	20
06	EMI 372 3211	A MATTER OF LIFE AND DEATH (2xLP, picture disc, gatefold, inner sleeves)	20

(see also Bruce Dickinson, A.S.A.P., Di'Anno, Gogmagog, Samson, Urchin, Xero, Lionheart, Pat Travers, Stratus, Nicko McBrain, Money, White Spirit, McEnroe & Cash, Speed)

IRON VIRGIN
74	Deram DM 408	Jet/Midnight Hitcher	10
74	Deram DM 416	Rebels Rule/Ain't No Clown	25

NEVILLE IRONS
68	Blue Cat BS 104	Soul Glide/DYNAMICS: My Friends	40

(see also Neville Hinds)

IRRESTIBLE FORCE
98	Ninja Tune ZEN 38	IT'S TOMORROW ALREADY (2xLP)	15

ANDY IRVINE
80	Tara 3002	RAINY SUNDAYS, WINDY DREAMS (LP, lyric insert)	15

ANDY IRVINE & PAUL BRADY
76	Mulligan LUN 008	ANDY IRVINE & PAUL BRADY (LP)	25

(see also Dr. Strangely Strange)

WELDON IRVINE
75	Strata East SES 19749	IN HARMONY (LP)	12

LONNIE IRVING
60	Melodisc MEL 1546	Pinball Machine/I Got Blues On My Mind	40

IRVING 6
70s	Port O Jam PJ4116	Ossie's Special/Trouble	20

(BIG) DEE IRWIN
64	Stateside SS 261	Donkey Walk/Someday You'll Understand Why	10
64	Colpix PX 11040	Heigh-ho/It's My Birthday	8
64	Colpix PX 11050	Personality/It's Only A Paper Moon	8
65	Stateside SS 450	You Satisfy My Needs/I Wanna Stay Right Here With You	125
65	Stateside SS 450	You Satisfy My Needs/I Wanna Stay Right Here With You (DJ copy)	200
68	Minit MLF 11013	I Can't Stand The Pain/My Hope To Die Girl (as Dee Irwin)	15

BIG DEE IRWIN & LITTLE EVA
63	Colpix PX 11010	Swinging On A Star/Another Night With The Boys (Little Eva uncredited)	5
64	Colpix PX 11021	I Wish You A Merry Christmas/Christmas Song	5
63	Colpix PXE 301	SWINGING ON A STAR (EP)	20
73	Golden Guinea GSGL 10497	SWINGING ON A STAR (LP)	15

(see also Little Eva, Suzi & Big Dee Irwin)

DAVID ISAACS
66	Island WI 261	I'd Rather Be Lonely/See That Man	50
68	Trojan TR 616	Place In The Sun/UPSETTER ALL STARS: Handy-Cap	15
69	Upsetter US 302	Good Father/SLIM SMITH: What A Situation	12
69	Upsetter US 305	I've Got Memories/I'm Leaving	12
69	Upsetter US 311	He'll Have To Go/Since You're Gone	12
69	Upsetter US 319	Who To Tell/BUSTY BROWN: I Can't See Myself Cry	12
69	Punch PH 6	I Can't Take It Anymore/LLOYD DOUGLAS: Anyway	10
71	Punch PH 84	You'll Be Sorry/Knock Three Times	8
71	Bullet BU 459	Just Enough/ROY PATIN: Standing (B-side actually by Roy Panton)	8
71	Tropical AL 006	Love Has Join Us/MAX ROMEO: Cross Over The Bridge (correct title for A-side is 'Love Has Joined Us').	5
73	Upsetter US 400	Stranger On The Shore/DILLINGER: John Devour	40
73	Bread BR 1118	Just Enough/We Are Neighbours	5
79	Attack TACK 13	Just Like A Sea (with Jah Thomas)/ WITTY'S ALL STARS: Just Like A Sea (Version) (12")	18

(see also Upsetters)

GREGORY ISAACS
70	Escort ERT 833	While There Is Life/HARRY YOUNG: Come On Over	15
70	Success RE 914	Too Late/KINGSTONIANS: You Can't Wine	25
70	Bullet BU 448	Set Back/SYDNEY'S ALLSTARS: Version II	15
71	Big Shot BI 584	Lonely Man/RUPIE EDWARDS ALL STARS: Lonely Man Version	12
73	Ackee ACK 522	I'm Coming Home/Version	5
73	Green Door GD 4054	Lonely Soldier/IMPACT ALL STARS: Version	12
74	Pyramid PYR 7012	Innocent People Cry/Version	8
74	Attack ATT 8066	Love Is Overdue Part 1/Love Is Overdue Part 2	8
74	Attack ATT 8081	Don't Go/Dubwise	8
74	Stop Points DL 0022	End Of The World/Gregory Shuffle	10
75	Black Wax WAX 9	Sunshine For Me/Version	8
75	Attack ATT 8095	Bad Da/Ad Dab	8
75	Attack ATT 8106	Fly Little Silver Bird/Dub	8
75	Camel CA 2008	Lonely Days/Version	8
75	Bullet BU 555	Lonely Days/Version	8
76	Third World TW 032	Look Before You Leap/K. SMILEY: Sata	15
76	Morpheus MOR 1017	Black Kill A Black/Version	25
77	Observer OBMM-1000	Soul On Fire/CHRISTINE: Saturday Night/TYRONE TAYLOR: Sufferation/ In Style (12")	40
78	Observer	Rock On/Murder Observer Style/DENNIS BROWN & DILLINGER: Jah Is Watching/Hustling (12")	60

616   Rare Record Price Guide 2014

78	DEB DEB 004	Mr Know It All/OSSIE HIBBERT & REVOLUTIONARIES: War Of The Stars (12").....................30
78	Hawkeye HE 008	John Public/LEGGO ALL STARS: Enemy No 1 8
78	Star PTP 1002	Lonely Days/U ROY: Nanny Skank (12")..15
79	Front Line FLS 12112	Soon Forward/Uncle Joe/Come Off Mi Toe (Feat. Prince Far I) (12").........................15
80	Pre PRES 8	Poor And Clean/Tribute To Wada 10
80	African Museum (no number)	If You See My Mary/Mary's Special (12", blue vinyl) 20
85	African Museum AF 0050	G.P./Version (12") 25
80	Solomonic SM 002	Sunday Morning/DENNIS BROWN: Running Around (12")......................................25
88	Greensleeves GRED 221	Rumours/More Rumours (12") 30
88	Greensleeves GRED 225	Rough Neck/Version (12" with the Mighty Diamonds) 30
89	Greensleeves GRED 256	Report To Me/Report To Me (continued) (12") 30
75	Trojan TRLS 102	IN PERSON (LP) 15
76	Trojan TRLS 121	ALL I HAVE IS LOVE (LP) 15
76	Shack BITE 200	EXTRA CLASSIC (LP) 20
78	Burning Sounds BS1010	SLUM - GREGORY ISAACS IN DUB (LP) 30
78	DEB DEB LP 04	MR ISAACS (LP) 30
78	Virgin Front Line FL 1020	COOL RULER (LP) 20
79	Virgin Front Line FL1044	SOON FORWARD (LP) 30
82	Island 9721	NIGHT NURSE (LP, blue vinyl with poster)..18
83	Burning Sounds BS 1051	SLUM DUB (LP) 25
83	Pre PREX1	THE LONELY LOVER (LP) 15

IKE ISAACS

| 68 | Morgan MR 116P | I LIKE IKE (LP) ....15 |

ISCA FAYRE

| 76 | Candle CAN 761 | THEN AROUND ME YOUNG AND OLD (LP) ....15 |

ISH

| 79 | TKS TKR 7540 | Faster Than A Speeding Bullet/Don't Stop..6 |

JON ISHERWOOD

| 70 | Decca LK/SKL 5051 | A LAUGHING CRY (LP) ....15 |

ISHMAEL & ANDY

| 73 | Myrrh MYR 1005 | READY SALTED (LP)..20 |

ISLANDERS

| 59 | Top Rank JAR 215 | The Enchanted Sea/Pollyanna ....8 |
| 60 | Top Rank JAR 305 | Blue Train/Tornado ....6 |

ISLANDERS

| 65 | Fontana TF 577 | It Ain't Me Babe/Four Strong Winds ....10 |
| 65 | Fontana TF 605 | Walkin' Away/Roberta Let Your Hair Hang Down ....5 |

JIMMY ISLE

59	London HLS 8832	Diamond Ring/I've Been Waiting 70
59	London HLS 8832	Diamond Ring/I've Been Waiting (78 rpm = £25)..25
60	Top Rank JAR 274	Billy Boy/Oh Judy...15

ISLEY BROTHERS

59	RCA RCA 1149	Shout (Parts 1 & 2) (tri centre) 30
59	RCA RCA 1149	Shout (Parts 1 & 2) (round centre)...25
59	RCA RCA 1149	Shout (Parts 1 & 2) (78) 200
60	RCA RCA 1172	Respectable/I'm Gonna Knock On Your Door 20
60	RCA RCA 1190	How Deep Is The Ocean/He's Got The Whole World In His Hands 20
60	RCA RCA 1213	Tell Me Who/Say You Love Me Too 20
62	Stateside SS 112	Twist And Shout/Spanish Twist 15
62	Stateside SS 132	Twistin' With Linda/Come Home...15
63	Stateside SS 218	Nobody But Me/I'm Laughing To Keep From Crying 20
63	United Artists UP 1034	Tango/She's Gone 18
64	United Artists UP 1050	Shake It With Me Baby/Stagger Lee 20
64	Atlantic AT 4010	The Last Girl/Looking For A Love 45
66	Tamla Motown TMG 555	This Old Heart Of Mine (Is Weak For You)/There's No Love Left (1st press with narrow print on label)...20
66	Tamla Motown TMG 555	This Old Heart Of Mine (Is Weak For You)/There's No Love Left (2nd re-press - 1968 - with wider print)..10
66	Tamla Motown TMG 566	Take Some Time Out For Love/Who Could Ever Doubt My Love 35
66	Tamla Motown TMG 572	I Guess I'll Always Love You/I Hear A Symphony (1st pressing with "sold subject to" on centre piece) 35
67	Tamla Motown TMG 606	Got To Have You Back/Just Ain't Enough Love 25
68	Tamla Motown TMG 652	Take Me In Your Arms (Rock Me A Little While)/Why When Love Is Gone 30
69	Tamla Motown TMG 683	I Guess I'll Always Love You/It's Out Of The Question 8
69	Tamla Motown TMG 693	Behind A Painted Smile/One Too Many Heartaches 7
69	Major Minor MM 621	It's Your Thing/Don't Give It Away 10
69	Tamla Motown TMG 708	Put Yourself In My Place/Little Miss Sweetness 7
69	Major Minor MM 631	I Turned You On/I Know Who You Been Socking It To 6
69	Tamla Motown TMG 719	Take Some Time Out For Love/Who Could Ever Doubt My Love (reissue) 7
70	Stateside SS 2162	Was It Good To You?/I Got To Get Myself Together 6
71	Stateside SS 2188	Warpath/I Got To Find Me One 6
71	Stateside SS 2193	Love The One You're With/He's Got Your Love 10
73	Tamla Motown TMG 877	Tell Me It's Just A Rumour, Baby/Save Me From This Misery 8
73	Epic EPC 1980	The Highways Of My Life/Don't Let Me Be Lonely Tonight 5
74	Epic EPC 2803	Need A Little Taste Of Love/If You Were There 5
76	DJM DJS 640	Twist And Shout/Time After Time (reissue) 5
79	RCA PC 9411	Shout/Respectable/Tell Me Who (12", p/s)...8
64	RCA RCX 7149	THE ISLEY BROTHERS (EP)..80
60	RCA RD 27165	SHOUT (LP, mono) 60
60	RCA SF 7055	SHOUT (LP, stereo) 100
64	United Artists ULP 1064	THE FAMOUS ISLEY BROTHERS - TWISTING AND SHOUTING (LP) 80
66	Tamla Motown TML 11034	THIS OLD HEART OF MINE (IS WEAK FOR YOU) (LP, mono).............................30
66	STML 11034	THIS OLD HEART OF MINE (IS WEAK FOR YOU) (LP, stereo).............................35
68	T. Motown TML 11066	SOUL ON THE ROCKS (LP, mono) 30
68	T. Motown STML 11066	SOUL ON THE ROCKS (LP, stereo) 35
69	Major Minor SMLP 59	IT'S OUR THING (LP) 25
69	T. Motown TML 11112	BEHIND A PAINTED SMILE (LP, mono) 25

69	T. Motown (S)TML 11112	BEHIND A PAINTED SMILE (LP, stereo)	22
70	Stateside SSL 10300	THE BROTHERS: ISLEY (LP)	22

ISOLATION
73	Riverside HASLP 2083	ISOLATION (LP, private pressing with insert)	300

ISOTOPE
74	Gull GULP 1002	ISOTOPE (LP)	15
74	Gull GULP 1006	ILLUSION (LP)	15
75	Gull GULP 1017	DEEP END (LP, 1976 on both labels)	15

(see also Brian Auger, Hugh Hopper)

ISRAELITES
69	Downtown DT 413	Moma Moma/Melody For Two	8
69	Downtown DT 421	Games People Play/AUDREY: One Fine Day	20
69	Downtown DT 433	Seven Books/Chaka Beat	8
70	J-Dan JDN 4410	Can't Help From Crying/Can't Get Used To Losing You	8

(see also Music Doctors)

ISRAEL VIBRATION
78	Harvest HAR 184	The Same Song/Weep And Moan	15
79	Harvest 12 HAR 5189	Crisis/Crisis Dub (12", feat. Augustus Pablo)	30
79	Harvest SHSP 4099	THE SAME SONG (LP, black and red Harvest label)	25
88	RAS RAS 3037	STRENGTH OF MY LIFE (LP)	30
90	RAS RAS 3054	PRAISES (LP)	25

HUGHY ISSACHAR
86	Melody Muzik MM 001	Mountain Rock/ORIGINAL ROCKERS: So Shall It Be (12")	50

ITALS (JAMAICA)
67	Giant GN 8	New Loving (with Soul Brothers)/I Told You Little Girl	30
67	Giant GN 12	Don't Throw It Away/Make Up Your Mind (both with Carib-Beats)	35
71	Big BG 325	Ba-Da-Doo-Ba-Dey/RUPIE EDWARDS ALL STARS: Version	10

(see also Alton Ellis, Honeyboy)

ITALS (U.K.)
71	Black Swan BW 1404	Dawn Patrol/Whiskey Bonga (DJ and Rhythm)	12
71	Black Swan BW 1407	Judgement Rock (actually by Charlie Ace)/Night West	12

ITHACA
73	Merlin HF 6	A GAME FOR ALL WHO KNOW (LP, with insert)	750
93	Background	A GAME FOR ALL WHO KNOW (LP, reissue)	25

(see also Friends, Alice Through The Looking Glass, Agincourt, Tomorrow Come Someday, BBC Radiophonic Workshop)

IT'S A BEAUTIFUL DAY
69	CBS 4457	White Bird/Wasted Union Blues	8
70	CBS 4933	Soapstone Mountain/Do You Remember The Sun	15
73	CBS 1625	Ain't That Lovin' You Baby/Time	5
69	CBS 63722	IT'S A BEAUTIFUL DAY (LP, gatefold sleeve)	25
70	CBS 64065	MARRYING MAIDEN (LP)	25
72	CBS 64314	CHOICE QUALITY STUFF - ANYTIME (LP)	20

IT'S IMMATERIAL
81	Inevitable Hit Machine IHM 002	Imitate The Worm/The Worm Turns (p/s)	10
84	Eternal JF 4	A Gigantic Raft In The Philipines/The Mermaid (p/s)	10

IVAN
58	Coral Q 72341	Real Wild Child/Oh, You Beautiful Doll	250
58	Coral Q 72341	Real Wild Child/Oh, You Beautiful Doll (78)	100

(see also Jerry Allison, Crickets)

IVAN D. JUNIORS
63	Oriole CB 1874	Catch You If I Can/On My Mind	20

IVANS MEADS
65	Parlophone R 5342	A Little Sympathy/The Sins Of A Family	70
66	Parlophone R 5503	We'll Talk About It Tomorrow/The Bottle	50

BURL IVES
54	Columbia SCMC 5	I've Got No Use For Women/River Of Smoke (export issue)	5
56	Brunswick 05510	Ballad Of Davy Crockett/Goober Peas	5
56	Brunswick 05551	Dying Stockman/Click Go The Shears	5
56	Brunswick 05604	The Bus Stop Song/That's My Heartstrings	5
56	Decca BM 31183	Marianne/Pretty Girl (with Trinidadies) (export issue)	10

IVEYS
68	Apple APPLE 5	Maybe Tomorrow/And Her Daddy's A Millionaire	55
69	Apple APPLE 14	Dear Angie/No Escaping Your Love (unreleased; Europe & Japan only)	0
68	Apple SAPCOR 8	MAYBE TOMORROW (LP, unissued; Europe & Japan only)	0
92	Apple SAPCOR 8	MAYBE TOMORROW (LP, reissue, gatefold sleeve & bonus 12" [SAPCOR 82])	25

(see also Badfinger, Pleasure Garden)

IVOR & SHEILA
81	Eron 027	CHANGING TIMES (LP, with insert)	30

IVORIES
85	Kent TOWN 103	Please Stay/TOMMY HUNT: The Work Song	10

(see also Tommy Hunt)

JACKIE IVORY
66	Atlantic AT 4075	Hi-Heel Sneakers/Do It To Death	20
65	Atlantic ATL 5046	SOUL DISCOVERY (LP)	60
65	Atlantic ATL 5046	SOUL DISCOVERY (LP, 1966 reissue)	25

IVORY SUN
70	Jupiter	Another Yesterday/ Rainy Tomorrow/Black Gold	60

IVY
94	Sarah SARAH 91	Wish You Would/Nowhere To Mourn (p/s)	12

94	Sarah SARAH 92	Avenge/Sound The Deep Waters	12

IVY LEAGUE

64	Piccadilly 7N 35200	What More Do You Want?/Wait A Minute	10
65	Piccadilly 7N 35228	That's Why I'm Crying/A Girl Like You	6
65	Piccadilly 7N 35267	Our Love Is Slipping Away/I Could Make You Fall In Love	6
66	Piccadilly 7N 35294	Running Round In Circles/Rain Rain Go Away	5
66	Piccadilly 7N 35326	Willow Tree/One Day	6
66	Piccadilly 7N 35348	My World Fell Down/When You're Young	10
67	Piccadilly 7N 35365	Four And Twenty Hours/Arrivederci Baby	7
67	Piccadilly 7N 35397	Suddenly Things/Tomorrow Is Another Day	7
67	Pye 7N 17386	Thank You For Loving Me/In The Not Too Distant Future	10
65	Piccadilly NEP 34038	FUNNY HOW LOVE CAN BE (EP)	18
65	Piccadilly NEP 34042	TOSSING AND TURNING (EP)	18
65	Piccadilly NEP 34046	THE HOLLY AND THE IVY LEAGUE (EP)	10
66	Piccadilly NEP 34048	OUR LOVE IS SLIPPING AWAY (EP)	25
65	Piccadilly NPL 38015	THIS IS THE IVY LEAGUE (LP)	30

(see also Carter-Lewis, White Plains, Edison Lighthouse, Flowerpot Men, Kestrels, One & One, Johnny Shadow, Perry Ford, First Class, Friends, Warm Sensations)

IVY THREE

60	London HLW 9178	Yogi/Was Judy There	22

DAFYDD IWAN

69	Welsh Teldisc WD 904	Croeso/Chwedeg Nain (p/s)	8

IWASACUBSCOUT

06	Fear And (No Cat. No.)	We Were Made To Love/That's Not A Crate, It's A Box Of Heaven Part Two (500 only, p/s)	6

IZZY POUND

69	Plexium PXM 9	Pumpkin Miny/Na Na Na Na	40

J

DAVID J. (& J. WALKERS)

81	4AD AD 112	Nothing/Armour (as David Jay & René Halkett) (p/s, with lyric sheet)	5
84	GLASS 12032	V For Vendetta: This Viscious Cabaret/V's Theme/Incidental/V's Theme (12" p/s)	8

(see also Bauhaus)

TONY J.

75	Stonehouse 001	Telephone Line/Telephone Version	5

JABBERWOCK

77	MCA MCA 264	Sneakin' Snaky/Fortune Teller	15

JABULA

76	Caroline CA 2009	THUNDER INTO OUR HEARTS (LP)	12
78	Jabula JBL 2003	AFRIKA AWAKE (LP)	18

JOY JACINTH

83	Zebratone ZTD 93	Baby Boy/Red Lights (12")	15

JACK (BERNARD) & BEANSTALKS

69	Supreme SUP 203	Work It Up/Chatty Chatty	12

(see also Kingstonians)

BILLY JACK (& CIMARONS)

70	Grape GR 3018	Let's Work Together/CORPORATION: Jam Monkey	10
70	Big Shot BI 558	Once A Man/Soul Mood (as Billy Jack & Cimarons)	7
70	Big Shot BI 559	Bet Your Life I Do/CANDY & CIMARONS: Ace Of Hearts	7

(see also Candy)

BOBBY JACK

59	Top Rank JAR 190	Tempting Me/Early Mornin'	8

JACKAL (1)

74	BASF BA 1009	The Year Of The Tiger/Big Star	10

JACKAL (2)

86	Crim. Damage CRI 12-134	Underneath The Arches/Thunder Machine (12", p/s)	15

(see also Renegade Soundwave)

JACKIE

78	Fashion FAD 002	It's Too Late Baby/Fashion On Fine Style (12")	20

JACKIE & BRIDIE

68	Major Minor MM 562	Come Me Little Son/We Only Needed Time	6
64	Fontana TL 5212	HOLD BACK THE DAWN (LP)	25
70	Concord CONS 1002	FOLK WORLD OF JACKIE AND BRIDIE (LP)	15
71	Galliard GAL 4009	THE PERFECT ROUND (LP)	15
70s	Nevis NEV LP 102	HELLO FRIEND (LP, as Jacqui & Bridie)	12
77	J & B CNN 5939	COME DAY GO DAY (LP)	12
77	J & B CNN 5949	HOW CAN YOU KEEP FROM SINGING WITH... (LP)	12

(see also Jacqueline & Bridie)

JACKIE & DOREEN

64	Ska Beat JB 168	Every Beat Of My Heart	20
65	Ska Beat JB 209	The New Vow/Adorable You	50

(see also Doreen Shaffer, Jackie Opel)

JACKIE (EDWARDS) & MILLIE (SMALL)

65	Island WI 253	This Is My Story/SOUND SYSTEM: Never Again	45

MINT VALUE £

66	Island WI 265	My Desire/MILLIE: That's How Strong My Love Is	15
67	Island WIP 6012	In A Dream/Ooh Ooh	20
67	Island ILP 941	PLEDGING MY LOVE (LP, as Jackie Edwards & Millie Small)	50
68	Island ILP 963	THE BEST OF JACKIE AND MILLIE VOLUME TWO (LP)	50
70	Trojan TTL 52	THE BEST OF JACKIE AND MILLIE VOLUME TWO (LP, reissue)	20
70	Trojan TBL 155	JACKIE & MILLIE (LP)	20

(see also Wilfred & Millicent, Jackie Edwards, Millie)

JACKIE & ROY

58	Vogue V 9101	You Smell So Good/Let's Take A Walk Around The Block	30
58	Vogue V 9101	You Smell So Good/Let's Take A Walk Around The Block (78)	10
59	Vogue VE 1-70131	JACKIE AND ROY (EP)	30
58	Vogue VA 1-60111	JACKIE AND ROY (LP)	40

DAVID JACKMAN

96	Speed Pig SP 001	TEN CUT (10" clear vinyl, serrated edge, signed, no'd 80 only)	50

JACKPOTS

69	Sonet SON 2006	Jack In The Box/Henbanes Sacrifice	25

ALEXANDER JACKSON & TURNKEYS

65	Sue WI 386	The Whip/Tell It Like It Is (actually "Flea Pot"/"Sweetie Lester" by Lala Wilson)	100

BULLMOOSE JACKSON & HIS ORCHESTRAO

53	Vogue V 2129	Nosey Joe/I Know Who Threw The Whisky In The Well (78)	20

CHRIS JACKSON

69	Soul City SC 112	I'll Never Forget You/Forever I'll Stay With You	35
70	444 Label	Since There's No Doubt/We Will Be Together (unissued, acetate only - 2 known copies)	0

CHUBBY JACKSON'S BIG BAND

60	Top Rank TR 5015	A Ballad For Jai/Hail, Hail, The Herd's All Here	5

CHUCK JACKSON

61	Top Rank JAR 564	I Don't Want To Cry/Just Once	40
62	Top Rank JAR 607	The Breaking Point/My Willow Tree	40
62	Stateside SS 102	Any Day Now/The Prophet	30
62	Stateside SS 127	I Keep Forgettin'/Who's Gonna Pick Up The Pieces	25
63	Stateside SS 171	Tell Him I'm Not Home/Getting Ready For The Heartbreak	25
64	Pye International 7N 25247	Beg Me/For All Time	25
64	Pye International 7N 25276	Any Day Now/The Prophet (reissue)	20
65	Pye International 7N 25287	Since I Don't Have You/Hand It Over	75
65	Pye International 7N 25287	Since I Don't Have You/Hand It Over (DJ Copy)	150
65	Pye International 7N 25301	I Need You/Chuck's Soul Brothers Twist	20
65	Pye International 7N 25321	If I Didn't Love You/Just A Little Bit Of Your Soul	25
66	Pye International 7N 25384	Chains Of Love/I Keep Forgettin'	100
66	Pye International 7N 25384	Chains Of Love/I Keep Forgettin' (DJ copy)	150
67	Pye International 7N 25439	Shame On Me/Candy	25
68	Tamla Motown TMG 651	Girls, Girls, Girls/(You Can't Let The Boy Overpower) The Man In You	30
70	Tamla Motown TMG 729	Honey Come Back/What Am I Gonna Do Without You	20
73	Probe PRO 595	I Only Get The Feeling/Slowly But Surely	10
74	Probe PRO 617	I Can't Break Away/Just A Little Tear	10
75	All Platinum 6146 310	I've Got The Need/Beautiful Woman	10
75	Disco Demand DDS 116	These Chains Of Love/Any Day Now	8
85	Kent TOWN 104	Hand It Over/CANDY & KISSES: Mr Creator (withdrawn)	30
86	Kent 6T2	MELBA MOORE: Magic Touch/CHUCK JACKSON: Little By Little	20
80s	Inferno SIN 1	Chains Of Love/Good Things Come To Those Who Wait/Hand It Over/ Any Day Now	20
92	Kent 8	Whats With This Loneliness	20
66	Pye Intl. NPL 28082	TRIBUTE TO RHYTHM AND BLUES (LP)	60
68	T. Motown (S)TML 11071	CHUCK JACKSON ARRIVES! (LP, mono/stereo)	45
69	T. Motown TML 11117	GOIN' BACK TO CHUCK JACKSON (LP, mono)	50
69	T. Motown STML 11117	GOIN' BACK TO CHUCK JACKSON (LP, stereo)	50
72	Probe SPB 1084	THROUGH ALL TIMES (LP)	25
74	Anchor ABCL 5040	THROUGH ALL TIMES (LP, reissue)	12

(see also Del[l]-Vikings)

CHUCK JACKSON & MAXINE BROWN

65	Pye International 7N 25308	Something You Got/Baby Take Me	20
65	Pye Intl. NPL 28091	SAYING SOMETHING (LP)	50

(see also Maxine Brown, Tammi Terrell)

DEON JACKSON

66	Atlantic AT 4070	Love Makes The World Go Round/You Said You Loved Me	45
66	Atlantic 584 012	Love Takes A Long Time Growing/Hush Little Baby	25
68	Atlantic 584 159	Ooh Baby/All On A Sunny Day	30
76	Contempo CS 9031	Love Makes The World Go Round/I Can't Go On	20

EARL JACKSON

76	ABC ABC 4110	Soul Self Satisfaction/Looking Thru' The Eyes Of Love	15

GEORGE JACKSON

69	Capitol CL 15605	Find 'Em, Fool 'Em And Forget 'Em/My Desires Are Getting The Best Of Me	25
72	London HLU 10373	Aretha, Sing One For Me/I'm Gonna Wait	12
73	London HLU 10413	Let 'Em Know You Care/Patricia	12

GORDON JACKSON

69	Marmalade 598 010	Me And My Zoo/A Day At The Cottage	20
69	Marmalade 598 021	Song For Freedom/Sing To Me Woman	25
69	Marmalade 608 012	THINKING BACK (LP)	200

(see also Hellions, Jane Relf, Traffic)

HAROLD JACKSON & TORNADOES

58	Vogue V 9105	Move It On Down The Line Parts 1 & 2	120
58	Vogue V 9105	Move It On Down The Line Parts 1 & 2 (78)	60

JACKIE JACKSON

74	T. Motown STML 11249	JACKIE JACKSON (LP)	15

(see also Jacksons, Jackson 5)

JANET JACKSON

87	Breakout USAD 601	Let's Wait A While/Nasty (Cool Summer Mix Pt. 1)/Nasty (Original Mix)/Control/Let's Wait A While (Remix)/Nasty (Cool Summer Mix Part 1 Fade) (picture disc/clear vinyl double pack in PVC foldout sleeve)	8
90	Breakout USAB 681	Come Back To Me (7" I'm Beggin' You Mix)/Alright (7" R&B mix) (box set with metal badge & foldout poster)	5
90	Breakout USAS 693	Alright (House Mix)/Vuelve A Mi (Come Back To Me) (shaped picture disc with plinth in printed PVC sleeve)	8

JANET JACKSON & CLIFF RICHARD

84	A&M AM 210	Two To The Power Of Love/JANET JACKSON: Rock'n'Roll (p/s)	12
84	A&M AMX 210	Two To The Power Of Love/JANET JACKSON: Rock'n'Roll/Don't Mess Up This Good Thing (12", p/s)	12

(see also Cliff Richard)

JERMAINE JACKSON

84	Epic JMJDJ 1	Tell Me I'm Not Dreamin' (Too Good To Be True) (with Michael Jackson)/ Come To Me/Oh Mother (promo only)	10

(see also Jacksons, Jackson 5, Michael Jackson)

JERRY JACKSON

63	London HLR 9689	Gypsy Eyes/Turn Back	40
66	Cameo Parkway P 100	It's Rough Out There/I'm Gonna Paint A Picture	175
66	Cameo Parkway P 100	It's Rough Out There/I'm Gonna Paint A Picture (DJ copy)	275

JIM JACKSON

66	RCA RCX 7182	R.C.A. VICTOR RACE SERIES VOL. 7 (EP)	10

JIMMY JACKSON('S ROCK 'N' ROLL SKIFFLE)

57	Columbia DB 3898	California Zephyr/I Shall Not Be Moved	20
57	Columbia DB 3937	Sittin' In The Balcony/Good Morning Blues	25
57	Columbia DB 3957	River Line/Lonely Road	15
57	Columbia DB 3988	White Silver Sands/Build Your Love (On A Strong Foundation) (solo)	5
58	Columbia DB 4085	Love-A Love-A Love A/Photographs (solo)	5
58	Columbia DB 4153	Swing Down, Sweet Chariot/This Little Light Of Mine (solo)	5
58	Columbia SEG 7750	ROCK 'N' SKIFFLE (EP)	75
58	Columbia SEG 7768	COUNTRY AND BLUES (EP)	75

J.J. JACKSON (& GREATEST LITTLE SOUL BAND IN THE LAND)

67	Polydor 56718	But It's Alright/Do The Boogaloo	20
67	Strike JH 329	Come See Me/Try Me	15
67	Warner Bros WB 2082	Sho Nuff (Got A Good Thing Going)/Here We Go Again	15
68	Warner Bros WB 2090	Down, But Not Out/Why Does It Take So Long?	15
68	Warner Bros WB 6029	Courage Ain't Strength/You Do It 'Cause You Wanna	15
69	Warner Bros WB 7276	Ain't Too Proud To Beg/But It's Alright	10
70	RCA RCA 1924	Bow Down To The Dollar/Indian Thing (as J.J.'s DILEMMA)	20
71	Mojo 2092 014	But It's Alright/Do The Boogaloo	10
67	Strike JLH 104	J.J. JACKSON WITH THE GREATEST LITTLE SOUL BAND (LP)	30
69	MCA SKA 100	GREATEST LITTLE SOUL BAND (LP)	25
70	RCA Victor SF 8093	J.J. JACKSON'S DILEMMA (LP)	30

(see also Greatest Little Soul Band)

J.J. JACKSON/LINDA JONES

77	Loma/Warners K 56271	THIS IS LOMA - VOL. 7 (LP, 1 side each)	15

LEVI JACKSON

71	Columbia DB 8807	This Beautiful Day/Don't You Be A Sinner	100
71	Columbia DB 8807	This Beautiful Day/Don't You Be A Sinner (DJ copy)	150

(see also Solomon King)

LLOYD JACKSON

71	Pama Supreme PS 308	Cracklin' Rosie/Little Deeds Of Kindness (B-side with Scorpions)	5

MAHALIA JACKSON

52	Vogue LDE 005	MAHALIA JACKSON (10" LP)	20
59	Philips BBL 7289	NEWPORT 1958 (LP, also stereo SBBL 547)	15
60	Top Rank 30/006	JUST AS I AM (LP)	15
60	Philips BBL 7362	GREAT GETTIN' UP MORNING (LP)	15
60	Philips BBL 7391	THE POWER AND THE GLORY (LP, also stereo SBBL 576)	15
60	Philips BBL 7435	COME ON CHILDREN LET'S SING (LP)	12
61	Philips BBL 7456	I BELIEVE (LP, also stereo SBBL 610)	12

MICHAEL JACKSON

SINGLES

72	Tamla Motown TMG 797	Got To Be There/Maria (You Were The Only One)	6
79	Epic 12EPC 7135	You Can't Win (Part 1)/You Can't Win (Part 2) (12")	10
79	Epic S EPC 7135	You Can't Win (Part 1)/You Can't Win (Part 2) (picture disc)	10
79	Epic 12EPC 7763	Don't Stop 'Til You Get Enough/I Can't Help It (12")	8
79	Epic 12EPC 8206	Rock With You/Get On The Floor/You Can't Win (Extended) (12")	8
81	Motown TMG 977	We're Almost There/We've Got A Good Thing Going (p/s)	8
81	Motown TMGT 977	We're Almost There (Album Version)/We've Got A Good Thing Going (12")	8
82	Epic EPCA 11-2729	The Girl Is Mine (with Paul McCartney)/ Can't Get Outta The Rain (picture disc)	15
83	Epic EPC 2906	GREATEST ORIGINAL HITS: Don't Stop 'Til You Get Enough/ She's Out Of My Life/Off The Wall/Rock With You (EP)	10
83	Epic EPCA 40-2906	GREATEST ORIGINAL HITS: Don't Stop 'Til You Get Enough/ She's Out Of My Life/Off The Wall/Rock With You (EP,)	8
83	Motown TMG 986	Happy (Love Theme From 'Lady Sings The Blues')/We're Almost There (poster p/s)	8
83	Motown EPCA 112729	Happy (Love Theme From 'Lady Sings The Blues')/We're Almost There (picture disc)	10
83	Epic EPCA 3643	Thriller/JACKSONS: Things I Do For You (live) (poster p/s)	8
83	Epic TA 3643	Thriller (Album Version)/Thriller (Remix Short Version)/JACKSONS: Things I Do For You (live) (12", 'calendar' p/s)	50
83	Epic MJ 1 (1-9)	MICHAEL JACKSON'S 9 SINGLES PACK (9 x 7", p/s, each on red vinyl, in PVC foldout wallet)	35
87	Epic 650 202-0	I Just Can't Stop Loving You (with Siedah Garratt)/Baby Be Mine (poster p/s)	10
87	Epic 650 202-6	I Just Can't Stop Loving You (with Siedah Garratt)/Baby Be Mine (12", p/s with poster)	15
87	Epic 651 155-6	Bad (Dance Extended Mix With False Fade)/Bad (7" Single Mix)/Bad (Dance Radio Edit)/Bad (Dub)/Bad (A Cappella) (12", p/s, red vinyl)	8

MINT VALUE £

87	Epic 651 275-7	The Way You Make Me Feel/The Way You Make Me Feel (Instrumental) (p/s, with competition leaflet, stickered sleeve)	5
87	Epic 651 275-3	The Way You Make Me Feel (7" Mix)/(A Cappella)/(Dance Radio Edit)/ (Dub)/(Get Into The Groove -Put Either Side On The Turntable, Lower The Arm And See Which Your Needle Pix) (12", p/s double-groove)	12
87	Epic 651 275-9	The Way You Make Me Feel (Dance Extended Mix)/The Way You Make Me Feel (Dub Version)/The Way You Make Me Feel (A Cappella) (CD, card p/s)	12
88	Epic 651 388-9	Man In The Mirror (Single Mix)/Man In The Mirror (Instrumental) (square-shaped picture disc)	15
88	Epic 651 388-2	Man In The Mirror (4.55)/Man In The Mirror (Album Mix)/ Man In The Mirror (Instrumental) (CD, card sleeve)	10
88	Epic 651 388-2	Man In The Mirror/Man In The Mirror (Album Mix)/ Man In The Mirror (Instrumental) (3" CD with adaptor, card sleeve)	12
88	Epic 651 546-7	Dirty Diana/Dirty Diana (p/s, with 13" cardboard figure)	12
88	Epic 652 864-6	Dirty Diana/Dirty Diana (Instrumental)/Bad (Extended Dance Mix With False Fade) (12", with tour poster p/s)	15
88	Epic 651 546-9	Dirty Diana (4.42)/Dirty Diana (Instrumental)/Bad (Dance Extended Mix Includes "False Fade") (CD, card p/s)	10
88	Epic 651 546-2	Dirty Diana (4.42)/Dirty Diana (Instrumental)/Dirty Diana (Album Version) (3" CD with adaptor, card p/s)	12
88	Epic MJ 5	THE MICHAEL JACKSON BAD SOUVENIR SINGLES PACK (5 x 7" square picture discs in foldout PVC wallet, with lyric book)	40
88	Epic 652 844-9	Another Part Of Me/(Instrumental) (p/s, with Bad tour backstage pass)	12
88	Epic 652 844-0	Another Part Of Me/Another Part Of Me (Instrumental) (poster p/s)	8
88	Epic 652 844-2	Another Part Of Me (Extended Dance Mix)/(Radio Edit)/(Drum Mix)/ (A Capella) (CD, card p/s)	10
88	Epic 652 844-3	Another Part Of Me (Extended Dance Mix)/(Radio Edit)/(Dub Mix)/ (Instrumental) (3" CD with adaptor, card p/s)	12
88	Epic 653 004-2	Another Part Of Me (Extended Dance Mix)/Another Part Of Me (Radio Edit) Another Part Of Me (Drum Mix)/Another Part Of Me (A Capella) (CD, pic disc)	12
88	Epic 653 026-0	Smooth Criminal/Smooth Criminal (Instrumental) (pack with 4 postcards)	15
88	Epic 653 170-6	Smooth Criminal (Extended Dance Mix)/ Smooth Criminal Extended (Dance Mix Dub Mix)/Smooth Criminal (A Cappella) (12" with "Moonwalker" advert calendar)	20
88	Epic 653 026-2	Smooth Criminal (Extended Dance Mix)/Smooth Criminal ("Annie" Mix)/ Smooth Criminal (A Cappella) (CD, card p/s)	10
89	Epic 654 672-0	Leave Me Alone/Human Nature (pop-up pic/s)	15
89	Epic 654 672-2	Leave Me Alone (4.40)/Don't Stop 'Til You Get Enough (3.55)/Human Nature (4.05)/Wanna Be Startin' Something (Extended 6.30) (CD, card sleeve)	10
89	Epic 654 672-3	Leave Me Alone (4.40)/Don't Stop 'Til You Get Enough (6.04)/ Human Nature (4.05) (3" CD, gatefold card sleeve)	18
89	Epic 654 947-9	Liberian Girl (Edit)/Girlfriend (star mobile foldout card pack)	15
89	Epic 654 947-2	Liberian Girl (Edit 3.39)/Girlfriend/The Lady In My Life/Get On The Floor (CD, card p/s)	10
89	Epic 654 947-3	Liberian Girl (Edit 3.39)/Get On The Floor/Girlfriend (3" CD, g/fold card p/s)	10
92	Epic 658 360-7	Jam (7" Edit)/Beat It (Moby's Sub Mix) ('picture frame' pack with 2 prints)	5
92	Epic MJ 4 (658 281-1/4)	TOUR SOUVENIR PACK (CD, 4-picture disc, box set with booklet)	40
95	Epic 662 127	Scream (Def Radio Mix)/Scream (Single Edit) (limited edition poster sleeve)	5
95	Epic 662 022	Scream (Single Edit)/Childhood (p/s, with 2 page lyric insert)	5
97	Epic 665 130 6	Smile/It It Scary (Deep Dish Dark And Scary Remix)/Is It Scary (Eddie's Rub-a-Dub Mix)/Is It Scary (Eddie's Love Mix)/Off The Wall (Junior Vasquez Remix) (12" p/s withdrawn. Beware of counterfeits with poor print quality on label, sleeve and especially the barcode)	200
03	Epic XPR 3744	TWELVES (7 x 12" p/s in box with insert)	60

ALBUMS

79	Epic EPC 83458/83468	OFF THE WALL (LP, gatefold sleeve, with 7" picture disc "You Can't Win (Parts 1)/(Part 2)" [S EPC 7135], some with information sheet)	25
79	Epic SXPR 1207	EPIC HITS FROM THE JACKSONS & MICHAEL JACKSON (LP, promo only, stickered sleeve)	12
82	Epic EPC 11-85930	THRILLER (LP, picture disc in PVC sleeve)	25
83	MCA MCA 70000	E.T. - THE EXTRA TERRESTRIAL (LP, box set with booklet & poster, narration & "Someone In The Dark", with music by John Williams)	30
87	Epic 450 290-8	BAD GIFT PACK (pack, with note pad, highlighter pen & calendar)	15
87	Epic 450 290-0	BAD (LP, picture disc)	25
87	Epic 450 290-9	BAD (CD, picture disc, sealed in long PVC blister pack)	45
87	Epic 450 290-9	BAD (CD, picture disc, unsealed in long PVC blister pack)	25
92	Epic 465 802-9	DANGEROUS (CD, gold disc, 10"x10" pop-up 'Collectors Edition First Printing')	15
08	Sony 88697233441	THRILLER (2-LP 25th Anniversary special edition)	20
09	Sony 88697616541	THIS IT IT (4-LP box set with 36 page book, numbered)	45

PROMOS

92	Epic XPR 1733	Remember The Time: (12" Main Mix)/(New Jack Mix)/(New Jack Main Mix)/ (Silky Soul 12" Mix)/(Silky Soul Dub)/(E-Smoov's Late Nite Mix) (12" company sleeve)	8
92	Epic XPR 1814	Jam: (More Than Enuff Mix)/(Roger's Club Mix)/(E-Smoov Jazzy Jam)/ (Atlanta Techno Mix)/(Roger's Underground Mix)/(Silky 12")/(More Than Enuff Dub)/(Maurice's Jammin' Dub Mix)/(Roger's Club Dub)/(Atlanta Techno Dub)/(Roger's Slam Jam Mix)/(Silky Dub)/(A Capella Mix) (12", double pack, black & orange stickered white sleeve)	15
92	Epic XPR 1797	Who Is It (Patience Mix)/(Patience Beats)/(Most Patient Mix)/(HIS Mix)/(The P-Man Mix) (12", company sleeve)	10
95	Epic XPR 2184	Scream: (Classic Club Mix)/(DM R&B Extended Mix)/(Def Radio Mix)/ (Naughty Main Mix)/(Naughty Main Mix No Rap)/(Dave 'Jam' Hall's Extended Urban Remix)/(Pressurised Dub Part 1)/(Pressurised Dub Part 2)/(Album Version)/(Single Edit No. 2)/(Naughty Pretty-Pella)/(Naughty A Capella) (12" double pack, red title sleeve)	20
95	Epic XPR 2266	DMC Megamix (15.40)/(11.18) (12", custom sleeve)	12
95	Epic XPR 2265	The Classic Remix Series: Wanna Be Startin' Something (Brothers In Rhythm Mix)/(Tommy D's Main Mix) (12", plain sleeve, sealed with title sticker)	10
95	Epic XPR 2229	The Classic Remix Series: Rock With You (Frankie's Favorite Club Mix)/ (The Masters At Work Remix) (12", plain sleeve, sealed with title sticker)	12
95	Epic XPCD 7222	The Classic Remix Series: Rock With You (Frankie's Favorite Club Mix Radio Edit)/(Frankie's Favorite Club Mix) (CD)	20
96	Epic XPR 3033	The Classic Remix Series: Don't Stop Til You Get Enough (Roger's Underground Solution Mix)/Beat It (Moby's Sub Mix) (12", plain sleeve sealed with title sticker)	8
96	Epic XPR 2207	Mj Club Megamix (MJ Mega Remix)/(MJ Urban Megamix) (12", blue & purple title sleeve)	15
96	Epic XPR 3020	They Don't Care About Us (The Love To Infinity Mixes): Classic Paradise Mix/ Anthem Of Love/Classic Dub/Anthem Of love Dub/Hacienda Mix (12", p/s)	8
96	Epic XPR 3030	They Don't Care About Us (The R&B Mixes): Track Masters Remix/ Dallas Austin Main Mix/Charles' Full Dirty Mix/LP Edit/Love To Infinity's Walk In The Park/Track Master's Instrumental (12" p/s)	10

97	Epic XPR 3159	HIStory (Tony Moran's HIStory Lesson)/(Tony Moran's HIStorical Dub) Is It Scary (Eddie's Love Mix)/(Eddie's Rub-A-Dub Mix)/(Eddie's Love Mix)/ (Radio Edit) (12", white embossed title p/s)	20
97	Epic XPR 3149	HIStory (Marks! Philly Vocal)/(Marks! Future Dub) (12", yellow title sleeve)	8
97	Epic XPR 3169	HIStory (Ummah Urban Mix)/(Ummah Radio Mix)/(Tony Moran's 7" HIStory Lesson Edit)/(Ummah DJ Mix) (12", green title sleeve)	8
97	Epic XPR 3125	Blood On The Dancefloor (TM's Switchblade Mix)/(TM's O-Postive Dub) (12", blue title p/s)	8
97	Epic XPR 3136	Blood On The Dancefloor (Refugee Camp Mix)/(7" Version) (12", green title p/s)	8
97	Epic XPR 3196	Is It Scary (Deep Dish Dark & Scary Remix)/(Deep Dish Double-Dry Dub)/ (Deep Dish Dark & Scary Remix)/(Radio Edit) (12", black embossed title p/s)	35
97	Epic XPCD 2989	Cheater (1-track promo CD)	15

(see also Jackson 5, Diana Ross & Michael Jackson, Paul McCartney, Jacksons, Jermaine Jackson)

MILLIE JACKSON

72	Mojo 2093 011	A Child Of God/You're The Joy Of My Life	15
72	Mojo 2093 015	Ask Me What You Want/I Just Can't Stand It	8
72	Mojo 2093 022	My Man, A Sweet Man/I Gotta Get Away (From My Own Self) (paper label)	10
73	Polydor 2066 317	Breakaway/Strange Things	5
75	Polydor 2066 536	If Loving You Is Wrong/The Rap	5
75	Polydor 2006 612	Loving Arms/Left Over	5
76	Spring 2066 713	A House For Sale/There You Are	20
72	Mojo 2918 005	MILLIE JACKSON (LP)	20

(see also Elton John)

MILT JACKSON

53	Vogue LDE 044	MILT JACKSON AND HIS NEW GROUP (10" LP)	20
55	Esquire 20-042	MILT JACKSON QUINTET (10" LP)	20
55	London Jazz LZ-C 14006	MILT JACKSON QUARTET (10" LP)	20
57	London Jazz LTZ-K 15064	BALLADS AND BLUES (LP)	12
57	London Jazz LTZ-K 15074	THE JAZZ SKYLINE (LP)	12
57	London Jazz LTZ-K 15091	JACKSONSVILLE (LP)	12
57	Vogue LAE 12046	WIZARD OF THE VIBES (LP)	12
59	London Jazz LTZ-K 15141	PLENTY, PLENTY SOUL (LP)	12
59	London Jazz LTZ-T 15172	BAGS' OPUS (LP, also stereo SAH-T 6049)	12
60	London Jazz LTZ-T 15177	BAGS AND FLUTES (LP)	12
60	London Jazz LTZ-K 15196	BEAN BAGS (LP, also stereo SAH-K 6095; with Coleman Hawkins)	12
61	London Jazz LTZ-K 15220	THE ARTISTRY OF MILT JACKSON (LP, also stereo SAH-K 6163)	12
61	London Jazz LTZ-K 15232	BAGS AND TRANE (LP, with John Coltrane; also stereo SAH-K 6192)	12
61	Philips BBL 7459	MILT JACKSON (LP)	12
62	Esquire 32-134	MILT JACKSON MODERN JAZZ QUARTET/QUINTET (LP)	12
62	Riverside RLP (9)407	BAGS MEETS WES (LP, with Wes Montgomery)	12
63	Realm RM 119	THE MILT JACKSON QUARTET (LP)	12
63	HMV CLP 1589	STATEMENTS (LP, also stereo CSD 1455)	12
63	Realm RM 156	ROLL 'EM BAGS (LP)	12
64	HMV CLP 1888	JAZZ 'N' SAMBA (LP, featuring Joe E. Ross)	15
64	Atlantic ATL/SAL 5012	VIBRATIONS (LP)	12
65	Mercury LML/SML 4008	IN A NEW SETTING (LP)	12
65	Mercury LML/SML 4016	AT THE MUSEUM OF MODERN ART (LP)	12
66	Mercury LML/SML 4028	BORN FREE (LP)	12
73	CTI CTL 8	CHERRY (LP, with Stanley Turrentine)	12

(see also Ray Charles, Modern Jazz Quartet, Stanley Turrentine, Miles Davis/Art Blakey, Coleman Hawkins)

PAPA CHARLIE JACKSON

50	Tempo R 30	Long Gone Lost John/I'm Looking For A Woman Who Knows How To Treat Me Right (78)	15
60	Heritage R 100	PAPA CHARLIE JACKSON (EP) 99 only	80
60	Heritage HLP 1011	PAPA CHARLIE JACKSON (LP) 99 only	100

(see also Paramount Allstars, Blind Blake)

POOCH JACKSON

72	Sioux SI 013	You Just Gotta Get Ready/BROTHER DAN: Django's Valley	5
72	Sioux SI 017	King Of The Road/Circles/Mammy Blue	12
72	Sioux SI 016	Once Bitten (with Harry J. Allstars)/KING REGGAE: Slave Driver	5

(see also Circles)

PYTHON LEE JACKSON

70	Young Blood YB 1002	In A Broken Dream/Doing Fine (p/s)	6
72	Young Blood YB 3001	IN A BROKEN DREAM (LP, featuring Rod Stewart who is not credited on front or rear sleeve)	20

(see under 'P')

RALPH 'SOUL' JACKSON

69	Atlantic 584258	'Cause I Love You/Sunshine Of Your Love	25

RAY JACKSON

76	EMI EMI 2514	Take Some Time/Working On	5
80	Mercury MER 3	In The Night/Waiting For The Time (p/s)	5
80	Mercury MER 8	Little Town Flirt/Make It Last (p/s)	5
80	Mercury 9109 831	IN THE NIGHT (LP, with inner sleeve)	12

(see also Lindisfarne)

ROOT & JENNY JACKSON

69	Beacon BEA 110	Lean On Me/Please Come Home	10
69	Beacon BEA 136	Let's Go Somewhere/If I Didn't Love You	8

(see also Roots and Jenny Jackson)

SHIRLEY JACKSON

63	Decca F 11612	Don't Play Me A Love Song/You Gotta Love And Be Loved	7
63	Decca F 11661	The Boy Of The Year/I Miss You Most Of All	10
63	Decca F 11788	Broken Home/No Greater Love Than Mine	7

SHOVELVILLE K. JACKSON

60s	Melodisc MEL 1683	Be Careful Of Stones That You Throw/Kentucky Blues	12

SIMONE JACKSON

62	Piccadilly 7N 35087	Pop Pop Pop Pie/He Ain't Got No Time For Love	12
63	Piccadilly 7N 35124	Ain't Gonna Kiss Ya/Slow Motion	12

63	Piccadilly 7N 35149	Tell Me What To Do/Doing What You Know Is Wrong	12

JACKSON & SMITH

65	Polydor 56051	Ain't That Loving You Baby/Every Day I Have The Blues	10
66	Polydor 56086	Party '66/And That's It	10

STONEWALL JACKSON

59	Philips PB 941	Waterloo/Smoke Along The Track (78)	15

TONY JACKSON (& VIBRATIONS)

64	Pye 7N 15685	Bye Bye Baby/Watch Your Step	25
64	Pye 7N 15745	This Little Girl Of Mine/You Beat Me To The Punch	40
65	Pye 7N 15766	Love Potion No. 9/Fortune Teller	55
65	Pye 7N 15876	Stage Door/That's What I Want (as Tony Jackson Group)	35
66	CBS 202039	You're My Number One/Let Me Know (as Tony Jackson Group)	40
66	CBS 202069	Never Leave Your Baby's Side/The One She Really Thinks A Lot Of (solo)	40
66	CBS 202297	Follow Me/Walk Walk Walk Walk (solo)	65
66	CBS 202408	Anything Else You Want/Come On And Stop (solo)	40
91	Strange Things STZ 5005	JUST LIKE ME (LP)	15

(see also Searchers)

VIVIAN JACKSON & THE PROPHETS

78	Nationwide PRO 001	CHANT DOWN BABYLON KINGDOM (LP)	50

(See also Yabby U.)

WALTER JACKSON

65	Columbia DB 7620	Welcome Home/Blowin' In The Wind	40
66	Columbia DB 7949	Tear For Tear/It's An Uphill Climb To The Bottom	75
66	Columbia DB 7949	Tear For Tear/It's An Uphill Climb To The Bottom (DJ copy)	125
66	Columbia DB 8054	A Corner In The Sun/Not You	30
67	Columbia DB 8154	Speak Her Name/They Don't Give Medals (To Yesterday's Heroes)	30
70	Atlantic 584 311	Any Way That You Want Me/Life Has Its Ups And Downs	10
73	Brunswick BR 5	Easy Evil/I Never Had It So Good	8

WANDA JACKSON

59	Capitol CL 15033	You're The One For Me/A Date With Jerry	20
59	Capitol CL 15090	Reaching/I'd Rather Have You	20
60	Capitol CL 15147	Let's Have A Party/Cool Love	25
61	Capitol CL 15176	Mean Mean Man/Honey Bop	30
61	Capitol CL 15223	Right Or Wrong/Funnel Of Love	15
62	Capitol CL 15234	In The Middle Of A Heartache/I'd Be Ashamed	10
62	Capitol CL 15249	If I Cried Every Time You Hurt Me/Let My Love Walk In	10
58	Capitol EAP1 1041	WANDA JACKSON (EP)	75
62	Capitol EAP1 20353	A LITTLE BITTY TEAR (EP)	60
58	Capitol T 1041	WANDA JACKSON (LP)	150
60	Capitol T 1384	ROCKIN' WITH WANDA (LP)	120
61	Capitol T 1511	THERE'S A PARTY GOIN' ON (LP, mono)	80
61	Capitol (S)T 1511	THERE'S A PARTY GOIN' ON (LP, stereo)	90
61	Capitol T 1596	RIGHT OR WRONG (LP, mono)	50
61	Capitol (S)T 1596	RIGHT OR WRONG (LP, stereo)	60
62	Capitol T 1776	WONDERFUL WANDA (LP)	30
64	Capitol T 2030	TWO SIDES OF WANDA (LP, mono)	50
64	Capitol (S)T 2030	TWO SIDES OF WANDA (LP, stereo)	55
64	Capitol (S)T 2306	BLUES IN MY HEART (LP)	15
66	Capitol (S)T 2438	SINGS COUNTRY SONGS (LP, black label)	15
67	Capitol (S)T 2606	SALUTES THE COUNTRY MUSIC HALL OF FAME (LP, black label)	15
67	Capitol (S)T 2812	YOU'LL ALWAYS HAVE MY LOVE (LP)	15
69	Capitol (S)T 2976	CREAM OF THE CROP (LP, with Party Timers)	15
73	Word WST 9514	COUNTRY GOSPEL (LP)	15

JACKSON BROTHERS

59	London HLX 8845	Tell Him No/Love Me	25
59	London HLX 8845	Tell Him No/Love Me (78)	20

JACKSON 5

SINGLES

70	Tamla Motown TMG 724	I Want You Back/Who's Loving You	6
70	Tamla Motown TMG 738	ABC/The Young Folks (promo only p/s)	60
70	Tamla Motown TMG 738	ABC/The Young Folks	6
70	Tamla Motown TMG 746	The Love You Save/I Found That Girl	6
70	Tamla Motown TMG 758	I'll Be There/One More Chance	5
71	Tamla Motown TMG 769	Mama's Pearl/Darling Dear (promo only p/s)	60
71	Tamla Motown TMG 769	Mama's Pearl/Darling Dear	6
71	Tamla Motown TMG 778	Never Can Say Goodbye/She's Good	5
72	Tamla Motown TMG 809	Sugar Daddy/I'm So Happy	5
72	Tamla Motown TMG 825	Little Bitty Pretty One/Maybe Tomorrow	5
72	Tamla Motown TMG 833	Lookin' Through The Windows/Love Song (promo only p/s)	15
72	Tamla Motown TMG 833	Lookin' Through The Windows/Love Song	5
72	Tamla Motown TMG 837	THE CHRISTMAS EP: Santa Claus Is Coming To Town/ Someday At Christmas/Christmas Won't Be The Same This Year	12
73	Tamla Motown TMG 842	Doctor My Eyes/My Little Baby	5
73	Tamla Motown TMG 856	Hallelujah Day/To Know	5
73	Tamla Motown TMG 865	Skywriter/Ain't Nothin' Like The Real Thing (promo only p/s)	20
73	Tamla Motown TMG 865	Skywriter/Ain't Nothin' Like The Real Thing	5
73	Tamla Motown TMG 878	Get It Together/Touch	5
74	Tamla Motown TMG 895	The Boogie Man/Don't Let Your Baby Catch You	5
74	Tamla Motown TMG 904	Dancing Machine/It's Too Late To Change The Time	5
74	Tamla Motown TMG 927	The Life Of The Party/Whatever You Got I Want	5
74	Lyntone LYN 2639	Talk And Sing Personally To Valentine Readers (33rpm flexidisc free with 'Valentine' magazine)	15
75	Rice Krispies (no cat. Nos.)	Sugar Daddy/Goin' Back To Indiana/Who's Loving You/Mama's Pearl/ ABC/The Love You Save (6 different Rice Krispies cut-out card discs, price is for each)	30
75	Tamla Motown TMG 942	I Am Love (Part 1)/I Am Love (Part 2)	5
75	Tamla Motown TMG 1001	Forever Came Today/I Can't Quit Your Love	5
77	Motown TMG 1081	JUKEBOX GEMS: Skywriter/I Want You Back/The Love You Save (EP)	8

| 80 | Motown SPTMG 2 | THE MOTOWN 20TH ANNIVERSARY SINGLES BOX (15 x 7") | 30 |

ALBUMS

70	Tamla Motown TML 11142	DIANA ROSS PRESENTS THE JACKSON 5 (flipback sleeve, mono)	30
70	Tamla Motown (S)TML 11142	DIANA ROSS PRESENTS THE JACKSON 5 (flipback sleeve, /stereo)	20
70	Tamla Motown TML 11156	ABC (flipback sleeve, mono, existence unconfirmed)	40
70	Tamla Motown STML 11156	ABC (flipback sleeve, stereo)	20
70	Tamla Motown STML 11168	THE JACKSON 5 CHRISTMAS ALBUM (flipback sleeve)	25
71	Tamla Motown STML 11174	THIRD ALBUM (original with flipback sleeve)	20
71	Tamla Motown STML 11188	MAYBE TOMORROW	20
72	Tamla Motown STML 11214	LOOKIN' THROUGH THE WINDOWS	20
73	Tamla Motown STML 11231	SKYWRITER	12
73	Tamla Motown STML 11243	GET IT TOGETHER (with photo insert)	20
74	Tamla Motown STML 11275	DANCING MACHINE	18
75	Tamla Motown STML 11290	MOVING VIOLATIONS	18
76	Motown STML 12046	JOYFUL JUKEBOX MUSIC	12
77	Tamla Motown TMSP 6004	THE JACKSON 5 ANTHOLOGY (2-LP, original issue)	15
77	Motown STMX 6006	MOTOWN SPECIAL - THE JACKSON 5	15
79	MFP MFP 50418	ZIP-A-DEE-DOO-DAH	15
81	Motown PR 84	JACKSON 5: HISTORY OF MOTOWN (4-LP box set, with 1 Michael Jackson LP)	30
82	Motown/Pickwick TMS 3505	THE JACKSON 5	12

(see also Michael Jackson, Jermaine Jackson, Jacksons)

JACKSON HEIGHTS

70	Charisma JH 1	Doubting Thomas/Insomnia	6
72	Vertigo 6059 068	Maureen/Long Time Dying	25
70	Charisma CAS 1018	KINGS PROGRESS (LP, pink 'scroll' label)	40
72	Vertigo 6360 067	5TH AVENUE BUS (LP, gatefold sleeve, swirl label)	150
72	Vertigo 6360 077	RAGAMUFFIN'S FOOL (LP, swirl label, with poster)	150
72	Vertigo 6360 077	RAGAMUFFIN'S FOOL (LP, swirl label, without poster)	50
73	Vertigo 6360 092	BUMP AND GRIND (LP, 'spaceship label')	30

(see also Nice)

JACKSONS

77	Epic S EPC 5063	Enjoy Yourself (Extended Version 5.48)/Style Of Life (12", p/s)	12
80	Epic EPC 12-9391	Heartbreak Hotel (Album Version)/Different Kind Of Lady (12")	12
81	Epic EPC A 1294	Walk Right Now/Your Ways (picture disc)	10
79	Epic S XPR 1207	EPIC HITS FROM THE JACKSONS & MICHAEL JACKSON (LP, promo only)	20
84	Epic EPC 86303	VICTORY (LP, picture disc)	30
85	Epic SAI 7561	A TASTE OF VICTORY (LP, picture disc, promo only via Kelloggs offer)	50

(see also Jackson 5, Michael Jackson, Jermaine Jackson)

JACKSON SISTERS

73	Mums SMUM 1591	(Why Can't We Be) More than Just Friends/Rockin' On My Porch	10
73	Mums SMUM 1829	I Believe In Miracles/Day In The Blue	50
87	Urban URB 4	I Believe In Miracles/Boy You're Dynamite	8
87	Urban URBX 4	I Believe In Miracles/Boy You're Dynamite (12", p/s)	20
87	Urban URBX 4	I Believe in Miracles/MACEO & THE MACS: Across The tracks/URBAN ALL STARS: It All Began In Africa (12" promo)	25

JACKSON SISTERS

| 00 | Fab FAB 004 | Rocksteady/STOVELLS: Hang On In There | 5 |

JACK THE LAD

73	Charisma CB 206	One More Dance/Draught Genius (Polka) (p/s)	6
73	Charisma CB 218	Why Can't I Be Satisfied/Make Me Happy	5
75	Charisma CB 242	Home Sweet Home/Big Ocean Liner	5
75	Charisma CB 253	Gentleman Soldier/Oakey Strike Evictions	5
75	Charisma CB 264	My Friend The Drink/Rocking Chair	5
74	Charisma CAS 1085	IT'S JACK THE LAD (LP, small 'Mad Hatter' label)	15
74	Charisma CAS 1094	OLD STRAIGHT TRACK (LP, with lyric sheet, Charsima inner)	15
75	Charisma CAS 1110	ROUGH DIAMONDS (LP)	12

(see also Lindisfarne)

JACKY

68	Philips BF 1647	White Horses/Too Many Chiefs (Not Enough Indians)	10
68	Philips BF 1689	We're Off And Running/Well That's Loving You	6
69	Page One POF 122	Love Is Now/Never Will I Be	7
68	Philips SBL 7851	WHITE HORSES (LP)	35

(see also Jackie & Raindrops, Raindrops, Jackie Lee, Emma Rede, Vince Hill)

DICK JACOBS (& HIS ORCHESTRA)

56	Vogue Coral Q 72147	Saxophone/Never Come Sunday	5
56	Vogue Coral Q 72154	The Man With The Golden Arm Theme/Butternut	5
56	Vogue Coral Q 72204	Petticoats Of Portugal/East Of Eden	5
57	Vogue Coral Q 72245	The Big Beat/The Tower Trot	15
57	Vogue Coral Q 72260	Rock-a-billy Gal/The Golden Strings	15
57	Vogue Coral Q 72260	Rock-a-billy Gal/The Golden Strings (78)	10
57	Vogue Coral LVA 9076	THE SKIFFLE SOUND (LP, as Dick Jacobs & His Skiffle Group)	30
59	Coral LVA 9102	THEMES FROM HORROR MOVIES (LP)	25

HANK JACOBS

| 64 | Sue WI 313 | So Far Away/Monkey, Hips And Rice | 40 |
| 83 | Sue ENS 5 | SO FAR AWAY EP: So Far Away/Out Of Sight/Hank's Groove/Summertime | 10 |

JIMMY JACOBS & NITESPOTS

| 60s | Gargoyle ADV 305011 | SWINGIN' SOHO - JIMMY SINGS, THE NITESPOTS SWING (LP) | 15 |

JACQUELINE & BRIDIE

| 64 | Fontana TF 473 | Roses/Roving Jack | 6 |
| 64 | Fontana TL 5212 | HOLD BACK THE DAWN (LP) | 20 |

(see also Jackie & Bridie)

CHUCK JACQUES & LYNN TAITT & COMETS

| 67 | Ska Beat JB 264 | Dial 609/VIBRATORS & TOMMY McCOOK & COMETS: Wait For Me | 20 |

(see also Wilbert Francis & Vibrators)

ILLINOIS JACQUET & HIS ORCHESTRA

56	Vogue V 2387	Blow Illinois Blow/Destination Moon	6
53	Vogue LDE 026	ILLINOIS JACQUET (10" LP)	15
56	Columbia Clef 33C 9018	ILLINOIS JACQUET (10" LP)	15
57	Columbia Clef 33CX 10085	GROOVIN' WITH JACQUET (LP)	12
50s	Melodisc MLP 12-301	JAZZ AT THE PHILHARMONIC (LP)	12

JADE

70	DJM DJS 227	Alan's Song/Amongst Anemones	15
70	DJM DJLPS 407	FLY ON STRANGE WINGS (LP, gatefold sleeve)	130

JADE WARRIOR

72	Vertigo 6059 069	The Demon Trucker/Snake	15
78	Island JAD 1	Way Of The Sun/Sun Ra	5
71	Vertigo 6360 033	JADE WARRIOR (LP, gatefold sleeve, swirl label)	100
71	Vertigo 6360 062	RELEASED (LP, multi-poster sleeve, small swirl label)	400
72	Vertigo 6360 079	LAST AUTUMN'S DREAM (LP, gatefold sleeve, swirl label)	110
74	Island ILPS 9290	FLOATING WORLD (LP, pink rim palm tree label)	20
75	Island ILPS 9318	WAVES (LP, pink rim palm tree label)	20
76	Island ILPS 9393	KITES (LP)	18
78	Island ILPS 9552	WAY OF THE SUN (LP)	12
79	Butt BUTT 001	REFLECTIONS (LP)	18

(see also July, Joe O'Donnell)

JADIS

84	Private pressing	BABOON ENQUIRIES EP	12
87	Private pressing DEM 1	G13/Out Of Reach	8
88	Private pressing DEM 2	Don't Keep Me Waiting/In The Dark	8
89	Private pressing	Lost For Words/This Changing Face	8
90	Back Beat 004-12	THE JADIS ALBUM (LP, numbered)	15

MAX JAFFA (& HIS ORCHESTRA)

56	Columbia SCM 5226	China Boogie/Slap Happy	5

JAFFREY

76	Tank	ALICE AT JAFFREY (LP)	100

CHRIS JAGGER

73	GM GMS 3	Something New/Joy Of The Ride	6
73	GM GML 1003	CHRIS JAGGER (LP)	15

MICK JAGGER

70	Decca F 13067	Memo From Turner/Natural Magic (in export p/s)	40
70	Decca F 13067	Memo From Turner/Natural Magic	12
84	CBS TA 4431	State Of Shock/Your Ways (picture disc)	6
87	CBS 651028-0	Let's Work/Catch As Catch Can (poster p/s)	6
87	CBS THROW P1	Throwaway/Peace For The Wicked (picture disc)	10
70	United Artists UAS 29108	NED KELLY (LP, soundtrack)	35
70	Warner Bros WS 2554	PERFORMANCE (LP, first pressing, orange label, soundtrack)	45
70	Warner Bros WS 2554	PERFORMANCE (LP, second pressing, green label, soundtrack)	30

(see also Rolling Stones, Jacksons, Jack Nitzsche)

JAGO

72	Duke DU 134	Rebel Train/Babylon Version	10

JAGS

61	Decca F 11397	The Hunch/Cry Wolf	8
80	Island WIP 6683	The Sound Of G-O-O-D-B-Y-E/The Hurt (no p/s)	10

JAGS

79	Island WIP 6501	Back Of My Hand/Double Vision (p/s)	6
79	Island 12SWIP 6501	Back Of My Hand/Double Vision/Single Vision/What Can I Do? (12", p/s)	8
80	Island WIP 6531	Woman's World/Dumb Blonde (p/s)	8
80	Island WIP 6587	Party Games/She's So Considerate (p/s)	10
80	Island WIP 6666	I Never Was A Beach Boy/Tune Into Heaven (p/s)	18
79	Island ILPS 9603	EVENING STANDARDS (LP)	12
81	Island ILPS 9655	NO TIE LIKE A PRESENT (LP)	12

JAGUAR

81	Heavy Metal HEAVY 10	Back Street Woman/Chasing The Dragon (p/s)	40
82	Neat NEAT 16	Axe Crazy/War Machine (p/s)	20
83	Neat NEAT 1007	POWER GAMES (LP, some on purple vinyl)	30
83	Neat NEAT 1007	POWER GAMES (LP, black vinyl)	18
84	Roadrunner RR 9851	THIS TIME (LP)	15

JAGUARS

63	Impression IMP 101	Opus To Spring/The Beat (1,000 only)	35
65	Contest RGJ 152	We'll Live On Happily/Now You Wonder Why	300

(see also Dave Mason)

JAH BUNNY

77	Mainline ML2	Six And Seven Books/Version (actually by Reggae Scientist)	12
80	White Label	DUBBS INTERNATIONAL (LP)	40

JAH FATTA & THE BLACK BROTHERS

79	Rite Sound RS DD 002	Free Rasta Free/BLACK BROTHER ALL STARS: Free Dub (12")	60

JAH FISH

72	Grape GR 3034	Vampire Rock/MOD STARS: El-Sisco Rock	8

JAH FRANKIE JONES

77	Third World TWS 916	SATTA & PRAISE JAH (LP)	35

JAH FREE

93	Jah Free	Lightning Clap/Lightning Dub/Jubilation/Jubilation Dub (12")	20

JAH LION

83	Congo COS 2	Melody For Negus/Negus Dub	30
76	Island ILPS 9386	COLUMBIA COLLY (LP)	30

83	Kongo KLP 001	PRAISE JAH (LP)	100

(see also Jah Lloyd)

JAH LLOYD

73	Jaguar JAG 102	Channel One (with Douglas Boothe)/SOUL SYNDICATES:Channel Two	6
73	Jaguar JAG 104	Psalm Two/SOUL SYNDICATES: Channel Two	6
75	Treble C CCC 02	Once Bitten/CHARLEY ACE & INSWINGS: Real Red	6
76	Attack ATT 8121	World Class/World Class (Version)	6
74	DIP PL DL 1001	HERBS OF DUB...MORE HERBS (LP)	60
79	Virgin Frontline FL 1031	BLACK MOSES (LP)	15
70s	His Majesty MH 1004	REGGAE STICK (LP)	20
70s	His Majesty MH 1003	DREAD LION DUB (LP)	40

(see also Jah Lion)

JAH PALM

79	Soul And Fire SF 7	Cumbaya/Version (12")	45

JAH RUBY

77	Dynamic DYLP 3011	DREAD AFFAIR (LP)	25

JAH SCOUSE

85	Better Things BETS 1	Merge/Vegan Mix (foldout p/s)	5

JAH SHAKA

82	Jah Shaka 821	Revelation 18/Revelation Dub (12", red vinyl)	20
82	Jah Shaka 823	Jah Children (with Sister Pat)/SHAKA RIDIM SECTION : Jah Works (12")	30
82	Jah Shaka 828	Lion Youth/MAD PROFESSOR : Beyond The Realms (12")	20
82	Jah Shaka LP 824	THE COMMANDMENTS OF DUB (LP)	25
82	Rough trade ROUGH 50	COMMANDMENTS OF DUB (LP)	15
83	Jah Shaka 833	REVELATION SONGS (LP)	15
84	Jah Shaka 847	COMMANDMENTS OF DUB PART 2 (LP)	15
84	Ariwa SALP 84	JAH SHAKA MEETS MAD PROFESSOR (LP)	15
85	Jah Shaka	COMMANDMENTS OF DUB PART 3 (LP)	12
85	Jah Shaka 850	JAH SHAKA MEETS ASWAD (LP)	12
89	Jah Shaka SHAKA 87	DISCIPLES (LP)	20
89	Mango MPLM 1001	PRESENTS DUB MASTERS VOL. 1 (LP)	15
90	Jah Shaka SHAK 872	CORONATION DUB (LP)	20
94	Jah Shaka SHAK 947	JAH SHAKA MEETS HORACE ANDY (LP)	12

JAH SHAKA VS FATMAN

80	Live & Love LP 10	LIVE (LP)	30

JAH STITCH

77	Third World TW 73	Black Harmony Killer/Natty on Top (12")	12
78	Aries PFUS 6000	Combination Three/Combine Version	8
75	Third World TWS 401	NO DREAD CAN'T DEAD (LP)	30
78	Cancer CANSLP 002	MY PRECIOUS LOCKS (LP)	25

JAH THOMAS

78	Greensleeves GRE 12	Stop Yu Loafin'/Bicycle Skank	10
78	Greensleeves GREL 3	STOP YU LOAFIN' (LP)	25
80	Daddy Kool DKLP 16	DANCE HALL STYLEE (LP)	20
83	Silver Camel SCLP 03	DANCE HALL CONNECTION (LP)	15

JAH WALTON

81	Music Force MFLP 02	TOUCH HERE WHERE SHE WANT IT MOST (LP)	80

JAH WOBBLE

78	Virgin VOLE 9	Dreadlock Don't Deal In Wedlock/Pthilius Pubis (p/s)	5
78	Virgin 12VOLE 9	Dreadlock Don't Deal In Wedlock/Pthilius Pubis (12", p/s)	8
80	Virgin VS 337	Betrayal/MR. X: Battle Of Britain (p/s)	5
80	Virgin VS 337-12	Betrayal/MR. X: Battle Of Britain (12", p/s)	8
82	Jah Wobble JAH 1	Fading/Nocturnal (p/s, as Jah Wobble With Animal)	5
82	Jah Wobble JAH 2	Long Way/Nocturnal (12", p/s)	8
78	Virgin VS 239-12	STEEL LEG MEETS THE ELECTRIC DREAD (12 EP, p/s)	8
92	East West OVAL 103 T	VISIONS OF YOU (12" EP, some with p/s)	8
80	Virgin V 2158	THE LEGEND LIVES ON (mini-LP)	12

(see also Bartok)

JAH WOBBLE, THE EDGE & HOLGER CZUKAY

83	Island WOB 1	Snake Charmer/Hold On To Your Dreams (p/s)	5

(see also Don Letts & Jah Wobble, Dan MacArthur, Joolz, Public Image Ltd, The Edge, Orb, Can)

JAH WOOSH

74	Cactus CT 39	Judy Drownded/Crooked Skank	8
75	Lucky DL 5096	Don't Do That/That Dub	5
75	Lucky DL 5094	Rocking Blues/Version	5
75	Tropical AL 057	Iffie This Life/Iffie Version	8
76	Sunshot SS002	Religious Dread/Religious Dub	8
76	Sunshot SS005	Ital Feast/Dub Feast	8
76	Angen ANG 116	Set Up Yourself Dread/Version	8
76	Attack ATT 8124	I'm Alright/Version	10
76	Attack ATT 8129	Show I The Way/Show I The Way (Version)	8
77	Sunshot SS009	Whip Them Jah/Version	8
78	Grove Music GMDM 7	Pay Them Dues/Diverse Doctrine (with Ras Ibuna) (12")	15
78	Freedom Sounds FSD 001	Ales Skank/Different Style (12")	15
78	Attack ATT 8137	Marcus Say/Take Heed	8
79	Yard International YI 02	Jah Is The Ruler/Ruling Power/Jammys At The Control (12")	15
74	Cactus CTLP 103	JAH WOOSH (LP)	25
76	Student STULP 1003	CHALIS BLAZE (LP)	25
76	Black Wax WAX LP2	PSALMS OF WISDOM (LP)	100
76	Cactus CTLP 116	JAH JAH DEY DEY (LP)	25
77	K&B KBLP 002	LICK HIM WITH THE DUSTBIN (LP)	25
78	Trojan TRLS 157	RELIGIOUS DREAD (LP)	30
79	Creation Rebel CRBLP900	MARIJUANA WORLD TOUR (LP)	20
79	Dread & Dread 002	GATHERING ISRAEL (LP, multi-coloured vinyl)	35

MINT VALUE £

JAH YOUTH
76	Caribbean CBN 307	Little Natty Dread/Little Natty Dread Version	6

JAHFA CULTURE & THE OFFBEAT POSSE
86	Jah Tubbys JT 017	Listen To We/Listen Mix (12")	150

JAILHOUSE
72	Pye 7N 45172	Ya Hoo Hoo/Bad End	12

(see also Hamlett)

JAILHOUSE RECIPES
89	First Strike FS 01	ENERGY IN AN EMPTY TANK WORLD (LP)	15
91	First Strike FST 006	TWO YEARS OF TOOTHACHE (LP, as Jailcell Recipes)	12

JAKE & FAMILY JEWELS
70	Polydor 2425 027	JAKE AND THE FAMILY JEWELS (LP)	15

JAKLIN
69	Stable SLE 8003	JAKLIN (LP, laminated sleeve, black/silver labels)	350

JAM

SINGLES : ORIGINAL SINGLES
73	Fanfare	Some Kinda Lovin'/Making My Way Back Home (acetate 6 copies only)	2500
77	Polydor 2058 866	In The City/Takin' My Love	5
77	Polydor 2058 903	All Around The World/Carnaby Street	5
77	Polydor 2058 945	The Modern World/Sweet Soul Music/Back In My Arms Again/ Bricks And Mortar (Part) (B-sides live at 100 Club 11.9.77)	5
78	Polydor 2059 054	David Watts/"A" Bomb In Wardour Street (double-A-sided 7"; A-side songwriter miscredited as "Ray Davis" without an "e")	15
78	Polydor 2059 054	David Watts/"A" Bomb In Wardour Street (double-A-sided 7"; plastic moulded label, those with white paper labels are worth £8)	5
78	Polydor POSP 8 (2059 068)	Down In The Tube Station At Midnight/So Sad About Us/The Night (7"; misprinted with erroneous B-side ref. to All Mod Cons)	15
78	Polydor POSP 8 (2059 068)	Down In The Tube Station At Midnight/So Sad About Us/The Night)	5
78	Polydor 2058 995	News Of The World/Aunties And Uncles (Impulsive Youths)/Innocent Man	5

(The above singles were reissued in 1980 in picture sleeves; early originals have curved edges on sleeve openings wheras reissues are straight. Lettering on the reissue labels tends to be fatter, reissues are worth £2-3)

79	Polydor POSP 83	The Eton Rifles/See Saw	5
80	Polydor POSPJ 113 2816 024	Going Underground/The Dreams Of Children/Away From The Numbers/The Modern World/Down In The Tube Station At Midnight	8

Note: All 7" singles prior to 'Beat Surrender' were re-pressed on 14th January 1983 in their picture sleeves, the second reissue for singles prior to 'Going Underground'.

80	Polydor 2059 266	Start/Liza Radley	5
82	Polydor POSPX 540	Beat Surrender/Shopping/Move On Up/Stoned Out Of My Mind/War (12")	8

SINGLES : REISSUES & RETROSPECTIVE SINGLES
83	Polydor 2059 482/POSP 482	That's Entertainment/Down In The Tube Station At Midnight (Live Version) (UK reissue of earlier import)	5
83	Polydor POSP 483	Just Who Is The 5 O'Clock Hero/The Great Depression (UK reissue of earlier import)	5
89	Old Gold OG 9895	Beat Surrender/The Bitterest Pill (I Ever Had To Swallow) (generic Old Gold sleeve)	5
89	Old Gold OG 9896	The Eton Rifles/Down In The Tube Station At Midnight (in p/s)	7
89	Old Gold OG 9896	The Eton Rifles/Down In The Tube Station At Midnight	5
89	Old Gold OG 9897	Going Underground/Start! (in p/s)	7
89	Old Gold OG 9897	Going Underground/Start!	5
89	Old Gold OG 9894	Town Called Malice/Absolute Beginners (in p/s)	7
89	Old Gold OG 9894	Town Called Malice/Absolute Beginners	5
92	Polydor PO 199	The Dreams Of Children/Away From The Numbers (live)	6
92	Polydor POCS 199	The Dreams Of Children/Away From The Numbers (live) (, withdrawn)	6
92	Polydor PZ 199	The Dreams Of Children/Away From The Numbers (live)/The Modern World (live) (12")	8
92	Polydor PZCD 199	The Dreams Of Children/Away From The Numbers (live)/The Modern World (live) (CD)	10

ALBUMS
77	Polydor 2383 447	IN THE CITY (LP)	12
77	Polydor 2383 475	THIS IS THE MODERN WORLD (LP)	12
82	Polydor POLD 5055	THE GIFT (LP, 12/3/82, initially in pink/white striped paper bag)	12
83	Polydor SNAP 1/ SNAPL 45	SNAP! (2-LP, gatefold sleeve, with bonus 7" EP: Live! Wembley Arena 2 & 3.12.82 [SNAPL 45])	18
91	Receiver RRLP 141	LIVE AT THE ROXY (LP, unreleased, white label test pressings exist with printed proof sleeve shelved before release as the recording was actually only half a show from the 100 club 11/9/77)	150
92	Polydor 513 177-1	EXTRAS (2-LP, single sleeve with picture inners)	25
93	Polydor 519 667-1	LIVE JAM (2-LP, single sleeve with picture inners)	20
96	Polydor 531 493-1	THE JAM COLLECTION (2-LP, single sleeve, picture inners)	15
02	Simply Vinyl SVLP 108	ALL MOD CONS (LP, 180g vinyl, PVC sleeve, 2002)	18
02	Simply Vinyl SVLP 209	SETTING SONS (LP, 180g vinyl, PVC sleeve, 2002)	18
06	Polydor 9877182	SNAP! (3-CD, limited edition with bonus live EP [9818340])	18

PROMOS
78	Polydor 2059 054DJ	David Watts/'A' Bomb In Wardour Street	25
82	Polydor POSP 400	Precious (1-sided 7", company sleeve)	25
82	Polydor DEN 1	Town Called Malice (Live at Hammersmith Palais 14.12.81)/ Precious (Extended Version) (12", white label promo)	30
82	Polydor PODJ 540	Beat Surrender (Censored)/Shopping (7", radio promo)	15
82	Polydor POSPX 540	Beat Surrender/Shopping/Move On Up/Stoned Out Of My Mind/War (12", white label promo)	15
83	Polydor SNAPL 45	LIVE! WEMBLEY ARENA (bonus Snap! EP, white label promo)	30
97	Polydor 2058 266/	In The City (1-sided 7", "20th anniversary party invite", co. sleeve; some copies with 'tax disc'-style card invite (ADMITS 1)	25
97	Polydor 2058 266/ ADMITS 1	In The City (1-sided 7", "20th anniversary party invite", co. sleeve; some copies with 'tax disc'-style card invite (ADMITS 1)	15
02	Polydor JAMPCD 1	THE COMPLETE JAM: 3-TRACK CD SAMPLER (card sleeve)	15
02	Polydor JAMDVD 1	THE COMPLETE JAM (2-DVD)	25
02	Polydor JAMBBC 1	A SELECTION FROM ... THE JAM AT THE BBC (CD)	20

MISPRESSINGS
78	Polydor 2058 995	News Of The World/Aunties And Uncles (Impulsive Youths)/ Innocent Man (plays B-side on both sides)	40

78	Polydor POSP 8	Down In The Tube Station At Midnight/So Sad About Us/The Night (A-side plays John Travolta's "Sandy") 30
78	Polydor POSP 6	Sandy/Can't Let You Go (by John Travolta, B-side mispressed with "So Sad About Us").......30
79	Polydor POSP 69	When You're Young/Smithers-Jones (plays B-side both sides) 40
80	Polydor 2059 266	Start!/Liza Radley (A-side plays Village People's "Can't Stop The Music") 10
82	Polydor POSP 400	Town Called Malice/Precious (7", both sides play "Precious") 30

FLEXIDISCS

80	Lyntone (no cat. no.)	When You're Young (live) (1-sided fan club flexi) 25
80	Lyntone LYN 9048	Boy About Town/Pop Art Poem (hard vinyl white label test pressing, same tracks both sides, without mailer, 1980) 40
80	Lyntone LYN 9048	Boy About Town/Pop Art Poem (hard vinyl white label test pressing, same tracks both sides, with mailer, 1980)..............50
82	Lyntone (no cat. no.)	Tales From The Riverbank (re-recorded) (1-sided fan club flexi)..............15

(see also Style Council, Paul Weller, Bruce Foxton, Time U.K., Sharp)

JAM TODAY
80s	Stroppy Cow SCJT 1	Stereotyping/Song About Myself (p/s, with insert) 50

JAMAICA BAND
73	Action ACT 4611	Sticky Fingers Part 1/Part 2 10

JAMAICA FATS
66	Blue Beat BB 368	Jacqueline/Please Come Home (actually by Al T. Joe & Celestials) 22

(see also Al T. Joe)

JAMAICA JUBILEE STOMPERS
67	Amusicon AMU 1002	Give Your Love To Me/I Cry To My Heart 15

JAMAICAN ACTIONS
68	Coxsone CS 7070	Catch The Quinella/JACKIE MITTOO: Songbird 40

JAMAICAN EAGLES
73	Harry J HJ 6661	Country Living/Country Living (Version) 5

(see also Eagles)

JAMAICAN FOUNDATIONS
68	Coxsone CS 7036	Take It Cool/VICEROYS: Try Hard To Leave 150

JAMAICANS

66	Doctor Bird DB 1109	Cool Night/Ma And Pa 60
67	Trojan TR 007	Dedicated To You/The Things I Said To You 35
67	Treasure Isle TI 7007	Things You Say You Love/I've Got A Pain 35
67	Treasure Isle TI 7012	Baba Boom (Festival Song 1967) (actually by Baba Boom)/ TOMMY McCOOK & SUPERSONICS: Real Cool 20
67	Treasure Isle TI 7037	Peace And Love/Woman Gone Home 35
69	Escort ES 806	Early In The Morning/Mr. Lonely 12
70	Harry J. HJ 6604	Fire Parts 1 & 2 10
71	Dynamc DYN 410	Love Uprising/My Love For You 7
71	Dynamic DYN 417	Mary/CONSCIOUS MINDS: Soldier Boy 7
71	New Beat NB 084	Mary/CONSCIOUS MINDS: Soldier Boy 7
72	Dynamic DYN 430	I Believe In Music/Music (Version) 5
72	Dynamic DYN 442	Are You Sure/Are You Sure (Version) 5
72	Dynamic DYN 456	Sunshine Love/Sunshine Version 5
74	Dragon DRA 1029	My Heart Just Keeps On Breaking/My Heart Just Keeps On Breaking (Inst'l) 5

(see also Norris Weir & Jamaicans, Tommy Cowan)

JAMAICAN SHADOWS
67	Coxsone CS 7005	HUGH GODFREY : Have Mercy/Blending Love 40
69	Upsetter US 320	Dirty Dozen (actually by Upsetters)/Crying Too Long 40

JAMAICA'S OWN VAGABONDS
64	Decca DFE 8588	BEHOLD (EP) 30
64	Decca LK 4617	SKA TIME (LP) 50

(see also Vagabonds, Jimmy James & Vagabonds)

AHMED JAMAL

59	London Jazz LTZ-M 15162	BUT NOT FOR ME (LP) 15
59	London Jazz LTZ-M 15170	AHMED JAMAL (LP) 20
62	Pye Jazz NJL 38	ALHAMBRA (LP) 15
62	Pye Jazz NJL 47	ALL OF YOU (LP) 15
63	Pye Jazz NJL 50	Q (LP) 15
63	Pye Jazz NJL 50	MACANUDO (LP) 15
63	Pye Jazz NJL 52	POINCIANA (LP) 15
64	Chess CRL 4001	NAKED CITY THEME (LP) 15

JAMES

86	Sire JIM 3	Chain Mail/Hup Springs (p/s) 10
86	Sire JIM 4	So Many Ways/Withdrawn (p/s) 10
86	Sire JIM 4T	So Many Ways/Just Hipper/Withdrawn (12", p/s) 18
88	Blanco Y Negro NEG 26	Yaho/Mosquito (p/s) 6
88	Blanco Y Negro NEG 26T	Yaho/Mosquito/Left Out Of Her Will/New Nature (12", p/s) 12
88	Blanco Y Negro NEG 31	What For/Island Swing (p/s) 6
88	Blanco Y Negro NEG 31T	What For (Climax Mix)/Island Swing/Not There (12", p/s) 15
88	Blanco Y Negro NEG 31C	What For (Climax Mix)/Island Swing/Not There (, in video-style box) 10
89	Rough Trade RT 225	Sit Down/Sky Is Falling (p/s) 8
89	Rough Trade RTT 225	Sit Down/Goin' Away/Sky Is Falling (12", p/s, 1st 500 with postcard) 12
89	Rough Trade RTT 225	Sit Down/Goin' Away/Sky Is Falling (12", p/s, without postcard) 8
89	Rough Trade RTT 225 CD	Sit Down/Goin' Away/Sky Is Falling (3" CD, card sleeve) 12
89	Rough Trade RT 245	Come Home/Promised Land (p/s) 6
89	Rough Trade RTT 245	Come Home (Long Version)/Come Home (7" Version)/Promised Land/ Slow Right Down (Demo Version) (12", p/s) 10
90	Fontana JIMM 512	How Was It For You?/How Was It For You? (Different Mix)/Lazy/ Undertaker (12", p/s, with stencil) 12
90s	Lyntone	Weather Change (Demo Version) (flexidisc, with tour programme) 12
84	Factory FAC 78	JIMONE EP: What's The World/Fire So Close/Folklore 12
85	Factory FAC 138	VILLAGE FIRE: What's The World/Fire So Close/Folklore/Hymn From A Village/If Things Were Perfect (12" EP) 12

MINT VALUE £

85	Factory FAC 119	JAMES II: Hymn From A Village/If Things Were Perfect (p/s)	12
86	Sire JIM 3T	SIT DOWN EP: Chain Mail/Uprising/Hup Springs (12", p/s)	15
91	Fontana JIM 812	SIT DOWN (12" EP, recorded live at G-Mex)	10
89	Rough Trade ONEMAN 1LP	ONE MAN CLAPPING (LP, with inner sleeve)	18
94	Fontana 5228271	WAH WAH (LP)	25
94	Fontana 5228272	WAH WAH (CD, digipak)	20

BARNABY JAMES

| 71 | Decca F 13198 | Feeling Alright/Gone Fishing | 6 |

B.B. JAMES

| 70 | Upsetter US 328 | Consider Me/Consider Me Version | 12 |

BOB JAMES

75	CTI CTI 6043	BOB JAMES ONE (LP)	12
75	CTI CTI 6057	BOB JAMES TWO (LP)	12
76	CTI 6063	THREE (LP, gatefold)	20

BOBBY JAMES & DAVE (BARKER)

| 71 | Smash SMA 2314 | You Said It/AGGRO BAND: Hot Sauce | 40 |

BRIAN JAMES

| 68 | Olga OLE 005 | Come Back Silly Girl/It Just Happened That Way | 8 |

CALVIN JAMES

| 65 | Columbia DB 7516 | Some Things You Never Get Used To/Remember | 25 |

DANNY JAMES

| 72 | Southern Sound BT 100 | Your Gravy Train/Devil Made Me Say That | 7 |

DAVID JAMES

| 69 | Crystal CR 7008 | Nothing Left To Lose/Go With The Times | 25 |

DICK JAMES

53	Parlophone MSP 6039	Mother Nature And Father Time/Don't You Care	5
53	Parlophone MSP 6047	The Joker/Guessing	5
55	Parlophone MSP 6170	Unchained Melody/Come Back (Come Back To Me)	5
55	Parlophone MSP 6190	He/So Must I Love You	5
56	Parlophone MSP 6199	Robin Hood/The Ballad Of Davy Crockett	10
56	Parlophone MSP 6230	Summer Sing-Song Medley	5
56	Parlophone R 4220	I Only Know I Love You/Mirabelle	5
56	Parlophone R 4241	Sing Song Time (No. 3) Medley	5
57	Parlophone R 4255	The Garden Of Eden/I Accuse	5
57	Parlophone R 4314	Westward Ho The Wagons!/The Gay Cavalier	5
57	Parlophone R 4375	Skiffling Sing Song Medley	6
58	Parlophone R 4498	Daddy's Little Girl/When You're Young	5
59	Parlophone R 4606	There But For Your Love Go I/Minus One Heart	5
64	Parlophone R 5212	Sing A Song Of Beatles With Dick James Medley (Parts 1 & 2)	12

ELMORE JAMES

64	Sue WI 335	Dust My Blues/Happy Home (as Elmore James & Broom Dusters)	50
65	Sue WI 383	It Hurts Me Too/Bleeding Heart	40
65	Sue WI 392	Knocking At Your Door/Calling The Blues (B-side actually by Junior Wells & Earl Hooker)	120
66	Sue WI 4007	I Need You/Mean Mistreating Mama	40
65	Sue ILP 918	THE BEST OF ELMORE JAMES (LP)	70
65	Sue ILP 927	THE ELMORE JAMES MEMORIAL ALBUM (LP)	70
68	Bell MBLL/SBLL 104	SOMETHING INSIDE OF ME (LP)	45
68	Ember EMB 3397	THE LATE FANTASTICALLY GREAT ELMORE JAMES (LP)	25
70	United Artists UAS 29109	THE LEGEND OF ELMORE JAMES (LP)	50
70	Blue Horizon 7-66230	TO KNOW A MAN (2-LP)	60
70	Blue Horizon 7-63204	TOUGH (LP, with 4 tracks by John Brim)	65
73	Polydor 2383 200	COTTON PATCH HOTFOOTS (LP, shared with Walter Horton)	20
75	DJM DJLMD 8008	ALL THEM BLUES (2-LP)	18
83	Ace CH 68	KING OF THE SLIDE GUITAR (LP, yellow vinyl)	12

ETTA JAMES

60	London HLM 9139	All I Could Do Was Cry/Tough Mary	50
60	London HLM 9234	My Dearest Darling/Girl Of My Dreams	30
61	Pye International 7N 25079	At Last/I Just Want To Make Love To You	40
61	Pye International 7N 25080	Trust In Me/Anything To Say You're Mine	20
61	Pye International 7N 25113	Dream/Fool That I Am	20
62	Pye International 7N 25131	Something's Got A Hold On Me/Waiting For Charlie To Come Home	30
62	Pye International 7N 25162	Stop The Wedding/Street Of Tears	20
63	Pye International 7N 25205	Pushover/I Can't Hold It In Any More	25
65	Sue WI 359	Roll With Me Henry/Good Rockin' Daddy	60
67	Chess CRS 8052	I Prefer You/I'm So Glad (I Found Love In You)	20
67	Chess CRS 8063	Tell Mama/I'd Rather Go Blind	25
67	Chess CRS 8069	Security/I'm Gonna Take What He's Got	15
68	Chess CRS 8076	I Got You Babe/I Worship The Ground You Walk On	15
68	Chess CRS 8082	You Got It/Fire	15
72	Chess 6145 016	Tell Mama/I'd Rather Go Blind/I Found A Love	15
74	Chess 6145 033	Out On The Streets Again/Come A Little Closer	8
78	Warner Brothers K 17173	Piece Of My Heart/Lovesick Blues	8
85	Kent 6T1	MARY LOVE: Hey Stoney Face/IKETTES: It's Been So Long/ETTA JAMES: Wallflower	20
65	Chess CRL 4502	ETTA JAMES ROCKS THE HOUSE (LP)	75
67	Chess CRL 4524	AT LAST (LP)	70
68	Ember EMB 3390	THE SOUL OF ETTA JAMES (LP)	50
68	Chess CRL 4536	TELL MAMA (LP)	40
73	Chess 6671 003	PEACHES (2-LP)	25

(see also Etta & Harvey)

ETTA JAMES & SUGAR PIE DESANTO

| 65 | Chess CRS 8025 | Do I Make Myself Clear/Somewhere Down The Line | 25 |

(see also Sugar Pie DeSanto)

GARY JAMES
68	Polydor 56134	Nicole/You're Gone	20
67	Polydor S6208	Teddy Bear/In The Rain	15

GRAHAM JAMES
63	Columbia DB 7128	You Could Have Fooled Me/Why Can't You See It My Way?	8

HARRY JAMES & HIS ORCHESTRA
65	Dot DS 16729	Love Theme From In Harm's Way/Green Onions	5

(see also Rosemary Clooney)

JASON JAMES
67	CBS 2705	Miss Pilkington's Maid/Count Me Out	40

JERRY JAMES & BANDITS
64	Solar SRP 101	Sweet Little Sixteen/Three Steps To Heaven	15

JESSE JAMES
54	Vocalion V 1037	Southern Casey Jones/Lonesome Day Blues (78)	20
71	Mojo 2092 016	Don't Nobody Want To Get Married/(Pt. 2)	5

JIMMY JAMES (& THE VAGABONDS)
62	Dice CC 4	Bewildered And Blue/I Don't Want To Cry (solo)	20
63	R&B JB 112	Jump Children/Tell Me (solo)	25
64	Black Swan WI 437	Thinking Of You/Shirley (solo)	30
65	Columbia DB 7653	Shoo Be Doo You're Mine/We'll Never Stop Loving You	20
66	Ska Beat JB 242	Your Love/Someday (solo)	20
66	Piccadilly 7N 35298	I Feel Alright/I Wanna Be Your Everything (p/s)	75
66	Piccadilly 7N 35298	I Feel Alright/I Wanna Be Your Everything	30
66	Piccadilly 7N 35320	Hi Diddley Dee Dum Dum (It's A Good Good Feelin')/Come To Me Softly	20
66	Piccadilly 7N 35331	This Heart Of Mine/I Don't Wanna Cry (p/s)	100
66	Piccadilly 7N 35331	This Heart Of Mine/I Don't Wanna Cry	75
66	Piccadilly 7N 35349	Ain't Love Good, Ain't Love Proud/Don't Know What I'm Gonna Do	20
67	Piccadilly 7N 35360	I Can't Get Back Home To My Baby/Hungry For Love (solo)	12
67	Piccadilly 7N 35374	No Good To Cry/You Showed Me The Way	12
68	Pye 7N 17579	Red Red Wine/Who Could Be Loving You	10
69	Pye 7N 17719	Close The Door/Why (solo)	5
71	Trojan TR 7806	Help Yourself/Why	25
72	Bamboo BAM 67	Riverboat Jenny/If I Wasn't Black	5
72	Stateside SS 2209	A Man Like Me/Survival	15
72	Stateside SS 2209	A Man Like Me/Survival (DJ copy)	35
75	Pye 7N 45524	Whatever Happened To The Love We Knew/Let's Have Fun	5
75	Pye 7N 45472	Hey Girl/I Am Somebody	50
66	Piccadilly NEP 34053	JIMMY JAMES AND THE VAGABONDS (EP)	40
66	Piccadilly NPL 38027	THE NEW RELIGION (LP)	40
68	Marble Arch MAL 823	THIS IS JIMMY JAMES AND THE VAGABONDS (LP)	12
68	Pye N(S)PL 18231	OPEN UP YOUR SOUL (LP)	25
70	Marble Arch MAL 1244	THE NEW RELIGION (LP, reissue)	12

JIMMY JAMES & THE VAGABONDS/ALAN BOWN SET
67	Pye N(S)PL 18156	LONDON SWINGS - LIVE AT THE MARQUEE CLUB (LP, 1 side each)	30

(see also Vagabonds, Jamaica's Own Vagabonds, Alan Bown Set)

JOHN JAMES
70	Transatlantic TRA 219	MORNING BRINGS THE LIGHT (LP)	20
71	Transatlantic TRA 242	JOHN JAMES (LP)	20
72	Transatlantic TRA 250	SKY IN MY PIE (LP)	12
75	Transatlantic TRA 305	HEAD IN THE CLOUDS (LP)	12
76	Kicking Mule SNKF 128	DESCRIPTIVE GUITAR INSTRUMENTALS (LP)	15
78	Kicking Mule SNKF 136	LIVE IN CONCERT (LP)	18
84	Stoptime STOP 101	ACOUSTICA ECLECTICA (LP, signed)	35
84	Stoptime STOP 101	ACOUSTICA ECLECTICA (LP)	20

JONI JAMES
53	MGM SP 1013	Why Don't You Believe Me?/Wishing Ring	10
53	MGM SP 1025	Have You Heard/Purple Shades	5
53	MGM SP 1026	Your Cheatin' Heart/I'll Be Waiting For You	5
53	MGM SP 1041	Almost Always/Is It Any Wonder?	5
53	MGM SP 1064	I'll Never Stand In Your Way/Why Can't I	5
54	MGM SP 1081	I Need You Now/You're Nearer	5
54	MGM SP 1089	I'll Be Seeing You/Am I In Love	5
54	MGM SP 1094	You're My Everything/Maybe Next Time	5
54	MGM SP 1100	In A Garden Of Roses/Every Day	5
54	MGM SP 1105	Pa Pa Pa/Mama, Don't Cry At My Wedding	5
55	MGM SP 1125	This Is My Confession/How Important Can It Be?	5
55	MGM SP 1135	When You Wish Upon A Star/Is This The End Of The Line?	5
56	MGM SP 1149	You Are My Love/My Believing Heart	5
57	MGM MGM 918	Give Us This Day/How Lucky You Are	5
57	MGM MGM 954	Only Trust Your Heart/I Need You So	5
58	MGM MGM 973	My Funny Valentine/My Darling, My Darling	5
58	MGM MGM 978	Never 'Till Now/Love Works Miracles	5
58	MGM MGM 991	There Goes My Heart/Funny	5
59	MGM MGM 1002	There Must Be A Way/I'm Sorry For You, My Friend	5
60	MGM MGM-EP 728	THE SONGS OF HANK WILLIAMS (EP, mono)	10
60	MGM MGM-ES 3501	THE SONGS OF HANK WILLIAMS (EP, stereo)	10
54	MGM MGM-D 127	LET THERE BE LOVE (10" LP)	15

MARK JAMES
67	Liberty LIB 55953	Bimbo Knows/I Can't Let You Go	5

NICKY JAMES (MOVEMENT)
63	Pye 7N 15560	My Colour Is Blue/Take Me Back	70
65	Columbia DB 7747	Stagger Lee/I'm Hurtin' Inside (as Nicky James Movement)	30
67	Philips BF 1566	I Need To Be Needed/So Glad We Made It	7
68	Philips BF 1635	Would You Believe/Silver Butterfly	18
68	Philips BF 1694	Lookin' Through Windows/Nobody But Me	7

MINT VALUE £

69	Philips BF 1755	Time/Little Bit Of Paper	8
69	Philips BF 1804	Reaching For The Sun/No Life At All	7
72	Threshold TH 12	Why/Foreign Shore	6
73	Threshold TH 16	Black Dream/She Came To Me	6
73	Threshold TH 17	I Guess I've Always Loved You/My Style	8
71	Philips 6308 069	NICKY JAMES (LP, black/silver labels)	90
73	Threshold THS 10	EVERY HOME SHOULD HAVE ONE (LP, gatefold sleeve)	30
76	Threshold THS 19	THUNDERTHROAT (LP)	15

(see also Move)

OSCAR JAMES
| 64 | Carnival CV 7007 | Louisa/Go 'Way | 7 |

PHILIP JAMES & BLUES BUSTERS
| 65 | Island WI 219 | Wide Awake In A Dream/MAYTALS: Tell Me The Reason | 75 |

(see also Blues Busters)

RICKY JAMES
| 57 | HMV POP 306 | Knee Deep in The Blues/Bluer Than Blue | 30 |
| 57 | HMV POP 334 | Party Doll/Ninety-Nine Ways | 30 |

ROGER JAMES FOUR
65	Columbia DB 7556	Letter From Kathy/Leave Me Alone	10
66	Columbia DB 7813	Better Than Here/You're Gonna Come Home Cryin' (withdrawn)	70
66	Columbia DB 7829	Better Than Here/You're Gonna Come Home Cryin'	100

(see also Danny Storm)

ROGER JAMES
71	NEMS 563719	If I Didn't Have You/I Know It's Love	20
72	Chapter 1 SCH 165	Gold/Something Wonderful	7
71	Chapter One CHS 807	RIDING FREE (LP, red/silver labels)	25

(see also Danny Storm, Prestons)

RUBY JAMES
| 69 | Fontana TF 1051 | Gettin' Mighty Crowded/Don't Play That Song | 20 |

SALLY JAMES
| 74 | Philips 6006 418 | Isn't It Good/Wake Me When It's Over (p/s) | 7 |

SIDNEY JAMES (& DEAN ROGERS/LIZ FRASER)
61	Decca F 11328	The Ooter Song/Double Bunk (with Liz Fraser)	5
61	HMV POP 886	Kids/One Last Kiss (with Dean Rogers)	5
73	Pye 7N 4528	Our House/She's Gone (solo) (p/s)	5

(see also Tony Hancock)

SKIP JAMES
65	Vanguard VSD 79219	SKIP JAMES TODAY (LP)	40
67	Private PR3	1964-67 (LP, 99 copies only)	80
68	Vanguard VSD 79273	DEVIL GOT MY WOMAN (LP)	45
70	Spokane SPL 1003	THE ORIGINAL 1930/31 RECORDINGS (LP)	50
78	Vanguard VDP 20001	I'M SO GLAD (LP)	20
70s	Storyville 670 185	THE GREATEST OF THE DELTA BLUES SINGERS (LP)	15

SONNY JAMES
56	Capitol CL 14635	The Cat Came Back/Hello Old Broken Heart	25
56	Capitol CL 14664	Twenty Feet Of Muddy Water/For Rent (One Empty Heart)	15
57	Capitol CL 14683	Young Love/You're The Reason I'm In Love	15
57	Capitol CL 14708	First Date, First Kiss, First Love/Speak To Me	15
57	Capitol CL 14742	Dear Love/Lovesick Blues	10
57	Capitol CL 14788	Love Conquered (Love Came, Love Saw)/A Mighty Lovable Man	10
57	Capitol CL 14814	Uh-Huh-Mm/Why Can't They Remember?	30
57	Capitol CL 14814	Uh-Huh-Mm/Why Can't They Remember? (78)	10
58	Capitol CL 14848	Kathaleen/Walk To The Dance	15
58	Capitol CL 14879	Are You Mine/Let's Play Love	5
58	Capitol CL 14915	You Got That Touch/I Can See It In Your Eyes	6
58	Capitol CL 14952	I Can't Stay Away From You/Let Me Be The One To Love You	5
59	Capitol CL 14991	Yo-Yo/Dream Big	10
59	Capitol CL 14991	Yo-Yo/Dream Big (78)	20
59	Capitol CL 15022	Talk Of The School/The Table	5
59	Capitol CL 15046	Pure Love/This Love Of Mine	5
59	Capitol CL 15079	Red Mud/Who's Next In Line	5
60	London HL 9132	Jenny Lou/Passin' Through	10
65	Capitol CL 15377	You're The Only World I Know/Tying The Pieces Together	5
57	Capitol EAP1 827	YOUNG LOVE (EP)	20
64	Capitol EAP1 20654	YOU'RE THE ONLY WORLD I KNOW (EP)	10
57	Capitol T 779	SOUTHERN GENTLEMAN (LP)	15
57	Capitol T 867	SONNY (LP)	15
63	London HA-D 8049	YOUNG LOVE (LP)	20

STU(ART) JAMES (& MOJOS)
65	Decca F 12231	Wait A Minute/Wonder If She Knows (as Stu James & Mojos)	12
74	Bradleys BRAD 7406	I Only Wish I Had The Time/Back To Basingstoke (Part 1)	5
76	Bradleys BRAD 7614	I'm In The Mood/Firefly (as Stuart James)	8

(see also Mojos)

SULLIVAN JAMES BAND
| 66 | Parlophone R 5465 | Goodbye Mr. Heartache/We're Gonna Make It | 10 |

TOMMY JAMES & SHONDELLS
66	Roulette RK 7000	Hanky Panky/SHONDELLS: Thunderbolt	15
66	Pye International 7N 25398	It's Only Love/Ya! Ya!	10
67	Major Minor MM 511	I Think We're Alone Now/Gone Gone Gone	12
67	Major Minor MM 548	Out Of The Blue/Love's Closing In On Me	5
68	Major Minor MM 558	Wish It Were You/Get Out Now	8
68	Major Minor MM 567	Mony Mony/One, Two, Three And I Fell	7
68	Roulette RO 500	Do Something To Me/Somebody Cares	8
69	Roulette RO 502	Crimson And Clover/Some Kind Of Love	10

69	Roulette RO 506	Sweet Cherry Wine/Breakaway	5
69	Roulette RO 507	Crystal Blue Persuasion/I'm Alive	12
69	Roulette RO 511	Ball Of Fire/Makin' Good Time	6
70	Roulette RO 513	She/Loved One	5
70	Roulette RO 516	Come To Me/Talkin' And Signifyin'	5
70	Roulette RO 518	Ball And Chain/Candy Makers (solo)	5
68	Major Minor MMLP/SMLP 27	SOMETHING SPECIAL (LP)	35
68	Roulette RRLP/SRLP 1	MONY MONY (LP)	30
68	Roulette RRLP/SRLP 2	CRIMSON AND CLOVER (LP)	40
69	Roulette RRLP/SRLP 3	CELLOPHANE SYMPHONY (LP)	20
72	Roulette 2432 002	THE BEST OF TOMMY JAMES & THE SHONDELLS (LP)	15
72	Roulette 2432 005	MY HEAD, MY BED AND MY RED GUITAR (LP, solo)	12

TONY JAMES
| 68 | Jolly JY 002 | Treat Me Right/Me Donkey's Dead | 12 |

WINSTON JAMES
70	Hot Rod HR 106	Prison Sentence/JANET FERRON: Darling I Need You	20
70	Torpedo TOR 6	I May Never/Longest Day	35
70	Torpedo TOR 4	Gal You Think You Nice/White Silver Sands	12

JAMES BOYS
68	Direction 58-3721	The Mule (Instrumental)/The Horse (Vocal)	15
73	Penny Farthing PEN 806	Over And Over/Same Old Way	7
74	Penny Farthing PEN 846	I Love You/Pick A Bale Of Cotton	7
74	Penny Farthing PEN 857	Up Until Now/Pick A Bale Of Cotton	7

JAMES BROTHERS
68	Page One POF 077	I Forgot To Give You Love/The Truth About It	8
68	Page One POF 088	Does It Have To Be Me/You Don't Really Love Me	8
74	Penny Farthing PEN 857	Up Until Now/Pick A Bale Of Cotton	6
(see also Wheels)

JAMES GANG
70	Stateside SS 2158	Funk No. 48/Collage	15
70	Stateside SS 2173	Stop/Take A Look Around (withdrawn)	15
70	Probe PRO 502	Funk 49/Thanks	8
71	Probe PRO 533	Walk Away/Yadig?	8
70	Stateside SSL 10295	YER' ALBUM (LP)	20
70	Probe SPB 6253	RIDES AGAIN (LP)	18
71	Probe SPB 1038	THIRDS (LP)	15
71	Probe SPB 1045	LIVE IN CONCERT (LP, textured sleeve, flipback sleeve)	15
72	Probe SPB 1056	STRAIGHT SHOOTER (LP)	12
72	Probe SPB 1065	PASSIN' THRU (LP, textured sleeve)	12
(see also Tommy Bolin)

BOBBY JAMESON
64	Decca F 12032	All I Want Is My Baby/Each And Every Day	40
64	London HL 9921	I Wanna Love You/I'm So Lonely	30
65	Brit WI 1001	Rum-Pum/Please Mr. Mailman	20
69	Joy JOYS 193	TOO MANY MORNINGS (LP)	90

STEPHEN JAMESON
70	Pye 7N 45189	Margie Make It March/Happiness Road	5
73	Dawn DNS 1035	Don't Say/Back Together Once Again	5
73	Dawn DNLS 3044	STEPHEN JAMESON (LP)	15

JAMESON RAID
80	Blackbird BRAID 001	The Hypnotist/The Raid/Gettin' Hotter/Straight From The Butchers (p/s)	40
81	GBH GBH 1	Seven Days Of Splendour/It's A Crime/Catcher In The Rye (p/s, with lyric sheet, white sleeve)	35
81	GBH GBH 1	Seven Days Of Splendour/It's A Crime/Catcher In The Rye (p/s, with lyric sheet, later pressing with black sleeve)	30

JAMIE JON & JERRY
| 67 | Decca F12642 | You've Still Got A Place In My Heart/One Time Lover (All Time Fool) | 6 |

JAMIES
| 58 | Fontana H 153 | Summertime Summertime/Searching For You | 40 |
| 62 | Columbia DB 4885 | Summertime Summertime/Searching For You (reissue) | 20 |

JAMIROQUAI
93	Acid Jazz JAZID 46	When You Gonna Learn/Too Young To Die (p/s)	10
93	Acid Jazz JAZID 46T	When You Gonna Learn/Didgin' Out (12", p/s)	15
93	Sony 474069 1	EMERGENCY ON PLANET EARTH (2-LP)	25
94	Sony 477813 - 1	THE RETURN OF THE SPACE COWBOY (2-LP)	25
96	Sony 4839991	TRAVELLING WITHOUT MOVING (2xLP with bonus track Do You Know Where You're Coming From)	30
99	Sony S2 494517 1	SYNKRONIZED (2-LP)	20
01	Sony 504069 1	A FUNK ODYSSEY (LP)	25
05	Epic BL 96532	DYNAMITE (LP)	20
10	Mercury 2754292	ROCK DUST LIGHT STAR (2-LP)	20

JAMME
| 70 | Stateside-Dunhill SSL 5024 | JAMME (LP) | 25 |

JOE JAMMER
| 73 | Regal Zono. SRZA 8514 | BAD NEWS (LP, gatefold sleeve, red/silver labels) | 25 |
(see also Mitchell/Coe Mysteries)

JAN & ARNIE
| 58 | London HL 8653 | Jennie Lee/Gotta Getta Date | 50 |
| 58 | London HL 8653 | Jennie Lee/Gotta Getta Date (78) | 35 |
(see also Jan & Dean)

JAN & DEAN
| 59 | London HLN 8936 | Baby Talk/Jeanette, Get Your Hair Done | 30 |
| 59 | London HLN 8936 | Baby Talk/Jeanette, Get Your Hair Done (78) | 40 |

59	London HLU 8990	There's A Girl/My Heart Sings	25
59	London HLU 8990	There's A Girl/My Heart Sings (78)	40
60	London HLU 9063	Clementine/You're On My Mind	20
61	London HLH 9395	Heart And Soul/Midsummer Night's Dream	20
62	Liberty LIB 55397	A Sunday Kind Of Love/Poor Little Puppet	20
63	Liberty LIB 55531	Linda/When I Learn How To Cry	15
63	Liberty LIB 55580	Surf City/She's My Summer Girl	10
63	Liberty LIB 55613	Honolulu Lulu/Someday You'll Go Walkin' By	10
64	Liberty LIB 55641	Drag City/Schlock Rod Pt 1	15
64	Liberty LIB 55672	Dead Man's Curve/The New Girl In School	10
64	Liberty LIB 55704	The Little Old Lady From Pasadena/My Mighty GTO	10
64	Liberty LIB 55724	Ride The Wild Surf/The Anaheim, Azusa And Cucamonga Sewing Circle, Book Review And Timing Association	10
65	Liberty LIB 55727	Sidewalk Surfin'/When It's Over	10
65	Liberty LIB 55766	(Here They Come) From All Over The World/Freeway Flyer	12
65	Liberty LIB 55792	You Really Know How To Hurt A Guy/It's As Easy As 1, 2, 3	12
65	Liberty LIB 55833	I Found A Girl/It's A Shame To Say Goodbye	10
66	Liberty LIB 10225	Norwegian Wood/A Beginning From An End	20
66	Liberty LIB 55860	Batman/Bucket 'T'	25
66	Liberty LIB 10244	Popsicle/The Joker Is Wild	25
66	Liberty LIB 55923	The New Girl In School/School Day (Ring Ring Goes The Bell)	8
66	Liberty LIB 10252	Tennessee/Horace The Swinging School Bus Driver	12
67	CBS 202630	Yellow Balloon/A Taste Of Rain	25
65	Liberty LEP 2213	SURF 'N' DRAG HITS (EP)	30
66	Liberty LEP 2258	THE TITANIC TWOSOME (EP)	30
76	United Artists REM 402	REMEMBER JAN & DEAN (EP)	10
63	Liberty LBY 1163	SURF CITY AND OTHER SWINGING CITIES (LP)	30
64	Liberty LBY 1220	DEAD MAN'S CURVE/NEW GIRL IN SCHOOL (LP)	35
64	Liberty LBY 1229	RIDE THE WILD SURF (LP)	30
65	Liberty LBY 1279	GOLDEN HITS (LP)	20
65	Liberty LBY 1304	FOLK 'N' ROLL (LP)	25
66	Liberty LBY 1309	JAN AND DEAN MEET BATMAN (LP)	40
66	Liberty LBY 1339	FILET OF SOUL (A LIVE ONE) (LP)	30

(see also Legendary Masked Surfers, Fantastic Baggys, Jan & Arnie)

JAN & KELLY

62	Philips 326 567 BF	Ooh! 'E Didn't/Prepare To Meet Your Fate Mate	5
62	Philips BF 1253	I Could Have Died/Make Me A Doormat	7
63	Philips BF 1265	Ooh! I Can't/Write Me A Letter	7
64	Philips BF 1323	And Then He Kicked Me/My Country And Western Lover	8
64	Philips BF 1377	There Was A Girl/There Was A Boy/And Then There Was Nothing	6
63	Philips BE 12536	TIME FOR A LAUGH (EP)	15

JAN & KJELD

59	Pye International 7N 25013	Buona Sera/Tiger Rag	6
60	Ember EMB S 101	Banjo Boy/Don't Raise A Storm (in p/s)	20
60	Ember EMB S 101	Banjo Boy/Don't Raise A Storm	10
60	Qualiton PSP 7127	Sweet Sue/Oh! Mein Papa (as Jan & Keld)	6
60	Ember EMB S 109	Down By The Riverside/I Shall Not Be Moved	6
60	Ember EMB 3312	THE KIDS FROM COPENHAGEN (LP, label states "The Boys From Copenhagen")	15

BRUCE JANAWAY

78	Deep Range SRT/CUS/216	PURITANICAL ODES (LP, with insert)	35

JAN DUKES DE GREY

70	Decca Nova (S)DN 8	SORCERERS (LP)	250
71	Transatlantic TRA 234	MICE AND RATS IN THE LOFT (LP, gatefold sleeve, plastic inner/foam opening)	250

(see also Noy's Band)

JANE'S ADDICTION

88	WEA W 7520	Mountain Song/Jane Says (p/s)	6
88	WEA W 7520T	Mountain Song/Jane Says/Had A Dad (live) (12", p/s)	8
91	WEA W 0031TP	Classic Girl/No One's Leaving (live)/Ain't No Right (live) (12", picture disc, die-cut sleeve)	8

PETER JANES

67	CBS 203004	Emperors And Armies/Go Home Ulla (in p/s)	10
67	CBS 203004	Emperors And Armies/Go Home Ulla	6
68	CBS 3299	Do You Believe/For The Sake Of Time	20

BUSTER JANGLES' FLYING MATTRESS

72	RCA RCA 2112	Love Has Taken Over My Brain/The Little World I Knew	25

JANIE

61	Capitol CL 15180	You Better Not Do That/Only Girls Can Tell	12
70	President PT 309	Back On My Feet Again/Psycho	20

(see also Jeanne Black)

JANINE

81	Stiletto JAN 001	Crazy On You/Candy (p/s)	170

JOHNNY JANIS

58	London HLU 8650	The Better To Love You/Can This Be Love	10
60	Philips PB 1090	Gina/If The Good Lord's Willin'	6
58	HMV 7EG 8365	JOHNNY JANIS (EP)	30
66	London HA-U 8270	ONCE IN A BLUE MOON (LP)	20

BERT JANSCH

67	Big T BIG 102	Life Depends On Love/A Little Sweet Sunshine	12
73	Reprise K 14234	Oh My Father/The First Time Ever I Saw Your Face	7
74	Charisma CB 240	In The Bleak Midwinter/One For Jo	6
75	Charisma CB 267	Dance Lady Dance/Build Another Band	5
79	Kicking Mule SCK 44	Time And Time/Una Linea Di Dolcezza (as Bert Jansch Conundrum)	5
82	Logo GO 409	Heartbreak Hotel/Up To The Stars (p/s)	5
66	Transatlantic EP 145	NEEDLE OF DEATH (EP)	40
65	Transatlantic TRA 125	BERT JANSCH (LP)	50

65	Transatlantic TRA 132	IT DON'T BOTHER ME (LP)	45
66	Transatlantic TRA 143	JACK ORION (LP)	50
67	Transatlantic TRA 157	NICOLA (LP)	35
69	Transatlantic TRA 179	BIRTHDAY BLUES (LP)	30
69	Vanguard VSD 79292	STEPPING STONES (LP)	30
69	Transatlantic TRASAM 10	THE BERT JANSCH SAMPLER (LP)	15
71	Transatlantic TRA 235	ROSEMARY LANE (LP)	25
72	Transatlantic TRASAM 27	BOX OF LOVE - THE BERT JANSCH SAMPLER VOL. 2 (LP)	20
73	Reprise K 44225	MOONSHINE (LP, with lyric insert)	20
74	Charisma CAS 1090	L.A. TURNAROUND (LP, with lyric insert)	35
75	Charisma CAS 1107	SANTA BARBARA HONEYMOON (LP)	15
77	Charisma CAS 1127	A RARE CONUNDRUM (LP, lyric inner)	15
79	Charisma CLASS 6	AVOCET (LP)	12
80	Kicking Mule SNKF 162	THIRTEEN DOWN (LP, as Bert Jansch Conundrum)	30
85	Konexion KOMA 788006	FROM THE OUTSIDE (LP, 500 only)	12

BERT JANSCH & JOHN RENBOURN

| 66 | Transatlantic TRA 144 | BERT AND JOHN (LP) | 50 |

(see also Conundrum, Pentangle, John Renbourn)

JANUARY

| 69 | CBS 4465 | It Sings For Me/Julie | 10 |

JAPAN

78	Ariola Hansa AHA 510	Don't Rain On My Parade/Stateline (solid or press-out centre, no p/s)	15
78	Ariola Hansa AHA 525	The Unconventional/Adolescent Sex (with p/s)	20
78	Ariola Hansa AHA 525	The Unconventional/Adolescent Sex	6
78	Ariola Hansa AHA 529	Sometimes I Feel So Low/Love Is Infectious (p/s, initial pressing on blue vinyl)	10
78	Ariola Hansa AHA 529	Sometimes I Feel So Low/Love Is Infectious (p/s)	8
79	Ariola Hansa AHA 540	Life In Tokyo (Short Version)/Life In Tokyo Pt 2 (p/s, red vinyl)	8
79	Ariola Hansa AHAD 540	Life In Tokyo (Long Version)/(Short Version) (12", p/s, red vinyl)	12
80	Ariola Hansa AHA 559	I Second That Emotion/Quiet Life (dull red vinyl, card p/s)	8
80	Ariola Hansa AHA 559	I Second That Emotion/Quiet Life (dull red vinyl, paper p/s)	6
80	Virgin VS 379	Gentlemen Take Polaroids/The Experience of Swimming (fully autographed by band, p/s)	75
80	Virgin VS 379	Gentlemen Take Polaroids/The Experience of Swimming//The Width Of A Room/Burning Bridges (double pack, gatefold p/s)	12
82	Virgin VSY 472	Ghosts/The Art Of Parties (Version) (picture disc, stickered PVC cover)	5
80	Virgin V 2180	GENTLEMEN TAKE POLAROIDS (LP, with misprinted sleeve with sticker, Some Kind Of Fool listed instead of "Burning Bridges")	12

(see also David Sylvian)

JOHNNY JAPES & HIS JESTICLES

| 87 | Viz VIZ 1 | Bags Of Fun With Buster/Scrotal Scratch Mix (p/s) | 5 |

(see also XTC, John Otway, Mr. Partridge)

JIMMY JAQUES

| 58 | Fontana H 131 | In My Life/Never Let You Go | 6 |

JARMELS

| 61 | Top Rank JAR 560 | She Loves To DanceLittle Lonely One | 30 |
| 61 | Top Rank JAR 580 | A Little Bit Of Soap/The Way You Look Tonight | 40 |

COOK E. JARR

| 69 | RCA RCA 1820 | Pledging My Love/If I Were A Carpenter | 5 |

JEAN-MICHEL JARRE

78	Polydor POSP 20	Equinoxe 5/Equinoxe 1 (p/s, with etched autograph on run-off)	8
79	Polydor 2001 896	Equinoxe 4 (Remix)/Equinoxe 3 (p/s)	6
80	Polydor 2001 968	Jarre At The Concorde: Equinoxe 7 (live)/Equinoxe 8 (live) (p/s)	10
81	Polydor POSP 292	Magnetic Fields 2 (Remix)/Magnetic Fields 1 (Excerpt) (p/s)	5
81	Polydor POSP 363	Magnetic Fields 4 (Remix)/Magnetic Fields 1 (Excerpt) (p/s)	10
82	Polydor POSP 430	Orient Express/Fishing Junks At Sunset (p/s)	8
84	Polydor POSPX 718	Zoolook (Remix)/Wooloomooloo/Zoolook (Extended)/Zoolook (Effects) (12", p/s)	15
85	Polydor POSP 740	Zoolookologie (Remix)/Ethnicolor 2 (p/s)	8
85	Polydor POSPG 740	Zoolookologie (Remix)/Ethnicolor 2//Oxygene 4/Oxygene 6 (double pack)	12
85	Polydor POSPX 740	Zoolookologie (Extended Remix)/(Remix)/Ethnicolor 2 (12", p/s)	15
86	Polydor POSPX 788	Rendezvous 4 (Special Remix)/Rendezvous 4/Moon Machine (12", 'face' or 'city skyline' p/s)	20
88	Polydor PZ 25	Revolutions (Extended Mix)/Revolutions (LP Mix)/Industrial Revolution 2 (12", p/s)	8
88	Polydor PZCD 25	Revolutions (Extended Mix)/Revolutions/Revolutions (Single Remix) (CD, jewel case)	20
88	Polydor PZCD 32	London Kid (Full Version) (featuring Hank Marvin)/ Industrial Revolution 3/Revolutions (Remix) (CD, card sleeve)	20
89	Polydor PZCD 55	Oxygene IV (Single Version)/Industrial Revolution Overture/ Oxygene IV (live)/September (CD, card sleeve)	15
90	Polydor PZ 84	Calypso (Extended)/Calypso/Calypso Pt 2 (12", p/s)	10
87	Polydor 833 737-2	THE JEAN-MICHEL JARRE 10TH ANNIVERSARY CD BOX SET (7-CD, 5,000 only)	40
88	Polydor C88 1-3	OXYGENE (LP, HMV-only box set with booklet, 3,300 only)	15
88	Polydor C88-1-3	OXYGENE (CD, HMV-only box set with booklet, 3,500 only)	20

MAURICE JARRE

63	Pye Intl. NPL 28023	LAWRENCE OF ARABIA (LP, soundtrack)	12
65	Fontana (S)TL 5259	THE COLLECTOR (LP, soundtrack)	25
66	MGM MGM-CS 8037	GRAND PRIX (LP, soundtrack)	12
66	CBS (S)BPG 62843	IS PARIS BURNING? (LP, soundtrack)	18
67	RCA RD 7848	NIGHT OF THE GENERALS (LP, soundtrack)	30
67	RCA Victor RD/SF 7876	THE PROFESSIONALS (LP, soundtrack)	50
68	Dot (S)LPD 515	VILLA RIDES (LP, soundtrack)	15
76	EMI SLCW 1033	THE MESSAGE (LP, soundtrack, gatefold sleeve)	12
77	Pye NSPH 28504	JESUS OF NAZARETH (LP, soundtrack, gatefold sleeve)	15

ECCLETON JARRETT

| 86 | CF CFD 010 | Greedy Girl/Fling It Up (12") | 40 |

WAYNE JARRETT

80	Greensleeves GRED 41	Saturday Night Jamboree (12")	20
81	Greensleeves GRED 61	Chip In/You Were On My Mind (12")	12
82	Echo ECHO 011	Satta Dread/Sadat (12")	35

MINT VALUE £

81	Greensleeves GREL 28	CHIP IN (LP)	12
82	Wackies W 191	BUBBLE UP (LP)	25

WINSTON JARRETT
77	Carib Gems CG 012	Sleepers/Sleepers Version (with the Righteous Flames)	6
78	Write Sounds WTS 1002	Spanish Town Road/Version	8
80	Warrior WAR 144	Wise Man/I Shen Galore (12")	20

MARIAN JARVIS
75	Chelsea 2005 038	A Penny For Your Thoughts/A Good Man To Wake Up To	30

JASMIN T
69	Tangerine DP 13	Some Other Guy/Evening (with p/s)	50
69	Tangerine DP 13	Some Other Guy/Evening	20

JASMINE MINKS
84	Creation CRE 004	Think/Work For Nothing (p/s)	8

JASON & THE SCORCHERS
85	EMI EA 200	Shop It Around/Change The Tune (p/s)	5
85	EMI 12EA 200	Shop It Around/Absolutely Sweet Marie/Change The Tune (12", p/s)	8

JASON CREST
68	Philips BF 1633	Turquoise Tandem Cycle/Good Life (in export p/s)	160
68	Philips BF 1633	Turquoise Tandem Cycle/Good Life	60
68	Philips BF 1650	Juliano The Bull/Two By The Sea	40
68	Philips BF 1687	(Here We Go Round) The Lemon Tree/Patricia's Dream	60
69	Philips BF 1752	Waterloo Road/Education	40
69	Philips BF 1809	A Place In The Sun/Black Mass	180

(see also Holy Mackerel, High Broom)

JASON'S GENERATIONS
66	Polydor BM 56042	It's Up To You/Insurance Co.'s Are Very Unfair	80

JASPER
69	Spark SRLP 103	LIBERATION (LP, laminated front sleeve, blue/silver labels)	400

JEROME JASPER
82	NYC 1	I'll Do Anything/I'll Do Anything (Instrumental) (12" promo white label)	25
82	Rak 12RAK 354	I'll Do Anything For You/Treasure The Moment (12")	15

JAVELLS
77	Pye Disco Demand DDS 2003	Goodbye Nothin' To Say/Nothin' To Say	6

JAWBONE
70	Carnaby CNS 4007	How's Ya Pa?/Mister Custer	10
70	Carnaby CNS 4020	Way Down Down/Bulldog Goes West	10
72	B&C CB 190	Gotta Go/Automobile Blues	6
70	Carnaby CNLS 6004	JAWBONE (LP)	150

(see also Mirage, Portobello Explosion)

BOB JAXON (& HI-TONES)
55	London HL 8156	Ali Baba/Why Does A Woman Cry (as Bob Jaxon & Hi-Tones)	45
55	London HL 8156	Ali Baba/Why Does A Woman Cry (as Bob Jaxon & Hi-Tones) (78)	20
57	RCA RCA 1019	Beach Party/(Gotta Have Something In The) Bank Frank	80
57	RCA RCA 1019	Beach Party/(Gotta Have Something In The) Bank Frank (78)	20

FRANKIE JAXON/HOUNDHEAD HENRY
60	Jazz Collector JEL 10	THE MALE BLUES VOLUME 6 (EP)	10

JAY (BLACK)
64	Coral Q 72471	I Rise, I Fall/How Sweet It Is	35
67	United Artists UP 1174	What Will My Mary Say/Return To Me (as Jay Black)	10

(see also Jay & The Americans)

ABNER JAY
63	London HLN 9791	Cleo/Thresher	40

ERIC JAY
59	London HL 9004	The Little Drummer Boy/Blue Champagne Cha Cha	6
59	London HL 9004	The Little Drummer Boy/Blue Champagne Cha Cha (78)	10

LAURIE JAY COMBO
62	Ember JBS 710	Shades Of Red/Nevada Sunsets	8
63	HMV POP 1234	Teenage Idol/Think Of Me	15
64	HMV POP 1300	Love In My Heart/'Til You're Mine	8
64	HMV POP 1335	Maybe/Be Good To Me	8
65	Decca F 12083	A Song Called Soul/Just A Little Bit	25

(see also Nero & Gladiators)

LONNIE JAY & JAYNES
63	Stateside SS 197	Around And Around We Go/Somewhere	10

PETER JAY (& BLUE MEN)
60	Triumph RGM 1000	Just Too Late/Friendship (as Peter Jay & Blue Men)	40
60	Pye 7N 15290	Paradise Garden/Who's The Girl?	45

(see also Blue Men)

PETER JAY & JAYWALKERS
62	Decca F 11531	Can Can '62/Redskins	6
63	Decca F 11593	Totem Pole/Jaywalker	7
63	Decca F 11659	Poet And Peasant/Oo La La	10
63	Decca F 11757	Kansas City/The Parade Of Tin Soldiers	10
64	Decca F 11840	You Girl/If You Love Me	10
64	Piccadilly 7N 35199	Where Did Our Love Go/Caroline	8
64	Piccadilly 7N 35212	Tonight You're Gonna Fall In Love/Red Cabbage	10
65	Piccadilly 7N 35220	Parchman Farm/What's Easy For Two Is So Hard For One	20
65	Piccadilly 7N 35259	Before The Beginning/Solitaire	15

(see also Terry Reid, Miller, Big Boy Pete)

JAY (JOHN HOLT) & JOYA (LANDIS)

68	Trojan TR 633	I'll Be Lonely/SUPERSONICS: Second Fiddle	12

(see also John Holt, Joya Landis)

JAY & TECHNIQUES

67	Philips PB 1597	Apples, Peaches, Pumpkin Pie/Stronger Than Dirt	25
67	Philips PB 1618	Keep The Ball Rollin'/Here We Go Again	15
67	Mercury 6052 302	Apples, Peaches, Pumpkin Pie/Contact	7
68	Philips PB 1644	Strawberry Shortcake/Still (In Love With You)	12
68	Mercury MF 1034	Baby Make Your Own Sweet Music/Help Yourself To All My Lovin'	12
75	Polydor 2066 473	I Feel Love Comin' On/This World Of Mine	10
71	Mercury MCF 127360	Baby Make Your Own Sweet Music/Help Yourself To All My Lovin' (reissue)	6
67	Philips (S)BL 7834	APPLES, PEACHES, PUMPKIN PIE (LP)	30

JAY & THE AMERICANS

62	HMV POP 1009	She Cried/Dawning	40
63	United Artists UP 1002	This Is It/It's My Turn To Cry	8
63	United Artists UP 1018	What's The Use/Strangers Tomorrow	8
64	United Artists UP 1039	Come Dance With Me/Look Into My Eyes Maria	18
64	United Artists UP 1069	Come A Little Bit Closer/Goodbye Boys Goodbye	8
65	United Artists UP 1075	Let's Lock The Door (And Throw Away The Key)/I'll Remember You	10
65	United Artists UP 1088	Think Of The Good Times/If You Were Mine Girl	8
65	United Artists UP 1094	Cara Mia/When It's All Over	10
65	United Artists UP 1108	Some Enchanted Evening/Girl	8
66	United Artists UP 1119	Sunday And Me/Through This Doorway	12
66	United Artists UP 1129	Why Can't You Bring Me Home/Baby Stop Your Crying	20
66	United Artists UP 1132	Crying/I Don't Need A Friend	8
66	United Artists UP 1142	Livin' Above Your Head/She's The Girl (That's Messing Up My Mind)	30
66	United Artists UP 1162	(He's) Raining In My Sunshine/Reason For Living	7
67	United Artists UP 1178	You Ain't As Hip As All That Baby/Nature Boy	10
67	United Artists UP 1191	(We'll Meet In The) Yellow Forest/Got Hung Up Along The Way	60
68	United Artists UP 2211	French Provincial/Shanghai Noodle Factory	12
69	United Artists UP 2268	This Magic Moment/Since I Don't Have You	10
69	United Artists UP 35008	When You Dance/So Much In Love	10
69	United Artists UP 35026	Hushabye/No I Don't Know Her	6
70	United Artists UP 35074	Walkin' In The Rain/For The Love Of A Lady	12
65	United Artists UEP 1003	COME A LITTLE BIT CLOSER (EP)	50
66	United Artists UEP 1017	LIVING WITH JAY AND THE AMERICANS (EP)	50
66	United Artists (S)ULP 1117	JAY AND THE AMERICANS (LP)	45
66	United Artists (S)ULP 1128	SUNDAY AND ME (LP)	40
67	United Artists (S)ULP 1150	LIVIN' ABOVE YOUR HEAD (LP)	60
67	United Artists (S)ULP 1164	TRY SOME OF THIS (LP)	40

(see also Jay, Chapter Four)

JAYBIRDS

66	Sue WI 4013	Somebody Help Me/The Right Kind	150

JAYBIRDS (U.K.)

64	Embassy WB 672	What Have They Done To The Rain/BUD ASHTON & HIS GROUP: Genie With The Light Brown Lamp	5
65	Embassy WB 673	Go Now/TERRY BRANDON: Ferry 'Cross The Mersey	5

(see also Ray Pilgrim & Beatmen)

JAY BOYS

69	Trojan TR 665	Splendour Splash/TREVOR SHIELD: Please	40
70	Harry J. HJ 6602	The Dog (Parts 1 & 2)	8
70	Harry J. HJ 6607	Jack The Ripper/Don't Let Me Down	8
70	Harry J. HJ 6609	Jay Moon Walk/Elcong	8
70	Harry J. HJ 6610	Je T'Aime/It Ain't Me Babe	8
70	Harry J. HJ 6617	Del Gago/Killer Song	40
70	Harry J. HJ 6618	Can't Get Next To You/(Part 2) (both actually by Charmers)	5
71	Harry J. HJ 6628	The Arcade Walk/The Arcade Walk Vers. II	6
72	Harry J. HJ 6644	African People/HARRY J. ALL STARS: African (Version)	8
72	Ashanti AHS 407	Rough Road/TREVOR SHIELD: Rough Road	12

(see also Roy Panton, Bob & Marcia, Cables)

JERRY JAYE

67	London HLU 10128	My Girl Josephine/Five Miles From Home	40

JAYE SISTERS

59	London HLT 9011	Sure Fire Love/G-3	60
59	London HLT 9011	Sure Fire Love/G-3 (78)	30

JAYHAWKS (1)

56	Parlophone R 4228	Stranded In The Jungle/My Only Darling	800
56	Parlophone R 4228	Stranded In The Jungle/My Only Darling (78)	140

JAYHAWKS (2)

92	Def American 512.986-1	HOLLYWOOD TOWN HALL (LP, with inner)	100

JAYLADS

71	Punch PH 95	Royal Chord (actually by Melodians)/Version (actually "In The Spirit" by Lloyd Charmers)	12

(see also Melodians)

JAYNETTS

63	Stateside SS 227	Sally Go Round The Roses/Sally Go Round The Roses (Instrumental)	15

JAYS

63	Parlophone R 4764	Shock A Boom/Across The Sea	10

JAYWALKERS

76	Cream CRM 5003	Can't Live Without You/Heartbroken Memories	10

JAZZ BUTCHER

83	Glass GLASS 027	Southern Mark Smith/Jazz Butcher Meets Count Dracula (p/s)	20
85	Glass GLASS 12041	Real Men/The Jazz Butcher V The Prime Minister/Southern Mark Smith (Original) (12", p/s)	20

MINT VALUE £

86	Glass HMMM 001	Christmas With The Pygmies (p/s, promo freebie, given away at gigs)	10

(see also Institution)

JAZZ COMPOSERS ORCHESTRA

74	JCOA/Virgin JDA 3001	JAZZ COMPOSERS ORCHESTRA (2-LP, gatefold sleeve)	20

(see also Carla Bley, Mike Mantler, Don Cherry, Larry Coryell)

JAZZ COURIERS

50s	(no cat. no.)	Top Spot Blues/Monk Was Here/Last Minute Blues (square flexi)	100
57	Tempo EXA 75	JAZZ COURIERS (EP)	60
59	Tempo EXA 87	JAZZ COURIERS (EP)	60
58	Tempo TAP 22	IN CONCERT (LP)	400
59	Tempo TAP 26	THE LAST WORD (LP)	350
60	London Jazz LTZ-L 15188	THE COURIERS OF JAZZ! (LP)	200
67	M. For Pleasure MFP 1072	IN CONCERT (LP)	15
80s	Jasmine JASM 2004	THE JAZZ COURIERS (LP, reissue)	20
80s	Jasmine JASM 2024	THE LAST WORD (LP, reissue)	15

(see also Tubby Hayes, Ronnie Scott)

JAZZ CRUSADERS

66	Fontana 688 149 ZL	THE THING (LP)	20
66	Fontana 688 117 ZL	LOOKIN' AHEAD (LP)	18

(see also Crusaders)

JAZZ DEFEKTORS

87	Factory FACT 205	THE JAZZ DEFEKTORS (LP)	15

JAZZ FIVE

61	Tempo TAP 32	THE FIVE OF US (LP)	300

(see also Vic Ash Quartet, Harry Klein Quartet)

JAZZ HIP TRIO

67	Major Minor MMLP 8	JAZZ IN RELIEF (LP)	100

JAZZ MAKERS

66	Ember FA 2023	SWINGIN' SOUNDS (LP)	20

JAZZ MODES

60	London Jazz LTZ-K 15191	THE MOST HAPPY FELLA (LP)	20

JAZZ ROCK EXPERIENCE

70	Deram Nova SDN 19	JAZZ ROCK EXPERIENCE (LP)	100

JAZZATEERS

83	Rough Trade RT 138	Sixteen Reasons/Show Me The Door (p/s)	5
84	Rough Trade ROUGH 46	JAZZATEERS (LP, with insert)	12

J & B

66	Polydor 56095	Wow Wow Wow/There She Goes	50

(see also State Of Micky & Tommy, Foreigner)

J BLAST & 100% PROOF

92	Geek Street GEEK666JC001/DJ D Zire	2 The Break Of Dawn (12")	18

J.B.'S

71	Mojo 2001 155	These Are The J.B.'s (Parts 1 & 2)	8
71	Mojo 2027 002	The Grunt (Parts 1 & 2)	8
72	Mojo 2093 007	Gimme Some More/The Rabbit Got The Gun	8
72	Mojo 2093 016	Hot Pants Road/Pass The Peas	8
72	Mojo 2093 021	Givin' Up Food For Funk (Parts 1 & 2)	8
72	Mojo 2918 004	PASS THE PEAS (LP)	30
72	Polydor 2391 034	FOOD FOR THOUGHT (LP)	30
74	Polydor 2391 087	DOING IT TO DEATH (LP)	30
75	Polydor 2391 194	HUSTLE WITH SPEED (LP)	30
76	Polydor 2391 204	GIVIN' UP FOOD FOR FUNK - THE BEST OF THE JB's (LP)	30

(see also Fred Wesley & JB's, James Brown, Bobby Byrd)

J.B'S ALLSTARS

85	2 Tone CHSTT29	The Alphabet Army/Al arm (p/s)	30
85	2 Tone CHSTT1229	The Alphabet Army (extended mix)/The Alphabet Army (string mix)/The Alphabet Army/Al Arm (12" p/s)	35

JC001/DJ D ZIRE

88	Furious Fish FFDJD 001	No MC No Comment (12")	12
88	Furious Fish FFJC001	I Dis Therefore I Am (12")	8
91	White JCDZ001	Favourite Breaks (12")	18

J.D. (THE ROC)

72	Sioux SI 008	Superbad/MONTEGO MELON: Lucky Dip	8

(see also Jeff Dixon)

BOBBI JEAN

65	Mercury MF 921	Dry Your Tears/Pity The Man	10

JEAN & GAYTONES

71	Trojan TR 7817	I Shall Sing (actually by Judy Mowatt & Gaytones)/GAYTONES: Target	12

LANA JEAN

63	Pye International 7N 25214	It Hurts To Be Sixteen/Bad Boy	25

CATHY JEAN & ROOMATES

61	Parlophone R 4764	Please Love Me Forever/Canadian Sunset	60

JEAN & STATESIDES

64	Columbia DB 7287	Putty In Your Hands/One Fine Day	40
64	Columbia DB 7439	You Won't Forget Me/Cold, Cold Winter	30
65	Columbia DB 7651	Mama Didn't Lie/Just Let Me Cry	30

JEAN-ETTES

59	Pye 7N 15185	May You Always/I Saw A Light	10

59	Pye 7N 15185	May You Always/I Saw A Light (78) 10

JEANNIE (& BIG GUYS)
63	Piccadilly 7N 35147	Don't Lie To Me/Boys (as Jeannie & Big Guys) 15
64	Piccadilly 7N 35164	I Want You/Sticks And Stones (as Jeannie & Big Guys) 15
65	Parlophone R 5343	I Love Him/With Any Other Girl 10

(see also Cindy Cole)

JEANNIE & REDHEADS
64	Decca F 11829	Animal Duds/ANDREW OLDHAM GROUP: Funky And Fleopatra.....................30

(see also Andrew Oldham Orchestra)

AUDREY JEANS
56	Decca F 10768	Ticky Ticky Tick (I'm Gonna Tell On You)/Will You, Willyum 10
56	Decca F 10788	It's Better In The Dark/The Bus Stop Song (A Paper Of Pins) 10
58	Decca F 11035	Send A Letter To Jeanette - Yet!/Bad Pianna Rag 7
61	HMV POP 876	How Lovely To Be A Woman/What Did I See In Him 5

JEDDAH
83	Death RIP 2001	Eleanor Rigby/Ghosts (with poster, no p/s) 25

JEDI KNIGHTS
95	Clear CLR 406	MAY THE FUNK BE WITH YOU (12" EP, p/s) 10
95	Clear CLR 406X	MAY THE FUNK BE WITH YOU (12" EP, clear vinyl, embossed sleeve) 15

(see also Global Communications)

JEEPS
66	Strike JH 308	He Saw Eesaw/The Music Goes Round 15
66	Strike JH 315	Ain't It A Great Big Laugh/I Put On My Shoes 15

JEFFERSON
68	Pye 7N 17634	Montage/Did You Hear A Heartbreak Last Night 15
69	Pye 7N 17706	The Colour Of My Love/Look No Further 8
69	Pye 7N 17810	Baby Take Me In Your Arms/I Fell Flat On My Face 8
69	Pye 7N 17855	Love And All The World/I've Got To Tell Her 8
71	Pye 7N 45022	Spider/Can't Get You Out Of My Mind 30
75	Alaska ALA 1016	Workin' My Way Back To You/Baby You've Got Everything I Need 10
69	Pye NSPL 18316	THE COLOUR OF MY LOVE (LP) 15
73	Philips 6308 166	I LOVE YOU THIS MUCH (LP, blue/silver labels) 20

(see also Rockin' Berries, Sight & Sound)

JEFFERSON AIRPLANE
67	RCA Victor RCA 1594	Somebody To Love/She Has Funny Cars 15
67	RCA Victor RCA 1631	White Rabbit/Plastic Fantastic Lover 15
67	RCA Victor RCA 1647	Ballad Of You And Me and Pooneil/Two Heads 15
68	RCA Victor RCA 1711	Greasy Heart/Share A Little Joke (With The World) 12
68	RCA Victor RCA 1736	If You Feel Like China Breaking/Triad...10
70	RCA RCA 1933	Volunteers/We Can Be Together 6
70	RCA RCA 1964	Somebody To Love/White Rabbit 8
70	RCA RCA 1989	Mexico/Have You Seen The Saucers? 8
72	Grunt 65-0500	Pretty As You Feel/Wild Turkey 7
72	Grunt 65-0506	Long John Silver/Milk Train 5
67	RCA Victor RD 7889	SURREALISTIC PILLOW (LP, black label, mono) 70
67	RCA Victor SF 7889	SURREALISTIC PILLOW (LP, black label, stereo) 40
68	RCA Victor RD 7926	AFTER BATHING AT BAXTERS (LP, black label, mono) 70
68	RCA Victor SF 7926	AFTER BATHING AT BAXTERS (LP, black label, stereo) 40
68	RCA Victor RD 7976	CROWN OF CREATION (LP, black label, mono) 70
68	RCA Victor SF 7976	CROWN OF CREATION (LP, black label, stereo) 30
69	RCA RD/SF 8019	BLESS ITS POINTED LITTLE HEAD (LP) 20
69	RCA Victor SF 7889	SURREALISTIC PILLOW (LP, repressing, orange label) 35
69	RCA Victor SF 7926	AFTER BATHING AT BAXTERS (LP, repressing, orange label) 25
69	RCA Victor SF 7976	CROWN OF CREATION (LP, repressing, orange label) 40
70	RCA SF 8076	VOLUNTEERS (LP, gatefold sleeve) 20
71	RCA SF 8164	THE WORST OF JEFFERSON AIRPLANE (LP, textured sleeve) 12
71	Grunt FTR 1001	BARK (LP, bag cover with lyric sheet & brown inner sleeve)..........................15
71	RCA SF 8195	JEFFERSON AIRPLANE TAKES OFF (LP)..18
72	Grunt FTR 1007	LONG JOHN SILVER (LP, open-out box cover with inner lyric sleeve) 15
73	Grunt FTR 0147	30 SECONDS OVER WINTERLAND (LP, with inner sleeve) 12

(see also Jefferson Starship, Great Society, Paul Kantner, Papa John Creach, Hot Tuna)

BLIND LEMON JEFFERSON
50	Tempo R 38	Weary Dog Blues/Change My Luck Blues (78)...25
50	Tempo R 39	Lock Step Blues/Hangman's Blues (78) 25
51	Tempo R 46	Shuckin' Sugar Blues/Rabbit Foot Blues (78) 25
52	Tempo R 54	Gone Dead On You Blues/One Dime Blues (78) 25
53	Jazz Collector L 91	Shuckin' Sugar Blues/Rabbit Foot Blues (78) 20
53	Jazz Collector L 103	Jack O'Diamonds Blues/Clock House Blues (78) 20
54	Jazz Collector L 126	Gone Dead On You Blues/One Dime Blues (78) 20
50s	Poydras 99	BLIND LEMON JEFFERSON (10" LP) 50
53	London Jazz AL 3508	FOLK BLUES OF BLIND LEMON JEFFERSON (10" LP).......................................50
55	London Jazz AL 3546	PENITENTIARY BLUES (10" LP) 50
57	London Jazz AL 3564	SINGS THE BLUES (10" LP) 50
69	CBS 63738	THE IMMORTAL (LP)..20
70s	Roots Matchbox RL 301	BLIND LEMON JEFFERSON VOLUME 1 (LP)...20
70s	Roots Matchbox RL 306	BLIND LEMON JEFFERSON VOLUME 2 (LP)...18
70s	Roots Matchbox RL 331	BLIND LEMON JEFFERSON VOLUME 3 (LP)...18

(see also Paramount Allstars)

BLIND LEMON JEFFERSON/ED BELL
60	Jazz Collector JEL 13	THE MALE BLUES VOLUME 7 (EP) 10

BLIND LEMON JEFFERSON/BUDDY BOY HAWKINS
59	Jazz Collector JEL 8	THE MALE BLUES VOLUME 5 (EP) 10

BLIND LEMON JEFFERSON/LEADBELLY
61	Jazz Collector JEL 24	THE MALE BLUES VOLUME 8 (EP) 10

MINT VALUE £

BLIND LEMON JEFFERSON & RAMBLING THOMAS
50s	Heritage HLP 1007	BLIND LEMON JEFFERSON AND RAMBLING THOMAS (LP, 99 only)	100

EDDIE JEFFERSON
67	Stateside SS 591	Some Other Time/When You Look In The Mirror	20

GEORGE PAUL JEFFERSON
68	Fontana TF 923	Looking For My Mind/Out Of Place	45

MARSHALL JEFFERSON
88	ffrr FFRX 18	Open Your Eyes (Celestial Mix)/(Spiritual Mix)/ (Marshall's Elevated Dub) (12", p/s)	15

JEGA
96	Skam SKA 6	Phlax/Nortom Midgate/Bluette/Ionic/Evil Lee Kirtcele/ Steel Drum/In With The In (12", custom sleeve)	45
97	Skam SKA 9	Card Hore/Oak Hanger/Nausicaa/Stainless Steel Drum/Star/Houdini (12", p/s)	10
98	Planet Mu ZIQ 001	TYPE XERO EP (12")	20
99	Planet Mu ZIQ 009	Unity Gain/KID SPATULA: Hard Love (12", clear vinyl, p/s)	8
00	Planet Mu ZIQ 012	GEOMETRY (2-LP)	20

JEHST
99	Y n R Productions YNR 001	PREMONITIONS EP: (12", stickered (white die-cut sleeve, first pressing blue text on label)	40
99	Y n R YNR 1	PREMONITIONS (EP, second pressing black text on label)	15
01	Lowlife LOW 12	THE HIGH PLAINS DRIFTER (EP, p/s)	15
01	Lowlife LOW 12 PRO	The Trilogy Remix (1-sided 12", 2 mixes 500 pressed)	20
02	Y n R YNR008	Alcoholic Author/Night Breed (12", p/s)	10
02	Lowlife LOW 18	The Return Of The Drifter/People Under The Weather (12", p/s, 3 mixes each)	8
04	White B8080 1	Stand Up/Wake Up (12")	8
03	Lowlife LOW30	FALLING DOWN (LP)	12

JELLY
72	Mother MOT9	I'll Meet You Half Way/Chicago Calling	40

JELLYBEAN
84	EMI America 12EAX 210	Sidewalk Talk (featuring Madonna)/Was Dog A Doughnut/Sidewalk Talk (featuring Madonna)/Was Dog A Doughnut (12" remix, p/s)	10

(see also Madonna)

JELLY BEANS
64	Pye International 7N 25252	I Wanna Love Him So Bad/So Long	30
64	Red Bird RB 10011	The Kind Of Boy You Can't Forget/Baby Be Mine	30
75	Right On R 102	You Don't Mean Me No Good/I'm Hip To You	10

JELLYBREAD
69	Blue Horizon 57-3162	Chairman Mao's Boogaloo/No One Else	12
70	Blue Horizon 57-3169	Comment/Funky Wasp	12
70	Blue Horizon 57-3174	Rockin' Pneumonia And The Boogie-Woogie Flu/Readin' The Meters	12
70	Blue Horizon 57-3180	Old Man Hank/Faded Grace	15
71	Blue Horizon 2096 001	Creepin' And Crawlin'/The Loser/The Clergyman's Daughter	12
72	Blue Horizon 2096 006	Down Along The Cove/Sister Lucy	15
72	Liphook 1	JELLYBREAD (mini-LP)	300
69	Blue Horizon 7-63853	FIRST SLICE (LP)	80
71	Blue Horizon 2431 002	SIXTY-FIVE PARKWAY (LP, with lyric insert)	100
71	Blue Horizon 2431 002	SIXTY-FIVE PARKWAY (LP, without lyric insert)	60
72	Blue Horizon 2931 004	BACK TO THE BEGINNING AGAIN (LP, gatefold sleeve)	150

JELLYS
98	Mission Impossible MIRVL1	WELCOME TO OUR WORLD (LP, with inner sleeve, mail-order only)	12

(see also Honeycrack, Wildhearts)

DIANNE JENKINS
76	Crystal CR 7025	Tow-A-Way-Zone/Anniversary (as Diane Jenkins)	10

JOHNNY JENKINS
69	Atco 226 009	The Voodoo In You/Backside Blues	10
71	Atco 2400 033	TON-TON MACOUTE (LP)	25

LEROY JENKINS
76	JCOA/Virgin J 2005	FOR PLAYERS ONLY (LP)	15

JENNIFER (WARNES)
69	London HLU 10278	Let The Sun Shine In/Easy To Be Hard	7
70	London HLU 10312	Cajun Train/Old Folks (Les Vieux)	8

JENNIFERS
92	Nude NUD 2T	Just Got Back Today/Rocks And Boulders/Danny's Song/Tomorrow's Rain (12")	30
92	Nude NUD 2CD	Just Got Back Today/Rocks And Boulders/Danny's Song/Tomorrow's Rain (CD)	40

(see also Supergrass)

BILL JENNINGS
55	Parlophone MSP 6146	Stuffy/Solitude (as Bill Jennings-Leo Parker Quintet)	6
55	Parlophone MSP 6156	Soft Winds/What's New? (as Bill Jennings Quartet)	6

WAYLON JENNINGS
69	RCA RCA 1866	The Days Of Sand And Shovels/Delia's Gone	5
80	RCA PB 9561	The Dukes Of Hazzard Theme/Storms Never Last (p/s)	5

JENNORS
67	Coxsone CS 7024	Pressure And Slide (actually by Tennors)/SOUL BROTHERS: One Stop	30

(see also Tennors)

KRIS JENSEN
62	Fontana 267 241 TF	Torture/Let's Sit Down	20
63	Fontana 267 267 TF	Don't Take Her From Me/Claudette	15
64	Hickory 45-1224	Donna Donna/Big As I Can Dream	20
64	Hickory 45-1243	Lookin' For Love/In Time	12
64	Hickory 45-1256	Come Back To Me/You've Only Got Me To Lose	10
65	Hickory 45-1285	The Little Wind-Up Doll/Somebody's Smiling While I'm Crying	10
65	Hickory 45-1311	What Should I Do/That's A Whole Lotta Love	10

KRIS JENSEN/SUE THOMPSON
65   Hickory LPE 1507   INTRODUCING KRIS JENSEN AND SUE THOMPSON (EP, 2 tracks each) 12
(see also Sue Thompson)

PAUL JENSEN & CAR THIEVES
78   Albatross TIT 3   Holiday In Spain/Always Arrive On Time (p/s)..................................6

JENSENS
68   Philips BF 1686   Deep Thinking/Marguerite 12
(see also Tempus Fugit)

BILL JENTIES
70   Smash SMA 2307   Stop Them (actually by Bill Gentles)/MAXINE: I Don't Care 6
(see also Bill Gentles/Bill Jentles)

BILL JENTLES
70   Pama PM 809   True True Train/JEFF BARNES: Give And Take.............................15
70   Pama PM 801   What A Woman/Sleepy Cat 10
(see also Bill Jenties)

JEREMIAHS
85   No Label or catalogue number   Over The Stove/Wipe Away Your Tears/Never Come Back (printed insert and photo stuck on cover 25-50 copies only)................................150
87   Abstract ABCT 112   DRIVING INTO THE SUN (12" EP) 45
87   Abstract ABS 053   DRIVING INTO THE SUN EP 25

JERICHO (JONES)
71   A&M AMS 833   Time Is Now/Freedom 5
72   A&M AMS 883   Don't Let Me Down/Mona Mona 10
72   A&M AMS 7017   Hey Man/Champs 10
72   A&M AMS 7037   Mama's Gonna Take You Home/So Come On 10
71   A&M AMLH 68050   JUNKIES, MONKEYS & DONKEYS (LP, as Jericho Jones, gatefold, brown label)........150
72   A&M AMLS 68079   JERICHO (LP, beware of counterfeits with slightly thicker sleeves) 170

JERKS
78   Underground URA 1   Get Your Woofing Dog Off Me/Hold My Hand (p/s) 35
78   Lightning GIL 549   Cool/Jerkin' (p/s) 20
80   Laser LAS 25   Come Back Bogart (I Wish You Would)/Are You Strong Enough?/ The Strangest Man Of All (p/s) 15
97   Overground OVER 65   JERK OFF (LP, 600 only pressed in U.K. for export to Japan) 20

JERMZ
78   One Way EFP 1   Power Cut/Me And My Baby (with p/s) 200
78   One Way EFP 1   Power Cut/Me And My Baby (without p/s) 80

JERRY JEROME
55   MGM SP 1118   Honey/In A Little Spanish Town 5

JERONIMO
70   Major Minor MM695   Hey Ya/Na Na Hey Hey Kiss Him Goodbye 8

JERRY THE FERRET
78   Jerry The Ferret EGH 919   One Step Forward/I Think You're Lyin' (1000 only, no p/s) 50
80   Dead Horse   THE MUSIC GOES ON AND ON (EP) 20

JERRY & THE BLUEBELLS
75   Torpedo TOR 44   Girls/Girls Version..15

JERRY & FREEDOM SINGERS
70   Banana BA 308   It's All In The Game (pseudonym for Winston Francis)/ IM: The Way To My Heart (pseudonym for Cedric Brooks) 60
(see also Winston Francis)

JERRY O
67   London HLZ 10162   Karate Boo-ga-loo/The Pearl 12
71   Jay Boy BOY 33   Karate Boo-ga-loo/The Pearl (reissue) 6
72   Jay Boy BOY 62   Dance What 'Cha Wanna/Afro-Twist Time 8

JERUSALEM (1)
79   Praise PLP 4   JERUSALEM (LP, with insert)..................................12
80   Myrrh MYR 1097   VOLUME 2 (LP, with insert) 12
82   Myrrh MYR 1113   WARRIOR (LP)..12

JERUSALEM (2)
72   Deram DM 358   Kamakazi Moth/Frustration 40
72   Deram SDL 6   JERUSALEM (LP, gatefold sleeve, white/brown label with large 'Deram' logo) 250
72   Deram SDL 6   JERUSALEM (LP, gatefold sleeve, later red/white label) 100
(see also Pussy, Ian Gillan)

JESS & JAMES
68   MGM MGM 1389   Move/What Was I Born For 25
68   MGM MGM 1420   Something For Nothing/I Let The Day Go By (with J.J. Band) 20
68   MGM MGM 1454   Thank You Show Biz/Motherless Child 10

STEVE JESSE
President PT 502   Shifting Sands/Post Hall Life 6

JESSUP
72   Beacon BEA 108   Little Friend/On The Run......................................15

JESTERS
62   R&L RL 15/16   Little Girl/Casa Pedro (early labels blue and white) 30
73   Jam JAM 35   Fool For A Day/Can't Live Without You............................15

JESUS & MARY CHAIN
84   Creation CRE 012   Upside Down/Vegetable Man (black & white wraparound p/s in poly bag with address on rear & name in red) 20
84   Creation CRE 012   Upside Down/Vegetable Man (red & white wraparound p/s in poly bag with address on rear & name in black) 20
84   Creation CRE 012   Upside Down/Vegetable Man (pink, blue or yellow wraparound p/s in poly bag; with small T-shirt offer insert)......................................12

84	Creation CRE 012	Upside Down/Vegetable Man (pink, blue or yellow wraparound p/s in poly bag; without small T-shirt offer insert) 8
85	Fierce FRIGHT 004	RIOT (EP, with 'LSD bar' & badge; 2 different sleeves) 25
85	Blanco Y Negro NEG 008	Never Understand/Suck (p/s) 5
85	Blanco Y Negro NEG 17F	Just Like Honey/Head//Inside Me/Just Like Honey (Demo Oct 84) (double pack, gatefold p/s) 8
86	Creation CRE 012	Upside Down/Vegetable Man (reissue, different printed p/s) 5
86	Creation CRE 012T	Upside Down/Vegetable Man/Upside Down (demo) (12" white label, no sleeve) 60
86	Blanco Y Negro NEG 19	SOME CANDY TALKING EP: Some Candy Talking/Psychocandy/Cut Dead/Psychocandy (acoustic)/You Trip Me Up/Some Candy (acoustic) (2x7" double pack) 6
87	Blanco Y Negro NEGB 25	Happy When It Rains/Everything Is Alright When You're Down (box set with postcards) 7
89	Blanco Y Negro NEG 41TE	Blues From A Gun/Shimmer/Penetration/Break Me Down (10", gatefold p/s) 8
89	Blanco Y Negro NEG 42/XB/Y/Z	Head On/Terminal Beach//Head On/Deviant Slice//Head On//I'm Glad I Never/Head On/In The Black (4 x 7" box set; each single sold separately) 12
91	Strange Fruit SFPMA210	PEEL SESSIONS (12") 15
92	Blanco Y Negro NEG 57T	Almost Gold/Teenage Lust (Acoustic Version)/Reverberation (Doubt)/Don't Come Down (12", with poster) 8
94	Blanco Y Negro NEG 73	Come On/I'm In With The Out Crowd (orange vinyl, numbered limited edition) 6
85	Creation CRE(T) 1	LIVE (100 only, numbered, with press sheet) 100
85	Blanco Y Negro BYN 7	PSYCHOCANDY (LP, with inner) 20
87	Blanco Y Negro BY 11	DARKLANDS (LP, with inner) 15
89	Blanco Y Negro BYN 20W	AUTOMATIC (LP, gatefold sleeve, with insert) 15
92	Blanco Y Negro BYN 26	HONEY'S DEAD (LP) 15
94	Warner Bros. 4509-96717-4	STONED & DETHRONED (LP) 30
98	Creation CRELP 232	MUNKI (2-LP) 20
00	Strange Fruit SFRSLP092	THE COMPLETE PEEL SESSIONS (LP) 15

(see also Acid Angels, Primal Scream, Meat Whiplash)

JESUS IS
| 70s | Myrrh MYR 1049 | JESUS IS (LP) ....12 |

JESUS LIZARD
92	Own label	Gladiator (Marquee gig freebie) 10
93	Touch & Go TG 83	Puss/NIRVANA: Oh, The Guilt (p/s, blue vinyl, with poster) 40
93	Touch & Go TG 83	Puss/NIRVANA: Oh, The Guilt (p/s, blue vinyl, without poster) 25
93	Touch & Go TG 83	Puss/NIRVANA: Oh, The Guilt (p/s, black vinyl) 5
93	Touch & Go TG 83CD	Puss/NIRVANA: Oh, The Guilt (CD) 10
90	Touch & Go T&GLP 54	HEAD (LP, grey vinyl, numbered sticker on sleeve, 1500 only) 18
91	Touch & Go T&GLP #43	PURE (LP, purple vinyl, numbered sticker on sleeve, 1500 only) 18
91	Touch & Go T&GLP #68	GOAT (LP, orange vinyl, numbered stickeer on sleeve, 1000 only) 40
91	Touch & Go TG68P	GOAT (LP, picture disc) 18
92	Touch & Go TGLP 100	LIAR (LP, maroon vinyl, stickered no'd sleeve) 15
92	Tough & Go TG100 PD	LIAR (LP, picture disc in PVC sleeve) 12

(see also Nirvana)

JET
75	CBS S CBS 3317	Nothing To Do With Us/Brian Damage 8
75	CBS S CBS 3143	My River/Quandary 8
75	CBS 80699	JET (LP, with lyric insert) 20

(see also Andy Ellison, John's Children, Nice, Radio Stars, Sparks)

JET (AUSTRALIA)
| 03 | Warner Bros 7559 628861 | DIRTY SWEET EP: Take It Or Leave It/Cold Hard Bitch/Move On/Rollover DJ (12", p/s) ....10 |
| 03 | Elektra 7559-62956-1 | GET BORN (2xLP, white vinyl, stickered, gatefold with inners) ....20 |

JETHRO TULL
SINGLES
68	MGM MGM 1384	Sunshine Day/Aeroplane (miscredited to 'Jethro Toe'; counterfeits credit 'Jethro Tull') 500
68	Island WIP 6043	A Song For Jeffrey/One For John Gee 40
68	Island WIP 6048	Love Story/A Christmas Song (2 different pink label designs) 10
68	Island WIP 6048	Love Story/A Christmas Song (mispressing, B-side or both sides credited to Ian Henderson) 18
69	Island WIP 6056	Living In The Past/Driving Song (2 different pink labels) 15
69	Chrysalis WIP 6070	Sweet Dream/17 (push-out or large centre hole) 7
70	Chrysalis WIP 6077	The Witch's Promise/Teacher (in p/s) 20
70	Chrysalis WIP 6077	The Witch's Promise/Teacher 15
70	Chrysalis WIP 6081	Inside/Alive And Well And Living In 10
71	Chrysalis WIP 6098	Lick Your Fingers Clean/Up To Me (unissued) 0
71	Chrysalis WIP 6106	Life Is A Long Song/Up The 'Pool/Dr. Bogenbroom/From Later/Nursie (EP, p/s) 8
74	Chrysalis CHS 2054	Bungle In The Jungle/Back Door Angels 6
75	Chrysalis CHS 2075	Minstrel In The Gallery/Summerday Sands 5
76	Chrysalis CHS 2135	Too Old To Rock'n'Roll: Too Young To Die/Rainbow Blues 5
76	Chrysalis CXP 2275	Ring Out Solstice Bells/March The Mad Scientist/A Christmas Song/Pan Dance (EP) 8
77	Chrysalis CHS 2135	The Whistler/Strip Cartoon (some in p/s) 25
77	Chrysalis CHS 2135	The Whistler/Strip Cartoon 8
78	Chrysalis CHS 2214	Moths/Life Is A Long Song (p/s) 10
78	Chrysalis CHS 2260	A Stitch In Time (3.30 Version)/Sweet Dream (p/s, white vinyl) 12
78	Chrysalis CHS 2260	A Stitch In Time (3.30 Version)/Sweet Dream (p/s, black vinyl) 8
78	Chrysalis CHS 2260	A Stitch In Time (4.20 Version)/Sweet Dream (p/s, white vinyl) 12
78	Chrysalis CHS 2260	A Stitch In Time (4.20 Version)/Sweet Dream (p/s, black vinyl) 8
79	Chrysalis CHS 2378	North Sea Oil/Elegy (p/s) 10
79	Chrysalis CHS 2394	Home/King Henry's Madrigal (Theme From Mainstream)/Warm Sporran (p/s) 12
79	Chrysalis CHS 2468	Working John, Working Joe/Flyingdale Flyer (p/s) 8
80	Chrysalis CHS 2619	Broadsword/Fallen On Hard Times (p/s) 6
80	Chrysalis CHSP 2619	Broadsword/Fallen On Hard Times (picture disc) 12
84	Chrysalis TULLD 1	Lap Of Luxury/Astronomy//Automotive Engineering/Tundra (double pack, gatefold p/s) ...10
84	Chrysalis TULL X 1	Lap Of Luxury/Astronomy//Automotive Engineering/Tundra (12", p/s) 10
86	Chrysalis TULL 2	Coronach (with David Palmer)/Jack Frost And The Hooded Crow (p/s) 7
86	Chrysalis TULLX 2	Coronach (with David Palmer)/Jack Frost And The Hooded Crow/ Living In The Past/Elegy (12", p/s) 40
87	Chrysalis TULLP 3	Steel Monkey/Down At The End Of Your Road (die-cut picture disc) 20
87	Chrysalis ZTULL 3	Steel Monkey/Down At The End Of Your Road/Too Many Too/I'm Your Gun (numbered edition of 3,000 with competition pack & badge) 15
87	Chrysalis TULLX 3	Steel Monkey/Down At The End Of Your Road/Too Many Too/I'm Your Gun (12", p/s) 10

88	Chrysalis TULLX 4	Said She Was A Dancer/Dogs In The Midwinter/The Waking Edge (p/s) 8
88	Chrysalis TULLP 4	Said She Was A Dancer/Dogs In The Midwinter (shaped picture disc) 10
88	Chrysalis TULLX 4	Said She Was A Dancer/Dogs In The Midwinter (12", p/s) 8
88	Chrysalis TULLCD 4	Said She Was A Dancer/Dogs In The Midwinter/Down At The End Of The Road/Too Many Too (CD, picture disc, limited issue)..............25
88	Chrysalis TULPCD 1	Part Of The Machine (Edit)/Stormy Monday Blues (live)/Lick Your Fingers Clean/ Minstrel In The Gallery (live)/Farm On The Freeway (live) (CD, picture disc)...........15
89	Chrysalis TULL 5	Another Christmas Song (p/s) 10
89	Chrysalis TULLCD 5	Another Christmas Song/Intro - A Christmas Song (live)/Cheap Day Return - Mother Goose (live)/Outro - Locomotive Breath (live) (CD) 10
89	Chrysalis TULLX5	Another Christmas Song/Intro-A Christmas Song/Cheap Day Return-Mother Goose/Outro-Locomotive Breath (12" p/s) 20
91	Chrysalis TULLX 6	This Is Not Love/Night In The Wilderness/Jump Start (12", p/s) 8
92	Chrysalis TULLCD 7	Rocks On The Road/Jack-A-Lynn (Home Demo)/Tall Thin Girl (live)/Fat Man (live)/Rocks On The Road/Bouree (live)/Mother Goose-Jack-A-Lynn (live)/Aqualung-Locomotive Breath (live) (2-CD boxed)...............8
92	Chrysalis TULLX 7	Rocks On The Road/Jack-A-Lynn (home demo)/ Aqualung-Locomotive Breath (live) (12", picture disc)...............10
93	Chrysalis 12CHS 3970	Living In The Past (Club Mix)/Living In The Past (7" mix) Living In The Past (Dub Ravey Master)/Living In The Past (Dub N.Y. Mix) (12", p/s)...............10
93	Chrysalis 23970/1	Living In The (Slightly More Recent) Past (live)/Silver River Turning/Rosa On The Factory Floor/I Don't Want To Be Me/Living In The Past/Truck Stop Runner/Piece Of Cake/Man Of Principle (2-CD set) 8
99	Papillon BTFLYS 0001	Bends Like A Willow (edit)/Dot Com (edit)/It All Trickles Down (CD) 15

ALBUMS

68	Island ILP 985	THIS WAS (1st pressing, pink label/black & orange 'circle' logo, mono) 300
68	Island ILPS 9085	THIS WAS (1st pressing, pink label/black & orange 'circle' logo, stereo, flipback sleeve, some sleeves as mono issues with stereo stickers) 120
69	Island ILPS 9103	STAND UP (1st pressing, gatefold sleeve pop-up inside, pink label/black & orange 'circle' logo)...............200
70	Chrysalis ILPS 9123	BENEFIT (green Chrysalis or Island pink rim label)...............100
70	Chrysalis ILPS 9123	BENEFIT (Island pink rim label 'palm tree' logo)...............45
71	Island ILPS 9145	AQUALUNG (1st pressing, Matrixes ILPS 9145 A//1U and ILPS B//3U, Chrysalis labels with white 'i' at top of label, with textured E.J. Day Group gatefold sleeve with ILPS 9145 on top right hand corner, inner bag)...............80
71	Island ILPS 9145	AQUALUNG (pink rim palm tree label, gatefold sleeve)...............150
72	Chrysalis CHR 1003	THICK AS A BRICK (LP, 1st pressing with white 'i' at top of label, Matrixes: CHR1003 A-3U/CHR1003 B-2U, 'Porky' etched into dead wax side 1, 'Pecko' etched into dead wax side 2, textured sleeve with fold-out newspaper sleeve)...............80
72	Chrysalis CJT 1	LIVING IN THE PAST (2-LP, with hard sleeve & booklet)...............30
73	Chrysalis CHR 1040	A PASSION PLAY (gatefold sleeve with matt finish, with Linwell theatre booklet, Matrix CHR1040 A4U/B4, green label without small white "i", later presses have red wording on rim and A2U matrix)...............45
74	Chrysalis CHR 1067	WARCHILD (with lyric inner sleeve)...............12
76	Chrysalis CHR 1111	TOO OLD TO ROCK 'N' ROLL...............12
77	Chrysalis CJT 4	LIVE - BURSTING OUT (2-LP, gatefold sleeve with inners)...............15

(First pressings of all above Chrysalis LPs have a white 'I' logo on the label. Second pressings without this are worth slightly less.)

78	Chrysalis CHR 1175	HEAVY HORSES (LP, with insert)...............15
84	Chrysalis CDLP 1461	UNDER WRAPS (picture disc)...............15
88	Chrysalis Tbox1	20 YEARS OF JETHRO TULL (5-LP box set with 24-page booklet)...............75
88	Chrysalis Tbox CD1	20 YEARS OF JETHRO TULL (3-CD box set with 24-page booklet)...............50
89	Chrysalis CHRP 0018	ROCK ISLAND (Picture disc)...............18
91	Chrysalis DCHR 1886	CATFISH RISING (Ltd edn. With 3-track 12" and lyric sheet inner sleeve) 20
93	Chrysalis CDCHR 6004	JETHRO TULL 25th ANNIVERSARY (4-CD cigar box set with 48-page booklet) 55

ALBUMS : LP REPRESSINGS

68	Island ILP 985	THIS WAS (pink label/'i' logo, mono)...............50
69	Island ILPS 9085	THIS WAS (pink label/black 'block' logo, 1st mix)...............25
70	Island ILPS 9085	THIS WAS (pink label/'i' logo)...............20
70	Chrysalis ILPS 9103	STAND UP (pop-up sleeve, pink label/black 'block' logo or pink label/'i' logo)...............18
73	Chrysalis CHR 1044	AQUALUNG (LP, repressing)...............12
96	Chrysalis LP25AQUA1	AQUALUNG (2-LP, 25th anniversary edition)...............50

PROMOS

76	Chrysalis CHS 3 PDJ	Ring Out/Solstice Bells/March, The Mad Scientist/Christmas Song/ Pan Dance (12", p/s) ...25
79	Chrysalis CHS018-PDJ	Dark Ages (Special edited version) 12" promo...............15
84	Chrysalis AS 1967	Under Wraps#1 (electric)/Under Wraps#2 (acoustic) (12" promo)...............12
87	Chrysalis VAS 1039	Budapest (Special Radio Edit) (12" promo with illustrated sticker)...............12
87	Chrysalis VAS 2796	Steel Monkey (12" promo)...............12
87	Chrysalis VAS 2866	Farm On The Freeway (Special Rock Radio Edit) (12" promo)...............15
88	Chrysalis VAS 1170	Part Of The Machine/Part Of The Machine (Edit) (12" promo with tour dates sticker)...........18
99	Fuel 2000 FLDPRO 1119	Bends Like A Willow (Radio Edit) (CD, 1-track promo)...............10
03	RandM RR Promo 743	'Live In Europe 2003' With You There To Help Me (live)/Someday The Sun Won't Shine For You (live) (CD)...............12

(see also Mick Abrahams, Blodwyn Pig, Wild Turkey, The John Even Band)

JETLINERS

| 66 | Blue Beat BB 367 | Meditation (actually by Sugar & Dandy)/GIRL SATCHMO: Nature Of Love (actually with Jetliners)...............35 |

JETS (1)

| 73 | Cube BUG 35 | Yeah!/Rusty Corinthian Pillar ....15 |
| 78 | Soho SH 3 | Rockabilly Baby/James Dean...............7 |

JETS (2)

| 79 | Decca FR 13867 | Tearaway/Impossible ....100 |

JET SET

| 62 | Delta DW 5001 | VC 10/Cruising 600 (some in p/s) ....15 |
| 64 | Parlophone R 5199 | You Got Me Hooked/True To You ....25 |

JETSET

84	Dance Network NET 1	BEST OF THE JETSET (EP) 10
85	Dance Network NET 3	APRIL, MAY, JUNE AND THE JETSET (12" EP) 12
85	Dance Network WORK 1	THERE GOES THE NEIGHBOURHOOD (LP, pink sleeve, poster)...............20
86	Dance Network WORK 4	4 GO BANANAS (LP, with lyric insert)...............20

(see also Paul Bevoir)

MINT VALUE £

JETSTREAMS
| 59 | Decca F 11149 | Bongo Rock/Tiger | 20 |
| 59 | Decca F 11149 | Bongo Rock/Tiger (78) | 15 |

JEVUTSHTA
| 78 | Zel-La JHSPS 226 | Fight Your Way Out/Stomp | 30 |

JEWELLS (JAMAICA)
| 77 | Observer OB 005 | Black is The Highest Culture (Culture Version)/One Little Lick Version (12") | 25 |
| 77 | Observer OB 1101 | Jah I/LEROY SMART: Jah Is My Light/I-ROY: Wicked Eat Dirt (12") | 25 |

JEWELS
| 64 | Colpix PX 11034 | Opportunity/Gotta Find A Way | 30 |
| 65 | Colpix PX 11048 | But I Do/Smokey Joe | 18 |

JIGSAW
68	Polydor 56241	I Need Your Love/I've Gotta Get Me Some Money (as Jig-Saw Band)	15
68	Music Factory CUB 4	Mister Job/Great Idea	15
68	Music Factory CUB 6	Let Me Go Home/Tumblin'	80
68	MGM MGM 1410	One Way Street/Then I Found You	100
70	Philips 6006 112	One Way Street/Coffucious Confusion	70
70	Fontana 6007 017	Lollipop And Goody Man/Seven Fishes	40
71	Philips 6006 131	Jesu Joy Of Man's Desiring/No Questions Asked	10
71	Philips 6006 182	Keeping My Head Above Water/It's Nice But It's Wrong	7
74	BASF BA 1002	I've Seen The Film I've Read The Book/Mention My Name	7
75	BASF BA 1013	Baby Don't Do It/Stand Next To Me	7
75	Spalsh CPI 1	Sky High/Brand New Love Affair	5
71	Philips 6308 033	LETHERSLADE FARM (LP)	60
72	Philips 6308 072	AURORA BOREALIS (LP)	40
73	BASF 29106-5	BROKEN HEARTED (LP, gatefold sleeve)	15
74	BASF BAP 5051	I'VE SEEN THE FILM, I'VE READ THE BOOK (LP)	12
75	Spash CPLP 1001	SKY HIGH (LP)	12

JIH
| 88 | Jungle JUNG 32T/BOV 3 | Take Me To The Girl/Come Summer Come Winter/Wake Up (12", unissue, Mayking test pressings only, white proof p/s) | 20 |
| 88 | Jungle JUNG 32T/BOV 3 | Take Me To The Girl/Come Summer Come Winter/Wake Up (12", 'small photos' p/s, later blue art p/s) | 10 |

(see also Associates)

JILL & BOULEVARDS
| 62 | Columbia DB 4823 | And Now I Cry/Eugene | 25 |

JILL & Y'VERNS
| 60s | Oak RGJ 503 | My Soulful Dress/Anything He Wants Me To Do | 100 |

JILTED JOHN
78	Rabid TOSH 105	Jilted John/Going Steady (p/s)	12
78	EMI International INT 567	Jilted John/Going Steady (p/s, reissue)	6
78	EMI International INT 577	True Love/I Was A Pre-Pubescent (p/s)	7
78	EMI International INT 587	The Birthday Kiss/Baz's Party (p/s)	7
78	EMI Intl. INS 3024	TRUE LOVE STORIES (LP, with board game insert)	18
78	EMI Intl. INS 3024	TRUE LOVE STORIES (LP)	12

(see also Going Red?)

JIM & JEAN
| 68 | Verve Folkways VLP 5017 | CHANGES (LP) | 40 |

JIM & JOE
| 64 | London HL 9831 | Fireball Mail/Daisy Mae | 20 |

(see also James Burton)

JIM & MONICA
| 64 | Stateside SS 266 | Slippin' And Slidin'/Sing Along Without Jim & Monica | 20 |

(see also Jimmy Gilmer & Fireballs)

JIMBILIN
| 71 | Bamboo BAM 68 | Human Race/Let Love In (both actually by Herman Chin-Loy & Aquarians) | 15 |
| 75 | Ashanti ASH 421 | Balaclava/Tacku | 12 |

JOSE JIMINEZ
| 61 | London HLR 9434 | The Astronaut Part 1/Part 2 | 6 |

JIMMIE & NIGHT HOPPERS
| 59 | London HLP 8830 | Cruisin'/Night Hop | 30 |
| 59 | London HLP 8830 | Cruisin'/Night Hop (78) | 30 |

JIMMY AND THE DIMENSIONS
| 69 | Youngblood YB 1008 | Sugar Man/Slow Down | 12 |

(see also Jimmy Powell & Red Alligator)

JIMMY J & CRU-L-T
| 94 | Knifeforce KF 027 | Take Me Away (Slipmatt Remix)/FUTURE PRIMITIVE: Life Me Up (Slammin' VInyl Remix) (12", p/s) | 15 |

JIVA
| 75 | Dark Horse AMLH 22003 | JIVA (LP, with inner sleeve) | 12 |

JIV-A-TONES
| 58 | Felsted AF 101 | Flirty Gertie/Fire Engine Baby | 200 |
| 58 | Felsted AF 101 | Flirty Gertie/Fire Engine Baby (78) | 70 |

JIVE FIVE
61	Parlophone R 4822	My True Story/When I Was Single	150
62	Stateside SS 133	What Time Is It?/Begging You Please	90
65	United Artists UP 1106	I'm A Happy Man/Kiss Kiss KIss	45

JIVERS (JAMAICA)
| 68 | Trojan TR 604 | Wear My Crown/Down On The Beach | 8 |

(see also Brother Dan Allstars)

JIVERS (U.S.)
56	Vogue V 9060	Little Mama/Cherie	650
56	Vogue V 9060	Little Mama/Cherie (78)	150
57	Vogue V 9068	Ray Pearl/Dear Little One	600
57	Vogue V 9068	Ray Pearl/Dear Little One (78)	150

JIVING JUNIORS
60	Blue Beat BB 4	Lollipop Girl/Dearest Darling	30
60	Blue Beat BB 5	My Heart's Desire/I Love You	40
60	Starlite ST45 028	Lovers Line/Tu-Woo-Up-Tu-Woo	40
61	Starlite ST45 049	Slop & Mash/My Sweet Angel	40
61	Blue Beat BB 36	Over The River/Hip Rub (with Hersan & His City Slickers)	30
62	Island WI 003	Sugar Dandy/Valerie	25
62	Island WI 027	Andrea/Don't Leave Me	25
63	Island WI 129	Sugar Dandy/Valerie (reissue)	20
73	United Artists UP 35494	Stay/Call Me	5

(see also Duke Reid)

J.J. ALLSTARS
68	Duke DU 3	One Dollar Of Music/CARL DAWKINS: I'll Make It Up	30
69	Trojan TR 691	Memphis Underground (Parts 1 & 2)	20
70	Duke DU 94	Collecting Coins/Cabbage Leaf	15
70	Duke DU 95	This Land (actually by Carl Dawkins)/Land Version	12
70	Escort ES 821	Mango Tree/The Removers (both actually by Winston Wright & J.J. All Stars)	20
71	Big Shot BI 570	Perseverence Version/CARL DAWKINS: Perseverance	12
71	Explosion EX 2051	I Feel Good (Version 2)/CARL DAWKINS: I Feel Good	10
71	Duke DU 135	Soup/Soup (Version)	10

(see also Lloyd Young, Bleechers, Ethiopians)

J.J. BAND
| 71 | CBS S 64396 | THE J.J. BAND (LP) | 25 |

JJ72
| 01 | Lakota LAK 70019 | Snow/Wounded (p/s) | 5 |
| 00 | Lakota LAKLP 0017 | JJ72 (LP) | 20 |

JJ'S POWERHOUSE
| 83 | Sillysybin COX 1657 | Running For The Line/Blackrods (no p/s) | 250 |

MARCY JO & EDDIE RAMBEAU
| 63 | Stateside SS 235 | Lover's Medley/When You Wore A Tulip | 10 |

(see also Eddie Rambeau)

JOANIE, JOHNNY & HAL
| 60 | Capitol CL 15126 | When You Lose The One You Love/Miracles Are Always Happening | 6 |

ANTONIO CARLOS JOBIM
| 70 | Paramount SPFL 260 | THE ADVENTURERS (LP, soundtrack) | 12 |
| 72 | CTI CTL 3 | STONE FLOWER (LP) | 12 |

JOBRIATH
73	Elektra K 12129	Take Me I'm Yours/Earthling	5
74	Elektra K 12156	Ooh La La/Gone Tomorrow	5
74	Elektra K 12156	Ooh La La/Gone Tomorrow (demo)	20
73	Elektra EKS 75070	JOBRIATH (LP)	15
74	Elektra K 42163	CREATURES OF THE STREET (LP)	15

JO'BURG HAWK
| 72 | Charisma CB 194 | Orang Utang/Dark Side Of The Moon | 5 |
| 73 | Charisma CAS 1064 | JO'BURG HAWK (LP, gatefold sleeve, large 'Mad Hatter' label) | 20 |

JOCELYNE JOCYA
| 69 | CBS 4177 | I Have Loved Me A Man/Time | 60 |
| 69 | CBS 4177 | I Have Loved Me A Man/Time (DJ copy) | 150 |

JODEY
| 79 | Elliejay EJSP 9242 | The Rocker/Front Man | 150 |

JODIMARS
56	Capitol CL 14518	Well Now, Dig This/Let's All Rock Together	75
56	Capitol CL 14518	Well Now, Dig This/Let's All Rock Together (78)	20
56	Capitol CL 14627	Rattle My Bones/Lotsa Love	75
56	Capitol CL 14627	Rattle My Bones/Lotsa Love (78)	20
56	Capitol CL 14641	Rattle Shakin' Daddy/Eat Your Heart Out Annie	75
56	Capitol CL 14641	Rattle Shakin' Daddy/Eat Your Heart Out Annie (78)	20
56	Capitol CL 14642	Dance The Bop/Boom, Boom My Bayou Baby	75
56	Capitol CL 14642	Dance The Bop/Boom, Boom My Bayou Baby (78)	20
56	Capitol CL 14663	Midnight/Clarabella	75
56	Capitol CL 14663	Midnight/Clarabella (78)	20
57	Capitol CL 14700	Cloud 99/Later	80
57	Capitol CL 14700	Cloud 99/Later (78)	25
70s	Bulldog BD 16	Well Now, Dig This/Dance The Bop	5
72	Specialty SPE 6608	WELL NOW DIG THIS (LP)	20

(see also Bill Haley & Comets)

JODY GRIND
| 69 | Transatlantic TRA 210 | ONE STEP ON (LP, gatefold sleeve, lilac label with 't' logo) | 125 |
| 70 | Transatlantic TRA 221 | FAR CANAL (LP, white/lilac label with 't' logo) | 125 |

(see also Vinegar Joe, Hummingbird, Heads, Hands & Feet)

JODY ST
| 81 | Lips LIPS1 | Fight Back/Granny Did It (private pressing) | 150 |
| 81 | Private Pressing | STREET (LP, private pressing) | 75 |

AL T. JOE (& CELESTIALS)
62	Dice CC 9	Rise Jamaica/I'm On My Own	15
62	Blue Beat BB 126	You Cheated On Me/This Heart Of Mine (as Al T. Joe & Celestials)	12
63	Blue Beat BB 166	Goodbye Dreamboat/Please Forgive Me	12

MINT VALUE £

63	Blue Beat BB 169	Fatso/Slow Boat	12
70	Duke DU 70	It's A Shame/Desertion	8
72	Duke DU 148	Vision/Young And Unlearned	5
72	Dynamic DYN 429	Oh What A Price/The Prisoners Song	5

(see also Jamaica Fats)

JOE & ANN
65	Black Swan WI 468	Gee Baby/Wherever You May Be	20

BILLY JOE & CHECKMATES
61	London HLU 9502	Percolator/Round & Round & Round & Round	8

CALYPSO JOE
69	Escort ES 801	Adults Only/Calalue	8

JOE COOL (& THE KILLERS)
77	Ariola ARO 105	I Just Don't Care/My Way (p/s)	25

JOE CROW
82	Cherry Red CHERRY 48	Compulsion/Absent Friends	12

JOE & DELLA
65	Doctor Bird DB 1043	So Close/BABA BROOKS : Eight Games	20

JOE & EDDIE
59	Capitol CL 15038	Green Grass/And I Believed	7
64	Vocalion V 9215	There's A Meetin' Here Tonight/Lonesome Traveller	5
65	Vocalion V 9238	Gabrielle/He's Got The Whole World In His Hands	5
65	Vocalion V 9242	Depend On Yourself/With You In Mind	5
65	Vocalion V-N 9246	Farewell/Hey Nelly Nelly	5
65	Vocalion V-P 9250	Walkin' Down The Line/It Ain't Me Babe	12
65	Vocalion VAN 8046	WALKIN' DOWN THE LINE (LP)	40

JOE 9T & THUNDERBIRDS
80s	Gemme JOE 9T/LYN 6526	Joe 9T Theme/THEY MUST BE RUSSIANS: Psycho Analysis (p/s, stamped white label)	7

(see also They Must Be Russians)

JOE 90
92	Full Effect FERT 112	Good Times/New Found Strength (12")	20

JOE PUBLIC
70s	Wavelength HURT 3	Herman's Back/Travelling With Raymond/Like It (p/s)	8

JOE PUBLIC
85	Capital CLA 55	Anti CND	20

(see also Long Tall Shorty)

JOE (MANSANO) THE BOSS
70	Joe JRS 6	Son Of Al Capone/All My Enemies	25
70	Joe JRS 10	If Life Was A Thing/LLOYD KINGPIN: Daisy Bothering	120

(see also Joe's Allstars, Joe Mansano, Dice The Boss, Pama Dice)

BILLY JOEL
72	Philips 6078 001	She's Got A Way/Everybody Loves You Now	8
74	Philips 6078 018	The Ballad Of Billy The Kid/If I Only Had The Words (To Tell You) (in p/s)	35
74	Philips 6078 018	The Ballad Of Billy The Kid/If I Only Had The Words (To Tell You)	25
79	CBS 7150	Honesty/Root Beer Rag (withdrawn)	20
72	Philips 6369 150	COLD SPRING HARBOR (LP)	15
73	Philips 6369 160	PIANO MAN (LP, withdrawn)	20
73	Philips 6078 018	BALLAD OF BILLY THE KID (LP)	12
78	CBS H 82311	THE STRANGER (LP, half-speed master version)	15

(see also Hassles)

JOE'S ALLSTARS
69	Joe/Duke DU 24	Hey Jude/Musical Feet	15
69	Joe/Duke DU 28	Battle Cry Of Biafra/Funky Reggae Part 1	15
69	Joe/Duke DU 50	Brixton Cat/Solitude	50
70	Joe JRS 9	Tony B's Theme/JOE THE BOSS: Skinhead Revolt	125
72	Sioux SI 012	Tony B's Theme/RAY MARTELL: She Caught The Train	12
70	Trojan TBL 106	BRIXTON CAT (LP)	35

(see also Joe The Boss, Dice The Boss, King Horror, Pattie La Donne)

JOE SOAP
73	Polydor 2383 233	KEEP IT CLEAN (LP, laminated sleeve, correction sticker on rear)	150

JOEY & CONTINENTALS
70	Polydor 56520	She Rides With Me/Rudy Vadoo	85

(see also G.T.O.'s)

JOEY & GENTLEMEN
64	Fontana TF 444	Like I Love You/I'll Never Let You Go	10
64	Fontana TF 485	Dummy Dum Song/Goodbye Little Girl	6

JOHANNE & JIMMY
64	Fontana TF 447	Everybody Knows/I Still Love you	8

HENRIK JOHANSEN'S JAZZ BAND
55	Tempo EXA 23	THE TRADITIONAL DANES (EP)	10
57	Tempo EXA 64	HENRIK JOHANSEN'S JAZZ BAND (EP)	10

(see also City Ramblers Skiffle Group, Al Fairweather)

JOHN
71	Capitol CL 15678	The Ten Lost Tribes Of Israel/Good Morning Old Man Time	10

ALEXSANDER JOHN
70s	Myrrh MYR 1010	DAYS GO BY (LP)	18

ANDREW JOHN
71	CBS 7017	Streets Of London/Rick Rack	10
72	CBS 64835	THE MACHINE STOPS (LP)	20

BASIL JOHN

60s	Planetone RC 12	Drink And Drive/MIKE ELLIOTT: J.K. Shuffle	10

CLIVE JOHN

75	United Artists UAS 29733	YOU ALWAYS KNOW WHERE YOU STAND WITH A BUZZARD (LP)	25

(see also Man)

DAVID JOHN & MOOD

64	Vocalion V 9220	To Catch That Man/Pretty Thing	220
65	Parlophone R 5255	Bring It To Jerome/I Love To See You Strut	250
65	Parlophone R 5301	Diggin' For Gold/She's Fine	250

(see also Gagalactyca, Astral Navigations, Little Free Rock)

ELTON JOHN

SINGLES

68	Philips BF 1643	I've Been Loving You/Here's To The Next Time	250
69	Philips BF 1739	Lady Samantha/All Across The Havens	50
69	DJM DJS 205	It's Me That You Need/Just Like Strange Rain (in p/s)	100
69	DJM DJS 205	It's Me That You Need/Just Like Strange Rain	50
70	DJM DJS 217	Border Song/Bad Side Of The Moon	25
70	DJM DJS 222	Rock And Roll Madonna/Grey Seal	30
71	DJM DJS 233	Your Song/Into The Old Man's Shoes	5
71	DJM DJS 244	Friends/Honey Roll	10
72	DJM DJX 501	Rocket Man/Holiday Inn/Goodbye (gatefold p/s)	10
72	DJM DJX 501	Rocket Man/Holiday Inn/Goodbye (plain p/s)	5
72	DJM DJS 269	Honky Cat/Lady Samantha/It's Me That You Need	6
72	DJM DJS 271	Crocodile Rock/Elderberry Wine	5
73	DJM DJS 275	Daniel/Skyline Pigeon	5
73	DJM DJ X502	Saturday Night's Alright For Fighting/Jack Rabbit/Whenever You're Ready (We'll Go Steady Again) (non-laminated p/s)	20
73	DJM DJX 502	Saturday Night's Alright For Fighting/Jack Rabbit/Whenever You're Ready (We'll Go Steady Again) (laminated p/s)	8
73	DJM DJS 290	Step Into Christmas/Ho! Ho! Ho! (Who'd Be A Turkey At Christmas)	8
73	DJM DJS 10705	Benny And The Jets/Rock 'N' Roll Madonna	6
74	DJM DJS 297	Candle In The Wind/Benny And The Jets	5
74	DJM DJS 302	Don't Let The Sun Go Down On Me/Sick City	5
74	DJM DJS 322	The Bitch Is Back/Cold Highway	5
74	DJM DJS 340	Lucy In The Sky With Diamonds (featuring Dr. Winston O'Boogie [John Lennon] & His Reggae Guitars)/One Day At A Time	5
75	DJM DJS 354	Philadelphia Freedom/I Saw Her Standing There (as Elton John Band; B-side featuring John Lennon with Muscle Shoals Horns) (p/s)	6
75	DJM DJS 610	Island Girl/Sugar On The Floor (p/s)	6
77	DJM DJR 18001	FOUR FROM FOUR EYES (EP)	8
78	DJM DJS 10902	Your Song/Border Song (p/s)	5
78	DJM DJS 10903	Honky Cat/Sixty Years On (p/s)	5
78	DJM DJS 10904	Country Comfort/Crocodile Rock (p/s)	5
78	DJM DJS 10905	Rocket Man/Daniel (p/s)	5
78	DJM DJS 10908	Candle In The Wind/I Feel Like A Bullet (In The Gun Of Robert Ford) (p/s, limited edition)	10
78	DJM DJS 10910	Island Girl/Saturday Night's Alright For Fighting (p/s, limited edition)	5
78	DJM DJS 10911	Philadelphia Freedom/Lucy In The Sky With Diamonds (reissue)	5
78	DJM DJS 10912	Pinball Wizard/Benny And The Jets (p/s)	5
78	DJM EJ 12	THE ELTON JOHN SINGLES COLLECTION (12 x 7" box set [DJS 10901-12])	50
78	DJM DJT 15000	FUNERAL FOR A FRIEND (12" EP)	10
80	DJM DJS 10961	Harmony/Mona Lisas And Mad Hatters (glossy p/s)	8
77	Rocket GOALD 1	The Goaldigger Song/Jimmy, Brian, Elton, Eric (mail-order, signed, 500 only, solid centre copies are counterfeits)	250
77	Rocket GOALD 1	The Goaldigger Song/Jimmy, Brian, Elton, Eric (mail-order, unsigned, 500 only, solid centre copies are counterfeits)	150
79	Rocket XPRES 20	Mama Can't Buy You Love/Strangers (p/s; withdrawn, misspelt "Mamma")	350
79	Rocket XPRES 21	Victim Of Love/Strangers (p/s)	7
79	Rocket XPRES 2412	Johnny B. Goode/Thunder In The Night (12", p/s)	10
80	Rocket XPRES 45	Dear God/Tactics (company sleeve)	40
80	Rocket ELTON 1	Dear God/Tactics//Steal Away Child/Love So Cold (double pack, p/s)	6
82	Rocket XPPIC 77	Empty Garden/Take Me Down To The Ocean (picture disc)	6
82	Rocket XPRPO 88	All Quiet On The Western Front/Where Have All The Good Times Gone (poster p/s)	10
83	Rocket XPRES 91	That's Why They Call It The Blues/Lord Choc Ice Goes Mental ('raised musical note' sleeve with shorter A-side title)	15
83	Rocket EJPIC 1	I'm Still Standing/Earn While You Learn (piano-shaped picture disc)	15
83	Rocket EJS 2/FREEJ 2	Kiss The Bride/Dreamboat//Ego/Song For Guy (double pack)	10
83	Rocket EJS 3/2	Cold As Christmas/Crystal//Don't Go Breaking My Heart/Snow Queen (double pack, gatefold p/s, 2nd 45 with Kiki Dee)	12
84	Rocket PHPIC 7	Sad Songs (Say So Much)/Simple Man (hat-shaped picture disc)	5
85	Rocket EJS 8	Act Of War (Part 1)/(Part 2) (with Millie Jackson, 'concertina pack' of video stills)	8
85	Rocket EJS 10/EJS 9	Wrap Her Up/Restless (live)//Nikita/The Man Who Never Died (double pack, stickered gatefold PVC wallet with 2 separate p/s's)	10
85	Rocket EJSP 10	Wrap Her Up/Restless (live) (with George Michael, oblong-shaped picture disc, with pictures on wrong sides)	25
85	Rocket EJS 1012/ELTON 1	Wrap Her Up (Extended Remix) (with George Michael)/Restless (live)// Nikita/Cold As Christmas (12", double pack in stickered PVC sleeve)	10
86	Rocket EJSP 13	Slow Rivers (with Cliff Richard)/Billy & The Kids (picture disc)	30
86	Rocket EJS 13-12	Slow Rivers (with Cliff Richard)/Billy & The Kids/Lord Of The Flies (12", p/s)	12
88	Rocket EJSP 15	Candle In The Wind (live)/Sorry Seems To Be The Hardest Word (live) (picture disc)	8
88	Rocket EJS 1512	Candle In The Wind (live)/Sorry Seems To Be The Hardest Word (live)/ Your Song (live)/Don't Let The Sun Go Down On Me (live) (12", p/s)	12
88	Rocket EJSCD 15	Candle In The Wind (live)/Sorry Seems To Be The Hardest Word (live)/ Your Song (live)/Don't Let The Sun Go Down On Me (live) (CD, card sleeve)	18
88	Rocket EJSIP 16	I Don't Wanna Go On With You Like That/Rope Around A Fool/ (Radio 1 interview) (33rpm, poster sleeve)	10
88	Rocket EJS 1612	I Don't Wanna Go On With You Like That (Remix)/(7" Version)/ Rope Around A Fool (12", blue vinyl factory custom pressing, no p/s)	150
90	Rocket EJS 21	Club At The End Of The Street/Give Peace A Chance (p/s, withdrawn)	200
90	Rocket EJS 2112	Club At The End Of The Street/Give Peace A Chance (12", p/s, withdrawn)	500
90	Rocket EJSCD 21	Club At The End Of The Street/Give Peace A Chance/ I Don't Wanna Go On With You Like That (Live in Verona) (CD withdrawn with "Made In England" credit)	20

MINT VALUE £

| 97 | Rocket EJSCD 41 | Something About The Way You Look Tonight (Edited Version)/ I Know Why I'm In Love/No Valentines/Something About The Way You Look Tonight (Album Version) (CD, card sleeve, unreleased) | 40 |
| 97 | Rocket EJSCX 41 | Something About The Way You Look Tonight (Edited Version)/ I Know Why I'm In Love/You Can Make History (Young Again)/Something About The Way You Look Tonight (Album Version) (CD, digipak, unreleased) | 75 |

ALBUMS

69	DJM DJLP 403	EMPTY SKY (gatefold sleeve, mono)	150
69	DJM DJLPS 403	EMPTY SKY (gatefold sleeve, stereo, with 'stereo' sticker on sleeve)	25
70	DJM DJLPS 406	ELTON JOHN (textured gatefold sleeve)	18
70	DJM DJLPD 406	ELTON JOHN (later smooth gatefold sleeve)	15
73	DJM DJLP 1001	GOODBYE YELLOW BRICK ROAD (2 x LP, gatefold)	15
76	DJM DJLPH 473	HERE AND THERE (with inner)	12
76	DJM DJE 29001	GOODBYE YELLOW BRICK ROAD (2-LP, yellow vinyl, triplefold sleeve)	20
78	DJM DJV 2300	CAPTAIN FANTASTIC AND THE BROWN DIRT COWBOY (picture disc)	40
78	DJM LSP 14512	ELTON JOHN (5-LP, box set)	40
70	Warlock Music WMM 101/2	WARLOCK MUSIC SAMPLER (untitled publishing sampler, 7 tracks by Elton, 4 by Linda Peters)	1000
91	Rocket 848 236-2	TO BE CONTINUED ... THE VERY BEST OF ELTON JOHN (4-CD, 12" x 8" box set with large colour booklet)	100
93	Happenstance HAPP 001	PLAYS THE SIRAN (private pressing, 50 only)	1000
93	Happenstance HAPP 002	THE FISHING TRIP (4-CD set, private pressing, 100 only, existence unconfirmed)	700
97	Rocket ELTON 50	CELEBRATING ELTON JOHN'S 50TH BIRTHDAY (promo only)	50
99	Mercury ADV 1999/1	AIDA (with Sir Tim Rice) (box set with wallet, plinth stand, interview CD, booklet and calender cards, promo only)	50
99	Mercury ADV 1999/1	AIDA PRESS KIT (card box set with wallet, plinth stand, interview CD, booklet, calender cards, scented candle and broadcast CD-R, promo only)	50
99	Rocket STAR 3	ELTON JOHN'S AIDA (export CD, card p/s, promo only)	20

(see also [Stu Brown &] Bluesology, Bread & Beer Band, Neil Sedaka, Kiki Dee, Aretha Franklin, Dionne Warwick Radio Heart, Argosy)o

JOHN LEE'S GROUNDHOGS

| 66 | Planet PLF 104 | Over You Baby/I'll Never Fall In Love Again | 100 |

(see also Groundhogs, Tony McPhee)

LITTLE WILLIE JOHN

56	Parlophone DP 510	All Around The World/Don't Leave Me Dear (78, export issue)	30
56	Parlophone R 4209	Fever/Letter From My Darling	200
56	Parlophone R 4209	Fever/Letter From My Darling (78)	50
58	Parlophone R 4396	Uh, Uh, Baby/Dinner Date (With His Girl Friend)	60
58	Parlophone R 4396	Uh, Uh, Baby/Dinner Date (With His Girl Friend) (78)	35
58	Parlophone R 4432	Talk To Me, Talk To Me/Spasms	50
58	Parlophone R 4432	Talk To Me, Talk To Me/Spasms (78)	45
58	Parlophone R 4472	Let's Rock While The Rockin's Good/You're A Sweetheart	75
58	Parlophone R 4472	Let's Rock While The Rockin's Good/You're A Sweetheart (78)	40
59	Parlophone R 4571	Leave My Kitten Alone/Let Nobody Love You	60
60	Parlophone R 4674	Heartbreak (It's Hurtin' Me)/Do You Love Me	30
60	Parlophone R 4699	Sleep/There's A Difference	30
61	Parlophone R 4728	Walk Slow/HANK BALLARD: The Hoochie Coochie Coo	40
59	Parlophone PMC 1163	SURE THINGS (LP)	250
64	London HA 8126	COME ON AND JOIN LITTLE WILLIE JOHN (LP)	100

MABLE JOHN

66	Atlantic 584 022	It's Catching/Your Good Thing (Is About To End)	15
67	Stax 601 010	Same Time Same Place/Bigger And Better (dark blue label)	15
67	Stax 601 010	Same Time Same Place/Bigger And Better (light blue label)	10
68	Stax 601 034	Able Mable/Don't Get Caught	15

ROBERT JOHN

68	CBS 3436	If You Don't Want My Love/Don't	15
68	CBS 3730	Don't Leave Me/Children	5
68	A&M AMS 835	Raindrops Love And Sunshine/When The Party Is Over	50

SAMMIE JOHN

| 67 | Stateside SS 585 | Little John/Boss Bag | 25 |

JOHN & JOHNNY

| 63 | Decca F 11719 | I Want You To Be My Girl/It's You | 6 |

JOHN & PAUL

| 65 | London HLU 9997 | People Say/I'm Walkin' | 15 |

JOHNNIE & JOE

| 58 | London HLM 8682 | Over The Mountain, Across The Sea/My Baby's Gone, On, On | 350 |
| 58 | London HLM 8682 | Over The Mountain, Across The Sea/My Baby's Gone, On, On (78) | 75 |

JOHNNY DANGEROUSLY

| 90 | Village (no cat no) | Introducing Jane/Tear It Down/Subway Life (12" p/s) | 20 |
| 89 | Village (no cat no) | YOU, ME AND THE ALARM CLOCK (mini LP p/s with photo insert, 1,000 only) | 35 |

(see also I Am Kloot)

LITTLE JOHNNY JONES

| 73 | Pressure Beat PB 5515 | More Dub/More Dub - Chapter Two | 8 |

(see also Johnny Lover)

JOHNNY RONDO TRIO

| 78 | Chiltern Sound RONDO 1 | Las Bicicletas/Frog Dance (p/s, trio of Lol Coxhill, Chris Wood and Dave Holland) | 10 |

(see also Lol Coxhill)

JOHNNY (OSBORNE) & ATTRACTIONS

| 67 | Doctor Bird DB 1118 | Young Wings Can Fly/DUDLEY WILLIAMSON: I'm Moving On | 150 |
| 68 | Doctor Bird DB 117 | Coming On The Scene/Anything You Want | 200 |

JOHNNY & THE ATTRACTIONS

| 68 | Doctor Bird DB 1118 | Young Wings Can Fly/DUDLEY WILLIAMSON: I'm Moving On | 150 |

JOHNNY (STEVENS) & THE BLUE BEATS

| 64 | Blue Beat BB 229 | Shame/Ball And Chain | 15 |

JOHNNY & CHARLEY
65	Pye Int. 7N 25326	La Yenka/Baila La Yenka	10

JOHNNY & CHAZ & GUNNERS
61	Decca F 11365	Bobby/Out Of Luck	22

JOHNNY & THE COPYCATS
64	Norco AB 102	I'm A Hog For You Baby/I Can Never See You	60

(see also My Dear Watson)

JOHNNY & THE HURRICANES
59	London HL 8899	Crossfire/Lazy (triangular-centre)	20
59	London HL 8899	Crossfire/Lazy (later round centre)	10
59	London HL 8899	Crossfire/Lazy (78 rpm)	20
59	London HL 8948	Red River Rock/Buckeye (triangular-centre)	10
59	London HL 8948	Red River Rock/Buckeye (later round centre)	5
59	London HL 8948	Red River Rock/Buckeye (78)	30
59	London HL 9017	Reveille Rock/Time Bomb (triangular-centre)	10
59	London HL 9017	Reveille Rock/Time Bomb (later round centre)	5
59	London HL 9017	Reveille Rock/Time Bomb (78)	40
60	London HLI 9072	Beatnick Fly/Sand Storm	5
60	London HLI 9072	Beatnick Fly/Sand Storm (78)	40
60	London HLX 9134	Down Yonder/Sheba	5
60	London HLX 9134	Down Yonder/Sheba (78)	50
60	London HLX 9190	Rocking Goose/Revival	5
60	London HLX 9190	Rocking Goose/Revival (78)	90
60	London HL 7099	The Hep Canary/Catnip (export issue)	45
61	London HLX 9289	Ja-Da/Mr. Lonely	6
61	London HLX 9378	High Voltage/Old Smokie	10
62	London HLX 9491	Farewell, Farewell/Traffic Jam	10
62	London HLX 7116	You Are My Sunshine/Farewell, Farewell (export issue)	30
62	London HLX 9536	Salvation/Misirlou	18
62	London HLX 9617	Minnesota Fats/Come On Train	15
63	London HLX 9660	Whatever Happened To Baby Jane/Greens And Beans	12
64	Stateside SS 347	Money Honey/That's All	15
61	London REX 1284	ROCKING GOOSE (EP)	20
62	London REX 1347	JOHNNY AND THE HURRICANES (EP)	20
64	London REX 1414	JOHNNY AND THE HURRICANES VOL. 2 (EP)	20
60	London HA 2227	RED RIVER ROCK (LP, plum label)	50
60	London HA-I 2269	STORMSVILLE (LP)	30
61	London HA-X 2322	THE BIG SOUND OF JOHNNY AND THE HURRICANES (LP)	40
61	London HA 2227	RED RIVER ROCK (LP, reissue, black label)	25

JOHNNY & JACK
54	HMV 7MC 21	Honey, I Need You/Goodnight, Well It's Time To Go (export issue)	20
55	HMV JO 440	Beware Of "It"/Kiss Crazy Baby (78, export)	10
56	HMV JO 456	Weary Moments/S.O.S. (78, export)	10
59	RCA RCA 1145	Sailor Man/Wild And Wicked World	5
59	RCA RCA 1145	Sailor Man/Wild And Wicked World (78)	12
59	RCA RCX 176	COUNTRY GUITAR VOL. 10 (EP)	10

JOHNNY & JAMMERS
79	Big Beat NS 55	School Day Blues/You Know I Love You (p/s)	5

(see also Johnny Winter)

JOHNNY & JOHN
66	Polydor 56087	Bumper To Bumper/Scrape My Boot	30

(see also Johnny Gustafson, Big Three)

JOHNNY & JUDY
59	Vogue Pop V 9128	Bother Me Baby/Who's To Say	650
59	Vogue Pop V 9128	Bother Me Baby/Who's To Say (78)	150

(see also John Walker)

JOHNNY & THE SELF ABUSERS
77	Chiswick NS 22	Saints And Sinners/Dead Vandals (p/s)	25

(see also Simple Minds)

JOHNNY & VIBRATONES
63	Warner Bros WB 107	Bird Stompin'/Movin' The Bird	12

JOHNNY F & KLM
92	Liberty Grooves LIB003	TAKIN' LIBERTIES VOL 1 (LP)	20

JOHNNY MOPED
76	Chiswick PROMO 3	BASICALLY, THE ORIGINAL JOHNNY MOPED TAPE (33rpm, no p/s)	20
77	Chiswick S 15	No-One/Incendiary Device (p/s)	7
78	Chiswick NS 27	Darling, Let's Have Another Baby/Something Else/It Really Digs (p/s)	6
78	Chiswick NS 41	Little Queenie/Hard Lovin' Man (p/s)	8
78	Chiswick WIK 8	CYCLEDELIC (LP, with free single [PROMO 3])	30
78	Chiswick WIK 8	CYCLEDELIC (LP, without free single [PROMO 3])	12
90	Deltic DELTLP 6	THE SEARCH FOR XERTES (LP)	20

(see also Slime, Maxim's Trash)

JOHNNY'S BOYS
59	Decca F 11156	Sleep Walk/Ciao Ciao Bambina	10

JOHNNY'S JAZZ
56	Decca FJ 10663	R.J. Boogie/Get Happy (featuring Johnny Hawksworth)	6

(see also Johnny Hawksworth)

JOHN'S CHILDREN
66	Columbia DB 8030	The Love I Thought I'd Found/Strange Affair (very few in p/s)	500
66	Columbia DB 8030	The Love I Thought I'd Found/Strange Affair	300
67	Columbia DB 8124	Just What You Want - Just What You'll Get/But She's Mine	160
67	Track 604 003	Desdemona/Remember Thomas A'Beckett (in p/s)	150
67	Track 604 003	Desdemona/Remember Thomas A'Beckett	60

MINT VALUE £

67	Track 604 005	Midsummer Night's Scene/Sara Crazy Child (withdrawn)	4000
67	Track 604 005	Come And Play With Me In The Garden/Sara Crazy Child (in p/s)	200
67	Track 604 005	Come And Play With Me In The Garden/Sara Crazy Child	90
67	Track 604 010	Go Go Girl/Jagged Time Lapse	80
82	Cherry Red BRED 31	ORGASM (LP, with inner)	20
87	Bam Caruso KIRI 095	MIDSUMMER NIGHT'S SCENE (LP)	30

(see also Marc Bolan, Andy Ellison, Radio Stars, Jook, Tyrannosaurus Rex)

GLYN JOHNS
62	Decca F 11478	January Blues/Sioux Indian	5
63	Decca F 11753	Old Deceiver Time/Dancing With You	5
65	Immediate IM 013	Mary Anne/Like Grains Of Yellow Sand	25
65	Pye 7N 15818	I'll Follow The Sun/I'll Take You Dancing	5
60s	Westcot LYN 827/828	Today You're Gone/Such Stuff Of Dreams (freebie with jeans offer)	5

GLYNIS JOHNS
| 54 | Columbia SCM 5149 | I Can't Resist Men/Always You | 8 |

LYNDON JOHNS (& ISRAELITES)
| 69 | Downtown DT 444 | Don't Gamble With Love/Song Bird | 5 |
| 69 | Downtown DT 451 | Oh Mama Oh Papa/Bring Back The Night (with The Israelites) | 5 |

AL JOHNSON & JEAN CARN
| 80 | CBS 8545 | I'm Back For More/You Are My Personal Angel | 10 |

(see also Jean Carn)

ALEC JOHNSON
| 79 | RFP RFP 001 | Busman's Holiday (no p/s) | 12 |

(see also Nightwing)

ANTHONY JOHNSON
82	Rusty R 005	Dread Locks Fight/ANTHONY JOHNSON & RANKING TOYAN: Babyloving (12"	35
81	Greensleeves GRED 76	Let Go This One/BILLY BOYO: One Spliff A Day (12")	20
83	Rusty RILP 003	I'M READY (LP)	25
82	Midnight Rock MRLP 002	GUN SHOT (LP)	30

BETTY JOHNSON
56	London HLU 8307	I'll Wait/Please Tell Me Why	40
56	London HLU 8326	Honky Tonk Rock/Say It Isn't So, Joe	100
56	London HLU 8326	Honky Tonk Rock/Say It Isn't So, Joe (78)	50
57	London HLU 8365	I Dreamed/If It's Wrong To Love You	40
57	London HLU 8432	1492/Little White Lies	25
57	London HLU 8432	1492/Little White Lies (78)	12
58	London HLE 8557	Little Blue Man/Song You Heard When You Fell In Love	25
58	London HLE 8557	Little Blue Man/Song You Heard When You Fell In Love (78)	12
58	London HLE 8678	Dream/How Much	15
58	London HLE 8678	Dream/How Much (78)	20
58	London HLE 8701	There's Never Been A Night/Mr. Brown Is Out Of Town	40
58	London HLE 8701	There's Never Been A Night/Mr. Brown Is Out Of Town (78)	25
58	London HLE 8725	Hoopa Hoola/One More Time	25
58	London HLE 8725	Hoopa Hoola/One More Time (78)	25
59	London HLE 8839	Does Your Heart Beat For Me?/You And Only You	20
59	London HLE 8839	Does Your Heart Beat For Me?/You And Only You (78)	30
59	London RE-E 1221	DREAM (EP)	75
59	London HA-E 2163	THE SONG YOU HEARD WHEN YOU FELL IN LOVE (LP)	40

BLIND WILLIE JOHNSON
50s	Square M1	Dark Was The Night, Cold Was The Ground/Lord I Just Can't Keep From Crying (78)	10
58	Fontana TFE 17052	TREASURES OF NORTH AMERICAN NEGRO MUSIC NO. 2 (EP)	20
70	Xtra XTRA 1098	BLIND WILLIE JOHNSON (LP)	20

BOB JOHNSON & PETE KNIGHT
| 77 | Chrysalis CHR 1137 | THE KING OF ELFLAND'S DAUGHTER (LP, lyric insert, green label) | 15 |

(see also Steeleye Span, Mary Hopkin)

BOBBY JOHNSON & ATOMS
| 67 | Ember EMB S 245 | Do It Again A Little Bit Slower/Tramp (in p/s) | 20 |
| 67 | Ember EMB S 245 | Do It Again A Little Bit Slower/Tramp | 10 |

BROWNIE JOHNSON
| 62 | Longhorn BLH 0004 | Best Dressed Beggar/Just Pretending (estimated that atound 1000 pressed) | 20 |

BRYAN JOHNSON
| 60 | Decca F11213 | Looking, High, High, High/Each Tomorrow | 6 |

BUBBER JOHNSON
| 57 | Parlophone R 4259 | Confidential/Have A Little Faith In Me | 35 |
| 57 | Parlophone R 4259 | Confidential/Have A Little Faith In Me (78) | 12 |

BUDDY JOHNSON
55	Mercury MB 3231	Upside Your Head/ELLA JOHNSON: Crazy About A Saxophone (78)	12
59	Mercury ZEP 10009	BUDDY JOHNSON WAILS (EP, with Ella Johnson)	80
57	Mercury MPT 7515	ROCK AND ROLL (10" LP, with Ella Johnson)	175

BUNK JOHNSON (& HIS NEW ORLEANS BAND)
55	HMV 7M 141	When The Saints Go Marching In/Darktown Strutters' Ball	5
50s	Melodisc EPM7 52	ONE YOU LOVE (EP)	10
52	Jazz Man no cat. no.	MANDADISC (LP, with the Original Superior Band)	15
54	Goodtime Jazz LDG 110	BUNK JOHNSON AND THE YERBA BUENA JAZZ BAND (10" LP)	15
59	Melodisc MLP 12-112	BUNK JOHNSON AND HIS NEW ORLEANS JAZZ BAND (LP, w/ George Lewis)	15

CAREY JOHNSON
| 72 | Banana BA 369 | Correction Train/SOUL DEFENDERS: Version | 18 |

DOMINO JOHNSON
| 72 | Green Door GD 4045 | Summertime/SWANS: Grazing | 5 |

DOMINO JOHNSON & CHAMPIONS
| 70 | Duke DU 89 | You Broke My Heart/TONY & CHAMPIONS: Tell Me The Reason | 8 |

GENERAL JOHNSON

73	Invictus INV 531	Only Time Will Tell/Only Time Will Tell (Instrumental Version)	8
76	Arista ARIST 45	All In The Family/Ready, Willing And Able	6
73	Invictus SVT 1008	GENERALLY SPEAKING (LP)	20

(see also Norman Johnson, Showmen, Chairmen Of The Board)

GINGER JOHNSON AND HIS AFRICAN MESSENGERS

| 67 | Masquerade SM 02001 | AFRICAN PARTY (LP) | 125 |

HOWARD JOHNSON

| 71 | Jay Boy BOY 47 | The Slide/That Magic Touch Can Send You Flying | 15 |

JAMES P. JOHNSON

54	Columbia SCM 5127	Feeling Blues/Riffs	8
57	HMV 7EG 8215	LOUISIANA SUGAR BABIES (EP, with Fats Waller)	8
54	London AL 3511	EARLY HARLEM PIANO (10" LP)	15
55	London AL 3540	EARLY HARLEM PIANO VOLUME 2 (10" LP)	15

JIMMY JOHNSON

| 65 | Sue WI 387 | Don't Answer The Door Parts 1 & 2 | 30 |

J.J. JOHNSON

55	Vogue LDE 124	J.J. JOHNSON SEXTET (10" LP)	15
55	Vogue LDE 162	J.J. JOHNSON QUINTET (10" LP)	15
60	Fontana TFL 5041	J.J. IN PERSON (LP)	12
61	Fontana TFL 5137	BLUE TROMBONE (LP, also stereo STFL 559)	12
73	United Artists UAS 29451	ACROSS 110TH STREET (LP, soundtrack, with Bobby Womack)	20

(see also Sonny Stitt)

(JOHNNY JOHNSON &) THE BANDWAGON

68	Direction 58-3520	Baby Make Your Own Sweet Music/On The Day We Fall In Love (as Bandwagon)	6
68	Direction 58-3670	Breaking Down The Walls Of Heartache/Dancin' Master (as Bandwagon)	6
69	Direction 58-3923	You/You Blew Your Cool And Lost Your Fool	6
69	Direction 58-4180	Let's Hang On/I Ain't Lying (withdrawn)	12
69	Direction 58-4180	Let's Hang On/Don't Let It In	6
70	Bell BLL 111	Sweet Inspiration/Pride Comes Before A Fall	5
72	Stateside SS 2207	Honey Bee/I Don't Know Why	20
74	EMI EMI 2114	Strong Love, Proud Love/Fast Running Out Of World	25
69	Direction 8-63500	JOHNNY JOHNSON AND THE BANDWAGON (LP)	30
70	Bell SBLL 138	SOUL SURVIVOR (LP)	25

JUDI JOHNSON (& PERFECTIONS)

| 64 | HMV POP 1371 | My Baby's Face/Make The Most Of It (solo) | 15 |
| 65 | HMV POP 1399 | How Many Times/A Way Out (as Judi Johnson & Perfections) | 20 |

LARRY JOHNSON

| 70 | Blue Horizon 7-63851 | PRESENTING THE COUNTRY BLUES (LP) | 150 |

LAURIE JOHNSON ORCHESTRA

56	HMV 7MC 47	Buttercup/Lullaby Of The Leaves (export issue)	10
57	HMV POP 404	The Moonraker/Call Of The Casbah	7
60	Pye 7N 15251	No Hiding Place/The Deputy	6
64	Pye 7N 15599	Dr Strangelove Theme/Nevada	6
64	Pye 7N 15715	Call Me Irresponsible/The Beauty Jungle	6
65	Pye 7N 15933	Latin Quarter/M1 (in p/s)	8
65	Pye 7N 15933	Latin Quarter/M1	6
65	Pye 7N 17015	The Avengers/Minor Bossa Nova (in p/s)	50
65	Pye 7N 17015	The Avengers/Minor Bossa Nova	30
69	MGM MGM 1457	There Is Another Song/Caesar Smith	25
71	Columbia DB 8826	The Jason King Theme/There Comes A Time	50
76	EMI EMI 2562	The New Avengers Theme/A Flavour Of The Avengers (in p/s)	10
76	EMI EMI 2562	The New Avengers Theme/A Flavour Of The Avengers	6
80	Unicorn Kachana MCPS 5	The Professionals Main Title/On Target/The New Avengers Main Title (p/s, by Laurie Johnson & London Studio Orchestra)	6
57	Parlophone GEP 8604	THE GOOD COMPANIONS (EP)	15
58	Pye Nixa NEP 24083	OPERATION ORCHESTRA (EP)	8
58	Pye Nixa NPL 18017	SONGS OF THREE SEASONS (LP)	15
63	Pye NPL 18088	THE NEW BIG SOUND OF THE LAURIE JOHNSON ORCHESTRA (LP)	20
65	Pye NPL 18103	THE BIG NEW SOUND STRIKES AGAIN (LP)	20
66	Pye NPL 18136	TWO CITIES SUITE (LP)	12
67	Marble Arch MAL 695	THE AVENGERS AND OTHER FAVOURITES (LP)	25
68	Columbia S(C)X 6206	SOMETHING'S COMING (LP, mono/stereo)	12
69	MGM C(S) 8104	THEMES AND ... (LP)	25
70	Columbia SCX 6412	LAURIE JOHNSON/LONDON JAZZ ORCHESTRA - SYNTHESIS (LP, with Joe Harriott, Tubby Hayes, Stan Tracey & Tony Coe)	60
71	Columbia SCX 6464	CONQUISTADORS (LP)	12
73	Ronco RR 2006	THE BELSTONE FOX (LP, soundtrack, gatefold sleeve)	12
80	Unicorn Kachana KPM 7009	MUSIC FROM THE AVENGERS, THE NEW AVENGERS AND THE PROFESSIONALS (LP, gatefold sleeve, with London Studio Orchestra)	20

(see also Polka Dots)

LINTON KWESI JOHNSON

78	Virgin VX 1002	DREAD BEAT AN' BLOOD (LP, as Poet & The Roots)	15
79	Island ILPS 9566	FORCES OF VICTORY (LP, with inner sleeve)	15
80	Island ILPS 9505	BASS CULTURE (LP)	15

LONNIE JOHNSON

51	Vogue V 2015	Drunk Again/Jelly Roll Baker (78)	30
51	Vogue V 2079	Happy New Year/Little Rockin' Chair (78)	30
51	Melodisc MEL 1138	Rocks In My Bed/Solid Blues (78)	30
51	Melodisc MEL 1186	Blues For Everybody/In Love Again (78)	30
52	Melodisc MEL 1221	Blues In My Soul/Keep What You Got (78)	30
57	Parlophone GEP 8635	LONESOME ROAD (EP)	30
57	Parlophone GEP 8663	LONNIE'S BLUES (EP)	30
58	Parlophone GEP 8693	LONNIE'S BLUES NO. 2 (EP)	30
64	Storyville SLP 162	PORTRAITS IN BLUES VOL. 6 (LP)	30

Lou JOHNSON

64	Storyville 616 010	SEE SEE RIDER (LP, with Otis Spann)	40
60s	Xtra XTRA 1037	LONNIE JOHNSON (LP)	25

(see also Eddie Lang & Lonnie Johnson)

LOU JOHNSON
63	London HLX 9805	Reach Out For Me/Magic Potion	50
63	London HLX 9805	Reach Out For Me/Magic Potion (DJ copy)	100
64	London HLX 9917	(There's) Always Something There To Remind Me/Wouldn't That Be Something	25
64	London HLX 9929	A Message To Martha (Kentucky Bluebird)/The Last One To Be Loved	15
65	London HLX 9965	Please Stop The Wedding/Park Avenue	20
65	London HLX 9994	A Time To Love, A Time To Cry/Unsatisfied	80
65	London HLX 9994	A Time To Love, A Time To Cry/Unsatisfied (DJ copy)	150
69	London HLX 10269	(There's) Always Something There To Remind Me/Message To Martha	10
64	London REX 1438	THE MAGIC POTION OF LOU JOHNSON (EP)	150

LUTHER 'GEORGIA BOY SNAKE' JOHNSON
69	Transatlantic TRA 188	THE MUDDY WATERS BLUES BAND (LP, credits Muddy Waters on label)	30

MARV JOHNSON
59	London HLT 8856	Come To Me/Whisper	100
59	London HLT 8856	Come To Me/Whisper (78 rpm = £75)	75
59	London HLT 9013	You Got What It Takes/Don't Leave Me	15
59	London HLT 9013	You Got What It Takes/Don't Leave Me (tri centre)	25
59	London HLT 9013	You Got What It Takes/Don't Leave Me (78)	65
60	London HLT 9109	I Love The Way You Love/Let Me Love You	20
60	London HL 7095	I Love The Way You Love/Let Me Love You (export issue)	20
60	London HLT 9165	Ain't Gonna Be That Way/All The Love I've Got	20
60	London HLT 9187	(You've Got To) Move Two Mountains/I Need You	20
61	London HLT 9265	Happy Days/Baby, Baby	20
61	London HLT 9311	Merry-Go-Round/Tell Me That You Love Me	45
65	Tamla Motown TMG 525	Why Do You Want To Let Me Go/I'm Not A Plaything	115
69	United Artists UP 35010	I Love The Way You Love/You Got What It Takes	6
68	Tamla Motown TMG 680	I'll Pick A Rose For My Rose/You Got The Love I Love	6
69	Tamla Motown TMG 713	I Miss You Baby (How I Miss You)/Bad Girl	10
70	Tamla Motown TMG 737	So Glad You Chose Me/I'm Not A Plaything	12
60	London HA-T 2271	MARVELLOUS MARV JOHNSON (LP)	150
69	T. Motown TML 11111	I'LL PICK A ROSE FOR MY ROSE (LP, mono)	30
69	T. Motown STML 11111	I'LL PICK A ROSE FOR MY ROSE (LP, stereo)	25

MATT JOHNSON
81	4AD CAD 113	BURNING BLUE SOUL (LP, original 'psychedelic eye' cover)	18

(see also Gadgets, The The)

MIRRIAM JOHNSON
61	London HLW 9337	Lonesome Road/Young And Innocent	15

NORMAN JOHNSON (& SHOWMEN)
69	Action ACT 4529	You're Everything/Our Love Will Grow	50
69	Action ACT 4545	Take It Baby/In Paradise	50
71	Action ACT 4601	You're Everything/Our Love Will Grow (reissue)	30

(see also General Johnson, Chairmen Of The Board, Showmen)

PETE JOHNSON
51	Vogue V 2007	J.J. Boogie/Yancey Special (78, red label)	10
51	Vogue V 2007	J.J. Boogie/Yancey Special (78, orange label)	12
51	Vogue V 2008	Swanee River Boogie/St. Louis Boogie (78, red label)	12
51	Vogue V 2008	Swanee River Boogie/St. Louis Boogie (78, red orange label)	15
51	Vogue V 2019	Hollywood Boogie/Central Avenue Drag (78, orange label)	15
56	Vogue V 2007	J.J. Boogie/Yancey Special	35
56	Vogue V 2008	Swanee River Boogie/St. Louis Boogie	30
55	Vogue EPV 1039	PETE JOHNSON (EP)	30
59	Top Rank JKR 8009	ROLL 'EM BOY (EP)	25
55	London AL 3549	JUMPIN' WITH PETE JOHNSON (10" LP)	50
55	Vogue Coral LRA 10016	BOOGIE WOOGIE MOOD (LP)	30

(see also Joe Turner & Pete Johnson, Albert Ammons & Meade Lux Lewis)

PHILIP JOHNSON
82	Namedrop NR3	YOUTH IN MOURNING (LP, with 4 double sided A4 sheets)	20

PLAS JOHNSON (ORCHESTRA)
57	Capitol CL 14772	The Big Twist/Come Rain Or Come Shine	20
57	Capitol CL 14816	Swanee River Rock/You Send Me	20
58	Capitol CL 14836	Popcorn/Hoppin' Mad	20
58	Capitol CL 14903	Little Rockin' Deacon/Dinah	20
59	Capitol CL 14973	Robbins Nest Cha Cha/Plaz Jazz	10
57	London HB-U 1078	BOP ME DADDY (10" LP)	60

PROFESSOR JOHNSON & HIS GOSPEL SINGERS
51	Vocalion V 1013	Give Me That Old Time Religion/Where Shall I Be (78)	20
58	Brunswick OE 9352	PROFESSOR JOHNSON AND HIS GOSPEL SINGERS (EP)	20

RAY JOHNSON
57	Vogue V 9073	If You Don't Want Me Baby/Calypso Joe	40
57	Vogue V 9073	If You Don't Want Me Baby/Calypso Joe (78)	15
58	Vogue V 9093	Calypso Blues/Are You There	40
58	Vogue V 9093	Calypso Blues/Are You There (78)	15

ROBERT JOHNSON
62	Philips BBL 7539	ROBERT JOHNSON 1936-1937 (LP)	100
65	CBS BPG 62456	KING OF THE DELTA BLUES SINGERS (LP)	45
67	Kokomo K 1000	ROBERT JOHNSON (LP)	80
60s	Smokestack SS/LP 1	BLUES LEGEND 1936-1937 (LP)	50
70	CBS 64102	KING OF THE DELTA BLUES SINGERS VOL. 2 (LP)	30

ROY LEE JOHNSON
69	Action ACT 4518	So Anna Just Love Me/Boogaloo No. 3 (Red label)	35
69	Action ACT 4518	So Anna Just Love Me/Boogaloo No. 3 (Yellow label)	30

RUBY JOHNSON
67	Stax 601 020	If I Ever Needed Love (I Sure Do Need It Now)/Keep On Keeping On 25

SPIDER JOHNSON & POPEYE BAND
63	Riverside RIF 106904	Doin' The Popeye/The Gospel Truth...............5

SYL JOHNSON
73	London HL 10403	We Did It/Anyway The Wind Blows...............10
73	London HL 10438	Back For A Taste Of Your Love/Wind Blow Her Back My Way...............6
75	London HL 10476	Let Yourself Go/Please Don't Give Up On Me 6

(see also Lula Reed)

T J JOHNSON
83	Switch DSW 003	I Can Make It/Good For You (12")...............50

THEO JOHNSON
65	Aladdin WI 604	Masters Of War/The Water Is Wide 15

TOMMY JOHNSON
60s	Saydisc SDM 224	THE LEGACY OF TOMMY JOHNSON (LP) 20

WILKO JOHNSON & SOLID SENDERS
78	Virgin V 2105	SOLID SENDERS (LP, with free LP "Live" [VDJ 26]) 12

(see also Dr. Feelgood, Ian Dury & Blockheads)

DEBRA JOHNSON
98	Kent 6T 19	To Get Love/DIPLOMATS: I Really Love You 30

DANIEL JOHNSON (1)
65	Island WI 250	Come On My People/Brother Nathan 15

DANIEL JOHNSON (2)
99	Pickled Egg EGG 6	Dream Scream/Funeral Girl...............5
03	For Us FU 020	Mountain Top/Living It For The Moment...............6
03	Sketchbook SKETCH XX2	Fish/Living It For The Moment...............7
93	Ay Carramba! EL BARTO 001	RESPECT (10" LP)...............15
02	Pickled Egg EGG 22	REJECTED UNKNOWN (2-LP)...............20
06	Coppertree CTR 007	FEAR YOURSELF (LP, 1000 only)...............12

BRUCE JOHNSTON
77	CBS 5324	(Meet You On A) Rendezvous/I Write The Songs 6
77	CBS 5514	Pipeline/Disney Girls 7
77	CBS 5703	Deirdrie/Thank You Baby 6
77	CBS 61854	GOING PUBLIC (LP, with insert) 20

(see also Beach Boys)

BRUCE JOHNSTON COMBO
63	London HL 9780	Original Surfer Stomp/Pajama Party 60

(see also Beach Boys, California Music, Fantastic Baggys, Sagittarius)

DANIEL JOHNSTON
92	Seminal Twang TWANG 13	Laurie/The Monster Inside Of Me/Whiz Kid/The Lennon Song (p/s)...............10

KEVIN JOHNSTON
74	UK UKR 84	Rock And Roll (I Gave You The Best Years Of My Life)/Life Is What You Make It 5

JOHNSTON BROTHERS
54	Decca F 10234	The Creep/Crystal Ball 10
54	Decca F 10286	Oh Baby Mine I Get So Lonely/My Love, My Life, My Own 10
54	Decca F 10302	The Bandit/KEYNOTES: A Dime And A Dollar...............10
54	Decca F 10364	Sh-Boom (Life Could Be A Dream)/Crazy 'Bout Ya Baby 15
54	Decca F 10401	Mambo In The Moonlight/Papa Loves Mambo (with Ted Heath Music)...............5
54	Decca F 10414	Join In And Sing Medley (both sides)...............5
55	Decca F 10451	Majorca/Heartbroken 5
55	Decca F 10490	The Right To Be Wrong/Hot Potato Mambo 5
55	Decca F 10513	Chee Chee-Oo Chee (Sang The Little Bird)Hubble Bubble 5
55	Decca F 10526	Dreamboat/Jim, Johnny And Jonas 5
55	Decca F 10608	Hernando's Hideaway/Hey There 15
55	Decca F 10636	Join In And Sing Again Medley (both sides)...............10
56	Decca F 10721	No Other Love/Flowers Mean Forgiveness...............10
56	Decca F 10747	How Little We Know/The Street Musician 6
56	Decca F 10781	In The Middle Of The House (with Keynotes)/Stranded In The Jungle...............10
56	Decca F 10814	Join In And Sing, No. 3 Medley (both sides)...............10
56	Decca F 10828	Give Her My Love (When You Meet Her)/A Rose And A Candy Bar 10
57	Decca F 10860	Whatever Lola Wants (Lola Gets)/Heart...............10
57	Decca F 10939	I Like Music - You Like Music/Seven Bar Blues 7
57	Decca F 10962	Join In And Sing, No. 4 Medley (both sides)...............7
56	Decca DFE 6249	JOIN THE JOHNSTON BROTHERS (EP) 10

(see also Dennis Lotis, Vera Lynn, Joan Regan, Lita Roza, Suzi Miller, Ted Heath, Keynotes)

JOHNSTONS
68	Transatlantic TRA 169	THE JOHNSTONS (LP) 22
68	Transatlantic TRA 184	GIVE A DAMN (LP) 18
68	Transatlantic TRA 185	THE BARLEYCORN (LP)...............18
70	Transatlantic TRA 211	BITTER GREEN (LP) 20
71	Transatlantic TRA 231	COLOURS OF THE DAWN (LP) 15
72	Transatlantic TRA 251	IF I SANG MY SONG (LP, gatefold sleeve) 12

(see also Adrienne Johnston)

JOINER, ARKANSAS, JUNIOR HIGH SCHOOL BAND
60	London HLG 9147	Big Ben/National City...............7

JO JO GUNNE (U.K.)
68	Decca F 12807	Every Story Has An End/Should Live Like That 7
69	Decca F 12906	Beggin' You Baby/Bad Penny...............7

JO JO GUNNE (U.S.)
72	Asylum AYM 501	Run Run Run/Shake That Fat or Take It Easy as B-side (withdrawn) 10
72	Asylum AYM 507	Shake That Fat/I Make Love 5

JOKER (1)

MINT VALUE £

73	Asylum AYM 518	Ready Freddy/Wait A Lifetime	5
73	Asylum AYM 521	Rock Around The Symbol/Take Me Down Easy	5
74	Asylum AYM 528	I Wanna Love You/Neon City	5
74	Asylum AYM 534	Where Is The Show/Single Man	5

(see also Spirit)

JOKER (1)
| 84 | Lost Moment LM 018 | Back On The Road/Pusher (p/s) | 10 |

JOKER (2)
| 93 | Skanna 06 | The Joker/Roots (12") | 40 |

(see also Skanna)

JOKERS
| 62 | Salvo SLO 1806 | Blue Moonbeam/Dog Fight (99 only) | 35 |

JOKER'S WILD
| 66 | Regent Sound RSR 0031 | Don't Ask Me/Why Do Fools Fall In Love (handwritten labels, 50 only) | 500 |
| 66 | Regent Sound RSLP 007 | JOKER'S WILD: Don't Ask Me/Why Do Fools Fall In Love/You Don't Know What I Know/That's How Strong My Love Is (12", 1-sided, 50 copies only) | 1000 |

(see also Dave Gilmour, Pink Floyd)

JOHN JOLLIFFE
| 79 | Rocket XPRESS 9 | Follow The Wind/Dream Love | 6 |

JOLLIVER ARKANSAS
| 69 | Bell SBLL 119 | HOME (LP) | 30 |

(see also Leslie West, Mountain)

JOLLY BOYS
| 70 | Moodisc MU 3504 | On The Water/MUDIES ALL STARS: Cash Register | 15 |

JOLLY BROTHERS
| 78 | Ballistic FORCE 2002 | Conscious Man/PRODIGAL CREATOR: Life (actually dub to Lee Perry's Ne Jah Go Run) (12") | 15 |

JOLT
77	Polydor 2058 936	You're Cold/All I Can Do (p/s)	15
78	Polydor 2059 008	What'cha Gonna Do About It/Again And Again (die-cut p/s)	12
78	Polydor 2059 039	I Can't Wait/Route 66 (p/s)	12
79	Polydor 2229 215	Maybe Tonight/I'm In Tears/See Saw/Stop Look (p/s)	12
79	Polydor 2229 215DJ	Maybe Tonight/See Saw (promo only, no p/s)	12
78	Polydor 2383 504	THE JOLT (LP)	30

JON
67	Parlophone R 5604	So Much For Mary/Polly Sunday (in p/s)	50
67	Parlophone R 5604	So Much For Mary/Polly Sunday	25
67	Columbia DB 8249	Is It Love/Sing Out	150

(see also Titus Groan, Still Life)

JON & ALUN
| 63 | Decca LK 4547 | RELAX YOUR MIND (LP, mono) | 22 |
| 63 | Decca SKL 4547 | RELAX YOUR MIND (LP, stereo) | 30 |

JON & DAVE
| 97 | Earworm SS 1 | Land Beyond The Sun/Instrumental For Silence (p/s, pale green vinyl, 500 copies only) | 8 |

JON & JEANNIE
| 68 | Beacon 3-105 | Lover's Holiday/Something You Got | 10 |
| 69 | Beacon BEA 113 | Don't Sign The Papers/We Got Lovin' | 10 |

JON & ROBIN & IN-CROWD
| 67 | Stateside SS 2027 | Do It Again A Little Bit Slower/If I Need Someone It's You | 15 |

JON & VANGELIS
81	Polydor JV 1	I'll Find My Way Back Home/Back To School	5
81	Polydor POSPX 323	State Of Independence/Beside (12", in blue plastic film canister, promo only)	40
84	Polydor JV 5/POSP 246	State Of Independence/The Friends Of Mr. Cairo/Chariots Of Fire/ Eric's Theme (p/s doublepack, stickered shrinkwrapped p/s)	6
81	Polydor POLD 5039	THE FRIENDS OF MR. CAIRO (LP, promo issue with b&w sleeve, raised figures & logo in left corner)	15

(see also Jon Anderson, Vangelis)

JONAH
| 85 | MW MW 7853 | Tough/This Is Love (no p/s) | 280 |

JONATHAN & CHARLES
| 69 | Herald LLR 566 | ANOTHER WEEK TO GO (LP) | 30 |

A JONES
| 04 | Jah Tubbys JT 10020 | Jah Bless I/MA-KAYA CREW: Iron Dub | 25 |

AL JONES
58	HMV POP 451	Mad, Mad, World/Lonely Traveller	200
58	HMV POP 451	Mad, Mad, World/Lonely Traveller(78)	40
69	Parlophone PMC/PCS 7081	ALUN ASHWORTH JONES (LP, black/yellow label with "Sold in U.K..." text)	150
72	Village Thing VTS 19	JONESVILLE (LP)	140

ALLAN JONES
53	HMV 7M 111	Why Do I Love You/Make Believe	7
53	HMV 7M 135	I Believe/I Talk To The Trees	7
53	HMV 7M 161	Poppa Piccolino/Why?	7

BARBARA JONES
72	Bullet BU 516	Sad Movies/SIR HARRY: Deejay Version	8
74	Count Shelley CS 045	Baby I'm Yours/Don't Turn Your Back On Me	5
74	attack ATT 8077	Changing Partners/Part 2	6
75	Dip DL 5085	Where Do I Turn/G.G. ALL STARS: Version	5

BETTY HALL JONES
| 50 | Capitol CL 13266 | This Joint's Too Hip For Me/You've Got To Have What It Takes (78) | 15 |

BEVERLEY JONES (& PRESTONS)
63	HMV POP 1109	The Boy I Saw With You/When It Comes To Love	10
63	HMV POP 1140	Why Do Lovers Break Each Other's Heart/I'm Just An In-Between	20
63	HMV POP 1201	Wait 'Til My Bobby Gets Home/A Boy Like You	15
64	Parlophone R 5189	Heatwave/Hear You Talking (with Prestons)	20

(see also Roger James)

B-LOU JONES & HIS JUPITERS
| 61 | London HLU 9373 | Anchors Aweigh (Parts 1 & 2) | 10 |

BRENDA LEE JONES
| 75 | UK USA 8 | You're The Love Of My Life/Thread Your Needle (paper label) | 8 |

(see also Dean & Jean)

CARMELL JONES
| 62 | Fontana 688 125 ZL | BUSINESS MEETIN' (LP) | 12 |

CAROL JONES
| 60 | Triumph RGM 1012 | The Boy With The Eyes Of Blue/I Gave Him Back His Ring | 125 |

CASEY JONES & THE ENGINEERSO
| 63 | Columbia DB 7083 | One Way Ticket/I'm Gonna Love | 35 |

CASEY JONES & THE GOVERNERS
| 64 | Golden 12LP 106 | DON'T HA HA (LP) | 60 |

(see also Casey Jones & The Engineers)

CURTIS JONES
66	RCA RCX 7184	R.C.A. VICTOR RACE SERIES VOL. 9 (EP)	15
64	Decca LK 4587	CURTIS JONES IN LONDON (LP)	100
68	Blue Horizon 7-63207	NOW RESIDENT IN EUROPE (LP)	60

DAVEY JONES
| 65 | Philips BF 1410 | For Your Love/Love Bug | 10 |

DAVIE JONES & THE KING BEES
64	Vocalion V 9221	Liza Jane/Louie, Louie Go Home (Demo copy)	1600
64	Vocalion Pop V 9221	Liza Jane/Louie, Louie Go Home (beware of counterfeits without centres)	1250
78	Decca F 13807	Liza Jane/Louie, Louie Go Home (reissue)	25

(see also David Bowie, Davy Jones, Manish Boys, Calvin James)

DAVY JONES (U.K.) (1)
| 65 | Parlophone R 5250 | You've Got A Habit Of Leaving/Baby Loves That Way (Demo) | 700 |
| 65 | Parlophone R 5315 | You've Got A Habit Of Leaving/Baby Loves That Way | 800 |

(see also David Bowie)

DAVY JONES (U.K.) (2)
65	Colpix PX 784	What Are We Going To Do/This Bouquet	10
67	Pye 7N 17302	It Ain't Me Babe/Baby It's Me (in p/s)	10
67	Pye 7N 17302	It Ain't Me Babe/Baby It's Me	5
67	Pye 7N 17380	Theme For A New Love/Dream Girl (in p/s)	10
67	Pye 7N 17380	Theme For A New Love/Dream Girl	6
67	Pye International 7N 25432	Theme For A New Love/Dream Girl (reissue, withdrawn)	20
71	Bell BLL 1163	Rainy Jane/Welcome To My Love	5
77	MCA MCA 348	Life Line/It's A Jungle Out There/Gotta Get Up (from 'The Point') (p/s, last track with Micky Dolenz)	5
78	Warner Bros K 17161	(Hey Ra Ra) Happy Birthday Mickey Mouse/You Don't Have To Be A Country Boy To Sing A Country Song (p/s)	5
83	J.J. 2001	I'll Love You Forever/When I Look Back On Christmas	12
67	Pye NPL 18178	DAVY JONES (LP)	20

(see also Davy Jones & Micky Dolenz, Monkees)

DAVY JONES (U.K.) & MICKY DOLENZ
| 71 | Bell BLL 986 | Do It In The Name Of Love/Lady Jane | 12 |

(see also Monkees, Davey Jones)

DAVY JONES (U.K.) & THE LOWER THIRD/MANISH BOYS
79	EMI 2925	You've Got A Habit Of Leaving/Baby Loves That Way/MANISH BOYS: I Pity The Fool/Take My Tip (Demo copy, p/s)	20
79	EMI EMI 2925	You've Got A Habit Of Leaving/Baby Loves That Way/MANISH BOYS: I Pity The Fool/Take My Tip (p/s)	6
82	Charly CYM 1	You've Got A Habit Of Leaving/Baby Loves That Way/MANISH BOYS: I Pity The Fool/Take My Tip (10", p/s)	20

(see also David Bowie, Davie Jones & King Bees, Manish Boys, Calvin James)

DAVY JONES (U.S.)
60	Pye 7N 15254	Amapola/Mighty Man	10
61	Pye 7N 15318	Shenandoah/Scenery	25
61	Pye International 7N 25072	Model Girl/Scarlet Woman	12
61	Pye International 7N 25095	Bonnie Banks/Baby Baby	10
62	Piccadilly 7N 35038	Jezebel/Don't Come Crying To Me	10

(see also Thelonious Monk)

DILL JONES TRIO
56	Jazz Today JTE 104	PIANO MOODS VOL. 2 (EP)	25
56	Pye Jazz NJE 1024	PIANO MOODS VOL. 5 (EP)	25
57	Columbia SEG 7764	TOP OF THE POLL (EP)	10
59	Columbia SEG 7893	DILL JONES PLUS FOUR (EP)	8
60	Columbia 33SX 1336	JONES THE JAZZ (LP)	60
78	77 77SEU 12/45	UP JUMPED YOU WITH LOVE (LP)	20

DOROTHY JONES
| 61 | Philips 322 794 BF | Takin' That Long Walk Home/It's Unbearable | 30 |

(see also Cookies)

GARY JONES
| 62 | Piccadilly 7N 35084 | It's Over/Little Miss Nose In The Air | 8 |

GEORGE JONES

59	Mercury AMT 1021	The Treasure Of Love/If I Don't Love You (Grits Ain't Groceries)	10
59	Mercury AMT 1021	The Treasure Of Love/If I Don't Love You (Grits Ain't Groceries) (78)	20
59	Mercury AMT 1036	White Lightning/Long Time To Forget	50
59	Mercury AMT 1058	Who Shot Sam/Into My Arms Again	30
59	Mercury AMT 1078	Big Harlan Taylor/Money To Burn	15
60	Mercury AMT 1100	Sparkling Brown Eyes/Accidentally On Purpose	15
61	Mercury AMT 1124	Candy Hearts/The Window Up Above	15
62	United Artists POP 1037	She Thinks I Still Care/Geronimo	15
63	United Artists UP 1015	I Saw Me/Not What I Had In Mind (as George Jones with Jones Boys)	10
64	United Artists UP 1044	Your Heart Turned Left (And I Was On The Right)/My Tears Are Overdue	10
65	United Artists UP 1080	The Race Is On/She's So Lonesome Again	15
69	Stateside SS 2145	If My Heart Had Windows/Taggin' Along	8
71	Pye International 7N 25547	It's Been A Good Year For The Roses/Let A Little Come In	7
80	Epic EPC 8560	Stranger In The House (with Elvis Costello)/A Drunk Can't Be A Man (p/s)	6
59	Mercury ZEP 10036	GEORGE JONES (EP)	100
59	Melodisc EPM7 109	COUNTRY SONG HITS (EP)	40
64	Mercury 10009 MCE	C & W ACES (EP)	20
64	Ember EMB 4548	THE BEST OF AMERICAN COUNTRY MUSIC VOL. 4 (EP)	15
62	United Artists ULP 1007	THE NEW FAVOURITES OF GEORGE JONES (LP)	20
63	United Artists ULP 1014	MY FAVOURITES OF HANK WILLIAMS (LP)	20
63	Ember CW 101	THE CROWN PRINCE OF COUNTRY MUSIC (LP, original pressings have grey & orange label)	20
63	United Artists ULP 1037	HITS OF HIS COUNTRY COUSINS (LP)	15
64	United Artists ULP 1050	I WISH TONIGHT WOULD NEVER END (LP)	15
64	London HA-B 8125	GEORGE JONES SINGS HIS GREATEST HITS (LP)	15
64	United Artists ULP 1070	WHAT'S IN OUR HEARTS (LP, with Melba Montgomery)	18
64	Ember CW 109	THE FABULOUS COUNTRY MUSIC SOUND OF JONES (LP, original pressings have grey & orange label)	15
64	United Artists ULP 1074	MORE NEW FAVOURITES (LP)	20
65	United Artists ULP 1077	BLUE GRASS HOOTENANNY (LP, with Melba Montgomery)	20
65	United Artists ULP 1091	I GET LONELY IN A HURRY (LP)	20
65	United Artists ULP 1082	JONES SINGS LIKE THE DICKENS (LP)	20
65	United Artists ULP 1101	TROUBLE IN MIND (LP)	22
65	Stateside SL 10147	GEORGE JONES AND GENE PITNEY (LP, with Gene Pitney)	18
65	Stateside SL 10157	MR. COUNTRY AND WESTERN MUSIC (LP)	15
66	London HA-B 8259	GEORGE JONES (LP, with Tommy Hill's Band)	20
66	United Artists (S)ULP 1136	THE GREAT GEORGE JONES (LP)	15
66	United Artists (S)ULP 1137	BLUE MOON OF KENTUCKY (LP, with Melba Montgomery)	20
66	Stateside SL 10173	IT'S COUNTRY TIME AGAIN (LP, with Gene Pitney)	15
67	London HA-B 8340	THE GEORGE JONES SONG BOOK (LP)	18
68	Mercury SMWL 21003	THE GREAT GEORGE JONES (LP)	20

(see also Gene Pitney, Elvis Costello)

GEORGE JONES/JIMMIE SKINNER

59	Mercury ZEP 10012	COUNTRY AND WESTERN (EP, 2 tracks each)	10

JONES GIRLS

82	Philadelphia Intl. PIR 2031	Nights Over Egypt/Love Don't Ever Say Goodbye	5
82	Phil. Intl. PIR 12-2031	Nights Over Egypt/Love Don't Ever Say Goodbye (12")	15

GLORIA JONES

66	Capitol CL 15429	Heartbeat (Parts 1 & 2)	45
66	Stateside SS 555	Finders Keepers/Run One Flight Of Stairs	70
74	Tamla Motown TMG 910	Tin Can People/So Tired (Of The Way You're Treating Our Love Baby)	10
76	EMI EMI 2437	Get It On/Get It On (Version)	6
76	EMI EMI 2522	I Ain't Going Nowhere/Simplicity Blues	10
77	EMI EMI 2570	Go Now/Drive Me Crazy	6
77	EMI EMI 2720	Bring On The Love/Cry Baby	6
74	Tamla Motown STML 11254	SHARE MY LOVE (LP)	25
76	EMI EMC 3159	VIXEN (LP)	15

(see also Marc Bolan & Gloria Jones)

GRANDPA JONES

57	Brunswick 05676	Eight More Miles To Louisville/Dark As A Dungeon	25
59	Brunswick OE 9455	MOUNTAIN MUSIC VOL. 3 (EP)	15
57	Parlophone GEP 8666	MEET GRANDPA JONES (EP)	20
58	Parlophone GEP 8766	COUNTRY AND WESTERN (EP)	15
59	Parlophone GEP 8781	COUNTRY ROUND UP (EP)	15
64	London RE-U 1417	GRANDPA SINGS JIMMIE RODGERS (EP)	15
62	London HA-U/SH-U 8010	MAKES THE RAFTERS RING (LP)	25
64	London HA-U/SH-U 8119	YODELLING HITS (LP)	25

(see also Brown's Ferry Four)

HEATHER JONES

74	Sain SAIN 1008M	MAE'R OLWYN YN TROI (LP)	50

HUW JONES

69	Welsh Teldisc WD 912	Y ffoadur/Dewch I Ganu (La, La, La) (p/s)	10
69	Sain SAIN 1	Dwr/Fy Ngwlad Fy Hun	20
70	Sain SAIN 3	Paid Digalonni/Ffoi (p/s)	10

INDIGO JONES

70	Columbia DB 8744	Noel Highway/Prodigal Son	12

JACK JONES

58	Capitol CL 14969	Laffin' At Me/Deeply Devoted	10
62	London HLR 9525	Lillipops And Roses/Julie	5
63	London HLR 9806	Wives And Lovers/Toys In The Attic	5
65	London HLR 9956	The Race Is On/I Can't Believe I'm Losing You	5
79	Polydor POSP 92	The Love Boat/Wives And Lovers	6

JAKE JONES

71	MCA MVPS 432	JAKE JONES (LP)	25

JANET JONES
| 74 | Midas MR 005 | SING TO ME LADY (LP)..200 |
| 74 | Midas MFHR 059 | JANET JONES (LP, released on Folk Heritage label)..200 |

JANIE JONES (& LASH)
65	HMV POP 1495	Witches Brew/Take-A My Tip 15
66	HMV POP 1514	Gunning For You/Go Go Away From Me 15
67	Columbia DB 8173	Tickle Me Tootsie Wootsies/High And Dry 12
68	Pye 7N 17550	Charlie Smith/Nobody's Perfect 10
68	Major Minor MM 577	The Girl's Song/I've Never Met A Boy Like You 10
70	President PT 309	Back On My Feet Again/Psycho 10
83	Big Beat NS 91	House Of The Ju-Ju Queen/Sex Machine (as Janie Jones & Lash, p/s) 6

(see also The Clash, Janie)

JERRY JONES
70	Banana BA 316	Still Waters (Love)/SOUND DIMENSION: Wig Wam 18
71	Bamboo BAM 65	Still Waters (Love)/SOUND DIMENSION: Wig Wam (reissue) 15
71	Bamboo BALPS 213	LIVE AT THE KINGSTON HOTEL, JAMAICA (LP)..50

JIMMY JONES
60	MGM MGM 1051	Handy Man/The Search Is Over..7
60	MGM MGM 1051	Handy Man/The Search Is Over (78)...80
60	MGM MGM 1078	Good Timin'/Too Long Will Be Too Late..7
60	MGM MGM 1078	Good Timin'/Too Long Will Be Too Late (78) 80
60	MGM MGM 1091	I Just Go For You/That's When I Cried...12
60	MGM MGM 1103	Ready For Love/For You 15
61	MGM MGM 1123	I Told You So/You Got It 15
61	MGM MGM 1133	Dear One/I Say Love 12
61	MGM MGM 1146	Mr Music Man/Holler Hey 15
62	MGM MGM 1168	You're Much Too Young/Nights Of Mexico 12
65	Columbia DB 7592	Walkin'/Pardon Me..30
65	Cameo Parkway P 988	Don't You Just Know It 15
67	Stateside SS 2041	39-21-46/Personal Property...18
60	MGM MGM-EP 745	JIMMY HANDYMAN JONES (EP) 40
61	MGM MGM-EP 787	ORIGINAL HITS (EP)...30
60	MGM MGM-C 832	GOOD TIMIN' (LP) 60

JO JONES TRIO
| 59 | Top Rank 25/039 | JO JONES (LP)...18 |

JOE JONES
| 60 | Columbia DB 4533 | You Talk Too Much/I Love You Still ....15 |

JOHN PAUL JONES
| 64 | Pye 7N 15637 | Baja/A Foggy Day In Vietnam (B-side by Andrew Oldham Orchestra, white label promo) ..150 |
| 64 | Pye 7N 15637 | Baja/A Foggy Day In Vietnam (B-side actually by Andrew Oldham Orchestra) ....150 |

(see also Led Zeppelin, Tony Meehan, Andrew Oldham Orchestra)

JOHNNY JONES & KING CASUALS
68	MCA MU 1031	Soul Poppin'/Blues For The Brothers 10
76	Cream CRM 5004	Purple Haze/Horsing Around 10
76	Brunswick BR 37	Purple Haze/FRED HUGHES: Baby Boy..8
80	Sonet SNTF 821	JOHNNY JONES WITH BILLY BOY ARNOLD (LP)...12

JONAH JONES (QUARTET)
58	Capitol CL 14939	Night Train/Lots Of Luck Charley 7
59	Capitol 15085	I Dig Chicks/Cherry 5
62	Ember JBS 704	Down By The Riverside/Stars Fell On Alabama 7

JUSTIN JONES
| 61 | London HLU 9463 | Dance By Yourself/Love ....150 |

KEN JONES (& HIS ROCK'N'ROLLERS)
60	Parlophone R 4628	Two Way Stretch/Paper Chase 8
61	Parlophone R 4763	Bluesville/On The Rebound..7
61	Parlophone R 4788	Joxville/Just Rollin'...6
58	Embassy WEP 1004	ROCK'N'ROLL TIME (EP, as Ken Jones & His Rock'n'Rollers) 15

KENNEY JONES
| 74 | GM GMS 027 | Ready Or Not/Woman Trouble...8 |

(see also Small Faces, Faces, Who)

LESLIE JONES
| 59 | Pye NSEP 85004 | FOUR FARNON FAVOURITES (EP, stereo)..10 |
| 59 | Pye NSPL 83008/9 | THE MUSIC OF ROBERT FARNON (2-LP) ....20 |

LINDA JONES
67	Warner Bros WB 2070	Hypnotised/I Can't Stop Lovin' My Baby 50
72	London HLU 10368	For Your Precious Love/Don't Go..15
75	Warner Bros WB 16621	I Just Can't Live My Life/My Heart Will Understand...20

LINDA JONES/J.J. JACKSON
| 77 | Loma/Warners K 56271 | THIS IS LOMA - VOL. 7 (LP, 1 side each)..15 |

LLOYD JONES
| 70 | Bullet BU 429 | Rome/RHYTHM RULERS: Version ....30 |

LOUIS JONES ROCK & ROLL BAND
| 50s | Vogue VE1 70111 | ROCK AND ROLL (EP)..100 |

MAE JONES ENSEMBLE
| 54 | Decca 45-F 10486 | Tenderly He Watches/I Walked Into The Garden ....7 |

MAGGIE JONES
| 70 | VJM VLP 23 | COLUMBIA RECORDINGS IN CHRONOLOGICAL ORDER VOL. 1 (LP)......................15 |
| 70 | VJM VLP 25 | COLUMBIA RECORDINGS IN CHRONOLOGICAL ORDER VOL. 2 (LP)......................15 |

NIC JONES
| 70 | Trailer LER 2014 | BALLADS AND SONGS (LP, white label)..50 |

MINT VALUE £

Nigel MAZLYN JONES

70	Trailer LER 2014	BALLADS AND SONGS (LP, red label)	40
70	Trailer LER 2014	BALLADS AND SONGS (LP, later pressing with 'highway' label)	15
71	Trailer LER 2027	NIC JONES (LP, yellow label)	35
71	Trailer LER 2027	NIC JONES (LP, red label)	35
77	Trailer LER 2091	NOAH'S ARK TRAP (LP)	35
77	Trailer LER 2091	NOAH'S ARK TRAP (LP, reissue with Highway label)	15
78	Transatlantic LTRA 507	FROM THE DEVIL TO A STRANGER (LP)	30
80	Topic 12TS411	PENGUIN EGGS (LP)	30

(see also Jon Raven, Halliard)

NIGEL MAZLYN JONES

76	Isle Of Light IOL 666/1	SHIP TO SHORE (LP)	50
78	Avada AVA 105	SENTINEL (LP, with inner sleeve, b/w picture label)	20
82	Isle Of Light IOL 0230	BREAKING COVER (LP)	20
91	Isle Of Light 1OL 0232LP	MAZLYN JONES (LP)	20

PALMER JONES

68	Direction 58-3603	The Great Magic Of Love/Dancing Master	25

PATSY JONES

67	RCA 1600	Colours Of Love/There's A time And Place For Everything	7

PAUL JONES

66	HMV POP 1554	High Time/I Can't Hold On Much Longer	5
67	HMV POP 1576	I've Been A Bad Bad Boy/Sonny Boy Williamson	5
67	HMV POP 1602	Thinkin' Ain't For Me/Softly (La Vita)	5
67	HMV PSR 5307	Privilege (1-sided demo)	20
67	Columbia DB 8303	Sons And Lovers/Three Sisters	8
68	Columbia DB 8379	And The Sun Will Shine/The Dog Presides	25
68	Columbia DB 8417	When I Was Six Years Old/You Have No Idea	10
68	Columbia DB 8514	Aquarius/Pisces	6
69	Columbia DB 8567	It's Getting Better/Not Before Time	8
71	Vertigo 6059 053	Life After Death/The Mighty Ship	8
73	Philips 6006 282	Perfect Roadie/Mouth Organ	6
78	RSO RSO 003	Sheena Is A Punk Rocker/Pretty Vacant (p/s)	5
67	HMV 7EG 8975	PRIVILEGE (EP)	20
66	HMV CLP 3586	MY WAY (LP, mono)	25
66	HMV CSD 3586	MY WAY (LP, stereo)	30
67	HMV CLP 3602	LOVE ME, LOVE MY FRIENDS (LP, mono)	25
67	HMV CSD 3602	LOVE ME, LOVE MY FRIENDS (LP, stereo)	30
67	HMV CLP/CSD 3623	PRIVILEGE (LP, soundtrack, with George Bean Group & Mike Leander)	40
69	Columbia SX/SCX 6347	COME INTO MY MUSIC BOX (LP, mono/stereo)	18
71	Vertigo 6360 059	CRUCIFIX IN A HORSESHOE (LP, gatefold sleeve, swirl label)	70
70	President PTLS 1068	DRAKE'S DREAM (LP, soundtrack)	25

(see also Manfred Mann, Blues Band)

POPPA JONES

66	Parlophone R 5404	Birthday Cake Walk/The Street Parade	6

QUINCY JONES

62	Mercury AMT 1195	Soul Bossa Nova/On The Street Where You Live	20
65	Mercury MF 844	Seaweed/Golden Boy Theme	5
69	RCA RCA 1850	MacKenna's Gold/Soul Full Of Gold	5
70	A&M AMS 781	Killer Joe/Oh Happy Day	5
72	A&M AMS 888	Ironside/Cast Your Fate To The Wind	15
72	Reprise K 14150	Money Runned	8
72	Atlantic K 10172	Listen To The Melody/Hot Rock Theme	5
60	Mercury ZEP 10047	BIG BAND BASH (EP)	10
61	Mercury ZEP 10109	THE BIRTH OF A BAND (EP, mono)	10
61	Mercury SEZ 19017	THE BIRTH OF A BAND (EP, stereo)	15
61	Columbia SEG 8088	DOUBLE SIX MEET QUINCY JONES (EP)	12
61	Mercury ZEP 10119	THE BIRTH OF A BAND PT. 2 (EP, mono)	10
61	Mercury SEZ 19021	THE BIRTH OF A BAND PT. 2 (EP, stereo)	12
60	Mercury MMC 14038	THE BIRTH OF A BAND (LP, mono)	20
60	Mercury CMS 18026	THE BIRTH OF A BAND (LP, stereo)	25
60	Mercury MMC 14046	THE GREAT WORLD OF QUINCY JONES (LP, mono)	12
60	Mercury CMS 18031	THE GREAT WORLD OF QUINCY JONES (LP, stereo)	15
61	Mercury MMC 14080	I DIG DANCERS (LP, also stereo CMS 18055)	15
62	HMV CLP 1581	THE QUINTESSENCE (LP, also stereo CSD 1452)	15
62	Mercury MMC 14098	AROUND THE WORLD (LP, also stereo CMS 18064)	15
63	Mercury MMC 14125	BIG BAND BOSSA NOVA (LP, also stereo CMS 18080)	15
63	Mercury MMC 14128	PLAYS HIP HITS (LP)	15
64	Mercury MCL 20016	EXPLORES THE MUSIC OF HENRY MANCINI (LP, also stereo SMCL 20016)	15
65	Columbia 33SX 1637	QUINCY'S HOME AGAIN (LP)	15
65	Mercury 20047 MCL	GOLDEN BOY (LP)	15
65	Mercury 20063 SMCL	THE PAWNBROKER (LP, soundtrack)	30
66	Mercury 20072 (S)MCL	MIRAGE (LP, soundtrack)	25
66	Mercury 20073 MCL	PLAYS FOR PUSSYCATS (LP)	15
66	Mercury 20078 (S)MCL	QUINCY'S GOT A BRAND NEW BAG (LP)	15
66	Fontana FJL 127	FAB! (LP)	15
67	Mercury SMWL 30003	TRAVELLIN' ON THE QUINCY JONES BANDWAGON (LP)	15
68	RCA Victor RD/SF 7931	IN COLD BLOOD (LP, soundtrack)	15
68	United Artists (S)ULP 1181	IN THE HEAT OF THE NIGHT (LP, soundtrack, with Ray Charles)	25
69	Uni UNLS 103	LOST MAN (LP, soundtrack)	25
69	Paramount SPFL 256	THE ITALIAN JOB (LP, soundtrack, with Matt Monro)	75
69	RCA Victor SF 8017	MACKENNA'S GOLD (LP, soundtrack, with Jose Feliciano)	12
70	United Artists UAS 29128	THEY CALL ME MISTER TIBBS (LP, soundtrack)	15
71	A&M AMLS 63037	SMACKWATER JACK (LP)	12
72	WEA K 44168	THE HEIST (LP, soundtrack, with Little Richard)	15
72	Atlantic K 40371	HOW TO STEAL A DIAMOND IN FOUR UNEASY LESSONS (LP, soundtrack)	15
85	Nimbus/A&M AMLH 64485	SOUNDS AND STUFF LIKE THAT (LP, Nimbus Supercut, mail order only from Practical Hi Fi magazine)	40

(see also Annie Ross, Eddie Barclay & Quincy Jones, Diana Ross & Quincy Jones, John & Joan Shakespeare)

RICK JONES
72	Argo AFW106	Theme From The Aeronauts/Lovebug	10
73	Argo ZDA 156	HIYA MAYA (LP)	15

ROBIN JONES & HIS QUINTET
71	Apollo Sound APPS 5012	DENGA (LP)	40
71	Apollo Sound APP S 5016	EL MAJA (LP, as Robin Jones Seven)	50

RONNIE JONES
64	Decca F 12012	Let's Pin A Rose On You/I Need Your Loving (B-side with Night Timers)	20
65	Decca F 12066	My Love/It's All Over	40
65	Decca F 12146	Anyone Who Knows What Love Is/Nobody But You	20
65	Parlophone R 5326	You're Lookin' Good/I'm So Clean (with Blue Jays)	40
67	CBS 2699	Little Bitty Pretty One/Put Your Tears Away	18
67	Polydor 56222	In My Love Mind/Mama Come On Home	15
68	CBS 3304	Without Love (There Is Nothing)/Little Bitty Pretty One	12

(see also Night-Timers)

SALENA JONES
66	Columbia DB 7818	A Walk In The Black Forest (Our Walk Of Love)/As Long As I Live	7
66	Columbia DB 7991	I Am Yours/I Only Know I Love You	7
67	Columbia DB 8212	When I Tell You (That I Love You)/Respect	8
67	Decca F 12708	I've Got The Blues/The Glory Of Love	25
70	CBS 4767	This Is Love/Everybodys Talkin'	6
71	CBS 7542	Baby Don't Ya Get Crazy/Fire And Rain	15
73	Indigo GOPOP	Live And Let Die/Some Other World (in p/s)	15
73	Indigo GOPOP	Live And Let Die/Some Other World	6
75	DJM DJS 381	In Love Like You And Me/Tell It Like It Is	6
69	CBS 63613	THE MOMENT OF TRUTH (LP)	35
70	CBS 63901	EVERYBODY'S TALKIN' ABOUT SALENA JONES (LP)	30
71	CBS 64435	PLATINUM (LP)	20
73	RCA Victor SF 8335	ALONE & TOGETHER (LP)	20
74	RCA LPL 1 5025	THIS'N'THAT (LP)	20

SALINA JONES
65	Polydor 56012	Longing/Too Late	7

SAM JONES
60	Riverside 12-324	SOUL SOCIETY (LP)	20

SAMANTHA JONES
65	United Artists UP 1072	It's All Because Of You/I Woke Up Crying	15
65	United Artists UP 1087	Don't Come Any Closer/Just Call And I'll Be There	15
65	United Artists UP 1105	Chained To A Memory/Just For Him	10
66	United Artists UP 1139	That Special Way/Somebody Else's Baby	10
67	United Artists UP 1185	Surrounded By A Ray Of Sunshine/How Do You Say Goodbye	80
67	United Artists UP 1185	Surrounded By A Ray Of Sunshine/How Do You Say Goodbye (DJ Copy)	150
67	United Artists UP 1200	Why Can't I Remember/Live For Life	8
68	United Artists UP 2248	Lonely Lonely Man/Doll On A Music Box	10
68	United Artists UP 2258	And Suddenly/Go Ahead And Love Me	50
80	Ford SLE 19	Ford Leads The Way/Go Ahead And Love Me (p/s, Ford cars promo disc)	25
69	Penny Farthing PEN 703	Today (Without You)/The Feelin' That I Get	10
69	Penny Farthing PEN 708	Do I Still Figure In Your Life?/I'm Sorry, But I Think I Love You	10
70	Penny Farthing PEN 734	My Way/Darling Be Home Soon	10
70	Penny Farthing PEN 746	Best Of Both Worlds/Guilty Of Loving You	10
74	Columbia DB 9031	I Believed It All/This I Find Is Beautiful	8
68	United Artists	CALL IT SAMANTHA (LP)	25
72	Contour 2870 303	MY WAY (LP)	15

(see also Vernons Girls, Krimson Kake)

SAMMY JONES
70	Gas GAS 123	You're My Girl/HONEYBOY MARTIN: Unchained Melody	10
72	Sioux SI 002	Mendicino/RUM RUNNERS: Sugar Brown	5
72	Sioux SI 003	Little Caesar/TWINKLE BROTHERS: Happy Song	5
72	Sioux SI 011	You're My Girl/HONEYBOY MARTIN: Unchained Melody	8

SANDIE JONES
72	Polydor 2058 223	Music Of Love/Ceol An Ghra	12

SOLOMON JONES
70	Bullet BU 452	Be Strong/Version	5
70	Pama PM 812	Here Comes The Night/RECO RODRIGUEZ: Jaded Ramble	8

SPIKE JONES
53	HMV 7M 121	Hot Lips/Hotter Than A Pistol (as Spike Jones & His Country Cousins)	10
53	HMV 7M 160	I Saw Mommy Kissing Santa Claus/Winter (as Spike Jones & His City Slickers)	10
54	HMV 7MC 3	Deep Purple/Dragnet (as Spike Jones & His City Slickers)	10
54	HMV 7MC 17	I Wanna Go Back To West Virginia/Little Bo-Beep Has Lost Her Sheep (as Spike Jones & His City Slickers, export issue)	10
55	HMV 7M 324	Secret Love/I'm In The Mood For Love (as Spike Jones & His City Slickers)	10
61	Warner Bros WB 34	Monster Movie Babe/Teenage Brain Surgeon	6
57	HMV 7EG 8286	FUN IN HI FI (EP)	10
59	RCA RCX 1030	SPIKE JONES NO. 1 (EP)	10
59	RCA RCX 1037	SPIKE JONES NO. 2 (EP)	10
60	London HAG 2270	OMNIBUST (LP)	15
60	Warner Brothers WM 4004	IN HI-FI (LP)	15
60	Warner Bros. EB 8004	SPIKE JONES IN STEREO (LP)	15
61	London SAHG 6109	SIXTY YEARS OF MUSIC AMERICA HATES BEST (LP)	15

STAN JONES
58	Pye Disneyland DPL 39000	CREAKIN' LEATHER (LP)	15

STEVE JONES (1)
84	P flight PFD 01	I Need You (12")	80

STEVE JONES (2)
87	MCA MCA 1184	Mercy/Through The Night (p/s)	5

MINT VALUE £

87	MCA MCF 3384	MERCY (LP)	12

(see also Sex Pistols, Professionals)

TAMIKO JONES
76	Contempo CX 15	Let It Flow/DORIS DUKE: Woman Of The Ghetto	15

TAMMY JONES
68	CBS 3744	Come Back My Love/Say No More	6
69	CBS 4387	Don't Call Me Back/Tell Me Tell Me	6
69	CBS 4594	All The Love In The World/Time Will Come	6
70	CBS 5198	But At Night/I'm Still Looking For The Right One	6
75	CBS Epic EPC 3211	Let Me Try Again/Just One Woman	5
76	Epic SEPC 3990	Love's A Carousel/Amazing Grace	6
75	Epic 80853	LET ME TRY AGAIN (LP)	12

THAD JONES
57	Esquire 32-065	OLIO (LP)	40
58	Esquire 32-080	AFTER HOURS (LP)	60
59	Pye Nixa NJL 13	MAD THAD (LP)	70

THELMA JONES
68	Sue WI 4047	Stronger/Never Leave Me	50
69	Soul City SC 110	The House That Jack Built/Give It To Me Straight	30
76	CBS 4711	Salty Tears/You're The Song	15

THUNDERCLAP JONES
56	Oriole CB 1320	Hurricane Boogie/The Laughing Rag (78)	12
56	Oriole CB 1328	Sound Barrier Boogie/Ask For Joe (78)	12

TOM JONES
64	Decca F 11966	Chills And Fever/Breathless	60
65	Columbia DB 7566	Little Lonely One/That's What We'll All Do	20
65	Decca F 12191	With These Hands/Untrue	5
65	Decca F 12203	What's New Pussycat?/Rose	6
65	Columbia DB 7733	Lonely Joe/I Was A Fool	20
65	Decca F 12292	Thunderball/Key To My Heart	8
66	Decca F 12315	To Make A Big Man Cry/I'll Never Let You Go (export issue)	10
66	Decca F 12349	Stop Breaking My Heart/Never Give Away Love	10
66	Decca F 12390	Once There Was A Time/Not Responsible	6
66	Decca F 12461	This And That/City Girl	10
66	Decca F 12516	Green, Green Grass Of Home/If I Had You (export issue)	5
67	Decca F 22555	Detroit City/If I Had You	5
67	Decca F 22563	Detroit City/Ten Guitars (export issue)	10
68	Decca F 12854	A Minute Of Your Time/Looking Out My Window	10
71	Decca FR 13236	Till//The Sun Died (export issue)	5
71	Decca FR 13237	Till/One Day Soon (export issue)	10
65	Columbia SEG 8464	TOM JONES (EP)	20
65	Decca DFE 8668	WHAT A PARTY (EP)	15
65	Decca SKL 4743	A-TOM-IC JONES (LP, stereo)	12

JONES TOWN MALE QUARTET/FRANKLIN LADIES TOWN TRIO
62	Son TD 104	We'll Never Say Goodbye/Living For J (split 45 rpm single)	25

U.K. JONES
69	Deram DM 231	Let Me Tell Ya/And The Rains Came Down	15
70	Ember EMB S 298	Take Me For What I Am/Love Is Here To Stay	6

(see also Mike Berry)

VIVIAN JONES
79	White Rum/Red Stripe 101 PROOF	Jah Music/Vibes (as V. Jones)	10
87	Jah Shaka SHAKA 861	JAH WORKS (LP)	15

WINSTON JONES
73	Gayfeet GS 208	You Make Me Cry/Version	6

WIZZ JONES
69	United Artists (S)ULP 1209	WIZZ JONES (LP)	150
70	Village Thing VTS 4	LEGENDARY ME (LP)	100
72	CBS 64809	RIGHT NOW (LP)	100
74	Village Thing VTS 24	WHEN I LEAVE BERLIN (LP)	90
77	Plant Life PLR 009	MAGICAL FLIGHT (LP, with insert)	25

(see also Pete Stanley & Wizz Jones, Accolade)

JONES BOYS
57	Columbia DB 4046	Cool Baby/Rock-A-Hula Baby (Ukulele Lady)	15
58	Columbia DB 4170	A Certain Smile/Kathy-O	5
58	Columbia DB 4217	The Day The Rains Came/Hideaway	7
59	Columbia DB 4278	Dream Girl/Straight As An Arrow	6

(see also Four Jones Boys)

JONES BROTHERS
69	Pye Intl. 7N 25696	Lucky Lady/Good Old Days	75

JONESY
73	Dawn DNS 1030	Ricochet/Every Day's The Same	20
72	Dawn DNLS 3042	NO ALTERNATIVE (LP, gatefold sleeve)	60
73	Dawn DNLS 3048	KEEPING UP (LP, with lyric insert, lilac label)	70
73	Dawn DNLS 3048	KEEPING UP (LP, without lyric insert, lilac label)	50
73	Dawn DNLS 3055	GROWING (LP, gatefold sleeve, with lyric insert, pink 'sun' label)	65
73	Dawn DNLS 3055	GROWING (LP, gatefold sleeve, without lyric insert, pink 'sun' label)	50

(see also Alan Bown, Ray Thomas)

JONIE D
89	Positive Beat PBEP 001	WHICH BASE (EP)	15

HARLEM JONNS RESHUFFLE
68	Fontana TF 970	You Are The One I Love/Good Lovin'	30

| 69 | Fontana TF 1004 | Everything Under The Sun/Let Love Come Between Us | 20 |
| 69 | Fontana (S)TL 5509 | HARLEM JONNS RESHUFFLE (LP) | 40 |

JONSTON MCPHILBRY
| 66 | Fontana TF 663 | She's Gone/Woke Up At Eight | 90 |

JON THE POSTMAN
| 78 | Bent BIG BENT 2 | PUERILE (12" EP, stamped brown paper bag p/s, with inserts) | 20 |
| 78 | Bent BIG BENT 4 | PSYCHEDELIC ROCK'N'ROLL FIVE SKINNERS (12" EP, white label, foldover p/s in bag) | 20 |

JOOK
72	RCA RCA 2279	Alright With Me/Do What You Can	15
73	RCA RCA 2344	Shame/City And Suburban Blues	20
73	RCA RCA 2368	Oo-Oo-Rudi/Jook's On You	15
73	RCA RCA 2431	King Capp/Rumble	12
74	RCA RCA 5024	Bish Bash Bosh/Crazy Kids	18

(see also John's Children, Sparks)

JANIS JOPLIN
69	CBS 3683	Turtle Blues/Piece Of My Heart (withdrawn)	30
71	CBS 7019	Me And Bobby McGee/Half Moon	6
71	CBS 7217	Cry Baby/Mercedes Benz	7
71	CBS 9136	Move Over/Cry Baby/Try/Piece Of My Heart (maxi-single)	8
72	CBS 8241	Down On Me/Bye Bye Baby	6
76	CBS 3960	Piece Of My Heart/Kozmic Blues (p/s)	7
69	CBS 63546	I GOT DEM OL' KOZMIC BLUES AGAIN, MAMA! (LP)	30
74	CBS CQ 30322/Q 64188	PEARL (LP, quadrophonic)	25

(see also Big Brother & Holding Company)

JORDAN BROTHERS
59	London HLW 8908	Never, Never/Please Tell Me Now	30
59	London HLW 8908	Never, Never/Please Tell Me Now (78)	25
60	London HLW 9235	Things I Didn't Say/Polly Plays Her Kettle Drum	10
61	London HLW 9308	No Wings On My Angel/Living For The Day	10

DANNY JORDAN
| 61 | Mercury AMT 1159 | Jeannie/Boom Ditty Boom | 10 |

DICK JORDAN
60	Embassy WB 384	Let It Be Me/Running Bear (78)	10
60	Embassy WB 394	Cathy's Clown/Don't Throw All Those Teardrops (78)	10
60	Oriole CB 1534	Hallelujah, I Love Her So/Sandy	50
60	Oriole CB 1534	Hallelujah, I Love Her So/Sandy (78)	30
60	Oriole CB 1548	Little Christine/I'll Love You Forever	35
60	Oriole CB 1548	Little Christine/I'll Love You Forever (78)	30
60	Oriole CB 1566	Garden Of Eden/Alive, Alive Oh!	10
60	Oriole CB 1591	Angel On My Shoulder/The Next Train Home	15
61	Piccadilly 7N 35035	Some Of These Days/I Want Her Back	75
62	Piccadilly 7N 35057	Fortune Teller/My Angel	10
63	Columbia DB 7016	Stop The Music/Dream Chaser	10
66	Parlophone R5475	Progress/Something's Going On In There	25

(see also Don Duke)

EARL JORDAN
| 72 | Sovereign SVN 6501 | JORDAN (LP, textured sleeve with flipbacks) | 60 |

FRED JORDAN
| 66 | Topic 12T 150 | SONGS OF A SHROPSHIRE FARM WORKER (LP, blue label) | 15 |

JACK JORDAN - HIS MUSIC
| 60 | Parlophone R 4677 | Golden Girl/Beauty And The Beach | 7 |

LOUIS JORDAN (& HIS TYMPANY FIVE)
54	Melodisc 1031	Dad Gum Ya Hide Boy/Whiskey Do Your Stuff (78)	15
56	Melodisc 1349	Messy Bessy/I Seen What'cha Done (78)	20
60	Downbeat CHA 3	Ooo-Wee/I'll Die Happy	20
50s	Melodisc EPM7 66	LOUIS JORDAN (EP, as Louis Jordan Tympany Five, 3 different covers)	90
57	Mercury MPT 7521	SOMEBODY UP THERE DIGS ME (10" LP, with Tympany Five)	100
58	Mercury MPL 6541	MAN, WE'RE WAILIN' (LP, with Tympany Five)	60
64	HMV CLP 1809	HALLELUJAH, LOUIS JORDAN IS BACK (LP)	40

(see also Louis Armstrong)

LOUIS JORDAN & CHRIS BARBER'S BAND
| 63 | Melodisc 45-1616 | Is She Is Or Is She Ain't Your Baby/Fifty Cents | 18 |

(see also Chris Barber)

JORDANAIRES
57	Capitol CL 14687	Sugaree/Baby, Won't You Please Come Home?	80
57	Capitol CL 14687	Sugaree/Baby, Won't You Please Come Home? (78)	15
57	Capitol CL 14773	Summer Vacation/Each Day	20
57	Capitol CL 14773	Summer Vacation/Each Day (78)	15
58	Capitol CL 14921	Little Miss Ruby/All I Need Is You	25
63	Capitol CL 15281	Don't Be Cruel/Don't Worry	20
71	Ember EMB S 313	Kentucky/Teach The World To Sing	6
62	Capitol T 1742	SPOTLIGHT ON THE JORDANAIRES (LP)	40

(see also Elvis Presley, Patsy Cline, Don Gibson, Marty Robbins)

JORGE
| 69 | Aurora 7984 | Everybody Wants To Be Loved/Tic Tac Toe | 10 |

JOSEF K
79	Absolute ABS 1	Chance Meeting/Romance (p/s, 1,000 only)	30
80	Postcard 80-3	Radio Drill Time/Crazy To Exist (live) (hand-coloured foldaround p/s, blue labels)	30
80	Postcard 80-3	Radio Drill Time/Crazy To Exist (live) (brown sleeve & labels)	10
80	Postcard 80-3	Radio Drill Time/Crazy To Exist (live) (cream/yellow sleeve & labels)	8
80	Postcard 80-5	It's Kinda Funny/Final Request (in poly bag, with picture insert)	25
80	Postcard 80-5	It's Kinda Funny/Final Request (in poly bag, without picture insert)	10

MINT VALUE £

80	Postcard 80-5	It's Kinda Funny/Final Request (2nd issue, brown label and brown company sleeve)) 5
81	Postcard 81-5	Chance Meeting/Pictures (die-cut sleeve, with postcard)......................................25
81	Postcard 81-5	Chance Meeting/Pictures (die-cut sleeve, without postcard).................................8
81	Postcard 81-4/TWI 023	Sorry For Laughing/Revelation (p/s)..15
87	Supreme Intl. Edit. 87-7	Heaven Sent/Radio Drill Time/Heads Watch/Fun'n'Frenzy (12", p/s) 8
81	Postcard 81-1	SORRY FOR LAUGHING (LP, unreleased, a few with proof sleeve) 0
81	Postcard 81-7	THE ONLY FUN IN TOWN (LP, with inner sleeve) 40
87	Supreme Intl. Edit. 87-6	YOUNG AND STUPID (LP) 15
90	Supreme Intl. Edit.	YOUNG AND STUPID (CD)..18

(see also Orange Juice, Paul Haig, Happy Family, Rhythm Of Life)

IRVING JOSEPH
| 60 | London HLT 9027 | I Left My Love/Lorena ....8 |

MARGIE JOSEPH (& BLUE MAGIC)
72	Stax 2025 052	Medicine Bend/Same Thing 15
74	Atlantic K 10460	Sweet Surrender/My Love 6
75	Atlantic K 10649	What's Come Over Me/You And Me (as Margie Joseph & Blue Magic) 6
72	Stax 2362 008	MAKES A NEW IMPRESSION (LP)...12
73	Atlantic K 40462	MARGIE JOSEPH (LP)..12

JOSH
| 69 | Duke DU 41 | Judge/RON: Soul Of Joemel ....10 |
| 70 | Hot Rod HR 111 | Leaving Everything/HOT ROD ALL STARS : Psychedelic Bird ....20 |

(see also Girlie)

JOSH & HERBIE
| 60s | Kalypso AB 107 | I'm Nobody's Child/How Can I Believe In You ....6 |

JOSHUA
| 73 | Key KL 014 | JOSHUA (LP)..140 |

MARVA JOSIE
| 66 | Polydor 56711 | Crazy Stockings/I'll Get By..15 |

JOURNEY
| 82 | CBS CBS 11A 1728 | Don't Stop Believin'/Natural Thing (12", picture disc) ....8 |
| 92 | Columbia 4728102 | TIME3 (3-CD) ....25 |

JOY & DAVID/DAVE
58	Parlophone R 4477	Whoopee!/My Oh My! (as Joy & David)..40
58	Parlophone R 4477	Whoopee!/My Oh My! (78, as Joy & David)...30
59	Decca F 11123	Rocking Away The Blues/If You Pass Me By (as Joy & David) 40
59	Decca F 11123	Rocking Away The Blues/If You Pass Me By (78, as Joy & David).............................35
60	Triumph RGM 1002	Let's Go See Gran'ma/Believe Me (as Joy & Dave)..45
60	Decca F 11291	My Very Good Friend The Milkman/Doopey Darling (as Joy & Dave)..........................25
61	Parlophone R 4855	Joe's Been A-Gittin' There/They Tell Us Not To Love (as Joy & Dave) 20
61	Parlophone R 4855	Joe's Been A-Gittin' There/They Tell Us Not To Love (demo copies with alternate take of B-side)...45

MABEL JOY
| 75 | Real RR 2004 | MABEL JOY (LP)..20 |

RODDIE JOY
| 65 | Red Bird RB 10021 | Come Back Baby/Love Hit Me With A Wallop...60 |

JOHNNY JOYCE
| 76 | Freedom FLP 99003 | JOYCE'S CHOICE MIXTURE (LP) ....22 |

(see also Velvet Opera, Levee Breakers)

JOYCE'S ANGELS
| 67 | Major Minor MM 526 | Flowers For My Friends/Rodney Reginald Smithfield Harvey Jones ....15 |

(see also Chris White)

JOY DE VIVRE
| 81 | Crass CR & SS ENVY 1 | Our Wedding (flexidisc, white vinyl, no p/s, with mailer) ....300 |
| 81 | Crass CR & SS ENVY 1 | Our Wedding (flexidisc, white vinyl, no p/s, without mailer) ....200 |

(see also Crass)

JOY DIVISION
SINGLES
78	Enigma PSS 139	AN IDEAL FOR LIVING (Warsaw/No Love Lost/Leaders Of Men/Failures) (EP, 1,000 only, foldout p/s; beware of counterfeits) 1200
78	Anonymous ANON 1	AN IDEAL FOR LIVING (Warsaw/No Love Lost/Leaders Of Men/Failures) (12" EP reissue, 1,200 only) 600
79	Factory FAC 13	Transmission/Novelty (p/s)..10
80	Factory FAC 23	Love Will Tear Us Apart/These Days 8
80	Factory FACUS T2	She's Lost Control/Atmosphere..15
80	Factory FAC23.12	Love Will Tear Us Apart/These Days (12", with flexi) 15
80	Factory FAC 28	Komakino/Incubation/As You Said (flexi) 10
80	Factory FACUS2/UK	Atmosphere/She's Lost Control (UK variant, 12", red vinyl)...............................15
82	Factory FAC 13 12	Transmission/Novelty (12")...12
88	Factory FAC 213/7	Atmosphere/The Only Mistake (p/s)...5
88	Factory FAC213	Atmosphere/The Only Mistake/Sound Of Music (12", p/s).................................10
86	Strange Fruit SFPS 013	PEEL SESSIONS (12", p/s recorded 31/01/79) 12
87	Strange Fruit SFPS 033	PEEL SESSIONS (12" EP)...15
95	London YOJX 1	Love Will Tear Us Apart (Original Version)/Love Will Tear Us Apart (Radio Version)/Love Will Tear Us Apart (Arthur Baker Remix)/Atmosphere (12", stickered p/s)...8
11	Rhino FAC 33	Ceremony (Original Version)/In A Lonely Place (12" Version)//Ceremony (Heart & Soul Rehearsal Version)/In A Lonely Place (Unreleased Rehearsal Version) (12")...15

ALBUMS
79	Factory FACT 10	UNKNOWN PLEASURES (LP with inner sleeve, textured sleeve, 1st press turns a deep translucent red when held up to a light) 50
79	Factory FACT 10	UNKNOWN PLEASURES (LP with inner sleeve, textured sleeve, 2nd non transluscent issue) 40
80	Factory FACT 6	CLOSER (LP, hard textured sleeve & inner)...40

81	Factory FACT 40	STILL (2-LP, hessian sleeve, card inners & white/blue ribbon) 70
80	Factory FAC 40	STILL (2-LP, gatefold) 30
85	Factory FACT 10c	UNKNOWN PLEASURES (reissue, cassette in box with insert) 25
85	Factory FACT 25c	CLOSER (reissue, cassette in box with insert)...25
85	Factory FACT 40c	STILL (reissue, cassette in box with insert) 25
88	Factory FACT 250	SUBSTANCE (LP) 25
90	Strange Fruit SFRLP 111	PEEL SESSIONS (LP, reissue of both EPs) 20
95	London 828624 1	PERMANENT (2-LP, insert) 30
01	Strange Fruit SFRSLP 094	THE COMPLETE BBC RECORDINGS (LP) 30
07	London 2564699291	JOY DIVISION (4xLP boxed set, 3000 only) 100
07	Ozit Morpheus OZIT 8797	MARTIN HANNETT'S PERSONAL MIXES (2-LP) 20

(see also New Order)

COL JOYE & JOYBOYS
59	Brunswick 05806	(Rockin' Rollin') Clementine/Bye Bye Baby Goodbye 25
59	Brunswick 05806	(Rockin' Rollin') Clementine/Bye Bye Baby Goodbye (78) 20
60	Top Rank JAR 529	Be My Girl/Yes Sir, That's My Baby 10

JOYFUL SOUND
| 73 | SRT SRT 73278 | IT WILL BE WORTH IT ALL (LP) ....300 |

JOY GUESSING
| 70 | Crimson N 034 | The Blue Midget/Officer Bud Babe ....6 |

JOY OF COOKING
| 72 | Capitol E-ST 11050 | CASTLES (LP, laminated front cover. flipback sleeve).......................................12 |

JOYRIDE
| 69 | RCA SF 8027 | FRIEND SOUND (LP) ....20 |

JOY UNLIMITED
69	Page One POF 147	Daytime Night Time/Mister Pseudonym 30
69	Page One POF 160	Oh Darlin'/Feelin' 40
70	Page One POLS 028	TURBULENCE (LP).......................................80

J P SUNSHINE
| 95 | Uncle Glitch Records UG 1 | UNCLE GLITCH PRESENTS (LP, 500 only).......................................30 |

JR. WILSON
| 89 | Blue Trac BTRD 035 | Speak Softly (with T. Sparks and Mystic Man)/CONROY SMITH: Problems (12") ....40 |

J.S.D. BAND
73	Cube BUG 29	Sarah Jane/Paddy Stacks (p/s) 6
71	Regal Zono. SRLZ 1018	COUNTRY OF THE BLIND (LP, textured sleeve, first press with flipbacks).......................................80
71	Regal Zono. SRLZ 1018	COUNTRY OF THE BLIND (LP, textured sleeve, later press without flipbacks)..................40
72	Cube HIFLY 11	J.S.D. BAND (LP).......................................15
73	Cube HIFLY 14	TRAVELLING DAYS (LP, fully laminated sleeve) 15

JUAN & JUNIOR
| 67 | CBS 2949 | The Chase/Nothing ....6 |
| 68 | CBS 3223 | To Girls/Andurina ....15 |

JUBILEE STOMPERS
| 70 | Trojan TR 7725 | Luciana/I Really Like It ....6 |

JUDAS JUMP
70	Parlophone R 5828	Run For Your Life/Beer Drinking Woman 15
70	Parlophone R 5838	This Feelin' We Feel/Hangman's Playing.......................................8
70	Parlophone R 5873	Beer Drinking Woman/I Have The Right 6
70	Parlophone PAS 10001	SCORCH (LP, gatefold sleeve, black/silver label with boxed logo)...................50

(see also Herd, Amen Corner, Andy Bown)

JUDAS PRIEST
74	Gull GULS 6	Rocka-Rolla/Never Satisfied 25
76	Gull GULS 31	The Ripper/Island Of Domination 25
77	CBS S CBS 5222	Diamonds And Rust/Dissident Aggressor 7
78	CBS S CBS 6077	Better By You, Better Than Me/Invader 5
78	CBS S CBS 6794	Before The Dawn/Rock Forever 5
79	CBS S CBS 12-6915	Take On The World/White Heat Red Hot (12", p/s).......................................8
79	CBS S CBS 7312	Evening Star/Beyond The Realms Of Death 5
79	CBS 12-7312	Evening Star/The Green Manalishi/Beyond The Realms Of Death (12", clear vinyl with picture insert) 8
79	Gull GULS 71	The Ripper/Victims Of Change 8
79	Gull GULS 7112	The Ripper/Never Satisfied/Victim Of Changes (12", p/s) 12
80	CBS TA 4298	United/Grinder (poster p/s) 12
81	CBS A12 1153	Hot Rockin'/Steeler/You Don't Have To Be Old To Be Wise (12", no p/s) 8
82	CBS A 112611	You've Got Another Thing Comin'/Exciter (live) (picture disc) 6
82	CBS A 2822	(Take These) Chains/Judas Priest Audio File (p/s) 5
83	Gull GULS 7612	Tyrant/Rocka-Rolla/Genocide (12", p/s, white vinyl).......................................8
84	CBS TA 4298	Some Heads Are Gonna Roll/Green Manalishi (Live)/Jawbreaker (12", p/s) 8
86	CBS QTA 7144	Locked In (Extended)/Reckless/Desert Plains (live)/Freewheel Burning (live) (12", poster p/s).......................................10
90	Columbia 656273 6	Painkiller/United/Better By You, Better Than Me (12" red vinyl, p/s) 8
91	Columbia 656589 0	A Touch Of Evil/Between The Hammer And The Anvil (shaped disc) 12
91	Columbia 656589 6	A Touch Of Evil/Between The Hammer And The Anvil/ You've Got Another Thing Coming (Live) (12", p/s, with giant poster) 8
74	Gull GULP 1005	ROCKA ROLLA (LP, original issue, 'bottle top' sleeve) 30
76	Gull GULP 1015	SAD WINGS OF DESTINY (LP) 15
76	Gull PGULP 1015	SAD WINGS OF DESTINY (LP, picture disc).......................................20
77	CBS 82008	SIN AFTER SIN (LP) 15
78	CBS 82430	STAINED CLASS (LP) 15
78	Gull PGULP 1026	THE BEST OF JUDAS PRIEST (LP, picture disc) 12
78	CBS 83135	KILLING MACHINE (LP, red vinyl) 15
79	CBS 83852	UNLEASHED IN THE EAST (LP, with free single "Rock Forever"/ Hell Bent For Leather"/"Beyond The Realms Of Death" [SJP 1]).......................................25
79	CBS 66357	BOX SET (3-LP, reissue of "Sin After Sin"/"Stained Class"/"Killing Machine") 25
80	CBS 84160	BRITISH STEEL (LP) 12
86	Shanghai PGLP 1026	JUDAS PRIEST (LP, picture disc).......................................12

MINT VALUE £

93	CBS 473050	METAL WORKS (2xLP, gatefold sleeve)	18
98	SPV 0891 8542	98 LIVE MELTDOWN (2xLP)	18
04	Sony 5128933	METALOGY (4xCD, DVD, booklet, leather studded box set)	45

(see also Trapeze, Fancy)

JUDD
| 70 | Penny Farthing PEN 709 | Snarlin' Mumma Lion/Stronger Than A Man | 6 |
| 70 | Penny Farthing PELS 504 | JUDD (LP, die-cut sleeve, insert, red/black/yellow labels) | 150 |

(see also Kris Ife)

F.C. JUDD
60	Castle EFX 1	ELECTRONIC SOUNDS AND MUSIC (EP)	50
60	Castle EFX 2	ELECTRONIC THEMES AND MUSIQUE CONCRETE (EP)	50
60	Castle EFX 3	RHYTHMIC ELECTRONIC MUSIC (EP)	50
60	Castle HMX 1	HAUNTED HOUSE, MYSTERY SOUNDS AND MUISIC (EP)	25
67	(No label or cat no)	ELECTRONIC SOUNDS AND EFFECTS (flexi, free with Practical Electronics)	15

JUDGE HAPPINESS
| 85 | Mynah SCS 8501 | Hey Judge/Pig In Pink (very few with p/s) | 25 |
| 85 | Mynah SCS 8501 | Hey Judge/Pig In Pink | 10 |

(see also Mock Turtles)

TERRY JUDGE & THE BARRISTERS
63	Oriole CB 1896	Hey Look At Her/Kind Of Girl You Can't Forget	15
64	Oriole CB 1938	I Don't Care/Try To Forget	15
65	Fontana TF 599	Come With Me And Love Me/Waitin' For The Night To Come	15

JUGGERNAUTS
| 84 | Supreme Int. Editions 84-2 | Come Throw Yourself/My First Million (p/s) | 10 |

(see also Paul Haig)

JUICE CREW
08	Diggers With Gratitude DWG 002	THE JUICE CREW (EP, 125 only, black vinyl)	60
08	Diggers With Gratitude DWG 003	THE JUICE CREW (EP, 75 only, white vinyl)	80
08	Diggers With Gratitude DWG 004	THE JUICE CREW (EP, 75 only, blue vinyl)	80
08	Diggers With Gratitude DWG 004	THE JUICE CREW (EP, 75 only, red vinyl)	80

JUICE ON THE LOOSE
| 81 | Juice JJOS 1 | JUICE ON THE LOOSE (LP) | 12 |

JUICY LUCY
70	Fontana TF 1068	Who Do You Love/Walking Down The Highway (unissued)	0
70	Vertigo V1/6059 001	Who Do You Love/Walking Down The Highway	10
70	Vertigo 6059 015	Pretty Woman/I'm A Thief	18
72	Polydor 2001 279	It Ain't Easy/Promised Land	7
69	Vertigo VO 2	JUICY LUCY (LP, first press with 'Philips' credit on large swirl label, gatefold sleeve)	120
69	Vertigo VO 2	JUICY LUCY (LP, later press without 'Philips' credit on large swirl label, gatefold sleeve)	70
70	Vertigo 6360 014	LIE BACK AND ENJOY IT (LP, large swirl label, gatefold poster sleeve)	70
71	Bronze ILPS 9157	GET A WHIFF OF THIS (LP, textured sleeve, Island credit on label)	30
72	Polydor 2310 160	PIECES (LP)	25

(see also Misunderstood, Van Der Graaf Generator, Ray Owen, Paul Williams' Big Roll Band)

JIMMY JUKEBOX
| 75 | Sonet SON 2057 | Motorboat/25 Hours A Day | 15 |
| 77 | Sonet SON 2057 | Motorboat/25 Hours A Day (1977 re-issue with new Savage Pencil p/s sleeve but original 1975 records inside) | 20 |

(see also Kim Fowley)

JULIAN (SCOTT)
| 59 | Pye Nixa 7N 15236 | Sue Saturday/Can't Wait | 30 |
| 59 | Pye Nixa N 15236 | Sue Saturday/Can't Wait (78) | 20 |

(see also Brian Bennett)

JULIAN (JUDY MOWATT) & CHOSEN FEW
| 71 | High Note HS 054 | Joy To The World/Joyful Version | 8 |

JULIAN (JUDY MOWATT) & GAYTONES
| 72 | High Note HS 059 | She Kept On Talking/Version | 15 |

JULIAN'S TREATMENT
| 70 | Young Blood YB 1009 | Phantom City/Alda, Dark Lady Of The Outer Worlds | 25 |
| 70 | Young Blood SYB 2/3 | A TIME BEFORE THIS (2-LP, laminated gatefold sleeve, white/red labels) | 350 |

(see also Julian Jay Savarin)

JULY
68	Major Minor MM 568	My Clown/Dandelion Seeds	200
68	Major Minor MM 580	Hello, Who's There?/The Way	80
68	Major Minor MMLP 29	JULY (LP, laminated front sleeve, red/white/black labels)	800
87	Bam Caruso KIRI 097	DANDELION SEEDS (LP, reissue of above LP with extra tracks & different sleeve)	25
95	Essex 1011LP	JULY (LP, reissue with bonus 7": "Hello Who's There?"/"The Way" [p/s, 10117])	20

(see also Jade Warrior, Tom Newman, Tomcats)

JUMBLE LANE
| 71 | Holyground HG 115 | JUMBLE LANE (LP, 99 copies only) | 600 |

JUMP
| 80 | Caveman CLUB 1 | Shake Up/All In Vain (p/s) | 25 |

JUMPIN' JACKS
| 58 | HMV POP 440 | My Girl, My Girl/Tried And Tested | 25 |

JUMPLEADS
| 82 | Ock OC 001 | THE STAG MUST DIE (LP, with insert) | 15 |

JUMP SQUAD

81	101 UR 2	Lord Of The Dance/Debt (p/s)	20

(see also Embryo)

JUNCO PARTNERS

65	Columbia DB 7665	As Long As I Have You/Take This Hammer	70
79	Rigid JUNK 1028	Swinging Sixties Boys/Peepin' And Hidin'	6
81	Energy NRG 4	Tall Windows/Noizez In My Head (p/s)	5
81	Energy NRGX 4	Tall Windows (Extended)/Noizez In My Head (Extended) (12", stickered white label, plain sleeve, promo only)	10
71	Philips 6308 032	JUNCO PARTNERS (LP, laminated sleeve, black/silver labels)	120

JUNCTION 32

75	Holyground HGS 119	JUNCTION 32 (LP, 100 copies only)	650

JUNCUNO

71	Banana BA 361	The End (as Joncuno)/HORACE ANDY: See A Man's Face	30

(see also Jon Cundo)

ROSANNE JUNE

56	London HLU 8352	The Charge Of The Light Brigade/Broken Windows	20
56	London HLU 8352	The Charge Of The Light Brigade/Broken Windows (78)	10
58	Oriole CB 1430	When A Woman Cries/The Great Chicago Fire	8

ROSEMARY JUNE

59	Pye International 7N 25005	I'll Be With You In Apple Blossom Time/Always A Bridesmaid	6

JUNE BRIDES

84	Pink PINKY 1	In The Rain/Sunday To Saturday (p/s)	10
84	Pink PINKY 2	Every Conversation/Disneyland (die-cut sleeve, with insert)	8
84	Pink PINKY 2	Every Conversation/Disneyland (die-cut sleeve)	7

(see also Phil Wilson)

JUNG COLLECTIVE

02	Nanny Tango NT 1	Injustice/Street Preacher (Plaid Mix) (clear vinyl, poly sleeve w/sticker insert)	20

CARL GUSTAV JUNG

63	Piccadily FTF 38505	FACE TO FACE (LP)	20

JUNGLE JIM

71	Pye 7N 4509	Big Fat Oranguman/Neasden Melody	5
72	Pye7N 45185	Linda Love/Baby Go Down/Baby Go Down	8

JUNIOR (SIMPSON)

68	Giant GN 18	I'm Gonna Leave You Girl/I Love You I Love You	8
68	Giant GN 25	Come Cure Me/I Want Your Loving	8

JUNIOR B

92	Eastern Sher ES 001	Meditation/Black And White (12")	40

JUNIOR BROWN

78	Tempus TEMD 01	Jah Find Babylon Guilty (feat. Ranking Ruben)/Dub (12")	15
80	Jah Shaka 829	Fly Me Away/Travelling Dub (12")	30

JUNIOR DELGADO

77	Deb TIC 1001	Tiction/Tiction Volume 2	15
78	Deb DEB 001	Tonight & Tune In/Armed Robbery (12")	20
78	Deb DEB 019	Trickster/CARLTON & HIS SHOES: Better Days (12")	12
79	Greensleeves GRED 15	Love Tickles Like Magic/PRINCE JAMMY & AGGROVATORS : Prince Jammy's Magic (12")	20
79	Burning Sounds BRD 005	Raiders/Warrior	20
80	Niagra NIADD 108	Fort Augustus/Escape Prisioners (12")	25
82	Incredible Jux IJ 04	Trouble Part 1/Trouble Part 2 (12")	20
86	Incredible IM001	Poverty/Version (12")	30
88	Mango IS 368	Hanging Tree/Hey Good Looking (12")	20
89	Fashion FAD 066	Dub School/We A Blood (12")	25
79	Deb DEBLP 05	TASTE OF THE YOUNG HEART (LP)	25
82	Incredible Jux HBLP 001	BUSHMAN REVOLUTION (LP)	40
95	Incredible Music IMLP 001	TREAURE FOUND (LP)	12

JUNIOR DISPROL

01	SFDB AO27658	Fight Club/Junq Waffle	15

JUNIOR ENGLISH

79	Ethnic Fight ETH 1328	Keep On Trying/HORSEMOUTH: Herb Vendor (12")	20

JUNIOR'S EYES

69	Regal Zonophone RZ 3009	Mr. Golden Trumpet Player/Black Snake	30
69	Regal Zonophone RZ 3018	Woman Love/White Light Part 2 (withdrawn B-side)	30
69	Regal Zonophone RZ 3018	Woman Love/Circus Days	20
69	Regal Zonophone RZ 3023	Star Child/Sink Or Swim	20
69	Regal Zono. SLRZ 1008	BATTERSEA POWER STATION (LP, laminated front, flipbacks, "Sold in U.K..." label text)	125

(see also David Bowie, Tickle, Bunch Of Fives, Outsiders)

JUNIOR GEE

83	Masterfunk MF 005	Caveman Rock/Scratch The Rock (12")	10
86	Scorcher 1032	The Truth (12")	90

JUNIOR GEE & THE CAPITAL BOYS

84	Tai Wan 1948	Check Us Out/The Break (12")	25

HUGH ROY JUNIOR

71	Big BG 329	Papcito/RUPIE EDWARDS: I'm Gonna Live Some Life	8
71	Supreme SUP 211	Double Attack/MURPHY'S ALL STARS: Puzzle	12
72	Ashanti ASH 405	King Of The Road/ROOSEVELT ALL STARS: Version	10
72	Jackpot JP 806	Two Ton Guletto/Version	10

(see also U Roy Junior)

JUNIOR KEITHING

80	Grand Masters GM 001	Jah Wrote Me A Letter/Letter Dub (12")	20

MINT VALUE £

JUNIOR MCCANTS
98	Kent 6T 16	Try Me For Your New Love/GARLAND GREEN: Come Through Me	30

JUNIOR MURVIN
68	Doctor Bird DB 1112	Miss Cushie/LYNN TAITT & JETS: Dr. Paul	150
68	Big Shot BI 503	Chattie Chattie/The Magic Touch	200
69	Big Shot BI 527	The Hustler/The Magic Touch	200
70	Gayfeet GS 205	Jennifer/Slipping	8
76	Island WIP 6316	Junior Murvin/Grumblin Dub	8
77	Island IPR 2001	Tedious/Memories	30
77	Island 12WIP 2010	Upsetter Revue Feat. Junior Murvin: Dread Locks In Moonlight/Closer Together (12")	12
82	Dread At The Controls DATCD 009	Bad Man Posse/Riddim Request To All Posse Smoker Posse (12")	18
86	Greensleeves GRED 199	Apartheid/Jack Slick (12")	15
77	Island MLPS 9499	POLICE AND THIEVES (LP)	12
82	Dread At The Controls	BADMAN POSSE (LP)	30
84	Greensleeves GREL 70	MUGGERS IN THE STREET (LP)	20

JUNIOR REID
80	Negus Roots NERT 02	Sister Dawn/Dub Version (12")	20
81	Negus Roots NERT 09	IF I/Versions (12")	40
82	King Imperial KG 008	Jail House/We Got To Leave (12")	40

JUNIOR ROOTS
81	Black Roots BR 24	Natty Dread Time/BLACK TRAP: Into The Light (12")	12

TREVOR JUNIOR
84	Tonos TON 002	Ghetto Living/Have Faith In Jah (12")	50

U ROY JUNIOR
72	Big BG 313	Uncle Charley/Socialise	20
72	Attack ATT 8030	This Is A Pepper/JOHN HOLT: Justice	8
72	Sioux SI 024	The Wedding/LLOYD'S ALL STARS: Buttercup	8
73	Randy's RAN 532	Froggie/RHYTHM RULERS: Version	10
73	Techniques TE 928	Aunt Kereba/DON RECO: Waterloo Rock (B-side actually by Reco Rodriquez)	12

(see also Hugh Roy Junior, U Roy)

JUNIORS
64	Columbia DB 7339	There's A Pretty Girl/Pocket Size	55

JUNIPER GREEN
71	Columbia DB 8809	Dreams In The Sky/Cascade Of Ice	20

LENA JUNOFF
68	Olga OLE 8	Yesterday Has Gone/Good Kind Of Hurt	40

JUNO'S CLAW
79	MPA EMP 081	Barbara/The Master/Big City (EP, no p/s)	90

JUPITER
72	Parlophone R 5967	The Meteor Song/Life Is Getting Better Every Day	25

ERIC JUPP & HIS ORCHESTRA
53	Columbia SCM 5070	Jog Trot/Doina Voda	7
54	Columbia SCM 5081	Ooop De Ooh (Lazy Mambo)/Footsteps In The Fog	7
54	Columbia SCM 5140	They Were Doin' The Mambo/Skokiian (with Coronets)	7
56	Columbia DB 3817	Theme From 'East Of Eden'/When The Lilac Blooms Again	7
57	Columbia DB 4030	Bleep! Bleep!/Three-Two-One-Zero!	12
55	Columbia SEG 7589	ERIC JUPP AND HIS ORCHESTRA (EP)	10
56	Columbia SEG 7603	RHYTHM AND BLUES (EP)	10
56	Columbia 33S 1097	LET'S DANCE (10" LP)	15

(see also Coronets, Rockin' Strings)

MICKEY JUPP
83	A&M AM 128	Stormy Sunday Lunchtime/Reading Glasses	5
83	A&M AM 145	Boxes And Tins/Reading Glasses (p/s)	5

(see also Rossi & Frost, Legend)

JUS BADD
87	Tuff GrooveTUFF001	Freestyle/Proud (12")	100

JUST A HE HE
84	PRT JH 1	Lucky Day/Take Time (p/s)	8

JUST MEASURES
83	It's War Boy £5	FLAGELLATION (LP)	20

JUST BROTHERS
80s	Soul City SC 127	Carlena/IVORIES: Please Stay (die-cut company sleeve)	8

SAMANTHA JUSTE
66	Go AJ 11402	No One Needs My Love Today/If Trees Could Talk	20

JUST FOUR MEN
64	Parlophone R 5186	That's My Baby/Things Will Never Be The Same (withdrawn, as Four Just Men)	80
64	Parlophone R 5208	That's My Baby/Things Will Never Be The Same	60
65	Parlophone R 5241	There's Not One Thing/Don't Come Any Closer	60

(see also Wimple Winch, Four Just Men, Pacific Drift)

JUST FRANK
80	Rok ROK III/IV	You/SPLIT SCREENS: Just Don't Try (die-cut company sleeve)	35

JIMMY JUSTICE
60	Pye 7N 15301	I Understand Just How You Feel/Bloodshot Eyes (as Jimmy Justice & Jury)	25
61	Pye 7N 15351	When Love Has Left You/The Teacher	25
61	Pye 7N 15376	A Little Bit Of Soap/Little Lonely One	15
62	Pye 7N 15443	Ain't That Funny/One (with p/s)	12
62	Pye 7N 15443	Ain't That Funny/One	6
62	Pye 7N 15457	Spanish Harlem/Write Me A Letter	7
62	Pye 7N 15469	Parade Of Broken Hearts/Dawning	6

63	Pye 7N 15502	The World Of Lonely People/I Wake Up Crying	6
63	Pye 7N 15509	Little Cracked Bell/Lighted Windows	7
63	Pye 7N 15528	The Guitar Player/Don't Let The Stars Get In Your Eyes	7
63	Pye 7N 15558	You're Gonna Need My Lovin'/Since You've Been Gone (with Exchequers)	8
63	Pye 7N 15601	Don't Say That Again/Green Leaves Of Summer	7
69	Decca F 12899	Running Out Of Time/There Goes My World	7
65	Pye 7N 15963	Only Heartbreak For Me/Everything In The Garden	5
68	RCA Victor RCA 1681	I'm Past Forgetting You/Walking Away With My Heart	25
72	B&C CB 172	English Rose/Burgundy Port And Wine	10
63	Pye NEP 24159	HIT PARADE (EP)	20
62	Pye NPL 18080	TWO SIDES OF JIMMY JUSTICE (LP)	40
62	Pye NPL 18085	SMASH HITS (LP)	30

JUSTIFIED ANCIENTS OF MU MU (J.A.M.S)

87	KLF Comm. JAMS 23	All You Need Is Love (Original) (12", white label, 1-sided, 500 only)	50
87	KLF Comm. JAMS 23(s)	All You Need Is Love (Me Ru Con Mix)/(Ibo Version) (1,000 only, plain sleeve)	10
87	KLF Comm. JAMS 23T	All You Need Is Love/Ivum Naya/Rap, Rhyme And Scratch Yourself (12", 'James Anderton' p/s, 5,000 only)	15
87	KLF Comm. JAMS 24T	Whitney Joins The JAMs (120 bpm) (12", 1-sided, 'Scottish' issue, 500 only)	15
87	KLF Comm. JAMS 25T	1987 - The 45 Edits (12", p/s)	15
87	KLF Comm. JAMS 26T	BURN THE BEAT (12" EP, 5,000 for export only)	10
87	KLF Comm. JAMS 27	Down Town/118 BPM 27 (p/s)	8
87	KLF Comm. JAMS 27	Down Town (A-side Mix) (12", 1-sided, white label, 500 only)	12
87	KLF Comm. JAMS 27	Down Town (B-side Mix) (12", 1-sided, white label, 500 only)	12
87	KLF Comm. JAMS 27	Down Town (A-side Mix)/(B-side Mix) (12", white label)	12
87	KLF Comm. JAMS 27T	Down Town (118 bpm)/Down Town (12", JAMs label, generic sleeve)	10
87	KLF Comm. JAMS 27T	Down Town (118 bpm)/Down Town (12",mispressed 'album' label, generic sleeve)	15
88	KLF Comm. JAMS 28T	It's Grim Up North (Original Vocal Mix) (12", grey vinyl, 1-sided, 350 only)	100
87	KLF Comm. JAMS DS 1	Deep Shit (flexidisc, unreleased)	150
91	KLF Comm. JAMS 028R	It's Grim Up North (Original Vocal Mix) (12", black vinyl, 1-sided promo)	8
88	Fierce FRIGHT 34(T)	20 GREATEST HITS (12" EP; not actually by J.A.M.s!)	12
87	KLF Comm. JAMS LP 1	1987 (WHAT THE FUCK IS GOING ON?) (LP, withdrawn)	100
88	KLF Comm. JAMS LP 2	WHO KILLED THE JAMS? (LP, stickered sleeve with insert)	20
89	KLF Comm. JAMS DLP 3	SHAG TIMES (2-LP)	50
89	KLF Comm. JAMS CD 3	SHAG TIMES (CD)	40

(see also KLF, Timelords, Disco 2000, Space, Orb, Bill Drummond)

JUSTIN CASE

80	Rok ROK XIX	TV/STRAIGHT UP: One Out All Out (die-cut company sleeve)	40

DAVE JUSTIN

67	Polydor 56221	Everybody's Gone Home/Lincoln Green	12
68	Polydor 56253	You Outside/Thinking Twice	12

JAY JUSTIN

60	HMV POP 801	Nobody's Darlin' But Mine/Sweet Sensation	7
63	HMV POP 1183	Proud Of You/Love, Love Me, Baby Darling	6
68	Columbia DB 8439	I Sell Summertime/Time (withdrawn)	10

JUSTIN & KARLSSON

66	Piccadilly 7N 35295	Somewhere They Can't Find Me/What More Do You Want	40

JUSTINE

69	Dot DOT 121	Leave Me Be/Clown	20
69	Buffalo BFS 1001	Right Now/Place Where Sorrow Hides	20
70	Uni UNS 528	She Brings Back The Morning With Her/Back To Boulder	12
70	Uni UNLS 111	JUSTINE (LP)	120

JUSTINS

71	Punch PH 65	Cholera/LLOYD ALL STARS: Black Bird	8

BILL JUSTIS & HIS ORCHESTRA

57	London HLS 8517	Raunchy/The Midnight Man	25
57	London HLS 8517	Raunchy/The Midnight Man (78)	10
58	London HLS 8614	College Man/The Stranger (B-side with Spinners)	25
58	London HLS 8614	College Man/The Stranger (B-side with Spinners) (78)	10
63	Mercury AMT 1201	I'm Gonna Learn To Dance/Tamoure	10
69	Sun 6094 003	Raunchy/Flip, Flop And Bop	10

JUST PLAIN JONES

71	CBS CBS 7480	Crazy, Crazy/Should Have Stayed With Mary	20

(see also Just Plain Smith, Dave Ballantyne, Esprit De Corps)

JUST PLAIN SMITH

69	Sunshine SUN 7702	February's Child/Don't Open Your Mind (with p/s)	135
69	Sunshine SUN 7702	February's Child/Don't Open Your Mind	60

(see also Just Plain Jones, Esprit De Corps)

JUST US

66	CBS 202068	I Can't Grow Peaches On A Cherry Tree/I Can Save You	7

JUST WILLIAM

68	Spark SRL 1018	I Don't Care/Cherrywood Green	30

JUVENILES

66	Pye International 7N 25349	Bo Diddley/Yes I Believe	100

JYNX

64	Columbia DB 7304	How/Do What They Don't Say	75

MINT VALUE £

JOHNNY K
63   Fontana TF 408   Lemonade/Come Closer Melinda 12

MOSES K & PROPHETS
65   Decca F 12244   I Went Out With My Baby Tonight/So Long 25
(see also Them)

SIMON K
69   B&C CB 111   You Know I Do/Bring Your Love Back..40

KABBALA
82   Red Flame RF 1211   Ashewo Ara/Voltan Dance (12") 25

KABUKI
82   Kabaret Noir KAB 1   I Am A Horse/My Hair (p/s) 30

KADDO STRINGS
80   Grapevine GRP 146   Nothing But Love/Crying Over You 15
(see also Duke Browner, Tartans)

KADENZA
82   PRT 12P 247   Let's Stay Together (Night Club Mix)/Let's Stay Together (Vocal 2)/Instrumental
                                       Version (12")..30

KADETTES
82   Blank GET 1   Fireball XL5/Mission Impossible..8

BERT KAEMPFERT
66   Brunswick LAT/STA 8651   A MAN COULD GET KILLED (LP, soundtrack) 22

KAINE & ABEL
66   Philips BF 1472   Then You Must Know My Love/Crying In The Rain..8

KAISER CHIEFS
04   Drowned In Sound DIS0003   Oh My God/Born To Be A Dancer/Caroline, Yes (CD, 500 only) 20
04   B-Unique BUN088-7   I Predict A Riot/Take My Temperature (p/s) 6
04   B-Unique BUN088-7   I Predict A Riot/Take My Temperature (150 signed 7" with p/s)..............................20
05   KAISERCRIBS001   KAISER CHIEFS: Another Number/THE CRIBS: Modern Way (Double 'A' Side sold at
                                       gigs during 2005 tour dates. 1000 copies)...10
05   No Label   You Can Have It All (1-sided Xmas 2005 single sent out to first 2000 website
                                       subscribers. Christmas card fold-out sleeve. B side with 'I predict Some Quiet'
                                       label 10
07   No Label   The Angry Mob/The Angry Mob (Paul Emmanuel Off The Streets Mix) (mail-order
                                       only, with poster, 1,000 only) 10

(see also Parva)

KAISERS
94   No Hit Records NO HIT 14   IN STEP WITH THE KAISERS (LP) 15
93   No Hit NO HIT 012   SQUAREHEAD STOMP! (LP) 18

KAJANUS/PICKETT
72   Signport SGA 5001   HI HO SILVER (LP, sleeve with cut flap) 20

KAKKO
90   CBS 656023   What Kind Of Fool (mixes)/I Pledge You My Heart (12", p/s) 12
90   CBS 655 710 6   We Should Be Dancing (mixes) (12", p/s) 12
90   CBS 655 710 8   We Should Be Dancing (mixes) (12", p/s) 18
90   CBS 655 710 2   We Should Be Dancing (mixes) (CD) 20

KALA
73   Bradleys BRAD 302   Travelling Home/Still Got Time 5
73   Bradleys BRADL 1002   KALA (LP) 15
(see also Quintessence)

ALAN KALANI
59   Vogue V 9147   A Touch Of Pink/SURFERS: Mambo Jambo 20
59   Vogue V 9147   A Touch Of Pink/SURFERS: Mambo Jambo (78) 20

KALASANDRO!
60   Warner Bros WB 13   Chi Chi/Forbidden City 12

KALEIDOSCOPE (U.K.)
67   Fontana TF 863   Flight From Ashiya/Holidaymaker (in p/s) 100
67   Fontana TF 863   Flight From Ashiya/Holidaymaker 60
68   Fontana TF 895   A Dream For Julie/Please Excuse My Face 40
68   Fontana TF 964   Jenny Artichoke/Just How Much Are You 35
69   Fontana TF 1002   Do It Again For Jeffrey/Poem 50
69   Fontana TF 1048   Balloon/If You So Wish 110
69   Decca (No Cat. No.)   Black Fjord (1-sided) 130
67   Fontana (S)TL 5448   TANGERINE DREAM (LP, unlaminated sleeve, flipbacks, black/silver label) 700
69   Fontana STL 5491   FAINTLY BLOWING (LP, laminated gatefold sleeve; without watermark on beginning
                                       of each side) 1000
69   Fontana STL 5491   FAINTLY BLOWING (LP, laminated gatefold sleeve; with watermark on beginning of
                                       each side) 300
87   5 Hours Back TOCK 005   TANGERINE DREAM (LP, stereo reissue)...18
87   5 Hours Back TOCK 006   FAINTLY BLOWING (LP, reissue, single sleeve) 18
03   Circle CPWL 104   PLEASE LISTEN TO THE PICTURES (2-LP, BBC sessions, split LP with Fairfield Parlour) 20
(see also Fairfield Parlour, I Luv Wight)

KALEIDOSCOPE (U.S.)
70   CBS 64005   BERNICE (LP, as American Kaleidoscope) 30
76   Island ILPS 9462   WHEN SCOPES COLLIDE (LP) 12

KALIN TWINS

58	Brunswick D5751	When/Three O'Clock Thrill	10
58	Brunswick 05759	Forget Me Not/Dream Of Me (some B-side labels list "Dream Of You")	10
59	Brunswick 05775	Oh! My Goodness/It's Only The Beginning	8
59	Brunswick 05797	Cool/When I Look In The Mirror	8
59	Brunswick 05803	Moody/Sweet Sugar Lips	8
59	Brunswick 05814	The Meaning Of The Blues/Why Don't You Believe Me?	10
59	Brunswick 05814	The Meaning Of The Blues/Why Don't You Believe Me? (78)	15
60	Brunswick 05826	Chicken Thief/Loneliness	10
60	Brunswick 05844	Zing! Went The Strings Of My Heart/No Money Can Buy	10
61	Brunswick 05848	Momma Poppa/You Mean The World To Me...	10
61	Brunswick 05862	One More Time/I'm Forever Blowing Bubbles	10
58	Brunswick OE 9383	WHEN (EP)	25
59	Brunswick OE 9449	THE KALIN TWINS (EP)	25

KITTY KALLEN

54	Brunswick 05261	Are You Looking For A Sweetheart/In The Chapel In The Moonlight	20
54	Brunswick 05287	Little Things Mean A Lot/I Don't Think You Love Me Anymore	20
54	Brunswick 05357	Heartless Heart/The Spirit Of Christmas	20
54	Brunswick 05359	I Want You All To Myself/(Don't Let The) Kiddy Geddin'	12
55	Brunswick 05394	A Little Lie/Take Everything But You	7
55	Brunswick 05402	Polly Pigtails/I'm A Lonely Little Petunia (In A Potato Patch)	7
55	Brunswick 05431	Kitty Who?/By Bayou Bay	7
55	Brunswick 05447	Forgive Me/Lonely	7
55	Brunswick 05475	Let's Make The Most Of Tonight/Just Between Friends	6
55	Brunswick 05494	How Lonely Can I Get?/Sweet Kentucky Rose	6
56	Brunswick 05536	Go On With The Wedding (with Georgie Shaw)/Only Forever	6
56	Brunswick 05612	True Love/Will I Always Be Your Sweetheart?	6
57	Brunswick 05705	Long Lonely Nights/Lasting Love	6
58	Brunswick 05734	Crying Roses/I Never Was The One	5
59	Philips PB 971	If I Give My Heart To You/The Door That Won't Open	5

DICK KALLMAN

56	Brunswick 05608	Two Different Worlds/Love Me As Though There Were No Tomorrow	6
60	Vogue V 9162	Born To Be Loved/Just Squeeze Me But Don't Teeze Me	10
63	HMV POP 1118	Say It Isn't So/From This Day On (A-side with John Barry & His Orchestra)	5
63	HMV CLP 1642	SPEAK SOFTLY (LP)	20

BOBBY KALPHAT

68	Nu Beat NB 007	Rhythm And Soul/BUNNY & RUDDY: True Romance	12
74	Faith FA 008	Zion Hill/Dub Hill	10
73	Tropical AL 049	Natty Rock/Natty Dub	10

BOBBY KALPHAT & PHIL PRATT

76	Terminal TERM 001	ZION HILL DUB (LP)	200

CAROL KALPHAT

78	Hit Run HIT DD 1	African Land (featuring Clint Eastwood)/ DOCTOR PABLO AND THE CRYTUFF ALLSTARS -African Melody (12", title sleeve)	70

KAMARAS

69	CBS 4199	Let This Moment Pass Away/I Just Can't Break Away From This Lovin'	25

KAMIKAZE PILOTS

85	Lowther HCW 003	Sharon Signs To Cherry Red/It Goes Boing (p/s)	8

KANDAHAR

74	Sounds Superb 4M048-97401	LONG LIVE THE SLICED HAM (LP)	40

AMORY KANE

70	UNI UNS 518	You Were On My Mind/All The Best Songs And Marches	6
68	MCA MUP(S) 348	MEMORIES OF TIME UNWOUND (LP, with insert)	45
70	CBS 63849	JUST TO BE THERE (LP)	30

(see also Ron Geesin)

EDEN KANE

60	Pye 7N 15284	Hot Chocolate Crazy/You Make Love So Well	30
61	Decca F 11353	Well I Ask You/Before I Lose My Mind	5
61	Decca F 11381	Get Lost/I'm Telling You	5
62	Decca F 11418	Forget Me Not/A New Kind Of Lovin'	5
62	Decca F 11460	I Don't Know Why/Music For Strings	5
62	Decca F 11504	House To Let/I Told You	5
63	Decca F 11568	Sounds Funny To Me/Someone Wants To Know	6
63	Fontana TF 398	Tomorrow Night/I Won't Believe You (some in p/s)	6
63	Fontana TF 413	Like I Love You/Come Back (with Earl Preston's TTs)	8
64	Fontana TF 438	Boys Cry/Don't Come Crying To Me	6
64	Fontana TF 462	Rain Rain Go Away/Guess Who It Is	6
64	Fontana TF 508	Hangin' Around/Gonna Do Something About You	10
65	Fontana TF 582	If You Want This Love/Have I Done Something Wrong	10
66	Decca F 12342	Magic Town/The Whole World Was Crying	20
69	Fontana TF 1023	Boys Cry/Don't Come Cryin' To Me (p/s, reissue)	20
70	Bell BLL 1102	Reason To Believe/I Played It Like A Fool	8
62	Decca DFE 6696	WELL I ASK YOU! (EP)	20
62	Decca DFE 8503	HITS (EP)	20
64	Decca DFE 8567	SIX GREAT NEW SWINGERS (EP)	25
64	Fontana TFE 17424	IT'S EDEN (EP)	20
62	Ace Of Clubs ACL 1133	EDEN KANE (LP)	20
64	Fontana TL 5211	IT'S EDEN (LP)	30
66	Wing WL 1218	SMOKE GETS IN YOUR EYES (LP)	12

(see also Brothers Kane, Sarstedt Brothers)

GARY KANE

67	Pye 7N 17334	Too Good To Miss/Guilty Of Dreaming	5

HELEN KANE

55	MGM EP 549	THE BOOP BOOP A DOOP GIRL (EP)	25

MINT VALUE £

JEFF KANE

| 69 | Tangerine DP 0006 | Pretty Young Lady/On My Darkest Day ....35 |

JON KANE

| 69 | Warner Bros WB 8003 | Soulful Lady/In Ancient Times (Jerusalem) ....20 |

LEE KANE

| 55 | Capitol CL 14297 | Ev'ry Day/How Would You Have Me? ....8 |
| 55 | Capitol CL 14328 | Around And Around/Merci Beaucoup ....8 |

MARIA KANE

| 65 | Decca F 12184 | Love Is Slipping Away/Love Is Strange ....10 |

STEPHANIE KANE

| 64 | Oriole CB1908 | It's Love/Think Of Me ....25 |

KAN KAN

| 80 | Kabaret Music TRAIN 1 | Film Noir/The Watchmaker ....20 |

KANSAS

| 76 | Epic SEPC 4932 | Carry On Wayward Son/Questions Of My Childhood ....6 |

KANSAS HOOK

| 70 | UNI UNI 5515 | Echo Park/Manhattan Woman ....10 |
| 71 | Decca F13117 | Nervous Shaking/Mr. Universe ....25 |

PAUL KANTNER

71	RCA Victor SF 8163	BLOWS AGAINST THE EMPIRE (LP, gatefold sleeve with booklet, as Paul Kantner & Jefferson Starship) 20
71	Grunt FTR 1002	SUNFIGHTER (LP, gatefold sleeve with booklet & inner sleeve; as Paul Kantner, Grace Slick & Jefferson Starship) 15
73	Grunt BFL 1 0148	BARON VON TOLBOOTH (LP, with Grace Slick & David Freiberg) 12

(see also Jefferson Airplane/Starship)

KAPLAN

| 68 | Philips BF 1636 | Do You Believe In Magic/I Like ....18 |
| 68 | Philips BF 1699 | I Love It/Trousers Down ....6 |

KAPT. KOPTER & FABULOUS TWIRLY BIRDS

| 73 | Epic EPC 65381 | KAPT. KOPTER & THE FABULOUS TWIRLY BIRDS (LP) ....15 |

(see also Spirit)

ANTON KARAS

60	Decca F 9235	The "Harry Lime" Theme/The Cafe Mozart Waltz 5
55	Decca DFE 6035	ANTON KARAS ZITHER SOLOS (EP) 10
51	Decca LF 1053	ANTON KARAS (10" LP) 15

KAREEM

| 97 | Exploding Plastic EXP8 | Never Give Up On Love/Restless Soul (Peaktime Radio Mix)/Hipster Mix ....30 |

THE KARELIA

| 97 | The All Blacks B.V RR88232 | DIVORCE AT HIGH NOON (CD, 2005 re-issue has different p/s) ....40 |

(see also Franz Ferdinand, The Amphetameaniest)

KENNY KAREN

| 61 | Philips PB 1213 | Oh Susie Forgive Me/The Light In Your Window ....15 |

KARIBS

| 70s | Karibs KA1 | Aching Heart/Sugar Lips ....8 |

KARINA

| 71 | United Artists UP 35205 | Tomorrow I'm Coming Your Way/Something ....15 |

KARLINS

66	Parlophone R5457	You Mean Nothing To Me/Walkin' Away 6
66	Parlophone R5550	The Spinning Wheel/It's Good To Be Around 6
67	Parlophone R5607	The Hawk Moth And The Flame/Water Or The Wine 6
68	Columbia DB8394	Everybody Wants To Go To Heaven/Stay On The island 7
73	Enterprise ENTM 503	OUR KIND OF MUSIC (LP) 12

BILLY KARLOFF (& EXTREMES)

| 78 | Wanted CULT-45-001 | Crazy Paving/Back Street Billy (p/s) ....10 |
| 81 | Warner Bros K 17753 | Headbangers/Don't Keep Me Down (p/s) ....5 |

(see also Tom Robinson Band, Stiff Little Fingers)

BORIS KARLOFF

| 60 | Caedmon CAL 102/1 | HANS CHRISTIAN ANDERSEN (LP) ....15 |
| 67 | Brunswick LAT 8678 | AN EVENING WITH BORIS KARLOFF AND FRIENDS (LP) ....30 |

KARMA SUTRA

| 87 | Paradoxical PARODY 1 | DAYDREAMS OF A PRODUCTION LINE WORKER (LP, with booklet) ....40 |

STEVE KARMEN BIG BAND

| 75 | United Artists UP 35770 | Breakaway/Breakaway (Vocal Version) (featuring Jimmy Radcliffe) ....10 |

(see also Jimmy Radcliffe)

KAROO

| 65 | Oak RGJ 193 | Mamma's Out Of Town/Lonely Weekend ....200 |

KARRIER

84	Unit TRANS 101	I'm Back/Dreaming (no p/s) 30
86	Status JEMS 101	Poor Little Rich Girl/Endless Shadow 30
85	Unit	WAY BEYOND THE NIGHT (LP) 15

KARYN KARSH

| 66 | RCA Victor RCA 1740 | I Wasn't Born To Follow/Musty Dusty ....5 |

KASABIAN

03	BMG Paradise 02	Processed Beats (10" 45 rpm screen print sleeve with elastic bands) 25
04	BMG Paradise 04	Reason Is Treason (10" p/s 1,000 only) 15
04	BMG Paradise 06	Club Foot (Jagz Kooner mix) (12" with man-shaped hole sleeve) 20
04	BMG Paradise 09	Club Foot/(Jagz Kooner Vocal Mix)/(Paradise Mix) (with poster p/s) 8

04	BMG Paradise 15	L.S.F (Lost Souls Forever)/Club Foot (Live @ Cabinet War Rooms)/(Jagz Kooner Mix (Full Version) (10" poster p/s) 12
06	Paradise PARADISE 45	Shoot The Runner/(Shakes Remix) 8
07	No label	Fast Fuse/Thick As Thieves (10" 200 only die-cut sleeve, stamped labels given away at Somerset House gig 2007) 30
11	Sony BMG 88697523092	Days Are Forgotten/Pistols At Dawn (10") 12
04	BMG Paradise 18	KASABIAN (LP, 2 x 10") 25
06	Paradise PARADISE 38	EMPIRE (LP, 2x10") 20
09	Paradise PARADISE 59	WEST RYDER PAUPER LUNATIC ASYLUM (LP, 2x10") 20

MURRAY KASH
| 68 | RCA 1767 | Sleeping Beauty/Everything's OK ....6 |

AL KASHA
| 60 | Coral Q 72410 | Teardrops Are Falling/No Matter Where You Are ....5 |

EDWARD KA-SPEL
| 84 | In Phaze PHA 6 | EYES CHINA DOLL (LP) ....25 |
| 84 | In Phazw HAZ 6 | DANCE CHINA DOLL (EP 12") ....20 |

KATATONIA
| 96 | Misanthropy AMAZON 010 | Scarlet Heavens/PRIMORDIAL: To Enter Pagan MCMXCVI (10", p/s) ....18 |

KATCH-22
66	Fontana TF 768	Major Catastrophe/Hold Me 90
67	Fontana TF 874	Makin' Up My Mind/While We're Friends 25
68	Fontana TF 930	The World's Gettin' Smaller/Don't Bother 20
68	Fontana TF 984	Pumpkin Mini/100,000 Years 25
69	Fontana TF 1005	Out Of My Life/Baby Love 15
69	CBS 4644	It's The Sunshine/Mrs. Jones 20
68	Saga EROS 8047	IT'S SOFT ROCK & ALLSORTS (LP, with insert, Daga inner sleeve) 25

KATCH 22
| 91 | Kold Sweat KSLP1 | DIARY OF A BLACKMAN LIVING IN THE LAND OF THE LOST (LP) ....12 |
| 93 | Kold Sweat KSLP4 | DARK TALE OF TWO CITIES (LP) ....12 |

KATE
68	CBS 3631	Strange Girl/I Don't Make A Sound 70
68	CBS 3815	Hold Me Now/Empty World 20
69	CBS 4123	Shout It/Sweet Little Thing 60
(see also Viv Prince, Pretty Things)		

KATHY
| 69 | Morgan MR 14 | Bonjour Monsieur/Long Night ....5 |

KATINA
| 72 | Cactus CT 3 | Don't Stroke My Pussy/Don't Stroke My Pussy (Version) ....5 |

KATMANDU
| 86 | Nightflite NTFL 2001 | A CASE FOR THE BLUES (LP) ....12 |
| *(see also Peter Green, Ray Dorset, Crane/Farlowe)* | | |

KATZ (1)
| 60s | Tetlow TET 118 | LIVE AT THE RUM RUNNER (EP) ....75 |

KATZ (2)
| 79 | SRTS/79/CUS/533 | Talkin' About You/I'm So Nasty (no p/s, 200 only) ....250 |

ARTHUR KAY'S ORIGINALS
80	Red Admiral NYMPH 1	Ska-Wars/Warska (p/s) 8
80	Red Admiral NYMPH 2	Sooty Is A Rudie/Play My Record (p/s) 10
88	Skank MLP 105	RARE 'N' TASTY (mini-LP) 12

BARBARA KAY
65	Columbia DB 8009	The Power And The Glory/I Wanna Walk In Your Sun 5
65	Pye 7N 15774	That's What Angels Are For/What's The Good Of Loving 6
65	Pye 7N 15914	Yes I'm Ready/Someone Has To Cry 20
66	Pye 7N 15997	Chips With Everything/A Lot About Love 5

JANET KAY
| 77 | Stonehouse SH 003 | Loving You/Version ....8 |

JANET K(AY)
| 78 | Bushays BFM 108 | Silhouette (with Rico)/PRINCE JAZEBO & RICO: Silhouette Gone Clear (12") ....20 |

JOHN KAY
73	Probe PRO 601	Easy Evil/Dance To My Song 5
78	Mercury 6167 683	Give Me Some Good News I Can use/Business Is Business 5
72	Probe SPB 1054	FORGOTTEN SONGS AND UNSUNG HEROES (LP) 15
73	Probe SPBA 6274	MY SPORTIN' LIFE (LP) 12
(see also Steppenwolf)		

KAYAK
| 74 | Harvest SHSP 4033 | SEE SEE THE SUN (LP) ....20 |
| 74 | Harvest SHSP 4036 | KAYAK (LP) ....20 |

CAB KAYE
| 61 | Melodisc MEL 1584 | Everything Is Go/Don't You Go Away ....5 |

DANNY KAYE
53	Brunswick 05031	The Ugly Duckling/The king's New Clothes 8
59	Brunswick DE 9022	CHILDREN'S FAVOURITES (EP) 8
(see also Bing Crosby, Groucho Marx)		

DANNY KAYE & LOUIS ARMSTRONG
| 60 | London HL 7092 | The Five Pennies Saints/Bill Bailey Won't You Please Come Home (export issue) ....5 |
| *(see also Louis Armstrong)* | | |

DAVE KAYE (& DYKONS)
| 64 | Decca F 11866 | A Fool Such As I/It's Nice Isn't It (as Davy Kaye) ....35 |
| 65 | Decca F 12073 | In My Way/All The Stars In Heaven (as Dave Kaye) ....25 |

MINT VALUE £

69	Major Minor MM 641	Yesterday When I Was Young/Say You Love Me (as Dave Kaye & Dykons)	12

KATHIE KAY(E)

55	HMV 7M 335	Suddenly There's A Valley/Teddy Bear	8
56	HMV 7M 363	Jimmy Unknown/Dreams Can Tell A Lie	10
56	HMV POP 265	A House With Love In It/To Be Sure	7
57	HMV POP	We Will Make Love/Wind In The Willow	8

LINDA KAYE

66	Columbia DB 7915	I Can't Stop Thinking About You/When We Meet Again	25

PETER KAYE

60s	Aral PS 116	Do Me A Favour/You Doll (in p/s)	10
60s	Aral PS 116	Do Me A Favour/You Doll	5

SHIRLEY KAYE

68	Trojan TR 015	Make Me Yours/We Have Happiness	75

TONY KAYE & HEARTBEATS

67	Pye International 7N 25412	Hey, Hey Little Orphan Annie/Dream World	8

KAYES

67	Major Minor MM 515	It's No Secret/Remember Me	8

(see also Kaye Sisters)

KAYE SISTERS

58	Philips PB 806	Are You Ready, Freddy?/The Pansy	15
58	Philips PB 832	Stroll Me/Torero	10
59	Philips PB 892	Jerri-Lee (I Love Him So)/Deeply Devoted	10
60	Philips PB 1024	Paper Roses/If Only You'd Be Mine (in p/s)	8
60	Philips PB 1024	Paper Roses/If Only You'd Be Mine (in p/s)	5
60	Philips PB 1088	Come To Me/A Whole Lot Of Lovin' (in p/s)	5
57	Philips BBE 12166	PRESENTING THE KAYE SISTERS (EP)	8
59	Philips BBE 12256	THE KAYES AT THE COLONY (EP)	8

(see also Three Kayes/Three Kaye Sisters, Kayes, Frankie Vaughan)

KAY GEES

76	Polydor 2310 467	HUSTLE WIT' EVERY MUSCLE (LP)	15

LAINIE KAZAN

69	MGM MGM 1476	Window Of My Mind/It's You	30

KCF & SKELLA TON

91	Kold Sweat KS112	Taken To Heart/In Session (12")	10

ERNIE K-DOE

61	London HLU 9330	Mother-In-Law/Wanted, $10,000.00 Reward	15
61	London HLU 9390	Te-Ta-Te-Ta-Ta/Real Man	20
65	Vocalion VP 9233	My Mother In Law (Is In My Hair Again)/Looking Into The Future	20
68	Action ACT 4502	Dancing Man/Later For Tomorrow	25
68	Action ACT 4512	Gotta Pack My Bags/How Sweet You Are	25

PHIL KEAGGY BAND

70s	Myrrh MYR 1046	WHAT A DAY (LP)	20
70s	Myrrh MYR 1066	EMERGING (LP)	20
70s	Underground Bird 151	PRIVATE COLLECTION VOL 1 (LP)	20

KEANE

00	Zoomorphic (No cat. no)	Call Me What You Like/Rubbernecking/Closer Now (CD, 500 only)	80
01	Zoomorphic ZOO12101	Wolf At The Door/Call Me What You Like/She Has No Time (CD, 50 only p/s)	80
05	Island KEANE2	The Sun Ain't Gonna Shine Anymore/Your Eyes Open (Fan club issue 1000 only p/s)	40
06	Island (no cat no)	Nothing In My Way (512MB memory stick, 1500 only, numbered in title sleeve)	20
06	Island 1723054	A Bad Dream (512MN memory stick, numbered in title sleeve)	20
07	Island 1723058	A Bad Dream/She Sells Sanctuary (with fold-out sleeve, numbered)	15
04	Island ILPS 8145	HOPES AND FEARS (LP, 1000 only, numbered)	35
04	Island (no cat no)	HOPES AND FEARS (CD promo, 200 only, numbered)	30
04	Island (no cat no)	HOPES AND FEARS (DVD sampler, jewel case, promo)	25
05	Island	SINGLES BOX SET (1000 only, 5x 7" from HOPES AND FEARS LP)	100
06	Island (no cat no)	THE VIDEOS (Fan club issue only)	50
06	Island (no cat no)	UNDER THE IRON SEA (CD promo and A5 lyric booklet)	20

SHAKE KEANE

55	HMV 7MC 38	Akinla/Fire, Fire (export issue)	15
62	Columbia SEG 8140	IN MY CONDITION (EP)	40
64	Airborne MBP 002	A CASE OF JAZZ (EP, as Shake Keane and Michael Garrick Quartette, 99 copies only)	100
65	Decca SKL 4720	SHAKE KEANE WITH THE KEATING SOUND (LP)	20
66	Ace Of Clubs ACL 1219	THAT'S THE NOISE (LP)	25
69	Phase 4 Stereo PFS 4154	DIG IT (LP, with Ivor Raymonde Orchestra)	40
70	Pama SECO 30	RISING STARS AT EVENING TIME (LP with Gordon Langford and Hastings Girl Choir)	30

(see also Marie Bryant)

JOHNNY KEATING ORCHESTRA

62	Piccadilly 7N 35033	Theme From Z Cars/Lost Patrol	5
63	Piccadilly 7N 35113	The Preacher/Whoop Up (with the Z men)	10
62	Piccadilly NEP 34011	Z-CARS (EP, with Z-Men)	8
57	Oriole MG 20011	BRITISH JAZZ (LP)	75
58	London LTZ-15122	SWINGIN' SCOTS (LP)	25
64	Ace Of Clubs ACL 1160	SIXTEEN HITS FOR YOUR DANCE PARTY (LP)	20
64	Decca PFS 4038	SWING REVISITED (LP)	25
64	Decca PFS 4078	STRAIGHT AHEAD (LP)	30
72	Studio Two TWO 393	SPACE EXPERIENCE (LP)	15
72	Studio Two Q4 TWO 393	SPACE EXPERIENCE (LP, quadrophonic)	25
75	Studio Two TWOX 1044	SPACE EXPERIENCE 2 (LP)	15

KEEFERS KIDS

67	King KG 1068	Millions Of Hearts/KEEFERS: Lonely Hill	5

KEELE ROW & KEELE UNIVERSITY STUDENTS

64	Flexi	STANLEY MATTHEWS (EP, flexi)	20

KEEN
90	Scaredy Cat PUR 003	FELINE GROOVY EP (12")	30

JOHN KEEN
72	Track 2094 103	Old Fashioned Girl/That's The Way It Is	8
73	Track 2094 108	Let Us In/Keep On The Grass	8

(see also Speedy Keen, Thunderclap Newman)

SPEEDY KEEN
71	Track 2406 105	PREVIOUS CONVICTIONS (LP)	15

(see also John Keen, Thunderclap Newman)

MARION KEENE
56	HMV 7M 395	Fortune Teller/A Dangerous Age	7
57	HMV POP 375	In The Middle Of An Island/It's Not For Me To Say	6

NELSON KEENE
60	HMV POP 771	Image Of A Girl/Ocean Of Love	15
60	HMV POP 814	Keep Loving Me/Teenage Troubles	15
61	HMV POP 916	Miracles Are Happening To Me/Poor Little Rich Boy	15

(see also Guv'ners)

REX KEENE
56	Columbia DB 3831	Rebel In Town/Happy Texas Ranger	10

KEETY ROOTS
94	Black Legacy BL 003	African Blood/TENASTELIN: Spirit of	80

ACE KEFFORD STAND
69	Atlantic 584 260	For Your Love/Gravy Booby Jam (small centre hole)	50
69	Atlantic 584 260	For Your Love/Gravy Booby Jam (large centre hole)	40

(see also Move, Cozy Powell, Young Blood, Big Bertha, Bedlam, Carl Wayne)

KEITH
66	Mercury MF 940	Ain't Gonna Lie/It Started All Over Again	8
67	Mercury MF 955	98.6/The Teeny Bopper Song	10
67	Mercury MF 968	Tell Me To My Face/I Can't Go Wrong	10
67	Mercury MF 989	Daylight Savin' Time/Happy Walking Around	15
67	Mercury MF 1002	Sugar Man/Easy As Pie (in p/s)	12
67	Mercury MF 1002	Sugar Man/Easy As Pie	6
67	Mercury MCL 20103	98.6/AIN'T GONNA LIE (LP)	30

BRIAN KEITH
68	Page One POF 072	The Shelter Of Your Arms/C'est La Vie	7
68	Page One POF 103	When The First Tear Shows/When My Baby Smiles At Me	8
69	Page One POF 152	Till We Meet Again/Lady Butterfly	7

(see also Plastic Penny)

BRYAN KEITH
63	London HLU 9707	Sad Sad Song/Mean Woman	20

RON KEITH
76	A&M AMS 7217	Party Music/Gotta Go By What You Tell Me	80

KEITH (STEWART) & ENID (CUMBERLAND)
60	Blue Beat BB 6	Worried Over You/Everything Will Be Alright	10
60	Blue Beat BB 11	Send Me/TRENTON SPENCE GROUP: People Will Say We're In Love	10
61	Starlite ST45 047	Never Leave My Throne/Only A Pity (as Keith & Enid with Caribs)	12
61	Starlite ST45 067	You're Gonna Break My Heart/What Have I Done	12
62	Blue Beat BB 125	When It's Spring/True Love (with Sonny Bradshaw Orchestra)	10
63	Dice CC 14	Sacred Vow/My Dreams	8
63	Dice CC 20	Just A Closer Walk/Don't Yield To Temptation	8
64	Black Swan WI 429	Lost My Love/I Cried	10
63	Island ILP 901	KEITH & ENID SING (LP)	50
70	Trojan TTL 37	KEITH & ENID SING (LP, reissue)	15

KEITH (POPPIN) & IMPACT ALL STARS
71	Randy's RAN 515	Down By The Riverside/IMPACT ALL STARS: Version Two	6

KEITH (LYN) & KEN (LAZARUS)
65	London HA-R/SH-R 8229	YOU'LL LOVE JAMAICA (LP)	40

KEITH (ROWE) & TEX (DIXON)
67	Island WI 3085	Tonight/LYN TAIT & JETS: You Have Caught Me	125
68	Island WI 3091	Stop That Train/BOBBY ELLIS: Feeling Peckish (with Desmond Miles Seven)	150
68	Island WI 3137	Hypnotizing Eyes/Lonely Man	60
70	Explosion EX 2008	Tighten Up Your Gird/Look To The Sky	12

KEITHY
77	Xamayca XAD 002	Struggling In A Babylon (with Imperial Hudson)/XAMAYCA BAND: Togetherness	25

ROGER KELLAWAY
67	Liberty LBS 583061E	SPIRIT FEEL (LP)	25

JERRY KELLER
59	London HLR 8890	Here Comes Summer/Time Has A Way (triangular centre)	10
59	London HLR 8890	Here Comes Summer/Time Has A Way (round centre)	5
59	London HLR 8890	Here Comes Summer/Time Has A Way (78)	15
59	London HLR 8980	If I Had A Girl/Lovable	5
59	London HLR 8980	If I Had A Girl/Lovable (78)	20
60	London HLR 9106	Now, Now, Now/Lonesome Lullaby	7
60	London HA-R 2261	HERE COMES JERRY KELLER (LP, mono)	25
60	London SAH-R 6083	HERE COMES JERRY KELLER (LP, stereo)	50

PAT KELL(E)Y
68	Giant GN 37	Little Boy Blue/You Are Not Mine (as Pat Kelley & Uniques)	80
68	Island WI 3121	Somebodies Baby (as Pat Kelly)/BEVERLY SIMMONS: Please Don't Leave Me	45
69	Gas GAS 110	The Workman Song/Never Give Up (as Pat Kelly)	10
69	Gas GAS 115	How Long/Try To Remember (as Pat Kelly)	5

MINT VALUE £

69	Gas GAS 124	Festival Time (Parts 1 & 2) (as Pat Kelley)	8
69	Gas GAS 125	If It Don't Work Out/I Am Coming Home (as Pat Kelley)	5
70	Gas GAS 144	Tammy/I Am Not Your Guy (as Pat Kelley)	15
70	Gas GAS 145	Striving For The Right/When A Boy Fall In Love (as Pat Kelley)	15
70	Gas GAS 157	I Just Don't Know What To Do With Myself/What's He Got That I Ain't Got (B-side actually titled 'Lorna') (as Pat Kelley)	8
70	Jackpot JP 734	I Just Don't Know What To Do With Myself/Lorna (as Pat Kelley)	8
71	Camel CA 65	Talk About Love (as Pat Kelley)/PHIL PRATT ALL STARS: Version	15
71	Gas GAS 171	Love/With All Your Heart (as Pat Kelley)	6
71	Punch PH 88	Soulful Love (as Pat Kelly)/HUGH ROY & PARAGONS: One For All	10
72	Pama Supreme PS 353	I'm Gonna Give Her All The Love I've Got (as Pat Kelley)/ MAYTONES: As Long As You Love Me	8
73	Pama Supreme PS 379	Twelfth Of Never (as Pat Kelley)/JERRY LEWIS: 5000 Watts	6
73	Pama Supreme PS 384	I Wish It Could Rain (as Pat Kelley)/PAT KELLY SINGERS: Hallelujah	6
75	Black Wax WAX 1	Sunshine/Sunshine Version	6
77	Rainbow Stepper RK 231	Carefree Girl/Version	8
69	Pama PMLP 12	PAT KELLEY SINGS (LP)	45
71	Pama PMP 2013	COOL BREEZING (LP)	60
77	Burning Rockers BR 007LP	SO PROUD (LP)	25
78	Burning Sounds BS1001	LONELY MAN (LP)	20

(see also Wonder Boy)

PETER KELLEY
| 69 | London HAK 8402 | PATH OF THE WAVE (LP) | 40 |
| 71 | Polydor 2310 119 | DEALIN' BLUES (LP) | 25 |

MURRAY KELLUM
| 64 | London HLU 9830 | Long Tall Texan/GLEN SUTTON: I Gotta Leave This Town | 15 |

KELLY
| 66 | RCA RCA 1507 | Be My Man/Here Comes My Baby | 6 |
| 69 | Deram DM 277 | Mary Mary/Reverend Richard Baily | 30 |

CHARLIE KELLY
| 68 | Island WI 3155 | So Nice Like Rice/STRANGER & GLADDY: Over Again | 25 |

CHRIS KELLY
| 71 | CBS 7331 | Red Bird/Sweet Albuquerque | 7 |

DAVE KELLY
| 69 | Mercury 20151 SMCL | KEEPS IT IN THE FAMILY (LP, laminated sleeve, black/silver labels) | 200 |
| 71 | Mercury 6310 001 | DAVE KELLY (LP, with Jo-Ann Kelly & Brunning-Hall Sunflower Band) | 250 |

(see also John Dummer Blues Band, Brunning-Hall Sunflower Blues Band)

FRANK KELLY & HUNTERS
62	Fontana 267 242 TF	Send Me The Pillow That You Dream On/'Cept Me	15
63	Fontana 267 261 TF	I Saw Linda Yesterday/Good And True	15
63	Fontana 267 277 TF	What Do You Wanna Do/She Loves Me So	15
64	Fontana TF 454	Some Other Time/Why Baby Why	15

GENE KELLY
53	MGM SP 1012	Singin' In The Rain/All I Do Is Dream Of You	8
53	MGM SP 1015	'S Wonderful (with Georges Guetary)/I Got Rhythm (with Children's Choir)	7
53	MGM MGM-D 117	SONG AND DANCE MAN (10" LP)	15
55	MGM MGM-D 133	S'WONDERFUL (10" LP)	15

JO-ANN KELLY
64	GW EP 1	BLUES AND GOSPEL (EP, live at the Bridge House Club)	150
66	Harlequin HAL 1/HW 349	NEW SOUNDS IN FOLK (LP, with other artists)	100
69	CBS 63841	JO-ANN KELLY (LP, laminated front sleeve)	200
76	Red Rag RRR 006	DO IT (LP, with Peter Emery)	35

(see also Chilli Willi & Red Hot Peppers, Dave Kelly, Tramp)

JO-ANN KELLY & TONY MCPHEE
| 72 | Sunset SLS 50209 | THE SAME THING ON THEIR MINDS (LP) | 30 |

(see also Tony McPhee, Dave Kelly)

JONATHAN KELLY
69	Parlophone R 5805	Denver/Son John	10
70	Parlophone R 5830	Make A Stranger Your Friend/Daddy Don't Take Me Down Fishing No More	10
70	Parlophone R 5851	Don't You Believe It?/Billy (Eric Clapton on guitar)	40
70	Parlophone PCS 7114	JONATHAN KELLY (LP, black/silver labels with boxed logo)	100
72	RCA SF 8262	TWICE AROUND THE HOUSES (LP, laminated cover)	30
73	RCA SF 8353	WAIT TILL THEY CHANGE THE BACKDROP (LP, gatefold sleeve)	30

(see also John Ledingham)

KEITH KELLY
60	Parlophone R 4640	(Must You Always) Tease Me/Ooh-La-La	25
60	Parlophone R 4676	Listen Little Girl/Uh-Huh	30
60	Parlophone R 4713	With You/You'll Break My Heart	20
61	Parlophone R 4797	Cold White And Beautiful/When You First Fall In Love	20
65	CBS 201794	Laurie/Save Your Love For Me	10

MIKE KELLY
| 73 | Decca F 13397 | Catalina/You Made My World | 6 |

MONTY KELLY
| 60 | London HLL 9035 | Summer Set/Amalia (as Monty Kelly Orchestra) | 6 |

PAUL KELLY
65	Atlantic AT 4053	Chills And Fever/Only Your Love	45
67	Philips BF 1591	Sweet Sweet Lovin'/Cryin' For My Baby	25
72	Atlantic K 10272	Chills And Fever/Only Your Love (reissue)	10

PETE KELLY'S SOULUTION
| 68 | Decca F 12755 | Midnight Confessions/If Your Love Don't Swing | 30 |
| 68 | Decca F 22829 | Midnight Confessions/BERNIE & BUZZ BAND: The House That Jack Built (export issue) | 20 |

(see also Bernie & Buzz Band, Rhythm & Blues Inc.)

PETER D KELLY
74	DJM DJS 333	Rock To The Juke Box/Brotherhood Within (promo p/s)	10
74	DJM DJS 333	Rock To The Juke Box/Brotherhood Within	6

SALLY KELLY
59	Decca F 11175	Little Cutie/Come Back To Me	10
60	Decca F 11238	He'll Have To Stay/Honey That's Alright	7

SEYMOUR KELLY
68	Columbia DB8445	Indian Scene/Worlds Apart	15

STAN KELLY
60s	Transatlantic TRASP 21	The Ballad Of Armagh Jail/Kelly The Boy From Killang	5
60	Topic TOP 27	LIVERPOOL PACKET (EP)	10
60	Topic TOP 60	SONGS FOR SWINGING LANDLORDS TO (EP, with Leon Rosselson)	10

WYNTON KELLY TRIO
65	Verve VLP 9103	UNDILUTED (LP)	15

KELLY BROTHERS
67	Sue WI 4034	Falling In Love Again/Crying Days Are Over	80
68	President PT 143	You Put Your Touch On Me/Hanging In There	25
70	Blue Horizon 57-3177	That's What You Mean To Me/Comin' On In	30
68	President PTL 1019	SWEET SOUL (LP)	100

REV. (SAMUEL) KELSEY (& CONGREGATION)
56	Brunswick OE 9256	REV. KELSEY (EP)	20

(see also Sister Rosetta Tharpe)

WAYNE KEMP
66	Atlantic 584 006	Watch That First Step/Little Home Wrecker	12

KEMPION
77	Broadside BRO 123	KEMPION (LP)	18
77	Sweet Folk & C. SFA 044	CAM YE O'ER FRAE FRANCE (LP)	15

BOB KEN
80	Square S2SP	Keep Me Warm This Winter/More Than Life	6

KEN & NEW ESTABLISHMENT
73	Fab FAB 264	Soul Mood/Golden Locks	10

KEN & STEPPING TONY
78	Rama RMD 005	Sticks Man Affair/ROCKA & DAVE & GIRL WONDER: Skip-A Dip (12")	30

JOHNNY KENDALL & HERALDS
64	RCA RCA 1416	St. James Infirmary/Little Girl	10

KENDALL SISTERS
58	London HLM 8622	Won't You Be My Baby/Yea, Yea	35
58	London HLM 8622	Won't You Be My Baby/Yea, Yea (78)	20

GRAHAM KENDRICK
73	Key KL 011	FOOTSTEPS ON THE SEA (LP)	12
73	Key KL 016	BRIGHT SIDE UP (LP)	12
74	Key KL 024	PAID ON THE NAIL (LP)	12

LINDA KENDRICK
66	Polydor 56076	It's The Little Things/When Your Love Is Warm	30
66	Polydor 56076	It's The Little Things/When Your Love Is Warm (DJ copy)	50
69	Philips BF 1750	I Will See You There/Inside My Heart	8
69	Philips BF 1816	Hold On/Fa La La La La La Le	8
71	Philips 6006-078	Generation (Light Up The Sky)/Come With The Beautiful People	25
70	Philips SBL 7921	LINDA KENDRICK (LP)	15

NAT KENDRICK & SWANS
60	Top Rank JAR 351	(Do The) Mashed Potatoes Parts 1 & 2	30
60	Top Rank JAR 387	Dish Rag Parts 1 & 2	20

(see also James Brown)

LORETTA KENDRICK
01	Hayley HR004	Neither One Of Us/My Feelings Keep Getting In The Way	12

EDDIE KENDRICKS
73	Tamla Motown TMG 873	Keep On Truckin' Part 1/Part 2	15
71	T. Motown STML 11186	ALL BY MYSELF (LP)	18

KENICKIE
95	Slampt U.O. SLAMPT 1	CATSUIT CITY (EP)	20
96	Fierce Panda NING 16	SKILLEX (EP)	8

CALUM KENNEDY
62	Ember EMB 5167	The Celtic Chorus/Danny Boy	25

CHERYL KENNEDY
67	Columbia DB 8271	Thoroughly Modern Millie/Cradle Song	5
68	Columbia DB 8347	Love Is Blue/I Could Be Happy With You	6

DOUG KENNEDY
65	Columbia DB 7707	Julie/Jailbreak Man	5

GENE KENNEDY
65	Hickory 45-1314	You Better Take Home/Stand In Line	5

JOHN F. KENNEDY
64	Stateside SL 10064	THE PRESIDENTIAL YEARS 1960-1963 (LP)	15

JON KENNEDY
01	Tru Thoughts TRU LP 017	WE'RE JUST WAITING FOR YOU NOW (2xLP)	15

LOU KENNEDY
55	Columbia SCM 5198	Stars Shine In Your Eyes/The Kentuckian Song	10
56	Columbia SCM 5216	Whisper/Sincerely Yours	10

MINT VALUE £

MIKE KENNEDY
69	Major Minor MM 614	I'll Never Forget/I'll Never Get You	6
69	Major Minor MM 629	Johnny Rebel/Golden Memories	6
72	Youngblood YB 1035	Louisiana/Look Up In The Sky	20

(see also Los Bravos)

CHRIS KENNER
61	London HLU 9410	I Like It Like That Parts 1 & 2	35
65	Sue WI 351	Land Of 1,000 Dances/That's My Girl	35
66	Atlantic 587 008	LAND OF 1000 DANCES (LP)	40

JAMES KENNEY
| 58 | Pye 7N 15150 | The Shrine On The Second Floor/Expresso Party | 10 |

TONY KENNY & SANDS SHOWBAND
67	Major Minor MM 555	Help Me Rhonda/Some Enchanted Evening	5
68	Major Minor MM 573	Yummy Yummy Yummy/Peanuts	5
71	Hit HIT 1	Knock Three Times/See You In September	5

(see also Sands)

KENNY (EVERETT) & (DAVE) CASH
| 65 | Decca F 12283 | Knees/The B Side | 6 |

KENNY & DENY
| 65 | Decca F 12138 | Try To Forget Me/Little Surfer Girl | 70 |

(see also Jimmy Page, Tony Rivers & The Castaways, Harmony Grass, Capability Brown)

KENNY & WRANGLERS
| 64 | Parlophone R 5224 | Somebody Help Me/Who Do You Think I Am? | 25 |
| 65 | Parlophone R 5275 | Doobie Doo/Moonshine | 25 |

(see also Kenny Bernard & Wranglers)

JERRI BO KENO
| 75 | Phil Spector Intl. 2010 001 | Here It Comes (And Here I Go)/I Don't Know Why | 20 |

AL KENT
| 67 | Track 604 016 | You Got To Pay The Price/Where Do I Go From Here | 50 |
| 71 | Mojo 2092 015 | You Got To Pay The Price/Where Do I Go From Here (unissued) | 0 |

BILL KENT
| 58 | Decca F 10975 | The Prettiest Girl In School/Hasty Words | 5 |
| 58 | Decca F 10997 | Oh-Oh, I'm Falling In Love/In Love | 5 |

CINDY KENT
| 73 | York FYK 418 | I AM YOUR SERVANT (LP) | 150 |

ENOCH KENT
59	Top Rank JAR 238	The Ballad Of Johnny Ramensky/The Bonny Lass Of Fyvie	5
60	Top Rank JAR 386	The Smashing Of The Van/Sean South Of Garryowen	5
62	Topic TOP 81	SINGS THE BUTCHER BOY AND OTHER BALLADS (EP)	10

KLARK KENT
| 78 | Kryptone KK 1 | Don't Care/Thrills/Office Girls (p/s, green or rarer black vinyl) | 5 |
| 78 | Kryptone KMS 7390 | Too Kool To Kalypso/Theme For Kinetic Ritual (p/s, green vinyl) | 5 |

MARY KENT
| 69 | CBS 4510 | Lost Generation/Gentle Moments | 10 |

PAUL KENT
71	B&C CB 165	Do You/Helpless Harry	6
70	RCA SF 8083	P.C. KENT (LP)	40
71	B&C CAS 1044	PAUL KENT (LP)	30

RICHARD KENT STYLE
66	Columbia DB 7964	No Matter What You Do/Go, Go Children	200
66	Columbia DB 8051	You Can't Put Me Down/All Good Things	150
67	Columbia DB 8182	Marching Off To War/I'm Out	120
68	MCA MU 1032	Love Will Shake The World Awake/Crocodile Tears	40
69	Mercury MF 1090	A Little Bit O' Soul/Don't Tell Lies	40

SHIRLEY KENT
80	Tadpole TAD 001	My Dad/Marianne	6
66	Keele University 103	THE MASTER SINGERS AND SHIRLEY KENT SING FOR CHAREC 67 (EP)	35
89	Magic Spell 0001	FOREVER A WILLOW (LP)	12

(see also Ghost, Virginia Tree)

SONIA KENT
| 66 | Parlophone R 5401 | This Is My Wonderful Day/Somebody Must Care | 7 |

(see also Diamond Twins)

KENT (BROWN) & DIMPLE (HINDS)
| 63 | Island WI 046 | Day Is Done/Linger A While | 20 |

KENT (BROWN) & JEANNIE WITH CITY SLICKERS
| 62 | Blue Beat BB 98 | Daddy/Hello Love | 20 |

(see also Kent Brown & Rainbows)

RIK KENTON
| 74 | Island WIP 6214 | Bungalow Love/Lay It On You (no p/s) | 5 |
| 76 | EMI EMI 2443 | The Libertine/Messin' Round | 6 |

(see also Woody Kern, Roxy Music)

KEN-TONES
| 56 | Parlophone MSP 6229 | Get With It/In Port Afrique | 12 |
| 57 | Parlophone R 4257 | I Saw Esau/Yaller, Yaller Gold | 8 |

(see also Benny Lee)

KENTUCKY BOYS
| 55 | HMV 7M 312 | Don't Fetch It/A Little Fella Like Me | 12 |

KENTUCKY COLONELS
74	United Artists UAS 29514	THE KENTUCKY COLONELS (LP)	18

(see also Byrds)

BILL KENWRIGHT (& RUNAWAYS)
67	Columbia DB 8239	I Want To Go Back There Again/Walk Through Dreams (with Runaways)	10
68	MGM MGM 1430	Giving Up/Love's Black And White (solo)	6
69	MGM MGM 1463	Tiggy/House That Fell On Its Face	5
69	MGM MGM 1478	Baby I Could Be So Good At Loving You/A Boy And A Girl	6
69	Fontana TF 1065	Sugar Man/Epitaph (When Times Were Good)	6

BOB KERR'S WHOOPEE BAND
76	Whoopee WP 102 LP	THE WHOOPEE BAND (LP)	15

MOIRA KERR
69	Beltona MBE 102	FOLK WARM AND GENTLE (LP, also stereo [SBE 102])	15
71	Beltona SBE 118	SHADOWS OF MY CHILDHOOD (LP)	15

PATRICK KERR
65	Decca F 12069	Magic Potion/It's No Trouble To Love You	30

RICHARD KERR
66	Decca F12478	Concrete Jungle/You Got Nothing To Loose	12
66	Decca F12538	Hard Lovin'/Auntie's Insurance Policy	15
67	Deram DM 138	Happy Birthday Blues/Mother's Blue-Eyed Angel	20
69	RCA RCA 1785	Colour My World/For The Rest Of My Life	5
75	Epic SEPC 3662	Somewhere In The Night/In The End	5
73	Warner Bros K 46206	FROM NOW UNTIL THEN (LP, laminated cover, foldout lyric insert)	15

JOHN KERRUISH
70	A&M AMS 604	Time To Wander/Today, Tonight And Tomorrow Morning	70

CHRIS KERRY
65	Mercury MF 957	Seven Deadly Sins/The Place	15
66	Mercury MF 985	Watermelon Man/I've Got My Pride	25

DOUG KERSHAW
69	Warner Bros WB 7304	Feed It To The Fish/You Fight Your Fight (I'll Fight Mine)	8
70	Warner Bros WB 7413	Orange Blossom Special/Swamp Rat	6
71	Warner Bros WS 1906	DOUG KERSHAW (LP)	12
73	Warner Bros K 46196	DEVIL'S ELBOW (LP)	12

(see also Rusty & Doug)

MARY & HARVEY KERSHAW
76	Topic 12TS 302	LANCASHIRE SINGS AGAIN! (LP)	12

KEN KESEY
83	Psycho PSYCHO 4	THE ACID TEST (LP, 300 only)	30

BARNEY KESSEL
69	Polydor 56765	Frank Mills/Quail Bait	5
54	Vogue LDE 085	BARNEY KESSEL (10" LP)	20
55	Contemporary LDC 153	BARNEY KESSEL VOLUME 2 (10" LP)	20
59	Contemporary LAC 12206	SOME LIKE IT HOT (LP)	12
59	Contemporary LAC 12214	BARNEY KESSEL PLAYS CARMEN (LP)	12
77	Phil Spector Intl. 2307 011	SLOW BURN (LP)	15

(see also Rick Nelson)

LARRY KESSLER
96	Lissey's LISS 5S	Radar Eyes/Godz Mix (p/s)	10

KESTREL
75	Cube HIFLY 19	KESTREL (LP)	300

(see also Spiders From Mars)

KESTRELS
59	Pye 7N 15234	There Comes A Time/In The Chapel In The Moonlight	10
60	Pye 7N 15248	I Can't Say Goodbye/We Were Wrong	6
61	Decca F 11391	All These Things/That's It	6
62	Piccadilly 7N 35056	Wolverton Mountain/Little Sacka Sugar	6
62	Piccadilly 7N 35079	Don't Want To Cry/Love Me With All Your Heart	6
63	Piccadilly 7N 35104	Walk Right In/Moving Up The King's Highway	7
63	Piccadilly 7N 35126	There's A Place/Little Star	7
63	Piccadilly 7N 35144	Love Me With All Your Heart/Lazy River	6
60s	Donegal MAU 500	THE KESTRELS (EP)	20
63	Piccadilly NPL 38009	SMASH HITS (LP)	20

(see also Ivy League, Flowerpot Men, White Plains)

JACK KETCH & CROWMEN
87	Hangmen HANG 19 UP	BRIMFULL OF HATE (LP)	35

KEY CHAINS
66	London HLU 10055	Morgan's Song/Scruggs	5

EBONY KEYES
66	Piccadilly 7N 35358	Sitting In The Ring/If You Knew	100
67	Piccadilly 7N 35375	Cupid's House/If Our Love Should End	10
67	Piccadilly 7N 35390	Country Girl/How Many Times	10
67	Piccadilly 7N 35407	Don't/Sweet Mary (Sweeter Than A Rose)	12

KAROL KEYES
64	Fontana TF 517	You Beat Me To The Punch/No-One Can Take Your Place (in p/s)	30
64	Fontana TF 517	You Beat Me To The Punch/No-One Can Take Your Place	20
67	Fontana TF 846	Can't You Hear The Music/The Sweetest Touch	12
66	Columbia DB 7899	A Fool In Love/The Good Love, The Bad Love	20
66	Columbia DB 8001	One In A Million/Don't Jump	75

(see also Volunteers)

TROY KEYES
68	Stateside SS 2087	Love Explosions/I'm Crying (Inside)	22
69	Stateside SS 2149	Love Explosions/I'm Crying (Inside) (reissue)	10

KEY LARGO
71	Blue Horizon 57-3178	Voodoo Rhythm/As The Years Go Passing By	20
70	Blue Horizon 7-63859	KEY LARGO (LP)	50

KEY MASSIVE
89	Hat Music HT 001	Oh Girl/Sweet Sensi (12")	25
97	Wild Bunch WBRTDJ8	Risingson/Instrumental/Single Mix/Neanderthal Mix/Darren Emerson Mix/Underdog Mix/Underdog Instrumental (2 x 122, clear vinyl promo)	18

KEYMEN
59	HMV POP 584	Gazackstahagen/Miss You	6
62	Columbia DB 4902	Five Weeks In A Balloon/Secretly	8
57	Vogue Coral LVA 9048	THE VOCAL SOUNDS OF THE KEYMEN (LP)	15

KEYNOTES
54	Decca F 10302	A Dime And A Dollar/JOHNSTON BROTHERS: Bandit	10
55	Decca F 10643	Relax-Ay-Voo/Steam Heat	10
56	Decca F 10745	Let's Go Steady/Chincherinchee	8

(see also Bobbie Britton, Johnston Brothers, Dave King, Suzi Miller)

KEYNOTES
63	Planetone 14	I'm In Love/In The Valley	15

BOBBY KEYS
75	Ring O' Records 2017 102	Gimmie The Key/Honky Tonk	7
72	Warner Bros K 46141	BOBBY KEYS (LP)	25

EBONY KEYS
71	Parlophone R 5909	Brother Joe/Under The Apple Tree	8

KEYS (1)
64	Oriole CB 1968	Sleep Sleep My Baby/Colour Slide	20
65	CBS 201804	Go Get Her/My Everything	10

KEYS (2)
81	A & M	THE KEYS ALBUM (LP)	15

KEYTONES
85	Keytone KEY 3	Good To Be Alive/Now's The Time	15

KEYWI
83	Virgin VS 623	Lets Get It Right/Dub Version/Short Version (12")	15

K GROOVE
91	The White Label KG 1	The Future/On FB/10 To 10/BYS (12")	60

KHAN
72	Deram SDL 11	SPACE SHANTY (LP, gatefold, white/red label, small logo)	60
72	Deram SDL 11	SPACE SHANTY (LP, gatefold, white/red label, small logo, later stickered sleeve)	30

(see also Steve Hillage, Egg, Nick Greenwood, Arzachel, Hatfield & The North)

ASHISH KHAN
68	Liberty LBL 83083E	ASHISH KHAN (LP)	15
73	Elektra K 42129	JUGAL BANDI (LP, with John Barham)	12

USTAD ALI AKBAR KHAN
69	HMV ASD 2367	MUSIC FROM INDIA NO. 5 (LP)	15
69	Transatlantic TRA 183	DHUN PALAS KAFI (LP)	20
71	Mushroom 100 MR 14	THE PEACEFUL MUSIC OF USTAD ALI AKBAR KHAN (LP)	35

(see also Ravi Shankar)

USTAD VILAYET KHAN
69	RCA SF 8025	THE GURU (LP, soundtrack)	12
70	Transatlantic TRA 239	RAGA TILAKKAMOD (LP)	15

STEVE KHAN
85	Nimbus AN 3023	EVIDENCE (LP, Nimbus Supercut, mail order only from Practical Hi Fi Magazine)	25

KHANDARS
65	Blue Beat BB 332	Don't Dig A Hole For Me/BUSTER'S ALL STARS: Skara	60

KHANS
62	London HLU 9555	New Orleans, 2 AM/Blue Mist	18

KHARTOMB
83	Whaam! WHAAM 14	Swahili Lullaby/Teekon Warriors	6

KICK
84	Footwear FWR 01	Let's Get Back Together/A Shot In The Dark/Don't Ever Change (p/s)	6
86	Countdown VAIN 03	I Can't Let Go/Armchair Politician (p/s)	8

KICKS
80	Carrere CAR 138	Get Off The Telephone/Big Boys Don't Cry (p/s)	30
81	Blue Chip BC 102	If Looks Could Kill/Don't She Look Fab	70

JOHNNY KIDD (& PIRATES)
59	HMV POP 615	Please Don't Touch/Growl	30
59	HMV POP 674	Feelin'/If You Were The Only Girl In The World (solo)	25
60	HMV POP 698	You Got What It Takes/Longin' Lips	18
60	HMV POP 753	Shakin' All Over/Yes Sir, That's My Baby	15
60	HMV POP 790	Restless/Magic Of Love	18
61	HMV POP 853	Linda Lu/Let's Talk About Us	20
61	HMV POP 919	Please Don't Bring Me Down/So What	20
62	HMV POP 978	Hurry On Back To Love/I Want That (with The Mike Sammes Singers)	25
62	HMV POP 1088	A Shot Of Rhythm And Blues/I Can Tell (blue or black label)	15
63	HMV POP 1173	I'll Never Get Over You/Then I Got Everything	6
63	HMV POP 1228	Hungry For Love/Ecstasy	8
64	HMV POP 1269	Always And Ever/Dr. Feelgood	12

64	HMV POP 1309	Jealous Girl/Shop Around	15
64	HMV POP 1353	Whole Lotta Woman/Your Cheatin' Heart	20
65	HMV POP 1397	The Birds And The Bees/Don't Make The Same Mistake As I Did	20
65	HMV POP 1424	Shakin' All Over '65/Gotta Travel On	40
65	HMV POP 1520	It's Got To Be You/I Hate To Get Up In The Morning (solo)	20
66	HMV POP 1559	Send For That Girl/The Fool	30
60s	HMV JO 674	Feelin'/If You Were The Only Girl In The World (export issue, black label)	30
97	Cruisin' 50 CASB 005	Shakin' All Over/Please Don't Touch (78rpm, 300 only)	30
60	HMV 7EG 8628	SHAKIN' ALL OVER (EP)	40
64	HMV 7EG 8834	JOHNNY KIDD AND THE PIRATES (EP)	70
71	Starline SRS 5100	SHAKIN' ALL OVER (LP)	15

(see also Pirates)

KIDDA BAND
79	Carrere CAR 119	Fighting My Way Back/Saturday Night Fever	70

KID DYNAMITE
73	Pye 7N 45274	Call Me Sunshine Superman/Breaking The Ice	15

KID GUNGO
69	Escort ES 801	Hold The Pussy/KING CANNON: Wha Pen (B-side actually by Carl Bryan)	7

KIDNAPPED
79	Decca FR 13841	David's Song/Melancholy Catriona	5

KID 'N' PLAY
88	Cooltempo COOLXR 175	2 Hype (12" promo)	20

KIDROCK
73	Youngblood YB 1058	Ice Cream Man/Dream Dream	35

KIDS
75	Atlantic K 50143	ANVIL CHORUS (LP, with inner, stickered sleeve)	25

(see also Heavy Metal Kids, Gary Holton)

KIDS NEXT DOOR
65	London HLR 9993	Inky Dinky Spider/Goodbye Don't Cry	7

KIDZ NEXT DOOR
79	Warner Bros K 17492	What's It All About?/The Kidz Next Door (p/s)	50

KILBURN & HIGH ROADS
74	Dawn DNS 1090	Rough Kids/Billy Bentley	10
75	Dawn DNS 1102	Crippled With Nerves/Huffety Puff	12
78	Warner Bros K 17225	Billy Bentley/Pam's Moods	8
75	Dawn DNLS 3065	HANDSOME (LP, pink 'sun' label)	40

(see also Ian Dury & Blockheads, 999, Nine Days Wonder)

ROY KILDARE
64	Blue Beat BB 226	I Won't Leave/What About It	12

JUDY KILEEN
56	London HLU 8328	Just Walking In The Rain/A Heart Without A Sweetheart	35
56	London HLU 8328	Just Walking In The Rain/A Heart Without A Sweetheart (78)	10

KILFENORA CEILI BAND
74	Transatlantic TRS 108	KILFENORA CEILI BAND (LP)	12

MERLE KILGORE
54	London HL 8103	Seeing Double, Feeling Single/It Can't Rain All The Time	300
54	London HL 8103	Seeing Double, Feeling Single/It Can't Rain All The Time (78)	50
57	London HLP 8392	Ernie/Trying To Find (Someone Like You)	200
57	London HLP 8392	Ernie/Trying To Find (Someone Like You) (78)	50
60	Melodisc MEL 1545	Dear Mama/Jimmie Bring Sunshine	15
62	Mercury AMT 1193	42 In Chicago/A Girl Named Liz	15
65	London HA-B 8244	THERE'S GOLD IN THEM THAR HILLS (LP)	12

THEOLA KILGORE
67	Sue WI 4035	I'll Keep Trying/He's Coming Back To Me	40

KILLA INSTINCT
92	Music Of Life NOTE061	The Bambi Murders (12")	10
92	Music Of Life NOTE063	Den Of Thieves/Ununited Kingdom (12")	10
93	European Rhyme ERR02	WHISPERS OF HATRED (EP)	18
94	Move MOVE7013 1	ESCAPISM (EP)	8
96	Move MOVE7017 5	THE PENULTIMATE SACRIFICE (EP)	10

(see also Total Fiasco)

LOUIS KILLEN
62	Topic TOP 75	NORTHUMBRIAN GARLAND (EP)	10
66	Topic 12T 126	BALLADS AND BROADSIDES (LP, blue label)	20

LOUIS KILLEN & JOHNNY HANDLE
62	Topic TOP 74	THE COLLIER'S RANT (EP)	10
65	Topic 12T 122	TOMMY ARMSTRONG OF TYNESIDE (LP, with Colin Ross & Tom Gilfellon, blue label with booklet)	15
68	Topic 12T 189	ALONG THE COALY TYNE (LP, with Colin Ross, blue label with booklet)	20

(see also Johnny Handle)

KILLER
77	Ariola ARL 5003	KILLER (LP)	35

(see also Joe Cool & The Killers)

KILLERHERTZ
91	Evasion EVA 1	The Enforcer/X.XS (12", p/s)	12
92	FX FXUKT 9	Distant Dream (X-Static Mix)/Love Byte (Apocalypse Mix)/Love Byte (Stronthium Mix)/Distant Dream (Flying Fader Mix) (12")	40

KILLERMETERS
79	Psycho P 2620	Why Should It Happen To Me/Cardiac Arrest (in p/s)	100
79	Psycho P 2620	Why Should It Happen To Me/Cardiac Arrest	30

MINT VALUE £

80	Gem GEMS 22	Twisted Wheel/SX 225 (p/s, demo copies £50)	90
98	Detour DR 065	ARE YOU READY (EP, blue vinyl, 100 only)	8
97	Detour DRLP 013	METRIC NOISE (2xLP, gatefold, 'sparkly' clear vinyl)	18

KILLERS (1)

| 78 | Satril SAT 129 | Killer (On The Dancefloor)/No Surrender (no p/s) | 5 |

KILLERS (2)

03	Lizard King LIZARD007	Mr Brightside/On Top/Smile Like You Mean It/Who Let You Go (CD)	30
03	Lizard King LIZARD007X	Mr Brightside/Smile Like You Mean It (white vinyl, 500 only p/s)	80
04	Lizard King LIZARD009X	Somebody Told Me/The Ballad Of Michael Valentine (pink vinyl, 2,000 only, p/s and poster)	30
04	Lizard King LIZARD010X	Mr Brightside/Who Let You Go (red vinyl, p/s and poster)	25
04	Lizard King LIZARD 010CD2	Mr Brightside/Somebody Told Me (Remix)/Midnight Show (live)/Video (CD single)	12
04	Lizard King LIZARD 012X	All These Things That I've Done/Andy, You're A Star (Radio 1 session) yellow vinyl, 2000 only, with poster)	15
04	Lizard King IND1ERR	Glamorous Indie Rock & Roll (1-sided promo, 400 only)	15
05	Lizard King LIZARD 014X	Somebody Told Me (Mylo Remix)/Somebody Told Me (Glimmers Mix) (12")	12
05	Lizard King LIZARD 015X	Smile Like You Mean It/Ruby, Don't Take Your Love To Town (Radio 1 Session) (p/s, red vinyl)	8
05	Lizard King LIZARD 015Y	Smile Like You Mean It (Remix)/Mr Brightside (Dub Mix) (12")	8
06	Vertigo 170 672-1	When You Were Young/Where The White Boys Dance (numbered p/s)	6
07	Vertigo 17245686	Read My Mind/Steve Bays Remix (numbered p/s)	10
04	Lizard King LIZARD011X	HOT FUSS (LP, blue vinyl)	50
05	Lizard King	HOT FUSS : SINGLES BOX SET (5,000 only. 11 x 7" album box set)	45
07	Island TKREADVPX1	READ MY MIND REMIXES (2x12")	10

KILLER WATT

| 87 | Raglan RGS 312 | DEATH (EP) | 25 |

JOHN KILLIGREW

| 71 | Penny Farthing PELS 513 | JOHN KILLIGREW (LP, with Pete Dello, red/black/yellow labels) | 150 |

(see also Pete Dello)

KILLING FLOOR

70	Penny Farthing PEN 745	Call For The Politicians/Acid Bean	20
69	Spark (S)RLP 102	KILLING FLOOR (LP, blue/silver labels)	400
70	Penny Farthing PELS 511	OUT OF URANUS (LP, gatefold sleeve, red/black/yellow label)	300
73	Spark Replay SRLM 2004	ORIGINAL KILLING FLOOR (LP, reissue)	30

(see also Rory Gallagher)

KILLING JOKE

79	Malicious Damage MD 410	Nervous System/Turn To Red/Are You Receiving (10" EP in bag, with picture & 4 cards)	20
79	Malicious Damage MD 410	Nervous System/Turn To Red/Are You Receiving (10" EP in bag, without picture & 4 cards)	10
80	Island WIP 6550	Turn To Red/Nervous System (p/s)	5
80	Island WIP 6550	Turn To Red/Nervous System ('A' label)	15
80	Island 12 WIP 6550	Almost Red/Nervous System/Are You Receiving/Turn To Red (12", p/s)	10
80	Malicious Damage MD 540	Wardance/Psyche (p/s, with 'call up paper' insert)	15
80	Malicious Damage MD 540	Wardance/Psyche (p/s, without 'call up paper' insert)	5
80	Malicious Damage MD 540	Wardance/Psyche (Mispressed B-side plays 'unknown artist', p/s)	25
80	E.G. EGMD 1.00	Requiem/Change (p/s)	5
80	E.G. EGMX 1.00	Requiem/Change/Change/Requiem (12", stamped sleeve)	10
80	E.G. EGMX 1.00	Requiem/Change/Change/Requiem (12", later pressing in p/s)	8
82	E.G. EGOX 10	Birds Of A Feather/Flock The B-Side (12", p/s)	8
83	E.G. EGOD 14/KILL 1/2	Me Or You/Wilful Days//Feast Of Blaze (double pack, gatefold p/s)	5
83	E.G. EGOXD 14	Me Or You/Feast Of Blaze/Wilful Days//Let's All Go (To The Fire Dances)/The Fall Of Because (live)/Dominator (Version) (12", sealed double pack)	15
84	E.G. EGOX 16	Eighties (Serious Dance Mix)/Eighties/Eighties (Coming Mix) (12", p/s)	8
84	E.G. DJ17	A New Day/Dance Day (DJ promo)	12
85	E.G. EGOY 20	Love Like Blood (Gestalt Mix)/Love Like Blood/Blue Feather (12", p/s)	10
85	E.G. EGOY 21	Kings And Queens (Knave Mix) (12", p/s)	10
85	E.G. EGOX 21	Kings And Queens (The Right Royal Mix)/The Madding Crowd/Kings And Queens (12", different withdrawn p/s)	10
86	E.G. EGOD 27	Adorations/Exile//Ecstasy/Adorations (Instrumental Mix) (double pack)	5
90	ODIC1	Beautiful Dead (1-sided fan club flexi)	10
80	E.G. EGM5.45	KILLING JOKE (LP)	18
81	E.G. EGMD 5.50	WHAT'S THIS FOR? (LP)	12
82	E.G. EGMD 3	REVELATIONS (LP)	12
83	E.G. EGMD 5	FIRE DANCES (LP)	12
90	AG -54-1	EXTREMITIES DIRT AND VARIOUS REPRESSED EMOTIONS (2-LP)	15

(see also Youth, Peyr, Heavy Duty Breaks)

KILLJOYS (1)

| 77 | Raw RAW 3 | Johnny Won't Get To Heaven/Naive (p/s, 4 different label designs) | 30 |
| 91 | Dam. Goods FNARR LP10 | NAIVE (LP, green vinyl) | 20 |

(see also Girlschool)

KILLJOYS (2)

| 82 | Clay CLAY 18 | This Is Not Love/In Your Light (p/s) | 5 |

KILLS

02	Rug RUG 158	Fuck The People (1-sided, stamped card sleeve, 500 only)	8
03	Domino RUG 154	Fried My Little Brains/Jewel Thief (p/s, insert)	6
03	Domino RUG 165	Pull A U/The Search For Cherry Red	6
03	Domino WIGLP 124	KEEP ON YOUR MEAN SIDE (LP, with fold-out insert)	18
05	Domino WIGLP 140	NO WOW (LP, with DVD)	18
08	Domino WIGLP 184	MIDNIGHT BOOK (LP)	15

(see also Dead Weather)

KILOWATTS

| 68 | Doctor Bird DB 1140 | Bring It On Home/What A Wonderful World | 20 |

(see also West Indians)

PAT KILROY

| 67 | Elektra EKL 311 | LIGHT OF DAY (LP) | 40 |

KILTIES
56	Beltona BL 2666	Teach You To Rock/Giddy-Up-A Ding Dong	15

ANDY KIM
69	Dot DOT 125	Baby I Love You/Gee Girl	12

KIM & KINETICS
60s	Mortonsound 3032/3033	Without A Song/Stormy Monday	60
60s	Mortonsound 3036/3033	Wee Wee Hours/Stormy Monday	60

(see also Kim Davis)

WILLIAM KIMBER
56	EFDSS LP 1001	WILLIAM KIMBER (LP, with booklet)	15
74	Topic 12T 249	THE ART OF WILLIAM KIMBER (LP, with booklet)	15

WILLIAM E. KIMBER
68	Parlophone R 5690	Shilo/Emptiness	5
68	Parlophone R 5735	Kilburn Towers/Goodbye (withdrawn)	8
69	Parlophone R 5796	Black Sheep Boy/And The Sun Began To Shine	6

(see also E William)

STEVIE KIMBLE
66	Decca F 12378	Some Things Take A Little Time/All The Time In The World	18

KINCADE
72	Penny Farthing PEN 796	Jenny Jenny Dreams Are Ten A Penny/Counting Trains	5

KINDNESS
70	RCA 1942	Light Of Love/Lindy Lou	7

KINESPHERE
76	Kinesphere KIN 5001	ALL AROUND YOU (LP)	100

KINETIC EFFECT
93	Insane 1201	Borderin' Insanity/Beyond The Parameters (12" green vinyl, 500 pressed)	30
93	Insane 1201	Borderin' Insanity/Beyond The Parameters (12")	18
97	Insane 1202	Man Bites Dog/The Effect Of Fear (12")	12

(see also 2 The Top and Insane Macbeth)

AL KING
68	Sue WI 4045	Think Twice Before You Speak/The Winner	40

ALBERT KING
67	Atlantic 584 099	Crosscut Saw/Down Don't Bother Me	18
67	Stax 601 015	Born Under A Bad Sign/Personal Manager	10
68	Stax 601 029	Cold Feet/You Sure Drive A Hard Bargain	10
68	Stax 601 042	(I Love) Lucy/You're Gonna Need Me	8
73	Stax 2025 162	Breaking Up Somebody's Home/Little Brother (Make A Way)	5
67	Polydor 2343 026	TRAVELLIN' TO CALIFORNIA (LP)	40
68	Stax (S)XATS 1002	LIVE WIRE - BLUES POWER (LP)	40
69	Atlantic 588 173	KING OF THE BLUES GUITAR (LP)	40
69	Stax SXATS 1017	KING DOES THE KING'S THINGS (LP)	35
69	Stax SXATS 1022	YEARS GONE BY (LP)	35
71	Stax 2363 003	LIVE WIRE - BLUES POWER (LP, reissue)	15
71	Stax 2325 042	LOVEJOY (LP)	20
73	Stax 2325 089	I'LL PLAY THE BLUES FOR YOU (LP)	18
74	Stax STX 1003	I WANNA GET FUNKY (LP)	18

(see also Steve Cropper & Albert King)

ALLAN KING
73	Duke DU 151	Africa Wants Us All/JOE GIBBS: Liberation (B-side actually by Joe Gibbs' All Stars)	6

ANNA KING
65	Philips BF 1402	If Somebody Told You/Baby, Baby, Baby (as Anna King & Bobby Byrd)	15
65	Philips BBE 12584	BACK TO SOUL (EP)	40
65	Philips (S)BL 7655	BACK TO SOUL (LP)	60

(see also Bobby Byrd)

ANTHONY KING
70s	Peer Intl.	ELECTRICAL BAZAAR - SYNTHESIZERS UNLIMITED (LP, library issue)	25

B.B. KING
62	HMV POP 1101	Tomorrow Night/Mother's Love	25
64	Ember EMB S 196	Rock Me Baby/I Can't Lose	25
65	Sue WI 358	The Letter/You Never Know	30
66	HMV POP 1568	Don't Answer The Door Parts 1 & 2	15
67	HMV POP 1580	Night Life/Waitin' On You	12
67	HMV POP 1594	I Don't Want You Cuttin' Your Hair/Think It Over	15
67	Polydor 56735	Jungle/Long Gone Baby	15
68	Stateside SS 2112	Paying The Cost To Be The Boss/Having My Say	10
68	Blue Horizon 57-3144	The Woman I Love/Blues For Me	20
69	Stateside SS 2141	Don't Waste My Time/Get Myself Somebody	6
69	Blue Horizon 57-3161	Everyday I Have The Blues/Five Long Years	20
70	Stateside SS 2161	The Thrill Is Gone/You're Mean	8
70	Stateside SS 2169	So Excited/Confessin' The Blues	5
70	Stateside SS 2176	Hummingbird/Ask Me No Questions	5
71	Probe PRO 516	Chains And Things/King's Special	5
71	Probe PRO 528	Ask Me No Questions/Help The Poor/Humming Bird	5
71	Probe PRO 546	Ain't Nobody Home/Alexis' Boogie (with Alexis Korner)	10
72	Probe PRO 573	Summer In The City/Found What I Need	5
65	HMV CLP 1870	LIVE AT THE REGAL (LP)	50
66	HMV CLP 3514	CONFESSIN' THE BLUES (LP)	40
67	HMV CLP 3608	BLUES IS KING (LP)	30
67	Ember EMB 3379	THE R&B AND SOUL OF B.B. KING (LP)	20
68	Stateside (S)SL 10238	BLUES ON TOP OF BLUES (LP)	35
68	Blue Horizon 7-63216	THE B.B. KING STORY CHAPTER 1 (LP)	60
69	Stateside (S)SL 10272	LUCILLE (LP)	30

MINT VALUE £

69	Stateside SSL 10284	HIS BEST - THE ELECTRIC B.B. KING (LP)	25
69	Blue Horizon 7-63226	THE B.B. KING STORY CHAPTER 2 - BEALE STREET BLUES (LP)	75
70	Stateside SSL 10297	LIVE AND WELL (LP)	25
70	Stateside SSL 10299	COMPLETELY WELL (LP)	25
70	Probe SPBA 6255	INDIANOLA MISSISSIPPI SEEDS (LP)	15
71	Blue Horizon 2431 004	TAKE A SWING WITH ME (LP)	100
71	Probe SPB 1032	LIVE IN COOK COUNTY JAIL (LP)	20
71	Probe SPB 1041	IN LONDON (LP)	15

(see also U2)

B.B. KING & BOBBY BLAND

74	ABC ABCD 605	TOGETHER FOR THE FIRST TIME (2-LP)	18

(see also Bobby Bland)

KING BEE

90	Big One RUFF6X	Back By Dope Demand/Oral Excitement (12")	15
90	1st Bass Ruff6r	Back By Dope Demand/Feel The Flow (12")	15

BEN E. KING

61	London HLK 9258	Spanish Harlem/First Taste Of Love	10
61	London HLK 9358	Stand By Me/On The Horizon	15
61	London HLK 9416	Amor, Amor/Souvenir Of Mexico	10
61	London HLK 9457	Here Comes The Night/Young Boy Blues	15
62	London HLK 9517	Ecstasy/Yes	10
62	London HLK 9544	Don't Play That Song (You Lied)/The Hermit Of Misty Mountain (later copies have Atlantic labels instead of London Atlantic, this price is for both pressings)	10
62	London HLK 9586	Too Bad/My Heart Cries For You	15
63	London HLK 9631	I'm Standing By/Walking In The Footsteps Of A Fool	15
63	London HLK 9691	How Can I Forget/Gloria, Gloria	15
63	London HLK 9778	I (Who Have Nothing)/The Beginning Of Time	10
63	London HLK 9819	I Could Have Danced All Night/Gypsy	10
64	London HLK 9840	Around The Corner/Groovin'	20
64	Atlantic AT 4007	It's All Over/Let The Water Run Down	22
65	Atlantic AT 4018	Seven Letters/River Of Tears	22
65	Atlantic AT 4025	The Record (Baby I Love You)/The Way You Shake It	20
65	Atlantic AT 4043	Cry No More/(There's) No Place To Hide	30
66	Atlantic AT 4065	Goodnight My Love, Pleasant Dreams/Tell Daddy	12
66	Atlantic AT 4065	Goodnight My Love, Pleasant Dreams/I Can't Break The News To Myself (demos with blank label on different B-side)	400
66	Atlantic 584 008	So Much Love/Don't Drive Me Away	12
66	Atlantic 584 046	I Swear By The Stars Above/Get In A Hurry	12
67	Atlantic 584 069	What Is Soul?/They Don't Give Medals To Yesterday's Heroes	12
67	Atlantic 584 090	Save The Last Dance For Me (as Ben E. King & Drifters)/Stand By Me	8
67	Atlantic 584 106	Tears, Tears, Tears/A Man Without A Dream	15
68	Atlantic 584 149	Seven Letters/Goodnight My Love	10
68	Atlantic 584 184	Don't Take Your Love From Me/Forgive This Fool	25
68	Atlantic 584 205	It's Amazing/Where's The Girl	12
69	Atlantic 584 238	'Till I Can't Take It Any More/It Ain't Fair	12
70	Crewe CRW 2	Goodbye My Old Gal/I Can't Take It Like A Man	5
71	Atlantic 2091 100	It's Amazing/Tears, Tears, Tears	10
71	CBS 7397	White Moon/All Of Your Sorrows	6
72	CBS 7785	Take Me To The Pilot/I Guess It's Goodbye	6
75	Atlantic K 10565	Supernatural Things (Parts 1 & 2)	10
75	Atlantic K 10618	Happiness Is Where You Find It/Drop My Heart Off	10
63	London REK 1361	BEN E. KING (EP)	40
63	London REK 1386	I'M STANDING BY (EP)	40
64	Atlantic AET 6004	WHAT NOW MY LOVE (EP)	40
61	London HA-K 2395	SPANISH HARLEM (LP, mono)	50
61	London SAH-K 6195	SPANISH HARLEM (LP, stereo)	70
62	London HA-K 8012	DON'T PLAY THAT SONG! (LP)	50
63	London HA-K 8026	SONGS FOR SOULFUL LOVERS (LP, cover credits Sings For Soulful Lovers; mono)	50
63	London SH-K 8026	SONGS FOR SOULFUL LOVERS (LP, cover credits Sings For Soulful Lovers; stereo)	70
65	Atlantic ATL 5016	GREATEST HITS (LP, plum label)	40
65	Atlantic ATL 5024	SEVEN LETTERS (LP)	50
66	Atlantic 587/588 055	SONGS FOR SOULFUL LOVERS (LP, cover credits Sings For Soulful Lovers; reissue)	18
67	Atlantic 590 001	SPANISH HARLEM (LP, reissue)	12
67	Atlantic 587 072	WHAT IS SOUL? (LP)	25
68	Atlantic 588 125	SEVEN LETTERS (LP, reissue)	12
70	Crewe CRWS 203	ROUGH EDGES (LP)	15

(see also Drifters, Soul Clan)

BOB KING & THE COUNTRY KINGS

59	Oriole CB 1497	My Petite Marie/Hey Honey	100
59	Oriole CB 1497	My Petite Marie/Hey Honey (78)	30

BRENTON KING

73	Downtown DT 505	Why Do People Have To Cry/Version	6

BUZZY KING

60	Top Rank JAR 278	Schoolboy Blues/Your Picture	20

CANNON BALL KING

69	Camel CA 14	Danny Boy/Reggae Happiness	10
70s	Junior JR 103	Reggay Got Soul/Land Of Love (actually by Soul Cats)	10

(see also Carl Bryan, King Cannon, Cannon Ball & Johnny Melody)

CARL KING

66	CBS 202407	Out Of My Depth/Keep It Coming	25
67	CBS 202553	You And Me/Satin Doll	8

CAROLE KING

62	London HLU 9591	It Might As Well Rain Until September/Nobody's Perfect	10
66	London HLU 10036	Road To Nowhere/Some Of Your Lovin'	40
71	A&M AMS 849	It's Too Late/I Feel The Earth Move	5
72	Ode ODS 66031	Been To Canaan/Bitter With The Sweet	5

70	A&M AMLS 996	WRITER - CAROLE KING (LP)	15
72	Ode ODE 77016	RHYMES AND REASONS (LP)	12

CLAUDE KING

61	Philips PB 1173	Big River Big Man/Sweet Loving	7
61	Philips PB 1199	The Comancheros/I Can't Get Over The Way You Got Over Me	7
62	CBS AAG 108	Wolverton Mountain/Little Bitty Heart	8
62	CBS AAG 119	Burning Of Atlanta/Don't That Moon Look Lonesome	7
65	CBS EP 6067	TIGER WOMAN (EP)	12
62	CBS BPG 62114	MEET CLAUDE KING (LP)	12

CLYDIE KING

69	Minit MLF 11014	One Part, Two Part/Love Now Pay Later	5

(see also Jimmy Holiday & Clydie King, Raelets)

DANNY KING('S MAYFAIR SET)

64	Columbia DB 7276	Tossin' And Turnin'/Young Blood	35
65	Columbia DB 7456	Pretty Things/Outside Of My Room	40
65	Columbia DB 7792	Amen (My Teenage Prayer)/It's Such A Shame (as Danny King's Mayfair Set)	25

(see also Trevor Burton, Lemon Tree, Roy Wood)

DAVE KING

56	Decca F 10684	Memories Are Made Of This (& Keynotes)/I've Changed My Mind A 1000 Times	6
56	Decca F 10720	You Can't Be True To Two/A Little Bit Independent	6
56	Decca F 10741	The Birds And The Bees/Hot Chocolatta (with Keynotes)	6

DAVE KING REGGAE BAND

70	Attack ATT 8014	Hey Little Girl/Why Don't You Try Me	6

DEE KING

66	Piccadilly 7N 35316	Sally Go Round The Roses/It's So Fine	12

DENNIS KING

74	EMI 2247	Galloping Home/Within These Walls/Screen Scene	6
77	EMI EMI 2578	Regan's Theme From The Film 'Sweeney'/F.J.'s Tune	20
79	Columbia DB 9061	Dick Turpin/Belinda (as Denis King Orchestra)	6

(see also King Brothers)

DR. MARTIN LUTHER KING

68	Pama PM 732	I Have A Dream/Top Of The Mountain	5
68	Tamla Motown TML 11076	THE GREAT MARCH TO FREEDOM (LP)	60
68	Hallmark CHM 631	IN THE STRUGGLE FOR FREEDOM (LP)	12

EARL (CONNELLY) KING

56	Parlophone DP 511	Gratefully/Don't Take It So Hard (78, export issue)	20

EDDIE KING

65	Columbia DB 7572	Always At A Distance/If You Wish	8
65	Columbia DB 7654	I Wanna Love Her So Bad/If All You Need	10

KING FLOYD

71	Atlantic 2091-051	Groove Me/What Our Love Needs	10

FREDDY/FREDDIE KING

61	Parlophone R 4777	Hideaway/I Love The Woman	50
65	Sue WI 349	Driving Sideways/Hideaway	40
69	Atlantic 584 235	Play It Cool/Funky	15
73	A&M AMS 7076	Woman Across The River/Help Me Through The Day	5
69	Atlantic 588 186	FREDDIE IS A BLUES MASTER (LP)	45
69	Polydor 2343 009	KING OF R&B VOL. 2 (LP)	15
69	Python PLP-KM 5	FREDDY KING VOLUME 1 (LP, 99 copies only)	100
69	Python PLP-KM 7	FREDDY KING VOLUME 2 (LP, 99 copies only)	100
69	Python PLP-KM 11	FREDDY KING VOLUME 3 (LP, 99 copies only)	100

(Pre-1970 releases are usually credited to Freddy King, post-1970 releases to Freddie King.)

72	Polydor 2343 047	HIS EARLY YEARS VOLUME 1 (LP)	12
72	A&M AMLS 68113	TEXAS CANNONBALL (LP)	15
72	Black Bear 904	LIVE PERFORMANCES VOLUME 1 (LP)	15
72	Black Bear 905	LIVE PERFORMANCES VOLUME 2 (LP)	15
73	A&M AMLS 68919	WOMAN ACROSS THE RIVER (LP)	12

(see also Lula Reed & Freddy King)

HAMILTON KING

64	HMV POP 1289	Not Until/I Wanna Live	10
64	HMV POP 1356	Ain't It Time/Money, Money	20
65	HMV POP 1425	Bird Without Wings/Shoppin'	20
69	Toast TT 511	This Love Of Mine/The Cup Is Fuller	5

HANK KING

63	Starlite STEP 41	COUNTRY AND WESTERN (EP)	25
66	Starlite GRK 510	COUNTRY AND WESTERN (EP, reissue)	10

JAY W. KING

66	Stateside SS 505	I'm So Afraid/I Don't Have To Worry (Not Anymore)	22

JONATHAN KING

65	Decca F12950	Everyone's Gone To The Moon/Round Round	5
67	Decca LK/SKL 4908	OR THEN AGAIN... (LP)	15

(see also Weathermen, Hedgehoppers Anonymous, Pleasure Garden)

MORGAN KING

93	OM Records 12OM006	I Am Free (12" promo)	10
93	OM Records OM006	I Am Free (12")	10
93	OM Records 12OM0006 T	I Am Free (8 Mixes) (2 x12")	40

KING OLIVER

53	London AL 3510	PLAYS THE BLUES (10" LP)	15
53	Columbia 33S 1065	KING JOE (10" LP)	15
55	Vogue/Coral LRA 10020	DIXIE SYNCOPATORS (10" LP)	15

MINT VALUE £

P. KING
83   Red Bus RBUS 79   Hey Rosalyn/Lyin' Again 6
(see also Paul King)

P. RUFUS KING
73   Dawn DNS 1031   Look At Me Now/Nobody Knows 25
(see also Paul King, Mungo Jerry)

PAUL KING
72   Dawn DNS 1023   Whoa Buck/Zoe 7
72   Dawn DNLS 3035   BEEN IN THE PEN TOO LONG (LP, textured sleeve with lyric insert) 40
(see also Mungo Jerry, P. King, P. Rufus King, King Earl Boogie Band, D'Jurann Jurran, Jigilo Jug Band, Russian Roulette)

PEE WEE KING & HIS BAND
54   HMV 7MC 14   Bimbo/Changing Partners (export issue) 7
(see also Hank Snow)

PETE KING CHORALE & ORCHESTRA
61   London HLR 9437   Hey! Look Me Over/Tall Hope 5

PETER KING (1)
68   Crab CRAB 3   Reggae Limbo/DERRICK MORGAN: River To The Bank 8

PETER KING (2)
78   Miles Music MM 076   BROTHER BERNARD (LP, with Alan Skidmore) 20

PETER KING (3)
75   Orbitone OTLP 007   MILIKI SOUND (LP) 75
76   Orbitone OTLP 010   OMU LEWA (LP) 100
77   Orbitone OLP 012   A SOULFUL PETER KING (LP) 20

PETER KING (4)
85   Fashion FAD 029   Step On The Gas/Ten Commandments Of An MC (12") 30
85   Fashion FAD 045   Bad Memory/Rewind/Jack It Up (12") 30

RAMONA KING
64   Warner Bros WB 125   It's In His Kiss/It Couldn't Happen To A Nicer Guy 25

RAY KING SOUL BAND
67   Piccadilly 7N 35394   Behold/Soon You'll Be Gone 20
68   Direction 8-63394   LIVE AT THE PLAYBOY CLUB (LP) 20

REG KING
71   United Artists UP 35204   Little Boy/10,000 Miles (as Reg King & B.B. Blunder) 25
71   United Artists UAG 29157   REG KING (LP) 80
(see also Action, Andy Leigh, B.B. Blunder, Mark Charig, Elton Dean, Mighty Baby)

ROBERT KING
82   Charisma PRE 23   Paper Heart/Theme For Love 10
(see also Scars)

SAMMY KING (& VOLTAIRS)
64   HMV POP 1285   What's The Secret/Great Balls Of Fire (as Sammy King & Voltairs) 10
64   HMV POP 1330   Rag Doll/We're Through 8
65   HMV POP 1384   Only You (And You Alone)/A Kiss, A Promise 10
66   HMV POP 1540   If You Can Find Someone To Love You/Past Caring (with Voltairs) 8

SID KING & FIVE STRINGS
56   Philips PB 589   Booger Red/Oobie-Doobie (78) 100

SOLOMON KING
67   Columbia DB 8306   She Wears My Ring/Try Try (withdrawn B-side) 10
70   Columbia DB 8676   Say A Prayer/This Beautiful Day 100
70   Columbia DB 8676   Say A Prayer/This Beautiful Day (demo copy) 150
68   Columbia S(C)X 6250   SHE WEARS MY RING (LP) 18
71   Columbia SCX 6458   YOU'LL NEVER WALK ALONE (LP) 15
72   Polydor 2058258   When You Gotta Go/Life Child 30
(see also Levi Jackson)

KING SPORTY
70   Banana BA 321   Inspiration/Choice Of Music 15
70   Banana BA 322   Lover's Version (as Sporty & Wilson)/DUDLEY SIBLEY: Having A Party 22
70   Punch PH 44   For Our Desire/WINSTON WRIGHT: Version 15
71   Banana BA 323   D.J. Special/RICHARD & MAD: Creation Version 20
73   Green Door GD 4063   Yearful Of Sundays/Version 6
86   Dancefloor DFLP 3002   MEET ME AT THE DISCO (LP) 15

TEDDI KING
56   Vogue Coral Q 72142   My Funny Little Lover/I'll Never Be The Same 5
57   Vogue EPV 1204   STORYVILLE PRESENTS MISS TEDDI KING (EP) 12
55   Vogue LDE 142   MISS TEDDI KING WITH RUBY BRAFF (10" LP) 15
57   Vogue VA 160109   NOW IN VOGUE (LP) 15
(see also George Shearing)

TEDDY KING & BUSTER'S ALLSTARS
67   Fab FAB 27   Mexican Divorce/SOUL TOPS: Baby I Got News 18

TOBY KING
75   President PT 430   First Man To Die From The Blues/Country Bump 6

TONY KING (& HIPPY BOYS)
69   Trojan TR 667   Proud Mary/My Devotion (as Tony King & Hippy Boys) 6
70   Gas GAS 156   Daddy, Daddy Don't Cry/I Like It 6
(see also Maytals)

TONY KING SOUND
75   BBC Records REC 201   MUSIC THROUGH MIDNIGHT (LP) 15

KINGBEES
66   Tempo TPO 103   I'm A Kingbee/My Little Red Book (Irish-only, in p/s) 350

| 66 | Tempo TPO 103 | I'm A Kingbee/My Little Red Book (Irish-only) .... 250 |

KING BISCUIT BOY
| 70 | Paramount SPFL 270 | OFFICIAL MUSIC (LP) .... 18 |
| 71 | Paramount SPFA 7001 | GOODUNS (LP) .... 18 |

(see also Bobby Bland)

KING BISCUIT TIME
| 00 | Regal REG 49 | NO STYLE EP (12") .... 8 |

(see also Beta Band)

KING BROTHERS
57	Parlophone R 4288	Marianne/Little By Little 10
57	Parlophone R 4310	A White Sport Coat (And A Pink Carnation)/Minne-Minnehaha! 6
57	Parlophone R 4338	In The Middle Of An Island/Rockin' Shoes 6
57	Parlophone R 4367	Wake Up Little Susie/Winter Wonderland 6
57	Parlophone R 4389	Put A Light In The Window/Miss Otis Regrets 5
58	Parlophone R 4410	Hand Me Down My Walking Cane/6-5 Jive 5
58	Parlophone R 4438	Torero/Moonlight And Roses 6
58	Parlophone R 4469	Sitting In A Tree House/Father Time 5
59	Parlophone R 4513	Leaning On A Lamp-Post/Thank Heaven For Little Girls 5
59	Parlophone R 4554	Hop, Skip And Jump/Civilization (Bongo, Bongo, Bongo) 10
59	Parlophone R 4577	Makin' Love/Caribbean 5
61	Parlophone R 4825	The Next Train Out Of Town/Sabre Dance 5
61	Parlophone R 4861	The Language Of Love/Got Tell Her For Me 5
64	Oriole CB 1978	Real Live Girl/Every Time It Rains 8

(see also Jim Dale, Dennis King)

KING CANNON
69	Trojan TR 663	Soul Scorcher/GLEN & DAVE: Lucky Boy 40
69	Harry J TR 664	Soul Special/TREVOR SHIELD: Moon Is Playing Tricks On Me 40
69	Crab CRAB 6	Mellow Trumpet/VAL BENNETT: Reggae City 45
71	Hillcrest HCT 2	Reggay Got Soul/SOUL CATS: Land Of Love 7
71	Moodisc HME 109	Raw Deal (as King Cannon Allout; actually by Carl Bryan)/ MUDIE'S ALL STARS: Shirley's Hide Out 12

(see also Cannon Ball & Johnny Melody, Carl Bryan, Max Romeo, Lester Sterling, Kid Gungo, Erroll Dunkley)

KING CANNON (BALL)
| 68 | Trojan TR 636 | Thunderstorm/BURT WALTERS: Honey Love .... 40 |

KING CHUBBY
| 70 | Pama Supreme PS 297 | What's The World Coming To/Live As One .... 10 |
| 70 | Supreme PS 297 | What's The World Coming To/Live As One (reissue) .... 10 |

(see also Junior Byles)

KING CRIMSON
69	Island WIP 6071	The Court Of The Crimson King (Parts 1 & 2) 25
70	Island WIP 6080	Cat Food/Groon (in p/s) 25
70	Island WIP 6080	Cat Food/Groon 10
74	Island WIP 6189	The Night Watch/The Great Deceiver 7
76	Island WIP 6274	21st Century Schizoid Man/Epitaph (in p/s) 30
76	Island WIP 6274	21st Century Schizoid Man/Epitaph 10
69	Island ILPS 9111	IN THE COURT OF THE CRIMSON KING (LP, gatefold sleeve, 1st pressing, pink label/'i' logo) 450
70	Island ILPS 9111	IN THE COURT OF THE CRIMSON KING (LP, gatefold sleeve, 2nd pressing, pink rim label/'palm tree' logo) 70
70	Island ILPS 9127	IN THE WAKE OF POSEIDON (LP, textured gatefold sleeve made by E.J. Day, 1st pressing, A1/B1 matrixes deep pink lightly texttured label with 'i' logo) 100
70	Island ILPS 9127	IN THE WAKE OF POSEIDON (LP, 2nd pressing, pink rim label/'palm tree' logo) ... 30
70	Island ILPS 9141	LIZARD (LP, 1st pressing with E. J. Day Co sleeves, Matrix ILPS9141 A-2U/B-2U, laminated gatefold sleeve, pink rim label/'palm tree' logo) 50
70	Island ILPS 9141	LIZARD (LP, 2nd pressing with Robor sleeves, laminated gatefold sleeve, pink rim label/'palm tree' logo) 30
71	Island ILPS 9175	ISLANDS (LP, pink rim label/'palm tree' logo, gatefold sleeve with inner) 40
72	Island HELP 6	EARTHBOUND (LP, black/pink label) 30
73	Island ILPS 9230	LARKS' TONGUES IN ASPIC (LP, pink rim label/'palm tree' logo, with inner) 30
74	Island ILPS 9275	STARLESS AND BIBLE BLACK (LP, textured gatefold sleeve printed by Robor, palm tree' logo, matrixes: A/3U, B/3U, 'Garc' etched into dead wax side A, 'Sean & Ray' etched into dead wax side B, with inner) 50
74	Island ILPS 9308	RED (LP, pink rim label/'palm tree' logo, with inner sleeve) 45
75	Island ILPS 9316	U.S.A. (LP, pink rim label/'palm tree' logo, with inner) 15
76	Island ISLP 7	A YOUNG PERSON'S GUIDE (2-LP, gatefold sleeve, with booklet) 20
77	Polydor 2683-080	IN THE COURT OF THE CRIMSON KING/LARKS TONGUES IN ASPIC (2-LP) 20
81	EG EGLP 49	DISCIPLINE (LP) 20
82	EG EGLP51	BEAT (LP) 20
95	EG/Virgin CDVKCX 13	THRAK (CD, in metal box, with tour programme) 20

(see also Giles Giles & Fripp, Fripp & Eno, Andy Summers & Robert Fripp, Gordon Haskell, Shame, McDonald & Giles, Emerson Lake & Palmer, Uriah Heep, Boz, Trendsetters Ltd., Pete Sinfield)

KING CRY CRY (PRINCE FAR I)
| 71 | Banana BA 356 | I Had A Talk/BURNING SPEAR: Zion Higher .... 25 |

KING CURTIS
62	London HLU 9547	Soul Twist/Twistin' Time (as King Curtis & Noble Knights) 20
64	Capitol CL 15346	Soul Serenade/More Soul 20
67	Atlantic 584 109	Good To Me/Hold On I'm Comin' 12
67	Atlantic 584 134	Memphis Soul Stew/Blue Nocturne 15
68	Speciality SPE 1000	Wiggle Wobble/Night Train 8
69	Atlantic 584 287	Little Green Apples/La Jeanne 10
70	Atco 2091 012	Teasin'/Soulin' (as King Curtis & Delaney Bramlett, Eric Clapton & Friends) 15
60	London RE-K 1307	HAVE TENOR SAX, WILL BLOW (EP) 40
60	London HA-K 2247	HAVE TENOR SAX, WILL BLOW (LP) 70
62	RCA RD 27252	ARTHUR MURRAY'S MUSIC FOR DANCING - THE TWIST (LP) 30
62	Esquire 32-161	THE NEW SCENE OF KING CURTIS (LP) 40
67	Atlantic 587 067	PLAYS THE GREAT MEMPHIS HITS (LP) 20
68	Ember SPE/LP 6600	SOUL SERENADE (LP) 18

68	Atlantic 587 093	KINGSIZE SOUL (LP, as King Curtis & Kingpins)	18
68	Atlantic 587/588 115	SWEET SOUL (LP)	18
69	Atco 228 027	INSTANT GROOVE (LP)	15
69	Atco 228 002	BEST OF KING CURTIS (LP)	12

(see also Champion Jack Dupree, Eric Clapton)

KING CURTIS, OLIVER NELSON & JIMMY FORREST
| 63 | Esquire 32-189 | SOUL BATTLE (LP) | 30 |

KING DIAMOND
89	Roadrunner RR 9461-1	CONSPIRACY (LP, inner)	15
89	Roadrunner RR 94616	CONSPIRACY (LP, picture disc)	20
89	Roadrunner RR 2455-1	THE DARK SIDES (LP)	12

KINGDOM
| 70 | United Artists UP 35145 | All I Need/Nothing Could Be Better | 25 |

BOBBY KINGDOM/BLUE BEATS
| 61 | Bluebeat BB 44 | Honey Please/BLUE BEATS: That's My Girl | 25 |
| 62 | Blue Beat 45/BB/77 | Spanish Town Twist/Brand New Automobile | 12 |

KINGDOM COME (U.K.)
71	Polydor 2001 234	Eternal Messenger/I D Side To B Side The C Side	10
72	Polydor 2001 416	Spirit Of Joy/Come Alive	10
72	Polydor 2310 130	GALACTIC ZOO DOSSIER (LP, gatefold sleeve, with poster)	50
72	Polydor 2310 130	GALACTIC ZOO DOSSIER (LP, gatefold sleeve, without poster)	20
72	Polydor 2310 178	KINGDOM COME (LP)	25
73	Polydor 2310 254	JOURNEY (LP)	20

(see also Arcadium. Arthur Brown, Kiki Dee, Spirit Of John Morgan, Arcadium)

KING-EARL BOOGIE BAND
72	Dawn DNS 1024	Plastic Jesus/If The Lord Don't Get You	6
72	Dawn DNS 1028	Starlight/Goin' To Germany	6
72	Dawn DNLS 3040	TROUBLE AT MILL (LP, with poster)	30
72	Dawn DNLS 3040	TROUBLE AT MILL (LP, without poster)	20

(see also Mungo Jerry, Paul King, Skeleton Crew)

KING EDWARDS ALL STARS
| 66 | Rio R 077 | North Coast/Kingston 11 | 150 |

(KING) EDWARDS GROUP
63	Island WI 040	Dear Hearts/Oh Mary (B-side actually by Ransford Barnett)	25
63	Island WI 047	Russian Roulette (actually by King Edwards All Stars)/You're Mine (actually by Douglas Brothers)	30
63	Island WI 082	He Gave You To Me/Kings Priests And Prophets (both actually by The Schoolboys)	20
63	Island WI 087	Hey Girl/Skies Are Grey (both actually by Ransford Barnett)	18

KING FIGHTER
| 60s | Jump Up JU 518 | People Will Talk/Same Thing | 8 |

KINGFISH
| 76 | United Artists UAG 29922 | KINGFISH (LP) | 15 |
| 77 | United Artists UAG 30080 | LIVE AND KICKIN' (LP, early copies with picture inner sleeve) | 15 |

(see also Grateful Dead, Bob Weir)

KING GEORGE
| 67 | RCA RCA 1573 | Drive On James/I'm Gonna Be Somebody Someday | 30 |

KING HARVEST
| 73 | Pye Int. 7N 25605 | Dancing in The Moonlight/Marty And The Captain | 8 |
| 73 | Pye NSPL 28174 | DANCING IN THE MOONLIGHT (LP) | 15 |

KING HORROR
69	Joe/Duke DU 34	Dracula Prince Of Darkness/JOE'S ALL STARS: Honky	30
69	Grape GR 3003	Cutting Blade/Vampire	45
69	Grape GR 3006	The Hole/WINSTON GROOVY: Lover Come Back	25
69	Grape GR 3007	Lochness Monster/VISIONS: Zion I	40
69	Jackpot JP 713	Wood In The Fire/The Naked City	15
69	Jackpot JP 714	Police/PAMA DICE: Honky Tonk Popcorn	30
70	Nu Beat NB 051	Frankenstein/WINSTON GROOVY: I Can't Stand It	60
70	Reggae REG 3005	Slave Driver	20

(see also Laurel Aitken)

KING KONG
| 86 | Greensleeves GRED 206 | Paro Them Paro/BUBBLERS COMPUTER STARS : Paranoia (12") | 30 |
| 85 | Now Generation NG 013 | Predominant/Version (12") | 12 |

KING KOSS
| 69 | Polydor 56329 | Spinning Wheel/Louisiana | 8 |

KING KURT
| 86 | Stiff SEEZ 62 | SECOND ALBUM (BIG COCK) (LP) | 12 |
| 82 | Thin Sliced TSR 2 | Zulu Beat/Rockin' Kurt (various sleeve designs and coloured vinyl) | 15 |

KINGLY BAND
| 69 | Decca F 12926 | The Bitter And The Sweet/Standing At The Crossroads | 7 |

KING MIGUEL
| 73 | Bullet BU 524 | The Word Is Black/Town Talk | 10 |

KING OF LUXEMBOURG
| 86 | él GPO 14 | Valleri/Sketches Of Luxembourg (p/s) | 12 |

KINGPINS (U.K.)
| 65 | Oriole CB 1986 | Two Right Feet/That's The Way It Should Be | 35 |

KINGPINS (U.S.)
| 58 | London HLU 8658 | Ungaua Parts 1 & 2 | 15 |
| 58 | London HLU 8658 | Ungaua Parts 1 & 2 (78) | 10 |

KING ROCK & WILLOWS
67	Caltone TONE 111	You Are The One/ALVA LEWIS: Return Home	55

KING ROCKY
68	Studio One SO 2045	The King Is Back/THREE TOPS: Vex Till Yuh Buss	40

(see also Leroy & Rocky, Clancy Eccles, Heptones)

KINGS IV
59	London HLT 8914	Some Like It Hot/The World Goes On	12
59	London HLT 8914	Some Like It Hot/The World Goes On (78)	10

KINGS COUNTY CARNIVAL
69	United Artists UP 2267	Don't Vote For Luke McCabe/The Proof Of The pudding	18

KING SCRATCH
70s	Ethnic ETH 16	Spiritual Whip/Version	20
70s	Ethnic ETH 30	Mash Finger/Version	20

(see also Lee Perry/Upsetters, Skatalites)

KINGSFOLK FOLK GROUP
67	Outlet OUT 008	Black Velvet Band/Love Is Teasin	10

KING'S HENCHMEN
59	Coral FEP 2025	ALAN FREED PRESENTS VOL. 1 (EP)	150

KING SISTERS
57	Capitol CL 14711	While The Lights Are Low/In Hamburg (When The Nights Are Long)	10
57	Capitol CL 14729	Imagination/You're My Thrill	5
57	Capitol CL 14777	Easy To Love/That Old Feeling	5
58	Capitol CL 14865	Deep Purple/Unbelievable	5
58	Capitol CL 14893	What's New?/The Thrill Was New	5
58	Capitol CL 14934	Autumn In Pleasant Grove/The Guy In The Foreign Sports Car	5
59	Capitol CL 15012	Keep Smiling (Keep Laughin', Be Happy)/The Maids Of Cadiz	5
59	Capitol CL 15069	Lovin' Up A Storm/What Would I Do Without You	5
59	Capitol CL 15096	Over The River (And Through The Woods)/Holiday Of Love (with Their Family)	5
57	Capitol EAP1 919	IMAGINATION (EP)	8

PADDY KINGSLAND
74	EMI 2110	Spinball/Wobulator Rock	6
74	Studio 2 TWOX 1024	SUPERCHARGED (LP)	20

CHARLES KINGSLEY CREATION
65	Columbia DB 7758	Summer Without Sun/Still In Love With You	70

EVELYN KINGSLEY & TOWERS
58	Capitol CL 14944	To Know Him Is To Love Him/FRANK PERRY & TOWERS: Let Me Be The One	20

(see also Towers)

KINGSMEN (1)
58	London HLE 8735	Better Believe It/Week-End	30
58	London HLE 8735	Better Believe It/Week-End (78)	20
59	London HLE 8812	Conga Rock/The Cat Walk	30
59	London HLE 8812	Conga Rock/The Cat Walk (78)	30
59	London REE 1211	THE KINGSMEN (EP)	100

(see also Bill Haley & Comets)

KINGSMEN (2)
63	Pye International 7N 25231	Louie Louie/Haunted Castle	30
64	Pye International 7N 25262	Little Latin Lupe Lu/David's Mood	15
64	Pye International 7N 25273	Death Of An Angel/Searching For Love	10
65	Pye International 7N 25292	The Jolly Green Giant/Long Green	8
65	Pye International 7N 25311	The Climb/Waiting	10
65	Pye International 7N 25322	Annie Fanny/Something's Got A Hold On Me	10
66	Pye International 7N 25366	Little Latin Lupe Lu/Louie Louie	15
66	Pye International 7N 25370	Killer Joe/Little Green Thing	10
67	Pye International 7N 25406	Daytime Shadows/Trouble	10
71	Wand WN 14	Louie Louie/If I Needed Someone	8
64	Pye Intl. NEP 44023	THE KINGSMEN (EP)	30
65	Pye Intl. NEP 44040	MOJO WORKOUT (EP)	30
66	Pye Intl. NEP 44063	FEVER (EP)	30
63	Pye Intl. NPL 28050	THE KINGSMEN IN PERSON (LP, live)	25
64	Pye Intl. NPL 28054	THE KINGSMEN VOLUME II (LP)	25
65	Pye Intl. NPL 28068	THE KINGSMEN ON CAMPUS (LP)	25
66	Pye Intl. NPL 28085	15 GREAT HITS (LP)	25
68	Marble Arch MAL 829	THE KINGSMEN'S GREATEST HITS (LP)	15

(see also Touch)

KINGS OF LEON
03	Handmedown HMD 28	Molly's Chambers/Holy Roller Novocaine (10", limited issue, numbered p/s)	35
03	Handmedown HMD 31	Wasted Time/Molly's Hangover (10", silver vinyl, numbered p/s)	15
03	Handmedown HMD 20	HOLY ROLLER NOVOCAINE EP: Molly's Chambers/California Waiting/Holy Roller Novocaine (10", clear red vinyl, numbered p/s, 1000 only)	40
03	Handmedown HMD 21	HOLY ROLLER NOVOCAINE EP (CD, digipak, 1000 only)	40
03	Handmedown HMD 22	WHAT I SAW EP: Red Morning Light/Wicker Chair (10", blue vinyl, numbered p/s)	20
03	Handmedown HMD 24	What I Saw/Red Morning Light/Introducing The Band (audio/visual DVD single)	20
04	Handmedown HMD 43	The Bucket/Trani (Live) (numbered p/s)	8
05	Handmedown HMD 47	Four Kicks/Head To Toe (numbered p/s)	8
05	Handmedown HMD 50	King Of The Rodeo/Soft (Live) (numbered p/s)	8
07	Handmedown HMD 51	On Call/My Third House (p/s)	8
07	Handmedown HMD 53	Fans/Woo Hoo (p/s)	8
07	Handmedown HMD 54	Charmer/My Party (Chad Hugo/Kenna Remix) (p/s)	8
08	RCA 88697 36890 7	Sex On Fire/Beneath The Surface (p/s)	10
03	Handmedown HMD	YOUTH & YOUNG MANHOOD (LP, 2 x 10", p/s with picture inners)	50
04	Handmedown HMD 40	AHA SHAKE HEARTBREAK (2-LP, 10" white vinyl, gatefold sleeve)	20
10	RCA 88697 78241 1	COME AROUND SUNDOWN (LP, gatefold, inners)	15

KING SOUNDS

78	Grove Music GMDM5	Spend One Night In Babylon (feat. Trinity)/Keep Us Down In Poverty (feat. Jah Woosh) (12")	25
79	Grove Music GMDM 11	They That Hate Us (wrongfully)/Ungrateful Bretheren (12")	15
79	Grove Music GMDM 20	Kill Them Dead/Look Into Youself (12")	20
79	Grove GMLP 22	COME ZION SIDE HAPPINESS (LP)	15
82	Grove ILPS 9663	FORWARD (LP, with the Israelites)	12

KING SPARROW

58	Melodisc MEL 1447	Leading Calypsonians/BILLY MOORE: Love Is Everywhere	10
58	Melodisc MEL 1475	Familysize Cokes/Clara Honey Bunch	10
59	Melodisc MEL 1491	Goaty/I Confess	10
66	Island WI 285	Beggars Have No Choice (actually by Leonard Dillon & Wailers)/ MARCIA GRIFFITHS: Funny	50

(see also Mighty Sparrow, Sparrow)

KING STITT

69	Clandisc CLA 200	Who Yea/DYNAMITES: Mr Midnight	12
69	Clandisc CLA 202	Vigerton Two/On The Street	12
69	Clandisc CLA 203	On The Street/CYNTHIA RICHARDS: Foolish Fool	15
69	Clandisc CLA 206	The Ugly One/CLANCY ECCLES: Dance Beat	25
70	Clandisc CLA 207	Herbsman Shuffle (with Andy [Capp])/HIGGS & WILSON: Don't Mind Me	12
70	Clandisc CLA 223	King Of Kings/DYNAMITES: Reggaedelic	12
71	Clandisc CLA 235	Merry Rhythm/CLANCY ECCLES: John Crow Skank	10
71	Banana BA 332	Back Out Version/VEGETABLES: Holly Rhythm	15
71	Banana BA 334	Rhyming Time/Reality	12

(see also Kurass)

KINGSTON JOE

64	Blue Beat BB 253	Time Is On My Friend (actually by Lloyd Barnes)/Wear And Tear (B-side actually by Lascelles Perkins)	30

KINGSTON PETE & BUSTER'S ALL STARS

67	Blue Beat BB 403	Little Boy Blue/I'm A Lover Try Me (actually by Larry Marshall)	150

(see also Larry Marshall)

KINGSTON ALLSTARS

66	Dice CC 25	Happy Hunter/LITTLE NORMA: Ten Commandments Of Woman	70

KINGSTONIANS

67	Rio R 140	Winey Winey/I Don't Care	30
68	Coxsone CS 7066	Mother Miserable/I Make A Woman	150
68	Doctor Bird DB 1120	Put Down Your Fire/Girls Like Dirt	150
68	Doctor Bird DB 1123	Mummy And Daddy/False Witness	100
68	Doctor Bird DB 1126	Fun Galore/Crime Don't Pay	100
68	Trojan TR 627	Mix It Up/I'll Be Around	40
69	Big Shot BI 508	Sufferer/Kiss A Little Finger	65
69	Big Shot BI 526	Nice Nice/I'll Be Around	30
69	Crab CRAB 19	Hold Down/BARRY YORK: Who Will She Be	150
69	Bullet BU 409	I Am Just A Minstrel/Yesterday	25
69	Songbird SB 1011	The Clip/BRUCE ANTHONY: Little Miss Muffett	20
70	Songbird SB 1019	Singer Man/CRYSTALITES: Version	15
70	Songbird SB 1041	Rumble Rumble/CRYSTALITES: Version	20
70	Songbird SB 1045	Out There/CRYSTALITES: Out There Version II	25
70	Trojan TR 7708	I'll Need You Tomorrow/I'm Gonna Make It	10
70	Duke DU 88	You Can't Wine/RUPIE EDWARDS ALLSTARS: Bee Sting	15
72	Duke DU 126	Lion's Den/Version	15
70	Trojan TBL 113	SUFFERER (LP)	50

(see also Jack (Bernard) & Beanstalks, Gregory Isaacs)

KINGSTON TRIO

58	Capitol CL 14918	Scarlet Ribbons/Three Jolly Coachmen	5
58	Capitol CL 14951	Tom Dooley/Ruby Red	5
59	Capitol CL 14985	Raspberries, Strawberries/Sally	5
59	Capitol CL 15002	The Tijuana Jail/Oh Cindy	5
59	Capitol CL 15073	San Miguel/A Worried Man	7
63	Capitol CL 15287	Greenback Dollar/The New Frontier	7

(see also John Stewart)

KING TRUMAN

89	Acid Jazz JAZID 9T	Like A Gun (Safe Sax Mix)/(Dub Version)/(Radio Edit) (12", p/s)	75

(see also Style Council, Paul Weller)

KING TUBBY

94	Blood & Fire BAFLP 002	DUB GONE CRAZY (LP)	15
99	Blood & Fire SVLP 260	DUB LIKE DIRT (2-LP)	25

KING TUBBY & THE AGGROVATORS

82	Black Music BMLP 804	DUBBING IN THE BACKYARD (LP)	50

KING TUBBY & LEE PERRY

75	Live & Love LALP 02	MEETS THE AGROVATORS AT THE DUB STATION (LP)	75
76	Prophets (no. cat. no.)	PROPHECY OF DUB (LP, in plain sleeve)	120
76	Fay FMLP 307	SURROUNDED BY DREAD AT THE NATIONAL ARENA (LP)	55
76	Klik KLIP 9002	SHALOM DUB (LP)	40
77	Fay Music FMLP 304	KING TUBBY MEETS THE UPSETTER AT THE GRASS ROOTS OF DUB (LP)	50
78	Studio 16 WE 102	SURROUNDED BY DREAD AT THE NATIONAL ARENA (LP, re-issue)	35
79	Star PTLP 1029	MAJESTIC DUB (LP)	25
81	Live & Love LAP 015	UPSETS THE UPSETTER (LP)	35

KING TUBBY, PRINCE JAMMY & SCIENTIST

81	K&G Imperial KGLP 002	FIRST, SECOND AND THIRD GENERATION OF DUB (LP)	35

KING TUBBY MEETS ROOTS RADICS

81	Copasetic COPLP 5002	DANGEROUS DUB (LP)	30

KINKS

SINGLES : PYE SINGLES

64	Pye 7N 15611	Long Tall Sally/I Took My Baby Home	120
64	Pye 7N 15611	Long Tall Sally/I Took My Baby Home (Demo copy)	100
64	Pye 7N 15636	You Still Want Me/You Do Something To Me	200
64	Pye 7N 15636	You Still Want Me/You Do Something To Me (Demo copy)	125
64	Pye 7N 15673	You Really Got Me/It's All Right	10
64	Pye 7N 15714	All Day And All Of The Night/I Gotta Move	10
65	Pye 7N 15759	Tired Of Waiting For You/Come On Now	8
65	Pye 7N 15813	Everybody's Gonna Be Happy/Who'll Be The Next In Line	10
65	Pye 7N 15854	Set Me Free/I Need You	8
65	Pye 7N 15919	See My Friend/Never Met A Girl Like You Before	8
65	Pye 7N 15981	Till The End Of The Day/Where Have All The Good Times Gone	8
66	Pye 7N 17064	Dedicated Follower Of Fashion/Sittin' On My Sofa	8
66	Pye 7N 17125	Sunny Afternoon/I'm Not Like Everybody Else	8
66	Pye 7N 17222	Dead End Street/Big Black Smoke (some labels list "Deadend")	8
67	Pye 7N 17321	Waterloo Sunset/Act Nice And Gentle	10
67	Pye 7N 17400	Autumn Almanac/Mr. Pleasant	10
68	Pye 7N 17468	Wonderboy/Polly	15
68	Pye 7N 17573	Days/She's Got Everything	15
69	Pye 7N 17724	Plastic Man/King Kong	15
69	Pye 7N 17776	Drivin'/Mindless Child Of Motherhood	25
69	Pye 7N 17812	Shangri-La/Last Of The Steam-Powered Trains (unissued, acetates only)	0
69	Pye 7N 17812	Shangri-La/This Man He Weeps Tonight	25
69	Pye 7N 17865	Victoria/Mr Churchill Says	12
70	Pye 7N 17961	Lola/Berkeley Mews	6
70	Pye 7N 45016	Apeman/Rats	8
71	Pye PMM 100	You Really Got Me/Set Me Free/Wonder Boy/Long Tall Shorty (maxi-single, no p/s)	8
71	Pye 7NX 8001	PERCY (33rpm 4-track maxi-single, p/s)	20
74	Pye 7N 45313	Where Have All The Good Times Gone/Lola (p/s)	20
83	PRT KPD 1	You Really Got Me/Misty Water (picture disc)	10
84	PRT KIS 003	All Day And All Of The Night/I Gotta Move (picture disc)	10

SINGLES : EXPORT SINGLES

65	Pye 7N 15981	Till The End Of The Day/Where Have All The Good Times Gone (export p/s)	150
66	Pye 7N 17100	Well Respected Man/Milk Cow Blues	110
67	Pye 7N 17314	Mr. Pleasant/This Is Where I Belong	90
67	Pye 7N 17405	Autumn Almanac/David Watts	90
71	Pye 7N 8001	God's Children/Moments (in p/s)	60
71	Pye 7N 8001	God's Children/Moments	30

SINGLES : RCA SINGLES

72	RCA RCA 2211	Supersonic Rocket Ship/You Don't Know My Name	6
72	RCA RCA 2299	Celluloid Heroes/Hot Potatoes	8
73	RCA RCA 2387	Sitting In The Midday Sun/One Of The Survivors	8
73	RCA RCA 2418	Sweet Lady Genevieve/Sitting In My Hotel	8
74	RCA RCA 5015	Mirror Of Love/Cricket	12
74	RCA RCA 5042	Mirror Of Love/He's Evil	12
74	RCA RCA 2478	Holiday Romance/Shepherds Of The Nation	10
75	RCA RCA 2546	Ducks On The Wall/Rush Hour Blues	10
75	RCA RCA 2567	You Can't Stop The Music/Have Another Drink	10
76	RCA RCM 1	No More Looking Back/Jack The Idiot Dunce/The Hard Way (p/s)	12

SINGLES : ARISTA SINGLES

79	Arista ARIS 12240	I Wish I Could Fly Like Superman/Low Budget	5
77	Arista ARIST 153	Father Christmas/Prince Of The Punks (p/s)	10
78	Arista ARIST 189	A Rock'n'Roll Fantasy/Artificial Light	8
78	Arista ARIST 210	Black Messiah/Misfits (p/s)	8
79	Arista ARIST 300	Moving Pictures/In A Space (p/s)	8
80	Arista ARIST 404	Lola (live)/Celluloid Heroes (live) (export only)	12
81	Arista ARIST 415	Better Things/Massive Reductions (p/s)	10
81	Arista ARIST 415/KINKS 1	Better Things/Massive Reductions//Lola (live)/David Watts (live) (double pack, gatefold p/s)	8
81	Arista ARIPD 426	Predictable/Back To Front (picture disc)	8
83	Arista ARIST 524	Don't Forget To Dance/Bernadette (p/s)	7
83	Arista ARIST 524	Don't Forget To Dance/Bernadette//Predictable/Back To Front (shrinkwrapped with free picture disc)	12

SINGLES : OTHER SINGLES

84	Music Week LONF119	How Are You/The Video (freebie with Music Week magazine)	7
86	London LON 119	How Are You/Killing Time (p/s)	12
87	London LONX 132	Lost And Found/Killing Time (p/s, shrinkwrapped with bonus 7" The Official Ray Davies Interview/"Extracts From The LP 'Think Visual'")	12
88	London LON 165	The Road (7" Edit)/Art Lover (p/s)	8
89	London LONCD 239	Down All The Days (Til 1992)/You Really Got Me (live)/Entertainment (CD)	12
89	London LON 239	Down All The Days (Til 1992)/You Really Got Me (live) (p/s)	6
90	London LONCD 250	How Do I Get Close/War Is Over (CD, card sleeve)	10
90	London LON 250	How Do I Get Close/War Is Over (p/s)	6
91	Columbia COL 657593-2	Did Ya/Gotta Move (live)/New World/Days/Look Through Any Doorway (1991) (CD)	12

EPs

64	Pye NEP 24200	KINKSIZE SESSION	30
64	Pye NEP 24203	KINKSIZE HITS	40
65	Pye NEP 24221	KWYET KINKS	45
66	Pye NEP 24258	DEDICATED KINKS	120
68	Pye NEP 24296	THE KINKS	275
75	Pye AMEP 1001	THE KINKS ('Yesteryear' export issue, red or blue vinyl)	22

ALBUMS : PYE ALBUMS

64	Pye NPL 18096	THE KINKS (mono)	150
64	Pye NSPL 83021	THE KINKS (stereo, export only)	225
65	Pye NSPL 18096	THE KINKS (stereo, export only, reissue)	260
65	Pye NPL 18112	KINDA KINKS	150
65	Pye NPL 18131	THE KINK KONTROVERSY	100

MINT VALUE £

65	Pye NSPL 18131	THE KINK KONTROVERSY (reprocessed stereo with stickered catalogue number, export only)	270
66	Pye NPL 18149	FACE TO FACE (mono)	120
66	Pye NSPL 18149	FACE TO FACE (stereo, stickered sleeve "export only")	200
66	Pye ZCP 18149	FACE TO FACE (LP original issue)	25
67	Golden Guinea GGL 0357	THE KINKS (reissue, mono)	12
67	Golden Guinea GGGL 10357	THE KINKS (reissue, stereo)	15
67	Pye NPL 18191	LIVE AT KELVIN HALL (mono)	100
67	Pye N(S)PL 18191	LIVE AT KELVIN HALL (stereo)	150

(The Pye LPs listed above were originally issued with laminated flipback sleeves, pink labels & light blue labels.)

67	Pye NPL 18193	SOMETHING ELSE BY THE KINKS (mono)	200
67	Pye N(S)PL 18193	SOMETHING ELSE BY THE KINKS (stereo)	140
68	Pye N(S)PL 18233	THE KINKS ARE THE VILLAGE GREEN PRESERVATION SOCIETY (unissued, 12-track version, 2 test pressings only)	800
68	Pye NPL 18233	THE KINKS ARE THE VILLAGE GREEN PRESERVATION SOCIETY (15-track version, mono)	200
68	Pye N(S)PL 18233	THE KINKS ARE THE VILLAGE GREEN PRESERVATION SOCIETY (15-track version, stereo)	150
69	Pye NPL 18317	ARTHUR (mono, gatefold sleeve "Quiien Victoria" insert)	150
69	Pye N(S)PL 18317	ARTHUR (stereo, gatefold sleeve "Quiien Victoria" insert)	80
70	Pye NPL 18326	THE KINKS (2-LP, gatefold sleeve)	20
70	Pye NSPL 18359	THE KINKS PT 1 - LOLA VS POWERMAN & THE MONEY-GO-ROUND (gatefold sleeve)	22
71	Pye NSPL 18365	SOUNDTRACK FROM THE FILM 'PERCY' (soundtrack)	40
73	Pye 11PP 100	ALL THE GOOD TIMES (4-LP, box set)	50
83	PRT KINK 1	GREATEST HITS (with bonus 10" EP of unreleased material)	40

ALBUMS : OTHER ALBUMS

71	RCA SF 8243	MUSWELL HILLBILLIES (gatefold sleeve)	40
72	RCA DPS 2035	EVERYBODY'S IN SHOWBIZ, EVERYBODY'S A STAR (2-LP, gatefold sleeve)	22
73	RCA SF 8392	PRESERVATION ACT 1	20
74	RCA LPL2 5040	PRESERVATION ACT 2 (2-LP, gatefold sleeve)	25
75	RCA SF 8411	SOAP OPERA (gatefold sleeve)	15
75	RCA RS 1028	SCHOOLBOYS IN DISGRACE	12
76	RCA RS 1059	CELLULOID HEROES	15
93	Sony 472489-1	PHOBIA (omits 2 tracks from CD)	35
94	Konk Grapevine KNK LP 1	TO THE BONE	12

(see also Dave Davies, Ray Davies, Maple Oak, Leapy Lee, Phoenix)

TONY KINSEY (QUARTET)

55	Decca F 10548	She's Funny That Way/Fascinatin' Rhythm	20
55	Decca F 10606	Close Your Eyes/Pierrot	15
55	Decca F 10648	Hey! There/Ballet	25
56	Decca F 10708	Stompin' At The Savoy/China Boy (with Dill Jones)	6
56	Decca F 10709	Moonglow/One O'Clock Jump	6
56	Decca FJ 10725	Starboard Bow/Body And Soul	6
56	Decca FJ 10760	Lullaby Of The Leaves/Isolation	12
56	Decca FJ 10773	In A Ditch/A Smooth One	8
57	Decca FJ 10851	Mean To Me/Supper Party	12
57	Decca F 10952	The Midgets/Blue Eyes	6
62	Ember JBS 707	Girl In Blue/Weber The Great	20
56	Decca DFE 6282	PRESENTING THE TONY KINSEY QUARTET NO. 1 (EP)	40
56	Decca DFE 6285	PRESENTING THE TONY KINSEY QUARTET NO. 2 (EP)	40
58	Decca DFE 6461	MY FAIR LADY (EP)	15
59	Parlophone SGE 2004	RED BIRD - JAZZ AND POETRY (EP, mono [GEP 8765]/stereo, with Christopher Logue)	25
59	Parlophone SGE 2008	FOURSOME (EP, stereo, also mono GEP 8895)	15
57	Decca LK 4186	INTRODUCING THE QUINTET (LP)	100
57	Decca LK 4207	JAZZ AT THE FLAMINGO (LP)	150
58	Decca LK 4274	TIME GENTLEMEN PLEASE (LP)	80
61	Ember EMB 3337	AN EVENING WITH ... (LP)	70
63	Decca LK 4534	HOW TO SUCCEED IN BUSINESS WITHOUT REALLY TRYING (LP, with Gordon Beck)	50

TONY KINSEY TRIO & JOE HARRIOTT

54	Esquire EP 36	TONY KINSEY TRIO & JOE HARRIOTT (EP)	40
54	Esquire EP 52	TONY KINSEY TRIO & JOE HARRIOTT (EP)	40
54	Esquire EP 82	TONY KINSEY TRIO & JOE HARRIOTT (EP)	40

(see also Joe Harriott)

KINSMEN

| 68 | Decca F 22724 | Glasshouse Green, Splinter Red/It's Started To Rain Again | 45 |
| 68 | Decca F 22777 | It's Good To See You/Always The Loser | 10 |

(see also Four Kinsmen)

KIPPINGTON LODGE

67	Parlophone R 5645	Shy Boy/Lady On A Bicycle	40
68	Parlophone R 5677	Rumours/And She Cried	35
68	Parlophone R 5717	Tell Me A Story/Understand A Woman	40
68	Parlophone R 5750	Tomorrow Today/Turn Out The Light	40
69	Parlophone R 5776	In My Life/I Can See Her Face	90
78	EMI NUT 2894	KIPPINGTON LODGE (EP)	12

(see also Brinsley Schwartz, Nick Lowe)

KIRBY

76	Anchor ANC 1031	Love Letters/Flasher	12
78	Hot Wax WAX 1/ANCHO 1	Bottom Line/That's Some Dream	10
78	Hot Wax HW 2	COMPOSITION (LP)	75
94	Backtrack Archive HW 2	COMPOSITION (LP, reissue)	30

(see also Curved Air, Stretch)

KATHY KIRBY

60	Pye 7N 15313	Love Can Be/Crush Me	15
61	Pye 7N 15342	Danny/Now You're Crying	15
62	Decca F 11506	Big Man/Slowly	10
63	Decca F 11682	Dance On/Playboy	5
63	Decca F 11759	Secret Love/You Have To Want To Touch Him	5
64	Decca F 11832	Let Me Go, Lover!/The Sweetest Sounds	5
64	Decca F 11892	You're The One/Love Me Baby	5

64	Decca F 11992	Don't Walk Away/No Regrets	5
65	Decca F 12087	I Belong/I'll Try Not To Cry	5
65	Decca F 12177	The Way Of Love/Oh Darling, How I Miss You	5
65	Decca F 12280	Where In The World?/That Wonderful Feeling Of Love	5
66	Decca F 12338	Spanish Flea/Till The End Of Time	5
66	Decca F 12432	The Adam Adamant Theme/Will I Never Learn?	25
67	Columbia DB 8139	No One's Gonna Hurt You Anymore/My Yiddishe Momme	5
67	Columbia DB 8192	In All The World/Time	6
67	Columbia DB 8302	Turn Around/Golden Days	5
68	Columbia DB 8400	I Almost Called Your Name/Let The Music Start	8
68	Columbia DB 8521	Come Back Here With My Heart/Antonio	8
69	Columbia DB 8559	I'll Catch The Sun/Please Help Me I'm Falling	8
69	Columbia DB 8634	Is That All There Is?/Knowing When To Leave	8
70	Columbia DB 8682	Wheel Of Fortune/Lucky	8
70	Columbia DB 8721	My Way/Little Green Apples	8
71	Columbia DB 8795	So Here I Go/Yes - I've Got (A-side titled "Here I Go Again" on demos)	10
71	Decca F 13228	Bill/Can't Help Lovin' Dat Man	10
72	Columbia DB 8910	Do You Really Have A Heart/Dream On, Dreamer	10
73	Columbia DB 8965	Little Song For You/Here, There And Everywhere	10
73	Orange OAS 216	Singer With The Band/Hello Morning	60
76	President PT 455	My Prayer/Nobody Loves Me Like You Do	10
81	President PT 491	He/Nobody Loves Me Like You	8
63	Decca DFE 8547	KATHY KIRBY (EP)	15
65	Decca DFE 8596	KATHY KIRBY VOL. 2 (EP)	20
65	Decca DFE 8611	A SONG FOR EUROPE (EP)	20
67	Decca LK 4746	MAKE SOMEONE HAPPY (LP)	30
67	Ace Of clubs ACL 1235	BEST OF (LP)	15
68	Columbia S(C)X 6259	MY THANKS TO YOU (LP)	60

LARRY KIRBY & ENCORES

59	Top Rank JAR 143	My Baby Don't Love Me/My Rose Of Kentucky	15
59	Top Rank JAR 143	My Baby Don't Love Me/My Rose Of Kentucky (78)	10

PAT KIRBY

56	Brunswick 05560	Happiness Is A Thing Called Joe/Don't Tell Me Not To	7
56	Brunswick 05575	What A Heavenly Night For Love/Greensleeves	7
57	Brunswick 05697	Tammy/Don't Keep Silent	7
58	Brunswick 05731	Sayonara/Please Be Gentle With Me	7

BASIL KIRCHIN (BAND)

57	Parlophone R 4344	White Silver Sands/Waiting For The Robert E. Lee	5
58	Parlophone R 4511	Cha Cha Bells/Oh Dear What Can The Cha Cha Be (with Rock-A-Cha Cha Band)	5
59	Parlophone R 4527	Rock-A-Conga/Skin Tight (as Basil Kirchin Band)	6
71	Columbia SCX 6463	A WORLD WITHIN WORLDS (LP)	300
74	Island HELP18	A WORLD WITHIN WORLDS (not a reissue but second LP)	80
03	Trunk JBH 003 LP	QUANTUM LP, hand numbered, 500 only)	30
04	Trunk JBH 005 LP	CHARCOAL SKETCHES/STATES OF MIND (LP, 500 only)	40
05	Trunk JBH 012 LP	ABSTRACTIONS OF THE INDUSTRIAL NORTH (LP)	20
06	Trunk JBH 021 LP	PARTICLES (LP)	20

(see also Basil Kirchin, London Studio Group)

(IVOR & BASIL) KIRCHIN BAND

54	Parlophone MSP 6144	Mambo Macoco/Tangerine (as Kirchin Band)	10
55	Decca F 10434	Minor Mambo/Mother Goose Jumps (as Kirchin Band)	15
56	Parlophone R 4222	The Roller/St. Louis Blues (as Ivor & Basil Kirchin)	7
56	Parlophone R 4237	Rockin' & Rollin' Thru The Darktown Strutters' Ball/Ambush	20
57	Parlophone R 4266	Rock Around The World Medley (with Shani Wallis)	18
57	Parlophone R 4284	Calypso!!/Jungle Fire Dance (as Ivor & Basil Kirchin with Wendy Windows)	5
57	Parlophone R 4335	Teenage World/So Rare (as Kirchin Band & Bandits)	10
55	Parlophone GEP 8531	KIRCHIN BANDBOX (EP)	15
56	Parlophone GEP 8569	THE IVOR AND BASIL KIRCHIN BAND (EP)	30

DEE KIRK

62	Salvo SLO 1809	I'll Cry/My Used To Be (99 copies only)	15

KEVIN KIRK

62	Columbia DB 4909	Sweet/Don't Waste Your Tears On Him	6
62	Columbia DB 4863	Teenage Heartache/Midnight	7

RICHARD H. KIRK

81	Industrial IRC 34	DISPOSABLE HALF TRUTHS (cassette)	20

(see also Cabaret Voltaire, Peter Hope & Richard H. Kirk)

(RAHSAAN) ROLAND KIRK

64	Mercury 10015 MCE	THE KIRK QUARTET MEETS THE BENNY GOLSON ORCHESTRA (EP)	10
65	Mercury 10016 MCE	ROLAND SPEAKS (EP, with Benny Golson Orchestra)	10
62	Esquire 32-164	KIRK'S WORK (LP, with Jack McDuff)	25
63	Mercury MMC 14126	WE FREE KINGS (LP)	25
64	Mercury MCL 20002	THE KIRK QUARTET MEETS THE BENNY GOLSON ORCHESTRA (LP)	20
64	Mercury MCL 20021	KIRK IN COPENHAGEN (LP)	20
64	Mercury SMWL 21020	GIFTS & MESSAGES (LP)	15
65	Mercury MCL 20037	WE FREE KINGS (LP, reissue)	12
65	Mercury MCL 20045	DOMINO (LP)	20
65	Fontana FJL 114	HIP! (LP)	20
66	Mercury (S)LML 4005	I TALK WITH THE SPIRITS (LP)	15
66	Mercury (S)LML 4015	RIP, RIG AND PANIC (LP)	15
67	Mercury (S)LML 4019	SLIGHTLY LATIN (LP)	20
67	Verve 9193	NOW PLEASE DON'T YOU CRY BEAUTIFUL EDITH (LP)	18
71	Atlantic 2400 110	RAHSAAN, RAHSAAN (LP, as Rahsaan Roland Kirk)	12
72	Atlantic K 40358	BLACKNUSS (LP)	12
73	Atlantic K 40457	MEETING OF THE TIMES (LP, with Al Hibbler)	12
70	Atlantic 588178	LEFT & RIGHT (LP)	25
69	Atlantic 588 207	VOLUNTEERED SLAVERY (LP)	20

MINT VALUE £

KIRKBYS

66	RCA RCA 1542	It's A Crime/I've Never Been So Much In Love	150

(see also 23rd Turnoff, Jimmy Campbell, Rockin' Horse, Merseybeats)

KEN KIRKHAM

56	Columbia SCM 5244	It's Almost Tomorrow/No Not Much	10
58	Columbia DB 4116	Now And For Always/Cathy	6

JOHN KIRKPATRICK (& SUE HARRIS)

72	Trailer LER 2033	JUMP AT THE SUN (LP, with Sue Harris, first pressing with red/black label)	25
75	Trailer LER 2033	JUMP AT THE SUN (LP, with Sue Harris, repressing with yellow label)	15
76	Topic 12TS 295	AMONG THE MANY ATTRACTIONS AT THE SHOW WILL BE A REALLY HIGH-CLASS BAND (LP, with Sue Harris)	20
76	Free Reed FRR 010	PLAIN CAPERS (LP, with booklet)	12
77	Topic 12TS 355	SHREDS AND PATCHES (LP, with Sue Harris)	12

(see also Jon Raven)

JULIAN KIRSCH

69	Columbia DB 8541	Clever Little Man/The Adventures Of A Young Cuckoo	40

DANNY KIRWAN

75	DJM DJS 10783	Hot Summer's Day/Love Can Always Bring You Happiness (demo in p/s)	8
75	DJM DJS 10783	Hot Summer's Day/Love Can Always Bring You Happiness	6
75	DJM DJLPS 454	SECOND CHAPTER (LP, gatefold sleeve)	15

(see also Fleetwood Mac, Tramp)

KISS

SINGLES

75	Casablanca CBX 503	Nothin' To Lose/Love Theme From Kiss	25
75	Casablanca CBX 510	Rock And Roll All Nite/Anything For My Baby	25
76	Casablanca CBX 516	Shout It Out Loud/Sweet Pain	15
76	Casablanca CBX 519	Beth/God Of Thunder	18
77	Casablanca CAN 102	Hard Luck Woman/Calling Dr Love/Beth (in p/s)	40
77	Casablanca CAN 102	Hard Luck Woman/Calling Dr Love/Beth	10
77	Casablanca CAN 110	Then She Kissed Me/Hooligan/Flaming Youth	15
77	CAN110	Then She Kissed Me/Hooligan/Flaming Youth (12")	10
77	Casablanca CANL 110	Then She Kissed Me/Hooligan/Flaming Youth (12", company sleeve)	10
78	Casablanca CAN 117	Rocket Ride/Love Gun (live)	8
78	Casablanca CANL 117	Rocket Ride/Detroit Rock City (live)/Love Gun (live) (12", company sleeve)	12
78	Casablanca CAN 126	Rock And Roll All Nite/C'Mon And Love Me (in p/s)	25
78	Casablanca CAN 126	Rock And Roll All Nite/C'Mon And Love Me	8
79	Casablanca CAN 152	I Was Made For Lovin' You/Hard Times	8
79	Casablanca CANL 152	I Was Made For Lovin' You (extended)/Charisma (12", p/s)	18
79	Casablanca CAN 163	Sure Know Something/Dirty Livin' (no p/s)	6
80	Casablanca NB 1001	2000 Man/I Was Made For Lovin' You/Sure Know Something (p/s)	15
80	Casablanca NBL 1001	2000 Man/I Was Made For Lovin' You/Sure Know Something (12", co. sleeve)	12
80	Casablanca MER 19	Talk To Me/She's So European (p/s)	10
80	Casablanca KISS 1	What Makes The World Go 'Round/Naked City (p/s)	10
81	Casablanca KISS 2	A World Without Heroes/Mr Blackwell (p/s)	5
81	Casablanca KISSP 002	A World Without Heroes/Mr Blackwell (picture disc)	8
82	Casablanca KISS 3	Killer/I Love It Loud (pull-out tongue p/s)	12
82	Casablanca KISS 312	Killer/I Love It Loud/I Was Made For Lovin' You (12", p/s)	15
82	Casablanca KISS 4	Creatures Of The Night/Rock And Roll All Nite (live) (p/s, picture label)	10
82	Casablanca KISS 4	Creatures Of The Night/Rock And Roll All Nite (live) (p/s, silver label)	8
82	Casablanca KISS 412	Creatures Of The Night/War Machine/Rock And Roll All Nite (live) (12", p/s)	15
82	Casablanca KISSD 4	Creatures Of The Night/Rock And Roll All Nite (live) (12", double groove, autographs engraved on 1 side)	20
83	Vertigo KISS 5	Lick It Up/Not For The Innocent (p/s)	5
83	Vertigo KISSP 5	Lick It Up/Not For The Innocent (poster p/s)	12
83	Vertigo KPIC 5	Lick It Up/Not For The Innocent (tank-shaped picture disc)	20
83	Vertigo KISS 512	Lick It Up/Not For The Innocent/I Still Love You (12", p/s)	8
84	Vertigo VER 12	Heaven's On Fire/Lonely Is The Hunter (p/s)	5
84	Vertigo VERX 12	Heaven's On Fire/Lonely Is The Hunter/All Hell's Breakin' Loose (12", p/s with poster)	10
84	Vertigo VERX 12	Heaven's On Fire/Lonely Is The Hunter/All Hell's Breakin' Loose (12", p/s with poster)	8
88	Mercury 080 100-1	EXPOSED (12" CD video)	20
89	Mercury 080 044-2	Lick It Up/Dance All Over Your Face/Gimme More/Fits Like a Glove (CD video)	15
89	Vertigo 080 059-2	Tears Are Falling/Anyway You Slice It/Who Wants To Be Lonely/ Secretly Cruel (CD Video)	15

ALBUMS

75	Casablanca CBC 4003	KISS (blue 'Bogart' label)	25
75	Casablanca CBC 4004	DRESSED TO KILL (blue 'Bogart' label, embossed sleeve)	20
76	Casablanca CBC 4008	DESTROYER (blue 'Bogart' label with inner sleeve)	20
76	Casablanca CBC 4011/2	ALIVE! (2-LP, blue 'Bogart' label, gatefold sleeve with insert, sleeve also lists CBSP 401)	20
77	Casablanca CALH 2001	ROCK AND ROLL OVER ('lovegun' label, red vinyl)	40
77	Casablanca CAL 2006	KISS (reissue, 'lovegun' label, red vinyl)	40
77	Casablanca CAL 2007	HOTTER THAN HELL ('lovegun' label, red vinyl)	40
77	Casablanca CAL 2008	DRESSED TO KILL (reissue, 'lovegun' label, red vinyl)	40
77	Casablanca CAL 2009	DESTROYER (reissue, different sleeve, 'lovegun' label, red vinyl)	40
77	Casablanca CALD 5001	ALIVE! (2-LP, reissue, 'lovegun' label, red vinyl)	50
77	Casablanca CALH 2017	LOVE GUN ('lovegun' label, with picture inner sleeve)	12
77	Casablanca CALH 2017	LOVE GUN ('lovegun' label, red vinyl with picture inner sleeve)	40
77	Casablanca CALD 5004	KISS ALIVE II (2-LP, 'lovegun' label, with colour booklet & transfer sheet)	25
77	Casablanca CALD 5004	KISS ALIVE II (2-LP, 'lovegun' label, red vinyl with colour booklet)	50
78	Casablanca CALD 5005	DOUBLE PLATINUM (2-LP, 'lovegun' label, silver foil embossed sleeve & insert; sleeve & insert pressed in U.S. with U.K. cat. no. sticker)	20
79	Casablanca CALH 2051	DYNASTY ('lovegun' label, black vinyl, colour inner sleeve & poster)	15
80	Mercury 6302 032	UNMASKED (with poster)	15
81	Casablanca 6302 163	(MUSIC FROM) THE ELDER (single sleeve or gatefold)	15
82	Casa. CANL 4/6302 219	CREATURES OF THE NIGHT ('make-up' sleeve)	12
87	Vertigo 832 903-1	CRAZY NIGHTS (picture disc in stickered PVC wallet)	12

98	Mercury PLP 31453 8137-2	PSYCHO CIRCUS (LP, promo only picture disc)	30

(see also Gene Simmons, Ace Frehley, Peter Criss, Paul Stanley)

KISSING SPELL
93	Essex DELUJO 1001LP	LOS PAJAROS (LP, reissue of Chilean LP, 500 only)	12

KATIE KISSOON
83	Jive T37	You're The One/You're The One (Instrumental) (12")	15
69	Columbia DB 8525	Don't Let It Rain/Will I Never See The Sun	6

(see also Peanut, Marionettes, Rag Dolls [U.K.])

MAC KISSOON
60s	Boulevard (no cat. no.)	Wear It On Your Face/In A Dream	10
69	Youngblood YB 1005	Wear It On Your Face/In A Dream (reissue)	5

(see also Marionettes, Rag Dolls [U.K.])

KISS THE BLADE
85	Incision CUT 1	The Party's Begun/The Night Comes Down/The Bridge (12", p/s)	25
86	Incision CUT 3	Young Soldier/The Love I Give (12" p/s)	40

KIT KATS
66	London HLW 10075	Won't Find Better Than Me/That's The Way	18

(see also New Hope)

EARTHA KITT
54	HMV 7M 191	Under The Bridges Of Paris/Lovin' Spree	8
54	HMV 7M 198	Somebody Bad Stole De Wedding Bell/Sandy's Tune	8
54	HMV 7M 234	Santa Baby/Let's Do It (Let's Fall In Love)	8
54	HMV 7M 246	Easy Does It/Mink Shmink	7
55	HMV 7M 282	Monotonous/African Lullaby	7
55	HMV 7M 288	C'est Si Bon (with Henri René)/Senor	7
56	HMV 7M 422	Honolulu Rock-A-Roll-A/Je Cherche Un Homme (I Want A Man)	30
56	MGM SP 1153	Please Do It/Lady Loves	7
56	MGM SP 1178	Diamonds Are A Girl's Best Friend/Good Little Girls	7
57	HMV POP 309	Just An Old-Fashioned Girl/If I Can't Take It With Me When I Go (gold label)	10
57	HMV POP 309	Just An Old-Fashioned Girl/If I Can't Take It With Me When I Go (silver label)	6
57	HMV POP 346	There Is No Cure For L'Amour/Hey Jacque	10
58	RCA RCA 1037	Take My Love/Proceed With Caution	6
58	RCA RCA 1093	I Want To Be Evil/Oh John!	5
63	London HL 7119	Shango/In The Evening (When The Sun Goes Down) (export issue)	8
70	Spark SRL 1039	Hurdy Gurdy Man/Catch The Wind	20
71	CBS 7626	A Knight For My Nights/Summer Storm	5
55	HMV DLP 1067	THAT BAD EARTHA (10" LP)	15
55	HMV DLP 1087	DOWN TO EARTHA (10" LP)	15
58	RCA RD 27076	ST. LOUIS BLUES (LP)	15

KITTENS
64	Decca F 12036	Round About Way/Don't Stop Now	15

KIX
80	Creole CR 205	Fear Of Flying/Werewolf Walking (p/s)	6

KLAN
62	Palette PG 9052	Fifi The Fly/Already Mine	10

KLAXON 5
86	él GPO 20	Never Underestimate The Ignorance Of The Rich/Great Railway Journeys (p/s)	8

KLAXONS
06	Angular ARC 012	Gravity's Rainbow/The Bouncer (500, white label, numbered)	18
06	Merok ME 001	Atlantis To Interzone/4 Horsemen of 1012 (p/s)	8
06	Merok ME 003/4	Atlantis To interzone (Remixes) (6 Mixes on 12" and one 7", white labels)	10
07	Dim Mak DM 111	Gravity's Rainbow (Soulwax Remix) (12" 1-sided, etched)	8
07	RINSELP1T	MYTHS OF THE NEAR FUTURE (2-LP, 1 side etched)	25
10	RINSEELP2T	SURFING THE VOID (2-LP, 500 only, white vinyl)	18

SUSIE KLEE
66	Polydor BM 56082	Mr Zero/Punch And Judy Girl	15

KLEENEX
79	Rough Trade/Sunrise RT 9	Ain't You/Hedi's Head (poster p/s)	12
79	Rough Trade RT 014	You/U (p/s)	10

(see also Liliput)

ALAN KLEIN
62	Oriole CB 1719	Striped Purple Shirt/You Gave Me The Blues	20
62	Oriole CB 1737	Three Coins In The Sewer/Danger Ahead	20
65	Parlophone R 5292	It Ain't Worth The Lonely Road Back/I've Cried So Many Tears	6
65	Parlophone R 5370	Age Of Corruption/I'm Counting On You	5
69	Page One POF 119	Honey Pie/You Turned A Nightmare Into A Dream	8
70	Decca F 13033	Dinner's In The Ice Box/Here I Am, There You Are	7
64	Decca LK 4621	WELL, AT LEAST IT'S BRITISH (LP)	20

(see also New Vaudeville Band)

HARRY KLEIN QUARTET
56	Jazz Today JTE 105	BRASH BARITONE (EP)	25
56	Nixa NJE 1009	NEW SOUND (EP)	25
56	Nixa NJE 1022	HARRY KLEIN QUARTET (EP)	25
57	Columbia SEG 7647	BARITONE SAX (EP)	15

(see also Jazz Five)

KLEPTOMANIA
92	Hypno-Genesis HG 001	Amadeus (Martini Mix)/Amadeus (Stringi Wingi Mix)/ Morf (Plastascene Mix)/Morf (Scratchi Waxi Mix) (12")	70

DEAN KLEVATT
74	Decca F 13495	Don't Bury Molly/The Story Of His Life	10

KLF

89	KLF Comms 004M	What Time is Love (Monster Attack Mix) (1-sided 12", 3 only)	300
89	KLF Comms. KLF 004T	What Time Is Love? (Trance Mix)/What Time Is Love? (Mix 2) (12", 'Pure Trance 1', original issue with black/green p/s)	12
89	KLF Comms. KLF 004R	What Time Is Love? ('89 Primal Remix)/What Time Is Love? (Techno Slam)/ What Time Is Love? (Trance Mix 1) (12", stickered p/s)	12
89	KLF Comms KLF 010IR	Deep Shit Deep Shit Part 3 (the Illegal Remix)/Deep Shit Part 2/The Lovers' Side (unreleased 12", 6 copies only)	700
90	KLF Comms. KLF 004P	What Time Is Love? (Live At Trancentral)/Wandafull Mix (12", w/l, 1,500 only)	10
90	KLF Comms. KLF 004X	What Time Is Love? (Live At Trancentral)/Techno Gate Mix (12", p/s, mispressing, B-side actually plays "Wandafull Mix", matrix no.: KLF 004X-B)	25
90	KLF Comms. KLF 004CD	What Time Is Love? (Radio)/(Live At Trancentral)/(Trance Mix 1) (CD, mispressing playing part of Knebworth '90 live CD)	15
90	KLF Comms. KLF 005R	3AM Eternal 'Single Edit'/Blue Danube Orbital Mix/Moody Boys Version/ 3PM Electro (12", original issue with stickered p/s)	10
91	KLF Comms. KLF 005S	3AM Eternal (Live At The S.S.L.) (Radio Freedom Edit) (white label, 500 only)	12
91	KLF Comms. KLF 005	3AM Eternal (Live At The S.S.L.)/Guns Of Mu Mu (12" promo)	8
91	KLF Comms. KLF 005Y	3AM Eternal (Moody Boys mixes) (12", white label, promo only)	8
92	KLF Comms. KLF 5 TOTP	3AM Eternal (Xmas Top Of The Pops Version) (1-sided, w/Extreme Noise Terror, mail-order only, with insert & mailing envelope; beware of bootlegs!)	30
92	KLF Comms. KLF 5 TOTP	3AM Eternal (Xmas Top Of The Pops Version) (1-sided, w/Extreme Noise Terror, mail-order only, without insert & mailing envelope; beware of bootlegs!)	8
89	KLF Comms. KLF 008R	Last Train To Trancentral (Remixes 1 & 2) (12", p/s, 'Pure Trance 5', 2,000 pressed, some warped, price is for unwarped copy)	40
89	KLF PROMO 2	Kylie Said To Jason (Full Length)/Kylie Said Trance (12", promo & press sheet)	15
89	KLF Comms. KLF 010(S)	Kylie Said To Jason (Edit)/Kylie Said Trance (p/s)	8
89	KLF Comms. KLF 010T	Kylie Said To Jason (Full Length)/Kylie Said Trance (12", stickered p/s & pstr)	15
89	KLF Comms. KLF 010R	Kylie Said To Jason (Trance Kylie Express)/Kylie In A Trance/ Kylie Said Harder (12" remix, p/s, export issue)	15
89	KLF Comms. KLF 010RR	Kylie In A Trance/Kylie Said Mu (12", p/s, export edition, 500 only, shrinkwrapped with KLF 010R)	70
89	KLF Comms. KLF 010RR	Kylie In A Trance/Kylie Said Mu (12", p/s, export edition, 500 only)	40
89	KLF Comms. KLF 010CD	Kylie Said To Jason (Full Length)/Madrugada Eterna/Kylie Said Trance (CD)	40
89	KLF Comms. KLF 006T	Love Trance/What Time Is Love (12", p/s, 3 copies known)	500
90	KLF Comms. KLF 011T	Madrugada Eterna (Club Mix)/Madrugada Eterna (Edit)/Madrugada Eterna (Ambient House Mix) (12", 20 only, beware of counterfeits!)	150
90	KLF Comms. ETERNA 1	Madrugada Eterna (Club Mix) (12", 1-sided, white label, 6 pressed, beware of counterfeits!)	200
91	KLF Comms. CHOC ICE 1	Justified And Ancient (All Bound For Mu Mu Land)/Justified And Ancient (Make Mine A '99') (12", white label promo)	8
91	KLF Comms. CHOC ICE 2	Justified And Ancient (Stand By The J.A.M.s)/Justified And Ancient (Let Them Eat Ice Cream) (12", white label promo)	12
91	KLF Comms. CHOC ICE 3	Justified And Ancient (Anti-Acapella Version) (12", 1-sided, w/l, 200 only)	50
91	KLF Comms. LP PROMO 1	Make It Rain/No More Tears (12", promo only, 1,729 pressed)	20
91	KLF Comms. 92PROMO 1	America: What Time Is Love/America No More (12", white label)	8
91	KLF Comms. 92PROMO 2	America: What Time Is January? (12", 1-sided, white label promo, 50 - 250 only)	100
91	KLF Comms. 3AM 1	3AM Eternal (feat. Extreme Noise Terror) (p/s, mail order only)	20
92	KLF Comms. 92PROMO 3	What Time Is Love (Acid Mix) (12", 1-sided, w/l promo, perhaps 20 only)	300
92	KLF Comms. USA 4X/ CHOC ICE 2	Justified And Ancient/America: What Time Is Love? (12", 'longboat' picture disc, export edition, 4,000 only)	30
97	KLF Comms.	Fuck The Millennium (4-track CD, in white carrier bag Fuck The Millennium kit, with T-shirt, window sticker, certificate)	50
89	KLF Comms. JAMS LP 4	THE WHAT TIME IS LOVE STORY (LP)	20
89	KLF Comms. JAMS CD 4	THE WHAT TIME IS LOVE STORY (CD)	30
89	KLF Comms. JAMS LP 5	CHILL OUT (LP)	20
89	KLF Comms. JAMS CD 5	CHILL OUT (CD)	20
89	KLF Comms. JAMS LP 6	(TUNES FROM) THE WHITE ROOM (LP, 9-track white label, unreleased, promo only, beware of counterfeits!)	50

(see also J.A.M.s, Timelords, Disco 2000, Bill Drummond, Space, Orb)

TONY KLINGER & MICHAEL LYONS

72	Deram SML 1095	EXTREMES (LP, soundtrack)	50

PETER KLINT (QUINTET)

66	Mercury MF 997	Walkin' Proud/Shake	20
68	Atlantic 584 208	Hey Diddle Diddle/Just Holding On (solo)	15

KLO

83	International INTER 1	Fun/Weirdo	6

ANNETTE KLOOGER

56	Decca F 10701	The Rock And Roll Waltz/Rock Around The Island (with Ted Heath Music)	15
56	Decca F 10733	The Magic Touch/We'll Love Again (with Four Jones Boys)	15
56	Decca F 10738	Why Do Fools Fall In Love?/Lovely One (with Four Jones Boys)	15
56	Decca F 10776	Mama, Teach Me To Dance/Mama, I Long For A Sweetheart (with Edmundo Ros Orchestra)	10
57	Decca F 10844	The Wisdom Of A Fool/Tra La La	10

(see also Four Jones Boys, Ted Heath Orchestra)

KLUBS

68	Cam CAM 681	I Found The Sun/Ever Needed Someone	200

EARL KLUGH

85	Blue Note UAG 20009	LIVING INSIDE YOUR LOVE (LP, Nimbus Supercut, mail order only with Hi Fi Today magazine)	50

KNACK (U.K.)

65	Decca F 12234	She Ain't No Good/Who'll Be The Next In Line	60
65	Decca F 12278	It's Love Baby (24 Hours A Day)/Time Time Time	50
66	Piccadilly 7N 35315	Did You Ever Have To Make Up Your Mind?/Red Hearts	15
66	Piccadilly 7N 35322	Stop! (Before You Get Me Going)/Younger Girl	15
66	Piccadilly 7N 35347	Save All My Love For Joey/Take Your Love	15
67	Piccadilly 7N 35367	(Man From The) Marriage Guidance And Advice Bureau/ Dolly Catch Her Man	15

(see also Gun, Sky)

KNACK (U.S.)

79	Capitol E-ST 11948	GET THE KNACK (LP, limited white cover, unissued)	12

BERNIE KNEE QUARTETTE

55	HMV 7M 306	Chocolate Whiskey And Vanilla Gin/Scrape Off De Bark	7

(see also Bernie Nee)

KNEES

74	United Artists UP 35773	Day Tripper/Slow Down	10

(see also Brinsley Schwarz)

KNICKERBOCKERS

66	London HLH 10013	Lies/The Coming Generation	20
66	London HLH 10035	One Track Mind/I Must Be Doing Something Right	20
66	London HLH 10061	High On Love/Stick With Me	30
66	London HLH 10093	Rumours, Gossip, Words Untrue/Love Is A Bird	15
67	London HLH 10102	Can You Help Me/Please Don't Love Him	15
73	Elektra K 12102	Lies/ELECTRIC PRUNES: I Had Too Much To Dream (Last Night)	5
66	London HA-H 8294	THE FABULOUS KNICKERBOCKERS (LP)	60

KNIFE

06	Brille BRILLP105	DEEP CUTS (2xLP, inners)	70

KNIFE EDGE

80	No Hessle F001	Favourite Girl/Say You Will	75

BAKER KNIGHT

66	Reprise RS 20465	Would You Believe It/Tomorrow's Good Time Girl	12

CURTIS KNIGHT (& ZEUS)

69	RCA RCA 1888	Fancy Meeting You Here/Love In	12
70	RCA RCA 1950	Down In The Village/No Point Of View	15
74	Dawn DNS 1049	Devil Made Me Do It/Oh Rainbow	7
74	Dawn DNS 1065	People Places And Things/Mysterious Lady	7
74	Dawn DNLS 3060	THE SECOND COMING (LP, laminated sleeve, lyric insert, pink 'sun' label)	100
74	Dawn DNLS 3060	THE SECOND COMING (LP, laminated sleeve, no lyric insert, pink 'sun' label)	45

(see also Jimi Hendrix, Blue Goose)

GLADYS KNIGHT (& PIPS)

SINGLES

64	Stateside SS 318	Giving Up/Maybe Maybe Baby	30
64	Stateside SS 352	Lovers Always Forgive/Another Love	30
65	Sue WI 394	Letter Full Of Tears/You Broke Your Promise	40
66	Tamla Motown TMG 576	Just Walk In My Shoes/Stepping Closer To Your Heart	55
66	Tamla Motown TMG 576	Just Walk In My Shoes/Stepping Closer To Your Heart (DJ copy)	150
67	Tamla Motown TMG 604	Take Me In Your Arms And Love Me/Do You Love Me Just A Little Honey	15
67	Tamla Motown TMG 619	Everybody Needs Love/Stepping Closer To Your Heart (demo-only B-side)	90
67	Tamla Motown TMG 619	Everybody Needs Love/Since I've Lost You	20
67	Tamla Motown TMG 629	I Heard It Through The Grapevine/It's Time To Go Now	15
68	Tamla Motown TMG 645	The End Of Our Road/Don't Let Her Take Your Love From Me	20
68	Tamla Motown TMG 660	It Should Have Been Me/You Don't Love Me No More	18
68	Tamla Motown TMG 674	I Wish It Would Rain/It's Summer	18
69	Tamla Motown TMG 714	The Nitty Gritty/Got Myself A Good Man	10
70	Tamla Motown TMG 728	Didn't You Know (You'd Have To Cry Sometime)/Keep An Eye	12
70	Tamla Motown TMG 756	Friendship Train/You Need Love Like I Do (Don't You)	10
71	Tamla Motown TMG 765	If I Were Your Woman/The Tracks Of My Tears	8
72	Tamla Motown TMG 805	Make Me The Woman That You Go Home To/I Don't Want To Do Wrong	15
72	Tamla Motown TMG 813	Just Walk In My Shoes/I'm Losing You	10
73	Ember EMB S 326	Every Beat Of My Heart/Room In Your Heart	6
68	Tamla Motown TMG 844	The Look Of Love/You're My Everything	6
73	Tamla Motown TMG 864	Take Me In Your Arms And Love Me/No One Could Love You More	60
74	Contempo CS 2021	Why Don't You Leave Me/Maybe Baby	6
75	Tamla Motown TMG 945	You've Lost That Loving Feeling/This Child Needs A Father	15
89	MCA MCASP 1339	Licence To Kill/MICHAEL KAMEN: Pain (p/s with postcards & lyric sheet)	6
89	MCA MCAT 1339	Licence To Kill (Extended Version)/MICHAEL KAMEN: Pain (12", picture sleeve)	8

ALBUMS

67	Music F. Pleasure MFP 1187	GLADYS KNIGHT AND THE PIPS	15
67	T. Motown TML 11058	EVERYBODY NEEDS LOVE (mono)	35
67	T. Motown STML 11058	EVERYBODY NEEDS LOVE (stereo)	40
68	Bell MBLL 103	TASTIEST HITS	40
68	T. Motown TML 11080	FEELIN' BLUESY (mono)	30
68	T. Motown STML 11080	FEELIN' BLUESY (stereo)	35
69	T. Motown TML 11100	SILK 'N' SOUL (mono)	40
69	T. Motown STML 11100	SILK'N'SOUL (stereo)	35
69	T. Motown TML 11135	THE NITTY GRITTY (mono)	30
69	T. Motown (S)TML 11135	THE NITTY GRITTY (stereo)	22
70	Tamla Motown STML 11148	GREATEST HITS (original with flipback sleeve)	20
71	Tamla Motown STML 11187	IF I WERE YOUR WOMAN	20

(see also Pips, Dionne Warwick)

JASON KNIGHT

67	Pye 7N 17399	Love Is Getting Stronger/Standing In My Shoes	120
67	Pye 7N 17399	Love Is Getting Stronger/Standing In My Shoes (DJ copy)	200
73	Pye 7N 45287	Love Is Getting Stronger/Standing In My Shoes (reissue)	5

JEAN KNIGHT

71	Stax 2025 049	Mr Big Stuff/Why Do I Keep Living These Memories	8
72	Stax 2025 103	Carry On/Do You Think You're Hot Stuff	5
73	Stax 2025 161	Do Me/Save The Last Kiss For Me	5
72	Stax 2362 022	MR. BIG STUFF (LP)	20

MARIE KNIGHT

61	Fontana H 354	Nothing/Come Tomorrow	20
65	Stateside SS 419	Cry Me A River/Comes The Knight	20
85	Kent TOWN 102	That's No Way To Treat A Girl/JACK MONTGOMERY: Dearly Beloved	15

(see also Sister Rosetta Tharpe & Sister Marie Knight)

MINT VALUE £

PETER KNIGHT & KNIGHT RIDERS
| 61 | Pye 7N 15388 | Lucky Stars/Double Trouble | 7 |
| 64 | Pye 7N 15687 | Wonderful Day Like Today/It Isn't Enough | 8 |

PETER KNIGHT ORCHESTRA/SINGERS
| 55 | Parlophone MSP 6183 | Twenty Minutes South (Medley) (both sides, as Peter Knight Singers) | 6 |
| 67 | Mercury SML 30023 | SGT. PEPPER'S LONELY HEARTS CLUB BAND (LP) | 15 |

ROBERT KNIGHT
62	London HLD 9496	Free Me/The Other Half Of Man	30
68	Monument MON 1008	Everlasting Love/Somebody's Baby	15
68	Monument MON 1016	Blessed Are The Lonely/It's Been Worth It All	8
68	Monument MON 1017	The Power Of Love/Love On A Mountain Top	30
68	Bell BLL 1029	Isn't It Lonely Together/We'd Better Stop	8
68	Monument LMO/SMO 5015	EVERLASTING LOVE (LP)	20

SONNY KNIGHT
57	London HLD 8362	Confidential/Jail Bird (gold label print)	350
57	London HLD 8362	Confidential/Jail Bird (silver label print)	100
57	London HLD 8362	Confidential/Jail Bird (78 rpm)	60
57	London HL 7016	Confidential/Jail Bird (export issue)	100
59	Vogue Pop V 9134	But Officer/Dear Wonderful God	250
59	Vogue Pop V 9134	But Officer/Dear Wonderful God (78)	100

TERRY KNIGHT & PACK
| 66 | Cameo Parkway C 102 | I (Who Have Nothing)/Numbers | 75 |

(see also Grand Funk Railroad)

TONY KNIGHT
| 64 | Decca F 11989 | Did You Ever Hear The Sound?/I Feel So Blue (as Tony Knight & Live Wires) | 40 |
| 65 | Decca F 12109 | How Sweet/Surfer Street (as Tony Knight's Chessmen) | 35 |

KNIGHT BROTHERS
| 65 | Chess CRS 8015 | Sinking Low/Temptation 'Bout To Get Me | 30 |
| 66 | Chess CRS 8046 | That'll Get It/She's A1 | 30 |

KNIGHTRIDER
| 87 | Omega KS 1299 | Shout Out Loud | 25 |

KNIGHTS OF THE ROUND TABLE
| 68 | Pama PM 734 | Lament To Bobby Kennedy/If You Were My Girl | 7 |

KNIGHTSBRIDGE STRINGS
| 61 | Top Rank JAR 532 | The Singer Not The Song/Anacleto's Theme | 12 |
| 59 | Top Rank JKR 8040 | ROCKING STRINGS (EP) | 8 |

K9'S
| 79 | Dog Breath WOOF 1 | The K9 Hassle/Idi Amin/Sweeney Todd (1st issue in numbered blue p/s, with insert, 1000 only; reissue in white p/s with insert, 500 only) | 40 |

KNOCKER JUNGLE
| 70 | Ember EMB S 293 | I Don't Know Why/Reality (p/s) | 6 |
| 71 | Ember NR 5052 | KNOCKER JUNGLE (LP, gatefold sleeve) | 50 |

KNOCKOUTS
| 60 | Top Rank JAR 279 | Riot In Room 3C/Darling Lorraine | 25 |

MARK KNOPFLER
84	Vertigo DSDJ 7	Joy (from 'Comfort And Joy') (unissued, 1-sided promo only)	12
84	Vertigo DSTR 712	Joy (from 'Comfort And Joy')/Fistful Of Ice Cream (12", p/s)	12
84	Vertigo MARK ONE	Comfort And Joy (12", 1-sided promo)	25
02	Mercury 063292	THE RAGPICKERS DREAM (2-LP, numbered)	60

(see also Dire Straits, Randy Newman, Chet Atkins)

KNOPOV'S POLITICAL PACKAGE
| 80 | White label | Misadventure/You're In The Army Now | 6 |

(see also Mission)

KNOTT SISTERS
| 58 | London HLX 8713 | Undivided Attention/SHADES with KNOTT SISTERS: Sun Glasses | 40 |
| 58 | London HLX 8713 | Undivided Attention/SHADES with KNOTT SISTERS: Sun Glasses (78) | 10 |

KNOWLEDGE
| 78 | A&M AMLH 68500 | HAIL DREAD (LP) | 30 |

SONNY KNOWLES
| 72 | Rex RH079 | Do I Love You/I'm Just A Country Boy | 7 |

BOBBY KNOX
| 70 | Penny Farthing PEN 714 | Kissin Walkin/Down A Back Street | 12 |

BUDDY KNOX
57	Columbia DB 3914	Party Doll/My Baby's Gone (gold label print)	100
57	Columbia DB 3914	Party Doll/My Baby's Gone (gold label print) (78)	20
57	Columbia DB 3952	Rock Your Little Baby To Sleep/Don't Make Me Cry (as Lieutenant Buddy Knox, gold label print)	100
57	Columbia DB 3952	Rock Your Little Baby To Sleep/Don't Make Me Cry (as Lieutenant Buddy Knox, gold label print) (78)	25
57	Columbia DB 4014	Hula Love/Devil Woman	40
57	Columbia DB 4014	Hula Love/Devil Woman (78)	25
58	Columbia DB 4077	Swingin' Daddy/Whenever I'm Lonely	40
58	Columbia DB 4077	Swingin' Daddy/Whenever I'm Lonely (78)	25
58	Columbia DB 4180	Somebody Touched Me/C'mon Baby	30
58	Columbia DB 4180	Somebody Touched Me/C'mon Baby (78)	25
59	Columbia DB 4302	To Be With You/I Think I'm Gonna Kill Myself	20
61	London HLG 9268	Lovey Dovey/I Got You	15
61	London HLG 9331	Ling Ting Tong The Kisses (They're All Mine)	15
61	London HLG 9472	Three-Eyed Man/All By Myself	12
62	Liberty LIB 55411	Chi-Hua-Hua/Open Your Loving Arms	15
62	Liberty LIB 55473	She's Gone/Now There's Only Me	20

63	Liberty LIB 55592	Shadaroom/Tomorrow Is Coming	10
64	Liberty LIB 55694	All Time Loser/Good Loving	10
69	United Artists UP 35019	God Knows I Love You/Night Runners	7
70	United Artists UP 35100	Party Doll/God Knows I Love You	5
57	Columbia SEG 7732	ROCK-A-BUDDY KNOX (EP)	100
62	Liberty LBY 1114	GOLDEN HITS (LP)	25
71	Sunset SLS 50206	ROCK REFLECTIONS (LP)	15

KNUCKLEHEAD
93	Saucerman ART 01	Red Eye, Dead Eye/Spirit Matter (p/s, hand-painted label, 150 copies only)	15

FRANKIE KNUCKLES
89	FFRR FX 102	Tears (Classic Vocal)/(Accapella)/(Classic Instrumental) (with Satoshi Tomiie, 12", die-cut p/s (12")	10
89	Radical Records TRAXT 3	Your Love/ Baby Wants To Ride (12", p/s)	25
90	World Dance DJLTD1	Move Your Body (Original)/('90 Remix)/(Jackmaster Remix)/Original Acapella Dub)/Your Love/Baby Wants To Ride 12")	8

KOBALT 60
91	Music Of Life NOTE57	Chaos From Order/Concrete Show (12")	20

KOCK
83	Hard ON 11	One-Eyed Giant/Hickory Dickory Kock (p/s)	6

KODIAKS
69	Decca F 12942	All Because You Wanna See Me Cry/Tell Me Rhonda	20

(SPIDER) JOHN KOERNER
63	Palette PG 9035	Cool Ghoul/Sapphire	7
67	Elektra EKSN 45005	Won't You Give Me Some Love/Don't Stop	25
69	Elektra EKSN 45063	Friends And Lovers/Magazine Lady (with Willie Murphy)	10
66	Elektra EKL 267	(LOTS MORE) BLUES RAGS AND HOLLERS (LP, with Dave Ray and Tony Glover, US sleeve but UK pressed record with golden Elektra "guitar player" logo)	45
65	Elektra EKL 290	SPIDER BLUES (LP)	50
68	Elek. EKL 4041/EKS 74041	RUNNING JUMPING STANDING STILL (LP, with Willie Murphy)	30
71	Elektra K 42026	RUNNING JUMPING STANDING STILL (LP, reissue)	12

MOE KOFFMAN
58	London HLT 8549	Swingin' Shepherd Blues/Hambourg Sound	10
74	CBS S 73245	FOUR SEASONS IN ROCK (LP)	15

KOKOMO
60	London HLU 9305	Asia Minor/Roy's Tune	7

KO KO TAYLOR
66	Chess CRS 8035	Wang Dang Doodle/Blues Heaven	25
66	Chess CRS 8035	Wang Dang Doodle/Blues Heaven (DJ copy)	50
72	Chess 6145 018	Violent Love/The Egg Or The Hen/Wang Dang Doodle	8

KOLETTES
64	Pye International 7N 25278	Who's That Guy?/Just How Much	50
73	Chess 6145 021	Who's That Guy?/Just How Much (reissue)	10

BONNIE KOLOC
72	London HLO 10377	Jazz Man/Got To Get What You Can	6
72	London HLO 10392	Burgundy Wine/We Are Ships	6
72	London SHO 8432	AFTER ALL THIS TIME (LP)	25
72	London SHO 8440	HOLD ON TO ME (LP)	20

JIMMIE KOMACK
54	Vogue Coral Q 2031	Cold Summer Blues/The Nic-Name Song	10
55	Vogue Coral Q 72061	Wabash 4-7473/An Old Beer Bottle	10
55	Vogue Coral Q 72087	Rock-A-Bye Your Baby With A Dixie Melody/This Is The Place	10

CHRISTOPHER KOMEDA
66	Polydor 580001	CUL DE SAC (soundtrack EP)	150
68	Dot (S)LPD 519	ROSEMARY'S BABY (LP, as Kryzstophe Komeda)	35

JOHN (T.) KONGOS
66	Piccadilly 7N 35341	I Love Mary/Goodtime Party Companion (as John T. Kongos)	10
69	Dawn DNS 1002	Flim Flam Pharisee/Blood	6
71	Fly BUG 8DJ	He's Gonna Step On You Again/Sometimes It's Not Enough (DJ copy in p/s)	10
71	Fly BUG 8	He's Gonna Step On You Again/Sometimes It's Not Enough	5
69	Dawn DNLS 3002	CONFUSIONS ABOUT A GOLDFISH (LP, with sticker)	40
69	Dawn DNLS 3002	CONFUSIONS ABOUT A GOLDFISH (LP, without sticker)	30
71	Fly HIFLY 7	KONGOS (LP, gatefold sleeve, insert, Fly label)	30

(see also Scrugg, Floribunda Rose)

V. KONGS
63	Halagala HG 18	Tomorrow Will Soon Be Here/Pretty Little Girl	20

KONRADS
65	CBS 201812	Baby It's Too Late Now/I'm Over You	50

KONSTRUKTIVITS
83	Flowmotion FM 001	VOLUME 1 (cassette)	60
83	Flowmotion FM 002	A DISSEMBLY (LP)	35
83	Third Mind TM 02	PSYKO GENETIKA (LP)	35
84	Third Mind TMLP 05	BLACK DECEMBER (LP)	30
85	Sterile SR 10	GLENNASCAUL (LP)	15

(see also Whitehouse)

KOOBAS
65	Pye 7N 17012	Take Me For A Little While/Somewhere In The Night	50
66	Pye 7N 17087	You'd Better Make Up Your Mind/A Place I Know	60
66	Columbia DB 7988	Sweet Music/Face	60
67	Columbia DB 8103	Sally/Champagne And Caviar	35
67	Columbia DB 8187	Gypsy Fred/City Girl	30
68	Columbia DB 8419	The First Cut Is The Deepest/Walking Out	55
69	Columbia S(C)X 6271	THE KOOBAS (LP, black/silver label, boxed logo, "Sold in U.K..." text)	1500

MINT VALUE £

88	Bam Caruso KIRI 047	BARRICADES (LP)	18

(see also Kubas, Van Der Graaf Generator, Gary & Stu, Juicy Lucy, March Hare)

KOOGA

88	Kooga KO 001	Don't Break My Heart/Lay Down Your Love (p/s, private pressing)	8

(see also Skin)

KOOKS

05	Private Pressing	Slave To The Game (1-sided, stamped label, tour single, 500 only)	10

KOOL

67	CBS 203003	Look At Me, Look At Me/Room At The Top	20
69	CBS 2865	Step Out Of Your Mind/Funny (What A Fool A Man Can Be)	80
69	MCA MU 1085	Lovin'/Baby's Out Of Reach	12

KOOL KEITH/PHAROE MONCH/AKINYELLE

95	Liberty Grooves	Freestyle Frenzy/Gotta Go Down (7")	45

KOOL & THE GANG

70	London HLZ 10308	Kool And The Gang/Raw Hamburgers	15
71	Mojo 2027 005	Funky Man/Kool And The Gang/Let The Music Take Your Mind	10
71	Mojo 2027 006	Love The Life You Live/The Penguin	10
72	Mojo 2027 009	Music Is The Message (Parts 1 & 2)	10
73	Polydor 2001 474	Funky Stuff/More Funky Stuff	6
74	Polydor 2001 500	Jungle Boogie/North, South, East, West	6
71	Mojo 2347 001	LIVE AT P.J.'S (LP)	30
71	Mojo 2347 002	THE BEST OF KOOL AND THE GANG (LP)	20
72	Mojo 2347 003	LIVE AT THE SEX MACHINE (LP)	15
73	Mojo 2347 004	MUSIC IS THE MESSAGE (LP)	15
74	Polydor 2310299	WILD AND PEACEFUL (LP)	15

AL KOOPER

65	Mercury MF 885	Parchman Farm/You're The Lovin' End (as Alan Kooper)	20
69	CBS 4011	You Never Know Who Your Friends Are/Soft Landing On The Moon	6
69	CBS 4160	Hey Western Union Man/I Stand Alone	8
71	CBS 5146	Brand New Lady/The Landlord (Love Theme)	5
71	CBS 7376	John The Baptist (Holy John)/Back On My Feet	5
72	CBS 8084	Monkey Time/Bended Knees (Please Don't Let Me Down)	10
69	CBS 63538	I STAND ALONE (LP, orange label)	22
69	CBS 63651	YOU NEVER KNOW WHO YOUR FRIENDS ARE (LP, orange label)	20
70	CBS 63797	KOOPER SESSION - WITH SHUGGIE OTIS (LP, orange label)	20
70	CBS 66252	EASY DOES IT (2-LP, orange label)	18
71	United Artists UAS 29120	THE LANDLORD (LP, soundtrack, with Staple Singers & Lorraine Ellison)	20
71	CBS 64340	NEW YORK CITY (YOU'RE A WOMAN) (LP, gatefold sleeve, orange label)	15
72	CBS 64208	A POSSIBLE PROJECTION OF THE FUTURE/CHILDHOOD'S END (LP, orange label)	15
73	CBS 65193	NAKED SONGS (LP)	15

(see also Blues Project, Blood Sweat & Tears, Shuggie Otis)

AL KOOPER, MIKE BLOOMFIELD & STEPHEN STILLS

68	CBS 3770	Season Of The Witch/Albert's Shuffle	12
68	CBS 63396	SUPER SESSION (LP)	20
73	CBS CQ 30991	SUPER SESSION (LP, quadrophonic)	25

(see also Mike Bloomfield & Al Kooper, Stephen Stills)

KOPPYKATS

68	Fontana SFT 13052/3	BEATLES' BEST (2-LP)	40

(see also Ian [Edward] & Zodiacs)

TAMARA KORAN WITH PERCEPTION

68	Domain D 7	Veils Of Mourning Lace/Don't Throw Our Love Away	350

TOMMY KÖRBERG

69	Sonet SON 2005	Dear Mrs. Jones/Bird You Must Fly	8

PAUL KORDA

66	Columbia DB 7994	Go On Home/Just Come Closer To Me	30
69	Parlophone R 5778	Seagull (West Coast Oil Tragedy Of '68)/Night Of The Next Day	5
71	MAM MAM 20	Between The Road/English Country Garden	5
71	MAM AS 1003	PASSING STRANGER (LP, gatefold sleeve)	75

(see also Tim Andrews & Paul Korda, Dada, Fresh)

KORN

96	Epic 6638450	No Place To Hide/Proud (white vinyl, 7,500 only)	8

ALEXIS KORNER (BLUES INCORPORATED)

58	Tempo A 166	I Ain't Gonna Worry No More/County Jail (as Alexis Korner Skiffle Group)	100
58	Tempo A 166	I Ain't Gonna Worry No More/County Jail (78)	50
63	Lyntone LYN 299	Blaydon Races/Up-Town (as Blues Incorporated With Alexis Korner, free with women's magazine Trio)	100
63	Parlophone R 5206	I Need Your Loving/Please Please Please (as Alexis Korner's Blues Inc.)	30
65	Parlophone R 5247	Little Baby/Roberta (as Alexis Korner's Blues Inc.)	25
65	King KG 1017	See Rider/Blues A La King(as Alexis Korner's All Stars)	45
66	Fontana TF 706	River's Invitation/Everyday (I Have The Blues)	25
67	Fontana TF 817	Rosie/Rock Me	25
75	CBS 3520	Get Off My Cloud/Strange'n'Deranged	10
76	CBS 3877	Ain't That Peculiar/Tree Top Fever	8
58	Tempo EXA 76	BLUES FROM THE ROUNDHOUSE VOL. 1 (EP, as Alexis Korner Skiffle Group)	175
59	Tempo EXA 102	BLUES FROM THE ROUNDHOUSE VOL. 2 (EP, as Alexis Korner's Blues Inc.)	300
62	Topic TOP 70	3/4 A.D. (EP, with Davy Graham, first pressing in mauve sleeve with cream label)	90
62	Topic TOP 70	3/4 A.D. (EP, with Davy Graham, later pressing with lilac sleeve and blue label)	60
62	Topic TOP 70	3/4 A.D. (EP, with Davy Graham, later pressings with bronze sleeve and blue label)	30
57	'77' LP/2	BLUES FROM THE ROUNDHOUSE (10" LP, 99 only, as Alexis Korner Blues Breakdown Group)	1000
62	Ace of Clubs ACL 1130	R&B FROM THE MARQUEE (LP, claret labels, with Long John Baldry)	120
64	Transatlantic TRA 117	RED HOT FROM ALEX (LP, with Herbie Goins)	150
64	Oriole PS 40058	AT THE CAVERN (LP, live, with Herbie Goins, laminated sleeve with flipbacks)	375
65	Ace of Clubs ACL 1187	ALEXIS KORNER'S BLUES INCORPORATED (LP)	100
65	Spot JW 551	SKY HIGH (LP, featuring Duffy Power)	400

67	Fontana TL 5381	I WONDER WHO (LP, mono) 150
67	Fontana (S)TL 5381	I WONDER WHO (LP, stereo) 200
67	Polydor Special 236 206	BLUES INCORPORATED (LP, 1st issue, listing 4 tracks on Side A on sleeve/label) 80
67	Polydor Special 236 206	BLUES INCORPORATED (LP, 2nd issue, listing 5 tracks on Side A on sleeve/label) 50
68	Liberty LBL/LBS 83147	A NEW GENERATION OF BLUES (LP)...90
69	Transatlantic TRASAM 7	ALEXIS KORNER'S ALL STAR BLUES INCORPORATED (LP, reissue of "Red Hot From Alex", different cover) 30
71	Rak SRAK 501	ALEXIS KORNER (LP, textured sleeve)...45
72	Rak SRAKSP 51	BOOTLEG HIM! (2-LP, with booklet)..55
73	Transatlantic TRA 269	ACCIDENTALLY BORN IN NEW ORLEANS (LP, as Snape) 35
75	CBS 69155	GET OFF MY CLOUD (LP)..25

(see also Cyril Davies, C.C.S., Bob Hall & Alexis Korner, Herbie Goins, Duffy Power, Long John Baldry, Rocket 88, Davy Graham, Beryl Bryden, Jimmy Cotton, Ken Colyer, Jack Bruce, Snape & Little Brother Montgomery)

ARTIE KORNFELD'S TREE

72	Neighbourhood NBH 3	Island Song/Feel 5
70	Probe SPB 1022	A TIME TO REMEMBER (LP)..20

KORPERAYSHUN

89	BPM BP12007	K Factor/Non Stop (12")..40

KOSMIC KOMMANDO

94	Rephlex CAT 007EP	Cat 007 (I)/Cat 007 (II)/Cat 007 (III)/Cat 007 (IV) (12", clear vinyl) 20

(see also Aphex Twin)

PAUL KOSSOFF

73	Island ILPS 9264	BACK STREET CRAWLER (LP, pink rim palm tree label) 15
83	St. Tunes SDLP 0012PD	MR. BIG/BLUE SOUL (LP, picture disc)...12

(see also Free, Kossoff Kirke Tetsu & Rabbit, Creepy John Thomas)

KOSSOFF, KIRKE, TETSU & RABBIT

71	Island ILPS 9188	KOSSOFF, KIRKE, TETSU AND RABBIT (LP, gatefold sleeve, pink rim palm tree label) 50

(see also Paul Kossoff, Rabbit, Free)

CHIM KOTHARI

66	Deram DM 108	Sitar'N'Spice/Indian Bat 12
66	Deram DML 1002	SOUND OF THE SITAR (LP)..60

LEO KOTTKE

72	Sonet SNTF 629	LEO KOTTKE & HIS 6 & 12-STRING GUITAR (LP) 12
71	Capitol EST 682	MUDLARK (LP) 12

(see also John Fahey)

KOUMBA

82	Greensleeves GRED 105	We Are Leggo/Billy (12") 10

JENNIFER KRAAL

69	NEMS 56-4200	The Men In My Life/Sinful Davey 8

KRACKER

73	Rolling Stones RS 19106	A Song For Polly/Medicated Goo 12
74	Rolling Stones COC 49102	KRACKER BRAND (LP, gatefold sleeve) 20

KRAFTWERK

SINGLES

75	Vertigo 6147 012	Autobahn/Kometenmelodie 1 12
75	Vertigo 6147 015	Comet Melody 2/Kristallo 20
76	Capitol CL 15853	Radio Activity/Antenna (in p/s)..15
76	Capitol CL 15853	Radio Activity/Antenna..8
77	Capitol CL 104	Showroom Dummies/Europe Endless 8
77	Capitol CLX 104	Showroom Dummies (12", 'train station' p/s)..18
77	Capitol CL 15917	Trans-Europe Express/Franz Schubert 10
78	Capitol CL 15981	The Robots/Spacelab (foldout p/s)..15
78	Capitol CL 15981	The Robots (alternative mix)/Spacelab (foldout p/s) 30
78	Capitol CL 15998	Neon Lights/Trans-Europe Express/The Model 8
78	Capitol 12CL 15998	Neon Lights/Trans-Europe Express/The Model (12", luminous vinyl, dayglo sleeve) 35
78	Capitol 12CL 16098	Showroom Dummies/Spacelab/Europe Endless (12", reissue, 'red shirts' p/s) 15
81	EMI EMI 5175	Pocket Calculator/Dentaku (p/s) 8
81	EMI TCEMI 5175	Pocket Calculator/Numbers/Dentaku ('cigarette'-pack style box) 35
81	EMI 12EMI 5175	Pocket Calculator/Numbers/Dentaku (12", p/s) 12
81	Vertigo VER 3	Kometenmelodie 2/Vom Himmel Hoch (p/s)..15
81	EMI EMI 5207	Computer Love/The Model (p/s, original issue)..5
81	EMI 12EMI 5207	Computer Love/The Model (12", p/s, original issue) 12
82	EMI EMI 5272	Showroom Dummies/Numbers (p/s, some with mispressed B-side "The Model")....................8
82	EMI EMI 5272	Showroom Dummies/Numbers (p/s) 5
82	EMI 12EMI 5272	Showroom Dummies/Numbers/Pocket Calculator (12", p/s)..8
83	EMI EMI 5413	Tour De France/Tour De France (Instrumental) (p/s, red or yellow labels) 8
83	EMI TCEMI 5413	Tour De France/Tour De France (Short Version)/ Tour De France (2" Etape) () 15
83	EMI 12EMI 5413	Tour De France (Long Version)/(7" Version)/(2" Etape) (12", p/s, red or yellow labels)...18
84	EMI EMI 5413	Tour De France (Kevorkian Remix)/Tour De France (Original 7" Version) (reissue, 'Breakdance' p/s)...7
84	EMI 12EMI 5413	Tour De France (Kevorkian Remix)/Tour De France (Different Extended Version)/Tour De France (Original 7" Version) (12", reissue, 'Breakdance' p/s) 18
86	EMI EMI 5588	Musique Non-Stop/Musique Non-Stop (Different Version) (p/s) 5
86	EMI 12EMI 5588	Musique Non-Stop (6.15)/Musique Non-Stop (7" Version) (12", p/s).....................................15
87	EMI EMI 5602	The Telephone Call/Der Telefon Anruf (p/s) 6
87	EMI 12EMI 5602	The Telephone Call (Remix)/House Phone/Der Telefon Anruf (12", p/s).................................20
91	EMI EM 192	The Robots (re-recorded version)/Robotronik (p/s, red/black or white/black song title box) 5
91	EMI 12EM 192	Robotronik/The Robots (Single Mix)/The Robots (Album Version) (12", p/s, red/black or white/black song title box) 8
91	EMI CDEM 192	Robotronik/Robotnik/The Robots (Single Edit) (CD, white/black song title box)..................18
91	EMI EM 201	Radioactivity (Francois Kevorkian Remix)/(William Orbit Mix) (p/s)..6
91	EMI 12EM 201	Radioactivity (Francois Kevorkian 12" Remix)/ (Francois Kevorkian 7" Remix)/(William Orbit 12" Remix) (12", p/s)..8

MINT VALUE £

91	EMI CDEM 201	Radioactivity (Francois Kevorkian 7" Remix)/(Francois Kevorkian 12" Remix)/(William Orbit 12" Remix) (CD)	20
97	EMI KLANG BOX 101	KRAFTWERK (4 x 12" box set, including "Trans Europe Express", "Numbers", "Musique Non Stop & "Homecomputer"; without T-shirt, promo only)	80
97	EMI KLANG BOX 101	KRAFTWERK (4 x 12" box set, including "Trans Europe Express", Numbers, "Musique Non Stop" & "Homecomputer"; with separate white or black T-shirt, promo only)	150

ALBUMS

72	Vertigo 6641 077	KRAFTWERK (2-LP, gatefold sleeve, small 'swirl')	350
72	Vertigo 6641 077	KRAFTWERK (2-LP gatefold sleeve, 'spacecraft' labels)	100
74	Vertigo 6360 616	RALF AND FLORIAN (gatefold sleeve, 'spacecraft' label)	120
74	Vertigo 6360 616	RALF AND FLORIAN ('spacecraft' label, no gatefold sleeve)	50
74	Vertigo 6360 620	AUTOBAHN (embossed blue sleeve)	25
75	Vertigo 6360 629	EXCELLER 8 (some with stickered sleeve)	30
76	Capitol EST 11457	RADIOACTIVITY (with insert)	25
77	Capitol E-ST 11603	TRANS-EUROPE EXPRESS (LP)	20
78	Capitol E-ST 11728	MAN MACHINE (LP)	20
81	EMI EMC 3370	COMPUTER WORLD (LP)	15
81	Vertigo 6449 006	ELEKTROKINETIK (LP)	25
83	EMI EMC 3407	TECHNOPOP (unissued, sleeves only)	0
91	EMI EM 1408	THE MIX (2-LP, with inner sleeves)	20
03	EMI EMI 591 708 1	TOUR DE FRANCE SOUNDTRACKS (2-LP, single stickered sleeve with inners)	15
04	EMI KLANG BOX 001	THE CATALOGUE (8-CD, in card box, 1,000 only)	100
05	EMI 560 6111	MINIMUM - MAXIMUM (4-LP box set)	30

(see also Organisation, Elektric Music)

KRAFTY KUTS

99	Lacerba CERBAL 14	SLAM THE BREAKS IN (3-LP)	20
99	Southern Fried ECB17	Gimme The Funk (12")	10

KRAKEN

80	Knave EJSP 9370	FANTASY REALITY (EP, no p/s)	50

BILLY J. KRAMER

66	Parlophone R 5482	You Make Me Feel Like Someone/Take My Hand	8
67	Parlophone R 5552	Sorry/Going Going Gone	10
67	Reaction 591 014	Town Of Tuxley Toymakers/Chinese Girl	50
68	CBS 56-3396	1941/His Love Is Just A Lie	10
68	NEMS 56-3635	A World Without Love/Going Through It	8
69	MGM MGM 1474	The Colour Of My Love/I'm Running Away	10
73	Decca F 13426	A Fool Like You/I'll Keep You Satisfied	7
73	Decca F 13442	Darlin' Come To Me/Waiting	7
74	BASF BA 1006	Stayin' Power/Blue Jean Queen	7
77	EMI EMI 2661	San Diego/Warm Summer Rain	6
78	EMI EMI 2740	Ships That Pass In The Night/Is There Anymore At Home Like You	6
79	Hobo HOS 010	Blue Christmas/Little Love (p/s, blue vinyl)	10
80	JM JM 1005	Silver Dream/Lonely Lady	5
82	Runaway BJK 1	Rock It/Dum Dum	6
83	Rak RAK 359	You Can't Live On Memories/Stood Up (p/s)	5

BILLY J. KRAMER & THE DAKOTAS

63	Parlophone R 5023	Do You Want To Know A Secret/I'll Be On My Way	5
63	Parlophone R 5049	Bad To Me/I Call Your Name	5
63	Parlophone R 5073	I'll Keep You Satisfied/I Know	5
64	Parlophone R 5156	From A Window/Second To None	5
65	Parlophone R 5234	It's Gotta Last Forever/That's The Way I Feel	5
65	Parlophone R 5285	Trains And Boats And Planes/That's The Way I Feel	8
65	Parlophone R 5362	Neon City/I'll Be Doggone	10
66	Parlophone R 5408	We're Doing Fine/Forgive Me	10
63	Parlophone GEP 8885	THE BILLY J. KRAMER HITS (EP)	20
63	Parlophone GEP 8895	I'LL KEEP YOU SATISFIED (EP)	20
64	Parlophone GEP 8907	LITTLE CHILDREN (EP)	20
64	Parlophone GEP 8921	FROM A WINDOW (EP)	25
65	Parlophone GEP 8928	BILLY J. PLAYS THE STATES (EP)	50
63	Parlophone PMC 1209	LISTEN (LP, mono)	20
65	Regal REG 1057	BILLY J (LP, export only)	30

(see also Dakotas)

WAYNE KRAMER

78	Stiffwick DEA/SUK 1	Ramblin' Rose/Get Some (numbered p/s)	8
79	Radar ADA 41	The Harder They Come/East Side Girl (p/s)	6

(see also MC5)

KRAVIN AS

91	Hangman HANG 39 UP	KRAVE ON! (LP)	15

KRAY CHERUBS

88	Fierce FRIGHT 014	No (p/s, 1-sided)	20
89	Snakeskin SS 002	Rot In Hell Mom/SAUCERMAN: Motor Drag (numbered black p/s, 300 only)	12
89	Snakeskin SS 002	Rot In Hell Mom/SAUCERMAN: Motor Drag (later reissue in purple p/s)	8
89	Forced Exposure FE 18	Teen Camel/I Hate My Job (p/s)	15

(see also Art Attacks, Savage Pencil)

BILL KRENZ & HIS RAGTIMERS

56	London HLU 8258	There'll Be No New Tunes On This Old Piano/Goofus	35
56	London HLU 8258	There'll Be No New Tunes On This Old Piano/Goofus (78)	12

KREW KATS

61	HMV POP 840	Trambone/Peak Hour	20
61	HMV POP 894	Samovar/Jack's Good	30

(see also Shadows, Brian Bennett)

KREWMEN

91	Lost Moment LMLP 023	FINAL ADVENTURES OF THE KREWMEN (LP)	12

KRIMSON KAKE
69	Penny Farthing PEN 707	Feelin' Better/Waiter	30

(see also Samantha Jones, Vernons Girls)

KRISPY 3
91	Gumh 005	Hard Times (12")	10

DAVE KRISS
80s	private pressing	EMIGRATING (2-LP)	15

KRISSI K
74	People PEO110	Stick Up/Who Do You Think You Are?	10

SONJA KRISTINA
68	Polydor 56299	Let The Sunshine In/Frank Mills	15
80	Chopper CHOP 101	St Tropez/Mr Skin (p/s)	10
80	Chopper CHOPE 5	SONJA KRISTINA (LP)	35

(see also Curved Air)

KROKODIL
69	Liberty LBS 83306	KROKODIL (LP)	50
70	Liberty LBS 83417	SWAMP (LP)	50

KROME & TIME
92	Suburban Base SUBBASE 011	This Sound Is For The Underground/Manic Stampede (12", p/s)	25
92	Suburban Base SUBBASE 11R	This Sound Is For The Underground (E.5 Remix)/Manic Stampede (DJ Hype's Sandringham Road Mix) (12")	20
93	Suburban Base SUBBASE 26	The Slammer/Into The Night (12", p/s as DJ Krome & Mr Time)	20

KRONSTADT UPRISING
85	Dog Rock SD 108	Part Of The Game/The Horsemen (fold out p/s)	5
80s	Spider SDL 12	The Unknown Revolution (p/s)	10

HARDY KRUGER
59	Top Rank TR 5005	Blind Date (I'm A Lonely Man)/PINEWOOD ORCHESTRA: Blind Date (p/s)	8

GENE KRUPA (& HIS ORCHESTRA)
60	HMV POP 750	Cherokee/Indiana Montage	6
57	Columbia 335 1051	DRUMMIN' MAN (10" LP)	20
59	HMV 7EG 8595	DRUM BOOGIE (EP)	10
58	Columbia/Clef CX 10133	KRUPA ROCKS (LP)	15
61	Verve VLP/SVLP 9005	PERCUSSION KING (LP)	15

GENE KRUPA & BUDDY RICH
64	Verve VS 503	Perdido/Night Train	5
62	Verve SVLP 9014	BURNIN' BEAT (LP)	12

KRYPTON TUNES
78	Black & Red FIRE 1	Behind Your Smile/Coming To See You (p/s)	12
78	Lightning GIL 546	Limited Vision/All In Jail	12

KRYSIA (KOCJAN)
74	RCA LPL1 5052	KRYSIA (LP)	18

(see also Natural Acoustic Band, Fairport Convention)

KRYSTAL GENERATION
72	Mercury 6052 120	Wanted Dead Or Alive/Every Man Seems To Be For Himself	10

BOB KUBAN & INMEN
66	Stateside SS 488	The Cheater/Try Me Baby	60
66	Stateside SS 488	The Cheater/Try Me Baby (DJ copy)	110
66	Stateside SS 514	The Teaser/All I Want	20
68	Bell BLL 1027	The Cheater/Try Me Baby (reissue)	10

KUBAS
65	Columbia DB 7451	I Love Her/Magic Potion	60

(see also Koobas)

DAVE KUBINEC
69	Parlophone R5762	Schopi/The Lady Loves	20

KUF-LINX
58	London HLU 8583	So Tough/What'cha Gonna Do	100
58	London HLU 8583	So Tough/What'cha Gonna Do (78)	50

LENNY KUHR
69	Philips BF 1777	The Troubadour/Oh No Monsieur	10

KUKL
84	Crass 1984/1	THE EYE (LP, foldout sleeve)	20
85	Crass No. 4	HOLIDAYS IN EUROPE (LP, with inner sleeve)	20

(see also Sugarcubes)

KULA SHAKER
96	Columbia SHAKER 1LP	K (LP, inner)	35
99	Columbia SHAKER 2LP	PEASANTS, PIGS & ASTRONAUTS (LP, gatefold)	30

KULT
69	CBS 4276	No Home Today/Mister Number One	300

PRAMOD KUMAR
72	Philips 6460 854	THIS IS THE MUSIC OF INDIA (LP)	12

CHARLIE KUNZ
54	Decca F 10419	Charlie Kunz Piano Medley, No. 114	10

KURASS
70	Escort ES 825	Stampede/KING STITT: You Were Meant For Me (B-side actually by Lee Perry)	40

KUSTOM
82	Red Bus RBUS 71	Let The Girl Dance/Arrested	20

MINT VALUE £

FELA RANSOME KUTI (& AFRICA '70)

72	Regal Zonophone RZ 3052	Chop And Quench/Egbe Mi O (with Africa '70 & Ginger Baker)	10
72	Regal Zono. SLRZ 1023	FELI RANSOME-KUTI & THE AFRICA '70 WITH GINGER BAKER LIVE! (LP)	50
75	Decca/Aphrodisia DWAPS 2005	UPSIDE DOWN (LP)	25
75	Creole CRLP 501	SHAKARA (LP, with Africa '70)	20
77	Creole CRLP 511	ZOMBIE (LP, with Africa '70)	20
78	Phase 4 Stereo PFS 4412	YELLOW FEVER (LP)	20
79	Creole CRLP 502	GENTLEMEN (LP)	20
79	Creole CRLP 509	EVERYTHING SCATTER (LP)	20
81	Arista SPART 1167	BLACK PRESIDENT (LP)	30
82	Arista SPART 1177	ORIGINAL SUFFERHEAD (LP)	30
73	Regal Zono. SLR2 103Y	AFRODISIAC (LP, red/silver labels with EMI boxed logo)	200

(see also Ginger Baker)

BEN KWELLER
| 02 | 679 777201 | SHA SHA (LP) | 30 |

JIM KWESKIN JUG BAND
65	Fontana TFL 6036	JIM KWESKIN JUG BAND (LP)	20
67	Fontana (S)TFL 6080	SEE REVERSE SIDE FOR TITLE (LP)	18
68	Vanguard SVRL 19046	WHATEVER HAPPENED TO THOSE GOOD OLD DAYS AT CLUB 47 (LP)	18

KYDD
| 75 | Dart ASRT 2052 | Voodoo Magic/You Need Love Love Love | 8 |

(THE) KYDDS
| 69 | NEMS 56-4095 | The Sun Is A Laughing Child/Touch Of The Sun | 15 |

CHARLES KYNARD
| 73 | Mainstream MSL 1017 | YOUR MAMA DON'T DANCE (LP) | 25 |

KYODS
| 70 | President PT 289 | Judas In Blue/Where Did I Go Wrong | 6 |

KYTES
66	Pye 7N 17136	Blessed/Call Me Darling	15
66	Pye 7N 17179	Frosted Panes/I'll Give You Better Love	30
68	Island WI 6027	Running In The Water/The End Of The Day	70

KYTTOCK KYND
| 70 | Dorian 4782 | KYTTOCK KYND (LP) | 40 |

L

L.A.
| 70 | CBS 64109 | NEW DAY (LP) | 30 |

(see also Elastic Band, Love Affair)

LA BELLE EPOQUE
| 77 | Harvest SHSP 4074 | MISS BROADWAY (LP) | 12 |

PATTI LA BELLE (& BLUE BELLES)
64	Sue WI 324	Down The Aisle/C'est La Vie	30
65	Cameo Parkway P 935	Danny Boy/I Believe	20
65	Atlantic AT 4055	All Or Nothing/You Forgot How To Love (as Patty La Belle & Her Belles)	22
66	Atlantic AT 4064	Over The Rainbow/Groovy Kind Of Love (as Patty La Belle & Her Belles)	15
66	Atlantic 584 007	Patti's Prayer/Family Man (as Patti La Belle & Her Belles)	12
67	Atlantic 584 072	Take Me For A Little While/I Don't Want To Go On Without You	12
66	Atlantic 587 001	OVER THE RAINBOW (LP)	40

(see also Blue-Belles)

SLEEPY LABEEF
| 79 | Ace CH 16 | SLEEPY LABEEF AND FRIENDS (10" LP) | 12 |
| 79 | Charly CR 30172 | DOWNHOME ROCKABILLY (LP) | 12 |

LABRADFORD
95	Flying Nun FN 329	A STABLE REFERENCE (LP, reissue, numbered sleeve)	12
96	Blast First BFFP 136 LP	LABRADFORD (LP, die-cut sleeve)	12
97	Blast First BFFP 144	MI MEDIA NARANJA (LP)	15

LACE
| 68 | Columbia DB 8499 | People People/The Nun | 25 |
| 69 | Page One POF 135 | I'm A Gambler/Go Away | 10 |

(see also Universals, Pete Dello, Honeybus, Red Herring, Gary Walker & Rain)

DAVE LACEY & CORVETTES
| 65 | Philips BF 1419 | That's What They All Say/I've Had Enough | 10 |

LACKEY & SWEENEY
| 73 | Village Thing VTS 23 | JUNK STORE SONGS FOR SALE (LP) | 15 |

LACK OF KNOWLEDGE
81	LOK LOK 1	The Uninvited/Ritual (with A4 photocopied inserts)	20
83	Crass Records 121984/6	GREY (EP)	15
85	Chainsaw TEXT 7	SENTINEL (EP)	10
84	Corpus Christi CHRIST 15	SIRENS ARE BACK (LP)	20

JUNIOR LACY
| 70s | Aries ARI 003 | You Will See Jah Light/Jah Love Version (12") | 25 |

STEVE LACY
| 57 | Esquire 32 143 | SOPRANO TODAY (LP) | 40 |
| 72 | Emanem 301 | SOLO (LP) | 25 |

| 73 | Emanem 304 | THE CRUST (LP) .... | 35 |

STEVE LACY & DEREK BAILEY
| 76 | Incus 26 | COMPANY 4 (LP) .... | 25 |

(see also Derek Bailey)

LADDERS
| 83 | Statik TAK 2 | Gotta See Jane/Krugerrands (p/s) .... | 6 |
| 83 | Statik TAK 2-12 | Gotta See Jane/Krugerrands (12", p/s) .... | 10 |

LADD'S BLACK ACES
| 56 | London AL 3556 | LADD'S BLACK ACES (10" LP) .... | 15 |

LA-DE-DA BAND
| 69 | Parlophone R 5810 | Come Together/Here Is Love .... | 18 |

LADIES
| 80s | Music Of Life MOLIS 6 | Turned On To You/I Knew That Love (12") .... | 15 |

TOMMY LADNIER
| 54 | London AL 3524 | BLUES AND STOMPS VOLUME ONE - TOMMY LADNIER (10" LP) .... | 20 |
| 55 | London AL 3548 | PLAYS THE BLUES WITH MA RAINEY & EDMONIA HENDERSON (10" LP) ...... | 20 |

(see also Ma Rainey)

PATTIE LA DONNE
| 69 | Joe/Duke DU 23 | Friends And Lovers/JOE'S ALLSTARS: Hot Line .... | 12 |

LADY GAGA
| 08 | Interscope LGDANCEUP1 | JUST DANCE - THE REMIXES (LP, promo, pink vinyl) .... | 45 |

LADY JANE
| 84 | Schizoid SCHIZ 01 | For You Tonight/Out For The Count/Whisky And Leather (private pressing) .... | 50 |

LADY JANE & VERITY
| 59 | Pye International 7N 25036 | The Slow Look/Cry Baby .... | 8 |

LADY JUNE
| 74 | Caroline C 1509 | LADY JUNE'S LINGUISTIC LEPROSY (LP, with perforated lyric sheet) .... | 35 |

(see also Kevin Ayers, Eno)

LADY LEE
64	Decca F 11961	I'm Into Something Good/When Love Comes Along	12
65	Decca F 12147	99 Times Out Of 100/I Can Feel It	8
65	Columbia DB 7121	My Whole World (Seems To Be Tumbling Down)/Girl	10

LADY LUCK & LULLABIES
| 62 | Philips PB 1245 | Young Stranger/Dance .... | 5 |

LADYBIRDS
64	Columbia DB 7197	Lady Bird/I Don't Care Any More...	10
64	Columbia DB 7250	The White Cliffs Of Dover/It's Not The Same Without A Boy	10
64	Columbia DB 7351	Memories/Try A Little Love	10
65	Columbia DB 7523	I Wanna Fly/O.K. Fred	10
70	Decca F13014	Love As High As A Mountain/Stand Up And Be Counted............................	18

(see also Sharades, Russ Loader, Marion Davies, De Laine Sisters)

LADYTRON
00s	Telstar 7STAS 3311	Blue Jeans (Single Version)/Blue Jeans (Interpol Remix) (p/s, 1000 only)	6
02	Telstar 12STAR 3284	Seventeen (Soulwax Remixes) (12" die-cut sleeve)	8
01	Invicta Hi Fi LIQ 014	604 (2-LP, white vinyl)	20

LAFAYETTES
| 62 | RCA RCA 1299 | Life's Too Short/Nobody But You .... | 10 |
| 62 | RCA RCA 1308 | Caravan Of Lonely Men/I Still Do .... | 10 |

MARIE LAFORET
| 66 | Ember NR 5034 | THE GIRL WITH THE GOLDEN EYES (LP).. | 15 |

JACK LE FORGE
| 65 | Stateside SS 444 | Our Crazy Affair/Bossa Bossa Nova (withdrawn) .... | 25 |

FRANCIS LAI
67	United Artists (S)ULP 1185	VIVRE POUR VIVRE (LIFE FOR LIFE) (LP, soundtrack)...............................	12
67	Brunswick LAT/STA 8689	I'LL NEVER FORGET WHAT'S 'ISNAME (LP, soundtrack)............................	25
69	United Artists SULP 1231	HANNIBAL BROOKS (LP)..	30
69	Philips SBL 7876	MAYERLING (Francis Lai)	20
70	United Artists UAS 29137	RIDER IN THE RAIN (LP)	25
71	M. F. Pleasure MFP 50034	THE LEGEND OF FRENCHIE KING (LP)	12
76	Warner Bros K 56231	EMMANUELLE 2 (LP)	15
77	Warner Bros K 56375	BILITIS (LP, gatefold sleeve)	15

LAIBACH
84	L.A.Y.L.A.H. LAY 002	Boji/Sila/Brat Moj (12", p/s)	12
84	East West 12 EWS 3	Panarama/Decree (12", p/s)	10
85	Cherry Red 12CHERRY 91	Die Liebe/Die Liebe Ist Grösste Kraft, Die Alles Schafft (12", p/s)	10
87	Mute MUTE 62	Life Is Life/Germania (p/s)..	5
88	Mute PMUTE 80T	SYMPATHY FOR THE DEVIL (12" EP, picture disc)	10
86	Side Effects SER 08	OCCUPIED EUROPE TOUR '85 (LP)	15
92	Mute STUMM 82	KAPITAL (LP)	12
94	NSK NSK 2CDX	OCCUPIED EUROPE NATO TOUR (EPK, in numbered box, with CD, video & booklet)	20
96	Mute STUMM 136	JESUS CHRIST SUPERSTARS (LP)...	15
98	Mute STUMM 121	MCMXCIV (LP, with poster and inner)...	15

LAIKA
94	Too Pure PURE 42	SILVER APPLES ON THE MOON (LP)	25
97	Too Pure PURE 62	SOUNDS OF THE SATELLITES (2-LP)	20
03	Too Pure PURE 141	WHEREVER I AM I AM WHAT IS MISSING (LP)	12

CLEO LAINE
| 54 | Parlophone MSP 6107 | I Got Rhythm/I Know You're Mine (with Johnny Dankworth Orchestra) .... | 10 |
| 55 | Parlophone MSP 6147 | Ain't Misbehavin'/I Got It Bad, And That Ain't Good (with Johnny Dankworth Orchestra) ... | 10 |

57	Pye Jazz 7NJ 2013	I'm Beginning To See The Light/Jeepers Creepers	6
58	Pye 7N 15143	Hand Me Down Love/They Were Right	6
60	Fontana H 269	Let's Slip Away/Thieving Boy	12
61	Columbia DB 4723	It Was A Lover And His Lass/O Mistress Mine	8
61	Fontana H 326	You'll Answer To Me/I Only Have Eyes For You	6
62	Fontana TF 267257	You Gotta Have Love/I Can Dream, Can't I?	6
65	Fontana TF 532	Little Boat/The Exciting Mr. Fitch	5
65	Fontana TF 622	If We Live On The Top Of A Mountain/Don't You Pass Me By	5
66	Fontana TF 759	There Is Nothing Left To Say/Life Is A Wheel	5
70	Philips 6006 016	It Will Soon Be Spring/Feeling Good	5
71	Philips 6006 077	Model City's Programme/Night Owl	10
82	CBS 2947	Strictly For The Birds/Smilin' Through (with Dudley Moore)	8
57	Parlophone GEP 8613	I GOT RHYTHM (EP)	10
57	Pye Nixa Jazz NJE 1010	CLEO LAINE (EP)	10
57	Pye Nixa Jazz NJE 1026	THE APRIL AGE (EP, as Cleo Laine & Dave Lee Quintet)	20
57	Esquire EP 102	CLEO LAINE (EP, as Cleo Laine & Keith Christie Quintet)	20
57	Esquire EP 122	CLEO LAINE (EP, as Cleo Laine & Keith Christie Quintet)	20
59	Columbia SEG 7938	CLEO SINGS ELIZABETHAN (EP)	10
61	Fontana TFE 17381	THE FABULOUS CLEO (EP)	10
64	Fontana TFE 17404	CLEO (EP)	15
55	Esquire 15-007	CLEO LAINE (10" LP)	40
58	Pye Nixa NPT 19024	CLEO'S CHOICE (10" LP)	40
58	MGM MGM-C 765	SHE'S THE TOPS (LP)	25
62	Fontana 680 992 TL	ALL ABOUT ME (LP, also stereo 886 159 TY)	20
64	Fontana (S)TL 5209	SHAKESPEARE & ALL THAT JAZZ (LP)	20
66	Fontana (S)TL 5316	WOMAN TALK (LP)	15
68	Fontana STL 5483	SOLILOQUY (LP)	15

(see also Johnny Dankworth, Tubby Hayes & Cleo Laine, Dudley Moore)

DENNY LAINE

67	Deram DM 122	Say You Don't Mind/Ask The People	15
68	Deram DM 171	Too Much In Love/Catherine's Wheel	30
69	Deram DM 227	Say You Don't Mind/Ask The People (reissue)	10
73	Wizard WIZ 104	Find A Way Somehow/Move Me To Another Place	15
77	EMI 2588	Moondreams/Heartbeat	6
77	Palladin PAL 5014	Caroline/Blues	6
86	Preseident PT 555	Land Of Peace/If I Tried	6
73	Wizard SW2 2001	AHH...LAINE (LP, yellow labels)	20

(see also Moody Blues, Paul McCartney/Wings, Balls, Trevor Burton, Magic Christians, Ginger Baker's Airforce, BL&G)

FRANKIE LAINE

SINGLES

53	Columbia SCM 5016	The Ruby And The Pearl/The Mermaid	20
53	Columbia SCM 5017	Jealousy/The Gandy Dancers' Ball	25
53	Columbia SCM 5031	I'm Just A Poor Bachelor/Tonight You Belong To Me	20
53	Columbia SCM 5064	September In The Rain/Chow Willy	10
53	Columbia SCM 5073	The Swan Song/My Ohio Home	10
54	Columbia SCM 5085	Tomorrow Mountain/I'd Give My Life	10
56	Philips JK 1000	Moonlight Gambler/Only If We Love (jukebox issue)	20
57	Philips JK 1009	Love Is A Golden Ring (with Easy Riders)/There's Not A Moment To Spare	15
57	Philips JK 1017	Lonely Man/Without Him (jukebox issue)	15
57	Philips JK 1032	The Greater Sin/East Is East (jukebox issue)	10
58	Philips PB 797	Shine/Annabel Lee	5
58	Philips PB 821	The Lonesome Road/My Gal And A Prayer	5
58	Philips PB 836	Lovin' Up A Storm/A Kiss Can Change The World	5
58	Philips PB 848	Choombala Bay/I Have To Cry	5
58	Philips PB 886	When I Speak Your Name/Cottage For Sale	6
59	Philips PB 905	That's My Desire/In My Wildest Dreams	8
59	Philips PB 965	Rawhide/Journey's End	5
59	Philips PB 965	Rawhide/Journey's End (78)	15
60	Philips PB 1064	And Doesn't She Roll/Seven Women	7
61	Philips PB 1135	Gunslinger/Wanted Man	5
63	CBS AAG 144	Don't Make My Baby Blue/The Moment Of Truth	7
74	Warner Bros. K 16414	Blazing Saddles/I'm Tired	6

EPs

54	Columbia SEG 7505	JEZEBEL (company die-cut sleeve)	10

ALBUMS

52	Oriole/Mercury MG 10001	MR RHYTHM SINGS (10", stickered U.S. "Mr Rhythm" sleeve)	25
52	Oriole/Mercury MG 10002	SONGS BY FRANKIE LAINE (10")	20
54	Mercury MG 25097	MR. RHYTHM SINGS (10", reissue)	20
54	Mercury MG 25098	SONGS BY FRANKIE LAINE (10", reissue)	20
54	Columbia 33S 1047	ONE FOR MY BABY (10")	20
54	Philips BBR 8014	THE VOICE OF YOUR CHOICE (10")	20
55	Philips BBR 8068	MR. RHYTHM (10")	12
56	Mercury MPT 7007	CRY OF THE WILD GOOSE (10")	20
56	Philips BBL 7080	JAZZ SPECTACULAR (with Buck Clayton & His Orchestra)	15
57	Philips BBL 7155	ROCKIN'	30

(see also Jo Stafford & Frankie Laine, Four Lads, Doris Day, Easy Riders)

FRANKIE LAINE & JOHNNIE RAY

57	Philips JK 1026	Up Above My Head, I Hear Music In The Air/Good Evening Friends (jukebox issue)	10
57	Philips BBE 12153	FRANKIE AND JOHNNIE (EP, 1 track each, 2 together)	10

(see also Johnnie Ray)

LINDA LAINE (& SINNERS)

64	Columbia DB 7204	Doncha Know, Doncha Know, Doncha Know/Ain't That Fun	20
64	Columbia DB 7370	Low Grades And High Fever/After Today	20
65	Columbia DB 7549	Don't Do It Baby/All I Want To Do Is Run	20

(see also Sinners)

SCOTT LAINE
63   Windsor WB 114   Tearaway Johnnie/John Silver 40

DENZIL LAING
71   Songbird SB 1054   Medicine Stick/CRYSTALITES: Short Cut...12
(see also Soul Vendors, Dennis Alcapone)

LAKE
76   CBS 5015   Do I Love You/Key To The Rhyme 6

ALAN LAKE
70   Ember EMB S 278   Good Times/Got To Have Tenderness (p/s) 15

BONNIE LAKE & HER BEAUX
56   Brunswick 05622   Thirteen Black Cats/The Miracle Of Love..20
56   Brunswick 05622   Thirteen Black Cats/The Miracle Of Love (78)..10
(see also Jack Pleis)

GREG LAKE
75   Manticore K 13511   I Believe In Father Christmas/Humbug (p/s) 6
77   Atlantic K 10990   C'est La Vie/EMERSON, LAKE & PALMER: Jeremy Bender (p/s) 6
78   Atlantic K 11061   Watching Over You/EMERSON, LAKE & PALMER: Hallowed Be Thy Name (p/s) 6
81   Chrysalis CHS 2553   Love You Too Much/Someone (p/s)...5
82   Chrysalis CHS 2567   It Hurts/Retribution Drive 5
81   Chrysalis CHR1357   GREG LAKE (LP, inner sleeve) 12
83   Chrysalis CHR1392   MANEOVRES (LP)...12
(see also Emerson Lake & Palmer, King Crimson, Asia, Pete Sinfield, Gary Moore, Shy Limbs)

LEE LAMAR & HIS ORCHESTRA
57   London HLB 8508   Teenage Pedal Pushers/Sophia 75
57   London HLB 8508   Teenage Pedal Pushers/Sophia (78)..30

GENE LAMARR
72   Injun 112   You Don't Love Me Anymore/Crazy Little House On The Hill................................15

LAMB
96   Fontana PY 281   LAMB (2-LP, inner) 30

ANNABEL LAMB
83   A&M AMLH 68555   ONCE BITTEN (LP) 12

CHRIS LAMB & UNIVERSALS
65   Decca F 12176   Mysterious Land/If You Ask Me 15
(see also Universals, Gidian)

KEVIN LAMB
70   Concord CON 23   Who Is The Hero?/The Road To Antibes 6
73   Birth RAB 1004   Who Is The Hero?/Who Stole The Ice 5
72   Birth RAB 4   WHO IS THE HERO? (LP, white label with 'rabbit' child logo)............................40

LAMB LANCE
95   Long LENGTH 8   THE JOY OF JOUSTING (LP) 12

LAMBCHOP
96   City Slang 04974-45   The Man Who Loved Beer/Alumni Lawn/Burly & Johnson (p/s) 8
00   City Slang 20174-2   THE QUEEN'S ROYAL TRIMMA (CD EP, sold at gigs) 15
02   Virgin/City Slang   IS A WOMAN (2xLP with bonus CD EP)...20
10   City Slang SLANG 0680056   TOUR BOX (8-CD, 2-DVD in canvas box, 1000 only sold on 2010 tour)......................80

JEANNIE LAMBE
67   CBS 202636   Miss Disc/Montano Blues (with Gordon Beck Orchestra) 25
67   CBS 2731   Day After Day After Day/City At Night 20
67   CBS 3000   This Is My Love/Where Have All The Endings Gone (as Jeanne Lam) 8

DAVE LAMBERT, JON HENDRICKS & ANNIE ROSS
60   Philips BBL 7368   DAVE LAMBERT, JON HENDRICKS & ANNIE ROSS (LP, stereo SBBL 562) 15
(see also Jon Hendricks, Annie Ross)

TREVOR LAMBERT
72   Duke DU 132   Bald Head Teacher (act. by Max Romeo)/HEADMASTERS: Bald Head Version 5

LAMBRETTAS
79   Rocket XPRES 23   Go Steady/Listen Listen/Cortinas (p/s)..8
80   Rocket XPRES 25   Poison Ivy/Runaround (with '2-Stroke' die-cut sleeve & label) 12
80   Rocket XPRES 25   Poison Ivy/Runaround (with ROCKET die-cut sleeve & label).............................12
80   Rocket XPRES 333   Da-a-a-ance/(Can't You) Feel The Beat (picture disc; shades, red, white & blue)........5
80   Rocket XPRES 333   Da-a-a-ance/(Can't You) Feel The Beat (picture disc; shades, pink, white & blue) 8
80   Rocket XPRES 36   Page 3/Steppin' Out (Of Line) (withdrawn; one copy known to exist with p/s) 500
80   Rocket XPRES 36   Page 3/Steppin' Out (Of Line) (withdrawn)..300
80   Rocket XPRES 36   Another Day (Another Girl)/Steppin' Out (Of Line) ('emergency' p/s) 5
81   Rocket XPRES 48   Good Times/Lamba Samba (p/s)..5
81   Rocket XPRES 52   Anything You Want/Ambience (Rocket die-cut sleeve) 6
81   Rocket XPRES 62   Decent Town/Da-a-a-ance (p/s) 6
81   Rocket XPRES 6212   Decent Town/Da-a-a-ance/Total Strangers/Young Girls (12", p/s) 12
82   Rocket XPRES 74   Somebody To Love/Nobody's Watching Me (p/s) 8
82   Rocket XPRES 74   Somebody To Love/Nobody's Watching Me (p/s, mispressing, crediting Leap Before
                                 You Look on label & sleeve) 8
80   Rocket TRAIN 10   BEAT BOYS IN THE JET AGE (LP, with inner)..18

LAMELLA
80   Direct DO B1   When Julie Dances/Wasting Your Time (no p/s, 500 only) 50

TONI LAMOND
68   Philips BF 1722   Silent Voices/They Don't Give Medals (To Yesterday's Heroes) 15

DUNCAN LAMONT
67   Studio Two TWO 159   LATIN A LA LAMONT (LP)..12
68   Morgan MRSAM 2   THIS GUY (LP)..15

MINT VALUE £

LAMPLIGHTERS
55	Parlophone DP 416	Salty Dog/Ride Jockey Ride (78, export issue)	80

(see also Thurston Harris)

LAMP SISTERS
68	Sue WI 4048	A Woman With The Blues/I Thought It Was All Over	40

LANA SISTERS
58	Fontana H 148	Ring-A My Phone/Chimes Of Arcady	25
58	Fontana H 148	Ring-A My Phone/Chimes Of Arcady (78)	10
59	Fontana H 176	Buzzin'/Cry, Cry, Baby	25
59	Fontana H 176	Buzzin'/Cry, Cry, Baby (78)	15
59	Fontana H 190	Mister Dee-Jay/Tell Him No	25
59	Fontana H 190	Mister Dee-Jay/Tell Him No (78)	10
59	Fontana H 221	(Seven Little Girls) Sitting In The Back Seat (with Al Saxon)/ Sitting On The Sidewalk	20
59	Fontana H 221	(Seven Little Girls) Sitting In The Back Seat (with Al Saxon)/ Sitting On The Sidewalk (78)	15
60	Fontana H 235	My Mother's Eyes/You've Got What It Takes	20
60	Fontana H 235	My Mother's Eyes/You've Got What It Takes (78)	15
60	Fontana H 252	Someone Loves You, Joe/Tinatarella Di Luna	15
60	Fontana H 283	Two-some/Down South	15

(see also Al Saxon, Dusty Springfield, Chantelles)

CYNTHIA LANAGAN
54	Columbia SCMC 8	Body And Soul/I Can't Believe You're In Love With Me (export issue)	10
57	Parlophone R 4316	Jamie Boy/Silent Lips (as Cynthia Lanigan)	7
57	Parlophone R 4383	I'm Available/(Don't Stop, Don't Stop) Tell Me More	7

LANCASHIRE FAYRE
80	Folk Heritage FHR 113	LANCASHIRE FAYRE (LP)	20

STEVE LANCASTER
67	Polydor 56215	San Francisco Street/Miguel Fernando San Sebastian Brown	15

ALAN LANCASTER'S BOMBERS
96	P.J. Rocks PJR002CD	THE MATCHSTICKMEN EP (CD, 4 tracks, card p/s)	15

(see also Status Quo)

LANCASTRIANS
64	Pye 7N 15732	We'll Sing In The Sunshine/Was She Tall	25
65	Pye 7N 15791	Let's Lock The Door (And Throw Away The Key)/If You're Goin' To Leave Me	7
65	Pye 7N 15846	There'll Be No More Goodbyes/Never Gonna Come On Home	7
65	Pye 7N 15927	Lonely Man/I Can't Stand The Pain	7
66	Pye 7N 17043	The World Keeps Going Round/Not The Same Anymore	40
66	Pye 7N 17072	The Ballad Of The Green Berets/My Little Rose	5

MAJOR LANCE
63	Columbia DB 7099	The Monkey Time/Mama Didn't Know	30
63	Columbia DB 7099	The Monkey Time/Mama Didn't Know (DJ copy)	50
63	Columbia DB 7168	Hey Little Girl/Crying In The Rain	25
64	Columbia DB 7205	Um, Um, Um, Um, Um/Sweet Music	25
64	Columbia DB 7271	The Matador/Gonna Get Married	30
64	Columbia DB 7365	Rhythm/Please Don't Say No More	25
65	Columbia DB 7463	I'm So Lost/Sometimes I Wonder	25
65	Columbia DB 7527	Come See/You Belong To Me, My Love	30
65	Columbia DB 7609	Pride And Joy/I'm The One	60
65	Columbia DB 7688	Too Hot To Hold/Dark And Lonely	75
65	Columbia DB 7787	Everybody Loves A Good Time/I Just Can't Help It	30
65	Columbia DB 7787	Everybody Loves A Good Time/I Just Can't Help It (DJ Copy)	75
66	Columbia DB 7967	Investigate/Little Young Lover	75
66	Columbia DB 7967	Investigate/Little Young Lover (DJ copy)	125
67	Columbia DB 8122	Ain't No Soul (Left In These Ole Shoes)/You'll Want Me Back	60
67	Columbia DB 8122	Ain't No Soul (Left In These Ole Shoes)/You'll Want Me Back (DJ copy)	100
69	Atlantic 584 277	Follow The Leader/Since You've Been Gone	15
69	Atlantic 584 302	Sweeter As The Days Go By/Shadows Of A Memory	20
69	Soul City SC 114	The Beat/You'll Want Me Back	25
70	Buddah 2011 046	Gypsy Woman/Stay Away From Me	15
72	Stax 2025 124	I Wanna Make Up/That's The Story Of My Life	15
72	Epic EPC 8404	Um, Um, Um, Um, Um/Sweet Music (reissue)	6
73	Contempo C 1	The Right Track/Um, Um, Um, Um, Um	6
73	Contempo C 9	Ain't No Soul (Left In These Ole Shoes)/Investigate	8
73	Contempo C 26	Dark And Lonely/My Girl	20
73	Warner Bros K 16334	Sweeter/Wild & Free	8
74	Warner Bros K 16385	Without A Doubt/Open The Door To Your Heart	25
74	Contempo CS 2017	Gimme Little Sign/How Can You Say Goodbye	25
74	Contempo CS 9015	The Right Track/Ain't No Soul (Left In These Ole Shoes)	6
75	Contempo CS 2045	Don't You Know I Love You (Parts 1 & 2)	20
75	Pye 7N 45487	You're Everything I Need (Parts 1 & 2)	10
76	Pye International 7N 25705	Nothing Can Stop Me/Follow The Leader	10
64	Columbia SEG 8318	UM UM UM UM UM UM (EP)	100
65	Columbia 33SX 1728	THE RHYTHM OF MAJOR LANCE (LP)	170
73	Contempo COLP 1001	GREATEST HITS LIVE AT THE TORCH (LP, sitting under a tree is first pressing)	40
73	Contempo COLP 1001	GREATEST HITS LIVE AT THE TORCH (LP, second pressing with 'negative' b/w cover)	12
76	Epic EPC 81519	THE BEST OF MAJOR LANCE (LP)	12
78	Tamla Motown STML 12094	NOW ARRIVING (LP)	12

RICK LANCELOT & SEVEN KNIGHTS
66	RCA RCA 1502	Say Girl/Live Like A Lion	15

LANCERS
54	London HL 8027	Stop Chasin' Me Baby/Peggy O'Neil	40
54	London HL 8079	So High, So Low, So Wide/It's You, It's You I Love	40
54	Vogue Coral Q 2038	Mister Sandman/The Little White Light	25
55	Vogue Coral Q 72062	Timberjack/C-r-a-z-y Music	20
55	Vogue Coral Q 72081	Get Out Of The Car (as Lancers & Georgie Auld)/Close Your Eyes	20

55	Vogue Coral Q 72100	Jo-Ann/The Bonnie Banks Of Loch Lomon'	10
56	Vogue Coral Q 72128	Alphabet Rock/Rock Around The Island	40
56	Vogue Coral Q 72128	Alphabet Rock/Rock Around The Island (78)	15
56	Vogue Coral Q 72157	Little Fool/A Man Is As Good As His Word	8
56	Vogue Coral Q 72183	The First Travelling Saleslady/Free	5
57	Vogue Coral Q 72220	Never Leave Me/I Came Back To Say I'm Sorry	5
57	Vogue Coral Q 72254	It Happened In Monterey/Ramona/Freckled-Face Sara Jane	5
57	Vogue Coral Q 72282	Charm Bracelet/And It Don't Feel Bad	6
58	Coral Q 72300	The Stroll/Don't Go Near The Water	5
58	Coral Q 72300	The Stroll/Don't Go Near The Water (78)	10
60	Coral Q 72398	Joey, Joey, Joey/JOHNNY DESMOND: The Most Happy Fella	5
61	Warner Bros WB 39	Young In Love/Lonesome Town	5
55	London REP 1027	PRESENTING THE LANCERS (EP)	20
54	London H-APB 1029	OH SWEET MAMA (10" LP)	30
61	London HA-P 2307	CONCERT IN CONTRASTS (LP)	15

ELSA LANCHESTER

58	Vogue VA 160126	SONGS FOR A SMOKE-FILLED ROOM (LP, with Charles Laughton)	20
59	Vogue VA 160139	SONGS FOR A SHUTTERED PARLOUR (LP, with Charles Laughton)	20

BILLY LAND

62	Oriole CB 1750	I Go Walking/You're Too Much	10

HAROLD LAND

58	Contemporary LAC 12178	HAROLD IN THE LAND OF JAZZ (LP)	15

LAND OF BARBARA

93	Loble L02	Alcohol/Phosphorus For The Mutiny (p/s)	8

BOB LANDER & SPOTNICKS

62	Oriole CB 1784	Midnight Special/My Old Kentucky Home	15

(see also Spotnicks)

BILL & BRETT LANDIS

59	Parlophone R 4516	Since You've Gone/Bright Eyes	15
59	Parlophone R 4516	Since You've Gone/Bright Eyes (78)	10
59	Parlophone R 4551	By You, By You/Forgive Me	10
59	Parlophone R 4570	Baby Talk/Love Me True	15

JERRY LANDIS

62	Oriole CB 1930	Carlos Dominquez/He Was My Brother	40

(see also Paul Simon)

JOYA LANDIS

68	Trojan TR 620	Kansas City/Out The Light	10
68	Trojan TR 622	Angel Of The Morning/ALTON PHYLIS: Love Letters	15
69	Trojan TR 641	Moonlight Lover/I Love You True	12

(see also Jay & Joya, Hugh Roy)

LANDLORD

90	Debut DEBTX 3084	I Like It (12")	10

HOAGY LANDS

67	Stateside SS 2030	The Next In Line/Please Don't Talk About Me When I'm Gone	250
67	Stateside SS 2030	The Next In Line/Please Don't Talk About Me When I'm Gone (DJ copy)	400
68	Stateside SS 2085	I'm Yours/Only You	25
72	Action ACT 4605	Why Didn't You Let Me Know/Do You Know What Life Is All About	25
75	UK USA 13	Friends And Lovers Don't Go Together/True Love At Last	30
75	UK USA 14	The Next In Line/I'm Yours	10

NEIL LANDSTRUMM

95	Mosquito MSQ 02	PASCAL EP (12", custom sleeve)	20

(see also Blue Arsed Fly)

DES(MOND) LANE

56	Decca F 10821	Penny-Whistle Rock/Penny-Whistle Polka	8
57	Decca F 10847	Rock Mister Piper/Plymouth Rock	10
59	Top Rank JAR 203	Moonbird/The Clanger March (as Des Lane Orchestra, with John Barry)	6
68	Pye 7N 17546	Sadie/No More Wild Oats (as Des Lane)	5

(see also Cyril Stapleton, John Barry)

GARY LANE & GARRISONS

61	Fontana H 338	Start Walking Boy/How Wrong Can You Be	15
62	Fontana 267221 TF	I'm A Lucky Boy/A Love Like You	15

LOIS LANE

67	RCA RCA 1570	One Little Voice/Sing To Me	6
68	Mercury MF 1042	Punky's Dilemma/Lazy Summer Day	6
69	Mercury MF 1092	Brontasaurus Named Bert/Windmills Of Your Mind	5
69	Mercury MF 1115	Lovin' Time/Winds Of Heaven	6
70	Philips BF 1829	Putting My Baby To Sleep/Far From The Madding Crowd	5
70	DJM DJS 2280	Day By Day/Cloud Of Blue	5
68	Mercury SMCL 20125	LOIS LANE (LP)	25

(see also Caravelles)

MICKEY LEE LANE

64	Stateside SS 354	Shaggy Dog/Oo Oo	20
65	Stateside SS 456	Hey Sah-Lo-Ney/Of Yesterday	75
65	Stateside SS 456	Hey Sah-Lo-Ney/Of Yesterday (DJ copy)	150

PENNY LANE

68	Columbia DB 8377	Loving Or Losing You/Deep Down Inside	6
68	CBS 3718	The Boy Who Never Grew Up/I'm Going Back	6
70	CBS 4749	Bouzouki/Make Up Or Break Up	10
72	CBS 7916	Legend In Your Own Time/Driving Me Out Of My Mind	8
70	CBS 4905	Heartbreak House/He's Got A Hold Of My Heart	6
70	CBS 5311	Rock Me In The Cradle (Of Your Loving Arms)/I'm Free	10

MINT VALUE £

RONNIE LANE & SLIM CHANCE

73	GM GMS 011	How Come/Tell Everyone/Done This One Before (p/s)	8
77	Polydor 2058 944	Street In The City/Annie (with Pete Townshend)	6
77	Polydor 2058 944	Street In The City/Annie (12", with Pete Townshend)	8
79	Gem GEMS 12	Kuschty Rye/You're So Right (p/s)	8
74	GM GMS 024	The Poacher/Bye & Bye (Gonna See The King)	5
74	GM GMS 033	Roll on Babe/Anymore For Anymore	5
74	Island WIP 6216	What Went Down (That Night With You)/Lovely	7
75	Island WIP 6229	Brother Can You Spare A Dime/Ain't No Lady	7
76	Island WIP 6258	Don't Try And Change My Mind/Well, well, Hello (The Party)	7
80	GEM GEMS 19	One Step/Lad's Got Money	5
74	GML 1013	ANYMORE FOR ANYMORE (LP)	25
75	Island ILPS 9321	RONNIE LANE AND SLIM CHANCE (LP)	18
75	Island ILPS 9366	ONE FOR THE ROAD (LP)	15
76	Atlantic K 50308	MAHONEY'S LAST STAND (LP, with Ron Wood, soundtrack)	15
77	Polydor 2442 147	ROUGH MIX (LP, with Pete Townshend)	12
80	Gem GEMLP 107	SEE ME (LP, with insert)	12
88	Thunderbolt THBL 067P	MAHONEY'S LAST STAND (LP, reissue, picture disc)	12

(see also Small Faces, Faces, Pete Townshend & Ronnie Lane)

ROSEMARY LANE

60	Philips PB 1041	Down By The River/My First Love Letter	8

TONY LANE & DELTONES

64	Sabre SA-45-5	It's Great/Now She's Mine	30

PATTIE LANE

68	Polydor 56260	Paper Dreams/My Four Walls	25

LANE BROTHERS

60	London HLR 9150	Mimi/Two Dozen And A Half	10

LANE SISTERS

61	Columbia DB 4671	Peek A Boo Moon/Birmingham Rag	10

DON LANG (& HIS "FRANTIC" FIVE)

55	HMV POP 115	Coludburst/Seventeen (78)	10
56	HMV 7M 354	Four Brothers/I Want You To Be My Baby (solo)	30
56	HMV 7M 381	Rock Around The Island/Jumpin' To Conclusions (solo)	30
56	HMV 7M 416	Rock And Roll Blues/Stop The World I Wanna Get Off (solo)	30
56	HMV POP 260	Sweet Sue - Just You/Lazy Latin (solo)	20
56	HMV POP 260	Sweet Sue - Just You/Lazy Latin (solo) (78)	10
57	HMV POP 289	Rock Around The Cookhouse/Rock Mister Piper	30
57	HMV POP 289	Rock Around The Cookhouse/Rock Mister Piper (78)	12
57	HMV POP 335	Rock-A-Billy/Come Go With Me (B-side with Skifflers)	30
57	HMV POP 335	Rock-A-Billy/Come Go With Me (B-side with Skifflers) (78)	12
57	HMV POP 350	School Day (Ring! Ring! Goes The Bell)/Six-Five Special	30
57	HMV POP 350	School Day (Ring! Ring! Goes The Bell)/Six-Five Special (78)	12
57	HMV POP 382	White Silver Sands/Again 'N' Again 'N' Again	15
57	HMV POP 414	Red Planet Rock/Texas Tambourine	25
57	HMV POP 414	Red Planet Rock/Texas Tambourine (78)	12
58	HMV POP 434	Ramshackle Daddy/6-5 Hand Jive	25
58	HMV POP 434	Ramshackle Daddy/6-5 Hand Jive (78)	12
58	HMV POP 465	Tequila/Junior Hand Jive	25
58	HMV POP 465	Tequila/Junior Hand Jive (78)	15
58	HMV POP 488	Witch Doctor/Cool Baby Cool	10
58	HMV POP 510	Hey Daddy!/The Bird On My Head	10
58	HMV POP 510	Hey Daddy!/The Bird On My Head (78)	15
58	HMV POP 547	Queen Of The Hop/La-Do-Da-Da	15
58	HMV POP 547	Queen Of The Hop/La-Do-Da-Da (solo) (78)	20
59	HMV POP 585	Wiggle Wiggle/(You Were Only) Teasin' (solo)	15
59	HMV POP 585	Wiggle Wiggle/(You Were Only) Teasin' (solo) (78)	25
59	HMV POP 623	Percy Green/Phineas McCoy (solo)	15
59	HMV POP 623	Percy Green/Phineas McCoy (solo) (78)	30
59	HMV POP 649	A Hoot An' A Holler/See You Friday (solo)	8
59	HMV POP 649	A Hoot An' A Holler/See You Friday (78)	20
59	HMV POP 682	Reveille Rock/Frankie And Johnny	15
60	HMV POP 714	Sink The Bismarck!/They Call Him Cliff (solo)	30
60	HMV POP 805	Time Machine/Don't Open That Door	15
62	Decca F 11483	Wicked Women/Play Money (as Don Lang & Boulder Rollers)	10
57	HMV 7EG 8208	ROCK 'N' ROLL (EP)	100
57	HMV DLP 1151	SKIFFLE SPECIAL (LP, 10", by Don Lang & His Skiffle Group)	120
58	HMV DLP 1179	INTRODUCING THE HAND JIVE (LP, 10")	150
62	Ace Of Clubs ACL 1111	TWENTY TOP-TWENTY TWISTS (LP)	20

(see also Gordon Langhorn)

EDDIE LANG & LONNIE JOHNSON

67	Parlophone PMC 7019	BLUE GUITARS (LP)	25
70	Parlophone PMC 7106	BLUE GUITARS VOLUME 2 (LP)	25

(see also Blind Willie Dunn's Gin Bottle Four)

K.D. LANG

88	Sire W 7841	Sugar Moon/Honky Tonk Medley (p/s)	20
88	Sire W 7841T	Sugar Moon/Honky Tonk Medley/I'm Down To My Last Cigarette (12", p/s)	50
88	Sire W 7697	Our Day Will Come/Three Cigarettes In An Ashtray (live) (p/s)	20
88	Sire W 7697T	Our Day Will Come/Three Cigarettes In An Ashtray (live)/Johnny Get Angry (live) (12", p/s)	50
90	Warner Brothers W 9535	Ridin' The Rails (with Take Six)/DARLENE LOVE: Mr Fix-It (with p/s)	20
90	Warner Brothers W 9535	Ridin' The Rails (with Take Six)/DARLENE LOVE: Mr Fix-It	15
92	Sire W 0100T	Constant Craving (Edit)/Barefoot (Rhythmic Version)/ Season Of Hollow Soul (12", p/s)	8
92	Sire W 0100CD	Constant Craving (Edit)/Barefoot (Rhythmic Version)/ Season Of Hollow Soul (CD)	12

RAY LANG & JAMAICAN ROOM ORCHESTRA

57	Brunswick 05683	Last Train (Biddi-Biddi Bum-Bum)/Keetch (Hey! Bernice)	10
57	Brunswick 05683	Last Train (Biddi-Biddi Bum-Bum)/Keetch (Hey! Bernice) (78)	10

STEVIE LANGE

81	RCA RCA 152	Remember My Name/I Don't Want To Know (1st issue, p/s)	8
81	RCA LIM 1	Remember My Name/I Don't Want To Know (2nd issue, p/s)	6

GORDON LANGHORN

55	Decca F 10591	Give A Fool A Chance/Don't Stay Away Too Long	15

(see also Don Lang, Cyril Stapleton)

MARY LANGLEY

67	CBS 2862	Stay In My World/Summer Love	12
67	CBS 3032	It Always Rains On Sunday/All My Life Is You	6

(see also Perpetual Langley, Langleys)

PERPETUAL LANGLEY

66	Planet PLF 110	We Wanna Stay Home/So Sad	30
66	Planet PLF 115	Surrender/Two By Two	30

(see also Mary Langley, Langleys)

LANGLEYS

65	Fontana TF 544	Green Island/You Know I Love You	6

(see also Hawkwind, Widowmaker)

(HUW) LLOYD LANGTON (GROUP)

83	Flicknife FLS 021	Wind Of Change/Outside The Law (as Lloyd Langton Group, p/s)	5
83	Flicknife SHARP 015	OUTSIDE THE LAW (LP, 1,000 with bonus 7": "Working Time"/ I See You [FREE 001], as Huw Lloyd Langton)	15
83	Flicknife SHARP 015	OUTSIDE THE LAW (LP, 1,000 only without bonus 7")	12
86	Gas GAS 4014	LIKE AN ARROW (THROUGH THE HEART) (LP)	12

(see also Hawkwind, Widowmaker)

PHIL LANGTON TRIO

60s	Holyground	PHIL LANGTON TRIO (LP)	18

LESTER LANIN & HIS ORCHESTRA

62	Columbia 33SX 1442	TWISTIN' IN HIGH SOCIETY! (LP)	12

SNOOKY LANSON

50	London L 555	The Old Master Painter/Did You Ever See A Dream Walking? (78)	10
50	London L 682	Roses/Where Are You Gonna Be When The Moon Shines (78)	10
56	London HLD 8223	It's Almost Tomorrow/Why Don't You Write	100
56	London HLD 8223	It's Almost Tomorrow/Why Don't You Write (78)	12
56	London HLD 8236	Stop (Let Me Off The Bus)/Last Minute Love	200
56	London HLD 8236	Stop (Let Me Off The Bus)/Last Minute Love (78)	20
56	London HLD 8249	Seven Days/Tippity Top	200
56	London HLD 8249	Seven Days/Tippity Top (78)	20
56	London HL 7005	Seven Days/Tippity Top (export issue)	80

(see also Teresa Brewer)

LANZON & HUSBAND

75	Bradley's BRAD 7508	Do You Still Love Me/Ecstacy Express	6
75	Bradley's BRADL 1007	NOSTALGIA (LP)	15

JENNIFER LARA

79	Hitrun HIT DD 14	Jah Will Lead Us Home/RANKING PURPLE: Ah Fi We Jah (12")	60

LARD

89	Alternative Tentacles VIRUS 72T	POWER OF LARD (12" EP)	8
90	Alternative Tentacles VIRUS 84	LAST TEMPTATION OF REID (LP, with free 12")	15

PHILIP LARKIN

58	Mervell Press	LESS DECEIVED (LP, 100 only, numbered)	125
68	Listen	LESS DECEIVED (LP)	40
75	Argo PLP 1202	HIGH WINDOWS (LP)	25

LARKS

64	Pye International 7N 25284	The Jerk/Forget Me	50
64	Pye International 7N 25284	The Jerk/Forget Me (DJ copy)	80

LARKS

86	Exalation 12 LARX 2	All Or Nothing Girl/Whatever You Say/Teachers: Parents/Heartless (12", p/s)	12

SAM LARNER

61	Folkways FG 3507	NOW IS THE TIME FOR FISHING (LP)	15
74	Topic 12T 244	A GARLAND FOR SAM (LP, blue label)	15

LARO

60	Kalypso XX 21	Jamaican Referendum Calypso/Wrong Impressions Of A Soldier	8

WINSTON LARO

70	Downtown DT 461	Goodnight My Love/BOYSIE: I Don't Want To Be Hurt	5

JULIUS LA ROSA

55	London HL 8154	Mobile/Pass It On	30
55	London HLA 8170	Domani/Mama Rosa	35
55	London HLA 8193	Suddenly There's A Valley/Everytime I Kiss Carrie	40
56	HMV 7M 384	Lipstick And Candy And Rubber-Sole Shoe/Winter In New England	10
56	London HLA 8272	No Other Love/Rosanne	25
56	London HLA 8353	Jingle Bells (Campanelle)/Jingle Dingle	10
58	RCA RCA 1063	Torero/Milano	5
60	London HLR 9092	Green Fields/Caress Me (Accaressama)	5
54	London RE-P 1005	SINGS (EP)	10
57	London HA-A 2031	JULIUS LA ROSA (LP)	30

LARRY'S ALL STARS

71	Ackee ACK 125	In The Fields/Teardrops Got The Feeling	10
71	Ackee ACK 130	Pre-Fight/The Prayer	5

(see also Larry Lawrence, Delroy Wilson, Hugh Roy, Sensations)

LARRY (MARSHALL) & ALVIN

68	Studio One SO 2065	Nanny Goat/Smell You Crep	20
68	Studio One SO 2067	Can't You Understand/Hush Up	50
69	Studio One SO 2080	Lonely Room (No One To Give Me Love)/You Mean To Me	40
69	Coxsone CS 7081	Love Got Me/BOB ANDY: Lady With The Bright Light (both sides actually by Glen [Brown] & Dave [Barker])	25
70	Bamboo BAM 22	Girl Of My Dream/SOUND DIMENTION: Give It Away	50

(see also Larry Marshall, Sound Dimension, Vincent Gordon)

LARRY & JOHNNY

| 65 | Outasite 45 501 | Beatle Time Parts 1 & 2 (99 copies only) | 150 |

(see also Larry Williams & Johnny 'Guitar' Watson)

LARRY & LINDA

| 70 | Beacon BEA 146 | Most Peculiar Girl/Magnificent Opupouring | 10 |

LARRY & TOMMY

| 68 | Polydor 56741 | You've Gotta Bend A Little/Yo-Yo (A side written and produced by John Cale) | 35 |

KIM LARSEN & JUNGLE DREAMS

| 82 | CBS A 2232 | Rock 'N' Roll City/Time Bomb | 20 |

JACK LARSON

| 61 | Top Rank JAR 573 | I Love The Way She Laughs/The Hammer Bell Song | 8 |

DANNY LA RUE

| 63 | Page One POD 108 | On Mother Kellys Doorstep/The Impossible Dream | 5 |

LA'S

87	Go! Discs GOLAS 1	Way Out/Endless (p/s)	6
87	Go! Discs GOLAS 112	Way Out/Knock Me Down/Endless (12", red & silver p/s)	15
87	Go! Discs GOLAR 112	Way Out/Knock Me Down/Endless/Liberty Ship (Demo)/Freedom Song (Demo) (12", blue & silver stickered p/s listing 4 tracks)	15
87	Go! Discs GOLAR 112	Way Out/Knock Me Down/Endless/Liberty Ship (Demo)/Freedom Song (Demo) (12", blue & silver stickered p/s listing 5 tracks)	15
88	Go! Discs LASEP 2	There She Goes/Way Out/Who Knows/Come In Come Out (EP, blue p/s, 5,000 only)	15
88	Go! Discs GOLAS 2	There She Goes/Come In Come Out (red p/s)	10
88	Go! Discs GOLAS 212	There She Goes/Come In Come Out/Who Knows/ Man I'm Only Human (12", red sleeve)	10
89	Go! Discs GOLAS 3	Timeless Melody/Clean Prophet (p/s, unissued; 10 test pressings only)	60
89	Go! Discs LASEP 3	Timeless Melody (10", unissued)	0
89	Go! Discs LASDJ 312	Timeless Melody/Clean Prophet/All By Myself/Ride Yer Camel (12", promo, 500 only)	30
89	Go! Discs GOLAS 4	Timeless Melody/Clean Prophet (blue p/s)	5
89	Go! Discs GOLAS 412	Timeless Melody/Clean Prophet/Knock Me Down/Over (12", purple p/s)	8
90	Go! Discs GOLAB 5	There She Goes/Freedom Song (numbered box set with badge & 3 stickers)	10
90	Go! Discs GOLAS 5	There She Goes/Freedom Song (reissue, white sleeve)	5
90	Go! Discs GOLAS 512	There She Goes/Freedom Song/All By Myself (12", reissue, white p/s)	8
91	Go! Discs GOLAS 6	Feelin'/Doledrum (p/s)	8
91	Go! Discs GOLAB 6	Feelin'/IOU (Alternate Version)/Feelin' (Alternate Version)/Doledrum (numbered box set with badge & 3 stickers)	8
91	Go! Discs 828 202-1	THE LA'S (LP)	30
99	Viper VLP 002	LOST LA's 1984-1986 BREAKLOOSE (LP)	12
01	Viper VLP 008	LOST LA's 1986-1987: CALLIN' ALL (LP)	12
10	Polydor 5326495	CALLIN' ALL (4-CD 'book' box set)	20

(see also Cast)

BONGO LES (CHEN) & BUNNY (HERMAN)

| 72 | Attack ATT 8041 | Feel Nice (Version)/WINSTON SCOTLAND: Quick And Slick | 8 |

(see also Bongo Herman)

DENISE LASALLE

| 71 | Janus 6310206 | TRAPPED BY A THING CALLED LOVE (LP) | 15 |

COUNT LASHER

| 60s | Kalypso 100 AB | Calypso Cha Cha Cha/Perseverance | 5 |
| 60s | Kalypso 105 AB | Slide Mongoose/Miss Constance | 5 |

LASSIES & RAY CHARLES SINGERS

| 56 | Brunswick 05571 | Sleepy Head/This I Offer You | 5 |

LAST BANDITS

| 89 | Solid ROK 722 | The Angels Are Calling/The Dalkey Rake (p/s) | 5 |

(see also Swell Maps, Nikki Sudden)

LAST CHANT

| 81 | Chicken Jazz JAZZ 4 | Run Of The Dove/Strength Alone/Tradition (p/s) | 8 |

(see also Waterboys)

LAST EXIT

| 75 | Wudwink WUD 01 | Whispering Voices/Evensong (no p/s) | 35 |
| 75 | Wudwink WUD.C.101 | FIRST FROM LAST EXIT (cassette only, pink card insert, sold at gigs, only 3 copies known to exist) | 500 |

(see also Newcastle Big Band, Police, Sting)

LAST FLIGHT

| 81 | Heavy Metal HEAVY 5 | Dance To The Music/I'm Ready (p/s) | 8 |

LAST MAN IN EUROPE

| 85 | Cocteau CO 22 | A Certain Bridge/TV Addict (p/s) | 15 |

LAST POETS

| 72 | Douglas DGL 69012 | THIS IS MADNESS (LP) | 40 |

LAST RESORT (1)

| 78 | Red Meat RMRS 01 | Having Fun?/F.U.2 (die-cut printed paper sleeve) | 20 |

LAST RESORT (2)

82	Last Resort LR 1	SKINHEAD ANTHEMS (LP, red vinyl)	30
82	Last Resort LR 1	SKINHEAD ANTHEMS (LP, white vinyl)	30
82	Last Resort LR 1	SKINHEAD ANTHEMS (LP, blue vinyl)	30
82	Last Resort LR 1	SKINHEAD ANTHEMS (LP, black vinyl)	40

LAST RITES
83	Flicknife FLS 219	We Don't Care/Step Down (p/s) 20
84	Essential 004	FASCISM MEANS WAR (No Right To Take/Convicted Without Trial/Protest And Survive/The Dreams Of Many) (EP, gatefold p/s) 20
84	Essential 001	THIS IS THE REACTION (LP) 30

LAST ROUGH CAUSE
85	LRC 001	THE VIOLENT FEW (EP, with lyric sheet)................40

LAST STAND
81	Silly Symbol SJP 825	Just A Number/Caviare (p/s) 30

LAST STRAW
78	Solent SS 049	Oh Lady/Fly By Night (p/s) 50

LAST WORD
74	Polydor 2066 429	Keep On Bumping Before You Run Out Of Gas/Funky And Some 8

LAST WORDS
79	Rough Trade RT 022	Animal World/No Music In The World Today (p/s) 8
79	Remand REMAND 2	Todays Kidz/There's Something Wrong (p/s) 6
81	Armageddon ARM 2	THE LAST WORDS (LP) 12

BILL LASWELL
88	Venture VE12	HEAR NO EVIL (LP) 25

LATE OF THE PIER
07	Wow 02	Space And The Woods/Heartbeat, Flicker, Line (7", 500 only)................10

LATE SHOW
78	Decca F 13777	Drop Dead/Ain't Gonna Stamp On His Face (p/s) 15
78	Decca F13788	I Like It/I Wrote A Book 6
79	Decca F 13835	Chains/Screws On You (p/s) 7
79	Decca F 13822	BRISTOL STOMP EP (p/s) 8

YUSEF LATEEF
58	Esquire 32-069	THE SOUNDS OF YUSEF (LP) 40
58	Columbia Clef 33CX 10124	BEFORE DAWN (LP) 50
59	Esquire 32-139	CRY! TENDER (LP) 60
64	Realm RM 228	FABRIC OF JAZZ (LP) 25
64	Transatlantic PR 7319	EASTERN SOUNDS (LP) 30
72	Atlantic K 40359	GENTLE GIANT (LP) 15
73	Prestige PR 24007	YUSEF LATEEF (LP) 15
74	Atlantic K 50041	PART OF THE SEARCH (LP) 15
74	Milestone ML 47009	THE MANY FACES OF YUSEF LATEEF (LP) 12
76	Impulse IMPL 8013	CLUB DATE (LP) 15

LATIMORE
73	President PTLS 1058	S.T. (LP) 20
74	President PTLS 1062	MORE MORE MORE (LP) 20

LATIN QUARTER
89	Arista	SWIMMING AGAINST THE STREAM (CD) 25

MARCEL LATOUR
69	United Artists UP 350058	Women In Love/Kes 8

GENE LATTER
66	Decca F 12364	Just A Minute Or Two/Dream Lover 30
66	Decca F 12397	Mother's Little Helper/Please Come Back To Me Again 25
67	CBS 202483	Something Inside Me Died/Don't Go 8
67	CBS 202655	Always/A Woman Called Sorrow 8
67	CBS 2843	A Little Piece Of Leather/Funny Face Girl 30
67	CBS 2843	A Little Piece Of Leather/Funny Face Girl (DJ copy)................50
67	CBS 2986	With A Child's Heart/Ways 10
68	Direction 58-3245	A Tribute To Otis/Bring Your Love Home 10
68	Spark SRL 1015	My Life Ain't Easy/Angie (as Gene Latter & Detours) 6
69	Spark SRL 1022	Sign On The Dotted Line/I Love You................15
69	Spark SRL 1031	The Old Iron Bell/Holding A Dream 170
69	Parlophone R 5800	Help Me Judy, Help Me/On The Highway 7
69	Parlophone R 5815	Tiger Bay/We Can Make Out 10
70	Parlophone R 5853	Someday You'll Need My Love/Come On Home 6
71	Parlophone R 5896	Catch My Soul/Happiness 10
71	Parlophone R 5913	Sing A Song Of Freedom/Too Busy Thinking About My Baby 10

(see also Detours)

STANLEY LAUDAN
58	Oriole CB 1434	Two Guitars/Blue Shawl................10
57	Oriole CB 1397	Marushka/Bucharest 6

THE LAUGHING APPLE
81	Autonomy AUT 001	HA HA HEE HEE (EP) 8
81	Autonomy AUT 002	Participate!/Wouldn't You? (foldover p/s) 6
82	Essential ESS 001	Precious Feeling/Celebration (p/s) 8

(see also Biff Bang Pow!, Revolving Paint Dream)

LAUGHING GAS
70	RCA RCA 2006	All Shapes And Sizes/Opus No. 1 6

CYNDI LAUPER
84	Portrait WA 4290	Time After Time/I'll Kiss You (picture disc) 6
84	Portrait WA 4620	She Bop/Witness (Cyndi-shaped picture disc) 5

(see also Blue Angel)

LAUREL & HARDY
75	United Artists UAG 29676	THE GOLDEN AGE OF HOLLYWOOD COMEDY (LP, gatefold)................12

LAUREL (AITKEN) & OWEN (GRAY)
62	Blue Beat BB 149	She's Going To Napoli/Have Mercy Mr Percy................10

(see also Laurel Aitken, Owen Gray)

LAURELS
68	RCA Victor RCA 1741	Sunshine Thursday/Threepence A Tune	15
69	RCA Victor RCA 1836	Making It Groovy/Rainmaker	40
70	Pye 7N 17980	Shame Shame/Make Believe	10
71	Pye 45034	The Devil's Well/Underground	60

ROD LAUREN
| 59 | RCA RCA 1165 | If I Had A Girl/No Wonder | 10 |
| 59 | RCA RCA 1165 | If I Had A Girl/No Wonder (78) | 10 |

ZACK LAURENCE (ORCHESTRA)
61	Parlophone R 4802	Teenage Concerto/Saratoga	5
63	Parlophone R 5000	Tempo Seven/Sleeve Shaker	7
66	HMV 7EG 8968	BEATLE CONCERTO (EP)	8

LAURENT
| 71 | Pye 7N 25566 | Sing Sing Barbara/Le Temple Bleu | 8 |

JOHN LAURENZ
55	London HL 8138	Goodbye, Stranger, Goodbye/Red Roses	30
55	London HL 8138	Goodbye, Stranger, Goodbye/Red Roses (78)	10
65	Decca F 12147	99 Times Out Of 100/I Can Feel It	5

LAURI
| 78 | Thelopian THEO1 | If We Can't Have It Neither Can You/Reconciling Trades (p/s) | 6 |

LAURIE
| 66 | Decca F 12347 | He Understands Me/Fools Never Learn | 10 |
| 66 | Decca F 12424 | I Love Onions/I Want Him | 5 |

CY LAURIE JAZZ BAND
| 55 | Esquire 20-037 | CY LAURIE JAZZ BAND (10" LP) | 20 |
| 50s | Esquire 32-008 | CY LAURIE JAZZ BAND (LP) | 15 |

LAURIE SISTERS
| 60 | MGM MGM 1083 | Don't Forget (To Sign Your Name With A Kiss)/I Surrender Dear | 5 |
| 61 | MGM MGM 1128 | Live It Up/Lonesome And Sorry | 5 |

MISS LAVELL
| 65 | Vocalion VP 9236 | Everybody's Got Somebody/The Best Part Of Me | 25 |

JUNE LAVERICK
| 60 | Oriole CB 1537 | Stop/JOHNNY WEBB: Concertino | 6 |

(see also Dickie Henderson & June Laverick, Johnny Webb)

ROGER LA VERN & MICRONS
| 63 | Decca F 11791 | Christmas Stocking/Reindeer Ride | 40 |
| 75 | SRT SRTS/CUS/042 | Sing-A-Long Piano Party Parts 1 & 2 (maxi-single, p/s) | 8 |

(see also Tornados)

BETTY LAVETTE
67	Stateside SS 2015	I Feel Good All Over/Only Your Love Can Save Me	60
67	Stateside SS 2015	I Feel Good All Over/Only Your Love Can Save Me (DJ copy)	75
68	Pama PM 748	Only Your Love Can Save Me/I Feel Good All Over (reissue)	40
70	Polydor 56786	He Made A Woman Out Of Me/Nearer To You	10
72	Mojo 2092 030	Let Me Down Easy/I Feel Good All Over/What I Don't Know Won't Hurt Me	10
73	Atlantic K 10299	Your Turn To Cry/Soul Tambourine	10
78	Atlantic K 11198	Doin' The Best I Can Parts 1 & 2	6

DALIAH LAVI
70	Pye Intl. 7N 25533	Won't You Join Me/Love Is	5
71	Pye Intl. 7N 25582	I'm Leaving/Here's To You	6
70	Pye Intl. NSPL 28141	DALIAH LAVI (LP)	15
72	Pye Int. NSPL 28167	WOULD YOU FOLLOW ME (LP)	12

PETER LAW
| 67 | Major Minor MM 522 | Lingering On/Memories Of You | 6 |

LAW (THE)
| 79 | Smile SR011 | Be My Girl/Dead City Kicks/I Just Want Your Body (500 pressed) | 50 |

DEE LAWAL
| 89 | Play Hard DEC 26 | The D Don't Stop/Stop Skeezin' (12") | 8 |

GASPAR LAWAL
| 80 | Cap | AJOMASE (LP) | 20 |

AZIE LAWRENCE
59	Mezzotone ME 7001/7002	West Indians In England/Jump Up	12
59	Mezzotone ME 7004	Love In Every Land/No Dice	8
60	Starlite ST45 022	West Indians In England/Jump Up (with Carib Serenaders)	15
61	Starlite ST45 041	No Dice/Love In Every Land	10
61	Melodisc M 1563	Jamaica Blues/Come Rumble & Tumble With Me	8
61	Melodisc M 1572	You Didn't Want To Know/I Want To Be In Love	8
61	Blue Beat BB 71	So Far Apart/Palms Of Victory (with Melobeats)	12
64	Blue Beat BB 222	Pempelem/Lovers Understand	400

DIANE LAWRENCE
| 67 | Doctor Bird DB 1075 | I Won't Hang Around Like A Hound Dog/Read It Over | 35 |
| 68 | Jolly JY 005 | Treat Me Nice/I've Been Loving You | 12 |

EDDIE LAWRENCE
| 59 | Coral Q 72361 | The Salesman's Philosopher/Mother Philosopher | 5 |

ELLIOTT LAWRENCE BAND
| 51 | Vogue V 9024 | Sixty-Minute Man/Quick (78) | 10 |
| 58 | Vogue LAE 12057 | PLAYS GERRY MULLIGAN ARRANGEMENTS (LP) | 12 |

GENE LAWRENCE
| 67 | Jump Up JU 505 | Longest Day Meringue/Bachelor Boy | 8 |
| 67 | Jump Up JU 510 | Meringue Triniana/Devil Woman | 8 |

LARRY LAWRENCE (JAMAICA)
| 63 | Island WI 091 | Garden Of Eden/DERRICK MORGAN: Sendin' This Message | 12 |

(see also Larry's Allstars, McBean Scott & Champions)

LARRY LAWRENCE (U.S.)
59	Pye International 7N 25042	Goofin' Off/Bongo Boogie (as Larry Lawrence & Band Of Gold)	10
59	Pye International 7N 25042	Goofin' Off/Bongo Boogie (as Larry Lawrence & Band Of Gold) (78)	10
60	Ember EMB S 106	Squad Car Theme/Jug-A-Roo (with Beatniks, in art p/s)	15
60	Ember EMB S 106	Squad Car Theme/Jug-A-Roo (with Beatniks)	10

LEE LAWRENCE (& CORONETS)
54	Decca F 10285	The Little Mustard Seed/My Love For You	10
54	Decca F 10367	The Story Of Tina/For You My Love	10
54	Decca F 10408	The Things I Didn't Do/You Still Mean The Same To Me	6
55	Decca F 10422	My Own True Love (Tara's Theme)/Beware Now!	6
55	Decca F 10438	Lights Of Paris/A Love Like Ours	6
55	Decca F 10485	Wedding Bells And Silver Horse-Shoes/Will You Be Mine Alone?	7
55	Columbia SCM 5175	Beyond The Stars/Give Me Your Word	6
55	Columbia SCM 5181	My World Stood Still/Don't Worry	6
55	Columbia SCM 5190	More Than A Millionaire/Overnight	7
55	Columbia SCM 5201	Suddenly There's A Valley/Mi Muchacha (Little Girl)	15
56	Columbia SCM 5228	Young And Foolish/Don't Tell Me Not To Love You	7
56	Columbia SCM 5254	We Believe In Love/Welcome To My Heart	7
56	Columbia SCM 5283	Come Back, My Love/Valley Valparaiso	6
56	Columbia DB 3830	From The Candy Store On The Corner/High Upon A Mountain	6
57	Columbia DB 3855	Rock 'n' Roll Opera/Don't Nobody Move	12
57	Columbia DB 3885	Your Love Is My Love/By You, By You, By You	6
57	Columbia DB 3922	Sold To The Man With The Broken Heart/Chapel Of The Roses	6
57	Columbia DB 3981	His Servant/Lonely Ballerina	5
59	Top Rank JAR 175	The Man I Could Be/Be My Love	6
58	Columbia SEG 7780	LEE LAWRENCE (EP)	15
53	Decca LF 1132	PRESENTING LEE LAWRENCE (10" LP)	25

STEVE LAWRENCE
53	Parlophone MSP 6038	Say It Isn't True/This Night (Madalena) (as Steve & Bernie Lawrence)	15
54	Parlophone MSP 6080	Remember Me (You Taught Me To Love)/Too Little Time	15
54	Parlophone MSP 6106	You Can't Hold A Memory In Your Arms/King For A Day	15
55	Vogue Coral Q 72114	Open Up The Gates Of Mercy/My Impression Of Janie	15
56	Vogue Coral Q 72133	Speedo/The Chicken And The Hawk	25
56	Vogue Coral Q 72133	Speedo/The Chicken And The Hawk (78)	10
57	Vogue Coral Q 72228	The Banana Boat Song/If You Would Say You're Mine	10
57	Vogue Coral Q 72243	Party Doll/Pum-Pa-Lum (The Bad Donkey)	20
57	Vogue Coral Q 72264	Fabulous/Can't Wait For The Summer (with Dick Jacobs Band)	20
57	Vogue Coral Q 72281	Fraulein/Blue Rememberin' You	15
57	Vogue Coral Q 72286	Never Mind/Long Before I Knew You	15
58	Coral Q 72304	Geisha Girl/I Don't Know	6
58	Coral Q 72335	Those Nights At The Round Table (with Guinevere)/Stranger In Mexico	6
59	Coral Q 72353	These Things Are Free/I Only Have Eyes For You	7
59	Coral Q 72353	These Things Are Free/I Only Have Eyes For You (78)	10
59	HMV POP 604	Only Love Me (Angelina)/Loving Is A Way Of Living	6
60	HMV POP 689	Pretty Blue Eyes/You're Nearer	6
60	HMV POP 689	Pretty Blue Eyes/You're Nearer (78)	15
60	HMV POP 726	Footsteps/You Don't Know	6
60	HMV POP 726	Footsteps/You Don't Know (78)	10
60	Top Rank JAR 416	Say It Isn't True/My Shawl	6
60	HMV POP 763	Why, Why, Why/You're Everything Wonderful	5
60	London HLT 9166	Girls, Girls, Girls/Little Boy Blue	15
60	HMV POP 795	Going Steady/Come Back, Silly Girl	5
61	HMV POP 914	In Time/Oh How You Lied	6
61	HMV POP 950	Somewhere Along The Way/While There's Still Time	6
62	CBS AAG 127	Go Away Little Girl/If You Love Her Tell Her So	6
63	CBS AAG 150	Poor Little Rich Girl/More	6
63	CBS AAG 166	Walking Proud/House Without Windows	6
60	HMV CLP 1326	SWING SOFTLY WITH ME (LP)	15
60	Top Rank BUY 033	STEVE LAWRENCE (LP)	15
61	HMV CSD 1374	THE STEVE LAWRENCE SOUND (stereo)	12
62	HMV CSD 1404	PORTRAIT OF MY LOVE (stereo)	12

STEVE LAWRENCE & EYDIE GORMÉ
55	Vogue Coral Q 72044	Make Yourself Comfortable/EYDIE GORME: Chain Reaction	8
55	Vogue Coral Q 72085	Besame Mucho/Take A Deep Breath	8
61	London HLT 9290	The Facts Of Life/I'm A Girl, You're A Boy	5
63	CBS AAG 163	I Want To Stay Here/Ain't Love (in p/s)	8
63	CBS AAG 163	I Want To Stay Here/Ain't Love	5

(see also Eydie Gorme)

TERRY LAWRENCE
| 71 | Pye Int. 7N 25558 | Medicine Man/Let Me Be Free | 7 |

VALERIE ANN LAWRENCE
| 65 | DECCA F 12273 | My Love Loves Me/12A Heartache Square | 7 |

VICKI LAWRENCE
| 73 | Stateside SS 2210 | The Night The Lights Went Out In Georgia/Dime A Dance | 7 |

ZACK LAWRENCE
| 73 | Pemini Organisation | ASSASSIN EP (with p/s) | 70 |
| 73 | Pemini Organisation | ASSASSIN EP (without p/s) | 30 |

BILLY (M.) LAWRIE
69	Polydor 56363	Roll Over Beethoven/Come Back Joanna (as Billy M. Lawrie)	25
73	RCA RCA 2439	Rock And Roller/Shalee Shala	6
73	RCA SF 8395	SHIP IMAGINATION (LP, die-cut gatefold sleeve)	25

JULIET LAWSON

72	Sovereign SOV 111	Only A Week Away/Weeds In The Yard	7
72	Sovereign SVNA 7257	BOO (LP, textured gatefold sleeve)	200

(see also Trees)

SHIRLEY LAWSON
68	Soul City SC 108	The Star/One More Chance	150

LAWSON-HAGGART ROCKIN' BAND
59	Brunswick OE 9451	BOPPING AT THE HOP (EP)	30
53	Brunswick LA 8576	JELLY ROLL'S JAZZ (10" LP)	15
53	Brunswick LA 8580	BLUES ON THE RIVER (10" LP)	18
53	Brunswick LA 8593	KING OLIVER'S JAZZ (10" LP)	15
54	Brunswick LA 8635	RAGTIME JAMBOREE (10" LP)	15
54	Brunswick LA 8639	WINDY CITY JAZZ (10" LP)	15
55	Brunswick LA 8703	SOUTH OF THE MASON-DIXON LINE (10" LP)	15
59	Brunswick STA 3010	BOPPING AT THE HOP (LP)	60

JOHN LAWTON FEATURING ROGER GLOVER & GUESTS
75	Purple PUR 128	Little Chalk Blue/RONNIE DIO: Sitting In A Dream	10

(see also Roger Glover, Ronnie Dio, Deep Purple, Uriah Heep, Lucifer's Friend)

LOU LAWTON
67	Ember EMB S 232	Doin' The Philly Dog/I Am Searching	30
68	Speciality SPE 1005	I'm Just A Fool/Wrapped In A Dream	30

LAXTON & OLIVER
69	Blue Cat BS 168	Wickeder/Stay In My Arms	20

OSSIE LAYNE
65	R&B MRB 5006	Come Back/Never Answer That 'Phone	35

EDDIE LAYTON
58	Mercury 7MT 221	Over The Waves/Bright Lights Over Brussels	5
59	Mercury AMT 1064	Duck Walk/Doodles	10

PAUL LAYTON
68	Paradox PAR 45901	Mister Mister/Sing Sadman Sing (p/s)	25

KEN LAZ(A)RUS (& CREW)
65	Island WI 220	Funny (as Ken Lazrus & Byron Lee Orchestra)/ BYRON LEE ORCHESTRA: Walk Like A Dragon	15
70	London HLJ 10301	Monkey Man/Bongo Nyah	5
71	Explosion EX 2056	Girl/TOMORROW'S CHILDREN: Sister Big Stuff	8
72	Explosion EX 2064	Hail The Man/Where Do I Go	7
72	London HLH 10379	Hail The Man/Where I Go	6
70	London HA-J 8412	REGGAE SCORCHER (LP, unissued)	0
70	London LGJ/ZGJ 102	REGGAE SCORCHER (LP)	12
70	London ZGJ 107	REGGAE - GREATEST HITS VOL. 1 (LP)	20

PETER LAZONBY
96	Brainiak BRAINK 40R	Wavespeech (12")	30

LAZY LATINS
67	Morgan MR 110 P	LAZY LATIN (LP)	15

LAZY SMOKE
80s	Heyoka	CORRIDOR OF FACES (LP, reissue of U.S. LP)	15

LCD SOUNDSYSTEM
05	DFA DFAEMI2138LP	LCD SOUNDSYSTEM (2xLP)	25
07	EMI 0946 3 85114 1 0	SOUND OF SILVER (2xLP)	20

BARBARA LEA
56	London HB-U 1058	A WOMAN IN LOVE (10" LP)	20
56	Esquire 32/043	NOBODY ELSE BUT ME (LP)	20
57	Esquire 32/063	IN LOVE (LP)	20

JIMMY LEA
85	Trojan KANE 001	Citizen Kane/Poland (p/s)	15

(see also Slade)

LEADBELLY (HUDDIE LEDBETTER)

78s
50	Capitol CL 13282	Eagle Rock Rag/Backwater Blues	20
51	Melodisc 1140	How Long/Good Morning Blues	20
51	Melodisc 1151	Goodnight Irene/Ain't You Glad	20
51	Melodisc 1187	On A Monday/John Henry	20
54	Jazz Collector L 108	New Black Snake Moan/Fore Day Worry Blues	20
55	Jazz Collector L 124	Pig Meat Papa/Becky Beem	20
55	HMV MH 190	Alabama Bound/Pick A Bale Of Cotton	20

EPs
56	Melodisc EPM7 63	HOW LONG BLUES	10
58	Melodisc EPM7 77	LEADBELLY	10
58	Melodisc EPM7 82	SEE SEE RIDER	10
59	Melodisc EPM7 87	PARTY PLAYS AND SONGS	10
59	RCA RCX 146	ROCK ISLAND LINE	10
61	Capitol EAP1 1821	HUDDIE LEDBETTER'S BEST NO. 1	10
61	Capitol EAP4 1821	HUDDIE LEDBETTER'S BEST NO. 2	10
61	Capitol EAP1 20111	LEADBELLY	10
61	Storyville SEP 337	LEADBELLY	10
62	Storyville SEP 387	STORYVILLE BLUES ANTHOLOGY VOL. 7	15

ALBUMS
53	Capitol LC 6597	LEADBELLY SINGS CLASSICS IN JAZZ (10")	40
57	Melodisc MLP 511	LEADBELLY VOL. 1 (10", green & silver labels)	25
57	Melodisc MLP 512	LEADBELLY VOL. 2 (10", green & silver labels)	25

58	Melodisc MLP 515	LEADBELLY VOL. 3 (10", green & silver labels)	25
58	Melodisc MLP 517	PLAYS PARTY SONGS (10", green & silver labels)	25
58	Melodisc MLP 12-107	THE SAGA OF LEADBELLY (green & silver or blue & black labels)	20
59	Melodisc MLP 12-113	LEADBELLY'S LAST SESSIONS VOLUME 2 PART 1	20
59	Melodisc MLP 12-114	LEADBELLY'S LAST SESSIONS VOLUME 2 PART 2	20
62	Storyville SLP 124	A DEMON OF A MAN - BLUES ANTHOLOGY	20
63	Storyville SLP 139	LEADBELLY 2 - T.B. BLUES	20
63	Capitol T 1821	HIS GUITAR, HIS VOICE, HIS PIANO: HUDDIE LEDBETTER'S BEST	15
63	RCA Victor RD 7567	GOOD MORNING BLUES	20
65	Verve (S)VLP 5002	TAKE THIS HAMMER	20
66	Elektra EKL 301/2	THE LIBRARY OF CONGRESS RECORDINGS (3-LP)	30
67	Verve (S)VLP 5011	KEEP YOUR HANDS OFF HER	15
69	Xtra XTRA 1046	LEADBELLY SINGS FOLK SONGS	18
69	Xtra XTRA 1126	SHOUT ON	15

LEADBELLY & BLIND LEMON JEFFERSON
| 61 | Jazz Collector JEL 124 | THE MALE BLUES VOLUME 8 (EP) | 10 |

(see also Blind Lemon Jefferson)

HARRY LEADER BAND
| 65 | Parlophone R 5386 | Dragon Fly/Rush Hour | 5 |

LEADERBEATS
| 60 | Top Rank JAR 405 | Dance, Dance, Dance/Washington Square | 12 |

LEADERS (JAMAICA)
| 68 | Amalgamated AMG 804 | Tit For Tat (actually by Lynn Taitt & Jets)/MARVETTS: You Take Too Long | 25 |

(see also Pioneers, Stranger Cole, Versatiles)

LEADERS (U.K.)
| 65 | Fontana TF 602 | Night People/Love Will Find A Way | 10 |

LEADING FIGURES
| 67 | Deram DML/SML 1006 | OSCILLATION 67! (LP) | 40 |
| 67 | Ace Of Clubs SCL 1225 | SOUND AND MOVEMENT (LP) | 40 |

(see also Jon Lord, Deep Purple)

LEAF HOUND
| 71 | Decca SKL-R 5094 | GROWERS OF MUSHROOM (LP) | 2500 |

(see also Brunning Sunflower Blues Band, Black Cat Bones, Atomic Rooster, Cactus)

LEAGUE
| 67 | President PT 167 | Nothing On/Hey Conductor | 25 |

LEAGUE OF GENTLEMEN (1)
| 65 | Columbia DB 7666 | Each Little Falling Tear/And I Do Now | 70 |
| 66 | Planet PLF 109 | How Can You Tell/How Do They Know (with Planet company sleeve) | 70 |

LEAGUE OF GENTLEMEN (2)
| 80 | EG/Virgin EGEDS 1 | Heptaparaparshinokh/Marriagemuzic | 6 |

(see also Giles Giles & Fripp, Brain)

LEAH
| 73 | GM GMS 10 | Arise Sir Henry/Uptight Basil | 7 |

(see also Pete Dello, Red Herring)

JOE LEAHY (ORCHESTRA)
55	Parlophone MSP 6149	Desiree/Milano	5
55	Parlophone MSP 6168	Green Fire/Secretly Mine	5
57	London HBZ 1072	LOVELY LADY (10" LP)	12

JOE LEAHY
| 65 | Capitol CL 15417 | Life/Pink Powder Puff | 8 |

MIKE LEANDER ORCHESTRA
| 69 | MCA MUPS 383 | MIGRATION (LP) | 12 |

VICKY LEANDROS
| 72 | Philips 6000 025 | I Am/Love Tell Me Where Is Your Home | 8 |
| 71 | Philips 6303 019 | I AM VICKY LEANDROS (LP) | 12 |

(see also Vicky)

BOB LEAPER
65	Pye 7N 15700	High Wire (Theme From 'Danger Man')/The Lost World	40
64	Decca LK 4639	BIG BAND, BEATLE SONGS (LP)	20
71	Pye NSLP 18339	TRY THIS ONE FOR SIZE (LP)	12

LEAPERS CREEPERS SLEEPERS
| 66 | Island WI 275 | Precious Words/Ba Boo | 30 |

KEVIN 'KING' LEAR
67	Polydor 56203	Count Me Out/Pretty Woman	40
68	Page One POF 087	Power Of Love/Mr. Pearly	20
68	Page One POF 109	Cry Me A River/Shoe Shine Sam	20
69	Page One POF 132	The Snake/Man In The Funnies	20

TIMOTHY LEARY MEETS THE GRID
| 90 | Evolution EVO 1 | Origins Of Dance (Electronic Future Mix)/(Hi-Tec Pagan Mix) (12") | 10 |

(see also the Grid)

LEATHERCOATED MINDS
| 67 | Fontana (S)TL 5412 | A TRIP DOWN THE SUNSET STRIP (LP) | 80 |

(see also J.J. Cale)

LEATHERFACE
90	Roughneck HYPE 1	Razor Blades And Asprin/Colorado Joe, Leningrad Vlad/Post War Product Of A Fat Man's Wallet	15
91	Roughneck HYPE 14	I Want The Moon/You Are My Sunshine/Dreaming	10
92	Clawfist XPIG 15	Hops And Barley/Discipline/A Public House/Not Superstitious/James Whale (split release with Wat Tyler 2 x 7")	10

90	Meantime COXEP 3	BEERPIG (EP, with insert) 30
90	Roughneck HYPE 6T	SMOKEY JOE (12" EP) 10
91	Roughneck HYPE 9T	NOT SUPERSTITIOUS (12" EP) 10
92	Roughneck HYPE 17T	COMPACT AND BIJOU (10" EP) 10
89	Meantime COX 017	CHERRY KNOWLE (LP) 20
90	Roughneck NECKLP 1	FILL YOUR BOOTS (LP, with insert) 25
91	Roughneck NECKLP 5	MUSH (LP, inner) 50
93	Roughneck NECKLP 11	MINX (LP) 30
93	Roughneck NECK 11LPS	MINX (LP, with bonus 7" Can't Help Falling In Love/Dreaming (HYPE 24) 40

(see also Frankie Stubbs)

LEATHERHEAD

74	Philips 6006 371	Gimme Your Money Please/Epitaph (die-cut 'Leatherhead' sleeve) 20

LEATHER NUN

79	Industrial IR 0006	SLOW DEATH (EP) 20
84	Subterranean SUB 40	Prime Mover/F.F.A. (p/s) 5

LEA VALLEY SKIFFLE GROUP

58	Esquire EP 163	LEA VALLEY SKIFFLE GROUP (EP) 40

LEAVES

66	Fontana TF 713	Hey Joe/Funny Little World 40

OTIS LEAVILL(E)

70	Atlantic 2091 015	I Love You/I Need You 8
70	Atlantic 2091 035	Love Uprising/Glad I Met You 8
71	Atlantic 2091 160	There's Nothing Better/I'm So Jealous 8

LE CHEILE

78	Inchecronin INC 7423	AIRIS (LP) 12
78	Inchecronin INC 7424	LORD MAYO (LP) 12

LECUONDA CUBAN BOYS

55	Columbia 33S 1075	BENEATH THE CUBAN MOON (10" LP) 15

JOHN LEDINGHAM

68	Pye 7N 17488	Love Is A Toy/Thank You Mrs. Gilbert 6

(see also Jonathan Kelly)

LED ZEPPELIN

SINGLES

69	Atlantic 584 268	Good Times, Bad Times (unissued, 1-sided EMIdisc and LDC acetates only) 2000
69	Atlantic 584 269	Communication Breakdown/Good Times, Bad Times (unissued, promo only) 700
69	Atlantic/Emidisc	Whole Lotta Love (Edit)/Whole Lotta Love (Edit) (Acetate) 2000
69	Atlantic 584 309	Whole Lotta Love (Edit)/Livin' Lovin' Maid (She's A Woman) (withdrawn, large centre hole, clean label or "5th Dec 1969" stamp on label) 600
69	Atlantic 584 309	Whole Lotta Love (Edit)/Livin' Lovin' Maid (She's A Woman) (withdrawn, solid centre with small centre hole, 1 copy known) 1500
69	Atlantic 584 309	Whole Lotta Love (Edit)/Living Loving Maid (She's A Woman) (withdrawn, large centre hole, mispressing with Living Loving Maid labels on both sides) 600
70	Emidisc	Immigrant Song (unissued one sided acetate, scheduled to be released as Atlantic 2091 043 on 27th November 1970) 3000
73	Trident	D'Yer Mak'er (Unissued one sided acetate) 1200
73	Atlantic K 10296	D'Yer Mak'er/Over The Hills And Far Away (unreleased, promo only) 350
75	Swan Song DC 1	Trampled Underfoot/Black Country Woman (white label test pressing) 350
75	Swan Song DC 1	Trampled Underfoot/Black Country Woman (Red label test pressing) 500
75	Swan Song SSK 19403	Trampled underfoot/Black Country Woman (withdrawn first pressing) 150
75	Swan Song DC 1	Trampled Underfoot/Black Country Woman (Limited edition dealer incentive promo, die-cut title sleeve) 25
75	Swan Song SSK 19403	Trampled Underfoot/Black Country Woman (push mispressed cat. no.) 150
79	Swan Song SSK 19421	Wearing And Tearing/Darlene (cancelled Knebworth 45, existence unconfirmed) 0
90	Atlantic LZ 3	Stairway To Heaven/Whole Lotta Love (white label test pressing) 350
90	Atlantic LZ 2	Stairway To Heaven/Immigrant Song/Whole Lotta Love/ Good Times Bad Times (10", p/s, promo only) 30
90	Atlantic LZ 2	Stairway To Heaven/Immigrant Song/Whole Lotta Love/ Good Times Bad Times (10", test pressing, white labels) 350
90	Atlantic CD LZ 1	Stairway To Heaven/Immigrant Song/Whole Lotta Love/ Good Times Bad Times (CD, promo only, in Zeppelin-design long box) 30
90	Atlantic LZ 3	Stairway To Heaven/Whole Lotta Love (with East West Records internal memo, 150 copies only, promo) 150
90	Atlantic LZ 3 LC	Stairway To Heaven/Whole Lotta Love (jukebox single, push-out centre) 30
97	Atlantic PRCD 923	BBC SESSIONS SAMPLER: The Girl I Love/Whole Lotta Love/ Communication Breakdown (CD, promo only) 20
97	Atlantic AT 0031CD	Whole Lotta Love (Edit)/Baby Come On Home/Travelling Riverside Blues (CD, numbered digipak) 10
97	Atlantic AT 0031LC	Whole Lotta Love (Edit)/Whole Lotta Love (Edit) (jukebox issue, with pushout centre) 15
03	Warner Vision PR 03945	What Is And What Should Never Be/In My Time Of Dying/Rock And Roll (DVD, promo sampler) 25

ALBUMS

69	Atlantic 588 171	LED ZEPPELIN (LP, 1st pressing, red/maroon label, turquoise sleeve lettering, "Superhype" publishing credit) 1500
69	Atlantic 588 171	LED ZEPPELIN (LP, 2nd pressing, red/maroon label, orange sleeve lettering, "Warner Bros" publishing credit) 150
69	Atlantic 588 171	LED ZEPPELIN (LP, 2nd pressing, red/maroon label, orange sleeve lettering, "Superhype" publishing credit) 120
69	Atlantic 588 198	LED ZEPPELIN II (LP, 1st pressing, red/maroon label, with "Living Loving Wreck" miscredit, light brown gatefold sleeve with blue-green edge) 400
69	Atlantic 588 198	LED ZEPPELIN II (LP, 1st pressing, red/maroon label, with "The Lemon Song" credit, light brown gatefold sleeve with blue-green edge) 80
70	Atlantic 588 198	LED ZEPPELIN II (LP, light brown sleeve, 2nd pressing, credits "Killing Floor" instead of "The Lemon Song" on label) 40
70	Atlantic Deluxe 2401 002	LED ZEPPELIN III (LP, first pressing, red/maroon label, gatefold rotating-wheel sleeve, 'Do What Thou Wilt' in run-off side 1, "Produced by Jimmy Page" and "Executive Producer Peter Grant" on top of label. Catalogue number "2401002" on label) 200
70	Atlantic Deluxe 2401 002	LED ZEPPELIN III (LP, second pressing, red/maroon label, gatefold rotating-wheel sleeve, no Peter Grant Credit. Catalogue number 2401 002 on label) 50

71	Atlantic Deluxe 2401 012	LED ZEPPELIN IV (FOUR SYMBOLS) (LP, gatefold sleeve, red/maroon label with 2 'stickers' covering Peter Grant credit and also revised publishing details to "Kinney Music Ltd/Superhype Music Inc.") 300
71	Atlantic Deluxe 2401 012	LED ZEPPELIN IV (FOUR SYMBOLS) (LP, gatefold sleeve, red/maroon label with Peter Grant credit, 'Led Zeppelin' at bottom) 250
71	Atlantic Deluxe 2401 012	LED ZEPPELIN IV (FOUR SYMBOLS) (LP, gatefold sleeve, red/maroon label without Peter Grant credit, 'Led Zeppelin' at top) 70
73	Atlantic K 50014	HOUSES OF THE HOLY (LP, original pressing, unlaminated sleeve with 'obi' around the sleeve, textured inner sleeve with thumb notch, matrix A2/B2) 100
75	Swan Song SSK 89400	PHYSICAL GRAFFITI (2-LP, First pressing MATRIXES: SSK89400 A1/B5/C1/D1 (There are some with A1/B4/C1/D1). (Sleeve must have "Swan Song/484 Kings Road, London SW10", inner wraparound on thick card with a matt finish and a spine at the bottom, inner sleeves on thick card, labels have "Made in UK" at 9 "o" clock and NO Warners logo at 3 "o" clock. die-cut sleeve, inner sleeve, folded insert) 50
76	Swan Song SSK 59402	PRESENCE (LP, shrinkwrapped gatefold sleeve) 18
76	Swan Song SSK 59402	THE SONG REMAINS THE SAME (2-LP, textured gatefold sleeve with booklet) 30
78	Atlantic K 50008	LED ZEPPELIN IV (FOUR SYMBOLS) (LP, purple vinyl testpressing or mispressing of lilac vinyl reissue) 250
78	Atlantic K 50008	LED ZEPPELIN IV (FOUR SYMBOLS) (LP, lilac vinyl reissue) 50
79	Swan Song SSK 59410 A-F	IN THROUGH THE OUT DOOR (LP, 6 different covers with inner sleeves; set labelled 'A' to 'F', each in individual paper outer; available separately with paper outer £25 each) 350
88	Atlantic K 50008/C 88 1-4	FOUR SYMBOLS (LP, HMV 'Classic Collection' box set, with booklet, numbered) 25
88	Atlantic 250008/C 88 1-4	FOUR SYMBOLS (CD, HMV 'Classic Collection' box set, with booklet, numbered) 30
90	Atlantic ZEP 1	REMASTERS (3-LP, triple gatefold sleeve) 30
90	Atlantic 7567 82144-1	LED ZEPPELIN (5-LP, box set) 60
97	Atlantic 7567 83061-1	BBC SESSIONS (4-LP, box set) 80
99	Atlantic 7567 83268-1	EARLY DAYS - THE BEST OF LED ZEPPELIN VOLUME 1 (LP) 15
00	Atlantic 7567 83278-1	LATTER DAYS - THE BEST OF LED ZEPPELIN VOLUME 2 (LP) 25
08	Rhino/Atlantic/Swan Song 8122799489	SOUNDTRACK FROM 'THE SONG REMAINS THE SAME' (4-LP, 180gm expanded edition) 50
08	Rhino/Atlantic/Swan Song 8122799489	SOUNDTRACK FROM 'THE SONG REMAINS THE SAME' (4-LP 180 gm expanded edition, white vinyl, 200 only) 600
08	Rhino/Atlantic/Swan Song 8122799513	MOTHERSHIP (4-LP, 180gm vinyl) 70

(see also Jimmy Page, Robert Plant, John Paul Jones, Dansette Damage, Listen, Family Dogg, Ian Whitcomb, P.J. Proby, Lord Sutch,Yardbirds)

ALVIN LEE

74	Chrysalis CHS 2020	The World Is Changing/Riffin' (with Myron Le Fevre) 6
73	Chrysalis CHR 1054	ON THE ROAD TO FREEDOM (LP, with Myron Le Fevre) 20
75	Chrysalis CHR 1094	PUMP IRON! (LP) 12
78	Chrysalis CHR 1190	LET IT ROCK (LP) 12

(see also Ten Years After)

LEE & CLARENDONIANS

72	Green Door GD 4038	Night Owl/Night Owl Version 10

LEE (PERRY) & JIMMY (RILEY)

75	Dip DL 5075	Rasta Train/Yagga Yagga 18

LEE (PERRY) & JUNIOR (BYLES)

75	Dip DL 5060	Dreader Locks/Militant Rock 12

LEE & PAUL

59	Philips PB 912	The Chick/Valentina, My Valentina 7

ARTHUR LEE

72	A&M AMLS 64356	VINDICATOR (LP) 20

(see also Love)

BENNY LEE (& KEN-TONES)

56	Parlophone MSP 6214	Love Plays The Strings Of My Banjo (with Ken-Tones)/Born To Sing The Blues 6
56	Parlophone MSP 6252	Sweet Heartaches/How Long Has This Been Going On? 6
56	Parlophone R 4245	Rock 'N' Rollin' Santa Claus/Life Was Made For Livin' (with Ken-Tones) 20

(see also Ken-Tones)

BRENDA LEE

78s

56	Brunswick 05628	I'm Gonna Lasso Santa Claus/Christy Christmas (as Little Brenda Lee) 40
57	Brunswick 05685	Dynamite/Love You Til I Die 40
57	Brunswick 05720	Ain't That Love/One Teenager To Another..50
58	Brunswick 05755	Ring-A-My-Phone/Little Jonah (Rock On Your Little Steel Guitar)..............................50
59	Brunswick 05780	Bill Bailey, Won't You Please Come Home/Hummin' The Blues Over You 40
60	Brunswick 05819	Sweet Nuthin's/Weep No More My Baby...70

SINGLES

56	Brunswick 05628	I'm Gonna Lasso Santa Claus/Christy Christmas (triangular centre) 200
57	Brunswick 05685	Dynamite/Love You Til I Die (with Anita Kerr Singers, triangular centre) 150
57	Brunswick 05720	Ain't That Love/One Teenager To Another (w/ Anita Kerr Singers, tri-centre) 150
58	Brunswick 05755	Ring-A-My-Phone/Little Jonah (Rock On Your Little Steel Guitar) (tri-centre)...............150
58	Decca BM 31186	Fairyland/One Step At A Time (export issue, triangular centre) 50
59	Brunswick 05780	Bill Bailey, Won't You Please Come Home/Hummin' The Blues Over You (triangular centre)...20
59	Brunswick 05780	Bill Bailey, Won't You Please Come Home/Hummin' The Blues Over You (round centre) 10
60	Brunswick 05819	Sweet Nuthin's/Weep No More My Baby (round centre) 10
60	Brunswick 05823	Let's Jump The Broomstick/Rock-A-Bye Baby Blues...10
60	Brunswick 05833	I'm Sorry/That's All You Gotta Do 5
60	Brunswick 05839	I Want To Be Wanted/Just A Little 5
61	Brunswick 05847	Emotions/I'm Learning About Love 8
61	Brunswick 05854	Dum Dum/Eventually 6
62	Brunswick 05864	Break It To Me Gently/So Deep 8
62	Brunswick 05867	Speak To Me Pretty/Lover, Come Back To Me 6
62	Brunswick 05871	Here Comes That Feeling/Everybody Loves Me But You 6
62	Brunswick 05876	It Started All Over Again/Heart In Hand 6
62	Brunswick 05880	Rockin' Around The Christmas Tree/Papa Noel 7
63	Brunswick 05886	Losing You/He's So Heavenly 6
63	Brunswick 05896	Sweet Impossible You/The Grass Is Greener..5
64	Brunswick 05903	Think/The Waiting Game 5

MINT VALUE £

64	Brunswick 05915	Is It True/What'd I Say	10
66	Brunswick 05957	Too Little Time/Time And Time Again	35
66	Brunswick 05963	Ain't Gonna Cry No More/It Takes One To Know One	10
66	Brunswick 05967	Coming On Strong/You Keep Coming Back To Me	15
67	Brunswick 05970	Ride, Ride, Ride/Lonely People Do Foolish Things	5
67	Brunswick 05976	Where's The Melody?/Born To Be By Your Side	20
68	Decca AD 1003	That's All Right/Baby, Won't You Please Come Home (export issue)	5

EPs

59	Brunswick OE 9462	ROCK THE BOP (green p/s & tri-centre)	100
59	Brunswick OE 9462	ROCK THE BOP (blue p/s & round centre)	50
62	Brunswick OE 9482	PRETEND	30
62	Brunswick OE 9488	SPEAK TO ME PRETTY	30
63	Brunswick OE 9492	ALL ALONE AM I	15
64	Brunswick OE 9499	BRENDA LEE'S TRIBUTE TO AL JOLSON	15
65	Brunswick OE 9510	FOUR FROM '64	20

ALBUMS

59	Brunswick LAT 8319	GRANDMA WHAT GREAT SONGS YOU SANG	50
60	Brunswick LAT 8347	MISS DYNAMITE	40
61	Brunswick LAT 8360	THIS IS BRENDA	40
61	Brunswick STA 3044	EMOTIONS (stereo)	15
61	Brunswick STA 3048	ALL THE WAY (stereo)	15
61	Brunswick STA 3056	SINCERELY (stereo)	15
62	Brunswick LAT/STA 8516	BRENDA, THAT'S ALL (mono/stereo)	18
65	Brunswick LAT/STA 8603	TOP TEEN HITS (mono/stereo)	15

BUNNY LEE ALLSTARS

70	Camel CA39	Three Stooge/Isle Of Love	20
70	Pama PM 803	Annie Pama/Mr Magoo	12
71	Smash SMA 2304	Stanley (Parts 1 & 2) (as Bunnie Lee Allstars)	10
78	Jamaica Sound JS 013	SUPER DUB DISCO STYLE (LP, with the Aggrovators)	50

(see also Lloyd Charmers, Sonny Binns & Rudies, Copy Cats, John Holt, Lloyd & Doreen, Delroy Wilson)

BYRON LEE & DRAGONAIR(E)S

60	Blue Beat B 2	Dumplin's/Kissin' Gal (vocal: Buddy Davidson) (white label, blue print)	20
60	Blue Beat BB 2	Dumplin's/Kissin' Gal (vocal: Buddy Davidson) (2nd pressing, blue label, silver print)	15
61	Blue Beat BB 28	Mash! Mr. Lee/Help Me Forget (vocal: Keith Lyn)	15
61	Starlite ST45 045	Joy Ride/Over The Rainbow	15
64	Parlophone R 5124	River Bank/Musical Communion	15
64	Parlophone R 5125	Sour Apples/Hanging Up My Heart	15
64	Parlophone R 5140	Sammy Dead/Say Bye Bye (both actually by Eric Morris with Byron Lee)	15
64	Parlophone R 5177	Beautiful Garden/Too Late	15
64	Parlophone R 5182	Come Back/Jamaica Ska	18
64	MGM MGM 1256	Night Train From Jamaica/Ska Dee Wah (with Danny Davis)	20
66	Doctor Bird DB 1003	Sloopy/Gold Finger	20
67	Pyramid PYR 6015	Sloopy/Gold Finger (reissue)	10
68	Trojan TR 624	Soul Limbo/The Whistling Song	8
68	Trojan TR 631	Mr Walker/Sunset Jump Up	8
69	Major Minor MM 615	Every Day Will Be Like A Holiday/Oh What A Feeling	5
70	Trojan TR 7731	Squeeze Up (Parts 1 & 2)	12
70	Trojan TR 7736	Birth Control/Love At First Sight	6
70	Trojan TR 7747	Bond In Bliss/Musical Scorcher	6
70	Trojan TR 7761	Julianne/We Five	5
70	Duke DU 39	Elizabethan Reggae/Soul Serenade	10
70	Duke DU 91	Cashbox/WINSTON WRIGHT: Strolling Thru' The Park	6
71	Dynamic DYN 405	Hitching A Ride/Hitching A Ride Version	8
71	Dynamic DYN 409	My Sweet Lord/Shock Attack	7
71	Dynamic DYN 414	Way Back Home/Version	6
72	Dynamic DYN 435	Make It Reggae/DENNIS ALCAPONE: Go Johnny Go	8
73	Dragon DRA 1008	In The Mood/Black On	6
65	Atlantic AET 6014	SKA TIME (EP, as Byron Lee Ska Kings)	35
64	Island ILP 905	CARIBBEAN JOY RIDE (LP)	35
66	Atlantic 587018	JUMP UP (LP)	35
69	Trojan TTL 5	ROCKSTEADY EXPLOSION (LP)	40
69	Major Minor SMLP 53	BYRON LEE & THE DRAGONAIRES (LP)	20
70	Trojan TRLS 18	REGGAE WITH BYRON LEE (LP)	18
73	Dragon DRLS 5001	REGGAE ROUND THE WORLD (LP)	12

(see also Mighty Avengers, Ken Lazarus, Hopeton Lewis, Danny Davis Orchestra, Good Guys, Neville Hinds, Hubcaps & Wheels, Mighty Sparrow, Blues Busters)

LITTLE MR. LEE & CHEROKEES

| 66 | Vocalion VP 9268 | Young Lover/I Don't Want To Go | 40 |

CHRISTOPHER LEE

| 74 | Studio Two TWOA 5001 | HAMMER PRESENTS DRACULA (LP, gatefold sleeve) | 12 |
| 74 | Studio Two TWOA Q4 5001 | HAMMER PRESENTS DRACULA (LP, gatefold sleeve, quadrophonic) | 15 |

CURTIS LEE

60	Top Rank JAR 317	With All My Heart (I Love You)/Pure Love	60
61	London HLX 9313	Pledge Of Love/Then I'll Know	25
61	London HLX 9397	Pretty Little Angel Eyes/Gee How I Wish You Were Here	20
61	London HLX 9445	Under The Moon Of Love/Beverly Jean	20
62	London HLX 9533	A Night At Daddy Gee's/Just Another Fool	20
67	CBS 2717	Get My Bag/Everybody's Going Wild (as Curtis Lee & K.C.P.s)	40
67	CBS 2717	Get My Bag/Everybody's Going Wild (as Curtis Lee & K.C.P.s) (DJ copy)	70
72	Stateside SS 2208	Under The Moon Of Love/Beverly Jean (reissue)	6

DAVE LEE (& STAGGERLEES)

63	Decca F 11600	Take Four/Five To Four On	15
63	Oriole CB 1864	Dance Dance Dance/Love Me (as Dave Lee & Staggerlees)	15
63	Oriole CB 1907	Sweet & Lovely/Forever And Always (as Dave Lee & Staggerlees)	15
66	Fontana TF 723	Adam Adamant/Georgie's Theme (as Dave Lee & His Orchestra)	20

DAVE LEE
66	Colpix PXL 550	OUR MAN CRICHTON (LP, with Tubby Hayes)	80

(see also Tubby Hayes)

DAVID H. LEE
65	Pye 7N 15809	Heaven With No Angel	8
69	Morgan MR 1	Johnny's Eyes/You're The Only One	7

DEBBIE LEE
64	Decca F 11931	For Every Man There's A Woman/Can't You See	8

DEREK LEE
66	Parlophone R 5468	Girl/You've Done Something To My Heart	10

DICK LEE
53	Columbia SCM 5066	All I Want Is A Chance/The Show Is Ended	10
53	Columbia SCM 5078	I Thought You Might Be Lonely/Happy Bells	10
54	Columbia SCM 5094	The Book/(Stay In My Arms)Cinderella	12

DICKIE/DICKEY LEE
59	MGM MGM 1013	A Penny A Kiss - A Penny A Hug/Bermuda (as Dick Lee)	7
62	Mercury AMT 1190	Patches/More Or Less	15
62	Mercury AMT 1196	I Saw Linda Yesterday/The Girl I Can't Forget	15
62	Mercury AMT 1200	Don't Wanna Think About Paula/Just A Friend	10
65	Stateside SS 433	Laurie (Strange Things Happen)/Party Doll (as Dickey Lee)	10
65	Stateside SS 464	The Girl From Peyton Place/A Girl I Used To Know (as Dickey Lee)	7

DINAH LEE
65	Aladdin WI 606	I'll Forgive You Then Forget You/Nitty Gritty	30
65	Aladdin WI 608	I Can't Believe What You Say/Pushin' A Good Thing Too Far	40

DON (TONY) LEE
68	Big Shot BI 504	It's Reggae Time (as Don Tony Lee)/ERROL DUNKLEY: The Clamp Is On	30
68	Doctor Bird DB 1106	Lee's Special (as Don Tony Lee)/LLOYD & GROOVERS: My Heart And Soul	30
68	Island WI 3160	It's Reggae Time (as D. Tony Lee)/ERROL DUNKLEY: The Clamp Is On	30
69	Unity UN 519	Peyton Place/Red Gal In The Ring (as Don Tony Lee)	12
70	Gas 163	Work Out/Too Long (as Donald Lee)	25

EDNA LEE
68	President PT 175	I Really Think I'm Crying 'Cause I Love You/Don't Let My Friends See What You Do	7

(FREDDIE) 'FINGERS' LEE (& UPPER HAND)
65	Fontana TF 619	The Friendly Undertaker/Little Bit More (as 'Fingers' Lee)	25
66	Fontana TF 655	I'm Gonna Buy Me A Dog/I Can't Drive (as 'Fingers' Lee)	40
66	Columbia DB 8002	Bossy Boss/Don't Run Away (as Fingers Lee & Upper Hand)	40
77	Beeb 020	Down On the Farm/My Bucket's Got A Hole In It	8

(see also At Last The 1958 Rock & Roll Show)

GEORGE LEE (& MUSIC DOCTORS)
69	Downtown DT 443	Talking Boss/Jungle Fever (solo)	8
70	J-Dan JDN 4407	Johnny Dollar/Tough Of Poison (with Music Doctors)	8

(see also Desmond Riley)

HUBERT LEE
73	Ackee ACK 504	I Love Verona/Version	5
73	Downtown DT 498	Something On Your Mind/IMPACT ALL STARS: Mind Version	8
73	Green Door GD 4050	High School Dance/PRINCE TONY'S ALL STARS: Version	5
74	Ackee ACK 524	Tonight Will You Still Love Me/IMPACT ALL STARS: Version	6

JACKIE LEE (U.K.) (FEMALE)
55	Decca F 10550	I Was Wrong/For As Long As I Live	12
65	Decca F 12068	I Cry Alone/Cause I Love Him	12
65	Columbia DB 7685	Lonely Clown/Love Is Gone	12
66	Columbia DB 7860	I Know, Know, Know I'll Never Love/So Love Me	10
66	Columbia DB 8052	The Town I Live In/You Too	12
67	Decca F 12663	Born To Lose/Saying Goodbye	10
69	Pye 7N 17829	Love Is A Gamble/Something Borrowed, Something Blue	10
70	Pye 7N 45003	Rupert/Going To The Circus	6

(see also Jacky, Jackie Lee & Raindrops, Emma Rede)

JACKIE LEE & RAINDROPS (U.K.) (FEMALE)
62	Oriole CB 1702	I Was The Last One To Know/There's No One In The Whole World	10
62	Oriole CB 1727	There Goes The Lucky One/I Built My Whole World Around You	10
62	Oriole CB 1757	Party Lights/Midnight	15
63	Oriole CB 1800	The End Of The World/Goodbye Is Such A Lonely Word	10
63	Philips BF 1283	Down Our Street/My Heart Is Your Heart (as Jackie & Raindrops)	10
64	Philips BF 1328	Here I Go Again/Come On Dream Come On (as Jackie & Raindrops)	10

(see also Jacky, Jackie Lee [U.K.], Raindrops [U.K], Emma Rede)

JACKIE LEE (U.S.) (MALE)
60	Top Rank JAR 286	Rancho/Like Sunset	10

JACKIE LEE (U.S.) (MALE)
65	Fontana TF 646	The Duck/Let Your Conscience Be Your Guide	40
66	Jay Boy BOY 28	Would You Believe/You're Everything	10
68	London HLM 10233	The Duck/Dancing In The Street	15
70	Jay Boy BOY 26	Do The Temptation Walk/The Shotgun And The Duck	10
72	Jay Boy BOY 66	Oh! My Darlin'/Don't Be Ashamed	15
72	Jay Boy BOY 66	Oh! My Darlin'/Don't Be Ashamed (DJ copy)	30
72	Jay Boy BOY 76	African Boo-Ga-Loo/Bring It Home	8
73	Contempo CR 5	The Duck (Parts 1 & 2)	5
85	Kent TOWN 107	Darkest Days/EDDIE BISHOP: Call Me	25
67	London HA-M 8336	THE DUCK (LP)	50
71	Joy JOYS 192	THE DUCK (LP, reissue)	20

(see also Bob & Earl, Earl Nelson, Jackie Lee & Delores Hall)

JACKIE LEE & DELORES HALL
69	B&C CB 105	Whether It's Right Or Wrong/Baby I'm Satisfied	10

MINT VALUE £

| 72 | Jay Boy BOY 52 | Whether It's Right Or Wrong/Baby I'm Satisfied (reissue) | 6 |

(see also Jackie Lee [U.S.], Delores Hall)

JAMIE LEE & ATLANTICS
| 63 | Decca F 11571 | In The Night/Little Girl In Blue | 45 |

JIMMY LEE
| 61 | Starlite ST45 059 | All My Life/Chicago Jump | 30 |

JOHN LEE
| 72 | Explosion EX 2060 | Stagger Lee/Musical Version (both sides actually by John Holt) | 5 |

JOHNNIE LEE
59	Pye 7N 15201	Echo/It's-A Me, It's-A Me, It's-A Me My Love	8
59	Pye 7N 15233	I'm Finally Free/I Fell (with The King's Men)	8
60	Fontana H 257	They're Wrong/Cindy Lou	8
60	Fontana H 280	Poetry In Motion/Let It Come True	10
61	Fontana H 306	Lonely Joe/Nobody	8
67	CBS 202591	Kiss Tomorrow Goodbye/Love No Longer Sounds	5
67	CBS 2802	I Forgot What It Was Like/Lonely Is The Willow	5
67	CBS 3112	Because You're Mine/I'll Not Forget	5

RICKIE LEE JONES
| 84 | arner Bros. K56628 | RICKIE LEE JONES (LP, Nimbus Supercut, mail order only through Practical Hi-Fi magazine) | 80 |

JULIA LEE (& HER BOYFRIENDS)
50	Capitol CL 13321	Nobody Knows You When You're Down And Out/Decent Woman Blues (78)	10
50	Capitol CL 13323	Cold Hearted Daddy/Snatch And Grab It (78)	10
51	Capitol LC 6535	PARTY TIME (10" LP, 2 different sleeves)	50

LAURA LEE (U.K.)
60	Triumph RGM 1030	Tell Tommy I Miss Him/I'm Sending Back Your Roses	50
62	Decca F 11513	Too Young To Be In Love/Brand New Heartbeat	15
68	Columbia DB 8495	Love In Every Room/Master Jack	12
71	Columbia DB 8770	Someone To Love Me/Look Left-Look Right	8

LAURA LEE (U.S.)
67	Chess CRS 8062	Dirty Man/It's Mighty Hard	10
68	Chess CRS 8070	As Long As I Got You/A Man With Some Backbone	10
72	Tamla Motown TMG 831	To Win Your Heart/So Will I (	15
72	Tamla Motown TMG 831	To Win Your Heart/So Will I (DJ copy)	30
72	Hot Wax HWX 115	Rip Off/Two Lovely Pillows	8
73	Hot Wax HWX 118	Wedlock Is A Padlock/Since I Fell For You	7
73	Hot Wax HWX 119	You've Got The Love To Save Me/Crumbs Off The Table	15
74	Invictus INV 2654	I Need It Just As Bad As You/If I'm Good Enough To Love	7
71	Hot Wax SHW 5006	WOMEN'S LOVE RIGHTS (LP)	20
73	Hot Wax SHW 5009	TWO SIDES OF LAURA LEE (LP)	20

LEAPY LEE
65	Pye 7N 17001	It's All Happening/In The Meantime	5
66	Decca F 12369	King Of The Whole Wide World/Shake Hands (featuring the Kinks)	65
67	CBS 202550	The Man On The Flying Trapeze/My Mixed-Up Mind	5
68	Pye 7N 17619	It's All Happening/It's Great	5

MANDY LEE
| 69 | Dandelion S 4494 | Bottle Up And Go (Parts 1 & 2) | 6 |

MICHELLE LEE
| 68 | CBS 3350 | L. David Sloan/Everybody Loves My Baby | 6 |

MICKEY LEE
| 73 | Smash SMA 2332 | Hello My Little Queen/AUGUSTUS PABLO: African Queen | 10 |

NICKIE LEE
| 69 | Deep Soul DS 9103 | And Black Is Beautiful/Faith Within | 25 |

NORMA LEE
| 67 | CBM CBM 002 | Hurt/Rollin' On | 6 |

PEGGY LEE
SINGLES
62	Capitol CL 15279	I'm A Woman/Big Bad Bill (Is Sweet William Now)	6
54	Brunswick 05286	Johnny Guitar/I Didn't Know What Time It Was	8
54	Brunswick 05345	Love, You Didn't Do Right By Me/Sisters	8
55	Brunswick 05360	Let Me Go, Lover/Bouquet Of Blues	8
55	Brunswick 05368	Straight Ahead/It Must Be So (with Mills Brothers)	8
55	Brunswick 05421	Baubles, Bangles And Beads/Summer Vacation	8
55	Brunswick 05435	I Belong To You/How Bitter, My Sweet	8
55	Brunswick 05461	Ooh That Kiss/Oh! No! (Please Don't Go)	8
55	Brunswick 05471	Sugar/What Can I Say After I Say I'm Sorry	8
55	Brunswick 05472	He Needs Me/Sing A Rainbow	8
55	Brunswick 05482	He's A Tramp (with Pound Hounds)/The Siamese Cat Song (with Oliver Wallace)	8
55	Brunswick 05483	Bella Notte/La La Lu	8

(Originally issued with gold label lettering; silver reissues are worth two-thirds these values.)

56	Brunswick 05549	Three Cheers For Mister Magoo/Mister Magoo Does The Cha Cha Cha (with Jim Backus)	7
56	Brunswick 05554	The Come Back/You've Got To See Mama Every Night	7
56	Brunswick 05593	That's All Right Honey/Love You So	7
56	Brunswick 05625	We Laughed At Love/They Can't Take That Away From Me	7
57	Brunswick 05671	Mr. Wonderful/The Gypsy With Fire In His Shoes	8
57	Brunswick 05714	I Don't Know Enough About You/Where Flamingo's Fly	8
57	Capitol CL 14741	Baby, Baby Wait For Me/Every Night	6
58	Capitol CL 14902	Fever/You Don't Know	7
61	Capitol CL 15184	Till There Was You/Bucket Of Tears	5
65	Capitol CL 15394	Bewitched/Sneakin' Up On You	15
65	Capitol CL 15413	I Go To Sleep/Stop Living In The Past	5
69	Capitol CL 15614	Is That All There Is?/I'm A Woman (2nd pressing with different A-side)	10

EPs

| 55 | Brunswick OE 9153 | PETE KELLY'S BLUES NO. 1 ....8 |

ALBUMS

53	Capitol LC 6584	CAPITOL PRESENTS PEGGY LEE (10") 20
53	Brunswick LA 8629	BLACK COFFEE (10") 20
55	Brunswick LA 8717	SONGS IN AN INTIMATE STYLE (10")..20
55	Brunswick LAT 8078	PETE KELLY'S BLUES (with Ella Fitzgerald) 20
56	Brunswick LA 8731	SONGS FROM 'LADY AND THE TRAMP' (10")......................................20
56	Capitol LC 6817	MY BEST TO YOU (10") 15

(see also Bing Crosby, George Shearing)

ROBERT LEE

| 87 | Josiah KJ 008 | Easy Norman/MICHAEL MARTIN ALLSTARS: Version (12") ....40 |

ROBERTA LEE

52	Brunswick 04876	The Little White Cloud That Cried/Tell Me Why (78, with Grady Martin) 8
53	Brunswick 05076	Sixty Minute Man (with Hardrock Gunter)/RED FOLEY: Hot Toddy (78)....15
54	HMV 7M 261	True Love And Tender Care/When The Organ Played At Twilight 10
55	Brunswick 05388	Ridin' To Tennessee/I'll Be There If Ever You Want Me 10

(see also Red Foley, Hardrock Gunter)

ROBIN LEE

| 62 | Reprise R 20068 | Gambling Man/An Angel With A Broken Wing ....12 |

ROY LEE

| 61 | Decca F 11406 | Two Initials/Honey Lies..6 |

TONY LEE

| 68 | Doctor Bird DB 1106 | Lee's Special/LLOYD & GROOVERS: My Heart My Soul ....40 |

TONY LEE TRIO

71	Contour 2870142	ELECTRIC PIANO (LP) 15
76	Lambert 3416	TONY LEE TRIO (LP) 15
79	Lambert LAM105	STREET OF DREAMS (LP) 15

VINNY LEE & RIDERS

| 61 | HMV POP 856 | Mule Train/Gambler's Guitar ....15 |

WARREN LEE

| 69 | Pama PM 762 | Underdog Backstreet/Come Put My Life In Order..............................15 |

WILMA LEE & STONEY COOPER

| 64 | Hickory 45-1257 | Big John's Wife/Pirate King ....7 |

BRAD LEEDS

| 60 | Pye International 7N 25050 | A Teenage Love Is Born/I'm Walking Behind You ....6 |

PHIL LEEDS

| 66 | London HLR 10044 | Would You Believe It?/FRANK GALLOP: The Ballad Of Irving ....8 |

LEEDS UNITED FOOTBALL CLUB

| 72 | Chapter 1 SCH 168 | Leeds United/Leeds, Leeds, Leeds ....5 |

MARK LEEMAN FIVE

65	Columbia DB 7452	Portland Town/Gotta Get Myself Together 20
65	Columbia DB 7648	Blow My Blues Away/On The Horizon 25
66	Columbia DB 7812	Forbidden Fruit/Goin' To Bluesville 25
66	Columbia DB 7955	Follow Me/Gather Up The Pieces 20

(see also Cheynes)

THOMAS LEER

78	Oblique ER 101	Private Plane/International (folded photocopied p/s, hand-stamped labels)....15
78	Company/Oblique OBCO 1	Private Plane/International (reissue, printed p/s) 8
82	Cherry Red CHERRY 52	All About You/Saving Grace (p/s) 5
82	Cherry Red 12CHERRY 52	All About You/Saving Grace (12", p/s) 8
82	Cherry Red ERED 26	CONTRADICTIONS EP (12", double pack)..8
79	Industrial IR 0007	THE BRIDGE (LP, with Robert Rental) 40

(see also Act, Robert Rental)

JOHN LEES

74	Polydor 2058 513	Best Of My Love/You Can't Get It 15
77	Harvest HAR 5132	Child Of The Universe/Kes (A Major Fancy) 5
73	Harvest SHVL 811	A MAJOR FANCY (LP, released as SHSM 2018) 20

(see also Barclay James Harvest)

RAYMOND LEFEVRE & HIS ORCHESTRA

| 68 | Major Minor MM 559 | Soul Coaxing (Ame Caline)/When A Man Loves A Woman ....8 |

LEFT BANKE

66	Philips BF 1517	Walk Away Renee/I Haven't Got The Nerve 12
67	Philips BF 1540	Pretty Ballerina/Lazy Day...12
67	Philips BF 1575	Ivy Ivy/And Suddenly 10
67	Philips BF 1614	Desiree/I've Got Something On My Mind..7
87	Bam Caruso OPRA 023	Walk Away Renee/Ivy Ivy (DJ/jukebox issue) 6
67	Philips (S)BL 7773	WALK AWAY RENEE/PRETTY BALLERINA (LP) 60

LEFTFIELD

90	Outer Rhythm FOOT 3	Not Forgotten (12") 15
90	Outer Rhythm FOOT 9R	More Than I Know (10K Remix)/(More Mix)/(Even More Mix) (12") 8
91	Outer Rhythm FOOT 009	More Than I Know (12" Mix)/Not Forgotten (Hard Hands Mix) (12") 8
92	Hard Hands HAND 001T	Release The Pressure/Release The Pressure (Instrumental)/Release The Pressure (with Earl Sixteen) (12") 8
92	Hard Hands HAND 001R	Release The Dubs (Dub 1)/(Dub 2)/(Dub 3)/(Dub 4) (12") 8
92	Hard Hands HAND 002R	Song Of Life (Remixes)/Release The Horns (12") 10
92	Hard Hands HAND 002T	Song Of Life/Dub Of Life/Fanfare Of Life (12") 10
93	Hard Hands HAND 009T	Open Up (Full Vocal Mix)/Open Up (Dervish Overdrive) (12") 8
93	Hard Hands HAND 009R	Open Up (Remixes) (12") 8
95	Hard Hands HAND 23T	AFRO LEFT EP (12")..8

MINT VALUE £

95	Hard Hands/Columbia HAND 018T/6613486	Original (12")	8
99	Hard Hands HAND 057T	Afrika Shox (VW Remix)/Afrika Shox (Jedis Elastic Bass Mix)/Phat Planet (12")	8
95	Hard Hands HANDLP 2	LEFTISM (2-LP, gatefold sleeve)	20
95	Hard Hands HANDLP 2T	LEFTISM (3-LP, gatefold sleeve)	25
99	Hard Hands HANDLP 4	RHYTHM AND STEALTH (2-LP)	20
99	Hard Hands HANDLP 4T	RHYTHM AND STEALTH (5 x 10" box set, limited edition)	25

(see also A Man Called Adam, Curve)

LEFT HAND DRIVE
77	Bancrupt Records BECK 611	Jailbait/Motorway Crow (1,000 only, no p/s)	50
79	Bankcrupt BAN 012	Who Said Rock & Roll Is Dead/I Know Where I Am (p/s)	10

LEFT-HANDED MARRIAGE
67	Private pressing	ON THE RIGHT SIDE OF THE LEFT-HANDED MARRIAGE (LP)	500
96	Tenth Planet TP 022	ON THE RIGHT SIDE OF THE LEFT-HANDED MARRIAGE (LP, reissue, gatefold sleeve)	15

(see also Queen)

LEFT SIDE
69	Columbia DB 8575	Welcome To My House/This Little Village	6

LANCE LE GAULT
68	United Artists UP 2255	Billie/Louisiana Swamp Fox	5

LEGAY
69	Fontana TF 904	No-One/The Fantastic Story Of The Steam Driven Banana	160

(see also Gypsy)

LEGEND!
83	Creation CRE 001/Lyntone LYN 12903	'73 In '83/You (Chunka Chunka) Were Glamorous (foldaround p/s in poly bag, with 33rpm flexidisc "I Wonder Why! (live)" by The Pastels/"Wouldn't You? By Laughing Apple)	15
84	Creation CRE 010	The Legend Destroys The Blues/Arrogant Bastards (foldaround p/s in poly bag)	6

TOBI LEGEND
78	RK RK 1004	Time Will Pass You By/DEAN PARRISH: I'm On My Way/ JIMMY RADCLIFFE: Long After Tonight Is All Over (with p/s)	10
78	RK RK 1004	Time Will Pass You By/DEAN PARRISH: I'm On My Way/ JIMMY RADCLIFFE: Long After Tonight Is All Over	6

LEGEND (1)
69	Bell BLL 1048	National Gas/Wouldn't You	20
69	Bell BLL 1082	Georgia George Part 1/July	15
70	Vertigo 6059 021	Life/Late Last Night	15
71	Vertigo 6059 036	Don't You Know/Someday	15
69	Bell MBLL/SBLL 115	LEGEND (LP, blue/silver labels with "Sold in U.K..." text)	150
71	Vertigo 6360 019	LEGEND ('RED BOOT') (LP, gatefold sleeve, large swirl label)	250
72	Vertigo 6360 063	MOONSHINE (LP, gatefold sleeve, small swirl label)	300

(see also Procol Harum, Fingers, Mickey Jupp)

LEGEND (2)
81	Legend LEG 1	Hideaway/Heaven Sent (p/s)	70

LEGEND (3)
82	Workshop WR 3478	FRONTLINE EP (Frontline/Sabre & Chatila/ Stormers Of Heaven/Open The Skies (12")	25
81	Workshop WR 2007	LEGEND (LP)	90
82	Workshop WR 3477	DEATH IN THE NURSERY (LP, with insert)	20

LEGENDARY HEARTS
88	Surfin' Pict	IN A WORLD LIKE THIS (12" EP)	30

LEGENDARY LONNIE
81	Nervous NER 002	Constipation Shake/Devil's Guitar (p/s)	6

LEGENDARY MASKED SURFERS
73	United Artists UP 35542	Gonna Hustle You/Summertime, Summertime	18

(see also Beach Boys, Jan & Dean)

LEGENDARY PINK DOTS
81	Mirrordot MD 01	ONLY DREAMING (cassette, all different hand-made covers)	100
81	Mirrordot MD02/03	CHEMICAL PLAYSCHOOL 1/2 (double cassette, 24 copies all different handmade covers)	120
81	Cassetteking CK04	DOTS ON THE EYE (cassette)	45
82	Flowmotion FMC 09	PREMONITION (cassette, around 60 copies)	45
82	Mirrordot MD/03/II	CHEMICAL PLAYSCHOOL 2 EDITION 2 (cassette, 9 copies, different handmade copies)	120
82	Mirrordot MD 02-03	CHEMICAL PLAYSCHOOL 3/4 (double cassette, 120 copies, different covers)	75
82	Mirrordot MD 04	KLEINE KRIEG (cassette, 120 copies, individual hand-made covers)	80
82	In Phaze 4	BRIGHTER NOW (cassette, 300 copies, different mixes on some tracks)	45
82	In Phaze IPNER 1	BRIGHTER NOW (LP)	25
83	Third Mind TMT 08	BASILISK (cassette, 1000 copies)	30
83	In Phaze PHA 2	CURSE (LP, 2500 copies)	20
84	In Phaze PHA	THE TOWER (LP, 2500 copies)	20

LEGENDS
65	Pye 7N 15904	I've Found Her/Something's Gonna Happen	20
67	Parlophone R 5581	Tomorrow's Gonna Be Another Day/Nobody Laughs Anymore	40
67	Parlophone R 5613	Under The Sky/Twenty-Four Hours A Day	20

(see also First Impressions)

B. LEGGS
71	Green Door GD 4004	Drums Of Passion/Love And Emotion (Version)	6

(see also Morgan's All Stars)

LEGION OF PARASITES
84	Fight Back FIGHT 2	UNDESIRABLE GUESTS (12" EP)	15
85	Thrash THRASH 1	THE PRISON OF LIFE! (LP)	15

LEGO FEET
91	Skam SKAM 1	Untitled1/Untitled 2 (12", black die cut sleeve)	100

MICHEL LEGRAND

73	Tamla Motown TMG 848	Love Theme From "Lady Sings The Blues"/Any Happy Home (with Gil Askey)	5
73	Tamla Motown TMG 848	Love Theme From "Lady Sings The Blues"/Any Happy Home (demo in p/s)	15
58	Philips SBBL 510	LEGRAND JAZZ (LP)	12
64	Philips BL 7605	PLAYS RICHARD ROGERS (LP)	12
64	Mercury SML 30020	VIOLENT VIOLINS (LP)	12
66	Philips (S)BL 7792	THE YOUNG GIRLS OF ROCHEFORT (LP, soundtrack)	25
68	United Artists SULP 1218	THE THOMAS CROWN AFFAIR (LP, soundtrack)	35
68	Sunset SLS 50519	THE THOMAS CROWN AFFAIR (LP, reissue)	20
69	MGM MGM-C(S) 8101	ICE STATION ZEBRA (LP, soundtrack)	12
70	United Artists UAS 29084	THE HAPPY ENDING (LP, soundtrack)	20
73	Bell BELLS 235	THE THREE MUSKETEERS (LP, soundtrack)	18

LE GRIFFE

83	Bullet BOL 1	Fast Bikes/Where Are You? (p/s)	8
83	Bullet BOLT 1	Fast Bikes/Where Are You?/The Actor (12", p/s)	15
84	Bullet BOL 7	You're Killing Me (p/s)	8
83	Bullet BOLT 7	You're Killing Me/E.T.A. (12", p/s)	15
84	Bullet BULP 2	BREAKING STRAIN (mini-LP)	20

LEGS

74	Warner Bros K 16317	So Many Faces/You Bet You Have	15

(see also Curved Air, Stretch)

TOM LEHRER

60	Decca F 11243	Poisoning Pigeons In The Park/The Masochism Tango (in p/s)	5

LEIBER-STOLLER ORCHESTRA

62	HMV 1050	Cafe Expresso/Blue Baion	25

LEIBSTANDARTE SS MB

81	Come Organisation WDC 881015	TRIUMPH OF THE WILL (LP, 500 only)	100
81	Come Organisation WDC 881018	WELTANSCHAUUNG (LP)	100
82	Come Organisation WDC 883023	MENSES (cassette)	70

ANDREW LEIGH

70	Polydor 2343 034	MAGICIAN (LP)	60

(see also Reg King, Spooky Tooth)

ROBERTA LEIGH

58	HMV EH 8339	THE ADVENTURES OF TWIZZLE (EP)	15

BERNIE LEIGHTON

63	Pye International 7N 25177	Lawrence Of Arabia Theme/The Wonderful World We Live In (in p/s)	8

LEISURE ADDICTS

80	Addictive ADIC 1	Subway Suicide/Prefab 13 (no p/s)	20

LE MAT

82	Whaam 008	Waltz For A Fool/Every Dream	10

GARY LEMEL

67	London HLM 7124	Beautiful People/Take Me With You (export issue)	20

JOHN LE MESURIER

76	Reprise K54080	WHAT IS GOING TO BECOME OF US ALL (LP)	20

LEMMINGS

65	Pye 7N 15837	Out Of My Mind/My Little Girl	20
65	Pye 7N 15899	You Can't Blame Me For Trying/Bring Your Heart With You	20

(see also Honeycombs, Martin Murray)

LEMMY & UPSETTERS WITH MICK GREEN

90	Sunnyside STYLE 777	Blue Suede Shoes/Paradise (p/s)	6

(see also Motorhead, Rockin' Vickers, Sam Gopal)

LEMON D

92	Planet Earth PEDJ 01	DJ ON WAX (12" EP)	25
93	Planet Earth PDJ 02	PURSUIT OF A VISION (12" EP)	20
93	Planet Earth PDJ 03	TOXIC RHYTHMS (12" EP)	10
93	Planet Earth PDJ 05	THE REMIXES? (12" EP)	10
95	Conqueror OC 7	I Feel It/Don't Make Me Wait/Bad Man (12")	10
95	Conqueror OC 9	VOL II (12" EP)	15
95	Metalheadz METH 014	Urban Style Music/This Is LA (12")	8

LEMON DIPS

69	De Wolfe DW/LP 3114	WHO'S GONNA BUY? (10" LP, library issue)	75

LEMONHEADS

96	Warner Bros	CAR BUTTON CLOTH (CD, includes track 'Purple Parallelagram', promo-only)	15
90	Atlantic 82137	LOVEY (LP)	18
93	Atlantic 82537	COME ON FEEL (LP)	20

LEMON INTERRUPT

93	Junior Boys Own JBO 12002	Eclipse/Bigmouth (12")	15
93	Junior Boys Own JBO 712	Dirty/Minneapolis/Minneapolis (Airwaves) (12")	15

(see also Underworld)

LEMON JELLY

01	Soft Rock SOFTROCK 001	Soft/Rock (blue vinyl, denim sleeve with condom, 1000 only)	40
02	XL IFXLT 147P	Space Walk/Return To Patagonia (10", leather title sleeve, 3000 only)	15
03	Rolled Oats RO 01	Rolled/Oats (gold vinyl, hessian sleeve, 1200 only)	20
98	Impotent Fury IF 001	THE BATH EP: In The Bath/Nervous Tension/A Tune For Jack (10", 1000 only, stickered cardboard sleeve, 1st 250 hand-printed p/s)	130
98	Impotent Fury IF 001	THE BATH EP: In The Bath/Nervous Tension/A Tune For Jack (10", 1000 only, stickered)	40
99	Impotent Fury IF 002	THE YELLOW EP: His Majesty King Raam/The Staunton Lick/Homage To Patagonia (10", 1000 only, stickered cardboard sleeve, 1st 240 in hand-printed p/s)	100

99	Impotent Fury IF 002	THE YELLOW EP: His Majesty King Raam/The Staunton Lick/Homage To Patagonia (10", 1000 only, stickered cardboard sleeve)	40
00	Impotent Fury IF 003	THE MIDNIGHT EP: Kneel Before Your God/Page One/Come (10", 1000 only, stickered cardboard sleeve, 1st 350 in hand-printed p/s)	70
00	Impotent Fury IF 003	THE MIDNIGHT EP: Kneel Before Your God/Page One/Come (10", 1000 only, stickered cardboard sleeve)	25
00	XL IXXLLP 139	KY (2-LP gatefold sleeve with insert)	50
02	XL IFXLLP 160	LOST HORIZONS (2-LP, gatefold sleeve, with booklet)	15

LEMON KITTENS

79	Step Forward SF 10	SPOONFED AND WRITHING (EP)	25
81	United Dairies UD 07	CAKE BEAST (12" EP, with inner sleeve & insert)	25
80	United Dairies UD 02	WE BUY A HAMMER FOR DADDY (LP, with inner sheet)	35
83	Illuminated JAMS 131	THE BIG DENTIST (LP)	35

(see also Danielle Dax, Shock Headed Peters, Underneath, Gland Shrouds, Karl Blake, Fur Fur)

LEMON LINE

67	Decca F 12688	For Your Precious Love/You Made Me See The Light	15

LEMON MEN

69	Polydor 56365	I've Seen You Cut Lemons/Lemon Strip/Lemon Walk	7

LEMON PIPERS

68	Pye International 7N 25444	Green Tambourine/No Help From Me	7
68	Pye International 7N 25454	Rice Is Nice/Blueberry Blue	10
68	Pye International 7N 25464	Jelly Jungle (Of Orange Marmalade)/Shoeshine Boy	6
68	Pye Intl. NPL 28112	GREEN TAMBOURINE (LP)	30
68	Pye Intl. NSPL 28118	JUNGLE MARMALADE (LP)	20
69	Marble Arch MAL 1120	THE LEMON PIPERS (LP)	15

(see also Ram Jam)

LEMON PIPERS/1910 FRUITGUM CO.

68	Pye Intl. NEP 44091	PRESENTING ... (EP, 1 side each)	15

(see also 1910 Fruitgum Co.)

LEMONS

81	RCAE RB 004	My Favourite Band/English Summer	20

LEMON TREE

68	Parlophone R 5671	I Can Touch A Rainbow/William Chalker's Time Machine	50
68	Parlophone R 5739	It's So Nice To Come Home/Come On Girl	50

(see also Idle Race, Uglys, Danny King's Mayfair Set, Balls)

LEN & HIS SEXTET

63	Melotone ME 100	Blowin' The Top/Don't Stop	25

LEN & HONEYSUCKERS

66	Rio R 75	One More River/Emergency Ward	10

FREDDIE LENNON

66	Piccadilly 7N 35290	That's My Life (My Love And My Home)/The Next Time You Feel Important	50

(see also Loving Kind)

JIMMY LENNON & ATLANTICS

64	Decca F 11825	Louisiana Mama/I Learned To Yodel	35

JOHN LENNON/PLASTIC ONO BAND

SINGLES

69	Apple APPLE 13	Give Peace A Chance/Remember Love (p/s, as Plastic Ono Band; with Parlophone catalogue number, dark green label, only second pressings have R5795 added to catalogue number)	18
69	Apple APPLE 13	Give Peace A Chance/Remember Love (p/s, as Plastic Ono Band, first press with "sold in UK..." label text)	40
69	Apple APPLES 1001	Cold Turkey/Don't Worry Kyoko (Mummy's Only Looking For A Hand In The Snow) (p/s, as Plastic Ono Band)	15
69	Apple APPLES 1002	You Know My Name (Look Up The Number)/What's The New Mary Jane? (as Plastic Ono Band, unreleased; vinyl test pressings only with typed Apple 'Custom Recording' labels & hand written catalogue number)	3000
70	Apple APPLES 1003	Instant Karma!/Who Has Seen The Wind? (p/s as Lennon/Ono with Plastic Ono Band)	12
71	Apple R 5892	Power To The People (as John & Yoko/Plastic Ono Band: Open Your Box (p/s, full apple label both sides or full/half apple label)	15
72	Apple R 5970	Happy Xmas (War Is Over) (as John & Yoko/Plastic Ono Band with Harlem Community Choir)/YOKO ONO & PLASTIC ONO BAND: Listen, The Snow Is Falling (p/s green vinyl)	15
72	Apple R 5953	Woman Is The Nigger Of The World/Sisters O Sisters (unreleased, test pressings only)	2500
73	Apple R 5994	Mind Games/Meat City (p/s)	7
74	EMI PSR 369	Interview With John Lennon By Bob Mercer And Message To The Salesmen/Whatever Gets You Thru' The Night (promo only)	2000
75	Apple R 6003	9 Dream (Edited Version)/What You Got (demo only)	80
75	Apple R 6009	Imagine/Working Class Hero (p/s)	12
80	WEA Geffen K 79186	(Just Like) Starting Over/ YOKO ONO : Kiss Kiss Kiss (Green vinyl, promo)	500
81	WEA K 79207	Watching The Wheels/YOKO ONO: I'm Your Angel (Pink vinyl "in house" promo)	500
84	Polydor PODJ 700	Nobody Told Me (1-sided white label promo)	60
84	Polydor POSP 712	Every Man Has A Woman Who Loves Him/SEAN ONO LENNON: It's Alright (p/s, with poster)	10
84	Polydor POSP 712	Every Man Has A Woman Who Loves Him/SEAN ONO LENNON: It's Alright (p/s)	5
84	Polydor PODJ 701	Borrowed Time (Edited Version)/YOKO ONO: Your Hands (promo only)	25
88	Parlophone RP 6199	Imagine/Jealous Guy (picture disc)	15
88	Parlophone 12R 6199	Imagine/Jealous Guy/Happy Xmas (War Is Over) (12" p/s)	18
97	Parlophone IMAGINE 001	Imagine (CD, 1-track, card p/s, promo only)	10
97	Parlophone IMAGINE 002	Happy Xmas (War Is Over) (CD, 1-track, card p/s, promo only)	10
98	Parlophone LENNON 002	Happy Xmas (War Is Over) (Rough mix)/Be Bop A Lula (CD, card p/s, promo only)	15

ALBUMS

68	Apple APCOR 2	UNFINISHED MUSIC NO. 1: TWO VIRGINS (with Yoko Ono, mono; black inner, no track listing, with "Merrie In England..." blurb on front sleeve)	3000
68	Apple SAPCOR 2/Track 613 012	UNFINISHED MUSIC NO. 1: TWO VIRGINS (with Yoko Ono, stereo; black inner, with track listing & "Merrie In England..." blurb on back sleeve & Track Records logo on label, dark green label, "Sold in U.K..." "Mfd in UK" label text)	600

69	Zapple ZAPPLE 01	UNFINISHED MUSIC NO. 2: LIFE WITH THE LIONS (with Yoko Ono, with inner sleeve, dark green label, "Sold in U.K..." "Mfd in UK" label text)	250
69	Apple SAPCOR 11	WEDDING ALBUM (with Yoko Ono; gatefold sleeve in box set, includes wedding certificate glued to inside box lid, press booklet, poster, white 'Bagism' bag, passport photographs, postcard & picture of wedding cake)	600
69	Apple CORE 2001	LIVE PEACE IN TORONTO 1969 (as Plastic Ono Band, with stapled calendar, sealed, 1st pressing with rough surface label and Apple publishing credit on side 2, dark green label with "Sold in U.K..." text)	175
69	Apple CORE 2001	LIVE PEACE IN TORONTO 1969 (as Plastic Ono Band, with stapled calendar, unsealed)	40
70	Apple PCS 7124	JOHN LENNON : PLASTIC ONO BAND (LP, with inner)	50
72	Apple PAS 10004	IMAGINE (LP, with inner sleeve, poster & postcard, 1st pressing with laminated sleeve/'sniped' spine edges)	40
72	Apple PAS 10004	IMAGINE (LP, with inner sleeve, without poster & postcard)	30
72	Apple Q4PAS 10004	IMAGINE (LP, quadrophonic, with inner sleeve, poster & postcard)	150
72	Apple PCSP 716	SOMETIME IN NEW YORK CITY (2-LP, gatefold, inner sleeve & postcard)	40
72	Apple PCSP 716	SOMETIME IN NEW YORK CITY (2-LP, gatefold, inner sleeve & without postcard)	20
74	Apple PCTC 253	WALLS AND BRIDGES (LP, gatefold, with booklet and inner sleeve)	25
75	Apple PCS 7173	SHAVED FISH (LP)	30
81	Parlophone JLB 8	THE JOHN LENNON BOX (9-LP set, with insert)	100
84	Polydor POLH P5	MILK AND HONEY (picture disc, original pressing, thin vinyl, 2,000 only)	40
84	Polydor POLH P5	MILK AND HONEY (picture disc, 2nd pressing, thicker vinyl, 1,000 only)	50
86	Parlophone PCS 7301	LIVE IN NEW YORK CITY (LP, with inner)	15
86	Parlophone PCS 7308	MENLOVE AVENUE (LP, with inner)	20
88	Parlophone PCSP 722	IMAGINE : JOHN LENNON (2xLP with inner)	20
90	Parlophone CDS 79 5220	LENNON (4 x CD set)	70
97	Parlophone 8 21954 2	LENNON LEGEND (2 x LP with inner)	40
98	Parlophone 8306142	ANTHOLOGY (4-CDR, jewel cases with Abbey Road studio inlays, incorrect track listing and missing "Grow Old With Me" from CD4, promo only)	80
99	Capitol 497 6391	WONSAPONEATIME (2 x LP with inner)	50

(see also Beatles,Yoko Ono, Bill Elliott/Elastic Oz Band, Elephant's Memory, Musketeer Gripweed, Elton John)

JOHN LENNON & BLEECHERS (JAMAICA)

| 70 | Punch PH 23 | Ram You Hard/UPSETTERS: Soul Stew | 60 |

LENNON SISTERS

56	Vogue Coral Q 72176	Graduation Day/Toy Tiger	8
57	Vogue Coral Q 72259	Young And In Love/Teenage Waltz	8
57	Vogue Coral Q 72285	Shake Me I Rattle/Pocohontas	8
61	London HLD 9417	Sad Movies/I Don't Know Why	15

MIKE LENNOX

| 68 | Decca F 12736 | Images Of You/Words I Like | 7 |

J.B. LENOIR (& AFRICAN HUNCH RHYTHM)

65	Sue WI 339	I Sing Um The Way I Feel/I Feel So Good (with His African Hunch Rhythm)	50
65	Bootleg 503	Man Watch Your Woman/Mama Talk To Your Daughter (99 copies only)	60
66	Blue Horizon 45-1004	Mojo Boogie/I Don't Care What Nobody Say (99 copies only)	150
68	Python PLP 25	J.B. LENOIR (LP, 99 copies only)	75
70	Polydor 2482 014	CRUSADE (LP)	40
75	Rarity LP 2	J.B. LENOIR (LP)	25
70s	CBS 62593	ALABAMA BLUES (LP)	40

ROBIN LENT

| 71 | Nepentha 6347 002 | SCARECROW'S JOURNEY (LP, gatefold sleeve, with Focus) | 150 |

(see also Focus, Jan Akkerman)

VAL LENTON

| 65 | Immediate IM 008 | Gotta Get Away/You Don't Care | 80 |

LEON (SILVERA) & OWEN (GRAY)

| 62 | Blue Beat BB 117 | Murder (with Drumbago All Stars)/ROY PANTON: Forty Four | 15 |

(see also Owen & Leon, Owen & Millie)

CHRIS LEON

| 72 | Dynamic DYN 450 | (Last Night) I Didn't Get To Sleep At All/DYNAMITES: Instrumental Version | 5 |

DEKE LEONARD

| 73 | United Artists UAG 29464 | ICEBERG (LP, gatefold sleeve) | 15 |
| 74 | United Artists UAG 29544 | KAMIKAZE (LP, gatefold sleeve) | 15 |

(see also Man, Marty Wilde, Help Yourself, Pete Brown's Piblokto, Gary Pickford-Hopkins & Friends)

LEONARD FAMILY

| 72 | Beacon BEA 186 | Once You Understand/It Won't Happen Again | 6 |

ANN LEONARDO

57	Capitol CL 14723	Straws In The Wind/Travelling Stranger	15
57	Capitol CL 14755	Lottery/One And Only	10
57	Capitol CL 14797	Three Time Loser/I'll Wait Till Monday	5

LEONIE & JOE NOLAN BAND

| 68 | Jolly JY 015 | Move And Groove/Don't Let Me Do It | 8 |

LE ORME

| 73 | Charisma CAS 1072 | FELONA AND SORONA (LP, gatefold sleeve, large 'Mad Hatter' label) | 60 |

(see under 'O')

LEO'S SUNSHIPP

| 79 | Grapevine RED 3 | Give Me The Sunshine/I'm Back For More | 8 |
| 79 | Grapevine REDC 3 | Give Me The Sunshine/I'm Back For More (12") | 10 |

LEPRECHAUN

| 81 | Excalibur EXC 508 | Loc It Up/Party Freaks (12") | 8 |

LE RITZ

| 77 | Breaker BS 2001 | Punker/What A Sucker (p/s) | 15 |

MIKE LEROY

| 64 | Columbia DB 7316 | Five Hundred Miles/The Big City | 6 |

LEROY & ROCKY (ELLIS)

| 68 | Studio One SO 2042 | Love Me Girl/WRIGGLERS: Reel Up | 30 |

(see also King Rocky)

LE ROYS
64	HMV POP 1274	Gotta Lotta Love (Ciribiribin)/Don't Cry Baby	10
64	HMV POP 1312	Chills/Lost Out On Love	15
64	HMV POP 1368	I Come Smiling On Through/California GL 903	10

(see also Mike Sarne, Simon Scott, John Leyton, Mike Berry, Grazina, Billie Davis, Billy Boyle, Don Spencer)

LES & MITCH
63	Fontana 267265 TF	Why Can't We Love/Don't Wake Me Up	5

LES & SILKIE
70	Torpedo TOR 13	I Don't Want To Tell You/DENZIL DENNIS: Come On In	5

LES KITTIES
81	Camille CAM 1	What's That?/Little Claw (500 only, no p/s)	15

BILL LE SAGE
60s	Philips BL 7625	DIRECTIONS IN JAZZ (LP)	15
64	World Records T/ST 346	PRESENTING THE BILL LESAGE/RONNIE ROSS QUARTET (LP, stereo sticker on front)	40

(see also Ronnie Ross)

LORNE LESLEY
59	Parlophone R 4518	Some Of These Days/When Love Has Let You Down	5
59	Parlophone R 4567	Warm/You Ought To Be Mine	6
59	Parlophone R 4581	So High, So Low/I Don't Know	7
60	Polydor NH 66928	Take All My Love/Ritroviamoci (Till We Meet Again)	6
60	Polydor NH 66956	Bloodshot Eyes/We're Gonna Dance	7
65	Philips BF 1403	Someone Like You/Where My Heart Never Wandered	5
65	Philips BF 1434	Rainy Days Were Made For Lonely People/Fire Down Below	5
66	Philips BF 1487	Somebody's Gonna Be Sorry/(I'm Afraid) The Masquerade Is Over	5

DESMOND LESLIE
05	Trunk JBH 014 LP	MUSIC OF THE FUTURE (LP)	20

JOHN & CHRIS LESLIE
76	Cottage COT 901	THE SHIP OF TIME (LP)	15

MICHAEL LESLIE
65	Pye 7N 15835	Momma Didn't Know/I Don't Wanna Know	6
65	Pye 7N 15908	Penny Arcade/Bye Bye Baby	12
65	Pye 7N 15959	Make Up Or Break Up/She Can't See Me	25
66	Decca F 12531	Right Or Wrong/Office Girl (credited to Michael Leslie)	5

LESTER & DENWOOD
73	Atlantic K10381	America (What Have You Done)/Song For Joanne	10

HEDDY LESTER
77	Sonet SON 2013	The World Keeps Turning/Never Saw Him Laughing (p/s)	6

KETTY LESTER
62	London HLN 9527	Love Letters/I'm A Fool To Want You	10
62	London HLN 9574	But Not For Me/Moscow Nights	10
62	London HLN 9608	You Can't Lie To A Liar/River Of Salt	7
62	London HLN 9635	This Land Is Your Land/Love Belongs To Everyone	6
63	London HLN 9698	A Warm Summer Day/I'll Never Stop Loving You	7
64	RCA Victor RCA 1394	Some Things Are Better Left Unsaid/The House Is Haunted	60
64	RCA Victor RCA 1394	Some Things Are Better Left Unsaid/The House Is Haunted (DJ copy)	100
64	RCA Victor RCA 1403	Roses Grow With Thorns/Please Don't Cry Anymore	40
64	RCA Victor RCA 1421	I Trust You Baby/Theme From "The Luck Of Ginger Coffey"	15
65	RCA Victor RCA 1460	Looking For A Better World/Pretty Eyes	7
65	Capitol CL 15427	West Coast/I'll Be Looking Back	30
66	Capitol CL 15447	When A Man Loves A Woman/We'll Be Together Again	8
62	London RE-N 1348	KETTY LESTER (EP)	40
63	London HA-N 2455	LOVE LETTERS (LP)	60
64	RCA Victor RD 7669	THE SOUL OF ME (LP)	40
65	RCA Victor RD 7712	WHERE IS LOVE (LP)	40
67	Stateside S(S)L 10196	WHEN A MAN LOVES A WOMAN (LP)	80

LAZY LESTER
64	Stateside SS 277	I'm A Lover Not A Fighter/Sugar Coated Love	40
71	Blue Horizon 2431 007	MADE UP MY MIND (LP)	150
77	Flyright FLYLP 526	THEY CALL ME LAZY (LP)	15
79	Flyright FLYLP 544	POOR BOY BLUES (LP)	15

ROBIE LESTER
62	Polydor NH 66963	Ballad Of Cheating John/Miracle Of Love	5

LES YPER SOUND
69	Philips TFE 8004	MASS FOR THE PRESENT TIME (LP)	100

LETHAL
94	White BAD 1	Portrait Of A Young Man As An Artist (12")	20

JOE LETHAL
78	Lethal CI 200526	Don't Come Back/You Ain't Free (no p/s)	35

LETIMOV
85	Reconciliation RECONCILE 2	To The Suffering/The Gift Of Life (p/s)	15

LETTERMEN
61	Capitol CL 15222	The Way You Look Tonight/That's My Desire	7
62	Capitol CL 15248	Come Back Silly Girl/Song For Young Love	8
68	Capitol CL 15526	Goin' Out Of My Head/Can't Take My Eyes Off You - I Believe	5
69	Capitol CL 15609	Hurt So Bad/Traces	5
61	Capitol EAP 41669	THE LETTERMEN (EP)	8
62	Capitol (S)T 1669	A SONG FOR YOUNG LOVE (LP)	12

LETTERMEN
74	Stag SG 10075	FIRST CLASS (LP, private pressing)	90

LETTERS
79	Heartbeat PULSE 9	Nobody Loves Me/Don't Want You Back (p/s)	90

DON LETTS & JAH WOBBLE
79	Virgin VS 239	Steel Leg: Stratetime & The Wide Man/Electric Dread: Haile Unlikely (p/s)	10
79	Virgin VS 239-12	Steel Leg: Stratetime & The Wide Man/Electric Dread: Haile Unlikely (12", p/s)	12

(see also Jah Wobble, PiL)

LEVEE BREAKERS
65	Parlophone R 5291	Babe I'm Leaving You/Wild About My Loving	25

(see also Beverley, Johnny Joyce)

LEVEE CAMP MOAN
69	County	LEVEE CAMP MOAN (LP, private pressing)	750
69	County	PEACOCK FARM (LP, private pressing)	750

LEVEL 42
79	Elite DAZZ 4	Sandstorm/Journey To The Powerline (Remix) (12", white label test pressing, no p/s)	75
80	Elite DAZZ 5	Love Meeting Love/Instrumental Love (7", unreleased)	0
80	Elite DAZZ 5	Love Meeting Love/Instrumental Love (12", company die-cut stickered sleeve)	25
91	Polydor 511 635-2	THE COMPLETE LEVEL 42 (9-CD box set)	40

LEVELLERS
91	On The Fiddle OTF EP 1	Police On My Back/Where The Hell Are We Going To Love?/Travelogue (4am Mix) (12", fan club issue, p/s)	12
92	On The Fiddle OTF LP 2	LIVE 1992 (LP, fan club issue, 2,000 only)	15

GERRY LEVENE (& AVENGERS)
64	Decca F 11815	It's Driving Me Wild (solo)/Dr. Feelgood	40

(see also Moody Blues)

ANNABEL LEVENTON
69	Morgan MR 20	Easy To Be Hard/My Dear Friend	8

LEVERS
79	Bead Records BEAD 10	LEVERS (LP)	25

CARL LEV(E)Y & CIMARRONS
70	Hot Rod HR 100	Walk The Hot Street/PEGGY & CIMARRONS: You Say You Don't Love Me	25
70	Hot Rod HR 101	Remember Easter Monday/PEGGY & JIMMY: Pum Pum Lover	20

(see also Hot Rod Allstars, Rita Alston, Peggy)

IJAHMAN LEVI
76	Concrete CJ 756	I Am A Levi/Part 2	60
80s	Jahmani JMI 304	Moulding (as Ijahman)/HIS MAJESTERIANS: Jah Is Coming Again (12")	50
85	Jahmani JMI 501	Moulding/Africa (12")	50
78	Island ILPS 9521	HAILE I HYMN (LP)	18

FRANKIE LEVI
86	Firm (no cat no)	Steady Rock/KEVIN GAD: Bloodlines Connections (12")	150

LEVIATHAN
68	Elektra EKSN 45052	Remember The Times/Second Production	40
69	Elektra EKSN 45057	The War Machine/Time	25
69	Elektra EKSN 45052/45057	(WAY IN) THE FOUR FACES OF LEVIATHAN (Remember The Times/ Second Production/The War Machine/Time)(2 x 7" press pack, A4 folder sleeve, some overprinted with 'Harrods' logo, with bio & photo, promo, some commercial)	250
69	Elektra EKSN 45075	Flames/Just Forget Tomorrow	30
90s	(no cat.no.)	ELEKTRA DAZE (CD EP, private pressing)	25
69	Elektra EKS 74046	LEVIATHAN (2-LP, unissued, acetates only, 1 copy known)	1500

(see also Mike Stuart Span, High Broom)

HANK LEVINE ORCHESTRA
61	HMV POP 947	Image (Parts 1 & 2)	10
65	HMV POP 1390	Image (Parts 1 & 2) (reissue)	7

LEVITTS
69	ESP Disk/Fontana STL 5518	WE ARE THE LEVITTS (LP)	25

LEVON & HAWKS
65	Atlantic AT 4054	The Stones I Throw/He Don't Love You	55

(see also Band)

BARRINGTON LEVY
79	JB JBD	Call You On The Phone/RANKING TOYAN: London Girl (12")	10
79	Burning Rockers BRD 029	Hunting Man (with Jah Thomas)/LAWES ROCKERS: Hunter Dub (12")	20
79	Bushays BFM 128	Sister Debby/Blacksin Dub (12", with Jah Thomas)	20
70s	Burning Vibrations BVD 003	A Ya We Deh/Give Thanks And Praise (12", with Trinity)	20
79	Burning Rockers BRD 033	Shine Eye Gal/Dub version (12". Jah Thomas toasts on A-side but is uncredited)	12
79	Burning Sounds BRD 029	Hunting Man (feat. Jah Thomas)/Hunting Dub (12")	25
79	Greensleeves GRED 27	Lose Respect (feat. Trinity)/ROMAN STEWART & TRINITY: Since You're Gone (12")	15
80	Greensleeves GRED 40	Crucifixion/Eventide Fire A Disaster (red vinyl 12")	20
80	Cha Cha CHAD 22	Warm and Sunny Day/GENERAL SAINT - DJ cut (12")	50
80	His Majesty HMD 004	Shaolin Temple/Version (12")	20
80	Strong Like Sampson SLSD8	Wicked Intention/ROD TAYLOR (12")	40
80	Lovelinch LL 03	Skylarking/HORTENSE ELLIS - You Done Me Wrong (12")	40
82	Greensleeves GRED 80	Tomorrow Is Another Day/PAPA TULLO: Delaware (12")	20
82	Oak Sounds OSD 008	Open Book/Open version (12")	20
84	Greensleeves GRED 136	Prison Oval Rock (master mix)/Prison Oval Rock (dub plate mix) (12")	12
84	Greensleeves GRED 145	Pon Your Toe/Girl I Love You (12")	18
85	MGR MGR 4	Get Up Stand Up/Do The Dance (12")	10
87	Live & Learn LLD014	Juggling Soldier/Version (12")	15
87	Time I TR 026	Living Dangerously/Version	8
87	Time I 7TR 0200	Struggler/Version	8
79	Greensleeves GREL 9	ENGLISHMAN (LP)	30
79	Burning Sounds BS 1039	SHINE EYE GAL (LP)	30
80	JB JBLP 01	DOH RAY ME (LP)	40
80	Jah Guidance JA CC 14	ROBIN HOOD (LP)	40

83	GG's GG 0032	BARRINGTON LEVY'S LIFE STYLE (LP)	40
83	Burning Sounds BS 1050	HUNTER MAN (LP)	20
85	Time Records TRLP 003	HERE I COME (LP)	20

BEN LEVY
| 66 | Ska Beat JB 245 | Doreen/Never Knew Love | 10 |
| 66 | Ska Beat JB 255 | I'll Make You Glad/Keep Smiling | 10 |

JONA LEWIE
74	Sonet SON 2048	Piggy Back Sue/Papa Don't Go	6
75	Sonet SON 2056	The Swan/Custer's Last Stand	5
76	Sonet SON 2081	Hallelujah Europe Parts 1 & 2	5
77	Sonet SON 2117	Rocking Yobs/After We Swum	5
78	Stiff BUY 37	Halleluja Europe/Police Trap (Unreleased, test pressings only)	50
80	Stiff BUY 85-5	Big Shot - Momentarily/I'll Get By In Pittsburg (5" single)	6

(see also Brett Marvin & Thunderbolts)

CARL LEWIN
| 71 | Bullet BU 456 | Knock Three Times/SIDNEY ALL STARS: The Whealing Mouse | 8 |
| 71 | Punch PH 98 | Nobody Told Me/WING: Don't Play That Song Again (version) | 7 |

ALVA (REGGIE) LEWIS
67	Caltone TONE 111	Return Home/KING ROCK & WILLOWS: You Are The One	80
67	Island WI 3080	I'm Indebted/GROOVERS: You've Got To Cry	40
68	Jolly HY 009	Hang My Head And Cry/COOL CATS: Hold Your Love	80
72	Upsetter US 391	Natty Natty (as Alva Reggie Lewis)/UPSETTERS: Version	12

(see also Reggae Boys, Webber Sisters, Lester Sterling, Cool Cats)

ANDY LEWIS & KENI BURKE
| 90s | Acid Jazz AJX 147S | (Love Is Alive) In Your Heart (pink vinyl, p/s) | 12 |

LEWIS & CLARKE EXPEDITION
| 67 | RCA 1633 | Blue Revelations/I Feel Good (I Feel Bad) | 20 |

ANDY LEWIS & PAUL WELLER
| 97 | Acid Jazz AJX 193S | Are You Trying To Be Lonely?/Tell Me Once Again You Love Me (7", blue vinyl, numbered blue-ish p/s, 1,000 only) | 5 |
| 97 | Acid Jazz AJX 193P | Are You Trying To Be Lonely?/Tell Me Once Again You Love Me (7" promo, A-label in Acid Jazz sleeve, 50 copies only) | 40 |

BARBARA LEWIS
63	London HLK 9724	Hello Stranger/Think A Little Sugar	25
63	London HLK 9724	Hello Stranger/Think A Little Sugar (DJ Copy)	60
63	London HLK 9779	Straighten Up Your Heart/If You Love Her	25
64	London HLK 9832	Snap Your Fingers/Puppy Love	25
64	Atlantic AT 4013	Pushin' A Good Thing Too Far/Come Home	40
65	Atlantic AT 4031	Baby I'm Yours/Hello Stranger	18
65	Atlantic AT 4041	Make Me Your Baby/Love To Be Loved	18
66	Atlantic AT 4068	Don't Forget About Me/It's Magic	20
66	Atlantic 584 037	Make Me Belong To You/Girls Need Loving Care	15
67	Atlantic 584 061	Baby What Do You Want Me To Do/I Remember The Feeling	55
68	Atlantic 584 153	Hello Stranger/Baby I'm Yours (reissue)	8
68	Atlantic 584 174	Sho Nuff (It's Got To Be Your Love)/Thankful For What I Got	20
71	Atlantic 2091 143	Someday We're Gonna Love Again/Baby I'm Yours	15
72	Atlantic K 10128	Someday We're Gonne Love Again/Baby I'm Yours (reissue)	10
65	Atlantic AET 6015	SNAP YOUR FINGERS (EP)	70
66	Atlantic ATL 5042	BABY I'M YOURS (LP)	40
66	Atlantic 587 002	IT'S MAGIC (LP, mono)	50
66	Atlantic 588 002	IT'S MAGIC (LP, stereo)	60
70	Stax SXATS 1035	THE MANY GROOVES OF BARBARA LEWIS (LP)	40

BOBBY LEWIS
61	Parlophone R 4794	Tossin' And Turnin'/Oh Yes, I Love You	20
61	Parlophone R 4831	One Track Mind/Are You Ready	25
62	Stateside SS 126	I'm Tossin' And Turnin' Again/Nothin' But The Blues	25

CAPPY LEWIS
| 61 | Vogue V 9184 | Bullfight/OLYMPICS: Little Pedro | 20 |

(see also Olympics)

DAVE LEWIS (1)
| 66 | Pye Intl. NEP 44057 | GIVIN' GAS (EP) | 40 |
| 64 | Pye Intl. NPL 28053 | LITTLE GREEN THING(LP) | 30 |

DAVE LEWIS (2)
| 76 | Polydor 2383 420 | FROM TIME TO TIME (LP, with lyric sheet) | 18 |

DAVID LEWIS
| 70 | AX 1 | SONGS OF DAVID LEWIS (LP, private pressing, paste-on sleeve) | 400 |

(see also Andwella['s Dream], David Baxter)

FURRY LEWIS
69	Blue Horizon 7-63228	PRESENTING THE COUNTRY BLUES (LP)	80
70	Matchbox SDR 190	IN MEMPHIS (LP)	30
71	Xtra XTRA 1116	FURRY LEWIS (LP)	20
71	Spokane SPL 1004	THE EARLY YEARS 1927-1929 (LP)	30

(see also John Estes)

GARY LEWIS & PLAYBOYS
65	Liberty LIB 10187	This Diamond Ring/Tijuana Wedding	15
65	Liberty LIB 55778	Count Me In/Little Miss Go-Go	15
65	Liberty LIB 55809	Save Your Heart For Me/Without A Word Of Warning	10
65	Liberty LIB 55818	Everybody Loves A Clown/Time Stands Still	7
66	Liberty LIB 55846	She's Just My Style/I Won't Make That Mistake Again	20
66	Liberty LIB 55865	Sure Gonna Miss Her/I Don't Wanna Say Goodnight	8
66	Liberty LIB 55880	Green Grass/I Can Read Between The Lines	8
66	Liberty LIB 55898	My Heart's Symphony/Tina	20
66	Liberty LIB 55914	(You Don't Have To) Paint Me A Picture/Looking For The Stars	10

67	Liberty LIB 55933	Where Will The Words Come From/The Best Man	7
67	Liberty LIB 55949	Loser (With A Broken Heart)/Ice Melts In The Sun	7
67	Liberty LIB 55971	Girls In Love/Let's Be More Than Friends	7
67	Liberty LBF 15025	Jill/Needles And Pins	10
68	Liberty LBF 15131	Sealed With A Kiss/Pretty Thing	5
70	Liberty LBF 15335	Orangutan/Something Is Wrong	5
75	United Artists UP 35780	My Heart's Symphony/I Won't Make That Same Mistake Again (reissue)	6
65	Liberty LBY 1259	THIS DIAMOND RING (LP)	40
66	Liberty LBY 1322	JUST OUR STYLE (LP)	30

GEORGE LEWIS & HIS NEW ORLEANS STOMPERS/BAND

56	Vogue V 2051	Climax Rag/Deep Bayou Blues	8
56	Vogue V 2052	Millenberg Joys/Two Jim Blues	8
56	Vogue V 2053	Just A Closer Walk With Thee/Just A Little While To Stay Here	8
56	Vogue V 2054	Fidgety Feet/Dauphine Street Blues	8
56	Vogue V 2055	Don't Go 'Way Nobody/Careless Love Blues	8
60	HMV POP 707	South Rampart Street Parade/Chinatown My Chinatown (with Band)	7
52	Vogue LDE 012	GEORGE LEWIS AND HIS NEW ORLEANS ALLSTARS (10" LP)	15
54	Vogue LDE 082	GEORGE LEWIS JAM SESSION (10" LP)	15
55	Vogue LAE 12005	GEORGE LEWIS AND HIS NEW ORLEANS STOMPERS (LP)	20
57	Tempo TAP 13	GEORGE LEWIS RAGTIME BAND (LP)	20
50s	'77' LA 12/28	SMILE, DARN YA, SMILE (LP, as George Lewis with Barry Martyn's Band)	20

GEORGE LEWIS/FREDDIE KOHLMAN

| 53 | Brunswick LA 8627 | NEW ORLEANS JAZZ CONCERT (10" LP) | 15 |

HOPETON LEWIS

67	Island WI 3054	Rock Steady/Cool Collie	150
67	Island WI 3055	Finder's Keepers/ROLAND ALPHONSO: Shanty Town Curfew	50
67	Island WI 3056	Let Me Come On Home/Hardships Of Life (with Merritone All Stars)	50
67	Island WI 3057	Run Down/Pick Yourself Up	30
67	Island WI 3059	Let The Little Girl Dance/This Music Got Soul	50
67	Island WI 3068	Rock A Shacka/I Don't Want Trouble	100
68	Island WI 3076	Everybody Rocking/Stars Shining So Bright	50
68	Fab FAB 43	Skinny Leg Girl/Live Like A King (as Hopetown Lewis & Glenmore Brown)	25
70	Duke Reid DR 2505	Boom Shaka Lacka/TOMMY McCOOK QUINTET: Dynamite	15
70	Duke Reid DR 2516	Testify/TOMMY McCOOK: Super Soul	15
71	Duke DU 112	Grooving Out Of Life (with Byron Lee & Dragonaires) (actually titled Grooving Out On Life)/BYRON LEE & DRAGONAIRES: Fire Fire	8
71	Treasure Isle TI 7060	To The Other Man/TOMMY McCOOK: Stampede	12
72	Treasure Isle TI 7071	Judgement Day (actually by Hopeton Lewis & Dennis Alcapone)/ EARL LINDO: Version Day	10
72	Attack ATT 8035	Starting All Over Again/DYNAMITES: Instrumental Version	5
72	Dynamic DYN 436	Come Together/Going Back To My Hometown	5
72	Dynamic DYN 447	Good Together/Version	5
73	Dragon DRA 1001	City Of New Orleans/The Wind Cries Mary	5
73	Dragon DRA 1011	Groovin' Out On Life/God Bless Whoever Sent You	5
67	Island ILP 957	TAKE IT EASY: ROCKSTEADY WITH HOPETON LEWIS (LP)	200
71	Trojan TRL 36	GROOVING OUT ON LIFE (LP)	30

(see also Glenmore Brown & Hopeton Lewis)

HUGH X. LEWIS

66	London HLR 10032	Looking In The Future/Too Late	10
66	London HA-R 8293	THE HUGH X. LEWIS ALBUM (LP)	15
67	London HA-R 8303	JUST BEFORE DAWN (LP)	15

JEFFREY LEWIS

01	Rough Trade RTRADES 20	he Chelsea Hotel Oral Sex Song (1-sided promo, stamped label, without comic)	5
01	Rough Trade RTRADES 20	The Chelsea Hotel Oral Sex Song (1-sided promo, stamped label, with comic)	10
02	Rough Trade RTRADES 055	Back When I was 4/3.4 Moon (p/s)	5

JENNIFER LEWIS & ANGELA STRANGE

| 65 | Columbia DB 7662 | Bring It To Me/You Know | 10 |
| 66 | Columbia DB 7814 | I've Heard It All Before/Bad Storm Coming | 12 |

JERRY LEWIS

| 56 | Capitol CL 14626 | Buckskin Beauty/Pardners (with Dean Martin) | 5 |
| 57 | Brunswick 05636 | Rock-A-Bye Your Baby With A Dixie Melody/Come Rain Or Come Shine | 5 |

(see also Dean Martin)

JERRY LEWIS (JAMAICA)

| 72 | Pama PM 862 | The Godfather/ALTON ELLIS: Some Day | 15 |
| 73 | Explosion EX 2077 | Rhythm Pleasure/AGGROVATORS: Doctor Seaton | 12 |

(see also I Roy)

JERRY LEE LEWIS

78s

57	London HLS 8457	Whole Lotta Shakin' Goin' On/It'll Be Me	18
57	London HLS 8529	Great Balls Of Fire/Mean Woman Blues	20
58	London HLS 8559	You Win Again/I'm Feelin' Sorry	20
58	London HLS 8592	Breathless/Down The Line	20
58	London HLS 8700	Break-Up/I'll Make It All Up To You	35
59	London HLS 8780	High School Confidential/Fools Like Me	50
59	London HLS 8840	Lovin' Up A Storm/Big Blon' Baby	50
59	London HLS 8941	Let's Talk About Us/The Ballad Of Billy Joe	60
59	London HLS 8993	Little Queenie/I Could Never Be Ashamed Of You	100
96	Cruisin' The 50s CASB 002	Wild One/Old Black Joe (numbered, 300 only)	35

SINGLES

57	London HLS 8457	Whole Lotta Shakin' Goin' On/It'll Be Me	30
57	London HLS 8529	Great Balls Of Fire/Mean Woman Blues	20
58	London HLS 8559	You Win Again/I'm Feelin' Sorry	25
58	London HLS 8592	Breathless/Down The Line	20
58	London HLS 8700	Break-Up/I'll Make It All Up To You	20
59	London HLS 8780	High School Confidential/Fools Like Me	20

MINT VALUE £

59	London HLS 8840	Lovin' Up A Storm/Big Blon' Baby	20
59	London HLS 8941	Let's Talk About Us/The Ballad Of Billy Joe (no triangular centre)	20
59	London HLS 8993	Little Queenie/I Could Never Be Ashamed Of You (no triangular centre)	20

(Originally issued with triangular centres; round-centre pressings are worth two-thirds of these values.)

60	London HLS 9083	I'll Sail My Ship Alone/It Hurt Me So	20
60	London HLS 9131	Baby, Baby, Bye Bye/Old Black Joe	20
60	London HLS 9202	John Henry/Hang Up My Rock And Roll Shoes	20
61	London HLS 9335	What'd I Say?/Livin' Lovin' Wreck	10
61	London HLS 9414	It Won't Happen With Me/Cold Cold Heart	10
61	London HLS 9446	As Long As I Live/When I Get Paid	10
62	London HLS 9526	I've Been Twistin'/Ramblin' Rose	10
62	London HLS 9584	Sweet Little Sixteen/How's My Ex Treating You	10
63	London HLS 9688	Good Golly Miss Molly/I Can't Trust Me (In Your Arms Anymore)	10
63	London HLS 9722	Teenage Letter/Seasons Of My Heart (B-side with Linda Gail Lewis)	10
63	Mercury AMT 1216	Hit The Road Jack/Pen And Paper	10
64	Philips BF 1324	I'm On Fire/Bread And Butter Man	10
64	London HLS 9867	Lewis Boogie/Bonnie B	20
65	Philips BF 1371	Hi-Heel Sneakers/You Went Back On Your Word	7
65	Philips BF 1407	Baby Hold Me Close/I Believe In You	8
65	Philips BF 1425	Rockin' Pneumonia And The Boogie Woogie Flu/This Must Be The Place	10
65	London HLS 9980	Carry Me Back To Old Virginia/I Know What It Means	8
66	Philips BF 1521	Memphis Beat/If I Had It All To Do Over	10
67	Philips BF 1594	It's A Hang-Up Baby/Holdin' On	8
67	Philips BF 1615	Turn On Your Love Light/Shotgun Man	10
68	Mercury MF 1020	Another Place, Another Time/Walking The Floor Over You	6
69	Mercury MF 1088	To Make Love Sweeter For You/Let's Talk About Us	5
69	Mercury MF 1105	Long Tall Sally/Jenny, Jenny (some in p/s)	10
69	Mercury MF 1105	Long Tall Sally/Jenny, Jenny (some in p/s)	5
69	Mercury MF 1110	Great Balls Of Fire/Whole Lotta Shakin' Goin' On (in p/s)	10
73	Mercury 6052 260	Drinking Wine Spo Dee O Dee/Rock And Roll Medley	6
73	Mercury 6052 378	(Taking My) Music To The Man/Jack Daniels (Old No. 7) (in p/s)	8
79	Elektra K 12374	Rocking My Life Away/Rita May (p/s)	5
80	Elektra K 12399	Everyday I Have To Cry/Who Will The Next Fool Be	5
80	Elektra K 12432	Rockin' Jerry Lee/Good Time Charles Got The Blues	5
72	Mercury 6052 14 1	Chantilly Lace/Think About It Darlin'	7

SINGLES : EXPORT SINGLES

58	London HL 7050	High School Confidential/Fools Like Me	20
62	London HL 7117	Save The Last Dance For Me/Hello Josephine	30
63	London HL 7120	Good Golly Miss Molly/I Can't Trust Me (In Your Arms Anymore)	20
63	London HL 7123	In The Mood/I'm Feelin' Sorry	40

EPs

58	London RE-S 1140	JERRY LEE LEWIS - NO. 1 (with triangular centre)	40
58	London RE-S 1140	JERRY LEE LEWIS - NO. 1	35
59	London RE-S 1186	JERRY LEE LEWIS - NO. 2 (with triangular centre)	40
59	London RE-S 1186	JERRY LEE LEWIS - NO. 2	35
59	London RE-S 1187	JERRY LEE LEWIS - NO. 3 (with triangular centre)	40
59	London RE-S 1187	JERRY LEE LEWIS - NO. 3	35
61	London RE-S 1296	JERRY LEE LEWIS - NO. 4	30
62	London RE-S 1336	JERRY LEE LEWIS - NO. 5	30
63	London RE-S 1351	JERRY LEE LEWIS - NO. 6	30
63	London RE-S 1378	FOUR MORE FROM JERRY LEE LEWIS	30
66	Philips BE 12599	COUNTRY STYLE	30
84	Sun JLL EP 001	THE FABULOUS JERRY LEE LEWIS VOL. 1 (Fan Club issue)	15
84	Sun JLL EP 002	THE FABULOUS JERRY LEE LEWIS VOL. 2 (Fan Club issue)	15

ALBUMS

59	London HA-S 2138	JERRY LEE LEWIS	100
62	London HA-S 2440	JERRY LEE'S GREATEST	50
64	Philips (S)BL 7622	GOLDEN HITS	20
65	Philips (S)BL 7646	LIVE AT THE STAR CLUB, HAMBURG (with Nashville Teens)	25
65	Philips BL 7650	THE GREATEST LIVE SHOW ON EARTH	15
65	Philips BL 7668	THE RETURN OF ROCK	15
65	London HA-S 8251	WHOLE LOTTA SHAKIN' GOIN' ON	50
66	Philips BL 7688	COUNTRY SONGS FOR CITY FOLKS	15
66	Philips (S)BL 7706	MEMPHIS BEAT	15
67	London HA-S 8323	BREATHLESS	30

(Originally issued with plum labels; later black label reissues are worth £15-£20.)

69	Mercury 21047 SMCL	SHE STILL COMES AROUND (TO WHAT'S LEFT OF ME) (stereo only)	12
79	Elektra K52132	JERRY LEE LEWIS (LP)	12
84	Sun SUN 102	THE SUN YEARS (12-LP, box set with booklet)	40

(see also Nashville Teens)

JIMMY LEWIS

68	Minit MLF 11002	The Girls From Texas/Let Me Know	20

JOE 'CANNONBALL' LEWIS

51	MGM MGM 430	Train Whistle Nightmare/Trust Me Again (78)	10

JOHN LEWIS

60	London Jazz LTZ-K 15186	IMPROVISED MEDITATIONS AND EXCURSIONS (LP)	15
61	London Jazz LTZ-K 15218	THE GOLDEN STRIKER (LP, also stereo SAH-K 6152)	15

(see also Modern Jazz Quartet)

JOHN LEWIS AND SACHA DISTEL

59	UK Oriole MG20036	AFTERNOON IN PARIS (LP)	25

LEW LEWIS (REFORMER)

76	Stiff BUY 5	Caravan Man/Boogie On The Street (p/s, with Dr. Feelgood)	5
77	United Artists UP 36217	Out For A Lark/Watch Yourself (p/s)	5
78	Lew Lewis LEW 1	Lucky Seven/Night Talk (500 only, plain white sleeve, handwritten-style white label)	20
78	Stiff LEW 1	Lucky Seven/Night Talk (handwritten-style green label)	10
78	Stiff LEW 1	Lucky Seven/Night Talk (yellow label, p/s)	5

| 79 | stiff BUY 48 | Win Or Lose/Photo Finish ("A" label promo. p/s) | 5 |

(see also Oil City Sheiks, Dr. Feelgood, Eddie & the Hot Rods)

LINDA LEWIS

67	Polydor 56173	You Turned My Bitter Into Sweet/Do You Believe In Love	50
71	Reprise K 14096	We Can Win/Hampstead Way	6
72	Reprise K 14209	Old Smokey/It's The Frame	6
75	Arista ARIST 17	It's In His Kiss/Walk About (p/s)	6
73	Raft RA 18502	Rock A Doodle Doo/Reach For The Truth	6
71	Reprise K 44130	SAY NO MORE (LP)	20
72	Reprise K 44208	LARK (LP, textured gatefold sleeve)	15
73	Raft RA 48501	FATHOMS DEEP (LP, die-cut sleeve with inner)	12
79	Ariola ARL 5033	HACIENDA VIEW (LP)	12

(see also Ferris Wheel)

MARGARET LEWIS

| 62 | Starlite ST45 081 | Sometin's Wrong Baby/John De Lee | 30 |

MEADE 'LUX' LEWIS

50	Melodisc 1130	Boogie Tidal/Yancey's Pride (78)	10
50	Melodisc 1136	Glendale Glide/Denapas Parade (78)	10
51	Melodisc 1153	Randini's Boogie/Lux's Boogie (78)	10
52	Vogue V 2123	Blues Whistle/Chicago Flyer (78)	10
54	Vogue V 2229	Six Wheel Chaser Boogie/Bass On Top Boogie (78)	10
55	Vogue EPV 1065	MEADE 'LUX' LEWIS (EP)	20
56	Melodisc EPM7 107	BOOGIE WOOGIE AND BLUES (EP)	20
56	Columbia Clef SEB 10030	BOOGIE WOOGIE PIANO AND DRUMS NO. 1 (EP)	10
56	Columbia Clef SEB 10052	BOOGIE WOOGIE PIANO AND DRUMS NO. 2 (EP)	10
57	Columbia Clef 33CX 10094	YANCEY'S LAST RIDE (LP)	12
57	HMV DLP 1176	OUT OF THE ROARING TWENTIES (10" LP)	12

(see also Albert Ammons, [Big] Joe Turner)

MEADE 'LUX' LEWIS & SLIM GAILLARD

| 56 | Columbia Clef 33C 9021 | JAZZ AT THE PHILHARMONIC (10" LP) | 20 |

(see also Slim Gaillard)

MIA LEWIS

65	Decca F 12117	Wish I Didn't Love Him/This Is The End	10
65	Decca F 12240	It's Goodbye Now/The Luckiest Girl	8
66	Parlophone R 5526	Nothing Lasts Forever/(Baby) I'm Feeling Good	12
67	Parlophone R 5585	No Time For Lovin'/Onion	6
67	Parlophone R 5617	Woman's Love/You Won't Get Away	6

MICHAEL LEWIS

| 73 | United Artists UP 35569 | Theatre Of Blood Theme/Edwina's Theme | 15 |

MONICA LEWIS

| 56 | Parlophone R 4224 | I Wish You Love/Stay After School | 5 |

NIGEL LEWIS

| 86 | Media Burn MB10 | WHAT I FEEL NOW (LP) | 20 |

PATTI LEWIS

56	Columbia DB 3825	Earthbound/Happiness Street (Corner Sunshine Square)	10
57	Columbia DB 3923	Your Wild Heart/A Poor Man's Roses (Or A Rich Man's Gold)	8
57	Columbia DB 3967	Pull Down De Shade/Speak For Yourself John	8

PHILLIPPA LEWIS

| 65 | Decca F 12152 | Just Like In The Movies/Get Along Without You | 10 |

RAMSEY LEWIS (TRIO)

65	Chess CRS 8020	The 'In' Crowd/Since I Fell For You (as Ramsey Lewis Trio)	15
65	Chess CRS 8025	Hang On Sloopy/Movin' Easy (as Ramsey Lewis Trio)	8
66	Chess CRS 8029	A Hard Day's Night/'Tout A Doubt (as Ramsey Lewis Trio)	8
66	Chess CRS 8031	Hi-Heel Sneakers (Parts 1 & 2) (as Ramsey Lewis Trio)	10
66	Chess CRS 8041	Wade In The Water/Ain't That Peculiar (as Ramsey Lewis Trio)	40
66	Chess CRS 8041	Wade In The Water/Ain't That Peculiar (as Ramsey Lewis Trio) (DJ copy)	120
66	Chess CRS 8044	Uptight (Everything's Alright)/Money In The Pocket	10
67	Chess CRS 8051	Day Tripper/Hurt So Bad	20
67	Chess CRS 8055	1-2-3/Down By The Riverside	8
67	Chess CRS 8058	Function At The Junction/Hey Mrs. Jones	10
67	Chess CRS 8060	Saturday Night After The Movies/China Gate	8
67	Chess CRS 8061	Girl Talk/Dancing In The Street	8
67	Chess CRS 8064	Soul Man/Struttin' Lightly	10
69	Chess CRS 8096	Cry Baby Cry/Wade In The Water	20
69	Chess CRS 8096	Cry Baby Cry/Wade In The Water (DJ copy)	45
70	Chess CRS 8104	Julia/Do What You Wanna	10
72	Chess 6145 004	Wade In The Water/Ain't That Peculiar (paper label)	15
72	Chess 6145 013	The 'In' Crowd/Soul Man	6
72	CBS 8280	Slipping Into Darkness/Collage	8
66	Chess CRE 6019	A HARD DAY'S NIGHT (EP, as Ramsey Lewis Trio)	30
65	Pye Jazz NJL 55	AT THE BOHEMIAN CAVERNS (LP)	20
65	Chess CRL 4511	THE 'IN' CROWD (LP)	25
65	Chess CRL 4518	CHOICE! THE BEST OF RAMSEY LEWIS (LP)	25
66	Chess CRL 4520	HANG ON RAMSEY! (LP)	20
66	Chess CRL 4522	WADE IN THE WATER (LP)	40
67	Chess CRL 4528	GOIN' LATIN (LP)	25
67	Chess CRL 4531	THE MOVIE ALBUM (LP)	20
68	Chess CRL(S) 4533	DANCIN' IN THE STREET (LP)	25
68	Chess CRLS 4535	UP POPS RAMSEY LEWIS (LP)	25
68	Chess CRLS 4539	MAIDEN VOYAGE (LP)	25
69	Chess CRLS 4545	MOTHER NATURE'S SON (LP)	30
68	Fontana SFJL 962	DOWN TO EARTH (LP)	20
72	Chess 6310 106	BACK TO THE ROOTS (LP)	15
72	Chess 6310 114	THE BEST OF RAMSEY LEWIS (LP)	15
72	Chess 6310 124	TOBACCO ROAD (LP)	15

Richard LEWIS & HIS BAND

72	CBS 64718	UPENDO NI PAMOJA (LP)	12
73	CBS 65307	FUNKY SERENITY (LP)	20
73	CBS CQ 31096	UPENDO NI PAMOJA (LP, quadrophonic)	15
74	CBS S80677	SUN GODDESS (LP)	18

(see also Young-Holt Unlimited)

RICHARD LEWIS & HIS BAND
60	Downbeat CHA 1	Hey, Little Girl/Hey, Little Boy	40

SHIRLEY LEWIS
83	High Energy	Loves Warming Up/Dub Mix (12")	15

SMILEY LEWIS
53	London L 1189	Big Mamou/Play Girl (78, some copies miscredited to Smiley Davis)	100
56	London HLU 8312	One Night/Ain't Gonna Do It	800
56	London HLU 8312	One Night/Ain't Gonna Do It (78)	100
56	London HLU 8337	Down Yonder We Go Ballin'/Don't Be That Way (Please Listen To Me)	800
56	London HLU 8337	Down Yonder We Go Ballin'/Don't Be That Way (Please Listen To Me) (78)	100
57	London HLP 8367	Shame, Shame, Shame/No, No (gold lettering)	500
57	London HLP 8367	Shame, Shame, Shame/No, No (silver lettering)	400
57	London HLP 8367	Shame, Shame, Shame/No, No (78)	70
70	Liberty LBF 15337	I Hear You Knocking/Play Girl	10
70	Liberty LBS 83308	SHAME, SHAME, SHAME (LP)	25
78	United Artists UAS 30167	I HEAR YOU KNOCKING (LP)	15

STEVIE LEWIS
65	Mercury MF 871	Take Me For A Little While/My Whole World Seems To Be Tumbling Down	22
65	Mercury MF 919	Sometimes When You're Lonely/Under The Smile Of Love	5
65	Polydor 56003	Heard It All Before/Wild	7
69	RCA RCA 1840	Take A Little Warning/I Can Try	5

TAMALA LEWIS
79	Destiny DS 1010	You Won't Say Nothing/If You Can Stand Me	8
79	Destiny DS 1010	You Won't Say Nothing/If You Can Stand Me (DJ)	15

TINY LEWIS
60	Parlophone R 4617	Too Much Rockin'/I Get Weak	150

VIC LEWIS
63	HMV POP 1127	Bossa Nova Scotia/Vic's Tune	5
68	NEMS 56-3893	Goodnight/Julia (as Vic Lewis, his Orchestra and singers)	10
69	NEMS 56 3712	Sunshine Superman/Mellow Yellow	8
69	NEMS 56-4057	Blackbird/I Will	20
62	Columbia SEG 8202	SWINGS NELSON RIDDLE (EP)	8
55	Decca LF 1216	PROGRESSIVE JAZZ (10" LP)	30
62	HMV CLP 1641	PLAY BOSSA NOVA HOME AND AWAY (LP, features Tubby Hayes)	50
70	Ember CJS 807	AT THE BEAULIEU FESTIVAL (LP)	25
60s	Ember SE 8018	BIG BAND EXPLOSION (LP)	30
70s	DJM SPECB 103	MY LIFE MY WAY (LP)	15

LEWIS SISTERS
65	Tamla Motown TMG 536	You Need Me/Moonlight On The Beach	120
65	Tamla Motown TMG 536	You Need Me/Moonlight On The Beach (DJ Copy)	150

DAVE LEWRY
72	Westwood WRS 019	ALL I WANT TO DO IS PLAY GUITAR (LP)	35

MONIQUE LEYRAC
68	SNB 55-3309	Time Time/Love Is Blue	7

LEYTON BUZZARDS
78	Small Wonder SMALL 7	19 And Mad/Villain/Youthanasia (p/s)	6
79	Chrysalis CHS 2288	Saturday Night Beneath The Plastic Palm Trees/Through With You (p/s)	5
79	Chrysalis CHS 2328	I'm Hanging Around/I Don't Want To Go/No Dry Ice And Flying Pigs (p/s, green vinyl)	5
79	Chrysalis CHR 1213	JELLIED EELS TO RECORD DEALS (LP, as Buzzards)	12

JOHN LEYTON
60	Top Rank JAR 426	Tell Laura I Love Her/Goodbye To Teenage Love	40
60	HMV POP 798	The Girl On The Floor Above/Terry Brown's In Love With Mary Dee	70
61	Top Rank JAR 577	Johnny Remember Me/There Must Be	5
61	Top Rank JAR 585	Wild Wind/You Took My Love For Granted	5
61	HMV POP 956	Son This Is She/Six White Horses	5
62	HMV POP 992	Lone Rider/Heart Of Stone	10
62	HMV POP 1014	Lonely City/It Would Be Easy	10
62	HMV POP 1054	Down The River Nile/I Think I'm Falling In Love	10
62	HMV POP 1076	Lonely Johnny/Keep On Loving You	8
63	HMV POP 1122	Cupboard Love/Land Of Love	5
63	HMV POP 1175	I'll Cut Your Tail Off/The Great Escape	10
63	HMV POP 1204	On Lover's Hill/Lovers Lane	8
63	HMV POP 1230	I Guess You Are Always On My Mind/Beautiful Dreamer	6
64	HMV POP 1264	Make Love To Me/Missing You (as John Leyton & Le Roys)	15
64	HMV POP 1338	Don't Let Her Go Away/I Want A Love I Can See	15
64	HMV POP 1374	All I Want Is You/Every Day Is A Holiday (with Grazina Frame & Mike Sarne)	15
73	York SYK 551	Dancing In The Graveyard/Riversong	10
74	York YR 210	Rock 'N' Roll/Highway Song	10
62	Top Rank JKP 3016	JOHN LEYTON (EP)	40
62	HMV 7EG 8747	HIT PARADE (EP)	25
64	HMV 7EG 8843	BEAUTIFUL DREAMER (EP)	25
64	HMV 7EG 8854	TELL LAURA I LOVE HER (EP)	40
61	HMV CLP 1497	THE TWO SIDES OF JOHN LEYTON (LP)	40
62	HMV CLP 1664	ALWAYS YOURS (LP, with Charles Blackwell's Orchestra)	50
73	York FYK 416	JOHN LEYTON (LP)	30

(see also Le Roys)

L.F.O.
90	Warp/Outer WAP5R	LFO Remix/Mentok 1/Quijard (12")	10
90	Warp WAP 5	L.F.O. (The Leeds Warehouse Mix)/L.F.O. (Track 4)/Probe (The Cuba Edit) (12", p/s)	15

91	Warp WAP 14	We Are Back/Nurture (12")	10
92	Warp WAP 17	What Is House (LFO Remix)/Push/Tan Ta Ra (Moby Remix) (12")	10
91	Warp WARPLP1	FREQUENCIES (LP)	25
96	Warp WARPLP39	ADVANCE (2-LP)	20
03	Warp WARPLP110	SHEATH (LP)	15

LG & LOPEZ

| 01 | Sit Tight STR001 | Life Long/Tempered Waters/Storming (EP) | 10 |
| 02 | Sit Tight STR002 | Rocket Fuel/City Breaks (EP) | 10 |

LIAISON

82	Catweazle CR 001	Play It With A Passion/Caught In A ... (grey p/s)	35
82	Catweazle CR 001	Play It With A Passion/Caught In A ... (yellow p/s)	10
84	Liaison LSN 0020	Only Heaven Knows/Ease The Pain Away (p/s)	5

LIAR

| 79 | Bearsville K 55524 | SET THE WORLD ON FIRE (LP, picture disc) | 15 |

LIARS

05	Mute MUTE 39	It Fit When I Was A kid/Don't Techno For An Answer Mix (7", picture disc in p/s, 500 only)	5
02	Blast First BFFP 172	THEY THREW US ALL IN A TRENCH AND STUCK A MONUMENT ON TOP (LP)	15
04	Mute STUMM 225	THEY WERE WRONG SO WE DROWNED (LP, gatefold, white vinyl, booklet)	20
05	Mute STUMM 246	DRUM'S NOT DEAD (LP with DVD)	20
07	Mute STUMM 287	LIARS (LP, white vinyl, inner)	15

SVEN LIBAEK

| 06 | Trunk JBH 020 LP | INNER SPACE: THE LOST FILM MUSIC OF SVEN LIBAEK (LP) | 20 |

LIBERACE

| 56 | Columbia DB 3834 | I Don't Care (As Long As You Care For Me)/As Time Goes By | 5 |

LIBERATION SUITE

| 75 | Myrrh MYR 1027 | LIBERATION SUITE (LP) | 20 |

LIBERATORS

| 65 | Stateside SS 424 | It Hurts So Much/You Look So Fine | 15 |

(see also Pinkerton's Assorted Colours)

EVE LIBERTINE & CRASS

| 84 | Crass 1984/4 | ACTS OF LOVE (LP, with book) | 15 |

(see also Crass)

LIBERTINES

02	Rough Trade RTRADES 054	What A Waster/I Get Along (p/s, 2000 only)	25
02	Rough Trade RTRADES 064	Up The Bracket/Boys In The Band (p/s)	10
03	Rough Trade RTRADES 074	Time For Heroes/The 7 Deadly Sins (demo version) (p/s)	10
03	Rough Trade RTRADS 119	Don't Look Back Into The Sun/Death On The Stairs (blue vinyl, fold-out poster sleeve in PVC slipcase, 3000 only)	20
04	Rough Trade RTRADS 163	Can't Stand Me Now/The Tide That Left Never Came Back/(I've Got) Sweets (p/s)	5
04	Rough Trade RTRADS 215	What Became Of The Likely Lads?/(Reworked)/Boys In The Band (Live at Brixton Sat 6/3/04) (Free LP poster p/s)	15
02	Rough Trade RTRADELP 065	UP THE BRACKET (LP)	20
04	Rough Trade RTRADELPX166	THE LIBERTINES (LP, gatefold 3000 only)	30
04	Rough Trade RTRADELP166	THE LIBERTINES (White label test pressing, 10 only)	50
07	Rough Trade RTRADLP 421	TIME FOR HEROES - THE BEST OF THE LIBERTINES (LP)	12

(see also Babyshambles, Wolfman)

RAY LIBERTO

| 61 | HMV CSD 1435 | MOTION PICTURE THEMES A LA DIXIELAND (LP) | 12 |

LIBERTY

| 80s | Mortarhate MORT 19 | Our Voices Tomorrow's Hope | 12 |
| 80s | Mortarhate MORT 25 | THE PEOPLE WHO CARE ARE ANGRY (LP) | 20 |

LIBERTY BELLES

| 71 | Jay Boy BOY 40 | Shing-A-Ling Time/Just Try Me | 10 |

LIBIDO 1

| 73 | Mooncrest MOON 2 | Hold On To Your Fire/Weren't Born A Man | 20 |

LICKS

| 79 | Stortbeat BEAT 8 | 1970S EP | 15 |

(see also Epileptics, Flux Of Pink Indians)

JAMIE LIDELL

| 97 | Mosquito MSQ 08 | FREAKIN' THE FRAME (12" EP) | 20 |

BUNNY LIE LIE

| 81 | Greensleeves GRED 52 | Babylonian/WAYNE WADE: Poor And Humble (12") | 20 |

LIEUTENANT PIGEON

73	Decca SKL 5154	MOULDY OLD MUSIC (LP)	20
73	Decca SKL 5174	PIGEON PIE (LP)	20
74	Decca SKL 5196	PIGEON PARTY (LP)	25

(see also Shel Naylor, Stavely Makepeace, Heavy Cochran)

LIFE

72	Phillips 6006247	Hold On (I'll Find You)/Love Nest	40
69	Polydor 56778	Hands Of The Clock/Ain't I Told You Before	22
74	Polydor 2058 500	Woman/Bless My Soul	6
74	Polydor 2383 295	LIFE AFTER DEATH (LP)	60
73	Philips 6006 280	Cats Eyes/Death In The Family (paper label)	20
73	Philips 6006 280	Cats Eyes/Death In The Family (moulded label)	10

LIFE AFTER LIFE

| 85 | Timetrack SRTSKL 453 | LIFE AFTER LIFE (LP, private pressing) | 120 |

LIFE 'N' SOUL

| 67 | Decca F 12659 | Ode To Billy Joe/Peacefully Asleep | 25 |
| 68 | Decca F 12851 | Here Comes Yesterday Again/Dear Paul | 15 |

MINT VALUE £

LIFE SUPPORT
79	Slug SLUG 1	Leader Deceiver/Confusion (p/s, white labels)	6

LIFE WITHOUT BUILDINGS
00	Tugboat TUGS 019	Is Is & The IRS/Let's Get Out (p/s)	8
00	Tugboat TUGS 016	The Leanover/New Town (p/s)	8
01	Tugboat TUGS 026	Young Offenders/Daylighting (p/s)	5
00	Tugboat TUGLP 023	ANY OTHER CITY (LP)	30

LIFETIME
70	Polydor 2066 050	One Word/Two Worlds	20

(see also Tony Williams [Lifetime], Jack Bruce, John McLaughlin)

JOE LIGES
63	Blue Beat BB 172	Spit In The Sky/Tell Me What (both actually by Delroy Wilson)	25

(see also Delroy Wilson)

JOE LIGGINS & HONEYDRIPPERS
50	Parlophone R 3309	I've Got The Right To Cry/Blue Moods (78)	30
76	Specialty SDN 5006	Pink Champagne/Honey Dripper	5

(THE) LIGHT
96	AAA Recordings TRIP 002	Dusk (12")	15

BEN LIGHT
56	HMV 7M 350	Bring Me A Bluebird/You	10

ENOCH LIGHT
59	Top Rank JAR 134	With My Eyes Wide Open/I Cried For You (as Enoch Light & Light Brigade)	5
59	Top Rank JAR 234	Scarlet Ribbons/Greensleeves (as Enoch Light & His Vibrant Strings)	5
69	Studio Two TWO 312	SPACED OUT (LP)	25
70	Project 3	PERMISSIVE POLYPHONICS (LP)	25
65	Pye Command PCLS 873	DISCOTHEQUE (LP)	25

LIGHT FANTASTIC
73	MAM R 105	Love Is Everywhere/Gone Are The Days	10
73	MAM 112	Alley Oop/Peace And Love To The World	8
73	RCA RCA 2331	Jeanie/You Don't Care	20
74	Blue Jean BJS 701	Take Me, Shake Me/Don't Let Go	8
75	Blue Jean BJS 704	We Are The Song/Raining	6

J.J. LIGHT
69	Liberty LBF 15228	Heya/On The Road Now	10

LIGHT OF THE WORLD
82	EMI EMC 3410	CHECK US OUT (LP)	20
80	Ensign ENVY 14	ROUND TRIP (LP)	12

GORDON LIGHTFOOT
62	Decca F 11527	(Remember Me) I'm The One/Daisy-Doo (as Gord Lightfoot)	20
63	Fontana 267 275TF	Negotiations/It's Too Late, He Wins (as Gordie Lightfoot)	10
63	Fontana TF 405	The Day Before Yesterday/Take Care Of Yourself (as Gordie Lightfoot)	6
65	United Artists UP 1109	Just Like Tom Thumb's Blues/Ribbon Of Darkness	5
66	Warner Bros WB 5621	I'm Not Sayin'/For Lovin' Me	5
68	President PT 138	Adios Adios/Is My Baby Blue Tonight (as Gordie Lightfoot)	5
68	United Artists UP 2216	Black Day In July/Pussy Willow's Cat Tails	5
69	United Artists UP 2272	The Circle Is Small/Does Your Mother Know	5
69	United Artists UP 35020	Bitter Green/May I	5
68	United Artists SULP 1199	DID SHE MENTION MY NAME (LP)	12
69	United Artists SULP 1239	BACK HERE ON EARTH (LP)	12
70	Reprise RS 20974	If You Could Read My Mind/Poor Little Alison	5

PADDY LIGHTFOOT
50s	Melodisc EPM7 100	PADDY LIGHTFOOT (EP)	10

PAPA (GEORGE) LIGHTFOOT
69	Liberty LBF 15176	Wine Whiskey And Woman/SLIM HARPO: Something Inside Me	25
60s	Jan & Dil JR 451	MORE DOWN HOME BLUES (EP)	35
71	Liberty LBS 83353	NATCHEZ TRACE (LP, as Papa George Lightfoot)	30

TERRY LIGHTFOOT'S (NEW ORLEANS) JAZZMEN
61	Columbia 33SX 1290	TRAD PARADE (LP, with New Orleans Jazzmen, also stereo SCX 3354)	12
61	Columbia 33SX 1353	WORLD OF TRAD (LP)	15
62	Columbia 33SX 1449	LIGHTFOOT AT LANSDOWNE (LP)	12

LIGHTHOUSE
69	RCA RCA 1884	Eight Miles High/If There Ever Was A Time	7
71	Vertigo 6073 150	Hats Off (To The Strangers)/Sing Sing Sing	12
72	Philips 6073 152	One Fine Morning/Little Kind Words	12
72	Philips 6073 153	Take It Slow/Sweet Lullaby	20
70	RCA SF 8103	SUITE FEELING (LP)	15
70	RCA SF 8121	PEACING IT ALL TOGETHER (LP)	12
71	Vertigo 6342 010	ONE FINE MORNING (LP, gatefold sleeve, swirl label)	80
71	Vertigo 6342 011	THOUGHTS OF MOVIN' ON (LP, gatefold sleeve, swirl label)	80
70	RCA RCA 1982	The Chant (Nam Myo-Ho Renge' Kyo)/Could You Be Concerned	10

LIGHTNIN' SLIM
72	Blue Horizon 2096 013	Just A Little Bit/You're Old Enough To Understand/Mind Your Own Business	30
65	Stateside SL 10135	A LONG DRINK OF BLUES (LP, with Slim Harpo)	80
69	Python PLP 8	THE DOWNHOME BLUES PART 1 (LP, 99 copies only)	60
70	Blue Horizon 7-63863	ROOSTER BLUES (LP)	85
72	Blue Horizon 2931 005	LONDON GUMBO (LP)	130
78	Flyright FLYLP 533	TRIP TO CHICAGO (LP)	18
79	Flyright FLYLP 583	THE FEATURE SIDES 1954 (LP)	15
80	Flyright FLYLP 612	WE GOTTA ROCK TONIGHT (LP)	18

(see also Slim Harpo)

LIGHTNING LEON
60s   Jan & Dil JR 450   DOWN HOME BLUES - SIXTIES STYLE (EP) 35

LIGHTNING RAIDERS
80   Arista ARIST 341   Psychedelik Musik ('adult' version)/Views (p/s) 18
80   Arista ARIST 341DJ   Psychedelik Musik ('censored' version)/Views (promo only, no p/s) 35
81   Revenge REVS 200   Criminal World/Citizens (p/s) 10
81   Revenge RSS 39   Sweet Revenge/Rowdies/Addiction/Soul Rescue (12", promo only)..............45
(see also Pink Fairies, Professionals)

LIGOTAGE
84   Picasso PIKM005   FORGIVE AND FORGET (LP, lyric insert)..............................15

LIKE A SONG
73   De Wolfe DW/LP 3273   LIKE A SONG (LP, library issue) 18

LIL LOUIS
89   Rough TOUGH 4   Frequency (Remix) (12", 3,000 copies) 15
89   Ffrr FX 115   French Kiss/Wargames (12") 8

LILAC TIME
88   Swordfish LILAC 1   Return To Yesterday/Trumpets From Montparnasse (no p/s)..............8
88   Swordfish 12 LILAC 1   Return To Yesterday/Railway Bazaar/Trumpets From Montparnasse/Reunion Ball (12", p/s)..............12
88   Fontana LILCD 2   Return To Yesterday/Rooftrees/Gone For A Burton/ Reunion Ball (CD, card sleeve)...........12
88   Fontana LILAC 4   Black Velvet/Black Dawn (p/s in Xmas card folder)..............5
90   Caff CAFF 12   Madresfield/Bird On The Wire (p/s, with insert) 25
88   Swordfish SWF LP 6   THE LILAC TIME (LP, original issue) 15
88   Swordfish SWF CD 6   THE LILAC TIME (CD, original issue) 40
(see also Hawks, Stephen Duffy)

LILIPUT
80   Rough Trade RT 047   Spilt/Die Matrosen (p/s)..............................8
81   Rough Trade RT 062   Eisiger Wind/When The Cat's Away Then The Mice Will Play 10
82   Rough Trade ROUGH 43   LILIPUT (LP)..............................20
(see also Kleenex)

BEATRICE LILLIE
61   Decca F 11377   Typically English/Mr Perfect..............................6

LILYS
96   Ché CHE 51   Returns Every Morning/Touch The Water (white vinyl, p/s, 500 only) 6
96   Ché CHE 65   A Nanny In Manhattan/More Than Is Deserved (coffee-coloured vinyl, p/s, 500 only)...........6

LIMELIGHT (1)
75   United Artists UP 35779   I Should Have Known Better/Tell Me Why 12
84   Mausoleum SKULL 9309   ASHES TO ASHES (LP) 12
(see also Brinsley Schwarz)

LIMELIGHT (2)
80   Future Earth FER 006   Metal Man/Hold Me Touch Me (p/s)..............................12
82   Future Earth FER 010   Ashes To Ashes/Knife In Your Back (p/s, with insert)..............12
82   Future Earth FER 010   Ashes To Ashes/Knife In Your Back (p/s, some with insert)..............10
80   Future Earth FER 008   LIMELIGHT (LP)..............................22
81   Avatar AALP 5005   LIMITED LIMELIGHT (LP, with bonus single)..............................20
81   Avatar AALP 5005   LIMITED LIMELIGHT (LP)..............................15

ALISON LIMERICK
90   Arista 614 208   Where Love Lives: (Classic/Red Zone/Cut To The Bone Mixes) (12") 15

LIMEYS
65   Pye 7N 15820   I Can't Find My Way Through/Don't Cry (My Love) 8
65   Pye 7N 15909   Some Tears Fall Dry/Half Glass Of Wine 8
66   Decca F 12382   Cara-Lin/Feel So Blue 30
66   Decca F 12466   The Mountain's High/Lovin' Yourself..............................8

LIMIT
78   Private Stock PVT 156   Please Please Me/My World At Night (company sleeve) 40

LIMMIE
78   Psycho P 2604   Saturday Night's The Night/Party 50

LIMPS/NO SUPPORT
79   Matchbox Classics MC 1   OPPOSITE SIDES EP (Split 7" with 2 tracks by Limps and 2 tracks by No Support, p/s)...........20
79   Matchbox Classics MC 2   ANOTHER MATCHBOX CLASSIC? (Split EP, 2 tracks by Limps and 2 by No Support, with folded p/s)..............40
79   Matchbox Classics MC 2   ANOTHER MATCHBOX CLASSIC? (Split EP, 2 tracks by Limps and 2 by No Support, without folded p/s, just die-cut stamped sleeve)..............15

PETER LINCOLN
67   Major Minor MM 520   In The Day Of My Youth/My Monkey Is A Junkie 30
(see also Peter Sarstedt, Sarstedt Brothers, Brothers Kane)

PHILAMORE LINCOLN
68   NEMS 56-3711   Running By The River/Rainy Day 70
70   CBS 5007   The County Jail Band/You're The One 30

LINCOLN TURNPIKE
71   Polydor 2058109   Green On The Other Side Of The Mountain/You Can Call Everybody Your Friend..............8

LINCOLN X
63   Oriole CB 1823   Heartaches And Happiness/Stand In For Her Past 5

LINCOLNS
66   Parlophone R 5418   Mister Loneliness/Only Love Will Break Your Heart..............................6

BOB LIND
66   Fontana TF 670   Elusive Butterfly/Cheryl's Goin' Home..............................5
66   Fontana TF 702   Remember The Rain/Truly Julie's Blues (I'll Be There) 6
66   Fontana (S)TL 5340   DON'T BE CONCERNED (LP)..............................15
66   Verve F'ways (S)VLP 5015   THE ELUSIVE BOB LIND (LP)..............................15

LINDA LAURIE
59	London HL 8807	Ambrose/Ooh, What A Lover	8
60	Top Rank JAR 277	Stay With Me/All Winter Long	6

ROSA LINDA
53	London L 1215	Flight 88/Taboo (78)	12

DADDY LINDBERG
67	Columbia DB 8138	Shirl/Wade In The Shade	120

(see also Crocheted Doughnut Ring, Fingers)

ANITA LINDBLOM
62	Fontana 267223 TF	Uptown/Mr Big Wheel	10

DENNIS LINDE
73	Elektra K 42149	DENNIS LINDE (LP)	12
74	Elektra K 52013	TRAPPED IN THE SUBURBS (LP)	12

KATHY LINDEN
58	Felsted AF 102	Billy/If I Could Hold You In My Arms	6
58	Felsted AF 105	You'd Be Surprised/Why Oh Why	6
58	Felsted AF 108	Oh! Johnny, Oh! Johnny Oh!/Georgie	7
58	Felsted AF 111	Kissin' Conversation/Just A Sandy Haired Boy Called Sandy	8
59	Felsted AF 122	Goodbye Jimmy, Goodbye/Heartaches At Sweet Sixteen	5
59	Felsted AF 124	So Close To My Heart/You Don't Know Girls	8
60	Felsted AF 130	Think Love/Mary Lou Wilson And Johnny Brown	8
59	Felsted GEP 1001	KATHY (EP)	20
59	Felsted GEP 1002	KATHY'S IN LOVE VOLUME ONE (EP)	20
59	Felsted GEP 1004	KATHY'S IN LOVE VOLUME TWO (EP)	20

LINDISFARNE
70	Charisma CB 137	Clear White Light Part II/Knackers Yard Blues	15
71	Charisma CB 153	Lady Eleanor/Nothing But The Marvellous Is Beautiful (with p/s)	6
70	Charisma CAS 1025	NICELY OUT OF TUNE (LP, pink 'scroll' label)	35
70	Charisma CAS 1025	NICELY OUT OF TUNE (LP, 'mad hatter' label)	12
71	Charisma CAS 1050	FOG ON THE TYNE (LP, gatefold sleeve, pink 'scroll' label)	25
71	Charisma CAS 1050	FOG ON THE TYNE (LP, gatefold sleeve, later 'Mad Hatter' label)	12
72	Charisma CAS 1057	DINGLY DELL (LP, with inner sleeve & poster)	12

(see also Alan Hull, Jack The Lad, Chosen Few, Radiator, Ray Jackson)

WILLIE LINDO
78	Black Wax WAX 21	Midnight/After Midnight	35

JIMMY LINDSAY AND THE BEANS
70	Q 2203	Peace To You Brother/Tribute To Jimi Hendrix	10

JIMMY LINDSAY
77	Black Swan BS 8	Easy/FABIAN: Prophecy (12")	25
78	Music Hive MH002	Ain't No Sunshine/EXODUS : Take Six/DIMBALA : And Ting (12")	30
82	Music Hive MH004	Turn Out The Lights/Dole Queue (12")	30
80	Gem GEMLP 110	CHILDREN OF RASTAFARI (LP)	15

MARK LINDSAY
69	CBS 4699	Arizona/Man From Houston	10
70	CBS 5055	Silver Bird/So Hard To Leave You	8
70	CBS 5219	And The Grass Won't Pay No Mind/Funny How Little Men Care	8
71	CBS 5408	Problem Child/Bookends	8
71	CBS 7330	Been Too Long On The Road/All I Really See Is You	8
71	CBS 7551	Are You Old Enough/Don't You Know	8
71	CBS 7690	Something Big/Pretty Pretty	8

(see also Paul Revere & Raiders)

TERRY LINDSEY
69	President PT 232	It's Over/One Day Up, Next Day Down	15

DAVID LINDUP ORCHESTRA
66	Columbia DB 7979	Informer Theme/Blue Mountain	10
66	Polydor 56106	Survival Theme/New Forest	20
70	Aristocrat AR 1021	WHEN THE SAINTS GO (LP)	20

LINDYS
60	Decca F 11253	The Train Of Love/You Know How Things Get Around	15
60	Decca F 11272	Boy With The Eyes Of Blue/Someone Else's Roses	15

LINES
78	Linear SJP 782	White Night/Barbican (p/s)	7
79	Illegal ILS 0011	White Night/Barbican (p/s, reissue)	5
80	Red Linear RL 007	Nerve Pylon/Over The Brow (screen-printed p/s)	5
80s	Red Linear RL12 005	COOL SNAP EP (12")	15

LING FAMILY
77	Topic 12TS 292	SINGING TRADITIONS OF A SUFFOLK FAMILY (LP)	12

BUZZY LINHART
72	Kama Sutra 2013049	You Got What It Takes/Tell Me True	5
69	Philips SBL 7885	BUZZY (LP, laminated gatefold sleeve, black/silver labels)	40
71	Kama Sutra 2319011	THE TIME TO LIVE IS NOW (LP, textured gatefold sleeve, yellow/red labels)	25

LINK
92	Evolution EVO 05	THE FIRST LINK EP (12", plain sleeve)	30
93	Symbiotic SYM 001	THE LINK EP (12", plain sleeve, no credits on label)	8
95	Warp WAP 59	ANTACID EP (12", p/s)	15
95	Warp WAP 59R	ANTACID REMIXES EP (12", p/s as Link & E621)	10

(see also Reload, Global Communications, Mystic Institute)

LINKERS
71	Big Shot BI 567	Bongo Man/FUD CHRISTIAN ALLSTARS: Creation Version	6

(see also Links)

ANSEL LINKERS & FUD CHRISTIAN ALL STARS
73	Summit SUM 8540	Memories By The Score/FUD CHRISTIAN ALL STARS: Scorer	7

(see also Links)

LINKS
72	Tropical AL 0010	Sing A Song Of Freedom/TROPICAL ALL STARS: Love Rhythm (A-side actually by Linkers)	6

LINN COUNTY
68	Mercury SMCL 20142	PROUD FLESH SOOTHSEER (LP)	25
69	Mercury SMCL 20165	FEVER SHOT (LP)	20
70	Philips SBL 7923	TILL THE BREAK OF DAWN (LP)	18

ELMO LINN
63	Starlite ST45 101	Another Man's Arms/Sam Houston	18

JOE LINTHECOME
50s	Poydras 87	Pretty Mama Blues/Hummingbird Blues	15

LION (& HIS CALYPSO CUBS)
51	Sagomes SG 117	Ugly Woman/The Lost Watch (78)	10
52	Parlophone MP 114	Mary Ann/Little Mary Had No Lamb (export 78)	10
52	Parlophone MP 115	Tick! Tick!/Ugly Woman (export 78)	10
53	Melodisc 1236	Coronation Of Elizabeth 2/Crosby Cavalcade (78, with Caribbean Rhythm)	10
54	Parlophone MP 129	The Royal Tour/The Weather Man (export 78)	10
54	Parlophone MP 132	I Ain't Gonna Do It No More/Trinidad, The Land Of Calypso (export 78)	10
55	Parlophone MP 135	Bananas/The Devil Fly (export 78, with His Calypso Cubs)	10

LIONHEART
85	Epic A 5001	Die For Love/Dangerous Games (p/s)	7
84	Epic EPC26214	HOT TONIGHT (LP)	15

(see also Iron Maiden, Wildfire)

LIONROCK
92	M.E.R.C. 002	Roots'n'Culture (Part One)/Lionrock (12", original issue)	10
92	De Construction 74321124381	Lionrock - The Remixes: (Most Excellent Mix)/ (Roots 'n' Culture)/(A Trumpet Jamboree In Edinburgh)/(A Dubtastic Jamboree In Edinburgh) (12")	10
93	De Construction 74321144371	Packet Of Peace (Prankster Sound System Mix)/(Instrumental)/ (No More Fucking Trumpets) (12")	8
93	Distort & Cavort	Dub Plate No. 1 (12")	10
94	De Construction DUB PLATE 1	The Guide/Don't Be Foolish (12")	8
98	Concrete HARD 3112	Rude Boy Rock/Best Foot Forward/Push Button Cocktail (p/s)	8

LIONS
69	Polydor 56757	Twisted Nerve/My Friend The Blackbird	30

LIONS (JAMAICA)
77	Truth & Right L 001	Natty Congo 1/Version	15

LIONS OF JUDAH
69	Fontana TF 1016	Our Love's A Growin' Thing/Katja	20

LION TAMERS
68	Polydor 56283	Speak Your Mind/Light	50

LION YOUTH
81	Virgo Stomach VG104	Rat Cut A Bottle/Rub A Dub (12")	15
81	Virgo Stomach VGLP 001	LOVE COMES AND GOES (LP)	18

LIP MOVES
79	Tichonderoga HP 1	Guest/What Is (p/s with insert, stickered white labels, signed)	35
79	Tichonderoga HP 1	Guest/What Is (p/s with insert, stickered white labels)	30

JOE LIPMAN ORCHESTRA
54	MGM SP 1108	Looking Back To See/Stop	5

LIQUID CRYSTAL
91	Bizarre BIZZ 2	Inner Sense/Dischord (12")	25
92	Bizarre BIZZ 3	The Power Within/Let It Go/Inner Sense ('92 remix) (12")	25
92	Bizarre BIZZ 3R T	The Power Within (Remix)/Radiate/Inner Sense (Original) (12", p/s)	25
92	Ruff On Wax ROWT 1	CHROMATIC EP (12", stickered plain sleeve)	70
92	Ruff On Wax ROWTR 1	CHROMATIC 2 EP: (12", stickered plain sleeve)	60

LIQUID LIQUID
97	Mo Wax MW 078LP	LIQUID LIQUID (2-LP)	20

LIQUID SMOKE
75	Pye Int. 7N 25677	Dance Dance Dance/Where Is Our Love	8
70	Avco Embassy 646 6003	LIQUID SMOKE (LP)	25

LIQUID STONE
81	Liquid Stone LIQ 001	Here Comes The Weekend/Because Of You (no p/s, hand stickered labels)	300

LIQUORICE
78	Perno PER 1	It's Gonna Turn You On/This Is The B-Side	10

DAVID LISBON
61	Philips BBE 12469	LIKE LISBON (EP)	8

LISTEN
65	CBS 202456	You'd Better Run/Everybody's Gonna Say	250

(see also Robert Plant, Led Zeppelin)

LITTER
69	Probe CLPS 4504	EMERGE (LP)	60

'BIG' TINY LITTLE
57	Vogue Coral Q 72263	School Day/That's The Only Way To Live	40
57	Vogue Coral Q 72263	School Day/That's The Only Way To Live (78)	20
60	Coral FEP 2058	HONKY TONK PIANO VOL. 1 (EP)	10
60	Coral FEP 2059	HONKY TONK PIANO VOL. 2 (EP)	10

MINT VALUE £

LITTLE BOB STORY
78	Chiswick SW7	LITTLE BOB STORY (EP)	8

LITTLE FEAT
86	Nimbus 80027	FEAT DON'T FAIL ME NOW (LP, Nimbus Supercut, mail order only through Practical Hi Fi magazine)	70

LITTLE JOHN ANTHONY
60	Ember EMB 3302	TEENAGE DANCE PARTY (LP)	20

KENNY LITTLE & LITTLE PEOPLE
65	United Artists UP 1074	A Shot In The Dark/Never On A Sunday	5

SHARON LITTLE
78	One Love (no number)	Don't Mash Up Creation/Version (12")	90

LITTLE ANGELS
87	Little Angels LAN 001	LITTLE ANGELS '87 (12" EP)	30
89	Polydor LTLCD 2	THE BIG BAD EP (CD)	10
87	Powerstation AMP 14	TOO POSH TO MOSH (mini-LP)	18

LITTLE ANN
98	Kent TOWN 111	What Should I Do/O.C. TALBOT: I'm Shooting High (I Reach For The Sky)	15
99	Kent TOWN 112	Who Are You Trying To Fool/I Got To Have You	20

LITTLE ANTHONY & IMPERIALS
58	London HLH 8704	Tears On My Pillow/Two People In The World	50
58	London HLH 8704	Tears On My Pillow/Two People In The World (78)	40
59	London HL 8848	So Much/Oh Yeah	50
59	London HL 8848	So Much/Oh Yeah (78)	40
59	Top Rank JAR 256	Shimmy, Shimmy, Ko-Ko Bop/I'm Still In Love With You	30
60	Top Rank JAR 366	My Empty Room/Bayou, Bayou, Baby	25
64	United Artists UP 1065	I'm On The Outside Looking In/Please Go	20
64	United Artists UP 1073	Goin' Out Of My Head/Make It Easy On Yourself	20
65	United Artists UP 1083	Hurt So Bad/Reputation	25
65	United Artists UP 1098	Take Me Back/Our Song	20
65	United Artists UP 1112	I Miss You/Get Out Of My Life	15
66	United Artists UP 1126	Hurt/Never Again	40
66	United Artists UP 1137	Better Use Your Head/The Wonder Of It All	80
66	United Artists UP 1137	Better Use Your Head/The Wonder Of It All (DJ copy)	150
66	United Artists UP 1151	Gonna Fix You Good (Every Time You're Bad)/You Better Take It Easy Baby	75
67	United Artists UP 1189	My Love Is A Rainbow/You Only Live Twice	5
68	United Artists UP 2260	Let The Sunshine In/The Gentle Rain (as Anthony)	10
69	United Artists UP 35017	Anthem/Goodbye Goodtimes (as Anthony & Imperials)	5
72	United Artists UP 35345	Gonna Fix You Good (Every Time You're Bad)/You Better Take It Easy Baby (reissue)	10
76	United Artists UP 36118	Better Use Your Head/Gonna Fix You Good (Every Time You're Bad)	10
76	United Artists REM 405	Goin' Out Of My Head/I'm On The Outside Looking In/Hurt So Bad/ Gonna Fix You Good (Every Time You're Bad)	10
65	United Artists UEP 1004	LITTLE ANTHONY AND THE IMPERIALS (EP)	140
64	United Artists ULP 1089	I'M ON THE OUTSIDE LOOKING IN (LP)	150
66	United Artists ULP 1100	GOIN' OUT OF MY HEAD (LP)	100

LITTLE ARCHIE
68	Atlantic 584 209	I Need You/I Am A Carpet	40

LITTLE BEAVER
72	President PTLS 1060	JOEY (LP)	25

LITTLE BEVERLEY
68	Pama PM 731	What A Guy/You're Mine	5

(see also Beverley Simmons)

LITTLE BIG HORN
70	Polydor 2058042	Another Man's Song/Just A Game	40

LITTLE BILL & BLUE NOTES
59	Top Rank JAR 176	I Love An Angel/Bye, Bye Baby	25
59	Top Rank JAR 176	I Love An Angel/Bye, Bye Baby (78)	25

(see also Blue Notes)

LITTLE BIRD
84	Magus MGB 1	Zola/Reaching Out For Gold (p/s)	5

LITTLE BO BITCH
79	Cobra COB 1	It's Only Love/I'm Confused (p/s)	5
80	Cobra COB 4	Take It Easy (Lights Out Over London)/Lorraine, Lorraine (p/s)	5
79	Cobra CBR 1002	LITTLE BO BITCH (LP)	12

LITTLE BOOTS
08	50 Bones 4BONES	Meddle/Meddle (Toddla T & Ross Orton Mix) (green vinyl with tattoo set, 500 only)	40

LITTLE BOY BLUE
69	Jackpot JP 701	Dark End Of The Street/MR VERSATILE: Apple Blossoms	20

LITTLE CLARKIE & THE OFFBEAT POSSE
86	Jah Tubbys JT 015	Selector Him Good/COLONEL MITE: Bless The Selector/JAH TUBBY: Select The Rhythm (12")	100
86	Jah Tubbys JT 20	Live Stock Party/Bounty Hunter (12")	50
87	Y&D YDD 0107	Bubble-N-Rock/Cowboy Stylee (12")	50
88	Y&D YDD 0134	Can't Come A Dance And Stand Up/Never Give You Up (12")	30

LITTLE DARLING
65	Blue Beat BB 325	No One/BUSTER'S ALL STARS: Congo Revolution	120

LITTLE DARLINGS
65	Fontana TF 539	Little Bit O' Soul/Easy To Cry	100

LITTLE DES
70	J-Dan JDN 4400	Somebody's Baby/Spy Man	7

LITTLE DIPPERS
60	Pye International 7N 25051	Forever/Two By Four	12
61	London HLG 9269	Lonely/I Wonder, I Wonder, I Wonder	25

LITTLE EVA
62	London HL 9581	The Locomotion/He Is The Boy	6
62	London HLU 9633	Keep Your Hands Off My Baby/Where Do I Go	10
63	London HLU 9687	Let's Turkey Trot/Old Smokey Locomotion	6
63	Colpix PX 11013	The Trouble With Boys/What I Gotta Do (To Make You Jealous)	12
63	Colpix PX 11019	Please Hurt Me/Let's Start The Party Again	15
64	Colpix PX 11035	Run To Her/Making With The Magilla	15
65	Stateside SS 477	Stand By Me/That's My Man	20
82	London LOCOX1	The Locomotion (Extended Version)/He Is The Boy/Keep Your Hands Off/ Let's Turkey Trot (12" p/s)	8
63	London HA-U 8036	L-L-L-L-LOCO-MOTION (LP, original with plum label & laminated sleeve)	50
72	London SH-U 8437	L-L-L-L-LOCO-MOTION (LP, stereo reissue, plum label, boxed label logo)	15

(see also Big Dee Irwin & Little Eva)

LITTLE FISH
72	Plant Life PLR 011	HERTFORDSHIRE FOLK SONGS (EP, with insert)	50

LITTLE FOLK
71	Studio Republic CR 1001	LEAVE THEM A FLOWER (LP)	18

LITTLE FRANKIE (& COUNTRY GENTLEMEN)
65	Columbia DB 7490	The Kind Of Boy You Can't Forget/I'm Not Gonna Do It	20
65	Columbia DB 7578	Make-A-Love/Love Is Just A Game (with Country Gentlemen)	20
65	Columbia DB 7681	It Doesn't Matter Anymore/Happy, That's Me	20

(see also Chimes featuring Denise)

LITTLE FREDDY (MCGREGOR)
70	Unity UN 551	Why Did My Little Girl Cry/PETER AUSTIN: Change Partners	8

(see also Freddie McGregor, Ernest Wilson)

LITTLE FREE ROCK
69	Transatlantic TRA 208	LITTLE FREE ROCK (LP, laminated sleeve, white/lilac labels, 't' logo)	150

(see also David John & Mood)

LITTLE GEORGE
64	Rio R 45	Mary Anne/EDWARDS ALLSTARS: Blue Night	18

LITTLE GRANT
70	Torpedo TOR 27	Baby Don't Let Me Down/Brother Strong Man	20

(see also Equals, Pyramids, Eddy Grant)

LITTLE GRANTS & EDDIE (GRANT)
67	President PT 159	Rudy's Dead/Everything's Alright	10
67	President PT 172	Rock Steady '67/Bingo	7

(see also Equals, Pyramids, Eddy Grant)

LITTLE HANK
66	London HLU 10090	Mr. Bang Bang Man/Don't You Know (withdrawn)	150
66	London HLU 10090	Mr. Bang Bang Man/Don't You Know (withdrawn) (DJ copy)	150
70	Monument MON 1045	Mr. Bang Bang Man/Don't You Know (reissue)	15

LITTLE HOWIE
85	Look to Afrika LTAF 03	Original Love Me/EARL ANTHONY Sensi Man Rock (12")	100

LITTLE JOE (JAMAICA)
70	Torpedo TOR 15	Bad Blood/Maxi-Mini War	6

(see also Sexy Girls)

LITTLE JOE (& THRILLERS)
57	Philips PB 759	Peanuts/Lilly Lou (78)	15
60	Fontana H 281	Stay (as Little Joe & Thrillers)/Cherry	25
63	Reprise R 20142	Peanuts/No No I Can't Stop	20

LITTLE JOEY & FLIPS
62	Pye International 7N 25152	Bongo Stomp/Lost Love	12

LITTLE JOHN
67	Pama PM 702	Let's Get Married/Around The World	6
70	Unity UN 561	No Love/A Little Tear (both sides actually by John Holt)	8
84	greensleeves GRELD 139	Form A Line/YELLOWMAN: Rub & Go Down (12")	15

(see also John Holt)

LITTLE JOHN
84	Vista VSLP 4061	UNITE (LP)	20

ALAN LITTLEJOHN BAND
62	Oriole CB 1734	Out Of The Blue/There Ain't No Sweet Man Worth The Salt Of My Tears	10

LITTLE JOHN & BILLY BOYO
82	Greensleeves GRELD 86	Connection/BILLY BOYO: Little Girl (12")	18
82	Greensleeves GRED 92	Janet Sinclair/Agony Column Dub (12")	25

LITTLE JOHNNY & THREE TEENAGERS
58	Decca F 10990	Baby Lover/Rickety Rackety Rendezvous	20

LITTLE KIRK
70s	Ruddys RM 004	Ghetto People Broke/Version (12")	40
70s	Ruddys RM 001	Weed Them Out/Version (12")	50

LITTLE LEMMY & BIG JOE
58	Decca F 11054	Little Lemmy Kwela/Kwela No. 5 (78)	10

LITTLE LULU
72	FAB FAB 21	Love & Obey/AL CAMPBELL & FREDDIE MCGREGOR: Free Man	200

LITTLE LUMAN
64	Rio R 44	Hurry Harry/R. ALPHONSE: Hucklebuck (B-side actually by Roland Alphonso)	15

MINT VALUE £

LITTLE LUTHER

| 64 | Pye International 7N 25266 | Eenie Meenie Minie Moe/Twirl | 70 |

LITTLE MACK & BOSS SOUNDS

| 66 | Atlantic 584 031 | In The Midnight Hour/You Can't Love Me (In The Midnight Hour) | 25 |

MARIE LITTLE

71	Argo ZFB 19	FACTORY GIRL (LP)	150
73	Trailer LER 2084	MARIE LITTLE (LP)	50
87	private pressing	MY ELDORADO (LP)	12

LITTLE MILTON

65	Pye International 7N 25289	Blind Man/Blues In The Night	15
65	Chess CRS 8013	We're Gonna Make It/Can't Hold Back The Tears	20
65	Chess CRS 8013	We're Gonna Make It/Can't Hold Back The Tears (demo copy)	35
65	Chess CRS 8018	Who's Cheating Who?/Ain't No Big Deal On You	15
66	Sue WI 4021	Early In The Morning/Bless Your Heart (actually by Roy Milton)	40
69	Chess CRS 8087	Grits Ain't Groceries/I Can't Quit You Baby	25
69	Chess CRS 8100	Let's Get Together/I'll Always Love You	15
72	Stax 2025 095	That's What Love Will Make You Do/I'm Living Off The Love You Give	8
74	Stax STXS 2003	Behind Closed Doors/Bet You I Win	8
75	Stax STA 100	If That Ain't A Reason/Mr. Mailman	6
69	Chess CRLS 4552	GRITS AIN'T GROCERIES (LP)	80
72	Chess 6310 120	GOLDEN DECADE (LP)	15
74	Stax STX 1013	BLUES 'N' SOUL (LP)	25

LITTLE NELL

| 75 | A&M AMS 7351 | Do The Swim/Stilettos And Lipstick/Tropical Isle (red vinyl, p/s) | 8 |

LITTLE RICHARD

78s

56	London HLO 8336	Rip It Up/Ready Teddy	20
57	London HLO 8366	Long Tall Sally/Tutti Frutti	20
57	London HLO 8382	The Girl Can't Help It/She's Got It	20
57	London HLO 8446	Lucille/Send Me Some Lovin' (as Little Richard & His Band)	20
57	London HLO 8470	Jenny, Jenny/Miss Ann (as Little Richard & His Band)	20
57	London HLO 8509	Keep A Knockin'/Can't Believe You Wanna Leave	15
58	London HLU 8560	Good Golly Miss Molly/Hey-Hey-Hey-Hey	25
58	London HLO 8647	Ooh! My Soul/True, Fine Mama	30
58	London HLU 8770	Baby Face/I'll Never Let You Go	20
59	London HLU 8831	By The Light Of The Silvery Moon/Early One Morning	30
59	London HLU 8868	Kansas City/She Knows How To Rock	50
60	London HLU 9065	Baby/I Got It	90

SINGLES

56	London HLO 8336	Rip It Up/Ready Teddy (gold label print)	150
56	London HLO 8336	Rip It Up/Ready Teddy (later pressing with silver label print)	50
50s	London HLO 8336	Rip It Up/Ready Teddy (repressing, silver-top label, round centre)	25
57	London HLO 8366	Long Tall Sally/Tutti Frutti (gold label print)	150
57	London HLO 8366	Long Tall Sally/Tutti Frutti (later silver label print)	40
50s	London HLO 8366	Long Tall Sally/Tutti Frutti (repressing, silver-top label, round centre)	20
57	London HLO 8382	The Girl Can't Help It/She's Got It (gold label print)	150
57	London HLO 8382	The Girl Can't Help It/She's Got It (later silver label print)	40
50s	London HLO 8382	The Girl Can't Help It/She's Got It (repressing, silver-top label, round centre)	20
57	London HLO 8446	Lucille/Send Me Some Lovin' (as Little Richard & His Band)	30
57	London HLO 8470	Jenny, Jenny/Miss Ann (as Little Richard & His Band)	30
57	London HLO 8509	Keep A Knockin'/Can't Believe You Wanna Leave	30
58	London HLU 8560	Good Golly Miss Molly/Hey-Hey-Hey-Hey	30
58	London HLO 8647	Ooh! My Soul/True, Fine Mama	15
58	London HLU 8770	Baby Face/I'll Never Let You Go	8
59	London HLU 8831	By The Light Of The Silvery Moon/Early One Morning	8
59	London HLU 8868	Kansas City/She Knows How To Rock	15

(The above 45s were originally issued with triangular centres; later round-centres are worth around half to two-thirds these values.)

60	London HLU 9065	Baby/I Got It	15
61	Mercury AMT 1165	Joy Joy Joy (Down In My Heart)/He's Not Just A Soldier	8
62	Mercury AMT 1189	He Got What He Wanted (But He Lost What He Had)/ Why Don't You Change Your Ways?	10
63	London HLK 9708	Crying In The Chapel/Hole In The Wall	10
63	London HLK 9756	Travelin' Shoes/It Is No Secret	8
64	London HL 9896	Bama Lama Bama Loo/Annie's Back	10
64	Fontana TF 519	Blueberry Hill/Cherry Red	10
64	Stateside SS 340	Whole Lotta Shakin' Goin' On/Goodnight Irene	10
64	Mercury MF 841	Joy, Joy, Joy (Down In My Heart)/Peace In The Valley	10
66	Fontana TF 652	I Don't Know What You've Got But It's Got Me (Parts 1 & 2)	30
66	Stateside SS 508	Holy Mackeral/Baby, Don'tcha Want A Man Like Me?	20
66	Sue WI 4001	Without Love/Dance What You Wanna	40
66	Sue WI 4015	It Ain't Watcha Do (It's The Way How You Do It)/Crossover	40
66	Columbia DB 7974	Poor Dog/Well	25
66	Columbia DB 8058	I Need Love/The Commandments Of Love	20
67	Columbia DB 8116	Get Down With It/Rose Mary	25
67	Columbia DB 8240	A Little Bit Of Something/Money	50
67	Columbia DB 8240	A Little Bit Of Something/Money (DJ copy)	75
67	Columbia DB 8263	I Don't Want To Discuss It/Hurry Sundown	50
67	Columbia DB 8263	I Don't Want To Discuss It/Hurry Sundown (DJ copy)	85
68	MCA MU 1006	She's Together/Try Some Of Mine	10
68	London HLU 10194	Good Golly Miss Molly/Lucille	10
68	President PT 201	Whole Lotta Shakin' Goin' On/Lawdy Miss Clawdy	10
69	Action ACT 4528	Baby What Do You Want Me To Do (Parts 1 & 2)	10
70	Reprise RS 20907	Dew Drop In/Freedom Blues	10
71	President PT 329	Without Love/Talkin' 'Bout Soul	5
71	Reprise K 14124	Green Power/Dancing In The Street	10
72	Reprise K 14150	Money Is/Money Runner	5

SINGLES : EXPORT SINGLES

57	London HL 7022	Jenny, Jenny/Miss Ann (as Little Richard & His Band)	30
58	London HL 7049	Ooh! My Soul/True, Fine Mama	15
58	London HL 7056	Baby Face/I'll Never Let You Go	15
59	London HL 7074	She Knows How To Rock/Early One Morning	20
59	London HL 7079	By The Light Of The Silvery Moon/Kansas City	20
59	London HL 7085	Whole Lotta Shakin' Goin' On/All Around The World	40
68	Decca AD 1006	She's Together/Try Some Of Mine	25

EPs

57	London RE-O 1071	LITTLE RICHARD AND HIS BAND VOL. 1 (gold tri-centre)	50
57	London RE-O 1071	LITTLE RICHARD AND HIS BAND VOL. 1 (later silver label)	30
57	London RE-O 1074	LITTLE RICHARD AND HIS BAND VOL. 2 (later silver label)	40
57	London RE-O 1074	LITTLE RICHARD AND HIS BAND VOL. 2 (gold tri-centre, later silver)	30
57	London RE-O 1103	LITTLE RICHARD AND HIS BAND VOL. 3	30
57	London RE-O 1106	LITTLE RICHARD AND HIS BAND VOL. 4	30
59	London RE-U 1208	LITTLE RICHARD AND HIS BAND VOL. 5	30
60	London RE-U 1234	LITTLE RICHARD AND HIS BAND VOL. 6	40
60	London RE-U 1235	LITTLE RICHARD AND HIS BAND VOL. 7	50

(The above EPs were originally issued with triangular centres; later round-centre pressings are worth between half to two thirds of these listed values.)

62	Summit LSE 2049	FOUR DYNAMIC NUMBERS (2 each by Little Richard & Brock Peters)	8
63	London REK 1400	HE'S BACK	40
64	Vocalion VEP 170155	MEMPHIS SLIM AND LITTLE RICHARD	80
66	Stateside SE 1042	DO YOU FEEL IT	60

ALBUMS

57	London HA-O 2055	HERE'S LITTLE RICHARD (flipback, rear sleeve in gloss red)	100
57	London HA-O 2055	HERE'S LITTLE RICHARD (flipback)	50
57	London HA-O 2055	HERE'S LITTLE RICHARD (small flipback sleeve)	55
57	London HA-O 2055	HERE'S LITTLE RICHARD (non-flipback sleeve)	35
58	London HA-U 2126	LITTLE RICHARD VOL. 2 (flipback sleeve)	75
58	London HA-U 2126	LITTLE RICHARD VOL. 2 (non-flipback sleeve)	40
59	RCA Camden CDN 125	LITTLE RICHARD (8 tracks only; others by Buck Ram Orchestra, picture of Richard in "frame" on sleeve, brown wooden effect is first pressing)	25
59	London HA-U 2193	THE FABULOUS LITTLE RICHARD (flipback sleeve)	75
59	London HA-U 2193	THE FABULOUS LITTLE RICHARD (non-flipback sleeve)	40
60	Top Rank 25/025	PRAY ALONG WITH LITTLE RICHARD VOL. 1: A CLOSER WALK WITH THEE (plain white sleeve, mail-order only)	40
60	Top Rank 25/026	PRAY ALONG WITH LITTLE RICHARD VOL. 2: I'M QUITTING SHOW BUSINESS (plain white sleeve, mail-order only)	80
64	Stateside SL 10054	SINGS GOSPEL	25
64	Coral LVA 9220	COMING HOME	25
65	Mercury MCL 20036	IT'S REAL	15
65	Fontana TL 5235	IS BACK!	20
67	Columbia SX/SCX 6136	THE EXPLOSIVE LITTLE RICHARD	40
68	Fontana SFL 13010	KING OF THE GOSPEL SINGERS	15
70	Reprise RSLP 6406	THE RILL THING	15

(see also Canned Heat, Sister Rosetta Tharpe, Buck Ram's Ramrocks)

LITTLE ROOSTERS

79	Pye 7P 152	She Cat Sister Floozie/Roostering With Intent (p/s)	6
80	Ami AIS 101	That's How Strong My Love Is/Suspicious (p/s)	6
80	Ami AIS 107	I Need A Witness/The Age Of Reason (p/s)	6

(see also Cocksparrer, Alison Moyet)

LITTLE ROY

69	Crab CRAB 39	Without My Love (actually by Roy & Joy)/WINSTON SAMUELS: Here I Come Again	25
70	Bullet BU 445	Keep Trying/Version (actually by the Matadors)	10
81	Copasetic COP 5001	COLUMBUS SHIP (LP)	20

LITTLE ROYS

69	Camel CA 36	Bongonyah/CREATIONS: Dad Name (B-side actually "Bad Name")	10
70	Camel CA 42	Gold Digger (actually by Wailing Soul)/MATADORS: The Mine	15
70	Camel CA 57	Selassie Want Us Back/ROY AND JOY: Make It With You	10

(see also Little Roy, Hippy Boys)

LITTLE SAL WITH DANDY & SUPERBOYS

| 68 | Giant GN 19 | I'm In The Mood/I'm A Lover | 8 |

(see also Dandy & Superboys, Superboys)

LITTLE SISTERS

| 63 | MGM MGM 1192 | Goin' To Boston/Where Does It Lead | 7 |

LITTLE SONNY

| 71 | Stax 2363 005 | NEW KING OF THE BLUES HARMONICA (LP) | 20 |

LITTLE SUZIE

| 61 | Warner Bros WB 35 | Young Love/The Boy I Left Behind | 12 |

LITTLE TONY

| 75 | RCA 2638 | Shakin' All Over/Together | 6 |

LITTLE TONY & HIS BROTHERS

59	Durium DC 16639	Who's That Knockin'/The Beat	25
59	Durium DC 16639	Who's That Knockin'/The Beat (78)	30
59	Durium DC 16657	Four An' Twenty Thousand Kisses/Bella Marie	20
59	Decca F 11164	I Can't Help It/Arrivederci Baby	10
59	Decca F 11164	I Can't Help It/Arrivederci Baby (78)	40
59	Decca F 11169	The Hippy Hippy Shake/Hey Little Girl	10
59	Decca F 11169	The Hippy Hippy Shake/Hey Little Girl (78)	40
59	Decca F 11190	Too Good/Foxy Little Mama	8
59	Decca F 11190	Too Good/Foxy Little Mama (78)	40
60	Decca F 21218	I Love You/The Magic Of Love	8
60	Decca F 21223	Princess/I Love You	8
61	Durium DC 16657	Bella Marie/Four An' Twenty Thousand Kisses	8

LITTLE WALTER

MINT VALUE £

60	Decca F 21247	Teddy Girl/Kiss Me, Kiss Me	10
66	Durium DRS 54008	Let Her Go/What Did I Do	7
67	Durium DRS 54012	Long Is The Lonely Night/People Talk To Me About You (as Little Tony)	7
58	Durium U 20058	PRESENTING LITTLE TONY AND HIS BROTHERS (EP)	40
65	Durium DRL 50006	I SUCCESSI DI LITTLE TONY (LP)	15
66	Durium DRL 50020	LET HER GO (LP)	12

LITTLE WALTER

60	London HLM 9175	My Babe/Blue Midnight	50
64	Pye International 7N 25263	My Babe/You Better Watch Yourself	20
56	London RE-U 1061	LITTLE WALTER AND HIS JUKES (EP)	200
64	Pye Intl. NPL 28043	LITTLE WALTER (LP)	70
67	Chess CRL 4529	SUPER BLUES (LP, with Bo Diddley & Muddy Waters)	45
68	Marble Arch MAL 815	LITTLE WALTER (LP, reissue)	15
69	Python PLP-KM 20	LITTLE WALTER AND HIS DUKES (LP, 99 copies only)	55

LITTLE WILBUR (& PLEASERS)

57	Vogue V 9091	Plaything/I Don't Care	500
57	Vogue V 9091	Plaything/I Don't Care (78)	100
58	Vogue V 9097	Heart To Heart/Alone In The Night (solo)	600
58	Vogue V 9097	Heart To Heart/Alone In The Night (solo) (78)	170

(see also Wilbur Whitfield)

LITTLE WILLIE (FRANCIS)

63	Blue Beat BB 151	Settle Down/I'm Ashamed	8

(see also Wilbert Francis & Vibrators)

LIVE HUMAN

98	Fat Cat 12FAT 005	IMPROVISESSIONS (12" EP, custom sleeve)	8
99	Fat Cat 12FAT 019	ORANGEBUSHMONKEYFLOWER (12" EP, custom sleeve)	8

LIVELY ONES

63	London HA 8082	SURF DRUMS (LP)	70
63	London HA 8107	SURF RIDER (LP, mono)	70
63	London SH 8107	SURF RIDER (LP, stereo)	85

LIVELY SET

65	Pye 7N 15880	Don't Call My Name/What Kind Of Love	6
66	Capitol CL 15472	Let The Trumpets Sound/The Green Years	6

LIVERPOOL ECHO

73	Spark	LIVERPOOL ECHO (LP)	20

(see also Mandrake Paddle Steamers)

LIVERPOOL EXPRESS

76	Warner Brothers K 56281	TRACKS (LP)	15

LIVERPOOL F.C.

78	Logo GO 339	Hail To The Kop/We Are Liverpool (p/s)	5
80	no label	Liverpool's FA Cup Finals (gold flexi)	10
83	Mean MEAN 102	Liverpool We're Never Gonna Stop/Liverpool Anthem (red vinyl)	5
77	State STAT 50	LIVERPOOL FOOTBALL TEAM 76/77 (EP)	10
65	Seddon SED 100	EE AYE ADDIO: SEVENTY YEARS WAITING (LP)	50
84	Extra-Terrestrial KOP 1	CONQUERING LIONS OF ANFIELD (LP, picture disc, gatefold sleeve, with booklet, stickers & photographs)	25

LIVERPOOL F.C. & LIVERPOOL SUPPORTERS

72	Penny Farthing PEN 794	Sing A Song For Liverpool/Liverpool, Liverpool	8

LIVERPOOL FISHERMEN

71	Mushroom 150 MR 9	SWALLOW THE ANCHOR (LP)	50

LIVERPOOL SCENE

68	RCA RCA 1762	Son Son/Baby	6
69	RCA RCA 1816	The Woo-Woo/Love Is	6
67	CBS BPG 63045	THE INCREDIBLE NEW LIVERPOOL SCENE (LP)	40
68	RCA SF 7995	THE AMAZING ADVENTURES OF THE LIVERPOOL SCENE (LP)	20
68	RCA SF 7995	THE AMAZING ADVENTURES OF THE LIVERPOOL SCENE (LP, unlaminated cover)	20
69	RCA SF 8057	BREAD ON THE NIGHT (LP)	20
70	RCA SF 8100	ST. ADRIAN AND CO. BROADWAY & 3RD (LP)	20
70	RCA SF 8134	HEIRLOON (LP)	20
72	Charisma CS 3	RECOLLECTIONS (LP, pink scroll label with B&C reference)	12

(see also Clayton Squares, Adrian Henri, Brian Patten, Mike Hart, Andy Roberts, Grimms)

LIVERPOOL SPINNERS

61	Topic TOP 69	SONGS SPUN IN LIVERPOOL (EP)	10

(see also Spinners [U.K.])

RICKY LIVID & TONE DEAFS

64	Parlophone R 5136	Tomorrow/Nuts And Bolts	8

(see also Bill Oddie)

LIVING DAYLIGHTS

67	Philips BF 1561	Let's Live For Today/I'm Real (B-side actually titled "It's Real")	30
79	E.S.R. S/79/CUS 523	HEARTSTOP EP (Personality Changes/Outdoor Girl/Don't Fit/Let Me Know (33 rpm, die-cut p/s, also listed as ESR 3)	45
67	Philips BF 1613	Always With Him/Baila Maria	40

(see also Greatest Show On Earth, Naturals)

LIVING FORCE

84	Chapter 1 SCH 161	Ride Ride Ride/Some People	20

DANDY LIVINGSTONE

72	Horse HOSS 16	Suzanne Beware Of The Devil/Right On Brother	6
79	More Cuts RIC 109	Instant Music/Living In Sus	8
80	Mint Music MMD2	Fever/Righteous Man (12")	40
72	Trojan TRLS 45	DANDY LIVINGSTONE (LP)	12

J C LIVINGSTONE
73	Penny Farthing Pen 808	Let's Spend The Summer Together/Viva La Eva..6
73	Penny Farthing Pen 824	Momma Was A Steamroller Lady/OO La La Me...25

R D LIVINGSTONE
76	B&C CB 291	Roots Man/Mo' Roots..10

LIZA & JET SET
65	Parlophone R 5248	How Can I Know?/Dancing Yet 15

(see also Liza Strike, Jet Set)

LIZZARD
76	Attack ATT 8130	Fight Down/Jah Jah Bless I 8
76	Black Wax WAX 14	Satta I/I And Eye 10
76	Trojan TRLS 138	SATTA (LP)..25

LIZZIE & DELROY WILSON
71	Jackpot JP 771	Double Attack/AGGRAVATORS: The Sniper 18

LIZZY
70	Harry J HJ 6625	More Heartaches/HARRY J ALL STARS: Version...8
70	Pressure Beat PB 5508	Ten Feet Tall (actually "Wear You From The Ball"/JOE GIBBS & DESTROYERS: Chapter (actually "Harmony Hall" by Mr Nigel) 10
73	Duke DU 161	Love Is A Treasure/FREDDIE McKAY: Love Is A Treasure 7

LIZZY & DENNIS (ALCAPONE)
70	Ackee ACK 114	Happy Go Lucky Girl/BOBBY & DAVE: Sammy 12

LIZZY & PARAGONS
71	Ackee ACK 118	On The Beach/DAVE BARKER: Maria 15

LJ IV
69	CBS 63512	AN ELIZABETHAN SONGBOOK (LP) 150

(see also London Jazz Four)

LLAN
66	CBS 202405	Realise/Anytime 40

(see also Vogues)

BARRY LLEWELLYN
73	Downtown DT 515	Meaning Of Life/MORWELL ESQ: Version Of Life 25

(see also Heptones, Sound Dimension)

A.L. LLOYD
62	Topic TOP 71	A.L. LLOYD EWAN MACCOLL (EP) 12
57	Topic T7	A.L. LLOYD EWAN MACCOLL (8" LP with insert) 25
57	Topic T8	THE BLACK BALL LINE (8" EP, insert, with Ewan MaCColl) 25
60	Topic 12T 51	OUTBACK BALLADS (LP, blue label)...40
64	Topic 12T 103	ENGLISH AND SCOTTISH FOLK BALLADS (LP, with Ewan MacColl, with blue label & booklet) 30
64	Topic 12T 103	ENGLISH AND SCOTTISH FOLK BALLADS (LP, with Ewan MacColl) 20
65	Topic 12T 135	BIRD IN THE BUSH (LP, with Anne Briggs & Frankie Armstrong, blue label) 75
66	Topic 12T 118	FIRST PERSON (LP, blue label) 30
67	Topic 12T 174	LEVIATHAN! (LP, blue label with booklet) 35

(see also Frankie Armstrong, Anne Briggs)

A.L. LLOYD & MARTYN WYNDHAM-READ
71	Topic 12TS 203	THE GREAT AUSTRALIAN LEGEND (LP, blue label with booklet) 65

(see also Ewan MacColl, Peggy Seeger, Martin Wyndham-Read)

LLOYD ALEXANDER REAL ESTATE
67	President PT 157	Whatcha Gonna Do/Gonna Live Again 100

LLOYD & BARBARA
73	Grape GR 3045	Dear Lonely Hearts/LLOYD BANTAM: I Tried To Love You...................................6

LLOYD & CAREY WITH G.G. ALL STARS
72	Attack ATT 8029	Scorpion/MAYTONES: Hands And Feet..5

(see also Carey & Lloyd, Pat Satchmo)

LLOYD & CLAUDETTE
70	Big Shot BI 546	Queen Of The World/PROPHETS: Top Of The World 40

LLOYD (ROBINSON) & DEVON (RUSSELL)
69	Punch PH 14	Love Is The Key/VIRTUES: High Tide 30
69	Blue Cat BS 151	Out Of The Fire/Can't Understand (B-side actually by Austin Faithful)..................75

(see also Cobbs, Derrick Morgan)

LLOYD & DOREEN
71	Jackpot JP 762	Midnight/BUNNY LEE'S ALL STARS: Midnight - Version 7

(see also Lloyd Clarke/Doreen Shaeffer)

LLOYD (ROBINSON) & GLEN (BROWN)
67	Coxsone CS 7011	That Girl/You Got Me Wrong 100
67	Doctor Bird DB 1058	Jezebel/TOMMY McCOOK & SUPERSONICS: Jam Session 45
67	Doctor Bird DB 1071	Keep On Pushing/BOBBY AITKEN & CARIBBEATS: You Won't Regret (B-side actually by Lloyd & Glen) 45
67	Doctor Bird DB 1099	Feel Good Now/What You've Got 25
68	Doctor Bird DB 1105	Successful Man/I'll Give You Love 30

LLOYD (JACKSON) & GROOVERS
67	Caltone TONE 108	Do It To Me Baby/DIPLOMATS: Meet Me At The Corner 35
68	Caltone TONE 109	My Heart My Soul/DIPLOMATS with TOMMY McCOOK & SUPERSONICS: Going Along 40
68	Caltone TONE 112	Listen To The Music/DIPLOMATS: Strong Man...40

(see also Groovers, Don Lett, Tony Lee)

LLOYD & JOHNNY
68	Island WI 3158	My Argument (actually by Lloyd Terrell)/JOHNNY MELODY: Foey Man (actually by George Dekker)..250

(see also Lloyd Terrell)

LLOYD & KEN
72	Punch PH 110	Have I Sinned/Version	7

(see also Lloyd Charmers/Ken Boothe)

LLOYD & LARRY
70s	New Beat NB 080	Monkey Spanner/LLOYD & LARRY'S ALL STARS: Version	6

LLOYD & THE PROPHETS
70	Big Shot BI 553	Bush Beat/PATRICK & PROPHETS: Please Come Come	10
70	Big Shot BI 556	Jaco/Soul Reggae	10

(see also Prophets [Jamaica], Patrick & Lloyd)

CHARLES LLOYD (QUARTET)
67	Atlantic 584 125	Sombrero Sam (Parts 1 & 2)	6
66	Atlantic 588025	DREAMWEAVER (LP)	20
67	Atlantic 587/588 077	LOVE-IN (LP)	20
68	Atlantic 587/588 101	JOURNEY WITHIN (LP)	20
68	Atlantic 588 108	IN EUROPE (LP)	15
70	MCA MUPS 421	MOON MAN (LP)	15
71	Atlantic 2400 108	IN THE SOVIET UNION (LP)	20

LLOYD, DICE & THE BARRISTER
70	Joe JRS 14	Appeal Of Pama Dice/BOSS ALL STARS: Young And Strong Version 2	20

LLOYD, DICE & HIS MUM
70	Joe JRS 5	Trial Of Pama Dice/NYAH SHUFFLE: Jughead Returns Version 1	20

FRED LLOYD
65	Polydor BM 56055	Girl From Chelsea/You Kissed Him	8

IAN LLOYD
74	Kama Sutra KSS 702	Another Love/THE STORIES: Love Is In Motion	6

JIMMY LLOYD
58	Philips PB 795	The Prince Of Players/Ever Since I Met Lucy	10
58	Philips PB 827	Witch Doctor/For Your Love	8
58	Philips PB 871	The End/Street In The Rain	6
59	Philips PB 909	I Kneel At Your Throne/Sapphire	10
59	Philips PB 909	I Kneel At Your Throne/Sapphire (78)	10
59	Philips PB 978	That's Why I Dream/Take A Giant Step	10
60	Philips PB 1010	Teenage Sonata/Falling	10
60	Philips PB 1055	I Double Dare You/Just For A Thrill	8
61	Philips PB 1120	Pony Time/Three Handed Woman	10
61	Philips PB 1201	I'm Coming Home/You Are My Sunshine	5
62	Philips 326 527 BF	True Love/Mother Nature And Father Time	5
63	Philips 326 568 BF	Call On Me/Humma Humma Humma Humming Bird	5
59	Philips BBE 12186	FOCUS ON JIMMY LLOYD (EP)	12
62	Philips BBE 12509	YOU ARE MY SUNSHINE (EP)	12

(see also Jimmy Logsdon)

LLOYD & JOY
71	Explosion EX 2047	Back To Africa (actually by Alton Ellis)/Born To Lose	15

KATHY LLOYD
54	Decca F 10386	It Worries Me/Tomorrow Night	5
54	Decca F 10418	Teach Me Tonight/It's A Woman's World	5
55	Decca F 10464	Our Future Has Only Begun/Unsuspecting Heart	5
55	Decca F 10567	Experience Unnecessary/This Must Be Wrong (with Ted Heath Music)	5

LLOYD (CAMPBELL) THE MATADOR
72	Sioux SI 010	The Train/Julia Sees Me (Exodus)	8

RUE LLOYD
72	Green Door GD 4033	Loving You/Version	7
72	Green Door GD 4036	Cheer Up/Version	7

(see also Joe White)

TREVOR LLOYD
70	Explosion EX 2018	Chinee Brush/DICE & CUMMIE: Real Colley	10
70	Explosion EX 2019	Give Me Back Your Love/Hold Me	5

ANDY LLOYD
78	Ariola/Hansa AHA 519	Back To School/It's Up To You	12

LLOYDIE & LOWBITES
73	Harry J HJ 6660	Pussy Cat/Skanky Pussy	6
71	Lowbite LOW 001	CENSORED! (LP, green/silver label)	20

(see also Lloyd Tyrell/Charmers)

LLOYD'S ALLSTARS
69	Doctor Bird DB 1178	Love Kiss Blue/UNIQUES: Secretly	45

(see also Justins, U Roy Junior, Jimmy Green, Victors)

ELERI LLWYD
71	Sain 15	ELERI LLWYD (EP)	8
72	Cambrian CSP 730	Mae Bywyd Yn Galed/Breuddwyn (p/s)	8
77	Sain 1073	AM HEDDIW MAE NGHAN (LP)	40

LLYGOD FFYRNIG
78	Llygod Ffyrnig PWDWR 1	N.C.B. (EP, p/s)	70
78	Pwdwr PWDWR 1	N.C.B./Sais/Cariad Y Bus Stop (p/s, stamped labels)	100
78	Pwdwr PWDWR 1	N.C.B./Sais/Cariad Y Bus Stop (p/s, printed white labels)	130

LOADED FORTY-FOURS
81	X-S TL 44/1	Thunderbirds (Are Go!)/T.V. Child (p/s)	5

DICKIE LOADER
61	Palette PG 9015	Heatwave/Happiness	20

RUSS LOADER
65	Columbia DB 7522	When Your Heart Is Broken/That Girl Of Mine (with Breakaways Orchestra)	10
65	Columbia DB 7643	Just Lies/Mona Lisa	8
65	Columbia DB 7696	Count The Stars/Triyng Too Hard (with Ladybirds)	10
66	Columbia DB 7839	Too Soon/Just A Little Step To Heaven	10
69	Conquest CXT 2	Just Lies/Take Me Tonight	5

(see also Mark Wirtz)

LOBO
71	Phillips 6073 802	She Didn't Do Magic/I'm The Only One	6

EDU LOBO
71	A&M AMLS63035	SERGIO MENDES PRESENTS (LP)	20

LOCAL HEROES
80	Junior Records	Blast The Pop!/Tomorrow	50

LOCH NESS MONSTER
85	Hamster 17	INDUSTRIAL POPPIES (LP)	12

JOSEF LOCKE
92	EMI 78EM 231	Hear My Song, Violetta/Charmaine/Count Your Blessings/Goodbye (12" 78)	5

LOCKETS
63	Pye International 7N 25232	Don't Cha Know/Little Boy	40

LOCKJAW
77	Raw RAW 8	Radio Call Sign/The Young Ones (p/s)	20
78	Raw RAW 19	Journalist Jive/I'm A Virgin/A Doonga Doonga (p/s, beware of counterfeits)	80

(see also the Cure)

HANK LOCKLIN
60	RCA RCA 1188	Please Help Me, I'm Falling/My Old Home Town (78)	20
60	RCA RCA 1188	Please Help Me, I'm Falling/My Old Home Town	5
61	RCA RCA 1252	You're The Reason/Happy Birthday To Me	5
62	RCA RCA 1273	From Here To There To You/This Song Is Just for You	5
62	RCA RCA 1305	We're Gonna Go Fishin'/Welcome Home, Mr. Blues	5
63	RCA RCA 1336	Flyin' South/Behind The Footlights	5
67	RCA 1641	The Country Hall Of Fame/Evergreen	5
66	RCA 1510	I Feel A Cry Coming On/Insurance	5
58	RCA RCX 115	COUNTRY GUITAR VOL. 3 (EP)	8
62	RCA RCX 217	SEVEN DAYS (EP)	8
63	Parlophone GEP 8875	ENCORES (EP)	12

GERRY LOCKRAN
69	Decca F 12873	Hey Jude/This Train	6
69	Decca F 12919	Standing On Your Own/You're Not There	20
67	Planet PLL 1002	HOLD ON, I'M COMING (LP)	150
68	Waverley ZLP 2091	BLUES VENDETTA (LP)	60
69	Spark SRLP 104	THE ESSENTIAL GERRY LOCKRAN (LP)	50
72	Polydor 2383 122	WUN (LP)	60
76	Decca SKL-R 5257	RAGS TO GLADRAGS (LP)	40
80	BML 2536	ACROSS THE TRACKS (LP)	15

ANNA LOCKWOOD
70	Tangent TGS 104	THE GLASS WORLD OF ANNA LOCKWOOD (LP)	40

MALCOLM LOCKYER ORCHESTRA
54	Decca F 10304	I'm Gonna Rock, Rock, Rock/Changing Partners (78, as Malcolm Lockyer & His Strict Tempo Music For Dancing)	10
61	HMV POP 929	The Pursuers T.V. Theme/Stranger Than Fiction	10
65	Columbia DB 7552	The Intelligence Men/Brighton Run	20
65	Columbia DB 7663	The Eccentric Dr. Who/Daleks And Thals	60

LOCOMOTIVE
67	Direction 58-3814	Rudy A Message To You/Broken Heart	20
68	Parlophone R 5718	Rudi's In Love/Never Set Me Free	20
69	Parlophone R 5758	Mr. Armageddon/There's Got To Be A Way (in promos p/s)	30
69	Parlophone R 5758	Mr. Armageddon/There's Got To Be A Way	15
69	Parlophone R 5801	I'm Never Gonna Let You Go/You Must Be Joking	20
70	Parlophone R 5835	Movin' Down The Line/Roll Over Mary	10
71	Parlophone R 5915	Rudi's In Love/You Must Be Joking	20
69	Parlophone PCS 7093	WE ARE EVERYTHING YOU SEE (LP, laminated front sleeve)	900
95	Shoestring BL004	WE ARE EVERYTHING YOU SEE (CD reissue)	25

(see also Norman Haines Band, Dog That Bit People, Steam-Shovel)

LOEFAH
04	Big Apple BAM 006	Jungle Infiltrator/Jazz Lick/Indian Dub/Life Dub (12")	60
05	DMZ DMZ 006	Root/The Goat Stare (12")	40
05	Tectonic TEC 003	28g/Fearless (12")	15
06	DMZ DMZ 009	Mud/Rufage (12")	50
06	Six6Six SIx 001	Voodoo/Voodoo (Omen Mix)	25
06	Tectonic TEC 008	System/DIGITAL MYSTIKZ: Molten (10")	30

NILS LOFGREN
79	A&M AMS 7455	Shine Silently/Kool Skool (p/s, coloured or black vinyl)	5

(see also Grin, Crazy Horse, Bruce Springsteen)

LOFT
84	Creation CRE 009	Why Does The Rain/Like (foldaround p/s in poly bag)	15
85	Creation CRE 015	Up The Hill And Down The Slope/Lonely Street (foldaround p/s in poly bag)	6
06	Static Caravan VAN 116	Model Village/Rickety Frame (p/s)	6

(see also Weather Prophets, Wishing Stones)

CRIPPLE CLARENCE LOFTON
59	Vogue EPV 1209	CRIPPLE CLARENCE LOFTON (EP)	50
54	London AL 3531	A LOST RECORDING DATE (10" LP)	50
55	Vogue LDE 122	JAZZ IMMORTALS NO. 1 (10" LP)	50

MINT VALUE £

LOFTUS ROADRUNNERS
77　QPR QPR 1　　　　　Queens Park Rangers/Drive Me Down To QPR 10

LOGIC CONTROL MCS
90　Conscious CONN2　　High Pursuit/Gangster Trip (12")...12

JIMMY LOGSDON
54　Brunswick 05226　　Pa-Paya Mama/In The Mission Of St. Augustine (78)..10

L.O.K.
79　Fetish FET 001　　　Fun House/Starlet Love/Tell Me (p/s)..7

LOLA PAYOLA
81　Epic EPC 1499　　　Schoolgirl Song/I Got Married To A Man From Space (P/S)...6

LOLITA
60　Polydor NH 66818　Sailor (Your Home Is The Sea)/La Luna (Quanda La Luna) 10

LOLITA STORM
99　Rabid Badger NANG 09　Goodbye America/Get Back (I'm Evil) (p/s) 5

LOLLIPOP SHOP
85　Big Beat WIK36　　　JUST COLOUR (LP) 15

LOLLIPOPS
71　Atlantic 2091 114　　Nothing's Gonna Stop Our Love/I Believe In Love...10

LAURIE LOMAN
54　London HL 8101　　Whither Thou Goest/I Was The Last One To Know (gold triangular centre)........................50
54　London HL 8101　　Whither Thou Goest/I Was The Last One To Know (78) 10

ALAN LOMAX (& RAMBLERS)
56　Decca F 10787　　　Dirty Old Town/Hard Case (as Alan Lomax & Ramblers) 10
56　Decca DFE 6367　　OH LULA (EP) 10
58　Pye Jazz NJE 1055　SINGS (EP, with Dave Lee's Bandits) 12
58　Pye Jazz NJE 1062　MURDERER'S HOME PT. 1 (EP) 12
58　Pye Jazz NJE 1063　MURDERER'S HOME PT. 2 (EP) 12
58　Pye Jazz NJE 1064　MURDERER'S HOME PT. 3 (EP) 12
58　Pye Jazz NJE 1065　MURDERER'S HOME PT. 4 (EP) 12
59　Melodisc EPM7 88　SONGS FROM TEXAS (EP) 12
57　Nixa Jazz NJL 8　　PRESENTS BLUES IN THE MISSISSIPPI NIGHT (LP, with others + insert) 15
57　Nixa Jazz NJL 11　　MURDERER'S HOME (LP)...15
58　Pye Nixa NPL 18013　PRESENTS AMERICAN SONG TRAIN VOLUME ONE (LP) 12
58　HMV CLP 1192　　GREAT AMERICAN BALLADS (LP, with Alexis Korner & Guy Carawan)..........................25

LOMAX ALLIANCE
67　CBS 2729　　　　Try As You May/See The People 50
(see also Jackie Lomax)

JACKIE LOMAX
68　CBS 2554　　　　Genuine Imitation Life/One Minute Woman 20
68　Apple APPLE 3　　Sour Milk Sea/The Eagle Laughs At You 30
69　Apple APPLE 11　New Day/I Fall Inside Your Eyes..15
70　Apple APPLE 23　How The Web Was Woven/Thumbin' A Ride (in p/s) 30
70　Apple APPLE 23　How The Web Was Woven/Thumbin' A Ride 15
69　Apple APCOR 6　IS THIS WHAT YOU WANT (LP, with inner sleeve, mono)......................................125
69　Apple (S)APCOR 6　IS THIS WHAT YOU WANT (LP, with inner sleeve, stereo)......................................80
91　Apple SAPCOR 6　IS THIS WHAT YOU WANT (LP, reissue, gatefold sleeve with bonus 12" [SAPCOR 62]) 25
(see also Lomax Alliance, Undertakers, Takers, Heavy Jelly, Badger)

GUY LOMBARDO (& ROYAL CANADIANS)
55　Brunswick 05372　No More/Pupalina 5
55　Brunswick 05412　Softly Softly/(I'm Always Hearing) Wedding Bells 5
55　Brunswick 05413　Hey, Mr. Banjo/Blue Mirage 5
55　Brunswick 05443　Cherry Pink And Apple Blossom White/Marty 5
56　Capitol CL 14585　Charleston Parisien/Rinka Tinka Man..5

AL LOMBARDY & HIS ORCHESTRA
54　London HL 8076　The Blues/The Boogie 40
55　London HL 8127　In A Little Spanish Town/Flying Home 20

LONDON
77　MCA MCA 305　　Everyone's A Winner/Handcuffed 5
77　MCA MCA 336　　Animal Games/Us Kids Cold..5
77　MCA 12 MCA 319　SUMMER OF LOVE (12" EP, p/s)..10
78　MCA MCF 2823　ANIMAL GAMES (LP)...15

EDDIE LONDON & CHIMES
57　Decca F 10859　　Song Of The Moonlight/I'll Thank You 5

FRANCO LONDON ORCHESTRA
66　Philips BF 1470　　Theme From Robinson Crusoe/Adrift...15

JIMMY LONDON
71　Randy's RAN 514　Shake A Hand/CARL MURPHY: Lick I Pipe 6
71　Randy's RAN 517　Bridge Over Troubled Waters/RANDY'S ALLSTARS: War 20
71　Randy's RAN 518　Hip Hip Hooray/IMPACT ALLSTARS: Version 5
71　Randy's RAN 520　A Little Love/IMPACT ALLSTARS: Version 8
72　Randy's RAN 521　It's Now Or Never/IMPACT ALLSTARS: Version 5
72　Randy's RAN 527　Jamaica Festival '72 (with Rocking Horse)/IMPACT ALLSTARS: Version......................5
73　Explosion EX 2080　I'll Never Find Another You/IMPACT ALLSTARS: Version 5
73　Dragon DRA 1010　Jennie/I Wonder If I Care As Much (as Jimmi London) 5
74　Dragon DRA 1019　No Letter Today/The Road Is Rough 5
74　Ackee ACK 531　Till I Kiss You/Version 5
75　Black Wax WAX 4　Am I That Easy To Forget/100 Years Of Dub 8
72　Trojan TRL 39　　BRIDGE OVER TROUBLED WATERS (LP)...20
80　JB JBLP 03　　　CHILDREN CRYING IN THE GHETTO (LP) 15
(see also Jimmy Green, The Inspirations)

JOE LONDON

59	London HLW 9008	Lonesome Whistle/It Might Have Been	15

JULIE LONDON

SINGLES

56	London HLU 8240	Cry Me A River/S'Wonderful (gold label print)	80
56	London HLU 8240	Cry Me A River/S'Wonderful (later silver label print)	30
56	London HLU 8240	Cry Me A River/S'Wonderful (gold label print, later silver) (78)	15
56	London HLU 8279	Baby, Baby All The Time/Shadow Woman (gold label print)	40
56	London HLU 8279	Baby, Baby All The Time/Shadow Woman(78)	15
57	London HLU 8394	The Meaning Of The Blues/Now! Baby, Now! (gold label print)	30
57	London HLU 8394	The Meaning Of The Blues/Now! Baby, Now! (later silver label print)	15
57	London HLU 8394	The Meaning Of The Blues/Now! Baby, Now! (78)	10
57	London HLU 8414	The Boy On A Dolphin/Tall Boy	15
58	London HLU 8602	Saddle The Wind/It Had To Be You	10
58	London HLU 8657	My Strange Affair/It's Easy	10
58	London HLU 8769	Man Of The West/Blue Moon	10
58	London HLU 8769	Man Of The West/Blue Moon (78)	15
59	London HLU 8891	Come On-A My House/Must Be Catchin'	15
59	London HLU 8891	Come On-A My House/Must Be Catchin' (78)	35
61	London HLG 9360	Sanctuary/Every Chance I Get	5
63	Liberty LIB 10078	There'll Be Some Changes Made/Love On The Rocks	5
63	Liberty LIB 55605	I'm Coming Back To You/When Snowflakes Fall In The Summer	6
64	Liberty LIB 55666	I Want To Find Out For Myself/Guilty Heart	5
65	Liberty LIB 10189	Send For Me/Bye Bye Blackbird	5
65	Liberty LIB 10205	Charade/Wives And Lovers	10
67	Liberty LIB 10274	Girl Talk/The Mickey Mouse March	5

EPs

57	London RE-U 1076	JULIE SINGS FILM SONGS (gold label print)	20
57	London RE-N 1092	LONDON'S GIRL FRIENDS VOL. 1	20
58	London RE-U 1151	MAKE LOVE TO ME - PART ONE	12
58	London RE-U 1152	MAKE LOVE TO ME - PART TWO	12
58	London RE-U 1153	MAKE LOVE TO ME - PART THREE	12
59	London RE-U 1180	JULIE - PART ONE	10
59	London RE-U 1181	JULIE - PART TWO	10
59	London RE-U 1182	JULIE - PART THREE	10
63	Liberty LEP 2103	DESAFINADO	10
66	Liberty LEP 2260	ALL THROUGH THE NIGHT	10

ALBUMS

56	London HA-U 2005	JULIE IS HER NAME	30
57	London HA-U 2038	CALENDAR GIRL	30
58	London HA-U 2083	MAKE LOVE TO ME	30
58	London HA-U 2091	ABOUT THE BLUES	30
58	London HA-U 2112	JULIE	30
59	London HA-U 2171	LONDON BY NIGHT	25
59	London HA-U 2186	JULIE IS HER NAME VOL. 2 (also stereo SAH-U 6042)	30
60	London HA-W 2225	SWING ME AN OLD SONG	20
60	London HA-W 2229	YOUR NUMBER PLEASE	20
60	London HA-G 2280	JULIE AT HOME (mono)	18
60	London SAH-G 6097	JULIE AT HOME (stereo)	20
61	London HA-G 2299	AROUND MIDNIGHT	20
61	London HA-G 2353	SEND FOR ME (mono)	18
61	London SAH-G 6154	SEND FOR ME (stereo)	20
62	London HA-G 2405	WHATEVER JULIE WANTS (mono)	18
62	London SAH-G 6205)	WHATEVER JULIE WANTS (stereo)	20
62	Liberty (S)LBY 1083	LOVE LETTERS	12
63	Liberty (S)LBY 1113	LOVE ON THE ROCKS	20
63	Liberty (S)LBY 1136	SINGS LATIN IN A SATIN MOOD	15
66	Liberty (S)LBY 1281	FEELING GOOD (with Gerald Wilson Big Band)	12
66	Liberty (S)LBY 1300	ALL THROUGH THE NIGHT	12
67	Liberty (S)LBY 1334	FOR THE NIGHT PEOPLE	12
67	Liberty (S)LBY 1364	NICE GIRLS DON'T STAY FOR BREAKFAST	15
69	Liberty LBL/LBS 83183E	YUMMY, YUMMY, YUMMY	15

LAURIE LONDON

57	Parlophone R 4359	He's Got The Whole World In His Hands/The Cradle Rock	10
57	Parlophone R 4388	Handed Down/She Sells Sea Shells	5
58	Parlophone R 4408	The Gospel Train/Boomerang	5
58	Parlophone R 4426	I Gotta Robe/Casey Jones	5
58	Parlophone R 4450	Basin Street Blues/Joshua (Fit The Battle Of Jericho)	5
58	Parlophone R 4474	My Mother/Darktown Strutters' Ball	5
58	Parlophone R 4499	Up Above My Head/Three O'Clock	7
59	Parlophone R 4557	Pretty-Eyed Baby (with Gitte)/Boom-Ladda-Boom-Boom	8
59	Parlophone R 4601	Old Time Religion/God's Little Acre	5
60	Parlophone R 4662	Banjo Boy/Hear Them Bells	7
61	Parlophone R 4747	Todays Teardrops/Darling Sue	8
57	Parlophone GEP 8664	LAURIE LONDON (EP)	15
58	Parlophone GEP 8689	LITTLE LAURIE LONDON No. 2 (EP)	30

MARK LONDON

65	Pye 7N 15825	Stranger In The World/Moanin'	15

MICHAEL LONDON

62	HMV POP 1026	Miracles Sometimes Happen/Stranger On The Shore (with Acker Bilk)	8
62	HMV POP 1085	Mutiny On The Bounty Love Song/For The Very Young	5

PETER LONDON

65	Pye 7N 15957	Bless You/Baby I Like The Look Of You	50

(see also Peter Cook)

LONDONAIRES

66	Decca F12379	Dearest Emma/Bugles A Go-Go	15

MINT VALUE £

LONDON BALALAIKA ENSEMBLE
68	Deram DML/SML 712	LONDON BALALAIKA ENSEMBLE (LP)	12

LONDON & BRIDGES
66	CBS 202056	It Just Ain't Right/Leave Her Alone	40

LONDON FUNK ALLSTARS
96	Ninja Tune ZEN 24	FLESH EATING DISCO ZOMBIES VERSUS THE BIONIC HOOKERS FROM MARS (3xLP)	30

LONDON HOSPITAL
60s	Private Pressing WAD 9-1	LONDON HOSPITAL CHRISTMAS FACTOR (EP)	60

LONDON JAZZ CHAMBER GROUP
72	Ember CJS 823	ADAM'S RIB SUITE (LP)	20

(see also Ken Moule's London Jazz Chamber Group, Ken Moule Seven)

LONDON JAZZ COMPOSERS ORCHESTRA
70s	Incus 7	ODE (LP, with insert)	50

LONDON JAZZ FOUR
66	Polydor 56092	Norwegian Wood/I Feel Fine	25
67	Polydor 56214	It Strikes A Chord/Song For Hilary	30
67	Polydor 582 005	TAKE A NEW LOOK AT THE BEATLES (LP)	60

(see also London Jazz Quartet, LJ IV)

LONDON JAZZ QUARTET
66	Polydor 56092	Norwegian Wood/I Feel Fine	15
60	Tempo TAP 28	LONDON JAZZ QUARTET (LP, with Tubby Hayes & Tony Crombie)	350
60s	Ember EMB 3306	LONDON JAZZ QUARTET (LP)	150

(see also London Jazz Four, Tubby Hayes, Tony Crombie)

LONDON POPS ORCHESTRA
68	Pye 7N 17630	Eleanor Rigby/If I Only Had Time	6
68	Pye NSPL 18241	THE LONDON POPS ORCHESTRA (LP)	15

LONDON POSSE
88	Justice JT003	Money Mad (12")	30
87	Big Life BLR2T	London Posse/My Beatbox Reggae Style (12")	10
93	Bullet BULT2	How's Life In London?/Shut The Fuck Up/How I Make Papes (12")	8
95	Bullet BULT 4	Fedz/Live Like The Other Half Do (12")	8
96	Bullet BULT 5	Style (12")	10
90	Mango MLPS1066	GANGSTER CHRONICLE (LP)	12

(see also Rodney P)

LONDON PX
80	New Puritan NP 1	Orders/Eviction (p/s)	25
82	Terrapyn SYD 1	Arnold Layne/Indian Summer (1-sided flexidisc)	12

LONDON STRING CHORALE
72	Polydor 2058 280	Galloping Home/Vicky	6

LONDON STUDIO GROUP
66	De Wolfe DW/LP 2974	THE WILD ONE (10" LP, tricolour label)	60

(see also Ivor & Basil Kirchen Band)

LONDON UNDERGROUND
81	Situation Two SIT 9	Train Of Though/All Too Many (p/s)	6
82	On-U Sound ON-U 4	WATCHING WEST INDIANS IN THE COLD (10" EP)	8
83	On-U Sound ON-U 5	STRANGE (10" EP)	8
83	On-U Sound LP 22	AT HOME WITH THE LONDON UNDERGROUND (LP)	20

LONDON WAITS
66	Immediate IM 030	Softly Softly/Serenadio	30

LONDON ZOO
80	Gramaphone STB 80	Who's Driving This Car?/You And Your Great Ideas (stamped white labels, no p/s)	6
80	Zoom ZUM 12	Receiving End/London Zoo (p/s)	5

LONE PIGEON
01	Sketchbook SKETCH 001	CONCUBINE RICE (LP)	15
10	Domino REWIGCD77X	TIME CAPSULE (7-CD box set)	40

(see also Beta Band)

LONE RANGER
79	Island WIPDJ 6517	Barnabus Collins/Dub Part 2	8
82	Greensleeves GRED 85	Johnny Make You Bad So/TAXI GANG: Outside Right (12")	12

LONE WOLF (1)
80	Wolf Music LW 001	Cash For Candy/Pipedream Mary (p/s)	150
82	Guardian GRC 144	Leave Me Behind/High Class Hooker	20
84	Neat NEAT 44-12	Nobody's Move/Town To Town/Leave Me Behind (12")	20

LONE WOLF (2)
81	Kai KR 02	Fighting For Sommerlund/Vonotar The Traitor (p/s)	15

LONELY HEARTS
84	Tenacity TROIA	FM Fantasy/Young Girl (p/s)	10

LONESOME DRIFTER
70	Injun 104	Eager Boy/Teardrop Valley	10

JOHNNY LONESOME
61	HMV POP 837	Marie Marie/Doctor Heartache	20

LONESOME PINE FIDDLERS
64	London HA-B 8143	MORE BLUEGRASS (LP)	15

LONESOME STONE
73	Reflection RL 306	LONESOME STONE (LP, stage production recording)	18

(see also Sheep)

LONESOME SUNDOWN
71	Blue Horizon 7-63864	LONESOME LONELY BLUES (LP)	100
70s	Flyright LP 529	BOUGHT ME A TICKET (LP)	18
70s	Flyright LP 587	LONESOME WHISTLER (LP)	18

LONESOME TONE
81	Stiff BUY DJ 111	Mum Dad Love Hate And Elvis/Ghost Town (promo only)	20
81	Silent SSH 5	Mum Dad Love Hate And Elvis/Ghost Town (p/s)	5

LONESOME TRAVELLERS
70	Tradition TSR 004	THE LONESOME TRAVELLERS (LP)	25
70s	Nebula NEB 100	THE LOST CHILDREN (LP)	15

LONG & SHORT
64	Decca F 11964	The Letter/Love Is A Funny Thing	35
64	Decca F 12043	Choc Ice/Here Comes The Fool	40

LONG BLONDES
04	Thee Sheffield SPC 005	New Idols/Long Blonde (p/s pink vinyl, playing card & newsletter insert)	30
04	Angular Recording ARC 007	Giddy Stratospheres/Polly/Darts (p/s, 500 only)	30
04	Flithy Little Angels FILTHY 004	No Tomorrow/I Love You//THE BOYFRIENDS: Autonomy Boy/Long Blonde (tour 7" orange vinyl, 750 copies)	8
05	Angular Recording ARC 009	Appropriation (By Any Other Name)/Lust In The Movies (p/s, numbered)	5

LONG COLD STARE
90	Rise Above RISE 3	TIRED EYES (LP)	12

FITZROY D. LONG & BUSTER ALL STARS
68	Fab FAB 32	Get A New Girl/BUSTER'S ALL STARS: Come And Do It With Me	20

(see also Larry Marshall)

LONG HELLO
73	Private pressing	THE LONG HELLO (LP, mail-order only, numbered white sleeve)	20

(see also Van Der Graaf Generator)

SHORTY LONG
65	Tamla Motown TMG 512	Out To Get You/It's A Crying Shame	125
65	Tamla Motown TMG 512	Out To Get You/It's A Crying Shame (DJ copy)	200
66	Tamla Motown TMG 573	Function At The Junction/Call On Me	45
66	Tamla Motown TMG 573	Function At The Junction/Call On Me (DJ copy)	60
67	Tamla Motown TMG 600	Chantilly Lace/Your Love Is Amazing	20
68	Tamla Motown TMG 644	Night Fo' Last (Vocal)/Night Fo' Last (Instrumental)	20
68	Tamla Motown TMG 663	Here Comes The Judge/Sing What You Wanna	18
68	T. Motown (S)TML 11086	HERE COMES THE JUDGE (LP, mono/stereo)	45
70	T. Motown STML 11144	THE PRIME OF SHORTY LONG (LP)	35

(see also Art Mooney)

LONG TALL SHORTY
79	Warner Bros K 17491	By Your Love/1970's Boy (p/s, withdrawn)	100
81	Dr Creation LYN 9904	If I Was You/That's What I Want (flexidisc)	12
81	Ramkup CAC 007	Win Or Lose/Ain't Done Wrong (p/s)	100
85	Diamond DIA 002	On The Streets Again/I Fought The Law/Promises (p/s, with poster)	25
85	Diamond DIA 002	On The Streets Again/I Fought The Law/Promises (p/s, without poster)	12
86	Diamond DIA 005	What's Going On/Steppin' Stone/Win Or Lose/England (p/s)	15
88	no label or cat. no.	ROCKIN' AT THE SAVOY (LP, official bootleg, with poster)	18
88	no label or cat. no.	ROCKIN' AT THE SAVOY (LP, official bootleg, without poster)	15

(see also Case, Joe Public, Rage, Charlie Harper)

LONG TALL TEXANS
89	Razor RAZZ 44	FIVE BEANS IN THE WHEEL (LP)	12

LONGBOATMEN
66	Polydor 56115	Take Her Any Time/Only In Her Home Town	500

LONGDANCER
73	Rocket PIG 1	If It Was So Simple/Silent Emotions (p/s)	15
74	Rocket PIG 11	Puppet Man/Cold Love	15
77	Rocket PIGL 6	TRAILER FOR A GOOD LIFE (LP, die cut gatefold sleeve)	15

CLAUDINE LONGET
67	A&M AMS 708	Good Day Sunshine/The Look Of Love	8
67	A&M AML 903	CLAUDINE (LP)	20

LOOKING GLASS
72	Philips BF 1837	Can You Believe/Freedom In Our Time	8
72	Epic 65041	LOOKING GLASS (LP)	20

LOOP
86	Head HEAD 5	16 Dreams/Head On/Burning World (12", p/s)	18
87	Head HEAD 7L	Spinning Parts 1 & 2 (large centre, plain black die-cut sleeve)	15
87	Head HEAD 7	Spinning/Deep Hit/I'll Take You There (12", p/s)	20
88	Chapter 22 12 CHAP 27	COLLISION EP (12")	10
88	Chapter 22 12 CHAP 32	BLACK SUN EP (12")	8
88	Chapter 22 CAT 065	Torched (flexidisc, with The Catalogue magazine no. 65)	12
89	Situation 2 SIT 64T	ARC LITE EP (12", p/s)	8
87	Head HEAD LP 1	HEAVEN'S END (LP, with inner sleeve)	15
88	Chapter 22 CHAPLLP 34	FADE OUT (LP, 2 x 45rpm 12", gold stickered gatefold sleeve, signed)	30
88	Chapter 22 CHAPLLP 34	FADE OUT (LP, 2 x 45rpm 12", gold stickered gatefold sleeve)	15
90	Situation 2 SITU 27	A GILDED ETERNITY (2-LP with free 7")	15
91	Reactor REACTORLP 3	WOLF FLOW - JOHN PEEL SESSIONS 1987-90 (2-LP)	18
92	Reactor LP 5	DUAL (LP, blue vinyl)	20
92	Reactor CD5	DUAL (CD)	25

LOOPFLESH
91	Clawfist XPIG 07	Like Rats/FLESHLOOP: Straight To Your Heart (foldover p/s in poly bag, actually by Loop and Godflesh)	10

LOOSE ENDS (1)
66	Decca F 12437	Send The People Away/I Ain't Gonna Eat My Heart Out Anymore	40

66	Decca F 12476	Taxman/That's It	100

LOOSE ENDS (2)

82	Virgin VS 497-12	In The Sky/Only A Day Away/In The Sky (Instrumental) (12", p/s, as Loose End)	8
82	Virgin VS 542-12	We've Arrived (U.S. Mix)/(U.K. Mix)/(Dangerous Dub Version) (12", p/s as Loose End)	12
83	Virgin VS 588-12	Don't Hold Back Your Love/No Stranger To Darkness/Don't Hold Back Your Love (Instrumental) (12", p/s)	8
92	Ten TEN 408	Hanging On A String/Hanging On A String (Frankie Knuckles Mix)	8

LOOSE TALK

82	Jet JET 7025	Dan Dare/Home Planet (p/s)	8

LOOT

66	Page One POF 013	Baby Come Closer/Baby	15
67	Page One POF 026	I've Just Gotta Love You/You Need Someone To Love	20
67	CBS 2938	Whenever You're Ready/I Got What You Want	18
68	Page One POF 095	She's A Winner/Radio City (withdrawn B-side)	30
68	Page One POF 095	She's A Winner/Save Me	22
68	CBS 3231	Don't Turn Around/You Are My Sunshine Girl	25
69	Page One POF 115	Try To Keep It A Secret/Radio City	40

(see also Soul Agents, Hookfoot)

LINDA LOPEZ MAMBO ORCHESTRA

55	Parlophone MSP 6179	Limehouse Blues Mambo/Nursery Mambo	7

TRINI LOPEZ

63	London HL 9808	Jeanie Marie/Love Me Tonight	6
65	Stateside SE 1013	SINNER NOT A SAINT (EP)	30

DENISE LOR

54	Parlophone MSP 6120	If I Give My Heart To You/Hallo Darling	10
55	Parlophone MSP 6148	Every Day Of My Life/And One To Grow On	12

KENNY LORAN

59	Capitol CL 15081	Mama's Little Baby/Magic Star	30

L'ORANGE MECHANIK

86	Art Pop POP 44	Symphony/Intermezzo (Sprechstimme)/Scherzo (p/s)	15

(see also Times)

JON LORD

76	Purple PUR 131	Bourée/Aria	7
82	Harvest HAR 5220	Bach Onto This/Going Home (p/s)	6
84	Safari SAFE60	The Country Diary Of An Edwardian Lady (main theme)/Love Theme (p/s)	7
71	Purple TPSA 7501	GEMINI SUITE (LP, textured gatefold sleeve)	22
82	Harvest SHSP 4123	BEFORE I FORGET (LP)	12
74	Purple TPSA 7513	WINDOWS (LP, gatefold sleeve)	20
76	Purple TPSA 7516	SARABANDE (LP, die-cut sleeve)	15

(see also Artwoods, Deep Purple, [Paice] Ashton & Lord, Bernie Marsden, Wizard's Convention, Episode Six, Leading Figures, Whitesnake, Cozy Powell)

TONY LORD

66	Planet PLF 102	World's Champion/It Makes Me Sad	25

JERRY LORDAN

59	Parlophone R 4588	I'll Stay Single/Can We Kiss	8
60	Parlophone R 4627	Who Could Be Bluer?/Do I Worry?	10
60	Parlophone R 4653	Sing Like An Angel/Ev'ry Time	12
60	Parlophone R 4695	Ring, Write Or Call/I've Still Got You	12
61	Parlophone R 4748	You Came A Long Way From St. Louis/Let's Try Again	15
62	Parlophone R 4903	One Good Solid 24 Carat Reason/Second Hand Dress	20
70	CBS 5057	The Old Man And The Sea/Harlequin Melodies	30
61	Parlophone PMC 1133	ALL MY OWN WORK (LP, mono)	90
61	Parlophone PCS 3014	ALL MY OWN WORK (LP, stereo)	120

(see also Lee & Jay Elvin)

LORD BEGINNER

50	Melodisc 1131	Joe Louis Calypso/Trinidad Blues (78)	10
50	Melodisc 1133	Victory Test Match - Calypso/Sergeant Brown (78)	10
50	Melodisc 1134	Straight Hair Girl/Calinda (78)	10
51	Melodisc 1164	Gold Coast Victory/Family Scandal (78)	10
51	Melodisc 1167	Family Scandal/Gold Coast Champion (78)	10
51	Melodisc 1183	Jamaica Hurricane/Pretty Woman (78)	10
51	Melodisc 1193	John Goddard Calypso/Some Girl (78)	10
51	Parlophone MP 112	Federation/Rum, More Rum (78, export)	10
51	Melodisc 1211	Australia V. West Indies/One Morning (78)	10
51	Esquire 5-034	Randolph Turpin's Victory/West Indians And The Steel Band (78, with Kenny Graham's Afro-Cubists)	15
51	Esquire 5-041	Fifty Women To One Man/1951 Festival Of Britain (78, with Kenny Graham's Afro-Cubists)	15
53	Esquire 5-091	England Regains The Ashes/Nobody Wants To Grow Old (78)	15
54	Melodisc 1333	Sir Winston Churchill Calypso/Rhythm Dance (78)	15
54	Melodisc 1334	She Walks Like You/Tambourine (78)	12
50s	Parlophone MP 144	Africa/Syncopation (export 78)	12
60s	Melodisc CAL 1	Victory Test Match - Calypso/Sergeant Brown (reissue)	10

(see also Lord Kitchener)

LORD BRISCO(E)

64	Rio R42	Fabulous Eyes/What You See	20
64	Black Swan WI 447	Spiritual Mambo/BABA BROOKS: Fly Right	25
64	Black Swan WI 450	My Love Has Come/BABA BROOKS: Sweet Eileen	25
64	Black Swan WI 454	Trojan/I Am The Least	12
64	Island WI 131	Praise For I/Tell You The Story	15
65	Island WI 187	Jonah (The Master)/Mr. Cleveland	15

LORD BRYNNER & SHEIKS

66	Island WI 266	Congo War/Teach Me To Ska	18

(see also Roland Alphonso)

LORD BUCKLEY
62	Fontana 688 010ZL	IN CONCERT (LP)	30
67	Fontana TL 5396	BLOWING HIS MIND (AND YOURS, TOO) (LP)	30
70	Elektra 2410 002	THE BEST OF LORD BUCKLEY (LP)	18

LORD BURGESS & HIS SUN ISLANDERS
67	Pye Intl. NPL 28109	CALYPSO GO-GO (LP)	12

LORD CHARLES & HIS BAND
70s	Sound Of Jamaica JA 1	Jamaican Bits And Pieces/JA Island Soul	8

LORD COMIC
70	Bamboo BAM 66	Rhythm Rebellion/ROY RICHARDS: Reggae Children	20
70	Pressure Beat PR 5507	Jack Of My Trade/CYNTHIA RICHARDS: United We Stand	18

(see also Sir Lord Comic)

LORD CREATOR
62	Island WI 001	Independant [sic] Jamaica Calypso/Remember (B-side is actually Remember Your Mother And Father)	20
63	Kalypso XX 24	Peeping Tom/Second Hand Piano	25
64	Port-O-Jam PJ 4005	Rhythm Of The Blues/Simple Things	12
64	Port-O-Jam PJ 4119	Jamaica's Anniversary/Mother's Love	22
64	National Calypso NC 2001	Drive With Care/Sweet Jamaica	20
65	Blue Beat BB 292	Evening News/Good For Creator	45
65	Black Swan WI 463	Wicked Lady/MAYTALS: My Little Ruby	25
66	Doctor Bird DB 1029	Obeah Wedding/BERTRAM ENNIS COMBO: Part Two	10
67	Jump Up JU 503	Jamaica Jump Up/Laziest Man	8
67	Jump Up JU 524	Big Bamboo/Marjorie And Harry	8
76	Island WIP 6344	Big Pussy Sally/UPSETTERS: Big Pussy Dub	6

(see also Kentrick Patrick, Fabulous Flames)

LORD CRISTO
67	Jump Up JU 515	Dumb Boy And The Parrot/General Hospital	8
67	Jump Up JU 517	Election War Zone/Bad Luck Man	8

LORD DANIEL
60s	Kalypso XX 26	Small Island Gal	6

LORD FLEA & HIS CALYPSONIANS
57	Capitol CL 14704	The Naughty Little Flea/Shake Shake Senora	5

LORD GANDA
57	Melodisc MEL 1417	Everybody Is Rockin' & Rollin'/Landlady Don't Steal My Clothes (78)	15

LORD KITCHENER
50	Parlophone MP 102	Nora/LORD BEGINNER: The Dollar And The Pound (export 78)	12
50	Parlophone MP 103	Underground Train/LORD BEGINNER: I Will Die A Bachelor (export 78)	12
52	Melodisc MEL 1160	Kitch/Food From The West Indies (78)	10
52	Melodisc MEL 1222	Two Timing Josephine/The Tongue Mopsie (78)	10
53	Lyragon J 717	Alec Bedser Calypso/Mistress Jacob (78)	10
55	Melodisc MEL 1325	My Wife's Nightie/Sweet Home (78)	10
56	Melodisc MEL 1400	Rock 'n' Roll Calypso/Life Begins At Forty (78)	10
56	Melodisc MEL 1401	Romeo/Kitch's Calypso Medley (78)	10
59	Melodisc MEL 1498	Black Puddin'/Piccadilly Folk	7
59	Melodisc MEL 1538	If You're Brown/Come Back In The Morning	7
60	Melodisc MEL 1577	Jamaica Turkey/Edna What You Want	7
63	Melodisc CAL 2	Kitch/Rebound Wife	6
63	Melodisc CAL 3	Muriel And The Bug/Nora And The Yankee	6
63	Melodisc CAL 4	Kitch Take It Easy/Redhead	6
63	Melodisc CAL 5	Drink A Rum/Your Wife	15
63	Melodisc CAL 6	Too Late Kitch/Saxophone Number Two	6
63	Melodisc CAL 7	Wife And Mother/Mango Tree	6
64	Melodisc CAL 10	Kitch Mambo Calypso/Ghana	6
64	Melodisc CAL 11	Life Begins At Forty/Short Skirts	6
64	Melodisc CAL 12	Romeo/Kitch Calypso Medley	6
64	Melodisc CAL 14	Federation/Alfonso In Town	6
64	Melodisc CAL 19	Black Puddin'/Piccadilly Folk	6
64	Melodisc CAL 21	Come Back In The Morning/If You're Brown	6
64	Melodisc CAL 22	Jamaica Turkey/Edna What You Want	6
64	Melodisc CAL 23	Carnival/More Rice	6
60s	Jump Up JU 504	Love In The Cemetery/Jamaica Woman	6
60s	Jump Up JU 506	Road/Neighbour	6
64	Jump Up JU 511	Dr. Kitch/Come Back Home Meh Boy	10
65	Jump Up JU 530	Kitch You So Sweet/Ain't That Fun	6
65	Aladdin WI 612	Dr. Kitch/Come Back Home Meh Boy (reissue)	8
71	Duke DU 115	Dr. Kitch/Love In The Cemetary	5
55	Melodisc MLP 500	KITCH - KING OF CALYPSO (10" LP)	22
57	Melodisc MLP 510	KING OF CALYPSO VOL. 2 (10" LP)	22
60s	Melodisc 12-129	CALYPSOS TOO HOT TO HANDLE (LP)	30
60s	Melodisc 12-130	CALYPSOS TOO HOT TO HANDLE VOL. 2 (LP)	20
60s	Melodisc 12-199	CALYPSOS TOO HOT TO HANDLE (LP, reissue with extra tracks)	20
60s	Melodisc 12-200	CALYPSOS TOO HOT TO HANDLE VOL. 2 (LP, reissue with extra tracks)	20

(see also Lord Beginner)

LORD KITCHENER/FITZROY COLEMAN BAND
56	no label	City And United 1956/The Manchester Football Double (78)	60

LORD LARGE (FEATURING DEAN PARRISH)
06	Acid Jazz AJX 185S	Left Right & Centre/Sun In The Sands (7", co. sleeve)	6

LORD LEBBY
58	Kalypso RL 101	Dr Kinsey Report/Ethiopia	15
58	Kalypso XX 05	Sweet Jamaica/Mama Want No Rice No Peas)	10
60	Starlite ST45 018	Caldonia/One Kiss For My Baby	100

LORD MELODY
58	Melodisc MEL 1440	The Devil/No, No	6

LORD NELSON

58	Melodisc MEL 1440	The Devil/No, No (78)	10
58	Melodisc MEL 1449	Robbery/Men Company	8
58	Melodisc MEL 1449	Robbery/Men Company (78)	10
58	Melodisc MEL 1474	Do Able/Happy Holiday	6
58	Melodisc MEL 1474	Do Able/Happy Holiday (78)	12
59	Melodisc MEL 1491	I Confess/MIGHTY SPARROW: Goaty	8
59	Melodisc MEL 1503	Tom Dooley/Jealous Woman	6
59	Melodisc MEL 1504	Romeo/Knock On Any Door	6
60	Kalypso XX 14	Rock 'N' Roll Calypso/Bo Bo Man	5
60s	Melodisc CAL 16	Happy Holiday/Do Able	5

LORD NELSON

63	Stateside SS 189	I Got An Itch/Problems On My Mind	12
64	Stateside SS 281	It's Delinquency/Proud West Indian	15
68	Direction 58-3909	Michael/No Hot Summer	10
64	Stateside SE 1024	PROUD WEST INDIAN (EP)	30

LORD POWER

57	Kalypso XX 02	Chambolina/Penny Reel (78)	12
58	Maracas M 20001	Special Amber Calypso/Mambo La-La (78)	12
69	Coxsone CS 7079	Temptation/AL & VIBRATORS: Change Everything	45

LORD RIGBY

60s	Kalypso XX 29	The Milkman/Old Veterans	6
64	National Calypso NC 1001	Carnival Jamiaca/Music Teacher	20

LORD ROCKINGHAM'S XI

58	Decca F 11024	The Squelch/Fried Onions	10
58	Decca F 11059	Hoots Mon/Blue Train	8
59	Decca F 11104	Wee Tom/Lady Rockingham, I Presume?	12
59	Decca F 11139	Ra-Ra Rockingham/Farewell To Rockingham	15
59	Decca F 11139	Ra-Ra Rockingham/Farewell To Rockingham (78)	10
62	Decca F 11426	Newcastle Twist/Rockingham Twist	15
58	Decca DFE 6555	OH BOY! (EP)	30
68	Columbia S(C)X 6291	THE RETURN OF LORD ROCKINGHAM'S XI (LP, mono/stereo)	30

(see also Robinson Crew, Harry Robinson)

LORD ROSE

60s	Kalypso XX 25	Independent Jamaica/Twistin' Uncle	40

LORDS

67	Columbia DB 8121	Don't Mince Matters/No One Knows	140
68	Columbia DB 8367	Gloryland/Gypsy Boy	18

LORDS OF RAP

92	Mad Dog MADDOG001	STIX 'N' STONES (EP)	12

LORD SASSAFROST

82	Star Light SDLP 911	HORSE MAN CONNECTION (LP)	20

LORD SITAR

68	Columbia SX/SCX 6256	LORD SITAR (LP)	40

LORD SPOON

70	Escort ERT 839	Woman A Love In The Night Time/World On A Wheel	6

LORD TANAMO

60	Kalypso XX 20	Blues Have Got Me Down/Sweet Dreaming	20
64	Rio R 21	I Had A Dream/OSBOURNE GRAHAM: Be There	12
64	Ska Beat JB 177	Night Food Ska/My Business	20
65	Ska Beat JB 217	Mattie Rag/BABA BROOKS BAND: Mattie Rag	30
65	Ska Beat JB 224	I'm In The Mood For Ska/You Never Know	100
66	Ska Beat JB 243	Mother's Love/Downtown Gal	20
60s	Caribou CRC 3	I Love You Truly/If You Were Only Mine	80
70	Bamboo BAM 45	Rainy Night In Georgia/KEN PACKER: When You're Gone	15
71	Banana BA 319	Keep On Moving/JACKIE MITTOO: Totaly [sic] Together	70

LORELEI

74	CBS 2048	S.T.O.P. (Stop)/I'll Never Let You Down	15

SOPHIA LOREN

58	Philips PB 857	Love Song From "Houseboat"/Bing! Bang! Bong!	6

(see also Peter Sellers & Sophia Loren)

LORENZO

69	Harry J HE 6687	Saturday Vocal Night/Instro	10
69	Beacon BEA 134	I Ain't Afraid/Beggar	12
71	New Beat NB 094	I Will Never Let You Down/This Magic Moment	5

(see also Laurel Aitken)

LORI & CHAMELEONS

78	Zoo CAGE 006	Touch/Love On The Ganges (p/s)	5
81	Korova KOW 20T	Touch/The Lonely Spy/Love On The Ganges (12", p/s)	8

(see also Teardrop Explodes, Bill Drummond)

GARY & JOHN LORRAINE

65	Pye 7N 15836	I'm Not To Blame/Alone Again	10

MYRNA LORRIE

55	London HLU 8187	Underway/I'm Your Man, I'm Your Gal (B-side with Buddy DeVal)	25
56	London HLU 8294	Life's Changing Scene/Listen To My Heartstrings	25

LORRIES

79	Redball RR 016	The Night/Steal You Anyway/Pushover/Idiot Dances (p/s)	6

DICK LORY

56	London HLD 8348	Cool It Baby/Ball Room Baby	600
56	London HLD 8348	Cool It Baby/Ball Room Baby (78)	100
61	London HLG 9284	My Last Date/Broken Hearted	30
62	Liberty LIB 55415	Handsome Guy/The Pain Is Here	10

63	Liberty LIB 55529	Welcome Home Again/I Got Over You	10

LOS DOURADOS
70	EMI Regal/Starline SRS 5018	INTRODUCING LOS DOURADOS (LP)	15

JOE LOSS (& HIS ORCHESTRA)
66	HMV POP 1500	Thunderbirds Theme/"The Avengers" Theme	15
66	HMV POP 1517	The England World Cup March/Auld Lang Syne (March)	10

LOST CHEREES
83	Riot RIOT 3	No Fighting No War (EP)	10
84	Mortarhate MORT 3	A MAN'S DUTY ... A WOMAN'S PLACE (EP)	8
85	Mortarhate MORT 12	UNWANTED CHILDREN (12" EP, with inner)	10
84	Fight Back FIGHT 6	ALL PART OF GROWING UP (LP, with lyric inner)	12

LOST DOG
71	Phoenix SNIX 143	Latch Key Child/One More Time	59

LOST JOCKEY
82	Operation Twilight OPT 11	Professor Slack/Rise And Fall/Animal/Behaviour And Crude Din (10" p/s)	10

LOT 39 (STRANGERS)
60s	Eyemark EMS 1004	I'll Get Over You/I Still Love You	12

LOTHAR & THE HAND PEOPLE
69	Capitol CL 15610	Sdrawkcab (Backwards)/Today Is Only Yesterday's Tomorrow	20
69	Capitol E-ST 247	SPACE HYMN (LP)	60

DENNIS LOTIS
54	Decca F 10287	Such A Night/Cuddle Me (with Ted Heath Music & Johnston Brothers)	25
54	Decca F 10392	Honey Love/Manhattan Mambo (with Ted Heath Music)	20
55	Decca F 10469	Face Of An Angel, Heart Of A Devil/The Golden Ring	10
55	Decca F 10471	Chain Reaction/Go, Go, Go (with Ted Heath Music)	10
56	Pye 7N 15053	Green Grows The Grass/No Other Love Can Take Your Place	7
57	Columbia DB 3993	Tammy/I Complain	7
57	Columbia DB 4056	Valentina/Good Mornin' Life	7
58	Columbia DB 4090	I May Never Pass This Way Again/Gretna Green	7
58	Columbia DB 4158	The Only Man On The Island/Guessing What The Neighbours'll Say	6
68	Polydor 56266	Funny One/One Man's Life	20
68	Polydor 56298	Celebration/Why Do They Have To Fall In Love	30
68	Polydor 56346	One Woman Man/The Finger Points At you	30
56	Pye NEP 24017	PRESENTING DENNIS LOTIS (EP)	10
57	Pye NEP 24043	LET'S BE HAPPY (EP)	10
57	Pye NEP 24046	HOW ABOUT YOU (EP)	10
57	Pye NEP 24053	HOW ABOUT YOU PT. 2 (EP)	10
57	Pye NEP 24055	HOW ABOUT YOU PT. 3 (EP)	10
59	Columbia SEG 7955	HALLELUJAH IT'S DENNIS LOTIS (EP)	10
57	Nixa NPL 18002	HOW ABOUT YOU (LP)	25
58	Columbia 33SX 1089	BIDIN' MY TIME (LP)	25

(see also Johnstone Brothers)

PETER LOTIS
60	Ember EMB S 110	Doo-Dah/You're Singing Our Love Song To Somebody Else (with p/s)	6

LOTUS CRUISE
83	Armbury ARM 603	Billy's Got A Gun/Tonight	50

LOTUS EATERS
84	Sylvan SYL 2	You Don't Need Someone New/Two Virgins Tender (picture disc)	5
84	Sylvan SYL 4	Out Of Your Own/Endless (picture disc)	5
85	Arista FS 5	It Hurts/Evidence//The Soul In Sparks/Church At Llanbadrig (double pack)	5
84	Sylvan 206 263	NO SENSE OF SIN (LP)	12

(see also Wild Swans, Care)

BONNIE LOU
53	Parlophone MSP 6021	Seven Lonely Days/Dancin' With Someone	50
53	Parlophone MSP 6036	Hand-Me-Down Heart/Scrap Of Paper	50
53	Parlophone MSP 6048	Tennessee Wig Walk/Just Out Of Reach	50
53	Parlophone MSP 6051	Pa-Paya Mama/Since You Said Goodbye	40
54	Parlophone MSP 6072	The Texas Polka/No Heart At All	30
54	Parlophone MSP 6095	Don't Stop Kissing Me Goodnight/The Welcome Mat	30
54	Parlophone MSP 6108	No One/Huckleberry Pie	30
54	Parlophone MSP 6117	Blue Tennessee Rain/Wait For Me, Darling	30
54	Parlophone MSP 6132	Two Step - Side Step/Please Don't Laugh When I Cry	30
55	Parlophone MSP 6151	Tennessee Mambo/Train Whistle Blues	40
55	Parlophone MSP 6157	Tweedle Dee/The Finger Of Suspicion Points At You	40
55	Parlophone MSP 6173	Drop Me A Line/Old Faithful And True Love	25
55	Parlophone MSP 6178	The Barnyard Hop/Tell The World	20
55	Parlophone MSP 6188	Dancin' In My Socks/Daddy-O	40
56	Parlophone MSP 6223	Darlin' Why/Miss The Love (That I've Been Dreaming Of)	20
56	Parlophone MSP 6234	Bo Weevil (A Country Song)/Chaperon	20
56	Parlophone MSP 6253	Lonesome Lover/Little Miss Bobby Sox	25
56	Parlophone R 4215	No Rock 'N' Roll Tonight/One Track Love	25
57	Parlophone R 4350	Teenage Wedding/Runnin' Away	25
58	Parlophone DP 545	I'm Available/Waiting In Vain (export issue)	20

BONNIE LOU & RUSTY YORK
58	Parlophone R 4409	Let The School Bell Ring Ding-A-Ling/La Dee Dah	80
58	Parlophone R 4409	Let The School Bell Ring Ding-A-Ling/La Dee Dah (78)	30

BUBBA LOU & THE HIGHBALLS
81	Stiff BUY 114	Love All Over The Place/Over You (Unissued)	25
81	Silent SSH3	Love All Over The Place/Over You	10

LOU & KEVIN
78	Bushays BFM 103	Reunited/Reunited Stepping Out (12")	10

(see also Rusty York)

MINT VALUE £

LOUDER ANIMAL GROUP
80	Ears Pop POP 701	Pip Pop/Six Magnificent Cathedrals (p/s)	10
80	Ears Pop POP 702F	The Fossil Record (1-sided flexi on cardboard with 2 posters & inserts in poly bag)	12

JOHN D. LOUDERMILK
61	RCA RCA 1269	The Language Of Love/Darling Jane	8
62	RCA RCA 1287	Thou Shalt Not Steal/Mister Jones	8
62	RCA RCA 1323	Angela Jones/Road Hog	10
68	RCA RCA 1761	Sidewalks/The Odd Folks Of Okracoke	7
62	RCA RD 27248/SF 5123	THE LANGUAGE OF LOVE (LP)	25
62	RCA Victor RD/SF 7515	TWELVE SIDES OF JOHN D. LOUDERMILK (LP)	25
67	RCA Victor RD/SF 7890	SINGS A BIZARRE COLLECTION OF SONGS (LP)	25

(see also Johnny Dee)

LOUDNESS
84	Music For Nations MFN 22	DISILLUSION (LP)	12
85	Music For Nations MFN 38	THUNDER IN THE EAST (LP)	12

(THE) LOUDWATER TURN
68	Morgan MR 6S	Senorita/I'll Be Where You Are	40

JOE HILL LOUIS
65	Bootleg 502	Heartache Baby/I Feel Like A Million (99 copies only)	40
67	Advent LP 2803	MEMPHIS BLUES AND BREAKDOWNS (LP)	70
74	Polydor 2383 214	BLUE IN THE MORNING (LP)	30

LOUISIANA RED
64	Columbia DB 7270	Keep Your Hands Off My Woman/Don't Cry	40
64	Sue WI 337	I Done Woke Up/I Had A Feeling	40
64	Columbia 33SX 1612	LOWDOWN BACK PORCH BLUES (LP)	45
72	Atlantic K 40436	SINGS THE BLUES (LP)	20
72	Carnival 2941 002	THE SEVENTH SON (LP)	20

LOUISIANA SUGAR BABIES
57	HMV 7EG 8215	LOUISIANA SUGAR BABIES (EP, with Fats Waller & James P. Johnson)	12

LOUVIN BROTHERS
59	Capitol CL 14989	Knoxville Girl/I Wish It Had Been A Dream	20
59	Capitol CL 15078	You're Learning/My Curly Headed Baby	10
56	Capitol EAP1 769	TRAGIC SONGS OF LIFE (EP)	10
58	Capitol EAP1 910	IRA AND CHARLIE (EP)	10
59	Capitol EAP1 1106	COUNTRY LOVE BALLADS (EP)	10

LOVABLES
68	Stateside SS 2108	You're The Cause Of It/Beautiful Idea	25

ALAN LOVE AND MERLIN
74	CBS 3452	Too Too Much/Gettin' Involved	6

CHRISTOPHER LOVE
69	London HLU 10263	The Curse Goes On/You May Be The Next	18

DARLENE LOVE
63	London HLU 9725	(Today I Met) The Boy I'm Gonna Marry/Playing For Keeps	40
63	London HLU 9765	Wait 'Til My Bobby Gets Home/Take It From Me	40
63	London HLU 9815	A Fine Fine Boy/Marshmallow World	50
69	London HLU 10244	Wait 'Til My Bobby Gets Home/(Today I Met) The Boy I'm Gonna Marry	15
74	Warner Bros/Spector K 19011	Christmas (Baby Please Come Home)/Wait Till My Bobby Comes Home (blue vinyl)	6
77	Phil Spector Intl. 2010 019	Lord If You're A Woman/Johnny Baby Please Come Home	20
77	Phil Spector Intl. 2010 019	Lord If You're A Woman/Johnny Baby Please Come Home (12", some copies 1-sided)	15
88	CBS 6529357	He's Sure The Man I Love (New Version)/Everybody Needs (p/s)	5
88	CBS 6529356	He's Sure The Man I Love/My Heart Is A clock/Everybody Needs (12" p/s)	8
90	Warner Brothers W 9535	Mr Fix-It/K.D. LANG with TAKE SIX: Ridin' The Rails (with p/s)	20
90	Warner Brothers W 9535	Mr Fix-It/K.D. LANG with TAKE SIX: Ridin' The Rails	20
64	London RE-U 1411	WAIT TILL MY BOBBY GETS HOME (EP)	250

(see also Bob B. Soxx & Blue Jeans, Crystals, Phil Spector, Blossoms, Allisons [U.S.], Date With Soul, Cinders)

GARFIELD LOVE & JIMMY SPRUILL
69	Blue Horizon 57-3150	Next Time You See Me/Part Time Love	35

GEOFF LOVE ORCHESTRA
61	Columbia DB 4627	Coronation Street Theme/Sophia	6
62	Columbia DB 4881	Steptoe And Son/Over The Backyard Fence	5
70	Columbia DB 8707	Coronation Street Theme/ALIRIO DIAZ: Aranjuez Mon Amour (Rodgigo)	5
74	EMI EMI 2105	Match Of The Day/Bless This House	6

(see also Mandingo, Manuel & Music Of The Mountains)

MARY LOVE
65	King KG 1024	You Turned My Bitter Into Sweet/I'm In Your Hands	250
67	Stateside SS 2009	Lay This Burden Down/Think It Over Baby	75
67	Stateside SS 2009	Lay This Burden Down/Think It Over Baby (DJ copy)	125
68	Stateside SS 2135	The Hurt Is Just Beginning/If You Change Your Mind	15
82	Kent TOWN 501	You Turned My Bitter Into Sweet/SWEETHEARTS: This Couldn't Be Me (green vinyl)	10
85	Kent 6T1	Hey Stoney Face/IKETTES: It's Been So Long/ETTA JAMES: Wallflower	20

MIKE LOVE
83	Creole CR 61	Jingle Bell Rock/Let's Party (p/s)	8

(see also Beach Boys)

LOVE PARADE
90	Turntable Friend TURN 03	GUILT CHEST (EP)	25

PRESTON LOVE
00s	Beat Goes Public BGPS 009	Cissy Popcorn/BRENDA GEORGE: I Can't Stand It	8

RONNIE LOVE
61	London HLD 9272	Chills And Fever/Pledging My Love	50
78	Grapevine GRP 108	Let's Make Love/Nothing To It	8

WILLIE LOVE/WILLIE NIX
66	Highway 51 H 700	THE TWO WILLIES FROM MEMPHIS (LP, 99 copies only)	75

(see also Willie Nix)

LOVE (1)
SINGLES
66	London HLZ 10053	My Little Red Book/Hey Joe	40
66	London HLZ 10073	7 And 7 Is/No. Fourteen	40
67	Elektra EKSN 45010	She Comes In Colours/Orange Skies	30
67	Elektra EKSN 45016	Softly To Me/The Castle	30
68	Elektra EKSN 45024	Alone Again Or/Bummer In The Summer	30
68	Elektra EKSN 45026	The Daily Planet/Andmoreagain	30
68	Elektra EKSN 45038	Laughing Stock/Your Mind And We Belong Together	30
70	Elektra EKSN 45086	I'm With You/Robert Montgomery	15
70	Harvest HAR 5014	Stand Out/Doggone	10
70	Harvest HAR 5030	The Everlasting First/Keep On Shining	15
70	Elektra 2101 019	Alone Again Or/Bummer In The Summer (reissue, red label)	10
73	Elektra K 12113	Alone Again Or/Andmoreagain	6
75	RSO 2090 151	Time Is Like A River/You Said You Would	6

ALBUMS : ORIGINAL ALBUMS
66	Elek. EKL 4001/EKS 74001	LOVE (LP, gold label, U.K disc in U.S. sleeve)	150
67	Elek. EKL 4005/EKS 74005	DA CAPO (LP, orange label, with U.K. or U.S. sleeve)	120
67	Elek. EKL 4005/EKS 74005	DA CAPO (LP, with U.K. printed sleeve laminated front and back)	120
67	Elek. EKL 4013	FOREVER CHANGES (LP, mono orange label)	200
67	Elek. EKS 74013	FOREVER CHANGES (LP, stereo orange label)	150
69	Elektra EKL 4049	FOUR SAIL (LP, orange label, mono, existence unconfirmed)	70
69	Elektra EKS 74049	FOUR SAIL (LP, orange label, stereo)	70
70	Harvest SHDW 3/4	OUT HERE (2-LP, gatefold sleeve)	70
71	Harvest SHVL 787	FALSE START (LP, gatefold sleeve)	70
71	Elektra 2469 009	LOVE REVISITED (LP, gatefold sleeve)	18
73	Elektra K 32002	LOVE MASTERS (LP)	15
74	RSO 2394 145	REEL TO REAL (LP)	15

ALBUMS : REPRESSINGS
67	Elek. EKL 4001/EKS 74001	LOVE (LP, orange label, with U.K. or U.S. sleeve)	60
72	Elektra K 42068	LOVE (LP, 'butterfly' label)	25
71	Elektra EKS 74005	DA CAPO (LP, 'butterfly' label)	18
72	Elektra K 42011	DA CAPO (LP, 'butterfly' label)	15
72	Elektra K 42015	FOREVER CHANGES (LP, 'butterfly' label)	20
72	Elektra K 42030	FOUR SAIL (LP, 'butterfly' label)	15

(see also Arthur Lee)

LOVE (2)
90	Fierce FRIGHT 036	Welsh Girl (1-sided, p/s in bag, hand-finished labels, mail-order only)	20

LOVE AFFAIR
67	Decca F 12558	She Smiled Sweetly/Satisfaction Guaranteed	50
67	CBS 3125	Everlasting Love/Gone Are The Songs Of Yesterday	6
68	CBS 3366	Rainbow Valley/Someone Like Me (in p/s, says 'Someone Like Us' on p/s)	20
68	CBS 3366	Rainbow Valley/Someone Like Us	8
68	CBS 3674	A Day Without Love/I'm Happy	6
69	CBS 3994	One Road/Let Me Know	8
69	CBS 4300	Bringing On Back The Good Times/Another Day	8
69	CBS 4631	Baby I Know/Accept Me For What I Am	15
70	CBS 4780	Lincoln County/Sea Of Tranquility	15
70	Pye 7N 45218	Let Me Dance/Love's Looking Out At You	8
71	Parlophone R 5887	Wake Me I Am Dreaming/That's My Home	12
71	Parlophone R 5918	Help (Get Me Some Help)/Long Way Home	12
72	CBS 5017	Speak Of Peace Speak Of Joy/Brings My Whole Life Tumbling Down	10
73	CBS 33967	Everlasting Love/Bringing On Back The Good Times (p/s, 'Hall Of Fame Hits' series)	5
77	Creole CR 146	Private Lives/Let A Little Love Come In	6
68	CBS 63416	THE EVERLASTING LOVE AFFAIR (LP, mono/stereo)	30
70	CBS 64109	NEW DAY (LP)	20

(see also L.A., Ellis, Steve Ellis, Elastic Band, Widowmaker, Morgan, Phillip Goodhand-Tait, English Rose, Rainbow Ffolly)

LOVE & UNITY
80	Studio 16 (no. Cat. No.)	Put It On/(feat Ranking Bogart)/Dub	40
80	Studio 16 WE N1	Just Don't Care/Cut From The Master Tape (12")	30
80	Studio 16 WEA 347	I Adore You/CAPTAIN DESMOND : Lover In Dance (12")	25
79	Studio 16 WE 0014	Can't Let You Go/Dub Version (12")	30

LOVE AND WAR
80s	SRT SRT9KS 2323	Touch Of Class (p/s)	100

LOVE CHILDREN
69	Deram DM 268	Easy Squeezy/Every Little Step	15
70	Deram DM 303	Paper Chase/My Turkey Snuffed It	20

LOVE COMMITTEE
76	Ariola AA 105	Can't Win For Losing/Love Wins Every Time	8

LOVE CONNECTION
77	Strong Like Sampson SLS01	It's My House/Fall In Love (12")	20

LOVECUT D.B.
91	Suburbs Of Hell SOH 009EP	Heartspin/Heartspin (Dripping Clock Mix)/(Marisco Disco Mix)/(Porn Cable Mix) (12", p/s)	10
92	Suburbs Of Hell SOH 011EP	JOURNEY TO THE CENTRE OF LOVE EP (12")	10

(see also Sarah Cracknell, St. Etienne)

LOVE DIMENSION
79	Black Bear BLA 2010	You Stepped Into My Life/The Game	15

LOVE GENERATION (JAMAICA)
73	Grape GR 3046	Money Raper/HEPTONES: The Magnificent Heptones 3 In One	6

MINT VALUE £

| 73 | Grape GR 3041 | Warrika Hill/Battlefield (Third And Fourth Generation) | 6 |

LOVE GENERATION (U.S.)
| 67 | Liberty LBF 15018 | She Touched Me/The Love In Me | 10 |
| 68 | Liberty LBL/LBS 83121E | LOVE GENERATION (LP) | 25 |

JOY LOVEJOY
| 72 | Chess 6145 010 | In Orbit/Uh! Hum (paper label/moulded label) | 20 |

LOVELACE GREEN
| 69 | Concord CON 003 | Sister George/Pauper Millionaire | 20 |

LOVELITES
| 78 | Grapevine GRP 107 | Get It Off My Conscience/Oh, What A Day | 8 |

LOVE OF LIFE ORCHESTRA
| 80 | Infidelity JMB 227 | EXTENDED NICETIES (12" EP) | 8 |

(see also David Byrne)

JOHNNY LOVER
| 70 | Amalgamated AMG 871 | Pumpkin Eater/Version | 15 |
| 70 | Amalgamated AMG 873 | Two Edged Sword/Version | 20 |

(see also Little Johnny Jones, Heptones)

LOVERS
| 58 | Vogue Pop V 9111 | Let's Elope/I Wanna Be Loved | 500 |
| 58 | Vogue Pop V 9111 | Let's Elope/I Wanna Be Loved (78) | 150 |

LOVERS DUB
| 80 | Venture | CUT 7 (LP) (actually by Eargasm) | 40 |

(see also Tradition)

LOVE SCULPTURE
68	Parlophone R 5664	River To Another Day/Brand New Woman	20
68	Parlophone R 5731	Wang-Dang-Doodle/The Stumble	20
68	Parlophone R 5744	Sabre Dance/Think Of Love	5
69	Parlophone R 5807	Seagull/Farandole	15
70	Parlophone R 5831	In The Land Of The Few/People People	20
68	Parlophone PMC 7059	BLUES HELPING (LP, 1st pressing, yellow/black label, mono)	70
68	Parlophone PCS 7059	BLUES HELPING (LP, 1st pressing, yellow/black label, stereo)	50
69	Parlophone PCS 7090	FORMS AND FEELINGS (LP, 1st pressing, yellow/black label)	50
70	Parlophone PCS 7059	BLUES HELPING (LP, 2nd pressing, silver/black label)	20
70	Parlophone PCS 7090	FORMS AND FEELINGS (LP, 2nd pressing, silver/black label)	20

(see also Human Beans, Dave Edmunds)

EDDIE LOVETTE
69	Big Shot BI 519	You're My Girl/Let Them Say	15
70	London HLU 10298	Boomerang/Together	5
70	London HLJ 10311	Too Experienced/Little Blue Bird	10
70	London HA-J 8413	TOO EXPERIENCED (LP, unissued)	0
70	London LGJ/ZGJ 103	TOO EXPERIENCED (LP)	12

LENE LOVICH
76	Polydor 2058 812	I Saw Mommy Kissing Santa Claus/The Christmas Song (Merry Christmas To You)/Happy Christmas	12
78	Stiff BUYJ 32	I Think We're Alone Now (Japanese)/Lucky Number (mail-order promo only)	20
78	Stiff BUY 32 PLUG	I Think We're Alone Now/Lucky Number ("plug" copy on label. p/s)	10
78	Stiff BUY 32	I Think We're Alone Now/Lucky Number (p/s)	5
78	Stiff BUY 35	Home/Lucky Number (unreleased, test pressings only)	100
79	Stiff BUY 46 DJ	Say When (1-sided promo, black vinyl)	7

LOVIN'
| 67 | Page One POF 035 | Keep On Believing/I'm In Command | 35 |
| 67 | Page One POF 041 | All You've Got/Do It Again | 75 |

(see also Nerve)

LOVIN' SPOONFUL
65	Pye International 7N 25327	Do You Believe In Magic?/On The Road Again	12
66	Pye International 7N 25344	You Didn't Have To Be So Nice/My Gal	15
66	Kama Sutra KAS 200	Summer In The City/Bald Headed Lena	8
66	Kama Sutra KAS 201	Rain On The Roof/Warm Baby	7
67	Kama Sutra KAS 204	Nashville Cats/Full Measure	7
67	Kama Sutra KAS 207	Darling Be Home Soon/Darlin' Companion	12
67	Kama Sutra KAS 208	Six O'Clock/The Finale	10
67	Kama Sutra KAS 210	She Is Still A Mystery/Only Pretty, What A Pity	8
67	Kama Sutra KAS 211	Money/Close Your Eyes	8
68	Kama Sutra KAS 213	Never Going Back/Forever	12
66	Kama Sutra KEP 300	DID YOU EVER HAVE TO MAKE UP YOUR MIND (EP)	20
66	Kama Sutra KEP 301	JUG BAND MUSIC (EP)	20
66	Kama Sutra KEP 302	SUMMER IN THE CITY (EP)	20
67	Kama Sutra KEP 303	DAY BLUES (EP)	20
67	Kama Sutra KEP 304	NASHVILLE CATS (EP)	25
67	Kama Sutra KEP 305	LOVIN' YOU (EP)	30
67	Kama Sutra KEP 306	SOMETHING IN THE NIGHT (EP)	35
65	Pye Intl. NPL 28069	DO YOU BELIEVE IN MAGIC? (LP)	25
66	Pye Intl. NPL 28078	DAYDREAM (LP)	35
67	Kama Sutra KLP 401	HUMS OF THE LOVIN' SPOONFUL (LP)	20
67	Kama Sutra KLP 402	YOU'RE A BIG BOY NOW (LP, soundtrack)	18
67	Kama Sutra KLP 403	THE BEST OF THE LOVIN' SPOONFUL (LP)	12
68	Kama Sutra KLP 404	EVERYTHING PLAYING (LP)	15
68	Kama Sutra K(S)LP 405	THE BEST OF THE LOVIN' SPOONFUL VOL. 2 (LP)	15
69	Kama Sutra 602 009	REVELATION: REVOLUTION '69 (LP)	15

(see also John Sebastian, Mugwumps, Zalman Yanovsky, Even Dozen Jug Band)

LOVING AWARENESS
| 76 | More Love ML 001 | LOVING AWARENESS (LP, gatefold sleeve with 2 posters) | 15 |

(see also Glencoe, Skip Bifferty, Ian Dury)

LOVING KIND
66	Piccadilly 7N 35299	Accidental Love/Nothing Can Change This Love	15
66	Piccadilly 7N 35318	I Love The Things You Do/Treat Me Nice	18
66	Piccadilly 7N 35342	Ain't That Peculiar/With Rhyme And Reason	25

(see also Noel Redding Band, Freddie Lennon)

LOW
96	Vernon Yard YARD 24	Over The Ocean/Violence	10
96	Vernon Yard YARD 22	FINALLY... (EP)	20
98	Tugboat TUGS 001	Joan Of Arc/Long Long Long	6
02	Rough Trade RTRADES 0558	Canada/Fearless (p/s)	6
98	Rough Trade RTRADELP 061	TRUST (2-LP)	15
99	Tugboat TUGLP 007	SECRET NAME (2-LP)	18
01	Tugboat TUGLP 027	THINGS WE LOST IN THE FIRE (2 x LP, 4th side etched with lyrics)	25
04	Rough Trade RTRADCDX 195	A LIFETIME OF TEMPORARY RELIEF (3-CD and DVD box set)	20
05	Rough Trade RTRADELP 206	THE GREAT DESTROYER (2-LP)	20

BRUCE LOW
56	HMV JO 464	Just Walking In The Rain/Cindy Oh Cindy (export issue)	20

LOW NOISE
81	Happy Birthday UR 5	Jungle Line/Urban Tribal/Jungle Line (Instrumental) (12", p/s)	8

LOW NUMBERS
79	Warner Brothers K 17493	Keep In Touch/Nine All Out (p/s)	25

LOW PROFYLE
80	Ellie Jay EJSP 9434	Hangin' Around/Substitute (p/s)	50

LOWBITES
70	Black Swan BW 1403	I Got It/I Got It (Version)	6
80	Black Joy DH 800	Can I Go With You?/BOBBY DODSON & TRINITY: Having My Baby (12")	15

DENNIS LOWE
70	Downtown DT 465	What's Your Name/MUSIC DOCTORS: Mr Locabe	10
70	Downtown DT 468	Stand Up For The Sound/OWEN & DENNIS: Old Man Trouble	6

EARL LOWE
75	Tafari WL 708	Jah Can Count On I/Bongo Nyah (12")	70

JEZ LOWE
80	Fellside FE 034	JEZ LOWE (LP, textured sleeve, light green label, large 'Rams Horn' logo)	15
83	Fellside FE 034	THE OLD DURHAM ROAD (LP)	15
85	Fellside FE 049	GALLOWAYS (LP, with lyric insert)	15
86	Fellside FE 055	TWO A ROUE (LP, with Jake Walton, lyric insert)	12

JIM LOWE
55	London HLD 8171	Close The Door/Nueva Laredo (gold label print)	50
55	London HLD 8171	Close The Door/Nueva Laredo (gold label print) (78)	15
56	London HLD 8276	Blue Suede Shoes/Maybellene (silver label print)	100
56	London HLD 8276	Blue Suede Shoes/Maybellene (silver label print) (78)	30
56	London HLD 8288	Love Is The $64,000 Dollar Question/Rene La Rue (gold label print)	75
56	London HLD 8288	Love Is The $64,000 Dollar Question/Rene La Rue (gold label print) (78)	15
56	London HLD 8317	The Green Door/The Little Man In Chinatown (as Jim Lowe & High Fives, gold label print)	50
56	London HLD 8317	The Green Door/The Little Man In Chinatown (as Jim Lowe & High Fives, later silver print label)	25
57	London HLD 8368	I Feel The Beat/By You, By You, By You (gold label print)	50
57	London HLD 8368	I Feel The Beat/By You, By You, By You (later silver print label)	30
57	London HLD 8431	Four Walls/Talkin' To The Blues	25
58	London HLD 8538	Roc-A-Chicka/The Bright Light (with Billy Vaughan's Orchestra)	150
58	London HLD 8538	Roc-A-Chicka/The Bright Light (with Billy Vaughan's Orchestra) (78)	40
60	London HLD 9043	He'll Have To Go/(This Life Is Just A) Dress Rehearsal	25
65	United Artists UP 1096	Mr Moses/Make Your Back Strong	5
58	London HA-D 2108	SONGS THEY SING BEHIND THE GREEN DOOR (LP)	50
59	London HA-D 2146	WICKED WOMEN (LP)	30

(see also John Barry Seven)

MUNDELL LOWE QUARTET
56	London American LTZ U 15020	MUNDELL LOWE QUARTET (LP)	15

NICK LOWE
76	Stiff BUY 1	So It Goes/Heart Of The City, (push-out centre)	10
77	Stiff LAST 1-12	Bowi EP (Born A Woman//Marie Provost/Endless Sleep, 12" promo, 50 only)	100

LOWLIFE
88	LOLIF DEMO 1	THE DEMOS (LP, white label test pressings only, hand-written white sleeve)	18

LOW/PIANO MAGIC/TRANSIENT WAVES
98	Rocket Girl RGIRL 4	Sleep At The Bottom/TRANSIENT WAVES: Green Acres (p/s)	6

LOWRELL
79	AVI AVISL 108	Mellow Mellow Rich On (Four Mixes) (12")	10

PHILIP LOWRIE
63	Ember EMB S 179	I Might Have Known (Before)/I Might Have Known (After)	10

ART LOWRY
54	Columbia SCMC 1	The Curse Of An Aching Heart/Heart Of My Heart (export issue)	10

HENRY LOWTHER BAND
70	Deram SML 1070	CHILD SONG (LP)	150

(see also Manfred Mann, John Mayall & Bluesbreakers, Keef Hartley Band, Ricotti & Albuquerque)

MARK LOYD
65	Parlophone R 5277	I Keep Thinking About You/Will It Be The Same	10
65	Parlophone R 5332	Everybody Tries/She Said No	60
66	Parlophone R 5423	When Evening Falls/When I'm Gonna Find Her	200
66	Parlophone R 5423	When Evening Falls/When I'm Gonna Find Her (DJ copy)	300

L7
92	Slash L30780	BRICKS ARE HEAVY (LP, green marbled vinyl)	18

JEREMY LUBBOCK
58	Parlophone R 4399	Catch A Falling Star/The Man Who Invented Love	5
58	Parlophone R 4421	Lemon Twist/Tonight	5
58	Parlophone R 4473	Odd Man Out/Too Bad You're Not Around	5
58	Parlophone GEP 8745	JUST FOR THE FUN OF IT (EP)	10

LUCAS (& MIKE COTTON SOUND)
66	Polydor 56114	I Saw Pity In The Face Of A Friend/Dance Children Dance (solo)	20
67	Pye 7N 17313	Step Out Of Line/Ain't Love Good, Ain't Love Proud	50
68	MGM MGM 1398	Soul Serenade/We Got A Thing Going Baby	45
68	MGM MGM 1427	Jack And The Beanstalk/Mother-In-Law	30

(see also Mike Cotton Sound, Artwoods)

BUDDY LUCAS BAND
53	London L 1181	Organ Grinder's Swing/Laura (78, as Buddy Lucas & His Orchestra)	10
60	Pye International 7N 25045	I Want To Know/Deacon John	20
60	Pye International 7N 25045	I Want To Know/Deacon John (78)	10

CARRIE LUCAS
79	Solar FC 1482	Dance With You/Simpler Days (12")	10

TREVOR LUCAS
66	Reality RE 505	Waltzing Matilda/It's On	20
66	Reality RY 1002	OVERLANDER (LP)	275

(see also Eclection, Fotheringay, Fairport Convention, Bronco, Bunch, Sandy Denny)

LUCID DREAM
91	Euphoric E 9999T	DRIPPY EP (12", p/s, 1st pressing of 500 came with numbered insert)	8

JON LUCIEN
74	RCA ALP1-0493	MINDS EYE (LP)	30

LUCIFER
71	Lucifer L 001	Don't Care/Hypnosis	15
72	Lucifer L 003/004	Fuck You/Bad	8
72	Lucifer L 005/006	Prick/Want It	8
72	Lucifer L 005/006/L 003/004	Prick/Want It/Fuck You/Bad (double pack, black box set)	40
73	Lucifer L007	Mr Jack/Mr Jack	50
72	Lucifer LLP 1	BIG GUN (LP, private pressing, with poster/inserts, sold via Oz mag)	100
72	Lucifer LLP 1	BIG GUN (LP, private pressing, without poster/inserts, sold via Oz mag)	60
72	Lucifer LLP 2	EXIT (LP, private pressing, with poster, sold via Oz magazine)	140
72	Lucifer LLP 2	EXIT (LP, private pressing, without poster, sold via Oz magazine)	70

LUCIFER'S FRIEND
71	Philips 6003 092	Ride The Sky/Horla	15
71	Philips 6305 068	LUCIFER'S FRIEND (LP)	250

(see also John Lawton, Uriah Heep)

JOHNNY LUCK
58	Fontana H 110	Play Rough/Buzz, Buzz, Buzz (78)	20

LUCY SHOW
83	Shout XS 007	Leonardo Da Vinci/Kill The Beast (p/s)	5
85	A&M AMY 261	Ephemeral/White Space (12", p/s)	20

TOM LUCY
82	Bridgehouse BHS 15	Paris, France/Man Found Dead In Graveyard (no p/s)	6

(see also Wasted Youth)

LUCY (1)
69	Major Minor MM667	Georgie/With Him	8

LUCY (2)
77	Lightning GIL 516	Never Never/Feel So Good (p/s)	20
78	B&C BCS 8	Really Got Me Goin'/Oy (p/s)	10

(see also Def Leppard)

LUDDITES
83	Xcentric Noise SECOND 1	STRENGTH OF YOUR CRY (EP, black foldout p/s)	15
83	Xcentric Noise SECOND 1	STRENGTH OF YOUR CRY (EP, pink foldout p/s)	10

LUDLOWS
61	Pye NEP 24252	THE SEA AROUND US (EP)	20
66	Pye NPL 18150	THE WIND AND THE SEA (LP)	18

(see also Jim McCann)

LUDUS
80	New Hormones ORG 4	The Visit/Lullaby Cheat/Unveil (12", p/s with insert)	8
81	New Hormones ORG 8	My Cherry Is In Sherry/Anatomy Is Not Destiny (p/s)	5
81	New Hormones CAT 1	PICKPOCKET (C-30 cassette pack with A4 book & button in PVC bag)	12
81	New Hormones ORG 12	Mother's Hour/Patient (p/s, with poster)	5
81	New Hormones ORG 16	THE SEDUCTION (2 x 12" EP, each in p/s; whole package in poly bag)	12
80s	New Hormones	LINDER SINGS BARDOT (cassette)	12
82	New Hormones ORG 20	DANGER CAME SMILING (LP)	12

LUGWORM
97	Guided Missile GUIDE 11	Rococo Negro/BIS: Pop Song (p/s)	5

LUKE & BLAKE
66	CBS 202467	Just You/Wandering Man	8

ROBIN LUKE
58	London HLD 8676	Susie Darlin'/Living's Loving You	12
58	London HLD 8676	Susie Darlin'/Living's Loving You (78)	10
58	London HLD 8771	Chicka Chicka Honey/My Girl	30
58	London HLD 8771	Chicka Chicka Honey/My Girl (78)	20
59	London RED 1222	ROBIN LUKE (EP)	100

LULU (& LUVVERS)

71	Atco 2091049	Move To My Rhythm/Got To Believe In Love	8
64	Decca F 11884	Shout/Forget Me Baby (as Lulu & Luvers)	8
64	Decca F 11965	Can't Hear You No More/I Am In Love	15
64	Decca F 12017	Here Comes The Night/That's Really Some Good	15
65	Decca F 12128	Satisfied/Surprise Surprise (as Lulu & Luvers)	18
65	Decca F 12169	Leave A Little Love/He Don't Want Your Love Anymore	10
65	Decca F 12214	Try To Understand/Not In This Whole World	8
65	Decca F 12254	Tell Me Like It Is/Stop Fooling Around	20
66	Decca F 12326	Call Me/After You	7
66	Decca F 12491	What A Wonderful Feeling/Tossin' And Turnin'	12
67	Columbia DB 8169	The Boat That I Row/Dreary Days And Nights	8
67	Columbia DB 8221	Let's Pretend/To Sir With Love	10
67	Columbia DB 8295	Love Loves To Love/You And I	12
68	Columbia DB 8358	Me, The Peaceful Heart/Lookout	5
68	Columbia DB 8425	Boy/Sad Memories	10
68	Columbia DB 8500	I'm A Tiger/Without Him	5
69	Columbia DB 8550	Boom Bang-A-Bang/March!	5
69	Atco 226 008	Oh Me, Oh My (I'm A Fool For You Baby)/Sweep Around Your Own Backyard	10
65	Decca DFE 8597	LULU (EP)	35
65	Decca LK 4719	SOMETHING TO SHOUT ABOUT (LP)	60
67	Ace Of Clubs ACL 1232	LULU! (LP)	60
67	Fontana (S)TL 5446	TO SIR, WITH LOVE (LP, soundtrack, with Ron Grainer & Mindbenders)	60
67	Columbia S(C)X 6201	LOVE LOVES TO LOVE LULU (LP)	35
69	Columbia S(C)X 6365	LULU'S ALBUM (LP)	25
69	Atco 228 031	NEW ROUTES (LP)	25
70	Atco 2400	MELODY FAIR (LP)	15

(see also Luvvers, Scotland World Cup Squad)

LULU BELLE & SCOTTY

50	London L 833	Have I Told You Lately That I Love You/Schrudle Du (78)	10
65	London HA-B 8277	SWEETHEART STILL (LP)	15

BOB LUMAN

60	Warner Bros WB 12	Dreamy Doll/Buttercup	25
60	Warner Bros WB 28	Why, Why, Bye, Bye/Oh, Lonesome Me	15
61	Warner Bros WB 37	The Great Snow Man/The Pig Latin Song	15
61	Warner Bros WB 49	Private Eye/You Turned Down The Lights	10
62	Warner Bros WB 60	Louisiana Man/Rocks Of Reno (unissued)	0
62	Warner Bros WB 75	Hey Joe/The Fool	12
64	Hickory 45-1238	The File/Bigger Men Than I	10
64	Hickory 45-1266	(Empty Walls) A Lonely Room/Run On Home Baby Brother	6
64	Hickory 45-1277	Old George Dickel/Fire Engine Red	6
65	Hickory 45-1289	Bad Bad Day/Tears From Out Of Nowhere	10
65	Hickory 45-1410	Come On And Sing/It's A Sin	6
68	CBS 3602	Ain't Got Time To Be Unhappy/I Can't Remember To Forget	10
61	Warner Bros WEP 6046	LET'S THINK ABOUT LIVIN' (EP, mono)	40
61	Warner Bros WSEP 2046	LET'S THINK ABOUT LIVIN' (EP, stereo)	45
62	Warner Bros WEP 6055	LET'S THINK ABOUT LIVIN' NO. 2 (EP, mono)	35
62	Warner Bros WSEP 2055	LET'S THINK ABOUT LIVIN' NO. 2 (EP, stereo)	40
62	Warner Bros WEP 6102	LET'S THINK ABOUT LIVIN' NO. 3 (EP, mono)	35
62	Warner Bros WSEP 2102	LET'S THINK ABOUT LIVIN' NO. 3 (EP, stereo)	40
60	Warner Bros WM 4025	LET'S THINK ABOUT LIVIN' (LP, mono)	40
60	Warner Bros WS 8025	LET'S THINK ABOUT LIVIN' (LP, stereo)	60
64	Hickory LPM 124	LIVIN' LOVIN' SOUNDS (LP)	35

(see also Sue Thompson & Bob Luman)

BOB LUMAN/BOBBY LORD

64	Hickory LPM 121	CAN'T TAKE THE COUNTRY FROM THE BOYS (LP, 1 side each)	15

(see also Bobby Lord)

RUFUS LUMLEY

66	Stateside SS 516	I'm Standing/Let's Hide Away (Me And You)	200
66	Stateside SS 516	I'm Standing/Let's Hide Away (Me And You) (DJ copy)	380
78	EMI International INT 556	I'm Standing/Let's Hide Away (Me And You) (reissue)	15

LUNA C

93	Kn+feforce KF 001	THE LUNA C PROJECT EP (12")	40
93	Knifeforce KF 002	LUNA C PROJECT 2 - MISSION OF MADNESS (12")	40
93	Knifeforce KF 012	Death Of A Psychopath/Bass Drum Jungle Music (12")	10
94	Knifeforce KF 025	Piano Progression (Double Whopper Mix)/Onward (Extra Pepperami Mix) (12")	10

LUNACHICKS

89	Blast First BFFP 44	SUGAR LUV EP (7" double pack)	8

LUNAR TWO

60s	Spot JWS 551	Get It Take It/Don't Ever Leave Me	20

LUNATIC FRINGE

82	Resurrection	Keep In Touch	8
84	COR 1	CRINGE WITH THE FRINGE (EP)	12

LYDIA LUNCH

91	UFO UFOPF 1	Spooky (mono)/Spooky (stereo) (no p/s, promo only)	6
93	Clawfist X-PIG 19	Unearthly Delights/Busted (p/s)	8
80	Celluiod CEL 2 6561	QUEEN OF SIAM (LP)	25
82	Situation 2 SITU 6	13.13 (LP, with inner sleeve)	20
84	Doublevision DVR 5	IN LIMBO (LP, red vinyl with inner sleeve)	20
86	Widowspeak SWP 01/07	THE INTIMATE DIARIES OF THE SEXUALLY INSANE (cassette, box set with book, signed)	25
87	Widowspeak WSP 8	HYSTERIE (2-LP, with inners and poster)	20

(see also Eight-Eyed Spy, Roland S. Howard, No Trend)

ART LUND

53	MGM SP 1042	If I Were A Bell/JOHNNY DESMOND: A Bushel And A Peck	5
65	United Artists UP 1100	Branded/Gonna Have A Little Talk	7

MINT VALUE £

| 57 | Vogue Coral LVA 9056 | THIS IS ART (LP) | 20 |

TED LUNE
| 60 | Philips PB 1068 | Mr Custer/Time Machine | 6 |

(see also Michael Medwin 8 Army Game Cast)

LUNGFISH
| 97 | Dischord DIS 106V | INDIVISIBLE (LP, insert) | 12 |
| 99 | Dischord DIS 117 | UNANIMOUS HOUR (LP, inner) | 12 |

LARRY LUREX
| 73 | EMI EMI 2030 | I Can Hear Music/Goin' Back (demo) | 300 |
| 73 | EMI EMI 2030 | I Can Hear Music/Goin' Back (press-out centre; beware of solid-centered counterfeits) | 200 |

(see also Queen)

LURKERS
77	Beggars Banquet BEG 1	Free Admission Single: Shadow/Love Story (p/s, black vinyl)	10
77	Beggars Banquet BEG 1	Free Admission Single: Shadow/Love Story (p/s, reissue, red, blue or white vinyl)	12
77	Beggars Banquet BEG 2	Freak Show/Mass Media Believer (p/s)	10
78	Beggars Banquet BEG 6	Ain't Got A Clue/Ooh Ooh I Love You (p/s, 15,000 with gold flexidisc, 'Chaos Brothers Fulham Fallout Firty Free' [BEG 61/2])	6
78	Beggars Banquet BEG 6	Ain't Got A Clue/Ooh Ooh I Love You (p/s)	5
78	Beggars Banquet BEG 6	Ain't Got A Clue/Ooh Ooh I Love You (reissue, different p/s, with clear vinyl picture flexidisc)	5
79	Beggars Banquet BACK 1	Shadow/Love Story//Freak Show/Mass Media Believer (reissue double pack)	5
79	Beggars Banquet BACK 3	I Don't Need To Tell Her/Pills//Just Thirteen/Countdown (double pack)	5
82	Clay CLAY 17P	Drag You Out/Heroin (It's All Over) (picture disc)	5
78	Beggars Banquet BEGA 2	FULHAM FALLOUT (LP, gatefold sleeve, some with picture disc flexi 'Chaos Brothers Fulham Fallout Firty Free' [BEG 6 ½] & stickered sleeve)	20
78	Beggars Banquet BEGA 2	FULHAM FALLOUT (LP, gatefold sleeve)	12
79	Beggars Banquet BEGA 8	GOD'S LONELY MEN (LP, with inner)	12
89	Link LP 103	LIVE & LOUD! (LP)	12
85	Sin 006	FEAR AND WHISKEY (LP)	12

(see also Pete Stride & John Plain, Fulham Furies, Rowdies)

LUSH
90	4AD CAD 0013	SWEETNESS AND LIGHT EP (12")	8
89	4AD CADD 2002	SPOOKY (2x10" LP)	25
90	4AD CAD 0017	GALA (LP)	18
94	4AD CAD 4011	SPLIT (LP)	20
96	4AD CAD 6004	LOVELIFE (LP, clear vinyl)	15

DON LUSHER BAND
55	Decca F 10560	Rock 'n' Roll/On With The Don	20
56	Decca F 10740	Fast And Furious/Let's Do It	8
67	CBS 62883	FROM LUSHER WITH LOVE (LP)	15

LUSTMØRD
| 82 | Sterile SR 3 | LUSTMØRD (LP, with odorous label) | 35 |

NELLIE LUTCHER (& HER RHYTHM)
54	Brunswick 05352	Blues In The Night/Breezin' Along With The Breeze	10
55	Brunswick 05437	It's Been Said/Please Come Back	8
55	Brunswick 05497	Whose Honey Are You?/If I Didn't Love You Like I Do	8
60	Capitol CL 15106	My Mother's Eyes/The Heart Of A Clown	6
60	Capitol EAP 20066	REAL GONE (EP)	20
56	Philips BBE 12045	NELLIE LUTCHER (EP)	20
51	Capitol LC 6506	REAL GONE! (10" LP)	35
57	London HA-U 2036	OUR NEW NELLIE (LP)	35

LUTHER & LITTLE EVA
| 57 | Parlophone R 4292 | Love Is Strange/Ain't Got No Home | 400 |
| 57 | Parlophone R 4292 | Love Is Strange/Ain't Got No Home (78) | 100 |

LUV BUG
| 86 | Roxy!-Ritz TEASE 2 | You Can Count On Me/You Can't Have It (p/s) | 7 |

LUV MACHINE
| 71 | Polydor 2058 080 | Witches Wand/In The Early Hours | 30 |
| 71 | Polydor 2460 102 | LUV MACHINE (LP) | 200 |

LUVVERS
| 66 | Parlophone R 5459 | The House On The Hill/Most Unlovely | 70 |

(see also Lulu)

MICK LUVZIT
| 66 | Decca F 12421 | Long Time Between Lovers/Though I Still Love You | 20 |

GARY LUX
| 85 | Global LUX 2 | Children Of The World/Movies (p/s) | 5 |

LUXURY
| 91 | Spare Beat SBRR 001 | LUXURY EP 1 (12") | 15 |
| 92 | Spare Beat SBRR 003 | The Silencer/You And Me (12") | 15 |

L-VOAG
| 79 | Sesame Songs MOVE 1 | MOVE (EP, p/s with handmade labels & insert) | 30 |
| 81 | Axis No. 9 | THE WAY OUT (LP, with booklet & poster) | 40 |

(see also Homosexuals)

LYDS
| 96 | Dig The Fuzz DIG 014 | Fly Away With Me/Seperations (p/s) | 15 |

ARTHUR LYMAN GROUP
61	Vogue V 9183	Yellow Bird/Havah Magila	6
59	Vogue VA 160142	TABOO VOL. 1 (LP, mono)	15
59	Vogue SAV 8002	TABOO VOL. 1 (LP, stereo)	18
61	Vogue VA 160174	TABOO VOL. 2 (LP, also stereo SAV 8003)	15

FRANKIE LYMON (& TEENAGERS)

56	Columbia SCM 5265	Why Do Fools Fall In Love?/Please Be Mine (as Teenagers featuring Frankie Lymon)	60
56	Columbia SCM 5285	I Want You To Be My Girl/I'm Not A Know It All	50
56	Columbia SCM 5285	I Want You To Be My Girl/I'm Not A Know It All (78)	12
56	Columbia DB 3819	Who Can Explain?/I Promise To Remember	50
56	Columbia DB 3819	Who Can Explain?/I Promise To Remember (78)	10
56	Columbia DB 3858	Share/The A.B.C.'s Of Love	50
56	Columbia DB 3858	Share/The A.B.C.'s Of Love (78)	12
57	Columbia DB 3878	I'm Not A Juvenile Delinquent/Baby, Baby	30
57	Columbia DB 3910	Teenage Love/Paper Castles	40
57	Columbia DB 3910	Teenage Love/Paper Castles (78)	10
57	Columbia DB 3942	Miracle In The Rain/Out In The Cold Again	40
57	Columbia DB 3942	Miracle In The Rain/Out In The Cold Again (78)	10
57	Columbia DB 3983	Goody Goody/Creation Of Love	20
57	Columbia DB 4028	My Girl/So Goes My Love	25
57	Columbia DB 4028	My Girl/So Goes My Love (78)	15
58	Columbia DB 4073	Thumb Thumb/Footsteps (solo)	30
58	Columbia DB 4073	Thumb Thumb/Footsteps (solo) (78)	15
58	Columbia DB 4134	Mama Don't Allow It/Portable On My Shoulder (solo)	20
58	Columbia DB 4134	Mama Don't Allow It/Portable On My Shoulder (solo) (78)	15
59	Columbia DB 4245	Melinda/The Only Way To Love (solo)	20
59	Columbia DB 4245	Melinda/The Only Way To Love (solo) (78)	25
59	Columbia DB 4295	Up Jumped A Rabbit/No Matter What You've Done (solo)	25
60	Columbia DB 4499	Little Bitty Pretty One/Creation Of Love (solo)	25
66	King KG 1042	Why Do Fools Fall In Love?/I'm Not A Juvenile Delinquent	5
57	Columbia SEG 7662	TEENAGE ROCK (EP)	50
57	Columbia SEG 7694	THE TEENAGERS FEATURING FRANKIE LYMON (EP)	60
57	Columbia SEG 7734	FRANKIE LYMON AND THE TEENAGERS (EP)	60
58	Columbia 33S 1127	FRANKIE LYMON IN LONDON (10" LP, solo)	100
58	Columbia 33S 1134	ROCKIN' WITH FRANKIE LYMON (10" LP, solo)	300
75	Pye International NSPL 28251	WHY DO FOOLS FALL IN LOVE (LP)	19

LEWIS LYMON & TEENCHORDS

58	Oriole 45-CB 1419	Too Young/Your Last Chance	500
58	Oriole CB 1419	Too Young/Your Last Chance (78)	100

DERMOTT LYNCH

68	Blue Cat BS 101	Hot Shot/I've Got Your Number	60
68	Blue Cat BS 122	I Got Everything/Echo	40
68	Doctor Bird DB 1115	Adults Only/Cool It	40

(see also Trevor, Carl Dawkins, Joe White)

E D LYNCH

66	Fontana TF688	Sad Songs/Shoe Of True Love	15

JOE LYNCH

69	Spectrum SP 107	King Child/Johnny Appleseed	5

KENNY LYNCH

60	HMV POP 751	Mountain Of Love/Why Do You Treat Me This Way?	10
60	HMV POP 786	Slowcoach/You Make Love So Well	6
61	HMV POP 841	So/Love Me	6
61	HMV POP 900	The Story Behind My Tears/Steady Kind	6
61	HMV POP 985	There's Never Been A Girl/Doll Face	6
62	HMV POP 1005	It Would Take A Miracle/Strolling Blues	6
62	HMV POP 1057	Puff/Happy That's Me	15
62	HMV POP 1090	Up On The Roof/Jump On Your Broomstick	10
63	HMV POP 1136	Misery/Shut The Door	6
63	HMV POP 1165	You Can Never Stop Me Loving You/Crazy Crazes	6
63	HMV POP 1229	For You (There's Not A Thing I Wouldn't Do)/With Somebody	6
63	HMV POP 1260	Shake And Scream/Harlem Library	6
64	HMV POP 1280	Stand By Me/Baby It's True	6
64	HMV POP 1321	That's What Little Girls Are Made For/What Am I To You?	6
64	HMV POP 1367	My Own Two Feet/So Much To Love You For	30
65	HMV POP 1430	I'll Stay By You/For Loving You Baby	7
65	HMV POP 1476	Nothing But The Real Thing/Don't Ask Me To Stop Loving You	6
65	HMV POP 1496	Get Out Of My Way/One Look At You	10
66	HMV POP 1534	The World I Used To Know/Come On Come On	7
67	HMV POP 1577	I Just Wanna Love You/It's Too Late	8
67	HMV POP 1604	Movin' Away/Could I Count On You	150
68	Columbia DB 8329	Mister Moonlight/The Other Side Of Dreamland	15
68	Columbia DB 8498	Along Comes Love/Sweet Situation	15
69	Columbia DB 8599	The Drifter/Did I Stay Too Long?	40
70	Columbia DB 8703	In Old Kentucky/Loving You Is Sweeter Than Ever	15
63	HMV 7EG 8820	HEY GIRL (EP)	10
64	HMV 7EG 8855	KENNY LYNCH (EP)	10
65	HMV 7EG 8881	WHAT AM I TO YOU (EP)	10
63	HMV CLP 1635	UP ON THE ROOF (LP, mono)	45
63	HMV CSD 1489	UP ON THE ROOF (LP, stereo)	50

LEE LYNCH (& BLUE ANGELS)

66	Decca F 12375	You Won't See Me/You Know There's Me (as Lee Lynch & Blue Angels)	10
69	Ember EMB S 262	Stay Awhile/Bad Time To Stop Loving Me (p/s)	10
70	Ember EMB S 271	Sweet Woman/Can't Take My Eyes Off You (p/s)	10
70	Ember EMB S 282	Joe Poor Loves Daphne Elizabeth Rich/It's Love (p/s)	10
67	Pye 7N 17363	I'll Hold You In My Heart/Looking Through My Teardrops	10

LINDA LYNDELL

68	Stax 601 041	Bring Your Love Back To Me/Here I Am	50

BARBARA LYNN

64	London HLW 9918	Oh! Baby (We Got A Good Thing Goin')/Unfair	40
65	Immediate IM 011	You Can't Buy My Love/That's What A Friend Will Do	45
66	London HLU 10094	You Left The Water Running/Until I'm Free	35

MINT VALUE £

67	Sue WI 4028	Letter To Mommy And Daddy/Second Fiddle Girl	50
67	Sue WI 4038	You'll Lose A Good Thing/Lonely Heartaches	55
71	Atlantic 2091 133	Take Your Love And Run/(Until Then) I'll Suffer	20
75	Oval OVAL 1006	Letter To Mommy And Daddy/You'll Lose A Good Thing	10
67	Sue ILP 949	THE BARBARA LYNN STORY (LP)	200

BOBBI LYNN

68	Stateside SS 2088	Earthquake/Opportunity Street	50
68	Stateside SS 2088	Earthquake/Opportunity Street (DJ copy)	75
71	Bell BLL 1168	Earthquake/Opportunity Street (reissue)	8

CHERYL LYNN

79	CBS CBS 12-6967	Got To Be Real/Come In From The Rain (12")	10
84	Streetwave KHAN 23	Encore/Got To Be Real (12")	10

JESSE LYNN DEAN

79	Creole CR 176	Do It/My Boyfriend's Back In Town (p/s)	20

(see also the Wasps)

DONNA LYNN

64	Capitol CL 15359	Silly Girl/There Goes The Boy I Love With Mary	6

KARI LYNN

61	Oriole CB 1632	Yo Yo/Summer Day	15
61	Oriole CB 1644	You've Got To See Mamma Every Night/Lonesome And Sorry	15

LORETTA LYNN

68	MCA MUP 338	LORETTA LYNN (LP)	12

(see also Conway Twitty)

PATTI LYNN

62	Fontana H 370	I See It All Now/Someone Else's Valentine	15
62	Fontana H 391	Johnny Angel/Tonight You Belong To Me	15
62	Fontana 267 247 TF	Tell Me Telstar/Big Big Love	20
62	Fontana TFE 17392	PATTI (EP)	40

TAM(M)I LYNN

66	Atlantic AT 4071	I'm Gonna Run Away From You/The Boy Next Door	70
66	Atlantic AT 4071	I'm Gonna Run Away From You/The Boy Next Door (DJ Copy)	100
71	Mojo 2092 001	I'm Gonna Run Away From You/The Boy Next Door (reissue)	10
71	Mojo 2092 012	That's Understanding/Never No More	6
75	Contempo CS 9026	I'm Gonna Run Away From You/The Boy Next Door (2nd reissue)	6
71	Mojo 2916 007	LOVE IS HERE AND NOW YOU'RE GONE (LP)	25

VERA LYNN

52	Decca F 9927	Auf Wiederseh'n, Sweetheart/From The Time You Say Goodbye	10
54	Decca F 10372	My Son, My Son/Our Heaven On Earth (with Frank Weir & His Saxophone)	15

(see also Johnstone Brothers, Frank Weir & His Orchestra)

GLORIA LYNNE

64	London HLY 9846	I Wish You Love/Through A Long And Sleeping Night	8
64	London HLY 9888	I Should Care/Indian Love Call	8
69	Fontana TF 1017	Problem Child/I've Got To Be Someone	8
59	Top Rank JKP 2024	MEET GLORIA LYNNE (EP, with Wild Bill Davis)	20
60	Top Rank BUY 031	LONELY AND SENTIMENTAL (LP)	25
64	London HA-Y 8112	AT THE LAS VEGAS THUNDERBIRD (LP, with Herman Foster Trio)	15
65	Fontana TL 5315	INTIMATE MOMENTS (LP)	15
72	Mojo 2916 016	HAPPY AND IN LOVE (LP)	25

SUE LYNNE

68	RCA Victor RCA 1724	Reach For The Moon/All Alone	10
69	RCA Victor RCA 1822	You/Don't Pity Me	150
69	RCA Victor RCA 1822	You/Don't Pity Me (DJ copy)	200
69	RCA Victor RCA 1874	Baby Baby Baby/You Lose Again	7

PHIL LYNOTT

80	Vertigo LYNT 1	King's Call/Yellow Pearl (12", p/s)	8
80	Vertigo SOLO 2	King's Call/Ode To A Black Man (p/s)	5
81	Vertigo SOLO 3	Yellow Pearl/Girls (p/s, clear vinyl)	5
85	Vertigo SOLO 5	Old Town/Beat Of The Drum (p/s)	6
85	Polydor POSPD 777	19/19 (Dub Version)//THIN LIZZY: Whiskey In The Jar (live) (double pack, 2nd disc 1-sided)	8
80	Vertigo PHIL 1	SOLO IN SOHO (LP, picture disc, die-cut sleeve)	15

(see also Thin Lizzy, Gary Moore & Phil Lynott, John Sykes, Rockers)

JACKIE LYNTON

61	Piccadilly 7N 35012	Over The Rainbow/High In The Sky	8
62	Piccadilly 7N 35055	Don't Take Away Your Love/Wishful Thinking	8
62	Piccadilly 7N 35064	All Of Me/I'd Steal	7
63	Piccadilly 7N 35107	I Believe/The Girl In The Wood	7
63	Piccadilly 7N 35140	Jeannie With The Light Brown Hair/Teddy Bear's Picnic	7
63	Piccadilly 7N 35156	I'm Talkin' About You/Lawdy Miss Clawdy	7
64	Piccadilly 7N 35177	Little Child/Never A Mention	7
64	Piccadilly 7N 35190	Laura/Ebb Tide	7
65	Decca F 12052	Three Blind Mice/Corrina Corrine	6
67	Columbia DB 8097	He'll Have To Go/Only You	10
67	Columbia DB 8180	Decision/Sporting Life	10
67	Columbia DB 8224	Answer Me/I Never Loved A Girl Like You	25
79	Thumb TR003	Dan (The Hedgehog Song)/Farting With The Famous	8

(see also Savoy Brown Blues Band)

LYNX

78	ST Products SRTS/78/CUS 112	See The Light/C.I.A. (no p/s, 500 only)	250

LYNYRD SKYNYRD

74	MCA MCA 136	Don't Ask Me No Questions/Take Your Time	5
74	MCA MCA 160	Sweet Home Alabama/Take Your Time	5
75	MCA MCA 199	Saturday Night Special/Made In The Shade	5

76	MCA MCA 229	Double Trouble/Roll Gypsy Roll..5
76	MCA MCA 251	Free Bird/Sweet Home Alabama/Double Trouble (p/s) 8
76	MCA MCA 275	Free Bird (Edit)/Gimme Three Steps (p/s)...8
74	MCA MCG 3502	PRONOUNCED LEH-NERD SKIN-NERD (LP, gatefold sleeve) 18
77	MCA MCG 3525	STREET SURVIVORS (LP, gatefold sleeve with tour dates on inner sleeve) 15

BARBARA LYON

55	Columbia SCM 5186	I Love To Dance With You/Yes You Are..10
55	Columbia SCM 5207	Whisper/Where You Are..10
56	Columbia SCM 5232	Band Of Gold/Such A Day..8
56	Columbia SCM 5276	Puppy Love/The Birds And The Bees 8
56	Columbia DB 3826	It's Better In The Dark/A Heart Without A Sweetheart 6
56	Columbia DB 3865	Falling In Love/Letter To A Soldier 15
57	Columbia DB 3931	C'est La Vie/Fire Down Below 5
57	Columbia DB 4026	Thanks For The Loan Of A Dream/Third Finger - Left Hand 5
58	Columbia DB 4137	Red Was The Moon/Ring On A Ribbon 5
60	Triumph RGM 1027	My Charlie/Tell Me 40
56	Columbia SEG 7640	MY FOUR FRIENDS (EP) 20

RICHARD LYON

| 59 | Fontana H 206 | All My Own/Private Eye ....22 |
| 59 | Fontana H 206 | All My Own/Private Eye (78) ....12 |

SUE LYON

| 62 | MGM 1159 | Lolita Ya Ya/LEROY HOLMES : Main Theme From Lolita ....10 |

(See also Leroy Holmes)

LYONS & MALONE

| 69 | Jay Boy BOY 9 | Doctor Gentle/She's Alright ....60 |

LYRICS

67	Coxsone CS 7003	A Get It/KEN PARKER: How Strong 50
68	Coxsone CS 7067	Music Like Dirt/TONETTES: I Give It To You..60
70	Randy's RAN 504	Give Thanks And Praises/TOMMY McCOOK: Get Ready 15
71	Randy's RAN 511	Give Thanks/RANDY'S ALL STARS: Give - Version 15

(see also Randy's All Stars, Viceroys, Jackie Mittoo, Fred Locks)

LARS LYSTEDY SEXTET

| 64 | Realm REP 4004 | LARS LYSTEDY SEXTET (EP)..10 |

JIMMY LYTELL

| 59 | London HL 8873 | Hot Cargo/A Blues Serenade ....10 |

JOHNNY LYTLE

| 68 | Minit MLF 11006 | Gonna Get That Boat (Parts 1 & 2) ....12 |

HUMPHREY LYTTELTON (& HIS BAND)
SINGLES

51	Saturn EGX 105	When The Saints Go Marching In/Careless Love (78, picture disc) 60
53	Parlophone MSP 6001	Out Of The Gallion/The Old Grey Mare 10
53	Parlophone MSP 6023	Muskrat Ramble/Mamzelle Josephine (as Lyttelton Paseo Band, B-side with George Brown)..5
53	Parlophone MSP 6033	Maryland, My Maryland/Blue For Waterloo 5
53	Parlophone MSP 6034	Shake It And Break It/Jail Break 10
54	Parlophone MSP 6076	East Coast Trot/Breeze 10
54	Parlophone MSP 6093	Just Once For All Time/Joshua, Fit The Battle Of Jericho 5
54	Parlophone MSP 6097	Mainly Traditional/Oh! Dad (with 'Melody Maker' All Stars) 5
54	Parlophone MSP 6128	Mezzy's Tune/Jelly Bean Blues 5
56	Tempo A 10	When The Saints Go Marching In/Careless Love 8
57	Parlophone R 4333	Early Call (Bermondsey Bounce)/Creole Serenade 10
58	Parlophone CMSP 41	Bad Penny Blues/Baby Doll (export issue) 20
58	Decca F 11058	La Paloma/Bodega 5
59	Parlophone R 4519	Saturday Jump/The Bear Steps Out..8
59	Parlophone R 4519	Saturday Jump/The Bear Steps Out (78) 10

EPs

| 55 | Tempo EXA 1 | HUMPHREY LYTTELTON & HIS BAND (EP) ....10 |

ALBUMS : LPS

53	Parlophone PMD 1006	JAZZ CONCERT (10" LP) 30
54	Parlophone PMC 1012	HUMPH AT THE CONWAY (LP) 30
55	Parlophone PMD 1032	JAZZ AT THE ROYAL FESTIVAL HALL (10" LP) 20
56	Parlophone PMD 1035	JAZZ SESSION WITH HUMPH (10" LP) 15
56	Parlophone PMD 1044	HUMPH SWINGS OUT (10" LP) 25
57	Parlophone PMD 1049	HERE'S HUMPH (10" LP) 15
58	Parlophone PMD 1052	KATH MEETS HUMPH (10" LP, with Kathy Stobart) 20
58	Parlophone PMC 1070	HUMPH IN PERSPECTIVE (LP) 20
58	Decca LK 4276	I PLAY AS I PLEASE (LP) 20
59	Parlophone PMC 1110	TRIPLE EXPOSURE (LP) 70
54	Esquire 32-007	HUMPHREY LYTTELTON AND HIS BAND (LP) 20
60	Columbia 33SX 1239	BLUES IN THE NIGHT (LP) 25
60	Columbia 33SX 1305	HUMPH PLAYS STANDARDS (LP) 25
60	Columbia 33SX 1364	HUMPH MEETS CAB (LP) 40
61	Columbia 33SX 3382	HUMPH RETURNS TO THE CONWAY (LP) 20
62	Columbia 33SX 1484	LATE NIGHT FINAL (LP) 20

(see also Shirley Abicair, Sidney Bechet, George Brown, Buck Clayton, Helen Shapiro, Radiohead)o

MABEL
78	Sonet SON 2147	Boom Boom/FBI On The Nail (p/s)	6

MOMS MABLEY
69	Mercury MF 1127	Abraham, Martin And John/Sunny	12
71	Mercury 6052 109	That's Pops/I Surrender Dear	6

WILLIE MABON
64	Sue WI 320	Got To Have Some/Why Did It Happen To Me	50
65	Sue WI 331	Just Got Some/That's No Big Thing	50
65	Sue WI 382	I'm The Fixer/Some More	50

MABRAK
78	Different GET A101	DRUM TALK (mixed by King Tubby) (LP)	100

SPENCER MAC
70	Penny Farthing PEN 723	Blues Up In Down Town/Ka Ka Kabya Mow Mow	90
70	Penny Farthing PEN 742	Commuter/Better By You - Better By Me	60

MACABRE
87	Vinyl Solution SOL 18	GRIM REALITY (LP, with insert)	18
89	Vinyl Solution SOL 020	GLOOM (LP)	15

GLO MACARI
65	Piccadilly 7N 35218	He Knows I Love Him Too Much/I've Lost You	15
71	Columbia DB 8821	Looking For Love/People Like You	15

DAN MACARTHUR
79	Virgin VS 275-12	DAN MacARTHUR (12" EP)	8

(see also Jah Wobble, PiL)

NEIL MACARTHUR
69	Deram DM 225	She's Not There/World Of Glass	25
69	Deram DM 262	Don't Try To Explain/Without Her	15
69	Deram DM 275	It's Not Easy/12.29	15

(see also Colin Blunstone, Zombies)

MACARTHUR PARK
70	Columbia DB 8683	Taffeta Rose/Sammy	12
71	Philips 6006 086	Lottie Lottie/Love Is Coming	6

(see also Shadows)

MACATTACK
86	Baad! Records 12HIP1AZ	ART OF DRUMS (12" EP)	15

DAVID MACBETH
59	Pye Nixa 7N 15231	Mr. Blue/Here's A Heart	7
60	Pye 7N 15250	Tell Her From Me/Livin' Dangerously	5
62	Piccadilly 7N 35072	Have I Told You Lately That I Love You/A Brother Like You	6
63	Piccadilly 7N 35092	A Very Good Year For Girls/Broken Hearts	5

MACC LADS
89	Renegade RS 1	Jingle Bells/Even Uglier Women (p/s)	5
90	FM Revolver VHF 42	Barrels Round/Jingle Bells (p/s)	5
85	FM Revolver FMLP 56	BEER AND SEX AND CHIPS'N'GRAVY (LP, white vinyl)	15
88	FM Revolver WKFMLP 115	LIVE AT LEEDS (LP, blue vinyl)	15

EWAN MACCOLL
58	Topic 10T 26	BARRACK ROOM BALLADS (10" LP)	30
58	Topic 10T 36	BOLD SPORTSMEN ALL (10" LP, with A.L. Lloyd)	30
58	Topic 10T 50	STILL I LOVE HIM (10" LP with booklet, with Isla Cameron)	35
60	Topic 12T 41	STREETS OF SONG (LP, with Dominic Behan, with booklet and original blue label)	20
61	PRE 13004	THE BEST OF EWAN MacCOLL (LP)	12
62	Topic 12T 79	THE JACOBITE REBELLIONS (LP, with original blue label)	18
64	Topic 12T 103	ENGLISH AND SCOTTISH FOLK BALLADS (LP, with A.L. Lloyd, initial pressing with blue label & booklet)	25
64	Topic 12T 103	ENGLISH AND SCOTTISH FOLK BALLADS (LP, with A.L. Lloyd)	15
67	Topic 12T 130	BUNDOOK BALLADS (LP, originally with blue label)	18
67	Argo ZFB 12	SOLO FLIGHT (LP; reissued 1972)	30
67	Xtra 1052	BLOW BOYS BLOW - SONGS OF THE SEA (LP, with A.L. Lloyd)	15
68	Argo (Z)DA 85	THE WANTON MUSE (LP, with booklet)	25
72	Argo (Z)DA 85	THE WANTON MUSE (LP, reissue)	12

(see also A.L. Lloyd)

EWAN MACCOLL & PEGGY SEEGER (& CHARLES PARKER)
60s	AUEW AUEW 1	We Are The Engineers/I'm Gonna Be An Engineer (p/s)	6
57	Topic 10T 13	SHUTTLE AND CAGE (10" LP)	40
61	Topic 12T 16	CHORUS FROM THE GALLOWS (LP, original pressing with blue label, insert)	20
61	Topic 12T 16	CHORUS FROM THE GALLOWS (LP,)	15
64	Topic 12T 104	STEAM WHISTLE BALLADS (LP, blue label)	20
64	Topic 12T 104	STEAM WHISTLE BALLADS (LP, later reissue with booklet)	15
65	Argo RG 474	THE BALLAD OF JOHN AXON (LP, by Ewan MacColl & Charles Parker)	25
67	Topic 12T 147	THE MANCHESTER ANGEL (LP, original pressing with blue label)	18
67	Topic 12T 147	THE MANCHESTER ANGEL (LP)	12
67	Argo DA 140	THE BIG HEWER - A RADIO BALLAD BY EWAN MacCOLL, PEGGY SEEGER, CHARLES PARKER (LP, documentary with music)	30
67	Argo (Z)DA 66	LONG HARVEST 1 (LP)	15
67	Argo (Z)DA 67	LONG HARVEST 2 (LP)	15
67	Argo (Z)DA 68	LONG HARVEST 3 (LP)	15

67	Argo (Z)DA 69	LONG HARVEST 4 (LP)	15
67	Argo RG 502	SINGING THE FISHING (LP, with Charles Parker)	25
67	Argo DA 142	SINGING THE FISHING (LP, reissue, with Charles Parker)	18
68	Argo (Z)DA 70	LONG HARVEST 5 (LP)	15
68	Argo (Z)DA 71	LONG HARVEST 6 (LP)	15
68	Argo (Z)DA 72	LONG HARVEST 7 (LP)	15
68	Argo (Z)DA 73	LONG HARVEST 8 (LP)	15
68	Argo (Z)DA 74	LONG HARVEST 9 (LP)	15
68	Argo (Z)DA 75	LONG HARVEST 10 (LP)	15
68	Argo (Z)DA 84	THE AMOROUS MUSE (LP)	15
68	Argo (Z)DA	THE ANGRY MUSE (LP)	15
69	Argo (Z)DA 98	THE PAPER STAGE 1 (LP, with booklet)	15
69	Argo (Z)DA 99	THE PAPER STAGE 2 (LP)	15
60s	XTRA 1054	SCOTS BALLADS (LP)	35
60s	Folkways FW 8958	SONGS OF ROBERT BURNS (LP)	45
70	Argo SPA-A 102	THE WORLD OF EWAN MacCOLL & PEGGY SEEGER (LP)	20
70	Argo SPA-A 216	THE WORLD OF EWAN MacCOLL & PEGGY SEEGER VOL. 2 - SONGS FROM THE RADIO BALLADS (LP)	15
70	Argo DA 133	THE TRAVELLING PEOPLE (LP, with Charles Parker)	25
71	Argo DA 136	ON THE EDGE (LP)	15

(see also Peggy Seeger, A.L. Lloyd, Isla Cameron)

KIRSTY MACCOLL

83	Stiff BUY DJ 190	Terry/Quietly Alone (Grey promo. "A" label)	5
83	Stiff BUY DJ 190	Terry/Quietly Alone (Pink promo. "A" label)	15
84	Stiff BUY 216	A New England/Patrick (British flag p/s)	10
84	Stiff BUY 216	A New England/Patrick (Kirsty close-up p/s)	5
79	Stiff BUY 47	They Don't Know/Motor On (yellow label, push-out centre p/s)	7
79	Stiff PBUY 47	They Don't Know/Motor On (picture disc)	10
79	Stiff BUY 57	You Caught Me Out/Boys (with Boomtown Rats, unreleased, demos only)	50
81	Polydor POSP 225	Keep Your Hands Off My Baby/I Don't Need You (p/s)	7
81	Polydor POSP 368	You Still Believe In Me/Queen Of The High Teas (p/s)	15

(see also Drug Addix)

FINN MACCUILL

79	Radio Edinburgh REL 460	SINK YE - SWIM YE (LP)	200

GALT MACDERMOT

73	Decca SKLR 5164	TWO GENTLEMEN OF VERONA (LP)	30

AIMI MACDONALD

70	Philips 6308 011	WHAT'S LOVE ALL ABOUT (LP)	12

GAVIN MACDONALD

72	Regal Zono. SLRZ 1027	LINES (LP, red/silver label)	20

(see also Country Joe & Fish)

MACEO & ALL THE KING'S MEN

72	Pye International 7N 25571	Got To Get 'Cha/Thank You For Letting Me Be Myself Again (Part 1)	15
72	Mojo 2916 017	FUNKY MUSIC MACHINE (LP)	30
75	Contempo CRM 114	FUNKY MUSIC MACHINE (LP, reissue)	15

(see also Maceo & The Macks, James Brown)

BIG MACEO

62	RCA RCX 203	KINGS OF THE BLUES (EP)	20

MACEO & THE MACKS

87	Urban URB 1	Cross The Tracks (We Better Go Back)/Soul Power (printed die-cut sleeve)	8
87	Urban URBX 1	Cross The Tracks (We Better Go Back) (Extended Version)/Party Part 1/ Soul Power (12", printed die-cut sleeve)	15
74	Polydor 2391 122	US (LP)	30

(see also Maceo & All The King's Men, James Brown)

TEO MACERO

57	Esquire 32-113	TEO (LP)	30

MACEYS WINDOW

72	Parlophone R 5893	It's Getting Harder/Pray For Sister Sunshine	75

MACHINE (1)

67	Granta GR 7STD	Stupidity/Please Stay (private pressing)	40

MACHINE (2)

69	Polydor 56760	Spooky's Day Off/Nobody Wants You	20

(see also Swinging Soul Machine)

MACHINES

78	Wax EAR 1	True Life/Everything's Technical/You Better Hear/Evening Radio (stamped p/s, white labels)	100

MACHITO

57	Columbia SEB 10012	MACHITO JAZZ (EP)	10
58	Columbia SEB 10069	MACHITO JAZZ NO. 2 (EP)	10
50s	Columbia	KENYA (LP)	15

ALURA MACK

50s	Poydras 84	Everybody's Man Is Mine/Monkey Blues	8

FREDDY MACK

67	Rayrik TPMLP 143	LIVE AT TOFT CLUB FOLKSTONE (LP, as Freddy Mack Show, 99 copies only)	200

JOHNNY MACK

70	Columbia Blue Beat DB 116	Reggae All Night Long/A Million Marvellous Feelings	12

LONNIE MACK

63	Stateside SS 207	Memphis/Down In The Dumps	25
63	Stateside SS 226	Wham!/Susie-Q	25
64	Stateside SS 312	Lonnie On The Move/Say Something Nice To Me	18
65	Stateside SS 393	Sa-Ba-Hoola/Chickin' Pickin'	20
67	President PT 127	Where There's A Will/Baby What's Wrong?	7

MINT VALUE £

67	President PT 142	Save Your Money/Snow On The Mountain	7
68	President PT 198	Soul Express/I Found A Love	10
69	Elektra EKSN 45044	Memphis/Why (Edited Version)	10
69	Elektra EKSN 45060	Save Your Money/In The Band	8
71	Elektra EK 45715	Lay It Down/She Even Woke Me Up To Say Goodbye	6
67	President PTL 1004	THE WHAM OF THAT MEMPHIS MAN (LP)	30
69	Elektra EKL 4040	GLAD I'M IN THE BAND (LP, orange label, also stereo EKS 74040)	30
69	Elektra EKS 74050	WHATEVER'S RIGHT (LP, orange label)	30
70	Elektra 2410 007	FOR COLLECTORS ONLY (LP, reissue of "The Wham Of That Memphis Man")	12
72	Elektra K 42097	THE HILLS OF INDIANA (LP)	12

MACK SISTERS
| 56 | London HLU 8331 | Long Range Love/Stop What You're Doing | 60 |

WARNER MACK
58	Brunswick 05728	Roc-A-Chicka/Since I Lost You (with Anita Kerr Quartet)	200
58	Brunswick 05728	Roc-A-Chicka/Since I Lost You (with Anita Kerr Quartet) (78)	70
58	Decca	Roc-A-Chicka/Since I Lost You (export issue, with Anita Kerr Quartet)	90
62	London HA-R/SH-R 8002	GOLDEN COUNTRY HITS (LP)	15
63	London HA-R/SH-R 8025	GOLDEN COUNTRY HITS VOL. 2 (LP)	15

ANDY MACKAY
| 75 | Island WIP 6243 | Wild Weekend/Walking The Whippet (in promo p/s) | 6 |

(see also Roxy Music, Rock Follies)

MAHNA MACKAY
| 69 | Parlophone R 5808 | Mah Na Mah Na/Daydream | 6 |

RABBIT MACKAY
| 68 | MCA MU 1041 | Hard Time Woman/Candy | 8 |
| 68 | MCA MUPS 351 | BUG CLOTH (LP) | 15 |

BILLY MACKENZIE
| 01 | Rhythm Of Life ROL 006 | Wild Is The Wind/Mother Earth/Baltimore/Give Me Time (Version) (CD, internet-only release) | 75 |
| 92 | Circa CIRCD 22 | OUTERNATIONAL (CD) | 75 |

(see also Associates, Orbidoig,Yello, B.E.F., Sweden Through The Ages)

GISELE MACKENZIE
| 55 | HMV 7M 318 | Hard To Get/Boston Fancy | 8 |

MACKENZIE JET COMBO
| 70 | Torpedo TOR 18 | Milkman's Theme/Capadulah Recipe | 8 |

JUDY MACKENZIE
| 70 | Key KL 005 | JUDY (LP) | 22 |
| 71 | Key KL 009 | PEACE AND LOVE AND FREEDOM (LP, with poster) | 22 |

MACKENZIES
| 86 | Ron Johnson ZRON 9 | New Breed/Dog's Breakfast (7" p/s) | 6 |

MACKERAL
| 66 | Columbia DB 8013 | Funny Fish/This Is Mine | 5 |
| 68 | Columbia DB 8388 | Trying Again/White Man's Burden | 5 |

KEN MACKINTOSH (& HIS ORCHESTRA)
56	HMV 7M 343	Creeping Tom/Lovers In The Dark	10
56	HMV 7M 359	Start Walking/Curtain Call	10
56	HMV 7M 379	Blues In The Night/Come Next Spring (B-side with Kenny Bardell)	10
56	HMV 7M 403	Sleepwalker/The Berkeley Hunt	5
56	HMV 7M 417	Dizzy Fingers/The Policeman's Holiday	5
56	HMV POP 270	Soft Summer Breeze/Highway Patrol	5
57	HMV POP 287	The Buccaneers/Regimental Rock	10
57	HMV POP 300	Apple-Jack/Slow Walk	10
57	HMV POP 327	Almost Paradise/Rock Man Rock	15
57	HMV POP 358	Poni Tail/Keep It Movin'	12
57	HMV POP 396	Marching Along To The Blues/Six-Five Blues	8
57	HMV POP 426	Raunchy/Mojo	10
58	HMV POP 441	The Stroll/The Swingin' Shepherd Blues	8
58	HMV POP 464	Big Guitar/Squatty	5
58	HMV POP 506	The Swivel/Muchacha	5
58	HMV POP 543	Ulterior Mofif/That Old Cha Cha Feeling	5
59	HMV POP 592	Rock-A-Conga/Hampden Park	5
59	HMV POP 656	Sleep Walk/Morgen (One More Sunrise)	5
60	HMV POP 713	No Hiding Place/Tally Ho!	6
56	HMV 7EG 8170	TEENAGER'S SPECIAL (EP)	15
55	HMV DLP 1093	KEN MACKINTOSH (10" LP)	15
58	HMV DLP 1178	ONE NIGHT STAND (10" LP)	15

PETE MACLAINE & CLAN
| 63 | Decca F 11699 | Yes I Do/U.S. Mail | 15 |

DOUGIE MACLEAN
| 80 | Plant Life PLR 022 | SNAIGOW (LP, with lyric insert) | 12 |
| 88 | Dunkeld DUN 008 | REAL ESTATE (LP) | 20 |

(see also Alan Roberts)

JOHN MACLEOD SOUND
| 67 | Spectrum SP 12 | Russian Roulette/West Wind | 6 |
| 60s | Transatlantic TRASP 12 | Russian Roulette/West Wind | 6 |

JOHN MACLEOD'S FIRST XI
| 66 | Fontana TF 696 | Don't Shoot The Ref/Tomato Crisps | 15 |

ANGUS MACLISE
| 87 | Fierce FRIGHT 010 | Trance (1-sided, with 'Dopechoc' & badge) | 10 |

PATRICK MACNEE & HONOR BLACKMAN
| 64 | Decca F 11843 | Kinky Boots/Let's Keep It Friendly | 35 |

(see also Honor Blackman)

FLORA MACNEIL
77	Tangent TGS 124	CROABH NAN UBHAL (LP, with insert)	12

MADELINE MACNEIL
60s	Skyline DD 103	PATCHWORK (LP)	30

MACON JUG
70	Saga FID 8157	IN THE SUMMERTIME (LP, with tracks by Good Earth)	12
72	Boulevard BLVD 4078	RAY DORSET'S BEST (LP, 4 tracks by Good Earth, 6 tracks by Macon Jug)	12

(see also Ray Dorset, Mungo Jerry)

UNCLE DAVE MACON
63	RCA RCX 7112	UNCLE DAVE MACON NO. 1 (EP)	15
63	RCA RCX 7113	UNCLE DAVE MACON NO. 2 (EP)	15

GORDON MACRAE
54	Capitol CL 14168	How Do You Speak To An Angel?/C'est Magnifique	5
54	Capitol CL 14193	Count Your Blessings Instead Of Sheep/Never In A Million Years	5
55	Capitol CL 14222	Here's What I'm Here For/Love Can Change The Stars	5
55	Capitol CL 14276	Stranger In Paradise/High On A Windy Hill	5

(see also Jo Stafford, Ray Anthony, Jonathan & Darlene Edwards)

JOSH MACRAE
60	Top Rank JAR 290	Talkin' Army Blues/Talkin' Guitar Blues	6
60	Pye 7N 15306	Original Talkin' Blues (Talkin' Southern Blues)/Talkin' Thro' The Mill	6
60	Pye 7N 15307	Let Ramensky Go/Sky High Joe	6
60	Pye 7N 15308	Wild Side Of Life/Dear John	6
61	Pye 7N 15319	Messing About On The River/High Class Feeling	6
61	Pye 7N 15360	Arkansas Rambler/Never Never Man	7
61	Pye 7N 15384	Do It Yourself/Special Place Of Yorn	7
60	Pye NEP 24131	WALKIN', TALKIN', SINGIN' (EP)	12
60	Top Rank JKP 2061	JOSH MACRAE (EP)	10
66	Transatlantic TRA 150	JOSH MACRAE (LP)	15
66	Golden Guinea GGL 0335	MESSING ABOUT ON THE RIVER (LP)	12

MAD DOG (1)
74	Chappell LPC 1053	POP SOUNDS (LP, library edition)	30

MAD DOG (2)
85	Brainy CUTN 1	Sheriff (p/s)	50

JOHNNY MADARA
57	HMV POP 389	Be My Girl/Lovesick	10

OSIBERT MADDO
84	Sunsplash SNS 003	King In The Ring/PAPA SAN: Ghetto Life (12")	100

JOHNNY MADDOX (& HIS ORCHESTRA)
55	London MSD 1503/1504	Nickelodeon Tango/Solitude (unissued, demos only)	50
55	London HL 8134	The Crazy Otto - Medley/Humoresque	25
55	London HLD 8203	Do, Do, Do/When You Wore A Tulip (And I Wore A Big Red Rose)	15
56	London HLD 8277	Hop Scotch Boogie/Hands Off	35
56	London HLD 8277	Hop Scotch Boogie/Hands Off (78)	10
56	London HLD 8347	Heart And Soul/Dixieland Band	20
58	London HLD 8540	Yellow Dog Blues/Sugar Train	15
59	London HLD 8826	The Hurdy Gurdy Song/Old Fashioned Love	10
59	London HLD 8826	The Hurdy Gurdy Song/Old Fashioned Love (78)	12
55	London RE-P 1020	PRESENTING JOHNNY MADDOX AND THE RHYTHMASTERS (EP)	10
55	London RE-P 1040	PRESENTING JOHNNY MADDOX AND THE RHYTHMASTERS NO. 2 (EP)	10
58	London RE-D 1150	HONKY TONK JAZZ (EP)	10

ROSE MADDOX
59	Capitol CL 15023	Gambler's Love/What Makes Me Hang Around	10

MADE IN BRITAIN
91	White MIB001	Break The Crunch/Mellow Infection (12")	40

MADE IN ENGLAND (1)
81	Gargoyle GARG 1	Dance Of The Warriors/The Quest (p/s)	40

MADE IN ENGLAND (2)
86	Red Bus RBUS 2208	Prospects/Stay Sharp (A-side with Ray Dorset, p/s)	6

(see also Ray Dorset)

MADE IN SHEFFIELD
67	Fontana TF 871	Amelia Jane/Right Satisfied	30

(see also Joe Cocker, Grease Band, Chris Stainton)

MADE IN SWEDEN
69	Sonet SLP 71	MADE IN SWEDEN (LP)	40
69	Sonet SLP 2504	SNAKES IN A HOLE (LP)	30
70	Sonet SLP 2506	LIVE AT THE GOLDEN CIRCLE (LP)	30
70	Sonet SLP 2512	MADE IN ENGLAND (LP)	35
71	Sonet SNTF 621	MAD RIVER (LP)	45

MAD HATTERS
76	Epic EPC 4151	The Humphrey Song/Loving You Ain't Easy	6
76	Epic EPC 460	Love Potion No. 9/Loser	8

BETTY MADIGAN
54	MGM SP 1109	Always You/That Was My Heart You Heard!	5
55	MGM SP 1119	And So I Walked Home/Be A Little Darlin'	5
55	MGM SP 1131	Salute/The Wheels Of Love	5
55	MGM SP 1137	I Had A Heart/Wonderful Words	5
55	MGM SP 1138	Teddy Bear/Strangers	5
69	MGM MGM 1482	I'm Gonna Make You Love Me/Goodnight	5

MINT VALUE £

MAD JOCKS & ENGLISHMEN

| 80 | Wild Dog DOGLP 18 | TONGUE IN CHEEK (LP) | 18 |
| 80s | Wild Dog DOGLP 50 | THUD & BLUNDER (LP) | 18 |

MAD LADS (JAMAICA)

| 69 | Coxsone CS 7099 | Losing You/WINSTON JARRETT: Peck Up A Pagan | 30 |

MAD LADS (U.S.)

65	Atlantic AT 4051	Don't Have To Shop Around/Tear Maker	15
66	Atlantic AT 4083	I Want Someone/Nothing Can Break Through	15
66	Atlantic 584 038	Sugar Sugar/Get Out Of My Life Woman	15

MADNESS

SINGLES

79	2-Tone TT 3	The Prince/Madness (paper label, company sleeve)	15
79	2-Tone TT 3	The Prince/Madness (second pressing, silver label, company sleeve)	5
79	2-Tone TT 3	The Prince/Madness (later blue plastic label, company sleeve)	45
79	Stiff BUY IT 56	One Step Beyond/Mistakes/Nutty Theme (12", p/s)	15
79	Stiff MAD 1	Don't Quote Me On That/Swan Lake (12", promo only)	45
80	Stiff BUY IT 62	My Girl/In The Rain/Stepping Into Line (12" p/s)	8
80	Stiff BUY 71	WORK, REST & PLAY EP (P/s, mispress, white 'Madness' lettering instead of blue)	8
80	Stiff BUY 84	Baggy Trousers/The Business (p/s, blue labels instead of green, Mike Barson not credited as songwriter)	75
81	Stiff BUY IT 108	The Return Of The Los Palmas 7/My Girl (Demo)/That's The Way To Do It/ Swan Lake (live) (12", p/s, with M.I.S. Nutty Boys comic)	8
81	Stiff BUY IT 112	Grey Day/Baggy Trousers/Take It Or Leave It/Un Paso Adelante (12", p/s, white or yellow labels)	20
81	Stiff BUY 112	Grey Day/Memories (p/s, rare edition with legs instead of feet on label)	15
82	Stiff BUY IT 134	It Must Be Love/Mrs. Hutchinson/Shadow On The House (12", p/s credits Limited Edition Special 12 Dance Mix", record plays standard mix)	8
82	Stiff PBUY 146	House Of Fun/Don't Look Back (picture disc)	5
82	Stiff PBUY 153	Driving In My Car/Animal Farm (picture disc)	5
82	Stiff BUY 153	Driving In My Car/Animal Farm (poster p/s)	5
82	Stiff GRAB 1	THE MADNESS PACK (6 x 7" in clear plastic folder)	20
83	Stiff PBUY 169	Tomorrow's (Just Another Day)/Madness (Is All In The Mind) (picture disc)	5
83	Stiff BUY IT 169	Tomorrow's (Just Another Day) (Warped Mix)/Blue Skinned Beast (warped mix)/Tomorrow's (Just Another Day) (Elvis Costello vocal) (12", p/s)	8
84	Stiff BUY IT 196	Michael Caine (extended version)/Michael Caine/ If You Think There's Something (12", p/s)	8
84	Stiff PBUY 196	Michael Caine/If You Think There's Something (picture disc)	12
84	Stiff PBUY 201	One Better Day/Guns (poster p/s)	5
84	Stiff PBUY 201	One Better Day/Guns (picture disc)	7
85	Zarjazz JAZZ SD5	Yesterday's Men/All I Knew (square picture disc)//Yesterday's Men (Harmonica Mix)/It Must Be Love (double pack, gold PVC wallet)	12
85	Zarjazz JAZZF 7	Uncle Sam/Please Don't Go ('flag bag' edition)	20
85	Zarjazz JAZZY 7	Uncle Sam/Please Don't Go/Insanity Over Christmas (picture disc)	18
86	Zarjazz JAZZ B9-12	(Waiting For) The Ghost-Train/Maybe In Another Life/Seven Year Scratch (12", p/s with 8-page booklet)	10
86	Zarjazz JAZZS 9	(Waiting For) The Ghost Train/Maybe In Another Life (square picture disc)	45
86	Strange Fruit SFPS 0007	THE PEEL SESSIONS (12" p/s, brown label)	10
86	80s	Sweetest Girl/Jenny (A Portrait Of) (picture disc, stickered PVC sleeve)	18
87	Virgin VS 876	Our House/Walking With Mr. Wheeze	15
88	Virgin VSX 1054	I Pronounce You/4BF/Patience/11th Hour (as The Madness, box with badge, 2 cards & sticker)	8
88	Virgin VS 1078	What's That/Be Good Boy (p/s)	8
88	Virgin VS 1078	What's That/Be Good Boy (p/s)	8
88	Virgin VST 1078	What's That/Be Good Boy/Flashings (12", p/s)	10
88	Virgin VSJ 1078	What's That/Flashings ('Jig' disc, 1st of 2 interlocking shaped picture discs)	30
88	Virgin VSS 1078	What's That/Be Good Boy 'Saw' disc, 2nd of 2 interlocking shaped picture discs)	30
92	Go! Discs GOD 93	The Harder They Come/Tomorrow's Just Another Day/Take It Or Leave It (p/s, blue labels)	8
99	Virgin VSLH 1737	Love Struck/We Are Love (Jukebox issue)	10
99	Virgin VSLH 1740	Johnny The Horse/I Was The One (Jukebox issue)	12
05	V2 VVR55033247	Shame And Scandal/Shame And Scandal (Dub Mix) p/s, 2500 only)	6

ALBUMS

79	Stiff SEEZ 17	ONE STEP BEYOND (LP, first pressing, sleeve lists 'Bed & Breakfast' not 'Bed & Breakfast Man')	15
80	Stiff SEEZ 29	ABSOLUTELY (LP, first pressing with slightly different front cover image)	15
82	M.I.S. (no cat. no)	THIRTY MINUTES OF CULTURE (fan club cassette)	25
84	Stiff PSEEZ 53	KEEP MOVING (LP, picture disc, U.S. running order)	15
85	Zarjazz JZLP1	MAD NOT MAD (LP, withdrawn edition, alternative sleeve omitting gold on front)	75
86	M.I.S. (no cat. no)	SONGS FROM AROUND THE PLONET (fan club cassette, live compilation)	35
90	Virgin VVIP 107	IT'S MADNESS (LP, 1000 copies)	70
90	Virgin TPAK 8	ONE STEP BEYOND/ABSOLUTELEY/RISE & FALL (3-CD box set, picture discs)	50
92	Virgin 463 166	DIVINE (Digital compact cassette)	20
92	Virgon MDV 2692	DIVINE (Mini disc)	20
92	Go! Discs 828 367-1	MADSTOCK (LP, with picture inner sleeve)	20
94	Simply Vinyl SVLP 309	DIVINE (LP, Simply Vinyl reissue)	15
99	Virgin MADBOX 2	THE LOT (6-CD box set of first 6 studio albums)	40
09	Lucky 7 003SE	THE LIBERTY OF NORTON FOLGATE (LP, 3-CD box set including poster, membership card, rule book, letter & badge)	40

FLEXIDISCS

81	Lyntone LYN 10208	Take It or Leave It (free with Take It Or Leave It magazine)	10
81	Lyn. LYN 10353/EVENT 2	Event - The Madness (with Event magazine)	10
82	Lyntone LYN 11546	My Girl (Ballad) (hard vinyl test pressing of Flexipop free flexi)	200
82	Lyntone LYN 10719	Carols On 45 (fan club disc)	10
84	Lyntone LYN 15280/1	Insanity Over Christmas/Visit To Castle Dracstein (fan club disc)	10
85	Lyntone LYN 16981	Merry Christmas: Samantha (live)/Mad Not Mad (live)	10
85	Lyntone LYN 16676	From Us ... To You (Mad Not Mad tour disc, with tour programme)	18
86	Lyntone LYN 18251	Last Christmas With Madness:Ghost Train (The Demo)/The Final Goodbye (fan club disc)	20

(see also Argonauts, Fink Brothers)

RUTH MADOC

86	Sain 1375	Our Song Of Love/The Colours Of Christmas (with Bill Tarmey) (p/s)	5

MADONNA
SINGLES : SIRE SINGLES

82	Sire W 9899	Everybody/Everybody (Dub Version) (WEA sleeve, no p/s)	150
82	Sire W 9899T	Everybody/Everybody (Dub Version) (12", WEA sleeve, no p/s)	125
83	Sire W 9522	Lucky Star (Edit)/I Know It ('sunglasses' p/s with no Jellybean credit on label)	1000
83	Sire W 9522T	Lucky Star (Full Length Version)/I Know It (12", 'sunglasses' p/s)	50
83	Sire W 9522TV	Lucky Star (U.S Remix)/I Know It (12", stickered plain white die-cut sleeve)	35
83	Sire W 9405	Holiday (Edit)/Think Of Me ('train' p/s)	6
83	Sire W 9405T	Holiday (Full Length Version 6.08)/Think Of Me (12", 'train' p/s)	8
84	Sire W 9522	Lucky Star (Edit)/I Know It (reissue, 'bangles & stars' Jellybean credit on label, p/s)	5
84	Sire W 9522T	Lucky Star (Full Length Version)/I Know It (12" reissue, stickered 'TV screen' p/s)	10
84	Sire W 9522T	Lucky Star (Full Length Version)/I Know It (12" reissue, stickered 'TV screen' p/s, with poster)	30
84	Sire W 9260	Borderline (Edit)/Physical Attraction (p/s, large 'A' on paper A-side label)	5
84	Sire W 9260F	Borderline (Edit)/Physical Attraction/Holiday (Edit)/Think Of Me ('map' p/s, double pack with European p/s, copies of "Holiday", shrinkwrapped & stickered: beware of counterfeits with less than Mint picture sleeves)	100
84	Sire W 9210T	Like A Virgin (U.S. Dance Remix)/Stay (12", p/s, with poster & sticker)	35
85	Sire W 9083	Material Girl/Pretender (p/s)	5
85	Sire W 9083T	Material Girl (Jellybean Dance Mix)/Pretender (12", with poster p/s)	35
85	Sire WA6323	Crazy For You/Sammy Hagar "I'll Fall In Love Again" (7" Madonna shaped picture Disc in stickered PVC sleeve. No p/s.)	50
85	Sire WA6323	Crazy For You/Sammy Hagar "I'll Fall In Love Again" (Uncut 7" Picture disc on 10" vinyl in PVC sleeve. No p/s)	800
85	Sire W 8934P	Into The Groove/Shoo-Be-Doo (heart-shaped picture disc with 2 stickers)	40
85	Sire W 8934T	Into The Groove/Shoo-Be-Doo (12" uncut heart-shaped picture disc, very few copies)	1000
85	Sire W 8934T	Into The Groove/Everybody/Shoo-Be-Doo (12", p/s, with poster)	25
85	Sire W 9405T	Holiday (Full Length Version 6.08)/Think Of Me (12", 'cross earring' p/s reissue)	15
85	Sire W 9405P	Holiday (Full Length Version 6.08)/Think Of Me (12", picture disc)	30
85	Sire W 8881P	Angel (Edit)/Burning Up (shaped pic disc, with cardboard plinth)	45
85	Sire W 8881P	Angel (Edit)/Burning Up (shaped pic disc)	35
85	SireW8881P	Angel (Edit)/Burning Up (Uncut 7" pic disc on 12" vinyl in PVC sleeve, no p/s)	1000
85	Sire A6585	Gambler/Black 'n' Blue:Nature Of The Beach (7" p/s)	7
85	Sire QA6585	Gambler/Black 'n' Blue:Nature Of The Beach (7" foldout poster p/s)	30
85	Sire TA6585	Gambler (Extended Dance Mix)/(Instrumental Remix) Black 'n' Blue: Nature Of The Beach (12" p/s)	20
85	Sire W 8848T	Dress You Up (12" Formal Mix)/(Casual Instrumental)/I Know It (12", p/s)	8
85	Sire W 8848TF	Dress You Up (12" Formal Mix)/(Casual Instrumental)/I Know It (12", foldout p/s with Virgin Tour Video Advert on back)	35
85	Sire W 8848P	Dress You Up/I Know It ('Xmas tree star'-shaped picture disc)	35
85	Sire W 8848P	Dress You Up (Uncut 7" picture disc on 12" vinyl, no p/s)	750
86	Sire W 9560P	Borderline/Physical Attraction (Madonna-shaped picture disc in pvc sleeve no p/s)	50
86	Sire W 9560P	Borderline/Physical Attraction (Uncut 7" picture disc on 12" vinyl,pvc sleeve no p/s)	1000
86	Sire W 8717T(W)	Live To Tell (LP Version)/(Edit)/(Instrumental) (12", p/s, with poster)	20
86	Sire W8636T	Papa Don't Preach(Extended Version)/(LP Vesion) Ain't No Big Deal (12" with poster in stickered p/s)	20
86	Sire W 8636T(W)	Papa Don't Preach (Extended Version)/Papa Don't Preach (LP Version)/ Ain't No Big Deal (12", p/s, initially with free poster)	15
86	Sire W 8636T(W)	Papa Don't Preach (Extended Version)/Papa Don't Preach (LP Version)/ Ain't No Big Deal (12", p/s, initially with free poster)	8
86	Sire W 8636TP	Papa Don't Preach (Extended Remix)/Ain't No Big Deal (LP Version)/ Papa Don't Preach (LP version) (12", picture disc)	20
86	Sire W 8550TP	True Blue (Extended Dance Version)/Holiday (Full Length Version) (12" picture disc)	20
86	Sire W 8480TP	Open Your Heart (Extended Version)/Open Your Heart (Dub Mix)/ Lucky Star (Full Length Version) (12", picture disc)	10
87	Sire W 8378TP	La Isla Bonita (Extended Remix)/(Extended Instrumental) (12", picture disc)	20
87	Sire W 8341TX	Who's That Girl (Extended Version)/Who's That Girl (Dub Mix)/ White Heat (12" Remix) (12", p/s)	20
87	Sire W 8341TP	Who's That Girl (Extended Version)/White Heat (12", picture disc; beware of original decaying PVC sleeves)	40
87	Sire W 8224	Causing A Commotion (Silver Screen Single Mix)/Jimmy Jimmy (p/s, with badge shrinkwrapped to p/s)	50
87	Sire W 8224TP	Causing A Commotion (Silver Screen Mix)/Causing A Commotion (Movie House Mix)/Jimmy Jimmy (Fade) (12", picture disc)	15
87	Sire W 8115TW	The Look Of Love/Love Don't Live Here Anymore/I Know It (12", p/s & poster)	15
87	Sire W 8115TP	The Look Of Love/Love Don't Live Here Anymore/I Know It (12", picture disc)	20
89	Sire 925 681-2	Papa Don't Preach (7" Version)/(12" Version)/Pretender (Video)(5" CD-Video p/s)	40
89	Sire W 7539TX	Like A Prayer (12" Dance Mix)/(Churchapella)/(7"Remix Edit) (12", p/s)	10
89	Sire W 7539TP	Like A Prayer/(12" Extended Remix)/(12" Club Version)/Act Of Contrition (12", picture disc)	15
89	Sire W 7539CD	Like A Prayer/(12" Extended Remix)/(12" Club Version)/Act Of Contrition (3" Gatefold CD)	12
89	Sire W 2948X	Express Yourself (7" Remix)/The Look Of Love (LP) (poster p/s)	25
89	Sire W 2948C	Express Yourself (7" Remix)/The Look Of Love (LP) ('jeans zipper' p/s)	30
89	Sire W 2948CX	Express Yourself (Non-Stop Express Mix)/Stop + Go Dubs (cassette)	20
89	Sire W 2948TP	Express Yourself/(Non-Stop Express Mix)/(Stop + Go Dubs) (12", 'nude' picture disc)	15
89	Sire W 2948 CD	Express Yourself/(Non-Stop Express Mix)/(Stop + Go Dubs) (3" CD)	15
89	Sire W 2883TP	Cherish (Extended Version)/(7" Version)/Supernatural (12")	10
89	Sire W 2883 CD	Cherish (extended)/Cherish/Supernatural (3" CD)	15
89	Sire W 2668P	Dear Jessie/Till Death Do Us Part (picture disc)	12
89	Sire W 2668TW	Dear Jessie/Till Death Do Us Part/Holiday (12" Version) (12", poster p/s)	12
89	Sire W 2268CDX	Dear Jessie/Till Death Do Us Part/Holiday (12" Version) (CD, picture disc)	125
89	Sire 925 681-2	Papa Don't Preach (7" Version)/(12" Version)/Pretender (LP Version)/ Papa Don't Preach (CD Video)	35
90	Sire W 9851P	Vogue/Keep It Together (Single Remix) (picture disc)	12
90	Sire W 9851TW	Vogue (12" Version)/Keep It Together (12" Remix) (12", p/s, with 'Face of the 80s' poster)	15
90	Sire W 9851TX	Vogue (12" Version)/Vogue (Strike-A-Pose Dub) (12", p/s, with 'X-rated' 30" x 20" poster)	20
90	Sire W 9851TP	Vogue (12" Version)/Keep It Together (12" Remix) (12", picture disc)	20
90	Sire W 9789TP	Hanky Panky (Bare Bottom 12" Mix)/(Bare Bones Single Mix)/More (LP Version) (12", picture disc with gatefold insert & foldout poster)	15

MINT VALUE £

90	Sire W 9000TP	Justify My Love (William Orbit Remix)/Justify My Love/Express Yourself (Shep's 'Spressin' Himself Remix) (12", picture disc with insert)	10
90	Sire 7599382253	Justify My Love/Vogue (Live at MTV Awards 1990) (video single, p/s)	8
91	Sire W 0008P	Crazy For You (Remix)/Keep It Together (Single Remix) (shaped picture disc with plinth & insert)	15
91	Sire W 0008CD	Crazy For You (Remix)/Keep It Together (Shep Pettibone Remix)/ Into The Groove (Shep Pettibone Remix) (CD, picture disc)	8
91	Sire W0024	Rescue Me/Spotlight (7" p/s)	5
91	Sire W0024TW	Rescue (Titanic Mix)/(Houseboat Mix)/(Titanic Mix) (12" with free poster, p/s)	10
91	Sire W 0037TP	Holiday/True Blue (12", clear vinyl picture disc with insert in PVC sleeve)	15

SINGLES : MAVERICK SINGLES

92	Maverick W 0138TP	Erotica (Album Version 5.12)/Erotica (Instrumental 5.12)/Erotica (Radio Edit 4.31) (12", picture disc with gold insert, withdrawn, 138 only)	2500
92	Maverick W 0138TW	Erotica (Album Version 5.12)/Erotica (Instrumental 5.12)/Erotica (Radio Edit 4.31) (12", Free Poster, p/s)	10
92	Maverick W 0146TP	Deeper And Deeper (Shep's Classic 12")/(Shep's Deep Makeover Mix)/ (Shep's Deep Beats)/(David's Klub Mix)/(David's Deep Mix)/(Shep's Deeper Dub) (12", picture disc)	15
93	Maverick W0154TW	Bad Girl (Edit)/Erotica (William Orbit 12")/Erotica (William Orbit Dub)/ Erotica (Madonna's In My Jeep Mix) (12", Free Poster, p/s)	10
93	Maverick W 0168P	Fever (Edit)/Fever (Radio Edit Remix) (picture disc with numbered insert)	10
93	Maverick W0168T	Fever (Hot Sweat 12")/(Extended 12")/(Shep's Remedy Dub)/(Murk Boys Miami Mix)/(Murk Boys Deep South Mix)/(Oscar G's Dope Dub) (12" stickered, p/s)	10
94	Maverick W 0268P	Secret (Edit)/Let Down Your Guard (Rough Mix Edit) (picture disc w/insert)	12
95	Maverick W 0278P	Take A Bow (Edit)/Take A Bow (picture disc with insert)	8
95	Maverick W 0285CDX	Bedtime Story (Junior's Single Mix)/Secret (Allstar Mix)/Secret (Some Bizarre Mix)/Secret (Some Bizarre Single Mix) (CD, booklet sleeve)	10
95	Warner Bros W0285TX	Bedtime Story (Junior's Sound Factory Mix)/(Junior's Sound Factory Dub/ (Orbital Mix)/Junior's Wet Dream Mix) (12" Glitter Holographic Sleeve)	15
95	Warner Bros W0285CDX	Bedtime Story (Junior's Single Mix)/Secret (Allstar Mix)/Secret (Some Bizarre Mix)/ Secret/(Some Bizarre Single Mix) (CD, 'Bedtime Storybook' Digipack, p/s)	15
03	Warner Bros W634T	Love Profusion (Passengerz Club Mix)/Nobody Knows Me (Above & Beyond 12" Mix) (12" stickered, p/s)	8

SINGLES : OTHER SINGLES

| 92 | Receiver RRSP 1007 | Shine A Light/On The Ground (picture disc, withdrawn) | 12 |
| 92 | Reciever RRSPT 1007 | Shine A Light/On The Ground/Little Boy (12", picture disc) | 15 |

ALBUMS

85	Sire WX 20P	LIKE A VIRGIN (LP, picture disc in die-cut sleeve)	50
86	Sire WX 54	TRUE BLUE (LP, with tour poster)	15
87	Sire WX 76	YOU CAN DANCE (LP, with poster & gold 'obi')	15
90	Sire 7599 264932	ROYAL BOX (box set with "Immaculate Collection" CD in satin digipak, video, poster & postcards)	75
92	Sire WX49	EROTICA (Dirty Version) (2xLP, gatefold, stickered)	15
92	Sire WX49	EROTICA (Clean Version) (2xLP, gatefold, stickered)	15
94	Sire 9362 45767 1	BEDTIME STORIES (LP)	35
95	Sire 9362 46100-1	SOMETHING TO REMEMBER (LP)	35
98	Sire 9362 46847-1	RAY OF LIGHT (2xLP with inner sleeve, stickered)	15
00	Sire 9362 47865-1	MUSIC (2xLP with gold die-cut inners, stickered)	15
03	Sire 9362 48454-1	AMERICAN LIFE (2xLP, inner sleeve gatefold)	15
04	Sire 9362 46847-1	RAY OF LIGHT (Reissue, 2xLP with inner sleeve 180 gram deluxe vinyl, stickered)	20
06	Sire 9362 494601	CONFESSIONS ON A DANCE FLOOR (2-LP, gatefold, pink vinyl)	30

PROMOS

85	Sire SAM 251	Into The Groove (Edit) Holiday (Edit) (12" white label, die-cut sleeve, stickered	100
87	Sire SAM 412	Spotlight (Dub)/Holiday (Dub)/Over And Over (Dub)/Into The Groove (Dub) 12" white label, die-cut WEA sleeve, no p/s)	50
89	Sire SAM 641	Keep It Together (12" Remix)/(Dub)/(Extended Remix)/(12" Mix)/ (Bonus Beats)/(Instrumental) (12")	15
90	Sire SAM 659	Vogue (12" Version)/Vogue (Strike A Pose Dub) (12")	15
90	Sire SAM 738	Justify My Love (Remix) (One-sided 12" die-cut sleeve, p/s)	15
91	Sire SAM 800	Holiday (Edit) (CD)	50
92	Sire SAM 1103	Erotica (Album Version) (12")	25
92	Sire SAM 1118	Deeper And Deeper (Edit)/Shep's Deep Makeover Mix/Shep's Classic 12") David's Klub Mix)/David's Love Dub)/David's Deeper Dub) 12" white label no p/s	25
93	Sire SAM 1131	Fever (Hot Sweat 12" Mix)/(Shep's Remedy Dub)/(Dub One)/(Dub Two)/ (Bugged Out Bonzai Mix)/(Peggy's Nightclub Mix)/(Radio Edit)/(Murk Boys Miami Mix)/(Murk Boys Deep South Mix)/(Album Version)/(Oscar G's Dope Dub)/(Back To The Dub One) (2x12")	50
94	Warner Bros W 0278 CDDJ	Take A Bow (Edit) (CD with insert, no p/s)	12
94	Warner Bros SAM 1526	Bedtime Story (Junior's Sound Factory Mix)/(Mixes) (12")	15
94	Warner Bros SAM 1653	Human Nature: The Remixes/(Mixes) (12", stickered title sleeve)	15
94	Warner Bros W0300CDDJ	Human Nature (4'30" Radio Edit) (CD)	12
95	Warner Bros SAM 1526	Bedtime Story (Junior's Sound Factory Mix)/(Junior's Sound Factory Dub)/ (Orbital Mix)/Junior's Wet Dream Mix)/(Junior's Wet Dream Dub) (12")	15
95	Warner Bros W 0285 CDDJ2	Bedtime Story (Junior's Singles Mix) (CD in standard p/s)	25
95	Warner Bros W 0326 CDDJ	Oh Father (Edit) (12")	20
96	Sire SAM 1880	Love Don't Live Here Anymore (Mark!s It's A Girl Dub)/(Mark!s It's A Boy Dub)/(Mark!s Full On Vocal) (12")	20
96	Warner Bros SAM 1982	Don't Cry For Me Argentina (Miami Mix)/(Mixes) (12", title sleeve)	25
96	Warner Bros W0384CDDJ2	Don't Cry For Me Argentina (Miami Mix Edit)/Miami Mix) (CD)	15
96	Warner Bros W0388CDDJ	Another Suitcase In Another Hall (CD, title inlay)	10
96	Warner Bros W0337CDDJ	One More Chance (Album Version) (CD)	10
98	Warner Bros 3331000037	Drowned World/Substitute For Love (BT & Sasha's Bucklodge Ashram Remix)/ Sky Fits Heaven (Sasha Remix)/Substitute For Love (Victor Calderone Remix Edit) (12")	20
98	Sire SAM 3173	Frozen (Extended Club Mix)/(Stereo MC's Mix)/(Meltdown Mix - Long Version) (12" no p/s)	15
98	Warner Bros SAM 3247	Ray Of Light (Sasha's Ultra Violet Mix)/(William Orbit's Liquid Mix) (12")	15
98	Warner Bros SAM 3248	Ray Of Light (Calderone Club Mix)/(Album Version) (12" no p/s)	15
98	Warner Bros SAM 3268	Ray Of Light (Sasha's Twilo Mix)/(Victor Calderone Drum Mix) (12")	15
98	Warner Bros SAM 3269	Ray Of Light (Sasha's Strip Down Mix)/(Orbit's Ultra Violet Mix) (12")	15
98	Warner Bros 0444 CDDJ	Ray Of Light (Album Version) (CD, stickered p/s)	15
98	Warner Bros W 459 CDDJ	Little Star (CD)	15
99	Warner Bros W 471CDDJ	Nothing Really Matters (Album Version)/Nothing Really Matters (Club 69 Radio Mix) (CD, slimline jewel case)	10

00	Warner Bros PR01802	American Pie (Album Version)/(Richard 'Humpty' Vission Radio Mix) (CD)	15
00	Warner Bros PRO 6584	Music (mixes) (12" doublepack, title-stickered sleeve)	15
00	Warner Bros PR02054	Music (Album Version) (CD)	10
01	Warner Bros PR02296	Don't Tell Me (Thunderpuss Radio Mix)/(mixes) (CD)	15
01	Warner Bros MADZ 01	What It Feels Like For A Girl (Perfecto Mix)/(Above & Beyond Remix) (12" stickered white label, A4 press release, die-cut sleeve no p/s)	25
01	Warner Bros	GHV2 (CD, slimline jewel case, 'collage' insert)	25
01	Warner Bros SAM 00586	GHV2 (CD, 10" x 10" gatefold p/s)	50
02	Warner Bros SAM 00721	Die Another Day (Dirty Vegas Main Mix)/(mixes) (12" double pack, stickered title sleeve)	15
03	Warner Bros SAM 00824	Hollywood (Oakenfold 12" Full Remix)/Jacques Lu Cont Thin White Duck Mix) /Album Version/(Deepsky Home Sweet Home Vocal Remix) (12")	10

PROMOS : ALBUM PROMO

89	Sire MER 0120	LIKE A PRAYER (Box set in 10" x 7" x 1" box, includes CD, sealed cassette, press Release, badge, slides Rolling Stone re-print, 2 photos)	200

(see also Jellybean)

MADONNA & MISSY (ELLIOTT)

03	Maverick RRCG 0301	Into The Hollywood Groove/Hollywood (Jack Lu Cont's Thin White Dick Mix) (GAP in-store promo)	25

MAD PROFESSOR

82	Ariwa ARILP 001	DUB ME CRAZY (LP)	25
83	Ariwa ARILP 005LP	THE AFRICAN CONNECTION - DUB ME CRAZY PART 3 (LP)	25
83	Ariwa ARILP 011	ESCAPE TO THE ASYLUM OF DUB (LP)	20
85	Ariwa ARILP 025	CARIBBEAN TASTE OF TECHNOLOGY GONE CRAZY (LP)	25
86	Ariwa ARILP 030	SCHIZOPHRENIC DUB ME CRAZY VOL. 6 (LP)	15
93	Ariwa ARILP 095	BLACK LIBERATION DUB (LP)	15
94	Ariwa ARILP 057	PSYCHEDELIC DUB DUB - DUB ME CRAZY PART 10 (LP)	12

MADRIGAL

71	Decca F13110	Blue Eyes In Paradise/Wendy	12
72	Sovereign SOV 1071	Time Of The Season/Tapestry	20
73	Madrigal MAD 100	BENEATH THE GREENWOOD TREE (LP, private pressing)	60

MAD RIVER

69	Capitol (S)T 2985	MAD RIVER (LP)	80

JOHNNY MAESTRO

61	HMV POP 875	What A Surprise/The Warning Voice	30
61	HMV POP 909	Mr. Happiness/Test Of Love	30
64	United Artists UP 1004	Before I Love Her/Fifty Million Heartbeats	30
71	Buddah 2011 061	Rain Came/Never Knew This Kind Of Hurt Before	10

(see also Crests, Brooklyn Bridge)

MAGAZINE

78	Virgin VS 200	Shot By Both Sides/My Mind Ain't So Open (card p/s)	6
78	Virgin VS 200	Shot By Both Sides/My Mind Ain't So Open (paper p/s)	5
78	Virgin VS 207	Touch And Go/Goldfinger (p/s)	5
78	Virgin VS 237	I Love You You Big Dummy/Give Me Everything	6
78	Virgin VS 237	Give Me Everything/I Love You You Big Dummy	6
79	Virgin VS 219	Rhythm Of Cruelty/TV Baby	5
78	Virgin V2100	REAL LIFE (LP, original blue labels)	15
79	Virgin V2121	SECONDHAND DAYLIGHT (LP, gatefold)	15
80	V2156	THE CORRECT USE OF SOAP (LP)	12
80	Virgin V 2184	PLAY (LP)	12
82	Virgin VM 1	AFTER THE FACT (LP)	12

(see also Buzzcocks)

MAGENTA

78	Cottage COT 821	CANTERBURY MOON (LP, with insert)	40
80	Little Stan LSP 811	RECOLLECTIONS (2-LP, gatefold sleeve with insert)	35
81	Little Stan LSP 831	WOT'S NEXT THEN (LP, with insert)	25

MAGGIE

68	Columbia DB 8389	L. David Sloane/Too Young To Get Married	6

MAGIC CARPET

72	Mushroom 200 MR 20	MAGIC CARPET (LP, white/brown labels)	150

(see also Clem Alford)

MAGIC CHRISTIANS

69	Major Minor MM 673	If You Want It/Nuts	12
69	Major Minor MM 673	Come And Get It/Nuts (2nd pressing with correct title)	20
70	Major Minor SMLP 71	THE MAGIC CHRISTIANS (LP)	40

(see also Trevor Burton, Gary Wright, Denny Laine, Steve Gibbons)

MAGIC LANTERNS

66	CBS 202094	Excuse Me Baby/Greedy Girl	7
66	CBS 202250	Rumplestiltskin/I Stumbled	55
67	CBS 202459	Knight In Rusty Armour/Simple Things	10
67	CBS 202637	Auntie Grizelda/Time Will Tell (If I'm A Loser)	10
67	CBS 2750	We'll Meet Again/What Else Can It Be But Love?	10
68	Camp 602 007	Shame Shame/Baby I Gotta Go Now	10
69	Camp 602 009	Melt All Your Troubles Away/Bossa Nova 1940 - Hello You Lovers	10
70	Polydor 2038 058	One Night Stand/Frisco Annie	6
73	Polydor 2058 322	Stand For Our Rights/Pa Bradley	5
67	CBS (S)BPG 62935	LIT UP WITH THE MAGIC LANTERNS (LP)	30

MAGIC MICHAEL

80	Atomic MAGIC 1	Millionaire/My Friend And I (p/s)	5

(see also Damned, Captain Sensible)

MAGIC MIXTURE

68	Saga FID 2125	THIS IS MAGIC MIXTURE (LP, black/silver labels)	200

MAGIC MUSCLE

88	Five Hours Back TOCK 009	THE PIPE, THE ROAR, THE GRID (LP, with booklet)	15
89	One Big Guitar OBGLP 9005	100 MILES BELOW (LP)	15
90	Pilgrim (no cat. no.)	LIVING WEEDS FROM ANCIENT SEEDS (cassette, box set, autographed with booklet, posters & postcard)	15
91	Woronzow WOO 17	GULP! (LP)	20

(see also Keith Christmas, Hawkwind, High Tide, Twink)

MAGIC MUSHROOM BAND

85	Magick Eye MUSH 001	THE MAGIC MUSHROOM BAND (cassette EP)	12
85	Magick Eye MUSH 002	FEED YOUR HEAD (cassette)	12
86	Pagan PM 003	THE POLITICS OF ECSTASY (LP, 100 with A1 poster)	50
86	Pagan PM 003	THE POLITICS OF ECSTASY (LP, 500 with A3 insert)	25
87	Aftermath AFT 3	BOMSHAMKAR (LP)	15
90	Fungus FUN 003	PROCESS OF ILLUMINATION (LP, signed with insert & foldaround sleeve & comic in printed PVC sleeve)	12
91	Fungus FUN 005	SPACED OUT (LP, foldout sleeve with A4 booklet)	15

MAGIC NIGHT

75	Pye 7N 25698	If You And I Had Never Met/(version)	10

MAGIC NOTES

60	Blue Beat BB 9	Album Of Memory/Why Did You Leave Me	8
61	Blue Beat BB 51	Rosabel/I'm Not Worthy2	8

THE MAGIC NUMBERS

04	Heavenly HVN 143	Hymn For Her/Oh Sister (500 only, with 2 stickers of different band members p/s)	10
05	Heavenly HVN 147	Anima Sola/HAL: Keep Love As Your Golden Rule (Tour single - 500 only p/s)	7
05	Heavenly HVN 155P	Cold Fingers/THE WEBB BROTHERS : Try (Tour 7", 1000 only)	15

MAGIC SAM

69	Python PEN 701	Twenty One Days In Jail/Easy Baby (99 copies only)	50
69	Rooster 707	MEAN MISTREATER (EP)	20
70	Blue Horizon 7-63223	MAGIC SAM: 1937-1969 (LP)	90
70	Delmark DS 615	WEST SIDE SOUL (LP, blue label)	30
71	Delmark DS 620	BLACK MAGIC (LP, blue label)	35

MAGIC VALLEY

69	Penny Farthing PEN 701	Taking The Heart Out Of Love/Uptight Basil	10

(see also Pete Dello, Honeybus)

MAGICIAN

79	Hobo	MAGICIAN (LP)	40

MAGICIANS

66	Decca F 12361	Wet Your Whistle/Take The A Train	5
66	Decca F 12374	The Liars/Poggy Goes Pop	6
67	Decca F 12602	The Tarzan March/What A Day For A Metamorphosis	10
68	MCA MU 1046	Painting On Wood/Slow Motion	40

MAGISTRATES

68	MGM MGM 1425	Here Comes The Judge/Girl	10
68	MGM MGM 1437	After The Fox/Tear Down The Walls (with Jean Hillary)	10

(see also Jane Hillery)

MAGITS

79	Outer H. SRTS/79/CUS/401	Fragmented/Disconnected/Disjointed/Detached (p/s, with 3 page magazine insert)	125
79	Outer H. SRTS/79/CUS/401	Fragmented/Disconnected/Disjointed/Detached (p/s, without 3 page magazine insert)	100

(see also Rudimentary Peni)

MAGMA

74	A&M AMS 7119	Mekanik Machine/Mekanik Machine (Version)	20
70	Philips 6359 051/2	MAGMA (2-LP)	60
71	Philips 6397 031	1001 CENTIGRADE (LP)	40
74	A&M AMLH 64397	MEKANIK DESTRUCTIW KOMMANDOH (LP, gatefold sleeve, lyric insert)	40
74	A&M AMLH 68260	KOHN TARKOSZ (LP)	20

MAGNA CARTA

69	Fontana TF 1060	Romeo Jack/7 O'Clock Man	20
69	Mercury MF 1096	Mid-Winter/Spinning Wheels Of Time	20
70	Vertigo 6059 013	Airport Song/Elizabethan	10
71	Vertigo 6059 043	Time For The Leaving/Wayfarin'	8
72	Vertigo 6059 073	All My Life/Falkland Green	12
73	Vertigo 6059 092	Give Me Luv/Song Of Evening	10
70s	London Borough of Camden	When You're Young (charity issue for ROSPA)	5
69	Mercury MCL 20166 S	MAGNA CARTA (LP, laminated sleeve, black/silver labels)	150
70	Vertigo 6360 003	SEASONS (LP, 1st pressing, gatefold sleeve, large swirl label, "Vertigo" at base of label)	80
70	Vertigo 6360 003	SEASONS (LP, 2nd pressing, gatefold sleeve, small swirl label, "Vertigo" beneath swirl above centre hole)	25
71	Vertigo 6360 040	SONGS FROM WASTIES ORCHARD (LP, multifold sleeve, large swirl label)	100
72	Vertigo 6360 068	IN CONCERT (LP, gatefold sleeve, small swirl label)	18
73	Vertigo 6360 093	LORD OF THE AGES (LP, 1st pressing, side 1 matrix, 1 (crossed out 2) Y//1 1 1 1, gatefold sleeve, lyric insert, spaceship label)	15
76	GTO GTLP 012	PUTTING IT BACK TOGETHER (LP)	12
77	GTO GTLP 112	TOOK A LONG TIME (LP)	12

MAGNA JAZZ BAND

57	Parlophone R 4387	Buddy's Habits/Flat Foot	7

(see also Brian White & Magna Jazz Band)

MAGNET

69	CBS 4472	Let Me Stay/Mr Guy Fawkes	30
70	CBS 4844	Something To Remember Me By/Everything	6

MAGNETICS

02	Grapevine G2K 34-119	I'll Keep Holding On/Jackie Baby	12

MAGNETS
| 79 | Hurricane FIRE 1 | Who's The Fool (Me Or You)/Best (with insert, round white cut-out sheet) | 22 |

MAGNIFICENT MEN
66	Capitol CL 15462	Peace Of Mind/All Your Lovin's Gone To My Head	30
68	Capitol CL 15530	Sweet Soul Medley Parts 1 & 2	10
68	Capitol CL 15570	Save The Country/So Much Love Waiting	6

MAGNIFICENT MERCURY BROTHERS
| 74 | Transatlantic BIG 532 | New Girl In School/What About Us | 8 |
| 74 | Transatlantic BIG 536 | Why Do Fools Fall In Love/(I'm Not A) Juvenile Delinquent | 8 |

(see also Decameron)

MAGNOG
| 90s | Enraptured RAPT 4508 | Mist Waves Riding The Hills/Moving Ahead Again/Ghost States (p/s) | 6 |

MAGNUM
75	CBS S CBS 2959	Sweets For My Sweet/Movin' On (no p/s)	45
78	Jet SJET 116	Kingdom Of Madness/In The Beginning	6
78	Jet SJET 128	Invasion/Universe	6
79	Jet JET 155	Changes/Lonesome Star (silver p/s, with sew-on patch)	10
79	Jet JET 155	Changes/Lonesome Star (silver p/s)	8
79	Jet JET 163	Foolish Heart/Baby Rock Me (p/s)	6
80	Jet JET 175	Magnum Live [All Of My Life (live)/Great Adventure (live)//Invasion (live)/Kingdom Of Madness (live)] (double pack, stickered p/s)	6
80	Jet JET 188	Changes (live Remix)/Everybody Needs/Changes (live) (black p/s)	7
81	Jet JET 7007	Black Nights (possibly promo only)	12
82	Jet JET 7020	The Lights Burned Out/Long Days Black Nights (p/s)	6
82	Jet JET 7027	Back To Earth (live)/Hold Back Your Love (live)//Soldier Of The Line (live)/Sacred Hour (live) (double pack)	8
86	Polydor POSP 798	Lonely Night/Les Morts Dansant (live) (p/s)	5
86	Polydor POSPG 798	Lonely Night/Les Morts Dansant (live)//All England's Eyes (live)/Hit And Run (live) (double pack)	7
86	Polydor POSPP 833	Midnight (Remix)/Back Street Kid/Kingdom Of Madness (live) (12", picture disc)	10
87	Polydor POSP 850	When The World Comes Down (Edit)/Vigilante (live) (p/s)	5
88	Polydor POSPG 910	Days Of No Trust/Maybe Tonight ('oct-o-pack', gatefold p/s)	8
88	Polydor POSPP 910	Days Of No Trust/Maybe Tonight (p/s, with sew-on patch)	7
88	Polydor POSPG 920	Start Talking Love/C'est La Vie (gatefold pop-up p/s)	5
88	Polydor POSPG 930	It Must Have Been Love/Crying Time ('prismatic' pack)	5
78	Jet JETLP 210	KINGDOM OF MADNESS (LP, original 'king' sleeve)	18
83	FM WKFMPD 111	THE ELEVENTH HOUR (LP, picture disc)	15
85	FM WKFM LP 34	ON A STORYTELLER'S NIGHT (LP, with bonus single)	15
85	FM WKFM G/C LP 34	ON A STORYTELLER'S NIGHT (LP, gold or clear vinyl, with poster)	15
85	FM WKFM PD 34	ON A STORYTELLER'S NIGHT (LP, picture disc, with poster)	18
86	Polydor POLD 5198	VIGILANTE (LP, with inner)	12
87	FM Revolver WKFMHP 106	MIRADOR (LP, blue vinyl, gatefold sleeve, poster and Blue vinyl 12" [12HP106])	15
88	Polydor POLDP 5221	WINGS OF HEAVEN (LP, picture disc with extra track, die-cut sleeve)	12
88	FM Revolver WKFMPD 110	MAGNUM II (LP, reissue, picture disc)	15
90	FM Revolver WKFMBX 145	FOUNDATION (6-LP box set)	45

TEDDY MAGNUS
| 71 | Green Door GD 4008 | Flying Machine/VERSION BOYS: Machine Version | 5 |

MAGOO
| 95 | Noisebox NBX 013 | MUDSHARK EP: Tom, Lou And Me/Elsie's Skinny Arms/Hop Your Mouth (orange vinyl, numbered p/s, 500 only) | 10 |
| 98 | Fierce Panda NING 47 | Black Sabbath/MOGWAI: Sweet Leaf (p/s) | 7 |

MAGPIES
| 68 | Doctor Bird DB 1129 | Lulu/Must I Be Lonely | 12 |
| 68 | Doctor Bird DB 1132 | Blue Boy/I Guess I'm Crazy | 12 |

MAG SPIES/MAGAZINE SPIES/MAGSPIES
| 79 | Dance Fools Dance GLITCH 1 | LIFEBLOOD (12" EP, 2 tracks by Mag Spies/2 by Obtainers) | 400 |

(see also The Cure)

ALEX MAGUIRE
| 87 | Incus INCUS 52 | LIVE AT OSCARS (LP) | 35 |

LEO MAGUIRE
| 62 | Parlophone R 4917 | Small World/Crying For The Moon | 8 |

MAGUS
| 80 | Northern Sound NSR 200 | BREEZIN' AWAY (LP, private pressing) | 50 |

(see also Blue Epitaph)

TAJ MAHAL
68	Direction 58-3547	Everybody's Got To Change Sometime/Statesboro Blues	12
69	Direction 58-4044	Ee Zee Rider/You Don't Miss Your Water	12
70	Direction 58-4586	Give Your Woman What She Wants/Further On Down The Road	8
71	CBS 7413	Diving Duck Blues/Fishin' Blues	10
67	Direction 8-63279	TAJ MAHAL (LP)	30
69	Direction 8-63397	THE NATCH'L BLUES (LP)	30
69	Direction 8-66226	GIANT STEP/DE OLE FOLKS AT HOME (2-LP)	25
71	CBS 66288	THE REAL THING (2-LP)	18
72	CBS 64447	HAPPY JUST TO BE LIKE I AM (LP)	12
73	CBS 65090	RECYCLING THE BLUES AND OTHER RELATED STUFF (LP)	12
73	CBS 65814	OOOH SO GOOD 'N BLUES (LP)	12
73	CBS 70123	SOUNDER (LP, soundtrack)	12

MAHAVISHNU ORCHESTRA
75	CBS 3007	Can't Stand Your Funk/Eternity's Breath Part 1	6
72	CBS 64717	THE INNER MOUNTING FLAME (LP, with insert)	15
74	CBS CQ 31996	BIRDS OF FIRE (LP, quadrophonic)	20

(see also John McLaughlin)

MITCH MAHON & EDITIONS
| 69 | Pye 7N 17844 | You've Got What I Need/I've Thrown Our Love Away | 5 |

MINT VALUE £

SKIP MAHONEY & CASUALS
76	Contempo CLP 539	LAND OF LOVE (LP)	20

MAIL
71	Parlophone R 5916	Omnibus/Life Goes On	20

MAIN INGREDIENT
74	RCA APBO 0205	Just Don't Want To Be Lonely/Goodbye My Love	8
74	RCA APBO 0305	Happiness Is Just Around The Bend/Why Can't We All Unite	8
71	RCA LSA 3020	TASTEFUL SOUL (LP)	15
72	RCA APL0335	EUPHRATES RIVER (LP)	20

MAINFRAME
84	YYY	INTO TROUBLE WITH THE NOISE OF ART (12", 7-track EP)	10

MAINHORSE
71	Polydor 2383 049	MAINHORSE (LP)	45

MIKE MAINIERI
69	Solid State USS 7006	INSIGHT (LP)	20

MAINLAND
79	Christy ACML 0200	EXPOSURE (LP)	15

MAINLINER
03	Remorse LP 01	MELLOW OUT (LP, red vinyl)	15

(see also Acid Mothers Temple)

JULIE MAIRS & CHRIS STOWELL
77	Cottage COT 211	SOFT SEA BLUE (LP)	25

MAISON ROUGE
85	Red Barn RBR 0001	Questions (p/s)	5

MAJAMOOD
66	Doc. Bird/W.I.R.L. DB 1052	Two Hundred Million Red Ants/Faces Amassed	30

MAJESTERIANS
81	Daddy Kool DKR 125	So Many Times/Flute On Fire (12")	20

MAJESTIC CHOIR AND SOUL STIRRERS
69	Chess CRS 8101	Why Am I Treated So Bad/We Can All Walk A Little Prouder	15

MAJESTICS
73	Cube BUG 34	Living It All Again/She Troubles My Mind	25

MAJOR ACCIDENT
82	M. Melodies MAME 1001	Warboots/Terrorist Gang (unissued, test pressings only)	40
83	Step Forward SF 23	Mr. Nobody/That's You (p/s)	12
83	Flicknife FLS 216	Fight To Win/Free Man (p/s)	12
83	Flicknife FLS 023	Leaders Of Tomorrow/Dayo/Breakaway (p/s)	12
84	Flicknife FLS 026	Respectable/Man On The Wall (p/s)	12
83	Step Forward SFLP 9	MASSACRED MELODIES (LP)	30
84	Syndicate SYNLP 9	TORTURED TUNES LIVE (LP)	25
85	Flicknife SHARP 027	PNEUMATIC PNEUROSIS (LP)	25

(see also Accident)

MAJORETTES
63	Lyntone LYN 982	White Levi's (flexidisc)	15

MAJOR FORCE
94	Mo' Wax MW 082LP	Return Of The Original Artform/(Mixes) (5 x 12" box set)	18

(see also Major Force West)

MAJOR FORCE WEST
94	Mo' Wax MWMFWCD 001	HEADTURNER (CD)	20

(see also Major Force)

MAJORINE
69	Pyramid 6069	Loving Shrine/I Live	20

MAJORITY
65	Decca F 12186	Pretty Little Girl/I Don't Wanna Be Hurt No More	20
65	Decca F 12271	A Little Bit Of Sunlight/Shut 'Em Down In London Town	25
66	Decca F 12313	We Kiss In A Shadow/Ring The Bells	15
66	Decca F 12453	Simplified/One Third	100
66	Decca F 12504	To Make Me A Man/Tears Won't Help	15
67	Decca F 12573	I Hear A Rhapsody/Wait By The Fire	20
67	Decca F 12638	Running Away With My Baby/Let The Joybells Ring	20
68	Decca F 12727	All Our Christmases/People	25

MAJORS
62	London HLP 9602	A Wonderful Dream/Time Will Tell	25
62	London HLP 9627	She's A Troublemaker/A Little Bit Now	25
63	London HLP 9693	What In The World/Tra La La	25
64	Liberty LBF 66009	Ooh Wee Baby/I'll Be There	22
63	London RE-P 1358	MEET THE MAJORS (EP)	100
63	London HA-P 8068	MEET THE MAJORS (LP)	150

MAJOR SURGERY
77	Next 104	NEXT CUT (LP)	15

MAJOR TOM
76	Satril SAT 113	Spaceman Boy/Spaceman Boy (Instrumental)	25

MAKADOPOLOUS
60	Palette PG 9005	Never On Sunday/Yasou (p/s)	10
60	Palette PG 9005	Never On Sunday/Yasou	6

PETER MAKANA & HIS RHYTHM BOYS
58	Oriole CB 1445	Baboon Shepherd (with Black Duke)/Black John	5
58	Oriole CB 1446	Cool Mood/Sweet Baby	5

MIRIAM MAKEBA
63	London HL 9747	The Click Song/Mbube	5
67	Reprise RS 20606	Pata Pata/The Ballad Of The Sad Young Men	7
60	London HA 2332	MIRIAM MAKEBA (LP)	12

CARMEN MAKI
| 69 | CBS 4298 | (Sometime I Feel Like) A Lonely Baby/Anata Ga Hoshii | 7 |

MAKIN' TIME
85	Countdown VAIN 1	Here Is My Number/Nothing Else (p/s)	8
86	Countdown TVAIN 1	Here Is My Number/Nothing Else (picture disc)	8
86	Countdown VAIN 5	Pump It Up/Walk A Thin Line (p/s)	8
86	Countdown 12 VAIN 5	PUMP IT UP EP: Once Again/Walk A Thin Line/Eating Up The Cold	8
85	Countdown DOWN 1	RHYTHM 'N' SOUL (LP)	15
86	Ready To Eat READY 1	NO LUMPS OF FAT OR GRISTLE GUARANTEED (LP)	18
87	Re-Elect/President ELECT 1	TIME, TROUBLE AND MONEY (LP)	18

(see also Charlatans)

MAKKA BEES
| 77 | Congo CO 1 | Nation Fiddler/Fire | 20 |

MAL & PRIMITIVES
| 65 | Pye 7N 15915 | Every Minute Of Every Day/Pretty Little Face | 80 |

(see also Primitives, Mal Ryder & Spirits)

MALA
05	DMZ DMZ 003	Da Wrath Souljahz Vip Mix/LOEFAH: Twisup Vip (12")	25
06	DMZ DMZ 010	Left Leg Out/Vlue Notez (12")	20
07	DMZ DMZ 011	Bury Da Bwoy/Hunter (12")	25
07	DMZ DMZ 012	Lean Forward/Learn (12")	30

MALAGON SISTERS & CHA CHA RHYTHM BOYS
| 59 | Pye International 7N 25008 | In A Little Spanish Town/Lessons In Cha-Cha-Cha | 5 |

MALARIA!
| 82 | Jungle JUNG 3 | NEW YORK PASSAGE (12" EP) | 8 |

MALCOLM & ALWYN
| 73 | Pye NSPL 18404 | FOOL'S WISDOM (LP, textured sleeve with poster) | 15 |
| 74 | Key KL 022 | WILDWALL (LP) | 15 |

CARL MALCOLM
| 75 | Black Wax WAX 7 | Miss Wire Waist/SKIN, FLESH & BONES: Wire Dub | 10 |
| 77 | Grove Music GMDM 1 | Repatriation (feat. Ranking Trevor)/Take A Tip From Me (feat. Ranking Trevor) (12") | 40 |

CARLOS MALCOLM & AFRO CARIBS
| 65 | Island WI 173 | Bonanza Ska/Papa Luiga | 20 |

GEORGE MALCOLM
| 53 | Parlophone MSP 6058 | Bach Goes To Town/Bach Before The Mast | 5 |

HUGH MALCOLM
| 68 | Amalgamated AMG 827 | Good Time Rock/LYNN TAITT & JETS: Sleepy Ludy | 35 |
| 68 | Amalgamated AMG 829 | Mortgage/CANNONBALL BRYAN TRIO: Man About Town | 45 |

MALLARD
77	Virgin VS 168	Harvest/Green Coyote	7
76	Virgin V 2045	MALLARD (LP)	15
77	Virgin V 2077	IN A DIFFERENT CLIMATE (LP)	12

(see also Captain Beefheart & His Magic Band)

MALLET
| 80 | Rox ROX 014 | C C Rider/Route 66 | 25 |

STEPHEN MALLINDER
| 81 | Fetish FE 12 | Temperature Drop/Cool Down (12", p/s) | 8 |
| 82 | Fetish FM 2010 | POW-WOW (LP) | 12 |

(see also Cabaret Voltaire)

SIW MALMKVIST
59	Oriole CB 1486	Sermonette/The Preacher	5
61	Parlophone R 4765	Wedding Cake/Red Roses And Little White Lies	6
64	Columbia DB 7411	Sole Sole Sole/Sabato Sera (as Siw Malmkvist & Umberto Marcato)	5
68	Atlantic 584 229	The Man Who Took The Valise Off The Floor Of Grand Central Station/Sadie The Cleaning Lady	6

CINDY MALONE
| 61 | RCA RCA 1254 | Weird Beard/Young Marriage | 8 |

WIL MALONE
| 70 | Fontana STL 5541 | WIL MALONE (LP) | 1500 |
| 10 | Morgan Bluetown BT 5005 | WIL MALONE (LP, reissue, 750 only with signed certificate) | 35 |

(see also Barnaby Rudge, Motherlight, Wilson Malone Voiceband)

WILSON MALONE VOICEBAND
| 68 | Morgan MR 112P | FUNNY SAD MUSIC (LP) | 40 |

(see also Motherlight, Wil Malone)

RICHARD MALTBY
| 56 | HMV 7M 393 | Man With The Golden Arm Theme/Heart Of Paris | 8 |
| 61 | Columbia DB 4606 | The Rat Race/Walkie Talkie | 15 |

MAMA LAPATO
| 82 | Bead Records BEAD 20 | MAMA LAPATO (LP) | 20 |

MAMA LION
| 72 | Philips 6078002 | Ain't Too Proud To Beg/Mr. Invitation | 6 |
| 72 | Philips 6369 153 | MAMA LION (LP) | 15 |

MAMAS & PAPAS
| 66 | RCA Victor RCA 1503 | California Dreamin'/Somebody Groovy | 10 |

MAMA'S BOYS

66	RCA Victor RCA 1516	Monday, Monday/Got A Feelin'	5
66	RCA Victor RCA 1533	I Saw Her Again/Even If I Could	6
66	RCA Victor RCA 1551	Look Through My Window/Once There Was I Time I Thought	5
67	RCA Victor RCA 1564	Words Of Love/I Can't Wait	7
67	RCA Victor RCA 1576	Dedicated To The One I Love/Free Advice	5
67	RCA Victor RCA 1613	Creeque Alley/No Salt On Her Tail	6
67	RCA Victor RCA 1630	12.30/Young Girls Are Coming To The Canyon/Straight Shooter	6
67	RCA Victor RCA 1649	Glad To Be Unhappy/Hey Girl	7
68	RCA Victor RCA 1710	Safe In My Garden/Too Late	7
68	RCA Victor RCA 1726	Dream A Little Dream Of Me/Midnight Voyage (as Mama Cass and the Mamas & Papas)	6
68	RCA Victor RCA 1744	For The Love Of Ivy/Strange Young Girls	8
66	RCA Victor RD 7803	IF YOU CAN BELIEVE YOUR EYES AND EARS (LP)	20
66	RCA Victor RD/SF 7834	CASS, JOHN, MICHELLE, DENNY (LP)	20
67	RCA Victor RD/SF 7880	DELIVER (LP)	20
68	RCA Victor RD/SF 7960	THE PAPAS AND THE MAMAS (LP)	20
68	Stateside (S)SL 5002	THE MAMAS AND THE PAPAS GOLDEN ERA VOL. 2 (LP)	15
70	Probe SPB 1013/14	A GATHERING OF FLOWERS (LP)	20
71	Probe SPB 1048	PEOPLE LIKE US (LP)	15
78	St. Michael MO 101225	CALIFORNIA DREAMIN' (LP, exclusive to Marks & Spencer)	15

(see also Mama Cass [Elliot], John Phillips, Michelle Phillips, Scott McKenzie, Barry McGuire, Mugwumps, Big Three [U.S], Spanky & Our Gang)

MAMA'S BOYS

83	Spartan 12SP 6	Too Little Of You To Love/Freedom Fighters (12", p/s, with free "Official Bootleg" LP)	10
84	Spartan SP 11	Midnight Promises (p/s)	5
84	Spartan 12SP 11	MIDNIGHT PROMISES (12" EP)	8
85	Jive JIVEP 96	Needle In The Groove/Don't Tell Mama (shaped picture disc)	8
82	Ultra Noise ULTRA 1	PLUG IT IN (LP)	12
85	Jive HIP 24	POWER AND PASSION (LP, with 12" interview picture disc)	12

MAMA'S PRIDE

75	Atlantic K 10709	Blue Mist/Missouri Skyline	6

MAMMATH

84	Neat NEAT 42	Rock Me/Rough 'N' Ready (p/s)	7

MAMMOTH

89	Jive MOTHX 4	All The Days/Fatman/Bet You Wish (12", picture disc, PVC sleeve, withdrawn)	20

(see also John McCoy, Gillan, Samson, Tiger, Nicky Moore Band, Hackensack)

MAN

69	Pye 7N 17684	Sudden Life/Love	30
71	Liberty LBF 15448	Daughter Of The Fireplace/Country Girl	18
74	United Artists UP 35643	Don't Go Away (possibly unissued)	15
74	United Artists UP 35703	Taking The Easy Way Out Again/California Silks And Satins	6
74	United Artists UP 35739	Day And Night/A Hard Way To Live	5
76	MCA MCA 236	Out Of Your Head/I'm A Love Taker	5
76	United Artists REM 408	BANANAS (EP)	8
69	Pye N(S)PL 18275	REVELATION (LP, mono, original pressing with sky blue label with black at top)	70
69	Pye N(S)PL 18275	REVELATION (LP, stereo, original pressing with sky blue label with black at top)	40
69	Pye N(S)PL 18275	REVELATION (LP, mono/stereo, reissues with blue label but black on the side)	12
69	Dawn DNLS 3003	2 OZ'S OF PLASTIC WITH A HOLE IN THE MIDDLE (LP, orange label, gatefold sleeve)	45
69	Dawn DNLS 3003	2 OZ'S OF PLASTIC WITH A HOLE IN THE MIDDLE (LP, later pressings with lilac then pink 'sun' labels, gatefold sleeve)	20
70	Liberty LBG 83464	MAN (LP, gatefold textured sleeve)	40
72	United Artists UAS 29236	DO YOU LIKE IT HERE NOW (ARE YOU SETTLING IN ALRIGHT?) (LP)	30
72	United Artists USP 100	LIVE AT THE PADGET ROOMS, PENARTH (LP)	30
72	United Artists UAG 29417	BE GOOD TO YOURSELF AT LEAST ONCE A DAY (LP, fold out 'map' in gatefold sleeve with 'family tree' inner)	30
73	United Artists UDX 205/6	CHRISTMAS AT THE PATTI (LP, 2 x 10", with other artists)	22
73	Utd Artists UAD 60053/4	BACK INTO THE FUTURE (2-LP, gatefold sleeve, some stickered)	20
74	United Artists UAG 29631	RHINOS WINOS AND LUNATICS (LP, laminated gatefold)	15
74	United Artists UAG 29675	SLOW MOTION (LP, lyric inner sleeve)	15
75	United Artists UAG 29872	MAXIMUM DARKNESS (LP, gatefold sleeve, with poster)	15
77	MCA MCF 2815	ALL'S WELL THAT ENDS WELL (LP, initial batch with History Of Man booklet)	20
77	MCA MCF 2815	ALL'S WELL THAT ENDS WELL (LP)	12

(see also Bystanders, Eyes Of Blue, Ancient Grease, Big Sleep, Clive John, Alkatraz, Help Yourself, Deke Leonard, Neutrons, Gary Pickford-Hopkins & Friends, Wild Turkey)

T. MAN & T. BONES

72	Sioux SI 007	True Born African (actually by Winston Jarrett & Righteous Flames)/ Tropical Chief	5

MAN UPSTAIRS

82	Clock House CH 0502	Summa/The Gospel According To Mark (p/s)	15
85	Sideline SIDE 1	Sad In My Heart/Country Boy (p/s)	15
85	Sideline 1SIDE12	CONSUMERS EP (12", p/s)	40

(STEPHEN STILLS') MANASSAS

72	Atlantic K 60021	MANASSAS (2-LP, with 2 inner sleeves & lyric poster)	25
73	Atlantic K 40440	DOWN THE ROAD (LP, with inner sleeve)	18

(see also Stephen Stills, Crosby Stills & Nash, Flying Burrito Brothers)

MANASSEH

77	Genesis 12	MANASSEH (LP, with insert)	20

JUNIOR MANCE

60	HMV CLP 1342	JUNIOR (LP)	25
71	Atlantic 2400 028	WITH A LOTTA HELP FROM MY FRIENDS (LP)	20

STEVE MANCHA/J.J. BARNES

69	Stax SXATS 1012	RARE STAMPS (LP)	50

(see also J.J. Barnes)

MANCHESTER CITY F.C.

72	RCA 2200	Boys In Blue/Funky City	6

MANCHESTER MEKON
79	Newmarket NEW 102	No Forgetting/Have A Go-Go/Jonathan Livingstone Seafood (hand-painted p/s with insert, 1,000 only)	25

MICKY MANCHESTER
75	Rainbow RBW 2001	Have You Seen Your Daughter, Mrs Jones?/Chamberlain Said	10

MANCHESTER MOB
67	Parlophone R 5552	Bony Maronie At The Hop/Afro Asian	40

(see also Graham Gouldman, High Society, 10cc, Friday Browne)

MANCHESTER UNITED F.C.
78	Jet 775	Just One Of Those Teams/Na Na Hey Hey Kiss Him Goodbye (As Manchester United Supporters Club)	6
81	Goldspinners GOLD 1	Manchester United/Tribute To The Fans (as Manchester United)	6
86	Columbia DB 9107	We All Follow Man. United/They're The Best/Southbound Glory Glory Man. United (as Manchester United Football Team)	6

MANCHESTER UNITED FOOTBALL SQUAD
76	Decca F 13633	Manchester United/MARTIN BUCHAN: Old Trafford Blues	8
79	RCA MAN 1	Onward Sexton's Soldiers/Come On You Reds (red vinyl)	8
94	PolyGram TV MANUP 12	Come On You Reds/(Instrumental) (12" picture disc, with insert)	15

(see also Status Quo)

MANCHESTERS
66	Ember	TRIBUTE TO THE BEATLES (LP)	20

MANCHESTER'S PLAYBOYS
66	Fontana TF 745	I Feel So Good/I Close My Eyes	175

MANCINI & FOX
72	Polydor 2066 170	Light Song/The Colours Are Still There	8

HENRY MANCINI & HIS ORCHESTRA
59	RCA RCA 1134	Peter Gunn Theme/The Brothers Go To Mother's	10
61	RCA RCA 1256	Moon River/Breakfast At Tiffanys	5
62	RCA RCA 1285	Experiment In Terror/Tooty Twist	10
62	RCA RCA 1312	Man Of The World Theme/Fluter's Ball	6
64	RCA RCA 1431	Dear Heart/A Shot In The Dark	5
68	RCA RCA 1689	Wait Until Dark/Norma De Guadalajara	5
70	RCA RCA 1934	Z-Theme/Midnight Cowboy	5
57	Brunswick LAT 8162	ROCK, PRETTY BABY (LP, soundtrack, with Rod McKuen)	80
59	RCA RD 27123/SF 5033	PETER GUNN (LP, soundtrack)	15
63	RCA SF 7620	CHARADE (LP, soundtrack)	20
64	RCA RD 7667	THE BEST OF MANCINI (LP)	12
65	RCA RD 7759	THE GREAT RACE (LP, soundtrack)	15
66	RCA RD 7818	WHAT DID YOU DO IN THE WAR, DADDY? (LP, soundtrack)	15
66	RCA RD 7817	ARABESQUE (LP, soundtrack)	15
67	RCA RD/SF 7891	TWO FOR THE ROAD (LP, soundtrack)	15
67	RCA RD/SF 7899	GUNN (LP, soundtrack)	18
70	CBS 70061	ME, NATALIE (LP, soundtrack, with Rod McKuen)	12
70	Avco Embassy 6466 002	SUNFLOWER (LP, soundtrack)	12
70	United Artists UAS 29122	MASTER OF THE ISLANDS (LP, soundtrack)	15
70	RCA SF 8138	DARLING LILI (LP, soundtrack, gatefold sleeve)	12
72	RCA Victor SF 8127	FILM THEMES A TO Z (LP)	15
73	Elektra K 46239	THE THIEF WHO CAME TO DINNER (LP, soundtrack)	15
75	RCA Red Seal RS 1010	THE RETURN OF THE PINK PANTHER (LP, soundtrack)	15
75	MCA MCF 2707	THE GREAT WALDO PEPPER (LP, soundtrack)	15

MANDALABAND
75	Chrysalis CHR 1095	MANDALABAND (LP)	20
78	Chrysalis CHR 1181	THE EYE OF WENDOR: PROPHECIES (LP, with booklet)	20

MANDARIN KRAZE
70	Carnaby CNS 4008	How Long Does It Take/Magazine Cottage	10

HARVEY MANDEL
74	Janus 6146 024	Uno Ino/Shangrenade	6
68	Philips SBL 7873	CRISTO REDENTOR (LP)	25
69	Philips SBL 7904	RIGHTEOUS (LP)	20
70	Philips SBL 7915	GAMES GUITARS PLAY (LP)	15
71	Dawn DNLS 3015	BABY BATTER (LP)	20
71	Philips 6336 009	CRISTO REDENTOR (LP, reissue)	12
72	London SH-O 8426	GET OFF IN CHICAGO (LP)	12
72	Janus 6310 210	THE SNAKE (LP)	15
73	Janus 6499 831	SHANGRENADE (LP)	12

(see also Canned Heat, Dewey Terry)

RICHARD MANDEL
69	London HL 10256	Loneliness/Young And Warm And Wonderful	20

NELSON MANDELA
64	Ember CEL 905	WHY I'M READY TO DIE (LP, spoken word, narrated by Peter Finch)	20

MANDINGO
73	EMI EMI 2014	Medicine Man/Black Rite	15
73	EMI 2062	Fever Pitch/The Cheetah	10
73	EMI EMC 3010	MANDINGO 1: SACRIFICE (LP)	15
73	Studio Two TWO 400	MANDINGO 2: PRIMEVAL RHYTHM OF LIFE (LP)	40
73	Studio Two Q4TWO 400	MANDINGO 2: PRIMEVAL RHYTHM OF LIFE (LP, quadrophonic)	40
75	EMI EMC 3038	MANDINGO 3: STORY OF SURVIVAL (LP)	30
77	EMI EMC 3217	MANDINGO 4: SAVAGE RITE (LP)	25

(see also Geoff Love, Manuel & Music Of The Mountains)

MANDRAGORA
89	SAB 01	OVER THE MOON (LP, 1st pressing with white label/cream sleeve)	50
89	Babbleon Bab 1	OVER THE MOON (LP, 2nd pressing with blue label/yellow/blue/white/cream sleeve)	30
95	Mystic Stones RUNE 14	TEMPLE BALL (LP)	15

MINT VALUE £

| 93 | Mystic Stones RUNE 13 | EARTHDANCE (LP) | 15 |
| 91 | Resonance 33-9133 | HEAD FIRST (LP) | 20 |

MANDRAKE
| 60 | Philips PB 1093 | Mandrake/The Witch's Twist | 12 |
| 61 | Philips BF 1153 | Thank Goodness It's Friday/Queen Of Sheba | 7 |

MANDRAKE MEMORIAL
| 69 | RCA SF 8028 | MEDIUM (LP) | 100 |
| 70 | RCA/Poppy PYS 11003 | PUZZLE (LP) | 100 |

MANDRAKE PADDLE STEAMERS
| 69 | Parlophone R 5780 | Strange Walking Man/Steam | 130 |
| 88 | Bam Caruso NRIC 033 | Strange Walking Man/Steam (reissue, gatefold p/s) | 12 |

(see also Liverpool Echo)

MANDRILL
73	Polydor 2066 320	Mandrill/Hang Loose	5
73	Polydor 2066 357	Fencewalk/Polk Street Carnival	5
72	Polydor 2391 030	MANDRILL IS (LP, gatefold)	20
73	Polydor 2391 061	COMPOSITE TRUTH (LP)	15
73	Polydor 2391 092	JUST OUTSIDE OF TOWN (LP)	18
73	United Artists UAS 29923	SOLID (LP)	12

MANDY (SMITH)
87	PWL PWLP 1	I Just Can't Wait/Instrumental/You're Never Alone (12" picture disc)	10
88	PWL PWCD 11	Boys & Girls/Mandy's Theme (I Just Can't Wait) (The Cool & Breezy Jazz Mix)/ He's My Boy (3" CD)	15
88	PWL PWCD 18	Victim Of Pleasure (Red Rooster Mix)/Say It's Love/Victim Of Pleasure (Instrumental) (3" CD)	15
88	PWL HFCD 2	MANDY (CD)	30

MANEATERS
| 82 | Editions EG EGO 8 | Nine To Five/SUZI PINNS: Jerusalem (withdrawn 'Adam & Toyah' p/s) | 100 |
| 82 | Editions EG EGO 8 | Nine To Five/SUZI PINNS: Jerusalem (title p/s) | 5 |

(see also Adam & The Ants)

MAN FRIDAY & JIVE JUNIOR
| 83 | Malaco MAL 011 | Picking Up Sounds/Picking Up Sounds (Radio Mix) (p/s, features John Deacon) | 30 |
| 83 | Malaco MAL 1211 | Picking Up Sounds (Extended)/Picking Up Sounds (Radio Mix) (12", p/s, features John Deacon) | 50 |

(see also Queen)

MAN FROM DELMONTE
87	Ugly Man UGLY 3	Drive Drive Drive (22 And Still In Love With You)/Sun Serious (p/s)	25
87	Ugly Man UGLY 5	Water In My Eyes/Bored By You (p/s)	12
87	Ugly Man UGLY 5T	Water In My Eyes/Bored By You/The Country (12", p/s)	18
88	Ugly Man UGLY 7	(Will Nobody Save) Louise/Good Things In Life (p/s)	10
88	Ugly Man UGLY 7T	(Will Nobody Save) Louise/Good Things In Life/Like A Millionaire (12", p/s)	25
89	Bop Cassettes BIP 502	WAITING FOR ANN (12" EP)	15

MANGO GREEN
| 70 | Ackee ACK 109 | Birds Of A Feather/Run Down | 15 |

MANHATTANS
65	Sue WI 384	I Wanna Be (Your Everything)/Searchin' For My Baby	50
66	Carnival CAR 100	Baby I Need You/Teach Me (The Philly Dog)	20
66	Carnival CAR 101	That New Girl/Can I	20
74	CBS 2117	Soul Train/I'm Not A Run Around	6
73	London SHB 8449	A MILLION TO ONE (LP)	30
76	CBS 81513	THE MANHATTANS (LP)	12
78	CBS 81828	IT FEELS GOOD (LP)	12

MANIAC
| 85 | Rentaracket Recordings RKT 1 | KILLING FOR PLEASURE EP (p/s, with booklet) | 6 |

MANIACS
| 77 | United Artists UP 36327 | Chelsea 1977/Ain't No Legend (p/s) | 20 |
| 77 | United Artists UP 36327 | Chelsea 1977/Ain't No Legend (p/s, green labels, demo versions different mixes) | 30 |

(see also Rings, Physicals)

MANIAX
| 66 | White Label WLR 101/102 | Out Of Reach/The Devil's Home | 20 |

MANIC JABS
| 81 | Waldo's MS 009 | Autophagus/The Injuns Are Comin'/Thing Wild (p/s) | 10 |

MANIC STREET PREACHERS
SINGLES
88	SBS SBS 002	Suicide Alley/Tennessee (I Get Low) (hand-made p/s with press-cuttings glued to plain card cover)	750
88	SBS SBS 002	Suicide Alley/Tennessee (I Get Low) (blue p/s, 200 only)	400
88	SBS SBS 002	Suicide Alley/Tennessee (I Get Low) (no p/s, 100 only)	200
90	Hopelessly Devoted 1	UK Channel Boredom/LAURENS: I Don't Know What The Trouble Is (p/s flexidisc, free with Hopelessly Devoted fanzine; later repressed)	60
90	Hopelessly Devoted 1	UK Channel Boredom/LAURENS: I Don't Know What The Trouble Is (p/s flexidisc, without Hopelessly Devoted fanzine; later repressed)	45
90	Damaged Goods YUBB 4	NEW ART RIOT EP: New Art Riot/Strip It Down/ Last Exit On Yesterday/Teenage 20/20 (12", white label, 100 copies, plain sleeves rubber stamped with "Made In Wales")	35
90	Damaged Goods YUBB 4	NEW ART RIOT EP: New Art Riot/Strip It Down/Last Exit On Yesterday/Teenage 20/20 (12" EP, p/s, 1st 1,000 black & white label)	20
90	Damaged Goods YUBB 4	NEW ART RIOT EP: New Art Riot/Strip It Down/Last Exit On Yesterday/Teenage 20/20 (12" EP, p/s, 2nd 1,000 on black-on-yellow labels)	15
90	Damaged Goods YUBB 4	NEW ART RIOT EP: New Art Riot/Strip It Down/Last Exit On Yesterday/Teenage 20/20 (12" EP, p/s, later pressing on red, orange & silver & green labels)	10
91	Damaged Goods YUBB 004P	NEW ART RIOT EP: New Art Riot/Strip It Down/Last Exit On Yesterday/Teenage 20/20 (12" EP, reissue on pink vinyl)	25
91	Heavenly HVN 812	Motown Junk/Sorrow 16/We Her Majesty's Prisoners (12", withdrawn p/s)	35
91	Heavenly HVN 8CD	Motown Junk/Sorrow 16/We Her Majesty's Prisoners (CD, withdrawn sleeve)	80

91	Heavenly HVN 10	You Love Us/Spectators Of Suicide (p/s)..15
91	Heavenly HVN 1012	You Love Us/Spectators Of Suicide/Starlover/Strip It Down (live) (12", p/s) 20
91	Heavenly HVN 10CD	You Love Us/Spectators Of Suicide/Starlover/Strip It Down (live) (CD) 25
91	Columbia 657337 6	Stay Beautiful/R.P. McMurphy/Soul Contamination (12", p/s) 10
91	Columbia 657337 8	Stay Beautiful/R.P. McMurphy/Soul Contamination (12", stickered poster p/s)..................10
91	Columbia 657582 6	Repeat (U.K.)/Love's Sweet Exile/Democracy Coma (12", p/s).......................................12
91	Columbia 657582 8	Repeat/Democracy Coma/Love's Sweet Exile/Stay Beautiful (live) (12", gatefold, stickered p/s)...12
91	Caff CAFF 15	FEMININE IS BEAUTIFUL: Repeat After Me/New Art Riot (p/s, 500 only) 150
92	Columbia 657724 6	You Love Us/A Vision Of Dead Desire/It's So Easy (live) (12" gatefold p/s)......................10
92	Columbia 657873 7	Slash'N'Burn/Motown Junk (p/s)..6
92	Columbia 657873 6	Slash'N'Burn/Motown Junk/Ain't Goin' Down (12", with print, stickered p/s)..................12
92	Columbia 657873 2	Slash'N'Burn/Motown Junk/Ain't Goin' Down (gold CD, digipak) 15
92	Columbia 658083 6	Motorcycle Emptiness/Bored Out Of my Soul/Under My Wheels 15
92	Columbia 658083 6	Motorcycle Emptiness/Bored Out Of My Mind/Under My Wheels (12", picture disc, stickered PVC sleeve)...18
92	Damaged Goods YUBB 4CD	New Art Riot/Strip It Down/Last Exit On Yesterday/Teenage 20/20 (CD, picture disc, reissue, 3,000 only)..10
92	Columbia 658382 7	Theme From MASH EP (Suicide Is Painless)/FATIMA MANSIONS: Everything I Do (I Do It For You) (p/s)...6
92	Columbia 658382 6	Theme From MASH EP (Suicide Is Painless)/FATIMA MANSIONS/ Everything I Do (I Do It For You)/Sleeping With The NME (12", p/s) 8
93	Columbia 6597277	Roses In The Hospital/Us Against You/Donkeys (red vinyl, p/s) 8
93	Columbia 6597272	Roses In The Hospital/Us Against You/Donkeys/Wrote For Luck (CD) 10
93	Columbia 6597337 6	From Despair To Where/Hibernation/Spectators Of Suicide (Heavenly Version) (12", p/s) 8
93	Columbia 659477 6	La Tristesse Durera/Patrick Bateman/Repeat (live)/Tennessee (12", poster p/s)................8
07	Columbia 8697075597	Underdogs (1-sided, p/s)..20

ALBUMS

92	Epic 471060 1	GENERATION TERRORISTS (2-LP)..30
92	Columbia 471060 0	GENERATION TERRORISTS (2-LP, picture discs, inner sleeves, 5,000 only) 40
92	Columbia 471060 9	GENERATION TERRORISTS (CD, picture disc, 5,000 only) 40
93	Columbia 474064 1	GOLD AGAINST THE SOUL (LP, inner sleeve, in custom carrier-bag)...............................15
93	Columbia 4740649	GOLD AGAINST THE SOUL (gold CD) 20
94	Epic 477421 0	THE HOLY BIBLE (LP, picture disc) 30
94	Epic 4774219	THE HOLY BIBLE (CD, picture disc) 20
96	Epic 483930	EVERYTHING MUST GO (LP)..30
98	Epic 4917031	THIS IS MY TRUTH TELL ME YOURS (LP) 30
03	Sony 5123861	LIPSTICK TRACES (3 x LP, 1,000 only with tactile sleeve)...45

PROMOS

91	Heavenly HVN 10P	You Love Us (Radio Edit) (promo-only, some with stickered p/s, 1-sided white label, 500 only) 30
92	Columbia XPCD 185	Motorcycle Emptiness/Motorcycle Emptiness (Radio Edit) (CD)....................................20
93	Columbia/Damont XPS 272	Symphony Of Tourette (1-sided, white label, no p/s)..70
92	Columbia XPCD 171	GENERATION TERRORISTS (CD, 5-track sampler, digipak)...15
93	Columbia XPCD 285	GOLD AGAINST THE SOUL (CD, 4-track sampler, digipak)...20
94	Columbia	DONE AND DUSTED (12", Chemical Brothers Remixes)...20
96	Columbia XPR 3043	A Design For Life (Stealth Sonic Orchestra Remix)/(Instrumental) (12").........................20
96	Columbia XPR 3049	Kevin Carter (Stealth Sonic Orchestra Remix) (12", white label, 1-sided, stickered card sleeve, 30 only)..30
96	Columbia XPR 3094	Australia (Lionrock Remix) (12", white label, 1-sided, stickered card sleeve, 20 only)...60
97	Columbia MANIC 1-6CD	SIX SINGLES FROM GENERATION TERRORISTS (6-CD box set) 90
99	Epic XPR 3320	Tsunami (Cornelius Remix)/(Electron Ray Tube Mix by Stereolab) (12", p/s, sealed with sticker, promo only) 10

MANICURED NOISE

| 80 | Pre PRE 003 | Metronome/Moscow (die-cut p/s with postcard) ....5 |
| 80 | Pre PRE 006 | Faith/Free Time (p/s) ....5 |

(see also Weatherman & Friends)

MANISH BOYS

| 65 | Parlophone R 5250 | I Pity The Fool/Take My Tip ....900 |
| 65 | Parlophone R 5250 | I Pity The Fool/Take My Tip (Demo copy) ....500 |

(see also David Bowie)

MANISH BOYS/DAVY JONES & LOWER THIRD

79	EMI 2925	I Pity The Fool/Take My Tip/DAVY JONES You've Got A Habit Of Leaving/Baby Loves That Way (Demo copy p/s)...20
79	EMI 2925	I Pity The Fool/Take My Tip/DAVY JONES You've Got A Habit Of Leaving/Baby Loves That Way (Demo copy p/s)...20
79	EMI EMI 2925	I Pity The Fool/Take My Tip/DAVY JONES & LOWER THIRD: You've Got A Habit Of Leaving/Baby Loves That Way (p/s) 6
82	Charly CYM 1	I Pity The Fool/Take My Tip/DAVY JONES & LOWER THIRD: You've Got A Habit Of Leaving/Baby Loves That Way (10", p/s, reissue) 7

(see also David Bowie, Davy Jones, Davie Jones & King Bees)

MANIX

91	Reinforced RIVET 1209	Manic Minds (12", die-cut p/s)..8
91	Reinforced RIVET 1209R	Manic Minds EP (Remixes) (12") 8
94	Reinforced RIVET 1275	Intelligent Hoodlums EP (2x12")..12

EARLE MANKEY

| 78 | Bronze BRO 53 | Mau Mau/Crazy ....15 |

MANKIND

| 78 | Pinnacle PIN 71-12 | Dr. Who/Time Traveller (12", p/s, blue vinyl) ....10 |
| 78 | Motor Records MTR 001/12 | Dr. Who/Time Traveller (12", p/s, blue vinyl, p/s)..12 |

SYDNEY MANKIND

| 82 | Musical Ambassador MAPD 001 | The Truth/EDI FITZROY: Chant It To The Rhythm (12") ....40 |

ABEL MANN

| 70 | Trend TNY 51 | The Sun In The Morning/It's So Easy ....7 |

BARRY MANN

| 61 | HMV POP 911 | Who Put The Bomp (In The Bomp Bomp)/Love True Love ....20 |

MINT VALUE £

61	HMV POP 949	Little Miss U.S.A./Find Another Fool	20
62	HMV POP 1084	Hey Baby I'm Dancin'/Like I Don't Love You	15
63	HMV POP 1108	Bless You/Teenage Has Been	18
64	Colpix PX 776	Talk To Me Baby/Amy	15
66	Capitol CL 15463	Angelica/Looking At Tomorrow	15
68	Capitol CL 15538	The Young Electric Psychedelic Hippy Flippy Folk And Funky Philosophic Turned On Groovy 12 String Band/Take Your Love	10
63	HMV CLP 1559	WHO PUT THE BOMP IN THE BOMP BOMP BOMP? (LP)	125
72	CBS 64805	LAY IT ALL OUT (LP, gatefold)	20

CARL MANN

59	London HLS 8935	Mona Lisa/Foolish One	50
59	London HLS 8935	Mona Lisa/Foolish One (78)	40
59	London HLS 9006	Pretend/Rockin' Love	40
59	London HLS 9006	Pretend/Rockin' Love (78)	50
60	London HLS 9170	South Of The Border/I'm Comin' Home	25
60	London HA-S 2277	LIKE MANN - CARL MANN SINGS (LP)	300

GARY MANN ORCHESTRA

| 73 | Penny Farthing PEN 820 | The Original 'Big Match' Theme/Newscoop (The Original 'Grandstand' Theme) | 12 |

GEOFF MANN

| 84 | Food For Thought GRUB 4 | I MAY SING GRACE (LP) | 12 |
| 85 | Wobbly WOB 1 | PSALM ENCHANTED EVENING (LP) | 12 |

GLORIA MANN

| 56 | Brunswick 05569 | Why Do Fools Fall In Love/Partners For Life | 20 |
| 56 | Brunswick 05610 | It Happened Again/My Secret Sin | 10 |

HERBIE MANN

66	Atlantic 584 058	Love Theme (From 'Is Paris Burning')/Happy Brass	7
66	Atlantic 584 052	Philly Dog/DAVE PIKE: Sunny	10
66	A&M AMS 719	Unchain My Heart/Glory Of Love	10
67	Atlantic 584112	The Beat Goes On/Free For All	10
69	Atlantic 584 297	Memphis Underground/New Orleans	10
72	Atlantic K 10179	Philly Dog/Memphis Underground/It's A Funky Thing	6
75	Atlantic K 10580	Hijack/Orient Express	15
75	Atlantic SAM 26	Hijack (Disco Cut)/Bertha Boogie Part 1 (12", "Disco Special Cut" on label)	60
58	Fontana TFL 5013	SALUTE TO THE FLUTE (LP)	15
60	Top Rank 25/015	FLUTE FOR ETERNITY (10" LP, with Buddy Collette)	20
63	London HA-K/SH-K 8043	RIGHT NOW (LP)	20
64	Atlantic ATL 5008	HERBIE MANN AT NEWPORT (LP)	15
65	Atlantic ATL/SAL 5035	THE ROAR OF THE GREASE PAINT (LP)	20
66	CBS (S)BPG 62585	LATIN MANN (LP)	20
66	Atlantic ATL/SAL 5038	STANDING OVATION AT NEWPORT (LP)	15
66	Atlantic 587/588 003	MONDAY NIGHT AT THE VILLAGE GATE (LP)	15
66	Atlantic 587/588 028	NIRVANA (LP, with Bill Evans)	15

LORIE MANN

59	Top Rank JAR 116	A Penny A Kiss, A Penny A Hug/Dream Lover	6
59	Top Rank JAR 148	Just Keep It Up/You Made Me Care	8
59	Top Rank JAR 237	So Many Ways/I Wonder	7
61	Pye Int. 7N 25069	Happy Feet/The Busker	6

MANFRED MANN

63	HMV POP 1189	Why Should We Not/Brother Jack	35
63	HMV POP 1225	Cock-A-Hoop/Now You're Needing Me	25
64	HMV POP 1252	5-4-3-2-1/Without You	8
64	HMV POP 1282	Hubble Bubble (Toil And Trouble)/I'm Your Kingpin	8
64	HMV POP 1320	Do Wah Diddy Diddy/What You Gonna Do?	5
64	HMV POP 1346	Sha La La/John Hardy	6
65	HMV POP 1381	Come Tomorrow/What Did I Do Wrong?	5
65	HMV POP 1413	Oh No Not My Baby/What Am I Doing Wrong	6
65	HMV POP 1466	If You Gotta Go, Go Now/Stay Around	6
66	HMV POP 1541	You Gave Me Somebody To Love/Poison Ivy	10
65	HMV 7TEA 2124	There's No Living Without Your Loving/Tired Of Trying, Bored With Lying, Scared Of Dying (demo-only EP sampler)	30
66	Fontana TF 730	Just Like A Woman/I Wanna Be Rich	6
66	Fontana TF 757	Semi-Detached, Suburban Mr. James/Morning After The Party	5
67	Fontana TF 812	Ha! Ha! Said The Clown/Feeling So Good (in p/s)	8
67	Fontana TF 828	Sweet Pea/One Way	10
67	Fontana TF 862	So Long, Dad/Funniest Gig	7
68	Fontana TF 908	Up The Junction/Sleepy Hollow (in p/s)	18
68	Fontana TF 908	Up The Junction/Sleepy Hollow	5
68	Fontana TF 943	My Name Is Jack/There Is A Man	5
68	Fontana TF 985	Fox On The Run/Too Many People	5
69	Fontana TF 1013	Ragamuffin Man/A 'B' Side	8
64	HMV 7EG 8848	MANFRED MANN'S COCK-A-HOOP WITH 54321 (EP)	25
65	HMV 7EG 8876	GROOVIN' WITH MANFRED MANN (EP)	20
65	HMV 7EG 8908	THE ONE IN THE MIDDLE (EP)	10
65	HMV 7EG 8922	NO LIVING WITHOUT LOVING (EP)	18
66	HMV 7EG 8942	MACHINES (EP)	25
66	HMV 7EG 8949	INSTRUMENTAL ASYLUM (EP, with Jack Bruce)	25
66	HMV 7EG 8962	AS WAS (EP)	25
66	Fontana TE 17483	INSTRUMENTAL ASSASSINATION (EP)	12
64	HMV CLP 1731	THE FIVE FACES OF MANFRED MANN (LP)	80
64	Odeon PCLP 1731	THE FIVE FACES OF MANFRED MANN (LP, export issue gold/red odeon sticker on cover)	90
65	HMV CLP 1911	MANN MADE (LP, mono)	30
65	HMV CSD 1628	MANN MADE (LP, stereo)	40
66	HMV CLP 3559	MANN MADE HITS (LP)	35
66	Fontana TL 5377	AS IS (LP, 'alcove' cover, mono)	20
66	Fontana (S)TL 5377	AS IS (LP, 'alcove' cover, stereo)	30
66	Fontana (S)TL 5377	AS IS (LP, 'locomotive' cover, mono/stereo)	60
67	HMV CLP 3594	SOUL OF MANN (LP, mono)	50
67	HMV CSD 3594	SOUL OF MANN (LP, stereo)	70

68	Fontana (S)TL 5460	UP THE JUNCTION - ORIGINAL SOUNDTRACK RECORDING (LP)	60
68	Fontana SFL 13003	WHAT A MANN (LP)	18
68	Fontana TL 5470	MIGHTY GARVEY! (LP, mono)	25
68	Fontana (S)TL 5470	MIGHTY GARVEY! (LP, stereo)	15
70	Fontana 6852 005	UP THE JUNCTION - ORIGINAL SOUNDTRACK RECORDING (LP, reissue)	25

(see also Paul Jones, Blues Band, Mike Hugg, Henry Lowther, Mike D'Abo, McGuinness Flint, Jack Bruce, Coulson & Dean, Lyn Dobson, Paddy Klaus & Gibson)

MANFRED MANN & MIKE HUG(G)

71	Ski SKI 1	Ski 'Full-Of-Fitness' Theme/Baby Jane (in p/s)	15
71	Ski SKI 1	Ski 'Full-Of-Fitness' Theme/Baby Jane	7
71	Michelin MIC+01	The Michelin Theme (Go Radial, Go Michelin) (1-sided, gatefold p/s)	15

MANFRED MANN'S CHAPTER III

70	Vertigo 6059 012	Happy Being Me/Devil Woman	10
69	Vertigo VO 3	MANFRED MANN CHAPTER III (LP, 1st pressing, "Manfred Mann Chapter Three" and VO 3 847 902 VTY" in large type on B side, gatefold sleeve, large swirl label)	125
70	Vertigo VO 3	MANFRED MANN CHAPTER III (LP, 2nd pressing, "Manfred Mann Chapter Three" and VO 3 847 902 VTY" in smaller type on B side, gatefold sleeve, large swirl label)	80
70	Vertigo 6360 012	MANFRED MANN CHAPTER III VOL. 2 (LP, gatefold sleeve, large swirl label)	100

MANFRED MANN'S EARTH BAND

71	Philips 6006 122	Living Without You/Tribute (as Manfred Mann)	6
71	Philips 6006 159	Mrs Henry/Prayer (as Manfred Mann)	6
72	Philips 6006 251	Meat/Glorified Magnified (as Earth Band)	6
73	Vertigo 6059 078	Get Your Rocks Off/Sadjoy (as Earth Band)	7
79	Bronze BPO 77	Don't Kill It Carol/Blinded By The Light (picture disc)	7
71	Philips 6308 062	STEPPING SIDEWAYS (LP, unissued)	0
72	Philips 6308 086	MANFRED MANN'S EARTH BAND (LP, black/silver labels)	40
72	Philips 6308 125	GLORIFIED MAGNIFIED (LP, gatefold sleeve, 1st pressing, black/silver labels)	50
72	Philips 6308 086	GLORIFIED MAGNIFIED (LP, gatefold sleeve, 2nd pressing, blue/silver labels)	20
73	Vertigo 6360 087	MESSIN' (LP, die cut gatefold sleeve, 'spaceship' label)	25
73	Bronze ILPS 9265	SOLAR FIRE (LP, gatefold sleeve, lyric inner sleeve, Island label credit)	20
74	Bronze ILPS 9306	THE GOOD EARTH (LP, lyric inner sleeve with uncut corner, Island label credit)	20
75	Bronze ILPS 9337	NIGHTINGALES AND BOMBERS (LP, 1st pressing with Island matrix numbers ILPS 9337 A-2U/B-2U, "MELYS I.B.C" etched into dead wax)	20

(see also Australian Playboys, Trifle, AC/DC, Thin Lizzy, Alan Parsons Project, Skeleton Crew, Jeff Wayne)

ROBERTO MANN ORCHESTRA

| 69 | Deram DM 249 | Theme From The Film "Baby Love" (Guai Guai)/Serenade To Summertime | 6 |
| 68 | Decca F13904 | Love Theme From Witchfinder General/Both Sides Now | 30 |

SHADOW MANN

| 69 | Roulette RO 504 | Come Live With Me/One By One | 12 |

SHELLY MANNE

68	Atlantic 584 180	Daktari/Out On A Limb	12
54	Vogue LDE 072	SHELLY MANNE AND HIS MEN VOL. 1 (10" LP)	15
55	Contemporary LDC 143	SHELLY MANNE VOL. 2 (10" LP, with Andre Previn & Leroy Vinegar)	15
56	Contemporary LDC 190	SHELLY MANNE, SHORTY ROGERS AND JIMMY GIUFFRE - THE THREE (10" LP)	15
56	Contemporary LDC 192	SHELLY MANNE AND RUSS FREEMAN (10" LP)	15
56	Contemporary LAC 12075	SHELLY MANNE AND HIS FRIENDS (LP, with Andre Previn & Leroy Vinegar)	15
61	Contemporary LAC 12305/6	AT THE MANNE HOLE (2-LP)	15
65	Stateside SL 10125	SHELLY MANNE AND CO. (LP)	12
62	Contemporary LAC12315	CHECKMATE (LP)	15

(see also Gerry Mulligan & Shelly Manne, Shorty Rogers & His Orchestra)

MANNIN FOLK

| 76 | Kelly MAN 2 | KING OF THE SEA (LP) | 35 |
| 70s | Kelly KEP 1 | MANNIN FOLK SING (LP) | 20 |

BOB MANNING

54	Capitol CL 14190	I'm A Fool For You/It's All Right With Me	5
55	Capitol CL 14220	The Very Thought Of You/Just For Laughs	5
55	Capitol CL 14256	Majorca (Isle Of Love)/It's My Life	5
55	Capitol CL 14234	My Love Song To You/After My Laughter Came Tears	5
55	Capitol CL 14288	The Mission San Michel/You Are There	5
55	Capitol CL 14318	What A Wonderful Way To Die/Why Didn't You Tell Me?	5

LINDA MANNING

| 66 | King KG 1039 | Buy Me Something Pretty, Joey/Downtown Lonely Girl Blues | 7 |

MARTY MANNING & CHEETAHS

| 67 | CBS 2721 | Tarzan March/Sunny | 10 |

MICHAEL MANNING

| 03 | Ai AI 007 | THE LOST ABERRANT DRAGONFLY EP (12", p/s) | 8 |

EDDIE MANNION

| 60 | HMV POP 804 | Just Driftin'/Quiet Girl | 50 |

MAN ON THE MOON

| 69 | Philips 88457 DE | MAN ON THE MOON (EP, spoken word, 2-part tri-foldout p/s with insert, 'historic souvenir' available via News Of The World newspaper) | 10 |

WINGY MANONE ORCHESTRA

| 57 | Brunswick 05655 | Party Doll/Real Gone | 20 |

MAN...OR ASTROMAN

96	One Louder LOUDER 12	EXPERIMENTAL ZERO (LP, yellow vinyl, with poster)	15
94	One Louder LOUDER 4	YOUR WEIGHT ON THE MOON (10 LP", pink, silver or luminous vinyl)	12
95	Clawfist XPIG 28	WELCOME TO THE SONIC SPACE AGE EP (p/s)	10
95	One Louder LOUD 5	RETURN TO CHAOS EP (string-sealed 'folder' p/s)	8

MANOWAR

83	M. F. Nations 12 KUT 102	Defender (featuring Orson Welles)/Gloves Of Metal (12", p/s)	15
84	10 TEN 3012	All Men Play On 10/Mountains (12", p/s, gatefold)	18
84	10 TEN 3012	All Men Play On 10/Mountains (12", p/s)	12
87	Atlantic B 9463	Blow Your Speakers/Violence And Bloodshed (p/s)	7

MINT VALUE £

87	Atlantic BT 9463	Blow Your Speakers/Violence And Bloodshed (12", embossed p/s, with poster)	12
87	Atlantic BT 9463	Blow Your Speakers/Violence And Bloodshed (12", embossed p/s, without poster)	8
83	Music For Nations MFN 6	INTO ORION RIDE (LP, with inner)	12
84	Music For nations MFN 19	HAIL TO ENGLAND (LP, inner)	12
07	SPV 85601	GODS OF WAR (3-LP)	20

(see also Orson Welles)

MAN PARRISH

| 82 | Polydor POSPX 575 | Hip Hop Be Bop (Don't Stop)/Heatstroke (12") | 8 |
| 82 | Polydor POLD 5101 | MAN PARRISH (LP) | 15 |

JOE MANSANO

69	Blue Cat BS 150	Life On Reggae Planet/RECO & RHYTHM ACES: Z.Z. Beat	40
72	Sioux SI 022	The Trial Of Pama Dice/JACKIE ROWLAND: Lonely Man	15
70	Trojan TBL 106	BRIXTON CAT (LP)	35

(see also Joe The Boss, Joe's Allstars, Dice The Boss)

TONY MANSELL

54	Parlophone MSP 6130	The High And The Mighty/Hold My Hand (with Johnny Dankworth Orchestra)	8
56	Parlophone MSP 6222	Zambesi (Sweet African)/11th Hour Melody (with Johnny Dankworth Orchestra)	8
58	Parlophone R 4471	Impossible/Who Are They To Say	5

(see also Johnny Dankworth)

JAYNE MANSFIELD

| 67 | London HL 10147 | As The Clouds Drift By/Suey (with Jimi Hendrix, demos more common, £35) | 50 |
| 62 | World Record Club TP 262 | JAYNE MANSFIELD IN LAS VEGAS (LP) | 60 |

(see also Jimi Hendrix)

KEITH MANSFIELD ORCHESTRA

68	CBS 3895	Beautiful//Soul Thing	20
68	CBS 63426	ALL YOU NEED IS KEITH MANSFIELD (LP)	40
69	CBS 64666	RACE ON THE WIND (LP)	12
70	CBS 70073	LOOT (LP, soundtrack, with Steve Ellis)	60
72	2066 170	Beautiful/The Colours Are Still There	8

MANSFIELD ORGANISATION

| 67 | President PT131 | Daddy Russian Stoned/Ol' Nick | 20 |

CHARLES MANSON

80	Come Org. WDC 883008	LIE (cassette)	50
86	Fierce FRIGHT 006	Rise/Sick City (p/s, 1 side etched, handwritten labels)	20
88	Fierce FRIGHT 012	It's Comin' Down Fast (Helter Skelter) (p/s, 1 side etched, hand-made labels)	20
86	Fierce FRIGHT 001	LOVE AND TERROR CULT (LP)	30

EDDY MANSON

| 55 | HMV 7M 325 | Oh! No!/The Lovers | 8 |

JEANE MANSON

| 79 | CBS S CBS 7222 | I've Already Seen It In Your Eyes/J'ai Deja Vu Ca Dans Tes Yeux | 15 |

MARILYN MANSON

97	Interscope INVP 95541	The Horrible People/The Not So Beautiful People (10" picture disc)	12
97	Interscope INVP 95552	Tourniquet/(remix) (10" picture disc)	12
98	Nothing INVP 95610	The Dope Show/The Dope Show (10" picture disc, same track on both sides)	12
99	Interscope SAM 175 CD	I Don't Like Drugs (But The Drugs Like Me) (radio edit)/(album version) (CD, card sleeve, promo only)	10
00	Nothing/Universe 4974581	Disposable Teens/Five To One/Diamonds & Pollen (12" picture disc, PVC sleeve.)	10
01	Universal 4974911	The Fight Song/(Slipknot Remix)/(Love Song Remix) (12" picture disc, stickered sleeve)	10
03	Universal 9807728	Mobscene/Paranoiac (poster p/s)	10
03	Universal 9810794	This Is The New Shit/(Goldfrapp Version) (10" picture disc)	10
12	FRY 509	No Reflection (Edit)/No Reflection (Album Version) (white vinyl, p/s)	8
95	Simply Vinyl SVLP 208	SMELLS LIKE CHILDREN (LP, 180 gm vinyl)	18
96	Interscope IND 90086	ANTICHRIST SUPERSTAR (CD, in slipcase)	18
98	Simply Vinyl SVLP 195	MECHANICAL ANIMALS (2-LP, 180 gm vinyl)	20
98	Interscope IND 90273	MECHANICAL ANIMALS (CD, in slipcase)	18
99	Interscope ADV 490 394-2	MECHANICAL ANIMALS (CD, promo, numbered, card sleeve, with comic, PVC slipcase)	45
02	Simply Vinyl SVLP 055	ANTICHRIST SUPERSTAR (2-LP, 180 gm vinyl, gatefold sleeve)	25

MANSUN

95	Polygram no cat. no.	Take It Easy Chicken (Demo)/Naked Twister/Drastic Sturgeon (cassette, promo only, with title inlay)	25
95	Sci Fi Hi Fi MANSON 1	Take It Easy Chicken/Take It Easy Chicken (as Manson, same track both sides, die-cut sleeve, 500 only; promos with "Manson Promo" on label £30)	15
95	Regal REG 3	Skin Up Pin Up/Flourella (white vinyl)	6
96	Parlophone CDRS 6453	Wide Open Space/The Gods Of Not Very Much/Moronica (Acoustic Version)/Lemonade Secret Drinker (Acoustic Version) (CD, fold-out card p/s)	10
99	fan club MANSUN 001	Taxloss/Everyone Must Win (live) (fanclub-only release)	20
96	Parlophone R 6430	ONE EP (p/s)	12
96	Parlophone R 6437	TWO EP (p/s)	8
97	Parlophone CPCS 7387	ATTACK OF THE GREY LANTERN (2-LP, gatefold sleeve, with inners and poster)	30

JOHN MANTELL

| 65 | CBS 201783 | Remember Child/I'll See You Around | 10 |

MIKE MANTLER

| 75 | Watt WATT 3 | 133/4 (LP, with Carla Bley; with insert) | 20 |

(see also Carla Bley, Jazz Composers Orchestra)

BOB MANTON

| 81 | Mainstreet MS 101 | No Trees In Brixton Prison/Brixton Walkabout (p/s) | 8 |

(see also Purple Hearts)

MANUELLA

| 65 | Decca F 22275 | The Nitty Gritty/Two Shadows | 150 |

MANUFACTURED ROMANCE

| 81 | Fresh FRESH 16 | The Time Of My Life/Room To Breathe (various coloured p/s) | 5 |

MANYANA
80	Modello AVR 1938	LIVE CARROTS (LP, cat. no MHR 101 on sleeve)	15

PHIL MANZANERA (& 801)
76	Island ILPS 9444	801 LIVE (LP)	12

(see also Roxy Music, Quiet Sun, 801)

RAY MANZAREK
74	Mercury SRM 1703	THE WHOLE THING STARTED WITH ROCK'N'ROLL (LP)	15
83	A&M AMLX 64945	CARMINA BURANA (LP, with Philip Glass)	12

(see also Doors, Philip Glass)

MAP OF AFRICA
05	Whatever We Want WEWW 004	Black Skin Blue Eyed Boys (12")	30

MAPLEOAK
70	Decca F 13008	Son Of A Gun/Hurt Me So Much	20
71	Decca SKL 5085	MAPLEOAK (LP, blue/silver label, boxed logo)	160

LUCILLE MAPP
57	Columbia DB 3916	Mangos/On Treasure Island	10
57	Columbia DB 3949	Jamie Boy/Moonlight In Vermont	7
57	Columbia DB 4040	I'm Available/Lovin' Ya, Lovin' Ya, Lovin' Ya	8
58	Columbia DB 4071	Love Is/The Early Birdie	7
58	Columbia DB 4168	Remember When/I'm A Dreamer, Aren't We All?	7
59	Columbia DB 4261	Chinchilla/Follow Me	15
57	Columbia SEG 7726	STREET OF DREAMS (EP)	8
57	Columbia SEG 7773	LUCILLE MAPP (EP)	10

TOMMY MARA
55	MGM SP 1128	Pledging My Love/Honey Bunch	10
58	Felsted AF 109	Where The Blues Of The Night/What Makes You So Lonely	10
59	Felsted AF 116	You Don't Know/Marie	5
59	Felsted AF 123	Until I Hear From You/Now Is The Hour	5
58	Felsted GEP 1003	PRESENTING TOMMY MARA (EP)	12

MARABAR CAVES
85	Tiki MBAR 1	Sally's Place Crew/Seeds That Never Grew	10

(JOSEPH) MARAIS & MIRANDA
53	Columbia SCM 5025	Old Johnnie Goggabie/The Zulu Warrior	5
59	Fontana H 225	I-Ha-She/The Queen Bee (as Marais & Miranda))	5

MARATHONS
61	Pye International 7N 25088	Peanut Butter/Down In New Orleans	20
61	Vogue V 9185	Peanut Butter/Talkin' Trash	20

MARAUDERS
63	Decca F 11695	That's What I Want/Hey What D'ya Say	15
63	Decca F 11748	Always On My Mind/Heart Full Of Tears	15
64	Decca F 11836	Lucille/Little Egypt	15
65	Fontana TF 609	Baby I Wanna Be Loved/Somebody Told My Girl	20

(see also Danny Davis)

MARBLE STAIRCASE
83	Whaam! WHAAM 11	Still Dreaming/Dark Ages (p/s)	12

MARBLES
68	Polydor 56272	Only One Woman/The Light Of a Burning Candle	5
69	Polydor 56310	The Walls Fell Down/Love You	10
70	Polydor 56378	Breaking Up Is Hard To Do/I Can't See Nobody	6

(see also Graham Bonnet, Fut)

MARBOO
76	EMI 2424	What About Love?/I Remember Sunday Morning	25

MARC & MAMBAS
82	Some Bizzare BZS 512	Fun City/Sleaze (Take It, Shake It)/Taking It And Shaking It (12", p/s, fan club issue, mail-order only)	20
82	Some Bizzare BZS 15	Big Louise/Empty Eyes (unreleased, artwork only)	0
82	Some Bizzare BZS 1512	Big Louise/Empty Eyes/The Dirt Behind The Neon (Sleaze Revisited) (12", unreleased, artwork only)	0
83	Some Bizzare BZS 19	Black Heart/Your Aura (p/s, with postcard insert)	7
83	Some Bizzare BZS 1912	Black Heart/Your Aura/Mamba (12", p/s)	8
83	Some Bizzare BZSDJ 21	Torment/You'll Never See On Sunday (promo)	15
83	Some Bizzare BZS 2112	Torment/First Time/You'll Never See Me On A Sunday/ Megamillionmania - Multimaniamix (12", p/s)	10
82	Some Bizzare B2A 4	UNTITLED (2-LP, gatefold sleeve)	15
83	Some Bizzare BZA 13	TORMENTS & TOREROS (2-LP)	15
84	Gutterhearts GH 1	BITE BLACK AND BLUES - RAOUL & THE RUINED LIVE (LP, fan club issue)	30
92	Some Bizzare 510 298-2	UNTITLED (CD)	18
92	Some Bizzare 812 872-2	TORMENT AND TOREROS (2 x CD)	30

(see also Soft Cell, Marc Almond)

LYDIA MARCELLE
66	Sue WI 4025	Another Kind Of Fellow/I've Never Been Hurt Like This Before	80

MUZZY MARCELLINO
56	London HLU 8355	Mary Lou/MR. FORD & MR. GOON-BONES: Ain't She Sweet	25

MARCELS
61	Pye International 7N 25073	Blue Moon/Goodbye To Love	8
61	Pye International 7N 25083	Summertime/Teeter Totter Love	10
61	Pye International 7N 25105	You Are My Sunshine/Find Another Fool	12
61	Pye International 7N 25114	Heartaches/My Love For You	15
62	Pye International 7N 25124	My Melancholy Baby/Really Need Your Love	15
63	Pye International 7N 25201	I Wanna Be The Leader/Give Me Back Your Love	30
61	Pye Intl. NPL 28016	BLUE MOON (LP)	70

MINT VALUE £

(see also Tommy Regan)

GLORIA MARCH

| 58 | London HLB 8568 | Baby Of Mine/Nippon Wishing Well | 25 |

HAL MARCH

| 58 | London HLD 8534 | Hear Me Good/One Dozen Roses | 25 |

JO MARCH

58	London HLR 8696	Dormi, Dormi, Dormi (Sleep, Sleep, Sleep)/Fare Thee Well, Oh Honey	12
58	London HLR 8696	Dormi, Dormi, Dormi (Sleep, Sleep, Sleep)/Fare Thee Well, Oh Honey (78)	12
58	London HLR 8763	The Virgin Mary Had One Son/I, Said The Donkey	5

(LITTLE) PEGGY MARCH

63	RCA RCA 1338	I Will Follow Him/Wind Up Doll (as Little Peggy March)	10
63	RCA RCA 1350	My Teenage Castle/I Wish I Were A Princess (as Little Peggy March)	10
63	RCA RCA 1362	Hello Heartache, Goodbye Love/Boy Crazy (as Little Peggy March)	10
64	RCA RCA 1426	Watch What You Do With My Baby/Can't Stop (Peggy March)	10
65	RCA RCA 1472	Let Her Go/Your Girl	10
68	RCA RCA 1687	If You Loved Me/Thinking Through My Tears	30
68	RCA RCA 1687	If You Loved Me/Thinking Through My Tears (DJ copy)	60
68	RCA RCA 1752	I've Been Here Before/Time And Time Again	7
69	RCA RCA 1809	What Am I Going To Do Without You/Lilac Skies	7

BOBBY MARCHAN

| 68 | Atlantic 584 155 | Get Down With It/Half A Mind | 12 |
| 69 | Action ACT 4533 | Ain't No Reason For Girls To Be Lonely Parts 1 & 2 | 20 |

(see also Huey 'Piano' Smith & Clowns)

VICTOR MARCHESE

| 53 | MGM SP 1018 | Fandango/Flamingo | 5 |

MARCH HARE

| 68 | Chapter One CH 101 | Cry My Heart/With My Eyes Closed | 20 |
| 69 | Deram DM 258 | I Could Make It There With You/Have We Got News For You | 30 |

(see also Gary & Stu, Koobas)

MARCHING GIRLS

| 81 | Pop:Aural POP 011 | True Love/First In Line (p/s) | 5 |

MARCH VIOLETS

| 82 | Merciful Release MR 013 | Religious As Hell/Fodder/Children On Stun/Bon Bon Babies (p/s) | 20 |
| 83 | Merciful Release MR 017 | Grooving In Green/Stream (p/s) | 8 |

MARCIA & JEFF

| 68 | Studio One SO 2047 | Words/SHARKS: How Could I Live | 40 |

MARCO

| 74 | Torpedo 31 | Do Me Bump/Bump On | 12 |
| 75 | Torpedo 33 | I'm Coming Home/Instrumental Version | 20 |

MARCUS

| 76 | United Artists UAS 30000 | MARCUS (LP) | 15 |

MARCY JO

| 63 | Stateside SS 235 | Lover's Medley : The More I See You/When I Fall In Love/When You Wore A Tulip | 8 |

(see also Eddie Rambeau)

GUY MARDEL

| 65 | Vogue VRS 7000 | V'Avoue Jamais (actually "N'Avoue Jamais")/Si Tu N'y Crois Pas | 5 |

JANIE MARDEN

55	Decca F 10600	Soldier Boy/Hard To Get	10
55	Decca F 10605	I'll Come When You Call/Thank You For The Waltz (with Frank Weir & His Saxophone)	10
55	Decca F 10673	You Are My Love/A Teen Age Prayer	10
56	Decca F 10765	Allegheny Moon/Magic Melody	10
63	Piccadilly 7N 35128	Make The Night A Little Longer/Walk Alone	10
65	Decca F 12101	They Long To Be Close To You/This Empty Place	15
65	Decca F 12155	You Really Didn't Mean It/Only The One You Love	10

MARDEN HILL

86	él GPO 18	Curtain/Let's Make Shane & MacKenzie (p/s)	10
87	él GPO 30	Robe/Hangman (p/s)	8
88	el GPOT 36	Oh Constance/The Execution Of Emperor Maximillian/Bar Roof Fly (10", p/s)	8

ARIF MARDIN

68	Atlantic 584201	Lullaby From "Rosemary's Baby"/The Blue Bull	6
69	Atlantic 584 295	Glass Onion/How Can I Be Sure	8
73	Atlantic K10309	Theme From Brother Sun, Sister Moon/Yester Year	10

ERNIE MARESCA

62	London HLU 9531	Shout Shout Knock Yourself (Out) /Crying Like A Baby Over You	15
62	London HLU 9579	Mary Jane/Down On The Beach	30
63	London HLU 9720	Love Express/Lorelei	22
64	London HLU 9834	Rovin' Kind/Please Be Fair	15
65	London HLU 10008	It's Their World/I Can't Dance	10
66	Stateside SS 560	Rockin' Boulevard Street/Am I Better Off Than Them	25

MARGAH MAN

| 93 | Margah MMTB1 | Funky Bumpkin (12") | 40 |

MARGARET AND ANGLE

| 72 | Zella JHLPS 128 | KNOCK GOD UP (LP) | 75 |

MARGO

| 69 | Deram DM 274 | The Spark That Lights The flame/Left Over Love | 20 |

MARGO & MARVETTES

64	Parlophone R 5154	Say You Will/Cherry Pie	18
64	Parlophone R 5227	Copper Kettle/So Fine	15
67	Piccadilly 7N 35387	Seven Letters/That's How Love Goes	12

| 67 | Pye 7N 17423 | When Love Slips Away/I'll Be Home (When You Call) ....50 |
| 67 | Pye 7N 17423 | When Love Slips Away/I'll Be Home (When You Call) (DJ copy) ....75 |

(see also Liza Dulittle)

MARGUERITA
| 64 | Black Swan WI 431 | Woman Come/ERIC MORRIS: Number One ....30 |

CHARLES MARGULIS
| 59 | London HLL 8774 | Gigi/Malaguena ....6 |

MARI GRIFFITH
| 73 | Rediffusion ZS131 | MARI GRIFFITH'S WELSH FOLK (LP, with laminated front cover) ....12 |

VERA MARIA
| 69 | NEMS 56-4043 | Martha My Dear/Goodbye Yesterday ....10 |

MARIANNE
| 68 | Columbia DB 8420 | As For Marionettes/You Know My Name ....18 |
| 68 | Columbia DB 8456 | You Had Better Change Your Evil Ways/Like A See Saw ....25 |

MARIANNE & MIKE
| 64 | Vocalion V 9218 | As He Once Was Mine/MARIANNE: Go On ....8 |
| 64 | Vocalion V 9225 | You're The Only One/One Good Turn Deserves Another ....8 |

(see also Friday Brown. These records do not feature Mick Jagger or Marianne Faithfull)

CHARLIE MARIANO
| 56 | London LTZN15031 | CHARLIE MARIANO QUARTET (LP)...70 |

ANNE MARIE
| 65 | Fontana TF 523 | Runaround/There Must Be A Reason ....10 |

MARIE CELESTE
| 71 | Private pressing | AND THEN PERHAPS (LP)...400 |

TEENA MARIE
| 80 | Tamla Motown 12TMG 1203 | I Need Your Lovin'/Behind The Groove (12")..12 |
| 81 | Tamla Motown 12TMG 1251 | Portuguese Love/The Ballad Of Cradle Rob And Me (12") ....15 |

MARIETTA
| 82 | Polydor POSP 305 | You're Only Lonely/Making Up My Mind (p/s, with Rick Parfitt & Andy Bown)........6 |
| 82 | Polydor POSP 483 | Do You Wanna Dance/Only In Your Eyes (p/s, with Rick Parfitt & Andy Bown) ....6 |

(see also Status Quo)

MARILLION
82	EMI EMI 5351	Market Square Heroes/Three Boats Down From The Candy (p/s) 5
82	EMI 12 EMI 5351	Market Square Heroes/Three Boats Down From The Candy/Grendel (12", p/s)........8
82	EMI 12 EMIP 5351	Market Square Heroes/Three Boats Down From The Candy/Grendel (12", picture disc, 3,000 only)........25
83	EMI EMI 5362	He Knows, You Know/Charting The Single (p/s, originally with blue plastic label & paper sleeve) 5
83	EMI 12 EMI 5362	He Knows, You Know/Charting The Single/He Knows, You Know (Full Length Version) (12", p/s)........8
83	EMI 12 EMIP 5362	He Knows, You Know/Charting The Single/He Knows, You Know (Full Length Version) (12", picture disc, unreleased)........0
83	EMI EMI 5393	Garden Party/Margaret (live) (p/s)..5
83	EMI EMIP 5393	Garden Party/Margaret (live) ('jester'-shaped picture disc)................................15
83	EMI 12 EMIS 5393	Garden Party (Extended Version)/Charting The Single (live)/ Margaret (Extended Live Version) (12", p/s with poster) 10
84	EMI 12 MARILP 1	Punch And Judy/Market Square Heroes (New Version)/ Three Boats Down From The Candy (New Version) (12", picture disc) 10
84	EMI MARIL 2	Assassing/Cinderella Search (p/s)..5
84	EMI 12 MARIL 2	Assassing (Full Length Version)/Cinderella Search (Full Length Version) (12", p/s) 15
84	EMI 12 MARILP 2	Assassing (Full Length Version)/Cinderella Search (Full Length Version) (12", picture disc)........10
85	EMI MARILP 3	Kayleigh/Lady Nina (picture disc) 8
85	EMI 12 MARILP 3	Kayleigh (Alternative Mix)/Kayleigh (Extended Version)/ Lady Nina (Extended Version) (12", picture disc) 12
85	EMI 12 MARILP 4	Lavender (Remix)/Freaks/Lavender (12", picture disc) 10
85	EMI 12 MARILP 5	Heart Of Lothian (Full Length Version)/Chelsea Monday (live)/ Heart Of Lothian (7" Version) (12", picture disc) 12
87	EMI 12MARILP 6	Incommunicado (LP Version)/(Alternative Mix)/Going Under (12", picture disc) 8
87	EMI MARILP 7	Sugar Mice (Radio Edit)/Tux On (picture disc with poster)..................................8
87	EMI 12MARILP 7	Sugar Mice (Extended Version)/(Album Version)/Tux On (12", picture disc) 10
87	EMI CD MARIL 7	Sugar Mice (Radio Edit)/Tux On/Sugar Mice (Radio Edit)/ (CD, card p/s, 3,000 only, withdrawn) 15
88	EMI MARILP 9	Freaks (live)/Kayleigh (live) ('jester'-shaped picture disc) 8
99	Raw Power RAWP 2144	MARILLION.COM (CD, 3-track sampler, card p/s, promo only) 10
84	EMI EMCP 3429	SCRIPT FOR A JESTER'S TEAR (LP, picture disc) 20
84	EMI MRLP 1	FUGAZI (LP, picture disc) 18
85	EMI JESTP 1	REAL TO REEL (LP, picture disc) 18
85	EMI MRLP 2	MISPLACED CHILDHOOD (LP, picture disc) 15

(see also Fish, Chemical Alice)

MARINA & THE DIAMONDS
09	Neon Gold GOLD 004	CROWN JEWELS (EP)..30
09	679 Recordings 679L168	Mogwli's Road/Space And The Woods (20o only, in envelope, numbered and signed) 30
10	679 Recordings 679L173X	I Am Not A Robot/I Am Not A Robot (Clock Opera Remix) (p/s, signed edition)................10

MARINE GIRLS
82	In Phaze COD 2	On My Mind/The Lure Of The Rockpools (p/s, with insert) 15
82	Cherry Red CHERRY 40	On My Mind/The Lure Of The Rockpools (reissue, different p/s) 5
80	private release	A DAY BY THE SEA (cassette, 50 copies only)..50
81	In Phaze Tapes 002	BEACH PARTY (cassette, with photocopied drawings, game & handmade sleeve)........40
81	Whaam!/In Phaze COD 1	BEACH PARTY (LP, black & white sleeve & labels, with 2 inserts) 15

(see also Tracey Thorn, Everything But The Girl, Jane, Grab Grab The Haddock)

MARINERS
| 55 | London HLA 8201 | I Love You Fair Dinkum/(At The) Steamboat River Ball.......................................10 |
| 56 | London HA-A 2007 | SPIRITUALS (LP) ....12 |

MINT VALUE £

MARINO MARINI QUARTET

58	Durium DC 16632	Volare (Nel Blu Dip Into Di Blu)/Come Prima	5
59	Durium DC 16636	Ciao Ciao Bambina (Piove)/Alevamo La Stessa Eta'	5
60	Durium DC 16648	Mustapha/Abbracciami	5
59	Durium DLU 96034	COME PRIMA (10" LP)	12

MARION (FINLAND)

| 73 | Columbia DB 8987 | Tom Tom Tom/My Son John | 15 |

MARIONETTES (1)

65	Decca F 12056	Whirlpool Of Love/Nobody But You	10
65	Parlophone R 5300	Was It Me?/Under The Boardwalk	10
65	Parlophone R 5356	Raining It's Pouring/Pick Up Your Feet (withdrawn)	12
65	Parlophone R 5374	At The End Of The Day/Pick Up Your Feet	7
66	Parlophone R 5416	Like A Man/Tonight It's Going To Storm	20

(see also Rag Dolls [U.K.], Katie Kissoon, Mac Kissoon)

MARIONETTES (2)

| 90 | Maze Music DSMBC | AVE DEMENTIA (LP) | 20 |

MARK & JOHN

| 64 | Decca F 12044 | Walk Right Back/Karen | 6 |

MARK B

| 95 | Jazz Fudge JFR003 | ANY MORE QUESTIONS (EP) | 8 |
| 98 | K'Boro KBR 1002 | New School Dean/It's Impossible (12") | 12 |

MARK B/BLADE

| 98 | Jazz Fudge JFR011 | HITMEN FOR HIRE (EP) | 12 |

(see also Blade)

JON MARK

| 65 | Brunswick 5952 | Paris Bells/Little Town Girl | 12 |
| 69 | Philips BF 1772 | All Neat In Black Stockings/Run To Me | 10 |

(see also Johnny Almond Music Machine, John Mayall, Mark-Almond)

LOUISA MARK

75	Safari SF 1109	All My Loving/Sitting By The Wayside	10
77	Trojan TRO 9005	Keep It Like It Is/TROJANS: Fatty Bum Bum Gone To Jail	15
78	Bushays BFM 100	Even Though You're Gone/Gone Clear (12")	10
79	Bushays BFM 107	Six Street Six/Instrumental (12")	12
79	Safari SF1105	Caught You In A Lie/Caught Dubbing	20
79	Robot RRS 2	Six Street Six/Version	8
81	Bushays BFM LP 101	BREAKOUT (LP)	35

MARK-ALMOND

71	Harvest HAR 5044	The City/The Ghetto	12
71	Harvest SHSP 4011	MARK-ALMOND (LP, no EMI logo on label)	25
73	Harvest SHVL 809	RISING (LP, EMI logo on label)	20

(see also Johnny Almond Music Machine, Jon Mark, John Mayall)

MARKETTS

62	Liberty LIB 55401	Surfer's Stomp/Start (as Mar-kets)	15
62	Liberty LIB 55443	Balboa Blue/Stompede	15
64	Warner Bros WB 120	Out Of Limits/Bella Delana	30
64	Warner Bros WB 130	Vanishing Point/Borealis	20
66	Warner Bros WB 5696	The Batman Theme/Richie's Theme (with p/s)	40
66	Warner Bros WB 5696	The Batman Theme/Richie's Theme	20
67	Warner Bros WB 5847	Tarzan's March/Stirrin' Up Some Soul	50
67	Warner Bros WB 5847	Tarzan's March/Stirrin' Up Some Soul (DJ copy)	75
63	Warner Bros WM 8140	THE MARKETTS TAKE TO WHEELS (LP)	50
64	Warner Bros WM 8147	OUT OF LIMITS (LP)	40
66	Warner Bros W 1642	BATMAN (LP)	50

MAR-KEYS

61	London HLK 9399	Last Night/Night Before	25
61	London HLK 9449	Morning After/Diana	20
62	London HLK 9510	Foxy/One Degree North	20
66	Atlantic AT 4079	Philly Dog/Honey Pot	20
67	Atlantic 584 074	Last Night/Night Before	12
69	Stax STAX 132	Black/Jive Man	7
62	London HA-K 8011	DO THE POP-EYE (LP)	70
66	Atlantic 587/588 024	THE GREAT MEMPHIS SOUND (LP)	30
68	Atlantic 587/588 135	MELLOW JELLY (LP)	25
69	Stax SXATS 1021	DAMNIFIKNOW! (LP)	20
69	Stax 2363 008	DAMNIFIKNOW! (LP, reissue)	12

(see also Booker T. & M.G.'s)

MARK FIVE

| 64 | Fontana TF 513 | Baby What's Wrong/Tango | 60 |

(see also Nazareth)

MARK FOUR

64	Mercury MF 815	Rock Around The Clock/Slow Down	30
64	Mercury MF 825	Try It Baby/Crazy Country Hop	65
65	Decca F 12204	Hurt Me If You Will/I'm Leaving	70
66	Fontana TF 664	Work All Day (Sleep All Night)/Going Down Fast	100
85	Bam-Caruso OPRA 037	LIVE AT THE BEAT SCENE CLUB (EP, promo, 500 only)	12

(see also Creation)

PIGMEAT MARKHAM

| 68 | Chess CRS 8077 | Here Comes The Judge/The Trial | 12 |
| 68 | Chess CRS 8085 | Sock It To 'Em Judge/The Hip Judge | 15 |

MARK II

| 60 | Columbia DB 4549 | Night Theme/Confusion | 10 |

MARK IV

59	Mercury AMT 1025	Aah-Oo-Gah/I Got A Wife	10
59	Mercury AMT 1025	Aah-Oo-Gah/I Got A Wife (78)	12
59	Mercury AMT 1045	Move Over Rover/Dante's Inferno	10
59	Mercury AMT 1060	Ring, Ring, Ring Those Bells/Mairzy Doats	5

ALISON MARKLEW BAND

75	Pinnacle P 8412	Midnight Rider/Tumbledown	8

GUY MARKS

68	Stateside SS 2107	Loving you Has Made Me Bananas/Forgive Me My Love	6

MARKSMEN

63	Parlophone R 5075	Smersh/Orbit Three	20

(see also Mark Rogers & Marksmen, Houston Wells & Marksmen)

MIKE MARLAN

73	Bronze ILPS 9221	FAIR WARNING (LP, gatefold sleeve, label with Island credit)	20

BOB MARLEY/WAILERS
SINGLES

63	Island WI 088	Judge Not/Do You Still Love Me (as Robert Marley)	300
63	Island WI 128	ERNEST RANGLIN: Exodus/R. MARLEY: One Cup Of Coffee	300
65	Island WI 188	It Hurts To Be Alone/Mr. Talkative	90
65	Island WI 206	Play Boy/Your Love	90
65	Island WI 211	Hoot Nanny Hoot (actually by Peter Tosh & Wailers)/ BOB MARLEY: Do You Remember (actually with Wailers)	100
65	Island WI 212	Hooligan/Maga Dog (B-side actually by Peter Tosh & Wailers)	70
65	Island WI 215	Shame And Scandal (as Peter Touch [Tosh] & Wailers)/The Jerk	40
65	Island WI 216	Donna/Don't Ever Leave Me	40
65	Island WI 254	What's New Pussycat/Where Will I Find	50
65	Ska Beat JB 186	Simmer Down/I Don't Need Your Love	75
65	Ska Beat JB 211	Lonesome Feelings/There She Goes	70
65	Ska Beat JB 226	I Made A Mistake/SOUL BROTHERS: Train To Skaville	45
66	Ska Beat JB 228	Love And Affection/Teenager In Love	70
66	Ska Beat JB 230	And I Love Her/Do It Right	70
66	Ska Beat JB 249	Lonesome Tracks/Zimmerman	60
66	Island WI 260	Jumbie Jamboree/SKATALITES: Independent Anniversary Ska (I Should Have Known Better)	80
66	Island WI 268	Put It On/Love Won't Be Mine	30
66	Island WI 3001	He Who Feels It Knows It/Sunday Morning	90
66	Island WI 3009	Let Him Go (Rude Boy Get Bail)/Sinner Man (B-side matrix: WI-3009B+)	70
66	Island WI 3009	Let Him Go (Rude Boy Get Bail)/The Masher (actually by Beverley's All Stars or Soul Brothers) (B-side matrix: WI-3009 B+2)	70
66	Rio R 116	Dancing Shoes/Don't Look Back	35
66	Doctor Bird DB 1013	Rude Boy/ROLANDO AL & SOUL BROTHERS: Ringo's Theme (This Boy)	90
66	Doctor Bird DB 1021	Good Good Rudie (Jailhouse)/CITY SLICKERS: Oceans II	60
66	Doctor Bird DB 1039	Rasta Put It On/ROLAND AL & SOUL BROTHERS: Ska With Ringo	100
67	Island WI 3035	Baby I Need You (credited to Ken Boothe)/KEN BOOTHE: I Don't Want To See You Cry	90
67	Island WI 3042	I Am The Toughest (by Peter Touch [Tosh] & Wailers)/ MARCIA GRIFFITHS: No Faith	70
67	Island WI 3043	Bend Down Low/Freedom Time	70
67	Coxsone CS 7021	Oh My Darling/HAMLINS: Trying To Keep A Good Man Down	90
67	Doctor Bird DB 1091	Nice Time/Hypocrite	65
67	Studio One SO 2010	Have Faith In The Lord (with Heavenly Sisters; actually by Peter Austin)/ JOE HIGGS: Dinah	40
67	Studio One SO 2024	I Stand Predominate/NORMA FRAZER: Come By Here	250
68	Fab FAB 34	Pound Get A Blow/Funeral (white label only)	100
68	Fab FAB 36	Thank You Lord/Mellow Mood (white label only)	170
68	Fab FAB 37	Nice Time/Hypocrites (white label only)	80
68	Fab FAB 41	Burial/Bus Them Shut (existence unconfirmed)	0
68	Trojan TR 617	Stir It Up/This Train	45
70	Bamboo BAM 55	Jailhouse (Good Rudy)/JOHN HOLT: A Stranger In Love	40

(Credited to Wailers unless stated.)

70	Trojan TR 7759	Soul Shake Down Party/BEVERLY'S ALLSTARS: Version	25
70	Escort ERT 842	Run For Cover/To The Rescue	70
70	Unity UN 562	Duppy Conqueror/UPSETTERS: Duppy Conqueror (Version)	40
70	Jackpot JP 730	Mr Chatterbox (as Wailing Wailers)/DOREEN SHAEFFER: Walk Thru' This World	35
70	Upsetter US 340	My Cup (solo)/LEE PERRY & WAILERS: Son Of Thunder	35
70	Upsetter US 342	Version Of Cup (solo)/UPSETTERS: Dreamland	45
70	Upsetter US 348	Doppy Conqueror (song actually titled "Duppy Conqueror" but plays Runaway Child by Dave Barker)/UPSETTERS: Justice	20
70	Upsetter US 349	UPSETTERS: Upsetting Station (actually plays "Dig Your Grave" by Bob Marley & Wailers/UPSETTERS: Justice (Instrumental)	40
71	Upsetter US 354	Mr. Brown/UPSETTERS: Dracula	35
71	Upsetter US 356	Kaya/UPSETTERS: Version	35
71	Upsetter US 357	Small Axe/All In One	20
71	Upsetter US 368	Picture On The Wall (as Rass Dawkins & Wailers)/UPSETTERS: Version	22
71	Upsetter US 369	More Axe (as Bob Marley)/UPSETTERS: Axe Man	25
71	Upsetter US 371	Dreamland (as Wailers)/UPSETTERS: Version	25
71	Upsetter US 372	More Axe (as Bob Marley, different version)/UPSETTERS: Axe Man	25
71	Bullet BU 464	Soultown/Let The Sun Shine On Me	45
71	Bullet BU 493	Lick Samba/Samba	35
71	Punch PH 69	Small Axe/DAVE BARKER: What A Confusion	45
71	Punch PH 77	Down Presser (as Wailers)/JUNIOR BYLES: Got The Tip	40
71	Summit SUM 8526	Stop The Train/Caution (as Wailers)	35
71	Green Door GD 4005	Trench Town Rock/Grooving Kingston 12	25
71	Green Door GD 4022	Lively Yourself Up/TOMMY McCOOK: Lively	25
72	Green Door GD 4025	Guava Jelly/Redder Than Red	20
72	Upsetter US 392	Keep On Moving/African Herbsman	25
72	CBS 8114	Reggae On Broadway/Oh Lord, I Got To Get There (as Wailers)	20
73	Blue Mountain BM 1021	Baby Baby We've Got A Date/Stop That Train	15
73	Punch PH 101	Screw Face/Face Man	20
73	Punch PH 102	Lively Up Yourself/TOMMY McCOOK: Version	20
73	Supreme SUP 216	I Like It Like This (as Bob Marley)/(other artist)	45

Year	Label/Cat No	Title	Value
73	Island WIP 6164	Concrete Jungle/Reincarnated Soul	8
73	Island WIP 6167	Get Up, Stand Up/Slave Driver (as Wailers)	8
73	Island IDJ 2	I Shot The Sheriff/Pass It On/Duppy Conqueror (promo only)	30
74	Island 12WIP 6244	No Woman No Cry/Jamming (12", p/s)	8
74	Trojan TR 7911	Soul Shake Down Party/Caution	8
74	Trojan TR 7926	Mr Brown/Version	10
75	Island WIP 6212	So Jah Seh/Natty Dread	5
76	Island WIP 6478	Stir It Up/Rat Race (withdrawn, demos only)	15
77	Island WIP 6390	Exodus/Exodus (dub)	5
77	Island WIP 6402	Waiting In Vain/Roots	5
77	Island WIP 6402 1DJ	Promotional Advert For "Exodus" (handwritten label, same track both sides, with Marley commentary)	30
77	Island WIP 6410	Jamming/Punky Reggae Party (p/s)	5
77	Island IPR 2000	Exodus (7:38) / Exodus (3:08, inst. version)(12", pre-release Island sleeve)	8
78	Island WIP 6420	Is This Love?/Crisis (Version) (p/s)	5
78	Island WIP 6440	Satisfy My Soul/Smile Jamaica (p/s)	5
78	Island IPR 2026	War/No More Trouble/Jamming (12", p/s)	8
83	Island ISP 180	Waiting In Vain/Blackman Redemption (picture disc)	8
84	Daddy Kool DK 12101	Rainbow Country (Vocal)/Rainbow Country (Dub)/PABLO & UPSETTERS: Lama Lava (12", p/s)	15
84	Daddy Kool DK 12102	Natural Mystic/Natural Mystic Rhythm (12", p/s)	15
84	Island 12ISPX 169	One Love/One Love (Dub Version) (p/s)	7
84	Island 12ISP 169	One Love/One Love (Dub Version) (12", white label, p/s)	8
84	Island 12ISPP 169	One Love/One Love (Dub Version) (12", picture disc)	12
80s	Island 12 BMRM 1	Get Up Stand Up/Get Up Stand Up (live) ('Rasta' p/s, promo only)	8
99	Columbia XPR 2533	Turn Your Lights Down Low (with Lauryn Hill)/(original version) (die-cut p/s, promo only)	8

ALBUMS

Year	Label/Cat No	Title	Value
71	Upsetter TBL 126	SOUL REBEL	100
71	Trojan TBL 126	SOUL REBEL (reissue)	50
71	Trojan TTL 66A/B	SOUL REVOLUTION (LP, white label, test pressing only)	125
72	Island ILPS 9241	CATCH A FIRE (original 'pink rim' label, 'zippo lighter' sleeve)	150
73	Island ILPS 9256	BURNIN' (original label, gatefold sleeve with photos on innner)	20
73	Trojan TRLS 62	AFRICAN HERBSMAN (original issue with "12 Neasden Lane" address and rough orange/white paper labels)	40
73	BBC TS 133425/6	POP SPECTACULAR IN CONCERT (LP, in buff sleeve with printed sheets)	300
73	Black Power PW2	WAILERS (LP, no title, no sleeve, pink label)	40
74	Trojan TRLS 89	RASTA REVOLUTION (reissue of TBL 126 with 2 extra tracks)	20
75	Island ISS 3	BOB MARLEY & THE WAILERS RADIO SAMPLER (with photos & press release, promo only)	30
75	Island ISS 3	BOB MARLEY & THE WAILERS RADIO SAMPLER (promo only)	12
77	BBC	ROCK GOES TO COLLEGE IN CONCERT (LP, re-issue of BBC TS 133425/6)	80
83	Island PILPS 97690	CONFRONTATION (picture disc)	25
84	Island BMSP 100	THE BOX SET (All 9 Island albums in presentation box - 10,000 only)	125
84	Island PBMW 1	LEGEND - THE BEST OF BOB MARLEY (picture disc)	12

(see also Peter Tosh, Rita Marley, Ernest Ranglin, Interns, Skatalites, Rass Dawkins & Wailers, Family Man, Norma Frazer)

RITA MARLEY

Year	Label/Cat No	Title	Value
65	Island WI-226	One More Chance (as Rita and Soulettes)/SKALITES: Dick Tracey	75
67	Rio R 108	Pied Piper/It's Alright	80
67	Island WI 3052	Come To Me/SOUL BOYS: Blood Pressure	70

(see also Soulettes, Soul Brothers)

LAURA MARLING

Year	Label/Cat No	Title	Value
07	Way Out West WOW 003	LONDON TOWN EP (500 only)	45
07	Virgin VS 1956	MY MANIC AND I EP (with separate promotional booklet)	30
07	Virgin VS 1956	MY MANIC AND I EP (signed with booklet)	18
07	Virgin VS 1956	MY MANIC AND I EP (unsigned with booklet)	12
08	Virgin VS 1964	Ghosts/Man Sings About Romance	10
08	Virgin VS 1973	Cross Your Fingers/I'm A Fly	8
09	Virgin VS 1979	Night Terror/Alpha Shallows	15
09	Virgin VS 2004	Goodbye England (Covered In Snow) (1-sided)	15
10	Third Man TMR 044	Blues Run The Game/The Needle And The Damage Done (US pressing but 100 shipped over and sold in UK, 3 colour vinyl, signed)	50
08	Virgin V 3040	ALAS I CANNOT SWIM (LP, with bonus DVD)	30
08	Virgin CDVX 3040	ALAS I CANNOT SWIM (CD box with book and assorted printed ephemera)	20
10	Diverse DIV 028LP	I SPEAK BECAUSE I CAN (LP, gatefold)	18
11	Virgin CDVX 3091	A CREATURE I DON'T KNOW (Box set, picture disc LP, CD, DVD, postcard, slide viewer and booklet)	40

MICKI MARLO

Year	Label/Cat No	Title	Value
55	Capitol CL 14271	Prize Of Gold/Foolish Notion	15
57	London HL 8481	That's Right/What You've Done To Me (B-side with Paul Anka)	25

(see also Paul Anka)

MARLON

Year	Label/Cat No	Title	Value
74	Purple PUR 120	Let's Go To The Disco/Broken Man	7

(see also Roger Glover, Ray Fenwick)

ROBERT MARLOW

Year	Label/Cat No	Title	Value
83	Reset 7REST 1	Pictures Of Dorian Grey/The Tale Of Dorian Grey (p/s)	5
83	Reset 12REST 1	Pictures Of Dorian Grey/The Tale Of Dorian Grey (12", p/s)	10
83	Reset 7REST 3	I Just Want To Dance/No Heart (p/s)	5
83	Reset 7RESTP 3	I Just Want To Dance/No Heart (picture disc)	6
83	Reset 12REST 3	I Just Want To Dance/No Heart (12", p/s)	10
84	Reset 12REST 4	Claudette/This Happy World (12", p/s)	10
85	Reset 7REST 6	Calling All Destroyers/In Retrospect (p/s)	10
85	Reset 12REST 6	Calling All Destroyers/In Retrosepct (12", p/s, existence unconfirmed)	0

(see also Vince Clarke, Erasure)

MARION MARLOWE

Year	Label/Cat No	Title	Value
56	London HLA 8306	The Hands Of Time/Ring, Phone, Ring (withdrawn)	100
56	London HLA 8306	The Hands Of Time/Ring, Phone, Ring (78)	50

MARMALADE

66	CBS 202340	It's All Leading Up To Saturday Night/Wait A Minute Baby	20
67	CBS 202643	Can't Stop Now/There Ain't No Use In Hangin' On	25
67	CBS 2948	I See The Rain/Laughing Man	25
67	CBS 3088	Man In A Shop/Cry	15
68	CBS 3412	Lovin' Things/Hey Joe	6
68	CBS 3708	Wait For Me Mary-Anne/Mess Around	12
68	CBS 3892	Ob-La-Di, Ob-La-Da/Chains	5
69	CBS 4287	Baby Make It Soon/Time Is On My Side	6
69	CBS 4615	Butterfly/I Shall Be Released	6
68	CBS 63414	THERE'S A LOT OF IT ABOUT (LP)	20
70	CBS PR 36	THE BEST OF THE MARMALADE (LP)	15
70	Decca SKL 5047	REFLECTIONS OF THE MARMALADE (LP)	15
71	Decca SKL 5111	SONGS (LP)	15

(see also Dean Ford [& Gaylords], Gaylords, Junior Campbell, Chris McClure Section)

MARQUIS DE SADE

81	Xpose XP-02	Somewhere Up In The Mountain/Black Angel (p/s with insert)	200
82	Out Of Town HOOT 8	Crystal Grieff/Vampire Affair (p/s)	5

MARQUIS OF KENSINGTON

67	Immediate IM 052	Changing Of The Guard/Reverse Thrust	30

HANK MARR

60	Blue Beat BB 26	Tonk Game/Hob-Nobbin	15

RANDY MARR

70	Warner Bros WB 6115	I Wonder Who's Kissing Her Now/1941	6

MARRAKESH

73	Bell Bell 1325	The Prodigal Son Returns/Let Me Down Easy	12
73	Bell 1315	I Don't Wanna Say Goodnight/Stone	7

MARRATXI

79	Clubland SJP 901	Rock With Me/Swedish Lady	150

MARRIAGE

71	Decca F13178	Ever Find Yourself Running/She Follows The Band	6

A MARRIAGE OF CONVENIENCE

85	Stranglers Info Service SIS2	My Young Dreams/Two Sides To Every Story (no p/s, fan club issue)	5

(see also Stranglers)

STEVE MARRIOTT

63	Decca F 11619	Give Her My Regards/Imaginary Love	175
76	A&M AMS 7230	Star In My Life/Midnight Rollin'	8
85	Aura AUS 145	Wha'cha Gonna Do About It/All Shook Up	8
76	A&M AMLH 64572	MARRIOTT (LP)	20
85	Aura AUL 792	PACKET OF THREE (LP)	12

(see also Small Faces, Humble Pie, Spectrum, Pollcats)

MARS FENWICK BAND

86	President PT 556	Fire In The City/A Lover Not A Fighter	5
86	President PTLS 1083	FIRE IN THE CITY (LP)	12

JOHNNY MARS

81	Ace NS 73	Born Under A Bad Sign/Horses And Places/Mighty Mars (p/s, withdrawn)	5
72	Polydor 2460 168	BLUES FROM MARS (LP)	15

BERNIE MARSDEN

81	Parlophone R6047	Sad Clown/You And Me (p/s)	6
81	Parlophone R6050	Look At Me Now/Always Love You So (p/s)	6
81	Parlophone R6052	Shakey Ground/After All The Madness (p/s)	6
82	Parlophone R6053	Thunder And Lightning/Bylbo's Shack (p/s)	6
79	Parlophone PCS 7215	AND ABOUT TIME TOO (LP, with inner sleeve)	12
81	Parlophone PCS 7217	LOOK AT ME NOW (LP, with inner sleeve)	12

(see also Jon Lord, Whitesnake, Cozy Powell, Jack Bruce, Babe Ruth, Bogdon)

BERYL MARSDEN

63	Decca F 11707	I Know (You Don't Love Me No More)/I Only Care About You	15
64	Decca F 11819	When The Lovelight Starts Shining Through His Eyes/ Love Is Going To Happen To Me	20
65	Columbia DB 7718	Who You Gonna Hurt?/Gonna Make Him My Baby	35
65	Columbia DB 7797	Music Talk/Break-A-Way	30
66	Columbia DB 7888	What's She Got/Let's Go Somewhere	35

(see also Shotgun Express, She Trinity)

GERRY MARSDEN

67	CBS 2784	Please Let Them Be/I'm Not Blue	10
67	CBS 2946	Gilbert Green/What Makes Me Love You	15
68	CBS 3575	Liverpool/Charlie Girl (as Gerry Marsden & Derek Nimmo)	10
68	NEMS 56-3831	In The Year Of April/Every Day	10
69	NEMS 56-4229	Every Little Minute/In Days Of Old	6
71	Decca F 13172	I've Got My Ukelele/What A Day	6
72	Phoenix NIX 129	Amo Credo/Come Break Bread	5
76	DJM DJS 10708	My Home Town/Lovely Lady (p/s)	10
74	DJM DJS 314	They Don't Make Them Like That Any More/Can't You Hear The Song	6
76	DJM DJS 10708	My Home Town/Lovely Lady	6

(see also Gerry & Pacemakers)

LYNNE MARSDEN

84	Derelict DRL1	Cocktails For Two/Firefly	10

MARSEILLE

84	Ultra Noise ULTRA 3	TOUCH THE NIGHT (LP, with inner sleeve)	12

(see also Paul Dale)

BRENDA MARSH

68	Mercury MF 1044	Cross Town Bus/Close	7

STEVIE MARSH
59	Decca F 11181	If You Were The Only Boy In The World/Leave Me Alone 6
60	Decca F 11209	You Don't Have To Tell Me (I Know)/Wish 10
60	Decca F 11244	A Girl In Love/Over And Done With 10
62	Ember EMB S 139	I Shouldn't Be Kissing You/Time And Time Again 8

WARNE MARSH
| 57 | London LTZ-P 15080 | JAZZ OF TWO CITIES (LP) ....20 |

WAYNE MARSH
| 70 | Wave LP 6 | RELEASE RECORD SEND TAPE (LP) ....20 |
| 75 | Wave LP 10 | JAZZ FROM THE EAST VILLAGE (LP) ....20 |

CHUCK MASHALL & TWIST STARS
| 62 | Brunswick STA 3062 | TWIST TO SONGS EVERYBODY KNOWS (LP) ....15 |

GARY MARSHALL
| 61 | Parlophone R 4758 | One Twitchy Baby/Ev'ry Chance I Get ....12 |
| 60 | Parlophone R 4636 | Oh You Beautiful Doll/Large As Life ....6 |

JACK MARSHALL ORCHESTRA & CHORUS
| 58 | Capitol CL 14888 | Thunder Road Chase/Finger Poppin' ....10 |

JOY MARSHALL
68	Toast 512	And I'll Find You/I'm So Glad You're Back 15
64	Decca F 11863	When You Hold Me Tight /Rain On Snow 12
65	Decca F12189	Heartache Hurry On By/He's For Me 40
65	Decca F 12222	My Love Come Home/When A Girl Really Loves You 12
66	Decca F 12422	The More I See You/Taste Of Honey 20
65	Decca LK 4678	WHO SAYS THEY DON'T WRITE GOOD SONGS ANY MORE? (LP) 25

LARRY MARSHALL
67	Blue Beat BB 374	Move Your Feet/Find A New Baby 65
67	Blue Beat BB 380	Suspicion/Broken Heart 100
67	Doctor Bird DB 1008	Snake In The Grass/ROLAND ALPHONSO: V.C. 10 100
68	Caltone TONE 126	No One To Give Me Love/PHIL PRATT: Safe Travel 175
70	Bamboo BAM 22	Girl Of My Dreams/SOUND DIMENSON: Give It Away 15
70	Bamboo BAM 52	Man From Galilee/Give It Away (as Larry Marshall & Enid Cumberland) 15
70	Bamboo BAM 61	Let's Make It Up/BURNING SPEAR: Free 25
70	Banana BA 300	Stay A Little Longer/MAYTALS: He'll Provide 12
71	Banana BA 364	Maga Dog/OSSIE ROBINSON: Economical Heatwave 12
73	Pama PM 873	True Believer/FLAMES: Water Your Garden 6
75	Ocean OC 004	Can't You Understand/KING TUBBY : Locks Of Dub 18
75	Black & White CP 4326	I Admire You/KING TUBBY: Watergate Rock 10
79	Yard International YI 103	Birdsong/She's Gone (12") 15

(see also Larry & Alvin, Irving Brown, Fitzroy D. Long, Kingston Pete & Buster's Allstars, Max Romeo, Jackie Mittoo)

LOIS MARSHALL
| 59 | HMV ALP 1671 | BRITISH FOLK SONGS (LP) ....12 |

WAYNE MARSHALL
| 85 | Jah Tubbys JT 013 | Give Me The Mix/Mike In My Hand (12", with the Offbeat Posse) ....25 |

WILLIE MARSHALL
| 70 | Torpedo TOR 20 | Loosen Up Strong Man/Strong Man ....5 |

MARSHMALLOW WAY
| 69 | United Artists UP 35031 | C'mon Kitty Kitty/Michigan Mints ....8 |

MARSHMELLOW HIGHWAY
| 68 | London HLR 10204 | I Don't Wanna Live This Way/Loving You Makes Everything Alright ....18 |

MARSUPILAMI
| 70 | Transatlantic TRA 213 | MARSUPILAMI (LP, white/lilac label, 't' logo) ....150 |
| 71 | Transatlantic TRA 230 | ARENA (LP, white/lilac label, 't' logo) ....150 |

LENA MARTELL
| 67 | Pye 7N 17276 | The Pop Group Song/Reflections ....10 |

PIERA MARTELL
| 74 | CBS S CBS 2293 | My Ship Of Love/Mein Ruf Nach Dir ....12 |

RAY MARTELL
70	Joe JRS 3	She Caught The Train/PAMA DICE: Tea House From Emperor Rosko 100
70	Attack ATT 8015	Loving Lover/Cora 6
70	Doctor Bird DB 1503	This Little Light/Lover 6
70	Trojan TR 7787	This Little Light/Lover 6
72	Sioux SI 012	She Caught The Train/JOE'S ALLSTARS: Tony B.'s Theme 12
73	Rays RA 1	Working For My Love/King Fuzz - Downtown Rock 12
73	Rays RA 2	Lover/Dub 8
73	Rays RA 3	I Wish You Luck/Version 8
73	Rays RA 4	Angelina/Angelina Part 2 8
77	Rays RA 077	Falling In Love/Everlasting Love 8

MARTELLS
| 66 | Decca F 12463 | Time To Say Goodnight/The Cherry Song ....40 |

RALPH MARTERIE & HIS ORCHESTRA
| 57 | Mercury MEP 9517 | PRESENTING RALPH MARTERIE (EP) ....8 |

MARTHA & THE MUFFINS
| 80 | DinDisc DID 5 | TRANCE & DANCE (LP, with bonus 7" [WAS E 20]) ....12 |

MARTHA (REEVES) & VANDELLAS
63	Oriole CBA 1814	I'll Have To Let Him Go/My Baby Won't Come Back 450
63	Oriole CBA 1819	Come And Get These Memories/Jealous Lover 275
63	Stateside SS 228	Heatwave/A Love Like Yours (Don't Come Knockin' Every Day) 50
63	Stateside SS 228	Heatwave/A Love Like Yours (Don't Come Knockin' Every Day) (DJ copy) 150
64	Stateside SS 250	Quicksand/Darling, I Hum Our Song 55
64	Stateside SS 250	Quicksand/Darling, I Hum Our Song (DJ copy) 100

64	Stateside SS 272	Live Wire/Old Love (Let's Try It Again)	60
64	Stateside SS 272	Live Wire/Old Love (Let's Try It Again) (DJ copy)	100
64	Stateside SS 305	In My Lonely Room/A Tear For The Girl	80
64	Stateside SS 305	In My Lonely Room/A Tear For The Girl (DJ copy)	150
64	Stateside SS 345	Dancing In The Street/There He Is (At My Door)	20
64	Stateside SS 345	Dancing In The Street/There He Is (At My Door) (DJ copy)	100
65	Stateside SS 383	Wild One/Dancing Slow	50
65	Stateside SS 383	Wild One/Dancing Slow (DJ copy)	200
65	Tamla Motown TMG 502	Nowhere To Run/Motoring	25
65	Tamla Motown TMG 502	Nowhere To Run/Motoring (DJ copy)	120
65	Tamla Motown TMG 530	You've Been In Love Too Long/Love (Makes Me Do Foolish Things)	35
65	Tamla Motown TMG 530	You've Been In Love Too Long/Love (Makes Me Do Foolish Things) (DJ copy)	100
66	Tamla Motown TMG 549	My Baby Loves Me/Never Leave Your Baby's Side	40
66	Tamla Motown TMG 549	My Baby Loves Me/Never Leave Your Baby's Side (DJ copy)	120
66	Tamla Motown TMG 567	What Am I Going To Do Without Your Love/Go Ahead And Laugh	35
66	Tamla Motown TMG 567	What Am I Going To Do Without Your Love/Go Ahead And Laugh (DJ copy)	100
66	Tamla Motown TMG 582	I'm Ready For Love/He Doesn't Love Her Anymore	20
66	Tamla Motown TMG 582	I'm Ready For Love/He Doesn't Love Her Anymore (DJ copy)	50
67	Tamla Motown TMG 599	Jimmy Mack/Third Finger, Left Hand	12
72	Tamla Motown TMG 599	Jimmy Mack/Third Finger, Left Hand (reissue)	6
67	Tamla Motown TMG 621	Love Bug Leave My Heart Alone/One Way Out	35
67	Tamla Motown TMG 621	Love Bug Leave My Heart Alone/One Way Out (DJ copy)	75
68	Tamla Motown TMG 636	Honey Chile/Show Me The Way	18
68	Tamla Motown TMG 657	I Promise To Wait, My Love/Forget Me Not	18
68	Tamla Motown TMG 669	I Can't Dance To That Music You're Playing/I Tried	25
69	Tamla Motown TMG 684	Dancing In The Street/Quicksand	7
69	Tamla Motown TMG 694	Nowhere To Run/Live Wire	7
71	Tamla Motown TMG 762	Forget Me Not/I Gotta Let You Go	7
71	Tamla Motown TMG 794	Bless You/Hope I Don't Get My Heart Broke	7
73	Tamla Motown TMG 843	No One There/(I've Given You) The Best Years Of My Life	75
73	Tamla Motown TMG 843	No One There/(I've Given You) The Best Years Of My Life (DJ Copy)	150
65	Tamla Motown TME 2009	MARTHA AND THE VANDELLAS (EP)	120
66	Tamla Motown TME 2017	HITTIN' (EP)	125
63	Oriole PS 40052	COME AND GET THESE MEMORIES (LP)	400
65	Tamla Motown TML 11005	HEATWAVE (LP)	55
65	Tamla Motown TML 11013	DANCE PARTY (LP)	65
67	Tamla Motown TML 11040	GREATEST HITS (LP, original with flipback sleeve, mono)	25
67	Tamla Motown (S)TML 11040	GREATEST HITS (LP, original with flipback sleeve, stereo)	30
67	Tamla Motown (S)TML 11040	GREATEST HITS (LP, re-pressing non-flipback sleeve)	15
67	Tamla Motown TML 11051	WATCH OUT! (LP, mono)	40
67	Tamla Motown STML 11051	WATCH OUT! (LP, stereo)	45
68	Tamla Motown TML 11078	RIDIN' HIGH (LP, mono)	25
68	Tamla Motown STML 11078	RIDIN' HIGH (LP, stereo)	30
69	Tamla Motown (S)TML 11099	DANCING IN THE STREET (LP, mono/stereo)	25
70	Tamla Motown TML 11134	SUGAR N' SPICE (LP, mono)	25
70	Tamla Motown STML 11134	SUGAR N' SPICE (LP, stereo)	20
70	Tamla Motown STML 11166	NATURAL RESOURCES (LP)	22
72	Tamla Motown STML 11204	BLACK MAGIC (LP)	30

MARTIAN SCHOOLGIRLS

79	Red Planet RPR 1	Life In The 1980's/Lonely Nights (p/s)	10

MARTIN

68	Coxsone CS 7056	I Second That Emotion (actually by Martin Riley)/ROY TOMLINSON: I Stand For I	120

ALAN MARTIN

63	Rio R 3	The Party/Indeed	8
63	Rio R 6	You Came Late/Dreaming	8
63	Rio R 9	Secretly/Fame And Fortune	8
63	Rio R 10	Mother Brother/Tell Me	8
65	Rio R 66	Must Know I Love You/VIC BROWN'S COMBO: Rio Special	12
65	Rio R 67	Sweet Rosemarie/HONEY DUCKERS: Banjo Man	8
65	Rio R 68	Why Must I Cry/Shirley I Love You	8
65	Rio R 74	Since I Married Dorothy/You Promised Me	8
65	Venus VE 1	Cry Myself To Shame/Baby Don't Go	10
66	Rio R 94	Days Are Lonely/My Baby	8
66	Rio R 96	Rome Wasn't Built In A Day/I'm Hurt	8

MARTIN & DERRICK

61	Blue Beat BB 48	Times Are Going/I Love You Baby (with Cavaliers Combo)	15
62	Island WI 024	Come On/MONTY & CYCLONES: Organisation	20

(see also Derrick Morgan)

MARTIN & FINLEY

73	Tamla Motown TMG 867	It's Another Sunday/Best Friends (withdrawn, demo only)	250

BARRY MARTIN

61	RCA RCA 1234	Little Lonely One/Are You Sure	5

BENNY MARTIN

63	Realm RM 174	COUNTRY MUSIC'S SENSATIONAL ENTERTAINER (LP)	15

BOBBI MARTIN

64	Coral Q 72477	Don't Forget I Still Love You/On The Outside (Lookin' In)	5
65	Coral Q 72478	I Can't Stop Thinking About You/Million Thanks To You	6

CHRIS MARTIN

59	HMV POP 664	Lonely Street/Swing A Little Lover	10
60	HMV POP 692	Point Of No Return/I Don't Regret A Thing	6

DAVE MARTIN

64	Port-O-Jam PJ 4112	Let Them Fight/OSSIE IRVING SIX: Why I Love You	18
64	Port-O-Jam PJ 4115	All My Dreams/Take Your Belongings	18

DEAN MARTIN

SINGLES

54	Capitol CL 14123	Hey Brother, Pour The Wine/I'd Cry Like A Baby (green label)	30
54	Capitol CL 14123	Hey Brother, Pour The Wine/I'd Cry Like A Baby (purple label)	20
54	Capitol CL 14138	Sway/Pretty As A Picture	30
54	Capitol CL 14150	How Do You Speak To An Angel?/Ev'ry Street's A Boulevard In Old New York (with Jerry Lewis)	10
54	Capitol CL 14170	The Peddlar Man (Ten I Loved)/Try Again	10
54	Capitol CL 14180	One More Time/If I Could Sing Like Bing	10
55	Capitol CL 14215	Open Up The Doghouse (Two Cats Are Trying To Get In) (with Nat 'King' Cole)/Long, Long Ago	10
55	Capitol CL 14226	Let Me Go, Lover/The Naughty Lady Of Shady Lane	10
55	Capitol CL 14227	Mambo Italiano/That's All I Want From You	10
55	Capitol CL 14253	Belle From Barcelona/Confused	7
55	Capitol CL 14255	What Could Be More Beautiful/Under The Bridges Of Paris	7
55	Capitol CL 14311	Chee Chee-Oo Chee (Sang The Little Bird)/Ridin' Into Love	7
55	Capitol CL 14356	Relax-Ay-Voo/Two Sleepy People (with Line Renaud)	7
55	Capitol CL 14367	Simpatico/Love Is All That Matters	7
55	Capitol CL 14370	In Napoli/I Like Them All	7
	(Originally issued with triangular centres; round-centre reissues are worth around half these values.)		
56	Capitol CL 14505	When You Pretend/The Lucky Song	7
56	Capitol CL 14507	Inamorata/You Look So Familiar	7
56	Capitol CL 14519	Young And Foolish/Just One More Chance	6
56	Capitol CL 14523	Memories Are Made Of This/Change Of Heart	8
56	Capitol CL 14586	Watching The World Go By/The Lady With The Big Umbrella	10
56	Capitol CL 14624	The Test Of Time/I'm Gonna Steal You Away	5
56	Capitol CL 14625	Me 'N' You 'N' The Moon/The Wind, The Wind	5
56	Capitol CL 14626	Pardners (with Jerry Lewis)/Buckskin Beauty	5
59	Capitol CL 15015	Rio Bravo/My Rifle, My Pony And Me	10
64	Reprise R 20307	The Door Is Still Open/Every Minute, Every Hour	7
67	Pye DMA 1	I'm Not The Marrying Kind (Dean Martin Assoc. issue, 1-sided, promo only)	7

EPs

55	Capitol EAP 1-9123	DEAN MARTIN	10
56	Capitol EAP 1033	DEAN MARTIN AND JERRY LEWIS: "PARDNERS" (with Jerry Lewis)	10

ALBUMS

53	Capitol LC 6590	CAPITOL PRESENTS DEAN MARTIN (10")	30
56	Britone LP 1002	DEAN MARTIN SINGS, NICOLINI LUCCHESI PLAYS (10")	20
57	Capitol T 849	PRETTY BABY	20
58	Capitol T 1047	THIS IS DEAN MARTIN!	15

(see also Jerry Lewis, Line Renaud & Dean Martin, Frank Sinatra)

DEREK MARTIN

64	Sue WI 308	Daddy Rolling Stone/Don't Put Me Down Like This (credited as Derak Martin)	100
65	Columbia DB 7694	You Better Go/You Know	40
68	Stax 601 039	Soul Power/Sly Girl	30

DON MARTIN & DANDY (& SUPERBOYS)

67	Giant GN 6	Got A Feelin'/CONNECTIONS: At The Junction	12
68	Giant GN 24	Keep On Fighting/Rock Steady Boogie (with Superboys)	15

(see also Dandy & Superboys)

GEORGE MARTIN & HIS ORCHESTRA

64	Parlophone R 5135	I Saw Her Standing There/All My Loving	12
64	Parlophone R 5166	And I Love Her/Ringo's Theme (This Boy)	12
65	Parlophone R 5222	All Quiet On The Mersey Front/Out Of The Picture	15
65	Parlophone R 5256	I Feel Fine/The Niagara Theme	15
65	Parlophone R 5375	Yesterday/Another Girl	15
66	United Artists UP 1154	By George! - It's The David Frost Theme/Double Scotch	15
66	United Artists UP 1165	Love In The Open Air/Theme From "The Family Way"	20
67	United Artists UP 1194	Theme One/Elephants And Castles	20
72	United Artists UP 35423	Pulp - Theme/Pulp - Love Theme	10
65	Parlophone GEP 8930	MUSIC FROM "A HARD DAY'S NIGHT" (EP)	35
64	Parlophone PMC 1227	OFF THE BEATLE TRACK (LP, mono)	18
64	Parlophone PCS 3057	OFF THE BEATLE TRACK (LP, stereo)	20
65	Parlophone TA-PMC 1227	OFF THE BEATLE TRACK (reel-to-reel, mono only)	12
65	Columbia SX 1775	PLAYS HELP! (LP, mono)	20
65	Studio Two TWO 102	PLAYS HELP! (LP, stereo)	20
66	United Artists (S)ULP 1157	INSTRUMENTALLY SALUTES THE BEATLES GIRLS (LP)	30
66	Studio Two TWO 141	AND I LOVE HER (LP)	20
67	Decca LK 4847	THE FAMILY WAY (LP, mono, soundtrack)	70
67	Decca SKL 4847	THE FAMILY WAY (LP, stereo, soundtrack)	90
68	United Artists (S)ULP 1196	BRITISH MAID (LP)	25
70	Sunset SLS 50182	BY GEORGE! (LP)	20
73	United Artists UAS 29475	LIVE AND LET DIE (LP, soundtrack, gatefold sleeve)	25
74	Polydor Super 2383 304	BEATLES TO BOND AND BACH (LP)	15
78	St. Michael IMP 105	BEATLES TO BOND AND BACH (LP, exclusive to Marks & Spencer)	20
93	EMI RNB 1	THE BEATLES - GEORGE MARTIN INTERVIEW (CD, card sleeve, promo only)	12

(see also Beatles, Ray Cathode)

GRADY MARTIN & THE SLEWFOOT FIVE

56	Brunswick 05535	Nashville/Don't Take Your Love From Me	15

(see also Jane Turzy)

HONEYBOY MARTIN

67	Caltone TONE 103	Dreader Than Dread (and the Voices)/DANDY: In The Mood	45
70	Gas GAS 123	Unchained Melody/SAMMY JONES: You're My Girl	10
72	Sioux SI 011	Unchained Melody/SAMMY JONES: You're My Girl (reissue)	8
72	Harry J HJ 6643	Have You Ever Seen The Rain/Spanish Harlem	5

(see also Lynn Tait & Jets)

JACKI MARTIN

64	Fontana TF 487	Will You/Till He Tells Me	12

JANIS MARTIN
60	Palette PG 9000	Here Today And Gone Tomorrow Love/Hard Times Ahead	25
80	RCA PE 9494	JANIS MARTIN (EP)	10
80	RCA PL 43153	THE COMPLETE RCA JANIS MARTIN (2-LP)	25

JEAN MARTIN
| 63 | Decca F 11751 | Ain't Gonna Kiss Ya/Three Times Three Is Love | 10 |
| 64 | Decca F 11897 | Save The Last Dance For Me/Will You Still Love Me Tomorrow | 10 |

JERRY MARTIN
| 63 | London HLU 9692 | Shake-A Take-A/Exchange Student | 15 |

KERRY MARTIN
| 58 | Parlophone R 4449 | Stroll Me/Cold Hands, Warm Heart | 12 |

LUCIA MARTIN
| 62 | Parlophone R 4915 | Big Jim/Star From Heaven | 12 |

MARK MARTIN
| 67 | Page One POF 020 | Extraordinary Girl/Love Could Be Like Hell | 6 |

MARY MARTIN
| 64 | London HLR 9938 | A Spoonful Of Sugar/Feed The Birds | 5 |

MILES MARTIN FOLK GROUP
| 71 | Amber | MILES MARTIN FOLK GROUP (LP, private pressing) | 70 |

MILLICENT MARTIN
58	Columbia DB 4171	Our Language Of Love/Seriously	10
63	Parlophone R5033	Get Lost My Love/Gravy Waltz	8
63	Parlophone R 4998	That Was The Week That Was/Gotta Lotta Lovin' (with David Frost)	7
64	Parlophone R 5096	In The Summer Of His Years/If I Can Help Somebody	6
64	Parlophone R 5120	Suspicion/Nothing But The Best	6
59	Columbia 33SX 1145	MILLICENT (LP)	150
64	Philips BL 7591	MR & MRS (LP)	25

(see also Ronnie Carroll, David Frost)

PATRICK D. MARTIN
79	Deram DMR 432	I Like Electric Motors/Time (p/s)	5
80	Deram DM 433	Lucy 'Lectric/I Like Electric Motors/Mutant (p/s)	10
80	IRS/MCA ILS 0023	COMPUTER DATIN' EP	8

PAUL MARTIN
| 67 | Sue WI 4041 | Snake In The Grass/I've Got A New Love | 70 |

RAY MARTIN (& HIS) CONCERT ORCHESTRA
53	Columbia SCM 5001	Blue Tango/Belle Of The Ball	10
53	Columbia SCM 5002	The Marching Strings/The Waltzing Cat	10
53	Columbia SCM 5063	Swedish Rhapsody/Hi-Lili Hi-Lo	8
56	Columbia SCM 5264	The Carousel Waltz/ort Au Prince	8

(see also Ray Burns)

RICKY MARTIN & TYME MACHINE
| 68 | Olga OLE 4 | Something Else/Blue Suede Shoes | 15 |

RODGE MARTIN
| 67 | Polydor 56725 | When She Touches Me/Lovin' Machine | 20 |

RON MARTIN & JUBILEE STOMPERS
| 68 | Doctor Bird DB 1151 | Give Your Love To Me/I Cry My Heart | 20 |

RUPIE MARTIN('S ALLSTARS)
69	Ackee ACK 101	The Arena/Naturally	60
70	Torpedo TOR 24	Last Flight/Super Lotus	30
70	Torpedo TOR 26	Musical Container (Parts 1 & 2)	40
70	Punch PH 43	Death In The Arena (actually by Rupie Martin All Stars)/ MAN COMETH: Julia Caesar (actually by Charlie Ace)	30

SETH MARTIN
| 68 | Page One POF 073 | Another Day Goes By/Look At Me | 15 |
| 69 | Page One POF 134 | What A Lovely Way To Spend Forever/Mystery Lady | 5 |

SHANE MARTIN
| 68 | CBS 2894 | You're So Young/I Need You | 275 |
| 68 | CBS 2894 | You're So Young/I Need You (DJ copy) | 350 |

SKIP MARTIN VIDEO ALL-STARS
| 60 | Golden Guinea GGL 0060 | TV JAZZ THEMES (LP, mono) | 12 |
| 60 | Golden Guinea GGLS 10060 | TV JAZZ THEMES (LP, stereo) | 15 |

STEVE MARTIN
56	Columbia DB 3703	Only You/Lola	5
58	Philips PB 820	Stairway Of Love/Chanson D'Amour	5
58	Philips PB 853	The Man Inside/Blue-Eyed Sue	5

TONY MARTIN
53	HMV 7M 105	Tenement Symphony (both sides)	7
53	HMV 7M 136	The Golden Years/April In Portugal	7
54	HMV 7M 203	Here/I Could Write A Book	7
54	HMV 7M 258	I Love Paris/Boulevard Of Nightingales	5
55	HMV 7M 302	Stranger In Paradise/Vera Cruz	6
55	HMV 7M 320	Domani/What's The Time In Nicaragua	7
56	HMV 7M 414	Walk Hand In Hand/Flamenco Love	8
56	HMV 7MC 41	Walk Hand In Hand/Flamenco Love (export issue)	8
57	HMV POP 282	All Of You/Moderation	8
57	RCA RCA 1002	The Man From Idaho/One Is A Lonely Number	5
59	RCA RCA 1101	She Is Not Thinking Of Me/GOGI GRANT: Say A Prayer For Me Tonight	6
65	Stateside SS 394	Talkin' To Your Picture/Our Rhapsody	120
65	Tamla Motown TMG 537	The Bigger Your Heart Is (The Harder You'll Fall)/The Two Of Us	220
65	Tamla Motown TMG 537	The Bigger Your Heart Is (The Harder You'll Fall)/The Two Of Us (DJ copy)	300

MINT VALUE £

54	HMV 7EG 8006	TONY MARTIN (EP)	8
55	HMV 7EG 8124	TENEMENT SYMPHONY (EP)	8
55	Brunswick LA 8713	TONY MARTIN SINGS VOL. 1 (10" LP)	15
56	Mercury MPT 7005	TONY MARTIN FAVOURITES (10" LP)	15
57	Mercury MPT 7516	DREAM MUSIC (10" LP)	15
57	HMV DLP 1137	SPEAK TO ME OF LOVE (10" LP)	15

(see also Gogi Grant)

TRADE MARTIN
63	London HL 9662	Hula Hula Dancin' Doll/Something In The Wind	15

VINCE MARTIN
56	London HL 8340	Cindy Oh Cindy/Only If You Praise The Lord	18
59	HMV POP 594	Old Grey Goose (Aunt Rhodie)/Goodnight, Irene	10

(see also Tarriers)

MARTIN & THE BROWNSHIRTS
78	Lightning GIL 507	Taxi Driver/Boring	40

WINK MARTINDALE
59	London HLD 8962	Deck Of Cards/Now You Know How It Feels (tri centre)	10
59	London HLD 8962	Deck Of Cards/Now You Know How It Feels (78)	15
60	London HLD 9042	Life Gits Tee-Jus Don't It?/I Never See Maggie Alone	7
61	London HLD 9419	Black Land Farmer/Make Him Happy	8

TONY MARTINEZ QUINTET
54	HMV 7M 264	Cucusa Tune Mambo/Bernie's Tune Mambo	5

AL MARTINO
54	Capitol CL 14128	Wanted/There'll Be No Teardrops Tonight (Green label, tri centre)	20
54	Capitol CL 14128	Wanted/There'll Be No Teardrops Tonight (Purple label, tri centre)	15
54	Capitol CL 14148	On And On (In Love With You)/Give Me Something To Go With The Wine (Green label, tri centre)	20
54	Capitol CL 14148	On And On (In Love With You)/Give Me Something To Go With The Wine (Purple label, tri centre)	15
54	Capitol CL 14163	The Story Of Tina/Destiny (No One Can Change) (Green label, tri centre)	20
54	Capitol CL 14163	The Story Of Tina/Destiny (No One Can Change) (Purple label, tri centre)	15
54	Capitol CL 14192	I Still Believe/When?	5
54	Capitol CL 14202	Not As A Stranger/No One But You	5
55	Capitol CL 14224	Don't Go To Strangers/Say It Again	5
55	Capitol CL 14284	The Snowy, Snowy Mountains/Love Is Eternal	5
55	Capitol CL 14343	The Man From Laramie/To Please My Lady	5
55	Capitol CL 14379	Come Close To Me/Small Talk	5

(Originally issued with triangular centres; round-centre reissues are worth around half these values.)

67	Capitol 15516	More Than The Eye Can See/Red Is Red	20
61	Capitol EAP 1.20153	TO PLEASE MY LADY (EP)	10

MARTIN'S MAGIC SOUNDS
67	Deram DM 141	Mon Amour, Mon Amour/Midem Melody	6
67	Deram DML/SML 1014	MARTIN'S MAGIC SOUNDS (LP)	12

JOHN MARTYN
71	Island WIP 6116	May You Never/Just Now	20
77	Island WIP 6385	Over The Hill/Head And Heart	6
78	Island WIP 6414	Dancing/Dealer (Version)	6
78	Island WIP	Dancing/Dealer (Version) (promo)	8
80	Island WIP 6547	Johnny Too Bad/Johnny Too Bad (Version)	6
81	Island IPR 2046	Johnny Too Bad (Extended Dub Version)/Big Muff (Extended Mix) (12", promo)	10
82	WEA K 259987-7	Gun Money (US Remix)/Hiss On the Tape (live)	6
86	Island CID 265	Classic John Martyn: Angeline/Tight Connection To My Heart (Has Anybody Seen My Love)/May You Never/Solid Air/Glistening Glyndebourne (CD, foldout sleeve)	15
92	Permanent CDPERM 6	Sweet Little Mystery (CD)	12
67	Island ILP 952	LONDON CONVERSATION (LP, 1st pressing, with black & orange 'circle' logo)	300
69	Island ILP 952	LONDON CONVERSATION (LP, 3rd pressing, 'pink rim' label, 'orange' logo)	25
69	Island ILP 952	LONDON CONVERSATION (LP, 2nd pressing, pink label, white 'i' logo)	70
68	Island ILP 991	THE TUMBLER (LP, 1st pressing, with black 'circle' logo, mono)	200
68	Island ILPS 9091	THE TUMBLER (LP, 1st pressing, with black 'circle' logo, stereo)	40
70	Island ILPS 9091	THE TUMBLER (LP, 2nd pressing, 'pink rim' label, 'palm tree' logo, fully laminated sleeve)	20
71	Island ILPS 9167	BLESS THE WEATHER (LP, 'pink rim' label, 'palm tree' logo)	25
73	Island ILPS 9226	SOLID AIR (LP, gatefold sleeve with lyric sheet 'pink rim' label, 'palm tree' logo)	35
73	Island ILPS 9253	INSIDE OUT (LP, gatefold sleeve with inner, 'pink rim' label, 'palm tree' logo)	20
74	Island ILPS 9296	SUNDAY'S CHILD (LP, with lyric inner sleeve, 'palm tree' label)	15
75	Island ILPS 9343	LIVE AT LEEDS (LP, mail-order, 10,000 only, numbered & some signed)	30
86	Bodyswerve JMLP 001	PHILENTROPY (LP, red sleeve, matrix number etched on record only)	12
91	Permanent PERMLP 4	COOLTIDE (LP, with inner)	12

JOHN & BEVERLEY MARTYN
70	Island WIP 6076	John The Baptist/The Ocean	12
70	Island ILPS 9113	STORMBRINGER (LP, 1st pressing, pink label with 'i' logo)	90
70	Island ILPS 9113	STORMBRINGER (LP, 2nd pressing, 'pink rim' label, 'palm tree' logo)	12
70	Island ILPS 9133	THE ROAD TO RUIN (LP, 'pink rim' label, 'palm tree' logo)	22

(see also Beverley)

KID MARTYN
62	77 77LA 12/20	IN NEW ORLEANS WITH KID SHEIK'S BAND (LP)	15

MARVELETTES
61	Fontana H 355	Please Mr Postman/So Long Baby	55
62	Fontana H 386	Twistin' Postman/I Want A Guy	70
62	Oriole CBA 1764	Beechwood 4-5789/Someday Someway	155
63	Oriole CBA 1817	Locking Up My Heart/Forever	400
64	Stateside SS 251	As Long As I Know He's Mine/Little Girl Blue	60
64	Stateside SS 251	As Long As I Know He's Mine/Little Girl Blue (DJ copy)	90
64	Stateside SS 273	He's A Good Guy (Yes He Is)/Goddess Of Love	60
64	Stateside SS 273	He's A Good Guy (Yes He Is)/Goddess Of Love (DJ copy)	100
64	Stateside SS 334	You're My Remedy/A Little Bit Of Sympathy, A Little Bit Of Love	45

64	Stateside SS 334	You're My Remedy/A Little Bit Of Sympathy, A Little Bit Of Love (DJ copy)	100
65	Stateside SS 369	Too Many Fish In The Sea/Need For Love	40
65	Stateside SS 369	Too Many Fish In The Sea/Need For Love (DJ copy)	125
65	Tamla Motown TMG 518	I'll Keep Holding On/No Time For Tears	120
65	Tamla Motown TMG 518	I'll Keep Holding On/No Time For Tears (DJ copy)	400
65	Tamla Motown TMG 535	Danger Heartbreak Dead Ahead/Your Cheating Ways	50
65	Tamla Motown TMG 535	Danger Heartbreak Dead Ahead/Your Cheating Ways (DJ copy)	150
66	Tamla Motown TMG 546	Don't Mess With Bill/Anything You Wanna Do	50
66	Tamla Motown TMG 546	Don't Mess With Bill/Anything You Wanna Do (DJ copy)	85
66	Tamla Motown TMG 562	You're The One/Paper Boy	45
66	Tamla Motown TMG 562	You're The One/Paper Boy (DJ copy)	75
67	Tamla Motown TMG 594	The Hunter Gets Captured By The Game/I Think I Can Change You	30
67	Tamla Motown TMG 594	The Hunter Gets Captured By The Game/I Think I Can Change You (DJ copy)	60
67	Tamla Motown TMG 609	When You're Young And In Love/The Day You Take One, You Have To Take The Other	15
68	Tamla Motown TMG 639	My Baby Must Be A Magician/I Need Someone	22
68	Tamla Motown TMG 659	Here I Am Baby/Keep Off, No Trespassing	25
69	Tamla Motown TMG 701	Reachin' For Something I Can't Have/Destination Anywhere	15
73	Tamla Motown TMG 860	Reachin' For Something I Can't Have/Here I Am Baby	10
73	Tamla Motown TMG 860	Reachin' For Something I Can't Have/Here I Am Baby (DJ copy, plays "My Baby Must Be A Magician")	100
75	Tamla Motown TMG 1000	Finders Keepers, Losers Weepers/KIM WESTON: Do Like I Do	100
65	Tamla Motown TME 2003	THE MARVELETTES (EP)	110
65	Tamla Motown TML 11008	THE MARVELLOUS MARVELETTES (LP)	250
67	Tamla Motown TML 11052	THE MARVELETTES (LP, mono)	50
67	Tamla Motown STML 11052	THE MARVELETTES (LP, stereo)	55
69	Tamla Motown (S)TML 11090	SOPHISTICATED SOUL (LP, mono/stereo)	40
70	Tamla Motown STML 11145	IN FULL BLOOM (LP)	30
71	Tamla Motown STML 11177	THE RETURN OF THE MARVELETTES (LP, unissued)	0

MARVELOWS

65	HMV POP 1433	I Do/My Heart	30
65	HMV POP 1433	I Do/My Heart (DJ Copy)	40

MARVELS (JAMAICA)

62	Dice CC 8	Come To The Wedding/Angelo	10
63	Blue Beat BB 191	Sonia/The More We Are Together	12
64	Blue Beat BB 221	Millie/Saturday	12
70	Pama PM 813	Love One Another/Falling Rain	5
70	Pama PM 817	Don't Let Him Take Your Love From Me/A Little Smile	5
70	Gas GAS 138	Sail Away/Fight A Broke	12
70	Gas GAS 139	Someday We'll Be Together/MOHAWKS: The Rhythm	5
71	Pama PM 819	Oh Lord Why Lord/NEVILLE HINDS: Love Letter	5
71	Pama Supreme PS 338	Rocksteady/ Be My Baby	30
71	New Beat NB 081	Co Co/Hey Girl Don't Bother Me	5
72	Pama PM 832	Do You Know You Have To Cry/Love Power	5
72	Pama Supreme PS 348	What A Hurricane/If You Love Her	5
70s	Trojan TRLS 67	THE MARVELS (LP)	12

MARVELS (U.K.)

68	Columbia DB 8341	Keep On Searching/Heartache	100

MARVELS FIVE

65	HMV POP 1423	Bye Bye Baby Bunting/In Front Of Her House	7
65	HMV POP 1452	Don't Play That Song/(You Lied) I Forgive	15

MARVETTE

68	Amalgamated AMG 804	Tit For Tat (actually by Lyn Taitt & Jets)/You Take So Long To Know	50
68	Sacred Sound SS 001	We Are Not Divided/He Is So Real To Me	8
68	Sacred Sound SS 002	We Shall Have A Grand Time/Let The Power Fall On Me	8
68	Sacred Sound SS 003	I Was Once Lost In Sin/What A Wonderful Thing	8
68	Tabernacle TS 1001	I Want A Revival/Tell It	15
68	Tabernacle TS 1003	Sweet Jesus/When I Look Back	7
60s	Coxsone TLP 1002	IT'S REVIVAL TIME (LP)	60

MARVIN & FARRAR

73	EMI EMI 2044	Music Makes My Day/Skin Deep (with Olivia Newton-John)	10
75	EMI EMI 2335	Small And Lonely Light/Galadriel (Spirit Of Starlight)	7
73	EMI EMA 755	HANK MARVIN AND JOHN FARRAR (LP, with Olivia Newton-John on recorder)	20

(see also Shadows, Hank Marvin, Marvin Welch & Farrar)

MARVIN & JOHNNY

57	Vogue V 9074	Yak Yak/Pretty Eyes	500
57	Vogue V 9074	Yak Yak/Pretty Eyes (78)	150
58	Vogue V 9099	Smack, Smack/You're In My Heart	500
58	Vogue V 9099	Smack, Smack/You're In My Heart (78)	150
65	Black Swan WI 467	Cherry Pie/Ain't That Right	40

BRETT MARVIN & THUNDERBOLTS

70	Sonet SNTF 616	BRETT MARVIN AND THE THUNDERBOLTS (LP)	15
71	Sonet SNTF 619	12 INCHES OF BRETT MARVIN & THE THUNDERBOLTS (LP)	15
71	Sonet SNTF 620	BEST OF FRIENDS (LP)	12
72	Sonet SNTF 630	ALIAS TERRY DACTYL AND THE DINOSAURS (LP)	12

(see also Jona Lewie)

HANK (B.) MARVIN

68	Columbia DB 8326	London's Not Too Far/SHADOWS: Running Out Of World	15
69	Columbia DB 8552	Goodnight Dick/Wahine	12
69	Columbia DB 8601	Sacha/Sunday For Seven Days	12
69	Columbia DB 8628	Midnight Cowboy/SHADOWS: Slaughter On Tenth Avenue	18
70	Columbia DB 8693	Break Another Dawn/Would You Believe It? (demo-only, unissued B-side)	135
70	Columbia DB 8693	Break Another Dawn/Morning Star	15
78	EMI EMI 2744	Flamingo/Syndicated (as Hank Marvin Guitar Syndicate)	5
69	Columbia SCX 6352	HANK MARVIN (LP, blue/black label, mono)	35
69	Columbia SCX 6352	HANK MARVIN (LP, blue/black label, stereo)	30
70	Columbia SCX 6352	HANK MARVIN (LP, silver/black label re-pressing)	12

MINT VALUE £

77	EMI EMC 3215	GUITAR SYNDICATE (LP) 12

(see also Shadows, Marvin & Farrar, Marvin Welch & Farrar, Bruce Welch, Cliff Richard, Spaghetti Junction, Jean-Michel Jarre)

JOEL MARVIN
70	Explosion EX 2028	Too Late/Each Day (both actually by Gregory Isaacs).............................15

(see also Gregory Isaacs)

MARVIN, WELCH & FARRAR
71	Regal Zonophone RZ 3030	Faithful/Mr. Sun...8
71	Regal Zonophone RZ 3035	Lady Of The Morning/Tiny Robin 8
72	Regal Zonophone RZ 3048	Marmaduke/Strike A Light 10
71	Regal Zono. SRZA 8502	MARVIN, WELCH AND FARRAR (LP, fine textured gatefold sleeve, lyric insert) 15
71	Regal Zono. SRZA 8504	SECOND OPINION (LP, gatefold sleeve, lyric insert)..............................15
72	Regal Zono. Q4SRZA 8504	SECOND OPINION (LP, quadrophonic) 25

(see also Shadows, Marvin & Farrar, Bruce Welch [& Hank Marvin])

GROUCHO MARX
72	A&M AMS 7057	Show Me A Rose/Lydia The Tattooed Lady 7

(see also Danny Kaye, Jimmy Durante, Jerry Colonna & Groucho Marx)

MARY JANE WITH BARRY GRAY & SPACEMAKERS
63	Philips 326 587 BF	Robot Man/Just The Same As I Do (in p/s)..30
63	Philips 326 587 BF	Robot Man/Just The Same As I Do (no p/s)..18

(see also Barry Gray)

MARZ
80	Frozen Owl SRR 0023	Lady Of The Night/On The Road To Freedom/Daydreamer (p/s, with badge) 90

MARZIPAN
70	Trend 6099 007	My Kind Of Music/Sweet Water Mary..10

MASAI (1)
74	Contempo CS 2007	Across The Track (We Better Go Back) (Parts 1 & 2) 25

MASAI (2)
82	Turbo TURB 01	Stranger To Myself/Lightning (p/s) 8

MASCOTS
63	Pye International 7N 25189	Hey Little Angel/Once Upon A Love...20

HUGH MASEKELA
68	Uni UN 504	Grazing In The Grass/Bajabula Bonke 10
69	Uni UN 510	I Haven't Slept/Where Has All The Grass Gone? 6
68	Uni UNL(S) 101	ALIVE AND WELL AT THE WHISKEY (LP) 20
69	Fontana SFL 13056	HUGH MASEKELA (LP) 18
71	Rare Earth SRE 3002	HUGH MASEKELA AND THE UNION OF SOUTH AFRICA (LP) 25
72	Blue Thumb ICD 3	HOME IS WHERE THE MUSIC IS (LP) 30

MASHMAKAN
70	CBS S 5170	As The Years Go By/Days When We Are Free..15
74	Youngblood YB1063	Dance A Little Step/One Night Stand 6

MASKED PHANTOM
66	Parlophone R 5437	These Clogs Are Made For Walking/Fried Scampi 7

MASKMAN & AGENTS
69	Direction 58-4059	One Eye Open/Y'awll 10

MASON
73	Dawn DNS 1040	Fading/It's Alright 5
74	Antic K 11505	Follow Me/Peacefully 8
73	Dawn DNLS 3050	MASON (LP, export issue, do finished copies exist?) 20

BARBARA MASON
65	London HL 9977	Yes, I'm Ready/Keep Him 40
65	London HL 9977	Yes, I'm Ready/Keep Him (DJ copy) 75
68	Direction 58-3382	Oh How It Hurts/Ain't Got Nobody 40
69	Action ACT 4542	Slipping Away/Half A Love 25
72	Buddah 2011 133	Bed And Board/Yes It's You 10
73	Buddah 2011 154	Give Me Your Love/You Can Be With The One You Don't Love 7
75	Buddah BDS 425	From His Woman To You/When You Wake Up In Georgia 6
69	Action ACLP 6002	OH HOW IT HURTS (LP) 75
75	Buddah BDLP 4027	TRANSITION (LP) 20
75	Buddah BDLP 4032	LOVE'S THE THING (LP) 20

BARRY MASON
66	Decca F 12401	Misty Morning Eyes/Take Your Time 10
66	Deram DM 104	Over The Hills And Far Away/A Collection Of Recollections 45
67	MGM MGM 1356	Rowbottom Square/American Girl 12
69	Decca F 12895	I'm In Love With You, Pom Pom/Mister D.J. Play Me A Sad Song 7
70	MCA MK 5034	When You Do What You're Doing/Oh Baby 6
70	MCA MKS 5054	High Time/You Put Your Tears Away/Monte Carlo 6
75	Magnet MAG 40	Without You/Waiting In The Wings 5
76	Magnet MAG 5012	THE SONGWRITER (LP) 12

(see also Sounds Of Les & Barry)

BILL MASON BAND
79	Kingsway KMS 903	Out On The Streets/Mr. G (p/s) 15

DAVE MASON
68	Island WIP 6032	Just For You/Little Woman 15
70	Harvest HAR 5017	World In Changes/Can't Stop Worrying, Can't Stop Lovin' 5
70	Harvest HAR 5024	Only You Know And I Know/Sad And Deep As You 5
70	Harvest SHTC 251	ALONE TOGETHER (LP, gatefold sleeve, ' Gramophone Co' on label rim, no EMI logo, both matrix numbers end in -1 as well as crossed out matrix numbers SHVL 778 A-1/B-1)..35
72	Blue Thumb ILPS 9203	HEAD KEEPER (LP) 15
72	Island ICD 5	SCRAPBOOK (2-LP) 15
73	CBS 65258	IT'S LIKE YOU NEVER LEFT (LP, gatefold sleeve) 12

(see also Hellions, Revolution, Traffic, Fox, Jaguars)

DAVE MASON & CASS ELLIOT

71	Probe PRO 513	Something To Make You Happy/Next To You (as Mason & Cass, special sleeve)	6
71	Probe SPBA 6259	DAVE MASON AND CASS ELLIOT (LP, gatefold sleeve, pink label)	15

(see also Dave Mason, Mama Cass [Elliot])

GLEN MASON

56	Parlophone MSP 6240	Hot Diggity (Dog Ziggity Boom)/Baby Girl Of Mine	8
56	Parlophone R 4203	Love, Love, Love/Glendora	8
56	Parlophone R 4244	The Green Door/Why Must You Go, Go, Go	8
57	Parlophone R 4271	Don't Forbid Me/Amore	8
57	Parlophone R 4291	Round And Round/Walking And Whistling	6
57	Parlophone R 4334	Crying My Heart Out For You/Why Don't They Understand	6
57	Parlophone R 4357	By My Side/By The Fireside	5
58	Parlophone R 4390	What A Beautiful Combination/I'm Alone Because I Love You	5
58	Parlophone R 4415	I May Never Pass This Way Again/A Moment Ago	7
58	Parlophone R 4451	I Know Where I'm Going/Autumn Souvenir	6
58	Parlophone R 4485	The End/Fall In Love	6
59	Parlophone R 4562	The Battle Of New Orleans/I Don't Know	8
60	Parlophone R 4626	You Got What It Takes/If There's Someone	8
60	Parlophone R 4723	That's What I Want!/I Like It When It Rains	6
61	Parlophone R 4834	Don't Move/Shadrack	6
62	Parlophone R 4900	St. Louis Blues/That's Life	6

HARVEY MASON

77	Arista ARIST 12188	Till You Take My Love/What's Going On (12")	10
77	Arista SPART 1049	FUNK IN A MASON JAR (LP)	12

MARLIN MASON

56	Vogue Coral Q 72168	Don't Throw My Love Away/The Mystery Of Love	10

NICK MASON (& RICK FENN)

85	Harvest HAR 5238	Lie For A Lie/And The Address (with Rick Fenn, p/s)	5
85	Harvest 12 HAR 5238	Lie For A Lie (Extended 12" Version)/And The Address/ Mumbo Jumbo (with Rick Fenn) (12", p/s)	8
85	EMI MAF 1	PROFILES (LP, with Rick Fenn)	12
81	Harvest SHSP 4116	FICTITIOUS SPORTS (LP, solo, with inner sleeve)	12

(see also Pink Floyd, 10cc)

SPENCER MASON

67	Parlophone R 5555	Flugel In Carnaby Street/Albuferia	10

MASONICS

91	Hangman HANG 43 UP	MASONICS (LP)	20
02	Viny Japan ASKLP 133	THE MASONIC MACHINE TURNS YOU ON (LP)	12

(see also Milkshakes)

MASQUERADERS

68	Bell BLL 1023	I Ain't Got To Love Nobody Else/I Got It	8
70	Now! NOW 1001	Love Peace And Understanding/Tell Me You Love Me	8

(see also Lester Tipton)

MASS

80	4AD AD 14	You And I/Cabbage (with poster insert in die-cut sleeve)	12
80	4AD AD 14	You And I/Cabbage (in die-cut sleeve)	8
81	4AD CAD 107	LABOUR OF LOVE (LP, with inner sleeve)	15

(see also Models, Rema-Rema, Wolfgang Press)

MASSIEL

68	Philips BF 1667	La La La/He Gives Me Love (La La La)	7

MASSIVE ATTACK

88	Massive Attack MASS 001	Any Love/Any Love (Bonus)Any Love (Instrumental)/Any Love (Acapella) (12", stickered plain black die-cut sleeve)	20
90	Wild Bunch WBRT 1	Daydreaming/Daydreaming (Instrumental)/Any Love (12")	10
90	Wild Bunch WBRR 1	Daydreaming (Luv It Mix)/(Brixton Bass Mix)/(Luv It Dub) (12")	10
91	Wild Bunch WBRT 2	Unfinished Sympathy (Instrumental (12", p/s, as MASSIVE)	20
91	Wild Bunch WBRR 2	Unfinished Sympathy (Nellee Hooper 12" Mix)/ (Nellee Hooper Instrumental Mix)/(Original) (12", p/s)	20
91	Wild Bunch WBRR 3	Safe From Harm (7" Version)/(Original)/(Perfecto Mix) (12", p/s)	10
91	Wild Bunch WBRR 3	Safe From Harm (Perfecto Mix)/(Just A Dub)/(Instrumental) (12")	10
92	Wild Bunch WBRT 4	MASSIVE ATTACK EP (Hymn Of The Big Wheel (Nellee Hooper Mix)/Home Of The Whale/Be Thankful (Paul Oakenfold Mix)/Any Love (Larry Heard Mix) (12")	10
94	Wild Bunch WBRT 5	SLY EP (7" Edit)/(7 Stones Mix)/(Underdog Mix)/(Underdog Double Bass & Accapella) (12")	10
95	Wild Bunch WBRT 6	Protection: (Underdog's Angel Dust Mix)/(Radiation For The Nation Mix)/(The Eno Mix)/(J Swift Mix)/(Album Version) (12")	10
95	Wild Bunch WBRT 7	Karmacoma: (Portishead Experience)/(The Napoli Trip)/U.N.K.L.E. Situation)/(Blacksmith Daydreaming) (12")	10
97	Wild Bunch WBRT 8	Risingson: (Otherside)/(The Underdog Remix)/(Darren Emerson For Underground Remix)/(The Mad Professor Remix) (12" clear vinyl)	10
98	Circa/Virgin WBRT 10	Angel/(Remix)/Group Four (Mad Professor Remix) (12")	10
98	Circa/Virgin WBRTD11	Inertia Creeps: (LP Version)/(Manic Street Preachers Version)/Reflection/Reflection (Instrumental)/Inertia Creeps (Alpha Mix)/Back/She Comes/Inertia Creeps (State Of Bengal Mix) (2x12")	10
98	Wild Bunch WBRT 9	Teardrop: (LP Version)/Euro Zero Zero/Tear Drop (Scream Team Remix)/Teardrop (Mad Professor Remix) (12")	10
98	Wild Bunch WBRLH 9	Teardrop/Euro Zero Zero (jukebox issue)	20
98	Circa MASBOX 2	SINGLES 90/98 (11 x 12" singles in numbered heat sensitive box)	80
09	Vinyl Factory VF 006	SPLITTING THE ATOM EP (12", numbered p/s. 180 gram vinyl, 1000 only)	20
11	Vinyl Factory	Four Walls/Paradise Circus (12" as Massive Attack V Burial, silk-screened glitter sleeve, 1000 only)	80
91	Wild Bunch WBRLP1	BLUE LINES (LP, as Massive)	20
94	Wild Bunch WBRLP2	PROTECTION (LP)	20
96	Wild Bunch WBRLP3	NO PROTECTION (LP)	20
98	Wild Bunch WBRLP4	MEZZANINE (2-LP)	50
03	Virgin V2967	100th WINDOW (3-LP, gatefold)	18

MASSIVE DREAD
79	His Majesty HM 1001	MASSIVE DREAD (LP)	30

MASTER SINGERS
66	Parlophone R 5428	The Highway Code/Rumbletum Song	5
66	Parlophone R 5523	Weather Forecast/Roadilore	5

MASTERFLEET
73	Sussex LPSX 5	HIGH ON THE SEA (LP)	25

MASTERMINDS
65	Immediate IM 005	She Belongs To Me/Taken My Love	40

(see also Badfinger)

MASTERPLAN
78	Satril SAT 136	Love Crazy (Theme From 'Carry On Emmanuel')/ Since I've Been Away From My Love (p/s)	10

CARL MASTERS
72	Big Shot BI 604	Va Va Voom/GOD SONS: Rebel	15

(see also Max Romeo, Dennis Alcapone)

SAMMY MASTERS
60	Warner Bros WB 10	Rockin' Red Wing/Lonely Weekend	25
60	Warner Bros WB 10	Rockin' Red Wing/Lonely Weekend (78)	150
65	London HLR 9949	I Fought The Law (And The Law Won)/Big Man Cried	15

VALERIE MASTERS
58	Fontana H 132	Sharing/The Secret Of Happiness	8
58	Fontana H 145	(Well-a, Well-a) Ding-Dong/Merci Beaucoup	8
59	Fontana H 175	Dreams End At Dawn/Wonder	8
59	Fontana H 195	Jack O' Diamonds/Say When	8
59	Fontana H 224	If There Are Stars In My Eyes/Just Squeeze Me	8
60	Fontana H 238	Oh, Gee/No One Understands	8
60	Fontana H 253	Banjo Boy/Cow Cow Boogie	8
60	Fontana H 268	Sweeter As The Day Goes By/Fools Fall In Love	8
61	Fontana H 293	Too Late For Tears/I Got Rhythm	8
62	Fontana H 367	African Waltz/All Night Long	7
64	Columbia DB 7426	Christmas Calling/He Didn't Fool Me	75
65	Polydor 56056	It's Up To You/Next Train Out	15
66	Polydor 56135	Don't Ever Go/Say Hello	20
63	HMV POP 1125	The End Of The World/Sometime Kind Of Love	10

MASTER'S APPRENTICES
71	Regal Zonophone RZ 3031	I'm Your Satisfier/Because I Love Her	35
71	Regal Zono. SLRZ 1016	MASTER'S APPRENTICES (LP, red/silver labels with no EMI logo)	300
71	Regal Zono. SLRZ 1022	A TOAST TO PANAMA RED (LP, red/silver label with EMI logo)	250

MASTERS AT WORK
96	Talkin' Loud 578795-1	NUYORICAN SOUL (6-LP box set)	30

MASTERS OF REALITY
88	Def American DEFA 1	The Candy Song/The Blue Garden	10
88	Def American 838 474-1	THE MASTERS OF REALITY (LP)	20
88	Def American 838 474-2	THE MASTERS OF REALITY (CD)	20

MASTERSTROKE
80s	DTS DTS 043	Prisoner Of Love/Burning Heart (no p/s)	75

MASTERSWITCH
78	Epic S EPC 6259	Action Replay/Mass Media Meditation (no p/s)	25

MATADOR
71	Big Shot BI 594	Nyah Festival (actually "What Am I Living For" by Derrick Morgan)/Brixton Serenade	8

MATADORS
69	Crab CRAB 27	Death A Come (actually by Lloyd Robinson)/The Sword (actually "Zylon" by Lloyd Tyrell [Charmers])	20
70	Camel CA 45	Dark Of The Sun (actually by Jackie Mittoo)/Dreader Than Dread	30
71	Green Door GD 4017	I'm Sorry (actually by Tony Brevett)/JOE WHITE: I'm Sorry Version	10

(see also Emotions, Little Roys, Ethiopians)

MATATA (AIR-FIESTA)
72	President PT 380	Wanna Do My Thing/Wild River	20
73	President PT 406	I Feel Funky/I Want You	20
74	President PT 417	Return To You/Something In Mind (as Matata)	20
75	President PT 438	Good Good Understanding/Gimme Some Lovin' (as Matata)	20
72	President PTLS 1052	MATATA: AIR FIESTA (LP)	40
75	President PTLS 1057	INDEPENDENCE (LP)	80

MATAYO
75	RAK RAK 222	Matayo/I Like Rock 'N' Roll	20

MATCHBOX (1)
69	Polydor 56327	Run Much Faster/Every Little Thing She Does	150

MATCHBOX (2)
71	Rak 113	Don't Shut Me Out/Rod	10
78	Raw	Rock Rollin' Boogie/Troublesome Bay (p/s)	15
79	Magnet MAG 155	Rockabilly Rebel/I Don't Wanna Boogie Alone (p/s)	5
81	Dawn DNS 1104	Rock 'N' Roll Bank/Born To R 'N' R	12

(see also Cyclone)

MATCHING MOLE
72	CBS 8101	O Caroline/Signed Curtain	20
72	CBS 64850	MATCHING MOLE (LP)	45
72	CBS 65260	MATCHING MOLE'S LITTLE RED RECORD (LP, with inner sleeve)	50
79	CBS 32105	MATCHING MOLE (LP, reissue)	15

(see also Robert Wyatt, Soft Machine, Caravan, Hatfield & The North)

MATCHMAKERS
71	Chapter One	BUBBLEGUM A GO GO (LP)	25

(see also Mark Wirtz, Philwit & Pegasus, Fickle Finger)

KAREN MATHESON
96	Survival SURCD 020B	THE DREAMING SEA (CD, limited edition in box, with 6 postcards)	20

(see also Capercaillie)

MATHETAI
77	Cavs CAV 017	KNOWING (LP)	50

MIREILLE MATHIEU
66	Fontana TL 5363	MIREILLE MATHIEU (LP)	12

COUNTRY JOHNNY MATHIS
60	Top Rank JKP 2064	COUNTRY AND WESTERN EXPRESS NO. 5 (EP)	10

JODI MATHIS
75	Capitol CL 15827	Mama/Don't You Care Anymore	10

JOHNNY MATHIS
57	Philips JK 1029	The Twelfth Of Never/Chances Are (jukebox issue)	10
60	Fontana H 267	My Love For You/Oh That Feeling (in p/s)	5

MATIC 16
82	Music Hive (No cat. No)	Jahovah/Ten Man (12")	50
82	Regent RGTDS 1001	No Money Today/Matic Rock (12")	40

MATRIX RISE
92	Mutant 12 MUTATE 6	D.O.Y.L.E. Factor/Reality (12")	25
92	Mutant 12 MUTATE 8	Moments Of Pleasure/The Preacher (12")	40

BRIAN MATTHEW
61	Pye 7N 15403	Trad Mad/Sing With Me, Mates	7

BRIAN MATTHEW & PETE MURRAY
60	Decca F 11305	What's It All About Eh?/Gee Ma, I Wanna Go Home	7

AL MATTHEWS
75	CBS 3429	Fool/Don't Frun From My Love	12
78	Electric Co 23	Run To You/People Are People	15

IAN MATTHEWS
71	Vertigo 6059041	Hearts/Little Knows	12
73	Elektra K 12111	These Days/Same Old Man	7
71	Vertigo 6360 034	IF YOU SAW THRO' MY EYES (LP, 1st pressing textured gatefold sleeve, large swirl label)	125
71	Vertigo 6360 034	IF YOU SAW THRO' MY EYES (LP, 2nd LP textured gatefold sleeve, small swirl label)	30
72	Vertigo 6360 056	TIGERS WILL SURVIVE (LP, textured gatefold sleeve, small swirl label)	125
73	Elektra K 42144	VALLEY HI (LP, textured gatefold sleeve, 'butterfly' label)	30
74	Elektra K 42160	SOME DAYS YOU EAT THE BEAR, SOME DAYS THE BEAR EATS YOU (LP)	20
74	Mooncrest CREST 18	JOURNEYS FROM GOSPEL OAK (LP)	20
76	CBS 81316	GO FOR BROKE (LP)	18

(see also Pyramid, Fairport Convention, Matthews Southern Comfort, Plainsong, Hi-Fi)

JOE MATTHEWS
68	Sue WI 4046	Sorry Ain't Good Enough/You Better Mend Your Ways	80

MILT MATTHEWS
75	London HLF 10479	All These Changes/When Kids Rule The World	8

RANDY MATTHEWS
70s	Myrrh MXX 1035	NOW DO YOU UNDERSTAND (LP, gatefold sleeve)	40

TOBIN MATTHEWS
63	Warner Brothers WB 117	Can't Stop Talking About You/When You Came Along	6

WINSTON MATTHEWS
71	Banana BA 329	Sun Is Shining/INN KEEPERS: My Friend (B-side actually "The Pressure Is On" by Purpleites)	18

MATTHEWS SOUTHERN COMFORT
70	Uni UNS 513	Colorado Springs Eternal/The Struggle	12
70	Uni UNS 521	Ballad Of Obray Ramsey/Parting	7
70	Uni UNS 526	Woodstock/Scion	5
70	Uni UNLS 108	MATTHEWS SOUTHERN COMFORT (LP, gatefold, lyric insert, yellow swirl label)	40
70	Uni UNLS 112	SECOND SPRING (LP, textured sleeve, lyric insert, yellow swirl label)	30
70	Uni MKPS 2015	LATER THAT SAME YEAR... (LP, red/pink 'dogbone' label)	20

(see also Ian Matthews, Marc Ellington, Southern Comfort)

MATUMBI
73	G.G. GG 4540	Brother Louie Parts 1 & 2	10
77	Matumbi Music Corp. MA004	Music In The Air/Guide Us (12")	40
78	Matumbi Music MR 86	After Tonight/Take It From Me (12")	30
79	EMI 12RIC 101	This View/Another View (12" 'Matumbi' die cut sleeve)	8
78	EMI SHSP 4090	SEVEN SEALS (LP, red/black label with inner, some on green vinyl)	15
80	Extinguish MR 007	DUB PLANET ORBIT 1 (LP)	200

HARVEY MATUSOW'S JEWS HARP BAND
69	Head HDS 4004	Afghan Red/Wet Socks	8
69	Head HDLS 6001	WAR BETWEEN THE FATS & THE THINS (LP)	40

MAUDS
67	Mercury MF 1000	Hold On/C'mon And Move	10
67	Philips BL 7791	HEY, LOOK ME OVER (LP)	25

SUSAN MAUGHAN
61	Philips BF 1216	Mama Do The Twist/Blue Night In Yokohama	20
62	Philips BF 1236	Baby Doll Twist/Some Of These Days	20
62	Philips 326 533BF	I've Got To Learn To Forget/I Didn't Mean What I Said	10
62	Philips 326 544BF	Bobby's Girl/Come A Little Closer	10

63	Philips 326 562BF	Hand A Handkerchief To Helen/I'm A Lonely One Too	10
63	Philips 326 586BF	She's New To You/Don't Get Carried Away	10
63	Philips BF 1266	The Verdict Is Guilty/Bachelor Girl	7
64	Philips BF 1301	Hey Lover/Stop Your Foolin'	7
64	Philips BF 1336	Kiss Me Sailor/Call On Me	6
64	Philips BF 1363	Little Things Mean A Lot/That Other Place	12
64	Philips BF 1382	Make Him Mine/South American Joe	6
65	Philips BF 1399	You Can Never Get Away From You/Don't Be Afraid	6
65	Philips BF 1417	When She Walks Away/Come Along Down And See	6
65	Philips BF 1445	Poor Boy/Your Girl	6
66	Philips BF 1495	Come And Get Me/Don't Love Him Too Much	6
66	Philips BF 1518	Where The Bullets Fly/I'll Never Stop Loving You	5
67	Philips BF 1564	Don't Go Home (My Little Darlin')/Somebody To Love	6
68	Philips PF 1679	I Remember Loving You/Why Don't You Say You Love Me	8
68	Philips BF 1713	Cable Car For Two/Off My Mind	5
69	Philips BF 1824	We Really Go Together/I'll Never Forget You	5
62	Philips BBE 12525	HI, I'M SUSAN MAUGHAN AND I SING (EP)	15
63	Philips BBE 12549	FOUR BEAUX AND A BELLE (EP)	15
62	Philips 433 621 BE	EFFERVESCENT MISS MAUGHAN (EP)	15
63	Philips 433 641 BE	MORE OF MAUGHAN (EP)	15
63	Philips 632 300 BL	I WANNA BE BOBBY'S GIRL BUT ... (LP)	40
64	Philips BL 7577	SWINGIN' SUSAN (LP)	20
65	Philips BL 7637	SENTIMENTAL SUSAN (LP)	20

MAU-MAUS

82	Pax PAX 6	SOCIETY'S REJECTS (EP, black or blue sleeve)	18
82	Pax PAX 8	No Concern/Clampdown/Why Do We Suffer (p/s)	15
83	Pax/Paragon PAX 12	FACTS OF WAR (EP)	15
85	Rebellion REBEL 01	TEAR DOWN THE WALLS (EP)	15
85	Rebellion REBEL 1202	SCARRED FOR LIFE (12" EP)	15
83	Pax PAX 16	LIVE AT THE MARPLES (LP)	18
84	Pax PAX 20	RUNNING WITH THE PACK (LP)	30
85	Rebellion	FEAR NO EVIL (LP)	12

MAUREENY WISHFULL

| 68 | Moonshine WO 2388 | THE MAUREENY WISHFULL ALBUM (LP, 300 copies, beware of counterfeits) | 100 |

(see also Jimmy Page, Big Jim Sullivan, John Williams)

MAURICE & MAC

| 68 | Chess CRS 8074 | You Left The Water Running/You're The One | 12 |
| 68 | Chess CRS 8081 | Why Don't You Try Me/Lean On Me | 12 |

(see also Radiants)

MAWAMBA DUB

| 78 | Warrior DRLP 1001 | MAWANDA DUB (LP) | 60 |

(see also Dennis Bovell, Alton Ellis)

MAX

| 74 | Caroline C1506 | MAX (LP, black Virgin inner, black/red 'Twin' label, artist is Max Handley) | 20 |

MAX & ELAINE

| 73 | Ackee ACK 516 | I'm Leaving/Version | 5 |

(see also Max Romeo)

MAX & GREGORY

| 73 | Ackee ACK 525 | My Jamaican Collie/Push It Down, Rub It Up | 5 |

(see also Max Romeo)

MAX GROUP

| 69 | Fab FAB 110 | Abraham Vision/My Heart Was Breaking | 5 |

MAX HEADROOM & CARPARKS

| 80 | Parlophone R 6034 | Don't Panic/Rhythm And Bluebeat (p/s) | 6 |
| 82 | Bandwagon B001 | Soldier (no p/s) | 20 |

PAT MAX AND THE SPECIALISTS

| 68 | Pye 7N 17470 | Too Much/Girl From New Orleans | 12 |

SMILEY MAXEDON & HIS OKAW VALLEY BOYS

| 54 | Columbia SCMC 3 | Crazy To Care/In The Window Of My Heart (export issue) | 15 |

JOE S. MAXEY

| 73 | Action ACT 4607 | Sign Of The Crab/May The Best Man Win (actually plays Packers' "Hole In The Wall"/"Go Ahead On") | 20 |

MAXI

| 73 | Decca F 13394 | Do I Dream/Here Today And Gone Tomorrow | 6 |

MAXIE (ROMEO) & GLEN

| 71 | G.G. GG 4520 | Jordan River (actually by Max Romeo & Glen Adams)/ GLEN ADAMS:Version Two | 10 |

(see also Max Romeo, Ethiopians)

MAXIMILIAN

| 61 | London HLX 9356 | The Snake/The Wanderer | 35 |

MAXIMO PARK

| 03 | Billingham Records | Graffiti/Going Missing (red vinyl, 500 only, p/s) | 30 |
| 04 | Warp 7WAP183 | The Coast Is Always Changing/The Night I Lost My Head (500 only, p/s) | 15 |

MAXIM'S TRASH

| 79 | Gimp GIMP 1 | Disco Girls/Blu Shoes (plastic p/s & inner, hand-stamped white labels, tracks actually recorded in 1975) | 40 |

(see also Sunset Boys, Captain Sensible, Johnny Moped)

MAXIMUM BAND

| 68 | Fab FAB 51 | Cupid/Hold Me Tight | 5 |

MAXIMUM BREED

| 69 | Revolution REV 1 | Sitting In The Park/You've Got It | 5 |

MAXIMUM JOY
81	Y 11	Stretch/Silent Street (p/s)	20
81	Y Y 11	Stretch/Silent Street (12", p/s)	20
82	Y Y 15	White And Green Place/Building Bridges (12", p/s)	20
82	Y 28	STATION MXJY (LP)	25

ERNEST MAXIN
59	Top Rank JAR 267	On The Beach/Take A Giant Step	6
60	Top Rank JAR 335	Conspiracy Of Hearts/No Orchids For My Lady	6

MAXINE
70	Smash SMA 2301	My Boy Lollipop/Everybody Needs Love	6

BRIAN MAXINE
72	EMI Starline SRS 5140	BRIAN MAXINE SINGS (LP)	40
75	Columbia SCX 6575	RIBBON OF STAINLESS STEEL (LP)	30

(see also Fairport Convention)

HOLLY MAXWELL
69	Buddah 201 056	Suffer/No-One Else	8

MAXWELL PLUMM
75	Raven KS1007	WE CAN WORK IT OUT (LP)	12

BRIAN MAY
83	EMI EMI 5436	Starfleet (Single Version)/Son Of Starfleet (p/s)	15
91	Parlophone RDJ 6304	Driven By You (Edited Version)/(Pollarded Version)/(Special Version)/(Proper Version) (promo only, no stars on p/s)	70
91	Parlophone CDRDJ 6304	Driven By You (Edited Version)/(Pollarded Version)/(Special Version)/ (Proper Version) (CD, promo only, no stars on p/s)	100
92	Parlophone CDRS 6320	Too Much Love Will Kill You (Album Version)/I'm Scared (Single Version)/Too Much Love Will Kill You (Guitar Version)/Driven By You (New Version) (CD, red circular gatefold card p/s)	8
92	Parlophone MAYDJ 1	Too Much Love Will Kill You/Resurrection/Last Horizon/Driven By You (CD, promo only "Back To The Light" sampler, blue circular g/fold card p/s)	15
92	Parlophone RDJ 6329	Back To The Light (Radio Version)/Nothin' But Blue (Guitar Version) (promo only, p/s)	50
93	Parlophone 12RPF 6351	Resurrection/Love Token/Too Much Love Will Kill You (live) 12", picture disc with insert)	8
98	Parlophone R 6504	Why Don't We Try Again/Only Make Believe/F.B.I. (picture disc with poster)	6
83	EMI SFLT 1078061	STARFLEET PROJECT (mini-LP)	12
93	Parlophone 0 7777 80400 19	BACK TO THE LIGHT (LP, textured sleeve)	15
93	Parlophone CDPCSD X123	BACK TO THE LIGHT (Commemorative Issue) (gold CD, 10,000 only, stickered jewel case)	30
98	EMI 4949731	ANOTHER WORLD (LP, picture disc, with inner sleeve)	15

(see also Queen, MC Spy-D & 'Friends', Eddie Howell, Holly Johnson, Bad News, D-Rok, Ian & Belinda, Rock Aid Armenia, Cozy Powell, Black Sabbath)

DERRICK MAY
90s	R&S TMT 2	INNOVATOR (2xCD)	25

MARY MAY
63	Fontana 267266TF	Our Day Will Come/But I Know Now	8
64	Fontana TF 440	Anyone Who Had A Heart/They Say It's Wonderful	15

JOHN MAYALL (& BLUESBREAKERS)
SINGLES
64	Decca F 11900	Crawling Up A Hill/Mr. James (as John Mayall & Blues Breakers)	50
65	Decca F 12120	Crocodile Walk/Blues City Shakedown	45
65	Immediate IM 012	I'm Your Witchdoctor/Telephone Blues	50
66	Purdah 45-3502	Lonely Years/Bernard Jenkins (as John Mayall & Eric Clapton, 500 copies only)	400
66	Decca F 12490	Parchman Farm (solo)/Key To Love (B-side with Bluesbreakers)	25
66	Decca F 12506	Looking Back/So Many Roads (as John Mayall's Bluesbreakers & Peter Green)	15
67	Decca F 12545	Sitting In The Rain/Out Of Reach (as John Mayall's Bluesbreakers)	15
67	Decca F 12588	Curly/Rubber Duck (as Bluesbreakers)	12
67	Decca F 12621	Double Trouble/It Hurts Me Too (as John Mayall's Bluesbreakers)	20
67	Immediate IM 051	I'm Your Witchdoctor/Telephone Blues (reissue, as John Mayall with Eric Clapton)	25
67	Decca F 12684	Suspicions (Parts 1 & 2) (as John Mayall's Bluesbreakers)	15
68	Decca F 12732	Picture On The Wall/Jenny (as John Mayall)	12
68	Decca F 12792	No Reply/She's Too Young (as John Mayall's Bluesbreakers)	12
68	Decca F 12846	The Bear/2401	10
69	Polydor 56544	Don't Waste My Time/Don't Pick A Flower	12
70	Polydor 2066 021	Thinking Of My Woman/Plan Your Revolution	12
76	Decca F12120	Crocodile Walk/Blues City Shakedown (reissue, with boxed Decca logo, uninverted label matrix numbers, double A side)	15

EPs
67	Decca DFE-R 8673	THE BLUESBREAKERS WITH PAUL BUTTERFIELD (EP)	60

ALBUMS
65	Decca LK 4680	PLAYS JOHN MAYALL - LIVE AT KLOOKS KLEEK!	120
66	Decca LK 4804	BLUES BREAKERS WITH ERIC CLAPTON (original label, mono, "Beano" cover)	150
67	Decca LK/SKL 4853	A HARD ROAD (as John Mayall & Bluesbreakers)	50
67	Decca LK 4890	CRUSADE (Mono, as John Mayall & Bluesbreakers)	50
67	Decca SKL 4890	CRUSADE (Stereo, as John Mayall & Bluesbreakers)	30
67	Ace of Clubs ACL/SCL 1243	THE BLUES ALONE (LP, "A Hard Road" on back cover)	25
68	Decca LK/SKL 4918	THE DIARY OF A BAND VOL. 1	25
68	Decca LK/SKL 4919	THE DIARY OF A BAND VOL. 2	25
68	Decca LK/SKL 4945	BARE WIRES (gatefold sleeve, as John Mayall & Blues Breakers)	40
68	Decca LK/SKL 4972	BLUES FROM LAUREL CANYON (LP, unboxed logo, gatefold sleeve)	40

(The Decca LPs listed above were originally issued with unboxed Decca label logos.)

69	Polydor 583 571	THE TURNING POINT	18
69	Decca LK/SKL 5010	LOOKING BACK (gatefold sleeve)	25
69	Decca SKL 4804	BLUES BREAKERS WITH ERIC CLAPTON (reissue, original label, stereo)	40
70s	Decca LK 4804	BLUES BREAKERS WITH ERIC CLAPTON (reissue, boxed logo, mono)	20
70s	Decca SKL 4804	BLUES BREAKERS WITH ERIC CLAPTON (reissue, boxed logo, stereo)	15
70	Decca (S)PA 47	THE WORLD OF JOHN MAYALL	12
70	Polydor 583 580	EMPTY ROOMS (with lyric insert)	15

70	Polydor 2425 020	U.S.A. UNION	12
71	Decca SPA 138	THE WORLD OF JOHN MAYALL VOL. 2	12
71	Polydor 2657 005	BACK TO THE ROOTS (2-LP)	30
71	Polydor 2483 016	BEYOND THE TURNING POINT	15
71	Decca SKL 5086	THRU THE YEARS	25
71	Polydor 2425 085	MEMORIES	15
72	Polydor 2425 103	JAZZ-BLUES FUSION	15
73	Polydor 2391 047	MOVING ON	12
75	ABC ABCL 5115	NEW YEAR, NEW BAND, NEW COMPANY (gatefold sleeve)	12
76	Polydor 2482 272	JOHN MAYALL	12

(see also Paul Butterfield, Eric Clapton, Jack Bruce, Peter Green, McGuinness Flint, Johnny Almond Music Machine, Alan Skidmore, Mick Taylor, Dick Heckstall-Smith, Keef Hartley, Paul Williams, Ray Warleigh, Colosseum, Henry Lowther, Jon Mark, Aynsley Dun)

MAYBERRY MOVEMENT
| 06 | Kent 6T 21 | I See Him Making Love To You/THE DEVONNES: Doin' The Gittin' Up | 20 |

MAY BLITZ
| 70 | Vertigo 6360 007 | MAY BLITZ (LP, gatefold sleeve, large swirl label) | 250 |
| 71 | Vertigo 6360 037 | THE 2ND OF MAY (LP, gatefold sleeve, swirl label) | 350 |

(see also Jeff Beck,Boxer, Sounds Inc.)

MAYDAY
| 80 | Reddingtons R.R. DAN 2 | Day After Day/Love In The Spaceage (p/s) | 20 |
| 88 | Kool Kat KOOL T14 | NUDE PHOTO '88 EP (12", p/s) | 8 |

JOHN MAYER (GROUP)
66	Columbia DB 8037	Acka Raga (as John Mayer's I-J-7)/Gana (as John Mayer & Joe Harriott Quintet)	12
60s	National Petrol W 1	Music For People Who Go Your Own Way Themes 1 & 2 (p/s, with Frank Cordell)	10
67	Columbia SX 6122	INDO-JAZZ FUSIONS (LP)	35
69	Sonet SNTF 603	ETUDES (LP, as John Mayer Indo-Jazz Fusions)	15

(see also Joe Harriott & John Mayer, Radha Krishna)

NATHANIEL MAYER & FABULOUS TWILIGHTS
| 62 | HMV POP 1041 | Village Of Love/I Want A Woman | 50 |

CURTIS MAYFIELD
70	Buddah 2011 055	(Don't Worry) If There's A Hell Below We're All Going To Go (Edit)/ The Makings Of You	8
71	Buddah 2011 080	Move On Up/Give It Up/Beautiful Brother Of Mine (maxi-single)	8
71	Buddah 2011 101	We Got To Have Peace/People Get Ready	6
72	Buddah 2011 119	Keep On Keepin' On/Stone Junkie	6
72	Buddah 2011 141	Freddie's Dead (Theme From "Superfly")/Underground	6
72	Buddah 2011 156	Superfly/Give Me Your Love (Love Song)	6
73	Buddah 2011 187	Back To The World (edit)/The Other Side Of Town	6
74	Buddah BDS 402	Kung Fu/Right On For The Darkness	6
74	Buddah BDS 410	Move On Up/Give It Up	8
75	Buddah BDS 426	Mother's Son/Love Me Right In The Pocket	6
71	Buddah 2318 015	CURTIS (LP, gatefold sleeve)	25
71	Buddah 2659 004	CURTIS/LIVE (2-LP)	20
72	Buddah 2318 045	ROOTS (LP, gatefold sleeve)	15
72	Buddah 2318 065	SUPERFLY (LP, soundtrack, gatefold sleeve)	15
73	Buddah 2318 085	BACK TO THE WORLD (LP, gatefold sleeve)	12
73	Buddah 2318 091	CURTIS IN CHICAGO (LP, TV soundtrack, gatefold sleeve, with Impressions, Jerry Butler, Gene Chandler & Leroy Hutson)	15
74	Buddah BDLP 2001	CURTIS/LIVE (2-LP, reissue)	18
74	Buddah BDLP 4010	CLAUDINE (LP, soundtrack, with Gladys Knight)	15
74	Buddah BDLP 4015	MOVE ON UP (THE BEST OF CURTIS MAYFIELD) (LP)	12

(see also Impressions)

PERCY MAYFIELD
63	HMV POP 1185	The River's Invitation/Baby Please	10
76	Speciality SPE 5007	Please Send Me Someone To Love/The River's Invitation	6
67	HMV CLP/CSD 3572	MY JUG AND I (LP)	40

MAYFIELD'S MULE
69	Parlophone R 5817	Double Dealing Woman/(Drinking My) Moonshine (in p/s)	30
69	Parlophone R 5817	Double Dealing Woman/(Drinking My) Moonshine	15
70	Parlophone R 5843	I See A River/"Queen" Of Rock'n'Roll	15
70	Parlophone R 5858	We Go Rollin'/My Way Of Living	10

(see also Elastic Band, Sweet, Amen Corner, Andy Scott)

MAYFLY
| 73 | Bumble GE 121 | It's Elusive/Orphan Girl | 10 |

JUDY MAYHAN
| 71 | Atlantic 2466006 | MOMENTS (LP) | 15 |

MAYHEM
85	Vigilante VIG 1	Bloodrush/Addictive Risk (p/s)	6
85	Vigilante VIG 1T	Bloodrush/Addictive Risk (12", p/s)	10
96	Black Metal BMR 002	Freezing Moon/Carnage (12", picture disc)	20
97	Misanthropy HH 666	Ancient Skin/Necrolust (CD single in printed PVC sleeve, hand numbered insert, gig freebie, 500 only, beware of bootleg 7" singles of this)	40
97	Misanthropy Amazon 012	WOLF'S LAIR ABYSS (LP)	40
97	Misanthropy AMAZON CPD 012	WOLF'S LAIR ABYSS (LP, picture disc)	50

JENNY MAYNARD
| 68 | Inter-zel DR 001 | He Gives Me Love/Something Here In My Heart | 5 |

(TOOTS &) THE MAYTALS
63	Blue Beat BB 176	Hallelujah/Helping Ages Past	20
64	Blue Beat BB 215	He Is Real/Domino	20
64	Blue Beat BB 220	Pain In My Belly/BUSTER'S ALL STARS: City Riot	100
64	Blue Beat BB 231	Dog War/RECO & CREATORS: I'll Be Home	70
64	Blue Beat BB 245	Little Slea (song actually "Little Flea")/Don't Talk (song actually Pain In My Belly) (both sides miscredited as V. Maytals)	25
64	Blue Beat BB 254	Sweet Love/PRINCE BUSTER: Wings Of A Dove	30

64	Blue Beat BB 255	Judgement Day/Goodbye Jane	20
64	Blue Beat BB 270	You've Got Me Spinning/Lovely Walking	40
64	R&B JB 130	Hurry Up/Love Divide	20
64	R&B JB 141	Another Chance/FRANKIE ANDERSON: Always On A Sunday	20
64	R&B JB 153	Give Me Your Love/He Will Provide	20
64	R&B JB 164	Hello Honey/ROLAND ALPHONSO: Crime Wave	50
64	R&B JB 174	Christmas Feelings/Let's Kiss	25
65	Blue Beat BB 281	Looking Down The Street/PRINCE BUSTER: Blues Market	35
65	Blue Beat BB 299	Light Of The World/Lovely Walking	30
65	Blue Beat BB 306	Ska War (song actually "Treating Me Bad")/SKATALITES: Perhaps	70
65	Ska Beat JB 202	Let's Jump/Joy And Jean	20
65	Island WI 200	Never You Change/What's On Your Mind	25
65	Island WI 213	My New Name/It's No Use	25
65	Black Swan WI 464	John James/THEO BECKFORD: Sailing On	25
66	Doctor Bird DB 1019	If You Act This Way/SIR LORD COMIC & HIS COWBOYS: Ska-ing West	40
66	Doctor Bird DB 1038	Bam Bam/So Mad In Love (with Byron Lee and the Dragoniares)	35
68	Pyramid PYR 6030	54-46, That's My Number/ROLAND ALPHONSO: Dreamland	30
68	Pyramid PYR 6043	Struggle/ROLAND ALPHONSO: Stream Of Life	45
68	Pyramid PYR 6048	Just Tell Me/Reborn	20
68	Pyramid PYR 6050	Bim Today, Bam Tomorrow/Hold On	25
68	Pyramid PYR 6052	We Shall Overcome/DESMOND DEKKER & ACES: Fu Manchu	100
68	Pyramid PYR 6055	Schooldays/Big Man	15
68	Pyramid PYR 6057	Do The Reggay/BEVERLEY'S ALLSTARS: Motoring	35
68	Pyramid PYR 6064	Scare Him/In My Heart	20
69	Pyramid PYR 6066	Don't Trouble Trouble/BEVERLEY'S ALLSTARS: Double Action	20
69	Pyramid PYR 6070	Aldina/Hold On	30
69	Pyramid PYR 6073	Pressure Drop/BEVERLEY'S ALLSTARS: Express	25
69	Pyramid PYR 6074	Sweet And Dandy/Oh Yeah	15
69	Trojan TR 7709	Pressure Drop/BEVERLEY'S ALLSTARS: Smoke Screen	18
69	Nu Beat NB 031	My Testimony/JOHNSON BOYS: One Dollar Of Soul (actually by Ethiopians)	15
69	Trojan TR 7711	Monkey Man/Night And Day	15
70	Trojan TR 7726	Sweet And Dandy/54-46, That's My Number	8
70	Trojan TR 7741	Bla Bla Bla/Reborn	6
70	Trojan TR 7757	Water Melon/She's My Scorcher	12
70	Trojan TR 7786	Doctor Lester/Sun, Moon And Star	6
70	Summit SUM 8510	Peeping Tom/BEVERLEY'S ALLSTARS: Version	8
71	Trojan TR 7808	54-46 Was My Number/BEVERLEY'S ALLSTARS: 54-46 Instrumental	8
71	Trojan TR 7849	Johnny Cool Man/BEVERLEY'S ALLSTARS: Version	8
71	Summit SUM 8513	Monkey Girl/BEVERLEY'S ALLSTARS: Version	20
71	Summit SUM 8520	One Eye Enos/BEVERLEY'S ALLSTARS: Enos Version	6
71	Summit SUM 8527	It's You/BEVERLEY'S ALLSTARS: Version	6
71	Summit SUM 8529	Walk With Love/BEVERLEY'S ALLSTARS: Version	6
71	Summit SUM 8533	Never You Change/BEVERLEY'S ALLSTARS: Version	6
72	Attack ATT 8042	It Was Written Down/Sweet And Dandy	5
72	Summit SUM 8536	Thy Kingdom Come/BEVERLEY'S ALLSTARS: Version	6
72	Summit SUM 8537	It Must Be True Love/BEVERLEY'S ALLSTARS: Version	6
72	Blue Mountain BM 1020	Christmas Song/I Can't Believe	6
72	Dynamic DYN 438	Redemption Song	5
72	Trojan TR 7865	Louie Louie/Pressure Drop '72	5
73	Dragon DRA 1007	Sit Right Down/Screwface Underground/Pomps & Pride (as Toots & Maytals)	5
73	Dragon DRA 1013	Country Road/Funky Kingston (as Toots & Maytals)	12
73	Dragon DRA 1016	In The Dark/Sailing On (as Toots & Maytals)	5
73	Dragon DRA 1021	Fever/It Was Written Down	5
74	Dragon DRA 1024	Time Tough/Time Tough Version	5
74	Dragon DRA 1026	Sailing On/If You Act This Way (as Toots & Maytals)	5
11	Trojan THB 7008	Do The Boogaloo/Bim Today Bam Tomorrow (760 only)	10
64	Ska Beat JBL 1113	PRESENTING THE MAYTALS (NEVER GROW OLD) (LP)	225
66	Doctor Bird DLM 5003	THE SENSATIONAL MAYTALS (LP)	200
70	Trojan TBL 107	MONKEY MAN (LP, laminated front cover)	50
73	Trojan TRLS 65	FROM THE ROOTS (LP)	35
73	Dragon DRLS 5002	FUNKY KINGSTON (LP)	15
74	Dragon DRLS 5004	IN THE DARK (LP)	25
74	Prince Buster PB 11	ORIGINAL GOLDEN OLDIES VOLUME 3 (LP)	15
77	State ETAT16	TOOTS PRESENTS THE MAYTALS (LP)	15

(see also Vikings, Flames, Philip James & Blues Busters, Don Drummond, Stranger, Lord Creator, Larry Marshall, Derrick Morgan, Brentwood Road Allstars, Roland Alphonso, Charmers)

MAYTONES

68	Blue Cat BS 149	Billy Goat/Call You Up	40
69	Blue Cat BS 152	Loving Reggae/Musical Beat	40
69	Blue Cat BS 166	Copper Girl/Love	40
69	Blue Cat BS 173	We Nah Tek You Lick/Dig Away De Money	30
69	Camel CA 27	Sentimental Reason/Lover Girl	10
69	Songbird SB 1009	I've Been Loving You/Memphis Reggae	10
70	Punch PH 35	Serious Love/CHARLIE ACE: Musical Combination	10
70	Explosion EX 2012	Funny Man/G.G. ALLSTARS: Champion	10
70	Explosion EX 2013	Sentimental Reason/Lover Girl	7
70	Explosion EX 2014	Barrabus/G.G. ALLSTARS: Barrabus Part 2 (B-side actually "This Kind Of Life")	8
70	Explosion EX 2027	Cecelia (actually by Keeling Beckford)/Chariot Without Horse (B-side actually "Willie My Darling")	6
70	Explosion EX 2033	Another Festival/Happy Time	6
70	Bullet BU 446	I Don't Like To Interfere/Preaching Love	5
70	Camel CA 47	Black And White/GLORIA'S ALLSTARS: Jumbo Jet	10
70	Camel CA 49	Since You Left/GLORIA'S ALL STARS: Bird Wing	15
71	Duke DU 116	Babylon A Fall/TONY KING: Version Buggy	10
71	Camel CA 61	Judas (actually by Gladstone Anderson & Followers)/Mi Nah Tek	7
71	Camel CA 63	Cleanliness/Sister Hold On	20
71	G.G. GG 4508	Cleanliness/G.G. ALL STARS: Cleanliness Version 2	10
71	G.G. GG 4511	Let The Version Play/Lonely Nights	10
71	G.G. GG 4522	Black And White/TREVOR BROWN: Mr. Brown	6
71	G.G. GG 4525	Bongo Man Rise/ROY & BIM: Remember	6

MAZE (U.K.)

72	G.G. GG 4530	Donkey Face/G.G. ALL STARS: Donkey Face - Version 8
72	G.G. GG 4531	As Long As You Love Me (Side One)/As Long As You Love Me (Side Two).....................6
72	Attack ATT 8029	Hands And Feet/LLOYD & CAREY: Scorpion 6
72	Grape GR 3028	If Loving You Was Wrong/FLOWERS & ALVIN: In De Pum Pum 6
72	Pama PM 846	I'm Feeling Lonely/G.G. ALLSTARS: Version 6
72	Explosion EX 2076	Brown Girl/SHORTY PERRY: Half-Way-Tree Rock...6
73	Pama PM 871	All Over The World People Are Changing/Changing World (Dubwise)............................5
73	Bread BR 1114	All Over The World People Are Changing/Changing World (Dubwise)............................5
73	Bullet BU 528	People Get Funny/G.G. ALL STARS: Version 6
77	GG's GG 021	Money Trouble (with I Roy)/GG'S ALL STARS: Dub Part Two (12")..........................20

(see also Vern & Alvin, Vern & Son, Roland Alphonso, G.G. Rhythm Section, Cynthia Richards, Max Romeo, Charlie Ace, Dennis Alcapone)

MAZE (U.K.)

66	Reaction 591 009	Hello Stranger/Telephone 90
67	MGM MGM 1368	Catari Catari/Easy Street 40

(see also M.I. Five, Deep Purple)

MAZZY STAR

93	Rough Trade Singles Club 45 rev 19	Five String Serenade/Under My Car (p/s)...15
94	Capitol 10CL720	Fade Into You/Five String Serenade/Under My Car/ Bells Ring (Acoustic) (10" p/s) 20
96	Capitol CL 781	FLOWERS IN DECEMBER (EP, blue vinyl) 15
90	Rough Trade ROUGH 158	SHE HANGS BRIGHTLY (LP) 60
93	Capitol EST2206	SO TONIGHT THAT I MIGHT SEE (LP) 80
96	Capitol 8272241	AMONG MY SWAN (LP) 40

M.B.P. MIX

69	Major Minor MM66	Light My Fire/There's A Baby 25

MC KELZ

88	Three Stripe SAM 1113	Clash Of The Beats (12") 12

WINSTON MCANUFF

79	Third World	I Love Jah/FREDDIE McGREGOR : Massachusetts (12") 30

JACKIE MCAULEY

71	Dawn DNS 1011	Turning Green/It's Alright 8
72	Dawn DNS 1020	Rocking Shoes/One Fine Day 7
71	Dawn DNLS 3023	JACKIE McAULEY (LP, gatefold sleeve) 150

(see also Them, Belfast Gypsies, Trader Horne, Freaks Of Nature)

MCAULEY SCHENKER GROUP

90	EMI EMPD 127	Anytime/What We Need/Anytime (Edit) (uncut picture disc) 30
90	EMI EMPD 127	Anytime/What We Need/Anytime (Edit) (shaped picture disc)...............................8

(see also Michael Schenker, Michael Schenker Group, Grand Prix)

GERRY MCAVOY

79	Bridgehouse BHS 004	Street Talk/Many Rivers To Cross (p/s) 10

JIMMY MCBEATH

67	Topic 12T 173	WILD ROVER NO MORE (LP, blue label with booklet)......................................12
60	Collector JPSP	THY BALLADS (EP) 8

CECIL MCBEE

79	Inner City IC3023	MUSIC FROM THE SOURCE (LP) 15

NICKO MCBRAIN

91	EMI NICKO 1	Rhythm Of The Beast/Beehive Boogie (p/s) 6
91	EMI NICKOPD 1	Rhythm Of The Beast/McBrain Damage Interview (shaped picture disc with insert & plinth) 12

(see also Iron Maiden, Streetwalkers, Pat Travers)

DAN MCCAFFERTY

75	Mountain TOP 1	Out Of Time/Cinnamon Girl 6
75	Mountain TOP 5	Watcha Gonna Do About It/Nightingale 5
75	Mountain DAN 1	Stay With Me Baby/Out Of Time/Watcha Gonna Do About It (p/s) 7
79	Mountain TOP 47 DJ	Watcha Gonna Do About It/(7.30 maxi version)/Boots Of Spanish Leather (12" promo)......10
75	Mountain TOPS 102	DAN McCAFFERTY (LP, with inner sleeve) 12

(see also Nazareth, Sensational Alex Harvey Band, Mitchell/Coe Mysteries, Roger Glover)

JERRY MCCAIN

69	Python 02	Homogenised Love/728 Texas (99 copies only) 50

CASH MCCALL

63	Ember EMB S 173	Anytime/From The Very First Rose 10
65	Ember EMB S 204	Many Are The Words (I've Left Unspoken)/Buenos Noches 12
67	Chess CRS 8056	It's Wonderful (To Be In Love)/Let's Try It Over..20

DARRELL MCCALL

61	Capitol CL 15196	My Kind Of Lovin'/Beyond Imagination...8
63	Philips 304 002 BF	Dear One/I've Been Known 10
63	Philips BF 1259	Hud/No Place To Hide 7

TOUSSAINT MCCALL

67	Pye International 7N 25420	Nothing Takes The Place Of You/Shimmy 25
72	Mojo 2092 035	Nothing Takes The Place Of You/Shimmy (reissue) 5

DAVID MCCALLUM

66	Capitol CL 15439	Communication/My Carousel 12
66	Capitol CL 15474	In The Garden/The House On Breckenridge Lane 5
66	Capitol (S)T 2432	MUSIC ... A PART OF ME (LP) 25
66	Capitol (S)T 2498	MUSIC ... A BIT MORE OF ME (LP) 15

ALISON MCCALLUM

75	RCA 2608	Love Grows Cold/Lunatic Love (Part 2) 5

MCCALMANS

70	CBS 564145	TURN AGAIN (LP) 35
73	One Up OU 2161	McCALMANS' FOLK (LP) 15

JIM McCANN
72	Polydor 2489 053	McCANNED! (LP)	40

(see also Ludlows)

LES McCANN (LTD)
60	Vogue V 2417	Fish This Week/Vakushna (as Les McCann Ltd)	5
67	Mercury MF 973	All/Bucket O'Grease	15
69	Atlantic 584 284	With These Hands/Burnin' Coal	15
60	Vogue LAE 12238	THE TRUTH (LP)	12
66	Mercury LML 4026	PLAYS THE HITS (LP, mono)	12
69	Atlantic 588 176	MUCH LES (LP)	12
60s	Fontana 688 150ZL	THE WAILERS! (with Gerald Wilson Orchestra)	12

DON McCARLOS
80	Negus Roots NERT 003	I Don't Care/I Love Jah (12")	45

McCARTHY
86	Wall Of Salmon MAC 001	In Purgatory/The Comrade Era/Something Wrong Somewhere (foldover p/s in poly bag, white labels)	20
86	Pink PINKY 12	Red Sleeping Beauty/From The Damned (stickered p/s)	8
86	Pink PINKY 12T	Red Sleeping Beauty/The Comrade Era/From The Damned/ For The Fat Lady (12", p/s with foldover insert)	8
87	Pink PINKY 17	Frans Hals/The Fall (p/s)	5
87	Pink PINKY 17T	Frans Hals/The Fall (Remix)/Kill Kill Kill Kill/Frans Hals (Version) (12", p/s)	8
87	September SEPT 1	The Well Of Loneliness/Antiamericancretin/Unfortunately (p/s)	6
87	September SEPT 1T	The Well Of Loneliness/Bad Dreams/Someone Worse Off/ Antiamericancretin/Unfortunately (12", p/s)	8
88	September SEPTT 4	This Nelson Rockefeller (p/s)	10

(see also Stereolab)

KEITH McCARTHY
67	Coxsone CS 7014	Everybody Rude Now/BASES: Beware	30

LYN & GRAHAM McCARTHY
65	Columbia DB 7584	Seven Doves/Out After Ale	6
66	Columbia DB 7921	I Can't Help But Wonder/There's Got To Be Love	6
66	Columbia DB 8087	The Turkey's Trial/Bitter Withy	6
68	Columbia DB 8422	I Think It's Going To Rain/Once I Was	7
68	RCA RCA 1759	Scarborough Fair - Canticle/Wild Berries	5

MARY McCARTHY
67	CBS 2832	The Folk I Love/You Know He Did	100
67	CBS 2987	Happy Days And Lonely Night/Easy Kind Of Love	70

CECIL McCARTNEY
68	Columbia DB 8474	Hey Aleuthia I Want You/Liquid Blue	25
69	Columbia DB 8595	Orange And Green/Cloudy	15
68	Columbia S(C)X 6283	OM (LP, first pressing with blue/black label with "Sold in UK..." text)	150
68	Columbia S(C)X 6283	OM (LP, second pressing with black/silver label, boxed logo)	40

PAUL McCARTNEY/WINGS
SINGLES
71	Apple R 5889	Another Day/Oh Woman, Oh Why	8
71	Apple R 5914	The Back Seat Of My Car/Heart Of The Country (as Paul & Linda McCartney)	10
72	Apple R 5932	Love Is Strange/I Am Your Singer (unreleased)	1500
72	Apple R 5936	Give Ireland Back To The Irish/(Version) (as Wings, yellow 'Wings' die-cut sl.)	10
72	Apple R 5949	Mary Had A Little Lamb/Little Woman Love (p/s)	10
72	Apple R 5973	Hi Hi Hi/C Moon	6
73	Apple R 5985	My Love/The Mess (as McCartney's Wings, demos and early retail copies shipped in a plain red sleeve)	20
73	Apple R 5985	My Love/The Mess (credited to Paul McCartney/Wings)	5
73	Apple R 5987	Live And Let Die/I Lie Around	6
73	Apple R 5993	Helen Wheels/Country Dreamer	6
74	Apple R 5996	Jet/Let Me Roll It	6
74	Apple R 5997	Band On The Run/Zoo Gang	10
74	Apple R 5999	Juniors Farm/Sally G	8
75	Capitol R 6006	Listen To What The Man Said/Love In Song (p/s)	6
75	Capitol R 6008	Letting Go/You Gave Me The Answer	8
75	Capitol R 6010	Venus And Mars; Rock Show/Magneto And Titanium Man	8
76	Parlophone R 6015	Let 'Em In/Beware My Love	5
78	Parlophone R 6018	Mull Of Kintyre/Girls School (yellow juke box 'Best selling British single ever' p/s)	60
78	Parlophone R 6020	I've Had Enough/Deliver Your Children (p/s, as Wings)	10
79	Parlophone R6026	Old Siam Sir/Spin It On (die-cut p/s)	5
80	Parlophone 12R 6039	Temporary Secretary/Secret Friend (12", p/s)	30
82	Parlophone R 6054	Ebony And Ivory/Rainclouds (unreleased sepia-toned 'studio photo' p/s; beware of clever counterfeits)	50
82	Epic A 11-2729	The Girl Is Mine (with Michael Jackson)/MICHAEL JACKSON: Can't Get Outta The Rain (picture disc)	15
82	Parlophone R 6057	Tug Of War/Get It (p/s)	5
84	Parlophone 12RP 6080	No More Lonely Nights (Extended Version)/Silly Love Songs/ No More Lonely Nights (Ballad) (12", picture disc)	20
84	Parlophone R 6086	We All Stand Together/Humming Version (p/s)	5
84	Parlophone RP 6086	We All Stand Together/We All Stand Together (Humming Version) (with Frog Chorus, shaped picture disc, in printed PVC sleeve)	15
85	Parlophone RP 6118	Spies Like Us/My Carnival (shaped picture disc)	15
85	Parlophone 12RP 6118	Spies Like Us (Party Mix)/Spies Like Us (Alternative Mix)/Spies Like Us (DJ Version)/My Carnival (Party Mix) (12", picture disc)	20
86	Parlophone 10R 6133	Press/It's Not True/Press (Video Edit) (10", circular foldout p/s)	12
86	Parlophone R 6133	Press (video edit)/It's Not True (p/s)	10
86	Parlophone R 6145	Pretty Little Head/Write Away (p/s)	5
86	Parlophone R 6148/ R 6018	Only Love Remains/Tough On A Tightrope//Mull Of Kintyre/Girls' School (p/s, stickered double pack in PVC sleeve, no p/s on R 6018)	8
87	A&M FREE 21	Long Tall Sally (live)/I Saw Her Standing There (live) (p/s, free with "The Prince's Trust 10th Anniversary Birthday Party" LP (AMA 3906))	6
87	Parlophone CDR 6170	Once Upon A Long Ago/Back On My Feet/Don't Get Around Much Anymore/ Kansas City (CD, card sleeve with anti-static inner)	15
89	Parlophone 12RS 6235	Figure Of Eight/Ou Est Le Soleil? (12" etched vinyl)	25

MINT VALUE £

89	Parlophone RX 6223	This One/The Long And Winding Road (p/s, envelope pack with 6 postcards) 12
89	Parlophone R 6238	Party Party (1 side etched, p/s) 10
92	Parlophone R 6330	Hope Of Deliverance/Long Leather Coat (p/s) 5
97	Parlophone RP 6472	The World Tonight/Used To Be Bad (Picture disc) 6
97	Parlophone RP 6489	Beautiful Night/Love Come Tumbling Down (picture disc) 10
99	Parlophone R 6257	No Other Baby/Brown Eyed Handsome Man 5
01	Parlophone R 6567	From A lover To A Friend/Riding Into Jaipur (p/s) 5
04	Parlophone R6649	Tropic Island Hum/We All Stand Together (p/s, yellow vinyl) 5
05	Parlophone R 6673	Fine Line/Growing Up Falling Down (p/s, plus art print) 5
05	Parlophone R 6678	Jenny Wren/Summer Of '59 (red vinyl, p/s) 5
05	GRA2010	Really Love You/Lalula (1-side etched, McCartney remixes by TWIN FREAKS 2,500 only) 20
07	HearMusic 88072306219	Ever Present Past/House Of Wax (live) (p/s) 5

ALBUMS

70	Apple PCS 7102	McCARTNEY (LP, gatefold sleeve) 40
70	Apple TA 7102	McCARTNEY (reel-to-reel tape, jewel case, mono) 100
70	Apple TD-PCS 7102	McCARTNEY (reel-to-reel tape, jewel case, stereo) 50
71	Apple PAS 10003	RAM (LP, laminated gatefold sleeve) 40
71	Apple PCS 7142	WILDLIFE (LP, sleeve with 'sniped' spine edges, yellow inner) 40
73	Apple PCTC 251	RED ROSE SPEEDWAY (LP, gatefold sleeve, with booklet and poster) 70
73	Apple PCTS 251	RED ROSE SPEEDWAY (LP, gatefold sleeve, without booklet and poster) 25
73	Apple PAS 10007	BAND ON THE RUN (LP, with lyric inner sleeve & poster) 20
73	Apple PAS 1007	BAND ON THE RUN (LP, export edition, Apple logo on textured label above catalogue number, circle indent on label, etched not stamped matrix ZYEX-929-3/ZYEX-930-3, 'BLAIR' etched onto dead wax) 30
75	Capitol PCTC 254	VENUS AND MARS (LP, gatefold sleeve, inner sleeve) 12
75	Capitol PCTC 254	VENUS AND MARS (LP, gatefold sleeve, inner sleeve, 2 posters & stickers) 30
79	Parlophone PCTC 287	BACK TO THE EGG (LP, with inner) 20
80	Parlophone PCTC 258	MCCARTNEY II (LP, with inner) 20
80	Parlophone CHAT 1	MCCARTNEY INTERVIEW (LP) 30
84	Fame FA 413100-1	McCARTNEY (LP, gatefold sleeve) 15
84	Fame FA 416101-1	WINGS - WILD LIFE (LP, yellow inner) 12
84	Nimbus PAS 10007	BAND ON THE RUN (LP, with 'Nimbus' sticker) 200
87	Fame FA 3191	RED ROSE SPEEDWAY (LP, gatefold sleeve) 12
89	Parlophone PCSDX 106	FLOWERS IN THE DIRT (LP, World Tour pack with outer folder, 'Part' 7" single, poster, familty tree, sticker, postcards & tour itinary) 40
90	Parlophone PCST 7346	TRIPPING THE LIVE FANTASTIC (3-LP in slip sleeve with inners and 12" x 12" booklet) 40
91	EMI PAUL 1	LIVERPOOL ORATORIO (2-LP, box set with booklet) 20

(With Carl Davis and others. McCartney does not play on this record which is his first classical composition in collaboration with Carl Davis.)

93	Parlophone PCSD 125	OFF THE GROUND (LP, gatefold) 20
93	Parlophone PCSD 147	PAUL IS LIVE (2 x LP) 30
97	Parlophone PCSD 171	FLAMING PIE (LP, gatefold) 30
99	Parlophone 5223511	RUN DEVIL RUN (LP, gatefold) 30
99	Parlophone 5232291	RUN DEVIL RUN (8 x 7", box set with booklet) 50
99	EMI Classics 5568971	WORKING CLASSICAL (2 x LP, gatefold) 25
99	Parlophone 4991761	BAND ON THE RUN (2 x LP, gatefold, 25th Anniversary) 30
01	Parlophone 5355101	DRIVING RAIN (2 x LP) 35
01	Parlophone 5328501	WINGSPAN (4 x LP, gatefold) 25
05	Parlophone 3383452	CHAOS AND CREATION IN THE BACKYARD (LP, gatefold with 4 art prints) 35

PROMOS : PROMO SINGLES

74	EMI R 5997	Band On The Run (Edited Version)/(Full Version) (demo) 150
74	Apple R 5999	Junior's Farm (Edited Version)/Junior's Farm (Full Version) (demo) 100
75	Apple R 5999	Sally G/Junior's Farm (reversed sides, demo) 120
76	Parlophone R 6015	Let 'Em In (Edited Version)/Let 'Em In (Full Version) (demo) 55
76	Parlophone R 6014	Silly Love Songs (Edited Version)/Silly Love Songs (Full Version) (demo) 50
77	MPL Publishing MPL 1	We've Moved! (music publishing sampler with excerpts by Wings, Peggy Lee, Gene Vincent, Frank Sinatra, etc.; with press pack and insert) 350
77	MPL Publishing MPL 1	We've Moved! (music publishing sampler with excerpts by Wings, Peggy Lee, Gene Vincent, Frank Sinatra, etc.; without press pack and insert) 250
77	Capitol R 6018	Mull Of Kintyre (Edited Version)/Girls' School (Edited Version) (demo) 50
78	Parlophone R 6019	With A Little Luck (Edited Version)/Backwards Traveller-Cuff Link (demo) 40
80	Parlophone R 6037DJ	Waterfalls (3.22) (edit)/Check My Machine (demo) 40
80	Parlophone R 6039A	Temporary Secretary (1-sided demo, no p/s) 75
84	Parlophone 12RDJ 6080T	No More Lonely Nights (Mole Mix) (12", 1-sided, plain white numbered sleeve with plain white inner sleeve & insert, 250 only; beware of counterfeits with scratched [not stamped] matrix) 250
84	Parlophone 12R(DJ) 6080	No More Lonely Nights (Extended Version)/Silly Love Songs/No More Lonely Nights (Ballad) (12", promo, blue 'Give My Regards To Broad Street' label, black die-cut sleeve) 50
85	Parlophone RDJ 6118	Spies Like Us (DJ Version 3.46)/My Carnival (demo, white printed die-cut sleeve) 30
88	Parlophone PMBOX 11-19	ALL THE BEST! ('Special Edition') (9 x 7" box set, in black die-cut sleeves, with signed 7" print; with genuine signatures) 200
88	Parlophone PMBOX 11-19	ALL THE BEST! ('Special Edition') (9 x 7" box set, in black die-cut sleeves, with signed 7" print) 75
89	Parl. 12R LOVE 6223	This One (Lovejoy's Remix) (12", 1-sided, plain label, black die-cut sleeve) 35
89	Parlophone GOOD 1	Good Sign (6.51)/Good Sign (Groove Mix) (7.22) (12", black die-cut sleeve) 45
89	Parlophone RDJ 6235	Figure Of Eight (Edited Version 3.59)/Ou Est Le Soleil? (Edited Version 3.57) (demo, standard p/s) 30
89	Parlophone RDJ 6238	Party (Remix By Bruce Forest)/Party (different remix) (12", some listed as 'Party Party', with insert) 40
89	Parlophone RDJ 6238	Party (Remix By Bruce Forest)/Party (different remix) (12") 30
89	Parlophone R 6213	My Brave Face/Flying To My Home (promo in retro Parlophone sleeve) 20
90	Parlophone 12 SOL 1	Où Est Le Soleil? (Tub Dub Mix)/Où Est Le Soleil? (Instrumental Mix) (12", black die-cut stickered sleeve with insert) 40
90	Parlophone 12 SOL 1	Où Est Le Soleil? (Tub Dub Mix)/Où Est Le Soleil? (Instrumental Mix) (12", black die-cut stickered sleeve, some without insert) 20
90	Parlophone R 6271	Birthday Boy/Good Day Sunshine (promo in repro Parlophone sleeve) 20
90	Parlophone R 6278	All My Trials/C Moon (promo in repro Parlophone sleeve) 20
93	Parlophone CDRDJ 6338	C'mon People (Radio Edit)/C'mon People (CD) 30
93	Parlophone CDRS 6347	Biker Like An Icon/Things We Said Today/Mean Woman Blues/ Midnight Special (CD, unissued) 0
93	Parlophone CDRDJ 6347	Biker Like An Icon/Things We Said Today/Mean Woman Blues/ Midnight Special (CD, no inlay, jewel case with large sticker; beware of counterfeits with thicker blurred label print & smaller sticker on case) 70
93	Parlophone 12 DELIVDJ 1	Deliverance/Deliverance (Dub Mix) (12", green label, plain black die-cut sleeve) 20

Rare Record Price Guide 2014

99	Parlophone RDR03	Run Devil Run/Blue Jean Bop (mock 50's Parlophone label/sleeve)...................................30
01	WINDJ 002	Silly Love Songs (Loop Da Loop Mix)/Coming Up (Linus Loves Mix) (12" 50 copies) 150
03	Parlophone TEMPSEC 01	Temporary Secretary (Re-edited by Audioslave) (12", 1-sided) 20

PROMOS : PROMO ALBUMS

79	Parlophone PCTCP 257	BACK TO THE EGG (LP, as Wings, MPL in-house picture disc; die-cut sleeve, matrix numbers YEX 987-2 & YEX 988-4 or -1; beware counterfeits).....................................900
79	Parlophone PCTC 257	BACK TO THE EGG (LP, box set with badge, booklet, sticker, postcard & 5 cigarette cards; with or without T-shirt; beware of counterfeits with blurred printing)...300
79	Capitol (no cat. no.)	MPL PRESENTS (6-LP, box set, hand-numbered, 25 only) 700
93	Parlophone CDPMCOLDJ 1	PAUL McCARTNEY COLLECTION (CD, 18-track sampler) 25

(see also Beatles, Country Hams, Percy 'Thrills' Thrillington, Fireman, Mike McGear, Suzy & The Red Stripes, George Martin, Spirit Of Play, Ferry Aid, Michael Jackson)

CAROLINE MCCAUSLAND
| 60s | Happy Face MMLP 1022 | SONGS FOR GALA (LP) ....40 |

DAVE MCCLAREN
| 71 | Big BG 323 | Love Is What I Bring (actually by Dave Barker & Uniques)/ RUPIE EDWARDS ALL STARS: Love Version (with U Roy Junior) ....18 |

TOMMY MCCLENNAN
| 75 | Flyright LP 112 | TRAVELIN' HIGHWAY MAN (LP) ....15 |

DELBERT MCCLINTON
| 62 | Decca F 11541 | Hully Gully/Baby Heartbreak ....12 |

CHRIS MCCLURE (SECTION)
66	Decca F 12346	The Dying Swan/The Land Of The Golden Tree 10
68	Polydor 56227	Hazy People/I'm Just A Country Boy 15
68	Polydor 56259	Answer To Everything/Meditation 7
69	RCA RCA 1849	Our Song Of Love/Weather Vane 7
69	CBS 7646	You're Only Passing Time/Sing Our Song (as Chris McClure Section) 8

(see also Marmalade)

BRIAN MCCOLLOM FOLK GROUP
| 66 | Pye 7N 17198 | This Dusty Road/Henry Joy McCraken ....6 |

TOMMY MCCOOK (& SUPERSONICS)
63	Island WI 102	Adam's Apple/MAYTALS: Every Time (B-side actually by Tonettes) 25
63	Island WI 118	Below Zero/LEE PERRY: Never Get Weary 40
63	Island WI 124	Junior Jive/HORACE SEATON: Power 25
64	R&B JB 139	Sampson/ROY & ANNETTE: My Arms Are Waiting 50
64	R&B JB 163	Bridge View/NAOMI & CO: What Can I Do (B-side actually by Naomi & Clive) 45
64	Port-O-Jam PJ 4001	Exodus (& His Group)/LEE PERRY: Help The Weak 40
64	Port-O-Jam PJ 4003	Jam Rock/LEE PERRY: Band Minded People 40
64	Port-O-Jam PJ 4010	Road Bloack/LEE PERRY: Chatty Chatty Woman..70
64	Black Swan WI 422	Two For One/LASCELLES PERKINS: I Don't Know 25
65	Island WI 232	Rocket Ship/JUSTIN HINDS & DOMINOES: Turn Them Back 50
66	Rio R 100	Jerk Time (with Supersonics)/UNIQUES: The Journey 70
66	Rio R 101	Out Of Space (with Supersonics)/UNIQUES: Do Me Good 40
66	Rio R 103	Ska Jam/Smooth Sailing (with Supersonics) 90
66	Rio R 104	Riverton City/HEPTONES: Gunmen Coming To Town 70
66	Doctor Bird DB 1028	More Love/SILVERTONES: True Confession 35
66	Doctor Bird DB 1032	Naked City (with Supersonics)/NORMA FRASER: Heartaches 25
66	Doctor Bird DB 1047	Spanish Eyes (with Lynn Taitt)/STRANGER & HORTENSE: Loving Wine 20
66	Doctor Bird DB 1051	A Little Bit Of Heaven (& His Band)/LLOYD WILLIAMS: Sad World..................................25
66	Doctor Bird DB 1053	Indian Love Call (with Supersonics)/OWEN & LEON: How Would You Feel..............................25
66	Doctor Bird DB 1056	Danger Man (with Supersonics)/ERIC MORRIS: If I Didn't Love You 40
66	Doctor Bird DB 1061	What Now/Don't Stay Away 60
67	Doctor Bird DB 1058	Jam Session (with Supersonics)/LLOYD & GLEN: Jezebel 45
67	Island WI 3047	One Two Three Kick/TREASURE ISLE BOYS: What A Fool (B-side actually by Silvertones) 50
67	Island WI 3049	Saboo (with Supersonics)/MOVING BROTHERS: Darling I Love You....................................25
67	Treasure Isle TI 7017	Persian Cat/JUSTIN HINDS: Once A Man 20
67	Treasure Isle TI 7018	Saboo (with Supersonics)/MOVING BROTHERS: Darling I Love You (reissue) 25
67	Treasure Isle TI 7020	Shadow Of Your Smile/SILVERTONES: Cool Down 20
68	Treasure Isle TI 7027	Soul For Sale/SILVERTONES: In The Midnight Hour 20
68	Treasure Isle TI 7032	Venus/Music Is My Occupation (with Supersonics) 20
68	Treasure Isle TI 7039	Our Man Flint (with Supersonics)/SILVERTONES: Old Man River 50
68	Treasure Isle TI 7042	Moving (with Supersonics)/SILVERTONES: Slow And Easy 20
68	Doctor Bird DB 1135	Mad Mad World/Wonderful World (with Lloyd Williams) 30
68	Unity UN 501	Last Flight To Reggie (Reggae) City (with Stranger Cole)/Watch Dem Go 20
69	Trojan TR 642	Breaking Up/Party Time (with Supersonics) (both actually by Alton Ellis) 10
69	Trojan TR 652	Third Figure/You Should've Known Better..15
69	Trojan TR 657	When The Saints Go Marching In/SOUL OFROUS: Ease Me Up Officer (B-side actually by Righteous Flames)...15
69	Trojan TR 671	Moonshot/PHYLLIS DILLON: The Right Shot 15
69	Trojan TR 686	Tribute To Rameses/PHYLLIS DILLON: Lipstick On Your Collar 12
69	Trojan TR 7706	Black Coffee (with Supersonics)/VIC TAYLOR: Heartaches 15
69	Unity UN 506	The Avengers/LAUREL AITKEN: Donkey Man 20
69	Unity UN 534	Dream Boat/Tommy's Dream 20
69	Unity UN 535	Peanut Vendor/100,000 Tons Of Rock 20
70	Duke DU 76	The Rooster (with Supersonics) (actually by Jeff Barnes)/ PHYLLIS DILLON: Walk Through This World 10
70	Duke DU 77	Open Jaw (with Supersonics)/JOHN HOLT: The Working Kind 10
70	Duke DU 78	Key To The City (with Supersonics)/DOROTHY REID: Give It To Me 10
71	Treasure Isle TI 7058	My Best Dress/PHYLISS DILLON: One Life To Live 15
71	Treasure Isle TI 7061	Testify Version/JOHN HOLT: Let's Build Our Dreams 18
71	Treasure Isle TI 7065	Black River/JOHN HOLT: Sister Big Stuff 20
71	Treasure Isle TI 7066	Paragon's Medley Version/JOHN HOLT: Paragon's Medley 18
71	Treasure Isle TI 7070	Midnight Confession Version/PHYLISS DILLON: Midnight Confession 15
71	Big Shot BI 585	Psalm Nine To Keep In Mind (with Observers)/Psalm Nine (Version) 10
71	Spinning Wheel SW 109	Crying Everynight (with Supersonics) (actually by Stranger Cole)/ HERMAN MARQUIS: Tom's Version 40

Tommy McCOOK & GLEN BROWN

71	Spinning Wheel SW 110	Stupid Doctor (with Supersonics)/ROB WALKER: Grooving In Style (B-side actually by Ken Parker)	60
73	Technique TE 927	Rub It Down/Rub It Down (Version) (as Tommy McCook Stars)	6
73	G.G. GG 4539	Bad Cow Skank (with Bobby Ellis)/ GLADSTONE ANDERSON: Drummer Roach	5
75	Vulcan VUL 1002	Kojak/Cannon (with Aggrovators)	5
79	Grove Music GMDM 26	Sensimena/TONY TUFF: You Wrong (12")	20
70	Trojan TBL 111	GREATER JAMAICA (MOONWALK REGGAE) (LP, actually by various artists)	30
74	Attack ATLP 1007	TOMMY McCOOK (LP)	35
77	Third World TWS 920	HOT LAVA (LP)	25
77	Justice JUS LP 07	INSTRUMENTAL (LP)	45

(see also Denis Alcapone, Dave Barker, Dennis Brown, Chuck & Joe White, Shenley Duffas, Dennis & Lizzy, Dobby Dobson, Dynamics, Alton Ellis, Ethiopians, Eagles, Emotions, Herman, Heptones, Jamaicans, Lloyd Lewis, Lloyd & Glen, Lloyd & Groovers, Bob Marley, Maytals, Melodians, Mellodites, Millions, Paragons, Hugh Roy, Karl Walker Allstars)

TOMMY MCCOOK & GLEN BROWN
76	Groundation GROL 10	HORNY DUB (LP, white label)	300

TOMMY MCCOOK & BOBBY ELLIS
75	Grove Music GMLP 002	BLAZING HORNS (LP)	50

JASON MCCORD
65	Pye 7N 15925	It Was A Very Good Year/Song Of The Pine Tree	35

MCCORMICK BROTHERS
63	Polydor NH 66986	Red Hen Boogie/Blue Grass Express	50
66	Hickory LPE 1509	AUTHENTIC BLUEGRASS HITS (EP)	22

GEORGE MCCORMICK
55	MGM SPC 6	Don't Fix Up The Doghouse/Gold Wedding Band (export issue)	18

BUDD MCCOY
58	RCA RCA 1106	Hiawatha/The Midnight Ride Of Paul Revere	5

CHARLIE MCCOY
75	Monument MNT 5103	Stone Fox Chase/Honestly I Love You	6

CLYDE MCCOY
57	Mercury MEP 9513	DANCING TO THE BLUES (EP)	15

JOE MCCOY
59	Collector JDL 81	One In A Hundred/One More Greasing	30

(JOHN) MCCOY
83	Legacy LGY 9	Oh Well! (Edit)/Because You Lied (p/s)	5
84	Mausoleum SKULL 8373	THINK HARD (LP, with inner sleeve)	12

(see also Gillan, Samson, Mammoth, Zzebra, Split Knee Loons)

VIOLA MCCOY
50s	Ristic LP 27	VIOLA McCOY 1923-1927 (10" LP)	40

MCCOYS
65	Immediate IM 001	Hang On Sloopy/I Can't Explain It	8
65	Immediate IM 021	Fever/Sorrow	12
66	Immediate IM 028	Don't Worry Mother, Your Son's Heart Is Pure/Ko-Ko	10
66	Immediate IM 029	Up And Down/If You Tell A Lie	10
66	Immediate IM 034	Runaway/Come On Let's Go	10
66	Immediate IM 037	(You Make Me Feel) So Good/Every Day I Have To Cry	8
67	Immediate IM 046	I Got To Go Back/Dynamite	15
67	London HLZ 10154	Say Those Magic Words/I Wonder If She Remembers Me	25
68	Mercury MF 1067	Jesse Brady/Resurrection	8
69	Immediate IM 076	Hang On Sloopy/This Is Where We Came In	5
66	Immediate IMEP 002	HITS VOL. 1 (EP)	40
66	Immediate IMEP 003	HITS VOL. 2 (EP)	40
65	Immediate IMLP 001	HANG ON SLOOPY (LP)	55
68	Mercury (S)MCL 20128	THE INFINITE McCOYS (LP)	40
71	Joy JOYS 196	HANG ON SLOOPY (LP, reissue)	15

(see also Rick Derringer)

JIMMY MCCRACKLIN
58	London HLM 8598	The Walk/I'm To Blame (as Jimmy McCracklin & His Band)	50
58	London HLM 8598	The Walk/I'm To Blame (as Jimmy McCracklin & His Band) (78)	20
58	London HL 7035	The Walk/I'm To Blame (export issue, as Jimmy McCracklin & His Band)	30
62	Top Rank JAR 617	Just Got To Know/The Drag	25
65	R&B MRB 5001	I Got Eyes For You/I'm Gonna Tell Your Mother	25
66	Outasite 45 120	Christmas Time (Parts 1 & 2) (99 copies only)	50
65	Liberty LIB 66094	Every Night, Every Day/Can't Raise Me	12
66	Liberty LIB 66129	Think/Steppin' Up In Class	12
68	Minit MLF 11003	How Do You Like Your Love/Get Together	10
68	Minit MLF 11009	Pretty Little Sweet Thing/A And I	10
65	Vocalion VEP 170160	JIMMY McCRACKLIN (EP)	100
68	Minit MLL/MLS 40003	A PIECE OF JIMMY McCRACKLIN (LP)	40

GWEN MCCRAE
74	President PT 416	It's Worth The Hurt/90% Of Me Is You	22
82	Atlantic FLAM 1	Keep The Fire Burning/Funky Sensation	10
82	Atlantic FLAM 1T	Keep The Fire Burning/Funky Sensation (12")	25
75	President	GWEN McCRAE (LP)	20

DANNY MCCULLOCH
69	Capitol CL 15607	Blackbird/Time Of Man	8
70	Pye Intl./Festival 7N 25514	Colour Of The Sunset/Smokeless Zone	8
69	Capitol E-(S)T 174	WINGS OF A MAN (LP, black/silver label with boxed logo)	40

(see also Animals)

IAN MCCULLOCH
64	Decca F11855	Come On Home/Down By The River	40

HENRY MCCULLOUGH
75	Dark Horse AMLH 22005	MIND YOUR OWN BUSINESS! (LP, some with inner sleeve)	12

(see also Grease Band, Eire Apparent, Paul McCartney & Wings)

ED MCCURDY

66	Bounty BY 6017	BLOOD BOOZE N BONES (LP)	20
60s	Elektra ELK 110	WHEN DALLIANCE WAS IN FLOWER AND MAIDENS LOST THEIR HEADS (LP, with insert)	40
60s	Elektra ELK 140	WHEN DALLIANCE WAS IN FLOWER VOL 2 (LP)	40

GEORGE MCCURN

63	London HLH 9705	I'm Just A Country Boy/In My Little Corner Of The World	10

LUKE MCDANIEL

55	Parlophone CMSP 29	The Automobile Song/I Can't Steal Another's Bride (export issue)	40
55	Parlophone DP 407	The Automobile Song/I Can't Steal Another's Bride (78)	12

MAISIE MCDANIEL

61	Beltona BE 2744	Christmastime In Ireland/The Old Pigsty	5
63	Fontana TF 400	Something Special/This Song Is Just For You	5
63	Fontana TE 17397	MEET MAISIE McDANIEL! (EP, with The Hunters)	15
63	Fontana TE 17398	COUNTRY STYLE (EP, with The Hunters)	15
65	Fontana TL 5215	ARE YOU LONESOME TONIGHT (LP)	15

(see also Hunters)

EUGENE MCDANIELS

71	Atlantic 2465 022	OUTLAW (LP)	30

GENE MCDANIELS

61	London HLG 9319	A Hundred Pounds Of Clay/Take A Chance On Love	10
61	London HLG 9396	A Tear/She's Come Back	20
61	London HLG 9448	Tower Of Strength/Secret	10
62	Liberty LIB 55405	Chip Chip/Another Tear Falls	10
62	Liberty LIB 55480	Point Of No Return/Warmer Than A Whisper	15
63	Liberty LIB 55510	Spanish Lace/Somebody's Waiting	6
63	Liberty LIB 55541	The Puzzle/Cry Baby Cry	6
63	Liberty LIB 55597	It's A Lonely Town/False Friends	30
63	Liberty LIB 10130	Anyone Else/New Love In Old Mexico	8
64	Liberty LIB 55723	In Times Like These/Make Me A Present Of You	15
65	Liberty LIB 55752	(There Goes The) Forgotten Man	45
65	Liberty LIB 55805	Walk With A Winner/A Miracle	100
65	Liberty LIB 55805	Walk With A Winner/A Miracle (DJ copy)	250
61	London REG 1298	GENE McDANIELS (EP)	55
62	Liberty LEP 2054	A CHANGE OF MOOD (EP)	40
61	London HA-G 2384	A HUNDRED POUNDS OF CLAY (LP, mono)	80
61	London SAH-G 6184	A HUNDRED POUNDS OF CLAY (LP, stereo)	100
62	Liberty LBY 1003	... SOMETIMES I'M HAPPY (LP)	40
62	Liberty LBY 1021	TOWER OF STRENGTH (LP)	40
63	Liberty (S)LBY 1128	SPANISH LACE (LP)	40
63	Liberty LBY 1179	THE WONDERFUL WORLD OF GENE McDANIELS (LP)	40
68	Sunset SLS 50017E	FACTS OF LIFE (LP)	15

BILL MCDAVID

61	Starlite ST45 63	Kiss Me For Christmas/Little Shepherd Boy	8

MCDERMOTTS

89	Hag HAGLP 2	THE ENEMY WITHIN (LP)	12

CHAS MCDEVITT (SKIFFLE GROUP)

57	Oriole CB 1352	Freight Train (with Nancy Whiskey)/The Cotton Song	25
57	Oriole CB 1357	It Takes A Worried Man/The House Of The Rising Sun	15
57	Oriole CB 1371	Green Back Dollar (with Nancy Whiskey)/I'm Satisfied	12
57	Oriole CB 1386	Face In The Rain (with Nancy Whiskey)/Sporting Life (with Tony Kohn)	15
57	Oriole CB 1395	Sing, Sing, Sing/My Old Man	15
58	Oriole CB 1403	Johnny-O (with Nancy Whiskey)/Bad Man Stack-O-Lee	15
58	Oriole CB 1405	Across The Bridge (with Shirley Douglas)/Deep Down	15
58	Oriole CB 1457	Real Love (with Shirley Douglas)/Juke-Box Jumble	25
59	Oriole CB 1511	Teenage Letter (with Shirley Douglas)/SHIRLEY DOUGLAS: Sad Little Girl	12
59	Oriole CB 1511	Teenage Letter (with Shirley Douglas)/SHIRLEY DOUGLAS: Sad Little Girl (78)	15
60	Top Rank JAR 338	Dream Talk/Forever (with Shirley Douglas)	10
61	HMV POP 845	One Love/Can It Be Love (with Shirley Douglas)	5
61	HMV POP 928	Mommy Out De Light/I've Got A Thing About You (with Shirley Douglas)	5
62	HMV POP 999	Happy Family/Throwing Pebbles In A Pool (with Shirley Douglas)	5
65	Columbia DB 7595	The Most Of What Is Least/Don't Blame Me (with Shirley Douglas)	5
68	Fontana TF 957	City Smoke/One Man Band	5
57	Oriole EP 7002	CHAS AND NANCY (EP, with Nancy Whiskey)	25
57	Oriole MG 10018	THE INTOXICATING MISS WHISKEY (10" LP, with Nancy Whiskey)	45
65	Columbia 33SX 1738	SIXTEEN BIG FOLK HITS (LP, with Shirley Douglas)	15

(see also Nancy Whiskey, Cranes Skiffle Group, Coffee Bar Skifflers)

ALISTAIR MCDONALD

69	Major Minor MMLP 51	BATTLE BALLADS (LP)	15

(COUNTRY) JOE MCDONALD

71	Vanguard 6076 252	Hold On It's Coming Parts 1 & 2	6
70	Vanguard (S)VRL 19057	THINKING OF WOODY GUTHRIE (LP)	12
71	Vanguard 6359 004	TONIGHT I'M SINGING JUST FOR YOU (LP)	15
71	Sonet SNTF 622	QUIET DAYS IN CLICHY (LP, soundtrack)	15
71	Vanguard VSD 79314	HOLD ON - IT'S COMING (LP)	15
71	Vanguard VSD 79315	WAR WAR WAR (LP)	15
72	Vanguard VSD 79316	INCREDIBLE! LIVE! (LP)	12
73	Vanguard VSD 79328	PARIS SESSIONS (LP)	12

(see also Country Joe & The Fish)

LARRY MCDONALD & DENZIL LAING

71	Clandisc CLA 228	Name Of The Game/FABULOUS FLAMES: Holly Version	10

RITCHIE MCDONALD & GLEN BROWN

72	Duke DU 141	Boat To Progress/Boat To Progress - Version	10

MINT VALUE £

SHELAGH MCDONALD
70	B&C CAS 1019	THE SHELAGH McDONALD ALBUM (LP, textured sleeve)	100
71	B&C CAS 1043	STAR GAZER (LP, with inner sleeve)	100

(see also Keith Christmas)

SKEETS MCDONALD
56	Capitol CL 14566	Fallen Angel/It'll Take Me A Long, Long Time	10
56	Capitol CL 14566	Fallen Angel/It'll Take Me A Long, Long Time (78)	10
59	Capitol EAP1 1040	GOING STEADY WITH THE BLUES (EP)	80

TESFA MCDONALD
72	Dynamic DYN 455	Life Is The Highest/Recarnate (Re-Incarnate) (actually by Bobby Ellis and Tommy McCook)	18

MCDONALD & GILES
70	Island ILPS 9126	McDONALD AND GILES (LP, 1st pressing, pink label, with 'i' logo)	100
70	Island ILPS 9126	McDONALD AND GILES (LP, 2nd pressing, 'pink rim' label, 'palm tree' logo)	20
70	Polydor 2302 070	McDONALD AND GILES (LP)	12

(see also King Crimson; Giles, Giles & Fripp)

ROSE MCDOWALL
88	Rio Digital 7RDS 3	Don't Fear The Reaper/Crystal Days (p/s)	5
88	Rio Digital 12RDS 3	Don't Fear The Reaper/Crystal Days (12", p/s)	8

(see also Strawberry Switchblade, Ornamental, Psychic TV, Current 93, Death In June)

(MISSISSIPPI) FRED MCDOWELL
66	Bounty BY 6022	MY HOME IS IN THE DELTA (LP)	45
66	Fontana 688 806 ZL	MISSISSIPPI DELTA BLUES (LP)	40
69	CBS 63735	LONG WAY FROM HOME (LP)	30
69	Polydor 236 278	GOING DOWN SOUTH (LP)	30
70	Capitol E-ST 409	I DO NOT PLAY NO ROCK & ROLL (LP)	25
70	Transatlantic TRA 194	LONDON 1 (LP)	18
71	Transatlantic TRA 203	LONDON 2 (LP)	18
71	Revival RVS 1001	EIGHT YEARS RAMBLIN' (LP, with Johnny Woods)	18
74	Xtra XTRA 1136	MISSISSIPPI FRED McDOWELL 1904-1972 (LP)	15

FRED & ANNIE MAE MCDOWELL
64	Polydor 236 570	GOING DOWN SOUTH (LP)	18

BROTHER JACK MCDUFF
64	Stateside SS 275	Sanctified Samba/Whistle While You Work	10
64	Stateside SS 302	Rock Candy/Real Good 'Un	12
64	Stateside SS 328	Carpetbaggers (Main Theme)/The Pink Panther (Theme)	10
66	Atlantic 584 036	Down In The Valley/A Change Is Gonna Come	10
64	Stateside SL 10060	BROTHER JACK McDUFF LIVE! (LP)	15
64	Stateside SL 10101	THE DYNAMIC JACK McDUFF (LP, as Brother Jack McDuff Quartet)	15
65	Stateside SL 10121	BROTHER JACK McDUFF QUARTET LIVE! AT THE JAZZ WORKSHOP (LP)	20
65	Stateside SL 10142	PRELUDE (LP)	20
66	Stateside SL 10165	THE CONCERT McDUFF (LP)	18
66	Atlantic 587 030	A CHANGE IS GONNA COME (LP)	20
67	Transatlantic PR 7404	SILK AND SOUL (LP)	15
67	Transatlantic PR 7476	WALK ON BY (LP)	15
68	Transatlantic PR 7286	AT THE JAZZ WORKSHOP (LP)	15
68	Transatlantic ATRA 5056	DYNAMIC JACK McDUFF (LP)	15
72	York FYK 407	IF THE CAP FITS ... WEAR IT (LP, as Jack McDuff Band)	12
72	Prestige PR 24013	ROCK CANDY (LP)	12

(see also Roland Kirk, Kenny Burrell, Jimmy Witherspoon)

MCENROE & CASH WITH THE FULL METAL RACKETS
91	M. For Nations KUT 141	Rock'N'Roll (7" Version)/(Instrumental) (p/s)	5
91	M. For Nations 12KUT 141	Rock'N'Roll (Dance Mix)/(7" Version)/(Instrumental) (12", p/s)	8

(see also Iron Maiden, Roger Daltrey)

JOHNNY MCEVOY
67	Pye 17375	Funny Man/Was It You	6
73	Hawk HALPX 112	JOHNNY McEVOY (LP)	15
74	Hawk HALPX 117	SOUNDS LIKE JOHNNY McEVOY (LP)	20

(see also Rambler)

BOB MCFADDEN & DOR
59	Coral Q 72378	The Mummy/The Beat Generation (tri centre)	20
59	Coral Q 72378	The Mummy/The Beat Generation (round centre)	10
59	Coral Q 72378	The Mummy/The Beat Generation (78)	10

(see also Rod McKuen)

MC5
69	Elektra EKSN 45056	Kick Out The Jams/Motor City Is Burning	35
69	Elektra EKSN 45067	Ramblin' Rose/Borderline	35
69	Elektra EKL 4042	KICK OUT THE JAMS (LP, orange label, gatefold sleeve, mono)	200
69	Elektra EKS 74042	KICK OUT THE JAMS (LP, orange label, gatefold sleeve, stereo)	90
70	Atlantic 2400 016	BACK IN THE U.S.A. (LP)	75
71	Atlantic 2400 135	HIGH TIME (LP)	75
77	Atlantic K50346	BACK IN THE USA (LP, reissue)	25
77	Elektra K42027	KICK OUT THE JAMS (LP, reissue with 'Brothers & Sisters' edit)	30

(see also Wayne Kramer, Destroy All Monsters, Rob Tyner & Hot Rods)

MIKE MCGEAR
72	Island WIP 6131	Woman/Kill	15
74	Warner Bros K 16446	Leave It/Sweet Baby (p/s)	12
74	Warner Bros K 16446	Leave It/Sweet Baby	8
75	Warner Bros K 16520	Sea Breezes/Givin' Grease A Ride	8
75	Warner Bros K 16573	Dance The Do/Norton	10
75	Warner Bros K 16658	Simply Love You/What Do We Really Know (in p/s)	15
75	Warner Bros K 16658	Simply Love You/What Do We Really Know	8
76	EMI EMI 2485	Doing Nothing All Day/A To Z	6
80	Carrere CAR 144	All The Whales In The Ocean/I Juz Want What You Got - Money! (in p/s)	30

80	Carrere CAR 144	All The Whales In The Ocean/I Juz Want What You Got - Money!	15
81	Conn SRTS/81/CUS 1112	No Lardidar/God Save The Gracious Queen (in p/s)	55
81	Conn SRTS/81/CUS 1112	No Lardidar/God Save The Gracious Queen	35
72	Island ILPS 9191	WOMAN (LP, gatefold, pink rim palm tree label)	50
74	Warner Bros K 56051	McGEAR (LP, gatefold sleeve with folded lyric insert)	25
74	Warner Bros KMG 1	McGEAR'S LIMITED EDITION (7-track white label sampler & press kit)	45
80s	Centre Labs	McGEAR (LP, 6-track reissue, 500 only, numbered & signed)	60

(see also Grimms, Scaffold, McGough & McGear, Paul McCartney)

BROWNIE MCGHEE
51	Melodisc 1127	Secret Mojo Blues/Me And My Dog (78)	25
63	Columbia SEG 8226	BLUES ON PARADE NO. 1 (EP)	25
60s	Xtra 1021	BROWNIE McGHEE (LP)	20

BROWNIE MCGHEE & DAVE LEE
| 57 | Pye Jazz NJE 1060 | THE BLUEST (EP) | 22 |

(see also Sonny Terry & Brownie McGhee)

DONNA MCGHEE
| 78 | Anchor ANCT 1061 | Do As I Do/Mr Blindman (12") | 40 |
| 78 | Anchor ANCL 2027 | MAKE IT LAST FOREVER (LP) | 70 |

HOWARD MCGHEE
| 61 | Parlophone PMC 1811 | DUSTY BLUE (LP, black/gold label) | 50 |
| 61 | Fontana FJL906 | THE SHARP EDGE (LP) | 30 |

(see also Scaffold, Adrian Henri, Mike McGear, Jimi Hendrix, Grimms)

(ROGER) MCGOUGH & (MIKE) MCGEAR
68	Parlophone PMC/PCS 7047	McGOUGH AND McGEAR (LP, with phasing on "So Much"; black/yellow label with "Sold in U.K..." text)	250
89	Parlophone PCS 7332	McGOUGH AND McGEAR (LP, stereo reissue with inner sleeve, without phasing on "So Much")	15
89	RCA Neon CDP 7 91877-2	McGOUGH AND McGEAR (CD, without phasing on "So Much")	30

ROGER MCGOUGH & BRIAN PATTEN
| 75 | Argo ZPL 1190 | READ THEIR OWN VERSE - BRITISH POETS OF OUR TIME (LP) | 25 |

MAUREEN MCGOVERN
| 73 | Pye Intl. 7N 25603 | The Morning After/Midnight Storm (p/s) | 8 |

CHRIS MCGREGOR('S BROTHERHOOD OF BREATH)
68	Polydor 184 137	VERY URGENT (LP, as Chris McGregor Group)	75
68	Polydor 583 072	UP TO EARTH (LP, unreleased, test pressings only)	150
71	RCA Neon NE 2	CHRIS McGREGOR'S BROTHERHOOD OF BREATH (LP, gatefold sleeve)	60
72	RCA SF 8260	BROTHERHOOD (LP, gatefold sleeve, as Chris McGregor's Brotherhood Of Breath)	65
74	Ogun OG 100	LIVE, WILLISAU (LP)	15
77	Ogun OG 521	IN HIS OWN TIME (LP)	15
78	Ogun OG 524	PROCESSION (LP)	15

(see also Brotherhood Of Breath, Tunji)

FREDDIE MCGREGOR
73	Fab FAB 261	Wise Words/NEW ESTABLISHMENT: Version	20
79	Observer OBS 903	Run Come Rally (12")	40
81	Yashemabeth YM01	Wine Of Violence/Once A Man (12")	15
81	JB JBD 030	Leave Yah/20 Miles Blackstar Liner/U BROWN: Step It Up (12", blue/yellow vinyl)	40
83	Intense INT 007	Jumping Jack/Pretty Woman (12")	12
84	Real Authentic Sound RAS 7008	Across The Border/Version (12")	30
96	Blacker Dread BDTL 05	Mr. Pressure Man/CLIVE HYLTON: Babylon Keep On Knocking (12")	35
79	Jackal JALP 7000	FREDDIE McGREGOR (LP)	15

(see also Soul Brothers, Young Freddie)

JIMMY MCGRIFF
64	Sue WI 303	All About My Girl/M.G. Blues	40
64	Sue WI 310	Last Minute (Parts 1 & 2)	40
64	Sue WI 317	I've Got A Woman (Parts 1 & 2)	40
64	Sue WI 333	'Round Midnight/Lonely Avenue	40
66	United Artists UP 1170	See See Rider/Hallelujah	15
70	United Artists UP 35025	The Worm/What's That	30
64	Sue ILP 907	I'VE GOT A WOMAN (LP)	110
64	Sue ILP 908	GOSPEL TIME (LP)	100
65	London HA-C 8247	BLUES FOR MISTER JIMMY (LP)	60
66	London HA-C 8242	AT THE APOLLO (LP)	75
66	United Artists (S)ULP 1158	A BAG FULL OF SOUL (LP)	30
68	United Artists (S)ULP 1170	THE BIG BAND (LP)	25
69	Solid State USS 7012	I'VE GOT A NEW WOMAN (LP)	12
72	Groove Merchant GM 503	GROOVE GREASE (LP)	15
73	Groove Merchant GM 2205	GOOD THINGS DON'T HAPPEN EVERY DAY (LP, with Junior Parker)	12
74	People PLEO 14	FLY DUDE (LP)	15
74	People PLEO 19	LET'S STAY TOGETHER (LP)	15
74	People PLEO 23	IF YOU'RE READY COME GO WITH ME (LP)	15

BILL MCGUFFIE (TRIO)
53	Parlophone MSP 6040	Concerto For Boogie/Begin The Beguine (as Bill McGuffie Trio)	7
67	Philips BF 1550	Fugue For Thought (from the film 'Dalek Invasion Earth 2150AD')/ Fair's Fair	25
55	Philips BBR 8054	JAZZ WITH McGUFFIE (LP)	15
56	Philips BBR 8087	McGUFFIE MAGIC (LP)	20
56	Philips BBL 7072	MORE JAZZ WITH McGUFFIE (LP)	20
58	Philips BBL 7261	CONTINENTAL TOUR (LP)	20
61	Philips BBL 7450	PLAYING FOR PLEASURE (LP)	12
68	Philips LPS 16001	LATIN OVERTONES (LP)	12

ROGER MCGUINN
74	CBS 2649	Peace On You/Without You	6
77	CBS 5231	American Girl/Russian Hill	6
73	CBS 65274	ROGER McGUINN (LP)	12
74	CBS 80171	PEACE ON YOU (LP)	12
75	CBS 80877	ROGER McGUINN AND BAND (LP)	12

76	CBS 81369	CARDIFF ROSE (LP)	12

(see also Byrds)

McGUINNESS FLINT

70	Capitol EA-ST 22625	McGUINNESS FLINT (LP, gatefold sleeve)	20
71	Capitol ST 22794	HAPPY BIRTHDAY, RUTHY BABY (LP)	15
73	Bronze ILPS 9244	RAINBOW (LP, gatefold sleeve with inner, Island credit on label)	12

(see also Manfred Mann, Blues Band, John Mayall, Coulson Dean McGuinness Flint, Gallagher & Lyle, Paladin)

BARRY MCGUIRE

65	Ember EMB S 208	So Long Stay Well/Far Side Of The Hill	6
65	Ember EMB S 224	Greenback Dollar/One By One	5
65	RCA Victor RCA 1493	Child Of Our Times/Upon A Painted Ocean	5
66	RCA Victor RCA 1497	This Precious Time/Don't You Wonder Where It's At	5
66	RCA Victor RCA 1508	Walking My Cat Named Dog/I'd Have To Be Outta My Mind	5
66	RCA Victor RCA 1525	Cloudy Summer Afternoon/You've Got To Hide Your Love Away (B-side with Mamas & Papas)	15
67	RCA Victor RCA 1638	Masters Of War/Why Not Stop And Dig It While You Can	7
65	RCA Victor RD 7751	SINGS EVE OF DESTRUCTION (LP)	30
66	Ember EMB 3362	THE EVE OF DESTRUCTION (LP, with New Christy Minstrels)	12
71	A&M AMLS 2008	BARRY McGUIRE AND THE DOCTOR (LP, with Eric Hord)	12
70s	Sparrow BIRD 105	C'MON ALONG (LP)	15
70s	Sparrow BIRD 111	HAVE YOU HEARD? (LP)	15

(see also Mamas & Papas, New Christy Minstrels)

McGUIRE SISTERS

54	Vogue Coral Q 2028	Lonesome Polecat/Muskrat Ramble	15
55	Vogue Coral Q 72050	Sincerely/No More	10
55	Vogue Coral Q 72052	Melody Of Love/Open Up Your Heart	10
55	Vogue Coral Q 72082	Something's Gotta Give/It May Sound Silly	10
55	Vogue Coral Q 72108	Christmas Alphabet/He	10
56	Vogue Coral Q 72117	Young And Foolish/Doesn't Anybody Love Me?	10
56	Vogue Coral Q 72145	Missing/Be Good To Me (Baby, Baby)	10
56	Vogue Coral Q 72161	Delilah Jones/Picnic	10
56	Vogue Coral Q 72188	Weary Blues/In The Alps	10
56	Vogue Coral Q 72201	My Baby's Got Such Lovin' Ways/Endless	10
56	Vogue Coral Q 72209	Tip Toe Through The Tulips With Me/Do You Remember When?	10
56	Vogue Coral Q 72216	Goodnight My Love, Pleasant Dreams/Mommy	10
57	Vogue Coral Q 72238	Heart/Sometimes I'm Happy	10
57	Vogue Coral Q 72249	Kid Stuff/Without Him	10
57	Vogue Coral Q 72265	Rock Bottom/Beginning To Miss You	10
57	Vogue Coral Q 72272	He's Got Time/Interlude	10
57	Vogue Coral Q 72296	Forgive Me/Kiss Them For Me	10
58	Coral Q 72305	Sugartime/Banana Split	6
58	Coral Q 72327	Ding Dong/Since You Went Away To School	5
58	Coral Q 72334	Volare/Do You Love Me Like You Kiss Me?	5
59	Coral Q 72356	May You Always/Achoo-Cha-Cha	6
59	Coral Q 72370	Peace/Summer Dreams	8
59	Coral Q 72379	Red River Valley/Compromise	6
60	Coral Q 72387	Lovers' Lullaby/Livin' Dangerously	5
60	Coral Q 72399	The Unforgiven Theme (The Need For Love)/I Give Thanks	5
60	Coral Q 72406	Nine O'Clock/The Last Dance	5
60	Coral Q 72415	I Don't Know Why/To Be Loved	5
61	Coral Q 72427	Really Neat/Just For Old Time's Sake	6
61	Coral Q 72435	Will There Be Space In The Spaceship/Tears On My Pillow	10
61	Coral Q 72446	I Can Dream Can't I/Old Devil Moon	5
62	Coral Q 72452	Sugartime Twist/More Hearts Are Broken That Way	6
58	Coral FEP 2001	THE McGUIRE SISTERS (EP)	15
58	Coral FEP 2006	VOLARE (EP)	15
59	Coral FEP 2033	MAY YOU ALWAYS (EP)	15
56	Vogue Coral LVA 9024	DO YOU REMEMBER WHEN? (LP)	30
57	Vogue Coral LVA 9072	CHILDREN'S HOLIDAY (LP)	20
58	Coral LVA 9073	TEENAGE PARTY (LP)	20
58	Coral LVA 9082	WHILE THE LIGHTS ARE LOW (LP)	20
59	Coral LVA 9115	MAY YOU ALWAYS (LP)	20
60	Coral LVA 9133	OUR GOLDEN FAVORITES (LP)	15
61	Coral LVA 9140	HIS AND HERS (LP)	15
61	Coral LVA 9146	JUST FOR OLD TIME'S SAKE (LP)	15

KEN MCINTIRE

60	Esquire 32-133	LOOKING AHEAD (LP, with Eric Dolphy)	60

DAVID MCIVOR

69	Warner Bros WB8002	Closing My Eyes/Love That Burns	20

FREDDIE MCKAY

71	Banana BA 348	Picture On The Wall/SOUND DIMENSION: Version	25
71	Banana BA 353	Sweet You, Sour You/High School Dance	18
71	Banana BA 358	High School Dance/SOUND DIMENSION: High School Version	20
71	Moodisc HM 110	Old Joe/Too Much Fire	10
72	Banana BA 370	Drunken Sailor/SOUND DIMENSION: Version	18
73	Bullet BU 525	Go On This Way/SANTIC ALL STARS: Santic Dub	15
73	Dragon DRA 1012	Our Rendezvous/Black Beauty	15
73	Atra ATRA 003	I'm A Freeman/SWEET HARMONY: Santic Special	10
73	Grape GR 3060	Our Rendezvous/SOUL DYMAMITES: Version	10
74	Dragon DRA 1022	Dream My Life Over/YOUTH STARS: Version	5
78	Art & Craft ACD 004	A Love Like Mine/Version (12")	12
81	Greensleeves GRED 46	Another Weekend/EARL SIXTEEN: Live Together (12")	30
82	Greensleeves GRED 84	Roots Man Skanking/TOYAN: Version (12")	12
82	Live & Love LLDIS 2014	In Times Of Trouble/Version (12")	30
71	Banana BALPS 01	PICTURE ON THE WALL (LP)	45
73	Attack ATLP 1013	PICTURE ON THE WALL (LP, reissue)	15
74	Dragon DRLS 5005	LONELY MAN (LP)	12

(see also Lizzy)

SCOTT MCKAY
67	Columbia DB 8147	I Can't Make Your Way/Take A Giant Step	40

SCOTTY MCKAY
64	London HLU 9885	Cold Cold Heart/What You Wanna	10

TONY MCKAY
66	Polydor BM 56513	Nobody's Perfect/Detroit	8

LONETTE MCKEE
75	Sussex SXX 4	Save It/Do It To Me	12

MCKENDREE SPRING
69	MCA MUPS 277	McKENDREE SPRING (LP)	12
71	MCA MUPS 433	SECOND THOUGHTS (LP)	12
72	MCA MUPS 454	THREE (LP)	12

MAE MCKENNA
75	Transatlantic TRA 297	MAE McKENNA (LP)	12

(see also Contraband)

VAL MCKENNA
65	Piccadilly 7N 35237	Baby Do It/I Believe In Love	15
65	Piccadilly 7N 35256	Mixed Up Shook Up Girl/Now That You've Made Up Your Mind	25
66	Piccadilly 7N 35286	I Can't Believe What You Say/Don't Hesitate	15
69	Spark SRL 1005	House For Sale/I'll Be Satisfied	10
69	Spark SRL 1023	It's All In My Imagination/Sweet Sweet Lovin'	7
70	Spark SRL 1038	Love Feeling/It's All In My Imagination (silver label)	25

MCKENNA MENDELSON MAINLINE
69	Liberty LBF 15235	You Better Watch Out/She's Alright	6
69	Liberty LBF 15276	Don't Give Me No Goose For Christmas/Beltmaker	6
69	Liberty LBS 83251	STINK (LP)	30

CINDY MCKENZIE
10	Trojan THB 7003	Breakfast In Bed/Ice Cream	10

MERLENE MCKENZIE
68	Double D DD 106	Left Me For Another/BOBBY AITKEN & CARIBBEATS: Cell Block Eleven	20

SCOTT MCKENZIE
67	CBS 2816	San Francisco (Be Sure To Wear Some Flowers In Your Hair)/What's The Difference	5
67	Capitol CL 15509	Look In Your Eyes/All I Want Is You	20
67	CBS 3009	Like An Old-Time Movie/What's The Difference Chapter II	7
68	CBS 3393	Holy Man/What's The Difference (Chapter 3)	6
67	CBS (S)BPG 63157	THE VOICE OF SCOTT McKENZIE (LP)	22
70	A&M AMLS 999	STAINED GLASS MORNING (LP)	18

(see also Mamas & Papas)

TOMMY MCKENZIE
68	Pama PM 720	Fiddlesticks/Please Stay	15
71	Pama Supreme PS 327	Eastern Promise/Fiddlesticks (as Tommy McKenzie Orchestra)	7

MCKENZIE, DOUG & BOB
82	Mercury HOSER 1	Take Off/Elron McKenzie (p/s)	20

(see also Rush)

MCKENZIE & GARDINER
83	The Sound Of London TSOLL 501	From Time/From Time (Version) (12")	80

LESLIE MCKEOWN
79	Ego Trip EGOS 7	Shall I Do It (One More Number One)/Do It All Again (p/s)	7
79	Ego Trip EGO 001	ALL WASHED UP (LP, gatefold, with poster)	20

MCKINLEYS
64	Columbia DB 7230	Someone Cares For Me/A Million Miles Away	20
64	Columbia DB 7310	When He Comes Along/Then I'll Know It's Love	10
64	Parlophone R 5211	Sweet And Tender Romance/That Lonely Feeling	12
65	Columbia DB 7583	Give Him My Love/Once More	15

ROD MCKUEN
57	London HLU 8390	Happy Is A Boy Named Me/Jaydee	20
60	Brunswick 05828	Two Brothers/Time After Time	10
64	Capitol CL 15348	The World I Used To Know/Someplace Green	5
66	Ember EMB 223	Soldiers Who Want To Be Heroes/Wayfarin' Stranger	5
68	RCA Victor RCA 1734	Cat Named Sloopy/Where Are We Now	5
71	Buena Vista DF 482	Pastures Green/Theme From Scandalous John/Train To Quivira (p/s)	5

(see also Bob McFadden & Dor, Mike Redway, Mike Sarne, Henri Mancini)

HAL MCKUSICK SEXTET/QUINTET
57	Vogue Coral Q 72258	Kelly And Me (as Sextet)/When I Fall In Love (as Quintet)	6

IAN MCLAGAN
79	Mercury MER1	La De Da/Hold On (p/s)	5
80	Mercury 9100 072	TROUBLEMAKER (LP) (with poster)	12

(see also Faces)

TOMMY MCLAIN
66	London HL 10065	Sweet Dreams/I Need You So	10
66	London HL 10091	Think It Over/I Can't Take No More	10

(MAHAVISHNU) JOHN MCLAUGHLIN
69	Marmalade 608 007	EXTRAPOLATION (LP)	100
70	Polydor 02343 012	EXTRAPOLATION (LP, reissue)	15
71	Douglas DGL 65075	DEVOTION (LP, gatefold sleeve)	15
71	Douglas DGL 69014	MY GOAL'S BEYOND (LP, as Mahavishnu John McLaughlin, gatefold sleeve)	15
74	CBS Q 69037	LOVE, DEVOTION, SURRENDER (LP, quadrophonic issue)	12

JACKIE MCLEAN QUINTET
55	Esquire 32-041	LIGHTS OUT (LP)	30
56	Esquire 32-111	JACKIE'S PALS (LP)	50

(see also Lifetime, Tony Williams [Lifetime], Mahavishnu Orchestra, John Surman, Santana)

NANA MCLEAN
71	Banana BA 355	A Little Love/SOUND DIMENSION: Heavy Beat	30

PHIL MCLEAN
61	Top Rank JAR 597	Small Sad Sam/Chicken	6
62	Top Rank JAR 613	Big Mouth Bill/Come With Us	5

GERALD MCLEASH
71	G.G. GG 4516	False Reaper/G.G. ALL STARS: Reaping Version	10

LARIS MCLENNON
67	CBM 04	Confusion/Turn Me Loose	15

ENOS MCLEOD
68	Blue Cat BS 135	You Can Never Get Away/ENOS & SHEILA: La La La Bamba	25

(see also Enos & Sheila)

SEAN MCLEOD
69	Aurora 4594	Living Without You/Love Songs From Another Planet	20

VINCENT MCLEOD
69	Jackpot JP 711	Too Late/SIR COLLINS: Late Night	12

OSCAR MCLOLLIE & HIS HONEYJUMPERS
55	London HL 8130	Take Your Shoes Off, Pop/Love Me Tonight	250
55	London HL 8130	Take Your Shoes Off, Pop/Love Me Tonight (78)	40

EDDIE MCLOYD
75	Brunswick BR 27	Once You Fall In Love/Baby Get Down	22

BOBBY MCLURE
66	Chess CRS 8048	Peak Of Love/You Got Me Baby	45
66	Chess CRS 8048	Peak Of Love/You Got Me Baby (DJ copy)	75
75	Island USA 006	You Bring Out The Love In Me/SURVIVAL KIT: Daybreak	20

(see also Fontella Bass)

MCLYNNS
70	CBS 63836	OLD MARKET ST. (LP)	50

ROSS MCMANUS
64	HMV POP 1279	Patsy Girl/I'm The Greatest	10
66	HMV POP 1543	Stop Your Playing Around/Girlie Girlie	10
67	Decca F 12618	Can't Take My Eyes Off Of You/If I Were A Rich Man	6
72	Rediffusion ZS 122	THE LEAVING OF LIVERPOOL (LP)	12

(see also Day Costello)

MC MELLO
89	Republic LICT007	Bizzie Rhymin'/Comin' Correct/Wize (EP)	12
92	Funki Dreds PA6640	Gone Crazy/Talk Dem Way/Firm Stance (EP)	15
94	Natural Response MELLO 1	I Hear Voices/Live At Portland (promo only)	12

MARGARET MCMILLEN
65	Decca F 12272	You Can't Be True Dear/The Love Of My Man	6

IAN MCNABB
91	Way Cool WAY 147	Great Dreams Of Heaven/That's Why I Believe	8

BARBARA MCNAIR
66	Tamla Motown TMG 544	You're Gonna Love My Baby/The Touch Of Time	350
66	Tamla Motown TMG 544	You're Gonna Love My Baby/The Touch Of Time (DJ copy)	400
59	Coral FEP 2021	FRONT ROW CENTRE VOL. 1 (EP)	40
64	Warner Bros WEP 6129	I ENJOY BEING A GIRL (EP)	40

(see also Billy Williams & Barbara McNair)

HAROLD MCNAIR
68	RCA Victor RCA 1742	The Hipster/Indecision	100
65	Island ILP 926	AFFECTIONATE FINK (LP, with Ornette Coleman's Sidemen)	400
68	RCA SF 7969	HAROLD McNAIR (LP)	100
70	RCA Intl. INTS 1096	FLUTE AND NUT (LP)	60
70	B&C CAS 1016	THE FENCE (LP, gatefold with pink envelope containing balloon)	80
70	B&C CAS 1016	THE FENCE (LP, gatefold with pink envelope without balloon)	40
72	B&C CAS 1045	HAROLD McNAIR (LP)	70

(see also Ginger Baker's Airforce)

CHARLIE MCNAIR'S JAZZ BAND
60	Waverly SLP 504	Big House Blues/Fish Man	6

JOHN MCNALLY
69	CBS 4517	Mary In The Morning/My Love Forgive Me	5

TREVOR MCNAUGHTON
72	Hillcrest HCT 5	No Sins At All/No Sins At All Version	5

(see also The Melodians)

BIG JAY MCNEELY
59	Top Rank JAR 169	There Is Something On Your Mind/...Back...Shack...Track ('vocal: Little Sonny')	40
59	Top Rank JAR 169	There Is Something On Your Mind/...Back...Shack...Track ('vocal: Little Sonny') (78)	20
65	Sue WI 373	There Is Something On Your Mind/...Back...Shack...Track ('vocal: Little Sonny') (reissue)	35
64	Warner Bros WM 8143	BIG JAY'S PARTY (LP)	40

AARON MCNEIL
73	Action ACT 4619	Soul Of A Black Man/Reap What You Sow	12

DAVID MCNEIL
68	President PT 212	Don't Let Your Chance Go By/Space Plane	40

PAUL MCNEILL
66	Decca LK 4803	TRADITIONALLY AT THE TROUBADOUR (LP)	50

PAUL MCNEILL & LINDA PETERS
68	MGM MGM 1408	You Ain't Goin' Nowhere/I'll Show You How To Sing	6

(see also Linda Peters, Richard & Linda Thompson)

RONNIE MCNEIR
75	London HLA 10494	Wendy Is Gone/Give Me A Sign	10

MARIAN MCPARTLAND
55	Capitol EAP-1-574	AT THE HICKORY HOUSE PART 1 (EP, tri centre)	8
55	Capitol EAP-2-574	AT THE HICKORY HOUSE PART 2 (EP, tri centre)	8
55	Capitol LC 6828	AFTER DARK (10" LP)	15
57	Capitol T785	THE MARIAN MCPARTLAND TRIO (LP)	18

MCPEAKE FAMILY/FOLK GROUP
60s	Topic TOP 92	WILD MOUNTAIN THYME (EP)	12
60s	Topic	IRISH TRADITIONAL FOLK SONGS AND MUSIC (LP, blue label)	30
60s	Topic 12T 87	THE McPEAKE FAMILY (LP)	20
64	Fontana TL 5214	IRISH FOLK! (LP, as McPeake Family)	35
65	Fontana TL 5358	AT HOME WITH THE McPEAKES (LP)	20
67	Fontana TL 5433	PLEASANT AND DELIGHTFUL (LP, as McPeake Family)	20
69	Evolution Z 1002	WELCOME HOME (LP, as McPeake Folk Group)	40
72	Windmill WMD 151	IRISH TO BE SURE (LP, as McPeake Family)	25

CLYDE MCPHATTER
SINGLES
56	London HLE 8250	Seven Days/I'm Not Worthy Of You	400
56	London HLE 8250	Seven Days/I'm Not Worthy Of You (78)	30
56	London HL 7006	Seven Days/I'm Not Worthy Of You (export issue)	125
56	London HLE 8293	Treasure Of Love/When You're Sincere (gold label lettering)	150
56	London HLE 8293	Treasure Of Love/When You're Sincere (silver label lettering)	60
56	London HLE 8293	Treasure Of Love/When You're Sincere (78)	10
57	London HLE 8462	Just To Hold My Hand/No Matter What (triangular centre)	150
57	London HLE 8462	Just To Hold My Hand/No Matter What (78)	20
57	London HLE 8476	Long Lonely Nights/Heartaches (triangular centre)	100
57	London HLE 8476	Long Lonely Nights/Heartaches (triangular centre) (78)	20
57	London HLE 8525	Rock And Cry/You'll Be There (triangular centre)	90
57	London HLE 8525	Rock And Cry/You'll Be There (later round centre)	40
57	London HLE 8525	Rock And Cry/You'll Be There (78)	20
58	London HLE 8707	Come What May/Let Me Know (triangular centre)	60
58	London HLE 8707	Come What May/Let Me Know (78)	25
58	London HLE 8755	A Lover's Question/I Can't Stand Up Alone (triangular centre)	30
58	London HLE 8755	A Lover's Question/I Can't Stand Up Alone (78)	20
59	MGM MGM 1014	I Told Myself A Lie/(I'm Afraid) The Masquerade Is Over	20
59	London HLE 8878	Lovey Dovey/My Island Of Dreams (triangular centre)	30
59	London HLE 8878	Lovey Dovey/My Island Of Dreams (78)	25
59	London HLE 8906	Since You've Been Gone/Try Try Baby (triangular centre)	40
59	London HLE 8906	Since You've Been Gone/Try Try Baby (78)	30
59	MGM MGM 1040	Twice As Nice/Where Did I Make My Mistake	18
59	London HLE 9000	You Went Back On Your Word/There You Go	40
59	London HLE 9000	You Went Back On Your Word/There You Go (78)	40
59	MGM MGM 1048	Bless You/Let's Try Again	18
60	London HLE 9079	Just Give Me A Ring/Don't Dog Me	45
60	MGM MGM 1061	Think Me A Kiss/When The Right Time Comes Along	18
60	Mercury AMT 1108	I Ain't Givin' Up Nothin' (If I Can't Get Something)/Ta Ta	15
60	Mercury AMT 1120	You're For Me/I Just Want To Love You	18
61	Mercury AMT 1136	Tomorrow Is A-Comin'/I'll Love You Till The Cows Come Home	40
62	Mercury AMT 1174	Lover Please/Let's Forget About The Past	20
62	Mercury AMT 1181	Little Bitty Pretty One/Next To Me	20
66	Stateside SS 487	Everybody's Somebody's Fool/I Belong To You	18
66	Stateside SS 567	A Shot Of Rhythm And Blues/I'm Not Going To Work Today	30
67	Stateside SS 592	Lavender Lace/Sweet And Innocent	20
68	Deram DM 202	Only A Fool/Thank You Love	25
69	Deram DM 223	Baby I Could Be So Good At Loving You/Baby You've Got It	25
69	Pama PM 775	A Shot Of Rhythm And Blues/I'm Not Going To Work Today (reissue)	12
69	B&C CB 106	Denver/Tell Me	12

EPs
59	London RE-E 1202	CLYDE McPHATTER	250
60	London RE-E 1240	CLYDE MCPHATTER NO. 2 (unissued)	0
59	MGM MGM-EP 705	TWICE AS NICE	60
60	MGM MGM-EP 739	THIS IS NOT GOODBYE	60

ALBUMS
63	Mercury MMC 14120	LOVER PLEASE	100
64	Atlantic ATL 5001	THE BEST OF CLYDE McPHATTER	90
71	MCA MUPS 418	WELCOME HOME	20
73	Atlantic K 30033	A TRIBUTE TO CLYDE McPHATTER	20

(see also Drifters, Jackie Wilson, Dominoes, Billy Ward & Dominoes, Jackie Wilson/Clyde McPhatter)

TONY (T.S.) MCPHEE
66	Purdah 45-3501	Someone To Love Me/Ain't Gonna Cry No Mo' (as T.S. McPhee)	240
83	TS 001	Time Of Action/Born To Be With You (sold at gigs)	10
68	Liberty LBL/LBS 83190	ME AND THE DEVIL (LP)	60
71	Sunset SLS 50209	THE SAME THING ON THEIR MINDS (LP, with Jo-Ann Kelly)	30
73	World Wide Artists WWA 1	THE TWO SIDES OF TONY (T.S.) McPHEE (LP, with insert)	25

(see also Groundhogs, Champion Jack Dupree, Jo-Ann Kelly, John Dummer Blues Band, Hapshash & Coloured Coat, Herbal Mixture)

CHARLES MCPHERSON
65	Stateside SL 10151	BEBOP REVISITED (LP)	15
73	Mainstream MSL 1004	SIKU YA BIBI (LP)	12

MINT VALUE £

GILLIAN MCPHERSON
71	RCA Victor RCA 2089	It's My Own Way/Is Somebody In Tune With My Song	5
71	RCA Victor SF 8220	POETS AND PAINTERS AND PERFORMERS OF THE BLUES (LP)	60

KEVIN MCQUINN
62	Top Rank JAR 598	Every Step Of The Way/Keep Me On Your Mind	10

RON MCQUINN
77	Decca F13693	Look At Love Bleed/Banshee	20

CARMEN MCRAE
55	Brunswick 05502	Love Is Here To Stay/This Will Make You Laugh	5
56	Brunswick 05588	You Don't Know Me/Never Loved Him Anyhow	5
56	Brunswick 05632	Star Eyes/I'm A Dreamer (Aren't We All)	5
57	Brunswick 05652	Whatever Lola Wants (Lola Gets)/Ooh (What 'Cha Doin' To Me) (with Dave Lambert Quartet)	10
57	Brunswick 05723	It's Like Getting A Donkey To Gallop/The Party's Over	5
59	London HLR 8837	Play For Keeps/Which Way Is Love	10
68	Atlantic 584 178	Elusive Butterfly/I'm Always Drunk In San Francisco	6
57	London RE-N 1094	LONDON'S GIRL FRIENDS (EP)	15
56	Brunswick LAT 8133	TORCHY (LP)	15

(see also Sammy Davis Jnr.)

CARMEN MCRAE & DAVE BRUBECK FIVE
62	Fontana H 379	Take Five/It's A Raggy Waltz	6

(see also Dave Brubeck)

IAN MCSHANE
62	Columbia DB 4932	Harry Brown/The Tinker	6

JAY MCSHANN
55	Brunswick LA 8735	KANSAS CITY MEMORIES (10" LP)	15

MC SPY-D & 'FRIENDS'
95	Parlophone 12RDJ 6404	The Amazing Spider-Man (Solution Mix)/(Solution Chilled Mix)/(B&J White Trouser Mix) (12", no p/s, promo only)	25

(see also Brian May)

BLIND WILLIE MCTELL
66	Transatlantic PR 1040	LAST SESSION (LP)	35
67	Storyville 670 816	BLIND WILLIE McTELL 1940 (LP)	22
60s	Roots RL 324	BLIND WILLIE McTELL 1929-1935 (LP)	20
73	Atlantic K 40400	ATLANTA TWELVE STRING GUITAR (LP)	18

RALPH MCTELL
69	Big T BIG 125	Summer Comes Along/Girl On A Bicycle	8
70	Big T BIG 131	Kew Gardens/Father Forgive Them	8
70	Big T BIG 134	Spiral Staircase/Terminus	8
68	Transatlantic TRA 165	8 FRAMES A SECOND (LP, white/lilac label with 't' logo)	35
69	Transatlantic TRA 177	SPIRAL STAIRCASE (LP, laminated sleeve, with insert)	35
69	Transatlantic TRA 209	MY SIDE OF YOUR WINDOW (LP, textured sleeve)	25
70	Transatlantic TRA 227	REVISITED (LP)	20

MCTELLS
87	Frank TRUFFAUT 303	Jesse Man Rae/If Only/Rotten/M.T.B. (p/s in bag)	10

RAY MCVAY SOUND
65	Pye 7N 15777	Raunchy/Revenge (Promo copies have "Macvay" spelling)	45
65	Pye 7N 15816	Kinda Kinky/Kinkdom Come	50
66	Parlophone R 5460	Genesis/House Of Clowns (as Ray MacVay Band)	10
69	Mercury MF 1121	Destination Moon/Mexican Scavenger	10
71	Philips 6006 083	They Call Me Mr. Tibbs (as Ray McVay & Orchestra)	25

CHRISTINE MCVIE
84	Warner Bros W 9372T	Got A Hold On Me/Who's Dreaming This Dream (12", p/s)	8
84	Warner Bros W 9372PT	Got A Hold On Me/Who's Dreaming This Dream (12", picture disc)	10

(see also Christine Perfect, Fleetwood Mac, Chicken Shack)

CARL MCVOY
58	London HLU 8617	Tootsie/You Are My Sunshine	200
58	London HLU 8617	Tootsie/You Are My Sunshine (78)	70

DAVID MCWILLIAMS
66	CBS 202348	God And My Country/Blue Eyes	10
67	Major Minor MM 533	The Days Of Pearly Spencer/Harlem Lady	15
68	Major Minor MM 561	This Side Of Heaven/Mister Satisfied	8
69	Major Minor MM 592	The Stranger/Follow Me	10
69	Major Minor MM 616	Oh Mama Are You My Friend?/I Love Susie In The Summer	8
67	Major Minor MMLP 2	SINGING SONGS BY DAVID McWILLIAMS (LP, laminated sleeve, also stereo SMLP 2)	15
67	Major Minor MMLP 10	DAVID McWILLIAMS VOL. 2 (LP, laminated front cover, also stereo SMLP 10)	15
68	Major Minor MMLP 11	VOLUME III (LP, also stereo SMLP 11)	15
69	Major Minor MCP 5026	THE DAYS OF DAVID McWILLIAMS (LP)	15
71	Parlophone R 5886	Days Of Pearly Spencer/Harlem Lady (reissue)	6
72	Dawn DNLS 3039	LORD OFFALY (LP, textured gatefold sleeve)	20
73	Dawn DNLS 3047	THE BEGGAR AND THE PRIEST (LP)	20
74	Dawn DNLS 3059	LIVING'S JUST A STATE OF MIND (LP)	18

M.D.C.
83	Crass 121984/5	MULTI DEATH CORPORATION (EP)	10

(see also Millions Of Dead Children)

VAUGHN MEADER
63	MGM MGM 1239	No Hiding Place/The Elephant Song	6

MEAN MACHINE
76	Chrysalis CHS 2089	Boogie To The Drummer/Running With The Rat Pack	10

(see also Brian Bennett)

ME & THEM
64	Pye 7N 15596	Feels So Good/I Think I'm Gonna Kill Myself	18
64	Pye 7N 15631	Everything I Do Is Wrong/Show You Mean It Too	15
64	Pye 7N 15683	Get Away/Tell Me Why	15

MEANIES
79	Vendetta VD 002	Waiting For You/It's True (p/s)	80

MEAN STREET DEALERS
79	Graduate GRAD 5	Japanese Motorbikes/Tight Skirts (p/s)	20
79	Mean St. Dealers MSD 001	BENT NEEDLES (LP)	25
79	Graduate GRADLP 1	BENT NEEDLES (LP, reissue)	18

(see also Tea & Sympathy)

MEANWHILE BACK IN COMMUNIST RUSSIA...
00	Jitter JTR 1SP	No Cigar/Morning After Pill (p/s, 300 only)	7

MEASLES
65	Columbia DB 7531	Casting My Spell/Bye Birdie Fly	40
65	Columbia DB 7673	Night People/Dog Rough Dan	25
66	Columbia DB 7875	Kicks/No Baby At All	35
66	Columbia DB 8029	Walkin' In/Looking For Love	25

MEAT LOAF
75	Ode ODS 66304	Clap Your Hands, Stamp Your Feet/Stand By Me (withdrawn)	25
79	Epic S EPC 12-7018	Bat Out Of Hell/Heaven Can Wait (12", p/s, red vinyl)	8
81	Epic EPCA 11-1697	Dead Ringer For Love/More Than You Deserve (picture disc)	5
82	Epic EPCA 12-2251	MEAT LOAF IN EUROPE '82 (12" EP, clear vinyl, p/s, Irish issue)	10
83	Epic EPCA WA 3748	Midnight At The Lost And Found (Remix)/Fallen Angel/Bat Out Of Hell (Live)/ Dead Ringer For Love (Long Version) (picture disc)	5
84	Arista ARISDP 585	Modern Girl/Take A Number (bike-shaped picture disc, with poster & plinth)	5
84	Arista ARIST 12585D/	Modern Girl (Freeway Mix)/Take A Number (Extended)//Modern Girl (Freeway Mix)/Take A Number (Extended) (12", double pack, 2nd 12" is picture disc)	10
85	Arista ARISD 600	Nowhere Fast/Clap Your Hands (bike-shaped picture disc)	5
85	Arista ARISD 603	Piece Of The Action/Sailor To A Siren (jaw-shaped picture disc)	5
82	Epic EPC 11 82419	BAT OUT OF HELL (LP, picture disc)	15
79	S EPC 12-7018	Bat Out of Hell / Heaven Can Wait	8

(see also Stoney & Meat Loaf, Jim Steinman, Rocky Horror Show)

MEAT WHIPLASH
85	Creation CRE 020	Don't Slip Up/Here It Comes (foldaround p/s in poly bag; 1st pressing has photo of band by fence)	20
85	Creation CRE 020	Don't Slip Up/Here It Comes (foldaround p/s in poly bag; 2nd pressing has photo of band in field)	8

(see also Jesus & Mary Chain)

MECHANICAL HORSETROUGH
70s	Kap KAPS 96	Dogshit On Your Shoes/Jeremy Germoline/Horsetrough Hoedown (p/s)	5
75	Sonet SON 2068	When Santa Lost His Trousers/The Ballad Of Big Bruce	5

MECKENBURG ZINC
70	Orange OAS 205	Hard Working Woman/I'd Like To Help You	5

MEDDY EVILS
65	Pye 7N 15941	Find Somebody To Love/A Place Called Love	110
66	Pye 7N 17091	It's All For You/Ma's Place	150

(see also Stu James and the Mojos, the Quik)

MEDIA
79	Takeaway TA 001	TV Kids/Don't Sit Back/Just For You/Rose And Crown (500 only, p/s)	50

MEDIA
80	Brain Booster Music 4	Back On The Beach Again/South Coast City Rockers (p/s)	5

MEDIATORS
69	Success RE901	Look Whoa Bust Style/RUPIE EDWARDS : Same	15
70	Supreme SUP 210	When You Go To A Party (actually by Mediators)/ RUPIE EDWARDS ALLSTARS: Stop The Party	15

(see also Meditators)

MEDICINE HEAD
69	Dandelion S 4661	His Guiding Hand/This Love Of Old	20
70	Dandelion S 5075	Coast To Coast/All For Tomorrow	12
71	Dandelion DAN 7003	(And The) Pictures In The Sky/Natural Sight (also listed as K 19002) (in p/s)	10
72	Dandelion 2001 276	Kum On/On The Land	6
72	Dandelion 2001 325	Only To Do What Is True/Sittin' In The Sun	6
72	Dandelion 2001 383	How Does It Feel/Morning Light	6
69	Dandelion 63757	NEW BOTTLES, OLD MEDICINE (LP)	50
71	Dandelion DAN 8005	HEAVY ON THE DRUM (LP, gatefold sleeve, 1st pressing with lyric insert with DAN 8005 on sleeve, label and matrix)	100
71	Dandelion DAN 8005	HEAVY ON THE DRUM (LP, gatefold sleeve, later pressing listed as K 49005; without lyric insert)	40
71	Dandelion 2310 166	DARK SIDE OF THE MOON (LP, with insert)	30
73	Polydor 2310 248	ONE & ONE IS ONE (LP, fold-out sleeve)	15
74	Polydor 2383 272	THRU' A FIVE (LP)	12

(see also Ashton Gardner & Dyke, British Lions)

MEDITATIONS (1)
68	Liberty LBF 15045	Transcendental Meditation/Beautiful Experience	7

MEDITATIONS (2)
78	Island IPR 2022	Life Is Not Easy/Much Smarter (12")	10
77	United Artists UAS30178	MESSAGE FROM THE MEDITATIONS (LP)	20
78	Third World TWS 929	WAKE UP! (LP)	25
79	Tad's TRDLP 101579	GUIDANCE (LP)	20

MEDITATORS
69	Bullet BU 403	Duba Duba/CECIL NICKY THOMAS: Running Alone	12
69	Success RE 901	Look Who Bust A Style/RUPIE EDWARDS ALL STARS: Look Who Bust A Style	15

MINT VALUE £

70	Big BG 302	When You Go To A Party/Good Morning Mother Cuba	10
71	Big BG 305	Music Alone Shall Live/RUPIE EDWARDS AND ALL STARS: Music Alone - Version	10
73	Pyramid PYR 7010	Great Messiah/Nana Nana	8
73	Smash SMA 2331	Things Not Easy/BONGO HERMAN & BINGY BUNNY: Ration	10

(see also Busty Brown, Pat Satchmo)

MEDIUM
68	CBS 3404	Edward Never Lies/Colours Of The Rainbow	40

MEDIUM MEDIUM
80	APT SAP-01	Them Or Me/Freeze (p/s)	7
81	Cherry Red CHEER 18	Hungry, So Angry/Nadsat Dream (p/s)	7
81	Cherry Red BRED 19	THE GLITTERHOUSE (LP)	15

MEDIUM WAVE
69	Ember EMB 5265	Walk In The Sunshine/Looking Towards The Sky (p/s)	15

BILL MEDLEY
67	Verve VS 564	That Lucky Old Sun/My Darling Clementine	5
68	MGM MGM 1418	I Can't Make It Alone/One Day Girl	6
68	MGM MGM 1432	Brown Eyed Woman/Let The Good Times Roll	6
68	MGM MGM 1456	Peace Brother Peace/Winter Won't Come This Year	5
69	MGM MGM 1475	This Is A Love Song/Something's So Wrong	5
69	MGM MGM 1491	Someone Is Standing Outside/Reaching Back	5
71	A&M AMS 898	You've Lost That Lovin' Feelin'/We've Only Just Begun	5
69	MGM MGM-C(S) 8091	BILL MEDLEY 100% (LP)	20

(see also Righteous Brothers, Garnet Mimms)

JOE MEDLIN
59	Mercury AMT 1032	I Kneel At Your Throne/Out Of Sight, Out Of Mind	25
59	Mercury AMT 1032	I Kneel At Your Throne/Out Of Sight, Out Of Mind (78)	10

MICHAEL MEDWIN
58	HMV POP 490	The Army Game/What Do We Do In The Army? (with Bernard Bresslaw, Alfie Bass & Leslie Fyson)	5
59	HMV POP 645	Blankety-Blankety-Blank/Do It Yourself (with Norman Rossington)	5

KEITH MEEHAN
69	Marmalade 598 016	Darkness Of My Life/TONY MEEHAN: Hooker Street	30

TONY MEEHAN
64	Decca F 11801	Song Of Mexico/Kings Go Fifth	6

(see also Shadows, Jet Harris & Tony Meehan, Keith Meehan, John Paul Jones)

JOE MEEK ORCHESTRA
63	Decca F 11796	The Kennedy March/The Theme Of Freedom	30

(see also Blue Men)

MEGADETH
87	Capitol CL 476	Wake Up Dead/Black Friday (live) (p/s)	10
87	Capitol CLP 476	Wake Up Dead/Black Friday (live) (skull-shaped picture disc with insert)	18
87	Capitol 12CL 476	Wake Up Dead/Black Friday (live)/Devil's Island (live)/Wake Up Dead/Black Friday (live) (12", p/s, allegedly shrink-wrapped with 7" picture disc)	25
87	Capitol 12CL 476	Wake Up Dead/Black Friday (live)/Devil's Island (live)/Wake Up Dead/Black Friday (live) (12", p/s)	15
87	Capitol 12CL 476	Wake Up Dead/Black Friday (Tommy Vance Show)/Devil's Island (Tommy Vance Show) (12", stickered p/s, with 'Deth' certificate)	15
88	Capitol CL 480	Anarchy In The U.K./Liar (p/s)	10
88	Capitol CLP 480	Anarchy In The U.K./Liar (U.K.-shaped picture disc)	15
88	Capitol CLP 489	Mary Jane/Hook In Mouth (picture disc)	12
90	SBK SBKPD 4	No More Mr. Nice Guy/DEAD ON: "Different Breed" (chair-shaped pic disc)	15
90	SBK 12 SBKP 4	No More Mr. Nice Guy/DEAD ON: "Different Breed"/DANGEROUS TOYS: Demon Bell [The Ballad Of Horace Pinker] (12", poster p/s)	10
90	SBK CDSBK 4	No More Mr. Nice Guy/DEAD ON: "Different Breed")/(DANGEROUS TOYS: Demon Bell [The Ballad Of Horace Pinker]) (CD)	10
91	Capitol CLS 604	Hangar 18 (MJ 12 Edit)/The Conjuring (live) (p/s, shrinkwrapped with patch)	15
91	Capitol CLPD 604	Hangar 18 (MJ 12 Edit)/The Conjuring (live) (Vic-shaped picture disc)	20
91	Capitol CDCL 604	Hangar 18/Conjuring/Hangar 18 (version)/Hangar 18 (Live)/Hook In Mouth (CD)	15
92	Capitol 12CLS 662	Symphony Of Destruction/Breakpoint/Go To Hell (12", p/s, clear vinyl with giant autographed poster)	20
92	Capitol CLP 669	Skin O' My Teeth (LP Version)/Holy Wars... The Punishment Due (The General Schwarzkopf Mix)/High Speed Dirt (live)/The Passes (Mustaine Remarks On Game) (10" bronze Megadeth box with passes & game rules)	20
92	Capitol CL 669	Symphony Of Destruction/Skin O' My Teeth (yellow vinyl, p/s)	10
92	Capitol CLP 669	Symphony Of Destruction/Skin O' My Teeth (picture disc and card in PVC sleeve)	10
88	M. For Nations MFN 46P	KILLING IS MY BUSINESS ... AND BUSINESS IS GOOD (LP, picture disc with insert)	18
88	Capitol ESTP 2022	PEACE SELLS ... BUT WHO'S BUYING? (LP, picture disc with insert)	20
88	Capitol ESTP 2053	SO FAR, SO GOOD ... SO WHAT (LP, picture disc with insert)	25
90	Capitol ESTPD 2132	RUST IN PEACE (LP, picture disc, die cut sleeve)	25
94	Capitol ESTPD 2244	YOUTHANASIA (LP, picture disc)	25
94	Capitol ESTPD 2244	YOUTHANASIA (LP, blue vinyl)	30
95	Capitol CDESTS 2244	YOUTHANASIA/HIDDEN TREASURES (2-CD, card sleeve, 2,000 only)	25
07	EMI 50995 13187 28	WARCHEST ('ammo' box set with 4 CD's, DVD and booklet)	35

(see also Marty Friedman, Cacophony)

MEGATON
71	Deram DM-R 331	Out Of Your Own Little World/Niagara	30
81	Hot Metal HMM 69	Aluminium Lady/Diehard (p/s)	80
71	Deram SML-R 1086	MEGATON (LP, white/red label with small logo)	1000

MEGATONS (JAMAICA)
70	Downtown DT 464	Take It Easy/Funk The Beat	10
70	Downtown DT 469	Militant Man/MUSIC DOCTORS: Reggae Jeggae Version	10

(see also Revelation)

MEGATONS (U.S.)
65	Sue WI 325	Shimmy Shimmy Walk (Parts 1 & 2)	40

(see also Billy Lee Riley)

MEGATRONS

| 59 | Top Rank JAR 146 | Velvet Waters/The Merry Piper..6 |
| 59 | Top Rank JAR 236 | Tootie Flootie/Whispering Winds..6 |

GEORGE MEGGIE

| 72 | Bullet BU 504 | Hard To Believe/MAX ROMEO: Softie..7 |
| 72 | Punch PH 112 | People Like People/MAX ROMEO: Softie...7 |

JOHN MEHEGAN TRIO

| 56 | London EZC 19005 | THE FIRST MEHEGAN VOLUME ONE (EP) ....8 |
| 56 | London EZC 19015 | THE FIRST MEHEGAN VOLUME TWO (EP) ....8 |

MEKONS

78	Fast Products FAST 1	Never Been In A Riot/32 Weeks/Heart And Soul (p/s)..........................15
78	Fast Products FAST 7	Where Were You?/I'll Have To Dance Then (On My Own) (p/s) 10
80	Virgin SV 101	Teeth/Guardian//Kill/Stay Cool (double pack, gatefold p/s) 5
82	CNT CNT 1	This Sporting Life (6.12)/Frustration (6.21)/(mystery live track) (12", p/s) ...5
82	CNT CNT 008	This Sporting Life/Fight The Cuts (p/s)..5
82	CNT CNT 014	THE ENGLISH DANCING MASTER (12" EP)...8
82	CNT CNT 009	THE MEKONS STORY (LP)..18
79	Virgin V2143	THE QUALITY OF MERCY IS NOT STRNEN (LP) 15
90s	Virgin VCD 2143	THE QUALITY OF MERCY IS NOT STRNEN (CD) 15
87	Sin 006	HONKY TONKIN' (LP)..12
85	Sin 001	FEAR AND WHISKEY (LP) 12

(see also Batfish Boys, Sally Timms & Drifting Cowgirls, Ut)

MEL & DAVE

| 70 | Upsetter US 330 | Spinning Wheel/Version ....15 |

MEL & TIM

70	Concord CON 004	Backfield In Motion/Do Right Baby (pink label design)........................6
70	Concord CON 004	Backfield In Motion/Do Right Baby (multi design)...............................6
70	Concord CON 004	Backfield In Motion/Do Right Baby (egg design) 6
73	Stax 2025 125	Starting All Over Again/It Hurts To Want You So Bad 8
73	Stax 2025 171	What's Your Name/Free For All 8
73	Stax 2325 090	STARTING ALL OVER AGAIN (LP) 25

MELANIE

68	Buddah 2011 033	Alexander Beetle/Christopher Robin/Animal Crackers (p/s)...............10
69	Buddah 201 063	Tuning My Guitar/Beautiful People (withdrawn, demos may exist) 10
69	Buddah 203 019	BORN TO BE (LP, gatefold sleeve)..15
69	Buddah 203 028	AFFECTIONATELY MELANIE (LP, with inner lyric sheet) 15
70	Buddah 2318 009	CANDLES IN THE RAIN (LP, gatefold sleeve) 15
70	Buddah 2318 011	LEFTOVER WINE (LP, gatefold sleeve) 15
71	Buddah 2322 001	THE GOOD BOOK (LP, gatefold sleeve, with booklet) 12
71	Buddah 2322 002	GATHER ME (LP, gatefold sleeve) 12
72	Buddah 2318 054	GARDEN IN THE CITY (LP, scratch'n'sniff sleeve) 15
72	Buddah 2659 013	THE FOUR SIDES OF MELANIE (2-LP) 18

TERRY MELCHER

| 68 | Rex R 11039 | Indian Lake/Be My Girl ....8 |
| 74 | Reprise K 54016 | TERRY MELCHER (LP)...20 |

(see also Terry Day, The Rip Chords, Freeway)

GIL MELLE (QUINTET)

| 55 | Vogue LDE 141 | GIL MELLE QUINTET (10" LP) ....15 |

SUSAN MELLEN

| 75 | MAM MAMAS 1014 | THE MELLEN BIRD (LP, with insert) ....30 |

MELLODITIES

| 64 | R&B JB 179 | Vacation/TOMMY McCOOK: Music Is My Occupation ....45 |

MELLO & MELLOTONES

| 72 | Summit SUM 8538 | Haile Selasie/Old Man River..10 |

(see also Mellotones)

MELL(O)TONES

68	Amalgamated AMG 812	Fat Girl In Red/VERSATILES: Trust The Book.......................................20
68	Amalgamated AMG 817	Feel Good (actually maybe by Bleechers)/Soulful Mood (actually by Tommy McCook & Supersonics)...25
68	Doctor Bird DB 1136	None Such/VAL BENNETT: Popeye On The Shore................................20
68	Trojan TR 612	Uncle Charlie/What A Botheration...12
68	Pyramid PYR 6060	Let's Join Together/BEVERLEY'S ALLSTARS: I Don't Know....................12
69	Camel CA 18	Facts Of Life/TERMITES: I'll Be Waiting 20
70	Escort ERT 844	Work It/SOUL MAN: Good Lover 10

(see also Sexy Girls)

MELLOW CANDLE

68	SNB 55-3645	Feeling High/Tea With The Sun 100
72	Deram DM 357	Dan The Wing/Silversong (with promotional p/s) 500
72	Deram DM 357	Dan The Wing/Silversong...80
72	Deram SDL 7	SWADDLING SONGS (LP) 2000

MELLOW CATS WITH COUNT OSSIE & WARRICKAS

| 61 | Blue Beat BB 68 | Rock A Man Soul/MONTO & CYCLONES: Lazy Lou (B-side actually by Monty [Alexander] & Cyclones)..12 |

(see also Melo Cats)

MELLOW FRUITFULNESS

| 67 | Columbia S(C)X 6242 | MEDITATION (LP, mono/stereo) ....15 |

MELLOW LARKS

| 60 | Blue Beat BB 16 | Time To Pray (Alleluia)/Love You Baby ....10 |
| 61 | Blue Beat BB 38 | No More Wedding/Lite Of My Life ....8 |

(see also Basil Gabbidon)

MELLOW ROSE

| 80 | Studio 16 WE 348 | Imitation Love/SGT. PEPPER: Dub A Rub Ina Imitation Way (12") ......25 |

MINT VALUE £

GEORGE MELLY (& MICK MULLIGAN BAND)

51	Tempo A 96	Rock Island Line/Send Me To The 'Lectric Chair (78, as The George Melly Trio)	15
52	Tempo A 104	Kitchen Man/Jazzbo Brown From Memphis Town (78)	10
55	Decca F 10457	Frankie And Johnny/I'm Down In The Dumps	8
55	Decca F 10457	Frankie And Johnny/I'm Down In The Dumps (78)	10
56	Tempo A 144	Jenny's Ball/Muddy Water	8
56	Tempo A 147	Death Letter/Cemetery Blues	8
56	Tempo EXA 41	GEORGE MELLY WITH MICK MULLIGAN'S JAZZ BAND (EP)	10
56	Tempo EXA 47	GEORGE MELLY SINGS DOOM (EP, with Mick Mulligan's Jazz Band)	10
58	Decca DFE 6552	MICHIGAN WATER BLUES (EP)	10
58	Decca DFE 6557	ABDUL ABULBUL AMIR (EP)	10
61	Columbia SEG 8093	THE PSYCHOLOGICAL SIGNIFICANCE OF ANIMAL SYMBOLISM IN AMERICAN NEGRO FOLK MUSIC AND ALL THAT JAZZ (EP)	10

(see also Mick Mulligan Band)

MELO CATS

61	Blue Beat BB 54	Another Moses/ROLAND ALPHONSO & ALLEY CATS: Hully Gully Rock	10

(see also Mellow Cats)

MELODIANS

66	Island WI 3014	Lay It On/Meet Me	30
67	Coxsone CS 7004	I Should Have Made It Up/JOE HIGGS: Neighbour Neighbour	80
67	Treasure Isle TI 7006	You Don't Need Me/I Will Get Along	30
67	Treasure Isle TI 7022	You Have Caught Me/I Know Just How She Feels	50
67	Treasure Isle TI 7023	Last Train To Expo. '67/TOMMY McCOOK & SUPERSONICS: Expo	30
68	Treasure Isle TI 7028	Come On, Little Girl/TOMMY McCOOK & SUPERSONICS: Got Your Soul	30
68	Doctor Bird DB 1125	Little Nut Tree/You Are My Only Love	25
68	Doctor Bird DB 1139	Swing And Dine/I Could Be King	25
68	Fab FAB 61	Sweet Rose/It Comes And Goes	30
69	Gas GAS 108	Ring Of Gold/You've Got It	12
69	Gas GAS 116	Personally Speaking/LLOYD ROBINSON: Trouble Trouble	8
69	Crab CRAB 15	When There Is You/UNIQUES: My Woman's Love	30
69	Trojan TR 660	Everybody Bawlin'/TOMMY McCOOK: Kilowatt	8
69	Trojan TR 695	Sweet Sensation/It's My Delight	5
70	Trojan TR 7720	A Day Seems So Long/BEVERLEY'S ALLSTARS: Project	8
70	Trojan TR 7764	Say Darling Say/Come Rock It To Me	8
70	High Note HS 044	Love Is A Good Thing/No Nola	7
70	Summit SUM 8505	Walking In The Rain/Rivers Of Babylon	6
70	Summit SUM 8508	Rivers Of Babylon/BEVERLEY'S ALL STARS: Babylon Version	6
71	Duke DU 128	The Sensational Melodians (Parts 1 & 2)	6
71	Summit SUM 8512	It Took A Miracle/BEVERLEY'S ALLSTARS: Miraculous Version	5
71	Summit SUM 8522	Come Ethiopians, Come/BEVERLEY'S ALL STARS: Version Two	8
71	Summit SUM 8532	My Love, My Life/My Love, My Life - Version	6
72	Summit SUM 8534	The Time Has Come/BEVERLEY'S ALL STARS: McIntosh (B-side actually "No Sins At All" by Melodians)	6
72	Bullet BU 496	Tropical Land/HUGH ROY & SLIM SMITH: Love I Bring	6
72	Duke DU 130	The Mighty Melodians (Adapted) (Parts 1 & 2)	6
72	Attack ATT 8025	This Beautiful Land/MELODIOUS RHYTHMS: Version	6
72	Attack ATT 8031	Without You (What Would I Do)/DYNAMITES: Instrumental	6
72	Punch PH 111	Round And Round/UPSETTERS: Round Version	8
73	Randy's RAN 530	Passion Love/Love Makes The World Go Round	6

(see also Gentiles, Tony Brevett, Brent Dowe, Jaylads, Trevor McNaughton, Gaylads, Joe Grinne)

BOBBY MELODY

79	Hit Run HIT DD5	Anger & Strife (ft. Jah Lion)/JAH LION: Johnnie Walker (12")	30

JOHNNY MELODY

68	Pyramid PYR 6041	You Treating Me Bad/ROLAND ALPHONSO: Peace And Love	40
67	Pyramid PYR 6023	Govern Your Mouth (actually by George Dekker)/ ROLAND ALPHONSO: Peace And Love	30

(see also Lloyd & Johnny Melody under 'L', Lloyd Terrell)

RICKY MELODY

88	Wolrd Enterprise WED 61	What An Act/Version (12")	80

MELODY ENCHANTERS

63	Island WI 049	Enchanter's Ball/I'll Be True	20
63	R&B JB 117	Gone Gone/Blueberry Hill	18

MELODY FAIR

68	Decca F 12801	Something Happened To Me/Sittin', Watchin', Waitin'	6

MELO'S MARITIME

67	Philips BF 1602	Blow The Man Up/Maneater	5

KANSAS CITY MELROSE/CASINO SIMPSON

72	Chicago Piano 12-001	KANSAS CITY MELROSE/CASINO SIMPSON (LP)	15

MONIQUE MELSEN

71	Decca F 23170	The Love Beat/Pomme Pomme Pomme	12

JOE MELSON

61	Polydor NH 66959	Oh Yeah!/What's The Use I Still Love You	50
61	Polydor NH 66961	Hey Mister Cupid/No One Really Cares	40
64	Hickory 45-1229	Stay Away From Her/His Girl	5

MELTATIONS

87	Meltations MEL 701	32 Sweet Teeth/I'll Take It As A Compliment (p/s)	80

MELTING BEAR

85	Beggars Banquet BEG 144	It Makes No Difference/Nature's Way/Sea Song (unreleased, white label test pressings only)	6

(see also Icicle Works)

MELTON CONSTABLE

70s	SIS private pressing	MELTON CONSTABLE (LP)	150

HAROLD MELVIN & BLUE NOTES

72	CBS 8496	If You Don't Know Me By Now/Let Me Into Your World	5
75	Route RT 06	Get Out/You May Not Love Me	8
73	CBS 65350	HAROLD MELVIN & THE BLUES NOTES (LP)	12
73	CBS Q 65859	BLACK AND BLUE (LP, quadrophonic)	12

MELVINS

90	Tupelo TUPEP 10	Sweet Young Thing Ain't Sweet No More/STEEL POLE BATH TUB: I Dreamed I Dream (12", p/s, green vinyl, 600 only)	18

MEMBERS

78	Stiff/One Off OFF 3	Solitary Confinement/Rat Up A Drainpipe (p/s)	12
79	Virgin VS 242	The Sound Of The Suburbs/Handling The Big Jets (clear vinyl, window p/s)	5
80	Virgin VS 352	Flying Again/Disco Oui Oui//Live In A Lift/Rat Up A Drainpipe (double pack, gatefold p/s)	5
83	Albion ION1050	Working Girl/The Family (square coloured vinyl, p/s)	8

MEMO

74	Decca F13539	Kick A Tin Can/Attilah	8

MEMORIES

74	Rex R 11091	Lay It On Me/Did Ya Get It	20

MEMOS

59	Parlophone R 4616	The Biddy Leg/My Type Of Girl	60

MEMPHIS BEND

73	United Artists UP 35571	Louisiana Hoedown/Right String Baby But The Wrong Yo Yo	10
76	United Artists UP 36132	Ubangi Stomp/Tennessee	8
77	United Artists UAS 30036	GOOD ROCKIN' TONITE (LP)	12

MEMPHIS HORNS

71	Atlantic 2091 080	Woolly Bully/I Can't Turn You Loose	10
77	RCA PB 0836	Get Up And Dance/Don't Abuse It	6
71	Mojo 2466 010	THE MEMPHIS HORNS (LP)	25

MEMPHIS JUG BAND

55	HMV 7EG 8073	MEMPHIS JUG BAND (EP, withdrawn)	60
70s	Saydisc Matchbox RL 33	MEMPHIS JUG BAND (LP)	15
71	Saydisc Matchbox RL 337	MEMPHIS JUG BAND VOLUME 2 (LP)	15

MEMPHIS MINNIE

64	Heritage H 103	MEMPHIS MINNIE (EP)	75
69	Limited Edition (no cat. no.)	MEMPHIS MINNIE 1934-1936 (LP)	40
69	Limited Edition (no cat. no.)	MEMPHIS MINNIE 1934-1941 (LP)	40
69	Sunflower ET 1400	MEMPHIS MINNIE 1941-1949 (LP, 99 copies only)	50
74	Flyright LP 108	MEMPHIS MINNIE 1934-1941 (LP, reissue)	12
74	Flyright LP 109	MEMPHIS MINNIE 1941-1949 (LP, reissue)	12

MEMPHIS SLIM

53	Esquire 10-319	Harlem Bound/ST. LOUIS JIMMY R&B BAND: Holiday For Boogie (78)	30
60	Collector JDN 102	Pinetop's Blues/How Long	25
62	Storyville A 45055	Big City Girl/El Capitan (p/s)	15
61	Collector JEN 5	GOING TO KANSAS CITY (EP)	30
62	Storyville SEP 385	STORYVILLE BLUES ANTHOLOGY VOL. 5 - BOOGIE WOOGIE AND THE BLUES (EP)	22
63	Vocalion VEP 170155	MEMPHIS SLIM AND LITTLE RICHARD (EP)	80
63	Summit LSE 2041	WORLD'S FOREMOST BLUES SINGERS (EP)	12
61	Collector JGN 1004	MEMPHIS SLIM U.S.A. (LP)	45
61	Collector JGN 1005	MEMPHIS SLIM U.S.A. (VOL. 2) (LP)	45
62	Bluesville BV 1018	JUST BLUES (LP)	30
62	Storyville SLP 118	MEMPHIS SLIM (LP)	22
62	Storyville SLP 138	THIS IS A GOOD TIME TO WRITE A SONG (LP)	22
62	Fontana 688 302 ZL	NO STRAIN (LP)	25
63	United Artists ULP 1042	BROKEN SOUL BLUES (LP)	30
64	Storyville SLP 118	TRAVELLIN' WITH THE BLUES (LP)	22
64	Xtra XTRA 1008	MEMPHIS SLIM (LP)	18
64	Fontana 688 701	ALONE WITH MY FRIENDS (LP)	30
65	Fontana TL 5254	CLAP YOUR HANDS (LP)	25
65	Melodisc MLPS 12-149	FATTENIN' FROGS FOR SNAKES (LP)	25
66	Fontana 688 315 ZL	FRISCO BAY BLUES (LP)	30
67	Polydor 623 211	PINETOP'S BLUES (LP)	18
68	Polydor 623 263	BLUESINGLY YOURS (LP, with Mickey Baker)	18
68	Xtra XTRA 5060	ALL KINDS OF BLUES (LP)	15
69	Xtra XTRA 1085	CHICAGO BLUES (LP)	15
72	Barclay 920 214	BLUE MEMPHIS (LP, with Peter Green)	75
72	Barclay 920 332-3	OLD TIMES, NEW TIMES (2-LP)	18
70s	Xtra XTRA 5063	ALL KINDS OF BLUES (LP)	15

(see also Washboard Sam, Ivory Joe Hunter, Otis Spann)

MEMPHIS THREE

68	Page One POF 070	Wild Thing/She's A Yum Yum	7

MEN

79	Virgin VS 269	I Don't Depend On You/Cruel (p/s)	6
79	Virgin VS 269-12	I Don't Depend On You/Cruel (12", p/s)	8

(see also Human League)

MENACE

77	Illegal IL 004	Screwed Up/Insane Society (p/s)	15
77	Illegal IL 004	Screwed Up/Insane Society (12", p/s)	20
77	Small Wonder SMALL 5	G.L.C./I'm Civilized (p/s)	15
78	Illegal IL 008	I Need Nothing/Electrocutioner (p/s)	15
79	Small Wonder SMALL 16	Final Vinyl: Last Year's Youth/Carry No Banners (p/s)	8
82	Fresh FRESH 14	The Young Ones/Tomorrow's World/Live For Today (p/s)	15
86	Razor RAZ 18	GLC - RIP (LP)	25

(see also Aces, Vermilion & Aces)

MENACE
01	Plastica DPFT 004	Reap What You Sow (12")..	15

MENACE MAKES 3
92	Danse City DC 1203	Pure Hysteria (Give Me A Mother Mix)/Do You Feel What I'm Feeling? (Matrix Rise Remix)(12")..	50

CARLOS MENDES
72	Pye International 7N 25581	Shadows/Glow-Worm...	8

MENDES PREY
83	MP AM 076	On To The Borderline/Runnin' For You (p/s)...	20
86	Wag WAG 2	Wonderland/Can You Believe It (p/s)...	25
86	Wag 12 WAG 2	Wonderland/Can You Believe It (12", p/s)...	25

ENOCH & CHRISTY MENSAH
60	Melodisc M 1569	Rebecca/Dakuku Dum...	5

E.T. MENSAH & HIS TEMPO'S BAND
58	Decca WAL 1001	A SATURDAY NIGHT (10" LP)...	20
58	Decca WAL 1002	MORE MENSAH (10" LP)..	20

MENTAL
79	Kamikaze Pig RAM 1	God For A Day/18/Kill The Bill/Off The Rails (600 only, p/s)	80

MENTATZ
81	Naff N 001	Never Trust A Russian/Dead To The World (p/s)...................................	5

MEN WITHOUT HATS
85	Statik CDST 10	RHYTHM OF YOUTH (CD)...	15

IAN MENZIES
61	Pye Jazz 7NJ 2046	Auf Wiedersehn/Taboo...	8
58	Pye Jazz NJE 1049	MELODY MAKER ALL STARS (EP)..	8
60	Pye Nixa NJE 1071	SWINGIN' SEAMUS (EP)..	8
60	Pye Nixa NJL 23	HAVE TARTAN...WILL TRAD (LP)..	15
60	Pye Jazz NJL 26	IAN MENZIES AND THE CLYDE VALLEY STOMPERS (LP).................................	15

(see also Clyde Valley Stompers)

MIKE MERCADO
67	Parlophone 5589	Hey Mister Monk It's Page Nine/Popcorn..	15

MARY MAE MERCER
65	Decca DFE 8599	MARY MAE MERCER (EP)	50

MICKEY MERCIAN
84	Unity Sound UN 029	Ride The Rhythm/Go Anywhere (12")..	25

FREDDIE MERCURY
84	CBS WA 4735	Love Kills/GEORGIO MORODER: Rotwang's Party (picture disc)....................	30
85	CBS DA 6019	I Was Born To Love You/Stop All The Fighting//Love Kills (Extended)/ Stop All The Fighting (Extended) (double pack)	15
85	CBS A 6413	Made In Heaven (Remix 3.59)/She Blows Hot And Cold (p/s)......................	5
85	CBS WA 6413	Made In Heaven (Remix)/She Blows Hot And Cold (shaped picture disc)........	30
85	CBS WA 6413	Made In Heaven (Remix)/She Blows Hot And Cold (uncut shaped picture disc)..	500
85	CBS A 6725	Love Me Like There's No Tomorrow/Let's Turn It On (p/s)...........................	30
85	CBS TA 6725	Love Me Like There's No Tomorrow (Extended Version)/Let's Turn It On (Extended Version) (12", p/s)...	25
85	CBS DTA 6725	Love Me Like There's No Tomorrow (Extended Version)/Let's Turn It On (Extended Version)//Living On My Own (Extended 6.38)/My Love Is Dangerous (Extended 6.25) (12" double pack, shrinkwrapped with sticker)	50
85	CBS TA 6725	Love Me Like There's No Tomorrow (Extended Version)/Let's Turn It On (Extended Version) (12", promo, white card sleeve, with sticker)....................	50
86	EMI EMI 5559	Time (From The Musical)/Time (Instrumental) (p/s, with inner sleeve)	5
87	Parlophone RP 6151	The Great Pretender/Exercises In Free Love (Mercury Vocal) (shaped picture disc)...30	
87	Parlophone RP 6151	The Great Pretender/Exercises In Free Love (Mercury Vocal) (shaped picture disc, with unfolded or folded plinth)	60
87	Parlophone RP 6151	The Great Pretender/Exercises In Free Love (Mercury Vocal) (shaped picture disc, with unfolded or folded plinth)	40
87	Parlophone RP 6151	The Great Pretender/Exercises In Free Love (Mercury Vocal) (uncut shaped picture disc)..	350
87	Parlophone 10R 6151	The Great Pretender (Extended Version)/(7" Version)/Exercises In Free Love (7" Version) (10", 1-sided, printed white label, plain black die-cut sleeve, promo only)..	25
87	Polydor POSP 887	Barcelona/Exercises In Free Love (Caballé Vocal) (with Montserrat Caballé, with gatefold p/s)	6
87	Polydor POSPP 887	Barcelona (7" Version)/Exercises In Free Love (Caballé Vocal) (7" Version)/ Barcelona (Extended Version) (12", picture disc)...................................	30
87	Polydor POCD 887	Barcelona/Exercises In Free Love (Version 2) (Caballé Vocal)/ Barcelona (Extended) (CD, autographed card p/s, promo only)...........................	300
87	Polydor PO 23 DJ	The Golden Boy (with Montserrat Caballé) (radio edit) (1-sided DJ sampler, p/s, with sticker)..	100
88	Polydor POSPX 23	The Golden Boy/The Fallen Priest/The Golden Boy (Instrumental) (12", p/s)	20
88	Polydor PZCD234	The Golden Boy/The Fallen Priest/The Golden Boy (Instrumental) (CD).........	35
88	Polydor PO 29	How Can I Go On/Overture Piccante (with Montserrat Caballe) (p/s)............	15
88	Polydor POSX 29	How Can I Go On/Overture Piccante (with Montserrat Caballe) (picture disc) ...	45
89	Polydor PZ 29	How Can I Go On/Guide Me Home/Overture Piccante (12", p/s)...................	25
89	Polydor PZCD 29	How Can I Go On/Guide Me Home/Overture Piccante (CD, picture disc)	35
88	Polydor CD 3 125 211	The Golden Boy/La Japanese/Barcelona (CD promo, unreleased p/s, jewel case) ...	100
89	Polydor 0805 548-2	Ensueno/Barcelona/(Edit 4.24)/Exercises In Free Love/Barcelona (Extended Version 7.02)/Barcelona (CD Video)	40
89	Polydor 0805 580-2	The Fallen Priest/The Golden Boy (Album Version)/The Golden Boy (Instrumental Version)/The Golden Boy (Video) (CD Video)	40
92	Polydor PO 234	How Can I Go On/The Golden Boy (yellow p/s)	7
92	Polydor PZCD 234	How Can I Go On/The Golden Boy/The Fallen Priest (CD, yellow p/s)............	10
92	Parlophone R 6331	In My Defence/Love Kills (Wolf Euro Mix) (p/s)......................................	6
06	Parlophone KILLS 001	Love Kills (Glimmer Mix)/(Pixel 82 Mix)/I Was Born To Love You (George Demure Mix) (12" promo)	15
06	Parlophone KILLS 003	Living On My Own (mixes) (12" promo)	15
85	CBS CD 86312	MR. BAD GUY (CD, with 3 extended mixes; beware of counterfeits)............	25
94	Parlophone 7234 8 2814 10	FREDDIE MERCURY REMIXES (LP, unreleased)......................................	150

| 00 | Parlophone FMRARE001 | THE SOLO COLLECTION (10 CD & 2 DVD box set) | 80 |

(see also Queen, Larry Lurex, Eddie Howell, Billy Squier)

MERCURY REV
91	Mint Film MINT 5	Car Wash Hair/Coney Island Cyclone (4 track demo) (200 copies only, p/s)	10
91	Mint Film MINT 5 T	Car Wash Hair/Chasing A Bee (4 track demo)/Coney Island Cyclone (12", p/s)	8
93	Beggars Banquet BBQ 5 T	The Hum Is Coming From Her (as Mercury Theremin Sextet)/So There (as Mercury Rev Orchestra with Robert Creely) (10", p/s)	5
91	Mint Film MINTLP 4	YERSELF IS STEAM (LP, with bonus LP 'Lego My Ego')	25
93	Beggars Banquet BBQLP 140	BOCES (LP, clear red vinyl)	20
95	Beggars Banquet BBQLP 176 P	SEE YOU ON THE OTHER SIDE (LP, picture disc)	30
98	V2 VVR 1002771	DESERTERS SONGS (LP)	30

(see also Shady)

MERCY
| 69 | London HLZ 10273 | Love (Can Make You Happy)/Fireball | 25 |

MERCYFUL FATE
| 83 | Music For Nations MFN 10 | MELISSA (LP, inner) | 15 |
| 84 | Music For Nations MFN 28 | DON'T BREAK THE OATH (LP, inner) | 15 |

BURGESS MEREDITH
| 63 | Colpix PX 690 | Home In The Meadow/No Goodbye | 5 |

LOTTIE MERLE
| 72 | Flyright 001 | Howling In The Moonlight/Catfish | 10 |

MERLIN Q
| 69 | Pye 7N 17828 | The Secret/Love's Beautiful | 25 |

RAY MERRELL
60	Ember EMB S 113	Why Did You Leave Me?/Teenage Love (p/s)	10
60s	Aral PS 115	Battle Of Waterloo/Not Any More (p/s)	10
70	Jay Boy BOY 22	Tears Of Joy/Searchin' (withdrawn) (Beware of bootlegs!)	200
70	Jay Boy BOY 22	Tears Of Joy/Searchin' (withdrawn) (Beware of bootlegs!) (DJ copy)	350

TONY MERRICK
| 66 | Columbia DB 7913 | Lady Jane/Michelle | 10 |
| 66 | Columbia DB 7995 | Wake Up/It's For You | 6 |

BOB MERRILL
| 58 | Columbia DB 4086 | Nairobi/Jump When I Say Frog | 15 |

BUDDY MERRILL
| 66 | Vocalion VN 9261 | Sweet September/Sherk | 12 |

HELEN MERRILL
| 58 | Mercury MMB 12000 | THE NEARNESS OF YOU (LP, features Bill Evans) | 30 |

MAX MERRITT & METEORS
| 75 | Arista ARTY 108 | A LITTLE EASIER (LP) | 12 |
| 76 | Arista ARTY 134 | OUT OF THE BLUE (LP) | 12 |

MERRITTS
| 70 | Hot Rod HR 113 | I Don't Want To (Part 1)/HOT ROD ALL STARS: Version | 12 |

MERRY MAKER
| 76 | Western Kingston WK 505 | Untouchable Special/Straight To Music City Head | 10 |

MERRYMEN
66	Doctor Bird DB 1004	Big Bamboo/Island Woman	8
69	Trojan TR 7707	Little Drummer Boy/Mary's Boy Child	5
71	Duke DU 113	Big Bamboo/King Ja-Ja (both sides actually with Emille Straker)	5
68	Island ILP 984	CARIBBEAN TREASURE CHEST (LP)	30

(see also Soul Brothers)

JASON MERRYWEATHER
| 69 | Crystal CR 001 | My Summer Love/Abigail | 10 |

(see also Ricky Valance)

MERSEYBEATS
63	Fontana TF 412	It's Love That Really Counts/The Fortune Teller	12
64	Fontana TF 431	I Think Of You/Mister Moonlight	5
64	Fontana TF 459	Don't Turn Around/Really Mystified	6
64	Fontana TF 482	Wishin' And Hopin'/Milkman	5
64	Fontana TF 504	Last Night/See Me Back	10
65	Fontana TF 568	Don't Let It Happen To Us/It Would Take A Long Long Time	10
65	Fontana TF 607	I Love You, Yes I Do/Good Good Lovin'	8
65	Fontana TF 645	I Stand Accused/All My Life	10
69	Fontana TF 1025	I Think Of You/Wishin' And Hopin' (p/s)	10
81	Tudor CHEM 001	This Is Merseybeat (both sides) (p/s)	6
64	Fontana TE 17422	ON STAGE (EP)	40
64	Fontana TE 17423	I THINK OF YOU (EP)	30
64	Fontana TE 17432	THE MERSEYBEATS (EP)	30
64	Fontana TL 5210	THE MERSEYBEATS (LP)	70
69	Wing WL 1163	THE MERSEYBEATS (LP)	15
77	Look LKLP 6160	GREATEST HITS (LP)	12

(see also Merseys, Rockin' Horse, Tony Crane, Kirkbys, Quotations, Johnny Gustavson)

MERSEYBOYS
| 64 | Ace Of Clubs ACL 1169 | 15 GREAT SONGS BY JOHN, PAUL AND GEORGE (LP) | 20 |

MERSEYS
66	Fontana TF 694	Sorrow/Some Other Day	6
66	Fontana TF 732	So Sad About Us/Love Will Continue	15
66	Fontana TF 776	Rhythm Of Love/Is It Love?	10
67	Fontana TF 845	The Cat/Change Of Heart	25
68	Fontana TF 916	Penny In My Pocket/I Hope You're Happy	10
68	Fontana TF 955	Lovely Loretta/Dreaming	15
73	Philips 6006 258	Sorrow/MERSEYBEATS: I Think Of You	5

MINT VALUE £

MERSEYSIPPI JAZZ BAND

(see also Merseybeats, Crackers)

54	Esquire 20-063	WEST COAST SHOUT (LP)	12
55	Esquire 20-083	ALL THE GIRLS (LP)	12
55	Esquire 20-088	MERSEY TUNNEL JAZZ (LP)	12
56	Esquire 20-093	ANY OLD RAGS (LP)	12

WIM MERTENS

| 87 | Factory FACT 190c | EDUCES ME (cassette, in bespoke box with insert) | 200 |

MERTON PARKAS

79	Beggars Banquet BEG 22	You Need Wheels/I Don't Want To Know You (coloured p/s with patch)	10
79	Beggars Banquet BEG 22	You Need Wheels/I Don't Want To Know You (coloured p/s)	5
79	Beggars Banquet BEG 25	Plastic Smile/The Man With The Disguise (p/s)	5
79	Beggars Banquet BEG 30	Give It To Me Now/Gi's It (p/s)	5
80	Beggars Banquet BEG 43	Put Me In The Picture/In The Midnight Hour (p/s)	5
83	Well Suspect BLAM 002	Flat 19/Band Of Gold (p/s)	8
80s	Beggars Banquet BEG 22	You Need Wheels/I Don't Want To Know You (reissue, with silver Moulded label, black & white p/s)	7
79	Beggars Banquet BEGA 11	FACE IN THE CROWD (LP)	18

(see also Style Council)

MESCALINE UNITED

| 92 | R&S RS 92019 | We Have Arrived (Aphex Twin QQT Reconstruction Mix)/We Have Arrived (Aphex Twin TTQ Reconstruction Mix) (limited issue 12", also known as "PCP Remixed" plain paper sleeve) | 70 |

MESS

| 82 | Reasonable MEP 1 | Tried And Tested/I'm Falling | 12 |

MESSAGE (1)

| 70 | Doctor Bird DB 1503 | Rum-Bum-A-Loo/Drummer Boy | 90 |
| 72 | Reggae REG 3004 | Wrestling/Tricia | 60 |

(see also Boris Gardner)

MESSAGE (2)

| 75 | Decca SKL-R 5213 | MESSAGE (LP, blue/silver label) | 25 |

RICKY MESSENGER & SEMI PROFESSIONALS

| 80s | Kim 019 | Now Is The Time For Jah/Mr. Richman (12") | 20 |

MESSENGERS

| 64 | Columbia DB 7344 | I'm Stealin' Back/This Little Light Of Mine | 10 |
| 65 | Columbia DB 7495 | When Did You Leave Heaven/More Pretty Girls Than One | 8 |

MESSENGERS (JAMAICA)

73	Attack ATT 8057	Crowded City/Thula Thula	5
73	Bread BR 1116	Cherry Baby/B.B. SEATON: Summertime	5
73	Mirto MIR 100	Is It Because I'm Black/Just Like A Shelter	12

METABOLIST

79	Drömm DRO 1	Drömm/Slaves/Eulam's Beat (p/s, rough screen-printed & folded p/s)	20
79	Drömm DRO 1	Drömm/Slaves/Eulam's Beat (p/s, smooth printed & stapled p/s)	10
80	Drömm DRO 3	Identity/Tizhoznam (p/s)	15
79	Drömm NCN	GOATMANAUT (cassette)	50
80	Drömm DRO 2	HANSTEN KLORK (LP)	20
81	Cassetteking CK2	STAGMANAUT! (cassette)	50

METAL BOYS

| 79 | Rough Trade RT 016 | Sweet Marilyn/Fugue For A Darkening Island (p/s) | 8 |

(see also Metal Urbain)

METALLICA

SINGLES

84	Music For Nations 12 KUT 105	Jump In The Fire/Seek And Destroy (live)/Phantom Lord (live) (12", p/s, initial pressing with beige labels)	25
84	Music For Nations 12 KUT 105	Jump In The Fire/Seek And Destroy (live)/Phantom Lord (live) (12", p/s, later pressing with red/yellow labels)	20
84	Music For Nations CV12 KUT 105	Jump In The Fire/Seek And Destroy (live)/Phantom Lord (live) (12", red vinyl, p/s)	25
84	Music For Nations 12 KUT 105XP	Jump In The Fire/Seek And Destroy (live)/Phantom Lord (live) (12", stickered sleeve with sew-on patch)	30
84	Music For Nations 12 KUT 112	Creeping Death/Am I Evil?/Blitzkrieg (12", p/s, initial pressing with beige label)	20
84	Music For Nations 12 KUT 112	Creeping Death/Am I Evil?/Blitzkrieg (12", p/s, later pressing with red/yellow labels)	18
84	Music For Nations CV12 KUT 112	Creeping Death/Am I Evil?/Blitzkrieg (12", p/s, blue, red/yellow or 'Special Anniversary Edition' labels)	35
84	Music For Nations GV12 KUT 112	Creeping Death/Am I Evil?/Blitzkrieg (12", no p/s, 'Anniversary Gold Edition', gold vinyl, 3000 only; mispressing with 1 side gold, 1 side black vinyl)	75
84	Music For Nations GV12 KUT 112	Creeping Death/Am I Evil?/Blitzkrieg (12", no p/s, 'Anniversary Gold Edition', gold vinyl, 3000 only)	60
84	Music For Nations P12 KUT 112	Creeping Death/Am I Evil?/Blitzkrieg (12", picture disc, initially without barcode)	30
84	Music For Nations CD12 KUT 112	Creeping Death/Am I Evil?/Blitzkrieg Jump In The Fire/ Seek And Destroy (live)/Phantom Lord (live) (CD)	60
86	Music For Nations PKUT 105	Jump In The Fire/Phantom Lord (live) (shaped picture disc, initial pressing without barcode)	25
86	Music For Nations PKUT 105	Jump In The Fire/Phantom Lord (live) (shaped picture disc, later pressing with barcode)	20
86	Music For Nations PKUT 105	Jump In The Fire/Phantom Lord (live) (uncut picture disc)	150
87	Vertigo METAL 112	$5.98 EP - GARAGE DAYS RE-REVISITED: Helpless/Crash Course In Brain Surgery/The Small Hours/Last Caress - Green Hell (medley) (12" p/s, later copies add "The Wait")	35
88	Vertigo METAL 212	Harvester Of Sorrow/Breadfan/The Prince (12", p/s, some with 'skull' label)	18
88	Vertigo METAL CD 2	Harvester Of Sorrow/Breadfan/The Prince (CD, card sleeve)	20
89	Vertigo METAL 312	Jump In The Fire/Seek And Destroy (live)/Phantom Lord (live) (12", p/s, reissue)	10
89	Vertigo METAL 412	Creeping Death/Am I Evil?/Blitzkrieg (12", p/s, reissue)	10
89	Vertigo 842-219-2	Creeping Death/Am I Evil?/Blitzkrieg/Jump In The Fire/ Seek And Destroy (live)/Phantom Lord (live) (CD)	50
89	Vertigo METAP 5	One/Seek And Destroy (live) (card p/s, some stickered, with rolled poster)	15

89	Vertigo METPD 510	One/Seek And Destroy (live) (10", picture disc with card)	30
89	Vertigo METAL 5	One/Seek And Destroy (live) (silver/black labels, paper p/s)	10
89	Vertigo METAL 512	One (Demo Version)/For Whom The Bell Tolls (live)/Welcome Home (Sanitarium) (live) (12", p/s initial pressing with white labels)	12
89	Vertigo METAL 512	One (Demo Version)/For Whom The Bell Tolls (live)/Welcome Home (Sanitarium) (live) (12", p/s later pressing with yellow labels)	10
89	Vertigo METAL 512	One (Demo Version)/For Whom The Bell Tolls (live)/Welcome Home (Sanitarium) (live) (12", p/s mis-labelled as "Seek and Destroy" (live))	10
89	Vertigo METG 512	One (Demo Version)/For Whom The Bell Tolls (live)/Welcome Home (Sanitarium) (live) (12", gatefold p/s, with booklet, mispressed with B-side label on both sides)	20
89	Vertigo METCD 5	One/For Whom The Bell Tolls (live)/Welcome Home (Sanitarium) (live) (CD)	20
90	Vertigo 875 487 1	THE GOOD, THE BAD AND THE LIVE - THE 6½ YEARS ANNIVERSARY COLLECTION (6 x 12", with live 4-track EP [METAL 612])	80
91	Vertigo METAL 7	Enter Sandman/Stone Cold Crazy (p/s)	8
91	Vertigo METAL 7	Enter Sandman/Stone Cold Crazy (picture disc in p/s, stickered)	12
91	Vertigo METAL 712	Enter Sandman/Stone Cold Crazy/Holier Than Thou (Demo)/ Enter Sandman (Demo) (12", p/s, with stickered sleeve)	8
91	Vertigo METBX 712	Enter Sandman/Stone Cold Crazy/Enter Sandman (Demo) (12", box with 4 photo prints)	30
91	Vertigo METCD 7	Enter Sandman/Stone Cold Crazy/Enter Sandman (Demo) (CD, picture disc in box with room for 3 more CDs)	30
91	Vertigo METAP 812	The Unforgiven/Killing Time/The Unforgiven (Demo) (picture disc, card insert)	8
91	Vertigo METAL 812	The Unforgiven/Killing Time/So What/The Unforgiven (Demo) (12", p/s, some stickered)	8
92	Vertigo METAL 10	Nothing Else Matters/Enter Sandman (live) (p/s, black & white label)	8
92	Vertigo METCL 10	Nothing Else Matters - Live At Wembley 20/4/92: Enter Sandman/ Sad But True/Nothing Else Matters (CD)	25
93	Vertigo METAL 11	Sad But True/Nothing Else Matters (p/s, stickered, no labels)	5
93	Vertigo METAL 1112	Sad But True/Nothing Else Matters (Elevator Version)/Creeping Death (live)/ Sad But True (Demo) (12" picture disc with insert)	20
93	Vertigo METCH 11	Sad But True/Nothing Else Matters (live)/Sad But True (Live) (CD, picture disc)	20
96	Vertigo METJB 12	Until It Sleeps/Until It Sleeps (jukebox issue, no p/s)	10
96	Vertigo METAL 12	Until It Sleeps/2x4 (live)/Until It Sleeps (Moby Remix) (10" red vinyl, stickered)	8
96	Vertigo METAL 14	Mama Said/Ain't My Bitch (picture disc with insert)	8
97	Vertigo METJB 13	Hero Of The Day/Hero Of The Day (jukebox issue, no p/s)	8
97	Vertigo METJB 15	The Memory Remains/For Whom The Bell Tolls (Haven't Heard It Yet Remix) (Jukebox issue no p/s)	15
03	Columbia GABBA 1	53rd & 3rd/Outsider (by GREEN DAY)/I Wanna Be Sedated (by OFFSPRING) (blue vinyl, stickered p/s withdrawn single)	300
90s	Vertigo METJB 19	Whiskey In The Jar/Turn The Page (Jukebox issue no p/s)	15
10	Vertigo 00602527391100	Frantic (UNKLE Remix)/BLACK SABBATH: Paranoid (Alternative Vocal Version) (12", 1000 only)	20

ALBUMS

83	Music For Nations MFN 7	KILL 'EM ALL (LP, 1st issue with beige labels)	35
83	Music For Nations MFN 7	KILL 'EM ALL (LP, later pressing with red/yellow])	30
84	M. For Nations MFNCD 7	KILL 'EM ALL (CD)	25
84	Music For Nations MFN 27	RIDE THE LIGHTNING (LP, with inner sleeve, initial pressing with beige labels & without barcode)	25
84	M. For Nations MFN 27P	RIDE THE LIGHTNING (CD)	25
86	Music For Nations MFN 60	MASTER OF PUPPETS (LP, with inner sleeve & insert)	18
86	Music For Nations MFN 60	MASTER OF PUPPETS (LP, mispressing, Side 1 label on both sides)	30
86	Music For Nations MFN 60P	MASTER OF PUPPETS (LP, picture disc, initially without barcode)	25
86	Music For Nations MFN 60P	MASTER OF PUPPETS (LP, picture disc, with barcode)	20
86	M. For Nations MFNCD 60	MASTER OF PUPPETS (CD)	25
86	Music For Nations MFN 27P	RIDE THE LIGHTNING (LP, picture disc, initial pressing with no barcode)	30
86	Music For Nations MFN 27P	RIDE THE LIGHTNING (LP, picture disc, with barcode)	20
86	Music For Nations MFN 7P	KILL 'EM ALL (LP reissue, picture disc, lacking picture on 1 side, initially lacking barcode)	25
86	Music For Nations MFN 7P	KILL 'EM ALL (LP reissue, picture disc, with picture on 1 side and barcode)	22
87	Music For Nations MFN 7DM	KILL 'EM ALL (2-LP, 'direct metal mastered' reissue, gatefold sleeve)	35
87	Music For Nations MFN 60DM	MASTER OF PUPPETS (2-LP, 'direct metal mastered' reissue, gatefold sleeve with poster)	30
87	Music For Nations MFN 27DM	RIDE THE LIGHTNING (2-LP, 'direct metal mastered' reissue, gatefold sleeve with insert)	30
89	Vertigo 838-140-1	RIDE THE LIGHTNING (LP, reissue, mispressing, Side 1 lists Master Of Puppets tracks)	15
91	Vertigo MECAN 1/510-022-0	THE METALLICAN (CD, gold disc in metal 'paint can' with video & T-shirt; 35,000 only)	100
93	Vertigo 518-725-0	LIVE SHIT, BINGE & PURGE (3-CD box set with 3 videos & 72-page book)	80
96	Ekektra 532618	LOAD (2-LP)	30
97	Elektra 536409	RELOAD (2-LP)	30
08	Vertigo 00602517737310	DEATH MAGNETIC (Box set, 5x12")	50
08	Vertigo 00602517800502	DEATH MAGNETIC (LP, coffin-shaped box set, C CD, DVD, T-shirt, guitar picks, flag, poster and credit card)	75
08	Universal 0600753085271	KILL 'EM ALL (2-LP, reissue, gatefold with obi)	18
08	Universal 0600753085240	RIDE THE LIGHTNING (2-LP, reissue, gatefold with obi)	20
08	Universal 0600753101162	MASTER OF PUPPETS (2-LP, reissue, gatefold with obi)	20

PROMOS

88	Vertigo METDJ 2	Harvester Of Sorrow/Harvester Of Sorrow (unique p/s)	40
88	Vertigo MET CD 100	THE WHIPLASH SAMPLER (CD)	70
89	Vertigo METDJ 5	One/One (Edit) (unique blue cover, plus insert)	70
89	Vertigo METDJ 512	One (Demo Version)/For Whom The Bell Tolls (live)/Welcome Home (Sanitarium) (live) (12", unissued, promo-only p/s)	70
91	Vertigo METDJ 7	Enter Sandman (Radio Edit)/Stone Cold Crazy (p/s B-side actually silent)	15
93	Vertigo PRCD 8879-2	15 PIECES OF LIVE SH*T BINGE & PURGE (Promo CD, stickered card sleeve)	30
96	Mercury MM CJ-1	MANDATORY METALLICA (CD, 7-track sampler)	30
96	Vertigo MET INT 1	LOAD - THE INTERVIEW (CD, with cue booklet)	65
90s	Vertigo METDJ8	The Unforgiven (edit)/Killing Time (p/s)	20
97	Vertigo MMCJ-2	MANDATORY METALLICA 2 (2-CD, 17-track sampler)	40
03	Vertigo FRANTICDJ 1	Frantic (12" promo)	15
03	Vertigo SACDP 1	SAINT ANGER (2-CD promo)	20

METAL MIRROR

| 80 | M&M MM 001 | Rock 'N Roll Ain't Never Gonna Leave Us/English Booze (in p/s) | 80 |
| 80 | M&M MM 001 | Rock 'N Roll Ain't Never Gonna Leave Us/English Booze | 50 |

MINT VALUE £

METAL URBAIN
78	Radar ADA 20	Hysterie Connective/Pas Poubelle	10
77	Rough Trade RT 001	Paris Maquis/Cle De Contact (p/s)	12

METAPHORCE
95	Ill Gotten Gains FDN004	Recipes For Disaster/Behind Enemy Lines (12")	14

METEORS (1)
64	Polydor NH 52263	Get A Load Of This/Ruby Ann	10

METEORS (2)
79	EMI EMI 2987	It's Only You/Blitzkreig (p/s)	8
79	EMI EMI 5000	My Balls Ache/Action (p/s)	5

METEORS (3)
81	Ace SWT 65	METEOR MADNESS (10" EP, white label test pressings only, custom p/s)	200
81	Ace SW 65	METEOR MADNESS (EP, on blue vinyl)	25
81	Ace SW 65	METEOR MADNESS (EP)	15
81	Lost Souls LOST 101	The Crazed/Attack Of The Zorch Men (p/s)	12
81	Chiswick CHIS 147	Radioactive Kid/Graveyard Stomp (p/s)	12
81	Ace NS 74	Radioactive Kid/Graveyard Stomp (p/s, reissue, black vinyl)	8
81	Ace NS 74	Radioactive Kid/Graveyard Stomp (p/s, reissue, some clear or blue vinyl)	10
82	I.D. EYE 1	Johnny Remember Me/Fear Of The Dark/Wreckin' Crew (p/s)	8
82	I.D. EYE 1P	Johnny Remember Me/Fear Of The Dark/Wreckin' Crew (picture disc)	8
82	WXYZ ABCD 5	Mutant Rock/The Hills Have Eyes (p/s)	10
84	Mad Pig PORK 1	I'm Just A Dog/Electro Rock (p/s)	6
85	Mad Pig PORK 1T	I'm Just A Dog (Wild Hog Mix Down)/Hoover Rock/Electro (12", p/s)	8
85	Mad Pig PORK 2	Fire, Fire/Little Red Riding Hood (p/s)	5
85	Mad Pig PORK 2T	Fire, Fire/Little Red Riding Hood/Stampede (King Ray Bat Scalator In The Dark Mix) (12", p/s)	8
85	Mad Pig PORK 3	Bad Moon Rising/Rhythm Of The Bell (p/s)	5
85	Mad Pig PORK 3T	Hogs And Cuties /Bad Moon Rising/Rhythm Of The Bell (What? Another Cover Mix) (12", p/s)	8
86	I.D. EYE 10	MUTANT ROCK (EP, green vinyl)	8
86	I.D. EYET 10	MUTANT ROCK (12" EP, green or blue vinyl)	12
86	Anagram ANA 31	Surf City/The Edge (p/s)	10
86	Anagram 12ANA 31	Surf City (Has Beens From Outer Space Mix)/The Edge/Johnny's Here (12", p/s)	15
87	Anagram ANA 35	Go Buddy Go/Wildkat Ways (p/s)	7
87	Anagram ANA 35	Go Buddy Go (The Wonkey Donkey Mix)/Wildkat Ways/You Crack Me Up (12", p/s)	8
81	Ace MAD 1	THE METEORS MEET SCREAMIN' LORD SUTCH (mini-LP, 1 side each, 1,000 only, stickered cartoon print on plain card sleeve)	100
81	Lost Soul LOSTLP 3001	IN HEAVEN (LP)	20
86	Big Beat WIKA 47	TEENAGERS FROM OUTER SPACE (LP)	18
86	Big Beat WIKA 47CD	TEENAGERS FROM OUTER SPACE (CD)	18
86	Anagram GRAM 27	SEWERTIME BLUES (LP)	15
87	Dojo LP56P	NIGHT OF THE WEREWOLF (LP, picture disc)	12

(see also Tall Boys, Clapham South Escalators, [Screamin'] Lord Sutch, Deadbeats)

METERS
69	Stateside SS 2140	Sophisticated Cissy/Sehorn's Farm	10
70	Direction 58-4751	Look-Ka-Py-Py/This Is My Last Affair	10
74	Reprise K 14367	People Say/Africa	6
75	Reprise K 14405	Fire On The Bayou/They All Ask'd For You	6
72	Reprise K 44242	CABBAGE ALLEY (LP)	20
74	Reprise K 54027	REJUVENATION (LP)	20
74	Island ILPS 9250	CISSY STRUT (LP)	30
75	Reprise K 54044	FIRE ON THE BAYOU (LP)	15
76	Reprise K 54076	BEST OF THE METERS (LP)	15
76	Reprise K 54078	TRICK BAG (LP)	18
77	Reprise K 56378	NEW DIRECTIONS (LP)	12
79	Pye PKL 5578	GOOD OLD FUNKY MUSIC (LP)	12

METGUMBNERBONE
83	Aeon (No Cat. No.)	COPS OF MATTER (cassette)	40
83	Amission REV 13:15	LIGELIAHORN (LP, 500 only, with insert)	70
84	Private cassette	FOR THE RAVEN (cassette)	40

METHOD ACTORS
80	Armageddon AS 6	The Method/Can't Act (p/s)	7
81	Armageddon AS 11	Round World/Eye (p/s)	7

METHODS
70	DJM DJS 225	Chasing The Sun/And That Is Life	15

PETER METRO
82	Greensleeves GRED 97	Warn Them Teach Them (with Squiddly Ranking)/Carribean Connection (12")	10

METRO TRINITY
87	Cafeteria CAFF 1	DIE YOUNG EP (12")	60

METRONOME ALL STARS
51	Capitol CL 13545	Local 802 Blues/Early Spring (78, with Stan Getz & Miles Davis)	10

METROPAK
80	Metropak PAK 001	You're A Rebel/OK Let's Go/Run Run Run (numbered p/s)	6
80	Metropak PAK 002	Here's Looking At You/Walking (foldout card p/s)	5

METROPHASE
79	Neo London MS 01	In Black/Neo Beauty/Cold Rebellion (photocopied p/s with lyric insert)	8
79	Neo London MS 02	New Age/Frames Of Life (foldout p/s, stamped white labels)	8
81	Fresh FRESH 6	In Black/Neo Beauty/Cold Rebellion (reissue, better quality p/s with insert)	6

(see also Swell Maps)

METROPOLITAN POLICE BAND
66	Columbia DB 8095	Thunderbirds March/P.C. ALEXANDER MORGAN: Sussex By The Sea	8

METROTONE
97	Wurlitzer Jukebox WJ 40	Kiss Me Awake/Byddant Fel Y Ser/Four Continuous Tones (p/s, 1,000 only)	5

| 98 | Earworm WORM 21 | THE LESS YOU HAVE THE MORE YOU ARE (LP, 4 copies only on black vinyl) | 25 |

PAUL METSERS
| 81 | Highway SHY 7014 | CAUTION TO THE WIND (LP) | 18 |

M.E.V.
| 69 | Polydor 583 769 | MUSICA ELETTRONICA VIVA (LP) | 15 |

MEXICANO
| 75 | Angen ANG 111 | Cut Throat/Gorilla In Manilla | 5 |

MEXICANS
| 68 | Pye 7N 17613 | Alexander Higginbottom/Julie | 12 |
| 68 | Pye 7N 17657 | Without Your Love | 12 |

MEXICO RED
| 88 | Hummingbird | Eternal Flame/Follow Me To Heaven (p/s, insert) | 40 |

AUGIE MEYERS
| 70s | Sonet SNTF 883 | STILL GROWIN' (LP, with Doug Sahm) | 12 |
(see also Sir Douglas Quintet, Doug Sahm)

ANTHONY MEYNELL
| 82 | Hi-Lo LO 01 | HITS FROM 3000 YEARS AGO (LP, purple sleeve) | 15 |
(see also Squire)

LEE MEZA
| 67 | Stateside SS 589 | If It Happens/One Good Thing Leads To Another | 30 |

MEZZ MEZZROW
| 62 | Storyville SEP 394 | KING JAZZ STORY (EP) | 8 |
| 55 | Vogue LAE 12007 | PLEYEL CONCERT (LP) | 12 |
(see also Mezzrow-Bechet Quartet)

MEZZROW-BECHET QUINTET
| 56 | Vogue LAE 12017 | THE MEZZROW-BECHET QUINTET (LP) | 12 |
(see also Sidney Bechet)

M-G-M SINGING STRINGS
| 66 | MGM 1307 | Lara's Theme From "Dr Zhivago"/The Old And The New | 6 |

M-G-M STUDIO ORCHESTRA
| 55 | MGM SP 1144 | Rock Around The Clock/"Blackboard Jungle" Love Theme | 25 |

MIAMI
74	Jay Boy BOY 81	Party Freaks/(Part 2)	5
75	Jay Boy BOY 86	Hey Y'all We're Miami/Chicken Yellow	5
75	Jay Boy BOY 96	Funk It Up/Freak On Down My Way	5
76	Jay Boy BOY 111	Kill That Roach/Mr Notorious	5

MIAOW
85	Venus VENUS 1	Belle Vue/Fate (p/s)	6
86	Venus VENUST 1	Belle Vue/Fate/Grocer's Devil Daughter (12", p/s)	10
87	Factory FAC 189	Break The Code/Stolen Ears (p/s)	10

MICHA
| 65 | Pye 7N 15982 | Protest Singer/Serpent | 8 |

GEORGE MICHAEL
84	Epic A 4603	Careless Whisper/Careless Whisper (Instrumental) (poster p/s)	20
84	Epic QTA 4603	Careless Whisper (Extended Mix)/Careless Whisper (Special Version Wexler)/Careless Whisper (Instrumental) (12", title p/s)	25
84	Epic WA 4603	Careless Whisper (Extended Mix)/Careless Whisper (Instrumental) (12", picture disc, clear or black rim)	20
87	Epic EMUP 3	Faith/Faith (Instrumental)/Hand To Mouth (12", picture disc)	20
87	Epic EMU 4	Father Figure/Love's In Need Of Love Today (with calendar & stickered p/s)	8
87	Epic EMUT 4	Father Figure/Love's In Need Of Love Today/Father Figure (Instrumental) (12", stickered p/s with poster)	8
88	Epic EMUP 4	Father Figure/Love's In Need Of Love Today (oblong shaped picture disc)	10
88	Epic EMU B5	One More Try/Look At Your Hands (p/s, shrinkwrapped with badge)	8
88	Epic EMU G6	Monkey/Monkey (A Capella) (gatefold p/s, with photo insert)	8
88	Epic CD EMU 6	Monkey (Extended Version)/(A'Capella)/(Extra Bits)/(7" Edit) (CD)	12
90	Epic XPCD 140	Cowboys And Angels (Radio Edit 4.34)/(7.14) (CD single promo only)	30
87	Epic 460000 9	FAITH (CD, extra tracks, picture disc, PVC box)	40
90	Epic 467295 2	LISTEN WITHOUT PREJUDICE VOLUME 1 (CD, picture disc, stickered case)	20
(see also Wham!, Deon Estus, High, Elton John, Queen)

RAS MICHAEL & THE SONS OF NEGUS
75	Grounnation GRD 2037	None A Jah Children/Glory Dawn	10
75	Trojan TRSL 113	DADAWAH (PEACE & LOVE) (LP)	40
75	Vulcan VUL 005	RASTAFARI (LP)	25
75	Grounation GROL 505	RASTAFARI (LP)	25

MICHAEL SCHENKER GROUP
82	Chrysalis CHS 2636	Dancer/Girl From Uptown (picture disc)	5
82	Chysalis PCHR 1393	ASSAULT ATTACK (LP, picture disc)	15
83	Chysalis CHRP 1441	BUILT TO DESTROY (LP, picture disc, U.S. remixes)	15
(see also McAuley Schenker Group, Michael Schenker, Scorpions, UFO, Cozy Powell, Graham Bonnet, Alex Harvey Band)

CODY MICHAELS
| 79 | Grapevine GRP 121 | 7 Days - 52 Weeks/VIRTUE ORCHESTRA: Don't Look Back (Instrumental) | 8 |

MARILYN MICHAELS
| 60 | RCA RCA 1208 | Tell Tommy I Miss Him/Everyone Was There But You | 10 |

MICHIGAN RAG
| 72 | Blue Horizon 2096 009 | Don't Run Away/She's Looking Good | 20 |

MICHIGANS
| 63 | Vogue V 9207 | Intermission Riff/Tea For Two | 15 |

MICKEY & LUDELLA
95	Vinyl Japan ASKLP 52	BEDLAM A GO GO (LP)	30

(see also Milkshakes, Billy Childish, Del Monas, Thee Headcoatees)

MICKEY (BAKER) & KITTY (NOBLE)
60	London HLE 9054	Buttercup/My Reverie	35

MICKEY (BAKER) & SYLVIA
57	HMV POP 331	Love Is Strange/I'm Going Home	200
57	HMV POP 331	Love Is Strange/I'm Going Home (78)	50
58	RCA RCA 1064	Rock And Stroll Room/Bewildered	50
58	RCA RCA 1064	Rock And Stroll Room/Bewildered (78)	40
60	RCA RCA 1206	Sweeter As The Day Goes By/Mommy Out De Light	15
65	RCA Victor RCA 1487	Love Is Strange/Dearest	25
65	RCA Camden CDN 5133	LOVE IS STRANGE (LP)	200

(see also Mickey Baker, Sylvia [Robbins])

MICKEY FINN
64	Blue Beat BB 203	Tom Hark/Please Love Me (as 'Mickey Finn & the Blue Men')	25
64	Oriole CB 1927	Pills/Hush Your Mouth (as 'Mickey Finn & the Blue Men')	80
64	Oriole CB 1940	Reelin' & A'Rockin'/I Still Want You (as 'Mickey Finn')	50
65	Columbia DB 7510	The Sporting Life/Night Comes Down (as 'The Mickey Finn')	100
66	Polydor 56719	I Do Love You/If I Had You Baby (as 'The Mickey Finn')	100
67	Direction 58-3086	Garden Of My Mind/Time To Start Loving You (as 'The Mickey Finn')	200
95	Noiseburger 3	Ain't Necessarily So/God Bless The Child (foldaround p/s in poly bag, 1,000 only, 1st 500 signed)	8
95	Noiseburger 3	Ain't Necessarily So/God Bless The Child (foldaround p/s in poly bag, 1,000 only)	5

BOBBY "BOBCATS" MICKLEBURGH
55	Esquire EP 40	MICKLEBURGH'S BOBCATS (EP)	10
56	Esquire EP 73	MICKLEBURGH'S BOBCATS (EP)	10

MICROBE
69	CBS 4158	Groovy Baby/MICROBOP ENSEMBLE: Your Turn Now	5

MICRODISNEY
82	Kabuki KAMD 2	Hello Rascals/The Helicopter Of The Holy Ghost (p/s)	6
83	Kabuki KAMD 4	Pink Skinned Man/Fiction Land (p/s)	5
88	Virgin V2505	39 MINUTES (LP)	18
84	Rough Trade ROUGH 75	EVERYBODY IS FANTASTIC (LP)	15
84	Rough Trade ROUGH 85	THE CLOCK COMES DOWN THE STAIRS (LP)	12
84	Rough Trade RTM 155	WE HATE YOU SOUTH AFRICAN BASTARDS (LP)	20

MICRON
88	White SG045	Eastenders Rap (12")	10

(see Rebel MC)

STEPHAN MICUS
76	Caroline C 1517	ARCHAIN CONCERTS (LP)	15

MIDAS MOULD
72	Columbia DB 8868	Information Emily/Love Sweet Love	15

RAS MIDAS
77	Black Swan WIP 6371	Kude A Bamba/Congo Dub	10
79	Tribesman TM 24	Natty Dread Surprise/Good Old Days Original (with I-Roy) (12")	60
79	Warrior WAR 138	Can't Stop Rasta Now/Rain And Fire (12")	20

MIDAS (1)
70	Solar SL003	I've Seen A New Life/Visit The Sun	40

MIDAS (2)
83	Small Run SRR 0008	Can't Stop Loving You/Power In The Sky (p/s with insert)	200

MIDDLE OF THE ROAD
72	RCA 2264	Bottoms Up/See The Sky	5
73	RCA Camden CDS 1131	THE MIDDLE OF THE ROAD (LP)	12
74	RCA Camden CDS 1141	MIDDLE OF THE ROAD (LP)	12

MAX MIDDLETON & ROBERT AWWAI
79	Harvest SHSP 4103	ANOTHER SLEEPER (LP)	18

TONY MIDDLETON
65	London HLR 9983	My Little Red Book (as Burt Bacharach Orchestra with Tony Middleton)/BURT BACHARACH ORCHESTRA: What's New Pussycat	30
66	Polydor BM 56704	To The Ends Of The Earth/Don't Ever Leave Me	350
66	Polydor BM 56704	To The Ends Of The Earth/Don't Ever Leave Me (DJ copy)	500
78	Grapevine GRP 115	Paris Blues/Out Of This World	10

(see also Willows, Burt Bacharach)

MIDLAKE
08	Bella Union BELLAV117	THE TRIALS OF VAN OCCUPANTHER (LP)	30
10	Bella Union CD02245P	THE COURAGE OF OTHERS (Box set, 2-LP, DVD, CD & 32 page booklet)	50

MIDNIGHT
78	Ariola ATTA 514	Don't Bother To Knock/Keep Walking By (p/s)	15

MIDNIGHT CRUISER
77	It IT 2	Rich Bitch/Striker (p/s)	10

MIDNIGHT RAGS
80	Ace ACE 005	Public Enemy/Alcatraz/Mamma Said (p/s)	8
80	Velvet Moon VM 1	The Cars That Ate New York/Oscar Automobile (p/s, withdrawn)	8

(see also Paul Roland, Weird Strings)

MIDNIGHT SHIFT
66	Decca F 12487	Saturday Jump/Living Fast	30

MIDNIGHT SUN
71	MCA MKPS 2019	MIDNIGHT SUN (LP, red/pink 'dogbone' label)	60
72	MCA MKPS 2024	WALKING CIRCLES (LP, black/blue hexagon label)	60

MIDNIGHTERS

55	Parlophone DP 399	Work With Me Annie/Sexy Ways (78, export issue)	40
55	Parlophone DP 422	Annie Had A Baby/THUNDERBIRDS: Pledging My Love (78, export issue)	40

(see also Hank Ballard)

MIDNIGHTS

66	Ember EMB S 220	(Won'tcha) Show Me Around/Only Two Can Play	18
63	MEP 101/MN 1/EAG-EP-134	MIDNIGHTS (EP, private pressing)	130

MI5

80	Public PUB 002	Alright On The Night/Television Screen Heroes/Don't Make Waves (p/s)	7

M.I. FIVE

66	Parlophone R 5486	You'll Never Stop Me Loving You/Only Time Will Tell	100

(see also Maze, Deep Purple)

MIGHT OF COINCIDENCE

72	Entropia BM 0001	WHY COULDN'T PEOPLE WAIT (LP)	100

MIGHTY ABIJANS

80	No 1 Rock	Untamed(vocal & DJ Cut)/Dubwise (12")	10

MIGHTY AVENGERS (JAMAICA)

66	Rymska RA 101	Scatter Shot (actually by Byron Lee & Dragonaires)/BYRON LEE: Like You Do (B-side actually "No One" by Techniques)	20

MIGHTY AVENGERS (U.K.)

64	Decca F 11891	Hide Your Pride/Hey Senorita	18
64	Decca F 11962	So Much In Love/Sometime They Say	25
65	Decca F 12085	Blue Turns To Grey/I'm Lost Without You	25
65	Decca F 12198	(Walkin' Thru The) Sleepy City/Sir Edward And Lady Jane	35

(see also Andrew Oldham)

MIGHTY BABY

71	Blue Horizon 2096 003	Devil's Whisper/Virgin Spring	70
69	Head HDLS 6002	MIGHTY BABY (LP, gatefold sleeve, yellow label)	300
71	Blue Horizon 2931 001	A JUG OF LOVE (LP, with lyric insert)	600
71	Blue Horizon 2931 001	A JUG OF LOVE (LP)	300
84	Psycho PSYCHO 31	EGYPTIAN TOMB (LP, reissue of "Mighty Baby" in different sleeve)	30
06	Sunbeam SBRLP 5026	JUG OF LOVE (LP, reissue, gatefold)	12

(see also Action, Robin Scott, Habibiyya, Keith Christmas, Gary Farr, Stone's Masonry, Andy Roberts)

THEE MIGHTY CAESARS

86	Empire LWC 604	Ten Bears Of The Comanches/Baby What's Wrong (p/s)	15
86	Media Burn MB 5	Little By Little/The Swag/What You've Got/Cyclonic (12", p/s)	20
88	Swag SWG 001	She's Just Fifteen Years Old/The Swag (flexi in p/s with Pandora's Box fanzine)	15
95	Toe Rag RAG 1A	Billy B Childish/Dolli Bambi (Free single as FRAT SHACK, p/s)	8
85	Milkshakes NER - 0	S.T. (LP)	40
86	Milkshakes APOLL - 0	THEE CAESARS OF TRASH (LP)	30
86	Milkshakes PLAT - 0	ACROPOLIS NOW (LP)	30
86	Big Beat WIK45	BEWARE OF THE IDES OF MARCH (LP)	30
87	Hangman HANG 3 UP	DON'T GIVE ANY DINNER TO HENRY CHINASKI (LP)	35
87	Hangmen HANG 7 UP	PUNK ROCK SERENADE (LP)	25
87	Big Beat WIK 60	LIVE IN ROME (LP)	25
87	Ambassador AMBAS 2	WISE BLOOD (LP, colour sleeve)	35
89	Hangman HANG 26 UP	WISE BLOOD (LP, reissue, black and silver sleeve)	30
92	Hangman HANG 46 UP	CAESARS REMAINS (LP)	30

(see also Milkshakes, Prisoners, Billy Childish, Thee Headcoats)

MIGHTY DIAMONDS

75	Black Wax WAX13	I Need A Roof/Joe Joe Dub	8
75	Virgin VS 137	Have Mercy/Them Never Love Poor Marcus	8
75	Locks LOX 10	Back Weh (You No Mafia)/Mafia Dub	8
79	Virgin Frontline FLS 122 12	Bodyguard/One Brother Short (12", p/s)	10
80	Greensleeves GRED 45	Gates Of Zion/SLY AND ROBBIE - Zion In Dub (12", green vinyl)	40
76	Virgin V2052	RIGHT TIME (LP)	20
77	Virgin V 2078	ICE ON FIRE (LP)	15
79	Virgin Frontline FLD 6001	DEEPER ROOTS (LP, with bonus dub LP)	12
80	Mobiliser SRE 31	LEADER OF THE BLACK COUNTRY (LP)	20

MIGHTY DOUGLAS

60s	Jump Up JU 501	Laziest Man/Dance Me Lover	8
60s	Jump Up JU 508	Teacher Teacher/Split Me In Two	8
60s	Jump Up JU 509	Ugliness/My Wicked Boy Child	8

MIGHTY 'EM

73	Decca FR 13446	Jekyll And Hyde/What A Way To Go	30

MIGHTY ETHNICZ

88	Good Times EB20	Freestyle/B Style (12")	40
93	Lowdown LOWT01	Can I Get A Deal?/Bedrock (12")	15

MIGHTY FLEA & MICKEY BAKER

72	Polydor 2058 328	Bloodshot Eyes/Charley Stone	6
73	Polydor 2460 185	LET THE GOOD TIMES ROLL (LP)	22

MIGHTY FLYERS

74	Myrrh MYR 1016	LOW FLYING ANGELS (LP, with insert)	20

(see also Mick Abrahams)

MIGHTY HARD

70	Pye 7N 17878	Save The Life Of My Child/House Of The Rising Sun	30

MIGHTY MAYTONES

76	Mango MAN 1010	Madness/Madness Version	6
78	GG's GG 029	Searching In Disco (with Trinity)/Madness In Disco (with U Brown) (12")	20
76	Burning Sounds BS 1002	MADNESS (LP)	18
78	Burning Sounds BS 1022	BOAT TO ZION (LP)	25

MINT VALUE £

(see also Maytones)

MIGHTY MEN
62	Salvo SLO 1804	No Way Out/You Too Much (99 copies only)	30

MIGHTY MIGHTY
86	Girlie GAY 1	Everybody Knows The Monkey/You're On My Mind (foldover p/s, poly bag)	8
86	Girlie GAY 1	Everybody Knows The Monkey/You're On My Mind (standard p/s)	5
86	Girlie XGAY 2	IS THERE ANYONE OUT THERE? (12" EP)	8
87	Sha La La Ba Ba Ba Ba Ba 001	Throwaway (Throwaway Version)/CLOUDS: Jenny Nowhere (p/s, flexi)	10
87	Sha La La Ba Ba Ba Ba Ba 001	Throwaway (Throwaway Version)/CLOUDS: Jenny Nowhere (p/s, flexi, with Baby Honey Fanzine 1)	20

MIGHTY MO
72	Columbia DB 8851	Ape Call/Heavy Bear	10

MIGHTY POWER
67	Jump Up JU 513	You're Wasting Your Time/Smart Barbarian	8

MIGHTY SAM
66	Stateside SS 534	Sweet Dreams/Good Humor Man	15
66	Stateside SS 544	Fannie Mae/Badmouthin'	15
68	Stateside SS 2076	When She Touches Me/Just Like Old Times	15
70	Soul City SC 115	Papa True Love/I Need A Lot Of Lovin'	25
70	Soul City SCM 004	MIGHTY SOUL (LP)	85

MIGHTY SPARROW
59	Melodisc 1491	Goaty/LORD MELODY: I Confess (78)	10
60	Kalypso XX 22	Mr. Herbert/Simpson	6
68	NEMS 56-3558	Mr. Walker/Carnival In '68	6
60s	Jump Up JU 523	Village Ram/Pull Pistle Gang	6
69	Fab FAB 116	Mr. Walker/Jane	6
70	Fab FAB 147	I Don't Wanna Lose You/The Truth	6
60	Kalypso XXEP 1	THIS IS SPARROW (EP)	10
60	Kalypso XXEP 2	MAN, DIG THIS SPARROW (EP)	10
60	Kalypso XXEP 3	A PARTY WITH SPARROW (EP)	10
61	Kalypso XXEP 4	THIS IS THE SPARROW AGAIN (EP)	10
61	Kalypso XXEP 5	GREETINGS FROM SPARROW (EP)	10
62	Kalypso XXEP 6	SPARROW THE CONQUEROR (EP)	10
63	Island ILP 902	THE SLAVE (LP)	30
66	RCA RD 7516	SPARROW COME BACK (LP)	15
68	Melodisc MLPWI 12-146	CALYPSO CARNIVAL (LP)	25
68	Melodisc MLPWI 12-148	MR WALKER (LP)	30

(see also Sparrow, King Sparrow, Lord Melody)

MIGHTY TERROR & HIS CALYPSONIANS
50	Melodisc 1033	The Queen Is In/Chinese Children (78)	10
59	Pye N 15177	Women Police In England/Patricia Gone With Millicent (78)	10
59	Pye N 15178	Brown Skin Gal/Kitch Cavalcade (78)	10

MIGHTY VIKINGS
67	Island WI 3060	Do Re Mi/The Sound Of Music	15
67	Island WI 3074	Rockitty Fockitty/Give Me Back My Gal (both actually with Sammy Ismay)	15

MIGHTY WAH
00	Essental ESDCD 892	THE HANDY WAH! WHOLE (2 x CD)	20

MIGIL FIVE
64	Pye 7N 15597	Mockingbird Hill/Long Ago And Far Away	5
64	Pye 7N 15645	Near You/Don't Wanna Go On Shaking	6
64	Pye 7N 15677	Boys And Girls/I Saw Your Picture	6
65	Pye 7N 15757	Just Behind The Rainbow/Seven Lonely Days	7
65	Pye 7N 15874	One Hundred Years/I'm In Love Again	12
66	Pye 7N 17023	Pencil And Paper/Nevertheless (I'm In Love With You)	7
67	Columbia DB 8196	Together/Superstition	20
68	Jay Boy BOY 4	If I Had My Way/Somebody's Stolen The Moon	6
64	Pye NEP 24191	MEET THE MIGIL FIVE (EP)	22
64	Pye NPL 18093	MOCKING BIRD HILL (LP)	45

(see also Migil Four, Mike Felix)

MIGIL FOUR
63	Pye 7N 15572	Maybe/Can't I?	7

(see also Migil Five)

MIKA
06	Casablanca MIKA 7001	Relax (Take It Easy)/Billy Brown (die-cut p/s with printed inner sleeve, 500 only)	10

MIKE & MECHANICS
85	WEA U 8908P	Silent Running/I Get The Feeling (engine-shaped picture disc)	5

(see also Mike Rutherford, Genesis, Paul Carrack)

MIKE & MODIFIERS
62	Oriole CB 1775	I Found Myself A Brand New Baby/It's Too Bad	850

MIKE STUART SPAN
66	Columbia DB 8066	Come On Over To Our Place/Still Nights	100
67	Columbia DB 8206	Dear/Invitation	80
68	Jewel JL 01	Children Of Tomorrow/Concerto Of Thoughts	500
68	Fontana TF 959	You Can Understand Me/Baubles And Bangles	25
93	117 CPAT 1171	EXSPANSIONS: Second Production/Rescue Me/Remember The Times/World In My Head (EP)	15
95	Tenth Planet TP 014	TIMESPAN (LP, gatefold sleeve, numbered, 1,000 copies only)	25

(see also Leviathan, High Defenders, Tony's Defenders, High Broom)

BOBBY MILANO
55	Capitol CL 14252	A King Or A Slave/If You Cared	10
55	Capitol CL 14309	If Tears Could Bring You Back/Make Me A Present Of You	10

MILBURN
03	Private Pressing	Along Comes Mary (Disc only, no p/s)	5

AMOS MILBURN
57	Vogue V 9064	Every Day Of The Week/Girl Of My Dreams (triangular centre)	150
57	Vogue V 9064	Every Day Of The Week/Girl Of My Dreams (round centre)	75
57	Vogue V 9064	Every Day Of The Week/Girl Of My Dreams (78)	40
57	Vogue V 9069	Rum And Coca Cola/Soft Pillow (triangular centre)	250
57	Vogue V 9069	Rum And Coca Cola/Soft Pillow (triangular centre) (78)	85
57	Vogue V 9080	Thinking Of You Baby/If I Could Be With You (One Hour Tonight) (triangular centre)	200
57	Vogue V 9080	Thinking Of You Baby/If I Could Be With You (One Hour Tonight) (78)	70
60	Vogue V 9163	One Scotch, One Bourbon, One Beer/Bad, Bad Whiskey	150
57	Vogue VE 1-70102	ROCK AND ROLL (EP)	250
78	United Artists UAS 30203	CHICKEN SHACK BOOGIE (LP)	12

AMOS MILBURN JNR
63	London HLU 9795	Gloria/Look At Me Fool	20

MILDRED AND THE MICE
09	Third Man TMR 003	I Like My Mice (Dead)/Spider Bite (100 only, luminous vinyl)	40

PERCY MILEM
66	Stateside SS 566	Crying Baby, Baby, Baby/Call On Me	100
66	Stateside SS 566	Crying Baby, Baby, Baby/Call On Me (DJ copy)	150

ARTHUR MILES
90	Ffrr 148	Trippin On Your Love/Helping Hand	12

BERNARD MILES
56	HMV 7EG 8176	OVER THE GATE (EP)	8

BUDDY MILES (EXPRESS)
68	Mercury MF 1065	Train (Parts 1 & 2)	10
69	Mercury MF 1098	Miss Lady/'69 Freedom Special	8
70	Mercury 6052 036	Them Changes/Your Feeling Is Mine (solo)	6
69	Mercury 20137 SMCL	EXPRESSWAY TO YOUR SKULL (LP)	18
69	Mercury 20163 SMCL	ELECTRIC CHURCH (LP)	18
70	Mercury 6338 016	THEM CHANGES (LP)	15
71	Mercury 6338 028	WE GOT TO LIVE TOGETHER (LP)	15
71	Mercury 6338 048	A MESSAGE TO THE PEOPLE (LP)	12

(see also Electric Flag, Jimi Hendrix, Carlos Santana & Buddy Miles)

DICK & SUE MILES
79	Sweet Folk & Country SFA 106	THE DUNMOW FLITCH (LP)	18

GARRY MILES
60	London HLG 9155	Look For A Star/Afraid Of Love	10
60	London REG 1264	LOOK FOR A STAR (EP)	20

JOHN MILES
70	Orange OAS 508	Why Don't You Love Me?/If I Could See Through	20
71	Decca F 13196	Jose/You Make It So Hard	5
72	Orange OAS 207	Come Away Melinda/Walking With My Head Held High	5
72	Orange OAS 208	Yesterday (Was Just The Beginning)/Road To Freedom	5
73	Orange OAS 209	Hard Road/You're Telling Me Lies	5
73	Orange OAS 211	Jacqueline/Keep On Tryin'	5
73	Orange OAS 213	One Minute Every Hour/Hollywood Queen	5
74	Orange OAS 220	Fright Of My Life/Good Time Woman	5
74	Orange OAS 223	What's On Your Mind/Rock'n'Roll Band	5
74	Orange OAS 224	What's On Your Mind/To Be Grateful	5
78	Decca FR 13757	No Hard Feelings/Nice Man Jack	6
79	Decca FR 13827	I Can't Keep A Man Down/Sweet Lorraine	6

(see also Influence)

LENNY MILES
61	Top Rank JAR 546	Don't Believe Him Donna/Invisible	30

LIZZIE MILES
56	HMV 7EG 8178	THE BLUES THEY SANG (EP, 1 side by Billy Young, both with Jelly Roll Morton)	20

SARAH MILES
65	Fontana TF 552	Where Am I/Here Of All Places	5

MILITANT BARRY
79	Manic PFUL 1105	Pistol Boy/Green Valley (12")	8
77	Conflict COND 2000	Idi Amin Blood Up/Free Black People (12", die-cut p/s)	15
78	Conflict COND 2003	Ambition/Can't Stop Me (12")	15
79	Vista Sounds STLP 1012	GREEN VALLEY (LP)	20

MILK & COOKIES
75	Island WIP.6222	Little Lost And Innocent/Good Friends (as Milk 'n' Cookies)	12

MILKSHAKES
82	Havasong BILK-O	Please Don't Tell My Baby/It's You (p/s)	15
92	Damaged Goods DAMGOOD 3	Red Hot/Dull Knife (p/s)	8
83	Upright UP 6	Soldiers Of Love/Shimmy Shimmy (p/s)	20
84	Big Beat NS 94	Brand New Cadillac/Commanche/Jezebel/Jaguar And Thunderbird (p/s)	15
84	Big Beat SW 105	Ambassadors Of Love/No More/Gringles And Groyles Again/ Remarkable (p/s)	15
86	Empire UXF 228	Let Me Love You/She Tells Me She Loves Me (p/s)	25
83	Big Beat NED 4	14 RHYTHM AND BEAT GREATS (LP, red, lilac and blue sleeves)	25
83	Upright UPLP 1	AFTER SCHOOL SESSIONS (LP, laminated sleeve)	25
84	Milkshake GARB-O	THEE KNIGHTS OF TRASH (LP)	30
84	Milkshake HARP-O	NOTHING CAN STOP THESE MEN (LP)	20
84	Big Beat WIK22	SHOWCASE (LP)	25
84	Big Beat WIKM 20	ROCK 'N' ROLL HITS OF THE 50's AND 60's (LP)	12
85	Big Beat WIK 30	THEY CAME, THEY SAW, THEY CONQUERED (LP)	25
86	Media Burn MB 6	THE 107 TAPES (2-LP)	30
86	Milkshake MILK-O	TALKING 'BOUT MILKSHAKES (LP, with poster)	40

MINT VALUE £

86	Milkshakes MILK-0	TALKING 'BOUT MILKSHAKES (LP, without poster)	30
87	Hangman HANG 11 UP	LIVE FROM CHATHAM (LP)	20
87	Hangman HANG 1 UP	REVENGE - TRASH FROM THE VAULT (THE LEGENDARY MISSING 9th ALBUM) (LP)	25
92	Vinyl Japan ASKLP 10	STILL TALKING 'BOUT (LP)	25
05	Damaged Goods DAMGOOD 249LP	IN GERMANY (LP)	15

(see also Thee Mighty Caesars, Prisoners/Milkshakes, Pop Rivits, Len Bright Combo, Billy Childish, Thee Headcoats, Mickey & Ludella, Masonics)

MILK TEETH
74	Bead Records BEAD 1	A TOUCH OF THE SUN (LP)	150

MILLENIUM
84	Guardian GRC 2163	MILLENIUM (LP)	20

MILLER
65	Oak RGJ 190	Baby I've Got News For You/The Girl With The Castle	300
65	Columbia DB 7735	Baby I Got News For You/The Girl With The Castle	300

(see also Big Boy Pete, Peter Jay & Jaywalkers, Pete Miller, News)

BETTY MILLER
59	Top Rank JAR 115	Pearly Gates/Old Time Religion	6
59	Top Rank JAR 127	Jack O' Diamonds/(It Took) One Kiss	8

BOB MILLER & MILLERMEN
57	Columbia DB 4017	The Scamp/The Sack Line (as Bob Miller Music)	6
58	Columbia DB 4140	Square Bash/Muchacha (as Bob Miller Music)	5
59	Fontana H 181	Dig This!/The Poacher	10
59	Fontana H 192	Little Dipper/The Keel Row	5
59	Fontana H 228	In The Mood/Joey's Song	5
60	Fontana H 236	The Busker's Tune/My Guy's Come Back	5
60	Fontana H 245	77 Sunset Strip/Manhunt	5
60	Fontana H 284	Night Theme/Last Date	10
61	Parlophone R 4779	Trouble Shooter/Hootin'	10
61	Parlophone R 4854	The "Oliver" Twist/That's It	7
65	Mercury MF 947	Uptown And Downtown/Carnaby Street Parade	10
65	Polydor 56005	6-5 Special/Dick Van Dyke Theme	10
66	Columbia DB 7877	Get Smart/Bony's Blues (as Bob Miller & His Millermen)	8
72	Spiral DIT 3	Doin' The Slosh/Sloshing Around	8

BOBBIE MILLER
65	Decca F 12064	What A Guy/You Went Away	40
65	Decca F 12252	Every Beat Of My Heart/Tomorrow	15
66	Decca F 12354	Everywhere I Go/IAN STEWART & RAILROADERS: Stu-Ball	80

(see also Mongrels, Rolling Stones)

BRANKO MILLER
68	CBS 3955	Candy/Today Is Better Than Yesterday	8

CHUCK MILLER
56	Capitol CL 14543	Rogue River Valley/No Baby Like You	15
57	Mercury 7MT 153	The Auctioneer/Me Head's In De Barrel	20
58	Mercury 7MT 215	Down The Road A-Piece/Mad About Her Blues	100
58	Mercury MT 215	Down The Road A-Piece/Mad About Her Blues (78)	10
59	Mercury AMT 1026	The Auctioneer/Baby Doll	5
60	Mercury ZEP 10058	GOING GOING GONE (EP)	50

COUNT PRINCE (MILLER)
70	Downtown DT 460	I'm Gonna Keep On Trying/Girl I Need You (as Count Prince)	5
70	MCA MK 5042	Mule Train/Lucille (p/s)	5

(see also Jimmy James & The Vagabonds)

FRANKIE MILLER
59	Melodisc MEL 1519	True Blue/Black Land Farmer	15
59	Melodisc MEL 1519	True Blue/Black Land Farmer (78)	30
59	Melodisc MEL 1529	Poppin' Johnnie/Family Man	15
59	Melodisc MEL 1529	Poppin' Johnnie/Family Man (78)	30
60	Melodisc MEL 1552	Rain, Rain/Baby Rocked Her Dolly	15
62	Top Rank JKP 3013	COUNTRY MUSIC (EP)	30
64	Ember CW 107	THE TRUE COUNTRY STYLE OF FRANKIE MILLER (LP)	25

GARY MILLER
58	Pye 7N 15120	The Story Of My Life/Put A Light In The Window	5
58	Pye 7N 15136	Lollipop/Dancing With My Shadow	5
58	Pye Nixa 7N 15140	On The Street Where You Live/That's For Me	6
58	Pye Nixa 7N 15164	The First Christmas Day/Nearest And Dearest	6
60	Pye 7N 15277	Mission Bell/Happy Together	7
61	Pye 7N 15404	There Goes That Song Again/The Night Is Young	6
61	Pye 7N 15338	Dream Harbour/Goodnight Sweetheart	6
62	Pye 7N 15425	If You Were The Only Girl In The World/Dancing In The Dark	6
62	Pye 7N 15452	If I Had My Way/Moonlight Becomes You	6
62	Pye 7N 15474	Mr. Lonely/Sunday	6
63	Pye 7N 15497	I've Heard That Song Before/You Are Beautiful	6
63	Pye 7N 15592	Amor/Maria Elena	7
64	Pye 7N 15698	Aqua Marina/Stingray	12
64	Pye 7N 15651	The Way You Look Tonight/Dear Friend	6
56	Pye NEP 24013	YELLOW ROSE OF TEXAS (EP, 2 different sleeves)	10
57	Pye NEP 24047	HIT PARADE VOL. 1 (EP)	10
57	Pye NEP 24057	MEET MISTER MILLER PT. 1 - ON STAGE (EP)	8
57	Pye NEP 24058	MEET MISTER MILLER PT. 2 - FOR THE YOUNG IN LOVE (EP)	8
57	Pye NEP 24059	MEET MISTER MILLER PT. 3 - FOR THE YOUNG IN LOVE (EP)	8
57	Pye NEP 24123	FLOWER DRUM SONG (EP)	8
57	Nixa NPL 18008	MEET MISTER MILLER (LP)	20
61	Pye NPL 18059	GARY ON THE BALL (LP, with Kenny Ball)	15

GLEN MILLER
67	Doctor Bird DB 1089	Where Is The Love/Funky Broadway	300
68	Doctor Bird DB 1128	Rocksteady Party/Book Of Memories	25

GLENN MILLER & HIS ORCHESTRA

54	Columbia SCM 5086	I Got Rhythm/Sleepy Time Gal	5
54	HMV 7M 195	Little Brown Jug/Don't Sit Under The Apple Tree	5
59	Top Rank JAR 114	Boom Shot/You Say The Sweetest Things, Baby	6
54	HMV RLS 599	GLENN MILLER LIMITED EDITION (5-LP, presentation set, 'snakeskin' cover)	20
56	HMV CLPC 6-10/RLS 598	GLENN MILLER LIMITED EDITION VOL. 2 (5-LP, in presentation album)	20
56	HMV RLS 637	GLENN MILLER & THE ARMY AIRFORCE BAND (5-LP, presentation box, [CLP 1077-CLP 1081])	20

JACOB MILLER

75	Sound Tracs SK5	Dock Of The Bay/Version	8
76	Neville King NK 02	Tired Fe Lick Weed In A Bush/Chillum In A Gully	12
78	Hawkeye HD 009	Each One Teach One/Matthews Lane Dub/ TETRACK: Let's Get It Together/Black ArtsDub (12")	40

JAMES MILLER

| 70 | Trojan TR 7804 | You Got To Me/2001 | 12 |

JIMMY MILLER & (NEW) BARBECUES

57	Columbia DB 4006	Sizzlin' Hot/Free Wheelin' Baby (as Jimmy Miller & Barbecues)	80
57	Columbia DB 4006	Sizzlin' Hot/Free Wheelin' Baby (as Jimmy Miller & Barbecues) (78)	15
58	Columbia DB 4081	Jelly Baby/Cry, Baby, Cry (as Jimmy Miller & New Barbecues)	70
58	Columbia DB 4081	Jelly Baby/Cry, Baby, Cry (as Jimmy Miller & New Barbecues) (78)	30

(see also Station Skiffle Group)

JODY MILLER

64	Capitol CL 15335	He Walks Like A Man/Looking At The World Through A Tear	5
64	Capitol CL 15356	The Fever/In My Room	5
65	Capitol CL 15393	Queen Of The House/The Greatest Actor	15
65	Capitol CL 15404	Silver Threads And Golden Needles/Melody For Robin	6
65	Capitol CL 15415	Home Of The Brave/This Is The Life	15
66	Capitol CL 15482	If You Were A Carpenter/Let Me Walk With You	5
65	Capitol T 2416	HOME OF THE BRAVE (LP, mono)	20
65	Capitol (S) T 2416	HOME OF THE BRAVE (LP, stereo)	25
66	Capitol T 2446	JODY MILLER SINGS THE GREAT HITS OF BUCK OWENS (LP, mono)	20
66	Capitol (S) T 2446	JODY MILLER SINGS THE GREAT HITS OF BUCK OWENS (LP, stereo)	25

KENNY MILLER

| 65 | Stateside SS 405 | Restless/Take My Tip | 150 |

MITCH MILLER

60	Philips PB 1146	The Guns Of Navarone/Alouette March	6
62	CBS AAG 118	The Longest Day (Vocal Version)/The Longest Day (Instrumental Version)	6
63	CBS AAG 158	The Great Escape March/It's A Darn Good Thing	7

MRS MILLER

66	Capitol CL 15444	Downtown/A Lover's Concerto	10
66	Capitol T 2494	MRS. MILLER'S GREATEST HITS (LP)	25
66	Capitol T 2579	WILL SUCCESS SPOIL MRS. MILLER (LP)	25

MRS MILLER

| 69 | Jackpot JP 707 | Feel It/LYN BECKFORD: Kiss Me Quick (actually by Keeling Beckford) | 7 |

(see also Lloyd Terrell)

NED MILLER

63	Capitol CL 15301	Go On Back You Fool/Dark Moon	6
63	London HL 9658	From A Jack To A King/Parade Of Broken Hearts	5
63	London HL 9728	Just Before Dawn/Mona Lisa	5
63	London HL 9766	Another Fool Like Me/Magic Moon	5
64	London HL 9838	Sunday Morning Tears/Big Love	6
64	London HL 9873	Invisible Tears/Old Restless Ocean	6
64	London HL 9937	Do What You Do Do Well/Dusty Guitar	5
63	Capitol EAP1 20492	NED MILLER (EP)	15
63	London RE 1382	NED MILLER (EP)	15
63	London HA 8072	FROM A JACK TO A KING (LP)	20
66	Capitol T 2414	THE BEST OF NED MILLER (LP)	20
69	Capitol ST 2914	IN THE NAME OF LOVE (LP)	15

PAULETTE MILLER

| 79 | Rocerks PR 157 | Woman In Love/In Love Dub (12") | 20 |

PETE MILLER

| 97 | Tenth Planet TP 030 | SUMMERLAND (LP, numbered, 1000 only) | 15 |

(see also Miller, Big Boy Pete)

ROGER MILLER

64	Philips BF 1354	Dang Me/Got 2 Again	6
65	Philips BF 1390	Do-Wacka-Do/Love Is Not For Me	7
64	Philips BF 1365	Chug-A-Lug/Reincarnation	7
65	Stateside SS 445	Can't Stop Loving You/You're Forgetting Me	5

RUSS MILLER

| 57 | HMV POP 391 | I Sit In My Window/Wait For Me, My Love | 50 |
| 57 | HMV POP 391 | I Sit In My Window/Wait For Me, My Love (78) | 15 |

STEPHEN MILLER & LOL COXHILL

| 73 | Caroline C 1503 | COXHILL MILLER (LP, black/white/red 'Twin' label) | 25 |
| 74 | Caroline C 1507 | THE STORY SO FAR ... OH REALLY? (LP) | 30 |

(see also Lol Coxhill)

STEVE MILLER BAND

68	Capitol CL 15539	Sittin' In Circles/Roll With It	15
68	Capitol CL 15564	Living In The U.S.A./Quicksilver Girl	15
69	Capitol CL 15604	My Dark Hour/Song For Our Ancestors	15
69	Capitol CL 15618	Little Girl/Don't Let Nobody Turn You Around	6
70	Capitol CL 15656	Going To The Country/Never Kill Another Man	6
72	Capitol CL 15712	My Dark Hour/The Gangster Is Back/Song For Our Ancestors (33rpm)	5
73	Capitol CL 15765	The Joker/Something To Believe In	5

MINT VALUE £

74	Capitol CL 15786	Living In The U.S.A./Kow Kow Calqulator	5
68	Capitol (S)T 2920	CHILDREN OF THE FUTURE (LP, 'rainbow rim' label)	35
69	Capitol (S)T 2984	SAILOR (LP, 'rainbow rim' label)	20
70	Capitol E-(S)T 184	BRAVE NEW WORLD (LP)	18
70	Capitol E-ST 331	YOUR SAVING GRACE (LP)	12

(see also Boz Scaggs)

SUZI MILLER

54	Decca F 10389	Happy Days And Lonely Nights/Tell Me, Tell Me (with Johnston Brothers)	20
54	Decca F 10423	Two Step, Side Step (with Johnston Brothers)/ Hang My Heart On A Christmas Tree (with Keynotes)	10
55	Decca F 10475	Tweedlee-Dee (with Johnston Brothers)/That's All I Want From You	15
55	Decca F 10512	Dance With Me Henry (Wallflower) (with Johnston Brothers)/ Butterfingers (with Marilyn Sisters)	15
55	Decca F 10593	The Banjo's Back In Town/Go On By	10
56	Decca F 10677	Ay-Ay-Senores/Reckless	10
56	Decca F 10722	Get Up! Get Up! (You Sleepy Head)/The Key To My Heart	7
57	Decca F 10848	I Love My Baby/The Money Tree	5

(see also Johnston Brothers)

MILLER'S THUMB

| 76 | Tradition TSC 3 | SITTING ON THE RIGHT SIDE (LP, 100 copies only) | 20 |

MILLIE (SMALL)

63	Fontana TF 425	Don't You Know/Until You're Mine	10
64	Fontana TF 449	My Boy Lollipop/Something's Gotta Be Done	6
64	Fontana TF 479	Sweet William/Oh Henry	7
64	Fontana TF 502	I Love The Way You Love/Bring It On Home To Me	8
64	Cadbury's BNVT 01F	The Bournvita Song/Three Nights A Week (p/s)	25
65	Fontana TF 515	I've Fallen In Love With A Snowman/What Am I Living For	10
65	Fontana TF 529	See You Later Alligator/Chilly Kisses	12
65	Fontana TF 591	My Street/It's Too Late	10
65	Fontana TF 617	Bloodshot Eyes/Tongue Tied	18
65	Brit WI 1002	My Street/A Mixed Up, Fickle, Moody, Self-Centred, Spoiled Kind Of Boy	15
66	Fontana TF 740	Killer Joe/Carry Go Bring Come (as Millie Small)	8
67	Fontana TF 796	Chicken Feed/Wings Of A Dove (as Millie Small)	8
67	Island WIP 6021	You Better Forget/I Am In Love	10
68	Fontana TF 948	When I Dance With You/Hey Mr. Love	10
69	Decca F 12948	Readin' Writin' Arithmetic/I Want You Never To Stop	12
70	Pyramid PYR 6080	My Love And I/Tell Me About Yourself	10
70	Trojan TR 7744	Enoch Power/Mayfair	15
70	President PT 306	We're All In A Zoo/Piccaninny Man	10
70	Trojan TR 7801	Honey Hush/Sunday Morning	10
61	Blue Beat BBEP 302	MILLIE (EP, with Little Roy & Owen Gray; with sleeve)	140
61	Blue Beat BBEP 302	MILLIE (EP, with Little Roy & Owen Gray; without sleeve)	20
64	Fontana TE 17425	MY BOY LOLLIPOP (EP)	50
66	Island IEP 705	MILLIE AND HER BOYFRIENDS (EP)	40
64	Fontana TL 5220	MORE MILLIE (LP, mono)	40
64	Fontana (S)TL 5220	MORE MILLIE (LP, stereo)	50
65	Fontana TL 5276	MILLIE SINGS FATS DOMINO (LP)	60
67	Island ILP 953	THE BEST OF MILLIE SMALL (LP)	50
69	Trojan TTL 17	MILLIE AND HER BOYFRIENDS (LP)	15
69	Trojan TTL 49	THE BEST OF MILLIE SMALL (LP, reissue)	15
70	Trojan TBL 108	TIME WILL TELL (LP)	15

(see also Jackie & Millie, Roy & Millie, Owen & Millie)

SPIKE MILLIGAN

58	Parlophone R 4406	Wish I Knew/Will I Find My Love Today?	15
61	Parlophone R 4839	I'm Walking Out With A Mountain/The Sewers Of The Strand	15
62	Parlophone R 4891	Wormwood Scrubs Tango/Postman's Knock	15
64	Pye 7N 15720	The Olympic Team/Epilogue (with John Bluthal)	8
66	Parlophone R 5513	Purple Aeroplane/Nothing At All	10
66	Parlophone R 5543	Tower Bridge/Silent Night	10
69	Parlophone R 5771	The Q.5 Piano Tune/Ning, Nang, Nong	10
61	Parlophone PMC 1148	MILLIGAN PRESERVED (LP, mono)	15
61	Parlophone PCS 18	MILLIGAN PRESERVED (LP, stereo)	20
65	Decca LK 4701	MUSES WITH MILLIGAN (LP)	15
68	Pye NPL 18271	THE WORLD OF THE BEACHCOMBER (LP)	12

(see also Goons, Famous Eccles, Peter Sellers)

MARY MILLINGTON

| 99 | Trunk/Bonk B 01 | COME PLAY ME (EP) | 60 |

SIR EUGENE MILLINGTON-DRAKE

| 65 | Decca LK 4659 | MIXED GRILL (LP) | 60 |

JEB MILLION

| 86 | WEA YZ 82 | Speed Up My Heartbeat/Who Sent You (p/s) | 6 |
| 86 | WEA YZ 82T | Speed Up My Heartbeat (Extended Mix)/Speed Up My Heartbeat/ Who Sent You (12", p/s) | 12 |

MILLIONAIRES (IRELAND)

| 66 | Decca F 12468 | Wishing Well/Chatterbox | 100 |

MILLIONAIRES (U.S.)

| 67 | Mercury 6052301 | Never For Me/If I Had You Babe (paper labels) | 35 |
| 67 | Mercury 6052301 | Never For Me/If I Had You Babe (plastic labels) | 15 |

MILLIONS

| 73 | Duke DU 154 | Murmuring/TOMMY McCOOK & BOBBY ELLIS: Murmuring - Version | 6 |
| 73 | Downtown DT 516 | Love Of Jah Jah Children/Jah Jah Version | 7 |

BARBARA MILLS

65	Hickory 45-1323	Queen Of Fools/Make It Last, Take Your Time	400
65	Hickory 45-1323	Queen Of Fools/Make It Last, Take Your Time (DJ copy)	500
65	Hickory 45-1392	Try/Let's Make A Memory	15

75	London HLE 10491	Queen Of Fools/Make It Last, Take Your Time (reissue)	10

BETTY LOU MILLS
60s	Shal SHAL 1	Where Is My Star/Rock Him	30
60	Pilgrim JLPS 101	EVERYWHERE I LOOK (LP)	25

FREDDIE MILLS
57	Parlophone R 4374	One For The Road/One For The Band	7

GARRY MILLS
59	Top Rank JAR 119	Hey Baby (You're Pretty)/You Alone	25
59	Top Rank JAR 119	Hey Baby (You're Pretty)/You Alone (78)	10
59	Top Rank JAR 219	Seven Little Girls Sitting In The Back Seat/The Night You Became 17	10
59	Oriole CB 1529	Living Lord/Big Story Breaking	10
59	Oriole CB 1530	I Am The Great I Am/Rhythm In Religion	10
60	Top Rank JAR 301	Running Bear/Teen Angel	7
60	Top Rank JAR 336	Look For A Star/Footsteps	7
60	Top Rank JAR 393	Comin' Down With Love/I'm Gonna Find Out	10
60	Top Rank JAR 500	Top Teen Baby/Don't Cheat Me Again (in p/s)	10
60	Top Rank JAR 500	Top Teen Baby/Don't Cheat Me Again	8
61	Top Rank JAR 542	Who's Gonna Take You Home Tonight?/Christina	10
61	Decca F 11358	I'll Step Down/Your Way Is My Way	10
61	Decca F 11383	Bless You/Footprints In The Sand	10
61	Decca F 11415	Treasure Island/Sad Little Girl	10
62	Decca F 11471	Never Believed In Love/Save A Dream For Me	10
61	Top Rank JKP 3001	LOOK FOR A STAR (EP)	35

(see also Gary & Ariels)

HAYLEY MILLS
61	Decca F 21396	Let's Get Together/Cobbler Cobbler	6
62	Decca F 21442	Jeepers Creepers/Johnny Jingo	5
62	Decca LK 4426	LET'S GET TOGETHER (LP)	15

HAYLEY MILLS & EDDIE HODGES
63	HMV POP 1179	Flitterin'/Beautiful Beulah	7

(see also Eddie Hodges)

JEFF MILLS
61	Ember EMB S 133	Daddy's Home/TIMMY REYNOLDS: Lullaby Of Love	70

MAUDE MILLS
60s	Vintage Jazz VEP 34	MAUDE MILLS (EP)	8

RUDY MILLS
67	Island WI 3092	A Long Story/BOBBY ELLIS: Now We Know (actually. with Desmond Miles Seven)	40
68	Island WI 3136	I'm Trapped/BOBBY ELLIS & CRYSTALLITES: Dollar A Head	22
69	Big Shot BI 509	John Jones/A Place Called Happiness	45
69	Explosion EX 2007	Lemi Li/Goody Goody	10
69	Crab CRAB 20	Tears On My Pillow/I'm Trapped	10
69	Crab CRAB 24	A Heavy Load/Wholesale Love	12
69	Pama SECO 12	REGGAE HITS (LP)	100

STEPHANIE MILLS
74	Paramount PARA 3050	I Knew It Was Love/The Passion And The Pain	6
76	Tamla Motown TMG 1020	This Empty Place/I See You For The First Time (unissued)	70
76	Tamla Motown STML 12017	FOR THE FIRST TIME (LP)	20

MILLS BROTHERS
54	Brunswick 05325	How Blue?/Why Do I Keep Lovin' You?	7
55	Brunswick 05439	Smack Dab In The Middle/Opus One	7
55	Brunswick 05488	That's All I Ask Of You/Suddenly There's A Valley	7
55	Brunswick 05487	Mi Muchacha (Little Girl)/Gum Drop	10
56	Brunswick 05606	That's Right/Don't Get Caught	8
58	London HLD 8553	Get A Job/I Found A Million Dollar Baby	15
60	London HLD 9169	I Got You/Highways Are Happy Ways	8

(see also Louis Armstrong)

MILLWALL F.C.
72	Decca F1 3350	Millwall/The Ballad Of Harry Cripps	8

RONNIE MILSAP
66	Pye International 7N 25392	Ain't No Soul (Left In These Old Shoes)/ Another Branch From The Same Old Tree	60
66	Pye International 7N 25392	Ain't No Soul (Left In These Old Shoes)/ Another Branch From The Same Old Tree (DJ copy)	100
69	Pye International 7N 25490	Denver/Nothing Is As Good As It Used To Be	6
72	Wand WN 26	Ain't No Soul (Left In These Old Shoes)/ Another Branch From The Same Old Tree (reissue)	10

RONNIE MILSAP/ROSCOE ROBINSON
66	Pye Intl. NEP 44078	SOUL SENSATIONS (EP)	50

JOHNNY MILTON & CONDORS
61	Oriole CB 1588	Charleston Cocktail (medley) (as Johnny Milton Band)	5
64	Decca F 11862	A Girl Named Sue/Somethin' Else (as Johnny Milton & Condors)	8
64	Fontana TF 488	Cry Baby/Hurt	6

(see also Symbols)

MILVA
63	Oriole CB 1899	I Can't Believe You're Leaving Me/Loneliness Of Autumn	8
64	Oriole CB 1952	I'll Set My Love To Music/Come Sempre	8
67	Major Minor MM 510	Love Is A Feeling/Seasons Of Love	6

MILWAUKEE COASTERS
68	Pama PM 733	Treat Me Nice/Sick And Tired (Oh Babe)	5
68	Pama PMLP 2	WEST COAST ROCK'N'ROLL 1968 (LP)	15
69	Pama PSP 10	BEST PARTY ALBUM (LP, reissue of PMLP 2)	12

ILHAN MIMAROGLU
69	Turnabout TV34177S	ELECTRONIC MUSIC III (LP)	20

MINT VALUE £

GARNET MIMMS (& ENCHANTERS)

63	United Artists UP 1033	Cry Baby/Don't Change Your Heart (with Enchanters)	25
63	United Artists UP 1038	Baby Don't You Weep/For Your Precious Love (with Enchanters)	20
64	United Artists UP 1048	Tell Me Baby/Anytime You Want Me (with Enchanters)	25
65	United Artists UP 1090	It Was Easier To Hurt Her/So Close	30
66	United Artists UP 1130	I'll Take Good Care Of You/Looking For You	100
66	United Artists UP 1130	I'll Take Good Care Of You/Looking For You (DJ copy)	200
66	United Artists UP 1147	It's Been Such A Long Way Home/Thinkin'	20
66	United Artists UP 1153	My Baby/It Won't Hurt Half As Much	25
66	United Artists UP 1172	All About Love/The Truth Hurts	20
67	United Artists UP 1181	Roll With The Punches/Only Your Love	25
67	United Artists UP 1186	As Long As I Have You/Yesterday	40
68	Verve VS 569	I Can Hear My Baby Crying/Stop And Think It Over	20
68	Verve VS 569	I Can Hear My Baby Crying/BILL MEDLEY: That Lucky Old Sun (mispress)	10
68	Verve VS 574	We Can Find That Love/Can You Top This	35
76	United Artists REM 403	REMEMBER GARNET MIMMS (EP)	10
63	United Artists ULP 1067	CRY BABY AND 11 OTHER HITS (LP, with Enchanters)	120
66	United Artists (S)ULP 1145	WARM AND SOULFUL (LP)	50
67	United Artists (S)ULP 1174	LIVE (LP, as Garnet Mimms & Senate)	50

MINA

78	EMI EMC 3243	MINA (LP)	12

MINDBENDERS

66	Fontana TF 644	A Groovy Kind Of Love/Love Is Good	5
66	Fontana TF 697	Can't Live With You, Can't Live Without You/One Fine Day	8
66	Fontana TF 731	Ashes To Ashes/You Don't Know About Love	7
66	Fontana TF 780	I Want Her, She Wants Me/The Morning After	18
67	Fontana TF 806	We'll Talk About It Tomorrow/Far Across Town	8
67	Fontana TF 869	The Letter/My New Day And Age	10
67	Fontana TF 877	Schoolgirl/Coming Back	40
68	Fontana TF 910	Blessed Are The Lonely/Yellow Brick Road	20
68	Fontana TF 961	Uncle Joe, The Ice Cream Man/The Man Who Loved Trees	15
69	Fontana H 1026	A Groovy Kind Of Love/Ashes To Ashes (p/s)	7
66	Fontana TL 5324	THE MINDBENDERS (LP, mono)	45
66	Fontana (S)TL 5324	THE MINDBENDERS (LP, stereo)	55
67	Fontana (S)TL 5403	WITH WOMAN IN MIND (LP)	60
68	Fontana SFL 13045	THE MINDBENDERS (LP, reissue)	12

(see also Wayne Fontana & Mindbenders, Hotlegs, Lulu)

SAL MINEO

57	Philips JK 1024	Start Movin' (In My Direction)/Love Affair (jukebox issue)	40
58	Fontana H 118	Little Pigeon/Cuttin' In	50
58	Fontana H 118	Little Pigeon/Cuttin' In (78)	10
58	Fontana H 135	Seven Steps To Love/A Couple Of Crazy Kids	30
58	Fontana TFL 5004	SAL (LP)	70

CORINA MINETTE

60	HMV POP 752	He'll Have To Stay/TOMMY THOMAS ORCHESTRA: Young At Cha Cha	5

SEXTON MING

88	Hangman HANG-1-UP	OLD HORSE OF THE NATION (LP)	18
90	Hangman HANG 36 UP	BIRDS WITH TEETH (LP)	15
98	Hangman's Daughter HANG 018UP	6 MORE MILES TO THE GRAVEYARD (LP)	15

(see also Billy Childish)

SEXTON MING (& HIS DIAMOND GUSSETS)

96	D. Goods DAMGOOD 71	I'm In Love With Danny Edwards/Break His Spirit/Son Of Tractor Nits (p/s)	6

CHARLES/CHARLIE MINGUS

63	Parlophone GEP 8786	SCENES IN THE CITY (EP)	10
65	Mercury 10021 MCE	JAZZ MAKERS (EP, as Charlie Mingus Orchestra)	8
56	Vogue LDE 178	CHARLIE MINGUS PRESENTS JAZZ WORKSHOP VOL. 2 (10" LP)	20
59	Parlophone PMC 1092	EAST COASTING (LP)	25
59	Philips BBL 7352	MINGUS AH HUM (LP)	30
60	London Jazz LTZ-K 15194	BLUES AND ROOTS (LP, also stereo SAH-K 6087)	25
62	Atlantic SD 8005	CHARLES MINGUS PRESENTS CHARLES MINGUS (LP, U.K. issue of U.S. LP)	20
62	United Artists ULP 1004	JAZZ PORTRAITS (LP)	15
62	London HA-K/SH-K 8007	OH YEAH (LP, by Charlie Mingus & Jazz Group)	30
63	RCA RD/SF 7514	TIJUANA MOODS (LP)	20
63	Vocalion LAE 543	CHAZZ (LP)	20
64	HMV CLP 1694	THE BLACK SAINT AND THE SINNER LADY (LP)	30
65	United Artists ULP 1068	TOWN HALL CONCERT (LP)	15
65	Vocalion LAEF/SEAF 591	CHARLIE MINGUS QUINTET WITH MAX ROACH (LP)	15
65	HMV CLP 1742	MINGUS, MINGUS, MINGUS (LP, also stereo CSD 1545)	15
65	HMV CLP 1796	MINGUS PLAYS PIANO (LP)	15
65	Atlantic ATL/SAL 5019	CHARLIE MINGUS (LP)	15
66	Realm RM 211	JAZZ COMPOSERS WORKSHOP (NO. 1) (LP)	15
66	CBS (S)BPG 62261	MINGUS DYNASTY (LP)	15
68	Atlantic 587131	PITHECANTTHROPUS ERECTUS (LP)	25

MINIM

67	Polydor 582 011	WRAPPED IN A UNION JACK (LP)	22

MINISTRY

92	Sire W 0096	Jesus Built My Hotrod/T.V. Song (p/s)	10

MINISTRY OF SOUND

66	Decca F 12449	White Collar Worker/Back Seat Driver	40

MINNY POPS

81	Factory FAC 31	MINNY POPS EP: Dolphin Spurt/Goddess	10
82	Factory FAC 57	Secret Story/Island	15

KYLIE MINOGUE

SINGLES

87	PWL PWLT 8R	I Should Be So Lucky (Bicentennial Mix)/(Instrumental) (12", stickered p/s) 10
88	PWL PWLT 12R	Got To Be Certain (Extra Beat Boys Mix)/Got To Be Certain (7" Mix)/ Got To Be Certain (Out For A Duck Bill Platter Plus Dub Mix) (12", stickered p/s)..................12
88	PWL PWCD 12	Got To Be Certain (Extended Mix)/Got To Be Certain (Instrumental)/ I Should Be So Lucky (Extended Mix 6.03) (CD)...30
88	PWL PWLT 14R	The Loco-Motion (Sankie Mix)/I'll Still Be Loving You (12", stickered p/s).............15
88	PWL PWLT 21R	Je Ne Sais Pas Pourquoi (Revolutionary Mix)/Made In Heaven (Maid In England Mix) (12", stickered p/s)...15
88	PWL PWCD 21	Je Ne Sais Pas Pourquoi (Moi Non Plus Mix)/Made In Heaven (Maid In England Mix)/The Loco-Motion (Sankie Mix) (CD) 15
88	PWL PWCD 24	Especially For You (7" Mix)/Especially For You (Extended)/ All I Wanna Do Is Make You Mine (Extended) (with Jason Donovan) (CD) 15
89	PWL PWLT 35R	Hand On Your Heart (Heartache Mix)/Hand On Your Heart (Dub mix) Just Wanna Love You (12", with stickered p/s)...35
89	PWL PWCD 35	Hand On Your Heart (Great Aorta Mix)/Just Wanna Love You It's No Secret (Extended Mix) (CD)...15
89	PWL PWLT 42R	Wouldn't Change A Thing (Espagna Mix)/Wouldn't Change A Thing (7" Mix)/It's No Secret (Extended) (12", stickered p/s)..20
89	PWL PWCD 42	Wouldn't Change A Thing (7" Mix)/Wouldn't Change A Thing (Your Thang Mix)/ Je Ne Sais Pas Pourquoi (Revolutionary Mix) (CD) 15
90	PWL PWCD 64	Step Back In Time (7" Mix)/Step Back In Time (Walkin' Rhythm Mix)/ Step Back In Time (Extended instrumental) (CD) 12
91	PWL PWLP 72	What Do I Have To Do (New Mix)/What Do I Have To Do (Instrumental) (stickered p/s, with postcards) 12
91	PWL PWLT 72R	What Do I Have To Do (Between The Sheets Mix) (12", withdrawn, no p/s)................100
91	PWL PWCD 72	What Do I Have To Do (New Mix)/What Do I Have To Do (Pumpin Polly Mix)/ What Do I Have To Do (Extended Instrumental) (CD) 15
91	PWL PWL P81	Shocked (DNA 7" Mix)/Shocked (Harding & Curnow 7" Mix) (picture disc) 15
91	PWL PWCD 81	Shocked (DNA 7" Mix)/Shocked (DNA Extended Mix)/Shocked (Harding & Curnow Extended Mix) (CD)..15
91	PWL PWLT204R	Word Is Out (Summer Breeze Remix) (1-sided 12" Limited Edition with etched Kylie autograph on other side, p/s)..20
91	PWL PWCD 204	Word Is Out (Extended Mix)/Word Is Out (Instrumental)/ Say The Word - I'll Be There (CD) 12
91	PWL PWL 207	Keep On Pumpin' It (Angelic Remix Edit)/(Astral Flight Mix Edit) (with Vision Masters) (p/s)..5
91	PWL PWLT 207	Keep On Pumpin' It (Angelic Remix)/(Astral Flight Mix) (with Vision Masters) (12", p/s)..10
91	PWL PWCD 207	Keep On Pumpin' It (Angelic Remix Edit)/(Angelic Remix)/ (Astral Flight Mix) (with Vision Masters) (CD) 20
94	Polygram PSPMC 344	Hand On Your Heart/Give Me Just A Little More Time (Woolworths giveaway cassette) 10
95	MUTE MUTE185	Where The Wild Roses Grow (with Nick Cave)/The Ballad of Robert Moore & Betty Coltrane (non-Kylie track) (limited 7", p/s) 12
97	DeCon. 7432 1517257	Some Kind Of Bliss/Love Takes Over Me (numbered limited edition 7", die-cut p/s)...........25
00	Parlophone 12R 6542 A/B	Spinning Around (Sharp Vocal Mix)/(Sharp Double Dub)/ (7th Spinnin' Dizzy Dub)/(7th District Club Mix) (12" double-pack) 12
03	Parlophone 12R6625	Slow (Extended Mix)/Slow (Radio Slave Remix)/Slow (Medicine 8 Remix) (12" picture disc, PVC title sleeve, sealed with sticker)..8
03	BMG BMGSM94	Breathe/Where Is The Feeling? (Little Chef 'Music Collection' giveaway 2-track CD, Includes enhanced CD-Rom section, unique Kylie card p/s)...........................12
01	Parlophone 12RDJZ6562	Can't Get You Out Of My Head (Extended)/(Extended Instrumental)..........................8
04	Parlophone 12R6633	Red Blooded Woman (Whitey Mix)/Slow (Chemical Brothers Remix)/Red Blooded Woman (Narcotic Thrust Mix)..8
04	Parlophone 12R6639	Chocolate (Tom Middleton Cosmos Mix)/(Radio Edit)/(Emo Mix) (12" picture disc, PVC title sleeve, sealed with sticker) 8
04	Parlophone 12R6656	I Believe In You/(Mylo Dub)/(Skylark Dub) (12" picture disc, PVC title sleeve, sealed with sticker) 8
05	Parlophone 12R6661	Giving You Up (Riton Re-Rub Dub)/(Single Version)/(Alter Ego Remix) (12" picture disc, PVC title sleeve, sealed with sticker) 8

ALBUMS

88	PWL HFD 4	KYLIE (DAT) 150
90	PWL HF 18	RHYTHM OF LOVE (LP, with free poster) 12
90	PWL HFL 18	RHYTHM OF LOVE (LP, gold leaf sleeve, 100 only) 200
91	PWL HFCL 18	RHYTHM OF LOVE (cassette, with 3 bonus tracks, gold case) 8
91	PWL HFCDL 18	RHYTHM OF LOVE (CD, with 3 bonus tracks, gold case) 12
98	30DeCon. 74321 58715 1	MIXES (3xLP, inner sleeves, pink silhouette Kylie outer p/s)..25
98	20DeCon. 74321 58715 2	MIXES (2xCD, pink silhouette Kylie p/s)..15
07	Parlophone (Lc0299)	X (Very limited USB format in shape of Kylie robotic, house in a long pull-out box includes full album plus 'White Diamond' trailer and '2 Hearts' video etc)............30

PROMOS

88	PWL (no cat. no.)	Made In Heaven (3:26) PWL 1-track in-house promo cassette, custom PWL logo inlay typled/stickered, 1 only) 60
90	PWL PWLT 56R	Better The Devil You Know (KC Cohen 'US' Remix) (1-sided 12" promo, withdrawn, die-cut sleeve, 50 only)..100
91	PWL PWLT 72R	What Do I Have To Do (Between The Sheets Mix) (1-sided 12" promo, withdrawn die-cut sleeve) 50
91	PWL ZR-A1	Keep On Pumpin' It (12" white label issued under pseudonym of 'Angel K', includes Angelic Remix & 'Astral Flight Mix', handwritten/stamped labels, Some with 'I Guess I Like It' titles. Die-cut sleeve) 50
91	PWL (no cat. no.)	I Guess I Like It Like That (12" 1-sided white label issued under pseudonym of 'Angel K', includes 'Extended/Album Version', 200 only) 40
91	PWL ANGEL-2	Do You Dare (12" white label issued under pseudonym of 'Angel K', includes NRG Mix' & 'New Rave Mix', handwritten labels, die-cut sleeve, 100 only) 40
92	PWL PWLT 227	Finer Feelings (Brothers In Rhythm 12" Mix)/Closer (Pleasure Mix) ('Black Diamond' limited promo 12", black diamond label, die cut sleeve) 10
92	PWL PWLT 257	Celebration (Have A Party Mix)/Let's Get To It (Album Version) ('Black Diamond' limited promo 12", Christmas "leaving PWL" promo p/s, black diamond label).................25
94	DeCon. 21 227477 JB	Confide In Me (Radio Mix)/(Truth Mix) (7" jukebox issue, no p/s)..............................10
94	DeCon. 21 246577 JB	Put Yourself In My Place (Radio Mix)/(All Star Mix) (7" jukebox issue, no p/s).............15
94	DeCon. 21 293617 JB	Where Is The Feeling? (BIR Bish Bosh Mix Edit)/(BIR Dolphin Mix) (7" jukebox issue, no p/s) 10
95	DeConstruction FEEL2	Where Is The Feeling? (BIR Dolphin Mix)/(Morales Club Mix) (12", die-cut sleeve, limited quantities) 30
95	DeConstruction FEEL3	Where Is The Feeling? (Da Klubb Feelin' Mix)/(Aphroheadz Powerlite Mix)/(Three Rad Vid Clash Mix) (12", promo, no p/s, 200 only) 50
95	DeConstruction FEELING1	Where Is The Feeling? (UK 7" Edit) (UK export to Japan promo 1-track CD, unique Custom p/s) 50

MINT VALUE £

95	Deconstruction TIME1	Time Will Pass You By (Paul Masterson's 'Wand Silver Screen Remix') (1-sided 12" White Label, handwritten labels, unreleased mix, withdrawn, 20 only)	80
97	DeConstruction DID2	Did It Again (Trouser Enthusiasts' Goddess of Contortion Mix)/(Razor N Go Mix) (12" promo, custom Deconstruction die-cut sleeve, limited to 500 only)	35
97	DeCon. 21 535707 JB	Did It Again (Radio Edit)/Tears (7" jukebox issue, no p/s)	20
98	DeCon. 21 570137 JB	Breathe (Radio Edit)/(Tee's Radio Edit) (7" jukebox issue, no p/s)	20
98	DeConstruction BREATHE02	Breathe (3-track 'edits' promo CD, custom Deconstruction sleeve)	12
98	DeConstruction TOOFAR 1	Too Far (Brothers In Rhythm Mix)/(Junior Vasquez Remix) (12", promo, no p/s)	25
98	Arthrob ART021TJ	GBI (Sharp Boys Deee-Liteful Dub)/(Album Version)/(Kylie-Pella) (with Towa Tei) (UK promo 12" part 1, custom Arthrob sleeve)	15
98	Arthrob ART021TJX	GBI (Rekut/DJ Krust Mix)/(Ebony Boogie Down Mix)/Bold Line (not Kylie) (with Towa Tei) (UK promo 12" part 2, custom Arthrob sleeve)	15
98	Arthrob ART021CDJ	GBI (Radio Edit)/(Album Mix)/(Sharp Boys Deee-Liteful Dub) (with Towa Tei) (UK promo CD, custom Arthrob card slip case)	15
00	Parlophone BUTTERFLO1A	Butterfly (Sandstorm Dub) (12" 1-sided DJ white label, butterfly logo stamped die cut paper sleeve)	60
00	Parlophone 12MIND 1	Spinning Around (Messy Boyz Remix) (12" 1-sided promo featuring unreleased mix, die cut sleeve, Handwritten label, withdrawn, 10 only)	125
00	Parlophone SHARP DJ 1	Spinning Around (Sharp Vocal Mix)/Spinning Around (Sharp Double Dub) (12" Pink Promo DJ Vinyl, die-cut sleeve, 100 only)	60
00	Parlophone 12MIND JY 001	Spinning Around (7th District Dub Like This Mix)/Spinning Around (7th District Club-Mental Mix) (12" promo, p/s)	15
00	Parlophone 12MIND JX 001	Spinning Around (Sharp Vocal Mix)/Spinning Around (Sharp Double Dub Mix) (12" promo, p/s)	15
00	Parlophone CDMIND J 001	Spinning Around (CD promo, card insert)	15
00	Parlophone RLH6542	Spinning Around/Paper Dolls (7" jukebox issue, no p/s)	5
00	Parlophone RLH6546	On A Night Like This/Ocean Blue (7" jukebox issue, no p/s)	8
00	Parlophone 12MINDJ 002	On A Night Like This (Motiv8 Nocturnal Vocal Mix)/On A Night Like This (Bini & Martini Vocal Mix)/On A Night Like This (Rob Searle Mix)/Ypur Disco Needs You (Almighty Mix) (12" promo doublepack p/s)	18
00	Chrysalis CHSLH5119	Kids (with Robbie Williams)/United (not including Kylie) (7" jukebox issue, no p/s)	5
00	Parlophone RLH6551	Please Stay/Santa Baby (7" jukebox issue, no p/s)	5
00	Parlophone 12RDJ 6551	Please Stay (Metro Mix)/Please Stay (7th District Club Flava Mix)/ Please Stay (7th District Club Dub) (12" promo, p/s, with inner sleeve)	20
00	Parlophone 12MINWL 004	Please Stay (7th District Club Dub)/Please Stay (Hatiras Dreamy Dub)/ Please Stay (7th District Club Flava Mix) (12" promo, title-stickered sleeve)	15
00	Parlophone 12MINWL005	Please Stay (Hatiras Dreamy Dub Mix) (1-sided 12" promo, die-cut sleeve)	20
00	Parlophone CDRDJX6551	Santa Baby/Please Stay (Christmas 2000 promo CD, custom violet metallic slip case With large pink Kylie logo)	20
01	Parlophone RLH6562	Can't Get You Out Of My Head/Boy (7" jukebox issue, no p/s) NOTE: Clear 7" jukebox pressings carrying this 'RLH6562' catalogue number with 'Can't Get Blue Monday out Of my Head' as the B-side are unofficial bootlegs)	20
01	Parlophone 12RDJ 6562	Can't Get Into My Head (Plastika Mix)/Can't Get Into My Head (Tim Deluxe Inst.)/Can't Get Into My Head (Time Deluxe Dub) (12" promo, no p/s)	20
01	Parlophone 12RDJY 6562	Can't Get Out Of My Head (Superchumbo Todo Mamado Mix)/ Can't Get Out Of My Head (Superchumbo Leadhead Dub)/(Superchumbo Voltapella Mix) (12" promo issued under the pseudonym of 'Special K', die-cut sleeve)	20
01	Parlophone 12RDJX 6562	Can't Get You Out Of My Head (K&M Mindprint Mix)/Can't Get You Out Of My Head (Nick Faber Mix) (12" promo, p/s, frosted PVC outer title sleeve)	20
01	Parlophone 12RDJ6562	"Get Into My Head" - Can't Get You Out Of My Head (Plastika Mix)/(Deluxe's Dirty Dub Instrumental)/(Deluxe's Dirty Dub) (12" promo issued under pseudonym of 'Special K', Die-cut sleeve)	8
01	Parlophone 12RDJ6562	"Get Into My Head" - Can't Get You Out Of My Head (Plastika Mix)/(Deluxe's Dirty Dub Instrumental)/(Deluxe's Dirty Dub) (12" Limited Tastemaker white label issued under pseudonym of 'Special K', limited to 100 copies, die-cut sleeve)	20
01	Parlophone 12RDJY6562	"Get Out Of My Head" - Can't Get You Out Of My Head (Superchumbo Todo Mamado Mix)/(Superchumbo Leadhead Dub)/(Superchumbo Voltapella Mix) (12" promo issued under pseudonym of 'Special K', die-cut sleeve)	8
01	Parlophone KYLIE-6TRACKS	Can't Get You Out Of My Head 'Remixes' (UK export 6-track remix promo CD housed In custom card p/s)	20
01	Parlophone KBLUE1	Can't Get Blue Monday Out Of My Head (1-sided 12" promo, pink die-cut sleeve)	10
02	Parlophone 12RDJ 6569	In Your Eyes (Powder's Spaced Dub)/In Your Eyes (Powder's 12" Dub)/ In Your Eyes (Saeed & Palash Mix)/In Your Eyes (Saeed & Palash Nightmare Dub) (12" test pressing, white label, titled-stickered sleeve)	12
02	Parlophone 12RDJX 6569	In Your Eyes (The S Man's Release Mix)/In Your Eyes (Roger Sanchez Release The Dub Mix)/In Your Eyes (Jean Jacques Smoothie Dub) (12" promo, white sleeve, with title sticker)	8
02	Tripoli Trax 12RDJY 6569	In Your Eyes (Knuckleheadz Mix)/In Your Eyes (Mr. Bishi Mix) (12" promo, stickered title sleeve)	10
02	Parlophone RLH6569	In Your Eyes/Tightrope (7" jukebox issue, no p/s)	10
02	Parlophone RLH6577	Love At First Sight/Can't Get Blue Monday Out Of My Head (7" jukebox issue, No p/s)	6
02	Parlophone 12RDJX 6577	Love At First Sight (Twin Master Plan Mix)/(Ruff & Jam Vocal 7")/(Ruff & Jam Club Mix) (12" promo, p/s)	8
02	Parlophone 12RDJY 6577	Love At First Sight (Kid Crème Vocal Dub)/(Kid Crème Vocal-less Dub) (promo 12", custom label, die-cut sleeve, limited to 300 copies only)	8
02	Parlophone 12RDJY 6577	Love At First Sight (Kid Crème Vocal Dub)/(Kid Crème Vocal-less Dub) (promo white label 12", stamped label, die-cut sleeve, 50 only)	30
02	Parlophone RLH6590	Come Into My World (Single Version)/(Fischerspooner Mix) (7" jukebox issue, No p/s)	12
02	Parlophone RDJ 6590	Come Into My World (Fischerspooner Mix)/Come Into My World (Ashtrax Mix) (promo 7", die-cut title sleeve)	20
02	Parlophone 12RDJ 6590	Come Into My World (Robbie Rivera's Hard & Sexy Mix)/(Robbie Rivera's NYC Dub) (12" promo, title sleeve, 400 only)	10
03	Parlophone 12MINDJY 006	Slow (Chemical Brothers Remix) (1-sided 12", yellow vinyl promo, 200 only)	30
03	Parlophone (no cat. no.)	Slow (CD promo, in black card fold-out sleeve)	10
03	Parlophone RLH6625	Slow/Sweet Music (7" jukebox issue, no p/s)	10
04	Parlophone RLH6633	Red Blooded Woman/Almost A Lover) (7" jukebox issue, no p/s)	12
04	Parlophone RDJ6633	Red Blooded Woman (Promo 1-sided clear 7" vinyl featuring otherwise unreleased 'Play Paul Radio Edit', 50 only)	50
04	Parlophone 12RDJ6633	Red Blooded Woman (Narcotic Thrust Mix) (1-sided white label 12", stamped title, die cut sleeve)	10
04	Parlophone 12RDJZ6633	Red Blooded Woman (Whitey Mix) (1-sided white label 'DJ friendly' 180gm heavyweight black vinyl, stamped title)	12
04	Parlophone 12RDJY6633	Red Blooded Woman (Promo 1-sided 12" featuring otherwise unreleased 'Play Paul Extended Dub', die-cut sleeve, 50 only)	20
04	Parlophone 12RDJ6639	Chocolate (Tom Middleton Cosmos Mix)/(Emo Mix)/(Emo Dub) (white label 12" promo, stamped label, die-cut sleeve)	8
04	Parlophone (no cat. no)	Chocolate (Violanti's Remix) (1-sided 12" white label, unreleased remix, Withdrawn, hand-written label)	80
04	Parlophone 12RDJ6656	I Believe In You (Skylark Mix)/(Mylo Vocal)/(Mylo Dub) (12" promo pressed on 180gm heavy-weight vinyl, promo sleeve with stripes sticker in corner)	8
05	Parlophone 12RDJ6661	Giving You Up (Riton Re-Rub Vox)/(Riton Re-Rub Dub)/(Alter Ego Remix) (12" promo pressed on 180gm heavy-weight vinyl, promo sleeve with blue stripes in corner)	10

Year	Label / Cat. No.	Description	£
07	Parlophone (HEARTS002)	2 Hearts (Alan Braxe Remix)/(Studio Version)/(Mark Brown's Pacha Ibiza Upper Terrace Mix)/(Acapella) (Very limited heavyweight RED 12" promo, rubber-stamped)	12
94	Deconstruction KYLP1	KYLIE MINOGUE (10 track promo cassette, black p/s with titles)	12
94	DeConstruction KM 100	KYLIE MINOGUE (CD, promo, gatefold sl. in lilac slipcase with silver lettering)	70
97	DeConstruction KM001	KYLIE MINOGUE ('Impossible Princess' 6-track 'Interact' sampler cassette issued to People on the Kylie mailing list with a 'feedback' form to be completed. Snippets of 6 of the album tracks with a femail introducing each one, custom title inlay)	12
97	DeConstruction KYLIE 1	IMPOSSIBLE PRINCESS (CD, promo, with insert, withdrawn, some with Press Release from 'Hall Or Nothing' explaining about the withdrawal of the CD and title due to Princess Diana's death)	40
97	DeConstruction KM 002	AN INTERVIEW WITH KYLIE MINOGUE (Promo interview CD for 'Impossible Princess' album, unique p/s)	80
00	Parlophone LIGHT 001	LIGHT YEARS (CD promo, foldout 22" x 8" pack, does not include 'Kids')	30
00	Parlophone LIGHT 002 LIGHT YEARS (CD promo, foldout 22" x 8" pack, includes 'Kids')	LIGHT YEARS (CD promo, foldout 22" x 8" pack, includes 'Kids')	40
00	Parlophone LIGHTX 001	LIGHT YEARS (LP Promo, unique blue outer 'Kylie' logo sleeve, inner picture sleeve, does not include 'Kids' or 'Password', 100 only)	60
00	Parlophone LIGHTX 002	LIGHT YEARS (LP Promo, unique blue outer 'Kylie' logo sleeve, inner picture sleeve, includes 'Kids' but not 'Password', 100 only)	60
00	BMG HITS1	HITS+ (CD promo, original withdrawn artwork, card slip case, withdrawn at Kylie's request when she disliked the picture used, most copies incinerated, less than 5 copies exist)	150
01	Parlophone FEVER 01	FEVER (CD-Rom promo, DVD-style picture case)	30
01	Parlophone FEVER 02	FEVER (CD promo, card sleeve, frosted PVC outer title sleeve)	20
02	PWL9224680P	GREATEST HITS - THE REMIXES (12" Promo) Hand On Your Heart (WIP 2002 Mix)/ What Do I Have To Do? (Movers & Shakers 12" Mix)/Better The Devil You Know (Movers & Shakers Alternative 12" Mix)/'Greatest Hits 87-92 album, custom labels , die cut sleeve)	15
03	Parlophone BODYLANG01	BODY LANGUAGE (promo CD housed in picture card slip case with inner slip-case, Copy-control CD)	15
03	Parlophone MININT 02	BODY LANGUAGE INTERVIEW (CD interview promo)	20
04	Parlophone ULTIMATE01	ULTIMATE KYLIE (2xCD promo housed in glossy card slip case with 2 inner slip cases, copy-control CD)	20
04	Parlophone MININT003	ULTIMATE KYLIE - INTERVIEW DISC (promo 40-track interview CD with custom cover, Cues and questions, jewel case)	20
07	Parlophone (XINTER 001)	X 'The Interview' (promo 42-track interview CD with custom over etc)	20

MINORBOPS

| 58 | Vogue V 9110 | Need You Tonight/Want You For My Own | 800 |
| 58 | Vogue V 9110 | Need You Tonight/Want You For My Own (78) | 250 |

MINOR THREAT

| 85 | Discord DISCORD 15 | Salad Days/Stumped/Good Guys (p/s) | 15 |

MINSTRELS

| 67 | Studio One SO 2036 | People Get Ready/HAMLINS: Everyone's Got To Be There | 140 |
| 68 | Studio One SO 2050 | Miss Highty Tighty/WESTMORELITES: Let Me Be Yours Until Tomorrow | 70 |

MINT

| 69 | Tangerine 014 | Luv/Simone | 20 |
| 73 | Pye 7N.45299 | I'll Meet You Halfway/Three Score And Ten | 6 |

MINT JULEPS

| 87 | Stiff BUY DJ 264 | Docklands/Under Pressure (12" test pressing of last Stiff single for 20 years) | 30 |

DEREK MINTER

| 60 | Sound Stories EP 304 | STARS OF SPEED (EP) | 10 |

MINTS

| 57 | London HLP 8423 | Night Air/KEN COPELAND: Pledge Of Love | 150 |
| 57 | London HLP 8423 | Night Air/KEN COPELAND: Pledge Of Love (78) | 40 |

MINUCCI

| 56 | Vogue Coral LVA 9015 | GINA LOLLO BRIGIDA PRESENTS MUSIC OF GINO BY MINUCCI (LP, photo of Gina on cover) | 15 |

MINUTE MEN

| 61 | Capitol CL 15206 | Yankee Diddle/Blue Pearl | 6 |

MINUTEMEN

83	SST SST 002	PARANOID TIME (8-track EP)	18
84	SST SST 016	BUZZ OR HOWL UNDER THE INFLUENCE OF THE HEAT (12" EP)	20
85	Homestead REFLEX-L	TOUR SPIEL (EP, live 4-track)	10

MIRACLE MILE

| 86 | Miracle MIR 001 | Bless This Ship/Breaking Down The Barriers (p/s) | 35 |

(SMOKEY ROBINSON &) MIRACLES

61	London HL 9276	Shop Around/Who's Lovin' You	55
61	London HL 9366	Ain't It Baby/The Only One I Love	90
62	Fontana H 384	What's So Good About Goodbye/I've Been So Good To You	200
63	Oriole CBA 1795	You've Really Got A Hold On Me/Happy Landing	110
63	Oriole CBA 1863	Mickey's Monkey/Whatever Makes You Happy	80
64	Stateside SS 263	I Gotta Dance To Keep From Crying/Such Is Love, Such Is Life	55
64	Stateside SS 282	The Man In You/Heartbreak Road	40
64	Stateside SS 324	I Like It Like That/You're So Fine And Sweet	45
64	Stateside SS 353	That's What Love Is Made Of/Would I Love You	35
65	Stateside SS 377	Come On Do The Jerk/Baby Don't You Go	45

(Credited to The Miracles.)

65	Tamla Motown TMG 503	Ooo Baby Baby/All That's Good	40
65	Tamla Motown TMG 522	The Tracks Of My Tears/A Fork In The Road	45
65	Tamla Motown TMG 540	My Girl Has Gone/Since You Won My Heart	40
66	Tamla Motown TMG 547	Going To A Go-Go/Choosey Beggar	25
66	Tamla Motown TMG 569	Whole Lotta Shakin' In My Heart/Oh Be My Love	45
66	Tamla Motown TMG 584	(Come 'Round Here) I'm The One You Need/Save Me	25

(All of the singles listed above are credited to The Miracles.)

67	Tamla Motown TMG 598	The Love I Saw In You Was Just A Mirage/Swept For You Baby	25
67	Tamla Motown TMG 614	More Love/Swept For You Baby	25
67	Tamla Motown TMG 614	More Love/Come Spy With Me (withdrawn B-side)	80
67	Tamla Motown TMG 631	I Second That Emotion/You Must Be Love	12

68	Tamla Motown TMG 648	If You Can Want/When The Words From Your Heart Get Caught Up In Your Throat	15
68	Tamla Motown TMG 661	Yester-Love/Much Better Off	15
68	Tamla Motown TMG 673	Special Occasion/Give Her Up	15
69	Tamla Motown TMG 687	Baby, Baby Don't Cry/Your Mother's Only Daughter	15
69	Tamla Motown TMG 696	The Tracks Of My Tears/Come On Do The Jerk	7
70	Tamla Motown TMG 745	The Tears Of A Clown/You Must Be Love (with withdrawn B-side)	40
70	Tamla Motown TMG 745	The Tears Of A Clown/Who's Gonna Take The Blame	6
71	Tamla Motown TMG 761	(Come Round Here) I'm The One You Need/We Can Make It, We Can	6
71	Tamla Motown TMG 774	I Don't Blame You At All/That Girl	6
72	Tamla Motown TMG 811	My Girl Has Gone/Crazy 'Bout The La-La-La	6
73	Tamla Motown TMG 853	Going To A Go-Go/Whole Lotta Shakin' In My Heart/Yester-Love	6
76	Tamla Motown TMG 1023	Nightlife/The Miracle Workers: Overture (as The Miracles)	6
87	Motown ZB 41147 D	Just To See Her/Te Quiero Como Si No Hubiera Um Manana//Being With You/ What's In Your Life For Me? (solo, double pack)	6
61	London RE 1295	SHOP AROUND (EP, as The Miracles)	200
63	Oriole PS 40044	HI! WE'RE THE MIRACLES (LP)	250
64	Stateside SL 10099	THE FABULOUS MIRACLES (LP)	140
65	Tamla Motown TML 11003	I LIKE IT LIKE THAT (LP)	70
66	Tamla Motown TML 11024	GOIN' TO A GO-GO (LP, as Smokey Robinson & The Miracles, mono)	45
66	Tamla Motown TML 11024	GOIN' TO A GO-GO (LP, as Smokey Robinson & The Miracles, stereo)	55
66	Tamla Motown TML 11031	THE MIRACLES FROM THE BEGINNING (LP, mono)	50
66	Tamla Motown STML 11031	THE MIRACLES FROM THE BEGINNING (LP, stereo)	50
67	Tamla Motown TML 11044	AWAY WE A-GO-GO (LP, mono)	50
67	Tamla Motown STML 11044	AWAY WE A-GO-GO (LP, stereo)	65
68	Tamla Motown TML 11067	MAKE IT HAPPEN (LP, mono)	30
68	Tamla Motown STML 11067	MAKE IT HAPPEN (LP, stereo)	35
68	Tamla Motown (S)TML 11072	GREATEST HITS (LP, mono/stereo)	20
69	Tamla Motown (S)TML 11089	SPECIAL OCCASION (LP, mono/stereo)	25
69	Tamla Motown (S)TML 11107	SMOKEY ROBINSON & THE MIRACLES LIVE! (LP, mono/stereo)	25
70	Tamla Motown (S)TML 11129	TIME OUT FOR SMOKEY ROBINSON & THE MIRACLES (LP)	18
70	TamlaMotown STML 11151	FOUR IN BLUE (LP)	25
70	Tamla Motown STML 11163	WHAT LOVE HAS JOINED TOGETHER (LP, unissued)	0
71	Tamla Motown STML 11172	POCKETFUL OF MIRACLES (LP)	20
73	Tamla Motown STMA 8008	1957-1972 (LP, gatefold sleeve)	12
73	Motown STMA 8012	SMOKEY (LP, solo)	12

MIRAGE

65	CBS 201772	It's In Her Kiss/What Ye Gonna Do 'Bout It	20
65	CBS 202007	Go Away/Just A Face	20
66	Philips BF 1534	Tomorrow Never Knows/You Can't Be Serious	50
67	Philips BF 1554	Hold On/Can You Hear Me	50
67	Philips BF 1571	The Wedding Of Ramona Blair/Lazy Man	80
68	Page One POF 078	Mystery Lady/Chicago Cottage	12
68	Page One POF 111	Carolyn/World Goes On Around You	12

(see also Yellow Payges, Caleb, Jawbone, Spencer Davis Group, Portobello Explosion)

MIRETTES

68	Uni UN 501	In The Midnight Hour/To Love Somebody	5
68	Uni UN 505	The Real Thing/Take Me For A Little While	5
69	MCA Soul Bag BAG 8	Whirlpool/Ain't You Trying To Cross Over	8
72	Jay Boy BOY 65	Now That I've Found You Baby/He's Alright With Me	8
69	MCA MUP(S) 344	IN THE MIDNIGHT HOUR (LP)	20

(see also Ikettes)

MIRK

| 79 | Mother Earth MUM 1205 | MODDANS BOWER (LP) | 80 |
| 82 | Spring Thyme SPR 1009 | TAK A DRAM AFOR YE GO (LP) | 25 |

MIRKWOOD

| 71 | Flams Ltd PR 1067 | MIRKWOOD (LP) | 1000 |
| 93 | Tenth Planet TP 003 | MIRKWOOD (LP, reissue, numbered with insert, 500 only) | 30 |

STEVE MIRO & EYES

78	Object Music OM 03	Up And About/Smiling In Reverse (p/s)	6
79	Object Music OM 10	Dreams Of Desire/Queens Of The Sea (p/s)	5
80	Object Music OBF 008	RUDE INTRUSIONS (LP)	15
81	Object Music OBJ 015	SECOND SENTENCE (LP)	15

(see also Eyes, Noyes Bros)

MIRROR

| 68 | Philips BF 1666 | Gingerbread Man/Faster Than Light | 60 |

MIRRORS

| 78 | Lightning GIL 503 | Cure For Cancer/Nice Vice (p/s) | 15 |
| 79 | Lightning GIL 540 | Dark Glasses/999 (p/s) | 15 |

MISFITS (U.K.)

| 66 | A.S.C.C. PRI 101 | You Won't See Me/Hanging Around (Aberdeen Students Charities Campaign) | 10 |

(see also Complex)

MISFITS (U.S.)

| 81 | Plan 9/Cherry Red PLP 9 | BEWARE (12" EP) | 120 |

MISSING PRESUMED DEAD

79	Sequel PART 2	Say It With Flowers/Double Life/Driving Home/Family Tree (p/s)	5
80s	Sequel PART 4	MISSING PRESUMED DEAD (LP)	12
80s	Sequel PART 5	REVENGE (LP)	12

MISSING SCIENTISTS

| 80 | Rough Trade RT 057 | Big City, Bright Lights/Discotheque X (p/s) | 20 |

(see also Television Personalities, Slaughter)

MISSION

| 86 | Chapter 22 L12 CHAP 7 | Like A Hurricane/Garden Of Delight/Dancing Barefoot/The Crystal Ocean (12", autographed p/s) | 8 |
| 86 | Mercury MYSG 1 | Stay With Me/Blood Brother (autographed, gatefold p/s) | 5 |

87	Phonogram MYTHB 2	IV: Wasteland/Shelter From The Storm (Live)/Serpent's Kiss (Live)/1969 (Live) (doublepack, in box, with insert and photo's)	12
88	Mercury MYTHCD 6	Beyond The Pale/Tower Of Strength/Tadeusz (CD, card sleeve, numbered)	12
89	Mercury MYCDB 8	Butterfly On A Wheel (CD, in 12" x 12" collectors box)	10
80s	Mercury MYCDB 8	Butterfly On A Wheel (Complete 4 x CD set in box)	20
80s	Flexi FLEX 1	Crazy (1-track flexidisc)	12
90	Mercury MYTH 11	Hands Across The Ocean/Amelia/Love (p/s)	5
90	Phonogram MYTHB 912	Deliverance/(Sorceror's Mix)/METAL GURUS: Virginia Plain (12", in box with poster)	8
01	Playground PGND 001	Evangeline/Anyone But You//Melt/Swoon (Reprise) (doublepack, pink & blue vinyl, gatefold p/s)	8
02	Playground PGND003	Shine Like The Stars/Never Let Me Down/Spider And The Fly (In The Ointment)/ Never (2 x 7" on green and white vinyl, gatefold p/s)	8

(see also Sisters Of Mercy, Dead Or Alive, Pauline Murray, Artery, Red Lorry Yellow Lorry, Expelaires, Knopov's Political Package, TV Product)

MISSION BELLES
65	Decca F 12154	Sincerely/When A Girl Really Loves You	10

MISSISSIPPI
70	Fox FOX 1	Mr. Union Railway Man/Main Street	100

MISS JANE
68	Pama PM 704	Bad Mind People/My Heart Is Aching (B-side act. "Witch Doctor" by Coolers)	12

MISSPENT YOUTH
79	Big Bear BB20	Betcha Won't Dance/Birmingham Boys (p/s)	20

MISS X (JOYCE BLAIR)
63	Ember EMB S 175	Christine/S-E-X	10

MISTA CHARGE
76	Target TGT 112	Show Me What You're Made Of/Down On Arcturas	5

MISTAKEN IDENTITY
85	RAM 17CHP 7010	The Answer/The Answer (Club Version) (12")	25

MR. MOST
69	Downtown DT 408	Push Wood/Reggae Train	12

MISTER VERSATILE
69	Jackpot JP 701	Apple Blossom/LITTLE BOY BLUE: Dark End Of The Street (act. by Pat Kelly)	20
69	Jackpot JP 702	Devil's Disciples/ERROL DUNKLEY: Having A Party	8

(see also Lester Sterling)

MISTY
77	Cottage COT 511	MISTY (LP)	18

MISTY IN ROOTS
79	People Unite PU 001	See Them A Come/How Long Jah (12", p/s)	20
80	People Unite PU 002	Rich Man/Salvation (12", p/s)	10
81	People Unite PU 003	Peace And Love/BallOut (12")	15
83	People Unite PU 102	Follow Fashion/Earth/Own Them Control Them/New Day (12")	8
79	People Unite PU 003	LIVE AT THE COUNTER EUROVISION '79 (LP)	20
82	People Unite PU 101 ALB	WISE AND FOOLISH (LP)	20

MISTY MEADOWS
70	Rhone RH 002	Visions/We See The Sun	45

MISUNDERSTOOD
66	Fontana TF 777	I Can Take You To The Sun/Who Do You Love	55
69	Fontana TF 998	Children Of The Sun/I Unseen (small centre hole)	70
69	Fontana TF 998	Children Of The Sun/I Unseen (large centre hole)	50
69	Fontana TF 1028	You're Tuff Enough/Little Red Rooster (as Misunderstood featuring Glenn "Fernando" Campbell, in p/s)	60
69	Fontana TF 1028	You're Tuff Enough/Little Red Rooster (as Misunderstood featuring Glenn "Fernando" Campbell)	35
69	Fontana TF 1041	Never Had A Girl (Like You Before)/Golden Glass (as Misunderstood featuring Glenn "Fernando" Campbell)	45
81	Cherry Red CHERRY 22	Children Of The Sun/Who Do You Love/I'll Take You To The Sun (p/s)	7
82	Cherry Red B RED 32	BEFORE THE DREAM FADED (LP, with inner)	18

ADRIAN MITCHELL
68	Transatlantic TRA 171	POW! A LAUGH, A SONG AND A HAND GRENADE (LP, with Leon Rosselson)	15

BLUE MITCHELL
69	Blue Note BST 84300	COLLISION IN BLACK (LP)	15
73	Mainstream MSL 1002	BLUE'S BLUES (LP)	12

CHAD MITCHELL
62	London HLR 9509	Lizzie Borden/Super Skier	7

DENNY MITCHELL SOUNDSATIONS
64	Decca F 11848	I've Been Crying/For Your Love	25

(see also Preachers, Moon's Train)

GROVER MITCHELL
68	London HLU 10221	Turned On/Blue Over You	18
76	Vanguard VS 5003	What Hurts/Super Hero	40

GUY MITCHELL
SINGLES : SINGLES & EPS
53	Columbia SCM 5018	Feet Up (Pat Him On The Po-Po)/Jenny Kissed Me	20
53	Columbia SCM 5022	Cause I Love Ya, That's A-Why/Train Of Love (both with Mindy Carson)	20
53	Columbia SCM 5032	She Wears Red Feathers/Why Should I Go Home?	20
53	Columbia SCM 5037	Pretty Little Black-Eyed Susie/MITCH MILLER HORNS: Horn Belt Boogie	25
56	Philips JK 1001	Singing The Blues/Crazy With Love (jukebox issue)	15
57	Philips JK 1005	Knee Deep In The Blues/Take Me Back Baby (jukebox issue)	15
57	Philips JK 1015	Rock-A-Billy/Got A Feeling (jukebox issue)	15
57	Philips JK 1023	Sweet Stuff/In The Middle Of A Dark, Dark Night (jukebox issue)	15
57	Philips JK 1027	Call Rosie On The Phone/Cure For The Blues (jukebox issue)	15
58	Philips PB 766	C'mon Let's Go/The Unbeliever	8
58	Philips PB 798	Wond'rin' And Worryin'/If Ya Don't Like It, Don't Knock It	6

58	Philips PB 830	Hangin' Around/Honey Brown Eyes	10
58	Philips PB 858	Let It Shine, Let It Shine/Butterfly Doll	10
58	Philips PB 885	My Heart Cries For You (2nd Version)/Till We're Engaged	7
59	Philips PB 915	Alias Jesse James/Pride O' Dixie	7
59	Philips PB 964	Heartaches By The Number/Two (with triangular centre)	12
63	Pye International 7N 25179	Go, Tiger, Go/If You Ever Go Away (unreleased)	0
63	Pye International 7N 25185	Have I Told You Lately That I Love You/Blue Violet	5
66	CBS 202238	Singing The Blues/Rock-A-Billy	5
54	Columbia SEG 7513	PRETTY LITTLE BLACK EYED SUSIE (EP, plain sleeve)	15
55	Columbia SEG 7581	MY TRULY TRULY FAIR (plain sleeve)	10
55	Columbia SEG 7598	JENNY KISSED ME (plain sleeve)	15
55	Philips BBE 12008	GUY MITCHELL	10
56	Philips BBE 12093	GUY MITCHELL NO. 2	10
57	Philips BBE 12112	SINGING THE BLUES WITH GUY MITCHELL	10
58	Philips BBE 12215	GUY MITCHELL PHILIPS TV SERIES	10

JONI MITCHELL

68	Reprise RS 20694	Night In The City/I Had A King	15
69	Reprise RS 23402	Chelsea Morning/Both Sides Now	12
70	Reprise RS 20906	Big Yellow Taxi/Woodstock	5
72	Asylum AYM 511	You Turn Me On, I'm A Radio/Urge For Going	8
83	Geffen DA 3122	Chinese Cafe/Ladies Man (double pack, with bonus interview 7")	8
68	Reprise RSLP 6293	JONI MITCHELL (LP, gatefold sleeve, 'steamboat' label)	50
69	Reprise RSLP 6341	CLOUDS (LP, textured single sleeve, 'steamboat' label)	45
69	Reprise RSLP 6341	CLOUDS (LP, 2nd pressing, stickered U.S. gatefold sleeve, 'steamboat' label)	15
70	Reprise RSLP 6376	LADIES OF THE CANYON (LP, gatefold sleeve, 'steamboat' label)	30
71	Reprise K 44128	BLUE (LP, gatefold sleeve, with blue inner sleeve)	30
71	Reprise K 44128	BLUE (LP, gatefold sleeve)	15
73	Asylum SYLA 8753	FOR THE ROSES (LP, gatefold sleeve)	15
74	Asylum SYLA 8756	COURT AND SPARK (LP, gatefold sleeve)	20
75	Asylum SYLA 8763	THE HISSING OF SUMMER LAWNS (LP)	18
75	Asylum SYSP 902	MILES OF AISLES (2-LP, gatefold sleeve with inner flap)	20
79	Asylum K 53091	MINGUS (LP, gatefold sleeve)	12
70s	Asylum K 53053	HEJIRA (LP, gatefold sleeve)	15
82	Asylum/Nimbus K 53018	THE HISSING OF SUMMER LAWNS (LP, audiophile pressing, mail order issue)	60

MCKINLEY 'SOUL' MITCHELL

| 68 | President PT 125 | The Town I Live In/No Love Like Your Love | 10 |
| 68 | President PTL 1005 | McKINLEY 'SOUL' MITCHELL (LP) | 40 |

PHILIP MITCHELL

71	Jay Boy BOY 37	I'm Gonna Build California From All Over The World/ The World Needs More People Like You	30
71	Jay Boy BOY 37	I'm Gonna Build California From All Over The World/ The World Needs More People Like You (DJ copy)	50
72	Jay Boy BOY 57	Free For All/Flower Child	10
72	Jay Boy BOY 57	Free For All/Flower Child (DJ copy)	10
74	London HLU 10444	Ain't No Love In My Life/Turning Over The Ground	40

RED MITCHELL

| 62 | London LZ-N1 4017 | HAPPY MINORS (10" LP) | 15 |
| 63 | London SH-K 8027 | HEAR YE!! HEAR YE!! (LP) | 12 |

RONNIE MITCHELL

| 60 | London HLU 9220 | How Many Times/The Only Love | 8 |

SINX MITCHELL

| 64 | Hickory 45-1248 | This Weird Sensation/Love Is All I'm Asking For | 20 |

(see also Crickets, Earl Sinks)

VALERIE MITCHELL

65	Oak RGJ 160	There Goes My Heart Again/If I Didn't Love You (p/s)	60
65	HMV POP 1422	Bitter Tears/Forbidden	6
65	HMV POP 1462	There Goes My Heart Again/If I Didn't Love You	6
65	HMV POP 1490	Go My Way/Green Eyes	8
66	HMV POP 1509	Play With Me/Never Let It Be Said	10
66	HMV POP 1529	You Can Go/The Windmill Girls	8
67	Columbia DB 8186	Love Can Be The Sweetest Thing/I'm Sorry	6
67	Columbia DB 8265	Sunshine/You Belong To Me	6

WARREN MITCHELL

| 67 | CBS 2824 | The Writing On The Wall/Her Heart's In The Right Place (p/s) | 8 |
| 67 | CBS 2824 | The Writing On The Wall/Her Heart's In The Right Place (no p/s) | 6 |

WILLIE MITCHELL

64	London HLU 9926	20-75/Secret Home	20
64	London HLU 9926	20-75/Secret Home (DJ Copy)	40
65	London HLU 10004	Everything Is Gonna Be Alright/That Driving Beat (Boxed logo)	15
65	London HLU 10004	Everything Is Gonna Be Alright/That Driving Beat	20
65	London HLU 10004	Everything Is Gonna Be Alright/That Driving Beat (DJ copy)	50
66	London HLU 10039	Bad Eye/Sugar T.	10
66	London HLU 10085	Mercy/Sticks And Stones	10
68	London HLU 10186	Soul Serenade/Buster Browne	10
68	London HLU 10215	Prayer Meetin'/Rum Daddy	8
68	London HLU 10224	Up Hard/Beale Street Mood	10
70	London HLU 10313	Robbin's Nest/Six To Go	8
73	London HLU 10407	Last Tango In Paris/Six To Go	6
74	London HLU 10545	The Champion (2 parts) (DJ copy)	30
74	London HLU 10545	The Champion (2 parts)	5
67	London HA-U 8319	THE HIT SOUND OF WILLIE MITCHELL (LP)	30
68	London HA-U/SH-U 8365	SOUL SERENADE (LP)	20
68	London HA-U/SH-U 8368	LIVE (LP)	20
69	London HA-U/SH-U 8372	SOLID SOUL (LP)	20
70	London HA-U/SH-U 8388	ON TOP (LP)	20
70	London HA-U/SH-U 8408	SOUL BAG (LP)	20

MITCHELL/COE MYSTERIES
80	RCA PL 25297	EXILED (LP, with inner sleeve, with gatefold sleeve)	15
80	RCA PL 25297	EXILED (LP, with inner sleeve)	12

(see also Colin Blunstone, Lesley Duncan, Dan McCafferty, Francis Rossi & Berni Frost, Ray Russell, Joe Jammer, Complex, Monsoon)

ROBERT MITCHUM
57	Capitol CL 14701	What Is This Generation Coming To?/Mama Looka Boo Boo	5
62	Capitol CL 15251	The Ballad Of Thunder Road/My Honey's Lovin' Arms	5
67	Monument MON 1007	Little Ole Wine Drinker Me/Walker's Woods	5
55	Brunswick OE 9197	RACHEL AND THE STRANGER (EP)	10

MITHRANDIR
82	New Leaf SVC 570	Dreamers Of Fortune/After Tomorrow (p/s)	50
82	New Leaf SVC 01	MAGICK EP (p/s)	75

JACKIE MITTOO
66	Island WI 293	Killer Diller (as Jackie Mitto & Soul Brothers)/PATRICK HYTTON: Oh Lady	100
67	Rio R 114	Home Made/ETHIOPIANS: I'm Gonna Take Over Now	35
67	Rio R 123	Got My Buglaoo/ETHIOPIANS: What To Do	100
67	Coxsone CS 7002	Somebody Help Me/GAYLADS & SOUL VENDORS: The Sound Of Silence	25
67	Coxsone CS 7009	Ba Ba Boom/SLIM SMITH & FREEDOM SINGERS: Mercy Mercy	35
67	Coxsone CS 7019	Ram Jam/SUMMERTAIRES: You're Gonna Leave	20
67	Coxsone CS 7026	Something Stupid/LYRICS: Money Lover	25
68	Coxsone CS 7040	Norwegian Wood/GAYLADS: Most Peculiar Man	25
68	Coxsone CS 7042	Sure Shot/OCTAVES: The Bottle	35
68	Coxsone CS 7046	Man Pon Shot/BOP & BELTONES: Not For A Moment	25
68	Coxsone CS 7050	Napoleon Solo/CANNON BALL BRYAN: You're My Everything	60
68	Coxsone CS 7075	Mission Impossible/HEPTONES: Giddy Up (B-side actually by Actions)	50
68	Studio One SO 2043	Put It One/SOUL VENDORS: Chinese Chicken	25
68	Studio One SO 2056	Race Track/BASES: I Don't Mind	40
69	Studio One SO 2082	Hi-Jack/TREVOR CLARKE: Sufferer	40
69	Doctor Bird DB 1177	Dark Of The Sun/MATADOR ALL STARS: Bridge View	50
69	Bamboo BAM 6	Our Thing (with Sound Dimension)/C. MARSHALL: Tra La La Sweet '69	25
69	Bamboo BAM 15	Clean Up/Spring Time (as Jackie Mittoo & Sound Dimension)	18
70	Bamboo BAM 17	Dark Of The Moon/Moon Walk (as Jackie Mittoo & Sound Dimension)	30
70	Bamboo BAM 20	Gold Dust/SUPERTONES: Real Gone Loser	18
70	Bamboo BAM 31	Can I Change My Mind/BRENTFORD ALLSTARS: Early Duckling	18
70	Bamboo BAM 38	Baby Why/ETHIOPIANS: You'll Want To Come Back	25
70	Bamboo BAM 51	Dancing Groove/BLACK & GEORGE: Peanut Butter	25
70	Banana BA 315	Holly Holy/LARRY MARSHALL: I've Got To Make It	15
71	Banana BA 320	Peenie Wallie/ROY RICHARDS: Can't Go On	12
72	London HLU 10357	Wishbone/Soul Bird (as Jackie Mittoo - The Reggae Beat)	7
79	Justice DIS 001	Disco Jack/Disco Dub (12")	35
80	Rite Sound RTA 06	Mystic World/Version (12")	20
81	Black Roots BR20	These Eyes/Wall Street/Thriller The Killer (12", p/s)	30
67	Coxsone CSL 8009	IN LONDON (LP)	100
68	Coxsone CSL 8014	EVENING TIME (LP, with Soul Vendors)	125
69	Coxsone CSL 8020	KEEP ON DANCING (LP)	125
70	Bamboo BDLP 209	NOW (LP)	50
72	London SHU 8436	WISHBONE (LP)	25
79	Third World TWS 501	KEYBOARD KING (LP)	25

(see also Lord Tanamo, Jamaican Actions, Matadors, Jackie Opel, Soul Vendors, Winston Francis, Donna & Freedom Singers, Skatalites)

MIX BLOOD
80	Creole CR 201	Last Train To Skaville/Move And Move (p/s)	10

MIXED BAG
69	Decca F 12880	Potiphar (with Ramases III Orchestra)/Million Dollar Bash	6
69	Decca F 12907	Round And Round/Have You Ever Been In Love	6

MIXMAN
90	Citizen Kane 12KANE 2	Bright Child (Manmix)/Bright Child (Dancemix) (12", p/s)	15

MIXRACE & PRO-TON-ISOSPACE
94	Stronghold STRONG 3	The Endless Skies (Hyper-On-Experience Remix)/True Jungle (Brown & Dangerman Remix)/The Endless Skies/True Jungle (12")	20

MIXTURE
65	Fontana TF 640	One By One/Monkey Jazz	10
69	Parlophone R 5755	Sad Old Song/Never Trust In Tomorrow	7

MIXTURES
71	Polydor 205813	Never Be untrue/She's Gone Away	10

BILLY MIZE
60	Top rank JAR 391	Little Coco Palm/The Windward Isle	7

HANK MIZELL
76	Charly CEP 115	HANK MIZELL (EP)	10

VIC MIZZY, HIS ORCHESTRA & CHORUS
65	RCA RCA 1440	Addams Family Main Theme/Kentucky James Main Theme	20

M.J.6
60	Decca F 11212	Tracy's Theme/Private Eye	6

MO & STEVE
66	Pye 7N 17175	Oh What A Day It's Going To Be/Reach Out For Your Lovin' Touch	5

MO2VATION
93	No Noise NNDJ 008	Lowdown & Funky/That Ruff Track (with L Double, 12")	15
93	Pure Noise DASH 3	THE RHYTHM RIDE EP (12")	10

MO2VATION & APEX
92	Hypno Genesis HG 002	ANIMATION EP (12")	25

MOB (1)
68	Mercury MF 1026	Disappear/I Wish You Would Leave Me Alone	15
71	Polydor 2001 127	I Dig Everything About You/Love's Got A Hold On Me	15

71	Polydor 2001 169	Give It To Me/I'd Like To See More Of You	10
71	Polydor 2001 200	Money/Once A Man Twice A Child	5
73	MGM 2006 278	Tear The House Down/One Way Ticket To Nowhere	5
74	UK USA 4	Give It To Me/I'd LIke To See More Of You	8
75	Private Stock PVT 32	I Can't Stop This Love Song/Hot Music	8
71	Polydor 2344 001	MOB (LP)	15

MOB (2)

80	Kalida AKB 1/2	Send Me To Coventry/Mobbed (p/s)	8

MOB (3)

80	All The Madmen MAD 1	Youth/Crying Again (p/s)	40
80	All The Madmen MAD 002	Witch Hunt/Shuffling Souls/What's Going On (EP, handwritten white labels with sticker & foldout, stapled, gatefold p/s)	10
82	Crass 321984/7	No Doves Fly Here/I Hear You Laughing (foldout p/s)	10
83	All The Madmen MAD 6	The Mirror Breaks/Stay (screen-printed p/s, with lyric insert)	10
83	Cause For Concern CFC 2	LIVE AT THE LMC (LP, with the APOSTLES)	30
83	All The Madmen MAD 4	LET THE TRIBE INCREASE (LP, with lyric poster)	20
84	All The Madmen MAD 4	LET THE TRIBE INCREASE (LP, second pressing, blue cover)	12
86	All The Madmen MAD 13	CRYING AGAIN (EP)	30
80s	All/Madmen MADPACK 1	MAD PACK 1 (3 x 7" in 12" pack)	25

HANK MOBLEY

56	Esquire 32-029	MOBLEY'S MESSAGE (LP)	70

JOHN MOBLEY

62	Stateside SS 136	Tunnel Of Love/Work Out	15

MOBSTER

80	Ensign ENY 41	The Mobster Shuffle/Simmer Down (p/s)	6
81	Ensign ENY 209	Perfect Man/Trinidad (p/s)	5

MOBY

91	Outer Rhythm FOOT 15R	Go: (Demixes): (Analog Mix)/(Nightime Mix)/(Soundtrack Mix) (12")	8
91	Outer Rhythm FOOT 15	Go: (Woodstock Mix)/(Low Spirit Mix)/(Voodoo Child Mix) (12")	8
91	Outer Rhythm FOOT 15X	Go: (Rainforest Mix)/(Video Mix/Analog Mix) (12")	8

MOBY DICK

82	Ebony EBON 5	Nothing To Fear/Can't Have My Body Tonight	20

MOBY GRAPE

67	CBS 2953	Omaha/Hey Grandma	15
68	CBS 3555	Can't Be So Bad/Murder In My Heart For The Judge	15
69	CBS 3945	Trucking Man/Ooh Mama Ooh	8
67	CBS (S)BPG 63090	MOBY GRAPE (LP)	50
68	CBS 63271	WOW (LP, mono & stereo)	30
69	CBS 63430	69 (LP, mono & stereo)	30
69	CBS 63698	TRULY FINE CITIZEN (LP, mono & stereo)	30
72	Reprise K 44152	20 GRANITE CREEK (LP)	15
74	CBS 64743	GREAT GRAPE (LP)	15

MOCCA-SIN & THE TP'S

78	Alaska ALA 2013	Cherokee Dance/The Raindance	10

MOCEDADES

73	Bell BELL 1303	Touch The Wind/Eres Tu	6

MOCKINGBIRDS

65	Columbia DB 7480	That's How It's Gonna Stay/I Never Should Have Kissed You	50
65	Columbia DB 7565	I Can Feel We're Parting/The Flight Of The Mockingbird	50
65	Immediate IM 015	You Stole My Love/Skit Skat	150
66	Decca F 12434	One By One/Lovingly Yours	60
66	Decca F 12510	How To Find A Lover/My Story	50

(see also 10cc, Graham Gouldman, Whirlwinds, Doctor Father, Hotlegs, Godley & Greme)

M.O.D.

79	Vertigo 6059 233	M.O.D./M.O.D. (2) (p/s, allegedly mispressed on 2-Tone label)	30
79	Vertigo 6059 233	M.O.D./M.O.D. (2) (p/s)	7

(see also David Essex)

MOD '79

79	Casino Classics CC 13	Green Onions/High On Your Love	5

MODE

66	Private pressing	THE MODE (EP, white labels, no p/s)	400

MODEL MANIA

79	Boob MM1 A/MM 1AA	No Pride Slow Suicide/Epic Cowboy (250 with handmade stamped label)	100
79	Boob MM1 A/MM 1AA	No Pride Slow Suicide/Epic Cowboy (750 with black labels)	75

MODELS

77	Step Forward SF 3	Freeze/Man Of The Year (p/s)	20

(see also Adam & The Ants, Mass, Rema Rema, Wolfgang Press)

MODERATES

81	Hyped BMRB 53	Emile/For What It's Worth (not released in p/s)	10
80	Open Eye OEEP 1001	FETISHES (12" EP)	8

MODERN ART

84	Color Disc COLORS 1	Dreams To Live/Beautiful Truth (p/s)	25
86	Color Disc COLORS 5	Penny Valentine/One Way Ticket (1-sided, clear vinyl flexidisc, 1,000 only)	12
87	Color Disc COLOR 3	STEREOLAND (LP, hand-stencilled with insert, 300 only)	60
94	Acme 8007 LP	ALL ABOARD THE MIND TRAIN (LP, 500 only, numbered)	18

MODERN ENGLISH

79	Limp LMP 2	Drowning Man/Silent World (p/s)	16
80	4AD AD 6	Swans On Glass/Incident (p/s)	6
80	4AD AD 15	Gathering Dust/Tranquility Of A Summer Moment (p/s)	6
81	4AD AD 110	Smiles And Laughter/Mesh And Lace (p/s)	5
81	4AD CAD 105	MESH AND LACE (LP)	12

(see also This Mortal Coil)

MODERN EON
80	Modern Eon EON 001	PIECES (EP)	20
80	Inevitable INEV 3	Euthenics/Waiting For The Cavalry (p/s)	5
81	Dinsales 2	Euthenics/Choreography/Waiting For The Cavalry/The Real Hymn (12", white label LP sampler)	20

MODERN FOLK QUARTET (M.F.Q.)
64	Warner Bros WB 147	The Love Of A Clown/If You All Think	25
66	RCA RCA 1514	Night Time Girl/Lifetime (as M.F.Q.)	30
63	Warner Bros WM/WS 8135	THE MODERN FOLK QUARTET (LP)	20
85	Off Beat WIK 55	MOONLIGHT SERENADE (LP)	15

MODERN JAZZ QUARTET (M.J.Q.)
60	Decca F11212	Tracey's Theme/Private Eye	6
55	Esquire 20-069	MODERN JAZZ QUARTET (10" LP)	15
55	Esquire 20-038	MODERN JAZZ QUARTET VOL. 2 (10" LP)	15
55	Esquire 20-090	THE CLASSICAL PERFORMANCES OF... (10" LP)	15
57	London Jazz LTZK 15022	FONTESSA (LP, also stereo SAH-K 6031)	15
58	London Jazz LTZK 15085	AT THE MUSIC INN (LP)	12
58	London Jazz LTZ 15136	MODERN JAZZ QUARTET (LP)	12
59	London Jazz LTZ-K 15140	PLAYS ONE NEVER KNOWS (LP, also stereo SAH-K 6029)	15
59	London Jazz LTZK 15181	ODDS AGAINST TOMORROW (LP)	20
59	Columbia Clef 33CX 11028	MODERN JAZZ QUARTET & OSCAR PETERSON AT THE OPERA HOUSE (LP)	12
60	London Jazz LTZ-K 15193	PYRAMID (LP, also stereo SAH-K 6086)	15
61	London Jazz LTZ-K 15207	THIRD STREAM MUSIC (LP, with Beaux Arts String Quartet & Jimmy Giuffre Three)	15
61	London Jazz LTZK 15222	EUROPEAN CONCERT (LP)	12
61	Esquire 32-124	LOOKING BACK AT THE MODERN JAZZ QUARTET (LP)	12
63	London HA-K/SH-K 8016	LONELY WOMAN (LP)	15
63	London HA-K/SH-K 8046	THE COMEDY SUITE (LP)	12
64	London HA-K/SH-K 8161	THE SHERIFF (LP)	12
65	Stateside SL 10141	THE BEST OF THE MODERN JAZZ QUARTET (LP)	12
68	Apple APCOR 4	UNDER THE JASMINE TREE (LP, mono)	50
68	Apple SAPCOR 4	UNDER THE JASMINE TREE (LP, stereo)	35
69	Apple SAPCOR 10	SPACE (LP, gatefold sleeve, dark green label, black inner)	50
70s	Apple SAPCOR 10	SPACE (LP, later pressing, light green label, single sleeve, white 'Apple' inner)	75
93	Apple SAPCOR 4	UNDER THE JASMINE TREE (LP, reissue, gatefold sleeve with inner)	20
93	Apple SAPCOR 10	SPACE (LP, reissue)	20

(see also John Lewis, Milt Jackson, Sonny Rollins)

MODERN JAZZ SEXTET
56	Columbia Clef 33CX 10048	MODERN JAZZ SEXTET (LP)	15

MODERN JAZZ SOCIETY
56	Columbia Clef 33CX 10038	A CONCERT OF CONTEMPORARY MUSIC (LP)	12

MODERN TALKING
86	RCA PD 71133	READY FOR ROMANCE (CD)	30

MODERNAIRES (U.K.)
80	Illuminated ILL 2	Life In Our Times/Barbed Up (p/s)	5
81	Illuminated ILL 4	We Did It Again/And Again (p/s, red vinyl)	5

MODERNAIRES (U.S.)
54	Vogue Coral Q 2024	Teach Me Tonight/Mood Indigo (with Georgie Auld)	5
54	Vogue Coral Q 2035	New Juke Box Saturday Night/Bugle Call Rag	5
55	Vogue Coral Q 72069	Birds And Puppies And Tropical Fish/Mine! Mine! Mine!	5
55	Vogue Coral Q 72084	Wine, Women And Gold/Sluefoot (with Bob Crosby Bob Cats)	5
55	Vogue Coral Q 72112	At My Front Door/Alright, Okay, You Win	5

(see also Four Guys, Bing Crosby)

MO-DETTES
79	Mode/Rough Trade MODE 1	White Mice/Masochistic Opposite (pink [card or paper] or white p/s)	6
80	Deram DET 2	Deep Park Creeping/Two Can Play	5
80	Deram DET-R-1/MODE 11/2	Paint It Black/Bitta Truth (with free flexidisc "Twist And Shout" & insert, black & white or blue & white p/s)	6
81	Deram DET 3	Tonight/Waltz In Blue Minor (p/s, fold-out sleeve with postcards of each band member)	5
81	Human HUM 10	White Mice/Kray Twins (live) (p/s)	5
80	Deram SML 1120	THE STORY SO FAR (LP, with insert & free colour sticker)	15

MODIFIES
70	Punch PH 45	Bye Bye Happyness/Sufferation We Must Bear	6

MODS (1)
64	RCA RCA 1399	Something On My Mind/You're Making Me Blue	25

MODS (2)
80	Bootlegged Records 007	LOST TOUCH (LP; sold only in Portobello Market, London)	25

MODULATIONS
74	Buddah BDS 406	I Can't Fight Your Love/Your Love Has Locked Me Up	15
70s	Buddah	THE MODULATIONS (LP)	40

MOE
88	Times Five T5 01	There Were Four Other Guys/One Man Went To Moe (12", p/s)	8

PETER MOESSER'S MUSIC
70	Stateside SS 2182	Hello/Bye Bye (withdrawn)	7

MOFFAT ALL STARS
70	Jackpot JP 719	Riot/IMPERSONATORS: Girls And Boys	40

LEROY MOFFATT
74	Atra AR 20	What It Takes/I Love You Darling	20

MOGUL THRASH
70	RCA RCA 2030	Sleeping In The Kitchen/St. Peter	15
71	RCA SF 8156	MOGUL THRASH (LP)	100

(see also Colosseum, Eclection, Family, King Crimson)

MINT VALUE £

MOGWAI

96	Rock Action RAR 01	Tuner/Lower (p/s, 500 only)	50
96	Ché CHE 59	4 TRACK 3 BAND TOUR EP (with Urusei Yatsura & Backwater, p/s, 50 only)	50
96	Ché CHE 61	Angels Vs Aliens/DWEEB: Buzzsong (p/s, 1st 500 on green vinyl)	12
96	Ché CHE 61	Angels Vs Aliens/DWEEB: Buzzsong (p/s)	6
96	Love Train PUBE 014	Summer/Ithica 279 (p/s, 1,500 only)	20
97	Wurlitzer Jukebox WJ 22	New Paths To Helicon (Parts 1 & 2) (foldover p/s in polythene bag, 2 inserts,1,000 only)	15
97	Flotsam/Jetsam SHAG13.04	Stereo Dee/PH FAMILY: Club Beatroot Part 4 (p/s, 400 only)	20
01	Chrysalis 9460013221	FIVE TRACK TOUR SINGLE: Close Encounters/Drum Machine/D To E/You Don't Know Jesus/Helicon (tour CD, card sleeve)	20
98	Chemikal Underground CHEM 026	NO EDUCATION = NO FUTURE (FUCK THE CURFEW) EP (12")	8
99	Chemikal CHEM 036	EP (12")	12
01	Rock Action ROCKACT 10	My Father My King (1-sided 12")	15
04	14th Floor SAM 00967	In A Dream (1-sided 7" die-cut sleeve)	10
06	Pias PIAS X067T	Black Spider/Half Time (10")	8
97	Chemikal U'gnd CHEM 818LP	YOUNG TEAM (2 x LP)	30
98	Eye Q EYEUKLP 019	KICKING A DEAD PIG (2-LP)	18
99	Chemikal Underground CMEM 033	COME ON DIE YOUNG (2xLP)	35
01	Southpaw PAWLP1	ROCK ACTION (LP)	20
03	Pias PIASX 035LP	HAPPY SONGS FOR HAPPY PEOPLE (LP, silvered sleeve)	20
05	Pias PIAS051LP	GOVERNMENT COMMISSIONS : BBC SESSIONS 1996-2003 (2-LP)	20
06	Pias PIAS X067DLP	ZIDANE (2-LP)	20
07	Pias PIASX062DLP	MR BEAST (2-LP, one sided etched)	25
08	Wall Of Sund WOS 040DLP	THE HAWK IS HOWLING (2-LP)	20
10	Rock Action ROCKACT 48	SPECIAL MOVES (3-LP, CD, DVD and signed poster)	50

(see also Magoo)

ESSRA MOHAWK

75	Mooncrest CREST 24	ESSRA MOHAWK (LP, with insert)	15
77	Private Stock PVLP 1016	ESSRA (LP)	15

MOHAWKS

68	Pama PM 309	The Clock/Version	35
68	Pama PM 719	The Champ/Sound Of The Witchdoctors (blue label)	30
68	Pama PM 719	The Champ/Sound Of The Witchdoctors (purple label)	20
68	Pama PM 739	Baby Hold On (Parts 1 & 2)	20
68	Pama PM 751	Sweet Soul Music/Hip Jigger	20
68	Pama PM 757	Mony Mony/Pepsi	70
69	Pama PM 758	Ride Your Pony/Western Promise	25
69	Pama PM 798	Skinhead Shuffle/RICO: Red Cow	40
70	Supreme SUP 205	Wicked Lady/For Our Liberty	15
70	Pama PM 796	Landscape/Number 1	25
70	Supreme SUP 204	Let It Be/Looking Back	15
70	Supreme SUP 205	For Our Liberty/Wicked Lady	10
70	Supreme SUP 207	Give Me Some/(Instrumental)	50
72	Supreme PS 362	Storm/And I Love Her	40
73	Supreme PS 376	The Champ/Cherry Pink	40
70s	Star PTP 1011	Whiter Shade Of Pale/My One Desire	15
86	Pama PM (T) 1	The Champ/Landscape (12", p/s)	8
68	Pama PMLP 5	THE CHAMP (LP)	200

(see also Sid & Joe & Mohawks)

LOUIS MOHOLO

78	Ogun OG 520	SPIRITS REJOICE (LP)	30

MOIST

95	Chrysalis 12CHSS 5019	SILVER (12" EP, clear vinyl)	10

MOJO HANNAH

72	Kingdom KV 8004	St. Jeremy/You'll Be Alright	25
73	Kingdom KV 8008	Six Days On The Road/Moon Dog's Gonna Howl Tonight	5
73	Kingdom KVL 9001	SIX DAYS ON THE ROAD (LP, orange label)	35

MOJO MEN

65	Pye International 7N 25336	Dance With Me/Loneliest Boy In Town	30
66	Reprise RS 20486	Hanky Panky/She's My Baby	30
67	Reprise RS 20539	Sit Down I Think I Love You/Don't Leave Me Crying Like Before	20
67	Reprise RS 20580	Me About You/When You're In Love	15

MOJOS

63	Decca F 11732	They Say/Forever	15
64	Decca F 11853	Everything's Alright/Give Your Lovin' To Me	8
64	Decca F 11918	Why Not Tonight/Don;t Do It Any More	8
64	Decca F 11959	Seven Daffodils/Nothin' At All	10
65	Decca F 12127	Comin' On To Cry/That's The Way It Goes	15
67	Decca F 12557	Goodbye Dolly Gray/I Just Can't Let Her Go	25
68	Liberty LBF 15097	Until My Baby Comes Home/Seven Park Avenue	60
64	Decca DFE 8591	THE MOJOS (EP)	70

(see also Stu James & Mojos, Faron's Flamingos)

MOLDY PEACHES

01	Rough Trade RTRADES 016	Who's Got The Crack?/NYC's Like A Graveyard (p/s)	6

MOLES

68	Parlophone R 5743	We Are The Moles (Parts 1 & 2)	30

MOLESTERS

79	Small Wonder SMALL 14	Disco Love/Commuter Man (p/s)	5
79	Small Wonder SMALL 18	End Of Civilisation/Girl Behind The Curtain (p/s)	5

MOLOKO

95	Echo ECHLP 7	DO YOU LIKE MY TIGHT SWEATER (2-LP)	20
98	Echo ECHLP 21	I AM NOT A DOCTOR (2-LP, triple gatefold)	30

MOMENT

85	Diamond DIA 004	In This Town/Just Once	6
85	Diamond DIA 008	One, Two, They Fly/Karl's New Haircut	5
80s	Tenth Floor	Poor Mr. Diamond (Parts 1 & 2)	10
89	Big Stuff	Ready To Fall (promo only)	8
86	Rave RAVE UP 1	THE WORK GETS DONE (LP, coloured vinyl)	12

MOMENTS (1)

63	London HLN 9656	Walk Right In/Walk Right In (Instrumental)	12

MOMENTS (2)

72	London HLU 10378	Love On A Two Way Street/I Won't Do Anything	6
74	London HL 10449	Sexy Mama/Where Can I Find Her	5
74	All Platinum 6146 322	Next Time I See You/It Don't Rain In My Backyard	6
75	All Platinum 6146 309	Look At Me/French Version	6
76	All Platinum 6146313	Nine Times	7
75	All Platinum 9109 302	SHARP (LP)	15

MOMENTUM

89	Fierce FI 001	Bitter Herb Taste Sweet/Trojan Warrior (12")	8

MOMUS

86	Él GPO 9T	Nicky/Don't Leave/See A Friend In Tears (12")	20
87	Creation CRE 037 T	Murderers, The Hope Of Women (12", p/s)	12
88	Creation CRELP 036	TENDER PERVERT (LP, with free 7")	15
90	Creation CRELP 052	DON'T STOP THE NIGHT (LP)	15
91	Creation CRELP 059	MONSTERS OF LOVE (LP)	12
91	Creation CRELP 097	HIPPOPOTAMOMUS (LP, with "Michelin Man" track & Michelin Man style inlay, withdrawn)	15
91	Creation CRECD 097	HIPPOPOTAMOMUS (CD, with "Michelin Man" track & Michelin Man style inlay, withdrawn)	20
92	Creation CRECD 140	SPACEWALK EP (CD)	20
93	Creation CRECD 151	TIMELORD (CD)	18
94	Creation CRECD 052	DON'T STOP THE NIGHT (CD)	18
94	Creation CRECD 059	MONSTERS OF LOVE (CD)	18

(see also Happy Family)

STEPHEN MONAHAN

67	London HLR 10145	City Of Windsor/Lost People	12

MONARCHS

64	London HLU 9862	Look Homeward Angel/What's Made You Change Your Mind	30

GRACHAN MONCUR III

74	JCOA/Virgin J2003	ECHOES OF PRAYER (LP)	25

JULIE MONDAY

66	London HLU 10080	Come Share The Good Times With Me/Time Is Running Out For Me	8

MONDO KANE

86	Lisson DOLEQ 2	New York Afternoon (mixes)/Manhattan Morning (12", p/s)	10

(see also Georgie Fame)

MONEY (1)

69	Major Minor MM 571	Welcome Me Love/Breaking Her Heart	8
69	Major Minor MM 620	Come Laughing Home/Power Of The Rainbow	8

MONEY (2)

79	Gull GULL 64	Aren't We All Searching/Where Have All The Dancers Gone	8
80	Hobo HOS 011	FAST WORLD (EP, p/s)	80
79	Gull GULP 1031	FIRST INVESTMENT (LP)	18

(see also Iron Maiden)

MONEY JANGLE

72	President PT 362	Home/Away Away	20

MONEY PIT

97	Bluepose	Smile It's Sugar/Strange And Silent Staircase (P/S)	10

ZOOT MONEY('S BIG ROLL BAND)

64	Decca F 11954	The Uncle Willie/Zoot's Suit (solo)	50
65	Columbia DB 7518	Good/Bring It Home To Me	40
65	Columbia DB 7600	Please Stay/You Know You'll Cry	35
65	Columbia DB 7697	Something Is Worrying Me/Stubborn Kind Of Fellow	30
65	Columbia DB 7768	The Many Faces Of Love/Jump Back (as Paul Williams & Zoot Money Band)	30
66	Columbia DB 7876	Let's Run For Cover/Self-Discipline	30
66	Columbia DB 7975	Big Time Operator/Zoot's Sermon	20
66	Columbia DB 8090	The Star Of The Show (The La La Song)/The Mound Moves	35
67	Columbia DB 8172	Nick Knack/I Really Learnt How To Cry	15
70	Polydor 2058 020	No One But You/Prisoner	8
80	Magic Moon/MPL MACH 3	Your Feet's Too Big/Ain't Nothin' Shakin' But The Bacon (solo)	12
80	Magic Moon/MPL MACH 6	The Two Of Us/Ain't Nothin' Shakin' But The Bacon (solo)	30
66	Columbia SEG 8519	BIG TIME OPERATOR (EP)	200
66	Columbia S(C)X 6075	ZOOT! - LIVE AT KLOOK'S KLEEK (LP, mono)	100
66	Columbia S(C)X 6075	ZOOT! - LIVE AT KLOOK'S KLEEK (LP, stereo)	100
65	Columbia 33SX 1734	IT SHOULD'VE BEEN ME (LP)	150
68	Direction 8-63231	TRANSITION (LP)	100
70	Polydor 2482 019	ZOOT MONEY (LP)	80
80	Magic Moon/MPL LUNE 1	MR. MONEY (LP, solo)	12

(see also Paul Williams & Big Roll Band, Dantalian's Chariot, Eric Burdon & Animals, Grimms, Centipede, Ellis, Johnny Almond Music Machine)

MONGREL

73	Polydor 2058 318	Lonely Street/Sing A Little Song	5
73	Polydor 2058 347	Last Night/Twist Her Hand	5
73	Polydor 2383 182	GET YOUR TEETH INTO THIS (LP)	25

(see also Wizzard)

MONGRELS

64	Decca F 12003	I Long To Hear/Everywhere	30
65	Decca F 12086	My Love For You/Stewball	30

(see also Bobbie Miller)

MONITORS (1)

69	T. Motown TML 11108	GREETINGS WE'RE THE MONITORS (LP, mono)	100
69	T. Motown STML 11108	GREETINGS WE'RE THE MONITORS (LP, stereo)	90

MONITORS (2)

79	Monitor MON 1	Telegram/Compulsory Fun (p/s)	5

MONK BOUGHT LUNCH

91	Own Label	Love And Hate/Paint It White/The Sailor's Tilted Hat (p/s)	40

THELONIOUS MONK

56	Vogue EPV 1115	THELONIOUS MONK (EP)	10
55	Esquire 20-039	THELONIOUS MONK QUINTET (10" LP)	20
55	Esquire 20-049	THELONIOUS MONK (10" LP)	25
56	Esquire 20-075	THELONIOUS MONK PLAYS (10" LP)	25
57	London LTZU 15097	BRILLIANT CORNERS (LP)	25
60	Esquire 32-109	THELONIOUS MONK QUINTETS (LP)	25
61	Esquire 32-115	WORK! (LP, with Art Blakey & Sonny Rollins)	25
61	Esquire 32-119	MONK'S MOODS (LP)	20
61	Riverside RLP 12-201	MONK PLAYS ELLINGTON (LP)	20
61	Philips BBL 1510	THELONIOUS MONK VOL. 1 (LP)	20
61	Riverside RLP 12-226	BRILLIANT CORNERS (LP)	20
61	Riverside RLP 12-262	MONK IN ACTION (LP)	20
62	Riverside RLP 12-300	AT THE TOWN HALL (LP, also stereo RLP 1138)	20
62	Riverside RLP 12-323	AT THE BLACK HAWK (LP, also stereo RLP 1171)	20
62	Philips BBL 1511	THELONIOUS MONK VOL. 2 (LP)	20
62	Riverside RLP 12-242	MONK'S MUSIC (LP)	20
63	CBS (S)BPG 62135	MONK'S DREAM (LP)	20
63	Riverside RLP 12-235	THELONIOUS HIMSELF (LP)	20
63	Riverside JLP (9)46	THELONIOUS MONK AND JOHN COLTRANE (LP)	20
64	Riverside RLP 002	IN EUROPE (VOL. 1)	20
64	CBS (S)BPG 62173	CRISS-CROSS (LP)	20
64	Blue Note (B)BLP 1510	THE GENIUS OF MODERN MUSIC (VOL. 1) (LP)	20
64	Blue Note (B)BLP 1511	THE GENIUS OF MODERN MUSIC (VOL. 2) (LP)	20
64	Riverside RLP 279	MISTERIOSO (LP)	15
64	CBS (S)BPG 62248	BIG BAND AND QUARTET IN CONCERT (LP)	15
65	CBS (S)BPG 62391	IT'S MONK'S TIME (LP)	15
65	Riverside RLP 305	FIVE BY MONK BY FIVE (LP)	15
65	Riverside RLP 003	IN EUROPE (VOL. 2) (LP)	15
65	CBS (S)BPG 62497	MONK (LP)	15
65	Riverside RLP 312	ALONE IN SAN FRANCISCO (LP)	15
65	Fontana FJL 113	WAY OUT! (LP)	15
65	Realm RM 52223	NICA'S TEMPO (LP, with Gigi Gryce)	20
65	CBS (S)BPG 62549	SOLO (LP)	15
65	Stateside SL 10152	THE GOLDEN MONK (LP)	20
67	Transatlantic PR7169	WORK! (LP)	20

(see also John Coltrane, Sonny Rollins, Art Blakey, Miles Davis)

MONKEES

66	RCA Victor RCA 1560	I'm A Believer/(I'm Not Your) Stepping Stone	6
67	RCA Victor RCA 1580	A Little Bit Me, A Little Bit You/The Girl I Knew Somewhere	6
67	RCA Victor RCA 1604	Alternate Title/Forget That Girl	6
67	RCA Victor RCA 1620	Pleasant Valley Sunday/Words	7
67	RCA Victor RCA 1645	Daydream Believer/Goin' Down	7
68	RCA Victor RCA 1673	Valleri/Tapioca Tundra	6
68	RCA Victor RCA 1706	D.W. Washburn/It's Nice To Be With You	6
69	RCA RCA 1802	Teardrop City/Man Without A Dream	10
69	RCA RCA 1824	Someday Man/Listen To The Band	10
69	RCA RCA 1862	Daddy's Song/The Porpoise Song	10
69	RCA RCA 1887	Mommy And Daddy/Good Clean Fun	10
70	RCA RCA 1958	Oh My My/Love You Better	12
74	Bell BLL 1354	Monkees Theme/I'm A Believer	6
67	RCA Victor RD 7844	The MONKEES (LP, mono)	20
67	RCA Victor RD 7868	MORE OF THE MONKEES (LP, mono)	18
67	RCA Victor SF 7868	MORE OF THE MONKEES (LP, stereo)	20
67	RCA Victor RD 7886	HEADQUARTERS (LP, mono	20
67	RCA Victor SF 7886	HEADQUARTERS (LP, stereo)	22
67	RCA Victor RD/SF 7886	HEADQUARTERS (LP, with different 'beard' photo on back, mono)	25
67	RCA Victor SF 7886	HEADQUARTERS (LP, with different 'beard' photo on back, stereo)	30
67	RCA Victor RD/SF 7912	PISCES, AQUARIUS, CAPRICORN AND JONES LTD. (LP)	22
68	RCA Victor RD/SF 7948	THE BIRDS, THE BEES & THE MONKEES (LP)	22

(The above albums were originally issued with black labels; later orange label copies are worth the same value.)

69	RCA RD 8016	INSTANT REPLAY (LP, mono)	30
69	RCA SF 8016	INSTANT REPLAY (LP, stereo)	25
69	RCA RD 8051	HEAD (LP, soundtrack, mono)	90
69	RCA SF 8051	HEAD (LP, soundtrack, stereo)	60
73	M.F. Pleasure SPR 90032	THE MONKEES (LP, 'Sounds Superb' series, black 'circus' sleeve)	12
79	Arista MONK-1 1/2	MONKEEMANIA (LP)	20
89	Circus BOY 1	IDOLISED, PLASTICISED, PSYCHOANYLYSED, STERILISED (LP, spoken-word convention issue, white vinyl)	15
89	Circus BOY 1	IDOLISED, PLASTICISED, PSYCHOANYLYSED, STERILISED (LP, spoken-word convention issue, picture disc)	18

(see also Micky Dolenz, Davy Jones, Michael Nesmith, Tommy Boyce & Bobby Hart)

MONKS

74	Rex R11 095	Roller Coaster Rock N Roll/It's A crying Shame	10

MONOCHROME SET

79	Rough Trade RT 005	Alphaville/He's Frank (p/s)	8

79	Rough Trade RT 019	Eine Symphonie Des Grauens/Lester Leaps In (1st 1,000 with labels on wrong side with explanatory insert, p/s)............7
79	Rough Trade RT 019	Eine Symphonie Des Grauens/Lester Leaps In (p/s)............5
79	Disquo Bleu BL 1	He's Frank (Slight Return)/Silicon Carne/Fallout (all cuts live) (no p/s)............6
80	Dindisc DID 4	STRANGE BOUTIQUE (LP)............20
80	DinDisc DID 8	LOVE ZOMBIES (LP, with lithograph)............15
82	Cherry Red BRED 34	ELIGIBLE BACHELORS (LP)............15
83	Cherry Red MRED 47	VOLUME CONTRAST BRILLIANCE (LP)............15

(see also Art Attacks)

MONOGRAMS

59	Parlophone R 4515	Juke Box Cha Cha/The Greatest Mistake Of My Life............8
59	Parlophone R 4545	Crystal/Teach Me............5

MONOPOLY

67	Polydor 56164	House Of Lords/Magic Carpet............20
67	Polydor 56188	We're All Going To The Seaside/It Isn't Easy............6
70	Pye 7N 17940	We Belong Together/Gone Tomorrow............25

(see also Raymond Froggatt)

MONOS

79	RCA PB 5206	U.F.O./Teenage Confessions............6

MONOTONES (U.K.)

64	Pye 7N 15608	What Would I Do/Is It Right............10
64	Pye 7N 15640	It's Great/Anymore............10
65	Pye 7N 15761	No Waiting/Like A Lover Should............10
65	Pye 7N 15814	Something's Hurting Me/A Girl Like That............10

MONOTONES (U.S.)

58	London HLM 8625	Book Of Love/You Never Loved Me............50
58	London HLM 8625	Book Of Love/You Never Loved Me (78)............50

MATT MONRO

56	Decca F 10816	Ev'rybody Falls In Love With Someone/Out Of Sight, Out Of Mind............15
57	Decca F 10845	The Garden Of Eden/Love Me Do............10
57	Decca F 10870	My House Is Your House/The Bean Song............10
58	Fontana H 122	The Story Of Ireland/Another Time Another Place............7
58	Fontana H 167	Prisoner Of Love/Have Guitar, Will Travel............7
61	Ember EMB S 120	The Ghost Of Your Past/Quite Suddenly............15
64	Parlophone R 5103	I Love The Little Things/It's Funny How You Know............5
65	Parlophone R 5348	Yesterday/Just Yesterday (Mine Your Love Was Mine)............0
66	Capitol CL 15448	Honey On The Vine/My Best Girl............10
69	capitol CL 15603	On Days Like These/On A Clear Day (You Can See Forever)............15
70	Capitol CL 15643	We''re Gonna Change The World/You're Closer To Me............7
63	Parlophone GEP 8889	SINGS THE THEME FROM THE FILM 'FROM RUSSIA FROM LOVE' (EP)............10
57	Decca LF 1276	BLUE AND SENTIMENTAL (10" LP)............30

(see also John Barry)

BARRY MONROE

66	Polydor 56088	World Of Broken Hearts/Never Again............6

BILL MONROE (& HIS BLUE GRASS BOYS)

56	Brunswick 05567	New John Henry Blues/Put My Little Shoes Away............15
56	Brunswick 05567	New John Henry Blues/Put My Little Shoes Away (78)............15
57	Brunswick 05681	Four Walls/A Fallen Star............12
57	Brunswick 05681	Four Walls/A Fallen Star (78)............12
59	Brunswick 05776	Gotta Travel On/No One But My Darlin'............10
59	Brunswick 05776	Gotta Travel On/No One But My Darlin' (78)............10
66	Brunswick 05960	Blue Ridge Mountain Blues/John Hardy (solo)............10
55	Brunswick OE 9160	COUNTRY DATE (EP)............10
55	Brunswick OE 9195	COUNTRY WALTZ (EP)............10
63	RCA RCX 7105	COUNTRY GUITAR VOL. 16 (EP, 2 tracks by Monroe Brothers)............10
61	Brunswick LAT 8338	I SAW THE LIGHT (LP)............15
63	Brunswick LAT 8511	BLUEGRASS RAMBLE (LP, mono)............15
63	Brunswick STA 8511	BLUEGRASS RAMBLE (LP, stereo)............18

(see also Monroe Brothers)

MONROE BROTHERS

63	RCA RCX 7103	COUNTRY GUITAR VOL. 14 (EP)............8
63	RCA RCX 7104	COUNTRY GUITAR VOL. 15 (EP)............8
63	RCA RCX 7105	COUNTRY GUITAR VOL. 16 (EP, 2 tracks by Bill Monroe & Bluegrass Boys)............8

(see also Bill Monroe)

GERRY MONROE

70	Chapter 1 CH 122	Sally/You Always Hurt The One You Love............5
72	Chapter 1 CH 159	Girl Of My Dreams/When There's No You............7
70	Chapter 1 CHS 806	SALLY - PRIDE OF OUR ALLEY (LP)............12
71	Chapter 1 CHS 809	GERRY MONROE (LP)............12
72	Chapter 1 LRS 5011	BRING BACK THE GOOD TIMES (LP)............12

MARILYN MONROE

53	MGM MGM 663	Diamonds Are A Girl's Best Friend/Bye Bye Baby (78)............20
54	HMV 7M 232	The River Of No Return/I'm Gonna File My Claim............60
54	HMV B 10723	The River Of No Return/I'm Gonna File My Claim (78)............25
55	HMV B 10847	After You Get What You Want/Heat Wave (78)............40
59	London HLT 8862	I Wanna Be Loved By You/I'm Thru' With Love............40
59	London HLT 8862	I Wanna Be Loved By You/I'm Thru' With Love (78)............35
78	United Artists UP 36484	I Wanna Be Loved By You/Running Wild/I'm Thru With Love (gatefold p/s)............5
87	Zuma ZOOMP 6	When I Fall In Love/Heat Wave (picture disc)............5
55	HMV 7EG 8090	THERE'S NO BUSINESS LIKE SHOW BUSINESS - SOUNDTRACK EXCERPTS (EP, company sleeve)............40
59	London RET 1231	SOME LIKE IT HOT (EP, soundtrack; first pressing with triangular centre)............80
59	London RET 1231	SOME LIKE IT HOT (EP, soundtrack; later round centre)............50
60	Philips BBE 12414	LET'S MAKE LOVE - FILM SOUNDTRACK (EP, with Yves Montand & Frankie Vaughan; mono)............30

Vaughn MONROE (& HIS ORCHESTRA)

60	Philips SBBE 9031	LET'S MAKE LOVE - FILM SOUNDTRACK (EP, with Yves Montand & Frankie Vaughan; stereo)	40
53	MGM MGM-D 116	GENTLEMEN PREFER BLONDES (10" LP, soundtrack with other artists)	75
59	London HA-T 2176	SOME LIKE IT HOT (LP, soundtrack with other artists, mono)	50
59	London SAH-T 6040	SOME LIKE IT HOT (LP, soundtrack with other artists, stereo)	60
60	Philips BBL 7414	LET'S MAKE LOVE (LP, soundtrack, with Yves Montand & Frankie Vaughan, mono)	40
60	Philips SBBL 592	LET'S MAKE LOVE (LP, soundtrack, with Yves Montand & Frankie Vaughan; stereo)	40
63	Stateside S(S)L 10048	MARILYN (LP, soundtrack, mono)	40
63	Stateside S(S)L 10048	MARILYN (LP, soundtrack, stereo)	50
72	Pye Int. NSPH 28500	REMEMBER MARILYN (LP, gatefold)	15
83	Liberty UASP 30226	SOME LIKE IT HOT (LP, picture disc)	12

(see also Frankie Vaughan)

VAUGHN MONROE (& HIS ORCHESTRA)

53	HMV 7M 144	Less Than Tomorrow (But More Than Yesterday)/Ruby	10
54	HMV 7M 247	They Were Doin' The Mambo/Mister Sandman	10
56	HMV 7M 332	Black Denim Trousers And Motorcycle Boots/All By Myself	20
57	HMV POP 354	Wringle Wrangle/Westward Ho The Wagons!	7
59	RCA RCA 1124	The Battle Of New Orleans/Hercules	8
60	London HLT 9123	Ballerina/Love Me Forever	5

MONSOON (1)

71	Trojan TR 7831	Hot Honolulu Night/Come Back Jane	6
72	Blue Mountain BM 1006	Night Of The Fly/Caroline The Wine Was Good	40

MONSOON (2)

81	Indipop IND 1	Ever So Lonely/Sunset Over The Ganges/The Mirror Of Your Mind/ Shout! (Till You're Heard) (in plastic sleeve with insert)	8
83	Mobile Suit Dist. MOBIL 1	THIRD EYE (LP)	12

(see also Complex)

MONSTER MAGNET

93	A&M 580 280-7	Twin Earth/Nod Scene (live) (stickered p/s, sticker, insert)	10
93	A&M 580 281-1	Twin Earth/Nod Scene (live)/Medicine (live) (12" 1-sided etched sick, p/s)	10
93	A&M AMYDK 291	Twin Earth/Nod Scene (live)/Medicine (live) (12" promo)	10
95	A&M AMDJ 7	Negasonic Teenage Warhead/Eclipse This (12", promo, stickered die-cut black sleeve)	10
95	A&M AMDJ 10	Dopes To Infinity/I'm Five Years Ahead Of My Time (12" promo)	10
95	A&M 581 032-7	Dopes To Infinity/I'm Five Years Ahead Of My Time (shaped picture disc)	8
98	A&M 582822-7	Powertrip (1-sided picture disc)	5
98	A&M 563 274-7	Space Lord/The Game (picture disc)	5
95	A&M 540 315-1	DOPES TO INFINITY (2-LP)	40
98	A&M 540 908-1	POWERTRIP (2-LP)	40

MONTAG

03	Ai AI 006	OBJETS PERDUS EP (12", p/s)	8

MONTANAS

65	Piccadilly 7N 35262	All That Is Mine Can Be Yours/How Can I Tell	12
66	Pye 7N 17183	That's When Happiness Began/Goodbye Little Girl	50
67	Pye 7N 17282	Ciao Baby/Anyone There	10
67	Pye 7N 17338	Take My Hand/Top Hat	10
67	Pye 7N 17394	You've Got To Be Loved/Difference Of Opinion	20
68	Pye 7N 17499	A Step In The Right Direction/Someday (You'll Be Breaking My Heart Again)	12
68	Pye 7N 17597	You're Making A Big Mistake/Run To Me	10
69	Pye 7N 17697	Roundabout/Mystery	15
69	Pye 7N 17729	Ciao Baby/Someday (You'll Be Breaking My Heart Again)	6
70	MCA MK 5036	Let's Get A Little Sentimental/Hey Diddle Diddle	8
71	MAM R45	No Smoke Without Fire/Seaport	15
71	MAM MAMR62	Suzanne/Your Love Is Growing	15

(see also Trapeze)

MONTANA SEXTET

83	Virgin VS 600	Who Needs Enemies With A Friend Like You/Friendly Vibes (12")	15
87	10 TENT 204	Heavy Vibes pts. 1 & 2 (12")	8

MONTCLAIRS

74	Contempo CS 2008	Make Up For Lost Time/How Can One Man Live	8
75	Contempo CS 2036	Hung Up On Your Love/I Need You More Than Ever	20
01	Grapevine 114	Hey You Don't Fight It/Never Ending Love	10
74	Contempo CLP 503	DREAMING OF A SEASON (LP)	15

LOU MONTE

54	HMV 7M 176	A Baby Cried/One Moment More	7
54	HMV 7M 190	Darktown Strutters' Ball/I Know How You Feel	7
54	HMV 7M 249	Chain Reaction/Vera's Veranda	7

VINNIE MONTE

59	London HL 8947	Summer Spree/I'll Walk You Home	10
59	London HL 8947	Summer Spree/I'll Walk You Home (78)	10
63	Stateside SS 156	Joanie Don't Be Angry/Take Good Care Of Her	18

MONTEGO JOE

72	London HLP 10374	Stand Up And Be Counted/Glooey (with Seeds Of Life)	5
66	Stateside SL 10159	JARRIBA! CON MONTEGO JOE (LP)	12

MONTEGO MELON

68	Sioux SI 004	Swan Lake/HONG GANG: Reggae Mento	5

HUGO MONTENEGRO ORCHESTRA

62	Oriole CB 1765	Palm Canyon Drive/Dark Eyes	7
63	Oriole CB 1792	Get Off The Moon/Sherry	25
65	RCA 1462	Darlin' Jill/Candy's Theme	6
68	RCA Victor RCA 1727	The Good, The Bad And The Ugly/Fistful Of Dollars	5
68	RCA Victor RCA 1771	Hang 'Em High/Tomorrow's Love	8
69	RCA RCA 1807	Tony's Theme/Good Vibrations	5
65	RCA Victor RD 7758	THE MAN FROM U.N.C.L.E. (LP, soundtrack)	50
66	RCA Victor RD 7832	MORE MUSIC FROM THE MAN FROM U.N.C.L.E. (LP, soundtrack)	45

67	RCA Victor RD/SF 7877	HURRY SUNDOWN (LP, soundtrack)	20
69	RCA SF 8053	MOOG POWER (LP)	20
69	Stateside S(S)L 10267	LADY IN CEMENT (LP, soundtrack)	40
70	Pye Intl. NSPL 28136	DAWN OF DYLAN (LP)	15

BOBBY MONTEZ
60	Vogue V 9165	Holiday In Havana/Jungle Stars	8

CHRIS MONTEZ
63	London HLU 9764	My Baby Loves To Dance/In An English Towne	7
66	Pye International 7N 25348	Call Me/Go 'Head On	15
66	Pye International 7N 25369	The More I See You/You, I Love You	6
66	Pye International 7N 25381	There Will Never Be Another You/You Can Hurt The One You Love	7
66	Pye International 7N 23599	Time After Time/Keep Talkin'	5
67	Pye International 7N 25415	Because Of You/Elena	5
73	CBS S CBS 1291	Come On, Let's Go/Somebody Loves You	5
63	London REU 1392	LET'S DANCE (EP)	30
66	Pye Intl. NEP 44071	THE MORE I SEE YOU (EP)	15
66	Pye Intl. NEP 44080	CHRIS MONTEZ (EP)	15
63	London HA-U 8079	LET'S DANCE AND HAVE SOME KINDA FUN!!! (LP)	40
66	Pye Intl. NPL 28080	THE MORE I SEE YOU (LP)	15
67	Pye Intl. N(S)PL 28087	TIME AFTER TIME (LP)	15
68	A&M AML 906	FOOLIN' AROUND (LP)	15

JACK MONTGOMERY
85	Kent TOWN 102	Dearly Beloved/MARIE KNIGHT: That's No Way To Treat A Girl	20
80s	Soul City 124	My Dear Beloved/Do You Believe It	15

LITTLE BROTHER MONTGOMERY
50	Jazz Collector L 44	No Special Rider Blues/Vicksburg Blues (78)	15
61	Columbia DB 4595	Pinetop's Boogie Woogie/Cow Cow Blues	25
61	Columbia 33SX 1289	LITTLE BROTHER MONTGOMERY (LP, with Alexis Korner)	70
62	77' 77LA 12/21	LITTLE BROTHER MONTGOMERY/SUNNYLAND SLIM (LP)	30
65	Decca LK 4664	LITTLE BROTHER MONTGOMERY (LP)	30
66	Xtra XTRA 1018	LITTLE BROTHER MONTGOMERY (LP)	20
71	Xtra XTRA 1115	FARRO ST. JIVE (LP)	20
71	Saydisc SDR 213	LITTLE BROTHER MONTGOMERY 1930-1969 (LP)	20
72	Saydisc SDM 223	HOME AGAIN (LP)	20

MARIAN MONTGOMERY
65	Capitol CL 15375	When Sunny Gets Blue/Teach Me Tonight	5
67	Reaction 591 018	Love Makes Two People Sing/Monday Thru Saturday	25
68	Pye 7N 17533	Why Say Goodbye/Love Today - Cry Tomorrow	5
72	Polydor 2383 159	MARIAN IN THE MORNING (LP)	20

ROY MONTGOMERY
97	Enraptured RAPT 4510	Trajectory One/Trajectory Two (p/s, 27 in handmade p/s)	15
97	Enraptured RAPT 4510	Trajectory One/Trajectory Two (p/s, 280 clear vinyl)	8

STUART MONTGOMERY
69	Private pressing	CERTAIN SEA WORDS (LP, with insert)	15

WES MONTGOMERY
60	Fontana FJL 109	GO! (LP)	12
60	Riverside RLP 12-320	THE INCREDIBLE JAZZ GUITAR OF WES MONTGOMERY (LP, mono)	15
60	Riverside RLP 12-320	THE INCREDIBLE JAZZ GUITAR OF WES MONTGOMERY (LP, stereo)	20

MONTROSE
74	Warner Brothers K 16382	Bad Motor Scooter/One Thing On My Mind	5
74	Warner Brothers K 16428	Rock The Nation/One Thing On My Mind	5

(see also Sammy Hagar)

MONTY, DERRICK & PATSY
65	Blue Beat BB 280	Stir The Pot/Mercy	50

(see also Monty Morris, Derrick Morgan)

MONTY (MORRIS) & ROY
61	Blue Beat BB 61	In And Out The Window/Tra La La Boogie (with Dumbago's Orchestra)	12
61	Blue Beat BB 63	Sweetie Pie/ROLAND ALPHONSO'S GROUP: Green Door	18

(see also Monty Morris)

MONTY PYTHON('S FLYING CIRCUS)
72	Charisma CB 192	Spam Song/The Concert (as Monty Python's Flying Circus, p/s)	6
72	Charisma CB 200	Eric The Half A Bee/The Yangtse Song (Extended) (as Monty Python with Niel [sic] Innes)	5
72	Python Productions	Teach Yourself Heath (flexidisc free with Zig Zag magazine)	10
74	Charisma CB 268	Lumberjack Song/Spam Song (p/s)	5
74	NME/Charisma SFI 1259	Monty Python's Tiny Black Round Thing (D.P. Gumby Presents "Election '74"/ The Lumberjack Song) (live flexidisc free with NME)	10
75	Charisma MP PROMO 1	In Store Commercial (promo only, jukebox single)	5
79	Warner Bros K 17495	Always Look On The Bright Side Of Life/Brian (p/s)	15
80	Charisma CB 374	I Like Chinese/I Bet You They Won't Play This Song On The Radio/Finland (p/s)	15
83	CBS WA 3495	Galaxy Song/Every Sperm Is Sacred (goldfish bowl-shaped picture disc)	8
88	Warner Bros W 7653	Always Look On The Bright Side Of Life/Brian (p/s, reissue)	10
91	Virgin PYTH 2	Galaxy Song/Every Sperm Is Sacred (p/s, reissue)	5
76	Charisma MP 001	PYTHON ON SONG (EP, double pack (CBS 268/PY 2])	10
70	BBC REB 73M	MONTY PYTHON'S FLYING CIRCUS (LP, mono, mustard label)	18
70	Charisma CAS 1049	ANOTHER MONTY PYTHON RECORD (LP, inner sleeve, 3 inserts, 'scroll' label)	20
73	Charisma CAS 1063	MONTY PYTHON'S PREVIOUS RECORD (LP, with free flexidisc in p/s, Teach Yourself Heath & inner sleeve)	15
73	Charisma CAS 1080	MATCHING TIE AND HANDKERCHIEF (LP, parallel grooves on side 2, die-cut sleeve, 2 inserts)	15
74	Charisma CLASS 4	LIVE AT THE THEATRE ROYAL DRURY LANE (LP)	12
77	Charisma CAS 1134	THE MONTY PYTHON INSTANT RECORD COLLECTION (LP, foldout sleeve)	12
79	Warner Bros K 56751	LIFE OF BRIAN (LP, soundtrack, with inner sleeve)	12

(see also John Cleese, Rutles, Barry Booth)

MONUMENT

71	Beacon BEAS 15	THE FIRST MONUMENT (LP)	60

(see also Zior)

MONUMENTUM

95	Misanthropy AMAZON 007	IN ABSENTIA CHRISTI (LP)	20

MOOCHE

69	Pye 7N 17735	Hot Smoke And Sasafrass/Seen Through A Light	20

MOOD MOSAIC

66	Columbia DB 7801	A Touch Of Velvet, A Sting Of Brass/Bond Street P.M.	35
66	Columbia DB 7801	A Touch Of Velvet, A Sting Of Brass/Bond Street P.M.(DJ Copy)	50
67	Columbia DB 8149	Chinese Chequers/The Real Mr. Smith	25
68	Parlophone R 5716	The Yellow Spotted Capricorn/ELMER HOCKETT'S HURDY GURDY: Fantastic Fair	15
69	Columbia DB 8618	A Touch Of Velvet, A Sting Of Brass/Bond Street P.M. (reissue)	15
67	Columbia SX 6153	MOOD MOSAIC (LP, mono)	35
67	Studio Two TWO 160	MOOD MOSAIC (LP, stereo)	25

(see also Mark Wirtz Orchestra & Chorus, Keith West)

MOOD OF HAMILTON

67	Columbia DB 8304	Why Can't There Be More Love?/King's Message	25

MOOD REACTION

69	Gas 136	Too Much Loving/Roaring Twenties	8
70	Pama PSP 1007	LIVE AT THE CUMBERLAND (LP)	20

MOOD SIX

82	EMI EMI 5300	Hanging Around/Mood Music (p/s)	5
82	EMI EMI 5336	She's Too Far/Venus (unreleased; white label copies exist with p/s)	30
85	Psycho PSYCHO 2001	Plastic Flowers/It's Your Life (p/s)	5
85	Psycho PSYCHO 4001	PLASTIC FLOWERS (12" EP)	10
85	Psycho PSYCHO 33	THE DIFFERENCE IS... (LP)	12

AMEIL MOODIE

69	Blue Cat BS 143	Mello Reggae/Lifeline	20
69	Blue Cat BS 164	Ratchet Knife/Bend The Tree	20

MOODS

63	Starlite ST45 098	Duckwalk/Easy Going	22

MOODY BLUES

64	Decca F 11971	Steal Your Heart Away/Loose Your Money (But Don't Loose Your Mind) (as Moodyblues)	45
64	Decca F 12022	Go Now!/It's Easy Child	6
65	Decca F 12095	I Don't Want To Go On Without You/Time Is On My Side	7
65	Decca F 12166	From The Bottom Of My Heart (I Love You)/And My Baby's Gone	7
65	Decca F 12266	Everyday/You Don't (All The Time)	10
66	Decca F 12498	Boulevard De La Madelaine/This Is My House (But Nobody Calls)	12
67	Decca F 12543	Life's Not Life/He Can't Win (withdrawn)	60
67	Decca F 12607	Fly Me High/Really Haven't Got The Time	30
67	Decca F 12670	Love And Beauty/Leave This Man Alone	20
67	Deram DM 161	Nights In White Satin/Cities (1st issue, darker labels than later copies)	5
68	Deram DM 196	Voices In The Sky/Doctor Livingstone, I Presume	10
68	Deram DM 213	Ride My See-Saw/A Simple Game	8
69	Deram DM 247	Never Comes The Day/So Deep Within You	7
69	Threshold TH 1	Watching And Waiting/Out And In	8
81	Threshold THPD 29	Talking Out Of Turn/Veteran Cosmic Rocker (picture disc)	7
83	Threshold TH 30	Blue World/Going Nowhere (p/s, with free T-shirt)	6
65	Decca DFE 8622	THE MOODY BLUES (EP, original label)	30
65	Decca DFE 8622	THE MOODY BLUES (EP, reissue with boxed Decca logo)	10
65	Decca LK 4711	THE MAGNIFICENT MOODIES (LP, unboxed red/silver Decca label logo)	60
65	Decca LK 4711	THE MAGNIFICENT MOODIES (LP, boxed red/silver Decca label logo)	20
67	Deram DML 707	DAYS OF FUTURE PASSED (LP, originally with white band on sleeve & 'DSS' labels, mono)	30
67	Deram SML 707	DAYS OF FUTURE PASSED (LP, originally with white band on sleeve & 'DSS' labels, stereo)	15
68	Deram DML 711	IN SEARCH OF THE LOST CHORD (LP, gatefold sleeve, mono, 'DSS' label)	30
68	Deram SML 711	IN SEARCH OF THE LOST CHORD (LP, gatefold sleeve, stereo, 'DSS' label)	12
69	Deram DML 1035	ON THE THRESHOLD OF A DREAM (LP, gatefold sleeve with stapled booklet, mono. Label is white/brown with large logo)	30
69	Deram SML 1035	ON THE THRESHOLD OF A DREAM (LP, gatefold sleeve with stapled booklet, stereo)	20
69	Threshold THM 1	TO OUR CHILDREN'S CHILDREN'S CHILDREN (LP, gatefold, with insert, white/pink label, mono)	40
69	Threshold THS 1	TO OUR CHILDREN'S CHILDREN'S CHILDREN (LP, gatefold, with insert, white/lilac label, stereo)	20
70	Threshold THS 3	A QUESTION OF BALANCE (1st pressing, Matrixes 10009P-1W/10010P-1W, 'flap' gatefold sleeve with lyric sheet)	20
71	Threshold THS 5	EVERY GOOD BOY DESERVES A FAVOUR (LP, gatefold, lyric insert, white/blue label)	18
72	Threshold THS 7	SEVENTH SOJOURN (LP, gatefold sleeve, lyric insert, white/blue label)	18

(see also Justin Hayward, Denny Laine, Gerry Levene & Avengers, Ray Thomas)

GEORGE MOODY

65	Fontana TF 631	Bring A Little Sunshine (To My Heart)/Santa The Swagman	6

JAMES MOODY

55	Esquire 20-071	MOODY HI FI (10" LP)	20

MOOG MACHINE

69	CBS 63807	SWITCHED ON ROCK (LP)	20

(THE) MOOG

92	Delirious DELIS 2	Rush Hour/Jungle Muffin/Live Forever/Hopelessly Volatile/Subtone (12")	30
92	Delirious DELIS 4	THE MOOG REMIX EP: Jungle Muffin (Micky Finn Remix)/Rush Hour (Rotor Remix)/Live Forever (Mercy Remix)/Going Crazy (Justice Remix) (12")	12

MOOM

95	Delerium DELEC LP 031	TOOT (LP)	15

MOON

68	Liberty LBF 15076	Someday Girl/Mothers And Fathers	25
70	Liberty LBF 15333	Pirate/Not To Know	10
68	Liberty LBL/LBS 83146	WITHOUT EARTH (LP)	50

(see also Beach Boys)

KEITH MOON

75	Polydor 2058 584	Don't Worry Baby/Together	20
75	Polydor 2442 134	TWO SIDES OF THE MOON (LP)	30

LARRY MOON

63	Ember EMB 171	Tia Juana Ball/Bouquet Of Roses	20

PERRY MOON

63	Sway SW 002	Nine Five Baby/PLANTES: Water Front	10

TERRY MOON

63	Planetone RC 11	Moon Man/MIKE ELLIOT: This Love Of Mine	10

MOON BOYS

69	Amalgamated AMG 846	Apollo 11/PIONEERS: Love Love Everyday	80

(see also Hippy Boys)

MOONCHILD

75	Look LKSP 5010	Hourglass/War Orphan (Brother Of The Day)	20

MOONDANCE

70	A&M AMS 792	Lazy River/Anna St Claire	5

MOONDOG

54	London REP 1010	ON THE STREETS OF NEW YORK (EP)	30
59	Esquire 32-055	MOONDOG (LP)	150
69	CBS 63906	MOONDOG (LP, gatefold sleeve)	40

MOONDOGS (1)

78	Lyntone LT 002	Heads I Win/Two's A Crowd (p/s)	40

MOONDOGS (2)

79	Good Vibrations GOT 10	She's Nineteen/Ya Don't Do Ya (foldout p/s)	15
80	Real ARE 13	Who's Gonna Tell Mary/Overcaring Parents (p/s)	10
81	Real ARE 14	Talking In The Canteen/Make Her Love Me (p/s, with neckerchief)	35
81	Real ARE 14	Talking In The Canteen/Make Her Love Me (p/s)	10
81	Real ARE 16	Imposter/Baby Snatcher (p/s)	15

ART MOONEY (& HIS ORCHESTRA)

53	MGM SP 1037	I Played The Fool/I Just Couldn't Take It, Baby (with Cathy Ryan)	10
53	MGM SP 1045	Baby Don't Do It/Believe In Me (with Cathy Ryan)	10
54	MGM SP 1088	Oh Boy What Joy We Had/Silhouette D'Amour	8
55	MGM SP 1134	No Regrets/Honey Babe	8
55	MGM SP 1145	Give Me A Band And My Baby/The Girl I Left Behind Me	8
56	MGM SP 1166	Memories Of You/I'm Looking Over	8
56	MGM MGM 899	Tutti Frutti/OCIE SMITH & CLOVERLEAFS: Our Melody (78)	15
57	MGM MGM 923	Rebel Without A Cause Theme/"East Of Eden" Theme	15
57	MGM MGM 943	Giant/There's Never Been Anyone Else But You	15
57	MGM MGM 951	Rock And Roll Tumbleweed/Is There A Teenager In The House (with Ocie Smith)	22
57	MGM MGM 951	Rock And Roll Tumbleweed/Is There A Teenager In The House (with Ocie Smith) (78)	15

(see also Ocie Smith, Shorty Long, Cloverleafs, Cathy Ryan)

MOONGLOWS

57	London HLN 8374	I Knew From The Start/Over And Over Again	700
57	London HLN 8374	I Knew From The Start/Over And Over Again (78)	70

(see also Harvey & Moonglows, Etta & Harvey)

MOONI

73	Polydor 2058-367	Wine Ridden Talks/Nightmare	10

(see also Mott The Hoople)

MOONKYTE

71	Mother SMOT 1	COUNT ME OUT (LP, with insert, cover has a die-cut spire)	400

MOONLIGHTERS

63	Island WI 043	Going Out/Hold My Hands	20

MOONLIGHTERS

65	Columbia DB 7602	Come On Home/It's Too Late	10
66	Columbia DB 7910	We'll See It Through/Too Late To Come Home	10

MOONQUAKE

73	London HL 10446	Remember/This Winter	8

MOON ROCKS & PRINCE JAZZBO

78	Bushay's BFM 101	Unite Jah People/Have No Fear (12")	40

MICKY MOONSHINE

74	Decca F 13555	Baby Blue/Name It You Got It	20
74	Decca F 13555	Baby Blue/Name It You Got It (DJ copy)	40

MOONSHINE (1)

70	KJ Roberts ZDR56312	Susannah/Garden Of Men	60

MOONSHINE (2)

76	Moo Records MOO 1	MOONSHINE EP (EP)	10

MOONSHINERS

65	Stateside SL 10137	THE MOONSHINERS BREAKOUT! (LP)	18
67	Page One POLS 004	HOLD UP (LP)	22

MOONSTONES

65	Parlophone R 5331	Heaven Fell Last Night/Little Roses	6
66	Parlophone R 5497	Violets Of Dawn/Power Of Decision	6
67	Mercury MF 1011	How Many Times/Louisville	6

MOON'S TRAIN
67	MGM MGM 1333	Deed I Do/It's In My Mind	40

(see also Peter Frampton, Denny Mitchell, Preachers)

MOONTREKKERS
61	Parlophone R 4814	Night Of The Vampire/Melodie D'Amour	25
62	Parlophone R 4888	There's Something At The Bottom Of The Well/Hatashiai	30
63	Decca F 11714	Moondust/The Bogey Man	20

MICHAEL MOORCOCK('S DEEP FIX)
80	Flicknife FLS 200	Dodgem Dude/Star Cruiser (p/s)	5
82	Flicknife EJS P9831	Brothel In Rosenstrasse/Time Centre (numbered, 500 only, with autographed lyric sheet)	30
92	Cyborg (no cat. no.)	The Brothel In Rosenstrasse (cassette only)	20
75	United Artists UAG 29732	NEW WORLD'S FAIR (LP, with inner sleeve)	40

(see also Hawkwind)

ALEXANDER MOORE
60	77 77LA 12-7	WHISTLING ALEX MOORE (LP)	15

(see also Whistling Alexander Moore)

ALICE MOORE
50s	Poydras MC 66	Prison Blues/My Man Blues	22

ANTHONY MOORE
76	Virgin VS 144	Catch A Falling Star/Back To The Top	5
71	Polydor 2310 062	PIECES FROM THE CLOUDLAND BALLROOM (LP)	60
72	Polydor 2310 079	SECRETS OF THE BLUE BAG (LP)	40
76	Virgin V 2057	OUT (LP, unissued)	0
79	Quango HMS 98	FLYING DOESN'T HELP (LP)	12
81	Do It RIDE 7	WORLD SERVICE (LP, with inner)	12

BARBARA MOORE
67	CBS (S) BPG 62839	A LITTLE MOORE BARBARA (LP)	50

BOB MOORE & ORCHESTRA
61	London HLU 9409	Mexico/Hot Spot	5

BOBBY MOORE (& RHYTHM ACES)
66	Chess CRS 8033	Searching For My Love/Hey Mr D.J.	25
75	Pye International 7N 25691	Call Me Your Anything Man/Call Me Your Anything Man (Disco Version) (solo)	6
66	Chess CRL 4521	SEARCHIN' FOR MY LOVE (LP)	75

BUTCH MOORE
64	Piccadilly 7N 35170	Foolin Time/Too Soon To Know	10
64	Pye 7N 15727	Down Came The Rain/Bye Bye Till Then	8
64	Piccadilly 7N 35182	I Missed You/Touch Me	12
65	Pye 7N 15832	Walking The Streets In The Rain/I Stand Still	10
65	Pye 7N 15910	Our Love Will Go On/Words	8
67	Pye 7N 17368	Till Then My Love/The Incredible Miss Brown	7

CHRISTY MOORE
69	Mercury 20170 SMCL	PADDY ON THE ROAD (LP)	400
75	Polydor 2383 344	WHATEVER TICKLES YOUR FANCY (LP)	25
76	Polydor 2383 426	CHRISTY MOORE (LP)	25
70s	WEA WX 286	VOYAGE (LP)	15

CURLEY MOORE & THE COOL ONES
71	Pye 7N 25570	Shelly's Rubber Band/Funky Years	30

DUDLEY MOORE (TRIO)
61	Parlophone R 4772	Strictly For The Birds (solo)/Duddly Dell (B-side as Dudley Moore Trio)	10
68	Decca F 12850	30 Is A Dangerous Age, Cynthia/The Real Stuff	10
69	Decca F 12882	Keep It Up/Gently (as Dudley Moore Trio)	25
65	Decca LK 4732	THE OTHER SIDE OF DUDLEY MOORE (LP)	12
66	Decca LK 4788	GENUINE DUD (LP, as Dudley Moore Trio)	20
69	Decca SKL 4923	BEDAZZLED (LP, stereo, soundtrack)	90
69	Decca LK/SKL 4976	THE DUDLEY MOORE TRIO (LP)	30
72	Atlantic K 40397	TODAY (LP)	12

(see also Peter Cook & Dudley Moore, Cleo Laine)

G T MOORE
74	B&C CB 236	I'm Still Waiting/Judgement Day	8

GARY MOORE
78	MCA MCA 386	Back On The Streets/Track Nine (in p/s)	30
78	MCA MCA 386	Back On The Streets/Track Nine	5
79	MCA MCA 419	Parisienne Walkways/Fanatical Fascists (p/s)	12
79	MCA MCA 534	Spanish Guitar/Spanish Guitar (instrumental) (p/s)	12
81	Jet JET 12016	Nuclear Attack/Don't Let Me Be Misunderstood/Run To Your Mama (12", company sleeve, as Gary Moore & Friends)	10
82	Virgin VS 528	Always Gonna Love You/Cold Hearted (p/s)	7
82	Virgin VSY 528	Always Gonna Love You/Cold Hearted (picture disc)	8
83	Virgin VSY 564	Falling In Love With You/Falling In Love With You (Instrumental) (picture disc)	12
83	Virgin VS 564	Falling In Love With You/(Instrumental) (p/s, with comic)	10
83	Virgin VS 56412	Falling In Love With You/(Instrumental) (12", p/s)	15
84	10 TEN 13	Hold On To Love/Devil In Her Heart (poster p/s)	7
84	10 TENS 13	Hold On To Love/Devil In Her Heart (plectrum-shaped picture disc)	18
84	10 TEN 1312	Hold On To Love/Devil In Her Heart/Law Of The Jungle (12", p/s)	10
84	10 TEN 19	Shapes Of Things/Blinder (p/s, with patch)	12
84	10 TENS 19	Shapes Of Things/Blinder (explosion-shaped picture disc)	15
84	10 TEN 1912	Shapes Of Things/Blinder/(Interview) (12", p/s)	8
84	10 TEN 25	Empty Rooms/Nuclear Attack (live) (in poster p/s)	8
84	10 TEN 25-12	Empty Rooms (Ext. Mix)/Empty Rooms//Nuclear Attack (live)/ Empty Rooms (live)/Rockin' Every Night (live) (12", double pack, gatefold p/s with poster)	8
85	10 TEN D 58	Empty Rooms (Summer 85 Version)/Out Of My System with bonus single Parisienne Walkways (live)/Murder In The Skies (live)	7
85	10 TEN 58	Empty Rooms (Summer 85 Version)/Out Of My System (p/s)	5

86	10 TENS 134	Over The Hills And Far Away/Crying In The Shadows (guitar-shaped pic disc).............15
86	10 TENG 134	Over The Hills And Far Away (Extended Mix)/Over The Hills And Far Away (7" mix)/Crying In The Shadows/All Messed Up (12", p/s) 10
87	10 TENT 178	The Loner/Johnny Boy/The Loner (Extended Version)/The Loner (Live At Hammersmith Odeon (12", p/s)..10
88	Virgin GMSY 1	After The War/This Thing Called Love (picture disc, stickered PVC sleeve).....................8
73	CBS 65527	GRINDING STONE (LP, as Gary Moore Band)..20
78	MCA MCF 2853	BACK ON THE STREETS (LP, with inner sleeve) 12
81	Jet JETLP 245	LIVE AT THE MARQUEE (LP, withdrawn test pressing, white sleeve with Jet Info sticker)....100
82	Virgin V 2245	CORRIDORS OF POWER (LP, with free live EP [VDJ 34])..20
84	EMI OVED 206	VICTIMS OF THE FUTURE (LP, with inner & poster) 20
84	Jet JETLP 241	DIRTY FINGERS (LP) 12
86	10 DIXP 16	RUN FOR COVER (LP, picture disc, die-cut sleeve) 30
87	10 DIXG 56	WILD FRONTIER (2-LP, gatefold sleeve)...20

(see also Granny's Intentions, Dr. Strangely Strange, Skid Row, Thin Lizzy, Gary Moore & Phil Lynott, Greg Lake, Eddie Howell, G-Force, Cozy Powell, Jack Bruce. National Head)

GARY MOORE & PHIL LYNOTT

85	10 TENS 49	Out In The Fields/Military Man (2 1-sided interlocking shaped picture-disc set, stickered gatefold PVC sleeve)...25
85	10 TEND 49	Out In The Fields/Military Man//Still In Love With You/ Stop Messin' Around (live) (double pack) 7
85	10 TEN 49-12	Out In The Fields/Military Man/Still In Love With You (12", gatefold p/s, with poster)..10
85	10 TENC 49-12	Military Man (12", 1-sided, B-side etched with signatures, promo only)..........................12

JACKIE MOORE

71	Jay Boy BOY 35	Dear John/Here Am I 5
71	Atlantic 2091 054	Precious Precious/Will Power 5
71	Atlantic 2091 095	Sometimes It's Got To Rain (In Your Love Life)/Wonderful, Marvellous (with Dixie Flyers)...5
74	Atlantic K 10481	Both Ends Against The Middle/Willpower..7
79	CBS CBS 12-7722	This Time Baby/Let's Go Somewhere And Make Love (12") 10
74	Atlantic K40544	SWEET CHARLIE BABE (LP) 15

JACQUELINE MOORE

| 65 | Decca F 12165 | Queen Of The House/What's Going On Here ....7 |

JERRY MOORE

| 69 | Fontana STL 5502 | LIFE IS A CONSTANT JOURNEY HOME (LP) ....40 |

JOHNNY MOORE

| 67 | Caltone TONE 101 | Sound And Soul/ROY SHIRLEY: Get On The Ball ....40 |
| 69 | Doctor Bird DB 1180 | Big Big Boss/CARL CANNONBALL BRYON: Reggae This Reggae ....40 |

(see also Cannonball & Johnny Melody, Alton Ellis)

MATTHEW MOORE

| 66 | Capitol CL 15467 | A Face In The Crowd/St. James Infirmary ....6 |

MERRILL E. MOORE

54	Capitol CL 14057	Bell Bottom Boogie/The House Of Blue Lights (78) 15
54	Capitol CL 14130	Nola/Fly Right Boogie (78) 15
55	Capitol CL 14369	Five Foot Two, Eyes Of Blue/Hard Top Race (as Merrill Moore) 200
55	Capitol CL 14369	Five Foot Two, Eyes Of Blue/Hard Top Race (as Merrill Moore) (78)................................20
56	Capitol F 3397	King Porter Stomp/Rock Island Line (export only) 150
68	Ember EMB S 253	Down The Road A-Piece/Buttermilk Baby 15
69	B&C CB 100	Sweet Mama Tree Top Tall/Little Green Apples 8
70	Bulldog BD 20	House Of Blue Lights/Red Light 8
67	Ember EMB 3392	BELLYFUL OF BLUE-THUNDER (LP) 40
68	Ember EMB 3394	ROUGH-HOUSE 88 (LP; repressed 1973) 20
69	B&C CAS 1001	TREE TOP TALL (LP)..20

NICKY MOORE BAND

| 81 | Street Tunes STS 006 | Year Of The Lie ....10 |
| 81 | Street Tunes | 7 YEARS OF THE LIE (LP) ....12 |

(see also Tiger, Samson, Hackensack, Mammoth)

OSCAR MOORE TRIO

| 55 | London H-APB 1035 | KENYA (10" LP)..15 |

PETE MOORE'S SOLID ROCKIN' BRASS

| 74 | Gold Star 1500 009 | PETE MOORE'S SOLID ROCKIN' BRASS (LP) ....15 |

ROGER MOORE

| 65 | CBS 202014 | Where Does Love Go/Tomorrow After Tomorrow (in p/s) ....20 |
| 65 | CBS 202014 | Where Does Love Go/Tomorrow After Tomorrow ....10 |

SCOTTY MOORE

| 64 | Columbia 33SX 1680 | THE GUITAR THAT CHANGED THE WORLD! (LP) ....60 |

(see also Elvis Presley)

SHELLEY MOORE

| 55 | Columbia SCM 5197 | In The Wee Small Hours Of The Morning/ When You Lose The One You Love (solo) ....5 |

SHELLEY MOORE (& MOORE SESSIONEERS)

58	Starlite ST45 002	You've Tied Me Up/Gone On The Guy 7
58	Starlite ST45 003	Where Is The Bluebird?/Everything Is Gonna Be All Right..7
57	Starlite ST EP 1	PORTRAIT OF SHELLEY (EP) 8
58	Starlite ST EP 7	KOOOL KANARY (EP) 8

THURSTON MOORE & DON FLEMING

| 97 | Via Satellite V.SAT 6 | Telstar/E.A.R.: Sputnik ....20 |

TIM MOORE

| 75 | Mooncrest Moon 41 | A Fool Like You/Aviation Man ....12 |

MELBA MOORE

86	Kent 6T 2	Magic Touch/CHUCK JACKSON: Little By Little 20
87	Horace's 001	Magic Touch/TOMMY HUNT: The Pretty Part Of You 20
03	Kent TOWN 119	DEAN PARISH: Broken Bottles And Sticks/MELBA MOORE: Magic Touch.........................8

MINT VALUE £

ALAN MOORHOUSE ORCHESTRA
66	Pye 7N 17073	(The Ballad Of) The Green Berets/London Bridge	6
68	Page One POF 104	Stop Press/Chloe	7
70	Columbia DB 8674	Haunting Me/Soul Bossa	6

MOOSE
70	Escort ERT 840	Engine No. 9/KURASS: Do It	7

BIG MOOSE (WALKER)
68	Python PKM 1	Puppy Howl Blues/Rambling Woman (pressed with reversed labels)	35

MOPEDS
68	Col. Blue Beat DB 108	Whiskey And Soda/Do It	7

(see also Cindy Starr & Mopeds)

MOQUETTES
64	Columbia DB 7315	Right String, But The Wrong Yo-Yo/You Came Along	50

SANTOS MORADOS
68	Island WIP 6034	Tonopah/Anytime	6

NONO MORALES & HIS ORCHESTRA
54	HMV 7MC 5	Istanbul (Not Constantinople)/Am I Blue (export single)	6

MIKE MORAN
70s	Alba TAR 053	PENNY WHISTLES OF ROBERT LOUIS STEVENSON (LP)	20

MOYA MORAY
62	Piccadilly 7N 35023	My Heart Will Make A Fool Of Me/You're Running Out Of Kisses	12

MORBID ANGEL
94	Earache MOSH 112	LAIBACH REMIXES EP (God Of Emptiness/Sworn To The Black/Sworn To The Black [Laibach Remix]/God Of Emptiness [Laibach Remix]) (12", p/s)	25
89	Earache MOSH 11	ALTARS OF MADNESS (LP, pink splattered vinyl, stickered sleeve)	25
89	Earache MOSH 11P	ALTARS OF MADNESS (LP, picture disc)	30
91	Earache MOSH 31	BLESSED ARE THE SICK (LP)	18
91	Earache MOSH 31	BLESSED ARE THE SICK (LP on 6 x 7" in box with 4 page insert)	40
91	Earache MOSH 48	ABOMINATIONS OF DESOLATION (LP)	25
95	Earache MOSH 134 LP	DOMINATION (LP)	20

MORE
80	Atlantic K 11561	We Are The Band/Atomic Rock (with p/s)	6
80	Atlantic K 11561T	We Are The Band/Atomic Rock (12", p/s, with patch)	8
82	Atlantic K 11744	Trickster/Hey Joe (p/s)	15
81	Atlantic K 50775	WARHEAD (LP)	12
81	Atlantic K 50875	BLOOD & THUNDER (LP)	12

A. MORE
80	Quango HMGS 10	Judy/Lucia (p/s)	5

(see also Anthony Moore)

MANDY MORE
72	Philips 6006 199	Come With Me To Jesus/Alone In My Yellow	25
73	Philips 6006 277	San Francisco 5AM/Coffee Cups	25
73	Philips 6006 343	Every Mother's Child/Blue Seasons	25
75	Fresh Air 6121 119	Rose Coloured Window/If I Smiled On Saturday	25
72	Philips 6308109	BUT THAT IS ME (LP)	250

MORECAMBE & WISE
61	HMV POP 957	We're The Guys (Who Drive Your Baby Wild)/Me And My Shadow	5
63	HMV POP 1240	Boom Oo Yatta Ta Ta/Why Did I Let You Go	5
64	HMV POP 1373	A-Wassailing/The Happiest Christmas Of All	5
66	HMV POP 1518	Now That You're Here/That Riviera Touch	5
69	Columbia DB 8646	Bring Me Sunshine/Just Around The Corner	5
71	Columbia DB 8753	Bring Me Sunshine/Just Around The Corner (reissue)	5

JOE MORELLO
62	RCA LSP 2486	IT'S ABOUT TIME (LP, also stereo [SF 7502])	12

MORGAN
73	RCA SF 8321	NOVA SOLIS (LP, with insert)	40
78	Cherry Red ARED 1	THE SLEEPER WAKES (LP)	12

(see also Mott The Hoople, Love Affair, Humpy Bong)

AL MORGAN
58	London HLU 8741	Jealous Heart/Foolish Tears	12
50s	London BEP 6043	AL MORGAN (EP, export issue)	8
51	London H-APB 1001	JEALOUS HEART (10" LP)	12
51	London H-APB 1003	LITTLE RED BOOK (10" LP)	12

MORGAN AND THE MARK 7
66	Polydor BM 56083	I'm Gonna Turn My Life Around/Undercover Man	35

MORGAN BROTHERS
59	MGM MGM 1007	Nola/Guiding Star	5
59	MGM MGM 1026	Kissin' On The Red Light/Milk From The Coconut	6

DAVID/DAVY MORGAN
65	Columbia DB 7624	Tomorrow I'll Be Gone/Ain't Got Much More To See (as Davy Morgan)	45
68	Parlophone R 5692	True To Life/Dawning (as David Morgan)	25

(see also Wishful Thinking)

DERRICK MORGAN
60	Blue Beat BB 7	Fat Man/I'm Gonna Leave You	30
60	Blue Beat BB 12	Don't Cry/I Pray For You (as Derrick Morgan & Ebonies)	25
60	Blue Beat BB 18	Lover Boy/Oh My!	25
61	Blue Beat BB 31	Now We Know/Nights Are Lonely (with Trenton Spence Orchestra)	25
61	Blue Beat BB 35	Leave Earth/Wigger Wee Shuffle (with Clue J. & His Blues Busters)	25
61	Blue Beat BB 62	Shake A Leg/Golden Rule (as Derrick & Drumbago All Stars)	25
62	Blue Beat BB 76	Sunday, Monday/Be Still	25

62	Blue Beat BB 82	Don't You Know Little Girl (actually by Derrick & Basil)/ B. GABBIDON: Hully Gully Miss Molly	25
62	Blue Beat BB 85	Come On Over/Come Back My Darling (with Buster's Group)	25
62	Blue Beat BB 91	Headache/OWEN GRAY: Millie Girl	25
62	Blue Beat BB 94	Meekly Wait/Day In And Day Out (both sides with Yvonne [Sterling])	20
62	Blue Beat BB 100	In My Heart/BELL'S GROUP: Kingston 13	30
62	Blue Beat BB 110	Are You Going To Marry Me?/Troubles (as Derrick Morgan & Patsy)	25
62	Blue Beat BB 130	Should Be Ashamed/Marjorie (with Buster's Group)	20
62	Blue Beat BB 141	Joybells (with Duke Reid Group)/Going Down To Canaan (with Denzil Dennis)	20
62	Island WI 004	Travel On/Teach Me Baby	35
62	Island WI 006	The Hop/Tell It To Me	35
62	Island WI 011	Forward March/Please Don't Talk About Me (B-side actually with Eric Morris)	25
62	Island WI 013	Cherry Home/See And Blind	35
63	Blue Beat BB 148	Jezebell/Burnette	25
63	Blue Beat BB 177	Patricia My Dear/The Girl I Left Behind	25
63	Blue Beat BB 187	Tears On My Pillow/You Should Have Known	25
63	Blue Beat BB 196	Telephone/Life Is Tough (B-side actually "Tough Man Tough")	25
63	Island WI 037	Dorothy/Leave Her Alone	25
63	Island WI 051	Blazing Fire/DERRICK & PATSY: I'm In A Jam	20
63	Island WI 053	No Raise, No Praise/Loving Baby	25
63	Island WI 080	Angel With Blue Eyes/Corner Stone	25
63	Rio R 1	Blazing Fire/Edmarine	15
64	Black Swan WI 402	Street Girl/Edmarine	15
64	Black Swan WI 425	Cherry Pie (actually by Frederick Hibbert)/BOB WALLS: Beware	20
64	Blue Beat BB 233	Let Them Talk/Sleeping	20
64	Blue Beat BB 239	Miss Lulu/DERRICK & PALOY: She's So Young (B-side act. by Derrick & Patsy)	20
64	Blue Beat BB 261	The Soldier Man/BUSTER'S ALL STARS: Jet 707	100
64	Blue Beat BB 268	Katy Katy/Call On Me	18
65	Blue Beat BB 276	Weep No More/I Want A Girl	18
65	Blue Beat BB 283	Johnny Grave/BUSTER'S ALL STARS: Yeah Yeah	30
65	Blue Beat BB 311	Throw Them Away/Baby Face	25
65	Blue Beat BB 329	Sweeter Than Honey/You Never Know (with Prince Buster)	25
65	Ska Beat JB 185	Heart Of Stone/Let Me Go (with Baba Brooks Group)	25
65	Ska Beat JB 218	Don't Call Me Daddy/BABA BROOK'S BAND: Girl's Town Ska	30
65	Island WI 193	Two Of A Kind/I Want A Lover (both actually with Naomi)	30
65	Island WI 225	Starvation/I Am A Blackhead Again	30
66	Island WI 277	It's Alright/I Need Someone (both sides actually with Blenders)	30
66	Island WI 289	Ameletia (actually by Frank Cosmo)/Don't You Worry (B-side with Patsy Todd)	20
66	Island WI 3010	Gather Together Now (Jamaican Independence Song)/Soft Hand (actually "So Hard") (both sides actually with Blenders)	30
66	Rio R 122	Cool Off Rudies/Take It Easy	25
67	Island WI 3079	Someone (actually Derrick & Pauline Morgan)/Do You Love Me (with Pauline)	18
67	Pyramid PYR 6010	Tougher Than Tough/ROLAND ALPHONSO: Song For My Father	25
67	Pyramid PYR 6013	Greedy Gal/SOUL BROTHERS: Marcus Junior	20
67	Pyramid PYR 6014	Court Dismiss/FREDERICK McCLEAN: Fine Fine Fine	20
67	Pyramid PYR 6019	Judge Dread In Court/Last Chance	30
67	Pyramid PYR 6021	Kill Me Dead/Don't Be A Fool	20
67	Pyramid PYR 6024	No Dice/I Mean It	20
67	Pyramid PYR 6025	Do The Bang Bang/Revenge	15
68	Island WI 3094	Conquering Ruler/LLOYD & DEVON: Red Rum Ball	100
68	Island WI 3101	Gimme Back/VICEROYS: Send Requests	60
68	Island WI 3159	Hold You Jack/One Morning In May	40
68	Pyramid PYR 6029	I Am The Ruler/I Mean It	25
68	Pyramid PYR 6039	Woman A Grumble/Don't Be A Fool	25
68	Pyramid PYR 6040	Want More/ROLAND ALPHONSO: Goodnight My Love	25
68	Pyramid PYR 6045	Try Me/I'm Leaving (B-side with Pauline)	25
68	Pyramid PYR 6046	King For Tonight (with Pauline)/Last Chance	25
68	Pyramid PYR 6053	Me Naw Give Up/BEVERLEY'S ALLSTARS: Dreadnaught	45
68	Pyramid PYR 6056	Ben Johnson Day/MAYTALS: Ain't Got No Tip	40
68	Pyramid PYR 6061	What's Your Grouse/BEVERLEY'S ALLSTARS: I Don't Know	25
68	Pyramid PYR 6063	Johnny Pram Pram/Don't Say (B-side with Pauline Morgan)	40
68	Amalgamated AMG 824	I Want To Go Home/JACKIE ROBINSON: Let The Little Girl Dance	20
68	Crab CRAB 3	River To The Bank/PETER KING: Reggae Limbo	6
68	Trojan TR 626	Fat Man/VAL BENNETT: South Parkway Rock	25
68	Nu Beat NB 016	I Love You/JUNIOR SMITH: Searching	25
68	Big Shot BI 506	Shower Of Rain/VAL BENNETT: It Might As Well Be Spring	12
69	Crab CRAB 8	Seven Letters/TARTANS: Lonely Heartaches (B-side act. by Clarendonians)	15
69	Crab CRAB 11	My First Taste Of Love/TARTANS: Dance All Night	12
69	Crab CRAB 18	Don't Play That Song/How Can I Forget You?	12
69	Crab CRAB 23	Send Me Some Loving/Come What May	12
69	Crab CRAB 22	Mek It Tan Deah/Gimme Back	12
69	Crab CRAB 28	Hard Time/ROY RICHARDS: Death Rides A Horse	30
69	Crab CRAB 30	Man Pon Spot/What A Thing	25
69	Crab CRAB 32	Moon Hop/Harris Wheel	10
69	Jackpot JP 700	Seven Letters/Too Bad	5
69	Unity UN 507	Belly Woman/PAULETT & LOVERS: Please Stay	5
69	Unity UN 540	Derrick - Top The Pop/GLEN ADAMS: Capone's Revenge	20
70	Unity UN 546	Return Of Jack Slade/Fat Man	20
70	Unity UN 569	The Conquering Ruler/Bedweight	40
70	Crab CRAB 44	A Night At The Hop/Telephone	30
70	Crab CRAB 51	I Wish I Was An Apple/The Story	5
70	Crab CRAB 52	Take A Letter Maria/OWEN GRAY: Just A Little Loving	5
70	Crab CRAB 57	My Dickie/Brixton Hop	5
70	Crab CRAB 58	I Can't Stand It No Longer/Beyond The Wall	5
70	Crab CRAB 59	Endlessly/Who's Making Love	5
70	Crab CRAB 62	Hurt/Julia	5
70	Pama PM 822	Love Bug/My Dickie	5
71	Bullet BU 467	Nobody's Business/Standing By	5
71	Camel CA 84	I Am Just A Sufferer/We Want To Know	5
71	Crab CRAB 67	Searching So Long/MORGAN'S ALL STARS: Drums Of Passion	5
72	Grape GR 3032	Send A Little Rain/DERRICK MORGAN ALL STARS: A Little Rain (Version)	5

MINT VALUE £

72	Jackpot JP 793	Let Them Talk/Bringing In the Guns	5
72	Jackpot JP 794	Won't Be This Way/Ain't No Love	5
72	Jackpot JP 797	Me Naw Run/All Night Long	5
72	Jackpot JP 802	Festival 10/Festival 10 - Version	5
72	Punch PH 107	Forward March/Plenty Of One	5
72	Buster PB 60	Tears On My Pillow/KEITH REID: Worried Over You (actually by Keith & Enid)	5
73	Attack ATT 8048	Derrick's Big Eleven/My Ding A Ling	5
73	Big Shot BI 617	Housewives Choice/Don't You Worry (both sides with Hortense Ellis)	5
73	Bread BR 1119	I Who Have Nothing/I'm Not Home	5
73	Downtown DT 520	Hey Little Girl/Don't Blame The Man	5
73	Pama Supreme PS 387	I'll Never Give Up/I Who Have Nothing	5
75	Klik KL 603	Wet Dreams Part 1/Wet Dreams Part 2	5
63	Island ILP 903	FORWARD MARCH (LP)	200
69	Doctor Bird DLMB 5014	BEST OF DERRICK MORGAN (LP)	90
69	Island ILP 990	DERRICK MORGAN AND HIS FRIENDS (LP)	100
69	Pama ECO 10	DERRICK MORGAN IN LONDON (LP)	70
69	Pama PSP 1006	MOON HOP (LP)	70
69	Trojan TTL 5	SEVEN LETTERS (LP)	70
70	Trojan TTL 38	FORWARD MARCH (LP, reissue)	30
			20

(see also Roland Alphonso; Frank Cosmo; Copy Cats, Derrick & Lloyd; Derrick, Morris & Patsy; Derrick & Patsy; Derrick & Naomi; Derrick & Paulette; Derrick & Pauline; Morgan's All Stars; Martin & Derrick; Larry Lawrence; Matador, Jackie Robinson)

FREDDY MORGAN
| 59 | London HL 7077 | Side Saddle/64 Rue Blondell (export issue) | 8 |

GEORGE MORGAN
68	London HLB 10197	Barbara/Sad Bird	5
57	Philips BBE 12149	COUNTRY AND WESTERN SPECTACULAR (EP)	20
68	London HAB 8353	COUNTRY HITS BY CANDLELIGHT (LP)	22

MORGAN JAMES DUO
64	Philips BF 1462	Sweet Pussycat/Bye Bye Brown Eyes	7
64	Philips BF 1325	Sometimes I'm Happy/It Ain't Necessarily So	7
67	Philips BF 1630	If It Comes To That/Tell Me Where Our Love Went Wrong	7
68	Philips BF 1707	Let's Ride/After The Storm	25
66	Fontana SFL 13071	AT THE BAR OF MUSIC (LP)	50
66	Philips BL 7702	SHHHH...TALENT STRIKES AGAIN (LP)	30

JANE MORGAN (& TROUBADORS)
55	London HL 8148	Why - Oh Why/The Heart You Break (May Be Your Own)	40
57	London HLR 8395	From The First Hello To The Last Goodbye/ Come Home, Come Home, Come Home	30
57	London HLR 8436	Around The World/It's Not For Me To Say	20
57	London HLR 8468	Fascination (with Troubadors)/Why Don't They Leave Us Alone	15
58	London HLR 8539	I'm New At The Game Of Romance/It's Been A Long Long Time (with Troubadors)	15
58	London HLR 8611	I've Got Bells On My Heart/Only One Love	15
58	London HLR 8649	Enchanted Island/Once More, My Love, Once More	5
58	London HLR 8751	The Day The Rains Came/Le Jour Ou La Pluie Viendra	5
58	London HL 7064	The Day The Rains Came/I May Never Pass This Way Again (export issue)	10
59	London HLR 8810	If Only I Could Only Live My Life Again/To Love And Be Loved	5
59	London HLR 8925	With Open Arms/I Can't Begin To Tell You	5
59	London HLR 8999	Happy Anniversary/C'est La Vie, C'est L'Amour	5
59	London HLR 8999	Happy Anniversary/C'est La Vie, C'est L'Amour (78)	15
60	London HLR 9210	Lord And Master/Where's The Boy (I Never Met)	5
63	Colpix PX 700	Red Sails In The Sunset/My Special Dream	6
67	Columbia DB 7645	Maybe/Walking The Streets In The Rain	15
67	Columbia DB 8177	The Three Bells (Jimmy Brown Song)/I Want To Be With You	6
67	HMV POP 1608	This Is My World Without You/Somebody, Someplace	10
68	Stateside SS 2082	Masquerade/Smile	6
58	London RE-R 1161	ALL THE WAY PART 1 (EP, with Troubadours)	10
58	London RE-R 1162	ALL THE WAY PART 2 (EP, with Troubadours)	10
59	London RE-R 1204	THE DAY THAT THE RAINS CAME (EP, triangular centre)	10
61	London RE-R 1331	JANE MORGAN (EP)	10
57	London HA-R 2086	FASCINATION (LP)	15
58	London HA-R 2110	ALL THE WAY (LP, with Troubadors)	15
58	London HA-R 2133	SOMETHING OLD, SOMETHING NEW, SOMETHING BORROWED, SOMETHING BLUE (LP)	15
59	London HA-R 2158	THE DAY THE RAINS CAME (LP)	15
60	London HA-R 2244	JANE IN SPAIN (LP)	15
60	London HA-R 2316	THE BALLADS OF LADY JANE (LP)	15
61	London HA-R 2371	JANE MORGAN TIME (LP)	15
61	London SAH-R 6177	THE SECOND TIME AROUND (LP, stereo)	15
62	London SAH-R 6226	AT THE COCONUT GROVE (LP, stereo)	15
62	London HA-R/SH-R 8042	WHAT NOW MY LOVE (LP, stereo)	15

(see also Troubadors, Roger Williams)

JAYE P. MORGAN
55	HMV 7M 327	The Longest Walk/Swanee	15
56	HMV 7M 348	If You Don't Want My Love/Pepper Hot Baby	25
56	HMV POP 144	If You Don't Want My Love/Pepper Hot Baby (78)	25
56	HMV 7M 365	Not One Goodbye/My Bewildered Heart	10
56	Brunswick 05519	Have You Ever Been Lonely?/Baby Don't Do It	10
57	RCA RCA 1014	You, You Romeo/Graduation Ring	10
59	MGM MGM 1005	Are You Lonesome Tonight?/Miss You	5
59	MGM MGM 1005	Are You Lonesome Tonight?/Miss You (78)	10
59	MGM MGM 1021	(It Took) One Kiss/My Reputation	5
59	MGM MGM 1039	Somebody Loses, Somebody Wins/Somebody Else Is Taking My Place	5
60	MGM MGM 1093	I Walk The Line/Wondering Where You Are	6
62	MGM MGM 1182	Heartache Named Johnny/He Thinks I Still Ache	6
62	MGM MGM 1190	Brotherhood Of Man/Nobody's Sweetheart	6
54	London RE-P 1013	JAYE P. SINGS (EP)	12
59	MGM MGM-C 793	SLOW AND EASY (LP)	15

JOHN MORGAN
| 72 | Carnaby 6302 010 | KALEIDOSCOPE (LP, white label with red 'crab' logo) | 100 |
| 70s | SWP 1007 | LIVE AT DURRANT HOUSE (LP, private pressing) | 100 |

(see also Spirit Of John Morgan)

LEE MORGAN

61	Columbia 33SX 1399	THE BIRDLAND STORY VOL. 1 (LP)	15
62	Stateside SL 10016	EXPOOBIDENT (LP)	25

MACE MORGAN THUNDERBIRDS

63	Starlite STEP 36	SHAKE AND SWING (EP)	60

MARIA MORGAN

75	President PT 449	Touch Me Baby/Reaching Out For Your Love	7

MARY MORGAN

56	Parlophone MSP 6204	Jimmy Unknown/You Are My Love	10
56	Parlophone R 4227	From The Candy Store On The Corner/No-One Was There But You	10
57	Parlophone R 4348	A Call To Arms/One For Sorrow, Two For Joy	6

P.C. ALEXANDER MORGAN

66	Columbia DB 8095	Sussex By The Sea/METROPOLITAN POLICE BAND: Thunderbirds March	8

RAY MORGAN

70	B&C CB 128	Long And Winding Road/The Sweetest Wine	5

RUSS MORGAN ORCHESTRA

55	Brunswick 05464	Alabamy Bound/SCRANTON 7: The Popcorn Song	5
55	Brunswick 05493	Dog Face Soldier/Don't Cry Sweetheart	5
56	Brunswick 05537	The Poor People Of Paris (Poor John)/Silver Moon	5
56	Brunswick 05602	Lay Down Your Arms/My Best You You	5
55	Brunswick DE 9068	MOONLIGHT MUSIC (EP)	8

SAMMY MORGAN

70	Bullet BU 455	Get Out Of This Land/SYDNEY ALL STARS: Landmark	5
70	Punch PH 57	Get Out Of This Land/SYDNEY ALL STARS: Landmark	5

TONY MORGAN

69	Beacon BEA 115	Racial Segregation/Racial Segregation (instrumental)	15
72	Beacon BEA 188	Black Skin Blue Eyed Boys/Why Build A Mountain	15

MORGAN TWINS

58	RCA RCA 1083	T.V. Hop/Let's Get Going	60
58	RCA RCA 1083	T.V. Hop/Let's Get Going (78)	40

MORGAN'S ALL STARS

71	Camel CA 76	I Love You The Most (actually by Lloyd Clarke)/I Love You The Most - Version	5

(see also B. Leggs, Derrick Morgan, Marvels)

TIM MORGON

72	MCA MU 1173	Take A Look Around/For All We Know	6

(RON PAUL) MORIN & (LUKE P.) WILSON

72	Sovereign SVNA 7252	PEACEFUL COMPANY (LP)	20

JOHNNY MORISETTE

62	Stateside SS 107	Meet Me At The Twistin' Place/Any Time Any Day Any Where	15

ALANIS MORISSETTE

95	Maverick 9362 45901	JAGGED LITTLE PILL (LP, German pressing but imported into U.K.)	70

MORNIN

69	CBS 4883	Cheatin' On You/Let Me Love You	20

MORNING

70	Liberty LBS 83463	MORNING (LP)	40
72	United Artists UAS 29337	STRUCK LIKE SILVER (LP)	20

MORNING AFTER

71	Sky SKYLP 71014	BLUE BLOOD (LP)	80

MORNING GLORY

71	Chapter 1 CHS 148	Green On The Other side Of The Mountain/Marjory Daw	7
73	Island ILPS 9237	MORNING GLORY (LP, gatefold, pink rim palm tree label)	30

(see also John Surman)

GIORGIO MORODER

66	Page One POF 003	Full Stop/Believe Me	15
67	Page One POF 028	How Much Longer Must I Wait/Bla Bla Diddley	15
80	Polydor POSP 134	Night Drive/The Apartment	7
90s	Cause-N-Effect	I Wanna Rock You (Thee Maddcat Mix)/(Thee DrumDrum Mix) (12", no p/s)	15

(see also Giorgio)

ENNIO MORRICONE ORCHESTRA

67	RCA Victor RCA 1596	A Fistful Of Dollars/The Man With No Name	6
67	RCA Victor RCA 1634	For A Few Dollars More/La Resi Dei Conti	6
69	RCA RCA 1892	Once Upon A Time In The West (Jill's Theme)/Finale	6
69	United Artists UP 35004	A Professional Gun/Paco	6
67	RCA Victor RD/SF 7875	A FISTFUL OF DOLLARS (LP, soundtrack)	20
68	RCA Victor RD 7994	A FISTFUL OF DOLLARS/FOR A FEW DOLLARS MORE/ THE GOOD, THE BAD AND THE UGLY (LP, soundtrack)	15
68	United Artists (S)ULP 1197	THE GOOD, THE BAD AND THE UGLY (LP, soundtrack)	15
69	United Artists UAS 29005	A PROFESSIONAL GUN (LP, soundtrack)	25
70	CBS 70067	LOVE CIRCLE (LP, soundtrack)	50
70	MCA MKPS 2013	TWO MULES FOR SISTER SARA (LP, soundtrack)	30
72	United Artists UAS 29345	A FISTFUL OF DYNAMITE (LP, soundtrack)	40

CHRIS MORRIS

91	Flexi FLOP 1	THE SELECT FLOPPY DISC (EP, 33rpm, poly sleeve, with magazine)	10

ERIC MORRIS

61	Starlite ST45 052	Search The World/Buster's Shack	40
61	Blue Beat BB 53	Humpty Dumpty/Corn Bread And Butter (as Eric 'Humpty Dumpty' Morris & Drumbago All Stars; [B-side actually by Drumbago All Stars])	20

MINT VALUE £

62	Blue Beat BB 74	My Forty-Five/I've Tried Everybody (as Eric 'Humpty Dumpty' Morris & Drumbago All Stars)	20
62	Blue Beat BB 81	Sinners Repent And Pray/Now And Forever More (B-side act. by Alton Ellis)	20
62	Blue Beat BB 83	Money Can't Buy Life (with Buster's Group)/A. ELLIS: True Love	20
62	Blue Beat BB 105	Pack Up Your Troubles/Oh What A Smile Can Do (with D. Cosmo & Drumbago's All Stars)	20
62	Blue Beat BB 115	G.I. Lady/Going To The River	20
62	Blue Beat BB 128	Over The Hills/Lazy Woman (with Buster's Group)	20
62	Blue Beat BB 137	Miss Peggy's Grandmother/BUSTER'S GROUP: Megaton	10
62	Blue Beat BB 140	Seven Long Years/For Your Love	20
63	Blue Beat BB 153	Lonely Blue Boy/PRINCE BUSTER: Oh We	22
63	Blue Beat BB 184	Sweet Love/BUSTER, DEREK, ERIC: Country Girl	15
64	Blue Beat BB 218	Love Can Break A Man/Worried People	20
64	Blue Beat BB 273	Stitch In Time/For Ever	20
64	Black Swan WI 412	Sampson/BABA BROOKS: Jelly Beans	30
64	Black Swan WI 414	Solomon Grundie/BABA BROOKS: Key To The City	40
64	Black Swan WI 433	Supper In The Gutter/Words Of My Mouth	20
64	Black Swan WI 439	River Come Down/Seek And You'll Find	20
64	Black Swan WI 445	Home Sweet Home/LESTER STERLING: '64 Special	20
64	Island WI 142	Penny-Reel/DUKE REID'S GROUP: Darling When (B-side act. Dotty & Bonnie)	35
64	Island WI 147	Mama No Fret/FRANKIE ANDERSON: Santa Lucia (B-side w/Roland Alphonso)	20
64	Island WI 150	Drop Your Sword/Catch A Fire (B-side actually by Roland Alphonso)	25
64	Island WI 151	What A Man Doeth/DUKE REID'S GROUP: Rude Boy (B-side actually by Baba Brooks)	22
64	Port-O-Jam PJ 4006	Oh My Dear/Lena Belle	25
64	Rio R 39	Little District/True And Just	25
64	Rio R 48	Live As A Man/Man Will Rule	25
65	Rio R 72	By The Sea/I Wasn't Around	25
65	Island WI 177	Drop Your Sword/Catch A Fire	25
65	Island WI 183	Love Can Make A Mansion (actually "Love Can Break A Man")/ Ungodly People	15
65	Island WI 185	Suddenly/Many Long Years	25
65	Island WI 199	Fast Mouth/The Harder They Come	18
65	Island WI 234	Children Of Today/BABA BROOKS: Greenfield Ska	25
65	Blue Beat BB 298	Those Teardrops/DON DRUMMOND: Ska Town	50
66	Blue Beat BB 349	I'm The Greatest/BUSTER'S ALL STARS: Picket Line	60
60s	Fab BB 30	Humpty Dumpty (as Eric 'Humpty Dumpty' Morris & Buster All Stars)/ FOLKS BROTHERS: Carolina	7

(see also Monty Morris, Byron Lee & Dragonaires, Cool Sticky, Tommy McCook, Zoot Simms, Marguerita, Cool Cats)

HELMSLEY MORRIS
67	Caltone TONE 104	Love Is Strange/DON D. JUNIOR: Sir Pratt Special	90
68	Pama PM 720	Stay Loose Mama/You Think I'm A Fool (as Hainsley Morris)	7

JOE MORRIS & ORCHESTRA
54	London HL 8088	I Had A Notion/Just Your Way Baby (78)	25
54	London HL 8098	Travelin' Man/No, It Can't Be Done (78)	15

JOHNNY MORRIS
60s	Say Disc SAY 321	ANIMAL MAGIC (EP)	12
72	Decca PA 273	THE RAILWAY STORIES VOL 4 (LP)	12
72	BBC Roundabout 15	BEDTIME STORIES (LP)	12

LIBBY MORRIS
56	Parlophone R 4225	When Liberace Winked At Me/None Of That Now	6
65	RCA RCA 1499	One Of Those Songs/The Phoenix Love Theme (Senza Fine)	5
67	Polydor 56206	Bye, Yum, Pum, Pum/Ballad Of yesterday's Idol	5
66	RCA RD 7789	AD-LIBBY (LP)	15

MILTON MORRIS
69	Upsetter US 318	No Bread And Butter/UPSETTERS: Soulful I	12

MONTY MORRIS
67	Doctor Bird DB 1067	Play It Cool/BABA BROOKS' BAND: Open The Door	50
67	Doctor Bird DB 1081	Put On Your Red Dress/BABA BROOKS' BAND: Faberge	35
68	Doctor Bird DB 1162	Last Laugh/You Really Got A Hold On Me	30
68	Pama PM 721	Say What You're Saying/Tears In Your Eyes	20
68	Nu Beat NB 007	True Romance/BUNNY & RUDDY: Rhythm And Soul	15
68	Nu Beat NB 011	Simple Simon/BUNNY & RUDDY: On The Town	30
69	Doctor Bird DB 1176	Same Face/A Little Bit Of This (miscredited to Tennors)	60
69	Big Shot BI 513	Deportation/Say I'm Back	100
69	Camel CA 12	Can't Get No Peace/UPSETTERS: For A Few Dollars More	60
69	Camel CA 28	No More Teardrops/Love Me Or Leave Me (as Monty Morris & Maples)	20
70	Unity UN 557	Do It My Way/Where In The World (Are You Going)	12
70	Explosion EX 2016	Higher Than The Highest Mountain/G.G. ALL STARS: Musical Shot	12
73	Ackee ACK 527	I'm Ready To Go/TOMMY McCOOK: Flower Pot	7

(see also Eric Morris, Monty, Derrick & Patsy, Monty & Roy, Alton Ellis)

NAGGO MORRIS
79	Hit Run DD 111	Jah Will Explain/DOCTOR PABLO: Wicked Feel It (12")	25
82	S & G SG 12	A True You Na No/Going Places (12")	50
82	S & G SG 23	False Rasta/Two Time Girl (12")	70
82	Black Roots BR0036A	A True Them No Know/Version/Africa/Version (12")	30

RICHIE MORRIS
73	Satril SAT 11	Zimbabwa/Seasons Change	8

ROGER MORRIS
72	Regal Zono. SRZA 8509	FIRST ALBUM (LP, textured gatefold sleeve, red/silver label)	400

RUSSELL MORRIS
69	Decca F 22964	The Real Thing (Parts I & II)/It's Only A Matter Of Time	80
70	Decca F 23066	Rachel/Slow Joey	5

VICTOR MORRIS
68	Amalgamated AMG 813	Now I'm Alone/Rise And Fall	10

MORRIS & MINORS
80	Round MOR 1	STATE THE OBVIOUS (EP, p/s in poly bag)	10

MORRIS & MITCH

57	Decca F 10900	Cumberland Gap/I'm Not A Juvenile Delinquent	12
57	Decca F 10929	What Is A Skiffler?/The Tommy Rot Story	10
58	Decca F 11086	Highway Patrol/Bird Dog	10
68	Trend TRE 1010	The Magical Musherishi Tourists/Mister D.J. Man	15
58	Decca DFE 6486	SIX FIVE NOTHING SPECIAL (EP)	15

MORRIS FAMILY & GOSPEL JUBILEERS

60	Top Rank JAR 322	Wake Up Jonah/He Never Complained	7

CURLEY JIM MORRISON

61	Starlite ST45 065	Air Force Blues/Didn't I Tell You	80

DOROTHY MORRISON

69	Elektra EKSN 45070	All God's Children Got Soul/Put A Little Love In Your Heart	12

HAROLD MORRISON

65	Brunswick LAT 8639	HOSS HE'S THE BOSS (LP)	12

JAMES MORRISON & TOM ENNIS

80	Topic 12T 390	JAMES MORRISON & TOM ENNIS (LP)	12

PROFESSOR MORRISON'S LOLLIPOP

68	London HLU 10228	You Got The Love/Gypsy Lady	6
69	London HLU 10254	Oo-Poo-Pah Susie/You Take It	6

TOM MORRISON

60	MGM MGM-EP 709	THE ADVENTURES OF MIGHTY MOUSE AND HIS PALS (EP)	8

VAN MORRISON

67	London HLZ 10150	Brown-Eyed Girl/Goodbye Baby (Baby Goodbye)	45
70	Warner Brothers WB 7383	Come Running/Crazy Love	8
70	Warner Brothers WB 7434	Domino/Sweet Jannie	20
70	Warner Brothers WB 7434	Domino/Sweet Jannie (DJ Copy)	35
70	President PT 328	Brown-Eyed Girl/Goodbye Baby (Baby Goodbye) (reissue)	15
72	Warner Brothers K 16210	Jackie Wilson Said/You've Got The Power	10
74	London HLM 10453	Brown-Eyed Girl/Goodbye Baby (Baby Goodbye) (2nd reissue)	10
74	Warner Brothers K 16392	Caldonia/What's Up, Crazy Pup	10
77	Warner Brothers K 16939	The Eternal Kansas City/Joyous Sound	5
77	Warner Brothers K 16986	Joyous Sound/Mechanical Bliss	6
79	Mercury 6001 121	Bright Side Of The Road/Rolling Hills (p/s)	5
89	Polydor VANX 2	Whenever God Shines His Light (Album Version) (with Cliff Richard)/ Cry For Home/I'd Love To Write Another Song (12", p/s)	8
89	Polydor VANCD 2	Whenever God Shines His Light (7" Version) (with Cliff Richard)/ I'd Love To Write Another Song/Cry For Home/Whenever God Shines His Light (Album Version) (CD)	8
68	London HA-Z 8346	BLOWIN' YOUR MIND (LP)	150
69	Warner Brothers WS 1768	ASTRAL WEEKS (LP, laminated front sleeve, flipbacks, orange label)	250
69	Warner Brothers WS 1768	ASTRAL WEEKS (LP, green label)	25
70	Warner Brothers WS 1835	MOONDANCE (LP, orange label)	150
70	Warner Brothers WS 1835	MOONDANCE (LP, green label)	20
71	Warner Brothers WS 1884	HIS BAND AND STREET CHOIR (LP, green label)	35
71	President PTLS 1045	THE BEST OF VAN MORRISON (LP)	15
71	Warner Brothers K 46114	TUPELO HONEY (LP, gatefold sleeve, green label)	15
72	Warner Brothers K 46172	SAINT DOMINIC'S PREVIEW (LP, with folded insert, green label)	40
73	Warner Brothers K 46024	ASTRAL WEEKS (LP, reissue, 'Burbank' label)	15
73	Warner Brothers K 46040	MOONDANCE (LP, reissue, 'Burbank' label)	12
73	Warner Brothers K 46066	HIS BAND AND STREET CHOIR (LP, reissue, 'Burbank' label)	12
73	Warner Brothers K 46242	HARD NOSE THE HIGHWAY (LP, gatefold sleeve, 'Burbank' label)	12
74	London HSM 5008	T.B. SHEETS (LP, laminated front cover)	15
74	Warner Brothers K 86007	IT'S TOO LATE TO STOP NOW (2-LP, gatefold sleeve, 'Burbank' label)	15
74	Warner Brothers K 56068	VEEDON FLEECE (LP, 'Burbank' label)	20
77	Bang 6467 625	THIS IS WHERE I CAME IN (LP)	12
84	Mercury MERH 54	A SENSE OF WONDER (LP, white label test pressings with "Crazy Jane On God")	25
84	Mercury MERH 54	A SENSE OF WONDER (LP, credits but doesn't play "Crazy Jane On God")	12

(see also Them)

MORRISSEY

SINGLES

88	HMV TCPOP 1618	Suedehead/I Know Very Well How I Got My Name	20
88	HMV TCPOP 1618	Suedehead/I Know Very Well How I Got My Name/ Hairdresser On Fire/Oh Well, I'll Never Learn (cassette)	15
88	HMV TCPOP 1618	Suedehead/I Know Very Well How I Got My Name/Oh Well, I'll Never Learn (mispressed cassette, plays "Ordinary Boys" instead of I Know Very Well... withdrawn)	20
88	HMV 12 POP 1618	Suedehead/I Know Very Well How I Got My Name/Hairdresser On Fire (12", 1st pressings in brown p/s)	20
88	HMV CDPOP 1618	Suedehead/I Know Very Well How I Got My Name/Hairdresser On Fire/ Oh Well, I'll Never Learn (CD)	25
88	HMV POP 1619	Everyday Is Like Sunday/Disappointed (p/s)	5
88	HMV 12 POP 1619	Everyday Is Like Sunday/Sister I'm A Poet/Disappointed/ Will Never Marry (12", p/s)	8
88	HMV CDPOP 1619	Everyday Is Like Sunday/Sister I'm A Poet/Disappointed/ Will Never Marry (CD)	12
89	HMV 12 POP 1620	The Last Of The Famous International Playboys/Lucky Lisp/Michaels Bones (12")	10
89	HMV CDPOP 1620	The Last Of The Famous International Playboys/Lucky Lisp/ Michaels Bones (CD)	15
89	HMV POP 1621	Interesting Drug/Such A Little Thing Makes Such A Big Difference (p/s)	5
89	HMV 12 POP 1621	Interesting Drug/Such A Little Thing Makes Such A Big Difference/ Sweet And Tender Hooligan (live) (12", p/s)	10
89	HMV 12 POPS 1621	Interesting Drug/Such A Little Thing Makes Such A Big Difference (12", p/s, 1 side etched)	10
89	HMV CDPOP 1621	Interesting Drug/Such A Little Thing Makes Such A Big Difference/ Sweet And Tender Hooligan (live) (CD)	10
90	HMV POP 1622	Ouija Board, Ouija Board/Yes, I Am Blind (p/s)	6
90	HMV CDPOP 1622	Ouija Board, Ouija Board/Yes, I Am Blind (CD)	10
90	HMV POP 1623	November Spawned A Monster/He Knows I'd Love To See Him (p/s)	5
90	HMV 12 POP 1623	November Spawned A Monster/Girl Least Likely To/ He Knows I'd Love To See Him (12", p/s)	10
90	HMV POP 1624	Piccadilly Palare/Get Off The Stage (p/s)	6

Dick MORRISSEY

90	HMV 12 POP 1624	Piccadilly Palare/At Amber/Get Off The Stage (12, p/s)	10
90	HMV CDPOP 1624	Piccadilly Palare/At Amber/Get Off The Stage (CD)	12
91	HMV POP 1625	Our Frank/Journalists Who Lie (p/s)	5
91	HMV 12 POP 1625	Our Frank/Journalists Who Lie/Tony The Pony (12", p/s)	10
91	HMV POP 1626	Sing Your Life/That's Entertainment (p/s)	5
91	HMV POP 1627	Pregnant For The Last Time/Skin Storm (p/s)	5
91	HMV 12 POP 1627	Pregnant For The Last Time/Skin Storm/Cosmic Dancer (live)/ Disappointed (live) (12", p/s)	10
91	HMV CDPOP 1627	Pregnant For The Last Time/Skin Storm/Cosmic Dancer (live)/ Disappointed (live) (CD)	12
92	HMV 12POP 1629	We Hate It When Our Friends Become Successful/Suedehead/I've Changed My Plea To Guilty/Pregnant For The Last Time (12", p/s)	10
92	HMV CDPOP 1629	We Hate It When Our Friends Become Successful/Suedehead/I've Changed My Plea To Guilty/Alsatian Cousin (12", p/s)	10
92	EMI CDMOZBX 1	THE SINGLES COLLECTION 1986-1992 (13 x CD singles set hinged black/purple box with numbered insert)	90
92	HMV CDPOP 1629	Certain People I Know/You've Had Her/Jack The Ripper (CD)	15
94	Parlophone R 6372	The More You Ignore Me, The Closer I Get/Used To Be A Sweet Boy (poster, numbered p/s)	5
94	Parlophone 12R6372	The More You Ignore Me, The Closer I Get/Used To Be A Sweet Boy/I'd Love To (poster, numbered p/s)	8
94	Parlophone RDJ 6372	The More You Ignore, Me The Closer I Get/Used To Be A Sweet Boy (yellow p/s)	12
94	Parlophone 12 R6383	Hold Onto Your Friends/Moonriver (12", gatefold sleeve)	12
95	Parlophone R 6400	Boxers/Have-A-Go Merchant (p/s)	6
95	RCA 74321332947	Boy Racer/London (Live Version) (p/s)	6
95	RCA 74321332952	Boy Racer/Spring Heeled Jim/Why Don't You Find Out For Yourself (CD)	10
95	RCA Victor LC 0316	Dagenham Dave/Nobody Loves Us (p/s)	6
97	Island IS 667	Alma Matters/Heir Apparent (p/s)	20
97	Island IS 671	Roy's Keen/Lost (p/s)	20
97	Island 12 IS 671	Roy's Keen/Lost/The Edges Are No Longer Paralle (12")	40
97	Island IS 686	Satan Rejected My Soul/Now I Am A Was (p/s)	25
00	EMI EMI 8872932	SINGLES 88-91 (10 x CDs, card sleeves)	40
01	EMI EMI 8797452	SINGLES 91-95 (9 X CDs, card sleeves, in box)	40
06	Attack ATKTW 020	First Of The Gang To Die (12" 4-track EP)	8
06	Attack ATKTW 019	Irish Blood, English Heart (12" 4-track EP)	8
06	Attack ATKTW025	I Just Want To See The Boy Happy/Sweetie-Pie/I Want The One I Can't Have/ Speedway/Late Night, Maudlin Street (12" picture disc, 1,000 only)	8

ALBUMS

90	HMV CLP 3788	BONA DRAG (LP)	20
91	EMI CSD 3789	KILL UNCLE (LP, gatefold)	18
92	HMV CSD 3790	YOUR ARSENAL (LP)	30
93	HMV CSD 3791	BEETHOVEN WAS DEAF (LP)	25
94	Parlophone/EMI PCSD 148	VAUXHALL AND I (LP, gatefold)	60
95	RCA Victor 29953-1	SOUTHPAW GRAMMAR (LP, with limited edition booklet)	60
95	RCA 29953 1	SOUTHPAW GRAMMAR (LP)	30
95	Parlophone PCS 7374	BONA DRAG (LP, reissue)	20
95	Parlophone PCS 7375	KILL UNCLE (LP, reissue)	20
95	Parlophone PCS 7376	VIVA HATE (LP, reissue)	20
97	Island ILPS 8059	MALADJUSTED (LP)	40
97	EMI EMC 2771	SUEDEHEAD: THE BEST OF MORRISSEY (2-LP, gatefold)	50
97	Parlophone PCSD 163	WORLD OF MORRISSEY (LP, classic yellow/black Parlophone label)	50
04	Sanctuary ATKLP 001	YOU ARE THE QUARRY (LP, 5,000 only)	20
06	Attack ATKLP 016	RINGLEADER OF THE TORMENTORS (LP, gatefold)	40
09	Polydor/Decca SKL6014/ 4781581	YEARS OF REFUSAL (LP)	20

PROMOS

88	Factory FA 244+	I Know Very Well How I Got My Note Wrong (7" promo, as Vincent Gerrard and Stephen Patrick, 1,000 only)	40
88	Factory FACD 244+	I Know Very Well How I Got My Note Wrong (CD promo, as Vincent Gerrard and Stephen Patrick, 1,000 only)	40
88	HMV 12POP DJ 1618	Suedehead/I Know Very Well How I Got My Name/Hairdresser On Fire (12" promo)	20
88	HMV 12 POP DJ 1619	Everyday Is Like A Sunday (12", promo, 1-sided)	20
89	HMV 12POP DJ 1620	The Last Of The Famous International Playboys/Lucky Lisp/Michaels Bones (12" promo)	15
89	EMI SPM 29	Interesting Drug/Such A Little Thing Makes Such A Big Difference (12" die cut red sleeve, promo)	15
89	EMI SPM 29	Interesting Drug/etched B side (12", die cut black sleeve, promo)	60
90	HMV (No Cat. No)	November The Second (12" promo, white label 'Dance Mix' destroyed on order of Morrissey, i known copy)	2000
90	HMV POPDJ 1624	Piccadilly Palare/Get Off The Stage (promo, in die-cut HMV sleeve)	30
91	HMV POP DJ 1626	Sing Your Life/That's Entertainment (promo, die-cut HMV sleeve)	30
91	HMV POP DJ1627	Pregnant For The Last Time/Skin Storm (promo)	30
92	HMV POP DJ 1630	You're The One For Me, Fatty/You're The One For Me, Fatty (10", A-side plays at 45rpm, B-side at 78rpm, die-cut sleeve)	30
92	HMV POP DJ 1629	We Hate It When Our Friends Become Successful/We Hate It When Our Friends Become Sucessful (10", A-side plays at 45rpm, B-side at 78rpm, die-cut sleeve)	30
93	HMV POPDJ 1631	Certain People I Know/Jack The Ripper (die-cut 'Moz' p/s, 300 only)	75
93	HMV POPDJ 1632	Jack The Ripper/Sister I'm A Poet (p/s)	30
95	Parlophone CDRDJ 6243	Sunny/Black-Eyed Susan/A Swallow On My Neck (CD)	18
94	Parlophone CDRDJ 6372	The More You Ignore, Me Closer I Get/Used To Be A Sweet Boy/ I'd Love To (CD, yellow card p/s)	12
94	Parlophone CDRDJ 6372	The More You Ignore, Me Closer I Get (CD, with "45rpm" logo on disc, withdrawn)	45
94	Parlophone R 6383	Hold Onto Your Friends/Moonriver (promo in different p/s, 150 only)	100
94	Parlophone CDRDJ 6383	Hold On To Your Friends/Moonriver (CD, card p/s)	10
95	Parlophone RDJ 6400	Have-A-Go Merchant/Whatever Happens, I Love You (p/s)	25
95	Parlophone CDRDJ 6400	Have-A-Go Merchant/Whatever Happens, I Love You (CD, 'skinhead' card p/s)	25
95	Parlophone/EMI RDJ 6400	Have-A-Go Merchant/Whatever Happens, I Love You p/s, promo for unreleased single)	50
95	Parlophone CDRDJX 6400	Boxers/Have-A-Go Merchant/Whatever Happens I Love You (CD)	6
95	RCA SOLO 1	OUTSIDE TOUR SAMPLER (CD promo features Boy Racer)	60
04	Sanctuary (No Cat. No)	YOU ARE THE QUARRY (CD-R interview promo)	35

(see also Smiths, Durutti Column)

DICK MORRISSEY

61	77' LEU 12/8	HAVE YOU HEARD? (LP)	350
61	Fontana TFL 5149	IT'S MORRISSEY MAN! (LP)	400

67	Mercury 20093	HERE AND NOW AND SOUNDING GOOD (LP)	300
67	Mercury 20077MCL	STORM WARNING (LP)	350

(see also If, Morrissey-Mullen)

MORRISSEY-MULLEN
79	Harvest SHSP 4098	CAPE WRATH (LP)	12

(see also Dick Morrissey)

BUDDY MORROW & HIS ORCHESTRA
53	HMV 7M 145	Heap Big Beat/I Can't Get Started	6
53	HMV 7M 151	I Can't Get Started/Heap Big Beat (reissue)	6
53	HMV 7M 162	Dragnet/Your Mouth's Got A Hole In It	8
54	HMV 7M 216	Knock On Wood (with Shaye Cogan)/All Night Long	10
60	RCA RCA 1167	Staccato's Theme/Scraunchy	6
60	RCA RCX 174	IMPACT (EP)	10

ELLA MAE MORSE
53	Capitol CL 13960	Forty Cups Of Coffee/Oh! You Crazy Moon (78)	10
55	Capitol CL 14223	Bring Back My Baby To Me/Lovey Dovey	50
55	Capitol CL 14223	Bring Back My Baby To Me/Lovey Dovey (78)	20
55	Capitol CL 14303	Smack Dab In The Middle/Yes, Yes I Do	50
55	Capitol CL 14303	Smack Dab In The Middle/Yes, Yes I Do (78)	20
55	Capitol CL 14332	Livin', Livin', Livin'/Heart Full Of Hope	40
55	Capitol CL 14332	Livin', Livin', Livin'/Heart Full Of Hope (78)	20
55	Capitol CL 14341	Razzle-Dazzle/Ain't That A Shame (with Big Dave & His Music)	100
55	Capitol CL 14341	Razzle-Dazzle/Ain't That A Shame (with Big Dave & His Music) (78)	60
55	Capitol CL 14362	Seventeen/Piddily Patter Song (with Big Dave & His Music)	100
55	Capitol CL 14362	Seventeen/Piddily Patter Song (with Big Dave & His Music) (78)	60
55	Capitol CL 14376	Birmin'ham/An Occasional Man	40

(The 45s listed above were originally issued with triangular centres; later round-centres issues are worth around half to two-thirds of these values.)

55	Capitol CL 14376	Birmin'ham/An Occasional Man (78)	20
56	Capitol CL 14508	When Boy Kiss Girl (It's Love)/Sing-Ing-Ing-Ing	30
56	Capitol CL 14508	When Boy Kiss Girl (It's Love)/Sing-Ing-Ing-Ing (78)	15
56	Capitol CL 14572	Rock And Roll Wedding/Down In Mexico	40
56	Capitol CL 14572	Rock And Roll Wedding/Down In Mexico (78)	20
57	Capitol CL 14726	What Good'll It Do Me/Mister Money Maker	20
57	Capitol CL 14726	What Good'll It Do Me/Mister Money Maker (78)	10
57	Capitol CL 14760	I'm Gone/Sway Me	20
57	Capitol CL 14760	I'm Gone/Sway Me (78)	10
55	Capitol EAP1 513	BARRELHOUSE BOOGIE AND THE BLUES (EP)	20
54	Capitol LC 6687	BARRELHOUSE BOOGIE AND THE BLUES (10" LP)	40

(see also 'Tennessee' Ernie Ford)

ELLA MAE MORSE & FREDDIE SLACK
67	Ember SPE 6605	ROCKIN' BREW (LP)	25

MORTA SKULD
93	Peaceville CC 4	Sacrificial Rite/VITAL REMAINS: Amulet Of The Conquering (clear vinyl, p/s)	15
93	Deaf DEAF 11	DYING REMAINS (LP)	25
94	Deaf DEAF 15	HUMANITY FADES (LP)	20

AZIE MORTIMER
60	London HLX 9237	Lips/Wrapped Up In A Dream	100

MIKE MORTON CONGREGATION
70	Plexium PXM 19	Burning Bridges/You Gotta Be Mine	15

LIONEL MORTON
67	Philips BF 1578	What To Do With Laurie/I'll Just	7
67	Philips BF 1607	First Love Never Dies/Try Not To Cry	7
69	RCA RCA 1875	Waterloo Road/Floral Street	7

(see also Four Pennies)

MANDY MORTON (BAND)
79	Banshee BANS 791	Song For Me (Music Prince)/Little Inbetween (with Spriguns)	15
80	Polydor 2382 101	Ghost Of Christmas Past/Black Nights (p/s)	6
78	Banshee BAN 1011	MAGIC LADY (LP, with lyric insert, 1,000 only)	300
78	Banshee BAN 1011	MAGIC LADY (LP, with lyric insert, blue vinyl, 20 only)	500
80	Polydor 2382 101	SEA OF STORMS (LP, solo, with insert)	60
83	Banshee	VALLEY OF LIGHT (LP, private pressing)	100

MORWELLS
79	Attack TACK 5	Kingston Twelve Tuffie/PRINCE JAMMY: Jammin' For Survival (12")	12
79	Greensleeves GRED 17	Thief A Dub (12")	40
77	Burning Sounds BS 1006	CRAB RACE (LP)	50
79	Bushays BFMLP 100	COOL RUNNING (LP)	35
80	Trojan TRLS 193	A1 DUB (LP)	35

MOSAIC
71	Parlophone R5928	Blue Bird/Bird Of Fire	15

MOSAICS
66	Columbia DB 7990	Let's Go Drag Racing/Now That You're Here	35

MOSCOVITE FIVE
82	In Phaze	WINTER WEEKENDS (cassette)	20

ADRIAN MOSELY
68	Redcar RC001	Silent Night/Ellusive Face	60

JOSHUA MOSES
78	More Cut MCT 6001	Africa Is Our Land/Home (12", die-cut p/s)	70

PABLO MOSES
75	Treble C CCC 01	I Man A Grasshopper/Grasshopper (Part 2)	8
75	Treble C CCC 09	Blood Money/Version	8
76	Lizzard 001	We Should Be In Angola/Dubbing In Angola	25

MINT VALUE £

76	Klik KL 625	Give I Fe I Name/Version	8
80	Island 12WIP	Dubbing Is A Must/Revolutionary Step (12")	25
77	Klik KLP 9026	REVOLUTIONARY DREAM (LP)	45
78	Different GETL 104	REVOLUTIONARY DREAM (LP)	20
80	Island ILPS 9541	A SONG (LP)	12

MOSKOW
78	Moskow SRS 2103	Man From U.N.C.L.E./White Black (p/s)	8
79	Rialto TREB 107	Man From U.N.C.L.E./Too Much Commotion (reissue in different p/s)	5

BILL MOSS
69	Pama PM 765	Sock It To 'Em Soul Brother (Parts 1 & 2)	20
70	Pama PM 796	Number One/MOHAWKS: Lanscape	25

BUDDY MOSS
60s	Kokomo K 1003	GEORGIA BLUES VOLUME 2 (LP)	60

JENNY MOSS
63	Columbia DB 7061	Hobbies/Big Boys	40

STIRLING MOSS
60	HMV 7EG 8583	MOTOR RACING WITH STERLING MOSS (EP)	10
61	Redemption RLP 5004	THE STIRLING MOSS STORY (LP)	12

TEDDY MOSS/JOSH WHITE
62	Jazz Collector JEL 5	THE MALE BLUES (EP)	10

(see also Josh White)

GERRY MORRIS
72	york SYK 525	Come On Home/Nothing To Declare	20
73	York SYK 557	Sunlove/Only The Beginning	30
73	York FYK 415	ONLY THE BEGINNING (LP)	150

MOST
79	SRT SRTS/CUS/570	Carefree/In And Out (1,000 only stamped lyric insert)	60

ABE MOST OCTET
55	London RE-P 1028	PRESENTING THE ABE MOST OCTET (EP)	20

MOST DOMINANT
93	Kold Sweat KSEP210	PUSHED TO DA LIMIT (EP)	8

MICKIE MOST (& GEAR)
63	Decca F 11664	Mr. Porter/Yes Indeed I Do	30
63	Columbia DB 7117	The Feminine Look/Shame On You Boy	15
63	Columbia DB 7180	Sea Cruise/It's A Little Bit Hot	15
64	Columbia DB 7245	Money Honey/That's Alright (as Mickey Most & Gear)	20

(see also Most Brothers)

MOST BROTHERS
57	Decca F 10968	Whistle Bait/I'm Comin' Home	20
57	Decca F 10968	Whistle Bait/I'm Comin' Home (78)	15
58	Decca F 10998	Whole Lotta Woman/Teen Angel	20
58	Decca F 10998	Whole Lotta Woman/Teen Angel (78)	25
58	Decca F 11040	Don't Go Home/Dottie	20

(see also Mickie Most, Alex Murray)

MOTHER EARTH
69	Mercury MF 1081	Goodnight Melda Grebe The Telephone Company Has Cut Us Off/ I Did My Part	8
71	Reprise K 14089	Temptation Took Control Of Me/I'll Be Long Gone	5
68	Mercury SMCL 20143	LIVING WITH THE ANIMALS (LP)	12
69	Mercury SMCL 20173	MAKE A JOYFUL NOISE (LP)	12
69	Mercury SMCL 20179	TRACY NELSON COUNTRY (LP)	12
71	Mercury 6338 023	SATISFIED (LP)	12
71	Reprise K 44133	BRING ME HOME (LP)	12

MOTHER FREEDOM BAND
77	All Platinum 6146326	Beautiful Summer Day/Flick Of the Wrist	20

MOTHER GONG
81	Butt BUTT 003	ROBOT WOMEN (LP)	12
82	Shanghai HAI 100	ROBOT WOMEN 2 (LP)	12
83	Shanghai HAI 109	ROBOT WOMEN 3 (LP)	12

(see also Gong)

MOTHER NATURE
71	B & C CB 166	Orange Days And Purple Nights/Where Did She Go	12
72	Kingdom KV8003	Once There Was A Time/Clear Blue Sky	10

MOTHER NATURES CHILDREN
77	President PT468	Money Back Ride/Rollin Down	10

MOTHER YOD
97	Prescription DRUG 1	MOTHER YOD (LP, 99 copies only)	25

MOTHERLIGHT
69	Morgan Bluetown BT 5003	BOBAK, JONS, MALONE (LP)	600

(see also Will Malone [Voice Band], Orange Bicycle)

MOTHERLODE
69	Buddah 201 064	When I Die/Hard Life	6
69	Buddah 2318 043	WHEN I DIE (LP)	15

MOTHER'S RUIN
81	Spectra SPC 1	Streetfighters/Leaving You (in p/s)	55
81	Spectra SPC 1	Streetfighters/Leaving You	40
82	Spectra SPC 6	Street Lights/Turn A Corner (p/s)	20
82	Spectra SPC 7	Say It's Not True/It's Illogical (p/s)	35
81	Off Course G33303	WANT MORE (LP)	12
82	Spectra SPA 1	ROAD TO RUIN (LP)	12

MOTHER'S SONS
70	J-Dan JDN 4415	I Want To Tell The World/Underground Man	6

MOTHMEN
79	Absurd ABSURD 6	Does It Matter Irene?/Please Let Go (p/s)	5
81	Do It DUN 12	Show Me Your House And Car/People People (p/s, deleted after 1 day)	8
81	Do It DUNIT 12	Show Me Your House And Car/People People (12", p/s, deleted after 1 day)	10
81	Do It DUN 14	Temptation/People People (p/s)	5
82	Do It DUN 19	Wadada/As They Are (p/s)	5
82	Do It RIDE 9	ONE BLACK DOT (LP)	12
80s	On-U-Sound LP 2	PAY ATTENTION (LP)	15

(see also Alberto Y Lost Trios Paranoias)

MOTHS
69	Deroy	MOTHS (LP, private pressing in plain white sleeve)	500

MOTIFFE
72	Deroy 777	MOTIFFE (LP, private pressing in hand-illustrated white sleeve)	300

MOTION
79	DD Records DDLP04	MOTION (LP)	40

(see also Aswad)

MOTIONS
66	Pye International 7N 25390	Stop Your Crying/Every Step I Take	25

MOTIVATION
68	Direction 58-3248	Come On Down/Little Man	35

FRANK MOTLEY & KING HERBERT
99	Jazzman JM 002	Ya Ya/Ooga Boogaloo (as Frank Motley & The Bridge Crossing)	10
98	Jazzman JMANLP 001	CANADA'S MESSAGE TO THE METERS (THE BEST OF...) (LP)	20

MOTLEY CREW
68	MJB BEV 429	MOTLEY CREW (EP, hand made sleeve)	25

MÖTLEY CRÜE
84	Elektra E 9756T	Looks That Kill/Piece Of The Action/Live Wire (12", p/s with free tattoo)	15
84	Elektra E 9756TP	Looks That Kill/Piece Of The Action/Live Wire (12", picture disc)	20
84	Elektra E 9732T	Too Young To Fall In Love/Take Me To The Top (12", p/s, some with poster)	15
86	Elektra EKR 16TP	Smokin' In The Boys' Room/Use It Or Lose It (mask-shaped pic disc & sticker)	12
86	Elektra EKR 33P	Smokin' In The Boys' Room/Home Sweet Home (2 different interlocking mask-shaped picture disc set)	20
86	Elektra EKR 33T	Smokin' In The Boys' Room/Home Sweet Home/Shout At The Devil (12", p/s with poster)	8
87	Elektra EKR 59V	Girls, Girls, Girls/Sumthin' For Nuthin' ('X-rated' stickered p/s, 3,000 only)	8
87	Elektra EKR 59B	Girls, Girls, Girls/Sumthin' For Nuthin'/Smokin' In The Boys' Room (12", box set with patch)	8
87	Elektra EKR 59TP	Girls, Girls, Girls/Sumthin' For Nuthin'/Smokin' In The Boys' Room (12", picture disc)	8
88	Elektra EKR 65TB	You're All I Need/Wild Side/Home Sweet Home/Looks That Kill (12", box set with poster, tour pass & patch)	10
83	Elektra 9602 89-1	SHOUT AT THE DEVIL (LP, with bonus 12" picture disc & poster)	18
83	Elektra 9602 89-1	SHOUT AT THE DEVIL (LP, gatefold 'pentagram' black sleeve & inner)	12

MOTORCYCLE RIDE
93	Fierce FRIGHT 060	Union City Blue/Atomic (p/s)	12

(see also Ride)

MOTORDAMN
07	DJB66613	Over The Top (MotorDamn)/Ballroom Blitz (The Damned with Lemmy)	6

MOTÖRHEAD
76	Stiff BUY 9	Leaving Here/White Line Fever (Unreleased, but included in Stiff box set of first 10 singles and some also sold via mail order)	30
77	Chiswick S 13	Motörhead/City Kids (p/s)	10
77	Chiswick S 13A	Motörhead/City Kids (12", p/s)	12
78	Bronze BRO 60	Louie Louie/Tear Ya Down (p/s)	6
79	Bronze BRO 67	Overkill/Too Late, Too Late (p/s, iwith 'Overkill' badge)	10
79	Bronze BRO 67	Overkill/Too Late, Too Late (p/s)	5
79	Bronze 12 BRO 67	Overkill/Too Late, Too Late (12", p/s)	10
79	Bronze BRO 78	No Class/Like A Nightmare (3 different sleeves)	50
79	Bronze BRO 85	Bomber/Over The Top (p/s, on blue vinyl)	8
79	Big Beat NS 13	Motörhead/City Kids (p/s, black, pink, blue, orange or white vinyl)	5
80	Big Beat NSP 13	Motörhead/City Kids (p/s, black & white picture disc)	8
80	Big Beat NSP 13	Motörhead/City Kids (p/s, blue & white picture disc)	12
80	Bronze BRO 92 DJ	Leaving Here (live)/Stone Dead Forever (live) (2-track promo for Golden Years EP, no p/s)	40
80	Bronze BRO 106	Ace Of Spades/Dirty Love (p/s)	10
80	Bronze BROX 106	Ace Of Spades/Dirty Love (12", 'Xmas' sleeve)	8
81	Bronze BROP 124	Motörhead (live)/Over The Top (live) (picture disc)	6
82	Bronze BRO 146	Iron Fist/Remember Me I'm Gone (p/s, blue vinyl)	12
82	Bronze BRO 146	Iron Fist/Remember Me I'm Gone (p/s, red vinyl)	5
82	Bronze BRO 151	Stand By Your Man/No Class/Masterplan (p/s, as Lemmy & Wendy O. Williams)	8
83	Bronze BRO 165	I Got Mine/Turn You Round Again (p/s)	8
83	Bronze BROX 165	I Got Mine/Turn You Round Again (12", p/s)	8
83	Bronze BRO 167	Shine/Hoochie Coochie Man (live)	5
83	Bronze BROX 167	Shine/Hoochie Coochie Man (live)/Don't Need Religion (live) (12", p/s)	8
83	Bronze BROX 167/BROX 92	Shine/Hoochie Coochie Man (live)/Don't Need Religion (live)/ THE GOLDEN YEARS (12", p/s, stickered, shrinkwrapped double pack)	18
83	Lyntone LYN 4383	In Their Own Words/BRONZ: Taken By Storm (flexi free with Kerrang! mag)	10
84	Bronze BRO 185	Killed By Death/Under The Knife (p/s)	5
84	Bronze BROP 185	Killed By Death/Under The Knife (logo skull-shaped picture disc)	12
84	Bronze BROX 185	Killed By Death (Full Length Version)/Under The Knife/Under The Knife (12", stickered p/s, with poster)	10
88	GWR GWR 15	Ace Of Spades/Dogs/Traitor (sold at concerts & through fan club, no p/s)	15
90	Epic 656578 0	The One To Sing The Blues/Dead Man's Hand (shaped picture disc)	8
80	Big Beat SWT 61	BEER DRINKERS EP (12", p/s, scarce pink or orange vinyl)	8
80	Big Beat SWT 61	BEER DRINKERS EP (12", p/s, brown vinyl)	15

MOTORS

81	Bronze BROX 116	ST. VALENTINES DAY MASSACRE (10" EP, with Girlschool)	12
77	Chiswick WIK 2	MOTÖRHEAD (LP, black & white laminated sleeve with inner)	15
77	Chiswick WIK 2	MOTÖRHEAD (LP, black and silver sleeve with inner, 600 only)	100
77	Chiswick CWK 3008	MOTÖRHEAD (LP, white vinyl)	18
79	Bronze BRON 515	OVERKILL (LP, green vinyl)	30
79	Bronze BRON 523	BOMBER (LP, 3 different shades of blue vinyl)	15
80	Bronze BRONG 531	ACE OF SPADES (LP, gold vinyl, stickered sleeve)	15
80	Big Beat WIK 2	MOTÖRHEAD (LP, reissue, red or clear vinyl with inner sleeve)	15
81	Bronze BRONG 535	NO SLEEP 'TIL HAMMERSMITH (LP, gold vinyl, stickered sleeve)	20
84	Bronze/Pro MOTOR 1	NO REMORSE (2-LP, leather sleeve with inners)	20
86	GWR GWRLP 1	ORGASMATRON (LP, picture disc)	15
91	Epic 467481-0	1916 (LP, picture disc, stickered PVC sleeve)	15
91	Epic 467481 9	1916 (CD, 'tour' picture disc shrinkwrapped with booklet, stickered case)	18
93	Castle CTVLP 125	ALL THE ACES (2-LP, gatefold)	15
93	Castle/Bronze CTVCD 125	ALL THE ACES (CD, numbered promo, in box with metal skull, 10 only)	200
00	Metal-Is MISL 002	THE BEST OF...(3-LP, numbered with insert & bonus exclusive live EP)	45
04	SPV 22325	INFERNO (2xLP)	18

(see also Lemmy & Upsetters, Sam Gopal, Hawkwind, Girlschool, Wild Horses, Filthy Phil & Fast Eddie, Young & Moody, Rocking Vickers, Blue Goose, Motordamn, Persian Rise)

MOTORS

78	Virgin V 2089	APPROVED BY THE MOTORS (LP, withdrawn group photo sleeve & inner sleeve)	12

(see also Ducks Deluxe, Heroes, Snakes)

MOTORWAY

79	Neat NEAT 01	All I Wanna Be Is Your Romeo/It's Easy When You're Alone	10

MOTT THE HOOPLE

69	Island WIP 6072	Rock And Roll Queen/Road To Birmingham	25
71	Island WIP 6105	Midnight Lady/The Debt (in p/s)	18
71	Island WIP 6105	Midnight Lady/The Debt	6
71	Island WIP 6112	Downtown/Home	10
74	CBS 2439	Foxy Foxy/Trudi's Song (cherry vinyl)	5
76	CBS 3963	All The Young Dudes/Roll Away The Stone (p/s)	5
69	Island ILPS 9108	MOTT THE HOOPLE (LP, gatefold sleeve, pink label with white 'i' logo; with "Backsliding Fearlessly" in correct order)	100
69	Island ILPS 9108	MOTT THE HOOPLE (LP, pink label; mispress with 5 alternate mixes & Road To Birmingham in place of "Backsliding Fearlessly" or one alternative mix with "Road To Birmingham", and "Rock And Roll Queen" correctly credited. This price for each copy)	80
70	Island ILPS 9119	MAD SHADOWS (LP, pink label with pink 'i' logo, gatefold sleeve)	40
71	Island ILPS 9144	WILD LIFE (LP, gatefold, pink rim palm tree label)	40
71	Island ILPS 9178	BRAIN CAPERS (LP, pink rim palm tree label & inner sleeve, with mask)	90
71	Island ILPS 9178	BRAIN CAPERS (LP, pink rim palm tree label & inner sleeve, without mask)	20
72	CBS 65184	ALL THE YOUNG DUDES (LP, with inner sleeve)	30
72	Island ILPS 9215	ROCK AND ROLL QUEEN (LP, 'pink rim palm tree' label)	20
73	CBS 69038	MOTT (LP, die-cut gatefold sleeve with plastic flap, inner sleeve, orange label, stickered)	25
74	CBS 569062	THE HOOPLE (LP, with insert)	40
80	Island IRSP 8	TWO MILES FROM HEAVEN (LP, early copies listing "Moving On" on rear sleeve)	20
80	Island IRSP 8	TWO MILES FROM HEAVEN (LP)	12

(see also Mott, Ian Hunter, At Last The 1958 Rock & Roll Show, Morgan, Mick Ronson, British Lions, Luther Grosvenor, Charlie Woolfe)

TONY MOTTOLA

61	London HAZ 2442	STRING BAND STRUM-ALONG (LP, also stereo SAHZ 6231)	12

KEN MOULE'S LONDON JAZZ CHAMBER GROUP

70	Ember EMB S 275	Mae West/Zsa Zsa Gabor (in p/s)	15
70	Ember EMB S 275	Mae West/Zsa Zsa Gabor	5
69	Ember CJS 823	ADAM'S RIB SUITE (LP)	70

(see also London Jazz Chamber Group, Ken Moule Seven)

KEN MOULE SEVEN

55	Decca DFE 6261	ARRANGED BY KEN MOULE (EP)	8
57	Decca LK 4192	KEN MOULE ARRANGES FOR (LP)	25
58	Decca LK 4261	JAZZ AT TOAD HALL (LP)	30

(see also London Jazz Chamber Group)

MATTIE MOULTRIE

67	CBS 202547	That's How Strong My Love Is/The Saddest Story Ever Told	20
67	CBS 202547	That's How Strong My Love Is/The Saddest Story Ever Told (DJ Copy)	40

MOUND CITY BLUE BLOWERS

55	HMV 7EG 8096	MOUND CITY BLUE BLOWERS (EP)	8
60	Collector JEL 1	BLUES BLOWING JAZZ VOL. 1 (EP)	10

MOUNT RUSHMORE

68	Dot DOT 115	Stone Free/She's No Good To Me	10

MOUNTAIN

70	Bell BLL 1112	Mississippi Queen/The Laird	15
70	Bell BLL 1125	Sittin' On A Rainbow/To My Friend	20
71	Island WIP 6119	Roll Over Beethoven/Crossroader	15
70	Bell SBLL 133	MOUNTAIN CLIMBING! (LP)	25
71	Island ILPS 9148	NANTUCKET SLEIGHRIDE (LP, 'pink rim palm tree' label)	20
71	Island ILPS 9178	FLOWERS OF EVIL (LP, pink rim palm tree label)	12
72	Island ILPS 9199	LIVE - THE ROAD GOES EVER ON (LP, 'pink rim' label, 'palm tree' logo)	12

(see also West Bruce & Laing, Leslie West, Jolliver Arkansas)

MOUNTAIN ASH

75	Witches Bane LKLP 6036	THE HERMIT (LP, private pressing with insert)	200

MOUNTAIN GOATS

02	4AD AD 2208	See America Right/New Chevrolet In Flames (p/s)	5
03	4AD AD 2306	Palmcorder Yajna/Butter Teeth (p/s)	5

MOUNTAIN LINE

74	Xtra XTRA 1140	MOUNTAIN LINE (LP)	12

75	Xtra XTRA 1147	HORSEPOWER (LP)	12

MOUNTAIN MEN
65	Eos CE 717	Too Many People/Without You	250

VALERIE MOUNTAIN
61	Columbia DB 4660	Go It Alone/Gentle Christ	5
62	Pye 7N 15450	Some People/Yes You Did	5
62	Pye NEP 24158	SOME PEOPLE - SOUNDTRACK (EP, some tracks by Eagles)	8

(see also Eagles)

NORMAN MOURANT
79	Folk Heritage FHR 100	IT'S HARD TO LIVE ON DREAMS (LP)	12

MOURNING AFTER
94	Detour DR 017	Doin' Me In/Out For The Count (p/s, 100 blue vinyl)	6

MOURNING PHASE
71	Eden	MOURNING PHASE (LP, private pressing)	200
91	Eden EDEN 1	EDEN (LP, reissue of "Mourning Phase")	20

MOUSE
73	Sovereign SOV 122	We Can Make It/It's Happening To Me And You	20
74	Sovereign SOV 127	All The Fallen Teen Angels/Just Came Back	12
73	Sovereign SVNA 7262	LADY KILLER (LP, gatefold sleeve)	300

(see also Ginhouse, Ray Russell Quartet, Running Man)

MOUSE & TRAPS
68	President PT 174	L.O.V.E. Love/Beg Borrow And Steal	40
68	President PT 210	Sometimes You Just Can't Win/Crying Inside	20

MOUSEFOLK
80s	Tea Time SURFS UP 03	Grannie's Cake Crisis/Mrs Marr's Daughter (foldaround p/s, with badge)	5

MOUSEHOUSE
79	Fort FORT 001	Where Young Cats Fear To Tread/When Dave Says He Has He Hasn't	5

MOUSETRAP
71	Aurora AU 4324	Susie/Greenfields	35

MOUTH TO MOUTH
79	Mouth To Mouth MY 1	Gallery Of Dolls/Life In The Subbterain (white label stamped sleeve)	100

ALPHONSE MOUZON
76	United Artists UAG 20005	THE MAN INCOGNITO (LP)	12

ALPHONSE MOUZON & LARRY CORYELL
77	Atlantic K 50382	BACK TOGETHER AGAIN (LP)	12

(see also Larry Coryell)

MOVE
66	Deram DM 109	Night Of Fear/Disturbance	8
67	Deram DM 117	I Can Hear The Grass Grow/Wave The Flag And Stop The Train	10
67	Regal Zonophone RZ 3001	Flowers In The Rain/(Here We Go Round) The Lemon Tree	7
67	Regal Zonophone	Cherry Blossom Clinic/Vote For Me (unissued)	0
68	Regal Zonophone RZ 3005	Fire Brigade/Walk Upon The Water	7
68	Regal Zonophone RZ 3012	Wild Tiger Woman/Omnibus	12
69	Regal Zonophone RZ 3015	Blackberry Way/Something	7
69	Regal Zonophone RZ 3021	Curly/This Time Tomorrow	7
70	Regal Zonophone RZ 3026	Brontosaurus/Lightnin' Never Strikes Twice	7
70	Fly BUG 2	When Alice Comes Back To The Farm/What?	5
71	Harvest HAR 5036	Ella James/No Time (unissued)	0
71	Harvest HAR 5038	Tonight/Don't Mess Me Up	5
71	Harvest HAR 5043	Chinatown/Down On The Bay	5
72	MagniFly ECHO 104	Fire Brigade/I Can Hear The Grass Grow/Night Of Fear	5
72	Harvest HAR 5050	California Man/Do Ya/Ella James	5
74	Harvest HAR 5086	Do Ya/No Time	5
68	Regal Zono. TRZ 2001	SOMETHING ELSE FROM THE MOVE (EP, 33rpm)	60
68	Regal Zono. LRZ 1002	THE MOVE (LP, mono, red/silver labels with "Sold in the U.K..." text)	150
68	Regal Zono. SLRZ 1002	THE MOVE (LP, stereo, red/silver labels with "Sold in the U.K..." text)	100
68	Regal Zono. TA-LRZ 1002	THE MOVE (reel-to-reel, mono only)	15
70	Regal Zono. SLRZ 1012	SHAZAM (LP, many with pressing flaw on track "Don't Make My Baby Blue" that makes record skip on this track, red/silver label)	150
70	Fly HIFLY 1	LOOKING ON (LP, white label, 'Fly' logo)	40
71	Harvest SHSP 4013	MESSAGE FROM THE COUNTRY (LP, with EMI logo on label)	30
72	Fly TOOFA 5/6	THE MOVE/SHAZAM (2-LP reissue)	18
74	Harvest SHSP 4035	CALIFORNIA MAN (LP)	20

(see also Roy Wood, Jeff Lynne, ELO, Idle Race, Trevor Burton, Nicky James Movement, Ace Kefford Stand, Grunt Futtock, Rick Price, Uglys, Charlie Wayne)

MOVEMENT (1)
68	Pye 7N 17443	Tell Her/Something You've Got	120
68	Target 7N 17443	Something You've Got/Tell Her (Irish issue)	120
68	Big T BIG 112	Head For The Sun/Mister Mann	180

MOVEMENT (2)
80	Ballistic TRIF 2	No Man Is An Island/JAMDOWN PLAYERS: Levi's Choice (dubwise)/Togetherness/Deviate/Consolidate/Progression (12")	30

MOVERS (1)
65	Ska Beat JB 191	Jo-Anne/DON DRUMMOND: Don De Lion	45

MOVERS (2)
68	Capitol CL 15562	Birmingham/Leave Me Loose	25

MOVIES (1)
75	A&M AMLH 33002	THE MOVIES (LP)	12

(see also Ora, Public Foot The Roman)

MOVIES (2)
80	Gem GEMS 20	Love Is A Sacrifice/Fat Girl	6

MOVIETONE
94	Planet PUNK 003	She Smiled Mandarine Like/Orange Zero (p/s)	6
94	Planet PUNK 009	Mono Valley/Under The 3000 Foot Red Ceiling (p/s, 1,000 only)	5

MOVING BROTHERS
67	Island WI 3049	Darling I Love You/TOMMY McCOOK & SUPERSONICS: Saboo	30
67	Treasure Isle TI 7018	Darling I Love You/TOMMY McCOOK & SUPERSONICS: Saboo (reissue)	15

MOVING FINGER
68	Mercury MF 1051	Jeremy The Lamp/Pain Of My Misfortune	50
69	Mercury MF 1077	Higher And Higher/Shake And Fingerpop	70
73	Decca F 13406	So Many People/We're Just As Happy As We Are	8

(see also Anglians)

JUDY MOWATT
73	Gayfeet GS 207	Emergency Call/Emergency Call - Version	8
75	Torpedo 52	Too Good For Me/Cry To Me	10
80	Grove Muzik IPR 2041	Black Woman (feat. Joy Tulloch)/My My People (12")	25

(see also Jean & Gaytones)

MOWREY JNR. & WATSON
76	Riverdale RRL 1000	BUSKER (LP, with insert)	30

MP'S
80	Moving Plastic WSP 006	Housewives' Choice/Life On The Dole	5

MR. BLOE
70	DJM DJS 216	Groovin' With Mr. Bloe/Sinful	6
70	DJM DJLPS 409	GROOVIN' WITH MR. BLOE (LP)	18

(see also Harry Pitch)

MR. BUNGLE
91	London 828 276-1	MR BUNGLE (LP, picture disc)	40

MR. CALYPSON
71	Jump Up JU 40	Mohammed Ali/SAMSON DE LARK: Undemocratic Rhodesia	6

MR CHIPPS
77	Spiral SPF 7014	The Way I Am/Lady Elaine (no p/s)	30

MR. DYNAMITE
67	Sue WI 4027	Sh'mon/DYNAMITE ORCHESTRA: Sh'mon (Part Two)	300

MR. FINGERS
88	Jack Trax 12 J TRAX 10	SLAM DANCE EP (12")	50
94	Black Market BMI 022 LP	BACK TO LOVE (LP)	35
95	Black Market BMI 024 LP	CLASSIC FINGERS (2xLP)	20

MR. FLOOD'S PARTY
71	Ember EMB S 312	Compared To What/Unbreakable Toy	20
71	Ember EMB S 312	Compared To What/Unbreakable Toy (DJ copy)	40
75	Bulldog BD 6	Compared To What/Unbreakable Toy (reissue)	8

(see also Mike Corbett & Jay Hirsch)

MR. FORD & MR. GOON-BONES
56	London HLU 8355	Ain't She Sweet/MUZZY MARCELLINO: Mary Lou	25

(see also Mr. Goon-Bones & Cavaliers)

MR FOUNDATION
67	Studio One SO 2001	See Them A Come/KEN PARKER: Have A Good Time	35
67	Studio One SO 2003	All Rudies In Jail (actually by Zoot Sims/HORTENSE & ALTON Easy Squeeze	75
68	Studio One SO 2061	Time Oh/DUDLEY SIBLEY & PETER AUSTIN: Hole In Your Soul	40
68	Studio One SO 2069	Reggae Rumble/MARCIA GRIFFITHS : You Keep Me On The Move	40
69	Supreme SUP 201	Time To Pray (actually by Lloyd Robinson)/Young Budd (by Leonard Dillon)	12

(see also Sound Dimension)

MR. FOX
70	Big T BIG 135	Little Woman/Join Us In Our Game	8
70	Transatlantic TRA 226	MR FOX (LP)	75
71	Transatlantic TRA 236	THE GIPSY (LP, gatefold sleeve, plaatic inner with foam opening)	100
75	Transatlantic TRA 303	THE COMPLETE MR FOX (2-LP, reissue of "Mr Fox" & "The Gypsy")	20

(see also Bob Pegg, Bob & Carol Pegg)

MR. MO'S MESSENGERS
67	Columbia DB 8133	Feelin' Good/The Handyman	15

MISTER MOST
69	Downtown DT 409	Reggae Train/Pushwood	8

MR. PINK/MR. BLONDE
96	Resevoir BP1	Payin' The Price/Death Before Dishonour (12")	20
97	Resevoir BP2	Jamaica Crime Wave (12")	15

MR. REJECT
71	private pressing	MR. REJECT (LP)	40

MR. SCRUFF
99	Ninja Tune ZEN12 080	Get A Move On! (12")	8
01	Ninja Tune ZEN12 104	Get A Move On/Ug (12")	8
99	Ninja Tune ZEN 42	KEEP IT UNREAL (2xLP)	15
99	Ninja Tune ZEN 42	KEEP IT UNREAL (2xLP, purple sleeve)	15
99	Ninja Tune ZEN 65	TROUSER JAZZ (2xLP)	30

MR. TWISTER & TORNADOS
63	Starlite ST45 099	Big Twist (Parts 1 & 2)	15

MU
74	United Artists UAG 29709	LEMURIAN MUSIC (LP)	35

MU5

72	Crystal CR 7015	Mrs Watson/Rain Dance 50

MUCKRAM WAKES

76	Trailer LER 2093	MUCKRAM WAKES (LP) 20
73	Trailer LER 2085	A MAP OF DERBYSHIRE (LP, red/black or yellow label) 15

MUCKY DUCK

70	Deram DM314	Jefferson/Psycho's On The Run 15

MUD

67	CBS 203002	Flower Power/You're My Mother (in p/s) 50
67	CBS 203002	Flower Power/You're My Mother 35
68	CBS 3355	Up The Airy Mountain/Latter Days 30
69	Philips BF 1775	Shangri-La/House On The Hill 20
70	Philips 6006 022	Jumping Jehosaphat/Won't Let It Go 20
74	Rak RAK 187	Lonely This Christmas/I Can't Stand It (p/s) 5
75	Rak RAK 194	The Secrets That You Keep/Still Watching The Clock (p/s) 5
76	Rak RR 6	Tiger Feet/Oh Boy/Dynamite (p/s) 5
76	Private Stock PVT 65	Shake It Down/Laugh, Live, Love (p/s) 5
79	Carrere CAR 117	Drop Everything And Run/Taking The Easy Way Out (picture disc) 5

(see also Dum)

MUDHONEY

89	Blast First BFFP 46	Halloween/SONIC YOUTH: Touch Me I'm Sick (12", with tour/gig flyer) 12
89	Blast First BFFP 46	Halloween/SONIC YOUTH: Touch Me I'm Sick (12") 8
92	Reprise WO 137	Suck You Dry/Version/Over The Top/Underide (12") 10
92	Reprise WO 137T	Suck You Dry (LP Version)/Deception Pass (12") 10
95	Reprise 9362 458401	MY BROTHER THE COW (LP, with 6-track EP, [PRO S 7492]) 25

(see also Sonic Youth)

MUDIE'S ALL STARS

70	Moodisc HM 3503	Wha Who Wha - Version/G.G. RUSSELL: Wha Who Wha 12

(see also I Roy, Eternals, King Cannon, John Holt, Niney, Jolly Boys, Jo Jo Bennett)

MUDLARKS

58	Columbia DB 4064	Mutual Admiration Society/A New Love 10
58	Columbia DB 4099	Lollipop/Young Dove's Calling 7
58	Columbia DB 4133	Book Of Love/Yea, Yea 7
58	Columbia DB 4190	There's Never Been A Night/Lightnin' Never Strikes Twice 5
58	Columbia DB 4210	Which Witch Doctor/My Grandfather's Clock 5
59	Columbia DB 4250	Abdul The Bulbul Amer Cha Cha/The Love Game 5
59	Columbia DB 4291	Time Flies/Tell Him No 5
59	Columbia DB 4331	Waterloo/Mary 5
59	Columbia DB 4331	Waterloo/Mary (78) 15
59	Columbia DB 4374	Tennessee/True Love, True Love 5
60	Columbia DB 4417	Never Marry A Fishmonger/Candy 6
60	Columbia DB 4513	(You've Got To) Move Two Mountains/You're Free To Go 7
61	Columbia DB 4636	When Mexico Gave Up The Rumba/Toy Balloon 5
61	Columbia DB 4708	The Mountain's High/Don't Gamble With Love 5
62	Columbia DB 4788	Them Twistin' Bones/Coney Island Washboard 7
62	Columbia DB 4861	Mañana Pasado Mañana/March Of The Broken Hearts 5
62	Decca F 11537	I've Been Everywhere/Just The Snap Of Your Fingers 7
63	Decca F 11601	The Little Cracked Bell Of San Raquel/La De Da 6
64	Fontana TF 495	Walk Around/Here's Another Day 8
58	Columbia SEG 7854	THE MUDLARKS! (EP) 25

MUFF

71	Mother MOT 7	Hurdy Gurdy/Why Did You Leave Me 15
74	Bell Bell 1380	Sexy Sexy Lady/Burnin' 5
75	UA UP 3595	Do The Hand Jive/Discotheque King 5

MUFFIN

72	Dart ART 2018	Smokey Blues Away/Acapulco Gold 6

MUGWUMPS

64	Warner Bros WB 144	I'll Remember Tonight/I Don't Wanna Know 12
67	Warner Bros W 1697	THE MUGWUMPS - AN HISTORICAL RECORDING (LP) 35
70	Valiant VS 134	THE MUGWUMPS - AN HISTORICAL RECORDING (LP, reissue) 18

(see also Mamas & Papas, Mama Cass Elliot, Lovin' Spoonful, Zalman Yanovsky)

BOBBY MUIR & BLUEBEATS

60	Blue Beat BB 20	Baby What You Done Me Wrong/Go Pretty Baby Go (as Blue Beats) 12
61	Blue Beat BB 44	Honey Please/That's My Girl (as Bobby Kingdom & Blue Beats) 12
62	Blue Beat BB 77	Brand New Automobile/Spanish Town Twist (as Bobby Kingdom & Blue Beats) 12

JAMIE MUIR & DEREK BAILEY

81	Incus INCUS 41	DART DRUG (LP) 50

(see also Derek Bailey)

LINDSAY MUIR'S UNTAMED

66	Planet PLF 113	Daddy Long Legs/Trust Yourself A Little Bit (initial release with plain white white sleeve) 250
66	Planet PLF 113	Daddy Long Legs/Trust Yourself A Little Bit (with Planet company sleeve) 240

(see also Untamed)

MULCAYS

55	London HLF 8188	Harbour Lights/Dipsy Doodle 20
54	London REP 1016	MERRY CHRISTMAS (EP) 12
56	London REF 1046	HARMONICS BY THE MULCAYS (EP) 8

MULDOONS

65	Decca F 12164	I'm Lost Without You/Come Back Now Baby 30

MULESKINNERS

65	Fontana TF 527	Back Door Man/Need Your Lovin' 200
65	Keepoint KEE-EP-7104	MULESKINNERS (EP, private pressing, no p/s) 750

(see also Small Faces, Faces)

MULL HISTORICAL SOCIETY
01	Rough Trade RTRADES 021	Animal Cannabus/20 Days Of Sun (p/s)	10

BARBARA MULLANEY
73	Philips 6382 878	ON THE STREET WHERE I LIVE (LP)	12

ARTHUR MULLARD
67	Masquerade MA 5001	I Love You, You Love Me/Was It Something I said? (with Bill Shepherd Flock)	7
74	BASF BA 1012	Not Now Arthur/If I Had My Time Again	7

MOON MULLICAN
51	Vogue V 9013	Cherokee Boogie/Love Is The Light That Leads Me Home (78)	30
56	Parlophone DP 503	Yearning (Just For You)/Put Your Arms Around Me, Honey (export 78)	30
56	Parlophone DP 512	San Antonio Rose/Cedarwood Blues (export 78)	30
56	Parlophone MSP 6254	Seven Nights To Rock/Honolulu Rock-A Roll-A (with Boyd Bennett & His Rockets)	400
56	Parlophone R 4195	Seven Nights To Rock/Honolulu Rock-A Roll-A (with Boyd Bennett & His Rockets) (78)	50
59	Parlophone GEP 8794	COUNTRY ROUND UP (EP)	60
50s	Parlophone CGEP 13	MOON MULLICAN (EP, export issue)	40
50s	Parlophone CGEP 15	PIANO BREAKDOWN (EP, export issue, company sleeve)	40

(see also Boyd Bennett & His Rockets)

GERRY MULLIGAN
53	Capitol LC 6621	THE GERRY MULLIGAN TENTETTE - ROCKER (10" LP)	15
53	Vogue LDE 029	THE GERRY MULLIGAN QUARTET VOL. 1 (10" LP)	15
53	Vogue LDE 030	THE GERRY MULLIGAN QUARTET VOL. 2 (10" LP)	15
53	Vogue LDE 031	THE GERRY MULLIGAN QUARTET VOL. 3 (10" LP)	15
54	Vogue LDE 075	THE GERRY MULLIGAN QUARTET (10" LP)	15
54	Vogue LDE 083	THE GERRY MULLIGAN QUARTET VOL. 4 (10" LP)	15
54	Esquire 20-032	GERRY MULLIGAN ALLSTARS - MULLIGAN'S TOO (10" LP)	15
55	Vogue LDE 156	GERRY MULLIGAN QUARTET WITH LEE KONITZ (10" LP)	15
56	Esquire 32-014	GERY MULLIGAN ALLSTARS (LP)	15
56	Vogue LAE 12006	THE GERRY MULLIGAN QUARTET (LP)	15
56	Vogue LAE 12015	THE GERRY MULLIGAN QUARTET - PARIS JAZZ FAIR 1954 (LP)	15
56	Emarcy EJL 101	PRESENTING THE GERRY MULLIGAN SEXTET (LP)	15
57	Emarcy EJL 1259	MAINSTREAM OF JAZZ (LP, by Gerry Mulligan Sextet)	15
58	Columbia Clef 33CX 10113	GERRY MULLIGAN AND PAUL DESMOND QUARTET (LP)	15
58	HMV CLP 1204	PHIL SUNKEL'S "JAZZ CONCERTO GROSSO" (LP, with Bob Brookmeyer)	15
59	Philips SBBL 552	WHAT IS THERE TO SAY? (LP, stereo)	15
59	Vogue SEA 5006	GERRY MULLIGAN SONGBOOK (LP, stereo)	15
59	Vogue SEA 5007	REUNION WITH CHET BAKER (LP, stereo, as Gerry Mulligan Quartet)	15
59	London Jazz LTZT 15161	I WANT TO LIVE (LP, with Shelly Manne)	12
60	HMV CLP 1373	GERRY MULLIGAN MEETS BEN WEBSTER (LP)	12
61	HMV CLP 1432	THE CONCERT JAZZ BAND (LP, also stereo CSD 1351)	12
61	Vocalion LAE 12268	THE GENIUS OF GERRY MULLIGAN (LP)	12
62	HMV CLP 1465	GERRY MULLIGAN MEETS JOHNNY HODGES (LP, also stereo CSD 1372)	12
62	HMV CLP 1488	AT THE VILLAGE VANGUARD (LP, also stereo CSD 1396)	12
62	Riverside RLP 12-247	MULLIGAN MEETS MONK (LP, with Thelonious Monk)	15
62	HMV CLP 1549	A CONCERT IN JAZZ (LP, also stereo CSD 1432)	12
62	HMV CLP 1585	ON TOUR (LP, with Zoot Sims)	12

(see also Gerry Mulligan, Chet Baker, Shelly Manne, Annie Ross)

MICK MULLIGAN'S JAZZ BAND
50s	Saga STP 7020	YOUNG AND HEALTHY (EP)	10
55	Tempo EXA 25	MICK MULLIGAN'S JAZZ BAND (EP)	10
56	Tempo EXA 37	MICK MULLIGAN'S JAZZ BAND (EP)	10
56	Tempo EXA 41	GEORGE MELLY WITH MICK MULLIGAN'S JAZZ BAND (EP)	10
57	Tempo EXA 54	MICK MULLIGAN'S JAZZ BAND (EP)	10
58	Parlophone GEP 8750	MICK BLOWS (EP)	10
57	Tempo TAP 14	JAZZ AT THE RAILWAY ARMS (LP, with George Melly)	50
59	Pye Jazz NJL 21	MEET MICK MULLIGAN (LP)	20
59	Parlophone PMC 1103	THE SAINTS MEET THE SINNERS (LP, with George Melly & Saints Jazz Band)	15

(see also George Melly)

MUM
01	TMT TMT04CD	MUM REMIXED (CD)	20
02	Fat Cat FATLP 18	FINALLY WE ARE NO ONE (2 x 10")	35
07	Fat Cat FATLP46	GO GO SMEAR THE POISON IVY (LP, with bonus 7")	18

GENE MUMFORD
58	Philips PB 862	More Than You Know/Please Give Me One More Chance	8

MUMFORD & SONS
08	Chess Club CC 006	LEND ME YOUR EYES EP (10", p/s)	80
08	Chess Club CC 009	LOVE YOUR GROUND EP (10", p/s)	80
09	Chess Club CC 015	The Cave/My Heart Told My Head (Winter Winds) (1-sided 10", gatefold p/s, 300 only)	80
09	Island 2720975	Little Lion Man/To Darkness (p/s)	5
10	Chess Club WEDDING 1	FIRST DANCE EP (tour 10" as The Wedding Band)	50
09	V2 VVR 723601	SIGH NO MORE (LP)	20

MUMMIES
89	Hangman HANG 47 UP	FUCKS C.D.S.ITS...(LP)	20

MUMMY CALLS
83	MC 12	Mary I Swear/Unicorn Jones (p/s)	10

HUGH MUNDELL
78	Greensleeves GRE9	Let's All Unite/Unity Dub	15
79	Warrior WAR 131	Stop Them Jah/Push Dawta Push (12")	30
80	J&F 002	Jah Fire Will Be Burning/King Of Israel (12")	30
81	Greensleeves GRED 54	Can't Pop No Style/JUNIOR REID: Know Myself (12")	40
80	Live And Love LAP 13	JAH FIRE (LP, with Lacksley Castell and Augustus Pablo)	40
86	Message GREL 94	AFRICA MUST BE FREE BY 1983 (LP, reissue)	15

(see also Ray Dorset, Good Earth, King Earl Boogie Band, Horizon, Made In England, Jigilo Jug Band, P. King, Paul King, P. Rufus King, Russian Roulette, First Impression, Good Earth)

MUNGO JERRY

70	Dawn DNX 2502	In The Summertime/Mighty Man/Dust Pneumonia Blues (p/s)	5
70	Pye 7N 2502	In The Summertime/Mighty Man (jukebox issue)	8
71	Dawn DNX 2505	Baby Jump/The Man Behind The Piano/Live From Hollywood: Maggie/Midnight Special/Mighty Man (p/s)	5
71	Dawn DNX 2510	Lady Rose/Have A Whiff On Me/Milk Cow Blues/Little Louis (p/s, withdrawn)	5
71	Dawn DNX 2510	Lady Rose/She Rowed/Milk Cow Blues/Little Louis (re-pressing with different track, p/s)	5
83	Mach 1 MAGIC 008	There Goes My Heart Again/Thinking Of You (featuring Ray Dorset & Tarts)	5
85	Orbit TRIP 4	Sunshine Reggae/Nightlife (reissue of Horizon 45; as Mungo Jerry & Horizon)	6
87	Illegal MUNG 1	In The Summertime '87/Got A Job (as Mungo Jerry & Brothers Grimm, p/s)	5
96	Fan Club 12/1	Sugar In The Bowl/In The Summertime (fan club only, white label, autographed)	5
70	Dwn DNLS 3008	MUNGO JERRY (LP, gatefold sleeve, with 3-D glasses)	25
71	Dawn DNLS 3028	YOU DON'T HAVE TO BE IN THE ARMY (LP, gatefold sleeve, with lyric insert)	15
71	Dawn DNLS 3020	ELECTRONICALLY TESTED (LP, gatefold sleeve)	20
72	Dawn DNLS 3041	BOOT POWER (LP, with 'Dennis The Menace' or 'gun' gatefold sleeve)	15

(see also Ray Dorset, Good Earth, King Earl Boogie Band, Horizon, Made In England, Jigilo Jug Band, P. King, Paul King, P. Rufus King, Russian Roulette, First Impression, Good Earth)

RAY MUNNINGS

79	Tammi TAM 102	It Could Happen To You/Let's Boogie	30
79	Tammi TAM 103	Funky Nassau/Jump In The Water	25
79	Tammi TAM 103	Funky Nassau/Jump In The Water (12")	60

CAROLINE MUNRO

67	Columbia DB 8189	Tar And Cement/The Sporting Life	12

CAROLINE MUNRO

85	Numa NU 5	Pump Me Up/The Picture (p/s)	6
85	Numa NUM 5	Pump Me Up (Ext. 6.09)/The Picture/Pump Me Up (4.00 7" Version) (12", p/s)	10

(see also Gary Numan)

HAL MUNRO

58	Embassy WB 284	Breathless/Wear My Ring Around Your Neck	10
59	Embassy WB 336	C'mon Everybody/It's Late	10
59	Embassy WB 340	Dream Lover/Where Were You	10
59	Embassy WB 386	You Got What It Takes/California Here I Come	10
60	Embassy WB 401	Good Timin'/I Wanna Go Home	10
60	Embassy WB 401	Good Timin'/I Wanna Go Home (78)	10

(see also Neville Taylor)

JANET MUNRO & SEAN CONNERY

59	Top Rank JAR 163	Pretty Irish Girl/Ballamaquilty's Band	10
59	Top Rank JAR 163	Pretty Irish Girl/Ballamaquilty's Band (78)	10

ADRIAN MUNSEY

79	Virgin VS 266	C'Est Sheep (Part 1)/C'Est Sheep (Part 2) (p/s)	6
79	Virgin VS 266-12	C'Est Sheep (Part 1)/C'Est Sheep (Part 2) (12", p/s)	8

(see also Sparks)

STEPHAN MUNSON & FRIENDS

82	Rhythmic RMNS 2	And David Cried/And Dem Bahnhoff (fold-out photocopied p/s)	8

MURCOF

02	Leaf BAY 23	MARTES (2-LP)	25
05	Leaf BAY 47 V	REMEMBRANZA (2-LP)	20

MURDER INC.

80	MIL MIL 1	SOUNDS SO FALSE (EP)	8

(see also Business)

MURDER THE DISTURBED

79	Small Wonder	Walking Corpses The Ultimate System/Small Seventeen (P/S)	8

BILLY MURE (ORCHESTRA)

59	Felsted AF 120	Tea & Trumpets/A String Of Trumpets	5
59	RCA SRC 7032	SUPERSONICS IN FLIGHT (EP, also stereo SRC 7032)	10
60	MGM MGM-C 800	SUPERSONIC GUITARS (LP)	20
61	London HAR 2400	TOUGH STRINGS (LP)	15
64	MGM C976	FASCINATING SOUND OF THE AZTEC GUITARS (LP)	12

(see also Supersonics)

MURGATROYD BAND

71	Decca F 12809	Magpie (Theme From The TV Series)/Twice A Week (p/s)	40
71	Decca F 13256	Magpie (Theme From The TV Series)/Twice A Week (without p/s)	15
71	Decca F 13256	Magpie (Theme From The TV Series)/Twice A Week (with p/s)	25

(see also Spencer Davis Group, Ray Fenwick)

MURMAIDS

63	Stateside SS 247	Popsicles And Icicles/Comedy And Tragedy	20

MURMURS OF URMA

97	Dolly 001	Coloured Rice/Magic Shop/Vacuum Cleaner/Cloudwatch HQ (P/S)	12
99	Dolly 002	Banoffe Boy Writing To A Friend/Super Vacillation Day Snails Into Fast Food (P?S)	8

MICHAEL MURPHEY

72	Regal Zonophone RZ 3062	Boy From The Country/Geronimo's Cadillac	5
75	Epic EPC 3242	Wildfire/Night Thunder	6
73	EMI EMA 754	COSMIC COWBOY SOUVENIR (LP)	12

ARTHUR MURPHY

59	Parlophone R 4523	Sixteen Candles/Molly Malone	10

BRIAN MURPHY

78	Pye 7N 46086	Jogging/THe Great Gnome Robbery	7

DELIA MURPHY

57	HMV 7EG 8295	DELIGHTFUL DELIA (EP)	8

ELLIOT MURPHY
| 74 | Polydor 2391 100 | AQUASHOW (LP) | 12 |

KEITH MURPHY & THE DAZE
| 68 | Polydor 56542 | Slightly Reminiscent Of Her/Dirty Old Sam | 35 |

LYLE MURPHY
| 58 | Contemporary LAC 12135 | GONE WITH THE WOODWINDS (LP) | 20 |

MARK MURPHY
57	Brunswick 05701	Goodbye Baby Blues/The Right Kind Of Woman	6
58	Capitol CL 14962	Belong To Me/Don't Cry My Love	5
60	Capitol CL 15117	Send For Me/Come To Me	5
63	Riverside RIF 106901	Stoppin The Clock/Angel Eyes	5
63	Riverside RIF 106905	Like Love/Fly Away My Sadness	5
63	Riverside RIF 106908	Fly Me To The Moon/Why Don't You Do Right	30
65	Fontana TF 572	High On Windy Hill/Broken Heart	15
67	Fontana TF 803	(Ain't That) Just Like A Woman/Do You Wonder If I Love You	5
69	Pye 7N 17661	Come Back To Me/Dear Heart	5
57	Brunswick LAT 8172	MEET MARK MURPHY (LP)	12
60	Capitol (S)T 5011	HIT PARADE (LP)	12
64	Fontana (S)TL 5217	MARK TIME! (LP)	12
66	Immediate IMLP/IMSP 004	WHO CAN I TURN TO (LP)	25
69	Phoenix PMS 1001	THIS MUST BE EARTH (LP)	90
71	Riverside RLP 395	RAH (LP)	30

NOEL MURPHY
67	Fontana TL 5450	NYA-A-A-H! (LP)	15
73	Village Thing VTS 25	MURF (LP)	15
78	RCA PE 5090	THE BRICKLAYERS SONG (EP)	8

PETER MURPHY
| 92 | Beggars Banquet BEGA 123 | HOLY SMOKE (LP) | 12 |

(see also Bauhaus)

ROISIN MURPHY
| 05 | Echo ECHLP 63 | RUBY BLUE (2-LP, with booklet) | 40 |

(see also Moloko)

ROSE MURPHY
| 52 | Oriole/Mercury MG 10004 | SONGS BY ROSE MURPHY (10" LP) | 20 |

ALEX MURRAY
60	Decca F 11203	Teen Angel/Paper Doll	10
60	Decca F 11225	All On My Own/String Along	7
61	Decca F 11345	When You Walked Out/Send For Me	7

(see also Most Brothers)

LADY MURRAY
| 66 | Clan 597 002 | Mister Abercrombie Taught Me/In My Imagination | 10 |

(see also Grazina, Mr & Mrs Murray)

MARTIN MURRAY
| 66 | Pye 7N 17070 | I Know What I Want/Goodbye Baby | 10 |

MICKEY MURRAY
| 67 | Polydor 56738 | Shout Bama Lama/Lonely Room | 10 |

MISTER MURRAY
| 65 | Fontana TF 623 | Down Came The Rain/Whatever Happened To Music? | 8 |
| 66 | Fontana TF 674 | I Drink To Your Memory/I Was A Good Song | 6 |

(see also Mitch Murray Clan, Mr & Mrs Murray)

MITCH MURRAY CLAN
| 66 | Clan 597 001 | Skyliner/Cherokee | 15 |

MR & MRS MURRAY
| 68 | CBS 3633 | You're Outa Your Mind/A Little Bit Of You | 6 |

(see also Mitch Murray Clan, Lady Murray, Grazina, Mister Murray)

RUBY MURRAY
55	Columbia SCM 5162	Softly, Softly/What Could Be More Beautiful	25
55	Columbia SCM 5165	Spring, Spring, Spring/Goin' Co'tin (with Ray Burns, Diana Decker & Ronnie Harris)	8
55	Columbia SCM 5169	If Anyone Finds This, I Love You (with Anne Warren)/Before We Know It	15
60	Columbia ESG 7330/SEG 8502	LOVES OLD SWEET SONG (EP)	12
58	Columbia 33S 1135	ENDEARING YOUNG CHARMS (10" LP)	15
60	Columbia 33SX 1201	RUBY (LP, mono)	15
60	Columbia SCX 3289	RUBY (LP, stereo)	20

(see also Norman Wisdom & Ruby Murray, Ray Burns, Ronnie Harris, Diana Decker)

JOHN MURTAUGH
| 70 | Polydor 2482 015 | BLUES CURRENT (LP) | 20 |

MUSE
99	Mushroom MUSH 50S	Uno/Agitated (p/s, clear vinyl)	50
99	Mushroom MUSE 1	Uno/Jimmy Kane/Forced In/Agitated (minimax CD, with slipcase)	10
99	Mushroom MUSH 58S	Cave/Cave (Instrumental Remix) (clear vinyl, p/s)	35
99	Mushroom MUSH 66S	Muscle Museum/Escape (p/s)	20
99	Mushroom MUSH 66S	Muscle Museum/Minimum (clear vinyl, autographed p/s, 1000 only)	50
99	Mushroom MUSH 68S	Sunburn/(Live Acoustic Version) (stickered p/s, clear vinyl)	15
00	Mushroom MUSH 72S	Unintended/Sober (p/s, clear vinyl)	20
00	Mushroom MUSH 84S	Muscle Museum/Sober (The Saint Remix) (p/s)	12
01	Mushroom MUSH 89S	Plug In Baby/Nature 1 (p/s)	30
01	Mushroom MUSH 92S	New Born/Shrinking Universe (p/s, limited issue)	20
01	Mushroom MUSH 92T	New Born/Sunburn (Timo Maas Sunstroke Remix)/(Breakz Again Mix (12", p/s)	8
01	Mushroom MUSH 96S	Bliss/Hyper Chondriac Music (p/s)	15
01	Mushroom MUSH 96S	Bliss/The Gallery (p/s)	15

01	Mushroom MUSH 97S	Hyper Music/Feeling Good (numbered p/s)	30
01	Mushroom MUSH 104S	Dead Star/In Your World (p/s)	15
03	East West EW 272	Time is Running Uut/The Groove (clear vinyl, p/s)	15
03	East West EW 278	Hysteria/Eternally Missed (p/s)	10
04	East West EW 285	Sing For Absolution/Fury (p/s, clear vinyl)	8
04	Atlantic ATUK 003	Butterflies And Hurricanes/Butterflies And Hurricanes (Glastonbury 2004) (p/s, clear vinyl)	8
06	Warner Brothers HEL 3001	Supermassive Black Hole/Crying Shame (picture disc, stickered PVC sleeve)	6
06	Warner Brothers HEL 3003	Starlight/Supermassive Black Hole (Remix) (picture disc, stickered)	10
06	A & E HEL 3004	Knights of Cydonia/Assassion (picture disc, stickered)	20
07	Warner Brothers HEL3005	Invincible/Glorious (picture disc, stickered)	10
98	Dangerous DREX CDEP 103	MUSE EP (CD, 999 copies, numbered sticker)	400
98	Dangerous DREX CDEP 104	MUSCLE MUSEUM EP: Sober/Uno/Unintended/Instant Messenger/Muscle Museum # 2/Muscle Museum (CD, 999 copies, numbered sticker)	175
00	Mushroom MUSH 59LP	SHOWBIZ (2-LP, clear vinyl, gatefold sleeve, with inners, numbered)	150
01	Mushroom MUSH 93LP	ORIGIN OF SYMMETRY (2-LP, gatefold sleeve, with lyric inner sleeves, 1500 only)	70
01	Mushroom MUSE 14	ORIGIN OF SYMMETRY (CD promo, clear Perspex bolted case)	20
03	East West 5046 68587-1	ABSOLUTION (double LP, gatefold sleeve)	50
09	Warner Bros. 825646869664	THE RESISTANCE (Box set, CD, DVD, USB stick)	60

MUSHROOM

73	Hawk HASP 320	Devil Among The Tailors/Sun Ni Dhuibir/King Of Ireland's Daughter	25
74	Hawk HASP 340	Kings And Queens/Met A Friend	25
73	Hawk HALPX 116	EARLY ONE MORNING (LP, with poster inner)	600
73	Hawk HALPX 116	EARLY ONE MORNING (LP, without poster inner)	350

(see also Joe O'Donnell)

(THE) MUSIC

01	Fierce Panda NING 107	Take The Long Road And Walk It/The Walls Get Smaller (p/s, 1,000 only)	10
01	Fierce Panda NINGT 107	Take The Long Road And Walk It/The Walls Get Smaller (12", p/s, 250 only)	20

MUSIC BOX

72	Westwood MRS 013	SONGS OF SUNSHINE (LP)	110

MUSIC DOCTORS

69	Downtown DT 447	Music Doctor (Parts 1 & 2)	20
70	J-Dan JDN 4402	Electric Shock/KING DENNIS: Black Robin	8
70	J-Dan JDN 4403	Bush Doctor/Lick Your Stick	15
70	J-Dan JDN 4411	The Wild Bunch/ISRAELITES: Born To Be Strong	12
70	J-Dan JDN 4414	In The Summertime/Foundation Track	10
70	J-Dan JDN 4417	Discretion Version/Doctor Dan, Boy Friday And Friend	10
70	Trojan TBL 117	REGGAE IN THE SUMMERTIME (LP)	25

(see also Dennis Lowe, Audrey, Desmond Riley, Megatons, Prince Of Darkness, Gene Rondo)

MUSIC EMPORIUM

83	Psycho PSYCHO 11	MUSIC EMPORIUM (LP)	15

MUSIC EXPLOSION

67	Stateside SS 2028	A Little Bit O' Soul/I See The Light	25
67	Stateside SS 2054	Sunshine Games/Can't Stop Now	20
67	Philips BF 1547	Little Black Egg/Stay By My Side	10
69	London HLP 10272	A Little Bit O' Soul/Everybody	10
67	London HA-P/SH-P 8352	A LITTLE BIT O' SOUL (LP)	50

MUSIC MACHINE

67	Pye International 7N 25407	Talk Talk/Come On In	50
67	Pye International 7N 25414	The People In Me/Masculine Intuition	60

MUSIC MOTOR

70	Deram DM 282	Happy/Where Am I Going?	20

MUSIC SPECIALISTS

70	London HLJ 10309	Dynamic Pressure/Flip	7

MUSIC TAPES

98	Earworm WORM 32	The Television Tells Us/Freeing Song By Reindeer (p/s, pop-up sleeve with 2 inserts, 1,500 copies only)	5

MUSIC THROUGH SIX

68	Domain D3	Riff Raff/ROY DOCKER: Mellow Moonlight	30

(see also Jason Sims & Music Through Six)

MUSICAL THEATRE

70	Pye Intl. NSPL 28128	A REVOLUTIONARY REVELATION (LP)	12

MUSICIANS

66	King KG 1055	Jaunty Joe/The Chelsea Set	7

MUSICOLOGY

91	B12 B1201	Musicology (12")	40
91	B12 B1201	Musicology (12", clear vinyl)	100
92	B12 B1204	Outlook (12")	40
92	B12 B1206	Hall Of Mirrors (12")	15
92	B12 B1206	Hall Of Mirrors (12" Ltd, yellow vinyl)	40

MUSIQUE CONCRET

81	United Dairies UD 010	BRINGING UP BABY (LP, blue vinyl, 100 only)	120
81	United Dairies UD 010	BRINGING UP BABY (LP, black vinyl, 400 only)	100
87	United Dairies UDT 10	BRINGING UP BABY (cassette)	40

MUSKETEER GRIPWEED & THIRD TROOP

66	United Artists UP 1196	How I Won The War/Aftermath	175
66	United Artists UP 1196	How I Won The War/Aftermath (demo copy)	100

(see also John Lennon)

MUSKETEERS

69	Philips BF 1773	Fight/Magnifico	6

MUSKYTEERS

69	Upsetter US 309	Endlessly/Kidd-O	35

CHARLIE MUSSELWHITE BLUES BAND
69   Vanguard SVRL 19012   STONE BLUES (LP) 22

MUSTANG
67   Parlophone R 5579   Why/Here, There And Everywhere........25

MUSTARD
74   EMI EMI 2165   Good Time Comin'/I Saw I Heard 25

MUS-TWANGS
61   Mercury AMT 1140   Roch Lomond/Marie 12

MUTANTS
77   Rox ROX 002   Boss Man/Back Yard Boys (p/s) 12
78   Rox ROX 005   School Teacher/Hard Time/Lady (p/s, red vinyl) 10

MUTE DRIVERS
80s   Mute Drivers MD 001   MUTE DRIVERS (LP, with insert in handmade painted sleeve, 300 only)........15
(see also Anonymes)

MUTT 'N' JEFF
66   Decca F 12335   Don't Nag Me Ma/Strolling The Blues 12

Mm-ZIQ
93   Rephlex CAT 018   Bluff Limbo (remixes) (2 x 12", 800 only) 20
(see also Rude Ass Tinker)

MVP'S
71   Buddah BDS 469   Turnin' My Heartbeat Up/Every Man For Herself........20

M.W.A.B.
83   M.W.A.B. Records   Angus Young/Is Michael Bum An Apple? 10

MY BLOODY VALENTINE
86   Fever FEV 5X   No Place To Go/Moonlight (p/s) 100
86   Fever FEV 5   GEEK! (12" EP) 40
86   Kaleid. Sound KS 101   THE NEW RECORD BY MY BLOODY VALENTINE (12" EP) 60
87   Lazy LAZY 04   Sunny Sundae Smile/Paint A Rainbow (p/s) 30
87   Lazy LAZY 04T   Sunny Sundae Smile/Paint A Rainbow/Kiss The Eclipse/ Sylvie's Head (12", p/s)........50
87   Lazy LAZY 07   Strawberry Wine/Never Say Goodbye/Can I Touch You (12", p/s) 60
88   Creation CRE 055   You Made Me Realise/Slow (die-cut company sleeve)........8
88   Creation CRE 055T   You Made Me Realise/Slow/Thorn/Cigarette/Drive It All Over Me (12", p/s) 30
88   Creation CRE 061   Feed Me With Your Kiss/Emptiness Inside (plays "I Believe") (die-cut company sleeve)........20
88   Creation CRE 061T   Feed Me With Your Kiss/Emptiness Inside/I Need No Trust (12", p/s)........25
98   Creation CRESCD061   Feed Me With Your Kisses/I Believe/Emptiness Inside/I Need No Trust (CD single) 12
89   Creation CRE 085   Tremolo/To Hear Knows When (p/s) 10
89   Creation CRE 085T   Tremolo/To Hear Knows When (12", p/s) 20
89   Creation CRECD 085   Tremolo/To Hear Knows When (CD) 10
89   Lyntone CAT 067   Sugar/PACIFIC: December, With The Day (square flexidisc free with The Catalogue magazine, issue 67)........10
90   Creation CRE 073   Soon/Glider (p/s) 12
90   Creation CRE 073T   GLIDER EP (12", p/s) 20
90   Creation CRE 073X   GLIDER EP (12", remixed by Andy Weatherall, stickered die-cut sleeve) 25
87   Lazy LAZY 08   ECSTACY (mini-LP, 3,000 only) 70
88   Creation CRELP 040   ISN'T ANYTHING (LP, initial 3,000 copies with bonus 7", "Instrumental"/"Instrumental" [CRE FRE 4, no p/s] & stickered sleeve) 45
88   Creation CRELP 040   ISN'T ANYTHING (LP, without bonus 7") 25
89   Lazy LAZY 12   ECSTACY & WINE (LP, compilation of LAZY 07 & LAZY 08) 50
89   Lazy LAZY 12CD   ECSTACY & WINE (CD) 40
91   Creation CRELP 060   LOVELESS (LP) 50
(see also Primal Scream, Collapsed Lung, Snowpony, Dinosaur Jr.)

MY CAPTAINS
81   4AD AD 103   Fall/Converse/History/Nothing (EP) 8

MY CHEMICAL ROMANCE
03   20:20 TWENTY 7s 003   Honey, This Mirror Isn't Big Enough For The Two Of Us/This Is The Best Day Ever (p/s) 50
04   20:20 TWENTY 7S 004   Headfirst For Halos/Our Lady Of Sorrows (Live) (p/s) 40
04   20:20 TWENTY CDS 004   Headfirst For Halos/Our Lady Of Sorrows (Live) (CD) 15
04   Reprise W 661   Thank You For The Venom/Jack The Ripper (Live) (red vinyl, p/s) 40
05   Reprise W 666   I'm Not Okay (I Promise)/Bury Me In Black (Demo) (red vinyl, p/s) 5
05   Reprise W 671   Helena/I'm Not Okay (I Promise) (Live AOL Session) (picture disc)........5
05   Reprise W 683   The Ghost In You/Helena (live) (picture disc)........5
06   Reprise 116796-1   THE BLACK PARADE (2-LP box set) 30

MY DEAR WATSON
68   Parlophone R 5687   Elusive Face/The Shame Just Drained 30
68   Parlophone R 5737   Make This Day Last/Stop, Stop, I'll Be There 30
70   DJM DJS 224   Have You Seen Your Saviour/White Line Road 10
(see also Johnny & Copycats)

MY DYING BRIDE
90   private pressing   Towards The Sinister EP (4 track demo cassette) 40
92   Peaceville VILE 27   Symphonaire Infernus Et Spera Empyrium Act 1/ Symphonaire Infernus Et Spera Empyrium Act 2 (12", p/s)........25
92   Peaceville VILE 27   Symphonaire Infernus Et Spera Empyrium/God Is Alone/ De Sade Soliloquay (CD)........15
93   Peaceville VILE 44   I Am The Bloody Earth/Transcending (Into The Exquisite)/ Crown Of Sympathy (Remix) (CD)........12
93   Peaceville VILE 44T   I Am The Bloody Earth/Transcending (Into The Exquisite) (12", p/s)........20
93   Peaceville VILE 37T   The Thrash Of Naked Limbs/Le Cerf Malade/Gather Me Up Forever (12", p/s)........25
93   Unbridled Voyage (No Cat. No)   Unreleased Bitterness: The Bitterness And The Bereavement (1-sided flexidisc, fold-out p/s in poly sleeve, 1150 only)........20
94   Peaceville CC5   Sexuality Of Bereavement/Crown Of Sympathy (Remix) (p/s) 25
92   Peaceville VILE 30   AS THE FLOWER WITHERS (LP, gatefold sleeve) 15
93   Peaceville VILE 39   TURN LOOSE THE SWANS (LP, double) 35
94   Peaceville VILE 45   THE STORIES EP (box set, 1000 only) 75
95   Peaceville VILE 50   THE ANGEL AND THE DARK RIVER (LP, picture disc) 15

TIM MYCROFT
71	Parlophone R5919	Shadra/Bournemouth Rock	15

AMINA CLAUDINE MYERS
80	Leo LR 100	SONG FOR MOTHER E (LP)	20
80	Leo LR 103	AMINA CLAUDINE MYERS SALUTES BESSIE SMITH (LP)	45

ROWLAND MYERS
75	MSE MSE 2SSP/P	Give Them A Hand/Pandemonium	30

MY FRIENDS AND I
69	Marroo MR 001	Susan/Wake The Dead	40

MY KIND OF PEOPLE
70	CBS 555133	Somebodys Coming/Nobody Knows Why The Butterfly Died	25

BILLY MYLES
57	HMV POP 423	The Joker (That's What They Call Me)/Honey Bee	60
57	HMV POP 423	The Joker (That's What They Call Me)/Honey Bee (78)	15

MEG MYLES
56	Capitol CL 14555	Sing On, Baby/Will You Shed A Tear For Me?	7

MY LIFE STORY
86	Think Tank CHAPTER 1	HOME SWEET ZOO: Boring Dream/Sliding Bookcase (gatefold p/s, 500 only)	40

MY LORDE SHERIFFE'S COMPLAINTE
79	Frog FROG 1	MY LORDE SHERIFFE'S COMPLAINTE (LP, private pressing)	15

MYND MUZIC
94	Poor Person Prod.	IMAGINE THIS (LP, handmade sleeve, 500 only)	20

ROWLAND MYRES
74	Deroy DER 1063	JUST FOR THE RECORD (LP, private pressing, also listed as Music Sound Enterprise MSE 1)	120

MYRTELLES
63	Oriole CB 1805	Don't Wanna Cry Again/Just Let Me Cry	40

(see also Sue & Sunshine, Sue & Sunny, Stockingtops)

MYSTERE FIVE'S
80	Flicknife FLS 001	No Message/Shake Some Action (p/s)	5
81	Flicknife FLS 202	Never Say Thank You/Heart Rules The Head (p/s)	5

(see also Wayne County & Electric Chairs)

MYSTERIES
64	Decca F 11919	Give Me Rhythm And Blues/Teardrops	30

WILLIAM MYSTERIOUS
82	Mezzanine MEZ 1	Security Of Noise/Alright (p/s, with Fay Fife & Revettes)	6

(see also Rezillos, Revillos)

MYSTERY GIRLS
81	Strange HAM 002	I'm A Believer/Modern Mystery Pop/Walking Backwards (p/s)	6

MYSTERY GUESTS
80	Boys Own/Heater Volume BO 1	Wurlitzer Junction/The Merry Shark You Are (handmade stickered white labels)	6
81	Boys Own BO 3	The Sparrow That Ate New York/The Nude (p/s)	5

MYSTERY MAKER
77	Caves UHC 3	MYSTERY MAKER (LP, private pressing with booklet)	120

MYSTIC EMP
80	His Majesty HMD 006	Reality/JAH THOMAS: Throw Away Vanity/MYSTIC EMP & JAH THOMAS: Reality Dub (12")	20

MYSTIC EYES
79	Greensleeves GRED 11	Perilous Times (with Trinity)/REVOLUTIONARIES: Roots Man Version (12")	30
79	Warrior WAR 135	Elaine/MIKEY DREAD: Schoolgirls (12")	25
78	Burning Sounds BS 1033	MYSTERIOUS (LP)	45

MYSTIC INSTITUTE
92	Evolution EVO 06	CYBERDON EP (12")	18

(see also Global Communications, Reload, Link)

MYSTIC MATT & THE ANTHILL MOB
99	Love Peace & Unity LOVE 05	A SHOCK 2 DA SYSTEM EP (12", p/s)	25

(see also Anthill Mob)

MYSTIC MOODS
73	Warner Bros K 16265	Cosmic Sea/Awakening	7
74	Warner Bros K 46250	AWAKENING (LP)	15

MYSTIC NUMBER NATIONAL BANK
69	Probe SPB 1001	THE MYSTIC NUMBER NATIONAL BANK (LP)	25

MYSTIC TOUCH
75	Champagne 505	Get Yourself Together/Pary People	15

MYSTICS
59	HMV POP 646	Hushabye/Adam And Eve	30
59	Top Rank JAR 243	Don't Take The Stars/So Tenderly	40

MYSTICS (JAMAICA)
75	Grounation GRO 2049	God Bless The Youths/Dub	5

MYSTREATED
94	Twist TWIST 15	SHE'S GONE (EP)	6
95	Twist TWIST 18	LIVE AT THE BBC (EP)	6
96	Hangman's Daughter KETCH 7 UP	Never Question Why/Take A Look In The Mirror (p/s, 500 only)	8
97	Detour DR 054	(What's In) Your Mind Today/I'll Be There (p/s)	10
98	Detour DR 060	Contrasts (I've Got Plenty)/Right Here	10
92	Hangman TWISTBIG 4	10 BOSS CUTS (LP)	20

MINT VALUE £

94	Twist TWISTBIG 4	LOOKING RIGHT THROUGH (LP)	15
95	Twist TWISTBIG 5	10 BOSS CUTS (LP, reissue)	12
95	Twist TWISTBIG 7	EVERY QUESTIONING WHY (LP)	15
96	Twist TWISTBIG 8	THIS IS... (LP)	12

MYTHRO
| 00 | Deal Real DR001 | Kiss That Arse Goodnight/The Word's Out (12") | 8 |

MYTHRA
79	Guardian GRMA 16	DEATH & DESTINY: Death And Destiny/Killer/Overload/UFO (EP, no p/s)	12
80	Streetbeat LAMP 2	Death Or Destiny/Killer/U.F.O. (with p/s)	90
80	Streetbeat LAMP 2	Death Or Destiny/Killer/U.F.O.	10
80	Streetbeat 12 LAMP 2	Death Or Destiny/Killer/Overlord/U.F.O. (12", with p/s)	125
80	Streetbeat 12 LAMP 2	Death Or Destiny/Killer/Overlord/U.F.O. (12")	20

M ZONE & DJ GOLLUM
| 97 | UK44 UK44 EP3 | Harmony (Get Me)/Harmony (12") | 12 |

(see also DJ Gollum)

NABAY
| 80 | Grapevine GRP 143 | Believe It Or Not/Believe It Or Not (Instrumental) | 30 |

RICKY NADIR
| 75 | Charisma CB 345 | Birthday Special/Shingle Song | 10 |
| 79 | Charisma CB 339 | The Polaroid/PETER HAMMILL: The Old School Tie | 10 |

(see also Peter Hammill)

NA FILI
| 74 | Dolphin DOL 1008 | CHANTER'S TUNE (LP) | 12 |

NA H-ORGANAICH
| 73 | Beltona SBE 145 | THE GREAT GAELIC SOUND OF (LP) | 15 |
| 74 | Beltona SBE 160 | GAEL FORCE 3 (LP) | 15 |

NAKED LUNCH
| 81 | Ramkup CAC 003 | Rabies/Slipping Again (p/s) | 7 |

NAKED TRUTH
| 70 | Deram DM 287 | Two Little Rooms/Rag Doll Boy | 7 |

NAME
| 80 | Din Disc DIN 14 | Forget Art, Let's Dance/Misfits (p/s) | 10 |
| 87 | China WOK 15 | Jesus And The Devil/The Great Depression (P/S) | 8 |

NAMES
| 80 | Factory FAC 29 | Nightshift/I Wish I Could Speak Your Language (p/s) | 10 |

ZBIGNIEW NAMYSLOWSKI MODERN JAZZ QUARTET
| 64 | Decca LK/SKL 4644 | LOLA (LP) | 175 |

NANETTE
70	Columbia DB 8659	Flying Machine/You're Wasting Your Time	35
70	Columbia DB 8673	Every Night When I Cry Myself To Sleep/Jamie	10
70	Columbia DB 8733	Let Me Be The One/To Be Loved	10
71	Columbia DB 8751	Everybody's Singing Right Now/Could I Forget	10
70	Columbia SCX 6398	NANETTE (LP)	30

ED NANGLE
| 68 | Blue Cat BS 120 | Good Girl/ENFORCERS: Musical Fever | 30 |
| 68 | Coxsone CS 7038 | Whipping The Prince (actually by Ed Nangle & Alton Ellis & Soul Vendors)/HEPTONES: If You Knew | 40 |

NICK NANTOS & HIS FIREBALLERS
| 63 | Summit LSE 2042 | GUITARS ON FIRE (EP) | 15 |
| 64 | Summit ATL 4114 | GUITARS ON FIRE (LP) | 15 |

(see also Bill Haley & Comets)

NAOMI
| 70 | Gayfeet GS 207 | You're Not My Kind/GAYTONES: You're Not My Kind (Version II) | 10 |
| 70 | High Note HS 047 | Natural Woman/GAYTONES: Natural Woman - Version | 10 |

(see also Derrick Morgan, Tommy McCook)

NAPALM DEATH
87	Strange Fruit SFPS 049	THE PEEL SESSIONS (12", p/s)	10
89	Rise Above RISE 001	NAPALM DEATH EP (poster p/s, sold at gigs)	15
89	Earache 7MOSH 14	Mentally Murdered/Cause And effect (stickered p/s)	5
89	Earache MOSH 014	MENTALLY MURDERED EP (Rise Above/The Missing Link/Mentally Murdered Walls Of Confinement/Cause And Effect/No Mental Effort) (12", p/s)	15
90	Earache 7MOSH 24L	Suffer The Children/The Kill/Scum/Extremity Retained/Life? (stickered p/s, sticker sheet)	10
90	Earache MOSH 024	Suffer The Children/Siege Of Power/Harmony Corruption (12", p/s)	10
91	Earache 7MOSH 46	Mass Appeal Madness/Pride Assassin (p/s)	10
91	Earache MOSH 046	Mass Appeal Madness/Pride Assassin/Unchallenged Hate/Social Sterility (12", p/s)	10
92	Earache MOSH 65	THE WORLD KEEPS TURNING EP (12", p/s)	12
92	Earache MOSH 065CD	The World Keeps Turning/A Means To An End/Insanity Excursion (CD)	10
93	Earache 7MOSH 92	Nazi Punks Fuck Off/Aryanisms/Nazi Punks Fuck Off (Live)/Contemptuous (Xtreem Mix) (p/s)	10
95	Earache MOSH 146	GREED KILLING EP (Greed Killing/My Own Worst Enemy/Self Betrayal/Finer Truths White Lies/Antibody/All Links Severed/Plague Rages [Live]) (10", p/s)	15
96	Earache 7 MOSH 168	Food Chains/Upward And Uninterested (demo version)/COALESCE: A Safe Place/Harvest Of Maturity) (p/s, insert, purple vinyl)	15

96	Earache 7 MOSH 168	Food Chains/Upward And Uninterested (demo version)/COALESCE: A Safe Place/Harvest Of Maturity) (p/s, insert)	10
87	Earache MOSH 3	SCUM (LP, lyric insert, black/orange, black/green, black red or black/yellow cover)	15
88	Earache MOSH 8	FROM ENSLAVEMENT TO OBLITERATION (LP, gatefold sleeve, free 7" EP [7MOSH 8])	35
90	Earache MOSH 19/19L	HARMONY CORRUPTION (2-LP, with inserts)	25
90	Earache MOSH 19P	HARMONY CORRUPTION (LP, picture disc)	20
91	Earache MOSH 3	SCUM (LP, reissue, white and black swirl vinyl, black and gold sleeve, 2000 only)	15
91	Earache MOSH 51	DEATH BY MANIPULATION (LP, with insert)	12
92	Earache MOSH 53	UTOPIA BANISHED (LP, free 7" EP [MOSH 53L])	25
92	Earache MOSH8/19/51/67L	BOX SET (4-CD)	25
06	Earache MOSH 003PD	SCUM (LP, 2nd reissue, picture disc, stickered PVC sleeve, 1500 only)	15

MARTY NAPOLEON
55	London EZ-NI9001	NAPOLEON SINGS AND SWINGS (EP)	15

NAPOLEON XIV
66	Warner Bros WB 5831	They're Coming To Take Me Away Ha-Haa!/ !Aah-Ah Yawa Em Ekat Ot Gnimoc Er'Yeht	7
66	Warner Bros WB 5853	I'm In Love With My Little Red Tricycle/Doin' The Napoleon	12
66	Warner Bros W 1661	THEY'RE COMING TO TAKE ME AWAY HA-HA-A! (LP)	70

(see also Jerry Samuels, Kim Fowley)

RAYMOND NAPTALI AND ROY RANKING
81	KG Imperial KG 006	New Cross Fire/Brixton Incident (12", blue vinyl)	25

PETER NARDINI
80s	Kettle KS 701	I Think You're Great/Ma Maw's A Mod (in p/s)	15
80s	Kettle KS 701	I Think You're Great/Ma Maw's A Mod	8

NARNIA
74	Myrrh MYR 1007	NARNIA - ASLAN IS NOT A TAME LION (LP)	80

(see also After The Fire, Pauline Filby)

BILLY NASH
61	Philips PB 1181	Sunset/Nobody Loves Me Like You (as Billy Nash Combo)	7
63	Philips 370 406 BF	The Madison Step/Madison Rhythm (as Billy Nash Rock Band)	7

GENE NASH
59	Capitol CL 15042	I'm An Eskimo Too/Ja, Ja, Ja (Deutsche Rock 'N Roll)	15

GRAHAM NASH
71	Atlantic 2091 096	Chicago/Simple Man	6
71	Atlantic 2091 135	Military Madness/I Used To Be A King	6
71	Atlantic 2401 011	SONGS FOR BEGINNERS (LP)	18

(see also Hollies, Crosby Stills Nash & Young)

JOHNNY NASH
57	HMV POP 402	Ladder Of Love/I'll Walk Alone	10
57	HMV POP 402	Ladder Of Love/I'll Walk Alone (78)	12
58	HMV POP 435	Won't You Let Me Share My Love With You?/A Very Special Love	10
58	HMV POP 435	Won't You Let Me Share My Love With You?/A Very Special Love (78)	10
58	HMV POP 475	It's Easy To Say/My Pledge To You	10
58	HMV POP 475	It's Easy To Say/My Pledge To You (78)	10
58	HMV POP 553	Almost In Your Arms/Midnight Moonlight	7
58	HMV POP 553	Almost In Your Arms/Midnight Moonlight (78)	12
59	HMV POP 597	Walk With Faith In Your Heart/Roots Of Heaven	7
59	HMV POP 597	Walk With Faith In Your Heart/Roots Of Heaven (78)	10
59	HMV POP 620	As Time Goes By/Voice Of Love	7
59	HMV POP 651	And The Angels Sing/Baby, Baby, Baby	7
59	HMV POP 673	Take A Giant Step/Imagination	6
60	HMV POP 746	A Place In The Sun/Goodbye	6
60	HMV POP 822	Somebody/Kisses	6
62	Warner Bros WB 65	Don't Take Away Your Love/Moment Of Weakness	20
62	Warner Bros WB 76	Ol' Man River/My Dear Little Sweetheart	30
63	Warner Bros WB 93	Cigareets, Whuskey And Wild, Wild Women/I'm Moving On	15
64	Pye International 7N 25250	Love Ain't Nothin'/Talk To Me	60
65	Chess CRS 8005	Strange Feelin'/Rainin' In My Heart	25
66	Pye International 7N 25353	Let's Move And Groove (Together)/Understanding	20
66	Pye International 7N 25363	One More Time/Tryin' To Find Her	20
68	Regal Zono. RZ 3010	Hold Me Tight/Let's Move And Groove Together	10
68	Major Minor MM 586	You've Got Soul/Don't Cry	7
68	Major Minor MM 603	Cupid/People In Love	10
69	MGM MGM 1480	(I'm So) Glad You're My Baby/Stormy	35
71	MAM MAM R 9	Falling In And Out Of Love/People In Love	7
64	RCA Victor RCX 7163	PRESENTING JOHNNY NASH (EP)	125
59	HMV CLP 1251	JOHNNY NASH (LP)	40
59	HMV CLP 1299	QUIET HOUR WITH JOHNNY NASH (LP)	25
60	HMV CLP 1325	I GOT RHYTHM (LP, mono)	35
60	HMV CSD 1288	I GOT RHYTHM (LP, stereo)	45
62	Encore ENC 2005	LET'S GET LOST (LP)	15
69	Major Minor MMLP/SMLP 47	YOU GOT SOUL (LP)	15
69	Major Minor MMLP/SMLP 56	SOUL FOLK (LP)	15
69	Major Minor MMLP/SMLP 63	PRINCE OF PEACE (LP)	15

JOHNNY NASH & KIM WESTON
69	Major Minor SMLP 54	JOHNNY NASH AND KIM WESTON (LP)	20

(see also Kim Weston)

KATE NASH
07	Moshi Moshi MOMO 4	Caroline's A Victim/Birds	12

NASH THE SLASH
81	Dindisc DIN 28	Dead Man's Curve/Reactor No. 2 (p/s)	10

TONY NASH
70	Hot Rod HR 110	Keep On Trying/WINSTON JAMES: Just Can't Do Without Your Love	12

MINT VALUE £

NASHVILLE FIVE
62	Decca F 11427	Stand Up And Say That/Like Nashville	7
62	Decca F 11484	Some Other Love/Brainwave	7
62	Decca DFE 6706	LIKE NASHVILLE (EP)	40

NASHVILLE TEENS
64	Decca F 11930	Tobacco Road/I Like It Like That	8
64	Decca F 12000	Google Eye (some misspelled "Goggle Eye" on label)/T.N.T.	8
65	Decca F 12089	Find My Way Back Home/Devil-In-Law	8
65	Decca F 12143	This Little Bird/Whatcha Gonna Do?	8
65	Decca F 12255	I Know How It Feels To Be Loved/Soon Forgotten	8
66	Decca F 12316	The Hard Way/Upside Down	15
66	Decca F 12458	Forbidden Fruit/Revived 45 Time	25
66	Decca F 12542	That's My Woman/Words	18
67	Decca F 12580	I'm Coming Home/Searching	10
67	Decca F 12657	The Biggest Night Of Her Life/Last Minute	10
68	Decca F 12754	All Along The Watchtower/Sun-Dog	15
69	Major Minor MM 599	The Lament Of The Cherokee Reservation Indian/Looking For You	18
69	Decca F 12929	Tobacco Road/All Along The Watchtower	6
71	Parlophone R 5925	Ella James/Tennessee Woman	15
72	Parlophone R 5961	You Shouldn't Have Been So Nice/Tell The People (unissued)	0
73	Enterprise ENT S101	Lawdy Miss Clawdy/Rocking On The Railroad/Let It Rock	7
77	Sky 1007	Tobacco Road/Chips And Peas	5
65	Decca DFE 8600	THE NASHVILLE TEENS (EP)	50
75	New World NW 6002	THE NASHVILLE TEENS (LP)	40

(see also Arizona Swamp Company, Jerry Lee Lewis, Carl Perkins)

NASTY FACTS
81	5th Column FC 2	Drive My Car/Gotta Get To You/Crazy 'Bout you (p/s)	40

NASTY HABIT
92	Reinforced RIVET 1233	As Nasty As I Wanna Be (12")	25
92	Reinforced RIVET 1233R	As Nasty As I Wanna Be (Remixes) (12")	25

NASTY MEDIA
78	Lightning GIL 542	Spiked Copy/Winter (p/s)	20

NATCHBAND
78	Far In FARS 01	Cadillac (Made In USA)/Being From The Sky (p/s)	6

BARRY NATHAN TRIO
80	EMAL BNT 1	MORNING SONGRISE (LP)	50

NATIONAL
05	Beggars Banquet BBQ 385	Abel/Warm Singing Whores (p/s)	6
07	Beggars Banquet BBQ 405	Mistaken For Strangers/Blank Slate (p/s)	6
07	Beggars Banquet BBQ 407	Apartment Story/Mansion On The Hill (live) (yellow vinyl)	10
07	Beggars Banquet BBQ 408 CDP	EXTRAS EP (tour CD, 1000 only)	20
10	4AD AD3X50	Terrible Love/You Were A Kindness (purple vinyl, p/s)	6
10	4AD CAD 3X03X	HIGH VIOLET (2-LP, violet vinyl)	20
11	Beggars Banquet BBQLP 241	ALLIGATOR (LP, reissue, green vinyl)	15

NATIONAL ART HATE WEEK
09	No Cat no	God Save Marcel Duchamp/Silent Revolt (p/s, mail order only, 350 copies, numbered)	15

NATIONAL-ELLS
67	Parlophone R 5609	Mr. Moon/Dance, Dance	7

NATIONAL HEAD BAND
71	Warner Bros K 46094	ALBERT 1 (LP)	30

(see also Caravan, Gary Moore, Toe-Fat, Uriah Heep)

NATIONAL HEALTH
78	Affinity AFF 6	NATIONAL HEALTH (LP)	12
78	Charly CRL 5010	OF QUEUES AND CURES (LP)	12

(see also Hatfield & The North)

NATIONAL LAMPOON
78	Island HELP 8	RADIO DINNER (LP)	12

NATIONAL PINION POLE
66	Planet PLF 111	Make Your Mark Little Man/I Was The One You Came In With (in Planet sleeve)	18
66	Planet PLF 111	Make Your Mark Little Man/I Was The One You Came In With	12

NATIONWIDE ENGLAND SUPPORTERS CLUB
86	Peak PRIDE 1	Oh Sweet England/England Supporter (picture disc, with rosette & beermat)	5

NATURAL ACOUSTIC BAND
73	RCA RCA 2324	Echoes/Is It True Blue	5
72	RCA SF 8272	LEARNING TO LIVE (LP, textured gatefold sleeve)	35
72	RCA SF 8314	BRANCHING IN (LP, with lyric insert)	25

(see also Krysia)

NATURAL BRIDGE BUNCH
69	Atlantic 584 231	Pig Snoots (Parts 1 & 2)	10

CLIVE NATURAL
77	WIRL WIRL 1	Marridge Rekka/No Money (12")	40

NATURAL FOUR
75	Curtom 16583	Love's So Wonderful/What's Happening Here	15
75	Atlantic K 56142	HEAVEN RIGHT HERE ON EARTH (LP)	30

NATURAL GAS
76	Private Stock PVLP 1007	NATURAL GAS (LP, gatefold sleeve with inner sleeve)	15

(see also Badfinger, Blue Goose, Humble Pie, Uriah Heep, Quiver)

NATURAL IMPULSE
08	Soul Junction SJ 502	She Went Away/Time Was Right	10

THE NATURAL ITES AND THE REALISTICS
83	CSA 12CSA 501	Picture On My Wall/Jah Works Mama (12")	12

NATURAL MAGIC
75	Oyster OYR 102	Strawberry Fields Forever/Isolated Lady	10

(see also Roger Glover, Eddie Hardin)

NATURAL ROOTS
82	Fasim FS106	Know Yourself/Ain't Got No Money (12")	20

NATURAL VIBES
82	Starlight Records SDLP 907	LIFE HARD IN A YARD (LP)	35

NATURALITY
69	Ackee ACK 101	The Arena/Natural	50

NATURALLY
79	Bushays BFM 111	I'll Get By/All I Have Is Written In Your Eyes (12")	15

NATURALS (U.K.) (1)
64	Parlophone R 5116	Daisy Chain/That Girl	12
64	Parlophone R 5165	I Should Have Known Better/Didn' I?	15
64	Parlophone R 5202	It Was You/Look At Me Now	15
65	Parlophone R 5257	Blue Roses/Shame On You	15

(see also Living Daylights, Greatest Show On Earth)

NATURALS (U.K.) (2)
80	Refined RR2	STRANGE DAYS (EP, 500 only)	25
81	Just For The Records	Six Girls & Alice (fold-out cover)	12

NATURALS (U.S.)
55	MGM SP 1123	The Finger Of Suspicion Points At You/You Forgot To Remember	12
57	MGM MGM 939	The Buccaneers/The Ballad Of Sir Lancelot	8

(see also Debbie Reynolds)

FATS NAVARRO
56	London LZ-C 14015	MEMORIAL (LP)	15

NAVY BLUE
82	AP 572	THE PUSSERS (EP)	15

JERRY NAYLOR
61	Top Rank JAR 591	Stop Your Crying/You're Thirteen	25
67	Stateside SS 2029	Sweet Violets/Temptation Leads Me	6
70	CBS 4882	But For Love/Angeline	5

SHEL NAYLOR
63	Decca F 11776	How Deep Is The Ocean/La Bamba	20
64	Decca F 11856	One Fine Day/It's Gonna Happen Soon	150

(see also Lieutenant Pigeon, Stavely Makepeace)

NAZARETH
72	Pegasus PGS 2	Dear John/Friends	20
72	Pegasus PGS 2	Dear John/Friends (2nd issue, PEG label, B-side lists 'Occasional Failure')	25
72	Pegasus BCP 3	Dear John/Witchdoctor Woman/Morning Dew (unreleased, promo only, stamped white labels and insert)	50
72	Pegasus PGS 4	Morning Dew/Spinning Top (PEG label)	20
72	Pegasus BCP 8	Fool About You/Woke Up This Morning/Morning Dew (unreleased, promo only, handwritten white labels)	50
72	Pegasus PGS 5	If You See My Baby/Hard Living (PEG label)	20
73	Mooncrest MOON 9	Bad Bad Boy/Hard Living/Spinning Top (in p/s)	5
74	Mooncrest MOON 22	Shanghai'd In Shanghai/Love, Now You're Gone	5
74	Mooncrest MOON 37	Love Hurts/Down	5
75	Mooncrest MOON 44	Hair Of The Dog/Too Bad, Too Sad	5
75	Mooncrest MOON 47	My White Bicycle/My White Bicycle (A label promo only)	12
75	Mooncrest MOON 47	My White Bicycle/Miss Misery	5
76	Mountain PSLP191	I Don't Want To Go On Without You/Waiting For The Man (12" promo)	15
92	Mausoleum 3670010.7	Every Time It Rains/This Flight Tonight (p/s)	5
78	Mountain TOP 37	Place In Your Heart/Kentucky Fried Blues (mispressing, B-side plays Bee Gees track, company sleeve)	15
79	Mountain NAZ 4	Whatever You Want Babe/Telegram Parts 1, 2 & 3 (p/s, purple vinyl)	10
80	NEMS BSD 1	NAZARETH LIVE (2 x 7", gatefold)	6
71	Pegasus PEG 10	NAZARETH (LP, 1st issue, Pegasus picture label, textured matt sleeve)	75
72	Pegasus PEG 10	NAZARETH (LP, 2nd issue, PEG label/glossy sleeve)	40
72	Pegasus PEG 14	EXERCISES (LP, gatefold sleeve)	50
73	Mooncrest CREST 1	RAZAMANAZ (LP)	40
73	Mooncrest CREST 4	LOUD 'N' PROUD (LP)	40
74	Mooncrest CREST 15	RAMPANT (LP, inner sleeeve, sticker insert)	50
75	Mooncrest CREST 27	HAIR OF THE DOG (LP, with inner)	50
76	Mountain TOPS 109	CLOSE ENOUGH FOR ROCK 'N' ROLL (LP)	18
76	Mountain TOPS 113	PLAY 'N' THE GAME (LP, with inner sleeve)	18
77	Mountain TOPS 115	EXPECT NO MERCY (LP, with inner sleeve)	20
79	Mountain TOPS 123	NO MEAN CITY (LP, with inner sleeve)	15
85	Sahara SAH 130	SOUND ELIXIR (LP, Marimba label, withdrawn)	12

(see also Dan McCafferty, Mark Five, Sensational Alex Harvey Band, Tandoori Cassette, Billy Rankin)

NAZIS AGAINST FASCISM
79	Truth TRUTH 1	Sid Did It (Intelligible)/Sid Did It (Radio Version) (p/s, 2 different issues)	6

(see also Vibrators)

NAZZ
68	Screen Gems SGC 219001	Open My Eyes/Hello It's Me	20
69	Screen Gems SGC 219002	Hello It's Me/Crowded	10
69	Screen Gems SGC 219003	Not Wrong Long/Under The Ice	10
69	Screen Gems SGC 221001	NAZZ (LP)	65

(see also Todd Rundgren)

'N BETWEENS
66   Columbia DB 8080   You Better Run/Evil Witchman (demos credit In-Be-Tweens)............................420
(see also Slade, Vendors)

CHRIS NEAL
71   Fly BUG 15   Blame It All On Eve/All The Time In The World (p/s) 6

JOHNNY NEAL & STARLINERS
65   Pye 7N 15838   And I Will Love You/Walk Baby Walk..80
70   Parlophone R 5870   Put Your Hand In The Hand/Now 7
(see also Storyteller)

TOMMY NEAL
68   Vocalion VL 9290   Goin' To A Happening/Tee Ta 50
68   Vocalion VL 9290   Goin' To A Happening/Tee Ta (DJ copy) 125

NEARLY GOD
96   Durban Poison DPLP 1001   NEARLY GOD (LP) 12

NEAT
80s   Neatbeat LYN 6269   Hormones In Action/Take Your Chances (p/s)...50

NEAT CHANGE
68   Decca F 12809   I Lied To Auntie May/Sandman (in foldout p/s) 120
68   Decca F 12809   I Lied To Auntie May/Sandman 60
(see also Peter Banks, English Rose)

NEBULA II
91   Reinforced RIVET 1211   Seance/Atheama (12")..8
92   Reinforced RIVET 1232   Peace Maker/X-Plore H-Core (12")..8
92   Reinforced RIVET 1232R   X-Plore H-Core/Peace Maker (Remixes) (12")...15
93   Reinforced RIVET 1247   Eye Memory (12")...8

NECROMANDUS
90   Reflection MM 09   QUICKSAND DREAM (LP, 500 only) 18

BERNIE NEE
58   Philips PB 794   Lend Me Your Comb/Medal Of Honour 20
58   Philips PB 794   Lend Me Your Comb/Medal Of Honour (78) 10
(see also Bernie Knee)

NEEDLES
80   Ellie Jay EJSP 9340   Gotta Know You/Jayneski (no p/s) 150

LOUIS NEEFS
69   Columbia DB 8561   Jennifer Jennings/I Love You 25

ELGIN NEELY
65   Vogue V 9240   Four Walls/I Could Be 12

NEGATIVE FX
84   Fundamental HOLY 7   NEGATIVE FX (LP) 25

NEGATIVES
78   Look LK/SP 6478   Stakeout (50 copies with p/s)..200
78   Look LK/SP 6478   Stakeout (no p/s) 40
80   Aardvark STEAL 1   Electric Waltz/Money Talks (p/s) 5
81   Aardvark STEAL 3   Scene Of The Crime (p/s) 8

NEGATIVES IN COLOUR
90s   own label NEG 1   Caught In Possession...15

NEGAZIONE
85   Children Of The Revolution   MUCCHIO SELVAGGIO (split LP with DECLINO) 75
      GURT 7

NEGRIL
75   Torpedo TOR 51   I Shot The Sheriff/Negril 10
75   Klik KLP 9005   NEGRIL (LP) 30

NEGRO
80   Negro NEG 1   Unite/DJ A HUMBLE I: Unite Tonight 120

NEGUS DAWTAS
78   Natty Congo NATTY 001   I Speak The Truth/Hail Rastafari (Actually by Ranking Reuben) 15

NEGUS ROOTS MEETS THE MAD PROFESSOR
83   Negus Roots NERLP 009   DUB ROCKERS VOLUME 2 (LP)...80
(see also Lackley Castell)

FRED NEIL
69   Elektra EKSN 45036   Candy Man/The Water Is Wide 8
69   Capitol CL 15616   Everybody's Talkin'/Badi-Da..12
67   Elektra EKS 7293   BLEECKER & MACDOUGAL (LP)..60
70   Capitol E-ST 657   OTHER SIDE OF THIS LIFE (LP)..35

DON NEILSON
60   Philips BF 1058   The House Is Haunted/For All We Know 5
62   Piccadilly 7N 35044   Forgotten Dreams/These Things Remain 5
63   Piccadilly 7N 35103   I Will Live My Life For You/How Do You Keep From Crying..............................5

NEKTAR
73   United Artists NEK 1   What Ya Gonna Do?/Day In The Life Of A Preacher Pt. One (Edit) (p/s) 15
74   United Artists UP 35706   Fidgety Queen/Little Boy 10
75   United Artists UP 35853   Astral Man/Nelly The Elephant 10
73   United Artists UAD 60041/2   SOUNDS LIKE THIS (2-LP)..40
74   United Artists UAS 29499   A TAB IN THE OCEAN (LP, gatefold sleeve) 35
74   United Artists UAg 29545   REMEMBER THE FUTURE (LP, gatefold)..35
74   United Artists UAG 29680   DOWN TO EARTH (LP, gatefold sleeve) 30
76   Decca SKL-R 5250   RECYCLED (LP)...15
(see also Robert Calvert)

NELLIE
69	Gas GAS 126	I Who Have Nothing/You Send Me	25

BILL NELSON('S RED NOISE)
85	Cocteau JEAN 1	PERMANENT FLAME SINGLES BOX (box set of 5 singles)	10
71	Smile LAF 2182/HG 116	NORTHERN DREAM (LP, 250 only, numbered, in foldover gatefold sleeve with booklet)	35
71	Smile LAF 2182/HG 116	NORTHERN DREAM (LP, 250 second pressing unnumbered, (reissues on the Butt label, £15)	20
85	Cocteau JEAN 2	TRIAL BY INTIMACY (THE BOOK OF SPLENDOURS) (4-LP, box set, with book & postcards, initial copies misspelt as "The Book Splendours")	20
86	KPM/Themes TIM	CHAMELEON - THE MUSIC OF BILL NELSON (LP, library issue)	12
78	Harvest SHSP 4095	SOUND ON SOUND (LP)	15

(see also A - Austr, Astral Navigations, Gagalactyca, Be-Bop Deluxe)

CLARE NELSON
59	MGM MGM 1025	The Valley Of Love/You Are My Sunshine	8

EARL NELSON
59	London HLW 8950	No Time To Cry/Come On	30
59	London HLW 8950	No Time To Cry/Come On (78)	20

OLIVER NELSON
60	Esquire 32-148	SCREAMIN THE BLUES (LP, as the Oliver Nelson Sextet)	50
63	Verve VLP 9053	FULL NELSON (LP)	15
68	HMV CLP 1868	MORE BLUES AND THE ABSTRACT TRUTH (LP)	18

OZZIE & HARRIET NELSON
59	London HA-P 2145	OZZIE AND HARRIET NELSON (LP)	35

PETER NELSON
65	Piccadilly 7N 35278	Donna/I Want To Be Wanted	8
66	Piccadilly 7N 35314	Don't Make Promises (You Can't Keep)/No Need To Cry	7
72	Peacock PEA502	Good Scotch Whiskey/I Am A Ship	20

RICK(Y) NELSON
78s
57	HMV POP 355	I'm Walkin'/A Teenager's Romance	40
57	HMV POP 390	You're My One And Only Love/BARNEY KESSEL: Honey Rock	40
57	London HLP 8499	Be-Bop Baby/Have I Told You Lately That I Love You	20
58	London HLP 8542	Stood Up/Waitin' In School	20
58	London HLP 8594	Believe What You Say/My Bucket's Got A Hole In It	20
58	London HLP 8732	Someday/I Got A Feeling	20
58	London HLP 8738	Lonesome Town/My Babe	20
59	London HLP 8817	It's Late/Never Be Anyone Else But You	20
59	London HLP 8927	Just A Little Too Much/Sweeter Than You	25
60	London HLP 9021	I Wanna Be Loved/Mighty Good	60
60	London HLP 9121	Young Emotions/Right By My Side	30
60	London HLP 9188	Yes, Sir, That's My Baby/I'm Not Afraid	60

SINGLES
57	HMV POP 355	I'm Walkin'/A Teenager's Romance (gold label lettering)	150
57	HMV POP 355	I'm Walkin'/A Teenager's Romance (silver label lettering)	60
57	HMV POP 390	You're My One And Only Love/BARNEY KESSEL: Honey Rock	100
57	London HLP 8499	Be-Bop Baby/Have I Told You Lately That I Love You	30
58	London HLP 8542	Stood Up/Waitin' In School	25
58	London HLP 8594	Believe What You Say/My Bucket's Got A Hole In It	25
58	London HLP 8670	Poor Little Fool/Don't Leave Me This Way	8
58	London HLP 8732	Someday/I Got A Feeling	8
58	London HLP 8738	Lonesome Town/My Babe	8
59	London HLP 8817	It's Late/Never Be Anyone Else But You (all black or silver-top label)	8
59	London HLP 8894	Just A Little Too Much/Sweeter Than You (unreleased)	0
59	London HLP 8927	Just A Little Too Much/Sweeter Than You (triangular centre)	10

(The 45s listed above were originally issued with triangular centres; later round-centre copies are worth half to two-thirds these values.)

59	London HL 7081	Just A Little Too Much/Sweeter Than You (export issue)	10
60	London HLP 9021	I Wanna Be Loved/Mighty Good	10
60	London HLP 9121	Young Emotions/Right By My Side	5
60	London HLP 9188	Yes, Sir, That's My Baby/I'm Not Afraid	5
61	London HLP 9260	You Are The Only One/Milk Cow Blues	20
61	London HLP 9260	You Are The One And Only/Milk Cow Blues (with different label credit)	15
61	London HLP 9347	Hello Mary Lou Goodbye Heart/Travelin' Man (later copies as "Hello Marylou Goodbye Heart")	5
61	London HLP 9440	Everlovin'/A Wonder Like You	6

(The 45s listed above are credited to Ricky Nelson)

62	London HLP 9524	Young World/Summertime	10
62	London HLP 9583	Teen Age Idol/I've Got My Eyes On You (And I Like What I See)	10
63	London HLP 9648	It's Up To You/I Need You	5
63	Brunswick 05885	I Got A Woman/You Don't Love Me Anymore	5
63	Brunswick 05889	String Along/Gypsy Woman	5
63	Brunswick 05895	Fools Rush In/Down Home	5
64	Brunswick 05900	For You/That's All She Wrote	5
64	Liberty LIB 66004	Today's Teardrops/Thank You Darling	5
64	Brunswick 05908	The Very Thought Of You/I Wonder	5
64	Brunswick 05918	Lonely Corner/There's Nothing I Can Say	5
64	Brunswick 05924	A Happy Guy/Don't Breathe A Word	5
65	Brunswick 05939	Come Out Dancin'/Yesterday's Love	10
66	Brunswick 05964	Louisiana Man/You Just Can't Quit (as Ricky Nelson)	10
66	Liberty LIB 12033	I Need You/Wonder Like You	10
69	MCA MU 1106	She Belongs To Me/Promises	5
70	MCA MU 1124	Red Balloon/I Shall Be Released	5
71	MCA MU 1135	Life/California (with Stone Canyon Band)	5
72	MCA MU 1147	Love Minus Zero: No Limit/Gypsy Pilot (with Stone Canyon Band)	5
72	MCA MU 1165	Garden Party/So Long Mama	5
73	MCA MUS 1181	Palace Guard/A Flower Opens Gently By Itself	5
73	MCA MUS 1225	Lifestream/Evil Woman Child	5

Sandy NELSON

MINT VALUE £

74	MCA MCA 126	Windfall/Legacy (with Stone Canyon Band)	5
74	MCA MCA 144	One Night Stand/Lifestream (with Stone Canyon Band)	5
75	MCA MCA 198	Try (Try To Fall In Love)/Louisiana Belle (with Stone Canyon Band)	5
77	Epic S EPC 5821	You Can't Dance/It's Another Day	5

EPs

58	London RE-P 1141	RICKY PART 1	25
58	London RE-P 1142	RICKY PART 2	25
58	London RE-P 1143	RICKY PART 3	25
58	London RE-P 1144	RICKY PART 4	25
59	London RE-P 1168	RICKY NELSON PART 1	25
59	London RE-P 1169	RICKY NELSON PART 2	25
59	London RE-P 1170	RICKY NELSON PART 3	25
59	London RE-P 1200	RICKY SINGS AGAIN PART 1	25
59	London RE-P 1201	RICKY SINGS AGAIN PART 2	25
60	London RE-P 1238	I GOT A FEELING	30
60	London RE-P 1249	RICKY SINGS SPIRITUALS	25
61	London RE-P 1300	RICKY NELSON PART 4	25

(The EPs listed above are credited to Ricky Nelson)

62	London RE-P 1339	IT'S A YOUNG WORLD	30
63	London RE-P 1362	IT'S UP TO YOU	30
63	Brunswick OE 9502	ONE BOY TOO LATE	30
64	Liberty LEP 4001	SINGS FOR YOU	60
64	Liberty LEP 4019	THAT'S ALL	60
65	Liberty LEP 4028	I'M IN LOVE AGAIN	60
65	Brunswick OE 9512	HAPPY GUY	30

ALBUMS : LPS

57	London HA-P 2080	RICKY	50
58	London HA-P 2119	RICKY NELSON	50
59	London HA-P 2159	RICKY SINGS AGAIN	40
59	London HA-P 2206	SONGS BY RICKY	40
60	London HA-P 2290	MORE SONGS BY RICKY (gatefold sleeve, mono)	30
60	London SAH-P 6102	MORE SONGS BY RICKY (gatefold sleeve, stereo)	40
61	London HA-P 2379	RICK IS 21 (mono)	25
61	London SAH-P 6179	RICK IS 21 (stereo)	35

(Credited to Ricky Nelson)

62	London HA-P 2445	ALBUM SEVEN (mono)	25
62	London SAH-P 6236	ALBUM SEVEN (stereo)	30
63	London HA-P 8066	IT'S UP TO YOU	25
63	Brunswick LAT 8545	FOR YOUR SWEET LOVE (mono)	25
63	Brunswick STA 8545	FOR YOUR SWEET LOVE (stereo)	30
64	Brunswick LAT 8562	RICKY SINGS "FOR YOU" (mono)	25
64	Brunswick STA 8562	RICKY SINGS "FOR YOU" (stereo)	40
64	Liberty LBY 3027	MILLION SELLERS	25
64	Brunswick LAT/STA 8581	THE VERY THOUGHT OF YOU	25
64	Brunswick LAT/STA 8596	SPOTLIGHT ON RICK	25
65	Brunswick LAT 8615	BEST ALWAYS	25
65	Brunswick LAT/STA 8630	LOVE AND KISSES	25
66	Brunswick LAT/STA 8657	BRIGHT LIGHTS, COUNTRY MUSIC	25
67	Brunswick LAT/STA 8680	COUNTRY FEVER	25

SANDY NELSON

59	Top Rank JAR 197	Teen Beat/Big Jump	5
59	London HLP 9015	Drum Party/The Big Noise From Winnetka	10
59	London HLP 9015	Drum Party/The Big Noise From Winnetka (78)	50
60	London HLP 9214	I'm Walkin'/Bouncy (as Sandy Nelson & His Combo)	10
61	London HLP 9377	Get With It/Big Noise From The Jungle	10
61	London HLP 9466	Let There Be Drums/Quite A Beat (as Sandy Nelson On The Drums)	5
62	London HLP 9521	Drums Are My Beat/My Girl Josephine	7
62	London HLP 9558	Drummin' Up A Storm/Drum Stomp	8
62	London HLP 9612	...And Then There Were Drums/Live It Up	8
63	London HLP 9717	Ooh Poo Pah Doo/Feel So Good	8
64	Liberty LIB 66060	Teen Beat '65/Kitty's Theme	8
66	Liberty LIB 12062	Hey Joe/Come On Let's Go	5
70	President PT 294	Teen Beat/PRESTON EPPS: Bongo Rock	8
60	Top Rank JKP 2060	RUSHING FOR PERCUSSION (EP, 2 tracks by Preston Epps)	30
62	London REP 1337	LET THERE BE DRUMS (EP)	15
63	London REP 1371	IN THE MOOD (EP)	15
65	Liberty LEP 4033	SANDY NELSON PLAYS (EP)	15
60	London HA-P 2260	TEEN BEAT (LP, mono)	30
60	London SAH-P 6082	TEEN BEAT (LP, stereo)	35
61	London HA-P 2425	LET THERE BE DRUMS (LP, mono)	25
61	London SAH-P 6221	LET THERE BE DRUMS (LP, stereo)	30
62	London HA-P 2446	DRUMS ARE MY BEAT! (LP, mono)	25
62	London SAH-P 6237	DRUMS ARE MY BEAT! (LP, stereo)	30
62	London HA-P 8009	DRUMMIN' UP A STORM (LP, mono)	25
62	London SH-P 8009	DRUMMIN' UP A STORM (LP, stereo)	30
63	London HA-P/SH-P 8029	COMPELLING PERCUSSION (LP)	25
63	London HA-P/SH-P 8051	TEENAGE HOUSE PARTY (LP)	25
65	Liberty LBY 3007	SANDY NELSON PLAYS (LP)	20
65	Liberty LBY 3035	LIVE IN LAS VEGAS (LP)	20
66	Liberty LBY 3061	DRUMS A GO-GO (LP)	20
66	Liberty (S)LBY 3080	SUPERDRUMS (LP)	20
67	Liberty LBL/LBS 83043E	THE BEAT GOES ON (LP)	15
68	Liberty LBL/LBS 83094E	SOUL DRUMS (LP)	15
68	Liberty LBL/LBS 83110E	BOOGALOO BEAT (LP)	15
68	Liberty LBL/LBS 83131E	SUPERDRUMS (LP, reissue, different sleeve)	15
69	Liberty LBL/LBS 83165E	ROCK'N'ROLL REVIVAL (LP)	15
70	Liberty LBS 83302E	GROOVY (LP)	15

(see also Preston Epps)

TERRY NELSON (& FIREBALLS)

65	Dice CC 22	I'll Stand By You/Love On A Saturday Night	10
65	Dice CC 23	Run Run Baby/Bonita (as Terry Nelson & Fireballs)	12
65	Dice CC 25	Bulldog Push/Pretty Little Girl (as Terry Nelson & Fireballs)	12
65	Dice CC 27	Tomorrow Will Soon Be Here/My Blue Eyed Baby	8
65	Blue Beat BB 326	Help/PRINCE BUSTER: Johnny Dollar	25
66	Halagala HG 11	Take These Chains From My Heart/Let-Kiss	6
67	Halagala HG 19	That True Love Must Be Me/Bulldog Walk	5
69	Rude Boy RBH 002	Woman Whine And Grine/Dem CIty GIrls (actually the FIRE-BALLS)	20

WILLIE NELSON

63	Liberty LIB 55532	Half A Man/The Last Letter	10
64	Liberty LIB 55697	River Boy/Opportunity To Cry	10
69	RCA RCA 1867	My Own Peculiar Way/Natural To Be Gone	7
66	RCA Victor RD 7749	COUNTRY WILLIE (LP)	25
66	Liberty (S)LBY 1240	AND THEN I WROTE (LP)	20
69	RCA RD 7997	TEXAS IN MY SOUL (LP)	25

NELSON TRIO (U.K.)

57	Oriole CB 1360	Tear It Up/Roll The Carpet Up	8
57	Oriole CB 1360	Tear It Up/Roll The Carpet Up (78)	10

NELSON TRIO (U.S.)

60	London HLL 9019	All In Good Time/The Town Crier	15
60	London HLL 9019	All In Good Time/The Town Crier (78)	30

NEMO

71	Parlophone R 5927	The Sun Has Got His Hat On/Bernie's Song	6

NEO MAYA

67	Pye 7N 17371	I Won't Hurt You/U.F.O.	75

(see also Episode Six)

CHIITRA NEOGY

68	Gemini GMX 5030	THE PERFUMED GARDEN (LP)	22

NEON

78	Sensible FAB 3	Anytime Anyplace Anywhere/Bottles/I'm Only Little	5
78	Radar ADA 27	Don't Eat Bricks/Hanging Off An O (p/s)	5

NEON BOYS

90	Overground OVER 11	TIME (12" EP, 20 test pressings only)	20
91	Overground OVER 19	That's All I Know (Right Now)/Love Comes In Spurts/High Heeled Wheels/ Don't Die/Time (last 2 tracks credited to Richard Hell & Voidoids [Part III]) (12" p/s, 2,000 only, clear vinyl)	8

(see also Richard Hell, Television)

NEON DIOR

80	Diskatron DTRON 1	Kid At Heart/It's In Her Kiss (p/s)	10

NEON HEARTS

77	Neon Hearts NEON 1	Venus Eccentric/Regulations (8" p/s)	30
78	Satril SAT 133	Answers/Armchair Thriller (p/s)	8
79	Satril SAT 139	Popular Music/Pretty As A Picture (p/s)	8
79	Satril SATL 4012	POPULAR MUSIC (LP)	15

NEON NEON

07	Lex LEX 047	Trick For Treat/Instrumental (12" picture disc, 500 only)	8

(see also Super Furry Animals)

NEPTUNE'S EMPIRE

71	Polymax PXX 01	NEPTUNE'S EMPIRE (LP)	100

NERO & GLADIATORS

61	Decca F 11329	Entry Of The Gladiators/Boots	15
61	Decca F 11367	In The Hall Of The Mountain King/The Trek To Rome	15
61	Decca F 11413	Czardas/That's A Long Time Ago	20

(see also Laurie Jay, Gladiators, Screaming Lord Sutch & Savages, State Of Mickey & Tommy)

PETER NERO

69	CBS 4277	Soulful Strut/For Once In My Life	8
69	CBS 4464	Theme From Picasso Summer/Be In	6

PAUL NERO (SOUNDS)

68	Liberty LBL 83100	NERO'S SOUL PARTY (LP)	25

NERVE (1)

67	Page One POF 019	No. 10 Downing Street/Georgie's March	12
68	Page One POF 055	Magic Spectacles/Come The Day	20
68	Page One POF 081	It Is/Mystery Lady	18
68	Page One POF 097	Piece By Piece/Satisfying Kind	15

(see also Lovin')

NERVE (2)

95	Straw B001	Submarine/Seeds From The Electric Garden (p/s)	6

NERVES (1)

78	Lightning GIL 520	TV Adverts/Sex Education (p/s)	35

NERVES (2)

81	Good Vibrations BIG 3	NOTRE DEMO (LP, official bootleg, foldover sleeve with booklet)	20

NERVES (3)

94	Inflammable Material BURN 2	Bits/SUBSTANDARD: Rostock (p/s)	7

NERVE SENTA

81	Supermusic SUPLP 2002	NERVE SENTA (LP)	12

NERVOUS CHOIR

89	Cathexis CRN 5407	O'David/Tonight We Start On Witches/Alsatians/Introducing (p/s, with inserts)	5

MINT VALUE £

NERVOUS NORVUS

56	London HLD 8338	Ape Call/Wild Dog Of Kentucky (gold label print)	75
56	London HLD 8338	Ape Call/Wild Dog Of Kentucky (silver label print)	30
57	London HLD 8383	Dig/Bullfrog Hop (gold label print)	100
57	London HLD 8383	Dig/Bullfrog Hop (silver label print)	50
62	Salvo SLO 1812	Does A Chinese Chicken Have A Pigtail/ROD BARTON: Dear Old San Francisco	40
85	Big Beat NED 12	NERVOUS NORVUS (mini-LP)	12

JIM NESBIT

65	Vocalion V 9241	Tiger In My Tank/I Can't Stand This Living Alone	25

MICHAEL NESMITH (& FIRST/SECOND NATIONAL BAND)

70	RCA RCA 2001	Joanne/The Crippled Lion (with First National Band)	5
71	RCA RCA 2053	Silver Moon/Lady Of The Valley (with First National Band)	5
71	RCA RCA 2086	Nevada Fighter/Here I Am (with First National Band)	5
70	RCA SF 8136	MAGNETIC SOUTH (LP, with First National Band)	25
71	RCA SF 8209	NEVADA FIGHTER (LP, with First National Band)	25
72	RCA SF 8276	TANTAMOUNT TO TREASON VOLUME ONE (LP, with Second National Band)	20
73	RCA APL1 0164	PRETTY MUCH YOUR STANDARD RANCH STASH (LP, solo)	15
75	Island ILPS 9428	THE PRISON (LP, boxed with book, unreleased in U.K.)	0
76	RCA RS 1064	THE BEST OF MICHAEL NESMITH (LP)	15

(see also Monkees, Wichita Train Whistle)

NEU!

73	United Artists UP 35485	Super/Neuschnee (p/s)	20
73	United Artists UP 35485	Super/Neuschnee	20
75	United Artists UP 35874	Isi/After Eight	15
72	United Artists UAS 29396	NEU (LP, laminated cover)	70
73	United Artists UAS 29500	NEU II (LP, gatefold sleeve)	70
75	United Artists UAS 29782	NEU '75 (LP, gatefold sleeve)	60

(see also Kraftwerk, La Dusseldorf)

NEUROSIS

04	Neurot NR 033	THE EYE OF EVERY STORM (LP, gatefold, inner, poster, grey marbled vinyl)	30
07	Neurot NR 050	GIVEN TO THE RISING (LP, gatefold, inner, black/white splattered vinyl)	20

NEUROTICS

85	Jungle FREUD 7	REPERCUSSIONS (LP)	12

(see also Newtown Neurotics)

NEUTRAL MILK HOTEL

98	Blue Rose BRRC 10237	Holland, 1945/Engine (numbered fold-out poster in polythene bag	30

NEUTRONS

74	United Artists UP 35704	Dance Of The Psychedelic Lounge Lizard/Suzy And The Wonder Boy	5
74	United Artists UAG 29652	BLACK HOLE STAR (LP, with inner sleeve)	15
75	United Artists UAG 29726	TALES FROM THE BLUE COCOONS (LP, laminated gatefold sleeve)	15

(see also Clive John, Gentle Giant, Man)

NEVILLE (WILLOUGHBY)

72	Explosion EX 2057	I Love Jamaica/Marry Me Marie	5

(see also Whistling Willie)

AARON NEVILLE

67	Stateside SS 584	Tell It Like It Is/Why Worry	20
67	Stateside SS 584	Tell It Like It Is/Why Worry (DJ Copy)	40
69	B&C CB 107	Tell It Like It Is/Why Worry (reissue)	5
67	Liberty LBY 3089	LIKE IT 'TIS (LP)	50

ART NEVILLE

76	Specialty SON 5008	Cha-Dooky-Doo/Zing Zing	5

NEW YORK NEW YORK

83	Urchin NY 2001	Roger Wilson Said/Too Drunk To Drive (p/s)	8
85	Beach Culture 2 BC	I WANNA BE LIKE YOU (12" EP)	15
85	Izuma IZUMA LP 1	NEW YORK NEW YORK (LP)	18

(see also Higsons. Terry Edwards, Serious Drinking)

NEW AGE STEPPERS

80	On-U Sound ONU 1	Fade Away/LONDON UNDERGROUND: Learn A Language (p/s)	7
81	Statik 612	My Love/Love Forever (12")	20
11	For Us FU 047	Fade Away/Conquer (p/s, 600 only)	5
80	On-U Sound ONULP 1	NEW AGE STEPPERS (LP)	25
81	Statik/On U Sound STATLP 2	ACTION BATTLEFIELD (LP)	25
82	On U Sound ONULP 21	FOUNDATION STEPPERS (LP)	25

NEW ATLANTIC

91	3 Beat 38TT1	I Know: (Love Decade Mix)/(Flute Mix)/Yes To Satan (Bonus Techno Mix) (12")	8

NEWBEATS

64	Hickory 45-1269	Bread And Butter/Tough Little Buggy (pink or black/blue label)	7
64	Hickory 45-1282	Everything's Alright/Pink Dally Rue	10
65	Hickory 45-1290	Break Away/Hey O Daddy O	10
65	Hickory 45-1305	The Birds Are For The Bees/Better Watch Your Step	8
65	Hickory 45-1320	I Can't Hear You No More/Little Child	15
65	Hickory 45-1332	Run Baby Run/Mean Woolly Willie	30
65	Hickory 45-1332	Run Baby Run/Mean Woolly Willie (DJ copy)	70
66	Hickory 45-1366	Shake Hands (And Come Out Crying)/Too Sweet To Be Forgotten	20
66	Hickory 45-1387	Crying My Heart Out/Short Of Love	40
66	Hickory 45-1387	Crying My Heart Out/Short Of Love (DJ copy)	70
66	Hickory 45-1422	My Yesterday Love/Patent On Love	10
71	London HLE 10341	Run Baby Run (Back Into My Arms)/Am I Not My Brother's Keeper	6
65	Hickory LPE 1503	NEWBEATS (EP)	30
65	Hickory LPE 1506	AIN'T THAT LOVIN' YOU BABY (EP)	30
66	Hickory LPE 1510	OH! GIRLS GIRLS (EP)	30
65	Hickory LPM 120	BREAD AND BUTTER (LP)	35
72	London SHE 8428	RUN BABY RUN (LP)	15

(see also Dean & Mark, Larry Henley)

NEW BLOCKADERS
82	Private Pressing	CHANGEZ LES BLOCKEURS (LP, 100 only, white label A4 sheet as cover)	300
91	Hypnagogia GOG 01	SYMPHONIE IN X MAJOR (LP, 500 only, numbered)	20

PHINEAS NEWBORN
61	Columbia 33SX 1311	I LOVE A PIANO (LP, also stereo SCX 3370)	12

(see also Roy Haines)

NEWBOY
73	Count Shelly CS007	Sweet Talk/J ENGLISH: One And Only	20

NEW BREED
65	Decca F 12295	Friends And Lovers Forever/Unto Us	75

MICKEY NEWBURY
72	Elektra K 12047	An American Trilogy/San Francisco Mabel Joy	6

NEWBY
65	Pye 7N 15986	I Can't Grow Peaches On A Cherry Tree/The Children Sleep	7

NEWBY & JOHNSON
70	Mercury 6052 027	I Want To Give You My Everything/Sweet Happiness	25

NEWCASTLE BIG BAND
72	Impulse ISS NBB 106	NEWCASTLE BIG BAND (LP, white labels, 2,000 only)	150

(see also Last Exit, Police, Sting, Radio Actors)

NEW CENSATION
75	DJM DJS 10371	First Round Knockout/Everybody's Got A Story	8

NEW COLONY SIX
66	London HLZ 10033	I Confess/Dawn Is Breaking	75
66	Stateside SS 522	At The River's Edge/I Lie Awake	50
68	Mercury MF 1030	I Will Always Think About You/Hold Me With Your Eyes	12
69	Mercury MF 1086	Things I'd Like To Say/Come And Give Your Love To Me	10

NEWCOMERS
72	Stax 2025 063	Pin The Tail On The Donkey/Mannish Boy	8
75	Stax STXS 2023	Keep An Eye On Your Close Friends/(Instrumental Version)	10

NEW CUOREY
73	Taurus TR 101	Vietnam/The Girl I Had	25

NEW DAWN
69	private pressing	MAINLINE (LP)	80

NEW DEAL STRING BAND
69	Argo ZDA 104	DOWN IN THE WILLOW (LP, with insert)	40

NEW DECADE
92	Out Of Romford ROCC 002	Get The Message/ABC Remix (12", stamped white labels)	10

NEW DEPARTURES QUARTET
60s	Transatlantic TRA 134	THE NEW DEPARTURES QUARTET (LP, with Stan Tracey)	40

(see also Stan Tracey)

MARTIN NEWELL
80	Off Street OSR 001	Young Jobless/Sylvie In Toytown (p/s)	15
80	Liberty BP 392	Young Jobless/Sylvie In Toytown (p/s reissue)	8

(see also Gypp, Cleaners From Venus)

NEW ENGLAND
79	Infinity INF 110	P.U.N.K./Shoot (green vinyl, 'lightning' PVC sleeve)	5

DENNIS NEWEY
61	Philips PB 1134	Checkpoint/Title Unknown	10
61	Philips PB 1198	Border Patrol/Yes Yes	10
62	Philips 326 588 BF	The Nightriders/The Pied Piper	10

NEW FACES
65	Pye 7N 15842	So Small/Blue Mist	10
65	Pye 7N 15931	Never Gonna Love Again/You'll Be Too Late	8
66	Pye 7N 17029	Like A Man/Shake Up The Party (Myra)	15
67	Pye 7N 17335	Lace Covered Window/The Life That I Lead	10
68	Decca F 12746	We Can Get There By Candlelight/The Yellow Road	8
68	Decca F 12862	Someday/Biscuit Coloured Overcoat	7
69	Decca F 12933	Carnival Day/Grandfather Dugan	7
69	Decca F 12968	There Is An Island In The Sun/Happy The Heart That I Own	7
74	Ember MBS 334	Where Would I Find Another You/Lullaby	6

NEW FORESTERS
65	Lyntone LYN 932/933	Travel/LIZARDS: My Love Goes On (Sheffield Students Rag record)	30

NEW FORMULA
67	Piccadilly 7N 35381	Do It Again A Little Bit Slower/I'm On The Outside Looking In	18
67	Piccadilly 7N 35401	I Want To Go Back There Again/Can't You See That She Loves Me	18
68	Pye 7N 17552	My Baby's Coming Home/Burning In The Background Of My Mind	20
69	Pye 7N 17818	Stay Indoors/Hare Krishna	25

NEW GENERATION
69	Spark SRL 1000	Sadie And Her Magic Mister Garland/Digger	15
69	Spark SRL 1007	Smokey Blues Away/She's A Soldier Boy	10
70	Spark SRL 1019	Police Is Here/Mister C	35

NEW HEARTS
77	CBS 5800	Just Another Teenage Anthem/Blood On The Knife (p/s)	10
78	CBS 6381	Plain Jane/My Young Teacher (p/s)	10

(see also Secret Affair)

NEW HERITAGE
73	Westwood WRS 028	ALL MANNER OF THINGS (LP)	50

NEW HOPE
69	London HL 10296	Won't Find Better Than Me/They Call It Love	18

(see also Kit Kats)

NEW HORIZON
73	Decca F13463	Hullabaloo/Believe In Yourself	10

NEW INSPIRATION
67	Major Minor MM 539	You Made A Fool of Me/M.T.	25
73	Penny Farthing PEN 803	Medicine Man/Is It Really That Hard To Understand	10

NEW INSPIRATION
70	Penny Farthing PEN 719	Thinking About The Good Times/There You Go My friend	6

NEW JAZZ GROUP
56	Tempo EXA 39	MODERN JAZZ SCENE (EP)	40

NEW JAZZ ORCHESTRA
65	Decca LK 4690	WESTERN REUNION (LONDON 1965) (LP)	80
69	Verve SVLP 9236	DEJEUNER SUR L'HERBE (LP)	175

(see also Neil Ardley, Nucleus)

NEW JERSEY CONNECTION
82	Nitelife LIFE 1	Love Don't Come Easy/Love Don't Come Easy (Instrumental)	10
82	Nitelife LIFE 1	Love Don't Come Easy/Love Don't Come Easy (Instrumental) (12")	15

NEW JUMP BAND
68	Domain D 1	The Only Kind Of Girl/Seven Kinds Of Sweet Lovin'	25

ANTHONY NEWLEY
59	Decca F 11127	I've Waited So Long/Sat'day Night Rock-A-Boogie	6
59	Decca F 11137	Idle On Parade/Idle Rock-A-Boogie	6
59	Decca F 11142	Personality/My Blue Angel	5
59	Decca F 11163	Someone To Love/It's All Over	5
60	Decca F 11220	Do You Mind/Girls Were Made To Love And Kiss (78)	12
61	Decca F 11376	What Kind Of Fool Am I/Once In A Lifetime	5
62	Decca F 11486	That Noise/The Little Golden Clown	6
64	Decca F 11818	Tribute/Lament To A Hero	10
59	Decca DFE 6566	IDLE ON PARADE (EP)	10

ANDY NEWMAN
72	Track 2406 103	RAINBOW (LP, gatefold sleeve, black/silver label)	25

(see also Thunderclap Newman)

BRAD NEWMAN
62	Fontana H 357	Somebody To Love/This Time It's Love	15
62	Fontana H 369	Get A Move On/Here And Now And Evermore	10
62	Fontana 267 220TF	Stay By Me/Candy Lips	10
62	Fontana 267 243TF	Point Of No Return/Now I've Lost You	10
63	Fontana 267 273TF	I'll Find You Another Baby/No Man Should Ever Be Alone	10
64	Piccadilly 7N 35174	Please Don't Cry/Every Hour Of Living	8

COLIN NEWMAN
80	Beggars Banquet BEG 48	B/Classic Remains/Alone On Piano (p/s)	5
81	Beggars Banquet BEG 52	Inventory/This Picture (p/s)	5

(see also Wire)

DEL NEWMAN SOUND
67	Columbia SCX 6181	FLOWER GARDEN (LP)	20

JIMMY (C.) NEWMAN
57	London HLD 8460	A Fallen Star/I Can't Go On This Way	30
59	MGM MGM 1009	What'cha Gonna Do/So Soon	15
59	MGM MGM 1037	Grin And Bear It/The Ballad Of Baby Doe	10
60	MGM MGM 1085	A Lovely Work Of Art/What About Me	8
61	MGM MGM 1112	Now That You're Gone/Wanting You With Me Tonight	8
59	MGM MGM-EP 706	GRIN AND BEAR IT - COUNTRY AND WESTERN STYLE (EP)	30

JOE NEWMAN (SEXTET)
57	Vogue Coral Q 72244	Cocktails For Two/Later For The Happenings	5
57	Vogue Coral LVA 9052	HAPPY CATS (LP)	12
57	Pye/Vanguard PPT 12001	JOE NEWMAN (LP)	12

NANETTE NEWMAN
77	BAC BCS 0004	Fun Food Factory/Morris (The Studio Mouse)	6

PAUL NEWMAN
66	Mercury MF 969	Ain't You Got A Heart/Tears On My Pillow	50

RANDY NEWMAN
68	Reprise RS 20692	Love Story/I Think It's Going To Rain Today	5
70	Reprise RS 20945	Gone Dead Train/JACK NITZCHE: Harry Flowers	5
68	Reprise R(S)LP 6286	RANDY NEWMAN CREATES SOMETHING NEW UNDER THE SUN (LP)	15
70	Reprise RSLP 6373	12 SONGS (LP)	15

(see also Harry Nilsson, Tom Petty & Heartbreakers)

TOM NEWMAN
75	Virgin VS120	Sad Sing/Ali's Got A Broken Bone	8
75	Virgin VS130	Don't Treat Your Woman Bad/Why Does Love Hurt So Bad	5
75	Virgin VS133	Sleep/Darling Corey	6
75	Virgin V 2022	FINE OLD TOM (LP, features Mike Oldfield)	20
75	Virgin V 2042	LIVE AT THE ARGONAUT (LP, unreleased, test pressings only)	80
77	Decca TXS 123	FAERIE SYMPHONY (LP, gatefold sleeve)	30
88	Oceandisc	OZYMANDIAS (LP, unissued, 20 test pressings only in proof sleeve)	30

(see also Jade Warrior, July, Mike Oldfield)

TONY NEWMAN

68	Decca F 12795	Soul Thing/Let The Good Times Roll	30
70	Decca F 13041	Soul Thing/Let The Good Times Roll (reissue)	10

(see also Sounds Incorporated, Flying Machine, Pinkerton['s Assorted Colours], May Blitz, Three Man Army)

THE NEW MASTERSOUNDS

00	Blow It Hard BIH 017	One Note Brown/Burnt Black	20

NEWMENS

72	Parlophone R5941	Start My Life Again/A Million Tears	10

NEW MODEL

83	Mr. Clean MERC 001	Chilean Warning/The World Thru Our Eyes/Totalitarian Terror (p/s, in 7" x 10" folder)	10
83	Mr. Clean MERC 001	Chilean Warning/The World Thru Our Eyes/Totalitarian Terror (p/s)	6

NEW MONITORS

72	Buddah 2011 118	Fence Around Your Heart/Have You Seen Her	20

PETER NEWNHAM

77	B & C BCS 011	Rudi/Outside My Window (100 only)	200

NEW ORDER (1)

81	Come Org WDC 883011	BRADFORD RED LIGHT DISTRICT (cassette)	50
81	Come Org. CARA12	BRADFORD RED LIGHT DISTRICT (LP)	110

(see also Come)

NEW ORDER (2)

81	Factory FAC 33	Ceremony/In A Lonely Place (p/s)	12
81	Factory FAC 33T	Ceremony/In A Lonely Place (12")	10
81	Factory FAC 3312	Ceremony (Re-recording)/In A Lonely Place (Extended) (12", cream & blue p/s)	12
81	Factory FAC 53	Procession/Everything's Gone Green (9 different coloured sleeves : black, brown, red, orange, yellow, green, aquamarine, blue and purple)	10
81	Factory Benelux FBNL 8	Everything's Gone Green/Mesh/Cries & Whispers (12", yellow sleeve)	12
82	Factory FAC 51B	Rocking Carol/Ode To Joy (flexidisc, given away at Hacienda, 4,000 only)	25
82	Factory FAC 63	Temptation/Hurt	5
83	Factory FAC 7312	Blue Monday/The Beach (12", die-cut sleeve, silver insert)	15
83	Factory FAC 93	Confusion (Edit)/Confusion (Edit) (p/s, DJ promo only)	15
84	Factory FAC 103	Thieves Like Us (Edit)/Lonesome Tonight (Edit) (p/s, DJ promo only)	15
88	Factory FAC 73RD	Blue Monday 1988/Blue Monday (DJ-only mix) (12", p/s, DJ promo only)	10
87	Factory FACD 193	Touched By The Hand Of God (Twelve Inch Mix)/Confusion Dub 1987/Temptation (Original Mix))CD, gatefold card sleeve)	15
88	Factory FACD 73R	Blue Monday 1988 (12 Inch)/Beach Buggy (12 Inch)/Blue Monday 1988 (7 Inch) (CD)	10
88	Factory FACDV 73R	Blue Monday 1988 (12 Inch)/Blue Monday (7 Inch)/Beach Buggy/Blue Monday 1988 (Video) (CD Video)	50
88	Factory FACDV 183	True Faith (Remix 12 Inch)/Evil Dust/True Faith (7 Inch) (CD Video)/True Faith (CD Video)	30
89	Factory FAC 263DJ	Round & Round (Ben Grosse Mix)/(12" Mix)/(Detroit Mix) (12", p/s, DJ only)	12
89	Factory FAC 273/7	Run 2 (Edit)/MTO (Edit) (DJ promo only, 500 pressed)	10
11	Rhino FAC 33	Ceremony (Original Version)/In A Lonely Place (12" Version)//Ceremony (Heart & Soul Rehearsal Version)/In A Lonely Place (Unreleased Rehearsal Version) (12")	10
81	Factory FACT 50	MOVEMENT (LP)	20
83	Factory FACT 75	POWER CORRUPTION & LIES (LP, die cut sleeve)	15
85	Factory FACT 50c	MOVEMENT (reissue, cassette in box with insert)	12
85	Factory FACT 100c	LOW LIFE (cassette in box with inserts in rice paper gatefold)	10
85	Factory FACT 50c	MOVEMENT (reissue, cassette in box with insert)	10
85	Factory FACT 75c	POWER CORRUPTION AND LIES (reissue, cassette in box with insert)	10
86	Factory FACT 150SP	BROTHERHOOD (LP, limited metallic sleeve)	15
86	Factory FACD 150SP	BROTHERHOOD (CD with 'State Of The Nation' & metallic booklet)	20
87	Factory FACT 200	SUBSTANCE (LP, 2 inners)	18
86	Factory FACT 150c	BROTHERHOOD (cassette in box with insert)	10
87	Factory FACT 200	THE GATEFOLD SUBSTANCE (LP, numbered gatefold sleeve, 1,000 only)	20
87	Factory FACT 200c	SUBSTANCE (cassette, 200 only in box set with insert)	20
93	London 8284131	REPUBLIC (LP)	25
94	London 8285801	BEST OF (2-LP, with inner sleeve)	20
05	London 2564622021	WAITING FOR THE SIREN'S CALL (2-LP)	20

(see also Joy Division, Electronic)

NEW ORLEANS BOOTBLACKS

54	Columbia SCM 5090	Flat Foot/Mad Dog	8

NEW OVERLANDERS

69	RCA 1861	Thought Back/These Are Not My People	6
70	RCA 1953	Unchained Melody/Memories	6

NEW PENNIES

72	Chapter One SCH 166	Marianna/B-Boom	5

NEWPORT JAZZ FESTIVAL ALL STARS

61	London Jazz LTZ-K 15202	NEWPORT JAZZ FESTIVAL ALL STARS (LP, mono)	12
61	London Jazz SAH-K 6116	NEWPORT JAZZ FESTIVAL ALL STARS (LP, stereo)	15

NEW RELIGION

72	Bamboo BAM 70	In The Black Caribbean/Black Is Black	35
73	Ackee ACK 526	Walk Away Renee/What's It All About	5

NEWS

66	Decca F 12356	The Entertainer/I Count The Tears	18
66	Decca F 12477	This Is The Moment (from the TV series "Adam Adamant")/Ya Ya Da Da	12

(see also Patto, Glenn Hughes, Finders Keepers, Miller, Big Boy Pete)

NEWS FROM BABEL

86	Recommended RE 6116	NEWS FROM BABEL (LP, hand-screened sleeve)	15
89	ReR 6116 RE 6116	WORK RESUMED ON THE TOWER (LP)	18

NEW SETTLERS

74	York YR 218	She Didn't Forget Her Shoes/Lifelight	12

MINT VALUE £

NEWSFLASH
90	Newsflas 001	Nobodies Home/Mundane Me And You (p/s)	40

JOANNA NEWSOM
05	Drag City DC 303	YS (2-LP, gatefold, booklet)	20

BOBBY NEWSOME
72	Mojo 2093 018	Jody Come And Get Your Shoes/Post Office	10

OLIVIA NEWTON-JOHN
66	Decca F 12396	Till You Say You'll Be Mine/For Ever	150
71	Pye International 7N 25543	If Not For You/The Biggest Clown	6
80	Jet JET 10-185	Xanadu/Fool Country (10" pink vinyl, die-cut p/s, with ELO)	12
78	EMI EMAP 789	TOTALLY HOT (LP, picture disc)	20
85	Mercury 826 169-2	SOUL KISS (CD)	15

(see also Toomorrow, Marvin & Farrar)

NEWTOWN NEUROTICS
79	No Wonder A 45	Hypocrite/You Said No (no p/s, with insert & sticker)	80
79	No Wonder A 45	Hypocrite/You Said No	20
80	No Wonder NOW 4	When The Oil Runs Out/Oh No (p/s)	40
82	CNT 4/No Wonder NOW 56	Kick Out The Tories!/Mindless Violence! (p/s)	15
82	CNT CNT 010	Licensing Hours/No Sanctuary (p/s)	18
83	Razor RZS 107	Blitzkrieg Bop/Hypocrite (New Version)/I Remember You (p/s)	12
84	No Wonder NOW 6T	Suzi/Fools (p/s)	12
83	Razor RAZ 6	BEGGARS CAN BE CHOOSERS (LP)	20

NEW TRENDS
67	Columbia SX 6245	THE NEW TRENDS (LP)	20

NEW VICTORY BAND
78	Topic 12TS 382	ONE MORE DANCE AND THEN (LP)	15

NEW WALK
83	Web WEB 22	Pressure Point/Shape Of Things To Come (p/s)	12

NEW WANDERERS
79	Grapevine GRP 144	This Man In Love/Adam And Eve	15
79	Grapevine GRP 144	This Man In Love/Adam And Eve (DJ Copy)	30

NEW WORLD
68	Saga FID 2114	TRUMPET A GO-GO (LP)	12

NEW YORK DOLLS
73	Mercury 6052 402	Jet Boy/Vietnamese Baby	20
74	Mercury 6052 615	Stranded In The Jungle/Who Are The Mystery Girls	10
77	Mercury 6160 008	Jet Boy/Babylon/Who Are The Mystery Girls	10
85	Antler DOLLS 1	Personality Crisis/Subway Train (picture disc)	8
85	Antler DOLLS 2	Looking For A Kiss/Bad Girl (picture disc)	8
73	Mercury 6338 270	NEW YORK DOLLS (LP, laminated front and black sleeve)	60
74	Mercury 6338 498	TOO MUCH TOO SOON (LP)	40
77	Mercury 9286.996/7	NEW YORK DOLLS (LP)	20

(see also Johnny Thunders, Heartbreakers, Sylvain Sylvain, Idols)

NEW YORK PUBLIC LIBRARY
66	Columbia DB 7948	I Ain't Gonna Eat Out My Heart Anymore/Rejected	25
68	MCA MU 1025	Gotta Get Away/Time Wastin'	15
68	MCA MU 1045	Love Me Two Times/Which Way To Go	10
72	B & C CB 176	Whei Ling Ty Luu/Boozy Queen	8

NEW YORK ROCK ENSEMBLE
71	CBS 5292	Running Down The Highway/Law And Order	15
69	Atco 228 932	FAITHFUL FRIENDS (LP)	12
71	CBS 64126	ROLL OVER (LP)	12
72	CBS 64324	FREEDOMBURGER (LP)	12

NEXT BAND
78	Gannet SRTS/79/CUS 159	FOUR BY THREE EP (p/s)	50

NEXUS 21
89	Blue Chip BLUE C34R	(Still) Life Keeps Moving Remix (12")	10
89	Blue Chip BLUE C34T	(Still) Life Keeps Moving (12")	10
91	Network NWKT 35	I Know We Can Make It (12", white label)	10
89	Blue Chip BLUE TEC. 2	THE RHYTHM OF LIFE (LP)	15

NIADEM'S GHOST
86	Hibination HIDE 001	IN SHELTERED WINDS (LP)	25

(see also IQ)

NICE
67	Immediate IM 059	The Thoughts Of Emerlist Davjack/Angel Of Death	15
68	Immediate IM 068	America/The Diamond Hard Blue Apples Of The Moon (pink label, in p/s)	20
68	Immediate IM 068	America/The Diamond Hard Blue Apples Of The Moon (pink label)	10
68	Immediate IM 072	Brandenburger/Happy Freuds	10
70	Charisma CB 132	Country Pie/One Of Those People	6
70s	Immediate IM 068	America/The Diamond Hard Blue Apples Of The Moon (white label, reissue in p/s)	6
67	Immediate AS 2	ALBUM SAMPLER - THE THOUGHTS OF EMERLIST DAVJACK (1-sided LP, promo only)	60
67	Immediate IMLP 016	THE THOUGHTS OF EMERLIST DAVJACK (LP, mono)	70
67	Immediate IMSP 016	THE THOUGHTS OF EMERLIST DAVJACK (LP, stereo)	50
68	Immediate IMSP 020	ARS LONGA VITA BREVIS (LP, laminated front, flipbacks, pink label, "Sold in U.K..." text)	40
69	Immediate IMSP 026	THE NICE (LP, gatefold sleeve)	30
70	Charisma CAS 1014	FIVE BRIDGES (LP, pink label, gatefold sleeve)	20
71	Charisma CAS 1030	ELEGY (LP, gatefold sleeve pink 'scroll' label)	20

(see also Keith Emerson, Emerson Lake & Palmer, Jackson Heights, Habits, Brian Davison, Refugee, Attack, Jet, P.P. Arnold)

NICK NICELY
80	Voxette VOX 1001	D.C.T. Dreams/Treeline (p/s, reissue copies £4)	20
81	EMI EMI 5256	Hillyfields (1892)/49 Cigars (p/s)	15

| 04 | Tenth Planet TP 059 | PSYCHOTROPIA (LP, 1000 copies only) ....20 |

ALBERT NICHOLAS
| 56 | Tempo A 129 | How Long Blues (with Al Fairweather)/Rose Room (with Lise West) ....10 |

(see also Al Fairweather)

PAUL NICHOLAS
68	Polydor 56285	Where Do I Go/Here Comes The Clown..5
69	Polydor 56322	Who Can I Turn To/Sing A Sad Song For Sammy 5
70	Polydor 56374	Freedom City/Run Shaker Life (with p/s).....................................100
70	Polydor 56374	Freedom City/Run Shaker Life 70
71	Polydor 2058 086	The World Is Beautiful/Lamplighter 45

(see also Oscar, Paul Dean)

BILLY NICHOLLS
68	Immediate IM 063	Would You Believe/Daytime Girl (features Small Faces) 50
73	Track 2094 109	Forever's No Time At All/This Song Is Green (with Pete Townshend) 12
68	Immediate IMCP 009	WOULD YOU BELIEVE (LP, withdrawn) 4000
90s	Tenth Planet	WOULD YOU BELIEVE (LP, reissue, with insert) 40
07	Castle CMQLP 1523	WOULD YOU BELIEVE (LP, reissue, green vinyl) 35

JANICE NICHOLLS
| 63 | Decca F 11586 | I'll Give It Five/The Wednesbury Madison ....10 |

SUE NICHOLLS
| 68 | Pye 7N.17565 | Where Will You Be/Every Day ....5 |

PENNY NICHOLS
| 68 | Pye int 7N 2451 | Look Around Rock/Farina..35 |

ROSEMARY NICHOLS
| 70 | Gemini GM5013 | Once Upon A Time/Baby...10 |

LEA NICHOLSON
| 72 | Trailer LER 3010 | HORSEMUSIC (LP) ....20 |

ROGER NICHOLSON
| 72 | Trailer LER 3034 | NONSUCH FOR DULCIMER (LP, red label)....................20 |

NICKELSON
| 72 | Decca F13328 | Sitting On A Fence/Oh How Much ....8 |

STEVIE NICKS
| 89 | EMI EMD 1008 | THE OTHER SIDE OF THE MIRROR (LP, with hologram).............12 |

(see also Fleetwood Mac, Buckingham-Nicks, Tom Petty & Heartbreakers)

NICKY AND THE DOTS
| 78 | Small Wonder SMALL 12 | Never Been So Stuck/Linoleum Walk (p/s) ....15 |

NICO
65	Immediate IM 003	I'm Not Sayin'/The Last Mile (early copies in blue/white "immediate" sleeves)....85
65	Immediate IM 003	I'm Not Sayin'/The Last Mile (in standard black/white "immediate" sleeves)....75
81	Flicknife FLS 206	Vegas/Saeta (p/s) 8
82	Immediate IMS 003	I'm Not Saying/The Last Mile (p/s, reissue) 5
82	Half 1?2 1	Procession/All Tomorrow's Parties (p/s) 5
83	Aura AUS 137	Heroes/One More Chance (p/s) 5
85	Beggars Banquet BEG 139	My Funny Valentine/My Heart Is Empty (p/s, as Nico and the Faction)....5
10	Elektra 8122797856	Frozen Warnings/No One Is There (die-cut sleeve, 750 only) 8
68	Elektra EKL 4029	THE MARBLE INDEX (LP, orange label, mono) 45
68	Elektra EKS 74029	THE MARBLE INDEX (LP, orange label, stereo) 40
71	Reprise RSLP 6424	DESERT SHORE (LP, with John Cale) 35
71	Reprise K 44102	DESERT SHORE (LP, with John Cale, 2nd pressing).....25
71	MGM Select 2353 025	CHELSEA GIRL (LP)....................................35
74	Island ILPS 9311	THE END (LP)..25
81	Aura AUL 715	DRAMA OF EXILE (LP, colour cover) 18

(see also John Cale, Velvet Underground, Ayers Cale Nico & Eno)

NICODEMUS
81	Cha Cha CHAD 44	Gunman Connection/It Have To Ram (12") 20
81	Greensleeves GRED 75	BONE CONNECTION/LEROY SMART: All My Love (12") 15
82	Cha Cha CHALP 011	GUNMAN CONNECTION (LP) 35
82	Black Joy DHLP 2003	DANCE HALL STYLE (LP)......................50

JIMMY NICOL (& SHUBDUBS)
64	Pye 7N 15623	Humpty Dumpty/Night Train..........................25
64	Pye 7N 15666	Husky/Don't Come Back (solo) 18
64	Pye 7N 15699	Baby Please Don't Go/Shub Dubbery (possibly unissued)....20

(see also Sound Of Jimmy Nicol, Georgie Fame)

NICOLETTE
| 89 | Shut Up & Dance SUAD 14 | Waking Up (12") ....10 |

WATT NICOLL
| 71 | Xtra XTRA 1122 | NICE TO BE NICE (LP, laminated front cover)........15 |

NICRA
| 77 | Ogun OG 010 | LISTEN/HEAR (LP).....................................18 |

(see also Keith Tippett)

NIDDY GRIDDY BAND
| 68 | Pye 7N 17461 | Dinny Girgy/Summertime ....6 |

NIE ELECTRIKK
| 80 | Synesthesia SYN 1 | Cover Girl/Practically Isolate (p/s) ....8 |

NIEMEN
| 72 | CBS 564896 | STRANGE IS THIS WORLD (LP, orange/black label)........25 |

STEVE NIEVE
| 80 | Comb 1 | OUTLINE ON A HAIRDO (EP) ....20 |

NIGGY HOI!
80s   Deli K1Z   Theme From Niggy Hoi!/Titanium Kedi (p/s) 8

NIGHT DOCTOR
81   Race Records RB DIS 001   Romancin'/Menelik (12") 35

NIGHT MOVES
83   GC GCT 2   Transdance (New York Disco Mix)/Transdance (UK Disco Mix)/Nightdrive (12") 30
84   GC/MCA GCT 1001   Transdance (Robot Rock) (UK Club Mix)/You Can Take My Love/ Beat This/Nightdrive (12", p/s) 20

NIGHTBIRDS
59   Oriole CB 1490   Cat On A Hot Tin Roof/The Square 12
59   Oriole CB 1490   Cat On A Hot Tin Roof/The Square (78) 10

NIGHTBLOOMS
90   Fierce FRIGHT 041   Crystal Eyes/Never Dream At All (p/s) 10

NIGHTCRAWLERS
67   London HLR 10109   The Little Black Egg/You're Running Wild 60

NIGHT-HAWKS
58   Fontana H 120   Cool For Cats/Time Will Tell (78) 10

NIGHTIME FLYER
69   Pye 7N 17739   Talk To Me/Spinning Wheel 6
69   Pye 7N 17798   Don't Push Me Baby/Thru' Loving You 7
71   Pye 7N 45046   Love On Borrowed Time/It's A Hurtin' Thing 6
03   Phoenix NWOBHM 7007   Out With A Vengeance/Heavy Metal Rules (yellow vinyl reissue, numbered, 250 copies, 7.5 inch sleeve) 10

NIGHTIME FLYER
81   Red Eye EYE 2   Out With A Vengeance/Heavy Metal Rules (p/s) 20

TUNDE NIGHTINGALE & HIS HIGHLIFE BOYS
68   Melodisc MLPAS 12-142   THE BIRDS THAT SINGS ALL THE NIGHT (LP) 15

NIGHTINGALES
81   Rough Trade/Vindaloo RT 075/ UGH 4   Idiot Strength/Seconds 6
83   Cherry Red CHERRY 56   Urban Ospreys/Cakehole 5
83   Ink Records INK 1   HYSTERIC (LP) 12

NIGHTMARE
79   PVK PV 30   Great Balls Of Fire/Witch Woman (p/s) 10
83   PVK PV 119   I Wanna Be Shot/Ruth Ellis (P/S) 6
84   Ebony EBON 22   WAITING FOR THE TWILIGHT (LP) 12

NIGHTMARES IN WAX
79   Inevitable INEV 0002   BIRTH OF A NATION (EP, with wraparound p/s) 20
84   KY KY 9   Black Leather/Shangri-La (12", 'horror' p/s) 18
85   KY KY 9 1/2   Black Leather/Shangri-La/Girls Song (12", different p/s, 3,000 only) 20
(see also Dead Or Alive)

NIGHTMARES ON WAX
91   Warp WARPLP4   A WORD OF SCIENCE (THE 1st & FINAL CHAPTER) (LP) 20
95   Warp WARPLP 36   SMOKERS DELIGHT (2-LP) 20
99   Warp WARPLP 61   CARBOOT SOUL (2-LP) 20
06   Warp WARPLP 133   IN A SPACE OUTTA SOUND (2-LP) 25
08   Warp WARPLP 159   THOUGHT SO (2-LP) 12

NIGHTRIDERS
66   Polydor BM 56066   Love Me Right Now/Your Friend (withdrawn) 120
66   Polydor BM 56066   Love Me Right Now/Your Friend (promo copy) 85
66   Polydor BM 56116   It's The Dog/Your Friend 60
(see also Mike Sheridan & Nightriders, Mike Sheridan's Lot, Idle Race, Jeff Lynne)

NIGHTRIDERS
79   Stardust STR 1001   I Saw Her With Another Guy/London Town (picture insert) 15

NIGHTSHIFT
65   Piccadilly 7N 35243   Corrine Corrina/Lavender Tree 15
65   Piccadilly 7N 35264   That's My Story/Stormy Monday Blues 18

NIGHTSHIFT
79   Zum 9   Jetset 6

NIGHT-TIMERS
65   Parlophone R 5355   The Music Played On/Yield Not To Temptation (featuring Herbie Goins) 50
(see also Herbie Goins & Night-Timers, Ronnie Jones)

NIGHTWING
80   Ovation OVS 1209   Barrel Of Pain/Nightwing (p/s) 10
84   Gull GULS 75   Treading Water/Call Your Name (p/s) 6
84   Gull GULS 7512   Treading Water/Call Your Name/Barrel Of Pain (12", red vinyl, p/s) 10
84   Gull GULS 77   Night Of Mystery/Dressed To Kill (p/s) 10
84   Gull GULS 7712   Night Of Mystery/Dressed To Kill (12", p/s) 12
85   Gull GULS 80   Strangers Are Welcome/Games To Play//The Devil Walks Behind You/ Cell 151 (double pack, gatefold p/s) 5
80   Ovation OV 1757   SOMETHING IN THE AIR (LP) 12
83   Gull PGULP 1038   STAND UP AND BE COUNTED (LP, picture disc) 15
(see also Alec Johnson Band, Nutz)

NIGHTWISH
04   Back On Black BOBV 003 DPD   ANGELS FALL FIRST (2-LP picture discs, stickered bag) 20
04   Back On Black BOBV 004 DPD   OCEANBORN (2-LP picture discs, stickered bag) 20
04   Back On Black BOBV 007 DPD   OVER THE HILLS AND FAR AWAY (2-LP picture discs, stickered bag) 20
04   Back On Black BOBV 006 DPD   WISHMASTER (2-LP picture discs, stickered bag) 20
04   Back On Black BOBV 008 DPD   CENTURY CHILD (2-LP picture discs, stickered bag) 20
05   Back On Black BOBV 035 DPD   ONCE (2-LP picture discs, stickered bag) 20

NIHILIST SPASM BAND
85	United Dairies UD 016	1X - X = X (LP)	20

BILL NILES
67	Decca F 12661	Pashionella Grundy/Bric-A-Bric Man	15

WILLY NILLY
84	Ad Hoc AH 1	On The Spur Of The Moment/Half A Job (p/s, with 'time-table' insert)	45

(see also Randy Newman, Ringo Starr, Cher)

(HARRY) NILSSON
67	RCA Victor RCA 1632	You Can't Do That/Ten Little Indians	6
68	RCA Victor RCA 1675	One/Sister Marie	6
68	RCA RCA 1707	Everybody's Talkin'/Don't Leave Me	5
68	RCA RCA 1764	Mourning Glory/Rainmaker	6
69	RCA RCA 1864	Maybe/The Puppy Song	6
69	RCA RCA 1876	Everybody's Talkin'/One	5
72	RCA RCA 2266	You're Breaking My Heart/Spaceman (possibly withdrawn, Demo stamped copy)	12
68	RCA Victor RD/SF 7928	PANDEMONIUM SHADOW SHOW (LP, mono)	18
68	RCA Victor RD/SF 7928	PANDEMONIUM SHADOW SHOW (LP, stereo)	15
68	RCA RD/SF 7973	AERIAL BALLET (LP, mono)	18
68	RCA RD/SF 7973	AERIAL BALLET (LP, stereo)	15
69	RCA SF 8010	SKIDOO (LP, soundtrack)	20
69	RCA SF 8046	HARRY (LP)	15
73	RCA SF 8326	AERIAL PANDEMONIUM BALLET (LP)	12
74	Rapple/RCA APL1-0220	SON OF DRACULA (LP, soundtrack, with Ringo Starr, fold-out sleeve)	15

NILSSON TWINS
57	Capitol CL 14698	Rain On My Window/I Dance When I Walk	5

NIMBO
71	Pye 7N 450097	Maisie Jones/Forget Her	8
72	Pye 7N 45174	When The Swallows Fly/Noticeingly By	15

LEONARD NIMOY
68	Dot (S)LPD 511	MR. SPOCK PRESENTS MUSIC FROM OUTER SPACE (LP)	25
72	Rediffusion ZS 156	MUSIC FROM OUTER SPACE (LP, reissue of DOT (S) LPD 511)	20

NINA
69	CBS 4681	Do You Know How Christmas Trees Are Grown?/The More Things Change	12

NINE BELOW ZERO
81	A&M AMS 8127	Ain't Comin' Back/Liquor Lover (p/s)	5
81	A&M AMS 8110	Three Times Enough/Doghouse (p/s, yellow vinyl)	5
82	A&M AMSX 8210	Wipe Away Your Kiss/True Life Is A Crime (12")	8

NINE DAYS WONDER
71	Harvest SHSP 4014	NINE DAYS WONDER (LP, textured sleeve, EMI logo on label)	80

(see also Gnidralog)

NINE INCH NAILS
90	Island 12IS 482	Down On It (Skin)/Terrible Lie (Sympathetic Mix)/Down On It (Shred)/Down On It (Singe)/Terrible Lie (Empathetic Mix)/Down On It (Demo) (12", numbered limited edition)	20
91	Island IS 484	Head Like A Hole/Head Like A Hole (Copper Mix) (p/s)	5
91	Island 10ISP 484	Head Like A Hole (Slate)/Head Like A Hole (Copper) (10", poster p/s)	8
91	Island 12IS 484	Head Like A Hole (Slate)/Head Like A Hole (Copper)/Head Like A Hole (Opal) (12", ps)	10
91	Island ISDJ 484	Head Like A Hole (Radio Edit) (promo, stickered p/s, same track both sides)	20
91	Island ISDJ 508	Sin (Radio Edit)/(same) (promo only, stickered p/s)	12
91	Island 9IS 508	Sin (Long)/Sin (Dub)/Get Down Make Love (9", p/s)	10
92	Island IS 552DJ	Wish (Radio Edit) (1-sided, stickered plain sleeve, promo only)	12
94	Island IS 592	March Of The Pigs/A Violent Fluid (p/s, etched disc)	5
94	Island 9IS 592	March Of The Pigs/A Violent Fluid/All The Pigs, All Lined Up/Underneath The Skin (9",numbered p/s)	10
94	Island 12IS 596	Closer (Deviation)/Closer (Further Away)/Closer (6.26)/Closer (Precursor)/Closer (Internal) (12", p/s)	10
94	Island 12ISX 596	Closer to God/March Of The Fuckheads/Heresy (Blind)/Memorabilia (12", p/s)	10
90	Island CID 482	DOWN IN IT (mixes) (CD EP, numbered case)	20
90	Island CID 484	HEAD LIKE A HOLE (CD EP)	10
91	Island ILPS 9973	PRETTY HATE MACHINE (LP)	12
92	Interscope ILPM 8004	BROKEN (1-sided 6 track mini LP with free 7" 'Physical [your'e so]' / 'Suck')	30
92	Island ILPM 8005	FIXED (remix mini LP)	20
94	Island ILPSD 8012	THE DOWNWARD SPIRAL (double LP, gatefold sleeve)	18
99	Island ILPST 8091	THE FRAGILE (triple LP, inners, booklet)	30

NINE INCH WORMS
97	Martian BEER 05	A NIGHT ON THE TOWN WITH THE NINE INCH WORMS (9" LP)	12

999
77	Labritain LAB 999	I'm Alive/Quite Disappointing (p/s)	10
77	United Artists UP 36299	Nasty Nasty/No Pity (p/s, green vinyl)	10
77	United Artists UP 36299	Nasty Nasty/No Pity (p/s, black vinyl)	5
77	United Artists FREE 7	Nasty Nasty/No Pity (78rpm promo, 50 copies only)	250
78	Labritain 12 FREE 10	Waiting/Action (12", mail-order freebie)	8
78	United Artists UP 36399	Emergency/My Street Stinks (p/s)	5
78	United Artists UP 36376	Me And My Desire/Crazy (p/s)	5
78	United Artists UP 36435	Feelin' Alright With The Crew/Titanic (My Over) Reaction (p/s)	5
78	United Artists UP 36467	Homicide/Soldier (p/s, green vinyl)	5
79	Radar ADA 46	Found Out Too Late/Lie, Lie, Lie (p/s)	5
81	Albion ION 1011	Obsessed/Change/Lie, Lie, Lie (live) (p/s, with laminated sleeve, shrinkwrapped with patch)	6
81	Albion ION 1017	Li'l Red Riding Hood/Waiting For Your Number To Be Called/I Ain't Gonna Tell Ya (live) (p/s, with stencil; shrinkwrapped)	6
81	Albion ION 1023	Indian Reservation/So Greedy (Remixed)/Taboo (Remix) (p/s, clear vinyl, with sticker)	5
78	United Artists UAG 30199	999 (LP, with inner sleeve)	12
78	United Artists UAG 30209	SEPARATES (LP, with inner sleeve)	15
80	United Artists POLS 1013	BIGGEST PRIZE IN SPORT (LP)	12
86	Castle DOJOLP 31	999 IN CASE OF EMERGENCY (LP)	12

MINT VALUE £

(see also Kilburn & High Roads)

SADIE NINE
81	Precious AVE 3	If You Take A Morning From My Life/Kiss Me Not Him	6

9.30 FLY
72	Ember NR 5062	9.30 FLY (LP, textured gatefold sleeve)	200

NINESENSE
76	Ogun OG 900	OH! FOR THE EDGE (LP)	20
77	Ogun OG 910	HAPPY DAZE (LP)	20

(see also Elton Dean, Julie Tippetts, Keith Tippett, Mark Charig, Harold Beckett, Alan Skidmore)

1984
69	Big T BIG 117	This Little Boy/Rosalyn	12
69	Big T BIG 120	Got To Have Your Love/Here We Are	8
71	Decca F23159	Little Girl/Laramee	12

1919
82	Red Rhino RED 22	Repulsion/Tear Down These Walls (white hand-written labels, 500 only)	25

1910 FRUITGUM CO.
68	Pye International 7N 25447	Simon Says/Reflections From The Looking Glass	5
68	Pye International 7N 25458	May I Take A Giant Step (Into Your Heart)/(Poor Old) Mr. Jensen	5
68	Pye Intl. 7N 25468	1,2,3, Red Light/Sticky Sticky	6
68	Pye Int. 7N.25478	Pop Goes The Weasel/The Year 2001	6
68	Pye Intl. N(S)PL 28115	SIMON SAYS (LP)	15
69	Buddah 203 014	GOODY GOODY GUMDROPS (LP)	15
70	Buddah 2359 006	HARD RIDE (LP)	15

1910 FRUITGUM CO./LEMON PIPERS
68	Pye Intl. NEP 44091	PRESENTING... (EP, 1 side each)	10

90 DEGREES
79	Virgin VS 311	No Doctor/Fantasy Woman (p/s)	8

NINEY (& DESTROYERS/OBSERVERS)
70	Amalgamated AMG 856	Niney Special/Danger Zone	18
70	Pressure Beat PR 5501	Honey No Money/INSPIRATIONS: This Message To You	8
71	Big BG 317	You Must Believe/You Must Believe Version	12
71	Big Shot BI 568	Blood And Fire/Mud And Water	15
71	Big Shot BI 586	Message To The Ungodly/Message To The Ungodly - Version	8
71	Supreme SUP 214	You Must Believe Me/RUPIE EDWARDS ALLSTARS: Funk The Funk	12
71	Gas GAS 167	Blood And Fire/ROLAND ALPHONSO: 33 66	20
71	Moodisc HME 111	People Let Love Shine/MUDIES ALL STARS: Too Much	6
72	Big Shot BI 607	Hiding By The Riverside/The Red Sea	5
72	Big Shot BI 609	Beg In The Gutter/Beg In The Gutter Version	5
72	Big Shot BI 610	Everyday Music (by The Observers)/Observing The Avenue	6
72	Bullet BU 503	Aily And Ailaloo (& Max)/Version	5
72	Downtown DT 494	Get Out My Life/Get Out My Life - Version (with the Observers)	5
72	Downtown DT 495	Hi Diddle/Hi Diddle - Version	5

(see also Niney's All Stars, Observers)

NINEY'S ALL STARS
70	Unity UN 563	Skankee/Skankee - Version	10

(see also Niney, Observers)

NING
71	Decca F 23114	Machine/More Ning	25

NINJAMAN & FLOURGON
90	Sure Delight 23 SDT	ZIG IT UP - MAIN ATTRACTION: Zig It Up (Radio/Freestyle/Funke-Club/Funke-Instrumental Mixes) (12", p/s)	10

NINO & EBBTIDES
61	Top Rank JAR 572	Those Oldies But Goodies/Don't Run Away	30

9TH CREATION
76	Pye 7N 45622	Sexy Girl/Falling In Love	15

NIPPLE ERECTORS
78	Soho SH 1/2	King Of The Bop/Nervous Wreck (with glossy p/s)	40
78	Soho SH 1/2	King Of The Bop/Nervous Wreck (later matt p/s)	20

(see also Nips, Pogues)

NIPS
78	Soho SH 4	All The Time In The World/Private Eyes (foldover p/s)	30
80	Soho SH 9	Gabrielle/Vengeance	18
80	Soho SH 9	Gabrielle/Vengeance (tour copy with 'licensed to cool' stamp)	30
80	Chiswick CHIS 119	Gabrielle/Vengeance (reissue, p/s)	15
81	Test Pressing TP 5	Happy Song/Nobody To Love (p/s)	30
80	Soho HOHO 1	ONLY AT THE END OF THE BEGINNING (LP, with insert, white labels)	35

(see also Nipple Erectors, Pogues)

NIRVANA (U.K.)
67	Island WIP 6016	Tiny Goddess/I Believe In Magic	25
67	Island WIP 6020	Pentecost Hotel/Feelin' Shattered	20
68	Island WIP 6029	Rainbow Chaser/Flashbulb	25
68	Island WIP 6038	Girl In The Park/C Side In Ocho Rios	25
68	Island WIP 6045	All Of Us (The Touchables)/Trapeze	15
69	Island WIP 6052	Wings Of Love/Requiem To John Coltrane	25
69	Island WIP 6057	Oh! What A Performance/Darling Darlene	30
70	Pye International 7N 25525	The World Is Cold Without You/Christopher Lucifer	20
71	Vertigo 6059 035	The Saddest Day Of My Life/(I Wanna Go) Home	25
71	Philips 6006 127	Pentecost Hotel/Lazy Day Drift	12
72	Philips 6006 166	Stadium/Please Believe Me	12
76	Bradleys BRAD 7602	Two Of A Kind/Before Midnight	6
76	Island WIP 6180	Rainbow Chaser/Tiny Goddess (p/s)	10
78	Pepper UP 36461	Love Is/Pascale	5

79	Pepper UP 36538	Restless Wind/Thank You And Goodnight	5
81	Zilch ZILCH 8	The Picture Of Dorian Gray/No It Isn't	5
82	Zilch ZILCH 15	Black And White Or Colour/Tall Trees And Mansions	5
88	Bam Caruso OPRA 45	Black Flower/WIMPLE WINCH: Save My Soul (jukebox issue, die-cut sleeve)	5
68	Island ILP 959	THE STORY OF SIMON SIMOPATH (LP, mono, pink label, black/orange circle logo)	250
68	Island ILPS 9059	THE STORY OF SIMON SIMOPATH (LP, stereo, pink label, black/orange circle logo)	350
68	Island ILPS 9087	ALL OF US (LP, pink label, black/orange circle logo)	200
70	Pye Intl. NSPL 28132	DEDICATED TO MARKOS III (LP)	200
71	Vertigo 6360 031	LOCAL ANAESTHETIC (LP, gatefold sleeve, swirl label)	200
72	Philips 6308 089	SONGS OF LOVE AND PRAISE (LP)	100
87	Bam-Caruso KIRI 061	BLACK FLOWER (LP)	12

(see also Patrick Campbell-Lyons, Ray Singer, Pica, Hat & Tie)

NIRVANA (U.S.)

89	Tupelo TUP EP8	Blew/Love Buzz/Been A Son/Stain (12", p/s)	40
89	Tupelo TUP CD8	Blew/Love Buzz/Been A Son/Stain (CD)	35
90	Tupelo TUP 25	Sliver/Dive (gatefold p/s, green vinyl only, 2,000 pressed)	25
91	Tupelo TUP EP25	Sliver/Dive/About A Girl (live)/Dive (12", p/s)	15
91	Tupelo TUP EP25	Sliver/Dive/About A Girl (live)/Dive (12", repressing, blue vinyl, p/s)	30
91	Tupelo TUP CDEP25	Sliver/Dive/About A Girl (live)/Spank Thru (live) (CD)	15
91	Geffen DGCT 5	Smells Like Teen Spirit (Edit)/Even In His Youth/Aneurysm (12", p/s)	20
91	Geffen DGCS 5	Smells Like Teen Spirit (Edit)/Drain You (p/s)	8
91	Geffen DGCTP 5	Smells Like Teen Spirit (Edit)/Drain You (LP Version)/Aneurysm (12", picture disc, p/s)	20
91	Geffen DGCCD 5	Smells Like Teen Spirit (Edit)/Drain You/Even In His Youth/Aneurysm (CD, digipak with tour dates)	12
92	Geffen DGCTP 7	Come As You Are/Endless Names/School (Live)	35
92	Geffen DGCTP 7	Come As You Are/Endless, Nameless/School (live) (12", picture disc, die-cut p/s)	20
92	Geffen DGCTP 9	Lithium/Been A Son (live)/Curmudgeon (12", picture disc, die-cut p/s)	20
92	Geffen DGCTD 9	Lithium/Been A Son (live)/Curmudgeon (CD, digipak)	10
92	Geffen GFS 34	In Bloom/Sliver (live)/Polly (live) (p/s)	12
92	Geffen DGCTP 34	In Bloom/Sliver (live)/Polly (live) (12", picture disc, die-cut p/s)	20
93	Touch & Go TG 83	Oh, The Guilt/JESUS LIZARD: Puss (p/s, blue vinyl, with poster)	25
93	Touch & Go TG 83	Oh, The Guilt/JESUS LIZARD: Puss (p/s, blue vinyl, without poster)	10
93	Touch & Go TG 83	Oh, The Guilt/JESUS LIZARD: Puss (p/s, black vinyl)	28
93	Touch & Go TGCD 83	Oh, The Guilt/JESUS LIZARD: Puss (CD)	10
93	Geffen GFST 54	Heart Shaped Box/Milk It/Marigold (12" p/s)	15
93	Geffen GFST 66	All Apologies/Rape Me/MV (12", p/s with 2 art prints)	15
94	Geffen (no cat. no.)	Penny Royal Tea (Scott Litt Mix)/Where Did You Sleep Last Night (live) (unreleased, 10 test pressings only)	500
94	Geffen NIRPRO (no cat. no.)	Penny Royal Tea (Scott Litt Mix) (CD, 1-track, no inlay, promo only)	500
95	Geffen GED 24901	SINGLES (6 x CD box set)	20
89	Tupelo TUP LP 6	BLEACH (LP, 300 on white vinyl)	200
89	Tupelo TUP LP 6	BLEACH (LP, 2,000 on green vinyl)	60
89	Tupelo TUP LP 6	BLEACH (LP, black vinyl)	20
89	Tupelo TUP CD 6	BLEACH (CD, original album with extra tracks "Love Buzz" & "Downer")	20
91	Geffen DGC 24425	NEVERMIND (LP, with inner sleeve)	15
91	Geffen DGCCD 24425	NEVERMIND (CD, without uncredited bonus track "Endless, Nameless")	15
94	Geffen GED 24727	UNPLUGGED IN NEW YORK (LP, white vinyl with inner sleeve)	35
96	Geffen GEF 25105	FROM THE MUDDY BANKS OF THE WISHKAH (2-LP)	25
02	Sub Pop 9878700341	BLEACH (LP, reissue, 13 tracks, white marbled vinyl)	20
02	Sub Pop 9878400341	BLEACH (LP, reissue, 11 tracks, white vinyl)	20
04	Geffen NIRVBOXCDP1	SELECTIONS FROM WITH THE LIGHTS OUT (CD card wallet, promo)	20
09	Simply Vinyl SVLP 0038	NEVERMIND (LP, reissue)	18

(see also Foo Fighters)

NITE-LITERS

72	RCA 2214	K-Jee/Tanga Boo Gonk	5
72	RCA SF 8282	INSTRUMENTAL DIRECTIONS (LP)	20

NITE PEOPLE

66	Fontana TF 747	Sweet Tasting Wine/Nobody But You	25
67	Fontana TF 808	Trying To Find Another Man/Stay As Sweet As You Are	20
67	Fontana TF 885	Summertime Blues/In The Springtime	60
68	Fontana TF 919	Morning Sun/Where You There	40
69	Page One POF 149	Love, Love, Love/Hot Smoke And Sassafras (with insert)	25
69	Page One POF 149	Love, Love, Love/Hot Smoke And Sassafras	15
69	Page One POF 159	Is This A Dream/Cream Tea	25
70	Page One POF 174	Season Of The Rain/P.M.	20
69	Page One POLS 025	P.M. (LP)	230

(see also Banana Bunch)

NITE ROCKERS

58	RCA RCA 1079	Nite Rock (Lonely Train)/Oh! Baby	50
58	RCA RCA 1079	Nite Rock (Lonely Train)/Oh! Baby (78)	30

NITESHADES

65	CBS 201763	Be My Guest/I Must Reveal	18
65	CBS 201817	Fell So Fast/I'm Not Gonna Worry	12

NITS

79	CBS 8049	Tutti Ragazzi/Harrow Accident	8

NITTY GRITTY

85	Greensleeves GRED 187	Hog In A Minty/Run Down The World	12

NITTY GRITTY DIRT BAND

67	Liberty LIB 55948	Buy Me For The Rain/Candy Man	10
68	Liberty LBF 15099	Collegiana/End Of Your Line	10
69	Liberty LBF 15275	Some Of Shelly's Blues/Yukon Railway	6
70	Liberty LBF 15358	Rave On/The Cure	6
68	Liberty LBL/LBS 83122	PURE DIRT (LP)	30
69	Liberty LBL/LBS 83286	DEAD AND ALIVE (LP)	25
71	Liberty LBG 83345	UNCLE CHARLIE AND HIS DOG TEDDY (LP, gatefold sleeve)	20
72	United Artists UAS 29284	ALL THE GOOD TIMES (LP)	15

74	United Artists USD 307/8	STARS AND STRIPES FOREVER (2-LP)	18

(see also Kaleidescope, Chris Darlow)

NITZER EBB
85	Own label	BASIC PAIN PROCEDURE (EP, cassette, given away at gig)	20

JACK NITZSCHE
63	Reprise R 20202	The Lonely Surfer/Song For A Summer Night	35
63	Reprise R 20237	Night Walker/Green Grass Of Texas	18
78	MCA MCA 366	Hard Workin' Man (featuring Captain Beefheart)/Coke Machine	15
74	Warner Bros K 41211	ST GILES CRIPPLEGATE (LP)	30

(see also Date With Soul, Mick Jagger, Captain Beefheart, Randy Newman, Crazy Horse)

NIVENS
89	Woosh WOOSH 5	Yesterday/I Hope You'll Always Be My Friend (p/s)	5

NIX-NOMADS
64	HMV POP 1354	You're Nobody (Till Somebody Loves You)/She'll Be Sweeter Than You (demos miscredited to Nix-Nomands)	80

MEL NIXON
72	Parlophone R5958	Pillars Of Straw/Ev'ry Little Beat Of Your Heart	6
75	Alaska ALA 26	Every Beat Of Your Heart/ASTRA NOVA ORCHESTRA: Soul Sleeper	6

NMONIC
00	YNR YNR002	REQUIEM (EP)	12

NO DOUBT
96	INTERSCOPE INSP 95515	Don't Speak/Greener Pastures (picture disc - p/s)	5

NO SUPPORT/LIMPS
79	Matchbox Classics MC 1	OPPOSITE SIDES EP (Split 7" with 2 tracks by Limps and 2 tracks by No Support, p/s)	20
79	Matchbox Classics MC 2	ANOTHER MATCHBOX CLASSIC? (Split EP, 2 tracks by Limps and 2 by No Support, with folded p/s)	40
79	Matchbox Classics MC 2	ANOTHER MATCHBOX CLASSIC? (Split EP, 2 tracks by Limps and 2 by No Support, without folded p/s, just die-cut stamped sleeve)	15

RAB NOAKES
78	Ring O' 2017 115	Waiting Here For You/Restless (in p/s)	18
78	Ring O' 2017 115	Waiting Here For You/Restless	12
78	Ring O' 2017 117	I Won't Let You Down/Long After Dark (unreleased)	0
70	Decca SKL 5061	DO YOU SEE THE LIGHTS (LP)	40
72	A&M AMLS 68119	RAB NOAKES (LP, with Stealers Wheel)	25
75	Warner Bros. K56114	NEVER TOO LATE (LP)	15
78	Ring O' 2339 201	RESTLESS (LP)	12

NOBELMEN
59	Top Rank JAR 155	Thunder Wagon/Dragon Walk	20
59	Top Rank JAR 155	Thunder Wagon/Dragon Walk (78)	15

BARRY NOBLE
68	Columbia DB 8438	I've Got My Eyes On You/I've Always Wanted You	5

KEITH NOBLE & RADO KLOSE
70	Eden EDEN LP 14	MR COMPROMISE (LP,, private pressing, handmade sleeve)	500

LISA NOBLE
58	Decca F 11006	Maggie! Yes Ma!/Who's Sorry Now	10

NICK NOBLE
60	Coral Q 72403	The Tip Of My Fingers/Sweet Love	6
60	Coral Q 72413	Island Farewell/Excuse Me (I Think I've Got A Heartache)	6

(see also Dick Noel)

PATSY ANN NOBLE
61	HMV POP 980	Good Looking Boy/The Guy Who Can Mend A Broken Heart	25
63	Columbia DB 4956	Don't You Ever Change Your Mind/Sour Grapes	15
63	Columbia DB 7008	Heartbreak Avenue/I'm Nobody's Baby	15
63	Columbia DB 7060	I Was Only Foolin' Myself/Ordinary Love	10
63	Columbia DB 7088	Accidents Will Happen/He Tells Me With His Eyes	15
63	Columbia DB 7148	It's Better To Cry Today/Don't Tell Him I Told You	10
64	Columbia DB 7258	I Did Nothing Wrong/Better Late Than Never	10
64	Columbia DB 7318	Private Property/Crack In The Door	10
64	Columbia DB 7386	Tied Up With Mary/Green Eyed People	10
65	Columbia DB 7472	Then You Can Tell Me Goodbye/If You Wanna Be More Than Friends	10
65	Polydor BM 56054	He Who Rides A Tiger/City Of Night	30

(see also Trisha Noble)

TRISHA NOBLE
67	MGM MGM 1371	Live For Life/The New Is Rarely Patchka	20

(see also Patsy Ann Noble)

WOODROW NOBLE
79	Baby Mother HIT DD10	Reggae A The Best (Feat. Prince Hammer)/Strike The Hammer Wild (12")	30

CLIFF NOBLES (& CO.)
68	Direction 58-3518	The Horse/Love Is Alright	8
68	Direction 58-3738	Judge Baby, I'm Back/Horse Fever (solo)	8
69	Direction 58-4205	Switch It On/Burning Desire	8
68	Direction 8-63477	THE HORSE (LP)	20

NO CHOICE
83	Riot City RIOT 20	SADIST DREAM (EP)	8

NO COVER
82	Guardian GRC 136	200 Voices/Seen Too Much	50

NOCTURNAL EMISSIONS
81	Sterile ION 2	FRUITING BODY (LP)	50
84	Sterile SR 6	NO SACRIFICE (12", p/s, 2,000 only)	12
84	CFC LP 2	CHAOS - LIVE AT THE RITZY (LP)	20

84	Illuminated JAMS LP 33	VIRAL SHEDDING (LP)	20
84	Sterile EMISS 001	TISSUE OF LIES (LP, 1st batch numbered)	50
84	Sterile EMISS 001	TISSUE OF LIES (LP, later pressing in blue sleeve)	25
84	Sterile SR 4	DROWNING IN A SEA OF BLISS (LP)	50
84	Sterile SR 5	BEFEHLSNOTSTAND (LP)	25
85	Sterile SRC 003	DEATHDAY (cassette)	15
85	Sterile SR 7	SONGS OF LOVE AND REVOLUTION (LP)	15
86	Sterile SR 9	SHAKE THOSE CHAINS, RATTLE THOSE CAGES (LP)	15
87	Earthly Delights EARTH 02	THE WORLD IS MY WOMB (LP)	20
88	Earthly Delights EARTH 04	SPIRITFLESH (LP)	20
89	Earthly Delights EARTH 03	STONEFACE (LP)	12
89	Earthly Delights EARTH 05	BEYOND LOGIC (LP, 250 signed)	25
89	Earthly Delights EARTH 05	BEYOND LOGIC (LP)	18
90	Earthly Delights EARTH 06	MOUTH OF THE BABES (LP)	30
93	Earthly Delights EARTH 08	THE QUICKENING (LP, 250 signed)	25
93	Earthly Delights EARTH 08	THE QUICKENING (LP)	18

(see also Caroline K)

NOCTURNES (1)

55	MGM SP 1120	Whodat? (Buck Dance)/Hey Punchinello	10
55	MGM SP 1148	Birmin'ham/Toodle-oo Igaloo	10

NOCTURNES (2)

64	Solar SRP 102	Trioka/Rawhide	15

NOCTURNES (3)

67	Columbia DB 8158	Wish You Would Show Me Your Mind/I Do, I Do	10
67	Columbia DB 8219	Why (Am I Treated So Bad?)/Save The Last Dance For Me	10
68	Columbia DB 8332	A New Man/Suddenly Free	10
68	Columbia DB 8453	Carpet Man/Look At Me	15
68	Columbia DB 8493	Montage/Fairground Man	40
68	Columbia S(C)X 6223	THE NOCTURNES (LP)	30
68	Columbia S(C)X 6315	WANTED ALIVE (LP)	30

(see also Lyn Paul)

NOCTURNS

64	Decca F 12002	Carryin' On/Three Cool Cats	10

PROFESSOR ERNEST NODE & HIS MUG & JUG BAND

67	Columbia DB 8100	The Egg Plant That Ate Chicago/I'm In The Doghouse	7

NODENS ICTUS

87	(No cat no)	THE GROVE OF SELVES (Cassette LP)	50

(see also Ozric Tentacles)

DICK NOEL

56	London HLH 8295	(The Same Thing Happens With) The Birds And The Bees/Birth Of The Blues	20

(see also Nick Nobel)

NOEL & THE FIREBALLS

70	Pama PM 807	Confussion (sic)/We Got To Have Loving	10
70	Pams PM 808	Can't Turn You Loose/Skinny Legs	10

NO FAITH

81	No Faith NF 001	Double Trouble/Only The Good Die Young (p/s, private pressing)	120

JACKY NOGUEZ

60	Pye Int. 7N.25063	Hover On Sunday/Chanson Du Jan Gadeiro	6

NOIR

71	Dawn DNLS 3029	WE HAD TO LET YOU HAVE IT (LP, with insert)	35

NOISE FACTORY

92	3rd Party 3RD#01	MY MIND EP (12")	20
92	3rd Party 3RD#02	THE FIRE EP (12")	50
92	3rd Party 3RD#03	ALIENATION EP (12")	25
92	3rd Party 3RD#04	The CAPSULE EP (12")	20
93	3rd Party 3RD#07	A NEW SOMETHING EP (12")	20

NOIZ BOIZ

81	Caveman CMR 03	Noiz Boiz/Flashback (p/s)	10

NO KIDDING

74	Wave	NO KIDDING (LP)	15

JOE NOLAN & HIS BAND

69	Jolly JY 013	Cool It With Reggae/Reggae With Me	150
69	Jolly JY 016	Confidential/Poison Reggae	40

(see also Bonnie Frankson)

NOLAN SISTERS/NOLANS

77	Hanover Grand HG 19751	THE NOLAN SISTERS (LP, sold only at London Room Club, Drury Lane)	12

TERRY NOLAND

58	Coral Q 72311	Oh Baby! Look At Me/Puppy Love	150
58	Coral Q 72311	Oh Baby! Look At Me/Puppy Love (78)	50

PIERRE NOLES

63	Oriole CB 1791	Jacqueline/Marilyn	7

NAZ NOMAD & NIGHTMARES

84	Big Beat NS 93	I Had Too Much To Dream (Last Night)/Cold Turkey (p/s)	5
84	Big Beat WIK 21	GIVE DADDY THE KNIFE CINDY (LP, purple vinyl)	20

(see also Damned)

NOMADS

65	Grampian NAN 1008	I'm Coming Home/Hey Little Girl	70

NOMADS

70	Pye 7N 17906	The Singer Sang His Song/Lovin' Him	6

NO-MAN

90s	Hidden Art HA4	Colours/Colours Remodelled (7", promo, fold-out cover, 8 page press sheet)	20
90	Probe Plus PP27T	COLOURS (EP) (12")	35
91	One Little Indian 57TP12	DAYS IN THE TREES EP (12")	20
92	One Little Indian 63TP12	OCEAN SONG EP (12")	20
91	One Little Indian TPLP 47M	LOVESIGHS - AN ENTERTAINMENT (LP)	20
93	One Little Indian 73TPCD	SWEETHEART RAW EP (CD)	20
93	One Little Indian 83TP12	ONLY BABY EP (12")	20
93	One Little Indian TPLP57	LOVEBLOWS AND LOVECRIES (CD)	25
93	One Little Indian TPLP 057	LOVEBLOWS & LOVECRIES - A CONFESSION (LP)	20
94	Hidden Art HI-ART 2	FLOWERMIX (CD)	20
94	One Little Indian TPLP 067	FLOWERMOUTH (2-LP)	50

(see also Porcupine Tree, Japan)

NO MAN IS AN ISLAND

89	Plastic Head	The Girl From Missouri/Forest Almost Burning/Night Sky Sweet Earth/ The Ballet Beast (uncedited) (12")	60

(see also No-Man, Porcupine Tree, Japan)

NON

80	Mute MUTE 7	I Can't Look Straight/SMEGMA: Flash Cards (p/s, with 2 centre holes)	15
81	Mute MUTE 015	NON EP (Rise/Out Out Out/Romance Fatal Dentro Deun Auto) (12", p/s)	15
00	Mute MUTE 250	Solitude/Receive The Flame (p/s, two centre holes, A-side plays at 45 rpm, B-side has closed grooves and plays at any speed, 700 copies only)	10

(see also Boyd Rice)

NO NAMES

65	Polydor NH 59080	All Because Of You/She Is Mine	40

NOOKIE

92	Absolute 2 ABS 005DJ	THE LOVE IS EP (12", p/s)	10
92	Absolute 2 ABS 005 DJR	THE LOVE IS EP (REMIX) (12")	8
92	Reflective REFLECT 003	ACCOUSTIC ASSAULT SQUAD EP (12")	40
94	Reinforced RIVET 1255	Give A Little Love/Give A Little Love (Manix Mix)/ Livin' Inside A Dream/T-Three (12")	15
94	Reinforced RIVET 1268	Only You/Celebrate Life (12")	10
93	Reinforced RIVET 1239	RETURN OF NOOKIE EP (12", p/s)	20
95	Reinforced RIVET LP 05	THE SOUND OF MUSIC (2xLP)	40

PETER NOONE

70	RAK 106	Lady Barbara/Don't Just Stand There	5
71	RAK 114	Oh You Pretty Things/Together Forever	5
71	RAK 121	Walnut Whirl/Right On Mother	6
72	RAK 129	Shoo Be Doo Ah/Because You're There	6
72	RAK 136	Should I/Each And Every Minute	6
76	Bus Stop BUS 1034	We Don't Need The Money/Love Don't Change	7
77	Bus Stop BUS 1057	Goodbye Sam Hello Samantha/Can I Put My Song In Your Heart	7

NO OTHER NAME

79	Daylight LD 500	DEATH INTO LIFE (LP, with insert)	25

NO QUARTER

83	Reel REEL 1	Survivors/Time And Space/Racing For Home (12", foldout p/s)	40
83	Bonzo Bear	BIRDS OF PREY EP (12")	30

NORA/BUNNY

72	Tropical AL 0015	Butterfly/TROPICAL ALL STARS: Fly Version	6

NORBITON SURFERS

80	Hut S/80/CUS 700	Ivor The Engine/My Ego Dies (DIY p/s)	20

KEN NORDINE

57	London RE-D 1091	KEN NORDINE READS (EP, with Billy Vaughn Orchestra)	10
59	London Jazz EZ-D 19040	WORD JAZZ (EP)	10
67	Philips BL 7785	COLOURS (LP)	25

(see also Billy Vaughn & His Orchestra)

NORFOLK & JOY

79	Dara MPA 031	SCOTSOUNDS (LP)	30

NO RIGHT TURN

83	Chelful CHL 001	NO (LP)	25

NORMA & TONY

69	(No Cat. No.)	YOU ARE ALWAYS WELCOME AT OUR HOUSE (LP, private pressing, 100 only)	80

NORMAL

78	Mute MUTE 001	Warm Leatherette/T.V.O.D (p/s)	10

(see also Robert Rental)

NORMAL

03	Ai AI 005	GREEN FUELS EP (12", p/s)	8

NORMAN CONQUEST

67	MGM MGM 1376	Two People/Upside Down	100

(see also Factory, Peter & Wolves, John Pantry)

NORMAN & HOOLIGANS

77	President PT 461	I'm A Punk/Re-Entry	15

NORMAN & INVADERS

64	United Artists UP 1031	Stacey/Our Wedding Day	12
64	United Artists UP 1058	Our Wedding Day/Stacey (reissue)	6
65	United Artists UP 1077	Night Train To Surbiton/Likely Lads	12

LARRY NORMAN

81	Solid Rock CS 103A	I Feel Like Dying/Alwyn Wall - Hold On	12
69	Key KL 010/Dove DOVE 64	UPON THIS ROCK (LP)	12
73	MGM 2315 135	I'M ONLY VISITING THIS PLANET (LP, with lyric sheet)	12
76	Solid Rock ROCKY 1	IN ANOTHER LAND (LP, gatefold sleeve)	15

MONTY NORMAN
55	HMV 7M 349	The Shifting, Whispering Sands/Bonnie Blue Gal	8
57	HMV POP 281	The Garden Of Eden/Priscilla	8
63	United Artists UEP 1010	DOCTOR NO SOUNDTRACK (EP)	25
63	United Artists ULP 1097	DOCTOR NO (LP, soundtrack, mono)	40
63	United Artists (S)ULP 1097	DOCTOR NO (LP, soundtrack, stereo)	50

OLIVER NORMAN
67	Polydor 56176	Down In The Basement/Drowning In My Own Despair	60
68	Polydor 56247	People People/You'll Find It Will Come	6

NORMIL HAWAIIANS
80	Dining Out TUX 13	The Beat Goes On/Ventilation (p/s)	6

NORTH BANK
72	Polydor 2058225	Arsenal We're On Your Side/Half Time	5

FREDDIE NORTH
72	Mojo 2092043	Sweeter Than Sweetness/I Did The Woman Wrong	10

ROY NORTH
63	Oak RGJ 107	Blues In Three/Blues In Five	50

NORTH STARS
65	Fontana TF 581	For My True Love/Nothing But The Best	10
66	Fontana TF 726	She's So Far Out She's In/Eeenie Meenie Minee Mo	30

TOM NORTHCOTT
68	Warner Bros WB 7160	1941/Other Times	12

NORTHERN LIGHT
75	CBS 3370	Minnesota/Minnesota (DJ Version)	25

NORTHERN LIGHTS
66	United Artists UP 1123	No Time/Time To Move Along	50
66	United Artists UP 1161	Through Darkness, Light/Baby Those Are The Rules	50

(see also Hooten[anny] Singers, Abba)

NORTHERN PICTURE LIBRARY
93	Vinyl Japan TASK 6	Love Song For The Dead Che/The Way That Stars Die (12", p/s)	15
94	Sarah SARAH 95	Last September's Farewell Kiss/Signs (p/s, insert)	18
93	Vinyl Japan ASKLP 23	ALASKA (LP)	20
94	Vinyl Japan TASK 25	BLUE DISSOLVE EP (12", p/s)	15
94	Sarah SARAH 94	Paris/Norfolk Windmills (p/s, insert)	18

NORTHWIND
71	Regal Zono. SLRZ 1020	SISTER, BROTHER, LOVER (LP)	300

(see also Elastic Band)

NORWICH CITY FOOTBALL CLUB
82	NCP NCFC 1	Something To Shout About/Supporters - Canary Celebration	7

NOSEBLEEDS
77	Rabid TOSH 12	Ain't Bin To No Music School/Fascist Pigs (p/s)	25

(see also Durutti Column, Ed Banger, Blue Orchids)

NO SECURITY
89	Peaceville VILE 11	BURY THE DEBT NOT THE DEAD (split LP with DOOM)	18

NOSMO KING
74	Pye 7N 45382	Goodbye (Nothing To Say)/Teenage Love	5

NO SPORTS
90	Unicorn PHZA-6	Stay Rude Say Rebel/Tour De France/Love Song/Girl (Tango) (12", p/s)	12

NO SWEAT
79	Rip Off RIP 4	Start All Over Again/You Should Be So Lucky (p/s)	20

NOTATIONS (U.K.)
72	Chapter One SCH 174	Need Your Love/Just Nothing Left To Give	22

NOTATIONS (U.S.)
76	Curtom K 16696	Think Before You Stop/I'm Losing	5
76	Curtom K 56212	NOTATIONS (LP)	30

FREDDIE NOTES & RUDIES
69	Downtown DT 427	I Don't Wanna Lose That Girl/Train From Vietnam	12
69	Grape GR 3010	Guns Of Navarone/Yester-Me, Yester-You	40
69	Grape GR 3011	Babylon Girl/Girl I've Got A Date	8
69	Trojan TR 7713	Shanghai/Rome Wasn't Built In A Day	12
70	Bullet BU 421	The Feeling Is Fine/Girl You're Killing Me	7
70	Trojan TR 7724	Rocco/Don't Tell Your Mama	8
70	Trojan TR 7734	Down On The Farm/Easy Street	30
70	Trojan TR 7791	Montego Bay/RUDIES: Blue Mountain	6
70	Trojan TR 7810	Walk A Mile In My Shoes/JOHNNY ARTHEY ORCHESTRA: Reggae Rouser	6
70	Duke DU 63	The Bull/River Ben Come Up	50
70	Duke DU 68	Chicken Inn/Chicken Scratch	12
70	B&C CB 125	It Came Out The Sky/Well Oh Well (p/s)	6
70	Trojan TBL 109	UNITY (LP)	25
70	Trojan TBL 152	MONTEGO BAY (LP)	20

NOTHINGS
65	CBS 201779	At Times Like This/Love So Sweet	15

NO TREND/LYDIA LUNCH
85	Widowspeak WSP 3	HEART OF DARKNESS (12" EP)	8

(see also Lydia Lunch)

NOTSENSIBLES
79	Redball RR 02	(I'm In Love With) Margaret Thatcher/Little Boxes/Gary Bushell's Band Of The Week (p/s)	15

— MINT VALUE £

80	Bent SMALL BENT 5	Death To Disco/Coronation Street Hustle/Lying On The Sofa (p/s)	18
80	Snotty Snail NELCOL 1	(I'm In Love With) Margaret Thatcher/Little Boxes/Gary Bushell's Band Of The Week (p/s, reissue)	10
80	Snotty Snail NELCOL 3	I Thought You Were Dead/I Make A Balls Of Everything I Do/Teenage Revolution (p/s)	10
81	Snotty Snail NELCOL 6	I Am The Bishop/The Telephone Rings Again (p/s)	8
80	Bent BIGBENT 6	INSTANT CLASSICS (LP)	50
80	Snotty Snail SSLP 1	INSTANT CLASSICS (LP, reissue)	30

NOTTINGHAM JAZZ ORCHESTRA

71	Swift SP 55	FESITVAL SUITE (LP)	50

NOTTS ALLIANCE

72	Tradition TSR 011	THE CHEERFUL 'ORN (LP, with Roy Harris)	15

NOUVELLE VAGUE

95	Peacefrog PFG 051	NOUVELLE VAGUE (LP, inner)	25
06	Peacefrog PFG 079	BANDE A PART (LP, poster)	30

NOVA LOCAL

69	MCA MUPS 377	NOVA 1 (LP)	35

PAUL NOVA

82	Exhibit 1 EX 001	Julie Ann/Video Age	60
83	Exhibit 1 EX 002	Famous Boys/Home Sweet Home	50
85	Exhibit 1 EX 004	FANTASY AND FEELING EP	60
84	Exhibit 1 EX 003	TREES WITHOUT LEAVES (LP)	200

NOVAK

97	Enraptured WORM 2	Silver Seas/Schmaltz (p/s in outer hand-sewn cloth sleeve with embroidered "Hand-knitted by Novak" label, 200 only, each different)	15
97	Enraptured WORM 2	Silver Seas/Schmaltz (p/s, 800 only)	8
97	Kitty Kitty CHOOSY 007	Rapunzel/Almost Chinook (hand crayoned p/s, 1,000 only)	8

NOVAS

63	RCA RCA 1360	Push A Little Harder/Oh, Gee Baby!	30
65	London HLU 9940	The Crusher/Take 7	45

NOW

69	NEMS 56-4125	Marcia/The Hands On My Clock Stand Still	35
73	President PT 401	I Wanna Be Free/People Are Standing	12

NOW

77	Ultimate ULT 401	Development Corporations/Why (p/s, blue vinyl)	35
77	Ultimate ULT 401	Development Corporations/Why (p/s)	20
79	Raw RAW 31	Into The 1980s/Nine O'Clock (p/s, 800 only)	40

NOW GENERATION

73	Green Door GD 4055	Alone Again, Naturally/MIND-BODY-SOUL: My Part (Version)	5
73	Pyramid PYR 7007	Baby Don't Do It/You'll Never Know	5
74	Trojan TRLS 78	FOR THE GOOD TIMES (LP)	20

(see also I Roy, B.B. Seaton, Audley Rollins)

NO WAY

78	Our Own IS/NW/1035	Breaking Point/TV Pox/30 Seconds (p/s)	100

NOYES BROTHERS

80	Object Music OBJ 009/010	SHEEP FROM GOATS (2-LP)	25

(see also Steve Miro & Eyes, Spherical Objects)

NOY'S BAND

74	Dawn 1075	Love Potion Number 9/Eldorado	10

(see also Jan Dukes De Grey)

NOYS OF US

60s	KPS KPS 502	He's Alright Jill/What Can I Do	30

NQB

72	Epic S EPC 2151	Long Long Weekend/Free The People	6

N.R.B.Q. (NEW RHYTHM & BLUES QUINTET)

69	CBS 4290	Stomp/I Didn't Know Myself	5
69	CBS 4501	C'mon Everybody/Rocket Number 9	5
69	CBS 63653	N.R.B.Q. (LP)	20
72	Buddah 2319 018	SCRAPS (LP)	12

(see also Carl Perkins)

N.S.U.

69	Stable SLE 8002	TURN ON OR TURN ME DOWN (LP)	180

NU SHOOZ

86	A9446T	I Can't Wait: (Long Dutch Mix)/Make Your mind Up (12")	8

GUITAR NUBBIT

64	Bootleg 501	Georgia Chain Gang/Hard Road (99 copies only)	45
60s	XX MIN 705	GUITAR NUBBIT (EP)	20

NUCHA

90	CBS 655885 7	Together/Ha Sempre Alguem	5

NUCLEAR ASSAULT

88	Under One Flaf 12 FLAG 107	GOOD TIMES, BAD TIMES (12" EP)	8
88	Under One Flag FLAG 21P	SURVIVE (LP, picture disc)	15
88	Under One Flag FLAG 21	SURVIVE (LP)	15
89	Under One Flag FLAG 35	HANDLE WITH CARE (LP)	12

NUCLEAR SOCKETTS

81	Subversive SUB 001	HONOUR BEFORE GLORY (EP, folded p/s, 33rpm)	25
81	Subversive SUB 002	Play Loud/Shadow On The Map	25
82	None	Riot Squad (magazine flexi-disc with fold out picture insert)	20

(IAN CARR'S) NUCLEUS

70	Vertigo 6360 008	ELASTIC ROCK (LP, die cut gatefold sleeve, large swirl label)	100

70	Vertigo 6360 008	ELASTIC ROCK (LP, die cut gatefold sleeve, later 'spaceship' label) 15
71	Vertigo 6360 027	WE'LL TALK ABOUT IT LATER (LP, die cut gatefold sleeve, large swirl label) 100
71	Vertigo 6360 027	WE'LL TALK ABOUT IT LATER (LP, die cut gatefold sleeve, 'spaceship' label) 15
71	Vertigo 6360 039	SOLAR PLEXUS (LP, as Ian Carr's Nucleus, 1st pressing, gatefold sleeve, large swirl label) 150
72	Vertigo 6360 076	BELLADONNA (LP, as Ian Carr, 1st pressing, Matrix side 1, 6360076 1Y//1 1 1 3 Side 2, 6360076 2Y//1 1 1 3, gatefold sleeve, swirl label) 150
74	Vertigo 6360 076	BELLADONNA (LP, as Ian Carr, 2nd pressing, Matrix side 1, 6360076 1Y//1 1 1 4 Side 2, 6360076 2Y//1 1 1 5, gatefold sleeve, swirl label) 80
73	Vertigo 6360 039	SOLAR PLEXUS (LP, as Ian Carr's Nucleus, 2nd pressing, gatefold sleeve, small swirl label) 40
73	Vertigo 6360 091	LABYRINTH (LP, 'spaceship' label, any with swirl are Italian pressings!) 25
73	Vertigo 6360 100	ROOTS (LP, 'spaceship' label) 35
74	Vertigo 6360 110	UNDER THE SUN (LP, 'spaceship' label) 25
75	Vertigo 6360 076	BELLADONNA (LP, as Ian Carr, gatefold sleeve, 'spaceship' label) 30
75	Vertigo 6360 119	SNAKE HIPS ETCETERA (LP, laminated sleeve, 'spaceship' label) 25
75	Vertigo 6360 124	ALLEY CAT (LP, 'spaceship' label) 25
76	Vertigo 9286 019	DIRECT HITS (LP, 'spaceship' label) 35
76	Vertigo 6360 039	SOLAR PLEXUS (LP, as Ian Carr's Nucleus, 3rd pressing gatefold sleeve, 'spaceship' label) 15
77	Capitol EST 11771	IN FLAGRANTI DELICTO (LP) 12
80	Mood 24000	AWAKENING (LP) 12

(see also Don Rendell & Ian Carr Quintet, Neil Ardley, Centipede, Michael Garrick, New Jazz Orchestra, Linda Hoyle)

TED NUGENT (& AMBOY DUKES)

74	Discreet K 19200	Sweet Revenge/Ain't It The Truth (as Ted Nugent & Amboy Dukes) 8
75	Epic S EPC 3900	Stormtroopin'/Hey Baby (some in p/s, orange label) 5
76	Epic S EPC 4796	Dog Eat Dog/Love You So I Told You A Lie 5
77	Epic S EPC 5482	Cat Scratch Fever/A Thousand Nights 5
78	Epic S EPC 9545	Homebound/Death By Misadventure (p/s) 5
75	Discreet K 59203	CALL OF THE WILD (LP) 15

(see also [American] Amboy Dukes)

NUGGETS

| 55 | Capitol CL 14216 | Quirl Up In My Arms/So Help Me, I Love You ....12 |
| 55 | Capitol CL 14267 | Shtiggy Boom/Anxious Heart ....12 |

GARY NUMAN

SINGLES

79	Beggars Banquet BEG 23	Cars/Asylum (p/s,orange plastic labels) 6
79	Beggars Banquet BEG 23	Cars/Asylum (p/s, 'mispressed' on dark red vinyl) 10
79	Beggars Banquet BEG 29	Complex/Bombers (live) (p/s, 'mispressed' on dark red vinyl) 18
80	Beggars Banquet BEG 35	We Are Glass/Trois Gymnopedies (First Movement) (p/s, custom factory pressings on green and yellow vinyl) 500
80	Beggars Banquet BEG 35	We Are Glass/Trois Gymnopedies (1st Movement) (p/s, 'mispressed' on dark red vinyl) 12
80	Beggars Banquet BEG 46	I Die, You Die/Down In The Park (Piano Version) (p/s, dark red vinyl 'mispress') 8
80	Beggars Banquet BEG 46	I Die, You Die/Down In The Park (Piano Version) (p/s, mispressing, plays Remember I Was Vapour & "On Broadway" [SAM 126]) 22
81	Beggars Banquet BEG 62	She's Got Claws/I Sing Rain (p/s, mispressing, plays Dollar's Hand Held In Black And White) 60
82	Beggars Banquet BEG 77	We Take Mystery (To Bed)/The Image Is (mispressed sleeve, no writing) 35
83	Beggars Banquet BEG 95P	Warriors/My Car Slides (aeroplane-shaped picture disc) 12
84	Beggars Banquet TUB 1	This Is My Life (unissued promo for "THE PLAN LP", 300 white label test pressings only) 100
84	Numa NUP 4	Berserker/Empty Bed, Empty Heart (head shaped picture disc) 5
85	Numa NUP 9	Your Fascination/We Need It (mispressed picture disc with pictures on the wrong side) 18
85	Numa NU PROMO 1002	WHITE NOISE (12", 4-track sampler Beserker/We Are Glass/Cars/Are "Friends" Electric?) ...30
85	Numa NUM 7	THE LIVE EP (12", p/s, custom factory pressing on multicoloured vinyl) 200
85	Numa NUM 7	THE LIVE EP (12", p/s, blue, white vinyl or black vinyl) 8
85	Numa NUM 13	Miracles (Extended)/The Fear (Extended) (12" mispressed sleeve: no red writing) 30
86	Numa NUMX 16	This Is Love/Survival//Call Out The Dogs (Extended)/No Shelter/This Ship Comes Apart (12", p/s, stickered double pack, shrinkwrapped) 10
86	Numa NUM 17 DJ	I Can't Stop (Special Club Mix) (12" 1-sided DJ promo) 10
86	Numa NUP 17	I Can't Stop/Faces (aeroplane-shaped picture disc) 8
87	B. Banquet BEG 199P	Cars ('E' Reg Model)/Are 'Friends' Electric? (picture disc) 6
88	Polydor POSPP 894	No More Lies (picture disc) 5
88	I.R.S. ILSP 1003	New Anger/I Don't Believe (poster p/s) 5
88	I.R.S. ILSCD 1003	New Anger/I Don't Believe/Creatures (live)/I Can't Stop (live) (CD) 15
88	I.R.S. ILSPD 1004	America/Respect (live) (Picture disc) 5
88	I.R.S. ILSPD 1004	America/Respect (live) (mispressed picture disc, 'Gary' picture both sides) 45
89	B. Banquet BBP 5CD	SELECTION (CD EP, sampler) 8
91	I.R.S. NUMAN 1	Heart/Icehouse (p/s, black vinyl) 6
91	Numa NU 22	Emotion/In A Glasshouse (p/s) 5
91	Numa NUCD 22	Emotion/In A Glass House/Hanoi/Emotion (CD mix) (CD, 'mispressed' disc) 12
92	Numa NU 23	The Skin Game/Dark Mountain (p/s) 5
92	Numa NU 24DJ	Machine & Soul/Machine & Soul (fan club issue, white label, mail-order only) 8
92	NUCD 124/NUCD224	Machine & Soul (2 x CD single set) 15
93	Beggars Banquet BEG 264T	Cars (Multivalve)/Cars (Endurance Model)/Cars (Top Gear Model) (12", black vinyl, promo only) 12
93	Beggars Banquet BEG 264	Cars ('93 Sprint)/Cars (Top Gear) (poster p/s) 6
93	Beggars Banquet BEG 264L	Cars ('93 Sprint)/Cars (Endurance) (McLaren F1-shaped picture disc) 8
93	Beggars Banquet	Cars ('93 Sprint)/(Multivalve)/(Classic)/(Endurance)/(Top Gear)/(Motorway Mix)/ ('E' Reg Version) (CD, withdrawn, Extended 'E' Reg Model replaces Motorway Mix) 30
93	Beggars Banquet BEG 264CD	Cars '93 Sprint)/(Multivalve)/(Classic)/(Endurance)/(Top Gear)/(Motorway Mix)/'E' Reg Model) (CD, Autosports Awards issue, 300 only) 40
94	Salvation SACD 1	THE RADIAL PAIR (CD EP, fan club issue, mail order only) 25
94	Numa NUM 26	A Question Of Faith (12", withdrawn, black labels with blue print) 25
94	Numa NU 26	A Question Of Faith/Whisper Of Truth (fan club issue, white label, mail-order only) ...25
95	Salvation Records SACD 2/1	BABYLON 1 (CD EP, fan club only, initial copies mailed out with withdrawn additional insert) 18
95	Salvation Records SACD 2/2	BABYLON 2 (CD EP, fan club only, initial copies mailed out with withdrawn additional insert) 18
96	The Record Label SPIND 6	Radio (with N.R.G.)/Radio (extended mix) (CD, withdrawn) 150
06	Mortal MORTAL VS 001	In A Dark Place (7" Edit)/Fold (Alternate Version) (picture disc in stickered sleeve, 1800 only) 6

MINT VALUE £

ALBUMS

			MINT VALUE £
80	Beggars Banquet BEGA 19	TELEKON (LP, dark red vinyl 'mispressing', with stickered sleeve.; with bonus single SAM 126 "Remember I Was Vapour [live]"/"On Broadway" [Live])	20
80	Beggars Banquet BEGA 19	TELEKON (LP, dark red vinyl 'mispressing', with stickered sleeve)	15
81	Beggars Banquet BEGA 28	DANCE (LP, gatefold sleeve with poster)	12
82	Beggars Banquet BEGA 40	I, ASSASSIN (LP, initial copies at Woolworths with colour poster and merchandise sheet)	20
84	B. Banquet BEGA 55P	THE PLAN (LP, picture disc)	15
85	Beggars Banquet BEGC 78/79	NUMAN/TUBEWAY ARMY 1978-79 (Cassette only, compiling NUMAN/TUBEWAY ARMY 1978 [BEG 92E], NUMAN/TUBEWAY ARMY 1978-79 [BEGA 123E] & NUMAN/TUBEWAY ARMY 1978-79 [BEGA 124E])	12
86	Numa NUMAP 1003	THE FURY (LP, mispress picture disc, "Your Fascination" 12" photo on A-side with lyric insert)	25
86	Numa GNFCDA 1	IMAGES 1 & 2 (2-LP, fan club issue with photo inserts, mail-order only, initial signed copies)	20
86	Numa CDNUMA 1003	THE FURY (CD, with original mixes and artwork)	18
86	Numa CDNUMA 1005	STRANGE CHARM (CD, with original artwork and mixes)	18
87	Numa GNFCDA 2	IMAGES 3 & 4 (2-LP, fan club issue with photo inserts, mail-order only, initial signed copies)	20
87	Numa GNFCDA 3	IMAGES 5 & 6 (2-LP, fan club issue with photo inserts, mail-order only, initial signed copies)	20
87	Numa GNF CDA 4	IMAGES 7 & 8 (2-LP, fan club issue with photo inserts, mail-order only, initial signed copies)	20
87	Numa GNFCDA 4	IMAGES 7 & 8 (2-LP, fan club issue with photo inserts, mail-order only)	15
89	Numa GNF CDA 5	IMAGES 9 & 10 (2-LP, fan club issue with photo inserts, mail-order only, initial signed copies)	20
89	Numa GNFCDA 5	IMAGES 9 & 10 (2-LP, fan club issue with photo inserts, mail-order only)	15
88	I.R.S. ILPPD 035	METAL RHYTHM (LP, picture disc)	12
88	IRS ILPCD 035	METAL RHYTHM (CD)	30
89	IRS EIRSACD 1021	METAL RHYTHM (CD, reissue)	30
89	IRS EIRSACD 1019	THE SKIN MECHANIC - LIVE (CD)	20
91	Numa NUMACD 1001	BERSERKER (CD, fan club issue, mail order only, blue text on CD & inlay)	25
91	Numa GNFCCD 11	IMAGES 11 (CD, fan club issue, mail order only)	20
92	Receiver RRLP 170	THE OTHER SIDE OF GARY NUMAN (LP, withdrawn)	12
92	Numa NUMA 1009	MACHINE & SOUL (LP)	12
92	Numa NUMACD 1009	MACHINE & SOUL (CD, mispressed plays 9 tracks instead of 13)	18
93	Numa NUMACDX 1009	MACHINE & SOUL (CD, mispressed with 9 tracks instead of 13)	20
94	Numa NUMA 1010	DREAM CORROSION (3-LP, autographed gatefold sleeve; copies bought at HMV with signed 10" x 8" photo)	20
94	Numa NUMA 1011	SACRIFICE (LP, with lyric sheet, stickered sleeve & bonus single: The Seed Of A Lie [5.26]/"The Seed Of A Lie [7.07]")	30
98	Eagle EAGBX025	THE NUMA YEARS (5-CD set of Beserker, The Fury, Strange Charm, Machine and Soul Sacrifice.)	30
03	Jagged Halo JHLP 5	HYBRID (2-LP, numbered gatefold sleeve)	18
06	Mortal Records LP001	JAGGED (1,000 only, white vinyl, first 250 copies hand signed, numbered and sold via offical Gary Numan website)	35
06	Mortal Records LP001	JAGGED (LP, 1,000 only, white vinyl)	20
08	OTB LP1	PURE (LP, 300 pressed in purple/red/clear vinyl (100 of each). Final 2 tracks pressed on separate yellow vinyl 7	20
08	OTB LP2	EXILE (LP, 300 copies, turquoise/white/orange vinyl (100 of each))	20
08	Beggars Banquet BBQCD 2057	REPLICAS REDUX (2-CD with additional 6 track of mixes and versions CD in card sleeve (GNCD 2008)	25
08	VIN 180 LP 001	THE PLEASURE PRINCIPLE (LP, reissue)	15

(see also Tubeway Army, Paul Gardiner, Dramatis, Claire Hamill, Radio Heart, Nicky Robson, Paper Toys, Caroline Munro, Generator, Bauhaus, Bill Sharpe, Sharpe & Numan, Battles)

NUMBER NINE BREAD STREET

67	Holy Ground HG 112/1109	NUMBER NINE BREAD STREET (LP, 250 copies only)	400

NUMBERS

79	Blasto SRTS 79/CUS/358	ROCK STARS (EP, with insert)	30

NUMBERS

80s	Homegrown HG 701	Here Today/Put 'Em All To Shame/Another Day/Tear You Down (photocopied or green & white sleeve; with poster)	6
80s	Homegrown HG 701	Here Today/Put 'Em All To Shame/Another Day/Tear You Down (photocopied or green & white sleeve; without poster)	5

NUMSKULLZ

96	High Noon NUM003	Enough Of That (12")	8
98	Hombre MEX003	Signs Of The End/The Difference (12")	8

NU NOTES

63	HMV POP 1232	Hall Of Mirrors/Fury	20
64	HMV POP 1311	Kathy/Sunset	20

(see also Russ Sainty & Nu Notes)

NUNS

81	Butt FUN 2	Wild/Suicide Child (p/s)	10

NURSE WITH WOUND

83	L.A.Y.L.A.H. LAY 3	GYLLENSKÖLD, GEIJERSTAM AND I AT RYDBERG'S (12" EP)	40
84	L.A.Y.L.A.H. LAY 7	BRAINED BY FALLING MASONRY (12" EP)	12
86	Torso 33016	SPIRAL INSANA (12" EP)	12
87	Crystal/Wisewound WW 01	Crank/TERMITE QUEEN: Wisecrack (numbered plain black sleeve with printed band, 500 only)	20
88	Yangki 002	FAITH'S FAVOURITES EP: Swamp Rat (with Current 93)/Ballad Of The Pale Girl (12", laminated p/s)	30
88	Idle Hole MIRROR 003	Cooloorta Moon/Great Empty Space (12", p/s)	20
90	Harbinger 001	The Burial Of The Stoned Sardine/CURRENT 93: No Hiding From The Blackbird	15
90	United Dairies UD 031	SORESUCKER EP: I Am The Poison/Journey Through Cheese (12", p/s, 2,000 only)	20
90	Shock SX 004	Sinister Senile: Human Human Human/Psychedelic Underground (45/33rpm, 1,000 only)	25
92	Clawfist 12	Steel Dream March Of The Metal Men/The Dadda's Intoxication ('singles club' release, 33rpm, foldover p/s in poly bag, 1,400 only)	15
93	Clawfist 20	CRUMB DUCK (10" EP, shared with Stereolab, 37 with handmade p/s (Gain/Sadier only)	100
93	Clawfist 20	CRUMB DUCK (10" EP, shared with Stereolab, 1450 regular without handmade p/s)	20
93	World Serpent WS 7003	Alien (1-sided, company sleeve 1,000 only)	25
95	WN 001	ALICE THE GOON (1-sided 12", p/s, 500 only)	75

79	United Dairies UD 01	CHANCE MEETING ON A DISSECTING TABLE OF A SEWING MACHINE AND AN UMBRELLA (LP, 500 only, originals have hand-painted numbers; beware of bootlegs with printed numbers) 200
80	United Dairies UD 03	TO THE QUIET MEN FROM A TINY GIRL (LP, numbered, 500 only, originals have hand-painted numbers; beware of bootlegs with printed numbers) 150
80	United Dairies UD 04	MERZBILD SCHWET (LP, numbered, 500 only, originals have hand-painted numbers; beware of bootlegs with printed numbers) 150
81	United Dairies UD 08	INSECT AND INDIVIDUAL SILENCED (LP, 1,000 only) 80
83	Mi Mort MI MORT iii	GYLLENSKÖLD, GEIJERSTAM & FRIENDS, LIVE AT BAR MALDOROR (LP, some with insert) 40
83	Third Mind TMR 03	OSTRANENIE 1913 (LP, 3,000 only) 60
85	L.A.Y.L.A.H. LAY 15	THE SYLVIE AND BABS HI-FI COMPANION (LP, gatefold sleeve) 25
85	United Dairies UD 110	DRUNK WITH THE OLD MAN OF THE MOUNTAINS (LP) 25
85	United Dairies UD 012	HOMOTOPY TO MARIE (LP, 5,000 only) 35
86	United Dairies UD 019	AUTOMATING VOL. 1 (LP, 3,000 only) 30
86	United Dairies UD 020	A MISSING SENSE (LP, 1 side only; other side by Organum; 2,000 only) 30
87	United Dairies UD 025	DRUNK WITH THE OLD MAN OF THE MOUNTAINS (LP, reissue, handmade custom sleeve, with insert, signed, 100 only) 150
88	United Dairies UD 027	ALAS THE MADONNA DOES NOT FUNCTION (mini-LP, 45/33rpm, 3,000 only) 25
88	Idle Hole MIRROR ONE	SOLILOQUY FOR LILITH (3-LP box set) 80
88	Idle Hole MIRROR 1C	SOLILOQUY FOR LILITH PTS 5/6 (LP, with insert) 25
89	Idle Hole MIRROR TWO	PRESENTS THE SISTERS OF PATAPHYSICS (LP, 1,000 only) 25
89	United Dairies UD 030	AUTOMATING VOL. II (LP) 20
89	United Dairies UD 032	A SUCKED ORANGE (LP, with full colour insert) 35
89	United Dairies UD 032	A SUCKED ORANGE (LP) 30
89	Yangki 003	LUMBS SISTER (LP) 30
90	United Dairies UD 134	PSILOTRIPITAKA (3-LP [UD 01, 03 & 04], with bonus LP "Registered Nurse" [UD 00], 1,000 only, in leather bag) 400
90	United Dairies UD 134	PSILOTRIPITAKA (3-LP [UD 01, 03 & 04], with bonus LP "Registered Nurse" [UD 00], 1,000 only) 150
90	United Dairies UD 134CD	PSILOTRIPITAKA (3-CD [UD 01, 03 & 04], with bonus CD "Registered Nurse" [UD 00CD], 1,000 only, 30 in 'leather bondage bag') 400
90	United Dairies UD 134CD	PSILOTRIPITAKA (3-CD [UD 01, 03 & 04], with bonus CD "Registered Nurse" [UD 00CD], 1,000 only)) 60
90	L.A.Y.L.A.H. LAY 30	BRAINED/GYLLENSKÖLD (LP, withdrawn) 35
91	United Dairies UD 038	CREAKINESS (LP, with Spasm) 20
91	United Dairies UD 09	THE 150 MURDEROUS PASSIONS (LP) 30
91	United Dairies UD 09CD	THE 150 MURDEROUS PASSIONS (CD, sealed in black plastic, 500 only) 30
93	United Dairies UD 059	CRUMB DUCK (LP, shared with Stereolab, reissue of Clawfist EP, 50 copies on pink vinyl) 50
93	United Dairies UD 059	CRUMB DUCK (LP, shared with Stereolab, reissue of Clawfist EP, 500 on fluorescent yellow vinyl) 25
94	United Dairies UD 043	SECOND PIRATE SESSION - ROCK'N'ROLL STATION - SPECIAL EDITION (LP, red vinyl, 500 only) 20
99	United Dairies UD 056	AN AWKWARD PAUSE (2-LP, translucent grey vinyl, 500 only, 1 side not available on CD) 40
00	United Dairies UD 081	ALICE THE GOON (1-sided reissue, 800 copies) 50
01	United Durtro UDOR 8	BRIGHT YELLOW MOON (CD, with Current 93, first 1,000 with bonus CD) 30
02	United Durtro UD 102	MAN WITH THE WOMAN FACE (LP, ltd. edition clear vinyl, poly sleeve, 2 inserts) 15
00s	United Dairies UDX 092	SOLILOQUY FOR LILITH (3-CD box set) 30
07	United Dairies UD 08.C	INSECT AND INDIVIDUAL SILENCED (CD, 120 copies numbered with "insect") 90
09	United Dirter DPROMOCD 72	THE SURVEILLANCE LOUNGE/THE MEMORY SURFACE (3-CD) 30

(see also Current 93, Organum/New Blockaders, Diana Rogerson, Sol Invictus, Steven Stapleton & David Tibet, Tibet & Stapleton, Whitehouse)

NU-SOUND EXPRESS LTD.
72	Pye Int'l 7N 25580	One More Time Y'all/A Rose For A Lady 20

NUTHIN' FANCY
80s	Dynamic Cat DC 1001	Looking For A Good Time/Too Much Rock'n'Roll (p/s) 250

(see also Terraplane, Thunder)

NU TORNADOS
58	London HLU 8756	Philadelphia U .S.A./Magic Record 15
58	London HLU 8756	Philadelphia U .S.A./Magic Record (78) 10

NUTRONS
60s	Melodisc M 1593	The Very Best Things/Stop For The Music 15

NUTSHELL
70s	Myrrh MYR 1056	FLYAWAY (LP) 18
75	Myrrh MYR 1029	IN YOUR EYES (LP, lyric inner sleeve) 20

MAY'F NUTTER
66	Vocalion VL 1282	Head Shrinker/Don't Know What To Do 15
73	London HLL 10414	I Don't Care/Hitch Hike Nightmare 6

NUTTY SQUIRRELS
59	Pye Int. 7N.25044	Uh! Oh! (Pts. 1 & 2) 7

NUTZ
74	A&M AMLS 68256	NUTZ (LP) 12
75	A&M AMLS 68306	NUTZ TOO (LP) 15

(see also Rage, Nightwing)

NYAH FEARTIES
86	Nya DOPLP 001	A TASTY HEIDFUL (LP) 25

NYAH SHUFFLE
70	Grape GR 3021	Sting Ray/Paradise 10
70	Grape GR 3019	Boot Lace/Honey Won't You Stay? 20

JUDY NYLON
82	On-U-Sound LP 16	PAL JUDY (LP) 15

(see also John Cale, Snatch)

NYLONS
82	Attic NYLON 1	A Million Ways/Up On The Roof (p/s) 8

NYMONIC
00	Y N R YNR02	REQIEM (EP) 18

MINT VALUE £

LAURA NYRO

67	Verve Forecast VS 1502	Wedding Bell Blues/Stoney End	15
68	CBS 3604	Eli's Coming/Sweet Blindness	8
68	CBS 4031	Once It Was Alright Now (Farmer Joe)/Woman's Blues	7
69	CBS 4719	Time And Love/The Man Who Sends Me Home	7
68	CBS 63346	ELI AND THE THIRTEENTH CONFESSION (LP, gatefold sleeve, orange label)	35
69	CBS 63510	NEW YORK TENDABERRY (LP, orange label)	20
69	Verve Forecast SVLP 6022	THE FIRST SONGS (LP)	25
70	CBS 64157	CHRISTMAS AND THE BEADS OF SWEAT (LP, orange label)	15

O

OAK TREE

70	President PT 316	The Sun It Always Shone/My Baby Don't Cry	6

OAKENSHIELD

82	Acorn OAK 001	ACROSS THE NARROW SEAS (LP)	18
85	Acorn OAK 002	AGAINST THE GRAIN (LP, with insert)	18

OASIS

SINGLES

94	Creation CRE 176	Supersonic/Take Me Away (p/s)	15
94	Creation CRE 182	Shakermaker/D'Yer Wanna Be A Spaceman? (p/s)	15
94	Creation CRE 185	Live Forever/Up In The Sky (Acoustic) (jukebox issue, large centre hole)	15
94	Creation CRE 185	Live Forever/Up In The Sky (Acoustic) (numbered foldover p/s in stickered poly bag)	15
94	Creation CRE 195	Whatever/(It's Good) To Be Free (no'd foldover p/s in stickered poly bag)	15
95	Creation CRE 215	Wonderwall/Round Are Way (p/s)	8
96	Creation CRE 221	Don't Look Back In Anger/Step Out (p/s, with poly outer)	10
97	Creation CRE 278	Stand By Me/I Got The Fever (p/s)	5
02	Big Brother RKID 23	The Hindu Times/Just Getting Older (p/s, limited edition)	6
06	Big Brother RKID37	Stop The Clocks EP (2 x 7", stickers, numbered)	15

ALBUMS

94	Creation CRELP 169	DEFINITELY MAYBE (2-LP, gatefold sleeve)	35
95	Creation CRELP 189	(WHAT'S THE STORY) MORNING GLORY? (2-LP, gatefold sleeve)	35
97	Creation CRELP 219	BE HERE NOW	25
98	Creation CRELP 241	THE MASTERPLAN (3-LP)	60
00	Big Brother RKID LP005	FAMILIAR TO MILLIONS (3-LP)	70
00	Big Brother RKID LP002	STANDING ON THE SHOULDER OF GIANTS	20
02	Big Brother RKID LP25	HEATHEN CHEMISTRY (2-LP)	20
05	Big Brother RKID LP30X	DON'T BELIEVE THE TRUTH (LP, numbered art print)	30
06	Big Brother RKID LP36	STOP THE CLOCKS (3-LP box-set)	50
09	Big Brother RKIDBOX 58	LP BOX SET (8-LP, numbered, 1,500 only)	300

PROMOS : PROMOS: SINGLES

93	Creation CTP 8	Columbia (Demo) (12", 1-sided, white label, 510 pressed)	200
94	Creation CRE 176TP	Supersonic/Take Me Away/I Will Believe (Live) (12", company sleeve)	40
94	Creation CRESCD 176P	Supersonic/Take Me Away/I Will Believe (Live)/ Columbia (White Label Demo) (CD)	15
94	Creation CRE 182TP	Shakermaker/D'Yer Wanna Be A Spaceman?/Alive (8 Track Demo) (12")	60
94	Creation CRESCD 182P	Shakermaker/D'Yer Wanna Be A Spaceman?/Alive (8 Track Demo)/ Bring It On Down (Live) (CD)	10
94	Creation CRE 185TP	Live Forever/Up In The Sky (Acoustic)/Cloudburst (12")	70
94	Creation CRESCD 185P	Live Forever/Up In The Sky (Acoustic)/Cloudburst/ Supersonic (Live April '94) (CD)	10
94	Creation CTP 190TP	I Am The Walrus (Live At Glasgow Cathouse June '94) (12", 250 only, co. sl.)	250
94	Creation CTP 190CL	Cigarettes & Alcohol (12", 1-sided)	75
94	Creation CTP 190CL	Cigarettes & Alcohol/I Am The Walrus (live Glasgow Cathouse June '94)/ Fade Away (12", 300 only)	75
94	Creation CRESCD 190P	Cigarettes & Alcohol/I Am The Walrus (live Glasgow Cathouse June '94)/ Listen Up/Fade Away (CD)	10
94	Creation CRE 195TP	Whatever (12", 1-sided)	75
94	Creation CRESCD 195P	Whatever/(It's Good) To Be Free/Half The World Away/Slide Away (CD)	10
94	Creation CTP 195	(It's Good) To Be Free (12", 1-sided, 360 only)	50
94	Creation CREDM 001	DEFINITELY MAYBE (4 x 7" box set, in silver cigarette-pack-shaped plastic box, with booklet & interview CD)	25
95	Creation CCD 169	Slide Away (CD, 1-track Brits Awards issue, 1,000 only; beware of counterfeits)	30
95	Creation CCD 204	Some Might Say (CD, 1-track, 350 only)	60
95	Creation CRESCD 204P	Some Might Say/Talk Tonight/Acquiesce/Headshrinker (CD)	10
95	Creation CREMG 001	(WHAT'S THE STORY) MORNING GLORY? (4 x 7" box set, in gold cigarette-pack-shaped plastic box,with booklet & interview CD)	25
95	Creation CTP 204	Acquiesce (12", 1-sided, 570 only)	100
95	Creation CCD 204P	Acquiesce (CD, 1-track, 300 only)	60
95	Creation CTP 212	Roll With It (12", 1-sided)	40
95	Creation CRESCD 212P	Roll With It/Better People/Rockin' Chair/ Live Forever (Live at Glastonbury '95) (CD, 3,078 only)	10
95	Creation CRESCD 215P	Wonderwall/Round Are Way/The Swamp Song/The Masterplan (CD, 2,320 only)	10
95	Creation CTP 215	Round Are Way (12", 1-sided, 843 only)	60
96	Creation CTP 221X	Cum On Feel The Noize/Champagne Supernova (Lynchmob Beats Mix) (12", 1,203 pressed, plain die-cut sleeve; beware of counterfeits)	40
96	Creation CCD 221	Cum On Feel The Noize (CD, pic. disc, 1-track, with football motif, no inlay, 500 only)	60
96	Creation CRESCD 221P	Don't Look Back In Anger/Step Out/Underneath The Sky/ Cum On Feel The Noize (CD)	10
96	Creation P 96/1	OASIS (Fade Away/Half The World Away/Acquiesce/The Masterplan) (CD sampler for singles box set)	15
97	Creation CTP 256	D'You Know What I Mean?/Heroes (12")	30
97	Creation CRESCD 256P	D'You Know What I Mean/Stay Young/Angel Child/Heroes (CD, digipak)	10
97	Creation CCD 256	D'You Know What I Mean (CD, 1-track, black card p/s)	15
97	Creation CCD 256X	D'You Know What I Mean?/Heroes (CD, 2-track, white card title p/s)	15
97	Creation CCD 219PL	Be Here Now (live)/Be Here Now (live with DJ intro) (CD)	15

97	Creation CTP 278	Stand By Me/I Got The Fever (12")	35
97	Creation CCD 278	Stand By Me (CD, 1-track, black card p/s)	15
97	Creation CCD 278X	Stand By Me (CD, 2-track, white card p/s)	15
97	Creation CRESCD 278P	Stand By Me/(I Got) The Fever/My Sister Lover/Going Nowhere (CD, digipak)	10
97	Creation CTP 282	All Around The World/Street Fighting Man (12", black die-cut sleeve)	25
97	Creation CCD 282	All Around The World (Edit) (CD, 1-track, black card sleeve)	15
97	Creation CCD 282X	All Around The World/Street Fighting Man (CD, blue card sleeve)	15
97	Creation CRESCD 282	All Around The World/The Fame/Flashbax/Street Fighting Man (CD)	10
97	Creation (no cat. no.)	VOX BOX (9-CD, wooden guitar-amp-shaped box set in outer box, with booklets from "Silver" & "Gold" CD box sets; contains commerical issues of "Supersonic" through to "Don't Look Back In Anger"; in house giveaway only)	500
98	Creation CCD 241	Acquiesce/Talk Tonight/Rockin' Chair/The Masterplan (CD sampler)	25
98	Creation CRELP 241P	THE MASTERPLAN SAMPLER (Acquiesce/Underneath The Sky/ I Am The Walrus/The Masterplan) (12" sampler)	25
00	Creation CTP 327	Go Let It Out (12", 1-track, 1-sided, p/s)	25
00	Big Brother FITB 001	Fuckin' In The Bushes (12", 1-sided, white label)	40
00	SINE 002CD	Who Feels Love (Acoustic)/Sunday Morning Call (Acoustic) (CD, white card p/s)	20
00	Big Brother RKID 004TP	Sunday Morning Call (12", 1-sided, flipback laminated p/s)	25
00	Big Brother RKID 03TP	Who Feels Love? (12", 1-sided, laminated p/s)	25
00	Big Brother RKIDSCD 005P	FAMILIAR TO MILLIONS (Gas Panic/Supersonic/Helter Skelter) (live CD, promo-only)	12
01	Own label OASIS 10	10 YEARS OF NOISE & CONFUSION (Columbia/Rock & Roll Star (Live)/Acquiesce/Fuckin' In The Bushes) (10", promo-only, custom labels, die-cut sleeve, 200 only, with press release)	35
01	Own label OASIS 10	10 YEARS OF NOISE & CONFUSION (Columbia/Rock & Roll Star (Live)/Acquiesce/Fuckin' In The Bushes) (10", promo-only, custom labels, die-cut sleeve, 200 only, without press release)	30
02	Big Brother RKID 23TP	The Hindu Times (Spike Mix) (12", promo-only, custom logo sleeve, 250 only)	25
02	Big Brother RKID 24TP	Stop Crying Your Heart Out (Spike Mix) (12", custom sleeve, 250 only)	20
02	Big Brother RKIDSCD 24PX	Stop Crying Your Heart Out (Spike Mix) (CD, custom sleeve, 250 only)	12
02	Big Brother RKID 25TP	Hung In A Bad Place (12", 1-track, custom mauve/pink or brown sleeve)	30
02	Big Brother RKID26TPX	My Generation (12" 1-sided promo with Union Jack Sleeve. 800 only)	35
02	Big Brother RKID27TP	Columbia (Live)/(You've Got) The Heart Of A Star (12", custom sleeve)	30
02	Big Brother (No cat. no)	Songbird (Demo) (CD-R promo, 25 only)	200
05	Big Brother RKID28TPX	Can You See It Now? I Can See It Now (12" 1-sided white label promo 50 only)	200
05	Big Brother RKID29TP	Lyla (12" 1-sided promo. 770 only)	25
05	Big Brother RKID31TP	Turn Up The Sun (12" 1-sided promo in card sleeve and inner sleeve. 1,120 only)	35
05	Big Brother RKID32TP	Mucky Fingers (12" 1-sided promo in double p/s. 950 copies)	30
05	Big Brother RKID1 NIL	Meaning Of Soul (CD-R promo)	150
05	Big Brother (No cat. no)	Cast No Shadow (UNKLE Beachhead Mix) (CD-R promo)	30
06	Big Brother RKIDSCD35TP	Champagne Supernova (Lynchmob Beats Mix) (12", promo-only)	20
06	Big Brother RKIDSCD35P	Champagne Supernova (Lynchmob Beats Mix) (CD-R, promo-only)	200
06	Big Brother RKIDSCD37P1	Acquiesce	10
06	Big Brother RKIDSCD37P2	The Masterplan	10
07	Big Brother RKID39TP	Lord Don't Slow Me Down (12", promo-only)	40
07	Big Brother RKIDSCD39P	Lord Don't Slow Me Down (CD-R, promo)	40

PROMOS : PROMOS: ALBUMS

94	Creation CRECD 169P	DEFINITELY MAYBE (CD)	50
95	Creation CRECD 189P	(WHAT'S THE STORY) MORNING GLORY? (CD, with "Step Out", black card p/s, withdrawn, beware of counterfeits)	45
95	Creation CRECD 189P	(WHAT'S THE STORY) MORNING GLORY? (CD, without "Step Out", black card p/s)	30
95	Creation C-CRE 189P	(WHAT'S THE STORY) MORNING GLORY? (cassette, with "Step Out", card p/s, withdrawn)	25
97	Creation (no cat. no.)	BE HERE NOW (LP, mail-order 12" box set, with The Making Of Be Here Now booklet, 1,000 only)	60
97	Creation (no cat. no.)	BE HERE NOW (CD, mail-order 12" box set, with The Making Of Be Here Now booklet, 1,000 only)	50
97	Creation CCD 219	BE HERE NOW (CD, black card sleeve, in custom picture sleeve)	30
97	Creation CCD 219	BE HERE NOW (CD, black card sleeve, not in custom picture sleeve)	25
98		THE MASTERPLAN (CD, slimline case, p/s)	35
98	Creation CRELX 241	THE MASTERPLAN (mail-order 7 x 10" single box set)	60
00	Big Brother RKIDCD 002P	STANDING ON THE SHOULDER OF GIANTS (CD, g/fold card sl. with insert)	15
02	Big Brother RKIDCD 25P	HEATHEN CHEMISTRY (CD, in promo-only hardback photobook, features hidden track)	20
06	Big Brother RKIDCD 36P	STOP THE CLOCKS (2-CD promo in gatefold custom sleeve)	20

*(see also Oas*s)*

OAS*S
95	Fierce Panda NING 12	WIBBLING RIVALRY (interview disc, stickered p/s, without barcode, 1000 only)	10

(see also Oasis)

OBERON
71	Acorn (no cat. no.)	A MIDSUMMER NIGHT'S DREAM (LP, private pressing)	600

OBITUARY
89	Roadracer RO 9489	SLOWLY WE ROT (LP)	18
90	Roadracer RO 9370	CAUSE OF DEATH (LP)	15

HUGH O'BRIAN
58	HMV DLP 1189	TV'S WYATT EARP SINGS (10" LP)	15

DERMOT O'BRIEN
66	Envoy ENV 016	The Merry Plough Boy/Off To Dublin/In The Green/Come Down the Mountain Katie Daly	8

JIMMY O'BRYANT
60	Heritage RE-101	FAMOUS ORIGINAL WASHBOARD BAND, VOL. 1 (99 copies only) (EP)	30
60	Heritage RE-106	FAMOUS ORIGINAL WASHBOARD BAND, VOL. 2 (99 copies only) (EP)	30

OBSERVERS
71	Big Shot BI 575	Brimstone And Fire/Lightning And Thunder	6
71	Big Shot BI 588	Keep Pushing/Hot Tip	8
72	Big Shot BI 610	Everyday Music/NINEY: Observing The Av	6
72	Songbird SB 1083	International Pum/Reggaematic	5

(see also Niney)

OBSERVERS ALL STARS & KING TUBBY
75	Attack ATLP 017	DUBBING WITH THE OBSERVER (LP)	40

OBTAINERS
79	Dance Fools Dance (No cat. no.)	Yeh Yeh Yeh/Pussy Wussy/MAG-SPYS: Lifeblood/Bombs (stickered plain sleeve, 100 only) 400

(see also Cure)

OCCASIONALLY DAVID
79	Oven Ready OD 77901	TWIST AND SHOUT (EP) 10
80	Oven Ready OD 1/98002	I Can't Get Used To Losing You (So I'm Coming Back)/Will You Miss Me Tonight? (foldout p/s) 10

OCCASIONAL WORD ENSEMBLE
69	Dandelion 63753	THE YEAR OF THE GREAT LEAP SIDEWAYS (LP) 40

OCCULT CHEMISTRY
80	Bikini Girl (no. cat. no.)	Water Earth Fire Air (Rough Version) (5" clear flexidisc in stamped envelope with Bikini Girl magazine) 15
81	Dining Out TUX 4	Water Earth Fire Air/Fire Air Water Earth (handmade p/s) 8

(see also Twilight Zonerz)

OCEAN COLOUR SCENE
90	!Phffft WAVE 1P	One Of These Days/Talk On (p/s, promo only) 15
90	!Phffft WAVE 1	One Of These Days/Talk On (12", p/s, promo only) 15
96	MCA OCS 2	You've Got It Bad (Full Length Demo Version)/Mona Lisa Eyes (featuring Jimmy Miller) (p/s, mail-order only) 8
97	MCA MCD 60034	B-SIDES, SEASIDES AND FREE RIDES (2-LP, with lyric booklet) 18
97	MCA MCA 60048	MARCHIN' ALREADY (2-LP, with booklet) 18

(see also Boys, Fanatics, Echo Base)

HUMPHREY OCEAN
78	Stiff BUY 29	Whoops A Daisy/Davy Crockett (p/s, blue, black, red, green, white and clear vinyl pressed, p/s) 6

OCEANS
82	Record Shack SHACK 129	Pacific Dreams/Pacific Dreams (Instrumental) (12", white label, stickered or stamped label) 150

PHIL OCHS
66	Elektra EKSN 45002	I Ain't Marching Any More/That Was The President 15
68	A&M AMS 716	Outside Of A Small Circle Of Friends/Miranda 8
65	Elektra EKL 269	ALL THE NEWS THAT'S FIT TO SING (LP, 'guitar player' label, UK record in US sleeve) 35
65	Elektra EKL 287	I AIN'T MARCHIN' ANYMORE (LP) 35
66	Elektra EKL 310	PHIL OCHS IN CONCERT (LP, gold label) 30
67	A&M AML(S) 913	PLEASURES OF THE HARBOR (LP) 25
68	A&M AMLS 919	TAPE FROM CALIFORNIA (LP) 25
69	A&M AMLS 934	REHEARSALS FOR RETIREMENT (LP) 25
70	A&M AMLS 973	GREATEST HITS (LP) 18

GENE OCTOBER
83	Illegal ILS 0034	Suffering In The Land/Suffering Love (p/s) 5

(see also Chelsea)

JOHNNY OCTOBER
59	Capitol CL 15070	Growin' Prettier/Young And In Love 15
60	Capitol CL 15121	So Mean/There'll Always Be A Feeling 15

OCTODRED
95	Acid Fever MDMA 9501	BIG FOOT EP (12") 40
95	Acid Fever MDMA 9502	DOUBLE DIPPED EP (12") 15
96	Acid Fever MDMA 9601	TECHNOLOGICAL ILLUSION VOL. 1 EP (12") 30
96	Acid Fever MDMA 9603	TECHNOLOGICAL ILLUSIONS VOL. 2 EP (12") 25
96	Acid Fever MDMA 9606	UNTITLED EP (12") 40
96	Acid Fever MDMA 9608	PSYCHIK MONK EP (12") 30

OCTOPUS
69	Penny Farthing PEN 705	Laugh At The Poor Man/Girl Friend 20
70	Penny Farthing PEN 716	The River/Thief 20
73	Mooncrest MOON 7	Hey Na Na/Future Feelings 6
70	Penny Farthing PELS 508	RESTLESS NIGHT (LP, gatefold sleeve, red/black label) 500
96	Essex ESSEX 1013LP	RESTLESS NIGHT (LP, reissue, gatefold sleeve) 15

(see also Cortinas)

RAY O'DANIEL
62	Longhorn BLH 0001	What Goes Up Always Comes Down/You're The Only Love For Me 8

ANITA O'DAY
56	HMV POP 245	You're The Top/Honeysuckle Rose 10
60	HMV POP 821	Tea For Two/Sweet Georgia Brown 10
55	Columbia Clef SEB 10042	ANITA O'DAY (EP) 8
56	HMV CLP 1085	ANITA (LP) 20
56	Columbia Clef 33C 9020	ANITA O'DAY COLLATES (10" LP) 25
57	Columbia Clef 33CX 10068	AN EVENING WITH ANITA O'DAY (LP) 20
58	Columbia Clef 33CX 10125	ANITA SINGS THE MOST (LP) 20
58	HMV DLP 1169	PICK YOURSELF UP (10" LP) 25
59	HMV DLP 1203	ANITA AT MISTER KELLY'S (10" LP) 20
60	HMV CLP 1332	ANITA O'DAY SWINGS COLE PORTER WITH BILLY MAY (LP) 12
63	Verve VLP 9125	THE JAZZ STYLINGS OF (LP) 12

PAT O'DAY
55	MGM SP 1129	Earth Angel (Will You Be Mine?)/A Rusty Old Halo 25
55	MGM SP 1142	Soldier Boy/Annie Oakley 15
60	Pye International 7N 25048	I'll Build A Stairway To Your Paradise/No One Understands 6

ODD
84	OK OK 007	Last Time I Saw You/Look Into My Eyes (p/s) 15

BILL ODDIE
64	Parlophone R 5153	Nothing Better To Do/Traffic Island 5
65	Parlophone R 5346	Knitting Song/Ain't Got Rhythm 5
66	Parlophone R 5433	I Can't Get Through/Because She Is My Love 5

| 69 | Decca F 12903 | We Love Jimmy Young/Irish Get Out (as Bill Oddie & Average Mothers) | 5 |
| 70 | Dandelion S 4786 | On Ilkla Moor Baht'at/Harry Krishna | 10 |

(see also Ricky Livid)

ODD NUMBERS
| 95 | Detour DR 032 | The Easy Life/Clubbin' (A Jazz Odyssey) (p/s, coloured vinyl) | 5 |

ODDS
80	Double R RED 001	Saturday Night/Not Another Love Song (p/s)	6
81	JSO EAT 1	Yesterday Man/So You Think (p/s)	20
81	JSO EAT 7	Dread In My Bed/Spare Rib (with press release)	10

ODDSOCKS
| 75 | Sweet Folk & C. SFA 030 | MEN OF THE MOMENT (LP) | 20 |

(see also Bevis Frond)

ANN ODELL
| 73 | DJM DJS 10280 | Swing Song/Everything's Fine Sunshine | 6 |
| 73 | DJM DJLPS 434 | A LITTLE TASTE (LP, gatefold) | 30 |

(see also Chopyn, Blue Mink, CMU)

DOYE O'DELL
| 57 | London HAP-B 1073 | DOYE (10" LP) | 12 |

MAC ODELL
| 54 | Parlophone CMSP 25 | The Stone Was Rolled Away/Heaven-Bound Gospel Train (export issue) | 8 |

RONNIE O'DELL & HIS ORCHESTRA
| 57 | London HLD 8439 | Melody Of Napoli/Struttin' Down Jane Street | 10 |

ODEONS
| 80 | Ellie Jay EJSP 9480 | Maybe Today/5.30 Anthem | 25 |

ODIN'S PEOPLE
| 67 | Major Minor MM 501 | From A Distance/I Need You | 7 |
| 67 | Major Minor MM 505 | Tommy Jones/I Need Your Hand In Mine | 7 |

JOE ODOM
| 69 | Capitol CL 15600 | Big Love/It's In Your Power | 15 |

AL O'DONNELL
| 72 | Trailer LER 2073 | AL O'DONNELL (LP, red label) | 20 |
| 78 | Transatlantic LTRA 501 | AL O'DONNELL 2 (LP) | 12 |

ALISON O DONNELL
| 08 | Fruits De Mer CRUSTACIAN 03 | Day Is Done/Frozen Warnings (p/s. coloured vinyl 300 only) | 20 |

JOE O'DONNELL
| 77 | Polydor 2383 465 | GAODHAL'S VISION (LP) | 22 |

(see also East of Eden, Mushroom, Rory Gallagher, Jade Warrior)

ROCK O'DOODLE
| 73 | Decca F 13450 | Queen Of Rock & Roll/Woman | 10 |

(see also Patrick Campbell-Lyons)

ODYSSEY (U.K.)
| 66 | Strike JH 312 | How Long Is Time/Beware | 22 |

(see also Sons Of Fred)

ODYSSEY (U.S.)
| 73 | Mowest MWS 7002 | ODYSSEY (LP) | 75 |

OEDIPUS COMPLEX
| 69 | Phillips BF 1771 | Up Down Round & Round/Empty Highways | 30 |

OF MONTREAL
| 01 | Jonathon Whisky 16 | Inside A Room Full Of Treasures, A Black Pygmi Horse's Head Pops Up Like A Periscope/LATE B.P. HELIUM: Song For Marie/Alright Yeah (P/s, 250 only) | 10 |
| 03 | Track & Field LANE 18 | Jennifer Louise/There Is Nothing Wrong With Hating Rock Critics (p/s) | 5 |

OFFICERS & GENTLEMEN
| 84 | Gap GAP 001 | That's Life And Love/Noise (no p/s) | 50 |

OFFSIDE
| 70 | Pye Intl. 25534 | Match Of The Day/Small Deal (p/s) | 20 |

OFFSPRING
| 84 | Offspring Records OP001/SRT4K5169 | One More Night/Nota Sad Song (this is how it is typed on B-side label) | 30 |

OFO
| 74 | Decca F13496 | Let's Go Where The Action Is/The Book | 10 |

OFO THE BLACK COMPANY
| 72 | London FL12261 | Allah Wakbarr/Beautiful Daddy | 75 |

JAMES O'GWYNN
| 59 | Mercury AMT 1052 | How Can I Think Of Tomorrow/Were You Ever A Stranger | 10 |

JOHN O'HARA
| 72 | Spark SRL 1075 | Hand Me Down Man/I Am The Candidate For Love | 12 |
| 77 | President PT 465 | Starsky And Hutch/Sister Rae | 5 |

O'HARA'S PLAYBOYS
66	Fontana TF 763	Start All Over/I've Been Wondering	6
67	Fontana TF 793	Spicks And Specks/One Fine Lady	8
67	Fontana TF 872	Ballad Of The Soon Departed/Tell Me Why	50
67	Fontana TF 893	Island In The Sun/Harry	6
68	Fontana TF 924	In The Shelter Of My Heart/Goodnight Mr. Nightfall	6
68	Fontana TF 974	I Started A Joke/Show Me	15
68	Fontana (S)TL 5461	GET READY (LP)	50

OHIO EXPRESS
| 68 | Pye Intl. TH25439 | Yummy Yummy Yummy/Zigzag | 5 |

68	Pye Intl. 7N 25469	Down At Lulu's/She's Not Coming Home	6
69	Pye Intl. NSPL 28117	OHIO EXPRESS (LP)	20
69	Buddah 203 015	CHEWY CHEWY (LP)	15

(see also Joey Vine)

OHIO KNOX
71	Reprise RSLP 6435	OHIO KNOX (LP, gatefold sleeve)	20

(see also Fifth Avenue Band)

OHIO PLAYERS
69	Capitol CL 15587	Here Today And Gone Tomorrow/Bad Bargain	10
72	Janus 6146 009	Pain (Parts 1 & 2)	5
72	Janus 6146 017	Got Pleasure/I Wanna Hear From You	5
73	Westbound 6146 100	Funky Worm/Paint Me	5
74	Mercury 6167 012	Skin Tight/Heaven Must Be Like This	5
75	Mercury 6167 058	Fire/Together	5
74	Mercury 6338 497	SKIN TIGHT (LP)	12
73	Westbound CDSEWM026	ECSTACY (LP)	12

OHR MUSIK
97	Prescription DRUG 2	OHR MUSIK (LP, 99 copies only)	20

(see also Spiral Sky)

OI POLLOI
86	EDR 5	RESIST THE ATOMIC MESSAGE (EP)	10
88	Words Of Warning WOW 5	OUTRAGE (EP)	10
89	Words Of Warning WOW 17	OMNICIDE (EP)	12
93	Ruptured Ambition	GUILTY (EP)	8
87	Oi! OIR 011	UNITE AND WIN (LP, with lyric sheet)	12
88	Words Of Warning WOW 13	OUTRAGED BY THE ATOMIC MESSAGE (LP, with lyric sheet)	12

OIL CITY SHEIKS
79	United Artists UP 36514	Don't Take But A Few Minutes/Blues Jam (p/s)	7

(see also Dr. Feelgood, Lew Lewis)

OISIN
80	Tara 2012	OVER THE MOOR TO MAGGIE (LP)	12
82	Tara 2013	THE JEANNIE C (LP)	12

O'JAYS
65	Liberty LIB 66102	Lipstick Traces/Think It Over Baby	40
65	Liberty LIB 66102	Lipstick Traces/Think It Over Baby (DJ copy)	75
66	Liberty LIB 66197	Stand In For Love/Friday Night	20
67	Stateside SS 2073	I'll Be Sweeter Tomorrow/I Dig Your Act	50
67	Stateside SS 2073	I'll Be Sweeter Tomorrow/I Dig Your Act (DJ copy)	100
68	Bell BLL 1020	Look Over Your Shoulder/I'm So Glad I Found You	30
68	Bell BLL 1020	Look Over Your Shoulder/I'm So Glad I Found You (DJ copy)	50
68	Bell BLL 1033	The Choice/Going Going Gone	15
70	Now! NOW 1002	Don't You Know A True Love/That's Alright	8
72	United Artists UP 35337	Working On Your Case/Hold On	15
73	CBS 1181	Love Train/Who Am I?	6
73	Mojo 2092 052	I Dig Your Act/I'll Be Sweeter Tomorrow (reissue)	8

O'KAYSIONS
68	Stateside SS 2126	Girl Watcher/Deal Me In	25
68	Stateside SS 2126	Girl Watcher/Deal Me In (DJ copy)	50

JOHNNY O'KEEFE (& DEE JAYS)
58	Coral Q 72330	Shake Baby Shake/Real Wild Child (as Johnny O'Keefe & Dee Jays)	150
58	Coral Q 72330	Shake Baby Shake/Real Wild Child (as Johnny O'Keefe & Dee Jays) (78)	60
60s	Zodiac ZR 0016	Sing/Tell The Blues So Long	10

(ROGER) EARL OKIN
67	Parlophone R 5644	Yellow Petals/I Can't Face The Animals (as Roger Earl Okin)	6
69	CBS 4495	Stop And You'll Become Aware/You're Not There At All (as Earl Okin)	22

OLA (& JANGLERS)
67	Decca F 12646	I Can Wait/Eeny Meeny Miney Moe	15
68	Big T BIG 108	What A Way To Die/That's Why I Cry (solo)	15
69	Sonet SON 2004	Let's Dance/Bird, Bird	10

BABATUNDE OLATUNJI
73	Paramount PARA 3038	Soul Makossa (Parts 1 & 2)	10
73	Paramount SPFL 289	SOUL MAKOSSA (LP)	15

OLD AND IN THE WAY
75	Round RX 103	OLD AND IN THE WAY (LP)	12

(see also Jerry Garcia, Seatrain, Rowan Brothers)

OLD SCHOOL TIE
80	Modello MHMS 195	Gambler/Oscar (p/s)	10

OLDEST PROFESSION
72	Midas Private Pressing	THE OLDEST PROFESSION (LP)	150

MIKE OLDFIELD
SINGLES
74	Virgin VS 101	Mike Oldfield's Single ("Tubular Bells" Theme)/ Froggy Went A-Courtin' (in p/s)	10
75	Virgin VS 117	Don Alfonso (with David Bedford)/In Dulci Jubilo (For Maureen)	5
76	Virgin VS 163	Portsmouth/Speak (Tho' You Only Say Farewell) (Roger Dean or blue/red label; reissued in brown wraparound p/s)	5
78	Virgin VS 238-12	Take 4 (12", white vinyl, stickered p/s)	8
79	Virgin VS 245	Guilty/Excerpt From Incantations (p/s, red/green or white/blue label)	5
79	Virgin VS 317	Blue Peter/Woodhenge (p/s, sudden or 'refined' ending (A7 matrix))	5
82	Virgin VSY 464	Five Miles Out/Live Punkadiddle (picture disc)	8
82	Virgin VSY 489	Family Man/Mount Teidi (picture disc)	8
82	Virgin VSY 541	Mistake/Waldberg (The Peak) (picture disc)	5
83	Virgin VSY 586	Moonlight Shadow/Rite Of Man (picture disc)	5

85	Virgin VSD 836	Pictures In The Dark/Legend/Moonlight Shadow/Rite Of Man (double pack in PVC gatefold stickered p/s) 8
86	Virgin VSS 863	Shine (with Jon Anderson)/The Path (uncut picture disc) 30
86	Virgin VSS 863	Shine (with Jon Anderson)/The Path (shaped picture disc) 10
89	Virgin VSCD 1189	Earth Moving (7" Version)/(Disco Mix)/Bridge To Paradise (3" CD, card p/s)..............12
89	Virgin VST 1214	Innocent (7" Version)/(12" Mix)/(Club Version) (12", p/s)..............8
89	Virgin VSCD 1214	Innocent (7" Version)/(12" Mix)/(Club Version) (3" CD, card p/s) 10
90	Virgin VS 1328	Etude (The Theme Music For The "Nurofen" TV Commercial)/ ONO GAGAKU KAï SOCIETY ORCHESTRA: Gakkain (p/s)..............6
90	Virgin AMACD 1	AMAROK X-TRAX 3 extracts from the Amarok album (3" CD EP, 'discount voucher CD' free with W.H. Smith's Insight magazine) 20

ALBUMS

73	Virgin V 2001	TUBULAR BELLS (LP, gloss laminate sleeve with "13 Notting Hill Gate" address, White/black 'Twin' label) 40
74	Virgin QV 2001	TUBULAR BELLS (LP, quadrophonic, with model plane noise at the end of side 2, stickered sleeve) 20
74	Virgin V2013	HERGEST RIDGE (LP, A-1U/B-1U matrixes, poor pressing and many returned, most other "girl/dragon" pressings £5) 15
75	Virgin V2043	OMMADAWN (LP, 1st pressing on beige "mirror" label) 12
75	Virgin QVQS 2043	OMMADAWN (LP, quadrophonic, stickered sleeve) 18
75	Virgin VD 2502	V (2-LP, compilation, includes long version of 'Don Alfonso') 20
76	Virgin 2043	OMMADAWN (LP, blue Virgin label with matt finish) 12
76	Virgin QV 2043	OMMADAWN (LP, different quadrophonic mix, stickered sleeve) 18
76	Virgin VBOX 1	BOXED (4-LP box set, with booklet) 20
78	Virgin VDT 101	INCANTATIONS (2-LP, some with 7" red vinyl of Julie Covington, & poster)..............30
78	Virgin VDT 101	INCANTATIONS (2-LP) 15
78	Virgin VP 2001	TUBULAR BELLS (LP, picture disc, die-cut sleeve, stereo remix of 1976 Boxed quadrophonic mix; with or without model plane noise) 12
79	Virgin V 2141	PLATINUM (LP, with inner sleeve & "Sally"; matrix reads "V 2141 B1" or B2, 30,000 copies, withdrawn) 20
79	Tellydisc TELLY 4	IMPRESSIONS (LP, mail-order only) 20
83	Virgin V 2262	CRISES (LP, with bonus 7" 'Moonlight Shadow') 12
83	Virgin V 2001	TUBULAR BELLS (LP, reissue at 1973 price, with sticker) 8
84	Virgin V 2328	THE KILLING FIELDS (LP, with 20 page film booklet) 15
93	Virgin CD BOX 2	ELEMENTS (4-CD, remastered best of in special plastic box with 64pp booklet) 30
97	Virgin LPCENT 18	TUBULAR BELLS (LP, coloured Dean label, audiophile pressing) 20
01	Simply Vinyl SVLP 322	OMMADAWN (LP, Audiophile pressing on 180g vinyl, with 2 stickers) 15
01	Virgin CD BOXY 2	ELEMENTS (4-CD remastered best of, revised "book" sleeve, 64pp booklet)..............25

PROMOS

74	Virgin VS 112	Hergest Ridge (1-sided white label) 100
75	Virgin VDJ 1	Extract from The Orchestral Tubular Bells/Extract from The Orchestral Tubular Bells 40
75	Virgin VDJ 117	Don Alfonso ('A' label) 15
75	Virgin VDJ 9	An Extract From Ommadawn Part 1/An Extract From Ommadawn Part 2 (On Horseback) (12") 50
75	Virgin VS 131	In Dulci Jubilo/On Horseback ('A' label) 5
76	Virgin VS 163	Portsmouth/Speak (Tho' You Only Say Farewell) (Roger Dean label) 5
77	Virgin VS 167	The William Tell Overture/Argiers (blue Virgin 'A' label) 8
79	Virgin VSDJ 317	Blue Peter (1-sided) 20
85	Virgin SWALLOW 1	Etude/Moonlight Shadow/Portsmouth/In Dulci Jubilo (p/s, promo-only for "The Complete Mike Oldfield") 30
87	Virgin CDEP 6	Islands/When The Night's On Fire/The Wind Chimes(Part One)/ Islands (Extended Version) (white gatefold stickered card p/s) 20
94	WEA YZ 880 T	Let There Be Light: BT's Pure Luminescence Remix/Hardfloor Remix/ Hardfloor Dub (12" p/s with 'promo not for sale' sticker) 8
90	Virgin AMACD 1DJ	Mike Oldfield Album Sampler (CD, 5 Extracts From Amarok) 20
92	WEA SAM 1085	Sentinel (Single Restructure) (CD, stickered p/s) 10
92	WEA SAM 1094	OLDFIELD V THE ORB: Sentinel (Total Overhaul/Sentinel Nobel Prize Mix/ Sentinel Orbular Bells/Sentinel 7" Mix (12") 15
92	WEA SAM 1150	SENTINEL RESTRUCTURE MIXES: Satoshi Tomii Interpretation/ Global Lust Mix/TranceMix/Tubular Beats (12", title stickered red sleeve) 15
92	WEA SAM 1470	A SHOT OF MOONSHINE: Jungle Mix (Featuring Rankin' Sean & Peter Lee)/ A Shot Of Moonshine (Jungle Instrumental)/A Shot of Moonshine (Solution Hoedown Mix) (12", lists artist as MOT2) 12
92	WEA YZ 708CDDJ	Tattoo (stickered p/s) 12
76	Virgin QVQS 2043	OMMADAWN (LP, unreleased different quadrophonic mix, promo stickered sleeve)..........30
76	Virgin V BOX 1	COLLABORATIONS (LP, green/yellow label in stamped white sleeve) 20
79	(no cat. no.)	THE SPACE MOVIE (4 x 1-sided acetates of unreleased LP containing music from soundtrack to the 'Space Movie' video; includes Orchestral Hergest Ridge, Orchestral Tubular Bells, Incantations, Ommadawn and Portsmouth, some extracts otherwise released) 400
92	WEA 4509-90618-2	TUBULAR BELLS 2 (CD, with unique back sleeve) 18
92	WEA WX 2002	TUBULAR BELLS 2 (LP, stickered sleeve) 15
94	WEA SAM 1477	THE SONGS OF DISTANT EARTH (CD in film can, with 2 inserts) 100
98	WEA 3331000043	TUBULAR BELLS III (CD, in special 'Waterside Inn' card sleeve) 20
98	WEA 3331000043	TUBULAR BELLS III (CD, in card sleeve, with bag, TB III tag, press releases and premiere concert details) 30
98	WEA 3331000043	TUBULAR BELLS III (CD, in card sleeve) 20
99	WEA (no cat. no.)	MILLENNIUM BELL (CD-R, some tracks with different samples to released album) 40
99	WEA (no cat. no.)	MILLENNIUM BELL (CD-R) 30

(see also Sallyangie, David Bedford, Kevin Ayers & Whole World, Pekka, Lea Nicholson, Tom Newman)

OLD GOLD

| 70 | Trend TNT 56 | It's Goodbye/Teachers Of Electricity..............25 |

ANDREW OLDHAM (ORCHESTRA)

64	Decca F 11878	365 Rolling Stones/Oh I Do Like To See Me On The 'B' Side 30
64	Decca F 11987	We Don't All Wear D'Same Size Boots/Right Of Way 30
64	Ace Of Clubs ACL 1180	16 HIP HITS (LP) 40
64	Decca LK 4636	LIONEL BART'S MAGGIE MAY (LP) 40
66	Decca LK/SKL 4796	THE ROLLING STONES SONGBOOK (LP)..............100
82	Decca 820 186-1	THE ROLLING STONES SONGBOOK (LP, reissue) 12

(see also Aranbee Pop Symphony, Rolling Stones, Cleo, Bo & Peep, Jeannie & Her Redheads, Gulliver's Travels, Mighty Avengers, John Paul Jones)

OLDHAM TINKERS

| 74 | Topic 12TS 237 | BEST O' T' BUNCH (LP, blue label) ....18 |

Will OLDHAM

75	Topic 12TS 276	FOR OLD TIMES SAKE (LP, blue label)	18
77	Topic 12TS 323	SIT THEE DOWN (LP)	15
79	Topic 12TS 399	THAT LANCASHIRE BAND (LP)	15

WILL OLDHAM
| 97 | Domino WIGLP 39 | JOYA (LP, insert) | 15 |
| 00 | Domino WIGLP 74 | GUARAPERO (LOST BLUES 2) (2-LP) | 20 |

(see also Bonnie 'Prince' Billy, Palace Brothers)

OLD SWAN BAND
71	Dingles DIN 322	GAMESTERS, PICKPOCKETS AND HARLOTS (LP)	15
80	Free Reed 028	OLD SWAN BAND (LP)	15
81	Free Reed FRR 011	NO REELS (LP)	15

OLD TIMERS SKIFFLE GROUP
| 58 | Fontana H 105 | The Woman Who Loved A Swine/The Lynching Of Jeff Buckner (78) | 12 |

TONY O'LEARY AND THE CAPITOL
| 71 | Dolphin DOS61 | She Meant Everything/Whole World Shaking | 6 |

JOHNNY OLENN & HIS BAND
57	London HLU 8388	I Ain't Gonna Cry No More/My Idea Of Love	250
57	London HLU 8388	I Ain't Gonna Cry No More/My Idea Of Love (78)	60
59	Mercury AMT 1050	Born Reckless/You Lovable You (as Johnny Olenn & Blockbusters)	150

O-LEVEL
78	Psycho PSYCHO 2	East Sheen/Pseudo Punk ('map' p/s)	50
78	Psycho PSYCHO 2	East Sheen/Pseudo Punk ('schoolboy' p/s)	40
78	Kings Road KR 002	THE MALCOLM EP (photocopied wraparound p/s)	30
78	Kings Road KR 002	THE MALCOLM EP (printed p/s)	15

(see also Teenage Filmstars, Times, Television Personalities)

JOHNNY OLIVER
| 56 | MGM SP 1165 | Chain Gang/These Hands | 25 |
| 60 | Mercury AMT 1095 | What A Kiss Won't Do/That's All I'm Living For | 12 |

OLIVER & TWISTERS
| 64 | Pye Intl. NPL 28018 | LOOK WHO'S TWISTIN' (LP) | 15 |

OLIVER (1)
69	CBS 4435	Good Morning Starshine/Can't You See	5
70	Crewe CRW 1	Jean/Good Morning Starshine (Arrangement) (p/s)	5
70	Crewe CRWS 201	OLIVER (LP)	12
70	Crewe CRWS 202	AGAIN (LP)	12

OLIVER (2)
74	Oliv OL 1	STANDING STONE (LP, private pressing, withdrawn blue sleeve)	1000
74	Oliv OL 1	STANDING STONE (LP, private pressing, withdrawn, later green sleeve)	800
92	Tenth Planet TP 001	STANDING STONE (LP, reissue, numbered, 500 only)	20

OLLIE & NIGHTINGALES
| 69 | Stax STAX 109 | You're Leaving Me/Showered With Love | 12 |

NIGEL OLSSONS DRUM ORCHESTRA & CHORUS
71	DJM DJS 239	Natures Way/Natures Way	10
72	DJM DJS 266	Alabama/Sunshine Looks Like Rain	10
71	DJM DJLP 5	NIGEL OLSSON'S DRUM ORCHESTRA AND CHORUS (LP, with poster)	20

(see also Elton John, Hookfoot, Plastic Penny)

OLYMPICS
58	HMV POP 528	Western Movies/Well!	12
58	HMV POP 528	Western Movies/Well! (78)	15
58	HMV POP 564	(I Wanna) Dance With The Teacher/Everybody Needs Love	20
58	HMV POP 564	(I Wanna) Dance With The Teacher/Everybody Needs Love (78)	10
59	Columbia DB 4346	Private Eye/(Baby) Hully Gully	25
60	Vogue Pop V 9174	I Wish I Could Shimmy Like My Sister Kate/Workin' Hard	15
61	Vogue Pop V 9181	Dance With A Dolly/Dodge City	25
61	Vogue Pop V 9184	Little Pedro/CAPPY LEWIS: Bullfight	20
62	Vogue Pop V 9196	The Twist/Everybody Likes To Cha Cha Cha	15
62	Vogue Pop V 9198	The Stomp/Mash Them 'Taters	20
62	Vogue Pop V 9204	Baby It's Hot/The Scotch	25
64	Sue WI 348	The Bounce/Fireworks	40
65	Warner Bros WB 157	Good Lovin'/Olympic Shuffle	15
66	Fontana TF 678	We Go Together (Pretty Baby)/Secret Agents	20
66	Fontana TF 778	Baby, Do The Philly Dog/Western Movies	20
69	Action ACT 4539	Baby, Do The Philly Dog/Mine Exclusively	20
70	Action ACT 4556	I'll Do A Little Bit More/Same Old Thing	25
71	Jay Boy BOY 27	Hully Gully/Big Boy Pete	8
72	Jay Boy BOY 56	Baby, Do The Philly Dog/Secret Agents	8
72	Jay Boy BOY 74	I'll Do A Little Bit More/Same Old Thing (reissue)	10
61	Vocalion VAH 8059	DANCE BY THE LIGHT OF THE MOON (LP)	100
67	London HA-M 8327	SOMETHING OLD, SOMETHING NEW (LP, unissued)	0
67	Fontana TL 5407	SOMETHING OLD, SOMETHING NEW (LP)	60
72	Jay Boy JSX 2008	THE OLYMPICS (LP)	20

(see also Cappy Lewis)

PATRICK O'MAGICK
| 74 | Chrysalis CHS 2041 | You're A Winner/The Proposal | 5 |

(see also Patrick Campbell-Lyons)

MICHAEL O'MARTIAN
76	Myrrh MYRA 1048	WHITE HORSE (LP, gatefold sleeve, with Larry Carlton)	12
77	Myrrh MYR 1073	SEASONS OF THE SOUL (LP, with Stormie)	12
78	Sparrow BIRD 141	MAINSTREAM (LP)	12

OMEGA RED STAR
| 69 | Decca LK/SKL 4974 | OMEGA RED STAR (LP, unboxed Decca on label) | 150 |

OMEGA TRIBE

82	Crass 221984/10	ANGRY SONGS (EP)	12
83	Corpus Christi CHRIST O5	NO LOVE LOST (LP)	12

(see also Pete Fender)

OMEGA (1)

75	Decca SKL-R 5219	HALL OF FLOATERS IN THE SKY (LP)	20
76	Decca SKL-R 5243	TIME ROBBER (LP)	20

OMEGA (2)

85	Rock Machine MACH 1	THE PROPHET (LP)	35

OMEN

69	Ackee ACK 102	Don't Leave Me Never/No More	15

OMEN SEARCHER

82	OCS 001	Too Much/Teacher Of Sin (p/s)	50
82	OCS 002	Teacher Of Sin/Too Much (p/s)	50

OMENKA BROTHERS

77	Ashiko	MR CROOKED CHIAUOTU (LP)	35

OMNIA OPERA

93	Delerium DELEC LP 011	OMNIA OPERA (LP)	60
97	Delerium DELECLP 044	RED SHIFT (LP)	20

ON A FRIDAY

88	(No label or cat no)	Happy Song/To Be A Brilliant Light/Sinking Ship (cassette)	250
90	(No label or cat no)	THE GREAT SHINDIG (Cassette, 15 tracks)	250
91	(No label or cat no)	What Is That You See?/Stop Whispering (Demo)/Give It Up (Cassette, 3 known different cover inlays)	150
91	(No label or cat no)	I Can't (Demo)/Nothing Touches Me/Thinking About You (EP Version)/Phillipa Chicken/You (Demo) (Cassette, known as "Manic hedgehog" demos)	150

(see also Radiohead)

ONDIOLINE BAND

66	London HL 10022	Last Bicycle To Brussels/Lovers Of Cologne	6

ONE

69	Fontana STL 5539	ONE (LP, gatefold sleeve, black/silver label)	175

ONE & ONE

64	Decca F 11948	I'll Give You Lovin'/It's Me	15

(see also Ivy League, Flowerpot Men)

ONE EYED JACKS

65	Ember EMBS 206	For Us There'll Be No Tomorrow/Soul Chart	8

ONE EYED JACKS

78	Pennine PSS 154	TAKE AWAY (LP, in "One Eyed Jacks" brown paper carrier bag)	25
78	Pennine PSS 154	TAKE AWAY (LP)	20

ONE GANG LOGIC

79	Stark 1	Alienate/Queue Here/Repeat Action/Who Killed Sex (numbered p/s)	12

ONE HIT WONDERS

72	CBS 7760	Hey Hey Jump Now/Goodbye	18

101'ERS

76	Chiswick (N)S 3	Keys To Your Heart/5 Star Rock & Rock Petrol (with p/s)	30
76	Chiswick (N)S 3	Keys To Your Heart/5 Star Rock & Rock Petrol	10
79	Big Beat NS 3	Keys To Your Heart/5 Star Rock & Rock Petrol (reissue, with p/s)	10
79	Big Beat NS 3	Keys To Your Heart/5 Star Rock & Rock Petrol	8
80	Big Beat NS 63	Sweet Revenge/Rabies (From The Dogs Of Love) (p/s)	5
81	Andalucia AND 101	ELGIN AVENUE BREAKDOWN (LP, with booklet)	35
81	Andalucia AND 101	ELGIN AVENUE BREAKDOWN (LP, without booklet)	25

(see also Clash, Alvaro)

100% PROOF

80	Smile SR 929	NEW WAY OF LIVIN' (EP)	25
81	Myrrh MYR 1107	100% PROOF (LP, with insert)	50

100% PROOF AGED IN SOUL

71	Hot Wax HWX 102	Somebody's Been Sleeping/I've Come To Save You	5
71	Hot Wax HWX 108	Somebody's Been Sleeping/I've Come To Save You (reissue)	5
72	Hot Wax HWX 113	Everything Good Is Bad/I'd Rather Fight Than Switch	5
72	Hot Wax HWX 120	Never My Love/Since You've Been Gone	5
71	Hot Wax SHW 5003	SOMEBODY'S BEEN SLEEPING IN MY BED (LP)	15

100% PURE POISON

74	EMI Untl. 501	You Keep Coming Back/(And When I Said) I Love You	20
77	EMI Intl. INS 3001	COMING RIGHT AT YOU (LP)	175

ONE IN A MILLION

67	CBS 202513	Use Your Imagination/Hold On	250
67	MGM MGM 1370	Fredereek Hernando/Double Sight	900

(see also Thunderclap Newman)

ONE MILLION FUZZTONE GUITARS

82	Monsters In Orbit TVEYE 3	Heaven/Annuese (foldover p/s, at least 2 different designs)	6
83	Monsters In Orbit TVEYE 10	26 (LP)	12

1 SYNTAX 1

84	Proteus PRT 101	Negatives/Feel No Touch (p/s)	25

MATTY O'NEIL

54	London L 1037	Don't Sell Daddy Any More Whiskey/Little Rusty (gold label, tri-centre)	40
54	London L 1037	Don't Sell Daddy Any More Whiskey/Little Rusty (silver label, tri-centre)	25
54	London L 1037	Don't Sell Daddy Any More Whiskey/Little Rusty (silver top, round centre)	10

ONE TAKES

80	No Choice NC 001	Accident/Street Kid/Backdoor Dump/Eviction Orders (p/s)	20

1,000 MEXICANS
83	Whaam! WHAAM 12	The Art Of Love/News For You (p/s, 1,500 only)	6

1,000 VIOLINS
85	Dreamworld DREAM 2	Halcyon Days/I Remember When Everybody Used To Ride Bikes ... Now We All Drive Cars (12", p/s, 1,000 only)	20
86	Dreamworld DREAM 8	Please Don't Sandblast My House/Time I Broke Down (p/s, 2,000 only)	12
86	Dreamworld DREAM 8T	Please Don't Sandblast My House/You Ungrateful Bastard/Though It Poured The Next Day, I Never Noticed The Rain (12", p/s)	12
87	Dreamworld DREAM 14	Locked Out Of The Love-In (p/s)	15
87	Report REPX 1	If I Were A Bullet (Then For Sure I'd Find A Way To Your Heart)/Poet (p/s)	8
88	Immaculate IMMACLP 1	HEY MAN, THAT'S BEAUTIFUL (LP)	40
00	Vinyl Japan ASKCD 119	LIKE ONE THOUSAND VIOLINS (CD)	15

(see also Page Boys)

ONE TWO & THREE
65	Decca F 12093	Black Pearl/Bahama Lullaby	15
65	Decca LK 4682	BLACK PEARLS AND GREEN DIAMONDS (LP)	200

ONE WAY SYSTEM
82	Lightbeat WAY 1	Stab The Judge/Riot Torn City/Me And You (p/s)	12
82	Anagram ANA 1	Give Us A Future/Just Another Hero (p/s)	5
83	Anagram ANA 5	Jerusalem/Jackie Was A Jackie (p/s)	10
83	Anagram ANA 9	Cum On Feel The Noise/Breakin' In (p/s)	6
83	Anagram ANA 14	This Is The Age/Into Fires (p/s)	5
84	Anagram ANA 19	Visions Of Angels/Shine Again (p/s)	5
83	Anagram GRAM 003	ALL SYSTEMS GO (LP, with lyric inner)	12
83	Anagram GRAM 008	WRITING ON THE WALL (LP, with lyric inner)	15

ONE WAY TICKET
78	President PTLS 1069	TIME IS RIGHT (LP, featuring tracks from "Five Day Rain" LP)	90

(see also Five Day Rain)

ONLOOKERS
82	Demon D 1012	You And I/Understand/Julia (p/s)	15

ONLY ONES
77	Vengeance VEN 001	Lovers Of Today/Peter And The Pets (p/s)	12
77	Vengeance VEN 001	Lovers Of Today/Peter And The Pets (12", with 7" x 7" sticker)	12
78	CBS S CBS 6228	Another Girl, Another Planet/Special View (p/s)	10
78	CBS S CBS 6576	Another Girl, Another Planet/As My Wife Says	10
78	CBS S CBS 12-6576	Another Girl, Another Planet/As My Wife Says (12", p/s)	6
78	CBS S CBS 7086	You've Got To Pay/This Ain't All (It's Made Out To Be) (p/s)	6
79	CBS S CBS 7285	Out There In The Night/Lovers Of Today	5
79	CBS S CBS 12-7285	Out There In The Night/Lovers Of Today/Peter And The Pets (12", p/s, blue vinyl, 2 slight sleeve variations)	10
79	CBS S CBS 7963	Trouble In The World/Your Chosen Life (withdrawn 'group' black & red p/s)	350
79	CBS S CBS 7963	Trouble In The World/Your Chosen Life (standard p/s)	5
80	CBS S CBS 8535	Fools/Castle Built On Sand (p/s, with Pauline Murray)	5
83	Vengeance VEN 002	Baby's Got A Gun/PETER PERRETT: Silent Night	5
78	CBS 82830	THE ONLY ONES (LP, orange label, with insert)	20
79	CBS 83451	EVEN SERPENTS SHINE (LP, embossed sleeve, orange label)	20
80	CBS 84089	BABY'S GOT A GUN (LP, with insert, orange label)	12
89	Strange Fruit SFRLP 102	PEEL SESSIONS ALBUM (LP)	15

(see also England's Glory)

YOKO ONO
71	Apple APPLE 38	Mrs. Lennon/Midsummer New York	18
72	Apple APPLE 41	Mind Train/Listen, The Snow Is Falling (p/s)	22
73	Apple APPLE 47	Death Of Samantha/Yang Yang	20
73	Apple APPLE 48	Run Run Run/Men Men Men	25
70	Apple SAPCOR 17	YOKO ONO/PLASTIC ONO BAND (LP, with inner sleeve)	50
71	Apple SAPTU 101/2	FLY (2-LP, laminated gatefold, inner sleeves, poster & postcard)	60
73	Apple SAPDO 1001	APPROXIMATELY INFINITE UNIVERSE (2-LP, with lyric inner sleeves)	25
73	Apple SAPCOR 26	FEELING THE SPACE (LP)	35

(see also John Lennon, Bill Elliott & Elastic Oz Band)

ONSLAUGHT
83	Complete Control TROL 1	First Strike/State Control/No More (p/s)	10
85	Children Of The Revolution GURT 2	POWER FROM HELL (LP, with inner)	20
86	Under One Flag FLAG 1	THE FORCE (LP, inner)	12

ON THE WATERFRONT
86	Wizz	The Kids Are Allright/Never Surrender/Far From The Madding Crowd/Mrs. Harrington (12", p/s)	60

ONYX
68	Pye 7N 17477	You've Gotta Be With Me/It's All Put On	30
68	Pye 7N 17622	My Son John/Step By Step	30
69	Pye 7N 17768	Tamaris Khan/So Sad Inside	60
69	CBS 4635	Time Off/Movin' In	20
71	Parlophone R 5888	Air/Our House	10
71	Parlophone R 5906	The Next Stop Is Mine/What's That You Say	10

(see also Salamander)

OO BANG JIGGLY JANG
71	President PT 356	Hanging Tree/1000 Leagues	15

OPAL
85	One Big Guitar OBG 002T	Northern Line/Empty Bottles/Soul Glver (12")	15
87	Rough Trade RTT 129	Fell From The Sun/Freight Train/Grains Of Sand (12")	15
87	Rough Trade ROUGH 116	HAPPY NIGHTMARE BABY (LP)	20
89	Rough Trade ROUGH 128	EARLY RECORDINGS (LP)	18

(see also Mazzy Star)

OPAL BUTTERFLY

68	CBS 3576	Beautiful Beige/Speak Up	35
69	CBS 3921	Mary Anne With The Shakey Hand/My Gration Or?	60
70	Polydor 2058 041	You're A Groupie Girl/Gigging Song	60

(see also Hawkwind, Motorhead, Mott The Hoople)

JACKIE OPEL

63	Jump Up JU 512	TV In Jamaica/Worrell's Captaincy	25
64	Black Swan WI 421	You're No Good/King Liges	40
64	R&B JB 138	Stand By Me (as Jackie Opel & Hortense Ellis)/Solid Rock	50
64	R&B JB 160	Pity The Fool/The Day Will Come	40
65	King KG 1011	Cry Me A River/Eternal Love	25
65	Island WI 203	Wipe Those Tears/Don't Take Your Love	30
65	Island WI 209	Go Whey/Shelter The Storm	125
65	Island WI 227	Old Rockin' Chair/SKATALITES: Song Of Love (B-side is actually "Ska In Vienna Woods")	200
65	Ska Beat JB 190	Done With A Friend/More Wood In The Fire	40
65	Ska Beat JB 227	The Lord Is With Thee/A Little More	150
66	Island WI 264	A Love To Share/ROLAND ALPHONSO: Devoted To You	25
66	Rio R 117	I Am What I Am/JACKIE MITTOO & SKATALITES: Devil's Bug	60
66	Rio R120	I Don't Want Her/SOUL BOYS: Rudie Get Wise	60

(see also Jackie & Doreen, Doreen & Jackie, Hortense & Jackie)

OPEN

03	Loog 9813076	NEVER ENOUGH EP (1,000 only, p/s)	12
04	Loog 9817238	Close My Eyes/The View (mail order only 12" p/s)	12

OPEN HOUSE

72	Nest NRS 102A	Mr Sparky/My Song	100

OPEN MIND

69	Philips BF 1805	Magic Potion/Cast A Spell (Demo copy)	400
69	Philips BF 1790	Horses And Chariots/Before My Time	100
69	Philips BF 1805	Magic Potion/Cast A Spell	600
69	Philips SBL 7893	OPEN MIND (LP, laminated sleeve, black/silver label)	1000
86	Antar ANTAR 2	OPEN MIND (LP, reissue)	20

(see also Drag Set)

OPEN ROAD

72	Greenwich GSS 102	Swamp Fever/Lost And Found	12
71	Greenwich GSLP 1001	WINDY HAZE (LP, gatefold sleeve)	50

(see also Warm Sounds, Denny Gerrard, Donovan)

OPERA

79	Bead records BEAD 13	OPERA (LP)	25

OPETH

01	Music For Nations MFSN 264	BLACKWATER PARK (2xLP)	35
02	Peaceville DLPVILE 78	STILL LIFE (2-LP, 1000 only)	40
03	Music For Nations MFSN 297	DAMNATION (LP)	45
10	Peaceville VILLELP78	STILL LIFE (2-LP, reissue, 2000 only)	30

OPPO

76	EMI 2541	Miracles (A Mini Epic)/The Flame	5

OPPRESSED

83	Oppressed OPPO 1	Work Together/Victims (p/s)	20
83	Firm NICK 1	NEVER SAY DIE (EP)	18
84	Oppressed OPLP 1	OI! OI! MUSIC (LP)	20
85	Skinhead CREW 1	FATAL BLOW (LP)	20
88	OIR 12	DEAD AND BURIED (LP)	15

OPTIMISTS

81	Armageddon AS 018	Mull Of Kintyre/The Plumbers Song (p/s)	18

OPUS

70	Columbia DB 8675	Baby, Come On/Angela Grey	15

ORA

69	Tangerine OPLOP 0025	ORA (LP)	350

(see also Byzantium, Movies)

ORAL EXCITERS

79	Three Elms TE 001	It's A Holiday/Tonight (p/s, 500 only)	35

ORAL SEX

82	Conquest Quest 6	ORAL SEX (LP)	15

DAPHNE ORAM

62	HMV 7EG8762	LISTEN, MOVE AND DANCE 3 - ELECTRONIC SOUND PATTERNS (EP)	20

ORANGE ALABASTER MUSHROOM

98	Earworm WORM 36	The Slug/Ethel Tripped A Mean Gloss (p/s, with sticker)	8

ORANGE BICYCLE

67	Columbia DB 8259	Hyacinth Threads/Amy Peate	35
67	Columbia DB 8311	Laura's Garden/Lavender Girl	25
68	Columbia DB 8352	Early Pearly Morning/Go With Goldie	20
68	Columbia DB 8413	Jenskadajka/Nicely	15
68	Columbia DB 8483	Sing This All Together/Trip On An Orange Bicycle	25
69	Parlophone R 5789	Tonight I'll Be Staying Here With You/Last Cloud Home	15
69	Parlophone R 5811	Carry That Weight/You Never Give Me Your Money/Want To B Side	12
70	Parlophone R 5827	Take Me To The Pilot/It's Not My World	20
70	Parlophone R 5854	Jelly On The Bread/Make It Rain	15
71	Regal Zonophone RZ 3029	Goodbye Stranger/Country Comforts	15
70	Parlophone PCS 7108	ORANGE BICYCLE (LP, laminated front sleeve, black/silver label)	200
88	M'n Blue Town MBT 5003	LET'S TAKE A TRIP ON AN ORANGE BICYCLE (LP)	15
11	Morgan Bluetown BT 5007	ORANGE BICYCLE (LP, reissue, 500 only, orange vinyl, with numbered certificate)	20

(see also Motherlight)

MINT VALUE £

ORANGE BLOSSOM
74 Westwood WRS 038 KEEP ON PUSHING (LP) 30

ORANGE DISASTER
80s Neuter OD 1 Something's Got To Give/Out Of The Room/Hiding From Frank...20
(see also Varicose Veins)

ORANGE GOBLIN
04 Rise Above RISE7/051 Some You Win, Some You Lose/White Night Cyanide (p/s) 6
00 The Music Cartel TMC 036LP THE BIG BLACK (LP) 20
04 Rise Above RISELP 46 THIEVING FROM THE HOUSE OF GOD (LP, orange vinyl, 1000 only) 25
07 Mayan MYNLP 058 HEALING THROUGH FIRE (LP) 18

ORANGE JUICE
80 Postcard 80-1 Falling And Laughing/Moscow Olympics/Moscow (foldover p/s in poly bag, with postcard; and with flexidisc "Felicity (live)" [I Wish I Was A Postcard 1], 963 only) 180
80 Postcard 80-1 Falling And Laughing/Moscow Olympics/Moscow (foldover p/s in poly bag, without postcard and without flexidisc, 963 only) 100
80 I Wish I Was A Postcard 1 Felicity (live) (freebie flexidisc, also given away with fanzines) 15
80 Postcard 80-2 Blue Boy/Lovesick (hand-coloured p/s in poly bag, blue labels)............................18
80 Postcard 80-2 Blue Boy/Lovesick (yellow labels/cream cover sleeve).......................................8
80 Postcard 80-2 Blue Boy/Lovesick (3rd issue, brown labels in brown company sleeve...............8
80 Postcard 80-6 Simply Thrilled Honey/Breakfast Time (p/s, with picture insert in poly bag)........40
80 Postcard 80-6 Simply Thrilled Honey/Breakfast Time (2nd issue, brown labels in brown company sleeve)..8
81 Postcard 81-2 Poor Old Soul/Poor Old Soul Pt. 2 (die-cut co. sleeve, with postcard) 30
81 Postcard 81-2 Poor Old Soul/Poor Old Soul Pt. 2 (die-cut co. sleeve, without postcard)..........5
81 Postcard 81-6 Wan Light/You Old Eccentric (unreleased)...0
83 Polydor POSP 547 Rip It Up/Snake Charmer (p/s, with free live 21/4/79 cassette) 6
84 Polydor OJ 5/JUICE 1 Bridge/Out For The Count (stickered p/s, with free flexidisc Poor Old Soul [live])..........6
84 Polydor OJ 6/OJC 6 What Presence?!/A Place In My Heart (Dub) (p/s, with free cassette The Felicity Flexi Session: The Formative Years)...6
92 Postcard DUBH 922 OSTRICH CHURCHYARD (LP, 1,000 with bonus 10" "Irritation Disc" [922TEN]) ...20
(see also Edwyn Collins, Paul Quinn & Edwyn Collins, Fun Four, Josef K)

ORANGE MACHINE
68 Pye 7N 17559 Three Jolly Little Dwarfs/Real Life Permanent Dream 200
69 Pye 7N 17680 You Can All Join In/Dr. Crippen's Waiting Room 150
(see also Danny Hughes)

ORANGE PEEL
71 Reflection HRS 5 I Got No Time/Searching For A Place To Hide 25

ORANGE SEAWEED
68 Pye 7N 17515 Stay Awhile/Pictures In The Sky 60
(see also Fadin' Colours)

ORB
SINGLES
89 Wau! Mr Modo MWS 010T KISS (12" EP, 949 only, die-cut company sleeve) 15
90 Wau! Mr Modo MWS 017T A Huge Ever-Growing Pulsating Brain That Rules From The Centre Of The Ultraworld: Loving You (Orbital Mix)/(Bucket And Spade Mix)/Why Is 6 Scared of 7? (12" p/s, B-side matrix states 'MWS 016T') 15
90 Big Life BLR 270T A Huge Ever-Growing Pulsating Brain That Rules From The Centre Of The Ultraworld : Loving You (edited)/(Bucket And Spade Mix)/(Why Is 6 Scared of 7?) (12" p/s, 8,000 only, B-side matrix 'MWS 016T') 10
90 Big Life BLR 270CD A Huge Ever-Growing Pulsating Brain That Rules From The Centre Of The Ultraworld : Loving You (Original Ambient House Mix) (CD) 12
90 Big Life BLR 27T A Huge Ever-Growing Pulsating Remix (Orbital Dance Mix)/(9am Radio Mix)/(Aubrey Mix I) (12", p/s, 8,000 only)..8
90 Big Life BLR 27CD A Huge Ever-Growing Pulsating Remix (Orbital Dance Mix)/(9am Radio Mix)/(Aubrey Mix I) (CD) 12

ALBUMS
91 Big Life BLRDLP 5 THE ORB'S ADVENTURES BEYOND THE UNDERWORLD (2-LP, with inner sleeve, 'classical pressing' sticker on sleeve)...20
91 Big Life BLRLP 14 THE ORB AUBREY MIXES: THE ULTRAWORLD EXCURSIONS (LP, with inner sleeve, deleted on day of release) 15
91 Strange Fruit SFRLP 118 PEEL SESSIONS (LP) 12
92 Big Life BLV 2 ADVENTURES BEYOND THE ULTRAWORLD: PATTERNS AND TEXTURES VERSION (video with 7-track live CD from Brixton Academy)..15
93 Island ILPSQ 8022 LIVE 93 (4-LP)..20
94 Island ORBLP 1 5240131 POMME FRITZ (LP) 12
95 Island ILPSD 8037 ORBUS TERRARUM (2-LP) 20
97 ILPSD 8055 OBLIVION (2-LP)...18
92 Big Life BLRLA 18 U.F.ORB (2xLP, 12" and 2 art prints in unopened blue plastic cover) 30
92 Big Life BLRLA 18 U.F.ORB (2xLP, 12" and 2 art prints in opened blue plastic cover) 15

PROMOS
90 Wau! Mr Modo MWS 017T A Huge Ever-Growing Pulsating Remix/From One Ear To Another/Why Is 6 Scared Of 7? (12", white label, 100 only) 20
90 Wau! Mr Modo MWS 017R A Huge Ever-Growing Pulsating Brain That Rules From The Centre Of The Ultraworld (Orbital Dance Mix)/(Orbital Radio Mix)/(Aubrey Mix Mk II) (12", stamped white label, 1,000 only) 15
90 Big Life ORB PROMO 1 A Huge Ever-Growing Pulsating Remix (Orbital Dance Mix)/(9am Radio Mix)/(Aubrey Mix Mk 1) (12") 8
90 Big Life ORB PROMO 2 Little Fluffy Clouds (Dance Mk 1)/Into The Fourth Dimension/Little Fluffy Clouds (Ambient Mk 1) (12")...10
91 Big Life ORB PICTURE 3 Perpetual Dawn: Ultrabass II (12", 1-sided picture disc, 400 only) 8
91 Big Life ORB PICTURE 3 Perpetual Dawn: Ultrabass II (12", 1-sided picture disc, mispressing, plays "Towers Of Dub (Ambient)", 400 pressed but 300 allegedly destroyed) 15
(see also System 7, KLF, J.A.M.s, Jah Wobble, Apollo XI, Space)

ORBIDÖIG
81 Situation 2 SIT 15 Nocturnal Operation/Down Periscope (p/s) 25
(see also Billy MacKenzie, Sensational Creed)

ROY ORBISON

SINGLES

60	London HLU 9149	Only The Lonely (Know How I Feel)/Here Comes That Song Again	6
60	London HLU 9149	Only The Lonely (Know How I Feel)/Here Comes That Song Again (78)	450
60	London HLU 9207	Blue Angel/Today's Teardrops	10
61	London HLU 9307	I'm Hurtin'/I Can't Stop Loving You	10
61	London HLU 7108	I'm Hurtin'/I Can't Stop Loving You (export issue)	15
61	London HLU 9342	Runnin' Scared/Love Hurts	7
61	London HLU 9405	Cryin'/Candy Man	5
62	London HLU 9511	Dream Baby/The Actress	5
62	London HLU 9561	The Crowd/Mama	5
62	London HLU 9607	Workin' For The Man/Leah	5
63	London HLU 9676	In Dreams/Shahdaroba	5
63	London HLU 9727	Falling/Distant Drums	5
63	London HLU 9777	Blue Bayou/Mean Woman Blues	5
64	London HLU 9845	Borne On The Wind/What'd I Say	5
64	London HLU 9882	It's Over/Indian Wedding	5
64	Ember EMB S 197	Rock House/You're My Baby	25
64	Ember EMB S 200	This Kind Of Love/I Never Knew (in p/s)	25
64	Ember EMB S 200	This Kind Of Love/I Never Knew	10
64	London HLU 9919	Oh, Pretty Woman/Yo Te Amo Maria	5
64	London HLU 9930	Pretty Paper/Summersong	5
65	London HLU 9951	Goodnight/Only With You	6
65	Ember EMB S 209	Sweet And Easy To Love/You're Gonna Cry (in p/s)	20
65	Ember EMB S 209	Sweet And Easy To Love/You're Gonna Cry	10
65	London HLU 9978	(Say) You're My Girl/Sleepy Hollow	7
65	London HLU 9986	Ride Away/Wondering	7
65	London HLU 10000	Crawling Back/If You Can't Say Something Nice	5
66	London HLU 10015	Breakin' Up Is Breakin' My Heart/Wait	6
66	London HLU 10034	Twinkle Toes/Where Is Tomorrow	6
66	London HLU 10051	Lana/House Without Windows	5

(London 45s from HLU 9676 to HLU 9978 and HLU 1051 were originally issued on the London Monument label as were later pressings of HLU 9149, 9495, 9511 and 9697.)

66	London HLU 10067	Too Soon To Know/You'll Never Be Sixteen Again	5
66	London HLU 10096	There Won't Be Many Coming Home/Going Back To Gloria	5
67	London HLU 10113	So Good/Memories	5
67	London HLU 10143	Cry Softly Lonely One/Pistolero	5
67	London HLU 10159	She/Here Comes The Rain Baby	5
68	London HLU 10176	Born To Be Loved By You/Shy Away	6
68	London HLU 10206	Walk On/Flowers	6
68	London HLU 10222	Heartache/Sugar Man	6
69	London HLU 10261	My Friend/Southbound Jerico Parkway	5
69	London HLU 10285	Penny Arcade/Tennessee Owns My Soul	6
69	London HLU 10294	Break My Mind (by Roy Orbison & Art Movement)/How Do You Start Over	12
70	London HLU 10310	So Young/If I Had A Woman Like You	12
71	London HLU 10339	(Love Me Like You Did It) Last Night/Close Again	10
72	Sun 6094 001	Ooby Dooby/Devil Doll	5
72	London HLU 10358	God Love You/Changes	8
72	London HLU 10388	Memphis Tennessee/I Can Read Between The Lines	6
72	London HLU 10388	Memphis Tennessee/I Can Read Between The Lines (export issue with alternate take of A-side: matrix no. MSC-8474-T2-IL)	8
74	Mercury 6167 014	Sweet Mama Blue/Heartache	7
85	ZTT DZTAS 9	Wild Hearts (...Time)/Wild Hearts (Voiceless)//Ooby Dooby/ Crying (double pack, p/s)	12

EPs

57	London RE-S 1089	HILLBILLY ROCK (orange p/s, mauve/silver label, triangular centre)	150
57	London RE-S 1089	HILLBILLY ROCK (orange p/s, mauve/silver label, round centre)	100
60	London RE-U 1274	ONLY THE LONELY	25
63	London RE-S 1089	HILLBILLY ROCK (re-pressing, yellow p/s, silver-top, round centre)	80
63	London RE-U 1354	ROY ORBISON	20

(Later pressings are on London Monument label as were later pressings of RE-U 1274 and RE-U 1354)

63	London RE-U 1373	IN DREAMS	10
64	Ember EP 4546	SWEET AND EASY TO LOVE	40
64	Ember EP 4563	TRYIN' TO GET TO YOU	40
64	London RE-U 1435	IT'S OVER	15
64	London RE-U 1437	OH PRETTY WOMAN	15
65	London RE-U 1439	ROY ORBISON'S STAGE SHOW HITS	15
65	Ember EP 4570	DEVIL DOLL	50
65	London RE-U 1440	LOVE HURTS	15

ALBUMS : LONDON LPS

61	London HA-U 2342	LONELY AND BLUE	40
62	London HA-U 2437	CRYIN' (mono)	30
62	London SAH-U 6229	CRYIN' (stereo)	35
63	London HA-U 8108	IN DREAMS (mono)	20
63	London SH-U 8108	IN DREAMS (stereo)	30
64	London HA-U 8207	OH, PRETTY WOMAN	20
65	London HA-U 8252	THERE IS ONLY ONE ROY ORBISON (mono)	20
65	London SH-U 8252	THERE IS ONLY ONE ROY ORBISON (stereo)	30
66	London HA-U 8279	THE ORBISON WAY (mono)	20
66	London SH-U 8279	THE ORBISON WAY (stereo)	30
66	London HA-U 8297	THE CLASSIC ROY ORBISON (mono)	20

(The London LPs listed above were originally issued with plum labels [mono] or blue labels [stereo]. Later copies were re-pressed with black labels [mono] or plum labels [stereo] with a boxed London logo)

66	London HA-U 8297	THE CLASSIC ROY ORBISON (black label mono)	20
66	London SH-U 8297	THE CLASSIC ROY ORBISON (blue label stereo)	25
67	London HA-U 8318	SINGS DON GIBSON (black label mono)	20
67	London SH-U 8318	SINGS DON GIBSON (blue label stereo)	25
68	London HA-U/SH-U 8357	CRY SOFTLY, LONELY ONE	20
68	London HA-U/SH-U 8358	SONGS FROM "THE FASTEST GUITAR ALIVE" FILM SOUNDTRACK	20
70	London HA-U 8406	THE BIG "O" (mono)	20
70	London SH-U 8406	THE BIG "O" (stereo)	15
72	London SH-U 8435	ROY ORBISON SINGS	15

MINT VALUE £

| 73 | London SH-U 8445 | MEMPHIS ....15 |

ALBUMS : OTHER ALBUMS

64	Ember NR 5013	THE EXCITING SOUNDS OF ROY ORBISON (original copies list 'Great Newport Street' address on cover; reissued 1972) 25
64	Ember NR 5013	THE EXCITING SOUNDS OF ROY ORBISON (reissued 1972) 18
65	Ember FA 2005	ROY ORBISON AND OTHERS (with 4 tracks by Orbison) 15

(see also Traveling Wilburys)

ORBIT FIVE

| 68 | Decca F 12799 | I Wanna Go To Heaven/Walking (in p/s) ....25 |
| 68 | Decca F 12799 | I Wanna Go To Heaven/Walking ....15 |

WILLIAM ORBIT

| 93 | Virgin VSCDT 1465 | WATER FROM A VINE LEAF (CD) ....20 |

ORBITAL

SINGLES

| 89 | Oh Zone ZONE 1 | Chime/Deeper (12", p/s) ....20 |
| 90 | Ffrr FRRFX 135 | Chime/Deeper (12", reissue, die-cut p/s) ....8 |

ALBUMS

91	FFRR 828248-1	ORBITAL (2-LP) 25
93	Internal TRULP 2	ORBITAL 2 (2-LP) 25
94	Internal TRULP 5	SNIVILISATION (2-LP, gatefold sleeve, poster) 18
96	Internal TRULP 10	IN SIDES (3-LP) 30
96	Internal PromoBox TRUCD 10/ LIECD 30	IN SIDES (2-CD, 245mm x 175mm burgundy box with "The Box" video)............15
97	Ffrr FRR PromoBox TRCDR10/ FCD 296	IN SIDES (2-CD, in 245mm x 175mm burgundy box with gold Orbital logo & The Saint second promo video by Activate, custom sleeve) 15
02	Ffrr 092746190	WORK 1989-2002 (2-LP) 20

PROMOS

90	Ffrr FRRXDJ 145	Omen (7")/Omen (12")/2 Deep/Open Mind (12") 8
91	Ffrr FRRXDJ 149	Satan (2 mixes)/LC1/Belfast (12") 8
91	Ffrr FRRDJ 163	Midnight (Radio Edit)/Choice (Radio Edit) 5
91	Ffrr FRRXDJ 163	Midnight/Midnight (Sasha Mix)/Choice/Choice Remix (12") 12
96	Internal ORB CD3	EVIL SANTA (3-CD set, including LIECD 37, LICDP 37 & LICDD 37, silver box)...........20

ORBITONES

| 73 | Explosion EX 207 | Memories Of Love/SONNY EARLE: In Peace ....5 |

ORCA

92	Micro Genetic 001	9 Lives/Shining Bright (12") 20
92	Lucky Spin LSR-ORC 1	DANCES WITH DOLPHINS EP NO. 1 (12", stickered, black die-cut sleeve) 30
92	Lucky Spin LSR 002	My Brothers/The Power (12") 30
93	Lucky Spin LRS 006	DANCES WITH DOLPHINS EP NO. 2 (12") 25
93	Lucky Spin LSR 011	4AM/Pure Bliss/Jungle Vibes/Pure Bliss (Remix) (100 on red vinyl) 50
93	Lucky Spin LSR 011	4AM/Pure Bliss/Jungle Vibes/Pure Bliss (Remix) (black vinyl) 30
93	Lucky Spin ORCA 6	BACK TO THE JUNGLE EP (12") 12
94	Lucky Spin STU 06	4AM (Remix 1)/4AM (Remix 2) (12") 12
94	Lucky Spin LSR 016	Intalect/Tranquility To Earth (12") 12

ORCHESTRA DEL ORO

| 62 | Pye Int 7N.25143 | Main Theme From Lolita/Lolita Ya Ya (in PS) ....8 |

ORCHESTRAL MANOEUVRES IN THE DARK (O.M.D.)

79	Factory FAC 6	Electricity/Almost (black 'braille' p/s) 60
79	Din Disc DIN 2	Electricity (Re-Recorded Version)/Almost (p/s, reissue) 5
80	Din Disc DIN 6	Red Frame-White Light/I Betray My Friends (p/s) 5
80	Din Disc DIN 15-10	Messages (Extended)/Waiting For The Man/Taking Sides Again (10", p/s) 6
80	Din Disc DIN 22-12	Enola Gay (Extended)/Annex (p/s) 5
80	Din Disc DIN 24-10	Souvenir (Extended)/Motion And Heart (Amazon Version)/Sacred Heart (10", p/s) ...8
82	Din Disc DIN 40-12	Maid Of Orleans (The Waltz Joan Of Arc)/Navigation/Of All The Things We've Made (12", 'coin' cover; incorrectly lists "Experiments In Vertical Take-Off") 12
82	Virgin VSY 527	Genetic Engineering/4-Neu (picture disc) 5
83	Virgin VSY 580	Telegraph/66 And Fading (picture disc) 5
84	Virgin VSS 660	Locomotion/Her Body In My Soul (train-shaped picture disc)..............................10
84	Virgin VSY 685	Talking Loud And Clear/Julia's Song (picture disc) 5
84	Virgin VSY 727	Never Turn Away/Wrappup (picture disc) 5
85	Virgin VS 766	So In Love/Concrete Hands//Maria Gallante/White Trash (live) (double pack, stickered gatefold p/s) 6
85	Virgin VS 796	Secret/Drift (poster p/s) 6
85	Virgin VSS 811	La Femme Accident/Firegun (shaped picture disc) 6
86	Virgin VSD 911	We Love You/(Dub)//If You Leave/88 Seconds In Greensboro' (double pack) 6
80	Din Disc DID 2	ORCHESTRAL MANOEUVRES IN THE DARK (LP, 12" x 12" grid sleeve, black, blue or grey outer sleeves with orange, pink or red inner) 25
80	Din Disc DID 6	ORGANISATION (LP, stickered sleeve, with insert & 7": "Introducing Radios"/ Distance Fades Between Us"/"Progress"/"Once When I Was Six" [DEP 2]) 15
91	Virgin V 2648	SUGAR TAX (LP, mispressing with extra track "All She Wants Is Everything" instead of "Neon Lights") 15
84	Virgin V 2310	JUNK CULTURE (LP, stickered sleeve, with free 7": "[Angels Keep Turning] The Wheels Of The Universe" [JUNK 1]) 15
96	Virgin V2807	UNIVERSAL (LP) 60

ORCHIDS (1)

63	Decca F 11743	Gonna Make Him Mine/Stay At Home 25
63	Decca F 11785	Love Hit Me/Don't Make Me Mad 20
64	Decca F 11861	I've Got That Feeling/Larry 25

(see also Exceptions)

ORCHIDS (2)

88	Sarah SARAH 002	I've Got A Habit/Give Me Some Peppermint Freedom/Apologies (foldover p/s with poster, 1,000 only) 60
88	Sarah SARAH 011	UNDERNEATH THE WINDOW, UNDERNEATH THE SINK EP (p/s) 10
88	Sha La La BaBaBaBaBa 5	From This Day/SEA URCHINS: Summertime (flexi, 2,500 only, 1,000 in p/s) 15
89	Sarah SARAH 023	WHAT WILL WE DO NEXT? EP (p/s) 12
90	Sarah SARAH 029	Something For The Longing/Farewell Dear Bonnie/On A Sunday (p/s, with inserts) 10

90	Caff CAFF 11	An Ill Wind That Blows/All Those Things (p/s, with insert)	20
91	Sarah SARAH 042	PENETRATION EP (12", p/s with insert)	12
92	Sarah SARAH 66	Thaumaturgy/I Was Just Dreaming/Between Sleeping And Waking (p/s, insert)	10
91	Sarah SARAH 605	UNHOLY SOUL (LP)	20
94	Sarah SARAH 617	STRIVING FOR THE LAZY PERFECTION (LP)	20
95	Sarah SARAH 401	LYCEUM (10" mini-LP)	12
95	Sarah SARAH 611 LP	EPICUREAN: A SOUNDTRACK (2-LP)	25

ORE
82	Bandit BR 003	Your Time Will Come/Yellow River (p/s)	100

CHARLES ORGANAIRE
64	Blue Beat BB 241	How Did Moses Cross The Red Sea/You May Not Believe (as Big Charlie)	18
64	R&B JB 149	Little Village/It Happens On A Holiday	35
64	Rio R 28	Little Village/It Happens On A Holiday (reissue)	15

ORGANISATION
70	RCA SF 8111	TONE FLOAT (LP)	300

(see also Kraftwerk)

ORGANISERS
66	Pye 7N 17022	Lonesome Road/The Organiser	80

ORGANUM
94	Aeroplane AR 15	Gloria (1-sided, numbered p/s, 113 only)	50
95	Aeroplane AR 16	Lysis (1-sided, 72 only)	50
95	Aeroplane AR 17	Kanroku (1-sided 12", black outer sleeve, illustrated, stamped, signed and no'd inner sleeve, 111 only)	60
95	Aeroplane AR 19	Rotor (1-sided, signed, no'd, 83 only, p/s)	60
95	Aeroplane AR 20	Arc (1-sided, signed, no'd, 85 only, p/s)	50
96	Aeroplane AR 23	Shovels (1-sided, signed, no'd, 91 only, p/s)	50
96	Aeroplane AR 24	Raw (1-sided, signed, no'd, 83 only, p/s)	50
88	United Dairies UN 023	SUBMISSION (LP, 1000 only)	40
94	Aeroplane AR 14	SPHYX (LP, black picture label, 546 only)	50
94	Aeroplane AR 14	SPHYX (LP, blue picture label, 509 only, reissue)	20

(see also David Jackman)

ORGANUM/NEW BLOCKADERS
84	Aeroplane AR 7	Pulp Parts 1 & 2 (gatefold p/s, 279 only)	60
85	Laylah/Antirecords LAY 19	IN EXTREMIS (LP)	20
88	Laylah LAY 012	TOWER OF SILENCE (LP)	20

(see also Current 93, Nurse With Wound, Eddie Prevost Band, David Jackman, New Blockaders)

ORIGINAL BARNSTORMERS SPASM BAND
59	Tempo A 168	That's All There Is/Stormin' The Barn	8
59	Tempo A 168	That's All There Is/Stormin' The Barn (78)	15
59	Tempo EXA 95	ORIGINAL BARNSTORMERS SPASM BAND (EP)	15

(see also Barnstormers Spasm Band)

ORIGINAL CHECKMATES
62	Pye 7N 15428	Hot Toddy/Tuxedo Junction	10
62	Pye 7N 15442	Checkmate Stomp/Begin The Beguine	15
63	Decca F 11688	Union Pacific/The Spy	30

(see also Checkmates)

ORIGINAL DOWNTOWN SYNCOPATORS
62	VJM VEP 14	ORIGINAL DOWNTOWN SYNCOPATORS (EP)	10
64	Columbia SEG 8293	IT'S JASS (EP)	10
63	J.R.T. Davies DAVLP 301/2	THE ORIGINAL DOWNTOWN SYNCOPATORS (10" LP, white labels only)	25

(see also Ron Geesin)

ORIGINAL DYAKS
67	Columbia DB 8184	Got To Get A Good Thing Going/Would You Love Me Too	10

ORIGINAL NEW ORLEANS RHYTHM KINGS
54	Columbia SCM 5113	Golden Leaf Strut/She's Crying For Me	10

ORIGINALS (1)
62	Top Rank JAR 600	Gimme A Little Kiss, Will Ya, Huh/At Times Like This	35
69	T. Motown STML 11116	GREEN GROW THE LILACS (LP, stereo)	55

ORIGINALS (2)
67	Tamla Motown TMG 592	Goodnight Irene/Need Your Lovin', Want You Back	80
67	Tamla Motown TMG 592	Goodnight Irene/Need Your Lovin', Want You Back (DJ copy)	150
70	Tamla Motown TMG 733	Baby I'm For Real/The Moment Of Truth	18
72	Tamla Motown TMG 822	God Bless Whoever Sent You/I Like Your Style/Baby I'm For Real	8
69	Tamla Motown TMG 702	Green Grow The Lilacs/You're The One	20
76	T. Motown TMGT 1038	Down To Love Town/Just To Be Closer To You (12")	8
76	Tamla Motown TMG 1066	Six Million Dollar Man/Mother Nature's Best (unreleased)	0
69	Tamla Motown TML 11116	GREEN GROW THE LILACS (LP, mono)	60
69	Tamla Motow STML 11116	GREEN GROW THE LILACS (LP, stereo)	55

ORIGINAL SIN
84	Sin S1N	The Shadow/Salvation (12", p/s, private pressing)	25

ORIGINAL TORNADOS
75	SRT SRTS 75350	Telstar/Red Rocket	10

(see also Tornados)

ORIGINATION
92	Rudeboy RUDE 001	Break Down/Bass/R.E.S.P.E.C.T. (12")	15
92	Rudeboy RUDE 002	Breakdown (Remix)/Breakdown (Original Edit)/ Breaking Out The B-Line/Gimme Ya Luv (12")	12
92	Rudeboy/Entity RUDE 003	NTT 12-33 Bass Remix/Sensation/Hardcore Yout/ Respect Remix/Funky Darkness (12")	8
93	Rudeboy RUDE 005	Sunrise/Sunrise (Ruff Mix)/Make Ya Wanna Do Right/Out Of This World (12")	10
93	Rudeboy RUDE 006	Music Takes Control/Signal To Noise/Music Takes Control (Remix) (12')	10
94	Rudeboy RUDE 007	Shine on '94/Shine On (Unreleased '92 Remix)/ Shine On '94 (Dub Version)/Shine On (Original '92 Mix) (12")	30

ORIGINELLS 4

64	Columbia DB 7259	My Girl/Kathy (as Origenells)	20
64	Columbia DB 7388	Nights/I Can Make You Mine	18

ORIGIN UNKNOWN

92	Ram RAMM 002	Untitled (6.03)/Untitled (5.01)/Untitled (5.22)/Untitled (6.12) (12", stamped white labels, promo only, not released)	20
93	Ram RAMM 004	The Touch/Valley Of The Shadows (12")	10
93	Ram RAMM 004R	The Touch (Part 2)/Valley Of The Shadows (Long Dark Remix) (12")	10
95	Ram RAMM 014	Truly one/Mission control (12")	12
90s	Ram RAMM 002	EASTERN PROMISE EP (12", stamped white label, 4 untitled tracks, promo only)	120
96	Ram RAMM 16	Valley Of The Shadows (original Mix)/Valley Of The Shadows (Awake '96 Remix) (12")	10

ORIOLES

53	London L 1180	Hold Me, Thrill Me, Kiss Me/Teardrops On My Pillow (78)	40
53	London L 1201	Crying In The Chapel/Don't You Think I Ought To Know (78)	40
54	London HL 8001	In The Mission Of St. Augustine/Write And Tell Me Why (78)	40

ORION THE HUNTER

84	Portrait PRT 25906	ORION THE HUNTER (LP)	12

(see also Boston)

ORION (1)

84	Lost Moment LM 02	Insane In Another World/Storm (p/s)	15

ORION (2)

87	Gypsy GYP 001	JACK ORION (LP)	30

TONY ORLANDO

61	Fontana H 308	Halfway To Paradise/Lonely Tomorrows	20
61	Fontana H 330	Bless You/Am I The Guy	10
61	Fontana H 350	Happy Times (Are Here To Stay)/Lonely Am I	10
62	Fontana H 366	Talkin' About You/My Baby's A Stranger	10
62	Columbia DB 4871	Chills/At The Edge Of Tears	20
63	Columbia DB 4954	Beautiful Dreamer/The Loneliest	25
63	Columbia DB 4991	Shirley/Joanie	8
64	Columbia DB 7288	Tell Me What Can I Do/She Doesn't Know It	10
63	Columbia SEG 8238	BLESS YOU (EP)	40
63	Fontana TFL 5167	BLESS YOU (LP, mono)	50
63	Fontana STFL 582	BLESS YOU (LP, stereo)	60

ORLANDO (1)

69	NEMS 56-4159	Am I The Same Guy/Poor Little Me	30

ORLANDO (2)

96	Blanco Y Negro 0630-19718-2	PASSIVE SOUL (CD)	30

ORLONS

62	Columbia DB 4865	The Wah Watusi/Holiday Hill	35
62	Cameo Parkway C 231	Don't Hang Up/The Conservative	25
63	Cameo Parkway C 243	South Street/Them Terrible Boots	20
63	Cameo Parkway C 257	Not Me/My Best Friend	15
63	Cameo Parkway C 273	Crossfire/It's No Big Thing	15
63	Cameo Parkway C 287	Bon Doo Wah/Don't Throw Your Love Away	20
63	Cameo Parkway C 295	Shimmy Shimmy/Everything Nice	15
64	Cameo Parkway C 319	Rules Of Love/Heartbreak Hotel	15
64	Cameo Parkway C 332	Knock Knock (Who's There)/Goin' Places	15
66	Planet PLF 117	Spinnin' Top/Anyone Who Had A Heart	150
72	Mojo 2092 029	Spinnin' Top/Anyone Who Had A Heart (reissue)	15
62	Cameo Parkway C 1033	ALL THE HITS (LP)	60
63	Cameo Parkway C 1061	BIGGEST HITS (LP)	60
78	London HA-U 8504	CAMEO PARKWAY SESSIONS (LP)	30

(see also Rosetta Hightower)

CYRIL ORNADEL (ORCHESTRA)

55	MGM SP 1141	King Of Kings (Theme From)/El Cid (Theme From)	6
61	MGM C841	THE MUSICAL WORLD OF COLE PORTER (LP)	12
62	MGM CD 6037	THE MUSICAL WORLD OF JEROME KERN (LP)	12

ORNAMENTAL

88	One Little Indian 18TP 7	Crystal Nights/Yonilingaphonics (p/s)	5

(see also Sugarcubes, Rose McDowall)

OROONIES

91	Demi Monde DMLP 1027	OF HOOF AND HORN (LP)	18

ORPHAN (1)

80	Orphan Records ORP-1	Little Mother/I Don't Want To Go (To Work Tomorrow), stamped inner sleeve and insert p/s)	20

ORPHAN (2)

85	Swoop RTLS 013	Nervous/Little England (p/s)	15

ORPHEUS

66	Red Bird RB 10-041	My Life/Music Minus Orpheus	40
68	MGM MGM 1413	I've Never Seen Love Like This/Lesley's World	12
68	MGM MGM C(S) 8072	ORPHEUS (LP)	25

RIZ ORTOLANI

71	United Artists UP 35278	The Hunting Party/CAROL CARMICHAEL: Where's Poppa?	8

BETH ORTON

96	Heavenly HVN 56	I Wish I Never Saw The Sunshine (p/s, 1-sided limited edition, 500 only)	20
96	Heavenly HVNLP 17	TRAILER PARK (LP, 100 copies only)	50
99	Heavenly HVNLP 22	CENTRAL RESERVATION (2-LP, gatefold sleeve, 1000 copies only)	35
02	Heavenly HVNLP 37	DAYBREAKER (LP)	25

(see also Spill)

EILEEN OSBORNE
| 75 | Seagull SG1 | SINGING SHORES (LP) | 15 |

MIKE OSBORNE
71	Turtle TUR 300	OUTBACK (LP)	60
73	Cadillac SGC 1002	ORIGINAL (LP, as Mike Osborne & Stan Tracey)	20
75	Ogun OG 300	BORDER CROSSING (LP)	15
76	Ogun OG 700	ALL NIGHT LONG (LP)	20
77	Ogun OG 210	TANDEM - LIVE AT BRACKNELL FESTIVAL (LP, with Stan Tracey)	18
77	Ogun OG 810	MARCEL'S MUSE (LP)	15

(see also Stan Tracey)

OZZY OSBORNE
80	Jet JET 197	Crazy Train/You Looking At Me Looking At You (p/s)	6
80	Jet JET 7003	Mr. Crowley (live)/You Said It All (live) (p/s)	8
80	Jet JET 12003	Mr. Crowley (live)/You Said It All (live)/Suicide Solution (live) (12", p/s)	10
80	Jet JETP 12003	Mr. Crowley (live)/You Said It All (live)/Suicide Solution (live) (12", picture disc)	15
81	Jet JET 7017	Over The Mountain/I Don't Know (p/s)	5
81	Jet JET 12017	Over The Mountain/I Don't Know (12", p/s)	8
82	Jet JET 7030	Symptom Of The Universe/N.I.B. (p/s)	6
82	Jet JETP 7030	Symptom Of The Universe/N.I.B. (picture disc)	10
82	Jet JET 12030	Symptom Of The Universe/N.I.B./Children Of The Grave (12", p/s)	8
83	Epic TA 3915	Bark At The Moon/One Up The B-Side (12", p/s, silver vinyl)	15
83	Epic WA 3915	Bark At The Moon/One Up The B-Side (12", picture disc, unreleased)	0
84	Epic DA 4452	So Tired/Bark At The Moon (live)//Waiting For Darkness/Paranoid (live) (double pack, gatefold sleeve)	8
84	Epic TA 4452	So Tired/Bark At The Moon (live)/Waiting For Darkness/Suicide Solution/Paranoid (live) (12", p/s with free patch)	8
84	Epic WA 4452	So Tired/Bark At The Moon (live)/Waiting For Darkness/Suicide Solution/Paranoid (live) (12", p/s, gold vinyl)	12
86	Epic A 6859	Shot In The Dark/Rock'n'Roll Rebel (p/s, with signature card)	6
86	Epic QA 6859	Shot In The Dark/Rock'n'Roll Rebel (poster p/s)	8
86	Epic A 7311	The Ultimate Sin/Lightning Strikes (p/s, with free patch)	5
88	Epic 653 063-9	Miracle Man/Crazy Babies (head-shaped picture disc)	8
88	Spiral Scratch 2/Ozzy 1	An Interview With... (no p/s, free with Spiral Scratch, issue 2, 5,000 only)	5
90	Adventure ADV TS 102	The Urpney Song/Whirlypad Launch (p/s, with poster, with Frank Bruno/Billy Connolly)	6
90	Adventure ADV TS 102	The Urpney Song/Whirlypad Launch (p/s, without poster, with Frank Bruno/Billy Connolly)	5
90	Adventure ADV TS 102	The Urpney Song/Whirlypad Launch (picture disc, with Frank Bruno/Billy Connolly)	10
91	Epic 657 4406	No More Tears (extended version)/S.I.N./Party With The Animals (12" pic. disc)	8
93	Epic 659 3406	Changes/Changes (extended version)/No More Tears (live)/ Desire (12" picture disc, with insert)	8
96	Epic 662 6391	Perry Mason/Living With The Enemy (picture disc)	6
86	Epic EPC 26404	THE ULTIMATE SIN (LP)	15
86	Epic EPC 11-26404	THE ULTIMATE SIN (LP, picture disc)	15
89	Epic 463 0862	DIARY OF A MADMAN (CD, promo-only, with diary)	18
91	Epic 467 8592	NO MORE TEARS (CD in embossed wallet)	18
95	Epic XP CD 2007	THE BALLADS OF OZ (CD, promo-only compilation)	20

(see also Black Sabbath, Lita Ford & Ozzy Osbourne, Billy Connolly)

TONY OSBORNE
| 62 | HMV POP 967 | Turkish Coffee/Tony's Tune | 10 |

OSBORNE BROTHERS
| 62 | MGM MGM 1184 | The Banjo Boys/Poor Old Cora | 5 |
| 59 | MGM MGM-EP 691 | COUNTRY PICKING AND HILLSIDE SINGING (EP) | 10 |

JOHNNY OSBOURNE (& SENSATIONS)
70	Big Shot BI 549	See And Blind (solo)/THE TECHNIQUES: Scar Face	12
72	Techniques TE 916	See And Blind/TECHNIQUES ALL STARS: Rema Skank	10
80	Jammys JM 002	Long Life Life/HIGH MUNDELL: Walk With Jah (12")	15
80	Cha Cha CHAD 27	Kiss Somebody/Version (12")	30
80	Black Joy DH 810	Purify Your Heart/Politician (blue vinyl)	30
80	Greensleeves GRED 34	Fally Ranking/Trench Town School (12")	30
81	Greensleeves GRED 50	Back Off (with PAPA TULLO).Dub (12")	35
81	Greensleeves GRED 60	Trying To Turn Me On/Turn On Dub (12")	15
81	Simba LION 1	13 Dead (Nothing Said)/Black Lion Band Murder (12")	25
81	Simba SIM 002	Don't Bite The Hand (with ASWAD)/Dub (10")	25
82	Oak Sounds OSD 006	Yo Yo/ECHO MINOTT : Man In Love (12")	15
86	Greensleeves GRED 208	Dub Plate Playing/COCOA TEA: Cocoa Tea Medley (12")	40
70	Trojan TTL29	COME BACK DARLING (LP)	40
73	Big Shot BILP 103	READY OR NOT (LP)	75
80	Greensleeves GREL 12	FALLY LOVER (LP, red vinyl)	30
81	Cha Cha CHALP 010	IN NAH DISCO STYLE (LP)	40
81	Black Joy DHLP 2001	WARRIOR (LP)	20
82	Arrival ALP 002	YO YO (LP)	15
84	Selection SELP 01	REALITY (LP)	25

BOB OSBURN
| 64 | London HLD 9869 | Bound To Happen/Think Of Me | 15 |

OSCAR BICYCLE
| 68 | CBS 3237 | On A Quiet Night/The Room Revolves Around Me | 60 |

OSCAR (1)
66	Reaction 591 003	Club Of Lights/Waking Up	60
66	Reaction 591 006	Join My Gang/Days Gone By	40
67	Reaction 591 012	Over The Wall We Go/Every Day Of My Life	40
67	Reaction 591 016	Holiday/Give Her All She Wants	30
68	Polydor 56257	Open Up The Skies/Wild Ones	30

(see also Paul Dean, Paul Nicholas)

OSCAR (2)
| 74 | Buk BULP 2001 | OSCAR (LP) | 15 |

OSCILLATORS
79	Warren Records WAR-SEP-465	Leonard Cheshire/Fast Breeder Reactor (p/s, with or without 'group' drawing, 1000 only)	20

PETER OSGOOD
70	Penny Farthing PEN 715	Chelsea/Stamford Bridge	10

OSIBISA
71	MCA MDKS 8001	OSIBISA (LP, gatefold, purple/red 'dogbone' label)	30
72	MCA MDKS 8005	WOYOYA (LP, gatefold, black/blue/white hexagon label)	20
72	MCA MDKS 8007	HEADS (LP, gatefold, black/blue/white label)	20
73	Buddah 2318 087	SUPER FLY T.N.T. (LP, soundtrack)	15

(see also Del Richardson)

OSMOSIS
70	RCA VICTOR LPS 4369	OSMOSIS (LP)	20

OSMOND BROTHERS
63	MGM MGM 1208	Be My Little Baby Bumble Bee/I Wouldn't Know	15
63	MGM MGM 1245	Travels Of Jamie McPheeters/Aura Lee	12
63	MGM MGM-C 1011	NEW SOUND OF THE BROTHERS (LP)	30

OSSIAN
77	Springthyme SPR 1004	OSSIAN (LP, textured sleeve)	12
79	Iona IR 001	ST. KILDA WEDDING (LP, with lyric insert)	12
81	Iona IR 002	SEAL SONG (LP, with lyric insert)	12

OSSIE & SWEET BOYS
67	Polydor 56167	Nothing Takes The Place Of You/Brixton Boo-Ga-Loo	15

OSSIE & UPSETTERS
66	Doctor Bird DB 1018	Turn Me On/True Love	20

(see also Upsetters, Desmond Dekkar)

AL OSTER
60s	Dominion LP 1321	ECHO OF THE YUKON (LP)	20

OSU
83	Shaka XAKA 2	Light Up My Fire/Merry Go Round (p/s)	10

GILBERT O'SULLIVAN
71	Columbia DB 8779	I Wish I Could Cry/Mr Moody's Garden	8

(see also Gilbert)

PETER O'SULLIVAN
76	Charisma CAS 1160	PETER O'SULLIVAN TALKS TURF (LP)	15

RAMON OTANO
64	Jump Up/Island JU 250	Fiesta En La Joya/Mambo Trinidad	10

OTHER BROTHERS
69	Pama PM 785	Let's Get Together/Little Girl	25

OTHER SIDE
87	Casual Sax SRT 8KS 1432	Is It Any Wonder/Let's Be Perfect (p/s)	40

OTHER TWO
64	Decca F 11911	I Wanna Be With You/Grumbling Guitar	12
65	RCA RCA 1465	Don't You Wanna Love Me Baby/Hold Back The Light Of Dawn	10
66	RCA RCA 1531	I'll Never Let You Go/Hot At Night	12

(see also Storyteller, J.J. Jackson)

OTHERS
64	Fontana TF 501	Oh Yeah/I'm Taking Her Home	60

(see also Sands, Sundragon)

JOHNNY OTIS SHOW
50	Parlophone R 3291	Harlem Nocturne (solo)/SLIM GAILLARD: Jam Man (78)	20
57	Capitol CL 14794	Ma (He's Makin' Eyes At Me)/Romance In The Dark	5
58	Capitol CL 14817	Bye Bye Baby (as Johnny Otis Show with Marie Adams)/Good Golly	15
58	Capitol CL 14817	Bye Bye Baby (as Johnny Otis Show with Marie Adams)/Good Golly (78)	10
58	Capitol CL 14837	The Light Still Shines In My Window/All I Want Is Your Love (with Marie Adams)	25
58	Capitol CL 14837	The Light Still Shines In My Window/All I Want Is Your Love (78, with Marie Adams)	10
58	Capitol CL 14854	Well, Well, Well!/You Just Kissed Me Goodbye (with Mel Williams)	25
58	Capitol CL 14854	Well, Well, Well, Well!/You Just Kissed Me Goodbye (with Mel Williams) (78)	10
58	Capitol CL 14875	Ring-A-Ling/The Johnny Otis Hand Jive	25
58	Capitol CL 14875	Ring-A-Ling/The Johnny Otis Hand Jive (78)	20
58	Capitol CL 14941	Crazy Country Hop/Willie Did The Cha Cha	25
59	Capitol CL 15008	You/My Dear (as Johnny Otis Show with Mel Williams)	18
59	Capitol CL 15018	Castin' My Spell/Telephone Baby (as Johnny Otis Show with Marci Lee)	25
59	Capitol CL 15057	Three Girls Named Molly Doin' The Hully Gully/I'll Do The Same Thing For You	20
60	Capitol CL 15112	Mumblin' Mosie/Hey Baby, Don't You Know?	15
64	Ember EMB S 192	Hand Jive One More Time/Baby I Got News For You	10
69	Sonet SON 608	Country Girl/Signifyin' Monkey	6
72	Epic EPC 7896	The Watts Breakaway/You Can Depend On Me	8
72	Epic EPC 8071	The Watts Breakaway/Willie And The Hand Jive	8
59	Capitol EAP1 1134	THE JOHNNY OTIS SHOW (EP)	40
65	Vocalion VEP 170162	JOHNNY OTIS (EP)	60
58	Capitol T 940	THE JOHNNY OTIS SHOW (LP)	90
69	Sonet SNTF 613	COLD SHOT (LP)	15
72	Ember SPE 6604	FORMIDABLE (LP)	15

(see also Marie Adams)

SHUGGIE OTIS
70	CBS 63996	HERE COMES SHUGGIE OTIS (LP)	35

(see also Al Kooper & Shuggie Otis)

NOIT OTNI & PITS
79	Automotive AERS 107	A Heart Can Only Be Broken Once/Moving Target (in p/s)	35

| 79 | Automotive AERS 107 | A Heart Can Only Be Broken Once/Moving Target .... 25 |

JOHN OTWAY

72	County COUN 215	Gypsy/Misty Mountain (private pressing, with duplicated lyric sheet) 25
76	Viking YRS CF 01	Louisa On A Horse/Beware Of The Flowers (private pressing) 15
78	Polydor 2059 001	Geneve/It's A Long Time Since I Heard Homestead On The Farm (p/s) 5
78	Polydor 2059 060	Baby's In The Club/Julie Julie Julie (p/s) 5
79	Polydor 2059 105	Frightened And Scared (instrumental)/Are You On My Side? (p/s, only 3 copies pressed!) 50
80	Stiff BUY 101	Green Green Grass Of Home/Wednesday Club (p/s) 5
82	Empire HAM 3	In Dreams/You Ain't Seen Nothing Yet (as John Otway Sweat, p/s) 5
86	'Warner Bros' OTWEAY 1	The New Jerusalem/The Tyger (private pressing) 20
82	Empire HAMLP 1	JOHN OTWAY (ALL BALLS AND NO WILLY) (LP, with Europeans) 12

JOHN OTWAY & WILD WILLY BARRETT

73	Track 2094 111	Murder Man/If I Did 8
76	Track 2094 133	Louisa On A Horse/Misty Mountain 5
77	Polydor 2058 916	Racing Cars (Jet Spotter Of The Track)/Running From The Law (p/s) 10
77	Polydor 2058 951	Really Free/Beware Of The Flowers (Cos I'm Sure They're Going To Get You Yeh) (p/s) 6
77	Polydor 2058 951	Really Free/Beware Of The Flowers (Cos I'm Sure They're Going To Get You Yeh) (die-cut 'review' sleeve) 5
82	Stiff Indie STIN 1	Headbutts/Live Version Headbutts (p/s) 5
82	Empire HAM 5T	12 STITCH EP (12" EP in polythene bag with jay-card) 15
87	VM VMS 6	The Last Of The Mohicans/Fashion (brown paper bag sleeve) 5
77	Extracted EXLP 1	JOHN OTWAY AND WILD WILLY BARRETT (LP, handmade stickered sleeve) 20
77	white label OBL 1	OTWAY AND BARRETT LIVE AT THE ROUNDHOUSE (private pressing LP, freebie, handwritten labels, plain sleeve, 250 numbered copies only) 35
81	Polydor POLS 1039	GONE WITH THE BIN (THE BEST OF OTWAY-BARRETT) (LP) 12
87	VM VM 7	THE WIMP AND THE WILD (LP, 1,000 only) 12

(see also Wild Willy Barrett)

OUR PLASTIC DREAM

| 67 | Go AJ 11411 | A Little Bit Of Shangrila/Encapsulated Marigold .... 90 |

COUSINS (BELGIUM)

61	Palette PG 9011	Kili Watch/Feugo 10
61	Palette PG 9017	Bouddha/Kana Kapila 10
62	Palette PG 9035	Anda/Danseuse 10

OUT

| 79 | Rabid TOSH 113 | Who Is Innocent/Linda's Just A Statue (p/s) .... 7 |

OUTCASTS

78	It IT 4	Frustration/Don't Want To Be No Adult/You're A Disease (p/s) 30
78	Good Vibrations GOT 3	Just Another Teenage Rebel/Love Is For Sops (poster p/s, various colours; 'band' p/s) 18
78	Good Vibrations GOT 3	Just Another Teenage Rebel/Love Is For Sops (poster p/s, various colours; 'type' p/s) 18
79	Good Vibrations GOT 17	Self Conscious Over You/Love You For Never (p/s) 12
81	GBH GBH 001	Magnum Force/Gangland Warfare (p/s) 20
81	Outcasts Only 0001	Programme Love/Beating And Screaming (Parts 1 & 2)/Mania (p/s) 5
79	Good Vibrations BIG 1	SELF CONSCIOUS OVER YOU (LP) 22

OUTER LIMITS

60s	Teldisc TD 154	Paradise For Two/Don't Ever Change 20
67	Deram DM 125	Just One More Chance/Help Me Please. 30
68	Instant IN 001	Great Train Robbery/Sweet Freedom 50
70s	Snow/Deroy 1049	(I'm Not) Your Stepping Stone/Great Balls Of Fire 400

OUTER LIMITS

67	Elephant LUR 100	When The Work Is Thru'/5 MAN CARGO: What A Wonderful Feeling (Leeds Students Charity Rag record) 55
68	Immediate IM 067	Great Train Robbery/Sweet Freedom (demo only) 70
71	Decca F 13176	The Dark Side Of The Moon/Black Boots 10

(see also Christie, Acid Gallery)

OUTLAW BLUES BAND

| 69 | Stateside SSL 10290 | BREAKING IN (LP) .... 30 |

OUTLAW POSSE

| 91 | Outlaw OP1 | Sonz Of The Devil (12") .... 12 |

OUTLAWS

61	HMV POP 844	Swingin' Low/Spring Is Near 15
61	HMV POP 877	Ambush/Indian Brave 15
61	HMV POP 927	Valley Of The Sioux/Crazy Drums 20
62	HMV POP 990	Ku-pow!/Last Stage West 20
62	HMV POP 1074	Sioux Serenade/Fort Knox 20
63	HMV POP 1124	The Return Of The Outlaws/Texan Spiritual 20
63	HMV POP 1195	That Set The Wild West Free/Hobo 20
63	HMV POP 1241	Law And Order/Do-Da-Day 20
64	HMV POP 1277	Keep-A-Knockin'/Shake With Me 40
61	HMV CLP 1489	DREAM OF THE WEST (LP, mauve label, gold print) 80
61	HMV CLP 1489	DREAM OF THE WEST (LP, later black label) 60

(see also Mike Berry, Ritchie Blackmore, Bobbie Graham, Chaps, Rally Rounders, Houston Wells [& Marksmen])

OUT OF DARKNESS

| 70 | Key KL 006 | OUT OF DARKNESS (LP, laminated front sleeve) .... 150 |

OUT OF ORDER

| 81 | Daviton SPEP 120 | OUT OF CONTROL (EP, export copy, 500 only) .... 40 |

OUTRAGE

| 70 | Kama Sutra 618 027 | The Letter/The Way I See It .... 5 |

OUTSIDERS (U.K.)

65	Decca F 12213	Keep On Doing It/Songs We Sang Last Summer 40
77	Raw Edge RER 002	ONE TO INFINITY (EP) 25
77	Raw Edge RER 001	CALLING ON YOUTH (LP, laminated sleeve) 40
78	Raw Edge RER 003	CLOSE UP (LP, with insert) 40

(see also Bunch Of Fives, Junior's Eyes, Tickle)

MINT VALUE £

OUTSIDERS (U.K.)
78	Xciting Plastic	Vital Hours/Take Up (unissued)	0

(see also Second Layer, Sound)

OUTSIDERS (U.S.)
66	Capitol CL 15435	Time Won't Let Me/Was It Really Real?	35
66	Capitol CL 15435	Time Won't Let Me/Was It Really Real? (DJ copy)	50
66	Capitol CL 15450	Girl In Love/What Makes You So Bad, You Weren't Brought Up That Way	15
66	Capitol CL 15468	Respectable/Lost In My World	20
66	Capitol CL 15480	Help Me Girl/You Gotta Look	10
67	Capitol CL 15495	I'll Give You Time/I'm Not Tryin' To Hurt You	20

OUTSKIRTS OF INFINITY
87	Woronzow WOO 7	LORD OF THE DARK SKIES (LP)	15
89	Infinity INF 001	SCENES FROM THE DREAMS OF ANGELS (LP)	12
89	Infinity INF 002	STONED CRAZY (LP)	12
94	Dark Skies DSKLP 2	INCIDENT AT PILATUS (2-LP)	18

OVALTINEES
83	BAA 021	BRITISH JUSTICE EP (p/s)	70

OVARY LODGE
73	RCA SF 8372	OVARY LODGE (LP)	100
76	Ogun OG 600	OVARY LODGE (LP)	25

(see also Keith Tippett)

OVATIONZ
81	Dread At The Controls DCD 005	Forever Love/Forever Dub (12")	15

OVERCOMERS
68	Bamboo BAM 64	Stop And Let Me Tell You/Take Courage Soul (unissued: white labels only)	50

OVERDRIVE
81	Boring Grantham BGR 1	ON THE RUN (EP)	80
90	Boring Grantham BGR 11	DISHONEST WORDS (LP)	12

OVERKILL
80	Killer EJSP 9357	Elemental/On My Own	75

OVERLANDERS
63	Pye 7N 15544	Summer Skies And Golden Sands/Call Of The Wild	12
63	Pye 7N 15568	Movin'/Rainbow	7
66	Pye NEP 24245	MICHELLE (EP)	25
66	Pye NPL 18138	MICHELLE (LP, laminated front sleeve with flipbacks)	35

(see also Paul Arnold, Cuppa T)

OVERLOAD
80	MCA MCA 618	Into Overload/Follow The Lines (p/s)	10
81	MCA MCA 656	Who Are You/Drift Away	10

OVERLORD
78	Airebeat ABT 3	Lucy/Guardsman/Johnny (p/s)	30

RUNE OVERMAN
63	Decca F 11605	Big Bass Boogie/Madison Piano	10

OVERNIGHT PLAYERS
80	Cha Cha CHALP 008	BABYLON DESTRUCTION (LP)	30

OVERTAKERS
68	Amalgamated AMG 803	That's The Way You Like It/The Big Take-Over	40
68	Amalgamated AMG 809	Girl You Ruff/KEITH BLAKE: Woo Oh Oh	40

BILL OWEN
81	Look LK/SP 6681	Compo Has Gone And Lost His Wellies/Friends (p/s)	5

OWEN (GRAY) & DANDY (LIVINGSTONE)
69	Downtown DT 428	Lovey Dovey/HERBIE GRAY & RUDIES: Kitty Wait	8

OWEN (DA SILVERA) & LEON
64	Island WI 146	Nextdoor Neighbour/ROLAND ALPHONSO: Feeling Fine	25
64	Island WI 163	My Love For You/How Many Times	25
64	Island WI 164	The Fits Is On Me/SKATALITES: Good News	25
64	Island WI 165	Running Around/SKATALITES: Around The World	30
65	Island WI 170	I Want My Cock/I Am Only Human (DERAK HARRIOTT) (probably withdrawn)	50
65	Ska Beat JB 189	Woman/BABA BROOKS with DON DRUMMOND: Doctor Decker	25

(see also Leon & Owen, Tommy McCook)

OWEN (GRAY) & MILLIE
62	Blue Beat BB 96	Sit And Cry/Do You Know (with City Slickers Orchestra)	8
62	Island WI 014	Sugar Plum/OWEN GRAY: Jezebel	15

(see also Owen Gray, Millie, Owen & Leon, Leon & Owen)

RAY OWEN('S MOON)
69	Fontana TF 1045	Tonight I'll Be Staying Here With You/Down, Don't Bother Me (solo)	6
71	Polydor 2058 095	Hey Sweety/Free Man (as Ray Owen's Moon)	7
71	Polydor 2066-119	Try My Love/Talk To Me	25
71	Polydor 2325 061	RAY OWEN'S MOON (LP, textured sleeve)	70

(see also Juicy Lucy)

REG OWEN & HIS ORCHESTRA
59	Pye International 7N 25009	Manhattan Spiritual/Ritual Blues	5
60	Palette PG 9004	Obsession/Sunday Morn.	10
56	Parlophone PMD 1045	SWING ME HIGH (10" LP)	20
59	Pye Intl. NPL 28000	MANHATTAN SPIRITUAL (LP, mono)	15
59	Pye Intl. NSPL 93000	MANHATTAN SPIRITUAL (LP, stereo)	20
58	RCA RD 27040	DREAMING (LP)	12

BUCK OWENS (& BUCKAROOS)
59	Capitol CL 15009	Everlasting Love/Second Fiddle	10

60	Capitol CL 15123	Above And Beyond/Til These Dreams Come True..7
60	Capitol CL 15162	Excuse Me (I Think I've Got A Heartache)/I've Got A Right To Know 7
61	Capitol CL 15187	Foolin' Around/High As The Mountain 5
62	Longhorn BLH 0006	Down On The Corner Of Love/Right After The Dance (estimated that 1000 pressed) 7
63	Capitol CL 15321	Love's Gonna Live Here/Getting Used To Losing You..5
64	Capitol CL 15364	Together Again/Ain't It Amazin' Gracie (as Buck Owens & Buckaroos)........................5
65	Capitol CL 15379	I've Got A Tiger By The Tail/Cryin' Time 5
66	Capitol CL 15452	Think Of Me/Heart Of Glass 5
67	Capitol CL 15501	Sam's Place/Don't Ever Tell Me Goodbye (as Buck Owens & Buckaroos) 5
63	Capitol EAP1 1550	FOOLIN' AROUND (EP) 10
65	Capitol EAP1 20602	ACT NATURALLY (EP) 10

DONNIE OWENS
58	London HLU 8747	Need You/If I'm Wrong 25
58	London HLU 8747	Need You/If I'm Wrong (78) 15
59	London HLW 8897	Ask Me Anything/Between Midnight And Dawn (unissued) 0

JAMIE OWENS
| 73 | Light LS 7012 | LAUGHTER IN YOUR SOUL (LP) ....15 |

OWL
| 68 | United Artists UP 2240 | Run To The Sun/Shades Of Blue And Green Water Flies ....20 |

O.W.L.
| 70s | Shebazz SHE 002 | Shady Tree/4TH STREET ORCHESTRA: Sun Hot ....8 |

TONY OXLEY (QUARTET)
69	CBS 52664	THE BAPTISED TRAVELLER (LP) 110
70	CBS 64071	4 COMPOSITIONS FOR SEXTET (LP, with Derek Bailey) 125
71	RCA SF 8215	ICHNOS (LP) 90
70s	Incus INCUS 8	TONY OXLEY (LP, with Derek Bailey, et al.)..100
70s	Incus INCUS 18	FEBRUARY PAPERS (LP) 40
80s	Bead BEAD 25	THE GLIDER & THE GRINDER (LP)...30
(see also Derek Bailey, Howard Riley)o

TONY OXLEY, WOLFGANG FUCHS, PHILIPP WACHSMANN & HUGH METCALFE
| 87 | Bead Records BEAD 25 | THE GLIDER AND THE GRINDER (LP) ....20 |

OXYM
| 80 | Cargo CRS 003 | Music Power/Mind Key (p/s) ....40 |

OYSTER BAND
86	Cooking Vinyl FRY 001	Hal-an-Tow/Ashes To Ashes (p/s)..6
89	Cooking Vinyl FRYX 012	Love Vigilantes/Polish Plain/I Fought The Law (Live)/Between The Wars (Live) (10", pink vinyl, poster sleeve) 10
82	Pukka YOP 01	ENGLISH ROCK 'N' ROLL, 1800-1850 (LP)..30
85	Pukka YOP 04	LIE BACK AND THINK OF ENGLAND (LP)..30
85	Pukka YOP 07	LIBERTY HALL (LP) 30

OYSTER CEILIDH BAND
| 80 | Dingles DIN 309 | JACK'S ALIVE (LP) ....20 |

OZARKS
| 63 | Vocalion V 9210 | Who Stole My Bird Dog/Any Waltz ....40 |

OZO
76	DJM DJS 628	Listen To The Buddah/Kites...6
77	DJM DJT 10764	Anambra (Edited Version)/Anambra (12")..35
82	Sphinx SPS 1201	Anambra River (Tranquil Rivers From The Floating Crystal City Of Budatan Shire Of Western Heaven)/Skintight (No Room To Move Up) (12")...................................15
76	DJM DJF 20488	LISTEN TO THE BUDDHA (LP) 40

OZRIC TENTACLES
91	Dovetail DOVEST 3	Sploosh!/Live Throbbe (12" P/s)...10
90	Dovetail Records DOVE LP1	ERPLAND (2-LP) 25
91	Dovetail DOVE LP 3	STRANGETUDE (LP) 15
92	Black Adder OZT 01	MUCK KICKER (LP)...20
93	Dovetail DOVELP6	JURASSIC SHIFT (LP)...15
94	Dovetail DOVE LP7	ARBORESCENE (2-LP) 25
94	Dovetail DOVEBOX 1	VITAMIN ENHANCED (6-CD box set) 30
98	Snapper SMALP 410	CURIOUS CORN (LP) 12
00	Strechy/Pancromatic PLP 2002	THE HIDDEN STEP (LP) 12
(see also Oroonies, Ullulators)

OZZ II
| 83 | Streamline | EXPLOITED (LP, red vinyl) ....12 |
| 84 | Zebra ZEB 2 | THE ASSASSIN (LP) ....12 |

P

PACESETTERS
70	Saga BC 101	Cool Coffee/Israelites..12
70	Escort ERT 829	Bits And Pieces/Nimrod Leap...8
74	Saga SAGA 8154	REGGAE MEETS POP (LP)..25

PACIFIC DRIFT
70	Deram Nova DN 13	FEELIN' FREE (LP, mono, blue/silver labels)..200
70	Deram Nova SDN 13	FEELIN' FREE (LP, stereo, red/silver labels)...150
70	Deram DM 304	Water Woman/Yes You Do 20
(see also Wimple Winch, Just Four Men)

PACIFIC GAS & ELECTRIC (P.G. & E.)

70	CBS 5039	Are You Ready?/Staggolee	6
70	CBS 5204	Father Come On Home/Elvira	5
69	B&C CAS 1003	GET IT ON (LP)	50
69	CBS 63822	PACIFIC GAS & ELECTRIC (LP, orange label)	20
70	CBS 64026	ARE YOU READY (LP, orange label)	15
71	CBS 64295	HARD BURN (LP, orange label)	15

PACIFIC SOUND
71	M&M FMSS 10012	Tribute To Jimi/Thick Fog	30

(see also Theatre Of Hate, Spear Of Destiny, Senate)

PACK (1)
65	Columbia DB 7702	Do You Believe In Magic?/Things Bring Me Down	40

PACK (2)
79	SS PAK 1	Brave New Soldiers/Heathen (p/s, 2,500 only)	12
79	Rough Trade RT 025	King Of Kings/Number 12 (p/s)	8
80	SS SS 1N2/SS 2N1	KIRK BRANDON AND THE PACK OF LIES (EP, with printed inner sleeve)	12
82	Cyclops CYCLOPS 1	LONG LIVE THE PAST (EP)	8

PACKABEATS
61	Parlophone R 4729	Gypsy Beat/Big Man	15
62	Pye 7N 15480	Evening In Paris/The Traitors	20
63	Pye 7N 15549	Dream Lover/Packabeat	20

PACKERS
66	Pye International 7N 25343	Hole In The Wall/Go 'Head On	20
69	Soul City SC 111	Hole In The Wall/Go 'Head On (reissue)	15
70	Soul City SCM 003	HOLE IN THE WALL (LP)	40

PAC-KEYS
68	Speciality SPE 1003	Stone Fox/Diggin'	20

PAD ANTHONY
87	Jammys JAM 7	Gotta Be Strong/Version//You Gonna Be Late/Version (12")	30

PADDINGTONS
04	Poptones MC5093S	21/Some Old Girl (p/s)	7

PADDY, KLAUS & GIBSON
65	Pye 7N 15906	I Wanna Know/I Tried	20
66	Pye 7N 17060	No Good Without You Baby/Rejected	50
66	Pye 7N 17112	Teresa/Quick Before They Catch Us	40

(see also Manfred Mann, Big Three, Rory Storm & Hurricanes, Kingsize Taylor)

PAGAN BEAU
82	RVNIC Records AMO 24	Odd Man Out/Natures Daughter (p/s)	15

BILLY PAGE
65	London HLU 10006	It's Pop/American Girl	12

CHRIS PAGE
66	Cameo Parkway CP 751	Wait And See/Mine Mine Mine	12

CLEO PAGE
79	JSP 4502	I Love To Eat It - Hamburger/Goodie Train	15

PAGE FIVE
66	Parlophone R 5426	Let Sleeping Dogs Lie/I Know All About Her	35

GENE PAGE
75	Atlantic K50105	HOT CITY (LP)	12

HOT LIPS PAGE & HIS ORCHESTRA
55	Parlophone MSP 6172	Ain't Nothing Wrong With That Boy/The Cadillac Song	20

JIMMY PAGE
65	Fontana TF 533	She Just Satisfies/Keep Moving (promo sticker on label)	750
65	Fontana TF 533	She Just Satisfies/Keep Moving	650
88	Geffen GEF 41	Wasting My Time/Writes Of Winter (p/s, withdrawn)	8
91	Fontana TF 533	She Just Satisfies/Keep Moving (reissue as part of Fontana box set)	15
91	Fontana TFCD 533	She Just Satisfies/Keep Moving (CD, in 'Led Zeppelin, A Celebration' promo book pack)	10

(see also Led Zeppelin, Page & Plant, Firm, Yardbirds, Paul, Carter-Lewis & Southerners, Neil Christian & Crusaders, Bobby Graham, Robert Plant, Honeydrippers, Brian Auger, Cartoone, Maureeny Wishfull, Jimmy Page with Puff Daddy, Coverdale-Page)

MALLY PAGE
66	Pye 7N 17105	The Life And Soul Of The Party/You Can Be Wrong About Boys	6

PATTI PAGE

SINGLES
58	Mercury 7MT 184	I'll Remember Today/My, How The Time Goes	8
58	Mercury 7MT 200	Bring Us Together/Belonging To Someone	8
58	Mercury 7MT 206	These Worldly Wonders/Another Time, Another Place	8
58	Mercury 7MT 223	Left Right Out Of Your Heart/Longing To Hold You Again	10
58	Mercury AMT 1000	Fibbin'/You Will Find Your Love (In Paris)	8
59	Mercury AMT 1022	Trust In Me/Under The Sun Valley Moon	8
59	Mercury AMT 1038	The Walls Have Ears/My Promise	8
59	Mercury AMT 1054	My Mother's Eyes/With My Eyes Wide Open I'm Dreaming	8
59	Mercury AMT 1054	My Mother's Eyes/With My Eyes Wide Open I'm Dreaming (78)	15
60	Mercury AMT 1089	Promise Me Thomas/Two Thousand, Two Hundred And Twenty-Three Miles	8
60	Mercury AMT 1102	One Of Us (Will Weep Tonight)/What Will My Future Be	8
60	Mercury AMT 1112	I Wish I'd Never Been Born/I Need You	6
61	Mercury AMT 1160	Broken Heart And A Pillow Full Of Tears/Dark Moon	8
62	Mercury AMT 1176	Most People Get Married/You Don't Know Me	6
63	CBS AAG 136	Just A Simple Melody/Pretty Lonely Boy	6

EPs
56	Mercury MEP 9502	PATTI PAGE	10

59	Mercury ZEP 10006	PATTI PAGE ONE	10
59	Mercury ZEP 10017	PATTI PAGE TWO	10
59	Mercury ZEP 10032	PATTI PAGE THREE	10
59	Mercury ZEP 10045	PATTI PAGE FOUR	10
60	Mercury ZEP 10073	PATTI PAGE FIVE	10
61	Mercury SEZ 19008	THIS LADY IS NO TRAMP (stereo, with Pete Rugolo All Stars)	10
61	Mercury SEZ 19020	MY KINDA LOVE (stereo)	10

ALBUMS

54	Mercury MG 25101	FOLK SONG FAVOURITES (10")	20
55	Mercury MG 25197	PATTI'S SONGS (10")	20
56	Mercury MPT 7510	CHRISTMAS WITH PATTI PAGE (10")	20
57	Mercury MPT 7531	I'M GETTING SENTIMENTAL OVER YOU (10")	20
57	Mercury MPT 7535	PATTI'S SONGS (10", reissue)	12

(see also Pete Rugolo)

PAGE & PLANT

94	Fontana PPDD 2	Gallows Pole/Four Sticks/What Is And What Should Never Be (CD, picture disc, part 2 of 2-CD set)	8
95	Fontana PPCDJ 3	Kashmir (CD promo, withdrawn)	30
95	Fontana PPCDJ 4	The Battle Of Evermore (CD promo)	12
98	Mercury 558 324 2	Walking Into Clarksdale (CD, limited issue digipak)	10
98	Mercury ADV 1998	Walking Into Clarksdale (CD promo, card sleeve)	40
94	Fontana PP ID 1	NO QUARTER UNLEDDED (CD, radio-promo only, with 'question' booklet)	50
94	Fontana 526 3621	NO QUARTER UNLEDDED (LP)	12
98	Mercury ADV 982	TBA (CD, advance promo for WALKING INTO CLARKSDALE)	30
98	Mercury PPTIC 1	WALKING INTO CLARKSDALE AN INTERVIEW (CD radio promo)	30
98	Mercury 558 025 1	WALKING INTO CLARKSDALE (LP)	25

(see also Jimmy Page, Robert Plant)

PAGE BOYS (U.K.)

83	Whaam! WHAAM 10	You're My Kind Of Girl/In Love With You (p/s, 1,000 only)	20

(see also 1,000 Violins)

PAGEBOYS (U.S.)

65	London HLU 9948	When I Meet A Girl Like You/I Have Love	10

PAGE ONE & THE OBSERVERS

76	Carib Gems CGLP 004	OBSERVATION OF LIFE DUB (LP)	40

LARRY PAGE (ORCHESTRA)

57	Columbia DB 3965	Cool Shake/Start Movin' (In My Direction)	25
58	Columbia DB 4012	That'll Be The Day/Please Don't Blame Me	25
58	Columbia DB 4080	Under Control/This Is My Life	20
59	Saga SAG 45-2902	Big Blon' Baby/I Vibrate	20
60	Saga SAG 45-2903	How'm I Doing, Hey Hey/Throw All Your Lovin' My Way	10
60	Saga SAG 45-2904	Little Old Fashioned You/Marylin	7
66	Decca F 12320	Waltzing To Jazz/Jo Jo (as Larry Page Orchestra)	5
66	Decca F 12368	Peyton Place Theme/Leanda's Theme (as Larry Page Orchestra)	5
68	Page One POF 068	Take Five/Michelle	5
68	Page One POF 096	Hey Jude/Those Were The Days (as Larry Page Orchestra)	5
69	Page One POF 125	Wichita Lineman/Scarboro Fair	6
60	Saga STP 1024	SINGS HIS PERSONAL CHOICE (EP)	8
65	Decca LK 4692	KINKY MUSIC (LP, as Larry Page Orchestra)	70
68	Page One POL(S) 002	EXECUTIVE SUITE (LP, as Larry Page Orchestra)	25

PAGE TEN

65	Decca F 12248	Boutique/Colour Talk	18

(see also Niney)

CARLOS PAIAO

81	EMI EMI 5174	Playback (English)/Playback (Portuguese)	7

PAICE, ASHTON & LORD

77	Polydor/Oyster 2391 269	MALICE IN WONDERLAND (LP, with inner sleeve)	15

(see also Deep Purple, Jon Lord, Ashton & Lord, Ashton Gardner & Dyke, Elf, Bernie Marsden)

MARTY PAICH

57	London LZ-U 14040	MARTY PAICH QUARTET (LP, with Art Pepper)	40

HAL PAIGE & WHALERS

60	Melodisc MEL 1553	Going Back To My Home Town/After Hours Blues	45

JOEY PAIGE

65	Fontana TF 554	Cause I'm In Love With You/Yeah Yeah Yeah	20

ROSALIND PAIGE

55	London HL 8120	When The Saints Go Marching In/Nobody's Sweetheart Now	30
57	MGM MGM 937	Love, Oh Careless Love/That Funny Melody	10

PAIN KILLER

91	Earache MOSH 45	GUTS OF A VIRGIN (LP)	15

PAINS OF BEING PURE AT HEART

08	Atomic Beat ABR 003	Kurt Cobain's Cardigan/PARALLELOGRAMS: 1 2 3 Go/Pop The Bubbles (p/s)	20
09	Fortuna Pop! FPOP 84	Young Adult Friction/Ramona (p/s)	6
10	Fortuna Pop FPOP 96	Say No To Love/Lost Saint (p/s)	6

PAINTBOX

70	Young Blood YB 1013	Get Ready For Love/Can I Get To Know You	10
71	Young Blood YB 1029	Get Ready For Love/Can I Get To Know You (reissue)	6

(see also Easybeats, Haffy's Whiskey Sour)

PAINTED SHIP

67	Mercury MF 988	Frustration/I Told Those Little White Lies	80

PAISLEYS

83	Psycho PSYCHO 7	COSMIC MIND AT PLAY (LP, reissue)	20

PALACE BROTHERS

93	Big Cat ABB 51 S	Ohio Riverboat Song/Drinking Woman (p/s) 8
94	Domino RUG 21T	AN ARROW THROUGH THE BITCH (12" EP, p/s) 15
95	Domino RUG 35T	The Mountain/Gulf Shores/(End Of) Travelling/West Palm Beach (12", stickered p/s as Palace) 18
93	Big Cat ABB 50	THERE IS NO ONE WHAT WILL TAKE CARE OF YOU (LP) 12
94	Domino WIG LP 18	HOPE (mini-LP as Palace Songs) 10
94	Domino WIG 14	PALACE BROTHERS (LP) 20
95	Domino WIGLP 21X	VIVA LAST BLUES (LP with 7" (RUG 39) stickered sleeve, as Palace Music) 40
95	Domino WIGLP 21	VIVA LAST BLUES (LP, as Palace Music, without 7") 20
98	Domino WIGLP 33	LOST BLUES AND OTHER SONGS (LP, gatefold, poster) 35

(see also Bonnie 'Prince' Billy, Will Oldham)

PALADIN

| 71 | Bronze ILPS 9150 | PALADIN (LP, textured sleeve, Island credit on label) ....30 |
| 72 | Bronze ILPS 9190 | CHARGE (LP, gatefold sleeve, Island credit on label) ....40 |

(see also Arthur Brown, Glass Menagerie, McGuinness Flint)

PALE FOUNTAINS

82	Operation Twilight OPT 09	(There's Always) Something On My Mind/Just A Girl (p/s) 25
82	Virgin VS 557	Thank You/Meadow Of Love (picture disc, stickered PVC sleeve) 5
82	Virgin VS 557-12	Thank You/Meadow Of Love/(There's Always) Something On My Mind (12", p/s) 8
83	Virgin VS 568	Palm Of My Hand/(Instrumental)/Love's A Beautiful Place (p/s) 5
85	Virgin VS 750	From Across The Kitchen Table/Bicycle Thieves//Thank You/ Just A Girl (double pack) 5
84	Virgin V 2274	PACIFIC STREET (LP) 12
85	Virgin V 2333	FROM ACROSS THE KITCHEN TABLE (LP, with inner sleeve) 12

(see also Shack, Michael Head & Strands)

PALE SAINTS

91	4AD AD 1009	Kinky Love/Hair Shoes (demo) (p/s) 10
90	4AD CAD 0002	THE COMFORTS OF MADNESS (LP, with postcards) 15
92	4AD CAD 2004	IN RIBBONS (LP, with free 7" "A Thousand Stars Burst Open"/A Revelation [RIB 1]) 12

TOM PALEY

| 69 | Argo ZFB 3 | SUE COW (LP) ....12 |
| 76 | Kicking Mule SNKF 119 | HARD LUCK PAPA (LP) ....18 |

(see also Peggy Seeger)

PALEY BROTHERS

| 78 | Sire SRE 4005 | Come On Let's Go/Magic Power (p/s) ....12 |
| 78 | Sire 6078 613 | Ecstacy/Rendezvous/Hide N' Seek/Come Out And Play (12", p/s) ....12 |

(see also Ramones)

PALI GAP

| 82 | Sinister SYN 001 | Under The Sun/The Knives Are Out (p/s, with insert) ....20 |

MORTY PALITZ & ACES

| 59 | London HLJ 8778 | The Grocer's Cha Cha Cha/Eso Es El Amor (This Is Love) ....8 |

PALLAS

82	Granite Wax GWS 1	Arrive Alive/Stranger (On The Edge Of Time) (two different p/s, with insert) 50
82	Granite Wax GWS 1	Arrive Alive/Stranger (On The Edge Of Time) (two different p/s, without insert) 40
83	Cool King CK010	Paris Is Burning/The Hammer Falls (p/s) 5
83	Cool King 12CK010	Paris Is Burning/The Hammer Falls/Stranger At The Edge Of Time (12", p/s) 12
84	EMI Harvest PLSP1	Eyes In The Night (Arrive Alive)/East West (picture disc) 10
84	EMI Harvest PLSP1	Eyes In The Night (Arrive Alive)/East West/Crown Of Thorns (12", p/s) 10
84	EMI Harvest PLS2	Shock Treatment/March On Atlantis (poster p/s) 5
84	EMI Harvest 12PLS2	Shock Treatment/March On Atlantis/Heart Attack (12", p/s) 10
78	Sue-i-cide PAL/101	THE PALLAS EP (stamped plain die-cut sleeve) 50
85	Harvest 12PLS3P	THE KNIGHT MOVES EP (12" picture disc) 12
85	Harvest 12PLS3D	THE KNIGHT MOVES EP (12" + free 7" Mad Machine / Stitch In Time, sealed in plastic sleeve) 15
83	Cool King CKLP002	ARRIVE ALIVE (LP) 15
84	Harvest SHSP2400 121	THE SENTINAL (LP, gatefold sleeve, with poster and sticker) 18
84	Harvest SHSP2400 121	THE SENTINAL (LP, gatefold sleeve) 12
86	Harvest SHVL 850	THE WEDGE (LP + inner sleeve) 15

EARL PALMER & HIS TEN PIECE ROCKIN' BAND

58	Capitol CL 14859	Drum Village (Parts 1 & 2) 10
58	Capitol EAP1 1026	SWINGIN' DRUMS (EP) 12
61	Liberty LBY 1008	DRUMSVILLE (LP) 20

EDDIE PALMER

| 57 | Decca F 10873 | The Sky/The Twilight Theme ....8 |

JERRY PALMER

| 66 | London 10026 | Walking The Dog/Don't Leave Me Baby ....25 |

MICHAEL PALMER

| 84 | Greensleeves GREL 155 | Done With It/Can't Take The Fuss (12") ....15 |
| 84 | Simba SM 08 | Me Nah Run/JACKIE PARRIS: When Your Are Young (12", with Aswad) ....25 |

MICHAEL PALMER AND JIM BROWN

| 83 | Greensleeves GRED 131 | Ghetto Dance/JAH THOMAS & ROOTS RADICS: Ghetto Dub (12") ....10 |

RICK PALMER

| 59 | London HLL 8900 | You Threw A Heart/My Greatest Wish (unreleased) ....0 |

ROY PALMER & STATE STREET RAMBLERS

| 54 | London AL 3518 | A CHICAGO SKIFFLE SESSION (10" LP) ....30 |

TRISTAN PALMER/PALMA

81	Greensleeves GRED 66	Entertainment/JAH THOMAS & TOYAN: Jah Guide (12") 15
82	Greensleeves GRED 93	Joker Smoker/PAPA BRUCE: Loafter Smoker (12") 25
82	Greensleeves GREL 43	JOKER SMOKER (LP) 20

PALMETTO KINGS

| 60 | Starlite ST45 021 | Ten Rum Bottles/Home Cookin' Mama ....15 |

CHARLIE PALMIERI
| 68 | Atlantic 588157 | LATIN BUGALU (LP) | 40 |

PAMA DICE
| 69 | Jackpot JP 715 | Bongo Man/Bear De Pussy | 18 |
| 69 | Jackpot JP 716 | Sin, Sun And Sex/Reggae Pop-Corn | 15 |

(see also Winston Groovy, King Horror, Ray Martell)

PAN
| 93 | Big Cat ABB 49 | HANGIN' OUT FOR JUNE (LP) | 15 |

PANACHE
| 83 | Mach 1 MAGIC 004 | I Wanna Dance/Crazy For Your Love (with Ray Dorset) | 7 |

(see also Ray Dorset)

PANAMA FRANCIS BLUES BAND
| 64 | Stateside SL 10070 | TOUGH TALK!! (LP) | 35 |

PANAMA LIMITED (JUG BAND)
69	Harvest HAR 5010	Lady Of Shallot/Future Blues	30
70	Harvest HAR 5022	Round And Round/Rotting Wooden In A White Collar's Grave	30
69	Harvest SHVL 753	PANAMA LIMITED JUG BAND (LP, laminated gatefold sleeve, "Sold in U.K..." text on 5 lines", no EMI on label)	200
70	Harvest SHVL 753	PANAMA LIMITED JUG BAND (LP, laminated gatefold sleeve, 2nd pressing, no "Sold in U.K..." no EMI on label)	50
70	Harvest SHVL 779	INDIAN SUMMER (LP, as Panama Limited, gatefold sleeve, no EMI on label)	350

(see also Ian (A) Anderson)

ALPHONSO PANCHO
| 79 | Attack TACK 3 | Love Is A Pleasure/Never Give Up In A Babylon | 20 |

(see also Pancho Alphonso)

GENE PANCHO
| 68 | Giant GN 21 | I Like Sweet Music/Seven Days (with Sandy & Superboys) | 8 |

(see also Gene Rondo)

PANDEMONIUM
67	CBS 202462	Season Of The Witch/Today I'm Happy	50
67	CBS 2664	No Presents For Me/The Sun Shines From His Eyes	300
68	CBS 3451	Chocolate Buster Dam/Fly With Me Forever	55

PANDIT PRAN NATH
| 69 | Transatlantic TRA 193 | EARTH GROOVE (LP) | 20 |

PANDORAS
| 67 | Liberty LIB 55954 | (I Could Write A Book) About My Baby/New Day | 18 |

PANHANDLE
| 72 | Decca SKL 5105 | PANHANDLE (LP, laminated cover, blue/silver label with boxed logo) | 30 |

(see also Chris Spedding)

PANIK
| 77 | Rainy City SHOT 1 | IT WON'T SELL (EP) | 15 |

PAN PIPERS
| 69 | Pye 7N 17699 | Stop/Money Or Love | 100 |

PANS PEOPLE
| 74 | Epic SEPC 2606 | You Can Really Rock N Roll Me/The Singer Not The Song | 8 |

PAN SONIC
| 00 | Blast First BFFP 166 | AALTOPIIRI (2-LP, print) | 20 |
| 04 | Blast first BFFP 180BX | KESTO (4-CD box set) | 30 |

PANT
| 79 | Redball RR019X | Mother Fo/Modern/No Possessions/Mummy Told You | 25 |

GARY PANTER & JAY COTTON
| 90 | Blast First FU 7 | ONE HELL SOUNDWICH (LP, picture disc) | 20 |

JAN PANTER
65	Oriole CB 1938	My Two Arms Minus You Equals Tears/Does My Heart Show	25
65	CBS 201810	Let It Be Now/Stand By And Cry	20
66	Pye 7N 17097	Scratch My Back/Put Yourself In My Place	250
69	President PT 241	Si Si Senor/Stella In Lights	10

PANTHER BURNS
| 81 | Rough Trade RT 077 | Train Kept A Rollin'/Red Headed Woman (p/s) | 10 |
| 81 | Rough Trade ROUGH 32 | BEHIND THE MAGNOLIA CURTAIN (LP) | 20 |

(see also Tav Falco's Panther Burns, Alex Chilton)

ROY PANTON
63	Blue Beat BB 182	Mighty Ruler/Run Old Man	30
64	Blue Beat BB 219	Good From The Bad/Hell Gate	30
64	Rio R 19	Cherita/Seek And You Shall Find	20
64	Rio R 33	You Don't Know Me/KING EDWARD'S ALLSTARS: Doctor No	35
64	Island WI 137	Goodbye Peggy Darling (actually "Goodbye Peggy" by Stranger Cole)/ BABA BROOKS: Portrait Of My Love	25
70	Harry J HJ 6624	The Same Old Life/JAYBOYS: Life Version	8

(see also Roy & Annette, Roy & Millie, Roy & Paulette, Roy & Yvonne, Roy & Duke Allstars, Roy & Patsy, Derrick Harriot, Leon & Owen, Charmers)

JOHN PANTRY
72	Philips 6006 250	Net Of Concern/Words	10
79	Kingsway KMS 902	Nothing Is Impossible/Jesus On The Airwaves	8
72	Philips 6308 129	JOHN PANTRY (LP)	40
73	Philips 6308 138	LONG WHITE TRAIL (LP)	18
80	Kingsway KMR 323	TO STRANGERS AND FRIENDS (LP)	15
80s	Tenth Planet TP 040	THE UPSIDE DOWN WORLD OF JOHN PANTRY (LP, limited edition, 1,000 only)	50

(see also Factory, Peter & Wolves, Norman Conquest, Sounds Around, Bunch)

PANZA DIVISION
82　Panza Traz PTO1　　　　We Will Rock The World/Standing On The Outside 10

PAPA CHARJAN
82　CF CF 006　　　　DJ Pumping/COURTNEY BARKELY: I Am Alright (12") 20

PAPA DOO RUN RUN
75　RCA RCA 2620　　　　Be True To Your School/Disney Girls 8

PAPA MICHIGAN & GENERAL SMILEY
81　Tuff Gong IPR 2035　　　　One Love Jame Down/FREDDIE MCGREGOR: Joggin' (12") 10

PAPA TULLO
81　Negus roots NERT 006　　　　Church And State/Righteous Rock (12") 15
82　Negus Roots NERLP 004　　　　TULLO AT HOME (LP)...40

NIKKI PAPAS
59　Parlophone R 4590　　　　49 State Rock/Try Again 45
60　Parlophone R 4652　　　　By The River/Don't Leave Me Alone 18

PAPER BLITZ TISSUE
67　RCA Victor RCA 1652　　　　Boy Meets Girl/Grey Man 400
(see also Cupid's Inspiration)

PAPER BUBBLE
70　Deram DML/SML 1059　　　　SCENERY (LP, white/red label) 100
(see also Dave Cousins)

PAPER DOLLS
68　Pye 7N 17456　　　　Something Here In My Heart/All The Time In The World 5
68　Pye 7N 17547　　　　My Life Is In Your Hands/There's Nobody I'd Sooner Love 8
68　Pye 7N 17655　　　　Someday/Any Old Time You're Lonely And Sad 7
70　RCA RCA 1919　　　　My Boyfriend's Back/Mister Good Time Friday 7
70　RCA RCA 2007　　　　Remember December/Same Old Story 7
68　Pye N(S)PL 18226　　　　PAPER DOLLS HOUSE (LP)...50

PAPER DRAGON
69　Bell BLL 1054　　　　April Fool/Get Something Going 12

PAPERHOUSE
91　Mystic Stones RUNE LP 11　　　　SPONGY COMESTIBLES (LP) 20

PAPERTOYS
90　Armada ARMAP 003　　　　Cold Surrender (Winston Club Mix)/Cold Surrender (D-Day 7" Radio Mix)/Cold
　　　　Surrender (Outland Mix) (12", numbered p/s, 500 only) 8

(see also Gary Numan)

PARADE
67　A&M AMS 701　　　　Sunshine Girl/This Old Melody 18
67　A&M AMS 720　　　　Radio Song/I Can See Love 15

VANESSA PARADIS
87　Polydor POSPG 902　　　　Joe Le Taxi/Varvara Pavlovna (poster p/s) 6
88　Polydor 080 466-2　　　　Joe Le Taxi/Manolo Manolete/Joe Le Taxi (Version Espagnole)/Joe Le Taxi (Version
　　　　Longue)/Joe Le Taxi (Video) (CD Video) 15
88　Polydor 080 468-2　　　　Marilyn And John (Version Français) (4.40)/Soldat/Marilyn And John
　　　　(Version Anglais)/Marilyn And John (Version Français) (5.44)/Marilyn And
　　　　John (Version Francais) (Video) (CD video) 18
88　Polydor 081 312-2　　　　Coup Coup (Remix)/Maxou/Marilyn And John/Coup Coup (Remix) (Video) (CD Video) 18

PARADISE
80　Ebony EB 701　　　　PARADISE (LP) 125
82　Ebony EB 702　　　　WORLD'S MIDNIGHT (LP) 100
83　Priority PLP 1　　　　LOVE IS THE ANSWER (LP) 100

PARADISE HAMMER
70　Polydor 2058048　　　　She Is Love/You Got Me In 25
71　Polydor 2058084　　　　1+1=2/To Live 15

PARADISE LOST
93　Music For Nations MFN 152　　　　LOST (LP)..18

PARDISE SQUARE
74　White label　　　　NEVER THOUGHT I'D SEE THE DAY (LP, plain white sleeve, 5 inserts) 500

PARADONS
60　Top Rank JAR 514　　　　Diamonds And Pearls/I Want Love 80

PARADOX (1)
68　Polydor 56275　　　　The Wednesday Theme/Ring The Changes 125
(see also David Walker)

PARADOX (2)
90　Ronin RDP10　　　　Revolutionary/Dedicated (12") 8

PARAFFIN JACK FLASH LTD
68　Pye NSPL 18252　　　　MOVERS AND GROOVERS (LP) 18

PARAGONS
66　Doctor Bird DB 1060　　　　Happy-Go-Lucky Girl/Love Brings Pain 35
67　Island WI 3045　　　　On The Beach/CAROL & TOMMY McCOOK: Sweet And Gentle (B-side actually by
　　　　Tommy McCook & Supersonics) 40
67　Island WI 3067　　　　Talking Love/If I Were You 40
67　Island WI 3093　　　　So Depressed/We Were Meant To Be 80
67　Treasure Isle TI 7009　　　　Only A Smile/The Tide Is High 25
67　Treasure Isle TI 7011　　　　Mercy, Mercy, Mercy/Riding On A High And Windy Day 25
67　Treasure Isle TI 7013　　　　The Same Song/TOMMY McCOOK & SUPERSONICS: Soul Serenade 28
67　Treasure Isle TI 7025　　　　Wear You To The Ball/You Mean The World To Me 30
68　Treasure Isle TI 7034　　　　Silver Bird/My Best Girl...25
68　Island WI 3138　　　　Memories By The Score/The Number One For Me 30
69　Studio One SO 2081　　　　Have You Ever Been In Love/Change Your Style 30
69　Duke DU 7　　　　Left With A Broken Heart/I've Got To Get Away 80

69	Crab 13	Take Your Hand From My Neck/Equality And Justice 40
67	Doctor Bird DLM 5010	ON THE BEACH (LP) 160
77	Wildflower WF 523	Do The Best Thing/Best Thing 8

(see also Rosalyn Sweat & Paragons, John Holt, Lester Sterling)

PARALEX
80	Reddingtons R.R. DAN 4	White Lightning/Travelling Man/Black Widow, (12", p/s, green vinyl) 50

PARALLELOGRAMS
08	Atomic Beat ABR 003	1 2 3 Go/Pop The Bubbles/PAINS OF BEING PURE AT HEART: Kurt Cobain's Cardigan (p/s) ..20

PARAMEDIC SQUAD
81	Gargoyle GRGL 2	Movement In Time/For You/Thinking Psychedelia (p/s) 25

PARAMETER
70	Deroy	GALACTIC RAMBLE (LP, 450 only, 4 page inner) 300

NORRIE PARAMOR & HIS ORCHESTRA
53	Columbia SCM 5051	April In Portugal/The Song From Moulin Rouge 8
54	Columbia SCM 5126	Johnny Guitar/Paramambo 8
54	Columbia SCM 5136	The High And The Mighty/Rip Van Twinkle 8
56	Columbia SCM 5251	Theme From Threepenny Opera/Poor John 7
56	Columbia DB 3815	Autumn Concerto/Lullaby Of Birdland 7
60	Columbia DB 4419	Summer Place (Theme)/Half Pint 5
62	Columbia DB 4789	Z Cars (Theme)/Ballad Of A Soldier (Theme) 5
63	Columbia DB 8430	Soul Coaxing/Autumn In London Town 7
64	Columbia DB 7114	Dream Of Tomorrow/Laramie 7
65	Columbia DB 7446	Dance Of The Warriors/Dragon Dance 6
70	Polydor 56375	Randall And Hopkirk (Deceased)/A Summer Palace 65

(see also Harry Gold)

PARAMORE
06	Fueled By Ramen ATUK 037	Emergency/O'Star (poster sleeve) 10
07	Fueled By Ramen ATUK 0279	Misery Business/My Hero (Electronic Mix) (Clear vinyl, poster sleeve) 6
07	Fueled By Ramen AT 0279X	Misery Business (Album Version)/Sunday Bloody Sunday (Bonus Version) 6
07	Fueled by Ramen AT 0284	Hallelujah (Album Version)/Decoy (Bonus Version) (gatefold p/s, poster) 6
07	Fueled By Ramen AT 0284X	Hallelujah (Album Version) (1-sided etched disc, poster sleeve) 6
07	Fueled By Ramen AT 0295	Crush Crush Crush (Album Version)/Misery Business (Live) (stickered p/s, sheet of stickers) 6
07	Fueled By Ramen AT 0295X	Crush Crush Crush (Album Version)/For A Pessimist I'm Pretty Optimistic (Live) (blue vinyl, printed PVC sleeve, insert) 6

PARAMOUNT ALL-STARS
50	Tempo R 20	Hometown Skiffle (Parts 1 & 2) (78) 20

(see also Blind Blake, Will Ezell, Georgia Tom, Alex Hill, Papa Charlie Jackson, Blind Lemon Jefferson, Charlie Spand)

PARAMOUNT FOUR
09	Kent 6T 26	Sorry Ain't The Word/GENE & GARY: Baby Without You...20

PARAMOUNTS
63	Parlophone R 5093	Poison Ivy/I Feel Good All Over 15
64	Parlophone R 5107	Little Bitty Pretty One/A Certain Girl 20
64	Parlophone R 5155	I'm The One Who Loves You/It Won't Be Long 25
64	Parlophone R 5187	Bad Blood/Do I 25
65	Parlophone R 5272	Blue Ribbons/Cuttin' In 20
65	Parlophone R 5351	You Never Had It So Good/Don't Ya Like My Love 50
64	Parlophone GEP 8908	THE PARAMOUNTS (EP) 200

(see also Procol Harum)

PARANOIA
84	Rot ASS 8	Dead Man's Dreams/Man In Black (p/s) 8
84	Rot ASS 11	SHATTERED GLASS (LP) 25

PARANOIDS
79	Hurricane FIRE 8	Stupid Guy/Road To Ruin (p/s) 10
80	Hurricane FIRE 14	The Love Job/Theme From Gravity's Rainbow (p/s)...10

PARCHMENT
73	Pye 7N 45261	You Are My Morning/Getting Out Of This Town 5
72	Pye 7N 45178	Light Up The Fire/Let There Be Light (p/s) 5
73	Pye 7N 45214	Where Can I Find You/Working Man 8
72	Pye NSPL 18388	LIGHT UP THE FIRE (LP, textured sleeve with poster insert)..20
73	Pye NSPL 18409	HOLLYWOOD SUNSET (LP) 12
75	Myrrh MYR 1028	SHAMBLEJAM (LP) 18
77	Pilgrim GRAPEVINE 106	REHEARSAL FOR A REUNION (LP) 12

WALTER PARDON
75	Leader LED 2063	A PROPER SORT (LP) 20

TONY PARENTI
57	London EZ V 19022	RAGTIME (EP) 10
57	London LTZU 15072	RAGTIME (LP) 12

PAULA PARFITT
69	Beacon BEA 135	I'm Gonna Give You Back Your Ring/Love Is Wonderful (Beware of bootlegs! - originals have anti-slip grips around the label) 150
70	Up Front UPF4	Peace Of Mind/Baby You Give Me A Good Song To Sing 10

TINY PARHAM
50s	Audubon AAC	TINY PARHAM (10" LP) 25

PARIS
72	Avalanche AV 67312	I've Lost The Way/Long Time 8
76	Thunderbird THE 114	Circles/Liar 5
84	Bluebird BRT 9	I Choose You/Punkin' Funkin' (12", p/s) 8

BOBBY PARIS
68	Polydor 56747	Per So Nal Ly/Tragedy 80
69	Polydor 56762	Let The Sun Shine In/You 22
77	London HLU 10553	Night Owl/YVONNE BAKER: You Didn't Say A Word 10

MICA PARIS
91	4th & Broadway 12BRWDJ207	A STAND FOR LOVE EP (12" promo p/s. Mispress, plays Prince's vocal version of 'A Stand For Love')	100

PRISCILLA PARIS
74	Rak RAK 184	I Love How You Love Me/Over You	10

(see also Paris Sisters)

PARIS SISTERS
61	Top Rank JAR 588	I Love How You Love Me/I'll Be Crying Tomorrow	50
64	MGM MGM 1240	Dream Lover/Lonely Girl	50

(see also Date With Soul, Priscilla Paris)

JOHN PARISH & POLLY JEAN HARVEY
96	Island IS 648	That Was My Veil/Losing Ground (p/s)	12
96	Island HEELCD1	Heela (Promo-only CD, unreleased single)	15
96	Island CIDX 8051	DANCE HALL AT LOUSE POINT (CD, 5,000 in digipak with insert)	20
96	Island ILPS 8051	DANCE HALL AT LOUSE POINT (LP)	35

(see also P.J. Harvey)

PARISH HALL
70	Liberty LBS 83374	PARISH HALL (LP)	60

SIMON PARK
74	EMI EMC 3059	SOMETHING IN THE AIR (LP)	20
75	EMC 3085	VENUS FLY TRAP (LP)	12

ALAN PARKER
70	Aristocrat AR 1022	GUITAR FANTASY (LP)	18
73	MCA MUPS 471	BAND OF ANGELS (LP)	20

(see also Hungry Wolf, Ugly Custard)

BENNY PARKER & DYNAMICS
64	Decca F 11944	Boys And Girls/You'll Be On Your Way	45

BILLY PARKER
63	Decca F 11668	Thanks A Lot/Out Of Your Heart	7

BOBBY PARKER
61	London HLU 9393	Watch Your Step/Steal Your Heart Away	60
64	Sue WI 340	Watch Your Step/Steal Your Heart Away (reissue)	55
69	Blue Horizon 57-3151	It's Hard But It's Fair/I Couldn't Quit My Baby	45

CHARLIE PARKER
EPs
55	Vogue EPV 1011	CHARLIE PARKER PLAYS	10
56	Columbia Clef SEB 10026	NOW'S THE TIME	8
50s	Esquire EP 57	CHARLIE PARKER QUINTET	8
60	Vogue EPV 1264	ALL STAR SEXTET	8
60	HMV 7EG 8626	CHARLIE PARKER BIG BAND	8

ALBUMS
52	Vogue LDE 004	CHARLIE PARKER VOLUME ONE (10")	60
53	Vogue LDE 016	CHARLIE PARKER VOLUME TWO (10")	60
56	Vogue LAE 12002	CHARLIE PARKER MEMORIAL ALBUM (gatefold sleeve w/ 2 inserts)	20
55	Melodisc MLP 12-105	BIRD AT ST. NICK'S	30
55	Columbia Clef 33CX 10004	CHARLIE PARKER BIG BAND	40
56	Columbia Clef 33C 9026	BIRD AND DIZ (10", with Dizzy Gillespie)	40
57	Columbia Clef 33CX 10081	APRIL IN PARIS (as Charlie Parker With Strings)	35
57	Columbia Clef 33CX 10090	CHARLIE PARKER PLAYS COLE PORTER	25
58	Columbia Clef 33CX 10117	CHARLIE PARKER JAZZ PERENNIAL	15
58	London Jazz LTZ-C 15104	THE IMMORTAL CHARLIE PARKER VOL. 1	15
58	London Jazz LTZ-C 15105	THE IMMORTAL CHARLIE PARKER VOL. 2	15
58	London Jazz LTZ-C 15106	THE IMMORTAL CHARLIE PARKER VOL. 3	15
58	London Jazz LTZ-C 15107	THE IMMORTAL CHARLIE PARKER VOL. 4	15
58	Mercury MPL 12-105	BIRD AT NICK'S	15
60	Collector JGN 1002	CHARLIE PARKER IN SWEDEN	30
61	HMV/Verve CLP 1538	THE ESSENTIAL CHARLIE PARKER	15
62	Verve VLP 9105	BIRD SYMBOLS (with insert for Egmont AJS 3)	15
62	Storyville SLP 27	IN SWEDEN 1950	15
62	Esquire 32-157	'BIRD' IS FREE	15

(see also Dizzy Gillespie & Charlie Parker, Sir Charles Thompson)

DAVID PARKER
71	Polydor 2460 101	DAVID PARKER (LP)	50

(see also Andwella's Dream)

DEAN PARKER & REDCAPS
62	Decca F 11555	Stormy Evening/Blue Eyes And Golden Hair	45

DYON PARKER
69	Marble Arch MAL 787	OUT ON THE HIGHWAY (LP)	20

EDDIE PARKER
55	Columbia SCM 5211	Far Away From Everybody/Bella Notte	8
56	Columbia DB 3804	Love Me As Though There Were No Tomorrow/Rich In Love	8

EULA PARKER
58	Oriole CB 1411	Silhouettes/Hedgehopper	20

(see also Frank Weir)

EVAN PARKER
75	Incus INCUS 19	SAXOPHONE SOLOS (LP)	40
78	Incus INCUS 27	MONOCEROS (LP)	30
80	Incus INCUS 39	SIX OF ONE (LP)	30
86	Incus INCUS 49	THE SNAKE DECIDES (LP)	50
89	Cadillac (no cat no)	COLLECTED SOLOS (4 x LP and cassette hand numbered to 200)	60

EVAN PARKER, DEREK BAILEY, HAN BENNINK
70	Incus INCUS 1	THE TOPOGRAPHY OF THE LUNGS (LP)	100

EVAN PARKER, BARRY GUY & PAUL LYTTON
83	Incus INCUS 42	TRACKS (LP)	40

EVAN PARKER & GEORGE LEWIS
80	Incus INCUS 35	FROM SAXOPHONE & TROMBONE (LP)	40

EVAN PARKER, GEORGE LEWIS, BARRY GUY & PAUL LYTTON
83	Incus INCUS 45	HOOK, DRIFT & SHUFFLE (LP)	50

EVAN PARKER & PAUL LYTTON
72	Incus INCUS 5	COLLECTIVE CALLS (URBAN) (TWO MICROPHONES) (LP)	40
75	Incus INCUS 14	AT THE UNITY THEATRE (LP)	40

(see also Derek Bailey & Evan Parker, Derek Bailey Evan Parker & Han Bennink)

FESS PARKER
57	Oriole CB 1378	Wringle Wrangle/Ballad Of John Colter	10

JIMMY PARKER
62	Top Rank JAR 608	We Gonna/No Word From Betty	10

(LITTLE) JUNIOR PARKER
61	Vogue V 9179	Stand By Me/I'll Forget About You (as Little Junior Parker)	30
62	Vogue V 9193	Mary Jo/Annie Get Your Yo-Yo (as Little Junior Parker)	30
66	Vocalion VP 9256	These Kind Of Blues (Parts 1 & 2)	40
66	Vocalion VP 9256	These Kind Of Blues (Parts 1 & 2) (DJ copy)	60
66	Vocalion VP 9275	Goodbye Little Girl/Walking The Floor Over You	30
67	Mercury SMCL 20097	LIKE IT IS (LP)	50
72	Groove Merchant GM 502	BLUE SHADOWS FALLING (LP)	15
73	Groove Merchant GM 2205	GOOD THINGS DON'T HAPPEN EVERY DAY (LP, with Jimmy McGriff)	15
73	Vogue LDM 30163	MEMORIAL (LP)	15
73	People PLEO 4	YOU DON'T HAVE TO BE BLACK TO LOVE THE BLUES (LP)	20

KEN PARKER
67	Island WI 3082	How Could I/SONNY BURKE: Choo Choo Train	45
67	Studio One SO 2001	See Them A-Come/MR FOUNDATION: Have A Good Time	35
68	Island WI 3096	Down Low/Sad Mood	45
68	Island WI 3105	Lonely Man/ERROL DUNKLEY: I Am Going Home	100
68	Giant GN 34	Change Is Gonna Come/VAL BENNETT: Jumping With Val	125
69	Bamboo BAM 1	My Whole World Is Falling Down/The Chokin' Kind	30
69	Amalgamated AMG 847	It's Alright/COBBS: One One	40
69	Amalgamated AMG 853	Only Yesterday/COBBS: Joe Gibbs Mood	30
70	Duke DU 79	I Can't Hide/TOMMY McCOOK: Kansas City	10
70	Unity UN 553	When You Were Mine/CLAREDONIANS: The Angels (song actually "The Angels Listened In")	8
71	Duke Reid DR 2504	Sugar Pantie (as Ken Parker & Tommy McCook; actually by Andy Capp)/ TOMMY McCOOK: All Afire	10
71	Duke Reid DR 2521	Jimmy Brown/Version	6
71	Big BG 332	Ain't Misbehaving/Genuine Love	6
72	Jackpot JP 805	Guilty/AGGROVATORS: Guilty (Version)	6
72	Pama PM 844	Shake It Loose/TOMMY McCOOK: Shake It Loose - Version (actually titled "Help Me Make It Through The Night")	6
72	Treasure Isle TI 7073	Help Me Make It Through The Night/TOMMY McCOOK & ALLSTARS (Version)	8
73	Dragon DRA 1003	Will The Circle Be Unbroken/DYNAMITES: Instrumental	6
73	Dragon DRA 1015	Say Wonderful Things/It's True	6
74	Attack ATT 8063	Kiss An Angel/TOMMY McCOOK: Inez	8
74	Attack ATT 8073	Count Your Blessings/Count Your Blessings (Version)	6
74	Trojan TRLS 80	JIMMY BROWN (LP)	18

(see also Lyrics, Scotty)

LEWIS PARKER
95	White JED1	B BOY ANTICS (EP, different recording to Bite It! version - first batch with a black and white sticker, later batch has coloured sticker)	50
96	Bite It! BITEDJ10	B BOY ANTICS (EP)	30
96	Bite It! BITE11	Rise/Visions Of Splendour/Sea Freestyle (12")	25
97	White LEWIS1	Wonderwall (7", 100 only)	40
98	Melankolic SADTDJ3	Shadows Of Autumn/101 Pianos (12")	10
00	M'lic LEWISTDJ1LC03098	THE OPTIONS (EP)	25
01	White SADTDJ13	It's All Happening Now/Schemes/What The Ancients Say (remixes) (EP, 50 copies only)	30
03	Dusty Vinyl DV1JEDI	Mr Parker's Siesta/Blood (12")	18
98	Melankolic SADT4	MASQUERADES AND SILHOUETTES (LP)	30
02	Melankolic LPSAD14	IT'S ALL HAPPENING NOW (LP)	30
06	Dusty Vinyl DVJEDI008	MASQUERADES AND SILHOUETTES INSTRUMENTALS (LP, 200 only with unreleased track)	40

RAYMOND PARKER
66	Sue WI 4024	Ring Around The Roses/She's Coming Home	40

ROBERT PARKER
66	Island WI 286	Barefootin'/Let's Go Baby (Where The Action Is)	20
66	Island WI 3008	Happy Feet/The Scratch	20
74	Island USA 001	Get Ta Steppin'/Get Right On Down	8
74	Contemporaries CS 9010	Barefootin'/I Caught You In A Lie	10
66	Island ILP 942	BAREFOOTIN' (LP)	80

(see also Huey 'Piano' Smith & Clowns)

SONNY PARKER
56	Vogue V 2392	My Soul's On Fire/Disgusted Blues	400
56	Vogue V 2392	My Soul's On Fire/Disgusted Blues (78)	100

(see also Lionel Hampton)

EDDIE PARKER (U.S.)
79	Grapevine GRP 119	Love You Baby (Parts 1 & 2) (in p/s)	15
79	Grapevine GRP 119	Love You Baby (Parts 1 & 2) (in p/s) (DJ copy)	20

WILLIE PARKER
67	President PT 171	You Got Your Finger In My Eye/I Live The Life I Love	15

MINT VALUE £

WINFIELD PARKER
72	Mojo 2093 019	Stop Her On Sight/I'm On My Way	8

GRAHAM PARKER
80	Stiff BUY 72	Stupefaction/Women In Charge (p/s)	5
80	Stiff BUY 72	Stupefaction/Paralysed (p/s)	10

PARKING LOT
69	Parlophone R 5779	Carpet Man/World Spinning Sadly	45

PARKINGSON'S LAW
72	RCA RCA 2291	Daughter Of Thunder And Lightning/I Need Your Loving And I Can't Let Go	8

JIMMY PARKINSON
56	Columbia SCM 5236	The Great Pretender/Hand In Hand	30
56	Columbia SCM 5267	Walk Hand In Hand/Cry Baby	10
56	Columbia DB 3808	Gina/A Lover's Quarrel	8
56	Columbia DB 3833	In The Middle Of The House/You To Me	8
57	Columbia DB 3876	But You/Together (You And I)	6
57	Columbia DB 3912	Round And Round/Whatever Lola Wants (Lola Gets)	6
57	Columbia 33S 1109	SOLO (10" LP)	20

BERNICE PARKS
55	Coral Q 72056	Lovin' Machine/Only Love Me	15

LLOYD PARKS
70	Harry J. HJ 6603	Feel A Little Better/I'll Be Your Man	10
72	Randy's RAN 524	Stars/Stars - Version	12
74	Fab FAB 273	Schooldays/Version	7
75	Cactus CT 75	Mafia/Mafia Version (Dub)	8

(see also L. Sparks)

SONNY PARKS
63	Warner Bros WB 100	New Boy In Town/Us Kids Have Got To Make Up Our Minds	10

VAN DYKE PARKS
66	MGM MGM 1301	Number Nine/Do What You Wanta	12
69	Warner Bros W(S) 1727	SONG CYCLE (LP)	35

PARLET
79	Casablanca CAL 2052	INVASION OF THE BOOTY SNATCHERS (LP)	15

(see also Parliament)

PARLIAMENT
71	Invictus INV 513	The Silent Boatman/Livin' The Life	10
72	Invictus INV 522	Come In Out Of The Rain/Little Ole Country Boy	8
75	Casablanca CBX 505	Up On The Down Stroke/Presence Of A Brain	8
76	Casablanca CBX 518	Tear The Roof Off The Sucker (Give Up The Funk)/P. Funk	5
77	Casablanca CAN 103	Tear The Roof Off The Sucker (Give Up The Funk)/Dr. Funkenstein/P. Funk	5
78	Casablanca CAN 115	Bop Gun/I've Been Watching You	5
78	Casablanca CAN 136	Aqua Boogie/Water Sign	5
79	Casablanca CAN 154	Deep/Flashlight	5
71	Invictus SVT 1004	OSMIUM (LP)	80
74	Casablanca NBLP 7002	UP ON THE DOWN STROKE (LP)	15

(see also Parliaments, Funkadelic, Parlet, Bootsy's Rubber Band, P-Funk Allstars)

PARLIAMENTS
67	Track 604 013	I Wanna Testify/I Can Feel The Ice Melting	30
69	Track 604 032	I Wanna Testify/I Can Feel The Ice Melting (reissue)	20

(see also Parliament, Funkadelic)

PARLOPHONE POPS ORCHESTRA
56	Parlophone R 4250	Giddy Up A Ding Dong/(We're Gonna) Rock Around The Clock	15

(see also Ron Goodwin)

PARLOUR BAND
72	Deram SDL 10	IS A FRIEND? (LP, laminated gatefold sleeve, white/red label)	500

CHRIS PARMENTER ORCHESTRA
66	Polydor 56107	Cul De Sac/Donkey	20

JACK PARNELL (ORCHESTRA)
53	Parlophone MSP 6009	Waltzing The Blues/Catherine Wheel (as Jack Parnell Band)	10
53	Parlophone MSP 6031	Night Train/Hawk Talks (as Jack Parnell & His Music Makers)	10
53	Parlophone MSP 6046	Cotton Tail/April In Paris	10
53	Parlophone MSP 6054	Dragnet/Fuller Bounce (as Jack Parnell & His Music Makers)	10
54	Parlophone MSP 6066	Route 66/The Creep	10
54	Parlophone MSP 6078	Skin Deep/Devil's Eyes (B-side with Dennis Hale)	20
54	Parlophone MSP 6094	Knock Out/Blowin' Wild (B-side with Dennis Hale)	12
54	Parlophone MSP 6102	The Bandit (with Dennis Hale)/Annie's Blues (with Annie Ross)	18
54	Parlophone MSP 6138	Sky Blue Shirt And Rainbow Tie/Trip To Mars	10
58	Parlophone R 4500	Topsy/Cha Cha Rock	8
59	HMV POP 630	Kansas City/The Golden Striker	10
60	Philips PB 1005	77 Sunset Strip/Teen Ride	10
64	Decca F 11958	The Kiss/The Hidden Truth	10
55	Parlophone GEP 8532	JACK PARNELL AND HIS ORCHESTRA (EP)	10
55	Parlophone GEP 8564	PARNELL ON PARADE (EP)	10
58	Parlophone GEP 8707	KICK OFF! (EP)	10
66	Hanover HR 1001	MY FAIR LADY (EP)	8
52	Decca LF 1065	THE JACK PARNELL QUARTET (10" LP)	25
58	Parlophone PMD 1053	TRIP TO MARS (10" LP)	80

(see also Dennis Hale)

CATHERINE PARR
65	Decca F 12210	You Belong To Me/He's My Guy	12

JACKIE PARRIS AND BIG YOUTH
79	Book Of Psalms BP 001	Let Him Try/Really Together (12")	15

BRIAN PARRISH

69	United Artists UP 35049	In Good Time (Love Chant)/I Wanna Go To Sleep	10

DEAN PARRISH

66	Stateside SS 531	Tell Her/Fall On Me	60
66	Stateside SS 531	Tell Her/Fall On Me (DJ copy)	100
66	Stateside SS 550	Turn On Your Lovelight/Determination	100
66	Stateside SS 550	Turn On Your Lovelight/Determination (DJ copy)	150
67	Stateside SS 580	Skate (Parts 1 & 2)	60
67	Stateside SS 580	Skate (Parts 1 & 2) (DJ copy)	100
75	UK USA 2	I'm On My Way/Watch Out	10
75	UK USA 2	I'm On My Way/Watch Out (DJ copy)	15
03	Kent TOWN 119	Broken Bottles And Sticks/MELBA MOORE: Magic Touch	8

PARRISH & GURVITZ

71	Regal Zono. SRZA 8506	PARRISH & GURVITZ (LP, textured gatefold sleeve)	35

(see also Baker Gurvitz Army, Three Man Army, Frampton's Camel)

GAYLORD PARRY

67	CBS 2685	I'm On The Way Up/I'm Coming Home	10

SAM PARRY

73	Argo ZDA 155	IF SADNESS COULD SING (LP)	250

PARSON & SMITH

72	Polydor 2058229	The Letter/When It Rains	20

BILL PARSONS & HIS ORCHESTRA

59	London HL 8798	The All American Boy/Rubber Dolly (78)	15

(see also Bobby Bare)

GENE PARSONS

74	Warner Bros K 46257	KINDLING (LP)	18

(see also Byrds, Flying Burrito Brothers)

GRAM PARSONS

73	Reprise K 14245	The New Soft Shoe/She	8
73	Reprise K 44228	GP (LP, gatefold sleeve)	30
74	Reprise K 54018	GRIEVOUS ANGEL (LP, with Emmylou Harris)	30
76	A&M AMLH 65478	SLEEPLESS NIGHTS (LP, with Flying Burrito Brothers & Emmylou Harris)	25
82	Sundown SDLP 003	GRAM PARSONS AND THE FALLEN ANGELS (LP, featuring Emmylou Harris)	15

(see also Byrds, Flying Burrito Brothers)

PARTICULAR PEOPLE

68	Big T BIG 105	Boys Cry/What's The Matter With Juliet	6

PARTISANS (1)

82	No Future OI 2	Police Story/Killing Machine (p/s, with lyric insert)	12
82	No Future OI 12	17 Years Of Hell/The Power And The Greed/Bastards In Blue (p/s)	10
83	Cloak & Dagger PART 1	Blind Ambition/Come Clean (p/s)	15
83	No Future PUNK 4	PARTISANS (LP)	22
84	Cloak & Dagger PARTLP 1	THE TIME WAS RIGHT (LP, with inner)	35

PARTISANS (2)

88	Hotwire HWS 863	Open Your Eyes/Partisan (p/s)	8

(see also Blades)

PARTNERS IN CRIME

84	Epic A 4803	Hold On/She's Got Eyes For You (p/s)	6
84	Epic TX 4803	Hold On (Extended)/She's Got Eyes For You (12", p/s)	8
85	Epic A 5040	Miracles/What You Gonna Do? (p/s)	6
85	Epic TX 5040	Miracles (Extended)/What You Gonna Do? (12", p/s)	8
85	Epic A 6170	Hollywood Dreams/She's Got Eyes For You (p/s)	7
85	Epic TX 6170	Hollywood Dreams (Extended)/She's Got Eyes For You (12", p/s)	10
85	Epic EPC 26356	ORGANISED CRIME (LP)	12

(see also Status Quo)

PART ONE

82	Paraworm	FUNERAL PARADE (EP)	12

DON PARTRIDGE

68	Columbia DB 8484	Top Man/We Have Ways Of Making You Laugh	5
69	Columbia DB 8538	Breakfast On Pluto/Stealin'	5
69	Columbia DB 8583	Colour My World/Homeless Bones	6
69	Columbia DB 8617	Going To Germany/Ask Me Why	6
70	Columbia DB 8723	We're All Happy Together/Following Your Fancy	5
60s	CFP CFP 001/002	SINGING SOHO STYLE (EP)	15
68	Columbia S(C)X 6280	DON PARTRIDGE (LP)	12

(see also Accolades)

PARTRIDGE FAMILY

72	Bell SBLL 143	THE PARTRIDGE FAMILY ALBUM (LP)	12
72	Bell SBLL 143	UP TO DATE (LP)	12
73	Bell BELLS 220	THE PARTRIDGE FAMILY NOTEBOOK (LP)	12
74	Bell BELLS 234	CROSSWORD PUZZLE (LP)	12

(see also David Cassidy)

MR. PARTRIDGE

80	Virgin V 2145	TAKEAWAY - THE LURE OF THE SALVAGE (LP)	12

(see also XTC, Three Wise Men, Dukes Of Stratosphere, Colonel)

PARTY BOYS

87	Epic 651230 0	He's Gonna Step On You Again/She's A Mystery (shaped picture disc)	12

(see also Status Quo)

PARVA

01	Mantra MNT 66	Heavy/Panic Attack (p/s, 500 only)	12

(see also Kaiser Chiefs)

PASADENA ROOF ORCHESTRA
78   CBS CBS 12-637   Pennies From Heaven/Back In Your Own Back Yard/Pennies From Heaven (10" p/s, 2nd side plays at 78 rpm) 15

PASHA
69   Liberty LBF 15199   Someone Shot The Lollipop Man/Pussy Willow Dragon 120
(see also Searchers)

JOE PASS
60s   Fontana 688 137 ZL   CATCH ME (LP) 20

PASSAGE
78   Object Music OMO 2   Love Song/The Competition/Slit Machine/New Kind Of Love (p/s) 10
80   Object Music OBJ 11   PINDROP (LP) 12
(see also Contact)

PASSENGERS
95   Island IS 625   Miss Sarajevo/One (live) (7", with poster in 12" card in PVC p/s) 10
95   Island CID 625   Miss Sarajevo/One (live)/Bottoms (Zoo Station Remix)/Via Davidoff (CD, with shrinkwrapped poster, withdrawn) 20
96   Island OST 3   Your Blue Room (CD, 1-track promo, card sleeve, export issue) 50
95   Island OST 2   ORIGINAL SOUNDCHAT 1 (2-CD, music & interview disc, fold-out digipaks, with cue sheet, promo only) 60
95   Island ILPS8043   ORIGINAL SOUNDTRACKS (LP) 40
(see also U2, Brian Eno)

PASSION BLADES
83   Caprice CAP 1   Living In A Lighthouse/Dub Version (no p/s) 8

PASSIONS (1)
58   Capitol CL 14874   My Aching Heart/Jackie Brown 80

PASSIONS (2)
59   Top Rank JAR 224   Just To Be With You/Oh Melancholy Me 60
60   Top Rank JAR 313   I Only Want You/This Is My Love 70

PASSIONS (3)
79   Soho SH5   Needles And Pills/Body And Soul 10
79   Fiction FICS 008   Hunted/Oh No, It's You 5
70   Fiction FIX 003 LP   MICHAEL & MIRANDA (LP, with gold embossed stamp "Limited Edition £2.99 Pay No More") 12

PAST AND PRESENT
79   Rook CUS 423   FIRST TIME OUT (LP, private pressing) 30

PAST SEVEN DAYS
86   4AD AD 102   Raindance/So Many Others/Nothing (p/s) 10

PASTELS
82   Whaam! WHAAM 005   Songs For Children: Heavens Above!/Tea Time Tales (p/s) 22
83   Rough Trade RT 137   I Wonder Why/Supposed To Understand (p/s) 18
84   Creation CRE 005   Something Going On/Stay With Me Till Morning (foldaround p/s in poly bag) 18
84   Creation CRE 011T   A Million Tears/Baby Honey/Surprise Me (12", p/s) 8
85   Villa 21 VILLA 3   Heavens Above!/Tea Time Tales/I Wonder Why (live)/Tea Time Tales (live) (p/s) 25
87   Glass PASTEL 001   Truck Train Tractor/Truck Train Tractor (2)/Breaking Lines//Crawl Babies/ Empty House/The Day I Got Certified (12", double pack) 8
90   Overground OVER 06   Heavens Above!/Tea Time Tales/Something Going On (demo)/ Until Morning Comes (demo) (p/s; 200 clear vinyl) 5
90   Overground OVER 06   Heavens Above!/Tea Time Tales/Something Going On (demo)/Until Morning Comes (demo) (p/s; 157 green vinyl) 6
93   Glass 12053   Comin' Through/Sit On It Mother/Lonely Planet Boy/Not Unloved (12") 10
87   Glass GLAL P021   UP FOR A BIT WITH THE PASTELS (LP, with inner) 20
(see also Buba & Shop Assistants, Jad Fair, Vaselines)

PASTEL SIX
63   London HLU 9651   The Cinnamon Cinder/Bandido 20

PASTORAL SYMPHONY
68   President PT 202   Love Machine/Spread A Little Love Around 20

PAT
71   Gas GAS 158   Teach Me (actually "Words Of Temptation" by Earl Lawrence)/RHYTHM RULERS: Sea Breeze (actually by Im & David) 8

PAT & MARIE
66   Ska Beat JB 234   I Try Not To Tell You/PAT RHODEN: Don't Blame It On Me 15
66   Ska Beat JB 235   You're Really Leaving/PAT RHODEN: Broken Heart 15
(see also Pat Rhoden)

PAT & ROXIE
65   Caribou CRC 2   Sing To Me/Things I Used To Do 7

PATCHES
72   Warner Bros K 16201   Living In America/Quicksand 8
75   Bradley BRAD 7516   Telltale/Chug-A-Lug 5

PATCHWORK
72   Decca FR 13346   Laughing Sam (On The Phone)/Afrodisiac 40

JOHNNY PATE ORCHESTRA
58   Parlophone 4437   I'm Stepping Out Of The Picture/Muskeeta 12
59   Parlophone PMD 1057   JAZZ GOES IVY LEAGUE (10" LP) 12
59   Parlophone PMD 1072   SWINGIN' FLUTE (10" LP) 12
60s   MGM   OUTRAGEOUS (LP) 18
73   Probe SPB 1077   SHAFT IN AFRICA (LP, soundtrack, with Four Tops) 20
74   ABC ABCL 5035   SHAFT IN AFRICA (LP, soundtrack, reissue) 12

KELLEE PATERSON
76   Mint CHEW 10   I'm Gonna Love You Just A Little More Baby/You Are So Beautiful.....................60

PAMELA PATERSON
72   Polydor 2001 278   Finally (Theme From 'Gumshoe')/OLYMPIC STUDIO CONCERT ORCHESTRA: Music From 'Gumshoe' (p/s) 20

PATHETIX
78   No Records NO 001   Aleister Crowley/Don't Touch My Machine/Snuffed It (p/s, with insert).......................30
79   TJM TJM 12   THE PATHETIX EP (no p/s) 25

PATHFINDERS
64   Decca F 12038   I Love You Caroline/Something I Can Always Do..18

PATHFINDERS
64   Hayton SP 138/139   What Do You Do/What'd I Say (private pressing)..20

PATHFINDERS
65   Parlophone R 5372   Don't You Believe It/Castle Of Love 20
(see also [White] Trash, Poets)

PATHWAY TO YOUR MIND
68   Major Minor SMLP 19   PREPARING THE MIND AND BODY FOR MEDITATION (LP, spoken word).........................25

PATIENCE & PRUDENCE
56   London HLU 8321   Tonight You Belong To Me/A Smile And A Ribbon (Gold label)).............................30
56   London HLU 8321   Tonight You Belong To Me/A Smile And A Ribbon (Silver label) 15
57   London HLU 8369   Gonna Get Along Without Ya Now/The Money Tree (Gold label)...........................30
57   London HLU 8369   Gonna Get Along Without Ya Now/The Money Tree (Silver label) 15
57   London HL 7017   Gonna Get Along Without Ya Now/The Money Tree (export issue) 20
57   London HLU 8425   Dreamer's Bay/We Can't Sing Rhythm And Blues 15
57   London HLU 8493   You Tattletale/Very Nice Is Bali Bali 15
58   London HLU 8773   Tom Thumb's Tune/Golly Oh Gee 8
57   London REU 1087   A SMILE AND A SONG (EP) 40

LEON PATILLO
70s   Maranatha MM 0049   DANCE CHILDREN, DANCE (LP) 18
70s   Myrrh MYR 1136   LIVE EXPERIENCE (LP) 18

SANDY & CAROLINE PATON
60   Topic TOP 57   HUSH LITTLE BABY (EP) 10
(see also Beat Brothers, Tony Sheridan & Beat Brothers)

BOBBY PATRICK BIG SIX
64   Decca F 11898   Shake It Easy Baby/Wildwood Days 40
64   Decca F 12030   Monkey Time/Sweet Talk Me Baby 30
64   Decca DFE 8570   TEENBEAT 3 (FROM STAR CLUB, HAMBURG) (EP)...120

DAN PATRICK
67   Stateside SS 2004   Tiger Lee/Call Of The Wild 10

KENTRICK PATRICK
63   Island WI 066   Man To Man/ROLAND ALFONSO: Blockade (B-side actually "Hit And Run") 30
63   Island WI 079   Don't Stay Out Late/Forever And Ever 30
63   Island WI 104   The End Of The World/Little Princess 25
63   Island WI 119   Golden Love/Beyond 40
64   Island WI 132   Take Me To The Party/I'm Sorry 25
64   Island WI 140   I Am Wasting Time/RANDY'S GROUP: Royal Charley 120
(see also Lord Creator)

PATRICK & LLOYD
70   Big Shot BI 550   Return Of The Pollock/PROPHETS: Concorde...25
(see also Lloyd & Prophets)

PATRIOTS
66   Fontana TF 650   Prophet/I'll Be There...20

PATRON OF THE ARTS
66   Page One POF 012   The True Patron Of The Arts/Eleanor Rigby (USA release credits it as Queen City Show Band) 60

PATSY
68   Doctor Bird DB 1113   A Man Is Two Faced/LENNIE HIBBERT & COUNT OSSIE: Pure Soul 120
68   Doctor Bird DB 1122   Little Flea/The Retreat Song 45
68   High Note HS012   We Were Lovers/DELANO STEWART : Give Me A Chance.....................................35
(see also Patsy Todd, Derrick & Patsy, Stranger & Patsy, Emotions)

PATSY & PEGGY
70   Hot Rod HR 107   Dog Your Woman/Strictly Invitation..10

BRIAN PATTEN
70   Caedmon TC 1300   BRIAN PATTEN (LP)..20
76   Tangent TGS 116   VANISHING TRICK (LP)..20
77   Argo ZSW 607   SLY CORMORANT (LP) 12
(see also Liverpool Scene, Roger McGough & Brian Patten)

PATTERN PEOPLE
68   MGM MGM 1429   Love Is A Lover/Loving To Be Loved 8

PATTERNS IN PERU
86   Vernon Bros/WEA   This Is The Night/Playing Games 60

BOBBY PATTERSON (& MUSTANGS)
68   Pama PM 735   Broadway Ain't Funky No More/I Met My Match (with Mustangs)........................10
68   Pama PM 743   The Good Ol' Days/Don't Be So Mean 15
68   Pama PM 754   Busy Busy Bee/Sweet Taste Of Love (with Mustangs) 20
69   Pama PM 763   T.C.B. Or T.Y.A./What A Wonderful Night For Love (with Mustangs).....................20
69   Pama PM 773   My Thing Is Your Thing/Keep It In The Family 20
72   Action ACT 4604   I'm In Love With You/Married Lady 80
77   Contempo 2115   I Got To Get Over/If He Hadn't Slipped And Got Caught 20
72   Mojo 2092 037   How Do You Spell Love/She Don't Have To See You 10

DON PATTERSON
64   Transatlantic PR 733   THE EXCITING NEW ORGAN SOUND OF (LP) 12

Manley PATTERSON

| 67 | Transatlantic PR 7349 | HIP CAKE WALK (LP) | 18 |
| 67 | Transatlantic PR 7430 | SATISFACTION! (LP) | 12 |

MANLEY PATTERSON
| 72 | Pama Supreme PS 337 | I Stayed Away Too Long/Country Boy | 5 |

MARY-ANNE PATTERSON
| 70 | Joy JOYS 162 | ME (LP) | 300 |

OTTILIE PATTERSON
55	Decca F 10472	I Hate A Man Like You/Reckless Blues (with Chris Barber's Jazz Band)	10
55	Decca F 10621	Weeping Willow Blues/Nobody Knows You When You're Down And Out	10
57	Pye 7N 15109	Kay-Cee Rider/I Love You Baby	10
58	Pye Jazz 7NJ 2015	Jailhouse Blues/Beale Street Blues	10
58	Pye Jazz 7NJ 2025	Trombone Cholly/Lawdy, Lawdy Blues	10
61	Columbia DB 4760	Blueberry Hill/I'm Crazy 'Bout My Baby	10
62	Columbia DB 4834	I Hate Myself/Come On Baby	12
63	Columbia DB 7140	Jealous Heart/Won't Be Long	10
63	Columbia DB 7208	Baby Please Don't Go/I Feel So Good (with Sonny Boy Williamson)	40
65	Columbia DB 7332	Tell Me Where Is Fancy/Oh Me What Eyes	10
69	Marmalade 598 016	Spring Song/Sound Of The Door As It Closes	25
69	Marmalade 598 020	Bitterness Of Death/Spring Song	25
55	Jazz Today JTE 102	THAT PATTERSON GIRL (EP)	10
56	Decca DFE 6303	BLUES (EP)	15
56	Pye Jazz Today NJE 1023	THAT PATTERSON GIRL VOL. 2 (EP)	12
59	Columbia SEG 7915	OTTILIE (EP)	8
60	Columbia SEG 7998	SWINGS THE IRISH (EP)	10
59	Pye NPL 18028	OTTILIE'S IRISH NIGHT (LP)	15
69	Marmalade 608 011	3000 YEARS WITH OTTILIE (LP)	100
69	Polydor 2384 031	SPRING SONG (LP)	35

(see also Chris Barber)

ROBERT PATTERSON SINGERS
| 60s | United Artists UAS 29003 | THE SOUL OF GOSPEL (LP) | 25 |
| 65 | Fontana 688 516 ZL | I'M SAVED (LP) | 18 |

PATTERSONS
68	CBS 63335	TRAVELLING PEOPLE (LP)	12
69	CBS M 63532	AGAIN (LP, mono)	18
69	CBS 63522	AGAIN (LP, stereo)	15
70	CBS 5083	I Can Fly/An Cailin Deas	15

PATTERSON'S PEOPLE
| 66 | Mercury MF 913 | Shake Hands With The Devil/Deadly Nightshade | 35 |

PATTIE
| 69 | Columbia DB 8542 | Gravitation/Let The Music Start | 12 |

PATTI & PATETTES
| 75 | Dart ART 2053 | Bill/It's My Party | 8 |
| 76 | United Artists UP 36077 | Summer Heartbreak/Too Much | 12 |

HUBERT PATTISON
| 66 | Pye 7N 17207 | Bare Back Rider/The Baby 1 & 2 Problem | 5 |
| 67 | Fontana TF 859 | My Home's In My Pocket/Saturday Morning Bride | 10 |

LITTLE JOHN PATTISON
| 64 | Giv-A-Disc LYN 510 | Needles And Pins/All My Loving (flexidisc with Giv-A-Disc booklet) | 10 |

(MIKE) PATTO
66	Columbia DB 8091	Can't Stop Talking About My Baby/Love (as Mike Patto)	100
74	Goodear EAR 106	Sitting In The Park/Get Up And Dig It (as Mike Patto)	10
70	Vertigo 6360 016	PATTO (LP, textured gatefold sleeve, large swirl label)	200
71	Vertigo 6360 032	HOLD YOUR FIRE (LP, 3-flap gatefold, small swirl label)	400
72	Island ILPS 9210	ROLL 'EM SMOKE 'EM PUT ANOTHER LINE OUT (LP, pink rim/palm tree label)	50

(see also Bo Street Runners, Breakaways, Boxer, News, Chicago Line, Timebox, Felder's Orioles, Steve York, Centipede, Grimms, Spooky Tooth, V.I.P.s)

ALEXANDER PATTON
| 66 | Capitol CL 15461 | A Lil Lovin' Sometimes/No More Dreams | 250 |
| 66 | Capitol CL 15461 | A Lil Lovin' Sometimes/No More Dreams (DJ copy) | 350 |

CHARLIE PATTON
| 50s | Heritage REU 4 | CHARLIE PATTON (EP, 99 only) | 60 |

JOHN PATTON
| 64 | Blue Note 45-1889 | I'll Never Be Free/Along Came John | 8 |

PATTY & EMBLEMS
| 64 | Stateside SS 322 | Mixed Up Shook Up Girl/Ordinary Guy | 50 |
| 64 | Stateside SS 322 | Mixed Up Shook Up Girl/Ordinary Guy (DJ copy) | 100 |

PATTY FLABBIE'S COUGHED ENGINE
| 69 | Stateside SS 2136 | Billy's Got A Goat/Tin Can Eater | 6 |

PAUL
| 65 | Polydor BM 56045 | Will You Follow Me/Head Death | 80 |

(see also Jimmy Page)

ANDREW PAUL
| 85 | Fashion FAD 038 | Hustle Them A Hustle/Bad Boys (12") | 25 |
| 85 | Y&D YDD 0126 | Under Me Sensima/Can't Take It No Longer (12", with the Offbeat Posse) | 30 |

ANDY PAUL
| 84 | Proto ENA 117 | Anna Mari-Elena (Greek)/Anna Mari-Elena (English)/Bistepsememe (p/s, all copies mispressed with Greek version of A-side included twice) | 12 |

BILLY PAUL
| 73 | Epic EPC 65351 | 360 DEGREES OF BILLY PAUL (LP) | 15 |
| 73 | Epic EPC 65456 | EBONY WOMAN (LP) | 15 |

74	Phil. Intl. PIR 65861	WAR OF THE GODS (LP, gatefold sleeve)	15

BUNNY PAUL
54	Columbia SCM 5102	New Love/You'll Never Leave My Side	10
54	Columbia SCM 5112	Such A Night/I'm Gonna Have Some Fun	20
54	Columbia SCM 5131	Lovey Dovey/Answer The Call	20
54	Columbia SCM 5151	You Came A Long Way From St. Louis/You Are Always In My Heart	12
55	Capitol CL 14279	Please Have Mercy (On A Fool)/These Are The Things We'll Share	12
55	Capitol CL 14304	Leave My Heart Alone/Two Castanets	12
55	Capitol CL 14368	Song Of The Dreamer/For The Very First Time	10

DARLENE PAUL
64	Capitol CL 15344	Act Like Nothing Happened/Little Bit Of Heaven	30

DEREK PAUL
73	Youngblood YB 1006	Drugtaker/Riverboat	8

DON PAUL
68	RCA 1666	Wise/Ways Of The World	12

EUGENE PAUL
70	Pama Supreme PS 303	Don't Let The Tears Fall/Another Saturday Night	6
70	Pama Supreme PS 305	I Found A Man In My Bed/So Many Things	6
71	Pama Supreme PS 317	Farewell My Darling/Whole Lot Of Woman	6
71	Pama Supreme PS 329	Somebody's Changing My Sweet Baby's Mind/Hard Minded Neighbour	6
72	Pama PM 838	Beautiful Sunday/Take Care Son	6
72	Pama Supreme PS 357	I'll Take You There/Beautiful Baby	6
73	Pama Supreme PS 382	Power To All Our Friends/RANNY WILLIAMS ALLSTARS: Wicked And Dreadful	7

EUGENE PAUL & PILOTS
70	Torpedo TOR 17	Sugar Dumpling/I May Dwell	7

FRANKIE PAUL
85	Greensleeves GRED 189	Fools Fighting/Fighting Dub (12")	12
85	Tonos TON 007	Shining Star/If I Am Wrong (12")	30

JASON PAUL
69	Pye 7N 17710	Shine A Little Light Into My Room/Paradise Pudding	20

(see also Svensk)

JOHN E. PAUL
67	Decca F 12685	Prince Of Players/I Wanna Know (DJ copy with curved Decca logo inverted matrix)	200
67	Decca F 12685	Prince Of Players/I Wanna Know (Boxed Decca logo, inverted matrix)	100
67	Decca F 12685	Prince Of Players/I Wanna Know (Matrix number 41387 correct way up)	20

LES PAUL (& MARY FORD)
54	Capitol CL 14185	Mandolino/Whither Thou Goest	15
55	Capitol CL 14212	Mister Sandman/That's What I Like	20
55	Capitol CL 14233	Someday Sweetheart/Song In Blue	12
55	Capitol CL 14300	No Letter Today/Genuine Love	12
55	Capitol CL 14342	Goodbye My Love/Hummingbird	12
56	Capitol CL 14502	Alabamy Bound/Texas Lady	8
56	Capitol CL 14521	Magic Melody/Amukiriki (The Lord Willing)	5
56	Capitol CL 14534	Theme From "The Threepenny Opera" (Moritat) (as Les Paul)/Nuevo Laredo	5
56	Capitol CL 14577	Send Me Some Money/Say The Words I Love To Hear	5
56	Capitol CL 14593	San Antonio Rose/Cimarron (Roll On)	5
56	Capitol CL 14665	Runnin' Wild/Blow The Smoke Away	5
57	Capitol CL 14710	Cinco Robles (Five Oaks)/Ro-Ro-Robinson	5
57	Capitol CL 14776	Strollin' Blues/I Don't Want You No More	5
57	Capitol CL 14809	(I'm Keeping My Heart Away From) Fire/A Pair Of Fools	5
58	Capitol CL 14839	Bewitched/The Night Of The Fourth (as Les Paul solo)	5
58	Philips PB 873	Put A Ring On My Finger/Fantasy	5
58	Philips PB 882	Jealous Heart/Big Eyed Girl	5
59	Philips PB 906	At The Sav-A-Penny Super Store/All I Need Is You	5
55	Capitol EAP1 9121	PRESENTING LES PAUL AND MARY FORD (EP)	10
55	Capitol EAP1 540	SITTING ON TOP OF THE WORLD (EP)	10
60	Capitol EAP1 20048	MR AND MRS MUSIC (EP)	10
61	Capitol EAP1 20145	NOLA (EP)	10
65	Capitol EAP1 20540	JAZZ ME BLUES (EP)	10
51	Capitol LC 6514	THE NEW SOUND (LP, 10")	20
53	Capitol LC 6581	THE NEW SOUND VOL. 2 (LP, 10")	20
54	Capitol T 416	HIT MAKERS (LP)	15
55	Capitol LC 6701	LES AND MARY (LP, 10")	20
55	Capitol LC 6704	LES AND MARY PART 2 (LP, 10")	15
56	Capitol LC 6806	BYE BYE BLUES! (LP, 10")	15

LYN PAUL
74	Polydor 2058 472	Sail The Summer Winds/Lay Me Down (with John Barry)	7
75	Polydor 2383 340	GIVE ME LOVE (LP)	15

(see also Nocturnes)

PAUL RICH
62	Embassy WB 494	Rock-A-Hula-Baby/Walk On By	5

RIM D. PAUL
68	Philips BF 1737	Thousand Hours/Downstairs To Meet Her	5

SHELLEY PAUL
69	Jay Boy BOY 10	Clowns Are Coming In/Take Me To Your Heart	6

PAULA & JETLINERS
66	Rainbow RAI 102	The Great Pretender/The Legend Of The Man From U.N.C.L.E.	15
66	Rainbow RAI 105	I Know Someday/Something On My Mind (B-side with Carols)	8

PAUL & LINDA
69	Page One POF 140	You're Taking My Bag/When I Hear Your Name	10

PAUL & PAULA
63	Philips 304 012 BF	Hey Paula/Bobby Is The One	5

PAUL AND RITCHIE & CRYING SHAMES

63	Philips 304 016 BF	Young Lovers/Ba-hey-be	5
63	Philips BF 1256	First Quarrel/School Is Thru	5
63	Philips BF 1269	Something Old, Something New/Flipped Over You	5
63	Philips BF 1281	First Day Back At School/A Perfect Pair	5
64	Philips BF 1380	No Other Baby/Too Dark To See	7
63	Philips BBE 12639	YOUNG LOVERS (EP)	20
63	Philips 652 026BL	SING FOR YOUNG LOVERS (LP)	25
63	Philips BL 7573	WE GO TOGETHER (LP)	25
63	Philips BL 7587	HOLIDAY FOR TEENS (LP)	20

PAUL AND RITCHIE & CRYING SHAMES

| 66 | Decca F 12483 | September In The Rain/Come On Back (more common demos are worth, £80) | 120 |

(see also Cryin' Shames, Gary Walker & Rain)

PAULETTE (WILLIAMS)

| 68 | Major Minor MM 565 | One Love In My Heart/Must We Say Goodbye | 6 |
| 73 | Summit SUM 8543 | Every Day Is The Same Kind Of Thing/ SHORTY PERRY: The Sweat Of Your Brow | 6 |

(see also Paulette & Gee)

PAULETTE & DELROY

| 63 | Island WI 120 | Little Lover/Lovin' Baby | 20 |

(see also Paulette, Paulette & Gee)

PAULETTE & GEE

| 70 | G.G. GG 4506 | Hold On Tight/G.G. ALL STARS: Tight Version | 8 |

(see also Paulette, Sister, Winston Wright)

PAULETTE SISTERS

55	Capitol CL 14294	Dream Boat/Leave My Honey Be	12
55	Capitol CL 14310	Ring-A-Dang-A-Doo/Lonely One	12
55	Capitol CL 14347	You Win Again/Mama, El Baion	12

PAULINE (& BROWN SUGAR)

| 80 | Studio WE 706 | I Am So Proud/NATTY LOCKS: Studio 16 Workshop (12") | 25 |
| 80 | Isis 1 | Lion, Me And My Dread/Revelation Side (12") | 40 |

(see also Brown Sugar)

PAUL'S DISCIPLES

| 65 | Decca F 12081 | See That My Grave Is Kept Clean/Sixteen Tons | 35 |

PAUL'S TROUBLES

| 67 | Ember EMB S 233 | You'll Find Out/You've Got Something | 25 |

PAUPERS

68	Verve Forecast VS 1514	Think I Care/White Song	15
69	Verve Forecast VS 1520	Southdown Road/Numbers	15
68	Verve Forecast (S)VLP 6017	ELLIS ISLAND (LP, mono/stereo)	30

(see also Lighthouse)

PAVEMENT

92	Big Cat ABB 35S	Trigger Cut/Sue Me Jack/So Stark (You're A Skyscraper) (p/s)	8
94	Big Cat ABB 55S	Cut Your Hair/Camera/Stare (p/s)	6
94	Big Cat UK ABB 55T	Cut Your Hair/Camera/Stare (uncredited track) (12")	12
95	Big Cat ABB 86S	Rattled By La Rush/False Skorpion/Easily Fooled (p/s)	5
95	Big Cat ABB 91S	Father To A Sister Of Thought/Kris Kraft/Mussle Rock Is A Horse In Transition (p/s)	6
96	Big Cat ABB 110 S	Give It A Day/Gangsters & Pranksters/Saganaw/I Love Perth (p/s)	10
92	Big Cat ABB 38P	WATERY, DOMESTIC (12" EP, picture disc, stickered poly sleeve)	12
91	Big Cat ABB 34	SLANTED AND ENCHANTED (LP, with lyric sheet)	30
94	Big Cat ABB 56L	CROOKED RAIN CROOKED RAIN (LP, with inner sleeve, some with free 7": "Haunt You Down"/"Jam Kids")	40
95	Big Cat LC 5661	WOWEE ZOWEE (2xLP, 3-sided gatefold cover)	30

RITA PAVONE

63	RCA 1354	Il Ballo Del Mattone Part 1/Part 2	10
64	RCA RCA 1415	Remember Me/Just Once More	6
66	RCA RCA 1553	Heart/The Man Who Makes The Music	10
66	RCA RCA 1561	You Only You/Before You Go	5
73	Decca F 13462	He (Didn't Remember My Name)/(Vado Via) Last Summer	6
64	RCA RD 7657	RITA PAVONE (mono)	15
64	RCA SF 7657	RITA PAVONE (stereo)	18

PAX EXTERNAL

| 71 | Decca F 13167 | A Second Chance Mr. Jones/You See Him As Your Brother | 6 |

GARY PAXTON

| 62 | Liberty LIB 55485 | Stop Twistin' Baby/Alley Oop Was A Two Dab Man | 15 |

(see also Skip & Flip)

TOM PAXTON

66	Elektra EKSN 45001	The Last Thing On My Mind/Goin' To The Zoo	20
66	Elektra EKSN 45003	One Time And One Time Only/Bottle Of Wine	5
67	Elektra EKSN 45006	Leaving London/All The Way Home	5
69	Elektra EKSN 45021	Jennifer's Rabbit/The Marvellous Toy	5
69	Elektra EKSN 45049	Victoria Dines Alone/Clarissa Jones	5
67	Elektra EPK 802	TOM PAXTON (EP)	20
66	Elektra EKL 277/EKS 7277	RAMBLIN' BOY (LP, U.K. pressing in U.S. sleeve)	12
66	Elektra EKL 298/EKS 7298	AIN'T THAT NEWS (LP, U.K. pressing in U.S. sleeve)	20
66	Elektra EKL 317/EKS 7317	OUTWARD BOUND (LP)	12
68	Elek. EKL 4019/EKS 74019	MORNING AGAIN (LP, red label)	12

DAVEY PAYNE & MEDIUM WAVE

| 69 | Ember EMB S 265 | Walk In The Sunshine/Looking Towards The Sky (p/s) | 30 |

FREDA PAYNE

62	HMV POP 1091	He Who Laughs Last (Desafinado)/Slightly Out Of Tune	20
70	Invictus INV 502	Band Of Gold/ The Easiest Way To Fall	6
70	Invictus INV 505	Deeper And Deeper/Unhooked Generation	6
71	Invictus INV 509	Cherish What Is Dear To You (While It's Near To You)/ The World Don't Owe You A Thing	6

71	Invictus INV 512	Rock Me In The Cradle (Of Your Lovin' Arms)/ Now Is The Time To Say Goodbye	6
71	Invictus INV 515	Bring Home The Boys/Odds And Ends	6
71	Invictus INV 518	You've Got To Love Somebody/Mama's Gone	8
72	Invictus INV 520	You Brought Me Joy/Suddenly It's Yesterday	6
72	Invictus INV 526	Unhooked Generation/Come Back	5
73	Invictus INV 529	I Shall Not Be Moved/Thru' The Memory Of My Mind	5
73	Invictus INV 533	Band Of Gold/The Easiest Way To Fall (reissue, withdrawn)	30
75	ABC ABC 4087	You/Lost In Love	5
70	Invictus SVT 1001	BAND OF GOLD (LP)	12
71	Invictus SVT 1005	CONTACT (LP)	12
70s	MGM 2351 004	FREDA PAYNE (LP)	12

JACKIE PAYNE
77	Barak 4	I Found Myself/Instrumental	25

LEON PAYNE
64	London HA-B 8136	AMERICANA (LP)	12

LAWRENCE PAYTON
74	ABC 4021	Tell Me You Love Me/Instrumental	15

(see also the Four Tops)

PAZ
79	Magnus 2	PAZ AT CHICHESTER (LP)	25
83	Spotlight SPJ 507	KANDEEN LOVE SONG (LP)	12

(see also Lol Coxhill)

P BROTHERS
01	White (Heavy Bronx) PBHB 01	HEAVY BRONX EXPERIENCE VOL. 1 (EP)	40
01	White (Heavy Bronx) PBHB 002	HEAVY BRONX EXPERIENCE VOL. 2 (EP)	20

PC LTD
69	Fontana TF 1032	Sunny Was A Fool/Here We Come	6

DAVE PEABODY
73	Village Thing VTS 22	PEABODY HOTEL (LP, with insert)	50

DAVE PEACE QUARTET
69	Saga FID 2155	GOOD MORNING MR. BLUES (LP)	15

(see also Birmingham)

DIXIE PEACH AND THE OFFBEAT POSSE
86	Jah Tubby's JT 018	Slaughter/Slaughter Mix (12")	25
87	Y&D YDD 0102	Raggamuffin And Rambo/Version (12")	10

PEACHES
02	Kitty Yo XLLP 163	TEACHES OF PEACHES (5x7")	25
03	Kitty Yo XLLP 171	FATHERFUCKER (LP, pink vinyl)	18

PEACHES & HERB
67	CBS 202509	Let's Fall In Love/We're In This Thing Together	30
67	CBS 202509	Let's Fall In Love/We're In This Thing Together (DJ copy)	40
67	CBS 2711	Close Your Eyes/I Will Watch Over You	8
67	CBS 2866	For Your Love/I Need Your Love So Desperately	25
67	CBS 2866	For Your Love/I Need Your Love So Desperately (DJ copy)	40
67	Direction 58-3096	Love Is Strange/Two Little Kids	10
68	Direction 58-3415	Let It Be Me/I Need Your Love So Desperately	10
68	Direction 58-3548	United/Thank You	8
68	Direction 58-3829	Let's Make A Promise/Me And You	10
69	Direction 58-4085	When He Touches Me/Thank You	7
70	Direction 58-4909	Satisfy My Hunger/It's Just A Game, Love	8
70	Direction 58-5249	Soothe Me With Your Love/We're So Much In Love	8
71	CBS 5249	Soothe Me With Your Love/We're So Much In Love (reissue)	6
77	Epic EPC 4903	Soothe Me With Your Love/Satisy My Hunger (coloured vinyl)	6
67	CBS 62966	LET'S FALL IN LOVE (LP)	15
67	CBS 63119	FOR YOUR LOVE (LP)	15
68	Direction 8-63263	GOLDEN DUETS (LP)	15

PEACOCK
71	Famous FAM 109	Sun Was In Your Eyes/Just A Lonely Man	20

ANNETTE PEACOCK
72	RCA SF 8255	I'M THE ONE (LP)	22
79	Aura	LIVE IN PARIS (LP)	18

ANNETTE PEACOCK & PAUL BLEY
73	Freedom 2383 105	DUAL UNITY (LP)	15

(see also Paul Bley, Bley-Peacock Synthesiser Show, Annette Peacock)

ROGER PEACOCK
65	Columbia DB7764	Everybody's Talking About My Baby/Times Have Changed	20

TREVOR PEACOCK
61	Decca F 11414	I Didn't Figure On Him To Come Back/Can I Walk You Home	22

PEANUT
65	Pye 7N 15901	Thank Goodness For The Rain/I'm Not Sad	10
65	Pye 7N 15963	Home Of The Brave/I Wanna Hear It Again	30
66	Columbia DB 8032	I'm Waiting For The Day/Someone's Gonna Be Sorry	22
67	Columbia DB 8104	I Didn't Love Him Anyway/Come Tomorrow	20

(see also Katie Kissoon, Ragdolls U.K.)

PEANUT BUTTER CONSPIRACY
67	CBS 2981	It's A Happening Thing/Twice Is Life	15
68	CBS 3543	Turn On A Friend/Captain Sandwich	10
69	London HLH 10290	Back In L.A./Have A Little Faith	10
68	CBS 63277	THE GREAT CONSPIRACY (LP)	40
80s	Drop Out DO 2000	TURN ON A FRIEND (LP)	12

PEANUTS
71	Philips 6006087	Goldendays/Headin Straight For You	10

BOB PEARCE BLUES BAND
74	Westwood WRS 040	LET'S GET DRUNK AGAIN (LP)	18
79	Forest Tracks FT 3015	COLOUR BLIND (LP)	12

(see also Brother Bung)

PEARL JAM
92	Epic 657 572-7	Alive/Once (white/red vinyl p/s)	12
92	Epic 657 572-6	Alive/Once/Wash (12", poster p/s)	10
92	Epic 657 867-7	Even Flow/Oceans (p/s)	5
92	Epic 657 857-8	Even Flow/Dirty Frank/Oceans (12", white vinyl, p/s)	15
92	Epic 658 258-7	Jeremy/Alive (live) (white vinyl, p/s)	10
92	Epic 658 258-6	Jeremy/Alive (live)/Footsteps (12", picture disc, with card insert)	25
92	Epic 658 258-2	Jeremy/Yellow Ledbetter/Alive (live) (CD, picture disc)	15
93	Epic 660 020-6	Daughter/Blood (Live)/Yellow Ledbetter (Live) (12", ltd. ed. poster sleeve)	15
93	Epic 659 795-6	Go/Alone/Elderly Woman Behind The Counter In A Small Town (Acoustic) (12", with free cassette [plays 'Animal' (Live)])	12
93	Epic 660 020-7	Daughter/Blood (live) (red vinyl p/s)	5
94	Epic 660 441-7	Dissident/Rearviewmirror (live) (stickered poster p/s)	5
92	Epic 468 884-0	TEN (LP, picture disc)	20
94	Epic 477861-1	VITALOGY (LP, embossed gatefold sleeve)	20
96	Epic 484448-1	NO CODE (LP, gatefold sleeve, inners, 8 cards)	25
98	Epic 489365-1	YIELD (LP, die-cut sleeve, inner sleeve)	25
98	Epic 429859-1	LIVE ON TWO LEGS (2-LP, stickered gatefold sleeve with inner sleeves)	40
00	Sony E263665	BINAURAL (2 x LP, 3-part fold out sleeve with booklet)	20
02	Epic 510000-1	RIOT ACT (2-LP, gatefold sleeve, inner sleeves)	80

(see also Temple Of The Dog)

PEARLS BEFORE SWINE
68	Fontana STL 5503	BALAKLAVA (LP)	30
68	Fontana STL 5505	ONE NATION UNDERGROUND (LP)	25
69	Reprise RSLP 6364	THESE THINGS TOO (LP)	20
70	Reprise RSLP 6405	THE USE OF ASHES (LP)	20
71	Reprise RSLP 6442	CITY OF GOLD (LP)	20
71	Reprise RSLP 6467	BEAUTIFUL LIES YOU COULD LIVE (LP)	15

PEARLS (1)
72	Bell BELL 1217	Third Finger, Left Hand/Little Lady Love Me	5
72	Bell 1372	Wizard Of Love/Playing Around	6
72	Bell BELL 1254	You Came, You Saw, You Conquered/Sing Out To Me	5
74	Bell BELL 1352	Guilty/I'll Say It Over Again	5
74	Bell 1394	Doctor Love/Pass It On	6

(see also Bud Ashton)

PEARLS (2)
75	Private Stock PVT39	The Cheater/I'm Gonna Steal Your Heart Away	8

BUSTER PEARSON BAND
73	Action ACT 4612	Big Funky/Pretty Woman	15
75	K&B 5516	Take It Easy/Instrumental	6

DUKE PEARSON
68	Polydor 583 723	ANGEL EYES (LP)	120

JOHNNY PEARSON
62	Oriole CB 1721	Doh La La/Johnny's Tune	7
62	Parlophone R 4977	Theme From The L-Shaped Room Part 1/Part 2	7
66	Columbia DB 7851	Rat Catcher's Theme/Weaver's Green Theme	20
73	BBC RESL 6	Spy Trap/Playgirl (with Quator)	10
70	Aristocrat AR 103	SOUNDS EXTRAVAGANZA (LP)	20

(see also John Barry Seven)

KEITH PEARSON'S RIGHT HAND BAND
76	Eron ER 014	KEITH PEARSON'S RIGHT HAND BAND (LP)	12

RONNIE PEARSON
58	HMV POP 489	Flippin' Over You/Teen-Age Fancy	700
58	HMV POP 489	Flippin' Over You/Teen-Age Fancy (78)	150

PEASANTS
65	Columbia DB 7642	Got Some Lovin' For You Baby/Let's Get Together	160

PEBBLES
78	Arawak AR 01	Positive Vibration (12")	30
68	Major Minor MM 574	40 Miles Inside Your Heart/Get Around	15
69	Decca F 22944	Incredible George/Playing Chess	15
70	Deram DM 305	Stand Up And Be Counted/May In The Morning	8
71	Parlophone R 5900	Goodnight Ma/Sadness Of A Summer's Afternoon	8
71	Parlophone R 5921	First Time Loving/Party	8

PEBBLES & BAMM BAMM / FLINTSTONES
65	Pye Int. 7N.25332	Daddy (mono)/The World Is Full Of Joys (For Girls And Boys)	7

PEDDLERS
64	Philips BF 1375	Let The Sunshine In/True Girl	8
65	Philips BF 1404	Whatever Happened To The Good Times/Song For The Blues	6
65	Philips BF 1455	Over The Rainbow/You Must Be Having Me On	6
66	Philips BF 1506	Adam's Apple/Anybody's Fool	6
66	Philips BF 1530	I've Got To Hold On/Gassin'	8
67	Philips BF 1557	What'll I Do/Delicious Lady	8
67	CBS 2947	Irresistable You/Murray's Mood	8
67	CBS 3055	You're The Reason I'm Living/Nine Miles High	8
68	CBS 3333	Handel With Care/Horse's Collar	8
68	CBS 3734	Comin' Home Baby/Empty Club Blues	25
68	CBS 4050	That's Life/Wasting My Time	8

69	CBS 4449	Birth/Steel Mill	8
69	CBS 4720	Girlie/P.S I Love You	6
70	Phillips 6006034	Tell The World We're Not In/Rainy Day In London	20
73	Philips 6006 283	Sing Me An Old Song/It's So Easy	30
66	Philips BE 12954	SWINGING SCENE (EP)	15
67	Philips (S)BL 7768	LIVE AT THE PICKWICK (LP, flipback sleeve)	15
67	CBS (S)BPG 63183	FREE WHEELERS (LP)	15
68	CBS 63411	THREE IN A CELL (LP)	15
68	Fontana SFL 13016	THE FANTASTIC PEDDLERS (LP)	12
70	CBS 63682	BIRTHDAY (LP)	12
70	Philips 6308 028	THREE FOR ALL (LP, flip top 'matchbox' cover)	12
71	Philips 6386 066	GEORGIA ON MY MIND (LP)	12
72	Philips 6308 102	SUITE LONDON (LP)	40

PEDESTRIANS
81	Metropolis MET 1	Communter Fantasy/1984	8

MIKE PEDICIN QUINTET
62	HMV POP 1001	When Cats Come Twistin' In/Gotta Twist	15

BOBBY PEDRICK
58	London HLX 8740	White Bucks And Saddle Shoes/Stranded	25
58	London HLX 8740	White Bucks And Saddle Shoes/Stranded (78)	18

ANN PEEBLES
70	London HLU 10322	Part Time Love/I Still Love You	6
71	London HLU 10328	I Pity The Fool/Heartaches, Heartaches	6
71	London HLU 10346	Slipped, Tripped And Fell In Love/99 lbs	5
72	London HLU 10361	Breaking Up Somebody's Home/Troubles, Heartaches And Sadness	5
72	London HLU 10385	Somebody's On Your Case/I've Been There Before	5
73	London HLU 10405	I'm Gonna Tear Your Playhouse Down/One Way Street	6
73	London HLU 10428	I Can't Stand The Rain/I've Been There Before	6
74	EMI 2106	(You Keep Me) Hangin On/Run Run Run	8
75	London HLU 10484	Beware/You Got To Feed The Fire	5
75	London HLU 10508	Come On Mama/I'm Leaving You	5
72	London SHU 8434	STRAIGHT FROM THE HEART (LP)	15
74	London SHU 8468	I CAN'T STAND THE RAIN (LP)	15
76	London SHU 8490	TELLIN' IT (LP)	15

PAUL PEEK
61	Pye International 7N 25102	Brother In Law/Through The Teenage Years	20
66	CBS 202073	Pin The Tail On The Donkey/Rockin' Pneumonia	12

(see also Gene Vincent & Blue Caps)

DAVID PEEL (& LOWER EAST SIDE)
68	Elektra EKL 4032	HAVE A MARIJUANA (LP, red label, mono)	40
68	Elektra EKS 74032	HAVE A MARIJUANA (LP, red label, stereo)	25
70	Elektra 2401 001	AMERICAN REVOLUTION (LP)	20

PEELERS
72	Polydor Folk Mill 2460 165	BANISHED MISFORTUNE (LP)	160

PEELS
66	Stateside SS 513	Juanita Banana/Fun	8
66	Audio Fidelity AFSP 527	Scrooey Mooey/Time Marches On	25

PEENUTS
67	Ember EMB S 242	The Theme For "The Monkees"/The World's Been Good To Me Tonight (in p/s)	20
67	Ember EMB S 242	The Theme For "The Monkees"/The World's Been Good To Me Tonight	10

PEEPERS
72	Bumble GE102	Ayeo/A Heavy Drinking Ego Shrinking	20

PEEPS
65	Philips BF 1421	Now Is The Time/Got Plenty Of Love	15
65	Philips BF 1443	What Can I Say?/Don't Talk About Love	15
66	Philips BF 1478	Gotta Get A Move On/I Told You Before	60
66	Philips BF 1509	Tra La La/Loser Wins	10

(see also Martin Cure & Peeps, Sabres, Rainbows)

PEEP SHOW
67	Polydor 56196	Your Servant, Stephen/Mazy	90
68	Polydor 52226	Esprit De Corps/Mino In A Mix Up	15

BEV PEGG (AND FRIENDS)
75	Beaujangle DB 0006	AWAY FROM THE SAND (LP, 50 copies only)	200

(see also Bev Pegg, Dave Cartwright, Brindley Brae)

BEV PEGG (& HIS GOIN' NOWHERE BAND)
78	Beaujangle DB 0007	NOSTALGIA IS A THING OF THE PAST (LP, private pressing, with booklet, 50 only; as Bev Pegg & His Goin' Nowhere Band)	150
80	Beaujangle DB 0008	THE FOUNDRY DITTY AND THE INDUSTRIAL AIR (LP, private pressing, 500 only, 150 destroyed so only 350 out there...)	45

(see also David Cartwright, Brindley Brae)

BOB PEGG
74	Transatlantic TRA 280	THE SHIPBUILDER (LP, with Nick Strutt, credited to Bob Pegg)	15
75	Transatlantic TRA 299	ANCIENT MAPS (LP, with lyric insert)	20

BOB & CAROL PEGG
71	Trailer LER 3016	HE CAME FROM THE MOUNTAIN (LP, red label, as Carole Pegg)	35
72	Galliard GAL 4017	AND NOW IT IS SO EARLY - THE SONGS OF SYDNEY CARTER (LP)	25

(see also Carol Pegg, Carolanne Pegg, Mr. Fox)

BOB PEGG & NICK STRUTT
73	Transatlantic TRA 265	BOB PEGG & NICK STRUTT (LP)	25

CAROL(ANNE) PEGG
73	Transatlantic TRA 226	CAROLANNE PEGG (LP, gatefold sleeve)	80

PEGGY

(see also Bob & Carol Pegg)

PEGGY
| 70 | Trojan TR 7752 | All Kinds Of Everything Part 1/CARL LEVEY: Instrumental Version | 6 |
| 70 | Hot Rod HR 103 | I Shall Follow The Star/CARL LEVEY: Gifted At The Top | 8 |

PEGGY & JIMMY
| 70 | Hot Rod HR 101 | Pum Pum Lover/CARL LEVEY: Remember Easter Monday | 8 |

PEGGY'S LEG
| 73 | Bunch BAN 2001 | GRINILLA (LP, with insert) | 400 |

(see also Skid Row, Jimi Slevin)

PEG LEG SAM
| 74 | Flyright LP 507/8 | THE LAST MEDICINE SHOW (2-LP) | 15 |

PEKKA
| 75 | Virgin V 2036 | B THE MAGPIE (LP as Pekka Pohjolo) | 20 |
| 77 | Virgin V 2084 | THE MATHEMATICIANS AIR DISPLAY (LP, features Mike Oldfield) | 15 |

PELICAN
| 04 | Hydra Head HHILP 07501 | AUSTRALASIA (2-LP, 290 only) | 18 |

DAVE PELL OCTET
54	London RE-P 1008	IRVING BERLIN GALLERY VOL. 1 (EP)	12
55	London RE-P 1018	RODGERS AND HART (EP)	12
54	London H-APB 1034	RODGERS AND HART GALLERY (10" LP)	15

LANA PELLAY
| 86 | Sublime LIMET 101 | Pistol In My Pocket/Dirty Harry Version (12", p/s) | 12 |

JACK PENATE
| 06 | Young Turks YT 001 | Second Minute Or Hour/Got My Favourite... (die-cut p/s with colour Numbered Polaroid photo initialled by artist, PVC bag, 1,000 only) | 8 |

TRACY PENDARVIS
| 60 | London HLS 9059 | A Thousand Guitars/Is It Too Late | 30 |
| 60 | London HLS 9213 | Is It Me/South Bound Line | 25 |

MIKE PENDER
| 86 | Sierra FED 23 | It's Over/Brothers And Sisters (p/s) | 6 |
| 86 | Sierra FED 23T | It's Over/Brothers And Sisters (12", p/s) | 8 |

(see also The Searchers)

PENDLEFOLK
| 70 | Folk Heritage FHR 007 | PENDLEFOLK (LP) | 18 |

PENDRAGON
87	Awareness AWS 101	Red Shoes/Searching/Contact (p/s)	5
89	Toff PENDS 7S	Saved By You/Lady Luck (p/s)	5
85	Elusive ARRLP 100	FIRE IN HARMONY (LP)	12
85	Elusive ARRLP 101	THE JEWEL (LP)	12

PENELOPES FRIEND
| 87 | MTG MTG 1 | THE GAP EP (12") | 40 |

PENETRATION
77	Virgin VS 192	Don't Dictate/Money Talks (p/s)	8
78	Virgin VS 213	Firing Squad/Never (p/s)	5
78	Virgin VS 226	Life's A Gamble/V.I.P. (p/s)	5
79	Virgin VS 257	Danger Signs/Stone Heroes (live) (p/s)	5
79	Virgin VS 268	Come Into The Open/Lifeline (p/s)	5
78	Virgin V 2109	MOVING TARGETS (LP, 15,000 on luminous vinyl)	15
78	Virgin V 2109	MOVING TARGETS (LP, black vinyl)	20

BOB PENFOLD
| 78 | A C Wall ACW 01 | Free/Mother Natures Child | 12 |

PENGUINS
55	London HL 8114	Earth Angel/Hey Senorita (gold label print, triangular centre)	1750
55	London HL 8114	Earth Angel/Hey Senorita (large centre hole, export issue)	500
55	London HL 8114	Earth Angel/Hey Senorita (78)	100

DAWN PENN
66	Rio R 113	Long Days Short Night/Are You There (label lists 'Dawn Tenn')	60
67	Studio One SO 2030	You Don't Love Me/SOUL VENDORS: Portobello Road	50
68	Island WI 3097	I'll Never Let You Go/MARK BROWN: Brown Low Special	45

(see also Max Romeo, Viceroys)

TONY PENN
| 62 | Starlite ST45 083 | That's What I Like/I Won't Cry Anymore | 30 |

LEONARD PENNARIO
| 54 | Capitol CL 14173 | Midnight On The Cliffs/Dream Rhapsody (with Les Baxter Orchestra) | 10 |

(see also Les Baxter)

PENNSYLVANIA SIXPENCE
| 67 | Pye 7N 17326 | Love Of The Common People/Midweek Excursion | 8 |

PENNY
| 61 | Piccadilly 7N 35009 | Who Does He Think He Is/Sparks | 8 |
| 62 | Piccadilly 7N 35045 | Shall I Take My Heart And Go/What'd I Do? | 8 |

PENNY CANDLES
| 89 | Red Eye RED 04 | THE TAJ MAHAL EP (12" p/s) | 20 |

GEORGE A. PENNY
| 68 | Trojan TR 625 | Win Your Love/VAL BENNETT: All In The Game | 12 |

HANK PENNY
| 56 | Parlophone MSP 6202 | Bloodshot Eyes/Wham! Bam! Thank You Ma'am | 100 |
| 56 | Parlophone R 4120 | Bloodshot Eyes/Wham! Bam! Thank You Ma'am (78) | 18 |

PENNY LANE
70	CBS 4903	Heartbreak House/He's Got A Hold Of My Heart	5

PENNY PEEPS
68	Liberty LBF 15053	Little Man With A Stick/Model Village	300
68	Liberty LBF 15114	I See The Morning/Curly, The Knight Of The Road	40

PENNY WAGER
72	Folk Heritage FHR 0256	LIGHT OF OTHER DAYS (LP)	75

PENNY ARCADE
70	Pye 7N.17943	The Two Of Us/Don't Need You Anymore	20

PENNYWORTH
69	CBS 4573	Malena Malena/Who Are You?	12

CHARLES PENROSE
72	Columbia DB 8959	Laughing Policeman/George Formby - Window Cleaner/Stanley Holloway - The Lion And Albert	6
57	Columbia SEG 7743	THE ADVENTURE OF THE LAUGHING POLICEMAN (EP)	10

PENTAD
65	Parlophone R 5288	Silver Dagger/Nothing But Love	25
65	Parlophone R 5368	Don't Throw It All Away/Too Many Ways	20
66	Parlophone R 5424	Something Other People Call Love/It Better Be Me	25

PENTAGONS
61	London HLU 9333	To Be Loved Forever/Down At The Beach	100

PENTAGRAM
87	Napalm FLAME 006	DAY OF RECKONING (LP)	40
92	Peaceville	1972-1979 (LP)	15
93	Peaceville VILE 40	DAY OF RECKONING (LP, reissue)	25
93	Peaceville VILE 38	RELENTLESS (LP, reissue of US self-titled debut)	30
94	Peaceville VILE 42	BE FOREWARNED (2-LP, insert)	50

PENTANGLE
68	Big T BIG 109	Travellin' Song/Mirage (in title die-cut sleeve)	10
68	Big T BIG 109	Travellin' Song/Mirage	6
69	Big T BIG 124	Once I Had A Sweetheart/I Saw An Angel	20
70	Big T BIG 128	Light Flight/Cold Mountain	6
73	Big T BIG 567	Light Flight/Market Song/The Time Has Come	6
68	Transatlantic TRA 162	THE PENTANGLE (LP, laminated sleeve)	30
68	Transatlantic TRA 178	SWEET CHILD (2-LP)	40
69	Transatlantic TRA 205	BASKET OF LIGHT (LP, gatefold sleeve)	30
70	Transatlantic TRA 228	CRUEL SISTER (LP, gatefold sleeve)	25
71	Transatlantic TRA 240	REFLECTION (LP, gatefold sleeve with inner sleeve)	20
72	Reprise K 44197	SOLOMON'S SEAL (LP, with lyric insert)	60
72	Transatlantic TRASAM 23	HISTORY BOOK (LP)	12
73	Transatlantic TRASAM 29	PENTANGLING (LP)	12
85	Spindrift SPIN 111	OPEN THE DOOR (LP)	20

(see also Bert Jansch, John Renbourn, Duffy's Nucleus)

PENTHOUSE
71	Penny Farthing PEN 765	40 Days Of Rain/I'm Nobody's Fool	8

PEOPLE
69	Capitol CL 15553	I Love You/Somebody Tell Me My Name	22
69	Capitol CL 15599	Ulla/Turnin' Me In	22
70	RCA RCA 2028	I Am (The Preacher)/September's Son	10
71	Deram DM 346	In Ancient Times/Glastonbury	45
70	Paramount SPFL 261	THERE ARE PEOPLE AND THERE ARE PEOPLE (LP)	25

PEOPLE BAND
70	Transatlantic TRA 214	THE PEOPLE BAND (LP, with Charlie Watts)	75

(see also Charlie Watts, Battered Ornaments)

PEPPELKADE 14
88	Top Shelf CAV 031	TIME FLIES EP (12")	40

PEPPER
68	Pye 7N 17569	We'll Make It Together/(Look Out) I'm On The Way Down	10

ART PEPPER
54	Vogue LDE 067	ART PEPPER QUARTET (10" LP)	50
57	London HLZ V 14038	ART PEPPER QUARTET (10" LP)	50
60	Contemporary LAC 12229	MODERN JAZZ CLASSICS (LP, as Art Pepper Eleven)	25

(see also Chet Baker)

JIM PEPPER
71	Atlantic 2400 149	PEPPER'S POW WOW (LP)	25

KEN PEPPER
61	Top Rank JAR 535	Just A Little At A Time/I Get The Blues When It Rains	7

DANNY PEPPERMINT (& JUMPING JACKS)
61	London HLL 9478	The Peppermint Twist/Somebody Else Is Taking My Place (with Jumping Jacks)	12
62	London HLL 9516	One More Time/La Dee Dah	10
62	London HLL 9614	Maybe Tomorrow (But Not Today)/Passing Parade	10
62	London HA-L 2438	TWIST WITH DANNY PEPPERMINT (LP)	75

PEPPERMINT CIRCUS
67	Olga OLE 007	All The King's Horses/It Didn't Take Long	10
68	Polydor 56288	I Won't Be There/Keeping My Head Above Water	6
69	Polydor 56312	Please Be Patient/Take My Love	6
70	A&M AMS 765	One Thing Could Lead To Another/It's So Easy	6

PEPPERMINT RAINBOW
68	MCA MU 1034	Walking In Different Circles/Pink Lemonade	12
69	MCA MU 1076	Will You Be Staying After Sunday/And I'll Be There	20

MINT VALUE £

| 69 | MCA MU 1091 | Don't Wake Up In The Morning, Michael/Rosemary | 10 |

PEPPERMINT TROLLEY COMPANY
| 68 | Dot DOT 110 | Baby You Come Rolling 'Cross My Mind/Nine O'Clock Business Man | 10 |

PEPPI
62	Decca F 11520	Stories/When I Think Of You	5
63	Decca F 11638	Can You Waddle/I Never Danced Before	10
64	Decca F 11991	Pistol Packin' Mama/Roll On Baby	5
64	Fontana TF 446	So Used To Loving You/Don't Trust My Friend	8
65	Decca F 12055	The Skip/Do The Skip	8

ARMANDO PERAZA
| 68 | Fontana STL 5525 | WILD THING (LP) | 20 |

PERCELLS
| 63 | HMV POP 1154 | What Are Boys Made Of?/Cheek To Cheek | 20 |

LANCE PERCIVAL
| 63 | Parlophone R 507 | The Beetroot Song/Dancing In The Streets Tonight | 5 |
| 65 | Parlophone R 5335 | Shame And Scandal In The Family/There's Another One Behind | 5 |

NORMAN PERCIVAL
| 67 | United Artists UP 1197 | Theme From "Billion Dollar Brain"/Shades Of Green | 5 |

PERCY PAVILION
| 84 | Dead Good Dolly P. DMS 2 | Gower Power/You're An Extra Baby (p/s) | 5 |

(see also Captain Sensible)

PEREGRINE
| 72 | Westwood WRS 016 | SONGS OF MINE (LP) | 100 |

RAY PEREIRA
| 70 | Baf BAF 5 | Don't Mess With Cupid/CATS: Falling In Love | 8 |
| 70 | Baf BAF 6 | On Broadway/Hey Chick | 30 |

PERERIN
| 80 | Gwerin SYWM 215 | HAUL AR YR EIRA (LP, with insert) | 180 |

CARLO PERETTI
| 60 | Society SOC 906 | MAMBOS AND CHA CHAS (LP) | 15 |

PERE UBU
79	Chrysalis CHS 2372	The Fabulous Sequel (Have Shoes Will Walk)/Humour Me (live)/ The Book Is On The Table (p/s)	8
80	Rough Trade RT 049	Final Solution/My Dark Ages (p/s)	8
81	Rough Trade RT 066	Not Happy/Lonesome Cowboy Dave (p/s)	8
78	Radar RDR 1	DATAPANIK IN THE YEAR ZERO (12" EP)	15
78	Blank BLANK 001	THE MODERN DANCE (LP)	30
78	Rough Trade ROUGHUS 14	DUB HOUSING (LP)	20
79	Rough Trade ROUGHUS 20	NEW PICNIC TIME (LP)	15
80	Rough Trade ROUGH 14	THE ART OF WALKING (LP, original with "Miles" & "Arabia")	18
81	Rough Trade ROUGH 22	THE MODERN DANCE (LP, reissue)	20
81	Rough Trade ROUGH 23	390° OF SIMULATED STEREO - UBU LIVE: VOLUME 1 (LP)	15
85	Rough Trade ROUGH 83	TERMINAL TOWER (LP, gatefold sleeve)	12

(see also David Thomas)

CHRISTINE PERFECT
69	Blue Horizon 57-3165	When You Say/No Road Is The Right Road	30
70	Blue Horizon 57-3172	I'm Too Far Gone (To Turn Around)/Close To Me	30
70	Blue Horizon 7-63860	CHRISTINE PERFECT (LP)	100

(see also Christine McVie, Fleetwood Mac, Illusive Dream, Chicken Shack, Rick Hayward)

PERFECT DISASTER
| 87 | Glass GLALP 027 | PERFECT DISASTER (LP) | 30 |

PERFECT END
| 81 | Hellfire HELL 1 | Sweet Dreams/Natural Causes/Puppets | 15 |

PERFECT PEOPLE
| 69 | MCA MU 1079 | House In The Country/Polyanna | 15 |

PERFECTORS
| 80 | Active ACT 4 | YT50295ID/Tiny Radios (p/s) | 100 |

PERFORMANCE
| 73 | Polydor 2058 324 | Funny Little Things/Rejoice | 6 |

PERFORMERS
| 69 | Action ACT 4552 | I Can't Stop You/L.A. Stomp | 22 |

PERFORMING FERRET BAND
| 80 | Dead Hippy DHR3 | Brow Beaton/Hoo-Shar/Disco One (EP, p/s) | 18 |

PERISHERS
| 68 | Fontana TF 965 | How Does It Feel/Bye Bye Baby | 40 |

(see also Seftones)

CARL PERKINS
78s
56	London HLU 8271	Blue Suede Shoes/Honey Don't	30
57	London HLS 8408	Matchbox/Your True Love	40
57	London HLS 8527	Glad All Over/Forever Yours	60
58	London HLS 8608	Lend Me Your Comb/That's Right	60
59	Philips PB 983	I Don't See Me In Your Eyes Anymore/One Ticket To Loneliness	70

SINGLES
56	London HLU 8271	Blue Suede Shoes/Honey Don't	200
57	London HLS 8408	Matchbox/Your True Love	200
57	London HLS8527	Glad All Over/Forever Yours	90
58	London HLS 8608	Lend Me Your Comb/That's Right	90

59	Philips PB 983	I Don't See Me In Your Eyes Anymore/One Ticket To Loneliness	20
61	Philips PB 1179	Anyway The Wind Blows/The Unhappy Girls	15
64	Brunswick 05905	Help Me Find My Baby/I Wouldn't Have You	15
64	Brunswick 05909	Big Bad Blues/Lonely Heart (with Nashville Teens)	15
64	Brunswick 05923	The Monkey Shine/Let My Baby Be	15
67	Stateside SS 599	A Country Boy's Dream/If I Could Come Back	15
68	London HLP 7125	A Country Boy's Dream/Shine Shine Shine (export issue)	15
68	Spark SRL 1009	Lake County, Cotton Country/It's You	10
68	London HLS 10192	Blue Suede Shoes/Matchbox	10
69	CBS 3932	Restless/11.43	10
70	CBS 4991	All Mama's Children/Step Aside (with N.R.B.Q.)	6

ALBUMS

59	London HA-S 2202	THE DANCE ALBUM OF CARL PERKINS (plum label, flipback sleeve)	150
59	London HA-S 2202	THE DANCE ALBUM OF CARL PERKINS (plum label, non-flipback sleeve)	50
66	Ember NR 5038	SUNSTROKE (shared with Jerry Lee Lewis)	25
66	CBS Realm 52305	WHOLE LOTTA CARL PERKINS (original pressing with boxed square logo)	50
66	CBS Realm 52305	WHOLE LOTTA CARL PERKINS	25
68	CBS 63309	KING OF ROCK	15
68	London HA-P/SH-P 8366	COUNTRY BOY'S DREAM	20
69	CBS 63676	CARL PERKINS' GREATEST HITS	12
70	CBS 63826	BOPPIN' THE BLUES (with N.R.B.Q.)	12
82	Sun BOX 101	THE SUN YEARS (3-LP, box set with booklet)	20

(see also N.R.B.Q.)

JOE PERKINS

72	Mojo 2092 047	Wrapped Up In Your Love/Looking For A Woman	8

LASCELLES PERKINS

61	Blue Beat BB 41	Creation/Lonely Robin	12
63	Island WI 038	Tango Lips (with Yvonne)/DENNIS SINDREY: Rub Up (B-side actually plays "Jamaica's Song")	25
64	R&B JB 175	I Am So Grateful/When I Survey	20
70	Escort ES 814	Please Stay/MATADORS: Voyage From The Moon	25
71	Banana BA 317	Tell It All Brothers/SOUND DIMENSION: Polkadots	15

(see also Tommy McCook)

POLLY PERKINS

63	Decca F 11583	I Reckon You (as Polly Perkins & Bill)/The Girls Are At It Again	10
63	Oriole CB 1869	Sweet As Honey/I've Gotta Tell You	10
63	Oriole CB 1929	Young Lover/You Too Can Be A Beatle	10
63	Oriole CB 1979	Faling In Love Again/I Went By Your House Today	10
73	Chapter One CMS 1018	LIBERATED WOMAN (LP)	25
77	Greasepaint GP3/6575/SMB	POLLY (LP)	12

(see also Academy)

TONY PERKINS

57	RCA RCA 1018	Moonlight Swim/First Romance	12

KATIE PERKS

83	Plastichead PLAS 001	Small/Cold Stone (p/s)	8

PERMANENTS

63	London HLU 9803	Oh Dear, What Can The Matter Be/Let Me Be Baby	12

JEAN-JACQUES PERREY

72	Vanguard VAN 1005	Gossipo Perpetuo/Moog Indigo	10
73	Vanguard VAN 1008	Minuet Of The Robots/Porcupine Rock	10
71	Vanguard VSD 6525	KALEIDOSCOPIC VIBRATIONS - SPOTLIGHT ON THE MOOG (LP, 'kaleidoscope' sleeve, with Gershon Kingsley)	18
72	Vanguard VSD 6549	MOOG INDIGO (LP, title sleeve)	25
73	Vanguard VSD 79222	THE IN SOUND FROM WAY OUT! (LP, green/black 'starburst' sleeve, with Gershon Kingsley)	20
73	Vanguard VSD 79286	THE AMAZING NEW ELECTRONIC POP SOUND OF... (LP)	15
74	Vanguard DPS 2051	THE BEST OF THE MOOG (2-LP)	18

PAT PERRIN

68	Island WI 3115	Over You/LLOYD TERRELL: Lost Without You	25

PERRI'S

59	Oriole CB 1481	Jerri-Lee/Ballad Of A Happy Heart	15
59	Oriole CB 1481	Jerri-Lee/Ballad Of A Happy Heart (78)	15

BARBARA PERRY

70	Pama PM 795	Say You Need Me/Unloved	15

JEFF PERRY

76	Arista ARIST 51	Love Don't Come No Stronger/I've Got To See You Right Away	25

LEE 'SCRATCH' PERRY (& UPSETTERS)

63	R&B JB 102	Prince In The Black/Don't Copy	50
63	R&B JB 104	Old For New/Prince And Duke	50
63	R&B JB 106	Mad Head/Man And Wife	50
63	R&B JB 135	Royalty/Can't Be Wrong	50
63	Island WI 118	Never Get Weary/TOMMY McCOOK: Below Zero	40
64	Port-O-Jam PJ 4001	Help The Weak/TOMMY McCOOK: Exodus	40
64	Port-O-Jam PJ 4003	Bad Minded People/TOMMY McCOOK & HIS GROUP: Jam Rock	40
64	Port-O-Jam PJ 4010	Chatty Chatty Woman/TOMMY McCOOK & HIS GROUP: Road Block	70
65	Island WI 210	Please Don't Go/Bye, St. Peter (both sides with Soulettes)	40
65	Island WI 223	Country Girl/Strange Country (as Upsetters; both act. by Ossie & Upsetters)	25
65	Ska Beat JB 201	Roast Duck/Hand To Hand, Man To Man	45
65	Ska Beat JB 203	Trail And Crosses/Jon Tom	50
65	Ska Beat JB 212	Wishes Of The Wicked/Hold Down	60
65	Ska Beat JB 215	Open Up/ROLAND ALPHONSO: Twin Double	50
66	Ska Beat JB 251	The Woodman/Give Me Justice	40
66	Island WI 259	Just Keep It Up/ROLAND ALPHONSO: James Bond	150
66	Island WI 292	Doctor Dick (as King Perry)/SOUL BROTHERS: Magic Star	40

Mal PERRY

66	Island WI 298	Rub And Squeeze (as King Perry & Soulettes)/SOUL BROTHERS: Here Comes The Minx	40
67	Doctor Bird DB 1073	Run For Cover/Something You've Got (as Lee 'King' Perry & Sensations)	30
67	Doctor Bird DB 1098	Whop Whop Man/Wind-Up Doll (with Dynamites)	50
68	Amalgamated AMG 808	The Upsetter/Thank You Baby	50
68	Doctor Bird DB 1146	People Funny Boy/BURT WALTERS: Blowing In The Wind	35
68	Trojan TR 629	Sentence (as Danny & Lee)/LEE PERRY: You Crummy	20
68	Trojan TR 644	Uncle Desmond/Bronco (with Upsetters)	20
69	Upsetter US 303	People Funny Fi True/UPSETTERS: Ten To Twelve	20
69	Upsetter US 324	Yakety Yak/Tackio (with Upsetters)	20
70	Upsetter US 325	Kill Them All/Soul Walk (with Upsetters)	20
71	Bullet BU 461	All Combine Pts 1& 2 (as Lee Perry & Upsetters)	12
72	Upsetter US 385	French Connection (with Upsetters)/UPSETTERS: Version	15
72	Upsetter US 389	Back Biter (with Dennis Alcapone)/UPSETTERS: Version	15
73	Upsetter US 397	Jungle Lion/Freakout Skank	100
73	Upsetter US 398	Cow Thief Skank (actually by Lee Perry & Charlie Ace)/Seven And Three Quarters Skank	18
73	Bread BR 1111	Station Underground/CARLTON & SHOES: Better Days	25
73	Downtown DT 513	Bucky Skank/Mid East Rock	25
73	Jackpot JP 812	Justice To The People/UPSETTERS: Version	20
74	Dip DL 5037	Dub A Pum Pum (with Silvertones)/Version	8
74	Dip DL 5060	Dreader Locks (& Junior Byles)/Militant Rock	8
76	Island WIP 6370	Dreadlocks In Moonlight/Cut Throat	6
79	Black Art BH 001	Reggae Music (actually by Hugo Blackwood)/DOC ALIMANTADO: Rastaman Train (12")	35
73	SRNO 8002	CLOAK & DAGGER (LP, as Scratch The Upsetter)	70
75	Cactus CTLP 112	REVOLUTION DUB (LP)	50
75	DIP DLPD 6002	KUNG FU MEETS THE DRAGON (LP, as The Mighty Upsetter)	50
70s	Jet Star PTLP 1023	THE BEST OF (LP)	30
85	Trojan PERRY 1	UPSETTER BOX SET (3-LP)	30
98	Pressure Sounds PSLP19	PRODUCED & DIRECTED BY UPSETTER (2-LP)	20
99	Pressure Sounds PSLP32	DIVINE MADNESS DEFINITELY (2-LP)	20

(see also Upsetters, Defenders, Roland Alphonso, Bob Marley/Wailers, King Scratch, Punchers, Roy Shirley, Pioneers, Desmond Dekker)

MAL PERRY

58	Fontana H 133	That's When Your Heartaches Begin/Make Me A Miracle	8
58	Fontana H 149	Too Young To Love/Who Are They To Say	8
58	Fontana H 157	Things I Didn't Say/The Girl Next Door	8
59	Fontana H 172	Richer Than I/Willingly	8

MARK PERRY

80	NB NB 7	You Cry Your Tears/Music Death? (with Dennis Burns, p/s in poly bag)	5
80	Deptford Fun City DFC 12	Whole World's Down On Me/I Live - He Dies (p/s)	5
80	Deptford Fun City DLP 06	SNAPPY TURNS (LP)	12

(see also Alternative TV)

SHORT(L)Y PERRY

72	Attack ATT 8043	Musical Goat/WINSTON GRENNON & J. JACKSON: Stinging Dub	8
72	Explosion EX 2067	Sprinkle Some Water/FLOWERS & ALVIN: Howdy And Tenky	7
72	Bullet BU 512	Sprinkle Some Water/FLOWERS & ALVIN: Howdy And Tenky	7
73	Bullet BU 529	Yama Skank/U ROY JUNIOR: Doctor Run Come Quick	10
73	Downtown DT 517	Dedicated To Illiteracy/G.G. ALL STARS: Illiteracy Dub	7
73	Grape GR 3052	Abusing And Assaulting (by Flowers & Alvin)/Food Control	7
73	Green Door GD 4043	President Mash Up The Resident/President Mash Up The Resident Part Two	7

(see also Shorty, Cornell Campbell, Maytones, Paulette Williams)

STEVE PERRY

60	HMV POP 745	Step By Step/Because They're Young	15
62	Decca F 11462	Ginny Come Lately/Two Of A Kind	10
62	Decca F 11526	Young And In Love/Let It Come True	6
63	Decca F 11656	Find Me A Girl/My Dad	6
64	Decca F 11895	Crooked Little Man/Day Dreams	6

PERRY SISTERS

59	Brunswick 05802	Fabian/Willie Boy	25

PERSIAN FLOWERS

84	Fourth Dimension FDS 02	Somebody Else's Sin/Summer Of Love (1000 only, p/s)	7

(see also Wasted Youth)

PERSIAN RISK

81	SRT SRTS/81/CUS/1146	Calling For You/Chasing The Dragon (p/s)	140
83	Neat NEAT 24	Ridin' High/Hurt You (p/s)	18
86	Metal Masters METALLP 2	RISE UP (LP)	18

(see also Motorhead)

PERSIANS

69	Pama PM 772	I Only Have Eyes For You/The Sun Gotta Shine In Your Heart	12
72	Capitol CL 15726	Baby Come Back Home/I Want To Go Home	8

PERSIMMON'S PECULIAR SHADES

68	Major Minor MM 554	Watchmaker/Coplington	30

PERSONALITIES

65	Dice CC 30	I Remember/Suffering	15
65	Ska Beat JB 222	Hey Little Girl/Teardrops	20
66	Blue Beat BB 354	Push It Down/BUSTER'S ALL STARS: Blues Market	50

PERSONS UNKNOWN

81	Po 1	Addiction (p/s)	25

PERSUADERS!

93	Detour DR 001	Finished Forever/In The Night (p/s, 300 only)	20
94	Detour DR 011	Waiting For The Nowhere Express/Girl/The Paperchase (p/s, 100 on red vinyl)	8
94	Detour DR 011	Waiting For The Nowhere Express/Girl/The Paperchase (p/s)	5

PERSUADERS (U.S.)

72	Atlantic K 40370	THE THIN LINE BETWEEN LOVE AND HATE (LP)	20
73	Atlantic K 40476	THE PERSUADERS (LP)	15

PERSUASIONS
65	Columbia DB 7560	I'll Go Crazy/Try Me	30
65	Columbia DB 7700	Big Brother/Deep Down Love	30
66	Columbia DB 7859	La, La, La, La, La/Opportunity	30

PERSUASIONS (U.S.)
69	Minit MLF 11017	Party In The Woods/It's Better To Have Loved And Lost	20
73	MCA MUS 1222	Good Old Acappella/You Must Believe Me	7
70	Straight STS 1062	A CAPPELLA (LP)	40
72	Island ILPS 9201	STREET CORNER SYMPHONY (LP)	20

MORRIS PERT
75	Chantry ABM 21	LUMINOS/CHROMOSPHERE/4 JAPANESE VERSES (LP)	40
80	Chantry CHT 001	LUMINOS/CHROMOSPHERE/4 JAPANESE VERSES (LP, reissue)	30
82	Chantry CHT 007	BOOK OF LOVE/FRAGMENTI I/ULTIMATE DECAY (LP)	30

JON PERTWEE
72	Purple PUR 111	Who Is The Doctor/Pure Mystery	20
85	Safari DOCTOR 1	Who Is The Doctor/Doctor Blood Donor (p/s)	6
62	Phillips BBL 7558	SONGS FOR VULGAR BOATMEN (LP)	20
80	Decca CROW 1	WORZEL GUMMIDGE SINGS (LP)	12

(see also Rupert Hine, Derek Roy, BBC Radiophonic Workshop)o

PESKY GEE!
69	Pye 7N 17708	Where Is My Mind/A Place Of Heart Break	50
69	Pye N(S)PL 18293	EXCLAMATION MARK (LP, textured sleeve)	150

(see also Black Widow, Agony Bag)

PEST
03	Ninja Tune ZEN 74	NECESSARY MEASURES (2-LP)	20

PETALS
63	Decca F 11650	Let's Do The Tamoure/Look At Me	8

PETER
70	Sonet SON 2012	Peace/Values	15

PETER & ALEX
70	Carnaby 4018	Big Beat/On The Loose	7

PETER & GORDON
65	Columbia DB 7729	Baby I'm Yours/When The Black Of Yout Eyes Turns To Grey	6
66	Columbia DB 7834	Woman/Wrong From The Start	7
66	Columbia DB 7951	Don't Pity Me/To Show I Love You	5
66	Columbia DB 8003	Lady Godiva/Morning's Calling	6
66	Columbia DB 8075	Knight In Rusty Armour/The Flower Lady	8
67	Columbia DB 8159	Sunday For Tea/Start Trying Someone Else	8
67	Columbia DB 8198	The Jokers/Red, Cream And Velvet	6
68	Columbia DB 8398	I Feel Like Going Out/The Quest For The Holy Grail	20
68	Columbia DB 8451	You've Had Better Times/Sipping My Wine	6
69	Columbia DB 8585	I Can Remember (Not Too Long Ago)/Hard Time, Rainy Day	10
64	Columbia SEG 8337	JUST FOR YOU (EP)	15
64	Columbia SEG 8348	NOBODY I KNOW (EP)	20
64	Columbia 33SX 1630	PETER AND GORDON (LP, mono)	20
64	Columbia SCX 3518	PETER AND GORDON (LP, stereo)	25
64	Columbia 33SX 1660	IN TOUCH WITH PETER AND GORDON (LP, mono)	20
64	Columbia SCN 3532	IN TOUCH WITH PETER AND GORDON (LP, stereo)	25
65	Columbia 33SX 1761	HURTIN' 'N' LOVIN' (LP, mono)	20
65	Columbia SCX 3565	HURTIN' 'N' LOVIN' (LP, stereo)	25
66	Columbia SX 6045	PETER AND GORDON (LP, mono)	20
66	Columbia SCX 6045	PETER AND GORDON (LP, stereo)	25
66	Columbia SX 6097	SOMEWHERE... (LP, mono)	20
66	Columbia SCX 6097	SOMEWHERE... (LP, stereo)	25
65	Columbia SCXC 25	I GO TO PIECES (LP, export issue)	30
66	Columbia SCXC 29	WOMAN (LP, export issue)	30
66	Columbia SCXC 33	LADY GODIVA (LP, export issue)	35

(see also Gordon Waller)

PETER & HEADLINES
64	Decca F 11980	Don't Cry Little Girl/It Was Love	15
64	Decca F 12035	Tears And Kisses/I've Got My Reasons	15

(see also Count Downe & Zeros)

PETER & MARY
54	Columbia SCMC 6	Crazy Mix Up Song/What Shall We Do With The Lonesome Lover (export issue)	6

(see also Peter Lind Hayes)

PETER & PAUL
66	Blue Beat BB 364	Hosana/Schoolgirl	18

PETER & PERSUADERS
65	Oak RGJ 197	The Wanderer/Wine Glass Rock/Oh My Soul/Cross My Heart (EP)	50

PETER & TEST TUBE BABIES
81	No Future OI 4	Banned From The Pubs/Moped Lads/Peacehaven Wild Lads (p/s)	8
82	No Future OI 15	Run Like Hell/Up Yer Bum (p/s)	8
83	Trapper EARS 1	Zombie Creeping Flesh/No Invitation/Smash And Grab (p/s)	6
83	Trapper EARS 2	The Jinx/Trapper Ain't Got A Bird (p/s)	5
82	No Future Punk 3	PISSED AND PROUD (LP)	15
83	Trapper THIN 1	MATING SOUNDS OF SOUTH AMERICAN FROGS (LP, with lyric inner)	15

PETER & WOLVES
67	MGM MGM 1352	Little Girl Lost And Found/Is Me	35
68	MGM MGM 1374	Lanternlight/Break Up-Break Down	30
68	MGM MGM 1397	Julie/Birthday	20
68	MGM MGM 1452	Woman On My Mind/Old & The New	35
70	UPC UPC 104	Something In The Way She Moves/The Lady And Me	10

(see also Factory, Norman Conquest, John Pantry, Sounds Around, Bunch)

PETER B'S
66	Columbia DB 7862	If You Wanna Be Happy/Jodrell Blues	70

(see also Tony Colton, Peter Bardens, Peter Green, Cheynes, Shotgun Express)

PETER, PAUL & MARY
63	Warner Bros WB 95	Puff/Pretty Mary	6
63	Warner Bros WB 104	Blowing In The Wind/Flora	5
64	Warner Bros WB 142	The Times They Are A-Changin'/Blue	5

see also Mary Travers

PETER'S FACES
64	Piccadilly 7N 35178	Why Did You Bring Him To The Dance/She's In Love	10
64	Piccadilly 7N 35196	Try A Little Love My Friend/I Don't Care	10
64	Piccadilly 7N 35205	Just Like Romeo And Juliet/Wait	25
65	Piccadilly 7N 35225	De-Boom-Lay-Boom/Suzie Q	10

(see also Flowerpot Men, White Plains)

JANICE PETERS & PLAYBOYS
58	Columbia DB 4222	This Little Girl's Gone Rockin'/Kiss Cha Cha	30
58	Columbia DB 4222	This Little Girl's Gone Rockin'/Kiss Cha Cha (78)	20
59	Columbia DB 4276	A Girl Likes/You're The One	30
59	Columbia DB 4276	A Girl Likes/You're The One (78)	15

JO PETERS
61	Pye 7N 15350	I Love The Long Light Evenings/I May Be Wrong	6
62	Pye 7N 15413	When Opportunity Knocks/Never Cheat Your Sweetheart	7

JOHNNY PETERS
65	Decca F 12172	When You Ask About Love/People Say	25

LENNIE PETERS
63	Oriole CB 1887	And My Heart Cried/For A Lifetime	7
64	Oriole CB 1956	Let The Tears Begin/Love Me, Love Me (Love Me, Love Me)	7

LINDA PETERS
70	Warlock Music WMM 101/2	WARLOCK MUSIC SAMPLER (LP, sampler, 7 tracks by Elton John)	1000

(see also Paul McNeill & Linda Peters, Richard & Linda Thompson)

MARK PETERS & SILHOUETTES
63	Oriole CB 1836	Fragile (Handle With Care)/Janie	30
64	Oriole CB 1909	Cindy's Gonna Cry/Show Her	30
64	Piccadilly 7N 35207	Don't Cry For Me/I Told You So	15

(see also Rats)

PETER'S PRIVATE ARMY
83	Spartan SP 9	The Gaol Song (Hip For The Day)/Bounce Back	6

SCOTT PETERS
61	Pye 7N 15343	Kookie Talk/Game Of Love	7
61	Pye 7N 15363	Bobbie Allen/It's The Natural Thing To Do	6
61	Columbia DB 8244	Go Tell The World/More And More	6

WENDY PETERS
68	Saga OPP 1	Morning Dew/I Don't Understand	18

JENNY PETERS
79	Redball RR008	JENNY PETERS (EP)	12

CLIVE PETERSEN
61	Columbia DB 4687	For Every Boy/If No One Tells You	15

PAUL PETERSEN
62	Pye International 7N 25153	Keep Your Love Locked/Be Everything To Anyone You Love	7
62	Pye International 7N 25163	Lollipops And Roses/Please Mr Sun	10
63	Pye International 7N 25173	My Dad/Little Boy Sad	10
63	Pye International 7N 25196	Amy/Goody Goody	8
68	Tamla Motown TMG 670	A Little Bit For Sandy/Your Love's Got Me Burnin' Alive	35

PAUL PETERSEN & SHELLEY FABARES
62	Pye International 7N 25133	She Can't Find Her Keys/Very Unlikely	10

(see also Shelley Fabares)

BOBBY PETERSON (QUINTET)
59	Top Rank JAR 232	The Hunch/Love You Pretty Baby (as Bobby Peterson Quintet)	15
64	Sue WI 342	Rockin' Charlie (Parts 1 & 2) (solo)	30
65	Sue WI 346	Piano Rock/One Day (solo)	30

OSCAR PETERSON
55	Columbia 33C 1037	PLAYS PRETTY (10" LP)	20
55	Columbia Clef 33C 9012	PLAYS PRETTY (10" LP, reissue)	15
55	Columbia 33C 1038	THE OSCAR PETERSON QUARTET (10" LP)	15
55	Columbia 33C 1039	OSCAR PETERSON SINGS (10")	15
55	Columbia Clef 33CX 10012	PLAYS DUKE ELLINGTON (LP)	15
55	Columbia Clef 33CX 10016	PLAYS COLE PORTER (LP)	12
55	Columbia Clef 33CX 10028	PLAYS RICHARD RODGERS (LP)	12
55	Columbia Clef 33CX 10039	PLAYS COUNT BASIE (LP)	12
56	Columbia Clef 33C 9025	OH LADY BE GOOD (10" LP)	15
56	HMV CLP 1086	IN ROMANTIC MOOD (LP)	12

(see also Louis Armstrong, Lester Young, Ella Fitzgerald, Sonny Stitt)

RAY PETERSON
59	RCA RCA 1131	The Wonder Of You/I'm Gone	12
59	RCA RCA 1131	The Wonder Of You/I'm Gone (78)	12
59	RCA RCA 1154	Shirley Purley/Come And Get It	12
59	RCA RCA 1154	Shirley Purley/Come And Get It (78)	12
60	RCA RCA 1175	Answer Me/Goodnight My Love, Pleasant Dreams	15
60	RCA RCA 1195	Tell Laura I Love Her/Wedding Day	10

60	London HLX 9246	Corrine, Corrina/Be My Girl	10
61	London HLX 9332	Sweet Little Kathy/You Didn't Care	10
61	London HLX 9379	Missing You/You Thrill Me	10
62	London HLX 9489	I Could Have Loved You So Well/Why Don't You Write Me	15
62	London HLX 9569	You Didn't Care/You Know Me Much Too Well	8
63	London HLX 9746	Without Love/Give Us Your Blessing	8
64	MGM MGM 1249	Oh No/If You Were Here	5
64	MGM MGM 1258	Across The Street/When I Stop Dreaming	5
65	MGM MGM 1273	House Without Windows/Wish I Could Say No To You	5
65	MGM MGM 1288	I'm Only Human/One Lonesome Rose	7
66	MGM MGM 1303	Everybody/Love Hurts	5
61	London REX 1293	CORRINE CORRINA (EP)	25

PETER, SUE & MARC & PFURI, GORPS & KNIRL

| 79 | EMI EMI 2940 | Second Hand Company/Troedler & Co. | 6 |

PETEY, PATTY, PEGGY & BRUCE

| 59 | Top Rank JAR 250 | The Happy Penguins/IRVING KRASE ORCHESTRA: The Happy Penguin Waltz | 5 |

PET HATE

| 83 | FM 12VHF 2 | Roll Away The Stone/Caught/Playing With My Heart (12", p/s) | 12 |
| 84 | Heavy Metal HMRLP 23W | BAD PUBLICITY (LP, white vinyl) | 12 |

(see also Silverwing)

PETITES

| 60 | Philips PB 1035 | Get Your Daddy's Car Tonight/Sun Showers | 10 |

PETR & PAVEL

| 68 | Page One POF 112 | Laska/Wencelas Square | 6 |

PETS

58	London HL 8652	Cha-Hua-Hua/Cha-Kow-Ski	25
58	London HL 8652	Cha-Hua-Hua/Cha-Kow-Ski (78)	20
59	Pye International 7N 25004	(You Wandered) Beyond The Sea/Wow-ee!!!	10
59	Pye International 7N 25004	(You Wandered) Beyond The Sea/Wow-ee!!! (78	10

(see also Seph Acre & Pets)

PET SHOP BOYS

SINGLES

84	Epic A 4292	West End Girls/Pet Shop Boys (p/s)	20
84	Epic TA 4292	West End Girls (Extended)/Pet Shop Boys (12", p/s)	30
85	Parlophone R 6097	Opportunities (Let's Make Lots of Money)/In The Night (matrix: A-3-1-2) (1st mix, white p/s)	12
85	Parlophone 12R 6097	Opportunities (Let's Make Lots of Money) (Dance Mix)/In The Night (Extended) (12", white p/s)	20
85	Parlophone 12RA 6097	Opportunities (Let's Make Lots of Money) (Version Latina)/(Dub For Money Remix)/In The Night (Extended Mix) (12", large picture labels, die-cut p/s)	40
85	Parlophone 12R 6097	Opportunities (Let's Make Lots of Money) (Dance Mix)/ In The Night (Extended) (12", p/s, mispressing, B-side plays "Opportunities [Dub For Money] Remix")	30
85	Parlophone 12R 6097	Opportunities (Let's Make Lots of Money) (Dance Mix)/ In The Night (Extended) (12", p/s, 2nd mispressing, A-side plays "Opportunities [Version Latina]")	30
85	Parlophone 10R 6115	West End Girls (Untitled Mix)/A Man Could Get Arrested (4.09 Mix)/ West End Girls (7" Mix) (10", round foldout p/s; sealed with sticker)	60
85	Parlophone 12R 6115	West End Girls (Dance Mix)/A Man Could Get Arrested (4.09 Mix)/ West End Girls (7" Mix) (12", with 6" die-cut holes in p/s, 6" picture labels)	8
86	Parlophone 12RA 6115	West End Girls (Shep Pettibone Mastermix)/West End Dub/A Man Could Get Arrested (4.09 Mix) (12", black/blue/red p/s, standard labels)	10
86	Parlophone 12RA 6115	West End Girls (Shep Pettibone Mastermix)/West End Dub/A Man Could Get Arrested (4.09 Mix) (12", same as above with 6" yellow circle on sleeve)	10
86	Parlophone 12RA 6115	West End Girls (Shep Pettibone Mastermix)/West End Dub/A Man Could Get Arrested (4.09 Mix) (12", stickered black/blue/red p/s with 6" die-cut hole & 6" yellow picture labels)	10
86	Parlophone 10R 6116	Love Comes Quickly (Dance Mix)/That's My Impression (Disco Mix) (10", PVC sleeve with poster)	60
86	Parlophone 12R 6116	Love Comes Quickly (Dance Mix)/That's My Impression (Disco Mix) (12", large picture labels, die-cut white sleeve)	10
86	Parlophone RD 6140	Suburbia/Paninaro/Love Comes Quickly (Shep Pettibone Remix)/Jack The Lad/Suburbia Part Two (double pack, gatefold p/s)	6
87	Parlophone 12RX 6158	It's A Sin (Ian Levine Remix)/You Know Where You Went Wrong (Rough Mix) (12", 'video still' p/s)	8
87	Parlophone 12RX 6171	Always On My Mind (Phil Harding Remix)/Do I Have To?/ Always On My Mind (Dub) (12", title sleeve)	8
88	Parlophone CDR 6177	Heart (Disco Mix)/I Get Excited (You Get Excited Too)/Heart (Dance Mix)	8
88	Parlophone 12RX 6190	Domino Dancing (Remix)/Don Juan (Demo)/Domino Dancing (Demo) (12", 'hotel' p/s)	8
89	Parlophone 10R 6220	It's Alright (Alternative Mix)/It's Alright (Extended Dance Mix) (10", black title sleeve with poster)	8
89	Parlophone 12RS 6220	It's Alright (Extended)/One Of The Crowd/Your Funny Uncle (12", p/s, with obi)	8
93	Parlophone R 6348	Can You Forgive Her? (7" Version)/Hey Headmaster (red or blue vinyl, factory custom pressing, p/s)	600
96	Parlophone 12RX 6431	Before (Underground Mix)/(Bonus Dub)/(Underground Instrumental)/(Bonus Beats)/(Classic Paradise Mix)/(Afrodisiac Mix)/(Hedboys Mix)/(Hedboys Dub)/(Joey Negro Extended Mix) (3 x 12", each in p/s, boxed set)	8
96	Parlophone 12RD 6443	Se A Vida É (That's The Way Life Is) (Mark's Deep And Dark Vocal)/ (Mark's Deep And Dark Instrumental)/(Mark's Shelter Dub)/(Deep Dish Liquid Remix)/(Pink Noise Mix)/(Deep Dish Dub)/(7" Version) (12" double pack, yellow & green vinyl, p/s 2 inner sleeves)	8
97	Parlophone Fan Club	It Doesn't Often Snow At Christmas (CD, fan club issue, in sealed silver bubble wrap)	125
06	Parlophone R6690	I'm With Stupid/Girls Don't Cry (picture disc, p/s)	5
06	Parlophone R6708	Minimal/In Private (clear vinyl, p/s)	5
06	Parlophone R6723	Numb/Party Song (p/s)	5
10	Parlophone R 6810	Love Life/A Powerful Friend (Jukebox centre, blue parlophone sleeve, 1000 only)	12

ALBUMS

93	Parlophone CDPSDX 143	VERY (CD, with 6-track bonus CD "Relentless" in foldout 'bubble' wallet)	25
00	Parlophone 724352185719	NIGHTLIFE (LP)	20
87	Parlophone PCSDX 104	ACTUALLY (LP, with U.S. import "Always On My Mind" 12", stickered sleeve)	12
87	Parlophone CDPCSDX 104	ACTUALLY (CD, with U.S. import "Always On My Mind" CD single)	25
88	Parlophone PCSX 7325	INTROSPECTIVE (LP, 3 x clear vinyl 12" factory custom pressing, with wraparound paper strip, 10 copies only)	800

MINT VALUE £

88	Parlophone PCSX 7325	INTROSPECTIVE (LP, 3 x black vinyl 12", with picture labels & wraparound paper obi strip) 15
93	Parlophone PCSD 143	VERY (LP) 15
96	Parlophone PCSD 170	BILINGUAL (LP) 15
02	Parlophone 538150-1	RELEASE (LP, white vinyl) 12
02	Parlophone 0 724358146	DISCO 3 (3-LP) 25
09	Vinyl Factory	YES (11 x 12" in smoked perspex box with gold-plated 'tick' on cover, with art print, signed and numbered by both band members, 300 only) 500

PROMOS

85	Parlophone R 12R 6097	Opportunities (Let's Make Lots of Money)/In The Night (12", "photocopy" sl.) 30
86	Parlophone R 6116	Love Comes Quickly (1-sided, p/s) 40
86	Parlophone 12R 6129	Opportunities (Let's Make Lots of Money) (7.18 Shep Pettibone Mastermix)/Opportunities (4.27 Reprise)/Opportunities (6.44 Original Dance Mix)/Was That What It Was (12", autographed black die-cut sleeve, with press release) 35
86	Parlophone 12R 6129	Opportunities (Let's Make Lots of Money) (7.18 Shep Pettibone Mastermix)/Opportunities (4.27 Reprise)/Opportunities (6.44 Original Dance Mix)/Was That What It Was (12", autographed black die-cut sleeve, without press release) 35
86	Parlophone 12R 6140	Suburbia (The Full Horror)/Paninaro/Jack The Lad (12", 1-sided) 8
88	Parlophone 12RDJ 6198	Left To My Own Devices (The Disco Mix)/Left To My Own Devices/ The Sound Of The Atom Splitting (12", unique title sleeve) 12
90	Parlophone 12RXDJ 6275	Being Boring (Remix)/We All Feel Better In The Dark (After Hours Climax)/ We All Feel Better In The Dark (Ambient) (12", black die-cut sleeve) 8
91	Parlophone 12R 6283A	Lose My Mind (Disco Version) (12", 1-sided) 8
91	Parlophone 12RDJ 6301A	D.J. Culture (12", 1-sided) 8
91	Parlophone MFB 1	Music For Boys (12", 3 untitled mixes, hand-stamped white label) 25
91	Parlophone 12MFBX 1	Music For Boys (12", 2 untitled mixes, white label) 12
92	Parlophone CDRX 6332	Go West (7" Version)/West End Girls (Sacha Mix)/Forever/Go West (Extended Dance Mix) (cassette, title sleeve) 150
93	Parlophone 12RXDJ 6348	Can You Forgive Her? (MK Remix)/(MK Bicycle Dub)/I Want To Wake Up (Johnny Marr 1993 Remix)/(Johnny Marr Groove Mix) (12") 10
93	Abbey Road	COMPILED EP (CD-R, Abbey Road title sleeve; autographed by The Boys, 20 only) 800
94	Parlophone 12RDJ 6386	Yesterday When I Was Mad (Jam & Spoon Mix)/(Junior Vasquez Dub)/(Junior Vasquez Fabulous Dub)/(Junior Vasquez Body Dub)/(Coconut 12" Mix)/(RAF Zone Mix)/(RAF Dub Zone)/Euroboy/Some Speculation (12", double pack unique p/s) 15
96	Parlophone 12RDJD 6431	Before (Classic Paradise Mix)/(Afrodisiac Mix)/(Hedboys Mix)/ (Dub)/(Extended Mix) (2 x 12", blue 'penis' p/s) 25
96	Parlophone 12RJD 6431	Before (Underground Mix)/(Bonus Dub)/(Underground Instrumental)/(Bonus Beats) (12", red 'penis' p/s) 25
96	Parlophone CDIN 103	BILINGUAL THE INTERVIEW (CD) 20
97	Parlophone 12 BARDJ 2	The Truck Driver & His Mate/Before (Love To Infinity Classic Paradise Mix) (12", 'two knobs' p/s, 150 copies) 150
97	Parlophone 12RDJ 6460	A Red Letter Day (Trouser Enthusiasts Autoerotic Decapitation Mix)/(Trouser Enthusiasts Congo Dongo Dubstramental) (12") 10
97	Parlophone 12BOYDJ 101	The Boy Who Couldn't Keep His Clothes On (Main Vocal)/(INT... Club Mix)/(Banji Girlfriend Beats)/(On Stage At Twilo)/(Radio Edit) (12", die-cut sleeve) 60
97	Parlophone 12RDJD 6470	Somewhere (Forthright Club Mix)/(Trouser Enthusiasts Mix)/To Step Aside (Brutal Bill Mix)/Somewhere (Forthright Dub)/To Step Aside (Ralph's Old School Dub)/To Step Aside (Davidson Ospina Dub) (12", double pack, title p/s) 8
97	PSB 97	PET SHOP BOYS TALK (interview CD, promo-only) 15
99	Parlophone (no cat. no.)	NIGHTLIFE (10" x 10" box in PVC slip case, contains interview CD, music CD, book, EPK & 3 photographs) 50
01	10th Planet/PSBP/RUG	FIVE TITLES FROM CLOSER TO HEAVEN: Positive Role Model/Friendly Fire/ Shameless/K-Hole/For All Of Us (CD-R, title sleeve, all sung by Neil Tennant) 150
03	Parlophone 12RDJ 6620	Miracles (Extended Version) (12", 1-sided white label test pressing) 8
03	Parlophone 12RDJX 6620	Miracles (Lemon Jelly Remix) (12", 1-sided white label test pressing) 8
03	Parlophone LONDON 001	London/(Remix) (12", white label) 8
06	Parlophone FUNDA001	Fundamentalism Part 1 (12", promo) 15
06	Parlophone FUNDA002	Fundamentalism Part 2 (12", promo) 15
06	Parlophone PSB002	Psychological (1-sided 12" promo no Pet Shop Boys credit on label) 25
06	Parlophone REMIXES01	Psychological (Ewan Pearson Mixes) (12" promo) 25
06	Parlophone 0094636497921	I'm With Stupid Remixes (CD, 6-track promo, card p/s) 25
06	Parlophone STUPID002	I'm With Stupid Remixes 1 (12" promo) 25
06	Parlophone STUPID001	I'm With Stupid Remixes 2 (12" promo) 15
06	Parlophone STUPID003	I'm With Stupid Remixes 3 (12" promo) 15
06	Parlophone 0094637114421	Minimal Remixes (CD, 10-track, promo card p/s) 25
06	Parlophone NUMB01	Numb (CD, 2-track, promo p/s) 10
06	Parlophone PRIVATE001	In Private (Tomcraft Mixes) (12" promo) 20
07	Parlophone INTEGRAL001	Integral (CD, 2-track promo p/s) 15
89	Parlophone CDPCSD 113	BEHAVIOUR (CD, commercial issue, different inlay, in white monogrammed pouch, with full-album cassette & chronology) 50
91	Parlophone CDPSBDJ 1	DISCOGRAPHY (CD, with Mark Goodyear spoken-word introductions) 12
93	Parlophone DF 118	RELENTLESS (3 x 12", on pink/yellow/blue vinyl) 30
96	Parlophone BILING 1	BILINGUAL (A4 yellow box set, including "A Taste Of Bilingual" CD: (Discoteca/Electricity/A Red Letter Day/It Always Comes As A Surprise/Se A Vida E) (with 2 photos & inset in transparent PVC box) 50
96	Parlophone PSBCDDJ 1	BILINGUAL (A4 pale blue launch party promo box set including "A Taste Of Bilingual" CD [Before/Se A Vida E], & album cassette, unique inlay) 200
99	Parlophone CDIN 126	INTERVIEW (CD, slipcase, for NIGHTLIFE album) 15
01	Really Useful Group	CLOSER TO HEAVEN (CD-R, title sleeve; 19 tracks, all sung by Neil Tennant) 250
02	Parlophone RELEASE 01	RELEASE (CD, white card sleeve sealed with title sticker) 15
02	Parlophone RELEASE02	RE: RELEASE (CD, interview, sitckered card sleeve) 15
03	Parlophone POPART 02	THE INTERVIEW (interview CD for 'PopArt', with cue sheet) 15
06	Parlophone 009463661421	FUNDAMENTAL INTERVIEW (CD, p/s with cues) 15
07	Parlophone DISCO004	DISCO 4 ALBUM SAMPLER (12" 4-tracks) 20
07	Parlophone (no cat. No.)	DISCO FOUR (Promo CD-R, 5-track album sampler and press sheet, 30 copies) 40
01	Parlophone PSB 001	SAMPLER (CD, 13-track sampler, includes six previously unreleased versions, part-laminated card sleeve) 15

(see also Eighth Wonder, Dusty Springfield, Absolutely Fabulous, Electronic, Liza Minnelli, Ian Wright)

MARY PETTI

61	RCA RCA 1239	Hey! Lawdy Lawdy/Gee, But It Hurts 40

PETTICOATS

80	Bla Bla Bla 01	Normal/Allergy/I'm Free (with insert) 20

FRANK PETTY TRIO

53	MGM SP 1010	St. Louis Blues (Boogie Woogie)/Somebody Stole My Girl 20

53	MGM SP 1033	Side By Side/Who's Sorry Now	7
53	MGM SP 1038	Sugar/Sioux City Sue	7
53	MGM SP 1053	Sweet Jenny Lee/Yes Sir That's My Baby	6
54	MGM SP 1092	Loch Lomond/Pino Pantaloni	6
54	MGM SP 1112	Mr Pogo/Sunday	6

NORMAN PETTY TRIO
54	HMV 7M 274	Mood Indigo/Petty's Little Polka	10

TOM PETTY (& HEARTBREAKERS)
77	Shelter WIP 6377	American Girl/Wild One Forever (some in p/s)	5
77	Shleter WIP 12-6396	Anything That's Rock'n'Roll/Fooled Again (I Don't Like It) (live) (12")	8
77	Shelter WIP 12-6403	American Girl/Luna (live) (12")	8
76	Shelter 1DJ 24A	OFFICIAL LIVE BOOTLEG (LP, with Heartbreakers, 1-sided 5-track, promo only)	20

(see also Stevie Nicks, Randy Newman, Traveling Wilburys, k.d. lang & Roy Orbison)

P.F.M.
73	Manticore K 43502	PHOTOS OF GHOSTS (LP, laminated gatefold sleeve)	25
74	Manticore K 53502	THE WORLD BECAME THE WORLD (LP, die-cut sleeve with inner)	20
74	Manticore K 53506	COOK (LP)	15
76	Manticore K 53508	CHOCOLATE KINGS (LP, gatefold sleeve with lyric sheet)	12

PHANTOM
78	Cool Ghoul COOL 1	Lazy Fascist/Power Dub	6

(see also Tom Robinson, Blazing Sons)

PHANTOM BAND
71	Polydor 2058-176	Loop-Di-Love/Funkin' About	30
72	Polydor 2058-290	Silhouettes/Drummitt	15

PHANTOM CHORDS
92	Camden Town GNAR 003	Town Without Pity/She's A Bad Motorcycle (p/s, 2,000 only)	5

(see also Damned)

PHANTOMS
61	Palette PG 9014	Phantom Guitar/Cachina	20
60s	Arc ARC	GREAT GUITAR HITS (LP)	30

PHARAOHS
58	Decca DFE 6522	THE PHARAOHS (EP)	800
86	Ace SW 116	THE PHARAOHS (EP, reissue)	8

RORY PHARE
88	Parlophone RP 1	Laughing Inside/Laughing Inside (actually by Roy Harper; p/s, promo only)	7

(see also Roy Harper)

PHASE 4
66	Decca F 12327	What Do You Say About That/Think I'll Sit Down And Cry (1st issue)	25
66	Fab FAB 1	What Do You Say About That/I'm Gonna Sit Down And Cry (2nd issue)	20
67	Fab FAB 6	Man Am I Worried?/Listen To The Blues	50

PHASE 5
70	Polydor 2058 063	Star Trek/Enterprise	30

PHASE 3
71	Mushroom SMR 5	Walkin' Free/Bill Bailey	10

JAMES PHELPS
72	Paramount PARA 3019	Check Yourself/My Lover's Prayer	12

PHENOMENA
85	Bronze BRO 193	Dance With The Devil/Hell On Wings (p/s)	7
85	Bronze BROX 193	Dance With The Devil (MIdnight Mix)/Hell On Wings (12", p/s with poster)	10

(see also Trapeze, Whitesnake, Cozy Powell, Black Sabbath, Thin Lizzy, Budgie, A-Ha)

PHEON BEAR
73	Pye 7N 45232	War Against War/87th Precinct	22

PHIL & FLINTSTONES
64	Bedrock PR 5371	Love Potion No. 9/Honey Don't (private pressing)	80

PHI LIFE CYPHER
98	Compressed Knowledge CK001	Baddest Man/Da Shinn/Rap 'N' Bullshit/Forever (12")	12

PHILIP & HIS FOETUS VIBRATIONS
82	Self Immol. WOMB KX 07	Tell Me, What Is The Bane Of Your Life/Mother I've Killed The Cat (p/s)	25

(see also You've Got Foetus On Your Breath, Foetus Art Terrorism, Foetus Äœber Frisco, Foetus Under Glass, Scraping Foetus Off The Wheel)

LOUIS PHILIPPE
86	él GPO 15	Like Nobody Do/Twangy Twangy (p/s)	6
88	él ACME 15	IVORY TOWER (LP)	20
89	el ACME 23	AN APPOINTMENT WITH VENUS (LP)	30
89	él ACME 36	YURI GAGARIN (LP)	20

BRENDAN PHILIPS
66	Mercury MF 896	Is It Worth A Try/When She's Kissing Me	25

NOEL PHILIPS
71	CBS 7036	Eternal Loner/Snowman	10

TONY PHILIPS & THE HAYSEEDS
66	CBS 202337	Shropshire Lad/Situation Vacant	12

PHILL MOST CHILL
06	Diggers With Gratitude DWG 001	BE INTELLIGENT (EP, 100 only)	300
11	Diggers With Gratitude DWG 008	ALL CUTS RECORDED RAW (LP)	45
11	Diggers With Gratitude DWG 008	ALL CUTS RECORDED RAW (LP, 25 copies only, alternative pressing, white stickered cover)	350
11	Diggers With Gratitude DWG 008	ALL CUTS RECORDED RAW (LP, coloured vinyl, alternative pressing EP and 7")	200

ANTHONY PHILLIPS
79	Arista SPART 1085/AFLP 1	SIDES (LP, 1st 500 copies sealed with free LP "Private Parts & Pieces")	20

(see also Genesis)

CONFREY PHILLIPS (TRIO)
56	Columbia SCM 5223	Love And Marriage/The Others I Like	5
57	Decca F 10835	Am I Going Out Of My Mind?/Afterglow	5
57	Decca F 10866	Shotgun Rock 'n' Roll/Hokey-Kokey Rock 'n' Roll (as Confrey Phillips Trio)	20
57	Decca F 10866	Shotgun Rock 'n' Roll/Hokey-Kokey Rock 'n' Roll (as Confrey Phillips Trio) (78)	10

EDDY/EDWIN PHILLIPS
76	Charisma CB 283	Limbo Jimbo/Change My Ways (as Eddy Phillips)	5

(see also Creation, Mark Four, Spectrum)

(LITTLE) ESTHER (PHILLIPS)
62	Stateside SS 140	Release Me/Don't Feel Rained On	25
63	Ember EMB S 174	Am I That Easy To Forget/I Really Don't Want To Know (as Little Esther Phillips)	15
65	Sue WI 395	The Chains/Feel Like I Wanna Cry (as Esther Phillips)	40
65	Atlantic AT 4028	And I Love Him/Shangri-La	18
65	Atlantic AT 4048	Let Me Know When It's Over/I Saw Me	15
66	Atlantic AT 4077	I Could Have Told You/Just Say Goodbye	80
66	Atlantic AT 4077	I Could Have Told You/Just Say Goodbye (DJ Copy)	100
66	Ember EMBS 221	Release Me/Be Honest With Me (as Little Esther Phillips)	12
66	Atlantic 584 013	When A Woman Loves A Man/Ups And Downs	15
67	Atlantic 584 062	Someone Else Is Taking My Place/When Love Comes To The Human Race	10
67	Atlantic 584 103	And I Love Him/Shangri-La (reissue)	8
67	Atlantic 584 126	I'm Sorry/Cheater Man	15
69	Roulette RO 505	Too Late To Worry, Too Blue To Cry/I'm In The Mood For Love (Moody's Mood For Love)	8
69	Roulette RO 508	Tonight I'll Be Staying Here With You/Sweet Dreams	6
72	Atlantic K 10168	Catch Me I'm Falling/Release Me	15
72	Kudu KUS 4000	Home Is Where The Hatred Is/Til My Back Ain't Got No Bone	20
73	Kudu KUS 4002	I've Never Found A Man/Cherry Red	15
75	Kudu 925	What A Difference A Day Made/Turn Around, Look At Me	5
63	Ember CW 103	REFLECTIONS OF GREAT COUNTRY AND WESTERN STANDARDS (LP)	50
65	Atlantic ATL 5030	AND I LOVE HIM (LP)	50
67	Atlantic 587/588 010	ESTHER PHILLIPS SINGS (LP)	30
72	Kudu KUL 2	FROM A WHISPER TO A SCREAM (LP)	20
73	Kudu KUL 6	ALONE AGAIN, NATURALLY (LP)	12
75	Kudu KU 18	PERFORMANCE (LP)	12
76	Atlantic K 50521	CONFESSIN' THE BLUES (LP, gatefold sleeve)	12

FLIP PHILLIPS
56	Columbia/Clef 33C 9003	FLIP PHILLIPS QUARTET (10" LP)	12

GLENN PHILLIPS
75	Caroline C 1519	LOST AT SEA (LP)	20
77	Virgin V 2087	SWIM IN THE WIND (LP)	12

GREGORY PHILLIPS
63	Pye 7N 15546	Angie/Please Believe Me	12
64	Pye 7N 15593	Everybody Knows/Closer To Me (with Remo Four)	8
64	Pye 7N 15633	Don't Bother Me/Make Sure That You're Mine	8
65	Immediate IM 004	Down In The Boondocks/That's The One	30

(see also Remo Four)

JOHN PHILLIPS
70	Stateside SS 8046	Mississippi/April Anne	6
70	Stateside-Dunhill SSL 5027	JOHN PHILLIPS: THE WOLFKING OF L.A. (LP)	35

(see also Mamas & Papas)

LESLIE PHILLIPS
59	Parlophone R 4610	The Navy Lark/The Disc	7
62	Parlophone R 4912	Jolly Old Spring/I Must Resist Temptation	6
69	Columbia DB 8562	The Man Most Likely To/Marigold	6

MICHELLE PHILLIPS
76	A&M AMS 7250	No Love Today/Aloha Louie	7
77	A&M AMS 7340	Victim Of Romance/Lady Of Fantasy	15
77	A&M AMLS 64651	VICTIM OF ROMANCE (LP)	30

(see also Mamas & Papas)

NOEL PHILLIPS
80	Jammys JM001	Youth Man/Living In The Ghetto (12")	25

PHIL PHILLIPS & TWILIGHTS
59	Mercury AMT 1059	Sea Of Love/Juella	35
60	Mercury AMT 1072	Take This Heart/Verdi Mae	30
60	Mercury AMT 1093	Your True Love Once More/What Will I Tell My Heart	30
61	Mercury AMT 1139	I Love To Love You/No One Else But You	30

SHAWN PHILLIPS
65	Columbia DB 7611	Hey Nelly Nelly/Solitude	12
65	Columbia DB 7699	Doesn't Anybody Know My Name?/Nobody Listens	12
65	Columbia DB 7789	Little Tin Soldier/London Town	8
66	Columbia DB 7956	Summer Came/Storm	8
67	Parlophone R 5606	Stargazer/Woman Mine	80
70	A&M AMS 819	Christmas Song/Lovely Lady	6
65	Columbia 33SX 1748	I'M A LONER (LP)	140
66	Columbia S(C)X 6006	SHAWN (LP)	250
70	A&M AMLS 978	CONTRIBUTION (LP)	18
71	A&M AMLS 2006	SECOND CONTRIBUTION (LP, with insert)	18
72	A&M AMLS 64324	COLLABORATION (LP)	18
73	A&M AMLS 64363	FACES (LP)	18
74	A&M AMLH 68278	FURTHERMORE (LP)	12
77	A&M AMLH 64650	SPACED (LP, with inner sleeve)	12

SID PHILLIPS BAND
56	HMV POP 269	Farewell Blues (Rock 'N' Roll Style)/It Goes Like This	6
55	HMV DLP 1102	HORS D'OEUVRES (10" LP)	15

STU PHILLIPS
58	London HL 8673	The Champlain And St. Lawrence Line/The Priest Who Slept 100 Years	10
60	Pye International 7N 25062	Strangers When We Meet/BOB MERSEY ORCHESTRA: Song Of India	6
67	RCA RCA 1601	Angel Of Love/The Great El Tigre	5
59	Pye Intl. NEP 44001	STU PHILLIPS (EP)	12

TEDDY PHILLIPS & HIS ORCHESTRA
54	Parlophone CMSP 4	Down Boy/Meet "Miss Pippin" (export issue)	12
54	Parlophone CMSP 12	The Old Red Barn/JIMMY BLUE CREW: The Old Shoe Cobbler (export issue)	8
54	Parlophone CMSP 28	Life Is Like A Slice Of Cake/One-Sided Love Affair (export issue)	12

WARREN PHILLIPS & THE ROCKETS
69	Decca (S)PA 43	THE WORLD OF ROCK 'N' ROLL (LP)	15

(see also Savoy Brown, Foghat)

WOOLF PHILLIPS & HIS ORCHESTRA
54	Decca F 10416	Count Your Blessings Instead Of Sheep/Your Heart, My Heart (B-side with Dennis Morley - Vocal)	6

PHILLY DOG
74	Penny Farthing PEN 581	You Got The Gun/Hijack	10

PHILOSOPHERS
69	Pye 7N 17740	The Lovedene Girls/I Believe Forever	25

VINCE PHILPOTT & DRAGS
64	Decca F 11997	The Cramp/Eenie Meenie Miny Mo	15

PHILWIT & PEGASUS
70	Chapter One CHR 130	And She Came - Final Thought/Pauper's Son	8
70	Chapter One CHR 131	And I Try/Pauper's Son	8
70	Chapter One CHR 137	The Elephant Song/Pseudo Phoney Mixed Up Croney	40
70	Chapter One CHSR 805	PHILWIT AND PEGASUS (LP)	40

(see also Mark Wirtz)

PHOENIX
69	President PT 246	Tour De France/Time To Go	5
81	Rising PR 433032	PHOENIX RISING EP (Lonely Attack/The Minstrel/Understanding/Phoenix Rising 'Av An 'Am) (12" EP)	35

PAT PHOENIX
62	HMV POP 1030	The Rovers Chorus/Coronation Street Monologue	12

PHONES SPORTSMAN BAND
81	Rather GEAR 9	I REALLY LOVE YOU (EP)	8

(see also Swell Maps)

PHOTOGRAPHED BY LIGHTNING
86	Fierce FRIGHT 008	Sleep's Terminator/Winter Trees (foldaround p/s, hand-coloured labels)	30

PHUTURE PHANTASY
88	Low Fat Vinyl LFV 1	SLAM (12")	15

PHUTURE PRIMITIVE
93	Knifeforce KF 006	Full Metal Jacket/Twinkle (12")	30
94	Knifeforce KF 026	Lift Me Up/Infect Me (12")	15

PHYSICALS
79	Big Beat NS 58	Be Like Me/Pain In Love (p/s)	6

(see also Maniacs)

PIANO MAGIC
96	i IRE 1071	Wrong French/Non-Fiction/General Electric With Fairylights (12", p/s)	10
97	i IRE 2031	Wintersport/Cross Country/Angel Pie/Magic Tree/Magnetic North (12", p/s)	10
97	Wurlitzer Jukebox WJ 26	For Engineers A/For Engineers AA (p/s)	7
98	Lissy's LISS 32	Music For Rolex/MATMOS: The Soldering Social (p/s)	6
98	Debut DEBT 001SP	French Mittens/Icebreaker: Melody For Nato (p/s)	8
98	Bad Jazz BEBOP 9	Music For Annahbird/Music For Wasps/Me At 19 (p/s)	8
98	Piao! PIAO! 12	The Fun Of The Century/The Sharpest Knife In The Drawer/Industrial Cutie/I Am The Sub-Librarian (12", p/s)	12
99	Rocket Girl RGIRL 12	There's No Need For Us To Be Alone/The Canadian Brought Us Snow (p/s)	5
00	Morr MUSIC 008	Panic Amigo - Piano Magic Remixed (12" EP)	10

PIANO RED
52	HMV B 10244	Rockin' With Red/Red's Boogie (78)	20
52	HMV B 10246	Just Right Bounce/Hey, Good Lookin' (78)	20
52	HMV B 10316	Count The Days I'm Gone/Bouncin' With Red (78)	20
52	HMV JO 244	Rockin' With Red/Red's Boogie (78, export issue)	18
52	HMV JO 276	Layin' The Boogie/Baby What's Wrong (78, export issue)	18
52	HMV JO 296	My Gal Jo/Let's Have A Good Time (78, export issue)	18
53	HMV JO 334	Voo Doopee Doo/Everybody's Boogie (78, export issue)	18
53	HMV 7M 108	Rockin' With Red/Red's Boogie	150
64	RCA RCX 7138	RHYTHM AND BLUES VOL. 2 (EP)	15

(see also Dr. Feelgood [U.S.])

PICA
70	Polydor 2058 056	Take The Barriers Down/Insurance Man	10
71	Philips 6006 129	Rainbow Chaser/Ad Lib	150

(see also Nirvana [UK])

PICADILLY LINE
67	CBS 2785	At The Third Stroke/How Could You Say You're Leaving Me	30
67	CBS 2958	Emily Small (The Huge World Thereof)/Gone Gone Gone	25
68	CBS 3595	Yellow Rainbow/Evenings With Corrina	30
68	CBS 3595	Yellow Rainbow/I Know, She Believes (reissue with different B-side)	25
68	CBS 3743	Evenings With Corrina/My Best Friend	20

MINT VALUE £

| 67 | CBS (S)BPG 63129 | THE HUGE WORLD OF EMILY SMALL (LP, laminated front sleeve)...........................300 |
| 67 | CBS (S)BPG 63129 | THE HUGE WORLD OF EMILY SMALL (LP, laminated front sleeve, promo insert)................350 |

(see also Edwards Hand)

PIC & BILL
67	Page One POF 024	All I Want Is You/It's Not You 15
67	Page One POF 037	This Is It/Nobody But My Baby..15
68	Page One POF 052	Sad World Without You/Just A Tear 15

PICARDY
| 68 | Statside SIDE 8004 | Montage/How Sweet It Is ....5 |

PIERO PICCIONI
| 67 | Fontana TF 898 | Main Theme From 'The Tenth Victim'/Part 2 (mono)................................12 |

BUSTER PICKENS
| 60s | Heritage HLP 1008 | TEXAS PIANO (LP, 99 only) ....60 |

J.B. PICKERS
| 71 | London HLU 10334 | Super Soul Sounds/KIM & DAVE: Nobody Knows ....15 |

BOBBY (BORIS) PICKETT & CRYPT-KICKERS
| 62 | London HLU 9597 | Monster Mash/Monsters' Mash Party...10 |
| 73 | London ZGU 133 | MONSTER MASH (LP)...20 |

DAN PICKETT
| 60s | XX MIN 710 | DAN PICKETT (EP) ....15 |

KENNY PICKETT
| 80 | F Beat PRO 2 | Got A Gun/Same...15 |

(see also The Creation)

NICK PICKETT
| 72 | Warner Bros K 14156 | America/Lady Luck ....6 |
| 72 | Reprise K 44172 | SILVERSLEEVES (LP) ....30 |

(see also John Dummer Blues Band)

WILSON PICKETT
63	Liberty LIB 10115	It's Too Late/I'm Gonna Love You 25
65	Atlantic AT 4036	In The Midnight Hour/I'm Not Tired 20
65	MGM MGM 1286	Let Me Be Your Boy/My Heart Belongs To You............................50
65	MGM MGM 1286	Let Me Be Your Boy/My Heart Belongs To You (DJ copy).................100
65	Atlantic AT 4052	Don't Fight It/It's All Over 12
66	Atlantic AT 4072	634-5789/That's A Man's Way 12
66	Atlantic 584 023	99 And A Half (Won't Do)/Danger Zone 12
66	Atlantic 584 039	Land Of 1000 Dances/You're So Fine 10
66	Atlantic 584 066	Mustang Sally/Three Time Loser 10
67	Atlantic 584 101	Everybody Needs Somebody To Love/Nothing You Can Do 10
67	Atlantic 584 107	New Orleans/Soul Dance III 10
67	London HLU 10146	Billy The Kid/I Don't Want No Part-Time Love (with Falcons).......10
67	Atlantic 584 130	Funky Broadway/I'm Sorry About That 10
67	Atlantic 584 142	Stag-O-Lee/I'm In Love.................................10
68	Atlantic 584 150	In The Midnight Hour/Danger Zone 7
68	Atlantic 584 173	That Kind Of Love/I've Come A Long Way 8
68	Atlantic 584 183	She's Looking Good/We've Got To Have Love 10
68	Atlantic 584 203	I'm A Midnight Mover/Deborah 5
68	Atlantic 584 221	I Found A True Love/For Better Or Worse 5
69	Atlantic 584 236	Hey Jude/Night Owl....................................8
69	Atlantic 584 261	Mini-Skirt Minnie/Back In Your Arms 10
69	Atlantic 584 281	Hey Joe/Born To Be Wild.................................5
70	Atlantic 584 313	You Keep Me Hangin' On/Now You See Me, Now You Don't...............8
70	Atlantic 2091 005	Sugar, Sugar/Cole, Cooke And Redding.................................5
70	Atlantic 2091 032	(Get Me Back On Time) Engine No. 9/International Playboy.............5
71	Atlantic 2091 086	Fire And Water/Don't Let The Green Grass Fool You...............5
71	Atlantic 2091 124	Don't Knock My Love (Parts 1 & 2) 5
72	Atlantic K 10166	Don't Let The Green Grass Fool You/Covering The Same Old Ground 5
72	President PT 319	If You Need Me/I'm Gonna Love You 5
73	President PT 322	I Can't Stop/Down To My Last Heartbreak 5
65	Atlantic ATL 5037	IN THE MIDNIGHT HOUR (LP).................................50
66	Atlantic 587/588 029	THE EXCITING WILSON PICKETT (LP)..............................20
66	Atlantic 587 032	IN THE MIDNIGHT HOUR (LP, reissue)...............................20
67	Atlantic 587/588 057	THE WICKED PICKETT (LP).................................20
67	Atlantic 587/588 080	THE SOUND OF WILSON PICKETT (LP)..............................20
68	Atlantic 587/588 092	THE BEST OF WILSON PICKETT (LP)...............................20
68	Atlantic 587/588 107	I'M IN LOVE (LP)...................................20
68	Atlantic 587/588 111	MIDNIGHT MOVER (LP).................................20
69	Atlantic 588 170	HEY JUDE (LP) 20
70	Atlantic 2465 002	RIGHT ON (LP).................................20
70	Joy JOYS 181	IF YOU NEED ME (LP)................................15
71	Atlantic 2400 026	ENGINE NO. 9 - IN PHILADELPHIA (LP)...............................15

(see also Falcons)

GARY PICKFORD-HOPKINS & FRIENDS
| 83 | Spartan SP 143 | Why? (The Song)/Why? (The Story) (p/s) ....8 |
| 83 | Spartan SP 143T | Why? (The Song)/Why? (The Story) (12", p/s) ....10 |

(see also Deke Leonard, Man, Andy Fairweather-Low, Alan Ross, Big Sleep, Eyes Of Blue, Wild Turkey)

PICKWICKS
64	Decca F 11901	Apple Blossom Time/I Don't Wanna Tell You Again 18
64	Decca F 11957	You're Old Enough/Hello Lady............................15
65	Warner Bros WB 151	Little By Little/I Took My Baby Home 100

PICTURE FRAME SEDUCTION
84	SOSO 33	I'm Good Enough For Me/Sabotage The Classes/Fur Queue 40
87	PFS 2	Try With A Little Help From My Friends/And Entertainment USA 40
85	Rot PFS 1	HAND OF THE RIDER (LP) 40

PIED PIPERS (1)
54	Parlophone CMSP 21	Kissin' Drive Rock/Please Understand (export issue)	15

PIED PIPERS (2)
66	Columbia DB 7883	Ragamuffin/Fat Marie	30

BILLY & DEDE PIERCE/JIM ROBINSON
64	London HA-K/SH-K 8163	JAZZ AT PRESERVATION HALL VOL. 2 (LP)	12

WEBB PIERCE
50s	Decca BM 311368	We'll Find A Way/Any Old Time (export issue)	30
56	Brunswick 05630	Teenage Boogie/Any Old Time	150
56	Brunswick 05630	Teenage Boogie/Any Old Time (78)	30
57	Brunswick 05682	Bye, Bye Love/Honky Tonk Song	40
57	Brunswick 05682	Bye, Bye Love/Honky Tonk Song (78)	20
59	Brunswick 05809	I Ain't Never/Shanghaied	20
59	Brunswick 05809	I Ain't Never/Shanghaied (78)	20
60	Brunswick 05820	No Love Have I/Whirlpool Of Love	10
60	Brunswick 05842	Drifting Texas Sand/All I Need Is You	10
56	Brunswick OE 9253	WEBB PIERCE PT. 1 (EP)	20
56	Brunswick OE 9254	WEBB PIERCE PT. 2 (EP)	20
56	Brunswick OE 9255	WEBB PIERCE PT. 3 (EP)	20
62	Ember EMB 4520	COUNTRY AND WESTERN FAVOURITES VOL. 1 (EP)	15
59	Parlophone GEP 8792	COUNTRY ROUND UP (EP)	40
55	Brunswick LA 8716	THE WONDERING BOY (10" LP)	50
60	Brunswick LAT 8324	WEBB! (LP)	25
65	Brunswick LAT 8540	HIDEAWAY HEART (LP)	25
65	Brunswick LAT 8551	CROSS COUNTRY (LP)	15

(see also Red Sovine & Webb Pierce)

CLIVE PIG & THE HOPEFUL CHINAMEN
79	Pinnacle PIN 21	Happy Birthday Sweet Sixteen/Our Movement (p/s)	10

(see also Trixie's Big Red Motorbike)

PIGEON DETECTIVES
06	Dance To The Radio DTTR 08	I'm Not Sorry/I'm Always Right (p/s)	10

PIGEON FLYERS
68	Columbia DB 8449	The Heaven We Shared Together/Keep On Sayin'	8

BILLY PIGG
71	Leader LEA 4006	THE BORDER MINSTREL (LP, gatefold sleeve with booklet)	12

PIGGLESWICK FOLK
77	Acorn CF 256	PIG IN THE MIDDLE (LP)	12

PIGS
77	Bristol Recorder NBR 01	Youthenasia/They Say/Psychopath/National Front (p/s)	10

PIGSTY HILL LIGHT ORCHESTRA
70	Village Thing VTS 1	PHLOP! (LP)	15
72	Village Thing VTS 8	PIGGERY JOKERY (LP)	15

DAVE PIKE
63	Starlite ST45 094	Melvalita/Ginha - Bossa Nova	5
66	Atlantic 584 052	Sunny/HERBIE MANN: Philly Dog	15
66	Atlantic 588 005	JAZZ FOR THE JET SET (LP)	25
62	Esquire32-150	BOSA NOVA CARNIVAL (LP)	15

RAY PILGRIM (& BEATMEN)
60	Oriole CB 1557	Baby Doll/Gambler's Guitar (solo)	15
61	Oriole CB 1616	Little Miss Makebelieve/Granada (solo)	8
64	Embassy WB 645	Kissin' Cousins (with Beatmen)/ JAYBIRDS: Some Day We're Gonna Love Again	5

(see also Bud Ashton, Jaybirds, Typhoons)

PILGRIM FATHERS
69	Tangerine 009	Love And The World Will Love/Come A Day	7

PILOT
74	EMI 2217	Magic/Just Let Me Be	5
74	EMI 2250	January/Never Give Up	5

PILTDOWN MEN
60	Capitol EAP1-20155	PILTDOWN MEN RIDE AGAIN (EP)	8
60	Capitol CL 15149	McDonald's Cave/Brontosaurus Stomp	8
61	Capitol CL 15175	Piltdown Rides Again/Bubbles In The Tar	8
61	Capitol CL 15186	Goodnight Mrs Flintstone/The Great Imposter	8
61	Capitol CL 15211	Gargantua/Fossil Rock	10
62	Capitol CL 15245	A Pretty Girl Is Like A Melody/Big Lizard	20
61	Capitol EAP1 20155	GOODNIGHT MRS. FLINTSTONE (EP)	25

SIR HUBERT PIMM
55	London HL 8155	Goodnight And Cheerio/Honky Tonk Train Blues	50
55	London RE-U 1032	PIMM'S PARTY (EP, with Ellen Sutton)	20

(see also Duke & Duchess)

COURTNEY PINE
88	Island 10ISB 301	CHILDREN OF THE GHETTO (LP, 2 x 10", with 4 prints)	20

PINEAPPLE CHUNKS
65	Mercury MF 922	Drive My Car/Dream About	15

PINEAPPLE THIEF
00	Obtuse OBT 001	Shertbert Gods/Perpetual Flying Objects (wraparound p/s in poly bag)	40
05	Cyclops CYCLS 150	4 STORIES DOWN EP (CD)	20
01	Cyclops CYCL 079	ABDUCTING THE UNICORN (CD)	25

PINEWOOD STUDIO ORCHESTRA
59	Top Rank JAR 112	Sapphire/Tiger Bay	6
62	Parlophone R 4906	The Waltz Of The Toreadors/Picture Parade	6

PINEWOOD TOM/TOM TALL
59	Jazz Collector JEL 5	THE MALE BLUES VOLUME 4 (EP)	18

'PING PING' & AL VERLANE
60	Oriole CB 1589	Sucu Sucu/Maria Della Montagna	8

RICHARD PINHAS
80	Pulse 500	West Side/Houston 69 (p/s)	5

PINK ELEPHANT
72	Pye 7N 45143	Down In The Valley/I'm Living In This World Just For You	15

PINK FAIRIES
71	Polydor 2058 089	The Snake/Do It	25
72	Polydor 2059 302	Well Well Well/Hold On	25
76	Stiff BUY 2	Between The Lines/Spoiling For A Fight (p/s)	7
71	Polydor 2383 045	NEVERNEVERLAND (LP, printed PVC outer & gatefold card inner, in yellow bag with photos & notes)	200
71	Polydor 2383 045	NEVERNEVERLAND (LP, printed PVC outer & gatefold card inner, pink vinyl & "pink plastic" in text on rear sleeve, around 100 pressed)	500
71	Polydor 2383 045	NEVERNEVERLAND (LP, black vinyl, standard sleeve)	40
72	Polydor 2383 132	WHAT A BUNCH OF SWEETIES (LP)	22
73	Polydor 2383 212	KINGS OF OBLIVION (LP, with poster)	35
75	Polydor 2384 071	FLASHBACK (LP)	18

(see also Twink, Larry Wallis, Deviants, Lightning Raiders, Shagrat)

PINK FLOYD
SINGLES
67	Columbia DB 8156	Arnold Layne/Candy And A Currant Bun	80
67	Columbia DB 8214	See Emily Play/Scarecrow	60
67	Columbia DB 8310	Apples And Oranges/Paintbox	120
68	Columbia DB 8401	It Would Be So Nice/Julia Dream	80
68	Columbia DB 8511	Point Me At The Sky/Careful With That Axe, Eugene	100
79	Harvest HAR 5194	Another Brick In The Wall (Part 2)/One Of My Turns (initial pressing, plain B-side label without 'window' picture)	5
81	Harvest HAR 5217	Money (Edit)/Let There Be More Light (unreleased, die-cut sleeve)	0
81	Harvest 12HAR 5217	Money (Full Length)/Let There Be More Light (12", unreleased)	0
82	Harvest HAR 5222	When The Tigers Broke Free/Bring The Boys Back Home (gatefold p/s)	7
82	Harvest HAR 5222	When The Tigers Broke Free/Bring The Boys Back Home (standard p/s)	8
87	EMI EM 34	On The Turning Away (Album)/Run Like Hell (Live Version) (p/s)	5
87	EMI EMP 34	On The Turning Away (Album)/Run Like Hell (Live Version) (p/s, pink vinyl, 1000 only)	8
87	EMI 12EMP 34	On The Turning Away (Album)/Run Like Hell (Live Version)/On The Turning Away (Live Version) (12", poster p/s)	12
87	EMI CDEM 34	On The Turning Away/Run Like Hell (Live Version)/On The Turning Away (Live Version) (CD)	15
87	EMI 12EMP 34	On The Turning Away (Album)/Run Like Hell (Live Version)/On The Turning Away (Live Version)	12
87	EMI EMDJ 26	Learning To Fly (Edited Version)/One Slip (Edited Version)/Terminal Frost (no p/s, mispressing without "One Slip", 50 on black vinyl)	20
87	EMI CDEM 26	Learning To Fly (Edited Version)/One Slip (Edited Version)/Terminal Frost (no p/s, mispressing without "One Slip", 1,000 only on pink vinyl)	12
87	EMI CDEM 26	Learning To Fly (Edited Version)/One Slip (Edited Version)/Terminal Frost (Album Version)/Terminal Frost (DYOL Version) (CD, card sleeve & inner)	15
88	EMI EMG 52	One Slip/Terminal Frost (pink vinyl, gatefold p/s with ticket application)	8
88	EMI 12EMP 52	One Slip/Terminal Frost/The Dogs Of War (live) (12", poster p/s)	8
88	EMI CDEM 52	One Slip/Terminal Frost/The Dogs Of War (live) (CD)	12
94	EMI EM 309	Take It Back (Edit)/Astronomy Domine (live) (jukebox issue, black vinyl)	8
94	EMI EM 309	Take It Back (Edit) /Astronomy Domine (Live) (p/s)	7
94	EMI EM 309	Take It Back (Edit)/Astronomy Domine (Live) (red vinyl, p/s)	7
94	EMI EM 342	High Hopes (Radio Edit)/Keep Talking (Radio Edit) (clear vinyl, poster p/s)	8
94	EMI 12EM 342	High Hopes (Album Version)/Keep Talking (Album Version)/One Of These Days (live) (12", 1-sided, laser-etched blue vinyl, p/s in outer gtefold p/s with 7 postcards)	12

ALBUMS
67	Columbia SX 6157	THE PIPER AT THE GATES OF DAWN (LP, mono, blue/black label, with "Sold in U.K..." text)	700
67	Columbia SCX 6157	THE PIPER AT THE GATES OF DAWN (LP, stereo, blue/black label, with "Sold in the U.K..." text)	400

(Second pressings have "File Under Pop" on the right of the flipback; first pressings do not have this. Second pressing worth half to a third less)

68	Columbia SX 6258	A SAUCERFUL OF SECRETS (LP, mono, blue/black label, "Sold in U.K..." text)	500
68	Columbia SCX 6258	A SAUCERFUL OF SECRETS (LP, stereo, blue/black label, "Sold in U.K..." text)	400
69	Columbia SCX 6346	SOUNDTRACK FROM THE FILM 'MORE' (LP, laminated flipback sleeve, 'couple facing west' photo on green-tinted rear sleeve. 1st pressing with black/silver label, boxed logo and "Sold in UK..." text)	70
69	Harvest SHDW 1/2	UMMAGUMMA (2-LP, without EMI logo, laminated gatefold sleeve)	100
69	Harvest SHDW 1/2	UMMAGUMMA (2-LP, with EMI logo, laminated gatefold sleeve)	40
69	Harvest SHDW 1/2	UMMAGUMMA (2-LP, with EMI logo, laminated gatefold sleeve)	40
70	Columbia SCX 6157	THE PIPER AT THE GATES OF DAWN (LP, re-pressing, laminated sleeve, silver & black label with boxed EMI logo)	50
70	Columbia SCX 6258	A SAUCERFUL OF SECRETS (LP, re-pressing, silver & black label)	25
70s	Columbia SCX 6346	SOUNDTRACK FROM THE FILM 'MORE' (LP, laminated non-flipback sleeve, 'couple facing west' photo on black-tinted rear sleeve)	45
70s	Columbia SCX 6346	SOUNDTRACK FROM THE FILM 'MORE' (LP, laminated non-flipback sleeve, 'couple facing east' photo on black-tinted rear sleeve)	50
70	MGM 2315 002	ZABRISKIE POINT (LP, soundtrack, with Jerry Garcia/Kaleidoscope, et al.)	30
70	Harvest SHVL 781	ATOM HEART MOTHER (LP, gatefold sleeve, no EMI logo)	90

(First pressing Harvest LPs of UMMAGUMMA and ATOM HEART MOTHER have "The Gramophone..." text on label rim and "Harvest" on the left side of the label; second pressings have "The Gramophone..." text with a boxed EMI logo above "Harvest")

71	Harvest SHVL 795	MEDDLE (LP, textured inside/outside gatefold sleeve)	40
71	Harvest SHVL 795	MEDDLE (LP, textured outside gatefold sleeve)	20
71	Starline SRS 5071	RELICS (LP, white textured sleeve)	15
72	Harvest SHSP 4020	OBSCURED BY CLOUDS (LP, rounded sleeve, EMI logo on label)	25
73	Harvest SHVL 804	THE DARK SIDE OF THE MOON (LP, first pressing, solid light blue triangle label, black inner, 2 posters & 2 stickers, gatefold sleeve, only one side opening)	500
73	Harvest SHVL 804	THE DARK SIDE OF THE MOON (LP, blue & black label, gatefold sleeve with black inner, 2 posters & 2 stickers, with stickered sleeve)	20

73	Harvest SHVL 804	THE DARK SIDE OF THE MOON (LP, blue & black label, gatefold sleeve with black inner, 2 posters & 2 stickers, without stickered sleeve)	15
73	Harvest Q4 SHVL 804	THE DARK SIDE OF THE MOON (LP, quadrophonic, gatefold sleeve, no inserts)	40
70s	Harvest SHVL 804	THE DARK SIDE OF THE MOON (LP, repressing, blue & silver label, gatefold sleeve with black inner, 2 posters & 2 stickers)	20
73	Harvest Q4 SHVL 781	ATOM HEART MOTHER (LP, quadrophonic, gatefold sleeve, with 'quadrophonic' logo on front sleeve)	35
73	Harvest Q4 SHVL 781	ATOM HEART MOTHER (LP, quadrophonic, gatefold sleeve, without 'quadrophonic' logo on front sleeve, logo is inside)	25
73	Harvest SHDW 403	A NICE PAIR (2-LP, gatefold sleeve, with 2 inner sleeves; early copies with 'Mr Phang' dentist cover)	35
73	Harvest SHDW 403	A NICE PAIR (2-LP, gatefold sleeve, with 2 inner sleeves)	15
75	Harvest SHVL 814	WISH YOU WERE HERE (LP, with inner sleeve, postcard & black cellophane wraparound with sticker, sealed)	200
75	Harvest SHVL 814	WISH YOU WERE HERE (LP, with inner sleeve, postcard & black cellophane wraparound with sticker, unsealed)	50
76	Harvest Q4 SHVL 814	WISH YOU WERE HERE (LP, quadrophonic, with inner sleeve)	75
70s	Harvest SHVL 814	WISH YOU WERE HERE (LP, audiophile edition, Nimbus supercut sold through Hi-Fi Today magazine)	300
77	Harvest SHVL 815	ANIMALS (LP, 1st pressing, picture labels, non-barcode gatefold sleeve printed by 'Garrod & Lofthouse', with card inner with rounded edges, large thumb notch at top and catalogue number on bottom right of inner, Matrix numbers: SHVL 815 A-2U/B-2U)	100
78	Harvest SHDW 4111/4112	THE WALL (2-LP, First press, MATRIXES: SHSP 4111 A-2U/B-3U/SHSP 4112 A-1U/B-5U: TML-M/TML-X/TML-M/TML-M stamped into dead wax. Creamy coloured sleeve, bricks do not align right to bottom of sleeve, inner surface of sleeve is heavyweight card and creamy in colour, 8th brick states "produced by David Gilmour" then "written by Roger Waters". 9th brick "words and music Roger Waters except "Young Lust", "Comfortably numb"" etc. Inner sleeve has rounded edges and thumb notch along top edge. "SHDW 4111/1" in bottom right corner. Gatefold sleeve with 'static transparant "title" sticker)	80
78	Harvest SHDW 4111/4112	THE WALL (2-LP, later pressings, lighter inner card browner in colour,. Inside gatefold on right hand side 9th brick "Bob Ezrin, Roger Waters", 10th brick: no text, then Pink Floyd, names of the band. Square inner sleeve - usually - with OC-15863411/SHSP4111/2 catalogue numbers. Gatefold sleeve)	20
79	Harvest PF 11	THE FIRST XI (11-LP set, original sleeves, plus exclusive "Dark Side Of The Moon" & "Wish You Were Here" picture discs, 1,000 only)	200
83	Harvest SHPF 1983	THE FINAL CUT (LP, gatefold sleeve with title sticker)	20
87	EMI EMD 1003	A MOMENTARY LAPSE OF REASON (LP, gatefold sleeve with inner)	20
93	EMI CDDSOM 20	THE DARK SIDE OF THE MOON (CD, 20th anniversary box set with booklet & 5 art cards)	18
92	EMI CDS 7805572	SHINE ON (9-CD box set, with book and postcards)	90
94	EMI EMD 1055	THE DIVISION BELL (LP, gatefold sleeve, with inner)	70
95	EMI EMD 578	PULSE (4-LP box set in slipcase with hardback book)	100
97	EMI 859 857-1	THE PIPER AT THE GATES OF DAWN (LP, reissue, gatefold sleeve with inner, mono)	25
97	EMI CDEMD 1110	THE PIPER AT THE GATES OF DAWN (CD, mono, 30th anniversary box set with prints)	18
97	EMI SIGMA 630	'97 VINYL COLLECTION (7-LP set, die-cut box, includes "The Piper At The Gates Of Dawn" [EMD 1110], "The Wall" [EMD 1111], "Atom Heart Mother" [EMD 1112], "Relics" [EMD 1113], "The Dark Side Of The Moon" [EMD 1114], "Wish You Were Here" [EMD 1115], each in)	80
97	EMI CDEMD 1118	THE FIRST THREE SINGLES (CD, mono, mini album in card gatefold sleeve)	20
97	EMI EMD 1133	RELICS (LP, gatefold with poster)	40

PROMOS

67	Columbia DB 8156	Arnold Layne/Candy And A Currant Bun (demo copy in promo-only p/s)	1500
67	Columbia DB 8214	See Emily Play/Scarecrow (demo copy in promo-only p/s)	1500
67	Columbia DB 8310	Apples And Oranges/Paintbox (demo copy in promo-only p/s)	1500
68	Columbia DB 8401	It Would Be So Nice (1-sided demo)	1000
68	Columbia DB 8511	Point Me At The Sky/Careful With That Axe, Eugene (demo, with newsletter)	900
68	Columbia DB 8511	Point Me At The Sky/Careful With That Axe, Eugene (demo, with postcard)	750
69	Emidisc no cat. no.	The Narrow Way (acetate, different version, 1 copy only)	500
81	Harvest HAR 5217	Money (1-sided pink vinyl promo in p/s, 200 only)	100
81	Harvest HAR 5217	Money (Edited Version) (1-sided, pink vinyl, 200 only)	40
81	Harvest HAR 5217	Money (Edited Version) (1-sided, pink vinyl, mispressing with "Let There Be More Light" label on B-side)	50
87	EMI EMDJ 34	On The Turning Away (edit)/On The Turning Away (album) (stickered p/s)	10
88	EMI 12PF 1	Delicate Sound Of Thunder Sampler: Another Brick In The Wall Part 2/ One Of These Days/Run Like Hell (12", black & pink sleeve)	20
88	EMI PSLP 1026	Pink Floyd In Europe '88: Money/Shine On/Another Brick In The Wall Part 2/ One Slip/On The Turning Away/Learning To Fly (12", with "Another Brick...Part 1" miscredit on rear p/s)	20
88	EMI CDPINK 1	Wish You Were Here/Learning To Fly/Run Like Hell (CD)	20
92	EMI SHINE 1	SELECTED TRACKS FROM "SHINE ON" (CD, card sleeve)	20

(see also Syd Barrett, Roger Waters, David Gilmour, Rick Wright, Nick Mason, Joker's Wild, Ron Geesin)

PINK INDUSTRY

82	Zulu ZULU 1	Is This The End?/47/Don't Let Go/Final Cry (12", p/s)	8
85	Zulu ZULU RA 8	What I Wouldn't Give	6
83	Zulu ZULU 2	LOW TECHNOLOGY (LP)	12
83	Zulu ZULU 4	WHO TOLD YOU - YOU WERE NAKED (LP)	12

(see also Pink Military, Big In Japan)

PINK MILITARY

79	Last Trumpet LT 001	BUDDHA WALKING DISNEY SLEEPING (EP, foldout sleeve)	8
79	Eric's ERIC'S 002	BLOOD AND LIPSTICK (12" EP, die-cut p/s)	8
80	Eric's ERIC'S 005	Did You See Her/Everyday (p/s)	7
80	Virgin/Eric's ERIC'S 004	DO ANIMALS BELIEVE IN GOD? (LP)	15

(see also Pink Industry, Big In Japan, Ambrose Reynolds)

PINK PEOPLE

| 64 | Philips BF 1355 | Psychologically Unsound/Cow Catcher | 50 |
| 64 | Philips BF 1356 | Indian Hate Call/I Dreamt I Dwelt In Marble Halls | 20 |

(see also Four Squares)

PINK RHYTHM

| 85 | Beggars Banquet BEG 136T | Can;t Get Enough Of Your Love/Can't Get Enough Of Your Dub (12", p/s) | 15 |
| 85 | Beggars Banquet BEG 149T | India/Trust Me/More And More/India (Instrumental) (12", p/s) | 15 |

PINKERTON'S ('ASSORTED' COLOURS)

| 65 | Decca F 12307 | Mirror Mirror/She Don't Care (as Pinkerton's 'Assorted' Colours) | 8 |

PINKOES

66	Decca F 12377	Don't Stop Loving Me Baby/Will Ya? (as Pinkerton's 'Assorted' Colours)	15
66	Decca F 12493	Magic Rocking Horse/It Ain't Right (as Pinkerton's Colours)	35
67	Pye 7N 17327	Mum And Dad/On A Street Car (as Pinkerton's Colours)	18
67	Pye 7N 17414	There's Nobody I'd Sooner Love/Look At Me (as Pinkerton's)	40
68	Pye 7N 17574	Kentucky Woman/Behind The Mirror (as Pinkerton's)	18

(see also Flying Machine, Liberators, Tony Newman)

PINKOES

79	Popular POP1	INTO THE RED (EP)	12

PINKY (& FELLAS)

65	Polydor BM 56009	All Cried Out/Back Where I Belong	10
68	Decca F 12748	Manchester And Liverpool/Come Back Again (as Pinky & Fellas)	5
69	Polydor BM 56338	Let The Music Start/Oh, A Beautiful Day (as Pinky & Fellas)	5

PINKY & PERKY

58	Decca F 11095	Tom Dooley/The Velvet Glove (Pinky & Perky Theme) (in p/s)	10
59	Decca F 11116	The Little Mountaineer/Does Your Chewing Gum Lose Its Flavour (some in p/s)	15
59	Decca F 11174	Pinky And Perky's Sing Song Medley (both sides)	6
63	Columbia 33SX 1550	PINKY & PERKY'S MELODYMASTER (LP)	25

PINNACLE

74	Stag HP 125	ASSASSIN (LP, laminated sleeve, black/silver label)	150

DELROY PINNOCK

81	SG 5	Babylon Walls/MIKEY RANKS : I Want To Be	70

PINPOINT

79	Albion CEL 8	Richmond/Love Substiture (p/s)	25
80	Albion ALB103	THIRD STATE (LP, with free 12")	20

PIONEERS

66	Rio R 102	Good Nannie/Doreen Girl	40
66	Rio R 106	Too Late/Give Up	40
68	Blue Cat BS 100	Shake It Up/Rudies Are The Greatest	45
68	Blue Cat BS 103	Give It To Me/LEADERS: Someday Someway	40
68	Blue Cat BS 105	Whip Them/Having A Bawl	40
68	Blue Cat BS 139	Reggae Beat/Miss Eva	60
68	Caltone TONE 119	I Love No Other Girl/MILTON BOOTHE: I Used To Be A Fool	60
68	Amalgamated AMG 811	Give Me A Little Loving/This Is Soul (B-side actually by Lyn Tait & Jets)	18
68	Amalgamated AMG 814	Long Shot/Dip And Fall Back	30
68	Amalgamated AMG 821	Jackpot/CREATORS: Kimble (B-side actually by Lee Perry)	25
68	Amalgamated AMG 823	No Dope Me Pony/LORD SALMONS: Great - Great In '68	35
68	Amalgamated AMG 826	Tickle Me For Days/VERSATILES: The Time Has Come	15
68	Amalgamated AMG 828	Catch The Beat/SIR GIBB'S ALLSTARS: Jana (B-side actually Immortals' "Jane Anne")	20
68	Amalgamated AMG 830	Sweet Dreams/DON DRUMMOND JUNIOR: Caterpillar Rock	20
68	Pyramid PYR 6062	Easy Come, Easy Go/BEVERLEY'S ALLSTARS: Only A Smile (B-side actually by Lyn Tait & Jets)	55
69	Pyramid PYR 6065	Pee Pee Cluck Cluck/BEVERLEY'S ALLSTARS: Exclusively	15
69	Amalgamated AMG 833	Don't You Know/Me Naw Go A Believe	40
69	Amalgamated AMG 835	Mama Look Deh/BLENDERS: Decimal Currency	35
69	Amalgamated AMG 840	Who The Cap Fits/I'm Moving On	60
69	Amalgamated AMG 850	Alli Button/HIPPY BOYS: Death Rides	60
69	Trojan TR 672	Long Shot Kick The Bucket/RICO: Jumping The Gun	15
69	Trojan TR 685	Black Bud/Too Late	10
69	Trojan TR 698	Poor Rameses/BEVERLEY'S ALLSTARS: In Orbit	5
70	Trojan TR 7781	Money Day/BEVERLEY ALL STARS: Ska Ba Do	8
71	Summit SUM 8511	Starvation/BEVERLEY'S ALLSTARS: Version	7
72	Summit SUM 8535	Story Book Children/SIDNEY, GEORGE AND JACKIE: Gorgeous, Marvellous	5
74	Trojan TR 7923	Honey Bee/Hot Blooded Man	25
76	Mercury 6198061	Feel The Rhythm Of You and I/Version	8
77	Mercury 6007147	My Good Friend James/Secrets Of You	125
78	Ice GUY 14	My Good Friend James/Secrets Of You (reissue)	100
68	Amalgam. AMGLP 2003	GREETINGS FROM THE PIONEERS (LP)	70
70	Trojan TBL 103	LONGSHOT (LP)	30
70	Trojan TBL 139	BATTLE OF THE GIANTS (LP)	25
71	Trojan TRL 24	YEAH! (LP)	15

(see also Sir Gibbs, Rebels [Jamaica], Jackey Robinson, Moonboys, Sidney George & Jackie)

PIPE DREAM

70	Penny Farthing PEN 710	If You Do What You Gotta Do/Here We Go Again	5

PIPES OF PAN

67	Page One POF 038	Monday Morning Rain/Monday Morning Rain (Instrumental Mix)	20
71	Rolling Stones COC 49100	BRIAN JONES PRESENTS THE PIPES OF PAN AT JOUJOUKA (LP, gatefold sleeve with foldout insert; "Presents" sticker on misprinted cover)	70

PIPES OF PAN

71	Rolling Stones COC 49100	BRIAN JONES PLAYS WITH THE PIPES OF PAN AT JOUJOUKA (LP, gatefold sleeve with foldout insert; front cover with misprinted title)	90
71	Rolling Stones COC 49100	BRIAN JONES PRESENTS THE PIPES OF PAN AT JOUJOUKA (LP, gatefold sleeve with foldout insert; corrected title on front cover)	65

(see also Rolling Stones)

PIPETTES

04	No label or cat no	In The Bleak Midwinter (CD, gig freebie, 200 only)	30
05	Unpopular UNPOP 6	I Like A Boy In Uniform/It Hurts To See You Dance So Well (hand-numbered p/s, insert, 500 only)	20
05	Transgressive TRANS 005	ABC/Judy/Simon Says (white vinyl, p/s, 500 only)	15
06	Memphis Industries MI 071S1	Pull Shapes/Guess Who Ran Off With The Milkman (white vinyl, p/s)	5
06	Memphis Industries MI 071S2	Pull Shapes/Magician Man (yellow vinyl, p/s)	5
06	Memphis Industries MI 077S1	Judy (Single Mix)/Feminist Complaints (white vinyl, die-cut p/s)	5
06	Memphis Industries MI 077S2	Judy (Single Mix)/The Burning Ambition Of The Early Diuretics (blue vinyl, die-cut p/s)	5

PIPP

70	Decca F 23030	Otaki/Which Way Did She Go	12

PIPS

61	Top Rank JAR 574	Every Beat Of My Heart/Room In Your Heart	45

(see also Gladys Knight & Pips)

PIRATES

64	HMV POP 1250	My Babe/Casting My Spell	60
66	Polydor BM 56712	Shades Of Blue/Can't Understand	25
77	Warner Bros K 17002	Sweet Love On My Mind/You Don't Own Me (p/s)	15
78	Warner Bros K 17113	All In It Together/Dr. Feelgood (p/s)	10
78	Warner Bros K 17231	Shakin' All Over/Saturday Night Shoot Out	5
79	Cube Hi Fly 33	HAPPY BIRTHDAY ROCK N' ROLL (LP, with flexidisc [PIR 2])	12
99	Diamond	OUT OF THEIR SKULLS...PLUS (CD)	20

(see also Johnny Kidd & Pirates, [Billy J. Kramer &] Dakotas)

PISCES

71	Trailer LER 2025	PISCES (LP)	30

PISTONS

81	Humdrum ZIT 1	Solitary Reality/Hyper Active (p/s and insert)	70

HARRY PITCH

68	MOR MR 101P	HARMONICA JEWEL BOX (LP)	20

(see also Mr. Bloe)

PITCH SHIFTER

92	Earache MOSH 66	SUBMIT EP (12")	8

PITMAN

02	Son HM001	Phone Pitman/Pitman Sez	6

GENE PITNEY
SINGLES

61	London HL 9270	(I Wanna) Love My Life Away/I Laughed So Hard I Cried	10
61	HMV POP 933	Every Breath I Take/Mr Moon, Mr Cupid & I	30
61	United Artists POP 952	Town Without Pity/Air Mail Special	10
62	United Artists POP 1018	The Man Who Shot Liberty Valance/Take It Like A Man	10
62	United Artists UP 1005	If I Didn't Have A Dime/Only Love Can Break A Heart	5
63	United Artists UP 1012	Half Heaven, Half Heartache/Tower Tall	5
63	United Artists UP 1021	Mecca/Teardrop By Teardrop	8
63	United Artists UP 1030	True Love Never Runs Smooth/Donna Means Heartbreak	5
63	United Artists UP 1035	24 Hours From Tulsa/Lonely Night Dreams (blue or black label)	5
64	United Artists UP 1045	That Girl Belongs To Yesterday/Who Needs It?	7
64	United Artists UP 1055	I'm Gonna Find Myself A Girl/Lips Are Redder On You	10
64	United Artists UP 1063	It Hurts To Be In Love/Hawaii	7
64	Stateside SS 358	I'm Gonna Be Strong/Aladdin's Lamp	6
64	Stateside SS 365	It Hurts To Be In Love (reissue)	5
65	Stateside SS 390	I Must Be Seeing Things/Save Your Love	5
65	Stateside SS 420	Lookin' Thru The Eyes Of Love/Last Chance To Turn Around	5
65	Stateside SS 471	Princess In Rags/Amore Mio	5
66	Stateside SS 490	Backstage/In Love Again	5
66	Stateside SS 518	Nobody Needs Your Love/Dream World	5
66	Stateside SS 558	Just One Smile/The Boss's Daughter	5
67	Stateside SS 597	(In The) Cold Light Of Day/Flower Girl	8
67	Stateside SS 2060	Something's Gotten Hold Of My Heart/Building Up My Dream World (withdrawn)	20
67	Stateside SS 2060	Something's Gotten Hold Of My Heart/Where Did The Magic Go	5
68	Stateside SS 2103	Somewhere In The Country/Lonely Drifter	5
68	Stateside SS 2118	Love Grows/Conquistador	5
68	Stateside SS 2131	Yours Until Tomorrow/She's A Heartbreaker	15
68	Stateside SS 2131	Yours Until Tomorrow/She's A Heartbreaker (DJ copy)	30
69	Stateside SS 2142	Maria Elena/The French Horn	6
70	Stateside SS 2177	Shady Lady/Billy, You're My Friend	5
71	Pye International 7N 25564	Run Run Road Runner/Rain Maker	10
72	Pye International 7N 25579	I Just Can't Help Myself/Beautiful Sounds	5

EPs

63	HMV 7EG 8832	TOWN WITHOUT PITY	20
64	United Artists UEP 1001	TWENTY FOUR HOURS FROM TULSA	10
64	United Artists UEP 1002	THAT GIRL BELONGS TO YESTERDAY	10
65	Stateside SE 1030	I MUST BE SEEING THINGS	8
65	Stateside SE 1032	GENE ITALIANO	10
66	Stateside SE 1036	GENE PITNEY SINGS JUST FOR YOU	10

ALBUMS : LPS

62	HMV CLP 1566	THE MANY SIDES OF GENE PITNEY	30
63	United Artists ULP 1028	ONLY LOVE CAN BREAK A HEART (mono)	20
63	United Artists (S)ULP 1028	ONLY LOVE CAN BREAK A HEART (stereo)	30
63	United Artists ULP 1043	GENE PITNEY SINGS JUST FOR YOU	20
64	United Artists ULP 1061	BLUE GENE	20
64	United Artists ULP 1064	GENE PITNEY MEETS THE FAIR YOUNG LADIES OF FOLKLAND	20
64	United Artists ULP 1073	GENE PITNEY'S BIG SIXTEEN	15
65	Stateside SL 10120	I'M GONNA BE STRONG	15
65	Stateside SL 10132	GENE PITNEY'S MORE BIG SIXTEEN (VOL. 2)	18
65	Stateside SL 10147	GEORGE JONES AND GENE PITNEY (with George Jones)	18
65	Stateside SL 10148	LOOKING THRU THE EYES OF LOVE	15
65	Stateside SL 10156	SINGS THE GREAT SONGS OF OUR TIME	18
66	Stateside SL 10173	IT'S COUNTRY TIME AGAIN (with George Jones)	15
67	Stateside S(S)L 10199	GENE PITNEY'S BIG SIXTEEN (VOL. 3)	12
67	Stateside S(S)L 10212	JUST ONE SMILE	12
68	Stateside S(S)L 10242	PITNEY TODAY	12

(see also Marc Almond & Gene Pitney, George Jones)

RICHIE PITTS

73	Contempo C3	Every Couple's Not A Pair/I Refuse To Know Your Name	10
78	Magnet 113	(Love Is) One Step Away/Looks Like It's Gonna Rain Again	8

TERRY PITTS JAZZ BAND

61	Oriole CB 1621	A Drop Of The Hard Stuff/Show Me The Way To Go Home	6

PIXIES

88	4AD BAD 805	GIGANTIC EP (12", p/s)	10
89	4AD BAD 904	THIS MONKEY'S GONE TO HEAVEN EP (12")	8
89	4AD BAD 909	HERE COMES YOUR MAN EP (12", p/s)	10
90	4AD BAD 0014	DIG FOR FIRE EP (12", p/s)	8
88	4AD BAD 805CD	Gigantic/River Euphrates/Vamos (live)/In Heaven (Lady In The Radiator Song) (live) (CD)	12
89	4AD PIX ONE	DOOLITTLE SAMPLER: Debaser/Wave Of Mutilation/I Bleed/Gouge Away (12", 1-sided, title sleeve, promo only)	15
89	4AD PIX 2	Into The White/Wave Of Mutilation (U.K. Surf) (12", 1-sided, promo only)	10
90	4AD PIX 3	EXTRACTS FROM BOSSANOVA: Allison/Rock Music/Down To The Well/The Happening (12", 1-sided, promo only)	15
90	4AD AD 0014	Dig For Fire/Velvety (p/s)	6
91	4AD PIX 4	EXTRACTS FROM TROMPE LE MONDE: U-Mass/Letter To Memphis/Subbacultcha (10", same track both sides, promo only)	15
04	4AD PIX 2004CD	BEST OF PIXIES (CD, 5-track sampler, promo only)	20
87	4AD MAD 709	COME ON PILGRIM (mini-LP)	18
88	4AD CAD 803	SURFER ROSA (LP, with inner)	20
89	4AD CAD 905	DOOLITTLE (LP, with lyric booklet & postcard, in carrier bag)	40
89	4AD CAD 905	DOOLITTLE (LP, with lyric booklet & postcard)	20
90	4AD CAD 0010	BOSSANOVA (LP, with booklet)	25
90	4AD CAD 1014	TROMPE LE MONDE (LP)	15
97	4AD DADD 7011	DEATH TO THE PIXIES (4-10" LP, box set)	50
02	Cooking Vinyl COOK 234	PIXIES - THE PURPLE TAPE (LP, inner)	18

(see also Breeders, Frank Black)

PIXIES THREE

63	Mercury AMT 1214	Birthday Party/Our Love	25

PLACEBO

95	Fierce Panda NING 13	Bruise Pristine/SOUP: M.E.L.T.D.O.W.N. (foldover p/s, 1500 only)	35
96	Deceptive BLUFF 024	Come Home/Drowning By Numbers (p/s)	10
96	Deceptive BLUFF 024	Come Home/Drowning By Numbers (CD)	25
96	Elevator FLOOR 001	36 degrees/Dark globe (p/s)	10
96	Hut FLOOR 3	Teenage Angst/Hug Bubble/Been Smoking Too Long (part 1 0f 2, p/s)	8
96	Hut FLOORCD 3	Teenage Angst/Hug Bubble/Been Smoking Too Long (CD, card sleeve)	12
96	Hut FLOOR 4	Nancy Boy (Sex Mix)/Slackerbitch (p/s)	6
97	Hut FLOOR 5	Bruise Pristine/(One Punch Remix) (p/s)	12
98	Hut SILVER 1	THE ORIGINAL DEMOS: Nancy Boy/Teenage Angst/36 Degrees/Bruise Pristine (CD, fan club issue, card sleeve)	15
99	Hut FLOOR TP 10	Without You I'm Nothing (with David Bowie) (UNKLE Remix)/(Flexirol Mix)/(Brothers In Rhythm Club Mix) (12" promo, 500 only, stickered die-cut sleeve)	15
99	Hut FLOOR CD 10	Without You I'm Nothing (Single Mix)/(UNKLE Remix)/(Flexirol Mix)/(Brothers In Rhythm Club Mix) (multimedia CD, gatefold card sleeve)	10
03	Virgin 7432547480743	Special Needs/English Summer Rain (p/s)	8
04	Virgin 724381618776	Twenty Years/Detox 5	8
96	Hut LPFLOORY 2	PLACEBO (LP)	45
96	Hut CD FLOOR 2	PLACEBO (CD, digipak, 5000 only)	20
98	Elevator FLOORLP 8	WITHOUT YOU I'M NOTHING (LP, gatefold)	25

PLAGUE (1)

68	Decca F 12730	Looking For The Sun/Here Today, Gone Tomorrow	225

PLAGUE (2)

80	Evolution EV 4	Out With Me All Night/Er/Don't Want To Be Like Jimmy	50
79	Psycho P2615	In Love/Wimpey Bar Song (silk screened fold-out cover)	50
79	Psycho P 2615	In Love/Wimpey Bar Song (2nd pressing, printed sleeve, pink vinyl)	20

PLAID

92	GPR GENP(X) 7	Scoobs In Columbia (remixes) (12", custom sleeve)	30
94	Clear CLR 409	ANDROID (12" EP, p/s, clear vinyl)	20
94	Clear CLR 409	ANDROID (12" EP, p/s, black vinyl)	15
95	Rumble RUMBLE 01	MIND OVER RHYTHM MEET THE MEN FROM PLAID (3 x 10" in p/s)	15
92	Black Dog Prods. LP 1	MBUKI MVUKI (LP)	80

(see also Black Dog)

PLAINSONG

72	Elektra K 12976	Even The Guiding Light/Yoko Man/Call The Tune	7
72	Elektra K 42120	IN SEARCH OF AMELIA EARHART (LP, gatefold sleeve with lyric insert)	25
73	Elektra K 42136	PLAINSONG II (LP, white label, promo only)	120

(see also Andy Roberts, Ian Matthews)

PLANET EARTH

78	Pye NSPL 18556	PLANET EARTH (LP)	25

PLANET GONG

77	Affinity AF 5101	Opium For The People/Poet For Sale (p/s)	8
78	Charly CYX 202	Opium For The People/Stoned Innocent Frankenstein (10", p/s)	18
78	Charly CRM 2000	FLOATING ANARCHY - LIVE 1977 (LP)	18

(see also Daevid Allen, Gong)

PLANET P PROJECT

83	Geffen A3205	Why Me/Only You And Me (p/s)	6
83	Geffen GEF25367	PLANET P PROJECT (LP + inner sleeve)	12
85	MCA MCSP311	PINK WORLD (2LP, gatefold sleeve)	18

(see also Tony Carey, Rainbow)

PLANETS (1)

60	Palette PG 9008	Like Party/Ippy Yippy Beatnik (only this value if in p/s)	25

PLANETS (2)

60	HMV POP 818	Chunky/Screwball	20
61	HMV POP 832	Jam Roll/Delaney's Theme	25
61	HMV POP 895	Jungle Street/The Grasshopper	25

PLANETS (3)
73	Bullet BU 528	People Get Funny/DOCBIRD ALL STARS : Funny Version	10

ROBERT PLANT
67	CBS 202656	Our Song/Laughin', Cryin', Laughin'	300
67	CBS 202656	Our Song/Laughin' Cryin' Laughin' ('A' label demo)	250
67	CBS 202858	Long Time Coming/I've Got A Secret	300
67	CBS 202858	Long Time Coming/I've Got A Secret ('A' label demo)	250
82	Swan Song SSK 19429T	Burning Down One Side/Far Post (12", p/s)	10
82	Swan Song SAM154	PICTURES AT ELEVEN (LP, promo interview disc with cue sheet)	18
82	Es Paranza SAM 169	THE PRINCIPLE OF MOVEMENTS (LP, promo interview disc with cue sheet)	18
88	Es Paranza PR 2244	NON STOP GO! (LP, two disc set interview promo for NOW AND ZEN album)	15
90	Es Paranza WX 339X	MANIC NIRVANA (LP, gatefold)	15
02	Mercury 063094-1	DREAMLAND (2 x LP, numbered)	35
05	Sanctuary SANLP 356	MIGHTY REARRANGER (LP)	45

(see also Led Zeppelin, Listen, Jimmy Page, Robert Plant & The Strange Sensation, Page & Plant, Honeydrippers)

PLASMATICS
80	Stiff BUY 76	Butcher Baby/Tight Black Pants (splatter vinyl)	5
80	Stiff BUY 76	Butcher Baby/Tight Black Pants (black vinyl, p/s)	8
80	Stiff BUY 91	Monkey Suit/Squirm (splatter vinyl, p/s)	5

PLASTIC BERTRAND
78	Sire 9103258	AN 1 (LP, gatefold)	20

PLASTIC GANGSTERS
83	Secret SHH 144	Plastic Gangster/Sretsgnag Citsalp (7", 12", no p/s on 12" stamped p/s on 7", unissued, 10 DJ copies only)	250
11	Secret SHH 144	Plastic Gangster (I Could Be So Good For You)/Sretsgnag Citsalp (reissue, on red, white or blue vinyl)	7

(see also 4 Skins)

PLASTIC PENNY
67	Page One POF 051	Everything I Am/No Pleasure Without Pain My Love	5
68	Page One POF 062	Nobody Knows It/Just Happy To Be With You	10
68	Page One POF 079	Your Way To Tell Me Go/Baby You're Not To Blame	20
69	Page One POF 107	Hound Dog/Currency	20
69	Page One POF 146	She Does/Genevieve	20
68	Page One POL(S) 005	TWO SIDES OF THE PENNY (LP, laminated front sleeve, flipbacks)	100
69	Page One POLS 014	CURRENCY (LP, laminated front sleeve, flipbacks)	140
70	Page One POLS 611	HEADS YOU WIN, TAILS I LOSE (LP)	65

(see also Universals, Circles, Brian Keith, Mick Grabham)

PLASTIC SANDWICHES
81	Ellie Jay EJSP 9746	Bayonets And Colours/Parties At War (p/s is two separate 7" pieces of paper)	20

PLASTICS
81	Island ILPS 9627	WELCOME BACK (LP, first copies came with free limited edition 7" full colour flexidisc "Paté/Last Train To Clarksville".	12

PLASTIKMAN
94	NovaMute L NO MU 37	MUSIK (2-LP, with bonus 1-sided etched 12")	15

PLATFORM SIX
65	Piccadilly 7N 35255	Money Will Not Mean A Thing/Girl Down Town	70

EDDIE PLATT
58	Columbia DB 4101	Tequila/Pop Corn	25

PLATTERS
78s
55	Parlophone DP 433	Voo-Vee-Ah-Bee/STRANGERS: Just Don't Care (export issue)	30
56	Parlophone DP 506	Beer Barrel Boogie/Roses Of Picardy (export issue)	30
56	Mercury MT 107	(You've Got) The Magic Touch/Winner Takes All	15
58	Mercury MT 197	Helpless/Indiff'rent	15
58	Mercury MT 205	Don't Let Go/Are You Sincere?	10
58	Mercury MT 227	You're Making A Mistake/My Old Flame (sung by Zola Taylor)	15
58	Mercury AMT 1001	I Wish/It's Raining Outside	12
58	Mercury AMT 1016	Smoke Gets In Your Eyes/No Matter What You Are	15
59	Mercury AMT 1039	Enchanted/The Sound And The Fury	20
59	Mercury AMT 1053	Remember When/Love Of A Lifetime (featuring Tony Williams)	30
60	Mercury AMT 1081	Harbour Lights/(By The) Sleepy Lagoon	40

SINGLES
56	Mercury MT 117	The Great Pretender/Only You (And You Alone) (export issue)	40
58	Mercury 7MT 197	Helpless/Indiff'rent	40
58	Mercury 7MT 205	Don't Let Go/Are You Sincere?	30
58	Mercury 7MT 214	Twilight Time/Out Of My Mind	10
58	Mercury 7MT 227	You're Making A Mistake (featuring Tony Williams)/My Old Flame	20
58	Mercury AMT 1001	I Wish/It's Raining Outside	18
58	Mercury AMT 1016	Smoke Gets In Your Eyes/No Matter What You Are	5
59	Mercury AMT 1039	Enchanted/The Sound And The Fury	6
59	Mercury AMT 1053	Remember When/Love Of A Lifetime (featuring Tony Williams)	10
59	Mercury AMT 1066	My Blue Heaven/Wish It Were Me	6
60	Mercury AMT 1076	My Secret/What Does It Matter	5
60	Mercury AMT 1081	Harbour Lights/(By The) Sleepy Lagoon	5
60	Mercury AMT 1098	Ebb Tide/(I'll Be With You In) Apple Blossom Time (featuring Tony Williams)	5
60	Mercury AMT 1106	Red Sails In The Sunset/Sad River (featuring Tony Williams)	5
60	Mercury AMT 1118	To Each His Own/Down The River Of Golden Dreams	5
61	Mercury AMT 1128	If I Didn't Care/True Lover	5
61	Mercury AMT 1154	I'll Never Smile Again/You Don't Say	5
62	Ember JBS 701	Only You/Tell The World	125
66	Stateside SS 511	I Love You 1000 Times/Hear No Evil, Speak No Evil, See No Evil	25
66	Stateside SS 568	I'll Be Home/(You've Got) The Magic Touch	12
67	Stateside SS 2007	With This Ring/If I Had A Love	25
67	Stateside SS 2042	Washed Ashore (On A Lonely Island In The Sea)/What Name Shall I Give You My Love	25

67	Stateside SS 2042	Washed Ashore (On A Lonely Island In The Sea)/What Name Shall I Give You My Love (DJ copy)	60
67	Stateside SS 2067	Sweet Sweet Lovin'/Sonata	20
67	Stateside SS 2067	Sweet Sweet Lovin'/Sonata (DJ copy)	60
69	Stateside SS 2150	With This Ring/If I Had A Love (reissue)	8
71	Pye Intl. 7N 25559	Sweet Sweet Lovin'/Going Back To Detroit	15
71	Pye Intl. 7N 25569	With This Ring/I Washed Ashore (On A Lonely Island In The Sea)	8
87	Kent 6T3	SAMMY AMBROSE: Welcome To Dreamsville/PLATTERS: Not My Girl	25

EPs

56	Mercury MEP 9504	THE FABULOUS PLATTERS	10
57	Mercury MEP 9514	THE FABULOUS PLATTERS VOL. II	10
57	Mercury MEP 9524	THE FABULOUS PLATTERS VOL. III	12
58	Mercury MEP 9526	THE FLYING PLATTERS VOL. I	15
58	Mercury MEP 9528	THE FLYING PLATTERS VOL. II	15
58	Mercury MEP 9537	THE PLATTERS	15
59	Mercury ZEP 10000	PICK OF THE PLATTERS NO. 1	12
59	Mercury ZEP 10008	PICK OF THE PLATTERS NO. 2	12
59	Mercury ZEP 10025	PICK OF THE PLATTERS NO. 3	12
59	Mercury ZEP 10031	PICK OF THE PLATTERS NO. 4	15
59	Mercury ZEP 10042	PICK OF THE PLATTERS NO. 5	12
60	Mercury ZEP 10056	PICK OF THE PLATTERS NO. 6	12
60	Mercury ZEP 10070	PICK OF THE PLATTERS NO. 7	12
61	Mercury ZEP 10112	HARBOUR LIGHTS	15
62	Mercury ZEP 10126	THE PLATTERS ON A PLATTER	25

ALBUMS : LPS

57	Mercury MPL 6504	THE PLATTERS	35
57	Mercury MPL 6511	THE PLATTERS VOL. 2	30
58	Mercury MPL 6528	THE FLYING PLATTERS	30
58	Parlophone PMD 1058	THE PLATTERS (10")	250
59	Mercury MMC 14009	AROUND THE WORLD WITH THE FLYING PLATTERS	30
59	Mercury MMC 14010	THE PLATTERS ON PARADE	30
59	Mercury MMC 14014	REMEMBER WHEN?	30
60	Mercury MMC 14045	REFLECTIONS	25
61	Mercury MMC 14072	LIFE IS JUST A BOWL OF CHERRIES	25
64	Mercury MCL 20000	THE PLATTERS SING LATINO	12
67	Stateside S(S)L 10208	GOING BACK TO DETROIT	25

(see also Buck Ram's Ramrocks, Linda Hayes)

PLAYBOYS (JAMAICA)

71	Tropical AL 007	Change Change/TROPICAL ALL STARS: Version 2	5

PLAYBOYS (U.S.)

58	London HLU 8681	Over The Weekend/Double Talk	50
58	London HLU 8681	Over The Weekend/Double Talk (78)	15

PLAYBOYS (U.S.)

69	Capitol CL 15621	Let's Get Back To Rock And Roll/Homemade Cookin'	6

(see also Rad Bryan)

PLAY DEAD

81	Fresh FRESH 29	Poison Takes A Hold/Introduction (p/s)	7
81	Fresh FRESH 38	T.V. Eye/Final Epitaph (p/s)	7

PLAYERS

63	Oriole CB 1861	Mockingbird/Bizet As It May	25

PLAYERS ASSOCIATION

80	Vanguard VSL 5017	The Get Down Mellow Mellow Sound/Version	15

PLAYGIRLS (JAMAICA)

65	Black Swan WI 456	Looks Are Deceiving/BABA BROOKS: Dreadnaught	30

PLAYGIRLS (U.S.)

59	RCA RCA 1133	Hey Sport/Young Love Swings The World	15
59	RCA RCA 1133	Hey Sport/Young Love Swings The World (78)	15

PLAYGROUND

67	MGM MGM 1351	At The Zoo/Yellow Balloon	20
69	NEMS 56-4019	I Could Be So Good/The Girl Behind The Smile	10
69	NEMS 56-4442	Things I Do For You/Lazy Days	10

PLAYING AT TRAINS

87	Idea IDT 001	A World Without Love/Just Around The Mountain/Playing At Trains/A Japanese Intervention (12" p/s)	85

(see also Waving At Trains)

PLAYMATES

57	Columbia DB 3941	Pretty Woman/Barefoot Girl	10
57	Columbia DB 4033	Island Girl/Darling, It's Wonderful	10
58	Columbia DB 4084	Jo-Ann/You Can't Stop Me From Dreaming	10
58	Columbia DB 4127	Let's Be Lovers/Give Me Another Chance	10
58	Columbia DB 4224	Beep Beep/Your Love	8
59	Columbia DB 4288	Star Love/The Thing-A-Ma-Jig	5
58	Columbia SEG 7864	AT PLAY WITH THE PLAYMATES (EP)	10
59	Columbia SEG 7949	PARTY PLAYMATES NO. 1 (EP)	10
59	Columbia SEG 7966	PARTY PLAYMATES NO. 2 (EP)	10

PLAYMATES (IRELAND)

70	Emerald MD 1150	Don't Fight It/Jodi	10

PLAYTHINGS

70	Pye 7N 45212	Stop What You're Doing To Me/Sad (light blue label)	6
70	Pye 7N 45212	Stop What You're Doing To Me/Sad	10
73	Pye 7N 45399	Surrounded By A Ray Of Sunshine/Dance The Night Away	5

BOBBY PLEASE
57	London HLB 8507	Your Driver's Licence, Please/Heartache Street (unissued, 2x 1-sided demos - price is for BOTH demos together) 300
57	London HLB 8507	Your Driver's Licence, Please/Heartache Street (78) 40

PLEASERS
77	Solid Gold SGR 104	You Know What I'm Thinking/Hello Little Girl 8
77	Arista ARIST 21	Girl I Know/Don't Go Breaking My Heart (p/s) 5
77	Arista ARIST 152	You Keep Tellin' Lies/I'm In Love/Who Are You (p/s, silver label) 5
77	Arista ARIST 152	You Keep Tellin' Lies/I'm In Love/Who Are You (p/s, blue label) 10
78	Arista ARIST 180	The Kids Are Alright/Stay With Me (p/s) 12
96	Lost Moment LMCD 032	THAMESBEAT (CD) 25

PLEASURE
76	Fantasy FTC 138	Ghettos Of The Mind/I'm Mad (12") 10

PLEASURE BEACH
90s	Acid Jazz AJX 124S	Rollercoaster/Smells Like Teen Spirit (p/s) 6

PLEASURE FAIR
68	Uni UN 500	Morning Glory Blues/Fade Out Fade In 12
67	Uni UNL(S) 100	PLEASURE FAIR (LP) 25

(see also Bread)

PLEASURE GARDEN
68	Sound For Industry SFI 31H/32H	Permissive Paradise/EMPEROR ROSKO & JONATHAN KING: Young London (flexidisc, art sleeve) 100

(see also Iveys)

PLEASURES
65	Sue WI 357	Music City/If I Had A Little Money 45

PLEBS
64	Decca F 12006	Bad Blood/Babe I'm Gonna Leave You 80
60s	Oak	THE PLEBS (LP, 1-sided, private pressing) 1000

PLEXUS
78	Look LKLP 6175	PLEXUS (LP) 65
79	Hill & Dale HD004	LIFE UP THE CREEK (LP) 55

PLUGS
79	Cathedral CATH 1	Too Late/UFO/Sally (gatefold p/s) 20
80	Pop 1	CRACKIN' UP EP 12

JEAN PLUM
76	London HLU 10514	Look At The Boy/Back At You 10

JON PLUM
69	SNB 55-3971	Alice/Sunshine 20
69	SNB 55-4317	You Keep Changing Your Mind/An Apple Falls 15

PLUM & YOUTH
80s	Checkmount CHK 1	I Got You Babe/Got To Be Moving On (p/s, withdrawn) 15

(see also Cozy Powell, Rainbow, Bernie Marsden, Big Bertha)

PLUMMERS
64	Blue Beat BB 260	Johnny/Little Stars (actually by Plamers) 22

PLUNDER
08	Lolarox ROX 1	Hellion Castle/I Spy On Love (p/s, booklet, 200 only) 5

PLUS
70	Probe SPB 1009	SEVEN DEADLY SINS (LP, laminated front sleeve, flipbacks) 120

PLUTO
71	Dawn DNS 1017	Rag A Bone Joe/Stealing My Thunder 20
72	Dawn DNS 1026	I Really Want It/Something That You Loved 30
71	Dawn DNLS 3030	PLUTO (LP, laminated sleeve, lilac label) 200

(see also Dry Ice, Foundations)

PNEUMONIA (1)
68	Oak RGJ 625	I Can See Your Face 400

PNEUMONIA (2)
79	Plastic PLAS 001	Exhibition/Coming Attack/U.K. DECAY: U.K. Decay/Carcrash (folded p/s) 25

POACHER
79	RK 1022	Star Love/Question Of Trust 5

POCKETS
77	CBS 5780	Come Go With Me/Pt. 2 8

POCO
71	Epic EQ 30209	DELIVERIN' (LP, quadrophonic) 12

(see also Buffalo Springfield, Au Go-Go Singers)

POEMSO
81	Polka DOT 1	ACHIEVING UNITY (EP, initially with booklet) 10

(see also Strawberry Switchblade)

POET & ONE MAN BAND
69	Verve Forecast SVLP 6012	THE POET AND THE ONE MAN BAND (LP, laminated front sleeve, flipbacks) 100

(see also Tony Colton, Nicky Hopkins, Heads Hands & Feet)

POETS
64	Decca F 11995	Now We're Thru/There Are Some 20
65	Decca F 12074	That's The Way It's Got To Be/I'll Cry With The Moon 50
65	Decca F 12195	I Am So Blue/I Love Her Still 60
65	Immediate IM 006	Call Again/Some Things I Can't Forget 90
66	Immediate IM 024	Baby Don't You Do It/I'll Come Home 90
67	Decca F 12569	Wooden Spoon/In Your Tower 450
71	Strike Cola SC 1	Heyla Hola/Fun Buggy 50

MINT VALUE £

88	Bam Caruso OPRA 088	I Love Her Still/GHOST: Time Is My Enemy (company sleeve, promo only)..........................12

(see also Pathfinders, [White] Trash, Blue)

POETS (IRELAND)

68	Pye 7N 17668	Locked In A Room/Alone Am I...240
68	Target 7N 17668	Locked In A Room/Alone Am I (Irish issue, different label) 240

POGUE MAHONE

84	Pogue Mahone PM 1	Dark Streets Of London/The Band Played Waltzing Mathilda 10
84	Pogue Mahone PM 1	Dark Streets Of London/The Band Played Waltzing Mathilda (white label tour copy with 'harp' stamp, 237 only)...50

(see also Pogues)

POGUES

84	Stiff BUY DJ 212	The Irish Rover/DUBLINERS: Rare Old Mountain Dew (promo, dirty verse taken out for airplay)..15
84	Stiff BUY 207	Dark Streets Of London/The Band Played Waltzing Mathilda (reissue of Pogue Mahone)....10
84	Stiff BUY 212	Boys From The County Hell/Repealing Of The Licensing Laws (green-tinted p/s) 10
84	Stiff BUY 212	Boys From The County Hell/Repealing Of The Licensing Laws (A-label promos in blue-tinted p/s)..15
84	Stiff BUY 207/BUY 212	Dark Streets Of London/The Band Played Waltzing Mathilda//Boys From The County Hell/Repealing Of The Licensing Laws (shrinkwrapped double pack) 20
85	Stiff DBUY 220	A Pair Of Brown Eyes/Whiskey You're The Devil (picture disc) 15
85	Stiff BUYIT 220	A Pair Of Brown Eyes/Whiskey You're The Devil/Muirshin Durkin (12", p/s)........................15
85	Stiff BUY 212/BUY 220	Boys From The County Hell/Repealing Of The Licensing Laws//A Pair Of Brown Eyes/Whiskey You're The Devil (shrinkwrapped double pack) 15
85	Stiff BUY 224	Sally MacLennane/Wild Rover (wraparound poster p/s, green vinyl) 10
85	Stiff BUY 224	Sally MacLennane/Wild Rover (wraparound poster p/s) 7
85	Stiff BUY 224	Sally MacLennane/Wild Rover (standard p/s) 5
85	Stiff PBUY 229	Dirty Old Town/A Pistol For Paddy Garcia (picture disc)...10
85	Stiff BUYIT 229	Dirty Old Town/A Pistol For Paddy Garcia/The Parting Glass (12", with poster & stickered p/s)...20
85	Stiff BUYIT 229	Dirty Old Town/A Pistol For Paddy Garcia/The Parting Glass (12", without poster & stickered p/s)...15
85	Stiff MAIL 3	Dirty Old Town (live)/Sally MacLennane (live)/(interview) (12", mail-order) 12
86	Stiff PBUY 243	POGUETRY IN MOTION (EP, picture disc) 5
87	Stiff/Hell BLOOD 1	The Good, The Bad & The Ugly/Rake At The Gates Of Hell (unreleased) 0
87	Stiff/Hell BLOODY 1	The Good, The Bad & The Ugly/Rake At The Gates Of Hell (12", unreleased) 0
89	WEA SAM 553	Misty Morning Albert Bridge/(same track) (12" promo, green vinyl) 8

(see also Pogue Mahone, Nips, Nipple Erectors, Radiators From Space)

POGUES FEATURING KIRSTY MACCOLL

87	Pogue Mahone CDNY 7	A Fairytale Of New York/The Battle March Medley/Shane Bradley (CD) 12

POINDEXTER BROTHERS

66	Verve VS 550	(Git Your) Backfield In Motion/(Grandma) Give That Girl Some Slack 20

POINT BLANK MCS

92	Kold Sweat KS120	Planting Semtex/Revenge Of The Ghetto Child (12") 12

POINTED STICKS

79	Stiff BUY 59	Out Of Luck/What Do You Want Me To Do/Somebody's Mom ("Plug Copy on label, p/s) 10
79	Stiff BUY 59	Out Of Luck/What Do You Want Me To Do/Somebody's Mom (p/s) 7
79	Stiff BUY 59	Out Of Luck/What Do You Want Me To Do/Somebody's Mom (12", p/s) 10

BONNIE POINTER

78	Motown TMG 1125	Free Me From My Freedom/Tie Me To A Tree 8
78	Motown TMG 1134	I Wanna Make It In Your World/Heaven Must Have Sent You 15

POINTS PROVEN

92	Payday PD002	Pass The Mic/Noisy Music Part 2/Funky Rhymes, Funky Style (EP) 12
93	Payday PD003	ONLY FOOLS AND HORSES (EP)..8

POISON GIRLS

79	Small Wonder WEENY 4	HEX (12" EP, with lyric insert)..15
80	Crass/Xntrix 421984/1	Persons Unknown/CRASS: Bloody Revolutions (folded 21" x 14" poster p/s)......................5
81	Crass 421984/10	Pretty Polly/Bully Boys (live) (square red or clear flexidisc free with In The City fanzine, with magazine) 10
81	Crass 421984/8	All Systems Go/Promenade Immortelle/Dirty Work (p/s with lyrics) 5
83	Illuminat ed ILL 23	One Good Reason/Cinnamon Gardens (p/s)..5
83	Illuminated ILL 25	Are You Happy Now?/Cream Dream (p/s) 5
80	Crass 421984/2	CHAPPAQUIDICK (LP, with free flexidisc "Statement" [421984/7])..................................12
81	Xentrix XN 2003	WHERE'S THE PLEASURE? (LP)...12
84	Xentirx RM 101	7 YEAR SCRATCH (2-LP) 15

(see also Crass, Fatal Microbes/Poison Girls)

POISON IDEA

89	In Your Face FACE 06	IAN MACKAYE (EP) 15
91	Vinyl Solution VS 29	Plastic Bomb/We Got The Beat/Harder They Come/Lawdy Miss Clawdy (double pack, p/s) ..8
91	Vinyl Solution VS325	Punish Me/Mario The Cop (p/s, purple vinyl)..8
93	Dirtier Promotions 7DPROMS 11	Feel The Darkness (Remix)/Feel The Darkness (Remix) (foldover p/s in poly bag, same track both sides free with Fear & Loathing fanzine)..8
90	Vinyl Solution SOL 025	FEEL THE DARNESS (LP) 15
92	Vinyl Solution SOL 033	BLANK BLACKOUT VACANT (LP, poster and free 7" [FART 4]) 20
92	Vinyl Solution SOL 033	BLANK BLACKOUT VACANT (LP)..12
93	Vinyl Solution SOL 037	WE MUST BURN (LP)..12
94	Vinyl Solution SOL 040	WAR ALL THE TIME (LP)..12

POISON IVY

64	Granta GR 7EP 1011	CLINGING MEMORIES (EP) 110

POISONED ELECTRIC HEAD

89	Dead Fly ACAD 002	Cap Of Flies/Trickeroo (p/s) 10

POLARBEAR

97	Electric Honey EHRCD007	Starfighter Pilot/Holy Cow/Safety (CD single) 30

(see also Snow Patrol)

POLECAT

76	DJM DJF 20475	MONEY TALKIN' (LP) 12

POLECATS
81	Nervous NER 001	Rockabilly Guy/Chicken Shack (p/s)	6
81	Mercury POLE 1	John I'm Only Dancing/Big Green Car (P/S)	5
81	Nervous NERD 001	CULT HEROES (LP, with Robin Scott aka Boorer)	12

POLES
88	Warm WARM 1	Letters To Send/Grow Old	8

ROLO POLEY
69	Jackpot JP 704	Zapatoo The Tiger/Music House (both sides actually by Lester Sterling)	45

POLICE
77	Illegal IL 001	Fall Out/Nothing Achieving (black & white p/s, red & black label, various designs)	10
78	A&M AMS 7348	Roxanne/Peanuts (2.52) ('telephone' p/s, typed matrix no., 'All Rights ...' on top half of label)	5
78	A&M AMS 7348	Roxanne/Peanuts (12", 'telephone' p/s)	15
78	A&M AMS 7381	Can't Stand Losing You/Dead End Job (glossy p/s, original issue, label credited to 'Police', rarer black vinyl)	10
78	A&M AMS 7381	Can't Stand Losing You/Dead End Job (glossy p/s, original issue, label credited to 'Police', mid-blue vinyl)	7
78	A&M AMS 7402	So Lonely/Time This Time (p/s, miscredited flip, label credited to 'Police')	5
79	A&M AMS 7348	Roxanne/Peanuts (3.54) (reissue, 'group' p/s, handwritten matrix number, blue vinyl)	6
79	A&M AMS 7348	Roxanne/Peanuts (2.52) (reissue, 'group' p/s, typed matrix number, blue)	6
79	A&M AMSP 7348	Roxanne/Peanuts (12", reissue, 'group' p/s)	10
79	A&M AMS 7381	Can't Stand Losing You/Dead End Job (reissue, label credited to 'The Police'; dark blue or light blue vinyl)	10
79	A&M AMS 7381	Can't Stand Losing You/Dead End Job (p/s, reissue, red, yellow, green or white vinyl)	10
79	A&M AMS 7381	Can't Stand Losing You/Dead End Job (p/s, mispressed B-side, plays "No Time This Time")	20
79	AMSP 7474	Message In A Bottle (Test pressing of unreleased 12")	700
79	Illegal IL 001	Fall Out/Nothing Achieving (reissue, various label designs, green/black p/s)	5
79	Illegal IL 001	Fall Out/Nothing Achieving (reissue, various label designs, purple/blue p/s)	15
79	Illegal IL 001	Fall Out/Nothing Achieving (reissue, various label designs, black & orange p/s)	30
80	A&M AMPP 6001	POLICE PACK (6 x 7" printed foldout PVC pack [AMS 7348, 7381, 7402, 7474 & 7494] & "The Bed's Too Big Without You"/"Truth Hits Everybody" [AMPP 6001/E]; on blue vinyl with 6 inserts)	25
80	A&M SAMP 5	SIX-TRACK RADIO SAMPLER (custom p/s, promo radio sampler)	15
80	A&M AMS 7564	Don't Stand So Close To Me/Friends (poster p/s)	7
81	A&M AMS 8194	Spirits (In The Material World)/Low Life (poster p/s, with badge)	8
83	A&M AM 117	Every Breath You Take/Murder By Numbers (p/s, with free badge)	5
83	A&M AM 117/AM 01	Every Breath You Take/Murder By Numbers//Truth Hits Everybody/ Man In A Suitcase (double pack, gatefold p/s)	10
83	A&M AMSP 117	Every Breath You Take/Murder By Numbers (picture disc)	10
83	A&M AMP 127	Wrapped Around Your Finger/Someone To Talk To (Sting picture disc)	8
83	A&M AMP 127	Wrapped Around Your Finger/Someone To Talk To (Andy Summers or Stewart Copeland picture disc, 1,000 each)	10
78	A&M AMLN 68502	OUTLANDOS D'AMOUR (LP, blue vinyl)	25

(see also Sting, Radio Actors, Zoot Money's Big Roll Band, Last Exit, Newcastle Big Band, Eberhard Schoener, Andy Summers & Robert Fripp)

POLIPHONY
73	Zella JHLPS 136	POLIPHONY (LP, private pressing)	150

POLITICIANS
72	Hot Wax HWX 114	Love Machine/Free Your Mind	15
72	Hot Wax SHW 5007	THE POLITICIANS FEATURING MCKINLEY JACKSON (LP)	30

FRANK POLK
65	Capitol CL 15389	Trying To Keep Up With The Joneses/Welcome Home, Baby	60
65	Capitol CL 15389	Trying To Keep Up With The Joneses/Welcome Home, Baby (DJ copy)	125

POLKA DOTS
59	Columbia SEG 7894	SINGIN' AND SWINGIN' (EP)	8
63	Philips BL 7576	NICE WORK AND YOU CAN BUY IT (LP)	12

(see also Teddy Johnson, Laurie Johnson)

RAY POLLARD
65	United Artists UP 1111	The Drifter/Let Him Go (And Let Me Love You)	200
65	United Artists UP 1111	The Drifter/Let Him Go (And Let Me Love You) (DJ Copy)	300
66	United Artists UP 1133	It's A Sad Thing/All The Things You Are	100
66	United Artists UP 1133	It's A Sad Thing/All The Things You Are (DJ Copy)	200

(see also Wanderers)

POLLCATS
90	Community Charge AXT 1	Poll Tax Blues/Poll Tax Blues (same track both sides, p/s)	10

(see also Steve Marriott)

POLYGON WINDOW
93	Warp WARP 33	QUOTH (12" EP, clear vinyl)	20
92	Warp WARP LP 7	SURFING ON SINE WAVES (2-LP)	30
92	Warp WARP LP 7LTD	SURFING ON SINE WAVES (LP, clear vinyl)	50

(see also Aphex Twin)

POLYPHEMUS
92	Placebo PILL 001	GREAT VILLAGE TRIP EP (10")	8
93	BB 212	Masses Of Tiny Dots/Fire Breathing Annabella (p/s)	10
95	Beggars Banquet BBQ 57CD	Stonecutter (p/s)	8
95	Acme AC 8010LP	SCRAPBOOK OF MADNESS (LP, reissue with insert, 500 only)	18
95	Acme AC 8016LP	STONEHOUSE (LP, gatefold sleeve, 700 only)	18

POLYPHONIC SPREE
02	679 679LO14	ORCHESTRAL: Light And Day/Soldier Girl (p/s, 500 only)	15
02	Good Records 679L011TLP	BEGINNING STAGES OF (LP)	12

HERB POMEROY BIG BAND
57	Columbia SX 1091	LIFE IS A MANY SPLENDOURED GIG (LP)	12

POMPHEY
72	Green Door GD 4029	Jamaica Skank/JOHNNY MOORE: Bing Comes To Town	10

MINT VALUE £

PONI-TAILS

58	HMV POP 516	Born Too Late/Come On Joey, Dance With Me (as Pony-Tails)	10
58	HMV POP 558	Close Friends/Seven Minutes In Heaven	15
58	HMV POP 558	Close Friends/Seven Minutes In Heaven (78)	12
59	HMV POP 596	Early To Bed/Father Time	15
59	HMV POP 596	Early To Bed/Father Time (78)	10
59	HMV POP 644	Moody/Oom Pah Polka	15
59	HMV POP 663	I'll Be Seeing You/I'll Keep Tryin'	25
58	HMV 7EG 8427	THE PONI-TAILS (EP)	125

JEAN-LUC PONTY

69	Liberty LBL/LBS 83262	ELECTRIC CONNECTION (LP)	20
70	Liberty LBL/LBS 83375	KING KONG (LP)	20

(see also Frank Zappa)

PONY

73	Pye 7N 25663	It's Gonna Be So Easy/Til I Met You	25

POOGY

74	EMI EMI 2136	She Looked Me In The Eye (I Gave Her My Life)/Morris And His Turtle	8

POOH

72	CBS 7930	I'll Close The Door Behind Me/The Suitcase	20

POOH STICKS

88	Fierce FRIGHT 011	On Tape (p/s, 1-sided, etched)	40
88	Fierce FRIGHT 011	On Tape (p/s, 1-sided, with unetched B-side)	35
88	Fierce FRIGHT 021	1-2-3 Red Light (p/s, 1-sided)	20
88	Fierce FRIGHT 023	Heartbreak (1-sided, etched B-side, hand-coloured promo p/s, with insert)	40
88	Fierce FRIGHT 021-025	FIERCE BOX SET (5 x 1-sided etched discs, hand-coloured labels, with insert)	50
88	Fierce FRIGHT 026	ALAN McGEE (CD EP, with FRIGHT 021-025 tracks plus "On Tape"/Please Hue, Please, in 7" box with booklet)	20
88	Fierce FRIGHT 026	ALAN McGEE (CD EP, with FRIGHT 021-025 tracks plus "On Tape"/Please Hue, Please)	10
88	Fierce FRIGHT 028	HEROES AND VILLAINS (LP, with inner)	18
89	Fierce FRIGHT 034	Dying For It (p/s, sold at U.L.U. gig, 300 only, signed)	25
89	Fierce FRIGHT 034	Dying For It (p/s, sold at U.L.U. gig, 300 only, unsigned)	15
89	Fierce FRIGHT 034	Dying For It (1-sided, different p/s to above)	15
89	Woosh WOOSH 007/WOOSH 6	Hard On Love (yellow flexi with Pooh Sticks fanzine)//GROOVE FARM: Heaven Is Blue/ESMERALDA'S KITE: Vampire girl (red flexi) (with Woosh fanzine 3)	12
92	Fierce/BMG FRIGHT 42	Million Seller (1-sided)	6
89	53rd & 3rd AGAMC 5	ORGASM (LP, pink vinyl with insert for export)	12
89	Fierce FRIGHT 025	THE POOH STICKS (mini-LP, with inner, black & white sleeve, 1-sided, side 2 etched)	12
89	Fierce FRIGHT 035	TRADE MARK OF QUALITY (LP, mail-order only, plain stickered sleeve with insert, numbered)	18
91	Cheree 18LP	GREAT WHITE WONDER (LP)	12
93	Zoo 11043	MILLION SELLERS (LP)	12

(see also Dumb Angels)

BRIAN POOLE

66	Decca F 12402	Hey Girl/Please Be Mine	10
66	CBS 202349	Everything I Touch Turns To Tears/I Need Her Tonight	22
67	CBS 202661	That Reminds Me Baby/Tomorrow Never Comes	6
67	CBS 3005	Just How Loud/The Other Side Of The Sky	20
69	President PT 239	Send Her To Me/Pretty In The City (as Brian Poole & Seychelles)	5
69	President PT 264	What Do Women Most Desire/Treat Her Like A Woman (with Seychelles)	5
75	Pinnacle P 8407	Satisfied/Red Leather (with Carousel)	6
83	Outlook OUT 100K	Do You Love Me/Twist And Shout/Time And Tide (with Tramline)	6

(see also Brian Poole & Tremeloes)

BRIAN POOLE & TREMELOES

62	Decca F 11455	Twist Little Sister/Lost Love	15
62	Decca F 11515	That Ain't Right/Blue	12
63	Decca F 11567	A Very Good Year For Girls/Meet Me Where We Used Meet	10
63	Decca F 11616	Keep On Dancing/Run Back Home	10
63	Decca F 11694	Twist And Shout/We Know	6
63	Decca F 11739	Do You Love Me/Why Can't You Lover Me	5
63	Decca F 11771	I Can Dance/Are You Loving Me At All	6
64	Decca F 11823	Candy Man/I Wish I Could Dance	6
64	Decca F 11951	Twelve Steps To Love/Don't Cry	6
65	Decca F 12124	After A While/You Know	6
65	Decca F 12197	I Want Candy/Love Me Baby	10
65	Decca F 12274	Good Lovin'/Could It Be You	6
64	Decca DFE 8566	BRIAN POOLE AND THE TREMELOES (EP)	25
65	Decca DFE 8610	BRIAN POOLE AND THE TREMELOES (EP)	25
63	Ace of Clubs ACL 1146	BIG BIG HITS OF '62 (LP)	25
63	Decca LK 4550	TWIST AND SHOUT WITH BRIAN POOLE AND THE TREMELOES (LP)	40
65	Decca LK 4685	IT'S ABOUT TIME (LP)	40

(see also Brian Poole, Tremeloes)

GLYN POOLE

73	York SYK 565	Milly Molly Mandy/Beautiful City	5

LOU & LAURA POOLE

72	Jay Boy BOY 63	Only You And I Know/Look At Me	15

POOR SOULS

65	Decca F 12183	When My Baby Cries/My Baby She's Not There	25
66	Alp ALP 595 004	Love Me/Please Don't Change Your Mind	50

POOR THINGS

66	CBS 202431	We Trust In A Better Way Of Life/Danny Boy	50

GROOVY JOE POOVEY

70	Injun 100	Ten Long Fingers On The 88 Keys/Thrill Of Love	15
71	Injun 101	Move Around/BILL REEDER: Till I Waltz Again With You	15
81	President PR 497	Lightning From The Sky/You Are My Sunshine	10

IGGY POP

77	RCA PB 9093	China Girl/Baby	5
77	RCA PB 9160	Success/The Passenger	5
77	RCA PB 9160	Some Weird Sin/The Passenger	5
78	RCA PB 9213	I Got A Right/Sixteen (some in b/w picture sleeve)	10
78	Radar ADA 4	Kill City (with James Williamson)/I Got Nothin' (p/s)	5
79	Arista ARISP 274	Five Foot One/Pretty Flamingo (picture disc)	5
79	Arista ARIST 255	I'm Bored/African Man	5
79	Arista ARIST 274	Five Foot One/Pretty Flamingo	5
80	Arista ARIST 327	Loco Mosquito/Take Care Of Me (p/s)	5
81	Arista ARIST 407	Bang Bang /Sea Of Love	5
88	A&M AMCD 909	COMPACT HITS (EP)	8
73	CBS 65586	RAW POWER (LP, with inner, orange label, as Iggy & Stooges)	30
78	Radar RAD 2	KILL CITY (LP, as Iggy Pop & James Williamson)	12
77	RCA PL12275	THE IDIOT (LP)	12
77	RCA PL12488	LUST FOR LIFE (LP)	15
84	RCA NL82488	LUST FOR LIFE (LP, reissue)	12
93	Virgon VUSLP 64	AMERICAN CAESAR (2-LP)	25

(see also Stooges)

POPCORNS

63	Columbia DB 4968	Zero Zero/Chinese Twist	15

DAVE POPE

70s	Myrrh MYR 1003	TIME TO TAKE ACCOUNT (LP)	12

TIM POPE

84	Fiction FICS 21	I Want To Be A Tree/The Double Crossing Of Two Faced Fred (p/s)	15
84	Fiction FICSX 21	I Want To Be A Tree/(Elephant) Song/The Double Crossing Of Two Faced Fred (12", p/s)	25

(see also Cure)

POP GROUP

79	Radar ADA 29	She Is Beyond Good And Evil/3.38 (p/s)	10
79	Radar ADA 1229	She Is Beyond Good And Evil/3.38 (12", p/s)	15
79	Rough Trade RT 023	We Are All Prostitutes/Amnesty International Report On British Army Torture Of Irish Prisoners (p/s)	10
80	Rough Trade RT 039/ Y Y1	Where There's A Will There's A Way/SLITS: In The Beginning There Was Rhythm (p/s)	8
79	Radar RAD 20	Y (LP, with foldout colour poster)	30
80	Rough Trade ROUGH 9	FOR HOW MUCH LONGER DO WE TOLERATE MASS MURDER? (LP, with 4 black-and-white posters)	20
80	Y/Rough Trade ROUGH 12	WE ARE TIME (LP, plain black sleeve)	15

(see also Slits)

FRANK POPP ENSEMBLE

01	Blow Up BU026	Hip Teens Don't Wear Blue Jeans/The Catwalk	8
03	Expansion SCEX 7	Breakaway/You've Been Gone Too Long	5

POPPIES

66	Columbia DB 7879	Lullaby Of Love/I Wonder Why	30

KEITH POPPIN

73	Randy's RAN 531	Kick The Bucket/I'm A Man Of My Word	6
75	Sunshot SS001	Envious/Fed Up	10
76	Sunshot SS004	Who Are You/Dub Heavier Than Lead	8
76	Sunshot SS006	It's Too Late/Part 2	8
76	Sunshot SS012	Someday Girl/Version	8
76	Mango 1002	Time Slipping Away/King Tubby's Time	12
79	JB Music JBD 006	Hold Not Thy Peace/Birdie (12")	80

POPPY FAMILY

69	Decca F 22976	Which Way You Going Billy/Endless Sleep	8
70	Decca F13092	That's Where It Went Wrong/Shadows On The Wall	10
71	Decca F 13132	I Was Wondering/Where Evil Grows	6
70	Decca KL-R 5022	WHICH WAY YOU GOING BILLY? (LP, mono)	15
70	Decca SKL-R 5022	WHICH WAY YOU GOING BILLY? (LP, stereo)	12
72	Decca SKL 5114	POPPY SEEDS (LP)	12

POPPYHEADS

88	Sarah SARAH 006	Cremation Town/Pictures You Weave/Dreamboat (foldaround p/s with large poster in poly bag)	10

POP RIVETS

79	M.T. Sounds HEP 001	BACK FROM NOWHERE (EP, no p/s)	25
79	M.T. Sounds HEP 002	BACK FROM NOWHERE (EP, split single with SULFATE, no p/s)	25
79	Hypocrite JIM 1	FUN IN THE U.K. (EP, no p/s, double pack)	30
02	(No label) HAD 1	Kray Twins/BUFFS: All My Feelings Denied (no p/s, 450 free with Chatham's Burning fanzine)	25
02	(No label) HAD 01	Kray Twins/BUFFS: All MY Feelings Denied (no p/s, without Chatham's Burning fanzine)	10
79	Hypocrite HIP 007	THE POP RIVETS GREATEST HITS (LP, printed sleeve, stamped white labels)	30
79	Hypocrite HIP 007	THE POP RIVETS GREATEST HITS (LP, title sleeve with Pop Rivets printed repeatedly across white sleeve, stamped white labels, 50 only)	100
79	Hypocrite HIP-O	EMPTY SOUNDS FROM ANARCHY RANCH (LP, coloured back, stamped labels)	30
80	Hypocrite HIP 007	THE POP RIVETS GREATEST HITS (LP, screen printed sleeve, 2 inserts, 50 only)	150
89	Hangman HANG 27 UP	ORIGINAL FIRST ALBUM!!! (LP)	18
90	Hangman HANG 35 UP	LIVE IN GERMANY '79 (LP)	18
90s	Damaged Goods DAMGOOD 142	CHATHAM'S BURNING (LP, brown vinyl)	12

(see also Milkshakes)

POPSICLES

65	Vocalion VH 9243	I Don't Want To Be Your Baby Anymore/Baby I Miss You	50

(see also Ellie Greenwich, Raindrops)

POP TOPS

72	A&M AMS 7001	Suzanne Suzanne/Oh Lord Why Lord	15
69	Major MInor MM 594	That Woman/The Man I m Today (Adagio Cardinal)	10

POPULAR 5
| 68 | Minit MLF 11011 | I'm A Lovemaker/Little Bitty Pretty One ....15 |

POP WORKSHOP
| 68 | Page One POF 091 | Fairyland/When My Little Girl Is Happy ....30 |
| 69 | Page One POF 129 | Punch And Judy Man/Love Is A One Way Highway ....10 |

PORCUPINE TREE
92	Delerium DELEC EP 010	VOYAGE 34 (12" EP) 45
90	Private (No Cat. No.)	LOVE, DEATH AND MUSSOLINI (EP, 10 copies, plain black cassette with 3 page booklet)....400
92	Delerium DELEC EP 007	VOYAGE 34 (Astralasia Remix) (12" EP) 15
92	Delerium DELECD EP 010	VOYAGE 34 (CD EP, first 100 with blue not green artwork) 60
94	Delerium DELEC EP 032	Stars Die/Moonloop (12", p/s) 15
98	Chromatic CHR 003	METANOIA (EP, 2 x 10", 1,000 only) 60
99	K-Scope/Snapper SMAS 103	Piano Lessons/Oceans Have No Memory (p/s, 1,000 copies) 15
99	K-Scope/Snapper SMAS 107	Stranger By The Minute/Hallogallo (p/s, 1,000 only) 15
99	K-Scope/Snapper SMAS 110	Pure Narcotic/Nine Cats - Acoustic (p/s) 15
00	K-Scope/Snapper SMAS 120	Shesmovedon/Novak (p/s, 1000 only) 10
00	K-Scope/Snapper SMAS 7111	4 Chords That Made A Million/Orchidia (p/s, 1,000 only) 12
01	Delerium (No Cat. No.)	TRANSMISSION IV - MOONLOOP EP (Free to Transmission Subscribers, 500 only) 80
89	Delerium DELC 0002	TARQUIN'S SEAWEED FARM (cassette, 1st issue, around 50 only) 300
92	Delerium DELEC 008	ON THE SUNDAY OF LIFE (2-LP, gatefold sleeve, 1,000 only) 80
92	Delerium DELEC CD 008	ON THE SUNDAY OF LIFE (CD) 25
93	Delerium DELEC 020	UP THE DOWN STAIR (LP) 60
94	Delerium DELEC PROMO CASS 5	SPIRAL CIRCUS (cassette give away free with Transmission newsletter) 150
94	Magic Gnome MG 4299325	YELLOW HEADGROW DREAMSCAPE (CD, 2,500 only) 100
95	Delerium DELEC LP 028	THE SKY MOVES SIDEWAYS (LP, 2,000 on blue vinyl with poster) 40
96	Delerium DELECLP 045	SIGNIFY (double LP, gatefold sleeve) 40
97	Chromatic CHR 002	SPIRAL CIRCUS (LP, 500 only) 130
99	Gates Of Dawn GOD 005	YELLOW HEDGEROW DREAMSCAPE (2-LP reissue, gold vinyl) 40
01	K-Scope/Snapper SMACD840	RECORDINGS (CD, numbered slipcase, 20,000 only) 50
06	Delerium DELECLP999	MOONLOOP (LP, 500 black vinyl in screen printed blue vinyl bag) 25
06	Delerium DELECLP 999	MOONLOOP (LP, 99 clear vinyl in screen printed blue vinyl bag) 50
06	Delerium DELECLP 999	MOONLOOP (LP, 500 white vinyl in screen printed blue vinyl bag) 30
06	Gates Of Dawn GOD 011	STUPID DREAM (2-LP, black/grey 'marbled' vinyl) 70
07	Tonefloat TF40	FEAR OF A BLANK PLANET (2-LP, gatefold) 18
07	Tonefloat TF40	FEAR OF A BLANK PLANET (2-LP, 1000 only special edition with poster, booklet and slipcase) 40

(see also No Man, Steve Wilson)

PORK DUKES
77	Wood WOOD 9	Bend And Flush/Throbbing Gristle (p/s) 10
77	Wood BRANCH 9	Making Bacon/Tight Pussy (12", p/s, yellow vinyl) 12
78	Wood Standard WOOD 56	Telephone Masturbator/Melody Makers (p/s) 10
78	Wood PORK 001	THE PORK DUKES (LP, pink vinyl with warning sticker & postcard) 25
80	Wood PORK 2	PIG OUT OF HELL (LP) 25

PORNO CASSETTES
| 82 | Heresy Records DOC 1 | You're Face, A Fucking Disgrace/Dead End Yobs ....25 |

DAVID PORTER
70	Stax STAX 150	One Part - Two Parts/Can't I See You When I Want To 8
70	Stax SXATS 1034	GRITTY, GROOVY AND GETTIN' IT (LP) 15
71	Stax STX 1030	VICTIM OF THE JOKE (LP) 20
71	Stax 2362 006	INTO A REAL THING (LP) 15

NOLAN PORTER
72	Probe PRO 580	If I Could Only Be Sure/Work It Out In The Morning 75
72	Probe PRO 580	If I Could Only Be Sure/Work It Out In The Morning (DJ copy) 100
72	Probe SPB 1067	NOLAN (LP) 25

ROBIE PORTER
| 66 | MGM 1306 | Here In My Arms/I've Often Wondered ....6 |
| 66 | MGM 1313 | Either Way I Lose/That's The Way Love Goes ....20 |

PORTER CUNNINGHAM
| 72 | Folk Heritage FHR 027 | OBSERVATIONS (LP) ....130 |

PORTION CONTROL
82	In Phaze POR CON 006	Surface And Be Seen/Spinola (Blotch)/Terror Leads To Better Days/Simple As ABC/Monstrous Bulk/He Is A Barbarian (12" p/s, with plastic outer sleeve) 60
83	Illuminated ILL 2612	Raise The Pulse/Collapse/Bite My Head 8
83	Illuminated ILL 2612	Raise The Pulse/Collapse/Bite My Head (12", p/s) 10
84	Illuminated ILL 3212	Rough Justice/The Man Who Did Backwards Somersaults (12", p/s with inner) 8
85	Illuminated ILL 4312	Go-Talk/Upside Down/Drag Down (12", p/s) 8
85	Rhythmic/Havoc 7RMIC 7	The Great Divide/Totall Recall (p/s) 5
85	Rhythmic/Havoc 12RMIC 7	The Great Divide/Divided/Bolt It Down (12", p/s) 8
85	Rhythmic/Havoc 12RMICX 7	The Great Divide (Julian Mendelsohn Remix)/Divided/Bolt It Down (12", p/s) 12
86	Dead Man's Curve DMC 1	PRESENT PURGE (12" EP) 8
81	In Phaze PORCON 002	DINING ON THE FLESH (cassette box set with free flexi 7") 70
81	In Phaze PORCON 002	GAINING MOMENTUM (cassette) 40
82	In Phaze CP 007	I STAGGERED MENTALLY (LP) 50
82	In Phase NCN	WITH MIXED EMOTION (cassette) 40
82	Third Mind TMT 07	SHOT IN THE BELLY (cassette) 40
83	In Phaze EZ 2	HIT THE PULSE (mini-LP, 45/33rpm) 18
84	Illuminated JAMS 44	STEP FORWARD (LP) 12
85	In Phaze PHA 5	SIMULATE SENSUAL (LP, clear vinyl, PVC sleeve with insert) 25
86	Dead Man's Curve DMC 8	PSYCHO-BOD SAVES THE WORLD (LP, with inner sleeve) 12

PORTISHEAD
94	Go! Beat GODX 116	Sour Times/Sour Sour Times/Lot More/Sheared Times (12") 12
94	Go! Beat GODX 114	Numb/Numbed In Moscow/Revenge Of The Number/Earth - Linger Remix/A Tribute To Monk & Canatella (12") 12
94	Go Beat GODX 120	Glory Box/Toy Box/Scorn/Sheared Box (12", p/s) 12
97	Go Beat 571 597-1	All Mine/Cowboys/Cowboys (Instrumental) (12", p/s) 10

94	Go Beat 828 522	DUMMY (LP)	30
97	Go Beat 539189-1	PORTISHEAD (LP, gloss sleeve)	20
98	Go Beat 559 424-1	ROSELAND NYC LIVE (2-LP, with poster)	20
08	Island 1766390	THIRD (2-LP, etched 12", print, with USB stick, numbered)	45

(see also Jimi Entley Sound)

PORTOBELLO EXPLOSION
| 69 | Carnaby CNS 4001 | We Can Fly/Hot Smoke And Sasafrass (label credits Portebello Explosion) | 30 |

(see also Mirage, Jawbone, Spencer Davis Group)

PORTRAIT
| 71 | Pye 7N 45043 | Tokaido Lines/Cuddle Me Closer | 6 |

PORTRAIT OF DAN TRACY
| 94 | Direct Lite 726 | Silly Girl/I Know Where Syd Barrett Lives/Remember Bridget Riley A Picture Of Dorian Grey (p/s) | 10 |

PORTSMOUTH FOOTBALL PLAYERS
| 70s | Solent SS 046 | Sing Along With Pompey/Pompey City With A Heart | 8 |

PORTWAY PEDLARS
| 84 | Greenwich Village GVR 229 | IN GREENWOOD SHADES (LP) | 15 |

SANDY POSEY
66	MGM MGM 1321	Born A Woman/Caution To The Wind	5
66	MGM MGM 1330	Single Girl/Blue Is My Best Colour	6
67	MGM MGM 1335	What A Woman In Love Won't Do/Shattered	8
67	MGM MGM 1342	I Take It Back/The Boy I Love	8
67	MGM MGM 1364	Are You Never Coming Home/I Can Show You How To Live	8
67	MGM MGM-C(S) 8035	BORN A WOMAN (LP)	25
67	MGM MGM-C(S) 8042	SINGLE GIRL (LP)	20
68	MGM MGM-C(S) 8051	SANDY POSEY (LP)	20
68	MGM MGM-C 8060	THE BEST OF SANDY POSEY (LP, original with blue label)	20
68	MGM MGM-C(S) 8073	LOOKING AT YOU (LP)	20

POSH
| 81 | Marathon RUN 1 | Letter To Linda/Racey Tracey (p/s) | 10 |

POSITIVE FORCE
| 79 | Sugarhill SH 102 | We Got The Funk/Tell Me What You See (12") | 8 |

POSITIVE SIGNALS
| 80 | Yob YOB 001 | Media Man/Only For A Day/STRAND: Here Today Gone Tomorrow/Changing World (split EP, p/s) | 15 |

POSSESSED
| 86 | Under One Flag FLAG 3 | BEYOND THE GATES (LP) | 15 |
| 87 | Under One Flag M FLAG 16 | THE EYES OF HORROR EP (12", p/s) | 15 |

HOWIE POST & SWIFTIES
| 63 | Fontana TF 421 | Tom Swift/The Elephant | 10 |

POST MORTEM
| 83 | Regime FM 006 | BETER OFF DEAD (EP) | 25 |

ADRIENNE POSTER/POSTA
63	Oriole CB 1890	Only Fifteen/There's Nothing You Can Do About That	30
63	Decca F 11797	Only Fifteen/There's Nothing You Can Do About That (reissue)	20
64	Decca F 11864	Shang A Doo Lang/When A Girl Really Loves You	25
65	Decca F 12079	He Doesn't Love Me/The Way You Do The Things You Do	25
65	Decca F 12181	The Winds That Blow/Back Street Girl	25
66	Decca F 12329	Something Beautiful/So Glad You're Mine	35
66	Decca F 12455	They Long To Be Close To You/How Can I Hurt You (as Adrienne Posta)	20
73	DJM DJS 286	Dog Song/Express Yourself	12

POTATOES
| 66 | Fontana TF 756 | The Bend/Bend Ahead | 7 |

POTENTIAL BAD BOY
| 06 | Sublogic/Ninety-Two Retro SLVR 001/9T2RX | Everyday Child (1-sided 12", 100 only, stamped and hand-numbered labels) | 40 |

POTENTIAL THREAT
82	Out Of Town HOOT 7	WHAT'S SO GREAT BRITAIN! (EP)	30
84	Children Of The Revolution COR 6	Brainwashed/Turn A Blind Eye/A Cry For Help/Conflict (p/s)	15
80s	Mortarhate MORT 24	DEMAND AN ALTERNATIVE (LP)	30

KEITH POTGER
| 69 | Mercury MF 1073 | The World Would Never Turn Again/Santa Marie (in p/s) | 8 |
| 69 | Mercury MF 1073 | The World Would Never Turn Again/Santa Marie | 6 |

(see also Seekers, Judith Durham)

POTLIQUOR
72	Janus 6146 011	Cheer/Chatanooga	8
70	Dawn DNLS 3016	FIRST TASTE (LP, withdrawn)	90
72	Janus 6310 202	LEVEE BLUES (LP)	30
72	Janus 6310 203	FIRST TASTE (LP, reissue)	12

PHIL POTTER
76	Genesis GEN 10	MY SONG IS LOVE UNKNOWN (LP)	20
79	Dove DOVE 61	THE RESTORER (LP)	15
70s	Kingsway KMR 321	LEAD ME ON (LP)	12

POTTERS
| 72 | Trent JT 100 | We'll Be With You/Theme For A Team | 20 |

POUND HOUNDS
| 55 | Brunswick 05484 | Home Sweet Home/MELLOMEN: Lady | 5 |

(see also Peggy Lee)

MINT VALUE £

POUND OF FLESH
75	Creole CR 106	Funky March/Part 2	10

ALLEN POUND'S GET RICH
66	Parlophone R 5532	Searchin' In The Wilderness/Hey You (rare stock copy)	900
66	Parlophone R 5532	Searchin' In The Wilderness/Hey You (more common demo)	500

FRANCK POURCEL
59	HMV POP 622	Only You/Rainy Night In Paris	8

ANDREW POWELL & THE PHILHARMONIC ORCHESTRA
83	EMI CDP 7 46006 2	THE BEST OF THE ALAN PARSONS PROJECT (CD)	15

(see also Alan Parsons Project)

BUD POWELL (TRIO)
55	Vogue EPV 1030	BUD POWELL TRIO (EP)	15
55	Vogue EPV 1033	BUD POWELL'S MODERNISTS (EP)	15
55	Vogue EPV 1036	BUD POWELL TRIO (EP)	15
55	Columbia Clef SEB 10013	BUD POWELL (EP)	15
57	Columbia Clef SEB 10074	GENIUS OF BUD POWELL (EP)	15
58	Columbia Clef SEB 10094	GENIUS OF BUD POWELL NO. 2 (EP)	15
52	Vogue LDE 010	THE BUD POWELL TRIO (10" LP)	20
54	Vogue LDE 053	JAZZ AT THE MASSEY HALL VOL. 2 (10" LP)	20
56	Columbia Clef 33C 9016	BUD POWELL TRIO (10" LP)	25
57	Columbia Clef 33CX 10069	JAZZ ORIGINAL (LP)	30
58	Columbia Clef 33CX 10123	BLUES FOR BUD (LP)	30
59	HMV CLP 1294	THE LONELY ONE (LP)	30
63	Vogue LAE 558	THE BUD POWELL TRIO (LP)	15
63	Columbia 33SX 1575	THE BUD POWELL TRIO FEATURING MAX ROACH (LP)	25
64	Fontana FJL 903	HOT HOUSE (LP)	25
68	Fontana SFJL 901	BLUES FOR BOUFFEMONT (LP)	25
73	Mainstream MSL 1007	UPS 'N' DOWNS (LP, gatefold)	12

COZY POWELL
73	Rak RAK 164	Dance With The Devil/And Then There Was Skin (export copy, European diff p/s)	10
73	Rak 4C 006 94962	Dance With The Devil/And Then There Was Skin (export issue, p/s, RAK 164 in run out groove, blue or yellow vinyl)	20
73	Rak 4C 006 94962	Dance With The Devil/And Then There Was Skin (export issue, p/s, RAK 164 in run out groove)	12
74	Rak RAK 4C006-95491	The Man In Black/After Dark (export issue, p/s)	10
79	Ariola ARO 189	Theme One/Over The Top pt. 1 (p/s, red vinyl)	5
79	Ariola ARPD 189	Theme One/Over The Top (full version) (12")	5
79	Ariola ARO 205	The Loner/El Sid (p/s, blue vinyl)	5
80	Ariolo ARO 222	Heidi Goes To Town / Over The Top part 2 (p/s, clear vinyl)	5
92	Old Gold OG 6177	Dance with The Devil/Na Na Na/The Man In Black (CD, single)	10

(see also Rainbow, Young Blood, Big Bertha, Ace Kefford Stand, Bedlam, Bernie Marsden, Phenomena, Black Sabbath, Jeff Beck, Whitesnake, Michael Schenker Group, Donovan, Gary Moore, Young & Moody, Brian May, Chick Churchill, Graham Bonnet, Forcefield, Emerson Lake & Powell, Jack Bruce, Plum & Youth, Suzi Quatro)

JANE POWELL
53	MGM SP 1061	Something Wonderful/I Whistle A Happy Tune	5
53	MGM SP 1062	Hello, Young Lovers/We Kiss In A Shadow	5
56	HMV POP 267	True Love/Mind If I Make Love To You	6
59	MGM MGM-EP 701	JANE POWELL SINGS (EP)	8
54	Capitol LC 6665	THREE SAILORS AND A GIRL (10" LP)	25
57	HMV CLP 1131	JANE POWELL (LP)	25

(see also Marilyn Monroe)

JIMMY POWELL (& DIMENSIONS)
62	Decca F 11447	Sugar Babe (Parts 1 & 2) (solo)	15
62	Decca F 11544	Tom Hark/Dance Her By Me (solo)	10
63	Decca F 11570	Remember Them/Everyone But You (solo)	8
64	Pye 7N 15663	That's Alright/I'm Looking For A Woman	60
64	Pye 7N 15735	Sugar Babe/I've Been Watching You (as Jimmy Powell & 5 Dimensions)	20
66	Strike JH 309	I Can Go Down/Love Me Right	15
67	Decca F 12664	Unexpected Mirrors/Time Mends Broken Hearts (with Dimensions)	15
68	Decca F 12751	I Just Can't Get Over You/Real Cool (with Dimensions)	20
68	Decca F 12793	Sugar Babe (Parts 1 & 2)	10

JUDITH POWELL
67	RCA RCA 1569	Greener Days/No Goodbyes	6

KEITH POWELL (& VALETS)
63	Columbia DB 7116	The Answer Is No!/Come On And Join The Party (with Valets)	15
64	Columbia DB 7229	Tore Up/You Better Let Him Go (with Valets)	25
64	Columbia DB 7366	I Should Know Better (But I Don't)/Too Much Monkey Business (with Valets)	35
65	Piccadilly 7N 35235	People Get Ready/Paradise	15
65	Piccadilly 7N 35249	Come Home Baby/Beyond The Hill	15
66	Piccadilly 7N 35275	Goodbye Girl/It Was Easier To Hurt Her	15
66	Piccadilly 7N 35300	Victory/Some People Only	15
66	Piccadilly 7N 35353	It Keeps Rainin'/Song of The Moon	20

(see also Move, Carl Wayne & Vikings)

KEITH (POWELL) & BILLIE (DAVIES)
66	Piccadilly 7N 35288	When You Move, You Lose/Tastes Sour, Don't It? (as Keith & Billie)	15
66	Piccadilly 7N 35321	You Don't Know Like I Know/Two Little People	15
66	Piccadilly 7N 35340	Swingin' Tight/That's Really Some Good	15

(see also Keith Powell, Billie Davis)

MARILYN POWELL
64	Fontana TF 448	All My Loving/After The Party	7
65	Fontana TF 526	Please Go Away/Where Did I Go Wrong	5
65	Fontana TF 557	As Long As You Come Back To Me/Go Away	5
65	Fontana TF 687	Showdown/Came The Day	5
68	CBS 2331	Something To Hold On To/Kiss Me Again	5
69	CBS 4440	Have Another Dream On Me/Afraid To Love You	5

RAY POWELL
74	RCA 2490	King Kong/Rock Ness Monster	5

POWER
82	Malaco MAL1	Groovin'/Instrumental	8

POWER CUT/CASH CREW
88	Vinyl Lab VL 004T	Mission Impossible/Microphone Maniac (12")	35

DUFFY POWER
59	Fontana H 194	Dream Lover/That's My Little Suzie	15
59	Fontana H 194	Dream Lover/That's My Little Suzie (78)	20
59	Fontana H 214	Kissin' Time/Ain't She Sweet	15
59	Fontana H 214	Kissin' Time/Ain't She Sweet (78)	20
59	Fontana H 230	Starry-Eyed/Prettier Than You	15
59	Fontana H 230	Starry-Eyed/Prettier Than You (78)	20
60	Fontana H 279	Whole Lotta Shakin' Goin' On/If I Can Dream	30
61	Fontana H 302	I've Got Nobody/When We're Walking Close	15
61	Fontana H 344	No Other Love/What Now	12
63	Parlophone R 4992	It Ain't Necessarily So/If I Get Lucky Someday	12
63	Parlophone R 5024	I Saw Her Standing There (with Graham Bond Quartet)/Farewell Baby	40
63	Parlophone R 5059	Hey Girl/Woman Made Trouble	15
64	Parlophone R 5111	Parchman Farm/Tired, Broke And Busted (with Paramounts)	40
64	Parlophone R 5169	Where Am I?/I Don't Care	40
67	Parlophone R 5631	Davy O'Brien (Leave That Baby Alone)/July Tree	30
70	CBS 5176	Hell Hound/Hummingbird	15
71	Epic EPC 7139	Hummingbird/Hell Hound (reissue)	6
73	GSF GSZ 6	River/Little Soldiers	5
73	GSF GSZ 8	Liberation/Song About Jesus	5
71	Transatlantic TRA 229	INNOVATIONS (LP)	50
73	GSF GS 502	DUFFY POWER (LP)	20
73	Spark SRLM 2005	DUFFY POWER (LP)	20
76	Buk BULP 2010	POWERHOUSE (LP, revised reissue of GSF GS 502)	15

(see also Alexis Korner, John McLaughlin, Jack Bruce, Graham Bond, Duffy's Nucleus)

JIMMY POWER
76	Topic 12TS 306	IRISH FIDDLE PLAYER (LP)	12

POWER CUT CREW
89	Vinyl Lab VL 007T	You Get Down (12")	8
88	PowerCut PC001	Power Cut 1/African Beats (12")	40

POWERHOUSE
66	Decca F 12471	Chain Gang/Can You Hear Me?	20
66	Decca F 12507	Raindrops/La Bamba	10

POWERLINE
81	Elite DAZZ 7	Journey (6.54)/Double Journey (13.05) (12", stickered die cut sleeve)	25

POWERPACK
66	CBS 202335	It Hurts Me So/What You Gonna Do	40
67	CBS 202551	I'll Be Anything For You/The Lost Summer	20
69	Polydor 56319	Hannibal Brooks/Juliet Simkins	8
70	Polydor 2001 077	Oh Calcutta/Soul Searchin'	20
69	Polydor 583 057	SOUL CURE (LP)	60

(see also Procol Harum, Emperor Rosko & Power Pack)

POWERPILL
92	ffrreedom TABX 110	PAC MAN EP: Powerpill Mix/Ghost Mix/Choci's Hi Score Mix/Mickey Finn's Yum Yum Mix (12", limited edition yellow vinyl)	30
92	ffrreedom TABX 110	PAC MAN EP: Powerpill Mix/Ghost Mix/Choci's Hi Score Mix/Mickey Finn's Yum Yum Mix (12")	20
92	ffrreedom TABX 110	PAC MAN EP: Powerpill Mix/Ghost Mix/Choci's Hi Score Mix/Mickey Finn's Yum Yum Mix (CD)	30

(see also Aphex Twin)

JETT POWERS
70	Liberty LBS 83320	CALIFORNIA LICENCE (LP)	40

(see also P.J. Proby)

JOEY POWERS
63	Stateside SS 236	Midnight Mary/Where Do You Want The World Delivered	10

KID CONGO POWERS
89	Night Shift NISHI 208T	In The Heat Of The Night/Cat Tabu/La Historia Des Un Amour (12", p/s)	8

(see also Gun Club)

POWERS OF BLUE
67	CBS 62953	FLIP OUT! (LP)	20

POWER STATION
85	Parlophone 12 RP 6091	Some Like It Hot (Full Length Version)/The Heat Is On/ Some Like It Hot (12", picture disc)	8

(see also Duran Duran, Robert Palmer)

P.P. & PRIMES
96	Nice (no cat. no.)	Understanding/STEVIE'S BUZZ (i.e. Buzzcocks): Autumn Stone (promo only)	10

(see also Primal Scream, P.P. Arnold)

PEREZ 'PREZ' PRADO & HIS ORCHESTRA
54	HMV 7M 255	Skokiaan - Mambo/The High And The Mighty	8
55	HMV 7M 295	Cherry Pink And Apple Blossom White/Maria Elena	10
55	HMV 7MC 29	Mambo De La Telefonista/En Las Calles De La Habana (export issue)	5
58	RCA RCA 1067	Patricia/Why Wait	7
58	RCA RCA 1082	Guaglione/Paris	10
59	RCA RCA 1129	Tic Toc Polly Woc/My Roberta	5
58	RCA RD 27102	DILO (LP)	15
60	RCA RD 27046	LATIN SATIN (LP)	15

64	Parlophone PMC 1226	A CAT IN LATIN (LP)	15
74	Contour 2870 385	NOW (LP)	15

PRAG VEC
78	Spec SP 001	Wolf/Cigarettes/Existential/Bits! (p/s)	10
79	Spec SP 002	Expert/The Follower! (p/s)	10
81	Spec RESPECT 1	NO COWBOYS (LP, with insert)	18

(see also Foetus etc.)

PRAISE
76	No Seven 001	BLESSED QUIETNESS (LP)	40

PRAISE SPACE ELECTRIC
91	Pop God PGTT 005	PRAISE SPACE ELECTRIC (LP)	15
94	Delerium DELEC LP 015	LEAVING DEMONS (LP)	20

PRAM
93	Too Pure PURE 17	IRON LUNG EP (12")	10
01	Too Pure PURE 41	HELIUM (LP)	20

PRAMS
81	Product/Ltd. Edition TAKE 3	Nowhere's Safe/TV PRODUCT: Jumping Off Walls (foldout p/s)	15
86	Classic Quotes CLASS 1	Black Sleep/Classic Quotes (p/s)	5
80s	Wabbit	WHAT'S THE TIME, MR WOLF? (LP)	20

PRATS
80	Rough Trade RT 042	1990's POP EP (p/s)	10

ANDY PRATT
69	Polydor 2489 003	RECORDS ARE LIKE LIFE (LP)	25

GRAHAM & EILEEN PRATT
78	Cottage Records	CLEAR AIR OF THE DAY (LP)	20
80	Dingle's DIN 308	TO FRIEND & FOE (LP)	20
81	Dingle's DIN	BANDSTAND (LP)	18
85	Plant Life PLR 068	HEIROGLYPHICS (LP)	15

PRATT & MCCLAIN
76	Reprise K 14435	Happy Days/Cruisin' With The Fonz (PS)	6

PHIL PRATT
69	Jolly JY 008	Sweet Song For My Baby/THRILLERS: I'm Restless	95

(see also Charlie Ace, Larry Marshall, Don Drummond)

PHIL PRATT ALL STARS
70	Jackpot JP 748	Cut Throat/KEN BOOTHE: You Left The Water Running	20
71	Punch PH 94	Winey Winey (actually "Kingstonians Medley" by Kingstonians)/There Is A Place (actually by Barrington Spence)	20

(see also Dennis Alcapone, Horace Andy, Dennis Brown, Ken Boothe, Erroll Dunkley, John Holt, Delroy Wilson)

PRAYING MANTIS
79	Ripper/Harvest HAR 5201	THE SOUNDHOUSE TAPES PART 2: Captured City/Johnny Cool (p/s)	60
79	Ripper/Harvest 12HAR 5201	THE SOUNDHOUSE TAPES PART 2 (12")	15
80	Gem GEMS 36	Praying Mantis/High Roller (p/s, with transfer)	20
80	Gem GEMS 36	Praying Mantis/High Roller (p/s)	18
81	Arista ARIST 397	All Day And All Of The Night/Beads Of Ebony (p/s)	12
81	Arista ARIST 478	Cheated/Thirty Pieces Of Silver/Flirting With Suicide/Panic In The Streets (2x7", gatefold sleeve)	8
82	Jet JET 7026	Tell Me The Nightmare's Wrong/A Question Of Time/Turn The Tables (p/s)	20
81	Arista SPART 1153	TIME TELLS NO LIES (LP, with inner sleeve)	25

(see also Stratus, Grand Prix, Uriah Heep)

PREACHERS
65	Columbia DB 7680	Hole In My Soul/Too Old In The Head	80

(see also Herd, Peter Frampton, Denny Mitchel & Soundsations, Moon's Train)

PRECIOUS LITTLE
80	Rock On ROR 2	Give It To Me Now/Clean Living Boy (p/s)	20

PRECISIONS
67	Track 604 014	If This Is Love (I'd Rather Be Lonely)/You'll Soon Be Gone	40
79	Grapevine GRP 129	Such Misery/A Lovers Plea	10

PREDATOR (1)
78	Bust! SOL 2	Punk Man/Paperboy Song (with insert)	60

PREDATOR (2)
85	CTM C 001	Don't Stop/Shotdown (in p/s)	80
85	CTM C 001	Don't Stop/Shotdown	30

PREDATORS
83	Ears And Eyes EER 012	SOCIAL DECAY (LP)	40

PREDATUR
82	Quicksilver QUICK 5	Take A Walk/Seen You Here (p/s)	75

PREFAB SPROUT
82	Candle CANDLE 1	Lions In My Own Garden (Exit Someone)/Radio Love	20

PREFECTS
79	Rough Trade TR 040	Going Through The Motions/Things In General	10
82	Variety BBY 402	Love Is All Around/I Saw The Night	6
87	Strange Fruit SFPS 025	PEEL SESSIONS (12")	8

PREFUSE 73
03	Warp WARPLP 105	ONE WORD EXTINGUISHER (2-LP)	20
03	Warp WAP 164	EXTINGUISHED: OUTTAKES (LP)	15

PREGNANT INSOMNIA
67	Direction 58-3132	Wallpaper/You Intrigue Me	50

PRELUDE (1)

72	Crotchet CME 18A/B	PRELUDE (LP, private pressing)	70
73	Dawn DNLS 3052	HOW LONG IS FOREVER (LP, textured gatefold sleeve)	20
74	Dawn DNLS 3061	DUTCH COURAGE (LP)	12

PRELUDE (2)

| 72 | Decca F13292 | Edge Of The Sea/Looking For Indians | 10 |

PRELUDE (3)

| 83 | Black Crow CROS 1 | Freedom/Prelude | 10 |

PREMIERS (U.K.)

| 64 | Silver Phoenix 1002 | Tears, Tears/Bye Bye Johnny | 45 |

PREMIERS (U.S.)

| 64 | Warner Bros WB 134 | Farmer John/Duffy's Blues | 15 |
| 64 | Warner Bros W 1565 | FARMER JOHN "LIVE" (LP) | 60 |

YVONNE PRENOSILOVA

| 65 | Pye 7N 15775 | When My Baby Cries/Come On Home | 45 |

PRESENCE (1)

| 76 | NC SLCW 1031 | PRESENCE (LP) | 35 |

PRESENCE (2)

| 91 | Reality LOL 1 | In Wonder/Soft (p/s, withdrawn) | 5 |
| 91 | Reality LOLX 1 | In Wonder/Soft/In Wonder (Didgeribdub Mix) (12", p/s, withdrawn) | 8 |

(see also Cure)

PRESIDENT REAGAN IS CLEVER

| 86 | Hyena HAHA 001 | FROM THIS TO THAT EP (12") | 8 |

PRESIDENTS (1)

| 64 | Decca F 11826 | Candy Man/Let The Sunshine In | 50 |

PRESIDENTS (2)

| 72 | A&M AMS 856 | 5-10-15-20 Years Of Love/Triangle Of Love | 5 |
| 72 | Sussex AMLS 65001 | 5-10-15-20-25-30 (LP) | 15 |

ELVIS PRESLEY

78S : HMV 78S

56	HMV POP 182	Heartbreak Hotel/I Was The One	20
56	HMV POP 213	Blue Suede Shoes/Tutti Frutti	25
56	HMV POP 235	I Want You, I Need You, I Love You/My Baby Left Me	25
56	HMV POP 249	Hound Dog/Don't Be Cruel	15
56	HMV POP 253	Love Me Tender/Anyway You Want Me (That's How I Will Be)	20
56	HMV POP 272	Blue Moon/I Don't Care If The Sun Don't Shine	30
57	HMV POP 295	Mystery Train/Love Me	40
57	HMV POP 305	Rip It Up/Baby, Let's Play House	40
57	HMV POP 330	Too Much/Playing For Keeps	30
57	HMV POP 359	All Shook Up/That's When Your Heartaches Begin	15
57	HMV POP 378	Paralyzed/When My Blue Moon Turns To Gold Again	30
57	HMV POP 408	Tryin' To Get To You/Lawdy, Miss Clawdy	40
58	HMV POP 428	I'm Left, You're Right, She's Gone/How Do You Think I Feel?	40

78S : RCA 78S

57	RCA RCA 1013	(Let Me Be Your) Teddy Bear/Loving You	15
57	RCA RCA 1020	Party/Got A Lot O' Livin' To Do	15
57	RCA RCA 1025	Santa Bring My Baby Back (To Me)/Santa Claus Is Back In Town	25
58	RCA RCA 1028	Jailhouse Rock/Treat Me Nice	15
58	RCA RCA 1043	Don't/I Beg Of You	25
58	RCA RCA 1058	Wear My Ring Around Your Neck/Doncha' Think It's Time	30
58	RCA RCA 1070	Hard Headed Woman/Don't Ask Me Why	30
58	RCA RCA 1081	King Creole/Dixieland Rock	30
58	RCA RCA 1088	All Shook Up/Heartbreak Hotel	100
58	RCA RCA 1095	Hound Dog/Blue Suede Shoes	100
59	RCA RCA 1100	One Night/I Got Stung	60
59	RCA RCA 1113	(Now And Then There's) A Fool Such As I/I Need Your Love Tonight	60
59	RCA RCA 1136	A Big Hunk O' Love/My Wish Came True	100
60	RCA RCA 1187	Stuck On You/Fame And Fortune	500
60	RCA RCA 1194	A Mess Of Blues/The Girl Of My Best Friend	750

SINGLES : HMV 45S: PURPLE LABEL/GOLD PRINT

56	HMV 7M 385	Heartbreak Hotel/I Was The One ('removable/replaceable' centre)	350
56	HMV 7M 385	Heartbreak Hotel/I Was The One (solid centre)	200
56	HMV 7M 405	Blue Suede Shoes/Tutti Frutti	300
56	HMV 7M 424	I Want You, I Need You, I Love You/My Baby Left Me ('removable/replaceable' centre)	300
56	HMV 7M 424	I Want You, I Need You, I Love You/My Baby Left Me ('solid centre')	200
56	HMV POP 249	Hound Dog/Don't Be Cruel	150
56	HMV POP 253	Love Me Tender/Anyway You Want Me (That's How I Will Be)	150
56	HMV POP 272	Blue Moon/I Don't Care If The Sun Don't Shine ('removable/replaceable' centre)	200
56	HMV POP 272	Blue Moon/I Don't Care If The Sun Don't Shine (solid centre)	150
57	HMV POP 295	Mystery Train/Love Me ('removable/replaceable' centre)	350
57	HMV POP 295	Mystery Train/Love Me (solid centre)	200
57	HMV 7MC 42	Mystery Train/I Forgot To Remember To Forget (U.K. issue of export single, gold label print only, smooth edge to labels)	300
57	HMV POP 305	Rip It Up/Baby, Let's Play House ('removable/replaceable' centre)	300
57	HMV POP 305	Rip It Up/Baby, Let's Play House (solid centre)	200
57	HMV POP 330	Too Much/Playing For Keeps	120
57	HMV POP 359	All Shook Up/That's When Your Heartaches Begin (push-out centre)	150
57	HMV POP 359	All Shook Up/That's When Your Heartaches Begin (solid centre)	100
57	HMV POP 378	Paralyzed/When My Blue Moon Turns To Gold Again	100

SINGLES : HMV 45S :PURPLE LABEL/SILVER PRINT

| 56 | HMV 7M 385 | Heartbreak Hotel/I Was The One | 200 |
| 56 | HMV 7M 405 | Blue Suede Shoes/Tutti Frutti | 250 |

MINT VALUE £

56	HMV 7M 424	I Want You, I Need You, I Love You/My Baby Left Me	150
56	HMV POP 249	Hound Dog/Don't Be Cruel	100
56	HMV POP 253	Love Me Tender/Anyway You Want Me (That's How I Will Be)	100
56	HMV POP 272	Blue Moon/I Don't Care If The Sun Don't Shine	100
57	HMV POP 295	Mystery Train/Love Me	150
57	HMV POP 305	Rip It Up/Baby, Let's Play House	150
57	HMV POP 330	Too Much/Playing For Keeps	150
57	HMV POP 359	All Shook Up/That's When Your Heartaches Begin ('removable/replaceable' centre)	150
57	HMV POP 359	All Shook Up/That's When Your Heartaches Begin (solid centre)	50
57	HMV POP 378	Paralyzed/When My Blue Moon Turns To Gold Again	50
57	HMV POP 408	Tryin' To Get To You/Lawdy, Miss Clawdy	50
58	HMV POP 428	I'm Left, You're Right, She's Gone/How Do You Think I Feel?	50

SINGLES : ORIGINAL RCA 45S: BLACK LABELS

57	RCA RCA 1013	(Let Me Be Your) Teddy Bear/Loving You	20
57	RCA RCA 1020	Party/Got A Lot O' Livin' To Do	20
57	RCA RCA 1025	Santa Bring My Baby Back (To Me)/Santa Claus Is Back In Town	20
58	RCA RCA 1028	Jailhouse Rock/Treat Me Nice	15
58	RCA RCA 1043	Don't/I Beg Of You	15
58	RCA RCA 1058	Wear My Ring Around Your Neck/Doncha' Think It's Time	15
58	RCA RCA 1070	Hard Headed Woman/Don't Ask Me Why	15
58	RCA RCA 1081	King Creole/Dixieland Rock	15
58	RCA RCA 1088	All Shook Up/Heartbreak Hotel	50
58	RCA RCA 1095	Hound Dog/Blue Suede Shoes	50
59	RCA RCA 1100	One Night/I Got Stung	15

(This RCA 45 was issued with a triangular centre, round-centre re-pressings are worth half to two-thirds these values. RCA Victor re-pressings are on a par with Triangular centre prices)

59	RCA RCA 1113	(Now And Then There's) A Fool Such As I/I Need Your Love Tonight	15
59	RCA RCA 1136	A Big Hunk O' Love/My Wish Came True	15

(The above 45s were issued with a triangular centre, round-centre re-pressings are worth half to two-thirds these values. RCA Victor re-pressings are on a par with Triangular centre prices)

60	RCA RCA 1187	Stuck On You/Fame And Fortune	5
60	RCA RCA 1194	A Mess Of Blues/The Girl Of My Best Friend	5
60	RCA RCA 1207	It's Now Or Never (O Sole Mio)/Make Me Know It	5
61	RCA RCA 1216	Are You Lonesome Tonight?/I Gotta Know	5
61	RCA RCA 1226	Wooden Heart/Tonight Is So Right For Love	5
61	RCA RCA 1227	Surrender (Torna A Surriento)/Lonely Man	5
61	RCA RCA 1244	Wild In The Country/I Feel So Bad	5
61	RCA RCA 1258	(Marie's The Name) His Latest Flame/Little Sister	5
61	RCA RCA 1270	Rock-A-Hula Baby/Can't Help Falling In Love	5
62	RCA RCA 1280	Good Luck Charm/Anything That's Part Of You	5
62	RCA RCA 1303	She's Not You/Just Tell Her Jim Said Hello	5
62	RCA RCA 1320	Return To Sender/Where Do You Come From	5

SINGLES : ORIGINAL RCA VICTOR 45S: BLACK LABELS

62	RCA Victor RCA 1280	Good Luck Charm/Anything That's Part Of You	5
62	RCA Victor RCA 1303	She's Not You/Just Tell Her Jim Said Hello	6
62	RCA Victor RCA 1320	Return To Sender/Where Do You Come From	6
63	RCA Victor RCA 1337	One Broken Heart For Sale/They Remind Me Too Much Of You	8
63	RCA Victor RCA 1355	(You're The) Devil In Disguise/Please Don't Drag That String Around	5
63	RCA Victor RCA 1374	Bossa Nova Baby/Witchcraft	6
62	RCA Victor RCA 1375	Kiss Me Quick/Something Blue	6
64	RCA Victor RCA 1390	Viva Las Vegas/What'd I Say	8
64	RCA Victor RCA 1404	Kissin' Cousins/It Hurts Me	6
64	RCA Victor RCA 1411	Such A Night/Never Ending	7
64	RCA Victor RCA 1422	Ain't That Loving You Baby/Ask Me	6
64	RCA Victor RCA 1430	Blue Christmas/White Christmas	8
65	RCA Victor RCA 1443	Do The Clam/You'll Be Gone	7
66	RCA Victor RCA 1509	Frankie And Johnny/Please Don't Stop Loving Me	15
66	RCA Victor RCA 1526	Love Letters/Come What May	7
66	RCA Victor RCA 1545	All That I Am/Spinout	10
66	RCA Victor RCA 1557	If Every Day Was Like Christmas/How Would You Like To Be?	8
67	RCA Victor RCA 1565	Indescribably Blue/Fools Fall In Love	20
67	RCA Victor RCA 1593	The Love Machine/You Gotta Stop	15
67	RCA Victor RCA 1616	Long-Legged Girl (With The Short Dress On)/That's Someone You Never Forget	20
67	RCA Victor RCA 1628	Judy/There's Always Me	40
67	RCA Victor RCA 1642	Big Boss Man/You Don't Know Me	20
68	RCA Victor RCA 1663	Guitar Man/Hi-Heel Sneakers	10
68	RCA Victor RCA 1688	U.S. Male/Stay Away	15
68	RCA Victor RCA 1714	Your Time Hasn't Come Yet Baby/Let Yourself Go	15
68	RCA Victor RCA 1747	You'll Never Walk Alone/We Call On Him	30
68	RCA Victor RCA 1768	A Little Less Conversation/Almost In Love	25

SINGLES : RCA VICTOR 45S: BLACK LABEL REISSUES

64	RCA Victor RCA 1020	Party/Got A Lot O' Livin' To Do	10
64	RCA Victor RCA 1025	Santa Bring My Baby Back (To Me)/Santa Claus Is Back In Town	15
64	RCA Victor RCA 1028	Jailhouse Rock/Treat Me Nice	15
64	RCA Victor RCA 1043	Don't/I Beg Of You	15
64	RCA Victor RCA 1058	Wear My Ring Around Your Neck/Doncha' Think It's Time	10
64	RCA Victor RCA 1070	Hard Headed Woman/Don't Ask Me Why	15
64	RCA Victor RCA 1081	King Creole/Dixieland Rock	15
64	RCA Victor RCA 1088	All Shook Up/Heartbreak Hotel	15
64	RCA Victor RCA 1095	Hound Dog/Blue Suede Shoes	15
64	RCA Victor RCA 1100	One Night/I Got Stung	10
64	RCA Victor RCA 1113	(Now And Then There's) A Fool Such As I/I Need Your Love Tonight	10
64	RCA Victor RCA 1136	A Big Hunk O' Love/My Wish Came True	10
64	RCA Victor RCA 1187	Stuck On You/Fame And Fortune	10
64	RCA Victor RCA 1194	A Mess Of Blues/The Girl Of My Best Friend	8
64	RCA Victor RCA 1207	It's Now Or Never (O Sole Mio)/Make Me Know It	8
64	RCA Victor RCA 1216	Are You Lonesome Tonight?/I Gotta Know	15
64	RCA Victor RCA 1226	Wooden Heart/Tonight Is So Right For Love	8
64	RCA Victor RCA 1227	Surrender (Torna A Surriento)/Lonely Man	8

64	RCA Victor RCA 1244	Wild In The Country/I Feel So Bad..8
64	RCA Victor RCA 1258	(Marie's The Name) His Latest Flame/Little Sister 6
64	RCA Victor RCA 1270	Rock-A-Hula Baby/Can't Help Falling In Love 7

SINGLES : RCA VICTOR 45S: ORANGE LABEL REISSUES

69	RCA Victor RCA 1088	All Shook Up/Heartbreak Hotel...15
69	RCA Victor RCA 1095	Hound Dog/Blue Suede Shoes 15
69	RCA Victor RCA 1207	It's Now Or Never (O Sole Mio)/Make Me Know It 15
69	RCA Victor RCA 1216	Are You Lonesome Tonight?/I Gotta Know 15
69	RCA Victor RCA 1226	Wooden Heart/Tonight Is So Right For Love 30
69	RCA Victor RCA 1688	U.S. Male/Stay Away 100
71	RCA MAXI 2104	Heartbreak Hotel/Hound Dog/Don't Be Cruel ('Maximillion' sleeve) 10
71	RCA MAXI 2153	Jailhouse Rock/Are You Lonesome Tonight?/(Let Me Be Your)Teddy Bear/ Steadfast, Loyal And True ('Maximillion' sleeve) 10
75	RCA MAXI 2601	Blue Moon/You're A Heartbreaker/I'm Left, You're Right, She's Gone ('Maximillion' sleeve)...20

SINGLES : ORIGINAL RCA VICTOR ORANGE LABEL 45S

69	RCA Victor RCA 1795	If I Can Dream/Memories 10
69	RCA Victor RCA 1831	In The Ghetto/Any Day Now 6
69	RCA Victor RCA 1869	Clean Up Your Own Backyard/The Fair's Moving On 6
69	RCA Victor RCA 1900	Suspicious Minds/You'll Think Of Me (p/s) 10
70	RCA Victor RCA 1916	Don't Cry Daddy/Rubberneckin' (p/s) 15
70	RCA Victor RCA 1949	Kentucky Rain/My Little Friend (p/s) 10
70	RCA Victor RCA 1999	I've Lost You/The Next Step Is Love 10
71	RCA Victor RCA 2060	There Goes My Everything/I Really Don't Want To Know (p/s) 10
71	RCA Victor RCA 2084	Rags To Riches/Where Did They Go, Lord (p/s) 10
71	RCA Victor RCA 2125	I'm Leavin'/Heart Of Rome 6
71	RCA Victor RCA 2158	I Just Can't Help Believin'/How The Web Was Woven...................................6
72	RCA Victor RCA 2188	Until It's Time For You To Go/We Can Make The Morning (p/s) 10
72	RCA Victor RCA 2229	American Trilogy/The First Time Ever I Saw Your Face 10
72	RCA Victor RCA 2267	Burning Love/It's A Matter Of Time...8
72	RCA Victor RCA 2304	Always On My Mind/Separate Ways 7
73	RCA Victor RCA 2359	Polk Salad Annie/See See Rider 7
73	RCA Victor RCA 2393	Fool/Steamroller Blues 7
73	RCA Victor RCA 2435	Raised On Rock/For Ol' Times Sake 7
74	RCA Victor APBO 0196	Take Good Care Of Her/I've Got A Thing About You Baby (solid centre, no p/s; most copies as U.S. imports with large centre hole in U.S. p/s)...........................200
74	RCA Victor APBO 0196	Take Good Care Of Her/I've Got A Thing About You Baby (solid centre, no p/s; most copies as U.S. imports with large centre hole in U.S. p/s)............................15
74	RCA Victor APBO 0280	If You Talk In Your Sleep/Help Me 10
74	RCA Victor RCA 2458	My Boy/Loving Arms 5
74	RCA Victor PB 10074	Promised Land/It's Midnight (1st pressing) 5
74	RCA Victor PB 10074	Promised Land/It's Midnight And I Miss You (2nd pressing with correct B-side title) 15
75	RCA Victor RCA 2562	T-R-O-U-B-L-E/Mr. Songman..5
75	RCA Victor RCA 2635	Green Green Grass Of Home/Thinking About You 5
76	RCA Victor RCA 2674	Hurt/For The Heart 10

SINGLES : RETROSPECTIVE RCA BLUE LABEL 45S

78	RCA PB 9265	Don't Be Cruel/Hound Dog (p/s) 5
78	RCA PB 9334	Old Shep/Paralysed (p/s) 5
80	RCA RCA 4	It's Only Love/Beyond The Reef (p/s) 5
80	RCA RCA 16	Santa Claus Is Back In Town/I Believe (p/s) 5
81	RCA RCA 43	Guitar Man/Faded Love (with matt U.K. p/s [cat. no. RCA 43]).......................50
81	RCA RCA 43	Guitar Man/Faded Love (with glossy U.S. p/s [cat. no. PB 12158])....................5
82	RCA RCA 196	Are You Lonesome Tonight? (Laughing Version)/From A Jack To A King (p/s) 6

SINGLES : OTHER RCA 45S

82	RCA RCAP 232	The Sound Of Your Cry/I'll Never Know (picture disc) 5
83	RCA RCAP 1028	Jailhouse Rock/The Elvis Medley (without "Hound Dog" credit on B-side) (reissue, picture disc) 5
83	RCA RCAP 1028	Jailhouse Rock/The Elvis Medley (with "Hound Dog" credit on B-side) (reissue, picture disc) 15
83	RCA RCAP 332	Baby, I Don't Care/One-Sided Love Affair/Tutti Frutti (picture disc) 5
83	RCA RCA 369	I Can Help/The Lady Loves Me (p/s) 5
83	RCA RCAP 369	I Can Help/If Every Day Was Like Christmas/The Lady Loves Me (10", picture disc in clear plastic sleeve) 15
84	RCA RCA 405	Green Green Grass Of Home/Release Me (And Let Me Love Again)/ Solitaire (p/s, with poster) 24
84	RCA RCA 405	Green Green Grass Of Home/Release Me (And Let Me Love Again)/ Solitaire (p/s) 5
84	RCA RCA 459	The Last Farewell/It's Easy for You (p/s) 5
84	RCA RCAT 459	The Last Farewell/It's Easy for You (10", p/s) 10
85	RCA RCA 476	The Elvis Medley/Blue Suede Shoes (p/s) 5
85	RCA PB 49943	Always On My Mind (Alternate Version)/Tomorrow Night (p/s) 5
87	RCA ARON 1	Bossa Nova Baby/Ain't That Loving You Baby (p/s) 5
87	RCA ARONT 1	Bossa Nova Baby/Ain't That Loving You Baby (12", p/s) 15
87	RCA ARON 2	Love Me Tender/If I Can Dream (p/s) 5
87	RCA ARONT 2	Love Me Tender/If I Can Dream (p/s) (12", p/s) 10
88	RCA PB 49177	Are You Lonesome Tonight/Reconsider Baby (p/s) 5
88	RCA PB 49177	Are You Lonesome Tonight/Reconsider Baby (12", p/s) 10
88	RCA PB 49473	Mean Woman Blues/I Beg Of Of You (p/s) 10
88	RCA PT 49474	Mean Woman Blues/I Beg Of Of You (12", p/s) 20
88	RCA PB 49545	Stuck On You/Any Way You Want Me (p/s) 5
88	RCA PT 49546	Stuck On You/Any Way You Want Me (12", p/s) 10
88	RCA PB 49943	Always On My Mind/Tomorrow Night (p/s) 10
88	RCA PT 49944	Always On My Mind/Tomorrow Night (12", p/s) 20
90	RCA TCB 1	(Now And Then There's) A Fool Such As I (Take 3)/Danny (promo only)..............12
04	BMG 82876 619211	That's All Right/Blue Moon Of Kentucky (10", brown die-cut sleeve, with 'Sun' labels) 25

SINGLES : SINGLES BOX SET

| 77 | RCA (no cat. no.) | PRESLEY GOLD - 16 NUMBER ONES (16 x 7", each in p/s, black box set) ....40 |

SINGLES : OTHER SINGLES AND FLEXIDISCS

| 57 | Weekend Mail (no cat. no.) | THE TRUTH ABOUT ME (1-sided 6" 78 rpm, mail-order only, in mailer)................40 |
| 57 | Weekend Mail (no cat. no.) | THE TRUTH ABOUT ME (1-sided 6" 78 rpm, mail-order only, not in mailer) ....25 |

MINT VALUE £

77	RCA Victor 2694-2709	GOLD 16 SERIES (16 x p/s 7" in foldout cardboard carrier)	30
79	RCA LB 1	The Wonder Of You/Noel Edmonds Introduces Record Year (Lever Brothers premium)	20
81	Chiswick NS 71	Press Conference 1957/DEKE RIVERS: Elvis Presley Medley (picture disc)	6

EXPORT SINGLES : HMV EXPORT 45S

57	HMV 7MC 42	Mystery Train/I Forgot To Remember To Forget (gold label print, serrated edge to labels)	300
57	HMV 7MC 45	I Want You, I Need You, I Love You/My Baby Left Me (gold label print)	200
57	HMV 7MC 50	Hound Dog/Don't Be Cruel (gold label print)	150
57	HMV JO 465	Love Me Tender/Anyway You Want Me (That's How I'll Be) (gold label print)	150
57	HMV JO 466	Too Much/Playing For Keeps (gold label print)	200
57	HMV JO 473	All Shook Up/That's When Your Heartaches Begin (gold label print)	150

EPS : HMV EPS

57	HMV 7EG 8199	LOVE ME TENDER (soundtrack, round centre)	120
57	HMV 7EG 8199	LOVE ME TENDER (soundtrack, removeable centre)	175
57	HMV 7EG 8256	GOOD ROCKIN' TONIGHT (round centre only)	200

EPS : RCA EPS: TRIANGULAR CENTRES

57	RCA RCX 101	PEACE IN THE VALLEY	30
57	RCA RCX 104	ELVIS PRESLEY	40
58	RCA RCX 106	JAILHOUSE ROCK (soundtrack)	40
58	RCA RCX 117	KING CREOLE VOL. 1 (soundtrack, black label, cream or white rear p/s)	30
58	RCA RCX 118	KING CREOLE VOL. 2 (soundtrack, cream or white rear sleeve)	30
58	RCA RCX 121	ELVIS SINGS CHRISTMAS SONGS (1st issue, single sleeve)	60
58	RCA RCX 131	ELVIS SAILS (interview record, sleeve laminated front & back)	40
59	RCA RCX 135	ELVIS IN TENDER MOOD (with red print on rear sleeve)	40

(Originally issued with laminated front and back sleeves; later copies with front-only laminate are worth three quarters of these values.)

59	RCA RCX 1045	A TOUCH OF GOLD (laminated front sleeve only)	50
59	RCA RCX 175	STRICTLY ELVIS	40
60	RCA RCX 1048	A TOUCH OF GOLD VOL. 2	80

EPS : RCA EPS : ROUND CENTRE REPRESSINGS

60s	RCA RCX 101	PEACE IN THE VALLEY	20
60s	RCA RCX 104	ELVIS PRESLEY	15
60s	RCA RCX 106	JAILHOUSE ROCK (soundtrack)	15
60s	RCA RCX 117	KING CREOLE VOL. 1 (soundtrack)	15
60s	RCA RCX 118	KING CREOLE VOL. 2 (soundtrack)	15
60s	RCA RCX 121	ELVIS SINGS CHRISTMAS SONGS (gatefold p/s)	60
60s	RCA RCX 131	ELVIS SAILS (interview record)	25
60s	RCA RCX 135	ELVIS IN TENDER MOOD	20
60s	RCA RCX 1045	A TOUCH OF GOLD	25
60s	RCA RCX 175	STRICTLY ELVIS	20
60s	RCA RCX 1048	A TOUCH OF GOLD VOL. 2	35

EPS : ORIGINAL RCA EPS : ROUND CENTRES

60	RCA RCX 190	SUCH A NIGHT	25
62	RCA RCX 211	FOLLOW THAT DREAM (soundtrack)	10
62	RCA RCX 211	FOLLOW THAT DREAM (mispressing, 2nd side features Jim Reeves)	100
62	RCA RCX 7109	KID GALAHAD (soundtrack)	10
64	RCA Victor RCX 7141	LOVE IN LAS VEGAS (soundtrack)	20
64	RCA Victor RCX 7142	ELVIS FOR YOU VOL. 1	50
64	RCA Victor RCX 7143	ELVIS FOR YOU VOL. 2	50
64	RCA Victor RCX 135	ELVIS IN TENDER MOOD	20
65	RCA Victor RCX 7173	TICKLE ME (soundtrack)	35
65	RCA Victor RCX 7174	TICKLE ME VOL. 2 (soundtrack)	35
67	RCA Victor RCX 7187	EASY COME, EASY GO (soundtrack)	40

EPS : RCA VICTOR EPS: BLACK LABEL RE-PRESSINGS

64	RCA Victor RCX 101	PEACE IN THE VALLEY	15
64	RCA Victor RCX 104	ELVIS PRESLEY	15
64	RCA Victor RCX 106	JAILHOUSE ROCK (soundtrack)	15
64	RCA Victor RCX 117	KING CREOLE VOL. 1 (soundtrack)	15
64	RCA Victor RCX 118	KING CREOLE VOL. 2 (soundtrack)	15
64	RCA Victor RCX 121	ELVIS SINGS CHRISTMAS SONGS (single p/s)	30
64	RCA Victor RCX 131	ELVIS SAILS (interview record)	25
64	RCA Victor RCX 1045	A TOUCH OF GOLD	15
64	RCA Victor RCX 175	STRICTLY ELVIS	15
64	RCA Victor RCX 1048	A TOUCH OF GOLD VOL. 2	25
64	RCA Victor RCX 190	SUCH A NIGHT	10
64	RCA Victor RCX 211	FOLLOW THAT DREAM (soundtrack)	10
64	RCA Victor RCX 7106	KID GALAHAD (soundtrack)	10

EPS : RCA VICTOR EPS: ORANGE LABEL RE-PRESSINGS

69	RCA Victor RCX 101	PEACE IN THE VALLEY (push-out centre)	10
69	RCA Victor RCX 101	PEACE IN THE VALLEY (solid centre)	8
69	RCA Victor RCX 104	ELVIS PRESLEY (push-out centre)	12
69	RCA Victor RCX 104	ELVIS PRESLEY (solid centre)	8
69	RCA Victor RCX 106	JAILHOUSE ROCK (soundtrack, solid centre)	10
69	RCA Victor RCX 117	KING CREOLE VOL. 1 (soundtrack, push-out centre)	15
69	RCA Victor RCX 117	KING CREOLE VOL. 1 (soundtrack, solid centre)	8
69	RCA Victor RCX 118	KING CREOLE VOL. 2 (soundtrack, push-out centre)	10
69	RCA Victor RCX 118	KING CREOLE VOL. 2 (soundtrack, solid centre)	8
69	RCA Victor RCX 131	ELVIS SAILS (interview record, push-out or solid centre)	10
69	RCA Victor RCX 135	ELVIS IN TENDER MOOD (push-out or solid centre, with different take of "Lover Doll")	10
69	RCA Victor RCX 1045	A TOUCH OF GOLD (push-out centre)	15
69	RCA Victor RCX 1045	A TOUCH OF GOLD (solid centre)	10
69	RCA Victor RCX 175	STRICTLY ELVIS (push-out or solid centre)	10
69	RCA Victor RCX 1048	A TOUCH OF GOLD VOL. 2 (push-out centre)	15
69	RCA Victor RCX 1048	A TOUCH OF GOLD VOL. 2 (solid centre)	10
69	RCA Victor RCX 190	SUCH A NIGHT (push-out centre)	10
69	RCA Victor RCX 190	SUCH A NIGHT (solid centre)	8

EPS : EP BOXED SETS

82	RCA EP 1	THE EP COLLECTION (11-EP box set, reissues, with booklet)	50
83	RCA EP 2	THE EP COLLECTION VOL. 2 (11-EP box set, reissues, with booklet)	50

ALBUMS : LPS: HMV ISSUES

56	HMV CLP 1093	ROCK 'N' ROLL	500
57	HMV CLP 1105	ROCK 'N' ROLL NO. 2	700
57	HMV DLP 1159	THE BEST OF ELVIS (10")	200

ALBUMS : LPS: ORIGINAL BLACK/SILVER SPOT RCA ISSUES

57	RCA RC 24001	LOVING YOU (10", soundtrack)	75
57	RCA RD 27052	ELVIS' CHRISTMAS ALBUM (laminated front & back covers with 4 pictures on back cover)	100
58	RCA RD 27088	KING CREOLE (soundtrack)	40
59	RCA RD 27120	ELVIS	75
59	RCA RD 27128	A DATE WITH ELVIS	60
60	RCA RD 27159	ELVIS' GOLDEN RECORDS VOL. 2	30
60	RCA RD 27171	ELVIS IS BACK! (gatefold sleeve, mono)	40
60	RCA SF 5060	ELVIS IS BACK! (gatefold sleeve, stereo)	60
60	RCA RD 27192	G.I. BLUES (soundtrack, mono)	18
60	RCA SF 5078	G.I. BLUES (soundtrack, stereo)	25
61	RCA RD 27211	HIS HAND IN MINE (mono)	25
61	RCA SF 5094	HIS HAND IN MINE (stereo)	45
61	RCA RD 27224	SOMETHING FOR EVERYBODY (mono)	20
61	RCA SF 5106	SOMETHING FOR EVERYBODY (stereo)	35
61	RCA RD 27238	BLUE HAWAII (soundtrack, mono)	15
61	RCA SF 5115	BLUE HAWAII (soundtrack, stereo)	20
62	RCA RD 27265	POT LUCK (mono)	20
62	RCA SF 5135	POT LUCK (stereo)	30

ALBUMS : LPS: SILVER SPOT/'RED SEAL' RCA ISSUES

58	RCA RB 16069	ELVIS' GOLDEN RECORDS (maroon 'silver spot' label, gatefold sleeve with stapled-in 4-page photo booklet)	100
60	RCA RB 16069	ELVIS' GOLDEN RECORDS ('Red Seal'/'silver spot' label, gatefold sleeve with stapled-in 2-page photo booklet)	30
63	RCA RB 16069	ELVIS' GOLDEN RECORDS ('Red Seal'/'black spot' label, no booklet, gatefold sleeve)	20
67	RCA RB 16069	ELVIS' GOLDEN RECORDS ('Red Seal'/'black spot' label, no booklet, single sleeve)	18

ALBUMS : LPS: ORIGINAL BLACK/SILVER SPOT RCA VICTOR ISSUES

63	RCA Victor RD 7534	GIRLS! GIRLS! GIRLS! (soundtrack, mono)	15
63	RCA Victor SF 7534	GIRLS! GIRLS! GIRLS! (soundtrack, stereo)	35
63	RCA Victor RD 7565	IT HAPPENED AT THE WORLD'S FAIR (soundtrack, mono)	18
63	RCA Victor SF 7565	IT HAPPENED AT THE WORLD'S FAIR (soundtrack, stereo)	35
63	RCA Victor RD 7609	FUN IN ACAPULCO (soundtrack, mono)	20
63	RCA Victor SF 7609	FUN IN ACAPULCO (soundtrack, stereo)	35

ALBUMS : LPS: ORIGINAL BLACK/RED SPOT RCA VICTOR ISSUES

64	RCA Victor RD 7630	ELVIS' GOLDEN RECORDS VOL. 3 (mono)	20
64	RCA Victor SF 7630	ELVIS' GOLDEN RECORDS VOL. 3 (stereo)	30
64	RCA Victor RD 7645	KISSIN' COUSINS (soundtrack, mono)	18
64	RCA Victor SF 7645	KISSIN' COUSINS (soundtrack, stereo)	30
64	RCA Victor RD 7678	ROUSTABOUT (soundtrack, mono)	15
64	RCA Victor SF 7678	ROUSTABOUT (soundtrack, stereo)	25
65	RCA Victor RD 7714	GIRL HAPPY (soundtrack, mono)	20
65	RCA Victor SF 7714	GIRL HAPPY (soundtrack, stereo)	30
65	RCA Victor RD 7723	FLAMING STAR AND SUMMER KISSES (soundtrack, mono only, black label)	75
65	RCA Victor RD/SF 7752	ELVIS FOR EVERYONE (mono, 'orange shirt' sleeve)	35
65	RCA Victor SF 7752	ELVIS FOR EVERYONE (stereo, 'orange shirt' sleeve)	45
65	RCA Victor RD 7767	HAREM HOLIDAY (soundtrack, mono)	20
65	RCA Victor SF 7767	HAREM HOLIDAY (soundtrack, stereo)	25
66	RCA Victor RD 7793	FRANKIE AND JOHNNY (soundtrack, mono)	20
66	RCA Victor SF 7793	FRANKIE AND JOHNNY (soundtrack, stereo)	30
66	RCA Victor RD 7810	PARADISE, HAWAIIAN STYLE (soundtrack, mono)	20
66	RCA Victor SF 7810	PARADISE, HAWAIIAN STYLE (soundtrack, stereo)	30
66	RCA Victor RD 7820	CALIFORNIA HOLIDAY (soundtrack, mono)	20
66	RCA Victor SF 7820	CALIFORNIA HOLIDAY (soundtrack, stereo)	30
67	RCA Victor RD 7867	HOW GREAT THOU ART (mono)	25
67	RCA Victor SF 7867	HOW GREAT THOU ART (stereo)	35
67	RCA Victor RD 7892	DOUBLE TROUBLE (soundtrack, mono)	15
67	RCA Victor SF 7892	DOUBLE TROUBLE (soundtrack, stereo)	20
68	RCA Victor RD 7917	CLAMBAKE (soundtrack, black/red dot labels, mono)	20
68	RCA Victor SF 7917	CLAMBAKE (soundtrack, black/red dot labels, stereo)	25
68	RCA Victor RD 7924	ELVIS' GOLD RECORDS VOLUME 4 (with "Never Ending" listed on sleeve instead of "Love Letters"; mono)	30
68	RCA Victor SF 7924	ELVIS' GOLD RECORDS VOLUME 4 (with "Never Ending" listed on sleeve instead of "Love Letters"; stereo)	40
68	RCA Victor RD 7924	ELVIS' GOLD RECORDS VOLUME 4 (corrected sleeve, mono)	25
68	RCA Victor SF 7924	ELVIS' GOLD RECORDS VOLUME 4 (corrected sleeve, stereo)	25
68	RCA Victor RD 7957	SPEEDWAY (soundtrack, with Nancy Sinatra, mono)	30
68	RCA Victor SF 7957	SPEEDWAY (soundtrack, with Nancy Sinatra, stereo)	25

ALBUMS : LPS: ORIGINAL ORANGE RCA VICTOR ISSUES

69	RCA Victor RD 8011	ELVIS ("TV Special" Soundtrack)	15
69	RCA Victor RD 8029	FROM ELVIS IN MEMPHIS (mono)	15
69	RCA Victor SF 8029	FROM ELVIS IN MEMPHIS (stereo)	12
70	RCA Victor SF 8080/1	FROM MEMPHIS TO VEGAS - FROM VEGAS TO MEMPHIS (2-LP, with 2 x 10" x 8" photos, glossy cover)	30
70	RCA Victor SF 8080/1	FROM MEMPHIS TO VEGAS - FROM VEGAS TO MEMPHIS (2-LP, with 2 x 10" x 8" photos, matt cover)	25
70	RCA SF 8128	ON STAGE, FEBRUARY 1970 (with 30" x 20" colour poster; glossy cover)	15
70	RCA SF 8128	ON STAGE, FEBRUARY 1970 (with 30" x 20" colour poster; matt cover)	12
70	RCA LPM 6401	WORLDWIDE 50 GOLD AWARD HITS VOL. 1 - A TOUCH OF GOLD (4-LP, box set with 20-page photo book)	30

MINT VALUE £

71	RCA LPM 6402	THE OTHER SIDES - WORLDWIDE 50 GOLD AWARD HITS VOL. 2 (4-LP, box with material patch & colour portrait)	30
71	RCA Victor SF 8162	THAT'S THE WAY IT IS (glossy cover)	15
71	RCA Victor SF 8162	THAT'S THE WAY IT IS (matt cover)	12
71	RCA Victor SF 8172	I'M 10,000 YEARS OLD - ELVIS COUNTRY (with colour print, glossy cover)	15
71	RCA Victor SF 8202	LOVE LETTERS FROM ELVIS	15
71	RCA Victor SF 8221	ELVIS SINGS THE WONDERFUL WORLD OF CHRISTMAS	15
72	RCA Victor SF 8266	ELVIS NOW	15
72	RCA Victor SF 8275	HE TOUCHED ME	15
72	RCA Victor SF 8296	ELVIS AS RECORDED AT MADISON SQUARE GARDEN	15
73	RCA Victor SF 8378	ELVIS (with "Fool" sticker, must be UK disc and UK cover!)	50
73	RCA DPS 2040	ALOHA FROM HAWAII VIA SATELLITE (2-LP)	20
73	RCA APL1 0388	RAISED ON ROCK/FOR OL' TIMES SAKE (U.K. disc in U.K. sleeve)	200
74	RCA CPL1 0341	ELVIS - A LEGENDARY PERFORMER VOL. 1	15
74	RCA APL1 0475	GOOD TIMES (back cover credits "Loving Arms" or "Lovin' Arms")	18
74	RCA APL1 0606	ELVIS AS RECORDED ON STAGE IN MEMPHIS	15
74	RCA LPL1 7527	HITS OF THE 70s	15
75	RCA APL1 0873	PROMISED LAND	15
75	RCA APM1 0818	HAVING FUN WITH ELVIS ON STAGE	20
75	RCA RS 1011	TODAY	18
76	RCA CPL1 1349	ELVIS - A LEGENDARY PERFORMER VOL. 2	15
76	RCA RS 1060	FROM ELVIS PRESLEY BOULEVARD, MEMPHIS, TENNESSEE	15
77	RCA LP 3021	MOODY BLUE	12
77	RCA PL 02587	ELVIS IN CONCERT	18
77	RCA PL 12274	WELCOME TO MY WORLD	15
77	RCA PL 12772	HE WALKS BESIDE ME	15
77	RCA PL 42003	ELVIS IN DEMAND	15
80	RCA CPL8 3699	ELVIS ARON PRESLEY (8-LP, box set)	60
83	RCA RCALPP 9020	JAILHOUSE ROCK/LOVE IN LAS VEGAS (picture disc)	12
84	RCA PLP 89287	I CAN HELP (picture disc)	12
84	RCA PL 85172	A GOLDEN CELEBRATION (6-LP box set with inserts)	30

ALBUMS : LPS: BLACK/SILVER SPOT RCA VICTOR RE-PRESSINGS

64	RCA Victor RC 24001	LOVING YOU (10" LP, mono only)	60
64	RCA Victor RD 27052	ELVIS' CHRISTMAS ALBUM (laminated front & back covers, no pictures on back cover, mono only)	60
64	RCA Victor RD 7528	ROCK 'N' ROLL NO. 2 (reissue of HMV LP, mono)	18
64	RCA Victor SF 7528	ROCK 'N' ROLL NO. 2 (reissue of HMV LP, stereo)	25
64	RCA Victor RD 27088	KING CREOLE (soundtrack, mono only)	35
64	RCA Victor RD 27120	ELVIS (mono only)	35
64	RCA Victor RD 27128	A DATE WITH ELVIS (mono only)	20
64	RCA Victor RD 27159	ELVIS' GOLDEN RECORDS VOL. 2 (mono only)	15
64	RCA Victor RD 27171	ELVIS IS BACK! (gatefold sleeve, mono)	30
64	RCA Victor SF 5060	ELVIS IS BACK! (gatefold sleeve, stereo)	40
64	RCA Victor RD 27192	G.I. BLUES (soundtrack, mono)	15
64	RCA Victor SF 5078	G.I. BLUES (soundtrack, stereo)	30
64	RCA Victor RD 27211	HIS HAND IN MINE (mono)	25
64	RCA Victor SF 5094	HIS HAND IN MINE (stereo)	30
64	RCA Victor RD 27224	SOMETHING FOR EVERYBODY (mono)	18
64	RCA Victor SF 5106	SOMETHING FOR EVERYBODY (stereo)	30
64	RCA Victor RD 27238	BLUE HAWAII (soundtrack, mono)	18
64	RCA Victor SF 5115	BLUE HAWAII (soundtrack, stereo)	25
64	RCA Victor RD 27265	POT LUCK (mono)	15
64	RCA Victor SF 5135	POT LUCK (stereo)	30

ALBUMS : LPS: BLACK/RED SPOT RCA VICTOR RE-PRESSINGS

64	RCA Victor RD 7528	ROCK 'N' ROLL NO. 2 (reissue of HMV LP, mono)	18
64	RCA Victor SF 7528	ROCK 'N' ROLL NO. 2 (reissue of HMV LP, stereo)	25

ALBUMS : LPS: 'SMALL' ORANGE RCA VICTOR MONO RE-PRESSINGS

69	RCA Victor RD 27052	ELVIS' CHRISTMAS ALBUM	40
69	RCA Victor RD 27088	KING CREOLE (soundtrack)	30
69	RCA Victor RD 27120	ELVIS	30
69	RCA Victor RD 27128	A DATE WITH ELVIS	30
69	RCA Victor RD 27159	ELVIS' GOLDEN RECORDS VOL. 2	30
69	RCA Victor RD 27171	ELVIS IS BACK! (gatefold sleeve)	30
69	RCA Victor RD 27192	G.I. BLUES (soundtrack)	30
69	RCA Victor RD 27211	HIS HAND IN MINE	15
69	RCA Victor RD 27224	SOMETHING FOR EVERYBODY	30
69	RCA Victor RD 27238	BLUE HAWAII (soundtrack)	30
69	RCA Victor RD 7528	ROCK 'N' ROLL NO. 2	30
69	RCA Victor RD 7630	ELVIS' GOLDEN RECORDS VOL. 3	30
69	RCA Victor RD 7723	FLAMING STAR AND SUMMER KISSES (soundtrack, orange label)	400
69	RCA Victor RD 7810	PARADISE, HAWAIIAN STYLE (soundtrack)	20
69	RCA Victor RD 7867	HOW GREAT THOU ART	20
69	RCA Victor RD 7917	CLAMBAKE (soundtrack)	30
69	RCA Victor RD 7924	ELVIS' GOLD RECORDS VOLUME 4	15
69	RCA Victor RD 7957	SPEEDWAY (soundtrack, with Nancy Sinatra)	20

ALBUMS : LPS: 'LARGE' ORANGE RCA VICTOR STEREO RE-PRESSINGS

72	RCA Victor SF 8232	ELVIS FOR EVERYONE ('blue shirt'/'TV Special' sleeve)	40

ALBUMS : LPS: GREEN RCA INTERNATIONAL ISSUES

70	RCA Intl. INTS 1103	LET'S BE FRIENDS	15
72	RCA Intl. INTS 1414	BURNING LOVE AND HITS FROM HIS MOVIES (U.K. disc in U.K. sleeve)	40

ALBUMS : OTHER LPS

71	Camden CDS 1088	YOU'LL NEVER WALK ALONE (LP, withdrawn)	150
78	St. Michael IMP 113	ELVIS (exclusive to Marks & Spencer)	60
78	St. Michael IMPD 204	THE WONDERFUL WORLD OF ELVIS PRESLEY (2-LP, via Marks & Spencer)	50
79	Hammer HMR 6002	THE KING SPEAKS (green sleeve)	30
84	Imperial Records DR 1124	AMERICAN TRILOGY (3-LP, box set)	25
85	Sunday 1	ELVIS: THE GOLDEN ALBUM (LP, available via Sunday Times magazine)	20

86	RCA AREP 1	ACUFF-ROSE PRESENTS ELVIS (promo-only, 300 copies)	150

ALBUMS : CDS

84	RCA PD 89061/2/3	THE LEGEND (3-CD, gold box set, with booklet, numbered, 5,000 only)	100
84	RCA PD 89061/2/3	THE LEGEND (3-CD, silver box set, 5,000 only, with booklet, numbered)	100

ALBUMS : CASTLE REISSUES

00	Castle Music/BMG ELVIS 102	THAT'S THE WAY IT IS (5-LP)	45
99	Castle Music/BMG ELVIS 100P	ARTIST OF THE CENTURY (box set, 5 x picture disc LPs & booklet, numbered)	40
99	Castle Music/BMG ELVIS 100	ARTIST OF THE CENTUY (5-LP box set & booklet, numbered)	40
99	Castle Music/BMG ELVIS 100R	ARTIST OF THE CENTURY (box set, 5-LP red vinyl & booklet, numbered)	50
99	Castle Music/BMG ELVIS 100X	ARTIST OF THE CENTURY (box set, 5-LP, blue vinyl & booklet, numbered, HMV exclusive)	50
99	Castle Music/BMG ELVIS 101X	THE SUN SINGLES COLLECTION (6 x 7" box set, yellow vinyl, numbered HMV exclusive)	35
99	Castle Music/BMG ELVIS 101	THE SUN SINGLES COLLECTION (6 x 7" box set with poster, numbered)	35
00	Castle Music/BMG ELVIS 103	THE UK NO. 1 SINGLES COLLECTION (17 x 7" box set with booklet)	50
00	Castle Music/BMG ELVIS 103X	THE UK NO. 1 SINGLES COLLECTION (17 x 7" box set with booklet, coloured vinyl)	75
00	Castle Music/BMG ELVIS 104X	PEACE IN THE VALLEY (5-LP box set, with bonus 10" EP)	40
00	Castle Music/BMG ELVIS 104	PEACE IN THE VALLEY (5-LP box set)	30
01	Castle Music/BMG ELVIS 105	THE INTERNATIONAL EP COLLECTION (11 x 7" box set with insert)	30
01	Castle Music/BMG ELVIS 106	G.I. BLUES (LP, with bonus EP)	15
01	Castle Music/BMG ELVIS 108	LIVE IN LAS VEGAS (5-LP box set)	60
01	Castle Music/BMG ELVIS 107	BLUE HAWAII (LP, with bonus EP)	15
02	Castle Music/BMG ELVIS 111	JAILHOUSE ROCK (LP, with bonus EP)	15
02	Castle Music/BMG ELVIS 112	KING CREOLE (LP, with bonus EP)	15
02	Castle Music/BMG ELVIS 113	TICKLE ME (LP, with bonus EP)	25
02	Castle Music/BMG ELVIS 110	LOVING YOU (LP, with bonus EP)	15

(see also Jordanaires, Scotty Moore, Bill Black's Combo)

REG PRESLEY

69	Page One POF 131	Lucinda Lee/Wichita Lineman	8
73	CBS 1478	'S Down To You Marianne/Hey Little Girl	5

(see also Troggs, Suzi Quatro)

PRESSGANG

89	Vox Pop VOX 022	ROGUES (LP)	15

RAY PRESSLEY

62	Longhorn BLH 0002	Living, Learning, Trying To Forget/Half A Love (estimated that around 1000 pressed)	15

PRESSURE 28

82	Helen Of Oi! HOO 01	Get Ready/Up Yours	8

PRESSURE CO.

82	Paradox SOLID 1	LIVE IN SHEFFIELD 19 JAN '82 (LP)	12

(see also Eric Random, Cabaret Voltaire)

PRESSURE GROUP

87	Poltroon POL 001	ONLY GOD IS PERFECT (EP, 300 only)	60

PRESTIGE BLUES SWINGERS

59	Esquire 32-082	BLUES GROOVE (Tiny Grimes & Coleman Hawkins as Prestige Blues Swingers (LP)	20
60	Esquire 32-110	OUTSKIRTS OF TOWN (LP)	20

BILLY PRESTON

66	Sue WI 4012	Billy's Bag/Don't Let The Sun Catch You Cryin'.	25
66	Capitol CL 15458	In The Midnight Hour/Advice	25
66	Capitol CL 15458	In The Midnight Hour/Advice (DJ copy)	50
66	Capitol CL 15471	Sunny/Let The Music Play	15
69	President PT 263	Billy's Bag/Don't Let The Sun Catch You Crying (reissue)	10
69	President PT 263	Billy's Bag/Goldfinger (different B-side)	15
69	Apple APPLE 12	That's The Way God Planned It/What About You (p/s)	10
69	Apple APPLE 19	Everything's Alright/I Want To Thank You	20
70	Apple APPLE 21	All That I've Got/As I Get Older (some in p/s)	25
70	Apple APPLE 21	All That I've Got/As I Get Older (some in p/s)	8
70	President PT 298	If I Had A Hammer/Ferry 'Cross The Mersey	5
70	Soul City SC 107	Greazee (Parts 1 & 2)	20
70	Soul City SC 107	Greazee (Parts 1 & 2) (DJ Copy)	100
67	Capitol (S)T 2532	THE WILDEST ORGAN IN TOWN (LP)	35
67	Sue ILP 935	THE MOST EXCITING ORGAN EVER (LP)	60
69	President PTLS 1034	APPLE OF THEIR EYE (LP)	18
69	Apple SAPCOR 9	THAT'S THE WAY GOD PLANNED IT (LP)	30
70	Apple SAPCOR 14	ENCOURAGING WORDS (LP)	60
70	Soul City SCM 002	GREAZEE SOUL (LP)	30
70	Joy JOYS 174	GOSPEL IN MY SOUL (LP)	20
91	Apple SAPCOR 9	THAT'S THE WAY GOD PLANNED IT (LP, gatefold sleeve, with bonus 12" [SAPCOR 92])	15
93	Apple SAPCOR 14	ENCOURAGING WORDS (LP, gatefold sleeve with bonus 12" [SAPCOR 142])	15

(see also Beatles)

EARL PRESTON

63	Fontana TF 406	I Know Something/Watch Your Step (as Earl Preston & T.T.'s)	20
64	Fontana TF 481	Raindrops/That's For Sure (as Earl Preston & Realms)	20

(see also Realm)

JOHNNY PRESTON

60	Mercury AMT 1079	Running Bear/My Heart Knows	8
60	Mercury AMT 1079	Running Bear/My Heart Knows (78)	40
60	Mercury AMT 1092	Cradle Of Love/City Of Tears (some in p/s)	20
60	Mercury AMT 1092	Cradle Of Love/City Of Tears (no p/s)	6
60	Mercury AMT 1104	Feel So Fine/I'm Starting To Go Steady	8
60	Mercury AMT 1114	Charming Billy/Up In The Air	8
61	Mercury AMT 1129	Leave My Kitten Alone/Do What You Did	20
61	Mercury AMT 1145	Big Chief Heartbreak/Madre De Dios (Mother Of God)	20
61	Mercury AMT 1164	New Baby For Christmas/Rock And Roll Guitar	25
61	Mercury AMT 1167	Free Me/Kissing Tree	25
60	Mercury ZEP 10078	RUNNING BEAR (EP)	70

60	Mercury ZEP 10098	RING TAIL TOOTER (EP)	70
61	Mercury ZEP 10116	TOKEN OF LOVE (EP)	80
60	Mercury MMC 14051	JOHNNY PRESTON - RUNNING BEAR (LP)	100

MIKE PRESTON

58	Decca F 11053	A House, A Car And A Wedding Ring/My Lucky Love	8
58	Decca F 11087	Why, Why, Why/Whispering Grass	8
59	Decca F 11120	Dirty Old Town/In Surabaya	8
59	Decca F 11167	Mr. Blue/Just Ask Your Heart	5
60	Decca F 11222	A Girl Like You/Too Old	5
60	Decca F 11222	A Girl Like You/Too Old (78)	10
60	Decca F 11255	I'd Do Anything/Where Is Love?	5
60	Decca F 11255	I'd Do Anything/Where Is Love? (78)	12
60	Decca F 11287	Togetherness/Farewell My Love	5
61	Decca F 11335	Marry Me/Girl Without A Heart	5
64	Decca F 11810	No Strings/Nobody Told Me	5
66	Emerald MD1028	Our Love Will Go On/Forgive Me	10
60	Decca DFE 6635	FOUR SONGS BY RAY NOBLE (EP)	15
61	Decca DFE 6679	MARRY ME (EP)	15

PRETTY BOY FLOYD & GEMS

| 79 | Rip Off RIP OFF 1 | Spread The Word Around/Hold Tight (p/s) | 15 |
| 79 | Rip Off RIP 10 | Sharon/The Instigator (p/s) | 20 |

PRETTY THINGS

64	Fontana TF 469	Rosalyn/Big Boss Man	15
64	Fontana TF 503	Don't Bring Me Down/We'll Be Together	12
65	Fontana TF 537	Honey I Need/I Can Never Say	12
65	Fontana TF 585	Cry To Me/Get A Buzz	20
65	Fontana TF 647	Midnight To Six Man/Can't Stand The Pain	20
66	Fontana TF 688	Come See Me/£.s.d.	30
66	Fontana TF 722	A House In The Country/Me Needing You	25
66	Fontana TF 773	Progress/Buzz The Jerk	30
67	Fontana TF 829	Children/My Time	20
67	Columbia DB 8300	Defecting Grey/Mr. Evasion	80
68	Columbia DB 8353	Talkin' About The Good Times/Walking Through My Dreams	80
68	Columbia DB 8494	Private Sorrow/Balloon Burning	40
69	Fontana TF 1024	Rosalyn/Don't Bring Me Down (p/s)	12
70	Harvest HAR 5016	The Good Mr. Square/Blue Serge Blues	10
70	Harvest HAR 5031	October 26/Cold Stone	10
71	Harvest HAR 5037	Stone-Hearted Mama/Summertime/Circus Mind	10
72	Warner Bros K 16225	Over The Moon/Havana Bound	5
64	Fontana TE 17434	THE PRETTY THINGS (EP)	60
65	Fontana TE 17442	RAININ' IN MY HEART (EP)	60
66	Fontana TE 17472	ON FILM (EP)	150
65	Fontana TL 5239	THE PRETTY THINGS (LP)	150
65	Fontana TL 5280	GET THE PICTURE (LP)	200
67	Wing WL 1164	BEST OF THE PRETTY THINGS (LP)	25
67	Fontana (S)TL 5425	EMOTIONS (LP, mono/stereo)	150
67	Wing WL 1167	THE PRETTY THINGS (LP, reissue)	40
68	Columbia SX 6306	S.F. SORROW (LP, gatefold sleeve, blue/black label, mono)	600
68	Columbia SCX 6306	S.F. SORROW (LP, gatefold sleeve, blue/black label, stereo)	351
70	Columbia SCX 6306	S.F. SORROW (LP, gatefold sleeve; silver/black label re-pressing, stereo)	40
70	Harvest SHVL 774	PARACHUTE (LP, gatefold sleeve)	100
72	Fontana Special SFL 13140	EMOTIONS (LP, reissue)	20
72	Warner Bros K 46190	FREEWAY MADNESS (LP, gatefold sleeve)	18
74	Swan Song SSK 59400	SILK TORPEDO (LP, gatefold sleeve with insert)	12
75	Harvest SHDW 406	S.F. SORROW/PARACHUTE (2-LP)	35
75	Swan Song SSL 59401	SAVAGE EYE (LP, gatefold sleeve with inner)	12
78	Butt Nott DO1	ELECTRIC BANANA THE SEVEN TIES (LP)	15
77	Harvest SHSM 2022	SINGLES A'S & B'S (LP)	20

(see also Electric Banana, Twink, Viv Prince, Sunshine, Fenmen, Kate, Zac Zolar & Electric Banana)

ANDRE PREVIN

| 74 | EMI 2222 | Theme From Jennie Churchill/Stanley Myers - Cavatina | 5 |

DORY PREVIN

| 70 | United Artists UAG 29176 | ON MY WAY TO WHERE (LP) | 12 |
| 71 | United Artists UAG 29186 | MYTHICAL KINGS & IGUNAS (LP, gatefold sleeve) | 12 |

EDDIE PREVOST BAND

| 78 | Matchless MR 1 | LIVE VOLUME 1 (LP, private pressing) | 15 |

(see also Amm, Organum)

JOEL PREVOST

| 78 | CBS SCBS 6300 | Somewhere Sometime/Il Y Aura Toujours Des Violins | 10 |

ALAN PRICE (SET)

65	Decca F 12217	Any Day Now (My Wild Beautiful Baby)/Never Be Sick On Sunday	12
66	Decca F 12367	I Put A Spell On You/Iechyd-Da	7
66	Decca F 12518	Willow Weep For Me/Yours Until Tomorrow	6
67	Decca F 12691	Shame/Don't Do That Again	8
68	Decca F 12774	When I Was A Cowboy/Tappy Turquoise (export issue)	20
68	Decca F 12808	Love Story/My Old Kentucky Home	6
69	Deram DM 263	Trimdon Grange Explosion/Falling In Love Again	6
70	Decca F 13017	Sunshine And Rain (The Name Of The Game)/ Is There Anybody Out There? (solo)	6
67	Decca DFE 8677	THE AMAZING ALAN PRICE (EP)	30
66	Decca LK 4839	THE PRICE TO PLAY (LP, laminate front cover, flipbacks)	35
67	Decca LK/SKL 4907	A PRICE ON HIS HEAD (LP, laminated front cover)	25
73	Warner Bros K 46227	O LUCKY MAN! (LP, soundtrack)	15

(see also Animals, Paul Williams Set, Johnny Almond Music Machine, Dave Greenslade)

BILL PRICE

| 72 | Folk Heritage FHR 038 | THE FINE OLD YORKSHIRE GENTLEMAN (LP) | 22 |

KENNY PRICE

66	Stateside SS 554	Walking On New Grass/Wasting My Time	6

LLOYD PRICE

57	London HL 8438	Just Because/Why (triangular centre)	150
57	London HL 8438	Just Because/Why (round centre)	80
57	London HL 8438	Just Because/Why (78)	20
59	HMV POP 580	Stagger Lee/You Need Love	15
59	HMV POP 580	Stagger Lee/You Need Love (78)	25
59	HMV POP 598	Where Were You (On Our Wedding Day)?/Is It Really Love?	12
59	HMV POP 598	Where Were You (On Our Wedding Day)?/Is It Really Love? (78)	25
59	HMV POP 626	Personality/Have You Ever Had The Blues?	10
59	HMV POP 626	Personality/Have You Ever Had The Blues? (78)	25
59	HMV POP 650	I'm Gonna Get Married/Three Little Pigs	10
59	HMV POP 650	I'm Gonna Get Married/Three Little Pigs (78)	60
59	HMV POP 672	Won't 'Cha Come Home/Come Into My Heart	10
60	HMV POP 712	Lady Luck/Never Let Me Go	15
60	HMV POP 712	Lady Luck/Never Let Me Go (78)	30
60	HMV POP 741	For Love/No If's - No And's	10
60	HMV POP 772	Question/If I Look A Little Blue (as Lloyd Price Orchestra)	10
60	HMV POP 772	Question/If I Look A Little Blue (as Lloyd Price Orchestra) (78)	40
60	HMV POP 799	Just Call Me (And I'll Understand)/Who Coulda' Told You (They Lied)	10
61	HMV POP 826	Know What You're Doin'/That's Why Tears Come And Go (as Lloyd Price Orchestra)	10
61	HMV POP 926	Boo Hoo/I Made You Cry	10
62	HMV POP 983	Be A Leader/'Nother Fairy Tale	10
62	HMV POP 1100	Under Your Spell, Again/Happy Birthday Mama	10
63	Liberty LIB 10127	Misty/Cry On	10
72	President PT 321	Ready For Betty/Beat In Trinidad	10
73	GSF GSZ 5	Love Music/Just For Baby	10
73	GSF GSZ 11	Trying To Slip Away/They Get Down	10
59	HMV 7EG 8538	THE EXCITING LLOYD PRICE (EP, mono)	80
59	HMV GES 5784	THE EXCITING LLOYD PRICE (EP, stereo)	100
59	HMV CLP 1285	THE EXCITING LLOYD PRICE (LP)	80
59	HMV CLP 1314	MR. PERSONALITY (LP)	65
60	London HA-U 2213	LLOYD PRICE (LP)	80
60	HMV CLP 1361	MR. PERSONALITY SINGS THE BLUES (LP)	50
60	HMV CLP 1393	THE FANTASTIC LLOYD PRICE (LP, mono)	50
60	HMV CSD 1323	THE FANTASTIC LLOYD PRICE (LP, stereo)	60
62	HMV CLP 1519	COOKIN' (LP, mono)	50
62	HMV CSD 1413	COOKIN' (LP, stereo)	60
63	Encore ENC 2004	PRICE SINGS THE MILLION DOLLAR SELLERS (LP)	25
69	Major Minor SMLP 57	LLOYD PRICE NOW (LP)	25

MALCOLM PRICE (TRIO)

61	Oak RGJ 106	PICKIN' ON THE COUNTRY STRINGS! (EP)	18
64	Decca LK 4627	COUNTRY SESSION (LP, as Malcolm Price Trio)	15
65	Decca LK 4665	WAY DOWN TOWN (LP)	15
69	Saga FID 2156	HIS SONGS, HIS GUITARS (LP)	12
75	Sweet Folk & C. SFA 017	THEN WE ALL GOT UP AND WALKED AWAY (LP)	12

RAY PRICE

57	Philips BBE 12137	RAY PRICE (EP)	25

(see also Cherry Wainer)

(ROCKIN') RED PRICE

56	Decca F 10822	Rocky Mountain Gal/Rock O' The North (as Red Price & His Rockin' Rhythm)	15
56	Decca F 10822	Rocky Mountain Gal/Rock O' The North (78)	10
57	Woodbine	Woodbine Rock (78, with picture on label, promo only)	40
57	Woodbine	Woodbine Rock (78, without picture on label, promo only)	15
58	Pye 7N 15169	Weekend/The Sneeze	20
58	Pye 7N 15169	Weekend/The Sneeze (78)	25
60	Pye 7N 15262	Wow!/My Baby's Door	10
61	Parlophone R 4789	Theme From "Danger Man"/Blackjack (as Red Price Combo)	30

RED PRICE & BLUE BEATS

64	Blue Beat BB 209	Blue Beats Over (The White Cliffs Of Dover)/Kiss The Baby (When You Grow Too Old To Dream)	10

RICK PRICE

70	Gemini GMS 012	Davey Has No Dad/Bitter Sweet	10
71	Gemini GMS 017	Top Ten Record/Beautiful Sally	10
71	Gemini GME 1017	TALKING TO THE FLOWERS (LP, laminated front sleeve)	40

(see also Move, Sheridan-Price, Sight & Sound)

RIKKI PRICE

58	Fontana H 162	Tom Dooley/(It Looks Like Rain In) Cherry Blossom Lane	6
59	Fontana H 171	Honey, Honey/The Very Thought Of You	8
59	Fontana H 217	Mr. Blue/Man On My Trail	6
62	Fontana H 371	You're For Real/When You Pass By	6
58	Fontana TFE 17100	RIKKI PRICE (EP)	20

(see also Sheridan-Price)

SAMMY PRICE

63	Storyville A 45 068	Boogieing With Big Sid/133 Street Boogie (with p/s)	30
63	Storyville A 45 068	Boogieing With Big Sid/133 Street Boogie	20
57	Columbia SEG 7679	ORIGINAL SAMMY BLUES (EP)	20
58	Vogue EPV 1146	SAMMY PRICE (EP)	60
58	Vogue EPV 1151	SAMMY PRICE'S BLUESICIANS (EP)	60
58	Vogue LAE 12027	SWINGIN' PARIS STYLE (LP)	40
62	London Jazz LTZ-R 15240	THE BLUES AIN'T NOTHIN' (LP, mono)	30
62	London Jazz SAH-R 6234	THE BLUES AIN'T NOTHIN' (LP, stereo)	40

(see also Sister Rosetta Tharpe)

VINCENT PRICE

77	EMI EMI 2659	The Monster Mash/The Bard's Own Recipe	10

| 59 | Columbia 33SX 1141 | VINCENT PRICE (LP) | 45 |

DICKIE PRIDE

59	Columbia DB 4283	Slippin' 'N' Slidin'/Don't Make Me Love You	45
59	Columbia DB 4296	Fabulous Cure/Midnight Oil	40
59	Columbia DB 4340	Frantic/Primrose Lane	25
60	Columbia DB 4403	Betty, Betty (Go Steady With Me)/No John	25
60	Columbia DB 4451	You're Singin' Our Love Song To Somebody Else/Bye Bye Blackbird	10
59	Columbia SEG 7937	SHEIK OF SHAKE (EP)	300
61	Columbia 33SX 1307	PRIDE WITHOUT PREJUDICE (LP, mono)	80
61	Columbia SCX 3369	PRIDE WITHOUT PREJUDICE (LP, stereo)	100

(see also Guvners)

LOUIS PRIMA (& HIS ORCHESTRA)

56	Capitol CL 14669	5 Months, 2 Weeks, 2 Days/Banana Split For My Baby	20
58	Capitol CL 14821	Buona Sera/Beep! Beep!	15
60	London HLD 9230	Ol' Man Moses (with Sam Butera's Witnesses)/Wonderland By Night	10
64	Prima PR 1001	Fee Fie Foo Part 1/Fee Fie Foo Part 2	6
58	Capitol T 908	THE WILDEST SHOW AT TAHOE (LP)	20
59	Capitol EAP1 1132	STRICTLY PRIMA (EP)	12
57	Capitol T 755	THE WILDEST (LP)	30
58	Capitol T 836	THE CALL OF THE WILDEST (LP)	20
58	Capitol T 1010	LAS VEGAS PRIMA STYLE (LP)	15
62	Ember EMB 3348	LOUIS PRIMA SWINGS (LP)	15

(see also Sam Butera's Witnesses)

LOUIS PRIMA & KEELY SMITH

54	Columbia SCM 5092	Take A Little Walk Around The Block/LOUIS PRIMA: Oh! Cumari	15
58	Capitol CL 14862	The Lip/KEELY SMITH: Foggy Day	8
58	Capitol CL 14948	That Old Black Magic/KEELY SMITH: You Are My Love	8
59	Capitol CL 14994	I've Got You Under My Skin/KEELY SMITH: Don't Take Your Love From Me	5
59	London HLD 8923	Bei Mir Bist Du Schon/I Don't Know Why	10
60	London HLD 9084	I'm Confessin' (That I Love You)/Night And Day	8
59	Capitol T 1160	HEY BOY! HEY GIRL! (LP)	25
60	London HA-D 2243	LOUIS AND KEELY (LP)	15
61	London HA-D 2350	ON STAGE (LP, also stereo SAH-G 6149)	15

(see also Keely Smith)

PRIMAL SCREAM

85	Creation CRE 017	All Fall Down/It Happens (foldaround p/s in poly bag)	25
86	Creation CRE 026	Crystal Crescent/Velocity Girl (p/s)	10
86	Creation CRE 026T	Crystal Crescent/Velocity Girl/Spirea X (12", p/s)	12
87	Elevation ACID 3	Gentle Tuesday/Black Star Carnival (p/s)	5
87	Elevation ACID 3T	Gentle Tuesday/Black Star Carnival/I'm Gonna Make You Mine (12", p/s)	8
87	Elevation ACID 5	Imperial/Star Fruit Surf Rider (p/s)	5
87	Elevation ACID 5T	Imperial/Star Fruit Surf Rider/So Sad About Us/Imperial (demo) (12", in poster p/s with 'special price' sticker)	8
87	Elevation ACID 5T	Imperial/Star Fruit Surf Rider/So Sad About Us/Imperial (demo) (12")	8
91	Creation DOCKERS 001	Come Together (Original Recording) (12" promo)	8
87	Elevation ELV 2	SONIC FLOWER GROOVE (LP)	12
89	Creation CRELP 054	PRIMAL SCREAM (LP, with bonus 45 "Split Wide Open 1"/ Lone Star Girl 1 [CREFRE 6, no p/s])	20
91	Creation CRELP 076	SCREAMADELICA (2 x LP)	25
94	Creation CRELP 146	GIVE OUT BUT DON'T GIVE UP (2-LP, inners)	25
97	Creation CREL 7224	ECHO DEK (5 x 7", box set)	20
98	Creation CRELP 178	VANISHING POINT (2-LP)	40
00	Creation CRELP 239	EXTERMINATOR (EXTMNTR) (2-LP)	35
02	Columbia 508923	EVIL HEAT (2-LP)	18
06	Columbia 82876831651	RIOT CITY BLUES (2-LP)	18

(see also Jesus & Mary Chain, Revolving Paint Dream, P.P. & Primes, Death In Vegas)

PRIME MOVERS

| 89 | Cyanide CND 001 | SINS OF THE FOURFATHERS (LP) | 25 |

PRIME RHYME MASTERS

| 91 | Kold Sweat KS115 | You Need Discipline/To Kill A Mockingbird (12") | 15 |

PRIME-MATES

| 69 | Action ACT 4530 | Hot Tamales (Versions 1 & 2) | 20 |

PRIMETTES

| 68 | Ember EMBS 3398 | LOOKING BACK WITH THE PRIMETTES AND EDDIE FLOYD (LP, 1 side each) | 50 |
| 73 | Windmill WMD 192 | THE ROOTS OF DIANA ROSS AND EDDIE FLOYD (LP, reissue) | 20 |

(see also Supremes, Eddie Floyd)

PRIMITIVE MAN

| 71 | Decca F13188 | Animal Love/Major Barmy From The Army | 30 |

PRIMITIVES

| 64 | Pye 7N 15721 | Help Me/Let Them Tell | 220 |
| 65 | Pye 7N 15755 | You Said/How Do You Feel | 250 |

(see also Mal & Primitives)

PRIMITIVES

86	Head HEAD 010	Thru The Flowers/Across My Shoulder/Lazy/She Don't Need You (12", unreleased, white label test pressings only)	30
86	Lazy LAZY 01	Thru The Flowers/Across My Shoulder/She Don't Need You/Lazy (12", p/s)	10
86	Lazy LAZY 02	Really Stupid/We Found A Way To The Sun (p/s)	5
86	Lazy LAZY 02T	Really Stupid/We Found A Way To The Sun/Where The Wind Blows (12", p/s)	8
86	Lazy LAZY 03	Stop Killing Me/Buzz Buzz Buzz (p/s, with postcard, sleeves printed back-to-front; with badge)	5
87	Lazy LAZY 05	Ocean Blue/Shadow (2,000 only, given away free at London Astoria gig)	6

PRIMO & HOPETON

| 67 | Rio R 139 | Your Safekeep/Loving And Kind | 10 |
| 68 | Pama PM 753 | Peace On Earth/SCHOOL BOYS: Love Is A Message | 12 |

PRIMROSE
69	NEMS 56-4129	Just For You/Nine Till Five	25

PRIMROSE CIRCUS
70	President PT 314	P.S. Call Me Lulu/In My Mind	10

PRINCE
SINGLES
79	Warner Bros K 17537	I Wanna Be Your Lover/Just As Long As We're Together	5
79	Warner Bros K 17537T	I Wanna Be Your Lover/Just As Long As We're Together (12", company sleeve)	15
80	Warner Bros K 17590	Sexy Dancer/Bambi (die-cut company sleeve)	25
80	Warner Bros K 17590T	Sexy Dancer (Remix)/Bambi (12", die-cut company sleeve)	50
81	Warner Bros K 17768	Do It All Night/Head (die-cut company sleeve)	25
81	Warner Bros K 17768T	Do It All Night/Head (12", die-cut company sleeve)	60
81	Warner Bros K 17819	Gotta Stop (Messin' About)/Uptown (p/s)	60
81	Warner Bros K 17819	Gotta Stop (Messin' About)/I Wanna Be Your Lover (p/s)	60
81	Warner Bros LV 47	Gotta Stop (Messin' About)/Uptown/Head (12", stickered p/s)	60
81	Warner Bros LV 47	Gotta Stop (Messin' About)/I Wanna Be Your Lover/Head (12", stickered, colour p/s)	60
81	Warner Bros K 17866	Controversy/When You Were Mine (p/s)	20
81	Warner Bros K 17866T	Controversy/When You Were Mine (12", p/s)	30
82	Warner Bros K 17922	Let's Work/Ronnie, Talk To Russia (p/s)	40
82	Warner Bros K 17922T	Let's Work (Extended)/Ronnie, Talk To Russia (12", p/s)	40
83	Warner Bros W 9896	1999/How Come U Don't Call Me Anymore (paper labels, p/s, with free cassette mini-album in card p/s: "1999 (Edit)"/"Uptown"/"Controversy"/"Dirty Minds"/"Sexuality")	40
83	Warner Bros W 9896	1999/How Come U Don't Call Me Anymore (paper labels, p/s)	8
83	Warner Bros W 9688	Little Red Corvette/Lady Cab Driver (p/s)	10
83	Warner Bros W 9688T	Little Red Corvette (Full Length Version)/Automatic/International Lover (12", stickered p/s, with poster insert)	40
83	Warner Bros W 9688T	Little Red Corvette (Full Length Version)/Automatic/International Lover (12", stickered p/s)	12
83	Warner Bros W 9688T	Little Red Corvette (Full Length Version)/Automatic/International Lover (12", 'negative image' p/s)	20
83	Warner Bros W 9436	Little Red Corvette/Horny Toad (poster calendar p/s)	55
83	Warner Bros W 9436	Little Red Corvette/Horny Toad (standard p/s)	40
83	Warner Bros W 9436T	Little Red Corvette (Full Length Version)/Horny Toad/D.M.S.R. (12", p/s)	15
83	Warner Bros W 9436T	Little Red Corvette (Full Length Version)/Horny Toad/D.M.S.R. (12", p/s, with spiral-bound calendar)	85
83	Warner Bros W 9436T	Little Red Corvette (Full Length Version)/Horny Toad/D.M.S.R. (12", p/s, with poster)	75
84	Warner Bros W 9286T	When Doves Cry/17 Days/1999/D.M.S.R. (12", stickered shrinkwrapped double pack)	20
84	Warner Bros W 9174P	Purple Rain/God (motorbike-shaped picture disc)	20
84	Warner Bros W 9174T	Purple Rain/God (instrumental)/God (12", p/s, initial pressing with poster)	15
84	Warner Bros W 9174T	Purple Rain/God (instrumental)/God (12", p/s)	8
84	Warner Bros W 9121TE	I Would Die 4 U (U.S. Remix)/Another Lonely Christmas (U.S. Remix) (12", p/s)	20
85	Paisley Park W 9052P	Paisley Park/She's Always In My Hair (shaped picture disc)	25
85	Paisley Park W 9052T	Paisley Park/She's Always In My Hair/Paisley Park (Remix) (12", p/s)	8
85	Paisley Park W 9052T	Paisley Park/She's Always In My Hair/Paisley Park (Remix) (12", mispressing with repeated 2nd track "She's Always In My Hair")	25
85	Paisley Park W 9286T	Raspberry Beret (Extended Remix)/Hello (Extended Remix) (12", p/s)	8
85	Paisley Park W 8858T	Pop Life (Extended)/Girl (12", p/s)	8
86	Paisley Park W 8751P	Kiss/Love Or Money (shaped picture disc with plinth)	30
86	Paisley Park W 8751T	Kiss (Extended)/Love Or Money (12", p/s, with poster)	15
86	Paisley Park W 8711TE	Mountains (Ext.)/Alexa De Paris (Extended) (10", white vinyl in PVC sleeve)	20
86	Paisley Park W 8711T	Mountains (Extended 9.56)/Alexa De Paris (12", p/s, with poster)	20
86	Paisley Park W 8586F	Girls And Boys (Edit)/Under The Cherry Moon/She's Always In My Hair/ 17 Days (double pack, gatefold p/s)	15
86	Paisley Park W 8586P	Girls And Boys (Edit)/Under The Cherry Moon (shaped picture disc)	15
86	Paisley Park W 8586T	Girls And Boys/Under The Cherry Moon/Erotic City (12", p/s, with poster advertising London gigs)	18
86	Paisley Park W 8521W	Anotherloverholenyohead/I Wanna Be Your Lover (paper or plastic labels, poster p/s)	12
86	Paisley Park W 8521T	Anotherloverholenyohead (Extended)/I Wanna Be Your Lover (12", p/s)	10
87	Paisley Park W 8399TP	Sign O' The Times (Extended)/La La La He He Hee (Extended) (12", picture disc)	10
87	Paisley Park W 8334W	If I Was Your Girlfriend/Shockadelica (poster p/s)	8
87	Paisley Park W 8334E	If I Was Your Girlfriend/Shockadelica (peach vinyl, PVC cover, with postcards & stickers)	15
87	Paisley Park W 8334TP	If I Was Your Girlfriend (Extended)/Shockadelica (12", picture disc)	12
87	Paisley Park W 8289TP	U Got The Look (Long Look)/Housequake (7 min MoQuake)/ U Got The Look (Single Cut) (12", picture disc)	8
87	Paisley Park W 8288TP	I Could Never Take The Place Of Your Man/Hot Thing (Remixed Edit)/ Hot Thing (Extended) (12", picture disc)	15
88	Paisley Park W 7900CD	Alphabet Street (Album Version)/This Is Not Music, This Is A Trip (Alphabet Street) (Extended) (3" CD, with adaptor, 5" case)	10
88	Paisley Park W 7806CD	Glam Slam (Edit)/Escape (Free Yo Mind) (Edit)/Glam Slam (Remix) (3" CD, with adaptor, 5" case)	10
88	Paisley Park W 7745	I Wish U Heaven (Edit)/Scarlet Pussy (Edit) (poster p/s)	5
88	Paisley Park W 7745TW	I Wish U Heaven (Parts 1/2/3)/CAMILLE: Scarlet Pussy (Edit) (12", p/s with poster)	8
88	Paisley Park W 7745CD	I Wish U Heaven (Parts 1/2/3)/CAMILLE: Scarlet Pussy (Edit) (3" CD, with adaptor, 5" case)	10
89	Paisley Park W 2814TP	Partyman (Video Mix)/Feel U Up (Long Stroke) (12", picture disc, PVC sleeve)	8
89	Paisley Park W 2814CDX	Partyman (Video Mix)/Feel U Up (Long Stroke) (3" CD, octagonal foldout sleeve with film stills)	15
88	Paisley Park W 8751TP	Kiss/Love Or Money (shaped picture disc, 're-promoted' edition with longer, extended version of B-side & without plinth)	10

ALBUMS
83	Warner Bros 923 809-1	1999 (LP, original issue, single disc)	18
84	Warner Bros 925 110-1	PURPLE RAIN - MUSIC FROM THE MOTION PICTURE (LP, purple vinyl with poster)	25
86	Paisley Park WX 39P	PARADE - MUSIC FROM "UNDER THE CHERRY MOON" (LP, pic. disc, die-cut sleeve)	35
89	Paisley Park 925 978-2	BATMAN (CD, picture disc in 'Bat' tin with booklet)	15
94	Warners 936245793-1	BLACK ALBUM (LP, title sticker)	15
95	NPG 6103-1	EXODUS (LP, as NPG)	15
96	NPG EMI CDEMO 1102	EMANCIPATION (3-CD, as ß)	25
98	NPG BCT 9871	CRYSTAL BALL (4-CD, import only, as ß)	40

PROMOS
81	Warner Bros SAM 172	Dance Music Sex Romance/Dance Music Sex Romance (12", p/s, promo only)	100

PRINCE ALLAH

84	Warner Bros	Purple Rain (promo only p/s, purple vinyl)	60
84	Warner Bros SAM 230	I Would Die 4 U/I would Die 4 U	30
91	Warner Brothers SAM 888	Gett Off (Urge Single Edit) (1-sided promo)	15
92	Paisley Park W 0113	Thunder (DJ Edit) (1-sided promo only white label, stickered company sleeve)	15
95	NPG 61225	Get Wild (Money Maker Radio Mix) (CD, as NPG, radio programmer's picture disc)	45
95	NPG 61047	Get Wild/Beautiful Girl (no p/s, as NPG)	6
96	NPG 60667	Lovesign/MARGIE COX: Standing At The altar (no p/s, as ß)	10
96	NPG 60600	Lovesign (Radio Edit Mix)/(1-800 New Funk Version)/(The Storyboard Video Mix) (12", as ß, most with title sticker)	35
96	NPG 60605	Lovesign (Radio Edit Mix)/(1-800 New Funk Version)/(The Storyboard Video Mix) (CD, as ß)	30
01	Warners PRO 2721	THE VERY BEST OF PRINCE: (When Doves Cry/Purple Rain/Kiss/Cream/1999/ Money Don't Matter) (CD, radio sampler)	20

PRINCE ALLAH

78	Freedom Sounds FSD 020	Bucket Bottom/FULL WOOD: Stop And Think Me Over (12")	25

PRINCE BROTHERS

77	Carib Gems CG 010	Ram Jam/REVOLUTIONARIES: Version To Jam	6

PRINCE BUSTER (& ALL STARS)

61	Starlite ST45 052	Buster's Shack (as Buster's Group)/ERIC MORRIS: Search The World	30
62	Blue Beat BB 101	My Sound That Goes Around/They Got To Go (with Torchlighters)	30
62	Blue Beat BB 116	Independence Song (with Bluebeats)/RICO & BLUEBEATS: August 1962	25
62	Blue Beat BB 133	Time Longer Than Rope/Fake King (with Voice Of The People)	30
62	Blue Beat BB 138	One Hand Washes The Other/Cowboy Comes To Town	30
63	Blue Beat BB 150	Run Man Run/Danny, Dane And Lorraine	25
63	Blue Beat BB 158	Open Up, Bartender/Enjoy It (B-side actually "Enjoy Yourself")	25
63	Blue Beat BB 162	Money/SCHOOL BOYS: Little Boy Blue	40
63	Blue Beat BB 163	King, Duke, Sir/I See Them In My Sight	30
63	Blue Beat BB 167	The Ten Commandments (with All Stars)/Buster's Welcome	20
63	Blue Beat BB 170	Madness/PRINCE BUSTER ALL STARS: Toothache	25
63	Blue Beat BB 173	Burning Creation/PRINCE BUSTER ALL STARS: Boop	30
63	Blue Beat BB 180	Three More Rivers To Cross/RAYMOND HARPER & PRINCE BUSTER ALL STARS: African Blood	30
63	Blue Beat BB 186	Fowl Thief/Remember Me	60
63	Blue Beat BB 189	Watch It Blackhead/Hello My Dear	30
63	Blue Beat BB 192	Rollin' Stone (with Charmers)/RICO & HIS BLUES BAND: This Day	30
63	Blue Beat BB 197	Window Shopping/Sodom And Gomorrah	35
63	Blue Beat BB 199	Spider And Fly/Three Blind Mice	30
63	Blue Beat BB 200	Wash All Your Troubles Away/RICO & BLUE BEATS: Soul Of Africa	18
63	Dice CC 6	They Got To Come/These Are The Times (with Voice Of The People)	15
63	Dice CC 11	Blackhead Chinaman/You Ask (I Had A Girl)	18
63	Dice CC 18	World Peace/The Lion Roars (as Prince Buster & Hazel)	15
64	Stateside SS 335	30 Pieces Of Silver/Everybody Ska	15
64	Blue Beat BB 210	Wash All Your Troubles Away/RICO & BLUE BEATS: Soul Of Africa (p/s reissue)	50
64	Blue Beat BB 211	Bluebeat Spirit/Beggars Are No Choosers	35
64	Blue Beat BB 216	You're Mine/Tongue Will Tell	35
64	Blue Beat BB 225	Three Blind Mice/I Know	35
64	Blue Beat BB 232	Sheep On Top (song actually titled "She Pon Top")/Midnight	50
64	Blue Beat BB 234	She Loves You/Healing	60
64	Blue Beat BB 243	Jealous/Buster's Ska	35
64	Blue Beat BB 248	Thirty Pieces Of Silver/The National Dance	35
64	Blue Beat BB 254	Wings Of A Dove/MAYTALLS: Sweet Love	30
64	Blue Beat BB 262	Old Lady/Dayo Ska	35
64	Blue Beat BB 271	No Knowledge In College/In The Middle Of The Night	45
64	Blue Beat BB 274	I May Never Love You Again/Hey Little Girl	35
65	Blue Beat BB 278	Blood Pressure/Islam	120
65	Blue Beat BB 281	Blues Market/MAYTALS: Looking Down The Street	35
65	Blue Beat BB 282	Big Fight/Red Dress	35
65	Blue Beat BB 293	Agua Fumar/Long Winter (with Charmers)	40
65	Blue Beat BB 302	Ling Ting Tong/Walk Along	100
65	Blue Beat BB 307	Bonanza/Wonderful Life	30
65	Blue Beat BB 309	Here Comes The Bride (with Patsy Todd, as Jamaica's Greatest)/ BUSTER'S ALLSTARS: Burkes' Law	40
65	Blue Beat BB 313	Everybody Yeah Yeah (as Jamaica's Greatest)/ BUSTER'S ALLSTARS: Gun The Man Down	50
65	Blue Beat BB 314	Float Like A Butterfly/Haunted Room	50
65	Blue Beat BB 316	Sugar Pop/Feel Up (as Prince & Jamaica's Greatest)	40
65	Blue Beat BB 317	Come Home/I Thank You (as Jamaica's Greatest)	45
65	Blue Beat BB 321	My Girl/BUSTER'S ALL STARS: The Fugitive	50
65	Blue Beat BB 324	Al Capone/One Step Beyond (as Prince Buster's Allstars) (blue label)	15
65	Blue Beat BB 324	Al Capone/One Step Beyond (as Prince Buster's Allstars) (other label colours)	15
65	Blue Beat BB 328	Ambition/BUSTER'S ALL STARS: Ryging	30
65	Blue Beat BB 330	Rum And Coca Cola/I Love Her	25
65	Blue Beat BB 334	The Ten Commandments/BUSTER'S ALL STARS: Sting Like A Bee (reissue)	15
65	Blue Beat BB 335	Respect/BUSTER'S ALL STARS: Virginia (B-side actually Dance Jamaica by Val Bennett & Prince Buster's All Stars)	45
66	Blue Beat BB 338	Big Fight (Prince Buster Versus Duke Reid)/Adios, Senorita	40
66	Blue Beat BB 339	Under Arrest (But Officer)/PRINCE BUSTER'S ALLSTARS: Say Boss Man	40
66	Blue Beat BB 343	Prince Of Peace/Don't Throw Stones	110
66	Blue Beat BB 352	Day Of Light (song actually "Dayo")/It's Too Late	25
66	Blue Beat BB 355	Sunshine With My Girl/Girl Answer Your Name	120
66	Blue Beat BB 357	I Won't Let You Cry/Hard Man Fe Dead	80
66	Blue Beat BB 359	The Prophet (actually "Feel The Spirit" with Slim Smith)/ BUSTER'S ALL STARS: Lion Of Judah	90
66	Blue Beat BB 362	To Be Loved/BUSTER'S ALLSTARS: Set Me Free	30
66	Rainbow RAI 107	Your Turn (Sad Song)/If You Leave Me (with Allstars)	25
67	Blue Beat BB 370	Shanty Town (Get Scanty)/BUSTER'S ALL STARS: Duppy	30
67	Blue Beat BB 373	Knock On Wood/And I Love Her	50
67	Blue Beat BB 377	Dark End Of The Street/Love Oh Love	45
67	Blue Beat BB 378	Drunkard's Psalm (Wise Man)/7 Wonders Of The World (as Prince Buster All Stars)	150
67	Blue Beat BB 382	Sit And Wonder (with His All Stars)/ROLAND ALFONSO: Sunrise In Kingston	60
67	Blue Beat BB 383	Sharing You/You'll Be Lonely On The Blue Train (as Prince Buster's Allstars; A-side actually by Prince Buster, B-side actually by Rico's Band)	30

67	Blue Beat BB 384	Take It Easy/Why Must I Cry (2nd issue, B-side actually by Hopeton Lewis)	20
67	Blue Beat BB 387	Judge Dread (Judge Four Hundred Years)/FITZROY CAMPBELL & PRINCE BUSTER ALL STARS: Waiting For My Rude Girl	25
67	Blue Beat BB 388	Dance Cleopatra/All In My Mind	100
67	Blue Beat BB 390	Soul Serenade/Too Hot	30
67	Blue Beat BB 391	Land Of Imagination/The Appeal (B-side actually "The Barrister Appeal")	30
67	Blue Beat BB 393	Johnny Dollar/Rude Boys Rude	45
67	Blue Beat BB 395	This Gun's For Hire/Yes, Daddy	30
67	Blue Beat BB 397	Quit Place/Rude Boys Rude	40
67	Blue Beat BB 400	All In My Mind/Judge Dread Dance (The Pardon)	30
67	Blue Beat BB 402	Vagabond/PRINCE BUSTER ALL STARS: Come Get Me	30
67	Philips BF 1552	The Ten Commandments/Don't Make Me Cry	15
67	Fab FAB 10	Shakin' Up Orange Street/Black Girl (with Allstars)	30
67	Fab FAB 11	Johnny Cool (Parts 1 & 2) (with Allstars)	30
67	Fab FAB 16	Bye Bye Baby/Human (with Allstars)	30
67	Fab FAB 25	Train To Girls Town/Give Love A Try (with Allstars)	30
67	Fab FAB 26	Going To The River (as Prince Buster & Allstars)/ PRINCE BUSTER'S ALLSTARS: Julie On My Mind	20
68	Fab FAB 31	Kings Of Old (My Ancestors)/Sweet Inspiration (with Allstars)	45
68	Fab FAB 35	Try A Little Tenderness/All My Loving (with Allstars)	250
68	Fab FAB 36	The Glory Of Love/Another Sad Nite	30
68	Fab FAB 37	This Is A Hold Up/Julie On My Mind (with Allstars)	30
68	Fab FAB 38	Free Love (with Allstars)/DALTONS: All Over The World	18
68	Fab FAB 40	Rough Rider (with Allstars)/PRINCE BUSTER: 127 Orange Street (B-side actually by Prince Buster Allstars)	20
68	Fab FAB 41	Shepherd Beng Beng (with Teddy King)/TENNORS: Ride Your Donkey	20
68	Fab FAB 47	Going To Ethiopia (as Prince Buster & Allstars)/ PRINCE BUSTER ALLSTARS: Shakin' Up Orange Street	20
68	Fab FAB 49	Glory Of Love/WAILERS: Mellow Mood (possibly white labels only)	100
68	Fab FAB 56	Intensified Dirt/Don't You Know I Love You (with Allstars)	35
68	Fab FAB 57	Green Green Grass Of Home (as Prince Buster's Allstars; actually by Prince Buster & Allstars)/SOUL MAKERS: Girls Like You	20
68	Fab FAB 58	We Shall Overcome/Keep The Faith (as Prince Buster's Allstars; actually by Prince Buster & Allstars)	15
68	Fab FAB 64	Cool Stroker/It's You I Love (B-side actually by Little Roy)	20
68	Fab FAB 80	Hypocrite/New Dance (B-side actually by Little Roy)	20
68	Fab FAB 81	Wine And Grind/The Scorcher (with Allstars)	20
69	Unity UN 522	30 Pieces Of Silver/Everybody Ska (reissue)	20
69	Fab FAB 82	Dr. Rodney (Black Power)/Taxation	35
69	Fab FAB 92	Pharaoh House Crash/Ob-La-Di, Ob-La-Da	20
69	Fab FAB 93	Ob-La-Di, Ob-La-Da/Wreck A Pum Pum	10
69	Fab FAB 94	Hey Jude/Django Fever	35
69	Fab FAB 102	Black Soul/CALEDONIANS: Oh Baby (B-side actually by Claredonians)	15
69	Fab FAB 108	Wine And Grind/The Scorcher (with Allstars) (reissue)	20
69	Fab FAB 118	Bull Buck/ROLAND ALPHONSO: One Heart	15
69	Fab FAB 119	Let Her Go/Tie The Donkey's Tail	15
69	Fab FAB 122	Stand Up/Happy Reggae (with Allstars)	10
70	Fab FAB 127	Young Gifted And Black/PRINCE BUSTER'S ALLSTARS: The Rebel	10
70	Fab FAB 131	That's All/The Preaching (B-side actually titled "The Preacher")	10
70	Fab FAB 132	Ganja Plant/Creation	10
70	Fab FAB 140	Hit Me Back/Give Peace A Chance	10
70	Fab FAB 150	Big Five/Musical College	10
70	Prince Buster PB 1	Big Five/Musical College (reissue)	8
70	Prince Buster PB 2	Rat Trap/Black Organ (B-side with Allstars but actually by Ansell Collins & Prince Buster's Allstars)	10
71	Fab FAB 162	Baby Version (with Jan Fender)/Holly	8
71	Fab FAB 176	Police Trim Rasta (with Allstars)/Smooth (B-side actually by Ansell Collins & Prince Buster Allstars)	10
71	Prince Buster PB 4	Fishey/More Fishey	7
71	Prince Buster PB 7	I Wish Your Picture Was You/PRINCE BUSTER ALLSTARS: It Mash Up - Version (B-side actually by Dennis Alcapone)	8
71	Prince Buster PB 8	Sons Of Zion (actually by Dennis Alcapone)/ANSELL COLLINS: Short Circuit	8
71	Prince Buster PB 9	My Happiness/Human (with Allstars)	7
71	Prince Buster PB10	Still/Version	10
72	Prince Buster PB 14	Big Sister Stuff/Satta Massagana (with Allstars)	12
72	Prince Buster PB 15	Protection/Cool Operator (with Allstars)	8
72	Prince Buster PB 16	I Stand Accused/My Heart is Gone (with Allstars)	7
72	Prince Buster PB 19	Four In One Medley/Drums Drums (as Prince Buster & Allstars, B-side actually by Prince Buster Allstars)	7
72	Prince Buster PB20	They Got To Come/Time Longer Than Rope	20
72	Prince Buster PB24	Giant/Science	20
72	Prince Buster PB 32	Still/Sister Big Stuff (with Allstars)	7
72	Prince Buster PB 36	South Of The Border/South Of The Border (Version) (with Allstars)	7
72	Fab FAB 36	South Of The Border/South Of The Border (Version) (with Allstars)	7
72	Prince Buster PB 47	Baldhead Pum Pum/Giver Her (with Allstars)	7
79	Blue Beat DDBB 324	Al Capone/One Step Beyond (12", p/s)	12
79	Blue Beat DDBB 334	THREE OF THE BEST (12" EP, p/s)	10
79	Blue Beat DDPB 1	Big Five/FOLK BROTHERS: Carolina/ PRINCE BUSTER: Shaking Up Orange Street (12", p/s)	8
79	Blue Beat DDPB 2	PICK OF THE PUNCH (12" EP, p/s, 2 tracks each by Tennors & Prince Buster)	8
79	Blue Beat DDPB 3	NAUGHTY BUT NICE (12" EP, p/s)	8
79	Blue Beat DDPB 4	BEHIND BARS (12" EP, p/s)	8
63	Blue Beat BBLP 802	I FEEL THE SPIRIT (LP)	120
65	Blue Beat BBLP 805	SKA-LIP-SOUL (LP, with His All Stars)	150
65	Blue Beat BBLP 806	IT'S BURKE'S LAW - JAMAICA SKA EXPLOSION! (LP, as Prince Buster All Stars; 2 different sleeves, laminated plain and unlaminated 'explosion')	250
67	Blue Beat BBLP 807	WHAT A HARD MAN FE DEAD - PRINCE BUSTER SINGS FOR THE PEOPLE (LP, with Baba Brooks)	300
67	Blue Beat BBLP 808	ON TOUR (LP)	120
67	Blue Beat BBLP 809	JUDGE DREAD (LP)	100
67	Blue Beat BBLP 820	SHE WAS A ROUGH RIDER (LP)	70
68	Fab BBLP 820	SHE WAS A ROUGH RIDER (LP, reissue on Fab label)	30
68	Fab BBLP 821	WRECK A PUM PUM (LP)	40
69	Fab BBLP 822	THE OUTLAW (LP, title listed as "Queen Of The Outlaws" on disc)	75

MINT VALUE £

70	Fab MS 1	FABULOUS GREATEST HITS (LP, original issue with 'West Brothers Printers' credit on rear of sleeve)	18
70	Fab MS 2	I FEEL THE SPIRIT (LP)	60
70	Fab MS 6	TUTTI FRUTTI (LP)	45
72	Melodisc MLP 12-156	SISTER BIG STUFF (LP)	45
72	Melodisc MLP 12-157	BIG FIVE (LP)	30
73	Prince Buster PB 9	ORIGINAL GOLDEN OLDIES VOLUME 1 (LP)	20
70s	Fab MS 7	THE MESSAGE DUBWISE (LP)	70

(see also Buster's Allstars, Buster's Group, Dennis Alcapone, Jim Dakota, Hortense Ellis, Heptones, Eric Morris, Terry Nelson, Schoolboys, Protegue, Vietnam All Stars)

PRINCE CHARLIE
| 69 | Coxsone CS 7101 | Hit And Run/Darling, There I Stand | 35 |

PRINCE FAR I
78	Virgin Front Line FLS 112	No More War/Version	10
82	On-U Sound DP 1	Virgin/Danger (10")	15
83	Pre PRE 11-12	83 Struggle (with ASHANTIE ROY)/KONGO ASHANTIE ROY/Weeping Waiing (12")	25
77	Virgin Front Line FL 1013	MESSAGE FROM THE KING (LP)	15
78	Virgin Front Line FL 1021	LONG LIFE (LP)	20
79	Virgin Front Line FLX 4002	CRY TUFF DUB ENCOUNTER PART 2 (LP)	35
79	Hit Run APLP 9006	DUB TO AFRICA (LP, as Prince Far I & the Arabs)	20
79	TRLS 205	CRY TUFF DUB ENCOUNTER CHAPTER IV (LP)	20
80	Daddy Kool DKLP 15	CRY TUFF DUB ENCOUNTER CHAPTER III (LP, as Prince Far I & the Arabs)	25
80	Pre PRE XF 3	SHOWCASE IN A SUITCASE (LP)	45
81	Pre PRE X 7	LIVITY (LP)	25

(see also Arabs)

PRINCE HAMMER
77	Baby Mother HIT DD 11	Them Must Fall/Ball Of Fire (12")	30
78	Hit Run HIT DP 15	Ten Thousand Lions/North London Thing (Carry The Swing) (12")	50
83	Saab (No catalogue number)	Warika Hill/Africa Dance Hall (12")	45
79	Hit Run APLP 9007	WORLD WAR DUB PART 1 (LP)	80
79	Miss Pat Walker PW1	ROOTS ME ROOTS (LP)	60

PRINCE HAROLD
| 66 | Mercury MF 952 | Forget About Me/Baby You've Got Me | 15 |

PRINCE JAMMY
| 79 | TRLS 174 | KAMIKAZI DUB (LP) | 20 |

PRINCE JAZZBO
73	Count Shelley CS 025	Wise Shepherd (with Linval Carthy)/ EARL GEORGE: Gonna Give Her All The Love I've Got	10
74	Cactus CT 31	Concubine Donkey/Part 2	8
74	Count Shelley CS 057	Step Forward Youth/Black Is Power	8
73	Grape GR 3047	Free From Chains/LLOYD & PATSY: Papa Do It Sweet	8
73	Techniques TE 921	Mr. Harry Skank/GLEN BROWN: Telavid Drums	8
74	Ackee ACK 532	Kick Boy Face/Version	8
74	Dip DL 5036	Penny Reel/Good Things	8
75	ABI AB 001	Bag A Wolf/Version	8
76	Attack ATT 8122	The Wormer/The Great Pablo	10
76	Third World TWLP 109	KICK BOY FACE (LP)	30
76	Black Wax WAXLP 1	NATTY PASSING THRU' (LP)	90

(see also Earl George)

PRINCE JAZZBO & I ROY
| 78 | Live & Love LAP 003 | STEP FORWARD YOUTH (LP) | 25 |

PRINCE LASHA ENSEMBLE
| 66 | CBS SBPG 62409 | INSIGHT (LP) | 30 |

PRINCE OF DARKNESS
69	Downtown DT 441	Burial Of Long Shot/MUSIC DOCTORS: Burial Of Long Shot	15
69	Downtown DT 448	Meeting Over Yonder/MUSIC DOCTORS: Ghost Rider	12
71	Downtown DT 467	Sound Of Today/MUSIC DOCTORS: Red Red Wine Version	12

PRINCE PATO EXPEDITION
| 70s | Beacon BEAS 18 | FIREBIRD (LP) | 30 |

PRINCE & PRINCESS
| 65 | Aladdin WI 609 | Ready Steady Go/Take Me Serious | 25 |

PRINCE SISTERS
| 55 | Decca 45-F1050 | A Rusty Old Halo/Love Love Beautiful Love | 8 |

PRINCE TALLIS & THE CHALLIS
| 72 | Upsetter US 383 | Who Feels It/THE UPSETTERS: He Who Feels It (Chapter 2) | 20 |

VIV PRINCE
| 66 | Columbia DB 7960 | Light Of The Charge Brigade/Minuet For Ringo | 40 |

(see also Pretty Things, Bunch Of Fives, Kate, Vamp, Chicago Line)

PRINCE WILLIAMS
| 73 | Atra ATRA 004 | Action Wood Part 1/Action Wood Part 2 | 8 |

PRINCESS
| 86 | Supreme SU 1 | PRINCESS (LP) | 12 |
| 86 | Supreme CDSU 1 | PRINCESS (CD) | 60 |

PRINCESS BALOU
| 81 | PB YYS 11 | Making Love To You/Making Love To You (Part II) (p/s) | 10 |

PRINCESS & SWINEHERD
| 68 | Oak RGJ 633 | PRINCESS AND THE SWINEHERD (LP, plain black sleeve) | 100 |

PRINCESS TINYMEAT
| 84 | Rough Trade RTT 160 | Sloblands/The Fairest Of Them All (12", some with sticker) | 15 |
| 87 | Rough Trade ROUGH 108 | HERSTORY (LP) | 20 |

(see laso Virgin Prunes, Daniel Figgis)

PRINCIPAL EDWARDS MAGIC THEATRE

69	Dandelion S 4405	Ballad Of The Big Girl Now/Lament For The Earth	10
73	Deram DM 391	Captain Lifeboy/Nothing	5
73	Deram DM 398	Weekdaze/Whizzmore Kid	15
69	Dandelion 63752	SOUNDTRACK (LP, gatefold sleeve)	50
71	Dandelion DAN 8002	THE ASOMOTO RUNNING BAND (LP, gatefold sleeve)	35
74	Deram SML 1108	ROUND ONE (LP, white/red label with small logo)	30

MADDY PRIOR

78	Chrysalis CHS 2232	Baggy Pants/Woman In The Wings	6
80	EMI EMI 5903	Wake Up England/Paradise (p/s, as Maddy Prior Band)	6
82	Plant Life PLRS 001	Face To Face/Half Listening (p/s, as Maddy Prior Band)	6
83	RCA/Spindrift RCA 379	Deep In The Darkest Night/Western Movies (p/s)	6
85	Making Waves SURF 108	Stookie/Incidental Music From Stookie (p/s)	6
85	Making Waves SURF 109	Deep In The Darkest Night/Western Movies (p/s, reissue)	6
78	Chrysalis CHR 1185	WOMAN IN THE WINGS (LP, with insert)	12
87	Saydisc SDL 366	A TAPESTRY OF CAROLS (LP)	20

(see also Steeleye Span,Tim Hart & Maddy Prior)

PRISONERS

83	Big Beat NS 90	Hurricane/Tomorrow (She Said) (p/s)	12
84	Big Beat SW 98	ELECTRIC FIT (EP)	12
82	Own Up OWN UP U2	A TASTE OF PINK (LP)	15
83	Big Beat WIK 19	THE WISERMISERDEMELZA (LP)	15
85	Own Up OWN UP U2	A TASTE OF PINK (LP, reissue in pink sleeve on pink vinyl)	30
85	Own Up OWN UP U3	THE LAST FOURFATHERS (LP)	20
86	Countdown DOWN 2	IN FROM THE COLD (LP)	20
89	Hangman HANG 23 UP	RARE AND UNISSUED (LP)	25
91	Cyanide CND 2	RARE AND UNISSUED (LP, reissue)	20

(see also James Taylor Quartet)

PRISONERS/MILKSHAKES

86	Empire MIC 001	THE LAST NIGHT AT THE MIC CLUB (LP, live, 1 side each)	18
86	Media Burn MB 17	THEE MILKSHAKES VS. THE PRISONERS (LP, live, 1 side each)	18

(see also Milkshakes, Thee Mighty Caesars)

PRIVATE DICKS

79	Heartbeat PULSE 6	She Said So/Private Dicks (p/s)	20

PRIVATE LIFE

72	Realm RM 3	Put Her Down/Chasing Dragons	400

PRIVATE PARTY

87	IMW 1201	Puppet Capers/Tennants Super Mix (12")	10

PRIVATE SECTOR

78	TJM TJM 8	Just Just (Wanna) Stay Free/Things Get Worse (p/s)	20

P.J. PROBY

62	Liberty LIB 55367	Try To Forget Her/There Stands The One	10
64	Decca F 11904	Hold Me/The Tips Of My Fingers	5
64	Decca F 11967	Together/Sweet And Tender Romance	5
64	Liberty LIB 10182	Somewhere/Just Like Him	5
65	Liberty LIB 10188	I Apologise/What's On Your Mind	5
65	Liberty LIB 10206	Let The Water Run Down/I Don't Want To Hear It Anymore	10
65	Liberty LIB 10215	That Means A Lot/My Prayer	10
65	Liberty LIB 10218	Maria/She Cried	5
66	Liberty LIB 10223	You've Come Back/It Ain't Necessarily So	5
66	Liberty LIB 10236	To Make A Big Man Cry/Wicked Woman	10
66	Fab FAB 2	You've Got Me Cryin'/I Need Love (in die-cut p/s)	20
66	Fab FAB 2	You've Got Me Cryin'/I Need Love	7
66	Liberty LIB 10250	I Can't Make It Alone/Sweet Summer Wine	12
67	Liberty LIB 55936	Nicki Hoeky/Good Things Are Coming My Way	15
67	Liberty LIB 55974	You Can't Come Home Again/Work With Me Annie	15
67	Liberty LIB 55974	You Can't Come Home Again/Work With Me Annie (DJ Copy)	30
68	Liberty LBF 15046	It's Your Day Today/I Apologise Baby	10
68	Liberty LBF 15046	It's Your Day Today/I Apologise Baby (DJ Copy)	30
68	Liberty LBF 15085	What's Wrong With My World/Why Baby Why	7
68	Liberty LBF 15152	The Day That Lorraine Came Down/Mery Hoppkins Never Had Days Like These (B-side features Led Zeppelin)	15
69	Liberty LBF 15245	Hanging From Your Loving Tree/Empty Bottles	15
70	Liberty LBF 15280	Today I Killed A Man/It's Too Good To Last	10
70	Liberty LBF 15386	It's Goodbye/Gift Of Love	10
70s	Rooster ROO 101	You've Got It All (with Polly Brown)/Starting All Over Again	20
72	Columbia DB 8874	We'll Meet Again/Clown Shoes	10
73	Ember EMB S 328	Put Your Head On My Shoulder/Momma Married A Preacher	7
74	Seven Sun SSUN 13	The Champ (Parts 1 & 2)	8
81	Rooster RONS 101	You've Got It All/Starting All Over Again (with Polly Brown)	5
64	Liberty LEP 2192	P. J. PROBY (EP)	15
65	Liberty LEP 2229	SOMEWHERE (EP)	15
65	Liberty LEP 2239	CHRISTMAS WITH P. J. (EP)	15
66	Liberty LEP 2251	P. J.'s HITS (EP)	20
67	Liberty LEP 2267	PROBY AGAIN (EP)	30
65	Liberty LBY 1235	I AM P. J. PROBY (LP)	20
65	Liberty LBY 1264	P. J. PROBY (LP)	20
66	Liberty LBY 1291	P. J. PROBY IN TOWN (LP)	20
67	Liberty LBY 1361	ENIGMA (LP)	15
67	Liberty LBL/LBS 83045	PHENOMENON (LP)	15
68	Liberty LBL/LBS 83087	BELIEVE IT OR NOT (LP)	15
69	Liberty LBS 83219E	THREE WEEK HERO (LP, featuring Led Zeppelin on "Jim's Blues")	60
73	Ember NR 5069	I'M YOURS (LP)	15
78	Astoria 1	ELVIS (LP, sold at theatres)	15

(see also Jett Powers, Marc Almond)

PROCESSION

68	Mercury MF 1053	Every American Citizen/Essentially Susan (p/s)	10
68	Mercury MF 1070	One Day In Every Week/Wigwam City	10
69	Mercury SMCL 20132	PROCESSION (LP)	30

PROCOL HARUM

67	Deram DM 126	A Whiter Shade Of Pale/Lime Street Blues (1st issue with darker labels)	5
67	Regal Zonophone RZ 3003	Homburg/Good Captain Clack	5
68	Regal Zonophone RZ 3007	Quite Rightly So/In The Wee Small Hours Of Sixpence	8
69	Regal Zonophone RZ 3019	A Salty Dog/Long Gone Geek	10
72	Fly Magni Fly ECHO 101	A Whiter Shade Of Pale/A Salty Dog/Homburg (p/s)	5
72	Chrysalis CHS 2003	Conquistador/Luskus Delph (PS)	6
79	RCA LB 6	A Whiter Shade Of Pale/Noel Edmonds Introduces Record Year (Lever Brothers premium)	5
67	Regal Zono. LRZ 1001	PROCOL HARUM (LP, laminated front sleeve, flipbacks, blue/silver label)	100
68	Regal Zono. LRZ 1004	SHINE ON BRIGHTLY (LP, mono), laminated front sleeve, blue/silver label)	150
67	Regal Zono. SLRZ 1004	SHINE ON BRIGHTLY (LP, stereo), laminated front sleeve, red/silver label)	70
69	Regal Zono. SLRZ 1009	A SALTY DOG (LP, laminated sleeve, red/silver label)	50
70	Regal Zono. SLRZ 1014	HOME (LP, with lyric sheet)	50
71	Chrysalis ILPS 9158	BROKEN BARRICADES (LP, gatefold sleeve, first pressing with a small white "i" at the top of the label)	15
71	Chrysalis ILPS 9158	BROKEN BARRICADES (LP, gatefold sleeve)	12
73	Chrysalis CHR 1037	GRAND HOTEL (LP, gatefold sleeve, booklet, green label)	25

(see also Paramounts, Legend, Matthew Fisher, Robin Trower, Matthew Ellis, Freedom, Mick Grabham, Power Pack)

JUDD PROCTOR

61	Parlophone R 4769	Rio Grande/Plainsman	10
61	Parlophone R 4809	Palamino/Nola	10
61	Parlophone R 4841	Speakeasy/Clearway	10
62	Parlophone R 4885	The Turk/Mad	10
62	Parlophone R 4920	Backfire/It's Bluesy	10
64	Parlophone R 5126	Better Late/Boots	10
68	Morgan MR 103P	GUITARS GALORE (LP)	40
70s	Gemini GMX 5004	GUITARS GALORE (LP, reissue)	25

see also Ray Ellington

MIKE PROCTOR

67	Columbia DB 8254	Mr. Commuter/Sunday, Sunday, Sunday	160

PRODIGY

91	XL XLT 17	WHAT EVIL LURKS EP (What Evil Lurks/We Gonna Rock/Android/ Everybody In The Place) (12", company sleeve)	30
91	XL XLS 21	Charly/Charly (Original Mix)	10
91	XL XLS 26	Everybody In The Place (Fairground Edit)/G-Force (Energy Flow)	8
92	XL XLS 30	Fire (Edit)/Jericho (Original Version)	8
92	XL XLS 35	Out Of Space/Ruff In The Jungle Bizness (Uplifting Vibes Remix)	8
93	XL XLS 39	Wind It Up (Rewound)/We Are The Ruffest	8
93	XL EB 1	EARTHBOUND 1 : One Love (original Mix)/Full Throttle (original Mix) (12")	50
93	XL XLT 47	One Love/Rhythm Of Life/Full Throttle/One Love (Jonny L Remix) (12")	8
94	XL XLT 54	Voodoo People (Haiti Island Remix)/(Dust Brothers Remix)/Goa (The Heat The Energy Part 2) (12")	8
94	XL XLT 51	No Good (Start The Dance)/(Bad For You Mix)/(C J Bollands Museum Mix) (12")	8
95	XL SC 1	SCIENIDE (12", white label, 500 hand-stamped promos only)	50
95	XL XLT 58	Poison (95 EQ)/Rat Poison/Scienide/Poison (Enviromental Science Dub Mix) (12")	8
96	XL XLT70CDPR	Firestarter Sampler (CD picture disc, promo only)	12
96	XL XLT 70	Firestarter/(Instrumental)/(Empirion Mix)/Molotov Bitch (12")	8
96	XL XLT 80	Breathe (Edit)/The Trick/Breathe (Instrumental)/Their Law (Live At Phoenix Festival '96) (12")	8
98	XL XLTV90DJ	Smack My Bitch Up/(DJ Hype Remix)/No Man Army/Minefields (Headrock Dub) (12" promo)	8
04	XL XLXV1501	What Evil Lurks/We Gonna Rock/Android/Everybody In The Place (12")	8
05	XL XLT 213	Spitfire (05 Version)Spitfire (Future Funk Squad's "Dogfight" Remix/Spitfire (Nightbreed Remix) (12" stickered p/s, with 2 stickers, 2000 only)	25
05	XL XLS 213 CDE	Spitfire (05 Version)/Spitfire (Nightbreed Remix)/Spitfire (Future Funk Squad's "Dogfight" Remix) (CD stickered digipak 500 only)	30
92	XL XLLP 110	THE PRODIGY EXPERIENCE (2-LP)	20
94	XL XLLP 114	MUSIC FOR THE JILTED GENERATION (LP)	15
97	XL XLLP 121	THE FAT OF THE LAND (2xLP)	20
04	XL XLLP 183	ALWAYS OUTNUMBERED, NEVER OUTGUNNED (3-LP)	20
09	Take Me To The Hospital HOSPLP001	INVADERS MUST DIE (2-LP)	20
09	Take Me To The Hospital HOSPBOX001	INVADERS MUST DIE (Box set, CD/DVD/5x7")	30

PROFESSIONALS

80	Virgin VS 353	Just Another Dream/Action Man (p/s)	5
80	Virgin VS 376	1-2-3/White Light White Heat/Baby I Don't Care (p/s, with giant foldout poster in stickered PVC sleeve)	5
80	Virgin VS 376	1-2-3/White Light White Heat/Baby I Don't Care (p/s, signed by Cook & Jones)	15
81	Virgin VS 426	Join The Professionals/Has Anybody Got An Alibi? (gatefold p/s)	7
81	Virgin V 2220	I DIDN'T SEE IT COMING (LP)	15

(see also Sex Pistols, Greedies, Lightning Raiders, Steve Jones)

PROFESSOR LONGHAIR

65	Sue WI 397	Baby Let Me Hold Your Hand/Looka' No Hair	40
78	Harvest HAR 5154	Mess Around/Tipitina	15
72	Speakeasy 10-78	NEW ORLEANS 88 (10" LP)	50
72	Atlantic K 40402	NEW ORLEANS PIANO (LP)	30
78	Harvest SHSP 4086	LIVE ON THE QUEEN MARY (LP)	30
80	Sonet SNTF 830	CRAWFISH SIESTA (LP)	15
83	Stateside SSL 6004	LIVE ON THE QUEEN MARY (LP, reissue)	18
81	JSP 1025	THE LONDON CONCERT (LP)	15

PROFESSOR LUDLOW & DR. SMITH

99	Fat Cat 12FAT 029	Professor's Saying Raas (12", custom sleeve)	8

FRANK PROFFITT
66	Topic 12T 162	NORTH CAROLINA SONGS AND BALLADS (LP)	20

PROFIL
80	CBS S CBS 8574	Hey Music Man/Jour De Chance (p/s)	10

PROFILE
65	Mercury MF 875	Haven't They Got Better Things To Do/Touch Of Your Hand	12
65	Mercury MF 981	Got To Find A Way/Don't Say Goodbye	12
69	Philips BF 1757	Politician Man/Where Is Love	8

(see also Karl Stuart & Profiles, Voice)

PROLES
79	Rock Against Racism RAR 1	Stereo Love/Thought Crime/CONDEMNED: Soldier Boys/ Endless Revolution (p/s)	45
79	Small Wonder SMALL 23	Softground/SMK (p/s)	6

PROMISE
69	NEMS 56-4129	Just For You/Nine To Five	90

PROPAGANDA
85	ZTT 12 ZTAS 2	Das Testaments Des Mabuse/Femme Fatale/The 9th Life (Of Dr. Mabuse) (12", white p/s, title sticker reads "13th Life New Mix")	15
85	ZTT P ZTAS 8	Duel/Jewel (Rough Cut) (ZTT logo-shaped picture disc)	10
85	ZTT DUAL 1	Duel/Jewel//Lied/The Lesson (double pack, gatefold sleeve)	8
85	ZTT PROP 1	Bejewelled (12", 1-sided, white label, stickered title sleeve, promo only)	12
85	ZTT ZTAS 12	P-Machinery/Frozen Faces (clear vinyl, printed PVC sleeve)	5
85	ZTT 12X ZTAS 12	P-Machinery (Beta)/Complete Machinery/Frozen Faces (12", 'sofa' p/s)	10
85	ZTT 12P ZTAS 12	P-Machinery (Polish)/P Machinery (Passive)/Frozen Faces (12", p/s, clear vinyl, printed PVC sleeve)	8
02	ZTT ZTT 180CDX	OUTSIDE WORLD (CD, with bonus DVD, digipak)	25

(see also Act, Ralph Dorper, Claudia Brucken)

PROPERTY
70	Staple ST01	My Mind Sleeps/Calling You	60

PROPHECY OF DOOM
89	Prophecy SRT 9KS 2178	Calculated Mind Rape/Hybrid Thought (p/s)	10
82	Deaf DEAF 02	ACKNOWLEDGE THE CONFUSION MASTER (LP, insert)	20
90	Strange Fruit SFPS 079	PEEL SESSIONS EP (12", p/s)	15

PROPHET
74	UK UK 64	Have Love Will Travel/Blues In B Sharp	40

MICHAEL PROPHET
79	Grove GMDM 17	Turn Me Loose/Praise You Jah Jah (12")	20
79	Grove GMDM 25	Warn Them Jah/Don't Interfere (12")	18
80	Greensleeves GRED 44	Help Them Please/WAILING SOULS : See Baba Joe	20
82	Greensleeves GRED 72	Here Comes The Bride/MYSTIC EYES: Bring The Kuchie Come	20
80	Island/Grove Music 12WIP 6583	Fight to The Top (Discomix)/Love And Unity/Mash Down Rome (12")	20
80	Lovelinch LL 002	True Born African (with Soul Syndicate)/RANKING TOYAN: What A Bam Bam (12")	30
80s	WLN WLN 003	Rock Me Baby/Don't Throw Stone (12")	20
81	Greensleeves GRED 59	Gunman/Cassandra (12")	15
82	Greensleeves GRED 87	Boom Him Up Now/Trouble Nobody (12")	15
82	Greensleeeves GRED 104	Just Talking/Thru Me (with Papa Dimes) (12")	15
80	Island ILPS 9606	SERIOUS REASONING (LP)	18
81	Greensleeves GRED 104	MICHAEL PROPHET (LP)	15

ORVAL PROPHET
63	London HLL 9729	Run Run Run/My Lois And Me	10

REX PROPHET
55	Brunswick OE 9144	CANADIAN PLOWBOY (EP)	10

PROPHETS
78	Grove Music GMDM 12	Give Thanks And Praise/Till I Kiss You (12")	30
79	Grover Music GMDM 4	Blessed Are The Meek (feat Trinity)/TOMMY MCCOOK: Stepping High (12")	25

PROPHETS (JAMAICA)
70	Big Shot BI 554	Crystal Blue Persuasion (Parts 1 & 2)	15
70	Big Shot BI 555	Tumble Time (Parts 1 & 2)	12
70	Big Shot BI 557	Revenge Of Eastwood Version One/Version Two	12
70	Jackpot JP 712	Let's Fall In Love/Purple Moon	30

(see also Lloyd & Prophets, Claudette, Lloyd & Claudette, Patrick & Lloyd)

PROPHETS (U.S.)
69	Mercury MF 1097	I Got The Fever/Soul Control	30
69	Mercury MF 1097	I Got The Fever/Soul Control (DJ copy)	50

(see also Creation [U.S.])

PROS & CONS
66	CBS 202341	Bend It/No Time	7

PROTECTORS
73	Live Wire SON 4004	Loretta/Jump The Sidewalk	15

PROTEGUE (& PRINCE BUSTER'S ALL STARS)
67	Blue Beat BB 398	Foul Dance/PRINCE BUSTER'S ALL STARS: This Is It	25

PROTEX
78	Good Vibrations GOT 6	Don't Ring Me Up/(Just Want) Your Attention/Listening In (wraparound p/s)	20
79	Rough Trade GOT 1	Don't Ring Me Up/(Just Want) Your Attention/Listening In (reissue, 1st pressing, text above telephone p/s)	10
79	Rough Trade GOT 1	Don't Ring Me Up/(Just Want) Your Attention/Listening In (reissue, 2nd pressing, text above telephone p/s)	8
79	Polydor 2059 124	I Can't Cope/Popularity (p/s)	12
79	Polydor 2059 167	I Can Only Dream/Heartache (p/s)	15
80	Polydor 2059 245	A Place In Your Heart/Jeepster (p/s)	15

MINT VALUE £

BRIAN PROTHEROE
| 74 | Chrysalis CHS 2043 | Pinball/Money Love | 5 |

PROTON
| 80 | Ballistic 12BP 264 | We're Funkin'/Make Your Move (Instrumental Version) | 20 |

PROTOS
| 82 | Airship AP 391 | ONE DAY A NEW HORIZON (LP) | 140 |

PROVIDENCE
| 73 | Threshold TH 14 | Fantasy Fugue/Island Of Light | 5 |
| 72 | Threshold THS 9 | EVER SENSE THE DAWN (LP, gatefold sleeve with insert) | 30 |

PROWLER (1)
| 73 | Parlophone R 5986 | Pale Green (Hnmmmm) Driving Man/Jaywick Cowboy | 25 |

PROWLER (2)
| 85 | SRT SRT5KS/368 | Alcatraz/So Lonely (p/s) | 70 |

PRUDES
| 89 | Yo Yo PRU 1 | P.S. I'm Leaving/Lighthouse Keeper's Daughter (p/s, white vinyl) | 5 |

JEANNE PRUETT
| 73 | MCA MU 1209 | Satin Sheeets/Sweet Sweetheart | 6 |

PRUNES
| 70 | Songbird SB 1023 | Come A Little Closer/Come A Little Closer Version II | 5 |
(see also Eric Donaldson, West Indians)

SNOOKY PRYOR
| 70 | Flyright LP 100 | SNOOKY PRYOR (LP) | 15 |

ARTHUR PRYSOCK
65	CBS 201820	It's Too Late, Baby Too Late/My Special Prayer	10
77	Polydor 2058842	When Love Is New/All I Need Is You Tonight	10
66	CBS EP 6076	AGAIN (EP)	15
67	Verve SVLP 9176	MISTER PRYSOCK (LP)	20

RED PRYSOCK
59	Mercury AMT 1028	Chop Suey/Margie	20
58	Mercury MPL 6535	THE BEAT (LP)	50
58	Mercury MPL 6550	FRUIT BOOTS (LP)	40
56	Mercury MPT 7517	JUMP RED JUMP (10" LP)	40

PSEUDO EXISTORS
| 80 | Dead Good DEAD 2 | Pseudo Existence/Coming Up For Air/New Modern Warfare (rubber-stamped folded p/s, pink/white label) | 60 |
| 80 | Dead Good DEAD 2 | Pseudo Existence/Coming Up For Air/New Modern Warfare (rubber-stamped folded p/s, later red/black label & stamped white sleeve) | 35 |

PSYCHEDELIC FURS
79	Epic EPC 8005	We Love You/Pulse (green, pink or orange p/s)	5
81	CBS A 1166	Dumb Waiters/Dash (1st 5,000 with playable p/s)	5
81	CBS A 13 1327	Pretty In Pink/Mack The Knife/Soap Commercial (12", shrinkwrapped with free T-shirt)	8
(see also Unwanted)

PSYCHEOUT
00	Discord DISCORD 002	BOOM EP (12")	15
00	Discord DISCORD 003	WARP EP (12") (12")	60
00	Discord DISCORD 004	TRAIN TRAX EP (12")	15
00	Discord DISCORD 005	SURGE EP (12")	10

PSYCHIC PHENOMENA
| 97 | Lowlife LOW05 | THE WHOLE CIRCUMFERENCE (12", EP) | 25 |

PSYCHIC TV
82	Some Bizzare PTV 1	Just Drifting/Breakthrough (p/s)	10
82	Some Bizzare PTV 1T	Just Drifting/Just Drifting (Midnight) (12", p/s)	15
84	Temple TOPY 001	Unclean/Mirrors (12", p/s)	10
86	Temple TOPYS 009	Godstar/Godstar (BJ Mix)/Discopravity/Yes It's The B Side (double pack, gatefold p/s)	8
86	Temple TOPIC 009	Godstar/Godstar (California Mix) (12", picture disc)	15
86	Temple TOPYD 023	Good Vibrations/Interzone/Roman P/Hex-Sex/Godstar (Ugly Mix)/Je T'Aime (double pack, gatefold p/s)	6
86	Temple TOPYT 023	Roman P (Fireball Mix)/Interzone/Good Vibrations (Kundalini Mix)/Hex-Sex (Voodoo Mix) (12", p/s)	10
88	Temple TOPY 037	Tune In (Turn On To Thee Acide House) (12", p/s, as (Psychic TV/Jack The Tab)	10
88	DC DC 23	Superman/Jack The Tab (12", p/s, no artist credit on label)	15
89	Temple TOPY 048	Love, War, Riot/Eve Of Destruction (Vocoder Mixes) (12", p/s, including sticker)	10
82	Some Bizzare PSY 1	FORCE THE HAND OF CHANCE (LP, with bonus LP & double-sided poster, featuring Marc Almond)	40
83	CBS 25737	DREAMS LESS SWEET (LP, with inner sleeve, some with free 12" EP [XPR 1251])	30
83	CBS 25737	DREAMS LESS SWEET (LP, with inner sleeve)	25
84	Temple TOPY 003	PAGAN DAY (LP, picture disc, 999 copies)	40
84	Gramm GRAMM 23	THOSE WHO DO NOT (2-LP, 5000 copies)	30
85	Temple TOPY 004	THEMES 2 (LP)	15
85	Temple TOPY 008	THEMES 3 (LP)	15
85	Temple TOPIC 010	MOUTH OF THE NIGHT (LP, picture disc)	18
86	Temple TOPIC 009	GODSTAR (LP, with picture disc)	15
87	Temple TOPY 029	LIVE IN GOTTINGEN (LP)	15
88	Temple TOPY 031	PSYCHIC TV (LP, picture disc)	15
88	Temple TOPY 032	ALBUM 10 (LP, picture disc)	15
88	Temple TOPY 038	ALLEGORY AND SELF (LP, blue vinyl)	15
88	Temple TOPY 036	LIVE AT MARDI GRAS (LP)	12
88	Temple TOPY 045	LIVE AT THEE CIRCUS (LP)	12
89	Temple TOPY 045	LIVE AT THEE RITY (LP)	12
89	Temple TOPY 046	KONDOLE / COPYCAT (LP)	12
89	Temple TOPY 047	LIVE AT THE PYRAMID NYC (LP, picture disc)	12
91	Temple TOPY 020	LIVE IN BRENGENZ (LP)	12

PSYCHOPATHS
| 91 | Elicit 12 ELIC 2 | NIGHTMARES (12", no p/s) ....8 |

PSYCHO'S MUM
| 89 | Woronzow W 011 | A SIBILANT SIN (LP, with insert) ....15 |

PSYCOMETRIC
| 97 | Acid Fever MDMA 9701 | Piano Dreams/Funk Bits/The Kaison Ogle/DJ CYCLONE: Spare Parts/Meltdown/Chaos (12") ....12 |

PSYKYK VOLTS
| 79 | Ellie Jay EJPS 9262 | Totally Useless/Horror Story No. 5 (p/s) ....20 |
| 79 | MHG GHM 109 | Totally Useless/Horror Story No. 5 ....35 |

PSYLONS
86	E Type ETYPE 1	The Mockery Of Decline/Clear Sky 10
87	Iron Lung IL 001	All The Things We Need (12", p/s) 15
90	Unsigned UN 001	No Choice (p/s) 8
91	Unsigned UN 002	SAND MAN EP 8

PTOLOMY PSYCON
| 71 | Hollick and Taylor HT/IPS 1306 | LOOSE CAPACITOR (10" LP, 50 only, silkscreened front sleeve, printed back) ....800 |

PUBLIC ENEMY
87	Def Jam 651 245-0	Rebel Without A Pause (Vocal Mix)/(Instrumental) (picture disc) 8
88	Def Jam 652 833-0	Don't Believe The Hype/Prophets Of Rage (p/s, with patch)................................5
88	Def Jam 653 089-7	Night Of The Living Baseheads/Terminator X To The Edge Of Panic (p/s, badge pack)...........5
87	Def Jam 450482-1	YO BUM RUSH THE SHOW (LP, with lyric sheet)..12

PUBLIC FOOT THE ROMAN
| 73 | Sovereign SVNA 7259 | PUBLIC FOOT THE ROMAN (LP, gatefold sleeve)..90 |

(see also Movies)

PUBLIC IMAGE LTD (PIL)
78	Virgin VS 228	Public Image/The Cowboy Song (foldout 'newspaper' p/s) 20
79	Virgin VS 274-12	Death Disco/And No Bird Do Sing (1/2 Mix)/Death Disco Megamix (12", p/s, 5,000 only) ...12
81	Virgin VS 397-12	Flowers Of Romance (Exended Version)/Home Is Where The Heart Is (12", p/s)................8
86	Virgin VSD 855	Home/Round//Rise/Rise (Instrumental) (double pack) 5
87	Virgin VS 988	Seattle/Selfish Rubbish (box set with 7", badge, postcard & sew-on patch) 6
78	Virgin V2114	FIRST ISSUE (with colour inner sleeve and PiL on both labels) 20
79	Virgin METAL 1	METAL BOX (LP, 3 x 12" with circular paper dividers & inner sheet in round tin) 80
79	Virgin VD 2512	SECOND EDITION (standard issue, of Metal Box, 2-LP, gatefold) 18
90	Virgin TPAK 5	METAL BOX (CD, in round tin with insert) 20

(see also Sex Pistols, Jah Wobble, Don Letts & Jah Wobble, Vivien Goldman, Time Zone, Cowboys International)

PUBLIC ZONE
| 77 | Logo GO 104 | Naive/Innocence (p/s) ....6 |

GARY PUCKETT (& UNION GAP)
68	CBS 3365	Young Girl/I'm Losing You (as Union Gap featuring Gary Puckett)............................5
68	CBS 3551	Lady Willpower/Daylight Stranger 5
68	CBS 3714	Over You/If The Day Would Come 7
69	CBS 4122	Don't Give In To Him/Could I 7
69	CBS 4505	This Girl Is A Woman Now/His Other Woman 8
68	CBS (S) 63342	YOUNG GIRL (LP)..20
68	CBS (S) 63429	INCREDIBLE (LP) 20
70	CBS 63794	THE NEW GARY PUCKETT AND THE UNION GAP ALBUM (LP)...........................20

PUDDING
| 67 | Decca F 12603 | The Magic Bus/It's Too Late ....50 |

TITO PUENTE
| 57 | RCA RD 27002 | LET'S CHA-CHA WITH PUENTE (LP) ....12 |
| 58 | RCA SF 5008 | MUCHO PUENTE (LP) ....12 |

PUFFIN CLUB
| 81 | Big Nob NOB 001 | Great Western Revival/Feel So Low/Anhedonia/Set A Table (no p/s, 50 only) ....15 |

DUDU PUKWANA
| 74 | Caroline C1504 | IN THE TOWNSHIPS (LP, as Dudu Pukwana & Spear)......................................20 |
| 83 | Jika ZL 2 | LIFE IN BRACKNELL & WILLISAU (LP, featuring Dinise Saul) ....25 |

LEROY PULLENS
| 66 | London HLR 10056 | I'm A Nut/Knee Deep ....12 |
| 77 | MCA 315 | I'm A Nut/Knee Deep (Reissue) ....5 |

VERNE PULLENS
| 72 | Injun 107 | Mama Don't Allow No Boppin'/Bop Crazy Baby ....15 |
| 72 | Injun 111 | Bop Crazy Baby/Would You Be Happy ....15 |

PULLOVERS
| 80 | Supermusic SUP 24/LYN 8613/4 | Peter Pan Pill/Spare Part Surgery (p/s, some with kidney donor card) ....20 |

PULP

SINGLES
83	Red Rhino RED 32	My Lighthouse (Remix)/Looking For Life (p/s) 60
83	Red Rhino RED 37	Everybody's Problem/There Was (p/s) 50
85	Fire BLAZE 5	Little Girl (With Blue Eyes)/Simultaneous/Blue Glow/The Will To Power (12", p/s) 30
85	Fire BLAZE 5	Little Girl (With Blue Eyes)/Simultaneous/Blue GLow/The Will To Power, 12" promo)...........50
86	Fire BLAZE 10	Dogs Are Everywhere/The Mark Of The Devil/97 Lovers/Aborigine/ Goodnight (12", p/s) ..40
87	Fire BLAZE 17	They Suffocate At Night (Edited Version)/Tunnel (Cut Up Version) (p/s) 15
87	Fire BLAZE 17T	They Suffocate At Night (Uncut Version)/Tunnel (Full Length Version) (12", p/s)............18
87	Fore BLAZE 21T	Masters Of The Universe (Sanitised Vresion)/Manon/Silence (12", promo).....................40
87	Fire BLAZE 21T	Masters Of The Universe (Sanitised Version)/Manon/Silence (12", p/s) 20
90	Fire BLAZE 44T	Is This House?/This House Is Condemned (12" promo, 1-sided) 50
90	Fire BLAZE 44T	My Legendary Girlfriend/Is This House?/This House Is Condemned (12", p/s) 10
91	Fire BLAZE 51T	Countdown/Death Goes To The Disco/Countdown (Radio Edit) (12", p/s) 10
92	Gift GIF 1	O.U. (Gone Gone)/Space/O.U. (Gone Gone) (Radio Edit) 12" promo & press sheet) 40
92	Gift GIF 1	O.U. (Gone Gone)/Space/O.U. (Gone Gone) (Radio Edit) (12", p/s) 8

92	Gift GIF 1CD	O.U. (Gone Gone) (Radio Edit)/Space/O.U. (Gone Gone) (CD) 15
92	Caff CAFF 17	My Legendary Girlfriend/Sickly Grin/Back In L.A. (foldover p/s with insert in poly bag, 500 only) 50
92	Fire BLAZE 44CD	My Legendary Girlfriend/Is This House?/This House Is Condemned (CD) 20
92	GIF 3	Babies/Styloroc (Nites Of Suburbia)/Sheffield : Sex City (12" promo with press sheet)........40
92	Gift GIF 3	Babies/Styloroc (Nites Of Suburbia)/Sheffield: Sex City (12", p/s) 15
92	Gift GIF 3CD	Babies/Styloroc (Nites Of Suburbia)/Sheffield: Sex City/ Sheffield: Sex City (Instrumental) (CD, card sleeve) 10
93	Gift 7GIF6	Razzmatazz/Inside Susan/59 Lyndhurst Grove (p/s) 8
93	Gidt GIF 6	Razzmatazz/Inside Susan : A Story In 3 Songs (Stacks/Inside Susan/59 Lyndhurst Grove) (12" promo with press sheet) 40
93	Gift GIF 6CD	Razzmatazz/Inside Susan: A Story In 3 Songs (Stacks/Inside Susan/ 59 Lyndhurst Grove) (CD) 10
93	Island IS 567	Lipgloss/You're A Nightmare (p/s) 6
94	Island IS 595	THE SISTERS EP 8
94	Island 12IS 595	THE SISTERS EP (12", p/s with print) 8
96	Island ISC 613	Common People/Underwear (reissue, yellow vinyl) 20
96	Island ISC 620	Sorted For E's And Whizz/Miss-Shapes (reissue, blue vinyl)...........................12
96	Island ISC 567	Lipgloss/You're A Nightmare (p/s, reissue, red vinyl)....................................6
96	Island ISC 574	Do You Remember The First Time/Street Lites (reissue, brown vinyl, p/s) 10
96	Island ISC 595	THE SISTERS EP (p/s, reissue, white vinyl) 8
96	Island ISC 623	Disco 2000/Ansaphone (orange vinyl) 15

ALBUMS

84	Red Rhino REDLP 29	IT (mini-LP) 40
87	Fire FIRELP 5	FREAKS (LP) 20
92	Fire FIRE 11026	SEPARATIONS (LP) 15
93	Island ILPM 2076	INTRO (LP) 20
94	Island ILPS 8025	HIS 'N' HERS (LP) 20
94	Fire FIRE LP 36	MASTERS OF THE UNIVERSE (PULP ON FIRE 1985-86) 50
94	Cherry Red CDMRED 112	IT (CD, with extra tracks, withdrawn, 1,000 only) 20
95	Island ILPS 8041	DIFFERENT CLASS (LP, die-cut sleeve with 12 inserts) 100
95	Island ILPS 8041	DIFFERENT CLASS (LP, with 1 insert) 50
96	Nectar NTMLP 521	COUNTDOWN 1992-1983 (LP) 20
98	Island ILPSD 8066	THIS IS HARDCORE (2 x LP, gatefold, with insert) 40
99	Cooking Vinyl COOK CD 178	PULPED 93-92 (4-CD box set with booklet) 30
01	Island ILPS 8110	WE LOVE LIFE (LP) 20

PULP MUSIC

79	Pulp Music PB 1	Low Flying Aircraft/Something Just Behind My Back/So Lo (blank labels, some numbered up to 2,000 & signed, with handmade sleeve) 25
79	Pulp Music PB 1	Low Flying Aircraft/Something Just Behind My Back/So Lo (blank labels, some numbered up to 2,000 & signed) 20
77	MCA 315	I'm A Nut/Knee Deep (Reissue) 5

PULSAR

| 76 | Decca SKL-R 5228 | POLLEN (LP) ....20 |
| 77 | Decca TXS 119 | STRANDS OF THE FUTURE (LP, gatefold sleeve)..25 |

PULSE

| 70 | Major Minor SMLP 64 | PULSE (LP)..50 |

PUMPHOUSE GANG

| 77 | Kitsch FAD 1 | Motorcity Fantasy/Cocaine (p/s) ....7 |

(see also Slush)

PUNCHERS

| 70 | Punch PH 46 | Sons Of Thunder (actually by Lee Perry & The Upsetters)/ Only If You Understand.............22 |

PUNCHIN' JUDY

| 73 | Transatlantic TRA 272 | PUNCHIN' JUDY (LP, laminated front sleeve) ....20 |

(see also Downliner Sect)

PUNCTURE

| 77 | Small Wonder SMALL 1 | Mucky Pup/Can't Rock'n'Roll (p/s)...20 |

PUNISHMENT OF LUXURY

78	Small Wonder SMALL 8	Puppet Life/The Demon (p/s)..8
79	United Artists UP 36507	Engine Of Excess/Jellyfish (p/s) 6
79	United Artists UP 36537	Secrets/Brainbomb (p/s) 6
80	United Artists BP 317	Laughing Academy/Baby Don't Jump (p/s) 6
79	United Artists UAG 30258	LAUGHING ACADEMY (LP, with inner sleeve)...15
83	Red Rhino REDLP 34	7 (LP)...12

PUNKETTES

| 77 | Response SR 511 | Going Out Wiv A Punk/Polythene ....25 |

PUPILS

| 66 | Wing WL 1150 | A TRIBUTE TO THE ROLLING STONES (LP) ....40 |
| 69 | Fontana SFL 13087 | A TRIBUTE TO THE ROLLING STONES (LP, reissue) ....15 |

(see also Eyes)

PUPPETS

63	Pye 7N 15556	Poison Ivy/Everybody's Talking 60
64	Pye 7N 15625	Shake With Me/Three Boys Looking For Love (existence unconfirmed) 0
64	Pye 7N 15634	Baby Don't Cry/Shake With Me...60

DANNY PURCHES

| 55 | Columbia SCM 5183 | Mama/Just One More Time ....8 |

(BERNARD) PRETTY PURDEY

68	Direction 58-3301	Funky Donkey/Caravan 15
68	Direction 58-3628	Soul Clappin'/Blow Your Lid 15
71	Philips 6073 708	Good Livin' Good Lovin'/Day Dreaming 6
68	Direction 8-63290	SOUL DRUMS (LP) 40
71	Philips 6369 421	SOUL IS ... (LP) 20

PURE GOLD

| 69 | President PT 250 | Fairground/You've Gotta Give It Time ....10 |

PURE HELL
| 78 | Golden Sphinx GSX 002 | These Boots Are Made For Walking/No Rules (p/s) | 20 |

PURE LOVE & PLEASURE
| 70 | Stateside SSL 5026 | A RECORD OF PURE LOVE AND PLEASURE (LP) | 30 |

PURE REASON REVOLUTION
| 04 | Poptones MC50896 | Apprentice Of The Universe/Nimos & Tambos (p/s) | 5 |

PURESSENCE
| 92 | Damn Loud 2DM01 | PETROL SKIN (EP, 1,000 only) | 30 |
| 93 | Damn Loud 2DM02 | OFFSHORE (EP, 1,000 only) | 30 |

PURGE
| 69 | Corn CP 101 | The Mayor Of Simpleton Hall/The Knave (p/s) | 200 |
| 69 | Corn CP 101 | The Mayor Of Simpleton Hall/The Knave (without p/s) | 90 |

JAMES & BOBBY PURIFY
66	Stateside SS 547	I'm Your Puppet/So Many Reasons	20
67	Stateside SS 595	Wish You Didn't Have To Go/You Can't Keep A Good Man Down	15
67	Stateside SS 2016	Shake A Tail Feather/Goodness Gracious	25
67	Stateside SS 2039	I Take What I Want/Sixteen Tons	12
67	Stateside SS 2049	Let Love Come Between Us/I Don't Want To Have To Wait	25
68	Stateside SS 2093	Do Unto Me/Everybody Needs Somebody	20
68	Bell BLL 1008	I Can't Remember/I Was Born To Lose Out	10
68	Bell BLL 1024	Help Yourself To All My Lovin'/Last Piece Of Love	10
69	Bell BLL 1043	Untie Me/We're Finally Gonna Make It	8
69	Bell BLL 1056	Let Love Come Between Us/Shake A Tail Feather	10
69	Bell BLL 1067	Do Unto Me/Wish You Didn't Have To Go	8
72	Mojo 2092 056	I'm Your Puppet/Wish You Didn't Have To Go	8
67	Stateside SL 10206	JAMES AND BOBBY PURIFY (LP)	60
67	Bell MBLL/SBLL 101	THE PURE SOUND OF THE PURIFYS (LP)	40

PURITAN GUITARS
| 80 | Riverside Records | £100 In 15 MInutes/Making It (p/s, stamped white labels) | 20 |

ALTON PURNELL
| 70 | Dixie DIX 4 | TRAVELLING LIGHT (LP) | 30 |

(see also Bonnie Raitt)

PURPLE ALGAE
| 95 | Poor Person Prod. PPPR 7 | ADRIFT ON A SEA OF SOUND (LP, handmade sleeve & 2 inserts, no'd, 500 only) | 15 |

PURPLE GANG
67	Big T BIG 101	Granny Takes A Trip/Bootleg Whisky	15
68	Big T BIG 111	Kiss Me Goodnight Sally Green/Auntie Monica	7
68	Transatlantic TRA 174	THE PURPLE GANG STRIKES (LP)	60

PURPLE HAZE
| 85 | S.R.S. SRS 6 | Hear It On The Radio (p/s) | 55 |

PURPLE HEARTS
79	Fiction FICS 003	Millions Like Us/Beat That! (p/s)	10
79	Fiction FICS 007	Frustration/Extraordinary Sensations (p/s)	10
80	Fiction FICS 9	Jimmy/What Am I Gonna Do (p/s)	10
80	Safari SAFE 30	My Life's A Jigsaw/The Guy Who Made Her A Star/Just To Please You (in foldout jigsaw p/s)	12
80	Safari SAFE 30	My Life's A Jigsaw/The Guy Who Made Her A Star/Just To Please You	8
82	Road Runner RR 1	Plane Crash/Scooby Doo/Gun Of Life (p/s)	12
86	UNICORN PHZ3	Friends Again/Head On Collision Time (p/s)	8
80	Fiction FIX 002/2383 568	BEAT THAT! (LP)	20
85	Razor RAZS 13	HEAD ON COLLISION TIME (LP)	12
85	Razor RAZS 19	POPISH FRENZY (LP)	12

(see also Bob Manton, Rage)

PURPLE WINE
| 71 | The Mental Health Council | It's My Mind/I'm Lonely/Friends (p/s) | 80 |

PURSUIT OF COLOUR
| 84 | Colour | LOVE PLAYS EGO: Can't Let You Go/Radomontade (b/w, p/s allegedly 50 copies only) | 200 |

GEOFF PURVIS
| 77 | Fellside FE 003 | THE BORDER FIDDLER (LP) | 12 |

PUSSY (1)
| 69 | Morgan Bluetown BT 5002 | PUSSY PLAYS (LP) | 1200 |
| 09 | Morgan Bluetown BT 5002 | PUSSY PLAYS (LP, reissue by Secret Records/Record Collector, 350 only with signed and numbered laminated insert) | 35 |

(see also Angel Pavement, Fortes Mentum)

PUSSY (2)
| 72 | Deram DM 368 | Feline Woman/Ska Child | 25 |

(see also Jerusalem)

PUSSYFOOT
66	Decca F 12474	Freeloader/Things That Still Remind Me	25
67	Decca F 12561	Mr Hyde/Hasty Words	30
67	Pye 7N 17395	Dee Dee Do Your Dance/Big Brown Eyes	30
68	Pye 7N 17520	Good Times/Till You Don't Want Me Anymore	25

(see also Rare Breed)

PUSSY GALORE
87	Vinyl Drip SUK 001	GROOVY HATE FUCK (LP)	20
87	Product Inc. 33PROD 19	RIGHT NOW (LP)	12
89	Product INCLP 1	DIAL M FOR MOTHERFUCKER (LP)	12

(see also Jon Spencer Blues Explosion)

ASHA PUTHLI
| 76 | CBS 4623 | The Devil Is Loose/Space Talk | 10 |
| 73 | CBS 65804 | ASHA PUTHLI (LP) | 20 |

MINT VALUE £

75	CBS 80978	SHE LOVES TO HEAR THE MUSIC (LP)	15
76	CBS 81443	THE DEVIL IS LOOSE (LP)	30

PUTNEY BRIDGE
71	Chapter One CH 145	Take A Ride/Road To Purity	10

PUZZLE
69	Stateside SS 2146	Hey Medusa/Make The Children Happy	25
72	Jam JAM 1	Houla/Do You Feel The Pain	40
69	Stateside SSL 10285	PUZZLE (LP)	40

PVC 2
77	Zoom ZUM 2	Put You In The Picture/Pain/Deranged, Demented and Free (p/s)	8

(see also Midge Ure, Zones)o

PYEWACKET
81	Dingles DIN 312	PYEWACKET (LP)	12
83	Familiar FAM 43	THE MAN IN THE MOON DRINKS CLARET (LP)	12

PYLON
80	Armageddon ARM 1	Cool/Dub/Driving School/Danger!! (10")	10

PYLONS
80	Hi Voltage HVVS 701	Marvel World/Spoof (p/s)	30

NATASHA PYNE
66	Polydor 56713	It's All In Your Head/I'm A Dreamer	15

PYRAMID
67	Deram DM 111	Summer Of Last Year/Summer Evening	50

(see also Fairport Convention, Ian Matthews)

PYRAMIDS (JAMAICA)
67	President PT 161	Train Tour To Rainbow City/John Chewey	20
68	President PT 177	Wedding In Peyton Place/Girls Girls Girls	10
68	President PT 195	All Change On The Bakerloo Line/Playing Games	10
68	President PT 206	Mexican Moonlight/Mule	10
68	President PT 225	Tisko My Darling/Movement All Around	10
69	President PT 243	Do-Re-Mi/I'm Outnumbered	10
69	President PT 274	I'm A Man/Dragon Fly	10
69	Doctor Bird DB 1307	Stay With Him/Chicken Mary	20
70	Duke DU 80	Geronimo/Feel Alright	10
70	Trojan TR 7755	Feel Alright/Telstar	8
70	Trojan TR 7770	To Sir With Love/Reggae Shuffle	8
71	Trojan TR 7803	All For You/All For You Version	8
71	Creole CR 1003	Mosquito Bite/Mother's Bath	8
68	President PTL 1021	THE PYRAMIDS (LP)	70

(see also Symarip, Equals, Little Grants & Eddie, Seven Letters, Bruce Ruffin)

PYRAMIDS (U.S.)
64	London HLU 9847	Penetration/Here Comes Marsha	50

PYTHAGORAS THEOREM
70	Pye 7N 17924	Give A Damn/London Bridge	12
70	Pye 7N 17990	Our House/Free Like Me	7

PYTHON LEE JACKSON
76	Young Blood YB 1077	The Blues/Cloud Nine	10
80	Young Blood YB 0089	In A Broken Dream/The Blues	6
80	Young Blood YEP 89	In A Broken Dream (mono)/In A Broken Dream (stereo)/The Blues/ Cloud Nine (EP, "Kelly Girl" Employment Agency advert on p/s)	10

(see also Rod Stewart)

Q

QPR
67	Eyemark EMS 1008	QPR The Greatest/Supporters Supprt Us	45

Q-PROJECT
92	QTIP 001	FREESTYLE FANATIC EP (12", stamped white label, 4 untitled tracks)	39
93	Legend LEG 001	Return Of Q Project/Champion Sound/Night Moves (12")	20

QRUUX ADU XA
82	Shooting Star STAR 007	Shakin' All Over/Robotics (p/s, as K.A.D.)	15

QTS
79	SRT SRTS/79/CUS 429	SAVAGE IN THE CITY EP	35

QUAD
97	Acme AC 8020LP	QUAD (LP, clear vinyl in printed clear PVC cover)	30
97	Prescription DRUG 3	QUAD (LP, 99 copies only, handmade sleeve with colour photo, mail-order only)	50

(see also Sun Dial)

QUADROPHONICS
75	Contempo 2054	Betcha If You Check It Out/Prove My Love To You	15

QUADS
80s	Big Bear BB29	UFO/Astronaut's Journey (p/s)	10

CHRISTINE QUAITE
62	Oriole CB 1739	Guilty Eyes/Oh My!	20
62	Oriole CB 1772	Your Nose Is Gonna Grow/Our Last Chance	20
63	Oriole CB 1845	Mister Heartache/Whisper Wonderful Words	20
63	Oriole CB 1876	In The Middle Of The Floor/Tell Me Mama	60

63	Oriole CB 1921	I Believe In Love/Here She Comes	20
64	Oriole CB 1945	Mister Stuck Up/Will You Be The Same Tomorrow	20
65	Stateside SS 435	If You've Got A Heart/So Near So Far	20
66	Stateside SS 482	Long After Tonight Is All Over/I'm Hoping	50
66	Stateside SS 482	Long After Tonight Is All Over/I'm Hoping (DJ copy)	100

QUAKER CITY BOYS

59	London HLU 8796	Teasin'/Won't Y' Come Out, Mary Ann	15
59	London HLU 8796	Teasin'/Won't Y' Come Out, Mary Ann (78)	12

QUAKERS

65	Oriole CB 1992	I'm Ready/Down The Road A Piece	200
65	Studio 36 KSP 109/110	She's Alright/Talk To Me (only 50 pressed)	600

QUALITY DRIVEL

81	No Cure WHOOP 1	SUBLIMINAL CUTS EP (p/s)	30

QUANDO QUANGO

84	Factory FAC 102	Atom Rock (p/s)	6
85	Factory FAC 137	Genius/This Feeling (p/s)	6
85	Factory FACT 110	PIGS & BATTLESHIPS (LP)	18
85	Factory FACT 110c	PIGS & BATTLESHIPS (cassette, with postcards)	18

QUANTIC

00	Breakin' Bread BNB 002	We Got Soul/Fresh Rhythm	25
01	Tru Thoughts TRU 014	Life In The Rain/Common Knowledge/Time Is The Enemy (12")	15
01	Tru Thoughts TRU LP 016	THE 5TH EXOTIC (2xLP)	40
02	Tru Thoughts TRU LP 034	APRICOT MORNING (2xLP)	30
04	Tru Thoughts TRU LP 062	MISHAPS HAPPENING (2xLP)	15

QUANTIC SOUL ORCHESTRA

01	Tru Thoughts TRU7 018	Super 8 (Part 1)/Super 8 (Part 2)	12
02	Tru Thoughts TRU7 023	Assassin (Part 1)/Assassin (Part 2)	5
03	Tru Thoughts TRU7 051	Pushin' On/Pushin' On My Thing	8
03	Tru Thoughts TRU7 055	Babarabatiri/The Conspirator	10
03	Tru Thoughts TRU LP 029	STAMPEDE (LP)	15
05	Tru Thoughts TRU LP 074	PUSHIN' ON (LP)	12

QUARRY MEN

58	'P.F. Phillips Kensington'	That'll Be The Day/In Spite Of All The Danger (78 rpm shellac acetate, handwritten labels, 1 copy only, owned by Paul McCartney)	200000
81	'Percy Philips, Kensington'	That'll Be The Day/In Spite Of All The Danger (78rpm, private pressing reproduction of 1958 demo disc, repro Parlophone co. sleeve, 25 only)	10000
81	'Percy Philips, Kensington'	That'll Be The Day/In Spite Of All The Danger (45rpm, private pressing reproduction of 1958 demo disc, repro Parlophone co. sleeve, 25 only)	10000

(see also Beatles, Trad Grads)

QUARTER NOTES

57	Parlophone R 4365	My Fantasy/Ten Minutes To Midnight	15

JOE QUARTERMAN & FREE SOUL

73	GSF GSZ 3	So Much Trouble In My Mind (Parts 1 & 2)	8
74	GSF GSZ 12	Thanks Dad Parts 1 & 2	5
73	GSF GS 504	JOE QUARTERMAN & FREE SOUL (LP)	50

QUARTET

69	Decca F12974	Now/Will My Lady Come	8
70	Decca F13072	Mama Where Did You Fail/Joseph	10

QUARTZ

77	Jet UP 36290	Sugar Rain/Street Fighting Lady/Mainline Riders	15
77	Jet UP 36317	Street Fighting Lady/Mainline Riders	12
80	Reddingtons R.R. DAN 1	Nantucket Sleighride/Wildfire (p/s, white or blue vinyl)	10
80	Reddingtons R.R. DAN 1	Nantucket Sleighride/Wildfire (p/s, black vinyl)	5
80	Jet SJET 189	Street Fighting Lady/Mainline Riders (p/s, reissue, demos £15)	10
80	Logo GO 387	Satan's Serenade/Bloody Fool (p/s)	5
80	Logo GOT 387	Satan's Serenade/Bloody Fool/Roll Over Beethoven (live) (12", p/s, blue vinyl)	25
80	Logo GOT 387	Satan's Serenade/Bloody Fool/Roll Over Beethoven (live) (12", p/s, red vinyl)	18
80	MCA MCA 642	Stoking The Fires Of Hell/Circles (p/s)	10
80	Logo MOGO 4007	LIVE QUARTZ (12" EP)	18
81	MCA MCA 661	Stand Up And Fight/Charlie Snow (p/s)	18
83	Heavy Metal HEAVY 17	Tell Me Why/Streetwalker (p/s)	7
77	Jet UAG 30081	QUARTZ (LP, with inner sleeve)	50
79	Jet JETLP 233	DELETED (LP, in sealed brown paper bag with insert. Reissue of 1st LP)	18
80	Reddingtons R.R. REDD 001	QUARTZ LIVE - COUNT DRACULA (LP, in b&w 'live' sleeve)	15
80	Reddingtons R.R. REDD 001	QUARTZ LIVE - COUNT DRACULA (LP)	12
80	Logo MOGO 4007	LIVE QUARTZ (LP)	12
80	MCA MCF 3080	STAND UP AND FIGHT (LP, with lyric insert)	25
83	Heavy Metal HMRLP 9	AGAINST ALL ODDS (LP, with inner sleeve)	12
83	Heavy Metal HMRPD 9	AGAINST ALL ODDS (LP, picture disc)	25

(see also Black Sabbath, Copperfield, Bandy Legs)

QUASAR

82	Q QUA 1	FIRE IN THE SKY (LP, with insert)	20

(see also Solstice)

QUATERMASS (1)

70	Harvest SVHL 775	QUATERMASS (LP, gatefold sleeve, no EMI logo on label)	200
75	Harvest SHSM 2002	QUATERMASS (LP, reissue, different sleeve)	25

(see also Ian Gillan Band, Episode Six, Hard Stuff)

QUATERMASS (2)

97	Metropolitan MM 027	The Judgement (12", no p/s)	15

QUATOR

72	BBC RESL 6	Spy Trap/Playgirl	30

QUATRAIN

69	Polydor 583 743	QUATRAIN (LP)	50

MINT VALUE £

SUZI QUATRO

72	Rak RAK 134	Rolling Stone/Brain Confusion (For All The Lonely People)	30
75	Rak RAK 200	I Bit Off More Than I Could Chew/Red Hot Rosie	5
75	Rak RAK 215	I May Be Too Young/Don't Mess Around	5
75	Rak RAK 256	Roxy Roller/I'll Grow On You	5
73	Rak PSR 355	Primitive Love/Shakin' All Over (promo only)	30
78	Rak RAK 285	Stumblin' In/Stranger With You (with Chris Norman) (2 different p/s)	5
79	Rak RAK 299	She's In Love With You/Space Cadets (p/s)	5
87	Hackenbacker HACK 101	Am I Dreaming/Who Needs Chairs/Will You Take This Woman (only available at pantomime show)	10

QUBISM

94	em:t 2294	QUBISM (CD, digipak)	50

QUEEN
SINGLES

98	Parlophone QUEEN PD28	Under Pressure (picture disc)	8
96	Parlophone 12QUEEN25	You Don't Fool Me (Remixes) 12"	8
73	EMI EMI 2036	Keep Yourself Alive/Son And Daughter	40
74	EMI EMI 2121	Seven Seas Of Rhye/See What A Fool I've Been	5
74	EMI EMI 2229	Killer Queen/Flick Of The Wrist	5
75	EMI EMI 2256	Now I'm Here/Lily Of The Valley	5
75	EMI EMI 2375	Bohemian Rhapsody/I'm In Love With My Car (p/s; beware counterfeits with 'computer-scanned' logo)	30
76	EMI EMI 2565	Somebody To Love/White Man (p/s, beware of counterfeit sleeves)	10
77	EMI EMI 2593	Tie Your Mother Down/You And I	8
77	EMI EMI 2623	QUEEN'S FIRST EP: Good Old Fashioned Lover Boy/Death On Two Legs/ Tenement Funster/White Queen (As It Began) (p/s)	10
77	EMI EMI 2708	We Are The Champions/We Will Rock You (p/s)	8
78	EMI EMI 2575	Spread Your Wings/Sheer Heart Attack (p/s)	6
78	EMI EMI 2870	Bicycle Race/Fat Bottomed Girls (p/s)	6
78	EMI EMI 2870	Bicycle Race/Fat Bottomed Girls (different p/s for export to Belgium)	200
79	EMI EMI 2910	Don't Stop Me Now/In Only Seven Days (p/s)	6
79	EMI EMI 2959	Love Of My Life (live)/Now I'm Here (live)	18
79	EMI EMI 5001	Crazy Little Thing Called Love/We Will Rock You (live) (p/s)	5
80	EMI EMI 5022	Save Me/Let Me Entertain You (live) (p/s)	5
80	EMI EMI 5076	Play The Game/A Human Body (p/s, beige label with red 'EMI' logo or white label with large black 'Queen' logo)	6
80	EMI EMI 5102	Another One Bites The Dust/Dragon Attack (p/s)	8
82	EMI EMI 5293	Body Language/Life Is Real (Song For Lennon) (p/s)	6
82	EMI EMI 5316	Las Palabras De Amor (The Words Of Love)/Cool Cat (p/s)	6
82	EMI EMI 5325	Backchat/Staying Power (p/s)	10
82	EMI 12EMI 5325	Backchat (Extended)/Staying Power (12", p/s)	20
84	EMI 12QUEEN 1	Radio Ga Ga (Ext. Version)/Radio Ga Ga (Instrumental)/I Go Crazy (12", p/s)	10
84	EMI QUEEN 2	I Want To Break Free (Remix)/Machines (Back To Humans) ('Freddie' p/s, gold lettering)	12
84	EMI QUEEN 2	I Want To Break Free (Remix)/Machines (Back To Humans) ('Freddie' p/s, white lettering)	8
84	EMI QUEEN 2	I Want To Break Free (Remix)/Machines (Back To Humans) ('Brian', p/s, with gold lettering)	12
84	EMI QUEEN 2	I Want To Break Free (Remix)/Machines (Back To Humans) ('Roger', p/s, with gold lettering)	15
84	EMI QUEEN 2	I Want To Break Free (Remix)/Machines (Back To Humans) ('John' p/s, with gold lettering)	18
84	EMI 12QUEEN 2	I Want To Break Free (Extended Remix)/Machines (Back To Humans) (12", p/s, with red background with gold lettering)	20
84	EMI 12QUEEN 2	I Want To Break Free (Extended Remix)/Machines (Back To Humans) (12", p/s, with red background with black lettering)	12
84	EMI 12QUEEN 2	I Want To Break Free (Extended Remix)/Machines (Back To Humans) (12", p/s, with white background)	10
84	EMI QUEEN 3	It's A Hard Life/Is This The World We Created...? (p/s)	6
84	EMI QUEEN 3	It's A Hard Life/Is This The World We Created...? ('Roger Taylor' overprinted photo p/s)	20
84	EMI 12QUEEN 3	It's A Hard Life (Extended)/It's A Hard Life/ Is This The World We Created...? (12")	25
84	EMI 12QUEENP 3	It's A Hard Life/Is This The World We Created...? (12", picture disc)	20
84	EMI QUEEN 4	Hammer To Fall (Edit)/Tear It Up ('live' p/s, withdrawn)	100
84	EMI QUEEN 4	Hammer To Fall (Edit)/Tear It Up (red p/s)	6
84	EMI 12 QUEEN 4	Hammer To Fall (The Headbangers Mix)/Tear It Up (12", 'live' p/s, withdrawn)	100
84	EMI 12 QUEEN 4	Hammer To Fall (The Headbangers Mix)/Tear It Up (12", red p/s)	12
84	EMI QUEEN 5	Man On The Prowl/Keep Passing The Open Windows (unreleased, white label test pressings only)	150
84	EMI QUEEN 5	Thank God It's Christmas/Man On The Prowl/ Keep Passing The Open Windows (p/s)	8
84	EMI 12QUEEN 5	Thank God It's Christmas/Man On The Prowl (Extended Version)/ Keep Passing The Open Windows (Extended Version) (12", p/s)	10
84	EMI G 45 1	You're My Best Friend/Killer Queen (re-issue, Golden 45's series)	20
85	EMI QUEEN 6	One Vision (7" Mix)/Blurred Vision (p/s, with red lyric inner sleeve)	7
85	EMI QUEEN 6	One Vision (7" Mix)/Blurred Vision (p/s)	5
85	EMI 12QUEEN 6	One Vision (Extended Vision)/Blurred Vision (12", p/s, with red lyric inner sleeve)	12
85	EMI 12QUEEN 6	One Vision (Extended Vision)/Blurred Vision (12", p/s)	10
85	EMI 12QUEEN 6	One Vision (Extended Vision)/Blurred Vision (12", printed PVC sleeve & red inner)	20
86	EMI 12QUEEN 7	A Kind Of Magic (Ext. Version)/A Dozen Red Roses For My Darling (12", p/s)	12
86	EMI 12QUEENP7	A Kind Of Magic (Extended Version)/Don't Lose Your Head (Instrumental Version) (12", picture disc)	35
86	EMI QUEEN 8	Friends Will Be Friends/Seven Seas Of Rhye (p/s)	6
86	EMI QUEEN P8	Friends Will Be Friends/Seven Seas Of Rhye (picture disc)	40
86	EMI 12QUEEN 8	Friends Will Be Friends (Extended Version)/Friends Will Be Friends (7" Version)/Seven Seas Of Rhye (12", p/s)	10
86	EMI QUEEN 9	Who Wants To Live Forever/Killer Queen (p/s)	8
86	EMI 12QUEEN 9	Who Wants To Live Forever (7" Version)/(Album Version)/Killer Queen/ Who Wants To Live Forever (Piano Version) (12", p/s)	15
89	Parlophone 12QUEEN 10	I Want It All (Single Version)/Hang On In There/ I Want It All (Album Version) (12", p/s)	12
89	Parlophone CDQUEEN 10	I Want It All (Album Version)/Hang On In There/I Want It All (Single Version) (CD, picture disc)	20
89	Parlophone QUEEN PD 11	Breakthru' (7" Mix)/Stealin' (shaped picture disc, 12" PVC sleeve with insert)	20
89	Parlophone QUEEN PD 11	Breakthru' (7" Mix)/Stealin' (uncut picture disc, 12" PVC sleeve with insert)	120

89	Parlophone 12QUEEN 11	Breakthru' (12" Version)/Breakthru' (Single Version)/Stealin' (12", p/s) 8
89	Parlophone CD QUEEN 11	Breakthru' (12" Version)/Stealin'/Breakthru' (7" Mix) (CD) 25
89	Parlophone QUEEN 12	The Invisible Man/Hijack My Heart (black vinyl, p/s)...............5
89	Parlophone QUEEN X12	The Invisible Man/Hijack My Heart (clear vinyl, p/s)...............12
89	Parlophone 12QUEEN 12	The Invisible Man (12" Version)/(7" Version)/Hijack My Heart (12", p/s) 12
89	Parlophone 12QUEENX12	The Invisible Man (12" Version)/The Invisible Man (7" Version)/ Hijack My Heart (12", clear vinyl, PVC sleeve with insert)...............20
89	Parlophone CD QUEEN 12	The Invisible Man (12" Version)/Hijack My Heart/ The Invisible Man (Single Version) (CD)...............30
89	Parlophone QUEEN 14	Scandal/My Life Has Been Saved (p/s)...............8
89	Parlophone QUEEN P14	Scandal/My Life Has Been Saved (poster p/s)...............20
89	Parlophone 12QUEEN 14	Scandal (12" Version)/Scandal (7" Version)/My Life Has Been Saved (12", p/s) 10
89	Parlophone 12QUEENS 14	Scandal (12" Version)/My Life Has Been Saved/Scandal (7" Version)/ (12", p/s, 1-sided, B-side etched with group's signatures)...............20
89	Parlophone CD QUEEN 14	Scandal (12" Version)/My Life Has Been Saved/Scandal (7" Version) (CD) 25
89	Parlophone QUEEN 15	The Miracle/Stone Cold Crazy (live) (p/s) 8
89	Parlophone QUEEN H15	The Miracle/Stone Cold Crazy (live) (orange hologram p/s) 15
89	Parlophone QUEEN H15	The Miracle/Stone Cold Crazy (live) (proof sleeve with negative hologram p/s)...............300
89	Parlophone 12QUEEN 15	The Miracle/Stone Cold Crazy (live)/My Melancholy Blues (live) (12", yellow p/s)...............15
89	Parlophone 12QUEENP 15	The Miracle/Stone Cold Crazy (live)/My Melancholy Blues (live) (12", turquoise p/s with insert print)...............18
89	Parlophone QUEENCD 15	The Miracle/Stone Cold Crazy (live)/My Melancholy Blues (live) (CD) 30
89	Parlophone QUEEN 16	Innuendo/Bijou (p/s) 6
91	Parlophone 12QUEEN 16	Innuendo (Explosive Version)/Under Pressure/Bijou (12", p/s)...............8
91	Parl. 12QUEEN PD16	Innuendo (Explosive Version)/Under Pressure/Bijou (12", picture disc, PVC sleeve with insert)...............20
91	Parlophone QUEEN 17	I'm Going Slightly Mad/The Hitman (p/s) 5
91	Parlophone QUEEN PD 17	I'm Going Slightly Mad/The Hitman (shaped picture disc with insert)...............20
91	Parlophone QUEEN PD 17	I'm Going Slightly Mad/The Hitman (uncut picture disc with insert) 125
91	Parlophone 12QUEEN 17	I'm Going Slightly Mad/The Hitman/Lost Opportunity (12", gatefold p/s) 15
91	Parlophone CDQUEEN 17	I'm Going Slightly Mad/The Hitman/Lost Opportunity (CD)...............10
91	Parlophone 12QUEEN PD18	Headlong/All God's People/Mad The Swine (12", clear vinyl picture disc, with insert in PVC sleeve)...............15
91	Parlophone CD QUEEN 18	Headlong/All God's People/Mad The Swine (CD) 10
91	Parlophone QUEEN 19	The Show Must Go On/Keep Yourself Alive (p/s)...............5
91	Parlophone QUEEN C19	The Show Must Go On/Keep Yourself Alive (cassette) 15
91	Parlophone 12QUEENSG 19	The Show Must Go On/Keep Yourself Alive/Queen Talks (12", 1-sided, B-side etched with group's signatures, gatefold p/s)...............18
91	Parlophone CDQUEEN 19	The Show Must Go On/Keep Yourself Alive/Queen Talks/Body Language (CD)...............10
91	Parlophone CDQUEENS 19	The Show Must Go On/Now I'm Here/Fat Bottomed Girls/Las Palabras De Amor (The Words Of Love) (CD, in box with foldout poster, 10,000 only)...............20
91	Parlophone QUEEN 19/20	The Show Must Go On/Bohemian Rhapsody (unissued, no p/s)...............500
93	Parlophone CDR 6340	FIVE LIVE EP: Killer/Papa Was A Rolling Stone (PM Dawn Remix)/ Somebody To Love/These Are The Days Of Our Lives (as Queen featuring George Michael & Lisa Stansfield) (CD, picture disc, silver inlay) 8
95	Parlophone QUEENLH 24	Let Me Live/Fat Bottomed Girls (Jukebox 45, black vinyl no p/s) 15
96	Parlophone QUEEN 23	Too Much Love Will Kill You/We Will Rock You/We Are The Champions (p/s, pink vinyl)...............6
96	Parlophone QUEENPD 24	Let Me Live/Fat Bottomed Girls/Bicycle Race (picture disc with poster) 6
96	Parlophone 12QUEEN25	You Don't Fool Me - Remixes (12", silver vinyl, p/s, numbered)...............8
97	parlophone QUEENLH 26	No-One But You/We Will Rock You (Original 1977 version) (unreleased) 20
97	Parlophone QUEEN 26	No-One But You (Only The Good Die Young)/Princes Of The Universe/ We Will Rock You (Rick Rubin 'Ruined' Remix)/Gimme The Prize (Instrumental 'Eye' Remix) (Unissued 7") 150
97	Parlophone QUEENPD 27	No-One But You (Only The Good Die Young)/We Will Rock You (Rick Rubin 'Ruined' Remix)/Tie Your Mother Down/Gimme The Prize (Instrumental 'Eye' Remix) (picture disc)...............6
99	Parlophone QUEENPD 28	Under Pressure (Rah Mix) 6
98	Parlophone QUEENPD28	Under Pressure - Rah Mix/Bohemian Rhapsody (picture disc) 8
11	Island	Stone Cold Crazy/Keep Yourself Alive (numbered picture disc in PVC sleeve, 2000 only)......12

SINGLES : 3" CD SINGLES

80s	Parlophone	QUEEN : THE 3" SINGLES (gatefold wallet, card insert) 150
88	Parlophone QUECD 1	Seven Seas Of Rhye/See What A Fool I've Been/Funny How Love Is 12
88	Parlophone QUECD 2	Killer Queen/Flick Of The Wrist/Brighton Rock...............12
88	Parlophone QUECD 3	Bohemian Rhapsody/I'm In Love With My Car/You're My Best Friend...............12
88	Parlophone QUECD 4	Somebody To Love/White Man/Tie Your Mother Down 12
88	Parlophone QUECD 5	QUEEN'S FIRST EP: Good Old Fashioned Lover Boy/Death On Two Legs/ Tenement Funster/White Queen (As It Began)...............12
88	Parlophone QUECD 6	We Are The Champions/We Will Rock You /Fat Bottomed Girls 12
88	Parlophone QUECD 7	Crazy Little Thing Called Love/Spread Your Wings/Flash 12
88	Parlophone QUECD 8	Another One Bites The Dust/Dragon Attack/Las Palabras De Amor 12
88	Parlophone QUECD 9	Under Pressure/Soul Brother/Body Language 12
88	Parlophone QUECD 10	Radio Ga Ga/I Go Crazy/Hammer To Fall 12
88	Parlophone QUECD 11	I Want To Break Free/Machines (Back To Humans)/It's A Hard Life 12
88	Parlophone QUECD 12	A Kind Of Magic/A Dozen Red Roses For My Darling/One Vision 12

ALBUMS

73	EMI EMC 3006	QUEEN (LP) 30
74	EMI EMA 767	QUEEN II (LP, laminated gatefold sleeve, lyric inner sleeve) 35
74	EMI EMC 3061	SHEER HEART ATTACK (LP, laminated sleeve, inner lyric sleeve) 25
75	EMI EMTC 103	A NIGHT AT THE OPERA (LP, gatefold sleeve) 25
76	EMI EMTC 104	A DAY AT THE RACES (LP, gatefold sleeve) 20
77	EMI EMA 784	NEWS OF THE WORLD (LP, gatefold with lyric inner sleeve) 20
78	EMI EMA 788	JAZZ (LP, gatefold sleeve with attached poster, inner sleeve has band shot on olne side and track listing on the other)...............40
81	EMI EMTV 30	GREATEST HITS (LP, mispress, side 2 plays "Anne Murray's Greatest Hits") 15
85	EMI QB 1	THE COMPLETE WORKS (14-LP box set including "Complete Vision" LP of non-LP tracks, 2 booklets & map, numbered; 600 autographed) 1000
85	EMI QB 1	THE COMPLETE WORKS (14-LP box set including "Complete Vision" LP of non-LP tracks, 2 booklets & map, numbered) 100
86	EMI EU 3509	A KIND OF MAGIC ('Princes Of The Universe' proof sleeve; unreleased) 400
89	Band Of Joy BOJLP 001	QUEEN AT THE BEEB (LP)...............15
91	Parlophone PCSD 115	INNUENDO (LP)...............20
91	Parlophone PMTV 2	GREATEST HITS 2 (2-LP, embossed gatefold sleeve)...............25
92	Parlophone PCSP 725	LIVE AT WEMBLEY (2-LP, gatefold sleeve) 25
92	Parlophone CDQTEL 0001	BOX OF TRIX (CD, box set, with video, book, poster, T-shirt, patch & badge)...............60

MINT VALUE £

92	Parlophone CQTEL 0001	BOX OF TRIX (cassette, box set, with video, book, poster, T-shirt, patch & badge) 50
95	Parlophone 724383608812	MADE IN HEAVEN (LP, gatefold with inserts) 40
95	Parlophone QUEEN BOX 20	ULTIMATE QUEEN (20 x CD set, in numbered glazed box and numbered cardboard outer box, with Freddie hologram and 2 booklets) 450
99	Parlophone 7243 5 23452 1 1	GREATEST HITS III (2-LP with inners)...25

PROMOS

73	EMI (no cat. no.)	QUEEN (LP, white label, EMI conference custom issue, die-cut sleeve, with/without outer envelope) 450
73	EMI (no cat. no.)	QUEEN (LP, white label, EMI conference custom issue, die-cut sleeve, with/without outer envelope) 250
77	EMI SP SLP 241 A1U	We Will Rock You/We Are The Champions/Spread Your Wings (12", 1-sided)...........400
77	EMI (no cat. no.)	NEWS OF THE WORLD (LP, box set, with factory sample sticker, 5 photos, bio, badge & demo copy of "We Are The Champions"/"We Will Rock You", 50 only) 500
78	EMI EMI 2375	Bohemian Rhapsody/I'm In Love With My Car (EMI 'Queen's Award For Export' in-house edition, blue vinyl, Queen crest label, hand-numbered, purple p/s., with invites, matches, pen, ticket, menu, outer card sleeve, scarf & EMI goblets in card box)..5000
78	EMI EMI 2375	Bohemian Rhapsody/I'm In Love With My Car (EMI 'Queen's Award For Export' in-house edition, blue vinyl, Queen crest label, hand-numbered, purple p/s., with outer 'EMI International' carrying envelope) 3800
78	EMI EMI 2375	Bohemian Rhapsody/I'm In Love With My Car (EMI 'Queen's Award For Export' in-house edition, blue vinyl, Queen crest label, hand-numbered, purple p/s. 3500

(The blue vinyl 'Bohemian Rhapsody' was limited to 200 numbered copies)

84	EMI QUEEN 1	Radio Ga Ga (Edit)/I Go Crazy ('video shoot' p/s, unreleased, proofs only) 450
84	EMI QUEENDJ 5	Man On The Prowl/Thank God It's Christmas 150
84	Flexi Ltd. (no cat. no.)	Excerpts From Their New Album 'The Works' (flexidisc sampler, p/s) 15
86	(no label or cat. no.)	A Message From Queen (cassette, 1st Fan Club Convention issue)..................................20
86	Parlophone EMCDV 2	THE HIGHLANDER SELECTION (CD Video, 50 only) 400
86	EMI/Channel 4 QUEEN 7	NETWORK QUEEN ('A Kind Of Magic' 7" housed in promotional fold-out sleeve that opens up to depict illustrated band playing to audience. 50 made to promote TV advertising for July 1986 Wembley Stadium concerts) 800
89	Flexi Ltd. (no cat. no.)	A Message From Queen (flexidisc, 4th Fan Club Convention issue) 25
89	Parlophone TEASER 1	THE TEASER TAPE (cassette, edits sampler for "The Miracle")..15
89	Parlophone QUEEN 10	I Want It All/Hang On In There (p/s in promo gatefold sleeve, press release, B&W photo) 20
91	Parlophone (no cat. no.)	A SAMPLE OF MAGIC (CD, segued excerpts from "Greatest Hits 2")..............................60
91	Parlophone (no cat. no.)	HINTS OF INNUENDO (cassette, edits/out-takes sampler for "Innuendo")....................30
91	EMI	INNUENDO (Promo boxed set with CD, cassette, calendar, folder, bio & photos) 45
91	Parlophone (no cat. no.)	EIGHT GOOD REASONS TO BUY GREATEST HITS 2 (cassette, segued excerpts) 30
94	EMI CD DIG 1	DIGITAL MASTER SAMPLER (CD, picture disc) 45
95	EMI QUEEN DJ95	Bohemian Rhapsody/I'm In Love With My Car (purple vinyl, hand numbered, p/s, 10th anniversary Fan Club Convention issue, 2,000 only) 150
95	Parlophone QUEENDJ 22	A Winter's Tale/Thank God It's Christmas (jukebox issue, plain white sleeve, with jukebox strip)...10
95	Parlophone CDD JUKE	Heaven For Everyone (single version)..10
95	Parlophone QUEENLHDJ 21	Heaven For Everyone (Album Version)/Heaven For Everyone (Single Version) (jukebox issue, plain white sleeve, with poster, fold-out card & jukebox strip)...20
96	Parlophone QUEENDJ 23	Too Much Love Will Kill You/We Are The Champions (jukebox issue, plain white sleeve, with jukebox strip) 10
96	Parlophone VIRGIN 1	Heaven For Everyone/Heaven For Everyone (12", white label, Virgin Radio 'Queen Day' competition prize, black 'Queen crest' p/s with handwritten details; mispressing with same tracks both sides, unreleased) 0
96	Parlophone VIRGIN 2	Heaven For Everyone (12", 1-sided, white labels, Virgin Radio 'Queen Day' competition prize, 'Queen crest' p/s w/ handwritten details, 15 copies only) 750
96	Parlophone VIRGIN 3	A Winter's Tale (12", 1-sided, white labels, Virgin Radio 'Queen Day' competition prize, 'Queen crest' p/s with handwritten details, 15 only) 750
96	Parlophone VIRGIN 4	Mother Love (12", 1-sided, white labels, Virgin Radio 'Queen Day' competition prize, 'Queen crest' p/s with handwritten details, 15 only)...........750
96	Parlophone VIRGIN 5	Let Me Live (12", 1-sided, white labels, Virgin Radio 'Queen Day' competition prize, 'Queen crest' p/s with handwritten details, 15 only) 750
96	Parlophone VIRGIN 6	You Don't Fool Me (12", 1-sided, white labels, Virgin Radio 'Queen Day' competition prize, 'Queen crest' p/s with handwritten details, 15 only) 750
96	Parlophone VIRGIN 7	It's A Beautiful Day (12", 1-sided, white labels, Virgin Radio 'Queen Day' competition prize, 'Queen crest' p/s with handwritten details, 15 only) 750
96	Parlophone VIRGIN 8	I Was Born To Love You (12", 1-sided, white labels, Virgin Radio 'Queen Day' competition prize, 'Queen crest' p/s with handwritten details, 15 only) 750
97	Parlophone CDQT 1	QUEEN ROCKS (CD, Brian May interview)...75
99	EMI QUEENWL 28	Under Pressure (Remixes) (with David Bowie) (12", white label, unreleased mix, promo only)..30
99	EMI QUEEN DJ 28	Under Pressure (Rah Mix)/(Mike Spencer Mix)/The Show Must Go On (CD, card p/s, promo only)..15

MISPRESSINGS

75	EMI EMI 2378	Bohemian Rhapsody/I'm In Love With My Car (2nd issue, with incorrect cat. no.)...............12
78	EMI EMI 2870	Bicycle Race/Fat Bottomed Girls (p/s, B-side plays Crystal Gayle's 3 O'Clock In The Morning or Dollar track)...10
79	EMI EMI 2975	CLIFF RICHARD: We Don't Talk Anymore/Count Me Out (A-side plays "Bohemian Rhapsody")..12
79	EMI EMI 5001	Crazy Little Thing Called Love/We Will Rock You (live) (p/s, both sides play "We Will Rock You")..15
80	EMI EMI 5076	Play The Game/A Human Body (p/s, both sides play "A Human Body")............................12
86	Parlophone RP 5452	BEATLES: Paperback Writer/Rain (picture disc, A-side plays Friends Will Be Friends) 75

(see also Freddie Mercury, Brian May, Roger Taylor, Larry Lurex, Cross, Immortals, Hilary Hilary, Eddie Howell, Man Friday & Jive Junior)

QUEENS OF THE STONE AGE

02	Interscope 497 812-7	No One Knows/Tension Head (Live From The Mean Fiddler) (p/s, grey vinyl) 15
98	Roadrunner RR 8674-2	QUEENS OF THE STONE AGE (LP)..20
00	Interscope 490 683-1	X (LP, gatefold sleeve) 25
02	Interscope 493435-2	SONGS FOR THE DEAF (2 x LP, gatefold, red vinyl)...35
03	Interscope 493 436-2	SONGS FOR THE DEAF (2-CD tour edition) 25
11	Music On Vinyl MOVLP 250	LULLABIES TO PARADISE (2-LP, one side etched)...15
11	Music On Vinyl MOVLP 250	LULLABIES TO PARADISE (2-LP, red vinyl, one side etched)..20

QUEENSRYCHE

83	EMI America 12EA 162	Queens Of The Reich/Nightrider/Blinded/Lady Wore Black (12", p/s) 8
84	EMI America EA 183	Take Hold Of The Flame/Nightrider (p/s)..6
86	EMI America EA 22	Gonna Get Close To You/Prophecy (p/s) 6

86	EMI America EAD 22	Gonna Get Close To You/Prophecy//Queen Of The Reich (live)/Deliverance (live) (double pack)	10
89	EMI USA 12MTG 65	Eyes Of A Stranger/Queen Of The Reich/Walk In The Shadows/Take Hold Of The Flame (12", gatefold p/s)	8
88	EMI Manhattan 10QR 1	OVERSEEING THE OPERATION (10" EP)	8

QUEERS
| 90 | Shakin Street YEAH HUP 010 | GROW UP (LP) | 30 |

? & THE MYSTERIANS
66	Cameo Parkway C 428	96 Tears/Midnight Hour	35
66	Cameo Parkway C 441	I Need Somebody/'8' Teen	45
67	Cameo Parkway C 467	Can't Get Enough Of You, Baby/Smokes	30
67	Cameo Parkway C 479	Girl (You Captivate Me)/Got To	25
67	Cameo Parkway C 496	Do Something To Me/Love Me Baby	25
76	London HLU 10534	96 Tears/'8' Teen	10

QUESTIONS
| 68 | Decca F 22740 | We Got Love/Something Wonderful | 30 |

TOMMY QUICKLY (& REMO FOUR)
63	Piccadilly 7N 35137	Tip Of My Tongue/Heaven Only Knows (solo)	30
63	Piccadilly 7N 35151	Kiss Me Now/No Other Love	8
64	Piccadilly 7N 35167	Prove It/Haven't You Noticed	6
64	Piccadilly 7N 35183	You Might As Well Forget Him/It's As Simple As That	6
64	Pye 7N 15708	The Wild Side Of Life/Forget The Other Guy	6
64	Pye 7N 15748	Humpty Dumpty/I'll Go Crazy	8

(see also Remo Four)

QUICKSAND
70	Carnaby CNS 4015	Passing By/Cobblestones	15
73	Dawn DNS 1046	Time To Live/Empty Street, Empty Heart	10
73	Dawn DNLS 3056	HOME IS WHERE I BELONG (LP, gatefold sleeve, pink 'sun' label)	60

(see also Man)

QUICKSILVER MESSENGER SERVICE
76	Capitol CL 15859	Gypsy Lights/Witches' Moon	5
68	Capitol (S)T 2904	QUICKSILVER MESSENGER SERVICE (LP, black label with rainbow rim)	40
69	Capitol E-(S)T 120	HAPPY TRAILS (LP)	25
70	Capitol E-ST 391	SHADY GROVE (LP)	18
70	Capitol EA-ST 498	JUST FOR LOVE (LP)	15
71	Capitol EA-ST 630	WHAT ABOUT ME? (LP)	15
72	Capitol E-SW 819	QUICKSILVER (LP)	12
72	Capitol EA-ST 11002	COMIN' THRU (LP, gatefold sleeve)	12
75	Capitol E-ST 11462	SOLID SILVER (LP, with insert)	12
83	Psycho PSYCHO 10	MAIDEN OF THE CANCER MOON (2-LP)	40

(see also Dino Valenti, Nicky Hopkins)

QUICKSPACE (SUPERSPORT)
| 94 | Love Train PUBE 04 | Found A Way/Do It My Own Way (12", p/s, 1,500 only) | 12 |

QUIET FIVE
65	Parlophone R 5273	When The Morning Sun Dries The Dew/Tomorrow I'll Be Gone (in p/s)	20
65	Parlophone R 5273	When The Morning Sun Dries The Dew/Tomorrow I'll Be Gone	10
65	Parlophone R 5302	Honeysuckle Rose/Let's Talk It Over	8
66	Parlophone R 5421	Homeward Bound/Ain't It Funny What Some Lovin' Can Do	18
66	Parlophone R 5470	I Am Waiting/What About The Time For Me	10
67	CBS 202586	Goodnight Sleep Tight/Just For Tonight	6

(see also Kris Ife, Patrick Dane, Richard Barnes)

QUIET SUN
| 75 | Island HELP 19 | MAINSTREAM (LP, black label with pink 'i' label) | 20 |

(see also Phil Manzanera, Roxy Music)

QUIET WORLD
69	Dawn DNS 1001	Miss Whittington/There Is A Mountain (as Quiet World Of Lea & John)	40
70	Dawn DNS 1005	Children Of The World/Love Is Walking	40
70	Pye 7N 45005	Rest Comfortably/Gemima	12
71	Pye 7N 45074	Visitor/Sam	10
70	Dawn DNLS 3007	THE ROAD (LP)	175

(see also Steve Hackett, Genesis)

QUIK
67	Deram DM 121	Love Is A Beautiful Thing/Bert's Apple Crumble	150
67	Deram DM 139	King Of The World/My Girl	50
67	Deram DM 155	I Can't Sleep/Soul Full Of Sorrow	70
98	Klooks Kleek 60	Bert's Apple Crumble/THE SONICS: The Witch (re-issue)	10

(see also Meddy Evils)

QUILL
| 79 | Kite KR 10 | LIVE (LP) | 15 |

QUILLER
| 75 | BBC RESL 25 | Quiller/General Direction | 7 |

QUINCEHARMON
| 71 | Columbia DB 8772 | Suddenly The Whole World Is Mine/Strange Feeling | 15 |
| 71 | Columbia DB 8798 | On The Buses/Don't Tell Me It's Over | 10 |

PAUL QUINCHETTE
| 57 | Esquire 32-057 | ON THE SUNNY SIDE (LP) | 40 |

QUINCICASM
| 73 | Saydisc SDL 249 | QUINCICASM (LP) | 20 |

MIKE QUINN
66	Fontana TF 761	Someone's Slipping Into My Mind/I Know What You Know	7
69	CBS 4506	Apple Pie/There's A Time	6
69	Jay Boy BOY 7	Toothbrush Nell/Fairy Cakes	5

PAUL QUINN

| 92 | Postcard DUBH 921 | THE PHANTOMS AND THE ARCHETYPES (LP) | 40 |

PAUL QUINN & EDWYN COLLINS

| 84 | Swamplands SWP 1 | Pale Blue Eyes (Edited Version)/Burro (p/s) | 5 |
| 84 | Swamplands SWX 1 | Pale Blue Eyes/Pale Blues Eyes (Western)/Burro (12", original pressing with 'film' p/s, inner sleeve & yellow obi) | 10 |

(see also Edwyn Collins, Orange Juice)

QUINTESSENCE

70	Island WIP 6075	Notting Hill Gate/Move Into The Light	7
71	Neon NE 1003	Sweet Jesus/You Never Stay The Same (in p/s)	15
71	Neon NE 1003	Sweet Jesus/You Never Stay The Same	6
69	Island ILPS 9110	IN BLISSFUL COMPANY (LP, gatefold, pink label with white 'i' logo)	80
70	Island ILPS 9128	QUINTESSENCE (LP, pink label with white 'i' logo)	60
71	Island ILPS 9143	DIVE DEEP (LP, inner sleeve, pink rim palm tree label)	50
72	RCA SF 8273	SELF (LP)	20
72	RCA SF 8317	INDWELLER (LP)	15

(see also Kala)

QUINTET MODERNE

| 87 | Bead Records BEAD 26 | IKKUNAN TAKANA (LP) | 20 |

QUINTET OF HOT CLUB OF FRANCE

| 53 | Decca LF 1139 | SWING FROM PARIS (10" LP) | 15 |

(see also Django Reinhardt)

QUINTET OF THE YEAR

| 54 | Vogue L.D.E. 087 | JAZZ AT THE MASSAY HALL VOL. 3 (10" LP) | 18 |

QUIREBOYS

| 90 | Parlophone RPD 6248 | I Don't Love You Anymore/Mayfair (Original Version) (uncut shaped picture disc) | 10 |

(see also Wildhearts)

DARYL QUIST

63	Pye 7N 15538	Thanks To You/Keep Moving (in p/s)	10
63	Pye 7N 15538	Thanks To You/Keep Moving	5
63	Pye 7N 15563	Goodbye To Love/All Through The Night	5
64	Pye 7N 15605	True To You/Above And Beyond	5
64	Pye 7N 15656	See The Funny Little Clown/When She Comes To You	5
65	Decca F 12058	Put Away Your Teardrops/Across The Street	5

QUIVER

72	Warner Bros K 16165	Green Tree/I Might Stumble	6
71	Warner Bros K 46089	QUIVER (LP)	20
72	Warner Bros K 46153	GONE IN THE MORNING (LP, gatefold sleeve)	12

(see also Bridget St. John, Natural Gas, Sutherland Brothers, Village)

QUODLING'S DELIGHT

| 76 | Fanfare FR 2179 | AMONG THE LEAVES SO GREEN (LP) | 25 |

QUOTATIONS (U.K.)

64	Decca F 11907	Alright Baby/Love You All Over Again	25
68	CBS 3716	Cool It/Mark Of Her Head	35
69	CBS 4378	Hello Memories/Pretend	10

(see also Fleur De Lys, Johnny B. Great, Johnny Gustafson, Merseybeats, Johnny Goodison)

QUOTATIONS (U.S.)

| 61 | HMV POP 975 | Imagination/Ala-Men-Sy | 100 |

QUOTING MARX

| 77 | Full Stop PUNC 28 | Opening And Closing/66 And 99 | 12 |

RABBIT

73	Island WIP6161	Broken Arrows/Blues My Guitar	5
73	Island ILPS 9238	BROKEN ARROWS (LP, gatefold sleeve, pink rim palm tree label)	18
74	Island ILPS 9289	DARK SALOON (LP)	15

(see also Free; Kossoff, Kirke, Tetsu & Rabbit)

RABBITS

| 79 | Stortbeat BEAT 4 | Kitchen Parties/Tonight (numbered p/s, 1000 only) | 12 |

MIKE RABIN (& DEMONS)

| 64 | Columbia DB 7350 | Head Over Heels/Leaving You (as Mike Rabin & Demons) | 85 |
| 65 | Polydor BM 56007 | If I Were You/What Do You Do | 25 |

STEVE RACE

| 61 | Parlophone R 4808 | Crosstrap/Stop Look Listen | 10 |

RACE FANS

| 68 | Trojan TR 610 | Bookie Man/UNIQUES: More Love | 30 |
| 68 | Trojan TR 637 | Time Marches On/SILVERTONES: Party Night | 40 |

YANK RACHELL TENNESSEE JUG BUSTERS

| 64 | '77' LA 12-23 | MANDOLIN BLUES (LP) | 22 |

RACONTEURS

08	XL XLS 227	Steady As She Goes/Store Bought Bones (1st issue, 1,000 only, p/s Jack White to right of cover)	15
06	XL XLLP 196X	BROKEN BOY SOLDIERS (LP)	25
08	XL XLLP 359	CONSOLERS OF THE LONELY (2-LP)	25

(see also White Stripes)

RADAR
83	House Of Wax WAX 1	Leave Her Alone/Reach For The Sky (p/s)	10

JIMMY RADCLIFFE
65	Stateside SS 374	Long After Tonight Is Over/What I Want I Can Never Have	35
65	Stateside SS 374	Long After Tonight Is Over/What I Want I Can Never Have (DJ copy)	150
73	Pye International 7N 25614	Long After Tonight Is Over/What I Want I Can Never Have (reissue)	8
77	DJM DJS 10772	Long After Tonight Is Over/What I Want I Can Never Have (2nd reissue) (P/S) (Promo)	7

(see also Steve Karmen Big Band)

RADHA KRISHNA
71	Columbia SCX 6462	RADHA KRISHNA (LP, composed & directed by John Mayer)	45

(see also John Mayer)

RADHA KRISHNA TEMPLE (LONDON)
69	Apple APPLE 15	Hare Krishna Mantra/Prayer To The Spiritual Masters (p/s, as Radha Krishna Temple [London], with insert)	30
69	Apple APPLE 15	Hare Krishna Mantra/Prayer To The Spiritual Masters (p/s, as Radha Krishna Temple [London], without insert)	20
69	Apple APPLE 15	Hare Krishna Mantra/Prayer To The Spiritual Masters (no p/s, as Radha Krishna Temple [London])	6
70	Apple APPLE 25	Govinda/Govinda Jai Jai (p/s)	40
70	Apple APPLE 25	Govinda/Govinda Jai Jai (in company sleeve)	12
70	Apple APPLE 25	Govinda/Govinda Jai Jai	5
71	Apple SAPCOR 18	THE RADHA KRISHNA TEMPLE (LP, gatefold sleeve, with insert)	50
71	Apple SAPCOR 18	THE RADHA KRISHNA TEMPLE (LP, gatefold sleeve, without insert)	40
93	Apple SAPCOR 18	THE RADHA KRISHNA TEMPLE (LP, reissue, gatefold sleeve with inner)	15
93	Apple SAPCOR 18	THE RADHA KRISHNA TEMPLE (CD)	18

RADIANTS
64	Chess CRS 8002	Voice Your Choice/If I Only Had You	40
64	Chess CRS 8002	Voice Your Choice/If I Only Had You (DJ copy)	60
68	Chess CRS 8073	Hold On/I'm Glad I'm The Loser	20
68	Chess CRS 8073	Hold On/I'm Glad I'm The Loser (DJ copy)	50

(see also Maurice & Mac, Caston & Majors)

RADIATORS (FROM SPACE)
77	Chiswick S 10	Television Screen/Love Detective (p/s, original issue)	8
77	Chiswick NS 19	Enemies/Psychotic Reaction (p/s)	5
78	Chiswick NS 24	Prison Bars/(Why Can't I Be A) Teenager In Love (unreleased, promo only white label in stamped white sleeve & loose printed labels)	40
79	Chiswick NS 45	Walkin' Home Alone Again/Try And Stop Me/The Huckelbuck (unreleased; white label test pressings exist with loose labels; as Radiators)	40
79	Chiswick CHIS 115	Kitty Ricketts/Ballad Of The Faithful Departed (company sleeve)	8
77	Chiswick WIK 4	TV TUBE HEART (LP)	15
79	Chiswick CWK 3003	GHOSTOWN (LP, inner sleeve)	12

(see also Pogues)

RADICAL DANCE FACTION
80	Earth Zone EZ 001	BORDERLAND CASES (LP, 1st pressing with white picture sleeve)	20
80	Earth Zone EZ 001	BORDERLAND CASES (LP, 2nd pressing with black picture sleeve)	15
81	Earth Zone EZ 003	WATERLAND (LP)	15

RADICALS
84	Bluetrac BTR 003	Rum Tree/Racids In Dub (12")	50

MARK RADICE
72	Paramount PARA 3024	Hey My Love/Your Love Is Like Fire	8
72	Paramount PARA 3025	New Day/Take Me To The Park	6
72	Paramount SPFA 7004	MARK RADICE (LP)	12

RADIO DEPT
02	Rex REKD 30S	Liebling/We Would Fall Against The Tide (die-cut Rex sleeve)	15
04	Rex REKD 41S	Why Don't You Talk About It?/I Don't Need Love, I've Got My Band (p/s)	15
04	XL XLS 196	Where Damage Isn't Already Done/You And Me Then?/Peace Of Mind (p/s)	12
04	XL XLS 203	Ewan/Slottet/The Things That Went Wrong (p/s)	12
04	XL XLLP 177	LESSER MATTERS (LP)	50

RADIOACTIVE
77	Beeb BEEB 021	Ten Years After/All Time Needletime Loser (no p/s)	30

RADIO ACTORS
79	Charly CYS 1058	Nuclear Waste/Digital Love (p/s, reissue of Fast Breeder & Radio Actors single, 2 slightly different label designs)	20
79	DB DBS 5	Nuclear Waste/Digital Love (different p/s, 2nd reissue)	5

(see also Fast Breeder & Radio Actors, Sting, Newcastle Big Band, Police, Gilli Smyth, Inner City Unit, Steve Hillage, Sphynx)

RADIO BIRDMAN
78	Sire 6078 617	What Gives/Anglo Girl Desire	10
78	Sire 9103 332	RADIOS APPEAR (LP, with inner sleeve)	25
78	Sire SRK 6050	RADIOS APPEAR (LP, reissue)	12

RADIO CITY
80	Media Wave MW 001	Love And A Picture/She's A Radio (p/s)	200

RADIOHEAD

SINGLES
92	Parlophone TCR 6312	DRILL EP (Prove Yourself/Stupid Car/You/Thinking About You) (cassette, 3,000 only)	40
92	Parlophone 12R 6312	DRILL EP (Prove Yourself/Stupid Car/You/Thinking About You) (12", p/s, 3,000 only)	120
92	Parlophone CDR 6312	DRILL EP (Prove Yourself/Stupid Car/You/Thinking About You) (CD, 3,000 only)	120
92	Parlophone 12R 6078	Creep/Lurgee/Inside My Head/Million $ Question (12", p/s, 6,000 only)	20
92	Parlophone CDR 6078	Creep/Lurgee/Inside My Head/Million $ Question (CD, 6,000 only)	20
93	Parlophone 12R 6333	Anyone Can Play Guitar/Faithless, The Wonder Boy/Coke Babies (12", p/s)	15
93	Parlophone CDR 6333	Anyone Can Play Guitar/Faithless, The Wonder Boy/Coke Babies (CD)	30
93	Parlophone 12R 6345	Pop Is Dead/Banana Co. (Acoustic)/Creep (live)/Ripcord (live) (12", g/fold p/s)	20
93	Parlophone CDR 6345	Pop Is Dead/Banana Co. (Acoustic)/Creep (live)/Ripcord (live) (CD)	30
93	Parlophone RS 6359	Creep/Yes I Am/Blow Out (Remix)/Inside My Head (live) (p/s, clear vinyl)	15

93	Parlophone 12RG 6359	U.S. LIVE EP (Creep [Acoustic KROQ]/You [live]/Vegetable [live]/Killer Cars [live]) (12", numbered gatefold p/s)	15
93	Parlophone CDR 6359	Creep/Yes I Am/Blow Out (Remix)/Inside My Head (live) (CD, digipak)	10
94	Parlophone 12R 6394	My Iron Lung/Punchdrunk Lovesick Singalong/The Trickster/ Lewis (Mistreated) (12", numbered p/s)	15
94	Parlophone CDRS 6394	My Iron Lung/Punchdrunk Lovesick Singalong/Lozenge Of Love (card sleeve, CD)	10
94	Parlophone CDR 6394	My Iron Lung/The Trickster/Lewis (Mistreated)/Permanent Daylight/ You Never Wash Up After Yourself (CD)	10
95	Parlophone 12R 6405	Planet Telex/(remixes)/High & Dry (12", limited edition, numbered p/s)	15
95	Parlophone CDR 6405	Planet Telex/High & Dry/Killer Cars/Planet Telex (LFO JD Mix) (CD,2 of 2-CD set)	10
95	Parlophone CDR 6411	Fake Plastic Trees/Fake Plastic Trees (Acoustic)/Bulletproof (...I Wish I Was) (Acoustic)/Street Spirit (Fade Out) (Acoustic) (CD, 2 of 2-CD set)	10
95	Parlophone CDR 6411	Fake Plastic Trees/Fake Plastic Trees (Acoustic)/Bulletproof (...I Wish I Was) (Acoustic)/Street Spirit (Fade Out) (Acoustic) (CD, with poster)	10
95	Parlophone CDR 6415	Just/Bones (live)/Planet Telex (live)/Anyone Can Play Guitar (live) (CD, box set with 2 postcards)	12
95	Parlophone 8 83115 2	The Bends/My Iron Lung (Live At Forum)/Bones (Live At Forum) (CD, for export to Ireland, slimline jewel case)	40
95	Parlophone 8 83115 2	The Bends/My Iron Lung (Live At Forum)/Bones (Live At Forum) (CD, for export to Ireland, mispressed with "Planet Telex" instead of "The Bends" slimline jewel case)	40
96	Parlophone R 6419	Street Spirit (Fade Out)/Bishop's Robes (die-cut p/s, white vinyl)	15
96	Parlophone R 6419LH	Street Spirit (Fade Out)/Bishop's Robes (jukebox issue, black vinyl)	10
96	Parlophone CDRS 6419	Street Spirit (Fade Out)/Bishop's Robes (CD, with poster)	10
96	Capitol 509996 93540	14 Spirit Street/Tak Show Host/Bishop's Robes (12")	12
97	Parlophone NODATA 01	Paranoid Android/Polyethelene (Parts 1 & 2) (blue vinyl, die-cut p/s)	20
97	Parlophone NODATALH 03	Karma Police (Album Version)/Lull (jukebox issue, black vinyl)	8
97	Parlophone 12NODATA 03	Karma Police/Meeting Up The Aisle/Climbing Up The Walls (Zero 7 Mix) (12", p/s)	12
97	Parlophone NODATALH 04	No Surprises/Palo Alto (jukebox issue, black vinyl)	10
97	Parlophone 12NODATA 04	No Surprises/How I Made My Millions (jukebox 7")	8
98	Parlophone 12NODATA 04	No Surprises/Palo Alto (12", p/s)	25
01	Parlophone 12FHEIT 45103	Knives Out/Cuttooth/Life In A Glasshouse (Full Length Version) (12")	8
05	Parlophone 7243 552 3360	There There/Paperbag Writer/Where Bluebirds Fly (12" p/s)	8
11	XL TICK 02	Supercollider/The Butcher (12" p/s, 2000 only, some with reversed labels)	12
11	Ticker Tape TICK 009	Bloom (Janie XX Rework)/Separator (Anstam RMX)/Lotus Flower (SBTRKT RMX) (12", p/s, 2000 only)	8

ALBUMS

93	Parlophone PCS 7360	PABLO HONEY (LP)	40
95	Parlophone PCS 7372	THE BENDS (LP)	35
97	Parlophone NODATA 02	OK COMPUTER (2-LP)	40
00	Parlophone LPKIDA	KID A (2xLP 10")	25
01	Parlophone LPFHEIT 45101	AMNESIAC (2xLP, 10")	15
01	Parlophone CDKIDA 4	KID A (CD, in 6"x 6" hardback book)	20
01	Parlophone 12FHEIT 45104	I MIGHT BE WRONG (mini-LP)	12
03	Parlophone 5848052	HAIL TO THE THIEF (CD, limited issue, with foldout map)	10
03	Parlophone 724358454314	HAIL TO THE THIEF (2xLP)	15
07	Parlophone 5.09995E+12	RADIOHEAD (Mail-order 4GB shaped USB stick, bespoke box, 7 albums as WAV files)	70
07	Xurbia Xendless Ltd X X001	IN RAINBOWS (box set, 2 x CD, 2-LP, 2xbooklets in presentation case)	70
11	Ticker Tape TICK 001S	THE KING OF LIMBS (2-10" clear vinyl LPs, with CD, newspaper, acid tab sheet, mail order only in sealed plastic bag)	35

PROMOS

92	Parlophone 12 R 6312	DRILL EP (White label promo in die cut sleeve)	100
92	Parlophone 12RDJ 6078	Creep/Lurgee/Inside My Head/Million Dollar Question (12", die-cut sleeve)	50
92	Parlophone CDRDJ 6078	Creep (Radio Version)/Lurgee/Inside My Head/Million Dollar Question (CD)	50
93	Parlophone CDRDJ 6345	Pop Is Dead/Banana Co. (live)/Creep (live)/Ripcord (live) (CD)	60
93	Parlophone CDRDJ 6359	Creep (CD, picture disc)	35
93	Parlophone 12RDJ 6369	Ripcord/Prove Yourself/Faithless, The Wonderboy/ Stop Whispering (Album Version) (12", p/s)	60
93	Parlophone 12RDJ 6333	Anyone Can Play Guitar/Faithless, The Wonder Boy/Coke Babies (12", die-cut sleeve)	80
93	Parlophone CDRDJ 6369	Stop Whispering (U.S. Version)/Prove Yourself/Lurgee (CD, promo only, card p/s & inner sleeve)	15
93	Parlophone (no cat. No.)	Stop Whispering (U.S. Version - Chris Sheldon Remix)/Creep (Acoustic)/Pop Is Dead/Inside My Head (Live) (CD)	25
94	Parlophone (no cat. no.)	PLANET TELEX: LFO & Hexidecimal mixes (12")	18
93	Parlophone CDRJ 6369	Stop Whispering/Prove Yourself/Lurgee (CD promo, p/s)	20
94	Parlophone 12RSDJ 6394	My Iron Lung/Lozenge Of Love/The Trickster/Punchdrunk Lovesick Singalong (12", die-cut red sleeve)	18
94	Parlophone 12RSDJ 6394	My Iron Lung/Lozenge Of Love/The Trickster/Punchdrunk Lovesick Singalong (12", die-cut blue sleeve)	18
94	Parlophone 12RSDJ 6394	My Iron Lung/Lewis (Mistreated)/Permanent Daylight/You Never Wash Up After Yourself (12" die-cut red sleeve)	15
94	Parlophone 12RSDJ 6394	My Iron Lung/Lewis (Mistreated)/Permanent Daylight/You Never Wash Up After Yourself (12" die-cut blue sleeve)	15
95	Parlophone 12RDJ 6405	CLUB MIX DJ: PLANET TELEX (Album version)/Hexadecimal Mix/L.F.O DJ Mix/Trashed Mix) (12")	12
95	Parlophone 12RDJ 6411	Fake Plastic Trees/India Rubber/How Can You Be Sure? (12", die-cut sleeve)	20
95	Parlophone 12RDJ 6411	Fake Plastic Trees (Edit) (Album Version) (CD)	10
95	Parlophone 12RDJ 6145	Just/Planet Telex/Killer Cars (12", die-cut sleeve)	15
95	Parlophone 12RDJ 6145	Just/Planet Telex (Karma Sun Ra Mix)Killer Cars (Mogadon Version) (12")	18
95	Parlophone HIGH-1	High & Dry (1-track CD, custom sleeve)	15
95	Parlophone RHEAD US 1	JUST FOR COLLEGE: India Rubber/Maquiladora/How Can I Be Sure?/Just (CD)	70
96	Parlophone 12RDJ 6419	Street Spirit (Fade Out)/Talk Show Host/Bishop's Robes (12", promo-only)	20
96	Parlophone CDRDJ 6419	Street Spirit (Fade Out)/Talk Show Host/Bishop's Robes (CD)	20
97	EMI (no cat. no.)	Airbag (1-track Abbey Road CD-R with mini bio and title sleeve)	20
98	Parlophone 12DATADJO3	Climbing Up The Walls (Zero 7 Mix)/(Fila Brazilia Mix) (1-sided 12", 200 only)	70
00	Parlophone 12KIDA 6	Idioteque (12", white label test pressing)	18
01	Parlophone AMNESIAC 01	4 SONGS FROM AMNESIAC: Pyramid Song/I Might Be Wrong/Packt Like Sardines In A Crushd Tin Box/Dollars & Cents (CD, card sleeve)	12
03	Parlophone 12RDJWL 6623	SKTTERBRAIN (Four Tet Mix)/REMYXOMOTOSIS (Super Collider Mix) (12", 100 only)	35
97	Parlophone 724385522925	OK COMPUTER (Stickered jewel case, printed disc, mispressing plays Deep Purple's 'The Collection')	40
97	Parlophone (no cat. no.)	OK COMPUTER (Cassette, in customized jiffy bag)	35
97	Parlophone (no cat. no.)	OK COMPUTER (promo Aiwa personal stereo, glued-in cassette, two stickers)	120
97	Parlophone CDPP 005	OK COMPUTER (CD, numbered title sleeve)	50

97	Parlophone NODATA 02	OK COMPUTER (EPK, with CD & video in polystyrene case in jiffy bag)	60
00	Parlophone CDKIDA 3	KID A (CD, card title sleeve)	18
01	Parlophone AMNESIAC 02	AMNESIAC (CD, in facsmile library book, with press release & inserts)	30
03	Parlophone LC 0299	INTERVIEW CD (p/s 22 track promo for HAIL TO THE THIEF)	20

(see also Headless Chickens, On A Friday, Thom Yorke, Jonny Greenwood)

RADIO HEART
| 87 | NBR NBRL 1 | RADIO HEART (LP, withdrawn) | 12 |

(see also Gary Numan)

RADIO MOSCOW
87	Status RM 100	Hand Of Freedom (p/s)	8
91	Status RMLP 103	WORLD SERVICE (LP)	15
92	Status RMLP 104	GET A NEW LIFE (LP)	15

RADIO 9
| 90s | Enraptured RAPT 1031 | Motorik/Fluid/Moving In Two Directions/Pianosong (10", 9 only) | 15 |

RADIOPHONIC WORKSHOP
| 73 | BBC RESL 13 | Moonbase 3/World Of Dr. Who | 20 |

(see also BBC Radiophonic Workshop)

RADIO RADIO
| 83 | Radio RAD 101 | Calling/Signed With A Star | 20 |

RADIO STARS
| 78 | Chiswick CWK 3001 | HOLIDAY ALBUM (LP, with inner sleeve) | 15 |

(see also John's Children, Andy Ellison, Trevor White)

RADIUM
| 81 | Isotope | THROUGH THE SMOKE (EP) | 75 |

RAELET(T)S
67	HMV POP 1591	One Hurt Deserves Another/One Room Paradise (as Raelets)	30
71	Tangerine 6121 002	Bad Water/That Goes To Show You	5
71	Tangerine 6121 003	Here I Go Again/Leave My Man (Woman) Alone	5

(see also Ray Charles, Clydie King, Merry Clayton)

GERRY RAFFERTY
| 71 | Transatlantic TRA 241 | CAN I HAVE MY MONEY BACK? (LP) | 12 |

(see also Humblebums, Fifth Column)

RAG DOLLS (U.K.)
| 67 | Columbia DB 8289 | Never Had So Much Loving/Any Little Bit | 10 |
| 68 | Columbia DB 8378 | My Old Man's A Groovy Old Man/They Didn't Believe Me | 10 |

(see also Marionettes, Peanut, Katie Kissoon, Mac Kissoon)

RAG DOLLS (U.S.)
| 64 | Cameo Parkway P 921 | Society Girl/Ragen (with Caliente Combo) | 35 |
| 65 | Stateside SS 398 | Dusty/Hey Hoagy | 40 |

RAGAMUFFIN
| 72 | Decca F13312 | Can I Have My Money Back/Fresh As A Daisy | 12 |

RAGE AGAINST THE MACHINE
93	Epic 658 492-6	Killing In The Name/Clear The Lane/Darkness Of Greed (12" white vinyl, p/s)	15
93	Epic 659 258-6	Bullet In The Head (Remix)/Bullet In The Head (Album Version) Settle For Nothing (live) (12" picture disc, p/s)	10
93	Epic 658 492-7	Killing In The Name/Clear The Lane/Darkness Of Greed (white vinyl, p/s)	10
93	Epic 659 258-7	Bullet In The Head/Bullet In The Head (Remix) (picture disc, p/s)	10
96	Epic 663 152-7	Bulls On Parade/Hadda Be Playing On The Jukebox (red vinyl)	10
96	Epic 481026	EVIL EMPIRE (LP)	20

RAGE (1)
80	Carrere CAR 159	Money/Thank That Woman (p/s)	8
80	Carrere CAR 159CT	Money/Thank That Woman (10", red vinyl, stickered clear sleeve)	12
81	Carrere CAR 182	Out Of Control/Double Dealer (p/s)	5
81	Carrere CAR 182CT	Out Of Control (Extended Version)/Double Dealer (12", yellow vinyl, PVC sleeve)	15
83	Carrere CAR 304	Cry From A Hill (p/s)	10
81	Carrere CAL 124	OUT OF CONTROL (LP)	12
82	Carrere CAL 138	NICE N' DIRTY (LP)	12
83	Carrere CAL 149	RUN FOR THE NIGHT (LP)	12

(see also Nutz)

RAGE (2)
| 86 | Diamond RAGE 1 | Looking For You/Come On Now (p/s) | 20 |
| 86 | Diamond RAGE 112 | Looking For You/Come On Now/Great Balls Of Fire/Hallelujah I Love Her So (12", unissued, test pressings only) | 25 |

(see also Case, Long Tall Shorty, Purple Hearts, Chords)

RAGGAMUFFINS
| 67 | London HLU 10134 | Four Days Of Rain/It Wasn't Happening At All | 15 |

RAGGED HEROES
| 83 | Celtic CM 013 | ANNUAL (LP) | 25 |

RAGING STORMS
| 62 | London HLU 9556 | The Dribble/Hound Dog | 25 |

LOU RAGLAND
| 73 | Warner Bros K 16312 | Since You Said You'd Be Mine/I Didn't Mean To Love You | 30 |

RAGPICKERS
| 59 | Saga SAG 45-2906 | Fifi/Cat On A Cool Tin Roof (p/s) | 5 |

(see also Bert Weedon)

RAH BAND
82	TNT RAH 1/RAH 2	Winter Love/Funk Me Down To Rio (82 Version)/Perfumed Garden (12")	10
82	TNT RAH 1/RAH 2	Winter Love/Funk Me Down To Rio (82 Version)/Perfumed Garden (12")	10
83	TMT TMTT 5	Messages From The Stars (Long Wave Mix)/(Astro Mix)/(Short Wave Mix) (12", blue vinyl)	15

MINT VALUE £

78	Ebony EBY 1001	THE CRUNCH AND BEYOND (LP)	12
81	DJM DJF 20573	RAH BAND (LP)	12
83	TMT RAH-1	GOING UP (LP)	20

(see also Richard Hewson Orchestra)

RAIDER OF THE LOST DUB
| 81 | Island ILPS 9705 | RAIDERS OF THE LOST DUB (LP) (withdrawn due to legal action) | 40 |

RAIDERS
70	CBS 4801	Just Seventeen/Sorceress With Blue Eyes	10
70	CBS 5015	Gone Movin' On/Interlude (to be Forgotten)	10
71	CBS 7474	Birds Of A Feather/The Turkey	6
72	CBS 7808	Country Wing/It's Hard Getting Up Today	6
72	CBS 8428	Song Seller/A Simple Song	10

(see also Paul Revere)

RAINBEAUS
| 60 | Vogue V 9161 | That's All I'm Asking Of You/Maybe It's Wrong | 170 |

(RITCHIE BLACKMORE'S) RAINBOW
74	Oyster OYR 103	Man On The Silver Mountain/Snake Charmer (as Ritchie Blackmore's Rainbow)	8
77	Polydor 2066 845	Kill The King (live)/Man On The Silver Mountain (live)/Mistreated (live) (p/s)	8
78	Polydor 2066 913	Long Live Rock'n'Roll/Sensitive To Light (p/s)	8
78	Polydor 2066 968	L.A. Connection/Lady Of The Lake (p/s, initial pressing on red vinyl)	12
78	Polydor 2066 968	L.A. Connection/Lady Of The Lake (p/s)	5
82	Polydor POSPX 421	Stone Cold/Rock Fever (12", on blue vinyl)	10
82	Polydor POSPX 421	Stone Cold/Rock Fever (12")	8
83	Polydor POSP 631	Street Of Dreams/Anybody There? (p/s)	5
83	Polydor POSPP 631	Street Of Dreams/Anybody There? (picture disc, 2000 only)	20
83	Polydor POSPX 631	Street Of Dreams/Anybody There?/Power (live) (12", p/s)	10
83	Polydor POSP 654	Can't Let You Go/All Night Long (live) (p/s)	5
83	Polydor POSPP 654	Can't Let You Go/All Night Long (live) (guitar-shaped picture disc)	15
83	Polydor POSPX 654	Can't Let You Go/All Night Long (live)/Stranded (live) (12", p/s)	10
75	Oyster OYA 2001	RITCHIE BLACKMORE'S RAINBOW (LP, gatefold sleeve, as Ritchie Blackmore's Rainbow)	40
77	Polydor 2808 010 010	RAINBOW ON STAGE (LP, music & interview disc, with insert, promo only)	100
79	Polydor POLD 5023	DOWN TO EARTH (LP, clear vinyl, with inner sleeve)	15

(see also Ritchie Blackmore, Deep Purple, Elf, Dio, Graham Bonnet, Cozy Powell, Roger Glover, Wild Horses, Tony Carey)

CHRIS RAINBOW
| 81 | EMI 5215-6 | Body Music/Girl In Collision (p/s) | 8 |
| 81 | EMI 12EMI 5215 | Body Music/Girl In Collision (12", p/s) | 15 |

RAINBOW FAMILY
| 72 | President PT 375 | Travellin' Lady/My Father | 80 |

RAINBOW FFOLLY
| 68 | Parlophone R 5701 | Go Girl/Drive My Car | 60 |
| 67 | Parlophone PMC/PCS 7050 | SALLIES FFORTH (LP, laminated front, flipbacks, black/yellow label, "Sold in U.K..." text) | 400 |

(see also Love Affair)

RAINBOW PEOPLE
68	Pye 7N 17582	Walk'll Do You Good/Dream Time	15
68	Pye 7N 17624	The Sailing Song/Rainbows	15
69	Pye 7N 17759	Living In A Dream World/Happy To See You Again	30

RAINBOWS
| 69 | CBS 3995 | Rainbows/Nobody But You | 20 |
| 69 | CBS 4568 | New Day Dawning/Days And Nights | 40 |

(see also Peeps, Martin Cure & Peeps)

RAINCHECKS
| 64 | Solar SRP 104 | Something About You/You're My Angel | 20 |
| 65 | R&B MRB 5002 | How Are You Boy/Bye Bye Baby | 40 |

RAINCOATS
79	Rough Trade RT 013	Adventures Close to Home/In Love/Fairytale In The Supermarket	18
82	Rough Trade TR 093	Running Away/No Ones Little Girl	18
83	Rough Trade RTT 153	Animal Rhapsody/Honey Mad Woman/No-Ones Little Girl (12")	18
79	Rough Trade ROUGH 3	THE RAINCOATS (LP, with lyric booklet)	30
81	Rough Trade ROUGH 13	ODYSHAPE (LP)	30
83	Rough Trade ROUGH66	MOVING (LP)	20

(see also Slits)

RAINDANCE
| 87 | Raindance X1S 121 | RAINDANCE (LP) | 40 |

RAINDROPS (U.K.)
59	Parlophone R 4559	Italian Style/Along Came Jones	10
60	Oriole CB 1544	Let's Make A Foursome/If I Had My Life To Live Over	5
60	Oriole CB 1555	Banjo Boy/Crazy Rhythm	5
61	Oriole CB 1595	Will You Love Me Tomorrow/Raindrops	10
62	Oriole CB 1707	Paintin' The Town With Teardrops/A Letter From Anne	5
67	CBS 202669	Foolman/Got To Find A Reason (credited to Raindrops '67)	10

(see also Jackie & Raindrops, Jackie Lee, Jacky, Emma Rede, Vince Hill)

RAINDROPS (U.S.)
63	London HL 9718	What A Guy/It's So Wonderful	25
63	London HL 9769	The Kind Of Boy You Can't Forget/Even Though You Can't Dance	30
64	London HL 9825	That Boy John/Hanky Panky	20
64	Fontana TF 463	The Book Of Love/I Won't Cry	25
64	London RE 1415	WHAT A GUY (EP)	125
64	London HA 8140	THE RAINDROPS (LP)	125

(see also Ellie Greenwich, Popsicles)

LORRY RAINE
| 54 | London HL 8043 | You Broke My Broken Heart/I'm In Love With A Guy | 25 |
| 55 | London HL 8132 | Love Me Tonight/What Would I Do | 40 |

MA RAINEY

50	Jazz Collector L 16	Don't Fish My Sea/Soon This Morning (78)	10
50	Jazz Collector L 20	Jealous Hearted Blues/See See Rider Blues (78)	10
50	Jazz Collector L 35	Blues The World Forgot (Parts 1 & 2) (78)	10
50	Jazz Collector L 42	New Bo-Weavil Blues/Moonshine Blues (78)	10
50	Jazz Collector L 48	Barrel House Blues/Walking Blues (78)	10
50	Jazz Collector L 52	Misery Blues/Dead Drunk Blues (78)	10
50	Jazz Collector L 57	Morning Hour Blues/Weepin' Woman Blues (78)	10
50	Jazz Collector L 66	Moonshine Blues/Southern Blues (78)	10
51	Jazz Collector L 73	Stack O'Lee Blues/Yonder Come The Blues (78)	10
52	Jazz Collector L 82	Honey Where Have You Been So Long/Ma Rainey's Mystery Record (78)	10
52	Jazz Collector L 87	Slave To The Blues/Oh My Babe Blues (78)	10
52	Jazz Collector L 98	Blues Oh Blues/Oh Papa Blues (78)	10
54	Jazz Collector L 107	Lawd Send Me A Man Blues/South Bound Blues (78)	10
55	Jazz Collector L 120	Gone Daddy Blues/Slow Driving Moan (78)	10
50s	Signature 908	Yonder Come The Blues/Stack O'Lee Blues (78)	10
53	London AL 3502	MA RAINEY VOLUME 1 (10" LP)	25
55	London AL 3538	MA RAINEY VOLUME 2 (10" LP)	25
56	London AL 3558	MA RAINEY VOLUME 3 (10" LP)	25
50s	Ristic LP 13	MA RAINEY (10" LP)	30
50s	Ristic LP 19	MA RAINEY (10" LP)	30
62	Riverside RL 12-108	MA RAINEY SINGS THE BLUES (LP)	20
64	Riverside RLP 8807	MOTHER OF THE BLUES (LP, gatefold sleeve with booklet)	20
70	CBS 52798	MA RAINEY AND THE CLASSIC BLUES SINGERS (LP)	15

MA RAINEY & IDA COX

60	Jazz Collector JEL 12	THE FEMALE BLUES VOL. 1 (EP)	10
64	Jazz Collector JEL 22	THE FEMALE BLUES VOL. 3 (EP, with Trixie Smith)	10

(see also Ida Cox, Tommy Ladnier)

MA RAINEY & PAPA CHARLIE JACKSON

50s	Poydras 11	Ma And Papa Poorhouse Blues/Big Feeling Blues	15

RAIN PARADE

83	Enigma BOB 4/LYN 15263	Sad Eyes Kill (3.16) (hard vinyl white label test pressing)	12

MARVIN RAINWATER

55	MGM SP 1150	Tennessee Houn' Dog Yodel/Albino (Pink-Eyed) Stallion	60
55	MGM 876	Tennessee Houn' Dog Yodel/Albino (Pink-Eyed) Stallion (78)	18
56	MGM MGM 929	What Am I Supposed To Do/Why Did You Have To Go And Leave Me	25
57	MGM MGM 961	Gonna Find Me A Bluebird/So You Think You've Got	15
58	MGM MGM 974	Whole Lotta Woman/Baby, Don't Go	5
58	MGM MGM 980	I Dig You Baby/Two Fools In Love (B-side with Sister Patty)	6
58	MGM MGM 988	Dance Me Daddy/Because I'm A Dreamer (B-side with Sister Patty)	6
59	MGM MGM 1030	Half-Breed/A Song Of New Love	5
59	MGM MGM 1030	Half-Breed/A Song Of New Love (78)	10
60	MGM MGM 1052	Nothin' Needs Nothin' (Like I Need You)/The Valley Of The Moon	10
61	London HLU 9447	Boo Hoo/I Can't Forget	80
58	MGM MGM-EP 647	MEET MARVIN RAINWATER (EP)	40
58	MGM MGM-EP 662	WHOLE LOTTA MARVIN (EP)	50
59	MGM MGM-EP 685	MARVIN RAINWATER SINGS (EP)	50
63	Ember EMB 4521	COUNTRY AND WESTERN FAVOURITES VOL. 2 (EP)	30
58	MGM MGM-D 152	SONGS BY MARVIN RAINWATER (10" LP)	70

(see also Connie Francis & Marvin Rainwater)

RAINY DAY

84	EMI EMI 5472	Painting Pictures/Welche Farbe Hat Der Sonnenschein (p/s)	12

RAINY DAZE

67	CBS 3200	What Do You Think/Autumn Leaves	18
67	Polydor 56731	That Acapulco Gold/In My Mind Lives A Forest	20
68	Polydor 56737	Blood Of Oblivion/Stop Sign	20
68	CBS 56731	THAT ACAPULCO GOLD (LP, unissued in U.K.)	0

RAISINS

68	Major Major MM 540	Ain't That Lovin' You Baby/Stranger Things Have Happened	15
69	Major Minor MM 602	I Thank You/Don't Leave Me Like This	8
68	Major Minor MMLP 20	THE RAISINS (LP, also stereo SMLP 20)	30

(see also Coloured Raisins)

BONNIE RAITT

75	Warner Bros. K 56160	HOME PLATE (LP)	12

(see also Roy Orbison, Alton Purnell)

RAKES

04	Trash Aesthetics TA 702	22 Grand Job/Something Clicked And I Fell Off The Edge (Pink vinyl, insert and Fold-out sleeve. 480 only)	10
04	City Rockers ROCKERS28	Strasbourg/Just Got Paid/Ausland Mission - Demo (p/s)	5

RALFI

75	Island USA 005	Wonderful Things/The Gambler	15

DON RALKE ORCHESTRA

59	Vogue V 9152	Maverick/Travellin' West	5
59	Vogue V 9152	Maverick/Travellin' West (78 rpm = £12)	12
60	Warner Brothers WB 2	77 Sunset Strip (as Big Sound Of Don Ralke)/ PETE CANDOLI & HIS ORCHESTRA: 77 Sunset Strip Cha-Cha	6
60	Warner Bros. WM 4007/WS8007	BUT YOU NEVER HEARD GERSHWIN WITH BONGOS (LP)	20
60	Warner Brothers WM 8014	DANCE CAPER IN HI-FI (LP) (& WS 8014)	20
60	Warner Brothers WS 8031	SAVAGE AND THE SENSUOUS BONGOS (LP)	20

RALLY ROUNDERS

64	Lyntone LYN 573/574	Bike Beat Part 1/Bike Beat Part 2 (actually by the Outlaws) (p/s, flexidisc)	50

(see also Outlaws, Ritchie Blackmore)

MINT VALUE £

RALPH & PONYTAILS
| 80 | Pony Tunes RATP 1 | James Bond/James Bond (Different Version) (p/s)..5 |

BUCK RAM'S RAMROCKS
| 63 | London HLU 9677 | Benfica/Odd Man Theme ....15 |

(see also Little Richard, Platters)

RAMA
| 69 | Polydor 56328 | God Created Love/Memory Of Love ....6 |

RAMA (4TH STREET ORCHESTRA)
77	Rama RM 001	AH WHO SHE? GO-DEH! (LP) 60
77	Rama RM 004	(SCIENTIFIC) HIGHER RANKING DUB (LP) 80
77	Rama RMLP 005	YUH LEARN! (LP) 80

(see also Dennis Bowell, Matumbi)

RAMASES
71	Philips 6113 001	Ballroom/Muddy Water...20
71	Philips 6113 003	Jesus Come Back/Hello Mister 10
71	Vertigo 6360 046	SPACE HYMNS (LP, foldout poster sleeve, small swirl label) 300
71	Vertigo 6360 046	SPACE HYMNS (LP, foldout sleeve, later 'spaceship' label) 40
75	Vertigo 6360 115	GLASS TOP COFFIN (LP, die-cut gatefold sleeve, 'spaceship' label) 35

(see also 10cc, Ramases & Seleka, Ramases & Selket)

RAMASES & SELEKA
| 70 | Major Minor MM 704 | Love You/Gold Is The Ring..50 |

(see also Ramases)

RAMASES & SELKET
| 68 | CBS 3717 | Crazy One/Mind's Eye ....80 |

(see also Ramases)

RAMATAM
| 72 | Atlantic K 40415 | RAMATAM (LP) ....15 |

(see also Iron Butterfly)

EDDIE RAMBEAU
62	Stateside SS 116	Summertime Guy/Last Night Was My Last Night 10
64	Stateside SS 301	Come Closer/She's Smilin' At Me 8
65	Stateside SS 448	My Name Is Mud/I Just Need Your Love 8
66	Stateside SS 486	The Train/Yesterday's Newspapers 8
66	Stateside SS 501	I'm The Sky/I Just Need Your Love 7
66	Stateside SS 561	The Clock/If I Were You...7

(see also Marcy Jo & Eddie Rambeau)

RAMBLER
| 66 | Pye 7N 17164 | Love Minus Zero No Limit/An Bonnan Bui ....7 |

(see also Johnny McEvoy)

RAMBLERS
| 63 | Decca F 11775 | Dodge City/Just For Chicks ....40 |

RAMBLERS TWO
| 65 | Pye 7N 15989 | Today Is The Highway/The Mountains And The Sea......................5 |

RAMBLETTES
| 65 | Brunswick 05932 | Thinking Of You/On Back Street ....20 |

RAMBLIN' JIMMY DOLAN
| 51 | Capitol CL 13600 | Wine, Women And Pink Elephants/GENE O'QUIN: Boogie Woogie Fever (78) ....18 |
| 53 | Capitol CL 13982 | Playin' Dominoes And Shootin' Dice/The Wheel That Does The Squeekin' (78) ....10 |

RAMBLING SYD RUMPO
| 67 | Parlophone R 5638 | The Ballad Of The Wogglers Moulie/Green Grow My Nadgers Oh! ....6 |
| 70 | Starline SRS 5034 | THE BEST OF RAMBLING SYD RUMPO (LP)......................................12 |

(see also Kenneth Williams)

SID RAMIN
| 70 | CBS 4813 | Stiletto/Sugar In The Rain ....20 |
| 69 | CBS 70062 | STILETTO (LP, soundtrack) ....30 |

LOUIE RAMIREZ
| 67 | Mercury 20113 | IN THE HEART OF SPANISH HARLEM (LP) ....20 |

RAM JAM BAND
| 65 | Columbia DB 7621 | Shake Shake Senora/Akinla..25 |

(see also Geno Washington & Ram Jam Band, Ram John Holder, Ram Holder Brothers)

RAMLEH
83	Broken Flag BF V4	THE HAND OF GLORY (EP, p/s)..30
87	Broken Flag BF 57	Redcap/AIN-TOW: Intolerant (cassette) 10
87	Broken Flag BF 70	Bite The Bolster/Fistfuck 2 (cassette) 10
91	Shock SX 013	Slammers/Black Moby Dick (p/s, numbered, 500 only) 8
92	Dying Earth DE 003	Loser Patrol/Tracers (p/s, numbered, 500 only, 1st 30 in red sleeve) 15
92	Dying Earth DE 003	Loser Patrol/Tracers (p/s, numbered, 500 only)..........................8
93	Dying Earth DE 007	Say Fuck/Slackjaw (wraparound p/s, numbered, 500 only) 8
94	Format Supremacy 1 Of EACH	Welcome/Pristine Womankind (cardboard p/s, 500 only) 8
94	Freek FRR 006	HOMELESS (CD-only EP)..15
95	Broken Flag BS 78	ADIEU ALL YOU JUDGES (CD-only live EP, features Skullflower, 500 only)........15
82	Broken Flag BF 01	31/5/1962 - 1982 (cassette) 70
83	Broken Flag BF V2	A RETURN TO SLAVERY (LP, with Libertarian Recordings) 30
83	Broken Flag BF 07	LIVE McCARTHY (cassette) 50
83	Broken Flag BF 20	LIVE NEW FORCE (cassette) 50
83	Broken Flag BF 24	LIVE PHENOL (cassette) 50
83	Broken Flag BF 25	LIVE PROSSNECK (cassette) 50
83	Broken Flag BF 28	LIVE AT MORDEN TOWER (cassette) 50
84	Broken Flag BF 37	104 WEEKS (cassette) 40
84	Broken Flag BF 38	AS I HAVE WON (cassette) 40

85	Broken Flag BF 40	AWAKE! (6 cassettes in lockable steel box with booklet)	400
87	Broken Flag BF 59	HOLE IN THE HEART (cassette)	40
94	Broken Flag BF 75	SOUNDCHECK CHANGLING (cassette)	20
95	Broken Flag BF 77	AIRBORNE BABEL (cassette)	20
95	Broken Flag BF 80	ELITE GYMNASTICS/LIVE 1983 (cassette)	20

(see also Skullflower)

RAMMALAMMA
75	Private Stock PVT 10	Roll It Over/Can't You Feel It	5

RAMMSTEIN
09	Pilgrim/Spinefar /Universal 2718498	Pussy (p/s, limited edition)	8

RAMON & CRYSTALITES
71	Songbird SB 1053	Golden Chickens/Stranger Version	18

DEE DEE RAMONE
97	Blackout BLK 5000-7	I Am Seeing UFOs (featuring Joey Ramone)/Bad Horoscope (2,500 copies only)	8

DEE DEE RAMONE & ICLC
94	Rough Trade/World Service RDT 157.1757.2	Chinese Bitch/I Don't Want To Get Involved With You/ That's What Everybody Else Does/We're A Creepy Family (CD)	10
94	World Service/Rough Trade RTD 157.1757.1	I HATE FREAKS LIKE YOU (LP, with inner)	15

(see also Ramones)

RAMONES
76	Sire 6078 601	Blitzkrieg Bop/Havana Affair (in rare p/s)	200
76	Sire 6078 601	Blitzkrieg Bop/Havana Affair	12
77	Sire 6078 603	I Remember You/California Sun (live)/I Don't Wanna Walk Around With You (live) (p/s)	40
77	Sire RAM 001 (6078 606)	Sheena Is A Punk Rocker/Commando/I Don't Care (12", with T-shirt offer on perforated centre of numbered p/s, 12,000 only)	20
77	Sire RAM 001 (6078 606)	Sheena Is A Punk Rocker/Commando/I Don't Care (12", without T-shirt offer on perforated centre of numbered p/s, 12,000 only)	10
77	Sire 6078 607	Swallow My Pride/Pinhead/Let's Dance (live) (p/s)	10
77	Sire 6078 611	Rockaway Beach/Teenage Lobotomy/Beat On The Brat (p/s)	10
77	Sire 6078 611	Rockaway Beach/Teenage Lobotomy/Beat On The Brat (12", p/s, with poster)	30
77	Sire 6078 611	Rockaway Beach/Teenage Lobotomy/Beat On The Brat (12", p/s, without poster)	12
78	Sire 6078 615	Do You Wanna Dance?/It's A Long Way Back To Germany/Cretin Hop (p/s)	15
78	Sire (no cat. no.)	Questioningly/Don't Come Close/Sedated/I Just Want To Have Something To Do (with p/s, promo only, with spoken intros by Joey Ramone)	45
78	Sire (no cat. no.)	Questioningly/Don't Come Close/Sedated/I Just Want To Have Something To Do (without p/s, promo only, with spoken intros by Joey Ramone)	15
78	Sire SRE 1031	Don't Come Close/I Don't Want You (p/s, yellow vinyl)	10
78	Sire SRE 1031	Don't Come Close/I Don't Want You (p/s)	5
78	Sire SRE 1031	Don't Come Close/I Don't Want You (12", p/s, yellow or red vinyl, red vinyl lacks p/s)	10
79	Sire SIR 4009	She's The One/I Wanna Be Sedated (p/s)	8
79	Sire SIR 4021	Rock'n'Roll High School/Rockaway Beach (live)/Sheena Is A Punk Rocker (live) (p/s)	7
80	Sire SIR 4037	Do You Remember Rock'n'Roll Radio/I Want You Around (p/s)	5
80	RSO RSO 70 (2090 512)	I Wanna Be Sedated/The Return Of Jackie And Judy (p/s)	18
80	Sire SREP 1	MELTDOWN WITH THE RAMONES: I Just Want To Have Something To Do/ Here Today Gone Tomorrow/I Wanna Be Your Boyfriend/Questioningly (EP)	15
81	Sire SIR 4051	We Want The Airwaves/You Sound Like You're Sick (p/s)	6
81	Sire SIR 4052	She's A Sensation/All Quiet On The Eastern Front (no p/s)	8
83	Sire W 9606	Time Has Come Today/Psycho Therapy (p/s)	15
83	Sire W 9606T	Time Has Come Today/Sheena Is A Punk Rocker/Teenage Lobotomy/ Rock'n'Roll Radio (12", p/s)	20
85	Beggars Banquet BEG 128	Howling At The Moon/Chasing The Night (p/s)	5
85	Beggars Banquet BEG 128D	Howling At The Moon//Smash You/ Chasing The Night/Street Fighting Man (double pack, gatefold sleeve)	8
85	Beggars Banquet	Howling At The Moon/Chasing The Night/ Smash You/Street Fighting Man (12", p/s)	8
85	Beggars Banquet BEG 140	Bonzo Goes To Bitburg/Go Home Ann (p/s)	7
85	Beggars Banquet BEG 140T	Bonzo Goes To Bitburg/Go Home Ann/Daytime Dilemma (12", p/s)	8
86	Beggars Banquet BEG 157	Somebody Put Something In My Drink/Something To Believe In (p/s)	5
86	Beggars Banquet BEG 157T	Somebody Put Something In My Drink/(You) Can't Say Anything Nice/ Something To Believe In (12", p/s, with promo poster)	15
86	Beggars Banquet BEG 157T	Somebody Put Something In My Drink/(You) Can't Say Anything Nice/ Something To Believe In (12", p/s, without promo poster)	8
86	Beggars Banquet BEG 167	Crummy Stuff/She Belongs To Me (p/s)	7
86	Beggars Banquet BEG 167T	Crummy Stuff/Something To Believe In/I Don't Want To Live This Life (12", p/s)	12
87	Beggars Banquet BEG 198	Real Cool Time/Life Goes On (p/s)	5
87	Beggars Banquet BEG 198T	Real Cool Time/Life Goes On/Indian Giver (12", p/s)	8
87	Beggars Banquet BEG 201	I Wanna Live/Merry Christmas (I Don't Want To Fight Tonight) (p/s)	5
87	Beggars Banquet BEG 201T	I Wanna Live/Merry Christmas (I Don't Want To Fight Tonight) (12", p/s)	8
89	Chrysalis CHS 3423	Pet Sematary/All Screwed Up (p/s)	5
92	Chrysalis CHS 3917	Poison Heart/Censorshit (p/s)	5
92	Chrysalis 0946 3 23917 66	Poison Heart/Chinese Rocks/Sheena Is A Punk Rocker (live)/ Rockaway Beach (live) (12", yellow vinyl, p/s)	8
76	Sire 9103 253	RAMONES (LP, with insert)	20
77	Sire 9103 254	RAMONES LEAVE HOME (LP, with "Carbona Not Glue" with inner sleeve)	15
77	Sire 9103 255	ROCKET TO RUSSIA (LP, with inner sleeve)	12
78	Sire SRK 6063	ROAD TO RUIN (LP, yellow vinyl)	20
79	Sire SRK 6077	END OF THE CENTURY (LP)	12
79	Sire SRK2 6074	IT'S ALIVE (2-LP)	18
81	Sire SRK 3571	PLEASANT DREAMS (LP)	12
85	Beggars Banquet BEGA 59	TOO TOUGH TO DIE (LP)	12
86	Beggars Banquet BEGA 70	ANIMAL BOY (LP, picture inner sleeve and poster)	15
87	Beggars Banquet BEGA 89	HALFWAY TO SANITY (LP, inner)	12
89	Chrysalis CHR 1725	BRAIN DRAIN (LP, inner)	12
90	Beggar's Banquet	END OF THE DECADE (6 x 12" singles, box set with t-shirt, postcards & poster, 2,500 copies only)	50
91	Chysalis CHR 1901	LOCO LIVE (LP)	15
92	Chrysalis 094632196019	MONDO BIZARRO (LP)	15
93	Chrysalis CHR 6052	ACID EATERS (LP)	15
95	Chrysalis 724383413614	ADIOS AMIGOS (LP)	15

MICHEL RAMOS
60s | London DEP 95013 | PLAYING THE CLASSICS (EP, export) | 30

RAMP
77 | ABC/Blue Thumb BT 6028 | COME INTO KNOWLEDGE (LP) | 40

RAM RAM GO GO SOUND
69 | Halagala HG 26 | Pep 77/USA Outcry | 15

RAM RAM KINO
85 | Temple TOPY 006 | Advantage - Tantric Routines 1-4 (3.23)/(Basket Mix) (4.00)/Into The Bush (3.26)/Special (3.56) (12", p/s) | 8

(see also Crispy Ambulance)

RAMRODS
65 | United Artists UP 1113 | Overdrive/Stalker | 15

RAMRODS (U.S.)
61 | London HLU 9282 | Riders In The Sky/Zig Zag | 6
61 | London HLU 9355 | Loch Lomond Rock/Take Me Back To My Boots And Saddle | 20
61 | London RE-U 1292 | RIDERS IN THE SKY (EP) | 70

BILL RAMSEY
62 | Polydor NH 66812 | Go Man Go/Rocking Mountain | 12

LEE RAMSEY
96 | Real Deal RD 001 | RISE TO SHINE (EP) | 12
96 | Real Deal RD002 | RD STYLE (EP) | 10

RANCHERS
65 | Cavern Sound IMSTL 2 | An American Sailor At The Cavern/Sidetracked | 25

(see also Phil Brady & Ranchers)

RANCID
95 | Out Of Step WOOS 8 S | Time Bomb/The War's End/Blast 'Em (p/s) | 6
96 | Epitaph 86464-7 | Ruby Soho/That's Entertainment/Disorder And Disarray (p/s) | 6
98 | Epitaph 1005-7 | Bloodclot/Endrine/Stop (p/s) | 6
98 | Epitaph 1009-7 | Hooligans/Cash, Culture and Violence (Bass Drop Mix)/Things to Come (Dance hall Mix) (p/s) | 6
00 | Epitaph 1040-7 | Let Me Go/Ben Zanotto/Dead And Fone (p/s) | 6
03 | Warner Brothers W 618 | Fall Back Down/Killing Zone (p/s) | 5
94 | Epitaph 86434-1 | LET'S GO (LP, 2 x 10", gatefold sleeve, white vinyl) | 12

ALAN RANDALL (& SHEP'S BANJO BOYS)
70 | Domino 110 | The Coventry City Song/Football Football | 6

RANDALL AND ANDY C.
94 | Ram RAMM 11 | Sound Control/Feel It (12") | 15

(see also Andy C)

ELLIOTT RANDALL
71 | Polydor 2489 004 | RANDALL'S ISLAND (LP) | 20

FREDDY RANDALL & HIS BAND
58 | Parlophone GEP 8715 | CHICAGO JAZZ (EP) | 10
58 | Parlophone PMD 1046 | DR JAZZ (LP) | 20

TONY RANDALL & JACK KLUGMAN
73 | Decca F 13439 | You're So Vain/When Banana Skins Are Falling (I'll Come Sliding Back To You) | 7
72 | Decca Phase Four PFS 4277 | THE ODD COUPLE SINGS (LP) | 15

ALAN RANDALL
68 | Electratone s1002 | The Meditating Hindoo Man/Why Don't Women Like Me | 8

TEDDY RANDAZZO (& DAZZLERS)
59 | HMV POP 578 | It's Magic/Richer Than I | 10
60 | HMV POP 806 | Journey To Love/Misery | 10
61 | HMV POP 866 | Happy Ending/But You Broke My Heart | 10
61 | HMV POP 925 | Let The Sunshine In/Broken Bell | 15
62 | HMV POP 1067 | Dance To The Locomotion/Cottonfields (as Teddy Randazzo & Dazzlers) | 15
63 | HMV POP 1119 | Echoes/It Wasn't A Dream | 5
63 | Pye International 7N 25181 | Big Wide World/Be Sure, My Love | 10
62 | HMV CLP 1527 | JOURNEY TO LOVE (LP, mono) | 60
62 | HMV CSD 1421 | JOURNEY TO LOVE (LP, stereo) | 75
63 | HMV CLP 1601 | TEDDY RANDAZZO TWISTS (LP, with Dazzlers) | 100

(see also Three Chuckles)

LYNNE RANDELL
67 | CBS 2847 | Ciao Baby/Stranger In My Arms (DJ Copy) | 250
67 | CBS 2847 | Ciao Baby/Stranger In My Arms | 200
67 | CBS 2927 | That's A Hoe Down/I Need You Boy | 30

RAN-DELLS
63 | London HLU 9760 | The Martian Hop/Forgive Me Darling (I Have Lied) | 25

BARBARA RANDOLPH
67 | Tamla Motown TMG 628 | I Got A Feelin'/You Got Me Hurtin' All Over | 50
67 | Tamla Motown TMG 628 | I Got A Feelin'/You Got Me Hurtin' All Over (DJ copy) | 100
71 | Tamla Motown TMG 788 | I Got A Feelin'/You Got Me Hurtin' All Over (reissue) | 7
79 | Tamla Motown TMG 1133 | Can I Get A Witness/You Got Me Hurtin' All Over/I Got A Feeling | 15

BOOTS RANDOLPH
62 | London HLU 9567 | Bluebird Of Happiness/Keep A Light In Your Window Tonight | 6
63 | London HLU 9685 | Yakety Sax/I Really Don't Want To Know | 10
63 | London HLU 9798 | Windy And Warm/Lonely Street | 5
64 | London HLU 9891 | Hey, Mr. Sax Man/Baby Go To Sleep | 5
66 | London HLU 10017 | Theme From A Dream/King Of The Road | 5
66 | London HLU 10028 | These Boots Are Made For Walking/Honey In Your Heart | 5
66 | Monument MON 1001 | The Shadow Of Your Smile/I'll Just Walk Away | 6

63	London RE-U 1365	THE YAKETY SAX OF BOOTS RANDOLPH (EP)	15
63	London HA-U 8106	YAKETY SAX (LP)	25
66	London HA-U 8280	MORE YAKETY SAX (LP, as Boots Randolph & His Combo)	15
67	Monument LMO/SMO 5002	HIP BOOTS (LP)	15

CHARLES RANDOLPH GREEN SOUND
| 69 | London HLD 10283 | Quintin's Theme/Number One At The Blue Whale | 6 |

ERIC RANDOM
| 80 | New Hormones CAT 4 | LIVE IN EUROPE (cassette) | 10 |

(see also Tiller Boys, Cabaret Voltaire, Free Agents, Pressure & Co.)

RANDOM HARVEST
| 82 | Random Harvest RH 501 | RANDOM HARVEST (LP) | 12 |

RANDY & RAINBOWS
| 63 | Stateside SS 214 | Denise/Come Back | 65 |

RANDY'S ALLSTARS
70	Randy's RAN 500	I'm The One, You're The One/End Us	12
70	Randy's RAN 501	Pepper Pot (act. with Count Machuki)/Same Thing (B-side actually by Gaylads)	80
70	Randy's RAN 502	Dixie/Five Cents (B-side actually "A Lover's Question" by Winston Samuels)	7
70	Randy's RAN 505	Emperor Waltz/War	10
70	Randy's RAN 506	Blue Danube Waltz/Together (B-side actually by Delroy Wilson)	8
70	Randy's RAN 507	Bridge Over Troubled Water (actually by Lyrics)/Waterfall	5
71	Explosion EX 2052	Hold On Girl (actually by Lyrics)/Hold On Girl (Version)	5

(see also Impact Allstars, Lyrics, Dave Barker, Ethiopians, Jimmy London)

RANEE & RAJ
| 68 | Fontana TF 920 | Feel Like A Clown/Rainbow Land | 20 |
| 68 | Fontana TF 941 | Don't Tell Me I Must Go/Razor Edge | 20 |

SUE RANEY
57	Capitol CL 14757	The Careless Years/What's The Good Word, Mr. Bluebird	6
57	Capitol CL 14792	Please Hurry Home/Don't Take My Happiness	6
58	Capitol T 964	WHEN YOUR LOVER HAS GONE (LP)	15

WAYNE RANEY (STRING BAND)
54	Parlophone CSMP 20	Adam/The Roosters Are Crowing (export issue)	25
55	Parlophone DP 413	Mama (Don't You Remember When You Were Young)/Trying To Live Without You (78, export issue)	8
58	Parlophone GEP 8746	COUNTRY AND WESTERN (EP)	45

RANGLERS
| 68 | Trend TRE 1007 | You Never Said Goodbye/Step Down | 60 |

ERNEST RANGLIN
62	Island WI 015	Harmonica Twist/Mitty Gritty (as Ernest Ranglin Orchestra)	40
63	Island WI 128	Exodus/ROBERT MARLEY: One Cup Of Coffee	300
66	Black Swan IEP 704	ERNEST RANGLIN & THE G.B.'s (EP, with p/s)	180
66	Black Swan IEP 704	ERNEST RANGLIN & THE G.B.'s (EP)	50
64	Island ILP 909	WRANGLIN' (LP)	150
64	Island ILP 915	REFLECTIONS (LP)	150
60s	Vista Sounds	FROM KINGSTON J.A. TO MIAMI U.S.A. (LP)	25

(see also Owen Gray, Graham Bond)

MASSIMO RANIERI
| 71 | CBS 7207 | Goodbye My Love/The Sun Shining Down On Me | 12 |

BILLY RANKIN
| 83 | A&M AM 172 | Baby Come Back/Part Of The Scenery (p/s) | 6 |

(see also Nazareth)

KENNY RANKIN
60	Brunswick 05845	As Sure As You're Born/Teasin' Heart	8
70	Mercury MF1128	Peaceful/The Dolphin	15
73	Atlantic K 10275	Comin' Down/Stringman	5
74	Little David	Carfish/Silver Morning	8

ROY RANKIN AND RAYMOND NAPTALI
| 81 | KG Imperial KG 004 | Go Deh In A Late Night Blues/Late Night Session/ Babylon Policy/Peacful Something (12", green vinyl) | 20 |

RANKING ANN
| 82 | Ariwa ARIL 002 | A SLICE OF ENGLISH TOAST (LP) | 20 |
| 82 | Ariwa ARILP 010 | SOMETHING FISHY GOING ON (LP) | 15 |

RANKING DREAD
78	Greensleeves GRE10	Dub Sister Dub It/Nine Months Belly	10
80	Art And Craft ACD 005	DISCO EP SHOWCASE: Honda Accord/ Joe Grine Girl/Baby Mother/Nice Up The Lawn (12")	15
80	Art & Craft AC006	DISCO EP SHOWCASE: My Liza/Same Thing/Hard Times Leave My Life/Jah Walk Through Galilee (12" green vinyl)	20
81	Greensleeves GRED 65	Fattie Boom Boom/SLY & ROBBIE : Dub Boom (12")	12
82	Greensleeves GRED 82	Shut Me Mouth/Shut Up Shut Up (Dub Version)	25
76	Burning Sounds BS 1025	GIRLS FIESTA (LP)	25
79	Burning Sounds BS 1037	KUNTA KINTE ROOTS (LP)	25
80	Freedom Sounds FSLP 001	LOTS OF LOVING (LP)	25

RANKING JOE
78	Greensleeves GREL 2	WEAKHEART FADEAWAY (LP)	30
79	Student NWLP 009	ROUND THE WORLD (LP)	50
80	Greensleeves GREL 16	SATURDAY NIGHT JAMDOWN STYLE (LP)	20
81	Copasetic COPLPS 003	DISCO SKATE (LP, blue or black vinyl)	20

PETER RANKING AND GENERAL LUCKY
| 82 | Greensleeves GRED 98 | Beverly Black/Walk And Talk (12") | 15 |

RANKING TREVOR
| 78 | Virgin Frontline FL1015 | IN FINE STYLE (LP) | 20 |

MINT VALUE £

RANKING TREVOR AND TRINITY
78	Cha Cha CHALP 001	THREE PIECE CHICKEN AND CHIPS (LP)	30

RANSOME HEAD
71	York SYK 506	Sing/Wide Wide River	30

PETER RANSOME
72	York FYK 402	PETER RANSOME (LP, blue/silver label)	25

RAOUL & RUINED
84	Gutter Hearts GH 1	BITE BACK + BLUES (LP, fan-club only issue)	50

(see also Marc Almond)

RAPED
78	Parole KNIT 1	PRETTY PAEDOPHILES (EP)	25
78	Parole PURL 1	Cheap Night Out/Foreplay Playground (p/s, with ad sheet)	12
84	Iguana PILLAGED 1	PHILES AND SMILES (LP, official bootleg, with booklet)	50

(see also Cuddly Toys)

RAPEMAN
88	Fierce FRIGHT 031	Hated Chinee/Marmoset (p/s)	20

(see also Big Black)

RAPHAEL
67	Hispa Vox HXS 303	Please Speak To Me Of Love/While I Live	8

JOHNNY RAPHAEL
58	Vogue V 9104	We're Only Young Once/The Lonely Road To Nowhere	90
58	Vogue V 9104	We're Only Young Once/The Lonely Road To Nowhere (78)	40

RAPIERS (1)
60s	Ilford Sound ILF 272	The Phantom Stage/Valencia	20

RAPIERS (2)
86	Off Beat NS 112A	The Closing Theme/Still I Cry	10
83	Red Door RA 001	THE RAPIERS VOL. 1 (EP)	18
84	Twang RA 002	THE RAPIERS VOL. 2 (EP)	12
85	Twang RA 003	THE RAPIERS VOL. 3 (EP)	12
86	Twang RA 004	THE RAPIERS VOL. 4 (EP)	12
91	Fury DEP 3018	THE RETURN OF THE RAPIERS (EP)	10
85	Off Beat WIK 40	STRAIGHT TO THE POINT (LP)	18
87	Off Beat WIK 67	1961 (LP)	18

BRIAN RAPKIN & KELVIN JONES
70s	MSR	DREAMS OF THE BEAST (LP)	20

RAPOLOGISTS
84	Billy Boy Whiz1	Kid's Rap/Party Rap (12")	8

RARE AMBER
69	Polydor BM 56309	Malfunction Of The Engine/Blind Love	30
69	Polydor 583 046	RARE AMBER (LP)	200

RARE BIRD
70	Charisma CB 120	Sympathy/Devil's High Concern (in p/s)	15
70	Charisma CB 138	What You Want To Know/Hammerhead	10
72	Charisma CB 179	Sympathy/Devil's High Concern/What Do You Want To Know/Hammerhead (p/s)	10
73	Polydor 2058 402	Virgina/Lonely Street	5
74	Polydor 2058 471	Body And Soul/Redman	5
74	Polydor SH 1041/2	Diamonds/BARCLAY JAMES HARVEST: Negative Earth (flexi, with Sounds)	10
69	Charisma CAS 1005	RARE BIRD (LP, laminated front sleeve, pink 'scroll label)	100
70	Charisma CAS 1011	AS YOUR MIND FLIES BY (LP, textured gatefold, pink 'scroll' label)	70
72	Polydor 2442 101	EPIC FOREST (LP & poster, with bonus EP "Roadside Welcome"/ Four Grey Walls/"You're Lost" [2814 011], p/s)	100
72	Polydor 2442 101	EPIC FOREST (LP, gatefold with free EP but no poster)	50
72	Polydor 2442 101	EPIC FOREST (LP with no poster or free EP)	20
73	Polydor 2383 211	SOMEBODY'S WATCHING (LP, gatefold sleeve)	20

(see also Fields, Fruit Machine)

RARE BREED
66	Strike JH 316	Beg, Borrow And Steal/Jeri's Theme	30

(see also Ohio Express)

RARE EARTH
70	Rare Earth RES 114	(I Know) I'm Losing You/When Joanie Smiles	7
71	Rare Earth RES 104	Hey Big Brother/Under God's Light	8
71	Rare Earth RES 102	I Just Want To Celebrate/The Seed	6
70	Tamla Motown TMG 742	Get Ready/Magic Key	20
70	Tamla Motown STML 11165	GET READY (LP)	20
71	Tamla Motown STML 11180	ECOLOGY (LP)	20
71	Rare Earth SREA 4001	ONE WORLD (LP, textured gatefold sleeve)	18
72	Rare Earth SRESP 301	IN CONCERT (2-LP satchel sleeve)	15
73	Rare Earth SRE 3008	WILLIE REMEMBERS (LP, gatefold sleeve)	12

RARE PLEASURE
76	DJM DJS 10738	Let Me Down Easy/Let Me Down Easy (Long Version) (Promo p/s)	10
76	DJM DJS 10738	Let Me Down Easy/Let Me Down Easy (Long Version)	7

HERMAN RAREBELL
81	Harvest HAR 5125	I'll Say Goodbye/Junk Funk	10
81	Harvest SHSP 4118	NIP IN THE BUD (LP)	12

RAS NATURAL
03	Unity Sound US006	Roar Like A Lion/Lion Chant/Version (10")	20

RASCALS
68	Atlantic 584 182	A Beautiful Morning/Rainy Day	8
68	Atlantic 584 210	People Got To Be Free/My World	8
69	Atlantic 584 255	Heaven/Baby I'm Blue	8

69	Atlantic 584 274	See/Away Away	8
69	Atlantic 584 292	Carry Me Back/Real Thing	7
70	Atlantic 584 307	Hold On/I Believe	8
70	Atlantic 2091 029	Glory, Glory/You Don't Know	6
71	CBS 7363	Love Me/Happy Song	6
71	CBS 7672	Lucky Day/Love Letter	6
68	Atlantic 587/588 098	ONCE UPON A DREAM (LP)	18
68	Atlantic 587/588 120	TIME PEACE - RASCALS' GREATEST HITS (LP)	12
69	Atlantic 588 183	FREEDOM SUITE (LP)	12
70	Atlantic 588 210	SEE (LP)	12
71	Atlantic 2400 113	SEARCH AND NEARNESS (LP)	12
71	CBS S 64406	PEACEFUL WORLD (2xLP)	18

(see also Young Rascals)

RENATO RASCEL
| 60 | RCA RCA 1177 | Romantica/Dimmelo Con Un Fiore | 5 |

(see also Royal Rasses)

(EMPRESS) RASHEDA
| 92 | Rasheda Lioness RLM 001 | Only Jah Worthy/Give Jah Praise (12") | 20 |
| 95 | Roots Music RRLP 011 | HAIL H.I.M (LP) | 25 |

RAS IMRU
| 80 | Jah Shaka KMD001 | Marshall/SHAKA RYDIM SECTION : Warrior Style (12") | 60 |

RAS MIDAS
| 78 | Tribesman TM24 | Good Old Days/Natty Dread Surprise (12") | 70 |

RASPBERRY PIRATES
| 68 | Atlantic 584 230 | Looky Looky My Cookie's Gone/Good Morning Baby | 6 |

RASTAFARI
| 73 | Satril SAT8 | Funky City/In The Garden | 40 |

THE RAT & THE WHALE
| 80 | Rewind REWIND 5 | Wheels On Fire/Wheels On Fire (Long Version) (p/s) | 5 |

(see also Alternative TV, Rat Scabies)

BASIL RATHBONE
| 60s | Caedmon TC 1028 | EDGAR ALLAN POE (LP) | 15 |

RATIO
| 70 | Big Chief BC 102 | Let There Be Peace In The World/Pharaoh's Walk | 7 |

RATIONAL ANTHEM
| 86 | Radio Humberside/HLS 001 | THE NORTHERN TRAWL (LP) | 50 |

ARMAN RATIP
| 70 | Columbia SCX 6532 | INTRODUCING THE ARMAN RATIP TRIO (LP) | 120 |
| 73 | Regal Zono. SLRZ 1038 | THE SPY FROM ISTANBUL (LP, gatefold sleeve) | 120 |

RATS (1)
64	Oak RGJ 145	Spoonful (1-sided, with foldout p/s)	400
64	Oak RGJ 145	Spoonful (1-sided)	250
65	Columbia DB 7483	Spoonful/I've Got My Eyes On You Baby	120
65	Columbia DB 7607	I Gotta See My Baby Everyday/Headin' Back (To New Orleans)	90
95	Tenth Planet TP	THE RISE AND FALL OF BERNIE GRIPPLESTONE & THE SPIDERS FROM HULL (LP, gatefold sleeve, 1,000 only)	15

(see also Beat Boys, Mark Peters)

RATS (2)
| 64 | Oriole CB 1967 | Parchman Farm/Every Day I Have The Blues | 100 |
| 65 | CBS 201740 | Sack Of Woe/Gimme That Wine | 85 |

RATS (3)
74	MAM MAM 113	Don't Let Go/Dragon Child	8
74	Goodear Records EAR. 101	Turtle Dove/Oxford Donna (with p/s)	25
74	Goodear EARLH 5003	FIRST (LP)	18

(see also World of Oz)

RATT
| 85 | Atlantic A 9546P | Lay It Down/Got Me On The Line (shaped picture disc) | 6 |
| 86 | Atlantic A 9502P | You're In Love/Between The Eyes (shaped picture disc) | 8 |

RATTLES
63	Philips BF 1277	The Stomp/Zip A Dee Doo Dah	20
64	Decca F 11873	Bye Bye Johnny/Roll Over Beethoven	25
64	Decca F 11936	Tell Me What I Can Do/Sunbeam At The Sky	25
65	Fontana TF 618	Come On And Sing/Candy To Me	25
66	Fontana TF 724	Say All Right/Love Of My Life	25
70	Decca F 23058	The Witch/Geraldine	6
71	Decca F 23119	You Can't Have Sunshine Everyday/Where Is The Friend	15
71	Decca FR 13243	The Devil's On The Loose/I Know You Don't Know	15
73	Decca FR 13390	Devils Son/What Do I Care	20
64	Decca DFE 8568	TEENBEAT FROM THE STAR CLUB HAMBURG (EP)	125
64	Philips BL 7614	TWIST AT THE STAR CLUB HAMBURG (LP)	100
67	Mercury MG 1127	GREATEST HITS (LP)	30
71	Decca SKL-R 5088	THE RATTLES (LP)	30

(see also Wonderland)

CARL RAVAZZA
| 51 | HMV B 10202 | Rock, Rock, Rock/Like A Dream (78) | 10 |

CHRIS RAVEL & RAVERS
| 63 | Decca F 11696 | I Do/Don't You Dig This Kind Of Beat | 20 |

(see also Chris Andrews)

RAVEN
| 80 | Neat NEAT 06 | Don't Need Your Money/Wiped Out (p/s) | 8 |
| 81 | Neat NEAT 11 | Hard Ride/Crazy World (p/s) | 6 |

Jon RAVEN

82	Neat NEAT 1512	CRASH BANG WALLOP (Crash Bang Wallop/Firepower/Run Them Down/ Rock Hard) (12" EP, mauve splattered vinyl)	15
86	WEA A 9453	Gimme Some Lovin' (no p/s)	8
81	Neat NEAT1001	ROCK UNTIL YOU DROP (LP + lyric insert)	12
81	Neat NEAT1004	WIPED OUT (LP + poster)	12
83	Neat NEATP1001	ROCK UNTIL YOU DROP (reissue picture disc LP)	15
83	Neat NEAT 1011	ALL FOR ONE (LP, inner)	12
88	Under One Flag FLAG 28	NOTHING EXCEEDS LIKE EXCESS (LP, inner)	12

JON RAVEN

70s	Broadside	HARVEST (LP, with book)	15
71	Argo ZFB 29	KATE OF COALBROOKDALE (LP, as Jon & Mike Raven with Jean Ward)	100
73	Trailer LER 2083	SONGS OF A CHANGING WORLD (LP, with Nic Jones & Tony Rose, red label with insert)	25
75	Tradition TSR 019	THE BOLD NAVIGATORS: THE STORY OF ENGLAND'S CANALS IN SONG (LP, with John Kirkpatrick, Sue Harris, & Gary & Vera Aspey)	20
76	Broadside BRO 117	HARVEST (LP)	50
76	Broadside BRO 118	THE ENGLISH CANALS (LP, with John Kirkpatrick & Sue Harris)	15
81	Dingles DIN 319	REGAL SLIP (LP)	30

(see also Halliard, Black Country Three, John Kirkpatrick)

PAUL RAVEN (1)

61	Parlophone R 4812	Walk On Boy/All Grown Up	8
61	Parlophone R 4842	Tower Of Strength/Livin' The Blues	8
77	EMI NUT 2855	PAUL RAVEN (EP)	8

PAUL RAVEN (2)

68	MCA MU 1024	Musical Man/Wait For Me	15
68	MCA MU1035	Soul Thing/We'll Go Where The World Can't	12

(see also Rubber Bucket)

SIMON RAVEN

66	Piccadilly 7N 35301	I Wonder If She Remembers Me/Sea Of Love	80

RAVENS

53	Oriole CB 1148	Rock Me All Night Long/Write Me One Sweet Letter (78)	30
53	Oriole CB 1149	Begin The Beguine/Looking For My Baby (78)	30
53	Oriole CB 1258	Who'll Be The Fool?/Rough Ridin' (78)	30

RAVENS

63	Oriole CB 1910	I Just Wanna Hear You Say/Send Me A Letter	30

RAVENS ROCK GROUP

61	Pye International 7N 25077	The Ghoul Friend/Career Girl	20

RAVE ONS

60s	Sounds Good MT 103	She's A Spoon/Keep Wrong	120

RAVERS

69	Upsetter US 312	Babam Bam/UPSETTERS: Medical Operation	100

RAW DEAL (1)

81	White Witch WIT 701	Out Of My Head/In The Mood (no p/s)	50
81	Neat NEAT 12	Lonewolf/Take The Sky (p/s)	10

RAW DEAL (2)

95	Mental Disorder MAD 666	THE LEGENDARY RAW DEAL (10" LP)	12

PETER RAWES

87	Official OFFA 5	Why Should I Ask Her To Stay?/Theme From Shark/Theme From Forever (with Jet Harris) (p/s)	6

(see also Jet Harris)

LOU RAWLS

65	Capitol CL 15398	Three O'Clock In The Morning/Nothing Really Feels The Same	10
66	Capitol CL 15465	Love Is A Hurtin' Thing/Memory Lane	10
67	Capitol CL 15488	You Can Bring Me All Your Heartaches/A Woman Who's A Woman	15
67	Capitol CL 15499	Dead End Street/Yes It Hurts Doesn't It	20
67	Capitol CL 15507	Show Business/When Loves Goes Wrong	25
67	Capitol CL 15515	Hard To Get Thing Called Love/(How Do You Say) I Don't Love You Anymore	10
67	Capitol CL 15522	Little Drummer Boy/Child With A Toy	8
68	Capitol CL 15533	My Ancestors/Evil Woman	8
68	Capitol CL 15548	You're Good For Me/Soul Serenade	10
68	Capitol CL 15560	Down Here On The Ground/I'm Satisfied	8
69	Capitol CL 15583	It's You/Sweet Charity	8
69	Capitol CL 15611	Your Good Thing (Is About To End)/Season Of The Witch	8
70	Capitol CL 15630	You've Made Me So Very Happy/Let's Burn Down The Cornfield	5
74	Bell BLL 1390	She's Gone/Hourglass	5
63	Capitol EAP-1 20646	LOST AND LOOKIN' (EP)	50
65	Capitol T 1824	BLACK AND BLUE (LP)	25
66	Capitol (S)T 2459	LIVE (LP)	20
67	Capitol (S)T 2566	SOULIN' (LP)	25
67	Capitol (S)T 2632	CARRYIN' ON! (LP)	20
68	Capitol (S)T 2864	FEELIN' GOOD (LP)	30
69	Capitol ST 2927	YOU'RE GOOD FOR ME (LP)	20
69	Capitol E-ST 215	THE WAY IT WAS THE WAY IT IS (LP)	20

RAW MATERIAL

69	Evolution E 2441	Time And Illusion/Bobo's Party	50
70	Evolution E 2445	Hi There Hallelujah/Days Of The Fighting Cock	35
70	Evolution E 24495	Travelling Man (Part 1)/Part 2	30
71	RCA Neon NE 1002	Ride On Pony/Religion	30
70	Evolution Z 1006	RAW MATERIAL (LP)	700
71	RCA Neon NE 8	TIME IS (LP, gatefold sleeve)	500

(see also Deep Feelings, Shoot)

ANNITA RAY

62	MGM 1177	Wouldn't It Be Lovely/I'm In Love With Jim	6

CONGO ASHANTI RAY
83	On U Sound DP5	Africa Blood/Hands And Hearts	15

DANNY RAY
76	Doctor DR 01	REVOLUTION ROCK (LP)	30

DANNY RAY & FALCONS
70	MCA MK 5037	Scorpion/I Love You Girl	10

DIANE RAY
63	Mercury AMT 1209	Please Don't Talk To The Lifeguard/That's All I Want From You	22

FROGGIE RAY
71	Big BG 313	Uncle Charlie/Party Version	8
71	Big BG 314	Half Moon/RUPIE EDWARDS ALL STARS: Full Moon	7

JAMES RAY
62	Pye International 7N 25126	If You Gotta Make A Fool Of Somebody/It's Been A Drag	25
62	Pye International 7N 25147	Itty Bitty Pieces/You Remember The Face	20

JOHNNIE RAY
53	Columbia SCM 5015	Walkin' My Baby Back Home/The Lady Drinks Champagne (B-side with the Four Lads)	20
53	Columbia SCM 5033	Ma Says, Pa Says/A Full Time Job (with Doris Day)	20
53	Columbia SCM 5041	Whiskey And Gin/Tell The Lady I Said Goodbye	20
53	Columbia SCM 5074	Please Don't Talk About Me When I'm Gone/Coffee And Cigarettes (B-side with the Four Lads)	20
54	Columbia SCM 5111	Nobody's Sweetheart/I Can't Escape From You	20
54	Columbia SCM 5122	She Didn't Say Nothin' At All/I'm Just A Shadow Of Myself	20
57	Philips JK 1004	You Don't Owe Me A Thing/Look Homeward, Angel (jukebox issue)	20
57	Philips JK 1011	So Long/I Miss You So (jukebox issue)	20
57	Philips JK 1016	Yes, Tonight, Josephine/No Wedding Today (jukebox issue)	30
57	Philips JK 1025	Build Your Love (On A Strong Foundation)/Street Of Memories (jukebox issue)	30
57	Philips JK 1026	Up Above My Head, I Hear Music On The Air/Good Evening Friends/ Memories (with Frankie Laine, jukebox issue only)	30
57	Philips JK 1033	Pink Sweater Angel/Texas Tambourine (jukebox issue)	30
58	Philips PB 785	Miss Me Just A Little/Soliloquy Of A Fool	5
58	Philips PB 808	Strollin' Girl/Plant A Little Seed	5
58	Philips PB 829	Lonely For A Letter/Endlessly	5
58	Philips PB 849	No Regrets/Up Until Now	5
58	Philips PB 884	What More Can I Say/You're The One Who Knows	5
59	Philips PB 901	When's Your Birthday, Baby/One Man's Love Song Is Another Man's Blues	5
59	Philips PB 918	Call Me Yours/Here And Now	5
59	Philips PB 918	Call Me Yours/Here And Now (78)	10
59	Philips PB 952	You're All That I Live For/I'll Never Fall In Love Again	6
59	Philips PB 952	You're All That I Live For/I'll Never Fall In Love Again (78)	20
60	Philips PB 990	When It's Springtime In The Rockies/Wagon Wheels	6
60	Philips PB 1025	Before You/I'll Make You Mine	6
60	Philips PB 1047	Tell Me/Don't Leave Me Now	5
60	London HLA 9216	In The Heart Of A Fool/Let's Forget It Now	5
61	Philips PB 1126	An Ordinary Couple/Cool Water	5
61	United Artists POP 902	How Many Nights How Many Days/I'll Bring Along My Banjo	15
62	London HLG 9484	I Believe (with Timi Yuro)/TIMI YURO: Smile	8
63	Brunswick 05884	Lookout Chatanooga/After My Laughter Came Tears	7
69	Pye 7N 17691	Wise To The Ways Of The World/Since I Lost You Baby	7
69	Pye 7N 17760	Long And Lonely Nights/Brokenhearted Me, Evilhearted You	8
76	EPIC MEPC 4533	Cry/The Little White Cloud That Cried	20
54	Columbia SEG 7511	JOHNNIE RAY (EP,company sleeve)	10
55	Philips BBE 12006	JOHNNIE RAY (EP)	10
57	Philips BBE 12115	WALKING AND CRYING (EP)	20
57	Philips BBL 7148	THE BIG BEAT (LP)	15
58	Philips BBL 7254	AT THE DESERT INN - LAS VEGAS (LP)	20
58	Philips BBL 7264	SHOWCASE OF HITS (LP)	

(see also Four Lads, Frankie Laine & Johnnie Ray, Timi Yuro)

RICARDO RAY
68	Roulette RO 501	Nitty Gritty/Mony Mony	11

WADE RAY
63	London HL 9700	Burning Desire/Two Red Red Lips	8

RAY & COLLUNEY
71	Westwood WRS 001	TYRANTS OF ENGLAND (LP)	40

RAY & HIS COURT
00	Jazzman JM 014	Soul Freedom/RAY & HIS FAMILY: Cookie Crumbs	5

CHRIS(TINE) RAYBURN
63	Parlophone R 5098	Slow Loving Woman/Same Old Places	10
64	Parlophone R 5144	I've Cried My Last Tear/You Forgot To Say When	10
66	Parlophone R 5422	I Wanna Be In Love Again/Another Night Alone	10
68	Music Factory CUB 2	One Way Ticket/Photograph Of Love	10
69	Pye 7N 17679	Skip A Rope/Starlight (as Christine Rayburn)	10
66	Parlophone PCS7001	CHRIS RAYBURN (LP)	25

MARGIE RAYBURN
56	Capitol CL 14532	The Wedding Song/That's The Chance I've Got To Take	10
57	London HLU 8515	I'm Available/If You Were	25
58	London HLU 8648	I Would/Alright, But It Won't Be Easy	18

CLYDE RAY
57	Columbia DB 3875	Follow Me/Steady As A Rock	10
58	Columbia DB 4106	Locked In The Arms Of Love/I'm Not Afraid Anymore	10

ANTHONY RAYE
80	Grapevine GRP 147	Give Me One More Chance/Hold On To What You've Got	8

SOL RAYE
63	Oriole CB 1855	Dear Michelle/I Love You Because	10

MINT VALUE £

67	Deram DM 154	While I'm Here/To Be With You	12

BILLY RAYMOND
58	HMV POP 503	Making Love/I Would	5
58	HMV POP 526	One In Particular/Seven Daughters	5
59	HMV POP 614	Charlie Is Their Darling/Loch Lomond	5

DANNY RAYMOND
71	Big Shot BI 587	Sister Big Stuff/BOY FRIDAY: Free Man	7

LEE RAYMOND WITH COSTELLO SISTERS
55	Brunswick 05438	Foolishly Yours/Baby Darling	10

MARK RAYMOND & CROWD
64	Columbia DB 7308	Girls/Remember Me To Julie	15

TONY RAYMOND
59	Fontana H 213	Broken-Hearted Melody/This Earth Is Mine	8
59	Fontana H 213	Broken-Hearted Melody/This Earth Is Mine (78)	10
62	Oriole CB 1708	Handful Of Songs/She'll Have To Go	6
62	Oriole CB 1777	The Infant King/Because Of You	6

IVOR RAYMONDE & HIS ORCHESTRA
65	Mercury MF 866	Feelin' Fruggy/Grotty	12

JULIE RAYNE
59	HMV POP 665	Waltz Me Around/Love Where Can You Be?	15
60	HMV POP 785	Bim Bam Bom/One More Time	15
61	HMV POP 868	Green With Envy Purple With Passion/My First Romance	15
63	Windsor WPS 123	Faithfully/Free To Love	12
64	Windsor WPS 128	You Can't Come Back/Straight To Your Arms	12

LISA RAYNE
65	Fontana TF 563	Don't Ever Change/It Had To Be You	10

MARTIN RAYNOR & SECRETS
65	Columbia DB 7563	Candy To Me/You're A Wonderful One	60

(see also Secrets, Simon's Secrets, Clifford T. Ward)

RAYS
57	London HLU 8505	Silhouettes/Daddy Cool	40
57	London HLU 8505	Silhouettes/Daddy Cool (78)	20

RAZAR
78	Polydor 2058 983	Ascension Day/Ain't No Mystery	30

(see also Third World War, Soho Jets)

RAZBERRY HOLIDAY BAND
89	Caleche LIS 001	Hangover Square/Promise	20

RAZORCUTS
86	Subway Org. SUBWAY 5	Big Pink Cake/I'll Still Be There (foldover p/s with insert, poly bag, 2,000 only)	18
86	Subway Org. SUBWAY 8	Sorry To Embarrass You/Summer In Your Heart (p/s, with insert, 2,000 only)	15
87	Sha La La BaBaBaBaBa 02	Sad Kaleidoscope/TALULAH GOSH: I Told You So (flexidisc p/s, 2,500 only)	10
80s	Caff CAFF 10	Sometimes I Worry About You/For Always/Sorry To Embarrass You/ Music From The Big Pink (foldaround p/s with insert, 500 only)	20
88	Creation CRELP 026	STORYTELLER (LP)	25
89	Creation CRELP 045	THE WORLD KEEPS TURNING (LP)	20
91	Creation CRECD 119	PATTERNS ON THE WATER (CD, compilation)	20
02	Matinee MATCD 12	R IS FOR RAZORCUTS (CD)	20

(see also Cinematics, Red Chair Fadeaway)

RAZORLIGHT
04	Vertigo 986 710-1	UP ALL NIGHT (LP)	15

RAZOR'S EDGE
66	Stateside SS 532	Let's Call It A Day, Girl/April	15

CHRIS REA
74	Magnet MAG 10	So Much Love/Born To Lose (no p/s)	25
79	Magnet MAGL 5028	DELTICS (LP, blue vinyl, stickered sleeve)	12

REACTA
79	Battery Operated WAC 1	Stop The World/SUS (p/s)	100

(see also Television Personalities)

REACTION
68	President PT 208	That Man/Falling In Love With You	12

REACTION
70	Columbia Blue Beat DB 119	Oh Me, Oh My/RECO: It's Love	12
70	Attack ATT 8022	You Yes You/CIMARONS: Be There	10

(see also Ezz Reco, Joe Higgs)

REACTION
78	Island WIP 6437	I Can't Resist/I Am A Case (p/s)	15

(see also Talk Talk)

AL READ
56	HMV POP 278	We Haven't Any Money/What Is A Home	5
59	HMV POP 575	That's Life/Our Maggie's Going To Get Married	5

PAT READER
60	Triumph RGM 1024	Ricky/Dear Daddy	60
62	Piccadilly 7N 35077	Cha Cha On The Moon/May Your Heart Stay Young Forever	30
63	Oriole CB 1903	Helpless/Lover's Lane	30

BERTICE READING
55	Parlophone R 4057	Songs From "Jazz Train" Parts 1 & 2 (with Edric Connor)	6
57	Decca F 10965	No Flowers By Request/September In The Rain	15
58	Parlophone R 4462	Rock Baby Rock/It's A Boy	60
58	Parlophone R 4462	Rock Baby Rock/It's A Boy (78)	20

58	Parlophone R 4487	My Big Best Shoes/No More In Life	10

WILMA READING
| 74 | Pye 7N 45380 | Play It Again/Two Can Have A Party | 5 |

REALISTICS
| 77 | Epic SEPC 5723 | So Sad/The Magic That You Do | 7 |

REALISTS
| 78 | Stiff OFF 4 | I've Got A Heart/Living in The City (p/s) | 5 |

REALITY
| 82 | Subversive SUB | BLIND TO THE TRUTH (EP, foldout sleeve and insert) | 8 |
| 84 | Fight Back FIGHT 3 | WHO KILLED THE GOLDEN GOOSE? (EP) | 8 |

REALITY FROM DREAM
| 75 | (no label) CP 109 | REALITY FROM DREAM (LP, private pressing) | 140 |

REAL KIDS
| 78 | Bronze BRO 54 | All Kindsa Girls/Common At Noon (p/s) | 8 |
| 78 | Bronze BRON 509 | REAL KIDS (LP) | 20 |

REALM
| 66 | CBS 202044 | Hard Time Loving You/Certain Kind Of Girl | 35 |

(see also Earl Preston & Realms)

REAL MCCOY
67	Fontana TF 794	Show Me How You Milk A Cow/I Paid For My Laughs	8
68	Target 7N 17669	Quick Joey Small/Happiness Is Love	20
68	Pye 7N 17618	I Get So Excited/Somebody's Taken Maria Away	8
69	Pye 7N 17669	Quick Joey Small/Happiness Is Love	8
69	Pye 7N 17704	Round The Gum Tree/I Will	8
69	Pye 7N 17772	Gitarzan/Anytime You Need Me	8
69	Pye 7N 17850	Many The Memories/She's Different, She's Beautiful	8
70	Marble Arch MAL 1251	THIS IS THE REAL McCOY (LP)	20
71	CBS 7065	I'll Give You Things/Baby, Go Home	8

(see also Tony Colton)

REALMS
| 70s | Summertime BUSS 11 | Happiness Is Your Name/Happiest Dread | 10 |

REAL THING
| 72 | Bell BLL 1232 | Vicious Circles Parts 1 & 2 | 5 |

(see also Chants)

REASONS
| 78 | Island WIP 6467 | Hard Day At The Office/Baby Bright Eyes (p/s) | 30 |

REBEL
| 81 | Bridge House BHS 2 | Rocka Shocka/Drift Away (p/s) | 12 |
| 86 | Flying Pig REBS 1 | Valentino/Lonely Traveller (p/s, with free single) | 12 |

REBEL ROUSERS
| 68 | Fontana TF 973 | Should I?/As I Look | 200 |

(see also Cliff Bennett & Rebel Rousers, Soul Sounds)

REBELS
| 78 | Rigid IS REB 1029 | Suicide/The Leader Of The Rebellion | 250 |

REBELS & ALLIES
| 79 | Brixton sound BS01234 | BROKEN HEART (LP) | 20 |

REBELS (JAMAICA)
76	Black Wax WAX 16	Rhodesia/Version	20
70	Bullet BU 440	Nice Grind/SIDNEY ALL STARS: Nice Grind - Version	10
70	Trojan TR 7779	It's All In The Game/Easy Come	12

(see also The Pioneers)

REBELS (U.K.)
| 67 | Page One POF 017 | Hard To Love You/Call Me | 40 |

REBOUNDS
| 64 | Fontana TF 461 | Help Me/The World Is Mine | 25 |

REBS
| 58 | Capitol CL 14932 | Bunky/Renegade | 15 |

RECKLESS
| 92 | Pulse-8 12LOSE 24 | Time To Make The Floor Burn (The Reckless Hypermix)/Take Me (Ruff Mix)/Take Me (Uplifting Piano Mix) (12", p/s) | 25 |

RECO
69	Downtown DT 417	Quando Quando/Reg 'A' Jeg (as Reco & Rudies)	12
69	Jackpot JP 710	Memory Of Don Drummond/THE TOBIES: Resting	15
69	Treasure Isle TI 7052	The Lion Speaks/ANDY CAPP: Pop A Top	10
69	Pama ECO 14	RECO IN REGGAE LAND (LP)	120

(see also Reaction, Don Reco, Rico Rodriguez, Father Sketto, Joe Monsano, Slim Smith, Laurel Aitken)

DON RECO
| 71 | Big Shot BI 597 | Waterloo Rock/LLOYD'S ALL STARS: Walls Soul | 15 |

(see also Reco)

EZZ RECO & LAUNCHERS
64	Columbia DB 7217	King Of Kings/Blue Beat Dance	12
64	Columbia DB 7222	Little Girl/The Bluest Beat	7
64	Columbia DB 7290	Please Come Back/At A Party	7
64	Columbia SEG 8326	JAMAICAN BLUE BEAT (EP)	30

(see also Reaction)

RECORD PLAYERS
| 78 | Wreckord WRECK 001 | DOUBLE C SIDE (EP, label also listed as Aerco AERO 1104) | 8 |
| 80 | Wreckord WRECK 002 | Give An Inch/Squirming In The Vermin By The Bonny Banks Of Clyde/ 67/Parasite (p/s) | 6 |

RECTIFY
| 88 | Taffcore TAFF 001 | 20TH CENTURY EP (foldout p/s) | 10 |

RED
| 83 | Jigsaw SAW 2 | RED (LP, private pressing) | 25 |

RED ALERT (1)
| 69 | Total TL3 | Witch Woman/Sabra | 35 |

RED ALERT (2)
80	Guardian GM-RA/B 61	BORDER GUARDS (EP)	250
82	No Future OI 5	In Britain/Screaming At The Nation/Murder Missile (p/s)	10
82	No Future OI 33	Take No Prisoners/Empire Of Crime/Sell Out (p/s)	10
83	No Future OI 20	City Invasion/Negative Reaction (p/s)	8
83	No Future OI 27	THERE'S A GUITAR BURNING (12" EP)	15
83	No Future PUNK 5	WE'VE GOT THE POWER (LP)	15

RED ALERT (3)
| 82 | Steel City AJS7R | Run To Ground/Wild You (no p/s) | 10 |

RED ALLIGATOR
| 69 | Youngblood YB1004 | Real Cool/Slow Down | 18 |

(see Jimmy Powell)

RED BALUNE
| 78 | MCCB 001 | Capitalist Kid/Spider In Love (p/s) | 12 |

RED DRAGON
| 86 | Redman Intl. RED 4 | Ease Off/ADMIRAL TIBET: New Tactics (12") | 20 |

RED PYJAMAS
| 88 | Ride SRT 8KS1750 | Hands Off, Hands On, Lucinda Loves You/Lets Get Happy (p/s) | 6 |

REDBEAT
| 80 | Malicious Damage MD 440 | Machines In Motion/More Or Less Cut (12", p/s) | 8 |

REDBONE
70	CBS 5061	Crazy Cajun Cakewalk Band/Night Come Down	5
70	CBS 5326	Maggie/New Blue Sermonette	6
70	CBS 64069	REDBONE (LP)	15
70	CBS 64198	POTLATCH (LP)	15
71	Epic EPC 64709	WITCH QUEEN OF NEW ORLEANS (LP)	12
72	Epic EQ 30815	MESSAGE FROM A DRUM (LP, quadraphonic)	15

REDCAPS
63	Decca F 11716	Shout/Little Things You Do	20
63	Decca F 11789	Talkin' 'Bout You/Come On Girl	20
64	Decca F 11903	Mighty Fine Girl/Funny Things	20

REDCELL
92	B12 B1205	REDCELL EP (12")	25
92	B12 B1205	REDCELL EP (12", purple vinyl)	80
92	B12 B1207	RETREAT FROM UNPLEASANT REALITIES EP (12")	40
92	B12 B1207	RETREAT FROM UNPLEASANT REALITIES EP (12", blue vinyl)	60
92	B12 B1207	RETREAT FROM UNPLEASANT REALITIES EP (12", red vinyl)	60
93	B12 B1208	INTERIM OUTERIM EP(12")	15
93	B12 B1208	INTERIM OUTERIM EP (12", white vinyl)	60
96	B12 B1215	Untitled (12", White label promo)	60

RED CHAIR FADEAWAY
89	Cosmic Eng. M. CTA 103	Let It Happen/Myra/Dragonfly/Grasshopper (12", p/s, 500 only)	15
90	Cosmic Eng. M. CTA 105	Mr Jones/Chimney Pots/Faraway Lights/Out Of The Grey (12", p/s, 450 only)	15
91	Waterbomb SPLAT 002	Never Remember/FUDGE: Girlwish (flexi, p/s)	12
91	Tangerine MM 10	CURIOUSER AND CURIOUSER (LP, foldaround sleeve with booklet, no'd)	20
93	Aural AUR 102	MESMERISED (LP, 500 only)	12

(see also Razorcuts)

RED CRAYOLA
| 78 | Radar ADA 22 | Wives In Orbit/Yik Yak (p/s, red vinyl) | 7 |
| 78 | Radar RAD 12 | THE PARABLES OF ARABLE LAND (LP, stickered sleeve) | 15 |

FREDDIE REDD
| 58 | Nixa NJL 19 | GET HAPPY (LP) | 200 |

GENE REDD & GLOBETROTTERS
| 59 | Parlophone R 4584 | Red River Valley Rock/Kentucky Home Rock | 15 |

NOEL REDDING BAND
| 75 | RCA RS 1030 | CLONAKILTY COWBOYS (LP) | 12 |

(see also Loving Kind, Jimi Hendrix, Fat Mattress, Lord Sutch, Road)

OTIS REDDING
SINGLES : SINGLES, EPS, LPS
64	London HLK 9833	Pain In My Heart/Something Is Worrying Me	25
64	London HLK 9876	Come To Me/Don't Leave Me This Way	25
65	Atlantic AT 4024	Mr Pitiful/That's How Strong My Love Is	25
65	Sue WI 362	Shout Bamalama/Fat Girl	30
65	Atlantic AT 4029	I've Been Loving You Too Long/Winter Wonderland (unissued, demos only)	75
65	Atlantic AT 4039	Respect/I've Been Loving You Too Long	18
65	Atlantic AT 4050	My Girl/Down In The Valley	15
66	Atlantic AT 4080	(I Can't Get No) Satisfaction/Any Ole Way	12
66	Atlantic 584 019	My Lover's Prayer/Don't Mess With Cupid	12
66	Atlantic 584 030	I Can't Turn You Loose/Just One More Day	10
66	Atlantic 584 049	Fa-Fa-Fa-Fa-Fa (Sad Song)/Good To Me	10
67	Atlantic 584 070	Try A Little Tenderness/I'm Sick Y'all	10
67	Atlantic 584 091	Respect/These Arms Of Mine	8
67	Atlantic 584 092	My Girl/Mr Pitiful	8
67	Stax 601 005	Day Tripper/Shake (dark blue labels)	10

67	Stax 601 007	Let Me Come On Home/I Love You More Than Words Can Say (dark blue labels)	10
67	Stax 601 011	Shake (live)/634-5789 (live)	10
67	Stax 601 017	The Glory Of Love/I'm Coming Home	8
67	Stax 601 027	(I Can't Get No) Satisfaction/I've Been Loving You Too Long	8
68	Stax 601 031	(Sittin' On) The Dock Of The Bay/My Sweet Lorene	8
68	Stax 601 040	The Happy Song/Open The Door	8
68	Pye International 7N 25463	She's All Right/Gama Lama	10
68	Atlantic 584 199	Hard To Handle/Amen	8
68	Atlantic 584 220	Champagne And Wine/I've Got Dreams To Remember	10
68	Atlantic 584 234	Papa's Got A Brand New Bag/Direct Me	8
69	Atlantic 584 249	A Lover's Question/You Made A Man Out Of Me	10
69	Atco 226 001	Love Man/That's How Strong My Love Is	10
69	Atco 226 002	Free Me/Higher And Higher	8
69	Evolution E 2442	She's All Right/Tuff Enuff	15
70	Atco 226 012	Look At That Girl/That's A Good Idea	8
70	Atco 2091 020	Wonderful World/Security	8
71	Atlantic 2091 062	I've Been Loving You Too Long/Try A Little Tenderness	5
71	Atlantic 2091 112	(Sittin' On) The Dock Of The Bay/Respect/Mr Pitiful (reissue)	5
72	Atlantic K 10206	White Christmas/Merry Christmas, Baby	5
05	Atco 002	Loving By The Pound/BENNY TROY: I Wanna Give You Tomorrow (promo, 500 only)	10
08	Kent Select CITY 008	Loving By The Pound/BARBARA AND THE BROWNS: I'm Gonna Start A War	10
66	Sue IEP 710	EARLY OTIS REDDING (EP)	100
65	Atlantic ATL 5029	THE GREAT OTIS REDDING SINGS SOUL BALLADS (LP)	50
66	Atlantic ATL 5041	OTIS BLUE: OTIS REDDING SINGS SOUL (LP)	40
66	Atlantic 587 011	THE SOUL ALBUM (LP)	30
66	Atlantic 587 035	THE GREAT OTIS REDDING SINGS SOUL BALLADS (LP, reissue)	20
66	Atlantic 587/588 036	OTIS BLUE: OTIS REDDING SINGS SOUL (LP, reissue, mono/stereo)	20
67	Atlantic 587/588 050	COMPLETE AND UNBELIEVABLE: THE OTIS REDDING DICTIONARY OF SOUL (LP)	25
67	Atlantic 587 042	PAIN IN MY HEART (LP)	25
67	Stax VOLT 418	THE HISTORY OF OTIS REDDING (LP)	25
68	Stax 589 016	OTIS REDDING IN EUROPE (LP)	20
68	Stax 230 001/231 001	THE DOCK OF THE BAY (LP)	20
68	Atlantic 587/588 113	THE IMMORTAL OTIS REDDING (LP)	25
68	Atlantic 587/588 148	OTIS REDDING AT THE WHISKEY A GO GO, LOS ANGELES (LP)	20
69	Atco 228 001	THE HISTORY OF OTIS REDDING (LP, reissue)	12
69	Atco 228 022	THE DOCK OF THE BAY (LP, reissue)	12
69	Atco 228 025	LOVE MAN (LP)	25
70	Atlantic 2464 003	REMEMBERING (LP)	18
71	Atco 2400 018	TELL THE TRUTH (LP)	18
71	Reprise K 40430	LIVE AT THE MONTEREY INTERNATIONAL POP FESTIVAL (LP, shared with Jimi Hendrix)	30

OTIS REDDING & CARLA THOMAS

67	Stax 601 012	Tramp/Oooh Carla, Oooh Otis (with Carla Thomas)	8
67	Stax 601 021	Knock On Wood/Let Me Be Good To You	8
68	Stax 601 033	Lovey Dovey/OTIS REDDING: New Year's Resolution	8
67	Stax 589 007	THE KING AND QUEEN OF SOUL	30

(see also Carla Thomas)

RED DIRT

70	Fontana STL 5540	RED DIRT (LP)	1500
10	Morgan Bluetown BT 5004	RED DIRT (LP, reissue, 500 only)	25

EMMA REDE

67	Columbia DB 8136	Just Like A Man/I Gotta Be With You	20

(see also Jacky, Jackie Lee, Jackie & Raindrops, Raindrops)

TEDDY REDELL

60	London HLK 9140	Judy/Can't You See	60

REDGEE SEEBOE

74	Bug 38	Please Don't Bring Your Sister/Daphnies Brains	15

VANESSA REDGRAVE

64	Topic STOP 111	Hanging On A Tree/Where Have All The Flowers Gone (in title sleeve)	6

MICHAEL REDGRAVE & JULIET MILLS

61	Parlophone R 4804	No My Darling Daughter/Blimp's Blues	7

REDHEAD

73	UK UK R 38	We Ran And We Ran/Lookin' For You	8

RED HERRING

87	Crystal 717	Albert Road/Harbour Lights	30

RED HOT & BLUE

85	Northwood NOR 1	RED HOT & BLUE (LP)	25

RED HOT CHILI PEPPERS

85	EMI America EA 205	Hollywood (Africa)/Never Mind (p/s)	10
85	EMI America 12EA 205	Hollywood (Africa) (Remix)/Hollywood (Africa) (Dub Mix)/Never Mind (12", p/s)	12
89	EMI 12MT 70	KNOCK ME DOWN EP (12", p/s)	15
89	EMI 12MT 75	Higher Ground/Catholic Schoolgirls Rule (p/s)	10
90	EMI 12MTX 85	TASTE THE PAIN EP (12", push-out sleeve with inner)	12
90	EMI 10MTX 85	TASTE THE PAIN EP (square disc, numbered)	12
90	EMI 12MTG 88	Higher Ground/Catholic Schoolgirls Rule/None As Weird As Me (12", gatefold sleeve)	15
90	EMI 12MTPD 88	Higher Ground/Catholic Schoolgirls Rule/None As Weird As Me (12", picture disc, card insert)	12
06	Warner Bros 9362499961	STADIUM ARCADIUM (4xLP box set with foil outer & 2 booklets)	60
06	Warner Bros 9362443911	STADIUM ARCADIUM (4xLP, standard edition)	20

RED HOUSE PAINTERS

94	4AD BAD 4004	Shock Me/Sundays And Holidays/Three-Legged Cat/Shock Me (12", p/s)	30
92	4AD CAD 2014	DOWN COLOURFUL HILL (LP)	70
93	4AD DAD 3008	RED HOUSE PAINTERS (2-LP, inner sleeves)	70
93	4AD CAD 3016	RED HOUSE PAINTERS (LP, different release from DAD 3008)	50
95	4A DADD 5005	OCEAN BEACH (LP, 2 x 10" with inner sleeves)	50

RED LETTERS
79	Burning Bing CPS 025	SACRED VOICES EP: Sacred Voices/Shot In The Dark/Science Has The Answer (folded p/s)..80

RED LIGHTS
78	Free Range PF 5	Never Wanna Leave/Seventeen (p/s) 60

RED LONDON
83	Razor RZS 105	Sten Guns In Sunderland/This Is England/Soul Train/Revolution Times (p/s)...........12
84	Razor RAZ 10	THIS IS ENGLAND (LP) 30

RED LORRY, YELLOW LORRY
82	Red Rhino RED 20	Beating My Head/I'm Still Waiting (p/s) 10
83	Red Rhino RED 28	Take It All/Happy (p/s) 5

RED MEAT
72	Worsley WR 1	She/My Mind Sleeps On (P/S) 50

RED ONION JAZZ BABIES
60	Collector JE 19	RED ONION JAZZ BABIES (EP) 10

(see also Louis Armstrong)

JEAN REDPATH
66	Bounty BY 6004	LOVE LILT AND LAUGHTER (LP) 20

RED RAGE
80	Flicknife FLS 203	Total Control/I Give You This (p/s) 40

RED RIVER BAND
70	Banana BA 35	I'm Gonna Use What I've Got/Shame Shame 8

REDS
79	A&M AMS 7454	Whatcha' Doin' To Me/Not You (p/s, green vinyl) 5

REDSKINS
82	CNT CNT 007	Lev Bronstein/The Peasant Army (p/s) 25
83	CNT CNT 016	Lean On Me!/Unionize! (p/s) 7
94	Dojo DOJOCD 188	REDSKINS LIVE (CD)..20

RED SQUARES
67	Columbia DB 8160	Mountain's High/Pity Me..20
67	Columbia DB 8257	True Love Story/Lollipop 12

RED TELEVISION
71	Brecht Times	RED TELEVISION (LP, private pressing with insert) 120

REDUCERS
78	Vibes XP 1/VR 001	Things Go Wrong/We Are Normal (p/s) 50
79	Vibes VR 003	Man With A Gun/Vengeance/Can't Stop Now (p/s) 50
80	EMI EMI 5028	Airways/Waiting For No One (p/s) 8

MIKE REDWAY
64	Oriole CB 1948	Many People/It's So Funny I Could Cry 8
65	CBS 201755	Darling Take Me Back/That's The Way Love Goes 5
65	CBS 202017	Magic Rocking Chair/When You Go 8
66	CBS 202092	One Day/Let Me Be The Someone 5
67	Deram DM 124	Have No Fear, Bond Is Here (Casino Royale)/My Poem For You..................................10
67	Deram DM 157	Don't Speak Of Me/Sometimes I Remember 5
69	RCA 1873	Through The Eyes Of Love/Love Me 6

(see also Rod McKuen, Typhoons, Bud Ashton)

REDWOODS
62	Columbia DB 4859	Please Mr Scientist/Where You Used To Be 25

DIZZY REECE QUINTET
56	Tempo A 140	Chorus/Basie Line 10
58	Tempo EXA 84	A VARIATION ON MONK (EP) 175
59	Tempo EXA 86	NOWHERE TO GO (EP, featuring Tubby Hayes)..175
59	Tempo EXA 89	ON THE SCENE (EP) 75
55	Tempo LAP 3	A NEW STAR... (10" LP) 250
57	Tempo TAP 9	PROGRESS REPORT (LP) 600
58	Esquire 32 185	ASIA MINOR (LP) 80
84	Jasmine JASM 2013	PROGRESS REPORT (LP, reissue) 20

(see also Victor Feldman, Ronnie Scott)

CHUCK REED
57	Brunswick 05646	Whispering Heart/Another Love Has Ended 15
58	Columbia DB 4113	No School Tomorrow/Let's Put Our Hearts Together 30
62	Stateside SS 108	Just Plain Hurt/Talking No Trash 15

DEAN REED
59	Capitol CL 14986	The Search/Annabelle 10
59	Capitol CL 15030	I Kissed A Queen/A Pair Of Scissors (And A Pot Of Glue).......................................10

DENNY REED
61	London HLK 9274	A Teenager Feels It Too/Hot Water...18

JERRY REED
58	Capitol CL 14851	Bessie Baby/Too Young To Be Blue 300
58	Capitol CL 14851	Bessie Baby/Too Young To Be Blue (78) 50
69	RCA RCA 1798	Oh What A Woman/Claw 5
70	RCA RCA 2025	Georgia Sunshine/Singing '69...5
71	RCA RCA 2063	Amos Moses/The Preacher And The Bear 5
69	RCA SF 8006	ALABAMA WILD MAN (LP) 18

JIMMY REED
60	Top Rank JAR 333	Baby What You Want Me To Do/Caress Me Baby 20
60	Top Rank JAR 394	Found Love/Where Can You Be 20
60	Top Rank JAR 533	Hush-Hush/Going By The River 20
63	Stateside SS 205	Shame Shame Shame/Let's Get Together 22
64	Stateside SS 330	Shame Shame Shame/Let's Get Together (reissue) 12

66	Sue WI 4004	Odds And Ends/Going By The River Pt. II (B-side actually Pt. I)	40
67	HMV POP 1579	Two Ways To Skin A Cat/Got Nowhere To Go	25
64	Stateside SE 1016	BLUES OF JIMMY REED (EP)	30
64	Stateside SE 1026	I'M JIMMY REED (EP)	30
62	Stateside SL 10012	JIMMY REED AT CARNEGIE HALL (LP)	20
64	Stateside SL 10055	JUST JIMMY REED (LP)	30
64	Stateside SL 10069	SINGS THE BEST OF THE BLUES (LP)	20
64	Stateside SL 10086	PLAYS 12-STRING GUITAR BLUES (LP)	20
64	Stateside SL 10091	THE BOSS MAN OF THE BLUES (LP)	30
65	Fontana 688 514 ZL	THINGS AIN'T WHAT THEY USED TO BE (LP)	20
67	HMV CLP/CSD 3611	THE NEW JIMMY REED (LP)	20
68	Stateside S(S)L 10221	SOULIN' (LP)	35
69	Action ACLP 6011	DOWN IN VIRGINIA (LP)	60

JOE REED
71	Dawn DNS 1012	Ain't That A Shame/Follow Me	6

LES REED
66	Fontana TF 765	Good King Went Ridiculous/Valley Of Kings	12
67	Deram DM 128	Imogene/Pay Off	10
69	Deram DM 244	Don't Linger With Your Finger On The Trigger/Big Drum	15

(see also Sounds of Les & Barry)

LOU REED
72	RCA RCA 2240	Walk And Talk It/Wild Child	8
72	RCA RCA 2303	Walk On The Wild Side/Perfect Day	5
73	RCA RCA 2318	Vicious/Satellite Of Love	5
73	MGM 2006 283	I'm Waiting For The Man/Run Run Run/Candy Says (with Velvet Underground)	8
74	RCA APBO 0221	Caroline Says (Parts 1 & 2)	5
74	RCA APBO 0238	Sweet Jane/Lady Day	5
74	RCA RCA 2467	Sally Can't Dance/Ennui	5
76	RCA RCA 2666	Charley's Girl/Nowhere At All	5
72	RCA SF 8281	LOU REED (LP, laminated sleeve, orange label)	15
72	RCA LSP 4807	TRANSFORMER (LP, 1st pressing, laminated sleeve)	40
73	RCA LSP 4807	TRANSFORMER (LP, 2nd pressing, non-laminated sleeve)	12
73	RCA RS 1002	BERLIN (LP, orange label with insert)	12
75	RCA CPL 2 1101	METAL MACHINE MUSIC (2-LP, U.S. import with U.K. sticker)	35

(see also Velvet Underground)

LULA REED
55	Parlophone CMSP 34	Troubles On Your Mind/Bump On A Log (export issue)	60
55	Parlophone DP 408	Troubles On Your Mind/Bump On A Log (78, export issue)	15

LULA REED & SYL JOHNSON
63	Ember EMB EP 4535	RHYTHM & BLUES BLUE BEAT STYLE (EP)	70

LULA REED & FREDDIE KING
63	Ember EMB 4536	LULA REED AND FREDDIE KING (EP)	60

(see also Freddie King)

OLIVER REED
61	Decca F 11390	The Wild One/Lonely For A Girl	15
62	Piccadilly 7N 35037	Sometimes/Ecstasy	10

TAWNY REED
65	Pye 7N 15935	Needle In A Haystack/I've Got A Feeling	50
66	Pye 7N 17078	You Can't Take It Away/My Heart Cries	30

VIVIEN REED
68	Direction 58-3574	I Wanna Be Free/Yours Until Tomorrow	8

WINSTON REED
72	Pama Supreme PS 365	Breakfast In Bed/RANNY WILLIAMS: Guitar Shuffle	7
73	Pama PM 863	Big Eight/RANNY WILLIAMS & CLASSICS: Big Eight - Version	7

WINSTON REEDY
82	SG SG 17	Daughter Of Zion/Zion Dub (12")	30
83	Carousel 12CAR 48	Dim The Light/Shower Of Rain (12")	20

VALA REEGAN & VALARONS
66	Atlantic 584 009	Fireman/Living In The Past	250
66	Atlantic 584 009	Fireman/Living In The Past (DJ copy)	300

TONY REES & COTTAGERS
75	Sonet SON 2059	Viva El Fulham/Rainbow	7

DELLA REESE
57	London HL 7024	I Cried For You (Now It's Your Turn To Cry Over Me)/And That Reminds Me (export issue)	10
58	London HLJ 8687	You Gotta Love Everybody/I Wish	10
59	London HLJ 8814	Sermonette/Dreams End At Dawn	10
59	RCA RCA 1160	Not One Minute More/Soldier Won't You Marry Me	7
66	HMV POP 1553	It Was A Very Good Year/Solitary Woman	30
68	Stateside SS 2128	It Was A Very Good Year/I Had To Know My Way Around	20
72	Avco Embassy 6105 010	If It Feels Good, Do It/Good Lovin' (Makes It Right) (paper label)	10
74	People PEO 106	Who Is She And What Is She To You/If Loving You Is Wrong	6
59	London LTZ-J 15163	THE HISTORY OF THE BLUES (LP)	30
60	RCA RD 27167/SF 5057	DELLA (LP)	15
61	RCA RD 27208/SF 5091	DELLA DELLA CHA-CHA-CHA (LP)	18
62	RCA RD 27234/SF 5112	SPECIAL DELIVERY (LP)	20
63	RCA Victor RD/SF 7508	ON STAGE (LP)	15
63	RCA Victor RD/SF 7584	WALTZ WITH ME, DELLA (LP)	12
64	RCA RD/SF 7628	AT BASIN STREET EAST (LP)	12
65	RCA RD 7695	MOODY (LP)	12
74	People PLEO 7	LET ME IN YOUR LIFE (LP)	30

TONY REESE
59	London HLJ 8987	Just About This Time Tomorrow/Lesson In Love	25

59	London HLJ 8987	Just About This Time Tomorrow/Lesson In Love (78)	12

DEL REEVES

65	United Artists UP 1092	Girl On The Billboard/Eyes Don't Come Crying To Me	7
66	United Artists UP 1122	Women Do Funny Things To Me/My Half Of Our Past	7
66	United Artists UP 1145	Gettin' Any Feed For Your Chickens/Plain As The Tears On My Face	7

EDDIE REEVES

62	London HL 9548	Cry Baby/Talk Talk	20

JIM REEVES

78s

54	London HL 8014	Bimbo/Gipsy Heart	20
54	London HL 8030	Mexican Joe/I Could Cry (with Circle O Ranch Boys)	25
54	London HL 8055	Butterfly Love/It's Hard To Love Just One (with String Band)	30
54	London HL 8064	Echo Bonita/Then I'll Stop Loving You (with Louisiana Hayride Band)	30
54	London HL 8105	Padre Of Old San Antone/Mother Went A-Walkin'	30
55	London HL 8118	Penny Candy/I'll Follow You (with Louisiana Hayride Band)	30
55	London HL 8159	Drinking Tequila/Red-Eyed And Rowdy	35
55	London HLU 8185	Tahiti/Give Me One More Kiss	30
56	London HLU 8351	The Wilder Your Heart Beats, The Sweeter You Love/ Where Does A Broken Heart Go	30
57	RCA RCA 1005	Four Walls/I Know And You Know	20
58	RCA RCA 1074	Blue Boy/Theme Of Love	25
59	RCA RCA 1144	Partners/I'm Beginning To Forget You	30
60	RCA RCA 1168	He'll Have To Go/In A Mansion Stands My Love	40

SINGLES

54	London HL 8014	Bimbo/Gipsy Heart	200
54	London HL 8030	Mexican Joe/I Could Cry (with Circle O Ranch Boys)	200
54	London HL 8055	Butterfly Love/It's Hard To Love Just One (with String Band)	200
54	London HL 8064	Echo Bonita/Then I'll Stop Loving You (with Louisiana Hayride Band)	200
54	London HL 8105	Padre Of Old San Antone/Mother Went A-Walkin'	120
55	London HL 8118	Penny Candy/I'll Follow You (with Louisiana Hayride Band)	120
55	London HLU 8185	Tahiti/Give Me One More Kiss	120
55	London HL 8159	Drinking Tequila/Red-Eyed And Rowdy	200

(The 45s listed above were issued with gold label print on black labels.)

56	London HLU 8351	The Wilder Your Heart Beats, The Sweeter You Love/ Where Does A Broken Heart Go	150
57	RCA RCA 1005	Four Walls/I Know And You Know	30
58	RCA RCA 1074	Blue Boy/Theme Of Love	20
59	RCA RCA 1144	Partners/I'm Beginning To Forget You (triangular or round centre)	20

EPs

54	London RE-P 1015	THE BIMBO BOY (EP)	100
55	London RE-P 1033	THE BIMBO BOY VOL. 2 (EP)	100

ALBUMS

60	RCA RD 27176	HE'LL HAVE TO GO (LP)	12
61	RCA RD 27193	THE INTIMATE JIM REEVES (LP, also stereo SF 5079)	12
62	London HA-U 8015	BIMBO (LP)	12

REFLECTION

68	Reflection RL 3015	THE PRESENT TENSE: SONGS OF SYDNEY CARTER (LP)	18

(see also Sounds Of Salvation)

REFLECTIONS A.O.B.

86	Keep KEEP 1 12	ONLY IN MY DREAMS EP (12")	40

REFLECTIONS (U.K.)

74	Purple PUR 124	Love And Affection/No More	7
75	Purple PUR 127	Moon Power/Little Star	7

REFLECTIONS (U.S.)

64	Stateside SS 294	(Just Like) Romeo & Juliet/Can't You Tell By The Look In My Eyes	60
64	Stateside SS 294	(Just Like) Romeo & Juliet/Can't You Tell By The Look In My Eyes (DJ copy)	100
65	Stateside SS 406	Poor Man's Son/Comin' At You	30
74	Tamla Motown TMG 907	(Just Like) Romeo & Juliet/Can't You Tell By The Look In My Eyes (reissue)	15
77	ABC ABC 4181	Like Adam And Eve/AUGUST & DENEEN: We Go Together	15
65	Stateside SE 1034	POOR MAN'S SON (EP)	125

(see also The High and Mighty)

REFUGEE

74	Charisma CAS 1087	REFUGEE (LP, with lyric inner sleeve, large 'Mad Hatter' label)	20

(see also Nice, Yes)

REGAL DEWY

78	RCA XB 1032	Love Music/Where Would I Be Without Me	8

JOAN REGAN

54	Decca F 10362	Wait For Me, Darling (with Johnston Brothers)/Two Kinds Of Tears (gold lettering)	30
54	Decca F 10362	Wait For Me, Darling (with Johnston Brothers)/Two Kinds Of Tears (silver lettering)	20
54	Decca F 10373	If I Give My Heart To You/Faded Flowers	12
54	Decca F 10397	This Ole House/Can This Be Love?	12
55	Decca F 10432	Prize Of Gold/When You're In Love	12
55	Decca F 10474	Open Up Your Heart And Let The Love In (with Rusty Regan)/ If You Learn To Love Each Other	12
55	Decca F 10505	Danger! Heartbreak Ahead/Don't Be Afraid Of Love	12
55	Decca F 10521	Just Say You Love Her/Nobody Danced With Me	12
55	Decca F 10598	The Shepherd Boy/The Rose And The Flame	8
56	Decca F 10659	Love And Marriage/Cross Of Gold (Croce Di Oro)	8
59	HMV POP 593	May You Always/Have You Ever Been Lonely	7
60	Pye Nixa 7n 15238	Happy Anniversary/So Close To My Heart	7
60	Pye 7N 15278	Papa Loves Mama/When You Know Somebody Loves You	7
60	Pye 7N 15303	Must Be Santa/Will Santa Come To Shanty Town	7
60	Pye 7N 15310	One Of The Lucky Ones/My Thanks to You	15
61	Pye 7N 15367	We Who Are In Love/My Foolish Heart	5
61	Pye 7N 15400	Surprisin'/In The Arms Of My Love (some with p/s)	8

66	CBS 202100	Don't Talk To Me About Love/I'm No Toy	25
66	CBS 202100	Don't Talk To Me About Love/I'm No Toy (DJ copy)	40
67	CBS 2657	No-One Beside Me/A Love So Fine	20
55	Decca DFE 6235	JOAN REGAN SUCCESSES (EP)	10
56	Decca DFE 6278	JOAN REGAN SUCCESSES VOL. 2 (EP)	10
54	Decca LF 1182	THE GIRL NEXT DOOR (10" LP)	50
56	Decca LK 4153	JUST JOAN (LP)	150
60	Pye NPL 18048	JOAN AND TED (LP, With Edmund Hockridge)	15

(see also Edmund Hockridge)

RUSS REGAN
| 59 | Capitol CL 15084 | Adults Only/Just The Two Of Us | 10 |

TOMMY REGAN
| 64 | Colpix PX 725 | I'll Never Stop Loving You/This Time I'm Losing You (DJ Copy) | 125 |
| 64 | Colpix PX 725 | I'll Never Stop Loving You/This Time I'm Losing You | 100 |

(see also Marcels)

REGENTS (U.K.) (1)
| 63 | Oriole CB 1912 | Bye Bye Johnny/Come Along | 40 |

(see also Buddy Britten)

REGENTS (U.K.) (2)
| 66 | CBS 202247 | Words/Worryin' Kind | 45 |

REGENTS (U.K.) (3)
| 79 | Rialto TREB 111 | 7 Teen (Uncensored Version)/Hole In The Heart (p/s) | 6 |

REGENTS (U.S.)
| 61 | Columbia DB 4666 | Barbara Ann/I'm So Lonely | 30 |
| 61 | Columbia DB 4694 | Runaround/Laura My Darling | 28 |

REGGAE BOYS
69	Amalgamated AMG 841	Me No Born Ya/The Wicked Must Survive	30
69	Amalgamated AMG 843	The Reggae Train/Dolly House On Fire	30
69	Gas GAS 135	Ba Ba/GLEN ADAMS: Power Cut	60
69	Unity UN 530	What You Gonna Do/HEDLEY BENNETT: Hot Coffee	70
70	Bullet BU 431	Pupa Live On Eye Top/Give Me Faith	35
70	Gas GAS 122	Phrases/Give Me Faith	50
70	Upsetter US 339	Hurry Up/Thanks We Get	20
70	Pressure Beat PR 5503	Walk By Day, Fly By Night/JOE GIBBS & DESTROYERS: Unknown Tongue	20

(see also Glen Adams, Alva Lewis, Upsetters)

REGGAE GEORGE
| 83 | Greensleeves GRED 114 | You'll Never Know/We Still Survive (12") | 15 |

REGGAE GIRLS
| 69 | Nu Beat NB024 | Rescue Me/SOULMATES: Unity Is Strength | 18 |

REGGAE REGULAR
77	Greensleeves GRE 001	Where Is Jah?/Jah Is Here	6
78	Greensleeves GRE 004	The Black Star Liner/It's Coming	6
78	Greensleeves GRE 2	The Black Star Liner/Where Is Jah? (12")	10
82	Greensleeves GRED 83	House Party (with Clint Eastwood)/Dub Party (12")	8

REGGAE STRINGS
| 73 | Trojan TRLS 54 | REGGAE STRINGS (LP) | 20 |

(see also Horace Faith)

LOU REICHNER BAND
| 80 | ESR Records S/80/CUS 733 | Photograph/I Sit And Stare/The End Of The World/Out On The Streets (also listed as ESR 4, 300 only, with insert) | 50 |
| 80 | ESR Records S/80/CUS 733 | Photograph/I Sit And Stare/The End Of The World/Out On The Streets (also listed as ESR 4, 300 only, without insert) | 20 |

AL REID
| 69 | Blue Cat BS 161 | Vietcong/MAX ROMEO: Me Want Man | 40 |
| 69 | Blue Cat BS 163 | Darling/MAX ROMEO: It's Not The Way | 50 |

ALTYMAN REID
| 72 | Green Door GD 4026 | A Sugar/A Sugar Part Two (with Roy Shirley) | 7 |

(see also Roy Shirley)

CARLTON REID
| 66 | Ska Beat JB 254 | Funny/Turn On The Lights | 20 |
| 69 | Blue Cat BS 162 | Leave Me To Cry/Warning | 100 |

DENNIS REID
| 77 | Greensleeves GRE 6 | Land Of The Rising Sun/DENNIS REID & REVOLUTIONARIES: Rising Sun Version | 8 |

DUKE REID (& HIS GROUP)
60	Blue Beat BB 24	Duke's Cookies (with His Group)/JIVING JUNIORS: I Wanna Love	20
62	Blue Beat BB 119	Twelve Minutes To Go (actually by Don Drummond)/ HORTENSE ELLIS: Midnight Train	30
63	Duke DK 1002	Pink Lane Shuffle (with His Group)/LAUREL AITKEN: Low Down Dirty Girl	20
67	Master's Time MT 003	Religious Service At Bond Street Gospel Hall/Religious Service At Bond Street Gospel Hall (Continued)	15
67	Trojan TR 001	Judge Sympathy (actually by Freedom Singers & Duke Reid All Stars)/ROLAND ALPHONSO: Never To Be Mine	45
60s	Doctor Bird DB 1028	True Confessions/TOMMY McCCOOK : More Love	35
72	Duke Reid DR 2522	Hurt Parts 1 & 2 (actually by Eagles [Jamaica])	15

(see also Chuck & Darby, Derrick Morris, Stranger)

LEYROY REID
| 68 | Blue Cat BS 125 | The Fiddler/LOVELETTES: Shook | 30 |
| 68 | Blue Cat BS 127 | Great Surprise/TEN(N)ORS: Khaki | 30 |

(see also Nehemiah Reed)

MARC REID
| 66 | CBS 202244 | For No One/Lonely City Blues | 15 |
| 67 | CBS 202581 | Magic Book/My World Turns Around | 15 |

67	CBS 2950	We Should Live Together/Sale By Auction	15

NEHEMIAH REID('S ALL STARS)
68	Island WI 3102	Family War/Give Me That Love	40
70	Hot Shot HS 03	Hot Pepper/Seawave (as Nehemiah Reid's All Stars)	30
70s	Torpedo TOR 23	Mafia/H.E.L.L. 5 (as Nehemiah Reid's All Stars)	12

(see also Leyroy Reid, Cynthia Richards)

NORVELLE REID
57	Brunswick 05725	All The Way/The World Won't End (export issue)	5

P. REID
65	Ska Beat JB 197	Redeemed/Goodbye World	18

PATTI REID
87	Fellside FE 061	PATTI REID (LP)	12

TERRY REID (& JAYWALKERS)
67	Columbia DB 8166	The Hand Don't Fit The Glove/This Time (as Terry Reid & Jaywalkers)	12
68	Columbia DB 8409	Better By Far/Fires Alive	18
69	Columbia PSRS 323	Superlungs (promo only, as "Terry Reid Is Superlungs")	25
76	ABC 4137	Oooh Baby/Brave Awakening	5
79	Capitol CL 16071	Ain't No Shadow/Bowangi	5
69	Columbia SCX 6370	TERRY REID (LP, laminated front, flipbacks)	50
69	M. For Pleasure MFP 5220	THE MOST OF TERRY REID (LP)	12
73	Atlantic K 40340	RIVER (LP, gatefold sleeve)	20
76	ABC ABCL 5162	SEED OF MEMORY (LP)	12

(see also Peter Jay & Jaywalkers)

REIGN
70	Regal Zonophone RZ 3028	Line Of Least Resistance/Natural Lovin' Man	90

(see also Yardbirds, Keith Relf, Renaissance, Armageddon, Illusion)

JOHN REILLY
78	Topic 12T 359	THE BONNY GREEN TREE (LP, with booklet)	12

TOMMY REILLY
60	Philips PB 1094	Theme From "The Sundowners"/Down Under	7
63	Philips PB 1248	So Little Time/Moon Fire	6

REINCARNATE
82	Zipp REIN 001	Take It Or Leave It/Metal In Disguise	70

REINDEER SECTION
02	Bright Star BSR 22V	You Are My Joy/Budapest (Demo)	6
01	Bright Star BSR 14V	Y'ALL GET SCARED NOW, YA HEAR! (LP)	20
02	Bright Star BSR 19V	SON OF EVIL REINDEER (LP)	15

(see also Arab Strap, Belle & Sebastian, Snow Patrol, Mogwai, Teenage Fanclub, Idlewild)

DJANGO REINHARDT
54	Oriole/Mercury MG 10019	DJANGO (10" LP)	12

(see also Quintet Of Hot Club Of France)

JOE REISMAN ORCHESTRA
56	HMV 7M 364	Robin Hood/His Name Was Judas	5
60	Columbia DB 4553	The World Of Suzi Wong (Theme)/Melodie D'Amour	5
61	Pye International 7N 25087	The Guns Of Navarone/Yassu	5

LOU REIZNER
69	Phillips	On Days Like This/Get A Bloomin' Move On	15

REJOICE!
69	Stateside SS 8010	November Snow/Quick Draw Man	5
69	Stateside S(S)L 5009	REJOICE! (LP)	20

BOB RELF
75	Black Magic BM 101	Blowin' My Mind To Pieces/PAULA RUSSELL: Blowin' My Mind To Pieces	5

(see also Bob & Earl)

JANE RELF
71	Decca F 13231	Without A Song From You/Make My Time Pass By	30
	Findus Frozen Foods SD/DS/7001	Gone Fishing/Gordon Jackson - Hints From The Findus Kitchen (P/S)	10

(see also Stairway, Renaissance, Gordon Jackson)

KEITH RELF
66	Columbia DB 7920	Mr. Zero/Knowing	60
66	Columbia DB 8084	Shapes In My Mind/Blue Sands	70

(see also Yardbirds, Jim McCarty, Renaissance, Reign, Together, Armageddon)

RELICT/THE CLIENTELE
01	Johnny Kane KANE 004	Held In Glass/(I Can't Seem) To Make You Mine	5

(see also Clientele)

RELIGIOUS OVERDOSE
80	Glass GLASS 004	Control Addicts/25 Minutes (p/s with green label)	5

RELOAD
92	Evolution EVO 01	RELOAD EP (12", plain sleeve)	20
92	Evolution EVO 02	AUTO RELOAD EP (12", with E 621)	30
92	Evolution EVO 03	RELOAD EP (12", 1-side credited to E 621)	40
93	Infonet INF 13	AUTO RELOAD EP VOLUME 2 (12", p/s)	10
93	Infonet INF 04LP	A COLLECTION OF SHORT STORIES (2-LP, with colour booklet)	50
93	Infonet INF 04LP	A COLLECTION OF SHORT STORIES (2-LP)	40
93	Infonet INF 04CD	A COLLECTION OF SHORT STORIES (CD, with colour booklet)	18
93	Infonet INF 04CD	A COLLECTION OF SHORT STORIES (CD, with no colour booklet)	15

(see also Global Communications, Link, Mystic Institute)

R.E.M.

SINGLES

83	I.R.S. PFP 1017	Radio Free Europe/There She Goes Again (p/s)	50
83	I.R.S. PFSX 1026	Talk About The Passion/Shaking Through/Carnival Of Sorts (Box Cars)/ 1,000,000 (12", p/s)	15
84	I.R.S. IRS 105	S. Central Rain (I'm Sorry)/King Of The Road (p/s)	8
84	I.R.S. IRSX 105	S. Central Rain (I'm Sorry)/Voice Of Harold/Pale Blue Eyes (12", p/s)	12
84	I.R.S. IRS 107	(Don't Go Back To) Rockville/Wolves (Lower) (p/s)	6
84	I.R.S. IRSX 107	(Don't Go Back To) Rockville/Wolves/9 - 9 (Live Version)/ Gardening At Night (live) (12", p/s)	10
85	I.R.S. IRM 102	Can't Get There From Here/Bandwagon (p/s)	6
85	I.R.S. IRT 102	Can't Get There From Here (sleeve states 'Extended Mix', label states 'LP Version', but actually 3.39 edit)/Bandwagon/Burning Hell (12", p/s, with printed banner crediting unissued tracks)	12
85	I.R.S. IRM 105	Wendell Gee/Crazy (p/s)	6
85	I.R.S. IRMD 105	Wendell Gee/Crazy//Ages Of You/Burning Down (double pack)	8
86	I.R.S. IRM 121	Fall On Me/Rotary Ten (p/s, blue, gold or silver label)	5
86	I.R.S. IRM 128	Superman/White Tornado (p/s, gold or silver label)	10
86	I.R.S. IRMT 128	Superman/White Tornado/Femme Fatale (12", p/s)	10
86	I.R.S. DIRM 128	Superman/White Tornado/Femme Fatale (CD, unissued)	0
87	I.R.S. IRM 145	It's The End Of The World As We Know It (And I Feel Fine) (2.59 edit)/ This One Goes Out (live) (p/s, gold or metallic blue label)	8
87	I.R.S. IRMT 145	It's The End Of The World As We Know It (And I Feel Fine)/This One Goes Out (live)/Maps And Legends (live) (12", p/s)	8
87	I.R.S. IRM 146	The One I Love/Last Date (bronze label, glossy p/s; silver label, matt p/s)	8
87	I.R.S. IRMT 146	The One I Love/Last Date/Disturbance At The Heron House (live) (12", p/s)	8
88	I.R.S. DIRM 161	Finest Worksong (LP Version)/Time After Time, Etc. (live)/ It's The End Of The World As We Know It (And I Feel Fine) (CD, numbered stencilled 7" box, 5,000 only)	15
88	I.R.S. IRM161	Finest Worksong/Time After Time Etc live (p/s)	8
88	I.R.S. IRMT161	Finest Worksong Lengthy Club Mix/Other Mix/Time After Time Etc medley (12", p/s)	10
88	I.R.S. IRM173	The One I Love /Fall On Me (p/s)	6
88	I.R.S. IRMT173	The One I Love/Fall On Me/So. Central Rain (12", p/s)	10
88	I.R.S. DIRM173	The One I Love/Fall On Me/So. Central Rain (CD)	12
91	I.R.S. DIRMX178	The One I Love/Driver Eight (Live)/Disturbance At The Heron House (Live)/Crazy (CD)	10
91	I.R.S. DIRMT 178	The One I Love/This One Goes Out (live)/Maps And Legends (CD, with 10-page insert)	10
92	I.R.S. DIRM 180	It's The End Of The World As We Know It (And I Feel Fine)/Radio Free Europe (Hib-Tone Version) (gold or silver labels, p/s, with Album version of 'Radio Free Europe')	8
92	I.R.S. DIRM 180	It's The End Of The World As We Know It (And I Feel Fine)/Radio Free Europe (Hib-Tone Version) (gold or silver labels, p/s)	5

SINGLES : WARNER BROS SINGLES

89	Warner Bros W 7577CD	Stand/Memphis Train Blues/(The Eleventh Untitled Song) (3" CD, card sleeve)	10
89	Warner Bros W 7577CDX	Stand/Memphis Train Blues/(The Eleventh Untitled Song)(3" CD, 'maple-leaf' pack)	12
89	Warner Bros W 2833W	Stand/Pop Song '89 (Acoustic) (stencil die-cut p/s)	12
89	Warner Bros W 2833CD	Stand/Pop Song '89 (Acoustic)/Skin Tight (live) (3" CD, gatefold card sleeve)	12
89	Warner Bros W 2833CDX	Stand/Pop Song '89 (Acoustic)/Skin Tight (live) (3" CD, black die-cut sleeve in Velcro seal envelope)	15
89	Warner Bros W 2960B	Orange Crush/Ghost Riders ('The Green Package' box set with poster)	8
89	Warner Bros W 2960CD	Orange Crush/Ghost Riders/Dark Globe (3" CD, gatefold card sleeve)	12
91	Warner Bros W 0072CDX	Radio Song (CD in 'Out Of Time' collectors box set)	12
93	Warner Bros W0184TP	Nightswimming (12" picture disc)	6
95	Warner Bros W0308X	Tongue/Instrumental (numbered tour booklet p/s)	5
95	Warner Bros W0290X	Strange Currencies/Strange Currencies Instrumental (p/s, Dayglo yellow/green vinyl + pin badge)	6
11	Warners 527426-1	THREE (Record Store Day box of 3 x 7")	15

ALBUMS

86	IRS ILP 4653811	LIFE'S RICH PAGEANT (LP)	12
90	IRS 46588-2	THE COLLECTION (5-CD box set)	50
94	Warners 9362-45740-1	MONSTER (LP)	18
96	Warners 9362-463210-1	NEW ADVENTURES IN HI-FI (2-LP, gatefold)	20
98	Warners 9362-47112-1	UP (2-LP)	25
03	Warners 9362 48381-1	IN TIME: THE BEST OF REM 1988-2003 (2-LP)	18
04	Warners 9362 48894-1	AROUND THE SUN (2-LP)	20
11	Warners 9362-49626-9	COLLAPSE INTO NOW (LP)	12

PROMOS

83	I.R.S. PFP 1026	Talk About The Passion/Talk About The Passion (plain sleeve, promo only)	15
88	I.R.S. WIRM(T) 161 DL	Finest Worksong (Lengthy Club Mix)/Finest Worksong (Other Mix)/Time After Time Etc. (12" in 'media' p/s)	18
92	I.R.S. CDREM 92	THE ALTERNATIVE RADIO SAMPLER (CD, 7-track promo, includes unreleased version of 'Gardening At Night')	50
92	Warner Bros REM 1	SAMPLER FROM THE BEST OF REM (CD, Brit Awards nomination issue)	25
03	Warners PR 04359	THE BEST OF REM - IN TIME 1980-2003 (promo box set containing 18 1-trackk CDs each housed in individual card sleeve in flip top box)	60

FLEXIDISCS : FLEXIDISCS & OTHER RELEASES

85	Bucketfull Of Brains BOB 5	Tighten Up (flexidisc [LYN 15742] with Bucketfull Of Brains magazine)	12
85	Bucketfull Of Brains BOB 5	Tighten Up (hard vinyl test pressing, 50 only)	50
92	Lyntone BOB 32	Academy Fight Song (live)/COAL PORTERS: Watching Blue Grass Burn (p/s, free with Bucketfull Of Brains magazine, double issue 39/40)	10
92	Lyntone BOB 32	Academy Fight Song (live)/COAL PORTERS: Watching Blue Grass Burn (white label test pressing)	20

(see also Full Time Men, Syd Straw)

REMA-REMA

80	4AD BAD 5	WHEEL IN THE ROSES: Feedback Song/Rema-Ream/Instrumental/ Fond Affections (12" EP, original pressing with blue labels)	20
80	4AD BAD 5	WHEEL IN THE ROSES: Feedback Song/Rema-Ream/Instrumental/ Fond Affections (12" EP)	15

(see also Adam & The Ants, Mass, Models, Wolfgang Press)

REMEMBER THIS

75	Penny Farthing PEN 862	Rock' N' Roll Revival/Over And Over Again	6

HERBIE REMINGTON

66	Fontana FJL 313	REMINGTON RIDES AGAIN (LP)	15

REMO FOUR

64	Piccadilly 7N 35175	I Wish I Could Shimmy Like My Sister Kate/Peter Gunn	25
64	Piccadilly 7N 35186	Sally Go Round The Roses/I Know A Girl	25
67	Fontana TF 787	Live Like A Lady/Sing Hallelujah	70

(see also Tommy Quickly, Johnny Sandon, Gregory Phillips, Ashton Gardner & Dyke, Mike Hurst, George Harrison)

RENAISSANCE (U.K.)

70	Island WIP 6079	Island/The Sea	15
75	Warner Bros. K 17177	Northern Lights/Opening Out	5
78	Sire SRE 1022	Northern Lights/Opening Out (picture disc, export issue)	15
79	Sire SIR 4019	Jekyll And Hyde/Forever Changing (withdrawn)	15
69	Island ILPS 9114	RENAISSANCE (LP, gatefold, pink label with white 'i' logo)	30
71	Island HELP 27	ILLUSION (LP, withdrawn, export only, black labeil with pink 'i' logo)	50
72	Sovereign SVNA 7253	PROLOGUE (LP, gatefold sleeve)	12
73	Sovereign SVNA 7261	ASHES ARE BURNING (LP, gatefold seeve)	12

(see also Jim McCarty, Keith Relf, Jane Relf, Yardbirds, Rupert's People, Reign, Stairway)

RENAISSANCE (U.S.)

68	Polydor BM 56736	Mary Jane (Get Off The Devil's Merry-Go-Round)/Daytime Lovers	35

RENAULTS

60	Warner Bros WB 11	Meloncolie/Stella	7

DIANE RENAY

64	Stateside SS 270	Navy Blue/Unbelievable Guy	15
64	Stateside SS 290	Kiss Me Sailor/Soft Spoken Guy	15
64	MGM MGM 1262	Watch Out Sally/Billy Blue Eyes	25
65	MGM MGM 1274	Troublemaker/I Had A Dream	25

(see also Laura Greene)

JOHN RENBOURN

65	Transatlantic TRA 135	JOHN RENBOURN (LP)	30
66	Transatlantic TRA 149	ANOTHER MONDAY (LP)	25
68	Transatlantic TRA 167	SIR JOHN ALOT OF MERRIE ENGLANDE'S MUSICK THYNGE AND YE GREENE KNIGHT (LP)	30
70	Transatlantic TRA 224	THE LADY AND THE UNICORN (LP)	20
72	Transatlantic TRA 247	FARO ANNIE (LP)	20
76	Transatlantic TRA 336	THE HERMIT (LP)	15
73	Transatlantic TRASAM 20	THE JOHN RENBOURN SAMPLER (LP)	12
73	Transatlantic TRASAM 28	SO CLEAR - THE JOHN RENBOURN SAMPLER VOL. 2 (LP)	15

(see also Pentangle, Bert Jansch & John Renbourn, Steve Tilston, Dorris Henderson)

JOHN RENBOURN & STEFAN GROSSMAN

70s	Kicking Mule SNKF 139	JOHN RENBOURN & STEFAN GROSSMAN (LP)	12
70s	Kicking Mule SNKF 161	UNDER THE VOLCANO (LP)	12

(see also Stefan Grossman)

JOHN RENBOURN'S SHIP OF FOOLS

88	Run River 009	SHIP OF FOOLS (LP)	20

DON RENDELL

55	Tempo A 108	Muskrat Ramble/Thames Walk	30
55	Tempo A 108	Muskrat Ramble/Thames Walk (78, as Don Rendell Sextet)	10
55	Tempo A 110	You Stepped Out Of A Dream/Slow Boat To China (78, as Don Rendell Quartet)	10
55	Tempo A 112	Didn't We/Dance Of The Ooblies (78, as Don Rendell Sextet)	10
55	Tempo A 114	From This Moment On/Blow Mr. Dexter (78, as Don Rendell Quartet)	10
55	Tempo EXA 11	DON RENDELL QUARTET (EP)	60
55	Tempo EXA 12	DON RENDELL SEXTET (EP)	40
55	Tempo EXA 16	DON RENDELL SEXTET/DAMIAN ROBINSON TRIO (EP, 2 tracks each)	50
55	Tempo EXA 20	DON RENDELL QUINTET (EP)	60
57	Pye Jazz NJE 1044	DON RENDELL JAZZ SIX (EP)	40
58	Decca DFE 6501	PACKET OF BLUES (EP, as Don Rendell Jazz Six)	20
54	Decca LK 4087	JAZZ AT THE FESTIVAL HALL (LP)	70
54	Vogue LDE 050	MUSIC IN THE MAKING (10" LP)	100
55	Vogue LDE 144	DON RENDELL IN PARIS (10" LP, with Bobby Jaspa)	100
55	Tempo LAP 1	MEET DON RENDELL (10" LP)	1000
56	Nixa NJL 4	TENORAMA (LP)	250
57	Nixa Jazz Today NJL 7	DON RENDELL PRESENTS THE JAZZ SIX (LP)	200
58	Decca LK 4265	PLAYTIME (LP, as Don Rendell Jazz 6)	100
62	Jazzland JLP 51	ROARIN' (LP, as Don Rendell New Jazz Quintet [with Graham Bond]	200
72	Columbia SCX 6491	SPACEWALK (LP, as Don Rendell Quintet)	150

(see also Frank Horrox)

DON RENDELL & IAN CARR QUINTET

65	Columbia 33SX 1733	SHADES OF BLUE (LP)	1000
66	Columbia S(C)X 6064	DUSK FIRE (LP, first pressing with blue label)	700
68	Columbia S(C)X 6064	DUSK FIRE (LP)	250
68	Columbia S(C)X 6214	PHASE III (LP)	250
69	Columbia S(C)X 6316	LIVE (LP)	175
69	Columbia SCX 6368	CHANGE IS (LP)	250

(see also Neil Ardley, Ian Carr, Nucleus)

DON RENDELL QUARTET/JOE HARRIOT QUARTET

57	MGM MGM-EP 615	JAZZ BRITANNIA (EP, 2 tracks each)	40

(see also Joe Harriott)

DON RENDES

76	Neville King NK 3	Beware/Dun Beware	8

RENDEZVOUS

71	Philron ADR	It Shouldn't Have Happened/I'll Give You Love	25

RENE & HIS ALLIGATORS

66	Decca F 22324	She Broke My Heart/I Can Wait	18

GOOGIE RENE COMBO

60	London HLY 9056	Forever/Ez-zee	20
66	Atlantic AT 4076	Smokey Joe's La La/Needing You	30

66	Atlantic 584 015	Chica-Boo/Mercy Mercy (Too Much For The Soul)	10

HENRI RENE
55	HMV 7M 308	Enchantment/Crystal Chandelier (with Hugo Winterhalter Orchestra)	7
59	London HLP 8960	La Shabla (The Shovel)/Destiny (with His Orchestra & Chorus)	7

RENE & RENE
65	HMV POP 1468	Chantilly Lace/I'm Not The Only One	10
67	Island WIP 6001	Loving You Could Hurt Me So Much/Little Diamonds	8

RENEGADE (1)
74	Dawn DNS 1067	A Little Rock 'N' Roll/My Revolution	20
73	Parlophone R 5981	Loving And Forgiving/never Let Me Go	20

RENEGADE (2)
80	White Witch WIT 1	LONELY ROAD (12" EP, with insert)	100

RENEGADES
66	Polydor BM 56508	Cadillac/Every Minute Of The Day	30
66	President PT 106	Thirteen Women/Walking Down The Street	200
67	Parlophone R 5592	Take A Message/Second Thoughts	25
68	Columbia DB 8383	No Man's Land/Sugar Loaf Mountain	25

RENIA
73	Transatlantic TRA 261	FIRST OFFENDERS (LP)	30

TONY RENIS
62	HMV POP 1036	Quando, Quando, Quando/Blu	6

JON RENNARD
70	Tradition TSR 003	BRIMBLEDON FAIR (LP)	12
71	Tradition TSR 010	THE PARTING GLASS (LP)	12

DON RENNIE
56	Parlophone MSP 6218	To Love, To Love Is Wonderful/One Girl - One Boy	7
56	Parlophone MSP 6237	Who Are We?/Can You Find It In Your Heart?	7

DON RENO & RED SMILEY
58	Parlophone GEP 8777	COUNTRY AND WESTERN (EP)	30
61	Melodisc MLP 12-123	HYMNS SACRED GOSPEL SONGS (LP)	15
64	Ember CW 104	SING SWEET BALLADS OF THE WEST (LP)	18

GERRY RENO
62	Decca F 11477	Don't Ever Change/What Would You Do	8
62	Decca F 11516	Who's Fooling You/Three Deadly Sins	8
63	Decca F 11774	It Only Happens In The Movies/One Lonely Guy	15

GINETTE RENO
69	Decca F 22972	Don't Let Me Be Misunderstood/Everything That I Am	8

PAUL RENO
63	Oriole CB 1872	Lonely Little Girl/Angela	10

CHRIS RENSHAW & THE KEEPERS
73	Pye 7N 45285	Banksie (A Tribute To Gordon Banks)/National (Health) Anthem (p/s)	6

ROBERT RENTAL
78	Regular ER 102	Paralysis/A.C.C. (photocopied black & white foldover p/s)	30
78	Company/Regular RECO 2	Paralysis/A.C.C. (reissue, card gatefold p/s)	20
80	Mute MUTE 010	On Location/Double Heart (p/s)	15
79	Industrial IR 0007	THE BRIDGE (LP, with Thomas Leer)	40
80	Rough Trade ROUGH 17	ROBERT RENTAL AND THE NORMAL (LP, 1-sided, plain red sleeve)	25
	(see also Thomas Leer, Normal)		

REPARATA & DELRONS
65	Stateside SS 382	Whenever A Teenager Cries/He's My Guy	30
65	Stateside SS 414	Tommy/Momma Don't Allow	25
68	Bell BLL 1002	Captain Of Your Ship/Toom Toom Is A Little Boy	12
68	RCA Victor RCA 1691	I Can Hear The Rain/Always Waitin'	30
68	Bell BLL 1014	Saturday Night Didn't Happen/Panic	40
68	Bell BLL 1014	Saturday Night Didn't Happen/Panic (DJ copy)	60
68	Bell BLL 1021	Weather Forecast/You Can't Change A Young Boy's Mind	20
72	Dart ART 2057	Your Life Is Gone/Octopus Garden (credited to Reparata)	10
76	Polydor 2058 688	Jesabee Lancer (The Belly Dancer)/We Need You	7
72	Avco 6467 250	ROCK AND ROLL REVOLUTION (LP)	40

REPLACEMENTS
86	Sire W 8727	Swingin' Party/Left Of The Dial	5
86	Sire W 8679	Kiss Me On The Bus/Little Mascara (p/s)	5
87	Sire W 8297	Alex Chilton/Election day (p/s)	5
84	Zippo ZONG 002	LET IT BE (LP)	15
85	Sire 925330	TIM (LP)	15
87	Sire 925557	PLEASED TO MEET ME (LP)	20
89	What Goes On GOES ON 17	SORRY MA, FORGOT TO TAKE OUT THE TRASH (LP)	12
89	What Goes On ON 20	STINK (mini-LP)	18

REPORTERS
81	Cloggtown CLOGGTOWN 1	Office Staff/Cinema/Lady Luck (p/s)	8

REPULSION
89	Necrosis NECRO 0002	HORRIFIED (LP)	30

REQUIEM
80	Sacrificial SAC 001	Angel Of Sin/Sacrificial Wanderer (no p/s)	80

RESCUE COMPANY NO 1
72	Jam JAM 14	I Want To Save You/Amanda	15
72	Jam JAM 27	I Stand Alone/You Shouldn't Have Been So Nice	15
73	Jam JAM 45	It's Only Words/Look Out	25

RESERVE
88	Sha La La Ba Ba Ba-Ba Ba 006	Wherever You Go/SIDDELEYS: The Sun Slid Down/Behind The Tower (flexidisc, foldover p/s)	10

RESIDENTS
80	Pre PRE 009	THE COMMERCIAL SINGLE (p/s)	5
84	Korova KOW 36	It's A Man's Man's Man's World/I'll Go Crazy (p/s, 5,000 only)	5
83	London RALPH 1	INTERMISSION (12" EP)	8
79	Virgin VR 3	NIBBLES (LP, stickered sleeve, 5,000 only)	12
80	Pre PRE X2	THE COMMERCIAL ALBUM (LP, 5,000 only, with incorrect song order)	12

RESISTANCE
81	Fontana KIT 1	Survival Kit/Big Flame (p/s)	6

RESISTANCE 77
82	Riot City RIOT 18	NOWHERE TO PLAY (EP)	15
84	Resistance RESIST 1	You Reds/Young And Wrong (p/s)	5
84	Rot ASS 6	Vive The Resistance	20
84	Rot ASS 14	THOROUGHBRED MEN (LP)	80

RESISTORS
80	Break SMASH 1	For Jeanie/Takeaway Love/End Of The Line (p/s)	10
83	DT 027	That's It/Steal My Love	25

REST
80	Shooting Star SSR 2	Raga/My House (screen printed p/s)	10

JOHNNY RESTIVO
59	RCA RCA 1143	The Shape I'm In/Ya Ya (with triangular centre)	35
59	RCA RCA 1143	The Shape I'm In/Ya Ya (later round centre pressing)	15
59	RCA RCA 1143	The Shape I'm In/Ya Ya (78)	20
59	RCA RCA 1159	I Like Girls/Dear Someone	20
59	RCA RCA 1159	I Like Girls/Dear Someone (78)	40
60	Ember EMB S 135	Look Here Now/Sweet Sweet Lovin'	15

RESTRICTED HOURS
79	Stevenage (no cat. no.)	Getting Things Done/Still Living Out The Car Crash/SYNDICATE: One Way Or Another/I Want To Be Somebody (white label, foldover p/s)	10

(see also Astronauts)

RETREADS
81	Eddi Osmo EO 101	Would You Listen Girl/One After 909/You Said You Knew (p/s, with mini-poster insert)	55

RETREAT FROM MOSCOW
80	Wicker Monkey WM 001/ MHMS 169/EJSP 9328	To The Night/Perception (p/s)	15

RETURN TO FOREVER
73	Polydor 2310 283	HYMN OF THE SEVENTH GALAXY (LP)	12

(see also Chick Corea)

MARTIN REV
85	New Rose ROSE 52	CLOUDS OF GLORY (LP, red vinyl)	12

(see also Suicide)

REVELATION (JAMAICA)
70	Trojan TR 7727	Suffering/MEGATONS: Crazy Elephant	7

REVELATION (1)
78	Write Sounds WTS 1003	With You Boy/Dub You	8
78	Write Sounds WTS 1003	Jah Feelings/With You Boy (12")	15
78	Write Sounds WTS 1004	Jah Feelings/Dub Feelings	8
81	Kingdom KV 8013	Tonight/Fussin' And Fightin'	6
81	Kingdom KV 8013-12	Tonight/Fussin' And Fightin' (12")	10
78	Burning Sounds BS 1030	BOOK OF REVELATION (LP)	25
79	Burning Vibrations BV 1007	VARIATION ON A THEM (LP)	20

REVELATION (2)
80	Handshake HANDS 1	Feel It/When I Fall In Love	8

REVELATION (3)
91	Rise Above RISE 6	SALVATIONS ANSWER (LP, stickered sleeve)	25

REVELLERS
66	Columbia DB 8093	Believe, Believe/Love Is The Greatest Thing	7
67	Spin SP2002	Yasmin/When I Needed A Neighbour	12
67	Spin LP 1703	REVELLERS AGAIN (LP)	35

REVELLS
71	CBS 7050	Mind Party/Indian Ropeman	50

DIGGER REVELL'S DENVERMEN
63	Decca F 11657	Surfside/Lisa Marie	20

REVELS
59	Top Rank JAR 235	Midnight Stroll/Talking To My Heart	50

REVENGE (1)
76	Normal QS 000	Go Away/Game	12
78	Loony LOO 1	Our Generation/I Love Her Way (counterfeits lack ridge around label)	400
70s	Blood CUS 614	Don't Tell Me Lies/Gimme The Good Times	10

REVENGE (2)
78	Loony LOO 2	We're Not Gonna Take It/Pornography (glossy p/s, counterfeits have matt sleeve, and lack ridge around label)	200

REVERB
94	Ochre OCH 001	Pedal/Swift (Foldover p/s in poly bag)	10

PAUL REVERE & THE RAIDERS (FEATURING MARK LINDSAY)
61	Top Rank JAR 557	Like Long Hair/Sharon	20
65	Sue WI 344	Like Long Hair/Sharon (reissue)	30

65	CBS 202003	Steppin' Out/Blue Fox	10
66	CBS 202027	Just Like Me/B F D R F Blues	20
66	CBS 202205	Kicks/Shake It Up	15
66	CBS 202253	Hungry/There She Goes	10
66	CBS 202411	The Great Airplane Strike/In My Community	12
67	CBS 202502	Good Thing/Undecided Man	12
67	CBS 202610	Ups And Downs/Leslie	10
67	CBS 2737	Him Or Her - What's It Gonna Be?/The Legend Of Paul Revere	10
67	CBS 2919	I Had A Dream/Upon Your Leaving	6
67	CBS 3186	Mo'reen/Oh! To Be A Man	10
68	CBS 3310	Too Much Talk/Happening '68 (featuring Mark Lindsay)	20
68	CBS 3586	Don't Take It So Hard/Observation From Flight 285 (featuring Mark Lindsay)	8
68	CBS 3757	Cinderella Sunshine/Theme From It's Happening (featuring Mark Lindsay)	6
69	CBS 4025	Mr. Sun, Mr. Moon/With You (featuring Mark Lindsay)	6
69	CBS 4260	Let Me/I Don't Know (featuring Mark Lindsay)	7
69	CBS 4504	We Gotta All Get Up Together/Frankfurt Side Street (featuring Mark Lindsay)	6
76	Jay Boy BOY 108	Ain't Nothin' Wrong/ou're Really Sayin' Something	7
66	CBS (S)BPG 62406	JUST LIKE US (LP)	25
66	CBS (S)BPG 62797	MIDNIGHT RIDE (LP)	25
67	CBS (S)BPG 62963	GOOD THING (LP)	20
68	CBS (S)BPG 63095	REVOLUTION (LP)	20
69	CBS 63265	GOIN' TO MEMPHIS (LP, mono/stereo)	20
69	CBS 63649	HARD 'N' HEAVY (LP)	20

(see also Mark Lindsay, Raiders)

REVIEW
80s	All The Madmen REV 1	England's Glory (stapled gatefold p/s with lyric insert)	8

REVILLOS
79	Snatzo/Dindisc DIN 1	Where's The Boy For Me/The Fiend (p/s)	5
79	Snatzo/Dindisc DIN 5	Motor Bike Beat/No Such Luck (p/s)	5
80	Snatzo/Dindisc DINZ 16	Scuba Scuba/Scuba Boy Bop (p/s)	5
80	Snatzo/Dindisc DINZ 20	Hungry For Love/Voodoo 2 (p/s, label also lists SP 703)	5
82	Superville SV 1001	She's Fallen In Love With A Monster Man/Mind Bending Cutie Doll (p/s)	10
82	Superville SV 2001	Bongo Brain/Hip City - You Were Meant For Me (p/s)	6
82	Aura AUS 135	Tell Him/Graveyard Groove (p/s)	6
83	EMI RVL 1	Bitten By A Love Bug/Cat Call	5
83	EMI 12 RVL 1	Bitten By A Love Bug (Extended Version)/Cat Call (12", p/s)	8
84	EMI RVL 2	Midnight/Z-X-7 (p/s)	5
84	EMI 12 RVL 2	Midnight (Extended Version)/Midnight (7" Version)/Z-X-7 (12", p/s)	8
80	Snatzo/Dindisc DID X 3	REV UP (LP, green or pink titles)	20
82	Superville SV 4001	ATTACK! (LP, withdrawn)	40

(see also Rezillos)

REVOLUTION
66	Piccadilly 7N 35289	Hallelujah/Shades Of Blue	65

(see also Hellions, Luther Grosvenor, Family, Traffic, Dave Mason & Cass Elliot, Spirit)

(THE) REVOLUTIONARIES
77	Sky Note SKY DD 002	Afro rock part 1/Afro rock part 2 (12")	40
77	Sky Note SKY 1002	El Bamba	20
78	Island IPR 2024	Headache/Bellyache/Toothache/Headache (12")	30
78	Ballistic FORCE 2003	FATAL DUB (12" EP)	20
75	Love LOV 01	GUN COURT DUB (LP)	40
76	Trenchtown TRELP 001	REVOLUTIONARY DUB (LP, with the We The People Band)	60
78	Hawkeye HALP 001	DREAD AT THE CONTROLS (LP)	40
78	Cha Cha CHALP 002	REACTION IN DUB (LP)	35
78	Cha Cha CHALP 005	JONKANOO DUB (LP)	30
79	Burning Vibrations BV 1002	DUTCH MAN DUB (LP)	30
79	Burning Vibrations BV 1004	GREEN BAY DUB (LP)	50
79	Burning Vibrations BV 1010	BURNING DUB (LP)	30
79	Trojan TRLS 169	OUTLAW DUB (LP)	25
80	Manzie DRS LP 002	KING'S DUB (LP)	25
82	Cha Cha CHALP 014	REVIVAL (LP)	40

REVOLUTIONARY ARMY OF INFANT JESUS
87	Probe Plus PROBE 12	THE GIFT OF TEARS (LP)	40

REVOLUTIONARY BLUES BAND
70	MCA MUP(S) 402	REVOLUTIONARY BLUES BAND (LP)	20

REVOLUTIONARY CORPS OF TEENAGE JESUS VS SUICIDE
96	Creeping Bent BENT 005	FRANKIE TEARDROP EP (Frankie Teardrop [126 b.p.m.]/U.S.A. '95/Frankie Teardrop [114 b.p.m.]/Womb 17) (12", p/s, 1,000 only)	10

(see also Suicide, Future Pilot A.KA.)

REVOLVER (1)
69	Young BLood YB 1006	Frisco Annie/Imaginations	20

REVOLVER (2)
78	Rockburgh ROCS 203	Silently Screaming/On The Run (p/s)	15

REVOLVING PAINT DREAM
84	Creation CRE 002	Flowers In The Sky/In The Afternoon (foldaround p/s in poly bag)	20

(see also Laughing Apple, Primal Scream)

REVS
91	Vinyl Japan TASK 9	Just Ask Why/We're So Modern/Stay With Me/Julie Got A Raise (12", p/s)	8

REVULSION
85	Radical Change RC 7	Ever Get The Feeling Of Utter... (12")	20

KIMBERLEY REW
80	Armageddon AS 004	Stomping All Over The World/Nothing's Going To Change In Your Life/Fighting Someone's War (p/s)	5
81	Armageddon AS 012	My Baby Does Her Hairdo Long/Fishing (p/s, with dB's)	5

(see also Soft Boys, Waves)

REX
| 77 | CBS 82186 | WHERE DO WE GO FROM HERE (LP) | 12 |

REX (MORRIS) & MINORS
| 60 | Triumph RGM 1023 | Chicken Sax/Snake Eyes | 50 |

ROBERTA REX
| 68 | Fontana TF 967 | Joey/I Can Feel It | 6 |

ALVINO REY
| 61 | London HLD 9431 | Original Mama Blues/Steel Guitar Rag | 10 |
| 62 | London HA-D 2414 | ALVINO REY'S GREATEST HITS (LP) | 20 |

CHICO REY & JET BAND
| 70 | Pye 7N 17899 | Stiletto/Midnight In Mexico | 40 |

LITTLE BOBBY REY & HIS BAND
| 60 | Top Rank JAR 525 | Rockin' "J" Bells/Dance Of The New Year | 8 |

REYNARD
| 76 | Pilgrim/Grapevine GRA 102 | FRESH FROM THE EARTH (LP) | 40 |

AMBROSE REYNOLDS
| 83 | Zulu ZULU 3 | GREATEST HITS (LP) | 12 |

(see also Pink Military)

DEBBIE REYNOLDS
55	MGM SP 1127	Carolina In The Morning/Never Mind The Noise In The Market (B-side as Debbie Reynolds' Naturals)	10
56	MGM SP 1155	(Love Is) The Tender Trap/Canoodlin' Rag	8
57	Vogue Coral Q 72274	Tammy/French Heels	5
58	MGM MGM 968	All Grown Up/Wall Flower	5
58	Coral Q 72324	This Happy Feeling/Hillside In Scotland	5
60	London HLD 9028	Am I That Easy To Forget?/Ask Me To Go Steady	5
60	London HLD 9128	City Lights/Just For A Touch Of Your Love	5
61	London HLD 9351	Lonely People/Just A Little Girl	5
58	MGM MGM-EP 670	DEBBIE REYNOLDS (EP)	20
58	MGM MGM-EP 671	SINGING IN THE RAIN (EP, with Gene Kelly & Donald O'Connor)	10
59	MGM MGM-EP 694	DELIGHTFUL DEBBIE REYNOLDS (EP)	15
60	MGM MGM-EP 725	FROM DEBBIE WITH LOVE (EP)	15
59	London HA-D 2200	DEBBIE (LP, mono)	40
59	London SAH-D 6051	DEBBIE (LP, stereo)	45
60	London HA-D 2294	AM I THAT EASY TO FORGET? (LP, mono)	20
60	London SAH-D 6106	AM I THAT EASY TO FORGET? (LP, stereo)	25
61	London HA-D 2326	FINE AND DANDY (LP)	20
63	London HA-D 8075	GREAT FOLK HITS (LP, mono)	20
63	London HA-D/SH-D 8075	GREAT FOLK HITS (LP, stereo)	25
69	Pye Int 7N 25507	With A Little Love (Just A Little Love)/I Think You're Gonna Be Alright	6

(see also Naturals [U.S.])

DONN REYNOLDS
58	MGM MGM 996	Blue Eyes Crying In The Rain/Bella Belinda	6
58	Pye 7N 15122	Swing Low Sweet Chariot/Ramona	6
59	Pye NEP 24098	THE DONN REYNOLDS SONGBAG (EP)	10

ELI REYNOLDS
| 70 | Punch PH 37 | Mr Car Man/Chiney Man | 10 |

JODY REYNOLDS
| 58 | London HL 8651 | Endless Sleep/Tight Capris | 25 |
| 58 | London HL 8651 | Endless Sleep/Tight Capris (78) | 15 |

TIMMY REYNOLDS
| 62 | Ember EMB S 133 | Lullaby Of Love/JEFF MILLS: Daddy's Home | 70 |

REZILLOS
77	Sensible FAB 1	Can't Stand My Baby/I Wanna Be Your Man (p/s, 15,000, 5,000 numbered)	15
77	Sensible FAB 1	Can't Stand My Baby/I Wanna Be Your Man (p/s, 15,000, 10,000 unnumbered)	10
77	Sensible FAB 2	Flying Saucer Attack/(My Baby Does) Good Sculptures (p/s, unissued)	0
77	Sire 6078 612	Flying Saucer Attack/(My Baby Does) Good Sculptures (p/s)	12
78	Sire 6198 215	Cold Wars/William Mysterious Overture (unissued, rare picture sleeve)	150
78	Sire SIR 4001	Top Of The Pops/20,000 Rezillos Under The Sea (p/s)	8
78	Sire SIR 4008	Destination Venus/Mystery Action (p/s)	6
79	Sire SIR 4014	Cold Wars (live)/Flying Saucer Attack (live)/Twist & Shout (live) (p/s)	12
79	Sensible FAB 1 (Mark 2)	Can't Stand My Baby/I Wanna Be Your Man (reissue, new p/s, run out groove reads "Come Back John Lennon")	7
79	Sensible FAB 1 (Mark 2)	Can't Stand My Baby/I Wanna Be Your Man (reissue, p/s, mispressing, B-side plays "(My Baby Does) Good Sculptures (live)", run-off groove reads "De-sire-able product?", 4,000 only)	6
78	Sire K 56530	CAN'T STAND THE REZILLOS (LP, with inner sleeve & postcard insert)	20
78	Sire SRK 6069	MISSION ACCOMPLISHED ... BUT THE BEAT GOES ON (LP, live)	18

(see also Revillos, Shake, Jo Callis, William Mysterious)

RHABSTALLION
| 81 | Rhab RHAB 001 | Day To Day/Breadline (p/s, with badge) | 30 |
| 81 | Rhab RHAB 001 | Day To Day/Breadline (p/s) | 20 |

RHINOCEROS
69	Elektra EKSN 45051	Apricot Brandy/I Don't Want To Discuss It	10
69	Elektra EKSN 45058	I Will Serenade You/Belbuekul	7
70	Elektra EKSN 45080	Back Door/In A Little Room	6
70	Elektra 2101 009	Old Age/Let's Party	6
69	Elektra EKL 4030	RHINOCEROS (LP, orange label, also stereo EKS 74030)	20
69	Elektra EKL 4056	SATIN CHICKENS (LP, also stereo EKS 74056)	20
70	Elektra 2469 006	BETTER TIMES ARE COMING (LP, gatefold sleeve)	15

RHODA WITH THE SPECIAL A.K.A.
| 82 | 2-Tone CHS TT 18 | The Boiler/Theme From The Boiler | 5 |
| 82 | 2-Tone CHS TT 1218 | The Boiler/Theme From The Boiler (12", p/s existence unconfirmed) | 20 |

(see also Special A.K.A.)

JAN RHODE & HIS COOL CATS
60	Qualiton Offbeat PSP 7128	Come Back Baby/So Shy	8

PAT RHODEN
65	Ska Beat JB 195	Jezebel/You Can Hold My Hand	20
66	Blue Beat BB 360	Send Your Love/Make Believe	15
68	Trojan TR 606	Woman Is Greedy/Endlessly	8
70	Pama PM 811	Maybe The Next Time/Got To See You	8
70	Pama Supreme PS 298	Do What You Gotta Do/Crying Won't Help You	8
70	Mary Lyn ML 101	Time Is Tight/MILTON & DENZIL: I Like It Like That	8
73	Pama Supreme PS 378	Out Of Time/Put A Little Rain Into My Life	8

(see also Pat Riden, Pat & Marie, Denzil & Pat)

EMITT RHODES
71	Probe PRO 520	Fresh As A Daisy/You Take The Dark Out Of The Night	7
71	Probe PRO 529	With My Face On The Floor/Somebody Made For Me	7
71	A&M AMS 865	You're A Very Lovely Woman/Till The Day After	6
72	Probe PRO 565	Tame The Lion/Golden Child Of God	7
71	Probe SPBA 6256	EMITT RHODES (LP, gatefold sleeve)	18
71	A&M AMLS 64254	AMERICAN DREAM (LP)	18
71	Probe SPBA 6262	MIRROR (LP)	15
72	Probe SPBA 6266	FAREWELL TO PARADISE (LP)	15

TODD RHODES ORCHESTRA
55	Parlophone MSP 6171	Specks/Silver Sunset	30

RHODESIANS
80	Period PER 001	Clock!!!/Postmortem (p/s)	15

RHUBARB RHUBARB
68	President PT 229	Rainmaker/Moneylender	160

RHYME AND REASON
77	Decca F 13711	Good Morning England/Night Life	6

GRUFF RHYS
11	Ovni OVNI 006	Y Baban Bach/Y Baban Back (instrumental) (tour 7", 300 only)	10

RHYTHM HAWKS
79	Redball RR 011	ZODIAC EP	25

RHYTHM ACES
61	Starlite ST45 061	A Thousand Teardrops/Wherever You May Go	20
61	Starlite ST45 066	Please Don't Go Away/Oh My Darling	20
62	Blue Beat BB 134	I'll Be There/DON DRUMMOND: Dewdrops	20
62	Island WI 032	C-H-R-I-S-T-M-A-S/TOP GRANT: A Christmas Drink	18

RHYTHM & BLUES INC.
65	Fontana TF 524	Louie Louie/Honey Don't	75

RHYTHMETTES
59	Coral Q 72358	Page From The Future/I'll Be With You In Apple Blossom Time	10

RHYTHM FORCE
72	Tropical AL 0013	Satta Call/Satta Version	6

RHYTHM KINGS
63	Vocalion POP V 9212	Blue Soul/Exotic	30

RHYTHM OF LIFE
81	Rational RATE 6	Soon/Summertime (p/s; label also lists Rhythm RHYTHM 1)	10
82	Rational RATE 7	Uncle Sam/Portrait Of The Heart (p/s; label also lists Rhythm RHYTHM 2)	15

(see also Josef K, Paul Haig)

RHYTHM RULERS
70	Bullet BU 447	Second Pressure/Sammy Dead	10

(see also Lloyd Jones, U Roy Junior, Matadors, Winston Groovy, Pat, Winston Wright)

RIBS
78	Aerco AERS 101	Man With No Brain/Long Time Coming (p/s)	25

BOYD RICE & FRIENDS
90	New European BADVC 1969	MUSIC, MARTINIS AND MISANTHROPY (LP, with inner sleeve)	25

(see also Non, Death In June, Current 93)

MACK RICE
69	Atlantic 584 250	Love's A Mother Brother/Coal Man	12

TIM RICE & WEBBER GROUP
69	RCA RCA 1895	Come Back Richard (Your Country Needs You)/Roll On Over The Atlantic	8

(see also Tales Of Justine, Nightshift)

MANDY RICE-DAVIES
64	Ember EMB 4537	MANDY (EP)	30

BOB RICH
70	Mother MOT 1	Christas In My Pants/My Woman	8
73	Mother MOT 5	Filthy Rich/Navy Blue Blues	10

BUDDY RICH
67	Fontana TF836	Norwegian Wood (This Bird Has Flown)/Monitor Theme	20
56	HMV CLP 1092	BUDDY RICH SINGS JOHNNY MERCER (LP)	12
56	Columbia Clef 33CX 10052	THE WAILING BUDDY RICH (LP)	12
57	Columbia Clef 33CX 10071	THIS ONE'S FOR BASIE (LP)	12
57	Columbia Clef 33CX 10080	BUDDY AND SWEETS (LP, with Harry 'Sweets' Edison)	12

CHARLIE RICH
60	London HLU 9107	Lonely Weekends/Everything I Do Is Wrong	50
62	London HLS 9482	Just A Little Bit Sweet/It's Too Late	40
65	RCA RCA 1433	Too Many Teardrops/It's All Over Now	10

Dave RICH

65	Philips BF 1432	Mohair Sam/I Washed My Hands In Muddy Water	10
67	London HLU 10104	Love Is After Me/Pass On By (silver-top label)	15
67	London HLU 10104	Love Is After Me/Pass On By (later boxed logo label)	10
67	London HLU 10104	Love Is After Me/Pass On By (DJ copy)	70
69	Mercury MF 1109	Mohair Sam/I Washed My Hands In Muddy Water (reissue)	10
65	RCA RD 7719	THAT'S RICH (LP)	40

DAVE RICH
| 58 | RCA RCA 1092 | Burn On Love Fire/City Lights | 15 |
| 66 | Polydor BM 56113 | Last Two People On Earth/I Just Wanna Dance | 6 |

JOHNNY RICH
| 64 | Mercury MF 836 | Dream On/Together | 6 |

LEWIS RICH
| 66 | Parlophone R 5434 | I Don't Want To Hear It Anymore/Shedding Tears | 15 |

RICHIE RICH
| 89 | ffrr FX 113 | Salsa House (Silver On Black Mix)/(Original Mix)/(Orbital Mix) (12") | 12 |
| 89 | ffrr FXR 156 | You Used To Salsa/You Used To Hold Me (12", remix) | 20 |

SKETTO RICH
| 70 | Pama PM 806 | Hound Dog/Black Girl | 7 |
| 71 | Big Shot BI 596 | Know Your Friend/Know Your Friend - Version | 5 |

(see Buddy & Sketto, Ruddy & Sketto, Father Sketto, Owen Gray)

TONY RICH
| 66 | Piccadilly 7N 35291 | Save Your Love/Don't Mention Your Name | 10 |
| 66 | Piccadilly 7N 35323 | It's All Up To You Now/See Saw | 15 |

(see also Tony Sheveton)

RICHARD
| 69 | Parlophone R 5754 | A Little Bit/Take Me | 15 |

CLIFF RICHARD (& DRIFTERS/SHADOWS)
78s
58	Columbia DB 4178	Move It!/Schoolboy Crush	35
58	Columbia DB 4203	High Class Baby/My Feet Hit The Ground	30
59	Columbia DB 4249	Livin' Lovin' Doll/Steady With You	80
59	Columbia DB 4290	Mean Streak/Never Mind	80
59	Columbia DB 4306	Living Doll/Apron Strings	40

(The above 78s were credited to Cliff Richard & Drifters)

| 59 | Columbia DB 4351 | Travellin' Light/Dynamite (as Cliff Richard & Shadows) | 45 |
| 60 | Columbia DB 4398 | A Voice In The Wilderness/Don't Be Mad At Me (credited to Cliff Richard & Shadows) | 100 |

SINGLES : COLUMBIA
58	Columbia DB 4178	Move It!/Schoolboy Crush (green label)	40
58	Columbia DB 4178	Move It!/Schoolboy Crush (later pressing with black label)	30
58	Columbia DB 4203	High Class Baby/My Feet Hit The Ground (green label)	40
58	Columbia DB 4203	High Class Baby/My Feet Hit The Ground (later pressing with black label)	30
59	Columbia DB 4249	Livin' Lovin' Doll/Steady With You (green label)	60
59	Columbia DB 4249	Livin' Lovin' Doll/Steady With You (later pressing with black label)	30
59	Columbia DB 4290	Mean Streak/Never Mind (green label)	30
59	Columbia DB 4290	Mean Streak/Never Mind (later pressing with black label)	20
59	Columbia DB 4306	Living Doll/Apron Strings (green label)	25
59	Columbia DB 4306	Living Doll/Apron Strings (later pressing with black label)	20
59	Columbia DB 4351	Travellin' Light/Dynamite	7
60	Columbia DB 4398	A Voice In The Wilderness/Don't Be Mad At Me	5
60	Columbia DB 4431	Fall In Love With You/Willie And The Hand Jive	5
60	Columbia DB 4479	Please Don't Tease/Where Is My Heart	5
60	Columbia DB 4506	Nine Times Out Of Ten/Thinking Of Our Love	6
60	Columbia DB 4547	I Love You/"D" In Love	5
61	Columbia DB 4593	Theme For A Dream/Mumblin' Mosie	5
61	Columbia DB 4667	A Girl Like You/Now's The Time To Fall In Love	5
61	Columbia DB 4716	When The Girl In Your Arms Is The Girl In Your Heart/ Got A Funny Feeling (solo)	5
62	Columbia DB 4761	The Young Ones/We Say Yeah (green label)	5
62	Columbia DB 4761	The Young Ones/We Say Yeah (later black label)	7
62	Columbia DB 4828	I'm Lookin' Out The Window/Do You Want To Dance?	5
62	Columbia DB 4886	It'll Be Me/Since I Lost You	6

(The above 45s were originally green labels; later black label copies are worth at least twice the listed values)

62	Columbia DB 4950	The Next Time/Bachelor Boy	5
63	Columbia DB 4977	Summer Holiday/Dancing Shoes	5
63	Columbia DB 7034	Lucky Lips/I Wonder	5
63	Columbia DB 7089	It's All In The Game/Your Eyes Tell On You (solo)	5
63	Columbia DB 7150	Don't Talk To Him/Say You're Mine	5
64	Columbia DB 7203	I'm The Lonely One/Watch What You Do With My Baby	5
64	Columbia DB 7272	Constantly (solo)/True True Lovin'	5
64	Columbia DB 7305	On The Beach/A Matter Of Moments	5
64	Columbia DB 7372	The Twelfth Of Never/I'm Afraid To Go Home (solo)	5
64	Columbia DB 7420	I Could Easily Fall (In Love With You)/I'm In Love With You	5

(The above singles credited to Cliff Richard & Shadows unless otherwise stated, those listed below are Cliff Richard solo unless otherwise stated)

64	Columbia DB 7435	This Was My Special Day/I'm Feeling Oh So Lovely (withdrawn, credited to Cliff Richard, Audrey Bayley, Joan Palethorpe & Faye Fisher)	20
65	Columbia DB 7496	The Minute You're Gone/Just Another Guy	5
65	Columbia DB 7596	On My Word/Just A Little Bit Too Late	6
65	Columbia DB 7660	The Time In Between/Look Before You Love (as Cliff Richard & Shadows)	6
65	Columbia DB 7745	Wind Me Up (Let Me Go)/The Night	6
66	Columbia DB 7866	Blue Turns To Grey/Somebody Loses (as Cliff Richard & Shadows)	6
66	Columbia DB 7968	Visions/What Would I Do (For The Love Of A Girl?)	6
66	Columbia DB 8017	Time Drags By/La La La Song (as Cliff Richard & Shadows)	7
66	Columbia DB 8094	In The Country/Finders Keepers (as Cliff Richard & Shadows)	5
66	Columbia PSRS 304	Finders Keepers (promo only, 1-sided, with spoken intro by Simon Dee)	30
67	Columbia DB 8150	It's All Over/Why Wasn't I Born Rich?	5
67	Columbia DB 8210	I'll Come Runnin'/I Get The Feelin'	7

67	Columbia DB 8245	The Day I Met Marie/Our Story Book 5
67	Columbia DB 8293	All My Love/Sweet Little Jesus Boy 5
68	Columbia DB 8376	Congratulations/High 'N' Dry 5
68	Columbia DB 8437	I'll Love You Forever Today/Girl, You'll Be A Woman Soon 10
68	Columbia DB 8476	Marianne/Mr Nice 6
68	Columbia DB 8503	Don't Forget To Catch Me/What's More (I Don't Need Her) 8
69	Columbia DB 8548	Good Times (Better Times)/Occasional Rain 7
69	Columbia DB 8581	Big Ship/She's Leaving You 7
69	Columbia DB 8615	Throw Down A Line (as Cliff & Hank)/Reflections 5
69	Columbia DB 8641	With The Eyes Of A Child/So Long 7
70	Columbia DB 8657	Joy Of Living (as Cliff & Hank)/CLIFF RICHARD: Leave My Woman Alone/ HANK MARVIN: Boogatoo..8
70	Columbia DB 8685	Goodbye Sam, Hello Samantha/You Never Can Tell 5
70	Columbia DB 8708	I Ain't Got Time Anymore/Monday Comes Too Soon 7
71	Columbia DB 8747	Sunny Honey Girl/Don't Move Away (with Olivia Newton-John)/ I Was Only Fooling Myself.7
71	Columbia DB 8774	Silvery Rain/Annabella Umbrella/Time Flies 8
71	Columbia DB 8797	Flying Machine/Pigeon 10
71	Columbia DB 8836	Sing A Song Of Freedom/A Thousand Conversations 6
72	Columbia DB 8864	Jesus/Mister Cloud 10
72	Columbia DB 8917	Living In Harmony/Empty Chairs 5
72	Columbia DB 8957	Brand New Song/The Old Accordion 6

SINGLES : EMI SINGLES

84	EMI 5457	Ocean Deep/Baby You're Dynamite (p/s) 20
73	EMI EMI 2012	Power To All Our Friends/Come Back Billie Joe 5
73	EMI EMI 2022	Help It Along/Tomorrow Rising/The Days Of Love/Ashes To Ashes (in p/s)......10
73	EMI EMI 2022	Help It Along/Tomorrow Rising/The Days Of Love/Ashes To Ashes 5
73	EMI EMI 2088	Take Me High/Celestial Houses 5
74	EMI PSR 368	Nothing To Remind Me/The Learning (promo only) 40
74	EMI EMI 2150	(You Keep Me) Hangin' On/Love Is Here 5
75	EMI EMI 2279	It's Only Me You've Left Behind/You're The One. 5
75	EMI EMI 2344	Honky Tonk Angel/(Wouldn't You Know It) Got Myself A Girl 15
76	EMI EMI 2376	Miss You Nights/Love Enough 6
76	EMI EMI 2376	Miss You Nights/Love Enough (with p/s in box set) 5
77	EMI EMI 2633	When Two Worlds Drift Apart/That's Why I Love You 6
78	EMI EMI 2730	Yes! He Lives/Good On The Sally Army 15
78	EMI EMI 2832	Please Remember Me/Please Don't Tease 5
78	EMI EMI 2885	Can't Take The Hurt Anymore/Needing A Friend (p/s) 10
79	EMI EMI 2920	Green Light/Imagine Love (in p/s) 15
79	EMI EMI 2920	Green Light/Imagine Love 5
79	EMI EMI 2975	We Don't Talk Anymore/Count Me Out (p/s, mispress, A-side plays Queen's "Bohemian Rhapsody")..12

EXPORT SINGLES

61	Columbia DC 756	Gee Whiz It's You/I Cannot Find A True Love 5
63	Columbia DC 758	What'd I Say/Blue Moon 150
65	Columbia DC 762	Angel/Razzle Dazzle 60

EPs

59	Columbia SEG 7895	SERIOUS CHARGE (soundtrack) 30
59	Columbia SEG 7903	CLIFF NO. 1 (mono) 25
59	Columbia ESG 7754	CLIFF NO. 1 (stereo) 30
59	Columbia SEG 7910	CLIFF NO. 2 (mono) 20
59	Columbia ESG 7769	CLIFF NO. 2 (stereo) 25
59	Columbia SEG 7971	EXPRESSO BONGO (soundtrack, mono) 20
59	Columbia ESG 7783	EXPRESSO BONGO (soundtrack, stereo) 30
60	Columbia SEG 7979	CLIFF SINGS NO. 1 (mono) 25
60	Columbia ESG 7788	CLIFF SINGS NO. 1 (stereo) 30
60	Columbia SEG 7987	CLIFF SINGS NO. 2 (mono) 25
60	Columbia ESG 7794	CLIFF SINGS NO. 2 (stereo) 30
60	Columbia SEG 8005	CLIFF SINGS NO. 3 (mono) 25
60	Columbia ESG 7808	CLIFF SINGS NO. 3 (stereo) 30
60	Columbia SEG 8021	CLIFF SINGS NO. 4 (mono) 25
60	Columbia ESG 7816	CLIFF SINGS NO. 4 (stereo) 30
60	Columbia SEG 8050	CLIFF'S SILVER DISCS 20
60	Columbia SEG 8065	ME AND MY SHADOWS NO. 1 (mono) 25
60	Columbia ESG 7837	ME AND MY SHADOWS NO. 1 (stereo) 30
61	Columbia SEG 8071	ME AND MY SHADOWS NO. 2 (mono) 25
61	Columbia ESG 7481	ME AND MY SHADOWS NO. 2 (stereo) 30
61	Columbia SEG 8078	ME AND MY SHADOWS NO. 3 (mono) 25
61	Columbia ESG 7843	ME AND MY SHADOWS NO. 3 (stereo) 30
61	Columbia SEG 8105	LISTEN TO CLIFF NO. 1 (mono) 25
61	Columbia ESG 7858	LISTEN TO CLIFF NO. 1 (stereo) 30
61	Columbia SEG 8119	DREAM (mono) 20
61	Columbia ESG 7867	DREAM (stereo) 25
61	Columbia SEG 8126	LISTEN TO CLIFF NO. 2 (mono) 25
61	Columbia ESG 7870	LISTEN TO CLIFF NO. 2 (stereo) 30
62	Columbia SEG 8133	CLIFF'S HIT PARADE 20
62	Columbia SEG 8151	CLIFF RICHARD 30
62	Columbia SEG 8159	HITS FROM 'THE YOUNG ONES' 20
62	Columbia SEG 8168	CLIFF RICHARD NO. 2 30

(The above EPs were originally issued with turquoise labels, later blue/black label copies are worth two-thirds these values.)

62	Columbia SEG 8203	CLIFF'S HITS 20
63	Columbia SEG 8228	TIME FOR CLIFF AND THE SHADOWS (mono) 20
63	Columbia ESG 7887	TIME FOR CLIFF AND THE SHADOWS (stereo, turquoise label) 20
63	Columbia ESG 7887	TIME FOR CLIFF AND THE SHADOWS (stereo, turquoise blue/black label) 25
63	Columbia SEG 8246	HOLIDAY CARNIVAL (mono) 20
63	Columbia ESG 7892	HOLIDAY CARNIVAL (stereo) 25
63	Columbia SEG 8250	HITS FROM 'SUMMER HOLIDAY' (mono) 15
63	Columbia ESG 7896	HITS FROM 'SUMMER HOLIDAY' (stereo) 20
63	Columbia SEG 8263	MORE HITS FROM 'SUMMER HOLIDAY' (mono) 20
63	Columbia ESG 7898	MORE HITS FROM 'SUMMER HOLIDAY' (stereo) 25

Cliff RICHARD (& DRIFTERS/SHADOWS)

63	Columbia SEG 8269	CLIFF'S LUCKY LIPS	20
63	Columbia SEG 8272	LOVE SONGS (mono)	20
63	Columbia ESG 7900	LOVE SONGS (stereo)	20
64	Columbia SEG 8290	WHEN IN FRANCE	20
64	Columbia SEG 8299	CLIFF SINGS 'DON'T TALK TO HIM'	20
64	Columbia SEG 8320	CLIFF'S PALLADIUM SUCCESSES	20
64	Columbia SEG 8338	WONDERFUL LIFE (mono)	20
64	Columbia ESG 7902	WONDERFUL LIFE (stereo)	25
64	Columbia SEG 8347	A FOREVER KIND OF LOVE	20
64	Columbia SEG 8354	WONDERFUL LIFE NO. 2 (mono)	20
64	Columbia ESG 7903	WONDERFUL LIFE NO. 2 (stereo)	25
64	Columbia SEG 8376	HITS FROM 'WONDERFUL LIFE' (mono)	20
64	Columbia ESG 7906	HITS FROM 'WONDERFUL LIFE' (stereo)	25
65	Columbia SEG 8384	WHY DON'T THEY UNDERSTAND?	20
65	Columbia SEG 8395	CLIFF'S HITS FROM 'ALADDIN AND HIS WONDERFUL LAMP'	20
65	Columbia SEG 8405	LOOK IN MY EYES, MARIA	20
65	Columbia SEG 8444	ANGEL	20
65	Columbia SEG 8450	TAKE FOUR	20
66	Columbia SEG 8474	WIND ME UP	20
66	Columbia SEG 8478	HITS FROM 'WHEN IN ROME'	20
66	Columbia SEG 8488	LOVE IS FOREVER	20
66	Columbia SEG 8510	THUNDERBIRDS ARE GO! (3 tracks by Cliff & Shadows, 1 solo)	50
66	Columbia SEG 8517	LA LA LA LA LA (1 track by Bruce Welch & Hank Marvin)	30
67	Columbia SEG 8527	CINDERELLA	70
67	Columbia SEG 8533	CAROL SINGERS	30
68	Columbia SEG 8540	CONGRATULATIONS	20
77	EMI PSR 410	EVERY FACE TELLS A STORY (promo, issued to shops only)	15
77	EMI PSR 414/415	40 GOLDEN GREATS (double pack promo, issued to shops only)	15

ALBUMS : COLUMBIA LPS

59	Columbia 33SX 1147	CLIFF (green labels)	50
59	Columbia 33SX 1147	CLIFF (later blue/black labels)	20
59	Columbia 33SX 1192	CLIFF SINGS (green labels)	50
59	Columbia 33SX 1192	CLIFF SINGS (later blue/black labels)	20
60	Columbia 33SX 1261	ME AND MY SHADOWS (mono)	30
60	Columbia SCX 3330	ME AND MY SHADOWS (stereo)	40
61	Columbia 33SX 1320	LISTEN TO CLIFF! (mono)	30
61	Columbia SCX 3375	LISTEN TO CLIFF! (stereo)	45
61	Columbia 33SX 1368	21 TODAY (mono)	30
61	Columbia SCX 3409	21 TODAY (stereo)	45
61	Columbia 33SX 1384	THE YOUNG ONES (soundtrack with inner, mono)	15
61	Columbia SCX 3397	THE YOUNG ONES (soundtrack with inner, stereo)	20
62	Columbia 33SX 1431	32 MINUTES AND 17 SECONDS WITH... (mono)	30
62	Columbia SCX 3436	32 MINUTES AND 17 SECONDS WITH..	40
63	Columbia 33SX 1472	SUMMER HOLIDAY (soundtrack with inner sleeve, mono)	12
63	Columbia SCX 3462	SUMMER HOLIDAY (first pressing, stereo, with green labels)	25
63	Columbia SCX 3462	SUMMER HOLIDAY (second pressing, stereo, with blue/black labels)	18
63	Columbia SX 1512	CLIFF'S HIT ALBUM	12
63	Columbia SX 1541	WHEN IN SPAIN (mono)	20
63	Columbia SCX 3488	WHEN IN SPAIN (stereo)	30
64	Columbia SX 1628	WONDERFUL LIFE (soundtrack, mono, gatefold sleeve with inner sleeve)	12
64	Columbia SCX 3515	WONDERFUL LIFE (soundtrack, stereo, gatefold sleeve with inner sleeve)	20
64	Columbia SX 1676	ALADDIN AND HIS WONDERFUL LAMP (with stage cast, gatefold sleeve, mono)	15
64	Columbia SCX 3522	ALADDIN AND HIS WONDERFUL LAMP (with stage cast, gatefold sleeve, stereo)	20
65	Columbia SX 1709	CLIFF RICHARD (mono)	25
65	Columbia SCX 3546	CLIFF RICHARD (stereo)	35
65	Columbia SX 1737	MORE HITS BY CLIFF (mono)	15
65	Columbia SCX 3555	MORE HITS BY CLIFF (stereo)	18
65	Columbia SX 1762	WHEN IN ROME	30
65	Columbia SX 1769	LOVE IS FOREVER (also stereo SCX 3569)	25
66	Columbia SX 6039	KINDA LATIN (mono)	30
66	Columbia SCX 6039	KINDA LATIN (stereo)	35
66	Columbia SX 6079	FINDERS KEEPERS (soundtrack, with inner, mono)	15
66	Columbia SCX 6079	FINDERS KEEPERS (soundtrack, with inner, stereo)	20
67	Columbia S(C)X 6103	CINDERELLA (with stage cast)	20
67	Columbia S(C)X 6133	DON'T STOP ME NOW	30
67	Columbia S(C)X 6167	GOOD NEWS	15
67	Columbia JSX 6167	GOOD NEWS (export issue)	35
68	Columbia S(C)X 6244	CLIFF IN JAPAN (blue/black labels)	30
68	Columbia S(C)X 6244	CLIFF IN JAPAN (later pressing with white/black labels)	20
68	Columbia S(C)X 6262	TWO A PENNY (blue/black labels)	20
68	Columbia S(C)X 6262	TWO A PENNY (later pressing with white/black labels)	15
68	Columbia SX 6282	ESTABLISHED 1958 (gatefold sleeve, half tracks by Shadows, mono)	15
68	Columbia SCX 6282	ESTABLISHED 1958 (gatefold sleeve, half tracks by Shadows, /stereo)	12

(The above Columbia LPs were originally issued with blue/black labels; white/black copies are worth half these values.)

69	Columbia SX 6357	SINCERELY CLIFF RICHARD (mono)	15
69	Columbia SCX 6357	SINCERELY CLIFF RICHARD (stereo)	12
70	Columbia SCX 6408	ABOUT THAT MAN (4 songs plus narration)	40
70	Columbia SCX 6435	TRACKS 'N' GROOVES	15
70	Columbia SCX 6443	HIS LAND (documentary soundtrack, with Cliff Barrows)	15

ALBUMS : EMI LPS

73	EMI EMC 3016	TAKE ME HIGH (soundtrack, with poster)	20
73	EMI EMC 3016	TAKE ME HIGH (soundtrack)	12
74	EMI EMA 768	HELP IT ALONG (gatefold sleeve)	20
74	EMI EMC 3048	THE 31ST OF FEBRUARY STREET	15
74	EMI TC EXSP 1601	THE MUSIC AND LIFE OF CLIFF RICHARD (6-cassette box set, music & interviews, with Brian Bennett, Olivia Newton-John, Cilla Black etc.)	15
82	EMI PSLP 350	CLIFF (promo-only sampler)	20
87	EMI EMDB 1004	ALWAYS GUARANTEED (box set, some in embossed sleeve with free 7" "Another Christmas Day")	15
87	EMI EMDB 1004	ALWAYS GUARANTEED (box set)	12

| 89 | EMI CR 1 | THE 30TH ANNIVERSARY PICTURE RECORD COLLECTION (2-LP, picture discs, gatefold sleeve, mail-order only) | 15 |

ALBUMS : OTHER LPS

63	Elstree Extra Range	SUMMER HOLIDAY (2-LP, full soundtrack recording, 80 copies only)	300
64	Elstree Extra Range	WONDERFUL LIFE (2-LP, full soundtrack recording, 150 copies only)	200
64	World Record Club T 643	HOW WONDERFUL TO KNOW (mono)	15
64	World Record Club (S)T 643	HOW WONDERFUL TO KNOW (stereo)	20
64	EMI Regal SREG 1120	ME AND MY SHADOWS (export issue)	70
69	World R. Club STP 1051	CLIFF RICHARD	30

FLEXIDISCS : FLEXIDISCS & OTHER RELEASES

60	Serenade Magazine/	Serenade Presents Cliff Richard's Personal Message To You (turquoise flexidisc with magazine)	20
60s	Serenade Magazine	Cliff's Rock Party (flexidisc with magazine)	20
60s	Boyfriend Magazine	untitled flexidisc with magazine	20
60s	Rainbow Magazine	Music From America (flexidisc with magazine)	20
90	EMI CRTBX 31	Miss You Nights (Acapella version) (1-sided 7" etched message and autograph on reverse)	10
60s	New Spotlight	Star Souvenir Greetings (208 Radio Luxembourg flexidisc)	20
73	Spree (no cat. no.)	Good News (plain black flexidisc with spoken/sung introduction from Cliff, other side by Johnny Cash)	20
98	Cruisin' The 50's CASB 007	Breathless/Lawdy Miss Clawdy (10" 78, p/s, with 6 inserts)	50

(see also Drifters [U.K.], Shadows, Olivia Newton-John, Sheila Walsh, Janet Jackson, Elton John, Phil Everly, Grazina)

WENDY RICHARD & DIANA BERRY

| 63 | Decca F 11680 | We Had A Dream/Keep 'Em Looking Around | 15 |

(see also Mike Sarne)

RICHARD & GLEN

| 72 | Duke DU 141 | Boat To Progress (Parts 1 & 2) | 15 |

RICHARD & YOUNG LIONS

| 66 | Philips BF 1520 | Open Up Your Door/Once Upon Your Smile | 50 |

RICHARD BROTHERS

| 63 | Island WI 060 | I Need A Girl/Desperate Lover | 12 |
| 63 | Island WI 109 | I Shall Wear A Crown/BABA BROOKS: Robin Hood | 20 |

(see also Joe White)

CYNTHIA RICHARDS

69	Clandisc CLA 203	Foolish Fool/KING STITT: On The Street	15
70	Clandisc CLA 210	Conversation/DYNAMITES: Conversation Version II	12
70	Clandisc CLA 216	Can't Wait/Promises	7
70	Clandisc CLA 220	Foolish Fool/CLANCY & STITT: Dance Beat	12
71	Clandisc CLA 229	Stand By Your Man (actually by Merlene Webber)/DYNAMITES: Version 2	6
71	Big Shot BI 581	I'm Moving On/HIPPY BOYS: I'm Moving On - Version	7
71	Escort ERT 861	Love & Unity/MAYTONES: Wah Noh Dead	7
71	G.G. GG 4528	Place In My Heart/You've Got A Friend (act. Irving [Brown] & Cynthia Richards)	8
72	Pama Supreme PS 366	Mr Postman/SKIN, FLESH AND BONES: Version	10
73	Attack ATT 8047	Aily I/REID'S ALL STARS: Aily I - Version	6
70	Trojan TBL 123	FOOLISH FOOL (LP, actually Clancy Eccles productions compilation)	35

(see also Bobby Aitken, Lord Comic, Sir Lord Comic)

JOHNNY RICHARDS

| 59 | Esquire 32-076 | THE RITES OF DIABLO (LP) | 25 |

KEITH RICHARDS

79	Rolling Stones RSR 102	Run Rudolph Run/The Harder They Come (p/s)	18
86	Arista ARIST 678P	Jumping Jack Flash/Integrity (with Aretha Franklin) (shaped pic disc & plinth)	12
88	Virgin VS 1125	Take It So Hard/I Could Have Stood You Up (p/s)	5
88	Virgin VST 1125	Take It So Hard/I Could Have Stood You Up/It Means A Lot (12", p/s)	8
89	Virgin VS 1179	Make No Mistake (Edit)/It Means A Lot (p/s)	6
89	Virgin VST 1179	Make No Mistake (Extended Version)/(LP Version)/It Means A Lot (12", p/s)	8
88	Virgin KEITH 1234	Make No Mistake/Locked Away/Struggle/Big Enough (4 x 1-sided 7", "Talk Is Cheap" sampler box set, promo only)	90
88	Virgin 2-91047 A/B/C	TALK IS CHEAP (3 x 3" CDs in tin)	40

(see also Rolling Stones, Aranbee Pop Symphony Orchestra, Dirty Strangers, Screamin' Jay Hawkins)

LISA RICHARDS

| 65 | Vocalion VP 9244 | Mean Old World/Take A Chance | 55 |
| 65 | Vocalion VP 9244 | Mean Old World/Take A Chance (DJ copy) | 70 |

LLOYD RICHARDS

| 64 | Port-O-Jam PJ 4004 | Be Good/I Need You | 25 |

ROY RICHARDS

66	Doctor Bird DB 1012	Contact/Maureen	20
66	Island WI 297	Green Collie/MARCIA GRIFFITHS: You No Good	25
66	Island WI 283	Double Trouble/FITSY & FREDDY: Why Did You Do It	25
66	Island WI 299	Western Standard Time/(JA) EAGLES: What An Agony	35
66	Island WI 3000	South Viet Nam/You Must Be Sorry (Vocal)	15
67	Island WI 3027	Rub-A-Dub/SHARKS: Baby Come Home	25
67	Tabernacle TS 1000	When I see Jesus/My Savior Come	20
67	Island WI 3037	Hopeful Village Ska/DELROY WILSON: Ungrateful Baby	35
67	Island WI 3050	Port-O-Jam/DELROY WILSON: Get Ready	45
67	Studio One SO 2020	Hanky Panky/ALTON ELLIS: I Am Still In Love	50

(see also Roland Alphonso, Lord Comic, Soul Vendors, Jackie Mittoo, Derrick Morgan, Righteous Flames)

RUSTY RICHARDS

| 60 | Top Rank JAR 297 | Middle Hand Road/Golden Moon (China Night) | 7 |

TRUDY RICHARDS

57	Capitol CL 14728	Wishbone/Hangin' Around	10
57	Capitol CL 14744	Weaker Than Wise/I Want A Big Butter And Egg Man	6
58	Capitol CL 14857	Somebody Just Like You/The Night When Love Was Born	6
57	Capitol T 838	CRAZY IN LOVE (LP)	15

MINT VALUE £

VIC RICHARDS
| 67 | Polydor 56163 | Jonathan Whatsit/Goodbye | 70 |

WINSTON RICHARDS
| 67 | Rio R 124 | Studio Blitz/Don't Up | 20 |

DEL RICHARDSON
| 73 | MCA MUPS 491 | PIECES OF A JIGSAW (LP, black/silver label) | 100 |

(see also Osibisa, Sundae Times)

JOE 'GROUNDHOG' RICHARDSON
| 69 | Major Minor MM 632 | Take It Off/Blues To Take It Off | 15 |

MARK RICHARDSON
| 65 | Stateside SS 440 | Baby, I'm Sorry/Blanket Fair | 7 |
| 65 | Stateside SS 467 | See It My Way/Think | 7 |

RICH FEVER
| 70 | Parlophone R5869 | Everything's Moving/King Of All The Kingdoms | 15 |
| 71 | Parlophone R 5894 | Song Of A Sad Man/Island Dreams | 12 |

RICH GYPSY
| 80 | Splash SP 016 | What Hit Me (no p/s) | 25 |

TONY RICHIE
| 68 | Beacon BEA 114 | Anybody At The Party Seen Jenny/You Can't Win | 40 |

RICH KIDS
78	EMI EMI 2738	Rich Kids/Empty Words (red vinyl, p/s)	5
78	EMI EMI 2803	Marching Men/Here Comes The Nice (p/s)	6
78	EMI EMC 3263	GHOSTS OF PRINCES IN TOWERS (LP)	15

(see also Sex Pistols, Ultravox, Spectres, Swingers, Visage)

JONATHAN RICHMAN & MODERN LOVERS
75	United Artists UP 36006	Road Runner/It Will Stand	7
77	Beserkley BZZ 1	Road Runner (Once)/Road Runner (Twice) (p/s)	5
77	Beserkley BSERK 9	ROCK 'N' ROLL WITH THE MODERN LOVERS (LP)	20
77	Beserkley BSERK 2	JONATHAN RICHMAN AND THE MODERN LOVERS (LP)	25
77	Beserkley BSERK 12	MODERN LOVERS LIVE (LP)	15
77	Beserkley BSERK 17	BACK IN YOUR LIFE (LP)	18
81	Mohawk LBOM 1	ORIGINAL (LP)	20
84	Rough Trade ROUGH 52	JONATHAN SINGS (LP)	15
85	Rough Trade ROUGH 72	ROCKIN' & ROMANCE (LP)	15

RICH MIX
| 83 | Satril 12 SAT 509 | I Got The Love/Version (12") | 15 |

RICHMOND
73	Dart ART 2008	Candy Dora/Willow Farm	12
73	Dart ART 2025	Frightened/Breakfast	8
73	Dart ART 2031	Raise Your Heads To The Wind/All I Really Need	5
74	Dart ART 2044	Peaches/Work For My Baby	6
73	Dart ARTS 65371	FRIGHTENED (LP, textured sleeve, lyric insert)	30

BEN RICHMOND
| 63 | Piccadilly 7N 35092 | Blue Bird/Bells All Started Ringing | 6 |
| 63 | Piccadilly 7N 35132 | You Gotta Have Love/I Don't Care | 6 |

FIONA RICHMOND
| 73 | Raymond PR 112 | FRANKLY FIONA (LP) | 50 |

JANET RICHMOND
60	Top Rank JAR 288	You Got What It Takes/Not One Minute More	10
60	Top Rank JAR 378	June Bride/My One And Only Love	7
61	Top Rank JAR 536	Senora/I Need You	10

RICHUS FLAMES
| 67 | Fab FAB 17 | Need To Be Loved/I Am Going Home | 25 |

(see also Righteous Flames)

RICK & KEENS
| 61 | Mercury AMT 1150 | Peanuts/I'll Be Home | 75 |

RICK & SANDY
| 65 | Decca F 12196 | Lost My Girl/I Can't Help It | 35 |
| 65 | Decca F 12311 | Creation/In A 100 Years From Now | 25 |

BERESFORD RICKETTS
60	Starlite ST45 025	Cherry Baby/I Want To Know	30
60	Starlite ST45 029	Baby Baby/When I Woke Up	30
61	Starlite ST45 048	Hold Me Tight/Dream Girl (as Ricketts & Rowe)	30
62	Starlite ST45 079	I'm Going To Cry/Waiting For Me	30
62	Blue Beat BB 107	You Better Be Going/I've Been Walking (as Beresford Ricketts & Blue Beats)	22
63	Dice CC 12	Oh Jean/Rivers Of Tears (as Lauren Aitken's Group)	20
66	Blue Beat BB 350	Jailer Bring Me Water/Careless Love	22

RICKY & THE MUTATIONS
| 83 | Cool Ghoul COOL 003 | Thatcher Rap (12") | 35 |

RICKY BAILEY
| 78 | K&B KB 5525 | Proud Mary/Proud Man | 6 |

RICO (RODRIGUEZ)
61	Blue Beat BB 56	Luke Lane Shuffle (as Rico Rodrigues & Buster's All Stars)/ BUSTER'S GROUP: Little Honey	20
62	Island WI 022	Rico Special (as Emanuel Rodrigues Orchestra; some copies may credit Reco & His Happy Orchestra)/BUNNY & SKITTER: A Little Mashin'	35
62	Planetone RC 1	London Here I Come/Midnight In Ethiopia	25
62	Planetone RC 4	Planet Rock/You Win	20
62	Planetone RC 5	Youth Boogie/Western Serenade (as Rico's Combo)	20
67	Fab FAB 12	Jingle Bells/Silent Night (with His Boys)	10

68	Pama PM 706	Soul Man/It's Not Unusual (as Reco Rodriguez)	12
68	Pama PM 715	Tender Foot Ska/Memories (as Reco Rodriguez)	15
69	Blue Cat BS 160	The Bullet/Rhythm In (as Reco Rodriguez & His Rhythm Aces)	25
69	Doctor Bird DB 1302	Baby Face (as Reco & Rudies)/RUDIES: News	25
69	Bullet BU 407	Tribute To Don Drummond/Japanese Invasion (as Rico Rodriquez)	60
71	Duke DU 96	Surprise Package (as Rico & Satch)/PETE JOHNSON: I'm Sorry	20
70s	Island IPR 2006	Ska-Wars/Ramble (12")	25
78	Island IPR 2002	Dial Africa/Dub (12")	25
79	Island IPR 2016	Take 5/Sound Check (12")	20
80	Island IPR 2030	Children Of Sanchez/You Really Got Me/Midnight In Ethiopia (12")	30
80	2-Tone CHS TT 15	Sea Cruise/Carolina	20
82	2-Tone CHS TT 19	Jungle Music/Rasta Call You (paper label, 2-Tone sleeve, with Special A.K.A.)	25
82	2-Tone CHS TT 1219	Jungle Music/Rasta Call You/Easter Island (12", p/s, with Special A.K.A.)	20
69	Trojan TTL 12	BLOW YOUR HORN (LP, as Rico & Rudies)	35
78	Island ILPS 9485	MAN FROM WARREIKA (LP)	12
78	Ghetto Rockers PRE 1	WARREIKA DUB (LP, white label, white sleeve, beware of bootlegs)	80
81	2 Tone CHR TT 5005	THAT MAN IS FORWARD (LP)	35
82	2 Tone CHR TT5006	JAMA RICO (LP)	50

(see also Special A.K.A., Reco, Andy Capp, Don Reco, Prince Buster, Pioneers, Stranger)

RICOCHET
| 80 | Heavy Rock HER 1 | Midas Light/Off The Rails (p/s) | 150 |

RICOCHET KLASHNEKOFF
| 02 | Y n R YNR09 | Daggo Mentality/Jankrowville (12") | 12 |

RICOTTI & ALBUQUERQUE
| 71 | Pegasus PEG 2 | FIRST WIND (LP) | 30 |

(see also Frank Ricotti, Henry Lowther)

FRANK RICOTTI QUARTET
| 69 | CBS 52668 | OUR POINT OF VIEW (LP) | 40 |

(see also Ricotti & Albuquerque, Chris Spedding)

NELSON RIDDLE ORCHESTRA
55	Capitol CL 14241	Vera Cruz/You Won't Forget Me	6
55	Capitol CL 14242	The Pendulum Song/Brother John	6
56	Capitol CL 14510	Robin Hood/In Old Lisbon (Lisboa Antigua)	6
63	Capitol CL 15253	Route 66 Theme/Lolita Ya Ya	5
63	Capitol CL 15309	Supercar/The Dick Van Dyke Theme	8
66	Stateside SS 517	Batman Theme (from the T.V. series)/Nelson's Riddler	8
59	Capitol EAP 1034	JOHNNY CONCHO (EP)	8
59	HMV GES 5792	NELSON RIDDLE PLAYS GERSHWIN (EP, stereo)	8
61	Capitol EAP4 1771	ROUTE 66 AND OTHER T.V. THEMES (EP)	8
62	Capitol (S)T 1771	ROUTE 66 AND OTHER GREAT T.V. THEMES (LP)	12
62	MGM MGM-C 896	LOLITA (LP, soundtrack)	25
64	Reprise R 2021	ROBIN AND THE SEVEN HOODS (LP, soundtrack)	20
66	Stateside S(S)L 10179	BATMAN (LP, TV soundtrack)	60
67	Columbia S(C)X 6155	EL DORADO (LP, soundtrack)	15

(see also Shirley Bassey)

RIDDLERS
| 66 | Polydor BM 56716 | Batman Theme/Weegie Walk | 30 |

RIDE
90	Creation CRE 075T	PLAY EP (12")	10
90	Creation CRE 087T	FALL EP (12")	8
91	No Label	Like A Snowflake (7" sold at London ULU gig 19/12/91)	20
94	Creation CRE 189T	I Don't Know Where It Comes From/Drive Blind/From Time To Time/How Does It Feel To Feel (p/s)	5
94	Creation CRE 155TC	Birdman/Rolling Thunder No. 2/Let's Get Lost/Don't Let It Die (12", cklear vinyl)	8
90	Creation CRELP 074	NOWHERE (LP)	30
92	Creation CRELP 124	GOING BLANK AGAIN (2-LP)	25
94	Creation CRELP 147	CARNIVAL OF LIGHT (2-LP)	40
96	Creation CRELP 180	TARANTULA (LP)	25

(see also Motorcycle Ride)

PAT RIDEN & BROTHER LLOYD'S ALL STARS
| 69 | Mercury MF 1072 | I Need Help/Let The Red Wine Flow (actually by Pat Rhoden) | 6 |

(see also Pat Rhoden)

JACKIE RIDING & IMESON SOUND
| 66 | Fab FAB 4 | Don't Wanna Leave/The Wave | 8 |

RIFF
| 64 | Blue Beat BB 242 | Oh What A Feeling/Primitive Man | 70 |

RIFF-RAFF
73	RCA RCA 2396	Copper Kettle/You Must Be Joking	5
73	RCA SF 8351	RIFF-RAFF (LP, with booklet)	45
73	RCA SF 8351	RIFF-RAFF (LP, without booklet)	25
74	RCA LPL1 5023	ORIGINAL MAN (LP)	25

RIFF RAFF
78	Chiswick SW 34	I WANNA BE A COSMONAUT (EP)	10
80	Geezer GZ 3	Little Girls Know/She Don't Matter (p/s)	10
80	Geezer GZ 3	Every Girl/You Shaped House (p/s)	10

RIFKIN
| 68 | Page One POF 071 | Continental Hesitation/We're Not Those People Any More | 70 |

THE RIFLES
| 05 | Blow Up BU 029 | Peace And Quiet/Breakdown (die-cut Blow Up sleeve) | 10 |
| 05 | Xtra Mile XMR 007 | When I'm Alone/ Holiday In The Sun (p/s) | 5 |

BRAM RIGG SET
| 67 | Stateside SS 2020 | Take The Time Be Yourself/I Can Only Give You Everything | 50 |

DIANA RIGG

72	RCA RCA 2178	Forget Yesterday/Sentimental Journey	20
02	Harkit HRKLP	DIANA RIGG SINGS (LP, test pressings only)	50

JACKIE RIGGS

56	London HLF 8244	The Great Pretender/His Gold Will Melt	40

RIGHTEOUS BROTHERS

63	London HL 9743	Little Latin Lupe Lu/I'm So Lonely	10
63	London HL 9814	My Babe/Fee-Fi-Fidily-I-Oh	10
64	London HL 9975	You've Lost That Lovin' Feelin'/There's A Woman	5
65	London HL 9975	Unchained Melody/Hung On You	6
65	London HL 10066	Just Once In My Life/The Blues	6
65	Pye International 7N 25297	Bring Your Love To Me/Try And Find Another Man	8
65	Pye International 7N 25304	Something's Got A Hold On Me/Night Owl	5
65	Pye Int. 7N 25323	Let The Good Times Roll/B Flat Blues	6
65	London HL 10011	Ebb Tide/(I Love You) For Sentimental Reasons	12
65	London HL 9962	Just Once In My Life/The Blues (withdrawn)	25
66	Pye International 7N 25358	Georgia On My Mind/My Tears Will Go Away	7
66	Verve VS 535	(You're My) Soul And Inspiration/B Side-Blues	7
66	Verve VS 537	He/He Will Break Your Heart	7
66	Sue WI 4018	You Can Have Her/Justine	20
66	London HL 10086	The White Cliffs Of Dover/Baby She's Mine	7
66	Verve VS 547	Island In The Sun/What Now My Love	8
67	Verve VS 560	Standing In The Middle Of No Place/Been So Nice	12
77	Phil Spector Int'l 2010 022	You've Lost That Lovin' Feelin'/RIGHTEOUS BROTHERS BAND: Rat Race (ins't)	5
65	Pye Intl. NEP 44043	THE RIGHTEOUS BROTHERS (EP)	15
66	Verve VEP 5024	SOUL AND INSPIRATION (EP)	15
66	Verve VEP 5025	THE RIGHTEOUS BROTHERS (EP, reissue)	10
65	Pye Intl. NPL 28056	SOME BLUE-EYED SOUL (LP)	20
65	London HA-U 8226	YOU'VE LOST THAT LOVIN' FEELIN' (LP)	20
65	Pye Intl. NPL 28059	RIGHT NOW! (LP)	15
65	London HA 8245	JUST ONCE IN MY LIFE (LP)	15
66	London HA 8278	BACK TO BACK (LP)	15
66	Verve (S)VLP 9131	SOUL AND INSPIRATION (LP)	15
66	Sue ILP 937	IN ACTION! (LP)	40
68	Verve (S)VLP 9190	SOULED OUT (LP)	15
67	Verve VLP 9168	SAYIN SOMETHIN' (LP)	15

(see also Bill Medley, Bobby Hatfield)

RIGHTEOUS FLAMES

67	Fab FAB 18	Gimme Some Sign Girl/Let's Go To The Dance (B-side act. by Prince Buster)	150
67	Fab FAB 30	When A Girl Loves A Boy	40
68	Coxsone CS 7061	You Don't Know/ROY RICHARDS & SOUL VENDORS: Summertime	200
71	High Note HS 052	Run To The Rock/GAYTONES: Run To The Rock Version	10
71	Nu Beat NB 083	Love And Emotion/Version	10

(see also Richus Flames, Alton Ellis, Flames, Soul Vendors)

RIGHTEOUS HOMES (FLAMES)

68	Coxsone CS 7049	I Was Born To Be Loved/NORMA FRAZER: Heartaches	40
68	Blue Cat BS 112	Seven Letters (actually by Winston Jarrett)/SOUL VENDORS: To Sir With Love	40

RIGHTEOUS SOULS

71	Supreme SUP 217	Mount Zion/ECCLE & NEVILL: All Over	10

RIGHTEOUS TWINS

69	Blue Cat BS 174	If I Could Hear My Master/Satan Can't Prevail	40

RIGOR MORTIS

73	Track 2094 107	Made In Japan/Hound Dog	8
73	Track 2406 106	RIGOR MORTIS SETS IN (LP, gatefold, inner sleeve)	20

(see John Entwistle, Who)

RIKKI & CUFFLINKS

79	Different HAVE 17	Nervous Breakdown/Steamin' On	5

RIKKI & THE LAST DAYS OF EARTH

77	(own label)	Oundle 29/5/77 (1-sided)	60
77	DJM DJS 10814	City Of The Damned/Victimized (p/s)	10
77	DJM DJF 20526	FOUR MINUTE WARNING (LP)	12

RILEY ALL STARS

76	Concrete Jungle CJDPLP	CONCRETE JUNGLE DUB (LP, 300 pressed)	400

BILLY LEE RILEY

65	King KG 1015	I've Been Searchin'/Everybody's Twistin'	8
69	Stax STAX 120	Going Back To Memphis/Family Portrait	10
72	CBS 8182	I Got A Thing About You Baby/You Don't Love Me A.K.A Shimmy Shimmy Walk	7

(see also Megatons)

BOB RILEY

58	MGM MGM 977	The Midnight Line/Wanda Jean	50
58	MGM MGM 977	The Midnight Line/Wanda Jean (78)	15

DESMOND RILEY

69	Downtown DT 432	Tear Them/GEORGE LEE & RUDIES: Chaka Ground	15
69	Downtown DT 435	Tears On My Pillow/RUDIES: Man Pon Spot	10
69	Downtown DT 436	If I Had Wings/AUDREY: You'll Lose A Good Thing	10
69	Downtown DT 438	Out Your Fire/No Return	12
69	Downtown DT 450	Skinhead, A Message To You/MUSIC DOCTORS: Going Strong	100
69	Downtown DT 454	If I Had Wings/AUDREY: You'll Lose A Good Thing (reissue)	6

HOWARD RILEY (TRIO)

68	Opportunity CP 2499	DISCUSSIONS (LP with insert, as Howard Riley Trio)	800
69	CBS 52669	ANGLE (LP)	50
70	CBS 64077	THE DAY WILL COME (LP)	60
71	Turtle TUR 301	FLIGHT (LP, gatefold sleeve)	140

| 76 | Incus INCUS 13 | SYNOPSIS (LP, as Howard Riley Trio with Tony Oxley & Barry Guy) | 100 |
| 79 | Spotlite | THE OTHER SIDE (LP) | 15 |

(see also Colosseum, Karyobin)

JIMI/JIMMY RILEY
71	Supreme SUP 217	Mount Zion (actually by Jimi Riley & Stranger Cole)/ ECCLE & NEVIL: All Over	7
75	Dip DL 5067	Ram Goat Liver/OMAR & MARSHA PERRY: Ram Goat Dub	5
76	Upsetter UP 101	Give Me A Love/UPSETTERS: Give Me A Dub	15
79	Attack TACK 1	Give Thanks And Praise/Feeling Is Believing (12")	20
78	Burning Sounds BS 1011	SHOWCASE (LP)	25
78	Burning Sounds BS 1029	MAJORITY RULE (LP)	25
79	Trojan TRLS 167	TELL THE YOUTHS THE TRUTH (LP)	20

(see also Martin Riley, Sensations, Uniques)

MARTIN RILEY
69	Gas GAS 114	Walking Proud/LLOYD CHARMERS: Why Baby	35
69	Punch PH 7	Trying To Be Free/I've Got It Bad	10
70	Camel CA 53	Catch This Sound/Suspense	10
70	Escort ES 823	It Grows (actually "It's Growing")/We Had A Good Thing Going	20
71	Camel CA 77	When Will We Be Paid/WILLIE FRANCIS: He's Got The Whole World In His Hands	8

(see also Slim Smith, Slickers)

TERRY RILEY
71	CBS 64259	CHURCH OF ANTHRAX (LP, with John Cale)	20
71	CBS 64564	A RAINBOW IN CURVED AIR (LP)	15
71	CBS 64665	IN "C" (LP)	18
72	Shandar 83501/2	PERSIAN SURGERY DERVISHES (2-LP)	30

(see also John Cale)

WINSTON RILEY
| 73 | Techniques TE 922 | Woman Don't You Go Astray/Travelling Man | 8 |

(see also Techniques)

RILEY'S ALLSTARS
| 71 | Banana BA 343 | Glory Of Love (actually "Mystic Blue" by Hugh Hendricks & Buccaneers)/ We'll Cry Together - Version | 15 |

(see also Bobby Davis, Techniques)

RIMBARA
| 85 | Cordelia | ON DRY LAND (LP, with free 7", 400 copies only) | 30 |

RIMINGTON
| 73 | Man MAM 95 | In The Grip Of The Mullah/Dragon Child | 20 |

SHANE RIMMER
| 59 | Columbia DB 4293 | (Roll Along) Wagon Train/A Touch Of Pink | 6 |
| 59 | Columbia DB 4343 | The Three Bells (Jimmy Brown Song) (as Shane Rimmer & Spinners)/ I Want To Take You Home | 6 |

RIMSHOTS
| 82 | Respond RESP 3 | Sweet Talk/What's The Matter Baby (p/s) | 6 |

RINGS
| 77 | Chiswick S 14 | I Wanna Be Free/Automobile (p/s) | 10 |

(see also Maniacs, Twink)

RINGS & THINGS
| 68 | Fontana TF 987 | Strange Things Are Happening/To Me: To Me: To Me | 150 |

RINKY DINK AND THE CRYSTAL SET
| 75 | Harvest SHSP 4047 | CAMEO ROLES (LP) | 12 |

RINKY DINKS
58	London HLE 8679	Early In The Morning/Now We're One (as Rinky-Dinks featuring Bobby Darin)	40
58	London HLE 8679	Early In The Morning/Now We're One (78)	20
59	London HLE 8793	Mighty Mighty Man/You're Mine (as Bobby Darin with Rinky Dinks)	30
59	London HLE 8793	Mighty Mighty Man/You're Mine (78)	20

(see also Bobby Darin)

BOBBY RIO (U.S.)
| 63 | Stateside SS 211 | Don Diddley/I Got You | 25 |

BOBBY RIO (& REVELLES)
65	Pye 7N 15790	Boy Meets Girl/Don't Break My Heart And Run Away	60
65	Pye 7N 15897	Everything In The Garden/When Love Was Young	50
65	Pye 7N 15958	Value For Love/I'm Not Made Of Clay	50
66	Piccadilly 7N 35303	Ask The Lonely/Be Lonely Little Girl (solo)	25
66	Piccadilly 7N 35337	Angelica/Lovin' You (solo)	12

RIO GRANDE
| 71 | RCA SF 8208 | RIO GRANDE (LP) | 15 |

RIO GRANDES
| 66 | Pyramid PYR 6001 | Soldiers Take Over/Moses | 15 |

RIOT
| 77 | Ariola ARL 5007 | ROCK CITY (LP) | 12 |
| 78 | Capitol E-ST 12081 | NARITA (LP) | 12 |

RIOT CLONE
82	Riot Clone RC 001	THERE'S NO GOVERNMENT LIKE NO GOVERNMENT (EP)	15
82	Riot Clone RC 002	DESTROY THE MYTH OF MUSICAL DESTRUCTION (EP)	12
84	Riot Clone RCR 004	BLOOD ON YOUR HANDS (EP)	8

RIOTOUS BROTHERS
| 80 | Riotous RI 001 | Vicki's Dancing/Operation Zero/Emotional Cripple (p/s) | 10 |

RIOTS
| 65 | Island WI 176 | Telling Lies/Don't Leave Me (actually by Techniques) | 40 |
| 65 | Island WI 195 | You Don't Know (actually by Techniques)/DON DRUMMOND & DRUMBAGO: Treasure Island | 40 |

| 65 | Island WI 197 | I Am In Love/When You're Wrong (actually by Techniques) | 40 |
| 65 | Island WI 247 | Yeah Yeah/BABA BROOKS: Virginia Ska | 40 |

(see also Techniques)

RIOT SQUAD & MATUMBI

| 82 | Extinguish EXT 004 | Why Do You Make Me Wait/Paraphrase (12") | 20 |

RIOT SQUAD (1)

65	Pye 7N 15752	Any Time/Jump	50
65	Pye 7N 15817	I Wanna Talk About My Baby/Gonna Make You Mine	55
65	Pye 7N 15869	Nevertheless/Not A Great Talker	55
66	Pye 7N 17041	Cry Cry Cry/How Is It Done	50
66	Pye 7N 17092	I Take It We're Through/Working Man	175
66	Pye 7N 17130	It's Never Too Late To Forgive/Try To Realise	50
67	Pye 7N 17237	Gotta Be A First Time/Bitter Sweet Love	60

(see also Graham Bonney, Jimi Hendrix Experience, Blue Aces)

RIOT SQUAD (2)

82	Rondelet ROUND 23	Fuck The Tories/Civil Destruction (p/s)	8
82	Rondelet ROUND 25	Riot In The City/Religion (p/s)	8
83	Rot ASS 1	DON'T BE DENIED (EP)	20
83	Rot ASS 2	I'm OK Fuck You/In The Future/Friday Night (p/s)	15
84	Rot ASS 13	NO POTENTIAL THREAT (LP, with free single [ASS3], stickered sleeve)	12

RIP CHORDS

| 78 | Cells SELL 1 | Ringing In The Streets/Music's Peace Artist/Television Television (p/s) | 18 |

RIP CHORDS (U.S.)

63	CBS AAG 143	Here I Stand/Karen	20
63	CBS AAG 162	Gone/She Thinks I Still Care	20
64	CBS AAG 181	Hey Little Cobra/The Queen	30
64	CBS AAG 202	Three Window Coupe/Hot Rod USA	35
64	CBS BPG 62228	HEY LITTLE COBRA (LP)	100

(see also Terry Day, Terry Melcher, Bruce Johnston)

RIPCORD

89	Raging Records RAGE 2	HARVEST HARDCORE (EP, foldout sleeve)	15
86	Raging RAGE 1	DAMAGE IS DONE (Flexi)	10
87	Manic Ears ACHE 005	DEFIANCE OF POWER (LP)	12
88	Raging RAGE 001	POETIC JUSTICE (LP, with inner)	15

MINNIE RIPERTON

| 74 | Epic SEPC 80426 | PERFECT ANGEL (LP) | 15 |

RIPLEY WAYFARERS

71	Tradition TSR 006	CHIPS AND BROWN SAUCE (LP, 500 only with front-laminated dark green and white flipback sleeve, title in blue)	30
72	Tradition TSR 013	FIVE WELLS (LP)	15
74	Tradition TSR 018	GENTLEMEN OF HIGH RENOWN (LP)	15
78	MWM MWM 1017	SONG AND DANCE TUNES (LP, as The Wayfarers)	12
73	Tradition TSR 006	CHIPS AND BROWN SAUCE (LP, reissue, plain green sleeve, title in black)	15

RIP 'N' LAW

| 71 | Crab CRAB 64 | In The Ghetto/Something Sweet | 20 |

RIPPERS

| 68 | Saga | HONESTLY (LP) | 30 |

RIP RIG & PANIC

| 81 | Virgin VZZ13 | GOD (2x12") | 15 |

RISAN

| 82 | Saffron | Eastern Palace/Part 2 | 30 |

RISING MOON

| 74 | Theatre Projects | RISING MOON (LP) | 30 |

RISING SONS (U.K.)

| 68 | Pye 7N 17554 | Hold Me Just A Little While Longer/Fountain Of Love | 10 |

RISING SONS (U.S.)

| 65 | Stateside SS 426 | You're My Girl/Try To Be A Man | 35 |

RITA

| 69 | Major Minor MM 653 | Erotica/Sexologie | 15 |

RITA (ALSTON)

| 69 | Jackpot JP 718 | Love Making/NAT COLE: My Love | 5 |

(see also Rita Alston)

RITA & TIARAS

79	Destiny DS 1002	Gone With The Wind Is My Love/Wild Times (with p/s)	5
79	Destiny DS 1002	Gone With The Wind Is My Love/Wild Times	5
79	Destiny DS 1002	Gone With The Wind Is My Love/Wild Times (DJ copy with p/s)	15
09	Kent CITY 009	Gone With The Wind Is My Love/DORE STRINGS: Gone With The Wind Is My Love	8

JEAN RITCHIE

53	Argo ARL 1012	SONGS FROM KENTUCKY VOL. 1 (10" LP)	30
53	Argo ARL 1013	SONGS FROM KENTUCKY VOL.2 (10" LP)	30
53	Argo TM.17	SONGS FROM KENTUCKY VOL. 1 (10" LP, reissue)	20
53	Argo TM.18	SONGS FROM KENTUCKY VOL. 2 (10" LP, reissue)	20
60s	Transatlantic XTRA 1030	JEAN RITCHIE (LP)	15

TEX RITTER

54	Capitol CL 14175	Is There A Santa Claus?/Old Tex Kringle	5
55	Capitol CL 14277	A Whale Of A Tale/High On A Mountain Top	5
55	Capitol CL 14335	Marshal Of Wichita/September Song	5
56	Capitol CL 14581	The Wayward Wind/Gunsmoke	5
56	Capitol CL 14605	The Searchers/Remember The Alamo	5
56	Capitol CL 14660	The Last Wagon/Paul Bunyan Love	5

57	Capitol CL 14684	Green Grow The Lilacs/The Touch Of The Masters Hand	5
52	Capitol LC 6552	COWBOY FAVOURITES (10" LP)	20
60	Capitol (S)T 1292	BLOOD ON THE SADDLE (LP)	15

BOB RITTERBUSH
| 59 | Top Rank JAR 118 | I Wish That You Were Mine/Darling Corey | 7 |

RITZ
| 74 | Dawn DNS 1070 | Jenny Gentle/Why Love | 15 |

(see also Paul Ryder & The Time Machine)

RIVAL SCHOOLS
| 02 | Island 548936 | UNITED BY FATE (LP) | 20 |

RIVALS (1)
| 74 | Decca F 13509 | Speedway/Hoskins Still Rides | 10 |

RIVALS (2)
| 78 | Sound On Sound SOS 100 | Skateboarding In The UK/Top Of The Pops | 35 |

RIVALS (3)
| 80 | Ace ACE 007 | Future Rights/Flowers (p/s) | 100 |
| 80 | Oakwood/Ace ACE 011 | Here Comes The Night/Both Sides (p/s) | 40 |

RIVAL SAVAGES
| 80 | Savage VC 1968 | Get Some (gatefold p/s) | 25 |

HECTOR RIVERA
| 67 | Polydor 65728 | At The Party/Do It To Me | 60 |

BLUE RIVERS & MAROONS
67	Columbia Blue Beat DB 103	Witchcraft Man/Searching For You Baby	25
68	Spectrum SP 105	Take It Or Leave It/I've Been Pushed Around	10
68	Columbia S(C)X 6192	BLUE BEAT IN MY SOUL (LP)	50

CLIFF RIVERS
| 63 | London HLU 9739 | True Lips/Marsha | 40 |

DANNY RIVERS
60	Top Rank JAR 408	Hawk/I Got	40
60	Decca F 11294	Can't You Hear My Heart/I'm Waiting For Tomorrow	25
61	Decca F 11357	Once Upon A Time/My Baby's Gone Away (with Alexander Combo)	40
64	Decca F 11865	There Will Never Be Anyone Else/I Don't Think You Know How I Feel	20
62	HMV POP 1000	We're Gonna Dance/Movin' In (as Danny Rivers & River Men)	50

DEEK RIVERS
| 62 | Oriole CB 1735 | One Kiss/Outsider | 25 |
| 81 | Chiswick NS 71 | Elvis Presley Medley/ELVIS PRESLEY: Press Conference Vancouver 1957 (picture disc) | 5 |

JOHNNY RIVERS
61	Pye Intl. 7n 25118	Blue Skies/That Someone Should Be Me	10
64	Liberty LIB 66032	Memphis/It Won't Happen With Me	10
64	Liberty LIB 66056	Maybellene/Walk Myself n Home	10
64	Liberty LIB 66075	Mountain Of Love/Moody River	12
65	Liberty LIB 66087	Midnight Special/Cupid	10
65	Liberty LIB 66112	The Seventh Son/Un-Square Dance	8
65	Liberty LIB 12021	He Don't Love You Like I Love You/Where Have All The Flowers Gone	7
66	Liberty LIB 12023	Secret Agent Man/Tom Dooley	15
66	Liberty LIB 66144	Under Your Spell Again/Long Time Man	7
66	Liberty LIB 66175	I Washed My Hands In Muddy Water/Roogalator	15
66	Liberty LIB 66205	Poor Side Of Town/A Man Can Cry	12
67	Liberty LIB 66227	Baby I Need Your Loving/Getting Ready For Tommorow	10
68	Liberty LIB 15078	Look To Your Soul/Something Strange	7
68	Liberty LBF 15163	Right Relations/A Better Life	7
69	Liberty LBF 15241	Muddy River/Resurrection	7
66	Liberty LEP 4049	MORE JOHNNY RIVERS (EP)	15
64	Liberty LBY 3031	AT THE WHISKY A GO-GO (LP)	15
65	Liberty LBY 3036	HERE WE A GO-GO AGAIN (LP)	15
65	Liberty LBY 3064	RIVERS ROCKS THE FOLK (LP)	15
68	Liberty LBS 83040	REWIND (LP)	12

MAVIS RIVERS
60	Capitol CL 15120	So Rare/Longing, Longing, Longing	5
63	Reprise RS 20115	Slightly Out Of Tune/Footsteps Of A Fool	15
60	Capitol ST 1408	THE SIMPLE LIFE (LP)	12

ROYD RIVERS & CLIFF AUNGIER
| 65 | Decca LK 4696 | WANDERIN' (LP) | 35 |

(see also Cliff Aungier)

TONY RIVERS & THE CASTAWAYS
63	Columbia DB 7135	Shake Shake Shake/Row Row Row	20
64	Columbia DB 7224	I Love The Way You Walk/I Love You	15
64	Columbia DB 7336	Life's Too Short/Tell On Me	15
65	Columbia DB 7448	She/Till We Get Home	15
65	Columbia DB 7536	Come Back/What To Do	15
66	Columbia DB 7971	God Only Knows/Charade	20
66	Parlophone R 5400	Nowhere Man/The Girl From New York City	25
66	Immediate IM 027	Girl Don't Tell Me/The Girl From Salt Lake City	50
68	Polydor 56245	I Can Guarantee Your Love/Pantomime	12

(see also Capability Brown, Grapefruit, Harmony Grass, Senators, Sugarbeats)

RIVIERA
| 69 | Pye 7N 17712 | Baby Won't Leave Me Alone/The Love Story | 5 |

RIVIERAS
| 60 | HMV POP 773 | Blessing Of Love/Moonlight Cocktails | 120 |

RIVIERAS (U.S.)
| 64 | Pye International 7N 25237 | California Sun/H B Goose Step | 45 |

RIVINGTONS
62	Liberty LIB 55427	Papa Oom Mow Mow/Deep Water	50
63	Liberty LIB 55553	The Bird's The Word/I'm Losing My Grip	60
66	CBS 202088	Rose Growing In The Ruins/Tend To Business	40

RIVVITS
79	Alien AUX 1	Saturday Night At The Dance/Girl Next Door (p/s, with flexi)	10

FREDDIE ROACH
67	Transatlantic PR 7490	THE SOUL BOOK (LP)	15

MAX ROACH
62	HMV CLP 1522	PERC 'N' BITTER SUITE (LP)	15

MAX ROACH (& CLIFFORD BROWN GROUP)
58	Emarcy ERE 1572	MAX ROACH AND CLIFFORD BROWN (EP, withdrawn)	12
55	Vogue LDE 117	MAX ROACH & CLIFFORD BROWN IN CONCERT VOL. 1 (10" LP)	12
55	Vogue LDE 128	MAX ROACH & CLIFFORD BROWN IN CONCERT VOL. 2 (10" LP)	12
58	Emarcy EJL 1282	JAZZ IN THREE-QUARTER TIME (LP)	12
59	Emarcy MMB 12005	MAX ROACH, NEWPORT (LP, by Max Roach)	12
59	Emarcy MMB 12009	THE MAX ROACH FOUR PLUS FOUR (LP, by Max Roach)	12

(see also Clifford Brown)

ROAD
73	Rare Earth SRE 3006	ROAD (LP)	50

(see also Noel Redding)

ROADHOUSE
92	Vertigo VERP 57	Hell Can Wait/Loving You/Jackson High/More Than I Want (12", picture disc)	8

ROADRUNNERS
65	Cavern Sound 2BSNL 7	PANTOMANIA (EP, with tracks by Chris Edwards & Clive Wood)	35

ROADSTER
81	Mayhem SRTS 81	Fantasy/45 MPH (p/s)	30

ROADSTERS
64	Stateside SS 293	Joy Ride/Drag	40

ROAMING DOG
72	Perfect PF 01	Sign Your Name/Eclipse	50

ROARING SIXTIES
66	Marmalade 598 001	We Love The Pirates/I'm Leaving Town	40

(see also Family, Ivy League)

ROBAN'S SKIFFLE GROUP
61	Storyville A45 062	Careless Love/Frankie And Johnny (with p/s)	35
61	Storyville A45 062	Careless Love/Frankie And Johnny	18

E.G. ROBB
63	Columbia DB 7100	Stage To Cimarron/Jezebel	15

MARTY ROBBINS
SINGLES
56	Philips PB 590	Long Tall Sally/Mr. Teardrop (78)	20
57	Philips PB 696	A White Sport Coat (And A Pink Carnation)/Grown-Up Tears (78)	20
57	Philips JK 1019	A White Sport Coat (And A Pink Carnation)/Grown-Up Tears (jukebox issue)	30
57	Philips PB 741	Please Don't Blame Me/Teen-Age Dream	15
57	Philips PB 741	Please Don't Blame Me/Teen-Age Dream (78)	10
58	Fontana H 102	The Story Of My Life/Once-A-Week Date (78)	10
58	Fontana H 128	Stairway Of Love/Just Married	15
58	Fontana H 128	Stairway Of Love/Just Married (78)	10
58	Fontana H 150	Sittin' In A Tree House/She Was Only Seventeen	15
58	Fontana H 150	Sittin' In A Tree House/She Was Only Seventeen (78)	10
59	Fontana H 184	The Hanging Tree (from film)/The Blues Country Style	7
59	Fontana H 212	Cap And Gown/Last Night About This Time	7
59	Fontana H 212	Cap And Gown/Last Night About This Time (78)	15
59	Fontana H 229	Big Iron/Cool Water	8
59	Fontana H 229	Big Iron/Cool Water (78)	30
59	Fontana H 233	El Paso/Running Gun	8
59	Fontana H 233	El Paso/Running Gun (78)	30
60	Fontana H 263	I Told My Heart/Is There Any Chance	5
60	Fontana H 270	Ballad Of The Alamo/Five Brothers (in p/s)	10
61	Fontana H 301	Don't Worry/Like All Other Times	6
61	Fontana H 324	Ghost Train/Jimmy Martinez	6
61	Fontana H 342	It's Your World/You Told Me So	6
62	CBS AAG 114	Devil Woman/April Fool's Day	6
63	CBS AAG 128	Ruby Ann/Won't You Forgive	8
63	CBS AAG 141	Cigarette And Coffee Blues/Teenager's Dad	8
65	CBS 201789	Ribbon Of Darkness/Little Robin	5

EPs
59	Fontana TFE 17161	MARTY'S BIG HITS	15
59	Fontana TFE 17168	WEDDING BELLS	10
60	Fontana TFE 17167	SONG OF THE ISLANDS	10
61	Fontana TFE 17224	GUNFIGHTER	10

ALBUMS : LPS
59	Fontana TFL 5063	GUNFIGHTER BALLADS AND TRAIL SONGS	20
60	Fontana TFL 5086	MARTY'S GREATEST HITS	15
61	Fontana TFL 5113	MORE GUNFIGHTER BALLADS AND TRAIL SONGS (stereo STFL 541)	20
61	Fontana TFL 5145	MORE GREATEST HITS (also stereo STFL 565)	15
61	Fontana TFL 5162	JUST A LITTLE SENTIMENTAL (with Jordanaires, also stereo STFL 579)	15
62	CBS (S)BPG 62041	MARTY AFTER MIDNIGHT	15
63	CBS (S)BPG 62113	DEVIL WOMAN (mono/stereo)	15
63	CBS BPG 62131	PORTRAIT OF MARTY (mono/stereo)	15

63	CBS BPG/SBPG 62169	HAWAII'S CALLING ME (LP)	15
63	CBS 62190	THE RETURN OF THE GUNFIGHTER (LP)	15
66	CBS (S)BPG 62782	THE DRIFTER	15
65	CBS BPG 62499	TURN THE LIGHTS DOWN LOW (LP)	15

(see also Jordanaires)

MEL ROBBINS

59	London HLM 8966	Save It/To Know You (initially pressing with triangular centre)	600
59	London HLM 8966	Save It/To Know You (later round centre)	320
59	London HLM 8966	Save It/To Know You (78)	150

SYLVIA ROBBINS

| 60 | London HLJ 9118 | Frankie And Johnny/Come Home | 35 |

(see also Mickey & Sylvia)

ROBERT & REMOULDS

| 79 | Black & White BW 1 | X No. 1/Do Eyes Ever Meet? (p/s) | 60 |

ALAN ROBERTS

| 70s | Plant Life PLR 012 | CALEDONIA (LP, with Dougie Maclean) | 12 |

(see also Dougie MacLean)

ANDY ROBERTS

73	Elektra K 12109	Baby Baby/All Around My Grandmother's Floor	5
70	RCA SF 8086	HOME GROWN (LP, laminated front sleeve, lyric insert)	80
71	Charisma CAS 1034	HOME GROWN (LP, reissue, different sleeve)	15
71	B&C	HOME GROWN (LP, reissue)	18
71	Pegasus PEG 5	NINA AND THE DREAM TREE (LP)	40
73	Elektra K 42139	URBAN COWBOY (LP, with insert, 'butterfly' label)	20
73	Elektra K 42151	ANDY ROBERTS AND THE GREAT STAMPEDE (LP, gatefold sleeve)	15

(see also Clayton Squares, Liverpool Scene, Everyone, Plainsong, Mighty Baby)

BOB ROBERTS

| 70 | Explosion EX 2021 | Stick By Me/TOMMY McCOOK: The Designer | 7 |

BOB ROBERTS (U.K.)

| 81 | Solent SS 054 | BREEZE FOR A BARGEMAN (LP) | 15 |

HUGH ROBERTS

| 70 | Explosion EX 2041 | California Dreaming/One Woman (both sides actually by Lloyd Charmers) | 8 |

J. ROBERTS

| 70 | Bamboo BAM 30 | Someday We'll Be Together/SOUND DIMENSION: Everyday People | 20 |

JOHN ROBERTS

| 68 | Sue WI 4042 | Sockin' 1, 2, 3, 4/Sophisticated Funk | 35 |
| 68 | Action ACT 4511 | I'll Forget You/Be My Baby | 30 |

KEITH ROBERTS

| 72 | Trailer LER 3031 | PIER OF THE REALM (LP, red label) | 15 |

KENNY ROBERTS

| 57 | Brunswick 05638 | I'm Looking For The Bully Of The Town/Broken Teenage Heart | 12 |
| 66 | Pye 7N 17054 | Run Like The Devil/Where Goes My Heart | 25 |

KENNY ROBERTS

| 65 | Pye 7N 15882 | Say, Do You Mean It/Since My Love Has Gone | 15 |

(see also Kenny Damon)

KIM ROBERTS

| 64 | Decca F 11813 | I'll Prove It/For Loving Me This Way | 80 |

MALCOLM ROBERTS

| 69 | Major Minor MMLP 49 | MALCOLM (LP) | 12 |

PADDY ROBERTS

| 62 | Decca F 11552 | Merry Christmas You Suckers/Got 'n' Idea | 6 |

RENEE ROBERTS

| 62 | Oriole CB 1731 | I Want To Love You/Aching Heart | 10 |

RICK ROBERTS

| 72 | A&M AMLH 64372 | WINDMILLS (LP) | 12 |

(see also Flying Burrito Brothers)

ROCKY ROBERTS

| 67 | Durium DRL 50026 | SABATO SERA (LP) | 30 |

STEVE ROBERTS

| 80s | EXPLP 2002 | DO YOU KNOW WHO I AM (LP) | 15 |

(see also U.K.Subs)

DALE ROBERTSON

| 60 | RCA SF 5064 | PRESENTS HIS ALBUM OF WESTERN CLASSICS (LP) | 20 |

DON ROBERTSON

50	London L 629	Gamblin' Fever/On The Hudson Bay Line (78, with Lou)	8
56	Capitol CL 14575	The Happy Whistler/You're Free To Go (B-side with Lou Dinning)	12
56	Capitol CL 14629	Every Day That I Live (with Lou Dinning)/You	5
59	Capitol CL 15088	Fine Day/The Merry Men	5

JEANNIE ROBERTSON

59	Topic 10T 52	I KEN WHERE I'M GOING (10" LP)	15
59	Topic 12T 96	JEANNIE ROBERTSON (LP, blue label, with card insert)	15
60	Collector JFS 4001	LORD DONALD (LP)	15

JIM ROBERTSON

| 55 | MGM SPC 7 | Pride Of My Heart/Walkin' And Talkin' With The Lord (export issue) | 15 |

IVO ROBIC

| 59 | Polydor NH 23923 | Morgen (One More Sunrise)/Ay Ay Ay Paloma (Currurrucucu Paloma) | 10 |

DAVE ROBIN
65	Eyemark EMS 1003	You I Don't Want To Share/Life's Too Short	6

EDE ROBIN
75	Crystal CR 7023	There Must Be A Love Somewhere/Soul Over Easy	8

RICHIE ROBIN
60	Top Rank JAR 262	Strange Dream/GERRY GRANAHAN: It Hurts	15

TINA ROBIN
57	Vogue Coral Q 72284	Over Somebody Else's Shoulder/Lady Fair	10
57	Vogue Coral Q 72294	Never In A Million Years/Ça C'est L'Amour	10
58	Coral Q 72309	Everyday/Believe Me)	20
58	Coral Q 72309	Everyday/Believe Me (78)	12
58	Coral Q 72323	No School Tomorrow/Sugar Blues	20
58	Coral Q 72323	No School Tomorrow/Sugar Blues (78)	15
62	Mercury AMT 1199	Get Out Of My Life/Why Did You Go	5

ROGER ROBIN
94	Saxon SAX 010	More Love/Version (12")	8
95	Sazon SHF 004	Do Right/Tell Me (12")	20
98	Saxon SAX 065	Unity/Mix 2//My Medication/Version (12")	15
06	Jah Shaka SHAKA 665	I SEE JAH (LP)	12

ROBIN HOODS
65	Mercury MF 865	Wait For The Dawn/Love You So	15

ROBINS
60	Vogue V 9168	Cherry Lips/Out Of The Picture	100
60	Vogue V 9173	Just Like That/Whole Lot Imagination	100

(see also H.B. Barnum)

JIMMY ROBINS
68	President PT 118	I Can't Please You/I Made It Over	150

ALVIN ROBINSON
64	Pye International 7N 25248	Something You Got/Searchin'	25
64	Red Bird RB 10010	Down Home Girl/Fever	30
66	Strike JH 307	You Brought My Heart Right Down To My Knees/Whatever You Had	20

ANDY ROBINSON
68	Philips SBL 7887	PATTERNS OF REALITY (LP, laminated sleeve, black/silver label)	30

BROTHER CLEOPHUS ROBINSON
57	Vogue EPV 1196	BROTHER CLEOPHUS ROBINSON (EP)	25

ROBINSON CREW
63	Decca F 11706	Taxi (Theme From TV Series)/Stormalong	7

(see also Lord Rockingham's XI)

DAVE ROBINSON
79	Bushays BFM 124	Ruby & Diamond (feat. Jah Thomas/Dub (12")	20

EDDIE ROBINSON
71	Ember EMB S 301	Hey Blackman Parts 1 & 2	5
74	Myrrh MYR 1013	REFLECTIONS OF THE MAN INSIDE (LP)	15

ELZADIE ROBINSON
50	Tempo R 33	The Santa Claus Crave/St. Louis Cyclone Blues (78)	10
50	Tempo R 36	Arkansas Mill Blues/Gold Mansion Blues (78, with Will Ezell)	10
50	Tempo R 37	Rowdy Man Blues/Going South Blues (78)	10

(see also Will Ezell)

FLOYD ROBINSON
59	RCA RCA 1146	Makin' Love/My Girl (initially with triangular centre)	7
59	RCA RCA 1146	Makin' Love/My Girl (later round centre)	5
60	RCA RCA 1179	I Believe In Love/Tattletale	8
60	RCA RD 27166	FLOYD ROBINSON (LP)	40

FREDDY ROBINSON
72	Stax 2325 085	AT THE DRIVE-IN (LP)	18

HARRY ROBINSON
60	Top Rank JAR 325	The Skirl/Wimoweh (as Harry Robinson "String Sound")	5
61	Decca F 11319	Heavy Date/Sentimental Journey (as Harry Robinson's XV)	5

(see also Lord Rockingham's XI)

JACKEY ROBINSON
70	Punch PH 50	Heart Made Of Stone (actually by Jackie Bernard)/BOB TAYLOR: I May Never See My Baby Anymore	20

(see also Jackie Robinson, Pioneers)

JACKIE ROBINSON
68	Amalgamated AMG 819	Over And Over/Woman Of Samaria	20
68	Amalgamated AMG 824	Let The Little Girl Dance/DERRICK MORGAN: I Want To Go Home	20
74	Harry J. HJ 6695	My Love For You/R.D. Livingstone: Smokey Mountains	5

JIM ROBINSON NEW ORLEANS BAND
61	Riverside RLP 369	NEW ORLEANS: THE LIVING LEGENDS (LP)	15
64	Riverside RLP 393	PLAYS SPIRITUAL AND BLUES (LP)	15

J.P. ROBINSON
72	Atlantic K 10149	George Jackson/Wall To Wall Love	10
72	Atlantic K 10209	What Can I Tell Her/Please Accept My Call	15

JUNE ROBINSON
56	Oriole CB 1319	45 Men In A Telephone Box/Oo-Shoo-Be-Doo-Be (78)	10

LLOYD ROBINSON
62	Blue Beat BB 122	Give Me A Chance/When You Walk	20
63	Blue Beat BB 159	I Need Your Love/You Told Me	20

69	Duke DU 5	Cuss Cuss/Lavender Blue	30
70	Camel CA 41	The Worm/NEVILLE HYNES: Afro (actually by Neville Hinds)	25
72	Green Door GD 4028	I Can't Forget/LLOYD AND THE NOW GENERATION: I Can't Forget - Version	5
77	Cactus CT 109	Rocky Road/Version	20

(see also Lloyd Clarke, Lloyd Charmers, Harry J. Allstars, Matadors, Melodians)

M. ROBINSON
| 64 | Port-O-Jam PJ 4114 | Who Are You/Follow You | 15 |

MARTEL ROBINSON
| 75 | Arrow AR 006 | Sunny Soil/Sunny | 8 |

PAUL ROBINSON
| 83 | King City KCD 006 | Come On Sister/Instrumental (12") | 80 |

ROSCO ROBINSON
66	Pye International 7N 25385	That's Enough/One More Time	50
66	Pye International 7N 25385	That's Enough/One More Time (DJ copy)	100
72	Wand WN 27	That's Enough/One More Time (reissue)	10
73	Contempo C 16	We're Losing It Baby/We Got A Good Thing Going	8

SANDRA ROBINSON
| 85 | Trojan TROT 9079 | Sensi For Sale (Part 1)/TUFF TONES: Boogie Mix (Part 2)/SANDRA ROBINSON & TUFF TONES: Depression/DAN AMBRASSA: Life's Riddle/TUFF TONES: Boogie Mix (12") | 20 |

SUGAR CHILE ROBINSON
| 53 | Capitol LC 6586 | CAPITOL PRESENTS SUGAR CHILE ROBINSON (10" LP) | 40 |

TOM ROBINSON (BAND)
| 75 | Chebel SRT/CUS 015 | GOOD TO BE GAY (EP, as Bradford Gay Liberation Front) | 15 |
| 79 | EMI EMI 2946 | All Right All Night/Black Angel (withdrawn, demo-only) | 8 |

(see also Cafe Society, Phantom, Billy Karloff [& Extremes])

CARSON ROBISON (& HIS PLEASANT VALLEY BOYS)
53	MGM SP 1004	Lady Round The Lady/Pokeberry Promenade	10
53	MGM SP 1024	Square Dance Jitterbug/Keep On Circlin' 'Round	18
58	MGM MGM-EP 669	LIFE GETS TEEJUS (EP)	15
61	MGM MGM-EP 755	SQUARE DANCE - WITH CALLS (EP)	10
52	MGM MGM-D 101	EIGHT SQUARE DANCES (10" LP)	15

RALPH ROBLES
| 69 | London HA/SH 8385 | TAKING OVER (LP) | 20 |

ROBOTIKS
| 85 | Ariwa ARILP 019 | MAN & MACHINE (LP) | 12 |
| 86 | Ariwa ARILP 027 | MY COMPUTER'S ACTING STRANGE (LP) | 12 |

JEREMY ROBSON
| 63 | Columbia SEG 8244 | BLUES FOR THE LONELY (EP, with Michael Garrick and Shake Keane) | 100 |

NICKY ROBSON
| 80 | Scratch SCR 006 | Stars/Eye To Eye (p/s) | 20 |
| 80 | Scratch SCRT 006 | Stars (Extended)/Eye To Eye (12") | 45 |

(see also Gary Numan)

ROCAMARS
| 65 | King KG 1031 | All In Black Woman/Give Me Time | 20 |

TONY ROCCO
| 62 | Parlophone R 4886 | Stalemate/Keep A Walking | 15 |
| 62 | Parlophone R 4946 | Competition/Torture | 15 |

HARRY ROCHE CONSTELLATION
67	CBS 202653	Casino Royale/In The Pad Of The Mountain King	10
67	CBS SBPG 63013	CASINO ROYALE (LP)	35
71	Studio Two TWO 340	SPINDRIFT (LP)	20
73	Pye Intl. NSPL 41024	SPIRAL (LP, laminated sleeve)	30
73	Pye QUAD 1022	SOMETIMES (LP, quadrophonic)	20

ROCHEE & SARNOS
| 85 | Nervous NERD 018 | UNDERSTANDING SARNO (LP) | 12 |

JACKIE ROCHELLE
| 68 | Olga OLE 011 | Till The End/Grown Up Games | 5 |

DICKIE ROCK & MIAMI SHOWBAND
63	Piccadilly 7N 35154	Boys/There's Always Me	5
64	Piccadilly 7N 35202	From The Candy Store/Twenty Flight Rock	7
64	Pye 7N 15729	Just For Old Times Sake/Me Not You	7
65	Pye 7N 15750	Round And Around/Little Baby	7
65	Pye 7N 15855	Every Step Of The Way/Rock And Roll Music	7
65	Pye 7N 17063	Come Back To Stay/Can't Make Up My Mind (p/s)	7
65	Pye NEP 24251	COME BACK TO STAY (EP)	8

JOHNNY ROCK
| 55 | Vogue VE170112 | JOHNNY ROCK (EP) | 40 |

ROCKABILLY PSYCHOSIS
| 84 | Big Beat WIK 18 | ROCKABILLY PSYCHOSIS AND THE GARAGE DISEASE (LP) | 12 |

ROCKABILLY REBS
| 79 | SRTS 79 CUS 524 | ROCKABILLY REBS (EP, no p/s) | 100 |

ROCK AID ARMENIA
89	Life Aid Armenia ARMEN 01	Smoke On The Water/BLACK SABBATH: Paranoid (1970) (p/s)	5
89	Life Aid Armenia ARMEN T01	Smoke On The Water/BLACK SABBATH: Paranoid (1970) (12", blue or white p/s)	8
89	Life Aid Armenia ARMENCD 01	Smoke On The Water (Radio Mix)/Smoke On The Water (Extended Mix)/ BLACK SABBATH: Paranoid (1970) (CD)	10
90	Life Aid Armenia ARMEN 002	Smoke On The Water '90 (Radio Edit)/BLACK SABBATH: Paranoid ('90) (p/s)	5

(see also Brian May, Roger Taylor, Ritchie Blackmore, Dave Gilmour, Black Sabbath, Rush, Bruce Dickinson,

ROCK-A-TEENS
59	Columbia DB 4361	Woo-Hoo/Untrue	40

ROCK BROTHERS
56	Parlophone MSP 6201	Dungaree Doll/Livin' It Up	90
56	Parlophone R 4119	Dungaree Doll/Livin' It Up (78)	30

ROCK CANDY
71	MCA MK 5069	Remember/Don't Put Me Down	6

ROCKERS
59	Oriole CB 1501	Get Cracking/Counter Melody	10
83	CBS TA 3929	We Are The Boys (Who Make All The Noise) (Extended Version)/Rockin' On Stage (12", p/s)	12

ROCKERS
83	CBS A 3929	We Are The Boys (Who Make All The Noise)/Rockin' On Stage (p/s)	8

(see also Phil Lynott, Roy Wood, Status Quo)

ROCKERS ALL STARS
78	Rough Trade RT 002	Pablo Meets Mr. Bassie/Mr. Bassie Special (basically, augustus Pablo)	10

ROCKERS HI-FI
96	Different Drummer 12 G 001	GOING UNDER (THE KRUDER & DORFMEISTER SESSIONS EP) (12" p/s)	12

ROCKET 88
81	Atlantic K 50776	ROCKET 88 (LP)	20

(see also Charlie Watts, Alexis Korner, Jack Bruce, Dick Heckstall-Smith)

ROCKET FROM THE CRYPT
93	Southern Studios PUS 007	Glazed/Pressures/Cut It Loose (white label test pressing, 5-10 copies only)	30
95	Elemental ELM 32S	Born in 69/Ciao Patsy (p/s)	8
96	Elemental ELM 33S	Young Livers/Burning Army Men (p/s)	8
96	Dinked 1	Used/Lose Your Clown (in-store giveaway)	25
98	Elemental ELM 47PIC	When In Rome/Tarzan/Tiger Feet Tonight (picture disc)	8
98	Elemental ELM 48S	Lipstick/Hot Heart (p/s)	10
98	Elemental ELM 49S	Break It Up/Turkish Revenge (p/s)	10
95	Elemental ELM 27LP	HOT CHARITY (LP)	15
08	One Little Indian ELM 50DMM	ROCKET FROM THE CRYPT (LP, 1000 only)	18

ROCKETS
60	Philips PB 982	Gibraltar Rock/Walkin' Home	20
60	Philips PB 982	Gibraltar Rock/Walkin' Home (78)	40
61	Zodiac ZR 0010	Warrior/Countdown	22

ROCKIN' BERRIES
63	Decca F 11698	Wah Wah Wah Woo/Rockin' Berry Stomp	25
63	Decca F 11760	Itty Bitty Pieces/The Twitch	20
64	Piccadilly 7N 35197	I Didn't Mean To Hurt You/You'd Better Come Home	10
64	Piccadilly 7N 35203	He's In Town/Flashback	6
65	Piccadilly 7N 35217	What The World's Come Over You/You Don't Know What To Do	6
65	Piccadilly 7N 35236	Poor Man's Son/Follow Me	6
65	Piccadilly 7N 35254	You're My Girl/Brother Bill	10
65	Piccadilly 7N 35270	The Water Is Over My Head/Doesn't Time Fly	10
66	Piccadilly 7N 35304	I Could Make You Fall In Love/Land Of Love	6
66	Piccadilly 7N 35327	Midnight Mary/Money Grows On Trees	6
67	Piccadilly 7N 35373	Sometimes/Needs To Be	6
67	Piccadilly 7N 35400	Smile/Breakfast At Sam's	6
67	Pye 7N 17411	Dawn (Go Away)/She's Not Like Any Girl	6
68	Pye 7N 17519	When I Reach The Top/Pain	10
68	Pye 7N 17589	Mr. Blue/Land Of Love	10
73	Satril SAT 9	Day To Day/Big Louie's Birthday	10
74	Pye 7N 45394	Rock-A-Bye Nursery Rhyme/Long Time Ago	10
75	Pye 7N 45439	Black Gold/Eve	5
75	Satril SAT 101	Lonely Summertime/Send Me No Letters	6
65	Piccadilly NEP 34039	I DIDN'T MEAN TO HURT YOU (EP)	35
65	Piccadilly NEP 34043	NEW FROM THE BERRIES (EP)	35
65	Piccadilly NEP 34045	HAPPY TO BE BLUE (EP)	50
64	Piccadilly NPL 38013	IN TOWN (LP)	50
65	Piccadilly NPL 38022	LIFE IS JUST A BOWL OF BERRIES (LP)	50

(see also Jefferson)

ROCKIN' DEVILS
75	Hot Stuff HSL 001	BRING BACK ROCK'N' ROLL (LP)	20
75	Hot Stuff HSL 003	WITH A LITTLE HELP FROM OUR FRIEND (LP)	20

ROCKIN' DUPSEE
76	Sonet SNTF718	DOIN' THE ZYDECO (LP)	20
82	Flyright FLY 592	ROCKIN' WITH DUPSEE (LP)	12

ROCKIN' FOO
70	Stateside SS 2168	Rochester River/Stranger In The Attic	6
70	Stateside SSL 10303	ROCKIN' FOO (LP)	22

ROCKIN' HENRI & HAYSEEDS
63	Decca F 11700	Sally/Sweet Adeline	7

ROCKIN' HORSE
71	Philips 6006 156	The Biggest Gossip In Town/You Say	12
72	Philips 6006 200	Julian The Hooligan/Stayed Out Late Last Night	12
70	Philips 6308 075	YES IT IS (LP, laminated sleve, black/silver label)	100

(see also Jimmy Campbell, 23rd Turnoff, Kirkbys, Merseys)

ROCKIN' RAMRODS
66	Polydor BM 56512	Don't Fool With Fu Manchu/Tears Melt The Stone	25

ROCKIN' REBELS
63	Stateside SS 162	Wild Weekend/Wild Weekend Cha Cha	22
63	Stateside SS 187	Rockin' Crickets/Hully Gully Rock (both sides actually by Hot-Toddys)	20

(see also Hot-Toddys)

ROCKIN' R'S
59	London HL 8872	The Beat/Crazy Baby	40
59	London HL 8872	The Beat/Crazy Baby (78)	30

ROCKIN' SAINTS
60	Brunswick 05843	Cheat On Me, Baby/Half And Half	100

ROCKIN' STRINGS
59	Columbia DB 4349	Red Sail In The Sunset/Autumn Leaves	7

ROCKIN' VICKERS
64	Decca F 11993	I Go Ape/Someone Like You (as Rocking Vickers)	40
66	CBS 202051	It's Alright/Stay By Me	55
66	CBS 202241	Dandy/I Don't Need Your Kind	40

(see also Sam Gopal, Motorhead)

ROCKING DEVILS
75	Hot Stuff HSL 002	THAT OLD ROCK MUSIC'S HERE TO STAY (LP, most copies signed on front cover)	25
79	Hot Stuff HS 007	GOT THEM BLUES (EP, red vinyl)	20

ROCKING HORSE
71	Camel CA 75	Running Back Home/SOUL SYNDICATE BAND: Running Back - Version	6
72	Randy's RAN 522	Hard Time/Change Your Ways	8
73	Randy's RAN 535	I'm So Fed Up/I'm So Fed Up - Version	5
74	Pyramid PYR 7009	New Situation/New Version	5
74	Sydna SYD 5026	Be Thankful/Thankful Dub	8

ROCKING RICHARD AND WHISTLING VIC TEMPLAR
87	Hangman HANG 14 UP	PRESENT: TEA AND BACCY (LP)	15

ROCKITS
73	Mowest MW 3012	Livin' Without You/Love My Love	6
74	Mowest MW 3016	Gimme True Love/I'm Losing You	8

ROCK MACHINE
73	T.I.M.	THEMES (LP)	60

(see also Ugly Custard)

ROCK 'N' ROLL ALLSTARS
72	B&C BCM 104	RED CHINA ROCKS (LP)	12

ROCK'N'ROLL REVIVAL SHOW
68	Decca F 12752	Midnight Train/Oh Boy (both sides featuring Tommy Bishop)	5

(see also Tommy Bishop's Ricochets)

ROCK-OLGA
60	Ember EMB S 105	Red Sails In The Sunset/My Dixieland Doll (in p/s)	10
60	Ember EMB S 105	Red Sails In The Sunset/My Dixieland Doll	5

ROCKSTAR
76	MCA MCA 265	Mummy/Over The Hill	15

ROCKSTEADYS
67	Giant GN 2	Squeeze And Freeze/JUNIOR SMITH: I'm A Good Boy	12

ROCKSTONES
70	Trojan TR 7762	A.B.C. Reggae/BEVERLEY'S ALLSTARS: Be Yours	6
70	Summit SUM 8501	Everything Is Beautiful/BEVERLEY'S ALLSTARS: Give Up	6

(see also Gaylads)

ROCK WORKSHOP
70	CBS 5046	You To Lose/Born In The City	6
71	CBS 7252	Very Last Time/Light Is Light	5
70	CBS 64075	ROCK WORKSHOP (LP, orange label)	40
71	CBS 64394	THE VERY LAST TIME (LP, gatefold sleeve, orange label)	40

(see also Bob Downes, Alex Harvey)

ROCKY FELLERS
63	Stateside SS 175	Killer Joe/Lonely Treardrops	20
63	Stateside SS 212	Like The Big Guys Do/Great Big World	18
63	Pye International 7N 25225	Ching A Ling Baby/Hey Little Donkey	22

ROCKY HORROR SHOW
75	Ode ODS 66305	Science Fiction Double Feature/Time Warp	8
87	Ode RHVX 1	ROCKY HORROR BOX SET (4-LP box, with inserts, numbered)	20
87	Ode RHBXLP 1	ROCKY HORROR BOX SET (4-LP box, with different inserts to above)	20
90	Ode RHBXCD 1	THE ROCKY HORROR PICTURE ALBUMS (15th ANNIVERSARY) (4-CD, with booklet)	40

(see also Tim Curry, Meat Loaf, Original Soundtracks)

ROCOCO
73	Deram DM 375	Ultrastar/Wildfire	6
76	Mountain TOP 9	Follow That Car/Lucinda	6

ROD & CAROLYN
63	Pye 7N 15519	How Can You Tell/What About The Teardrops	8
63	Pye 7N 15565	Bye-Bye My Lover/To Be Alone	8
64	Pye 7N 15629	Young Love/Talk To Me	8
64	Pye 7N 15706	Love Is Where You Are/I've Got You On My Mind	8

GENE RODDENBERRY
76	CBS 4692	Star Trek Theme/Star Trek Philosophy	12

RODD-KEN & CAVALIERS
60	Triumph RGM 1001	Magic Wheel/Happy Valley	40

(see also Blue Men)

TIM RODDY
82	Tiara 001	Frankly Fiona/Don't Turn The Light Out On Me	8

MINT VALUE £

CLODA(GH) RODGERS

62	Decca F 11534	Believe Me I'm No Fool/End Of The Line	10
63	Decca F 11607	Sometime Kind Of Love/I See More Of Him	10
63	Decca F 11667	To Give My Love To You/I Only Live To Love You	10
64	Decca F 11812	Mister Heartache/Time	10
65	Columbia DB 7468	Wanting You/Johnny Come Home	8
66	Columbia DB 7926	Every Day Is Just The Same/You'll Come A Running	8
66	Columbia DB 8038	Stormy Weather/Lonely Room	8
68	RCA 1684	Room Full Of Roses/Play The Drame To The End	20
68	RCA 1748	Rhythm Of Love/River Of Tears	8
69	RCA 1891	Biljo/Spider	6
69	RCA SF 8033 / RD 8033	CLODAGH RODGERS (LP)	20
69	RCA SF 8071	MIDNIGHT CLODAGH (LP)	20
71	RCA SF 8180	RODGERS AND HEART (LP)	20

EILEEN RODGERS

58	Fontana H 136	Careful, Careful/I'm Alone Because I Love You	12
58	Fontana H 156	Treasure Of Your Love/Little Bit Bluer	12
61	London HLR 9271	Sailor (Your Home Is The Sea)/Wait Till Tomorrow	15

JEAN RODGERS

65	Columbia DB 7637	Take What I Have/Baby What You Gonna Do?	6

JIMMIE RODGERS (THE BLUE YODELLER)

56	HMV MH 192	Blue Yodel No. 4/Waiting For A Train (78, export issue)	10
56	HMV MH 193	In The Jailhouse Now No. 2/Peach Picking Time Down In Georgia (78, export)	10
56	HMV MH 194	Blue Yodel No. 9/Jimmie The Kid (78, export issue)	10
58	HMV 7EG 8163	JIMMIE RODGERS (EP)	15
60	RCA RCX 1058	LEGENDARY JIMMIE RODGERS (EP)	15
59	RCA RD 27110	TRAIN WHISTLE BLUES (LP)	20
59	RCA RD 27138	NEVER NO MO' BLUES (JIMMIE RODGERS MEMORIAL ALBUM) (LP)	20
61	RCA RD 27203	MY ROUGH AND ROWDY WAYS (LP)	20
61	RCA RD 27241	JIMMIE THE KID (LP)	20
62	RCA RD 7505	COUNTRY MUSIC HALL OF FAME (LP)	20
63	RCA RD 7562	THE SHORT BUT BRILLIANT LIFE OF JIMMIE RODGERS (LP)	20
64	RCA RD 7644	MY TIME AIN'T LONG (LP)	20

JIMMIE RODGERS

58	Columbia DB 4130	Secretly/Make Me A Miracle	7
57	Columbia DB 3986	Honeycomb/Their Hearts Were Full Of Spring (as Jimmy Rodgers)	15
57	Columbia DB 4052	Kisses Sweeter Than Wine/Better Loved You'll Never Be	8
58	Columbia DB 4078	Oh-Oh, I'm Falling In Love Again/The Long Hot Summer	8
58	Columbia DB 4175	Are You Really Mine/The Wizard	5
58	Columbia DB 4206	Woman From Liberia/Girl In The Wood	5
59	Columbia DB 4235	Bimbombey/You Understand Me	5
59	Columbia DB 4281	Because You're Young/I'm Never Gonna Tell	5
59	Columbia DB 4327	Soldier, Won't You Marry Me?/Ring-A-Ling-A-Lario	5
59	Columbia DB 4362	Tucumcari/The Night You Became Seventeen	6
59	Columbia DB 4401	Waltzing Matilda/T.L.C Tender Love And Care	6
62	Columbia DB 4904	The Fox And The Goose/Soldier, Won't You Marry Me	6
62	London HLD 9582	No One Will Ever Know/Because	6
63	London HLD 9654	Rhumba Boogie/Rainbow At Midnight	7
63	London HLD 9697	Face In A Crowd/Lonely Tears	6
58	Columbia 33SX 1082	JIMMIE RODGERS (LP)	25
58	Columbia 33SX 1097	THE NUMBER ONE BALLADS (LP)	25
59	Columbia 33SX 1144	SINGS FOLK SONGS (LP)	20
59	Columbia 33SX 1176	JIMMIE RODGERS FAVOURITES (LP)	20
59	Columbia 33SX 1206	IT'S CHRISTMAS ONCE AGAIN (LP)	20
63	London HA-D 8040	NO ONE WILL EVER KNOW (LP)	20
65	London HA-D/SH-D 8116	HONEYCOMB (LP)	20
66	Dot DLP 3710	COUNTRY MUSIC 1966 (LP)	15

RODNEY & BRUNETTES

79	London/Bomp HLZ 10574	NEW YORK BLONDES featuring MADAME X: Little GTO/Holocaust On Sunset Boulevard(no p/s)	12

(see also Blondie, Debbie Harry)

RODNEY P (AKA RODDIE ROK)

01	Riddim Killah RK001	Murderer Style/Friction (12")	10
04	Riddim Killah RKP04LP	THE FUTURE (LP- Limited White Vinyl)	20

(see also London Posse)

RODS

79	Rods ROD 1	Like A Mirror/Hear I Am	10

TOMMY ROE (& ROEMANS)

62	HMV POP 1060	Sheila/Save Your Kisses	7
62	HMV POP 1092	Susie Darlin'/Piddle De Pat	8
63	HMV POP 1117	Gonna Take A Chance/Don't Cry Donna	5
63	HMV POP 1138	The Folk Singer/Count On Me	6
63	HMV POP 1174	Kiss And Run/What Makes The Blues (Want To Pick On Me)	6
63	HMV POP 1207	Everybody/There's A Great Day A-Coming	5
63	HMV POP 1259	Come On/There Will Be Better Years	6
64	HMV POP 1290	Be A Good Little Girl/Carol	6
64	HMV POP 1364	Little Miss Heartache/You Might As Well Forget Him	10
65	HMV POP 1368	Diane From Manchester Square/Part Girl	8
65	HMV POP 1469	Doesn't Anybody Know My Name/I'm A Rambler, I'm A Gambler	10
66	HMV POP 1539	Sweet Pea/Much More Love	10
69	Stateside SS 2143	Dizzy/The You I Need	5
69	Stateside SS 2152	Heather Honey/Money Is My Pay	8
63	HMV 7EG 8806	THE FOLK SINGER (EP)	20
63	HMV CLP 1614	SHEILA (LP)	40
64	HMV CLP 1704	EVERYBODY LIKES TOMMY ROE (LP)	30
65	HMV CLP 1860	BALLADS AND BEAT (LP)	30
69	Stateside S(S)L 10282	DIZZY (LP)	20

BOB ROGERS
71	Chapter One LRS 5005	SOUNDS (LP)	12

CE CE ROGERS
89	WEA A 8852T	Forever (12" Extended Mix)/Forever (Club Mix)/Someday (12" Extended Mix) (12", no p/s)	10

DANE ROGERS & NU BEATS
64	Pye 7N 15621	Mary Jane/Jeanette	10

DEAN ROGERS
60	Parlophone R 4732	End Of Time (as Dean Rogers & Hi-Fi's)/Keep The Miracle Going	10
61	Parlophone R 4835	Timber/High In A Misty Sky	10

(see also Sydney James)

ERIC ROGERS
63	Decca F 11585	The Iron Maiden/Fly-Wheel	7

JULIE ROGERS
64	Mercury MF 809	It's Magic/Without Your Love	5
64	Mercury MF 838	Like A Child/Our Day Will Come	5
65	Mercury MF 849	Hawaiian Wedding Song/Turn Around Look At Me	6
68	Philips BF 1727	Tar And Cement/The Muffin Man	7
64	Mercury 10023 MCE	JULIE ROGERS (EP)	10
65	Mercury 10028 MCE	THE SOUND OF JULIE (EP)	12
65	Mercury 20048 (S)MCL	THE SOUND OF JULIE (LP, mono/stereo)	12
66	Mercury 20086 (S)MCL	CONTRASTS (LP, mono/stereo)	20
67	Mercury 20100 (S)MCL	SONGS OF INSPIRATION (LP, mono/stereo)	12

KENNY ROGERS (& FIRST EDITION)
69	Reprise RSLP 6352	RUBY DON'T TAKE YOUR LOVE TO TOWN (LP)	12

(see also First Edition)

LINCOLN ROGERS
73	Phoenix NIX 137	Let Love Come Between Us/She Looked At Me With Love	15

LYNNE ROGERS
65	RCA RCA 1479	Sometimes/I Shouldn't Care	7

MARK ROGERS & MARKSMEN
63	Parlophone R 5045	Bubble Pop/Hold It!	25

(see also Marksmen, Mark Wirtz)

PAUL ROGERS
61	HMV POP 872	Four An' Twenty Thousand Kisses/Free To Love	10
63	HMV POP 1121	Always/Joanie Don't Be Angry	10

PAULINE ROGERS
54	Columbia SCM 5106	Spinnin' The Blues/But Good	20

PIERCE ROGERS & OVERLANDERS
61	Parlophone R 4838	Do You Still Love Me?/That Someone	12

SHORTY ROGERS & HIS ORCHESTRA
54	HMV 7EG 8044	THE WILD ONE (EP)	15
52	Capitol LC 6549	MODERN SOUNDS (10" LP, as Shorty Rogers & His Giants)	15
54	HMV DLP 1030	COOL AND CRAZY (10" LP, featuring Giants)	15
54	HMV DLP 1058	EIGHT SHORTY ROGERS' NUMBERS (10" LP)	15
56	Contemporary LDC 190	SHELLY MANNE, SHORTY ROGERS AND JIMMY GIUFFRE - THE THREE (10" LP, with Shelly Manne & Jimmy Giuffre)	18

(see also Boots Brown, Bud Shank, Shelly Manne, Jimmy Giuffre)

SIDNEY ROGERS
73	Techniques TE 923	Don't Throw Stones/Toughness	8
75	Ethnic EF 2222S	TIPPIN' IN (LP)	30

TIMMIE ROGERS
57	London HLU 8510	Back To School Again/I've Got A Dog Who Loves Me	80
57	London HLU 8510	Back To School Again/I've Got A Dog Who Loves Me (78)	25
58	London HLU 8601	Take Me To Your Leader/Fla-Ga-La-Pa	100
58	London HLU 8601	Take Me To Your Leader/Fla-Ga-La-Pa (78)	30

TRACY ROGERS
65	Polydor 56029	How Love Used To Be/When I Realise	7
65	Polydor 56037	Love Story/I Remember When I Loved You (p/s)	10
66	Polydor 56077	Baby/Through Thick And Thin	25
67	Polydor 56197	Back With You Baby/In The Morning	12

VERN ROGERS & HI-FI'S
62	Oriole CB 1785	That Ain't Right/Be Everything To Anyone You Love	20
63	Oriole CB 1826	He's New To You/Can't Complain	15
63	Oriole CB 1885	I Will/One Way Love Affair	20
63	Oriole CB 1923	Anna/Pride	15

DIANA ROGERSON
85	United Dairies UD 017	THE INEVITABLE CHRYSTAL BELLE SCRODD RECORD (LP)	25
86	United Dairies UD 021	CHRYSTAL BELLE SCRODD: BELLE DE JOUR (LP)	25

(see also Nurse With Wound)

ROGUES (U.K.)
67	Decca F 12718	Memories Of Missy/And You Let Her Pass By	30

ROGUES (U.S.)
65	CBS 201731	Everyday/Rogers Reef	20

(see also Terry Day, Terry Melcher, Bruce Johnston)

CHRIS ROHMANN
73	RCA Victor SF 8364	THE MAN I AM TODAY (LP)	22
77	Old Fangled OLDF 1	TECHNICOLOUR DREAM (LP)	12

ROKES
67	RCA RCA 1587	Let's Live For Today/Ride On	30
67	RCA RCA 1646	Hold My Hand/Regency Sue	50
68	RCA RCA 1694	When The Wind Arises/The Works Of Bartholemew	70

ROKKA
80	Rock Trax RT 01	Come Back/Touch & Go	10

CHERRY ROLAND
63	Decca F 11579	Handy Sandy/Stay As I Am	12
63	Decca F 11648	What A Guy/Just For Fun	12

(see also Cherry Rowland)

PAUL ROLAND
82	Aristocrat ARC 1389	Doctor Strange/Madelaine (p/s)	8
83	Aftermath AEP 12011	Blades Of Battenburg (Remix)/Captain Blood/Puppet Master/Cavalier (12", p/s)	10
85	Aftermath AEP 12012	Death Or Glory (Revamped Version)/The Great Edwardian Air Raid/Beau Brummel/The Curious Case Of Richard Fielding (12", p/s)	8
86	Aftermath AEP 12013	Gabrielle/Berlin/Sword & Sorcery (p/s)	8
86	Imaginary MIRAGE 002	Demon In A Glass Case/In The Opium Den (oversized p/s)	7
87	Bam Caruso PABL 094	Alice's House/Go Down You Murderers/Happy Families/Jumbee (demo) (p/s)	8
85	Aftermath SCOOP 2	BURNT ORCHIDS (mini LP)	12
80	Ace ACE 013	THE WEREWOLF OF LONDON (LP)	18
81	Armageddon ARM 9	THE WEREWOLF OF LONDON (Revamped Version) (LP, different sleeve)	12

(see also Weird Strings, Midnight Rags)

WALTER ROLAND/GEORGIA SLIM
59	Jazz Collector JEL 2	THE MALE BLUES VOL. 1 (EP)	22

BARRY ROLFE
73	Philips 6006 331	Look The Business/Molly Molly	25
73	Philips 6006 348	Beam Me Aboard, Mr. Spock/Boadecia	8
74	Philips 6006 381	Going Up/Johnny Bo Jangle	6

ROLFE, GIFFORD & ANDREW MULLINS
72	Look REM 104	Tutankamun/Sad Eyes	10

ROLLERS (1)
61	London HLG 9340	Continental Walk/I Want You So	18

ROLLERS (2)
79	Arista 259	Turn On The Radio/Washington's Birthday (p/s)	6

ROLLING STONES
SINGLES : DECCA SINGLES
63	Decca F 11675	Come On/I Want To Be Loved (demo copies £350)	50
63	Decca F 11742	Fortune Teller/Poison Ivy (solid centre, withdrawn)	1500
63	Decca F 11764	I Wanna Be Your Man/Stones (B-side mis-spelled)	35
63	Decca F 11764	I Wanna Be Your Man/Stoned	20
64	No Cat. No.	We Were Falling In Love (EMI disc acetate, unreleased single)	1000
64	Decca F 11845	Not Fade Away/Little By Little	12
64	Decca F 11934	It's All Over Now/Good Times, Bad Times	12
64	Decca F 12014	Little Red Rooster/Off The Hook	12
65	Decca F 12104	The Last Time/Play With Fire	15

(The above singles were originally issued with "Recording first published..." text and wide label lettering.)

65	Decca F 12220	(I Can't Get No) Satisfaction/The Spider And The Fly	15
65	Decca F 12263	Get Off Of My Cloud/The Singer Not The Song	15
66	Decca F 12331	19th Nervous Breakdown/As Tears Go By	10
66	Decca F 12395	Paint It, Black/Long Long While	15

(The above singles were originally issued with a round Decca logo; later boxed-logo pressings are worth £4 each.)

66	Decca F 12497	Have You Seen Your Mother, Baby, Standing In The Shadow?/ Who's Driving Your Plane	15
67	Decca F 12546	Let's Spend The Night Together/Ruby Tuesday	12
67	Decca F 12654	We Love You/Dandelion	15
68	Decca F 12782	Jumping Jack Flash/Child Of The Moon	15
69	Decca F 12952	Honky Tonk Women/You Can't Always Get What You Want (in demo-only p/s)	70
69	Decca F 12952	Honky Tonk Women/You Can't Always Get What You Want	12
71	Decca F 13203	Street Fighting Man/Surprise Surprise (jukebox edition)	30
71	Decca F 13195	Street Fighting Man/Surprise Surprise/Everybody Needs Somebody To Love (33rpm maxi-single)	10
73	Decca F 13404	Sad Day/You Can't Always Get What You Want	20
74	Decca F 13517	Paint It Black/It's All Over Now (release cancelled, demo-only)	220
75	Decca F 13584	I Don't Know Why I Love You (credited to either 'Jagger/Richard/Taylor'/Try A Little Harder	20
75	Decca F 13584	I Don't Know Why I Love You (credited Stevie Wonder')/Try A Little Harder	15
75	Decca F 13597	Out Of Time/Jiving Sister Fanny	8
76	Decca F 13635	Honky Tonk Women/Sympathy For The Devil	8
70s	Decca F 11934	It's All Over Now/Good Times, Bad Times (repressing, with stereo mix on A-side, [ZXDR instead of XDR matrix no.] boxed Decca logo)	8
87	Decca F 102	Jumping Jack Flash/Child Of The Moon (p/s, reissue)	8
87	Decca FX 102	Jumping Jack Flash/Child Of The Moon/Sympathy For The Devil (12", p/s, reissue)	20

SINGLES : SINGLES BOX SETS
80	Decca STONE 1-12	SINGLE STONES (12-single box set)	60
80	Decca BROWSE 1	SINGLE STONES (in-store, 3 x 12-single box set [STONE 1-12], with poster & badge, also available via mail-order)	150

SINGLES : ROLLING STONES LABEL SINGLES
71	Rolling Stones RS 19100	Brown Sugar/Bitch/Let It Rock (in p/s)	50
71	Rolling Stones RS 19100	Brown Sugar/Bitch/Let It Rock	7
74	Rolling Stones RS 19114	It's Only Rock 'N' Roll/Through The Lonely Nights	6
78	R. Stones 12EMI 2802	Miss You (8.26)/Faraway Eyes (12", p/s, pink vinyl)	12
81	Rolling Stones	Beast Of Burden/Everything Is Turning Gold (unreleased)	0
82	Rolling Stones RSR 111	Time Is On My Side (live)/Twenty Flight Rock (live) (p/s)	5
82	Rolling Stones 12RSR 111	Time Is On My Side (live)/Twenty Flight Rock (live) (repressing, with live)/ Under My Thumb (live) (12", p/s)	10
83	Rolling Stones 0-96978	Undercover Of The Night (Extended Version)/Feel On Baby (Instrumental) (12", p/s)	8
84	Rolling Stones RSR 114	She Was Hot/I Think I'm Going Mad (p/s)	5

84	Rolling Stones RSR 114	She Was Hot/I Think I'm Going Mad (yellow paper label, p/s) 5
84	Rolling Stones RSRP 114	She Was Hot/I Think I'm Going Mad (shaped picture disc) 10
84	Rolling Stones SUGAR 1	Brown Sugar/Bitch (p/s, reissue)...5
84	Rolling Stones SUGARP 1	Brown Sugar/Bitch (shaped picture disc)...5
93	Rolling Stone RS LH 1	Brown Sugar/Start Me Up (jukebox issue, no p/s) 15
93	Rolling Stone ORDER LH 1	Gimme Shelter (Live Version)/NEW MODEL ARMY FEATURING TOM JONES: Gimme Shelter (jukebox issue, no p/s) 15

SINGLES : OTHER SINGLES

72	Sound For Industry 107	Mick Jagger Introduces 'Exile On Main Street' (flexidisc free with NME) 15
74	Atlantic K 19107	Brown Sugar/Happy/Rocks Off (unissued) 100
02	Virgin VS1838	Don't Stop/New Rock Remix (Limited edition red vinyl, numbered) 12
03	Mercury 9810615	Sympathy For The Devil (Neptune's Full Length Remix)/Full Phatt - Full Length Remix/Fatboy Slim - Full Length Remix (12", p/s)...8
03	Abkco 0602498106136	Sympathy For The Devil (Neptune's Radio Edit)/Original Version (p/s) 8
10	Universal 273 547-7	Plundered My Soul/All Down The Line (p/s)...10
11	Universal 0602527643410	Brown Sugar/Bitch/Let It Rock (Live At Leeds 13th March 1971) (p/s) 7

SINGLES : CBS SINGLES

86	CBS QA 6864	Harlem Shuffle/Had It With You (poster p/s) 5
86	CBS TA 6864	Harlem Shuffle (N.Y. Mix)/(London Mix)/Had It With You (12", p/s)..8
86	CBS QTA 6864	Harlem Shuffle (N.Y. Mix)/(London Mix)/Had It With You (12", p/s)......................................10
86	CBS A 7160	One Hit (To The Body)/Fight (p/s) 5
86	CBS TA 7160	One Hit (To The Body) (London Mix)/Fight (12", p/s)...8
89	CBS 655 193-7	Mixed Emotions/Fancyman Blues (p/s) 8
89	CBS 655 193-2	Mixed Emotions (7" Version)/Mixed Emotions (Chris Kimsey's 12")/ Fancyman Blues (CD, picture disc, card sleeve) 8
89	CBS 655 193-6	Mixed Emotions (Chris Kimsey's 12")/Fancyman Blues (12", p/s) 8
89	CBS 655 193-5	Mixed Emotions (7" Version)/Fancyman Blues/Tumbling Dice/Miss You (CD, picture disc, in circular tin with 'tongue' logo sticker) 35
89	CBS 655 214-2	Mixed Emotions (7" Version)/Fancyman Blues/Shattered/Waiting On A Friend (CD, picture disc, in circular tin with 'tongue' logo sticker) 35
89	CBS 655 193-6	Mixed Emotions (Chris Kimsey's 12")/Fancyman Blues/ Mixed Emotions (7" Version) (12", p/s)...8
89	CBS 655 422-7	Rock And A Hard Place/Cook Cook Blues (p/s) 5
89	CBS 655 422-5	Rock And A Hard Place (Michael Brauer Mix)/Rock And A Hard Place (Bonus Beats Mix)/Rock And A Hard Place (Edited 7" Version) (2nd 12", p/s)...8
89	CBS 655 422-8	Rock And A Hard Place (Dance Mix)/(Hard Dub Mix)/Cook Cook Blues (3rd 12", p/s) 8
89	CBS 655 422-6	Rock And A Hard Place (Dance Mix)/Emotional Rescue/Some Girls/ Rock And A Hard Place (Hard Dub Mix)/Cook Cook Blues (12", p/s) 8
89	CBS 655 422-2	Rock And A Hard Place (7" Version)/(Dance Mix)/(Bonus Beats Mix)/ Cook Cook Blues (CD, picture disc, card sleeve) 15
89	CBS 655 448-2	Rock And A Hard Place (7" Version)/Cook Cook Blues/It's Only Rock'n'Roll (But I Like It)/Rocks Off (3rd CD, picture disc, 7" box set with poster) 25
89	CBS 655 448-5	Rock And A Hard Place (7" Version)/Cook Cook Blues/Emotional Rescue/ Some Girls (CD, tongue-shaped card sleeve) 15
90	CBS 656 065-7	Almost Hear You Sigh/Wish I'd Never Met You (p/s) 8
90	CBS 656 065-5	Almost Hear You Sigh/Miss You/Waiting On A Friend/Wish I'd Never Met You (CD, in tin with 'Urban Jungle' sticker) 30
90	CBS 656 065-6	Almost Hear You Sigh/Beast Of Burden/Angie/Fool To Cry (12", gatefold p/s) 8
90	CBS 656 065-2	Almost Hear You Sigh/Beast Of Burden/Angie/Fool To Cry (CD, gold disc) 25
90	CBS 656 1227	Terrifying/Rock And A Hard Place (p/s) 8
90	CBS 656 122-6	Terrifying (12" Dance Remix)/Rock And A Hard Place (Dance Mix)/ Harlem Shuffle (London Mix) (12", p/s)...8
91	CBS 656 756-7	Highwire/2000 Light Years Away (p/s) 8
91	CBS 656 756-6	Highwire/2,000 Light Years From Home (live)/Sympathy For The Devil (live)/ I Just Wanna Make Love To You (live) (12", gatefold p/s) 8
91	CBS 656 756-5	Highwire/Play With Fire (live)/Factory Girl (live) (CD) 10
91	CBS 656 892-6	Ruby Tuesday/Play With Fire (live)/You Can't Always Get What You Want (live)/Rock And A Hard Place (live) (12", p/s) 10
91	CBS 656 892-5	Ruby Tuesday/Harlem Shuffle (live)/Winning Ugly (CD) 10
91	CBS 656 892-2	Ruby Tuesday/Play With Fire (live)/You Can't Always Get What You Want (live)/Undercover Of The Night (live) (CD) 10
91	CBS 657 334-2	Sex Drive (single edit)/(Dirty Hands Mix)/(Club Version) (CD)...10

SINGLES : VIRGIN SINGLES

94	Virgin VS 1503	Love Is Strong/The Storm (numbered p/s, 7,000 only)...10
94	Virgin VCS 1503	Love Is Strong/The Storm (injection moulded jukebox copy) 12
94	Virgin VSCDX 1503	Love Is Strong (Album Version)/The Storm/So Young/Love Is Strong (Bob Clearmountain Remix) CD 1)//Love Is Strong (Teddy Riley Radio Remix)/Teddy Riley Extended Remix/Teddy Riley Extended Rock Remix/Teddy Riley Dub Remix/Joe The Butcher Club Mix/Teddy Riley Instrumental (CD2) (2-CD Special Edition)........................15
94	Virgin VST 1518	You Got Me Rocking (Perfecto Mix)/(Sexy Disco Dub Mix)/(Trance Mix) (12", p/s) 8
94	Virgin VS 1518	You Got Me Rocking/Jump On Top Of Me (numbered p/s, 7,000 only) 10
94	Virgin VS 1524	Out Of Tears/I'm Gonna Drive (numbered p/s, 7,000 only) 10
94	Virgin VSCDX 1524	Out Of Tears (Don Was Edit)/I'm Gonna Drive/Sparks Will Fly (Radio Clean)/ Out Of Tears (Bob Clearmountain Remix Edit) (CD, tear-shaped card p/s) 15
94	Virgin VSCDG 1524	Out Of Tears (Don Was Edit)/I'm Gonna Drive/So Young/The Storm/ Jump On Top Of Me (CD, digipak, numbered, 4,000 only, withdrawn) 250
94	Virgin VSP 1539	I Go Wild/I Go Wild (live) (numbered picture p/s) 20
96	Virgin VS 1578	Wild Horses/Tumbling Dice/Gimme Shelter (unreleased) 0
96	Virgin VSCDT 1578	Wild Horses/Tumbling Dice/Gimme Shelter (CD, unreleased) 0
97	Virgin VS 1653	Anyone Seen My Baby?/Anyone Seen My Baby (Soul Solution Remix) (7" picture disc).........5
97	Virgin VST 1653	Anybody Seen My Baby? (LP Edit)/(Soul Solution Remix)/(Bonus Roll) (12", p/s) 15
97	Virgin VS 1653	Anybody Seen My Baby? (LP Edit)/(Soul Solution Remix Edit) (numbered picture disc, p/s, 7,500 only) 15
98	Virgin VS 1667	Saint Of Me/Anyway You Look At It (7" picture disc) 10
98	Virgin VSY 1667	Saint Of Me (Radio Edit)/Anyway You Look At It (picture disc) 10
98	Virgin VSLH 1667	Saint Of me/Radio Edit/Anyway You Look At It (injection moulded jukebox labels) 8
98	Virgin VSTTDT 1667	Saint Of Me (remixes)/Anybody Seen My Baby? (remixes) (12", double pack, stickered p/s) 15
98	Virgin VSTX 1667	Saint Of Me (remixes)/Anybody Seen My Baby? (remixes) (12", double pack, stickered p/s) 15
98	Virgin VSCDX T 1667	Saint Of Me (Radio Edit)/Gimme Shelter/Anybody Seen My Baby? (Phil Jones Remix) ?Saint Of Me (Deep Dish Grunge Garage Dub) (CD 1) Saint Of Me (Radio Edit)/Anyway You Look At It/Saint Of Me (DeepDish Grunge Garage Remix (Parts 1 and 2) (CD 2)...15
98	Virgin VS 1700	Out Of Control/In Hand With Fluke Radio Edit (7" picture disc) 8

98	Virgin VS 1700	Out Of Control/Out Of Control (In Hand With Fluke Mix) (7" picture disc) 5
98	Virgin VSY 1700	Out Of Control (Album Radio Edit)/In Hand With Fluke Radio Edit (p/s) 10
98	Virgin VSY 1700	Out Of Control (Album Radio Edit)/(In Hand With Fluke Radio Edit) 10
02	Virgin VS 1838	Don't Stop (Edit)/New Rock Remix (red vinyl, numbered p/s) 12
05	Virgin VS 1905	Streets Of Love/Rough Justice (red vinyl, p/s) 10
05	Virgin VS 1907	Rain Fall Down (Will i Am Remix)/(Ashley Beedle's Heavy Vocal Re-Edit) (7", p/s)..............10
05	Virgin VST 1907	Rain Fall Down (Will i Am Remix)/(Ashley Beedle's Heavy Vocal Re-Edit) (12", p/s)............8
06	Virgin VS 1914	Biggest Mistake/Hand Of Fate (red vinyl, p/s) 10

EXPORT SINGLES

63	Decca AT 15005	I Wanna Be Your Man/Stoned 125
64	Decca AT 15006	Not Fade Away/Little By Little 125
64	Decca AT 15032	Come On!/Tell Me (You're Coming Back) 150
64	Decca AT 15035	Empty Heart/Around And Around...150
65	Decca AT 15039	Time Is On My Side/Congratulations 150
65	Decca AT 15040	Little Red Rooster/Off The Hook 110
65	Decca AT 15043	(I Can't Get No) Satisfaction/The Under Assistant West Coast Promotional Man (p/s).......150
65	Decca F 12104	The Last Time/Play With Fire (with Dutch or Scandinavian p/s)....................................85
65	Decca F 12220	(I Can't Get No) Satisfaction/The Under Assistant West Coast Promotional Man (with p/s)...75
65	Decca F 12220	(I Can't Get No) Satisfaction/The Under Assistant West Coast Promotional Man 30
65	Decca F 22180	Heart Of Stone/What A Shame (in p/s) 140
65	Decca F 22180	Heart Of Stone/What A Shame 100
65	Decca F 22265	Get Off My Cloud/I'm Free 30
65	Decca F 22265	Get Off My Cloud/I'm Free (in p/s) 75
66	Decca F 12395	Paint It, Black/Long Long While (p/s) 50
66	Decca F 12331	19th Nervous Breakdown/As Tears Go By (with Dutch p/s) 50
67	Decca F 12546	Let's Spend The Night Together/Ruby Tuesday (p/s) 50
67	Decca F 12654	We Love You/Dandelion (p/s) 50
67	Decca F 22706	2,000 Light Years From Home/She's A Rainbow..50
68	Decca F 22825	Street Fighting Man (remix)/No Expectations (in p/s)..50
68	Decca F 22825	Street Fighting Man (remix)/No Expectations 30
69	Decca F 12952	Honky Tonk Women/You Can't Always Get What You Want (p/s) 50
71	Decca F 13204	Street Fighting Man/Everybody Needs Somebody To Love (in p/s) 40
71	Decca F 13195	Street Fighting Man/Surprise Surprise/Everybody Needs Somebody To Love (33rpm maxi-single, p/s) 40
71	Decca F 13126	Little Queenie/Love In Vain (in p/s) 55
71	Decca F 13126	Little Queenie/Love In Vain 20
71	Decca F 13204	Street Fighting Man/Everybody Needs Somebody To Love 20

EPs

64	Decca DFE 8560	THE ROLLING STONES (with unboxed Decca logo) 40
64	Decca DFE 8560	THE ROLLING STONES (later boxed Decca logo) 12
64	Decca DFE 8590	FIVE BY FIVE (with unboxed Decca logo)...40
64	Decca DFE 8590	FIVE BY FIVE (later boxed Decca logo)..12
65	Decca DFE 8620	GOT LIVE IF YOU WANT IT! (with unboxed Decca logo)..40
65	Decca DFE 8620	GOT LIVE IF YOU WANT IT! (later boxed Decca logo)..12
83	Decca DFEX 8560	THE ROLLING STONES (12", reissue)..12
83	Decca DFEX 8590	FIVE BY FIVE (12", reissue)...12
83	Decca DFEX 8620	GOT LIVE IF YOU WANT IT (12", reissue)...12

EPS : EXPORT EPS

64	Decca SDE 7260	ROLLING STONES 120
64	Decca SDE 7501	THE ROLLING STONES VOLUME 2 110
65	Decca DFE 8620	GOT LIVE IF YOU WANT IT! (red label, some with yellow titles on p/s)............................110
65	Decca SDE 7502	GOT LIVE IF YOU WANT IT! 120
65	Decca SDE 7503	ROLLING STONES (with "Out Of Our Heads [U.K. version]" sleeve) 110

ALBUMS : DECCA ALBUMS

64	Decca LK 4605	ROLLING STONES (1st pressing, plays 2.52 version of "Tell Me"; Side 2 matrix: XARL 6272-1A) 1000
64	Decca LK 4605	ROLLING STONES (2nd pressing, plays 4.06 version of "Tell Me"; sleeves list "Mona").......350
64	Decca LK 4605	ROLLING STONES (2nd pressing, plays 4.06 version of "Tell Me"; more common, with sleeves that list "I Need You, Baby") 200
65	Decca LK 4661	ROLLING STONES NO. 2...200
65	Decca LK 4661	ROLLING STONES NO. 2 (with 'blind man' text pasted over on rear sleeve)........................250
65	Decca LK 4733	OUT OF OUR HEADS (mono) 110
65	Decca SKL 4733	OUT OF OUR HEADS (stereo) 110

(The above LPs were simultaneously pressed with both flipback and non-flipback sleeves. Values are the same.)

66	Decca LK 4786	AFTERMATH (mono) 110
66	Decca SKL 4786	AFTERMATH (stereo) 110
66	Decca LK 4786	AFTERMATH (mono, front cover title has purple shadow) 150
66	Decca SKL 4786	AFTERMATH (stereo, front cover title is shadowed) 125
66	Decca TXL 101	BIG HITS (HIGH TIDE AND GREEN GRASS) (1st pressing, gatefold sleeve, with stapled 12" x 12" picture booklet, mono) 80
66	Decca TXS 101	BIG HITS (HIGH TIDE AND GREEN GRASS) (1st pressing, gatefold sleeve, with stapled 12" x 12" picture booklet, stereo) 80
66	Decca TXL/TXS 101	COULD YOU WALK ON THE WATER (unreleased, proof sleeves exist) 0
67	Decca TXS 101	BIG HITS (HIGH TIDE AND GREEN GRASS) (2nd pressing, gatefold sleeve, without booklet, stereo) 50
67	Decca TXL 101	BIG HITS (HIGH TIDE AND GREEN GRASS) (2nd pressing, gatefold sleeve, without booklet, mono) 30
70s	Decca TXS 101	BIG HITS (HIGH TIDE AND GREEN GRASS) (2nd pressing, gatefold sleeve, later issue with foldout insert & later Decca logo, stereo only) 15
67	Decca LK 4852	BETWEEN THE BUTTONS (mono) 150
67	Decca SKL 4852	BETWEEN THE BUTTONS (stereo) 120
67	Decca TXL 103	THEIR SATANIC MAJESTIES REQUEST (3-D gatefold sleeve with red inner, mono) 200
67	Decca TXS 103	THEIR SATANIC MAJESTIES REQUEST (3-D gatefold sleeve with red inner, stereo) 150
68	Decca LK 4955	BEGGARS BANQUET (gatefold sleeve, with Stones Decca label insert, mono) 200
68	Decca SKL 4955	BEGGARS BANQUET (gatefold sleeve, with Stones Decca label insert, stereo) 150
69	Decca LK 5019	THROUGH THE PAST, DARKLY (BIG HITS VOL. 2) (octagonal gatefold sleeve, mono) 80
69	Decca SKL 5019	THROUGH THE PAST, DARKLY (BIG HITS VOL. 2) (octagonal gatefold sleeve, stereo)............65
69	Decca LK 5025	LET IT BLEED (mono, red inner, with poster, with stickered sleeve) 400
69	Decca LK 5025	LET IT BLEED (mono, red inner, with poster, without stickered sleeve)............................100

69	Decca SKL 5025	LET IT BLEED (stereo, blue inner, with poster, with stickered sleeve).................................	150
69	Decca SKL 5025	LET IT BLEED (stereo, blue inner, with poster, without stickered sleeve)	60
69	Decca TXL/TXS 103	THEIR SATANIC MAJESTIES REQUEST (2nd pressing, gatefold sleeve with red inner, stereo, stereo disc in stickered mono sleeve)	50

All of the above LPs were originally issued with Decca labels with a large-print logo without a box surrounding it; later pressings with smaller print & boxed logo are worth around two-thirds the value.)

69	Decca TXL/TXS 103	THEIR SATANIC MAJESTIES REQUEST (2nd pressing, gatefold sleeve with red inner, mono)..	50
70	Decca SKL 5065	GET YER YA-YA'S OUT! (1st pressing with fully laminated sleeve front and back, with "sleeve printed in England" XZAL 10076 1W/XZAL 10077 1W	60
70	Decca SKL 5065	GET YER YA-YA'S OUT! (2nd pressing with laminated front sleeve front and un-laminated rear sleeve with "sleeve printed in England by Clout & Baker Ltd.")	20
70s	Decca SKL 4733	OUT OF OUR HEADS (2nd pressing, light green sleeve, box Decca logo)	30
71	Decca SKL 5025	LET IT BLEED (LP, reissue, stereo only, no mono/stereo indicator hole on rear sleeve, poster and inner sleeve, boxed logo on label)....................................	50
71	Decca SKL 5084	STONE AGE..	15
71	Decca SKL 5101	GIMME SHELTER..	12
71	Decca NPS2	THEIR SATANIC MAJESTIES REQUEST (LP, gatefold, stereo reissue, boxed Decca logo)....	25
72	Decca SKL 5098	MILESTONES..	12
72	Decca SKL 5149	ROCK 'N' ROLLING STONES...	12
73	Decca SKL 5165	GOLDEN B-SIDES (unreleased, test pressings only)	1000
73	Decca SKL 5173	NO STONE UNTURNED...	15

(Except where noted, the above Decca LPs were originally issued with dark blue labels & laminated sleeves; later copies are worth two-thirds the value.)

75	Decca (no cat. no.)	THE HISTORY OF THE ROLLING STONES (3-LP box set; 3x12" pink label test pressings exist, no sleeves, matrices read: ZAL 12996/7, ZAL 12998/9 & ZAL 13000/1; release cancelled in favour of "Rolled Gold" 2-LP set)	1000
75	Decca SKL 5212	METAMORPHOSIS (dark blue label, matt sleeve).......................................	15
75	Decca TXS 103	THEIR SATANIC MAJESTIES REQUEST (3rd pressing, 3-D matt gatefold sleeve, stereo only) ..	25
75	Decca ROST 3/4	LIVE STONES (2-LP, compilation, pink label test pressings only, follow-up to "Rolled Gold", unreleased)	500
83	Decca ROLL 1	THE FIRST EIGHT STUDIO ALBUMS (8-LP set, with 192-page book; wraparound card box, each LP has star printed on rear sleeve).....................................	250

ALBUMS : EXPORT LPS

65	Decca SKL 4725	OUT OF OUR HEADS (with U.S. track listing & cover design, unboxed Decca label logo, stereo, withdrawn)	200
65	Decca LK 4725	OUT OF OUR HEADS (export, LP, with U.S. track listing & cover design, unboxed Decca label logo, mono, withdrawn)	170
66	Decca LK 4838	HAVE YOU SEEN YOUR MOTHER, LIVE (export LP, laminated sleeve & unboxed Decca label logo, mono)	125
66	Decca SKL 4838	HAVE YOU SEEN YOUR MOTHER, LIVE (export LP, laminated sleeve & unboxed Decca label logo, stereo)	150
67	Decca LK 4888	FLOWERS (export LP, mono, laminated sleeve, unboxed Decca label logo)	400
67	Decca SKL 4888	FLOWERS (export LP, stereo, laminated sleeve, unboxed Decca label logo).............	250
70	Decca SKL 4786	AFTERMATH (export LP, white label, black print, supposedly for export)	25
70	Decca SKL 5065	GET YER YA-YA'S OUT! (export LP, white label, black print, supposedly for export)	20
70	Decca TXS 103	THEIR SATANIC MAJESTIES REQUEST (export LP, gatefold sleeve, white label, black print, supposedly for export)	25
72	Decca LK/SKL 4838	HAVE YOU SEEN YOUR MOTHER, LIVE (export LP, later pressing, boxed logo, laminated sleeve)	80
72	Decca LK/SKL 4888	FLOWERS (export LP, later pressing, laminated sleeve, boxed Decca label logo)	100

ALBUMS : ROLLING STONES LABEL LPS

71	Rolling Stones COC 59100	STICKY FINGERS ('big' zip sleeve with insert)	60
71	Rolling Stones COC 59100	STICKY FINGERS (zip sleeve with insert)	40
72	Rolling Stones COC 69100	EXILE ON MAIN STREET (2-LP, gatefold, with inners, postcard inserts)	100
72	Rolling Stones COC 69100	EXILE ON MAIN STREET (2-LP, with inners, without postcard inserts).................	40
73	Rolling Stones COC 59101	GOAT'S HEAD SOUP (gatefold sleeve, with 2 inserts)	30
76	Rolling Stones COC 59106	BLACK AND BLUE (LP)...	15
78	Rolling Stones CUN 39108	SOME GIRLS (LP, die cut sleeve with uncensored inner sleeve, featuring Farrah Fawcett, Raquel Welch, Judy Garland and Marilyn Monroe)................................	35
78	Rolling Stones CUN 39108	SOME GIRLS (LP, die cut sleeve with censored inner sleeve, it is believed that those with the red 'Some Girls' title is the rarest with blue, green and yellow being more common)..	15
80	Rolling Stones CUN 39111	EMOTIONAL RESCUE (LP with poster)	12
81	Rolling Stones CUN 39114	TATTOO YOU (LP)...	15
82	R. Stones CUNP 39115	STILL LIFE (AMERICAN CONCERT 1981) (LP, picture disc, mispressed with wrong tracks)	140
82	R. Stones CUNP 39115	STILL LIFE (AMERICAN CONCERT 1981) (LP, picture disc)	25
84	Rolling Stones 450196	EXILE ON MAIN STREET (2-LP, reissue in single sleeve)	20

ALBUMS : OTHER ALBUMS

77	CBS 450 208	LOVE YOU LIVE (2-LP)	25
83	R. Digest GROLA 119	THE GREAT YEARS (4-LP, box set)..	25
86	CBS 86321	DIRTY WORK (LP, with inner)..	25
89	ABKCO 820900-1	ROLLING STONES SINGLES COLLECTION/LONDON YEARS (4-LP set)	45
89	CBS 466 918 2	COLLECTION 1971-1989 (15-CD box set, with bonus CD, 'Collector's Edition')	130
91	Sony 468 135-9/468 135-2	FLASHPOINT/INTERVIEW 1990 (2-CD pack, shrinkwrapped with tongue logo sticker, numbered)...	40
94	Virgin V2750	VOODOO LOUNGE (2-LP)	40
95	Virgin V 2801	STRIPPED (2-LP with inner sleeves)	35
97	Virgin V2840	BRIDGES TO BABYLON (2-LP, with inner sleeves)	40
02	Virgin CDVDXX2964	FORTY LICKS (Ltd edition CD box set)..	35
10	Eagle Rock ERELP 815	LADIES AND GENTLEMEN (2-LP)	20

PROMOS : PROMO SINGLES

76	Rolling Stones RS 19121 DJ	Fool To Cry/Crazy Mama (7" promo, mono mix, edited down to 3.59, no 'phased' electric piano intro)	70
83	R. Stones RSR 112 (DJ)	Let's Spend The Night Together (live)/Start Me Up (live)	20
91	CBS A 026/B 027	Highwire/Sympathy For The Devil (live) (12")..	15
93	EMI ORDERLH 1	Gimme Shelter (live) (1-sided jukebox issue)	20
93	Virgin STONES 1	JUMP BACK (EP)..	25
94	Virgin VSCDJ 1518	You Got Me Rocking (Original Version)/(Perfecto Mix) (CD)............................	15
95	Virgin VSCDJ 1562	Like A Rolling Stone (Edit)/(Album Version) (CD)	12
95	Virgin VSCDJ 1539	I Go Wild (CD, 1-track)...	15
96	Virgin VSCDJ 1578	Wild Horses (Edit) (CD, 1-track)	10
97	Virgin VSCDJ 1653	Anybody Seen My Baby? (LP Edit)/(Don Was Radio Remix) (CD)	10

97	Virgin VSCDXJ 1653	Anybody Seen My Baby? (Armand's Rolling Steelo Mix)/(Soul Solution Remix)/ (Bonus Roll) (CD)	10
98	Virgin VSTDJ 1667	Saint Of Me (Deep Dish Grunge Garage Remix) (Part 1)/(Part 2)/ (Grunge Garage Dub)/(Rolling Dub)/Anyone Seen My Baby? (Armand's Rolling Steelo Mix)/Anyone Seen My Baby? (Bonus Roll) (12" double pack, stickered sleeve)	20
98	Virgin VSTDJ 1700	Out Of Control (In Hand With Fluke)/(In Hand Full Version)/ (Bi-Polar's Fat Controller Mix)/(Bi-Polar At The Controls)	10
98	Virgin VSP 1700	Out Of Control (Bi-Polar At The Controls)/(Bi-Polar Outer Version) (withdrawn brown label)	30
98	Virgin VSTDDJ 1700	Out Of Control (In Hand With Fluke Instrumental)/(In Hand Full Version)/ (Bi-Polar's Fat Controller Mix)/(Bi-Polar At The Controls) (12")	10
98	Virgin VSP 1700	Out Of Control (Bi-Polar At The Controls)/(Bi-Polar Outer Version) (withdrawn silver label)	15
90s	Virgin VSCDY 1838	Don't Stop (1-track CD)	10
00s	Virgin DEVIL 666	Sympathy For The Devil (Fatboy Slim Remix)/(Neptunes Remix)//(Full Phat Remix)/ (Original Version) (2x12", with press sheet)	20

PROMOS : PROMO LPS

67	Decca TXL/TXS 103	THEIR SATANIC MAJESTIES REQUEST (LP, padded silk sleeve)	2000
69	Decca RSM. 1	PROMOTIONAL ALBUM (LP, U.K. disc in U.S. sleeve [lists RSD-1], 200 copies pressed [100 each for U.K. & U.S.], U.K. issues include a letter from Decca)	2000
86	CBS SAMP 1103	STONES ON CD - A RADIO SAMPLER (CD, poly sleeve)	200
89	CBS (no catalogue no.)	STEEL WHEELS - THE ALBUM OF THE TOUR (box set, with LP, CD, cassette and "Terrifying" 12", European tour dates & sticker)	150
89	CBS SAMPC 1347	SAY AHHH! (LP, promo-only compilation)	200
95	Virgin IVDG 2801	STRIPPED (2-CD, interview disc & album, fold-out digipak)	40
97	Virgin (no catalogue no.)	BRIDGES TO BABYLON (CD in promo press box, with "Anybody Seen My Baby?" promo CD, press release, bottle opener, notebook and sheet of stamps, 200 only)	150
97	Virgin IVDG 2840	BRIDGES TO BABYLON INTERVIEW (2-CD, interview disc & album, fold-out digipak)	30
97	Virgin CDVDJ 2840	BRIDGES TO BABYLON (CD, with spoken word intros, 200 only)	70
99	Virgin CDVDJ 2880	NO SECURITY ALBUM SAMPLER (CD, card p/s)	15
99	Virgin CDIDJ 2880	NO SECURITY (3-CD [2 interview discs], foldout digipak)	45
90s	Virgin CDVDY 2964	FORTY LICKS (CD)	45

(see also Mick Jagger, Keith Richards, Pipes Of Pan, Bill Wyman, Charlie Watts, Mick Taylor, Andrew Oldham, Bobbie Miller)

AUDLEY ROLLINS

72	Explosion EX 2062	Repatriation/HUGH ROY JUNIOR: Repatriation - Version	10
73	Attack ATT 8060	Without You In My World/It's Flowing (actually "It's Growing")	6
73	Harry J HJ 6654	What's Your Name/NOW GENERATION: What's Your Name - Version	6

(see also A. Boyne)

(HENRY) ROLLINS BAND

91	Vinyl Solution VS 30	Let There Be Rock/Carry Me Down (12", p/s, as Henry Rollins & Hard-Ons)	18
91	Vinyl Solution VS 30CD	Let There Be Rock/Carry Me Down (CD, as Henry Rollins & Hard-Ons)	18
92	Imago 72787250181	TEARIN' (12" EP, poster p/s)	8
92	Imago 72787250187	TEARIN' (CD EP, poster p/s)	10
94	Imago 7432323057	LIAR (EP, poster p/s)	10
92	Quarter Stick QS 13CD	DEEP THROAT (4-CD box set, spoken-word)	45

BIRD ROLLINS

| 72 | Mojo 2092 049 | Love Man From Carolina/She Needs Loving All The Time | 10 |

SONNY ROLLINS

58	Esquire EP 198	WAILING MISTER ROLLINS (EP)	12
56	Esquire 20-050	SONNY ROLLINS QUARTET (10" LP)	50
57	Esquire 20-080	SONNY ROLLINS QUINTET (10" LP)	35
57	Esquire 32-025	SONNY ROLLINS PLUS FOUR (LP)	50
57	Esquire 32-035	PERSPECTIVES (LP, with Modern Jazz Quartet)	40
58	Esquire 32-038	WORKTIME (LP)	50
58	Esquire 32-045	SAXOPHONE COLOSSUS (LP, as Sonny Rollins Four)	100
58	Contemporary LAC 12118	WAY OUT WEST (LP)	30
58	Esquire 32-058	TENOR MADNESS (LP)	50
59	Esquire 32-075	ROLLINS PLAYS FOR BIRD (LP)	50
59	Esquire 32-085	TOUR-DE-FORCE (LP)	40
59	MGM MGM-C 776	SONNY ROLLINS AND THE BIG BRASS (LP)	15
60	Contemporary SCA 5013	SONNY ROLLINS AND THE CONTEMPORARY LEADERS (LP, stereo only)	20
61	Riverside RLP 12-241	THE SOUND OF SONNY (LP)	15
62	Riverside RLP 12-258	FREEDOM SUITE (LP)	15
62	Esquire 32-155	MOVIN' OUT (LP)	50
62	RCA RD/SF 7504	THE BRIDGE (LP)	15
63	Esquire 32-175	SONNY BOY (LP)	30
63	RCA RD/SF 7524	WHAT'S NEW (LP)	15
63	RCA RD/SF 7546	OUR MAN IN JAZZ (LP)	15
64	RCA RD/SF 7593	SONNY MEETS HAWK (LP, with Coleman Hawkins)	15
64	RCA RD/SF 7626	SONNY ROLLINS & CO. (LP)	15
65	RCA RD 7670	NOW'S THE TIME (LP)	15
65	Fontana FJL 124	BLOW! (LP)	25
66	HMV CLP 1915	ROLLINS ON IMPULSE (LP)	15
66	Stateside SL 10164	SAXOPHONE COLOSSUS (LP, reissue)	15
67	RCA RD/SF 7736	STANDARD SONNY ROLLINS (LP)	15
67	HMV CLP/CSD 3529	SONNY PLAYS ALFIE (LP)	15
67	HMV CLP/CSD 3610	EAST BROADWAY RUNDOWN (LP)	15

(see also Modern Jazz Quartet, Thelonious Monk, Clifford Brown, Coleman Hawkins, Kenny Durham)

ROLL MOVEMENT

| 67 | Go AJ 11410 | I'm Out On My Own/Just One Thing | 35 |

ROLL-UPS

| 80 | Bridgehouse BHS 6 | Blackmail/Hold On (p/s) | 15 |
| 79 | Bridgehouse BHLP 004 | LOW DIVES FOR HIGHBALLS (LP) | 25 |

ROLO TOMASSI

| 07 | Danger! Laser! Phaser! Razor! DLPR 003 | ROLO TOMASSI (LP, 1000 only, blue vinyl) | 20 |

GLORIA ROMA

| 64 | Decca F 12001 | It Hurts Me So/I Didn't Know What Time It Was | 8 |

DICK ROMAN
59	MGM MGM 1004	Party Girl/My Greatest Mistake	5
65	London HLU 10007	The Truth Hurts/What Good Does It Do Me	5

MIMI ROMAN
61	Warner Bros WB 55	Johnny Will/Let It Be Me	8

MURRAY ROMAN
69	Track 613 007	YOU CAN'T BEAT PEOPLE UP AND HAVE THEM SAY I LOVE YOU (LP)	25
69	Track 613 015	A BLIND MAN'S MOVIE (LP)	30

SANDY ROMAN
66	Columbia DB 7931	Dale Anne/Home Is Where The Heart Is	5

TONY ROMAN
67	Stateside SS 2022	Shadows On A Foggy Day/Maggie	7

LYN ROMAN
67	Stateside SS2069	The Penthouse/Born To Lose	12

MAX ROMEO
68	Island WI 3104	Put Me In The Mood/My One Girl	25
68	Island WI 3111	Walk Into The Room/DAWN PENN: I'll Get You	40
68	Island WI 3124	Twelfth Of Never (actually by Pat Kelly)/VAL BENNETT: Caledonia	40
68	Unity UN 503	Wet Dream/She's But A Little Girl	10
69	Blue Cat BS 161	We Want Man/AL REID: Vietcong	40
69	Blue Cat BS 163	It's Not The Way/AL REID: Darling	50
69	Nu Beat NB 022	Blowing In The Wind/LARRY MARSHALL: Money Girl	12
69	Trojan TR 656	Sweet Chariot/Far Far Away (with Hippy Boys)	20
69	Unity UN 507	Belly Woman (actually by Derrick Morgan)/PAULETT & LOVERS: Please Stay	7
69	Unity UN 511	Twelfth Of Never (actually by Pat Kelly)/TARTONS: Solid As A Rock (actually by Tartans)	15
69	Unity UN 516	Wine Her Goosie/KING CANNON: Fire Ball	10
69	Unity UN 532	Mini-Skirt Vision/Far Far Away	20
70	Unity UN 544	Melting Pot/HIPPY BOYS: Death Rides A Horse	30
70	Unity UN 545	Clap Clap (with Hippy Boys)/Death Rides A Horse	30
70	Unity UN 547	What A Cute Man/Buy You A Rainbow	30
70	Unity UN 560	Fish In The Pot/Feel It	10
71	Bullet BU 478	Mother Oh Mother/Dreams Of Passion (actually "Judgement Rock" by Charlie Ace)	10
71	Pama Supreme PS 328	Ginal Ship/UPSETTERS: Version 2	10
71	Pama Supreme PS 306	Let The Power Fall On I/The Raid	7
71	Pama Supreme PS 318	Don't You Weep/Weeping (Version)	7
71	Punch PH 73	Chie Chie Bud/Version	7
71	Unity UN 571	Macabee (Version)/SOUL SYNDICATE: Music Book	6
71	Camel CA 66	Black Equality/Suffering	20
71	Camel CA 82	The Coming Of Jah/Watch And Pray	6
71	Prince Buster PB 11	Words Sounds And Power/Version	12
72	Camel CA 85	Rasta Bandwagon/When Jah Speaks	6
72	Camel CA 86	Public Enemy Number One/How Long Must We Wait	6
72	Big BG 334	Are You Sure/RUPIE EDWARDS ALL STARS: Are You Sure - Version	6
72	Dynamic DYN 444	We Love America/SOUL RHYTHM: We Love Jamaica Version	6
72	G.G. GG 4535	Is It Really Over?/MAYTONES: Born To Be Loved	6
72	High Note Hs 058	Pray For Me (with Gaytones)/GAYTONES: Pray For Me - Version	8
72	Pama PM 836	Wet Dream/("Bang Bang Lulu" by Lloyd Tyrell)/("Birth Control" by Lloyd Tyrell)/Sex Education by Classics) (Maxi-Single)	5
72	Pama Supreme PS 345	Pray For Me/Version	5
72	Pama Supreme PS 359	Are You Sure/CARL MASTERS: Va-Va-Voom	8
72	Prince Buster PB 11	River Jordan/Words Sound And Power	6
73	Dragon DRA 1028	No Joshua No/JOSHUA'S ALL STARS: No Joshua No (Version)	5
73	Magnet MA 032	Murder In The Place/Version	7
73	Magnet MA 032	I Woke Up In Love/Version	5
73	Pama PM 875	Pussy Watchman/You Are My Sunshine	5
73	Pama Supreme PS 383	Hide Away/SOUL SYNDICATE: Sweet And Gentle	6
73	Pama Supreme PS 385	Everyman Aught To Know/Version	6
73	Unity UN 572	Rent Crisis/Version	7
74	Ackee ACK 529	Sixpence/Eating Competition	5
75	Tropical Sound Tracs TST 107	Big Jack/Cross Over The Bridge/Please Help Me, I'm Falling	5
76	Island WIP 6305	One Step Forward/One Step Dub	10
76	Island WIP 6330	Chase The Devil/UPSETTERS FEAT. PRINCE JAZZBO: Croaking Lizard	40
69	Pama PMLP 11	A DREAM (LP)	60
71	Pama PMP 2010	LET THE POWER FALL (LP)	50
76	Island ILPS 9392	WAR INA BABYLON (LP)	30
76	Tropical TSL 1000	REVELATION TIME (LP)	50
92	Jah Shaka SHAKA 921	FAR I - CAPTAIN OF MY SHIP (LP)	12
95	Jah Shaka SHAKA 951	OUR RIGHTS (LP)	15
78	Mango MLPS 9503	RECONSTRUCTION (LP, blue rim)	30

(see also Max & Elaine, Maxie & Glen, Al Read, Henry & Lisa, Dennis Alcapone, George Meggie, David Isaacs)

ROMEO Z
66	CBS 202645	Come Back Baby/Since My Baby Said Goodbye	30

ROMEO & EMOTIONS
67	Caltone TONE 106	Don't Want To Let You Go/I Can't Do No More	80

CHAN ROMERO
59	Columbia DB 4341	The Hippy Hippy Shake/If I Had A Way	100
60	Columbia DB 4405	My Little Ruby/I Don't Care Now	200

ROMFORD STOMPERS
81	Rott ROTT 1	Dead Girls/MARY & KEN: Happy (stamped labels in stamped paper die-cut sleeve)	20

ROMI & JAZZ
90	Chrysalis CHSR 123545	One Love One World (Feel The Rhythm Mix)/One Love One World (Unity '90 Mix)/Love Crime (Sunrise Mix) (12", p/s)	12

RON AND MEL
65	Columbia DB 7469	In A Shabby Little Hut/I See Your Face	6

MINT VALUE £

RONALD & LLOYD
74	Magnet MG 042	Back In My Arms/HEPTONES: Drifting Away	8

RONALD & RUBY
58	RCA RCA 1053	Lollipop/Fickle Baby	30
58	RCA RCA 1053	Lollipop/Fickle Baby (78)	15

RONDELLS
58	London HLU 8716	Good Good/Dreamy (with Ned Jr.)	130
58	London HLU 8716	Good Good/Dreamy (with Ned Jr.) (78)	100

RONDELS
61	London HLU 9404	Back Beat No. 1/Shades Of Green	20

DON RONDO
57	London HLJ 8466	White Silver Sands/Stars Fell On Alabama	8
58	London HLJ 8567	What A Shame/Made For Each Other	10
58	London HLJ 8610	I've Got Bells On My Heart/School Dance	8
58	London HLJ 8641	Blonde Bombshell/Her Hair Was Yellow	6
59	London RE-J 1154	RONDO PT. 1 (EP)	8
59	London RE-J 1155	RONDO PT. 2 (EP)	8

GENE RONDO
68	Giant GN 39	Ben Nevis/Grey Lies	15
68	Jolly JY 004	Mary, Mary/Baby, Baby	10
69	Downtown DT 422	A Lover's Question/HERBIE GRAY & RUDIES: Blue Moon	12
69	Downtown DT 431	Sentimental Reasons/Then You Can Tell Me Goodbye	7
70	Downtown DT 459	Spreading Peace/MUSIC DOCTORS: Guitar Riff	7
72	Downtown DT 490	Wanna Be Like Daddy/STUDIO SOUND: A Little More	8
72	Count Shelly CS 005	Happy Birthday Sweet Sixteen/Meditation	5
73	Magnet MA 001	Prisoner Of Love/How Many Times Girl	5
73	Magnet MA 006	Each Moments/If You Do Want Me	5
73	Magnet MA 028	Oh Sweet Africa/This Is Love	8
73	Magnet MA 035	Valley Of Tears/He'll Break Your Heart	5

(see also Gene Pancho)

RONDO VENEZIANO
88	Fanfare CDRON 1	VENICE IN PERIL (CD)	20

RONETTES
63	London HLU 9793	Be My Baby/Tedesco And Pitman	10
64	London HLU 9826	Baby I Love You/Miss Joan And Mr Sam	10
64	London HLU 9905	(The Best Part Of) Breakin' Up/Big Red	20
64	London HLU 9922	Do I Love You?/When I Saw You	20
64	London HLU 9931	(Walking) In The Rain/How Does It Feel?	18
65	London HLU 9952	Born To Be Together/Blues For Baby	20
65	London HLU 9976	Is This What I Get For Loving You?/You Baby	30
66	London HLU 10087	I Can Hear Music/When I Saw You (withdrawn)	100
69	London HLU 10240	Be My Baby/Baby I Love You	8
69	A&M AMS 748	You Came, You Saw, You Conquered/I Can Hear Music	8
75	Phil Spector Intl. 2010 009	I'm A Woman In Love/When I Saw You	10
77	Phil Spector Intl. 2010 017	I Wonder/Walking In The Rain	10
64	London HA-U 8212	PRESENTING THE FABULOUS RONETTES FEATURING VERONICA (LP, original pressing on plum label)	100
64	London HA-U 8212	PRESENTING THE FABULOUS RONETTES FEATURING VERONICA (LP, later pressing on black label)	50
65	Colpix PXL 486	THE RONETTES (LP)	150
75	Phil Spector Intl. 2307 003	SING THEIR GREATEST HITS (LP)	15

(see also Ronnie Spector, Joey Dee & Starlighters)

RONNIE & DEL AIRES
64	Coral Q 72473	Drag/Wigglin' 'N' Wobblin'	35

RONNIE & HI-LITES
62	Pye International 7N 25140	I Wish That We Were Married/Twistin' And Kissin'	30

RONNIE & RAINBOWS
61	London HL 9345	Loose Ends/Sombrero	25

RONNIE & ROBYN
80	Grapevine GRP 137	As Long As You Love Me/Sidra's Theme (unissued)	0

RONNIE & ROY
59	Capitol CL 15028	Big Fat Sally/Here I Am	150

RONNO
71	Vertigo 6059 029	Fourth Hour Of My Sleep/Powers Of Darkness	65

(see also Mick Ronson, Rats)

RONNY
64	Decca F 21908	Oh! My Darling Caroline/Lu La Lu	10

RONNY & THE DAYTONAS
64	Stateside SS 333	G.T.O./Hot Rod Baby	25
64	Stateside SS 367	California Bound/Hey Little Girl	25
65	Stateside SS 391	Bucket T/Little Rail Job	30
65	Stateside SS 432	Beach Boy/No Wheels	30
66	Stateside SS 484	Sandy/Sandy (Instrumental)	20

(see also Buzz & Bucky)

MARK RONSON
05	Exit (No Cat. No.)	EXIT EP (12", 200 only, promo)	15
07	Sony BMG 88697186221	Valerie (Original Mix)/(Baby J Remix) (10")	8

MICK RONSON
74	RCA APBO 0212	Love Me Tender/Only After Dark	6
74	RCA 11474 XSP	Love Me Tender/Slaughter On 10th Avenue (1-sided red or black interview flexidisc, included in press kits)	15
74	RCA LPBO 5022	Slaughter On 10th Avenue/Leave My Heart Alone	6

75	RCA RCA 2482	Billy Porter/Seven Days	6
74	RCA Victor APL1-0353	SLAUGHTER ON 10th AVENUE (LP)	15
74	RCA APL1-0681	PLAY DON'T WORRY (LP, laminated gatefold sleeve)	15
94	Epic EPC 474742 1	HEAVEN AND HULL (LP, picture disc)	15

(see also Ronno, David Bowie, Mott The Hoople, Slaughter & The Dogs, Ian Hunter)

LINDA RONSTADT

69	Capitol E-ST 208	HOME SOWN, HOME GROWN (LP)	20
70	Capitol E-ST 407	SILK PURSE (LP)	15
72	Capitol EA-ST 635	LINDA RONSTADT (LP)	12

(see also Stone Poneys)

RONYSAN

| 88 | 2 Man MAN 1 | I Take Pictures Of You/In The Valley Of The Larne | 5 |

ROOFTOP SINGERS

63	Fontana 271 700 TF	Walk Right In/Cool Water	6
63	Fontana 271 702 TF	Tom Cat/Hey Boys	5
63	Fontana 680 999 TL	WALK RIGHT IN (LP)	15
66	Fontana TFL 6065	RAINY RIVER (LP)	15

(see also Tarriers)

ROOM 10

| 65 | Decca F 12249 | I Love My Love/Going Back | 15 |

ROOM 13

| 82 | Woronzow W 002 | Murder Mystery/Need Some Dub (12", p/s) | 25 |

(see also Bevis Frond)

ROOM (1)

| 70 | Deram SML 1073 | PRE-FLIGHT (LP, non-laminated sleeve, white/red label) | 900 |

ROOM (2)

| 80 | Box BOX 001 | Motion/Waiting Room (p/s) | 6 |
| 81 | Box BOX 003 | In Sickness And Health/Bated Breath (p/s) | 5 |

MARY ROOS

| 72 | CBS 7959 | Wake Me Early In The Morning/When You're Singing (Don't Forget) | 6 |

ROOSEVELT SINGERS

| 73 | Sioux SI 025 | Heavy Reggae/HONG GANG: Smoking Wild | 5 |

ROOT BOYS

| 70 | Columbia Blue Beat DB 115 | Please Don't Stop The Wedding/Your Love, Your Love | 10 |

ROOTS

| 78 | Greensleeves GRE 7 | Mash Down/Solja Man Skank | 20 |

ROOTS MANUVA

95	Sound Of Money SNM006	Next Typa Motion/Raw Uncut (12")	25
99	Big Dada BD009	Juggle Tings Proper/Strange Behaviour (12")	12
99	Big Dada BD011	Motion 5000/Skiver's Guide (12")	8
01	Big Dada BD022/7	Witness (1 Hope)/(Walworth Rockers Dub)	20
01	Big Dada BD022	Witness/Son Of The Soil (12")	8
01	Big Dada BD 24	Join The Dots/Ital Versions (12")	8
05	Big Dada BD073P	Colossal Insight (Royskopp remix)	6
99	Big Dada BD010	BRAND NEW SECOND HAND (LP)	12
01	Big Dada BDLP032	RUN COME SAVE ME (LP)	12
02	Big Dada BDLP040	DUB COME SAVE ME (LP)	12

(see also IQ Procedure)

ROOTS MANUVA/MC SKEME

| 96 | Wayward AHP01 | Fever/Herbman Hustling/Life's Funny (12") | 50 |

ROOTS MANUVA/SKITZ

| 96 | Ronin RDP5 | Where My Mind Is At/Blessed Be The Manner/Fuck Being Polite (12") | 12 |

ROOTS RADICS

84	Kingdom KV 8032	Earsay/I'm Not A King	10
79	Form BB1004	OUTERNATIONAL RIDDIM (LP, with Revolutionaries)	30
82	Cha Cha CHALP 012	RADICFATION (LP)	25

GEORGE ROPER & PIPEDREAM

| 70s | Goldspinners GOLD 1 | Manchester United/Tribute To The Fans | 5 |

RO RO

70	Parlophone R 5920	Here I Go Again/What You Gonna Do	20
72	Regal Zonophone RZ 3056	Goin' Round My Head/Down On The Road	10
73	Regal Zonophone RZ 3076	Blackbird/Feel It Coming	10
72	Regal Zono. SRZA 8510	MEET AT THE WATER (LP, textured gatefold sleeve, red/silver label)	200

(see also Ross)

ROSARIES

| 92 | Sarah SARAH 623 | FOREVER EP (p/s, insert) | 10 |

ANDY ROSE

| 58 | London HLU 8761 | Lov-A Lov-A Love/Just Young | 25 |

DAVID ROSE ORCHESTRA

53	MGM SP 1009	Harlem Nocturne (with Woody Herman)/Vanessa	5
56	MGM SP 1181	Forbidden Planet/The Portuguese Washerwomen	5
60	MGM MGM 1110	Bonanza/Gloria's Theme From Butterfield 8	5
62	MGM MGM 1158	The Stripper/Ebb Tide	5

(see also Woody Herman, Rush Adams)

DUSTY ROSE

| 55 | London HLU 8162 | The Birds And The Bees/It Makes Me So Mad | 50 |
| 57 | London RE-U 1078 | COUNTRY SONGS (EP) | 50 |

JOHNNY ROSE

| 60 | Capitol CL 15166 | Linda Lee/The Last One To Know | 18 |

TIM ROSE

67	CBS 202631	Morning Dew/You're Slipping Away From Me	8
68	CBS 3277	I Got A Loneliness/Long Time Man	30
68	CBS 3478	I Guess It's Over/Hello Sunshine	6
68	CBS 3598	Long-Haired Boy/Looking At A Baby	6
69	CBS 4209	Roanoke/Baby You Turn Me On	6
70	CBS 2631	Morning Dew/You're Slipping Away From Me (reissue)	6
70	Capitol CL 15664	I've Gotta Get A Message To You/Ode To An Old Ball	5
74	Dawn DN51085	You've Got To Hide Your Love Away/If I Were A Carpenter	8
67	CBS (S)BPG 63168	TIM ROSE (LP)	25
69	CBS 63636	THROUGH ROSE COLOURED GLASSES (LP)	25
71	Capitol ST 22673	LOVE - A KIND OF HATE STORY (LP)	20
74	Dawn DNLS 3062	TIM ROSE (LP)	18

TONY ROSE

70	Trailer LER 2013	YOUNG HUNTING (LP)	15
72	Trailer LER 2024	UNDER THE GREENWOOD TREE (LP)	15

ROSE GARDEN

68	Atlantic 584 163	Next Plane To London/Flower Town	10

ROSEHIPS

87	Subway Organisation SUBWAY 10	Room In Your Heart/Thrilled To Bits/Dead End (foldaround p/s with insert in poly bag)	10
87	Subway Organisation SUBWAY 10T	Room In Your Heart/Middle Of Next Week/Thrilled To Bits/So Naive/ Just Another Girl/Dead End (12", p/s)	12
87	Subway Organisation SUBWAY 16	I Shouldn't Have To Say/Loophole/Wastin' My Time/All Mine/ Sad As Sunday (p/s, with insert)	8
87	Subway Organisation SUBWAY 16T	I Shouldn't Have To Say/Loophole/Wastin' My Time/All Mine/ Sad As Sunday (12", p/s with insert)	12
88	Sweet William BILLY 001	Ask Johnny Dee/FAT TULIPS: You Opened My Eyes (33rpm flexi, p/s w/insert)	12

ROSEMARY'S CHILDREN

86	él GPO 012	Southern Fields/Whatever Happened To Alice	12
87	Cherry Red MRED 077	KINGS AND PRINCES EP (12", p/s)	12

LEONARD ROSENMAN ORCHESTRA

57	London HA-P 2040	A TRIBUTE TO JAMES DEAN (LP)	20

ROSE OF AVALANCHE

86	Fire BLAZE 14	Velveteen/Who Cares (p/s)	6
89	Avalanche AVE4T	A PEACE INSIDE (LP)	20

ROSE OF VICTORY

83	No Future OI 24	Suffragette City/Overdrive (p/s)	12

(see also Blitz)

ROSES ARE RED

79	Posthumous Petal PET 1	Can't Understand/Your Love Is Like A Ballistic Missile (p/s)	40

ROSE TATTOO

78	Carrere CAL 125	Bad Boy For Love/Tramp (p/s)	6
78	Carrere CAL 125	Bad Boy For Love/Tramp (12", p/s)	8
78	Epic EPC 9411	Rock 'N' Roll Outlaw/One Of The Boys (p/s)	5
80	Repeal PRS 2724	Release Legalise/COL PATERSON: Bong On Aussie (500 only)	40
81	Mirage PR 405	Rock 'N' Roll Is King/Sidewalk Sally (12", promo only)	10
81	Carrere CAR 200P	Rock 'N' Roll Outlaw/Remedy (picture disc)	5
81	Carrere CAR 220	Assault And Battery/Astra Wally//One Of The Boys/Manzil Madness (double pack, gatefold p/s)	5
83	Carrere CARP 263	It's Gonna Work Itself Out/Fightin' Sons (picture disc)	5
82	Albert Productions AP 854	We Can't Be Beaten/Fightin' Sons	5
82	Albert Productions AP 898	Branded/Dead Set	5
82	Albert Productions AP 1007	It's Gonna Work Itself Out/Sydney Girls	5
81	Carrere CAL 127	ASSAULT AND BATTERY (LP)	12

ROSETTA STONE

95	Whatever Got.H 000000 Ru 12	GENDER CONFUSION (CD, 500 only first pressing)	20

ROSIE (& ORIGINALS)

61	London HLU 9266	Angel Baby/Give Me Love (as Rosie & Originals)	30
61	Coral Q 72426	Lonely Blue Nights/We'll Have A Chance	40

ROSKO

70	Trojan TR 7758	Al Capone/Kaiser Bill	7
70	Philips 6009 070	Grab The Rabbit/Mohammed Ben Ali	15

(see also Emperor Rosko & Power Pack)

EMPEROR ROSKO & POWER PACK

69	Polydor 56316	Opposite Lock Parts 1 & 2	10
71	B&C CB 148	The Customs Man/Take It In Your Stride	12

(see also Rosko, Power Pack, Pleasure Garden)

FRANK ROSOLINO SEXTET

54	Capitol KC 65001	That Old Black Magic/Yo Yo	5

ROSS

74	RSO 2394 127	ROSS (LP)	12
75	RSO 2394 144	THE PIT AND THE PENDULUM (LP)	12

(see also Indian Summer, Gary Pickford-Hopkins, Ro Ro)

ANNIE ROSS

54	Esquire 10-344	Jackie/The Song Is You (78, with Quincy Jones)	10
55	Decca F 10514	Mama (He Treats Your Daughter Mean)/The Fish	12
55	Decca F 10637	I Want You To Be My Baby (with Tony Crombie)/TONY CROMBIE & HIS ORCHESTRA: Three Little Words	6
56	Decca F 10680	Cry Me A River/Only You	10
63	Ember EMB S 182	Bye Bye Blues/A Lot Of Livin' To Do	10
72	Columbia DB 8912	Straight On Till Morning/God Bless The Child	10
57	Pye Jazz NJE 1035	NOCTURNE FOR VOCALIST (EP)	60

54	Esquire EP 1	WITH THE TEACHO WILTSHIRE GROUP (EP)	30
58	Pieces Of Eight PEP 604	WITH THE TONY CROMBIE FOURTET (EP)	12
64	Transatlantic TRAEP 112	GO TO THE WALL (EP)	15
57	Nixa Jazz NJT 504	ANNIE BY CANDLELIGHT (10" LP)	125
59	Vogue LAE 12203	ANNIE ROSS (LP, with Gerry Mulligan Quintet)	60
60	Vogue LAE 12233	A GASSER (LP, with Zoot Sims)	60
63	Ember NR 5008	A HANDFULL OF SONGS (LP)	75
63	Transatlantic TRA 107	LOGUERRHYTHMS (LP)	60
65	Golden Guinea GGL 0316	ANNIE BY CANDLELIGHT (LP, reissue)	60
66	Xtra XTRA 1049	ANNIE ROSS WITH THE TONY KINSEY QUINTET (LP)	60
71	Decca SKL 5099	YOU AND ME BABY (LP)	20

(see also Tony Crombie, Dave Lambert, Gerry Mulligan, Zoot Sims, Jack Parnell, Teacho Wiltshire, Art Blakey, Quincy Jones)

DAVID ROSS
58	Oriole CB 1416	Pit-A-Patter Boom Boom/Everybody's Got A Girl But Tino (as Dave Ross)	6

DIANA ROSS
71	Tamla Motown TMG 792	Surrender/I'm A Winner (green/white demo, stereo, has YTMG on label and etched into dead wax))	15
71	Tamla Motown TMG 792	Surrender/I'm A Winner (stereo)	10
70	Tamla Motown TMG 743	Reach Out And Touch (Somebody's Hand)/Dark Side Of The World	6
70	Tamla Motown TMG 751	Ain't No Mountain High Enough/Can't It Wait Until Tomorrow	6
71	Tamla Motown TMG 768	Remember Me/How About You	6
71	Tamla Motown TMG 781	I'm Still Waiting/Reach Out I'll Be There	6
71	Tamla Motown TMG 792	Surrender/I'm A Winner (mono)	6
70	T. Motown STML 11159	DIANA ROSS (LP)	12
70	T. Motown STML 11178	EVERYTHING IS EVERYTHING (LP)	12
71	T. Motown STML 11193	I'M STILL WAITING (LP)	12

(see also Supremes)

DIANA ROSS & MICHAEL JACKSON
78	MCA MCA 396	Ease On Down The Road/QUINCY JONES: Poppy Girls (p/s)	5
78	MCA MCAT 12-396	Ease On Down The Road (U.S. Version)/THE WIZ: Poppy Girls (12", p/s)	8

(see also [Diana Ross &] Supremes, Michael Jackson, Quincy Jones)

DOCTOR (ISAIAH) ROSS
66	Blue Horizon LP 1	THE FLYING EAGLE (LP, 99 copies only)	1500
66	Xtra XTRA 1038	DOCTOR ROSS (LP, reissue of "The Flying Eagle")	40
66	Bounty BY 6020	CALL THE DOCTOR (LP)	60
72	Polydor 2460 169	LIVE AT MONTREUX (LP)	30
75	Big Bear BEAR 2	THE HARMONICA BOSS (LP)	25

ERROL ROSS
80	Carrere CAR 149	Round And Round In Circles/Reggae Music Of Today (p/s)	6

GENE ROSS
58	Parlophone R 4434	Endless Sleep/The Only One	25
58	Parlophone R 4434	Endless Sleep/The Only One (78)	10

JACK ROSS
62	London HLD 9534	Cinderella/Margarita	6

JACKIE ROSS
64	Pye International 7N 25259	Selfish One/Everything But Love	60
64	Pye International 7N 25259	Selfish One/Everything But Love (DJ copy)	100
64	Chess CRS 8003	Jerk And Twine/New Lover	40
64	Chess CRS 8003	Jerk And Twine/New Lover (DJ copy)	70

JOAN ROSS
70	Crab CRAB 61	Band Of Gold/HAMMERS: Midnight Sunshine	10

JOE E. ROSS
64	Columbia 335X1710	LOVE SONGS FROM A COP (LP)	18

RONNIE ROSS
58	Parlophone PMC 1079	DOUBLE EVENT (LP)	100
61	Ember EMB 3323	STOMPIN' WITH (LP)	80
65	Ember FA 2023	THE SWINGIN' SOUNDS OF THE JAZZ MAKERS (LP, with Allan Ganley)	60
69	Fontana SFJL 915	CLEOPATRA'S NEEDLE (LP)	200

(see also Bill Le Sage)

SONNY ROSS
71	Mojo 2093 001	Alakazam/The Piper Must Be Paid	10

SPENCER ROSS
60	Philips PB 992	Tracy's Theme/Thanksgiving Day Parade	6
60	London HLX 9141	Theme Of A Lonely Evening/Bobby's Blues	7

T.T. ROSS
75	Dip DL 5079	Single Girl/Funny What Love Can Do	5
76	Dip DL 5104	Last Date/I Am Sorry	5
76	Lucky LY 6000	No Charge/When I Was A Little Girl	5
76	Lucky LY 6014	Baby Why/TOUGH GANG: Part 2	5
76	Lucky LY 6017	Misty Blue/Version	5
76	House Of Eve 001	Let The World Go Away/Part 2	5
76	House Of Eve 002	Piece Of My Heart/Part 2	5
77	Lovers Rock CJ 622	I Will/I Will Dub	5

JOHN ROSSALL
75	Bel 1411	I Was Only Dreaming/Every Night And Every Day	6
75	Bell 1428	You'll Never know/Don't Beleive A Word	6

LEON ROSSELSON
62	Topic TOP 77	SONGS FOR CITY SQUARES (EP)	15
70	Acorn CF 206	SONGS FOR SCEPTICAL CIRCLES (EP)	20
66	BOUNTY BY 6029	SONGS FOR SCEPTICAL CIRCLES (LP)	100
71	Trailer LER 3015	THE WORD IS HUGGA MUGGA CHUGGA HUMBUGGA BOOM CHIT (LP, with Roy Bailey & Martin Carthy)	20
75	Acorn CF 249	PALACES OF GOLD (LP)	18

MINT VALUE £

| 75 | Acorn CF 251 | THAT'S NOT THE WAY IT'S GOT TO BE (LP, with Roy Bailey) | 18 |

(see also Three City Four, Roy Bailey)

NITA ROSSI

65	Piccadilly 7N 35258	Every Little Day Now/Untrue Unfaithful	40
66	Piccadilly 7N 35307	Here I Go Again/Something To Give	40
66	Piccadilly 7N 35307	Here I Go Again/Something To Give (DJ copy)	70
66	Piccadilly 7N 35354	The Daddy Christmas Song/Our Love Was Meant To Be	8
67	Piccadilly 7N 35384	Misty Blue/Come Around	12

(see also Status Quo, Bernie Frost, Boz Frost, Mickey Jupp, Mitchell/Coe Mysteries, Demis Roussos, Tokyo Olympics)

(FRANCIS) ROSSI & (BERNARD) FROST

85	Vertigo VER 17/FROS 1	Modern Romance (I Want To Fall In Love Again)/I Wonder Why (p/s)	5
85	Vertigo VERX 17/FROSX 1	Modern Romance (I Want To Fall In Love Again)/(Extended Remix)/I Wonder Why (Extended Remix) (12", p/s)	10
85	Vertigo VER 24	Jealousy/Where Are You Now? (p/s)	6
85	Vertigo VERX 24	Jealousy/Where Are You Now?/That's Alright (12", p/s)	12

JOHN HENRY ROSTILL

| 71 | Columbia DB 8794 | Funny Old World/Green Apples | 30 |

(see also Shadows)

STEVE ROSTRON

| 74 | Sweet Folk & Country SFA 009 | NO STRANGER'S FACE (LP) | 30 |

VINCENT ROSWELL

| 82 | Water Mount MW 001 | Apple Of My Eye/Going To A Dance (12") | 100 |

NINO ROTA

| 72 | Paramount PARA 3023 | Love Theme Form "The Godfather"/The Godfather Waltz | 6 |

ROTARY CONNECTION

68	Chess CRS 8072	Soul Man/Ruby Tuesday	6
69	Chess CRS 8103	The Weight/Respect	6
70	Chess CRS 8106	Want You To Know/Memory Band	10
68	Chess CRL 4538	ROTARY CONNECTION (LP)	15
69	Chess CRL(S) 4547	ALADDIN (LP)	15
69	Chess CRLS 4551	SONGS (LP)	15

ROTATION

| 70 | Polydor 2041-037 | Ra-Ta-Ta/Rotation | 15 |

ROTEN ROSEN

| 87 | Virgin VS 1031 | Itsy Bitsy Teenie Weenie Honolulu-Strand Bikini (German Version) Itsy Bitsy Teenie Weenie Honolulu-Strand Bikini (English Version) (p/s) | 100 |
| 87 | Virgin VST 1031 | Itsy Bitsy Teenie Weenie Honolulu-Strand Bikini (German Version) Itsy Bitsy Teenie Weenie Honolulu-Strand Bikini (English Version)/Agent X (12", p/s) | 150 |

DAVID LEE ROTH

| 86 | Warner Bros W 8656P | Yankee Rose/Shy Boy (pin-up shaped picture disc) | 10 |

(see also Van Halen)

ROTHCHILDS

| 66 | Decca F 12411 | You've Made Your Choice/It's Love | 10 |
| 66 | Decca F 12488 | Artificial City/I Let Her Go | 15 |

LINDA ROTHWELL

| 73 | Chapter One SCH 180 | Write Me A Letter/Tell Me | 8 |

ROOTS TRUNKS AND BRANCHES

| 79 | Splendor Heights WJWX 1945/2 | Just The Way You Are/Chicken Disco (12") | 20 |

ROTTEN TO THE CORE

| 73 | Pye 7N 45257 | Don't Let Me Wait Too Long/Let's Do It One More Time | 10 |

ROUGE

| 78 | SRT SRTSCUS 78104 | Have You Seen Gene (no p/s) | 75 |

ROUGH DIAMOND

| 90 | Bedrock BR 1 | Woman's Touch (p/s) | 12 |

ROUGH ELEMENT

| 92 | UAR UAR120020 | The Elements/Breaking The Silence/Unbound Rage (remix) (EP) | 60 |
| 94 | UAR 003 | Reflex Reaction/Criminal Behaviour (12") | 15 |

ROUGH JUSTICE

| 80s | Rough Justice RJ 001 | MILLION TO ONE (EP, p/s) | 200 |

ROUGH RIDERS

| 74 | Rare Earth RES 118 | Hot California Beach/Do You See Me | 20 |

ROULETTES

62	Pye 7N 15467	Hully Gully Slip 'N' Slide/La Bamba	15
63	Parlophone R 5072	Soon You'll Be Leaving Me/Tell Tale Tit	15
64	Parlophone R 5110	Bad Time/Can You Go	20
64	Parlophone R 5148	I'll Remember Tonight/You Don't Love Me	15
64	Parlophone R 5218	Stubborn Kind Of Fellow/Somebody	25
65	Parlophone R 5278	I Hope He Breaks Your Heart/Find Out The Truth	15
65	Parlophone R 5382	The Long Cigarette/Junk	25
66	Parlophone R 5419	The Tracks Of My Tears/Jackpot	20
66	Oak RGJ 205	I Can't Stop (1-sided, with p/s)	250
66	Oak RGJ 206	I Can't Stop (1-sided)	150
66	Parlophone R 5461	I Can't Stop/Yesterday, Today And Tomorrow	20
67	Fontana TF 822	Rhyme Boy, Rhyme/Airport People	40
67	Fontana TF 876	Help Me To Help Myself/To A Taxi Driver	20
65	Parlophone PMC 1257	STAKES AND CHIPS (LP, laminated front cover, flipbacks, black/yellow label with "Sold in the U.K..." text)	500

(see also Adam Faith, Unit 4 + 2, Argent)

ROUND ROBIN

| 64 | London HLU 9908 | Kick That Little Foot Sally Ann/Slauson Party | 30 |

64	London HLU 9908	Kick That Little Foot Sally Ann/Slauson Party (DJ copy)	70

ROUNDTABLE
69	Jay Boy BOY 18	Saturday Gigue/Scarborough Fair	20
69	Jay Boy JSL 2	SPINNING WHEEL (LP)	40

CHARLIE ROUSE QUINTET
60	Riverside/Jazzland JLP19	TAKIN' CARE OF BUSINESS (LP)	15

DEMIS ROUSSOS
80	Mercury MER 25	Sorry/Love Is The Answer (p/s, A-side written by & featuring Francis Rossi/ Bernie Frost)	5

(see also Aphrodite's Child, Forminx, Rossi & Frost)

ROUTERS
62	Warner Bros WB 77	Let's Go (Pony)/Mashy	10
63	Warner Bros WB 91	Make It Snappy/Half Time	10
63	Warner Bros WB 97	Stingray/Snap Happy	10
63	Warner Bros WB 108	Big Band/A Ooga	12
64	Warner Bros WB 139	Stamp And Shake/Ah Ya	12
73	Warner Bros K 16156	Let's Go/Mashy (reissue)	5
63	Warner Bros WM/WS 8126	LET'S GO! WITH THE ROUTERS (LP, features Scott Walker)	40
64	Warner Bros WM/WS 8144	PLAY 1963'S GREAT INSTRUMENTALS (LP)	25
65	Warner Bros WM/WS 8162	CHARGE! (LP)	30

(see also Scott Walker)

JONATHAN ROUTH
57	Nixa NPT 19016	CANDID MIKE (10" LP)	12
62	Pye NPL 18077	CANDID CAMERA (LP)	12

ROVERS
55	Capitol CL 14283	Ichi-Bon Tami, Dachi/Why Oh-h (Why Do You Lie To Me?)	500
55	Capitol CL 14283	Ichi-Bon Tami, Dachi/Why Oh-h (Why Do You Lie To Me?) (78)	90

ROVING KIND
65	Decca F 12264	Ain't It True/Don't Tell Me The Time	8
66	Decca F 12381	Lies A Million/How Many Times	7

ROWAN BROTHERS
72	CBS 1125	All Together/Lady Of Laughter	20

ROWAN & MARTIN
69	CBS 63490	ROWAN AND MARTIN'S LAUGH-IN (LP)	12
69	Atlantic 588 151	ROWAN AND MARTIN AT WORK (LP)	15

ROWDIES
78	Birds Nest BN 109	A.C.A.B. (All Coppers Are Bastards)/Negative Malfunction/Freeze Out	50
79	Teenage Depression TD 1/2	She's No Angel/Had Me A Real Good Time (p/s)	20

(see also Boys, Lurkers, Steve Sharp & Cleancuts)

KEITH ROWE
77	Black Swan WIP 6405	Groovy Situation/Groovy Dub	15
77	Black Swan BS 6	Groovy Situation/Groovy Dub	20
81	Seven Leaves SLD 02	Groovy Situation/Groovy Dub	15

NORMIE ROWE
66	Polydor 56132	It's Not Easy/Mary Mary	15
66	Polydor 56144	Ain't Nobody Home/Ooh La La	6
67	Polydor 56159	Going Home/I Don't Care (Just Take Me There) (in p/s)	10
67	Polydor 56159	Going Home/I Don't Care (Just Take Me There)	5
67	Polydor 56169	But I Know/Sunshine Secret	10

MAJOR ROWELY
65	Stateside SS 438	There's A Riot Going On/Do It The Right Way	15

JEFF ROWENA FIVE
63	Oriole CB 1797	Dance Baby Dance/Love Me once Again	10

CHERRY ROWLAND
63	Fontana TF 420	Nobody But Me/Boys	12
74	Decca F 13491	Here Is Where The Love Is/I Can Give You Back Yourself	6

(see also Cherry Roland)

JACKIE ROWLAND
72	Sioux SI 015	Indian Reservation/JUNIOR SMITH: I'm In A Dancing Mood	5
72	Sioux SI 022	Lonely Man/JOE MANSANO: The Trial Of Pama Dice	15

(see also Joe Higgs)

KEVIN ROWLAND
88	Mercury DEXYB 1412	Young Man/The Way You Look Tonight/Even When I Hold You/Walk Away (12", gatefold p/s)	8
99	Creation CRECD 216	MY BEAUTY (CD)	20

(see also Dexys Midnight Runners)

STEVE ROWLAND
67	Fontana TF 844	So Sad/I See Red	40

(see also Family Dogg)

JOHN ROWLES
68	MCA HUP 335	JOHN ROWLES (LP)	15
69	MCA MKPS 2001	THAT LOVIN' FEELING (LP)	12

ROX
82	Teenteeze ROX 100	HOT LOVE IN THE CITY (Hot Love In The City/Do Ya Feel Like Lovin'/Love Ya Like A Diamond (EP)	25
83	MFN 12KUT 103	KRAZY KUTZ (12" EP)	8
83	Music For Nations MFN 11	VIOLENT BREED (LP, with innersleeve)	15

ROXY MUSIC
72	Island WIP 6144	Virginia Plain/The Numberer (initially pink labels, later orange)	5
73	Island WIP 6159	Pyjamarama/The Pride And The Pain	5

Alvin ROY & THE SARATOGA JAZZ BAND

74	Island WIP 6173	Street Life/Hula Kula	5
74	Island WIP 6208	All I Want Is You/Your Application's Failed	5
78	Polydor/EG 2001 756	Do The Strand/Editions Of You (12", p/s)	8
86	E.G. EGOX 26	Love Is The Drug/Let's Stick Together (12", p/s, promo only)	15
72	Island ILPS 9200	ROXY MUSIC (LP, laminated gatefold sleeve, pink rim palm tree label)	20
73	Island ILPS 9232	FOR YOUR PLEASURE (LP, laminated gatefold, pink rim/palm tree label)	15
79	Polydor/E.G. EGPD 001	MANIFESTO (LP, picture disc, mispress, 1 side plays Gordon Giltrap's Fear Of The Dark LP)	12
81	Polydor/E.G. EGBS 001	THE FIRST SEVEN ALBUMS (7-LP box set plus insert)	80
81	Polydor/E.G. EGBS 001	THE FIRST SEVEN ALBUMS (7-cassette box set)	15

(see also Brian Eno, Bryan Ferry, Andy Mackay, Phil Manzanera, Dumbelles, 801, Fripp & Eno)

ALVIN ROY & THE SARATOGA JAZZ BAND
61	Interdisc INT 45001	Yogi/Broken Promises	5

D ROY BAND
70s	D Roy MFLP 1001	ORTHODOX DUB (white label LP in stamped, plain white sleeve)	150

DEREK ROY
57	Oriole CB 1415	Derek Roy's All-Star Party (with Bob Monkhouse, Richard Murdoch, Jon Pertwee, Ted Ray & others)	8

(see also Jon Pertwee, Bob Monkhouse)

HUGH ROY/U ROY
70	Supreme SUP 211	Double Attack/Puzzle	15
70	Explosion EX 2040	Whisper A Little Prayer (actually by Audley Rollins)/ Rain A Fall (actually by Melanie)	15
70	Punch PH 34	Scandal/Son Of The Wise	12
70	Duke Reid DR 2509	Wake The Town/Big Boy And Teacher	18
70	Duke Reid DR 2510	Rule The Nation/NORA DEAN: Ay Ay Ay Ay	20
70	Duke Reid DR 2513	Wear You To The Ball (with John Holt)/EARL LINDO: The Ball	20
70	Duke Reid DR 2514	You'll Never Get Away/TOMMY McCOOK QUINTET: Rock Away	12
70	Duke Reid DR 2515	Version Galore/TOMMY McCOOK: Nehru	25
71	Duke Reid DR 2516	Testify/TOMMY McCOOK: Super Soul	12
71	Duke Reid DR 2517	Tom Drunk (with Hopeton Lewis)/TOMMY McCOOK: Wailing	12
71	Duke Reid DR 2518	True True/On The Beach	12
71	Duke Reid DR 2519	Flashing My Whip/Do It Right	18
71	Treasure Isle TI 7059	Drive Home (Parts 1 & 2) (with Hopeton Lewis)	15
71	Treasure Isle TI 7062	Behold/Way Back Home (with Tommy McCook)	12
71	Treasure Isle TI 7064	Everybody Bawlin'/Ain't That Loving You	15
71	Upsetter US 375	Earthquake/Suspicious Minds	20
71	Duke DU 105	Love I Tender/JOYA LANDIS: When The Lights Are Low	12
71	Duke Reid DR 2517	Tom Drunk/Wailing (as U Roy, B-side actually by Tommy McCook)	12
72	G.G. GG 4532	Way Down South/BILLY DYCE: Be My Guest	12
72	Duke DU 137	Live It Up/DENNIS BROWN: Baby Don't Do It	12
72	Jackpot JP 806	Two Ton Gulleto/Version	10
72	Dynamic DYN 448	Festival Wise/Festival Wise Part 2	8
72	Banana BA 367	Keep On Running/LARRY'S ALL STARS: Version	12
72	Grape GR 3026	On Top The Peak/TYPHOON ALLSTARS: Race Attack	8
72	Pama PM 835	Way Down South/BILLY DYCE: Be My Guest	12
72	Punch PH 104	Nannyscrank (title actually "Nanny Skank")/PITTSBURG ALLSTARS: Scank Version	12
72	Green Door GD 4034	Hudson Affair/KEITH HUDSON: Hot Stick - Version	18
72	Trojan TR 7884	Hat Trick/Wet Vision	10
73	Green Door GD 4052	King Tubby's Special/Here Come The Heartaches	12
73	Gayfeet GS 210	Hard Feeling/Regular Style	12
73	Duke DU 157	Higher The Mountain/OLD BOYS INC.: Version	8
73	Harry J. HJ 6651	Treasure Isle Skank/Words Of Wisdom	12
73	Lord Koos KOO 25	Call On I (with D. Wilson)/DJ Special	8
75	Virgin VS 138	Runaway Girl/Chalice In The Palace	6
76	Soulfood SF 001	High Priest/London City Rock	15
71	Trojan TBL 161	VERSION GALORE (LP, as U Roy)	30
73	Attack ATLP 1006	U ROY (LP, as U Roy)	25
75	Virgin V2048	DREAD IN A BABYLON (LP)	20
76	Virgin V 2059	NATTY REBEL (LP)	20
77	Virgin V2092	RASTA AMBASSADOR (LP)	20
79	Virgin Frontline FLX 4004	WITH WORDS OF WISDOM (LP)	20

(see also Jeff Barnes, Melodians, Delroy Wilson)

HUGH ROY JUNIOR
71	Big BG 329	Papacito/RUPIE EDWARDS: I'm Gonna Live Some Life	12
71	Supreme SUP 211	Double Attack/MURPHY'S ALL STARS: Puzzle	12
72	Ashanti ASH 405	King Of The Road/ROOSEVELT ALL STARS: Version	8
72	Jackpot JP 806	Two Ton Guletto/Version	8

I ROY
71	Moodisc MU 3509	Musical Pleasure/JO JO BENNETT: Hot Pop	15
71	Moodisc MU 3510	Heart Don't Leap (as I. Roy & Dennis Walks)/ DENNIS WALKS & MUDIE'S ALLSTARS: Snow Bird	15
71	Moodisc MU 3512	Let Me Tell You Boy (with Ebony Sisters)/MUDIE'S ALLSTARS: Version	15
71	Moodisc HM 104	The Drifter (with Dennis Walks)/JO JO BENNETT: Snowbird	18
72	Green Door GD 4030	Hot Bomb (with Jumpers)/JUMPERS: The Bomb	12
72	Soferno B SOF 001	No Money/Version	10
72	Green Door GD 4044	Make Love/STAGE: Tic Toc Bill	10
73	Pyramid PYR 7001	Tip From The Prince/Fat Beef Skank	15
73	Attack ATT 8050	Space Flight/JERRY LEWIS: Burning Wire	15
73	Downtown DT 503	Blackman's Time/High Jacking	18
73	Downtown DT 519	Clapper's Tail/Live And Learn	18
73	Duke DU 156	Buck And The Preacher/PETE WESTON ALLSTARS: Preacher - Version	12
73	Smash SMA 2337	The Magnificent Seven/Leggo Beast	12
73	Smash SMA 2338	Rose Of Sheron/Slip Out	15
73	Techniques TE 926	Pauper And The King/GREGORY ISAACS: Loving Pauper	15
73	Techniques TE 930	Monkey Fashion/Medley Mood	10
73	Ackee ACK 503	Great Great Great (with Ken Parker)/RUPIE EDWARDS ALLSTARS: Version	22
73	Ackee ACK 510	Sound Education/AUGUSTUS PABLO: Cinderella In Black	18

73	Harry J HJ-6655	Musical Drum Sound/NOW GENERATION: Musical Drum - Version 12
73	Pama PM 854	Cowtown Skank/AUGUSTUS PABLO: Cowtown Skank Version 12
74	Atra ATRA 017	Yah Ma Ride/SWEET HARMONY: Mexican Rockin' 12
74	Ashanti ASH 412	Mood For Love (Parts 1 & 2) 12
75	Bullet BU 551	Step Right Up/ANDY'S ALLSTARS: Banjo Serenade 8
75	Lucky DL 5098	I Man Time/Version 12
75	Third World TW 015	Mr Benwood Dick/Mad Mad Hatter 8
75	Third World TW 85	New York City/CORNELL CAMPBELL: Blessed Are They 8
75	Student STU 1001	Jazz Bo Have Fe Run/Version 12
76	Dip DL 5107	Padlock/Lock And Key (copies also exist with Lucky label) 10
77	ATA ATA 1005	Roots Man/Observer Mix 10
77	Observer OB 002	Jamaican Girl/River Jordan/ OBSERVER IN FINE STYLE: First Cut/Second Cut (12", p/s) 25
78	Jungle Beat JBDC 805	Troubles/I Man (12" with FREDDY CLARKE) 80
78	GG's GG 011	Natty Get Ready/Version 6
79	Virgin Front Line FLS 124 12	Fire In A Wire/Hill And Gully (12") 12
70s	Nationwide NW 005	Tea Pot/Tea Cup 12
73	Trojan TRLS 63	PRESENTING I ROY (LP, original issue with "12 Neasden Lane" address and rough orange/white paper labels) 35
74	Trojan TRLS 71	HELL AND SORROW (LP, original issue with "12 Neasden Lane" address and rough orange/white paper labels) 30
74	Trojan TRLS 91	THE MANY MOODS OF I ROY (LP, original issue with "12 Neasden Lane" address and rough orange/white paper labels) 30
75	Grounation GROL 504	TRUTH & RIGHTS (LP) 25
76	Caroline CA 2011	CRISIS TIME (LP) 25
76	Klik 9020	DREAD BALDHEAD (LP) 45
77	Justice JUS LP 08	CAN'T CONQUER RASTA (LP) 30
78	Virgin Frontline FL 1028	TEN COMANDMENTS (LP) 15
78	Third World TWS 930	THE GODFATHER (LP) 20
77	Virgin V 2075	MUSICAL SHARK ATTACK (LP) 20
77	Virgin Frontline VF 1001	HEART OF A LION (LP) 20

(see also Keith Hudson & I Roy)

LEE ROY
| 65 | Island WI 251 | Oh Ee Baby/My Loving Baby Come Back ....10 |

LITTLE ROY
70	Bullet BU 445	Keep Trying/THE MATADORS: Version II 10
70	Camel CA 43	Scrooge/In The Days Of Old 12
70	Camel CA 46	You Run Come/THE LITTLE ROYS: Skank King (actually "Skank Me" by Little Roy) 12
70	Camel CA 52	Fight Them/Dreadlock 12
71	Escort ERT 850	Yester-Me Yester-You Yesterday/MATADOR ALL-STARS: Yes Sir 10
71	Punch PH 75	Hard Fighter/COUNT OSSIE: Back To Africa Version 12

(see also Roy & Joy, Little Roys)

MAD ROY
70	Banana BA 324	Nanny Version (actually by Dennis Alcapone)/BIGGER D: Freedom Version 20
71	Banana BA 326	Home Version (actually by Dennis Alcapone)/SOUND DIMENSION: One Time 15
71	Banana BA 327	Universal Love/ROLAND ALPHONSO: Shelly Belly 15
71	Banana BA 328	Duppy Serenade/Sunshine Version (both sides actually by Dennis Alcapone) 12

ROY REDMOND
| 67 | Warner Bros WB 2075 | Good Day Sunshine/That Old Time Feeling ....20 |

U ROY JUNIOR
72	Duke Reid DR 2520	Rock To The Beat/Love Is Not A Gamble (both actually by Dennis Alcapone) 12
72	Attack ATT 8030	This Is A Pepper (as U Roy Junior)/JOHN HOLT: Justice 12
72	Sioux SI 024	The Wedding (as U Roy Junior)/LLOYD'S ALL STARS: Buttercup 8
73	Randy's RAN 532	Froggie (as U Roy Junior)/RHYTHM RULERS: Version 10
73	Techniques TE 928	Aunt Kereba (as U Roy Junior)/DON RECO: Waterloo Rock (B-side actually by Reco Rodriquez) 12

(see also Hugh Roy, Dennis Alcapone, Sir Harry, Shorty Perry, Heptones, Herman Chin-Loy)

BILLY JOE ROYAL
62	Oriole CB 1751	Never In A Hundred Years/We Haven't A Moment To Lose 20
65	CBS 201802	Down In The Boondocks/Oh! What A Night 15
65	CBS 201983	You Make Me Feel Like A Man/I've Got To Be Somebody 6
65	CBS 202009	I Knew You When/Steal Away 6
66	CBS 202052	It's A Good Time/Don't Wait Up For Me Mama 6
66	CBS 202087	Heart's Desire/Everbody's Gotta Cry 40
66	CBS 202087	Heart's Desire/Everbody's Gotta Cry (DJ copy) 75
66	CBS 202400	High On A Hilltop/I'm Gonna Get Right Tonight 6
66	Atlantic 584 002	Never In A Hundred Years/We Haven't A Moment To Lose (reissue) 8
67	CBS 202548	Yo Yo/We Tried 10
67	CBS 3044	Hush/Watching From The Bandstand 8
68	CBS 3644	Storybook Children/Just Between Me And You 8
68	CBS 3859	Gabriel/Movies In My Mind 7
69	CBS 4470	Cherry Hill Park/Helping Hand 7
71	CBS 7302	Tulsa/Pick Up The Pieces 7
72	CBS 7727	We Go Back/Colorado Rain 7
66	CBS BPG 62590	INTRODUCING BILLY JOE ROYAL (LP) 25

BOBBY ROYAL
| 63 | HMV POP 1253 | Big Big Star/Little Word Of Love ....12 |
| 65 | Decca F 12097 | Within My Lonely Heart/When I Found You ....10 |

ROYAL HOLIDAYS
| 58 | London HLU 8722 | Margaret/I'm Sorry (I Did You Wrong) ....125 |
| 58 | London HLU 8722 | Margaret/I'm Sorry (I Did You Wrong) (78) ....50 |

ROBBIE ROYAL
| 65 | Mercury MF 923 | Only Me/I Don't Need You ....8 |
| 65 | Decca F 12097 | Within My Lonely Heart/When I Found You ....6 |

ROYAL BLUES
| 69 | Pye 7N 17670 | Mountain Of Love/Wishful Thinking ....6 |
| 69 | Pye 7N 17732 | Mendocino/Hi-Lili Hi-Lo ....5 |

ROYALETTES

| 69 | Pye 7N 17769 | Proud Mary/Sunny Girl Friend | 6 |
| 69 | Pye 7N 17847 | High As A Mountain/Wildwood Flower | 5 |

ROYALETTES

65	MGM MGM 1272	Poor Boy/Watch What Happens	15
65	MGM MGM 1279	It's Gonna Take A Miracle/Out Of Sight Out Of Mind	25
65	MGM MGM 1279	It's Gonna Take A Miracle/Out Of Sight Out Of Mind (DJ copy)	55
65	MGM MGM 1292	I Want To Meet Him/Never Again	18
66	MGM MGM 1302	You Bring Me Down/Only When You're Lonely	20
66	MGM MGM 1324	It's A Big Mistake/I Want To Meet Him	15
68	Big T BIG 106	River Of Tears/Something Wonderful	15
66	MGM MGM-C 8028	THE ELEGANT SOUND OF THE ROYALETTES (LP)	100

ROYAL GUARDSMEN

67	Stateside SS 2010	The Return Of The Red Baron/Sweetmeats Slide	7
67	Stateside S(S)L 10202	SNOOPY VS THE RED BARON (LP)	20
68	London HA-P/SH-P 8351	THE RETURN OF THE RED BARON (LP)	20

JAMES ROYAL (& HAWKS)

65	Parlophone R 5290	She's About A Mover/Black Cloud (as James Royal & Hawks)	25
65	Parlophone R 5383	Work Song/I Can't Stand It	35
67	CBS 202525	Call My Name/When It Comes To My Baby	20
67	CBS 2739	It's All In The Game/Green Days	7
68	CBS 2959	Take Me Like I Am/Sitting In The Station	5
68	CBS 3232	I Can't Stand It/Little Bit Of Rain	30
68	CBS 3450	Hey Little Boy/Thru' The Love	25
68	CBS 3624	A Woman Called Sorrow/Fire	20
69	CBS 3797	Time Hangs On My Mind/Anna-Lee	6
69	CBS 3915	House Of Jack/Which Way To Nowhere	30
69	CBS 4139	I've Something Bad On My Mind/She's Independent	6
69	CBS 4181	That Kind Of Girl/Will You Be Staying After Sunday	6
69	CBS 4463	Send Out Love/I've Lost You	30
70	CBS 5032	And Soon The Darkness/I'm Going Home	6
70	Carnaby CNS 4021	Carolina/Big Heat On The Loose	6
71	Carnaby 6151 002	Carolina/A Woman Called Sorrow	8
72	Carnaby 6151 006	Two Of Us/Who Are We (with Liz Christian)	5
69	CBS 63780	CALL MY NAME (LP)	30
70	Carnaby CNLS 6008	ONE WAY (LP)	50
72	Carnaby 6302 011	THE LIGHT AND SHADE OF JAMES ROYAL (LP)	40

ROYAL RASSES

76	Neville King NK 01	Love The Way It Should Be/Bud The Way It Should Be	10
77	Neville King NK 4	Kingston 11/Dub Up Kingston	10
79	12 Bakistuc 315	You Gotta Have Love (Jah Love)/Humanity (Love The Way It Should Be)/They Know Not Jah (12", clear vinyl)	12
79	Warrior BP 327	Royal Rasses - Aint' Nobody Here But Me/Kingston 11 (Ghetto Rock) (12")	15
79	Ballistic 12UP36496	Old Time Friend (Disco Style)/San Salvador (Disco Style) (12", clear vinyl, p/s)	8
78	Ballistic UAG 30259	EXPERIENCE (LP)	12
79	Ballistic PRE 1	GOD SENT DUB (white label/plain sleeve) (LP)	40
79	Warrior WARLP 2002	HARDER NA RASS! (LP)	40
80	Ballistic LBR 1031	HARDER NA RASS (LP)	20

ROYAL ROCKERS

| 60 | Top Rank JAR 326 | Jet II/Swinging Mambo | 20 |

ROYALS

64	Blue Beat BB 259	Save Mama/Out De Fire	30
68	Amalgamated AMG 831	Never See Come See/CANNONBALL BRYAN TRIO: Jumping Jack	45
69	Trojan TR 662	Pick Out Me Eye/Think You Too Bad	60
69	Duke DU 29	Never Gonna Give You Up/Don't Mix Me Up	20
73	Dip DL 5016	Promised Land/Every Jamaican Is A Rebel	20
79	Warrior WAR 143	Rising Sun/It's Real (Gone Sweet)	15
77	Magnum DEAD 1004	PICK UP THE PIECES (LP)	25
78	Ballistic UAG 30206	ISRAEL BE WISE (LP)	20
81	Kingdom KVLP 9006	MOVING ON (LP)	20

ROYAL SHOWBAND WATERFORD

62	HMV POP 1011	Come Down The Mountain Katie Daly/I Heard The Bluebirds Sing	6
63	HMV POP 1238	No More/Fountain Of Love	6
64	HMV POP 1377	Hucklebuck/Sorry (I Ran All The Way Home)	7
65	HMV POP 1444	Count Me In/She Was You Again	6
65	HMV POP 1460	Hucklebuck Shoes/The Hawaiian Wedding Song	6

ROYAL TEENS

58	HMV POP 454	Short Shorts/Planet Rock	35
58	HMV POP 454	Short Shorts/Planet Rock (78)	20
59	Capitol CL 15068	Little Cricket/Believe Me	30

ROYALTONES

58	London HLJ 8744	Poor Boy/Wail!	20
58	London HLJ 8744	Poor Boy/Wail! (78)	20
61	London HLU 9296	Flamingo Express/Tacos	20
64	Stateside SS 309	Our Faded Love/Holy Smokes	10

ROYAL TRUX

93	Domino RUG 8T	DOGS OF LOVE EP (12")	8
95	Hut 12790	LIVE IN DENVER EP (10" promo)	20
93	Domino WIGLP 6	CATS & DOGS (LP)	20
95	Hut HUTLP 23	THANK YOU (LP, purple vinyl)	20
97	Domino WIGLP 40	SINGLES, LIVES, UNRELEASED (3-LP box set)	20
98	Domino WIGLP 45	ACCELERATOR (LP)	20
99	Domino WIGLP 68	VETERANS OF DISORDER (LP)	18

ROYALTY

| 69 | CBS 4181 | That Kind Of Girl/Will You Be Staying After Sunday | 50 |

ROY & ANNETTE
63	R&B JB 107	My Baby/Go Your Ways	20

(see also Tommy McCook, Lester Sterling)

ROY & DUKE ALL STARS
68	Blue Cat BS 113	Pretty Blue Eyes Parts 1 & 2	40
68	Blue Cat BS 117	The Train Parts 1 & 2	40

(see also Roy Panton)

ROY & ENID
68	Coxsone CS 7063	Rocking Time/RALPH BLAKE: High Blood Pressure	100
68	Coxsone CS 7069	He'll Have To Go/CARLTON & SHOES: Love Is A Treasure	50
69	Coxsone CS 7088	Reggae For Days/SOUND DIMENSION: Holy Moses	30

(see also Little Roys)

(LITTLE) ROY & JOY
73	Camel CA 107	Rainy Weather/THE DEN BROTHERS: Version	8

ROY (PANTON) & MILLIE
62	Island WI 005	We'll Meet/ROLAND ALPHONSO: Back Beat (B-side act. with City Slickers)	25
63	Island WI 050	This World/Never Say Goodbye	25
63	Island WI 090	There'll Come A Day/I Don't Want You	20
63	Blue Beat BB 154	Over And Over/I'll Go (with Prince Buster All Stars)	20
64	Black Swan WI 409	Cherry I Love You/You're The Only One	30
64	Black Swan WI 410	Oh Merna/DON DRUMMOND: Dog War Bossa Nova	30
64	Black Swan WI 427	Oh Shirley/Marie	25

(see also Roy Panton, Millie [Small])

ROY (RICHARDS) & PAULETTE
63	Island WI 067	Have You Seen My Baby/Since You're Gone	25

ROY (PANTON) & YVONNE (HARRISON)
64	Blue Beat BB 258	Little Girl/No More	20
64	Black Swan WI 436	Two Roads/Join Together	20

(see also Roy Panton)

ROY (PANTON) & PATSY
62	Blue Beat BB 118	My Happy Home/In Your Arms Dear (with Hersang & His Combo)	25

(see also Roy Panton)

EARL ROYCE & OLYMPICS
64	Columbia DB 7433	Que Sera Sera/I Really Do	25
65	Parlophone R 5261	Guess Things Happen That Way/Sure To Fall (In Love With You)	25

ROY'S BOYS
64	Columbia DB 7425	Do Wah Diddy Diddy-I'm Into Something Good-I Want To Hold Your Hand/ Oh! Pretty Woman-Have I The Right?-It's All Over Now	7

LITA ROZA
53	Decca F 10070	(How Much Is) That Doggie In The Window/Tell Me We'll Meet Again (78)	20
53	Decca F 75082	(How Much Is) That Doggie In The Window/Tell Me We'll Meet Again (export issue)	70
54	Decca F 10240	Changing Partners/Just A Dream Or Two Ago (B-side with Stargazers)	15
54	Decca F 10269	Bell Bottom Blues (with Johnston Brothers)/Make Love To Me (both with Ted Heath Orchestra)	15
54	Decca F 10277	Young At Heart/Secret Love	15
54	Decca F 10393	Call Off The Wedding/The "Mama-Doll" Song	15
55	Decca F 10427	Heartbeat/Leave Me Alone	15
55	Decca F 10431	Let Me Go, Lover!/Make Yourself Comfortable	15
55	Decca F 10479	Tomorrow/Foolishly	15
55	Decca F 10536	Two Hearts, Two Kisses (Make One Love)/Keep Me In Mind	15
55	Decca F 10541	The Man In The Raincoat/Today And Ev'ry Day	12
55	Decca F 10611	Hey There/Hernando's Hideaway	15
56	Decca F 10679	Jimmy Unknown/The Rose Tattoo	15
56	Decca F 10728	Too Young To Go Steady/You're Not Alone	7
56	Decca F 10761	No Time For Tears/But Love Me (Love But Me)	7
56	Decca F 10792	Innismore/The Last Waltz	7
56	Decca F 10830	Hey! Jealous Lover/Julie	7
57	Decca F 10861	Lucky Lips/Tears Don't Care Who Cries Them	7
57	Decca F 10884	Tonight My Heart She Is Crying/Five Oranges, Four Apples	7
58	Pye Nixa 7N 15149	Hillside In Scotland/Sorry, Sorry, Sorry	5
58	Pye Nixa 7N 15155	Nel Blu Dipinto Di Blu (Volare)/It's A Boy	5
59	Pye Nixa 7N 15204	Allentown Jail/Once In A While	5
63	Ember EMB S 168	Mama (He Treats Your Daughter Mean)/(He's My) Dreamboat (as Lisa Rosa)	30
65	Columbia DB 7689	Keep Watch Over Him/Stranger Things Have Happened	8
57	Decca DFE 6386	LITA ROZA SELECTION (EP)	40
57	Decca DFE 6399	LITA ROZA (EP)	35
58	Decca DFE 6443	BETWEEN THE DEVIL AND THE DEEP BLUE SEA NO. 1 (EP)	35
54	Decca LF 1187	PRESENTING LITA ROZA (10" LP)	100
56	Decca LF 1243	LISTENING IN THE AFTER HOURS (10" LP)	120
57	Decca LK 4171	LOVE IS THE ANSWER (LP)	80
57	Decca LK 4218	BETWEEN THE DEVIL AND THE DEEP BLUE SEA (LP)	75
58	Pye Nixa NPL 18020	ME ON A CAROUSEL (LP, mono)	40
58	Pye Nixa NSPL 83003	ME ON A CAROUSEL (LP)	50
60	Pye NPL 18047	DRINKA LITA ROZA DAY (LP)	50
64	Ember NR 5009	LOVE SONGS FOR NIGHT PEOPLE (LP)	40
83	President PLE 509	YOU'RE DRIVING ME CRAZY (LP)	15

(see also Stargazers, Johnston Brothers)

ROZAA & WINE
76	Right On! 104	Disco Boogie Woman/Disco Boogie Woman Part 2	20

(see also David & Rozaa)

RT & B
79	Splendor Heights SH 1	Forward/Join Them (12")	20

MISTER JACK RUANE ESQUIRE
68 Pye 7N 17529   Everybody Wants To Go To Heaven/Just For Fun 7

RUB-A-DUBS WITH DANDY
65 Blue Beat BB 304   Without Love/I Know..25
(see also Dandy)

RUBAIYATS
68 Action ACT 4516   Omar Khayam/Tomorrow 40

GIDEON JAH RUBBAAL
77 Greensleeves GRE 003   Love Rasta/GIDEON JAH RUBBAAL ALL STARS: Rasta Version 8

RUBBER BAND
73 Youngblood YB 1052   Moonwalker/Wichita..6
69 Major Minor SMCP 5045   CREAM SONGBOOK (LP)...20
69 Major Minor SMCP 5048   HENDRIX SONGBOOK (LP)...20

RUBBER BOOTZ
67 Deram DM 134   Joy Ride/Chicano 30

RUBBER BUCKET
69 MCA MK 5006   We're All Living In One Place/Take Me Away 10
(see also Paul Raven)

JOHNNY RUBBISH
78 United Artists UP 36405   Living In NW3 4JR/Other Side (p/s) 10

RUBIN
75 MCA MU 196   You've Been Away/Baby, You're My Everything..10
75 MCA MU 196   You've Been Away/Baby, You're My Everything (DJ copy)............................20

RUBY
74 Chrysalis CHR 1061   RED CRYSTAL FANTASIES (LP, textured sleeve, green label) 20
(see also Procol Harum)

RUBY & GLORIA
71 Big Shot BI 583   Worried Over You/Worried Over You - Version...8
71 Black Swan BW 1409   Talk To Me Baby/LLOYD'S ALL STARS: Talk To Me Baby - Version 8

RUBY & ROMANTICS
63 London HLR 9679   Our Day Will Come/Moonlight And Music 15
63 London HLR 9734   My Summer Love/Sweet Love And Sweet Forgiveness 15
63 London HLR 9771   Hey There Lonely Boy/Not A Moment Too Soon 15
63 London HLR 9801   Young Wings Can Fly/Day Dreaming...15
64 London HLR 9881   Our Everlasting Love/Much Better Off Than I've Ever Been.........................30
64 London HLR 9916   Baby Come Home/Every Day's A Holiday 30
64 London HLR 9935   When You're Young And In Love/I Cry Alone 15
65 London HLR 9972   Your Baby Doesn't Love You Anymore/We'll Meet Again 15
69 A&M AMS 750   Hurting Each Other/Baby I Could Be So Good At Loving You 15
63 London RE-R 1389   OUR DAY WILL COME (EP)..75
64 London RE-R 1427   HEY THERE LONELY BOY (EP)..70
63 London HA-R 8078   OUR DAY WILL COME (LP)..70
66 London HA-R 8282   GREATEST HITS (LP)..65
(see also Danny Davis Orchestra)

RUBY PEARL & THE DREAMBOATS
74 MagnetMAG 7   The Shang-A-Lang Song/Will You Stop That! 5

RUDDY & SKETTO
62 Dice CC 2   Please Enid/ABC Boogie 12
62 Dice CC 7   Little Schoolgirl/Hush Baby 10
63 Dice CC16   Hold The Fire/Good Morning Mr Jones 15
71 Supreme SUP 218   Every Night/Ethiopia 8
(see also Sketto Rich)

RUD(D)Y (GRANT) & SKETTO (RICH)
62 Dice CC 5   Summer Is Just Around The Corner/Nothing Like Time (as Ruddy & Sketto & Reco's All Stars) 25
62 Dice CC 7   Little Schoolgirl/Hush Baby (as Ruddy & Sketto & Baron Twist & His Knights)..25
62 Dice CC 10   Mr Postman/Christmas Blues (as Rudy & Sketto with Laurel's Group) 25
63 Dice CC 16   Hold The Fire/Good Morning Mr Jones 25
63 Dice CC 19   Never Set You Free/Brothers And Sisters 20
63 Blue Beat BB 198   Was It Me/Minna Don't Deceive Me 20
64 Blue Beat BB 208   Show Me The Way To Go Home/Let Me Dream 20
64 Blue Beat BB 230   Ten Thousand Miles From Home/I Need Someone (as Ruddy & Sketto) 25
64 Blue Beat BB 252   I Love You/If Only Tomorrow 25
65 Blue Beat BB 297   See What You Done/Heart's Desire (as Ruddy & Sketto)...........................20
65 Blue Beat BB 310   Oh Dolly/You're Mine (as Ruddy & Sketto) 20
(see also Ruddy & Sketto)

RUDE AND DEADLY
95 Unity UNITY 002   Lightnin' and Tundra/Mash Dem Down (12") 40
95 No Smoking SMOKE 7   Give Me A Dub/Murder De boy (12", as Rude And Deadly Vs. The Dogz)..........15
97 Smokers Inc. SINC 1200   Give Me A Dubplate (97 Remix) (12", 1-sided, stamped white labels)...........15
97 Smokers Inc SINC 1200   Give Me A Dubplate (97 Remix)/Give Me A Dubplate (Original Mix) (12")........15

RUDE ASS TINKER
90s Deathchant DEATH 30   Imperial Break/Silk Ties (12", limited issue) 18
(see also Mu-Ziq, Tusken Raiders, U-Ziq)

RUDE BOY BUSINESS
90 Rude Boy Biz RBB001   I Play For Keeps (12") 8
90 Kold Sweat KS103   Chasing Competition/Cool Sailing (12")..8

RUDE BOYS
67 Island WI 3088   Rock Steady Massachusetts/Going Home...20

RUDI

78	Good Vibrations GOT 1	Big Time/Number 1 (folded p/s, 3,000 only)...30
79	Good Vibrations GOT 1	Big Time/No. 1 (reissue p/s) 10
79	Good Vibrations GOT 12	I Spy/Genuine Reply/Sometimes/Ripped In Two (p/s) 30
81	Jamming! CREATE 1	When I Was Dead/The Pressure's On (p/s) 5
82	Jamming! CREATE 3	Crimson/14 Steps (p/s) 5

RUDIES (FANATICS)

68	Blue Cat BS 107	The 7-11 Go To The Go Go Club (Parts 1 & 2) 120
68	Blue Cat BS 109	Cupid/RECO'S ALLSTARS: Wise Message 35
68	Nu Beat NB 001	Train To Vietnam/Skaville To Rainbow City 25
68	Nu Beat NB 005	Engine 59/My Girl 25
68	Fab FAB 46	I Wanna Go Home/La Mer 18
68	Fab FAB 70	Give Me The Rights/I Do Love You (as Rudies Fanatics) 18
68	Fab FAB 71	Mighty Meaty/Go (as Rudies Fanatics) 18
69	Doctor Bird DB 1301	Sin Thing/What's Your Name 15
69	Doctor Bird DB 1302	Boss Sound/RECO & RUDIES: Peace 25
69	Fab FAB 104	Brixton Rocket/Rudie's Joy 200
70	Pama PM 789	Give Peace A Chance/She 8
70	Trojan TR 7798	Patches/Split 10
70	Grape GA 3016	Henry The Great/Black Scorcher 45
71	Spinning Wheel SW 106	My Sweet Lord/Devil's Lead Soup 45

(see also Freddie Notes, Sonny, Binns & Rudies, Rico, Dandy, Owen & Dandy, Downtown All Stars, Desmond Riley)

RUDIMENTARY PENI

81	Outer Himalayan SRTS 81 CUS 1097	RUDIMENTARY PENI (EP, A4 foldout p/s with booklet) 30
81	Outer Himalayan BOOBOO 1	RUDIMENTARY PENI (EP, later 14" x 7" sleeve) 20
82	Crass 211984/2	FARCE (EP, initial pressing in 21" x 14" foldout black & white p/s) 20
97	Outer Himalayan BOOB 006	ECHOES OF ANGUISH (12", EP) 12
83	Corpus Christi CHRIST ITS 6	DEATH CHURCH (LP, fold put poster sleeve) 30
89	Corpus Christi BOOBOO 2	CACOPHONY (LP, with booklet) 20

(see also Magits)

RUEFREX

| 80 | Good Vibrations GOT 8 | One By One/Cross The Line/Don't Panic (foldover p/s, 2 different designs) ....12 |
| 83 | Kabuki KAR 7 | Capital Letters/April Fool (p/s) ....5 |

RAY RUFF & CHECKMATES

| 64 | London HLU 9889 | I Took A Liking To You/A Fool Again ....15 |

RUFF WITH THE SMOOTH

| 93 | Basement BRSS 023 | Art Of Intelligence/Sounds Superior (12") ....15 |
| 94 | Basement BRSS 037 | Twisted Girl/Who's Loving Me (12") ....10 |

(see also Jack Smooth)

RUFFIANS

| 71 | Banana BA 359 | Room Full Of Tears (actually by Sensations)/Black Soul (actually "Black And White - Version" by Riley's Allstars) ....12 |

(see Al Brown, Sensations)

BRUCE RUFFIN

69	Songbird SB 1002	Long About Now/Come See About Me (as Bruce Ruffin & Temptations).............20
69	Trojan TR 7704	Dry Up Your Tears/BEVERLEY'S ALLSTARS: One Way Street 15
70	Trojan TR 7737	I'm The One/Who's Gonna Be Your Man? 8
70	Trojan TR 7776	Cecelia/BEVERLEY ALL STARS: Stand Up 5
70	Summit SUM 8509	O-o-h Child/Bitterness Of Life 12
71	Summit SUM 8516	Candida/Are You Ready 10
71	Trojan TR 7814	Rain/THE PYRAMIDS: Geronimo (B-side actually by Pyramids) 8
71	Trojan TR 7814	Rain/THE PYRAMIDS: Off Limits (B-side actually by Aquarians) 8
71	Trojan TR 7832	One Big Happy Family (Parts 1 & 2) 5
72	Trojan TRM 9000	Songs Of Peace/You Are The Best/We Can Make It 12
72	Rhino RNO 101	Mad About You/Save The People 6
73	Rhino RNO 114	Tickle Me/I Like Everything About You 6
71	Trojan TRL 23	RAIN (LP) 15

(see also Bruce Downer)

DAVID RUFFIN

69	Tamla Motown TMG 689	My Whole World Ended (The Moment You Left Me)/ I've Got To Find Myself A Brand New Baby 20
69	Tamla Motown TMG 711	I've Lost Everything I've Ever Loved/We'll Have A Good Thing Going On 15
76	Tamla Motown TMG 1022	Heavy Love/Me And Rock And Roll Are Here To Stay 6
69	T. Motown (S)TML 11118	MY WHOLE WORLD ENDED (LP, mono/stereo) 30
70	T. Motown (S)TML 11139	FEELIN' GOOD (LP) 20
73	Tamla Motown STML 11228	DAVID RUFFIN (LP) 20

(see also Temptations)

JIMMY RUFFIN

66	Tamla Motown TMG 577	What Becomes Of The Broken-Hearted?/Baby I've Got It...................................18
66	Tamla Motown TMG 577	What Becomes Of The Broken-Hearted?/Baby I've Got It (DJ copy)....................85
67	Tamla Motown TMG 593	I've Passed This Way Before/Tomorrow's Tears 20
67	Tamla Motown TMG 593	I've Passed This Way Before/Tomorrow's Tears (DJ copy) 60
67	Tamla Motown TMG 603	Gonna Give Her All The Love I Got/World So Wide, Nowhere To Hide (DJ copy) 15
67	Tamla Motown TMG 603	Gonna Give Her All The Love I Got/World So Wide, Nowhere To Hide 50
67	Tamla Motown TMG 617	Don't You Miss Me A Little Bit Baby/I Want Her Love 15
67	Tamla Motown TMG 617	Don't You Miss Me A Little Bit Baby/I Want Her Love (DJ copy) 40
68	Tamla Motown TMG 649	I'll Say Forever My Love/Everybody Needs Love 15
68	Tamla Motown TMG 649	I'll Say Forever My Love/Everybody Needs Love (DJ copy) 45
68	Tamla Motown TMG 664	Don't Let Him Take Your Love From Me/Lonely Lonely Man Am I 18
68	Tamla Motown TMG 664	Don't Let Him Take Your Love From Me/Lonely Lonely Man Am I (DJ copy) 30
69	Tamla Motown TMG 703	I've Passed This Way Before/Tomorrow's Tears 7
70	Tamla Motown TMG 726	Farewell Is A Lonely Sound/If You Let Me, I Know I Can 6
70	Tamla Motown TMG 740	I'll Say Forever My Love/Everybody Needs Love 6
70	Tamla Motown TMG 753	It's Wonderful (To Be Loved By You)/Maria (You Were The Only One) 6
71	Tamla Motown TMG 767	Let's Say Goodbye Tomorrow/Living In A World I Created For Myself 7

71	Tamla Motown TMG 784	On The Way Out (On The Way In)/Honey Come Back	12
67	T. Motown TML 11048	THE JIMMY RUFFIN WAY (LP, mono)	40
67	Tamla Motown STML 11048	THE JIMMY RUFFIN WAY (LP, stereo)	45
69	Tamla Motown TML 11106	RUFF 'N' READY (LP, mono)	35
69	T. Motown STML 11106	RUFF 'N' READY (LP, stereo)	30
70	Tamla Motown STML 11161	JIMMY RUFFIN ... FOREVER (LP)	15
73	Polydor 2383 240	JIMMY RUFFIN (LP)	15
70s	Sounds Superb SPR 90041	I'VE PASSED THIS WAY BEFORE (LP)	12

(see also Council Collective)

JIMMY & DAVID RUFFIN

| 71 | Tamla Motown STML 11176 | I AM NOT MY BROTHER'S KEEPER (LP) | 25 |

(see also David Ruffin, Temptations)

RUFFNECK

| 93 | Represent REPREC 1 | Radford(You Get Me)/You And Me (12") | 15 |

RUFIGE CRU

92	Reinforced RIVET 1220	Krisp Biscuit (Power)/Killa Muffin (The Band Dog Mix) (12", die-cut title sleeve with tracks and artist mispelt)	15
92	Reinforced RIVET 1224	Darkrider/Believe/Menace/Jim Skreech (12", p/s)	30
93	Reinforced RIVET 1244	Terminator II Remix/Fabio's Ghost (The Edit)/ Ghosts Of My Life/High Rollerz Ghostin' Out (12", promo only)	25

RUFIGE KRU

| 07 | Exit EXIT 010 | Is This Real/This Real (I'm Not Sure Remix) (12", p/s, yellow vinyl, poster) | 25 |

RUFUS (& CHAKA KHAN)

74	ABC ABC 4022	You Got The Love/Rags To Rufus/Chaka Khan	5
75	ABC ABC 4055	Once You Get Started/Right Is Right (p/s)	5
79	MCA MCAT 575	Any Love (Full Length Version)/What Am I Missing (12", p/s as Rufus & Chaka)	20
75	ABC ABCL 5151	RUFUS WITH CHAKA KHAN (LP)	12

RUGBYS

| 69 | Polydor 56781 | You And I/Stay With Me | 45 |
| 70 | Polydor 56789 | Wendegahl The Warlock/Light | 20 |

PETE RUGOLO (& DIAMONDS)

| 60 | Warner Bros WM 4001 | BEHIND BRIGITTE BARDOT - COOL SOUNDS FROM HER HOT SCENES (LP, gatefold, also stereo WS 8001) | 25 |
| 58 | Mercury MPL 6512 | BRASS IN HI-FI (LP) | 12 |

(see also Diamonds, Patti Page)

RULERS

66	Rio R 105	Don't Be A Rude Boy/Be Good	15
66	Rio R 107	Copasetic/Too Late	20
67	Rio R 132	Wrong 'em Boyo/Why Don't You Change	25
67	Rio R 135	Well Covered/CARL DAWKINS: Help Time	15
67	Rio R 138	Be Mine/CARL DAWKINS: Hot And Sticky	15
69	Trojan TR 696	Got To Be Free/Situation	25

RUMBLE

| 70 | Warner Bros WB 8011 | Rich Man, Poor Man/Let Me Down | 30 |

RUMBLERS

63	London HLD 9684	Boss/I Don't Need You No More	40
65	King KG 1021	Soulful Jerk/Hey Did A Da Da	60
63	London RE-D 1396	BOSSOUNDS (EP)	150
63	London HA-D 8081	BOSSOUNDS (LP, mono)	90
63	London SH-D 8081	BOSSOUNDS (LP, stereo)	100

RUMOUR

| 79 | Stiff BUY 45 DJ | Emotional Traffic/Hard Enough To Show (1-sided promo, black vinyl) | 10 |
| 79 | Stiff BUY 45 DJ | Emotional Traffic/Hard Enough To Show (1-sided promo, blue vinyl) | 7 |

(see also Graham Parker)

RUMPLESTILTSKIN

70	Bell BLL 1101	Squadron Leader Johnson/Rumplestiltskin	20
71	Bell BLL 1157	Wimoweh/Through My Looking Glass	6
70	Bell SBLL 130	RUMPLESTILTSKIN (LP, gatefold sleeve)	50

(see also Clem Cattini)

RUN DMC

86	Profile LOXPD 104	Walk This Way/Walk This Way (instrumental)/My Adidas (12" picture disc)	10
84	4th & Broadway BRLP 506	RUN DMC (LP)	15
85	4th & Broadway BRLP 504	KING OF ROCK (LP)	12

RUN 229

| 80 | MM JR 7040S | Soho/Dance/In This Day And Age | 40 |

RUNAWAYS

76	Mercury 6167 392	Cherry Bomb/Blackmail	10
77	Mercury 6167 493	Queens Of Noise/Born To Be Bad	6
77	Mercury 6167 587	School Days/Wasted (p/s)	8
79	Cherry Red CHERRY 8	Right Now/Black Leather (p/s)	12
76	Mercury 9100 029	THE RUNAWAYS (LP, with gatefold sleeve & lyric sheet; U.S. pressing, with cat. no. SRM 1 1090, in U.K. sleeve)	18
77	Mercury 9100 032	QUEENS OF NOISE (LP, with lyric sheet)	15
77	Mercury 9100 046	LIVE IN JAPAN (LP)	15
77	Mercury 9100 047	WAITIN' FOR THE NIGHT (LP)	15
79	Cherry Red ARED 38	AND NOW ... THE RUNAWAYS (LP, 1,000 copies each in yellow, red, blue & orange vinyl, numbered)	25
80	Cherry Red BRED 9	FLAMING SCHOOLGIRLS (LP)	12

(see also Joan Jett, Lita Ford & Ozzy Osbourne)o

TODD RUNDGREN

| 72 | Bearsville K 15502 | I Saw The Light/Marlene | 6 |

RUNESTAFF

| 85 | FM VHF 5 | Road To Ruin/Last Chances (p/s) | 10 |

85	FM VHF 17	Do It!/Runestaff (no p/s)	6
85	Heavy Metal HMRLP 26	RUNESTAFF (LP)	15

RUNNER
79	Acrobat BAT 2	Run For Your Life/Gone Too Long	8
79	Acrobat ACRO1	RUNNER (LP, with inner)	15

RUNNING MAN
72	RCA Neon NE 11	THE RUNNING MAN (LP)	500

(see also Ray Russell Quartet, Mouse, Rock Workshop)

RUNNING RIOT
00	Rejected 001	RECLAIM THE STREETS (LP)	12

RUNRIG
83	Ridge RRS 003	Loch Lomond/Tuireadh Iain Ruaida (p/s)	15
84	Simple SIM 4	Dance Called America/Na H Uain A's T-Earrach (p/s)	30
84	Simple 12 SIM 4	Dance Called America/Na H Uain A's T-Earrach/Ribhinn (12", p/s)	20
84	Simple SIM 8	Skye/Hey Mandu (p/s)	15
86	Ridge RRS 006	The Work Song/This Time Of Year (p/s)	10
86	Ridge RRS 007	Alba/Worker For The Wind (p/s)	12
88	Chrysalis CHS 3284	Protect And Survive/Hearts Of Olden Glory (live) (p/s)	6
88	Chrysalis CHS 12 3284	Protect And Survive/Hearts Of Olden Glory (live)/Protect And Survive (live) (12", p/s)	10
88	Chrysalis CHSCD 3284	Protect And Survive/Hearts Of Olden Glory (live)/Protect And Survive (live) (CD)	15
89	Chrysalis CHS 3404	News From Heaven/Chi Mi'n Tir (p/s)	5
89	Chrysalis CHS 12 3404	News From Heaven/Chi Mi'n Tir/The Times They Are A'Changing (12", p/s)	8
89	Chrysalis CHS 12T 3404	News From Heaven/Chi Mi'n Tir/The Times They Are A'Changing (12", picture disc)	20
89	Chrysalis CHSCD 3404	News From Heaven/Chi Mi'n Tir/The Times They Are A'Changing (CD)	20
89	Chrysalis CHS 3451	Every River/This Time Of Year (p/s)	6
89	Chrysalis CHS 12 3451	Every River/This Time Of Year/Our Earth Was Once Green (12", p/s)	8
89	Chrysalis CHSCD 3451	Every River/This Time Of Year/Our Earth Was Once Green (CD)	15
90	Chrysalis CHSCD 3594	CAPTURE THE HEART EP: Stepping Down The Glory Road/Satellite Flood/Harvest Moon/The Apple Came Down (10", p/s)	8
90	Chrysalis CHSCD 1235941	CAPTURE THE HEART EP: Stepping Down The Glory Road/Satellite Flood/Harvest Moon/The Apple Came Down (12", p/s)	15
90	Chrysalis CHSCD 3594	CAPTURE THE HEART EP: Stepping Down The Glory Road/Satellite Flood/Harvest Moon/The Apple Came Down (CD)	15
90	Chrysalis CHS 38051	Flower Of The West/Ravenscraig/Ch Mi'n Greamhradh (p/s)	5
90	Chrysalis CHSCD 3805	Flower Of The West/Ravenscraig/Ch Mi'n Greamhradh/Harvest Moon (CD, digipak)	12
91	Chrysalis CHSG 123754	HEARTHAMMER EP (12", gatefold, with booklet)	8
91	Chrysalis CHS 123805	FLOWER OF THE WEST EP (12", numbered box set, with poster, discography & sticker)	10
93	Chrysalis CHSS 3952	Wonderful/April Come She Will (limited edition blue vinyl)	5
78	Neptune NA 105	RUNRIG PLAY GAELIC (LP)	15
79	Ridge RR 001	THE HIGHLAND CONNECTION (LP)	15
81	Ridge RR 002	RECOVERY (LP, with inner)	20

RUNS
80	Carrere CAR 139	Bun In The Oven (no p/s)	20

RUNT
71	Bearsville K 44505	RUNT (LP)	15
71	Bearsville K 44506	RUNT - THE BALLAD OF TODD RUNDGREN (LP)	15

(see also Todd Rundgren, Utopia, Nazz)

R.U.1.2.
78	SRTS/78/CUS 131	She's Gone/Purely Physical/Teenage Girl (p/s)	20

RUPERT'S PEOPLE
67	Columbia DB 8226	Reflections Of Charles Brown/Hold On	60

(this is the Fleur-De-Lys, they do not appear on the other 2 singles)

67	Columbia DB 8278	A Prologue To A Magic World/Dream In My Mind	100
68	Columbia DB 8362	I Can Show You/I've Got The Love	120

(see also Renaissance, Fleur-De-Lys, Gun, Sweet Feeling)

RUPIE AND SIDY
70	Success RE 910	Return Of Herbert Spliffington/RUPIE EDWARDS ALL STARS: Young, Gifted And Black	15

RUSH (AUSTRALIA)
67	Decca F 12614	Happy/Once Again	20
67	Decca F 12635	Make Mine Music/Enjoy It	20

RUSH (CANADA)
77	Mercury RUSH 7	Closer To The Heart/Bastille Day/Temples Of Syrinx (metallic blue label)	18
77	Mercury RUSH 7	Closer To The Heart/Bastille Day/Temples Of Syrinx (beige label)	8
78	Mercury RUSH 12	Closer To The Heart/Anthem/Bastille Day/Temples Of Syrinx (12", p/s)	10
80	Mercury RADIO 7	Spirit Of Radio/The Trees (p/s)	10
80	Mercury RADIO 12	Spirit Of Radio/The Trees/Working Man (12", p/s)	10
81	Mercury VITAL 7	Vital Signs/In The Mood (p/s)	8
81	Mercury VITAL 12	Vital Signs/In The Mood/A Passage To Bangkok/Circumstances (12", p/s)	8
81	Mercury EXIT 7	Tom Sawyer (live)/A Passage To Bangkok (live) (p/s)	6
81	Mercury EXIT 12	Tom Sawyer (live)/A Passage To Bangkok (live)/Red Barchetta (live) (12", p/s)	8
81	Mercury RUSH 1	Closer To The Heart (live)/The Trees (live) (p/s)	5
82	Mercury RUSH 8	New World Man/Vital Signs (live) (p/s)	5
82	Mercury RUSH 812	New World Man/Vital Signs (live)/Freewill (live) (12", p/s)	15
82	Mercury RUSH P9	Subdivisions/Red Barchetta (live) (picture disc)	10
82	Mercury RUSH 10 PD	Countdown/New World Man (shaped picture disc)	12
82	Mercury RUSH 1012	Countdown/New World Man/Spirit Of Radio (live)/Interview Excerpts (12", p/s)	10
84	Vertigo RUSH 11	The Body Electric/The Analog Kid (p/s)	5
84	Vertigo RUSH 1110	The Body Electric/The Analog Kid/Distant Early Warning (10", p/s, red vinyl)	12
84	Vertigo RUSH 1112	The Body Electric/The Analog Kid/Distant Early Warning (12", p/s)	50
78	Mercury 9100 059	HEMISPHERES (LP, mispressing, both sides play Side 1)	50
80	Mercury 9100 071	PERMANENT WAVES (LP, with newspaper and lyric inner)	12
85	Vertigo VERHP 31	POWER WINDOWS (LP, picture disc, with discography on sleeve)	20

(see also McKenzie Doug & Bob, Max Webster Band)

ED RUSH

92	Primavera PRIM 001	Edrush/Fat Girl (12", as Edrush)	20
92	ER 007	I wanna Stay In The Jungle/5AM/Touch Me/Keep On (12")	20
92	PSY 001	Look What They've Done/What If My Heart Stops?/Look What They've Done (Dub Mix) (12")	20
93	No U-Turn NUT 002	Bludclot Artattack/Bludclot Artattack (Dark Mix) (12")	20
94	No U-Turn NUT 007	BLUDCLOT ARTATTACK REMIXES (12")	8
94	Jet Star XCT 001	Selecta/Selecta (Remix) (12")	30
95	No U-Turn NUT 011	Gangsta Hardstep/The Force Is Electric (12")	8
95	No U-Turn NUT 012	Guncheck/The Force Is Electric (Remix) (12")	8

MERRILEE RUSH & TURNABOUTS

68	Bell BLL 1013	Angel Of The Morning/Reap What You Sow	6
68	Bell BLL 1026	That Kind Of Woman/Sunshine And Roses	6
69	Bell BLL 1041	Reach Out I'll Be There/Love Street	10
68	Bell MBLL/SBLL 109	MERRILEE RUSH (LP)	25

OTIS RUSH

66	Vocalion V-P 9260	Homework/I Have To Laugh	75
66	Vocalion V-P 9260	Homework/I Have To Laugh (DJ copy)	125
69	Blue Horizon 57-3159	All Your Love/Double Trouble	25
68	Blue Horizon 7-63222	THIS ONE'S A GOOD UN (LP)	100
69	Atlantic 588 188	MOURNING IN THE MORNING (LP)	40
70s	Atlantic K 40495	MOURNING IN THE MORNING (LP, reissue)	15
70	Python KM 3	GROANING THE BLUES (LP)	50
76	Delmark DS 63?	COLD DAY IN HELL (LP)	25
78	Sonet SNTF756	TROUBLES, TROUBLES (LP)	12

TOM RUSH

67	Elektra EKSN 45004	Who Do You Love/On The Road Again	8
67	Elektra EKSN 45015	On The Road Again/Love's Made A Fool Of You	8
68	Elektra EKSN 45025	No Regrets/Shadow Dream Song	7
68	Elektra EKSN 45032	Something In The Way She Moves/Rockport Sunday	8
66	Xtra XTRA 5024	BLUES, SONGS & BALLADS (LP)	30
66	Xtra XTRA 5053	I GOT A MIND TO RAMBLE (LP)	30
67	Elektra EKL 308	TAKE A LITTLE WALK WITH ME (LP, also stereo EKS 7308)	35
68	Elektra EKL 4018	THE CIRCLE GAME (also stereo EKS 74018) (LP, 1st issue black 'Elektra' on red label)	25
68	Elektra EKL 4018	THE CIRCLE GAME (also stereo EKS 74018) (LP, 2nd issue white 'Elektra' on redder label)	15
69	Elektra EKL 4062	CLASSIC RUSH (LP, red label, also stereo EKS 74062)	22
70	CBS 63940	TOM RUSH (LP)	15
70	CBS 64268	WRONG END OF A RAINBOW (LP)	15

JIMMY RUSHING (WITH ADA MOORE & BUCK CLAYTON)

57	Philips BBE 12150	CAT MEETS CHICK (EP, as Jimmy Rushing, Buck Clayton & Ada Moore)	20
57	Vanguard EPP 14003	LITTLE JIMMY ALL STAR BAND (EP)	15
57	Parlophone GEP 8597	JIMMY RUSHING (EP)	15
58	Parlophone GEP 8695	THE WAY I FEEL (EP)	15
63	Ember EMB 4523	JIMMY RUSHING (EP)	15
55	Vanguard PPT 12002	SINGS THE BLUES (10" LP)	50
57	Vanguard PPT 12016	SHOWCASE (10" LP)	45
57	Philips BBL 7105	CAT MEETS CHICK (LP, with Ada Moore & Buck Clayton)	20
57	Philips BBL 7166	THE JAZZ ODYSSEY OF JAMES RUSHING ESQ (LP, with Buck Clayton)	20
58	Vanguard PPL 11008	IF THIS AIN'T THE BLUES (LP)	20
58	Philips BBL 7252	LITTLE JIMMY RUSHING AND THE BIG BRASS (LP, also stereo SBBL 524)	20
60	Philips BBL 7360	RUSHING LULLABIES (LP)	18
61	Philips BBL 7484	THE SMITH GIRLS - BESSIE, CLARA (LP, mono)	20
61	Philips SBBL 631	THE SMITH GIRLS - BESSIE, CLARA (LP, stereo)	25
66	Ace Of Hearts AH 119	BLUES I LOVE TO SING (LP)	15
67	Golden Guinea GGL 0384	FIVE FEET OF SOUL (LP)	12

(see also Count Basie, Dave Brubeck, Buck Clayton)

JIMMY RUSHING/CHAMPION JACK DUPREE

64	Ember CJS 800	TWO SHADES OF BLUE (LP, 1 side each)	30

(see also Champion Jack Dupree)

BARBARA RUSKIN

65	Piccadilly 7N 35224	Halfway To Paradise/I Can't Believe In Miracles	10
65	Piccadilly 7N 35246	You Can't Blame A Girl For Trying/No More To Fall	12
66	Piccadilly 7N 35274	Well How Does It Feel/Wishing Your Life Away	10
66	Piccadilly 7N 35296	Song Without End/Love Came Too Late	10
66	Piccadilly 7N 35328	Light Of Love/At Times Like These Mama	10
67	Parlophone R 5571	Take It Easy/Sunshowers	10
67	Parlophone R 5593	Euston Station/Hear That Telephone	10
67	Parlophone R 5642	Come Into My Arms Again/Just A Little While Longer	10
68	Parlophone R 5685	Is This Another Way/The Night Of The Spanish Tightrope Walker	5
68	President PT 217	Pawnbroker Pawnbroker/Almost	25
69	President PT 238	Gentlemen Please/24th Of July	6
69	President PT 261	Hail Love/Lady Of Leisure	6
70	President PT 280	A Little Bit Of This (And A Little Bit Of That)/Where Are We	6
70	President PT 315	For The First Time In My Life/Merry-Go-Round	6
71	President PT 350	(I Wanna Be) Your Teddy Bear/It Really Doesn't Matter	6

ROGER RUSKIN SPEAR

74	United Artists UP 35683	On Her Doorstep Last Night/Frank The Ripper	12
74	United Artists UP 35721	I Love To Bumpity Bump/When Yuba Plays The Rhumba On The Tuba Down In Cuba	20
71	United Artists UP 35221	REBEL TROUSER: Trouser Freak/Trouser Press/Release Me/Drop Out (EP, without p/s)	10
71	United Artists UP 35221	REBEL TROUSER: Trouser Freak/Trouser Press/Release Me/Drop Out (EP, with p/s)	20
74	United Artists UAS 29508	UNUSUAL (LP)	20

(see also Bonzo Dog Doo-Dah Band, Topo D. Bill)

EDDIE RUSS

76	Impact IMP 5	Zauis/See The Light/Tea Leaves (12")	150

LONNIE RUSS
62	Fontana 267263 TF	Something Old Something New/My Wife Can't Cook	7

THANE RUSSAL (& THREE)
66	CBS 202049	Security/Your Love Is Burning Me (in p/s)	300
66	CBS 202049	Security/Your Love Is Burning Me	150
66	CBS 202403	Drop Everything And Run/I Need You (solo)	150

RUSSANT
82	Mach 1 MAGIC 003	It Happened Then/Synthamation (no p/s)	10

CHARLOTTE RUSSE
68	Fontana BF1683	Anyway The Wind Blows/High On A Roof Top	25

ROLAND RUSSEL
68	Nu Beat NB 019	Rhythm Hips/RHYTHM FLAMES: Deltone Special	40

ANDY RUSSELL
58	RCA RCA 1076	Seven Daughters/A Certain Smile	6

ARTHUR RUSSELL
87	Rough Trade ROUGH 114	WORLD OF ECHO (LP)	20
04	Soul Jazz SJRLP 083	THE WORLD OF ARTHUR RUSSELL (3-LP, original 2004 pressing)	20

BOBBY RUSSELL
68	Bell BLL 1019	Dusty/I Made You This Way	6
68	Bell BLL 1034	1432 Franklin Pike Circle Hero/Let's Talk About It	6
69	Bell BLL 1050	Carlie/Ain't Society Great?	6
71	United Artists UP 35283	Saturday Morning Confusion/Little Ole Song About Love	5

BRENDA RUSSELL
79	A&M AMSP 7515	In The Thick Of It/So Good So Right (12", p/s)	10
79	A&M AMLJ 739	BRENDA RUSSELL (LP)	12

CONNIE RUSSELL
54	Capitol CL 14171	No One But You/One Arabian Night	10
54	Capitol CL 14197	Love Me/Papa's Puttin' The Pressure On	10
55	Capitol CL 14214	Foggy Night In San Francisco/This Is My Love	10
55	Capitol CL 14236	Ayuh, Ayuh/I'm Making Believe	15
55	Capitol CL 14246	Snow Dreams/Green Fire	6
55	Capitol CL 14268	Farewell, Farewell/The Magnificent Matador	6
57	Capitol CL 14676	All Of You/This Is My Love	6

DAVE RUSSELL
66	Columbia DB 7828	When I Grow Too Old To Dream/All The Tears In The World	5

(see also Dave & Diamonds)

DOROTHY RUSSELL
71	Duke Reid DR 2524	You're The One I Love/Version	6

GEORGE RUSSELL
71	Flying Dutchman FD10124	ELECTRONIC SONATA FOR SOULS (LP)	20

JANE RUSSELL
51	London L 956	Dear Dear Dear/I Can't Get Started With You (78)	10
51	London L 969	Five Little Miles From San Berdoo/You'll Know (78)	10
53	Columbia SCM 5043	Please Do It Again/Two Sleepy People (B-side with Bob Lowery)	25
53	Columbia SCM 5043	Please Do It Again/Two Sleepy People (B-side with Bob Lowery) (78)	10
53	MGM MGM 662	A Little Girl From Little Rock/When Love Goes Wrong (78)	10
53	MGM MGM 664	Bye Bye Baby/Ain't There Anyone Here For Love? (78)	10
56	Capitol CL 14590	If You Wanna See Mamie Tonight/Keep Your Eyes On The Hands	10
59	MGM MGM-EP 702	JANE RUSSELL (EP)	45

JANET RUSSELL
88	Harbourtown HAR 003	GATHERING THE FRAGMENTS (LP)	20

JOHN RUSSELL/RICHARD COLDMAN
79	Incus INCUS 31	HOME COOKING/GUITAR SOLOS (LP, 1 side each)	35

JOHNNY RUSSELL
60	MGM MGM 1074	Lonesome Boy/Baby Won't You Tell Me So	10

KEITH RUSSELL
65	Piccadilly 7N 35235	People Get Ready/Paradise	10

KIT RUSSELL
73	Deram DM 399	Peppers Last Stand/Shuffle Back	15

LEON RUSSELL
65	Dot DS 16771	Everybody's Talkin' 'Bout The Young/It's Alright With Me	8

(see also Asylum Choir)

RAY RUSSELL QUARTET
68	CBS Realm 52586	TURN CIRCLE (LP)	40
69	CBS Realm 52663	DRAGON HILL (LP)	40
71	RCA SF 8214	JUNE 11TH 1971 (LP)	40
71	CBS 64271	RITES AND RITUALS (LP)	45
73	Black Lion BLP 12100	SECRET ASYLUM (LP, gatefold)	30

(see also Running Man, Mouse, Chopyn)

ROSALIND RUSSELL & EDITH ADAMS
55	Brunswick 05406	Ohio/Little Bit Of Love	5

IAN RUSSELL
70	Lucky LU 112	Love Locked Out/The Worm Song	10

RUSSELL FAMILY
75	Topic 12TS 251	OF DOOLIN COUNTY CLARE (LP, with insert)	12

RUSSIAN ROULETTE
84	Red Bus RBUS 86	Come Into My Room/Lyin' Again (p/s)	5

(see also Paul King, Mungo Jerry)

MINT VALUE £

CHARLIE RUSSO
63	Stateside SS 165	Preacherman/Teresa	8

WILLIAM RUSSO
63	Columbia 33SX 1508	RUSSO IN LONDON (LP)	20
66	Columbia 33SX 1758	STONEHENGE (LP, with the London Jazz Orchestra)	35

RUSTIKS
64	Decca F 11960	What A Memory Can Do/Hello Anne	10
65	Decca F 12059	I'm Not The Loving Kind/Can't You See	10

RUSTLERS
61	Pye 7N 15398	High Strung/Matter Of Who	12

RUSTY & DOUG (KERSHAW)
59	Oriole CB 1510	Hey Mae!/Why Don't You Love Me	150
59	Oriole CB 1510	Hey Mae!/Why Don't You Love Me (78)	50
59	London HL 8972	I Like You (Like This)/Dancing Shoes	30
59	London HL 8972	I Like You (Like This)/Dancing Shoes (78)	30
62	Polydor NH 66970	Hey Mae!/Sweet Thing	40
62	Fontana 267 238 TF	Cajun Joe (The Ballad Of The Bayou)/Sweet Sweet Girl To Me	15

(see also Doug Kershaw)

RUSTY HARNESS
70	Ember EMB S 283	Ain't Gonna Get Married/Goodbye (in p/s)	10
70	Ember EMB S 283	Ain't Gonna Get Married/Goodbye	5
73	Ember SE 8024	DISCOTHEQUE EXPLOSION (LP)	12

RUSTY NAIL
60s	Hi-Fi MEP 3093	RUSTY NAIL (EP, in p/s)	100
60s	Hi-Fi MEP 3093	RUSTY NAIL (EP, no p/s)	40

RUTH
67	Columbia DB 8218	Leaf In The Wind/Society's Child	7
68	Columbia DB 8386	Cherish/Until It's Time For You To Go	7

RUTH & BEAUTY
72	Montagu MONT 3000	29 Days To Doomsday/Cutting The Traces	18

MIKE RUTHERFORD
80	Charisma CB 364	Time And Time Again/At The End Of The Day (p/s, correct B-side & label)	5
80	Charisma CB 364	Time And Time Again/Overnight Job (p/s, with new label on B-side, credits & plays "Overnight Job")	5

(see also Genesis, Mike & Mechanics)

RUTHLESS RAP ASSASINS
87	White (Murdertone) AMC001	We Don't Care/Kiss AMC (12", 500 pressed)	50

RUTLES
78	Warner Bros K 17125	I Must Be In Love/Cheese And Onions/With A Girl Like You (p/s)	5
78	Warner Bros K 17180	Let's Be Natural/Piggy In The Middle	6
78	Warner Bros WB K56459	THE RUTLES (LP, gatefold, booklet and inner sleeve)	20
96	Virgin VUSLP 119	ARCHAEOLOGY (LP, inner)	20

(see also Dirk & Stig, Neil Innes, Monty Python, Beach Boys, Patto)

RUTS (D.C.)
79	People Unite SJP 795	In A Rut/H-Eyes (1,000 only, black-ringed label)	45
79	People Unite RUT 1	In A Rut/H-Eyes (repressing)	8
79	Virgin VS 271	Babylon's Burning/Society (p/s)	8
79	Virgin VS 298	Jah War/I Ain't Sofisticated (p/s)	5
79	Virgin VS 285	Something That I Said/Give Youth A Chance (p/s)	5
80	RSO RSO 71	Babylon's Burning/XTC: Take This Town (p/s)	5
81	Virgin VS 396	Different View/Formula Eyes (p/s, as Ruts D.C.)	5
82	Bohemian BO 2	Whatever We Do/Push Yourself - Make It Work (p/s, as Ruts D.C.)	5
83	Bohemian BO 3	Weak Heart/Militant (white label, with paper insert; as Ruts D.C., promo only)	15
83	Bohemian BO 4	Stepping Bondage/Lobotomy/Rich Bitch (p/s)	15
86	Strange Fruit SFPS 011	PEEL SESSIONS (12" EP)	12
82	Bohemian BOLP 4	RHYTHM COLLISION (LP)	20
79	Virgin V 2132	THE CRACK (LP, stickered sleeve with "Pay no more than £3.99")	15
87	Link LP 013	LIVE AND LOUD (LP)	12

(see also Laurel Aitken, Typhoons, Pete Zear)

BARRY RYAN (& MAJORITY)
68	MGM MGM 1423	Goodbye/I'm So Sad	10
68	MGM MGM 1442	Eloise/Love I Almost Found You (as Barry Ryan & Majority)	8
68	MGM MGM 1464	Love Is Love/I'll Be On My Way Dear	5
69	Polydor 56348	The Hunt/No Living Without Her	8
70	Polydor 56370	Magical Spiel/Caroline	8
70	Polydor 2001 035	Kitsch/Give Me A Sign	8
71	Polydor 2001 154	It Is Written/Annabella	8
71	Polydor 2001 256	Can't Let You Go/When I Was A Child (as Barry Ryan)	7
72	Polydor 2001 335	From My Head To My Toes/Alimony Money Blues	7
72	Polydor 2001 362	I'm Sorry Susan/L.A. Woman	7
75	Dawn DNS 1109	Do That/The Summers Over	12
76	Private Stock PVT 70	Where Were You/Making A Do	7
77	Private Stock PVT 87	Brother/Life's So Easy	7
69	MGM MGM-C(S) 8106	SINGS PAUL RYAN (LP)	40
69	Polydor 583 067	BARRY RYAN (LP)	25

(see also Paul & Barry Ryan)

CATHY RYAN
53	MGM SP 1051	Show Me The Way To Go Home/If I Had You	7

(see also Art Mooney)

KRIS RYAN (& QUESTIONS)
64	Mercury MF 818	Miss Ann/She Told Me Lies (as Kris Ryan & Questions)	10
64	Mercury MF 832	Don't Play That Song/If You Don't Come Back	10

64	Mercury MF 852	Marie Marie/I've Had Enough Of You Baby	10
65	Mercury MF 877	Tell Me How/She Belongs To Me	10
65	Mercury 10024 MCE	ON THE RIGHT TRACK (EP, as Kris Ryan & Questions)	40

MARION RYAN

58	Pye NIXA 7N 15121	Love Me Forever/Make The Man Love Me	7
58	Pye NIXA 7N 15130	Always And Forever/Oh Oh I'm Falling In Love Again	7
58	Pye NIXA 7N 15138	Stairway Of Love/I Need You	7
58	Pye 7NSR 15157	The World Goes Around And Around/Please Don't Say Goodnight (stereo)	10
59	Pye NIXA 7N 15184	Wait For Me (Ti Piro)/Jeepers Creepers	7
59	Pye 7N 15200	Jo-Jo The Dog Faced Boy/Doin' What Comes Naturally	6
60	Columbia DB 4448	Sixteen Reasons/Mangos	7
60	Columbia DB 4550	Somebody/It's You That I Love	6
68	Philips BF 1721	Better Use Your Head/The Seasons Change	40
57	Pye Nixa NEP 24041	THAT RYAN GIRL! (EP)	20
58	Pye NEP 24079	MARION RYAN HIT PARADE (EP)	30
59	Pye NPL 18030	A LADY LOVES! (LP, mono)	30
59	Pye NSPL 18030	A LADY LOVES! (LP, stereo)	40

(see also Ray Ellington, Gary Miller)

PAT RYAN

77	Folk Heritage FHR 094	LEABOY'S LASSIE (LP)	25

PAUL RYAN

72	Maple Annie MA 104	Born On A Beautiful Day/Come With Me	6
72	Maple Annie MA 107	Natural Gas/Hellow Hellow	6

PAUL & BARRY RYAN

65	Decca F 12260	Don't Bring Me Your Heartaches/To Remind You Of My Love	8
66	Decca F 12319	Have Pity On The Boy/There You Go	8
66	Decca F 12391	I Love Her/gotta Go Out To Work	8
66	Decca F 12445	I Love How You Love Me/Baby I'm Sorry	8
66	Decca F 12494	Have You Ever Loved Somebody?/I'll Tell You Later	12
66	Decca F 12520	Missy, Missy/Rainbow Weather	12
67	Decca F 12567	Keep It Out Of Sight/Who Told You?	10
67	Decca F 12633	Claire/I'll Make It Worth Your While	12
67	MGM 1354	Heartbreaker/Night Time	8
68	MGM 1385	Pictures Of Today/Madrigal	8
74	Polydor 2001511	Carry The Blues/Reincarnation Games	6
67	Decca LK 4878	THE RYANS - TWO OF A KIND (LP)	50
68	MGM MGM-C(S) 8081	PAUL AND BARRY RYAN (LP)	30

(see also Barry Ryan)

PHIL RYAN & CRESCENTS

64	Columbia DB 7406	Mary Don't You Weep/Yes I Will	8
65	Columbia DB 7574	Gypsy Woman/Be Honest With Yourself	20

BOBBY RYDELL

59	Top Rank JAR 181	Kissin' Time/You'll Never Tame Me	15
59	Top Rank JAR 181	Kissin' Time/You'll Never Tame Me (78)	45
59	Top Rank JAR 227	We Got Love/I Dig Girls	15
60	Columbia DB 4429	Wild One/Little Bitty Girl	8
60	Columbia DB 4471	Swingin' School/Ding-A-Ling	8
60	Columbia DB 4495	Volare/I'd Do It Again	8
60	Columbia DB 4545	Sway/Groovy Tonight	8
61	Columbia DB 4600	Good Time Baby/Cherie	8
61	Columbia DB 4651	Don't Be Afraid/That Old Black Magic	8
61	Columbia DB 4690	The Fish/The Third House	8
61	Columbia DB 4731	I Wanna Thank You/The Door To Paradise	8
62	Columbia DB 4785	I've Got Bonnie/Lose Her	8
62	Columbia DB 4858	I'll Never Dance Again/Gee, It's Wonderful	8
63	Cameo Parkway C 108	Forget Him/Hey Ev'rybody (in p/s)	15
63	Cameo Parkway C 108	Forget Him/Hey Ev'rybody	10
63	Cameo Parkway C 129	It's Time We Parted/Too Much too Soon	7
63	Cameo Parkway C 228	The Cha Cha Cha/The Best Man Cried	7
63	Cameo Parkway C 242	Butterfly Baby/Love Is Blind	7
64	Cameo Parkway C 309	Make Me Forget/Darling Jenny	7
65	Capitol CL 1537	I Can't Say Goodbye/Two Is The Loneliest Number	8
60	Top Rank JKP 2059	LOVINGEST (EP)	30
63	Cameo Parkway CPE 551	SWAY WITH BOBBY RYDELL (EP)	20
63	Cameo Parkway CPE 553	BOBBY RYDELL (EP)	20
63	Summit LSE 2036	BEST OF BOBBY RYDELL (EP)	10
60	Columbia 33SX 1243	WILD ONE (LP)	60
61	Columbia 33SX 1308	SINGS AND SWINGS (LP)	22
61	Columbia 33SX 1352	SALUTES "THE GREAT ONES" (LP)	25
62	Columbia 33SX 1425	RYDELL AT THE COPA (LP)	30
62	Cameo Parkway C 1019	ALL THE HITS (LP)	20
63	Cameo Parkway C 1040	ALL THE HITS VOL. 2 (LP)	20
63	Cameo Parkway C 1055	WILD (WOOD) DAYS (LP)	25
65	Capitol T 2281	SOMEBODY LOVES YOU (LP)	20

(see also Chubby Checker & Bobby Rydell)

RYDER

74	BUG 39	Ain't That Nice/Sugar Mama	10

FREDDIE RYDER

65	Mercury MF 864	To Get Your Love Back/A Little Thing Called Love	6
65	Mercury MF 879	Some Kind Of Wonderful/Slow Down	12
65	Mercury MF 935	Man Of The Moment/My Block	10
68	Columbia DB 8335	Shadows (I Can't See You)/Airport	6
68	Columbia DB 8427	Worst That Could Happen/World Of My Own	6

(see also Freddie Self, Trends)

MAL RYDER (& SPIRITS)

63	Decca F 11669	Cry Baby/Take Over (as Mal Ryder & Spirits)	20

MINT VALUE £

64	Vocalion V 9219	See The Funny Little Clown/Slow Down	70
64	Piccadilly 7N 35209	Your Friend/Forget It (as Mal Ryder & Spirits)	40
65	Piccadilly 7N 35234	Lonely Room/Tell Your Friend	22

(see also Mal & Primitives)

MITCH RYDER (& DETROIT WHEELS)

66	Stateside SS 481	Jenny Take A Ride/Baby Jane	25
66	Stateside SS 498	Little Latin Lupe Lu/I Hope	20
66	Stateside SS 521	Breakout/I Need Help	50
66	Stateside SS 521	Breakout/I Need Help (DJ copy)	100
66	Stateside SS 549	Devil With A Blue Dress On (Medley)/I Had It Made	20
67	Stateside SS 596	Sock It To Me Baby/I Never Had It Better	20
67	Stateside SS 2023	Too Many Fish In The Sea/Three Little Fishes/One Grain Of Sand	25
67	Stateside SS 2037	Joy/I'd Rather Go To Jail (solo)	10
67	Stateside SS 2063	What Now My Love/Blessing In Disguise (solo)	25
68	Stateside SS 2075	You Are My Sunshine/Wild Child (solo)	7
68	Stateside SS 2096	Personality/Chantilly Lace/I Make A Fool Of Myself (solo)	7
69	Dot DOT 129	Sugar Bee/I Believe (There Must Be Someone)	6
66	Stateside SE 1039	RIDIN' (EP)	60
66	Stateside S(S)L 10178	TAKE A RIDE ... (LP)	30
67	Stateside S(S)L 10189	BREAKOUT. . . !! (LP)	30
67	Stateside S(S)L 10204	SOCK IT TO ME (LP)	25
68	Stateside S(S)L 10229	WHAT NOW MY LOVE (LP, solo)	30
69	Bell MBLL/SBLL 114	ALL MITCH RYDER HITS (LP)	20

(see also Detroit)

PAUL RYDER & TIME MACHINE

| 74 | Penny Farthing PEN 834 | Are You Ready/If You Ever Get To Heaven | 8 |

TONY RYMOND

| 62 | Oriole 1708 | Handful Of Songs/She'll Have To Go | 12 |

S

SABICAS

| 70 | Polyor 2482 023 | ROCK ENCOUNTER (LP, with Joe Beck) | 30 |

PARK SABLE & JUNGLE 'N' BEATS

| 64 | Fontana TF 457 | Never Be Blue/Rave On | 40 |

SABOTAGE

| 80 | Optimistic OPT 001 | WHEN THE WAR IS OVER (EP) | 10 |
| 80 | Optimistic OPT 004 | SUBTERFUGE (EP) | 12 |

SABRE

| 83 | Neat NEAT 23 | Miracle Man/On The Loose (p/s) | 8 |

SABRES

| 66 | Decca F 12528 | Roly Poly/Will You Always Love Me? | 30 |

(see also Peeps)

SABRES OF PARADISE

93	Sabres Of Paradise PT 001	United (Andrew Weatherall Mix) (12", p/s, actually remix of Throbbing Gristle's "United", 800 only)	25
93	Sabres Of Paradise PT 009	Smokebelch II (Entry)/(Exit) (12", red p/s)	12
93	Sabres Of Paradise PT 009R	Smokebelch II (David Holmes Mix)/(Flute Mix) (12", yellow p/s)	10
94	Sabres Of Paradise PT 014	Theme/Return Of Carter & Edge 6 (Original Mix) (12")	10
94	Sabres Of Paradise PT 014R	Theme (Underdog Vs Sabres)/(Version) (10" remix)	10
94	Warp WAP 50	Wilmot/Rumble Summons (12")	15
94	Warp 10WAP 50	WILMOT II: Wilmot Meets Lord Scruffage/Wilmot's Last Skank (10", p/s)	8
95	Warp WARP 62	Tow Truck/(mixes) (12")	10
96	Emissions SEO 11	Ysaebud (PVC sleeve, 1-sided, etched B-side, 1,000 only)	10
90s	Sabres Of Paradise 002	Internal/Internment/Internalized/The Creator Speaks (12", blue vinyl)	8
93	Warp LP 16	SABRESONIC (2-LP, with unreleased 7", 5,000 only)	20

SACRED

| 93 | Twilight 7R5010A | You're The Only One/Lost In Time | 15 |

SACRED ALIEN

81	Greenwood GW 001	Spiritual Planet/Energy (stickered labels, in p/s)	30
81	Greenwood GW 001	Spiritual Planet/Energy (stickered labels)	10
83	Heighway Robbery SAD 001	Legends/VIRGIN: Sittin' In Front Row (gatefold p/s)	30

SACRILEGE

85	C.O.T.R. GURT 4	BEHIND THE REALMS OF MADNESS (6-track mini LP)	40
87	Under One Flag FLAG 15	WITHIN THE PROPHECY (LP)	15
90	Metalcore CORE 8	BEHIND THE REALMS OF MADNESS (Mini-LP, reissue)	20

SAD

| 72 | Phoenix NIX 124 | It Ain't Easy/Box | 10 |

SAD AFFAIR

| 71 | Lifelong LF 1 | Coloured Rice/Strange Sky | 30 |

SADDAR BAZAAR

98	Earworm WORM 13/WJ37	Crystalline/ELECTROSCOPE: Circus Heights/TRANSPARENT THING: Ahh (p/s, 1,500 in hand painted sleeve, 1st 176 embossed)	10
98	Earworm WORM 13/WJ37	Crystalline/ELECTROSCOPE: Circus Heights/TRANSPARENT THING: Ahh (p/s, 1,500 in hand painted sleeve)	5
95	Delerium DELEC LP 034	THE CONFERENCE OF THE BIRDS (LP)	15

SADIE'S EXPRESSION

| 69 | Plexium PXM 4 | Deep In My Heart/My Way Of Living | 7 |

SADISTIC MIKA BAND

74	Harvest SHSP 4029	SADISTIC MIKA BAND (LP)	12
75	Harvest SHSP 4043	BLACK SHIP (LP)	12
75	Harvest SHSP 4049	HOT MENU (LP)	12

BARRINGTON SADLER

69	Clandisc CLA 204	Soul Power/Rub It Down	12

S/SGT. BARRY SADLER

66	RCA RCA 1506	Ballad Of The Green Berets/I'm A Lucky One	7
66	RCA RCA 1520	The A Team/An Empty Glass	5

SAD LOVERS & GIANTS

81	Last Movement LM 003	CLE (EP)	50
82	Midnight DING 1	Lost In A Moment/The Tightrope Touch (p/s)	5
83	Last Movement LM 005	Colourless Dream/Things We Never Did	20
83	Midnight DING 5	Man Of Straw/Cow Boys (p/s)	5
83	Midnight DONG 5	Man Of Straw/Cow Boys (Version)/Close To The Sea (12", p/s)	8
87	Midnight DONG 31	Seven Kinds Of Sin/The Outsider/Ours To Kill (12", p/s)	10
87	Midnight DONG 34	White Russians/A Map Of My World/Life Under Glass (12", p/s)	10
88	Midnight DONG 36	Cow Boys (1988 Remix)/Lost In A Moment (1988 Remix)/The Best Film He Ever Made/Things We Never Did (Live) (12", p/s)	10
82	Midnight CHIME 01	EPIC GARDEN MUSIC (LP)	15
83	Midnight CHIME 03	FEEDING THE FLAME (LP)	15
84	Midnight CHIME 07	IN THE BREEZE (LP)	12
86	Midnight CHIME 022	TOTAL SOUND (LP)	12
87	Midnight CHIME 30	THE MIRROR TEST (LP)	12

JERRY SADOWITZ

88	Gobshite GOBSHITE 01	GOBSHITE (LP)	12

SAD PEOPLE

69	Chapter One CH113	Lonely Man/Turn Around	15

SAD SOCIETY

87	X Cert	Contaminate/Nothing ever Changes	12

SAFARI PARTY

85	Pure & Vain 1 PAV	Hope In Hell/Not There (p/s)	5

SAFARIS (& PHANTOM BAND)

60	Top Rank JAR 424	Image Of A Girl/Four Steps To Love	50
60	Top Rank JAR 528	The Girl With The Story In Her Eyes/Summer Nights (with Phantom Band)	40

SAFFIRE

76	Safari SFR 4	Lay You Boogy Down (Part One)/Lay Your Boogy Down (Part Two)	10

SAFFRON SUMMERFIELD

74	Mother Earth MUM 1001	SALISBURY PLAIN (LP)	60
76	Mother Earth MUM 1202	FANCY MEETING YOU HERE (LP)	50
76	Spectator	FANCY MEETING YOU HERE (LP, reissue)	20

SAGA

83	Portrait XPS 186	Don't Be Late/Careful Where You Step (p/s)	6
72	Westwood WRS 017	SAGA (LP)	50
73	Westwood WRS 036	SWEET PEG O'DERBY (LP)	100

MIKE SAGAR (& CRESTERS)

60	HMV POP 819	Deep Feeling/You Know (as Mike Sagar & Cresters)	20
61	HMV POP 988	The Brothers Three/Set Me Free	10

(see also Cresters, Richard Harding)

SAGE

80	Redball RR 032	GOING STRONG (LP)	45

SAGITTARIUS

67	CBS 2867	My World Fell Down/Libra	25
68	CBS 3276	Another Time/Virgo	25

(see also Bruce Johnston, Glen Campbell)

SAGRAM

72	Windmill WMD 118	POP EXPLOSION SITAR STYLE (LP)	20

(see also Clem Alford, Magic Carpet)

SAHARA

75	Dawn DNLS 3068	SUNRISE (LP)	35

DOUG SAHM

73	Atlantic K 10293	Is Anybody Going To San Antoine/Don't Turn Around	5
73	Atlantic K 40466	DOUG SAHM AND BAND (LP) (inc Dylan and Dr. John in his band)	18
74	Warner Bros K 56067	GROOVERS PARADISE (LP)	12
70s	Chrysalis CHR 1249	HELL OF A SPELL (LP)	12

(see also Sir Douglas Quintet, Augie Meyers)

OLIVER SAIN (& SHIRLEY BROWN)

72	Mojo 2092 031	St. Louis Breakdown/I Ain't Gonna Tell (with Shirley Brown)	5

(see also Shirley Brown, Fontella Bass)

ST. CHRISTOPHER

84	Bluegrass GM 001	Crystal Clear/My Fond Farewell (p/s)	10
86	Bluegrass GM 003	Go Ahead Cry/Charmelle (p/s)	8
89	Sarah SARAH 015	You Deserve More Than A Maybe/The Kind Of Girl/The Summer Of Love (foldaround p/s with poster in poly bag)	10
89	Sarah SARAH 020	All Of A Tremble/My Fortune/The Hummingbird	7
90	Sarah SARAH 34	Antoinette/Salvation (p/s, insert)	10
91	Sarah SARAH 46	Say Yes To Everything/It's Snowing On The Moon (p/s, insert)	10
90	Sarah SARAH 403	BACHARACH (10" LP)	20

CHERYL ST. CLAIR

66	CBS 202041	My Heart Is Not In It/We Want Love	15

MINT VALUE £

| 66 | Columbia DB 8077 | What About Me/I'll Forget You Tonight | 12 |

(see also Alison Wonder)

ISLA ST. CLAIR
| 81 | Clare ISLA 1 | THE SONG AND THE STORY (LP) | 20 |
| 85 | Topic 12TS 436 | SCOTCH MEASURE (LP) | 15 |

JERRY ST. CLAIR
| 69 | Philips BF 1796 | Summer Exodus/Mrs. Jensen Sits Alone | 15 |

SAINT DAVIDS ROAD
| 69 | Tangerine DP003 | Let The Sun Come In/Mama Ain't Gonna Like What She Sees | 15 |

SAINT ETIENNE
90	Heavenly HVN 2	Only Love Can Break Your Heart/Only Love Can Break Your Heart (Version) (p/s)	6
90	Heavenly HVN 212	Only Love Can Break Your Heart/Only Love Can Break Your Heart (Original Version) (12", p/s)	10
90	Heavenly HVN 212R	Only Love Can Break Your Heart (A Mix Of Two Halves)/The Official Saint Etienne World Cup Theme (12", die-cut p/s)	12
90	Heavenly HVN 4	Kiss And Make Up/Sky's Dead (p/s)	5
90	Heavenly HVN 412	Kiss And Make Up/Sky's Dead (12", p/s)	10
90	Heavenly HVN 412R	Kiss And Make Up (Midsummer Madness Remix)/Kiss And Make Up (Midsummer Dubness Mix) (12", p/s)	10
90	Heavenly HVN 4CD	Kiss And Make Up (7")/Kiss And Make Up (12")/Sky's Dead (CD)	12
91	Heavenly HVN 912R	Speedwell (Flying Mix)/Speedwell (Project Mix)/Nothing Can Stop Us (Instrumental)/3D Tiger (12", p/s)	10
91	Heavenly HVN 9CD	Nothing Can Stop Us/Speedwell/Nothing Can Stop Us (Instrumental) (CD)	10
92	Heavenly HVN 22	Live - Paris '92 (clear flexidisc, gig freebie, 1,000 only)	20
93	Heavenly HVN 2912	Hobart Paving/Who Do You Think You Are (12", p/s, mispressed with Hobart Paving & "Your Head My Voice" on both sides)	18
95	Heavenly HVN 41	XMAS '95: A Christmas Gift To You/Driving Home For Christmas/A Message In A Bottle (CD, signed fan club edition)	90
03	Mantra MNT 78	Soft Like Me/Gimp Crisis (p/s, limited edition)	8
93	Heavenly HVN 41	SO TOUGH (LP)	15
93	Heavenly HVNLP 6	YOU NEED A MESS OF HELP TO STAND ALONE (LP)	15
93	Heavenly HVNCDX 6	SO TOUGH/YOU NEED A MESS OF HELP TO STAND ALONE (2-CD)	25
95	Heavenly HVNLP 9CD	I LOVE TO PAINT (CD, fan club edition, 600 only)	140
95	Heavenly HVNCD 10	TOO YOUNG TO DIE (CD, with bonus CD "Too Young To Die - The Remix Album" [HVN LP 10CDR])	30
97	Heavenly HVN41-2	VALENTINES DAY (CD, EP fan club edition)	100
98	Fan Club SPCD 463	XMAS '98: I Don't Intend To Spend Christmas Without You/Kofi Annan (CD, fan club edition, in card sleeve)	80
98	Creation CRECD 225L	GOOD HUMOUR (CD, digipak with booklet and slipcase)	15
00	Mantra MNSTET 1	BUILT ON SAND: RARITIES 1994-1999 (CD, fan club edition)	120
03	Heavenly HVN136CD	XMAS 2003 (CD, EP fan club issue)	60
08	Foreign Office FOREIGN OFFICE 004	BOXETTE (4-CD, 3000 only)	80

(see also 50 Year Void, Sarah Cracknell, Lovecut D.B., Mike Vickers)

KIRK ST. JAMES
| 70 | Pye 7N 25518 | My Love Oh Linda/Tears I Cry | 60 |

BARRY ST. JOHN
64	Decca F 11933	A Little Bit Of Soap/Thing Of The Past	20
64	Decca F 11975	Bread And Butter/Cry To Me	20
65	Decca F 12111	Mind How You Go/Don't You Feel Proud	20
65	Decca F 12145	Hey Boy/I've Been Crying	20
65	Columbia DB 7783	Come Away Melinda/Gotta Brand New Man	15
66	Columbia DB 7868	Everything I Touch Turns To Tears/Sounds Like My Baby	65
66	Columbia DB 7868	Everything I Touch Turns To Tears/Sounds Like My Baby (DJ copy)	65
68	Major Minor MM 587	Cry Like A Baby/Long And Lonely Night	15
69	Major Minor MM 604	By The Time I Get To Phoenix/Turn On Your Light	15
75	Bradleys BRAD 7507	I Won't Be A Party/Do Me Good	7
69	M. Minor MMLP/SMLP 43	ACCORDING TO ST. JOHN (LP)	50

BERNIE ST. JOHN & BARTHOLEMEW
| 70 | Beacon BEA 167 | Believe In Your Love/Run Run | 5 |

BRIDGET ST. JOHN
69	Dandelion K 4404	To B Without A Hitch/Autumn Lullaby	15
70	Warner Bros WB 8019	If You've Got Money/Yep	12
72	Polydor 2001 280	Fly High/There's A Place I Know/Suzanne (p/s)	12
72	Polydor 2001 361	Nice/Goodbye Baby Goodbye	8
73	MCA MUS 1203	Passing Thru'/The Road Was Lonely On My Own	10
69	Dandelion 63750	ASK ME NO QUESTIONS (LP, gatefold sleeve)	70
71	Dandelion DAN 8007	SONGS FOR THE GENTLE MAN (LP, gatefold sleeve)	80
71	Dandelion K 49007	SONGS FOR THE GENTLE MAN (LP, gatefold sleeve, with cat no K 49007)	30
72	Dandelion 2310 193	THANK YOU FOR... (LP, gatefold sleeve)	100
74	Chrysalis CHR 1062	JUMBLE QUEEN (LP)	30

(see also Kevin Ayers, Ron Geesin, Mike Oldfield, Quiver)

PAUL ST. JOHN
| 70 | Pye 7N 45190 | Flying Saucers Have Landed/Spaceship Love | 80 |

TAMMY ST. JOHN
64	Pye 7N 15682	Boys/Hey Hey Hey Hey	15
65	Pye 7N 15762	He's The One For Me/I'm Tired Of Just Looking At You	15
65	Pye 7N 15948	Dark Shadows And Empty Hallways/I Mustn't Cry	15
66	Pye 7N 17042	Nobody Knows What's Goin' On (In My Mind But Me)/ Stay Together Young Lovers	50
66	Pye 7N 17042	Nobody Knows What's Goin' On (In My Mind But Me)/ Stay Together Young Lovers (DJ copy)	85
69	Tangerine DP 0007	Concerning Love/Sound Of Love	300

(see also Trends)

ST. LOUIS JIMMY
| 53 | Esquire 10-319 | Holiday For Boogie/MEMPHIS SLIM: Harlem Bound (78) | 20 |

ST. LOUIS UNION
| 66 | Decca F 12318 | Girl/Respect | 15 |

| 66 | Decca F 12386 | Behind The Door/English Tea | 50 |
| 66 | Decca F 12508 | East Side Story/Think About Me | 150 |

(see also Medicine Head)

SAINT ORCHESTRA
| 78 | Pye 7N 46127 | Return Of The Saint/Funko (p/s) | 12 |

OLIVER ST. PATRICK & DIAMONDS
| 67 | Trojan TR 005 | I Want To Be Loved By You/Tulips | 12 |

CRISPIAN ST. PETERS
65	Decca F 12080	At This Moment/Goodbye, You'll Forget Me	15
65	Decca F 12207	No No No/Three Goodbyes	15
66	Decca F 12287	You Were On My Mind/What I'm Gonna Be	5
66	Decca F 12359	The Pied Piper/Sweet Dawn My True Love	6
66	Decca F 12480	Changes/My Little Brown Eyes	15
66	Decca F 12525	But She's Untrue/Your Ever Changin' Mind	8
67	Decca F 12596	Almost Persuaded/You Have Gone	8
67	Decca F 12677	Free Spirit/I'm Always Crying	8
70	Decca F 13055	So Long/My Little Brown Eyes	10
74	Santa Ponsa PNS 17	Do Daddy Do/Every Time You Sinned	7
75	Route RT 18	Carolina/Samantha	7
67	Decca DFE 8678	ALMOST PERSUADED (EP)	55
66	Decca LK 4805	FOLLOW ME... (LP)	50
70	Square SQA 102	SIMPLY... CRISPIAN ST. PETERS (LP)	40

KIRBY ST. ROMAIN
| 63 | Stateside SS 199 | Summer's Comin'/Miss You So | 10 |

SAINT STEVEN
| 69 | Probe SPB 1005 | OVER THE HILLS/THE BASTICH (LP) | 75 |

ST. VALENTINE'S DAY MASSACRE
| 67 | Fontana TF 883 | Brother Can You Spare A Dime/Al's Party (with p/s) | 150 |
| 67 | Fontana TF 883 | Brother Can You Spare A Dime/Al's Party | 60 |

(see also Artwoods)

BUFFY SAINTE-MARIE
65	Fontana TF 574	Until It's Time For You To Go/The Flower And The Apple Tree	5
65	Fontana TF 614	The Universal Soldier/Cripple Creek	5
66	Fontana TF 695	Timeless Love/Lady Margret	5
71	RCA 2081	Soldier Blue/Moratorium (Bring Our Brothers Home)	5
72	Vanguard VRS 35143	I'm Gonna Be A Country Girl Again/The Piney Wood Hills	6
65	Fontana TFL 6040	IT'S MY WAY! (LP)	12
65	Fontana TFL 6047	MANY A MILE (LP)	12
71	Vanguard VSD 79311	SHE USED TO WANNA BE A BALLERINA (LP)	10

SAINTS (AUSTRALIA)
76	Power Exchange PX 242	I'm Stranded/No Time (p/s)	15
77	Power Exchange PXE 101	I'm Stranded/(STANLEY FRANK: 2 tracks) (p/s)	8
77	Harvest HAR 5123	Erotic Neurotic/One Way Street (with p/s)	150
77	Harvest HAR 5123	Erotic Neurotic/One Way Street	10
77	Harvest HAR 5130	This Perfect Day/L-I-E-S	6
77	Harvest 12 HAR 5130	This Perfect Day/L-I-E-S/Do The Robot (12", with 'disclaimer' stickered p/s)	10
77	Harvest HAR 5137	1, 2, 3, 4 (River Deep, Mountain High/Lipstick On Your Collar/One Way Street/Demolition Girl) (EP, double pack, gatefold p/s)	15
78	Harvest HAR 5148	Know Your Product/Run Down (no p/s)	10
78	Harvest HAR 5166	Security/All Times Through Paradise (p/s)	12
77	Harvest SHSP 4065	I'M STRANDED (LP)	30
78	Harvest SHSP 4078	ETERNALLY YOURS (LP, with inner sleeve)	25
78	Harvest SHSP 4094	PREHISTORIC SOUNDS (LP)	22
86	Razor RAZ 21	BEST OF (LP)	12

SAINTS (JAMAICA)
66	Doctor Bird DB 1009	Brown Eyes/BABA BROOKS & HIS BAND: King Size	30
69	Big Shot BI 522	Windy Part One/Windy Part Two	12
73	Count Shelley CS 043	How Long/Feeling Good	15

SAINTS (U.K.)
| 63 | Pye 7N 15548 | Wipe Out/Midgets | 25 |
| 63 | Pye 7N 15582 | Husky Team/Pigtails | 25 |

(see also Tornados, Heinz)

SAINTS (U.K.)
| 64 | MJB BEV 73/4 | SAINTS (10" LP, private pressing) | 300 |
| 64 | MJB BEVLP 127/8 | SAINTS ALIVE! (LP, private pressing) | 300 |

RUSS SAINTY (& NU NOTES)
60	Top Rank JAR 381	Happy-Go-Lucky-Me/Standing Around	15
60	Decca F 11270	Race With The Devil/Too Shy (solo)	18
61	Decca F 11325	Don't Believe Him, Donna/Your Other Love (solo)	10
62	HMV POP 1055	Keep Your Love Locked/I've Got A Girl (as Russ Sainty & Nu Notes)	10
62	HMV POP 1069	Send Me The Pillow That You Dream On/What Do You Know About That (solo)	10
63	HMV POP 1181	Unforgettable Love/The Twinkle In Your Eye (solo)	10
64	Parlophone R 5168	/Lonesome TownThat's How I'm Gonna Love You (as Russ Sainty & Nu-Notes)	7
64	Columbia DB 7394	This Is My Lovely Day/Bless You, Girl (as Russ Sainty & Nu-Notes)	7
65	Columbia DB 7521	It Ain't That Easy/And Then (solo)	6
65	Columbia DB 7708	Saving My Tears (For A Rainy Day)/She (solo)	6
65	Society SOC 1035	THE GENIUS OF LENNON AND McCARTNEY (LP)	15

(see also Nu Notes)

KYU SAKAMOTO
63	HMV POP 1171	Sukiyaki/Anoko No Namae Wa Nantenkana	8
63	HMV POP 1211	China Nights/Benkyo No Cha Cha Cha	8
64	HMV POP 1342	Rose Rose I Love You/Sayonara Tokyo	10
62	HMV CLP 1674	SUKIYAKI (LP)	50

MINT VALUE £

RYUICHI SAKAMOTO
80	Island IPR 2048	Riot In Lagos/Iconic Storage (12", company sleeve)	10
80	Island ILPS 9656	B-2 UNIT (LP)	12
90	Virgin VUSLP 14	BEAUTY (LP, with inner)	12

(see also David Sylvian, Yellow Magic Orchestra)

(BOB) SAKER
68	Polydor BM 56231	Still Got You/Imagination (as Bob Saker)	30
68	Parlophone R 5740	Foggy Tuesday/Ooh Nana Na (as Bob Saker)	40
69	Parlophone R 5752	Hey Joel/Christianity	15
71	CBS 7010	What A Beautiful World/City Of The Angels	6
71	CBS 7399	Even Though We Ain't Got Money/Wild Winds Are Blowing	6

SAL SALVADOR
55	KPL 105	SAL SALVADOR QUARTET (10" LP)	12

SALAMANDER
70	CBS 5102	Crystal Ball/Billy	15
71	Youngblood SSYB 14	THE TEN COMMANDMENTS (LP, gatefold poster sleeve)	400

(see also Onyx)

SALEM
82	Hilton FMR 056	Cold As Steel/Reach To Eternity	45

SALFORD JETS
78	WEA K 18008	Lookin' At The Squares/Dancing School (no p/s)	5
79	EMI INT 590	Manchester Boys/Last Bus (p/s)	20

SANDY SALISBURY
00	Poptones MC 5007	Do Unto Others/CURT BOETTCHER: That's The Way It's Gonna Be (numbered die-cut company sleeve)	6

SALLY & ALLEY CATS
64	Parlophone R 5183	Is It Something I Said/You Forgot To Remember	15

SALLYANGIE
69	Big T BIG 126	Two Ships/Colours Of The World	100
72	Philips 6006 259	Child Of Allah/Lady Go Lightly	100
68	Transatlantic TRA 176	CHILDREN OF THE SUN (LP, gatefold sleeve, purple/white textured label)	60
78	Transatlantic TRA 176	CHILDREN OF THE SUN (LP, reissue, different single sleeve)	20

(see also Mike Oldfield, Sally Oldfield)

DOUG SALMA & HIGHLANDERS
63	Philips BF 1279	Highland Fling/The Scavenger	18

SALMONTAILS
80	Oblivion OBL 001	SALMONTAILS (LP, with Dave Pegg)	20

SALOME
69	Page One POF 137	Vivo Cantando/Amigos Amigos	7

SALSOUL STRUT
96	Records Inc. no cat. no.	Better Days/(Mixes)	12

SALT
78	Grapevine GRA 111	BEYOND A SONG (LP, with insert)	18

SALT & PEPPER
61	London HLU 9338	High Noon/Come Softly To Me	15

SALVATION
69	United Artists UP 35048	Cinderella/The Village Shuck	15
69	United Artists UAS 29062	SALVATION (LP)	30

SALVATION
83	Merciful Release MR 025	Girlsoul/Evelyn (p/s)	12
83	Merciful Release MRX 025	Girlsoul/Evelyn/Dust Up (12", p/s)	15
86	Batfish Inc. BF 103	Jessica's Crime/The Shining (p/s)	12
86	Batfish Inc. USS 104	Jessica's Crime (Extended Mix)/The Shining/Shattered Sky (12", p/s)	8

SAMMY SALVO
58	RCA RCA 1032	Oh Julie/Say Yeah	30
58	RCA RCA 1032	Oh Julie/Say Yeah (78)	20
59	London HLP 8997	Afraid/Marble Heart	15
59	London HLP 8997	Afraid/Marble Heart (78)	20
62	Polydor NH 66974	Billy Blue/French Poodle	8

SAM
72	Pye 7N 45175	Johnny Rebel/He Loves Me, He Loves Me Not	6

SAM APPLE PIE
69	Decca F 22932	Tiger Man (King Of The Jungle)/Sometime Girl	15
72	DJM DJS 274	Call Me Boss/Old Tom	8
69	Decca LK-R 5005	SAM APPLE PIE (LP, mono, laminated front sleeve, unboxed logo label)	300
69	Decca SKL-R 5005	SAM APPLE PIE (LP, stereo, laminated sleeve, unboxed logo label)	250
73	DJM DJLPS 429	EAST 17 (LP)	30

SAM, ERV & TOM
68	Direction 58-3339	Soul Teacher/Hard To Get	12

(see also Diplomats)

SAM & BILL
66	Pye International 7N 25355	Fly Me To The Moon/Treat Me Right	15
67	Brunswick 05973	I Feel Like Cryin'/I'll Try	40
67	Brunswick 05973	I Feel Like Cryin'/I'll Try (DJ copy)	75

SAM & DAVE
66	King KG 1041	No More Pain/You Ain't No Big Thing Baby	50
66	Atlantic AT 4066	You Don't Know Like I Know/Blame Me, Don't Blame My Heart	20
66	Atlantic 584 003	Hold On I'm A Comin'/I Got Everything I Need	10
66	Atlantic 584 047	If You Got The Loving (I Got The Time)/Said I Wasn't Gonna Tell Nobody	12

67	Atlantic 584 064	You Got Me Hummin'/Sleep Good Tonight	12
67	Atlantic 584 086	You Don't Know Like I Know/Blame Me, Don't Blame My Heart (reissue)	10
67	Stax 601 004	Soothe Me/Sweet Pains (initial dark blue label)	25
67	Stax 601 004	Soothe Me/Sweet Pains (later light blue label)	20
67	Stax 601 006	When Something Is Wrong With My Baby/A Small Portion Of Your Love (initial dark blue label)	10
67	Stax 601 006	When Something Is Wrong With My Baby/A Small Portion Of Your Love (later light blue label)	8
67	Stax 601 023	Soul Man/May I Baby	8
68	Stax 601 030	I Thank You/Wrap It Up	8
68	Atlantic 584 192	You Don't Know What You Mean To Me/This Is Your World	7
68	Atlantic 584 211	Can't You Find Another Way/Still Is The Night	7
68	Atlantic 584 228	Everybody's Got To Believe In Somebody/If I Didn't Have A Girl Like You	8
69	Atlantic 584 237	Soul Sister, Brown Sugar/Come On In	8
69	Atlantic 584 247	You Don't Know Like I Know/Hold On I'm A Comin'	7
69	Atlantic 584 303	Ooh, Ooh, Ooh/Holdin' On	8
70	Atlantic 584 324	Baby, Baby, Don't Stop Now/I'm Not An Indian Giver	8
66	King KGL 4001	SAM AND DAVE (LP)	75
66	Atlantic 587/588 045	HOLD ON, I'M A COMIN' (LP)	50
67	Stax 589 003	DOUBLE DYNAMITE (LP)	50
68	Stax 589 015	SOUL MEN (LP)	40
68	Major Minor MCP 5000	SAM AND DAVE (LP)	22
69	Atlantic 588 154	I THANK YOU (LP)	25
69	Atlantic 588 155	THE BEST OF SAM AND DAVE (LP)	18
69	Atlantic 587/588 181	DOUBLE TROUBLE (LP)	22
69	Atlantic 588 185	SOUL MEN (LP, reissue)	15

SAM & KITTY
| 80 | Grapevine GRP 132 | I've Got Something Good/Love Is The Greatest | 20 |

SAME
79	Wessex WEX 267	Wild About You/Movements (p/s)	70
80	Blue Print BLU 2008	Movements/Wild About You (reissue with reversed sides & blue print on p/s)	30
80	Blue Print BLU 2008	Movements/Wild About You (reissue with reversed sides no p/s)	20

MIKE SAMMES SINGERS
| 68 | Davjon DJ 1006 | HYMNS A SWINGING (LP, with Ted Taylor Organisation) | 30 |
| 06 | Trunk JBH 109 LP | MUSIC FOR BISCUITS (LP) | 30 |

MICHAEL SAMMES SINGERS
| 59 | Top Rank JAR 166 | Upstairs And Downstairs/Ivor Raymonde - Mylene | 6 |

SAMMY
| 72 | Philips 6006 227 | Goo Ger Woogie/Big Lovin' Woman | 7 |
| 72 | Philips 6308 136 | SAMMY (LP, laminated sleeve, black/silver label) | 40 |

(see also Ian Gillan, Audience, Episode Six, Quatermass, Roy Young Band, Stackridge, Ginhouse)

SAMPLES
| 80 | Sample | VENDETTA (EP) | 20 |
| 84 | No Future OI 14 | Dead Hero/Fire Around Round/Suspicion (p/s) | 15 |

DAVE SAMPSON & HUNTERS
60	Columbia DB 4449	Sweet Dreams/It's Lonesome	20
60	Columbia DB 4502	If You Need Me/See You Around	20
61	Columbia DB 4597	Why The Chicken?/1999	15
61	Columbia DB 4625	Easy To Dream/That's All	15
62	Fontana H 361	Wide, Wide World/Since Sandy Moved Away (solo)	15
61	Columbia SEG 8095	DAVE (EP, mono)	60
61	Columbia ESG 7853	DAVE (EP, stereo)	80

(see also Hunters [U.K.])

TOMMY SAMPSON
58	Melodisc MEL 1411	Rockin'/Rock'n'Roll Those Big Brown Eyes (with His Strongmen)	22
58	Melodisc MEL 1411	Rockin'/Rock'n'Roll Those Big Brown Eyes (with His Strongmen) (78)	20
58	Parlophone R 4458	Lazy Train/Smooth Mood (as Tommy Sampson Orchestra)	7
58	Parlophone R 4458	Lazy Train/Smooth Mood (as Tommy Sampson Orchestra) (78)	10

SAM'S FRIENDS
| 66 | Decca F12519 | If I Gave You My Love/I Feel | 5 |

SAMSON (1)
| 69 | Instant INSP 004 | ARE YOU SAMSON (LP) | 70 |

(see also Strider)

SAMSON (2)
| 70 | Parlophone R5867 | Venus/Wool & Water | 8 |

SAMSON (3)
78	Lightning GIL 547	Telephone/Leavin' You (p/s)	35
79	Lightning GIL 553	Mr. Rock'n'Roll/Drivin' Music (p/s)	35
79	Laser LAS 6	Mr. Rock'n'Roll (remix)/Primrose Shuffle	10
80	EMI EMI 5061	Vice Versa (Edit)/Hammerhead (p/s, withdrawn, 1,000 demos only)	40
80	Gem GEMS 34	Vice Versa (Edit)/Hammerhead (reissue, p/s, with sticker)	8
80	Gem GEMS 34	Vice Versa (Edit)/Hammerhead (reissue, p/s)	5
80	Gem GEMS 38	Hard Times (Remix)/Angel With A Machine Gun (p/s)	5
81	RCA RCA 67	Riding With The Angels (Edit)/Little Big Man (no p/s)	10
81	RCA RCA 67	Riding With The Angels (Edit)/Little Big Man (picture disc)	10
82	Polydor POSPP 471	Losing My Grip/Pyramid To The Stars (picture disc)	6
82	Polydor POSPX 471	Losing My Grip/Pyramid To The Stars/Mr. Rock'n'Roll (live)/ Tomorrow Or Yesterday (live) (12" EP)	10
82	Polydor POSPG 519/	Life On The Run/Drivin' With ZZ!//Walking Out On You (live)/Bright Lights (live) (double pack, gatefold p/s)	7
82	Polydor SAM 2	Red Skies/Young Idea (unissued, promo only)	18
83	Polydor PODJ 554	Red Skies (DJ Edit) (1-sided promo)	12
83	Polydor POSPP 554	Red Skies/Livin', Lovin', Lyin' (picture disc)	6
83	Polydor POSPX 554	Red Skies/Livin', Lovin', Lyin'/Running Out Of Time (12", p/s)	10
84	Polydor POSP 670	Are You Ready?/Front Page News (p/s)	7

MINT VALUE £

84	Polydor POSPP 670	Are You Ready?/Front Page News (picture disc) 8
84	Polydor POSPX 670	Are You Ready?/Front Page News/La Grange (12", p/s)...................................8
84	Polydor POSP 680	The Fight Goes On/Riding With The Angels (re-recording) (p/s)......................5
84	Polydor POSPX 680	The Fight Goes On (Long Version)/Riding With The Angels (re-recording)/ Vice Versa (live) (12", p/s) 8
84	Thunderbolt THBE 1.003	Mr Rock'n'Roll/Primrose Shuffle/Telephone/Leavin' You (12", p/s)................8
86	Capitol CL 395	Vice Versa (Remix)/Losing My Grip (Remix) (p/s) 8
86	Capitol 12CLP 395	Vice Versa (Remix)/Losing My Grip (Remix) (12", picture disc) 15
87	Metal Hammer METAL 1	One Day's Heroes (as Paul Samson's Empire)/CHARIOT: Life On The Line/ HEAVY PETTIN': Heaven Sent/STRANGEWAYS: Never Gonna Lose It (EP with Metal Hammer magazine)...6
79	Laser LAP 1	SURVIVORS (LP) 15
80	Gem GEMLP 108	HEAD ON (LP, 2 different mixes, A1/B1 or A2/B2 in matrix; each with insert) 12
80	Gem GEMLP 108	HEAD ON (LP, mispress with A1/B2 or A2 matrix, without patch) 12
81	Gem GEMLP 113	SHOCK TACTICS (LP, release cancelled) 0
81	RCA LP 5031	SHOCK TACTICS (LP, with insert) 18
82	Polydor POLS 1077	BEFORE THE STORM (LP, with poster, stickered sleeve)................................20
82	Polydor POLS 1077	BEFORE THE STORM (LP, without poster, stickered sleeve) 12
84	Polydor POLD 5132	DON'T GET MAD, GET EVEN (LP, with insert) 15
84	Polydor POLD 5132	DON'T GET MAD, GET EVEN (2-LP, white labels, 2 different mixes of same album, promo only)..35
85	Metal Masters METALP 102	THANK YOU AND GOOD NIGHT (LP) 12

(see also Bruce Dickinson, Iron Maiden, John McCoy, Tiger, Colin Towns, Thunderstick, Nicky Moore, Mammoth, Egypt)

SAM THE SHAM & THE PHARAOHS

65	MGM MGM 1269	Woolly Bully/Ain't Gonna Move...12
65	MGM MGM 1269	Woolly Bully/Ain't Gonna Move (DJ Copy) 50
65	MGM MGM 1278	Ju Ju Hand/Big City Lights 10
65	MGM MGM 1285	Ring Dang Doo/Don't Try It 12
66	MGM MGM 1298	Red Hot/Long Long Way 15
66	MGM MGM 1315	Li'l Red Riding Hood/Love Me Like Before 10
66	MGM MGM 1326	The Hair On My Chinny Chin Chin/The Out Crowd..8
66	MGM MGM 1331	How Do You Catch A Girl/The Love You Left Behind......................................10
67	MGM MGM 1337	Oh That's Bad No That's Good/Take What You Can Get 10
67	MGM MGM 1343	Black Sheep/My Day's Gonna Come 15
68	MGM MGM 1379	Yakety Yak/Let Our Lovelight Shine 10
69	MGM MGM 1473	Woolly Bully/Ring Dang Doo 6
66	MGM MGM-EP 794	RED HOT (EP) 70
65	MGM MGM-C 1007	WOOLY BULLY (LP) 40
66	MGM MGM-C(S) 8032	LI'L RED RIDING HOOD (LP) 30

LEROY SAMUEL (ACTUALLY LEROY SMART)

| 72 | Punch PH 113 | Trying To Wreck My Life/JOHN HOLT: Pride And Joy ....12 |

(PHILLIP) SAMUEL THE FIRST

| 71 | Summit SUM 8515 | Sounds Of Babylon/BEVERLEY'S ALL STARS: Second Babylon Version ....10 |

JERRY SAMUELS

| 56 | HMV 7M 411 | Puppy Love/The Chosen Few ....15 |
| 56 | HMV 7M 411 | Puppy Love/The Chosen Few (78) ....10 |

(see also Napoleon XIV)

WINSTON SAMUELS

64	Columbia DB 7405	You Are The One/Angela 12
64	Rio R 26	Follow/I'm So Glad 12
64	Black Swan WI 419	Luck Will Come My Way/LLOYD BREVITT: One More Time 25
64	Black Swan WI 426	You Are The One/Gloria Love (B-side actually by Beltones) 15
65	Ska Beat JB 196	Be Prepared/Jericho Wall 20
65	Ska Beat JB 213	My Bride To Be/LLOYD PREVITT: Wayward Ska 25
65	Ska Beat JB 214	Never Again/My Angel 18
66	Ska Beat JB 238	What Have I Done/Broken Hearted 25
66	Ska Beat JB 241	Ups And Downs/Come What May 18
66	Ska Beat JB 244	Time Will Tell/I'm Sorry 18
67	Island WI 3051	The Greatest/FREDDIE & FITZY: Truth Hurts 40
67	Island WI 3053	I Won't Be Discouraged/FREDDIE & FITZIE: Why Did My Little Girl Cry............40
67	Fab FAB 21	Peace Of Mind/Shepherd Ben (by Prince Buster & Teddy King) 25
67	Fab FAB 14	Holding Out/To The Other Man 20
67	Fab FAB 28	Peace Of Mind/I'm Still Here 20
10	Randys THB 7002	Lick It Back/COUNT MACHUKI: Pepper Pot 10

SAMURAI (1)

| 68 | United Artists UP 2242 | Good Morning Starshine/Temple Of Gold ....35 |
| 71 | Greenwich GSLP 1003 | SAMURAI (LP, gatefold sleeve, white/brown label).....................................200 |

SAMURAI (2)

| 85 | Ebony EBON 25 | Fires Of Hell/Dreams Of The World (no p/s) ....12 |
| 84 | Ebony EBON 24 | SACRED BLADE (LP) ....15 |

SAN FRANCISCO TKO'S

| 98 | Kent 6T 14 | Make Up Your Mind/PEGGY GAINES: When The Boy That You Love...............25 |

SAND

| 71 | Philips 6006157 | Soft Lady/Babylon ....20 |

SANDEENO

| 03 | Wizkidz WK 011 | Ah Mankind/Preaching the Board ....12 |

ALEX SANDERS

| 70 | A&M AMLS 984 | A WITCH IS BORN (LP, foldout sleeve with warning sticker, withdrawn)...........125 |

GARY SANDERS

| 66 | Warner Bros WB 5676 | Ain't No Beatle/Ain't I Good To You ....12 |

GEORGE SANDERS

| 58 | HMV 7EG 8395 | THE GEORGE SANDERS TOUCH (EP)...8 |

PHARAOH SANDERS

| 66 | ESP Disk/Fontana SFJL 931 | PHARAOH SANDERS QUINTET (LP) ....35 |

71	Probe SPB 1019	DEAF, DUMB AND BLIND (LP)	25
70s	Impulse AS 9138	TAUHID (LP)	20
70s	Impulse AS 9199	SUMMUN BUKMUN UMYUN (LP)	25
70s	Impulse AS 9219	BLACK UNITY (LP)	25
70s	Impulse AS 9227	LIVE AT THE EAST (LP)	25
70s	Impulse AS 9229	THE BEST OF PHARAOH SANDERS (2-LP)	20
70s	Impulse 9233	WISDOM THROUGH MUSIC (LP)	20
70s	Impulse 9254	VILLAGE OF PHARAOHS (LP)	20
70s	Impulse 9261	ELEVATION (LP)	20
70s	Impulse 9280	LOVE IN US ALL (LP)	20
78	Arista SPART 1051	LOVE WILL FIND A WAY (LP)	15
82	Jasmine JAS 53	THEMBI (LP)	18

RAY SANDERS

60	London HLG 7106	A World So Full Of Love/A Little Bitty Tear (export issue)	12

TOMMY SANDERSON & SANDMEN

61	Ember EMB 131	Deadline/Candelglow	10
62	Ember EMB 152	Ding Dong Rag/Piano A-Go Go	10

CHRIS SANDFORD (& CORONETS)

63	Decca F 11778	Not Too Little - Not Too Much/I'm Lookin'	5
64	Decca F 11842	You're Gonna Be My Girl/Don't Leave Me Now (with Coronets)	6
65	Fontana TF 633	I Wish They Wouldn't Always Say I Sound Like The Guy From The U.S.A. Blues/Little Man, Nobody Cares	7

SANDGATE

75	Dawn DWS 1114	A Thousand Years/Such A Sad Song	6

GERRY SANDON

96	Twangsville TW 001	JUST GERRY (EP)	10

JOHNNY SANDON (& REMO FOUR)

63	Pye 7N 15542	Lies/On The Horizon (as Johnny Sandon & Remo Four)	15
63	Pye 7N 15559	Magic Potion/Yes (as Johnny Sandon & Remo Four)	15
64	Pye 7N 15602	Sixteen Tons/The Blizzard	10
64	Pye 7N 15665	Donna Means Heartbreak/Some Kinda Wonderful	10
64	Pye 7N 15717	The Blizzard/(I'd Be A) Legend In My Time	10

(see also Remo Four)

SAND PEBBLES

67	Track 604 015	Love Power/Because Of Love	20
68	Toast TT 505	If You Didn't Hear Me The First Time/Flower Power	8
69	Track 604 028	Love Power/Because Of Love (reissue)	15

SANDPIPERS

66	Pye Intl. 7N 25380	Guantanamera/What Makes You Dream, Pretty Girl	5
66	Pye International 7N 25396	Louie Louie/Things We Said Today	8
68	A & M AMS 723	Quando M'Immamoro (A Man Without Love)/I'll Remember You	8
76	Satril SAT 111	For The Last Time/Down By The River	8
76	Satril SAT 114	Hang On Sloopy/Skid Row Joe	5

SANDRA

86	10 TENY 78-12	(I'll Never Be) Maria Magdalena/Party Games/Little Girl (12", picture disc)	15
86	10 TEN 113-12/TENY 78-12	In The Heat Of The Night/Heatwave (Instrumental)//(I'll Never Be) Maria Magdalena/Party Games/Little Girl (12", double pack, including picture disc, gatefold PVC sleeve)	20
89	Siren SRNCD 85	Everlasting Love/Stop For A Minute/Everlasting Love (Remix)/ (I'll Never Be) Maria Magdalena (CD)	50
89	Siren SRNCD 104	Heaven Can Wait (Single Version 4.05)/(Dub Mix)/Heaven's Theme (Instrumental)/Heaven Can Wait (Extended Version) (3" CD, card sleeve)	20

SANDROSE

73	Polydor 2480 137	SANDROSE (LP)	250

SANDS (IRELAND)

69	Tribune TRS 122	Dance Dance Dance/The Cheater	20
69	Tribune TRS 129	Bubble Gum Music/Sherry	15
70	Major Minor MM 681	Venus/Cara Mia	10
69	Tribune	SAND DOIN'S (LP)	50
70s	Plough PLX 501	TIME OUT WITH THE SANDS (LP)	15

(see also Tony Kenny & Sands)

SANDS (U.K.)

67	Reaction 591 017	Mrs. Gillespie's Refrigerator/Listen To The Sky	350

(see also Others, Sundragon)

CLIVE SANDS

69	SNB 55-3955	Lo Mucho Que Te Quiro/Picture On The Wall	7
69	S.N.B. 55-4058	Hooked On A Feeling/Marie	7
69	S.N.B. 55-4431	Whitchi Tai Yo/In A Dream	12
69	CBS 4672	A Very Lonely Man/You Made Me What I Am	7

(see also Brothers Kane, Sarstedt Brothers, Wes Sands)

DAVEY SANDS & ESSEX

65	Decca F 12170	Please Me Mine/All The Time	20
67	CBS 202620	Advertising Girl/Without You I'm Nothing	25
71	Parlophone R5899	The Puppet Man/Oh What A Naughty Man	15

EVIE SANDS

65	Red Bird BC 118	Take Me For A Little While/Run Home To Mama	50
65	Red Bird BC 118	Take Me For A Little While/Run Home To Mama (DJ copy)	85
66	Cameo Parkway C 413	Picture Me Gone/It Makes Me Laugh	125
66	Cameo Parkway C 413	Picture Me Gone/It Makes Me Laugh (DJ copy)	200
68	A&M AMS 736	Shadow Of The Evening/Until It's Time For You To Go	10
69	A&M AMS 748	I'll Hold Out Of My Hand/One Fine Summer Morning	10
69	A&M AMS 760	Anyway That You Want Me/I'll Never Be Alone	10
75	Capitol CL 15818	You Brought The Woman Out In Me/Early Morning Sunshine	7

JODI(E) SANDS

57	London HL 8456	With All My Heart/More Than Only Friends (as Jodi Sands)	20
57	London HL 8530	Please Don't Tell Me (Sayonara)/If You're Not Completely Satisfied	20
57	London HL 8530	Please Don't Tell Me (Sayonara)/If You're Not Completely Satisfied (78)	15
58	Starlite ST45 005	All I Ask Of You/The Way I Love You	12
58	HMV POP 533	Someday (You'll Want Me To Want You)/Always In My Heart	10

SYLVIA SANDS

| 61 | Columbia DB 4579 | Autumn Tears/Steppin' Out With My Baby | 8 |

TOMMY SANDS

57	Capitol CL 14695	Teen-Age Crush/Hep Dee Hootie (Cutie Wootie)	25
57	Capitol CL 14724	Ring-A-Ding-A-Ding/My Love Song	25
57	Capitol CL 14724	Ring-A-Ding-A-Ding/My Love Song (78)	10
57	Capitol CL 14745	Goin' Steady/Ring My 'Phone	25
57	Capitol CL 14745	Goin' Steady/Ring My 'Phone (78)	10
57	Capitol CL 14781	Let Me Be Loved/Fantastically Foolish	10
57	Capitol CL 14811	Man, Like Wow!/A Swingin' Romance	20
57	Capitol CL 14811	Man, Like Wow!/A Swingin' Romance (78)	10
58	Capitol CL 14834	Sing, Boy, Sing/Crazy 'Cause I Love You	15
58	Capitol CL 14872	Hawaiian Rock/Teen-Age Doll	25
58	Capitol CL 14889	After The Senior Prom/Big Date	20
58	Capitol CL 14925	Blue Ribbon Baby/I Love You Because (as Tommy Sands & Raiders)	30
59	Capitol CL 14971	The Worryin' Kind/Bigger Than Texas	35
59	Capitol CL 15013	Is It Ever Gonna Happen/I Ain't Gittin' Rid Of You	30
59	Capitol CL 15047	Sinner Man/Bring Me Your Love	10
59	Capitol CL 15071	That's The Way I Am/I'll Be Seeing You	10
60	Capitol CL 15109	I Gotta Have You/You Hold The Future	10
60	Capitol CL 15143	The Old Oaken Bucket/These Are The Things You Are	8
61	Capitol CL 15219	Love In A Goldfish Bowl/I Love My Baby	7
63	HMV POP 1193	Connie/Young Man's Fancy	8
63	HMV POP 1247	Only 'Cause I'm Lonely/Cinderella	8
66	Liberty LIB 55842	The Statue/Lolita	45
66	Liberty LIB 55842	The Statue/Lolita (DJ copy)	85
57	Capitol EAP1 848	STEADY DATE WITH TOMMY SANDS PT. 1 (EP)	30
57	Capitol EAP2 848	STEADY DATE WITH TOMMY SANDS PT. 2 (EP)	30
57	Capitol EAP3 848	STEADY DATE WITH TOMMY SANDS PT. 3 (EP)	30
57	Capitol EAP1 851	TEENAGE CRUSH (EP)	30
59	Capitol EAP1 1081	SANDS STORM PART 1 (EP)	25
59	Capitol EAP2 1081	SANDS STORM PART 2 (EP)	25
59	Capitol EAP3 1081	SANDS STORM PART 3 (EP)	25
59	Capitol EAP1 1123	THIS THING CALLED LOVE (EP)	25
57	Capitol T 848	STEADY DATE WITH TOMMY SANDS (LP)	50
58	Capitol T 929	SING, BOY, SING (soundtrack) (LP)	50
59	Capitol T 1081	SANDS STORM! (LP)	80
59	Capitol T 1123	THIS THING CALLED LOVE (LP)	30
60	Capitol (S)T 1239	WHEN I'M THINKING OF YOU (LP, mono)	25
60	Capitol (S)T 1239	WHEN I'M THINKING OF YOU (LP, stereo)	20
61	Capitol T 1426	A DREAM WITH TOMMY SANDS (LP)	15

TONY SANDS & DRUMBEATS

| 60s | Studio 36 NSRS EP 1/22 | Shame Shame Shame/I Got A Feeling | 250 |

WES SANDS

| 63 | Columbia DB 4996 | There's Lots More Where This Came From/Three Cups | 45 |

(see also Brothers Kane, Sarstedt Brothers, Clive Sands)

SANDS OF TIME

| 66 | Pye 7N 17140 | Where Did We Go Wrong/When I Look Back | 10 |
| 67 | Pye 7N 17236 | One Day/Ev'ry Time We Say Goodbye | 8 |

PAT SANDY

| 69 | Attack ATT 8000 | Gentle On My Mind/BIG L: Soulful | 6 |

SANDY & TEACHERS

| 64 | Columbia DB 7244 | Listen With Mammy/Real Sweet | 5 |

(see also Sandy Brown)

SANDY COAST

71	Polydor 2121 046	True Love/That's A Wonder	7
73	Polydor 2001 457	Blackboard Jungle Lady/Don't Get Me Wrong	7
69	Page One POLS 020	FROM THE STEREO WORKSHOP (LP)	200
69	Page One MORS 201	SHIPWRECK (LP)	200
73	Polydor 2310 277	STONEWALL (LP)	20

SAN FRANCISCO EARTHQUAKE

| 68 | Mercury MF 1036 | Fairy Tales Can Come True (Have You Heard About Lucy)/Su Su | 10 |

CLAUDE SANG

| 70 | Sugar SU 105 | I'm In Love Again/You'll Never Fool Me Again | 6 |
| 70 | Sugar SUM 1 | THE WORLD OF REGGAE VOL. 1 (LP) | 15 |

SAN REMO STRINGS

71	Tamla Motown TMG 795	Festival Time/All Turned On	12
71	Tamla Motown TMG 795	Festival Time/All Turned On (DJ copy)	30
72	Tamla Motown TMG 807	Reach Out, I'll Be There/Hungry For Love	10
72	Tamla Motown TMG 807	Reach Out, I'll Be There/Hungry For Love (DJ copy)	30
73	Tamla Motown STML 11216	SAN REMO STRINGS SWING (LP)	20

SANS NOMS

| 71 | Decca Eclipse ECS 2095 | LARGELY LATIN (LP) | 12 |

BOBBY SANSOM (& GIANTS)

63	Oriole CB 1837	There's A Place/Lucille (as Bobby Sansom & Giants)	20
63	Oriole CB 1888	Where Have You Been/Do You Promise (as Bobby Sansom & Giants)	18
70	Decca F 13104	Lady One And Only/Handbags And Gladrags	8
71	Decca F 13151	I Believe In Music/The Valley Of The Shadows Of Tears	8

MONGO SANTAMARIA
63	Riverside RIF 106909	Watermelon Man/Don't Bother Me No More	20
65	CBS 201766	El Pussycat/Black Eyed Peas And Rice	20
69	Direction 58-4086	Cloud Nine/Son Of A Preacher Man	18
69	Direction 58-4430	Twenty Five Miles/El Tres	15
66	CBS SS 62123	HEY! LET'S PARTY (LP)	20
69	CBS S 233811	ALL STRUNG OUT (LP)	20
71	CBS 63904	WORKING ON A GROOVY THING (LP)	20
71	Atlantic 2400 140	MONGO'S WAY (LP)	20

SANTANA
69	CBS 4593	Persuasion/Savor	5
70	CBS 4940	Evil Ways/Jin-Go-Lo-Ba	5
70	CBS 5325	Black Magic Woman/Hope You're Feeling Better	5
69	CBS 63015	SANTANA (LP, laminated sleeve original, orange label)	20
70	CBS 63815	SANTANA (LP, non-laminated sleeve reissue, orange label)	12
70	CBS 64087	ABRAXAS (LP, orange label)	15
71	CBS 69015	SANTANA (III) (LP, gatefold sleeve, some stickered, orange label)	15
72	CBS CQ 30595	SANTANA (III) (LP, gatefold sleeve, quadrophonic)	18
72	CBS 65299	CARAVANSERAI (LP, gatefold sleeve, orange label)	12
73	CBS CQ 31610	CARAVANSERAI (LP, gatefold sleeve, quadrophonic)	15
74	CBS CQ 32445	WELCOME (LP, embossed gatefold sleeve, quadrophonic)	15
75	CBS CQ 30130	ABRAXAS (LP, gatefold sleeve, quadrophonic)	15
75	CBS Q 69081	GREATEST HITS (LP, quadrophonic)	15
75	CBS Q 69084	BORBOLETTA (LP, quadrophonic)	15
76	CBS Q 86005	AMIGOS (LP, quadrophonic)	15
85	CBS 69084	BORBOLETTA (LP, Nimbus Supercut, mail order only through Hi Fi Today magazine)	70

CARLOS SANTANA & BUDDY MILES
72	CBS 8338	Evil Ways/Them Changes	5
83	CBS A 3359	They All Went To Mexico (with Willie Nelson)/BUDDY MILES: Mudbone (p/s)	5
72	CBS 65142	CARLOS SANTANA & BUDDY MILES LIVE (LP, gatefold sleeve)	12
73	CBS CQ 31308	CARLOS SANTANA & BUDDY MILES LIVE (LP, quadrophonic)	15

(see also Santana, Buddy Miles, Mahavishnu Orchestra, John McLaughlin, John Lee Hooker)

SANTELLS
66	Sue WI 4020	So Fine/These Are Love	25

DAVID SANTO
68	London HLK 10219	Jingle Down A Hill/Rising Of Scorpio	8

SANTO & JOHNNY
59	Pye International 7N 25037	Sleep Walk/All Night Diner	20
59	Pye International N 25037	Sleep Walk/All Night Diner (78 rpm)	15
60	Parlophone R 4619	Tear Drop/The Long Walk Home	20
60	Parlophone R 4644	Caravan/Summertime	10
61	Pye International 7N 25111	Theme From Come September/Hopscotch	10
61	Parlophone R 4844	Bullseye!/Twistin' Bells	10
62	Parlophone R 4865	Birmingham/The Mouse	10
62	Stateside SS 110	Spanish Harlem/Stage To Cimarron	10
64	Stateside SS 253	Three Caballeros/Manhattan Spiritual	10
64	Stateside SS 292	In The Still Of The Night/Song For Rosemary	10
60	Parlophone GEP 8806	SANTO AND JOHNNY NO. 1 (EP)	30
60	Parlophone GEP 8813	SANTO AND JOHNNY NO. 2 (EP)	30
64	Stateside S(S)L 1008	HAWAII (LP)	20

SAPODILLA PUNCH
69	Mercury MF 1112	Hold On I'm Coming/Bach To Minor	8

SAPPHIRE
82	Sapphire Rocks SRR 001	Jealousy (p/s)	200
72	SRT SRT 72226	SAPPHIRE (LP)	180

SAPPHIRES
63	Stateside SS 223	Where Is Johnny Now/Your True Love	55
64	Stateside SS 267	Who Do You Love/Oh So Soon	65
65	HMV POP 1441	Gotta Have Your Love/Gee Baby I'm Sorry	180
65	HMV POP 1441	Gotta Have Your Love/Gee Baby I'm Sorry (DJ copy)	350
65	HMV POP 1461	Evil One/How Could I Say Goodbye	180
65	HMV POP 1461	Evil One/How Could I Say Goodbye (DJ copy)	300
72	Probe PRO 556	Gotta Have Your Love/Gee Baby I'm Sorry (reissue)	15
74	Probe PRO 609	Slow Fizz/Our Love Is Everywhere	12
78	ABC 4221	Gonna Be A Big Thing/EDDIE REGAN: Playin' Hide And Seek	8

SARABAND
73	Folk Heritage FHR 050	CLOSE TO IT ALL (LP)	22

SARACEN
82	Nucleus SAR 1	No More Lonely Nights/Rock Of Ages (p/s, with patch)	8
82	Nucleus SAR 1	No More Lonely Nights/Rock Of Ages (p/s)	6
83	Neat NEAT 30	We Have Arrived/Face In The Crowd (p/s)	7
82	Nucleus MPGR 492	HEROES, SAINTS AND FOOLS (LP)	15
84	Neat NEAT 1016	CHANGE OF HEART (LP)	12

SARAH JANE
66	Pye 7N 17114	Listen People/The World Is Round	7

SARASOTA
96	BIT Productions MIKE 004	We're Gettin' Hot (1-sided 12")	40
97	BIT Productions MIKE 009	Pleasure/We're Gettin' Hot (the Maximum Project pumped up remix) (stickered white label 12")	40

SARDONICUS
73	Country Recording Service COUN 240	Nymph/Evaporated Brain	350

DON SARGENT
60	Vogue Pop V 9160	St. James' Infirmary/Gypsy Boots (triangular centre)	500

SARI & SHALIMARS
68	United Artists UP 2235	It's So Lonely (Being Together)/You Walked Out On Me Before	30

DEREK SARJEANT
61	Oak RGJ 101	FOLK SONGS SUNG BY DEREK SARJEANT (EP)	20
61	Oak RGJ 103	SONGS WE LIKE TO SING (EP, with tracks by Lisa Turner & Mick Wells)	15
61	Oak RGJ 105	FOLK SONGS SUNG BY DEREK SARJEANT VOL. 2 (EP)	15
63	Oak RGJ 117	MAN OF KENT (EP)	18
61	Oak RGJ 7444	ENGLISH FOLK SONGS (EP)	20
61	Oak RGJ 7450	A SAILOR'S LIFE: SONGS OF THE SEA AND THE SHORE (EP)	20

MIKE SARNE
62	Parlophone R 4974	Just For Kicks/Don't You Phone Me, I'll Phone You	6
63	Parlophone R 5010	Code Of Love/Are You Satisfied	6
63	Parlophone R 5060	Please Don't Say/Now You've Moved	6
63	Parlophone R 5090	Hello Lover Boy/Baby I'm On My Way	8
64	Parlophone R 5129	Out And About/A Place To Go	8
64	Parlophone R 5170	Love Me Please/You've Got Something (as Mike Sarne & Le Roys)	10
63	Parlophone DP 558	Just Like Eddie/Slow Twistin' Round The Totem Pole (export issue)	80
63	Parlophone GEP 8879	MIKE SARNE HIT PARADE (EP)	30
62	Parlophone PMC 1187	COME OUTSIDE (LP)	30

(see also Wendy Richards, Le Roys, Billie Davis, Rod McKuen)

SAROFEEN & SMOKE
71	Pye International 7N 25556	Susan Jane/Tomorrow	15
71	Pye Intl. NSPL 28153	DO IT (LP)	25

SAROLTA
68	Island WIP 6035	Open Your Hands/L.O.V.E.	15
69	President PT248	I Am A Woman/Change Of Heart	10

SARR BAND
78	Calendar LDAY 115	Magic Mandrake/Double Action (12")	25

PETER SARSTEDT
68	Island WIP 6028	I Must Go On/Mary Jane	30
68	United Artists UP 2228	I Am A Cathedral/Blagged	10
69	United Artists UP 2262	Morning Mountain/Step Into The Candelight	10
69	United Artists UP 35021	Frozen Orange Sea/Arethusa Loser	15
69	United Artists UP 35041	As Though It Were A Movie/Take Off Your Clothes	8
69	United Artists UP 35075	Without Darkness (There's No Light)/Step Into The Candelight	8
69	United Artists (S)ULP 1219	PETER SARSTEDT (LP)	12
69	United Artists UAL 29037	AS THOUGH IT WERE A MOVIE (LP)	12
71	United Artists UAS 29247	EVERY WORD YOU SAY (LP, with inner sleeve)	12

(see also Sarstedt Brothers, Brothers Kane, Peter Lincoln)

SARSTEDT BROTHERS
73	Regal Zonophone RZ 3081	Chinese Restaurant/Beloved Illusions	7
73	Regal Zono. SRZA 8516	WORLDS APART TOGETHER (LP, gatefold sleeve with booklet)	20

(see also Brothers Kane, Peter Sarstedt, Eden Kane, Clive Sands, Wes Sands)

DAN SARTAIN
09	Third Man TMR 011	Bohemian Grove/Atheist Funeral (100 only, luminous vinyl)	40

SAS
85	No Label SAS4	SUAVE AND SOPHISTICATED? (7" EP, fold-out sleeve)	25

SASPARELLA
69	Decca F 12892	Spooky/Come Inside	30

SASSAFRAS
73	Polydor 2383 245	EXPECTING COMPANY (LP)	15

SASSENACHS
64	Fontana TF 518	That Don't Worry Me/All Over You	30

SATAN
82	Guardian GRC 145	Kiss Of Death/Heads Will Roll (with p/s)	200
82	Guardian GRC 145	Kiss Of Death/Heads Will Roll	50
85	Neat NEAT 1012	COURT IN THE ACT (LP)	30

SATANIC MALFUNCTIONS
86	Teacore TEACORE 1	WHO WANTS THE WORLD EP (wraparound p/s)	15
87	Looney Tunes TUNE 8	I'VE HAD JUST ABOUT ALL I CAN TAKE EP	8
89	Teacore TEA 3	REMEMBER EP (wraparound p/s)	12
88	Teacore TEA 2	HELLBOUND (LP, insert)	20
90	Teacore TEA 5	DISGRACE TO HUMANITY (LP, insert)	20

SATANIC RITES
81	Heavy Metal HEAVY 8	Live To Ride/Hit And Run (p/s)	12
85	Chub CHUBLP 001	WHICH WAY THE WIND BLOWS (LP)	25
87	Chub CHUBLP 002	NO USE CRYING (LP)	30

SATAN'S RATS
77	DJM DJS 10819	In My Love For You/Façade (p/s)	30
77	DJM DJS 10821	Year Of The Rats/Louise (p/s)	25
78	DJM DJS 10840	You Make Me Sick/Façade (p/s)	25
89	Overground OVER 01	Year Of The Rats/Louise (p/s, 600 yellow vinyl)	6
89	Overground OVER 01	Year Of The Rats/Louise (p/s, 400 white vinyl)	7
89	Overground OVER 01	Year Of The Rats/Louise (p/s, 25 gold vinyl, numbered test pressings)	15
89	Overground OVER 02	In My Love For You/Facade (p/s, 600 yellow vinyl)	12
89	Overground OVER 02	In My Love For You/Facade (p/s, 400 white vinyl)	12
89	Overground OVER 02	In My Love For You/Facade (p/s, 25 gold vinyl, numbered test pressings)	15
91	Overground OVER 14	You Make Me Sick/Louise (p/s, clear vinyl, 567 copies only)	7

YOUNG SATCH
70	Black Swan BW 1401	Bonga Bonga Bonga/HI-TALS: Ram Buck	40
70	Black Swan BW 1401	Bongo Bongo/BOYS: Ramba	12

GIRL SATCHMO

61	Blue Beat BB 45	Satchmo's Mash Potato/Darling	25
62	Blue Beat BB 79	Twist Around Town/My New Honey (with Karl Rowe & Bluebeats)	25
63	Blue Beat BB 156	Don't Be Sad/Brother Joe (with Les Dawson Combo)	25
64	Blue Beat BB 227	Rhythm Of The New Beat/Blue Beat Chariot	30
69	Fab FAB 111	Take You For A Ride/I'm Coming Home	20
69	Trojan TR 676	Taken For A Ride/I'm Coming Home	15

(see also Pat Satchmo, Sugar & Dandy)

PAT SATCHMO

69	Punch PH 9	Hello Dolly/ERIC DONALSON: Never Get Away	25
69	Upsetter US 316	Hello Dolly/King Of The Trombone	35
70	Punch PH 24	Wonderful World/MEDITATORS: Purple Mast	15
70	Songbird SB 1039	A Handful Of Friends/CRYSTALITES: Handful - Version	10
72	Attack ATT 8024	What's Going On/LLOYD & CAREY: Tubby's In Full Swing	30

SATELLITES

83	Brickyard EOR 1	Vietnam/Lucy Is A Prostitute/I Fell In Love With A Lesbian (p/s)	10
84	Brickyard	HERE IS TODAY'S NEWS (LP)	15

SATIN BELLS

68	Pye 7N 17531	Baby You're So Right For Me/When You're Ready	10
68	Pye 7N 17608	Da-Di-Da-Da/Oh No Oh Yes	6
69	Decca F 22937	I Stand Accused (Of Loving You)/Sweet Darlin'	20
70	Decca F 23044	The Power Of Love/Baby Come Back	6

(see also Three Bells)

SATIN STORM

91	Satin Storm SSP 201	Satin Storm 1999/Pleasurezone (inst)/Buzz/Feel The Spirit (12")	30
91	Satin Storm SSHC 1	See The Light/Call In The Hardcore/Kick Up A Sound Boy/Chill Out (12". As Satin Storm Dancers)	15
92	Satin Storm DJT DAPSS 1	Let's Get Together/Free My Mind (12". Artist not credited on labels)	40
92	Satin Storm ST 01	Sweat/Can't Wait/Can't Take No More/Tekno/Satin Storm/EBGB (12")	20
92	Satin Storm SSHC 2	What About What I Need /Drop That Bass/House Of My Dreams/Ram it (12" Artist not credited on labels)	15
92	Satin Storm SSHC 3	Think I'm Going Out Of My Head/Unknown/What Do You Do? (12")	15
93	Satin Storm SSHC 4	Return Of The Blopblingers/Rough And Smooth & The Driven) (12")	10
93	Satin Storm SSHC 5	Come On, Get Together/I'm A Technician/He's On It, All Night Long (12")	10

SATISFACTION (1)

71	Decca F 13129	Love It Is/Cold Summer	10
71	Decca F 13207	Don't Rag The Lady/Gregory Shan't	10
71	Decca SKL 5075	SATISFACTION (LP, laminated front sleeve, blue/silver boxed label)	50

(see also Mike Cotton Sound)

SATISFACTION (2)

79	Live & Love LAP 005	SATISFACTION IN DUB (LP)	40

SATISFIERS

57	Vogue Coral Q 72247	Where'll I Be Tomorrow Night?/Come Away, Love	12
57	Vogue Coral LVA 9068	THE SATISFIERS (LP)	20

LIZZARD SATTAI

76	Trojan TRLS 138	LIZZARD (LP)	30

LONNIE SATTIN

56	Capitol CL 14552	Trapped (In The Web Of Love)/Your Home Can Be A Castle	6
56	Capitol CL 14638	High Steel/What Time Does The Sun Go Down?	5
57	Capitol CL 14771	I'll Never Stop Loving You/Whoo-Pie Shoo-Pie	5
58	Capitol CL 14831	Ring Around The Moon/My Heart's Your Home	5
60	Warner Bros WB 15	I'll Fly Away/Any More Than I	5

SATURNALIA

71	Matrix TRIX 1	MAGICAL LOVE (LP, picture disc with 3D labels, with booklet & ticket)	150
71	Matrix TRIX 1	MAGICAL LOVE (LP, allegedly some copies in laminated sleeve, picture disc with 3D labels, with booklet & ticket)	500
73	Matrix TRIX 1	MAGICAL LOVE (LP, picture disc, reissue)	25

(see also Horse)

SATYR

79	Stardust STAR 001	Love Slide Boogie/Problem In The City	10

SAUCERMAN

88	Fierce FRIGHT 029	Scatterbrain/Beyond Repair (12", p/s with inner, 1 side etched, 1,000 only)	8
89	Fierce FRIGHT 035	I Will Be King/Sid James Rules (withdrawn)	25
80s	Fierce	WRESTLING (12", sampler, withdrawn)	12

(see also Kray Cherubs)

LARRY SAUNDERS

74	London HLU 10469	On The Real Side/Let Me Be The Special One	20
74	London HLU 10469	On The Real Side/Let Me Be The Special One (DJ copy)	40

MAHALIA SAUNDERS

71	Moodisc HME 112	Down The Aisle/IAN ROBINSON: Three For One	8
71	Upsetter US 374	Pieces Of My Heart/UPSETTERS: Version	10

KEVIN SAUNDERSON

88	Kool Kat DJ 5	Bounce Your Body To The Box (Mike 'Hitman' Wilson Acid Remix)/(Original Detroit Mix)/The Groove That Won't Stop (Detroit Special Mix)/Force Field (12")	15

TUPPER SAUSSY

63	London HAU 8127	DISCOVER TUPPER SAUSSY (LP)	15

LES SAUTERELLES

68	Decca F 22824	Heavenly Club/Dream Machine	45

SAVAGE

82	Ebony EBON 10	Ain't No Fit Place/China Run	8
83	Ebony EBON 12	LOOSE 'N' LETHAL (LP)	25
85	Zebra ZEB 4	HYPERACTIVE (LP)	12

MINT VALUE £

EDNA SAVAGE

55	Parlophone MSP 6175	Stars Shine In Your Eyes/A Star Is Born	7
55	Parlophone MSP 6181	Candlelight/In The Wee Small Hours Of The Morning	7
55	Parlophone MSP 6189	Arrivederci Darling/Bella Notte	7
56	Parlophone MSP 6217	Tell Me, Tell Me, Tell Me That You Love Me/Please Hurry Home	7
56	Parlophone R 4226	My Prayer/Me 'n' You 'n' The Moon	7
56	Parlophone R 4253	Never Leave Me/Don't Ever Go (I Need You)	6
57	Parlophone R 4301	Me Head's In De Barrel/Five Iranges Four Apples	6
57	Parlophone R 4360	Let Me Love/Diano Marina	6

(see also Michael Holliday)

JOAN SAVAGE

57	Columbia DB 3929	Five Oranges, Four Apples/Bamboozled	5
57	Columbia DB 3968	With All My Heart/Love Letters In The Sand	5
57	Columbia DB 4039	Shake Me, I Rattle/Lula Rock-A-Hula	20
58	Columbia DB 4159	Hello Happiness, Goodbye Blues/Left Right Out Of My Heart	5

SAVAGE PENCIL

88	Blast First FU 3LP	PRESENTS ANGEL DUST: MUSIC FOR MOVIE BIKERS (LP, picture disc, 1,000 only)	12

(see also Art Attacks, Kray Cherubs)

SAVAGE RESURRECTION

68	Mercury MF 1027	Thing In E/Fox Is Sick	60
68	Mercury SMCL 20123	SAVAGE RESURRECTION (LP)	175

SAVAGE ROSE

68	Polydor 184206	IN THE PLAIN (LP, red label)	40
69	Polydor 184316	TRAVELLIN' (LP, red label)	40
72	RCA Victor SF 8250	REFUGEE (LP, laminated front sleeve, orange label)	30
71	RCA Victor SF 8169	YOUR DAILY GIFT (LP, laminated front sleeve, orange label)	30

SAVAGES

63	Decca DFE 8546	EVERYBODY SURF! WITH THE SURFIN' SAVAGES (EP)	200

(see also Soul Sounds, Screaming Lord Sutch, Circles, Tony Dangerfield & Thrills)

JULIAN JAY SAVARIN

73	Lyntone LYN 3426	I Am You/Kizeesh (Corgi Books sampler)	30
73	Birth RAB 2	WAITERS ON THE DANCE (LP, textured sleeve with insert)	250
73	Birth RAB 2	WAITERS ON THE DANCE (LP, textured sleeve without insert)	150
87	Five Hours Back TOCK 002	WAITERS ON THE DANCE (LP, reissue)	20

(see also Julian's Treatment)

SAVATAGE

85	Music For Nations MFN 48	SIRENS (LP)	12
85	Music For Nations MFN 42	THE DUNGEONS ARE CALLING (LP)	12

JIMMY SAVILE

62	Decca F 11493	Ahab The Arab/Very Unlikely	10
63	Decca F 11576	The Bosa Nova/Don't Do Anything I'd Like	10

(see also Vernons Girls)

RONNIE SAVOY

61	MGM MGM 1122	And The Heavens Cried/Big Chain	15
61	MGM MGM 1131	Bewitched/It's Gotta Be love	10

SAVOY BROWN (BLUES BAND)

66	Purdah 45-3503	I Tried/Can't Quit You Baby (as Savoy Brown's Blues Band)	300
67	Decca F 12702	Taste And Try, Before You Buy/Someday People (as Savoy Brown Blues Band)	20
68	Decca F 12797	Walking By Myself/Vicksburg Blues	12
69	Decca F 12843	Train To Nowhere/Tolling Bells	15
69	Decca F 12978	I'm Tired/Stay With Me Baby	30
70	Decca F 13019	A Hard Way To Go/Waiting In The Bamboo Grove	15
70	Decca F 13098	Poor Girl/Master Hare	12
71	Decca F 13247	Tell Mama/Let It Rock	12
73	Decca F 13372	So Tired/The Saddest Feeling	7
73	Decca F 13431	Coming Down Your Way/I Can't Find You	7
67	Decca LK 4883	SHAKE DOWN (LP, mono, unboxed logo label)	150
67	Decca SKL 4883	SHAKE DOWN (LP, stereo, unboxed logo label)	90
68	Decca LK 4935	GETTING TO THE POINT (LP, mono, unboxed logo label)	100
68	Decca SKL 4935	GETTING TO THE POINT (LP, stereo, unboxed logo label)	75
68	Decca LK 4994	BLUE MATTER (LP, mono, unboxed logo label)	100
69	Decca SKL 4994	BLUE MATTER (LP, stereo, unboxed logo label)	50
69	Decca LK 5013	A STEP FURTHER (LP, mono, unboxed logo label)	100
69	Decca SKL 5013	A STEP FURTHER (LP, stereo, unboxed logo label)	40
70	Decca LK 5043	RAW SIENNA (LP, mono, laminated gatefold sleeve, boxed logo label)	100
70	Decca SKL 5043	RAW SIENNA (LP, stereo, laminated gatefold sleeve, boxed logo label)	30
70	Decca SKL 5066	LOOKING IN (LP, 1st pressing, dull laminated gatefold sleeve)	60
70	Decca SKL 5066	LOOKING IN (LP, 2nd pressing, glossy laminated gatefold sleeve)	30
71	Decca TXS 104	STREET CORNER TALKING (LP, gatefold sleeve)	20
72	Decca TXS 107	HELLBOUND TRAIN (LP, gatefold sleeve)	15
73	Decca SKL 5152	LION'S SHARE (LP)	15
73	Decca TXS 112	JACK THE TOAD (LP)	18
74	Decca SKL 5186	BOOGIE BROTHERS (LP)	12

(see also Warren Philips & The Rockets, Chris Youlden, Stone's Masonry, Jackie Lynton, Foghat)

SAVWINKLE AND TURNERHOPPER

70	Pye 7N 17913	Your Mother Thinks I'm A Hoodlum/Dirtyin' My Thing	20

TOM SAWYER

69	CBS 4243	Cookbook/Gates	10

(see also Unit 4 + 2)

'ACE' DINNING SAX

59	Top Rank JAR 184	Mulholland Drive/My Love	15
59	Top Rank JAR 184	Mulholland Drive/My Love (78)	10

MIKE SAX & IDOLS
65	Mercury MF 886	My Little One/Come Back To Me	10

(see also Idols)

AL SAXON
58	Fontana H 138	Where The Black Eyed Susans Grow/She Screamed	7
58	Fontana H 164	The Day The Rains Came (Le Jour Ou La Pluie Viendra)/You're The Top-Cha	12
59	Fontana H 188	Chattanooga Choo-Choo/Chip Off The Old Block	5
59	Fontana H 205	Only Sixteen/I'm All Right, Jack	12
59	Fontana H 222	Linda Lu/Heart Of Stone	8
59	Fontana H 231	Marina/Me Without You	6
61	Piccadilly 35002	Can You Keep A Secret/Promises	7
60	Fontana H 278	Blue-Eyed Boy/Don't Push Your Luck	15
61	Piccadilly 7N 35011	There I've Said It Again/You Came A Long Way From St. Louis	15
61	Piccadilly 7N 35021	Don't Get Around Much Anymore/Saturday Night	8
62	Parlophone R 4966	I Got A Girl/But I Do	7
63	Parlophone R 5016	The Man Who Broke The Bank At Monte Carlo/If You Want To Go To Dreamland	7
64	Mercury MF 801	Who Was That Girl?/All Night Long	7
64	Mercury MF 811	Another You/Hot And Bothered	7
68	President PT 183	Against The Wall/East Side 628	6
72	Phoenix NIX 125	Beautiful/Count To Ten	15

(see also Lana Sisters, Ella Stone & Moss)

SKY 'SUNLIGHT' SAXON
87	Fierce FRIGHT 009	Dog=God (p/s, with badge, piece of shirt, sugar 'skycubes' & inserts)	20
84	Psycho PSYCHO 29	STARRY EYED (LP, clear vinyl)	20
84	Psycho PSYCHO 29	STARRY EYED (LP)	12
90s	Water NOXAS 39	DRAGON SLAYER (LP, multicoloured vinyl)	12

(see also Seeds)

SKY SAXON & THE NEW SEEDS
90s	Expression EXP 777-3	In Love With Life/Starry Ride/Queen/Tired Of Being Poor	6

SAXON (1)
63	Ace Of Clubs ACL 1173	MEET THE SAXONS (LP)	80

SAXON (2)
79	Carrere SAM 109	Big Teaser/Stallions Of The Highway (12", promo only)	10
79	Carrere CAR 118	Big Teaser/Stallions Of The Highway (p/s)	7
79	Carrere CAR 129	Backs To The Wall/Militia Guard (p/s)	7
80	Carrere CAR 165	Suzy Hold On/Judgement Day (live)	6
81	Carrere CAR 180	And The Bands Played On/Hungry Years/Heavy Metal Thunder (7" picture disc)	6
83	Carrere CARP 284	Nightmare/Midas Touch (7" picture disc)	6
83	Carrere SAXON P1	Power And The Glory/See The Light Shining (live) (7" picture disc)	5
85	Parlophone RP 6103	Back On The Streets/Live Fast Die Young (7" shaped picture disc)	6
86	EMI EMIP 5587	Rock The Nations/747 (Strangers In The Night)/And The Bands Played On (7" shaped picture disc)	6
86	EMI 12EM15587	ROck The Nations/747 (Strangers In The Night)/And The Band Played On (12", clear vinyl)	8
88	EMI EMP 41	Ride Like The Wind/Red Alert (shaped 7" picture disc)	6
91	Virgin DINSY 105	We Will Remember/Altar Of The Gods (shaped 7" picture disc, insert)	6
82	Carrere CAL 137	THE EAGLE HAS LANDED (LP, picture disc)	15
83	Carrere CAL 147	THE POWER AND THE GLORY (LP, picture disc)	15
84	Carrere CALP 200	CRUSADER (LP, picture disc)	15
85	Parlophone SAXONP 2	INNOCENCE IS NO EXCUSE (LP, picture disc)	15
87	EMI EMS 1163	DENIM AND LEATHER (LP, blue vinyl reissue)	15

(see also Son Of A Bitch)

LINDA SAXONE
64	Pye 7N 15624	Love Is A Many Splendoured Thing/The Other Side Of The Street	10
65	Polydor BM 56015	I've Got To Say No/Another Day Another Night	6
65	Polydor BM 56032	Only Last Night/Lucky Girl	6

SAXONS
65	Decca F 12179	Saxon War Cry/Click-Ete-Clack	60

(see also Tornados)

JOHNNY SAYLES
66	Liberty LIB 12042	Deep Down In Your Heart/Anything For You	40

RAT SCABIES
84	Paradiddle Music HIT 1	Let There Be Rats/Wiped Out/Drums Drums Drums (mail-order only, no p/s)	8

(see also Damned, The Rat & The Whale, Pete Zear)

SCABS
79	Clubland Records SJP 799	Amory Building/Leave Me Alone/Don't Just Sit There/U.R.E. (blue/black or red/black fold out 'envelope' p/s, 2 inserts)	40

SCAFFOLD
66	Parlophone R 5443	2 Day's Monday/3 Blind Jellyfish	10
66	Parlophone R 5548	Goodbat Nightman/A Long Strong Black Pudding	10
67	Parlophone R 5643	Thank U Very Much/Ide B The First	5
68	Parlophone R 5734	Lily The Pink/Buttons On Your Mind	5
68	Parlophone R 5679	Do You Remember?/Carry On Krow	8
68	Parlophone R 5703	1-2-3/Today	6
69	Parlophone R 5784	Charity Bubbles/Goose	6
69	Parlophone R 5812	Gin Gan Goolie/Liver Birds	8
70	Parlophone R 5847	All The Way Up/Please - Sorry	8
70	Parlophone R 5866	Busdreams/If I Could Start All Over Again	8
71	Parlophone R 5922	Do The Albert/Commercial Break	8
74	Warner Bros K 16400	Liverpool Lou/Ten Years On After Strawberry Jam	6
68	Parlophone PMC/PCS 7051	SCAFFOLD ... - LIVE AT QUEEN ELIZABETH HALL (LP, black/yellow label with "Sold in U.K..." text)	40
69	Parlophone PMC/PCS 7077	L THE P (LP, black/yellow label with "Sold in U.K..." text)	30
73	Island ILPS 9234	FRESH LIVER (LP, gatefold sleeve, pink rim palm tree label)	20

(see also McGough-McGear, Roger McGough, Mike McGear, Liverpool Scene, Grimms, John Gorman)

MINT VALUE £

BOZ SCAGGS
69	Atlantic 588 205	BOZ SCAGGS (LP)	12
71	CBS 64248	MOMENTS (LP, plain orange label)	12

(see also Steve Miller Band, Steve York's Camelo Pardalis)

HARVEY SCALES & 7 SOUND
67	Atlantic 584 146	Get Down/Love It Is	15

SCAMPS
59	London HLW 8827	Petite Fleur/Naomi	12
62	Ace Of Clubs ACL 1116	TEEN DANCE AND SING ALONG PARTY (LP)	15

SCANDAL
79	Local LOC 1	Comic Book Hero/Casualty Of Love (p/s)	7

JOHNNY SCAR
85	Solomonic SM12 025	United Africa/Dub It In Africa (12")	200

SCARAB
80	Inferno HEADBANGER 1	Rock Night/Wicked Woman	30
84	Pharaoh PR-001	Poltergeist/Hell On Wheels (p/s)	50
03	Phoenix NWOBHM 7013	Rock Night/Wicked Woman (reissue, p/s, red vinyl 250 only, numbered)	15

SCARECROW
78	Spilt Milk SMFM 11278	SCARECROW (LP, numbered foldout sleeve with insert; beware of watermarked unnumbered copies)	100

SCARLET ALIVE
82	Jive Alive JA001	THE TERMINAL JIVE AND SCARLET ALIVE EP (2 tracks on one side, p/s, insert)	15
82	S.R.R. SRR011	On Earth And In Heaven/Always	15

SCARLETS
64	Philips BF 1376	Let's Go/Tambourine Shake	6

CHARLES FRANCIS SCARRATT III
59	Felsted AF 113	Two Innocent Lovers/Lovemobile	6

SCARS
79	Fast Product FAST 8	Horrorshow/Adult-ery (p/s)	10
80	Pre PRE 005	Love Song/psychomodo (p/s)	15
81	Pre PRE 014	All About You/Author Author (p/s)	10
81	Pre PREX 5	AUTHOR! AUTHOR! (LP)	15

SCENE (1)
80	Inferno BEAT 2	I've Had Enough/Show 'Em Now (p/s)	12

SCENE (2)
80	Hole In The Wall HS 1	Hey Girl/Reach The Top (p/s)	50

SCENE (3)
83	Diamond DIA 001	Looking For A Love/Let Me Know (p/s)	8
85	Diamond DIA 003	Something That You Said/Stop-Go (p/s)	7
85	Diamond DIA 007	Good Lovin'/2 Plus 2 (with p/s)	15
85	Diamond DIA 007	Good Lovin'/2 Plus 2	5

(see also Diplomats)

SCEPTRES
69	Spark SRL 1006	What's The Matter With Juliet/Something's Coming Along	30

SCHADEL
66	Parlophone R5899	The Puppet Man/Oh What A Naughty Man	8
68	Pye 7N 17528	With The Sun In My Eyes/Goodbye Thimble Mill Lane	30
70	United Artists UAS 29114	SCHADEL NO.1 (LP) (G/F)	12

HAL SCHAEFER ORCHESTRA & CHORUS
58	London HLT 8692	March Of The Vikings/March Of The Parisian Bakers	7

JANNE SCHAFFER
74	Vertigo 6360 107	THE CHINESE (LP, 'spaceship' label)	15
75	Vertigo 6360 118	SECOND LP (LP, 'spaceship' label)	15

SCHEER
93	Son BUACD 293	Wish You Were Dead/Green Room Sex Kitten/Don't Know Why (p/s)	20

SCHEME
82	No Label SS001	SCHEME SONGS (EP, 500 only, 2 inserts)	30
86	Scheme LP1	BLACK & WHITES (LP)	25

MICHAEL SCHENKER
94	EMI 724382861 1423	THE STORY OF MICHAEL SCHENKER (2-CD)	20

(see also McAuley Schenker Group, Michael Schenker Group, Scorpions, UFO)

SCHEREZADE
82	Tombstone SRT TOM/S82 CUS 1	Seventeen/Million Years	12

HANK SCHIFNER
69	Liberty LBF15244	Long John/How Or When	15

LALO SCHIFRIN
66	MGM MGM 1329	Our Venetian Affair/Venice After Dark	12
68	Dot DOT 103	Mission: Impossible/Jim On The Move	25
74	20th Century BTC 2150	Ape Shuffle (Theme From 'Planet Of The Apes')/Escape From Tomorrow	25
74	Warner Bros K16333	Theme From Enter The Dragon/The Big Battle	10
76	CTI CTSP 5	Jaws Theme/Quiet Village	5
77	CTI CTSP008	Theme From 'Most Wanted'/Roller Coaster	6
68	Dot (S)LPD 503	'MISSION: IMPOSSIBLE' - MUSIC FROM THE TV SERIES (LP, TV soundtrack)	40
69	Paramount SPFL 252	MORE 'MISSION: IMPOSSIBLE' (LP, TV soundtrack)	40
70s	Verve 2304 051	ROCK REQUIEM (LP)	12

SCHIZO FUN ADDICT
08	Fruits De Mer CRUSTACIAN 01	Theme One/Ogden's Nut Gone Flake (p/s, coloured vinyl, 300 only)	20

SCHMETTERLINGE
77   Pye International 7N 25743   Boom Boom Boomerang/Mr Moneymaker's Music Show 10

TOBIAS SCHMIDT
96   Mosquito MSQ 06   THE FINGERPRINT EP (12", p/s) 15

ZAPPATTA SCHMIDT
70   President PT 318   You Got The Love/Someone In The Crowd 40
70   Torpedo TOR 28   Let's Do It Together/Hey Man. Why 25
71   President PTLS 1041   IT'S GONNA GET YOU (LP) 90
(see also Equals, Eddy Grant)

OLIVER LINDSEY SCHMITT
72   private pressing   GRAFFENSTADDEN (LP) 30

WOLFGANG SCHMITT
69   RCA 1301   The Girl From the Monmouth County/Country Girl 6

EBERHARD SCHOENER
79   Harvest HAR 5196   Video Magic/Code Word Elvis (p/s)...8
79   Harvest SHSM 2030   VIDEO-FLASHBACK (LP) 20
(see also Police)

JOHN SCHOFIELD
84   Arista/Nimbus AN 3022   BAR TALK (LP, Nimbus Supercut, mail order only from Practical Hi-Fi magazine) 30

SCHOLARS
64   Stagesound SDE 29370/1   THE SCHOLARS (EP, no p/s) 15

SCHOOL TIES
81   School Ties SCF 01   No Future/Screw You 45

SCHOOL BOYS
63   Blue Beat BB 162   Little Boy Blue/PRINCE BUSTER: Money 40
63   Blue Beat BB 174   Little Dilly/The Joker (B-side actually by Prince Buster's Allstars)......................40
64   Port-O-Jam PJ 4000   Dream Lover/I Want To Know 40
(see also Bill Gentles)

SCHOOLBOYS
69   Junior JR 113   Do It Now/Blame It On The Children 10

SCHOOLERS
69   Doctor Bird DB 1170   Ugly Man (actually by Scorchers)/Whip Cracker (actually by Vincent Gordon) 40

SCHOOLGIRL BITCH
78   Garage!/Aerco AERS 102   Abusing The Rules/Thinking For Yourself (spray-painted p/s) 150
78   Garage!/Aerco AERS 102   Abusing The Rules/Thinking For Yourself ('gasmask' p/s) 100
78   Garage!/Aerco AERS 102   Abusing The Rules/Thinking For Yourself ('queen' p/s) 45
78   Garage!/Aerco AERS 102   Abusing The Rules/Thinking For Yourself (no p/s) 40

SCHOOL GIRLS
63   Blue Beat BB 168   Love Another Love/Little Keithie 20
63   Blue Beat BB 185   Live Up To Justice/Keith My Darling 20
64   Blue Beat BB 214   Sing And Shout/Last Time 20
64   Blue Beat BB 263   Never Let You Go/BUSTER'S ALL STARS: Supercharge 80

SCHOOL MEALS
80s   Edible EAT 001   Headmaster (with insert, re-labelled Defendents)......................................20

SCHOOL OF CULTURE
91   White CS12 01   Detonate To Activate/Come On 33 70

DON SCHROEDER
62   Philips BF 3040033   Quicksand/My Kind Of Woman..10

JOHN SCHROEDER ORCHESTRA
65   Piccadilly 7N 35240   The Fugitive Theme/Don't Break The Heart Of Kimble (in p/s) 15
65   Piccadilly 7N 35240   The Fugitive Theme/Don't Break The Heart Of Kimble 6
65   Piccadilly 7N 35253   You've Lost That Lovin' Feeling/Funny How Love Can Be 6
66   Piccadilly 7N 35280   Ave Maria No Morro/Peter Popgunn 5
66   Piccadilly 7N 35285   Hungry For Love/Soul Destroyer 30
65   Piccadilly 7N 35271   Agent 00 Soul/Night Rider 30
66   Piccadilly 7N 35319   On The Ball (Theme For The World)/The Britannia March 10
67   Piccadilly 7N 35362   Soul For Sale/Loving You Girl 30
69   Pye 7N 17862   The Virgin Soldiers' March/Sweet Soul Talk 12
71   Pye 7N 45108   One Way Glass/The Bird Has Flown 15
66   Piccadilly N(S)PL 38025   JOHN SCHROEDER'S WORKING IN THE SOULMINE (LP) 50
67   Piccadilly N(S)PL 38036   THE DOLLY CATCHER! (LP)..40
68   Marble Arch MAL 839   WORKING IN THE SOULMINE (LP, reissue) 25
71   Pye NSPL 18362   WITCHI-TAI-TO (LP, textured gatefold sleeve) 30
72   Polydor 2460 149   TV VIBRATIONS (LP) 20
71   Polydor 2460 134   DYLAN VIBRATIONS (LP)...20
71   Polydor 2460 135   PIANO VIBRATIONS (LP, with Rick Wakeman) 40
73   Polydor 2460 188   WAR AND PEACE & OTHER TELEVISION THEMES (LP) 12
96   Sequel NEM LP 769   SPACE AGE SOUL (LP) 12

IVY SCHULMAN & BOWTIES
57   London HLN 8372   Rock, Pretty Baby/BOWTIES: Ever Since I Can Remember......................................50
57   London HLN 8372   Rock, Pretty Baby/BOWTIES: Ever Since I Can Remember (78)................................25

KLAUS SCHULZE
74   Caroline CA 2003   BLACK DANCE (LP, gatefold, black/white/red 'twin' label) 15
75   Caroline CA 2006   TIMEWIND (LP) 12
76   Virgin V2064   MOONDAWN (LP, unissued) 0
(see also Tangerine Dream) (Voices Of)

(VOICES OF) WALTER SCHUMANN
54   HMV 7M 229   Haunted House/I Only Have Eyes For You...8
55   HMV 7M 323   The Man From Laramie/Let Me Hear You Whisper 8

SCHUNGE

72	Regal Zonophone RZ 3066	Misty/Joseph Demanio	7
73	Regal Zonophone RZ 3077	Ballad Of A Simple Love/Enter The Violins	7
72	Regal Zono. SLRZ 1033	BALLAD OF A SIMPLE LOVE (LP, unlaminated front sleeve)	30
72	Regal Zono. SLRZ 1033	BALLAD OF A SIMPLE LOVE (LP, laminated front sleeve)	25

SCHWARTZENEGGER

| 94 | Rugger Bugger SEEP 009 | THE WAY THINGS ARE AND OTHER STORIES (LP) | 20 |

SCIENCE POPTION

| 67 | Columbia DB 8106 | You've Got Me High/Back In Town | 80 |

SCIENTIST

69	Amalgamated AMG 848	Professor In Action/SUPERSONICS: Reflections Of Don D	60
80	JB JBLP 004	INTRODUCING (LP)	75
81	Starlight SLD 901	DUB LANDING (LP)	40
80	Greensleeves GREL 13	HEAVYWEIGHT DUB CHAMPION (LP)	25
81	Greensleeves GREL 25	RIDS THE WORLD OF THE EVIL CURSE OF THE VAMPIRE (LP)	40
81	Jah Guidance VPRLP 1007	IN DUB (LP)	25
82	Greensleeves GREL 37	WINS THE WORLD CUP (LP)	40
82	Greensleeves GREL 19	MEETS THE SPACE INVADERS (LP)	30
82	Greensleeves GREL 46	ENCOUNTERS PAC MAN (LP)	15
82	Kingdom KVL 9011	HIGH PRIEST OF DUB (LP)	30
89	Tamoki Wambesi TWP 1022	INTERNATIONAL HEROES DUB (LP, with The Forces Of Music)	25

SCIENTIST & PRINCE JAMMY

| 82 | Starlight SLDLP 903 | DUB LANDING VOL 2 (LP) | 20 |

SCIENTIST VERSUS PRINCE JAMMY

| 80 | Greensleeves GRED 10 | THE BIG SHOWDOWN 1980 (LP) | 35 |

SCIENTIST V THE PROFESSOR

| 83 | Kingdom KVL 9015 | DUB DUEL AT KING TUBBY'S (LP) | 25 |

(see also Scientist)

SCIENTISTS

85	Karbon KAR 007	You Only Live Twice/If It's The Last Thing I Do (p/s)	25
85	Karbon KAR 101 L	YOU GET WHAT YOU DESERVE (LP)	20
86	Karbon KAR 103 L	WEIRD LOVE (LP)	20
87	Karbon KAR 105 L	THE HUMAN JUKEBOX (LP)	20

SCIENTISTS OF SOUND

92	Bite It! BITE5	LIKE A SCIENTIST (EP, p/s)	10
96	Downlow DL3	LANDMINE SITUATION EP (12")	8
96	Downlow DLLP2	1.4.4. OR BUST - THE REPLENISHING (2-LP, with insert)	12

SCISSOR FITS

| 79 | Dubious DUB 1/SJP 793 | TAUT? TENSE? ANGULAR? AND OTHER BRITISH RAIL SANDWICHES (EP, gatefold sleeve) | 8 |

SCONEHEADS

| 81 | Linden Soun LS 01 | GO BUCKSKIN (EP, 700 pressed) | 30 |

SCOOP

| 80 | Sharp POINT 1 | You Can Do It/Disco/My Friend Tony/Anonymity (p/s) | 50 |

SCORCHED EARTH (1)

| 74 | Philips 6006422 | On The Run/Super Woman | 12 |

SCORCHED EARTH (2)

85	Carrere CAR 342	Tomorrow Never Comes/Questions (promo only)	35
85	Carrere CART 342	Tomorrow Never Comes/Questions/So Long/Where Do We Go From Here (12", initial black sleeve)	70
85	Carrere CART 342	Tomorrow Never Comes/Questions/So Long/Where Do We Go From Here (12", later red sleeve with insert)	60

ERROL SCORCHER

| 78 | Ballistic UAS 30198 | RASTAFIRE (LP, with the Revolutionaries) | 25 |

SCORCHERS

| 69 | Camel CA 17 | Hold On Tight/THE ROYALS: 100 Lbs Of Clay | 35 |
| 69 | Duke DU 26 | Hear Ya/VIBRATORS: Live Life | 15 |

(see also Neville Hinds)

SCORE

| 66 | Decca F 12527 | Please Please Me/Beg Me | 175 |

SCORN

| 95 | Earache SCORN 001 | ELLIPSIS (5 x 12" box set) | 18 |

SCORPION & BORIS GARDINER HAPPENING

| 73 | Dragon DRA 1002 | Deadly Sting/BORIS GARDINER HAPPENING: Boing Boing | 5 |

SCORPIONS (GERMANY)

77	RCA PB 5556	He's A Woman, She's A Man/Suspender Love	8
79	Harvest 5185	Is Anybody There?/Another Piece Of Meat (12", p/s)	10
79	Harvest 12HAR 5188	Love Drive/Coast To Coast (12", p/s)	8
79	RCA PC 9402	All Night Long/Fly To The Rainbow/Speedy's Coming/In Trance (12", p/s)	8
84	Harvest 12HARP 5231	Big City Nights/Bad Boys Running Wild (12" picture disc, die-cut sleeve)	12
85	Harvest 12HAR 5232	Still Loving You/Holiday/Big City Night (12", p/s)	8
85	Harvest 12HAR 5232	Still Loving You/Holiday/Big City Night (12" picture disc)	8
91	Vertigo VERXP 54	Wind Of Change (12", etched red vinyl)	8
91	Vertigo VERXP 54	Wind Of Change/Restless Nights/Hit Between The Nights/Blackout (live) (12", picture disc)	8
91	Vertigo VERX 58	Wind Of Change (12", white vinyl, 3-D sleeve)	12
93	Mercury MERX 395	Under The Same Sun/Ship Of Fools/Partners In Crime (12", yellow vinyl)	8
79	Harvest LP SHSP 4097	LOVE DRIVE (LP)	18
80	Harvest SHSP 4113	ANIMAL MAGNETISM (LP, inner sleeve)	15
82	H.M. worldwide HMILP 2	LONESOME CROW (LP, "castle" cover, clear vinyl)	20
82	H.M. Worldwide HMILP 2	LONESOME CROW (LP, "castle" cover, black vinyl)	15
82	H.M. Worldwide HMIPD 2	LONESOME CROW (LP, picture disc, re-issue)	15

82	Harvest SHVL 823	BLACKOUT (LP, black or green print on label, inner sleeve)	15
88	Harvest SHSP 4125	SAVAGE AMUSEMENT (LP)	12
88	Harvest SHSPP 4125	SAVAGE AMUSEMENT (LP, picture disc, with lyric sheet)	15

(see also Michael Schenker, Michael Schenker Group, UFO)

SCORPIONS (JAMAICA)
72	Green Door GD 4019	Breaking Your Heart/IN CROWD BAND: Breaking Your Heart Version	6

(see also Bill Gentles, Lloyd Jackson)

SCORPIONS (U.K.)
61	Parlophone R 4740	(Ghost) Riders In The Sky/Torquay	20
61	Parlophone R 4768	Rockin' At The Phil/Scorpio	20
93	Sting SITTEP 1	BACK TO THE TRACKS (EP)	12

COLIN SCOT
71	United Artists UP 35216	Hey! Sandy/Nite People	5
73	Warner Bros K 16330	Call Me Mr Blue/It's Gonna Be Alright	7
71	United Artists UAG 29154	COLIN SCOT WITH FRIENDS (LP, laminated gatefold sleeve, with Peter Hammill & Peter Gabriel)	25
73	Warner Bros. KY6236	JUST ANOTHER CLOWN (LP, gatefold sleeve)	12

(see also Peter Hammill, Peter Gabriel)

JOCK SCOT
80	Stiff MAX 1	A Souvenir To Commemorate The Wedding Of Dave (Robinson) And Rosemary. Featuring the dulcet tones Of Jock Scot (Promo Only)	150

WINSTON SCOTLAND
72	Green Door GD 4027	My (Girl) Little Filly/BUNNY BROWN: My Girl	7
72	Punch PH 100	Butter Cup/RONALD WILSON: I Care	7

(see also Bunny Flip, Big Youth, Bongo Les, Lennox Brown, Dennis Alcapone)

SCOTS OF ST. JAMES
66	Go AJ 111404	Gypsy/Tic Toc	200
67	Spot JW 1	Timothy/Eiderdown Clown	300

(see also Hopscotch, Forever More, Five Day Rain)

ANDY SCOT
75	RCA RCA 2629	Lady Starlight/Where D'Ya Go (p/s)	12
83	Static TAK 10	Krugerrands/Face (p/s)	8
84	Static TAK 24	Let Her Dance/Suck It And See (p/s)	10
84	Static TAK 24-12	Let Her Dance (Full Version)/(Instrumental)/Suck It And See (12", p/s)	10
84	Static TAK 31	Invisible/Never Too Young (clear vinyl, stickered PVC sleeve)	12
84	Statik TAK 31-12	Invisible (Single Version)/(Instrumental)/Invisible (Extended Version)/ Never Too Young (12", clear vinyl, stickered PVC sleeve)	12

(see also Sweet, Elastic Band, Mayfield's Mule)

ANITA SCOTT
61	Columbia DB 4623	A Million And One Tears/Come On And Dance With Me	15

ARTIE SCOTT ORCHESTRA
70	Major Minor MM 670	March Of The Skinheads/Love At First Sight	7

BILLY SCOTT
58	London HLU 8565	You're The Greatest/That's Why I Was Born	20
60	Top Rank JAR 270	Carole/Stairway To The Stairs	7

BOBBY SCOTT
56	London HL 8254	Chain Gang/Shadrack	40
55	London Jazz LZ-N 14001	BOBBY SCOTT TRIO (10" LP)	15

BOBBY SCOTT
70	Reflection RS2	Witness To A War/I Wish I Could Walk Away	6

BRUCE SCOTT
65	Mercury MF 857	I Made An Angel Cry/Don't Say Goodbye To Me	25
65	MGM MGM 1291	Once A Thief Twice A Thief/So Much To Live For	7

BUNNY SCOTT
75	Upsetter UP 100	I Am I Said/Let Love Us Now (as Bunny Ruggs)	12
75	KLIK KLP 9004	TO LOVE SOMEBODY (LP)	15

DEREK SCOTT ORCHESTRA
63	Pye 7N 15500	Hancock's Tune/Spying Tonight	5
67	Philips BF 1568	Honey Lane/Song Without Words	5

FREDDIE SCOTT
63	Colpix PX 692	Hey Girl/The Slide	35
63	Colpix PX 709	I Got A Woman/Brand New World	35
67	London HLZ 10103	Are You Lonely For Me/Where Were You	15
67	London HLZ 10123	Cry To Me/No One Could Ever Love You	15
67	London HLZ 10139	Am I Grooving You?/Never You Mind	10
67	London HLZ 10172	He Ain't Give You None/Run Joe	10
69	Roulette RO 509	Sugar Sunday/Johnny's Hill	6
71	Jay Boy BOY 34	Just Like A Flower/Spanish Harlem	10
72	Jay Boy BOY 59	Are You Lonely For Me Baby/The Woman Of My Love	10
72	Upfront UP 1	The Great If/Deep In The Night	10
71	Joy JOYS 215	ARE YOU LONELY FOR ME (LP)	25

HAZEL SCOTT
53	Capitol LC 6607	LATE SHOW (10" LP)	20

JACK SCOTT (& CHANTONES)
58	London HLU 8626	My True Love/Leroy	10
58	London HLU 8626	My True Love/Leroy (78)	15
58	London HLL 8765	With Your Love/Geraldine (as Jack Scott with Chantones)	20
58	London HLL 8765	With Your Love/Geraldine (as Jack Scott with Chantones) (78)	15
59	London HLL 8804	Goodbye Baby/Save My Soul (as Jack Scott with Chantones)	20
59	London HLL 8804	Goodbye Baby/Save My Soul (as Jack Scott with Chantones) (78)	20
59	London HL 7069	Goodbye Baby/Save My Soul (export issue)	20
59	London HLL 8851	I Never Felt Like This/Bella	20

MINT VALUE £

59	London HLL 8851	I Never Felt Like This/Bella (78)	30
59	London HLL 8912	The Way I Walk/Midgie (triangular or round centre)	25
59	London HLL 8912	The Way I Walk/Midgie (triangular or round centre) (78)	20
59	London HLL 8970	There Comes A Time/Baby Marie (triangular or round centre)	25
59	London HLL 8970	There Comes A Time/Baby Marie (78)	30
60	Top Rank JAR 280	What In The World's Come Over You/Baby, Baby	6
60	Top Rank JAR 375	Burning Bridges/Oh, Little One	10
60	Top Rank JAR 419	Cool Water/It Only Happened Yesterday	10
60	Top Rank JAR 524	Patsy/Old Time Religion	10
61	Top Rank JAR 547	Is There Something On Your Mind/Found A Woman	12
61	Capitol CL 15200	A Little Feeling/Now That I	12
61	Capitol CL 15216	My Dream Come True/Strange Desire	12
62	Capitol CL 15236	Steps 1 And 2/One Of These Days	12
63	Capitol CL 15302	All I See Is Blue/Meo Myo	12
62	Capitol CL 15261	I Can't Hold Your Letters In My Arms/Sad Story	15
59	London RE-I 1205	MY TRUE LOVE (EP, initial triangular centre)	70
59	London RE-I 1205	MY TRUE LOVE (EP, later round centre)	40
61	Top Rank JKP 3002	WHAT IN THE WORLD'S COME OVER YOU (EP)	40
61	Top Rank JKP 3011	I REMEMBER HANK WILLIAMS (EP)	50
58	London HA-L 2156	JACK SCOTT (LP)	100
60	Top Rank BUY 034	I REMEMBER HANK WILLIAMS (LP)	45
60	Top Rank 25-024	WHAT IN THE WORLD'S COME OVER YOU (LP)	40
61	Top Rank 35-109	THE SPIRIT MOVES ME (LP)	50
64	Capitol T 2035	BURNING BRIDGES (LP, mono)	40
64	Capitol ST 2035	BURNING BRIDGES (LP, stereo)	50

JANET SCOTT & JACKIE RAE

60	Fontana TFE 17203	SWEET TALK (EP, also stereo STFE 8009)	12
60	Fontana TFL 5102	WE LOVE LIFE! (LP, also stereo STFL 533)	15

(see also Jackie Rae)

JIMMY SCOTT

69	Revolution REV 002	Ob-La-Di, Ob-La-Da/Story Part 2 - Allulo & Doh	40
70	Revolution Soul REVS 505	Doh (Ob-La-Di-Ob-Lh-Da Story Part 2/Allulo (Part 1) Note: "lh" is how it is on the label	40
74	Deram DM 425	We All Need A Hero/Moonshine	7

JOHN SCOTT

60	Parlophone R 4697	Hi-Flutin' Boogie/Peace Pipe	6
65	Parlophone R 5333	Sailing By/The Song Of The Cuckoo (as Johnny Scott)	8
65	Parlophone R 5380	A Study In Terror/Punjab	10
67	Polydor 56184	Rocket To The Moon Theme/The Long Duel Theme	15
68	Spark SRL 1008	Amsterdam Affair Theme/Kathleen	8
66	Columbia SX 6026	LONDON SWINGS (LP)	15
67	Columbia S(C)X 6149	COMMUNICATION (LP)	30

JOHNNY SCOTT

70	Fontana 6383 002	PURCELL VARIATIONS FOR FIVE (LP)	25
73	JSD JSD 100	JOHN SCOTT DEMONSTRATION RECORD (LP, beware, many warped)	80

JUDI SCOTT

68	Page One POF 066	Billy Sunshine/Happy Song	25

JUDY SCOTT

57	Brunswick 05687	The Game Of Love (A-One And A-Two)/With All My Heart	10
57	Brunswick 05704	Parlour Piano Theme/A Tender Word	8

JULIAN SCOTT

61	Columbia DB 4571	My Steady Date/So Tired	7

LINDA SCOTT

60	Columbia DB 4638	I've Told Every Little Star/Three Guesses	8
61	Columbia DB 4692	Don't Bet Money, Honey/Starlight Starbright	15
61	Columbia DB 4748	I Don't Know Why/It's All Because	12
61	Columbia DB 4829	Count Every Star/Land Of Stars	12
62	Pye International 7N 25146	Never In A Million Years/Through The Summer	15
63	London HLR 9802	Let's Fall In Love/I Know It, You Know It	15
61	Columbia 33SX 1386	STARLIGHT, STARBRIGHT (LP)	70

LINDA SCOTT

69	CBS 4528	The Composer/You Made A Fool Out Of Me	15
69	CBS 4246	First Of All/The Answer's In My Eyes	5

MAUREEN SCOTT

63	HMV POP 1184	He's So Near/Ugly Bug Ball	6

MCBEAN SCOTT & CHAMPIONS

70	Jackpot JP 744	Top Of The World/LARRY LAWRENCE & CHAMPIONS: Everybody Reggae	8

MIKE SCOTT (1)

65	Mercury MF 906	I Am A Rock/I'm Gonna Be Somebody Someday	6

MIKE SCOTT (2)

95	Chrysalis CHR 6108	BRING'EM ALL IN (LP, gatefold with inner)	15

(see also Waterboys)

NEIL SCOTT

61	Pye International 7N 25096	Bobby/I Haven't Found It With Another	8

NICKY SCOTT

67	Immediate IM 044	Big City/Everything's Gonna Be Alright	50
67	Immediate IM 045	Backstreet Girl/Chain Reaction	50
69	Pye 7N 17688	Honey Pie/No More Tomorrow	7

(see also Diane Ferraz & Nicky Scott)

PEGGY SCOTT

69	Polydor 56722	Every Little Bit Hurts/You Can Never Get Something For Nothing	8
79	Pinnacle PIN 73	You've Got It All/Let Me Unite You (p/s)	5

(see also Peggy Scott & Jo Jo Benson)
PEGGY SCOTT & JO JO BENSON
68	Polydor 56745	Lover's Holiday/Here With Me	10
69	Polydor 56750	Pickin' Wild Mountain Berries/Pure Love And Pleasure	8
69	Polydor 56761	Soulshake/We Were Made For Each Other	10
69	Polydor 56773	We Got Our Own Bag/I Want To Love You Babe	8
71	Atlantic 2091 066	I Thank You/Spreadin' Love	5
69	Polydor 583 731	SOULSHAKE (LP)	25
70	Polydor 583 756	LOVER'S HEAVEN (LP)	25

(see also Peggy Scott)
ROBIN SCOTT
69	Head HDS 4003	The Sailor/Sound Of The Rain	40
69	Head HDLS 6003	WOMAN FROM THE WARM GRASS (LP, textured sleeve with insert, yellow/black label)	400
07	Sunbeam SBBLP 5009	WOMAN FROM THE WARM GRASS (LP, reissue)	15

(see also Mighty Baby, M)
RONNIE SCOTT
54	Esquire 10-335	Night And Day	10
56	Decca FJ 10712	Basie Talks/Flying Home (as Ronnie Scott Orchestra)	8
57	Tempo A 153	I'll Take Romance/Speak Low (as Ronnie Scott New Quintet)	35
55	Esquire EP 31	RONNIE SCOTT ORCHESTRA (EP)	25
55	Esquire EP 51	RONNIE SCOTT QUARTET (EP)	25
55	Esquire EP 61	RONNIE SCOTT ORCHESTRA (EP)	20
55	Esquire EP 65	RONNIE SCOTT QUINTET (EP)	25
56	Esquire EP 81	RONNIE SCOTT ORCHESTRA (EP)	25
56	Esquire EP 85	RONNIE SCOTT ORCHESTRA (EP)	30
56	Esquire EP 95	RONNIE SCOTT ORCHESTRA (EP)	25
56	Tempo EXA 45	RONNIE SCOTT BLOWS WITH THE DIZZY REECE QUARTET (EP)	100
52	Esquire 20-006	RONNIE SCOTT QUINTET (10" LP)	100
54	Esquire 32-001	THE RONNIE SCOTT JAZZ CLUB VOLUME 1 (LP)	50
54	Esquire 32-002	THE RONNIE SCOTT JAZZ CLUB VOLUME 2 (LP)	50
54	Esquire 32-003	THE RONNIE SCOTT JAZZ CLUB VOLUME 3 (LP)	50
54	Esquire 32-006	THE RONNIE SCOTT JAZZ CLUB VOLUME 4 (LP)	50
56	Decca LF 1261	AT THE ROYAL FESTIVAL HALL (10" LP)	45
57	Philips BBL 7153	PRESENTING THE RONNIE SCOTT SEXTET (LP)	90
66	Fontana TL 5332	THE NIGHT IS SCOTT AND YOU'RE SO SWINGABLE (LP)	40
69	CBS Realm Jazz 523661	LIVE AT RONNIE SCOTT'S (LP)	25
74	RCA Victor LPL1	SCOTT AT RONNIE'S (LP)	20
77	Pye NSPL 18542	SERIOUS GOLD (LP)	15

(see also Jazz Couriers, Tubby Hayes, Dizzy Reece)
SHIRLEY SCOTT
66	Transatlantic PR 7205	HIP SOUL (LP)	18
69	Atlantic 588 175	SOUL SONG (LP)	15
71	Chess 6310 109	MYSTICAL LADY (LP)	15

SIMON SCOTT (& LE ROYS)
64	Parlophone R 5164	Move It Baby/What Kind Of Woman (with Le Roys)	15
64	Parlophone R 5207	My Baby's Got Soul/MIdnight (with Le Roys)	12
65	Parlophone R 5298	Tell Him I'm Not Home (as Simon Scott & All Nite Workers)/Heart Cry	18
69	Polydor 56355	Brave New World/I'm The Universe	100

(see also Le Roys)
TOM SCOTT
77	Epic EPC 5589	Gotcha (Theme From 'Starsky & Hutch')/Smoothin' On Down	12

RAMBLIN' TOMMY SCOTT
54	Parlophone CMSP 15	Ain't Love Grand/What Do You Know - I Love Her (export issue)	20

TOMMY SCOTT
62	Decca F 11474	Angela/Did You (as Jay & Tommy Scott)	6
64	Decca F 11839	Who Will It Be?/If It's Me That You Want	5
64	Decca F 11942	Wrap Your Troubles In Dreams/Blueberry Hill	5

TONY SCOTT
69	Escort ES 805	What Am I To Do/Bring Back That Smile	10

SHEILA SCOTT WILKINGSON
68	SNB 55-4124	Down River/Quiet Man	10

SHARON SCOTT
96	Kent 6T 12	(Putting My Heart) Under Lock And Key/DEAN COURTNEY: Today Is My Day	35

GIL SCOTT-HERON (& BRIAN JACKSON)
73	Philips 6073 705	Lady Day And John Coltrane/When You Are Who You Are (with Pretty Purdie & The Playboys)	20
78	Arista ARIST 169	The Bottle (live)/Hello Sunday, Hello Road	8
78	Arista ARIST 169	The Bottle (live)/Hello Sunday, Hello Road (12")	20
79	Inferno HEAT 23	The Bottle (Drunken Mix)/The Bottle (Sober Mix) (with Brian Jackson)	10
79	Inferno HEAT 23-12	The Bottle (Drunken Mix)/The Bottle (Sober Mix) (12", with Brian Jackson)	15
81	Arista ARIST 452	Storm Music/Gun/B Movie	5
73	Philips 6369 415	PIECES OF A MAN (LP)	35
74	RCA SF 8428	THE REVOLUTION WILL NOT BE TELEVISED (LP)	25
75	Arista ARTY 106	FIRST MINUTES OF A NEW DAY (LP)	15
76	Arista DARTY 1	IT'S YOUR WORLD (LP, with Brian Jackson)	30

SCOTTY (DAVID SCOTT)
70	Songbird SB 1044	Sesame Street/CRYSTALITES: Version	20
71	Duke DU 106	Donkey Skank (with Tennors)/MURPHY'S ALLSTARS: Version	15
71	Songbird SB 1049	Riddle I This/Musical Chariot	12
71	Songbird SB 1051	Jam Rock Style/Jam Rock Style Version (with Crystalites)	10
71	Songbird SB 1056	Penny For Your Song/CRYSTALITES: Version	10
72	Songbird SB 1080	Clean Race/CRYSTALITES: Version Train	10
72	Harry J. HJ 6642	Skank In Bed/BONGO HERMAN: African Breakfast	8
73	Count Shelley CS 036	Salvation Train/KEN PARKER: Message To Mary	8

71	Trojan TRL 33	SCHOOLDAYS (LP)	45

(see also Lloyd Charmers, Joe White)

SCRAPING FOETUS OFF THE WHEEL

80s	Womb 12	Ramrod/Boxhead/Smut	5
81	Womb WOMB-OYBL-2	HOLE (LP, gatefold sleeve with lyrics, also listed as FDL 3)	15

(see also Foetus, You've Got Foetus On Your Breath, Philip & His Foetus Vibrations, Foetus Corruptus, Foetus Inc, Foetus Uber Frisco)

SCRAPYARD

58	Abbey APR 168	RECIPRICAL RHUMBAS (LP, private press, 250 copies, with insert)	200

SCRATCH ACID

86	Fundamental HOLY 1	SCRATCH ACID (Mini-LP)	20
87	Fundamental HOLY 2	BESERKER (LP)	15

SCRATCH AID

86	Fundamental SAVE 12	JUT KEEP EATING (LP)	15

SCREAMER

75	Arista ARISTA 18	City Or Bust/We Got Hairs	10

SCREAMING DEAD

82	Skull DEAD 1	Valley Of The Dead/Schoolgirl Junkie (p/s)	8
83	Skull DEAD 2	Paint It Black	10
83	No Future OI 25	NIGHT CREATURES EP (12")	10

DELTON SCREECHIE

80	Kim KIM 18	My Black Girl/Diamond & Pearl/B DONALDSON & U BLACK : You Are Mine (12")	15
80	Moa Anbessa MA004	She Is My Woman/Woman Version (12")	15
81	Moa Anbessa Intl MALP 001	LIVING IN THE GHETTO (LP)	25
81	Moa Anbessa Intl MALP 002	SUFFERING IN THE GHETTO (LP)	30

SCREECHING WEASEL

88	Wet Spots WETLP 005	BOOGADA BOOGADA BOOGADA (LP)	25
88	What Goes On GOES ON 18	SCREECHING WEASEL (LP, with insert)	20

SCREEMER

76	Bell Bell 1483	Interplanetary Twist/Billy	10

SCREEN

95	Muzic W'out Control MWC 021	I Wait For You (Sweep Sweep Mix)/I Wait For You (Radio Sweep Mix)/I Wait For You (Pink Noize Mix)/I Wait For You (T Rex Mix) (12', p/s)	60

SCREEN GEMS

79	Inflatable IN 001	I Just Can't Stand Cars/Teenage Teenage	200

SCREEN IDOLS

79	Cobra COB 2	Blindman/Hit Me Where It Hurts (p/s)	10

SCRITTI POLITTI

78	St. Pancras SCRIT 1	Skank Bloc Bologna/Is And Ought Of The Western World/28.8.78 (photocopied stapled foldout p/s, hand-stamped white labels)	10
79	Rough Trade RT 027T	4 A SIDES: Doubt Beat/Confidences/Bibbly O'Tek/P.A.s (12" EP)	10
79	Rough Trade	Songs To Remember/The Cassette Interview (cassette, with 12-page booklet & 2 photos, promo only)	10

SCROTUM POLES

79	Scrotum Poles ERECT 1	Revelation: Why Don't You Come Out Tonight?/Night Train/Pick The Cat's Eyes Out/Helicopter Honeymoon/Radio Tay (handwritten labels, 2p/s designs, with insert)	120
79	Scrotum Poles ERECT 1	Revelation: Why Don't You Come Out Tonight?/Night Train/Pick The Cat's Eyes Out/Helicopter Honeymoon/Radio Tay (handwritten labels, 2p/s designs, without insert)	100
80s	One-Tone ERECT 1	AUCHMITHY CALLING (cassette)	12

SCRUBS

86	Anubis ANU 003	Battle (p/s)	15
87	Flicknife FLS 035	Time For You (p/s)	10

SCRUGG

68	Pye 7N 17451	I Wish I Was Five/Everyone Can See	90
68	Pye 7N 17551	Lavender Popcorn/Sandwichboard Man	50
69	Pye 7N 17656	Will The Real Geraldine Please Stand Up/Only George	90

(see also Floribunda Rose, John T. Kongos)

EARL SCRUGGS

72	CBS 64777	EARL SCRUGGS: HIS FAMILY AND FRIENDS (LP, with Byrds, Joan Baez, Bob Dylan, etc.)	15

(see also Flatt & Scruggs, Byrds)

IRENE SCRUGGS

50s	Poydras 80	You've Got What I Want/My Back To The Wall	8

MR. JOHNNY SEA

60s	Fontana FJL 315	EVERYBODY'S FAVOURITE (LP)	15

SEA & CAKE

95	Lissy's LIS 1	Glad You're Right/Tiger Partner/Crimson Wing (p/s, 500 only)	6
94	Rough Trade THRILL 021	SEA & CAKE (LP)	20
97	Thrill Jockey THRILL LP 039UK	THE FAWN (LP, gatefold)	15

(see also Tortoise)

SEA-DERS

67	Decca F 22576	Thanks A Lot/Undecidedly	60
67	Decca DFE-R 8674	THE SEA-DERS (EP, export issue)	250

(see also Cedars)

DAVE SEALEY

69	DJM DJS 210	Picking Up The Pieces/I Can't Go On Living Without You	6

MILT SEALEY TRIO

60s	Duc. Thompson DEP 95017	MILTON SEALEY AND KANSAS FIELDS (EP)	8

PHIL SEAMAN

68	Verve (S)VLP 9220	PHIL SEAMAN NOW ... LIVE (LP)	175
60s	Decibel BSN 103	PHIL SEAMAN STORY (LP)	50
60s	Saga OPP 102	MEETS EDDIE GOMEZ (LP)	100
74	77 Records 77 SEU 12/53	PHIL ON DRUMS (LP)	50

SEARCHERS
SINGLES

63	Pye 7N 15533	Sweets For My Sweet/It's All Been A Dream	6
63	Philips BF 1274	Sweet Nuthins/What'd I Say	12
63	Pye 7N 15566	Sugar And Spice/Saints And Searchers (dark maroon label)	12
63	Pye 7N 15566	Sugar And Spice/Saints And Searchers (lighter pink label)	6
64	Pye 7N 15594	Needles And Pins/Saturday Night Out	5
64	Pye 7N 15630	Don't Throw Your Love Away/I Pretend I'm With You	5
64	Pye 7N 15670	Someday We're Gonna Love Again/No One Else Could Love You	5
64	Pye 7N 15694	When You Walk In The Room/I'll Be Missing You	5
64	Pye 7N 15739	What Have They Done To The Rain/This Feeling Inside (maroon label)	5
64	Pye 7N 15739	What Have They Done To The Rain/This Feeling Inside (lighter pink label)	5
65	Pye 7N 15794	Goodbye My Love/Till I Met You	6
65	Pye 7N 15878	He's Got No Love/So Far Away	6
65	Pye 7N 15950	When I Get Home/I'm Never Coming Back	8
65	Pye 7N 15992	Take Me For What I'm Worth/Too Many Miles (in export p/s)	25
65	Pye 7N 15992	Take Me For What I'm Worth/Too Many Miles	8
66	Pye 7N 17094	Take It Or Leave It/Don't Hide It Away	10
66	Pye 7N 17170	Have You Ever Loved Somebody/It's Just The Way	12
67	Pye 7N 17225	Popcorn, Double Feature/Lovers	20
67	Pye 7N 17308	Western Union/I'll Cry Tomorrow	15
67	Pye 7N 17424	Secondhand Dealer/Crazy Dreams	80
68	Liberty LBF 15159	Umbrella Man/Over The Weekend	50
69	Liberty LBF 15340	Kinky Kathy Abernathy/Suzanna	50
71	RCA RCA 2057	Desdemona/The World Is Waiting For Tomorrow	15
71	RCA RCA 2139	Love Is Everywhere/And A Button	10
72	RCA RCA 2231	Sing Singer Sing/Come On Back To Me	10
72	RCA RCA 2248	Needles And Pins/When You Walk In The Room/Come On Back To Me	10
72	RCA RCA 2288	Vahevala/Madman	15
73	RCA RCA 2330	Solitaire/Spicks And Specks	6
79	Sire SIR 4029	Hearts In Her Eyes/Don't Hang On (p/s)	10
80	Sire SIR 4036	It's Too Late/This Kind Of Love Affair (p/s)	7
81	Sire SIR 4041	Love's Melody/Changing (p/s)	12
81	Sire SIR 4049	Another Night/Back To The War (p/s)	10
80s	Private pressing	Don't Make Promises	10
80s	Private pressing	Four Strong Winds	10

EPs

63	Pye NEP 24177	AIN'T GONNA KISS YA	12
63	Pye NEP 24183	SWEETS FOR MY SWEET (some copies with white & maroon label)	15
64	Pye NEP 24184	HUNGRY FOR LOVE	20
64	Pye NEP 24201	THE SEARCHERS PLAY THE SYSTEM	15
64	Pye NEP 24204	WHEN YOU WALK IN THE ROOM	20
65	Pye NEP 24218	BUMBLE BEE	20
65	Pye NEP 24222	SEARCHERS '65	30
65	Pye NEP 24228	FOUR BY FOUR	35
66	Pye NEP 24263	TAKE ME FOR WHAT I'M WORTH	100

ALBUMS

63	Pye NPL 18086	MEET THE SEARCHERS	30
63	Pye NPL 18089	SUGAR AND SPICE	25
64	Pye NPL 18092	IT'S THE SEARCHERS	25
65	Pye NPL 18111	SOUNDS LIKE SEARCHERS	30
65	Pye NPL 18120	TAKE ME FOR WHAT I'M WORTH	40
67	Marble Arch MAL 640	SMASH HITS VOL. 1	12
67	Marble Arch MAL(S) 673	SMASH HITS VOL. 2 (mono/stereo)	12
72	RCA SF 8289	SECOND TAKE	18
79	Sire SRK 6082	SEARCHERS	15
80	Sire SRK 6086	THE SEARCHERS	12
81	Sire SRK 3523	PLAY FOR TODAY	12
83	PRT DOW 11	LOVE LIES BLEEDING (10")	12

(see also Chris Curtis, Pasha)

SEARGEANT SMILEY RAGS

70	Decca F13088	Smoke Smoke/Hey Na I Think I Love You	12

SEARS

84	Bluurg FISH 9	IF ONLY... (LP)	15

SEASICK STEVE

07	Bronzerat BR 006	It's All Good/Thunderbird (p/s)	8

SEA STONE

82	Plankton 02	AGAINST THE TIDE (EP, foldout sleeve)	40
78	Plankton PKN 101	MIRRORED DREAMS (LP, with insert)	80

SEATHROUGH

73	private pressing	LALA LAPLA (LP)	40

B.B. SEATON (HORACE SEATON)

63	Island WI 123	I'm So Glad/Tell Me	30
64	R&B JB 143	Hold On/LESTER STERLING: Peace And Love	30
72	Big BG 336	I Want Justice/RUPIE EDWARD'S ALL STARS: Justice (Version)	8
72	Bullet BU 514	I Miss My Schooldays/CONSCIOUS MINDS: School Days - Version	5
72	Camel CA 100	Lean On Me/NOW GENERATION: Samba Pati	8
72	Pama PM 864	I Want Justice/RUPIE EDWARD'S ALL STARS: Justice - Version	8
72	Pama Supreme PS 374	Sweet Caroline/Eleanor Rigby	5
73	Trojan TRLS 59	THE THIN LINE BETWEEN LOVE AND HATE (LP)	20

MINT VALUE £

74	Caroline CA 2002	DANCING SHOES (LP)	20

(see also Bibby, Winston & Bibby, Gaylads, Messengers)

SEA TRAIN

68	A&M AMS 737	Let The Duchess Know/As I Lay Losing	5
69	A&M AMLS 941	SEA TRAIN (LP)	30
71	Capitol EA-ST 659	SEA TRAIN (LP)	18
72	Capitol EA-ST 829	MARBLEHEAD MESSENGER (LP, gatefold sleeve)	15
73	Warner Bros K 46222	WATCH (LP)	15

(see also Blues Project, Old & In The Way)

SEA URCHINS

98	Sarah SARAH 33	A Morning Odyssey/Wild Grass Pictures	6
87	Kvatch KVATCH 001/	Clingfilm/GROOVE FARM: Baby Blue Marine (flexidisc, 1,000 only, 500 in p/s)	25
87	Sha La La Ba Ba Ba Ba 5	Summershine/ORCHIDS: From This Day (flexidisc, 2,500 only, 1,000 with p/s)	15
87	Sarah SARAH 001	Pristine Christine/Sullen Eyes/Everglades (foldaround p/s with 14" x 10" poster in poly bag, 1,600 only)	175
88	Sarah SARAH 008	Solace/Please Rain Fall (foldaround p/s in poly bag)	25
89	Fierce FRIGHT 032	30.10.88 (live) (1-sided, p/s)	10
91	Cheree CHEREE 15	Please Don't Cry/Time Is All I've Seen (die-cut company sleeve)	7
91	Cheree CHEREE 15T	Please Don't Cry/No matter What/Time Is All I've Seen (12")	10
92	Sarah SARAH 609	STARDUST (LP)	30

JOHN SEBASTIAN

54	London HL 8029	Inca Dance/Foolish Waltz	20
55	London HL 8131	Stranger In Paradise/Autumn Leaves	15

JOHN (B.) SEBASTIAN

69	Kama Sutra 618 026	She's A Lady/The Room Nobody Lives In	6
70	Reprise RS 20902	Magical Connection/Fa-Fana-Fa	5
70	Reprise RSLP 6379	JOHN B. SEBASTIAN (LP, gatefold sleeve)	20
70	Buddah 2361 003	JOHN SEBASTIAN SONGBOOK VOLUME ONE (LP, with Lovin' Spoonful)	12
71	Reprise K 44127	REAL LIVE JOHN SEBASTIAN (LP)	15
71	Reprise K 44149	THE FOUR OF US (LP, gatefold sleeve)	12
74	Reprise K 54028	TARZANA KID (LP)	12

(see also Lovin' Spoonful, Even Dozen Jug Band)

SECESSION

80s	Siren SRN12 23	Michael (12", p/s)	12
81	Beggars Banquet BEG 112	Fire Island/Fire Island (Instrumental)	10
88	Siren SRNLP 11	A DARK ENCHANTMENT (LP, with inner)	40

SECOND CITY SOUND

65	Decca F 12310	Tchaikovsky One/Shadows	6
66	Decca F 12366	Greig One/In A Mist	6
66	Decca F 12406	Love's Funny/Tell Me Where I'm Going	6
69	Major Minor MM 600	The Dream Of Olwyn/A Touch Of Velvet, A Sting of Brass	10

SECOND COMING

71	Mercury 6338 030	SECOND COMING (LP)	50

SECOND HAND

68	Polydor 583 045	REALITY (LP, early copies crediting band as Moving Finger)	300
68	Polydor 583 045	REALITY (LP, later copies not crediting band as Moving Finger)	200
72	Mushroom MR 2006	DEATH MAY BE YOUR SANTA CLAUS (LP, some copies omit "Funeral")	250

(see also Andreas Thomopoulos, Fungus, Chillum, Vulcans, Seventh Wave)

SECOND LAYER

79	Tortch TOR 001	FLESH AS PROPERTY (EP, white p/s, black printed labels)	30
80	Tortch TOR 006	State Of Emergency/I Need Noise/The Cutting Motion (p/s)	30
81	Tortch/Fresh FRESH 5	FLESH AS PROPERTY (EP, reissue, yellow p/s & white labels)	20
81	Cherry Red CHERRY 21	FLESH AS PROPERTY (EP, 2nd reissue, unreleased)	0
82	Cherry Red BRED 14	WORLD OF RUBBER (LP, with inner)	50

(see also Outsiders, Sound)

SECOND THOUGHTS

65	Recorded Sound Studios RSL 1596	Let's Stick Together/I'm Possessed	300

(see also July, Nirvana)

SECRET

77	Arista ARIST 142	The Young Ones/Handel A Vandel	10
78	Arista ARIST 173	Do You Really Care?/I Wanna Car Like That	15

SECRET AFFAIR

79	I-Spy SEE 1	Time For Action/Soho Strut (brown p/s, black print/paper labels)	10
79	I-Spy SEE 1	Time For Action/Soho Strut (black p/s, white print with plastic labels)	5
79	I-Spy SEE 3	Let Your Heart Dance/Sorry Wrong Number (p/s, paper label)	6
80	I-Spy SEE 5	My World/So Cool (paper labels)	6
80	I-Spy SEE 8	Sound Of Confusion/Take It Or Leave It (p/s, paper labels)	6
81	I-Spy SEE 10	Do You Know?/Dance Master (keyhole company sleeve, paper labels)	6
82	I-Spy SEE 11	Lost In The Night (Mack The Knife)/The Big Beat (p/s)	8
79	I-Spy I SPY 1	GLORY BOYS (LP, with 2 inserts)	15
80	I-Spy I SPY 2	BEHIND CLOSED DOORS (LP, with inner sleeve)	12
82	I-Spy I SPY 3	BUSINESS AS USUAL (LP, stickered sleeve)	15
90s	own label	CITY OF DREAMS (LP, handmade sleeve - this is a bootleg)	25

(see also New Hearts, Advertising, Innocents [U.K.])

SECRET OYSTER

74	CBS 80489	SEA SON (LP)	15

SECRET SERVICE

79	Sonet SON 2193	Oh Susie/Give Me Your Love	6

SECRET SHINE

91	Sarah SARAH 53	After Years/Snowfall Sorrow/Grey Skies (p/s)	12
92	Sarah SARAH 61	Honey Sweet/Secret Shine (p/s)	12
93	Sarah SARAH 71	Loveblind/Way Too High (p/s)	12

94	Sarah SARAH 89	GREATER THAN GOD EP (10" p/s)	25
93	Sarah SARAH 615	UNTOUCHED (LP)	20

SECRET SQUIRREL

92	Bogwoppa BOGWOPPA 05	E Drop/Come Rudeboy (12", handwritten white label, with AJ Flex)	60
92	Dance Bass DANCE BASS 01	Mu-Venom/DDT (12", stamped white label)	50
92	Dance Bass DANCE BASS 02	VOLUME 2 EP (12")	30
92	Dance Bass DANCE BASS 06	THE MAGIC FLUTE EP (12")	30

(See also Undercover Elephant and DJ Secret Squirrel)

SECRETS (U.K.)

66	CBS 202466	I Suppose/Such A Pity	35
67	CBS 202585	Infatuation/She's Dangerous	35
67	CBS 2818	I Intend To Please/I Think I Need The Cash	35

(see also Simon's Secrets, Clifford T. Ward, Martin Raynor & Secrets)

SECRETS (U.S)

64	Philips BF 1298	The Boy Next Door/Learnin' To Forget	30
64	Philips BF 1318	Hey Big Boy/Other Side Of Town	30

SECT (1)

81	Shoestring SHOE 1	This is Your Life/Private Eye (p/s)	5

SECT (2)

86	Insect NASTY 1	A Free England/Never Go (p/s)	20
80s		PLAYING WITH FIRE EP (12")	20
80s	Damaged Goods YUBB 2	SUMMER GIRL EP, blue vinyl)	20

SECTION A

82	Subversive SUB	TIME STANDS STILL EP	15

SECTION 5

85	Oi OIR 002	WE WON'T CHANGE (LP)	20
80s	OI	STREET ROCK 'N' ROLL (LP)	15
87	Link LP 08	FOR THE LOVE OF OI! (LP)	15

SECTION 25

87	Factory FAC 157	Bad News Week/Bad News Week 2 (The Cough Mix) (12", p/s)	8
84	Factory FAC 108	Looking From A Hilltop (Restructure)/(Megamix) (12")	10
83	Factory FAC 68	Back To Wonder/Beating Heart (p/s)	6
82	Factory FAC 66	The Beast/Sakura/Sakura (Matrixmix)/Trident (12")	10
80	Factory FAC 18	Girls Don't Count/New Noise/Up To You (tracing paper p/s, produced by Ian Curtis and Rob Gretton)	25
80	Factory FAC 18	Girls Don't Count/New Noise Up To You (12", 3 different p/s depicting band members girlfriends, produced by Ian Curtis and Rob Gretton)	15
81	Factory FACT 45	ALWAYS NOW (LP, in envelope/folder with poster)	25
81	Factory FACT 45	ALWAYS NOW (LP, in envelope/folder without poster)	20
84	Factory FACT 90	FROM THE HIP (LP, with inner)	25
86	Factory FACT 45c	ALWAYS NOW (reissue, cassette in box with insert)	100
86	Factory FACT 90c	FROM THE HIP (reissue, cassette in box with insert)	80
88	Factory FACT 160	LOVE & HATE (LP)	18

NEIL SEDAKA

59	RCA RCA 1099	The Diary/No Vacancy	20
59	RCA RCA 1099	The Diary/No Vacancy (78)	15
59	RCA RCA 1115	I Go Ape/Moon Of Gold	15
59	RCA RCA 1115	I Go Ape/Moon Of Gold (78)	15
59	RCA RCA 1130	You've Got To Learn Your Rhythm And Blues/Crying My Heart Out For You	15
59	London HLW 8961	Ring A Rockin'/Fly Don't Fly On Me	40

(The above 45s were originally issued with triangular centres; later round-centres are worth two-thirds these values.)

59	London HLW 8961	Ring A Rockin'/Fly Don't Fly On Me (78)	25
59	RCA RCA 1152	Oh! Carol/One Way Ticket (triangular centre)	12
59	RCA RCA 1152	Oh! Carol/One Way Ticket (round centre)	5
59	RCA RCA 1152	Oh! Carol/One Way Ticket (78)	40
60	RCA RCA 1178	Stairway To Heaven/Forty Winks Away	5
60	RCA RCA 1178	Stairway To Heaven/Forty Winks Away (78)	40
60	RCA RCA 1198	Run Samson Run/You Mean Everything To Me	10
60	RCA RCA 1198	Run Samson Run/You Mean Everything To Me (78)	40
62	Stateside SS 105	Oh Delilah/MARVELS: Neil's Twist	10
63	RCA RCA 1368	Bad Girl/Wait 'Til You See My Baby	15
65	RCA RCA 1475	World Through A Tear/High On A Mountain	6
59	RCA RCX 166	NEIL SEDAKA (EP)	40
60	RCA RCX 186	NEIL SEDAKA VOL. 2 (EP)	30
62	RCA RCX 212	NEIL SEDAKA VOL. 3 (EP)	30
59	RCA RD 27140	NEIL SEDAKA (LP)	60
60	RCA RD 27207	CIRCULATE (LP, mono)	40
60	RCA SF 5090	CIRCULATE (LP, stereo)	50

(see also Sam Cooke, Paul Anka, 10cc)

MIKE SEDGEWICK

68	Parlophone R 5694	The Good Guys In The White Hats Never Lose/Woman (She's Got To Be Treated Right)	5
71	President PT 348	Morning Has Broken/Pollution Song	8

(see also Adam Mike & Tim)

SEDUCER

83	Sticky SSR 0017	Call Your Name/Survivor (p/s)	60
84	Thunderbolt THBE 1007	Indecent Exposure/Down Down/No No Baby/DTs/Wild Joker (12", p/s)	10
85	Thunderbolt THBL 016	CAUGHT IN THE ACT (LP)	15
86	Stud STUDLP 2	'EADS DOWN - SEE YOU AT THE END (LP)	15

REDGIE SEEBOE

74	BUG 38	Please Don't Bring Your Sister/Daphne's Brains	10

RUDY SEEDORF

65	Island WI 189	One Million Stars/Mr. Blue	18

SEEDS

66	Vocalion VN 9277	Pushin' Too Hard/Try To Understand	60

MINT VALUE £

66	Vocalion VN 9277	Pushin' Too Hard/Try To Understand (DJ copy)	100
67	Vocalion VN 9287	Can't Seem To Make You Mine/Daisy Mae	40
88	Bam Caruso OPRA 091	Pushin' Too Hard/Greener Day	15
67	Vocalion VAN 8062	A WEB OF SOUND (LP)	120
67	Vocalion VAN 8070	FUTURE (LP, mono)	50
67	Vocalion SAVN 8070	FUTURE (LP, stereo)	60
78	Sonet SNTF 746	THE SEEDS (LEGENDARY MASTER RECORDINGS) (LP)	15
88	Strange Things STRANGEP 1	EVIL HOODOO (LP, picture disc)	15

(see also Sky Saxon, Ya Ho Wa 13)

SEEDS OF THE EARTH
| 75 | Contempo CS 2052 | Planting Seeds/Brother Bad | 20 |
| 75 | Contempo CS 2073 | Zion Plus/Phire | 20 |

MIKE SEEGER
| 65 | Fontana TFL 6039 | MIKE SEEGER (LP) | 15 |

(see also Peggy & Mike Seeger)

PEGGY SEEGER
57	Topic TRC 107	Freight Train/Cumberland Gap (78)	20
58	Topic TRC 108	Pretty Little Baby/Child Of God (78)	10
65	Decca F 12282	Pretty Little Baby/My Love And I Are One	6
57	Pye Jazz NJE 1043	ORIGINS OF SKIFFLE (EP)	20
57	Topic 7T 18	COME ALONG JOHN (EP, 33 rpm with insert)	20
58	Topic TOP 18	COME ALONG JOHN (EP, 45 rpm reissue, with insert)	15
60	Topic TOP 38	SHINE LIKE A STAR (EP)	10
61	Topic TOP 72	TROUBLED LOVE (EP)	10
61	Topic TOP 73	EARLY IN THE SPRING (EP)	10
50s	Topic 10T 9	PEGGY SEEGER (10" LP)	15
61	PRE 13005	THE BEST OF PEGGY SEEGER (LP)	15
64	Topic 12T 113	WHO'S GOING TO SHOE... (LP, with Tom Paley)	15
69	Argo (Z)DA 81	PEGGY ALONE (LP)	15

(see also Al Lloyd)

PEGGY SEEGER & GUY CARAWAN
| 58 | Nixa NPT 19029 | WE SING AMERICA (10" LP) | 30 |
| 58 | HMV CLP 1174 | AMERICA AT PLAY (LP) | 20 |

(see also Guy Carawan)

PEGGY & MIKE SEEGER
| 68 | Argo (Z)DA 80 | PEGGY 'N' MIKE (LP) | 15 |

(see also Ewan MacColl & Peggy Seeger, Mike Seeger)

PETE SEEGER
60	Top Rank TR 5020	Careless Love/LEON BIBB: Times Are Getting Hard (p/s)	10
63	CBS AAG 187	Little Boxes/Mail Myself To You	5
58	Melodisc EPM7 78	TRIBUTE TO LEADBELLY (EP)	8
58	Topic TOP 33	PETE AND FIVE STRINGS (EP)	8
59	Topic TOP 37	HOOTENANNY NEW YORK CITY (EP, with Sonny Terry)	15

(see also Big Bill Broonzy, Sonny Terry [& Brownie McGhee], Weavers)

PETE SEEGER & BIG BILL BROONZY
64	Xtra XTRA 1006	IN CONCERT - PETE SEEGER & BIG BILL BROONZY (LP)	20
66	Verve Folkways VLP 5006	IN CONCERT (LP, mono, reissue)	12
66	Verve Folkways ST SVLP 506	IN CONCERT (LP, stereo, reissue)	15

(see also Big Bill Broonzy)

SEEKERS
65	Oriole CB 1935	With A Swag On My Shoulder/Myra	10
65	Decca F 22167	Chilly Winds/Kumbaya	5
67	Columbia DB 8313	Emerald City/Music Of The World A Turnin'	10

SEEMON & MARIJKE
| 71 | A&M AMLS 64309 | SON OF AMERICA (LP) | 30 |

SEFTONS
| 66 | CBS 202491 | I Can See Through You/Here Today | 25 |

(see also Perishers)

VIVIENNE SEGAL & HAROLD LANG
| 54 | Columbia SCM 5114 | Den Of Iniquity/BARBARA ASHLEY: That Terrific Rainbow | 7 |

BOB SEGER (SYSTEM)
68	Capitol CL 15574	Ramblin' Gamblin' Man/Tales Of Lucy Blue (as Bob Seger System)	15
70	Capitol CL 15642	Lucifer/Big River (as Bob Seger System)	20
72	Reprise K 14208	If I Were A Carpenter/Jesse James	5
73	Reprise K 14243	Rosalie/Back In '72	5
74	Reprise K 14364	Get Out Of Denver/Long Song Comin'	5
72	Reprise K 44214	SMOKIN' O.P.'s (LP)	15

LLOYD SEIVRIGHT
| 70 | Creole CR 1001 | Mary's Boy Child/And Glory Walked Among Men | 5 |

SEIZE
| 81 | Why Not? NOT 001 | Grovelands Road/Why? (p/s) | 15 |
| 82 | Why Not? NOT 002 | EVERYBODY DIES EP (p/s) | 30 |

SEIZE THE CHAIR
| 11 | Too Pure PURE 272s | You Who/It Happens Periodically (all but 100 destroyed in PIAS fire) | 5 |

RICHARD SELANO
| 69 | Jolly JY 019 | All Of The Time/Broken Romance | 7 |

SELECTED FOUR
| 71 | Banana BA 351 | Selection Train/SOUND DIMENSION: Version Train | 12 |

SELECTER
| 79 | 2-Tone CHS TT 4 | On My Radio/Too Much Pressure (paper label, company sleeve) | 10 |
| 80 | 2-Tone CHS TT4 | On My Radio/Too Much Pressure (sliver plastic labels) | 6 |

80	2-Tone CHS TT 8	Three Minute Hero/James Bond (silver plastic label, company sleeve)	10
80	2-Tone CHS TT 8	Three Minute Hero/James Bond (paper labels, company sleeve)	10
80	2-Tone CHS TT 10	Missing Words/Carry Go Bring Home (paper label, company sleeve)	6
80	2-Tone CMS TT10	Missing Words/Carry Go Bring Home (sliver plastic labels)	5
80	2-TOne CHS TT 10	Nissing Words/Carry Go Bring Home (sliver plastic labels, misprint)	5
80	2-Tone CDLTT 5002	TOO MUCH PRESSURE (LP)	15

(see also Special A.K.A.)

FREDDIE SELF
64	Mercury MF 839	Don't Cry/Why Should I?	7

(see also Freddie Ryder, Trends)

RONNIE SELF
58	Philips PB 810	Bop-A-Lena/Ain't I A Dog (78)	200

SELF ABUSE
83	Radical Change RC 5	SOLDIERS (EP)	15

SELF DESTRUCT
91	Retch RR 12004	AFFRAY (12" EP)	8

BROTHER JOHN SELLERS
56	Vanguard EPP 14002	BLUES AND SPIRITUALS (EP)	15
57	Columbia SEG 7740	BLUES AND SPIRITUALS (EP)	15
57	Decca DFE 6457	BROTHER JOHN SELLERS IN LONDON (EP)	15
56	Vanguard PPT 12008	BROTHER JOHN SELLERS SINGS BLUES AND FOLK SONGS (10" LP)	25
57	Vanguard PPT 12017	JACK OF DIAMONDS AND OTHER FOLK SONGS AND BLUES (10" LP)	25

PETER SELLERS (& SOPHIA LOREN)
57	Parlophone R 4337	Any Old Iron/Boiled Bananas And Carrots	8
58	Parlophone R 4491	I'm So Ashamed/A Drop Of The Hard Stuff	5
59	Parlophone R 4605	Puttin' On The Smile/My Old Dutch	5
59	Parlophone R 4605	Puttin' On The Smile/My Old Dutch	15
60	Parlophone R 4702	Goodness Gracious Me! (with Sophia Loren)/Grandpa's Grave	5
61	Parlophone R 4724	Bangers And Mash (with Sophia Loren)/SOPHIA LOREN: Zoo Be Zoo Be Zoo	7
65	Parlophone R 5393	A Hard Day's Night/Help!	7
66	United Artists UP 1152	After The Fox (as Peter Sellers & Hollies)/BURT BACHARACH: The Fox-Trot	35
79	United Artists BP 335	There Are Camels Where The Taxis Used To Be/Night And Day	5
59	Parlophone PMC 1111	SONGS FOR SWINGIN' SELLERS (LP, mono, with Irene Handl)	12
59	Parlophone PCS 3003	SONGS FOR SWINGIN' SELLERS (LP, stereo)	12
60	Parlophone PMC 1131	PETER AND SOPHIA (LP, with Sophia Loren, mono)	15
60	Parlophone PCS 3012	PETER AND SOPHIA (LP, with Sophia Loren, stereo)	20

(Prices for Parlophone albums are for gold on black labels. Yellow and black labels are half of these prices)

74	Decca SKL 5194	HE'S INNOCENT OF WATERGATE (LP, with Spike Milligan)	15

PETER SELLERS, SPIKE MILLIGAN & HARRY SECOMBE
64	Philips AL 3464	HOW TO WIN AN ELECTION (LP)	12

(see also Goons, Spike Milligan, Sophia Loren, Hollies, Harry Secombe, Peter Ustinov)

SELOFANE
68	CBS 3413	Girl Called Fantasy/Happiness Is Love	15
68	CBS 3700	Shingle I.A.O./Chase The Face	30

SELWYN & JOHN
67	CBS 2708	Bogey Man/When God Gave Us Names	80

SEMA
82	Le Rey LR 06	THEME FROM HUNGER (EP)	60
82	Le Rey LR 04	NOTES FROM UNDERGROUND (LP)	150
83	Le Rey LR 101	EXTRACTS FROM ROSA SILBER (LP)	80
84	Le Rey LR 102	THREE SEASONS ONLY (LP)	60

SEMA 4
79	Pollen PBM 022	4 FROM SEMA 4 (EP, 2 different coloured sleeves, 500 only, numbered)	100
79	Pollen PBM 024	UP DOWN AROUND (EP, 1,000 only)	75

ARCHIE SEMPLE
60	Columbia 33SX 1240	JAZZ FOR YOUNG LOVERS (LP)	25
62	Columbia 33SX 1450	EASY LIVING (LP)	20
63	Columbia 33SX 1580	THE TWILIGHT COMETH (LP)	20
64	77 LEU 12/6	THE CLARINET OF ARCHIE SEMPLE (LP)	20

SENATE
67	Columbia DB 8110	I Can't Stop/Ain't As Sweet As You	60
68	United Artists (S)ULP 1180	THE SENATE SOCK IT TO YOU ONE MORE TIME (LP)	40

(see also Garnet Mimms)

SENATOR BOBBY
62	Cameo Parkway P 127	Wild Thing/SENATOR EVERETT McKINLAY: Wild Thing	5

SENATORS
64	Dial DSP 7001	She's A Mod/Lot About You	60
64	Oriole CB 1957	When Day Is Done/Breakdown	50
65	CBS 201768	The Tables Are Turning/Stop Wasting Time	30

(see also Tony Rivers & Castaways)

RAY SENDIT & HIS ROCKEY TEAM
57	Felsted SD 80052	Rocket 0869/Spike's Rock	8

LOS SENORS
63	Cameo Parkway C 290	Amapola/Acapulco	5

SENSATION
73	Sticky STY 1	Everybody Wants It/Lady Put Me Down	8
73	Sticky STY 5	Black Eyed Woman/Baby	10

SENSATIONAL CREED
84	Beggars Banquet BEG 125	Nocturnal Operation/Down Periscope (p/s, reissue of Orbidöig single)	15
84	Beggars Banquet BEG 125T	Nocturnal Operation/Down Periscope/Voyage Of The Titanic (12", p/s, reissue of Orbidöig single)	25

(see also Orbidoig)

SENSATIONS (JAMAICA)

67	Doctor Bird DB 1074	A Thing Called Soul/BOBBY LEE & SENSATIONS: I Was Born A Loser	35
67	Doctor Bird DB 1100	Right On Time/Lonely Lover	35
67	Doctor Bird DB 1102	Born To Love You/Your Sweet Love	60
68	Duke DU 2	Those Guys/I'll Never Fall In Love	80
68	Island WI 3110	Long Time Me No See You Girl/ROY SHIRLEY: Million Dollar Baby	25
69	Camel CA 31	The Warrior (actually by Johnny Osbourne & Sensations)/ JOHNNY ORGAN: Don Juan	20
70	Techniques TI 902	War Boat/Mr Blue	8
71	Duke DU 120	Remember/LARRY'S ALLSTARS: Madhouse	6
71	Duke DU 121	What Are You Doing Sunday/RUFFIANS: Sweet Dream	6

(see also Roy Shirley, Baba Dise, Winston Wright)

SENSATIONS (U.K.)

66	Decca F 12392	Look At My Baby/What A Wonderful Feeling	20
71	MCA MK 5078	Oh My Eli/Let's Get A Little Sentimental	30

SENSATIONS (FEATURING YVONNE) (U.S.)

61	Pye International 7N 25110	Music, Music, Music/A Part Of Me (as Sensations featuring Yvonne)	28
62	Pye International 7N 25128	Let Me In/Oh Yes I'll Be True	35

(see also Yvonne Baker)

SEONA DANCING

83	London LON 22	More To Lose/You're On My Side (p/s)	18
83	London LONX 22	More To Lose (Extended Mix)/You're on My Side (12", p/s)	10
83	London LON 32	Bitter Heart/Tell Her (p/s)	18
83	London LONX 32	Bitter Heart/Tell Her (12", p/s)	12

SEPTIC DEATH

88	Pusmort PUS 00703	KICHIGAI EP (p/s)	5
85	Pusmort 0012-01D	NOW THAT I HAVE THE ATTENTION... (LP, with inner sleeve, 18 tracks)	15

SEPULTURA

94	Roadrunner RR2377-8	Refuse/Resist (12", die cut sleeve)	10
96	Roadrunner RR 23145	Ratamahatta/War/Slave New World (Live)/Amen/Inner Self (Live) (CD, digipak)	15
91	Roadracer RO 93281	ARISE (LP)	15
91	Roadracer RO 9328-8	ARISE (LP, picture disc)	25
94	Roadrunner RR 90000 0	CHAOS A.D. (CD, limited edition tin box; CD has embossed cover & different sleeve, Brazilian flag & 2 bonus tracks, "Policia" & "Inhuman Nature")	50

SERENADERS

59	Top Rank JAR 111	Sudden Holiday/Tango Madeira	5

SERENDIPITY

68	CBS 3733	Through With You/I'm Flying	130
69	CBS 4428	If I Could/Castles	50

SERENDIPITY SINGERS

64	Philips BF 1333	Don't Let The Rain Come Down (Crooked Little Man)/Freedom's Star	6
64	Philips BL 7620	THE SERENDIPITY SINGERS (LP)	12
64	Philips BL 7651	TAKE YOUR SHOES OFF (LP)	12
65	Philips BL 7685	SING OF LOVE, LIES AND FLYING FESTOONS (LP)	12

SERFS

69	Capitol E-ST 207	THE SERFS (LP)	15

SERGEANT PEPPER

83	Ariwa ARILP 006	JUDGEMENT DAY (LP)	25

WILL SERGEANT

82	WEA K 19238	Favourite Branches/RAVI SHANKAR & BILL LOVEDAY: Himalaya (p/s)	8
95	Ochre OCH 003	Cosmos/Venus In Flares (as GLIDE, p/s, orange vinyl)	7
78	(no label or catt. no.)	WEIRD AS FISH (cassette, 7 copies only, each with a different cover)	30
83	92 Happy Cust. HAPLP 1	THEMES FOR "GRIND" (LP)	12

(see also Echo & Bunnymen)

SERGIO & ESTIBALIZ

75	Epic S EPC 3187	Love Come Home/Tu Volveras	12

SERIOUS DRINKING

83	Upright UP 5	Hangover/Don't Shoot Me Down/Baby I'm Dying A Death (p/s)	8
82	Upright YOURS 4	Love On The Terraces/Hypocrite/Bobby Moore Was Innocent (p/s)	8
84	Upright UP 8	Country Girl Became Drugs & Sex Punk/Go For The Burn	10
83	Upright UPLP 3	THE REVOLUTION STARTS AT CLOSING TIME (LP, with beer mat)	12
83	Upright UPLP 7	THEY MAY BE DRINKERS, ROBIN, BUT THEY'RE ALSO HUMAN BEINGS (mini-LP with bingo card)	12
90	Workers Playtime PLAYLP 14	STRANGER THAN TANNADICE (LP, some with free beer mat)	12

SERPENTINE

70	Decca F23001	Powerful Jim/I've Only Got Myself	20

JUAN MANUEL SERRAT

68	Philips BF 1654	She Gives Me Love (La La La)/La La La	6

SERVICEMEN

00	Grapevine 116	Are You Angry/I Need A Helping Hand	15
01	Grapevine 136	I'll Stop Loving You/Sweet Magic	15

NANCY SESAY & MELODAIRES

81	It's War Boys S 1	C'est Fab/The Ballad Of Hong Kong/National Honk (gatefold p/s)	5

(see also Homosexuals)

SESSION MEN

80	LKJ 001	THE SESSION MEN : Solitude/ABU BAKE : Introducing Abu Baka/ MICHAEL SMITH : Mi Cyaan Believe It/Roots (12")	25

(see also Michael Smith)

CAMILO SESTO

72	Pye Intl. 7N 25589	To Be A Man/Now Is My Time (Yo Soy Asi)	40

BOLA SETE
76	Sonet SNTF 695	OCEAN (LP)	15

SETTERS
70	Duke DU 65	Paint Your Wagon/Organ Man (both sides actually by Hot Rod All Stars)	140
70	Trojan TR 7738	Virgin Soldier/Brixton Reggae Festival (both actually by Hot Rod All Stars)	8

SETTING SUN
68	Oak RGI 840	Ob La De Ob La Da/Boy Who Was Only One/Homeward Bound/Fascinating Rhythm	40

SETTLERS
65	Pye 7N 159645	Woman Called Freedom/I Know I'm Right	6
66	Pye 7N 17065	Nowhere Man/Call Again	7
67	Pye 7N 17375	Major Minor/I Love 'Oo Kazoo ('Cos 'Oo Love Me)	6
70	Columbia DB 8695	Nessie The Monster/Jesus Met the Woman (At The Well)	6
71	York SYK 505	The Lightning Tree/Just This Side Of Nowhere	7
74	York YR 215	On Top Of The World/Let's Tell The World	6

SEVEN AGES OF MAN
72	Rediffusion ZS 115	SEVEN AGES OF MAN (LP, yellow/black label)	40

(see also Madeline Bell, Gordon Beck)

SEVEN LETTERS/SYMARIP
69	Doctor Bird DB 1189	People Get Ready/The Fit (as Seven Letters)	40
69	Doctor Bird DB 1194	Please Stay/Special Beat (as Seven Letters)	40
69	Doctor Bird DB 1195	Flour Dumpling/Equality (as Seven Letters [Symarip])	35
69	Doctor Bird DB 1206	Mama Me Want Girl/Sentry (as Seven Letters)	25
69	Doctor Bird DB 1207	Soul Crash/Throw Me Things (as Seven Letters)	40
69	Doctor Bird DB 1208	There Goes My Heart/Wish (as Seven Letters)	30
69	Doctor Bird DB 1209	Bam Bam Baji/Hold Him Joe (as Seven Letters [Symarip])	100
69	Doctor Bird DB 1306	Fung Sure/Tomorrow At Sundown (as Symarip)	40
69	Treasure Isle TI 7050	Skinhead Moonstomp/Must Catch A Train (as Symarip)	30
70	Treasure Isle TI 7054	Parson's Corner/Redeem (as Symarip)	30
70	Treasure Isle TI 7055	La Bella Jig/Holidays By The Sea (as Symarip)	10
70	Attack ATT 8013	I'm A Puppet/Vindication (as Symarip)	15
80	Trojan TRO 9062	Skinhead Moonstomp/Skinhead Jamboree (p/s)	8
70	Trojan TBL 102	SKINHEAD MOONSTOMP (LP, as Symarip)	30

(see also Pyramids, Equals, Laurel Aitken)

7 SECONDS
82	Alt. Tentacles VIRUS 15	SKIN, BRAINS AND GUTS (EP, with insert)	12
84	BYO BY008	CREW (LP)	12

SEVEN YEAR ITCH
81	Cargo CRS 007	I wanna Make Ya/Oo Ya Ha	10

SEVENTEEN
80	Vendetta VD 001	Don't Let Go/Bank Holiday Weekend (p/s)	100

(see also Alarm)

SEVENTH ANGEL
90	Under One Flag FLAG 51	THE TORMENT (LP)	15

SEVENTH SEAL
90	Mystic Red Corp MRC 8004	Sound Iration/Dub Seal (12")	50

SEVENTH SEAL
97	Acme ACLP 8018LP	THE SEVENTH SEAL (LP)	12

SEVENTH SON
82	Rising Son FMR 067	Man In The Street/Immortal Hours (in p/s)	75
82	Rising Son FMR 067	Man In The Street/Immortal Hours	20
84	Rising Son SRT4KS 282	Metal To The Moon/Sound And Fury (in gatefold p/s)	60
84	Rising Son SRT4KS 282	Metal To The Moon/Sound And Fury	30
87	Music Factory MF 0043	Northern Boots/The Harder You Rock (p/s)	18
89	Rising Son SRT9KLS	What More Do You Want/Sister Strange/Bitter Ashes (12", p/s)	12

SEVENTH WAVE
75	Gull GULS 14	Manifestations/Only The Beginning (Part 1)	5
89	SRT SRT9KS 2018	Tonight/Run (p/s)	20
74	Gull GULP 1001	THINGS TO COME (LP)	15
75	Gull GULP 1010	PSI-FI (LP)	18

(see also Second Hand, Fungus)

SEVENTH WONDER
80	Grapevine GRP 130	Captain Of My Ship/Pharaoh	12

SEVERE CARNAGE
90	White JC 002	The Struggle Continues/Back To Basics (12")	100

SEVERED HEAD
83	Plastic Canvas PC 002	Heavy Metal/Killin' The Kidz (p/s)	40

SEVERED HEADS
85	Ink INK 129	GOODBYE TONSILS (12" EP)	8
85	Ink INK 9	CITY SLAB HORROR (LP)	15

SEVERINE
71	CBS 7230	Chance In Time/Nothing Bad Can Be This Good	8
71	Philips 6009 135	Un Banc, Un Arbre, Une Rue/Viens	5
71	Philips 6009 152	La La Melodie/Je Ferme Les Yeux, Je Compte Dix	5

DAVID SEVILLE & HIS ORCHESTRA (& THE CHIPMUNKS)
64	Liberty 16170	All My Loving/Please Please Me	8
57	London HLU 8359	Armen's Theme/Carousel In Rome (initially gold label print)	20
57	London HLU 8359	Armen's Theme/Carousel In Rome (later silver label print)	10
57	London RE-U 1085	DAVID SEVILLE & HIS ORCHESTRA (EP)	15
59	London RE-U 1219	WITCH DOCTOR AND FRIENDS (EP)	15
59	London HA-U 2153	THE WITCH DOCTOR PRESENTS DAVID SEVILLE AND HIS FRIENDS (LP)	15

MINT VALUE £

60	London HAG 2268	SING AGAIN WITH THE CHIPMUNKS (LP)	15
64	Liberty LBY 1218	THE CHIPMUNKS SING THE BEATLES (LP)	15

(see also Alfi & Harry)

ALEC SEWARD
56	Vogue LDE 165	CITY BLUES (10" LP)	40

SEX
00	Grapevine 113	It's You Baby (It's You)/It's You Baby (Extended)	15

SEX AIDS
83	Riot City RIOT 23	BACK ON THE PISS AGAIN (EP)	15

(see also Vice Squad)

SEX BEATLES
79	Charly CYS 1061	Well You Never/Fatal Fascination (p/s)	8

SEX GANG CHILDREN
82	Illuminated ILL 1112	Beasts (12", EP)	30

SEXHURT
98	Dobbstown BOB 23	A ROMANTIC EVENING WITH BIG RED STRAPS (LP, with free straps)	12

SEX PISTOLS
SINGLES
76	EMI 401	Anarchy In The U.K (4.01 longer version)/No Fun (Abbey Road 2-sided acetate, only 3 known to exist)	7000
76	EMI	Anarchy In The U.K. (3.36 version) (1-sided Abbey Road Acetate)	5000
76	EMI EMI 2566	Anarchy In The U.K./I Wanna Be Me (black p/s, with Chris Thomas production credit on B-side)	120
76	EMI EMI 2566	Anarchy In The U.K./I Wanna Be Me ('Demo, not for sale'. Black p/s, Chris Thomas credit on both sides and with information slip)	300
76	EMI EMI 2566	Anarchy In The U.K./I Wanna Be Me (Dave Goodman production credit on B-side)	50
76	EMI EMI 2566	Anarchy In The U.K./I Wanna Be Me (Anarchy label on both sides)	150
77	(no label or cat. no.)	God Save The Queen/No Feelings (double sided 7" acetate on LTS - few copies pressed and used by Malcolm McLaren to get gigs and record deal)	10000
77	A&M AMS 7284	God Save The Queen/No Feelings (withdrawn, in brown envelope with press release)	8000
77	A&M AMS 7284	God Save The Queen/No Feelings (withdrawn, without brown envelope and press release)	7500
77	Virgin VS 181	God Save The Queen/Did You No Wrong (1st issue, with silver on blue sleeve and labels)	10
77	Virgin VS 181	God Save The Queen/Did You No Wrong (Plain blue no Queen's head sample sleeve - two known copies, Jamie Reid autograph added later to one)	1500
77	Virgin VS 181	God Save The Queen/Did You No Wrong (2nd issue, white on blue sleeve and labels)	8
77	Virgin VS 184	Pretty Vacant/No Fun (p/s)	10
77	Virgin VS 184	Pretty Vacant/No Fun (p/s with push-out centre)	30
77	Virgin VS 191	Holidays In The Sun/Satellite (withdrawn p/s)	20
77	Virgin/Lyntone LYN 3261	Lentilmas - A Seasonal Offering To You From Virgin Records (flexidisc, Xmas freebie to journalists; with Xmas card)	1500
77	Virgin/Lyntone LYN 3261	Lentilmas - A Seasonal Offering To You From Virgin Records (flexidisc, Xmas freebie to journalists; without Xmas card)	450
78	(No. Cat. No)	SID VICIOUS: My Way (1-sided Pye Studios Acetate)	700
78	Virgin VS 220	No One Is Innocent/SID VICIOUS: My Way (no p/s)	6
78	Virgin VS 220	No-One Is Innocent (mispress, plays Motors track)/SID VICIOUS: My Way (p/s)	35
78	Virgin VS 22012	The Biggest Blow (A Punk Prayer By Ronald Biggs)/(Interview)/SID VICIOUS: My Way (12", p/s [matrix: VS 22012A3], without interview [VS 22012 A1])	20
78	Virgin VS 22012	The Biggest Blow (A Punk Prayer By Ronald Biggs)/(Interview)/SID VICIOUS: My Way (12", p/s [matrix: VS 22012A3], with interview [VS 22012 A1])	10
78	(No label or cat no)	The Interview (recorded at Middlesborough Rock Garden August 1977, 7.30 minutes each side, 1000 pressed)	10
79	Virgin VS 240	Something Else/Friggin' In The Riggin' (p/s, black & white labels)	7
79	Virgin VS 256	Silly Thing/TENPOLE TUDOR: Who Killed Bambi (p/s)	6
79	Virgin VS 272	C'mon Everybody/The God Save The Queen Symphony/ Watcha Gonna Do About It (p/s)	5
79	Virgin VS 290	The Great Rock 'n' Roll Swindle/Rock Around The Clock (vocals by Tenpole Tudor) ('American Express' p/s)	6
79	Virgin VS 290	The Great Rock 'n' Roll Swindle (mispressing with 'lawyers' telephone conversation' track)/Rock Around The Clock ('American Express' p/s)	30
80	Virgin VS 339	(I'm Not Your) Stepping Stone/Pistols Propaganda (p/s, mispressing, B-side plays "Substitute")	25
80	Virgin VS 339	(I'm Not Your) Stepping Stone/Pistols Propaganda (p/s, mispressing, B-side plays Gillan track "No Laughing In Heaven")	30
80	Virgin SEX 1	PISTOLS PACK (6 x 7" in p/s; all in plastic wallet)	50
81	Virgin VS 443	Who Killed Bambi?/Rock Around The Clock (by Tenpole Tudor & Pistols, p/s)	10
85	Chaos DICK1	Submission/No Feelings (p/s, 5,000 only, blue vinyl)	7
85	Chaos DICK1	Submission/No Feelings (p/s, 5,000 only, pink vinyl)	15
85	Chaos DICK1	Submission/No Feelings (p/s, 5,000 only, yellow vinyl)	5
85	Chaos SUB 1	Submission (12", 1-sided test pressing, die-cut sleeve, label has big red 'A')	30
85	Chaos	Pretty Vacant (unreleased, 20 copies only)	75
85	Chaos CARTEL 1	Submission (12" 1-track promo)	25
86	Archive 4 TOF 104	THE ORIGINAL SEX PISTOLS LIVE (4-track 12", p/s, blue vinyl)	12
88	Virgin CDT 3	Anarchy In The U.K./No Fun/EMI (3" CD, card sleeve)	10
88	Virgin CDT 37	God Save The Queen/Did You No Wrong/Don't Give Me No Lip Child (3" CD, gatefold card sleeve)	10
88	Spiral Scratch SCRATCH 4	Pretty Vacant (Demo)/I Wanna Be Me (Demo) (with Spiral Scratch magazine, issue 4, B-side actually plays "Seventeen")	10
92	Virgin VS 1448	Pretty Vacant/No Feelings (p/s, Lady Di cover)	15
02	Virgin VS 1832	God Save The Queen/Did You No Wrong (reissue)	8
12	Universal	Anarchy In The U.K./I Wanna Be Me (picture disc, 3500 copies, numbered)	10

ALBUMS
77	Virgin V 2086/SPOTS 001	NEVER MIND THE BOLLOCKS, HERE'S THE SEX PISTOLS (LP, pink rear sleeve, with no track listing, with poster & 1-sided single, "Submission" [VDJ 24], shrinkwrapped, with orange or green-stickered versions extremely rare)	700
77	Virgin V 2086/SPOTS 001	NEVER MIND THE BOLLOCKS, HERE'S THE SEX PISTOLS (LP, pink rear sleeve, with no track listing, with poster & 1-sided single, "Submission" [VDJ 24], shrinkwrapped, with orange or green-stickered versions extremely rare)	125
77	Virgin V 2086	NEVER MIND THE BOLLOCKS, HERE'S THE SEX PISTOLS (LP, with track listing, no shrinkwrap)	25

77	Virgin V 2086	NEVER MIND THE BOLLOCKS, HERE'S THE SEX PISTOLS (LP, pink rear sleeve with no track listing)	25
78	Virgin VP 2086	NEVER MIND THE BOLLOCKS, HERE'S THE SEX PISTOLS (LP, picture disc)	40
79	Virgin VD 2510	THE GREAT ROCK 'N' ROLL SWINDLE (2-LP, including "Watcha Gonna Do About It", with paper insert)	30
79	Virgin VD 2510	THE GREAT ROCK 'N' ROLL SWINDLE (2-LP, "I Wanna Be Me" and "Who Killed Bambi?" replace "Watcha Gonna Do About It", with spoken overdubs on "God Save The Queen Symphony")	20
79	Virgin V2142	FLOGGING A DEAD HORSE (LP)	15
80	Factory FACT 30	THE HEYDAY (gold interview cassette in satin pouch with Xmas card)	50
80	Factory FACT 30	THE HEYDAY (cassette, in vinyl pouch without Xmas card)	20
86	Virgin CDV 2086	NEVER MIND THE BOLLOCKS, HERE'S THE SEX PISTOLS (CD, mispressing, plays country music titles)	20
89	Link LINKLP 063	LIVE AND LOUD (LP)	12
92	Virgin V2702	KISS THIS (2-LP)	25
98	Virgin VP 2087	NEVER MIND THE BOLLOCKS, HERE'S THE SEX PISTOLS (LP, pink vinyl reissue, numbered on rear sleeve)	15
06	Castle CMQLP 1395	SPUNK (LP, yellow vinyl)	15

(see also Public Image Ltd, Professionals, Rich Kids, Steve Jones, Cash Pussies, Spectres (UK), Swingers)

TONY SEXTON
78	Burning Sounds BSD 005	Desire (with Jah Son)/BOB DAVIS: World In My Arms (12")	15

SEXY GIRLS
69	Fab FAB 100	Pom-Pom Song/LITTLE JOE & BUSTER'S ALLSTARS: Hy There (B-side actually by Melltones)	15
69	Dice CC 100	Pom-Pom Song/LITTLE JOE & BUSTER'S ALLSTARS: Hy There (B-side actually by Melltones) (reissue)	15

DENNY SEYTON & SABRES
64	Mercury MF 800	Tricky Dicky/Baby What You Want Me To Do	20
64	Mercury MF 814	Short Fat Fanny/Give Me Back My Heart	20
64	Mercury MF 824	The Way You Look Tonight/Hands Off	25
65	Parlophone R 5363	Just A Kiss/In The Flowers By The Trees (as Denny Seyton Group)	35
65	Wing WL 1032	IT'S THE GEAR (14 HITS) (LP)	40

TONY SHABAZZ
79	Ethnic Fight FT DD 4436	Mr Fitzy/RUDDIE MOWATT: Public Enemy (12")	60

SHABBY TIGER
76	RCA Victor PL 25046	SHABBY TIGER (LP)	15

SHACK
88	Ghetto GTG B 1	Emergency/Liberation (p/s)	6
88	Ghetto GTG T 1	Emergency/Liberation/Faith (12", p/s)	12
88	Ghetto GTG CD 1	Emergency/Liberation/Faith/What's It Like (CD)	8
89	Ghetto GTG B 2	High Rise Low Life/Who Killed Clayton Square? (p/s)	5
89	Ghetto GTG T 2	High Rise Low Life/Who Killed Clayton Square?/High Rise Low Life (Bert Hardy Mix) (12", p/s)	10
90	Ghetto GTG B 11	I Know You Well/I Feel No Way (p/s)	5
90	Ghetto GTG 11T	I Know You Well (Extended Mix)/I Feel No Way/(If You Want It Mix) (12", p/s)	8
06	Sour Mash JDNC 007	Cup Of Tea/Lizzie Mallaly (p/s numbered)	5
88	Ghetto GHETT 1	ZILCH (LP, distributed by Epic)	15
88	Ghetto GHETT 1	ZILCH (LP, later independent issue)	25
88	Ghetto GHETT D 1	ZILCH (CD)	18
03	North Country NCLP 002	HERE'S TOM WITH THE WEATHER (LP)	18

(see also Pale Fountains, Michael Head & Strands)

SHADE JOEY & NIGHTOWLS
64	Parlophone R 5180	Bluebirds Over The Mountain/That's When I Need You Baby	90

SHADER
81	Piston Broke REDASH 1	Bad News Blues (no p/s)	100

SHADES
62	Starlite ST45 074	Weird Walk/Joe's Shuffle	20

SHADES (JAMAICA)
69	Gas GAS 119	Never Gonna Give You Up/Let Me Remind You (both actually by Techniques)	12

(see also Techniques)

SHADES OF BLUE (U.K.)
65	Parlophone R 5270	Voodoo Blues/Luceanne	50
65	Pye 7N 15988	Where Did All The Good Times Go/I Ain't No Use	15

SHADES OF BLUE (U.S.)
66	Sue WI 4022	Oh! How Happy/Little Orphan Boy	35

SHADES OF JOY
69	Fontana STL 5498	SHADES OF JOY (LP)	20

SHADES OF MACMURROUGH
73	Polydor 2908 007	CRAIG RIVER (LP, red label, Irish pressing)	150

SHADES OF MORLEY BROWN
68	Mercury MF1054	Silly Girl/Pretty Bluebird	120

SHADES (U.S.)
58	London HLX 8713	Sun Glasses (with Knott Sisters)/KNOTT SISTERS: Undivided Attention	40
58	London HLX 8713	Sun Glasses (with Knott Sisters)/KNOTT SISTERS: Undivided Attention (78)	10

SHADO
74	Montrose MON 1001	Evil City/Tell You I Know	60

JOHNNY SHADOW (& DANNY GAVAN)
63	Pye 7N 15506	Golli Golli/I'm Coming Home To You (with Danny Gavan) (in p/s)	15
63	Pye 7N 15506	Golli Golli/I'm Coming Home To You (with Danny Gavan)	5
63	Pye 7N 15529	Golli Guitar/Week (with Danny Gavan)	5
65	Parlophone R 5286	Kiss Me Now/What Colour Is The Wind	5
65	Parlophone R 5308	Atom Bomb Song Part 3/Talented Man	5

(see also Ivy League)

SHADOWFAX

79	BFD SFX 100	Really Into You (p/s)	50
80	Risky Discs RISK 1	The Russians Are Coming/Calling The Shots	8

SHADOWS (U.K.)

SINGLES

59	Columbia DB 4387	Saturday Dance/Lonesome Fella	50
59	Columbia DB 4387	Saturday Dance/Lonesome Fella (78)	200
60	Columbia DB 4484	Apache/Quartermaster's Stores (green label)	8
60	Columbia DB 4484	Apache/Quartermaster's Stores (later black label)	15
60	Columbia DB 4530	Man Of Mystery/The Stranger	5
61	Columbia DB 4580	F.B.I./Midnight	5
61	Columbia DB 4637	The Frightened City/Back Home	5
61	Columbia DB 4698	Kon-Tiki/36-24-36	5
61	Columbia DB 4726	The Savage/Peace Pipe	5
62	Columbia DB 4790	Wonderful Land/Stars Fell On Stockton	5
62	Columbia DB 4870	Guitar Tango/What A Lovely Tune	5

(The above 45s were originally issued with green labels; later black label copies are worth £10.)

62	Columbia DB 4948	Dance On!/All Day	5
63	Columbia DB 4984	Foot Tapper/The Breeze And I	5
63	Columbia DB 7047	Atlantis/I Want You To Want Me	5
63	Columbia DB 7106	Shindig/It's Been A Blue Day	5
63	Columbia DB 7163	Geronimo/Shazam	5
64	Columbia DB 7231	Theme For Young Lovers/This Hammer	5
64	Columbia DB 7261	The Rise And Fall Of Flingel Bunt/It's A Man's World	5
64	Columbia DB 7261	The Rise And Fall Of Flingel Bunt/It's A Man's World (mispressing with A-side on both sides)	8
64	Columbia DB 7342	Rhythm 'n' Greens/The Miracle	6
64	Columbia DB 7416	Genie With The Light Brown Lamp/Little Princess	10
65	Columbia DB 7476	Mary Anne/Chu-Chi	6
65	Columbia DB 7588	Stingray/Alice In Sunderland (in export p/s)	20
65	Columbia DB 7650	Don't Make My Baby Blue/My Grandfather's Clock (p/s)	20
65	Columbia DB 7769	The War Lord/I Wish I Could Shimmy Like My Sister Arthur	10
66	Columbia DB 7853	I Met A Girl/Late Night Set	10
66	Columbia DB 7952	A Place In The Sun/Will You Be There	10
66	Columbia DB 8034	The Dreams I Dream/Scotch On The Socks ('B' label demos worth £50)	30
67	Columbia PSR 305	Thunderbirds Are Go (1-sided advance promo)	60
67	Columbia DB 8170	Maroc 7/Bombay Duck	10
67	Columbia PSR 308	Maroc 7 (1-sided demo with spoken-word intro)	60
67	Columbia PSR 310	Chelsea Boot/Jigsaw (demo only)	80
67	Columbia DB 8264	Tomorrow's Cancelled/Somewhere	18
68	Columbia DB 8326	Running Out Of World/HANK MARVIN: London's Not Too Far	18
68	Columbia DB 8372	Dear Old Mrs. Bell/Trying To Forget The One You Love	18
69	Columbia DB 8628	Slaughter On Tenth Avenue/HANK MARVIN: Midnight Cowboy	18

EPs

61	Columbia SEG 8061	THE SHADOWS (mono)	10
61	Columbia ESG 7834	THE SHADOWS (stereo)	15
61	Columbia SEG 8094	THE SHADOWS TO THE FORE	10
62	Columbia SEG 8135	SPOTLIGHT ON THE SHADOWS	15
62	Columbia SEG 8148	THE SHADOWS NO. 2 (only some sleeves list "No. 2")	15
62	Columbia SEG 8166	THE SHADOWS NO. 3	15
62	Columbia SEG 8171	WONDERFUL LAND OF THE SHADOWS	15

(The above EPs were originally issued with turquoise labels; later blue/black label copies are worth two-thirds these values.)

62	Columbia SEG 8193	THE BOYS (mono)	10
62	Columbia ESG 7881	THE BOYS (stereo, turquoise labels)	30
62	Columbia ESG 7881	THE BOYS (stereo, later black/blue labels)	25
63	Columbia SEG 8218	OUT OF THE SHADOWS (mono)	10
63	Columbia ESG 7883	OUT OF THE SHADOWS (stereo, turquoise labels)	30
63	Columbia ESG 7883	OUT OF THE SHADOWS (stereo, black/blue labels)	25
63	Columbia SEG 8233	DANCE ON WITH THE SHADOWS	10
63	Columbia SEG 8249	OUT OF THE SHADOWS NO. 2 (mono)	10
63	Columbia ESG 7895	OUT OF THE SHADOWS NO. 2 (stereo ESG 7895)	25
63	Columbia SEG 8268	FOOT TAPPING WITH THE SHADOWS	10
63	Columbia SEG 8278	LOS SHADOWS (2 different sleeves)	10
63	Columbia SEG 8286	SHINDIG WITH THE SHADOWS	20
64	Columbia SEG 8321	THOSE BRILLIANT SHADOWS	20
64	Columbia SEG 8342	DANCE WITH THE SHADOWS	20
64	Columbia SEG 8362	RHYTHM AND GREENS (mono))	18
64	Columbia ESG 7904	RHYTHM AND GREENS (stereo)	30
64	Columbia SEG 8375	DANCE WITH THE SHADOWS NO. 2	20
65	Columbia SEG 8396	THEMES FROM "ALADDIN AND HIS WONDERFUL LAMP"	20
65	Columbia SEG 8408	DANCE WITH THE SHADOWS NO. 3	20
65	Columbia SEG 8445	ALICE IN SUNDERLAND	20
65	Columbia SEG 8459	THE SOUND OF THE SHADOWS	25
66	Columbia SEG 8473	THE SOUND OF THE SHADOWS NO. 2	25
66	Columbia SEG 8494	THE SOUND OF THE SHADOWS NO. 3	25
66	Columbia SEG 8500	THOSE TALENTED SHADOWS	22
66	Columbia SEG 8510	THUNDERBIRDS ARE GO! (with Cliff Richard)	60
67	Columbia SEG 8528	THE SHADOWS ON STAGE AND SCREEN	40

ALBUMS

61	Columbia 33SX 1374	THE SHADOWS (mono)	20
61	Columbia SCX 3414	THE SHADOWS (stereo)	40
62	Columbia 33SX 1458	OUT OF THE SHADOWS (mono)	20
62	Columbia SCX 3449	OUT OF THE SHADOWS (stereo)	30
63	Columbia 33SX 1522	GREATEST HITS (stereo SCX 1522)	15
64	Columbia 33SX 1619	DANCE WITH THE SHADOWS (mono)	20
64	Columbia SCX 3511	DANCE WITH THE SHADOWS (stereo)	22
65	Columbia 33SX 1736	THE SOUND OF THE SHADOWS (mono)	20
65	Columbia SCX 3554	THE SOUND OF THE SHADOWS (stereo)	20
65	Columbia 33SX 1791	MORE HITS! (stereo SCX 3578)	15

66	Columbia 33SX/SCX 6041	SHADOW MUSIC	15
67	Columbia S(C)X 6148	JIGSAW	18
67	Columbia S(C)X 6199	FROM HANK, BRUCE, BRIAN AND JOHN	18
68	Columbia SX 6282	ESTABLISHED 1958 (half by Cliff Richard, mono)	15
68	Columbia SCX 6282	ESTABLISHED 1958 (half by Cliff Richard, stereo)	12

(The above LPs were originally issued with blue/black labels; later silver/black label copies are worth half these values.)

70	Columbia SCX 6420	SHADES OF ROCK	18
72	World Records ALBUM 72	THE SHADOWS (6-LP box set)	20
73	EMI EMA 762	ROCKIN' WITH CURLY LEADS	15
77	EMI EMTV 3	TWENTY GOLDEN GREATS (mispressing, side 2 plays Pink Floyd's "Animals")	30

(see also Cliff Richard, Drifters, Five Chestnuts, Hank Marvin, Marvin Welch & Farrar, Bruce Welch, John Henry Rostill, Brian Bennett, Jet Harris, Tony Meehan, Vipers Skiffle Group, Marty Wilde, Krew Kats, Interns, Strangers, Wasp, MacArthur Park, Thunder Company, Alan Hawkshaw)

SHADOWS (U.S.)

58	HMV POP 563	Jungle Fever/Under Stars Of Love	100
58	HMV POP 563	Jungle Fever/Under Stars Of Love (78)	50

SHADOWS OF KNIGHT

66	Atlantic AT 4085	Gloria/Dark Side	40
66	Atlantic 584 021	Oh Yeah/Light Bulb Blues	35
66	Atlantic 584 045	Bad Little Woman/Gospel Zone	30
67	Atlantic 584 136	Someone Like Me/Three For Love	35
69	Buddah 201 024	Shake/From Way Out To Way Under	30
79	Radar ADA 11	GLORIA (LP)	15

SHADROCKS

67	Island WI 3061	Go Go Special/Count Down	12
68	Jay Boy BOY 2	There Is/Jigsaw	6

SHADY

98	Narcotic Candy BBQ 41 TT	Narcotic Candy/Micro Bodi Dot Con (10", p/s)	8

(see also Mercury Rev)

SHADY BARD

05	No label	Torch Song/Bobby/Memory Tree (CD-R in pvc sleeve, sold at gigs)	10
06	Static Caravan Van 108	TREEOLOGY EP (CD, hand wrapped in brown paper and string, 100 only)	15

DOREEN SHAFFER

69	Unity UN 536	No Matter What/Walk Through This World	8
69	Unity UN 538	How Much Is That Doggy In The Window/As Long As He Needs Me	6
70	Pama SECO 31	FIRST LADY OF REGGAE (LP)	80

(see also Bob Marley/Wailers, Lloyd Clarke, Doreen & Jackie)

JOHN SHAFT

72	Downtown DT 488	Forever Music/BLOSSOM JOHNSON: The Boy I Love	6

SHAFTESBURY

80	O.K. SRT CUS 025	Hit Man/Crazy Jane	5
80	O.K. OKA 001	THE LULL BEFORE THE STORM (LP, with insert)	15
81	O.K. OKA 002	WE ARE THE BOYS (LP)	12

BOBBY SHAFTO

62	Parlophone R 4870	Over And Over/I Want My Bed	5
62	Parlophone R 4958	Feel So Blue/I Haven't Got A Girl	5
64	Parlophone R 5130	She's My Girl/Wonderful You	5
64	Parlophone R 5167	Love, Love, Love (Don't Let Me Down)/I Don't Love You Anymore	5
64	Parlophone R 5184	Who Wouldn't Love A Girl Like That/I Remember	5
65	Parlophone R 5252	How Could You Do A Thing Like That To Me/Baby Then	5
66	Parlophone R 5403	Lonely Is As Lonely Does/The Same Old Room	15
66	Parlophone R 5481	A Little Like You/See Me Cry	5

SHAG 'N' SKOOB

92	WINTER 3	SKOOBY CHEWNZ VOL. 1 EP (12")	40

SHAG NASTY

79	Shag Nasty SN 1	No Bullshit Just Rock 'n' Roll/Looking For A Love? (p/s)	30

SHAGRAT

90	Shagrat ORC 001	Amanda/Peppermint Flickstick (p/s, 500 only, autographed)	10
90	Shagrat ORC 001	Amanda/Peppermint Flickstick (p/s, 500 only, some autographed)	6
91	Shagrat ENT 001	NOTHING EXCEEDS LIKE EXCESS (mini LP, as Steve Took's Shagrat, numbered, 400 only)	12

SHAKA FATMAN

80	Live And Love LAP 12	CONFRONTATION DUB - SHAKA (WARRIOR) VS. FATMAN (KILLER) (LP)	30

SHAKANE

70	UPC 110	Rhona/Find The Lady	15
72	Young Blood Int. YB 1004	Love Machine/Mr Jackson	6
76	United Artists UP 36087	Jenny/Gang Man	12

SHAKE

79	Sire SIR 4016	Culture Shock/Dream On	10
79	Sire SIR 4016-10	Culture Shock/Glass House/Dream On/(But) Not Mine (10", p/s)	12

(see also Rezillos, Jo Callis, TV 21)

SHAKE APPEAL

87	Notown NO 2	Gimme Fever/Mexico City SOS (p/s)	10
88	Jericho JR 001	Amphetamine/ANYWAYS: Well Of Hurt (no p/s)	15

SHAKEOUTS

65	Columbia DB 7613	Every Little Once In A While/Well Who's That	70

SHAKERS (U.K.)

63	Polydor NH 52158	Money/Memphis Tennessee	25
63	Polydor NH 52213	Hippy Hippy Shake/Dr. Feelgood	25
63	Polydor NH 66991	Hippy Hippy Shake/Dr. Feelgood	25
63	Polydor NH 52258	Money/Hippy Hippy Shake	25
63	Polydor NH 52272	Whole Lotta Lovin'/I Can Tell	25
63	Polydor 237 139	LET'S DO THE SLOP, TWIST, MADISON, HULLY GULLY WITH THE SHAKERS (LP)	70

(see also Kingsize Taylor & Dominoes)

SHAKERS (U.S.)
73	Probe PRO 582	One Wonderful Moment/Love, Love, Love	7
74	ABC ABC 4018	One Wonderful Moment/Love, Love, Love (reissue)	5

CHRIS SHAKESPEARE GLOBE SHOW
69	Page One POF 113	Ob-La-Di, Ob-La-Da/Tin Soldier	25

(see also Globe Show)

JOHN SHAKESPEARE
69	Decca F 12896	Number One Theme/Fade Out (with p/s)	30
69	Decca F 12896	Number One Theme/Fade Out	10

SHAKESPEARES
68	RCA Victor RCA 1695	Something To Believe In/Burning My Fingers	60

(see also Fynn McCool)

SHAKE THE TREE
88	Brickworks	SHAKE THE TREE (LP)	30

SHAKEY JAKE
69	Liberty LBL 83217E	FURTHER ON UP THE ROAD (LP)	40

SHAKEY VICK
69	Pye NPL 18276	LITTLE WOMAN, YOU'RE SO SWEET (LP mono)	50
69	Pye NSPL 18276	LITTLE WOMAN, YOU'RE SO SWEET (LP stereo, in mono sleeve with 'STEREO NSPL' sticker on rear)	35

SAM SHAM
69	Blue Cat BS 157	Drumbago's Dead/SPARTERS: Song Of The Year	15

SHAM 69
77	Step Forward SF 4	I Don't Wanna/Ulster/Red London (black & white photo p/s)	15
77	Step Forward SF 412	I Don't Wanna/Ulster/Red London (12", black & white photo p/s)	10
77	Polydor (no cat. no.)	Song Of The Streets/Fanx (1-sided concert freebie, red brick-wall label; white label copies are counterfeits)	20
78	Polydor 2058 966	Borstal Breakout/Hey Little Rich Boy (p/s)	15
78	Polydor 2059 023	Angels With Dirty Faces/The Cockney Kids Are Innocent (p/s)	8
78	Polydor 2059 050	If The Kids Are United/Sunday Morning Nightmare (p/s)	6
78		What Have We Got? (1-sided gig only 45, 500 only)	25
79	Step Forward SF 412	I Don't Wanna/Red London/Ulster (12" reissue, yellow p/s)	8
79	Step Forward SF 4	I Don't Wanna/Red London (reissue, p/s)	5
79		Hersham Boys/Day Tripper (Original "Pye Studios" acetate for 'Hersham' single, release withdrawn as unable to clear copyright)	250
79	Polydor POSP 64	Hersham Boys/I Don't Wanna (live)/Tell Us The Truth (live) (p/s)	5
79	Polydor POSPX 64	Hersham Boys/I Don't Wanna (live)/Rip Off (live)/I'm A Man, I'm A Boy (live)/Tell Us The Truth (live) (12", p/s)	8
79	Polydor POSP 82	You're A Better Man Than I/Give A Dog A Bone (p/s)	5
87	Legacy LGY 70	Ban The Gun/Ban The Gun	5
79	Polydor POLD 5025	THE ADVENTURES OF THE HERSHAM BOYS (LP, with 12" EP [2812 045], stickered sleeve)	12
80	Polydor 2383 596	THE FIRST, THE BEST AND THE LAST (LP, with live EP [RIOT 1/2816 028])	15

(see also Jimmy Edwards)

SHAMBLES
75	RCA RCA 2533	Hello Baby/Held Me Spellbound	40

(see also Mandrake Paddle Steramers, Prowler)

SHAME
67	MGM MGM 1349	Don't Go Away Little Girl/Dreams Don't Bother Me (with picture insert)	150
67	MGM MGM 1349	Don't Go Away Little Girl/Dreams Don't Bother Me (without picture insert)	90

(see also Shy Limbs, King Crimson, Gods, Emerson Lake & Palmer)

SHAMEN
86	One Big Guitar OBG 003T	THEY MAY BE RIGHT ... BUT THEY'RE CERTAINLY WRONG (12" EP)	12

(see also Alone Again Or, Stretchheads)

SHAMES
66	CBS 202344	Sugar And Spice/Ben Franklin's Almanac	25
66	CBS 202450	I Wanna Meet You/We Could Be Happy	18
67	CBS 2704	Mr Unreliable/Georgia	12
67	CBS 2929	It Could Be We're In Love/I Was Lonely When	22
68	CBS 3820	Greenburg, Glickstein, Charles, David, Smith And Jones/Warm	15

(see also Isaac Guillory)

SHAMPOO
93	Icerink DAV 06	Blisters & Bruises/Paydirt/I Love Little Pussy (p/s, pink vinyl)	20

SHAMROCKS
65	Polydor BM 56503	La La La La La/And I Need You	20

VALERIE SHAND
58	Philips PB 833	When The Boys Talk About Girls/Careful, Careful	8
58	Philips PB 879	Meet Me Tonight In Dreamland.One Billion Seven Million Thirty-Three	7
59	Philips PB 929	Make Love To Me/Baisez Moi	7

WINSTON SHAN(D)
69	Bullet BU 399	Throw Me Corn/Darling Remember (B-side actually by Pat Edwards)	25
69	Bullet BU 411	Matilda (as Wilston Shan)/HARMONIANS: Come To Me	25
70	Moodisc MU 3505	I'll Run Away/Time Is The Master	100
72	Camel CA 88	Audrey (as Winston Shan)/So Nice (as Winston Shan)	6

TRISTRAM SHANDY
74	Tiffany 6121 505	Saccharine Sandie, Fingers 'N Thumbs/Mr. Blue	6

LISA SHANE
66	Pye 7N 17124	Come And Get Me/Big Wide World	6

SHANE & SHANE GANG
64	Pye 7N 15662	Whistle Stop/Who Wrote That Song	35

SHANES
65	Columbia DB 7601	I Don't Want Your Love/New Orleans	70

SHANE SISTERS
60	Ember EMB S 115	My Mommy Told Me/Presents On The Christmas Tree	7

SHANGAANS
65	Columbia DB 7551	Genzene (What Have I Done)/Yeh Girl	15
65	Columbia Studio 2 TWO 109	JUNGLE DRUMS (LP)	25

SHANGO
69	A&M AMS 754	Mama Lion/Ljuba Ljuba	6

SHANGRI-LAS
64	Red Bird RB 10008	Remember (Walking In The Sand)/It's Easier To Cry	10
64	Red Bird RB 10014	Leader Of The Pack/What Is Love?	10
65	Red Bird RB 10018	Give Him A Great Big Kiss/Twist And Shout	15
65	Red Bird RB 10025	Out In The Streets/The Boy	15
65	Red Bird RB 10030	Give Us Your Blessings/Heaven Only Knows	15
65	Red Bird RB 10036	Right Now And Not Later/Train From Kansas City	35
66	Red Bird RB 10043	I Can Never Go Home Anymore/Bulldog	15
66	Red Bird RB 10048	Long Live Our Love/Sophisticated Boom Boom	15
66	Red Bird RB 10053	He Cried/Dressed In Black	15
66	Red Bird RB 10068	Past, Present, And Future/Paradise	20
66	Philips 6051027	Train From Kansas City/Past Present And Future	10
67	Mercury MF 962	The Sweet Sound Of Summer/I'll Never Learn	15
67	Mercury MF 979	Take The Time/Footsteps On The Roof	15
65	Red Bird RB 40 002	THE SHANGRI-LAS (EP)	60
66	Red Bird RB 40 004	I CAN NEVER GO HOME ANYMORE (EP, unreleased)	0
65	Red Bird RB 20 101	THE SHANGRI-LAS - LEADER OF THE PACK (LP)	80
66	Mercury MCL 20096	GOLDEN HITS OF THE SHANGRI-LAS (LP)	18

BUD SHANK
56	Vogue V 2376	Royal Garden Blues/It Had To Be You (with Bill Perkins Quintet)	5
56	Vogue V 2383	When Your Lover Has Gone/There's A Small Hotel (with Bob Brookmeyer)	5
56	Vogue V 2385	Shank's Pranks/Left Bank (with Shorty Rogers Quintet)	7
59	Vogue LAE 12248	LATIN CONTRASTS (LP)	20

(see also Shorty Rogers)

ANANDA SHANKAR
69	Reprise RSLP 6398	ANANDA SHANKAR (JUMPING JACK FLASH) (LP)	80
70	EMI	ANANDA SHANKAR AND HIS MUSIC (LP)	60
71	Reprise K 44092	ANANDA SHANKAR (LP, reissue)	30

RAVI SHANKAR
72	Apple APPLE 37	Joi Bangla/Oh Bhaugowan/Raga Mishri-Jhinjhoti (p/s)	40
71	Mushroom 300 MR 8	FOUR RAGA MOODS (2-LP)	30
72	United Artists UAG 29379	AT THE WOODSTOCK FESTIVAL (LP, gatefold)	15
73	Apple SAPDO 1002	IN CONCERT - 1972 (2-LP, with Ali Akbar Khan, gatefold sleeve)	90

(see also Ali Akbar Khan, Will Sergeant)

BILL SHANKLY
70s	Technical TECLP 001A	SHANKS ON SOCCER (2-LP)	20

JOHNNY SHANLY
60	Columbia DB 4526	I Wonder/It Happens That Way	6

SHANNON
75	Magnet MAG 38	Come Back And Love Me/She's A High Flyer	10

(See also Marty Wilde)

DEAN SHANNON
60	HMV POP 820	Blinded With Love/Jezebel	25
62	HMV POP 1103	Ubangi Stomp/Blowing Wild	35

DEL SHANNON
SINGLES
61	London HLX 9317	Runaway/Jody	6
61	London HLX 9317	Runaway/Jody (mispressed B-side, plays "The Snake" by Maximilian)	30
61	London HLX 9402	Hats Off To Larry/Don't Gild The Lily, Lily	5
61	London HLX 9462	So Long Baby/The Answer To Everything	5
62	London HLX 9515	Hey! Little Girl/You Never Talked About Me	5
62	London HLX 9587	Cry Myself To Sleep/I'm Gonna Move On	8
62	London HLX 9609	The Swiss Maid/Ginny In The Mirror	5
63	London HLX 9653	Little Town Flirt/The Wamboo	5
63	London HLX 9710	Two Kinds Of Teardrops/Kelly	5
63	London HLX 9761	Two Silhouettes/My Wild One	5
63	London HLU 9800	Sue's Gonna Be Mine/Since She's Gone	10
64	London HLU 9858	That's The Way Love Is/Time Of The Day	12
64	Stateside SS 269	Mary Jane/Stains On My Letter	10
64	Stateside SS 317	Handy Man/Give Her Lots Of Lovin'	10
64	Stateside SS 349	Do You Want To Dance/This Is All I Have To Give	10
64	Stateside SS 368	Keep Searching (We'll Follow The Sun)/Broken Promises	6
65	Stateside SS 395	Stranger In Town/Over You	12
65	Stateside SS 430	Break Up/Why Don't You Tell Him	12
65	Stateside SS 452	Move It On Over/She Still Remembers Tony	15
66	Stateside SS 494	I Can't Believe My Ears/I Wish I Wasn't Me Tonight	15
66	Liberty LIB 55866	The Big Hurt/I Got It Bad	12
66	Liberty LIB 55889	For A Little While/Hey Little Star	15
67	Liberty LIB 55939	She/What Makes You Run	15
67	Liberty LIB 10277	Mind Over Matter/Led Along	12
67	Liberty LBF 15020	Runaway/Show Me	12
68	Liberty LBF 15061	Thinkin' It Over/Runnin' On Back	15
68	Liberty LBF 15079	Gemini/Magical Musical Box	40
69	Stateside SS 8025	Comin' Back To Me/Sweet Mary Lou	12
70	Stateside SS 8040	Sister Isabelle/Colorado Rain	18

74	United Artists UP 35740	And The Music Plays On/In My Arms Again..8
83	Demon D1017	Cheat Love/Distant Ghost (p/s)..7

EPs

62	London RE-X 1332	RUNAWAY WITH DEL SHANNON 20
63	London RE-X 1346	DEL SHANNON NO. 2 20
63	London RE-X 1383	DEL'S OWN FAVOURITES 25
63	London RE-X 1387	FROM DEL TO YOU 25
67	Liberty LEP 2272	THE NEW DEL SHANNON...40
65	Stateside SE 1029	DEL SHANNON HITS 30

ALBUMS

61	London HA-X 2402	RUNAWAY WITH DEL SHANNON 40
63	London HA-X 8071	HATS OFF TO DEL SHANNON 35
63	London HA-X 8091	LITTLE TOWN FLIRT 35
65	Stateside SL 10115	HANDY MAN 50
65	Stateside SL 10130	DEL SHANNON SINGS HANK WILLIAMS 40
65	Stateside SL 10140	ONE THOUSAND SIX HUNDRED AND SIXTY-ONE SECONDS WITH DEL SHANNON 40
66	Liberty LBY 1320	THIS IS MY BAG (mono) 25
66	Liberty SLBY 1320	THIS IS MY BAG (stereo) 30
66	Liberty LBY 1335	TOTAL COMMITMENT (mono) 25
66	Liberty SLBY 1335	TOTAL COMMITMENT (stereo) 30
68	Liberty LBL/LBS 83114E	THE FURTHER ADVENTURES OF CHARLES WESTOVER..80
73	United Artists UAS 29474	LIVE IN ENGLAND..15
83	Demon FIEND 8	DROP DOWN AND GET ME (LP) 15

(see also Maximilian)

LINDA SHANNON

59	Parlophone R 4603	Goodbye Charlie/If You Only Knew 6

SHAPE

71	RCA RCA 2129	My Friend John/Yes 18

SHAPE OF THE RAIN

71	RCA Neon NE 1001	Woman/Wasting My Time 10
71	RCA RCA 2129	My Friend John/Yes 5
71	RCA Neon NE 7	RILEY, RILEY, WOOD & WAGGETT (LP, gatefold sleeve)...................................250

SHAPE & SIZES

66	Decca F 12441	A Little Lovin' Somethin'/Rain On My Face 10

SHAPES

79	Sofa SEAT 1/FRR 004	THE SHAPES (WOT'S FOR LUNCH, MUM?) (EP, no p/s, with insert) 12
79	Good Vibrations GOT 13	Blast Off/Airline Disasters (p/s)...15

HELEN SHAPIRO

SINGLES

61	Columbia DB 4589	Don't Treat Me Like A Child/When I'm With you 5
61	Columbia DB 4670	You Don't Know/Marvellous Lie 5
61	Columbia DB 4715	Walkin' Back To Happiness/Kiss 'N' Run 5
61	Columbia DB 4782	Tell Me What He Said/I Apologise 5
62	Columbia DB 4824	Let's Talk About Love/Sometime Yesterday 8
62	Columbia DB 4869	Little Miss Lonely/I Don't Care 5
62	Columbia DB 4908	Keep Away From Other Girls/Cry My Heart Out 8
63	Columbia DB 4966	Queen For Tonight/Daddy Couldn't Get Me One Of Those 15
63	Columbia DB 7026	Woe Is Me/I Walked Right In...5
63	Columbia DB 7072	Not Responsible/No Trespassing..5
63	Columbia DB 7130	Look Who It Is/Walking In My Dreams 10
64	Columbia DB 7190	Fever/Ole Father Time 25
64	Columbia DB 7266	Look Over Your Shoulder/You Won't Come Home 10
64	Columbia DB 7340	Shop Around/He Knows How To Love Me 100
64	Columbia DB 7395	I Wish I'd Never Loved You/I Was Only Kidding 10
65	Columbia DB 7517	Tomorrow Is Another Day/It's So Funny I Could Cry 10
65	Columbia DB 7587	Here In Your Arms/Only Once 12
65	Columbia DB 7690	Something Wonderful/Just A Line 12
66	Columbia DB 7810	Forget About The Bad Things/Wait A Little Longer 12
66	Columbia DB 8073	In My Calendar/Empty House 12
67	Columbia DB 8148	Make Me Belong To You/The Way Of The World 12
67	Columbia DB 8256	She Needs Company/Stop And You Will Become Aware...................................125
67	Columbia DB 8256	She Needs Company/Stop And You Will Become Aware (DJ copy) 150
68	Pye 7N 17600	You'll Get Me Loving You/Silly Boy (I Love You) 12
69	Pye 7N 17714	Today Has Been Cancelled/Face The Music 12
69	Pye 7N 17785	You've Guessed/Take Me For A While 20
70	Pye 7N 17893	Take Down A Note Miss Smith/Couldn't You See 12
70	Pye 7N 17975	Waiting On The Shores Of Nowhere/A Glass Of Wine.......................................12
75	DJM DJS 363	You're A Love Child/That's The Reason I Love You 10
77	Arista 131	Can't Break The Habit/For All The Wrong Reasons 10
78	Arista 178	Every Little Bit Hurts/Touchin' Wood 10

EPs

61	Columbia SEG 8128	HELEN (mono, 'smiling' or 'cross-armed' sleeve) 15
61	Columbia ESG 7872	HELEN (stereo, 'smiling' or 'cross-armed' sleeve) 20
61	Columbia SEG 8136	HELEN'S HIT PARADE 15
62	Columbia SEG 8170	A TEENAGER SINGS THE BLUES (mono) 20
62	Columbia ESG 7880	A TEENAGER SINGS THE BLUES (stereo) 25
62	Columbia SEG 8174	MORE HITS FROM HELEN 15
62	Columbia SEG 8209	EVEN MORE HITS FROM HELEN 15
63	Columbia SEG 8229	TOPS' WITH ME NO. 1 (mono) 20
63	Columbia ESG 7888	TOPS' WITH ME NO. 1 (stereo) 25
63	Columbia SEG 8243	TOPS' WITH ME NO. 2 (mono) 20
63	Columbia ESG 7891	TOPS' WITH ME NO. 2 (stereo) 25

ALBUMS

62	Columbia 33SX 1397	TOPS' WITH ME (mono) 15

62	Columbia SCX 3438	TOPS' WITH ME (stereo)	40
63	Columbia 33SX 1494	HELEN'S SIXTEEN (mono)	35
63	Columbia SCX 3470	HELEN'S SIXTEEN (stereo)	60
63	Columbia 33SX 1561	HELEN IN NASHVILLE	30
64	Columbia 33SX 1661	HELEN HITS OUT (mono)	35
64	Columbia SCX 3533	HELEN HITS OUT (stereo SCX 3533)	60
65	EMI Encore! ENC 209	12 HITS AND A MISS HELEN SHAPIRO	20
74	Columbia SCX 6565	THE VERY BEST OF HELEN SHAPIRO	12

(see also Ella Stone & Moss)

SHAPIROS
79	Now Records N 702	Waitress/Isolde (no p/s, 1000 only)	20

SHARADES
64	Decca F 11811	Dumb Head/Boy Trouble	85

(see also Ladybirds, Breakaways)

BILLY SHA RAE
71	Action ACT 4602	Do It/Crying Clown	15

BILLY SHARI
58	Decca F 11069	Going Home For Christmas/Count Every Star (as Shari)	5
68	United Artists UP 2235	It's So Lonely Being Together/You Walked Out On Me Before	5

SHARKS (1)
68	RCA RCA 1776	Goodbye Lorene/Funkology	20

(see also Marcisa & Jeff, Roy Richards)

SHARKS (2)
73	Island ILPS 9233	FIRST WATER (LP, 'pink rim palm tree' label with inner sleeve)	12
74	Island ILPS 9271	JAB IT IN YORE EYE (LP, 'palm tree' label with inner sleeve)	12

(see also Baker-Gurvitz Army, Chris Spedding, Andy Fraser Band, Free)

RALPH SHARON
53	Decca LF 1107	SPRING FEVER (10" LP)	12
53	Decca LF 1138	AUTUMN LEAVES (10" LP)	20
53	Lyragon AF 1	COCKTAIL TIME (10" LP)	15

(see also Tony Bennett)

SHARONETTES
75	Black Magic BM 102	Papa Ooh Mow Mow/Instrumental	5
75	Black Magic BM 104	Going To A Go Go/Instrumental	5

BOBBY SHARP & OTHERS
65	Stateside SS 404	Blues For Mr. Charlie (Parts 1 & 2) (with Paul Sindap, Joe Lee Wilson & Little Butler)	20

DEE DEE SHARP
62	Columbia DB 4818	Mashed Potato Time/Set My Heart At Ease	25
62	Columbia DB 4874	Gravy (For My Mashed Potatoes)/Baby Cakes	25
62	Cameo Parkway C 230	Ride/Night	40
63	Cameo Parkway C 244	Do The Bird/Lover Boy	25
63	Cameo Parkway C 260	Rock Me In The Cradle Of Love/You'll Never Be Mine	20
63	Cameo Parkway C 274	Wild/Why Doncha Ask Me	20
65	Cameo Parkway C 375	I Really Love You/Standing In The Need Of Love	80
65	Cameo Parkway C 375	I Really Love You/Standing In The Need Of Love (DJ copy)	125
65	Cameo Parkway C 382	It's A Funny Situation/There Ain't Nothing I Wouldn't Do (demo-only)	150
66	Atlantic 584 056	My Best Friend's Man/Bye Bye Baby	20
69	Action ACT 4522	What Kind Of Lady/You're Gonna Miss Me	60
79	London HA-U 8514	CAMEO PARKWAY SESSIONS (LP)	25

(see also Chubby Checker & Dee Dee Sharp)

STEVE SHARP & THE CLEANCUTS
80	Happy Face MM 122	We Are The Mods/He Wants To Be A Mod	125

(see also Rowdies)

BERNARD SHARPE
66	Parlophone R 5519	Lost In Space/Jorrocks	10
67	Parlophone R 5611	The Other Side Of The Sky/Where Do We Go	15

RAY SHARPE
59	London HLW 8932	Linda Lu/Red Sails In The Sunset (triangular centre)	50
59	London HLW 8932	Linda Lu/Red Sails In The Sunset (round centre)	40
59	London HLW 8932	Linda Lu/Red Sails In The Sunset (78)	30
63	United Artists UP 1032	Hey Little Girl/Day You Left Me	15

ROCKY SHARPE & THE REPLAYS
82	Chiswick DICE 9	Heart/Mary (Won't You Marry Me) (withdrawn, approx. 100 only)	10

SHARPE & NUMAN
85	Polydor PODJ 722	Change Your Mind (p/s, 1-sided 7" DJ promo)	10
88	Polydor POSPCD894	No More Lies (Extended Version)/Voices/Change Your Mind/No More Lies (7" Version) (CD single, initial copy signed by Gary Numan)	12
89	Polydor POPB 43	I'm On Automatic/No More Lies (New Version) (stickered poster sleeve)	6
89	Polydor 839-5201	AUTOMATIC (CD)	30

(see also Gary Numan)

SHARPEES
66	Stateside SS 495	Tired Of Being Lonely/Just To Please You	75
66	Stateside SS 495	Tired Of Being Lonely/Just To Please You (DJ copy)	150
73	President PT 389	Do The 45/Make Up Your Mind	15
73	President PT 399	Tired Of Being Lonely/Just To Please You (reissue)	15

BOB SHARPLES
56	Decca 45-F10707	Hurricane Boogie/Sadies Shawl (tri label)	5

SHARPS
57	Vogue V 9086	Lock My Heart/Love Is Here To Stay	750
57	Vogue V 9086	Lock My Heart/Love Is Here To Stay (78)	120

S-HATERS

58	Vogue V 9096	Shufflin'/What Will I Gain	750
58	Vogue V 9096	Shufflin'/What Will I Gain (78)	120

(see also Thurston Harris)

S-HATERS
81	Outer Himalayan OHR 02	Death Of A Vampire/Research (p/s)	30
82	Outer Himalayan OHR 005	STORIES AS COLD AS THE IRISH SEA (7" EP)	10

SHATTERED DOLLS
80	Rox ROX 1	Lipstick Killer/Talk To Me/Valley Of The Dolls 1 & 2	20

MIKE SHAUN
63	Decca F 11733	So Lonely/Let's Fall In Love	15

ADRIAN SHAW
96	Woronzow W0027	TEA FOR THE HYDRA (LP, 299 copies only, in hand-finished sleeves)	15

(see also Hawkwind, Bevis Frond)

MARLENA SHAW
67	Chess CRS 8054	Mercy Mercy Mercy/Go Away Little Boy	10
76	United Artists UP 36125	It's Better Than Walking Out/Be For Real	8

NINA SHAW
68	CBS 3239	Woven In My Soul/Love So Fine	7
68	CBS 3556	From Now Till Then/Window Of My Mind	8
69	CBS 4227	One Fine Day/Somewhere In The World	10

RICKY SHAW
62	London HLU 9606	No Love But Your Love/Be Still, Be Still, My Own	8

ROLAND SHAW ORCHESTRA
65	Decca LK 4730	JAMES BOND IN ACTION (LP)	12
67	Phase 4 Stereo PFS 4125	MORE JAMES BOND IN ACTION (LP)	12
60s	London BSP	DIAMONDS ARE FOREVER (LP, gatefold sleeve, export issue)	12

SANDIE SHAW
SINGLES
64	Pye 7N 15671	As Long As You're Happy Baby/Ya-Ya-Da-Da	40
64	Pye 7N 15704	(There's) Always Something There To Remind Me/Don't You Know	5
64	Pye 7N 15743	Girl Don't Come/I'd Be Far Better Off Without You	5
65	Pye 7N 15783	I'll Stop At Nothing/You Can't Blame Him	6
65	Pye 7N 15841	Long Live Love/I've Heard About Him	5
65	Pye 7N 15940	Message Understood/Don't You Count On It	5
65	Pye 7N 15987	How Can You Tell/If Ever You Need Me	5
65	Pye 7N 17036	Tomorrow/Hurting You	5
66	Pye 7N 17086	Nothing Comes Easy/Stop Before You Start	5
66	Pye 7N 17163	Run/Long Walk Home	8
66	Pye 7N 17212	Think Sometimes About Me/Hide All Emotion	10
67	Pye 7N 17239	I Don't Need Anything/Keep In Touch	10
67	Pye 7N 17272	Puppet On A String/Tell The Boys (pink label, later blue)	5
67	Pye 7N 17346	Tonight In Tokyo/You've Been Seeing Her Again	6
67	Pye 7N 17378	You've Not Changed/Make Me Cry	5
68	Pye 7N 17441	Today/London (pink label, later blue)	5
68	Pye 7N 17504	Don't Run Away/Stop	10
68	Pye 7N 17564	Show Me/One More Lie	10
68	Pye 7N 17587	Together/Turn On The Sunshine	10
68	Pye 7N 17611	Those Were The Days/Make It Go	8
69	Pye 7N 17675	Monsieur Dupont/Voice In The Crowd	5
69	Pye 7N 17726	Think It All Over/Send Me A Letter	12
70	Pye 7N 17954	Wight Is Wight/That's The Way He's Made	10
70	Pye 7N 45040	Rose Garden/Maybe I'm Amazed	10
84	Rough Trade RTT 130	Hand In Glove/I Don't Owe You Anything/Jeanne (12", p/s, with The Smiths)	10

EPs
64	Pye NEP 24208	(THERE'S) ALWAYS SOMETHING THERE TO REMIND ME	15
65	Pye NEP 24220	LONG LIVE LOVE	15
65	Pye NEP 24232	TALK ABOUT LOVE	15
65	Pye NEP 24234	SANDIE	15
66	Pye NEP 24236	MESSAGE UNDERSTOOD	15
66	Pye NEP 24247	TOMORROW	20
66	Pye NEP 24254	NOTHING COMES EASY	20
66	Pye NEP 24264	RUN WITH SANDIE SHAW	25
67	Pye NEP 24271	SANDIE SHAW IN FRENCH	30
67	Pye NEP 24273	SANDIE SHAW IN ITALIAN	30
67	Pye NEP 24281	TELL THE BOYS	20

ALBUMS
65	Pye NPL 18110	SANDIE SHAW	15
65	Pye NPL 18121	ME	15
69	Pye N(S)PL 18323	REVIEWING THE SITUATION	50

THOMAS SHAW
72	Xtra XTRA 1132	THOMAS SHAW (LP)	15

TIMMY SHAW & STERNPHONES
64	Pye International 7N 25239	Gonna Send You Back To Georgia/I'm A Lonely Guy	30

TREVOR SHAW
81	CMS PR 26	WHEELS IN MOTION (LP)	20

DOROTHY SHAY
53	Capitol LC 6618	THE PARK AVENUE HILLBILLIE (10" LP)	12

SHE
85	Neat NEAT 50	Never Surrender/Breaking Away (p/s)	5
85	Neat NEAT 5012	Never Surrender/Breaking Away/On My Way (12", p/s)	8

GEORGE SHEARING (QUINTET)

61	Capitol CL 15269	Baubles, Bangles And Beads/Cocktails For Two	5
51	Decca LF 1036	THE NEARNESS OF YOU (10" LP, as George Shearing Trio)	12
52	MGM MGM-D 103	YOU'RE HEARING GEORGE SHEARING (10" LP)	12
53	MGM MGM-D 118	I HEAR MUSIC (10" LP)	12

(see also Peggy Lee)

GARY SHEARSTON

74	Charisma CB241	Without A Song/Aborigini	6
74	Charisma CAS 1090	DINGO (LP)	12

BOBBY SHEEN

66	Capitol CL 15455	Dr. Love/Sweet, Sweet Love	125
66	Capitol CL 15455	Dr. Love/Sweet, Sweet Love (DJ copies)	175
72	Capitol CL 15713	Dr. Love/Sweet, Sweet Love (reissue)	20

(see also Bob B. Soxx & Blue Jeans)

SHEEP (U.K.)

73	Myrrh MYR 1000	SHEEP (LP, with insert)	20

(see also Lonesome Stone)

SHEEP (U.S.)

66	Stateside SS 493	Hide And Seek/Twelve Months Later	30
69	Stateside SS 2147	Hide And Seek/HAWKS: The Grissle	15

SHEEPHOUSE

71	Decca 13229	Juicy Lucy/Part 2	100

SHEEPS HEAD BAY

71	Parlophone R5897	My Name Is In The Wind/The River Song	8

IREEN SHEER

70	Bell BLL 1129	Hey Pleasure Man/You Walked Away	5
71	Parlophone R 5930	Many Rivers/Is It Me	5
74	Polydor 2041 533	Bye Bye I Love You/Roseberry Avenue	6

SHEER KHAN

84	SRT 4KS 140	Last Generation/Lady's Dance (p/s)	70
85	Mill	QUIET ENOUGH FOR LOVE (LP)	30

SHEFFIELDS

64	Pye 7N 15600	It Must Be Love/Say Girl	50
64	Pye 7N 15627	I Got My Mojo Working/Hey Hey Lover Boy	70
65	Pye 7N 15767	Bag's Groove (Skat Walking)/Plenty Of Love	75

SHEIKS (PORTUGAL)

66	Parlophone R 5500	Missing You/Tell Me Bird	15

SHEIKS (U.S.)

59	London HLW 9012	Très Chic/Little French Doll	15
59	London HLW 9012	Très Chic/Little French Doll (78)	30

SHEILA & JENNY

64	Ember EMB S 3202	When The Boy's Happy/Please Don't Break Her Heart (in p/s)	10
64	Ember EMB S 3202	When The Boy's Happy/Please Don't Break Her Heart	6

SHELBY

74	Santa Ponsa PNS 21	Dance With The Guitar Man/Jump Into The Fire	6
75	Route RT 02	Motorbike Girl/Cirrus	8

ALLEN SHELDON

70	Plexium PXM 14	Mirror Of My Mind/Old Windmill Tree	50

DOUG SHELDON

61	Decca F 11368	The Book Of Love/Play Me The Blues	10
61	Decca F 11398	Runaround Sue/Come With Me	10
61	Decca F 11416	Your Ma Said You Cried In Your Sleep/You're Only Fooling Yourself	10
62	Decca F 11433	My Kingdom For A Girl/You Never Had It So Good	10
62	Decca F 11463	A Big Big Baby/If You'd Be Mine	10
62	Decca F 11514	Lollipops And Roses/One Way To Say Goodbye	10
62	Decca F 11529	Live Now Pay Later/Me	15
63	Decca F 11564	I Saw Linda Yesterday/My Billy	8
63	Decca F 11654	Let's Make A Habit Of This/I Was Alone	10
63	Decca F 11790	Mickey's Monkey/Falling In Love With Love	10
65	Sue WI 332	Take It Like A Man/Lonely Boy	40
65	Pye 7N 17011	It's Because Of You/How Can I Tell Her?	7
63	Decca DFE 8527	HERE I STAND (EP)	50

SANDI SHELDON

76	Epic EPC 4186	You're Gonna Make Me Love You/Baby You're Mine	10

SHELL

66	Columbia DB 8082	Goodbye Little Girl/Little Bit Of Lovin'	15

SHELLEY

64	Pye 7N 15711	I Will Be Wishing/Why Won't You Say (That You Love Me)	15
65	Pye 7N 15773	Stairway To A Star/I Heard A Whisper	10
65	Pye 7N 15913	Where Has Your Smile Gone/Paradise	10

LIZ SHELLEY

65	Brunswick 05940	Make Me Your Baby/You Made Me Hurt	10
66	Brunswick 05953	No More Love/I Can't Find You	10

PETE SHELLEY

82	Lyntone 10952/53	Qu'est-Ce Que C'est, Qu'est Que Ça (Dub)/ANIMAL MAGNET: More (hard vinyl test pressing, numbered, with info sheet/letter)	15
82	Lyntone 10952/53	Qu'est-Ce Que C'est, Qu'est Que Ça (Dub)/ANIMAL MAGNET: More (hard vinyl test pressing, numbered)	12
80	Groovy STP 2	SKY YEN (mini-LP)	12

(see also Buzzcocks, Free Agents, Tiller Boys)

SHELLS
| 61 | London HLU 9288 | Baby, Oh Baby/Angel Eyes | 40 |
| 62 | London HLU 9644 | It's A Happy Holiday/Deep In My Heart | 45 |

SHELLY
| 95 | Sarah SARAH 98 | Reproduction Is Pollution/Prejudice/Here (p/s) | 12 |

ALAN SHELLY & MANU DIBANGO'S BROTHERS
| 69 | Philips BF 1709 | Lady Black Wife/Give Me Time | 12 |

ANNE SHELTON
53	HMV 7M 164	Answer Me/The Bridge Of Sighs	15
54	HMV 7M 186	The Book/Why Does It Have To Be Me	15
54	HMV 7M 197	Cross Over The Bridge/(Oh Baby Mine) I Get So Lonely	15
54	HMV 7M 240	Goodnight, Well It's Time To Go/If I Give My Heart To You	15
54	HMV 7M 279	My Gypsy Heart/Teach Me Tonight	15
57	Philips JK 1012	Absent Friends/Seven Ages Of Man (Jukebox issue)	15
59	Philips PB 969	The Village Of St. Bernadette/You're Not Living in Vain	6
61	Philips PB 1095	Sailor/A Souvenir Of Ireland (p/s)	6
56	Decca DFE 6321	FOUR STANDARDS (EP)	10
56	Philips BBE 12090	ANNE SHELTON (EP)	8
52	Decca LF 1023	FAVOURITES (10" LP)	25
53	Decca LF 1106	FAVOURITES VOL 2 (LP)	25
57	Philips BBL 7188	THE SHELTON SOUND (LP)	20
59	Philips BBL 7291	SONGS FROM THE HEART (LP)	20
60	Philips BBL 7393	SHOWCASE (LP)	20

JO SHELTON
| 59 | Top Rank JAR 124 | Tread Softly (You're Stepping On My Heart)/More More More Romancing | 6 |
| 59 | Top Rank JAR 245 | If There Are Stars In My Eyes/I Need Your Arms Around Me | 6 |

ROSCOE SHELTON
| 65 | Sue WI 354 | Strain On My Heart/Question (A- & B-side labels reversed) | 40 |

DEANNA SHENDEREY
| 65 | Decca F 12090 | Comin' Home Baby/I've Got That Feeling | 15 |

SHENLEY (DUFFAS) & ANNETTE
| 61 | Blue Beat BB 72 | Million Dollar Baby/The First Time I Met You | 20 |

SHENLEY (DUFFAS) & HYACINTH (BROWN)
| 66 | Rio R 80 | The World Is On A Wheel/ROY & CORNELL: Salvation | 15 |

(see also Baba Brooks)

SHENLEY (DUFFAS) & (LITTLE) LUNAN
| 65 | Rio R 52 | Something On Your Mind/The Rain Came Tumbling Down | 12 |

(see also Shenley Duffas)

SHEP & LIMELITES
| 61 | Pye International 7N 25090 | Daddy's Home/This I Know | 75 |
| 61 | Pye International 7N 25112 | Ready For Your Love/You'll Be Sorry | 100 |

JEAN SHEPARD
56	Capitol EAP 1030	SONGS OF A LOVE AFFAIR NO. 1 (EP)	8
56	Capitol EAP2 728	SONGS OF A LOVE AFFAIR NO. 2 (EP)	8
60	Capitol T 1253	THIS IS JEAN SHEPARD (LP)	12

BILLY SHEPHARD
| 59 | Felstad AF 117 | You Call Everybody Darling/Somebody Stole My Gal | 5 |

DAVE SHEPHERD QUINTET
| 69 | 77 LEU 12/35 | SHEPHERD'S DELIGHT (LP) | 20 |

PAULINE SHEPHERD
| 57 | Columbia DB 4010 | Love Me To Pieces/Just Between You And Me | 12 |

SHEPHERD BOYS (& GIRLS)
| 56 | Columbia SCM 5282 | Little Girls And Little Boys/Teenage Love (as Shepherd Boys & Girls) | 8 |
| 56 | Columbia DB 3816 | Summer Sweetheart/Song For A Summer Night | 6 |

TOM SHEPLEY'S BAND
| 78 | Tradition TSR 031 | HOW DO YOU DO? (LP) | 15 |

ARCHIE SHEPP
66	HMV CLP/CSD 3524	FOUR FOR TRANE (LP)	25
66	HMV CLP/CSD 3561	ON THIS NIGHT (LP)	25
67	HMV CLP/CSD 3600	LIVE IN SAN FRANCISCO (LP)	25
67	Polydor 623 235	ARCHIE SHEPP AND THE NEW YORK CONTEMPORARY FIVE (LP)	25
67	Fontana 681 014 ZL	RUFUS (LP, with John Tchicai)	25
68	Impulse MIPL/SIPL 508	MAMA TOO TIGHT (LP)	25
68	Polydor 623 267	NEW YORK CONTEMPORARY FIVE VOL. 2 (LP)	20
69	Impulse MILP/SIPL 512	THE MAGIC OF JU-JU (LP)	25
69	Impulse MIPL/SIPL 516	THE WAY AHEAD (LP)	25

(see also John Coltrane)

SHEPPARDS
| 71 | Jay Boy BOY 30 | How Do You Like It/Stubborn Heart | 40 |

SHEPHERD/SHEPPARD SISTERS
57	HMV POP 411	Alone (Why Must I Be Alone)/Congratulations To Someone	10
58	Mercury 7MT 196	Gettin' Ready For Freddy/Best Thing There Is (Is Love)(Sheppard Sisters)	15
58	Mercury 7MT 218	Eating Pizza/A Boy And A Girl (as Sheppard Sisters)	10
58	Mercury AMT 1005	Dancing Baby/Is It A Crime?	10
63	London HLK 9681	Don't Mention My Name/What Makes Little Girls Cry	20
63	London HLK 9758	Talk Is Cheap/Greatest Lover	15

SHEPPERTON FLAMES
| 69 | Deram DM 257 | Take Me For What I Am/Goodbye | 20 |

(see also Mike Berry)

SHERE KHAN
69	Tepee TPR 1007	Little Louise/No Reason	200
71	UPC 110	Rhone/Find The Lady	60

SHERIDAN
70	Gemini GMS 001	Follow Me Follow/When Love Breaks Your Heart	15

(see also Sheridan-Price, Mike Sheridan & Night Riders, Mike Sheridan's Lot)

DANI SHERIDAN
66	Planet PLF 106	Guess I'm Dumb/Songs Of Love	50

LEE SHERIDAN
73	Deram DM 373	Sweet Tasting Candy Sugar/Big Louis' Gun	8

MIKE SHERIDAN & NIGHT RIDERS
63	Columbia DB 7141	Tell Me What'cha Gonna Do/No Other Guy	30
63	Columbia DB 7183	Please Mr. Postman/In Love	30
64	Columbia DB 7302	What A Sweet Thing That Was/Fabulous	25
65	Columbia DB 7462	Here I Stand/Lonely Weekends	25

(see also Roy Wood, Idle Race, Mike Sheridan's Lot, Nightriders, Sheridan-Price, Sight & Sound)

MIKE SHERIDAN'S LOT
65	Columbia DB 7677	Take My Hand/Make Them Understand	50
66	Columbia DB 7798	Don't Turn Your Back On Me, Babe/Stop, Look, Listen	50

(see also Roy Wood, Idle Race, Mike Sheridan & Night Riders, Nightriders, Sheridan-Price, Sight & Sound)

TONY SHERIDAN & THE BEAT BROTHERS
64	Polydor NH 52315	Jambalaya/Will You Still Love Me Tomorrow (with The Beat Brothers)	12
64	Polydor NH 52927	Skinny Minny/You'd Better Move On (with The Beat Brothers)	12

(see also Bobby Patrick Big Six, Beat Brothers, Pete Best Four)

SHERIDAN-PRICE
70	Gemini GMS 009	Sometimes I Wonder (as Sheridan & Rick Price)/SHERIDAN: Lightning Never Strikes Twice	25
70	Gemini GME 1002	THIS IS TO CERTIFY THAT... (LP, gatefold sleeve)	35

(see also Rick Price, Mike Sheridan & Nightriders, Mike Sheridan's Lot, Idle Race, Sight & Sound, Sheridan)

ROGER SHERLOCK
78	Inchecronin INC 7419	MEMORIES OF SLIGO (LP)	12

BIM SHERMAN
77	Hawkeye HE 003	Ever Firm/GUSSIE ALLSTARS: Rigid	8
78	Yard International YI 1001	What Sweet You So/U BLACK: Pot A Bubble (12")	15
79	Hit Run DD6/7	Down In Jamtown (with Jah Lion)/TEEM ALL STARS: Version (12")	40
79	Hit Run HIT DD 11	Love Jah Only (with Jah Buzz)/CRYTUFF ALL STARS : Version (12")	45
79	Attack TACK 9	Lightning And Thunder/Why Don't You Come On? (12")	25
83	On-U Sound DP 10	Keep You Dancing (with Dub Syndicate)/Can't Stop Jumping (with Dub Syndicate and Augustus Pablo) (10", p/s)	15
77	Tribesman TM 007	LOVE FOREVER (LP)	80
88	On U Sound 17	ACROSS THE RED SEA (LP)	20
84	Century 200 C200	DANGER (LP)	15

BOBBY SHERMAN
69	Pye Intl. 7N 25508	La La La (If I Had You)/Time	10
70	CBS 5118	Hey, Mister Sun/Two Blind Minds	5
71	CBS 57468	Waiting At The Bust Stop/Runaway	12
71	CBS 7468	Waiting At The Bus Stop/Run Away	6

JOE SHERMAN
58	Fontana H 129	Miraculous Music Box/Make Me Laugh	6
58	Fontana H 147	Buttermilk/Please Don't Say Goodnight	6

BILLY SHERRILL
61	Mercury AMT 1131	Like Making Love/Rules Of The Game	8

SHERRYS
62	London HLW 9625	Pop Pop Pop-Pie/Your Hand In Mine	20
63	London HL 9686	Let's Stomp Again/Slop Time	25
63	London RE 1363	DO THE POPEYE (EP)	70

SHERWOOD
86	Sherwood SRT6KL 901	RIDING THE RAINBOW (12" EP)	50

BOBBY SHERWOOD
55	Vogue Coral Q 72097	The Kentuckian Song/Far Away Places	6

ROBERTA SHERWOOD
56	Brunswick 05572	Lazy River/This Train	10
57	Brunswick 05654	Tears Don't Care Who Cries Them/You're Nobody Till Somebody Loves You	5
57	Brunswick 05670	Mary Lou/What Does It Matter	5
63	Stateside SS 154	You Always Hurt The One You Love/In San Francisco	5
63	Stateside SL 10039	ON STAGE (LP)	20

TONY SHERWOOD TRIO
60s	Zodiac ZR 010	Piano Boogie Twist/Tom Dooley	15

SHERWOODS
61	Pye International 7N 25097	Nanette/El Scorpion	12

SHERWOODS
64	Solar SRP 105	Memories/Some Other Time	8

SHE TRINITY
66	Columbia DB 7874	He Fought The Law/The Union Station Blues	20
66	Columbia DB 7943	Have I Sinned/Wild Flower	10
66	Columbia DB 7959	Wild Flower/The Man Who Took The Valise Off The Floor Of Grand Central Station At Noon	7
66	Columbia DB 7992	Yellow Submarine/Promise Me You'll Never Cry	20
67	CBS 2819	Across The Street/Over And Over Again	8
70	President PT 283	Hair/Climb That Tree	40

(see also Shotgun Express, Beryl Marsden, Gilded Cage)

SHEVELLES
| 63 | Oriole CB 1915 | Ooh Poo Pa Doo/Like I Love You | 25 |

SHEVELLS
64	United Artists UP 1059	I Could Conquer The World/How Would You Like Me To Love You	30
65	United Artists UP 1076	Walking On The Edge Of The World/Not So Close	20
65	United Artists UP 1081	Watermelon Man/Taking Over Your Life	20
66	United Artists UP 1125	Come On Home/I Gotta Travel All Over	45
68	Polydor 56239	Big City Lights/Coffee Song	15

(see also Mike Stevens & Shevells)

TONY SHEVETON
62	Oriole CB 1705	Lullaby Of Love/I Have A Feeling	20
62	Oriole CB 1726	Lonely Heart/Foolish Doubts	20
62	Oriole CB 1766	Hey Little Girl/Kissing Date	25
63	Oriole CB 1788	Runaround Sue Is Getting Married/I Love The Girl Next Door	25
63	Oriole CB 1895	A Million Drums/Dance With Me	20
64	Oriole CB 1975	Excuses/Is It Me, Is It You?	18

(see also Tony Rich)

SHIDE & ACORN
| 73 | Private pressing | UNDER THE TREE (LP) | 400 |
| 94 | Acme AC 8006LP | UNDER THE TREE (LP, reissue, 500 only, numbered) | 15 |

(see also Jeremy Cahill)

SHIELA
| 71 | Nu Beat NB 079 | Only Heaven Knows/GRANT & RICHARDS: Freedom Psalm | 7 |

TREVOR SHIELD
69	Harry J TR 664	The Moon Is Playing Tricks On Me/KING CANNON: Soul Special	40
69	Trojan TR 665	Please/JAY BOYS: Splendour Splash	40
72	Ashanti ASH 407	Rough Road/JAY BOYS: Rough The Road	12

(see also Beltones, Trevor)

SHIELDS
| 58 | London HLD 8706 | You Cheated/That's The Way It's Gonna Be | 30 |
| 58 | London HLD 8706 | You Cheated/That's The Way It's Gonna Be (78) | 20 |

KEITH SHIELDS
67	Decca F 12572	Hey Gyp (Dig The Slowness)/Deep Inside Your Mind	70
67	Decca F 12609	The Wonder Of You/Run, Run, Run	30
67	Decca F 12666	So Hard Livin' Without You/Baby Do You Love Me	30

(see also Marty Wilde [& Wildcats])

BRUSH SHIELS (IRELAND)
| 77 | Hawk HASP 401 | Love At Love Bleed/Better Than I Expected | 8 |
| 77 | Hawk HASP 419 | Fight Your Heart Out/Coming Home | 12 |

ALLAN SHIERS
| 74 | Profile GMOR 003 | THE MAN IN ME (LP) | 40 |

SU SHIFRIN
| 76 | EMI 2442 | Over The Rainbow/When You Wish Upon A Star/Secrets | 6 |
| 78 | United Artists UP 36438 | We Must Believe In Magic/All I Wanna Do In Life | 6 |

SUSAN SHIFRIN
| 71 | Decca F13145 | To Love/25 Miles | 30 |

SAHIB SHIHAB QUARTET
| 70 | Youngblood SSYB 12 | SEEDS (LP) | 100 |

SHILLINGFORD MILL
| 71 | Mam | Frightened/Again | 12 |
| 71 | Mam MAM 15 | It's A Thing Called Love/Walking Along | 6 |

PETER SHILTON & JON SAMMELS
| 73 | Sports Talk ST 102 | SIMON SMITH INTERVIEWS.... 1973 (LP) | 12 |

YASUKI SHIMIZU
| 88 | Benelux Crammed MTM 12 | MUSIC FOR COMMERCIALS (LP) | 12 |

SHINDIGS
| 65 | Parlophone R 5316 | One Little Letter/What You Gonna Do | 40 |
| 65 | Parlophone R 5377 | A Little While Back/Why Say Goodbye | 40 |

SHINDOGS
| 67 | Fontana TF 790 | Who Do You Think You Are/Yes, I'm Going Home | 18 |

(see also Delaney & Bonnie, James Burton)

SHINE
| 74 | Fontana 6007041 | Candy Girl/I Wonder If Anything | 10 |

JOHNNY SHINES
| 69 | Blue Horizon 7-63212 | LAST NIGHT'S DREAM (LP, with Otis Spann, mono or stereo) | 80 |
| 74 | Xtra XTRA 1142 | COUNTRY BLUES (LP) | 25 |

DON SHINN (& THE SOUL AGENTS)
66	Polydor BM 56075	A Minor Explosion/Pits Of Darkness (with The Soul Agents)	70
69	Columbia S(C)X 6319	TEMPLES WITH PROPHETS (LP)	100
69	Columbia SCX 6355	DEPARTURES (LP)	150

(see also The Soul Agents)

SHINS
| 07 | Sub Pop | Sea Legs/Strange Powers (p/s) | 20 |
| 07 | Transgressive TRANS 046 | Phantom Limbs/Wincing The Night Away/Split Needles (p/s, double grooved b-side, 1000 only) | 8 |

SHINY TOO SHINY
| 83 | Red Flame RFB 29 | Waiting For Us/Ritual Hate (p/s) | 8 |

SHINY TWO SHINY
83	Red Flame RFB 29	Waiting For Us/Ritual hate (P/S)	8

SHIP
72	Elektra K 42122	THE SHIP - A CONTEMPORARY FOLK JOURNEY (LP, gatefold sleeve)	35

SHIRALEE
67	Fontana TF 855	I'll Stay By Your Side/Penny Wren	20

SHIRELLES
58	Brunswick 05746	I Met Him On A Sunday/I Want You To Be My Boyfriend	70
58	Brunswick 05746	I Met Him On A Sunday/I Want You To Be My Boyfriend (78)	30
60	London HL 9233	Tonight's The Night/The Dance Is Over	20
60	Top Rank JAR 540	Will You Love Me Tomorrow/Boys	8
61	Top Rank JAR 549	Dedicated To The One I Love/Look-A-Here Baby	18
61	Top Rank JAR 567	Mama Said/Blue Holiday	15
61	Top Rank JAR 578	What A Sweet Thing That Was/A Thing Of The Past	12
61	Top Rank JAR 590	Big John/Twenty One	12
62	Top Rank JAR 601	Baby It's You/The Things I Want To Hear	20
62	HMV POP 1019	Soldier Boy/Love Is A Swingin' Thing	12
62	Stateside SS 119	Welcome Home Baby/Mama Here Comes The Bride	15
62	Stateside SS 129	Stop The Music/It's Love That Really Counts	18
63	Stateside SS 152	Everybody Loves A Lover/I Don't Think So	12
63	Stateside SS 181	Foolish Little Girl/Not For All The Money In The World	15
63	Stateside SS 213	Don't Say Goodnight And Mean Goodbye/I Didn't Mean To Hurt You	15
63	Stateside SS 232	What Does A Girl Do/Don't Let It Happen To Us	15
63	Pye International 7N 25229	It's A Mad, Mad, Mad, Mad World/31 Flavours	20
64	Pye International 7N 25233	Tonight You're Gonna Fall In Love With Me/20th Century Rock And Roll	20
64	Pye International 7N 25240	Sha La La/His Lips Get In The Way	15
64	Pye International 7N 25279	Maybe Tonight/Lost Love	15
65	Pye International 7N 25288	Are You Still My Baby/I Saw A Tear	12
66	Pye International 7N 25386	Shades Of Blue/When The Boys Talk About The Girls	12
67	Pye International 7N 25425	Too Much Of A Good Thing/Bright Shiny Colours	20
69	Mercury MF 1093	There's A Storm Going On In My Heart/Call Me (If You Want Me)	22
71	United Artists UP 35192	Take Me/Dedicated To The One I Love	10
75	Pye Disco Demand DDs 115	Last Minute Miracle/March	15
61	Top Rank JKP 3012	THE SHIRELLES SOUND FEATURING "WILL YOU LOVE ME TOMORROW" (EP)	100
61	Top Rank 35-115	THE SHIRELLES SING - TO TRUMPET AND STRINGS (LP)	100
62	Stateside SL 10006	BABY IT'S YOU (LP)	80
63	Stateside SL 10041	THE SHIRELLES' HITS (LP)	50
70	Wand WNS 4	ETERNALLY SOUL (LP, with King Curtis)	25
71	Wand WCS 1001	TONIGHT'S THE NIGHT (LP)	18
72	RCA Victor SF 8237	HAPPY AND IN LOVE (LP)	15
72	RCA Victor SF 8279	THE SHIRELLES (LP)	15
72	Wand WCS 1009	REMEMBER WHEN VOL. 1 (LP)	15
72	Wand WCS 1010	REMEMBER WHEN VOL. 2 (LP)	15

(see also Shirley & Shirelles, Shirley Alston)

SHIRLEY
74	London HLA 10477	I Hear Those Church Bells Ringing/Chapel Of Love/I Do Love You	7

DON SHIRLEY
56	London HA-A 2003	PIANO PERSPECTIVES (LP)	15
56	London HA-A 2004	TONAL EXPRESSIONS (LP)	15
57	London HAA 2046	IMPROVISATIONS (LP)	15
62	London HAA 2448	DROWN IN MY OWN TEARS (LP, also stereo [SAHA 6238])	15

ROY SHIRLEY
66	Ska Beat JB 253	Paradise/Calling	20
66	Doctor Bird DB 1068	Hold Them/Be Good	25
67	Doctor Bird DB 1079	I'm A Winner/Sleeping Beauty	20
67	Doctor Bird DB 1088	Prophet/What To Do	20
67	Doctor Bird DB 1093	Musical Field/LEE PERRY & DYNAMITES: Trial And Crosses	35
67	Doctor Bird DB 1108	Thank You/Touch Them	18
67	Caltone CAL 101	Get On The Ball/JOHNNY MOORE: Sound And Soul	40
67	Island WI 3070	People Rock Steady/I'm Trying To Find A Home (actually by Uniques)	60
67	Island WI 3071	Musical War/Soul Voice	100
67	Island WI 3120	Girlie/GLEN ADAMS: She's So Fine	50
68	Doctor Bird DB 1165	Hush A Bye/Musical Dinner	15
68	Doctor Bird DB 1168	Dance The Reggae/The Agreement	20
68	Giant GN 32	Dance Hall Arena/The Musical Train	12
68	Giant GN 33	Warming Up The Scene/GLEN ADAMS: Lonely Girl	40
68	Island WI 3098	Thank You/Touch Them	25
68	Island WI 3108	Move All Day/Rollin' Rollin'	25
68	Island WI 3118	Million Dollar Baby/SENSATIONS: Long Time No See You Girl	25
68	Island WI 3119	Good Is Better Than Bad/Fantastic Lover	25
68	Island WI 3125	Facts Of Life/Lead Us Not Into Temptation (as Roy Shirley & Uniques; B-side actually by Roy Shirley & Slim Smith)	25
68	Island WI 3125	If I Did Know/Good Ambition	25
68	Amalgamated AMG 815	The World Needs Love/Dance The A	12
68	Fab FAB 54	Think About The Future/Golden Festival	10
69	Duke DU 18	Life/I Like Your Smile	8
71	Nu Beat NB 090	Hold Them One/Two Three Four	5
72	Punch PH 108	A Sugar/ALTYMAN REID: A Sugar - Version	6
72	Punch PH 103	Don't Be A Loser/Jamaican Girl	6
74	Arrow AR 001	Welcome Home/What Am I Loving For	10
74	Leroy LYW 001	Don't Destroy The World/Golden Festival	8
75	R&J 001	Heart Breaking Jepsey/Version	5
80s	Shirley SHIRLEY 1	For Everyone/Version (p/s)	5

(see also Val Bennett, Glen Adams, Shirley & Charmers, Sensations, Denzil, Errol & His Group, Ronsig, Stranger & Gladdy, Untouchables)

SUSAN SHIRLEY
68	Mercury MF 1038	Sun Shines Out Of Your Shoes/Tomorrow Today	5
69	Mercury MF 1087	Too Many Tears/Boy From Boston Massachusetts USA	5

MINT VALUE £

70	Philips 6006 037	Really Into Somethin'/My Friend The Clown	30
71	Columbia DB 8787	True Love And Apple Pie/To Find Out (p/s)	15
71	Columbia DB 8835	Jealous Guy/Oh Yoko	6
72	Columbia DB 8937	The Other Side Of Me/Imagine	5

SHIRLEY AND JOHNNY
| 64 | Parlophone R 5149 | I Don't Want To Know/It Must Be Love | 7 |
| 69 | Mercury MF 1074 | Don't Make Me Over/Baby, Baby, Baby | 7 |

SHIRLEY & CHARMERS
| 72 | Bullet BU 502 | Rum Rhythm/LLOYD CHARMERS: Rhythm (Version) | 6 |

(see also Roy Shirley)

SHIRLEY & LEE
56	Vogue V 9059	Let The Good Times Roll/Do You Mean To Hurt Me So	150
56	Vogue V 9059	Let The Good Times Roll/Do You Mean To Hurt Me So (78)	30
57	Vogue V 9063	I Feel Good/Now That It's Over	100
57	Vogue V 9063	I Feel Good/Now That It's Over (78)	30
57	Vogue V 9067	That's What I Wanna Do/When I Saw You	95
57	Vogue V 9067	That's What I Wanna Do/When I Saw You (78)	30
57	Vogue V 9072	Rock All Nite/Don't You Know I Love You	120
57	Vogue V 9072	Rock All Nite/Don't You Know I Love You (78)	30
57	Vogue V 9084	Rockin' With The Clock/The Flirt	130
57	Vogue V 9084	Rockin' With The Clock/The Flirt (78)	30
57	Vogue V 9088	I Want To Dance/Marry Me	80
57	Vogue V 9088	I Want To Dance/Marry Me (78)	30
57	Vogue V 9094	Feel So Good/You'd Be Thinking Of Me	80
57	Vogue V 9094	Feel So Good/You'd Be Thinking Of Me (78)	30
58	Vogue V 9103	I'll Thrill You/Love No One But You	85
58	Vogue V 9103	I'll Thrill You/Love No One But You (78)	30
58	Vogue V 9118	Everybody's Rockin'/Don't Leave Me Here To Cry	120
58	Vogue V 9118	Everybody's Rockin'/Don't Leave Me Here To Cry (78)	40
59	Vogue V 9129	All I Want To Do Is Cry/Come On And Have Your Fun	80
59	Vogue V 9129	All I Want To Do Is Cry/Come On And Have Your Fun (78)	30
59	Vogue V 9135	A Little Word/That's What I'll Do	80
59	Vogue V 9135	A Little Word/That's What I'll Do (78)	30
59	Vogue V 9137	I'll Do It/Lee's Dream	80

(The above 45s were originally issued with triangular centres; later round-centre issues are worth two-thirds of this value.)

| 59 | Vogue V 9137 | I'll Do It/Lee's Dream (78) | 30 |
| 59 | Vogue V 9156 | True Love/When Day Is Done | 80 |

(Later Vocalion pressings of the above 2 singles worth two-thirds of these values.)

59	Vogue V 9156	True Love/When Day Is Done (78)	40
60	London HLI 9186	I've Been Loved Before/Like You Used To Do	25
60	London HLI 9209	Let The Good Times Roll/Keep Loving Me	20
65	Island WI 257	Let The Good Times Roll/I'm Gone	20
57	Vogue VE 1-70101	ROCK 'N' ROLL (EP, triangular centre)	300
57	Vogue VE 1-70101	ROCK 'N' ROLL (EP, later round centre)	220
60	Vogue VE 1-70145	SHIRLEY AND LEE (EP)	250
71	Jay Boy JSX 2005	LET THE GOOD TIMES ROLL (LP)	20

SHIRLEY & RUDE BOYS
| 67 | Blue Beat BB 375 | Gently Set Me Free/BUSTER'S ALL STARS: Rock Steady | 150 |

SHIRLEY & SHIRELLES
69	Bell BLL 1049	Look What You've Done To My Heart/A Most Unusual Boy	10
69	Bell BLL 1065	Plaything/Looking Glass	6
72	Bell BLL 1251	Look What You've Done To My Heart/A Most Unusual Boy (reissue)	8

(see also Shirelles)

SHIRTS
78	Harvest HAR 5165	Tell Me Your Plans/Cyrinda	6
78	Harvest HAR 5170	Lonely Android/Running Through The Night (p/s)	5
78	SHSP 4089	THE SHIRTS (LP, blue vinyl)	15
79	Harvest SHSP 4104	STREET LIGHT SHINE (LP)	12

SHITMAT
| 03 | Planet Mu ZIQ 072 | Shopliftin' Gabba/Witness | 8 |
| 04 | Planet Mu ZIQ 089 | KILLABABYLONKUTZ (2-LP) | 20 |

SHIVA (1)
| 72 | D'art ART 2017 | The Legend Of Tutankhamun/Valley Of The Kings | 10 |

SHIVA (2)
82	Heavy Metal HEAVY 13	Rock Lives On/Sympathy For The Devil (p/s)	20
82	Heavy Metal HEAVY 16	Angel Of Mons/Stranger Lands (p/s)	10
82	Heavy Metal HMRLP 6	FIREDANCE (LP)	20

BUNNY SHIVEL
| 67 | Capitol CL 15487 | You'll Never Find A Love Like Mine/The Slide | 20 |

SHOC CORRIDOR
| 84 | Quiet QST 005 | Fever/That Sinking Feeling (12") | 12 |

SHOCK
| 81 | RCA RCAT 133 | Dynamo Beat/Dream Games (12") | 12 |

JOYCE SHOCK
58	Philips PB 824	Take Your Foot From The Door!/I've Got Bells On My Heart	6
58	Philips PB 872	Hoopa Hoola/You're Not Losing A Daughter, Mama	6
59	Philips PB 934	Personality/I Can't Love You Anymore	6
59	Philips PB 957	Cry, Baby, Cry/Dear Diary	6

SHOCK ABSORBERS
| 69 | Major Minor SMCP 5028 | GUITAR PARTY (LP) | 25 |

SHOCK HEADED PETERS
| 84 | él EL 1 | I, Blood Brother Be/Truth Has Come (p/s) | 7 |

(see also Lemon Kittens, Underneath, Karl Blake, Sol Invictus)

SHOCKING BLUE
69	Olga OLE 015	Send Me A Postcard/Harley Davidson (demo only)	60
69	Penny Farthing PEN 702	Venus/Hot Sand	5
70	Penny Farthing PEN 713	Mighty Joe/Wild Wind	5
70	Penny Farthing PEN 721	Never Marry A Railroad Man/Roll Engine Roll	5
70	Penny Farthing PEN 744	Sally Was A Good Old Girl/Long And Lonesome Road	6
70	Penny Farthing PELS 500	SHOCKING BLUE AT HOME (LP)	50
70	Penny Farthing PELS 510	SCORPIO'S DANCE (LP)	40
71	Penny Farthing PEN 748	Hello Darkness/Pickin' Tomatoes	5

SHOCK TREATEMENT
80s	Skull SKR 2001	The Mugger/Nuclear Warfare (p/s)	125

SHOES
67	Polydor 56739	Farewell In The Rain/What In The World Is Love	7

SHOES FOR INDUSTRY
79	Fried Egg EGG 001	Laughbeat/Can't Help It (p/s)	6
80	Fried Egg FRY 1	TALK LIKE A WHELK (LP)	20

SHOESTRING BAND
73	CBS SCBS 1284	Thingumajig/Don't It Make You Feel Good	6
86	Attack ATA 913	High In The Sky/When The Lights Go Down (p/s)	30
87	Jet JET 12049	Cloak And Dagger/Too Late For The Hunter/Tokyo Girl (12", p/s, red vinyl)	8
86	Attack ATA 006	SHOGUN (LP)	40

SHOGUN MC
89	Blue Chip C22T	Ready For Action (12")	15

TROY SHONDELL
61	London HLG 9432	This Time/Girl After Girl	8
62	Liberty LIB 55398	Island In The Sky/Tears From An Angel	15
63	London HL 9668	I Got A Woman/Some People Never Learn	12
64	London HAY 8128	MANY SIDES OF TROY SHONDELL (LP)	70

SHONDELLS
64	Ember EMB S 191	My Love/Don't Cry My Soldier Boy	50

SHOOT
73	EMI EMI 2026	On The Frontier/Ships And Sails	5
72	EMI EMA 73	ON THE FRONTIER (LP)	20
78	EMI Intl. INS 3020	SHOOTER (LP)	12

(see also Manfred Mann Chapter 3, Yardbirds, Raw Material)

SHOOTING PARTY
88	Lisson DOLER 9	Safe In The Arms Of Love (Phil's Extra Beat Update)/Safe In The Arms Of Love	12

SHOP ASSISTANTS
85	Subway Organisation SUBWAY 1	All Day Long/All That Ever Mattered/It's Up To You/Switzerland (red foldaround hand-coloured p/s in poly bag)	12
85	Subway Organisation SUBWAY 1	All Day Long/All That Ever Mattered/It's Up To You/Switzerland (later blue foldaround hand-coloured p/s in poly bag)	6
86	Blue Guitar AZLP 2	SHOP ASSISTANTS (LP)	15

(see also Buba & Shop assistants)

DINAH SHORE
53	HMV 7M 119	Keep It A Secret/Bella Musica	8
53	HMV 7M 139	Sweet Thing/Three-Cornered Tune	8
54	HMV 7M 183	Changing Partners/Think	8
54	HMV 7M 221	This Must Be The Place/Come Back To My Arms	8
54	HMV 7M 236	Three Coins In The Fountain/Pakistan	8
54	HMV 7M 250	If I Give My Heart To You/Let Me Know	8
56	HMV 7M 352	Love And Marriage/Compare	8
57	RCA RCA 1003	The Cattle Call/Promises, Promises (Skip Redwine)	7
58	RCA RCA 1054	Thirteen Men/I'll Never Say "Never Again" Again	5
58	RCA RD 27072	HOLDING HANDS AT MIDNIGHT (LP)	15

(see also Doris Day)

BRIAN SHORT
71	Transatlantic TRA 245	ANYTHING FOR A LAUGH (LP, textured gatefold sleeve)	30

(see also Black Cat Bones)

J.D. SHORT
73	Sonet SNTF 648	THE LEGACY OF THE BLUES VOL. 8 (LP)	12

KEVIN SHORT
79	EMI INT 574	Punk Strut/Short Cut (no p/s, demos only)	30

SHORT KUTS WITH EDDIE HARRISON
68	United Artists UP 2233	Your Eyes May Shine/Letting The Tears Tumbling Down	25

SHORTCAKES
71	Decca F13185	I Can Try/Save Me	10

ERROL SHORTER
81	Greensleeves GRED 58	Wild Inna Eighty-One Style/EEK A MOUSE : Wa Do Dem (12")	10

WAYNE SHORTER
79	Blue Note LBR 1021	THE SOOTHSAYER (LP)	15

SHORTWAVE (BAND)
75	RCA Victor SF 8400	SHORTWAVE BAND (LP, with lyric sheet)	12
77	Crescent/Avada ARS 111	GREATEST HATS (LP)	20
79	Pye 2CN 111	SHORTWAVE (LP)	12

SHORTY (THE PRESIDENT)
73	Ackee ACK 509	Aquarius Pressure/Halfway Tree Pressure (as Shorty The President)	10
73	Ackee ACK 517	Jelly-Belly-Nelly/Message Of Love (as Shorty)	6
75	Treble C CCC 03	Beast From The East/Version	8
76	Cactus CTLP	PRESENTING (LP)	25

79	Freedom Sounds FSLP 002	DUB CONFERENCE IN LONDON (LP)..	25

(see also Shorty Perry)

SHORTY & THEM
64	Fontana TF 460	Pills Or Love's Labours Lost/Live Laugh And Love	40

SHOTGUN EXPRESS
66	Columbia DB 8025	I Could Feel The Whole World Turn Round/Curtains........................	70
67	Columbia DB 8178	Funny 'Cos Neither Could I/Indian Thing	70
83	See For Miles CYM 2	I Could Feel The Whole World Turn Round/Curtains/Funny 'Cos Neither Could I/Indian Thing (10", p/s)	15

(see also Rod Stewart, Peter Bardens, Spencer Davis, Brian Auger, She Trinity, Beryl Marsden, Fleetwood Mac)

SHOTS
65	Columbia DB 7713	Keep A Hold Of What You've Got/She's A Liar	60

(see also Smoke)

SHOUT
72	Explosion 2058	Life Is Rough/Life Is Rough - Version..	5
92	Entity SHOUT	Is It Ever Going To End (Remix 1)/Is It Ever Going To End (Remix 2)/Is It Ever Going To End (Remix 3)/ Is It Ever Going To End (Radio Edit)/Is It Ever Going To End (Stiff Organ Mix)(12")	60

SHOUTS
64	React EA 001	She Was My Baby/That's The Way It's Gonna Be..........................	55

(see also Gene Vincent)

THE SHOVE
81	Shove Off PBM033/S/81	Raise The Roof Tonite/Violence/Pigs/Nutters Of York (foldover p/s, 500 only) ...	40
81	Shove Off Records	ROUGH AND READY EP (with p/s)	25
81	Shove Off Records	ROUGH AND READY EP	15

SHOW STOPPERS
68	Beacon 3-100	Ain't Nothing But A House Party/What Can A Man Do (red swirly label)	15
68	Beacon 3-106	Shake Your Mini/Heartbreaker...	40
68	MGM MGM 1436	Eeny Meeny/How Easy Your Heart Forgets Me	15
69	Beacon BEA 110	Don't Leave Me Standing In The Rain/Do You Need My Love	10
69	Beacon BEA 130	Just A Little Bit Of Lovin'/School Prom	15
69	Beacon BEA 100	Ain't Nothing But A House Party/What Can A Man Do (reissue, yellow label) ...	10
70	Beacon BEA 100	Ain't Nothing But A House Party/What Can A Man Do (reissue, green label)......	8
71	Beacon BEA 177	Reach In The Goody Bag/How Do You Feel	10
71	Beacon BEA 3-182	Actions Speak Louder Than Words/ Pick Up Your Smile................	30

SHOWBIZ KIDS
80s	Top Secret CON 1	She Goes To Finos/I Don't Want To Discuss That (p/s)	35

(see also Toy Dolls)

SHOW BOYS
69	Gas GAS 129	People Are Wondering/Long Time	10

SHOWMEN
62	London HLP 9481	It Will Stand/Country Fool	70
62	London HLP 9571	The Wrong Girl/I Love You Can't You See..................................	175
69	Pama PM 767	Action/What Would It Take...	15

(see also Norman Johnson, General Johnson, Chairmen Of The Board)

SHOWTIMERS
64	HMV POP 1328	You Must Be Joking/Don't Say Goodbye....................................	15

SHOX
80	Axis AXIS 4	No Turning Back/Lying Here (p/s)..	15
80	Beggars Banquet BEG 33	No Turning Back/Lying Here (p/s, reissue)	8

MARK SHREEVE
83	Uniton U 021	ASSASSIN (LP)	15

SHRIEKBACK
81	Y T104	Working On The Ground/Nightwork (12", p/s)	12

SHRINK
79	Oval AMS 7409	Valid Or Void/You Chauffeur Me (p/s)	6

SHRUG
95	Private Pressing	THE YOGURTS VS YOGURT DEBATE (Demo cassette, glued sleeve)........	80

(see also Snow Patrol)

SHUBERT
68	Fontana TF 942	Until The Rains Come/Let Your Love Go	20

SHUDDER TO THINK
90s	Dischord	Vacation Brain (p/s, with insert)...	12

SALMAN SHUKUR
77	Decca Headline HEAD 16	OUD (LP)..	18

MORT SHUMAN
59	Decca F 11184	Turn Me Loose/I'm A Man	50
59	Decca F 11184	Turn Me Loose/I'm A Man (78)	25
66	Fontana TF 685	Cry A Little/She Ain't Nothing But A Little Child..........................	10
67	Immediate IM 048	Monday Monday/Little Children	20

SHUTDOWNS
63	Colpix PX 11016	Four In The Floor/Beach Buggy	50

SHY LIMBS
69	CBS 4190	Reputation/Love	70
69	CBS 4624	Lady In Black/Trick Or Two	150

(see also Shame)

SHY ONES
63	Oriole CB 1848	Nightcap/Carry Me Back	20
64	Oriole CB 1924	La Route/Susanna..	18

(see also Spotnicks)

SHY (1)
74	Deram DM417	Disney Girls (1957)/The Time That I Love You The Most	7
87	RCA PT 41180	Break Down The Walls/Under Fire/Young Heart (12", gatefold p/s)	8

SHY (2)
83	Ebony EBON 15	ONCE BITTEN TWICE SHY (LP)	20

SHYSTER
68	Polydor 56202	Tick Tock/That's A Hoe Down	220

(see also Fleur-De-Lys)

SHYWOLF
82	MRS SW 001	Lucretia/California Jam (p/s)	40

LEROY SIBBLES & ROCKY ELLIS
68	Studio One SO 2042	Love Me Girl/WRIGGLERS: Reel Up	30
79	Warrior Records WAR 133	Ras-Tafari/MYSTIC EYES: Forward With Love/Dub (12")	30

(see also John Holt, King Rocky)

DON E SIBLEY & DIXIE PHOENIX
79	Hot Rock HR45-003	Punk Bashing Boogie/Rock With The Devil	7

DUDLEY SIBLEY
67	Coxsone CS 7010	Run Boy Run/Message Of Old (B-side actually by Joe Higgs & Ken Boothe)	45
67	Island WI 3034	Gun Man/Monkey Speaks His Mind (B-side actually by Dinsdell Thorpe)	50

(see also Delroy & Sporty, King Sporty, Mr. Foundation)

SICK THINGS
83	Chaos CHS 3	ANTI SOCIAL (EP)	25

SIDAN
75	Sain 1017	TEULU YNCL SAM (LP, laminated front cover)	40

SID & JOE & MOHAWKS
70	Pama PM 800	Down On The Cornere/Who Is That Stranger	20

(see also Mohawks)

SIDDELEYS
87	Sha La La Ba Ba Ba 006	Wherever You Go/RESERVE: The Sun Slid Down Behind The Tower (flexidisc with fanzines, p/s)	10
87	Medium Cool MC 005	What Went Wrong This Time?/No Names/My Favourite Wet Wednesday Afternoon (p/s)	35
88	Sombrero THREE	Sunshine Thuggery/Are You Still Evil When You're Sleeping/Falling Off My Feet Again (12", p/s)	25

SIDEKICKS
66	RCA RCA 1538	Suspicions/Up On The Roof	20

ANN SIDNEY
65	HMV POP 1411	The Boy In The Woolly Sweater/Lonely Doll (Miss World 1965)	5

SIDNEY, GEORGE & JACKIE
71	Summit SUM 8528	Lady Of My Complexion/No Sad Song	5
72	Summit SUM 8535	Story Book Children/Gorgeous Marvellous	5
74	Attack ATT 8054	At The Club/Reggae Fever	150

(see also Pioneers)

PAUL SIEBEL
70	Elektra EKSN 45085	Bride 1945/Miss Cherry Lane	5
70	Elektra EKS 74064	WOODSMOKE AND ORANGES (LP)	20
71	Elektra EKS 74081	JACK-KNIFE GYPSY (LP)	20

SIEGE
85	Siege THM 1	Goddess Of Fire (no p/s)	18
90	Revolution	Infest/Drop Dead (p/s)	20

SIEGEL-SCHWALL BAND
68	Vanguard SVRL 19044	SHAKE (LP)	20

CHRIS SIEVEY
79	Rabid TOSH 109	Baiser/Last (p/s)	10
79	Razz RAZZXEP 1	BAISER (33rpm EP, 2 tracks each by Sievey & Freshies, handwritten labels)	35
80	Razz RAZZ 4	My Tape's Gone/Moon Midsummer (with True Life Revealing Confessions Of Romance And Love fanzine)	10
80	Razz RAZZ 4	My Tape's Gone/Moon Midsummer (without True Life Revealing Confessions Of Romance And Love fanzine)	5
81	Razz RAZZ 5	Hey/FRESHIES: We're Like You (p/s)	6
82	Razz RAZZ 8	RED INDIAN MUSIC (EP)	8
82	Razz RAZZ 9	Skip The Flight/Jim Baiser ("Baiser"/"Last" with new labels & sleeve)	8

(see also Freshies, Going Red?)

LABI SIFFRE
71	Pye Intl. 7N 25572	It Must Be Love/To Find Love	6
70	Pye Intl. NSPL 28135	LABI SIFFRE (LP)	15
71	Pye Intl. NSPL 28147	THE SINGER AND THE SONG (LP, gatefold sleeve)	15
72	Pye Intl. NSPL 28163	CRYING, LAUGHING, LOVING, LYING (LP, gatefold sleeve with lyric insert)	12
73	Pye Intl. NSPL 28182	FOR THE CHILDREN (LP, gatefold sleeve, lyric insert)	12
75	EMI EMC 3065	REMEMBER MY SONG (LP)	60
98	EMI/Mr. Bongo MRBLP 011	REMEMBER MY SONG (LP, reissue)	12
06	EMI EMC 3065	REMEMBER MY SONG (LP, reissue)	12

RON SIG
71	Camel CA 58	1970's/Version	6
71	Camel CA 59	You Girl/ROY SHIRLEY & SLIM SMITH: Facts Of Life	8

SIGHT & SOUND
68	Fontana TF 927	Ebenezer/Our Love (Is In The Pocket)	40
68	Fontana TF 982	Alley Alley/Little Jack Monday	20

(see also Jefferson, Sheridan & Price, Mike Sheridan)

MINT VALUE £

BUNNY SIGLER
67	Cameo Parkway P 153	Let The Good Times Roll - Feel So Good/There's No Love Left	25
67	Cameo Parkway P 153	Let The Good Times Roll - Feel So Good/There's No Love Left (DJ copy)	60
76	Philadelphia SPIR 4935	Can't Believe That You Love Me/Woman, Woman	6
76	London HLU 10518	Let The Good Times Roll/Girl Don't Make Me Wait	12

SIGNS
66	Decca F 12522	Ain't You Got A Heart/My Baby Comes To Me	40

SIGUE SIGUE SPUTNIK
86	Parlophone PCSS 7305	FLAUNT IT (LP, box set with insert)	12

(see also Generation X, Sisters Of Mercy)

SIGUR RÓS
99	Fat Cat 12FAT 036	Svefn-G-Englar (12" EP, custom sleeve 2,000 only)	25
99	Fat Cat CD FAT 036	Svefn-G-Englar (CD, 2000 only)	20
00	Fat Cat 12FAT 039	NY BATTERY (mini-LP, 2,000 only)	40
00	Fat Cat CATCD FAT 039	NY BATTERY (CD, mini-LP, 2,000 only)	20
03	FAT KAT FATPK 01 A	Ineractive press kit for () album (2 x CD in DVD style case)	20
04	EMI 5496916	BA BA TI KI DI DO (12" EP)	8
05	EMI 17571	Hoppipolla/Meo Bloonasir/Hafsol (12")	8
06	EMI EMI 673	Hoppipolla/Heysatan (numbered p/s, 3000 only)	10
00	Fat Cat FATLP 11	AGAETIS BYRJUN (2-LP)	50
03	Fat Cat FATLP 22	() (LP)	40
05	EMI 3384632	TAKK (LP, special book edition)	25
05	EMI 337252	SIGUR RóS (2-LP, gatefold with inner sleeves and free 10")	30
07	EMI 5099951041991	HEIMA (Box set, CD, DVD, 116 page book)	50
09	Fat Cat FATLP 11X	AGAETIS BYRJUN (2-LP, reissue, 180 gm vinyl)	15
09	Fat Cat FATLP 22X	() (2-LP, reissue, 180 gm vinyl)	15

SILENT ECLIPSE
92	White (Mendoza) MEN018	How Many Miles Back To London/MCs (12")	100
92	Mendoza MEN018	How Many Miles Back To London/Mcs (12")	15
92	Dope Jams DJAM1	Take The Stage (3 Mixes, promo 12" only)	15

(see also Two Times Def)

SILENT MOVIES
79	ESR Records ESR 1	Ain't No Van Gough/What Did Ya Say? (p/s)	40

SILENT NOISE
79	Silent Noise/Easy ER 02	I've Been Hurt (Too Many Times Before)/Heart To Heart	75

SILENT ONES
70	Pulse P1	When It Rains/Lost Dreams (p/s)	50

SILHOUETTES (JAMAICA)
69	Sound System SSR 103	In Times Like These (act. by Lloyd Jackson & Groovers)/In Times Like These	6

SILHOUETTES (U.S.)
58	Parlophone R 4407	Get A Job/I Am Lonely	100
58	Parlophone R 4407	Get A Job/I Am Lonely (78)	50
58	Parlophone R 4425	Headin' For The Poorhouse/Miss Thing	150
58	Parlophone R 4425	Headin' For The Poorhouse/Miss Thing (78)	80

SILICON TEENS
79	Mute MUTE 003	Memphis Tennessee/Let's Dance (p/s, with poster)	10
79	Mute MUTE 003	Memphis Tennessee/Let's Dance (p/s)	5
80	Mute CC8AX	Sunflight/Just Like Eddie (P/S)	6
80	Mute STUMM 2	MUSIC FOR PARTIES (LP)	18

ERIC SILK (& HIS SOUTHERN JAZZ BAND)
57	Esquire 20-065	SOUTHERN JAZZ (LP)	12
58	Esquire 20-095	THE SILKEN TOUCH (LP)	12
67	Polydor 582 002	OFF THE CUFF (LP)	12

SILKIE
65	Fontana TF 556	Blood Red River/Close The Door Gently	5
65	Fontana TF 603	You've Got To Hide Your Love Away/City Winds	7
66	Fontana TF 659	Keys To My Soul/Leave Me To Cry	5
66	Fontana TF 709	Born To Be With You/So Sorry Now	5
65	Fontana TL 5256	THE SILKIE SING THE SONGS OF BOB DYLAN (LP)	20

JUDEE SILL
71	Asylum AYM 502	Jesus Was A Cross Maker/The Phantom Cowboy	7
72	Asylum AYM 509	Enchanted Sky Machines/My Man On Love	6
72	Asylum SYLA 8751	JUDEE SILL (LP, gatefold sleeve)	40
73	Asylum SYL 9006	HEART FOOD (LP)	25

SILLY SISTERS
76	Chrysalis CHR 1101	SILLY SISTERS (LP, with lyric insert)	12

(see also Steeleye Span, Maddy Prior, June Tabor)

SILVER EAGLE
67	MGM MGM 1345	Theodore/True As A Brand New Lie	30

SILVER (JAMAICA)
68	Jolly JY 006	Baby Oh Yeah/Rock Steady Is Here To Stay (as Silver & Magnets)	20
68	Jolly JY 012	Things/Sweet Lovin'	15
68	Jolly JY 017	I Need A Girl/Lost And Found	12
70	Columbia Blue Beat DB 117	Love Me Forever/Sugar, Sugar (B-side as Silver & Noreen)	5
71	Fab FAB 163	Change Has Got To Come/Magnet Stomp (as Silver & Magnets)	6

SILVER (U.S.)
76	Arista ARIST 79	Musician (It's Not An Easy Life)/Right On Time	6
76	Arista ARTY 144	SILVER (LP, U.S. disc & inner [AL 4076] in U.K. sleeve)	12

(see also Grateful Dead)

ANDEE SILVER
64	HMV POP 1297	Too Young To Go Steady/Sleeping Beauty	10

64	HMV POP 1344	The Boy I Used To Know/What Do You Do	10
66	Fontana TF 666	Only Your Love Can Save Me/Window Shopping	25
69	Decca F 22872	Go Now/You're Just What I Was Looking For Today	20
69	Decca F 22953	With A Little Love/Te Quiero (unreleased)	0
70	Decca F 23071	Love Me/You're Breaking My Heart (export issue)	10
70	Decca SKL-R 5059	A HANDFUL OF SILVER (LP)	50

EDDIE SILVER
58	Parlophone R 4439	Seven Steps To Love/Put A Ring On Her Finger	15
58	Parlophone R 4439	Seven Steps To Love/Put A Ring On Her Finger (78)	15
58	Parlophone R 4483	Rockin' Robin/The Ways Of A Woman In Love	20
58	Parlophone R 4483	Rockin' Robin/The Ways Of A Woman In Love (78)	20

HORACE SILVER QUINTET/TRIO
| 54 | Vogue LDE 065 | THE HORACE SILVER TRIO (10" LP) | 20 |
| 69 | Blue Note BST 84277 | SERENADE TO A SOUL SISTER (LP) | 25 |

LORRAINE SILVER
65	Pye 7N 15922	Lost Summer Love/I'll Know You'll Be There	75
65	Pye 7N 15922	Lost Summer Love/I'll Know You'll Be There (DJ copy)	75
66	Pye 7N 17055	The Happy Faces/When The Love Light Starts Shining Thru His Eyes	40

MIKE SILVER & MIKE BEASON
| 69 | Fontana STL 5506 | THE APPLICANT (LP) | 200 |

SILVER SCREEN GIRLS
| 81 | Siren SSG 1 | Photographs/Silver Screen Girls (p/s) | 15 |

SILVER APPLES
| 96 | Enraptured RAPT 4507 | Fractal Flow/Love Fingers (p/s) | 6 |
| 97 | Rocket Girl RGIRL 1 | I Have Known Love/WINDY & CARL: Crazy In The Sun (p/s, green vinyl) | 6 |

SILVER BIRCH
| 73 | Brayford BRO 2 | SILVER BIRCH (LP, private pressing) | 150 |

SILVERBIRD
| 72 | CBS 51279 | I See The Writing On The Wall/The Summer's Gone (And I'm Alone) | 8 |
| 73 | CBS 51800 | That's Why You Remember/You And Me | 8 |

SILVER BULLET
| 91 | Parlophone R 6290 | Ruff Karnage/Never Authorise Apocalypse (p/s) | 10 |

SILVER BYKE
| 68 | London HLZ 10200 | I've Got Time/Who Needs Tomorrow | 18 |

SILVERCHAIR
| 95 | Sony 480430 | FROGSTOMP (LP, green vinyl, inner, sleeve in PVC outer sleeve) | 20 |

SILVERGINGER 5
| 01 | Infernal INFERNAL 13CD/X | BLACK LEATHER MOJO (2-CD, in stickered leather-effect slipcase, 5000 only) | 25 |

(see also Ginger, Super$hit666, Wildhearts)

SILVERHEAD
72	Purple PUR 104	Ace Supreme/Oh No No No	10
72	Purple PUR 110	Rolling With My Baby/In Your Eyes	10
73	Purple TPSA 7506	SILVERHEAD (LP, gatefold)	30
73	Purple TPSA 7511	SIXTEEN AND SAVAGED (LP, gatefold sleeve)	25

(see also Michael Des Barres, Blondie)

SILVER JEWS
| 96 | Domino WIGLP 28 | THE NATURAL BRIDGE (LP) | 20 |
| 98 | Domino WIGLP 56 | AMERICAN WATER (LP) | 20 |

SILVER METRIC
| 71 | Department Of Health MET1 | Inch By Inch/Centimetre By Centimetre | 5 |

SILVER MOUNTAIN
| 83 | Road Runner RR 9884 | SHAKIN' BRAINS (LP) | 15 |

SILVERS
| 66 | Polydor BM 56094 | What A Way To Start A Day/Blue Blue Eyes | 7 |

PHIL SILVERS
| 57 | Fontana Fortune Z 4040 | BUGLE CALLS FOR BIG BAND (LP) | 15 |

SILVER SISTERS
| 60 | Parlophone R 4669 | Waiting For The Stars To Shine/When A Boy Meets A Girl | 10 |

DOOLEY SILVERSPOON
| 76 | Seville SEV 1022 | Game Players/Believe In Me | 5 |

SILVERSTARS
| 69 | Trojan TR 646 | Old Man Say/Promises | 12 |
| 70 | Bamboo BAM 23 | Love At first Sight/MAYTALS : Life Could Be A Dream | 35 |

SILVER STARS STEEL BAND
| 63 | Island ILP 904 | THE SILVER STARS STEEL BAND (LP) | 20 |

(see also Clancy Eccles)

SHEL SILVERSTEIN
| 73 | CBS 65452 | FREAKIN' AT THE FREAKER'S BALL (LP, with Dr. Hook) | 12 |

(see also Dr. Hook)

SILVERTONES
66	Doctor Bird DB 1028	True Confession (with Duke Reid)/TOMMY McCOOK & SUPERSONICS: More Love	35
66	RYMSKA RA 105	True Confession/Honky Tonky Ska (with Granville Williams)	30
66	Doctor Bird DB 1041	It's Real (with Lynn Tait & Boys)/LYNN TAIT & BOYS: Storm Warning	35
67	Treasure Isle TI 7020	Cool Down/TOMMY McCOOK & SUPERSONICS: Shadow Of Your Smile	25
68	Treasure Isle TI 7027	In The Midnight Hour/TOMMY McCOOK & SUPERSONICS: Soul For Sale	20
68	Treasure Isle TI 7039	Old Man River/TOMMY McCOOK & SUPERSONICS: Our Man Flint	50
68	Treasure Isle TI 7042	Slow And Easy/TOMMY McCOOK & SUPERSONICS: Moving	20
69	Trojan TR 7705	Intensified Change/Marie	12

MINT VALUE £

71	Clandisc CLA 234	Tear Drops Will Fall/DYNAMITES: Tear Drops - Version	6
73	Techniques TE 924	That's When It Hurts/I'll Take You Home	6
77	Trojan TRO 9013	African Dub/Version	25
71	Trojan TRLS 69	SILVER BULLETS (LP)	35

(see also Valentines, Tommy McCook, Vincent Gordon, Alton Ellis, Carl Bryon, Charmers)

SILVERWING

80	Mayhem SILVER 1	Rock'n'Roll Are Four-Letter Words/High Class Woman/Hot City Streets	7
82	Mayhem SILV 02	Sittin' Pretty/Teenage Love Affair (p/s)	8
82	Mayhem SILV 212	Sittin' Pretty/Teenage Love/Flashbomb Fever/Rock'n'Roll Mayhem (12")	10
82	Mayhem SILV 3	That's Entertainment/Flashbomb Fever (poster p/s)	8
83	Bullet BULP 1	ALIVE AND KICKING (LP)	15

(see also Pet Hate, Big Amongst Sheep)

VICTOR SILVESTER ORCHESTRA

| 62 | Columbia | World Cup Cha Cha Cha/Santiago | 5 |
| 66 | Columbia DB 7900 | The World Cup Waltz/The World Cup Cha Cha Cha | 10 |

VICTOR SILVESTER & HIS ROCK 'N' ROLL RHYTHM

| 57 | Columbia DB 3888 | Rockin' Rhythm Roll/Society Rock | 15 |
| 57 | Columbia DB 3907 | Alligator Roll/Off Beat Rock | 15 |

SIMBA

| 71 | Fire FIR 100 | Louie Louie/Movin' | 5 |

TYRONE SIMEON

| 79 | Burning Rockers BRD 010 | Do Good In This Time/Do Good Dub (12") | 15 |

SIMEONS

| 78 | Freedom Sounds FSLP 002 | DUB CONFERENCE IN LONDON (LP) | 25 |

LEO SIMMO

| 66 | Big Beat BB351 | I Love Her So/It's Good To Be Seen | 25 |

BEVERLEY SIMMON(D)S

68	Pama PM 716	Mr. Pitiful/That's How Strong My Love Is	15
73	Pama Supreme PS 380	You're Mine/What A Guy (as Beverley Simmonds)	8
69	Pama PMLP 1	PAYS TRIBUTE TO OTIS REDDING(LP)	50
69	Pama PMLP/PMSP 9	REMEMBER OTIS (LP)	30

(see also Little Beverly)

CHRIS SIMMONS

| 69 | MCA MK 5009 | Soraya/Gone Gone Gone | 6 |

DESMOND SIMMONS

| 81 | Dome 33.1 | ALONE ON PENGUIN ISLAND (LP) | 15 |

(JUMPIN') GENE SIMMONS

| 64 | London HLU 9913 | Haunted House/Hey, Hey Little Girl | 20 |
| 64 | London HLU 9933 | The Jump/The Dodo | 20 |

GENE SIMMONS

79	Casablanca CAN 134	Radioactive/When You Wish Upon A Star (p/s, red vinyl with mask, picture label, mispressed with black/red vinyl)	50
79	Casablanca CAN 134	Radioactive/When You Wish Upon A Star (p/s, red vinyl with mask, picture label)	20
79	Casablanca CAN 134	Radioactive/When You Wish Upon A Star (p/s, black vinyl)	8

(see also Kiss)

JEFF SIMMONS

| 69 | Straight STS 1057 | LUCILLE HAS MESSED UP MY MIND (LP) | 70 |

(see also Frank Zappa)

LITTLE MAC SIMMONS

| 66 | Outasite OSEP 1 | BLUES FROM CHICAGO (EP, 99 copies only) | 200 |

TONY SIMMONS

| 83 | Record Shack SOHOT 2 | I Can't Let You Go/I Can't Let You Go (Instrumental) (12" promo only) | 150 |

JAGO SIMMS

| 68 | Fontana TF 901 | In Too Deep/Conventional Fella | 45 |

JASON SIMMS & MUSIC THROUGH SIX

| 68 | Domain D 5 | It's Got To Be Mellow/MUSIC THROUGH SIX: Floppy Ears | 20 |

(see also Music Through Six)

(ZOOT) SIMMS & (LLOYD) ROBINSON

| 62 | Blue Beat BB 143 | White Christmas/Searching | 10 |

ZOOT SIMMS (JAMAICA)

63	Blue Beat BB 183	Press Along/PRINCE BUSTER ALLSTARS: 100 Ton Megaton (B-side actually "Mighty As A Rose" by Raymond Harper)	25
63	Blue Beat BB 193	Golden Pen/ERIC MORRIS: So You Shot Reds	35
64	Port-O-Jam PJ 4007	Please Don't Do It/Don't Do It (as Simms & [Lloyd] Robinson)	40
68	Blue Cat BS 118	Bye Bye Baby/AL & THRILLERS: Heart For Sale	70
69	Coxsone CS 7095	Tit For Tat/We Can Talk It Over (as Simms & Elmond)	40

SEIJA SIMOLA

| 78 | Sonet SON 2145 | Give Love A Chance/Little Smile (p/s) | 12 |

SIMON

67	RCA Victor RCA 1609	I Like The Way/Little Tin Soldier	10
68	RCA Victor RCA 1668	Dream Seller/Sweet Reflections Of You	15
69	Plum PLS 002	Mrs Lillyco/There's No More You	30

JOE SIMON

66	London HLU 10057	Teenager's Prayer/Long Hot Summer	30
67	Monument MON 1004	My Special Prayer/Travelin' Man	10
68	Monument MON 1010	Nine Pound Steel/The Girl's Alright With Me	20
68	Monument MON 1014	No Sad Songs/Come On And Get It	10
68	Monument MON 1019	You Keep Me Hangin' On/What Makes A Man Feel Good	7
68	Monument MON 1025	Message From Maria/I Worry About You	7

69	Monument MON 1029	Looking Back/Standing In The Safety Zone	7
69	Monument MON 1032	The Chokin' Kind/Come On And Get It	7
70	Monument MON 1042	Moon Walk (Parts 1 & 2)	5
70	Monument MON 1049	Yours Love/I Gotta Whole Lot Of Lovin'	25
70	Monument MON 1051	That's The Way I Want Our Love/When	15
71	Polydor 2066 066	Your Time To Cry/I Love You More (Than Anything)	8
74	Mojo 2093 030	Step By Step/Talk Don't Bother Me	6
67	Monument LMO/SMO 5005	SIMON PURE SOUL (LP)	20
68	Monument LMO/SMO 5017	NO SAD SONGS (LP)	20
69	Monument LMO/SMO 5026	SIMON SINGS (LP)	20
70	Monument LMO/SMO 5030	THE CHOKIN' KIND (LP)	20
70	Monument LMO/SMO 5033	BETTER THAN EVER (LP)	20
71	Mojo 2918 001	THE SOUNDS OF SIMON (LP)	15
72	Mojo 2918 003	DROWNING IN THE SEA OF LOVE (LP)	15

PAUL SIMON

65	CBS 201797	I Am A Rock/Leaves That Are Green	25
73	CBS 1545	Kodachrome (withdrawn, any pressed?)	15
65	CBS (S) 62579	THE PAUL SIMON SONGBOOK (LP, mono, flipback sleeve)	25
65	CBS (S) 62579	THE PAUL SIMON SONGBOOK (LP, stereo, flipback sleeve)	30
72	CBS CQ 30750/Q 69007	PAUL SIMON (LP, quadrophonic)	20
74	CBS CQ 32280/Q 69035	THERE GOES RHYMIN' SIMON (LP, quadrophonic)	18
75	CBS Q 86001	STILL CRAZY AFTER ALL THESE YEARS (LP, quadrophonic)	18

(see also Simon & Garfunkel, Jerry Landis, Tom & Jerry)

TONY SIMON

67	Track 604 012	Gimme A Little Sign/Never Too Much To Love	40

SIMON & GARFUNKEL

65	CBS 201977	The Sound Of Silence/We've Got A Groovy Thing Goin'	10
66	CBS 202045	Homeward Bound/Leaves That Are Green	10
66	CBS 202303	I Am A Rock/Flowers Never Bend With The Rainfall	10
66	CBS 202285	The Dangling Conversation/The Big Bright Green Pleasure Machine	15
66	CBS 202378	A Hazy Shade Of Winter/For Emily, Whenever I May Find Her	10
67	CBS 202608	At The Zoo/The 59th Street Bridge Song (Feelin' Groovy)	10
67	CBS 2911	Fakin' It/You Don't Know Where Your Interest Lies	20
68	CBS Special Prods. WB 73	The Sound Of Silence/GEORGIE FAME: By The Time I Get To Phoenix (p/s)	5
68	CBS Special Prods. WB 728	The 59th Street Bridge Song (Feelin' Groovy)/TREMELOES: Here Comes My Baby (p/s, mail-order only with Pepsi Cola tokens)	7
69	CBS 4162	The Boxer/Baby Driver (p/s)	7
70	CBS 4916	Cecelia/The only Living Boy In New York	6
65	CBS EP 6053	WEDNESDAY MORNING 3AM (EP)	20
66	CBS EP 6074	I AM A ROCK (EP)	20
67	CBS EP 6360	FEELING GROOVY (EP)	20
68	CBS EP 6400	MRS ROBINSON (EP)	15
66	CBS (S)BPG 62690	THE SOUNDS OF SILENCE (LP, mono)	12
66	CBS (S)BPG 62690	THE SOUNDS OF SILENCE (LP, stereo)	20
66	CBS (S)BPG 62860	PARSLEY, SAGE, ROSEMARY AND THYME (LP, mono)	12
66	CBS (S)BPG 62860	PARSLEY, SAGE, ROSEMARY AND THYME (LP, stereo)	20

(Originally issued with flipback sleeves & textured orange labels.)

67	Allegro ALL 836	SIMON AND GARFUNKEL (LP)	20
68	CBS (S) 70042	THE GRADUATE (LP, soundtrack, blue label, mono/stereo)	12
68	CBS (S) 63370	WEDNESDAY MORNING 3AM (LP, flipback sleeve, textured orange label, mono/stereo)	18
68	CBS (S) 63370	WEDNESDAY MORNING 3AM (LP, flipback sleeve, textured orange label, mono/stereo)	15
72	CBS CQ 30995	BRIDGE OVER TROUBLED WATER (LP, quadrophonic)	18

(see also Paul Simon, Art Garfunkel, Tom & Jerry)

NINA SIMONE

59	Parlophone R 4583	I Loves You Porgy/Love Me Or Leave Me	20
59	Pye International 7N 25029	Solitaire/Chilly Winds Don't Blow	10
63	Colpix PX 200	You Can Have Him/Return Home	10
64	Colpix PX 799	Exactly Like You/The Other Woman	10
65	Philips BF 1388	Don't Let Me Be Misunderstood/Monster	10
65	Philips BF 1415	I Put A Spell On You/Gimme Some	10
66	Philips BF 1465	Either Way I Lose/Break Down And Let It Out	15
69	RCA RCA 1903	Save Me/To Be Young Gifted And Black	15
61	Parlophone GEP 8844	MY BABY JUST CARES FOR ME (EP)	70
62	Parlophone GEP 8864	INTIMATE NINA SIMONE (EP)	25
64	Colpix PXE 303	FINE AND MELLOW (EP)	15
66	Colpix PXE 306	JUST SAY I LOVE HIM (EP)	15
66	Colpix PXE 307	I LOVE TO LOVE (EP)	15
65	Philips BE 12585	DON'T LET ME BE MISUNDERSTOOD (EP)	12
65	Philips BE 12589	STRANGE FRUIT (EP)	12
61	Pye Intl. NPL 28014	AT THE TOWN HALL (LP)	18
62	Pye Jazz NJL 36	FORBIDDEN FRUIT (LP)	20
64	Colpix PXL 419	FORBIDDEN FRUIT (LP, reissue)	15
64	Colpix PXL 421	NINA AT THE VILLAGE GATE (LP)	20
65	Colpix PXL 465	FOLKSY NINA (LP)	20
65	Fontana SFJL 954	TELL ME MORE (LP)	20
65	Philips BL 7662	BROADWAY . . . BLUES . . . BALLADS (LP)	20
65	Philips BL 7671	I PUT A SPELL ON YOU (LP)	20
65	Philips BL 7678	IN CONCERT (LP)	20
66	Philips BL 7683	PASTEL BLUES (LP)	20
66	Philips (S)BL 7722	LET IT ALL OUT (LP)	20
66	Philips (S)BL 7726	WILD IS THE WIND (LP)	20
67	Philips (S)BL 7764	HIGH PRIESTESS OF SOUL (LP)	20
67	RCA RD/SF 7883	SINGS THE BLUES (LP)	20
68	RCA RD/SF 7967	SILK AND SOUL (LP)	20
69	RCA Victor SF 7979	'NUFF SAID (LP)	20
69	RCA SF 8018	TO LOVE SOMEBODY (LP)	20

SUGAR SIMONE

68	Fab FAB 33	I Love My Baby/I'll Keep You Satisfied	18

66	Rainbow RAI 103	Is It Because/I Want To Know	20
67	Rainbow RAI 115	I Love My Baby/I'll Keep You Satisfied	8
67	Sue WI 4029	Suddenly/King Without A Throne	40
67	Go AJ 11409	It's Alright/Take It Easy	30
68	CBS 3250	The Vow/Spinning Wheel	18
69	Doctor Bird DB 1192	Black Is Gold/The Invitation	20
69	Doctor Bird DB 1193	The Squeeze Is On/Tell Me	20
69	Doctor Bird DB 1201	Come And Try/Don't Listen To What They Say	12
69	Fab FAB 106	Boom Biddy Boom/RUDIES: What Can I Do	8
69	Fab FAB 107	I Need A Witness/Johnny Dollar	10
69	Upfront UPF 1	Turns On The Heatwave/Crying Blues	7
70	Beacon BEA 156	Keep On Trying/Only The Lonely	7
70	Beacon BEA 174	Why Can't I Touch You/Gotta Get It Off My Mind	7
73	Smash SAM 2333	Rock And Cry/September	10

(see also Sugar & Dandy, Les Foster, Larry Foster & Soul Explosion, Lance Hannibal)

SIMON PLUG & GRIMES

70	Deram DM 296	Is This A Dream?/I'm Going Home	12
70	President PT 310	Way In, Way Out/Long Long Summer	5
71	President PT 354	Pull Together/I'll Keep Smiling	5

SIMON'S SECRETS

| 68 | CBS 3406 | Naughty Boy/Sympathy | 35 |
| 68 | CBS 3856 | I Know What Her Name Is/Keeping My Head Above Water | 40 |

(see also Secrets, Clifford T. Ward, Martin Raynor & Secrets)

SIMON SISTERS

| 64 | London HLR 9893 | Winkin', Blinkin' And Nod/So Glad I'm Here | 20 |
| 65 | London HLR 9984 | Cuddlebug/No One To Talk My Trouble To | 15 |

NIC SIMPER'S FANDANGO

| 83 | Paro PAR 0S4 | Just Another Day (In The Life Of A Fool)/Wish I'd Never Woke Up | 6 |
| 79 | Gull GULP 1033 | SLIPSTREAMING (LP) | 20 |

(see also Deep Purple, Warhorse)

SIMPLE IMAGE

| 70 | Carnaby CNS 4013 | Spinning Spinning Spinning/Shy Boy | 15 |

SIMPLE MINDS

79	Zoom ZUM 10	Life In A Day/Special View (p/s)	5
79	Zoom ZUM 11	Chelsea Girl/Garden Of Hate (p/s)	5
80	Arista ARIST 325	Changeling/Premonition (live) (p/s)	5
81	Arista ARIST 394	Celebrate/Changeling (p/s)	5
81	Virgin VS 451	Sweat In Bullet/20th Century Promised Land (original limited pressing,non-gatefold p/s)	30
88	Virgin VS 860/VS 817	All The Things She Said/Don't You Forget About Me (Live)//Alive And Kicking/Alive And Kicking (Intrumental) double single pack in PVC sleeve sealed by sticker that states "double pack 2 for the price of 1")	60

(see also Johnny & Self Abusers)

SIMPLICITY PEOPLE

| 73 | Grape GR 3062 | Murderer/BIG YOUTH: The Killer | 12 |
| 73 | Harry J HJ 6649 | Time Is Getting Harder/HARRY J ALLSTARS: Time Is Getting Harder | 6 |

SIMPLY RED

| 85 | Elektra EKT 27P | PICTURE BOOK (LP, picture disc, die-cut sleeve) | 15 |

(see also Frantic Elevators)

BILL SIMPSON

| 64 | Piccadilly 7N 35179 | I Love You For Sentimental Reasons/My Love Is Like A Red Red Rose (p/s) | 8 |

DANNY SIMPSON

| 69 | Trojan TR 653 | Outa Sight/JOHN HOLT: I Want You Closer | 30 |

DUDLEY SIMPSON & BRIAN HODGSON

| 73 | Polydor 2383 210 | IN A COVENT GARDEN (LP) | 25 |

(See also BBC Radiophonic Workshop)

HOKE SIMPSON

| 58 | HMV POP 442 | I Finally Found You/Gi-Gi | 8 |

JEANETTE SIMPSON

67	Giant GN 16	Rain/Whatcha Gonna Do About It	20
68	Giant GN 29	My Baby Just Cares For Me/Don't Let Me Cry No More (with Superboys)	40
68	Giant GN 35	Through Loving You/Send Me Some Lovin' (with Missions)	15

LEO SIMPSON

| 65 | Blue Beat BB 351 | I Love Her So/Good To Be Seen (as Leo Simmo) | 18 |
| 73 | Pyramid PYR 7004 | Waxy Doodle/Go Away | 6 |

(see also Lionel Simpson)

LIONEL SIMPSON

65	Ska Beat JB 205	Tell Me What You Want/Love Is A Game	15
65	Ska Beat JB 221	Red River Valley/Eight People	15
66	Ska Beat JB 233	Give Over/Never Before	15

(see also Leo Simpson)

MARTIN SIMPSON

76	Trailer LER 2099	GOLDEN VANITY (LP, yellow label)	20
81	Waterfront WF 008	SPECIAL AGENT (LP)	12
83	Topic 12TS 430	GRINNING IN YOUR FACE (LP, tan label)	12
85	Topic 12TS 438	SAD OR HIGH KICKING (LP, tan label)	12
86	Dambuster DAM 013	NOBODY'S FAULT BUT MINE (LP)	15

DUDLEY SIMPSON ORCHESTRA

| 78 | BBC RESL 58 | Blake's 7/The Federation March (p/s) | 8 |

RED SIMPSON

| 66 | Capitol ST 2468 | ROLL TRUCK ROLL (LP) | 12 |

VALERIE SIMPSON
72	Tamla Motown STML 11194	EXPOSED (LP)	22

(see also Ashford & Simpson)

CHUCK SIMS
58	London HLR 8577	Little Pigeon/Life Isn't Long Enough	300
58	London HLR 8577	Little Pigeon/Life Isn't Long Enough (78)	60

FRANKIE LEE SIMS
71	Specialty SPE 5009	Married Woman Blues/Lucy Mae Blues	5
71	Specialty SNTF 5004	LUCY MAE BLUES (LP)	15

JOAN SIMS
63	Parlophone R 5021	Oh Not Again Ken/Hurry Up Gran	8
63	Parlophone R 5089	Spring Song/Men	7
67	CBS 202635	Sweet Lovely Whatsisname/The Lass With The Delicate Hair	8

KELLY SIMS
60	Top Rank JAR 321	Betrayed By Love/A Girl In Love	6

SIMS TWINS/VALENTINOS
68	Soul City SCM 001	THE VALENTINOS/THE SIMS TWINS (LP, 1 side each)	60

ZOOT SIMS
57	Esquire EP 183	ZOOT! (EP)	20
57	Esquire EP 204	ZOOT'S CASE (EP)	20
52	Esquire 20-002	ZOOT SIMS QUARTET/QUINTET (10" LP)	40
53	Esquire 20-010	ZOOT SIMS ALLSTARS (10" LP)	35
53	Esquire 20-018	ZOOT SIMS QUARTET/QUINTET (10" LP)	35
54	Vogue LDE 056	ZOOT SIMS GOES TO TOWN (10" LP)	200
55	Esquire 20-040	ZOOT SIMS QUARTET/QUINTET (10" LP)	60
57	Esquire 32-040	ZOOT SIMS SEPTET (LP)	50
58	HMV CLP 1165	GEORGE HANDY COMPOSITIONS (LP)	25
58	HMV CLP 1188	PLAYS FOUR ALTOS (LP)	30
61	Vogue LAE 12309	CHOICE (LP)	30
61	Fontana TFL 5176	ZOOT AT RONNIE SCOTT'S (LP)	200
61	Parlophone PMC 1169	DOWN HOME (LP)	80
62	Fontana (S)TFL 588	ZOOT AT RONNIE SCOTT'S (LP, reissue)	100
62	Fontana 886 151 TY	SOLO FOR ZOOT (LP, also mono [680 982 TL], £50)	175
65	Fontana FJL 123	COOKIN'! (LP)	150
60s	Xtra XTRA 5001	TROTTING! (LP)	15

(see also Sims-Wheeler Vintage Jazz Band)

FRANK SINATRA
53	Columbia SCM 5052	Birth Of The Blues/Why Try To Change Me Now?	20
53	Columbia SCM 5060	You Do Something To Me/Lover	25
53	Columbia SCM 5076	Santa Claus Is Comin' To Town/My Girl	25
54	Capitol CL 14064	Young-At-Heart/Take A Chance	15
54	Capitol CL 14120	Three Coins In The Fountain/I Could Have Told You	20
54	Capitol CL 14174	White Christmas/The Christmas Waltz	15
54	Capitol CL 14188	When I Stop Loving You/It Worries Me	15
55	Capitol CL 14221	Someone To Watch Over Me/The Gal That Got Away	5
55	Capitol CL 14238	Melody Of Love/I'm Gonna Live Till I Die	5
55	Columbia SCM 5167	S'posin'/How Deep Is The Ocean	10
55	Capitol CL 14240	You, My Love/Just One Of Those Things	5
55	Capitol CL 14270	Don't Change Your Mind About Me/Why Should I Cry Over You	5
55	Capitol CL 14292	Two Hearts, Two Kisses (Make One Love)/From The Bottom To The Top	5
55	Capitol CL 14296	Learnin' The Blues/If I Had Three Wishes	5
55	Capitol CL 14326	Not As A Stranger/How Could You Do A Thing Like That To Me	5
55	Capitol CL 14352	My Funny Valentine/I Get A Kick Out Of You	5
55	Capitol CL 14360	It Never Entered My Mind/In The Wee Small Hours Of The Morning	5
55	Capitol CL 14373	Fairy Tale/Same Old Saturday Night	5

(Originally issued with triangular centre; later round-centre copies are worth half this value.)

54	Capitol LC 6654	SONGS FOR YOUNG LOVERS (10")	20
54	Capitol LC 6689	SWING EASY (10") Decca Pressing/EMIo	20
54	Philips BBR 8003	SING AND DANCE WITH FRANK SINATRA (10")	15
55	Capitol LC 6702	IN THE WEE SMALL HOURS VOL. 1 (10")	20
55	Capitol LC 6705	IN THE WEE SMALL HOURS VOL. 2 (10")	20
55	Philips BBR 8040	YOUNG AT HEART (10", with Doris Day)	12
55	Philips BBR 8038	FABULOUS FRANK (10")	12
56	Capitol LCT 6106	SONGS FOR SWINGIN' LOVERS	15
56	Capitol LCT 6111	FRANK SINATRA CONDUCTS TONE POEMS OF COLOUR	15
56	HMV DLP 1123	IT'S D-LOVELY (with Tommy Dorsey Orchestra)	15
57	Philips BBR 8114	CHRISTMAS DREAMING (10")	15
57	Philips BBL 7137	DORIS AND FRANK (6 tracks each by Doris Day & Frank Sinatra)	12
57	Philips BBL 7168	FRANKIE	12
57	Philips BBL 7180	THAT OLD FEELING	12
58	Fontana TFL 5000	THE VOICE	12
58	Fontana TFL 5006	ADVENTURES OF THE HEART	12
58	Fontana TFL 5030	THE FRANK SINATRA STORY	12
59	Fontana TFL 5048	PUT YOUR DREAMS AWAY	12
62	Reprise R(9) 1006	SINATRA SINGS GREAT SONGS FROM GREAT BRITAIN (mono)	20
62	Reprise R(9) 1006	SINATRA SINGS GREAT SONGS FROM GREAT BRITAIN (stereo)	30
83	Mobile Fidelity SC 1	THE SINATRA COLLECTION (16-LPs in silver box, with Swing Easy LP unavailable elsewhere)	60
85	Capitol SINATRA 20	FRANK SINATRA: THE CAPITOL YEARS (20-LP, box set)	40
90	Capitol C1-94777	THE CAPITOL YEARS (5-LP, box set)	12

(see also Nancy Sinatra, Count Basie, Tommy Dorsey, Dean Martin, Doris Day)

FRANK & NANCY SINATRA
67	Reprise REP 30082	SOMETHING STUPID (EP)	10
69	Reprise R(S)LP 1026	THE SINATRA FAMILY WISH YOU A HAPPY CHRISTMAS (LP)	15

NANCY SINATRA
61	Reprise RS 20017	Cuff Links And Tie Clips/Not Just Your Friend (with p/s)	20

MINT VALUE £

61	Reprise RS 20017	Cuff Links And Tie Clips/Not Just Your Friend	10
62	Reprise RS 20045	To Know Him Is To Love Him/Like I Do	12
63	Reprise RS 20144	I See The Moon/Put Your Head On My Shoulder	10
64	Reprise RS 20335	True Love/The Answer To Everything	8
65	Reprise RS 20407	So Long Babe/If He'd Loved Me	10
66	Reprise RS 20432	These Boots Are Made For Walkin'/The City Never Sleeps At Night	6
66	Reprise R 20461	How Does That Grab You Darlin'/I Move Around	7
66	Reprise RS 20491	Friday's Child/Hutchinson Jail	7
66	Reprise RS 20514	In Our Time/Leave My Dog Alone	7
67	Reprise RS 20527	Sugar Town/Summer Wine	7
67	Reprise RS 20559	Love Eyes/Coastin'	7
67	Reprise RS 20620	Lightning's Girls/Until It's Time For You To Go	8
69	Reprise RS 20869	The Highway Song/Are You Growing Tired Of My Love	7
77	Private Stock PVT 114	It's For My Dad/A Gentle Man Like You	7
66	Reprise REP 30069	RUN FOR YOUR LIFE (EP)	20
66	Reprise REP 30072	I MOVE AROUND (EP)	15
67	Reprise REP 30080	SORRY 'BOUT THAT (EP)	15
67	Reprise REP 30086	NASHVILLE NANCY (EP)	15
66	Reprise R 6202	BOOTS (LP)	25
66	Reprise R 6207	HOW DOES THAT GRAB YOU? (LP)	25
66	Reprise R(S)LP 6221	NANCY IN LONDON (LP)	30
67	Reprise RLP 6239	SUGAR (LP)	25
67	Reprise R(S)LP 6251	COUNTRY, MY WAY (LP)	20
68	Reprise R(S)LP 6277	MOVIN' WITH NANCY (LP)	20
69	Reprise RSLP 6333	NANCY (LP, flipback sleeve, laminated front)	20
73	RCA SF 8331	WOMAN (LP)	15
72	RCA DPS 2037	THIS IS (2-LP)	20

(see also Elvis Presley)

NANCY SINATRA & LEE HAZLEWOOD

67	Reprise RS 20629	Lady Bird/Sand	7
67	Reprise RS 23215	Some Velvet Morning/Tony Rome	8
71	Reprise K 14093	Did You Ever?/Back On The Road Again	6
67	Reprise REP 30083	JACKSON (EP)	15
68	Reprise R(S)LP 6273	NANCY & LEE (LP)	20
71	RCA Victor SF 8240	DID YOU EVER? (LP)	18

(see also Lee Hazlewood, Frank Sinatra)

BETTY SINCLAIR

70	Torpedo TOR 19	Why Why Why/HOT ROD ALL STARS: Fistful Of Dollars	45

JIMMY SINCLAIR

62	Wasp W005	To Prove My Love/Verona	12

JIMMY SINCLAIR & TRENTON SPENCE ORCHESTRA

61	Blue Beat BB 47	Verona/To Prove My Love	10

(see also Jimmy Sinclair)

PAUL SINCLAIR

76	Angen ANG 115	Jah Is My Saviour/Version	8

WINSTON SINCLAIR

69	Nu Beat NB 026	Another Heartache/Come On Little Girl	8

(see also Harmonisers)

SINDELFINGEN

73	Medway	ODGIPIG (LP, private pressing, with insert)	550
90	Cenotaph CEN 111	ODGIPIG/TRIANGLE (2-LP, reissue with live album, 300 only)	25

SINEWAVE

72	Chapter One SCH 172	Clochemerle/Star Trek	10

PETE SINFIELD

73	Manticore K 43501	STILL (LP, textured gatefold pink sleeve)	25
73	Manticore K 43501	STILL (LP, textured gatefold blue sleeve)	20

(see also Emerson Lake & Palmer, King Crimson, Greg Lake)

SINGAPORE

79	SRTS/79/CUS 274	Launching/A Bird With No Wings	200

SINGAROUND

69	G. Guinea GSGL 10436	SINGAROUND (LP)	15

JAMES SINGER

80	RTC 001	Black British/Wicked Man/CULTURE MARK: WIcked Babylon (12")	8

RAY SINGER

64	Ember EMB S 187	Tell Me Now/I'm Comin' Home	10
64	Ember EMB S 199	It's Gotta Be/Hey, Who?	10
65	Ember EMB S 215	I'm The Richest Man Alive/Pretty Little Rambling Rose (in p/s)	15
65	Ember EMB S 215	I'm The Richest Man Alive/Pretty Little Rambling Rose	10
65	Fontana TF 621	You'll Come Crying To Me/Who Can I Talk To About You	10
67	Ember EMB S 231	What's Done Has Been Done/Won't It Be Fine	60
66	Ember EMB 3364	RAY SINGER (LP)	40

(see also Nirvana [U.K.])

SUSAN SINGER

62	Oriole CB 1703	Gee It's Great To Be Young/Hello First Love	20
62	Oriole CB 1741	Bobby's Loving Touch/Johnny Summertime	150
62	Oriole CB 1778	Love Me With All Your Heart/Autumn Leaves	20
63	Oriole CB 1802	Lock Your Heart Away/Answer To A Prayer	20
63	Oriole CB 1882	I Know (You Don't Love Me No More)/That Old Feeling	20

(see also Susan Holiday)

SINGERS AND PLAYERS

81	Silent SSH3	Love All Over The Place/Over You (p/s)	15
81	On U Sound LP 5	WAR OF WORDS (LP)	15

83	On U Sound LP 23	STAGGERING HEIGHTS (LP) 15

SINGING BELLES

60	Top Rank JAR 350	The Empty Mailbox/Someone Loves You, Joe..........................8

SINGING DOGS

57	Pye NEP 24029	SINGING DOGS (EP) 10

SINGING LOINS

91	Hangman HANG 44 UP	SONGS FOR THE ORGAN (LP)...15
93	Hangman HANG 51 UP	STEAK AND GRAVY (LP) 15

(see also Billy Childish & Singing Loins)

SINGING POSTMAN

66	Parlophone R 5505	The Ladies Darts Team/Roundabout 7
67	Parlophone R 5584	Mind How You Go/Daddy's Trombone 7
67	Parlophone R 5632	Sound Barrier/Old North Walsham Line 7
64	Ralph Tuck Promotions Ltd. BEV EP 153	Come Along A Me/Moind Yer Hid Boy/Hev Yew Gotta Loight Boy/Miss From Diss (EP) 10
65	Ralph Tuck BEV EP 179	BBC SINGING POSTMAN (EP) 10

SINGING PRINCIPAL

73	Action ACT 4608	Thank You Baby/Women's Lib 60

SINGLE FACTOR

84	SF Records SINFAX 001	Fresh Upon Her Lips/I Think I'm Falling In Love (p/s, 2 inserts) 50

MARGIE SINGLETON

60	Melodisc 45-1544	Angel Hands/The Eyes Of Love 15
62	Mercury AMT 1197	Magic Star/Only Your Shadow Knows 20
68	Fontana TL 5456	SINGS COUNTRY WITH SOUL (LP) 18

SINISTER DUCKS

83	Situation 2 SIT 25	Suicide: March Of The Sinister Ducks/Homicide: Old Gangsters Never (foldout p/s) 10

(see also Bauhaus)

SINITTA

83	Midas 12MID 3	Never Too Late (Special Extended US Mix)/Never Too Late (Instrumental) (12", p/s) 40

EARL SINK(S)

61	Warner Bros WB 38	Look For Me, I'll Be There/Super Market (as Earl Sink) 15
61	Warner Bros WB 51	Superstitious/Little Suzie Parker 20
63	Capitol CL 15310	Looking For Love/Raining On My Side Of Town (as Earl Sinks) 15

(see also Crickets, Sinx Mitchell)

SINNER

79	Whitetower AMC 705	Need Your Love/Beggar/God's In His Heaven (foldout p/s)..........75

SINNERMAN & SARA

68	MGM 1450	Don't Think Twice It's Allright/Buffalo Boy 10
68	MGM MGM-C(S) 8099	SINNERMAN AND SARA (LP) 20

SINNERS

63	Columbia DB 7158	I Can't Stand It/If You Leave Me Now 10
64	Columbia DB 7295	It's So Exciting/Leave Him 10

(see also Linda Laine & Sinners)

SINS OF THE FLESH

90s	Plastic Head 014	In The Image Of Torture (12", p/s)..10

SIOUX

73	SRT SRT 73274	Prosmoe/Warlove/You're All I Need/Happiness In The Sky (EP) 75

SIOUXSIE & BANSHEES

78	Polydor 2059 052	Hong Kong Garden/Voices (10,000 only in gatefold p/s; beige plastic, silver plastic, red plastic or red paper label) 18
78	Polydor 2059 052	Hong Kong Garden/Voices (p/s) 5
79	Polydor 2059 151	Mittageisen (Metal Postcard)/Love In A Void (p/s).....................5
80	Polydor POSPX 205	Israel (Extended)/Red Over White (Extended) (12", a few with 'Made In England' credit, most with 'Made In France' credit)..........8
83	Fan Club FILE 1	Head Cut/Running Town (freebie)...30
85	Wonderland SHE 8	Overground/Placebo Effect (p/s)..6
85	Wonderland SHE 9	Cities In Dust/An Execution (poster p/s)...................................5
85	Wonderland SHEX 9	Cities In Dust/An Execution/Quarterdrawing Of The Dog (12", p/s, banned' picture label) 8
86	Wonderland SHEDP 10	Candyman/Lullaby (with free 2nd single, gatefold p/s, 2,000 only)..........8
87	Wonderland SHEPK 4	The Passenger/Hall Of Mirrors/You're Lost Little Girl/Sea Breezes/This Town Ain't Big Enough For Both Of Us/Gun (3 X promo 7" in plain black sleeves in foldout stickered and printed PVC wallet, single cat. no's SHESP 1/2/3) 20
87	Wonderland SHEG 11	This Wheel's On Fire/Shooting Sun/Sleepwalking (On The High Wire)/She's Cracked (numbered double pack, gatefold p/s) 6
88	Spiral Scratch SCRATCH 2	An Interview With... (free with Spiral Scratch mag, 5,000 only) 6
78	Polydor POLD 5009	THE SCREAM (LP, with inner sleeve; with labels reversed) 12
79	Polydor POLD 5024	JOIN HANDS (LP, gatefold. with inner sleeve) 12
87	Wonderland SHELP 4	THROUGH THE LOOKING GLASS (LP, mispressing, 1 side plays Jimi Hendrix's "War Heroes") 25
92	Polydor 517160	TWICE UPON A TIME - THE SINGLES (2-LP) 30

(see also Cure, Glove)

SIR ALEC & HIS BOYS

67	Deram DM 116	I'm A Believer/Green Green Grass Of Home 8

SIR ALICK & PHRASER

82	Recommended/Black Noise 7 NO 5	In Search Of The Perfect Baby/PROLIFIKURDS: Nursery Crymes (printed p/s in PVC sleeve or standard p/s) 10

(see also Homosexuals)

SIR BEANZ OBE

99	Mapache Chet002	MARS ATTACKS (EP) 8

SIR CHAUNCEY

60	Warner Bros. WB 9	Beautiful Obsession/Tenderfoot 5

MINT VALUE £

| 60 | Warner Bros. WB 36 | Midi-Midinette/Beyond Our Love | 5 |

SIR (CLANCY) COLLINS BAND

68	Collins Downbeat CR 005	Sock It Softly (with Bob Stackie)/LESTER STERLING, SIR COLLINS & BAND: Three Wise Men	45
68	Collins Downbeat CR 0011	Collins And The Boys/Bob Stackie In Soho (both with Bob Stackie)	40
68	Collins Downbeat CR 0017	Soul Feelings/SIR COLLINS: Hello Stella	70
69	Duke DU 46	Black Panther/I Want To Be Loved	200
69	Duke DU 47	Black Diamonds (with Diamonds)/DIAMONDS: I Remember	40
69	Duke DU 55	Brother Moses/Funny Familiar Feeling (both with Earthquakes)	40
69	Duke DU 69	Pair Of Wings/I Can't Stop Loving	50

(see also Bob Stackie, Earthquakes, Collins Band, Owen Gray)

SIR COXSONE SOUND (LLOYD COXON)

| 75 | Safari SFA 100 | KING OF DUB ROCK (LP) | 35 |
| 76 | Regal RLP 001 | KING OF DUB ROCK PART 2 (LP) | 20 |

SIR D'S GROUP

| 61 | Blue Beat BB 66 | Hey Diddle Diddle (with K. Brown)/Pocket Money (with Mossman & Zeddze) | 25 |

(see also Kent Brown & Rainbows)

SIR DOUGLAS QUINTET

65	London HLU 9964	She's About A Mover/We'll Take Our Last Walk Tonight	12
65	London HLU 9982	The Tracker/Blue Norther	12
65	London HLU 10001	The Story Of John Hardy/In Time	8
66	London HLU 10019	The Rains Came/Bacon Fat	8
69	Mercury MF 1079	Mendocino/I Wanna Be Your Mama Again	12
69	Mercury MF 1129	Dynamite Woman/Too Many Dociled Minds	8
69	London HLU 10248	She's About A Mover/The Rains Came (reissue)	6
65	London HA-U 8311	THE SIR DOUGLAS QUINTET (LP)	60
69	Mercury SMCL 20160	MENDOCINO (LP)	30
69	Mercury SMCL 20186	TOGETHER AFTER FIVE (LP)	30
75	Oval OVLM 5001	MENDOCINO (LP, with insert)	15

SIREN (1)

71	Dandelion DAN 7002	Strange Locomotion/I'm All Aching (label also lists K 19004)	6
69	Dandelion 63755	SIREN (LP, laminated front sleeve, black/red/silver labels)	45
71	Dandelion DAN 8001	STRANGE LOCOMOTION (LP, gatefold sleeve)	45
71	Dandelion DAN 8001	STRANGE LOCOMOTION (LP, with later label listing K 49001)	25

SIREN (2)

| 84 | Distant Cousins DC4R | Deceiving Lies/American Girl (white or black sleeve) | 10 |

SIR GIBBS

| 68 | Amalgamated AMG 822 | People Grudgeful/Pan Ya Machet (both sides actually by Pioneers) | 50 |

SIR HARRY

71	Duke DU 127	Last Call/ORGAN D: Hot Organ	10
72	Duke DU 136	Apples To Apples/DRUM BEAT ALL STARS: Good Life	10
72	Bullet BU 519	Mr. Parker's Daughter/U.ROY: On Top Of The Peak	12
72	Downtown DT 493	Meet The Boss/Musical Fight	12
73	Downtown DT 504	Apollo 17 (with Cables)/Uptown Rock	12

(see also Barbara Jones)

SIR HENRY (& HIS BUTLERS)

68	Columbia DB 8351	Camp/Pretty Style (as Sir Henry & His Butlers)	10
68	Columbia DB 8497	The Rolo Sensation (Camp)/Pretty Style (reissue, as Sir Henry & His Butlers)	10
70	Columbia DB 8740	Annie Got A Date/Like A Rose	8

SIR HORATIO

| 82 | Rock Steady/666 Mix 1T | Abracadubra/Sommadub (12", plain sleeve) | 15 |

(see also A Certain Ratio)

SIR LLOYD

| 71 | Lion LEO 1 | Mosi/Nursery Rhyme Version | 15 |

SIR LORD COMIC

67	Doctor Bird DB 1019	Ska-ing West/MAYTALS: If You Act This Way	40
67	Doctor Bird DB 1070	The Great Wuga Wuga (with Cowboys)/THREE TOPS: Feel So Lonesome	45
70	Pressure Beat PR 5507	Jack Of My Trade/CYNTHIA RICHARDS: United We Stand	70

(see also Lord Comic)

SIRUS

| 91 | White 002 | THE ONE AND ONLY (EP) | 60 |
| 93 | SBP SBPR004 | Clubland/DETT (12") | 8 |

SIR WASHINGTON

69	Star ST 1	Apollo 12/When You Kiss Me	12
70	Saga BC 100	Apollo 13/Space	10
70	Saga BC 102	Let There Be Peace in The World/Pharoah's Walk	10

SISTER

| 70 | Camel CA 55 | Feel It/MAYTONES: Serious | 12 |
| 73 | Camel CA 106 | Every Day Is The Same Kind Of Thing/Sweat Of Your Brow | 10 |

SISTER CANDY

| 83 | Vista Sounds VSLP 4026 | BLACK CULTURE (LP) | 20 |

SISTERHOOD

| 86 | Merciful Release SIS 010 | Giving Ground (RSV)/Giving Ground (AV) (p/s) | 5 |

(see also Sisters Of Mercy, James Ray & Performance)

SISTER RAIN

| 88 | A Serene | BURT REYNOLDS (12", EP) | 12 |

SISTERS

| 73 | Bell BELL 1307 | Kick Your Boots Off/Driving Me Home | 15 |
| 74 | Warner Brothers K 16445 | There's A Raver Coming Home/Help The Music | 8 |

SISTERS LOVE

70	A&M AMS 772	Forget It, I've Got It/Eye To Eye	5
70	A&M AMS 808	The Bigger Your Love/Piece Of My Heart	5
72	Tamla Motown TMG 828	Mr. Fix It Man/You've Got To Make Your Choice	8
73	Mowest MW 3009	I'm Learning To Trust My Man/Try It You'll Like It	10
75	Tamla Motown TMG 1002	I'm Learning To Trust My Man/Try It You'll Like It (reissue)	8

SISTERS OF MERCY

80	Merciful Release MR 7	The Damage Done/Watch/Home Of The Hitmen (p/s, 1,000 only; beware of counterfeits without 'MR 7' matrix number)	300
82	CNT CNT 002	Body Electric/Adrenochrome (p/s)	85
82	Merciful Release MR 015	Alice/Floorshow (white background p/s)	30
84	Merciful Release/WEA	ALICE/TEMPLE OF LOVE/REPTILE HOUSE/BODY AND SOUL (4 x 12" box set, promo only)	100
84	Merciful Release MR 033	Walk Away/Poison Door (p/s, with flexidisc "Long Train" [SAM 218])	15
84	Merciful Release MR 033T	Walk Away/Poison Door/On The Wire (12", p/s, with flexi "Long Train")	15
85	Merciful Release MR 335	No Time To Cry/Blood Money (p/s)	6
85	Merciful Release MR 035T	No Time To Cry/Blood Money/Bury Me Deep (12", p/s)	8
88	Merciful Release MR 43TB	Dominion (Extended)/Untitled/Sandstorm/Emma (12", box set with poster)	15
88	Merciful Release MR 43CD	Dominion (Extended)/Untitled/Sandstorm/Ozymandias (3" CD, black disc with adaptor, 5" case)	12
88	Merciful Release MR 44CD	Lucretia My Reflection (Extended 9.52)/Long Train (1984) (3" CD, with adaptor, 5" case)	12

(see also Mission, Sisterhood, Ghost Dance, Dead Or Alive)

SITUATION

66	CBS 202392	Situation Now/Time	30

SIVUCA

74	Vanguard VSD 79337	SIVUCA (LP)	30

SIX OF ONE

64	Mercury MF 812	He's The One You Love/I Love My Little Girl	10

SIX TEASERS

89	Kent 6T 5	Doing The Hundred/WALLY COX: This Man Wants You	15

SIX MINUTE WAR

80	(No label or cat no)	75P EP (7", fold-out p/s, 1st issue with 'soldier' sleeve)	10
80	(No label or cat no)	MORE SHORT SONGS (7" EP, fold-out p/s)	10
81	(No label or cat no)	SLIGHTLY LONGER SONGS (7" EP, fold-out, p/s)	10
81	(No label or cat no)	75P EP (7", fold-out p/s, 2nd issue with different black sleeve stating 33.3 rpm)	8

SIXPENCE

67	London HLJ 10124	You're The Love/What To Do	10

EARL SIXTEEN

79	Sufferers Heights SUFF 007	African Tribesman/MIKEY DREAD: Yoruba Dub (12")	20
79	Cha Cha CHAD 16	The World Has Begun (with the Heptones)/Make Up Your Mind (12")	20
81	DATC DCD 004	MR D.J./GILLY BUCHANAN: Ghetto Youths/DATC MUSIC STABLE : Dub (12")	25
81	Dread At The Controls DATCLP003	REGGAE SOUND (LP)	50
83	Vista VSLP 4023	SHINING STAR (LP)	25

SIX TEENS

56	London HLU 8345	A Casual Look/Teen Age Promise	350
56	London HLU 8345	A Casual Look/Teen Age Promise (78)	50

SIXTH COMM

87	Eyas Media EYAS 002	CONTENT WITH BLOOD/TURN OF THE WHEEL (LP, embossed, textured sleeve, 2,000 only)	20
87	Eyas Media EYAS 005	TASTE FOR FLESH (1st 2,000 in laminated, full-cover sleeve)	20
87	Eyas Media EYAS 005	TASTE FOR FLESH (LP)	12
88	Eyas Media EYAS 006	FRUITS OF YGGDRASIL (LP, limited issue, 669 copies only)	25
90	Eyas Media EYAS 013	ASYLUM (LP)	15
90	Eyas Media EYAS 071	COMING OF SEVEN (LP)	12

65 DAYS OF STATIC

06	monotreme MONO 21-7	Radio Protector/Asphalt & Trouble (p/s, 1500 only, 1000 with unique polaroid photos)	6

64 SPOONS

78	Bushbaby	LADIES DON'T HAVE WILLIES (EP)	10

SIZE SEVEN GROUP

64	Rendevous HS 1/PR 5020	Crying My Heart Out/So How Come	20
65	Mercury MF 845	Where Do We Go From Here/Till I Die	10
65	Mercury MF 896	In Time/Walking Proud	10
65	Mercury MF 896	It's Got To Be Love/I Met Her In The Rain	8

SKA CHAMPIONS

65	Blue Beat BB 305	My Tears/Yesterday's Dreams	20

SKA CITY ROCKERS

80	Inferno BEAT 1	Time Is Tight/Roadrunner/You Don't Know Like I Know (p/s)	6
80	Inferno BEAT 1	Time Is Tight/Roadrunner/You Don't Know Like I Know (12", p/s)	10

SKA-DOWS

80	Cheapskate CHEAP 1	Apache/The Tune That Time Forgot (p/s)	7
80	Cheapskate CHEAP 4	Telstar/Yes Yes Yes (p/s)	8
81	Cheapskate CHEAP 25	Yes Yes Yes/Twice (p/s)	8
81	Penthouse PENT 7	Ska's On 45/Rhapsody In Buh (plain stickered sleeve)	6
81	Penthouse PENT 127	Ska's On 45/The Ska-Dows Live (Let's Twist Again/Everybody Knows It's Shocking/Aye-Ho - Kinky Reggae) (12", p/s)	12
81	Cheapskate CHEAP 36	Ska's On 45/Rhapsody In Buh (p/s, reissue)	6
81	Cheapskate CHEAPT 36	Ska's On 45/The Ska-Dows Live (Let's Twist Again/Everybody Knows It's Shocking/Aye-Ho - Kinky Reggae) (12", p/s, reissue)	8
82	Cheapskate CHEAP 41	We Gotta Get Out Of This Place/Ska'd For Life	5
82	Cheapskate SKATE 3	SKA'D FOR LIFE (LP)	15

SKA KINGS

64	Atlantic AT 4003	Jamaica Ska (actually by Keith Lynn & Ken Lazarus, & Byron Lee/Dragonaires)/Oil In My Lamp (actually by Eric Morris with Byron Lee & Dragonaires)	30
65	Parlophone R 5338	Bimbo/Ska'ville	10

SKANNA

92	White House WYHS 010	Intimidator/Jungle Rain/Cease Fire/Dreamin' (12")	20
93	White House WYHS 013	The Future/Nightstalker/Intimidator (Technoid Mix)/Exit The Lights (12")	50
93	Skanna 03	NIGHT STALKER EP (12")	50
93	Skanna 04	Until The Night Is Morning/Untitled (12")	50
93	Skanna 05	Heaven/Run To Me/This Way (12")	30
94	Skanna 07	The Greatest Thing (Summertime Mix)/The Greatest Thing/Heaven (Remix) (12")	12
94	Skanna 08	All You Wanted/The Greatest Thing (Criminal Minds Mix) (12")	15
96	Skanna 09	Find Me/Find Me (Classic Skanna Mix) (12")	20

(see also The Joker)

SKAOS

88	Unicorn PHZA 24	BEWARE!...IS APPROACHING (LP)	12
90	Unicorn PHZA 56	CATCH THIS BEAT (LP)	12

SKATALITES (JAMAICA)

65	Island WI 161	Trip To Mars/DOTTIE & BONNIE: Bunch Of Roses	45
65	Island WI 164	Good News/OWEN & LEON: The Fits Is On Me	25
65	Island WI 168	Guns Of Navarone (actually by Roland Alphonso & Studio One Orchestra)/Marcus Garvey (actually "Where's Marcus Garvey" by Bongoman Byfield)	20
65	Island WI 175	Dragon Weapon/DESMOND DEKKER & FOUR ACES: It Was Only A Dream	100
65	Island WI 191	Dr. Kildare/Sucu Sucu	75
65	Island WI 207	Ball O' Fire/LINVAL SPENCER: Can't Go On	30
65	Island WI 226	Dick Tracy/RITA & SOULETTES: One More Chance	75
65	Island WI 228	Beardman Ska/BONNIE & RITA: Bless You	20
65	Island WI 244	Lucky Seven/JUSTIN HINDS & DOMINOES: Never Too Young	20
66	Island WI 260	Independent Anniversary Ska (I Should Have Known Better)/WAILERS: Jumbie Jamboree	80
65	Ska Beat JB 177	Latin Goes Ska/LORD TANAMO: Night Food Ska	35
65	Ska Beat JB 178	Silver Dollar/My Business	20
65	Ska Beat JB 182	Street Corner/DREAMLETS: Really Now	30
65	Ska Beat JB 206	Timothy/KING SCRATCH & DYNAMITES: Gumma	40
73	Trojan Maxi TRM 9008	Guns Of Navarone/Bonanza Ska/Napolean Solo	5
75	Tropical ALO64	Jumbo Malt/747 Dub (as Original Skatalites)	10
67	Studio One SOL 9006	SKA AUTHENTIC (LP)	300

(see also Justin Hinds, Deltas, Four Aces, Maytals, Jackie Opel, Joe White, Jackie Mittoo)

SKATALITES (U.K.)

68	Decca F 12743	Don't Knock It/I Know	10
69	Spark SRL 1034	Cos You're The One I Love/Please Let Me Hide	10

SKAVENGERS

80	Identity Discs ID 001	Party Girls/Go To Pieces/Happy	10

SK'BOO

70s	Cucumber CUE 1001	It's A Hard Road/Music Is Life/Talking Pictures/God's Peace In Mind	5

(see also Them)

BOBBY SKEL

64	London HLU 9942	Kiss And Run/Say It Now	15

SKELETAL FAMILY

83	Luggage RRP 00724	Trees/Just A Friend (foldout p/s)	12
86	Cave CAVE IN 1	Sharp Cheekbones In Black Clothing/Blood-Stained (p/s)	12
84	Red Rhino REDL LP 44	BURNING OIL (LP, picture inner and A5 booklet)	12
85	Red Rhino REDLP 57	FUTILE COMBAT (LP)	15

(see also Ghost Dance)

SKELETON CREW

87	B BS 1	BOOGIE-WOOGIE, SKIFFLE & BLUES (12" EP, p/s)	15
88	B BS 2	House Of The Rising Sun/Hurricane Janine (white label promo only)	15

(see also King Earl Boogie Band, Manfred Mann's Earth Band)

SKELLATON

94	Viceroy GREEB028	Bangers 'n' Mash (12")	20

SKEPTIX

82	Zenon SKEP 001	Routine Machine/Curfew (p/s)	15
83	Zenon SKEP 002	Scarred For Life/Born To Lose/Peaceforce (p/s)	15
83	Zenon SKEP 003	RETURN TO HELL (EP)	15

SKERNE

81	Guardian GRC 81	BETTER LATE THAN NEVER (LP, private pressing)	15

SKETTO

71	Big Shot BI 596	Know Your Friend/Three Sevens Version	15

(Father Sketto, Ruddy and Sketto)

FATHER SKETTO

73	Pama PM 877	Big Nine/RECO'S GROUP: Old Lady	5

(see also Sketto Rich, Ruddy & Sketto)

SKID

77	Galaxy GY 118	I Saw Her Standing There/Endless Sleep	15

SKIDDY & DETROIT

72	Grape GR 3030	The Exile Song/BUNNY GALE: In The Burning Sun Joh-Ho	8

ALAN SKIDMORE (QUINTET)

69	Deram Nova SDN 11	ONCE UPON A TIME (LP)	150
71	Philips 6308 041	T.C.B. (LP)	130

(see also John Mayall's Bluesbreakers, Brian Bennett, Centipede)

JIMMY SKIDMORE
72	DJM DJSL 026	SKID MARKS (LP)	50

SKID ROW (IRELAND)
70	Song SO 002	New Places Old Faces/Misdemeanour Dream Felicity (Irish pressing)	100
70	Song SO003	Saturday Morning Man (Irish pressing)	25
70	CBS 4893	Sandie's Gone (Parts 1 & 2)	15
71	CBS 7181	Night Of The Warm Witch/Mr. Deluxe	10
70	CBS 63965	SKID (LP, orange label, red & blue sleeve)	50
71	CBS 64411	34 HOURS (LP, gatefold sleeve, orange label)	40

(see also Gary Moore, Thin Lizzy, Peggy's Leg, UFO)

SKIDS
78	No Bad NB 1	Charles/Reasons/Test Tube Babies (p/s)	10
78	Virgin VS 227	Sweet Suburbia/Open Sound (p/s, white vinyl)	5
79	Virgin VS 262	Masquerade/Out Of Town//Another Emotion/Aftermath Dub (double pack)	5
79	Virgin VS 306	Working For The Yankee Dollar/Vanguard's Crusage//All The Young Dudes/Hymns From A Haunted Ballroom (double pack)	5
79	Virgin V 2116	SCARED TO DANCE (LP, blue vinyl, withdrawn)	300
79	Virgin V 2138	DAYS IN EUROPA (LP, with insert, 1st pressing with withdrawn cover featuring German 'gothic' lettering & 1936 Olympics picture)	12
80	Virgin V 2174	THE ABSOLUTE GAME (LP, with free LP "Strength Through Joy" [VDJ 33])	12

(see also Big Country)

BJORN SKIFS
78	EMI EMI 2785	When The Night Comes/Don't Stop Now	6
81	EMI EMI 5172	Haunted By A Dream/Fangad I En Drom	8

SKILLETS
70	Pantonic PAN 6303	BOTH SIDES NOW (LP)	15

SKIN
80s	Product Inc. 33 PROD 11	SHAME, HUMILITY, REVENGE (LP, with inner)	12

SKIN ALLEY
70	CBS 5045	Tell Me/Better Be Blind	20
72	Transatlantic BIG 506	You Got Me Danglin'/Skin Valley Serenade	8
72	Transatlantic BIG 511	In The Midnight Hour/Broken Eggs	8
73	Transatlantic BIG 514	If Only I Had The Time/Instrumental	10
69	CBS 63847	SKIN ALLEY (LP, laminated front sleeve, orange label)	110
70	CBS 64140	TO PAGHAM AND BEYOND (LP, gatefold sleeve, orange label)	50
72	Transatlantic TRA 260	TWO QUID DEAL (LP, laminated front with inner sleeve & poster)	45
73	Transatlantic TRA 273	SKIN TIGHT (LP)	18
75	Klik KLP 9007	BAG-O-WIRE (LP)	15

SKIN DEEP (1)
85	Enemy ENEMY 1	FOOTBALL VIOLENCE (EP)	200

SKIN DEEP (2)
88	Skank LP 103	MORE THAN SKIN DEEP (LP)	15

SKIN, FLESH & BONES
74	Pyramid PYR 7014	Butter Te Fish/Bammie And Fish	5
74	Opal PAL100	Man Come, Man Go/Guitar Rhythm	15
79	Love LPLV02	FIGHTING DUB (LP)	50

(see also Vincent Gordon, Cynthia Richards)

J SCOTT SKINNER
75	Topic 12T 280	STRATHSPEY KING (LP, blue label)	15

JIMMIE SKINNER
59	Mercury AMT 1030	Walkin' My Blues Away/Dark Hollow (78 rpm = £15)	15
59	Mercury AMT 1062	John Wesley Hardin/Misery Loves Company	10
60	Mercury AMT 1088	Riverboat Gambler/Married To A Friend	5
60	Mercury AMT 1117	Reasons To Live/I'm A Lot More Lonesome Now	5
64	London RE-B 1421	KENTUCKY COLONEL VOL. 1 (EP)	10
64	London RE-B 1422	KENTUCKY COLONEL VOL. 2 (EP)	10
64	London RE-B 1423	KENTUCKY COLONEL VOL. 3 (EP)	10

JIMMIE SKINNER/GEORGE JONES
59	Mercury ZEP 10012	COUNTRY AND WESTERN (EP, 2 tracks each)	10

SKINNYMAN/DJ FLIP
05	Netgroove NET7003	Forever Rangers/Not Bonny And Clyde (7" - 500 pressed)	5

SKIP BIFFERTY
67	RCA Victor RCA 1621	On Love/Cover Girl	30
67	RCA Victor RCA 1648	Happy Land/Reason To Live	40
68	RCA Victor RCA 1720	Man In Black/Mr. Money Man	55
68	RCA Victor RD/SF 7941	SKIP BIFFERTY (LP, black label)	300
68	RCA Victor RD/SF 7941	SKIP BIFFERTY (LP, later pressing with orange label)	150

(see also Chosen Few, Heavy Jelly, Griffin, Graham Bell, Arc, Bell & Arc, Every Which Way, Loving Awareness)

SKIP & FLIP
59	Top Rank JAR 156	It Was I/Lunch Hour	10
59	Top Rank JAR 248	Fancy Nancy/It Could Be	15
60	Top Rank JAR 358	Cherry Pie/(I'll Quit) Cryin' Over You	10

(see also Gary Paxton, Skip Battin, Hollywood Argyles)

SKI PATROL
80	Clever Metal VIN 1	Everything Is Temporary/Silent Screams (p/s)	10
80	Malicious Damage MD 2	Agent Orange/Driving (p/s, with insert)	12
81	Malicious Damage MD 3	Cut/Faith In Transition (p/s)	10

(see also Wall)

SKITZO
86	Nervous NERD 028	SKITZO MANIA (LP)	12
88	Nervous NERD 039	TERMINAL DAMAGE (LP)	12

MINT VALUE £

SAM SKLAIR
| 69 | Pye 7N 25488 | Zulu Warrior/Phata Phata | 15 |

YANI SKORDALIDIS
| 75 | Pinnacle P81413 | Little Drummer Boy/Here Pussy Pussy | 15 |

SKREAM
06	Big Apple BAM 007	Acid People/Get Mad/Who R Those Guys/Skunk Step (12")	25
06	Southside Dubstars DUBSTAR 008	SOUTHSIDE EP VOL 2 (12")	10
06	Southside Dubstars SSDUBSTAR 007	THE SOUTHSIDE EP (12", stickered white label)	8

SKREWDRIVER
77	Chiswick S 11	You're So Dumb/Better Off Crazy (green p/s)	50
77	Chiswick S 11	You're So Dumb/Better Off Crazy (orange p/s)	45
77	Chiswick NS 18	Anti-Social/19th Nervous Breakdown (p/s)	25
78	Chiswick NS 28	Streetfight/Unbeliever (unissued, Trident label)	300
80	TJM TJM 4	Built Up, Knocked Down/A Case Of Pride/Breakout (p/s)	25
82	Skrewdriver SKREW 1T	BACK WITH A BANG (12", p/s)	40
83	White Noise WN 1	White Power/Smash The I.R.A./Shove The Dove (p/s)	50
83	White Noise WN 2	Voice Of Britain/Sick Society (p/s)	50
77	Chiswick CH 3	ALL SKREWED UP (mini-LP, 12-track, 45rpm, 3 different colour sleeves)	50
77	Chiswick WIK 3	ALL SKREWED UP (LP, 15-track, 33rpm, unissued in U.K.; German-only)	100

SKROTEEZ
| 82 | Skroteez SPILL 1 | OVERSPILL (EP) | 15 |

SKULLFLOWER
86	Broken Flag BF V9	BIRTHDEATH (12" EP)	80
89	Shock SX 001	(I Live) In The Bottomless Pit/Bo Diddley's Shitpump (foldaround p/s in poly bag, 500 only, 75 copies in 'burns victim' sleeve)	20
89	Shock SX 001	(I Live) In The Bottomless Pit/Bo Diddley's Shitpump (foldaround p/s in poly bag, 500 only)	12
90	Toe Jam FLUF 005	Rotten Sun/Spook Rise (p/s, numbered, 500 only)	12
92	Dying Artefact DE 002	Bad Alchemy/Blues For H.M. (p/s in poly bag, numbered, 500 only)	10
94	Freak Records RR 001	White Fang 2/Glassy Essence (wraparound sleeve, stamped label)	8
89	Shock SX 008	XAMAN (LP, 1000 only)	20
89	Broken Flag BFV 10	FORM DESTROYER (LP)	30
92	HEADdIRT HD 01	IIIRD GATEKEEPER (CD)	20

(see also Ramleh)

SKULLS
| 89 | Snake Skin SS 001 | Graveyard Signal/Idols And Dolls (p/s, 300 only) | 10 |

SKULLSNAPS
| 73 | GSF GSZ 7 | My Hang Up Is You/It's A New Day | 65 |

SKUNKS
| 78 | Eel Pie EPS 001 | Good From The Bad/Back Street Fightin' (2,000 only, die-cut 'swirl' sleeve) | 12 |

(see also Craze, Hard Corps)

SKY
| 68 | United Artists UP 2234 | Air-O-Plane Ride/Weather Forecast | 7 |
| 69 | Decca F 12971 | On Our Way/The Singer Is Singing His Song | 7 |

(see also Knack)

SKY
| 71 | RCA RCA 2070 | Goodie Two Shoes/Make It On Time (as U.S. Sky) | 5 |
| 71 | RCA SF 8168 | DON'T HOLD BACK (LP, as U.S. Sky) | 12 |

PATRICK SKY
| 65 | Vanguard VSD 79179 | PATRICK SKY (LP) | 20 |
| 70 | Vanguard SVRL 19054 | A HARVEST OF GENTLE CLANG (LP) | 20 |

SKYBIRD
| 74 | Holyground HGS 118 | SUMMER OF '73 (LP, 250 copies only) | 60 |

SKY BLUES
| 67 | Centaur CPC 1003 | PLAYERS AT EASE: COVENTRY CITY (LP) | 12 |

SKYLARK
| 72 | Capitol CL 15747 | The Writings On The Wall/Wildflower | 8 |

SKYLINERS
59	London HLB 8829	Since I Don't Have You/One Night, One Night	200
59	London HLB 8829	Since I Don't Have You/One Night, One Night (78)	70
59	London HLU 8924	This I Swear/Tomorrow	80
59	London HLU 8924	This I Swear/Tomorrow (78)	70
59	London HLU 8971	It Happened Today/Lonely Way	75
59	London HLU 8971	It Happened Today/Lonely Way (78)	80
60	Polydor NH 66951	Pennies From Heaven/I'll Be Seeing You	15
61	Pye International 7N 25091	I'll Close My Eyes/The Door Is Still Open	20

SKY PONEY
| 70 | Decca F 23082 | Jubeldown/Chubby | 8 |

SKYSOUNDS
| 66 | Anglo TPMA 101/102 | Two Timer/No Matter Where I Wander (private pressing) | 10 |

SLACK ALICE
| 74 | Fontana 6007 038 | Motorcycle/Ridin' The Wind | 5 |
| 74 | Philips 6308 214 | SLACK ALICE (LP) | 15 |

(see also Sandra Alfred, Sandra Barry)

FREDDIE SLACK (& ORCHESTRA)
| 51 | Capitol LC 6529 | FREDDIE SLACK'S BOOGIE WOOGIE (10" LP) | 35 |

(see also Ella Mae Morse & Freddie Slack)

SLADE

SINGLES

69	Fontana TF 1056	Wild Winds Are Blowing/One Way Hotel (credited to The Slade)	100
70	Fontana TF 1079	Shape Of Things To Come/C'mon C'mon	60
70	Polydor 2058 054	Know Who You Are/Dapple Rose	80
71	Polydor 2058 112	Get Down With It/Do You Want Me/The Gospel According To Rasputin (with writing credit: Holder/Hill/Lea/Powell/Penniman; some copies repressed as "Get Down And Get With It")	5
74	Polydor 2058 453	Everyday/Good Time Gals (mispressed with Hollies' The Air That I Breathe on A-side)	6
75	Polydor 2058 547	How Does It Feel?/So Far So Good (p/s)	5
75	Polydor 2058 663	In For A Penny/Can You Just Imagine (in p/s)	5
76	Polydor 2058 716	Nobody's Fool/L.A. Jinx	5
77	Barn 2014 105	Gypsy Roadhog/Forest Full Of Needles	5
77	Barn 2014 106	Burning In The Heat Of Love/Ready Steady Kids	18
77	Barn 2014 114	My Baby Left Me; That's Alright/O.H.M.S. (p/s)	6
78	Barn 2014 121	Give Us A Goal/Daddio	8
78	Barn 2014 127	Rock'n'Roll Bolero/It's Alright By Me	15
79	Barn BARN 002	Ginny Ginny/Dizzy Mama (yellow vinyl only, with sticker)	10
79	Barn BARN 002	Ginny Ginny/Dizzy Mama (yellow vinyl only, without sticker)	8
79	Barn BARN 010	Sign Of The Times/Not Tonight Josephine	15
79	Barn BARN 011	Okey Cokey/My Baby's Got It	10
80	RSO RSO 051	Okey Cokey/My Baby's Got It (withdrawn reissue, existence unconfirmed)	0
80	S.O.T.B. SUPER 45 3	SIX OF THE BEST - NIGHT STARVATION (12" EP, die-cut sleeve)	15
80	Cheapskate CHEAP 5	ALIVE AT READING '80 (EP, die-cut sleeve)	7
80	Cheapskate CHEAP 11	Merry Xmas Everybody/Okey Cokey/Get Down And Get With It (as Slade & Reading Choir, some in die-cut p/s)	8
80	Cheapskate CHEAP 11	Merry Xmas Everybody/Okey Cokey/Get Down And Get With It (as Slade & Reading Choir, some in die-cut p/s)	5
81	Polydor 2058 422	Merry Xmas Everybody/Don't Blame Me (reissue, green background, holly leaf' design, colour group photo p/s)	5
81	Cheapskate CHEAP 16	We'll Bring The House Down/Hold On To Your Hats (p/s)	7
81	Cheapskate CHEAP 21	Wheels Ain't Comin' Down/Not Tonight Josephine (p/s)	7
81	Cheapskate CHEAP 24	Knuckle Sandwich Nancy/I'm Mad (p/s)	10
81	RCA	Tak Me Bak 'Ome/Gudbuy T'Jane) (12" EP, p/s)	10
82	RCA RCA 191	Ruby Red/Funk Punk And Junk (p/s)	10
82	RCA RCAD 191	Ruby Red/Funk Punk And Junk//Rock And Roll Preacher (live)/Take Me Bak 'Ome (live) (double pack, gatefold p/s)	5
82	RCA RCA 291	(And Now The Waltz) C'est La Vie/Merry Xmas Everybody (p/s)	5
82	Speed SPEED 201	Okey Cokey/Get Down And Get With It (no p/s)	8
82	Speed SPEEDP 201	Okey Cokey/Get Down And Get With It (picture disc)	5
83	RCA RCA 373	My Oh My/Merry Xmas Everybody (live)/Keep Your Hands Off My Power Supply (12", p/s)	8
84	RCA RCAT 455	All Join Hands/My Oh My/Here's To... (The New Year)/Merry Xmas (Live & Kickin') (12", stickered p/s)	8
85	RCA PB 40027	Mysterious Mizster Jones/Mama Nature Is A Rocker (picture disc, PVC sleeve)	6
85	Polydor POSPX 780	Merry Xmas Everybody/Don't Blame Me (12", p/s)	12
85	RCA PB 40449/PB 40549	Do You Believe In Miracles/My Oh My (Swing Version)//Santa Claus Is Coming To Town/Auld Lang Syne/You'll Never Walk Alone To Town/Auld Lang Syne/You'll Never Walk Alone	15
85	RCA PT 40450D	Do You Believe In Miracles/My Oh My (Swing Version)//Time To Rock/Santa Claus Is Coming To Town/Auld Lang Syne/You'll Never Walk Alone (12", 'Slade Xmas' double pack, separate sleeves in gatefold PVC cover)	10
87	RCA PB 41147D	Still The Same/Gotta Go Home//The Roaring Silence/Don't Talk To Me About Love (21st anniversary double pack, gatefold p/s)	8
88	Counterpoint CDEP 12 C	How Does It Feel/Far Far Away//(WIZZARD: 2 tracks) (CD)	10
80s	Polydor 2058 422	Merry Xmas Everybody/Don't Blame Me (export p/s from various artist box set, green background, 4 individual photos)	15
80s	SLADE 1	An Interview With Slade (picture disc, 2,000 only, PVC sleeve)	5
91	Polydor PZ 189	Universe/Red Hot/Gypsy Roadhog/Merry Xmas Everybody (12", stickered p/s)	8

ALBUMS : LPS

70	Polydor 2383 026	PLAY IT LOUD (LP, sleeve printed by E.J. Day)	40
70	Polydor 2383 026	PLAY IT LOUD (LP, later sleeve printed by Upton printers)	20
72	Polydor 2383 101	SLADE ALIVE (LP, gatefold sleeve)	20
72	Polydor 2283 163	SLAYED? (LP, laminated sleeve)	12
73	Polydor 2442 119	SLADEST (LP, gatefold sleeve with booklet)	20
73	Polydor 2383 261	OLD NEW BORROWED AND BLUE (LP, gatefold sleeve)	12
74	Polydor 2442 126	SLADE IN FLAME (LP, gatefold sleeve)	12
76	Polydor 2383 377	NOBODY'S FOOLS (LP, with inner sleeve)	15
77	Barn 2314 103	WHATEVER HAPPENED TO SLADE (LP, with lyric sheet)	18
78	Barn 2314 106	SLADE ALIVE VOLUME 2 (LP)	15
79	Barn NARB 003	RETURN TO BASE (LP)	30

PROMOS

72	Polydor 2814 008	Hear Me Calling/Get Down With It (33rpm sampler for "Slade Alive", 500 only)	125
74	Polydor 2058 492	The Bangin' Man/She Did It To Me (export p/s)	25
75	Polydor 2058 585	Thanks For The Memory (with altered lyrics)/Raining In My Champagne	25
77	Barn 2014 105	Gypsy Roadhog/Forest Full Of Needles (mono, DJ copy)	25
80	S.O.T.B. SUPER 3	Night Starvation/When I'm Dancing I Ain't Fightin'	45

FLEXIDISCS

72	Polydor/Sound For Industry SFI 122	The Whole World's Going Crazee/MIKE HUGG: Bonnie Charlie (33rpm with Music Scene magazine)	18
73	Lyntone LYN 2645	Slade talk to Melanie readers (with Melanie magazine)	15
74	Lyntone LYN 2797	Slade exclusive to all 19 readers (with 19 magazine)	15
75	Fan Club LYN 2645/2797	Slade talk to Melanie readers/Slade talk to 19 readers	10

(see also Ambrose Slade, Steve Brett, 'N Betweens, Vendors, Dummies, Jimmy Lea, Gary Holton, China Dolls, Clout, Gang Of Angels, Metal Gurus)

PAUL SLADE

69	Decca F12885	Odyssey/Sound Of Love	12
68	Decca F12840	Heaven Held/Remember Daphne	6

PRENTIS SLADE

61	Parlophone R 4850	I Can Tell/Looking For A Friend	6

SLADE BROTHERS

66	Pye 7N 17176	What A Crazy Life/For A Rainy Day	25
66	Pye 7N 17176	Peace In My Mind/Life's Great Race	80

SLAM CREEPERS
68	Olga OLE 009	Saturday/Hold It Baby	15
73	Sonet SON 2003	We Are Happy People/Yansbro Memories	5

SLAM DONAHUE
11	Too Pure PURE 268S	Where We Were On The Weekend/It's Scary (p/s, many destroyed in PIAS fire)	5

SLANES
65	Blue Beat BB 300	It Takes Time/LIGES: Have Mercy Baby (B-side actually by Frank Cosmo)	20

IVOR SLANEY ORCHESTRA
61	HMV POP 943	The Sir Francis Drake Theme/Midsummer Madness	6
64	HMV POP 1347	High Wire/Sacramento	10
66	Columbia DB 8020	Long Weekend/Eleven Up (as Slaney Strings)	8

SLAPP HAPPY
74	Virgin VS 105	Casablanca Moon/Slow Moon's Rose	12
75	Virgin VS 124	Johnny's Dead/Mr. Rainbow (p/s)	12
83	Half Cat HC 001	Everybody's Slimmin' (Even Men And Women!)/Blue-Eyed Villain (p/s)	12
72	Polydor 2310 204	SORT OF (LP, with German sleeve & insert)	400
74	Virgin V 2014	SLAPP HAPPY (LP)	30
75	Virgin V 2024	DESPERATE STRAIGHTS (LP, gatefold sleeve, with Henry Cow)	20
80	Recommended RR5	ACNALBASAC NOOM (LP, recorded 1973 with members of Faust)	20
81	Recommended RRS 5	SORT OF (LP, reissue)	20

(see also Henry Cow, Peter Blegvad, Anthony Moore, Art Bears)

MUTTER SLATER
76	Rocket ROKN 510	Dancing On Air/Solitude	5

FELIX SLATKIN
60	London HLG 9256	Theme From "The Sundowners"/Gaythers Gone	7

SLAUGHTER (& THE DOGS)
77	Rabid TOSH 101	Cranked Up Really High/The Bitch (p/s, blue, later cream plastic labels)	20
77	Rabid TOSH 101	Cranked Up Really High/The Bitch (p/s, repressings with b&w paper label)	15
77	Decca FR 13723	Where Have All The Boot Boys Gone/You're A Bore (paper label)	8
77	Decca LF 13723	Where Have All The Boot Boys Gone/You're A Bore (12", p/s, 10,000 only)	12
77	Decca FR 13743	Dame To Blame/Johnny T	12
78	Decca F 13758	Quick Joey Small/Come On Back (promo with self sealing 'spit proof' sticker on PVC sleeve)	75
78	Decca FR 13758	Quick Joey Small/Come On Back (with Mick Ronson)	6
79	TJM TJM 3	It's Alright/Edgar Allen Poe/Twist & Turn/UFO (12", p/s)	12
79	DJM DJS 10927	You're Ready Now/Runaway (p/s)	6
80	Decca FR	Where Have All The Boot Boys Gone/You're A Bore (reissue, p/s)	10
80	DJM DJS 10936	East Side Of Town/One By One (p/s, as Slaughter)	6
80	DJM DJS 10945	I'm The One/What's Wrong Boy? (live)/Hell In New York (p/s, as Slaughter)	5
82	Thrush THRUSH 1	HALF ALIVE (12" EP)	10
88	Damaged Goods FNARR 1	Where Have All The Boot Boys Gone/You're A Bore/Johnny T. (p/s, 1,000 only: 500 on green vinyl, 500 on red vinyl)	15
78	Decca SKL 5292	DO IT DOG STYLE (LP)	30
78	Rabid HAT 23	LIVE SLAUGHTER RABID DOGS (LP, plain white sleeve with large sticker)	12
80	DJM DJF 20566	BITE BACK (LP, as Slaughter)	12
89	Damaged Goods FNARR 2	DO IT DOG STYLE (LP, reissue, 1,000-only, multi-coloured vinyl, numbered, with 2 multi-coloured stickers)	12
89	Link LINK LP 092	THE SLAUGHTER TAPES (LP)	12

(see also Studio Sweethearts, Ed Banger)

SLAUGHTER JOE
85	Creation CRE 019	I'll Follow You Down/Napalm Girl (foldaround p/s in poly bag)	5
87	Kaleidoscope S. KLSLP 003	ALL AROUND MY HOBBY HORSE'S HEAD (LP)	12

(see also Television Personalities, Missing Scientists)

SLAVE
84	Cotillion BT 6955	Just A Touch Of Love/Wait For Me (12")	20

FRANK SLAY & HIS ORCHESTRA
61	Top Rank JAR 599	Flying Circle/Cincinnati	8

SLAYER
84	Roadrunner RR 2444 2	HAUNTING THE CHAPEL (12" EP)	25
87	London LON 133	Criminally Insane/Aggressive Perfector (Remix) ('cross' p/s, on red vinyl with patch)	35
87	London LONX 133	Criminally Insane/Postmortem/Aggressive Perfector (Remix) (12", red vinyl, no p/s)	30
89	Roadrunner RR 2444 2	Haunting The Chapel/Chemical Warfare/Captor Of Sin (CD, reissue)	15
91	DEF DEFAP 912	Seasons In The Abyss/Aggressive Perfector (7" picture disc)	20
87	Enigma 720151	LIVE UNDEAD (LP, picture disc)	25
86	London/Def Jam LONLP 34	REIGN IN BLOOD (LP, with inner)	20
87	London LONPP 34	REIGN IN BLOOD (LP, picture disc)	35
88	London/Def Jam LONLP 63	SOUTH OF HEAVEN (LP, stickered sleeve, inner)	30
90	Def American 846 871	SEASONS IN THE ABYSS (LP, with inner)	15
91	Phonogram 510605-1	DECADE OF AGGRESSION (2-LP, booklet, 6,500 copies only)	25
03	Universal B 00001519-02	SOUNDTRACK TO THE APOCALYPSE (4-CD set in 'ammo box' with Backstage laminate, flag, bonus DVD in 'blood pack' and booklet)	40
03	Universal B 00001619-02	SOUNDTRACK TO THE APOCALYPSE (3-CD set/1-DVD set in triple gatefold sleeve)	20

SLEAZ BAND
74	Fontana 6007034	All I Want Is You/Midnight Band	15

SLEAZE
75	No Cat no	SLEAZE (LP, white label private pressing, 50 only, insert)	175

F. SLEDGE
67	Blue Beat BB 386	Red Eye Girl/Try To Love Again (actually by "Go On Girl"/"Giving You A Try Girl" by Freddie McKay & Buster's Group)	40

PERCY SLEDGE
66	Atlantic 584 001	When A Man Loves A Woman/Love Me Like You Mean It	7
66	Atlantic 584 034	Warm And Tender Love/Sugar Puddin'	7
66	Atlantic 584 055	Heart Of A Child/My Adorable One	10
67	Atlantic 584 071	It Tears Me Up/Oh, How Happy	10

67	Atlantic 584 080	Baby, Help Me/You've Lost That Something Wonderful	10
67	Atlantic 584 108	Out Of Left Field/It Can't Be Stopped	10
67	Atlantic 584 140	Pledging My Love/You Don't Miss Your Water	10
68	Atlantic 584 177	Take Time To Know Her/It's All Wrong But It's Alright	10
68	Atlantic 584 225	Come Softly To Me/You're All Around Me	10
69	Atlantic 584 264	Any Day Now/The Angels Listened In	10
69	Atlantic 584 286	Kind Woman/Woman Of The Night	8
69	Atlantic 584 300	True Love Travels On A Gravel Road/Faithful And True	8
72	Atlantic K 10144	Rainbow Road/Standing on The Mountain	6
72	Atlantic K 10165	Baby, Help Me/Warm And Tender Love/Take Time To Know Her	6
74	Capricorn 2089 009	I'll Be Your Everything/Walkin' In The Sun	6
67	Atlantic 587/588 048	WARM AND TENDER SOUL (LP)	20
67	Atlantic 587/588 081	THE PERCY SLEDGE WAY (LP)	20
68	Atlantic 587/588 015	WHEN A MAN LOVES A WOMAN (LP)	20
69	Atlantic 587/588 153	THE BEST OF PERCY SLEDGE (LP)	15

SLEDGEHAMMER

79	Slammer SRTS79CUS 395	Sledgehammer/Feel Good (with p/s)	20
79	Slammer SRTS79CUS 395	Sledgehammer/Feel Good	10
80	Slammer CELL 2	Living In Dreams/Fantasia (p/s)	10
80s	Slammer MRSB 2	In The Middle Of The Night	10
80	Valiant STRONG 1	Sledgehammer/Feel Good (p/s, reissue)	10
80	Valiant ROUND 2	Sledgehammer/Feel Good (p/s, 2nd reissue)	6
85	Illuminated ILL 33	In The Queue/Oxford City (shaped picture disc)	25
83	Illuminated JAMS 32	BLOOD ON THEIR HANDS (LP)	30
83	Illuminated JAMS 32	BLOOD ON THEIR HANDS (LP)	25
84	Mausoleum LUST 834950	SLEDGEHAMMER (LP, with free 12")	30

SLEEPING DOGS

82	Crass 221984/11	BEWARE SLEEPING DOGS (EP)	8

SLEEPWALKERS

59	Parlophone R 4580	Sleep Walk/Golden Mile	15

SLEEPY

68	CBS 3592	Love's Immortal Fire/Is It Really The Same	275
68	CBS 3838	Rosie Can't Fly/Mrs. Bailey's Barbecue And Grill	60
68	No Cat No	You'll See Me/Time Gone (White label test pressing)	250

(see also Grapefruit, Fynn McCool)

SLENDER LORIS

76	Reverence DM 70	I'm Only Heavy When You Get Me Down/A Week Of A Day	6

SLENDER PLENTY

67	Polydor BM 56189	Silver Tree Top School For Boys/I've Lost A Friend And Found A Lover	80

SLENDER THREAD

80	Rock MHMS 193	I See The Light/Where Is The Beat	30

JIMI SLEVIN

82	Claddagh CCF 7	FREEFLIGHT (LP)	45

(see also Peggy's Leg)

GRACE SLICK

68	CBS 63476	CONSPICUOUS ONLY IN IT'S ABSENCE (LP, as Grace Slick And The Great Society)	40

RICKY SLICK

72	Dynamic DYN 449	Family Man/Family Man - Version	5

SLICKERS

68	Blue Cat BS 133	Wala Wala/LESTER STERLING: Super Special	35
68	Blue Cat BS 134	Nana (actually by George Dekker)/MARTIN RILEY: I May Never See My Baby Anymore	35
69	Blue Cat BS 154	Frying Pan/RARFIELD WILLIAMS: Code It	45
69	Amalgamated AMG 852	Man Beware/Matty Matty	20
69	Amalgamated AMG 866	Money Reaper/Man Beware	20
70	Bullet BU 449	Coolie Girl/BIGGIE: Bawling Baby	10
70	Trojan TR 7718	Run Fattie/Hoola Bulla (song actually "Bulla Man")	8
71	G.G. GG 4524	Oh My Baby/WINSTON WRIGHT: Change Of Love Version	8
71	Punch PH 59	Johnny Too Bad/Johnny Too Bad - Version	20
71	Dynamic DYN 406	Johnny Too Bad/ROLAND ALFONSO: Saucy Horde (act. by Roland Alphonso)	8
71	Dynamic DYN 419	You Can't Win/Don't Fight The Law	6
72	Explosion EX 2061	Bounce Me Johnny/Bounce Me 'Version' (actually "Say You")	6

(see also G.G. Allstars, Clancy Eccles, Viceroys)

SLIDE

80	Crash POW 4	Superman's Shoes/Meet Your New Neighbour (p/s)	50

SLIM

97	Em:t 0097	SLIM: 0097 (CD, digipak)	30

SLIM & FREEDOM SINGERS

70	Banana BA 304	Do Dang Do (actually by Leroy Sibbles)/JACKIE MITTOO & SOUND DIMENSION: Hot Milk	35

SLIME

78	Toadstool GOOD 1	Controversial/Loony (p/s)	8

(see also Johnny Moped)

SLINT

91	Touchh & Go T&GLP64	SPIDERLAND (LP)	20
93	Jennifer Hartman TG 138	TWEEZ (LP, reissue)	20

SLIPKNOT

00	Roadrunner RR 2090-7	Spit It Out/Surfacing (Live) (p/s, red vinyl)	10
04	Roadrunner RR 3988-7	Duality/Don't Get Close (picture disc)	5
00	Roadrunner RR 8655-6	SLIPKNOT (LP, picture disc)	15

SLITS

79	Island WIP 6505	Typical Girls/I Heard It Through The Grapevine (p/s)	10

MINT VALUE £

79	Island 12 WIP 6505	Typical Girls/I Heard It Through The Grapevine/Typical Girls (Brink Style)/Liebe And Romanize (12", p/s)	20
80	Rough Trade RT 039/Y Y 1	In The Beginning There Was Rhythm/POP GROUP: Where There's A Will There's A Way (p/s)	8
80	Rough Trade/Y RT044/Y4	Man Next Door/Man Next Door (Version p/s)	8
80	Human HUM 4	Animal Space/Animal Spacier (p/s)	12
81	CBS A1498	Earthbeat/Begin Again Rhythm (p/s)	8
81	CBS A 131498	Earthbeat/Earthdub/Begin Again Rhythm (12", p/s)	12
88	Strange Fruit SFPS 021	THE PEEL SESSIONS (Mini-LP)	12
79	Island ILPS 9573	CUT (LP, laminated cover with inner sleeve)	35
80	Rough Trade/Y Y 3	BOOTLEG RETROSPECTIVE (LP, plain sleeve, with SUBWAY SECT)	30
81	CBS 85269	THE RETURN OF THE GIANT SLITS (LP, some with bonus 45 American Radio Interview/"Face Dub" [XPS 125])	30
81	CBS 85269	THE RETURN OF THE GIANT SLITS (LP)	20

(see also Raincoats)

P.F. SLOAN

65	RCA Victor RCA 1482	Sins Of The Family/This Mornin'	12
67	RCA Victor RCA 1623	Sunflower Sunflower/The Man Behind The Red Balloon	12
72	Epic EPC 65179	RAISED ON RECORDS (LP)	25
80s	Big Beat WIK 73	SONGS OF OTHER TIMES (LP, some tracks as Grass Roots)	25

(see also Grass Roots, Fantastic Baggys, Willie & Wheels)

SAMMI SLOAN

68	Columbia DB 8480	Yes I Would/Be His Girl	20

SLOWBONE

74	Rare Earth RES 119	Oh Man/Get What You're Given	6

(see also Roll Ups)

SLOWBONE & THE WONDERBOYS

74	Rare Earth RES 116	Tales Of A Crooked Man/Happy Birthday Sweet Sixteen	8

SLOWBURNER

89	Burn BURN LP 001	AN EMOTIONAL BUSINESS (LP)	12

SLOW CLUB

07	Moshi Moshi	Because We're Dead/Sunday (500 only, p/s)	10
10	Moshi Moshi MOSHILP 29	YEAH SO (LP and CD, Record Store Day Release)	20

SLOWDIVE

90	Creation CRE 093T	Slowdive/Avalyn 1/Avalyn 2	15
90	Creation CRE093T	SLOWDIVE EP	15
91	Creation CRE 098T	Morningrise/She calls/Losing Today (12")	18
93	Creation CRE 119T	OUTSIDE YOUR ROOM EP (12")	20
91	Creation CRELP 094	JUST FOR A DAY (LP)	30
93	Creation CRELP 139	SOUVLAKI (LP, picture inner sleeve)	70
95	Creation CRELP 168	PYGMALION (LP)	50

SLOW DOG

72	Parlophone R5942	Walking Through The Blue Grass/Ain't Never Going Home	30

SLOWGUNS

79	MPA SMP 088	TV Movie/American Heartbeat	15
80	Cult 45 CULT 001	Karma/The Time Is Right For Us	12

SLOWLOAD

71	MAM MAM 27	On The Road Again/Big Boobs Boogie	35

(see also Fruit Eating Bears)

SLOW MOTION

79	RK RK 1024	Maybe/Xmas Charade	75

SLOWTRAIN

80	Spirit SR 1	Ronnie/Just One Way	30

SLR CREW

88	SLR XPR1536	Bass Drum/Life's A Bitch (12")	45

SL TROOPERS

88	Global Rhythm GR001	Debut (Unarmed And Dangerous) (12", 500 pressed)	40
89	Music Of Life NOTE32	Movement (12")	10
91	Kold Sweat KSEP201	SYSTEMATIC TERROR (EP)	8

SLUSH

78	Ember EMB 5367	White Christmas/Rich Man (no p/s)	70

(See also Pumphouse Gang)

SLY & THE REVOLUTIONARIES

80	Trojan TRLS 186	BLACK ASH DUB (LP)	20

SMACK

78	Asprin 001	Edward Fox/Came Again (p/s, original issue)	5

SMALL ADS

81	Bronze BRO 115	Small Ads/Motorway Madness (p/s)	5
81	Bronze BRO 125	HP Man/Radio Love (p/s)	5
81	Bronze BRO 135	Friday Nite Cowboy/I Wanna Fly Concorde (p/s)	5

SMALL IN A BIG WAY

84	Bedlam BLM 003	Katies Lips/Back To Zero (p/s)	8

JOAN SMALL

56	Parlophone MSP 6219	Change Of Heart/Come Next Spring	10
56	Parlophone R 4211	Love Is A Stranger/Autumn Concerto	10
57	Parlophone R 4269	Gonna Get Along Without You Now/You Can't Say I Love You To A Rock & Roll Tune	15
58	Parlophone R 4431	Afraid/How Many Times (Can I Fall In Love)	10
60	Parlophone R 4622	The Big Hurt/Ask Me To Go Steady	10

KAREN SMALL

66	Vocalion V 9281	To Get You Back Again/That's Why I Cry	30

MARY SMALL
56	Vogue Coral 45-Q-72196	Dino/None Of That Now	8

SMALL FACES
SINGLES
65	Decca F 12208	Whatcha Gonna Do About It?/What's A Matter, Baby?	20
65	Decca F 12276	I've Got Mine/It's Too Late	25
66	Decca F 12317	Sha-La-La-La-Lee/Grow Your Own	10
66	Decca F 12393	Hey Girl/Almost Grown	15
66	Decca F 12470	All Or Nothing/Understanding (curved or boxed Decca logo)	12
66	Decca F 12500	My Mind's Eye (alternate demo mix, matrix no. ends T1-1C)/I Can't Dance With You (withdrawn)	30
66	Decca F 12500	My Mind's Eye (matrix no. ends T2-1C)/I Can't Dance With You	10
67	Decca F 12565	I Can't Make It/Just Passing	25
67	Decca F 12565	I Can't Make It/Just Passing (in export p/s)	60
67	Decca F 12619	Patterns/E Too D (with export p/s)	140
67	Decca F 12619	Patterns/E Too D	70
67	Archive 4 TOF 103	Small Faces (1-sided sampler for "Small Faces", promo only)	200
67	Immediate AS 1	Here Comes The Nice/Talk To You	12
67	Immediate IM 050	Itchycoo Park/I'm Only Dreaming	12
67	Immediate IM 057	Tin Soldier/I Feel Much Better (in p/s)	80
67	Immediate IM 062	Tin Soldier/I Feel Much Better	15
67	Immediate IM 062	Lazy Sunday/Rollin' Over	12
68	Immediate IM 064	The Universal/Donkey Rides, A Penny A Glass (lilac label)	12
68	Immediate IM 069	The Universal/Donkey Rides, A Penny A Glass (later pink label)	8
68	Immediate IM 069	Afterglow (Of Your Love)/Wham Bam, Thank You Mam (demos [perhaps some copies] have demo version of B-side)	60
69	Immediate IM 077	Afterglow (Of Your Love)/Wham Bam, Thank You Mam (demos)	15
69	Immediate IM 077	Lazy Sunday/Rollin' Over (p/s, reissue with white label)	8
75	Immediate IM 077	Tin Soldier/Tin Soldier (live)/Rene	6
80	Virgin VS 367	Itchycoo Park/Lazy Sunday/Sha-La-La-La-Lee/Here Comes The Nice (12", p/s)	10
86	Archive 4 TOF 103	THE SMALL FACES (Itchycoo Park/Lazy Sunday/All Or Nothing (live)/Autumn Stone) (3" CD EP, with adaptor, 5" case, 5,000 only)	10
88	Castle Comms. Special Edition CD 3-9		

ALBUMS : LPS
66	Decca LK 4790	SMALL FACES (original red label)	250
67	Decca LK 4879	FROM THE BEGINNING (original red label)	280
67	Immediate IMLP 008	SMALL FACES (mono)	250
67	Immediate IMSP 008	SMALL FACES (stereo)	250
68	Immediate IMLP 012	OGDENS' NUT GONE FLAKE (lilac label, circular foldout sleeve, mono)	250
68	Immediate IMSP 012	OGDENS' NUT GONE FLAKE (lilac label, circular foldout sleeve, stereo)	150
68	Immediate IMLP 012	OGDENS' NUT GONE FLAKE (pink label, circular foldout sleeve, mono)	120
68	Immediate IMSP 012	OGDENS' NUT GONE FLAKE (pink label, circular foldout sleeve, stereo)	80
69	Decca LK 4790	SMALL FACES (boxed Decca label)	50
69	Decca LK 4879	FROM THE BEGINNING (boxed Decca label)	40
69	Immediate IMLP/IMSP 022	IN MEMORIAM (export issue [German copies more common, £60])	150
69	Immediate IMAL 01/02	THE AUTUMN STONE (2-LP, gatefold sleeve)	80
75	Immediate/NEMS IML 1001	OGDENS' NUT GONE FLAKE (reissue, round sleeve, white label)	40
76	NEMS AML 1008	MAGIC MOMENTS	15
77	Immediate/NEMS IML 2001	OGDENS' NUT GONE FLAKE (reissue, square sleeve)	15
77	Decca ROOTS 5	ROCK ROOTS - THE DECCA SINGLES	15
78	Charly CR 300005	OGDENS' NUT GONE FLAKE (export release, square sleeve)	15
78	Charly CR 300025	THE SMALL FACES - LIVE U.K. 1969 (export release)	15
80	Virgin/Immediate V 2166	SMALL FACES: BIG HITS (gatefold sleeve)	15
80	Virgin/Immediate V 2178	FOR YOUR DELIGHT, THE DARLINGS OF WAPPING WHARF LAUNDERETTE	25
91	Castle CLACT 016	OGDENS' NUT GONE FLAKE (CD, in round tin box with beer mats & booklet)	60
97	Castle CLA 016	OGDENS' NUT GONE FLAKE (reissue, round sleeve with obi)	15
01	Strange Fruit SFRSLP 087	BBC SESSIONS (LP)	20

(see also Faces, Steve Marriott, Humble Pie, Jimmy Winston & His Reflections, Winston's Fumbs, Billy Nicholls, Kenney Jones)

SMALL FOUR
66	Pye 7N 17191	One Up On Me/I'll Find Him	20

SMALL HOURS
80	Automatic K 17708	The Kid/Business In Town/Midnight To Six/End Of The Night (p/s)	30
80	Automatic K 17708X	The Kid/Business In Town/Midnight To Six/End Of The Night (10", p/s)	20

SMALL WONDER
75	Dawn DNS 1094	Ordinary Boy/Ride A Black Sheep	18

SMALL WORLD
81	Whaam! WHAAM 003	Love Is Dead/Liberty (p/s)	100
83	Valid VC 001	First Impressions/Stupidity Street/Tomorrow Never Comes (p/s)	100

SMART
82	Complex CPX 001	This Time (p/s)	35

SMART ALEC
79	B&C BCS 20	Scooter Boys/Soho (p/s)	100

LEROY SMART
70	Attack ATT 8012	Life Is A Funny Thing/TRINITY: Psalms	12
77	Conflict COND 2001	Jahovia/Dub (12")	20
78	Andinet AT 001	Zion/Version	10
78	Andinet AT 002	Faith/Version	10
78	Aries AR 003	It's A Long Time Now/Long Time Version	6
78	Write Sounds WTS 1001	Children Of The Getto [sic]/Version	8
78	Write Sounds WTS 001	What I Will Do/ROY SINCLAIR: Rite Mix/LEROY SMART: Jah Almighty (12")	25
79	Burning Sounds BDS 010	Find Your Destination/Jamaica In Peace (12")	15
79	Burning Sounds BDS 011	No One Remember Me/Don't Be Late (12")	15
70s	Aries ARI 002	Peace Is What We Want (with U. Brown)/Version (12", p/s)	30
80	Black Joy DH 803	Hooligan/HaveMercy (12")	10
82	Time One TR 0016	Money Comfort/If I Give My Love (12", with Barry Brown)	20
77	Conflict COLPD 2001	BALLISTIC AFFAIR (LP)	40
77	Dread Hot DHLP 1001	DREAD HOT IN AFRICA (LP)	30

MINT VALUE £

77	Third World TWS 601	SUPER STAR (LP)	20
78	Burning Sounds BS 1004	DREAD HOT IN AFRICA (LP)	25
78	Burning Sounds BS 1005	IMPRESSIONS OF LEROY SMART (LP)	15
78	Burning Sounds BS 1008	JAH LOVES EVERYONE (LP)	25
78	Dread Hot DHLP 1004	IMPRESSIONS (LP)	20
78	Burning Sounds BS 1009	PROPAGANDA (LP, clear vinyl)	25

LEROY SMART & BIG YOUTH
| 79 | Dub Vendor DVD 01 | Pride And Ambition (original style)/'78 Style (12") | 60 |

SMART PILLS
| 87 | Bluurg FISH 17 | NO GOOD NO EVIL (LP, with insert) | 12 |

SMART SYSTEMS
| 91 | Jumpin' & Pumpin' 12TOT18 | Tingler (Meltram Mix)/(Mingler Mix)/(State Side Swamp Mix) (12" p/s) | 10 |

SMASHING PUMPKINS
91	Hut	I Am One (1-sided blue flexidisc)	100
91	Caroline SMASH 1	Siva/Rhinoceros (no p/s, promo only)	80
91	Hut HUTT 6	Siva/Window Paine (12", p/s, 5,000)	30
92	Hut HUTT 10	LULL EP (Rhinoceros/Blue/Slunk/Bye June [Demo]) (12", p/s)	20
92	Hut CDHUT 10	LULL EP (Rhinoceros/Blue/Slunk/Bye June [Demo]) (CD)	12
92	Hut HUTT 017	PEEL SESSIONS: Siva/A Girl Named Sandoz/Smiley (12" EP, p/s)	12
92	Hut HUTEN 018	I Am One/Terrapin (live)/Bullet Train To Osaka (10", p/s, 6,000 only)	20
92	Hut HUTT 18	I Am One/Plume/Starla (12", p/s)	12
93	Sup Pop SP 90	Tristessa/La Dolly Vita (12", 5,000 only)	35
93	Hut HUT 31	Cherub Rock/Purr Snickety (p/s, clear vinyl, numbered, 5,000 only)	20
93	Hut HUTT 31	Cherub Rock/Pissant/French Movie Theme/(Star Spangled Banner) (12", p/s, last track uncredited)	8
93	Hut HUTT 37	Today/Apathy's Last Kiss (p/s, red vinyl, 5,000 only)	12
93	Hut HUTT 37	Today/Hello Kitty Kat/Obscured (12", p/s)	8
94	Hut HUT 43	Smile (Disarm/Siamese Dream) (stickered p/s, purple vinyl)	10
94	Hut HUTL 48	Rocket/Never Let Me Down (box set, salmon pink vinyl, 1,500 only)	40
93	Hut HUTTDJ 73	Zero (12", promo only)	12
94	Hut SPBOX 1	SIAMESE SINGLES (Rocket/Never Let Me Down/Cherub Rock/Purr Snickety//Today/Apathy's Last Kiss/Smile [Disarm/Siamese Dream]) (4 x 7" box set, black vinyl, 6,000 only)	50
94	Hut HUTLPX 2	GISH (LP, with inner)	18
95	Hut HUTDLP 30	MELLON COLLIE AND THE INFINITE SADNESS (3 x LP, 12 page booklet, numbered)	80
96	Hut HUTLP 41	PISCES ISCARIOT (LP, yellow vinyl)	20
96	Hut	THE AEROPLANE FLIES HIGH (5 x CD single box set with handle, lock & booklet)	50
00	HUTDLP 59	MACHINA/THE MACHINES OF GOD (2-LP)	35

ROY SMECK
| 54 | Brunswick LA 8649 | SONGS OF THE RANGE (10" LP) | 15 |
| 65 | London HAR 8273 | WIZARD OF THE STRINGS (LP) | 12 |

PHILIP LLOYD SMEE & DONATO CINICOLO III
| 71 | Deroy PLS 1 | DAS LUNE/SYNTHI-A (LP, private pressing, handmade sleeve, 2 copies only) | 400 |

SMIFFY
| 74 | Antic K 11501 | See You Later (Little Baby Love)/How Can You Be A Millionaire | 5 |

SMILE
| 72 | UNI UN 537 | A Year Every Night/Southbound | 10 |

SMILEY
| 72 | Philips 6006 206 | Penelope/I Know What I Want | 15 |

(see also Creation)

BRETT SMILEY
| 74 | Anchor ANC 70 | Va Va Va Voom/Space Age (with p/s) | 30 |
| 74 | Anchor ANC 70 | Va Va Va Voom/Space Age | 18 |

SMILEY CULTURE
| 86 | Top Notch TOP LP 001 | THE ORIGINAL (LP) | 15 |

K. SMILEY
| 72 | Pressure Beat PB 5514 | Tipatone/Do It To Me | 8 |

SMILIN' JOE
| 54 | London HL 8106 | A.B.C.'s Parts 1 & 2 (78) | 90 |

SMILING HARD
| 79 | Survival SUR 5 | Don't Call Us We'll Call You/Fire To The Galleon | 8 |

SMIRKS
| 78 | Besmirkly BZZ17 | OK UK/Streets (p/s) | 8 |

SMITH
69	Stateside-Dunhill SS 8028	Baby It's You/I Don't Believe	6
70	Stateside-Dunhill SS 8042	Take A Look Around/Mojalesky Ridge	6
70	Stateside-Dunhill SS 8055	What Am I Gonna Do/Born In Boston	6
70	Probe PRO 508	Comin Back To Me/Minus Plus	25
73	Probe Goldies GFF 115	The Weight/Baby It's You	12
69	Stateside-Dunhill SSL 5016	A GROUP CALLED SMITH (LP)	25
70	Stateside-Dunhill SSL 5031	MINUS PLUS (LP)	25

SMITH (U.K.)
| 81 | Rarn RARNS 1 | Here Comes My Baby/Just Another Line/Too Late (p/s) | 25 |

ADAM (ERIC) SMITH
| 62 | Island WI 057 | I Wonder Why/My Prayer | 20 |

A.S.A.P. (ADRIAN SMITH & PROJECT)
| 89 | EMI 12 EMPD 107 | Silver And Gold/Blood Brothers (12", silver & gold vinyl) | 10 |
| 90 | EMI EMPD 131 | Down The Wire (Crossed Line Mix)/When She's Gone (shaped picture disc) | 7 |

(see also Iron Maiden, Urchin)

ARTHUR 'GUITAR BOOGIE' SMITH (& HIS CRACKERJACKS)
| 53 | MGM SP 1008 | Guitar Boogie/Be Bop Rag | 25 |

53	MGM SP 1021	Five String Banjo Boogie/South..15
53	MGM SP 1039	Express Train Boogie/River Rag..15
53	MGM MGM 630	Recitation Sonny Smith: In Memory Of Hank Williams/HANK WILLIAMS & HIS DRIFTING COWBOYS: I Saw The Light (78)..6
54	MGM SP 1096	Oh, Baby Mine, I Get So Lonely/Outboard..15
54	MGM SP 1110	Redheaded Stranger/Texas Hop..20
55	MGM SP 1122	Hi Lo Boogie/Truck Stop Grill..5
54	MGM MGM-EP 510	ARTHUR 'GUITAR BOOGIE' SMITH AND HIS CRACKERJACKS (EP)............15
54	MGM MGM EPC 5	ARTHUR 'GUITAR BOOGIE' SMITH (EP, export issue)..............................15
59	MGM MGM-EP 695	ARTHUR 'GUITAR BOOGIE' SMITH AND HIS CRACKERJACKS (EP)............15
63	Stateside SE 1005	MISTER GUITAR (EP)..15
53	MGM MGM-D 111	FINGERS ON FIRE (10" LP)..25
54	MGM MGM-D 131	FOOLISH QUESTIONS (10" LP)...25

BEASLEY SMITH & HIS ORCHESTRA
| 56 | London HLD 8235 | Goodnight, Sweet Dreams/Parisian Rag..20 |
| 56 | London HLD 8273 | My Foolish Heart/Old Spinning Wheel...20 |

BESSIE SMITH
| 48 | Parlophone R 2146 | Gimme A Pigfoot/Take Me For A Buggy Ride (78)......................................20 |

BETTY SMITH SKIFFLE GROUP
| 57 | Tempo A 162 | There's A Blue Ridge Round My Heart, Virginia/Double Shuffle..............10 |
| 57 | Tempo A 162 | There's A Blue Ridge Round My Heart, Virginia/Double Shuffle (78)........10 |

(see also Betty Smith Quintet)

BETTY SMITH QUINTET
57	Tempo A 163	Sweet Georgia Brown/Little White Lies...20
58	Decca F 10986	Hand Jive/Bewitched (as Betty Smith Group)...10
58	Decca F 11031	Will The Angels Play Their Harps For Me/Betty's Blues...........................10
58	Decca F 11071	Begin The Beguine/Song Of The Boulevards...5
59	Decca F 11124	Song Of India/Stormy Weather..10
57	Tempo EXA 74	BETTY SMITH QUINTET (EP)...30
57	Decca DFE 6446	BETTY SMITH QUINTET (EP)...30
58	Decca DFE 6547	BETTY SMITH GROUP (EP)..30

(see also Betty Smith Skiffle Group)

BRODERICK SMITH
| 72 | Spark SRL 1087 | Going Down To The End Of The WOrld/She's Gone.....................................8 |

BUSTER SMITH
| 61 | London Jazz LTZ-K 15206 | THE LEGENDARY BUSTER SMITH (LP)..12 |

CAL SMITH
| 73 | MCA 143 | Country Bumpkin/It's Not The Miles You Travelled...................................5 |

CARL SMITH
| 56 | Philips PB 572 | Loose Talk/More Than Anything Else In The World (78)............................7 |
| 60 | Philips BBL 7437 | THE CARL SMITH TOUCH (LP)..12 |

CLARA SMITH
69	VJM VLP 15	CLARA SMITH VOLUME 1 (LP)..15
69	VJM VLP 16	CLARA SMITH VOLUME 2 (LP)..15
69	VJM VLP 17	CLARA SMITH VOLUME 3 (LP)..15

CLARA SMITH & FLETCHER HENDERSON
| 61 | Philips BBE 12491 | BLUES BY CLARA SMITH 1926-1928 (EP)..10 |

(see also Fletcher Henderson)

CONNIE SMITH
66	RCA Victor RD 7785	CUTE AND COUNTRY (LP)..15
71	RCA LSA 3042	WHERE IS MY CASTLE (LP)...12
73	RCA LSA 3150	IT AIN'T LOVE (LP)...12

DAVE SMITH & ASTRONAUTS
| 67 | Columbia Blue Beat DB 104 | A Lover Like You/Cup Of Love...15 |
| 67 | Amusicon SLE 10 | A Lover Like You/Cup Of Love...15 |

DAVE SMITH & JUDY DINNING
| 83 | Rubber RUB 043 | WAITING FOR THE CHANGE (LP)..20 |

DEREK SMITH TRIO
| 56 | Pye Nixa NJE 1036 | PIANO MOODS (EP)...80 |

DICK SMITH BAND
79	Smile SR 012	Body Heat/Motorway Madness (p/s)..75
80	Hol-O-Gram HOL 001	Way Of The World/Giving The Game Away (with p/s)...............................45
80	Hol-O-Gram HOL 001	Way Of The World/Giving The Game Away..25

EDDIE SMITH
| 55 | Parlophone MSP 6186 | Silver Star Stomp/Stumbling (as Eddie Smith & Chiefs)..........................15 |
| 60 | Top Rank JAR 285 | Upturn/Border Beat (as Eddie Smith & Hornets)......................................25 |

EDGEWOOD SMITH & FABULOUS TAILFEATHERS
| 67 | Sue WI 4037 | Ain't That Lovin'/Yeah..50 |

EFFIE SMITH
| 66 | Sue WI 4010 | Dial That Telephone Parts 1 & 2...20 |

ELLIOTT SMITH
98	Domino RUG 074	Ballad Of Big Nothing/Some Song (p/s)...15
98	Dreamworks DRMS 22347	Waltz No. 2/Our Thing (p/s)..10
99	Dreamworks DRMS 7	Baby Britain/Waltz No. 1 (p/s)..8
99	Dreamworks 459 037-2	Happiness/Son Of Sam (CD, digipak)..12
00	Dreamworks 450 949-7	Son Of Sam/A Living Will..8
98	Domino REWIGLP 001	ELLIOTT SMITH (LP)..60
98	Domino REWIGLP 002	ROMAN CANDLE (LP)..60
98	Domino WIGLP 51	EITHER/OR (LP)...30
04	Domino WIGLP 147	FROM A BASEMENT ON THE HILL (2-LP)..15
07	Domino WIGLP 198	NEW MOON (2-LP)..18

10	Domino WIGLP 265	AN INTRODUCTION TO (LP)	12

ELSON SMITH
61	Fontana H 291	Flip Flop/Are You Ready For That	30

ERNIE SMITH
71	Duke DU 119	Bend Down/Heaven Help Us All	6
71	Horse HOSS 6	Sunday Morning/One Three	5
74	Attack ATT 8071	Duppy Gunman/Duppy Gunman Version	8
73	London SHS 8442	ERNIE SMITH (LP)	12

(LITTLE) GEORGE (HARMONICA) SMITH
65	Blue Horizon 45-1002	Blues In The Dark/Telephone Blues (as Little George Smith)	90
70	Blue Horizon 57-3170	Someday You're Gonna Learn/Before You Do Your Thing (as George Smith)	20
69	Liberty LBL/LBS 83218E	BLUES WITH FEELING - A TRIBUTE TO LITTLE WALTER (LP, with Chicago Blues Band)	45
70	Blue Horizon 7-63856	NO TIME TO JIVE (LP)	100
71	Deram SML 1082	ARKANSAS TRAP (LP)	60

(see also Bacon Fat)

GLORIA SMITH
59	London HLU 8903	Playmates/Don't Take Your Love From Me	18
59	London HLU 8903	Playmates/Don't Take Your Love From Me (78)	12

GORDON SMITH
69	Blue Horizon 57-3156	Too Long/Funk Pedal	20
69	Blue Horizon 7-63211	LONG OVERDUE (LP)	80

(see also Kevin Coyne)

HAROLD SMITH'S MAJESTIC CHOIR
69	Chess CRS 8100	We Can All Walk A Little Bit Prouder/Why Am I Treated So Bad	8

HARVEY SMITH
75	Hankerchief Hanky 3	True Love/ End Of The World (p/s)	7

HOBART SMITH
69	Topic 12T187	THE OLD TIMEY RAP (LP)	20

HUEY 'PIANO' SMITH & THE CLOWNS
58	Columbia DB 4138	Don't You Just Know It/High Blood Pressure	85
58	Columbia DB 4138	Don't You Just Know It/High Blood Pressure (78)	50
60	Top Rank JAR 282	Don't You Just Know Kokomo/FRANKIE FORD: Cheatin' Woman	20
62	Top Rank JAR 614	Pop-Eye/Scald-Dog (as Huey Smith)	12
65	Sue WI 364	If It Ain't One Thing It's Another/Tu-Ber-Cu-Lucas And The Sinus Blues	25
65	Sue WI 380	Rockin' Pneumonia And The Boogie Woogie Flu (Parts 1 & 2)	25
78	Chiswick NS 43	Rockin' Pneumonia And The Boogie Woogie Flu (unissued)	0
82	Kent TOWN 502	Don't You Just Know It/MARY LOVE: Lay This Burden Down/DANNY MONDAY: Baby Without You	12
65	Sue ILP 917	ROCKIN' PNEUMONIA AND THE BOOGIE WOOGIE FLU (LP, titled "Havin' A Good Time" on labels)	40

(see also Frankie Ford, Lee Allen, Bobby Marchan, Robert Parker)

HURRICANE SMITH
71	Columbia DB 8735	Don't Let I Die/The Writer Sings His Songs	6
72	Columbia DB 8878	Oh Babe, What Would You Say/Getting To Know You	6
72	Columbia SCX 6510	DON'T LET IT DIE (LP)	15

IAN SMITH & INNER MIND
71	Bullet BU 490	Devil Woman/Nenn Street Rub	6

(see also Smithy All Stars)

JEFF SMITH
71	RAK RAK 120	Gypsy In My Blood/Going To A Party	30

JENNIE SMITH
59	Philips PB 924	Huggin' My Pillow (Sweet Side)/Huggin' My Pillow (Sweet Beat Side)	5

JIMMY SMITH
62	HMV POP 1025	Walk On The Wild Side Parts 1 & 2 (blue label)	10
62	HMV POP 1025	Walk On The Wild Side Parts 1 & 2 (black label)	5
65	Verve VS 509	Hobo Flats Parts 1 & 2	5
65	Verve VS 521	Who's Afraid Of Virginia Woolf Parts 1 & 2	5
65	Verve VS 523	The Cat/Basin Street Blues	20
65	Verve VS 531	The Organ Grinder's Swing/I'll Close My Eyes	6
66	Verve VS 534	Slow Theme From "Where The Spies Are" Parts 1 & 2	5
66	Verve VS 536	Got My Mojo Working Parts 1 & 2	10
66	Verve VS 540	I'm Your Hoochie-Coochie Man Parts 1 & 2	6
67	Verve VS 551	Cat In A Tree Parts 1 & 2	6
67	Verve VS 562	Mickey Mouse Parts 1 & 2	6
62	Verve CLP 1596/CSD 1462	BASHIN' THE UNPREDICTABLE (Verve label with HMV number)	15
63	Verve VLP 9039	HOBO FLATS	15
64	Verve VLP 9057	ANY NUMBER CAN WIN	15
64	Verve VLP 9068	WHO'S AFRAID OF VIRGINIA WOOLF	15
64	Verve (S)VLP 9079	THE CAT	25
65	Verve (S)VLP 9093	MONSTER	20
66	Verve (S)VLP 9108	ORGAN GRINDER SWING	15
66	Verve (S)VLP 9123	GOT MY MOJO WORKING	15
66	Verve (S)VLP 9159	HOOCHIE COOCHIE MAN	15
67	Verve (S)VLP 9159	PETER & THE WOLF	15
67	Verve (S)VLP 9160	THE DYNAMIC DUO (with Wes Montgomery)	15
67	Verve (S)VLP 9182	RESPECT	20
68	Verve (S)VLP 9218	STAY LOOSE	15
68	Verve (S)VLP 9227	LIVIN' IT UP	15
68	Verve (S)VLP 9231	CHRISTMAS COOKIN'	15
69	Verve (S)VLP 9241	FURTHER ADVENTURES OF JIMMY AND WES (with Wes Montgomery)	15
71	Verve 2304 020	I'M GON' GIT MYSELF TOGETHER	15
74	Verve 2304 167	PORTUGUESE SOUL	15

(see also Kenny Burrell)

JOEY SMITH & BABA BROOKS BAND
64	R&B JB 131	Maybe Once/Tell Me You're Mine	25

JUDI SMITH
65	Decca F 12132	Leaves Come Tumbling Down/Come My Way	15

JUNIOR SMITH
67	Giant GN 1	Cool Down Your Temper/I'm Groovin'	12
68	Giant GN 18	I'm Gonna Leave You Girl/I Love You, I Love You	10
68	Giant GN 25	Come Cure Me/I Want Your Lovin'	10
68	Gas GAS 132	Gimme Little/Trip To War Land	15
69	Crystal CR 7002	Put On The Pressure/I Don't Know	8
72	Sioux SI 019	Saturday Child/JUMBO STERLING: Hot Dog	8
72	Sioux SI 023	You Don't Know/JUMBO STERLING: My Sugar Ain't Sweet	6

(see also Stranger Cole, Derrick Morgan, Rocksteadys)

KATHY SMITH
70	Polydor 2310 081	SOME SONGS I'VE SAVED (LP)	60

KEELY SMITH (& LOUIS PRIMA)
57	Capitol CL 14717	Hurt Me/High School Affair	6
57	Capitol CL 14739	Young And In Love/You Better Go Now	6
57	Capitol CL 14754	Good Behaviour/You'll Never Know	6
57	Capitol CL 14803	Autumn Leaves/I Keep Forgetting	5
58	Capitol CL 14862	Foggy Day/The Lip (B-side with Louis Prima)	6
58	Capitol CL 14948	That Old Black Magic (with Louis Prima)/You Are My Love	6
59	Capitol CL 14994	I've Got You Under My Skin (with Louis Prima)/Don't Take Your Love From Me	6
59	London HLD 8984	If I Knew I'd Find You (I'd Climb The Highest Mountain)/Don't Let The Stars Get In Your Eyes	12
60	London HLD 9240	Here In My Heart/Close	8
65	Reprise R 20346	You're Breaking My Heart/Crazy	5
61	London RE-D 1269	YOU LOVERS (EP)	20
58	Capitol (S)T 914	I WISH YOU LOVE (LP, mono/stereo)	15
59	Capitol T 1160	HEY BOY! HEY GIRL! (LP, soundtrack, with Louis Prima)	25

(see also Louis Prima, Frank Sinatra)

LONNIE SMITH
67	CBS 63146	FINGER LICKIN' GOOD (LP)	25
70s	Blue Note BST 84290	THINK (LP)	25
70s	Blue Note BST 84313	TURNING POINT (LP)	25
70s	Blue Note BST 84326	MOVE YOUR HAND (LP)	30

LONNIE LISTON SMITH (& THE COSMIC ECHOES)
75	RCA RCA 2568	Expansions (Parts 1 & 2) (& Cosmic Echoes)	10
76	RCA RCA 2668	Chance For Peace/Sunset	5
76	RCA RCA 2727	Get Down Everybody/Inner Beauty	5
79	RCA PB 9450	Expansions/A Chance For Peace	6
79	RCA PC 9450	Expansions/A Chance For Peace (12")	35
83	Bluebird BRT 4	Expansions/Voodoo Woman (12")	15
75	RCA SF 8434	EXPANSIONS (LP, with Cosmic Echoes)	15
76	RCA SF 8461	VISIONS OF A NEW WORLD (LP)	15
76	RCA RS 1053	REFLECTIONS OF A GOLDEN DREAM (LP, with Cosmic Echoes)	12
77	RCA PL 11822	RENAISSANCE (LP, with Cosmic Echoes)	15

LORENZO SMITH
66	Outasite 45-503	(Too Much) Firewater/Count Down (99 copies only)	100

LOU SMITH
60	Top Rank JAR 520	Cruel Love/Close To My Heart	10

MARK E. SMITH
98	Artful ARTFULCD 14	THE POST NEARLY MAN (CD)	18

(see also The Fall)

MARTHA SMITH
65	Pye 7N 15778	As I Watch You Walk Away/It Always Seems Like Summer	20
65	Pye 7N 15860	Love Means Nothing To You/The Song Is Love	7

MARVIN SMITH
66	Coral Q 72486	Time Stopped/Have More Time	50
66	Coral Q 72486	Time Stopped/Have More Time (DJ copy)	100
74	Contempo CS 2034	Let The Good Times Roll/Ain't That A Shame	5

MEL SMITH
81	Mercury MEL 1	Mel Smith's Greatest Hits/Richard & Joey (p/s, with Roger Taylor)	15

MELODY SMITH
71	CBS CBS 7561	You Never Hear A Teardrop Fall/Rastus Ravel	10

MICHAEL SMITH
82	Island ILPS 9717	MI CYAAN BELIEVE IT (LP)	12

MICK SMITH
76	Midas MFHR 078	SOMEBODY NOBODY KNOWS (LP)	35
77	Alida Star AS 771	WORDS AND MUSIC (LP)	30
79	Repercussion RR 1000	RAINDANCE (LP, as Mike Smith)	25

MIKE SMITH
85	Proto ENA 130	Medley (7" version)/Bits And Pieces (in p/s)	7
85	Proto ENAT 130	Medley (12" version)/Glad All Over (12", p/s)	12
90	Mooncrest MOON 1010	You Gotta Play Rock'N'Roll/Operator	6

(see also Dave Clark 5, Smith & D'Abo)

O.C. (OCIE) SMITH
68	CBS 3918	Isn't It Lonely Together/I Ain't The Worryin' Kind	5
57	London HLA 8480	Lighthouse/Too Many (as Ocie Smith)	90
57	London HLA 8480	Lighthouse/Too Many (as Ocie Smith) (78)	60
68	CBS 3343	The Son Of Hickory Holler's Tramp/On A Clear Day You Can See Forever	8
68	CBS 3666	Main Street Mission/Long Black Limousine	5

MINT VALUE £

68	CBS 3767	Little Green Apples/Gas Food Lodgings	5
69	CBS 4514	Daddy's Little Man/If I Leave You Now	5
70	CBS 4657	Me And You/Can't Take Me Eyes Off You	5
70	CBS 5203	Baby I Need Your Loving/San Francisco Is A Lonely Town	5
68	CBS (S) 63147	THE DYNAMIC O.C. SMITH (LP)	20
68	CBS (S) 63362	HICKORY HOLLER REVISITED (LP)	15
69	CBS 63805	AT HOME (LP)	25

(see also Art Mooney)

OTELLO SMITH & TOBAGO BAD BOYS
| 67 | Direction 58-3082 | My Home Town/Trouble | 5 |
| 68 | Direction 8-63242 | THE BIG ONES GO SKA (LP) | 40 |

PATTI SMITH (GROUP)
76	Arista ARIST 47	Gloria (In Excelsis Deo) (Edit)/My Generation (p/s)	5
77	Arista ARIST 12135	Gloria (In Excelsis Deo)/My Generation (live) (12", Rough Trade copies in brown paper bag with titles in felt pen)	10
78	Arista ARIST 181	Because The Night/God Speed (p/s)	5
78	Sire 6078 614	Hey Joe (Version)/Piss Factory (p/s)	15
78	Arista ARIST 197	Privilege (Set Me Free)/Ask The Angels (p/s)	5
78	Arista ARIST 12197	Privilege (Set Me Free)/Ask The Angels/25th Floor (Live Version)/Babelfield (12", p/s)	10
79	Arista ARIST 264	Frederick/Fire Of Unknown Origin (p/s)	5
79	Arista ARIST 281	Dancing Barefoot/5-4-3-2-1 (live) (p/s)	5
79	Arista ARIST 291	So You Want To Be A Rock'n'Roll Star/Frederick (live) (p/s)	5
88	Fierce FRIGHT 017	Brian Jones/Stockinged Feet/Jesus Christ (1-sided, white label)	15
75	Arista ARTY 122	HORSES (LP, 1st pressing, 'Horses' written in white, blue label)	25
76	Arista SPARTY 1001	RADIO ETHIOPIA (LP, as Patti Smith Group, with lyric insert)	15
78	Arista SPART 1043	EASTER (LP)	12

PAUL SMITH
| 65 | Columbia DB 7636 | Piccadilly Paper Boy/Yakety Yak | 10 |

SMITH, PERKINS & SMITH
| 72 | Island ILPS 9198 | SMITH, PERKINS & SMITH (LP) | 12 |

PETER SMITH
| 70s | Pilgrim JLPS 148P | FAITH, FOLK & CLARITY (LP, with Kinfolk) | 18 |
| 70s | Galliard GAL 4016P | FAITH, FOLK & FESTIVITY (LP) | 12 |

RAY SMITH
| 60 | London HL 9051 | Rockin' Little Angel/That's All Right | 45 |

ROY SMITH (& THE STARGAZERS) (U.K.)
| 55 | Decca F 10529 | Red Roses (For My Lady Fair)/The Devil's In Your Eyes | 5 |
| 55 | Decca F 10644 | He/Glengarry (solo) | 5 |

(see also Stargazers)

ROY SMITH (JAMAICA)
| 70 | Grape GR 3013 | See Through Craze/TERRY CARL & DERRICK: I'm The One | 12 |
| 70 | Jackpot JP 723 | The Wedding/Air Balloon | 8 |

SLIM SMITH (& THE UNIQUES)
66	Island WI 3023	I've Got Your Number/The New Boss	55
67	Coxsone CS 7016	Hip Hug/FREEDOM SINGERS: I Want Money	70
67	Coxsone CS 7034	Rougher Yet/I'll Never Let Go	80
67	Coxsone CS 7009	Mercy Mercy/JACKIE MITTOO: Baba Boom	50
68	Trojan TR 619	Watch This Sound/Out Of Love (as Slim Smith & Uniques)	45
69	Unity UN 504	Everybody Needs Love/JUNIOR SMITH: Come Back Girl	10
69	Unity UN 508	For Once In My Life/Burning Desire	15
69	Unity UN 510	Zip A Dee Doo Dah/On Broadway	15
69	Unity UN 513	Let It Be Me/Love Makes Me Do Foolish Things (both with Paulette)	15
69	Unity UN 515	Somebody To Love/Confusion	15
69	Unity UN 520	Slip Away/Spanish Harlem	10
69	Unity UN 524	Sunny Side Of The Sea/A Place In The Sun	40
69	Unity UN 527	Blessed Are The Meek/Conversation	10
69	Unity UN 537	Keep That Light Shining On Me/Build My World Around You	10
69	Unity UN 539	Love Me Tender/This Feeling	10
69	Unity UN 542	Honey/There's A Light	10
69	Jackpot JP 703	If It Don't Work Out/Love Power	7
69	Gas GAS 132	The Vow (& Doreen Shaeffer)/JAMES NEPHEW: Why Don't You Say	5
70	Gas GAS 150	What Kind Of Life/MARTIN RILEY: It's All In The Game	7
70	Unity UN 570	Jenny/The Race	7
70	S&S SC 001	Strong Love/Strange World	15
71	Supreme SUP 219	Stay/You're My Everything	12
71	Pama Supreme PS 334	Send Me Some Loving/I'm Lost	10
71	Camel CA 81	Spanish Harlem/Slip Away	8
71	Escort ERT 851	My Love Come True/This Feeling	6
71	Escort ERT 852	Life Keeps Turning/My Girl	6
71	Escort ERT 859	My Girl/RECO: Plus One	10
71	Jackpot JP 779	Keep Walking/Will You Still Love Me Tomorrow	7
72	Jackpot JP 786	I Need Your Loving/You've Got What It Takes	7
72	Jackpot JP 788	Take Me Back/Where Do I Turn	6
72	Jackpot JP 789	Rain From The Skies/You're No Good	8
72	Jackpot JP 798	Closer Together/Blinded By Love	6
72	Jackpot JP 799	Turning Point/Money Lover	6
72	Dynamic DYN 428	Just A Dream/Send Me Some Loving	6
72	Pama PM 850	The Time Has Come/RECO & HIS BAND: Version	10
72	Pama Supreme PS 373	A Place In The Sun/Stranger On The Shore	6
72	Camel CA 89	Take Me Back/Where Do I Turn	6
72	Explosion EX 2074	The Time Has Come/Blessed Is The Man	6
73	Explosion EX 2078	Stand Up And Fight/The Sunny Side Of The Sea	8
73	Green Door GD 4058	Let Me Love You/If It Don't Work Out	8
73	Bullet BU 523	A Place In The Sun/Burning Fire	30
69	Pama ECO 9	EVERYBODY NEEDS LOVE (LP)	40
72	Trojan TBL 198	MEMORIAL (LP)	40

72	Trojan TBL 186	JUST A DREAM (LP)	40
73	Trojan TBL 198	GREATEST HITS (LP)	25
70s	Lord Koos KLP 1	SLIM SMITH (LP)	18
76	Angen ANGL 1	THE LATE AND GREAT (LP)	40
84	Pama PMLP 3240	TIME HAS COME (LP)	40

(see also Wonder Boy, Pioneers, Uniques, Roy Shirley, Ron Sig, Dakota Jim, Dennis Alcapone, David Isaacs, John Holt, (see also Wonder Boy, Pioneers, Uniques, Roy Shirley, Ron Sig, Dakota Jim, Dennis Alcapone, David Isaacs, John Holt,

SLIM SMITH & THE FREEDOM SINGERS

70	Banana BA 304	Do Dang DO/JACKIE MITTO: Hot Milk	60

SOMETHIN' SMITH & THE REDHEADS

58	Fontana TFR 6005	PUT THE BLAME ON ME (10" LP)	18

STUART SMITH

69	Polydor 56336	My Head Goes Around/Where Are You	6

TAB SMITH & HIS ORCHESTRA

56	Vogue V 2410	Jump Time/Rock City	15
59	London HLM 8801	Smoke Gets In Your Eyes/My Happiness Cha-Cha	10
59	London HLM 8801	Smoke Gets In Your Eyes/My Happiness Cha-Cha (78)	10

TERRY SMITH

69	Philips (S)BL 7871	FALL OUT (LP, laminated lseeve, black/silver label)	125
77	Lambert LAM 002	TERRY SMITH AND TONY LEE TRIO (LP)	20

(see also If)

TRIXIE SMITH

51	Tempo R 42	Black Bottom Stomp/He Likes It Slow (78)	25
52	Vocalion V 1006	Freight Train Blues/Trixie's Blues (78)	30
52	Vocalion V 1017	My Daddy Rocks Me (Parts 1 & 2) (78)	30
53	Jazz Collector L 102	The World's Jazz Crazy And So Am I/Railroad Blues (78)	12
50s	Poydras 101	TRIXIE SMITH (10" EP, 45 rpm)	15
50s	Ristic 12	TRIXIE SMITH (10" EP, 45 rpm)	15
50s	Audubon AAE	TRIXIE SMITH (10" LP)	30

TRIXIE SMITH/MA RAINEY

64	Jazz Collector JEL 22	FEMALE BLUES VOL. 3 (EP, 2 tracks each)	10

TRULY SMITH

66	Decca F 12373	My Smile Is Just A Frown Turned Upside Down/Love Is Me, Love Is You	25
66	Decca F 12415	I Love Him/Buttermilk Hill	5
66	Decca F 12489	You Are The Love Of My Life/The Merry Go Round Is Slowing	5
67	Decca F 12554	Windows And Doors/Take A Broken Heart	5
67	Decca F 12645	I Wanna Go Back There Again/Window Cleaner	35
67	Decca F 12700	The Boy From Chelsea/Little Man With A Stick	20
68	MGM MGM 1431	This Is The First Time/Taking Time Off	20

VERDELLE SMITH

66	Capitol CL 15234	In My Room/Like A Man	18
66	Capitol CL 15456	Tar And Cement/A Piece Of The Sky	12
66	Capitol CL 15481	I Don't Need Anything/If You Can't Say Anything Nice	12
67	Capitol CL 15516	There's So Much Love Around Me/Baby Baby	12

WARREN SMITH

60	London HL 7101	I Don't Believe I'll Fall In Love/Cave-In (export issue)	25
61	London HLG 7110	Odds And Ends/A Whole Lot Of Nothin' (export issue)	25
64	Liberty LIB 55699	Blue Smoke/Judge And Jury	10

WAYNE SMITH

81	Black Joy DH 815	Life Is A Moment In Space/Ain't No Me Without You (12")	40
82	Black Joy DHB 17	Isim Skism/Rose Marie (12", with Yellowman)	50
84	Greensleeves GRED 162	Come Along/Change Your Style (12")	30
85	Greensleeves GRED 169	Under Me Sleng Teng/MICHAEL BUCKLEY: Dance Gate (12")	30
85	Tonos TON 006	Dancing Machine/PATRICK ANDY: Leave The Door (12")	30
85	Greensleeves GRED 183	Ickie All Over/TONTO IRIE: Life Story (12")	30
80s	Unity UN 019	My Sweet Love/TONTO IRIE: Murder Commit (12")	12
85	Greensleeves GRED 177	Sleng Teng Mix Down Remix/PAD ANTHONY: Cry For Me (12")	20
81	Black Joy BHLP 2005	YOUTHMAN SKANKING (LP)	50

WHISPERING SMITH

72	Blue Horizon 2431 015	OVER EASY (LP)	120

WILLIE 'THE LION' SMITH

72	Polydor 2460 156	PORK AND BEANS (LP)	12

ORVILLE SMITH

91	Riz RIZ 001	Leaving Rome/BOMBASTIC CREW: Repatriation Dub	15

SMITH & MIGHTY

00	Studio !K7 !K700lp	BASS IS MATERNAL (LP)	20

SMITH & WESTON

73	Decca F 13441	A Shot Of Rhythm And Blues/Run Run Run	15

SMITH BROTHERS (U.S.)

78	Grapevine GRP 109	There Can Be A Better Way/Payback's A Drag	10

SMITHFIELD MARKET

73	Gloucester GLS 0435	LONDON IN 1665 (LP, private pressing, gatefold sleeve)	800
74	Globe/Gloucester GLS 0443	AFTER SHAKESPEARE (LP, private pressing, die-cut sleeve, with insert)	700

THE SMITHS

SINGLES

83	Rough Trade RT 131	Hand In Glove/Handsome Devil (p/s, original pressing with Manchester address on rear sleeve)	25
83	Rough Trade RT 131	Hand In Glove/Handsome Devil (p/s, second pressing with London address on rear label)	15
83	Rough Trade RT 131	Hand In Glove/Handsome Devil (p/s, third pressing with no address)	20
83	Rough Trade RT 131	Hand In Glove/Handsome Devil (later pressing with misprinted blue/negative p/s - beware of counterfeits!)	2000

MINT VALUE £

83	Rough Trade RT 136	This Charming Man/Jeane (unreleased first pressing with Rough Trade/Capitol logo and solid centre, p/s with Manchester address on rear)	50
83	Rough Trade RT 136	This Charming Man/Jeane (Rough Trade/Capitol logo or reissued 'stamped' logo, p/s)	10
83	Rough Trade RTT 136	This Charming Man (Manchester)/This Charming Man (London)/Accept Yourself/Wonderful Woman (12", p/s; later pressing with band title on sleeve)	30
83	Rough Trade RTT 136	This Charming Man (Manchester)/This Charming Man (London)/Accept Yourself/Wonderful Woman (12", p/s)	15
83	Rough Trade RTT 136NY	This Charming Man (New York Vocal)/This Charming Man (New York Instrumental) (12", p/s)	15
83	Rough Trade RTT 136NY	This Charming Man (New York Vocal)/This Charming Man (New York Instrumental) (12", p/s; later pressing with band title on sleeve)	50
84	Rough Trade RT 146	What Difference Does It Make?/Back To The Old House (Morrissey p/s)	10
84	Rough Trade RT 146	What Difference Does It Make?/Back To The Old House (Terence Stamp p/s)	10
84	Rough Trade RTT 146	What Difference Does It Make?/Back To The Old House/These Things Take Time (12", Morrissey or Terence Stamp p/s)	10
84	Rough Trade RTT 146	What Difference Does It Make?/Back To The Old House/These Things Take Time (Terence Stamp p/s, later pressing with band title on sleeve)	25
84	Rough Trade RT 156	Heaven Knows I'm Miserable Now/Suffer Little Children (p/s)	5
84	Rough Trade RTT 156	Heaven Knows I'm Miserable Now/Girl Afraid/Suffer Little Children (12", p/s)	8
84	Rough Trade RTT 156	Heaven Knows I'm Miserable Now/Girl Afraid/Suffer Little Children (mispressed 12" with extended version)	60
84	Rough Trade RTT 156	Heaven Knows I'm Miserable Now/Girl Afraid/Suffer Little Children (mispressed 12" with extended version)	60
84	Rough Trade RT 166	William, It Was Really Nothing/Please Please Please Let Me Get What I Want (original issue with green 'man on bed' p/s)	8
84	Rough Trade RTT 166	William, It Was Really Nothing/How Soon Is Now?/Please Please Please Let Me Get What I Want (12", original issue with green 'man on bed' p/s)	10
85	Rough Trade RT 176	How Soon Is Now?/Well I Wonder (p/s)	5
85	Rough Trade RTT 176	How Soon Is Now?/Well I Wonder/Oscillate Wildly (12", p/s)	8
85	Rough Trade RT 181	Shakespeare's Sister/What She Said (p/s)	5
85	Rough Trade RTT 181	Shakespeare's Sister/What She Said/Stretch Out And Wait (12", p/s, with yellow & blue inner)	8
85	Rough Trade RTT 181	Shakespeare's Sister/What She Said/Stretch Out And Wait (12", p/s, with misprinted red & green inner)	50
85	Rough Trade RT 186	That Joke Isn't Funny Anymore/Meat Is Murder (live) (p/s)	5
85	Rough Trade RTT 186	That Joke Isn't Funny Anymore/Nowhere Fast (live)/Stretch Out And Wait (live)/Shakespeare's Sister (live)/Meat Is Murder (live) (12", p/s)	8
85	Rough Trade RT 191	The Boy With The Thorn In His Side/Asleep (p/s)	5
85	Rough Trade RTT 191	The Boy With The Thorn In His Side/Rubber Ring/Asleep (12", p/s)	8
86	Rough Trade RT 192	Bigmouth Strikes Again/Money Changes Everything (p/s)	5
86	Rough Trade RTT 192	Bigmouth Strikes Again/Money Changes Everything/Unloveable (12", p/s)	8
86	Rough Trade RT 193	Panic/Vicar In A Tutu (p/s, with square sheet of 'Hang The DJ' stickers)	20
86	Rough Trade RT 193	Panic/Vicar In A Tutu (p/s, with round sheet of 'Hang The DJ' stickers)	15
86	Rough Trade RTT 193	Panic/Vicar In A Tutu/The Draize Train (12", p/s, with 'Hang The DJ' stickers)	15
86	Rough Trade RT 194	Ask/Cemetry Gates (p/s)	5
86	Rough Trade RTT 194	Ask/Cemetry Gates/Golden Lights (12", p/s)	8
86	Rough Trade RT 194C	Ask/Cemetry Gates/Golden Lights (cassette with picture inlay)	10
87	Rough Trade RT 195	Shoplifters Of The World Unite/Half A Person (p/s)	5
87	Rough Trade RTT 195	Shoplifters Of The World Unite/London/Half A Person (12", p/s; in carrier bag)	30
87	Rough Trade RTT 195	Shoplifters Of The World Unite/London/Half A Person (12", p/s)	8
87	Rough Trade RTT 195	Shoplifters Of The World Unite/London/Half A Person (12", p/s, mispressing, A-side plays "You Just Haven't Earned It Yet Baby")	70
87	Rough Trade RT 196	Sheila Take A Bow/Is It Really So Strange? (p/s)	5
87	Rough Trade RTT 196	Sheila Take A Bow/Is It Really So Strange?/Sweet And Tender Hooligan (12", p/s)	8
87	Rough Trade RT 197	Girlfriend In A Coma/Work Is A Four Letter Word (grey p/s)	5
87	Rough Trade RT 197	Girlfriend In A Coma/Work Is A Four Letter Word (misprinted green p/s, incorrectly shows additional 12" track 'I Keep Mine Hidden' on reverse of sleeve)	500
87	Rough Trade RTT 197	Girlfriend In A Coma/Work Is A Four Letter Word/I Keep Mine Hidden (12", green p/s; some in grey p/s)	35
87	Rough Trade RTT 197	Girlfriend In A Coma/Work Is A Four Letter Word/I Keep Mine Hidden (12", green p/s)	8
87	Rough Trade RTT 197C	Girlfriend In A Coma/Work Is A Four Letter Word/I Keep Mine Hidden (cassette with picture inlay)	10
87	Rough Trade RT 198	I Started Something I Couldn't Finish/Pretty Girls Make Graves (Troy Tate demo) (p/s)	5
87	Rough Trade RTT 198	I Started Something I Couldn't Finish/Pretty Girls Make Graves (Troy Tate demo)/Some Girls Are Bigger Than Others (Live) (12", p/s)	8
87	Rough Trade RTT 198C	I Started Something I Couldn't Finish/Pretty Girls Make Graves/Some Girls Are Bigger Than Others/What's The World (live) (cassette)	10
87	Rough Trade RT 200	Last Night I Dreamt That Somebody Loved Me/Rusholme Ruffians (John Peel version) (p/s)	5
87	Rough Trade RTT 200	Last Night I Dreamt That Somebody Loved Me/Rusholme Ruffians (John Peel version)/Nowhere Fast (John Peel Version) (12", p/s)	8
87	Rough Trade RTT 200CD	Last Night I Dreamt That Somebody Loved Me/Rusholme Ruffians (John Peel version)/Nowhere Fast (John Peel version)/William, It Was Really Nothing (John Peel Version) (CD)	20
87	Rough Trade RT 166	William, It Was Really Nothing/How Soon Is Now? (reissue, Billie Whitelaw p/s)	20
87	Rough Trade RTT 166	William, It Was Really Nothing/How Soon Is Now?/Please Please Please Let Me Get What I Want (12", reissue, Billie Whitelaw p/s)	30
88	Rough Trade CAT 063	London (Live) (Square 1-sided black flexi, 33rpm free with The Catalogue magazine, reverse has reproduction of hand-written poem for 'Poppycocteau' by Morrissey)	10
92	WEA YZ0001	This Charming Man/Jeane (p/s, reissue)	5
92	WEA YZ0002	How Soon Is Now? (p/s, reissue)	15
92	WEA YZ0003	There Is A Light That Never Goes Out/Handsome Devil (live) (p/s)	15

SINGLES : CD REISSUE SINGLES

88	Rough Trade RTT 146CD	What Difference Does It Make?/Back To The Old House/These Things Take Time	25
88	Rough Trade RTT 156CD	Heaven Knows I'm Miserable Now/Girl Afraid/Suffer Little Children	25
88	Rough Trade RTT 166CD	William, It Was Really Nothing/How Soon Is Now?/Please Please Please Let Me Get What I Want	30
88	Rough Trade RTT 171CD	Barbarism Begins At Home/Shakespeare's Sister/Stretch Out And Wait	35
88	Rough Trade RTT 191CD	The Boy With The Thorn In His Side/Rubber Ring/Asleep	25
88	Rough Trade RTT 193CD	Panic/Vicar In A Tutu/The Draize Train	25
88	Rough Trade RTT 194CD	Ask/Cemetry Gates/Golden Lights	15
88	Rough Trade RTT 215CD	The Headmaster Ritual/Nowhere Fast (live)/Stretch Out And Wait (live)/Meat Is Murder (live)	40
93	WEA YZ0003 CD1	There Is A Light That Never Goes Out/Hand In Glove (live)/Some Girls Are Bigger Than Others (live)/Money Changes Everything	10

| 93 | WEA YZ0003 CD2 | There Is A Light That Never Goes Out/Hand In Glove (Sandie Shaw)/I Don't Owe You Anything (Sandie Shaw)/Jeane (Sandie Shaw) | 10 |

ALBUMS

84	Rough Trade ROUGH 61	THE SMITHS (LP)	12
84	Rough Trade ROUGH 76	HATFUL OF HOLLOW (LP, original gatefold issue, with incorrect sleeve, no black dot appears between 'Accept Yourself' and 'Girl Afraid' on reverse of sleeve)	20
85	Rough Trade ROUGH 81	MEAT IS MURDER (LP, with lyric inner sleeve)	15
85	Rough Trade ROUGH CD 81	MEAT IS MURDER (CD, original issue)	18
85	Rough Trade ROUGH CD 76	HATFUL OF HOLLOW (CD, original blue sleeve)	60
86	Rough Trade ROUGH CD 61	THE SMITHS (CD, original issue)	18
86	Rough Trade ROUGH 96	THE QUEEN IS DEAD (LP, gatefold, inner sleeve)	15
86	Rough Trade ROUGH CD 96	THE QUEEN IS DEAD (CD, original issue)	18
87	Rough Trade ROUGH CD 101	THE WORLD WON'T LISTEN (CD, original issue)	18
87	Rough Trade ROUGH 106	STRANGEWAYS HERE WE COME (LP, embossed sleeve)	15
87	Rough Trade ROUGH CD 106	STRANGEWAYS, HERE WE COME (CD, original issue)	18
87	Rough Trade ROUGH 255	LOUDER THAN BOMBS (2-LP, gatefold sleeve)	20
87	Rough Trade ROUGH CD 255	LOUDER THAN BOMBS (CD)	20
88	Rough Trade ROUGH CD 76	HATFUL OF HOLLOW (CD, reissue sleeve)	18
88	Rough Trade ROUGH 126	RANK (LP, gatefold sleeve, with inner, ltd. edition with poster and cover sticker denoting amended catalogue number)	20
88	Rough Trade ROUGH 126D	RANK (DAT)	50
93	WEA SMITHS 1	THE SMITHS (10" LP, reissue)	12
93	WEA SMITHS 2	HATFUL OF HOLLOW (2-LP, 10" reissue)	12
93	WEA SMITHS 3	MEAT IS MURDER (10" LP reissue)	12
93	WEA SMITHS 4	THE QUEEN IS DEAD (10" LP reissue)	12
93	WEA SMITHS 5	THE WORLD WON'T LISTEN (10" LP reissue)	12
93	WEA SMITHS 6	STRANGEWAYS, HERE WE COME (10" LP)	12
93	WEA SMITHS 7	RANK (10" 2-LP reissue)	12

PROMOS : PROMOS & TEST PRESSINGS

83	Rough Trade RT 131	Hand In Glove (white label 1983 test pressing - approx. 5 only)	1800
83	N/A	3-Pack (Rough Trade promo cassette, promoting Hand In Glove and tracks by two other bands)	100
83	Rough Trade RT 136	Reel Around The Fountain/Jeane (unissued, white label test pressings only - beware of counterfeits!)	1000
83	Rough Trade RT 136	This Charming Man (London Version) (rejected white label test pressing)	800
83	Rough Trade RT 136	This Charming Man (Manchester) (one-sided white label test pressing)	300
83	Rough Trade RTT 136NY	This Charming Man (New York vocal)/(New York Instrumental) (12" white label test pressing)	300
84	Rough Trade RT 146	What Difference Does It Make?/Back To The Old House (white label test pressing)	30
84	Rough Trade RTT 146	What Difference Does It Make?/Back To The Old House/These Things Take Time (12" white label test pressing)	100
84	Rough Trade R 61 DJ	Still Ill/You've Got Everything Now (test pressing)	200
84	Rough Trade RT 61 DJ	Still Ill/You've Got Everything Now (promo)	25
84	Rough Trade ROUGH 61	THE SMITHS (white label test pressing)	30
84	Rough Trade RT 131	Hand In Glove (one-sided white label 1984 test pressing)	100
84	Rough Trade RT 131	Hand In Glove/Handsome Devil (white label test pressing for 1984 repressing)	100
84	Rough Trade RT 156	Heaven Knows I'm Miserable Now/Suffer Little Children (one-sided test pressing)	200
84	Rough Trade RT 156	Heaven Knows I'm Miserable Now/Suffer Little Children (rejected white label test pressing with extended version)	800
84	Rough Trade RTT 156	Heaven Knows I'm Miserable Now/Girl Afraid/Suffer Little Children (rejected 12" white label test pressing with extended version)	800
84	Rough Trade RT 156	Heaven Knows I'm Miserable Now/Suffer Little Children (standard white label test pressing)	20
84	Rough Trade RTT 156	Heaven Knows I'm Miserable Now/Girl Afraid/Suffer Little Children (standard 12" white label test pressing)	200
84	Rough Trade RT 166	William, It Was Really Nothing/Please Please Please Let Me Get What I Want (white label test pressing)	20
84	Rough Trade RTT 166	William, It Was Really Nothing/How Soon Is Now?/Please Please Please Let Me Get What I Want (12" white label test pressing)	100
84	Rough Trade ROUGH 76	HATFUL OF HOLLOW (white label test pressing)	30
84	Copymasters	HATFUL OF HOLLOW (cassette, early version with unreleased tracks)	100
85	Rough Trade RTT 171	Barbarism Begins At Home (12", 2 different 1-sided white label test pressings)	400
85	Rough Trade RTT 171	Barbarism Begins At Home (12" one-sided, promo)	50
85	Rough Trade RTT 171	Barbarism Begins At Home (edited version)/(long version)	45
85	Rough Trade RT 171	Barbarism Begins At Home (12", p/s, one-sided promo)	40
85	Rough Trade RT 176	How Soon Is Now?/Oscillate Wildly (white label test pressing with Oscillate Wildly instead of Well I Wonder on the B-side)	300
85	Rough Trade RTT 176	How Soon Is Now?/Well I Wonder/Oscillate Wildly (12" white label test pressing)	200
85	Rough Trade ROUGH 81	MEAT IS MURDER (white label test pressing)	300
85	Rough Trade RT 181	Shakespeare's Sister/What She Said (white label test pressing)	200
85	Rough Trade RT 186	Meat Is Murder/Nowhere Fast/Stretch Out And Wait (live EP, unissued, test pressings only)	1000
85	Rough Trade RT 186	Meat Is Murder/Nowhere Fast/Stretch Out And Wait (live EP, unissued, Mayking test pressings - beware of counterfeits!)	500
85	Rough Trade RTT 186	Meat Is Murder/William It Was Really Nothing/Nowhere Fast/Stretch Out And Wait /Miserable Lie (live 12" EP, unissued, test pressings only-beware of counterfeits!)	1000
85	Rough Trade RT 186	That Joke Isn't Funny Anymore/Meat Is Murder (live) (white label test pressing)	100
85	RT 186	That Joke Isn't Funny Anymore/Meat Is Murder (live) (Mayking test pressing)	300
85	Rough Trade RTT 191	The Boy With The Thorn In His Side/Rubber Ring/Asleep (white label test pressing)	20
86	Rough Trade RT 192	Bigmouth Strikes Again/Money Changes Everything (white label test pressing)	200
86	Rough Trade RTT 192	Bigmouth Strikes Again/Money Changes Everything/Unloveable (12" white label test pressing)	30
86	Rough Trade ROUGH 96	THE QUEEN IS DEAD (white label test pressing)	150
86	Rough Trade ROUGH 96	THE QUEEN IS DEAD (Mayking test pressing)	300
86	Rough Trade RTT 193	Panic/Vicar In A Tutu/The Draize Train (12" white label test pressing with promo posters)	50
86	Rough Trade RT 194	Ask/Cemetry Gates (white label test pressing)	200
87	Rough Trade RTT 195	You Just Haven't Earned It Yet Baby/London/Half A Person (12", white label test pressing)	800
87	Rough Trade ROUGH 101	THE WORLD WON'T LISTEN (white label test pressing)	20
87	Rough Trade RT 196	Sheila Take A Bow/Is It Really So Strange? (white label test pressing)	200
87	Rough Trade ROUGH 255	LOUDER THAN BOMBS (2-LP, white label test pressings)	200
87	Rough Trade RT 197	Girlfriend In A Coma/Work Is A Four Letter Word (white label test pressing)	200

			MINT VALUE £
87	Rough Trade ROUGH 106	STRANGEWAYS, HERE WE COME (white label test pressing)	20
87	Rough Trade RT 198	I Started Something I Couldn't Finish/Pretty Girls Make Graves (Troy Tate demo) (white label test pressing)	200
87	Rough Trade RT 198	I Started Something I Couldn't Finish/Pretty Girls Make Graves (Mayking test pressing)	400
87	Rough Trade RT 166-B	How Soon Is Now? (1-sided white label test pressing for B-side of re-issued William, It Was Really Nothing 7")	200
88	Rough Trade ROUGH 126	RANK (white label test pressing; in misprinted sleeve, no cover star or title on sleeve, just states 'The Smiths')	200
88	Rough Trade ROUGH 126	RANK (white label test pressing)	20

(see also Morrissey, Sandie Shaw, The The, Electronic)

SMITHY ALL STARS
71	Hillcrest HCT 3	Witchfinder General/Deserted	5

(see also Ian Smith & Inner Mind)

SMOG
95	City Slang EFAD 49517	A Hit/Wine Stained Lips (p/s, yellow vinyl)	6
97	Domino WIGLP 3	RED APPLE FALLS (LP)	18
00	Domino WIGLP 7	DONGS OF SEVOTION (2-LP)	18

SMOKE
67	Columbia DB 8115	My Friend Jack/We Can Take It	35
67	Columbia DB 8252	If The Weather's Sunny/I Would If I Could, But I Can't	35
67	Columbia DB 8252	If The Weather's Sunny/I Would If I Could, But I Can't (in export p/s)	80
67	Island WIP 6023	It Could Be Wonderful/Have Some More Tea	65
68	Island WIP 6031	Utterly Simple/Sydney Gill (unreleased)	0
70	Revolution Pop REVP 1002	Dreams Of Dreams/My Birth	50
71	Pageant SAM 101	Ride Ride Ride/Guy Fawkes	12
72	Regal Zonophone RZ 3071	Sugar Man/That's What I Want	25
74	Decca FR 13484	Shagalagalu/Gimme Good Loving	5
74	Decca FR 13514	My Lullaby/Looking High	15
70s	Gull 128 301	IT'S SMOKE TIME (LP, reissue of German-only LP)	20
88	M. Blue Town MBT 5001	MY FRIEND JACK (LP)	15

(see also Shots)

SMOKESTACK CRUMBLE
71	Dawn DNS 1013	Got A Bad Leg/Whiskey Macaroni	12

SMOKESTACK LIGHTNIN'
68	Bell BLL 1046	Light In My Window/Long Stemmed Eyes (John's Song)	15
69	Bell MBLL/SBLL 116	OFF THE WALL (LP)	30

SMOKEY BABE
62	77' LA 12-12	SMOKEY BABE AND HIS FRIENDS (LP)	25

SMOKEY CIRCLES
70	Carnaby CNS4011	Long Live Love/Love Me While You Can	5
70	Carnaby CNLS 6006	THE SMOKEY CIRCLES ALBUM (LP, union jack flag label)	60

SMOKEY SMOTHERS
69	Polydor 623 239	THE DRIVING BLUES (LP)	40

SMOKIE & HIS SISTER
67	CBS 202605	Creators Of Rain/In Dreams Of Silent Seas	10

THE SMOKIN' MOJO FILTERS
95	Go! Discs GOD 136	Come Together/THE BEAUTIFUL SOUTH: A Minute's Silence/DODGY: Is It Me/BLACK GRAPE: In The Name Of The Father (Crown Of Thorns Mix) (7")	5

(See also Paul Weller, Oasis)

SMOKIN' ROADIE
83	Zone To Zone ZON 3	Midnight/Ripp Off (p/s)	30

SMOOTH BUT HAZZARDOUS
92	Basement BRSS 007	Smooth But Hazzardous/Made U Dance/Violent Headrush (12")	20
93	Sound Entity SENT 1200	We Are The Creator/Push Up The Levels (12")	40
93	Sound Entity SENT 1205	Made You Dance (Carl Cox Remix)/Push Up The Levels (SBH Remix)/Push Up The Levels (Originla Mix) (12")	15
94	Sinister SNS 003	Help Me/DMX Override (12")	10

JACK SMOOTH
91	Sound Entity SE 001	WAVEFORMS EP (12")	15
91	Sound Entity SE 03	Untitled/Untitled/Untitled/Untitled (12", white label, hand-written labels, some in stamped sleeve)	15
93	Sound Entity SENT 1201	Tell Me Something/Happy Nonsense (12", with Spencer T)	20
93	Sound Entity SENT 120220	HURTS EP (12", with Alex Reece)	40

(see also Ruff With The Smooth, DJ Chemistry Meets Jack Smooth)

SMYLE
71	CBS 7225	Glory Glory/Will I Get Back Tomorrow	8

DES SMYTH & COLLEGEMEN
65	Pye 7N 15867	The Pillow That Whispers/Lonely Streets	5
65	Pye 7N 15996	Wedding Bells/All For The Love Of A Girl	5

GILLI SMYTH & MOTHER GONG
78	Charly CRL 5007	MOTHER (LP, with insert)	15

(see also Gong)

DONALD SMYTHE
71	Punch PH 83	Where Love Goes/HURRICANES: You Can Run	40

GLORIA SMYTHE
60	Vogue V 9159	I'll Be Over After A While/Gee Baby Ain't I Good To You	10

SNAFU
74	WWA WWS 007	Dixie Queen/Monday Morning	5
74	WWA WWA 003	SNAFU (LP, gatefold sleeve)	18
74	WWA WWA 013	SITUATION NORMAL (LP)	12

(see also Whitesnake, Freedom)

SNAKEBITE
83	Astor ASTOR 1	Blow You Away/Thin Ice (no p/s)	25

SNAKES
76	Dynamite DYR45006	Teenage Head/Lights Out (p/s)	8

(see also The Motors)

SNAPE
73	Transatlantic TRA 269	ACCIDENTALLY BORN IN NEW ORLEANS (LP)	22

(see also Alexis Korner)

SNAPPERS
59	Top Rank JAR 167	Big Bill/If There Were	18
67	CBS 2719	Upside Down Inside Out/Memories	40
59	Top Rank JAR 167	Big Bill/If There Were (78)	25

SNATCH (1)
75	Polydor 2058619	For Always And Ever/Hunting Kind	12

SNATCH (2)
78	Lightning LIG 502	Stanley/I.R.T. (p/s)	10
78	Lightning LIG 505	All I Want/When I'm Bored ('foil' p/s)	10
80	Fetish FET 004	Shopping For Clothes/Joey/Red Army (12", die-cut p/s)	20

(see also Johnny Thunders, Judy Nylon)

SNEAKERS
77	Petal PTL 010	Link Lady/Vapour Trails (no p/s, 500 only)	150

SNEAKY PETES
60	Decca F 11199	Savage (Parts 1 & 2)	15

SNEEKERS
64	Columbia DB 7385	I Just Can't Get To Sleep/Bald Headed Woman	150

SNEEKY FEELINS
79	Warped W102	Private Mail/Only The Rain (p/s with insert)	50

DAVID SNELL
66	Decca SKL 4745	THE SUBTLE SOUND OF DAVID SNELL (LP)	15

LEN SNIDER
63	London HLU 9790	Everyone Knows/I'll Be Coming Home Tonight	8

SNIFF 'N' THE TEARS
79	Chiswick NS 40	Driver's Seat (cancelled, test pressings only, picture sleeve)	15

SNIFTERS
78	Lightning GIL 534	I Like Boys/Baby Punker	15

SNIPERS
81	Crass 321984/4	THREE PEACE SUITE (EP)	12

SNIVELLING SHITS
77	Ghetto Rockers PRE 2	Terminal Stupid/I Can't Come (p/s, first pressing of 500,paper labels/black print)	60
77	Ghetto Rockers PRE 2	Terminal Stupid/I Can't Come (p/s, 2nd pressing, plastic labels/juke box centre)	25
89	Damaged Goods FNARR 4	Isgodaman?/Terminal Stupid/I Can't Come (p/s)	20
89	Dam. Goods FNARR4B	Isgodaman?/Terminal Stupid/I Can't Come (box set with badge & inserts, pink vinyl in stamped plain white sleeve)	25
90	Dam. Goods FNARR LP 3	I CAN'T COME (LP, brown vinyl)	12

(see also Doctor Dark)

SNOBS
64	Decca F 11867	Buckle Shoe Stomp/Stand And Deliver	15

SNOOKY & MOODY
66	Blue Horizon 45-1003	Snooky And Moody's Blues/Telephone Blues (99 copies only)	135

HANK SNOW (& RAINBOW RANCH BOYS)
54	HMV 7MC 7	Why Do You Punish Me (For Loving You)/When Mexican Joe Meets Jole Blon (with Rainbow Ranch Boys) (export issue)	15
54	HMV 7MC 15	Spanish Fire Ball/Between Fire And Water (with Rainbow Ranch Boys)(export issue)	15
54	HMV 7MC 24	My Arabian Baby/I Don't Hurt Anymore (with Rainbow Ranch Boys) (export issue)	15
54	HMV 7MC 25	My Religion's Not Old-Fashioned (But It's Real Genuine)/The Alphabet (with Rainbow Ranch Boys) (export issue)	15
54	HMV 7MC 31	Yellow Roses/Would You Mind (with Rainbow Ranch Boys) (export issue)	15
59	RCA RCA 1151	Old Shep/The Last Ride	10
61	RCA RCA 1248	Poor Little Jimmie/Beggar To A King	5
58	RCA RCX 116	COUNTRY GUITAR NO. 4 (EP)	8
59	RCA RCX 142	COUNTRY GUITAR NO. 7 (EP)	10
63	RCA RCX 7125	WHEN TRAGEDY STRUCK (EP)	10
64	RCA RCX 7154	THAT COUNTRY GENTLEMAN (EP)	12
59	RCA RD 27115	WHEN TRAGEDY STRUCK (LP)	15

(see also Chet Atkins)

SNOW PATROL
98	Jeepster JPR7004	Little Hide/Sticky Teenage Twin (1,000 only, p/s)	30
04	Polydor 9866356	Chocolate/One Night Is Not Enough (Live) (p/s orange vinyl)	10
04	Polydor FICTION 001	Run (Jacknife Lee Mix)/Run (Freelance Hellraiser Mix) (10" clear vinyl stickered poly bag)	8
06	Fiction 0602517043985	Chasing Cars/Play Me Like You Own Hand (p/s, with inner p/s)	12
98	Jeepster JPRLP004	SONGS FOR POLAR BEARS (LP)	30
03	Polydor 9866073	FINAL STRAW (LP)	15

(see also Shrug)

SNUFF
88	Deceptive	TWEET TWEET MY LOVELY (LP, with insert)	15

SNUGGY
71	Philips 6006138	Creole Jive/Jungle King	12

(see also Jade Warrior)

BILL SNYDER & HIS (MAGIC PIANO &) ORCHESTRA

54	London REP 1011	BEWITCHED (EP)	8
51	London H-APB 1004	BEWITCHED (10" LP)	12
54	Brunswick LA 8667	THE STARLIT HOUR (10" LP)	12

RON SNYDER
| 63 | Parlophone R 4993 | Oh My Twisted Bach/Narcissus | 6 |

SO WHAT!
| 86 | No label or Cat. No. | It Is All Over/Now I Don't Want You Around (no p/s) | 50 |
| 70 | CBS 5005 | Flowers/Tell Me Now | 10 |

S.O.B.
| 89 | Rise Above RISE 002 | THRASH NIGHT EP (p/s) | 8 |

ERROL SOBERS
| 70 | Beacon BEA 159 | Sugar Shaker/You're In Love | 12 |

(see also Bobby Bridger)

SOCIAL DISEASE
| 83 | Carnage | TODAY (EP) | 8 |

SOCIALITES
| 64 | Warner Bros WB 148 | Jive Jimmy/You're Losing Your Touch | 40 |

SOCIAL SECURITY
| 78 | Heartbeat PULSE 1 | I Don't Want My Heart To Rule My Head/Stella's Got A Fella/Cider/Choc Ice (p/s) | 30 |

SOCIETIE
| 67 | Deram DM 162 | Bird Has Flown/Breaking Down | 50 |

SO CONFUSING AND SO VERY CLEAR
| 76 | CFC 19776 | SO CONFUSING AND SO VERY CLEAR (LP) | 70 |

SOCRATES
| 72 | Deram DM 362 | Eating Momma's Cookin'/Dearest Agnes | 15 |

SODS (1)
| 79 | Tap TAP 1 | Mopey Grape/Negative Positive (p/s) | 30 |
| 79 | Stortbeat SB 5 | No Pictures Of Us/Plaything (p/s) | 40 |

SODS (2)
| 79 | Step Forward SFLP 3 | MINYUTES TO GO (LP) | 30 |

SOFERNO B
| 80 | Soferno B SOLP 001 | IN DUB (LP) | 75 |

SOFT BOYS
77	Raw RAW 5	GIVE IT TO THE SOFT BOYS (EP, acetate with withdrawn track, Vyrna Knowl Is A Headbanger in place of "Ventilator")	200
77	Raw RAW 5	GIVE IT TO THE SOFT BOYS (EP)	20
78	Radar ADA 8	(I Want To Be An) Anglepoise Lamp/Fat Man's Son (p/s)	15
79	Raw RAW 37	GIVE IT TO THE SOFT BOYS (EP, unreleased reissue)	0
79	Raw RAW 41	Where Are The Prawns (unreleased)	0
80	Armageddon AEP 002	NEAR THE SOFT BOYS (EP)	8
80	Armageddon AS 005	I Wanna Destroy You/I'm An Old Pervert (Disco) (p/s)	8
81	Armageddon AS 029	Only The Stones Remain/The Asking Tree (p/s)	8
82	Bucketfull Of Brains BOB 1	Love Poisoning/When I Was A Kid (p/s, with Bucketfull Of Brains magazine)	15
82	Bucketfull Of Brains BOB 1	Love Poisoning/When I Was A Kid (p/s, without Bucketfull Of Brains magazine)	12
83	Midnight Music DING 4	He's A Reptile/Song No. 4 (p/s, 2 different designs)	8
89	Overground OVER 4	The Face Of Death/The Yodelling Hoover (p/s, 600 yellow viny or 400 white vinyl)	6
89	Overground OVER 4	The Face Of Death/The Yodelling Hoover (p/s, 15 gold test pressings)	15
85	Delorean SOFT 1P	WADING THROUGH A VENTILATOR (12" EP, picture disc)	10
79	Two Crabs CLAW 1001	A CAN OF BEES (LP, original issue, black & white labels)	20
80	Aura AUL 709	A CAN OF BEES (LP, reissue)	12
80	Armageddon ARM 1	UNDERWATER MOONLIGHT (LP)	15
82	Armageddon BYE 1	TWO HALVES FOR THE PRICE OF ONE (LP)	12
83	M. Music CHIME 0002	INVISIBLE HITS (LP)	12
84	Two Crabs CLAW 1001	A CAN OF BEES (LP, 2nd reissue, black & red labels)	12

(see also Robyn Hitchcock, Kimberley Rew)

SOFT CELL
80	Big Frock ABF 1	MUTANT MOMENTS (EP, plain p/s with postcard; beware of counterfeits without postcard & in wraparound p/s!)	60
81	Some Bizzare HARD 1	A Man Can Get Lost/Memorabilia (p/s, 10,000 only)	10
81	Some Bizzare HARD 12	Memorabilia (Extended)/Persuasion (Extended) (12", p/s)	10
81	Some Bizzare BZS 212	Tainted Love/Where Did Our Love Go/Tainted Dub/Memorabilia (12", p/s, limited edition with 4 tracks)	10
81	Some Bizzare No Cat. No.	Metro Mr. X/B-MOVIE: Remembrance Day (white label test pressing)	60
82	Some Bizzare CELBX 1	THE 12" SINGLES (6 x 12" box set, with booklet)	50
83	Some Bizzare BZS 17	Numbers/Memorabilia (live) (foldout card p/s)	7
83	Some Bizzare BZS 2020	Soul Inside/You Only Live Twice/Loving You - Hating Me/Her Imagination (double pack)	8
83	Lyntone (no cat. no.)	Say Hello, Wave Goodbye (live) (flexidisc, blue vinyl, fan club issue, 500 only)	15
84	Lyntone (no cat. no.)	Ghostrider (live '83) (flexidisc, blue, black or green vinyl, fan club issue)	15
84	Some Bizzare BZSR 2212	Down In The Subway (Remix)/Disease And Desire/Born To Lose (12", p/s)	18
91	Some Bizzare SOFCP 1	Say Hello, Wave Goodbye - '91/Numbers/Torch (Original Extended Version) (CD, picture disc)	8
91	Some Bizzare (no cat no)	Megamix '91 (12", promo only, custom p/s)	12

(see also Marc Almond, Marc & Mambas, Anne Hogan)

SOFT PEDALLING
| 70 | Decca F 23034 | It's So Nice/Rolling On Home | 5 |

SOFT ROCK
| 72 | Philips 6308 | INVENTION (LP) | 15 |

SOFT DRINKS
| 82 | Outer Himalayan OH 4 | Pepsi Cola/Pop Stars In Their Pyjames (with booklet and sticker) | 30 |

SOFTIES
| 77 | Charly CYS 1036 | Suicide Pilot/C.I. Angel (p/s) ....5 |

(see also Captain Sensible)

MICK SOFTLEY
65	Immediate IM 014	I'm So Confused/She's My Girl 40
67	CBS 202469	Am I The Red One/That's Not My Kind Of Love 180
70	CBS 5130	Can You Hear Me Now/Time Machine 7
71	CBS 7337	Goin' Down The Road/Gypsy 7
72	CBS 8269	Lady Willow/From The Land Of The Crab 7
65	Columbia 33SX 1781	SONGS FOR SWINGIN' SURVIVORS (LP) 150
70	CBS 64098	SUNRISE (LP, gatefold sleeve) 50
71	CBS 64395	STREET SINGER (LP) 40
72	CBS 64841	ANY MOTHER DOESN'T GRUMBLE (LP) 40

SOFT MACHINE
67	Polydor 56151	Love Makes Sweet Music/Reelin' Feelin' Squeelin' 175
78	Harvest HAR 5155	Soft Space (Parts 1 & 2) (p/s) 8
69	Probe SPB 1002	THE SOFT MACHINE VOLUME TWO (LP, black/silver label) ...60
69	Probe SPB 1002	THE SOFT MACHINE VOLUME TWO (LP, second pressing, black/silver label, flipback sleeve) 40
70	CBS 66246	THIRD (2-LP, gatefold) 40
71	CBS 64280	FOURTH (LP, embossed textured sleeve) 25
72	CBS 64806	FIFTH (LP) 25
73	CBS 68214	SIX (2-LP, gatefold sleeve) 25
73	CBS 65799	SEVEN (LP, gatefold sleeve) 20
75	Harvest SHSP 4044	BUNDLES (LP, with inner sleeve) 12
76	Harvest SHSP 4056	SOFTS (LP) 15
77	Harvest SHTW 800	TRIPLE ECHO (3-LP, box set, with colour booklet) 50
78	Harvest SHSP 4083	ALIVE & WELL (LP) 15
79	CBS 31748	FIFTH (LP, reissue, embossed sleeve) 12
81	EMI EMC 3348	LAND OF COCKAYNE (LP) 12
88	Reckless RECKLP5	LIVE AT THE PROMS (LP) 15

(see also Robert Wyatt, Kevin Ayers, Hugh Hopper, Elton Dean, Daevid Allen, Matching Mole, 'Igginbottom, Lyn Dobson)

SOFT SHOE
| 78 | Aardvark AARD 1 | FOR THOSE ALONE (LP, with insert) ....100 |

SOFT TOUCH
| 67 | W+G WG 001 | A Silent Life/Ellusive Face (Private Pressing) ....300 |

SOHEP
| 81 | Merciful Release MR 3 | So Much Fun/You Could Be So Nice Dear (p/s) ....10 |

SOHO JETS
| 75 | Polydor 2058 525 | Hi Heel Tarzan/Night Flight ....20 |
| 75 | Polydor 2058 598 | Denim Goddess/Smile ....20 |

SOHO SKIFFLE GROUP
57	Melodisc 1403	Give Me A Big Fat Woman/The Midnight Special (78) 20
57	Melodisc 1421	Frankie And Johnny/Streamline Train (78) 20
57	Melodisc EMP 7 72	SOHO SKIFFLE GROUP (EP) 75

SOL INVICTUS
90	Cerne 004	Abbatoirs Of Love/CURRENT 93: This Ain't The Summer Of Love (live in Japan, gig freebie, 93 with insert & gig ticket) 50
90	Cerne 004	Abbatoirs Of Love/CURRENT 93: This Ain't The Summer Of Love (live in Japan, gig freebie, [200 without insert]) 25
91	Shock SX 016	See The Dove Fall/Somewhere In Europe (numbered foldover p/s in poly bag, 1,000 only) .15
91	World Serpent WS7 002	Looking For Europe (1-sided, etched B-side, foldover sleeve in poly bag, 963 only) 15
89	SVL SVL 009	IN THE JAWS OF THE SERPENT (LP, with insert) 20
90	Tursa 001	TREES IN WINTER (LP) 30
90	Tursa 002	LEX TALIONIS (CD, special edit in leather wallet) 30
91	Tursa 003	KILLING TIDE (LP) 25
91	Tursa 003	KILLING TIDE (CD, special edit in felt bag) 20
00	Tursa 026	EVE (picture disc, LP) 20
01	Tursa 029	HILL OF CROSSES (LP, 1,000 only, signed) 20
02	Tursa 030	THRONES (LP, 1,000 only, signed) 12
02	Tursa 014	THE BLADE (LP, 1,000 only, signed) 12

(see also Current 93, Death In June, Nurse With Wound, Karl Blake, Shock Headed Peters)

MARTIAL SOLAL
| 63 | RCA Victor RD/SF 7614 | AT NEWPORT '63 (LP) ....12 |

SOLAR PLEXUS
| 73 | Polydor 2383 222 | SOLAR PLEXUS (LP) ....35 |

SOLDIER
82	Heavy Metal HEAVY 12	Sheralee/Force (p/s, with postcard) 35
82	Heavy Metal HEAVY 12	Sheralee/Force (p/s, without postcard) 25
04	Killer Metal KMRS 001	Murderous Night/I'm Taken In (red vinyl, 500 copies, numbered) 7

SOLDIER DOLLS
| 83 | Scream 1 | WHAT DO THEY KNOW? (EP) ....8 |
| 84 | Scream 2 | A TASTE OF BLOOD (EP, red vinyl) ....8 |

SOLDIERS OF FORTUNE
| 83 | Total Darkness TD 1 | Stars/Autonomia (fold-out p/s) ....6 |

SOLENT
| 73 | Decca F 13375 | My World Fell Down/The Sound Of Summer's Over ....10 |

SOLID GOLD CADILLAC
| 73 | RCA SF 8311 | SOLID GOLD CADILLAC (LP) ....30 |
| 73 | RCA SF 8365 | BRAIN DAMAGE (LP) ....45 |

(see also Battered Ornaments, Chris Spedding, Mike Westbrook)

SOLID N MIND
| 92 | Liberty Grooves LIB 003 | Battle Tipped Rhyme (12") ....12 |

SOLID ROCK BAND

91	Liberty Grooves LIB 002 1/2	Centre Stage/Woke With Nothin' (12")	15
90	Liberty Grooves LIB001	An Original Break (12")	20
91	Liberty Grooves PPP001	Centre Stage/Woke With Nuthin' (Promo cassette)	15

SOLID ROCK BAND
78	Chapel Lane RWA 1	FOOTPRINTS ON THE WATER (LP, gatefold sleeve)	15

SOLID SPACE
82	In Phaze IP 011	SPACE MUSEUM (cassette)	150

SOLITAIRES
58	London HLM 8745	Walking Along/Please Kiss This Letter	150
58	London HLM 8745	Walking Along/Please Kiss This Letter (78)	60

JAKE SOLLO
79	Pye N 102	JAKE SOLLO (LP)	15

NORMAN SOLOMAN
81	Black Joy DH 816	Joy Bells Ringing/JAYS: Unity Call (12")	25

SOLSTICE (1)
84	Equinox EQRLP 001	SILENT DANCE (LP, gatefold sleeve)	18

SOLSTICE (2)
08	Iron Kodex IK 003	ONLY THE STRONG SURVIVE (2-LP with free 7")	20

SOLUTION
71	EMI 2023	Divergence/Fever	6
72	Decca SKL-R 5124	SOLUTION (LP)	25

SOME CHICKEN
77	Raw RAW 7	New Religion/Blood On The Wall (p/s)	20
78	Raw RAW 13	Arabian Daze/No. 7	15
78	Raw RAW 13	Arabian Daze/No. 7 (purple vinyl)	120
78	Raw RAWT 13	Arabian Daze/No. 7 (12")	8

SOMEONE'S BAND
70	Deram DM 313	Story/Give It To You	20
70	Deram SML 1068	SOMEONE'S BAND (LP)	200

GORDON SOMERS & HIS GROUP
64	Top Ten TPSX 101	THE SOUND OF THE BEATLES (EP)	8

SOMERVILLE GENTLEMAN'S BAND
80	Somerville PLR 026	FAR FROM HOME (LP, gatefold insert with sticker over 'Plant Life' logo)	25

SOMETHING HAPPENS!
86	Prophet PRS 002	TWO CHANCES (EP, p/s)	8

ELKE SOMMER
61	Columbia DB 4688	Be Not Notty/The Faithful Hussar	5

JOANIE SOMMERS
60	Warner Bros WB 23	Be My Love/Why Don't You Do Right?	7
60	Warner Bros WB 31	Ruby-Duby-Du/Bob White	7
60	Warner Bros WB 44	One Boy/I'll Never Be Free	7
61	Warner Bros WB 71	Johnny Get Angry/Theme From A Summer Place	10
62	Warner Bros WB 85	Goodbye Joey/Bobby Is Bobby	7
63	Warner Bros WB 105	Little Girl Bad/Wishing Well	7
64	Warner Bros WB 78	When The Boys Get Together/Passing Strangers	7
65	Warner Bros WB 150	If You Love Him/I Think I'm Gonna Cry	15
60	Warner Bros WEP 6013	POSITIVELY THE MOST (EP, also stereo WSEP 2013)	20
61	Warner Bros WEP 6047	THE VOICE OF THE SIXTIES (EP, also stereo WSEP 2047)	15

(see also Ed Byrnes)

SON OF JOHN
86	Individual AIRS 104	People Shouting/Your Interpretation	8

SONGSTERS
54	London HL 8100	Bahama Buggy Ride/It Isn't Right	18
54	London HL 8100	Bahama Buggy Ride/It Isn't Right (78)	18

SON HOUSE
60s	Saydisc Roots SL 504	THE VOCAL INTENSITY OF SON HOUSE (LP)	40
66	CBS (S)BPG 62604	THE LEGENDARY FATHER OF FOLK BLUES (LP)	35
70	Liberty LBS 83391	JOHN THE REVELATOR (LP)	30

SON HOUSE/J.D. SHORT
69	Xtra XTRA 1080	DELTA BLUES (LP)	20

SONIA
78	D Roy DRDD 006	Love Don't Live Here Any More/D ROY BAND: Version (12")	20
79	D Roy DRDD 18	Ooh Baby Baby/Back Street Dub (12")	12
79	Karn-Na KRN 002	Again (Suddenly You're Mine)/UNDIVIDED ROOTS: Version (12", purple vinyl)	12
81	S & S FERGY 001	Checking It Out/Version (12", with Creation Rebel)	20
80	Cha Cha CHAD 26	Easier To Love/That's The Way You Feel (12", with Earth & Stone)	15

SONIC ASSASSINS
81	Flicknife FLEP 101	SONIC ASSASSINS (12" EP, p/s)	8

(see also Hawkwind)

SONIC BOOM
90	Silvertone SONIC 1	Octaves/Tremeloes (10", orange vinyl PVC sleeve, mail-order only)	18
91	Silvertone SONIC 2	(I Love You) To The Moon And Back/Capo Waltz (live) (gig freebie in black die-cut sleeve, promo only, 33rpm)	12
91	Silvertone SONIC 2	(I Love You) To The Moon And Back/Capo Waltz (live) (gig freebie in black die-cut sleeve, promo only, 33rpm, p/s later available separately)	8
90	Silvertone ORE ZLP 506	SPECTRUM (LP, gatefold rotatable plastic disc sleeve with inner)	25

(see also Spacemen 3, Spectrum)

SONIC YOUTH
86	Blast First BFFP 3	Flower/Halloween (12", p/s, some on yellow vinyl)	15

86	Blast First BFFP 3	Flower/Rewolf (12", p/s, censored version) 25
86	Blast First BFFP 3(B)	(Savage Pencil etch)/Halloween II (12", p/s, A-side engraved, 1st 100 signed) 50
86	Blast First BFFP 3(B)	(Savage Pencil etch)/Halloween II (12", p/s, A-side engraved) 20
86	Blast First BFFP 3X	Flower/Halloween/Satan Supermix (12", unreleased) 0
86	Blast First BFFP 7	Starpower (edit)/Bubblegum (p/s, some with badge & poster) 25
87	Blast First BFFP 26 T	MASTER DIK (12" EP, with inner) 8
88	Fierce FRIGHT 015/016	Stick Me Donna Magick Momma/Making The Nature Scene (live) (p/s, 2 x 1-sided 7" with etched B-sides) 20
88	Fierce FRIGHT 015/016	Stick Me Donna Magick Momma/Making The Nature Scene (live) (p/s, single disc reissue).12
88	Catalogue CAT 064	Teenage Riot (square flexidisc sewn into 'The Catalogue' magazine)...............15
89	Blast First BFFP 46	Touch Me I'm Sick/MUDHONEY: Halloween (12", p/s)..................18
89	Blast First BFFP 48	Providence (stereo)/Providence (mono) (promo only) 5
90	Geffen GEF 81	KOOL THING EP: Kool Thing/That's All I Know (p/s).................8
92	Geffen DGCV 11	100% (10" EP, orange vinyl, numbered p/s) 10
92	Geffen DGCV 11	100% (10" EP, black vinyl promo) 30
92	Geffen DGCT 11	100% (12" EP, promo only, white label) 40
92	Geffen DGCTD 11	100% (CD EP, digipak)...................10
92	Geffen 7-19064 DJ	Personality Crisis/Dirty Boots (DJ promo only) 6
92	Geffen GFSV26	YOUTH AGAINST FASCISM (10" white vinyl EP, numbered p/s) 10
92	Geffen GFST 26	YOUTH AGAINST FASCISM EP (12", p/s)...................8
92	DGC DGCS 11	100%/Creme Brulee (p/s)...................5
93	Geffen GFSV37	SUGAR KANE (10" blue vinyl EP, numbered p/s) 10
94	Geffen GFSV 72	Bull In The Heather/Razor Blade/Doctor's Orders (10", silver vinyl, numbered p/s)......10
83	Neutral NEUTRAL 9	CONFUSION IS SEX (LP) 20
85	Blast First BFFP 1	BAD MOON RISING (LP, with lyric insert)..................20
85	NOT NOT 1/BUT 2	WALLS HAVE EARS (2-LP, 2,000 copies only, numbered).................50
86	Blast First BFFP 4	EVOL (LP) 25
87	Blast First CHAT 1	SISTER INTERVIEW DISC (LP) 18
87	Blast First BFFP 20	SISTER (LP)..................20
88	Blast First BFFP 34	DAYDREAM NATION (2-LP, 1st 1,000 with signed poster) 35
88	Blast First BFFP 34	DAYDREAM NATION (2-LP)..................20
90	WEA 7599 24297-1	GOO (LP) 15
92	Geffen GEF24485[2]	DIRTY (2-LP)..................15
93	Geffen424515	DAYDREAM NATION (2-LP, reissue, poster)..................25
94	Geffen GEF 24632	EXPERIMENTAL JET SET, TRASH & NO STAR (LP, blue vinyl) 20
95	Geffen GEF24825	WASHING MACHINE (2-LP)..................20

(see also Ciccone Youth, Mudhoney)

SONNY
| 71 | Ackee ACK 127 | Love And Peace/LARRY & ALVIN: Throw Me Corn ....10 |

SONNY (& SONNY'S GROUP)
65	Atlantic AT 4038	Laugh At Me/Tony (as Sonny & Sonny's Group) 10
65	Atlantic AT 4060	The Revolution Kind/Georgia And John Quetzal (as Sonny & Sonny's Group) 10
67	Atlantic 584 131	I Told My Girl To Go Away/Misty Roses (solo) 6

(see also Sonny & Cher)

SONNY & CHER
64	Reprise R 20309	Baby Don't Go/Walkin' The Quetzal 8
65	Atlantic AT 4035	I Got You Babe/It's Gonna Rain 5
65	Atlantic AT 4047	But You're Mine/Hello 5
65	Vocalion VL 9247	The Letter/Spring Fever (B-side by 'Sonny & Cher (Instrumental)') 7
66	Atlantic AT 4069	What Now My Love/I Look For You 5
66	Atlantic 584 018	Have I Stayed Too Long/Leave Me Be 6
66	Atlantic 584 040	Little Man/Monday 6
66	Atlantic 584 057	Living For You/Turn Around 5
67	Atlantic 584 078	The Beat Goes On/Love Don't Come 6
67	Atlantic 584 110	Podunk/Beautiful Story 7
67	Atlantic 584 129	It's The Little Things/Plastic Man 7
68	Atlantic 584 162	Good Combination/You And Me 10
68	Atlantic 584 168	Circus/SONNY BONO: I Would Marry You Today 8
68	Atlantic 584 215	You Gotta Have A Thing Of Your Own/I Got You Babe 8
65	Reprise R 30056	CAESAR AND CLEO (EP, 2 tracks each by Sonny & Cher, Caesar & Cleo) 25
64	Atlantic ATL 5036	LOOK AT US (LP, mono) 12
64	Atlantic STL 5036	LOOK AT US (LP, stereo).................15

(see also Caesar & Cleo, Cher, Sonny, Date With Soul)

SONNY & DAFFODILS
| 63 | Ember EMB EP 4538 | SONNY & DAFFODILS (EP) ....65 |

SONNY (BURKE) & YVONNE
| 64 | Island WI 134 | Life Without Fun/SONNY BURKE GROUP: Mount Vesuvius.................25 |

(see also Sonny Burke)

SON OF A BITCH
| 96 | Hengest SOABCDS 1 | Treacherous Times/Victim You (CD, stickered jewel case).................10 |

(see also Saxon)

SON OF A GUN
| 75 | RCA 2526 | La Maison De L'Amour/All Smoke And No Fire ....7 |

SON OF NOISE
91	Music Of Life NOTE53	Son Of Noise/Ill Justice (12") 10
91	Kold Sweat KS117	Master Of Menace/Milk In The Chocolate (12") 10
92	Kold Sweat KSEP207	NEGATIVE FORCES/THE MIGHTY SON/THE MISSION (EP) 15
92	Kold Sweat KSLP03	THE MIGHTY SON OF NOISE (LP) 20
95	Little Rascool MZE2711	ACCESS DENIED (LP) 15

(see also Hardnoise)

SONS & LOVERS
67	Camp 602 002	Matters/Peaceful Is The River 6
68	Beacon 3-101	Help Me (I'm On Top Of The World)/Feel Alright 5
68	Beacon 3-107	Happiness Is Love/Things You Do 5
68	Beacon BEA116	From Now On The Sunshine/How Could We Ever Get This Way.................12

SONS OF ALBATROSS
| 75 | Decca FR 13605 | Africa/Ha-ri-ah | 35 |

SONS OF CAIN
| 80 | Loppylugs LOPPY 1 | End Of Something/Kennedy Waltz (p/s) | 10 |

SONS OF DEMENTED CHILDREN
| 87 | Hatter MAD 003 | Spoof Dealer/Busking (p/s, with insert) | 18 |

SONS OF FRED
65	Columbia DB 7605	Sweet Love/I'll Be There	200
65	Parlophone R 5391	I, I, I (Want Your Lovin')/She Only Wants A Friend	100
66	Parlophone R 5415	Baby What Do You Want Me To Do/You Told Me	200

(see also Odyssey)

SONS OF GLORY
| 62 | Columbia 33SX 1474 | GOD GLORIFIES (LP) | 25 |

SONS OF JAH
| 75 | Bullet BU 557 | Nyah Chant/Rasta Waltz | 20 |

SONS OF JAH
| 79 | Natty Congo PFULP 3502 | BURNING BLACK (LP) | 25 |
| 82 | Natty Congo NCLP 001 | UNIVERSAL MESSAGE (LP) | 15 |

(see also Aubrey Small)

SONS OF MAN
| 67 | Oak RGJ 612 | SONS OF MAN (EP, no p/s) | 400 |

SONS OF MOSES
| 75 | MCA MCA 169 | Soul Symphony/Fatback | 5 |

SONS OF NUBIA
| 90 | White SON1 | RAPS THE LAST MEANS (EP) | 75 |

SONS OF PILTDOWN MEN
| 63 | Pye International 7N 25206 | Mad Goose/Be A Party | 20 |

SONS OF SOUL
| 66 | Doctor Bird DB 1037 | Yeah Yeah Baby/So Ashamed | 20 |

SONSONG
| 76 | Zebra ZM 5761 | SONSONG (LP) | 30 |

SOPHISTICATES
| 60s | Spectrum SPEEP 701 | AT THE WOODVILLE (EP) | 15 |

SOPHOMORES
| 60s | Seeco CELP 451 | THE SOPHOMORES (LP) | 30 |

SORE THROAT (1)
| 78 | Albion ION 3 | Zombie Rock/I Don't Wanna Go Home | 5 |
| 78 | Hubcap SPIN 1 | I Dunno/Complex | 7 |

SORE THROAT (2)
88	Acid Rain ARRGHHH001	DEATH TO CAPITALIST HARDCORE EP	20
88	Meantime COX	UNHINDERED BY TALENT (LP)	15
89	Manic Ears ACHE	INDESTROY (LP, with lyric poster, as SAW THROAT)	20
89	Earache MOSH 10	DISGRACE TO THE CORPSE OF SID (LP)	15
80s	Manic Ears ACHE	NEVER MIND THE NAPALM HERE'S SORE THROAT (LP)	20

SORROWS
65	Piccadilly 7N 35219	I Don't Wanna Be Free/Come With Me	35
65	Piccadilly 7N 35230	Baby/Teenage Letter	40
65	Piccadilly 7N 35260	Take A Heart/We Should Get Along Fine	25
66	Piccadilly 7N 35277	You've Got What I Want/No, No, No, No (export p/s)	35
66	Piccadilly 7N 35277	You've Got What I Want/No, No, No, No	20
66	Piccadilly 7N 35309	Let The Live Live/Don't Sing No Sad Songs For Me	40
66	Piccadilly 7N 35336	Let Me In/How Love Used To Be	40
67	Piccadilly 7N 35385	Pink, Purple, Yellow And Red/My Gal	140
66	Piccadilly N(S)PL 38023	TAKE A HEART (LP, mono)	225
66	Piccadilly N(S)PL 38023	TAKE A HEART (LP, stereo)	275

(see also Don Fardon)

SORT SOL
| 81 | 4AD AD 101 | Marble Station/Misguided (p/s) | 8 |

S.O.U.L. (SOUNDS OF UNITY & LOVE)
| 72 | Pye Intl. NSPL 28162 | CAN YOU FEEL IT (LP) | 30 |

HORATIO SOUL
| 68 | Island WI 3132 | Ten White Horses/Angela (Sweet Sweet) | 8 |
| 69 | Crystal CR 7006 | Nobody's Gonna Sleep Tonight/Turn Around Baby | 6 |

JIMMY SOUL
62	Stateside SS 103	Twistin' Matilda/I Can't Hold Out Any Longer	10
63	Stateside SS 178	If You Wanna Be Happy/Don't Release Me	20
64	Stateside SS 274	I Hate You Baby/Change Partners	10
64	Stateside SE 1010	IF YOU WANNA BE HAPPY (EP)	50

SHARON SOUL
| 65 | Stateside SS 411 | How Can I Get To You/Don't Say Goodbye Love | 75 |
| 65 | Stateside SS 411 | How Can I Get To You/Don't Say Goodbye Love (DJ copy) | 100 |

SOUL VENDORS
67	Coxsone CS 7028	You Troubled Me/BOP & BELTONES: Love	25
67	Coxsone CS 7029	Fat Fish/MARCIA GRIFFITHS: Call To Me	100
67	Studio One SO 2018	Rocking Sweet Pea/JOE HIGGS: Change Of Plans	45
67	Studio One SO 2022	Cool Shade/RICHARD ACE: I Need You	120
67	Studio One SO 2028	Just A Little Bit Of Soul/ALTON ELLIS: I Am Just A Guy	40
67	Studio One SO 2031	Take Me/DELROY WILSON: I'm Not A King	50

67	Studio One SO 2032	Pe Da Pa/ERNEST WILSON: Money Worries..40
67	Studio One SO 2034	Hot Rod/GAYLADS: Africa (We Want To Go) 100
67	Studio One SO 2035	Pupa Lick/ETHIOPIANS: Leave My Business Alone 40
68	Studio One SO 2038	Psychedelic Rock/GAYLADS: I'm Free 100
68	Studio One SO 2043	Chinese Chicken/JACKIE MITTOO: Put It On 25
68	Studio One SO 2044	Happy Ogan (actually titled "Happy Organ")/INVADERS: Soulful Music 100
68	Studio One SO 2048	Evening Time/RIGHTEOUS FLAMES: Ease Up 35
68	Studio One SO 2058	Frozen Soul/ERNEST WILSON: If I Were A Carpenter....................................40
68	Studio One SO 2066	Soul Joint/Soul Limbo 45
68	Studio One SO 2070	Captain Cojoe/JACKIE MITTOO: Drum Song..50
68	Coxsone CS 7037	Grooving Steady/ROY RICHARDS: Warm And Tender Ska 80
68	Coxsone CS 7038	Whipping The Prince (actually by Ed Hangle & Alton Ellis)/HEPTONES: If You Knew......30
68	Coxsone CS 7048	Last Waltz/HAMLINS: Sentimental Reasons 150
68	Coxsone CS 7057	Real Rock/AL CAMPBELL: Don't Run Away 90
68	Coxsone CS 7071	West Of The Sun/ALTON ELLIS: A Fool 50
69	Coxsone CS 7084	Sixth Figure/DENZIL LAING: Man Payaba 50
67	Coxsone CSL 8010	ON TOUR (LP) 300

(see also Dobby Dobson)

SOUL AGENTS
64	Pye 7N 15660	I Just Wanna Make Love To You/Mean Woman Blues 45
64	Pye 7N 15707	Seventh Son/Let's Make It Pretty Baby 75
65	Pye 7N 15768	Don't Break It Up/Gospel Train 70

(see also Loot, Don Shinn, Hookfoot)

SOUL AGENTS (JAMAICA)
67	Coxsone CS 7007	Get Ready It's Rocksteady/BOB & BELTONES: Smile Like An Angel (B-side actually by Bop & Beltones) 25
67	Coxsone CS 7018	For Your Education/SUMMERTAIRES: Tell Me 40
67	Coxsone CS 7027	Lecture/SOUL BOYS: Blood Pressure 40

SOUL BOYS
| 66 | Rio R120 | Rudie Get Wise/JACKIE OPEL: I Don't Want Her ....60 |
| 67 | Island WI 3052 | Blood Pressure/RITA MARLEY: Come To Me ....70 |

(see also Soul Agents [Jamaica])

SOUL BROTHERS
65	Mercury MF 916	Gotta Get A Good Thing Going/Good Lovin' Never Hurt 10
65	Decca F 12116	I Keep Ringing My Baby/I Can't Take It 18
65	Parlophone R 5321	I Can't Believe It/You Don't Want To Know 15

SOUL BROTHERS (JAMAICA)
65	Ska Beat JB 226	Train To Skaville/WAILERS: I Made A Mistake 45
66	Ska Beat JB 259	Bugaloo/I'll Come Back 50
66	Rio R 118	Crawfish/RITA MARLEY: You Lied..30
66	Rio R 121	Mr T.N.T./MARCIA GRIFFITHS: Mr Everything 50
66	Island WI 282	Green Moon/E Gal OK 20
66	Island WI 294	Ska-Bostello/DON DRUMMOND: Looking Through The Window 25
66	Island WI 296	Sound One/MARTINE: Grandfather's Clock (B-side actually by Emille Straker & Merrymen or Martinis) 20
66	Island WI 3013	More & More/DELROY WILSON: Dancing Mood..30
66	Island WI 3016	Mr Flint/Too Young To Love (B-side actually by Freddie McGregor) 30
67	Island WI 3036	Sound Pressure/ETHIOPIANS: For You 30
67	Island WI 3039	Hi-Life/DELROY WILSON: Close To Me 20
67	Coxsone CS 7001	Take Ten/HUGH GODFREY: Deh Pon Dem 80
67	Coxsone CS 7020	Hey Windell/KEN BOOTHE: Home Home Home..40
67	Coxsone CS 7024	One Stop/TENNORS: Pressure And Slide 30
67	Studio One SO 2006	Hot And Cold/TERMITES: Mercy Mr. Percy 80
67	Island WI 3038	Cherry/SOUL JUNIOR : Out Of My Mind (Some list Bumps Oakley as the B-side) 60
67	Studio One SO 2016	Honeypot/VICEROYS: Lose And Gain..50
70	Pressure Beat PR 5506	Pussy Catch A Fire (actually by Soul Twins)/DESTROYERS: Follow This Beat (B-side actually "Secret Weapon" by Ansell Collins)..15
67	Coxsone CSL 8001	HOT SHOT SKA (LP) 200
67	Coxsone CSL 8002	CARIB SOUL (LP) 120

(see also Earl Van Dyke & Soul Brothers, Soul Twins, Lee Perry, Tony Gregory, Ethiopians, Itals, Hortense & Delroy, Gaylads, Jennors, Derrick Morgan, Summertaires, Delroy Wilson)

SOUL BROTHERS SIX
67	Atlantic 584 118	Some Kind Of Wonderful/I'll Be Loving You..50
69	Atlantic 584 256	Some Kind Of Wonderful/Somebody Else Is Loving My Baby..........................12
72	Atlantic K 10204	Some Kind Of Wonderful/Check Yourself 6

SOUL CATS
69	Camel CA 23	Keep It Moving/Your Sweet Love 10
69	Gas GAS 109	Choo Choo Train/The Load (actually "Swinging For Joy" by Count Ossie Band) 10
71	Hillcrest HCT 2	Reggay Got Soul (actually by Carl Bryan)/Land Of Love 8
70s	Junior JR 103	Reggay Got Soul (actually by Carl Bryan)/Land Of Love (reissue) 8

SOUL CITY
| 62 | Cameo Parkway P 103 | Everybody Dance Now/Who Knows..75 |
| 62 | Cameo Parkway P 103 | Everybody Dance Now/Who Knows (DJ copy) ....125 |

SOUL CITY EXECUTIVES
| 69 | Soul City SC 109 | Happy Chatter/Falling In Love ....20 |

SOUL CLAN
68	Atlantic 584 202	Soul Meeting/That's How It Feels (in p/s) 15
68	Atlantic 584 202	Soul Meeting/That's How It Feels 8
68	Atlantic 587 127	SOUL MEETING (LP) 20

(see also Solomon Burke, Arthur Conley, Don Covay, Ben E. King, Joe Tex)

SOUL CONDOR
| 70 | Polydor 2344002 | CERTAIN LIONS & TIGERS (LP) ....30 |

SOUL DEFENDERS
| 71 | Banana BA 354 | Way Back Home/SOUL REBELS: Stand For Your Rights ....18 |
| 72 | Ackee ACK 147 | Sound Almighty/COUNT OSSIE: Meditation ....12 |

MINT VALUE £

(see also Eric Donaldson, Carey Johnson)

SOUL DESTROYERS
00	Stark Relaity STARK008	Blow Your Top Pt. 1/Blow Your Top Pt. 2	12

SOUL DIRECTIONS
70	Attack ATT 8011	Su Su Su/Better Hearing	200

GEORGE SOULE
75	United Artists UP 35771	Get Involved/Everybody's Got A Song To Sing	8

SOULETTES
65	Ska Beat JB 204	Opportunity/DIZZY JOHNNY & STUDIO 1 ORCHESTRA: Sudden Destruction	40
70	Upsetter US 337	Let It Be/UPSETTERS: Big Dog Bloxie	20
71	Jackpot JP 766	My Desire/Bring It Up	15
71	Jackpot JP 767	All Of Your Loving/LLOYD CLARKE: Love Me	15
73	Attack ATT 8044	This World/Same Thing	5

(see also Rita Marley, Ken Boothe, Roland Alphonso, Uniques)

SOUL EXPLOSION
69	Downtown DT 455	Let's Try It Again/Gumpton Rock	6
70	J-DAN JDN 4405	My Mother's Eyes/Gum Pot	7

SOUL FLAMES
68	Nu Beat NB 020	Mini Really Fit Dem/Soul Train	10

SOULFUL STRINGS
67	Chess CRS 8068	Burning Spear/Within You, Without You	30
67	Chess CRS 8068	Burning Spear/Within You, Without You (DJ Copy)	50
69	Chess CRS 8094	I Wish It Would Rain/Listen Here	10
69	Chess CRLS 4534	GROOVIN' WITH THE SOULFUL STRINGS (LP)	20

SOUL GENERATION
79	Grapevine GRP 131	Hold On/The Lonely Sea	8
73	Sticky SBL 135	BEYOND BODY AND SOUL (LP)	25

SOUL KINGS
69	Blue Cat BS 169	The Magnificent Seven/RUPIE EDWARDS: Long Lost Love	40

SOUL LEADERS
67	Rio R 134	Pour On The Sauce/Beauty Is Only Skin Deep	25

SOULMATES (JAMAICA)
69	Amalgamated AMG 836	Them A Laugh And A Ki Ki/The Hippys Are Here (B-side actually by Hippy Boys)	60
69	Amalgamated AMG 842	On The Move/Jump It Up (B-side actually by Viceroys)	70
69	Camel CA 33	Beware Of Bad Dogs/Short Cut (actually by Glen Adams)	50
70	Unity UN 555	Ten Cent/DOREEN SHAFFER: Stay With Me Forever	10

SOULMATES (U.K.)
65	Parlophone R 5334	Too Late To Say You're Sorry/Your Love	80
66	Parlophone R 5407	Bring Your Love Back Home (with Jet Set)/When Love Is Gone	15
66	Parlophone R 5506	Mood Melancholy/Sayin' Something	10
67	Parlophone R 5601	Is That You?/Time's Run Out	10

(see also Liza Strike)

SOUL MERCHANTS
67	President PT 166	Whole Lot Of Lovin'/Stormy Weather	7

SOUL ON DELIVERY
75	Decca F13601	Hustle/Crescent Boogie	10

SOUL PARTNERS
69	Pama PM 766	Walk On Judge/Lose The One You Love	20

SOUL PEOPLE
68	Island WIP 6040	Hummin'/Soul Drink	20

SOUL PROPRIETORS
65	Concord CON STD 74	All/Lonely Separation (private pressing)	300

SOUL REBELS
72	Banana BA 374	Listen And Observe/What's Love	45
72	Count Shelley CS 001	Judgement Day Is Near/Solid As A Rock	15
72	Count Shelley CS 003	I'm The One Who Loves You/I ROY: War Zone	10

(see also Soul Defenders)

SOUL RHYTHMS
69	Bullet BU 404	Work Boy Work/CECIL THOMAS: Girl Lonesome Fever	15
69	High Note HS 013	National Lottery/Round Seven	12
69	Gas GAS 113	Soul Call/Musical Gate	10

(see also Hippy Boys, Max Romeo)

SOUL RUNNERS
67	Polydor 56732	Grits 'n' Cornbread/Spreading Honey	10

SOUL SEARCHERS
74	Sussex SXX 2	Blow Your Whistle (Parts 1 & 2)	6
74	Sussex LPSX 4	SALT OF THE EARTH (LP)	25

SOUL SISTERS (JAMAICA)
69	Amalgamated AMG 839	Wreck A Buddy/VERSATILES: Push It In	25

(see also Dennis Brown)

SOUL SISTERS (U.S.)
64	Sue WI 312	I Can't Stand It/Blueberry Hill	40
64	Sue WI 336	Loop De Loop/Long Gone	50
65	London HLC 9970	Foolish Dreamer/Good Time Tonight	60
65	London HLC 9970	Foolish Dreamer/Good Time Tonight (DJ copy)	100
72	United Artists UP 35388	Good Time Tonight/Some Soul Food	10
64	Sue ILP 913	THE SOUL SISTERS (LP)	150

SOUL SOUNDS
67	Columbia S(C)X 6158	SOUL SURVIVAL (LP)	40

(see also Savages, Rebel Rousers)

SOUL STIRRERS
69	Duke DU 25	Come See About Me/LLOYD CHARMERS: 5 To 5	25

(see also Sam Cooke)

SOUL SURVIVORS
67	Stateside SS 2057	Expressway To Your Heart/Hey Gyp	30
68	Stateside SS 2094	Explosion (In Your Soul)/Dathon's Theme	18
69	Atlantic 584 275	Mama Soul/Tell Daddy	30

SOUL SYNDICATE
72	Green Door GD 4021	Riot (actually by Johnny Moore & Soul Syndicate)/Smoke Without Fire (actually by Keith Hudson)	25

(see also Rockin' Horse)

SOUL TONES
70	Pama PM 790	Dancing Time/BUNNY BARRETT: Love Locked Out	15

SOUL TOPS
67	Fab FAB 27	Baby I Got News/TEDDY KING & BUSTER'S ALL STARS: Mexican Divorce	20
68	Nu Beat NB002	Rain And Thunder/Swing Baby	20

SOUL TWINS (JAMAICA)
70	High Note HS 043	Little Suzie/Cherrie	8
72	Clandisc CLA 238	Don't Call Me Nigga/DYNAMITES: Joe Louis	6

SOUL TWINS (U.S.)
77	Grapevine GRP 101	Quick Change Artist/Give The Man A Chance	8

SOULWAX
04	Pias B060DLP	ANY MINUTE NOW (2-LP, inners)	20
07	Parlophone 50999 509247 1 4	MOST OF THE REMIXES WE'VE MADE... (2-LP)	20

SOUND
80	Korova KOW 10	Heyday/Brute Force (p/s)	5
81	Korova KOW 21	Sense Of Purpose/Point Of No Return (p/s)	5
79	Tortch TOR 003	PHYSICAL WORLD (EP)	35
79	Tortch TOR 008	THE SOUND (LP, possibly unissued)	0
80	Korova KODE 2	JEOPARDY (LP, with inner)	20
81	Korova KODE 5	FROM THE LIONS MOUTH (LP, gatefold)	35
82	Warner Bros. 240019	ALL FALL DOWN (LP)	18
85	Statik STAB 1	SHOCK OF DAYLIGHT (mini-LP)	12

(see also Outsiders, Second Layer)

SOUND BARRIER
68	Beacon BEA 109	She Always Comes Back To Me/Groovin' Slow	60

SOUND CEREMONY
89	Celestial Sound SRT 8KF	You're Breaking My Heart (p/s)	10
79	Celestial Sound RWG 001	GUITAR STAR (LP)	20
79	Celestial Sound RWG 002	RON WARREN GANDERTON & SOUND CEREMONY (LP)	40
81	Celestial Sound RWG 003	PRECIOUS AS ENGLAND (LP)	20

SOUND DIMENSION
69	Coxsone CS 7083	Scorcia/CECIL & JACKIE: Breaking Up (B-side actually "Hold Me Baby" by Basil Daley)	30
69	Coxsone CS 7085	Soul Trombone (Suffering Stink)/LARRY & ALVIN: Your Cheating Heart	50
69	Coxsone CS 7090	Soulful Strut/Breaking Up	120
69	Coxsone CS 7093	More Scorcha/LENNIE HIBBERT: Village Soul	40
69	Coxsone CS 7097	Time Is Tight/BARRY LLEWELLYN: Sad Song	40
69	Bamboo BAM 5	Doctor Sappa Too/Soul Eruption (B-side actually by Roy Richards & Sound Dimension)	45
69	Bamboo BAM 7	Baby Face/GLADIATORS: Anywhere	30
69	Bamboo BAM 9	Jamaica Rag/C. MARSHALL: I Need Your Loving	25
69	Bamboo BAM 13	Whoopee/NORMA FRAZER: Working (B-side actually by Marcia Griffiths)	25
69	Bamboo BAM 14	Black Onion/Bitter Blood	35
70	Bamboo BAM 18	Poison Ivy/Botheration - Version	20
70	Bamboo BAM 50	Soul Food/BURNING SPEAR: Door Peeper	50
70	Banana BA 313	In The Summertime/In The Summertime - Version	35
70	Banana BA 338	My Sweet Lord (Instrumental)/DENNIS BROWN: Silky (B-side actually by Monty Alexander & Cyclones)	15
70	Supreme SUP 202	More Games/MR. FOUNDATION: Maga Dog (actually by Invaders)	30
72	Ackee ACK 149	Solas/GLADIATORS: Sonia	15

(see also Brentford Road Allstars, Jackie Mittoo, Bob Andy, Horace Andy, John Holt, Larry Marshall, Irving Brown, Heptones, Freedom Singers, Winston Francis, Jerry Jones, Ethiopians, Cables, Alton Ellis, Gladiators, Ken Boothe, Soul Vendors)

SOUNDGARDEN
90	A&M AMX 560	Hands All Over/Come Together/Heretic/Big Dumb Sex (10", foldout pack)	8
90	A&M AMY 574	Loud Love/Big Dumb Sex/Get On The Snake/Fresh Deadly Roses (12", etched, stickered p/s)	8
92	A&M AMY 102	Outshined/I Can't Give You Anything/Homicidal Suicidal (12", p/s, limited ed.)	8
92	A&M AMY 723	Rusty Cage/Touch Me/Show Me (12", poster p/s, 5000 only)	12
96	A&M 5818457	Burden In My Hand/Karaoke (p/s, white vinyl, numbered, 5000 only)	15
94	A&M 540215-1	SUPERUNKNOWN (2 x LP, clear or blue vinyl, stickered, 2 lyric sheets)	18

SOUND IRATION
90s	Mystic Red Corp MRC 8888	Seventh Seal/Dub Seal (12")	30
89	Wau Mr. Modo MOWLP 001	IN DUB (LP)	35

SOUND NETWORK
65	Mercury MF 944	Watching/How About Now	25

SOUND OF JIMMY NICOL
65	Decca F 12107	Clementine/Bim Bam	25

(see also Jimmy Nicol)

SOUND OF SHA'BASS
| 91 | Guerilla GRRR16 | Take It Or Leave It (12")..8 |

SOUNDPROOF
| 71 | Look LKSP511-301 | Friday Every Friday/Lonely Boy Lonely Girl..............................100 |

SOUNDS AROUND
| 66 | Piccadilly 7N 35345 | What Does She Do?/Sad Subject.....................................25 |
| 67 | Piccadilly 7N 35396 | Red White And You/One Of Two......................................25 |

(see also Peter & Wolves, John Pantry, Norman Conquest, Factory)

SOUNDS COMBINE
| 71 | Escort ERT 862 | African Museum/African Museum - Version.............................8 |

SOUNDS GALACTIC
| 70 | Phase 4 Stereo PFS 4208 | AN ASTROMUSICAL ODYSSEY (LP)................................12 |

SOUNDS INCORPORATED
61	Parlophone R 4815	Mogambo/Emily..15
62	Decca F 11540	Sounds Like Locomotion/Taboo...8
63	Decca F 11590	Stop/Go..10
63	Decca F 11723	Order Of The Keys/Keep Moving...25
64	Columbia DB 7239	The Spartans/Detroit..7
64	Columbia DB 7321	Spanish Harlem/Rinky Dink...10
64	Columbia DB 7404	William Tell/Bullets..7
65	Columbia DB 7545	Time For You/Hall Of The Mountain King...............................7
65	Columbia DB 7676	My Little Red Book/Justice Neddi.......................................10
65	Columbia DB 7737	On The Brink/I'm Comin' Thru...40
67	Polydor 56209	How Do You Feel/Dead As You Go.......................................15
69	Decca 22883	Warmth Of The Sun/Apollo (export)...................................10
64	Columbia SEG 8360	TOP GEAR (EP)...25
64	Columbia 33SX 1659	SOUNDS INCORPORATED (LP, mono)..................................25
64	Columbia SCX 3531	SOUNDS INCORPORATED (LP, stereo)................................30
65	EMI Regal SREG 1071	RINKY DINK (LP, export issue)..20
66	Studio Two TWO 144	SOUNDS INCORPORATED (LP)...20

(see also Jeff Beck, May Blitz, Boxer, Tony Newman)

SOUNDS NICE
69	Parlophone R 5797	Love At First Sight/Love You Too ('featuring Tim Mycroft')...........8
69	Parlophone R 5821	Sleepless Night/Continental Exchange ('featuring Tim Mycroft')....6
69	Parlophone PMC/PCS 7089	LOVE AT FIRST SIGHT (LP)..25

(see also Third Ear Band, Chris Spedding, Clem Cattini Ork)

SOUNDS OF BOB ROGERS
| 67 | CBS 3018 | Among My Souveneirs/Dream With Me...............................20 |

SOUNDS OF JOHNNY HAWKSWORTH
| 66 | Columbia DB 8059 | Goal/"Goal - World Cup 1966" Theme.................................15 |

(see also Johnny Hawksworth)

SOUNDS OF LES AND BARRY
| 65 | Fontana TF 657 | Looie Girl/She Who Needs Me..6 |

SOUNDS OF MODIFICATION
| 68 | Stateside SL/SSL 10262 | SOUNDS OF MODIFICATION (LP).....................................20 |

SOUNDS OF REFLECTION
| 68 | Reflection RS6001SM | Brave New Day/Lord Of Believe (p/s)................................50 |

SOUNDS OF SALVATION
| 74 | Reflection RL 310 | SOUNDS OF SALVATION (LP, with booklet).........................90 |

(see also Reflection)

SOUNDS OF TIME
| 73 | Columbia DB 9000 | DANSE MACABRE (LP)..20 |

SOUNDS ORCHESTRAL
66	Piccadilly 7N 35284	Thunderball/Mr Kiss Kiss Bang Bang.................................10
68	Pye 7N 170507	When Love Has Gone/Fifth Avenue Breakdown.......................6
65	Pye NPL 38016	THUNDERBALL - SOUNDS ORCHESTRAL MEET JAMES BOND (LP, in gatefold sleeve)..........20
65	Pye NPL 38016	THUNDERBALL - SOUNDS ORCHESTRAL MEET JAMES BOND (LP)...........30

SOUNDS PROGRESSIVE
| 70 | Eyemark EMCL 1009S | KID JENSEN INTRODUCES SOUNDS PROGRESSIVE (LP)............40 |

SOUNDS SENSATIONAL
| 67 | HMV POP 1584 | Love In The Open Air/Night Cry...18 |

SOUND SCIENCE
| 91 | Sound Entity SE 0002 | HERT'Z SO GOOD EP (12")...15 |
| 91 | Sound Entity SE 0002 | HERT'Z SO GOOD EP (12")...15 |

SOUND SIXTY-SIX
| 66 | Decca F 12323 | Flight 4864/The Bouncer..12 |

SOUND STAGE ORCHESTRA
| 76 | BBC RESL 30 | Grandstand/Rugby Special...10 |

SOUND SYSTEM
| 65 | Island WI 258 | You Don't Know Like I Do/Take Me Serious...........................15 |

(see also Owen Gray)

EPIC SOUNDTRACKS
| 81 | Rough Trade RT 084 | Popular, Classical: Jelly Babies/A 3-Acre Floor/Pop In Packets (p/s)...........5 |

(see also Swell Maps, Thurston Moore Kim Gordon & Epic Soundtracks)

SOUND VISION
| 70s | Key KL 007 | IN CONCERT (LP, featuring Judy MacKenzie)........................25 |

SOUP DRAGONS

86	Subway Organisation SUBWAY 4	Whole Wide World/I Know Everything (with insert in poly bag, orange or blue foldaround p/s)	5
86	Raw TV Products RTV 1	Hang Ten!/Slow Things Down (p/s, blue or red vinyl)	7
86	Raw TV Products RTV 2	Head Gone Astray/Girl In The World/So Sad I Feel (PVC sleeve, with poster)	10
86	Subway Organisation SUBWAY 4	THE SUN IS IN THE SKY (EP, unreleased, 1,000 only, foldaround p/s in poly bag)	15
90	Raw TV SOUPLP 2	LOVEGOD (LP, with foiled sleeve & lyric sheet)	12

(see also BMX Bandits, Future PIlot A.K.A.)

SOUP GREENS

65	Stateside SS 457	That's Too Bad/Like A Rolling Stone	70

SOUPHERBS

65	Oak RGJ 601	SOUPHERBS (LP)	350

HARRY SOUTH ORCHESTRA

69	Philips BF 1770	Scarborough Fair/I'm Gonna Make You Love Me	25
75	EMI EMI 2252	The Sweeney (TV Theme) (Parts 1 & 2)	20
67	Mercury 20081 MCL	PRESENTING HARRY SOUTH (LP)	30

JOE SOUTH

62	Oriole CB 1752	Masquerade/I'm Sorry For You	20
63	MGM MGM 1206	Same Old Song/Standing Invitation	7
65	MGM MGM 1267	Concrete Jungle/Last One To Know	7
65	HMV POP 1474	I Want To Be Somebody/Deep Inside Me	7
68	Capitol CL 15535	Birds Of A Feather/It Got Away	6
69	Capitol CL 15568	Don't Throw Your Love To The Wind/Redneck	5
69	Capitol CL 15579	Games People Play/Mirror Of Your Mind	6
69	Capitol CL 15608	Don't It Make You Want To Go Home/Heart's Desire	15
70	Capitol CL 15666	Hush/Party People	5
69	Capitol E-(S)T 108	INTROSPECT (LP)	12
70	Capitol ST 21548	WALK A MILE IN MY SHOES (LP)	12

SOUTH COAST SKA STARS

80	Safari SAFE 27	South Coast Rumble/Head On (p/s)	8

(see also Ray Fenwick)

JERI SOUTHERN

54	Brunswick 05343	Remind Me/Little Boy Grown Tall	8
55	Brunswick 05367	The Man That Got Away/Speak Softly To Me	8
55	Brunswick 05490	An Occasional Man/It's D'Lovely	7
56	Brunswick 05529	Where Walks My True Love?/Don't Explain	10
57	Brunswick 05665	Fire Down Below/Smoke Gets In Your Eyes	8
57	Brunswick 05709	Scarlet Ribbons (For Her Hair)/Would I	5
57	Brunswick 05722	Bells Are Ringing/Just In Time	5
58	Brunswick 05737	I Waited So Long/The Mystery Of Love	5
59	Capitol CL 15054	Run/Don't Look At Me That Way	5
59	Brunswick OE 9438	CARESSES (EP)	10
59	Columbia SEG 7935	RIDIN' HIGH (EP)	10
55	Brunswick LA 8699	WARM (10" LP)	20
56	Brunswick LAT 8100	THE SOUTHERN STYLE (LP)	20
57	Brunswick LAT 8209	JERI GENTLY JUMPS (LP)	20
58	Columbia 33SX 1110	SOUTHERN BREEZE (LP)	20
58	Columbia 33SX 1134	COFFEE, CIGARETTES AND MEMORIES (LP)	20
59	Columbia 33SX 1155	JERI SOUTHERN MEETS JOHNNY SMITH (LP)	20
59	Capitol T 1278	AT THE CRESCENDO (LP)	12

JOHNNY SOUTHERN & HIS WESTERN RHYTHM KINGS

57	Melodisc MEL 1413	We Will Make Love/Crazy Heart	10
57	Melodisc MEL 1434	She's Long, She's Tall/Lonesome Whistle	10

SHEILA SOUTHERN

62	HMV POP 1089	White Wedding/LittleStar/Il Nostro Amore	5

SOUTHERN SOUND

66	Columbia DB 7982	Just The Same As You/I Don't Wanna Go	400

SOUTHERN TONES

64	Jazz Collector JEN 10	WAITING FOR THE LORD (EP)	10

SOUTHERN COMFORT

71	Harvest HAR 5035	Willie Urricane/Berkshire Berk	10
71	Harvest HAR 5047	Morning Has Broken/Cosmic Jig	10
71	Harvest SHSP 4012	FROG CITY (LP, no EMI logo on label)	20
72	Harvest SHSP 799	SOUTHERN COMFORT (LP, gatefold, EMI logo on label)	30
72	Harvest SHSP 4021	STIR DON'T SHAKE (LP, with EMI logo on label)	18

(see also Matthews Southern Comfort)

SOUTHERN DEATH CULT

83	Situation 2 SIT 19	Fatman/Moya (wraparound p/s)	20

(see also Death Cult, Cult)

SOUTHLANDERS

55	Parlophone MSP 6182	Ain't That A Shame/Have You Ever Been Lonely	10
56	Parlophone MSP 6236	Hush-A-Bye Rock/The Wedding Of The Lucky Black Cat	10
57	Decca F 10946	Alone/Swedish Polka	5
57	Decca F 10958	Peanuts/I Never Dreamed	5
58	Decca F 10982	Put A Light In The Window/Penny Loafers And Bobby Socks	10
58	Decca F 11032	I Wanna Jive Tonight/Torero	15
58	Decca F 11067	The Mole In A Hole/Choo-Choo-Choo-Choo Cha-Cha-Cha (tri-centre)	15
58	Decca F 11067	The Mole In A Hole/Choo-Choo-Choo-Choo Cha-Cha-Cha (tri-centre, repressing with solid centre)	7
58	Decca DFE 6508	THE SOUTHLANDERS NUMBER ONE (EP)	20

SOUTHSIDE JOHNNY & THE ASBURY JUKES

77	Epic EPC 5230	Little Girl So Fine/I Ain't Got The Fever (withdrawn)	20

SOUTHWEST F.O.B.
68	Stax STAX 107	Smell Of Incense/Green Skies	20

SOUTHWIND
70	Harvest HAR 5019	Boogie Woogie Country Girl/Honky Tonkin'	5

PHIL SOUTHWOOD
61	QRS 1-462	D's Dilemma/Sister Sadie (in p/s)	20
61	QRS 1-462	D's Dilemma/Sister Sadie	12

SOVEREIGNS
66	King KG 1050	Bring Me Home Love/That's The Way Love Is	15

RED SOVINE
56	Brunswick 05513	Why Baby Why? (with Webb Pierce)/Sixteen Tons	40
56	Brunswick 05513	Why Baby Why? (with Webb Pierce)/Sixteen Tons (78)	20
69	London HA-B 8379	TELL MAUDE I SLIPPED (LP)	15
75	RCA 2738	Teddy Bear/Daddy	8

(see also Webb Pierce)

SOWELL RADICS
81	Attack TACK 24	Caution/Bali-Hi Special (12")	40
81	Attack TACK 27	Fight Fight Fight/Aces Rock (12")	40
82	SG SG 15	Wheel O' Matlida/Rub Dis Ya One Ya (12")	45

SOWERS WITH EILEEN GREAVES
69	Galliard GAL 4002	SEEDS (LP)	30

SO WHAT
70	CBS 5005	Flowers/Tell Me Now	20

BOB B. SOXX & THE BLUE JEANS
63	London HLU 9646	Zip-A-Dee-Doo-Dah/Flip And Nitty	20
63	London HLU 9694	Why Do Lovers Break Each Other's Heart?/Dr Kaplan's Office	25
63	London HLU 9754	Not Too Young To Get Married/Annette	20
69	London HLU 10243	Zip-A-Dee-Doo-Dah/Why Do Lovers Break Each Other's Heart?	7
63	London HA-U 8121	ZIP-A-DEE-DOO-DAH (LP)	100
75	Phil Spector Intl. 2307 004	BOB B. SOXX & THE BLUE JEANS (LP)	25

(see also Darlene Love, Bobby Sheen, Blossoms, Crystals, Phil Spector)

CATHERINE SPAAK
65	Fontana TL 5282	NOI SIAMO I GIOVANI (LP)	15

SPACE
93	Hug HUG 1T	If It's Real/Lookin'/I'm Free (12", p/s with free 'fortune fish')	12

SPACE ART
77	Arista AHAL 8001	SPACE ART (LP)	15

SPACE (1)
78	PyeNSPH 28505	DELIVERANCE (LP)	20
79	Pye NSPH 28725	JUST BLUE (LP, picture disc)	20

(see also Madeline Bell)

SPACE (2)
90	Space LP 1	SPACE (LP)	50
90	Space CD 1	SPACE (CD, beware of counterfeits)	40

(see also J.A.M.S., KLF, Timelords, Disco 2000)

SPACED
92	Incite INC 1/123	Deeper (Original Mix)/Deeper (Remix) (12", stickered white label)	35
92	No Label PNI 001	Deeper (Mix 1)/(Mix 2)/Mix 3) (12", white label)	50

SPACEMEN
59	Top Rank JAR 228	The Clouds/The Lonely Jet Pilot	12

SPACEMEN 3
86	Glass GLAEP 105	Walkin' With Jesus (Sound Of Confusion)/Rollercoaster/Feel So Good (12" maxi-single, p/s, with numbered insert)	70
86	Glass GLAEP 105	Walkin' With Jesus (Sound Of Confusion)/Rollercoaster/Feel So Good (12" maxi-single, p/s, without numbered insert)	60
87	Glass GLAEP 108	Transparent Radiation/Ecstasy Symphony/Transparent Radiation (Flashback)/Things'll Never Be The Same/Starship (12" maxi-single, p/s)	50
88	Glass GLASS 12054	Take Me To The Other Side/Soul 1/That's Just Fine (12", p/s)	30
88	Fire BLAZE 29S	Revolution/Che (die-cut company sleeve)	6
88	Fire BLAZE 29T	Revolution/Che/May The Circle Be Unbroken (12")	12
89	Fire THREEBIE 3	Revolution/Suicide/Repeater/Love Intro Theme (Xtacy) (12", mail-order only, numbered p/s)	25
89	Sniffin' Rock SR 008	When Tomorrow Hits (with Sniffin' Rock magazine)	15
89	Sniffin' Rock SR 008	When Tomorrow Hits (without Sniffin' Rock magazine)	10
89	Fire BLAZE 36S	Hypnotized/Just To See You Smile (Honey Pt 2) (die-cut company sleeve)	8
89	Fire BLAZE 36T	Hypnotized/Just To See You Smile (Honey Pt 2)/The World Is Dying (12", with poster)	15
89	Fire BLAZE 36CD	Hypnotized/Just To See You Smile (Honey Pt 2)/The World Is Dying (3" CD, with adaptor, 5" case)	12
91	Fire BLAZE 41	Big City (Edit)/Drive (p/s)	5
89	Fire BLAZE 41T	Big City/Drive (12", p/s)	10
91	Fire BLAZE 41TR	Big City (Remix)/I Love You (Remix) (12", unissued, white label promo, 50 only)	50
91	Catalogue CAT 089	I Love You//Sometimes (2 x flexis, with The Catalogue magazine)	10
03	Earworm Gold EGS 01	Walking With Jesus/Take Me To The Other Side (Demo)/Walking With Jesus (Demo) (die-cut p/s, 'splatter' vinyl)	6
09	Great Pop Supplement GPS 50	Big City (demo)/WOODEN SHJIPS: I Believe It (red marbled vinyl, insert & sticker)	10
86	Glass GLALP 018	SOUND OF CONFUSION (LP)	25
87	Glass GLALP 026	THE PERFECT PRESCRIPTION (LP, gold/silver or bronze/silver sleeve)	60
88	Glass GLALP 030	PERFORMANCE (LP)	25
88	Glass GLACD 030	PERFORMANCE (CD)	20
88	Fire FIRELP 16	PLAYING WITH FIRE (LP, embossed sleeve)	30
90	Fire FIRE LP 23	RECURRING (LP)	30
90	Fire REFIRE 11	PERFORMANCE (LP, reissue)	20

(see also Sonic Boom, Spiritualized, Darkside, Spectrum)

SPACEPIMP
95	Clear CLR 415	The Pimp/Spacechace/K9 Law (12", p/s, on clear vinyl)	25
95	Clear CLR 415	The Pimp/Spacechace/K9 Law (12", p/s)	20

SPACE TURKEYS
81	Tavern Sound	Fun With A Social Worker/Disco Not Disco (p/s)	15

SPAGHETTI HEAD
75	RCA RCA 2513	Big Noise From Winnetka/Funky Axe	30

(see also Clem Cattini Ork, Tornados)

SPAGHETTI JUNCTION
72	Columbia DB 8935	Work's Nice - If You Can Get It/Step Right Up	25

(see also Hank Marvin)

SPANIELS
60	Joy JOYS 197	THE SPANIELS (LP)	20

MUGGSY SPANIER & DIXIELAND/RAGTIME BAND
56	Tempo A 36	Tin Roof Blues/Muskrat Rumble	7

(see also Sidney Bechet)

SPANISH BOYS
65	Blue Beat BB 331	I Am Alone/BUSTER'S ALL STARS: Vera Cruz	150

SPANISHTONIANS
67	Pyramid PYR 6005	Kisses/ROLAND ALPHONSO: Women Of The World	30
67	Pyramid PYR 6009	Suffer Me Not/ROLAND ALPHONSO: Guantanamera Ska	30
67	Pyramid PYR 6018	Rudie Gets Plenty/ROLAND ALPHONSO: Sock It To Me	100

SPANISHTOWN SKABEATS
65	Blue Beat BB 315	Oh My Baby (actually by Charmers)/Stop That Train	200
65	Blue Beat BB 320	King Solomon/BUSTER'S ALLSTARS: Devil's Daffodil	60

SPANKY & OUR GANG
67	Mercury MF 982	Sunday Will Never Be The Same/Distance	20
67	Mercury MF 999	Making Every Minute Count/If You Could Only Be Me	8
67	Mercury MF 1010	Lazy Day/It Ain't Necessarily Byrd Avenue	10
68	Mercury MF 1018	Sunday Mornin'/Echoes	8
68	Mercury MF 1023	Like To Get To Know You/Three Ways From Tomorrow	12
68	Mercury MF 1052	Give A Damn/The Swingin' Gate	10
69	Mercury MF 1123	And She's Mine/Leopard Skin Phone	7
76	Epic S EPC 3850	I Won't Brand You/When I Wanna	7
67	Mercury 20114 (S)MCL	SPANKY AND OUR GANG (LP)	35
68	Mercury 20121 SCML	LIKE TO GET TO KNOW YOU (LP)	35
69	Mercury 20150 SCML	ANYTHING YOU CHOOSE/WITHOUT RHYME OR REASON (LP)	35

(see also Mama & Papas)

OTIS SPANN
64	Decca F 11972	Stirs Me Up/Keep Your Hand Out Of My Pocket	20
68	Blue Horizon 57-3142	Bloody Murder/Can't Do Me No Good	15
69	Blue Horizon 57-3155	Walkin'/Temperature Is Rising (with Fleetwood Mac)	20
64	Decca LK 4615	THE BLUES OF OTIS SPANN (LP)	70
64	Storyville SLP 157	GOOD MORNING MR. BLUES (LP)	30
64	Storyville SLP 168	PIANO BLUES (LP, with Memphis Slim)	30
65	Decca LK 4661	BLUES NOW (LP)	65
66	Stateside SL 10169	THE BLUES NEVER DIE (LP)	35
67	HMV CLP/CSD 3609	BLUES ARE WHERE IT'S AT (LP)	35
67	Storyville 670 157	PORTRAITS IN BLUES VOL. 3 (LP, reissue of SLP 157)	15
67	Polydor 545 030	NOBODY KNOWS MY TROUBLES (LP)	35
67	Bounty BY 6037	NOBODY KNOWS MY TROUBLES (LP)	40
68	Stateside (S)SL 10255	BOTTOM OF THE BLUES (LP)	40
69	Chess CRLS 4556	FATHERS AND SONS (LP)	40
69	Blue Horizon 7-63217	BIGGEST THING SINCE COLOSSUS (LP, with Fleetwood Mac)	90
69	Deram DML/SML 1036	CRACKED SPANNER HEAD (LP)	45
69	Python KM 4	RAISED IN MISSISSIPPI (LP, 99 copies only, with Robert Jnr. Lockwood)	90
70	Vanguard VSD 6514	CRYIN' TIME (LP)	20

(see also Fleetwood Mac, Memphis Slim, Johnny Shines, Lonnie Johnson)

SPANNER THRU MA BEATBOX
87	Earthly Delights EARTH 3	SPANNER THRU MA BEATBOX (LP)	15

SPARKERS
69	Blue Cat BS 155	Dig It Up/DELROY WILSON: This Life Makes Me Wonder	175

(see also Samuel Edwards)

LOU SPARKES
69	Gayfeet GS 203	By The Time I Get To Phoenix/Lover Boy	8
70	Gayfeet GS 208	We Will Make Love/ROLAND ALPHONSO: Sticker	8

KRISTINE SPARKLE
74	Decca F 13485	Hokey Cokey/Baby I Love You	8

SPARKS
72	Bearsville K 15505	Wonder Girl/(No More) Mr. Nice Guy	15
74	Bearsville K 15516	Girl From Germany/Beaver O'Lindy (brown or white label)	10
74	Island WIP 6211	Never Turn Your Back On Mother Earth/Alabamy Right (p/s)	6
75	Island WIP 6221	Something For The Girl With Everything/Marry Me (title sleeve)	6
75	Island WIP 6236	Get In The Swing/Profile (title sleeve)	6
75	Island WIP 6239	Looks, Looks, Looks/Pineapple (title sleeve)	6
75	Island WIP 6249	Looks, Looks, Looks/Pineapple (DJ copy in promo p/s)	12
76	Island WIP 6282	I Want To Hold Your Hand/England (withdrawn after 1 day)	20
76	Island WIP 6357	I Like Girls/England	5
77	Island WIP 6282	I Want To Hold Your Hand/Under The Table With Her (promo only)	20
77	Island WIP 6193	This Town Ain't Big Enough For The Both Of Us/Barbecutie (reissue, orange sunset label)	20
79	Virgin VS 244	The No. 1 Song In Heaven/The No. 1 Song In Heaven (Version) (p/s, green vinyl)	5

79	Virgin VS 244-12	The No. 1 Song In Heaven/The No. 1 Song In Heaven (Long Version) (12", p/s, blue or red vinyl) 8
79	Virgin VS 270-12	Beat The Clock/Beat The Clock (Long Version) (12", black, blue, orange, yellow or pink vinyl, picture disc label, die-cut p/s) 8
79	Virgin VS 289-12	Tryouts For The Human Race/Tryouts For The Human Race (Long Version) (12", die-cut p/s, orange, yellow, blue or green vinyl, picture disc label) 8
79	Island WIP 6532	This Town Ain't Big Enough For The Both Of Us/Looks, Looks, Looks 7
80	Virgin VS 343-12	Young Girls (Disco Version)/Young Girls (Long Version)/Just Because You Love Me (12", p/s) 8
81	Why Fi WHYT 1	Tips For Teens/Don't Shoot Me (12", p/s) 8
83	Atlantic A 9866	Cool Places/Sports (no p/s) 5
85	London LONX 69	Change/This Town Ain't Big Enough For Both Of Us (Acoustic Version) (12", p/s) 5
85	Epic A 6671	Armies Of The Night/EVELYN KING: Give It Up (p/s) 5
85	Epic TA 6671	Armies Of The Night/EVELYN KING: Give It Up (12", p/s) 10
86	Consolidated TOON T2	Music That You Can Dance To (UK Extended Club Version)/Fingertips (Extended Club Version) (12", p/s) 8
87	Consolidated TOON T4	Rosebud (Extended Club Mix)/Theme For Rosebud (Cinematic Mix)/Rosebud (FM Mix) (12", p/s) 8
88	Carrere CART 427	So Important (Extremely Important Mix)/(Incredibly Important Mix)/(Single Version) (12", p/s) 8
93	Finiflex FF 1004	National Crime Awareness Week (13 Minutes In Heaven)/National Crime Awareness Week (Perkins Playtime) (12", p/s) 20
93	Finiflex FFCD 1004	National Crime Awareness Week (Psycho Cut)/National Crime Awareness Week (Highly Strung Hoedown)/National Crime Awareness Week (Complete Psycho)/National Crime Awareness Week (13 Minutes In Heaven) (CD) 20
94	Logic 7432 134461	When Do I Get To Sing My Way/(mixes) (12", doublepack, p/s) 12
94	Logic 74321 24302-2	Excerpts From Gratuitous Sax & Senseless Violins (CD, picture disc, gatefold card p/s, promo only) 20
97	Roadrunner RR 2262-6	The No. 1 Song In Heaven (Tin Tin Out Mix)/part 2/(Heavenly Dub) (with Jimmy Somerville) (12", die-cut p/s) 8
00	Recognition CDREC 14	The Calm Before The Storm (Radio Edit)/The Calm Before The Storm/It's Educational (CD, unreleased) 12
73	Bearsville K 45510	A WOOFER IN TWEETERS CLOTHING (LP) 18
74	Island ILPS 9272	KIMONO MY HOUSE (LP, pink rim label, sleeve laminated both sides, A-2U/B-1U matrixes) 20
76	Bearsville K 85505	TWO ORIGINALS OF SPARKS (2-LP, gatefold sleeve with 12-page booklet) 18
79	Virgin V 2115	NO. 1 IN HEAVEN (LP, yellow vinyl with lyric inner sleeve) 12
04	Universal LBRV001	LIL' BEETHOVEN (LP) 15

(see also Adrian Musey, Trevor White)

L. SPARKS
| 72 | Big Shot BI 601 | You Don't Care/TONY'S ALL STARS: Must Care (Version) ....6 |
| 72 | Pama PM 833 | You Don't Care/TONY'S ALL STARS: Must Care (Version) ....6 |

(see also Lloyd Parks, Termites)

SPARKY
| 72 | UK UK 13 | (Do You Remember) That Summertime Woman/You Gotta Have It Sometime ....8 |

SPARKY AND THE INNER CITIZENS
| 76 | Contempo CS2102 | Golden Gate Get Down (Short version)Golden Gate Get Down (Long Version) ....10 |

CANDY SPARLING
| 62 | Piccadilly 7N 35046 | When's He Gonna Kiss Me?/Lonely For You ....15 |
| 63 | Piccadilly 7N 35096 | Can You Keep A Secret/Charm Bracelet ....20 |

SPARROW
| 77 | Bronze BRO 38 | Half Of My Life/It's Alright Now ....5 |

SPARROW (JAMAICA)
60	Kalypso XX 10	Carnival Boycott/Gloria (with Lord Melody) 6
60	Kalypso XX 17	The Sack/Round And Around 5
60s	Melodisc CAL 15	Leading Calypsonians/Love Is Everywhere 6
60s	Melodisc CAL 17	Clara Honey Bunch/Family Sized Cokes 5
60s	Melodisc CAL 18	Goaty/I Confess 5

(see also Mighty Sparrow, King Sparrow)

SPARROW (U.S.)
| 66 | CBS 202342 | Tomorrow's Ship/Isn't It Strange ....75 |

(see also Steppenwolf)

JACK SPARROW
| 66 | Doctor Bird DB 1005 | Ice Water/ROLAND ALPHONSO: Ska-Culation ....150 |
| 66 | Doctor Bird DB 1027 | More Ice Water/ROLAND ALPHONSO: Miss Ska-Culation ....60 |

SPARTA
80	Suspect SUS 1	Fast Lane/Fighting To Be Free (in p/s) 50
80	Suspect SUS 1	Fast Lane/Fighting To Be Free 18
81	Suspect SUS 2	Angel Of Death/Tonight (wraparound p/s) 20

(see also Ethiopians)

SPARTANS
| 62 | Stateside SS 117 | Can You Waddle? (Parts 1 & 2) ....12 |

SPARTAN WARRIOR
| 83 | Guardian GRC 2164 | STEEL 'N' CHAINS (LP) ....20 |

SPAZZTIC BLUR
| 87 | Earache MOSH 5 | BEFO DA AWBUM (LP) ....15 |

ROGER RUSKIN SPEAR
| 72 | United Artists UAG 29381 | ELECTRIC SHOCKS (LP) ....25 |

(see also Bonzo Dog [Doo Dah] Band)

SPECIAL DUTIES
81	Charnel H. SARCOPHAGI 2	Violent Society/Colchester Council (wraparound p/s) 30
82	Rondelet ROUND 15	VIOLENT SOCIETY (EP) 15
82	Rondelet ROUND 20	POLICE STATE (EP) 10
82	Rondelet ROUND 24	Bullshit Crass/You're Doing Yourself No Good (p/s) 10
83	Expulsion OUT 1	Punk Rocker/Too Much Talking (p/s) 12
82	Rondelet ABOUT 9	77 IN 82 (LP) 20

SPECIALS (THE SPECIAL A.K.A.)

79	2-Tone TT 1/TT 2	Gangsters (as The Special A.K.A.)/THE SELECTER: The Selecter (paper label, in stamped plain white sleeve; matrix numbers TT1-3 & TT2-1)	45
79	2-Tone TT 1/TT 2	Gangsters (as The Special A.K.A.)/THE SELECTER: The Selecter (paper label)	15
79	2-Tone TT 1/TT 2	Gangsters (as The Special A.K.A.)/THE SELECTER: The Selecter (paper label, die-cut 2-Tone sleeve, 2nd issue with Chrysalis CHS TT 1/2 matrix no.)	6
79	2-Tone CHS TT 5	Message To You Rudy/Nite Klub (paper label, company sleeve, as The Specials featuring Rico)	8
79	2-TOne CHS TT 5	Message To You Rudy/Nite Klub (later pressing on moulded plastic labels)	5
80	2-Tone CHS TT 7	THE SPECIAL A.K.A. LIVE (EP, p/s, paper label)	10
80	2-Tone CHS TT 7	THE SPECIALS A.K.A. LIVE (EP, later pressing with plastic moulded labels)	5
80	2-Tone CHS TT 11	Rat Race/Rude Boys Outa Jail (company sleeve, paper label, as The Specials)	8
80	2-Tone CHS TT 11	Rat Race/Rude Boys Outa Jail (later pressing with plastic moulded labels)	5
80	2-Tone CHS TT 13	Stereotype/International Jet Set (company sleeve, paper label, as The Specials)	8
80	2-Tone CHS TT 13	Stereotype/International Jet Set (later pressing on plastic moulded labels)	5
80	2-Tone CHS TT 16	Do Nothing/Maggie's Farm (laminated p/s, paper label, as The Specials)	8
80	2-Tone CHS TT 16	Do Nothing/Maggie's Farm (later pressing, non laminated p/s with plastic moulded labels)	5
81	2-Tone CHS TT 17	Ghost Town/Why/Friday Night Saturday Morning (paper labels p/s)	8
81	2-Tone CHS TT 1217	Ghost Town (6.02 Extended Version)/Why/Friday Night, Saturday Morning (12", p/s)	15
81	2-Tone CHS TT 17	Ghost Town/Friday Night Saturday Morning (later pressing with plastic moulded labels, p/s)	6
82	2-Tone CHS TT 23	War Crimes (The Crime Is Still The Same)/War Crimes (p/s)	5
83	2-Tone CHS TPTT 25	Racist Friend/Bright Lights	5
83	2-Tone CHS TPTT 25	Racist Friend/Bright Lights (picture disc, as The Special A.K.A.)	6
84	2-Tone CHS TT 26	Nelson Mandela/Break Down The Door (p/s)	5
84	2-Tone CHS TT 1226	Nelson Mandela/Break Down The Door (12", p/s)	8
84	2-Tone CHS TT 27	What I Like Most About You Is Your Girlfriend/Can't Get A Break/War Crimes (The Crime Is Still The Same)/(Version) (double pack, as The Special A.K.A.)	8
84	2-Tone CHS TPTT 27	What I Like Most About You Is Your Girlfriend/Can't Get A Break (picture disc)	6
84	2-Tone CHS TT 1227	What I Like Most About You Is Your Girlfriend/Can't Get A Break (12", poster p/s with free single)	10
91	Two Tone CHSTT 30	Ghost Town/Ghost Dub '91 (p/s)	20
91	Two Tone CHSTT 12 30	Ghost Town/Ghost Dub '91 (12", p/s)	30
86	Strange Fruit SFPS 018	THE PEEL SESSIONS (EP)	10
79	2-Tone CDLTT 5001	SPECIALS (LP)	25
80	2-Tone CDL TT 5001	MORE SPECIALS (LP, with poster & bonus 7": Roddy Radiation & The Specials' "Braggin' And Tryin' Not To Lie"/Judge Roughneck's "Rude Buoys Outa Jail" [TT 999])	30
80	2-Tone CDL TT 5003	MORE SPECIALS (LP)	15
81	2-Tone CDL TT5001-P	SPECIALS (LP, picture disc)	12
84	2 Tone CHRTT 5008	IN THE STUDIO (LP)	12
91	2 Tone CHRTT 5010	SINGLES (LP)	15

(see also Colourfield, Selecter, Rhoda, Rico)

SPECIMEN

83	London LON 24	Returning From A Journey/Kiss Kiss Bang Bang (bat-shaped disc)	10
80s	Trust TRUE T 001	Sharp Teeth (12", p/s)	8

SPECKLED RED

60s	Storyville SEP 384	STORYVILLE BLUES ANTHOLOGY VOL. 4 (EP)	15
63	Esquire 32-190	THE DIRTY DOZENS (LP)	30
66	Storyville DL 601	THE DIRTY DOZENS (LP, reissue)	12
71	VJM LC 11	OH RED (LP)	20

PHIL SPECTOR

63	London HA-U 8141	A CHRISTMAS GIFT FOR YOU (LP, various artists, Spector as producer; plum label)	100
63	London HA-U 8141	A CHRISTMAS GIFT FOR YOU (LP, various artists, Spector as producer; later black label)	50
72	Apple APCOR 24	PHIL SPECTOR'S CHRISTMAS ALBUM (LP, reissue of London HA-U 8141)	30
74	Warner Bros K 59010	PHIL SPECTOR'S CHRISTMAS ALBUM (LP, 2nd reissue, with poster)	18
76	Phil Spector Intl. 2307 008	RARE MASTERS VOL. 1 (LP, various artists, Spector as producer)	35
76	Phil Spector Intl. 2307 009	RARE MASTERS VOL. 2 (LP, various artists, Spector as producer)	35
80	Phil Spector Intl. 2307 015	PHIL SPECTOR '74/'79 (LP, various artists, Spector as producer)	25
81	Phil Spector Intl. WOS 001	WALL OF SOUND (9-LP box set, various artists, Spector as producer)	130

(see also Ronettes, Crystals, Darlene Love, Bob B. Soxx & Blue Jeans, Teddy Bears)

RONNIE SPECTOR

71	Apple APPLE 33	Try Some, Buy Some/Tandoori Chicken (with p/s)	30
71	Apple APPLE 33	Try Some, Buy Some/Tandoori Chicken	10
77	Epic EPC 5185	Say Goodbye To Hollywood/Baby Please Don't Go (with E Street Band, p/s)	12
81	Red Shadow LP 002	SIREN (LP)	20

(see also Ronettes)

SPECTRES

66	Piccadilly 7N 35339	I (Who Have Nothing)/Neighbour, Neighbour	300
66	Piccadilly 7N 35352	Hurdy Gurdy Man/Laticia	300
67	Piccadilly 7N 35368	We Ain't Got Nothin' Yet/I Want It (beware bootlegs)	250

(see also Traffic Jam, Status Quo)

SPECTRES

80	Direct Hit DH 1	This Strange Effect/Getting Away With Murder (p/s)	7
81	Demon D 1002	Stories/Things (p/s)	5

(see also Rich Kids, Swingers)

SPECTRES (IRELAND)

65	Lloyd Sound UED QU 1	The Facts Of Life/Whirlpool	300

SPECTRUM (1)

65	Columbia DB 7742	Little Girl/Asking You	10
67	RCA RCA 1589	Samantha's Mine/Saturday's Child	10
67	RCA RCA 1619	Portobello Road/Comes The Dawn	10
67	RCA RCA 1651	Headin' For A Heatwave/I Wanna Be Happy With You	10
68	RCA RCA 1700	London Bridge Is Coming Down/Tables And Chairs	10
68	RCA RCA 1753	Little Red Boat By The River/Forget Me Not	10
68	RCA RCA 1775	Ob-La-Di, Ob-La-Da/Music Soothes The Savage Beast	10

MINT VALUE £

69	RCA RCA 1853	Free/The Tale Of Wally Toft	10
69	RCA RCA 1883	Glory/Nodnol	10
70	RCA RCA 1976	Portobello Road/Comes The Dawn (reissue)	10
71	Parlophone R 5908	I'll Be Gone/Launching Place - Pt II	20
69	RCA Intl. INTS 118	THE LIGHT IS DARK ENOUGH (LP)	30
00	Subway TRUMP 1	THE LIGHT IS DARK ENOUGH (LP, reissue)	20

SPECTRUM (2)

| 87 | Phoenix Modernist THE 1 | All Or Nothing (Contemporary Version)/All Or Nothing (Traditional Version) (12", p/s with 2 inserts & free 7", distributed by Nine Mile & Cartel) | 8 |

(see also Steve Marriott, Chris Farlowe, P.P. Arnold, Creation)

SPECTRUM (3)

94	Silvertone ORET 65	Undo The Taboo/In The Fullness Of Time/Turn The Tide (Sub Aqua)/Go To Sleep (12", p/s)	15
93	Silvertone ORET 56	Indian Summer/Baby Don't You Worry (California Lullaby)/It's Alright/True Love Will Find You In The End (12", p/s)	10
93	Silvertone ORE 56	Indian Summer/Baby Don't You Worry (California Lullaby) (numbered p/s)	6
92	Silvertone ORE 44	True Love Will Find You In The End (Radio Mix)/My Life Spins Round Your Every Smile (Remix) (yellow vinyl, printed plastic sleeve)	8
92	Silvertone ORE 41	How You Satisfy Me/Don't Go (Instrumental 2) (clear vinyl, printed plastic sleeve)	8
91	Silvertone SONIC 2	(I Love You)To The Moon And Back/Capo Waltz (Live) (die-cut p/s gig freebie)	8
91	Silvertone SONIC 2	(I Love You)To The Moon And Back/Capo Waltz (Live) (p/s, with Outer Limits fanzine)	20
92	Beechwood TT 015e	Taste The Ozone/MOONSHAKE: Night Tripper	5
94	Silvertone	Soul Kiss Glide Divine/STEREOLAB: Tone Burst (demo)/Tempter (demo) (unrel., with colour photocopied wraparound p/s, 25 test pressings only)	150
10	Great Pop Supplement GPS 54	Words May Shatter (with Tim "Love" Lee)/The Lonesome Death Of Johnny Ace (with Captain Memphis) (picture disc, printed plastic insert, PVC sleeve)	6
92	Silvertone ORELP 518	SOUL KISS (GLIDE DIVINE) (LP, inner)	30
92	Silvertone OREZLP 518	SOUL KISS (GLIDE DIVINE) (LP, clear vinyl, printed double walled PVC sleeve containing liquid)	30
94	Silvertone ORELP 532	HIGHS, LOWS AND HEAVENLY BLOWS (LP)	40
97	Space Age ORBIT 008LP	FOREVER ALIEN (2-LP)	20
97	Space Age ORBIT 008LP	FOREVER ALIEN (2-LP, yellow vinyl)	25

(see also Spacemen 3, Sonic Boom)

CHRIS SPEDDING

70	Harvest HAR 5013	Rock'n'Roll Band/BATTERED ORNAMENTS: Goodbye We Loved You (Madly)	25
75	Island WIP 6225	My Bucket's Got A Hole In It/I Can't Boogie	8
75	RAK RAK 210	Motor Bikin'/Working For The Union	5
76	RAK RAK 236	Guitar Jamboree/Sweet Disposition	5
76	RAK RAK 246	Pogo Dancing/Pose (p/s)	6
77	RAK RAK 261	Get Outa My Pagoda/Hey Miss Betty	5
70	Harvest SHSP 4004	BACKWOOD PROGRESSION (LP, flipback sleeve no EMI logo on label)	60
72	Harvest SHSP 4017	THE ONLY LICK I KNOW (LP, laminated sleeve, with EMI logo on label)	40

(see also Sharks, Nucleus, Sounds Nice, Panhandle, Solid Gold Cadillac, Matthew Ellis, Vibrators, Battered Ornaments, IOFR)

SPEED (JAMAICA)

| 71 | Bullet BU 477 | There's A Train/Blue Moon | 7 |

SPEED (1)

| 78 | It IT 1 | Big City/All Day And All The Night (in p/s) | 40 |
| 78 | It IT 1 | Big City/All Day And All The Night | 15 |

(see also Cobra, Tearjerkers)

SPEED (2)

| 80 | Speed GJS 001 | Man In The Street/Down The Road (p/s) | 100 |

(see also Bruce Dickinson, Iron Maiden)

SPEEDBALL(S)

| 80 | No Pap/Dirty Dick DD 1/2 | No Survivors/Is Somebody There? (miscredited as 'Speedballs' on label, in withdrawn printed die-cut sleeve) | 60 |
| 80 | No Pap/Dirty Dick DD 1/2 | No Survivors/Is Somebody There? (miscredited as 'Speedballs' on label) | 25 |

SPEEDOMETERS

| 78 | Mascot NICE 1 | Disgrace/Work (p/s) | 5 |
| 78 | Mascot NICE 2 | Liverpool Ladies (p/s) | 5 |

SPEEDY J

| 94 | Warp WAP 46 | Pepper (The Hot Mix)/Beam Me Up (The Pegasus Mix) (12") | 8 |

DAVEY SPEIRS

| 69 | Beltona LBA/LBS 61 | A MAN OF CONSTANT SORROW (LP) | 15 |

SPELLBINDERS

66	CBS 202453	Help Me (Get Myself Back Together)/Danny Boy	40
66	CBS 202453	Help Me (Get Myself Back Together)/Danny Boy (DJ copy)	85
67	CBS 202622	Chain Reaction/For You	40
67	CBS 202622	Chain Reaction/For You (DJ copy)	75
67	CBS 2776	Since I Don't Have You/I Believe	8
69	Direction 58-3970	Help Me/Chain Reaction	15

SPELLING MISSTEAKS

| 79 | Stortbeat BEAT 7 | POPSTAR (EP) | 50 |

BENNY SPELLMAN

| 62 | London HLP 9570 | Lipstick Traces/Fortune Teller | 50 |
| 62 | London HLP 9570 | Lipstick Traces/Fortune Teller (DJ Copy) | 100 |

BRUCE SPELMAN

69	Beacon BEA 112	Lady/Long Time Gone	8
72	Montagu MONT 3000	29 Years To Doomsday/Cutting The Traces	12
70	Beacon BES 3	YOU DON'T KNOW WHAT YOU'RE PADDLING IN (LP)	70
70	Montague MONS 1	YOU DON'T KNOW WHAT YOU'RE PADDLING IN (LP, different sleeve, blue/black label)	40

BARRINGTON SPENCE

86	Camara CAM002T	Hey Youthman/Version//K LEACOCK: Round And Round/Version (12")	30
88	Camara CAM 004T	Sons Of Far I/Far I Dub (12")	35
75	Grounation GRO 2009	For The Rest Of My Life/Version	5

| 76 | Student STU 1005 | Mash It Up/Straight To Radd Head | 10 |

JOHNNIE SPENCE
61	Parlophone R 4736	Wheels/First Romance	6
62	Parlophone R 4872	The Dr. Kildare Theme/The Midnight Theme	6
68	Verve (S)VLP 9222	WHY NOT? (LP, as Johnnie Spence Big Band)	12

BRINDLEY D SPENCER
| 68 | Domain D8 | The Company I Keep/On A Day Like Today | 10 |

DON SPENCER
62	HMV POP 1087	Fireball/I'm All Alone Again (blue or black labels)	12
63	HMV POP 1186	Busy Doing Nothing/The Joker	7
63	HMV POP 1205	Worried Mind/Give Give Give A Little	6
64	HMV POP 1306	Pride Is Such A Little Word/For Love (with Le Roys)	6
67	Talus TP1010	Uproar In The House/On The G.P.O Tower	20

(see also Le Roys)

DON SPENCER/XL5
| 63 | HMV 7EG 8802 | FIREBALL AND OTHER TITLES (EP, 2 tracks each) | 70 |

JEREMY SPENCER (BAND)
70	Reprise RS 27002	Linda/Teenage Darling	10
79	Atlantic K 11363	Travelling/Cool Breeze (as Jeremy Spencer Band)	5
70	Reprise RSLP 9002	JEREMY SPENCER (LP, label states K 44105 cat. no)	40
71	Reprise K 44105	JEREMY SPENCER (LP, reissue)	20
73	CBS 65387	JEREMY SPENCER AND THE CHILDREN OF GOD (LP)	12

(see also Fleetwood Mac)

JO SPENCER
| 71 | Dynamic DYN 415 | Bed Of Roses/Forgive Me | 5 |

JON SPENCER BLUES EXPLOSION
92	Clawfist 13	History Of Sex/Write A Song/Smoke Cigarettes (foldover p/s in poly bag)	12
94	Matador OLE 077	Afro/Relax Her (p/s)	8
91	Hut HUTLP 3	THE JON SPENCER BLUES EXPLOSION (LP)	15

(see also Pussy Galore)

SONNY SPENCER
| 59 | Parlophone R 4611 | Oh Boy/Gilee | 20 |

SPENCER & THE SAINTS
| 68 | Tabernacle TS 1005 | Something Within/When You Get To Heaven | 15 |

SPENCERS WASHBOARD KINGS
| 66 | Pye 7N 17245 | The Egg Plant That Ate Chicago/Somebody Stole My Gal | 7 |
| 69 | Parlophone R 5782 | Pimlico/Ordinary People | 15 |

SPERMICIDE
| 79 | No Wonder NOW 3 | Femme Prothèse/Belgique (p/s with lyrics) | 30 |

JIMMIE SPHEERIS
| 72 | CBS 8092 | Let It Flow/The Nest | 5 |

SPHERES
| 78 | Sphere | FESTIVAL AND SUNS (LP, with insert) | 25 |

(see also Jimmy Winston)

SPHERICAL OBJECTS
78	Object Music OM 01	The Kill/The Knot (p/s)	5
78	Object Music OM 04	Seventies Romance/Sweet Tooth (p/s)	5
78	Object Music PBJ 001	PAST & PARCEL (LP)	12
79	Object Music OBJ 004	ELLIPTICAL OPTIMISM (LP)	12

(see also Alternomen Unlimited, Noyes Brothers)

SPHYNKTA
83	Sultanic SUL 666	In The Shade Of The Gods/Jesus Bless My Upside-Down Cross (p/s, red vinyl, with 'devil' tattoo)	60
83	Sultanic SUL 999	Death And Violence/Ritual Slaughter (Of Your Daughter) (p/s, red vinyl)	40
84	Sultanic SUL 000	Spike Up My Sphynkta/No Pain No Gain (unissued)	100

SPHYNX
| 78 | Charisma CDS 4011 | XITINTODAY (LP, with booklet) | 30 |
| 78 | Charisma CDS 4011 | XITINTODAY (LP, without booklet) | 15 |

(see also Inner City Unit, Gong, Radio Actors)

SPICE (U.K.)
| 68 | United Artists UP 2246 | What About The Music?/In Love | 250 |

(see also Uriah Heep, Godz, Toe-Fat)

GEORGE SPICER
| 74 | Topic 12T 235 | BLACKBERRY FOLD (LP) | 15 |

SPIDELLS
| 66 | Sue WI 4019 | Find Out What's Happening/That'll Make My Heart Break | 40 |

SPIDER
| 66 | Decca F 12430 | The Comedown Song/Blow Ya Mind | 50 |

SPIDER
80	Alien ALIEN 14	Children Of The Street/Down 'N' Out (in p/s)	35
80	Alien ALIEN 14	Children Of The Street/Down 'N' Out	8
80	Alien ALIEN 16	College Luv/Born To Be Wild (in p/s)	35
80	Alien ALIEN 16	College Luv/Born To Be Wild	8

SPIDER-MAN
| 73 | Buddah 2318 075 | FROM BEYOND THE GRAVE (LP) | 12 |

SPIDERS
| 66 | Philips BF 1531 | Sad Sunset/Hey Boy | 55 |

SPIDERS (U.S.)
| 54 | London HL 8086 | I'm Slippin' In/I'm Searching (78) | 65 |

SPIDERS FROM MARS
| 75 | Pye 7N 45549 | White Man Black Man/National Poll | 6 |
| 76 | Pye NSPL 18479 | SPIDERS FROM MARS (LP) | 12 |

(see also David Bowie, Kestrel, Mick Ronson)

BERND SPIER
| 65 | Oriole CB 1987 | A Million And One Times/My Mistake | 10 |

SPILL
| 92 | Virgin VS 1141 | Don't Wanna Know About Evil (7" Wireless Road Mix)/(Saspelofiska Dub Mix) (p/s) | 12 |
| 92 | Virgin VST 1141 | Don't Wanna Know About Evil (Tumble Mix)/(Rumble Mix)/(Danny's Moto Mix)/(The Groovy Beats Mix) (12", p/s) | 15 |

(see also Beth Orton)

ARTHUR SPINK BAND
| 68 | Beltona BL 2766 | Beatles Och Aye/Harry Lauder Medley | 5 |

SPINNERS
| 66 | Fontana TE17468 | THE SINGING CITY (EP) | 8 |

(see also Liverpool Spinners, Shane Rimmer)

SPINNERS (U.S.)
61	Columbia DB 4693	That's What Girls Are Made For/Heebie Jeebies	200
61	Columbia DB 4693	That's What Girls Are Made For/Heebie Jeebies (DJ copy)	250
65	Tamla Motown TMG 514	Sweet Thing/How Can I? (demo with 'Spinners' credit)	300
65	Tamla Motown TMG 514	Sweet Thing/How Can I? (demos with 'Detroit Spinners' credit)	250
65	Tamla Motown TMG 514	Sweet Thing/How Can I? (stock copies credited to 'Spinners')	400

(see also Detroit Spinners)

SPINNING JENNY
| 71 | Midas MR004 | SPINNING JENNY (LP) | 100 |

SPINNING WHEEL
| 79 | private pressing | JACOB'S FLEECE (LP) | 15 |

(see also Dragonsfire)

SPINNING WHEELS
| 75 | Peter Dearden PD 205 | SPINNING WHEELS (EP) | 15 |

SPIRALS
| 58 | Capitol CL 14958 | The Rockin' Cow/Everybody Knows | 15 |

SPIRAL SKY
| 93 | Acme AC 8002LP | SPIRAL SKY (LP, numbered & sealed with insert, 500 only) | 25 |

(see also Sun Dial, Ohr Musik)

SPIRAL STAIRCASE
68	CBS 3507	Baby What I Mean/Makin' Your Mind Up	25
69	CBS 4187	More Today Than Yesterday/Broken Hearted Man	50
69	CBS 4187	More Today Than Yesterday/Broken Hearted Man (DJ copy)	75
69	CBS 4524	No One For Me To Turn To/Sweet Little Thing	25

SPIRAL TRIBE
92	Big Life BLRT 79	Breach The Peace/Do ET/Seven/23 Minute Warning (12", p/s)	25
92	Big Life BLRT 85	Forward the revolution/World Traveller Adventurer/Ragga Boom/Track 13 (criminal drug)(12", p/s)	25
92	Big Life BLRR 85	Forward The Revolution (the Youth remix) (1-sided, etched 12")	15
93	Butterfly BFLT 04	Sirius 23/Earthworm/Going All The Way/Predator (12", p/s, as Spiral Tribe Sound System)	20
93	Butterfly BFL LP 6	TECNO TERRA (2-LP)	50

SPIRIT
68	CBS 3523	Uncle Jack/Mechanical World	15
69	CBS 3880	I Got A Line On You/She Smiles	25
69	CBS 4511	Dark Eyed Woman/Ice	5
69	CBS 4565	Dark Eyed Woman/New Dope In Town	12
70	CBS 4773	1984/Sweet Stella Baby	8
70	CBS 5149	Animal Zoo/Red Light Roll On	6
70	Epic SEPC 7082	Mr Skin/Nature's Way	5
70	Epic SEPC 8083	Cadillac Cowboys/Darkness	6
68	CBS 63278	SPIRIT (LP, orange label)	35
68	CBS 63523	THE FAMILY THAT PLAYS TOGETHER (LP, orange label)	25
69	CBS 63729	CLEAR (LP, laminated cover, orange label)	30
70	Epic EPC 64191	THE TWELVE DREAMS OF DR. SARDONICUS (LP, g/fold sleeve, yellow label)	20
72	Epic EPC 64507	FEED-BACK (LP, gatefold sleeve, yellow label)	15
81	Beggars Banquet BEGA 23	POTATOLAND (LP, with cartoon book)	15

(see also Kapt. Kopter & Fabulous Twirlybirds, Jo Jo Gunne)

SPIRIT OF JOHN MORGAN
69	Carnaby CNS 4005	Ride On/Along Came John	10
71	RCA RCA 2085	Floating Opera Show/Never Let Go	10
69	Carnaby CNLS 6002	THE SPIRIT OF JOHN MORGAN (LP, union jack flag label)	150
70	Carnaby CNLS 6007	AGE MACHINE (LP, gatefold, union jack flag label)	130
71	Carnaby GOLD 6437 503	THE SPIRIT OF JOHN MORGAN (LP, reissue, 'crab' label logo)	50

(see also John Morgan)

SPIRIT OF MEMPHIS QUARTET
| 58 | Parlophone PMD 1070 | NEGRO SPIRITUALS (10" LP) | 25 |
| 65 | Vogue LAE 1033 | NEGRO SPIRITUALS (LP, reissue) | 15 |

SPIRIT OF PLAY
| 88 | Release KIDS 1988 | Children In Need/Children In Need (Instrumental) (with Paul McCartney) (in p/s) | 50 |
| 88 | Release KIDS 1988 | Children In Need/Children In Need (Instrumental) (with Paul McCartney) | 10 |

SPIRIT OF PROGRESS
| 71 | Philips 6006089 | Om Pa Pa/It's A Beautiful Day | 50 |

SPIRIT OF THE SECT
96	Garcia POUM 003	No Love Now/VIC GODARD: She's My Best Friend (1,000 only)	5

(see also Subway Sect, Vic Godard)

SPIRITBORN
84	Spearhead	Pity The Unborn Child/Sing To The Lord	20

SPIRITUALIZED
90	Dedicated ZB 43783	Anyway That You Want Me/Step Into The Breeze (p/s)	15
90	Dedicated ZT 43784	Anyway That You Want Me (Extended)/Step Into The Breeze 1 & 2 (12", p/s)	20
90	Dedicated ZT 43780	Anyway That You Want Me (Remix)/Step Into The Breeze 1 & 2 (12", p/s)	20
90	Dedicated ZD 43784	Anyway That You Want Me/Step Into The Breeze 1 & 2 (CD)	15
91	Fierce FRIGHT 053	Feel So Sad/I Want You (gig freebie, no p/s, stamped plain white sleeve with date & venue details)	30
91	Dedicated SPIRT 001T	Feel So Sad (Rhapsodies)/(Glides And Chimes) (12", p/s)	12
91	Dedicated SPIRT 002	Run/I Want You (p/s, with luminous sleeve & clear luminous vinyl)	20
91	Dedicated SPIRT 002	Run/I Want You (p/s)	8
91	Dedicated SPIRT 002T	Run/Luminescence (Stay With Me)/I Want You/Effervescent (Chimes) (12", with luminous sleeve)	18
91	Dedicated SPIRT 002T	Run/Luminescence (Stay With Me)/I Want You/Effervescent (Chimes) (12")	10
91	Dedicated SPIRT 002CD/ ZD 44846	Run/Luminescence (Stay With Me)/I Want You/Effervescent (Chimes) (CD)	15
91	Dedicated SPIRIT 003	Why Don't You Smile Now? (Edit)/Sway (clear vinyl, p/s)	10
91	Dedicated SPIRT 004	I Want You/You Know It's True (Instrumental)/100 Bars (Flashback) (p/s, mail-order with NME coupon only)	10
92	Dedicated SPIRT 004CD	I Want You/You Know It's True (Instrumental)/100 Bars (Flashback) (CD, no p/s, mail-order with NME coupon only)	12
92	Dedicated DEDCD 004	LAZER GUIDED MELODIES (CD EP, 4-track sampler of album)	10
92	Dedicated SPIRT 005	Medication/Smiles (p/s, red vinyl, 3000 only)	10
92	Dedicated SPIRT 005	Medication/Angel Sigh/Feel So Sad (white label test pressing, signed and inscribed by Jason Pierce in silver, limited availability through website)	30
92	Dedicated SPIRT 005T	Medication/Angel Sigh/Feel So Sad (12", p/s, with poster, 3000 only)	10
93	Dedicated SPIRT 006	Smiles (Live)/100 Bars (A Cappella) (7" flexidisc, fan-club only)	20
93	Greenpeace GR'NP'CE 001	Good Dope, Good Fun/MERCURY REV: 'Boys Peel Out (Live)' (gig 7", with booklet)	20
94	Dedicated SPIRT 009	Let It Flow/Don't Go/Stay With Me/Don't Go/Stay With Me (The Individual) (10", p/s)	8
95	Dedicated 7432 13 11782	Lay Back In The Sun/The Slide Song/Spread Your Wings/Lay Back In The Sun (CD)	15
96	Dedicated SPIRT 101T	Pure Phase Tones For DJs (12")	12
97	Dedicated SPIRT 011CD	Broken Heart (Instrumental) (CD, available via NME and Spiritualized Information Service, 500 only)	20
98	Dedicated SPIRT 014DJ	I Think I'm In Love/(Chemical Brothers Vocal Mix)/(Chemical Brothers Inst.) (12", DJ promo, 200 only)	15
98	Dedicated SPIRT 015DJ	Come Together (Death In Vegas Mix)/(Two Lone Swordsmen Mix) (12" promo, p/s)	8
92	Dedicated DEDLP 004S	LAZER GUIDED MELODIES (LP, limited Edition, with bonus 7" single 'Anyway That You Want Me'/'Why Don't You Smile Now?' [CWNN 7001])	40
92	Dedicated DEDLP 004S	LAZER GUIDED MELODIES (LP, limited. Edition, without bonus 7" single)	25
93	Dedicated no cat. no.	SUMMER EUROPEAN 93 BOX (3-CD promo set, with ribbon and insert)	80
93	Dedicated DEDLP 008	FUCKED UP INSIDE (LP, mail-order only)	70
93	Dedicated DEDCD 008	FUCKED UP INSIDE (CD, mail-order only)	50
93	Dedicated DEDLP 017	PURE PHASE (2-LP 45rpm)	20
93	Dedicated DEDCD 017S	PURE PHASE (CD in luminous slide out sleeve)	20
97	Dedicated DEDLP 034	LADIES AND GENTLEMEN WE ARE FLOATING IN SPACE (2-LP, limited issue)	100
97	Dedicated DEDCD 034S	LADIES AND GENTLEMEN WE ARE FLOATING IN SPACE (12 x 3" CDs, in blister packs in card box with insert, 1000 only, 200 with clear plastic backs)	100
97	Dedicated DEDCD 034S	LADIES AND GENTLEMEN WE ARE FLOATING IN SPACE (12 x 3" CDs, in blister packs in card box with insert, 1000)	70
97	Dedicated DEDCD 034P	LADIES AND GENTLEMEN WE ARE FLOATING IN SPACE (CD, 'Elvis version', given to Mercury Music Prize personnel, 50 copies only)	40
98	Deconstruction 74321 66285 1	ROYAL ALBERT HALL (2 x LP)	30
01	Dedicated OPM 001 CD	LET IT COME DOWN: RADIO INTERVIEW (CD, Jason Pierce speaks to Stuart Maconie plus 7 tracks)	20
08	Sanctuary 1768732	SONGS IN A&E (2-LP green vinyl, only availiable from Rough Trade)	35

(see also Spacemen 3)

SPIROGYRA
72	Pegasus PGS 3	Dangerous Dave/Captain's Log	12
73	Polydor 2001-419	I Hear You're Going Nowhere/Old Boot Wine	35
71	B&C CAS 1042	ST. RADIGUND'S (LP, with lyric inner)	130
72	Pegasus PEG 13	OLD BOOT WINE (LP, textured sleeve)	200
73	Polydor 2310 246	BELLS, BOOTS AND SHAMBLES (LP)	500

SPITERI
73	GM GML 1006	SPITERI (LP)	20

SPITFIRE (& BLACKFIRE BARMIES)
82	Carrere CAR 253	So You Want To Be A Rock'n'Roll Star/Spitfire Boogie	50

SPITFIRE BOYS
77	RK RK 1001	British Refugee/Mein Kampf (push-out centre)	75
77	RK RK 1001	British Refugee/Mein Kampf (reissue, solid centre, p/s)	60
79	Impeccable SRTS/79/CUS481	Funtime/Transedental Changing	35
83	RK RK 1001	British Refugee/Mein Kampf (2nd reissue to cash in on Frankie success p/s, no solid centre)	75

(see also Frankie Goes To Hollywood)

SPITZBROOK
79	Ace SPIT 1	Stranger/Looking At You (p/s)	60

SPIV
73	Pye 7N 45293	Oh You Beautiful Child/Little Girl	120

SPIZZ (OIL/ENERGI)
79	Rough Trade RTSO 1	6000 Crazy/1989/Fibre (p/s)	8
79	Rough Trade RTSO 2	Cold City/Red And Black/Solarisation (Shun)/Platform 3 (as Spizz Oil) (p/s)	5
79	Rough Trade RTSO 3	Soldier Soldier/Virginia Plain (as Spizz Energi) (p/s)	5
79	Rough Trade RTSO 4	Where's Captain Kirk?/Amnesia (as Spizz Energi) (p/s)	5
80	Rough Trade RTSO5	No Room/Spocks Missing (as Athletico Spizz 80)	5
80	AMS7550	Hot Deserts/legal Proceedings (as Athletico Spizz 80)	5

MINT VALUE £

S.P.K. (SEPPUKU/SURGICAL PENIS KLINIK)

80	Industrial IR 0011	MEAT PROCESSING SECTION (Mekano/Slogun) (p/s, labels list "Slogan"/Factory, with insert, as Surgical Penis Klinik) 40
83	Side Effekts SER 003	Dekompositiones (12", p/s, as Seppuku) 20
81	Side Effekts SER 01	INFORMATION OVERLOAD UNIT (LP, 1st 1,000 with booklet) 70
81	Side Effekts SER 01	INFORMATION OVERLOAD UNIT (LP) 50
83	Walter Ulbright WULP 002	AUTO-DA-FE (LP) 20
84	WEA WX 10	MACHINE AGE VOODOO (LP) 12
80s	Side Effekts SER 002	LEICHENSCHREI (LP) 30

SPLAT!
83	Ron Johnson RON 1	Yeah The Dum Dum/Bookface/Biggles Bloodbath (p/s) 6

SPLINTER
74	Dark Horse AMS 7135	Costafine Town/Elly May 5
75	Dark Horse AMS 5501	Drink All Day/Haven't Got Time (withdrawn) 12
75	Dark Horse AMS 5502	China Light/Drink All Day 10
75	Dark Horse AMS 5503	Which Way Will I Get Home/Green Bus Line 8
76	Dark Horse AMS 5506	Half Way There/What Is It (If You Never Ever Tried It Yourself) 8
77	Dark Horse K 17009	Round And Round/I'll Bend For You 7
77	Dark Horse K 17116	New York City (Who Am I)/Baby Love 7
78	Barn BARN 4	Danger Zone/Swear To God 8
76	Dark Horse DH 2	SPLINTER (LP, promo only, plain white sleeve) 130

(see also Elastic Oz Band)

SPLIT BEAVER
81	Heavy Metal HEAVY 7	Savage/Hound Of Hell (with p/s) 25
81	Heavy Metal HEAVY 7	Savage/Hound Of Hell 8
82	Heavy Metal HMRLP 3	WHEN HELL WON'T HAVE YOU (LP, silver label) 18
82	Heavy Metal HMRLP 3	WHEN HELL WON'T HAVE YOU (LP, red label) 15

SPLIT ENZ
76	Chrysalis CHS 2120	Late Last Night/Walking Down The Road (p/s) 5
77	Chrysalis CHS 2131	Another Great Divide/Stranger Than Fiction (p/s) 5
77	Chrysalis CHS 2170	My Mistake/Crosswords (p/s) 5
77	Chrysalis CHS 2170-12	My Mistake/Crosswords/The Woman Who Loves You (12", p/s) 8
79	Illegal ILS 19	I See Red/Give It A Whirl/Hermit McDermitt (p/s) 5
80	A&M AMLH 64822	TRUE COLOURS (LP, laser etched) 12

(see also Crowded House, Tim Finn)

SPLIT IMAGE
82	Heroes ER 01	Now That We've Parted 25

SPLIT KNEE LOONS
81	Avatar AAA 111	THE SPECIAL COLLECTORS EP (p/s, brown vinyl, with badge) 10
81	Avatar AAA 111	THE SPECIAL COLLECTORS EP (p/s, brown vinyl) 8

(see also Gillan, Bernie Torme, John McCoy, Colin Towns)

SPLIT SCREENS
78	Rok ROK III/IV	Just Don't Try/JUST FRANK: You (die-cut company sleeve) 10

SPLITCROW
84	Guardian GRC 21	ROCKSTORM (LP) 15

SPLODGENESSABOUNDS
80	Deram ROLF 1	Two Little Boys/Horse/Sox/Butterfly (p/s, with 'Splodge' boomerang) 15
81	Deram BUM 3	COWPUNK MEDIUM (EP, p/s, with free flexi [BUMF 3]) 8
81	Deram SML 1121	SPLODGENESSABOUNDS (LP) 15

SPODE
71	Decca F 13142	Singalong Song/Cincinatti Woman 20

SPOILERS
72	London HLU 10399	Turbo Rock/Sad Man's Land 20

SPOKESMEN
65	Brunswick 05941	The Dawn Of Correction/For You Babe 12
65	Brunswick 05948	It Ain't Fair/Have Courage Be Careful 12
66	Brunswick 05950	Michelle/Better Days Are Yet To Come 8
66	Brunswick 05958	Today's The Day/Enchanté 8

SPONOOCH
79	EMI EMI 2941	Crime Buster/Laserdance (12", p/s) 50
79	EMI EMI 2941	Crime Buter/Laserdance (p/s) 5

SPONTANEOUS COMBUSTION
71	Harvest HAR 5046	Lonely Singer/200 Lives/Leaving 15
72	Harvest HAR 5060	Gay Time Night/Spaceship 25
73	Harvest HAR 5066	Sabre Dance/Sabre Dance 10
72	Harvest SHVL 801	SPONTANEOUS COMBUSTION (LP, with EMI logo on label) 80
72	Harvest SHVL 805	TRIAD (LP, with 3 inserts, with EMI logo on label) 80

(see also Time)

SPONTANEOUS MUSIC ENSEMBLE
66	Eyemark EMP L1002	CHALLENGE (LP) 350
68	Island ILP 979	KARYOBIN ... ARE THE IMAGINARY BIRDS SAID TO LIVE IN PARADISE (LP, pink label) 200
69	Marmalade 608 008	SPONTANEOUS MUSIC ENSEMBLE (LP) 100
70	A A001	FOR YOU TO SHARE (LP) 100
71	Tangent TNGS 107	SOURCE FROM AND TOWARDS (LP) 35
72	Marmalade 2384 009	SPONTANEOUS MUSIC ENSEMBLE (LP, reissue) 25
73	Emanem 303	FACE TO FACE (LP) 30
73	Tangent TNGS 118	SO WHAT DO YOU THINK (LP) 35
77	Incus INCUS 24	BIOSYSTEM (LP) 50
82	Affinity AFF 81	1 2 ALBERT AYLER (LP) 20

(see also Howard Riley Trio)

SPONTANEOUS MUSIC ORCHESTRA
75	A A003	+ = (LP) 75

| 81 | Sweet Folk All SFA 112 | SME + SMO IN CONCERT (LP) .... | 50 |

(see also Spontaneous Music Ensemble)

SPOOKY TOOTH

67	Island WIP 6022	Sunshine Help Me/Weird	25
68	Island WIP 6037	Love Really Changed Me/Luger's Grove	15
68	Island WIP 6046	The Weight/Do Right People	10
69	Island WIP 6048	Nobody There At All/ART: Room With A View (unissued, white labels only)	40
69	Island WIP 6060	Son Of Your Father/I've Got Enough Heartache	7
73	Island WIP 6168	All Sewn Up/As Long As The World Keeps Turning	6
68	Island ILP 980/ILPS 9080	IT'S ALL ABOUT (LP, pink label)	120
68	Island ILP 980/ILPS 9080	IT'S ALL ABOUT (LP, palm tree label)	50
69	Island ILPS 9098	SPOOKY TWO (LP, 1st pressing with pink 'eye' label, matrix numbers ILPS 9098 +A & +B stamped into dead wax. No 'Porky' or 'Pecko' in dead wax (unlike reissues), gatefold 'E.J.Day' sleeve)	50
69	Island ILPS 9107	CEREMONY (LP, with Pierre Henry, pink label, gatefold sleeve)	50
70	Island ILPS 9117	THE LAST PUFF (LP, pink label)	40
73	Island ILPS 9227	YOU BROKE MY HEART SO I BUSTED YOUR JAW (LP, gatefold sleeve, lyric insert, pink rim label)	15
73	Island ILPS 9255	WITNESS (LP, pink rim label)	18
74	Good Ear EARL 2001	THE MIRROR (LP)	12
74	Island ILPS 9292	THE MIRROR (LP, export issue)	18

(see also Gary Wright, V.I.P.s, Art, Luther Grosvenor, Hellions, Revolution, State Of Mickey & Tommy, Mike Harrison, Foreigner)

SPOON FAZER

| 82 | Illuminated ILL 912 | Sunset/Ballad Of The Insectman/Flying Bodies/Fly On The Wall (12", p/s) .... | 60 |
| 82 | Project PROJECT 1 | MUSIC 2 DANCE 2 (12" EP, p/s) .... | 20 |

SPOONFUL

| 78 | Bunbury DCS 340 | Troubled Times/Country Blues (2 known copies p/s) .... | 300 |

SPORTS

78	Stiff LAST 5	WHO LISTENS TO THE RADIO EP: Who Listens To The Radio/Step By Step/So Obvious/Suspicious (originals have 'koala photo' p/s)	8
79	Sire SIR 6001	Who Listens To The Radio/Hit Single ('fireplace' p/s)	5
80	Sire SRUK 6001	WHO LISTENS TO THE RADIO (LP)	15

SPOTLIGHTERS

| 59 | Vogue Pop V 9130 | Please Be My Girlfriend/Whisper (with Bob Thompson & His Band) .... | 500 |
| 59 | Vogue Pop V 9130 | Please Be My Girlfriend/Whisper (with Bob Thompson & His Band) (78) .... | 100 |

SPOTLIGHTS

| 66 | Philips BF 1485 | Batman And Robin/Day Flower .... | 20 |

SPOTNICKS

62	Oriole CB 1724	Orange Blossom Special/The Spotnicks Theme	10
62	Oriole CB 1755	Galloping Guitars/The Rocket Man	10
63	Oriole CB 1790	Hava Nagila/High Flyin' Scotsman	8
63	Oriole CB 1818	Just Listen To My Heart/Pony Express	10
63	Oriole CB 1844	Valentina/Save The Last Dance For Me/No Yaga Daga Blues	10
63	Oriole CB 1886	Anna/The Sailor's Hornpipe	10
64	Oriole CB 1953	Lovesick Blues/The Space Creatures	15
64	Oriole CB 1981	Donner Wetter/Shamus O'Toole	15
63	Oriole EP 7075	ON THE AIR (EP)	20
64	Oriole EP 7078	SPOTNICKS IN PARIS (EP)	25
64	Oriole EP 7079	SPOTNICKS AT THE OLYMPIA PARIS (EP)	25
63	Oriole PS 40036	OUT-A SPACE: THE SPOTNICKS IN LONDON (LP, mono)	30
63	Oriole SPS 40037	OUT-A SPACE: THE SPOTNICKS IN LONDON (LP, stereo)	40
64	Oriole PS 40054	THE SPOTNICKS IN SPAIN (LP)	30
65	Oriole PS 40064	THE SPOTNICKS IN BERLIN (LP)	30

(see also Bob Lander & Spotnicks, Shy Ones)

JACK SPRATT & LEROY SIBBLES & HEPTONES

| 69 | Coxsone CS 7100 | Give Me Your Love/LARRY & ALVIN: Magic Moments .... | 70 |

SPREADEAGLE

72	Charisma CB 183	How Can We Be Lost/Nightmare (p/s, solid centre)	15
72	Charisma CB 183	How Can We Be Lost/Nightmare (four prong centre)	8
72	Charisma CAS 1055	THE PIECE OF PAPER (LP, pink 'scroll' label)	20

SPREDTHICK

| 78 | An Actual ACT 003 | SPREDTHICK (LP, with insert) .... | 18 |

SPRIGUNS (OF TOLGUS)

76	Decca F 13676	Nothing Else To Do/Lord Lovell	12
77	Decca F 13739	White Witch/Time Will Pass	12
75	Alida Star C'tage ASC7755	JACK WITH A FEATHER (LP, as Spriguns Of Tolgus)	1200
76	Decca SKL 5262	REVEL WEIRD & WILD (LP, with lyric insert)	250
77	Decca SKL 5286	TIME WILL PASS (LP, with lyric insert)	200
92	Kissing Spell KSLP 002	ROWDY DOWDY DAY (LP, reissue)	15

(see also Mandy Morton Band, Terra Cotta)

SPRING

| 71 | RCA Neon NE 6 | SPRING (LP, foldout sleeve, black inner sleeve) .... | 600 |

SPRINGBOARD

| 69 | Polydor 545007 | SPRINGBOARD (LP) .... | 100 |

(see also Ian Carr)

DUSTY SPRINGFIELD

63	Philips BF 1292	I Only Want To Be With You/Once Upon A Time	6
64	Philips BF 1313	Stay Awhile/Something Special	6
64	Philips BF 1348	I Just Don't Know What To Do With Myself/My Colouring Book	5
64	Philips BF 1369	Losing You/Summer Is Over	5
64	Philips BF 1381	Oh Holy Child/SPRINGFIELDS: Jingle Bells (with p/s)	6
64	Philips BF 1381	Oh Holy Child/SPRINGFIELDS: Jingle Bells	5
65	Philips BF 1396	Your Hurtin' Kinda Love/Don't Say It Baby	5
65	Philips BF 1418	In The Middle Of Nowhere/Baby Don't You Know	6

65	Philips BF 1430	Some Of Your Lovin'/I'll Love You For A While	6
66	Philips BF 1466	Little By Little/If It Hadn't Been For You	6
66	Philips BF 1482	You Don't Have To Say You Love Me/Every Ounce Of Strength	6
66	Philips BF 1502	Goin' Back/I'm Gonna Leave You	7
66	Philips BF 1510	All I See Is You/Go Ahead On (with p/s)	8
67	Philips BF 1553	I'll Try Anything/The Corrupt Ones	5
67	Philips BF 1577	Give Me Time/The Look Of Love	6
67	Philips BF 1608	What's It Gonna Be/Small Town Girl	15
68	Philips BF 1682	I Close My Eyes And Count To Ten/No Stranger Am I	6
68	Philips BF 1706	I Will Come To You/The Colour Of Your Eyes	5
68	Philips BF 1730	Son Of A Preacher Man/Just A Little Lovin'	10
69	Philips BF 1811	Am I The Same Girl/Earthbound Gypsy	15
69	Philips BF 1826	Brand New Me/Bad Case Of The Blues	7
70	Philips BF 1835	Morning Please Don't Come (with Tom Springfield)/TOM SPRINGFIELD: Charley	5
70	Philips 6006 045	How Can I Be Sure/Spooky	20
72	Philips 6006 214	Yesterday When I Was Young/I Start Counting	6
73	Philips 6006 295	Who Gets Your Love/Of All The Things	6
74	Philips 6006 325	Learn To Say Goodbye/Easy Evil	6
74	Philips 6006 350	What's It Gonna Be/Bring Him Back	10
75	Philips 6006 446	Yesterday When I Was Young/The Look Of Love	7
78	Mercury DUSTY 1	A Love Like Yours (Don't Come Knocking Every Day)/Hollywood Movie Girls	5
78	Mercury DUSTY 002	That's The Kind Of Love I've Got For You/Sandra	5
79	Mercury DUSTY 003	I'm Coming Home Again/Save Me Save Me	5
79	Mercury DUSTY 4	Baby Blue/Get Yourself To Love (p/s)	6
64	Philips BE 12560	I ONLY WANT TO BE WITH YOU	10
64	Philips BE 12564	DUSTY	12
65	Philips BE 12572	DUSTY IN NEW YORK	20
65	Philips BE 12579	MADEMOISELLE DUSTY	20
68	Philips BE 12605	IF YOU GO AWAY	10
64	Philips BL 7594	A GIRL CALLED DUSTY (mono)	15
64	Philips SBL 7594	A GIRL CALLED DUSTY (stereo)	20
65	Philips RBL 1002	EVERYTHING'S COMING UP DUSTY (gatefold sleeve with booklet, mono)	25
65	Philips SRBL 1002	EVERYTHING'S COMING UP DUSTY (gatefold sleeve with booklet, stereo)	30
67	Philips (S)BL 7820	WHERE AM I GOING?	25
68	Philips (S)BL 7864	DUSTY... DEFINITELY	15
69	Philips SBL 7889	DUSTY IN MEMPHIS	50
70	Philips SBL 7927	FROM DUSTY... WITH LOVE	20
80	Philips PRICE 83	IN MEMPHIS PLUS (LP)	30

(see also Lana Sisters, Springfields, Tom Springfield, Pet Shop Boys)

RICK SPRINGFIELD
72	Capitol EA-ST 80001	BEGINNINGS (LP)	12

TOM SPRINGFIELD (& HIS) ORCHESTRA
63	Philips BF 1294	The Moon Behind The Hill/The Londonderry Air	6
64	Philips BF 1331	Brazilian Shake/Brazilian Blues	6
69	Philips BF 1759	Theme From From The Troubleshooters/Homage To Spewdley Parsons (with p/s)	8
69	Philips BF 1759	Theme From From The Troubleshooters/Homage To Spewdley Parsons	6
68	Decca SKL 4967	SUN SONGS (LP)	80
69	Decca LK/SKL 5003	LOVE'S PHILOSOPHY BY... (LP, featuring Dusty Springfield)	30

(see also Springfields, Dusty Springfield)

SPRINGFIELD PARK
68	CBS 3775	Never An Everyday Thing/I Can See The Sun Shine	10

SPRINGFIELDS (1)
61	Philips PB 1145	Dear John/I Done What They Told Me To	6
61	Philips PB 1168	Breakaway/Good News	7
61	Philips PB 1178	Bambino/Star Of Hope (with p/s)	8
62	Philips PB 1220	Goodnight Irene/Far Away Places	5
62	Philips PB 1241	Silver Threads And Golden Needles/Aunt Rhody	5
62	Philips 326 536 BF	Swahili Papa/Gotta Travel On	5
62	Philips 326 557BF	Island Of Dreams/The Johnson Boys	5
63	Philips 326 577 BF	Say I Won't Be There/Little Boat	5
63	Philips BF 1263	Come On Home/Pit-A-Pat	7
64	Philips BF 1306	If I Was Down And Out/Maracabamba	7
61	Philips BBE 12476	THE SPRINGFIELDS (EP, mono)	12
61	Philips SBBE 9068	THE SPRINGFIELDS (EP, stereo)	15
62	Lyntone P125E	CHRISTMAS WITH THE SPRINGFIELDS (EP, mail-order via Woman's Own)	8
62	Philips 433 622 BE	KINDA FOLKSY (EP)	10
63	Philips 433 623 BE	KINDA FOLKSY No. 2 (EP)	10
63	Philips 433 624 BE	KINDA FOLKSY No. 3 (EP)	10
63	Philips BBE 12538	HIT SOUNDS (EP)	8
63	Philips 433 643 BE	FOLK SONGS FROM THE HILLS (EP)	10
62	Philips BBL 7551	KINDA FOLKSY (LP, mono)	15
62	Philips SBBL 674	KINDA FOLKSY (LP, stereo)	20
63	Philips 632 304 BL	FOLK SONGS FROM THE HILLS (LP)	15
69	Fontana SFL 13098	THE SPRINGFIELDS SING AGAIN (LP)	12

(see also Dusty Springfield, Lana Sisters, Tom Springfield, Mike Hurst)

SPRINGFIELDS (2)
88	Sarah SARAH 010	Sunflower/Clown/Are We Gonna Be Alright? (foldaround p/s with 14" x 10" poster in polyester bag; yellow p/s)	25
88	Sarah SARAH 010	Sunflower/Clown/Are We Gonna Be Alright? (foldaround p/s with 14" x 10" poster in polyester bag; later orange p/s)	18
91	Sarah SARAH 040	Wonder/Tomorrow Ends Today (p/s, with insert)	7

BRUCE SPRINGSTEEN
75	CBS A 3661	Born To Run/Meeting Across The River	15
76	CBS A 3940	Tenth Avenue Freeze-Out/She's The One	20
78	CBS A 6424	Prove It All Night/Factory	15
78	CBS A 6532	Badlands/Something In The Night	15
78	CBS A 6720	Promised Land/Streets Of Fire	65

80	CBS A 9309	Hungry Heart/Held Up Without A Gun (p/s, withdrawn first issue, black and white p/s, blue lettering)	25
80	CBS A 9309	Hungry Heart/Held Up Without A Gun	6
81	CBS A 9568	Sherry Darling/Independence Day (white label promo, 100 only 2 known copies with p/s listing 'Independence Day')	2500
81	CBS A 9568	Sherry Darling/Independence Day (white label promo, 100 only)	2000
81	CBS 9568	Sherry Darling/Be True (p/s)	15
81	CBS A 1179	The River/Independence Day (p/s)	15
81	CBS A 13-1179	The River/Born To Run/Rosalita (12", p/s, sleeves credit 'East Street Band')	15
81	CBS A 13-1179	The River/Born To Run/Rosalita (12", p/s)	12
81	CBS A 1557	Cadillac Ranch/Wreck On The Highway (p/s)	15
82	CBS A 2794	Atlantic City/Mansion On The Hill (p/s)	20
82	CBS A 2969	Open All Night/The Big Pay Back (p/s)	25
84	CBS WA 4436	Dancing In The Dark/Pink Cadillac (Cadillac-shaped picture disc)	20
84	CBS A 4662	Cover Me/Jersey Girl (live) (poster p/s)	5
84	CBS WA 4662	Cover Me/Jersey Girl (live) (Bruce-shaped picture disc with plinth)	25
84	CBS DA 4662/A 4436	Cover Me/Jersey Girl (live)//Dancing In The Dark/Pink Cadillac (shrinkable double pack, both 45s in p/s)	12
84	CBS DA 4662/A 7077	Cover Me/Jersey Girl (live)//Born To Run/Meeting Across The River (shrinkwrapped double pack, no p/s on 2nd 45)	12
84	CBS A 6561	I'm Going Down/Janey, Don't You Lose Heart (p/s)	7
85	CBS A 7077	Born To Run/Meeting Across The River (reissue, blue p/s, withdrawn)	25
85	CBS A 6342	I'm On Fire/Born In The U.S.A. (p/s, with competition postcard)	8
85	CBS WA 6342	I'm On Fire/Born In The U.S.A. (p/s, flag-shaped picture disc)	20
85	CBS QTA 6375	Glory Days/Stand On It/Sherry Darling/Racing In The Street (12", poster p/s)	8
85	CBS BRUCE 1	BORN IN THE U.S.A. - THE 12" COLLECTION (4 x 12" & 7", box with poster)	20
86	CBS 650 193-0	War/Merry Xmas Baby (live)/My Home Town (live)/Santa Claus Is Coming To Town (live) (shrinkwrapped double pack, both 45s in p/s)	10
86	CBS 650 193-6	War/Merry Xmas Baby (live)/Incident On 57th Street (live) (12", poster p/s)	8
87	CBS 650 381-6	Fire (live)/For You (live)/Born To Run (live)/No Surrender (live)/10th Avenue (live) Freeze-Out (live) (12", p/s)	12
87	CBS BRUCE B2	Born To Run/Spirit In The Night//Johnny 99/Because The Night (double pack box set)	8
87	CBS BRUCE C2	Born To Run (live)/Spirit In The Night (live)/Johnny 99 (live)/Seeds (live) (CD, card sleeve with gauze inner)	10
87	CBS 651 141-0	Brilliant Disguise/Lucky Man (gatefold p/s, with discography)	6
87	CBS 651 141-6	Brilliant Disguise/Lucky Man (12", p/s, with poster)	8
87	CBS 651 295-0	Tunnel Of Love/Two For The Road (postcard-shaped picture disc)	15
87	CBS 651 295-8	Tunnel Of Love/Two For The Road/Santa Claus Is Coming To Town (12", p/s with poster)	8
87	CBS 651 295-2	Tunnel Of Love/Santa Claus Is Coming To Town (live)/Two For The Road (CD, card sleeve)	20
88	CBS BRUCE Q4	Spare Parts/Cover Me (live)/Spare Parts (live)/I'm On Fire (live) (12", different p/s)	10
88	CBS BRUCE B4	Spare Parts/Pink Cadillac/Spare Parts (live)/Chimes Of Freedom (live) (CD, BRUCE C4 disc in silver tin)	20
92	Sony 658 138-5	57 Channels (And Nothin' On)/Stand On It/Janey, Don't You Lose Heart (CD, picture disc, digipak)	12
94	Columbia 660 065-8	Streets Of Philadelphia/If I Should Fall Behind/Growing Up/Big Muddy (12", picture disc)	10
73	CBS 65480	GREETINGS FROM ASBURY PARK, N.J. (cutaway gatefold sleeve, orange label)	20
74	CBS 65780	THE WILD, THE INNOCENT AND THE E STREET SHUFFLE (orange label, yellow lettering on sleeve; with "Ashbury" mis-spelling on label)	20
75	CBS 69170	BORN TO RUN (with "John Landau" misprint on rear sleeve)	20
79	CBS 66353	BRUCE SPRINGSTEEN (3-LP, box set)	18
82	CBS 25100	NEBRASKA (LP, inner)	12
84	CBS 11-86304	BORN IN THE U.S.A. (picture disc)	25
87	CBS 460 270-0	TUNNEL OF LOVE (picture disc)	15
87	CBS CDCBS 460 270-9	TUNNEL OF LOVE (CD, picture disc)	20
90	CBS LSP 980636 1	COLLECTED WORKS OF BRUCE SPRINGSTEEN (7 LP box set)	200
92	Sony 471 423-0	HUMAN TOUCH (picture disc)	12
92	Sony 471 424-0	LUCKY TOWN (picture disc, with side 1 on both sides)	75
92	Sony 471 424-0	LUCKY TOWN (picture disc)	12
93	Columbia 473860-1	IN CONCERT (2-LP, stickered sleeve)	40

(see also Nils Lofgren, Roy Orbison)

SPRINGTIME

78	Sonet SON 2143	Mrs Caroline Robinson/Honey Bye Bye (p/s)	6

SPRINGWATER (1)

71	Polydor 2058141	I Will Return/Stone Cross	12
72	Polydor 2058220	Listen Everybody/Guiding Light	12

SPRINGWATER (2)

80	Fabulous JC6	Move A Little Closer/Rescue Me (p/s)	5
70	Fabulous JC 2	Sailing/Captain Of The Sea	6

SPRINGWELL

71	London HLU 10345	It's For You/Our Question	15

SPROG & WIDGIT

72	Diddley Do DIDLP 02	32 ENGLISH FOLK SONGS IN THE SILLY TRADITION (2-LP, gatefold sleeve)	18

SPRONG & NYAH SHUFFLE

69	Grape GR 3001	Moonwalk/Think	30

BILLY SPROUD & ROCK 'N' ROLL SIX

57	Columbia DB 3893	Rock Mr. Piper/If You're So Smart (How Come You Ain't Rich)	25
57	Columbia DB 3893	Rock Mr. Piper/If You're So Smart (How Come You Ain't Rich) (78)	20

SPROUTS

58	RCA RCA 1031	Teen Billy Baby/Goodbye, She's Gone	40
58	RCA RCA 1031	Teen Billy Baby/Goodbye, She's Gone (78)	20

SPUD

75	Philips 9108 002	A SILK PURSE (LP)	20

SPUD AND THE FABS

80	Whitetower AMC 706	Your Place Or Mine (p/s)	25

MINT VALUE £

THE SPUNKY ONION
74	Contempo CS2006	Cookie Man (Part 1)/Cookie Man (Part 2)	6

THE SPUNKY SPIDER
73	Phoenix S-NIX 143	You Won't Come/Perchance	50

WILD JIMMY SPURRILL
60s	XX MIN 717	NOBLE 'THIN MAN' WATTS AND WILD JIMMY SPURRILL (EP)	20

(see also Noble 'Thin Man' Watts, Guitar Crusher)

SPURS
88	Outback OUT 1	Soldier (p/s)	12

SPYROGYRA
79	Infinity (no cat. no.)	MORNING DANCE (LP, picture disc, in-house issue, top-flap poly sleeve, 50 copies)	50

SPYS
79	No Bad NB 3	The Young Ones/Heavy Scene (p/s)	5

SQUAD
79	Squad SQS 1	Red Alert/£8 A Week (in die cut p/s)	40
79	Squad SQS 1	Red Alert/£8 A Week	20
79	Squad SQS 2	Millionaire/Brockhill Boys (p/s)	40

SQUADRONAIRES
54	Decca F 10248	Coach Call Boogie/Donegal Cradle Song	10
54	Decca F 10274	Wolf On The Prowl/Mudhopper	7
57	Columbia DB 3882	Rock And Roll Boogie/Right Now, Right Now	10
53	Decca LF 1141	CONTRASTS IN JAZZ (10" LP)	15

LESTER SQUARE & THE SQUARE DEAL SURFS
84	Thin Sliced TSR 4T	The Plug (12", p/s)	8

(see also Monochrome Set)

SQUARE SET
71	Decca FR 13197	That's What I Want/Come On	80

SQUARES (1)
78	Sire SIR 4003	No Fear/Nobodys Fool (p/s)	5

SQUARES (2)
93	Hangman HANG 52 UP	CURSE OF THE SQUARES (LP)	15
91	Hangman HANG 45 UP	TRAPPED IN A SQUARE (LP)	15

SQUEEK
72	Bronze BRO 130	Make Hay While The Sun Shines/L Amour D'un Apres Midi	20

SQUEEZE
77	BTM SBT 107	Take Me I'm Yours/No, Disco Kid, No (unreleased)	0
77	Deptford Fun City DFC 01	PACKET OF THREE (EP, red & blue photo p/s)	10
77	Deptford Fun City DFC 01	PACKET OF THREE (12" EP, plain pink die-cut sleeve, 500 only)	10
78	A&M AMS 7360	Bang Bang/All Fed Up (p/s, green vinyl)	5
78	A&M AMS 7398	Goodbye Girl/Saints Alive (3-D p/s)	5
79	A&M AMS 7426	Cool For Cats/Model (p/s, brilliant pink vinyl, 5,000 only)	6
79	A&M AMS 7426	Cool For Cats/Model (p/s, red vinyl, 1,000 only)	7
79	A&M AMSP 7426	Cool For Cats (12", p/s, pale pink vinyl)	8
79	A&M AMS 7495	Christmas Day/Going Crazy (p/s, white vinyl)	5
79	A&M AMS 7507	Another Nail In My Heart/Pretty Thing (p/s, clear vinyl)	5
81	A&M AMS 8147	Tempted/Yap Yap Yap (p/s, with free U.S. 5" single "Another Nail In My Heart"/"If I Didn't Love You", p/s, shrinkwrapped)	5
81	A&M AMS 8166	Labelled With Love/Squabs On Forty Five (withdrawn p/s)	12

SQUIBBY & REFLECTIONS
68	Direction 58-3453	Ragamuffin/For A Little While	7
68	Direction 58-3606	Loving You Has Made My Life Worthwhile/Better Off Without You	7
69	Direction 58-4073	You Got It/Come Back To Me	8

SQUIBS
81	Oily SLICK 1	On The Line (plain sleeve, with insert)	25
81	Oily SLICK 3	Parades/Out On The Town (p/s)	20

BILLY SQUIER
82	Capitol CL 261	Emotions In Motion/Catch 22 (p/s)	12
82	Capitol CL 261	Emotions In Motion/Catch 22 (picture disc)	15
84	Capitol SQD 1	Rock Me Tonite/Can't Get Next To You//She's A Runner/Listen To The Heart (double pack)	6
86	Capitol CL 433	Love Is The Hero/Learn How To Live (live) (p/s)	7
86	Capitol 12CL 433	Love Is The Hero (extended version with Freddie Mercury intro)/Learn How To Live (live) (12", p/s)	55

(see also Freddie Mercury, Roger Taylor)

SQUIRE
79	Rok ROK I/II	Get Ready To Go/COMING SHORTLY: Doing The Flail (company sleeve)	30
79	I-Spy SEE 2	Walking Down The King's Road/It's A Mod Mod Mod Mod World (company sleeve)	7
79	I-Spy SEE 4	The Face Of Youth Today/I Know A Girl (keyhole company sleeve, plastic labels)	6
80	Stage One STAGE 2	My Mind Goes Round In Circles/Does Stephanie Know? (p/s)	6
82	Hi-Lo HI 001	No Time Tomorrow/Don't Cry To Me (p/s)	5
82	Hi-Lo HI 002	Girl On A Train/Every Trick In The Book (p/s)	5
83	Hi-Lo HIT 003	Every Trick In The Book/Every Trick In The Book (Elastic Mix) (12", p/s)	8
83	Hi-Lo HI 004	Jesamine/When I Try, I Lie (p/s)	10
84	Hi-Lo HI 005/SFC 2	The Young Idea/It's Getting Better (Squire Fan Club issue)	10
94	Detour DR 020	The Place I Used To Live/Make Love To You/Over You (p/s, 900 only, 50 on white vinyl)	10
94	Detour DR 020	The Place I Used To Live/Make Love To You/Over You (p/s, 2nd pressing of 250 copies, white labels & purple print: 3rd pressing, 588 copies on clear splattered vinyl)	5
83	Hi-Lo LO 01	HITS FROM 3,000 YEARS AGO (LP)	18
83	Hi-Lo LO 02	GET SMART (LP, with poster)	15
85	Hi-Lo LO 03	THE SINGLES ALBUM (LP)	15

(see also Anthony Meynell)

JOHN SQUIRE
02	North Country Records NC001	Joe Louis/Home Sweet Home (p/s)	5

(see also Stone Roses)

SQUIRES
69	MCA MU 1060	Funky Bayswater/Games People Play	15

ROSEMARY SQUIRES
56	Decca F 10685	Band Of Gold/Where You Are	10
58	HMV POP 462	Happy Is The Bride/Give Me The Simple Life	8
58	HMV POP 541	There Goes My Lover/Please Be Kind	8
64	HMV POP 1288	Bluesette/Nothing's Changed	8
56	MGM MGM-EP 640	MY LOVE IS A WANDERER (EP)	40
60	HMV 7EG 8588	ROSEMARY (EP)	40
63	HMV CLP 1669	EVERYTHINGS COMING UP ROSY (LP, mono)	250
63	HMV CSD 1508	EVERYTHINGS COMING UP ROSY (LP, stereo)	400
65	HMV CLP 1832	SOMETHING TO REMEMBER ME BY (LP, mono)	80
65	HMV CSD 1586	SOMETHING TO REMEMBER ME BY (LP, stereo)	120

S.R.C.
69	Capitol CL 15576	Black Sheep/Morning Mood	35
87	Bam Caruso OPRA 063	Black Sheep/BRAIN: Nightmares In Red (jukebox issue, die-cut company sleeve)	5
69	Capitol (S)T 2991	S.R.C. (LP)	60
69	Capitol E-(S)T 134	MILESTONES (LP)	50
70	Capitol E-(S)T 273	TRAVELLER'S TALE (LP)	50

(See also Streamliners with Joanne)

ROY ST. JOHN
76	Caroline CA 2008	DECLARE IMMIGRATION (LP)	15

ASHBURY STABBINS DUO
76	Bead Records BEAD 4	FIRE WITHOUT STICKS (LP)	50

STACCATOS
61	Parlophone R 4828	Main Line/Topaz	15
68	NEMS 3003	Why Care About Today/Cry To Me	25
68	Fontana TF 966	Butchers And Bakers/Imitations Of Love	25

STACCATOS (U.S.)
66	Capitol CL 15478	Let's Run Away/Face To Face (With Love)	7
67	Capitol CL 15505	Half Past Midnight/Weatherman	7

CLARENCE STACEY
59	Pye International 7N 25025	Just Your Love/Lonely Guy	35
59	Pye International 7N 25025	Just Your Love/Lonely Guy (78)	20

GWEN STACEY
65	RCA RCX 7166	INTRODUCING GWEN STACEY (EP)	150

STACK OF HEARTS
86	SOH SOH 001	Danger Zone/Searching For A Spirit (no p/s)	25

BOB STACKIE
68	Collins Downbeat CR 009	Grab It Hold It Feel It (with Sir Collins Band)/DAN SIMMONDS: Way Out Sound	50

(see also Sir Collins [Band], Owen Gray)

STACKRIDGE
71	MCA MKS 5065	Dora, The Female Explorer/Everyman	5
72	MCA MKS 5091	Slark/Purple Spaceships Over Yatton	12
72	MCA MKS 5103	Anyone For Tennis?/Amazingly Agnes	5
71	MCA MDKS 8002	STACKRIDGE (LP, gatefold sleeve, pink/orange 'dogbone' label)	25
72	MCA MKPS 2025	FRIENDLINESS (LP, blue/black 'hexagon' label)	20
74	MCA MCG 3501	THE MAN IN THE BOWLER HAT (LP, gatefold sleeve)	12
74	Rocket PIGL 11	EXTRAVAGANZA (LP, gatefold label)	12
76	MCA MCF 2747	DO THE STANLEY (LP)	12
76	Rocket ROLL 3	MR. MICK (LP)	12

STACKWADDY
70	Dandelion S 5119	Roadrunner/Kentucky	12
72	Dandelion 2001 331	You Really Got Me/Willie The Pimp	10
71	Dandelion DAN 8003	STACKWADDY (LP, gatefold sleeve with lyric insert)	150
71	Dandelion DAN 8003	STACKWADDY (LP, gatefold sleeve with lyric insert, as K 49003)	40
72	Dandelion 2310 231	BUGGER OFF! (LP)	150

STADIUM DOGS
77	Audiogenic A 17	Easy Beat/Android Rocker/Media Withdrawal (die-cut p/s)	10

JIM STAFFORD
73	MGM 2006 374	Spiders & Snakes/Undecided	5

JO STAFFORD
53	Columbia SCM 5011	Star Of Hope/Somebody	10
53	Columbia SCM 5012	It Is No Secret/He Bought My Soul At Calvary	15
53	Columbia SCM 5013	You Belong To Me/Jambalaya (On The Bayou)	50
53	Columbia SCM 5026	Keep It A Secret/Once To Every Heart	15
53	Columbia SCM 5046	Something To Remember You By/Blue Moon	15
53	Columbia SCM 5064	September In The Rain/JO STAFFORD & FRANKIE LAINE: Chow, Willy	15
57	Philips JK 1003	On London Bridge/Perfect Love (jukebox issue)	25
58	Philips PB 818	With A Little Bit Of Luck/Wouldn't It Be Loverly	6
58	Philips PB 876	Hibiscus/How Can We Say Goodbye	5
59	Philips PB 898	My Heart Is From Missouri/It Won't Be Easy	5
59	Philips PB 935	Pine Top's Boogie Woogie/All Yours	8
59	Philips PB 935	Pine Top's Boogie Woogie/All Yours (78)	15
60	Philips PB 991	It Is No Secret/He Bought My Soul At Calvary (reissue)	5
60	Philips PB 1034	Candy/Indoor Sport	6
60	Pye Intl. 7N 25139	If My Heart Had A Window/Symphony	5
54	Columbia SEG 7516	WITH NELSON EDDY (plain sleeve)	10
54	Columbia SEG 7548	SHOW SONGS (plain sleeve)	10

MINT VALUE £

55	Philips BBE 12014	JO STAFFORD No. 1	10
57	Philips BBE 12138	JO STAFFORD No. 2	10
57	Philips BBE 12141	JO STAFFORD WITH THE ART VAN DAMME QUINTET	10
58	Philips BBE 12214	T.V. SERIES	10
60	Capitol EAP 20049	THE JO STAFFORD TOUCH	8
61	Capitol EAP 20154	SIMPLE MELODY	8
61	Philips BBE 12459	JO + JAZZ	10
50	Capitol LC 6500	AMERICAN FOLK SONGS (10")	20
51	Capitol LC 6515	KISS ME KATE (10", with Gordon MacRae)	15
53	Capitol LC 6575	CAPITOL PRESENTS JO STAFFORD (10")	15
53	Capitol LC 6611	SUNDAY EVENING SONGS (10", with Gordon MacRae)	12
54	Capitol LC 6635	CAPITOL PRESENTS JO STAFFORD, VOL. 2 (10")	15
54	Columbia 33S 1024	AS YOU DESIRE ME (10")	15
54	Philips BBR 8011	MY HEART'S IN THE HIGHLANDS (10")	12
56	Philips BBR 8076	THE VOICE OF YOUR CHOICE (10")	20
56	Philips BBL 7100	HAPPY HOLIDAY (soundtrack)	15
57	Philips BBL 7169	ONCE OVER LIGHTLY	15
57	Philips BBL 7187	SKI TRAILS	15
58	Philips BBL 7243	SWINGIN' DOWN BROADWAY	15
59	Philips BBL 7290	I'LL BE SEEING YOU	15
59	Philips BBL 7327	BALLAD OF THE BLUES	15
60	Philips BBL 7395	JO STAFFORD SHOWCASE	15
61	Philips BBL 7428	JO + JAZZ (also stereo SBBL 595)	15

(see also Jonathan & Darlene Edwards, Gordon MacRae, Tommy Dorsey)

JO STAFFORD & FRANKIE LAINE
| 53 | Columbia SCM 5014 | Settin' The Woods On Fire/Piece A-Puddin' | 25 |
| 55 | Philips BBR 8075 | FLOATIN' DOWN TO COTTON TOWN (10" LP) | 40 |

(see also Frankie Laine)

TERRY STAFFORD
63	Stateside SS 225	Heartache On The Way/You Left Me Here To Cry	15
64	London HLU 9871	Suspicion/Judy	10
64	London HLU 9902	I'll Touch A Star/Playing With Fire	10
64	London HLU 9923	Follow The Rainbow/Are You A Fool Like Me	12
64	London RE-U 1436	SUSPICION (EP)	40
64	London HA-U 8200	SUSPICION (LP)	60

STAGEFRIGHT
| 85 | STN STN 1 | Strangers In The Night/Heartless/Rock City (no p/s) | 150 |

ROSS STAGG
| 74 | Dawn DNS 1059 | I'll Never Be A Star (But I Might)/Oh Captain | 6 |

STAIFFI ET SES MUSTAFA'S
| 59 | Pye Intl. 7N 25057 | Mustafa Cha Cha Oriental/Zoubida Cha Cha Oriental | 10 |

STAINED GLASS
| 74 | Sweet Folk & C. SFA 019 | OPEN ROAD (LP) | 80 |

STAINS
| 79 | Redball RR 020 | Emotional Pills/Believer/Bored (p/s) | 100 |

CHRIS STAINTON & GLEN TURNER
| 76 | Decca SKL-R 5259 | TUNDRA (LP) | 12 |

STAIRS
| 92 | Imaginary MIRAGE 029 | Weed Bus (12", unissued, test pressings only, proof p/s) | 40 |

STAIRSTEPS
71	Buddah 2011 092	Stay Close To Me/I Made A Mistake	8
75	Dark Horse AMS 5505	From Us To You/Time (in USA p/s)	10
75	Dark Horse AMS 5505	From Us To You/Time	8
76	Dark Horse AMS 5507	Pasado/Throwin' Stones Atcha	10
71	Buddah 2359 021	STEP BY STEP BY STEP (LP)	20
71	Buddah 2365 015	STAY CLOSE TO ME (LP)	20
72	Buddah 2365 016	THE STAIRSTEPS (LP)	20
76	Dark Horse AMLH 22004	2ND RESSURECTION (LP)	20

(see also Five Stairsteps)

STAIRWAY
| 88 | New World NWCD 168 | MOONSTONE (CD) | 18 |

(see also Jane Relf, Yardbirds, Renaissance)

STAKKA AND SKYNET
00	Underfire UDFR 016	Knight Lore/Global Report (12")	10
01	Underfire UDFRLPS 04	CLOCKWORK SAMPLER EP: Decoy/Side Effects (Kemal and Rob Data remix)/9000 series/Side Effects (Teebee remix) (2 x 12", stickered, die-cut sleeve)	20
01	Underfire UDRFRLP 04	CLOCKWORK (LP, 5 discs)	40

STALAG 17
| 85 | Mortarhate/Warzone MORT 14 | THE TRUTH WILL BE HEARD (12", split EP with TOXIC WASTE) | 15 |

STALLION
| 75 | Flyright FLY 45 003 | Skinny Kid/Cobra | 45 |

STAMFORD BRIDGE
| 70 | Penny Farthing PEN 715 | Chelsea/Ossie | 12 |
| 71 | Penny Farthing PELS 515 | FIRST DAY OF YOUR LIFE (LP) | 25 |

TERRY STAMP
| 75 | A&M AMLH 68329 | FAT STICKS (LP, with lyric insert) | 30 |

(see also Third World War)

STAMPEDE
82	Polydor POSP 507	Days Of Wine And Roses/Photographs (p/s)	12
82	Polydor POSP 507	Photographs/Days Of Wine And Roses (A-side switched, no p/s)	30
82	Polydor POSPX 507	Days Of Wine And Roses/Movin' On/Photographs/Missing You (12", p/s)	20
83	Polydor POSP 592	The Other Side/The Runner (p/s)	10

82	Polydor ROCK 1	OFFICIAL BOOTLEG (LP)	15
83	Polydor POLS 1083	HURRICANE TOWN (LP)	15

STAMPEDERS
71	Stateside SS2197	Devil You/Giant In The Streets	8
72	Stateside SS 2202	Monday Morning Choo Choo/Then Came The White Man	5
73	Regal Zonophone RZ3083	Minstrel Gypsy/Mumbo Jumbo	5
72	Regal Zonophone RZ 3069	Johnny Lightning/Today's The Beginning Of The Rest Of Your Life	6
73	Regal Zonophone RZ 3079	Oh My Lady/No Destination	6
73	Regal Zonophone RZ3085	Ride In The Wind/Running Wild	20
72	Regal Zono. SLRZ 1032	THE STAMPEDERS (LP)	30
74	Regal Zono. SLRZ 1039	FROM THE FIRE (LP)	30

JOE STAMPLEY
73	Dot DOT 145	Soul Song/Not Too Long Ago	10

JEAN STANBACK
69	Deep Soul DS 9101	I Still Love You/If I Ever Needed Love	50

STANDELLS
64	Liberty LIB 55722	I'll Go Crazy/Help Yourself	35
66	Capitol CL 15446	Dirty Water/Rari	50
65	Liberty LBY 1243	THE STANDELLS IN PERSON AT P.J.'s (LP)	60

STANDING OVATION
92	Kold Sweat KS126	Shadows Of Mayhem (12")	12

STANDS
00s	Echo ECS 142	When This River Rolls Over You/She Speaks Of These Things (autographed p/s, 1000 only)	8

PAUL STANLEY
79	Casablanca CAN 140	Hold Me Touch Me/Goodbye (p/s, purple vinyl with mask & picture label, most with mispressed B-side: "Love In Chains")	20

PETE STANLEY & ROGER KNOWLES
70s	Xtra TRANS 1146	PICKING AND SINGING (LP)	25

PETE STANLEY & WIZZ JONES
65	Columbia DB 7776	The Ballad Of Hollis Brown/Riff Minor	20
66	Columbia SX 6083	SIXTEEN TONS OF BLUEGRASS (LP)	60

(see also Wizz Jones)

ROY STANNARD AND HIS MUSIC
87	SS SS 100	The Peanut Vendor/'Swingin' ' The Blues	5

LISA STANSFIELD
81	Devil DEV 2	Your Alibis/Thought Police (p/s)	5

VIV(IAN) STANSHALL
70	Liberty LBF 15309	Labio-Dental Fricative/Paper Round (with Sean Head Show Band featuring Eric Clapton)	40
71	Fly BUG 4	Suspicion (with Gargantuan Chums)/Blind Date (with biG GRunt)	15
74	Warner Bros K 16424	Lakonga/Baba Tunde	20
76	Harvest HAR 5114	Young Ones/Are You Havin' Any Fun/Question	15
80	Charisma CB 373	Terry Keeps His Clips On/King Cripple (p/s)	6
81	Charisma CB 382	Calypso To Colapso/Smoke Signals At Night (p/s)	5
74	Warner Bros K 56052	MEN OPENING UMBRELLAS AHEAD (LP, with inner)	70
78	Charisma CAS 1139	SIR HENRY AT RAWLINSON END (LP, soundtrack, with insert)	25
81	Charisma CAS 1153	TEDDY BOYS DON'T KNIT (LP)	25
84	Demon Verbals VERB 1	SIR HENRY AT NDIDDI'S KRAAL (LP)	25

(see also Bonzo Dog [Doo Dah] Band, Grimms)

STAPLE SINGERS
64	Riverside 106902 RIF	Hammer And Nails/Glory Land	10
67	Columbia DB 8292	For What It's Worth/Are You Sure?	30
69	Soul City SC 117	For What It's Worth/Are You Sure? (reissue)	18
69	Stax STAX 118	I See It/The Ghetto	5
71	Stax 2025 019	Heavy Makes You Happy/Love Is Plentiful	5
72	Stax 2025 068	Respect Yourself/You're Gonna Make Me Cry	5
72	Stax 2025 110	I'll Take You There/Just Another Soldier	5
62	Riverside REP 3220	THE SAVIOUR IS BORN (EP)	15
63	Stateside SL 10015	SWING LOW (LP)	30
63	Riverside RLP 3501	HAMMER AND NAILS (LP)	25
65	Fontana 688 515 ZL	UNCLOUDY DAY (LP)	20
66	Columbia SX 6023	FREEDOM HIGHWAY (LP)	20
69	Stax (S)XATS 1004	SOUL FOLK IN ACTION (LP)	15
69	Stax SXATS 1018	WE'LL GET OVER (LP)	15
71	Stax 2362 005	THE STAPLE SINGERS (LP)	15
71	Stax 2362 011	SOUL FOLK IN ACTION (LP, reissue)	12
72	Stax STX 1001	CITY IN THE SKY (LP)	12
72	Stax 2325 069	BEALTITUDE/RESPECT YOURSELF (LP)	12

CYRIL STAPLETON & HIS ORCHESTRA
54	Decca F 10293	Long Distance Love/There'll Be No Teardrops Tonight	5
55	Decca F 10456	Tango Mambo/Mexican Madness	8
55	Decca F 10470	Fanfare Boogie/Time After Time	6
55	Decca F 10488	Elephant Tango/Gabrielle	6
55	Decca F 10559	Blue Star (The "Medic" Theme) (with Julie Dawn)/Honey Babe (with Gordon Langhorn)	10
56	Decca F 10703	The Italian Theme/Come Next Spring	6
56	Decca F 10735	The Happy Whistler (with Desmond Lane)/Tiger Tango	6
56	Decca F 10793	Highway Patrol/Maids Of Madrid	6
57	Decca F 10883	Rock, Fiddle, Rock/Chantez, Chantez	5
57	Decca F 10912	Forgotten Dreams/It's Not For Me To Say	7
58	Decca F 10979	Monday Blues (Parts 1 & 2)	5
62	Decca F 11443	Afrikaan Beat/My Sad Girl	6
69	Pye 7N 17807	Department S (Theme)/W. Somerset Maugham TV Theme (in p/s)	10

(see also Gordon Langhorn, Desmond Lane)

MINT VALUE £

STEVEN STAPLETON & DAVID TIBET
91	United Dairies UD 037	THE SADNESS OF THINGS/THE GRAVE AND BEAUTIFUL NAME OF SADNESS (LP, one side each)	35

(see also Current 93, Nurse With Wound, Tibet & Stapleton)

STA-PREST
80	Avatar AAA 103	Schooldays/Tomorrow (p/s)	75

STAR
73	Bradley BRAD 315	Children Of the Sun/Your Day Will Come	12

STAR SPANGLES
02	Capitol R 6593	Which Of The Two Of Us Is Gonna Burn This House Down/Stain Glass Shoes (p/s)	10

STAR WITH PETER COLLINS
60s	SRT/Custom 10	Give It Up/Wake Up	10

STARBUCK
73	RCA RCA 2350	Wouldn't You Like It/Manana	8
73	Bradleys BRAD 312	Do You Like Boys?/You Never Wanna Rock 'N' Roll	15
74	Bradleys BRAD 7411	Heart Throb/Ricochet	8

(see also Mandrake Paddle Steamer, Shambles)

BUDDY STARCHER
64	London RE-B 1424	BUDDY STARCHER AND HIS MOUNTAIN GUITAR VOL. 1 (EP)	10
64	London RE-B 1425	BUDDY STARCHER AND HIS MOUNTAIN GUITAR VOL. 2 (EP)	10
64	London RE-B 1426	BUDDY STARCHER AND HIS MOUNTAIN GUITAR VOL. 3 (EP)	10

STARFIGHTERS
80	Motor City MCR 105	I'm Falling/Heaven And Hell (in p/s)	40
80	Motor City MCR 105	I'm Falling/Heaven And Hell	7
81	Jive JIV 003	Alley Cat Blues/Don't Touch Me (p/s)	7
81	Jive JIVET 003	Alley Cat Blues/Don't Touch Me (12", p/s)	15
81	Jive JIVET 6	Power Crazy/I Want You (p/s)	6
81	Jive JIVET 6	Power Crazy/I Want You/Get Out While You Can (12", p/s)	8
81	Jive HOP 200	STARFIGHTERS (LP, with inner)	22
82	Jive HOP 205	IN FLIGHT MOVIE (LP)	12

STARGAZERS
54	Decca F 10213	I See The Moon/Eh Cumpari	25
54	Decca F 10259	The Happy Wanderer/Till We Two Are One	15
54	Decca F 10379	365 Kisses/I Need You Now	6
54	Decca F 10412	Rose Of The Wildwood/Come The Morning	6
55	Decca F 10471	Somebody/(My Baby Don't Love Me) No More (& Sonny Farrar Banjo Band)	10
55	Decca F 10523	The Crazy Otto Rag/Hey, Mr. Banjo	10
55	Decca F 10569	At The Steamboat River Ball/I Love You A Mountain (with Sonny Farrar Banjo Band)	5
55	Decca F 10594	Close The Door/I've Got Four Big Brothers	12
55	Decca F 10626	Twenty Tiny Fingers/An Old Beer Bottle	15
55	Decca F 10668	(Love Is) The Tender Trap/When The Swallows Say Goodbye	5
56	Decca F 10696	Zambesi/When The Swallows Say Goodbye	10
56	Decca F 10731	Hot Diggity (Dog Ziggity Boom)/Rockin' And Rollin'	10
56	Decca F 10775	She Loves To Rock/John Jacob Jingleheimer Smith	10
57	Decca F 10867	You Won't Be Around/Mangos	5
57	Decca F 10898	Honky Tonk Song/Golly!	5
60	Palette PG 9003	Three Beautiful Words/Manhattan Spiritual	6
56	Decca DFE 6341	THE STARGAZERS (EP)	20
56	Decca DFE 6362	ROCKIN' AND ROLLIN' (EP)	20
54	Decca LF 1186	PRESENTING THE STARGAZERS (10" LP)	30
59	Decca LK 4309	SOUTH OF THE BORDER (LP)	30

(see also Roy Smith & Stargazers, Lita Roza, Dickie Valentine)

STARJETS
78	Epic S EPC 6902	Here She Comes Again/Watch Out	8
79	Epic S EPC 6968	It Really Doesn't Matter/Schooldays	5
79	Epic S EPC 7123	Run With The Pack/Watch Out	5
79	Epic S EPC 6968/7123	It Really Doesn't Matter/Schooldays//Run With The Pack/Watch Out (double pack, die-cut sleeves, promo only)	15
79	Epic S EPC 7417	Ten Years/One More Word (p/s)	5
79	Epic S EPC 7417	Ten Years/One More Word (Manchester gig issue, stamped white labels)	12
79	Epic S EPC 7770	War Stories/Do The Push (p/s)	5
79	Epic S EPC 7986	Schooldays/What A Life (p/s)	6
80	Epic S EPC 8276	Shiraleo/Standby 19 (p/s)	5
79	Epic EPC 83534	GOD BLESS STARJETS (LP)	15

STARK AND MCBRIAN
74	RCA 2586	Big Star/A Page Torn Out Of Me	5

STARLAND VOCAL GROUP
76	RCA RCA 2716	Afternoon Delight/Starland (as Starland Vocal Band)	6

STARLINGS
80s	Ruffin A-M 029	NEW BLOOD (EP)	8

STARLITES
73	Downtown DT 502	You're A Wanted Man/G.G. ALL STARS: Back To Dubwise	7
74	Big Shot BI 629	Mama Dee Part One/Mama Dee Part Two	8
75	Bullet BU 554	Healing In The Barnyard/G.G. ALL STARS: Version	6
68	Philips BF 1725	Good Morning Mr Milkman/Don't Break My Heart Again	12

(see also Bellfield)

CINDY STARR
68	Columbia Blue Beat DB 107	Pain Of Love/Hippy Ska (as Cindy Starr & Rude Boys)	20
68	Columbia Blue Beat DB 110	The Way I Do/Sad Movies (Make Me Cry) (as Cindy Starr & Mopeds)	15

(see also Mopeds, Teardrops)

EDWIN STARR
66	Polydor BM 56702	Stop Her On Sight (S.O.S.)/I Have Faith In You (demo)	500
66	Polydor BM 56702	Stop Her On Sight (S.O.S.)/I Have Faith In You	25

66	Polydor BM 56717	Headline News/Harlem	20
67	Polydor BM 56726	It's My Turn Now/Girls Are Getting Prettier	25
68	Polydor BM 56753	Stop Her On Sight (S.O.S.)/Headline News (reissue)	10
67	Tamla Motown TMG 630	I Want My Baby Back/Gonna Keep On Tryin' Till I Win	30
67	Tamla Motown TMG 630	I Want My Baby Back/Gonna Keep On Tryin' Till I Win (DJ copy)	50
68	Tamla Motown TMG 646	I Am The Man For You Baby/My Weakness Is You	30
68	Tamla Motown TMG 646	I Am The Man For You Baby/My Weakness Is You (DJ copy)	90
68	Tamla Motown TMG 672	25 Miles/Mighty Good Lovin'	12
68	Tamla Motown TMG 672	25 Miles/Mighty Good Lovin' (DJ copy)	45
69	Tamla Motown TMG 692	Way Over There/If My Heart Could Tell The Story	20
69	Tamla Motown TMG 692	Way Over There/If My Heart Could Tell The Story (DJ copy)	50
69	Tamla Motown TMG 720	Oh How Happy/O, O, O, Baby (demos only, unissued, with Blinky)	375
70	Tamla Motown TMG 725	Time/Running Back And Forth	20
70	Tamla Motown TMG 754	War/He Who Picks A Rose	7
71	Tamla Motown TMG 764	Stop The War Now!/Gonna Keep On Tryin' I Win	8
71	Tamla Motown TMG 790	Agent Double 0 Soul/Back Street	12
71	Tamla Motown TMG 790	Agent Double 0 Soul/Back Street (DJ copy)	40
72	Tamla Motown TMG 810	Funky Music Sho' Nuff Turns Me On/Cloud Nine	8
73	Tamla Motown TMG 875	Love The Lonely People's Prayer/You've Got My Soul On Fire	20
73	Tamla Motown TMG 930	Ain't It Hell Up In Harlem/Who's Right Or Wrong	8
75	Bradleys BRAD 7520	Stay With Me/I'll Never Forget You	15
75	Bradleys BRAD 7531	Pain/Party	10
76	GTO GT 65	Accident/Eavesdropper	8
70s	Tamla Motown TMG 905	Stop Her On Sight/Headline News (reissue)	6
70s	Tamla Motown TMG 1028	Time/Running Back And Forth (reissue)	10
69	T. Motown STML 11094	SOUL MASTER (LP, mono)	35
69	T. Motown STML 11094	SOUL MASTER (LP, stereo)	40
69	T. Motown TML 11115	25 MILES (LP, mono)	30
69	T. Motown STML 11115	25 MILES (LP, stereo)	25
70	T. Motown (S)TML 11131	JUST WE TWO (LP, as Edwin Starr & Blinky)	25
70	Tamla Motown STML 11171	WAR AND PEACE (LP)	20
72	Tamla Motown STML 11199	INVOLVED (LP)	20
72	Tamla Motown STML 11209	THE HITS OF EDWIN STARR (LP)	15
74	Tamla Motown STML 11260	HELL UP IN HARLEM (LP, soundtrack)	15

(see also Blinky & Edwin Starr, Holidays)

FRANK STARR

62	London HLU 9545	Little Bitty Feeling/Lost In A Dream	12

FREDDIE STARR & MIDNIGHTERS

63	Decca F 11663	Who Told You?/Peter Gunn Locomotion	25
63	Decca F 11786	It's Shaking Time/Baby Blue	25
64	Decca F 12009	Never Cry On Someone's Shoulder/Just Keep On Dreaming	40
71	A&M AMS 838	Naomi/Free To Carry On (solo)	5

(see also Howie Casey & Seniors)

JIMMY STARR

58	London HL 8731	It's Only Make Believe/Ooh Crazy	30
58	London HL 8731	It's Only Make Believe/Ooh Crazy (78)	15

KAY STARR

54	Capitol CL 14151	Am I A Toy Or A Treasure?/Fortune In Dreams	20
54	Capitol CL 14167	Fool, Fool, Fool/Allez-Vous En	20
55	HMV 7M 300	If Anyone Finds This, I Love You/Turn Right	15
55	HMV 7M 307	Foolishly Yours/For Better Or Worse	10
55	HMV 7M 315	Where, What Or When?/Good And Lonesome	10
56	HMV 7M 371	Rock And Roll Waltz/I've Changed My Mind 1,000 Times	20
56	HMV 7M 420	Second Fiddle/Love Ain't Right	10
57	HMV POP 345	A Little Loneliness/Touch And Go	8
57	HMV POP 357	Jamie Boy/The Things I Never Had	8
58	RCA RCA 1065	Stroll Me/Rockin' Chair	6
60	Capitol CL 15105	Riders In The Sky/Night Train	7
60	Capitol CL 15137	Wheel Of Fortune/If You Love Me (Really Love Me)	12
55	Vogue EPV 1014	KAY STARR	10
56	HMV 7EG 8165	WHAT A STAR IS KAY	10
56	HMV 7EG 8184	KAY STARR'S AGAIN	10
60	Top Rank JKP 2042	HEAVENLY KAY STARR	10
60	Capitol EAP1 1254	MOVING	10
60	Capitol EAP2 1254	MOVING PT. 2	10
60	Capitol EAP3 1254	MOVING PT. 3	10
61	Capitol EAP 1-20063	WHEEL OF FORTUNE	10
62	Capitol EAP 1-20210	WELL I ASK YOU	10
53	Capitol LC 6574	CAPITOL PRESENTS KAY STARR (10")	20
54	Capitol LC 6630	THE KAY STARR STYLE (10")	20
56	Capitol LC 6835	THE HITS OF KAY STARR (10")	20
57	Capitol T 580	IN A BLUE MOOD	20
57	London HA-U 2039	SWINGING WITH THE STARR	20
58	RCA RD 27056	BLUE STARR	20
60	Capitol (S)T 1254	MOVIN'!	12
60	Capitol (S)T 1303	LOSERS, WEEPERS	12
60	Capitol (S)T 1374	MOVIN' ON BROADWAY	12
61	Capitol T 1358	ONE MORE TIME	12
61	Capitol (S)T 1438	JAZZ SINGER	12

LUCILLE STARR

64	London HL 9900	The French Song/Sit Down And Write A Letter To Me	12

LUCKY STARR

62	Parlophone R 4963	I've Been Everywhere/Wrong	5

MAXINE STARR

63	London HLU 9712	The Wishing Star/Sailor Boy	8

RANDY STARR

57	London HL 8443	After School/Heaven High (Man So Low)	45

MINT VALUE £

57	London HL 8443	After School/Heaven High (Man So Low) (78)	18
58	Felsted AF 106	Pink Lemonade/Count On Me	15
58	Felsted AF 106	Pink Lemonade/Count On Me (78)	10
60	Top Rank JAR 264	Workin' On The Santa Fe/You're Growing Up	7

RINGO STARR

71	Apple R 5898	It Don't Come Easy/Early 1970 (p/s, B-side with Ringo or George Harrison production credit)	6
71	Apple R 5898	It Don't Come Easy/Early 1970 (p/s, B-side with Ringo or George Harrison production credit)	5
72	Apple R 5944	Back Off Boogaloo/Blindman (p/s, blue label)	6
73	Apple R 5992	Photograph/Down And Out (p/s)	6
74	Apple R 5995	You're Sixteen/Devil Woman (p/s)	5
74	Apple R 6000	Only You/Call Me (p/s)	5
75	Apple R 6004	Snookeroo/Oo-wee (stock EMI, not Apple sleeve)	12
76	Apple R 6011	Oh My My/No No Song (not in die-cut apple sleeve)	20
76	Polydor 2001 694	A Dose Of Rock 'N' Roll/Cryin'	15
76	Polydor 2001 695	You Don't Know Me At All/Cryin' (unissued in U.K., Europe only)	0
76	Polydor 2001 699	Hey Baby/Lady Gaye	15
77	Polydor 2001 734	Drowning In The Sea Of Love/Just A Dream	50
78	Polydor 2001 782	Lipstick Traces/Old Time Relovin' (unissued in U.K., Europe only)	0
78	Polydor 2001 795	Tonight/Heart On My Sleeve	100
72	R.O.R. ROR 2001	Steel (1-sided promo-only interview disc for 'Ringo Or Robin' reception at Liberty's department store; available for 1 week only, p/s)	2000
74	Parlophone PSR 374	Interview By Bob Mercer With Ringo For The Salesmen and Uxbridge Road/Only You (promo only)	1000
70s	Apple R 5944	Back Off Boogaloo/Blindman (green apple label)	250
84	Apple G45 13	It Don't Come Easy/Back Off Boogaloo (P/s EMI Golden 45s series)	20
99	Mercury 546 668-2	I Wanna Be Santa Claus (CD)	25
70	Apple PCS 7101	SENTIMENTAL JOURNEY (LP)	25
70	Apple TD-PCS 7101	SENTIMENTAL JOURNEY (reel-to-reel tape, jewel case)	20
70	Apple PAS 10002	BEAUCOUPS OF BLUES (LP, gatefold sleeve)	25
73	Apple PCTC 252	RINGO (LP, gatefold with 12" x 12" booklet)	15
74	Apple PCS 7168	GOODNIGHT VIENNA (LP, with inner)	15
74	Apple PCS 7170	BLAST FROM YOUR PAST (LP, with inner)	15
76	Polydor 2302-040 A	ROTOGRAVURE (LP, gatefold with inner)	15
78	Polydor 2310-599B	BAD BOY (LP, with inner)	15
78	Polydor 2480 429	SCOUSE THE MOUSE (LP, with Adam Faith, Donald Pleasance etc.; with stickered sleeve & printed [not photocopied] competition insert)	100
78	Polydor 2480 429	SCOUSE THE MOUSE (LP, with Adam Faith, Donald Pleasance etc.; without stickered sleeve & printed [not photocopied] competition insert)	50
90	EMI EMS 1375	RINGO STARR AND HIS ALL STARR BAND (LP)	35
00	Eagle Records EEECDO11	THE ANTHOLOGY...SO FAR (3xCD in slip case)	30

(see also Beatles, Harry Nilsson, Billy Connolly & Chris Cummings, Traveling Wilburys)

STELLA STARR

| 67 | Piccadilly 7N 35366 | Bring Him Back/Say It | 50 |
| 67 | Piccadilly 7N 35366 | Bring Him Back/Say It (DJ copy) | 80 |

TONY STARR

| 64 | Decca F 11847 | I'll Take A Rocket To The Moon/Next Train Leaving | 60 |

STARR BOUNDS

| 75 | Horse HOSS 95 | Heavenly (Parts 1 & 2) | 8 |

STARRY EYED

| 76 | CBS 4805 | Saturday/Believe | 6 |

STARSHIP

| 77 | Scratch SCH 01 | Vampire For Your Love/You Can Dance/Hey Girl/Never Thought I'd See The Day | 15 |

STARS OF HEAVEN

| 85 | Hotwire HWS 853 | Clothes Of Pride/All About You (beige or black label, with p/s) | 8 |
| 85 | Hotwire HWS 853 | Clothes Of Pride/All About You (beige or black label) | 6 |

STARTLED INSECTS

| 87 | Antilles ANCD 8708 | CURSE OF THE PHEREMONES (CD, plastic covered booklet) | 18 |

STATEN ISLAND FERRY

| 69 | Major Minor MM 643 | Candy Bar/Charlie Chan | 20 |

STATE OF GRACE

| 83 | PRT 12P266 | Touching The Times/Instrumental Mix (12") | 60 |

STATE OF MICKEY & TOMMY

| 67 | Mercury MF 996 | With Love From One To Five/I Know What I Will Do | 150 |
| 67 | Mercury MF 1009 | Frisco Bay/Nobody Knows Where You've Been | 150 |

(see also Spooky Tooth, Nero & Gladiators, Foreigner)

STATESMEN

63	Fontana TF 432	I've Just Fallen In Love/It's All Happening	8
63	Decca F11687	Look Around/I'm Wondering	8
63	Studio Republic	FIVE PLUS ONE (LP, private pressing)	100

STATE STREET SWINGERS/CHICAGO BLACK SWANS

| 73 | Collectors Items 003 | STATE STREET SWINGERS (LP) | 12 |

STATE TROOPER

| 85 | Neat 5212 | SHE GOT THE LOOK (12" EP) | 10 |

STATIC (1)

| 67 | Page One POF 039 | When You Went Away/Let Me Tell You | 7 |

STATIC (2)

| 81 | Eeyo EEYO 1 | Voice On The Line/Stealin' (no p/s, 1,000 only) | 15 |

(see also White Lightning)

STATIC (3)

| 01 | City Centre Offices BLOCK 013 | Headphones (plain sleeve with inserts, 1000 copies) | 8 |
| 02 | City Centre Offices BLOCK 016 | TURN ON SWITCH OFF (12" EP) | 8 |

03	City Centre Offices BLOCK 021	GHOST BOY (Feat. Ronald Lippok) (12" EP, custom sleeve)	8

STATION SKIFFLE GROUP

57	Esquire 10-503	Don't You Rock Me Daddy-O/Hugged My Honey (78)	15
57	Esquire 10-516	Steamboat Bill/Titanic (78)	22
58	Esquire EP 161	STATION SKIFFLE GROUP (EP)	50

(see also Jimmy Miller)

STATION 360

84	SRT STA 360	Optimist	30

STATLER BROTHERS

65	CBS 201976	Flowers On The Wall/Billy Christian	8
66	CBS BPG 62713	FLOWERS ON THE WALL (LP)	15

(see also Johnny Cash)

CANDI STATON

69	Capitol CL 15601	I'd Rather Be An Old Man's Sweetheart/For You	8
69	Capitol CL 15620	Heart On A String/I'm Just A Prisoner	8
70	Capitol CL 15646	Sweet Feeling/Evidence	8
70	Capitol CL 15658	Stand By Your Man/How Can I Put Out The Flame (When You Keep The Fire Burning)	8
75	United Artists UP 35823	Love Chain/I'm Gonna Hold On	6
70	Capitol ST 21631	I'M JUST A PRISONER (LP)	30

DAKOTA STATON

55	Capitol CL 14314	Don't Leave Me Now/A Little You	12
55	Capitol CL 14339	I Never Dreamt/Abracadabra	12
58	Capitol CL 14931	A Foggy Day/My Funny Valentine	7

STATUES

60	London HLG 9192	Blue Velvet/Keep The Hall Burning	45

STATUS QUO

SINGLES : PYE SINGLES

68	Pye 7N 17449	Pictures Of Matchstick Men/Gentleman Joe's Sidewalk Café (some with '75c Minimum' on B-side label credit)	12
68	Pye 7N 17497	Black Veils Of Melancholy/To Be Free	20
68	Pye 7N 17581	Ice In The Sun/When My Mind Is Not Live	8
68	Pye 7N 17650	Technicolor Dreams/Paradise Flat	600
69	Pye 7N 17665	Make Me Stay A Bit Longer/Aunt Nellie	22
69	Pye 7N 17728	Are You Growing Tired Of My Love/So Ends Another Life	20
69	Pye 7N 17825	The Price Of Love/Little Miss Nothing	30
70	Pye 7N 17907	Down The Dustpipe/Face Without A Soul (black, blue or reissue Precision labels)	5
70	Pye 7N 17998	In My Chair/Gerdundula (with p/s)	45
70	Pye 7N 17998	In My Chair/Gerdundula	8
71	Pye 7N 45077	Tune To The Music/Good Thinking	20
73	Pye 7N 45229	Mean Girl/Everything (blue labels)	5
73	Pye 7N 45253	Gerdundula/Lakky Lady (red label)	5
77	Pye BD 103	Down The Dustpipe/Mean Girl/In My Chair/Gerdundula (12", generic sleeve, reissued on PRT)	10
78	Pye 7N 46103	Pictures of Matchstick Men/Ice In The Sun (red labels, reissued on PRT)	5
79	Pye Flashbacks FBS 2	Pictures Of Matchstick Men/Down The Dustpipe (yellow vinyl, p/s)	6
79	Pye Flashbacks FBS 2	Pictures Of Matchstick Men/Down The Dustpipe (black vinyl, no p/s, reissued on PRT)	5
79	Pye 7P 103	In My Chair/Gerdundula (p/s)	5
79	Pye QUO 1/SFI 434	In My Chair (flexi, concert freebie, with Record Mirror Quo special)	10

SINGLES : VERTIGO SINGLES

72	Vertigo 6059 071	Paper Plane/Softer Ride (swirl label, solid centre)	6
73	Vertigo 6059 085	Caroline/Joanne (with B-side miscredited to Lancaster)	5
74	Vertigo 6059 101	Break The Rules/Lonely Night (mispressed, B-side labels on both sides)	7
76	Vertigo 6059 153	Wild Side Of Life/All Through The Night (brown plastic labels)	6
77	Vertigo 6059 184	Rockin' All Over The World/Ring Of A Change (p/s, with small poster)	15
77	Vertigo 6059 184	Rockin' All Over The World/Ring Of A Change (p/s)	5
78	Vertigo QUO 2	Accident Prone/Let Me Fly (p/s)	5
82	Vertigo QUO 9	Jealousy/Calling The Shots (unreleased in U.K.; Irish promos only)	150
82	Vertigo QUOP 10	Caroline (Live At The NEC)/Dirty Water (live) (picture disc)	5
83	Vertigo QUOP 14	Marguerita Time/Resurrection (picture disc)	5
83	Vertigo QUO 1414	Marguerita Time/Resurrection//Caroline/Joanne (double pack, stickered gatefold p/s)	10
84	Vertigo QUO 15	Too Close To The Ground/I Wonder Why (release cancelled)	0
85	Vertigo QUO 17	Naughty Girl (actually "Dreamin' ") (unreleased)	0
86	Vertigo QUOPD 18	Rollin' Home/Lonely ('Q'-shaped picture disc)	8
86	Vertigo QUOPD 18	Rollin' Home/Lonely (uncut picture disc)	150
86	Vertigo QUODP 19	Red Sky/Don't Give It Up/Rockin' All Over The World/Whatever You Want (double pack, gatefold p/s)	6
86	Vertigo QUOPB 191	Red Sky/Don't Give It Up/The Milton Keynes Medley (12", 'Wembley Souvenir Pack', poster p/s)	15
86	Vertigo QUO 20	In The Army Now/Heartburn (stickered p/s, with sew-on patch, shrinkwrapped)	10
86	Vertigo QUOPD 20	In The Army Now/Heartburn (picture disc)	15
86	Vertigo QUODP 20	In The Army Now/Heartburn//Marguerita Time/What You're Proposing (double pack, gatefold p/s)	6
86	Vertigo QUO 2012	In The Army Now (Military Mix)/Heartburn/Late Last Night (12", stickered p/s, with poster)	8
86	Vertigo QUOP 21	Dreamin'/Long-Legged Girls (p/s, with foldout poster/calendar)	6
88	Vertigo QUOCD 22	Ain't Complaining (Extended)/That's Alright/Lean Machine/In The Army Now (Remix) (CD, card sleeve)	15
88	Vertigo QUOCD 23	Who Gets The Love? (Extended)/Hallowe'en/The Reason For Goodbye/The Wanderer (Sharon The Nag Mix) (CD, card sleeve)	25
88	Vertigo QUACD 1	Running All Over The World (Extended)/Magic/Whatever You Want (CD, card sleeve)	20
88	Vertigo QUO 2512	Burning Bridges (On And Off And On Again) (Extended Version)/Whatever You Want/Marguerita Time (12", mispressing also including 7" edit)	10
88	Vertigo QUOCD 25	Burning Bridges (On And Off And On Again) (Extended Version)/Whatever You Want/Marguerita Time (CD)	15
89	Vertigo 080 322-2	Ain't Complaining (Extended)/That's Alright/Lean Machine/In The Army Now (Remix)/Ain't Complaining (Video) (CD Video)	20
89	Vertigo 080 630-2	Burning Bridges (On And Off And On Again) (Extended Version)/Whatever You Want (Extended Version)/Marguerita Time/Who Gets The Love?/Burning Bridges (Video) (CD Video)	0

MINT VALUE £

89	Vertigo QUOCD 26	Not At All/Everytime I Think Of You/Gone Thru The Slips (CD) 10
89	Vertigo QUOCD 27	Little Dreamer/Rotten To The Bone/Doing It All For You (CD) 10
90	Vertigo QUO 2812	The Anniversary Waltz/The Power Of Rock/Perfect Remedy (12", p/s, mispress, B-side plays "Little Lady" (live) & exclusive "Paper Plane" re-recording) 45
90	Vertigo QUO 2812	The Anniversary Waltz/The Power Of Rock/Perfect Remedy (12", p/s, mispress, A-side plays "The Power Of Rock [Full Version]") 45
91	Vertigo QUO 31	Fakin' The Blues (Edit)/Heavy Daze (p/s, swirl label, release cancelled, approximately 25 copies only) 450
91	Vertigo QUO 3112	Fakin' The Blues (Edit)/Fakin' The Blues (Album Version)/Heavy Daze/Better Times (12", swirl label, p/s, cancelled, approx. 25 copies only) 250
91	Vertigo QUOCD 31	Fakin' The Blues (Edit)/Fakin' The Blues (Album Version)/Heavy Daze/Better Times (CD, unissued, 2,000 later sent out by fan club, no inlay) 40
92	Vertigo QUO 3212	Rock 'Til You Drop/Medley/Forty-Five Hundred Times (12", p/s, mispressing, omits "Forty-Five Hundred Times") 15
92	Vertigo QUOCD 32	Rock 'Til You Drop/Medley/Forty-Five Hundred Times (CD in no'd guitar-shaped case) 12
88	Vertigo QUODJ 25	Burning Bridges (On & Off & On Again)/Burning Bridges (On & Off & On Again) 12

SINGLES : OTHER SINGLES

75	Lyntone LYN 3154/5	Down Down/Break The Rules (Smiths Crisps flexidisc, with 'Smiths' p/s) 15
80s	Lyntone QUO 1-4	Interview picture discs (4-single pack) 20
92	Polydor QUODD 33	Roadhouse Medley (Anniversary Waltz Part 25) (Radio Edit)/(Extended)/Don't Drive My Car (Live) (CD, numbered 4-fold digipak, 2nd CD card template) 10
94	Polydor QUO 34	I Didn't Mean It/Whatever You Want (p/s, blue vinyl) 5
94	Polydor QUODD 34	I Didn't Mean It (Acoustic Version)/(Hooligan Version)/Survival/She Knew Too Much (CD, numbered digipak, 2nd CD card template) 10
95	PolyGram TV 576262 7	Fun Fun Fun (with The Beach Boys)/Mortified (numbered picture disc) 5
96	PolyGram TV 5759447	All Around My Hat (with Maddy Prior)/I'll Never Get Over You (numbered picture disc) 6
99	From The Makers Of... FTMOCD1	FAKIN' THE BLUES (MILLENNIUM EDITION) (CD, fanclub mail order-only edition, hand-no'd exclusive p/s, contains unreleased Vertigo CD [QUOCD 31]) 50
00	PolyGram PSPCD464	NIGHT & DAY (CD EP, 4-track sampler, mail-order only via tokens from The Mail On Sunday, insufficient pressed to meet demand) 25

ALBUMS : LPS

68	Pye NPL 18220	PICTURESQUE MATCHSTICKABLE MESSAGES (mono) 180
68	Pye NSPL 18220	PICTURESQUE MATCHSTICKABLE MESSAGES (stereo) 120
69	Pye NPL 18301	SPARE PARTS (blue label, mono) 150
69	Pye NSPL 18301	SPARE PARTS (blue label, stereo) 70
69	Marble Arch MAL 1193	STATUS QUO-TATIONS (mono) 30
69	Marble Arch MAL(S) 1193	STATUS QUO-TATIONS (stereo, most copies exported) 50
70	Pye NSPL 18344	MA KELLY'S GREASY SPOON (very early copies with poster) 120
70	Pye NSPL 18344	MA KELLY'S GREASY SPOON 15
71	Pye NSPL 18371	DOG OF TWO HEAD (gatefold sleeve, blue labels, later reissued with red, black or PRT "Piccadilly Circus" labels) 25
72	Vertigo 6360 082	PILEDRIVER (swirl label, gatefold sleeve) 30
73	Vertigo 6360 098	HELLO! (spaceship label, with inner sleeve & poster) 20
74	Vertigo 9102 001	QUO (with paper/lyric sheet) 15
74	Record Club ACB 00217	QUO 25
77	Vertigo 9286 686/7	STATUS QUO LIVE (2-LP, spaceship label) 18
77	Pye FILD 005	THE FILE SERIES (2-LP, single sleeve with inner sleeves; repressed on Precision) 15
79	Pye NPSL 18607	JUST FOR THE RECORD (red vinyl) 15
79	Pye FILD 005	THE FILE SERIES (2-LP, reissue with different sleeve, inners; repressed on PRT) 15
82	Phonogram PRO BX 1	FROM THE MAKERS OF... (3-LP, with inserts in round metal tin, some numbered) 20
83	Vertigo VERH 10	BACK TO BACK (in-store promo copies with poster insert) 18
85	PRT Flashbacks FBLP 8082	NANANA 12
88	PRT PYX 4007	FROM THE BEGINNING (picture disc) 18
90	Essential! ESBLP 136	THE EARLY WORKS (5-LP box set with book) 30
91	Baktabak LINT 5003	INTROSPECTIVE (clear vinyl, 6 Pye-era tracks & interview) 20
92	Polydor 517 367-1	LIVE ALIVE QUO (with inner sleeve) 12
94	Polydor 523 607-1	THIRSTY WORK (with inner sleeve) 12

ALBUMS : CDS

83	Vertigo 800 035-2	1+9+8+2 18
83	Vertigo 800 053-2	NEVER TOO LATE 18
83	Vertigo 814 66-2	BACK TO BACK 18
85	PRT CDNSP 773	THE BEST OF STATUS QUO (THE EARLY YEARS) 18
86	PRT CDMP 8834	MA KELLY'S GREASY SPOON 18
86	PRT CDMP 8837	DOG OF TWO HEAD 12
89	Vertigo 842 098-2	PERFECT REMEDY (two different inlay designs) 30
98	Readers Digest RDCD1831-4	THE COMPLETE STATUS QUO (4-CD, mail-order only) 50
01	From The Makers Of ... FTMOCD2	FTMO LIVE! NO.1 (fanclub mail-order only, soundchecks & interviews) 50
02	Time Life TL SQC 069 827-2	THE ULTIMATE COLLECTION (4-CD, mail-order only) 35
03	From The Makers Of... FTMO LIVE 2-1/2 [matrix]	FTMO LIVE! NO.2 (2-CD, fanclub mail-order only) 25

PROMOS : PROMO ONLY SINGLES

68	Pye 7N 17449	Pictures Of Matchstick Men/Gentleman Joe's Sidewalk Café (75c Minimum) ('A' label) 60
68	Pye 7N 17497	Black Veils Of Melancholy/To Be Free ('A' label) 70
68	Pye 7N 17581	Ice In The Sun/When My Mind Is Not Live ('A' label) 60
68	Pye 7N 17650	Technicolor Dreams/Paradise Flat ('A' label) 400
69	Pye 7N 17665	Make Me Stay A Bit Longer/Aunt Nellie ('A' label) 70
69	Pye 7N 17728	Are You Growing Tired Of My Love/So Ends Another Life ('A' label) 70
69	Pye 7N 17825	The Price Of Love/Little Miss Nothing ('A' label) 70
70	Pye 7N 17907	Down The Dustpipe/Face Without A Soul ('A' label) 60
70	Pye 7N 17998	In My Chair/Gerdundula ('A' label) 60
71	Pye 7N 45077	Tune To The Music/Good Thinking ('A' label) 60
72	Phonogram DJ 005	Roadhouse Blues/BLACK SABBATH: Children Of The Grave (100 copies only) 400
72	Vertigo 6059 071	Paper Plane/Softer Ride ('A' label) 45
73	Pye 7N 45229	Mean Girl/Everything ('A' label) 50
73	Pye 7N 45253	Gerdundula/Lakky Lady ('A' label) 40
75	Lyntone LYN 3154	Down Down (Smiths Crisps 1-sided gold flexidisc test pressing, plays Bye Bye Baby by Bay City Rollers) 25
75	Lyntone LYN 3155	Break The Rules (Smiths Crisps 1-sided gold flexidisc test pressing, plays Bye Bye Baby by Bay City Rollers) 25

79	Pye 7P 103	In My Chair/Gerdundula ('A' label)	20
81	Vertigo QUO JB 6	Rock 'N' Roll/Hold You Back (jukebox issue, B-side at 33rpm)	10
86	Vertigo QUODJ 2112	Dreamin' (Wet Mix)/Long-Legged Girls/The Quo Xmas Cake Mix (12")	15
88	Vertigo QUOLP 99	Ain't Complaining (12" promo, 1-sided)	30
88	Vertigo QUODJ 2212	Ain't Complaining (Extended)/That's Alright/Lean Machine (12")	10
90	Vertigo (no cat. no.)	The Power Of Rock (Album Version)/(Single Edit)/Perfect Remedy (12" white label)	50

PROMOS : PROMO ONLY ALBUMS & ALBUM SAMPLERS

82	Phonogram PRO BX 1	FROM THE MAKERS OF... (3-LP, 20 copies in bronze tin for in-house use)	300
86	Vertigo MADDOX 18	IN THE ARMY NOW (LP, 4-track sampler, includes unreleased version of Dreamin')	50
88	Vertigo QUOLP 99	AIN'T COMPLAINING (LP, 4-track one-sided sampler)	25
88	Vertigo	AIN'T COMPLAINING (box set containing LP sampler [QUOLP 99], cassette, 1-track video, photo & press sheet)	70
88	Music & Media MM 1221	INTERVIEW (LP, uncut test pressing for unreleased saw-shaped picture disc)	50
89	Vertigo 842 077-9	LITTLE DREAMER (CD, card p/s, 4-track sampler for PERFECT REMEDY album)	40
90	Phonogram (no cat. no.)	ROCKING ALL OVER THE YEARS SNIPPETS (cassette, titles inlay)	20
90	Vertigo 846 797-2	ROCKING ALL OVER THE YEARS (CD, in Butlin's party pack containing Kiss Me Quo baseball cap, stick of Status Quo rock, and selection of party poppers, streamers, whistle, trumpet, silver Quo balloons & pack of condoms, all with "Anniversary Waltz" stickers)	75
97	PolyGram TV QUO 5-2	WHATEVER YOU WANT - THE VERY BEST OF STATUS QUO (CD, 5-track sampler different to above, no p/s, withdrawn)	18
02	Sanctuary CMRCD 490	SWEDISH RADIO SESSIONS (CD-R, titles insert, commercial release cancelled)	50

(see also Spectres, Traffic Jam, Rossi & Frost, Bob Young, Andy Bown, Alan Lancaster's Bombers, Partners In Crime, Party Boys, Rockers, John Du Cann, Manchester United Football Squad, Marietta, Stretch, Jimmy Sweep)

STAVELY MAKEPEACE

69	Pyramid PYR 6072	(I Want To Love You Like A) Mad Dog/Greasy Haired Woman	8
70	Pyramid PYR 6082	Tarzan Harvey/Reggae Denny (unissued, test pressings exist)	6
77	Unigram U6312	Baby Blue Eyes/Big Bad Baby Blonde	8

(see also Lieutenant Pigeon, Shel Naylor)

STAVERTON BRIDGE

70s	Saydisc SDL 266	STAVERTON BRIDGE (LP, with lyrics)	30

MARY STAVIN & GEORGE BEST

70s	Lifestyle LEG 22	IT TAKES TWO TO SHAPE UP (LP)	12

BONNIE ST. CLAIR

72	Philips 6012283	Clap Your Hands And Stamp Your Feet/Catch Me Driver	8
76	Sonet SON 2073	(Like A) Locomotion/Rocco	6

STEAK CATS

93	April 10 Records TEN 1	The Steak Song/Dead Real Soon/Fluffy's Lament/My Name Is Miguel (12")	12
94	April 10 Records TEN 2	Intergalactic Competition/Foxy Roxy (200 only, hand-written labels)	5
95	April 10 Records TEN 3	Ladyboy/Not Supposed To Love (200 only, hand-written labels)	5
96	April 10 Records TEN 4	Last Night In A Porn Stars Bed I Became A Man/From Behind (12" 200 only)	15
97	April 10 LP1	THE RISE OF ROSCOE (LP)	15

STEAM

69	Fontana TF 1058	Na Na Hey Hey Kiss Him Goodbye/It's The Magic In You Girl	5

STEAMHAMMER

69	CBS 4141	Junior's Wailing/Windmill	25
69	CBS 4496	Autumn Song/Blues For Passing People	18
71	Reflection HRS 9	Junior's Wailing/You'll Never Know	12
68	CBS (S) 63611	STEAMHAMMER (LP)	70
70	CBS (S) 63694	STEAMHAMMER MK. II (LP)	55
70	B&C CAS 1024	MOUNTAINS (LP, stickered gatefold sleeve)	40
70	Reflection REFL 1	STEAMHAMMER (LP, reissue, different sleeve)	40
71	Reflection REFL 12	STEAMHAMMER MK. II (LP, reissue)	40

(see also Armageddon, Rod Stewart)

STEAM-SHOVEL

68	Trojan/Big Bear TR 635	Rudi, The Red Nosed Reindeer/White Christmas	7
68	Decca F 22863	Rudi, The Red Nosed Reindeer/White Christmas (export issue)	12

(see also Locomotive)

STEEL

81	Neat NEAT 14	Rock Out/All Systems Go (p/s)	10

STEEL AN' SKIN

85	Cougar (no cat. no.)	STEEL AN' SKIN (LP)	20

GARY STEEL SOUND

72	Zel-La JHEPM 131	Go Go Girl/I've Got A Feeling Coming On	25

BETTE ANNE STEELE

55	Capitol CL 14315	Barricade/Give Me A Little Kiss Will Ya, Huh?	8

DAVY STEELE

83	Bracken BKN 1001	LONG TIME GETTING THERE (LP)	12

DORIS STEELE

59	Oriole CB 1468	Why Must I?/Never Again	6

JAN STEELE & JOHN CAGE

76	Obscure OBS 5	VOICES AND INSTRUMENTS (LP)	12

SONDRA & JON STEELE

55	Parlophone MSP 6166	I'm Crazy With Love/Fill My Heart With Happiness	8

TOMMY STEELE (& THE STEELMEN)

58	Weekend Mail (no cat. no.)	THE TRUTH ABOUT ME (6" in envelope, mail-order only) (78)	15
56	Decca F 10795	Rock With The Caveman/Rock Around The Town (with The Steelmen)	25
56	Decca F 10795	Rock With The Caveman/Rock Around The Town (with The Steelmen) (78)	15
56	Decca F 10808	Doomsday Rock/Elevator Rock	30
56	Decca F 10819	Singing The Blues/Rebel Rock (with The Steelmen)	20
57	Decca F 10849	Knee Deep In The Blues/Teenage Party (with The Steelmen)	10
57	Decca F 10877	Butterfingers/Cannibal Pot	5

MINT VALUE £

57	Decca F 10896	Shiralee/Grandad's Rock	5
57	Decca F 10923	Water Water/A Handful Of Songs	7
57	Decca F 10941	Hey You!/Plant A Kiss	5
58	Decca F 10976	Happy Guitar/Princess	5
58	Decca F 11072	Come On Let's Go/Put A Ring On Her Finger	6
59	Decca F 11152	Tallahassee Lassie/Give! Give! Give!	6
59	Decca F 11162	You Were Mine/Young Ideas (78)	15

(The above 45s were originally issued with triangular centres; later round-centre copies are worth two-thirds the values listed.)

59	Decca F 11177	Little White Bull/Singing Time (in p/s) (78)	10
56	Decca DFE 6388	YOUNG LOVE (EP)	12
56	Decca DFE 6389	SINGING THE BLUES (EP)	12

(The above 2 EPs were originally issued with triangular centres; later round-centre reissues are worth two-thirds this value)

| 58 | Decca DFE 6472 | THE DUKE WORE JEANS (EP) | 10 |
| 58 | Decca DFE 6551 | C'MON LET'S GO (EP) | 15 |

STEELERS
| 70 | Direction 58-4675 | Get It From The Bottom/I'm Sorry | 10 |

STEELEYE SPAN
71	B&C CB 164	Rave On/Reels/Female Drummer (p/s)	7
72	Pegasus PGS 6	JIGS AND REELS (maxi-single, with p/s)	10
72	Pegasus PGS 6	JIGS AND REELS (maxi-single)	6
72	Chrysalis CHS 2005	John Barleycorn/Bride's Favourite/Tansey's Fancy	5
70	RCA SF 8113	HARK! THE VILLAGE WAIT (LP, with lyric insert)	30
71	United Artists UAG 29160	HARK! THE VILLAGE WAIT (LP, reissue)	12
71	B&C CAS 1029	PLEASE TO SEE THE KING (LP, in 'hessian' textured sleeve, insert)	35
71	B&C CAS 1029	PLEASE TO SEE THE KING (LP)	12
72	Charisma CS 5	INDIVIDUALLY AND COLLECTIVELY (LP, large 'Mad Hatter' label)	12
71	Pegasus PEG 9	TEN MAN MOP, OR MR. RESERVOIR BUTLER RIDES AGAIN (LP, gatefold sleeve, initially with 8-page booklet)	30
72	Pegasus PEG 9	TEN MAN MOP, OR MR. RESERVOIR BUTLER RIDES AGAIN (LP)	12
72	Chrysalis CHR 1008	BELOW THE SALT (LP, gatefold, green label)	18

(see also Maddy Prior, Tim Hart & Maddy Prior, Gay & Terry Woods, Ashley Hutchings, Fairport Convention, Martin Carthy, Silly Sisters, Bob Johnson & Pete Knight)

STEEL MILL
71	Penny Farthing PEN 770	Green Eyed God/Zang Will	8
72	Penny Farthing PEN 783	Get On The Line/Summer's Child	20
75	Penny Farthing PEN 894	Green Eyed God/Zang Will (reissue)	8
71	Penny Farthing PELS 549	GREEN EYED GOD (LP)	450

STEEL PULSE
| 76 | Concrete Jungle CJ 602 | Kibudu Mansatta Abuku/Version | 35 |
| 77 | Anchor ANC 1046 | Nyah Luv/Luv Nyah (p/s) | 5 |

STEELY DAN
72	Probe PRO 562	Dallas/Sail The Waterway	5
73	Probe PRO 577	Do It Again/Fire In The Hole	5
73	Probe PRO 587	Reelin' In The Years/Only A Fool	7
73	Probe PRO 602	Show Biz Kids/Razor Boy	5
73	Probe PRO 606	My Old School/Pearl Of The Quarter	5
74	Probe PRO 622	Rikki Don't Lose That Number/Any Major Dude Will Tell You (gatefold sleeve, 1974 'Spacemen' tour logo)	50
82	MCA MCAT 786	FM EP	25
85	MCA MCAT 852	Reelin' In The Years/Rikki Don't Lose That Number/Do It Again/Haitian Divorce (12", p/s)	20
73	Probe SPB 1062	CAN'T BUY A THRILL (LP, original, with 'pink' label)	25
73	Probe SPD 1079	COUNTDOWN TO ECSTASY (LP, original)	12
80s	MCA 203 16009	GAUCHO (LP, audiophile pressing)	12
82	MCA MCF 3165	GOLD (LP, with free EP [MSAMT 21])	20

(see also Donald Fagen)

WOUT STEENHUIS
65	Columbia DB 7722	Desert Island/Teran Boelan	5
66	Columbia DB 8027	Nivram/Bay Of Paradise	5
63	Columbia DB 7021	Kassian/Minehaha	5

STEEPLECHASE
| 71 | Polydor 2489 001 | LADY BRIGHT (LP) | 15 |

(see also Dean Parrish)

STEERPIKE
| 68 | (no label credit) ADM 417 | STEERPIKE (LP, private pressing) | 550 |

BILL STEGMEYER & HIS ORCHESTRA
| 54 | London HL 8078 | On The Waterfront (From The Film)/We Just Couldn't Say Good-Bye | 20 |

LOU STEIN
| 57 | London HLZ 8419 | Almost Paradise/Soft Sands | 20 |
| 58 | Mercury 7MT 226 | Who Slammed The Door/Got A Match? | 8 |

JIM STEINMAN
81	Epic EPCA 13-1236	Rock And Roll Dreams Come Through/Love And Death And An American Guitar/The Storm (12", p/s, blue vinyl)	8
81	Epic EPCA 1561	Lost Boys And Golden Girls/Left In The Dark (p/s)	5
81	Epic EPCA 1707	Dance In My Pants/Dance In My Pants (unissued, promo only)	5
84	MCA MCA 889	Tonight Is What It Means To Be Young/Hold That Snake (p/s)	5
81	Epic EPC 11-84361	BAD FOR GOOD (LP, picture disc)	12

(see also Meat Loaf)

STEINWAYS
| 85 | Kent TOWN 106 | You've Been Leading Me On/JOHNNY CASWELL: You Don't Love Me No More | 20 |

MIKE STEIPHENSON
| 73 | Pye 7N 25577 | Rainbows/Dreams | 15 |

TENA STELIN
| 89 | Wau! Mr. Modo MWS 011T | Jah Equity/Jah Equity (Version) (12") | 50 |

89	Wau! Mr Modo MWS 015T	King Of Kings/Give Thanks And Praise (12")	50
00	Jah Tubbys JT 7005	Look After Yourself/DISCIPLES RHYTHM SECTION: Dub Yourself	20
89	Wai! Mr Modo MOWLP 002	WICKED INVENTION (LP)	40
92	Conscious Sounds DNC 001	SUN AND MOON (LP, as Tena Stelin Meets Century)	25

(see also Iration Steppas and Tena Stelin)

STELLA
82	President PT 504	Si Tu Aimes Ma Musique/If You Do Like My Music (p/s)	7

STENCH
82	Sticky PEEL OFF 5	MORAL DEBAUCHERY: Raspberry Cripple/Nonces/Adoption	15

STAN STENNETT
60s	Audio JDT 1	STYLE (EP)	8

MALCOLM STENT
70s	Starline SWL 2002	GO AND PLAY UP YOUR OWN END (LP)	15

STEP
80	Epic/Direction S DIR 8733	Love Letter/Land Of 1,000 Dances (p/s)	5
80	Epic/Direction S DIR 8944	Let Me Be The One/634 5789 (p/s)	5
80	Epic/Direction S DIR 9311	Tears That I Cry/Shake (p/s)	5
81	Epic EPC A 1291	Chain Gang/In The House (p/s)	5
81	Epic EPC A 1412	Model Soldiers/Hightime Havana (p/s)	5

STEPASIDE
80	Gale GALELP 01	SIT DOWN AND RELAPSE (LP)	20

STEPHEN
74	Antic K 11513	Right On Running Man/Epitath	8

ANN STEPHENS
56	HMV 7EG 8187	CHILDREN'S CHOICE (EP)	8

EWAN STEPHENS
71	Decca F 13219	Queen Of The Good Times/We Can Give It A Try	5
72	Decca F 13299	Brother, Surely We Can Work It Out/Long, Long Summer	5

(see also Turquoise)

LEIGH STEPHENS
69	Philips SBL 7897	RED WEATHER (LP)	60
71	Charisma CAS 1040	AND A CAST OF THOUSANDS (LP)	20

(see also Blue Cheer)

STEPPENWOLF
68	RCA RCA 1679	Sookie Sookie/Take What You Need	10
68	RCA RCA 1735	Born To Be Wild/Everybody's Next One	10
68	Stateside-Dunhill SS 8003	Magic Carpet Ride/Sookie Sookie	10
69	Stateside-Dunhill SS 8013	Rock Me/Jupiter Child	7
69	Stateside-Dunhill SS 8017	Born To Be Wild/Everybody's Next One (reissue)	8
69	Stateside-Dunhill SS 8027	Magic Carpet Ride/Sookie Sookie (reissue)	6
70	Stateside-Dunhill SS 8035	Monster/Move Over	6
70	Stateside-Dunhill SS 8038	The Pusher/Your Wall's Too High	6
70	Stateside-Dunhill SS 8049	Hey Lawdy Mama/Twisted	6
70	Stateside-Dunhill SS 8056	Screaming Night Hog/Spiritual Fantasy	6
70	Probe PRO 510	Who Needs Ya/Earschplittenloudenboomer	6
71	Probe PRO 525	Snowblind Friend/Hippo Stomp	6
71	Probe PRO 534	Ride With Me/For Madmen Only	6
71	Probe PRO 544	For Ladies Only/Sparkle Eyes	6
74	CBS MUM 2679	Straight Shootin' Woman/Justice Don't Be Slow	6
75	CBS MUM 3147	Smokey Factory Blues/A Fool's Fantasy	6
75	CBS MUM 3470	Caroline (Are You Ready)/Angel Drawers	6
68	RCA RD/SF 7974	STEPPENWOLF (LP, initial white sleeve)	50
68	RCA RD/SF 7974	STEPPENWOLF (LP, later silver sleeve)	30
68	Stateside SL 5003	STEPPENWOLF THE SECOND (LP, mono)	30
69	Stateside (S)SL 5003	STEPPENWOLF THE SECOND (LP, stereo)	25
69	Stateside SL 5011	AT YOUR BIRTHDAY PARTY (LP, mono)	25
69	Stateside(S)SL 5011	AT YOUR BIRTHDAY PARTY (LP, stereo)	20
69	Stateside (S)SL 5015	EARLY STEPPENWOLF (LP)	15
69	Stateside (S)SL 10276	CANDY (LP, soundtrack, 2 tracks by Steppenwolf, 1 track by Byrds)	30
70	Stateside-Dunhill SSL 5020	STEPPENWOLF (reissue)	15
70	Stateside-Dunhill SSL 5021	MONSTER (LP, gatefold sleeve)	18
70	Stateside-Dunhill SSL 5029	STEPPENWOLF 'LIVE' (LP, gatefold sleeve)	20
70	Probe SPBA 6254	STEPPENWOLF 7 (LP)	15
71	Probe SPBA 6260	FOR LADIES ONLY (LP)	15
71	Probe SPBA 1033	GOLD (LP)	12
72	Probe SPBA 1059	REST IN PEACE (LP)	12

(see also Sparrow, John Kay)

STEPPES
79	South Circular SGS 108	The Beat Drill/FIFTY FANTASTICS: God's Got Religion (p/s, white label)	10

(see also Fifty Fantastics, Disco Zombies)

STEPPING TALK
79	Eustone/Rough Trade TO1	Alice In Sunderland/Health And Safety/Common Problems/John Turtles (p/s, with stamped inner)	15

STEREOLAB
91	Duophonic DS 45-01	SUPER 45: The Light That Will Cease To Fail/Au Grand Jour/Brittle/Au Grand Jour! (10" EP, with insert, mail-order, sold at gigs and some record shops 40 with hand-painted p/s, in poly bag)	150
91	Duophonic DS 45-01	SUPER 45: The Light That Will Cease To Fail/Au Grand Jour/Brittle/Au Grand Jour! (10" EP, with insert, mail-order, sold at gigs and some record shops)	100
91	Duophonic DS 45-01	SUPER 45: The Light That Will Cease To Fail/Au Grand Jour/Brittle/Au Grand Jour! (25 test pressings, 10" cut into 12" discs)	175
91	Duophonic DS 45-02	STUNNING DEBUT ALBUM: Doubt/Clanger (20 black test pressings withdrawn due to pressing fault/warping, different cut of both tracks)	100

MINT VALUE £

91	Duophonic DS 45-02	STUNNING DEBUT ALBUM: Doubt/Clanger (p/s, mail-order, sold at gigs and some Record shops gatefold p/s with insert in poly bag; mulit coloured vinyl, unknown quantity but probably over 200)	175
91	Duophonic DS 45-02	STUNNING DEBUT ALBUM: Doubt/Clanger (p/s, mail-order, gigs and some record Shops, gatefold p/s with insert in poly bag; 985 copies on clear vinyl)	55
92	Duophonic DS 45-04	Harmonium/Farfisa (p/s, mail-order, gigs and some record shops 1,306 copies on transparent amber vinyl, with insert & fluorescent sticker)	35
93	Duophonic DS45-05/06	SHIMMIES IN SUPER 8 (2 x 7", green and white vinyl, foldout sleeve with inserts)	25
92	Too Pure PURE 14	Low Fi/Varoom!/Laissez-Faire/Elektro (He Held The World In His Iron Grip) (10", p/s, clear vinyl, 2,000 only, numbered)	25
93	Sub Pop SP107/283	Lo Boob Oscillator/Tempter (clear vinyl, p/s with US address on back cover)	20
93	Sub Pop SP107/283	Lo Boob Oscillator/Tempter (clear vinyl, p/s with German address on back cover)	15
93	Spacewatch FLX 2107	Ronco Symphony (demo)/Seeming And The Meaning (demo)/SUBMARINER: Lyricist Downer (clear vinyl flexi comes with Spacewatch fanzine in sleeve)	18
93	Duophonic D-UHF-D 01	Jenny Ondioline/Fruition/Golden Ball/French Disko (10", p/s)	10
93	Duophonic D-UHF-D 01	Jenny Ondioline (Part 1)/Golden Ball (Studio) (10", factory custom pressings; 3 on 'thick' clear vinyl, later endorsed & signed by band; no p/s)	220
93	Duophonic D-UHF-D 01	Jenny Ondioline (Part 1)/Golden Ball (Studio) (10", factory custom pressings; 5 copies on multicoloured vinyl; 25 on 'thin' clear vinyl, no p/s)	80
93	Duophonic D-UHF-CD 01	Jenny Ondioline/Fruition/Golden Ball/French Disko (CD)	12
93	Clawfist 20	CRUMB DUCK (10" EP, shared with Nurse With Wound; 37 with hand-drawn p/s (Gain/Sadier only)	120
93	Clawfist 20	CRUMB DUCK (10" EP, shared with Nurse With Wound; 1,450 regular p/s)	20
93	Duophonic D-UHF-D 03	French Disko/Jenny Ondioline ('teaser' single, p/s, 1,500 only, with hand printed sleeves)	25
93	Duophonic D-UHF-D 03	French Disko/Jenny Ondioline ('teaser' single, p/s, 1,500 only, regular printed sleeves)	15
93	Duophonic D-UHF-D 01P	French Disko/Jenny Ondioline (CD, 1,000 only, hand-made p/s)	15
94	Duophonic D-UHF-D 04S	Ping Pong/Moogie Wonderland (p/s, 2,150 on pink vinyl)	10
94	Duophonic D-UHF-D 04S	Ping Pong/Moogie Wonderland (p/s, 3,322 on green vinyl)	10
94	Silvertone	Tone Burst (demo)/Tempter (demo)/SPECTRUM: Soul Kiss Glide Divine (unreleased, with colour photocopied wraparound p/s, 25 test pressings only)	150
94	Duophonic D-UHF-07	Wow And Flutter/Heavy Denim (3,000 only with hand-painted p/s)	12
95	Wurlitzer Jukebox WJ 3	The Eclipse/Yes Sir! I Can Moogie/CAT'S MIAOW: Shoot The Moon (flexidisc, 1,000 only with insert and info sheet)	18
95	Duophonic Super 45s DS 45-10	Long Hair Of Death/YO LA TENGO: Evanescent Psychic Pez Drop (gig single, fluorescent yellow vinyl, plain white stickered card sleeve, 3,000 only)	12
95	Independent Project IP 060	Blue Milk/One Thousand Miles An Hour/Aluminum Tune (set of 4 singles all With same tracks in different coloured vinyl and different sets of gatefold sleeve. American Import. Singles worth £10 each)	50
95	Flying Nun STEREO 1	French Disko/Super Electric (CD, also listed as B 8595, promo only)	15
95	Duophonic STEREO 2	John Cage Bubblegum/Revox (CD, also listed as B 8895, promo only)	10
96	Duophonic D-UHF-D 10S	Cybele's Reverie/Brigitte (p/s, with insert)	5
96	Duophonic D-UHF-D 10	Cybele's Reverie/Les Yper Yper Sound/Brigitte/Young Lungs(25 black vinyl test pressing and 102 cut into 12" disc)	25
96	Duophonic D-UHF-D 10	Cybele's Reverie/Les Yper Yper Sound/Brigitte/Young Lungs(10", p/s, 2,000 only)	10
96	Lissy's LISS 15	You Used To Call Me Sadness/FUXA: Skyhigh (p/s, 400 on white vinyl)	20
96	Lissy's LISS 15	You Used To Call Me Sadness/FUXA: Skyhigh (p/s, 1,500 on black vinyl)	8
96	Duophonic D-UHF-D 12	Speedy Car/TORTOISE: Yaus (gig freebie, blue vinyl, p/s, 3,000 only)	15
96	Duophonic D-UHF-D 12	Speedy Car/TORTOISE: Yaus (orange vinyl export issue, p/s, 3,000 only)	15
96	Duophonic D-UHF-D 14S	Fluorescences/Pinball (p/s)	5
96	Duophonic D-UHF-D 14	Fluorescences/Pinball/You Used To Call Me Sadness/Soop Groove (12", p/s)	8
96	Duophonic D-UHF-D 15	Metronomic Underground (Wagon Christ Mix)/Percolations (12", plain red sleeve, 2,500 only)	12
97	Duophonic DS 4517	Splitting The Atom (Parts 1 & 2) (with Sonic Boom)/Monkey Brain (p/s, 2,500 only)	10
97	Duophonic D-UHF-D 18	Iron Man/The Incredible He Woman (red vinyl, p/s, gig single, 2,000 only)	5
97	Duophonic Super 45s DS 3311	Simple Headphone Mind/NURSE WITH WOUND: Trippin' With The Birds (12", 5,000 copies)	12
97	Duophonic Super 45s DS 3311	Simple Headphone Mind/NURSE WITH WOUND: Trippin' With The Birds (12", 1,000 copies on yellow vinyl, in sealed foil sleeve)	25
97	Duophonic Super 45s CD 3311	Simple Headphone Mind/NURSE WITH WOUND: Trippin' With The Birds (CD, sealed foil sleeve, 1,000 only)	35
98	Duophonic D-UHF-D 19	Refractions In The Plastic Pulse/Contronatura (12", die-cut stickered sleeve, black vinyl)	10
99	Duophonic D-UHF-D24	THE UNDERGROUND IS COMING: The Super-It/Monkey Jelly/Fried Monkey Eggs (Instrumental)/Fried Monkey Eggs (Vocal) (p/s)	10
01	Duophonic D-UHF 026	Captain Easychord (12")	10
03	Duophonic D-UHF-D 28S	INSTANT 0 IN THE UNIVERSE (3 x 7" box set)	12
01	Duophonic DS 45 30	Free Witch And No Bra Queen/Speck Voice (p/s, tour single)	15
04	Duophonic D-UHF-D 30S	Rose, My Pocket Brain!/Banana Monster Ne Repond Plus/University Microfilms International (p/s, tour single, 500 only)	15
06	Duophonic DS 45 38	Solar Throw Away/Jump Drive Shut Out (p/s, tour single)	8
90	Too Pure PURE 19	SPACE AGE BACHELOR PAD MUSIC (LP)	12
92	Too Pure PURELP 11	PENG! (LP, inner sleeve, insert)	18
92	Duophonic D-UHF-D 02	TRANSIENT RANDOM NOISE-BURSTS WITH ANNOUNCEMENTS (2-LP, with inner sleeves, poor playing-quality gold vinyl, with stickered sleeve, 1,500 only, numbered)	55
93	Duophonic D-UHF-D 02	TRANSIENT RANDOM NOISE-BURSTS WITH ANNOUNCEMENTS (2-LP, inners, black vinyl)	20
95	Duophonic D-UHF-D 05X	MARS AUDIAC QUINTET (2-LP, gatefold sleeve, 1st 1,000 copies with bonus coloured vinyl single "Klang Tone"/"Ulan Bator" [D-UHF-06])	55
94	Duophonic D-UHF-D 05	MARS AUDIAC QUINTET (2-LP, without single)	25
95	Duophonic D-UHF-D 08	MUSIC FOR THE AMORPHOUS BODY STUDY CENTRE (40 black vinyl test pressings 10" sides cut into 12" discs)	90
95	Duophonic D-UHF-D 08	MUSIC FOR THE AMORPHOUS BODY STUDY CENTRE (10" LP, 3,000 only, insert)	30
95	Duophonic D-UHF-CD 08	MUSIC FOR THE AMORPHOUS BODY STUDY CENTRE (CD, first issue with white cover & "1st edition" printed on disc available at Charles Long art exhibition; reissue has yellow sleeve)	0
95	Duophonic D-UHF LP 09	REFRIED ECTOPLASM - SWITCHED ON VOL 2 LP (2-LP, orange vinyl, card insert)	25
96	United Dairies UD 059	CRUMB DUCK (LP, shared with Nurse With Wound (2 extra tracks, reissue of Clawfist EP, 50 copies on pink vinyl)	70
96	United Dairies UD 059	CRUMB DUCK (LP, shared with Nurse With Wound (2 extra tracks, reissue of Clawfist EP, 500 on fluorescent green vinyl)	40
96	Duophonic UHF D-UHF-D11	EMPEROR TOMATO KETCHUP (2-LP, yellow glitter vinyl, gatefold sleeve)	60
96	Duophonic DUHFD11	EMPEROR TOMATO KETCHUP (2-LP, black vinyl)	25
97	Duophonic D-UHF-D 17	DOTS & LOOPS (2-LP, one green, one white vinyl)	25
98	Drag City CD 159	ALUMINIUM TUNES - SWITCHED ON VOL. 3 (3 x LP)	25
99	Duophonic D-UHF-D 23	COBRA & PHASES GROUP PLAY VOLTAGE IN THE MILKY NIGHT (2-LP)	20
00	Duophinic D-UHF-D 25	THE FIRST OF THE MICROBE HUNTERS (2-LP)	15

01	Duophonic D-UHF-D 27	SOUND-DUST (2-LP, hand-humbered, screenprinted heavy card sleeve, inners, 1200 only)	.40
01	Duophinic D-UHF-D 27	SOUND-DUST (2-LP, inners, 1800 only)	30
04	Duophinic D-UHF-D 29	MARGERINE ECLIPSE (2-LP, 3500 only)	20
06	(No Cat. No.)	FAB FOUR SUTURE (LP as 6 x 7" hand-stamped box)	20
06	Duophinic D-UHF-D 31	SERENE VELOCITY: A STEREOLAB ANTHOLOGY (2-LP, numbered sticker on sleeve, inners)	20

(see also McCarthy, Spectrum, Mouse On Mars, Clear Spot)

STEREOLAB & BRIGITTE FONTAINE
90s	Duophonic Super 45s DS 45-25	Caliméro/MONADE: Cache Cache (white vinyl, p/s)	8

STEREOPHONICS
96	V2 SPH 1	Looks Like Chaplin/More Life In A Tramp's Vest (p/s, 500 only)	60
96	V2 SPHD 1	Looks Like Chaplin/More Life In A Tramp's Vest/Raymond's Shops (CD)	30
96	V2 SPH 2	Local Boy In The Photograph/Too Many Sandwiches (p/s, 2,000 only)	12
97	V2 SPH 4	More Life In A Tramp's Vest/Raymond's Shop (p/s)	8
97	V2 VVR 500 0448	A Thousand Trees/Home To Me/Looks Like Chaplin/Summertime (CD, digipak)	12
99	V2 VVR 500 6777	Pick A Part That's New/Nice To Be Out (Demo) (p/s)	6
99	V2 no catalogue number	PERFORMANCE AND COCKTAILS (7 x 10" box set, with booklet and CD, promo mail order only)	40
97	Banana VVR 1000431	WORD GETS AROUND (LP, with bonus 12")	25
99	V2 VVR1004499	PERFORMANCE AND COCKTAILS (LP, gatefold)	25

STEREOS
61	MGM MGM 1143	I Really Love You/Please Come Back To Me	50
61	MGM MGM 1149	The Big Knock/Sweet Water	30
66	MGM MGM 1328	Sweet Water/The Big Knock (reissue)	7

STEREOTYPES
79	Hinterland/SRT no cat. no.	THE STEREOTYPES EP (no p/s)	500

STEREOTYPES
80	Art Theft AT 001	Calling All The Shots/Lovers Of The Future (p/s)	8

DEAN STERLING & TEENBEATS
61	Pye 7N 15345	Send Me A Girl/Lost Love	12

FITZROY STERLING
68	Gas GAS 102	Got To Play It Cool/Jezebel	12
70	Bullet BU 422	That's My Life/Queen Of Hearts	8
70	Bullet BU 438	Freedom Street/FITZROY ALL STARS: Freedom Street Version	8
71	Escort ERT 858	Girl Tell Me What To Do/Be Careful	8
71	Pama PM 820	My Sweet Lord/Darling That's Right	5

LESTER STERLING (& HIS GROUP)
63	Island WI 121	Clean The City/Long Walk Home (B-side actually by Charmers)	20
63	R&B JB 111	Air Raid Shelter/ROY & ANNETTE: I Mean It	25
63	R&B JB 115	Gravy Cool/WINSTON & BIBBY: Lover Lover Man	35
64	R&B JB 143	Peace And Love/HORACE SEATON: Hold On	30
64	R&B JB 150	Hot Cargo/MAYTALS: Marching On	30
64	R&B JB 155	Baskin' Hop (as Lester Sterling & His Group)/MAYTALS: Shining Light	20
64	R&B JB 172	Indian Summer (as Lester Sterling & His Group)/STRANGER & PATSY: I'll Forgive You	20
66	Doctor Bird DB 1057	Inez (with Tommy McCook & Supersonics)/GLORIA CRAWFORD: Sad Movies	40
67	Doctor Bird DB 1107	Soul Voyage/ALVA LEWIS: Revelation	40
67	Collins Downbeat CR 001	Sir Collins Special/Lester Sterling '67	50
68	Coxsone CS 7080	Africkaan Beat/PARAGONS: My Satisfaction	60
68	Blue Cat BS 116	Zigaloo/Wiser Than Solomon	40
68	Unity UN 502	Bangarang (with Stranger Cole)/STRANGER COLE: If We Should Ever Meet	12
69	Unity UN 505	Reggae On Broadway/CLIQUE: Love Can Be Wonderful	20
69	Unity UN 509	Spoogy/TOMMY McCOOK: Monkey Fiddle	15
69	Unity UN 512	Regina/Bright As A Rose	7
69	Unity UN 517	1,000 Tons Of Megaton/KING CANNON: Five Card Stud	10
69	Unity UN 518	Man About Town/Man At The Door	8
69	Unity UN 531	Lonesome Feeling/Bright As A Rose	6
69	Big Shot BI 507	Forest Gate Rock/RAVING RAVERS: Rock Rock And Cry	8
69	Gas GAS 103	Reggae In The Wind/SOUL SET: Try Me One More Time (B-side actually by Stranger & Gladdy)	6
70	Unity UN 562	Slip Up/DAVE BARKER: On Broadway	10
71	Nu Beat NB 095	Iron Side Part 1/COXSON'S ALL STARS: Iron Side Part 2	8
71	Nu Beat 96	War Is Not The Answer Part 2/Iron Side Part 2	15
71	Smash SMA 2321	Sir Collins Special/Version (actually "Heart Of The Knight" by Gaytones)	8
72	Ashanti ASH 409	Iron Side Part 1/COXSON'S ALL STARS: Iron Side Part 2	6
72	Ashanti ASH 410	War Is Not The Answer/COXSON'S ALL STARS: Version	6
69	Pama SECO 15	BANGARANG (LP)	55

(see also Mister Versatile, Bobby Aitken, Eric Morris, Sir Collins Band, Slickers, Uniques)

NINA STERN
65	Pye 7N 15823	Take It From Me/Please Come Back To Me	8

STEROID KIDDIES
70s	Steroid/Grundinga SK 001	THE KIDDIES EP	55

STEROID MAXIMUS
90s	Big Cat ABB 28	QUILOMBO (LP)	20

STEROIDS
78	Radar ADA 11	In The Colonies/Sha La La Loo Ley (p/s)	6

STEVE DARBYSHIRE
65	Decca F12261	That's The Reason Why/She's Got Quality	10
66	Decca F 12512	Trains Theme/Alma Jones	7
67	Decca F 12553	Just A Little Lovin' Changes Things/Holiday In Waikiki	6

STEVE 'N' BONNIE
72	Young Blood YB 1033	Brief Encounter/Don't/Lady	6
73	Sovereign SOV123	Me 'N' My Soul/A Screw Called Kirk	8
72	Young Blood SSYB 16	BRIEF ENCOUNTER (LP)	18

STEVE & STEVIE

68	Toast TT510	Merry-Go-Round/Remains To Be Seen	15
68	Toast TLP 2	STEVE AND STEVIE (LP)	30

(see also Tin Tin, Fut)

APRIL STEVENS

53	Parlophone MSP 6060	C'est Si Bon/Soft Warm Lips	10
54	Parlophone MSP 6088	How Could Red Riding Hood (Have Been...)/You Said You'd Do It	10
67	MGM MGM 1366	Falling In Love Again/Wanting You	100
67	MGM MGM 1366	Falling In Love Again/Wanting You (DJ copy)	200
76	MGM 2006 586	Wanting You/Falling In Love Again (reissue)	6

(see also Nino Tempo & April Stevens)

CAT STEVENS

66	Deram DM 102	I Love My Dog/Portobello Road	5
66	Deram DM 110	Matthew And Son/Granny	7
67	Deram DM 118	I'm Gonna Get Me A Gun/School Is Out	5
67	Deram DM 140	Bad Night/Laughing Apple	5
67	Deram DM 156	Kitty/Blackness Of The Night	10
68	Deram DM 178	Lovely City/Image Of Hell	7
68	Deram DM 211	Here Comes My Wife/It's A Supa (Dupa) Life	7
69	Deram DM 260	Where Are You/The View From The Top	7
70	Island WIP 6086	Lady D'Arbanville/Time/Fill My Eyes (in p/s)	8
70	Island WIP 6086	Lady D'Arbanville/Time/Fill My Eyes	5
67	Deram DML/SML 1004	MATTHEW AND SON (LP)	25
67	Deram DML/SML 1018	NEW MASTERS (LP)	25
67	Deram	CATS AND DOGS (LP, unreleased, test pressings only)	30
70	Island ILPS 9118	MONA BONE JAKON (LP, pink label with white 'i' logo)	80
70	Island ILPS 9135	TEA FOR THE TILLERMAN (LP, gatefold, pink label, with white 'i' logo)	60
71	Island ILPS 9154	TEASER AND THE FIRECAT (LP, pink rim label)	12

CHUCK STEVENS

57	Columbia DB 3883	Take A Walk/The Way I Do	7
57	Columbia DB 3938	My London/Couldn't Care More	7

CONNIE STEVENS

60	Warner Bros WB 3	Sixteen Reasons (with Don Ralke)/Little Sister (with Buddy Cole Trio)	10
60	Warner Bros WB 17	Too Young To Go Steady/A Little Kiss Is A Kiss, Is A Kiss	10
60	Warner Bros WB 25	Apollo/Why Do I Cry For Joey	10
61	Warner Bros WB 41	And This Is Mine/Make-Believe Lover	10
61	Warner Bros WB 47	The Greenwood Tree/If You Don't, Somebody Else Will	10
62	Warner Bros WB 63	Why'd You Wanna Make Me Cry/Just One Kiss	15
62	Warner Bros WB 73	Mr. Songwriter/I Couldn't Say No	10
64	Warner Bros WB 128	They're Jealous Of Me/A Girl Never Knows	10
60	Warner Bros WEP 6007	CONNIE STEVENS AS CRICKET (EP, mono)	15
60	Warner Bros WSEP 2007	CONNIE STEVENS AS CRICKET (EP, stereo)	18
63	Warners WEP 6105	CONNIE STEVENS AS CRICKET NO. 2 (EP, mono)	15
63	Warners WSE 6105	CONNIE STEVENS AS CRICKET NO. 2 (EP, stereo)	20
63	Warners WEP 6112	CONNIE STEVENS AS CRICKET NO. 3 (EP, mono)	15
63	Warners WSE 6112	CONNIE STEVENS AS CRICKET NO. 3 (EP, stereo)	18
62	Warner Bros WM 4060	CONNIE (LP, mono)	20
62	Warner Bros WS 8061	CONNIE (LP, stereo)	25
63	Warner Bros WM/WS 8111	THE HANK WILLIAMS SONG BOOK (LP)	15

(see also Edward Byrnes)

DEAN STEVENS

62	Philips 326540 BF	Sad And Lonely/I've Just Heard	10
64	Philips BF 1300	Only 'Cause I'm Lonely/Love Me Like I Love You	8
63	Philips 326580	Let Me Show You How/High On The Hill Of Hope	8

DODIE STEVENS

59	London HLD 8834	Pink Shoe Laces/Coming Of Age	20
59	London HLD 8834	Pink Shoe Laces/Coming Of Age	20
60	London HLD 9174	No/A-Tisket A-Tasket	10
61	London HLD 9280	Yes, I'm Lonesome Tonight/Too Young	10
63	London HLP 9672	Don't Send Me Roses/Daddy Couldn't Get Me One Of Those	10
64	Liberty LIB 83	I Wore Out Our Record/You Don't Have To Prove A Thing	8

JERRY STEVENS

66	CBS 2831	You Make My Life Worthwhile/So This Is Love	6

JIMMY STEVENS

66	Fontana TF 721	I Love You/Wharf 130	7

JOHN STEVENS AWAY

76	Vertigo 6059154	Can't Explain (Part 1)/Can't Explain (Part 2)	5
76	Vertigo 6360 131	JOHN STEVEN'S AWAY (LP)	20
76	Vertigo 6360 135	SOMEWHERE IN BETWEEN (LP)	20
77	Vertigo 6360 141	MAZIN ENNIT (LP, spaceship label)	12
78	Spotlite SPJ 508	NO FEAR! (LP)	30
78	Spotlite SPJ 513	APPLICATION INTERACTION AND... (LP)	30
82	Affinity AFF 101	FREEBOP (LP)	20
84	Affinity AYF 130	THE LIFE OF RILEY (LP, as John Steven's Solkus)	30

JOHNNY STEVENS & BLUE BEATS

64	Blue Beat BB 229	Shame/Ball And Chain	20

JOHNNY STEVENS & LES DAWSON SYNDICATE

62	Melodisc M 1586	Last Chicken In The Shop/Oh Yeah (some in p/s)	10

KIRK STEVENS

57	Decca F 10863	Once/This Silver Madonna	8

MEIC STEVENS

65	Decca F 12174	Did I Dream/I Saw A Field (as Mike Stevens)	40
70	Warner Bros WB 8007	Ballad Of Old Joe Blind/Blue Sleep	15
70	Wren WSP 2005	Nid Oes Un Gwydr Ffenestr/Rhywbeth Gwell I Ddod	40

68	Wren WRE 1045	MIKE STEVENS (EP, p/s)	50
68	Wren WRE 1053	RHIF 2 (EP, p/s)	50
69	Wren WRE 1073	MWG (EP, p/s)	50
70	Newyddion Da ND1	MEIC STEVENS (EP, p/s)	100
70	Sain SAIN 004	Y BRAWN HOUDINI (EP, p/s)	50
71	Wren WRE 1107	BYW YN Y WLAD (EP, p/s)	50
71	Sain SAIN 13	DIONCH YN FAWR (EP, p/s)	50
70	Warner Brothers WS 3005	OUTLANDER (LP, with insert)	300
72	Wren WRL 536	GWYMON (LP)	300
77	Sain SAIN 1065	GOG (LP)	120
79	Tic Toc no cat. no.	CANAEON CYNNAR (LP, private pressing)	220
82	Sain SAIN 1239	NOS DU NOS DA (LP)	50
83	Sain SAIN 1312	LAPIS LAZULI (LP)	50
97	Tenth Planet TP 028	GHOST TOWN (LP, gatefold sleeve, numbered, 1000 only)	12

(see also Gary Farr)

MICK STEVENS
79	Spaceeard SRS 030	THE ENGLISHMAN (LP, insert)	40
71	Deroy (no cat. no.)	SEE THE MORNING (LP, private pressing)	400
75	Deroy (no cat. no.)	NO SAVAGE WORD (LP, private pressing)	300

MIKE STEVENS
| 66 | Pye 7N 17243 | Cathy's Clown/Go-Go Train | 60 |
| 68 | Polydor 56269 | Guaranteed To Drive You Wild/Hog-Tied | 12 |

(see also Shevells)

MORT STEVENS & HIS ORCHESTRA
| 70 | Capitol CL 15655 | Hawaii Five-O Theme/McGarrett's Theme | 10 |

RAY STEVENS
58	Capitol CL 14881	Chickie-Chickie Wah Wah/Crying Goodbye	10
61	Mercury AMT 1158	Jeremiah Peabody's Polyunsaturated Quick Dissolving Fast Acting Pleasant Tasting Green And Purple Pills/Teen Years	7
62	Mercury AMT 1184	Ahab The Arab/It's Been So Long	9
63	Mercury AMT 1207	Harry The Hairy Ape/Little Stone Statue	7
68	Monument MON 1022	Mr Businessman/Face The Music	8

RICKY STEVENS
61	Columbia DB 4739	I Cried For You/I Am	10
62	Columbia DB 4778	Forever/Now, It's All Over	7
63	Columbia DB 4981	My Mother's Eyes/I'll Get By	7
62	Columbia SEG 8172	I CRIED FOR YOU (EP)	50

ROY STEVENS
| 66 | London HLU 10016 | Party People/ABC | 10 |

SHAKIN' STEVENS (& SUNSETS)
70	Parlophone R 5860	Spirit Of Woodstock/Down On The Farm	60
72	Polydor 2058 213	Sweet Little Rock'n'Roller/White Lightning	50
74	Emerald MD 1176	Honey Honey/Holey Moley 2001	35
76	Mooncrest MOON 51	Jungle Rock/Girl In Red	15
77	Track 2094 134	Never/You Always Hurt The One You Love	15
77	Track 2094 136	Somebody Touched Me/Way Down Yonder In New Orleans (in p/s)	20
77	Track 2094 136	Somebody Touched Me/Way Down Yonder In New Orleans	8
78	Track 2094 141	Justine/Wait And See	20
78	Epic SEPC 6567	Treat Her Right/I Don't Want No Other Baby	15
79	Epic SEPC 6845	Endless Sleep/Fire	15
79	Epic SEPC 7235	Spooky/I Don't Want No Other Baby	30
80	Epic SEPC 8090	Hot Dog/Apron Strings	6
80	Epic SEPC 8573	Hey Mae/I Guess I Was A Fool (in p/s)	60
80	Epic SEPC 8573	Hey Mae/I Guess I Was A Fool	5
80	Epic SEPC 9064	Shooting Gallery/Make It Right Tonight (p/s)	6
81	Battle Of The Bands BOB 2	Jungle Rock/Girl In Red (p/s, reissue, as Shakin' Stevens & Sunsets)	5
81	Mint CHEW 51	No Other Baby/Manhattan Melodrama (p/s)	5
81	Epic EPCA 11-1643	It's Raining/You And I Were Meant To Be (picture disc)	5
81	Solid Gold SGR 107	Shaky Sings Elvis (Parts 1 & 2) (medley) (p/s)	5
82	Epic EPCA 1742	Oh Julie/I'm Knocking (poster p/s)	5
82	Epic EPCA 2656	Give Me Your Heart Tonight/Thinkin' Of You (p/s, with poster)	5
82	Epic EPCA 2656	Give Me Your Heart Tonight/Thinkin' Of You (picture disc)	5
82	Everest/Premier EV 1000	Tiger/Sweet Little Sixteen/Give Me A Break (picture disc)	5
82	Everest/Premier EV 1000	Tiger/Sweet Little Sixteen/Give Me A Break	10
83	Epic WA 3565	It's Late/It's Good For You Baby (feet-shaped picture disc)	8
83	Epic WA 3774	Cry Just A Little Bit/Love Me Tonight (picture disc)	5
83	Kelloggs KELL 1	Oh Julie/ABBA: I Have A Dream (free with Kelloggs' 'Rice Krispies')	5
84	Epic A 4291	A Love Waiting For You/As Long As I Have You (live) (poster p/s)	5
84	Epic QA 4677	A Letter To You/Come Back And Love Me (p/s, with free post bag game)	5
84	Epic DA 4882	Teardrops/You Shake Me Up//Shakin' Stevens Party Mix (Parts 1 & 2) (double pack)	8
85	Epic GA 6072	Breakin' Up My Heart/I'll Give You My Heart (gatefold pop-up p/s)	5
86	Epic SHAKY 2	Because I Love You/Tell Me One More Time (2 picture sleeves, sealed together on edge with sticker, with autograph)	5
87	Epic SHAKY P5	What Do You Want To Make Those Eyes At Me For/You're Evil (picture disc)	5
81	Magnum Force MFEP 001	Memphis Earthquake/You Mostest Girl/Evil Hearted Ada/My Bucket's Got A Hole In It (EP, p/s)	8
82	Magnum Force MFEP 007	Frantic/Ready Teddy/Tear It Up/Monkey's Uncle (EP, p/s)	8
70	Parlophone PCS 7112	A LEGEND (LP)	55
71	CBS 52901	I'M NO J.D. (LP)	70
72	Contour 2870 152	ROCKIN' AND SHAKIN' (LP)	15
73	Emerald GES 1121	SHAKIN' STEVENS AND THE SUNSETS (LP)	18
78	Track 2406 011	SHAKIN' STEVENS (LP, with insert)	15
80	Epic EPC 84547	MARIE MARIE (LP, withdrawn)	18
83	Epic BX 86301	THE BOP WON'T STOP (LP & cassette, box set, with Shaky autograph book)	18

TERRI STEVENS
| 59 | Felsted AF 112 | My Wish Tonight/All Alone | 5 |
| 59 | Felsted AF 126 | Adonis/Vieni, Vieni | 6 |

MINT VALUE £

VIRGINIA STEVENS
77	Mulligan LUN A 332	TIOCFAIDH AN SAMHRADH - TRADITIONAL SONGS FROM THE WEST OF IRELAND (LP, with booklet)	15

RICHARD STEVENSEN
70	Pye 7N 45004	The Day That You Came Back/The Gates Of Me	8
70	Pye NSPL 18358	GATES OF ME (LP, textured sleeve)	25

MICKEY STEVENSON
72	Ember EMBS 320	Here I Am/Joe Poor Loves Daphne Elizabeth Richard	6
72	Ember NR 5063	HERE I AM (LP)	30

N A STEVENSON AND THE 4 ACES
73	Injun 103	Boogie Woogie Country Girl/Pins & Needles	10

STEVIE'S BUZZ
96	Nice no cat. no.	Autumn Stone/P.P. & THE PRIMES: Understanding (promo only, large centre)	8

(see also P.P. Arnold, Buzzcocks, Primal Scream)

AL STEWART
66	Decca F 12467	The Elf/Turn To Earth	60
67	CBS 3034	Bedsitter Images/Swiss Cottage Manoeuvres	12
70	CBS 4843	Electric Los Angeles Sunset/My Enemies Have Sweet Voices	8
70	CBS 5351	The News From Spain/Elvaston Place	15
72	CBS 7763	You Don't Even Know Me/I'm Falling	6
72	CBS 7992	Amsterdam/Songs Out Of Clay	6
73	CBS SCBS 1971	Terminal Eyes/Last Day Of June 1934	10
67	CBS (S)BPG 63087	BEDSITTER IMAGES (LP)	125
69	CBS (S) 63460	LOVE CHRONICLES (LP, gatefold sleeve)	25
70	CBS 63848	ZERO SHE FLIES (LP, gatefold sleeve)	22
70	CBS 64023	FIRST ALBUM (BEDSITTER IMAGES) (LP, remixed reissue, different track listing)	18
72	CBS 64730	ORANGE (LP)	12

(see also Jimmy Page)

BILLY STEWART
62	Pye International 7N 25164	Reap What You Sow/Fat Boy	15
63	Pye International 7N 25222	Strange Feeling/Sugar And Spice	15
65	Chess CRS 8009	I Do Love You/Keep Loving	10
65	Chess CRS 8017	Sitting In The Park/Once Again	10
66	Chess CRS 8028	Because I Love You/Mountains Of Love	10
66	Chess CRS 8038	Love Me/Why Am I Lonely	10
66	Chess CRS 8040	Summertime/To Love To Love	10
66	Chess CRS 8045	Secret Love/Look Back And Smile	10
66	Chess CRS 8050	Ole Man River/Every Day I Have The Blues	10
67	Chess CRS 8067	Cross My Heart/Why (Do I Love You So)	10
69	Chess CRS 8092	Summertime/I Do Love You	15
72	Chess 6145 017	Sitting In The Park/Summertime	8
65	Chess CRE 6010	IN CROWD (EP, with Ramsey Lewis Trio, et al)	30
67	Chess CRE 6024	I DO LOVE YOU (EP)	30
66	Chess CRL 4523	UNBELIEVABLE (LP)	30
72	Chess 6310 125	GOLDEN DECADE (LP)	12

BOB STEWART
55	MGM SP 1114	It's A Woman's World/I Went Out Of My Way	6

DAVID A. STEWART
92	Anxious ZT 43046	LILY WAS HERE (12", with 2 Orb mixes, featuring Candy Dulfer, p/s)	8

(see also Eurythmics, Longdancer, Stewart & Harrison)

DAVIE STEWART
78	Topic 12T 293	DAVIE STEWART (LP, with insert)	12

DELANO STEWART
68	Doctor Bird DB 1138	That's Life/Tell Me Baby	50
68	High Note HS 004	Let's Have Some Fun/Dance With Me	30
69	High Note HS 014	Rocking Sensation/GAYTONES: One Look	60
70	High Note HS 027	Got To Come Back/Don't Believe In Him	15
70	High Note HS 034	Hallelujah/I Wish It Could Last	10
70	High Hote HS 039	Wherever I Lay My Hat/Don't Believe Him (B-side actually by Gladstone Anderson & Gaytones)	12
70	High Note HS 041	Stay A Little Bit Longer/Stay A Little Bit Longer (Version II) (B-side actually by Gladstone Anderson & Gaytones)	12
70	Trojan TBL 138	STAY A LITTLE BIT LONGER (LP)	30

(see also Winston Stewart, Gaylads, Patsy Todd)

GRAHAM STEWART SEVEN
59	Tempo EXA 91	GRAHAM STEWART SEVEN (EP)	10

(DAVE) STEWART & HARRISON
70	Multicord MULT SH 1	GIRL (EP)	15

(see also Longdancer, Eurythmics, David A. Stewart)

JAMES STEWART
65	Brunswick 05938	The Legend Of Shenandoah/CHARLES 'BUD' DANT CHORUS: We're Ridin' Out Tonight	5

JAMES STEWART & HENRY FONDA
70	Stateside SS 2179	Rolling Stone/Theme From Cheyenne Social Club	8

JOHN STEWART
69	Capitol CL 15589	July, You're A Woman/Shackles And Chains	8
69	Capitol E-(S)T 203	CALIFORNIA BLOODLINES (LP)	12

(see also Kingston Trio, Cumberland Three, Scott Engel)

JOHNNY STEWART
58	HMV POP 480	Wishing For Your Love/Promise Me	7

PAUL STEWART (MOVEMENT)
67	Decca F12577	Saturday Mornin Man/Too Too Good (in export p/s)	40
66	Philips BF 1513	Queen Boadicea/Talkin'	7

| 67 | Decca F 12577 | Saturday Morning Man/Too Too Good (as Paul Stewart Movement) ....12 |

(see also Hamilton & [Hamilton] Movement)

RAPHAEL STEWART & HOT TOPS

| 71 | Punch PH 71 | Put Your Sweet Lips/JUSTINS: Stand By Me ....10 |

REX STEWART'S LONDON FIVE

| 55 | Tempo EXA 8 | REX STEWART'S LONDON FIVE (EP) ....15 |

ROD STEWART

64	Decca F 11996	Good Morning Little Schoolgirl/I'm Gonna Move To The Outskirts Of Town 160
65	Columbia DB 7766	The Day Will Come/Why Does It Go On? 150
66	Columbia DB 7892	Shake/I Just Got Some 200
68	Immediate IM 060	Little Miss Understood/So Much To Say 100
70	Vertigo 6086 002	It's All Over Now/Jo's Lament 15
72	Phonogram DJ004	Twisting the Night Away (EP 1-track on 4 track promo 7" also featuring Chuck Berry, Diane Davidson and the Stylistics) 20
73	Mercury 6052 371	Oh No Not My Baby/Jodie (tartan sleeve) 6
76	Mercury 6160 006	Maggie May/You Wear It Well/Twistin' The Night Away (p/s) 5
77	Mercury 6160 007	Mandolin Wind/Girl From The North Country/Sweet Little Rock'N'Roller 5
76	Mercury 6167 327	It's All Over Now/Handbags And Gladrags 7
77	Riva RIVA 1	You're Insane/You're Insane (DJ copy, 500 only) 25
77	Riva RIVA 3	Tonight's The Night/The First Cut Is The Deepest (withdrawn B-side) 10
78	Riva RIVA 9	Sailing/Stone Cold Sober (p/s) 5
78	Riva RIVA 9	Sailing/Stone Cold Sober(HMS Ark Royal Commemorative issue, blue vinyl, p/s) 150
78	Riva RIVA 15	Ole Ola/Que Sera Sera - I'd Walk A Million Miles For One Of Your Goals (p/s) 5
80	Riva RIVA 23	If Lovin' You Is Wrong/Last Summer (p/s)...5
80	Virgin VS 366	Little Miss Understood/So Much To Say (p/s, reissue) 5
80	Riva W 7929TP	Excerpts From "Foolish Behaviour" (flexidisc with London Evening News)................10
82	Riva RIVA 35	How Long/Jealous (p/s, with free sticker) 5
82	Decca F 11996	Good Morning Little Schoolgirl/I'm Gonna Move To The Outskirts Of Town (reissue) 8
82	Immediate IM 060	Little Miss Understood/So Much To Say (reissue, p/s) 5
83	Warner Bros W 9440P	Sweet Surrender/Ghetto Blaster (picture disc) 5
84	Warner Bros SAM 194	Infatuation (1-sided picture disc in wallet with interview cassette) 12
86	Warner Bros W 8668TP	Love Touch/Heart Is On The Line/Hard Lesson To Learn (12", picture disc) 8
88	Warner Bros WX 152TP	Lost In You (Extended Remix)/Lost In You (Fade)/Almost Illegal (12", pic disc).........8
89	Warner Bros W 2686P	This Old Heart Of Mine/Ain't Love A Bitch/Tonight I'm Yours (Don't Hurt Me) (with Ronald Isley, shaped picture disc) 8
70	Vertigo VO 4	AN OLD RAINCOAT WON'T EVER LET YOU DOWN (gatefold sleeve, large swirl label, original pressing with 'Philips' credit on label) 100
70	Vertigo VO 4	AN OLD RAINCOAT WON'T EVER LET YOU DOWN (gatefold sleeve, large swirl label, later pressing without 'Philips' credit on label) 20
70	Vertigo 6360 500	GASOLINE ALLEY (LP, 1st pressing, gatefold sleeve, large swirl label) 70
71	Vertigo 6360 500	GASOLINE ALLEY (LP, 2nd pressing, gatefold sleeve, small swirl label) 25
71	Mercury 6338 063	EVERY PICTURE TELLS A STORY (black label, with poster) 30
72	Mercury 6499 153	NEVER A DULL MOMENT (gatefold sleeve)...15
73	Mercury 6499 484	SING IT AGAIN, ROD 12
75	Riva RVLP 4	ATLANTIC CROSSING (gatefold sleeve, blue vinyl/orange vinyl) 25
76	Mercury 6672 013	THE VINTAGE YEARS..12
76	Philips SON 001	RECORDED HIGHLIGHTS & ACTION REPLAYS 12
78	St. Michael 21020 102	REASON TO BELIEVE (only available in Marks & Spencer) 20
84	Warner Bros 9250 951	CAMOUFLAGE (with bonus 1-sided picture disc "Infatuation" in wallet with interview tape [SAM 194]) 20

(see also Jeff Beck, Shotgun Express, Faces, Python Lee Jackson, Long John Baldry, Steamhammer, Ted Wood)

ROMAN STEWART

72	Songbird SB 1075	Changing Times (with Dave)/CRYSTALITES: Changing Times Version 12
73	Downtown DT 518	Try Me/BIG YOUTH: Rhythm Style..12
73	Techniques TE 932	Tonight I'm Staying Here (& Tennors)/Lady Love (& Tennors)............................5
75	Camel CA 2002	Wolverton Mountain/PITTERSON ALL STARS: Version 5
79	GGS 049	Don't Get Jumpy/GG ALL STARS: Dub Cut (12") 20
78	Pirate PIR 002	Herbalist/Version (12", various coloured vinyl) 35
78	Strong Like Sampson SLSD 06	Mr. Officer/Ain't Too Proud To Beg (12") 40
79	Thompson & Koots TK002	Rice & Peas/Breaking Up (12", with Linval Thompson) 40

SANDY STEWART

58	London HLE 8683	A Certain Smile/Kiss Me Richard 10
58	London HLE 8683	A Certain Smile/Kiss Me Richard (78) 12
63	Pye International 7N 25176	My Colouring Book/I Heard You Cried Last Night 5

SONNY STEWART & HIS SKIFFLE KINGS

| 57 | Philips PB 719 | The Northern Line/Black Jack (78)..20 |
| 57 | Philips PB 773 | Let Me Lie/Mama Don't Allow It (78) ....20 |

TINGA STEWART

71	Songbird SB 1048	Hear That Train/CRYSTALITES: Hear That Train - Version 7
72	Tropical AL 0018	A Brand New Me/BROWNS ALL STARS: Nice Version 6
74	Dragon DRA 1025	The Message/Dub 12
84	Londisc LDLP 003	KEY TO YOUR HEART (LP) 15

WINSTON STEWART

64	R&B JB 147	But I Do/MAYTALS: Four Seasons 35
64	Port-O-Jam PJ 4002	All Of My Life/How Many Times 30
65	Ska Beat JB 225	You Made Me Cry/CHECKMATES: Invisible Ska 40

(see also Andy & Clyde, Gaylads, Delano Stewart, Winston & Tonettes)

WYNN STEWART

| 60 | London HL 7087 | Wishful Thinking/Uncle Tom Got Caught (export issue).................................30 |

STEWPOT & SAVE THE CHILDREN FUND CHOIR

| 68 | MGM 1448 | I Like My Toys/Myrtles Birthday ....20 |

J.E. STICK & DRUMBAGO

| 61 | Blue Beat BB 64 | Boss Gill/COUNT OSSIE : Cassavuba ....20 |

STICKERS

| 71 | Bullet BU 492 | One Night Of Sin/Sin (Version) (both sides actually by Jackie Brown) ....5 |

(see also Jackie Brown)

STICK SHIFTS
| 80 | Chiswick CHIS 118 | Automobile/Parramatta Road (3 different p/s) | 12 |

ARBEE STIDHAM
| 70s | Mainstream MSL 1011 | A TIME FOR BLUES (LP) | 12 |

STIFF LITTLE FINGERS
78	Rigid Digits SRD-1	Suspect Device/Wasted Life (hand-made p/s, 500 only, red label with catalogue number on right-hand side)	100
78	Rigid Digits SRD-1	Suspect Device/Wasted Life (re-pressing, different machine-cut p/s, various colour labels/yellow labels)	18
78	Rough Trade RT 004	78 R.P.M./Alternative Ulster (p/s, A & B-sides reversed)	10
78	Rough Trade RT 004	Alternative Ulster/78 R.P.M. (p/s)	7
78	Rough Trade RT 006	Suspect Device/Wasted Life (reissue)	8
79	Rough Trade RT 015	Gotta Getaway/Bloody Sunday (p/s)	5
79	Chrysalis CHS 2368	Straw Dogs/You Can't Say Crap On The Radio (p/s)	7
81	SLFDJ1	Just Fade Away/Go For It (DJ promo)	10
82	Chrysalis CHSDJ 2580	Listen/Two Guitars Clash (p/s, jukebox issue)	12
89	Virgin SLFDJ1	St. Patrix, The Wild Rover/Johnny Was (DJ promo, unreleased as 7")	12
91	Essential ESSX 2007	Beirut Moon/Stand Up And Shout/Interview With Jake Burns (CD, limited edition)	30
89	Link 1203	THE LAST TIME (EP)	10
86	Strange Fruit SFPS 004	PEEL SESSIONS (12")	12
79	Rough Trade ROUGH 1	INFLAMMABLE MATERIAL (LP, with inner)	15
80	Chrysalis CHR 1270	NOBODY's HEROES (LP)	12
82	Chrysalis CHR 1400	NOW THEN... (LP, inner and poster)	12
88	Link LINK LP 026	LIVE AND LOUD (LP)	12
02	EMI Gold 7243 5 38560 21	LIVE IN ABERDEEN (CD)	35

(see also Billy Karloff & Extremes)

STIFFS
79	Dork UR 1	Standard English/S.C. Rip/Brookside Riot Squad (die-cut sleeve)	25
79	Dork UR 2	Inside Out/Kids On the Street (die cut sleeve or later Zonophone Z3 p/s)	20
80	Zonophone Z 14	Volume Control/Nothing To Lose (p/s)	10
80	Stiff BUY 86	Goodbye My Love/Magic Roundabout (p/s)	10
85	Dork UR 7(12)	The Young Guitars/Yer Under Attack (12", red p/s)	10
85	Dork UR 7(12)	The Young Guitars/Yer Under Attack (12", blue p/s)	8

STILETTOS
| 80 | Ariola ARO 200 | This Is The Way/Who Can It Be (p/s) | 20 |

STILL COOL
| 79 | Hit Run HITDD 22 | Insane Love/Stereo Version '79 (12") | 25 |

STILL LIFE
| 68 | Columbia DB 8345 | What Did We Miss/My Kingdom Cannot Lose | 70 |
| 71 | Vertigo 6360 026 | STILL LIFE (LP, gatefold sleeve, large swirl label) | 250 |

(see also Jon, Titus Groan)

STILL WATERS
| 78 | GTO 240 | Carry Me/World Of Fantasy | 5 |

STEPHEN STILLS
71	Atlantic 2091 046	Love The One You're With/To A Flame	5
71	Atlantic 2091 069	Sit Yourself Down/We Are Not Helpless	5
71	Atlantic 2091 117	Change Partners/Relaxing Town	5
71	Atlantic 2091 141	Marianne/Nothing To Do But Today	5
70	Atlantic 2401 004	STEPHEN STILLS (LP)	18
71	Atlantic 2401 013	STEPHEN STILLS 2 (LP, gatefold sleeve)	15
73	Atlantic K 40440	DOWN THE ROAD (LP)	15

(see also Buffalo Springfield, Al Kooper Mike Bloomfield & Stephen Stills, Crosby Stills Nash & Young, Manassas, Stills-Young Band)

STILLS-YOUNG BAND
76	Reprise K 14446	Long May You Run/12-8 Blues	5
76	Reprise K 14482	Like A Hurricane (edit)/Hold Back The Tears	5
76	Reprise K 54081	LONG MAY YOU RUN (LP)	15

(see also Stephen Stills, Manassas, Neil Young, Buffalo Springfield, Crosby Stills Nash & Young)

STILLWATER TRIO
| 70s | Sharon 330 | LIFE'S RAILROAD (LP) | 18 |

STING
82	A&M PARTY 1	Need Your Love So Bad/PAULINE BLACK : No Woman, No Cry (Promo)	10
85	A&M DREAMP 1	THE DREAM OF THE BLUE TURTLES (LP, picture disc, die-cut sleeve, insert)	15
91	A&M 397 171-2	ACOUSTIC LIVE IN NEWCASTLE (CD, box set with book)	18

(see also Police, Last Exit, [Fast Breeder &] Radio Actors, Newcastle Big Band)

STINGERS
| 72 | Upsetter US 395 | Preacher Man/UPSETTERS: Version | 12 |
| 72 | Explosion EX 2075 | Forward Up/UPSETTERS: Forward | 25 |

STING-RAYS
82	Big Beat SW 82	Dinosaurs/Math Of Trend/Another Cup Of Coffee/You're Gonna Miss Me (white label test pressing, 100 Club gig freebie, 80 only)	20
83	Big Beat SW 82	Dinosaurs/Math Of Trend/Another Cup Of Coffee/You're Gonna Miss Me (p/s)	5
84	Big Beat NS 95	Escalator/Loose Lip Synch Ship/Escalator (Instrumental) (p/s)	5
85	Big Beat NS 109	Don't Break Down/Don't Break Down (Version) (p/s)	5
87	Kaleidoscope Sound 7KS 102	Behind The Beyond/Perverted Justice (p/s)	10
86	Kaleidoscope Sound 102	BEHIND THE BEYOND (12" EP)	8
83	Big beat WIKM 16	DINOSAURS (LP)	12
84	Media Burn MB 1	LIVE RETALIATION (LP, white or black vinyl)	12
87	Kaleidoscope Sound KSLP 1	CRYPTIC AND COFFEE TIME (LP)	15
87	Big Beat WIK 61	THE ESSENTIAL EARLY STING-RAY RECORDINGS 1982 TO 1985 (LP)	15
87	Raucous FASTBUCK 1	LIVE & RAW (10")	15
88	Media Burn MB 18	GOODBYE TO ALL THAT - LIVE VOL. 2 (LP, red or black vinyl)	12

STINGRAYS (1)
80	Earache SRTS./80/CUS 809	Still In Love With You/Wasting Your Time/Couldn't Get It Right/Walking Down London Street (EP)	25
80	Fried Egg EGG 006	Countdown/Exceptions/Action (p/s)	20

STINGRAYS (2)
80	Fried Egg EGG 006	Countdown/Exceptions Action	40
82	Rocket XPRES 78	Radiator rock/Slap Bass Boogie (die cut sleeve)	8
81	Circus CIRC 0003	Never Do/Satellites	20

STINKY TOYS
77	Polydor 2056 630	Boozy Creed/Driver Blues (p/s)	15
77	Polydor 2393 174	STINKY TOYS (LP)	25

STIR
87	Spoonin SPOON 01	CHEEKY MONKEY (12", EP)	20

(PETER) LEE STIRLING (& BRUISERS)
63	Columbia DB 4992	My Heart Commands Me/Welcome Stranger (as Lee Stirling & Bruisers)	7
63	Parlophone R 5063	I Could If I Wanted To/Right From The Start (as Lee Stirling & Bruisers)	7
64	Parlophone R 5112	Now That I've Found You/I Believe (as Peter Lee Stirling & Bruisers)	7
64	Parlophone R 5158	Sad, Lonely And Blue/I'm Looking For Someone To Love (as Peter Lee Stirling & Bruisers)	10
64	Parlophone R 5198	Everything Will Be Alright/You'll Be Mine (as Peter Lee Stirling & Bruisers)	10
66	Decca F 12433	The Sweet And Tender Hold Of Your Love/Everybody Needs A Someone	7
66	Decca F 12535	Oh What A Fool/I'm Sportin' A New Baby	7
67	Decca F 12628	You Don't Live Twice/8.35 On The Dot	25
67	Decca F 12674	Goodbye Thimblemill Lane/Hey Conductor	12
69	MCA MU 1093	Big Sam/Mr. Average Man	6
70	MCA MK 5027	Goodbye Summer Girl/Judas In Blue	5

(see also Bruisers, Hungry Wolf)

STITCH
76	RCA 2526	La Maison De L'Amour/All Smoke & No Fire	5

GARY STITES
59	London HLL 8881	Lonely For You/Shine That Ring	25
59	London HLL 8881	Lonely For You/Shine That Ring (78)	15
59	London HLL 9003	Starry Eyed/Without Your Love	20
59	London HLL 9003	Starry Eyed/Without Your Love (78)	15
60	London HLL 9082	Lawdy, Miss Clawdy/Don't Wanna Say Goodbye	25

SONNY STITT
59	HMV 7EG 8532	SONNY STITT PLAYS JIMMY GIUFFRE (EP)	8
53	Esquire 20-013	SONNY STITT-BUD POWELL QUARTET (10" LP)	20
58	Esquire 32-049	S.P.J. JAZZ (LP, with Bud Powell & J.J. Johnson)	20
58	Columbia Clef 33CX 10114	NEW YORK JAZZ (LP)	20
59	Esquire 32-078	STITT'S BITS (LP)	20
59	HMV CLP 1280	ONLY THE BLUES (LP)	15
60	HMV CLP 1363	PERSONAL APPEARANCE (LP)	12
60	HMV CLP 1384	SONNY STITT WITH THE OSCAR PETERSON TRIO (LP)	12
61	HMV CLP 1420	BLOWS THE BLUES (LP, mono)	12
61	HMV CSD 1341	BLOWS THE BLUES (LP, stereo)	15
64	Chess CRL 4503	MY MAIN MAN (LP)	15
67	Marble Arch MAL 753	SONNY STITT (LP)	15

(see also Oscar Peterson, J.J. Johnson)

ALAN STIVELL
71	Philips 6009208	The Wind Of Ketta/Pop Plinn	8

STOCKER, GREENWOOD & FRIENDS
79	Changes CR1400	BILLY + NINE (LP)	25

(see also Slack Alice)

KARLHEINZ STOCKHAUSEN
65	CBS S72647	MIKROPHONIE I/MIKROPHONIE II (LP)	20
67	CBS 77209	COMPLETE PIANO MUSIC (2-LP, box set)	40
67	Vox STABY 615	PROZESSION (LP)	15
69	Vox VS 3184	STOCKHAUSEN (LP)	15
70	Deutsche Grammophon 2543003	STIMMUNG (LP)	20
74	Open University OP 15	TWENTIETH CENTURY MUSIC (LP)	25
75	Deutsche Grammophon 2530 582	PROZESSION (LP, reissue)	20

STOCK, HAUSEN & WALKMAN
96	Hot Air QRM SP 101	ORGAN TRANSPLANTS (EP)	10
97	Hot Air SPME 2	Buy Me/Sue Me (500 only on pink vinyl)	10
97	Hot Air SPME 2	Buy Me/Sue Me (300 on clear vinyl)	12
97	Hot Air SPME 2	Buy Me/Sue Me (200 on light blue vinyl)	15
99	Hot Air ALERT 01	Alert/Crash (500 only)	10
91	Hot Air SHWCASS 001	WHAT'S UP? (Cassette in small cereal box, various inserts)	20
95	Hot Air QRM CD 011	HAIRBALLS (CD, card sleeve)	18
96	Hot Air QRM LP 101	ORGAN TRANSPLANTS VOL 1 (LP)	15
00	Hot Air QRM LP 0000	ORGAN TRANSPLANTS VOL 2 (LP)	12

(see also Dummy Run)

STOCKHOLM MONSTERS
81	Factory FAC 41	Fairytales/Death Is Slowly (p/s)	15
82	Factory FAC 58	Happy Ever After/Soft Babies (p/s)	15
84	Factory FAC 107	All At Once (p/s)	10
87	Factory FAC 146	Partyline/Militia/Partylive (12")	8

STOCKINGTOPS
68	Toast TT 500	You're Never Gonna Get My Lovin'/You Don't Know What Love Is All About	18
68	CBS 3407	I Don't Ever Wanna Be Kicked By You/The World We Live In Is A Lonely Place	15

(see also Sue & Sunny, Sue & Sunshine, Myrtelles)

STOCKTON'S WING
78	Tara 2004	STOCKTON'S WING (LP, released in Irish Republic but imported into UK)	12

STOICS
68	RCA RCA 1745	Earth, Fire, Air And Water/Search Of The Sea	30

STOKES
65	London HLU 9955	Whipped Cream/Pie Crust	15

SIMON STOKES & NIGHTHAWKS
70	Elektra EKSN 45082	Voodoo Woman/Can't Stop Now	20

JOOP STOKKERMANS
71	Gemini GM 2017	THE MAGIC OF THE ARP SYNTHESISER (LP)	20

STOLEN POWER
81	Hornsey Rising POWER EP 1	The Wheel Is Turning/Family Snapshot/Sick And Tired/Little White Lies (p/s)	30

STOLEN PROPERTY
75	Live Wire SON 4012	Low Rider/Black Jack	8

RHET STOLLER (& HIS ECHOES)
60	Decca F 11271	Walk Don't Run/All Rhet	10
60	Decca F 11302	Chariot/Night Theme	10
63	Decca F 11738	Countdown/Over The Steppes (as Rhet Stoller & His Echoes)	10
64	Melodisc MEL 1595	Beat That/Treble Gold + One	15
64	Windsor PS 119	Caravan/Short Cut	20
64	Windsor PS 130	Ricochet/Knockout	20
66	Columbia DB 8013	Uncrowned King/Surf Ride (unissued, demos only)	20
69	Mosaic MOSAIC 1	SUNSHINE ANYTIME (EP, as Rhet Stoller & Music)	10
67	Coronet EC 101	THE INCREDIBLE RHET STOLLER (LP)	25

STOLLERS TEAM
72	Decca F13280	Sapporo/Mean	18

JACKIE STOLLINGS (& NASHVILLE BOYS)
62	Starlite ST45 092	Footsteps Of A Fool/And Then I Knew (B-side with Nashville Boys)	6

(See also Jess Conrad)

MORRIS STOLOFF (& COLUMBIA PICTURES ORCHESTRA)
56	Brunswick 05553	Moonglow/Theme From "Picnic"	7
56	Brunswick 05597	Theme From "The Solid Gold Cadillac"/Sweet Sue Just You	5
57	Brunswick 05666	Theme From "Fire Down Below"/Theme From "Full Of Life"	5
61	Warner Bros WB 48	Fanny/Panisse And Son	6

STOMPERS
62	Fontana H 385	Quarter To Four Stomp (Surf Stompin')/Foolish One	50

ALEXANDER STONE
70	Gemini GMS 003	I Try To Make You Good/Man In A Suitcase	10

CLIFFIE STONE & HIS ORCHESTRA
55	Capitol CL 14330	Barracuda/The Popcorn Song (with Billy Strange & Speedy West)	100
55	Capitol CL 14330	Barracuda/The Popcorn Song (with Billy Strange & Speedy West) (78)	20
56	Capitol CL 14666	Jingle Bells/Rudolph The Red Nosed Reindeer	5
58	Capitol CL 14928	Near You/Nobody's Darlin' But Mine	5
59	Capitol CL 14996	Blood On The Saddle/Cool Water	5
59	Capitol T 1080	THE PARTY'S ON ME (LP)	15

(see also Jeanne Gayle, Billy Strange)

ELLA STONE & MOSS
70s	Phoenix SNIX 128	The Prophet/Now Or Never	6

(see also Helen Shapiro, Al Saxon)

GEORGE STONE
65	Stateside SS 479	Hole In The Wall/My Beat	20

KIRBY STONE QUARTET/FOUR
56	Vogue Coral Q 72129	Honey Hush/Lassus Trombone	15
56	Vogue Coral Q 72129	Honey Hush/Lassus Trombone (78)	10
59	Philips PB 903	That "I Had A Dream, Dear" Rock/Sweet Nothings	5
63	Warner Bros WB 102	The Great Escape (March)/Fancy Dan	5
63	Warner Bros WB 118	Washington Square/Blue Guitar	7
59	London HA-A 2164	MAN, I FLIPPED WHEN I HEARD THE KIRBY STONE FOUR (LP)	15

MARK STONE
58	London HLR 8543	Ever Since I Met Lucy/The Stroll	70
58	London HLR 8543	Ever Since I Met Lucy/The Stroll (78)	30

SLY (& FAMILY) STONE
68	Columbia DB 8369	Dance To The Music/Let Me Hear It From You	100
68	Columbia DB 8369	Dance To The Music/Let Me Hear It From You (DJ copy)	150
68	Direction 58-3568	Dance To The Music/Let Me Hear It From You (reissue)	8
68	Direction 58-3707	M'Lady/Life	8
69	Direction 58-3938	Everyday People/Sing A Simple Song	8
69	Direction 58-4279	Stand!/I Want To Take You Higher	8
69	Direction 58-4471	Hot Fun In The Summertime/Fun	10
70	Direction 58-4782	Thank You (Falettinme Be Mice Elf Agin)/Everybody Is A Star	8
70	CBS 5054	I Want To Take You Higher/You Can Make It If You Try	6
71	Epic EPC 7632	Family Affair/Luv n' Haight	5
68	Direction 8-63412	DANCE TO THE MUSIC (LP)	25
68	Direction 8-63461	M'LADY (LP)	20
69	Direction 8-63655	STAND! (LP, CBS sleeve with Direction label)	20

STONE ANGEL
75	SSLP 04	STONE ANGEL (LP, private pressing, blue/silver label)	400
94	Acme AC 8008 LP	STONE ANGEL (LP, reissue, 500 only)	15

(see also Ken Saul)

STONEFIELD TRAMP
74   Acorn/Tramp CF 247   DREAMING (LP)..130
(see also Terry Friend, Rob Van Spyk)

STONE GRAPHICS
68   Parlophone R 5735   A Tale Of Long Ago/Travelling Man 12

STONEGROUND
71   Warner Bros K 16126   You Must Be One Of Us/It Takes A Lot To Laugh 5
71   Warner Bros K 46087   STONEGROUND (LP)...20
71   Warner Bros K 53999   FAMILY ALBUM (LP) 20

STONEGROUND BAND
70s   Nut   SUNSTRUCK!! (LP, stickered sleeve)...30

HARRY STONEHAM
76   One UP OU 2127   I FEEL GOOD, I FEEL FUNKY (LP)...15

HARRY STONEHAM & JOHNNY EYDEN
67   Tepee TPRLP 100   TWO GUYS TO FOLLOW (LP, mono [70s reissues credited soley to Harry Stoneham
                                  £15])...20

STONEHENGE MEN
62   HMV POP 981   Big Feet/Pinto...45

STONEHOUSE
71   RCA SF 8197   STONEHOUSE CREEK (LP, laminated front sleeve, orange label) 125

E.V. STONEMAN
63   London HA-B/SH-B 8089   E.V. STONEMAN AND THE STONEMAN FAMILY (LP) 12

STONE PONEYS
67   Capitol CL 15523   A Different Drum/I've Got To Know...10
(see also Linda Ronstadt)

STONE RISK
94   Stone Risk SR001   This Is Stone Risk (12")..8

STONE ROSES
SINGLES
85   Thin Line THIN 001   So Young/Tell Me (12", p/s, 1,200 only; beware of counterfeits!) 90
87   Black/Revolver 12 REV 36   Sally Cinnamon/Here It Comes/All Across The Sand (12", 'Printed In England' on
                                  rear p/s & no barcode, "All Across The Sands" listed on label; different
                                  mixes of 2 tracks to later reissue - increasingly difficult to find original) 30
88   Silvertone ORE 1   Elephant Stone/The Hardest Thing In The World (catalogue number in black print
                                  on rear of p/s)..8
88   Silvertone ORET 1   Elephant Stone (4.48)/Elephant Stone (7" Version) (3.00)/Full Fathom Five/The
                                  Hardest Thing In The World (12", p/s, cat. no. in black print on rear of p/s)
                                  (unique recording of Full Fathom Five on original pressing)..........................20
89   Silvertone ORE 2   Made Of Stone/Going Down (p/s, cat. no. in black print on rear of p/s) 7
89   Silvertone ORET 2   Made Of Stone/Going Down/Guernica (12", p/s, catalogue number in black print on
                                  rear of p/s) 20
89   Silvertone ORET 6   She Bangs The Drums/Mersey Paradise/Standing Here (12" with art print, stickered p/s) 8
89   Silvertone OREX 6   She Bangs The Drums/Standing Here (p/s, with postcard, 3,000 only)............10
89   Silvertone OREZ 6   She Bangs The Drums/Mersey Paradise/Standing Here (12", p/s with colour print (I
                                  Wanna Be Adored cover), 5,000 only)..15
89   Silvertone ORE 13   What The World Is Waiting For/Fools Gold 4.15 (paper label, with postcard
                                  stickered p/s credits "What The World Is Waiting For").............................8
89   Silvertone ORET 13   What The World Is Waiting For/Fools Gold 9.23 (12", stickered p/s credits What
                                  The World Is Waiting For, with print)..12
89   Black/Revolver 12 REV 36   Sally Cinnamon/Here It Comes/All Across The Sand (12" 'Printed in W Germany' on
                                  rear p/s – barcode) 8
89   Black/Revolver REV 36   Sally Cinnamon/Here It Comes (p/s)..8
90   Silvertone ORE 1   Elephant Stone (7" Version)/The Hardest Thing In The World (catalogue number in
                                  red print on rear of p/s) 8
90   Silvertone ORE 2   Made Of Stone/Going Down (p/s, cat. no. in blue print on rear of p/s) 5
90   Fierce FRIGHT 044   SPIKE ISLAND EP (fan interviews, P.A. announcements & fireworks, with
                                  cigarette, badge, bag of grass & banana sweet).....................................15
90   Silvertone OREZ 13   Fools Gold (The Top Won Mix!)/(The Bottom Won Mix!) (12") 12
90   Silvertone ORE 17   One Love/Something's Burning (p/s, with print) 8
90   Silvertone ORET 17   One Love/Something's Burning (12", p/s, with print) 8
91   Silvertone ORE 31   I Wanna Be Adored (3.28)/Where Angels Play (p/s) 6
91   Silvertone ORET 31   I Wanna Be Adored (4.52)/Where Angels Play/Sally Cinnamon (live at the Hacienda)
                                  (12" p/s)...10
91   Silvertone OREZ 31   I Wanna Be Adored (4.52)/Where Angels Play/Sally Cinnamon (live at the Hacienda)
                                  (12", stickered p/s with print) 18
92   Silvertone ORE 35   Waterfall (7" Version 3.31)/One Love (7" Version 3.40) (p/s).....................8
92   Silvertone OREZT 35   Waterfall (12" Version 5.23)/One Love (Adrian Sherwood 12" Version 7.10) (12",
                                  p/s with print) 15
92   Silvertone ORE 40   I Am The Resurrection (Pan And Scan Radio Version)/I Am The Resurrection (Highly
                                  Resurrected Dub) (p/s)...6
92   Silvertone ORET 40   I Am The Resurrection (Extended 19:9 Ratio Club Mix)/(Original LP Version)/Fools
                                  Gold (Bottom Won Mix) (12", with print) 30
92   Silvertone ORET 40   I Am The Resurrection (Extended 19:9 Ratio Club Mix)/(Original LP Version)/Fools
                                  Gold (Bottom Won Mix) (12", without print) 10
93   Silvertone ORECD 37   So Young/Tell Me (CD, from "CD Singles Collection")............................10
92   Silvertone SRBX 2   12" SINGLES COLLECTION (10 x 12" singles box set, numbered 1,000 only)........170
92   Silvertone SRBX 1   COMPACT DISC SINGLES COLLECTION (8 x CD singles box set, 1,000 only)......70
95   Geffen GFST 87   Ten Storey Love Song/Moses/Ride On (12", stickered/numbered p/s) 20
95   Geffen GFST 22060   Begging You (Album Version)/(Chic Mix)/(Cox's Ultimatum Mix)/(Stone Corporation
                                  Vox) (12" p/s with art print) 15
95   Geffen WGFSX 22060   Begging You (Album Version)/(Chic Mix)/(Stone Corporation Vox)/(Young American
                                  Primitive Remix) (12", no p/s) 8

ALBUMS : LPS
89   Silvertone ORE LP 502   THE STONE ROSES (LP, original pressing, embossed sleeve with gold lettering)........30
89   Silvertone ORE LP 502   THE STONE ROSES (LP, original pressing, not embossed gold lettering)............20
91   Silvertone OREZ LP 502   THE STONE ROSES (2-LP, reissue, numbered gatefold sleeve with silver lettering)........20
91   Silvertone OREZ CD 502   THE STONE ROSES (CD, reissue, numbered with silver lettering)...................18
92   Silvertone ORE LP 521   TURNS INTO STONE (LP, original pressing)...20

STONE'S MASONRY

94	Geffen GEF 24503	SECOND COMING (2-LP, original pressing, gatefold) 30
95	Silvertone ORE LP 535	THE COMPLETE STONE ROSES (2-LP) 20
95	Silvertone OREZ CD 535	THE COMPLETE STONE ROSES (2-CD includes two rare tracks on bonus disc)....................30
96	Garage Flower GARAGE LP 1	GARAGE FLOWER (LP, with print) 40
96	Garage Flower GARAGE LP 1	GARAGE FLOWER (LP, without print) 20
99	Geffen/Simply Vinyl SVLP 111	SECOND COMING (2-LP, limited edition, gatefold, heavy duty 180g vinyl)..................18
99	Silvertone 0591242	THE STONE ROSES - 10th Anniversary Edition (2-CD ltd edition in slipcase, enhanced with videos, booklet & sleeve notes) 25
10	Silvertone Sony/BMG 88697694171	THE STONE ROSES (LP, 1000 only, numbered, 2010 Record Store day release with 6 art prints) 30

PROMOS

85	Thin Line THIN 001	So Young/Tell Me (12" promo (pale) pink label test pressing, 100 pressed, this price without press pack)..250
85	Thin Line THIN 001	So Young/Tell Me (12" promo (pale) pink label test press) 100 pressed (in Cartel sleeve with press pack) 400
89	Silvertone ORE DJ 6	She Bangs The Drums (7" promo)...15
89	Silvertone ORE DJ T 13	Fools Gold 9.53/ What The World Is Waiting For (12" promo, b-side white label)...............20
89	Silvertone ORE DJ 13	Fools Gold 4.15/ What The World Is Waiting For (7" promo) 10
90	Silvertone ORE DJ T 17	One Love/Something's Burning (12" promo, b-side white label)............................10
90	Silvertone ORE DJ 17	One Love (7" edit) /Something's Burning (7" edit) (7" promo)..............................10
92	Silvertone ORE T DJ 34	Waterfall (12" Version 5.23)/One Love (Adrian Sherwood 12" Version 7.10) (12" promo) ...15
90	Silvertone STONE ONE	Fools Gold (A Guy Called Gerald Remix)/Elephant Stone (DJ Mix) (12", white label) this is actually a bootleg recording by Hard Tymez Productions 18
94	Geffen STONEPRO1	Love Spreads (Radio Edit, Album version) (CD promo, no p/s) 20
95	Silvertone OREDJ 71	Fools Gold (The Tall Paul Remix)/Fools Gold 9.23/Fools Gold (Cricklewood Ballroom Mix) (12")..8
95	Geffen WGFSX 22060	Begging You (Album Version)/(Chic Mix)/(Stone Corporation Vox)/(Young American Primitive Remix) (12", no p/s, with press sheet) 10

(see also Ian Brown, John Squire)

STONE'S MASONRY

| 66 | Purdah 45-3504 | Flapjacks/Hot Rock (99 copies only) ....200 |

(see also Action, Mighty Baby, Savoy Brown)

STONE TEMPLE PILOTS

| 92 | Atlantic 7567824 | CORE (LP) ....40 |
| 94 | Atlantic 82607 | PURPLE - 12 GRACIOUS MELODIES (LP, purple vinyl)....................................40 |

STONE THE CROWS

70	Polydor 2066 060	Mad Dogs & Englishmen/Sad Mary 5
72	Polydor 2058 301	Good Time Girl/On The Highway 5
70	Polydor 2425 017	STONE THE CROWS (LP) 50
70	Polydor 2425 042	ODE TO JOHN LAW (LP, gatefold sleeve) 30
71	Polydor 2425 071	TEENAGE LICKS (LP, gatefold sleeve) 25
72	Polydor 2391 043	ONTINUOUS PERFORMANCE (LP)..20

(see also White Trash)

STONEY BROOK PEOPLE

| 69 | CBS 4538 | Easy To Be Hard/There's Tomorrow ....30 |

STONEY & MEAT LOAF

71	Rare Earth RES 103	What You See Is What You Get/The Way You Do The Things You Do 12
79	Prodigal PROD 10	What You See Is What You Get/The Way You Do The Things You Do (reissue).............8
72	Rare Earth SRE 3005	STONEY AND MEAT LOAF (LP)...25
79	Prodigal PDL 2010	MEAT LOAF (FEATURING STONEY & MEAT LOAF) (LP, revised reissue of "Stoney And Meat Loaf" with different tracks) 15
86	Motown ZL 72217	MEAT LOAF (FEATURING STONEY & MEAT LOAF) (LP, 2nd reissue) 12

(see also Meat Loaf)

STOOGES

69	Elektra EKS 74051	THE STOOGES (LP, red label)..200
70	Elektra 2410 009	FUN HOUSE (LP, red label)..250
73	CBS 65586	RAW POWER (LP, as Iggy & Stooges, no name on front cover, plain orange label, with inner sleeve)..30
77	Elektra K 42032	THE STOOGES (LP, reissue, 'butterfly' label) 12
77	Elektra K 42051	FUN HOUSE (LP, reissue, 'butterfly' label)...12

(see also Iggy Pop)

STOP

| 80 | Elite CAB 101 | I Can Feel It/Lauwata (12")..8 |

STOPOUTS

| 78 | Skeleton LYN 5912 | Strange Thoughts/Just For You And Me (p/s) ....15 |

STOREY SISTERS

| 58 | London HLU 8571 | Bad Motorcycle/Sweet Daddy ....100 |
| 58 | London HLU 8571 | Bad Motorcycle/Sweet Daddy (78)...40 |

STORM/CUTMASTER SWIFT

| 91 | White SOLID001 | Playing The Field/Live In Spain (12") ....60 |

STORM/MIGHTY ETHNICZ

| 91 | Bite It! BITE 3 | You're Out There (12") ....10 |

BILLY STORM

59	Philips PB 916	I've Come Of Age/This Is Always 10
59	Philips PB 916	I've Come Of Age/This Is Always (78) 10
60	London HLK 9236	Sure As You're Born/In The Chapel In The Moonlight 10

DANNY STORM (& STROLLERS)

62	Piccadilly 7N 35025	Honest I Do/Sad But True (in p/s) 15
62	Piccadilly 7N 35025	Honest I Do/Sad But True...10
62	Piccadilly 7N 35053	Just You/I Told You So 10
62	Piccadilly 7N 35091	I Just Can't Fool My Heart/Thinking Of You 12
63	Piccadilly 7N 35143	Say You Do/Let The Sunshine In (as Danny Storm & Strollers) 15

GALE STORM

| 56 | London HLD 8222 | I Hear You Knocking/Never Leave Me ....50 |

56	London HLD 8232	Memories Are Made Of This/A Teen-Age Prayer 30
56	London HLD 8283	Ivory Tower/I Ain't Gonna Worry 30
56	London HLD 8286	Why Do Fools Fall In Love/I Walk Alone 30
56	London HL 7008	Why Do Fools Fall In Love/I Walk Alone (export issue) 20
56	London HLD 8311	Don't Be That Way (Please Listen To Me)/Tell Me Why..25
56	London HLD 8329	A Heart Without A Sweetheart/Now Is The Hour 15
57	London HLD 8393	Lucky Lips/On Treasure Island 30
57	London HLD 8413	Orange Blossoms/My Heart Belongs To You 15
57	London HLD 8424	Dark Moon/A Little Too Late 15
58	London HLD 8570	Love Theme From "Farewell To Arms"/I Get That Feeling 12
58	London HLD 8632	You/Angry 10
56	London HB-D 1056	PRESENTING GALE STORM (10" LP) 60
58	London HA-D 2104	SENTIMENTAL ME (LP) 40

RORY STORM & HURRICANES

| 63 | Oriole CB 1858 | Dr. Feelgood/I Can Tell ....45 |
| 64 | Parlophone R 5197 | America/Since You Broke My Heart ....25 |

(see also Keef Hartley, Paddy Klaus & Gibson)

STORMCLOUDS

| 96 | STORM 02 | NIGHTMARES IN THE SKY (LP, 500 only) ....12 |

ROBB STORME (& WHISPERS)

60	Decca F 11282	1000, 900 And When/I Don't Need Your Love Anymore 6
61	Decca F 11313	Music/Five Minutes More (as Robb Storme & Whispers) 6
61	Decca F 11364	Near You/Lonely Town (as Robb Storme & Whispers) 6
61	Decca F 11388	Transistor Sister/Earth Angel 12
62	Decca F 11432	Pretty Hair And Angel Eyes/A Mile Of Broken Hearts..8
63	Pye 7N 15515	Sixteen Years Ago Tonight/Surprise Surprise 7
63	Piccadilly 7N 35133	Happens Ev'ryday/Surprise Surprise 6
63	Piccadilly 7N 35160	To Know Her Is To Love Her/Bu Bop A Lu Bop A Lie..6
65	Pye 7N 15819	Love Is Strange/Shy Guy 10
65	Columbia DB 7756	Where Is My Girl?/Double Oh Seven (as Robb Storme & Whispers) 10
66	Columbia DB 7993	Here Today/Don't Cry (as Robb Storme Group) 20
62	Decca DFE 6700	WHEELS (EP) 100

STORMER

| 78 | Ring O' 2017 113 | My Home Town/Shake It Baby (in promo p/s) ....70 |
| 78 | Ring O' 2017 113 | My Home Town/Shake It Baby ....40 |

STORMQUEEN

| 82 | Real Fire RF 001 | Come Silent To The World/Raising The Roof (no p/s, 500 only)..400 |

STORMTROOPER (1)

| 78 | Solent SS 047 | I'm A Mess/It's Not Me (in stamped plain sleeve with insert)..30 |
| 78 | Solent SS 047 | I'm A Mess/It's Not Me ....12 |

STORMTROOPER (2)

| 80 | Heartbeat BEAT 1 | Pride Before A Fall/Still Comin' Home (p/s) ....25 |

STORMY PETREL

| 71 | CBS 7271 | Hello Hello Hello/The Light Of Day ....10 |

STORYTELLER (1)

71	CBS 7182	Remarkable/Laugh That Came Too Soon 5
70	Transatlantic TRA 220	STORYTELLER (LP, gatefold sleeve, white/lilac label, 't' logo) 60
71	Transatlantic TRA 232	MORE PAGES (LP, textured sleeve) 35

(see also Johnny Neal & Starliners, Terry Durham, Other Two, Andy Bown)

STORYTELLER (2)

| 79 | Alladin MDS 1002 | Just Another Cloud In The Sky/Weatherman ....20 |

STORYTELLER (3)

| 85 | Storyteller ZELSP 438 | Mystery Girl (p/s) ....50 |

LALLY STOTT

| 71 | Philips 6025029 | Jakaranda/Love Is Free Love Is Blind ....8 |
| 71 | Philips 6323 006 | CHIRPY CHIRPY CHEEP CHEEP (LP) ....12 |

WALLY STOTT ORCHESTRA/CHORUS

| 60 | Pye 7N 15271 | The Unforgiven/Mr. Lucky..6 |

BABE STOVALL

| 76 | Southern Sound SD 203 | THE BABE STOVALL STORY (LP) ....12 |

STOWAWAYS

| 79 | Supermusic SUP 27 | I Wanna Be Me/My Friends/You'll Tie Me Down (p/s)..25 |

STP 23

| 89 | Wau! Mr. Modo WMS 001R | Let Jimi Take Over/Let Jimi Take Over (Remix By Youth) (12", p/s)..10 |

STRAFE FÜR REBELLION

| 80s | Touch TO 6 | SANTA MARIA (LP, with inner)..15 |

STRAIGHT EIGHT

78	Eel Pie EPS 003	Modern Times/Tell Me If You Wanna Bleed (p/s) 10
79	Warner Bros K 18049	Spread It Around/It Ain't Easy/Oh No (p/s) 5
80	Logo DEAL 1	I'm Sorry/Satisfied (p/s) 6
80	Logo DEAL 2	Tombstone/On The Rebound (p/s) 5
82	Logo GO 416	Tomorrow/Faded Stars/You Are What You Are (with p/s)..10
82	Logo GO 416	Tomorrow/Faded Stars/You Are What You Are 8
79	Eel Pie EPRP 001	NO NOISE FROM HERE (LP) 15
80	Logo LOGO 1032	STRAIGHT TO THE HEART (LP) 12
80	Logo FLUSH 1	SHUFFLE'N'CUT (LP) 12

STRAIGHT UP

| 80 | Rok XX/XIX | One Out All Out/JUSTIN CASE: T.V. (die-cut company sleeve) ....10 |

STRAIGHT CORNERS

| 80 | SRTS/80/CUS 809 | Legal Executive/Berlin Wall (p/s)..15 |

STRAIGHTSHOOTER
79	Strolling Bone S 79 CUS 398	Straightshooter/She's So Fine (no p/s)	120

NICK STRAKER
83	Pinnacle PIN 100T	Turn Me Down/We Can Still Be Friends (12")	8

PETER STRAKER
69	Polydor 56345	Breakfast In Bed/The Right To Cry	5
69	Polydor 56362	I Never Thought I'd Fall In Love/Birdie Told Me	5
70	Polydor 2058 039	Carousel/It's A New Day	5
74	RCA LPBO 5011	From The Underworld/Love Motion	8
77	EMI EMI 2700	Ragtime Piano Joe/Saddest Clown	10
78	EMI EMI 2758	Jackie/I've Been To Hell And Back	12
77	EMI EMC 3204	THIS ONE'S ON ME (LP)	12

STRAND
80	Yob YOB 001	Here Today Gone Tomorrow/Changing World/POSITIVE SIGNALS: Mesdia Man/Only For A Day (split EP, p/s)	15

STRANDSMEN
67	Philips BF 1572	I Know/Stay Close To Me	10

BILLY STRANGE (& CHALLENGERS)
61	London HLG 9321	Where Your Arms Used To Be/Sadness Done Come	6
64	Vocalion V-N 9228	The James Bond Theme/007 Theme	15
64	Vocalion V-N 9231	Goldfinger/"Munsters" Theme	10
66	Vocalion V-N 9257	Thunderball/"Ninth Man" Theme	10
66	Vocalion V-N 9259	Get Smart/Run Spy, Run	15
67	Vocalion V-N 9289	A Few Dollars More Theme/You Only Live Twice	10
63	Vocalion VA/SVN 8022	12-STRING GUITAR (LP)	15
64	Vocalion VAN 8026	MR GUITAR (LP)	15
64	Vocalion VAN/SAVN 8032	THE JAMES BOND THEME (LP)	20
65	Vocalion VAN/SAVN 8038	GOLDFINGER (LP)	20
65	Vocalion VAN/SAVN 8042	ENGLISH HITS OF '65 (LP)	15
65	Vocalion VAN/SAVN 8045	STRANGE PLAYS THE HITS (LP)	15

(see also Cliffie Stone)

STRANGE BROTHERS SHOW
70	Polydor 2001-116	Right On/Shakey Jakes	15

GILES STRANGE
66	Stateside SS 570	Watch The People Dance/You're Goin' Up To The Bottom	70

STEVE STRANGE
82	Palace PALACE 1	In The Year 2525/Strange Connexions (white label, unreleased)	30
82	Palace PALACE 1	In The Year 2525/Strange Connexions (p/s, available separately)	20

(see also Visage)

STRANGE CRUISE
86	EMI 12EMI 5549	Rebel Blue Rocker/Love Addiction (12", p/s)	10
86	EMI EMC 3513	STRANGE CRUISE (LP)	18

STRANGE DAYS (1)
75	Retreat RTS 263	Monday Morning/Joe Soap	5
75	Retreat RTL 6005	NINE PARTS TO THE WIND (LP, lyric inner sleeve, blue label)	25

STRANGE DAYS (2)
83	Powerstation OHM 1	Within These Walls/Swimming Into The Doctor	6

STRANGE FOX
73	Parlophone R5978	Rock 'N' Roll Band/Tamarin Girl	15
70	Parlophone R5876	Bring It On HOme/Time And Tide	30

STRANGE FRUIT
71	Village Thing VTSX 1001	Cut Across Shorty/Shake That Thing	25

STRANGELOVE
94	Food FOODLP 11	TIME FOR THE REST OF YOUR LIFE (2-LP, numbered)	20
96	Food FOODLP 15	LOVE AND OTHER DEMONS (LP, with 12 page booklet)	20
97	Food FOODLPD 24	STRANGELOVE (2-LP)	20

STRANGELOVES
65	Stateside SS 446	I Want Candy/It's About My Baby	25
65	Immediate IM 007	Cara-Lin/Roll On Mississippi	30
66	London HLZ 10020	Night Time/Rhythm Of Love	35
66	London HLZ 10063	Hand Jive/I Gotta Dance	12
69	London HLZ 10238	Honey Do/I Wanna Do It	15

(see also Beach-Nuts)

STRANGE MOVEMENTS
79	Good Vibrations GOT 5	Dancing In The Ghetto/Amuse Yourself (foldout p/s)	25

STRANGER (COLE)
63	Blue Beat BB 165	Rough And Tough (with Duke Reid Band)/DUKE REID BAND: The Mood I Am In	20
63	Blue Beat BB 195	Miss Reamer/RICO & HIS BLUES BAND: Blues From The Hills	20

(see also Stranger Cole)

STRANGER (COLE) & GLADY (ANDERSON)
67	Island WI 3128	Love Me Today/Over Again	60
68	Amalgamated AMG 806	Seeing Is Knowing/ROY SHIRLEY: Music Is The Key	25
71	Clandisc CLA 230	Tomorrow (as Stranger & Gladdy)/DYNAMITES: Tomorrow Version	7
71	Supreme SUP 227	My Application (as Stranger & Gladdy)/TADDY & DIAMONDS: Oh No, My Baby	7
73	Count Shelley CS 015	Don't Give Up The Fight (as Stranger & Gladdy)/TIDALS: Stand Firm	5
73	Dragon DRA 1014	Conqueror/Conqueror (Instrumental Version)	5

(see also Stranger Cole, Gladdy & Followers, Gladstone Anderson, Gladdy & Stranger, Charlie Kelly)

STRANGER (COLE) & HORTENSE (ELLIS)
74	Count Shelley CS 049	Mocking Bird/Corra Bella Baby	6

STRANGER (COLE) & KEN (BOOTHE)
63	R&B JB 120	Thick In Love/All Your Friends	30

(see also Stranger Cole, Ken Boothe)

STRANGER (COLE) & PATSY (TODD)
63	Blue Beat BB 171	When I Call Your Name/Take My Heart (with Duke Reid All Stars)	20
63	Island WI 113	Senor And Senorita/DON DRUMMOND: Snowboy	30
64	Island WI 141	Oh Oh I Need You/DON DRUMMOND: J.F.K.'s Memory	35
64	Island WI 144	Tom, Dick And Harry/We Two, Happy People	20
64	Island WI 152	Yeah Yeah Baby/BABA BROOKS: Boat Ride	25
64	Island WI 160	Miss B/Thing Come To Those Who Wait	20
65	Black Swan WI 462	Hey Little Girl/CORNELL CAMBELL: Make Hay	30
66	Rio R 81	Give Me One More Chance/Fire In Cornfield	18
66	Doctor Bird DB 1050	Give Me The Right/Tonight	30
67	Doctor Bird DB 1084	Tell It To Me/Your Photograph	40
67	Doctor Bird DB 1087	Down The Trainlines/Sing And Pray	40
69	Escort ES 807	My Love/SWEET CONFUSION: Windsor Castle	15
69	Escort ES 811	Why Did You/Do You Remember	8

(see also Stranger Cole, Patsy)

STRANGERS (WITH MIKE SHANNON)
64	Philips BF 1335	One And One Is Two/Time And The River (as Strangers with Mike Shannon)	40
64	Philips BF 1378	Do You Or Don't You/What Can I Do	8

(see also Shadows)

STRANGERS
67	Pye 7N 17240	Look Out (Here Comes Tomorrow)/Mary Mary	40
67	Pye 7N 17351	You Didn't Have To Be So Nice/Daytime Turns To Night	15
68	Pye 7N 17585	I'm On An Island/Step Inside	20

STRANGER THAN FICTION
80s	Ellie Jay EJSP 9301	Into The Void/Darkness (p/s)	25
87	Constitution CON 3T	Prelude/Is She In Love With Love/The Realization (12", p/s)	25

STRANGE STONE
77	Own label DER 1399	STRANGE STONE (LP, private pressing, numbered sleeve with insert, 255 only)	500

STRANGEWAYS
78	Real ARE 2	Show Her you Care/You're On Your Own (p/s)	20
79	Real ARE 7	Wasting Time/All The Sounds Of Fear (p/s)	30

STRANGLERS
SINGLES
77	United Artists UP 36211	(Get A) Grip (On Yourself)/London Lady (card p/s)	5
77	United Artists UP 36248	Peaches/Go Buddy Go ('group' p/s with 'blackmail' lettering, withdrawn)	650
77	United Artists UP 36248	Peaches/Go Buddy Go ('peach' p/s)	7
77	United Artists UP 36277	Something Better Change/Straighten Out (p/s)	5
77	United Artists UP 36300	No More Heroes/In The Shadows (p/s, 'wreath' label)	6
80	United Artists 12-BP 344	Bear Cage (Extended)/Shah Shah A Go Go (Extended) (12", p/s)	10
82	Epic EPCA A-2893	The European Female/Savage Breast (p/s)	5
82	Epic EPCA 11-2893	The European Female/Savage Breast (picture disc)	5
84	Epic A 4738	Skin Deep/Here And There ('skin-feel' p/s, with 'Skin Deep' tattoo, 10,000 only)	6
84	Epic EPC GA 4921	No Mercy/In One Door/Hot Club (Riot Mix)/Head On The Line (gatefold)	6
84	Epic WA 4921	No Mercy/In One Door (ear-shaped picture disc)	6
86	Epic 650 055-0	Nice In Nice/Since You Went Away (shaped picture disc)	6
86	Epic SOLAR P1	Always The Sun/Norman Normal (shaped picture disc)	7
86	Epic SOLAR D1	Always The Sun/Norman Normal//Nice In Nice/Since You Went Away (double pack, shrinker & stickered)	8
86	Epic HUGE P1	Big In America/Dry Day (shaped picture disc)	7
86	Epic HUGE D1	Big In America/Dry Day//Always The Sun/Norman Normal (double pack, shrinkwrapped & stickered)	8
87	Epic SHEIK P1	Shakin' Like A Leaf/Hit Man (shaped picture disc)	7
88	Epic VICE 1	All Day And All Of The Night/¡Viva Vlad! ('Monica Coughlan' p/s, withdrawn sold via fan club)	7
88	Epic VICE P1	All Day And All Of The Night/¡Viva Vlad! (shaped picture disc)	5
89	Liberty EMR 84	Grip '89 - (Get A) Grip (On Yourself)/Waltzinblack (p/s, red vinyl with poster in gatefold PVC wallet, 5,000 only)	5

ALBUMS : LPS
77	United Artists UAG 30045	STRANGLERS IV - RATTUS NORVEGICUS (LP, 10,000 with 7" Choosey Susie/"Peasant In The Big Shitty" (Live At The Nashville, 12/76) [FREE 3, orange p/s,"What Do You Expect..." in run-off groove], some with sticker)	35
77	United Artists UAG 30045	STRANGLERS IV - RATTUS NORVEGICUS (LP)	12
78	United Artists UAK 30222	BLACK AND WHITE (LP, 75,000 with white vinyl 7" "Walk On By"/"Tits"/Mean To Me [FREE 9, black die-cut sleeve & card insert], mispressed on blue or beige vinyl)	65
78	United Artists UAK 30222	BLACK AND WHITE (LP, 75,000 with white vinyl 7" "Walk On By"/"Tits"/Mean To Me [FREE 9, black die-cut sleeve & card insert])	12
79	United Artists UAG 30262	THE RAVEN (LP, 20,000 with 3-D cover, cartoon on inner sleeve)	20
82	Liberty LBG 30353	THE COLLECTION '77-82 (LP, withdrawn plastic logo sleeve)	25
83	Epic EPC 25237	FELINE (LP, with bonus 1-sided 7" "Aural Sculpture" [XPS 167])	12
86	Epic EPC 26648	DREAMTIME (LP, picture disc)	12
92	United Artists SPEAKDLP 101	EARLY YEARS 74-75-76 RARE LIVE & UNRELEASED (2-LP, orange/green vinyl)	25

PROMOS : FREEBIES, PROMOS & MISCELLANEA
79	United Artists UAG 30262	THE RAVEN (LP, mispressing, 2nd side plays country & western [B-side matrix: UAK 30263])	25
82	Liberty LBG 30353	THE COLLECTION '77-82 (LP, Stranglers' own concept sleeve, unissued)	0
75	(no cat no)	My Young Dreams/Wasted (existence unconfirmed)	150
77	United Artists FREE 4	Peaches (radio version)/Go Buddy Go (promo only, p/s)	750
77	United Artists FREE 4	Peaches (radio version)/Go Buddy Go (promo only, no p/s)	120
77	United Artists UP 36262	Mony Mony/Mean To Me (p/s, as Celia And The Mutations)	7
77	United Artists UP 36277	Something Better Change/Straighten Out	25
77	United Artists FREE 8	No More Heroes (1-sided radio edit, promo only)	70
77	United Artists UP 36300	No More Heroes (1-sided, misprinted "No More Stheroes")	25
77	United Artists UP 36300	No More Heroes/In The Shadows (p/s, stamped, misprinted "No More Stheroes")	25

78	United Artists UP 36429	Walk On By (Promo Edit)/Old Codger/Tank	25
79	United Artists UA STR 1 DJ	Don't Bring Harry/HUGH CORNWELL: Wired (45rpm, promo only)	20
79	United Artists (no cat. no.)	Two Sunspots (unreleased)	30
80	Stranglers Info Service SIS 001	Tomorrow Was The Hereafter/Bring On The Nubiles (Cocktail Version) (numbered p/s, label has "Nublies")	8
82	SIS/Liberty FREE 3	Peasant In The Big Shitty (Live At The Nashville, 12/76)/Choosey Susie (fan club reissue, black p/s, with 'Ello 'Elen" in run-off groove)	5
82	Epic EPC A2893	The European Female (In Celebration Of)/(Promo Edit)	10
82	Liberty BP 410	La Folie (Promo Edit)/Waltzinblack	10
82	SIS/Liberty UP 36350	5 Minutes/Rok It To The Moon (reissue)	5
82	SIS/Liberty UP 36429	Walk On By/Old Codger/Tank (reissue, 33rpm)	5
82	SIS/Liberty FREE 18	Mony Mony/Mean To Me (reissue, as Celia & the Mutations)	5
78	United Artists UP 36248	Peaches/Go Buddy Go (p/s, mispressing, B-side plays Buzzcocks' "Oh Shit")	60
78	United Artists FREE 9	Walk On By/Mean To Me/Tits (EP [free with LP U.A. UAK 30222], mispressing, black die-cut sleeve & card insert, blue/clear vinyl)	30
78	United Artists FREE 9	Walk On By/Mean To Me/Tits (EP [free with LP U.A. UAK 30222], mispressing, black die-cut sleeve & card insert, pink/clear vinyl)	15
78	United Artists UP 36379	Nice 'N' Sleazy/Shut Up (p/s, mispressing, B-side plays tracks by other artist)	30
81	Liberty BP 393	Just Like Nothing On Earth/Maninwhite (p/s, mispressing, plays A-side both sides)	20
82	United Artists BP 407	Golden Brown/Love 30 (B-side plays "Everybody Salsa")	20

STRAPPS

76	Harvest SHSP 4055	STRAPPS (LP)	12

STRAPS

80	Donut DONUT 1	Just Can't Take Anymore/New Age (p/s)	6
82	Donut DONUT 3	Brixton/No Liquor (p/s)	8
83	Cyclops CYC 2	THE STRAPS ALBUM (LP)	15

(see also Public Image Ltd.)

STRATEGY

82	Ebony EBON 7	Technical Overflow/Astral Planes (in p/s)	60
82	Ebony EBON 7	Technical Overflow/Astral Planes	50

STRATE JACKET

70s	Wessex	You're A Hit (stamped plain sleeve)	12

STRATUS

85	Steel Trax STEEL 31001	THROWING SHAPES (LP)	18

(see also Grand Prix, Uriah Heep, Iron Maiden, Praying Mantis)

STRAWBERRY ALARM CLOCK

67	Pye International 7N 25436	Incense And Peppermints/The Birdman Of Alkatrash	25
68	Pye International 7N 25446	Tomorrow/Birds In My Tree	20
68	Pye International 7N 25456	Sit With The Guru/Pretty Song From Psych-Out	20
69	MCA MU 1080	Good Morning Starshine/Me And The Township	10
68	NPL 28106	INCENSE AND PEPPERMINTS (LP, mono)	150
68	Pye Intl. NSPL 28106	INCENSE AND PEPPERMINTS (LP, stereo)	100

STRAWBERRY CHILDREN

67	Liberty LBF 15012	Love Years Coming/One Stands Here	35

(see also Jim Webb)

STRAWBERRY JAM

69	Pye 7N 17711	Per-Son-Al-Ly/This Is To A Girl	10

STRAWBERRY PARK

82	Sonet 2245	Summer Is A Coming/Beach Party (in p/s)	8
82	Sonet 2245	Summer Is A Coming/Beach Party	7

STRAWBERRY SMELL

97	Detour DR 053	Penelope Bloomington/Kangeroo In My Garden (p/s, blue vinyl, 100 only)	6

STRAWBERRY SWITCHBLADE

85	Korova KODE 11	STRAWBERRY SWITCHBLADE (LP, with bonus 7" "Trees And Flowers", mispressed with some tracks playing twice & others out of order)	15
85	Korova KODE 11	STRAWBERRY SWITCHBLADE (LP, with bonus 7" "Trees And Flowers")	12

(see also Poems, Rose McDowall)

STRAWBS

68	A&M AMS 725	Oh How She Changed/Or Am I Dreaming	30
68	A&M AMS 738	The Man Who Called Himself Jesus/Poor Jimmy Wilson	8
70	A&M AMS 791	Forever/Another Day	8
71	A&M AMS 837	Witchwood/Keep The Devil Outside/We'll Meet Again Sometime (live) (withdrawn)	30
71	A&M AMS 874	Benedictus/Keep The Devil Outside	6
73	A&M AMS 7047	Part Of The Union/Will You Go (p/s)	5
69	private pressing	STRAWBERRY MUSIC SAMPLER NO. 1 (LP, publisher's sampler, 100 only)	500
69	A&M AMLS 936	STRAWBS (LP; disc inserted in middle of sleeve)	35
69	A&M AMLS 936	STRAWBS (LP; disc inserted at edge of sleeve)	20
70	A&M AMLS 970	DRAGONFLY (LP, textured sleeve, lyric insert, mustard label)	30
70	A&M AMLS 994	JUST A COLLECTION OF ANTIQUES AND CURIOS (LP, laminated gatefold sleeve, mustard label; 2 different rear sleeves)	15
71	A&M AMLH 64304	FROM THE WITCHWOOD (LP, gatefold sleeve)	15
72	A&M AMLH 68078	GRAVE NEW WORLD (LP, triple gatefold sleeve, with 12-page booklet)	15
73	A&M AMLH 68144	BURSTING AT THE SEAMS (LP, with inner sleeve)	12
73	Hallmark SHM 813	ALL OUR OWN WORK (LP, with Sandy Denny)	15

(see also Dave Cousins, Sandy Denny, Fire, Foggy, Monks, Davey & Morris, Hudson-Ford)

STRAY

70	Transatlantic PROMO 1	Only What You Make It/Time Machine	50
72	Big T BIG 141	Our Song/Mama's Coming Home	5
73	Transatlantic BIG 12	Hallelujah/Brand New Day	7
70	Transatlantic TRA 216	STRAY (LP, die-cut gatefold sleeve, white/lilac 't' logo label)	45
71	Transatlantic TRA 233	SUICIDE (LP, textured sleeve, white/lilac 't' logo label)	30
71	Transatlantic TRA 248	SATURDAY MORNING PICTURES (LP, gatefold sleeve)	20
73	Transatlantic TRA 268	MUDANZAS (LP, gatefold sleeve)	18
74	Transatlantic TRA 281	MOVE IT (LP, die-cut sleeve with inner)	12
75	Transatlantic TRA 3066	TRACKS (LP)	12

75	Dawn DNLS 3066	STAND UP AND BE COUNTED (LP, lyric insert, pink 'sun' label)	15
76	Pye NSPL 18482	HOUDINI (LP)	12
76	Pye NSPL 18512	HEARTS OF FIRE (LP)	12

STRAY DOG
73	Manticore K13502	Speak Of The Devil/A Letter	5
74	Manticore K 13508	Junkyard Angel/World Winds	6
73	Manticore K 43506	STRAY DOG (LP, textured sleeve, insert)	20
74	Manticore K 53504	WHILE YOU'RE DOWN THERE (LP)	20

(see also Emerson Lake & Palmer)

STREAK
72	A&M AME 602	Gonna Have A Good Time/Be Your Ryder/Hard Times (In New York City) (promo, b side plays at 33 rpm)	40
72	A&M AMS 7012	Gonna Have A Good Time/Be Your Ryder	15
73	Deram DM 376	Bang Bang Bullet/Black Jack Man	15

STREAKERS
74	Dawn DNS 1066	Turn Me Down/Wake Up Sunshine	6

STREAMLINERS (WITH JOANNE)
61	Columbia DB 4689	Frankfurter Sandwiches/Pachalata	5

(See also Rosemary Squires)

STREET
69	London HLU 10275	Apollo... Amen/Why Concern Yourself	5

DANNY STREET
63	Phillips BF 1250	Only Love Can Break A Heart/ Cold Cold Winter	5
64	Philips BF 1309	The Eyes Of The Young Ones/Someone As Wonderful As You	5
65	Philips BF 1387	Don't Go To Him/As It's Meant To Be	5
60s	Domino DO 114	Melanie/Birds An' Bees An' Things	5
71	London HLU 10342	My Little Guy/You Blew It	5

GARY STREET & FAIRWAYS
68	Domain D 2	Flipperty Flop/Hold Me Closer	20

(see also Fairways)

JOHN STREET & INMATES OF NO. 12
67	Deram DM 147	Keep A Little Love/My Kind Of Luck	10

JUDY STREET
78	Grapevine GRP 106	What/You Turn Me On	5
78	Grapevine GRP 106	What/You Turn Me On (DJ Copy)	10

STREET LEGAL
84	Weird Brothers SLW 1	Rollin' On/Mississippi Moonshine (p/s, initially with sticker over typo error in sleeve)	150
84	Weird Brothers SLW 1	Rollin' On/Mississippi Moonshine (p/s, without sticker)	150

STREETFIGHTER
82	J.R. JR 7049S	CRAZY DREAM (EP)	40

STREETFIGHTER (U.K.)
81	Streetfighter 749	STREETFIGHTER (12" EP)	25

STREET PEOPLE (1)
70	Stateside SS 2163	Jennifer Tomkins/All Night Long	10

STREET PEOPLE (2)
79	Ellie Jay Special Pressing EJSP 9276	PERSONAL VALUES EP (500 only, p/s)	75

STREET SERVICE
90	I Like It ILIT 01	JUST FOR YOU (LP)	18

STREETWALKERS
75	Vertigo 6360 123	DOWNTOWN FLYERS (LP, laminated gatefold sleeve, 'spaceship' label)	12
76	Vertigo 9102 010	RED CARD (LP, red vinyl with inner sleeve, numbered, 'spaceship' label)	15
77	Vertigo 9102 012	VICIOUS BUT FAIR (LP, lyric inner sleeve)	12
77	Vertigo 6641 703	LIVE (2-LP, gatefold sleeve)	15

(see also Family, Hummingbird, Nicko McBrain)

BARBRA STREISAND
62	CBS AAG 130	My Colouring Book/Lover Come Back To Me	7
63	CBS AAG 179	Happy Days Are Here Again/Down With Love	6
64	CBS AAG 223	People/Draw Me A Circle	6
64	CBS 201543	People/I Am A Woman You Are Man (p/s)	6
66	CBS 202025	Second Hand Rose/He Touched Me	5
70	CBS 5321	Stoney End/I'll Be Home	6
84	CBS TA 4754	Left In The Dark/Here We Are At Last/Woman In Love/Guilty Memory (12", p/s, withdrawn)	15
66	CBS EP 6150	SECOND HAND ROSE (EP)	10

TEXAS' BILL STRENGTH
55	Capitol CL 14357	Cry, Cry, Cry/The Yellow Rose Of Texas	15

STRESS
91	Eternal YZ 550	Flowers In The Rain/Flowers In The Rain (p/s)	6
85	Adventures In Reality ARR 14	THE BIG WHEEL (LP, with insert)	40

STRETCH
75	Anchor ANCL 2014	ELASTIQUE (LP)	15
76	Anchor ANCL 2016	YOU CAN'T BEAT YOUR BRAIN FOR ENTERTAINMENT (LP)	15
77	Anchor ANCL 2023	LIFE BLOOD (LP)	15
78	Hot Wax HW 1	FORGET THE PAST (LP)	30

(see also Elmer Gantry, Kirby, Status Quo, Clifford Davis, Legs, Curved Air)

STRETCHEADS
88	Moksha SOMALP2	FIVE FINGERS FOUR (LP)	20

WILLIAM R. STRICKLAND
69	Deram DML/SML 1041	WILLIAM R. STRICKLAND IS ONLY THE NAME (LP)	25

PETE STRIDE & JOHN PLAIN
80	Beggars Banquet BEGA 17	NEW GUITARS IN TOWN (LP, with inner sleeve)	12

(see also Lurkers)

STRIDER
73	GM GMS 002	Higher And Higher/Ain't Got No Love	5
74	GM GMS 023	Seems So Easy/Arthur Hydrogen	5
73	GM GML 1002	EXPOSED (LP, gatefold sleeve)	15
74	GM GML 1012	MISUNDERSTOOD (LP)	15

(see also Samson)

STRIFE
77	Outlaw OUT 1	School/Go/Feel So Good (p/s)	10
75	Chrysalis 1063	RUSH (LP)	15
78	Gull GULP 1029	BACK TO THUNDER (LP, on green vinyl with poster)	18
78	Gull 1029	BACK TO THUNDER (LP)	12

LIZA STRIKE
68	Parlophone R 5725	All's Quiet On West 23rd/Mr Daddy-Man	10

(see also Liza & Jet Set, Soulmates, Vice Versa)

STRIKER BLUE
76	Bootlegger 596	Get On Down/Loyalty To The Board	20

STRIKERS & CHILDREN OF SELSTON BAGTHORPE PRIMARY SCHOOL CHOIR
78	Eagle EGL 003	Good Old Charlie/Forest Fire	8

STRING-A-LONGS
61	London HLU 9278	Wheels/Am I Asking Too Much	5
61	London HLU 9354	Panic Button/Brass Buttons	5
61	London HLU 9394	Should I/Take A Minute	5
61	London HLU 9452	Scottie/Ming Bird	10
62	London HLD 9535	Sunday/Twistwatch	10
62	London HLD 9588	Spinning My Wheels/My Blue Heaven	10
63	London HLD 9652	Matilda/Replica	10
61	London RE-U 1322	THE STRING-A-LONGS (EP)	50
63	London RE-D 1350	THE STRING-A-LONGS (EP)	50
63	London RE-D 1398	STRINGALONG WITH THE STRING-A-LONGS (EP)	40
63	London HA-D 8054	THE STRING-A-LONGS (LP, mono)	45
63	London SH-D 8054	THE STRING-A-LONGS (LP, stereo)	50
69	London HAU/SHU 8371	WIDE WORLD HITS (LP)	40

STRING CHEESE
72	RCA SF 8222	STRING CHEESE (LP)	20

STRING DRIVEN THING
70	Concord CON 7	Another Night/Say What You Like	15
72	Charisma CB 195	Eddie/Hooked On The Road	5
70	Concord CON 1001	STRING DRIVEN THING (LP)	250
72	Charisma CAS 1062	STRING DRIVEN THING (LP, gatefold, insert,large 'Mad Hatter' label)	30
73	Charisma CAS 1070	THE MACHINE THAT CRIED (LP, gatefold sleeve, large 'Mad Hatter' label)	30
74	Charisma CAS 1097	PLEASE MIND YOUR HEAD (LP, lyric sheet, small 'Mad Hatter' label)	15
76	Charisma CAS 1112	KEEP YOUR 'AND ON IT (LP, insert)	12

STRIPES
82	Ellie Jay EJSP 9808/PINK01	One Step Ahead	20

STRIPES OF GLORY
62	Vogue V 9194	The Denial/O' Send The Fire	18

SYLVIA STRIPLIN
86	Music Of Love MOLS 8	Give Me Your Love/Will You Ever Pass This Way Again/Look Towards The Sky (12")	20

(THE) STROKES
01	Rough Trade RTRADES 010	The Modern Age/Last Night (die ct sleeve with barcode 2000 only)	30
01	Rough Trade RTRADES 023	Hard To Explain/New York City Cops (p/s, 2000 only)	8
01	Rough Trade RTRADES 041	Last Nite/When It Started (p/s)	10
02	Rough Trade RTRADES 063	Someday/Alone Together/Is This It (p/s, yellow vinyl)	10
01	Rough Trade RTRADELP030	IS THIS IT? (LP)	30

STROLLERS
58	Vogue V 9113	Jumping With Symphony Sid/Swinging Yellow Rose Of Texas	20
58	Vogue V 9124	Little Bitty Pretty One/Flute Cha-Lypso	20
58	Vogue V 9124	Little Bitty Pretty One/Flute Cha-Lypso (78)	10
61	London HLL 9336	Come On Over/There's No One But You	40

BARRETT STRONG
60	London HLU 9088	Money (That's What I Want)/Oh I Apologise	100
73	Epic S EPC 1778	Stand Up And Cheer For The Preacher/Instrumental	10
76	Capitol CL 15864	Man Up In The Sky/Gonna Make It Right	40

JOE STRUMMER
88	Epic TRASHP 1	Trash City/Theme From Permanent Record (picture disc)	8
89	Island STRUM T2	Island Hopping (12")	8
03	Hellcat 1137-7	Coma Girl/Yalla Yalla (Live) (with The Mescaleros, picture disc, stickered polythene sleeve)	10
03	Hellcat 1149-7	Redemption Song/Arms Aloft/Junco Partner (Live) (with the Mescaleros, picture disc,stickered polythene sleeve)	10
89	EPIC 465347	EARTHQUAKE WEATHER (LP, with inner)	20

(see also The Clash)

STRYDER
80	Quartz QS 010	Forcin' Thru'/Settle Down	20

GLEN STUART
60s	Honey Hit TB 126	Make Me An Angel/Walking To Heaven (with p/s)	7

GLEN STUART & CLANSMEN
59	Pye 7N 15232	Weepy Willow/Della Darling	10

KARL STUART & PROFILES
65	Mercury MF 870	Love Of My Eyes/Not A Girl In A Million	5
65	Mercury MF 875	Haven't They Got Better Things To Do/The Touch Of Your Hand	5

(see also Profile, Voice)

SHAWN STUART
74	Epic SEPC 2496	It's All Because Of YOu/Wise Old Man	8

FRANKIE STUBBS
90s	Sounds Of Subterrania S09	SECOND HAND SUIT (10" EP)	20
95	Rugger Bugger DUMP 025	UNHINGED (EP)	15

(see also Leatherface)

NAT STUCKEY
67	Pye International 7N 25403	Sweet Thang/Paralyze My Mind	6
69	RCA RCA 1833	Loving You/Joe And Mabel's 12th Street Bar And Grill	6
69	RCA RCA 1890	Cut Across Shorty/Understand, Little Man	7

STUD
70	Deram SML-R 1084	STUD (LP, laminated front sleeve, white/red label with small logo)	100

(see also Taste, Family, Blossom Toes, Eric Burdon & Animals)

STUDD PUMP
71	Penny Farthing PEN 757	Spare The Children/Floatin'	8

STUDIO G'S
70	LPSG 100	BETA GROUP (LP, library edition)	150
96	Tenth Planet TP 023	BEAT GROUP (LP, 600 only)	20

STUDIO ONE ALLSTARS
67	Island WI 3038	Sherry (actually by Bumps Oakley)/Out Of My Mind (actually by Soul Junior)	35

STUDIO SIX
66	Polydor 56131	When I See My Baby/Don't Tell Lies	15
67	Polydor 56162	Bless My Soul (I've Been And Gone And Done It)/People Say	10
67	Polydor 56174	Times Were When/I Can't Sleep	10
67	Polydor 56219	Strawberry Window/Falling Leaves	40
69	Polydor 56361	Bless My Soul/People Say	10

STUDIO SWEETHEARTS
79	DJM DJS 10915	I Believe/It Isn't Me (p/s)	20

(see also Cult, Slaughter & Dogs)

STUD LEATHER
73	Dart ART 2024	Cut Loose/Emma Louise	100

STUKAS
77	Sonet SON 2134	I Like Sport/I'll Send You A Postcard/Dead Lazy (p/s)	8
77	Chiswick NS 21	Klean Living Kids/Oh Little Girl (p/s)	10
78	Sonet SON 2159	Wash Machine Boogie/Motorbike	7

STUMPY
74	Dawn DNS 1080	Make Me A Superman/Keep It Coming	6

STUPIDS
85	Children Of Rev. COR 3	VIOLENT NUN (EP, some mispressed)	20
86	C.O.R. GURT 15	VAN STUPID (LP, insert)	12
88	C.O.R. GURT 9	PERUVIAN VACATION (LP, blue cover, lyric sheet)	12
88	Vinyl Solution SOL 2	JESUS MEETS THE STUPIDS (LP, insert with free 7")	15

STYLE COUNCIL
85	Polydor TSCX 8	Walls Come Tumbling Down!/Spin' Drifting/The Whole Point II/Blood Sports (12", limited edition with poster)	8
85	Polydor TSCDP 10/DP 1	The Lodgers (re-recorded)/You're The Best Thing/The Big Boss Groove//You're The Best Thing/Long Hot Summer (shrinkwrapped double pack)	6
86	Polydor CINE 1/ CINEC1	Have You Ever Had It Blue/Mr. Cool's Dream//Have You Ever Had It Blue (Uncut Version)/With Everything To Lose (Recorded Live In London Dec. '85) (7" with cassette single, printed PVC sleeve)	6
89	Polydor TSCB 17	Promised Land (Juan Atkins Mix)/Can You Still Love Me? (7", stickered box set with numbered 7" in p/s & poster)	6
89	Polydor TSCCD 17	Promised Land (Longer Version)/Promised Land (Pianopella Version)/Can You Still Love Me? (Dub)/Can You Still Love Me? (Vocal) (CD)	10
89	Polydor LHSCD 1	Long Hot Summer 89 Mix (Extended Version)/Everybody's On The Run/(Version One)/(Version Two) (CD)	10
89	Polydor TSC 18	Sure Is Sure/Love Of The World (unissued, acetates may exist)	0
88	PolyGram 080 206-2	À PARIS EP	12
88	PolyGram 080 336-2	Have You Ever Had It Blue (Uncut Version)/Mr. Cool's Dream/With Everything To Lose/Have You Ever Had It Blue	12
88	PolyGram 080 400-2	How She Threw It All Away /Love The First Time/Long Hot Summer (Tom Mix)/How She Threw It All Away	12
88	PolyGram 080 560-2	Life At A Top Peoples Health Farm (Extended Remix)/Spank!/Sweet Loving Ways/Life At A Top Peoples Health Farm	12
88	Polydor	CONFESSIONS OF A POP GROUP (box set, VHS & cassette;some with promo CD [CPGCD 1])	50
88	Polydor	CONFESSIONS OF A POP GROUP (box set, VHS & cassette;some without promo CD [CPGCD 1])	40
98	Polydor TSCLP 6	MODERNISM: A NEW DECADE (LP, promo only)	50
98	Polydor TSCLP 6	MODERNISM: A NEW DECADE (LP, 2 x 12" set, promo only)	60
00	Polydor 549135-1	GREATEST HITS (2-LP)	25

(see also Council Collective, Paul Weller, Jam, Merton Parkas, King Truman)

STYLOS
64	Liberty LBS 10173	Head Over Heels/Bye Bye, Baby, Bye Bye	100

POLY STYRENE
80	United Artists BP 370	Talk In Toytown/Sub Tropical (p/s)	5
80	United Artists UAG 30320	TRANSLUCENCE (LP, with lyric inner)	12

(see also X-Ray Spex, Mari Elliott)

STYVAR MANOR
70	Polydor 2058034	Just Dropped In/That's What I Need Most Of All	40

LAURIE STYVERS
72	Chrysalis CHR 1007	SPILT MILK (LP, green label, lyric inner sleeve)	12

STYX
75	RCA RCA 2518	Lady/Children Of The Land	5

SUBCULTURE
83	Essential ESS 002	Loud & Clear/Rogue Trooper/University City (p/s)	25

SUBHUMANS
81	Spiderleg SDL 3	Religious Wars/Love Is.../Work Experience/It's Gonna Get Worse (p/s)	8
82	Spiderleg SPIDL 5	Big City/Reason For Existence/Cancer/Peroxide (p/s)	7
82	Spiderleg SDL9	THE DAY THE COUNTRY DIED (LP, gatefold, original pressing with "Pay no more than £3.25" on front cover)	15
83	Bluurg Fish 8	FROM THE CRADLE TO THE GRAVE (LP, gatefold, original pressing with "Pay no more than £3.50" on front cover)	15

SUBMARINER
93	Spacewatch FLX 2107	Lyricist Downer/Seeming And The Meaning (demo)/STEREOLAB:Ronco Symphony (demo) (clear vinyl flexi with paper strip insert)	25

SUBMARINES
87	Head HEAD 4	Grey Skies Blue/I Saw The Children (p/s)	6

SUBS
78	Stiff OFF 1	Gimme Your Heart/Party Clothes (p/s)	5

(see also Larry Wallis)

SUBSTITUTE
79	Ignition IR 2	The One/Look Sharp (in p/s)	35
79	Ignition IR 2	The One/Look Sharp	20

(see also Vibrators)

SUB SUB
90s	Ten TENX 373	Space Face/Ecto-Jam-Sub (12", die-cut sleeve)	35
91	Ten TENX 373	Space Face (12")	8
91	Ten TENR 373	Space Face (Todd Terry Remix) (12")	8
90s	Robs Records 12ROB 07	Coast/Inside Of This/Past/Inside Out (12", p/s)	10
90s	Robs Records 7ROB 9	Ain't No Love/Parkside Mix (p/s)	8
90s	Robs Records 12ROB 9	Ain't No Love (Original Mix)/(Parkside Mix)/(Parkside Raw Dub) (12", die-cut p/s)	8
90s	Robs Records 12ROB 09R	Ain't No Love (On The Floor)/(On The House)/(On Yer Face) (12", die-cut p/s)	8
90s	Robs Records 7ROB 19	Respect (Radio Edit)/(Dasliva-McCready Mix)	8
90s	Robs Records 12ROB 19	Respect (Original Mix)/(Dasliva-McCready Mix)/(Dasliva's Acid Dub) (12", p/s)	8
90s	Robs Records 12ROB 29	Angel (Original Mix)/(Primetime Mix)/Senna/Southern Trees (Instrumental)(12", p/s)	8
90s	Robs Records 12ROB 29X	Angel (Primetime Dub)/(Deep Love Mix)/(Deep Love Instrumental)/(Pegasus (12", p/s)	8
90s	Robs Records 12ROB 39	Southern Trees/Jaggernath/Northern Trees (12", p/s)	8
90s	Robs Records 12ROB 53	This Time I'm Not Wrong/Heads Will Roll (Instrumental Demo)/Firesuite (12", p/s)	8

(see also Doves)

SUBTERRANEANS
87	Mother MUM 6	Slum/Maxi Joy (p/s)	5
87	Mother 12MUM 6	Slum/Maxi Joy/Head For The Light (12", p/s)	8

SUBURBAN STUDS
77	Pogo POG 001/LYN 44845	No Faith/Questions (no p/s, 'with horns' version)	15
77	Pogo POG 001/LYN 44845	No Faith/Questions (p/s)	6
78	Pogo POG 002	I Hate School/Young Power (p/s)	15
78	Pogo POW 001	SLAM (LP)	25

SUBWAYS
03	Bus Stop BS0502	No Heart, No Soul/We Get Around/Young For Eternity (live) (CD)	20
04	Private Pressing	DEMO (CD, sold at gigs, p/s)	30
04	Transgressive 58241H1	I Am/I Want To Hear What You Gotta Say/You Got Me (500 only, p/s)	12

SUBWAY SECT
78	Braik BRS 01	Nobody's Scared/Don't Split It (p/s)	15
79	Rough Trade RT 007	Ambition/A Different Story (initially in yellow text p/s)	10
79	Rough Trade RT 007	Ambition/A Different Story (later orange text p/s)	8

(see also Vic Godard [& Subway Sect], Spirit Of The Sect)

NIKKI SUDDEN
81	Rather GEAR 11	Back To The Start/Ringing On My Train (p/s)	5
82	Abstract ABS 009	Channel Steamer/Chelsea Embankment (p/s)	5
84	Pawn Hearts 1747-01	SHAME FOR THE ANGELS (12" EP)	8
84	Pawn Hearts 1747-01	SHAME FOR THE ANGELS (12" EP)	8
86	Glass GLAEP 102	PIN YOUR HEAR TO ME (12" EP, with Dave Kusworth & The Jacobites)	10
86	Creation CRE 033	Jangle Town/The Last Bandit (p/s)	8
82	ABSTRACT ABT 003	WAITING ON EGYPT (LP)	18
83	Flicknife SHARP 110	THE BIBLE BELT (LP)	18
84	Glass GLALP 008	JACOBITES (LP, with Dave Kusworth)	15
85	Hotwire HWLP 8504	THE LAST BANDITS IN THE WORLD (LP)	12
91	UFO UFO 4	THE JEWEL THIEF (LP)	15

(see also Swell Maps, Last Bandits, Jeremy Gluck)

(A) SUDDEN SWAY
80	Chant CHANT 1	Jane's Third Party/Don't Go (p/s, as A Sudden Sway)	15
81	Chant CHANT 2/EJSP 9692	TO YOU, WITH REGARD (12" EP, with insert)	20
84	Chant CHANT 3	The Traffic Tax Scheme (12" with badge & inserts in folder)	12
86	WEA BYN 8B	Spacemate (2 x 12" box set with stickers, info sheets, 2 booklets & poster)	12

SUDETEN CRECHE
83	Illuminated ILL 1712	Kindergarten/Dance (instrumental Version)/Dance/Asylums in Beiruit (12", p/s)	20

SUE & MARY
62	Decca F 11517	Traitor In Disguise/I Love You (Oh Yes I Do)	10

SUE & SUNNY

65	Columbia DB 7748	Every Ounce Of Strength/So Remember	15
67	Columbia DB 8099	You Can't By-Pass Love/I Like Your Style	25
68	CBS 3874	The Show Must Go On/Little black Book	20
68	Island WIP 6043	Set Me Free/NIRVANA ORCHESTRA: City Of The South	25
69	CBS 4567	Let Us Break Bread/Stop Messing About With My Heart	10
70	CBS 4757	You Devil, Cotton-Eyed Joe/Night In The City	10
70	Deram DM 318	Ain't That Telling You People/Didn't I Blow Your Mind	10
71	Deram DM 328	Freedom/Break Up	10
71	Reflection HRS 10	Let Us Break Bread Together/Michael From Mountains	6
72	Deram DM 355	I'm Gonna Make You Love Me/High On The Thought Of You	10
70	CBS 63740	SUE AND SUNNY (LP)	20
70	Reflection REFL 4	SUE AND SUNNY (LP)	20

(see also Sue & Sunshine, Myrtelles, Stockingtops, Brotherhood Of Man)

SUE & SUNSHINE

64	Columbia DB 7409	A Little Love/If You See Me Crying	10
65	Columbia DB 7533	We're In Love/Don't Look Behind	7

(see also Sue & Sunny, Myrtelles, Stockingtops)

SUEDE

91	RML RML 001	Be My God/Art (12", unissued, 250+ white label copies only, MPO pressings,no p/s; counterfeits have off-white labels with no MPO etchings)	100
92	Nude NUD 1 S	The Drowners (Radio Edit)/To The Birds (p/s, 1,000 copies only)	18
92	Nude NUD 3 T	Metal Mickey/Where Pigs Don't Fly/He's Dead (12", test pressing, plain sleeve)	30
93	Nude SUEDE 1	My Insatiable One (clear flexidisc, fan club/gig freebie)	12
94	Nude NUD 9T	Stay Together/The Living Dead/My Dark Star (12" numbered gatefold p/s)	10
94	Nude NUD 10 S	We Are The Pigs/Killing Of A Flash Boy (numbered gatefold p/s)	6
94	Nude NUD 11 T	The Wild Ones/Eno's Introducing The Band/Asda Town (12", photo insert, p/s)	10
96	Nude NUD 21S	Trash/Europe Is Our Playground (p/s, mail order only)	15
97	Nude SIS 1 CD	LIVE (CD EP, 6-track fan club-only issue)	25
97	Nude NUD 24 S	Saturday Night/Beautiful Ones (double pack, p/s, mail-order only)	10
97	Nude NUD SIS 1 CD	Film Star (live)/Rent (live)/Saturday Night (live) (CD, featuring Neil Tennant)	15
98	Nude SIS 2 CD	IMPLEMENT YEAH! (CD fan club-only issue)	15
99	Nude NUD 667043	ELECTRICITY EP (minidisc, withdrawn)	10
98	Nude SUEDE 1 CDF	ON FILM EP (CD EP, 6-track, promo only)	15
99	Nude INT 1 CD	Head Musing (CD, 2-track interview, promo only)	20
03	Fan Club (no cat. no.)	Attitude (2-CD with DVD, in numbered box)	20
02	Fan Club (no cat. no.)	Positivity (2-CD with DVD in numbered box)	20
02	Fan Club (no cat. no.)	Obsessions (2-CD with DVD in numbered box)	20
04	S.I.S. SIS4CD	SEE YOU IN THE NEXT LIFE (CD, fan club farewell, 2000 copies)	40
11	Edsel DROWN 1	The Drowners (Demo)/To The Birds (Demo) (p/s, Record Store Day release)	15
93	Nude NUDE 1LP	SUEDE (LP, with inner sleeve; with carrier bag from Chain With No Name stores)	40
93	Nude NUDE 1LP	SUEDE (LP, with inner sleeve)	15
94	Nude NUDE 3	DOG MAN STAR (LP, with poster)	80
96	Nude 4851212	COMING UP (LP, with inner sleeve)	30
99	NUDE 14LP	HEAD MUSIC (2-LP)	25

(see also Elastica, Tears)

SUEDE CROCODILES

83	No Strings NOSP 2	Pleasant Dreams/Stop The Rain	70

SUFFERER SOUND

78	Tempus TEMD 2	I A Sufferer/National Front (12")	12

SUGAR & SPICE (JAMAICA)

73	Stop Points DL 021	Indeed I Love You/Version	8

SUGAR MINOTT

83	SMP SMP 003	Come Again/BERTIE AT THE CONTROLS: Dubbing A Storm At Omega Studio (12")	150
79	Warrior WAR 124	Never Too Young/DON CARLOS: Hey Little Girl (12")	10
70s	Uptempo UT 1	SHOWCASE (10" mini LP, no ps)	15
83	PCJ PCJ 001	Can't Stop Jah Music/PCJ: Nah Stop Jah Music (12")	50
79	United Artists UAG 30310	GIVE THE PEOPLE (LP)	20
79	Island ILPS 9591	BLACK ROOTS (LP)	20
79	Trojan TRLS 173	GHETTO-OLOGY (LP)	15
79	Warrior WARLP20	BITTER SWEET (LP)	25
82	Black roots BRLP 001	MEET THE PEOPLE IN A LOVER DUBBER STYLE (LP)	15

SUGAR (1)

69	CBS 4226	It Was Yesterday Today/11AM Tuesday Morning Taxi	40

SUGAR (2)

92	Creation CRELP 129	COPPER BLUE (LP, lyric insert)	12

SUGAR (SIMONE) & DANDY (LIVINGSTONE)

63	Carnival CV 7006	One Man Went To Mow/Cryin'	8
64	Carnival CV 7009	Oh Dear What Can The Matter Be/Tra La La	8
64	Carnival CV 7015	What A Life/Time And Tide	8
64	Carnival CV 7016	I'm Not Crying Now/Blues Got A Hold On Me	8
65	Carnival CV 7023	Let's Ska/Only Heaven Knows	8
65	Carnival CV 7024	I'm Into Something Good/Crazy For You	8
65	Carnival CV 7027	Think Of The Good Times/Girl Come See	8
65	Carnival CV 7029	I Want To Be Your Lover/I Don't Know What I'm Going To Do Now	7
66	Blue Beat BB 367	Meditation (as Jetliners)/GIRL SATCHMO & JET LINERS: Nature Of Love	15
67	Page One POF 044	Let's Ska/Only Heaven Knows	8
64	Carnival CX 1000	THE SKA'S THE LIMIT (LP)	40
67	Page One FOR 006	THE SKA'S THE LIMIT (LP, reissue)	20

(see also Sugar Simone)

SUGAR & PEE WEE

58	Vogue Pop V 9112	One, Two, Let's Rock/Just A Few Little Words	750
58	Vogue Pop V 9112	One, Two, Let's Rock/Just A Few Little Words (78)	150

SUGAR & SPICE

69	London HLU 10259	Cruel War/Not To Return	10

SUGAR BEARS
72	Philips 6073 812	You Are The One/Someone Like You	5

SUGARBEATS
66	Polydor BM 56069	I Just Stand Here/The Ballad Of Ole Betsy	20
66	Polydor BM 56120	Alice Designs/Sunny Day Girl	20

(see also Tony Rivers & Castaways)

SUGARCUBES
87	One Little Indian 7z TP 7	Birthday/Birthday (Icelandic) (p/s)	6
87	One Little Indian 12 TP 7	Birthday/Birthday (Icelandic)/Cat (Icelandic) (12", p/s)	8
87	One Little Indian 7TP 7CD	Birthday/Motorcrash/Cat (Icelandic)/Birthday (Icelandic) (CD)	10
87	One Little Indian L12 TP 9	Cold Sweat (Remix)/Birthday (Original Demo Version)/Dragon (Icelandic)/Traitor (Icelandic) (12", p/s, 5,000 only)	8
88	One Little Indian 12TP 11L	BIRTHDAY CHRISTMAS MIX (12" EP, double groove, with Jesus & Mary Chain)	12
89	House Of Dolls HOD 010	Dark Disco/HOST: Homelands/MURRUMBRIDGE WHALERS: Giving Away To Trains/SHARK TABOO: Tinsel Town (live) (no p/s, with House Of Dolls mag)	6
89	One Little Indian OLI26TP7	Regina/Hot Meat/Hey/Regina (Propeller vs Jet) (with poster)	6
89	One Little Indian OLI26TP12	Regina/Hot Meat/Regina (Icelandic) (12")	8
91	One Little Indian OLI62TP12	Hit/Theft/Hit (Instrumental)/Leash Called Love (12")	8
92	One Little Indian OLI104TP12	Birthday (Justin Robertson 12" mix)/Tommy D Dub Mix/Christmas Eve Mix/Original 7" Mix/Tommy D 12" Mix/Justin Robertson Dub/Christmas Day Mix/Demo (12")	10
90	One Little Indian TP BOX 2	7.8 (8 x 7" box set)	25
90	One Little Indian TP BOX 1	12.11 (11 x 12" box set)	40
90	One Little Indian TP BOX 3	CD.6 (6 x CD box set)	45
88	One Little Indian TPLP 5	LIFE'S TOO GOOD (LP, green/blue/yellow/orange/pink sleeve)	15
88	One Little Indian DTPLP 5	LIFE'S TOO GOOD (LP)	20
89	One Little Indian TPLP 15SP	HERE TODAY, TOMORROW NEXT WEEK! (LP, silver vinyl, gatefold sleeve with sticker & inner)	20
89	One Little Indian TPLP 15L	SYKURMOLARNIR ILLUR ARFUR! (LP, as Sykurmolarnir, gatefold sleeve)	15
92	One Little Indian TPLP40	IT'S IT (2 x LP)	20

(see also Bjork, Kukl, Ornamental)

SUGAR DEE & THE OFFBEAT POSSE
89	YND YDD 0137	Danger/Having A Party (12")	25

SUGAR LOAF
70	RCA INTS 1113	SOUL STRUTTING (LP)	40

SUGARLOAF
70	Liberty LBF 15401	Green-Eyed Lady/West Of Tomorrow	12
71	Liberty LBS 83415	SUGARLOAF (LP)	15
74	United Artists UAS 29165	SPACESHIP EARTH (LP)	12
75	Polydor 2310 394	DON'T CALL US, WE'LL CALL YOU (LP, with Jerry Corbetto)	15

SUGAR LUMPS
69	Jay Boy BOY 16	Sugar Sugar/Can't We Be Friends	20

SUGARPLUMS
70	Fab FAB 160	Red River Reggae/Too Much	7

SUGAR SHOPPE
68	Capitol CL 15555	Skip-A-Long Sam/Let The Truth Come Out	20

SUGARGLIDERS
92	Sarah SARAH 63	Letter From A Lifeboat/Strong/What We Had Hoped (p/s, insert)	12
92	Sarah SARAH 67	Seventeen/Aloha Street/Fruitloopin' (p/s, insert)	12
93	Sarah SARAH 72	Ahprahan/Corn Circles/Theme From Boxville (p/s, insert)	20
93	Sarah SARAH 77	Trumpet Play/Unkind/Beloved (p/s, insert)	20
93	Sarah SARAH 83	Will We Ever Learn?/Dolly/Reinventing Penicillin (p/s, insert)	20
93	Sarah SARAH 86	Top 40 Sculpture/90 Days Of Moths And Rust/Yr. Jacket (p/s, insert)	20
94	Sarah SARAH 619	WE'RE ALL TRYING TO GET THERE (LP)	25

SUICIDAL TENDENCIES
87	Virgin VS 967-12	Possessed To Skate/Human Guinea Pig/Two Wrongs Don't Make A Right (12", picture disc)	15
88	Virgin VST 1039	Institutionalised/War Inside My Head/Cyco (12", p/s)	15
87	Virgin V 2495	SUICIDAL TENDENCIES (LP, with poster)	12
88	Virgin V 2551	HOW WILL I LAUGH TOMORROW WHEN I CAN'T EVEN SMILE TODAY? (LP)	15

SUICIDE
78	Red Star/Bronze BRO 57	Cheree/I Remember (p/s)	15
78	Red Star/Bronze 12 BRO 57	Cheree/I Remember (12", 'limited edition', p/s)	20
79	Island WIP 6543	Dream Baby Dream/Radiation (p/s)	10
79	Island 12 WIP 6543	Dream Baby Dream (Long Version)/Radiation (12", p/s)	20
86	Demon D 1046	Cheree/I Remember (promo only)	12
89	Chapter 22 12CHAP 36	Rain Of Ruin/Surrender (12")	10
89	Chapter 22 12CHAP 42	SUICIDE (12", unissued)	0
77	Red Star/Bronze BRON 508	SUICIDE (LP)	18
78	Red Star FRANKIE 1	24 MINUTES OVER BRUSSELS (LP, official bootleg, 1,000 only, no p/s)	30
80	Ze/Island ILPS 7007	SUICIDE: ALAN VEGA/MARTIN REV (LP, with printed inner sleeve)	20
89	Contempo CONTE 148	HALF ALIVE (LP, clear vinyl, 1,000 only)	12
98	Blast First BFFP 133 1/2	SUICIDE (2-LP)	30
99	Blast First BFFP 162	FIRST REHEARSAL TAPES (2-LP)	30

(see also Alan Vega, Martin Rev)

SUICIDE TWINS
86	Lick LICLP 9	SILVER MISSILES AND NIGHTINGALES (LP)	15

(see also Hanoi Rocks)

BIG JIM SULLIVAN
61	Decca F 11387	You Don't Know What You've Got/Hot Hiss Of Steam (as Big Jim Sullivan Combo)	12
65	Mercury MF 928	She Walks Through The Fair/Don't Know What I'm Doing (as Jim Sullivan Sound)	25
73	MAM MAM 100	Out Of The Question/Alone Again	6
67	Mercury SML 30001	SITAR BEAT (LP)	45
74	Retreat RTA 4001	BIG JIM'S BACK (LP, gatefold sleeve, blue/green label)	15

(see also Maureeny Wishfull, Brian Bennett, Tiger)

MAXINE SULLIVAN
| 54 | Parlophone MSP 6086 | Boogie Woogie Maxine/Piper In The Glen (with Vic Ash) ....15 |

PHIL SULLIVAN WITH LONZO & OSCAR'S PEAPICKERS
| 59 | Melodisc MEL 1512 | Love Never Dies/Luckiest Man In Town ....5 |

PETER SULLY
| 70 | Pye 7N 17935 | Row Row Row/Everybodys Talkin' About The War ....8 |
| 68 | Polydor 56291 | My Idea/Evil Woman (as Pete Sully And The Orchard)...35 |

YMA SUMAC
53	Capitol LC 6522	VOICE OF THE XTABAY (10" LP)...15
54	Capitol LC 6609	LEGEND OF THE SUN VIRGIN (10" LP)..15
59	Capitol T 1169	FUEGO DEL ANDE (LP) 20
64	Regal REG 2007	VOICE OF THE XTABAY (LP, export issue)...15
72	London HLU/SHU 8431	MIRACLES (LP) 25

HUBERT SUMLIN
| 65 | Blue Horizon 45-1000 | Across The Board/Sumlin Boogie (99 copies only) ....100 |

(see also Howlin' Wolf)

DONNA SUMMER
74	People PEO 115	The Hostage/Let's Work Together Now 7
79	Casablanca SANL 151	Hot Stuff/Journey To The Centre Of Your Heart (12", red vinyl) 10
82	Casablanca FEEL 12	I Feel Love (12", reissue) 10
89	WEA U 7780P	This Time I Know It's For Real/Whatever Your Heart Desires (shaped pic disc).......................5

(see also Donna Gaines, John Barry)

SUMMERHILL
| 69 | Polydor 583 746 | SUMMERHILL (LP) ....35 |

BOB(BY) SUMMERS
| 59 | Capitol CL 15063 | Rattle Rhythm/Excitement (as Bob Summers) ....15 |
| 60 | Capitol CL 15130 | Little Brown Jug/Twelfth Street Rag (as Bobby Summers) ....8 |

JOHN SUMMERS
| 65 | Pye 15918 | Don't Fool Yourself/Looking In Windows...30 |
| 66 | Pye 7N 17081 | That's A Magic Moment/One A Day ....10 |

SUMMER SET
66	Columbia DB 8004	Farmer's Daughter/Papa-Oom-Mow-Mow 40
66	Columbia DB 8004	Farmer's Daughter/What Are You Gonna Do (2nd issue with different B-side)...............40
67	Columbia DB 8215	Overnight Changes/It's A Dream 100

(see also Candy Choir)

SUMMERTAIR GIRLS
| 66 | Ska Beat JB 258 | My Heart Cries Out/SOUL BROTHERS: James Bond Girl ....50 |

(see also Jackie Mittoo, Soul Agents)

SUMMER WINE
72	Philips 6006 217	Why Do Fools Fall In Love/Ode To Steel Guitar 5
72	Philips 6006 238	Take A Load Off Your Feet/ Sound Of Summer's Over 5
73	Philips 6006 288	Living Right Next Door To An Angel/Sound Of Summer's Over 7
77	EMI EMI 2634	Why Do Fools Fall In Love/Sound Of Summer's Over 5

(see also Tony Rivers, John Perry)

SUMO GIANTS
| 81 | Metro 88 ELECS 1 | Tower Of Babel/Foolish Things...8 |

SUN ALSO RISES
| 70 | Village Thing VTS 2 | THE SUN ALSO RISES (LP, with insert) ....80 |

SUN DIAL
90	UFO 45 001T	Exploding In Your Mind/Otherside/Slow Motion (12", 1-sided, p/s) 15
91	Tangerine TANGERINE 111	Exploding In Your Mind (Colour Mix)/Otherside/Slow Motion (12", unreleased, 80 white label test pressings only) 30
90	Tangerine TAN 11145	Exploding In Your Mind/Other Side 50
91	UFO PF 2	Fireball/Only A Northern Song ('Pre-Flight' 7", promo only) 20
91	UFO UFO 45002 T	OVERSPILL EP (12", orange vinyl) 10
92	UFO UFO 45008 T	FAZER EP (12") 10
90	Tangerine MM 07	OTHER WAY OUT (LP, with insert, signed in silver ink) 40
90	Tangerine MM 07	OTHER WAY OUT (LP, with insert)...30
91	UFO UFO 1LP	OTHER WAY OUT (LP, reissue in gatefold sleeve)..12
92	UFO UFO 8	REFLECTOR (LP, with free 1-sided 7", Let It Go (live), TEX-4)...............................20
92	UFO UFO 8	REFLECTER (LP, clear vinyl) 18
93	Beggars Banquet BBQLP 138	LIBERTINE (LP, with poster) 12
94	Acme AC 8001	RETURN JOURNEY (LP, official bootleg; 200 promos with inserts) 30
94	Acme AC 8001	RETURN JOURNEY (LP, official bootleg; 500 numbered commercial copies) 20
95	Acme AC 8011LP	ACID YANTRA (LP, gatefold sleeve, some purple vinyl) 20
96	Acme AC 8015	LIVE DRUG (LP, red vinyl) 15
02	Ace Of Discs ACE 001	WILD DRUG (LP) 15
05	Third Eye TESLP 1001	OTHER WAY IN (LP) 15

(see also Modern Art, Spiral Sky, Quad)

SUN & MOON
| 88 | Geffen GEF 39 | The Speed Of Life/Death Of Imagination (p/s)..5 |
| 88 | Geffen GEF 39T | The Speed Of Life/Death Of Imagination/The Boy Who Sees Everything/I Love You, You Bastard (12", p/s) ....8 |

(see also Chameleons)

SUNBIRD
| 70 | Phillips 6011070 | Brother Bird/Love Of The Free ....18 |

(see also Nirvana)

SUNCHARIOT
| 72 | Decca F13317 | Rosemarie/Do You Wanna Know ....15 |
| 73 | Decca F13407 | Firewater/The Only Girl I Knew ....10 |

SUNDAE TIMES
68	President PT 203	Baby Don't Cry/Aba-Aba	5
68	President PT 219	Jack Boy/I Don't Want Nobody	10
70	President PT 285	Live Today/Take Me Higher Baby	5
70	Joy JOYS 159	US COLOURED KIDS (LP, laminated front sleeve, flipbacks)	40

(see also Osiba, Crosyby Stills Nash & Young, One)

SUNDANCE
73	Decca F 13423	Coming Down/Eagles	5
73	Decca F 13461	Stand By/Willie The Gambler	5
74	Decca F 13494	Loving You/Can You Feel It	5
73	Decca TXS 111	RAIN STEAM SPEED (LP, with insert)	18
74	Decca SKL 5183	CHUFFER (LP)	18

SUNDAY AFTERNOONS
70s	Longman	SUNDAY AFTERNOONS (LP)	90

SUNDAYS
89	Rough Trade RTX 218	Can't Be Sure/I Kicked A Boy (export issue, brown p/s)	6
89	Rough Trade RTTX 218	Can't Be Sure/I Kicked A Boy/Don't Tell Your Mother (12", export issue, brown p/s)	10
90	Catalogue CAT 076	I Won (square flexidisc with The Catalogue magazine)	10
90	Rough Trade ROUGH 148	READING WRITING AND ARITHMETIC (LP)	15
90	Rough Trade ROUGH 148P	READING, WRITING AND ARITHMETIC (LP, picture disc, stickered sleeve)	25
92	Parlophone PCSD 121	BLIND (LP)	30
97	Parlophone 724382121216	STATIC AND SILENCE (LP)	40

SUNDAY SING TRIO
70s	Sharon SHLP 1221	ONE OF THESE DAYS (LP)	15

SUNDERLAND FIRST TEAM SQUAD
73	RCA 2362	Sunderland All The Way/Bobby Knoxall - I'm Feeling Happy	7

SUNDOWNERS
63	Piccadilly 7N 35142	Baby Baby/House Of The Rising Sun	8
64	Piccadilly 7N 35162	Come On In/Shot Of Rhythm And Blues	8
65	Parlophone R 5243	Where Am I/Gonna Make The Future Bright	8
68	Columbia DB 8339	Dr. J. Wallace-Brown/Love Is In The Air	15
68	Spark SRL 1016	Gloria The Bosom Show/Don't Look Back	8

SUNDOWN PLAYBOYS
72	Apple APPLE 44	Saturday Nite Special/Valse De Soleil Couche (in p/s)	35
72	Apple APPLE 44	Saturday Nite Special/Valse De Soleil Couche	10
72	Apple APPLE 44	Saturday Nite Special/Valse De Soleil Couche (10", 78rpm, pink-patterned die-cut sleeve)	250

SUNDRAGON (1)
68	MGM MGM 1380	Green Tambourine/I Need All The Friends I Can Get	12
68	MGM MGM 1391	Blueberry Blue/Far Away Mountain	12
68	MGM MGM 1458	Five White Horses/Look At The Sun	30
68	MGM MGM-C(S) 8090	GREEN TAMBOURINE (LP, yellow/black 'lion' label)	100

(see also Sands, Others)

SUNDRAGON (2)
03	Y n R YNR014	The Path/Watching (12")	12

SUNFIGHTER
77	EMI EMI 2612	Café A Go-Go/Café A Go-Go (instrumental)	5
76	EMI EMI 2493	Drag Race Queen/Riding On Your Star	15
76	EMI EMI 2553	Such A Lovely Night/Don't Get Me Wrong	10

(see also Chris Rainbow)

SUNFIRE
82	Warner Bros.	Step In The Light/Lady (12")	15

SUNFLAYRE
70	Realm RM 1	The Passing Dream/RIch Woman (private pressing)	300

SUNFOREST
70	Deram Nova DN 7	SOUND OF SUNFOREST (LP, mono, laminated front sleeve)	350
70	Deram Nova SDN 7	SOUND OF SUNFOREST (LP, stereo, laminated front sleeve)	250

SUNN 0)))
04	Anti-Mosh 444	Candlewolff Ov Thee Golden Chalice (12")	35

SUNNY & HI-JUMPERS
65	Carnival CV 7022	Tarry Till You're Better/Dance Til You're Better	6
65	Carnival CV 7025	Going To Damascus/Sweet Potatoes	6

SUNNY & THE SUNGLOWS/SUNLINERS
63	London HL 9792	Talk To Me (as Sunny & the Sunglows)/Every Week, Every Month, Every Year (as Sunny & the Sunliners)	25

SUNNYLAND SLIM
65	77' LA 12-23	CHICAGO BLUES SESSION (LP, with Little Brother Montgomery)	30
65	Storyville SLP 169	I DONE YOU WRONG (LP)	20
68	Storyville 670 169	PORTRAITS IN BLUES (LP, reissue of SLP 169)	12
69	Liberty LBS 83237	SLIM'S GOT THIS THING GOIN' ON (LP)	30
69	Blue Horizon 7-63213	MIDNIGHT JUMP (LP)	100
74	Sonet SNTF 671	THE LEGACY OF THE BLUES VOL. II (LP)	12

SUNNYSIDERS
55	London HL 8135	Hey! Mr. Banjo/Zoom, Zoom, Zoom	50
55	London HL 8160	Oh Me Oh My Oh/(Let's Gather Round) The Parlour Piano	30
55	London HLU 8180	Banjo Woogie/She Didn't Even Say Goodbye	30
55	London HLU 8202	I Love You Fair Dinkum/Stay On The Sunny Side	25
56	London HLU 8246	Doesn't He Love Me/Humdinger	30

SUN RA ARKESTRA
74	Decca F 13542	Don't Go/Can We Change	20
82	Y 1 RA	NUCLEAR WAR (12" EP)	30

69	Fontana STL 5514	HELIOCENTRIC WORLDS VOL. 1 (LP)	40
69	Fontana STL 5499	HELIOCENTRIC WORLDS VOL. 2 (LP)	40
60s	Sonet 23 SPL	JAZZ BY SUN RA (LP)	30
71	Black Lion BLP 30103	PICTURES OF INFINITY - IN CONCERT (LP)	20
71	Byg 529 341	THE SOLAR MYTH APPROACH VOL. 2 (LP)	25
71	Polydor 2460 106	PICTURES OF INFINITY (LP)	25
78	Affinity AFF 10	S-M APPROACH (LP, with Solar-Myth Ark)	15
79	Cobra COB 37001	FATE IN A PLEASANT MOOD (LP)	15
80	Y Y 19	STRANGE CELESTIAL ROAD (LP)	15

SUN RA & MYTH SCIENCE ARKESTRA

| 90 | Blast First BFFP 60 | SUN RA & MYTH SCIENCE ARKESTRA (3 x 10", box set, with insert) | 35 |

SUNRAY

| 00 | Earworm WORM 68 | Music For The Dreammachine (Phase One) (Sonic Boom Remix)(1-sided 12", clear vinyl) | 10 |
| 06 | Earworm EGS 09 | OCEAN EP (12", p/s, with Sonic Boom) | 8 |

SUNRAYS

| 65 | Capitol CL 15416 | I Live For The Sun/Bye, Baby, Bye | 12 |
| 66 | Capitol CL 15433 | Andrea/You Don't Phase Me | 15 |

SUNRISE

| 76 | Grapevine GRA 105 | BEFORE MY EYES (LP) | 30 |

SUN SET

| 67 | Polydor BM 56193 | East Baby/You Can Ride My Rainbow | 15 |

SUNSET BOYS

| 79 | Gimp GIM 1234 | Wreck My Bed/Tutti Frutti/Copy Cat (Blues)/Wreck My Bed (Hippy Version) (p/s) | 5 |

(see also Maxim's Trash)

SUNSETS

| 61 | Ember EMB S 125 | Cry Of The Wild Goose/Manhunt | 15 |

SUNSHINE

| 72 | Warner Brothers K 46169 | SUNSHINE (LP, gatefold sleeve) | 15 |

(see also Pretty Things)

SUNSHINE COMPANY

67	Liberty LBF 15008	Happy/Blue May	12
67	Liberty LBF 15034	Back On The Street Again/A Year Of Janie's Time	10
68	Liberty LBF 15060	Look Here Comes The Sun/It's Sunday	8
68	Liberty LBF 15149	On A Beautiful Day/To Put Up With You	10
68	Liberty LBL/LBS 83120	THE SUNSHINE COMPANY (LP)	35
69	Liberty LBL/LBS 83159	SUNSHINE AND SHADOWS (LP)	35

SUNSHINE KID

| 73 | RCA RCA 2413 | My Linda/Get Your Rocks Off Baby | 18 |

MONTY SUNSHINE

63	London HLR 9822	Carnival/Charmaine E	5
63	London HAR 8037	MONTY SUNSHINE AND HIS BAND (LP, also stereo [SHR 8037])	12
64	London HAR 8158	BLACK MOONLIGHT & SUNSHINE (LP, also stereo [SHR 8158])	12

(see also Lonnie Donegan)

MR. SUNSHINE

| 56 | MGM SP 1160 | Along The China Coast/MRS. SUNSHINE: Two Car Garage | 7 |

SUNSPOTS

| 63 | Decca F 11672 | Paella/Vancouver | 5 |

SUNTREADER

| 73 | Island HELP 13 | ZIN ZIN (LP, innser sleeve, black label, pink 'i' logo) | 15 |

SUPER 8

| 95 | García POUM 001 | Billy The Kid/It Doesn't Matter/How Can I Understand The Flies? ('hairloss' p/s, 500 only, 37 sold, 35 returned for refund, the rest believed burned) | 25 |

(see also Sheds)

SUPER TONES

| 70 | Banana BA 312 | Freedom Blues/First Time I Met You | 40 |

SUPERBOYS

| 68 | Giant GN 22 | Ain't That A Shame/Do It Right Now | 8 |
| 68 | Giant GN 31 | You're Hurtin' Me/Funky Soul | 8 |

(see also Dandy & Superboys, Little Sal)

SUPER CAT

| 88 | Blue Trac BTRD 020 | Nuff Man Dead Ya/ABC (12") | 30 |

SUPERCHARGE

| 76 | Virgin VS 145 | Lonely And In Love/Give It The Nasty | 6 |
| 78 | Virgin VS 20212 | I Think I'm Gonna Fall In Love/Long Version (12") | 10 |

SUPER FURRY ANIMALS

95	SFAP1	Frisbee (12" promo, 1-sided, unreleased intended debut single. Not on a label)	40
96	Creation CRE 222	Hometown Unicorn/Don't Be A Fool Billy (p/s)	12
96	Creation CRESCD 231	God! Show Me Magic/Death By Melody/Dim Bendith (CD, picture disc)	8
96	Creation CRE 235	Something 4 The Weekend/Waiting To Happen (p/s)	8
96	Creation CRE 243	If You Don't Want Me To Destroy You/Guacamole (poster p/s)	8
96	Creation CRE 243	If You Don't Want Me To Destroy You (picture disc)	10
96	Creation CRE 247	The Man Don't Give A Fuck (p/s, 1-sided, blue vinyl)	20
96	Creation CRE 247 T	The Man Don't Give A Fuck/(Howard Marks Mix)/(Wishmountain Mix)/(Darren Price Mix) (12", p/s)	8
96	Creation CRESCD 247	The Man Don't Give A Fuck/(Howard Marks Mix)/(Wishmountain Mix) (CD, picture disc)	15
96	Creation CTP 229	The Man Don't Give A Fuck/Dim Brys Dim Chwys (12" 1-sided promo)	20
96	Debiel SS 01	(Nid) Hon Yw'r Gan Sy'n Mynd I Achub Yr Laith (1-sided gig freebie)	15
97	Creation CRE 275	Play It Cool/Pass The Time (fold out poster sleeve)	5
97	Creation CRE 283	Demons/Hit And Run (fold out poster sleeve)	5
98	Creation CRE 288	Ice Hockey Hair/Smokin' (stickered p/s, limited edition)	10

MINT VALUE £

00	Placid Casual PLC02	Ysbediau Heulog/Charge (White vinyl in PVC sleeve, 3000 only)	10
03	Epic 6739067	Golden Retriever/Summer Snow/Blue Fruit (picture disc, limited edition, numbered, stickered poly sleeve)	8
95	Ankst ANKST 057	LLANFAIRPWLLGWYNGYLLGOGERYCHWYRNDROBWLLANTYSILIOGOGOGOCHYNYGOFOD (IN SPACE) (EP) (1st issue/2nd issue, same cat no)	15
95	Ankst ANKST 057	LLANFAIRPWLLGWYNGYLLGOGERYCHWYRNDROBWLLANTYSILIOGOGOGOCHYNYGOFOD (IN SPACE) (EP) (1st issue/2nd issue, same cat no)	10
95	Ankst ANKST 057	LLANFAIRPWLLGWYNGYLLGOGERYCHWYRNDROBWLLANTYSILIOGOGOGOCHYNYGOFOD (IN SPACE) (EP) (CD, 1st issue/2nd issue, same cat no)1st.	20
95	Ankst ANKST 057	LLANFAIRPWLLGWYNGYLLGOGERYCHWYRNDROBWLLANTYSILIOGOGOGOCHYNYGOFOD (IN SPACE) (EP) (CD, 1st issue/2nd issue, same cat no)1st.	15
95	Ankst ANKST 62	MOOG DROOG EP (EP, 1st issue, p/s)	15
95	Ankst ANKST 62	MOOG DROOG EP (EP, 2nd issue, same cat no, p/s)	10
95	Ankst ANKST 62	MOOG DROOG EP (CD, 1st issue)	20
95	Ankst ANKST 62	MOOG DROOG EP (CD, 2nd issue, same cat no)	18
96	Creation CRELP 190	FUZZY LOGIC (LP, with insert)	25
97	Creation CRELP 214	RADIATOR (2 x LP)	40
98	Creation CRECD 229 L	OUT SPACED (CD, rubber pack [black, yellow or blue])	30
99	Creation CRELP 242	GUERRILLA (2xLP, gatefold, pop up sleeve)	25
00	Placid Casual PLC03LP	MWNG (LP, ltd white vinyl, p/s PVC sleeve. 2000 copies)	40
01	Sony/Epic 5024131	RINGS AROUND THE WORLD (2xLP, side 3 plays from inside out, with free 7" white label 7")	35
03	Epic 5123751	PHANTOM POWER (2xLP etched vinyl with insert, 3000 copies)	20
04	Placid Casual PL07CD	PHANTON PHORCE (2xLP ltd version with bonus 'Slow Life' EP disc, fold-out packaging. 3000 copies)	25
05	Epic 5176711	SONGBOOK - THE SINGLES VOLUME ONE (2x12" pop up gatefold sleeve)	25
05	Sony 5205011	LOVE KRAFT (2xLP, gatefold)	15

SUPERGRASS

94	Backbeat BEAT 4	Caught By The Fuzz/Strange Ones (hand-stamped labels, 1,000 only, later re-pressed)	10
94	Backbeat BEAT 6	Mansize Rooster/Sitting Up Straight (luminous green vinyl, printed green cardboard sleeve, 500 only)	15
94	Backbeat BEAT 6	Mansize Rooster/Sitting Up Straight (luminous green vinyl, plain die-cut sleeve, 500 only)	10
94	Backbeat BEAT 6	Mansize Rooster/Sitting Up Straight (marbled green vinyl, plain sleeve)	10
94	Parlophone R 6396	Caught By The Fuzz/Strange Ones (p/s, reissue)	8
94	Parlophone 12R 6396DJ	Caught By The Fuzz/Strange Ones (12", p/s, promo only)	10
95	Parlophone 12RDJ6402	Mansize Rooster (12" promo)	8
95	Parlophone R 6402	Mansize Rooster/Sitting Up Straight (p/s, red vinyl)	6
95	Parlophone RS 6410	Lenny/Wait For The Sun (p/s, light blue vinyl)	6
96	Parlophone R 6428	Going Out/Melanie Davis (p/s, burgundy vinyl)	5
97	Parlophone R 6461	Richard III/Nothing More's Gonna Get In My Way (p/s, yellow vinyl)	6
97	Parlophone R 6469	Sun Hits The Sky/Some Girls Are Bigger Than Others (numbered p/s, white vinyl)	6
99	EMI CDIN 125	INTERVIEW (CD, tri-fold digipak, promo only)	10
99	Parlophone R6518	Pumping On Your Stereo/You'll Never Walk Again (green vinyl), p/s)	5
99	Parlophone R6524	Moving/Believer (blue vinyl, p/s)	6
99	Parlophone R 6531	Mary/(Live Version) (p/s, silver vinyl)	5
02	Parlophone R 6586	Grace/Velvetine (pink vinyl, p/s)	6
97	Parlophone GRASS 9497	THE SINGLES 1994-1997 (8 x 7" black vinyl, 'grass'-covered box set, with signed & numbered insert, promo only)	50
95	Parlophone PCSX 7373	I SHOULD COCO (LP, with inner & bonus single "Stone Free"/"Odd?" [PCSS 7373])	35
97	Parlophone 724385522819	IN IT FOR THE MONEY (LP)	30
99	Parlophone 5220561	SUPERGRASS (LP, with poster)	30
02	Parlophone 724354180019	LIFE ON OTHER PLANETS (LP)	15
04	EMI 5789941	SUPERGRASS IS 10 : BEST OF 94-04 (2 x 10" LP, clear vinyl, gatefold)	20

(see also Jennifers, Hot Rats)

SUPERMAN AND SPIDERMAN

85	Kingdom KVL 9025	SUPERMAN AND SPIDERMAN (LP)	12

SUPERMATIX

81	MC 4	BAD TIMING EP (p/s)	20

SUPER$HIT666

00	Infernal INFERNAL003LP	SUPER$HIT666 (10" LP, with inner sleeve, purple or black vinyl)	10

(see also Backyard Babies, Hellacopters, Wildhearts)

SUPERSISTER

72	Polydor 2001 379	No Tree Will Grow/She Was Naked	12
71	Dandelion 2310 146	TO THE HIGHEST BIDDER (LP, gatefold sleeve)	100
71	Polydor 2419 030	SUPER STARSHINE 3 (LP)	30
72	Polydor 2419 061	PRESENT FROM NANCY (LP)	35
73	Polydor 2480 153	PUDDING & YESTERDAY (LP)	50
73	Polydor 2925 021	ISKANDER (LP, gatefold sleeve with lyric sheet)	25

SUPERTRAMP

70	A&M AMLS 981	SUPERTRAMP (LP, laminated sleeve, brown label)	20
71	A&M AMLH 64306	INDELIBLY STAMPED (LP, gatefold sleeve, brown label)	20
84	A&M AMLK63708	BREAKFAST IN AMERICA (LP, Nimbus Supercut mail order only through Practical Hi Fi magazine	80

SUPPORTERS

70	RCA 1972	Sing Your Own Team/On The Ball	30

(DIANA ROSS &) SUPREMES

64	Stateside SS 257	When The Lovelight Starts Shining Thru' His Eyes/Standing At The Crossroads Of Love	50
64	Stateside SS 257	When The Lovelight Starts Shining Thru' His Eyes/Standing At The Crossroads Of Love (DJ copy)	100

(Credited to Supremes.)

64	Stateside SS 327	Where Did Our Love Go/He Means The World To Me	12
64	Stateside SS 327	Where Did Our Love Go/He Means The World To Me (DJ copy)	100
64	Stateside SS 350	Baby Love/Ask Any Girl	12
64	Stateside SS 350	Baby Love/Ask Any Girl (DJ copy)	100
65	Stateside SS 376	Come See About Me/(You're Gone But) Always In My Heart	12

65	Stateside SS 376	Come See About Me/(You're Gone But) Always In My Heart (DJ copy)	100
65	Tamla Motown TMG 501	Stop! In The Name Of Love/I'm In Love Again	12
65	Tamla Motown TMG 501	Stop! In The Name Of Love/I'm In Love Again (DJ copy)	100
65	Tamla Motown TMG 516	Back In My Arms Again/Whisper You Love Me Boy	25
65	Tamla Motown TMG 516	Back In My Arms Again/Whisper You Love Me Boy (DJ copy)	85
65	Tamla Motown TMG 527	Nothing But Heartaches/He Holds His Own	25
65	Tamla Motown TMG 527	Nothing But Heartaches/He Holds His Own (DJ copy)	85
65	Tamla Motown TMG 543	I Hear A Symphony/Who Could Ever Doubt My Love	20
65	Tamla Motown TMG 543	I Hear A Symphony/Who Could Ever Doubt My Love (DJ copy)	75
66	Tamla Motown TMG 548	My World Is Empty Without You/Everything Is Good About You	25
66	Tamla Motown TMG 548	My World Is Empty Without You/Everything Is Good About You (DJ copy)	75
66	Tamla Motown TMG 560	Love Is Like An Itching In My Heart/He's All I Got	55
66	Tamla Motown TMG 560	Love Is Like An Itching In My Heart/He's All I Got (DJ copy)	150
66	Tamla Motown TMG 575	You Can't Hurry Love/Put Yourself In My Place	15
66	Tamla Motown TMG 575	You Can't Hurry Love/Put Yourself In My Place (DJ copy)	70
66	Tamla Motown TMG 585	You Keep Me Hangin' On/Remove This Doubt	15
66	Tamla Motown TMG 585	You Keep Me Hangin' On/Remove This Doubt (DJ copy)	60
67	Tamla Motown TMG 597	Love Is Here And Now You're Gone/There's No Stopping Us Now	12
67	Tamla Motown TMG 597	Love Is Here And Now You're Gone/There's No Stopping Us Now (DJ copy)	70
67	Tamla Motown TMG 607	The Happening/All I Know About You	12
67	Tamla Motown TMG 607	The Happening/All I Know About You (DJ copy)	75

(The above 45s are credited to the Supremes.)

67	Tamla Motown TMG 616	Reflections/Going Down For The Third Time	12
67	Tamla Motown TMG 616	Reflections/Going Down For The Third Time (DJ copy)	60
67	Tamla Motown TMG 632	In And Out Of Love/I Guess I'll Always Love You	12
67	Tamla Motown TMG 632	In And Out Of Love/I Guess I'll Always Love You (DJ copy)	40
68	Tamla Motown TMG 650	Forever Came Today/Time Changes Things	12
68	Tamla Motown TMG 650	Forever Came Today/Time Changes Things (DJ copy)	40
68	Tamla Motown TMG 662	Some Things You Never Get Used To/You've Been So Wonderful To Me	10
68	Tamla Motown TMG 662	Some Things You Never Get Used To/You've Been So Wonderful To Me (DJ copy)	40
68	Tamla Motown TMG 677	Love Child/Will This Be The Day?	10
68	Tamla Motown TMG 677	Love Child/Will This Be The Day? (DJ copy)	40
68	Tamla Motown PSRS 317	Love Child (special Royal Command Performance promo sent to journalists with Ken East "talking invite" with Love Child playing in the background)	70
69	Tamla Motown TMG 695	I'm Living In Shame/I'm So Glad I Got Somebody (Like You Around)	10
69	Tamla Motown TMG 695	I'm Living In Shame/I'm So Glad I Got Somebody (Like You Around) (DJ copy)	40
69	Tamla Motown TMG 704	No Matter What Sign You Are/The Young Folks	8
69	Tamla Motown TMG 704	No Matter What Sign You Are/The Young Folks (DJ copy)	35
69	Tamla Motown TMG 721	Someday We'll Be Together/He's My Sunny Boy	7
69	Tamla Motown TMG 721	Someday We'll Be Together/He's My Sunny Boy (DJ copy)	35

(The above 45s are credited to Diana Ross & Supremes.)

70	Tamla Motown TMG 735	Up The Ladder To The Roof/Bill, When Are You Coming Back	7
70	Tamla Motown TMG 735	Up The Ladder To The Roof/Bill, When Are You Coming Back (DJ copy)	30
70	Tamla Motown TMG 747	Everybody's Got The Right To Love/But I Love You More	8
70	Tamla Motown TMG 747	Everybody's Got The Right To Love/But I Love You More (DJ copy)	25
70	Tamla Motown TMG 760	Stoned Love/Shine On Me	6
71	Tamla Motown TMG 760	Stoned Love/Shine On Me (DJ copy)	30
71	Tamla Motown TMG 782	Nathan Jones/Happy (Is A Bumpy Road)	7
71	Tamla Motown TMG 782	Nathan Jones/Happy (Is A Bumpy Road) (DJ copy)	30

(The above 45s are credited to the Supremes and do not feature Diana Ross)

65	Tamla Motown TME 2008	THE SUPREMES HITS (with flipback sleeve & push-out centre)	30
65	Tamla Motown TME 2008	THE SUPREMES HITS	35
66	Tamla Motown TME 2011	SHAKE (EP)	75
64	Stateside SL 10109	MEET THE SUPREMES	35
65	Tamla Motown TML 11002	WITH LOVE - FROM US TO YOU	50
65	Tamla Motown TML 11012	WE REMEMBER SAM COOKE	55
65	Tamla Motown TML 11018	THE SUPREMES SING COUNTRY, WESTERN AND POP	55
65	Tamla Motown TML 11020	MORE HITS BY THE SUPREMES	30
66	T. Motown TML 11026	THE SUPREMES AT THE COPA (mono)	20
66	T. Motown STML 11026	THE SUPREMES AT THE COPA (stereo)	25
66	T. Motown TML 11028	I HEAR A SYMPHONY (mono)	20
66	T. Motown STML 11028	I HEAR A SYMPHONY (stereo)	25
66	T. Motown TML 11039	SUPREMES A-GO GO (mono)	25
66	Tamla Motown STML 11039	SUPREMES A-GO GO (stereo)	35
67	T. Motown TML 11047	THE SUPREMES SING MOTOWN (mono)	25
67	T. Motown STML 11047	THE SUPREMES SING MOTOWN (stereo)	30
67	T. Motown TML 11054	THE SUPREMES SING RODGERS AND HART (mono)	20
67	T. Motown STML 11054	THE SUPREMES SING RODGERS AND HART (stereo)	22

(The LPs listed above are credited to the Supremes, with flipback sleeves.)

68	T. Motown (S)TML 11063	GREATEST HITS (stereo/mono, original pressing with flipback laminated sleeve)	15
68	T. Motown (S)TML 11070	'LIVE' AT LONDON'S TALK OF THE TOWN (mono/stereo)	15
68	T. Motown (S)TML 11073	REFLECTIONS (mono/stereo)	25
69	T. Motown TML 11088	SING & PERFORM FUNNY GIRL (mono)	20
69	T. Motown STML 11088	SING & PERFORM FUNNY GIRL (stereo)	18
69	T. Motown TML 11095	LOVE CHILD (mono)	25
69	T. Motown STML 11095	LOVE CHILD (stereo)	20
69	T. Motown TML 11114	LET THE SUNSHINE IN (mono)	25
69	T. Motown STML 11114	LET THE SUNSHINE IN (stereo)	22
70	T. Motown TML 11137	CREAM OF THE CROP (mono)	20
70	T. Motown STML 11137	CREAM OF THE CROP (stereo)	18

(The above LPs are credited to Diana Ross & Supremes. Originally issued with flipback sleeves; later pressings are worth two-third of these values.)

70	T. Motown 11154	FAREWELL	12
70	Tamla Motown STML 11157	RIGHT ON (as Supremes)	15
70	Tamla Motown STML 11175	NEW WAYS BUT LOVE STAYS	15
71	Tamla Motown STML 11189	TOUCH (LP, as Supremes)	15
73	T. Motown STML 11222	PRODUCED AND ARRANGED BY JIMMY WEBB (LP, as Supremes)	15

(see also Primettes, Diana Ross, Temptations, Four Tops, Florence Ballard)

SUPREMES & FOUR TOPS

71	Tamla Motown TMG 777	River Deep, Mountain High/It's Gotta Be A Miracle (This Thing Called Love)	7
71	Tamla Motown TMG 793	You Gotta Have Love In Your Heart/I'm Glad About It	7

MINT VALUE £

| 71 | T. Motown STML 11179 | THE SUPREMES AND THE FOUR TOPS - MAGNIFICENT 7 (LP) | 18 |
| 71 | T. Motown STML 11192 | THE RETURN OF THE MAGNIFICENT 7 (LP) | 15 |

DIANA ROSS & THE SUPREMES & THE TEMPTATIONS

69	Tamla Motown TMG 685	I'm Gonna Make You Love Me/A Place In The Sun	7
69	Tamla Motown TMG 709	I Second That Emotion/The Way You Do The Things You Do	7
70	Tamla Motown TMG 730	Why (Must We Fall In Love)/Uptight (Everything Is Alright)	8
69	T. Motown TML 11096	DIANA ROSS & THE SUPREMES JOIN THE TEMPTATIONS (LP, mono)	20
69	T. Motown STML 11096	DIANA ROSS & THE SUPREMES JOIN THE TEMPTATIONS (LP, stereo)	18
69	T. Motown (S)TML 11110	THE ORIGINAL SOUNDTRACK FROM TCB (LP, gatefold laminated sleeve)	20
70	T. Motown TML 11122	TOGETHER (LP, flipback sleeve, mono)	18
70	T. Motown STML 11122	TOGETHER (LP, flipback sleeve, stereo)	15

SUPREME WARRIOR

| 83 | Supreme Warrior SW001 | Treading The Tightrope/Mad & Cynical | 50 |

ADAM SURF & PEBBLE BEACH BAND

| 76 | Paladin PAL 3 | Fun Fun Fun/Blue Surf | 10 |

SURFACE TENSION

| 83 | Spiv 2TS | Rotation/Don't Let Them/Traffic Accident (p/s) | 7 |

SURFARIS

63	London HLD 9751	Wipe Out/Surfer Joe	10
63	Brunswick 05894	Waikiki Run/Point Panic	15
64	Brunswick 05902	Scatter Shield/Bat Man	15
66	Dot DS 26756	Wipe Out/Surfer Joe (reissue)	10
63	London RE-D 1405	WIPE OUT (EP)	50
63	London HA-D 8110	WIPE OUT (LP)	50
63	Brunswick LAT 8561	THE SURFARIS PLAY (LP, mono)	50
63	Brunswick STA 8561	THE SURFARIS PLAY (LP, stereo)	60
64	Brunswick LAT 8567	HIT CITY '64 (LP, mono)	45
64	Brunswick STA 8567	HIT CITY '64 (LP, stereo)	50
64	Brunswick LAT 8582	FUN CITY (LP)	50
65	Brunswick LAT 8605	HIT CITY '65 (LP)	55
65	Brunswick LAT 8631	IT AIN'T ME BABE (LP, mono)	50
65	Brunswick STA 8631	IT AIN'T ME BABE (LP, stereo)	60
66	Dot DLP 3535	WIPE OUT (LP, reissue)	25
76	MCA MCF 2761	SURFERS RULE (LP)	12
77	MCA Coral CDL 8050	GONE WITH THE WAVE (LP)	12
87	MCA MCL 1842	WIPE OUT - THE SINGLES ALBUM 1963-1967 (LP, withdrawn)	35

SURFERS

| 59 | Vogue V 9147 | Mambo Jambo/ALAN KALANI: A Touch Of Pink | 10 |

LES SURFS

64	RCA RCA 1432	Just For The Boy/Stop	10
65	RCA RCA 1461	Go Your Way/Chained To A Memory	7
67	Fontana TF 832	When I Tell You (That I Love You)/I Want To Be Free	6

SURGEONS

| 79 | Surgery S-100 | Sid Never Did It/Breaking Rocks On Riker's Island | 50 |

SURGICAL SUPPORTS

| 81 | Industrious Youth CONSTRUCT 2 | WITHDRAWN FOR DISPOSAL EP | 30 |

JOHN SURMAN (TRIO)

79	Ogun OG 259	BY CONTRACT (LP)	18
69	Deram DM 224	Obeah Wedding/Can't Stop The Carnival	40
68	Deram DML/SML 1030	JOHN SURMAN (LP)	80
69	Deram DML-R/SML-R 1045	HOW MANY CLOUDS CAN YOU SEE? (LP)	100
70	Futura GER 12	ALORS! (LP)	45
71	Dawn DNLS 3006	THE TRIO (LP, with Stu Martin, poster)	70
71	Dawn DNLS 3018	WHERE FORTUNE SMILES (LP, with insert, with John McLaughlin, Karl Berger, Stu Martin & Dave Holland)	40
71	Dawn DNLS 3022	CONFLAGRATION (LP)	60
71	Deram SML 1094	TALES OF THE ALGONQUIN (LP, with John Warren)	90
72	Island HELP 10	WESTERING HOME (LP)	20
73	Island ILPS 9237	MORNING GLORY (LP)	20

(see also Morning Glory, Trio, Mike Westbook, John McLaughlin, Alan Skidmore/Mike Osborne/John Surman)

SURPLUS STOCK

| 79 | Outatune OUT 7911 | Spiv/Vips (p/s) | 7 |

SURPRISE SISTERS

| 76 | Good Earth GD1 | Seashore/La Booga Rooga | 8 |

SURPRISES

| 79 | Dead Dog DEAD 01 | Jeremy Thorpe Is Innocent/Flying Attack/Little Sir Echo (p/s) | 35 |

SURVIVORS (1)

| 65 | Rio R 55 | Take Charge/Ska-Ology | 10 |
| 65 | Rio R 70 | Rawhide Ska/OWEN GRAY: Girl I Want You | 10 |

SURVIVORS (2)

| 79 | Capitol PSR 436 | Pamela Jean/After The Game (Credits the Beach Boys on p/s, Survivors on disc) | 10 |

(see also The Beach Boys)

SURVIVORS (3)

| 79 | Tribesman TM 22 | Angel Of Love/Fashion Rock (12") | 15 |

SUSIE

| 71 | Decca F 13217 | I Feel The Earth Move/We Are All The Same | 20 |

SUSPECT

| 71 | Decca FR 13218 | Mariooka/Belinda | 20 |

SUSPEKT

| 93 | Union Hall UH002 | Under Suspicion (12") | 12 |

94	Union Hall UH004	BURY THE BULLSHIT (EP)	12
96	Move MV 7021-1	THE UNDERGROUND STRIKES BACK (LP)	12

SUSSED (1)
79	Shoestring LACE 002	I Like You/Tango/The Perv (p/s)	15
80	Graduate GRAD 7	I've Got Me A Parka/Myself, Myself And I Repeated (p/s, paper labels; later reissued [1986] with silver labels)	6

SUSSED (2)
86	Fusion FU 001	Harlem Spirit/Part Two	12

(SCREAMING) LORD SUTCH (& THE SAVAGES)
61	HMV POP 953	Till The Following Night/Good Golly Miss Molly	30
63	Decca F 11598	Jack The Ripper/Don't You Just Know It	15
63	Decca F 11747	I'm A Hog For You/Monster In Black Tights	15
64	Oriole CB 1944	She's Fallen In Love With A Monster Man/Bye Bye Baby	50
64	Oriole CB 1962	Dracula's Daughter/Come Back Baby	70
65	CBS 201767	The Train Kept A-Rollin'/Honey Hush (as Lord Sutch)	50
66	CBS 202080	The Cheat/Black And Hairy	50
70	Atlantic 584 321	Cause I Love You/Thumping Beat	15
70	Atlantic 2091 006	Cause I Love You/Thumping Beat (reissue)	6
70	Atlantic 2091 017	Election Fever/Rock The Election	10
72	Atlantic K 10221	Gotta Keep A-Rockin'/Flashing Lights/Hands Of Jack The Ripper	10
76	SRT SRTS 76361	Monster Ball/Rang-Tang-A-Lang	8
76	SRT SRTS 76375	I Drink To Your Health Marie (Parts 1 & 2)	8
77	Decca F 13697	Jack The Ripper/I'm A Hog For You	6
80	Ace SW 70	All Black A Hairy/London Rocker/Oh Well	8
89	Invitation KORNER 001	Creepy Christmas Party/Rap Up Christmas (no p/s)	10
81	Ridgemount RMR 45 010	LOONABILLY (EP, p/s, with bonus "Loon Party" single)	10
70	Atlantic 2400 008	LORD SUTCH AND HIS HEAVY FRIENDS (LP)	25
72	Atlantic K 40313	HANDS OF JACK THE RIPPER (LP, as Lord Sutch & Heavy Friends)	25
81	Ace MAD 1	THE METEORS MEET SCREAMING LORD SUTCH (mini-LP, 1 side each, stickered cartoon print on plain grey card sleeve, 1,000 only)	100
82	Ace CHA 65	ROCK A HORROR (LP, gatefold)	15

(see also Savages, Meteors, Led Zeppelin, Cliff Bennett & Rebel Rousers, Circles, Nero & Gladiators, Neil Christian & Crusaders)

SUTCLIFFE JUGEND
82	Come Org. WDC 883030	WE SPIT ON THEIR GRAVES (!0 x cassette box)	150
82	Come Org. WDC 883028	CAMPAIGN (cassette, beware of Japanese bootlegs)	75

SUTHERLAND BROTHERS BAND
71	Island ILPS 9181	THE SUTHERLAND BROTHERS BAND (LP, blue inner)	15

SUZANNE
77	Ring O' 2017 108	Born On Hallowe'en/Like No One Else (in promo p/s)	25
77	Ring O' 2017 108	Born On Hallowe'en/Like No One Else	12
78	Ring O' 2017 111	You Really Got A Hold On Me/You Could Be Right This Time	10
78	Ring O' 2017 115	single (unreleased)	0
78	Ring O' 2320 105	SUZANNE (LP, unreleased)	0

SUZI & BIG DEE IRWIN
66	Polydor BM 65715	Ain't That Lovin' You Baby/I Can't Get Over You	15

(see also Big Dee Irwin)

PAT SUZUKI
60	RCA RCA 1171	I Enjoy Being A Girl/Sunday	7

SUZY & THE RED STRIPES
77	A&M AMS 7461	Seaside Woman/B-side To The Seaside (yellow vinyl, die-cut p/s)	10
79	A&M AMSP 7461	Seaside Woman/B-side To The Seaside (yellow vinyl, die-cut p/s, in box set with badge & 10 'saucy' mini-postcards)	40
80	A&M AMS 7548	Seaside Woman/B-side To The Seaside (reissue, cartoon p/s, as Linda McCartney alias Suzy & Red Stripes)	10
80	A&M AMSP 7548	Seaside Woman/B-side To The Seaside (12", as Linda McCartney alias Suzy & Red Stripes)	12
86	EMI EMI 5572	Seaside Woman/B-side To The Seaside (p/s)	6
86	EMI 12EMI 5572	Seaside Woman/B-side To The Seaside (12", p/s)	10

(see also Paul McCartney [& Wings])

SVANTE
68	United Artists UP 2224	Baby I Need Your Lovin'/Just One Word From You	5

SVENSK
67	Page One POF 036	Dream Magazine/Getting Old	25
67	Page One POF 050	You/All I Have To Do Is Dream	18

(see also Jason Paul)

SWALLOWS
56	Vogue EPV 1113	RHYTHM AND BLUES (EP, 2 tracks by Dominoes)	350

SWALLOWS WITH SONNY THOMPSON
52	Vogue V 2136	Roll, Roll Pretty Baby/It Ain't The Meat (78)	50

(see also Sonny Thompson & His Rhythm & Blues Band)

SWAMP DOGG
74	Island USA 002	Did I Come Back Too Soon/I Wouldn't Leave Here	5
72	Mojo 2916 014	TOTAL DESTRUCTION TO YOUR MIND (LP)	20
73	President PTLS 1	GAG A MAGGOT (LP)	15

(see also Jerry Williams, Brooks & Jerry)

SWAMPFOXX
72	Polydor 2058251	I've Got A Thing About You Baby/On Your Side	5

SWAN ARCADE
82	Highway	SWAN ARCADE (LP, reissue)	12
73	Trailer LER 2032	SWAN ARCADE (LP)	20
84	Fellside FE 037	TOGETHER FOREVER (LP)	18

SWANEE RIVER BOYS
54	Parlophone CMSP 7	Do You Believe/Gloryland Boogie (export issue)	15

MINT VALUE £

| 54 | Parlophone DP 385 | Was He Quiet Or Did He Cry/I Have Desire (78, export issue) | 12 |

BETTYE SWANN

67	CBS 2942	Make Me Yours/I Will Not Cry	60
67	CBS 2942	Make Me Yours/I Will Not Cry (DJ copy)	100
67	CBS 2942	Make Me Yours/I Will Not Cry (DJ copy in p/s)	150
69	Capitol CL 15586	Don't Touch Me/(My Heart Is) Closed For The Season	30
72	Atlantic K 10174	Victim Of A Foolish Heart/Cold Day In Hell	10
72	Atlantic K 10273	Today I Started Loving You Again/I'd Rather Go Blind	6
73	Mojo 2092 059	Make Me Yours/I Will Not Cry (reissue)	6
75	Atlantic K 10622	Doing It For The One I Love/All The Way In Or All The Way Out	5
75	Contempo CS 9019	Make Me Yours/I Will Not Cry (reissue)	5
76	Atlantic K 10851	Heading In The Right Direction/Be Strong Enough To Hold On	5

(see also Sam Dees & Bettye Swann)

RUTH SWANN

| 75 | Spark SRL 1124 | Tainted Love/Boy, You'd Better Move On | 5 |

SWANS (1)

| 63 | Stateside SS 224 | He's Mine/You Better Be A Good Girl Now | 40 |
| 64 | Cameo Parkway C 302 | The Boy With The Beatle Hair/Please Hurry Home | 40 |

SWANS (2)

88	Product Inc. PROD 23	Love Will Tear Us Apart/Trust Me (red vinyl, 750 only, p/s)	10
86	K.422/Some Bizzare KDE 312	A Screw (Holy Money)/Blackmail/A Screw (12", p/s)	10
88	Product Inc. 12PROD 23	Love Will Tear Us Apart (Red Version)/Trust Me/Love Will Tear Us Apart (Black Version)/Our Love Lies (12", black vinyl, p/s)	15
84	K.422/Some Bizzare KCC 1	COPS (LP, with inner)	25
90	Young God	FILTH (LP, U.K. reissue, 500 only, numbered)	30
86	K. 422/Some Bizzare KCC 3	HOLY MONEY (LP)	15
87	Product Inc. 33PROD 17	CHILDREN OF GOD (2-LP)	50
86	K. 422/Some Bizzare KCC 2	GREED (LP, with inner)	15
86	No label BURN ONE	PUBLIC CASTRATION IS A GOOD IDEA (2-LP)	30
89	MCA MCG 6047	THE BURNING WORLD (LP, with lyric inner)	15
95	Young God YGLP 004	BODY TO BODY, JOB TO JOB (LP)	30
95	Young God YGLP 005B	LOVE OF LIFE (LP, in box)	50

BENRICE SWANSON

| 65 | Chess CRS 8008 | Lying Awake/Baby I'm Yours | 30 |
| 65 | Chess CRS 8008 | Lying Awake/Baby I'm Yours (DJ copy) | 50 |

DAVE SWARBRICK

67	Bounty BYI 6030	RAGS, REELS AND AIRS (LP, with Martin Carthy & Diz Disley)	40
67	Polydor Special 236 514	RAGS, REELS AND AIRS (LP, reissue, with Martin Carthy & Diz Disley)	25
76	Transatlantic TRA 337	SWARBRICK (LP)	12
77	Transatlantic TRA 341	SWARBRICK 2 (LP)	12
78	Sonet SNTF 763	LIFT THE LID AND LISTEN (LP)	12
78	Sonet SNTF 764	THE CEILIDH ALBUM (LP, as Dave Swarbrick & Friends)	12
81	Logo LOGO 1029	SMIDDYBURN (LP)	12

(see also Martin Carthy & Dave Swarbrick, Fairport Convention,Young Tradition, Vashti Bunyan, Ian Campbell)

DAVE SWARBRICK & SIMON NICOL

| 81 | White Bear WBR 001 | LIVE AT THE WHITE BEAR (LP) | 15 |
| 83 | Woodworm WR 006 | CLOSE TO THE WIND (LP) | 12 |

(see also Dave Swarbrick, Fairport Convention, Young Tradition)

SWARBRIGG (PLUS TWO)

| 75 | MCA MCA 179 | That's What Friends Are For/Love Is | 6 |

SWEAT

| 80 | Double D DDLP | NO MORE RUNNING (LP, insert) | 30 |

ROSALYN SWEAT & PARAGONS

| 73 | Duke DU 160 | Blackbird Singing/Always | 15 |
| 74 | Horse HRLP 703 | BLACKBIRD SINGING (LP) | 15 |

(see also Paragons)

SWE-DANES

60	Warner Bros WB 7	Scandinavian Shuffle/Hot Toddy	10
60	Warner Bros WB 22	Swe-Dane Shuffle/At A Georgia Camp Meeting	6
61	Warner Bros WEP 6017	THE SWE-DANES (EP; mono)	20
61	Warner Bros SWEP 2017	THE SWE-DANES (EP; stereo)	25

(see also Alice Babsi)

SWEDEN THROUGH THE AGES

| 86 | Snappy SW 001 | IT HELPS TO CRY EP (12", p/s) | 12 |

(see also Billy MacKenzie)

SWEDISH MODERN JAZZ GROUP

| 61 | Tempo TAP 31 | SAX APPEAL (LP) | 200 |

SWEENEY'S MEN

67	Pye 7N 17312	Old Maid In The Garrett/Derby Ram	10
68	Pye 7N 17459	Waxies Dargle/Old Woman In Cotton	10
69	Transatlantic TRASP 19	Sullivan's John/Rattlin' Roarin' Willy	8
68	Transatlantic TRA 170	SWEENEY'S MEN (LP)	90
69	Transatlantic TRA 200	THE TRACKS OF SWEENEY (LP)	90
76	Transatlantic TRASAM 37	SWEENEY'S MEN (LP, reissue)	20
77	Transatlantic TRASAM 40	THE TRACKS OF SWEENEY (LP, reissue)	18

(see also Gay & Terry Woods, Dr. Strangely Strange)

SWEENY BEAN

| 72 | Sonet SON 2028 | Rock 'N' Roll Wedding/Overcoat | 8 |

JIM SWEENY

| 58 | Philips PB 811 | The Midnight Hour/Till The Right One Comes Along | 20 |

SWEENY TODD

| 70s | London L2616 | Shut Up/Wastin' Time | 20 |

76	London HLU 10540	Roxy Roller/Rue De Chance	12

JIMMY SWEEP

81	Tamarin TAM 3	London Town/Bridgetown Girls (written, produced by & feat. Alan Lancaster)	10
82	PRT 7P 233	London Town/Bridgetown Girls (reissue)	8

(see also Status Quo)

SWEEPERS

73	Warner Bros K16318	Harlem Song/Something's Real	5

SWEET

68	Fontana TF 958	Slow Motion/It's Lonely Out There	350
69	Parlophone R 5803	The Lollipop Man/Time	100
70	Parlophone R 5826	All You'll Ever Get From Me/The Juicer	40
70	Parlophone R 5848	Get On The Line/Mr. McGallagher	70
71	RCA RCA 2051	Funny Funny/You're Not Wrong For Loving Me	6
71	RCA RCA 2087	Co Co/Done Me Wrong, All Right	5
71	Parlophone R 5902	All You'll Ever Get From Me/The Juicer (reissue)	15
71	RCA RCA 2121	Alexander Graham Bell/Spotlight	5
73	RCA RCA 2403	Ballroom Blitz/Rock & Roll Disgrace (mispressed at wrong speed, 49rpm; matrix: 2403-A-1E)	15
74	RCA RCA 2480	Turn It Down/Someone Else Will	5
75	RCA RCA 2578	Action/Sweet FA	5
76	RCA RCA 25410	The Lies In Your Eyes/Cockroach	5
76	RCA RCA 2748	Lost Angels/Funk It Up	5
77	RCA PB 5011	Fever Of Love/A Distinct Lack Of Ancient	6
77	RCA PB 5046	Stairway To The Stars/Why Don't You Do It To Me	8
78	Polydor POSP 5	California Nights/Show Me The Way (unreleased)	0
79	Polydor POSP 36	Call Me/Why Don't You	7
79	Polydor POSP 73	Big Apple Waltz/Why Don't You	35
80	RCA PE 5226	Fox On The Run/Hellraiser/Ballroom Blitz/Blockbuster (EP, p/s)	15
80	Polydor POSP 131	Give That Lady Some Respect/Tall Girls	7
80	Polydor POSP 160	Sixties Man/Oh Yeah	5
80	Polydor POSP 160	Sixties Man/Oh Yeah	15
80	Polydor POSP 160	Sixties Man/Oh Yeah (mispressing, B-side plays "Tall Girls")	20
81	RCA GOLD 524	Blockbuster/Hellraiser (pink 'Golden Groove' p/s)	5
81	RCA GOLD 551	Ballroom Blitz/Wig Wam Bam (pink 'Golden Groove' p/s)	5
84	Anagram ANA 27	The Sixteens/Action (p/s)	10
84	Anagram ANA 28	It's...It's... The Sweetest Mix/Fox On The Run (p/s)	5
84	Anagram 12 ANA 28	It's The Sweetest Mix/Fox On The Run (12" p/s; matrix no. 12 ANA 28 AI)	8
84	Anagram 12 ANA 28	It's The Sweetest Mix/Fox On The Run (12" p/s; matrix no. 12 ANA 28.A)	8
85	Anagram ANA 29	Sweet 2th - The Wig Wam-Willy Mix/The Teen Action Mix (p/s)	8
85	Anagram ANA 29	Sweet 2th - The Wig Wam-Willy Mix/The Teen Action Mix (12", p/s)	8
89	RCA PB 43337	Wig Wam Bam/Little Willy (p/s)	5
71	MFP MFP 5248	GIMME DAT DING (1 side each by Sweet & Pipkins)	12
71	RCA SF 8288	FUNNY HOW SWEET CO-CO CAN BE	25
74	RCA LPL 15039	SWEET FANNY ADAMS	18
74	RCA LPL 15080	DESOLATION BOULEVARD (LP, gatefold sleeve)	15
75	RCA SPC 0001	STRUNG UP (2xLP)	30
76	RCA RS 1036	GIVE US A WINK	12
77	RCA PL 25072	OFF THE RECORD (gatefold, with inner sleeve)	15
78	RCA Camden CDS 1168	THE SWEET	12
79	Polydor POLD 5022	CUT ABOVE THE REST (with inner sleeve)	15
70s	RCA SF 8316	THE SWEET'S BIGGEST HITS (LP, 1st pressing with laminated sleeve)	12
80	Polydor POLS 1021	WATER'S EDGE	18
82	Polydor 2311 1179	IDENTITY CRISIS	22
84	Anagram GRAM 16	SWEET SIXTEEN (LP)	15
84	Anagram P GRAM 16	SWEET SIXTEEN (LP, picture disc)	25

(see also Brian Connolly, Mayfield's Mule, Elastic Band, Andy Scott)

SWEET AIR

70	Chime CH 1	Pictures In A Puddle/Sally FInne	170

SWEET AROMA

73	Rhino RNO 113	Happiness/Rock Reggae (demos or stock copies)	5

SWEET TOOTH

90	Staindrop/Earache MOSH 26	SOFT WHITE UNDERBELLY (LP)	12

SWEET CHARIOT

69	MCA MK 5010	Heavenly Road/Wish I Were A Child	8
73	Columbia DB 8999	When I'm A Kid/Mozart '73	8
70s	T.O.G. SCEP 001	Angelina/Young At Heart/America	8
72	De Wolfe DWLP 3230	SWEET CHARIOT & FRIENDS (LP, library issue only)	40

SWEET CHARLES

88	Urban URBLP 9	FOR SWEET PEOPLE FROM SWEET CHARLES (LP)	12

SWEET CONFUSION

69	Escort ES 809	Elizabeth Serenade/Don At Rest	8
69	Escort ES 812	Hotter Scorcher/Conquer Lion	8

(see also Stranger & Patsy)

SWEET CORPORALS

59	Top Rank JAR 217	The Same Old Army/Warm And Willing	5

SWEET CREAM

78	Ember EMBS 368	I Don't Know What I'd Do.Skunk Funk	8

SWEET DREAMS

74	Bradleys BRADL 1008	WE'LL BE YOUR MUSIC (LP)	15

(see also Polly Brown, Jimmy Thomas)

SWEETEST ACHE

90	Sarah SARAH 36	If I Could Shine/Here Comes The Ocean (p/s, insert)	10
90	Sarah SARAH 39	Tell Me How It Feels/Heaven-Scented World (p/s, insert)	10
91	Sarah SARAH 47	Everlasting/Sickening (p/s, insert)	10

MINT VALUE £

91   Sarah SARAH 608   JAGUAR (LP) 20

SWEET FEELING
67   Columbia DB 8195   All So Long Ago/Charles Brown 180
(see also Rupert's People)

SWEETHEARTS
65   Blue Beat BB 389   Sit Down And Cry (actually with Clinton & Rufus)/PRINCE BUSTER: Ghost Dance 80

HARRY SWEETING
68   Coxsone CSL 8012   FROM JAMAICA WITH LOVE (LP) 100

SWEET INSPIRATIONS
67   Atlantic 584 117   Why (Am I Treated So Bad)/I Don't Want To Go On Without You.................10
67   Atlantic 584 132   Let It Be Me/When Something Is Wrong With My Baby 10
68   Atlantic 584 167   Sweet Inspiration/I'm Blue...10
68   Atlantic 584 233   What The World Needs Now Is Love/You Really Didn't Mean It 10
69   Atlantic 584 241   Sweet Inspiration/I'm Blue...6
69   Atlantic 584 279   Sweets For My Sweet/Get A Little Older 6
70   Atlantic 584 312   (Gotta Find) A Brand New Lover (Parts 1 & 2) 6
71   Atlantic 2091 073   Evidence/Change Me Not 5
68   Atlantic 587/588 090   THE SWEET INSPIRATIONS (LP) 20
69   Atlantic 587/588 137   WHAT THE WORLD NEEDS NOW IS LOVE (LP) 20
69   Atlantic 587/588 194   SWEETS FOR MY SWEET (LP) 20
70   Atlantic 2465 003   SWEET SWEET SOUL (LP) 20
(see also Cissy Houston)

SWEET JESUS
91   Chapter 22 CHAP 63   Cat Thing/Honey Loving Honey/Peach/Baby Blue (12" EP, ...10

SWEET LITTLE BUNTY
75   Ackee ACK 540   I (Who Have Nothing)/Oh Me Oh My 6

SWEET PAIN
71   United Artists UP 35268   Timber Gibbs/Chain Up The Devil 5
69   Mercury 20146 SMCL   SWEET PAIN (LP, laminated gatefold, black/silver label) 150
(see also Dick Heckstall-Smith)

SWEET PLUM
69   Middle Earth MDS 103   Lazy Day/Let No Man Steal Your Thyme 30
70   Middle Earth MDS 105   Set The Wheels In Motion/Catch A Cloud 30

SWEET REACTION
72   Satril SAT 5   Come Back My Dream/Call Me Maria 10

SWEET REVENGE
80s   SRS SRS 15   Feel The Bullets Bite/Inside Your Head 125

SWEET SAVAGE
81   Park PRK 1001   Take No Prisoners/Killing TIme (p/s, red and yellow label) 60
81   Park PRK 1001   Take No Prisoners/Killing TIme (p/s, black and yellow label) 40
80s   Crashed CAR 48   Straight Through The Heart/Teaser (no p/s) 150
80s   private pressing   The Raid/Prosecutors Of Greed (possibly unreleased) 50
(see also Dio, Whitesnake)

SWEETSHOP
68   Parlophone R 5707   Barefoot And Tiptoe/Lead The Way 25
(see also Mark Wirtz)

SWEET SLAG
71   President PTLS 1042   TRACKING WITH CLOSE-UPS (LP) 100

SWEET THUNDER
78   Fantasy FTC 158   Everybody's Singin' Love Songs/Joyful Noise 5

SWEET THURSDAY
69   Polydor 2310 051   SWEET THURSDAY (LP) 25
(see also Nicky Hopkins, Mark-Almond)

SWEGAS
70   Trend 6099 001   What You Gonna Do/There Is Nothing In It 10
71   Trend 6480 002   CHILD OF LIGHT (LP, gatefold sleeve) 20

SWELL
92   Mean MEAN LP 002   ...WELL? (LP, marble vinyl)...15
94   Beggars Banquet ARBLP 6   41 (LP) 12

SWELL MAPS
78   Rather GEAR ONE   Read About Seymour/Ripped And Torn/Black Velvet (p/s) 15
79   Rough Trade RT 010/Rather Read About Seymour/Ripped And Torn/Black Velvet (p/s, reissue, different back sleeve) 7
      GEAR ONE MK. 2
79   R. Trade RT 012/GEAR 3   Dresden Style/Mystery Track/Ammunition Train/Full Moon (Dub) (p/s) 7
79   R. Trade RT 021/GEAR 6   Real Shocks/English Verse/Monlogues (p/s, 2 different colours) 8
79   R. Trade RT 036/GEAR 7   Let's Build A Car/Big Maz In The Country/...Then Poland (p/s) 7
81   Rough Trade RT 012/Rather Dresden Style (new vocal)/Ammunition Train/Full Moon (Dub) (p/s, reissue,
      GEAR 3   different back sleeve)...7
79   Rough Trade ROUGH 2/Rather A TRIP TO MARINEVILLE (LP, with inner sleeve, with bonus EP in die-cut sleeve
      TROY 1   [Rather GEAR FIVE])..40
79   Rough Trade ROUGH 2/Rather A TRIP TO MARINEVILLE (LP, with inner sleeve, without bonus EP in die-cut sleeve
      TROY 1   [Rather GEAR FIVE])..25
80   Rough Trade ROUGH 15   SWELL MAPS IN 'JANE FROM OCCUPIED EUROPE' (LP) 30
81   Rough Trade ROUGH 21   WHATEVER HAPPENS NEXT... (2-LP) 18
84   Rough Trade ROUGH 41   SWELL MAPS IN 'COLLISION TIME' (LP) 12
(see also Cult Figures, Nikki Sudden, Steve Treatment, Phones Sportsman Band, Epic Soundtracks, Metrophase, Last Bandits)

SWERVEDRIVER
91   Creation CREF 009   Surf Twang/Deep Twang (p/s) 7
91   Creation CRE 079T   SON OF MUSTANG FORD EP (12") 8
91   Creation CRE 088T   RAVE DOWN EP (12")...8
91   Creation CRELP 093   RAISE (LP, with free 7")..30

91	Creation CRELP 093	RAISE (LP, without free 7")	20
93	Creation CRELP 143	MEZCAL HEAD (LP)	20
95	Creation CRELP 157	EJECTOR SEAT RESERVATION (LP, with free 7")	20
95	Creation CRELP 157	EJECTOR SEAT RESERVATION (LP, without free 7")	15

ANTHONY SWETE
69	RCA RCA 1905	Backfield in Motion/Soul Deep	8

JONATHAN SWIFT
71	CBS 64412	INTROVERT (LP, side opening gatefold, nude cover)	18
72	CBS 64751	SONGS (LP, with lyric insert)	15

TUFTY SWIFT
77	Free Reed FRR 017	HOW TO MAKE A BAKEWELL TART (LP, with booklet)	25
85	Shark SHARK 04	YOU'LL NEVER DIE FOR LOVE (LP, private pressing)	15

ALAN SWIMMER & DEE DAVIDSON
70s	Fab FAB 242	Take Me Back To Jamaica/Thousands Of Children	5

STEVE SWINDELLS
74	RCA LPL1 5057	MESSAGES (LP, with insert)	12

(see also Hawkwind)

SWINDLEFOLK
68	Deroy	A-ROVIN' (LP, private pressing)	75
69	Deroy	SWINDLED (LP, private pressing)	75

RAY SWINFIELD
68	Morgan MR 107P	ONE FOR RAY (LP)	45

SWINGERS
60	Vogue V 9158	Love Makes The World Go Round/Jackie	15
67	Blue Beat BB 379	Simpleton/FRANCIS: Warn The People	40

SWINGERS
81	Magnet MAG 202	Be My Baby/Swinging	5

(see also Spectres, Rich Kids)

SWINGING BLUE JEANS
63	HMV POP 1170	It's Too Late Now/Think Of Me	12
63	HMV POP 1206	Do You Know/Angie	15
63	HMV POP 1242	Hippy Hippy Shake/Now I Must Go	5
64	HMV POP 1273	Good Golly Miss Molly/Shakin' Feelin'	5
64	HMV POP 1304	You're No Good/Don't You Worry About Me	5
64	HMV POP 1327	Promise You'll Tell Her/It's So Right	7
64	HMV POP 1375	It Isn't There/One Of These Days	7
65	HMV POP 1409	Make Me Know You're Mine/I've Got A Girl	10
65	HMV POP 1477	Crazy 'Bout My Baby/Good Lovin'	8
66	HMV POP 1501	Don't Make Me Over/What Can I Do Today	8
66	HMV POP 1533	Sandy/I'm Gonna Have You	15
66	HMV POP 1564	Rumours, Gossip, Words Untrue/Now The Summer's Gone	15
67	HMV POP 1596	Tremblin'/Something's Coming Along	18
67	HMV POP 1605	Don't Go Out Into The Rain/One Woman Man	18
64	HMV 7EG 8850	SHAKE WITH THE SWINGING BLUE JEANS (EP)	40
64	HMV 7EG 8868	YOU'RE NO GOOD MISS MOLLY (EP)	40
64	HMV CLP 1802	BLUE JEANS A' SWINGING (LP, mono)	60
64	HMV CSD 1570	BLUE JEANS A' SWINGING (LP, stereo)	75
64	Regal SREG 1073	TUTTI FRUTTI (LP, export issue)	50
67	MFP MFP 1163	SWINGING BLUE JEANS (LP, reissue of HMV CLP 1802)	15
74	Dart BULL 1001	BRAND NEW AND FADED (LP)	18

(see also Ray Ennis & Blue Jeans, Blue Jeans, Escorts, Terry Sylvester)

SWINGING CATS
80	Two Tone CHS TT 14	Mantovani/Away (paper label, company sleeve)	7
80	Two Tone CHS TT 14	Mantovani/Away (silver plastic label, company sleeve)	15

SWINGIN' MEDALLIONS
66	Philips BF 1500	Double Shot Of My Baby's Love/Here It Comes Again	10
66	Philips BF 1515	She Drives Me Out Of My Mind/You Gotta Have Faith	10

SWINGING SAPERLIPOPETTE
79	Kitty 7	Little Claw/I'm Not A teddy Bear	30

SWINGING SOUL MACHINE
69	Polydor 56760	Spooky's Day Off/Nobody Wants You	15

(see also Machine)

SWISS MOVEMENT
00	Grapevine 118	I Wish Our Love Would Last Forever/One In A Million	10

SWORDEDGE
80	Swordedge 001	SWORDEDGE (LP)	250

SWORN LORD
90	Davy G DG003	The Vengeance Is Mine (12")	60

SWS
88	DTI MAC2	Boys From The Bec/Our Rhymes Are Fly (12")	15
90	Cue TCUE003	Overture/Empirical Expansions/Info Nation/Leaf In The Wind	10

SYD & JOE
72	Bullet BU 498	Three Combine/LES FOSTER : I'm The Nearest To Your Heart	5

SYDNEY (CROOKS) ALL STARS
70	Bullet BU 436	The Return Of Batman/In Action	10
70	Bullet BU 437	Outer Space/Full Moon	30

(see also Pioneers, Junior English, Sammy Morgan)

ERIC SYKES & HATTIE JACQUES
62	Decca F 11512	Doctor Kildare/Bedtime Story	5

(see also Eric & Hattie, Goons)

JOHN SYKES
82	MCA MCA 792	Please Don't Leave Me/(Instrumental) (with Phil Lynott, in p/s)	35
82	MCA MCA 792	Please Don't Leave Me/(Instrumental) (with Phil Lynott)	10

(see also Thin Lizzy, Phil Lynott, Tygers Of Pan Tang, Whitesnake)

SYKES & MEDINA
69	CBS 4529	Everything's Fine Fine Fine/I Can Feel The Thickness	10

ROOSEVELT SYKES
50	Jazz Collector L 40	Three, Six And Nine/We Can Sell That Thing (78)	10
56	Vogue V 2389	Fine And Brown/Too Hot To Hold	75
56	Vogue V 2389	Fine And Brown/Too Hot To Hold (78)	30
56	Vogue V 2393	Walkin' This Boogie/Security Blues	75
56	Vogue V 2393	Walkin' This Boogie/Security Blues (78)	30
66	Delmark DJB 2	BACK TO THE BLUES (EP)	30
62	Encore ENC 183	BIG MAN OF THE BLUES (LP)	25
61	Columbia 33SX 1343	FACE TO FACE WITH THE BLUES (LP)	30
62	Columbia 33SX 1422	THE HONEYDRIPPER (LP, with Alexis Korner)	60
65	Bluesville BVLP 1006	THE RETURN OF ROOSEVELT SYKES (LP)	25
67	77' 77LEU 12-50	BLUES FROM BAR ROOMS (LP)	30
67	Riverside RLP 8819	MR SYKES' BLUES 1929-1932 (LP)	22
67	Ember EMB 3391	ROOSEVELT SYKES SINGS THE BLUES (LP)	20
71	Barclay 920 294	THE HONEYDRIPPERS' DUKE'S MIXTURE (LP)	15
70s	Delmark DL 607	HARD DRIVIN' BLUES (LP, blue label)	15

(see also Robert Pete Williams)

SYKO & CARIBS
64	Blue Beat BB 213	Do The Dog/Jenny	15
64	Blue Beat BB 223	Big Boy/Sugar Baby	15

SYLTE SISTERS
63	London HLU 9753	Summer Magic/Well It's Summertime	15

SYLVAIN SYLVAIN
80	RCA PB 9500	Every Boy And Every Girl/Emily	5

(see also New York Dolls)

SYLVAN
65	Columbia DB 7674	We Don't Belong/Life's Colours Have Gone	20

GOOD PAUL SYLVAN
70	Polydor 2001 090	Ophelia/Stop Making A Fool Of Me	6

C. SYLVESTER & PLANETS
64	Blue Beat BB 206	Going South/LITTLE JOYCE: Oh Daddy	12

ROLAND SYLVESTER
64	Carnival CV 7018	Grandfather's Clock/SANDRA MURRAY: Nervous	6

TERRY SYLVESTER
74	Polydor 2383 394	I BELIEVE (LP, with insert)	12

(see also Escorts, Swinging Blue Jeans, Hollies)

SYLVESTER'S JUKE BOX
73	CBS 8419	Juke Box/It's Because	60

SYLVIA
67	Fontana TF 884	Make Me A Woman/Without Your Love	10
68	Fontana TF 932	Down Hill/A Few Sweet Moments Of Love	10
73	London SHU 8453	PILLOW TALK	12

SYLVIA (U.S.)
68	Soul City SC 103	I Can't Help It/It's A Good Life	20
75	London HLU 10415	Pillow Talk/My Thing	7

DAVID SYLVIAN
84	Virgin VSY 633	Red Guitar/Forbidden Colours (Version) (picture disc)	5
84	Virgin VS 717	Pulling Punches (7" Mix)/Backwaters (Remix) (p/s, with 3 postcards)	5
84	Virgin VSY 717	Pulling Punches (7" Mix)/Backwaters (Remix) (picture disc)	6
86	Virgin VSS 815	Taking The Veil/Answered Prayers (rectangular picture disc, stickered PVC sleeve)	8
88	Virgin CDT 23	Words With The Shaman: Part 1 - Ancient Evening/Part 2 - Incantation/Part 3 - Awakening (Songs From The Tree Tops) (3" CD, gatefold card p/s)	12
89	Virgin VSCD 1221	Pop Song/A Brief Conversation Ending In Divorce/The Stigma Of Childhood (Kin) (3" CD, card sleeve)	20
89	Virgin VSCDX 1221	Pop Song/A Brief Conversation Ending In Divorce/The Stigma Of Childhood (Kin) (CD, presentation card pack, with discography)	12
87	Virgin V2471	SECRETS OF THE BEEHIVE (LP)	15
89	Virgin DSCD 1	WEATHERBOX (5-CD box set, with poster & booklet)	100
04	Samadhisound SOUNDLP 1	BLEMISH (LP, gatefold sleeve, featuring Derek Bailey, 2000 only, extra track: Trauma)	60

(See also Japan, Virginia Astley)

DAVID SYLVIAN & ROBERT FRIPP
93	Virgin V2712	THE FIRST DAY (2-LP, inners)	40
94	Virgin DAMAGE 1	DAMAGE (gold CD in silver-coloured box)	20

SYLVIN & GLENROY
70	Torpedo TOR 25	What You Gonna Do 'Bout It/KEN JONES: Sad Mood	6

SYMBOL
79	Art & Craft AC 001	Motherless Children/RANKING CARETAKER: Take It Away (12")	40
79	Kebra Nagast KH 04	Black Man's Word/Mr. Oppressor (12")	15

SYMBOLICS
76	Angen ANG 119	Tell Them Jah Jah/Version	8

SYMBOLS
65	Columbia DB 7459	One Fine Girl/Don't Go	10
65	Columbia DB 7664	You're My Girl/Why Do Fools Fall In Love	10
66	President PT 104	See You In September/To Make You Smile Again	8

66	President PT 113	Canadian Sunset/The Gentle Art Of Loving	6
67	President PT 128	You'd Better Get Used To Missing Her/Hideaway	6
67	President PT 144	Bye Bye Baby/The Things You Do To Me	10
67	President PT 173	(The Best Part Of) Breaking Up/Again	10
68	President PT 190	Lovely Way To Say Goodnight/Pretty City	18
68	President PT 216	Do I Love You/Schoolgirl	20
75	Crystal CR 7021	Sound Of Sunset (Instrumental)/Canadian Sunset (Vocal Recording)	6
68	President PTL 1018	THE BEST PART OF THE SYMBOLS (LP)	25
72	CBS 7725	No No No/Woman	8

(see also Johnny Milton & Condors)

SYMON & PI
68	Parlophone R 5662	Sha La La La Lee/Baby Baby	25
68	Parlophone R 5719	Got To See The Sunrise/Love Is Happening To Me	12

DAVID SYMONDS
68	Philips BF 1652	Here Is The News/Don't Worry About A Thing	10

SYMPHONICS
73	Polydor 2058 341	Heaven Must Have Sent You/Using Me	15

SYMPHONIC SLAM
76	A&M AMLH 69023	SYMPHONIC SLAM (LP)	20

PAT SYMS
64	Oriole CB 1971	It's Got To Be You Or No One/Lost	7

SYLVIA SYMS
58	Brunswick 05771	The Night They Invented Champagne/The Nature Of Things	7

SYN
67	Deram DM 130	Created By Clive/Grounded	120
67	Deram DM 145	14-Hour Technicolour Dream/Flowerman	120

(see also Syndicats, Yes, Peter Banks)

SYNANTHESIA
69	RCA SF 8058	SYNANTHESIA (LP)	300

SYNCHROJAK
95	Ferox FER 014	SYNCHROJAK (12" EP, plain sleeve)	8
95	Ferox FER 108	PHAZE 11 (12" EP, plain sleeve)	8

SYNCHROMESH
80	Rok ROK XI/XII	October Friday/E.F. BAND: Another Day Gone (company die-cut sleeve)	40

SYNCOPATORS
61	Decca F 11359	Everything Stops For Tea/If I Had A Talking Picture Of You	7

SYNDICATE OF SOUND
66	Stateside SS 523	Little Girl/You	35
66	Stateside SS 538	Rumours/The Upper Hand	18
66	Stateside S(S)L 10185	LITTLE GIRL (LP)	50

SYNDICATE (1)
79	Stevenage/Rock Against Racism	One Way Or Another/I Want To Be Somebody/RESTRICTED HOURS: Getting Things Done/Still Living Out The Car Crash (white label, foldover p/s)	12

(see also Astronauts)

SYNDICATE (2)
81	EMI 12EMI 5182	Dance You To The Ground/Step On The Gas (12")	35

SYNDICATS
64	Columbia DB 7238	Maybellene/True To Me	150
65	Columbia DB 7441	Howlin' For My Baby/What To Do	250
65	Columbia DB 7686	On The Horizon/Crawdaddy Simone	650
65	Columbia DB 7686	On The Horizon/Crawdaddy Simone (demos)	420

(see also Peter Banks, Ray Fenwick, Syn, Tomorrow, Yes)

SYNYX
82	Reality Attack RAF 1	BLACK DEATH (EP, fold out sleeve, plain white labels)	20

SYRUP
70	Amity OTS 501	Gentlemen Joe's Sidewalk Café/Love Is Love	6

SYSTEM
77	Tash	THE OTHER SIDE OF TIME (LP, 250 copies only)	110

SYSTEM
82	Spiderleg SDL 4	THE WARFARE (EP)	10
82	Spiderleg SDL 11	THE SYSTEM IS MURDER (EP)	10

SYSTEM OF A DOWN
99	Columbia/American	Sugar/War (live)	25

SYZYGY
85	Taptag TAP 3	LADY IN GREY (mini-LP)	20

(see also Blackthorn)

GABOR SZABO
66	HMV CLP 3614	JAZZ RAGA (LP)	25
67	Impulse MILP 506	THE SORCERER (LP, mono)	30

BERNARD SZAJNER
80	IRC IRC 005	SOME DEATHS TAKE FOREVER (LP)	12

MINT VALUE £

ERROL T. & ROOSEVELT ALL STARS
72	Ashanti ASH 406	Jamaica Born And Bred/Version	7

JAMIE T.
05	Pacemaker PANICSDJ 001	So Lonely Was The Ballad/Back In The Game (p/s, 500 only)	10
07	Virgin 0094637885512	PANIC PREVENTION (LP)	18

T. & UNKNOWN
80	Carrere CAR 142	My Generation/Woodstock Rock (p/s)	12

TABLE
77	Virgin VS 176	Do The Standing Still/Magical Melon Of The Tropics (p/s)	8
78	Chiswick NS 28	Sex Cells/The Road Of Lyfe (p/s)	7

TABLE TOPPERS
62	Starlite ST45 069	Rocking Mountain Dew/My Wild Irish Rose Rock	20

CHARLIE TABOR
63	Island WI 061	Blue Atlantic/Red Lion Madison	20

JUNE TABOR
86	Strange Fruit SFPS 015	THE PEEL SESSIONS (12" EP)	15
76	Topic 12TS 298	AIRS AND GRACES (LP)	12
77	Topic 12TS 360	ASHES AND DIAMONDS (LP)	12

(see also Silly Sisters)

TACTICS
86	Red Flame RF 49	MY HOUDINI (LP)	12

TAD & SMALL FRY
62	London HLU 9542	Checkered Continental Pants/Pretty Blue Jean Baby	15

TADPOLES
69	High Note HS 032	Rasta/Like Dirt	8

TAG
75	Philips 6006 477	Off Down The Road/Guitar Love	15

TAGES
66	Columbia DB 8019	Crazy 'Bout My Baby/In My Dreams	15
66	HMV POP 1515	So Many Girls/I'm Mad	50
67	Parlophone R 5640	Treat Me Like A Lady/Wanting	15
68	Parlophone R 5702	There's A Blind Man Playin' Fiddle In The Street/Like A Woman	15
68	MGM MGM 1443	Halcyon Days/I Read You Like An Open Book	20

(see also Blond)

BLIND JOE TAGGART
52	Tempo R 55	Religion Is Something Within You/Mother's Love (78)	20
55	Jazz Collector L 129	Religion Is Something Within You/Mother's Love (78, reissue)	15

TAGMEMICS
80	Index INDEX 003	Chimneys/(Do The) Big Baby/Take Your Brain Out For A Walk (p/s, with insert)	12

(see also Art Attacks)

TAICONDEROGA
69	Beacon BEA 143	Whichi Tai To/Speakin' My Mind	70

JACQUELINE TAIEB
68	Fontana TF 952	Tonight I'm Going Home/7 A.M.	150

LYN(N) TAIT(T) (& THE JETS)
66	Doctor Bird DB 1006	Vilma's Jump Up (as Lyn Taitt & The Comets)/GLEN MILLER & HONEYBOY MARTIN: Dad Is Home	25
66	Doctor Bird DB 1047	Spanish Eyes (with Tommy McCook)/STRANGER & HORTENSE: Loving Wine	25
67	Island WI 3066	Something Stupid/Blue Tuesday (as Lyn Taitt & the Jets)	40
67	Island WI 3075	I Don't Want To Make You Cry/Nice Time (as Lyn Taitt & the Jets)	40
68	Island WI 3139	Napoleon Solo/Pressure And Slide (as Lyn Taitt & the Jets)	50
68	Amalgamated AMG 810	El Casino Royale/Dee's Special (as Lyn Taitt & the Jets)	35
68	Pama PM 723	Soul Food/Music Flames (as Lyn Taitt & the Jets)	30
68	Island ILP 969	SOUNDS ROCK STEADY (LP, as Lyn Taitt & the Jets)	200
68	Big Shot BBTL 4002	GLAD SOUNDS (LP, as Lynn Taitt & the Jets)	80

(see also Justin Hines, Mike Thompson Jnr, ALton Ellis, Ken Boothe, Baba Brooks)

TAKE FIVE
60s	D.S.C.A (no cat. no.)	MY GIRL (EP, oversized p/s; Dundee Students Charity Appeal record)	100

TAKE IT
80s	Fresh Hold TRI	Man Made World/Taking Sides/How It Is (p/s)	40
80	Fresh Hold FHR 1	Twenty Lines/Armchairs/Friends And Relations (foldout p/s with insert)	20

TAKE THAT
91	Dance U.K. DUK 2	Do What U Like/Waiting Around (p/s)	15
91	Dance U.K. 12DUK 2	Do What U Like (Club Mix)/Do What U Like (Radio Mix)/Waiting Around (12", p/s; most with wrong tracks listed on sleeve)	25
91	RCA PB 45085	Promises/Do What U Like (p/s)	5
91	RCA PB 45085P	Promises/Do What U Like (poster p/s)	8
91	RCA PT 45086	Promises (12" Mix)/Do What U Like (12" Mix) (12", p/s)	10
92	RCA PB 45257	Once You've Tasted Love/Guess Who Tasted Love (p/s)	5
92	RCA PB 45265	Once You've Tasted Love/Guess Who Tasted Love (spined p/s with pull-out hexagonal pop-up calendar)	15
92	RCA PB 45258	Once You've Tasted Love (Aural Mix)/Guess Who Tasted Love (Guess Who Mix)/Once You've Tasted Love (Radio Version) (12" picture disc, with insert)	12

92	RCA 74321 10100 7	It Only Takes A Minute/Satisfied (p/s, with Mark & Robbie prints) 15
92	RCA 74321 10101 7	It Only Takes A Minute/It Only Takes A Minute (Royal Rave Mix) (different p/s, with Jason & Howard prints & paper frame) 8
92	RCA 74321 10814 7	I Found Heaven (7" Radio Mix)/(Mr. F's Garage Mix) (poster p/s) 6
92	RCA 74321 10813 7B	I Found Heaven (7" Radio Mix)/I'm Out (picture disc) 6
92	RCA 74321 11600 7	A Million Love Songs/A Million Love Songs (The Lovers Mix) (p/s, with tattoos) 10

(see also Robbie Williams)

TAKE 3
| 84 | Elite DAZZ 32 | Music & Time/Music & Time (extended version) (12") ....15 |

TAKERS
| 64 | Pye 7N 15690 | If You Don't Come Back/Think..............25 |

(see also Undertakers, Jackie Lomax)

TALAN
| 89 | Talan SRT 9KS 2208 | Spellbinder/Underground Madness (p/s) ....20 |

TALBOT BROTHERS
| 59 | Melodisc MEL 1507 | Bloodshot Eyes/She's Got Freckles..............15 |
| 60s | Melodisc CAL 20 | Bloodshot Eyes/She's Got Freckles (reissue)..............6 |

ZIGGY TALENT
| 55 | Brunswick 05506 | Cheek To Cheek (Cha Cha)/Bozooki Blues..............7 |

TALES
| 73 | MAM 93 | Someone Like You/Rockin' Suzanna ....5 |

TALES OF JUSTINE
67	HMV POP 1614	Albert/Monday Morning (in p/s) 180
67	HMV POP 1614	Albert/Monday Morning..............60
97	Tenth Planet TP 034	PETALS FROM A SUNFLOWER (LP, gatefold sleeve, numbered, 1,000 only) 25

(see also Tim Rice)

TALION
| 89 | Major WADES 1 | KILLING THE WORLD (LP) ....12 |

TALISKER
| 75 | Caroline CA 1513 | DREAMING OF GLENISLA (LP)..............20 |

TALISMAN
73	Argo AFW 110	Stepping Stones/Dr Jazz..............5
72	Argo ZFB 33	PRIMROSE DREAMS (LP) 12
73	Argo ZDA 161	STEPPING STONES (LP) 12

TALISMEN
| 65 | Stateside SS 408 | Masters Of War/Casting My Spell ....70 |

TALKING HEADS
77	Sire 6078 604	Love Goes To Building On Fire/New Feeling (p/s) 7
77	Sire SAM 87	Love Goes To Building On Fire/New Feeling (limited edition, in p/s)..............12
77	Sire SAM 87	Love Goes To Building On Fire/New Feeling..............10
77	Sire 6078 610	Psycho Killer/I Wish You Wouldn't Say That (p/s) 10
77	Sire 6078 610	Psycho Killer/Psycho Killer (Acoustic)/I Wish You Wouldn't Say That (12", p/s) 12
78	Sire 6078 620	Pulled Up/Don't Worry About The Government (p/s) 10
79	Sire SIR 4004	Take Me To The River/Found A Job (p/s) 10
79	Sire SIR 4004/SAM 87	Take Me To The River/Found A Job//Love Goes To Building On Fire/ Psycho Killer (double pack, gatefold p/s) 15
79	Sire SIR 4027	Life During Wartime (live version)/Electric Guitar (p/s) 12
80	Sire SIR 4033	I Zimbra/Paper (p/s) 10
80	Sire SIR 4040	Cities/Cities (live) (p/s) 7
80	Sire SIR 4040T	Cities/Cities (live)/Artists Only (live) (12", p/s) 10
80	Sire SIR 4048	Once In A Lifetime/Seen And Not Seen (p/s) 5
80	Sire SIR 4050	Houses In Motion (Special Re-Mixed Version)/Air (p/s) 10
80	Sire SIR 4050T	Houses In Motion/Air/Houses In Motion (Live) (12") 10
84	Sire W 9451T/SAM 176	This Must Be The Place (Full Version)/Moon Rocks//Slippery People (Remix)/ Making Flippy Floppy (Remix) (12", p/s, double pack) 12
84	EMI 12EMI 5509	Girlfriend Is Better/Once In A Lifetime (12", p/s) 10
85	EMI 12EMID 5520	Lady Don't Mind/Give Me Back My Name//Slippery People (live)/ This Must Be The Place (Naive Melody) (live) (12", p/s, double pack) 10
85	EMI EMIP 5530	Road To Nowhere/Television Man (picture disc)..............5
85	EMI 12 EMID 5530/	Road To Nowhere/Television Man (Extended)//Slippery People (Long Live Version)/Naive Melody (live) (12", stickered double pack) 10
79	Sire K 56707	FEAR OF MUSIC (LP, with free single "Psycho Killer"/"New Feeling" [SAM 108])..............20
80	Sire SRK 6095	REMAIN IN LIGHT (LP, inner and insert) 15
83	EMI 9237711	SPEAKING IN TONGUES (LP, clear vinyl in special cover) 18

TALK TALK
82	EMI EMI 5265	Mirror Man/Strike Up The Band (p/s) 5
82	EMI 12EMI 5314	Today (Extended)/It's So Serious (12", p/s) 8
82	EMI EMIP 5352	Talk Talk (Remix)/Mirror Man (picture disc) 5
82	EMI EMIP 5352	Talk Talk (Extended)/Talk Talk (BBC Version) (12", p/s) 8
84	EMI EMI 5433	THE TALK TALK DEMOS (double pack, poster p/s [EMI 5433 & PSR 467]) 10
86	EMI 12EMID 5540	Life's What You Make It (Extended)/It's Getting Late In The Evening// It's My Life/Does Caroline Know? (12", p/s, double pack) 15
86	EMI EMIP 5551	Living In Another World/For What It's Worth (shaped picture disc) 10
91	Verve TALKD 1	After The Flood/Myrrhman (CD, picture disc in 3-CD box) 15
91	Verve TALKD 2	New Grass/Stump (CD, picture disc)..............10
91	Verve TALKD 3	Ascension Day/5.09 (CD, picture disc) 10
91	Verve TALKD1/2/3	After The Flood/Myrrhman//New Grass/Stump//Ascension Day/5.09 (3-CD, in die-cut box) 40
88	Parlophone PC50105	SPIRIT OF EDEN (LP) 40
98	Voiceprint	LONDON 1986 (CD) 30
91	Polydor 847 717-1	LAUGHING STOCK (LP) 70

(see also Reaction)

TOM TALL
| 55 | London HL 8150 | Are You Mine/Boom Boom Boomerang (as Ginny Wright & Tom Tall)..............30 |
| 55 | London HLU 8216 | Give Me A Chance/Remembering You..............50 |

55	London HLU 8216	Give Me A Chance/Remembering You (78)	10
56	London HLU 8231	Underway/Goldie Jo Malone	50
56	London HLU 8231	Underway/Goldie Jo Malone (78)	15
57	London HLU 8429	Don't You Know/If You Know What I Know (with Ruckus Taylor)	40
57	London HLU 8429	Don't You Know/If You Know What I Know (with Ruckus Taylor) (78)	22
55	London RE-U 1035	COUNTRY SONGS VOL. 2 (EP, as Tom Tall & Ginny Wright)	40

(see also Ginny Wright)

TALL BOYS

82	Big Beat NS 79	Island Of Lost Souls/Another Half Hour Till Sunrise (p/s)	6
84	Big Beat NED 8	WEDNESDAY ADDAM'S BOYFRIEND (12" EP)	8
85	Big Beat NST 107	Final Kick/Interceptor/Dragster/Action Woman (12" EP)	8
86	Big Beat NST 114	Brand New Gun/Last House On The Left/Took A Long Time (12" EP)	8

(see also Meteors)

TALMY/STONE BAND

| 62 | Decca F 11543 | Madison Time/Madison Time (A-side with Alan Freeman) | 10 |
| 62 | Ace Of Clubs ACL 1134 | ROSES ARE RED & OTHER HITS OF 1962 (LP) | 18 |

TALULAH GOSH

86	53rd & 3rd AGARR 4	Beatnik Boy/My Best Friend (p/s)	8
86	53rd & 3rd AGARR 5	Steaming Train/Just A Dream (p/s)	8
86	53rd & 3rd AGARR 4/5T	Beatnik Boy/My Best Friend/Steaming Train/Just A Dream (12", p/s)	8
87	53rd & 3rd AGARR 8	Talulah Gosh/Don't Go Away (p/s)	5
87	53rd & 3rd AGARR 8T	Talulah Gosh/Don't Go Away (12", p/s)	8
88	53rd & 3rd AGARR 14	Bringing Up Baby/The Girl With The Strawberry Hair (p/s)	6
88	53rd & 3rd AGARR 14T	Bringing Up Baby/I Can't Get No Satisfaction, Thank God/The Girl With The Strawberry Hair/Do You Remember?/Sunny Inside (12", p/s)	8
88	53rd & 3rd AGARR 16	Testcard Girl (p/s)	5
87	53rd & 3rd AGAS 004	ROCK LEGENDS VOL. 69 (LP, clear vinyl)	15
91	Sarah 064	THEY'VE SCOFFED THE LOT (LP)	12

TAMANGOES

| 79 | Grapevine GRP 122 | I Really Love You/You've Been Gone So Long | 20 |

TAMING THE OUTBACK

| 86 | Black Sun BS 1 | Blue Heart/Fire | 15 |

JAMES TAMLIN

| 65 | Columbia DB 7438 | Is There Time/Main Line Central Station | 20 |
| 65 | Columbia DB 7577 | Yes I Have/Now There Are Two | 10 |

TAMLINS

| 79 | Deb Music DEB 007 | Still Water/AUGUSTUS PABLO: Spirit Of Umoja (12") | 20 |

TAMPA RED

50	Jazz Collector L 58	Easy Rider Blues/Come On Mama Do That Dance (78)	15
52	HMV JO 301	Pretty Baby Blues/Since Baby's Been Gone (78, export issue)	40
50s	Square M 2	Moot It Boy/She Rocks Me (With One Steady Roll) (78)	40
64	RCA RCX 7160	R & B VOL. 3 (EP)	25
60s	Memory TR 1	TAMPA RED (LP)	35

TAMPA RED/GEORGIA TOM

| 59 | Jazz Collector JEL 3 | THE MALE BLUES VOLUME 2 (EP) | 20 |

TAMS

63	Stateside SS 146	Untie Me/Disillusioned	30
63	HMV POP 1254	What Kind Of Fool Do You Think I Am/Laugh It Off	20
64	HMV POP 1298	It's All Right, You're Just In Love/You Lied To Your Daddy	18
64	HMV POP 1331	Hey Girl Don't Bother Me/Take Away	150
64	HMV POP 1331	Hey Girl Don't Bother Me/Take Away (DJ copy)	200
65	HMV POP 1464	Concrete Jungle/Till The End Of Time	15
69	Stateside SS 2123	Be Young, Be Foolish, Be Happy/That Same Old Song	15
70	Capitol CL 15650	Too Much Foolin' Around/How Long Love	15
75	ABC ABC 4020	Hey Girl Don't Bother Me/Be Young, Be Foolish, Be Happy	8
68	Stateside (S)SL 10258	A LITTLE MORE SOUL (LP)	40
70	Stateside SSL 10304	BE YOUNG, BE FOOLISH, BE HAPPY (LP)	25

TANAMO

| 63 | Island WI 108 | Come Down/I Am Holding On (actually by Lord Tanamo) | 30 |

TANDOORI CASSETTE

| 83 | IKA IKA 001 | Angel Talk/Third World Brief Case (p/s, 5,000 only) | 20 |

(see also Nazareth, Alex Harvey, Tear Gas, Stone The Crows)

SHARON TANDY

65	Mercury MF 898	Love Makes The World Go Round/By My Side	30
65	Pye 7N 15806	Now That You've Gone/Hurtin' Me	40
65	Pye 7N 15939	I've Found Love/Perhaps Not Forever	15
67	Atlantic 584 098	Toe Hold/I Can't Get Over It	20
67	Atlantic 584 124	Stay With Me/Hold On	60
67	Atlantic 584 137	Our Day Will Come/Look And Find	20
68	Atlantic 584 166	Fool On The Hill/For No One	20
68	Atlantic 584 181	Love Is Not A Simple Affair/Hurry Hurry Choo-Choo	40
68	Atlantic 584 194	You've Gotta Believe It/Border Town	20
68	Atlantic 584 214	The Way She Looks At You/He'll Hurt Me	30
68	Atlantic 584 219	Hold On/Daughter Of The Sun	100
69	Atlantic 584 242	Gotta Get Enough Time/Somebody Speaks Your Name	80

(see also Fleur-De-Lys, Tony & Tandy)

NORMA TANEGA

66	Stateside SS 496	Walkin' My Cat Named Dog/I'm The Sky	6
66	Stateside SS 520	A Street That Rhymes At Six A.M./Treat Me Right	12
66	Stateside SS 537	Bread/Waves	7
71	RCA 2072	Nothing Much Is Happening Today/Antarctic Rose	6
66	Stateside S(S)L 10182	WALKIN' MY CAT NAMED DOG (LP)	25
71	RCA SF 8217	I DON'T THINK IT WILL HURT IF YOU SMILE (LP)	20

TANGERINE DREAM

74	Virgin PR 214	Phaedra (Edit)/Mysterious Semblance At The Strand Of Nightmares (promo)	30
76	Virgin VDJ 17	Stratosfear/The Big Sleep In Search Of Hades (promo only)	25
77	MCA PSR 413	Betrayal (Sorceror Theme)/Search (promo only)	25
77	Virgin VS 199	Encore/Hobo March	5
81	Virgin VS 444	Chronozon/Network 23 (p/s)	8
84	Jive Electro P 74	Warsaw In The Sun/Polish Dance (map-shaped picture disc)	20
84	Jive Electro T 74	Warsaw In The Sun (Parts 1 & 2)/Polish Dance/Rare Bird (12", p/s)	15
85	Jive JIVE 101	Streethawk/Tear Garden (p/s)	15
85	Jive Electro T 101	STREETHAWK (12" EP)	20
87	Jive Electro 143	Tyger/21st Century Common Man II (p/s)	6
87	Jive Electro T 143	Tyger/Tyger (7" Version)/21st Century Common Man II (12", p/s)	10
89	Private 663 747	ORANGES DON'T DANCE (CD EP, promo only)	30
74	Virgin V2010	PHAEDRA (LP, copies with A1U/B2U matrixes and catalogue number misprinted with catalogue number on top left hand of gatefold sleeve instead of rear)	20
74	Polydor Super 2383 297	ATEM (LP)	20
75	Polydor Super 2383 314	ALPHA CENTAURI (LP)	20
78	Virgin V2111	FORCE MAJEURE (LP, clear vinyl, textured stickered sleeve)	15
80	Virgin VBOX 2	TANGERINE DREAM '70-80 (4-LP box set)	20
80	Virgin TCVX 2	TANGERINE DREAM '70-80 (4-cassette box set)	25
81	Virgin V 2212	EXIT (LP, 1st 1,000 with poster)	12
84	MCA MCF 3233	FIRESTARTER (LP, soundtrack)	12
84	Jive HIP 22	POLAND - THE WARSAW CONCERT (2-LP, gatefold sleeve, with inners)	15
84	Jive Electro HIPX 22	POLAND - THE WARSAW CONCERT (2-LP, picture disc)	25
85	Heavy Metal HMI PD 29	FLASHPOINT (LP, soundtrack, picture disc)	12
85	Heavy Metal HMXD 29	FLASHPOINT (CD, soundtrack; playable CD [most copies faulty])	50
86	Jive Electro TANG 1	IN THE BEGINNING (6-LP box set, with booklet)	25
87	Jive HIP 26	LE PARC (LP)	12
90	Virgin TD AK 11	TANGERINE DREAM (3-CD, 'Collector's Edition' box set)	12
90s	TDI TDICD	LIVE-ARIZONA 92 (2xCD)	12
03	Virgin 724359612829	TANGENTS 1973 - 1983 (5-CD box set with booklet)	30

(see also Edgar Froese, Klaus Schulze)

TANGERINE PEEL

67	United Artists UP 1193	Every Christian Lion-Hearted Man Will Show You/Trapped	30
68	CBS 3402	Solid Gold Mountain/Light Across The River	130
68	CBS 3676	Talking To No One/Wishing Tree	20
69	MGM MGM 1470	Never Say Never Again/A Thousand Miles Away	15
69	MGM MGM 1487	Play Me A Sad Song And I'll Dance/Wish You Could Be Here With Me	15
70	RCA RCA 1936	Move Into My World/In Between	6
70	RCA RCA 1990	Soft Delights/Thinking Of Me	6
70	RCA RCA 2036	What Am I To Do?/Don't Let Me Be Misunderstood	6
70	RCA LSA 3002	SOFT DELIGHTS (LP)	25

TANGO

92	Formation FORM 12004	THE IMPACT EP (12", p/s)	15

TANGO PROJECT

92	White 004	Project 1/Untitled (12", white label test pressing)	50

TANK (1)

72	Bumble GE 105	Heads I Win, Tails You Lose/Burgundy, Port And Red Wine	20

TANK (2)

81	Kamaflage KAM 1	Don't Walk Away/Shellshock/Hammer On (p/s, with cover mounted patch)	10
81	Kamaflage KAM 1	Don't Walk Away/Shellshock/Hammer On (p/s)	8
82	Kamaflage KAM 3	Turn Your Head Around/Steppin' On A Landmine (p/s)	15
82	Kamaflage KAM 7	Crazy Horses/Filth Bitch Boogie (p/s)	5
82	Kamaflage KAP 1	(He Fell In Love With A) Stormtrooper/Blood Guts And Beer (picture disc)	7
83	MFN KUT 101	ECHOES OF A DISTANT BATTLE (EP)	8
82	Kamaflage KAMLP 1	FILTH HOUNDS OF HADES (LP, 1st pressing, with black & yellow sleeve)	15
82	Kamaflage KAMLP 1	FILTH HOUNDS OF HADES (LP, 2nd pressing, with bonus p/s 7" Don't Walk Away (live)/"The Snake" [KAM F1])	15
83	Music For Nations MFN 3P	THIS MEANS WAR (LP, picture disc)	20

(see also Damned, UK)

TANNAHILL WEAVERS

76	Plant Life PLR 001	ARE YE SLEEPING MAGGIE? (LP, with lyric insert)	20
78	Plant Life PLR 010	THE OLD WOMAN'S DANCE (LP)	12

HOLLY TANNEN & PETE COOPER

79	Plant Life PLR 015	FROSTY MORNING (LP)	15

PHIL TANNER

68	EDF SSLP 1005	PHIL TANNER (LP, with lyric book)	25

TAN TAN

81	Maccabees MPCLP TT1	MUSICAL NOSTALGIA FOR TODAY (LP)	40

TANTARA BLADE

88	King Dice	Seven Shades Of Shame/This Car Has Crushed (p/s)	50

TANTONES

57	Vogue V 9085	So Afraid/Tell Me	850
57	Vogue V 9085	So Afraid/Tell Me (78)	150

TANTRUM

80	Ovation OV 1247	RATHER BE ROCKIN' (LP)	12

TANZ DER YOUTH

78	Radar ADA 19	I'm Sorry, I'm Sorry/Delay (p/s)	5

(see also Brian James, Damned)

TAO JONES INDEX

97	RCA 512541	Pallas Athena (live)/V-2 Schneider (live) (12", p/s)	12

(see also David Bowie)

TAPESTRY
67	London HLZ 10138	Carnaby Street/Taming Of The Shrew	30
68	NEMS 56-3679	Like The Sun/Florence	20
69	NEMS 5639-64	Heart & Soul/Who Wants Happiness	60

DEMETRISS TAPP
64	Coral Q 72470	Lipstick Paint A Smile On Me/If You Find Love	40

TARA
70	Polydor 2062009	Happy/The Love Of A Woman	15

TARANTULA
70	A&M AMLS 959	TARANTULA (LP)	15

TARHEEL SLIM & LITTLE ANN
65	Sue WI 390	You Make Me Feel So Good/Got To Keep On Lovin' You	40

TARNEY BAND, ALAN
78	A&M AMS 7339	Takin Me Back/Set The Minstrel Free	6

DAVE TARRIDA
99	Mosquito MSQ 013	PLAYING THE GAME (12" EP)	10

TARRIERS
56	London HLN 8340	Cindy, Oh Cindy/Only If You Praise The Lord (gold label lettering, as Vince Martin & Tarriers)	15
56	London HLN 8340	Cindy, Oh Cindy/Only If You Praise The Lord (silver label lettering, as Vince Martin & Tarriers)	7
57	Columbia DB 3891	The Banana Boat Song/No Hidin Place	10
57	Columbia DB 3961	Tom Dooley/Everybody Loves Saturday Night	5
57	Columbia DB 4025	Dunya/Quinto (My Little Pony)	5
58	Columbia DB 4148	I Know Where I'm Going/Acres Of Clams	5
58	London HLU 8600	Lonesome Traveller/East Virginia	5
60	London RET 1237	HARD TRAVELIN' VOLUME 2 (EP)	8
57	Columbia 33S 1115	THE TARRIERS (10" LP)	15
62	London STA 8525	A LIVE PERFORMANCE AT THE BITTER END (LP)	15

(see also Vince Martin, Rooftop Singers)

TARTAN HORDE
75	United Artists UP 35891	Bay City Rollers, We Love You/Rollers Theme	15

(see also Nick Lowe, Rat Scabies, Roogalator)

TARTANS
67	Island WI 3058	Dance All Night/What Can I Do	20
68	Caltone TONE 115	Awake The Town (with Lynn Taitt's Band)/LYNN TAITT & JETS: The Brush	60
68	Caltone TONE 117	Coming On Strong/It's Alright (with Tommy McCook's Band)	50
71	Escort ERT 843	A Day Will Come/ROBI'S All STARS: Version	8

(see also Devon & Tartans, Kaddo Strings, Max Romeo, Derrick Morgan)

TARTS
81	If You Can't Take A Joke JOKE1	Tie Me Kangeroo Down/Gene Queenie	80

TASAVALLAN PRESIDENTTI
73	Sonet SNTF 636	LAMBERTLAND (LP)	30
74	Sonet SNTF 658	MILKY WAY MOSES (LP, with insert)	30

TASKFORCE
00	White(Lowlife)grafpromo1	Graf Da Bus Up (12" - One sided, 500 pressed)	20
00	White(Lowlife)no matrix	Wha Blow (12", 1-Sided white label, 200 only)	20
00	Lowlife LOW10	VOICE OF THE GREAT OUTDOORS (EP, 2000 only p/s)	15
01	Rehab RHB001	A LIFE WITHOUT INSTRUCTIONS (EP)	12
02	White no matrix	Graf Da Bus Up/Wha Blow (2 Mixes of A side, 12")	12
06	White WS01	The Bitches (3 versions) (12", 500 only)	12
99	K'Boro KBR1005	NEW MIC ORDER (LP)	30
03	MFTC MFTC 02	MUSIC FROM THE CORNER VOL 2 (2-LP)	15

TASSELS
59	London HL 8885	To A Soldier Boy/The Boy For Me	100
59	London HL 8885	To A Soldier Boy/The Boy For Me (78)	40
59	Top Rank JAR 229	To A Young Lover/My Guy And I	30

TASTE
68	Major Minor MM 560	Blister On The Moon/Born On The Wrong Side Of Time	70
69	Polydor 56313	Born On The Wrong Side Of Time/Same Old Story	10
70	Major Minor MM 718	Born On The Wrong Side Of Time/Blister On The Moon	10
69	Polydor 583 042	TASTE (LP, laminated sleeve)	35
70	Polydor 583 083	ON THE BOARDS (LP, textured sleeve)	30
71	Polydor 2310 082	LIVE TASTE (LP)	15
72	Polydor 2383 120	TASTE - LIVE AT THE ISLE OF WIGHT (LP)	20

(see also Rory Gallagher, Stud)

TASTE OF HONEY
69	Original Rim RIM 11	Goody Goody Gum Drops/Sunshine Rainbows	12
69	Rim RIM 19	8.05/Charleston	5

TASTY
77	DJM DJS 10751	Just A Little Too Much/You're A Heartbreaker (Promo p/s)	8

BUDDY TATE
58	Felsted FAJ 7004	SWINGING LIKE TATE (LP)	30

GRADY TATE
69	Fontana STL 5490	WINDMILLS OF MY MIND (LP)	15

HOWARD TATE
66	Verve VS 541	Ain't Nobody Home/How Come My Bulldog Won't Bark	15
67	Verve VS 549	Look At Granny Run Run/Half A Man	20
67	Verve VS 552	Get It While You Can/Glad I Knew Better	15
67	Verve VS 555	Baby I Love You/How Blue Can You Get	25
67	Verve VS 556	I Learned It All The Hard Way/Part Time Love	15

68	Verve VS 565	Stop/Shoot 'Em All Down	15
68	Verve VS 571	Night Owl/Every Day I Have The Blues	20
70	Major Minor MM 696	My Soul's Got A Hole In It/It's Too Late	10
67	Verve (S)VLP 9179	GET IT WHILE YOU CAN (LP)	70

TOMMY TATE
66	Columbia DB 8046	Big Blue Diamonds/A Lover's Reward	75
66	Columbia DB 8046	Big Blue Diamonds/A Lover's Reward (DJ Copy)	125

JACQUES TATI
58	Fontana TFE 17175	MY UNCLE (EP)	10

TATTY OLLITY
70s	Tatty TR 101	Punktuation	20

ART TATUM
51	Capitol LC 6524	ART TATUM (10" LP)	12
53	Capitol LC 6625	OUT OF NOWHERE (10" LP)	15
54	Vogue LDE 081	ART TATUM "JUST JAZZ" (10" LP)	15
55	Vogue Coral LRA 10011	THE ART TATUM TRIO (10" LP)	12
55	Columbia Clef 33CX 10005	THE GENIUS OF ART TATUM (LP)	12
55	Capitol LC 6638	ART TATUM ENCORES (10" LP)	12
56	Columbia Clef 33CX 10053	THE GENIUS OF ART TATUM (NO. 2) (10" LP)	12
57	Columbia Clef 33C 9033	THE GENIUS OF ART TATUM (NO. 3) (10" LP)	12
57	Columbia Clef 33C 9039	PRESENTING THE ART TATUM TRIO (10" LP)	12
57	Vogue Coral LVA 9047	HERE'S ART TATUM (LP)	12
58	Columbia Clef 33CX 10115	ART TATUM (LP)	12
59	Columbia Clef 33CX 10137	ART TATUM-BEN WEBSTER QUARTET (LP)	15
60	Top Rank 35/067	ART TATUM DISCOVERIES (LP)	12

BERNIE TAUPIN
71	DJM DJLPS 415	TAUPIN (LP, textured gatefold sleeve with booklet)	50
71	DJM DJLPS 415	TAUPIN (LP, textured gatefold sleeve without booklet)	20

TAVASCO
00	Grapevine 106	Love Is Trying To Get A Hold Of Me/(Radio Edit)	10

JOHN TAVENER
70	Apple SAPCOR 15	THE WHALE (LP, gatefold sleeve)	40
71	Apple SAPCOR 20	CELTIC REQUIEM (LP, gatefold sleeve, with insert & 'Apple' inner sleeve)	80
77	Ring O' 2320 104	THE WHALE (LP, reissue, different single sleeve)	45
92	Apple SAPCOR 15	THE WHALE (LP, 2nd reissue, gatefold sleeve with inner sleeve)	25
92	Apple SAPCOR 15	THE WHALE (CD)	25
93	Apple SAPCOR 20	CELTIC REQUIEM (LP, reissue, gatefold sleeve with inner sleeve)	25
93	Apple SAPCOR 20	CELTIC REQUIEM (CD)	25

TAVERNERS
69	Saga EROS 8146	SELDOM SOBER (LP)	12
73	Trailer LER 2080	BLOWING SANDS (LP, red label)	15
74	Folk Heritage FHR 062	TIMES OF OLD ENGLAND (LP)	15
78	Folk Heritage FHR 101	SAME OLD FRIENDS (LP, with insert)	12

TAW FOLK
75	Sentinel SENS 1030	DEVONSHIRE CREAM AND CIDER (LP)	12

CYRIL TAWNEY
62	HMV 7EG 8738	BABY LIE EASY (EP)	15
69	Polydor 236 577	THE OUTLANDISH KNIGHT (LP)	20
70	Argo ZFB 4	SINGS CHILDREN'S SONGS FROM DEVON AND CORNWALL (LP)	20
70	Argo ZFB 9	A MAYFLOWER GARLAND (LP)	25
72	Argo ZFB 28	TAWNEY IN PORT (LP)	12
73	Argo ZFB 87	I WILL GIVE MY LOVE (LP)	12

TAX DODGERS
93	TAX 2	Ragamuffin Bizness/Flying High (12", stamped white label)	20
94	TAX IT	Hot Off D Press/Rebel Without Applause (Two Mixes) (12", stamped white labels)	20

TAXMAN
93	Sir George SO 945	Well Armed And Dangerous/She Keeps Running Away (12")	30

ALLAN TAYLOR
71	Liberty LBF 15447	Sometimes/Song For Kathy	6
73	United Artists UP 35541	My Father's Room/Always You	6
71	Liberty LBS 83483	SOMETIMES (LP, gatefold sleeve)	50
72	United Artists UAS 29275	THE LADY (LP)	45
73	United Artists UAG 29468	THE AMERICAN ALBUM (LP, gatefold sleeve)	20

(see also Fairport Convention)

AUSTIN TAYLOR
60	Top Rank JAR 511	Push Push/A Heart That's True	20

BILLY TAYLOR (TRIO)
57	Esquire EP 115	MAMBO! (EP)	15
57	Esquire EP 169	THE MOON IN CONCERT (EP)	20
54	Felsted EDL 87009	JAZZ AT STORYVILLE (LP)	35
54	Esquire 20-053	AT THE TOWN HALL 1954 (LP)	30
54	Esquire 32-010	A TOUCH OF TAYLOR (LP)	30
57	HMV DLP 1181	MY FAIR LADY LOVES JAZZ (10" LP)	20
60	Vogue LAE 12192	TAYLOR MADE PIANO (LP)	20

BOBBY TAYLOR
64	Columbia DB 7282	Temptation/Mod Bod	15

BOBBY TAYLOR (& VANCOUVERS)
68	Tamla Motown TMG 654	Does Your Mama Know About Me/Fading Away (with Vancouvers)	50
73	Epic EPC 1720	I Can't Quit Your Love/Queen Of The Ghetto (solo)	8
69	Tamla Motown (S)TML 11093	BOBBY TAYLOR AND THE VANCOUVERS (LP. mono/stereo)	60
70	Tamla Motown (S)TML 11125	TAYLOR MADE SOUL (LP, stereo, solo)	140

MINT VALUE £

BRYAN TAYLOR
61	Piccadilly 7N 35018	The Donkey's Tale/Let It Snow On Christmas Day	25

CECIL TAYLOR
60	Contemporary LAC12216	LOOKING AHEAD! (LP)	20
88	Leo LR 152	CHINAMPAS (LP)	15
88	Leo LR 162	TZOTZIL MUMMERS TZOTZIL (LP)	15
88	Leo LR 404/405	LIVE IN BOLOGNA (2-LP)	25
88	Leo LR 408/409	LIVE IN VIENNA (2-LP)	25

CECIL TAYLOR JAZZ UNIT
62	Fontana SFJL 926	NEFERTITI, THE BEAUTIFUL ONE HAS COME (LP)	20

CECIL TAYLOR QUARTET
60	Contemporary LAC 12216	LOOKING AHEAD! (LP)	18

CHIP TAYLOR
62	Warner Bros WB 82	Here I Am/I Love You But I Know	6
73	Buddah 2011 151	Angel Of The Morning/Swear To God, Your Honor	5
73	Buddah 2318 074	GASOLINE (LP)	25
74	Warner Bros K 56032	CHIP TAYLOR'S LAST CHANCE (LP)	15

(see also Wes Voigt)

DEBBIE TAYLOR
76	Arista ARISTA 50	I Don't Wanna Leave You/Just Don't Pay	20

DREW TAYLOR
70s	One Up OU 2175	DREW'S BREW (LP)	12

DUFFY TAYLOR BLUES
69	Page One POF 130	You Wrecked My Life/I'll Be There	12

EDDIE TAYLOR
65	Big Bear BEAR 6	READY FOR EDDIE (LP)	12

ELIZABETH TAYLOR
63	Colpix PXL 459	IN LONDON (LP, TV soundtrack, music by John Barry, mono)	30
63	Colpix PXL 459	IN LONDON (LP, TV soundtrack, music by John Barry, stereo)	35

(see also John Barry)

FELICE TAYLOR
67	President PT 120	It May Be Winter Outside/BOB KEENE ORCHESTRA: Winter Again	8
67	President PT 133	I'm Under The Influence/BOB KEENE ORCHESTRA: Love Theme	8
67	President PT 155	I Feel Love Comin' On/BOB KEENE ORCHESTRA: Comin' On Again	8
68	President PT 193	Captured By Your Love/I Can Feel Your Love (Coming Down On Me)	10
68	President PT 220	Suree-Surrender/All I Want To Do Is Love You	8

GEOFF TAYLOR
55	Esquire EP 55	GEOFF TAYLOR SEXTET (EP)	10
57	Esquire EP 105	GEOFF TAYLOR ALL STARS (EP)	10
55	Esquire 20-060	GEOFF TAYLOR ALL STARS (10" LP)	50

GLORIA TAYLOR
70	Polydor BM 56788	You Gotta Pay The Price/Loving You And Being Loved By You	15

HOUND DOG TAYLOR
66	Outasite 45-504	Christine/Alley Music (99 copies only)	100

JAMES TAYLOR
70	Apple APPLE 32	Carolina In My Mind/Something's Wrong	15
68	Apple APCOR 3	JAMES TAYLOR (LP, gatefold sleeve, black inner, orange cover lettering, mono)	40
68	Apple SAPCOR 3	JAMES TAYLOR (LP, gatefold sleeve, black inner, orange cover lettering, stereo)	25
70	Apple SAPCOR 3	JAMES TAYLOR (LP, 2nd issue, gatefold sleeve, 'Apple' inner sleeve, black cover lettering)	25
70	Warner Bros WS 1843	SWEET BABY JAMES (LP, orange label, later green label)	20
71	Warner Bros WS 2561	MUD SLIDE SLIM AND THE BLUE HORIZON (LP, g/fold sleeve, green label)	18
72	Warner Bros K 46043	SWEET BABY JAMES (LP, reissue, green label)	15
72	Warner Bros K 46085	MUD SLIDE SLIM AND THE BLUE HORIZON (LP, reissue, gatefold sleeve, green label)	12
73	Warner Bros K 46185	ONE MAN DOG (LP, green label, with insert & stickered sleeve)	12
91	Apple SAPCOR 3	JAMES TAYLOR (LP, reissue, gatefold sleeve)	18
91	Apple SAPCOR 3	JAMES TAYLOR (CD)	18

JAMES TAYLOR QUARTET
92	Big Life JTQ 7 PROMO 1	Absolution (live) (gig freebie, plain black sleeve with postcard, 1 side etched)	5
90s	Big Life	Hope And Pray (p/s)	5
95	Acid Jazz JAZID 124S	Whole Lotta Love (white label, withdrawn)	50
96	Acid Jazz JAZID 139	Creation (10", p/s, mispressed with Hungarian porn music on A-side)	35
96	Acid Jazz JAZID 139	Creation (10", p/s)	8
96	Acid Jazz JTQ 1	Europa (Extended)/Redneck (12", company sleeve)	8
87	Re-Elect Pres. REAGAN 2D	MISSION: IMPOSSIBLE (mini-LP, with film dialogue, 500 only)	30
95	Acid Jazz JAZIDLP 115L	IN THE HANDS OF THE INEVITABLE (LP, with bonus 2-track 12")	10

(see also Prisoners, Daggermen, New Jersey Kings)

JEREMY TAYLOR
62	Decca F 11502	Ag Pleez Daddy/Jo'burg Talking Blues	8
66	Decca LK 4731	ALWAYS SOMETHING NEW (LP)	30
68	Fontana (S)TL 5475	HIS SONGS (LP)	20
69	Fontana (S)TL 5523	MORE OF HIS SONGS (LP)	20
72	Galliard GAL 4018	PIECE OF GROUND (LP)	15

JOHN TAYLOR
71	Turtle TUR 301	PAUSE AND THINK AGAIN (LP)	250

JOHNNIE TAYLOR
67	Stax 601 003	Ain't That Lovin' You/Outside Love (dark blue label)	30
67	Stax 601 003	Ain't That Lovin' You/Outside Love (light blue label)	20
68	Stax STAX 106	Who's Makin' Love/I'm Trying	8
69	Stax STAX 114	Take Care Of Your Homework/Hold On This Time	8
69	Stax STAX 122	(I Wanna) Testify/I Had To Fight With Love	10

69	Stax STAX 129	I Could Never Be President/It's Amazing	8
70	Stax STAX 141	Love Bones/Separation Line	8
70	Stax STAX 150	Steal Away/Friday Night	20
70	Stax STAX 156	I Am Somebody (Parts 1 & 2)	8
71	Stax 2025 021	Jody's Got Your Girl And Gone/A Fool Like Me	8
73	Stax 2025 083	Standing In For Jody/Shackin' Up	8
73	Stax 2025 194	I Believe In Love/Love Depression	8
75	Stax STXS 2021	It's September/Just One Moment	8
75	Stax STXS 2025	Friday Night/I Ain't Particular	10
76	CBS 4886	Disco Lady/Somebody's Gettin' It (blue vinyl)	8
67	Stax 589 008	WANTED, ONE SOUL SINGER (LP)	50
69	Stax (S)XATS 1006	WHO'S MAKING LOVE (LP)	20
69	Stax 228 008	LOOKING FOR JOHNNIE TAYLOR (LP)	25
69	Stax SXATS 1024	THE J.T. PHILOSOPHY CONTINUES (LP)	25
70	Soul City SCB 2	ROOTS OF JOHNNIE TAYLOR (LP)	75

(LITTLE) JOHNNY TAYLOR

65	Vocalion V 9234	Part Time Love/Somewhere Down The Line	50
65	Vocalion V 9234	Part Time Love/Somewhere Down The Line (DJ copy)	75
66	Vocalion VP 9264	One More Chance/Looking At The Future	30
72	Mojo 2092 033	Everybody Knows About My Good Thing (Parts 1 & 2)	8
72	Mojo 2092 044	It's My Fault Darling/There's Something On Your Mind	8
65	Vocalion VA-F 8031	LITTLE JOHNNY TAYLOR (LP)	100
72	Mojo 2916 015	EVERYBODY KNOWS ABOUT MY GOOD THING (LP)	30
73	Contempo COLP 1003	OPEN HOUSE AT MY HOUSE (LP)	15
74	Contempo CLP 502	SUPER TAYLORS (LP, with Ted Taylor)	15

JOSEPH TAYLOR

72	Leader LEA 4050	UNTO BRIGG FAIR (LP, gatefold sleeve with booklet)	20

KINGSIZE TAYLOR (& DOMINOS)

64	Polydor NH 66990	Memphis Tennessee/Money (reissue of Shakers single)	30
64	Polydor NH 66991	Hippy Hippy Shake/Dr. Feelgood (reissue of Shakers single)	30
64	Decca F 11874	Stupidity/Bad Boy	50
64	Decca F 11935	Somebody's Always Trying/Looking For My Baby (solo)	150
65	Polydor BM 56152	Thinkin'/Let Me Love You	40
63	Polydor EPH21 628	TWIST AND SHAKE (EP, manufactured in Germany)	110
64	Decca DFE 8569	TEENBEAT 2 - FROM THE STAR CLUB, HAMBURG (EP)	130

(see also Shakers, Paddy Klaus & Gibson)

LINDA TAYLOR

82	Groove Production GPLP 31	TAYLOR MADE (LP)	20

LIVINGSTON TAYLOR

70	Warner Bros WS 3006	LIVINGSTONE TAYLOR (LP)	12

MICK TAYLOR

65	CBS 201770	London Town/Hoboin'	40

MICK TAYLOR

79	CBS 82600	MICK TAYLOR (LP, with inner sleeve)	12
90	Maze 084 649	STRANGER IN THIS TOWN (LP)	12

(see also Rolling Stones, Gods, Institute Of Formal Research)

MIKE TAYLOR

65	Columbia SX 6042	PENDULUM (LP)	1000
66	Columbia SX 6137	TRIO (LP)	700
07	Trunk JBH 016 LP	MIKE TAYLOR REMEMBERED (LP)	25

(see also Jack Bruce)

NEVILLE TAYLOR (& CUTTERS)

58	Parlophone R 4447	House Of Bamboo/Mercy, Mercy, Percy (solo)	40
58	Parlophone R 4447	House Of Bamboo/Mercy, Mercy, Percy (solo) (78)	20
58	Parlophone R 4476	Tears On My Pillow/I Don't Want To Set The World On Fire (solo)	20
58	Parlophone R 4476	Tears On My Pillow/I Don't Want To Set The World On Fire (solo) (78)	10
58	Parlophone R 4493	A Baby Lay Sleeping/The Miracle Of Christmas (solo)	10
59	Parlophone R 4524	Crazy Little Daisy/The First Words Of Love (solo)	20
60	Oriole CB 1546	Dance With Dolly/Free Passes	20
60	Embassy WB 373	It Ain't Necessarily So/BOBBIE BRITTON: Woman Is A Sometime Love	6
60s	Honey Hit TB 127	Joshua Fit The Battle Of Jericho/It's Me, It's Me, It's Me, My Love (in p/s)	6

(see also Hal Munro, Bobbie Britton)

PEGGY TAYLOR

60	Top Rank JAR 421	(Don't You Come Home) Bill Bailey/So Similar	7

R. DEAN TAYLOR

68	Tamla Motown TMG 656	Gotta See Jane/Don't Fool Around	10
71	Tamla Motown TMG 763	Indiana Wants Me/Love's Your Name	7
71	Tamla Motown TMG 786	Ain't It A Sad Thing/Backstreet (unissued)	0
71	Rare Earth RES 101	Ain't It A Sad Thing/Backstreet (has TMG 786 matrix in run-out groove)	15
74	Tamla Motown TMG 896	There's A Ghost In My House/Let's Go Somewhere	5
74	Tamla Motown TMG 896	There's A Ghost In My House/Let's Go Somewhere (DJ Copy)	25
71	Tamla Motown STML 11185	INDIANA WANTS ME (LP)	18

ROD TAYLOR

78	Little Lute HITDD 311	If Jah Should Come Now/Africa Be Free/PRINCE HAMMER: Maccabee Bible (12")	30
78	Freedom Sounds FSD 004	Ethiopian King/PHILIP FRAZER: Come Ethiopians (12")	40
78	Hit Run APLP 9031	IF JAH SHOULD COME NOW (LP)	50
79	Hit Run DD 16	No One Can Tell I About Jah/ERROL HOLT : Yes Yes Yes (12")	60
81	Unity UP 003	Moving Out Ever/Version (12", with Ranking Dread)	20
80	Greensleeves GREL 17	WHERE IS YOUR LOVE MANKIND? (LP, green vinyl)	22

ROD TAYLOR & MIKEY DREAD & KING TUBBY

79	Sufferers Heights SUFF 006	Behold Him/Parrot Jungle/His Majesty/Dread All The Way (12")	30

ROGER TAYLOR

77	EMI EMI 2679	I Wanna Testify/Turn On The TV (demo copies £40)	30

MINT VALUE £

81	EMI EMI 5200	My Country (Edit)/Fun In Space (p/s)	20
84	EMI EMI 5478	Man On Fire/Killing Time (p/s)	10
84	EMI 12 EMI 5478	Man On Fire (Extended)/Killing Time (12", p/s)	25
84	EMI EMI 5490	Strange Frontier/I Cry For You (Remix) (p/s)	15
84	EMI 12 EMI 5490	Strange Frontier (Extended)/I Cry For You (Extended Remix)/ Two Sharp Pencils (Get Bad) (12", p/s)	20
94	Parlophone RR 6379	Nazis 1994/Nazis 1994 (Version) (red vinyl, numbered p/s)	5
94	Parlophone 12RC 6379	Nazis 1994 (Single Version)/(Radio Mix)/(Makita Mix - Extended)/ (Big Science Mix) (12" clear vinyl, numbered insert in PVC sleeve)	10
94	Parlophone NAZIS 1	Nazis 1994 (Radio Mix)/Nazis 1944 (Kick Mix) (12", black vinyl, p/s, promo only)	15
94	Parlophone NAZIS 3	Nazis 1994 (Radio Mix)/(Kick Mix)/(Big Science Mix)/(Makita Mix) (12", black vinyl, p/s, promo only)	15
94	Parlophone NAZIS 4	Nazis 1994 (Schindler's Mix)/(Big Science Mix)/(Makita Mix - Extended) (12", black vinyl, p/s, promo only)	10
94	Parlophone 12RDJ 6379	Nazis 1994 (Schindler's Mix)/(Big Science Mix)/(Makita Mix - Extended) (12", white label DJ promo)	30
94	Parlophone R 6389	Foreign Sand (Single Version)/You Had To Be There (as Roger Taylor & Yoshiki) (blue vinyl, numbered p/s)	5
94	Parlophone CDPCS 157	Happiness/Dear Mr. Murdoch/Everybody Hurts Sometime (live)/ Old Friends (live) (CD, numbered)	10
81	EMI EMC 3369	FUN IN SPACE (LP)	12
84	EMI RTA 1	STRANGE FRONTIER (LP)	12
93	Parlophone PCSD 157	HAPPINESS? (LP, some numbered)	25

(see also Queen, Cross, Hilary Hilary, Ian Hunter, Fox, Kansas, Camy Todorow, Mel Smith, Billy Squier)

ROSEMARY TAYLOR
75	JD 2009	TAYLORMAID (LP, private pressing with insert)	200

(see also Great Saturday Night Swindle)

SAM ('THE MAN') TAYLOR
54	MGM SP 1106	Please Be Kind/This Can't Be Love (as Sam 'The Man' Taylor & Cat Men)	30
56	MGM MGM-EP 531	SAM TAYLOR ORCHESTRA (EP)	35

(see also Claude Cloud)

TAYLOR SHARP & TAYLOR
70	CBS 5197	The Look Of Love/Mr Snow	15

TED TAYLOR FOUR
58	Oriole CB 1464	Son Of Honky Tonk/Farrago	15
58	Oriole CB 1464	Son Of Honky Tonk/Farrago (78)	10
60	Oriole CB 1573	M.1./You Are My Sunshine	10
61	Oriole CB 1574	Fried Onions/Yellow Rock Of Texas	10
61	Oriole CB 1628	Cat's Eyes/Canyon	10
61	Oriole CB 1630	Flyover/Haunted Pad	10
62	Oriole CB 1713	Jericho/Everytime We Say Goodbye	20
62	Oriole CB 1767	Surfrider/Spotlight	20

TYRONE TAYLOR
78	Observer OBMM 1000	Sufferation/Rock On/Christine (12")	35

VERNON TAYLOR
59	London HLS 8905	Today Is A Blue Day/Breeze (unreleased)	0
60	London HLS 9025	Mystery Train/Sweet And Easy To Love	100

VIC TAYLOR
67	Treasure Isle TI 7021	Heartaches/When It Comes To Loving You I'm Alright (B-side actually "Loving Pauper" by Dobby Dobson)	80
71	Trojan TRLS 38	DOES IT HIS WAY (LP)	20

(see also Tommy McCook)

VINCE TAYLOR (& HIS PLAYBOYS)
58	Parlophone R 4505	Right Behind You Baby/I Like Love (solo)	60
58	Parlophone R 4505	Right Behind You Baby/I Like Love (solo) (78)	40
59	Parlophone R 4539	Brand New Cadillac/Pledging My Love	50
60	Palette PG 9001	I'll Be Your Hero/Jet Black Machine	25
61	Palette PG 9020	Move Over Tiger/What'cha Gonna Do	25
76	Chiswick (N)S 2	Brand New Cadillac/Pledging My Love (no p/s)	5
97	Cruisin' 50 CASB 006	Brand New Cadillac/Right Behind You Baby (78, 300 only)	30

VINCENT TAYLOR
80	Live & Love LLDIS 115	Can't Seem To Forget You/Living A Lie (12")	50
80	Live & Love LLDIS 117	Got To Have You/TAYLOR PLAYERS: Got You Version (12")	30

WALTER TAYLOR
50s	Poydras 2	Thirty-Eight And Plus/Diamond Ring Blues	8

TAYLOR MAIDS
55	Capitol CL 14322	Po-Go Stick/Theme From "I Am A Camera" (Why Do I)	12

T-BONES
64	Columbia DB 7401	How Many More Times/I'm A Lover Not A Fighter	60
65	Columbia DB 7489	Won't You Give Him (One More Chance)/Hamish's Express Relief	35

(see also Gary Farr & T-Bones, Kevin Westlake)

JOHN TCHKAI
66	Fontana 881014/681 014ZL	RUFUS (LP, with ARCHIE SHEPP)	20

TDS MOB
10	Diggers With Gratitude DWG 006	THE DOPE COMMITTEE (EP, 75 only, burgundy vinyl)	90
10	Diggers With Gratitude DWG 006	THE DOPE COMMITTEE (EP, 275 only, black vinyl)	30
10	Diggers With Gratitude DWG 007	THE BOSTON CLASSICS (EP, 75 only, white vinyl)	40
10	Diggers With Gratitude DWG 007	THE BOSTON CLASSICS (EP)	12

TEA
74	Vertigo 6147 006	Good Times/Judy	5
75	Philips 6305 238	TEA (LP)	15

75	Philips 9118 001	THE SHIP (LP)	12

TEA & SYMPHONY
69	Harvest HAR 5005	Boredom/Armchair Theatre	20
69	Harvest SHVL 761	AN ASYLUM FOR THE MUSICALLY INSANE (LP, laminated gatefold sleeve. The name of the band appears above the "Harvest" logo. Those with 'An Asylum For The Musically Insane' above the Harvest Logo are Dutch pressings from 1969)	300
70	Harvest SHVL 785	JO SAGO (LP, gatefold sleeve no EMI logo on label)	650

TEACH YOURSELF TURNTABLISM
04	Pedestrian	TUTORITOOL - INTERACTIVE TURNTABLISM TUTORIAL (LP, gatefold with inserts and inner sleeves, 1000 only)	25

TEACHO & HIS STUDENTS
58	Felsted AF 104	Rock-et/Stop	60
58	Felsted AF 104	Rock-et/Stop (78)	30

TEA COMPANY
68	Mercury SMCL 20127	COME AND HAVE SOME TEA WITH THE TEA COMPANY (LP)	50

ANTHONY TEAGUE
62	Decca F 11548	Like I Don't Love You/My Guardian Angel	7

TEAM DOKUS
94	Tenth Planet TP 007	TEAM DOKUS (LP, numbered, 500 only)	15

TEA PARTY
94	Chrysalis CHR 6072	SPLENDOR SOILS (LP)	12
95	Chrysalis CHR 6108	THE EDGES OF TWILIGHT (LP)	12

TEARDROP EXPLODES
79	Zoo CAGE 003	Sleeping Gas/Camera Camera/Kirkby Workers' Dream Fades (red p/s)	15
79	Zoo CAGE 003	Sleeping Gas/Camera Camera/Kirkby Workers' Dream Fades (blue p/s)	12
79	Zoo CAGE 005	Bouncing Babies/All I Am Is Loving You (p/s)	10
80	Zoo CAGE 008	Treason (It's Just A Story)/Read It In Books (in blue & green p/s)	15
80	Zoo CAGE 008	Treason (It's Just A Story)/Read It In Books	6
80	Mercury TEAR 1	When I Dream/Kilimanjaro (p/s, limited pressing with paper labels not moulded plastic)	5
80	Mercury TEAR 2	Reward/Strange House In The Snow (p/s, limited pressing with paper labels not moulded plastic, textured sleeve)	6
81	Mercury TEAR 312	Treason (It's Just A Story) (Remix)/Traison (C'est Juste Une Histoire)/ Use Me (12", p/s)	8
81	Mercury TEAR 4	Ha Ha I'm Drowning/Poppies In The Field (in withdrawn p/s, limited pressing with paper labels not moulded plastic)	15
81	Mercury TEAR 44	Ha Ha I'm Drowning/Poppies In The Field/Bouncing Babies/Read It In Books (double pack, gatefold p/s, limited pressing with paper labels not moulded plastic)	6
81	Mercury TEAR 44	Ha Ha I'm Drowning/Poppies In The Field/Bouncing Babies/ Read It In Books (double pack, withdrawn gatefold p/s)	40
81	Mercury TEAR 5	Passionate Friend/Christ Versus Warhol (p/s, limited pressing with paper labels not moulded plastic)	6
81	Mercury TEAR 6	Colours Fly Away/Window Shopping For A New Crown Of Thorns (p/s & insert, limited pressing with paper labels not moulded plastic)	6
82	Mercury TEAR 7G	Tiny Children/Rachael Built A Steamboat (gatefold p/s, paper labels)	6
82	Mercury TEAR 7	Tiny Children/Rachael Built A Steamboat (p/s, paper labels)	5
83	Mercury TEAR 88	You Disappear From View/Suffocate//Ouch Monkey's/Soft Enough For You/ The In-Psychlopedia (double pack, gatefold, limited pressing with paper labels not moulded plastic)	6
89	Fontana DROP 112	Serious Danger/Sleeping Gas/Seven Views Of Jerusalem (p/s)	6
80	Mercury 6359 035	KILIMANJARO (LP, 1st pressing, light blue labels, 'group photo' on cover & inner sleeve)	20
80	Mercury 6359 035	KILIMANJARO (LP, 2nd pressing, dark blue labels)	12
81	Mercury 6359056	WILDER (LP)	12
90	Mercury 8424391	EVERYBODY WANTS TO SHAG THE TEARDROP EXPLODES (LP, with inner)	15

(see also Julian Cope, Rabbi Joseph Gordan, Lori & Chameleons)

TEARDROPS (JAMAICA)
71	Ackee ACK 126	Let Me Be Free/CINDY STARR: Sentimental Girl	7
71	Big Shot BI 582	Two In One/LAURIE'S ALL STARS: Rock-A-Boogie	7

TEARDROPS (1)
78	Bent BIGB 3	IN AND OUT OF FASHION (12" EP, foldout p/s in poly bag)	18
79	TJM TJM 9	Seeing Double/Teardrops And Heartaches (p/s)	20
80s	Illuminated JAMS 2	FINAL VINYL (LP)	15

TEARDROPS (2)
93	Kent 6T 9	Here Comes The Lonliness/CHUBBY CHECKER: You Can't Lose Something You've Never Had	20

TEAR GAS
70	Famous SFMA 5751	PIGGY GO-GETTER (LP, textured gtefold sleeve)	70
71	Regal Zono. SLRZ 1021	TEAR GAS (LP)	250

(see also Alex Harvey, Tandoori Cassette)

TEARJERKERS
80	Back Door DOOR 1	Murder Mystery/Heart On The Line (die cut p/s with insert)	8
81	Good Vibrations GOT 9	Love Affair/Bus Stop (p/s)	5

(see also Speed)

THE TEARS
05	Independiente ISOM49LP	HERE COME THE TEARS (LP, numbered)	12

(see also Suede)

TEARS FOR FEARS
81	Mercury IDEA 1	Suffer The Children/Wino (p/s, original issue with light labels)	10
81	Mercury IDEA 12	Suffer The Children (Remix)/Wino/Suffer The Children (Instrumental) (12", p/s)	12
82	Mercury IDEA 212	Pale Shelter (You Don't Give Me Love) (Extended)/Pale Shelter/ The Prisoner (12", original p/s)	8
82	Mercury IDEA 33	Mad World/Mad World (World Remix) (p/s)	5
82	Mercury IDEA 33	Mad World/Mad World (World Remix)//Suffer The Children/ Ideas As Opiates (double pack)	10
82	Mercury IDEA 4	Change/The Conflict (poster p/s)	7
82	Mercury IDEA 4	Change/The Conflict (withdrawn 'fishing net' sleeve)	50

MINT VALUE £

82	Mercury IDEA 412	Change/The Conflict (12" withdrawn 'fishing net' sleeve)	100
83	Mercury IDEA R/B 5	Pale Shelter/We Are Broken (p/s, red or blue vinyl)	10
83	Mercury IDEAG 5	Pale Shelter/We Are Broken (p/s, translucent green vinyl)	7
83	Mercury IDEAP 5	Pale Shelter/We Are Broken (picture disc)	12
83	Mercury IDEA 512	Pale Shelter/We Are Broken (12", p/s)	10
83	Mercury IDEA 6	(The) Way You Are/The Marauders (rumours of poster issue remain unconfirmed)	5
83	Mercury IDEAS 6	(The) Way You Are/The Marauders//Change (Live)/Start Of The Breakdown (live) (shrinkwrapped double pack)	8
84	Mercury IDEA 7	Mother's Talk/Empire Building (clear vinyl picture disc)	5
84	Mercury IDEA 7	Mother's Talk/Empire Building (green vinyl, p/s, with window sticker)	8
84	Mercury IDEA 12	Mother's Talk (Beat Of The Drum Mix)/Empire Building (12", p/s)	8
85	fan club ANTAR 4502	Mother's Talk/Interview	18
85	Mercury IDEC 8	Shout/The Big Chair (calendar pack with 6 cards)	7
85	Mercury IDEA 99	Everybody Wants To Rule The World/Pharoahs//Everybody Wants To Rule The World (Urban Mix)/Interview (double pack)	8
85	Mercury IDEA 910	Everybody Wants To Rule The World/Pharoahs (10", p/s)	7
85	Mercury RACE 112	Everybody Wants To Run The World/(Running Version) (12", p/s)	12
85	Mercury IDEAP 10	Head Over Heels (Remix)/When In Love With A Blind Man (poster p/s)	5
85	Mercury IDEP 10	Head Over Heels (Remix)/When In Love With A Blind Man (clover-shaped picture disc)	8
85	Mercury IDEA 11	I Believe/Sea Song (p/s, sealed with set of postcards, withdrawn)	8
85	Mercury IDEA 1111	I Believe (A Soulful Re-Recording)/Sea Song//I Believe (Original Version)/ Shout (Dub Version) (double pack, gatefold p/s)	5
85	Mercury IDEP 10	Head Over Heels/When In Love With A Blind Man (poster p/s)	8
89	Fontana IDCDL 12	Sowing The Seeds Of Love (Full Version)/Tears Roll Down/Shout (U.S. Remix) (3" CD, red/yellow plastic sunflower pack)	10
89	Fontana IDSUN 13	Woman In Chains/Always In The Past/My Life In The Suicide Ranks/ Woman In Chains (Instrumental) (3" CD, gold card 'sun' pack)	10
88	Mercury 080 032-2	Everybody Wants To Rule The World/The Marauders/When In Love With A Blind Man/Pharoahs/Everybody Wants To Rule The World (Video) (CD Video)	12
88	Mercury 080 064-2	Shout/Everybody Wants To Rule The World (Urban Mix)/Shout (U.S.A. Mix)/ Shout (Video) (CD Video)	10
88	Mercury 080 062-2	Head Over Heels/Sea Song/The Working Hour/Mother's Talk (U.S.A.)/ Head Over Heels (Video) (CD Video)	12
88	Mercury 080 068-2	I Believe (A Soulful Re-Recording)/Start Of The Breakdown/ Ideas As Opiates/Change/I Believe (Video) (CD Video)	12
89	Fontana IDPT 12	Sowing The Seeds Of Love/Tears Roll Down/Shout (US Remix) (12" picture disc, PVC sleeve)	8
89	Fontana IDEAB 13	Woman In Chains/Always In The Past (p/s, with badges)	6
92	Fontana IDEAP 16	Woman In Chains/Always In The Past/Woman In Chains (Instrumental) (12" picture disc, numbered, with poster)	8

(see also Graduate)

TEARS ON THE CONSOLE

75	Holyground HG 120	TEARS ON THE CONSOLE (LP, with booklet, 120 demo copies only)	150
90	Magic Mixture MM 3	TEARS ON THE CONSOLE (LP, reissue, 425 only, with insert)	20

TEASER

89	LTW 9KS 2049	Here Tonight (p/s)	20

TEA SET

66	King KG 1048	Join The Tea Set/Ready Steady Go!	25
79	Waldo's Beat PS 006	Parry Thomas/Tri-X Pan (gatefold p/s with poster 'mystery' envelope)	10
78	Waldo's Beat Series 003	CUPS AND SAUCERS (EP, with stapled lyric book sleeve)	10
80	Demon D 1009	South Pacific/The Preacher (foldout p/s with inserts)	10

TECHNIQUES (JAMAICA)

65	Island WI 231	Little Did You Know/DON DRUMMOND: Cool Smoke	25
67	Treasure Isle TI 7001	You Don't Care (with Tommy McCook & Supersonics Band)/ TOMMY McCOOK & SUPERSONICS BAND: Down On Bond Street	30
67	Treasure Isle TI 7019	Queen Majesty/Fighting For The Right	35
67	Treasure Isle TI 7026	Love Is Not A Gamble/Bad-Minded People	30
68	Treasure Isle TI 7031	My Girl/Drink Wine (with Tommy McCook & Supersonics)	25
68	Treasure Isle TI 7038	Devoted/Bless You (with Tommy McCook & Supersonics)	25
68	Treasure Isle TI 7040	It's You I Love/Travelling Man (with Tommy McCook & Supersonics)	60
68	Duke DU 1	I Wish It Would Rain/There Comes A Time	60
69	Duke DU 6	A Man Of My Word/The Time Has Come	60
69	Duke DU 22	What Am I To Do/You're My Everything	60
69	Duke DU 60	Where Were You/Just One Smile	18
69	Camel CA 10	Who You Gonna Run To/Hi There (B-side act. "Look Who's Back" by Carl Bryan)	30
69	Camel CA 19	Everywhere Everyone/Find Yourself Another Fool	25
70	Treasure Isle TI 7054	He Who Keepeth His Mouth/One Day (act. by Johnny Osborne & Sensations)	15
70	Techniques TE 904	Lonely Man/I Feel Alive	10
70	Techniques TE 906	Feel A Little Better (actually by Techniques Allstars)/You'll Get Left	10
70	Big Shot BI 536	He Who Keepeth His Mouth/One Day (act. by Johnny Osborne & Sensations)	12
71	Banana BA 350	Since I Lost You/RILEY'S ALLSTARS: Version	15

(see also Techniques All Stars, Riots, Tommy McCook, Mighty Avengers, Gaylads, Rad Bryan)

TECHNIQUES (U.S.)

58	Columbia DB 4072	Hey! Little Girl/In A Round About Way	45
58	Columbia DB 4072	Hey! Little Girl/In A Round About Way (78)	15

TECHNIQUES ALL STARS

70	Big Shot BI 543	Come Back Darling/Move Over (actually by Johnny Osborne & Sensations)	12
70	Big Shot BI 545	Elfrego Bacca (actually by Dave Barker)/TECHNIQUES: Iron Joe (B-side actually by Techniques All Stars)	35
70	Techniques TE 900	Something Tender/CANNONBALL: Bewitch	8
70	Trojan TR 7728	El Dora/TECHNIQUES: If It's Not True (B-side actually by Techniques All Stars)	8

(see also Dennis Alcapone, Ansell Collins)

TECHNO POP

79	Fairview SRTS 79424	Paint It Black/What Are You	7

TECHNOSAURUS

93	Invention TBH 1	YOU GAVE ME NOTHING EP (12", stamped white labels)	25

TED

74	Epic SPEC 3126	Gonna Make You My Angel/Can't Stop The Train	8

TEDDIE & THE TIGERS
67	Spin SP 2004	Hold On I'm Comin'/First Love Never Dies	20

TEDDY
71	Upsetter US 353	Elusion/UPSETTERS: Big John Wayne	15

TEDDY & THE CONQUERORS
71	High Note HS 053	Homebound/GAYTONES: Homebound Chapter 3	8

TEDDY & THE FRAT GIRLS
85	Alternative Tentacles VIRUS 19	I Wanna Be A Man/I Owe It All To The Girls/Clubnite/ Alophen Baby/The Eggman Don't Cometh (p/s)	5

TEDDY & THE TWILIGHTS
63	Stateside SS 167	I'm Just Your Clown/Bikini Bimbo	22

TEDDY BEARS
58	London HL 8733	To Know Him Is To Love Him/Don't You Worry, My Little Pet	8
58	London HL 8733	To Know Him Is To Love Him/Don't You Worry, My Little Pet (78)	10
59	London HLP 8836	I Don't Need You Anymore/Oh Why	25
59	London HLP 8836	I Don't Need You Anymore/Oh Why (78)	10
59	London HLP 8889	You Said Goodbye/If You Only Knew	30
59	London HLP 8889	You Said Goodbye/If You Only Knew (78)	15
59	London HA-P 2183	THE TEDDY BEARS SING! (LP)	250

(see also Phil Spector, Carol Connors)

WILLIE TEE
67	Atlantic 584 116	Thank You John/Walking Up A One-Way Street	35
71	Mojo 2092 025	Walking Up A One-Way Street/Thank You John/Teasin' You	8

TEEGARDEN & VAN WINKLE
70	Pye 7N 25535	God, Love And Rock And Roll/Work Me Tomorrow	6
69	Atco 228028	BUT ANYHOW (LP)	15

TEENAGE FANCLUB
90	Paperhouse PAPER 003	Everything Flows/Primary Education/Speeeder (1,500 only, die-cut p/s)	8
90	Paperhouse PAPER 005	The Ballad Of John And Yoko (p/s, 1-sided, 5,000 only, 2nd side engraved)	6
91	Creation CRESCD 105	Star Sign/(Demo Version)/Heavy Metal 6/Like A Virgin (CD, card sleeve)	12
91	Creation CRESCD 111	The Concept/What You Do To Me (Demo) (CD, card sleeve)	10
03	Creation POOLS 5	Did I Say/The Cabbage (p/s, 500 only)	5
90	Paperhouse PAPLP 004	A CATHOLIC EDUCATION (LP, gatefold sleeve)	12
91	Creation CRELP 096	THE KING (LP, available for 1 week only, sprayed plain sleeve)	20
91	Creation CRECD 096	THE KING (CD, available for 1 week only, sprayed plain sleeve)	15
91	Creation CRELP 106	BANDWAGONESQUE (LP, with inner)	25
93	Creation CRELP 144	THIRTEEN (LP)	25
95	Creation CRELP	GRAND PRIX (LP, with free 7")	30
97	Creation CRELP 196	SONGS FROM NORTHERN BRITAIN (LP)	25
00	Columbia 5006221	HOWDY! (LP)	20
10	Pema PEMA 007LP	SHADOWS (LP)	15

(see also Boy Hairdressers, BMX Bandits, Clouds, Eugenius)

TEENAGE FILMSTARS
79	Clockwork COR 002	(There's A) Cloud Over Liverpool/Sometimes Good Guys Don't Follow Trends (1st 150 with foldout p/s)	100
79	Clockwork COR 002	(There's A) Cloud Over Liverpool/Sometimes Good Guys Don't Follow Trends	25
80	Wessex WEX 275	The Odd Man Out/I Apologise	25
80	Blueprint BLU 2013	The Odd Man Out/I Apologise (reissue, p/s)	20
80	Fab Listening FL 1	I Helped Patrick McGoohan Escape/We're Not Sorry (p/s)	15

(see also Television Personalities, Times, O Level)

TEENAGERS
57	RCA RCX 102	THE TEENAGERS (EP)	60

TEENBEATS
79	Safari SAFE 17	I Can't Control Myself/I'll Never Win (p/s)	8
79	Safari SAFE 19	Strength Of The Nation/I'm Gone Tomorrow (in p/s)	15
79	Safari SAFE 19	Strength Of The Nation/I'm Gone Tomorrow	6

TEEN BEATS (U.S.)
60	Top Rank JAR 342	The Slop Beat/Califf Boogie (featuring Don Rivers & Califfs)	25

TEEN QUEENS
65	R&B MRB 5000	Eddie My Love/Just Goofed	30

TEEN STARLETS
61	Top Rank JAR 583	The Children's Picnic Song/Theme From 'Spinster'	5

TEE SET (1)
68	Pye 7N 25452	What Can I Do/Colours Of The Rainbow	15

TEE SET (2)
70	Major Minor MM 666	Ma Belle Amie/Angels Coming	8
70	Columbia DB 8375	Mr Music Man/In My House	5
70	Columbia SCX 6419	MA BELLE AMIE (LP)	15

TEESIDE FETTLER
74	Tradition TSR 016	RING OF IRON (LP, as Tee-side Fettler)	15
75	Tradition TSR 021	TRAVELLING THE TEES (LP, as Tee-side Fettlers)	12

TEETH
79	Soho SH 8	Say Hello To Suzy/Human Bondage (p/s)	5

JOHN TEJADA
98	Ferox 030	SONIC LIFE EP (12", plain sleeve)	8

TEK 9
91	Reinforced RIVET 1205	KINGDOM OF DUB EP(12")	10
92	Reinforced RIVET 1229	JUST A DREAM EP (12")	20
92	Reinforced RIVET 1229R	JUST A DREAM EP (Remixes) (12")	10
93	Reinforced RIVET 1238	THE RETURN OF TEK 9 EP (12")	15

93	Reinforced RIVET 1238R	THE RETURN OF TEK 9 (Rpt) (12")	10
93	Reinforced RIVET 1253	BREAKIN' THE SOUND BARRIERS EP (12")	15
94	Reinforced RIVET 1262	KILLING TIME EP (10")	12
94	Reinforced RIVET 1269	JUS' A LIKKLE SUMTIN' EP (2x12")	25

TELEGRAMS
| 78 | Creole CR 163 | Oh Baby Please/Hey Baby | 5 |

(See also Steve Allan, Alan Carvell, Carvells, Five Sapphires)

TELESCOPES
89	Cheree CHEREE 2	Kick The Wall/This Is The Last Of What's Coming Now (p/s, with insert, 1,000 only, light grey/blue p/s)	5
89	Cheree CHEREE 2	Kick The Wall/This Is The Last Of What's Coming Now (numbered re-pressing, 500 only, red wraparound p/s)	8
89	Cheree CHEREE 4	7th Disaster/Nothing/This Planet/Cold (12" p/s)	8
89	What Goes On WHAT GOES 15T	THE PERFECT NEEDLE EP (12")	8
89	What Goes On WHAT GOES ON 32	TASTE (LP)	15
90	Fierce FRIGHT 039	TRADE MARK OF QUALITY (LP)	12

TELEVISION
77	Elektra K 12252	Marquee Moon Parts 1 & 2	5
78	Elektra K 12287	Foxhole/Careful (12", red vinyl)	8
79	Ork/WEA NYC 1T	Little Johnny Jewel Parts 1 & 2/Little Johnny Jewel (live) (12", p/s)	15
77	Elektra K52046	MARQUEE MOON (LP, 1st pressing with quotation marks around title)	25
78	Elektra K52072	ADVENTURE (LP, red vinyl)	12

(see also Neon Boys)

TELEVISION PERSONALITIES
78	Teen '78 SRTS/CUS/77/089	14th Floor/Oxford Street W1 (p/s, various different sleeve designs)	80
78	Kings Road LYN 5976/7	WHERE'S BILL GRUNDY NOW? (EP, hand-stamped label, 2,000 only)	25
78	Kings Road LYN 5976/7	WHERE'S BILL GRUNDY NOW? (EP, white labels, various sleeves)	12
79	Rough Trade RT 033	WHERE'S BILL GRUNDY NOW? (EP, reissue, different p/s, printed labels)	10
80	Rough Trade RT 051	Smashing Time/King & Country (p/s)	15
81	Rough Trade RT 063	I Know Where Syd Barrett Lives/Arthur The Gardener (p/s)	15
82	Whaam! WHAAM 4	Three Wishes/Geoffrey Ingram/And Don't The Kids Just Love It (p/s, 2 different sleeve designs, 2,000 only)	15
82	Creation Artefact 002/Lyntone LYN 13546	Biff Bang Pow!/A Picture Of Dorian Gray (1-sided flexidisc, with Communication Blur fanzine)	25
82	Creation Artefact 002/Lyntone LYN 13546	Biff Bang Pow!/A Picture Of Dorian Gray (1-sided flexidisc, without Communication Blur fanzine)	18
83	Rough Trade RT 109	A Sense Of Belonging/Paradise Estate (p/s)	12
86	Dreamworld DREAM 4	How I Learnt To Love The Bomb/Then God Snaps His Fingers/ Now You're Just Being Ridiculous (12", p/s, 3,700 only)	15
86	Dreamworld DREAM 10	How I Learnt To Love The Bomb/Grocer's Daughter/Girl Called Charity (7", reissue, p/s, 1,000 only)	15
87	Dreamworld DREAM 13(T)	Privilege/Me And My Desires (unreleased)	0
89	Overground OVER 03	14th Floor/Oxford Street W1 (numbered p/s, 600 yellow vinyl)	6
89	Overground OVER 03	14th Floor/Oxford Street W1 (numbered p/s, 400 white vinyl)	7
89	Caff CAFF 5	I Still Believe In Magic/Respectable (p/s, in poly bag, 500 only)	35
89	Caff CAFF 5	I Still Believe In Magic/Respectable (p/s, 500 only)	25
90	Overground OVER 13	I Know Where Syd Barrett Lives/Arthur The Gardener (reissue, p/s, 2000 only)	6
90	Overground OVER 15	Silly Girl (unissued, 100 test pressings only)	18
91	Clawfist XPIG 8	Your Class/BMX BANDITS : Somebody To Share My Life With	12
92	Seminal Twang TWANG 15	We Will Be Your Gurus/Miro/An Exhibition By Jane/Love Is Better Than War (p/s)	7
81	Rough Trade ROUGH 24	AND DON'T THE KIDS JUST LOVE IT (LP, 1st 1,000 with insert)	60
81	Rough Trade ROUGH 24	AND DON'T THE KIDS JUST LOVE IT (LP)	35
81	Whaam! WHAAM 3	MUMMY YOU'RE NOT WATCHING ME (LP, 3,500 only, 1st 1,000 with insert)	60
81	Whaam! WHAAM 3	MUMMY YOU'RE NOT WATCHING ME (LP, 3,500 only, 2,500 without insert)	35
82	Whaam! BIG 5	THEY COULD HAVE BEEN BIGGER THAN THE BEATLES (LP, 2,500 only, hand-painted sleeve)	35
83	Whaam! BIG 10	TURN ON ... TUNE IN (LP, unreleased)	0
85	Illuminated JAMS 37	THE PAINTED WORD (LP)	25
86	Dreamworld BIG DREAM 2	THEY COULD HAVE BEEN BIGGER THAN THE BEATLES (LP, reissue with insert)	20
86	Dreamworld BIG DREAM 4	MUMMY YOU'RE NOT WATCHING ME (LP, reissue with insert)	20
87	Dreamworld BIG DREAM 6	PRIVILEGE (LP, unreleased)	0

(see also Teenage Filmstars, Times, O Level, Missing Scientists, Reacta, Dry Rib, Slaughter, Gifted Children)

TELEX
78	Sire SIR 4006	Twist A Saint-Tropez/Le Fond De L'Air (p/s)	5
79	Sire SIR 4017	Moskow Diskow/Twist A Saint-Tropez (p/s)	5
79	Sire SIR 4017T	Moskow Diskow (Disco Version)/Twist A Saint-Tropez (Disco Version) (12")	8
79	Sire SIR 4020	Rock Around The Clock/Moskow Diskow	5
82	Interdisc IN 2	L'amour Toujours/Cloche Et Sifflets (p/s)	5
79	Sire SRK 6072	LOOKING FOR ST. TROPEZ (LP, with lyric inner sleeve)	12
82	Interdisc INTO 1	BIRDS AND BEES (LP)	15

TELHAM TINKERS
| 84 | Eron ERON 031 | HOT IN ALICE SPRINGS (LP, with insert) | 12 |

TELLERS
| 74 | Pyramid PYR 7011 | No Work, No Pay/Version | 6 |
| 74 | Dragon DRA 1031 | Ta It Deh/Hit Dib | 6 |

TELSTARS
| 62 | Oriole CB 1754 | I Went A' Walkin'/A Rose And A Thorn | 20 |

TEMPERANCE SEVEN
| 61 | Argo EAF 14 | THE TEMPERANCE SEVEN INCH RECORD (EP) | 8 |
| 63 | Parlophone R 5070 | From Russia With Love/P.C.Q/Please Charleston Quietly | 7 |

(see also Ted Wood)

TEMPEST (1)
85	Magnet PEST 1	Always The Same/Love In The Wintertime (p/s)	50
85	Magnet 10PEST 1	Always The Same/The Physical Act (10")	25
85	Magnet PEST 2	Bluebelle/I Want To Live (p/s)	50
85	Magnet 10PEST 2	Bluebelle/I Want To Live (10")	25
86	Magnet LAZY 1	Lazy Sunday/You've Always Got Something To Say (p/s)	15

86	Magnet PEST 3	Didn't We Have A Nice Time?/The Physical Act	50

TEMPEST (2)
73	Bronze ILPS 9220	TEMPEST (LP, foldover cover with lyric inner sleeve)	50
74	Bronze ILPS 9267	LIVING IN FEAR (LP, die-cut cover with inner sleeve)	30

(see also Colosseum, Patto)

BOBBY TEMPEST
59	Decca F 11125	Love Or Leave/Don't Leave Me	12
59	Decca F 11125	Love Or Leave/Don't Leave Me (78)	10

BOB TEMPLE
57	Parlophone R 4264	Come Back, Come Back/Vim Vam Vamoose	100
57	Parlophone R 4264	Come Back, Come Back/Vim Vam Vamoose (78)	10

GERRY TEMPLE
61	HMV POP 823	No More Tomorrows/So Nice To Walk You Home	40
61	HMV POP 939	Seventeen Come Sunday/Tell You What I'll Do	30
63	HMV POP 1114	Angel Face/Since You Went Away	45
68	RCA Victor RCA 1670	Lovin' Up A Storm/Everything I Do is Wrong	20

RICHARD TEMPLE
70	Jay Boy BOY 31	That Beatin' Rhythm/Could It Be	15
70	Jay Boy BOY 31	That Beatin' Rhythm/Could It Be (DJ copy)	30

SHIRLEY TEMPLE
59	Top Rank JAR 139	On The Good Ship Lollipop/Animal Crackers In My Soup	5
59	Top Rank JAR 139	On The Good Ship Lollipop/Animal Crackers In My Soup (78)	10
59	Top Rank JKR 8003	I REMEMBER (EP)	20

TEMPLEAIRES
60s	Vogue V 2421	He Spoke/What Will Heaven Have In Store For Me	20

TEMPLE OF LIFE
91	T Life 001	EDP/Relax Your Soul/Slayer/Trancetone (12", stamped white labels)	50

TEMPLE OF THE DOG
92	A&M AM 0091	Hunger Strike/All Night Thing (picture disc)	15
92	A&M AMY 0091	Hunger Strike/Your Saviour/All Night Thing (12", p/s, with poster)	15
92	A&M AMCD 0091	Hunger Strike/Your Saviour/All Night Thing (CD, digipak)	20
91	A&M 395350-1	TEMPLE OF THE DOG (LP)	30

(see also Pearl Jam)

TEMPLE ROW
72	Polydor 2058254	King & Queen/One Of A Million Faces	50
73	Polydor 2058-329	Walk The World Away/Mystery Man	8

TEMPLETON TWINS
70	Liberty LBF 15379	Hey Jude/Macarthur Park	6

NINO TEMPO
57	London HLU 8387	Tempo's Tempo/June's Blues (as Nino Tempo & His Band)	300
57	London HLU 8387	Tempo's Tempo/June's Blues (as Nino Tempo & His Band) (78)	50
75	A&M AMS 7190	Come See Me Round Midnight/High On Music (as Nino Tempo & 5th Avenue)	5
58	London HB-U 1075	ROCK 'N' ROLL BEACH PARTY (10" LP)	300

(see also Nino Tempo & April Stevens, April Stevenso)

NINO TEMPO & APRIL STEVENS
62	London HLK 9580	Sweet And Lovely/TOP NOTES: Twist And Shout	15
63	London HLK 9782	Deep Purple/I've Been Carrying A Torch For You So Long That I Burned A Great Big Hole In My Heart	5
64	London HLK 9829	Whispering/Tweedle Dee	5
64	London HLK 9859	Stardust/1-45	5
64	London HLK 9890	Tea For Two/I'm Confessin' (That I Love You)	5
66	London HLU 10084	All Strung Out/I Can't Go On Living Baby Without You	6
67	Atlantic 584 048	Coldest Night Of The Year/Ooh La La (as April Stevens & Nino Tempo)	7
67	London HLU 10106	The Habit Of Lovin' Baby/You'll Be Needing Me Baby	6
67	London HLU 10130	My Old Flame/Wings Of Love	5
68	Atlantic 584 151	Deep Purple/Sweet And Lovely	5
68	London HLU 10209	Ooh Poo Pah Doo/Let It Be Me	5
69	London HLU 10245	All Strung Out/My Old Flame	8
69	Bell BLL 1087	Sea Of Love/On The Dock Of The Bay/Twilight Time	5
73	A&M AMS 7075	Put It Where You Want It/I Can't Get Over You Baby	5
64	London RE-K 1412	DEEP PURPLE (EP)	10
64	London HA-K 8168	NINO TEMPO AND APRIL STEVENS - DEEP PURPLE (LP)	35
64	Atlantic AL 5006	SING THE GREAT SONGS (LP, mono)	25
64	Atlantic SAL 5006	SING THE GREAT SONGS (LP, stereo)	30
66	Atlantic	HEY BABY (LP)	20
67	London HA-U/SH-U 8314	ALL STRUNG OUT (LP)	30

(see also Nino Tempo, April Stevens)

TEMPOS
59	Pye International 7N 25026	See You In September/Bless You My Love	100
59	Pye International 7N 25026	See You In September/Bless You My Love (78)	40

TEMPTATIONS (1)
60	Top Rank JAR 384	Barbara/Someday	30

TEMPTATIONS (2)
SINGLES
64	Stateside SS 278	The Way You Do The Things You Do/Just Let Me Know	70
64	Stateside SS 278	The Way You Do The Things You Do/Just Let Me Know (DJ copy)	120
64	Stateside SS 319	I'll Be In Trouble/The Girl's Alright With Me	80
64	Stateside SS 319	I'll Be In Trouble/The Girl's Alright With Me (DJ copy)	120
64	Stateside SS 348	Girl (Why You Wanna Make Me Blue)/Baby Baby I Need You	80
64	Stateside SS 348	Girl (Why You Wanna Make Me Blue)/Baby Baby I Need You (DJ copy)	240
65	Stateside SS 378	My Girl/(Talking 'Bout) Nobody But My Baby (DJ copy)	150
65	Tamla Motown TMG 504	It's Growing/What Love Has Joined Together	40

65	Tamla Motown TMG 504	It's Growing/What Love Has Joined Together (DJ copy)	100
65	Stateside SS 378	My Girl/(Talking 'Bout) Nobody But My Baby	45
65	Tamla Motown TMG 526	Since I Lost My Baby/You've Got To Earn It (DJ copy)	200
65	Tamla Motown TMG 526	Since I Lost My Baby/You've Got To Earn It	50
65	Tamla Motown TMG 541	My Baby/Don't Look Back (DJ copy)	100
65	Tamla Motown TMG 541	My Baby/Don't Look Back	45
66	Tamla Motown TMG 557	Get Ready/Fading Away	30
66	Tamla Motown TMG 557	Get Ready/Fading Away (DJ copy)	100
66	Tamla Motown TMG 565	Ain't Too Proud To Beg/You'll Lose A Precious Love (spelt "Previous")	30
66	Tamla Motown TMG 565	Ain't Too Proud To Beg/You'll Lose A Precious Love (spelt "Previous") (DJ copy)	130
66	Tamla Motown TMG 578	Beauty Is Only Skin Deep/You're Not An Ordinary Girl (DJ copy)	140
66	Tamla Motown TMG 578	Beauty Is Only Skin Deep/You're Not An Ordinary Girl	30
66	Tamla Motown TMG 587	(I Know) I'm Losing You/Little Miss Sweetness	25
66	Tamla Motown TMG 587	(I Know) I'm Losing You/Little Miss Sweetness (DJ copy)	80
67	Tamla Motown TMG 610	All I Need/Sorry Is A Sorry Word	20
67	Tamla Motown TMG 610	All I Need/Sorry Is A Sorry Word (DJ copy)	60
67	Tamla Motown TMG 620	You're My Everything/I've Been Good To You	20
67	Tamla Motown TMG 620	You're My Everything/I've Been Good To You (DJ copy)	50
67	Tamla Motown TMG 633	(Loneliness Made Me Realise) It's You That I Need/I Want A Love I Can See	40
67	Tamla Motown TMG 633	(Loneliness Made Me Realise) It's You That I Need/I Want A Love I Can See (DJ copy)	45
68	Tamla Motown TMG 641	I Wish It Would Rain/I Truly, Truly Believe	20
68	Tamla Motown TMG 641	I Wish It Would Rain/I Truly, Truly Believe (DJ copy)	30
68	Tamla Motown TMG 658	I Could Never Love Another (After Loving You)/Gonna Give Her All The Love I've Got	15
68	Tamla Motown TMG 658	I Could Never Love Another (After Loving You)/Gonna Give Her All The Love I've Got (DJ copy)	30
68	Tamla Motown TMG 671	Why Did You Leave Me Darling/How Can I Forget	15
68	Tamla Motown TMG 671	Why Did You Leave Me Darling/How Can I Forget (DJ copy)	30
69	Tamla Motown TMG 688	Get Ready/My Girl	7
69	Tamla Motown TMG 688	Get Ready/My Girl (DJ copy)	30
69	Tamla Motown TMG 699	Ain't Too Proud To Beg/Fading Away	7
69	Tamla Motown TMG 699	Ain't Too Proud To Beg/Fading Away (DJ copy)	25
69	Tamla Motown TMG 707	Cloud Nine/Why Did She Have To Go	7
69	Tamla Motown TMG 707	Cloud Nine/Why Did She Have To Go (Why Did She Have To Go) (DJ copy)	25
69	Tamla Motown TMG 716	Runaway Child, Running Wild/I Need Your Lovin'	8
70	Tamla Motown TMG 722	I Can't Get Next To You/Running Away (Ain't Gonna Help You)	7
70	Tamla Motown TMG 749	Ball Of Confusion (That's What The World Is Today)/It's Summer	7
70	Tamla Motown TMG 741	Psychedelic Shack/That's The Way Love Is	6
71	Tamla Motown TMG 773	Just My Imagination (Running Away With Me)/You Make Your Own Heaven And Hell Right Here On Earth	6
71	Tamla Motown TMG 783	It's Summer/Unite The World (Ungena Za Ulimwengu)	6
71	Tamla Motown TMG 783	Unite The World (Ungena Za Ulimwengu)/It's Summer (reissue)	8
72	Tamla Motown TMG 800	Superstar/Gonna Keep Tryin' Till I Win Your Love	6
72	Tamla Motown TMG 808	Take A Look Around/Smooth Sailing (From Now On)	6
72	Tamla Motown TMG 832	Smiling Faces Sometimes/Mother Nature	8
73	Tamla Motown TMG 839	Papa Was A Rolling Stone (Parts 1 & 2)	5
83	Tamla Motown TMG 1320	Papa Was A Rolling Stone/FOUR TOPS: Medley	35

EPs

65	Tamla Motown TME 2004	THE TEMPTATIONS (EP)	50
65	Tamla Motown TML 11009	MEET THE TEMPTATIONS	200
66	Tamla Motown TME 2010	IT'S THE TEMPTATIONS	40
71	Tamla Motown STML 11184	THE SKY'S THE LIMIT	15

ALBUMS : LPS

65	Tamla Motown TML 11016	SING SMOKEY	60
66	Tamla Motown STML 11023	THE TEMPTIN' TEMPTATIONS (stereo)	55
66	Tamla Motown TML 11023	THE TEMPTIN' TEMPTATIONS (mono)	45
66	Tamla Motown TML 11035	GETTIN' READY (mono)	40
66	Tamla Motown STML 11035	GETTIN' READY (stereo)	50
67	Tamla Motown STML 11057	WITH A LOT O'SOUL (stereo)	40
67	Tamla Motown STML 11053	THE TEMPTATIONS LIVE! (stereo)	25
67	Tamla Motown STML 11042	GREATEST HITS (stereo)	25
67	Tamla Motown TML 11042	GREATEST HITS (mono)	20
67	Tamla Motown TML 11053	TEMPTATIONS LIVE! (mono)	20
67	Tamla Motown TML 11057	WITH A LOT O'SOUL (mono)	35
68	Tamla Motown TML 11068	IN A MELLOW MOOD (mono)	30
68	Tamla Motown STML 11068	IN A MELLOW MOOD (stereo)	35
68	Tamla Motown TML 11079	WISH IT WOULD RAIN (LP, mono)	30
68	Tamla Motown STML 11079	WISH IT WOULD RAIN (LP, stereo)	35
68	T. Motown (S)TML 11079	THE TEMPTATIONS WISH IT COULD RAIN	40
69	Tamla Motown TML 11104	THE TEMPTATIONS LIVE AT THE COPA (mono)	30
69	Tamla Motown STML 11104	THE TEMPTATIONS LIVE AT THE COPA (stereo)	25
69	Tamla Motown (S)TML 11109	CLOUD NINE (mono/stereo)	25
70	Tamla Motown STML 11141	'LIVE' AT LONDON'S TALK OF THE TOWN (stereo, mono unconfirmed)	20
70	Tamla Motown TML 11133	PUZZLE PEOPLE (mono)	25
70	Tamla Motown STML 11133	PUZZLE PEOPLE (stereo)	22
70	Tamla Motown STML 11147	PSYCHEDELIC SHACK	20
70	Tamla Motown STML 11170	GREATEST HITS Vol. 2	15
72	Tamla Motown STML 11202	SOLID ROCK	15
72	Tamla Motown STML 11218	ALL DIRECTIONS	15
73	Tamla Motown STML 11229	MASTERPIECE	15

(see also David Ruffin, Diana Ross)

TEMPUS FUGIT

69	Philips BF 1802	Come Alive/Emphasis On Love	60

(see also Jensens)

10CC

72	UK UK 22	Johnny Don't Do It/4% Of Something	6
74	UK UK 57	The Worst Band In The World/18 Carat Man Of Means	6
73	UK UKAL 1005	10cc (LP, lyric insert)	12
80s	Mercury HS 9102 500	THE ORIGINAL SOUNDTRACK (LP, half-speed master)	12
80s	Mercury HS 9102 504	GREATEST HITS (LP, half-speed master)	12

95	Avex AVEXLP	MIRROR MIRROR (LP)	12

(see also Godley & Creme, Graham Gouldman, Mindbenders, Mockingbirds, Hotlegs, Whirlwinds, Tristar Airbus, Yellow Bellow Room Boom, Nick Mason & Rick Fenn, Frabjoy & Runcible Spoon, Manchester Mob, Ramases)

TENDER TONES
69	Crab CRAB 38	Devil Woman/Nobody Cares	10

TEN FEET
66	RCA RCA 1544	Got Everything But Love/Factory Worker	100
67	CBS 3045	Shoot On Sight/Losing Game	120

TEN FEET FIVE
65	Fontana TF 578	Baby's Back In Town/Send Me No More Lovin'	45

(see also Troggs)

TEN FOOT BONELESS
88	Fierce FRIGHT 027	Powerslide/Duane Peters Is God (12", yellow or white p/s, with inner)	12

(see also Pooh Sticks)

TENNENT & MORRISON
72	Polydor 2383 152	TENNENT & MORRISON (LP, with lyric insert)	150

(see also Joe Soap)

TENNESSEE JAY BIRDS
51	London L 1007	Sticks And Stones/Trouble Trouble (78)	10

TENNIS SHOES
78	Bonaparte BONE 3	(Do The) Medium Wave/Rolf Is Stranger Than Richard/So Large (p/s)	8

TEN(N)ORS
68	Doctor Bird DB 1152	Massy Massa/CLIVE ALLSTARS: San Sebastian	40
68	Doctor Bird DB 1175	Sufferer (Make It)/Little Things	40
68	Island WI 3133	Ride Your Donkey/I've Got To Get You Off My Mind	15
68	Island WI 3140	Copy Me Donkey (as Tenors)/The Stage (B-side actually by Ronnie Davis)	30
68	Island WI 3156	Grampa/ROMEO STEWART: While I Was Walking	30
68	Blue Cat BS 127	Khaki/LEYROY REID: Great Surprise (Pound Get A Blow)	30
68	Big Shot BI 501	Reggae Girl/CLIVE ALLSTARS: Donkey Trot	80
68	Fab FAB 41	Ride Your Donkey/I've Got To Get You Off My Mind	25
68	Fab FAB 50	Let Go Yah Donkey/ROMEO STEWART: While I Was Walking	25
69	Big Shot BI 514	You're No Good/Do The Reggae	40
69	Big Shot BI 517	Another Scorcher/My Baby	70
69	Duke Reid DR 2502	Hopeful Village/TOMMY McCOOK: The Village	15
69	Bullet BU 406	Greatest Scorcher/Making Love	10
69	Crab CRAB 26	Baff Boom/Feel Bad	30
69	Crab CRAB 29	True Brothers/Sign Of The Time	6
69	Crab CRAB 36	I Want Everything/Cherry	8
73	Explosion EX 2079	Weather Report/Weather Report - Version	8
73	Pyramid PYR 7000	Money Never Built A Mountain/My World	5

(see also Jennors, Prince Buster, Soul Brothers)

TENOR SAW
84	SKD SKD 092	Bad Bwoy/Dub (12")	18
84	Hawkeye HLD 0012	CLASH (LP, with Coco Tea)	15

TENPOLE TUDOR
80	Korova KOW 4	Real Fun/What's In A Word (p/s)	5

(see also Sex Pistols)

10,000 MANIACS
84	Reflex RE 1	My Mother The War (Remix)/Planned Obsolescence/National Education Week (12", p/s)	20
84	Press P 2010	HUMAN CONFLICT 5 (12" EP, gatefold p/s)	30
85	Lyntone LYN 15914	Grey Victory/SIMPLY RED: Something's Burning (33rpm 1-sided clear flexidisc free with Jamming! magazine, issue 29)	12
84	Press P 3001 LP	SECRETS OF THE I-CHING (LP, with insert)	25
84	Press P 3001 LP	SECRETS OF THE I-CHING (LP, with insert; later re-pressing in different 'Chinese Chicken' sleeve, some with insert)	15

TEN WHEEL DRIVE (WITH GENYA RAVAN)
71	Polydor 2066 034	Mornin' Much Better/Stay With Me	5
69	Polydor 583 577	CONSTRUCTION NO. 1 (LP)	20
70	Polydor 2425 002	BRIEF REPLIES (LP, with Genya Ravan)	20
71	Polydor 2425 065	PECULIAR FRIENDS (LP, with Genya Ravan)	20

(see also Goldie [& Gingerbreads])

TEN YEARS AFTER
68	Deram DM 176	Portable People/The Sounds	20
68	Deram DM 221	Hear Me Calling/I'm Going Home	8
70	Deram DM 299	Love Like A Man/Love Like A Man	6
71	Deram XDR 48532	She Lies In The Morning/Sweet Little Sixteen (demo only)	15
72	Chrysalis/Philips 6155 006	One Of These Days/Baby Won't You Let Me Rock 'n' Roll You	5
89	Chrysalis CHS 3477	Highway Of Love/Rock 'n' Roll Music To The World (p/s)	5
67	Deram DML 1015	TEN YEARS AFTER (LP, mono)	60
67	Deram SML 1015	TEN YEARS AFTER (LP, stereo)	40
68	Deram DML 1023	UNDEAD (LP, mono)	40
68	Deram SML 1023	UNDEAD (LP, stereo)	30
69	Deram DML 1029	STONEDHENGE (LP, gatefold sleeve, mono)	35
69	Deram SML 1029	STONEDHENGE (LP, laminated gatefold sleeve, stereo)	30
69	Deram DML/SML 1052	SSSSH! (LP, gatefold sleeve, mono/stereo)	30
70	Deram DML 1065	CRICKLEWOOD GREEN (LP, gatefold sleeve, with 'Alvin Lee' poster, mono)	60
70	Deram SML 1065	CRICKLEWOOD GREEN (LP, gatefold sleeve, with 'Alvin Lee' poster, stereo)	35
71	Deram SML 1078	WATT (LP, gatefold sleeve, with poster)	30
71	Chrysalis CHR 1001	A SPACE IN TIME (LP)	20
72	Deram SML 1096	ALVIN LEE AND COMPANY (LP)	15
72	Chysalis CHR 1009	ROCK & ROLL MUSIC TO THE WORLD (gatefold sleeve)	12
78	Deram SML 1023	UNDEAD (LP, reissue)	12

(see also Alvin Lee, Chick Churchill)

MINT VALUE £

WAYNE TENYUE
| 82 | Red Nail RN 0035 | Murderous Time/THE DUB BAND: Life Sentence (12") | 10 |

TERMINAL
| 80s | Cargo CRS 0081 | Hold On/We're Only Human (in p/s) | 100 |
| 80s | Cargo CRS 0081 | Hold On | 50 |

TERMINAL JIVE
| 82 | Jive Alive JA001 | THE TERMINAL JIVE AND SCARLET ALIVE EP (2 tracks on one side, p/s) | 15 |

TERMITES
| 65 | Oriole CB 1989 | Tell Me/I Found My Place | 40 |
| 65 | CBS 201761 | Every Day Every Day/No-One In The Whole Wide World | 20 |

TERMITES (JAMAICA)
67	Studio One SO 2006	Mercy Mr. Percy/SOUL BROTHERS: Hot And Cold	80
67	Studio One SO 2029	It Takes Two To Make Love/Beach Boy	80
67	Coxsone CS 7008	Sign Up/DELROY WILSON: Troubled Man	25
67	Coxsone CS 7025	Do It Right Now/SUMMERTAIRES: Stay (B-side actually by Gaylads)	25
68	Studio One SO 2040	Mr D.J. (actually by Delroy Wilson)/Tripe Girl (actually by Heptones)	40
68	Coxsone CS 7039	Mama Didn't Know/I Made A Mistake	100
68	Pama PM 729	Push It Up/Two Of A Kind (B-side act. by Clancy Eccles & Cynthia Richards)	80
68	Pama PM 738	Show Me The Way/What Can I Do	20
68	Trojan TR 634	Love Up Kiss Up/TOMMY McCOOK : Regay	30
69	Nu Beat NB 017	Push Push/Girls (actually by Hi Tones)	18
67	Studio One SO SOL 9003	DO THE ROCK STEADY (LP)	100

(see also L. Sparks, Ken Boothe, Upsetters)

PETE TERRACE
67	Pye International 7N 25427	At The Party/No! No! No!	30
67	Pye International 7N 25440	Shotgun Boo-Ga-Loo/I'm Gonna Make It	40
67	Pye Intl. NPL 28102	BOOGALOO (LP)	50

TERRA COTTA
| 78 | Terra Cotta TC 001 | To Be Near You (p/s, with insert) | 15 |

(see also Spriguns)

TERRAIN
| 83 | Terrain Musak TS 001 | Who's To Blame?/Vacation (no p/s) | 150 |

TERRAPLANE
| 85 | Epic 26439 | BLACK AND WHITE (LP) | 15 |
| 87 | Epic 460157 1 | MOVING TARGET (LP) | 12 |

(see also Thunder, Nuthin' Fancy)

LLOYD TERRELL
68	Island WI 3158	My Argument (as Lloyd & Johnny Melody)/JOHNNY MELODY: Foey Man (B-side actually by George Dekker)	250
68	Pama PM 710	Bang Bang Lulu/MRS MILLER: I Never Knew	5
68	Pama PM 740	How Come (actually by Lee Perry)/MRS MILLER: Oh My Lover	10
69	Pama PM 752	Lulu Returns/MRS MILLER: I Feel The Music	10
69	Nu Beat NB 023	Mr Rhya/After Dark	18
70	Pama PM 792	Birth Control/VAL BENNET: Return To Peace	5
70	Bullet BU 434	Exposure/Baby Huey	15
70	Bullet BU 443	Oh Me Oh My/I Did It	25
71	Escort ERT 855	One Woman/CHARMERS: What Should I Do (act. by Dave Barker & Charmers)	7
72	Bullet BU 508	Oily Sounds/Oily Version (as Lloyd Tyrell)	8
73	Pama PM 863	Big Eight/JUNIOR BYLES: Auntie Lu Lu	7

(see also Charmers, Lloyd Charmers, Lloyd & Johnny, Lloyd & Ken, Lloydie & Lowbites)

TAMMI TERRELL
66	Tamla Motown TMG 561	Come On And See Me/Baby Don'tcha Worry	120
66	Tamla Motown TMG 561	Come On And See Me/Baby Don'tcha Worry (DJ copy)	200
69	T. Motown (S)TML 11103	THE IRRESISTIBLE TAMMI TERRELL (LP, mono/stereo)	100

(see also Marvin Gaye & Tammi Terrell)

TAMMI TERRELL/CHUCK JACKSON
| 69 | Marble Arch MAL 1110 | THE EARLY SHOW (LP) | 20 |

(see also Chuck Jackson)

PHIL TERRELL
| 94 | Kent 6T 10 | Love Has Passed Me By/VIC & JOHN: Why Did She Lie | 35 |

TERRI & TERRORS
| 79 | Fresh FRESH 4 | Laugh At Me/Laugh At Me (Again) (folded p/s) | 5 |

TERRORIZER
| 89 | Earach MOSH 16 | WORLD DOWNFALL (LP, with inner) | 20 |

TERRORVISION
92	Total Vegas 12VEGAS 1	THRIVE EP (12" EP)	12
92	Total Vegas CDVEGAS 1	THRIVE EP (CD EP)	20
92	Total Vegas CDVEGAS 2	My House/Coming Up/Tea Dance (CD)	20
93	Total Vegas CDATVR 1	Problem Solved/Corpse Fly/We Are The Roadcrew/Sailing Home (CD)	25
93	Total Vegas CDPVEGAS 3	American TV/Psycho Killer/Hole For A Soul (CD)	15
92	Total Vegas ATVRLP 1	FORMALDEHYDE (LP, 14 tracks, green vinyl, 500 only, stickered sleeve)	40
92	Total Vegas ATVRCD 1	FORMALDEHYDE (CD, 14 tracks, 1,000 only)	20
93	Total Vegas VEGASLPS 1	FORMALDEHYDE (reissue LP, 12 tracks, 1,000 copies with 12-page booklet, stickered sleeve & lyric inner)	20
93	Total Vegas BOOT 1	LIVE AT THE DON VALLEY STADIUM (CD, picture disc, 250 promo copies only)	30

(see also Spoilt Bratz)

TERRY
| 66 | Fontana TF 751 | Spilt Milk/The Way That I Remember Him | 10 |

TERRY, CARL & DERRICK
| 69 | Grape GR 3012 | True Love/ROY SMITH: Another Saturday Night | 8 |

CLARK TERRY (& BOB BROOKMEYER)

61	Riverside RLP 12-246	DUKE WITH A DIFFERENCE (LP)	12
65	Fontana TL 5265	TONIGHT (LP, with Bob Brookmeyer)	12
66	Fontana TL 5290	POWER OF POSITIVE SWINGING (LP, with Bob Brookmeyer)	12
66	Fontana TL 5373	MUMBLES (LP)	12
67	Fontana (S)TL 5394	GINGERBREAD MEN (LP, with Bob Brookmeyer)	12
68	Impulse MIPL/SIPL 507	IT'S WHAT'S HAPPENIN' (LP)	12

(see also Coleman Hawkins)

DEWEY TERRY

73	Tumbleweed TW 3502	CHIEF (LP)	18

(see also Don & Dewey, Don Harris, Harvey Mandel)

GORDON TERRY

57	London REA 1098	COUNTRY CLAMBAKE (EP)	20

PAT TERRY (GROUP)

70s	Myrrh MYR 1031	PAT TERRY GROUP (LP)	18

SONNY TERRY (TRIO)

53	Parlophone MSP 6017	Hootin' Blues/TOMMY REILLY: Bop! Goes The Weasel	35
56	Vogue EPV 1095	SONNY TERRY (EP)	50
55	Vogue LDE 137	FOLK BLUES (10" LP)	40
55	Vogue LDE 165	CITY BLUES (10" LP)	40
58	Melodisc MLP 516	WHOOPIN' THE BLUES (10" LP)	40
58	Topic 10T 30	HARMONICA BLUES (10" LP)	40
65	Topic 12T 30	HARMONICA BLUES (12" LP, reissue)	35
66	Xtra XTRA 5025	SONNY'S STORY (LP)	25
67	Capitol T 20906	WHOOPIN' THE BLUES (LP, reissue)	12
69	Ember CW 136	BLIND SONNY TERRY & WOODY GUTHRIE (LP)	15
69	Xtra XTRA 1064	SONNY TERRY (LP)	15
60s	Mainstream MSL 1037	GOING DOWN SLOW (LP, with BROWNIE McGHEE & PEPPERMINT HARRIS)	18
70	Xtra XTRA 1099	BLUES FROM EVERYWHERE (LP)	15
71	Xtra XTRA 1110	ON THE ROAD (LP, with J.C. Burris)	15

(see also Woody Guthrie)

SONNY TERRY & BROWNIE MCGHEE

60	Columbia DB 4433	Talking Harmonica Blues/Rockin' And Whoopin'	35
64	Oriole CB 1946	Dissatisfied Woman/SONNY TERRY: Goin' Down Slow	20
50s	Melodisc EPM7 83	ME AND SONNY (EP)	10
58	Pye Jazz NJE 1060	THE BLUEST (EP)	10
59	Pye Jazz NJE 1073	SONNY TERRY & BROWNIE McGHEE & CHRIS BARBER'S JAZZ BAND (EP)	10
59	Pye Jazz NJE 1074	TERRY AND McGHEE IN LONDON PT. 1 (EP)	15
59	Topic TOP 37	HOOTENANNY NEW YORK CITY (EP, with Pete Seeger)	15
61	Top Rank JKP 3007	WORK-PLAY-FAITH-FUN-SONGS (EP)	15
64	Ember EP 4562	SONNY TERRY AND BROWNIE McGHEE (EP)	20
64	Topic TOP 121	R AND B FROM S AND B (EP)	15
64	Realm REP 4002	PAWNSHOP BLUES (EP)	15
64	Vocalion EPV 1274	SONNY TERRY AND BROWNIE McGHEE (EP)	20
65	Vocalion EPV 1279	I SHALL NOT BE MOVED (EP)	20
58	Topic 12T 29	BROWNIE McGHEE AND SONNY TERRY (LP)	30
58	Pye Nixa Jazz NJT 515	SONNY, BROWNIE AND CHRIS (10" LP, with Chris Barber)	45
58	Pye Nixa Jazz NJL 18	SONNY TERRY AND BROWNIE McGHEE IN LONDON (LP)	30
58	London Jazz LTZ-C 15144	BACK COUNTRY BLUES (LP)	50
60	Columbia 33SX 1223	BLUES IS MY COMPANION (LP)	50
61	World Record Club 7379	SONNY TERRY AND BROWNIE McGHEE (LP)	20
61	Vogue LAE 12247	BLUES IS A STORY (LP, mono)	30
61	Vogue SEA 5014	BLUES IS A STORY (LP, stereo)	40
63	Vogue LAE 12266	DOWN SOUTH SUMMIT MEETIN' (LP)	25
63	CBS 52165	BACK COUNTRY BLUES (LP)	25
64	Xtra XTRA 1004	BIG BILL BROONZY/SONNY TERRY/BROWNIE McGHEE (LP)	30
64	Vogue LAE 552	BROWNIE McGHEE AND SONNY TERRY (LP)	30
64	Realm RM 165	BACK COUNTRY BLUES (LP)	18
64	Stateside SL 10076	BLUES HOOT (LP, some tracks by Lightnin' Hopkins)	40
64	Fontana 688 006ZL	LIVIN' WITH THE BLUES (LP)	30
65	Society SOC 1015	BROWNIE & SONNY SING AND PLAY (LP)	12
66	Philips BL 7675	AT THE BUNK HOUSE (LP)	30
66	Verve VLP 5010	GUITAR HIGHWAY (LP, mono)	20
66	Verve SVLP 5010	GUITAR HIGHWAY (LP, stereo)	25
66	Fontana TL 5289	HOMETOWN BLUES (LP)	30
67	Ace Of Hearts (Z)AHT 182	HOMETOWN BLUES (LP, reissue)	12
69	Capitol T 20906	WHOOPIN' THE BLUES (LP)	30
69	Stateside SSL 10291	LONG WAY FROM HOME (LP)	12
69	Marble Arch MAL 843	SONNY TERRY AND BROWNIE McGHEE IN LONDON (LP)	12
70	Fontana SFJL 979	WHERE THE BLUES BEGAN (LP)	20
73	Mainstream MSL 1019	HOMETOWN BLUES (LP, gatefold sleeve)	15

(see also Brownie McGhee, Chris Barber, Pete Seeger, Big Bill Broonzy, Lightnin' Hopkins, Big Joe Turner)

SUSAN TERRY

62	Piccadilly 7N 35026	Along Came LOve/Looking For A Boy	15

TERRY & JERRY

65	R&B MRB 5009	People Are Doing It Every Day/Mama Julie	22

TERRY SISTERS

57	Parlophone R 4364	It's The Same Old Jazz/Broken Promises	6
58	Parlophone R 4509	Sweet Thing (Tell Me That You Love Me)/You Forgot To Remember	6

TESCO BOMBERS

82	Y Y14	Hernando's Hideaway/Break The Ice At Parties/Girl From Ipanema (p/s)	5

(see also Homosexuals)

TEST DEPARTMENT

83	Some Bizzare TEST 112	Compulsion/Pulsations (12", p/s)	10
87	Some Bizzare 12MOP 13	Victory (12", p/s)	10

MINT VALUE £

80s	Media City CMC 1	Gododdin (12", p/s, Welsh gig freebie with Brith Gof)	10
90	Mop MOP 5T	Jihad/(Desert Mix)/(Oil Mix) (12", p/s)	12
93	Mop MOP 8T	Bang On It/(Tao Systems Mix)/(TC Ruff House Remix) (12", die-cut p/s)	10
82	Test TEST ONE	HISTORY (cassette, with booklet in plastic bag)	15
85	Test TEST 33	BEATING THE RETREAT (LP, box set)	12
90s	Mop MOP 3	A GOOD NIGHT OUT (LP)	12

TEST ICICLES
05	Domino WIGLP 1	FOR SCREENING PURPOSES ONLY (LP)	15

TETRACK
77	Hawkeye HE 006	Let's Get Started/PABLO EXPERIENCE: Go it	10
78	Greensleeves GRE 8	Only Jah Knows/ROCKERS ALL STARS: Jah Jah Dub	20
78	Rockers APD 2	Love And Unity/JAH LEVE & JAH BULL: Two The Hard Way/ JUNIOR DAN: Jah Foundation (12")	30

ALAN TEW ORCHESTRA
76	Epic EPC 4676	The Sweeney/The Prowler	15
67	Decca Phase 4 PFS 4120	THIS IS MY SCENE (LP)	40
72	CBS 64665	LET'S FLY (LP)	25
76	Themes Int. Music TIM 1024	DRAMA SUITE PART 1 (LP)	100

JOE TEX
65	Atlantic AT 4015	Hold What You've Got/Fresh Out Of Tears	22
65	Atlantic AT 4021	You Better Get It/You Got What It Takes	20
65	Sue WI 370	Yum Yum Yum/You Little Baby Face Thing	40
65	Atlantic AT 4027	A Woman Can Change A Man/Don't Let Your Left Hand Know	15
65	Atlantic AT 4045	I Want To (Do Everything For You)/Funny Bone	15
65	Atlantic AT 4058	A Sweet Woman Like You/Close Your Door	15
66	Atlantic AT 4081	The Love You Save/If Sugar Was As Sweet As You	15
66	Atlantic 584 016	S.Y.S.L.J.F.M. (Letter Song)/I'm A Man	10
66	Atlantic 584 035	You Better Believe It/I Believe I'm Gonna Make It	25
67	Atlantic 584 068	Papa Was Too/The Truest Woman In The World	10
67	Atlantic 584 096	Hold What You've Got/A Sweet Woman Like You	10
67	Atlantic 584 102	Show Me/Woman Sees A Hard Time (When Her Man Is Gone)	15
67	Atlantic 584 119	Woman Like That, Yeah/I'm Going And Get It	10
67	Atlantic 584 144	Skinny Legs And All/Watch The One (That Brings The Bad News)	10
68	Atlantic 584 171	Men Are Getting Scarce/You're Gonna Thank Me Woman	10
68	Atlantic 584 212	Go Home And Do It/Keep The One You Got	10
69	Atlantic 584 296	We Can't Sit Down Now/It Ain't Sanitary	10
70	Atlantic 584 318	You're Alright Ray Charles/Everything Happens On Time	10
71	Mercury 6052 067	I Knew Him/Bad Feet	6
72	Mercury 6052 111	Give The Baby Anything/Takin' A Chance	6
72	Mercury 6052 129	I Got 'Cha/Mother Prayer	6
72	Mercury 6052 156	You Said A Bad Word/It Ain't Gonna Work Baby	6
65	Atlantic ATL 5043	THE NEW BOSS (LP)	40
66	Atlantic ATL 587 009	THE LOVE YOU SAVE (LP)	35
67	Atlantic 587 053	I'VE GOT TO DO A LITTLE BETTER (LP)	25
67	Atlantic 587/588 059	THE NEW BOSS (LP, reissue)	15
67	London HA-U 8334	THE BEST OF JOE TEX (LP)	40
67	Atlantic 587/588 079	GREATEST HITS (LP)	15
68	Atlantic 587/588 104	LIVE AND LIVELY (LP)	25
68	Atlantic 587/588 118	SOUL COUNTRY (LP)	20
69	Atlantic 587/588 130	YOU BETTER GET IT (LP)	20
69	Atlantic 588 193	BUYING A BOOK (LP)	15
72	Atlantic K 40239	FROM THE ROOTS CAME THE RAPPER (LP)	12
72	Mercury 6338 093	I GOTCHA (LP)	12
77	EPIC EPC 81931	BUMPS AND BRUISES (LP)	15

(see also Soul Clan)

TEXANS
64	Columbia DB 7242	Being With You/Wondrous Look Of Love	6

TEXAS BOYS' CHOIR
63	Brunswick LAT 8546	FOLKSONGS AND WESTERN BALLADS (LP)	12

TEXTONES
87	Enigma 3268-1	CEDAR CREEK (LP)	18

TEXTOR SINGERS
54	Capitol CL 14211	Sobbin' Women/Remember Me	10

RUDY THACKER & STRINGBEANS
62	Starlite ST45 087	The Ballad Of Johnny Horton/Tomorrow Is My Last Day	10

JAKE THACKRAY
67	Columbia SCX 6178	LAST WILL AND TESTAMENT (LP)	15

THAMESIDERS/DAVY GRAHAM
63	Decca DFE 8538	FROM A LONDON HOOTENANNY (EP, 2 tracks each)	50

(see also Davy Graham)

SISTER ROSETTA THARPE
52	Brunswick 04989	Cain't No Grave Hold My Body Down/Ain't No Room In Church For Liars (78)	12
57	Mercury MT 185	Up Above My Head There's Music In The Air/ Jericho (Joshua Fit The Battle Of Jericho) (78)	10
60	MGM MGM 1072	If I Can Help Somebody/Take My Hand, Precious Lord	6
57	Mercury MPL 6529	GOSPEL TRAIN (LP)	25
59	Brunswick LAT 8290	GOSPEL TRAIN (LP)	15
61	Mercury MMC 14057	THE GOSPEL TRUTH (LP)	20
63	Society SOC 900	HOT HOT HOT (LP)	15
65	Ember NR 5023	SPIRITUALS IN RHYTHM (LP)	20
60s	Gala 373	SPIRITUALS IN RHYTHM (LP, reissue)	12

(see also Little Richard)

SISTER ROSETTA THARPE & SISTER MARIE KNIGHT
51	Brunswick 04851	Didn't It Rain/SISTER ROSETTA THARPE: Two Little Fishes And Five Loaves Of Bread (78, with Sam Price Trio)	15

(see also Marie Knight, Rev. Kelsey, Sammy Price)o

THAT CORPORATE FEELING
84	Platform SOUL XX1	The Rain Has Gone/Industrial Backlash (die-cut Corporate Feeling sleeve)	50

T.H.C. ROLLER
94	Poor Person Prod. PPPR 4	CHAPTER IN THE LIFE OF T.H.C. ROLLER (LP, handmade sleeve with insert & king-size rolling papers, numbered, 500 only)	20
94	Poor Person Prod.	THIS MUST BE THE JOINT (LP, 500 only)	70

THEATRE OF HATE
80	S.S. SS 3	Original Sin/Legion (p/s)	10
81	Burning Rome BRR 1	Rebel Without A Brain/My Own Invention (p/s, mispress with 2 B-side labels)	10
81	Burning Rome BRR 1	Rebel Without A Brain/My Own Invention (p/s)	6
82	Burning Rome BRRT 4	Eastworld/Assegai (12")	8
85	Bliss TOH 1EP	The Wake/Love Is A Ghost/Poppies/Legion (EP, 33rpm, with T-shirt in stickered pack, sealed)	10
81	S.S. SSSSS 1P	HE WHO DARES WINS - LIVE AT THE WAREHOUSE, LEEDS (LP, white labels, some copies autographed)	12

(see also Pack, Spear Of Destiny, Senate, Cult, Crisis)

THEE
65	Decca F 12163	Each And Every Day/There You Go!	50

THEE HEADCOATEES
92	Damaged Goods DAMGOOD 4	Davey Crockett (Gabba Hey)/Young Blood (p/s, yellow vinyl, 2000 only)	8
92	Vinyl Japan PAD 1	My Girlfriend's Learning Karate/Mess Of Pottage (p/s)	5
92	Damaged Goods DAMGOOD 012	Santa Claus/Evil Thing (picture disc)	5
95	Vinyl Japan PAD 18	Ballad Of The Insolent Pup/Spineless Insolent Shit (p/s)	5
92	Vinyl Japan ASKLP 11	HAVE LOVE - WILL TRAVEL (LP)	20
94	Vinyl Japan ASKLP 45	BALLAD OF THE INSOLENT PUP (LP)	20
97	Vinyl Japan ASKLP 65	BOSTIK HAZE (LP)	18
99	Vinyl japan ASKLP 84	HERE COMES CESSATION (LP)	15
99	Damaged Goods DAMGOODLP 161	THE SISTERS OF SUAVE (LP)	12

THEE HEADCOATEES/THE HEADCOATS
92	Damaged Goods DAMGOOD 1	Headcoat Girl/THEE HEADCOATS: Lakota Woman (p/s, different coloured sleeves & vinyl)	8
95	Damaged Goods DAMGOOD 63	Johnny Jack!/THEE HEADCOATS: Sufference Wharf (p/s)	6
98	Damaged Goods DAMGOOD 155	Jackie Chan Does Kung Fu/THEE HEADCOATS: The Rise And Fall Of A Double (p/s)	8
93	Twist TWIST 5	strychnine/THEE HEADCOATS: Branded (p/s, different sleeve colours exist)	8

(see also Mickey & Ludella, Delmonas)

THEE HYPNOTICS
88	Hipsville HIP 1	Love In A Different Vein/All NIght Long (p/s)	6

THEE MIGHTY CAESARS
88	Crypt LP 014	ENGLISH PUNK ROCK EXPLOSION (LP)	12

(see also Milkshakes, Prisoners, Billy Childish, Thee Headcoatees)

HANS THEESINK
80	Kettle KOP 7	LATE LAST NIGHT (LP)	25

BOB THEIL
82	Private (no cat. no.)	SO FAR (LP, private pressing)	180
80	Ellie Jay EJSP 9459	ANOTHER FLIGHT (EP)	8

LLANS THELWELL & HIS CELESTIALS
66	Island WI 262	Choo Choo Ska/Lonely Night (B-side vocal: Busty Brown)	35

THEM
64	Decca F 11973	Don't Start Crying Now/One Two Brown Eyes	70
64	Decca F 12018	Baby Please Don't Go/Gloria	10
65	Decca F 12094	Here Comes The Night/All For Myself	10
65	Decca F 12175	One More Time/How Long Baby?	10
65	Decca F 12215	(It Won't Hurt) Half As Much/I'm Gonna Dress In Black	10
65	Decca F 12281	Mystic Eyes/If You And I Could Be As Two	10
66	Decca F 12355	Call My Name/Bring 'Em On In	10
66	Decca F 12403	Richard Cory/Don't You Know?	12
67	Major Minor MM 509	Gloria/Friday's Child	20
67	Major Minor MM 513	The Story Of Them (Parts 1 & 2)	25
73	Deram DM 394	Gloria/Baby Please Don't Go (reissue)	7
65	Decca DFE 8612	THEM (EP, unboxed decca logo)	130
65	Decca DFE 8612	THEM (EP, export-only 'band-on-ladder' p/s)	500
65	Decca LK 4700	(THE ANGRY YOUNG) THEM (LP, original label, with flipback sleeve)	150
65	Decca LK 4700	(THE ANGRY YOUNG) THEM (LP, original label)	120
66	Decca LK 4751	THEM AGAIN (LP, original label, with flipback sleeve)	150
66	Decca LK 4751	THEM AGAIN (LP, original label)	120
70	Decca LK 4700	(THE ANGRY YOUNG) THEM (LP, re-pressing, red label, boxed Decca logo)	40
70	Decca LK 4751	THEM AGAIN (LP, re-pressing, red label, boxed Decca logo)	40
70	Decca PA 86	THE WORLD OF THEM (LP, original issue, mono)	20
70	Decca (S) PA 86	THE WORLD OF THEM (LP, original issue, stereo)	15
73	Deram DPM 3001/2	THEM - FEATURING VAN MORRISON LEAD SINGER (2xLP, gatefold sleeve)	25
78	Sonet SNTF 738	BELFAST GYPSIES (LP, features Them without Van Morrison)	25

(see also Van Morrison, Trader Horne, Taste, Sk'boo, Belfast Gypsies, Moses K. & Prophets, Peter Barden, Jackie McCauley)

THEME
82	Creed CR 001	Sacred/Conflict	6

JOHN THEMIS
83	Coda CODS 1	Goblins In Sherwood/Post Hypnotic Suggestions (p/s)	6

THERAPY
72	CBS 69017	ALMANAC (LP, gatefold sleeve with inside centre opening)	25
73	Indigo IRS 5124	ONE NIGHT STAND (LP, private pressing)	15

THERAPY?

90	demo cassette	MEAT ABSTRACT (cassette sold at gigs, 150 only) 15
90	Multifuckingnational MFN 1	Meat Abstract/Punishment Kisses (p/s, labels on wrong sides, 1,000 only) 20
92	A&M (no cat. no.)	TEETHGRINDER (12", double pack, white labels in presentation pack) 30
92	A&M THX 1	Have A Merry Fucking Christmas: Teenage Kicks/With Or Without You (Xmas gig freebie) ..15
92	Wiiija WIJ 11	PLEASURE DEATH (mini-LP, 10 white labels) 35

THERMOMETERS

80	Fokker FEP 100	20th Century Girl/Newtown Refugees/Stole Your Drugs (in oversized p/s) 20
80	Fokker FEP 100	20th Century Girl/Newtown Refugees/Stole Your Drugs (p/s) 15

THE THE

80	4AD AD 10	Controversial Subject/Black And White (p/s) 30
81	Some Bizzare BZS 4	Cold Spell Ahead/Hot Ice (p/s) 25
86	Epic TRUTH Q3	Infected/Infected (Energy Mix)/Disturbed (12", uncensored 'wank' p/s) 15
82	private cassette	PORNOGRAPHY OF DESPAIR (LP, unreleased, cassettes exist) 0
83	Epic EPC 25525	SOUL MINING (LP, with inner sleeve, initially with 12" single Perfect/"Soup Of Mixed Emotions"/"Fruit Of The Heart") 15
86	Epic EPC 26770	INFECTED (LP, with poster & inner, 1st 25,000 with 'torture' sleeve) 15
86	Epic EPC 26770	INFECTED (LP, with poster & inner) 12
02	Sony 5079022	LONDON TOWN (5-CD box set) 30

(see also Matt Johnson, Gadgets)

THEY MUST BE RUSSIANS

80	No label	Nagasaki's Children/Nellie The Elephant/Circus/I Want To Hold You Now (mail-order only, p/s with poster insert) 10

(see also Joe 9T & Thunderbirds)

THICK PIGEON

80s	Factory FACT 85	TOO CRAZY COWBOYS (LP) 40

THIEVES

79	Arista ARIGV 266	400 Dragons/Headlights (green vinyl) 5

(see also Fairport Convention)

THIEVES LIKE US

80	Earlobe ELS 1	Mind Made/Strike Out (p/s) 8

THIGHPAULSANDRA

01	World Serpent ESKATON 27	Michel Publicity Window/Paralysed (p/s) 5

(see also Coil, Spiritualized)

THIN END OF THE WEDGE

81	Jungle JR 051S	Lights Are On Green/I'm Not Dead Yet (in p/s) 30
81	Jungle JR 051S	Lights Are On Green/I'm Not Dead Yet 6

(see also Damascus)

THINGS

80	Imperial IP 4301	Pieces Of You/Lost Love (p/s) 10
88	Epitaph E 86402	THINGS (LP) 12

(see also Buzzcocks)

THINGS FALL APART

72	President PT378	Bye Bye My Rose/Manna 20

THIN ICE

88	Blag It SJP 858	Freedom Road (p/s) 40

THIN LIZZY

SINGLES

70	Parlophone DIP 513	The Farmer/I Need You (Irish only, as Thin Lizzie) 1000
71	Decca F 13208	NEW DAY (EP, 33rpm, gatefold p/s) 300
71	Decca F 13208	NEW DAY (EP, 33rpm, without p/s) 150
72	Decca F 13355	Whiskey In The Jar/Black Boys On The Corner 8
72	Decca F 13355	Whiskey In The Jar/Black Boys On The Corner (demos in p/s) 30
73	Decca F 13402	Randolph's Tango/Broken Dreams (2 versions of A-side: matrices ZDR 53384 & ZCPDR 53312) 15
73	Decca F 13467	The Rocker/Here I Go Again (demos £25) 5
74	Decca F 13507	Little Darlin'/Buffalo Gal 8
74	Vertigo 6059 111	Philomena/Sha La La 8
75	Vertigo 6059 124	Rosalie/Half Caste 6
75	Vertigo 6059 129	Wild One/For Those Who Love To Die 8
76	Vertigo 6059 150	Jailbreak/Running Back (p/s) 25
77	Vertigo 6059 177	Dancing In The Moonlight/Bad Reputation (p/s) 10
78	Decca F 13748	Whiskey In The Jar/Vagabond Of The Western World/Sitamoia (p/s) 8
79	Vertigo LIZZY 3	Waiting For An Alibi/With Love (p/s, with cartoon lyric sheet) 8
79	Vertigo LIZZY 3	Waiting For An Alibi/With Love (p/s, without cartoon lyric sheet) 5
79	Decca THIN 1	Things Ain't Working Out Down At The Farm/The Rocker/Little Darling (10,000 with p/s) 8
79	Vertigo LIZZY 5	Sarah/Got To Give Up (3 different p/s designs) 5
70s	Vertigo DJ 016	It's Only Money/JANNE SCHAFFER: Dr Abraham (promo only, no p/s) 200
80	Vertigo LIZZY 7 701	Killer On The Loose/Don't Play Around//Got To Give It Up (live)/ Chinatown (live) (double pack) 8
82	Vertigo LIZZY 10	Hollywood (Down On Your Luck) (10", p/s, 1-sided, existence unconfirmed) 0
82	Vertigo LIZZY PD 10	Hollywood (Down On Your Luck)/Pressure Will Blow (picture disc) 6
83	Vertigo LIZZY 1111/22	Cold Sweat/Bad Habits//Angel Of Death (live)/Don't Believe A Word (live) (double pack) 8
83	Vertigo LIZZY 1112	Cold Sweat/Bad Habits/Angel Of Death (live) (12", p/s) 8
83	Vertigo LIZZY 1212	Thunder And Lightning/Still In Love With You (live) (12", p/s, some with poster) 10
83	Vertigo LIZZY 13	The Sun Goes Down/Baby Please Don't Go (p/s) 5
83	Vertigo LIZZY 1312	The Sun Goes Down (Remix)/The Sun Goes Down/Baby Please Don't Go (12", p/s) 8

ALBUMS

71	Decca SKL 5082	THIN LIZZY (dark blue/silver label, early copies with laminated sleeve) 100
71	Decca SKL 5082	THIN LIZZY (dark blue/silver label, later pressing with matt sleeve) 35
72	Decca TXS 108	SHADES OF A BLUE ORPHANAGE (gatefold sleeve, dark blue label) 51
73	Decca SKL 5170	VAGABONDS OF THE WESTERN WORLD (dark blue/silver label, with lyric insert) 40
73	Decca SKL 5170	VAGABONDS OF THE WESTERN WORLD (dark blue/silver label, without insert) 20

74	Vertigo 6360 116	NIGHT LIFE (LP, 'spaceship' label) 15
75	Vertigo 6360 121	FIGHTING (LP, 'spaceship' label) 15
76	Vertigo 9102 008	JAIL BREAK (LP, die-cut sleeve, 'spaceship' label) 20
76	Vertigo 9102 012	JOHNNY THE FOX (LP, inner sleeve, 'spaceship' label) 15
78	Vertigo 9199 645	LIVE & DANGEROUS (2-LP, inners) 25
76	Decca SKL 5249	REMEMBERING 12
83	Vertigo VERL 3	THUNDER AND LIGHTNING (with free 12") 18
83	Vertigo	LIFE - LIVE (2-LP, gatefold sleeve, with inners) 15
92	Windsong WINLP024	BBC RADIO 1 LIVE IN CONCERT (2xLP emerald green vinyl)........20

(see also Phil Lynott, Wild Horses, Phenomena, Eric Bell Band, Funky Junction, Greedies, John Sykes, Gary Moore)

THIN YOGHURTS
| 80 | Lowther Street Runner YOG 1 | Girl On The Bus/Drink Problem (p/s) ....25 |

THIRD & FOURTH GENERATION
| 72 | Punch PH 91 | Rudies Medley (actually by Peter Tosh & Soulmates)/Rude Boy - Version........10 |

(see also Peter Tosh)

3RD ARMY
| 81 | Elite DAZZ 10 | March Of 10,000 Soldiers (All Set To Go)/Step One (12") ....20 |

THIRD DIMENSION
| 70 | Unity UN 566 | Peace And Love/Peace And Love - Version ....6 |

THIRD EAR BAND
69	Harvest SHVL 756	ALCHEMY (LP, with "Sold in U.K..." label text on 4 lines) 80
69	Harvest SHVL 756	ALCHEMY (LP, later pressing without "Sold in U.K..." label text) 40
70	Harvest SHSP 773	THIRD EAR BAND: ELEMENTS (LP, no EMI logo on label) 60
72	Harvest SHSP 4019	MUSIC FROM MACBETH (LP, EMI logo on label) 35
76	Harvest SHSM 2007	EXPERIENCES (LP) 20

(see also High Tide, Sounds Nice)

THIRD EYE BAND
| 82 | Scarlet Quest 01 | Pass Myself/May The Circle Remain Unbroken (p/s) ....80 |

THIRD MEN
| 79 | SCHOOL 1 | You're So Fashionable/The Robot Age (p/s) ....20 |

THIRD QUADRANT
| 82 | Rock Cottage (no cat. no.) | SEEING YOURSELF AS YOU REALLY ARE (LP, private pressing, wraparound sleeve with handwritten insert, blank white label) ....40 |

3RD RAIL
| 92 | Delirious DELIS 5 | Look No Further/123 Break/Stand By For Fast Beats/Drop (KZ1 Remix) (12")........40 |

THIRD RAIL
| 67 | Columbia DB 8274 | Run, Run, Run/No Return ....30 |

THIRD WORLD
| 71 | CBS 7182 | Miracles/Baby Boeing ....6 |

THIRD WORLD ALL STARS
| 75 | Third World TWLP 103 | REBEL ROCK (LP) ....25 |

THIRD WORLD WAR
71	Fly BUG 7	Ascension Day/Teddy Teeth Goes Sailing (p/s) 8
71	Fly BUG 11	A Little Bit Of Urban Rock/Working Class Man 6
71	Fly FLY 4	THIRD WORLD WAR (LP, with lyric insert) 60
71	Fly FLY 4	THIRD WORLD WAR (LP, without lyric insert) 30
72	Track 2406 108	THIRD WORLD WAR II (LP) 60

(see also Terry Stamp)

13 AMP
| 75 | Power Exchange PX 114 | Need A Woman/Can You Feel The Music ....15 |

THIRTEEN SENSES
| 02 | Private Pressing | NO OTHER LIFE IS ATTRACTIVE EP (CD) ....35 |
| 04 | Vertigo 981633-4 | Thru The Glass/No Other Life Is Attractive (1,500 only p/s) ....8 |

13TH CHIME
81	Ellie Jay Records EJSP 9700	Cuts Of Love/Coffin Maker (foldout p/s) 50
82	13th Chime THC 1	Cursed (p/s) 25
82	13th Chime THC 2	Fire/Hide And Seek/Sally Ditch (p/s, 1,000 only) 25

13TH FLOOR ELEVATORS
78	Radar ADA 13	You're Gonna Miss Me/Tried To Hide (green vinyl) 6
78	Radar RAD 13	THE PSYCHEDELIC SOUNDS OF ... (LP) 18
78	Radar RAD 15	EASTER EVERYWHERE (LP) 15
89	Decal LIK 28	EASTER EVERYWHERE (LP, reissue) 20
88	Decal LIK 19	THE PSYCHEDELIC SOUNDS OF... (LP, reissue) 20
92	Xgarely/Decal LIKP 003	THE PSYCHEDELIC SOUNDS OF... (LP, picture disc) 12
92	Decal LIKP002	LIVE (picture disc with poster) 12
01	Get Back GET 594	EASTER EVERYWHERE (LP, reissue) 12

(see also Roky Erickson, Red Crayola)

31ST OF FEBRUARY
| 69 | Vanguard (S)VRL 19045 | THE 31ST OF FEBRUARY (LP) ....80 |

35MM DREAMS
| 81 | More Than This ASA 100 | More Than This/The Bearer (foldout p/s) ....5 |
| 81 | More Than This ASA 200 | Fasten Your Safety Belts/Corstorphine/Instamatic Dance (p/s) ....5 |

32ND TURN-OFF
| 69 | Jay Boy JSL 1 | 32ND TURN OFF (LP, textured sleeve, brown/black label) ....50 |

(see also Equals)

30 SECONDS TO MARS
07	Virgin 00946354474 77	The Kill/Attack (live) (picture disc, PVC stickered sleeve) 15
08	Virgin VUS 340	From Yesterday (red vinyl, 1-side etched) 15
09	Virgin 509993/0943315	THIS IS WAR (gatefold, 2-LP with CD) 18

THIS DRIFTIN'S GOTTA STOP
70s	private pressing	THIS DRIFTIN'S GOTTA STOP (LP)	15

THIS HEAT
80	Piano THIS 1201	Health And Efficiency/Graphic/Varispeed (12", p/s with insert)	25
79	Piano THIS 1	THIS HEAT (LP)	60
81	Rough Trade ROUGH 26	DECEIT (LP, 1st pressing)	45
88	These HEAT 1	THIS HEAT (reissue)	20
88	These HEAT 1	DECEIT (reissue)	20
98	These 12/6	REPEAT/HEALTH AND EFFICIENCY (2 x 12")	20
99	These HEAT 10	MADE AVAILABLE: PEEL SESSIONS (LP)	20
06	This Is LC 02677	OUT OF COLD STORAGE (6-CD box set)	40

THIS MORTAL COIL
83	4AD AD 310	Song To The Siren/16 Days (Reprise) (p/s)	5
83	4AD BAD 310	16 Days/Gathering Dust/Song To The Siren/16 Days (reprise) (12", p/s)	8
84	4AD AD 410	Kangaroo/It'll End In Tears (p/s, 2 different designs & label colours, 2,500 of each)	5
86	4AD BAD 608	Come Here My Love/Drugs (10", p/s with inner sleeve)	10
91	4AD TMC 1CD	Extracts From "Blood": Late Night/You And Your Sister/I Come And Stand At Every Door/With Tomorrow (CD, card sleeve, promo only)	20
84	4AD CAD 411	IT'LL END IN TEARS (LP)	12
86	4AD DAD 609	FILIGREE AND SHADOW (2-LP)	20
91	4AD DAD 1005	BLOOD (2-LP, with inners)	20

(see also Cocteau Twins, Modern English, Cindytalk)

THIS 'N' THAT
66	Mercury MF 938	Someday/Loving You	20
67	Strike JH 310	Get Down With It/I Care About You	10

(see also Cleo)

B.J. THOMAS
66	Hickory 45-1395	Never Tell/Billy & Sue	15
66	Pye International 7N 25374	Mama/Wendy	10
68	Pye International 7N 25467	The Eyes Of A New York Woman/I May Never Get To Heaven	5
69	Pye International 7N 25487	It's Only Love/You Don't Love Me Anymore (The Train Song)	5
69	Wand WN 1	Raindrops Keep Falling On My Head/Never Had It So Good	6
70	Wand WN 5	I Just Can't Help Believing/Send My Picture To Scranton, PA	5
72	Wand WN 24	Rock And Roll Lullaby/Are We Losing Touch? (feat. Duane Eddy)	5

CARLA THOMAS
61	London HLK 9310	Gee Whiz/For You	20
61	London HLK 9359	A Love Of My Own/Promises	15
62	London HLK 9618	I'll Bring It On Home To You/I Can't Take It	15
64	Atlantic AT 4005	I've Got No Time To Lose/A Boy Named Tom	18
66	Atlantic AT 4074	Comfort Me/I'm For You	12
66	Atlantic 584 011	Let Me Be Good To You/Another Night Without My Man	10
66	Atlantic 584 042	B-A-B-Y/What Have You Got To Offer Me	10
67	Stax 601 002	Something Good (Is Going To Happen To You)/It's Starting To Grow	10
67	Stax 601 008	When Tomorrow Comes/Unchanging Love (dark blue label)	15
67	Stax 601 008	When Tomorrow Comes/Unchanging Love (later light blue label)	8
68	Stax 601 032	Pick Up The Pieces/Separation	10
68	Stax STAX 103	Where Do I Go/I've Fallen In Love	8
69	Stax STAX 112	I Like What You're Doing To Me/Strung Out	8
69	Stax STAX 131	Unyielding/I've Fallen In Love	6
72	Stax 2025 082	Love Means/You've Got A Cushion To Fall On	6
91	Kent 6T 7	I'll Never Stop Loving/Prophets Band/Peaches Baby	40
67	Stax 589 004	CARLA THOMAS (LP)	30
67	Stax 589 012	THE QUEEN ALONE (LP)	20
69	Stax SXATS 1019	MEMPHIS QUEEN (LP)	40

(see also Otis Redding & Carla Thomas)

CHARLIE THOMAS (& DRIFTERS)
75	EMI International INT 506	I'm Gonna Take You Home/Run, Run, Roadrunner	8

CLAUDETTE THOMAS
68	Caltone TONE 116	Roses Are Red My Love/YVONNE HARRISON: Near To You	80

CREEPY JOHN THOMAS
69	RCA RCA 1912	Ride A Rainbow/Moon And Eyes Song	15
69	RCA SF 8061	CREEPY JOHN THOMAS (LP, laminated front sleeve)	250

(see also Paul Kossoff, Edgar Broughton Band)

DAVID THOMAS & THE PEDESTRIANS
84	Rough Trade ROUGH 30	THE SOUND OF THE SAND (LP)	12
85	Rough Trade ROUGH 80	MORE PLACES FOREVER (LP)	12

(see also Pere Ubu)

DON THOMAS
76	DJM DJS 670	Come On Train Parts 1 & 2 (Promos in p/s)	20
76	DJM DJS 10670	Come On Train Parts 1 & 2 (second pressing)	10

GENE THOMAS
64	United Artists UP 1047	Baby's Gone/Stand By Love	20

HERSAL THOMAS
50	Parlophone R 3261	Suitcase Blues/Hersal Blues (78)	50

IRMA THOMAS
64	Liberty LIB 66013	Breakaway/Wish Someone Would Care	25
64	Liberty LIB 66041	Anyone Who Knows What Love Is (Will Understand)/Time Is On My Side	20
65	Liberty LIB 66080	He's My Guy/True True Love	20
65	Liberty LIB 66095	Some Things You Never Get Used To/You Don't Miss A Good Thing (Until It's Gone)	20
65	Sue WI 372	Don't Mess With My Man/Set Me Free	30
65	Liberty LIB 66106	I'm Gonna Cry Till My Tears Run Dry/ Nobody Wants To Hear Nobody's Troubles	20
66	Liberty LIB 66137	Take A Look/What Are You Trying To Do	75
66	Liberty LIB 66137	Take A Look/What Are You Trying To Do (DJ copy)	125

MINT VALUE £

66	Liberty LIB 66178	It's A Man's-Woman's World	20
72	Atlantic K 10167	Full Time Woman/She's Taking My Part	6
72	United Artists UP 35402	Time Is On My Side/Anyone Who Knows What Love Is (Will Understand) (reissue)	8
65	Liberty LEP 4035	TIME IS ON MY SIDE (EP)	100
68	Minit MLL/MLS 40004E	TAKE A LOOK (LP)	75
76	Island HELP 29	LIVE (LP)	15
83	Kent 010	TIME IS ON MY SIDE (LP)	15

JAMO THOMAS & HIS PARTY BROTHERS ORCHESTRA

66	Polydor BM 56709	I Spy (For The FBI)/Snake Hip Mama	15
69	Polydor 56755	I Spy (For The FBI)/Snake Hip Mama (reissue)	8
69	Chess CRS 8098	I'll Be Your Fool/Jamo Soul	20
71	Mojo 2092 013	I Spy (For The FBI)/Snake Hip Mama (2nd reissue)	8

JIMMY THOMAS

69	Parlophone R 5773	The Beautiful Night/Above A Whisper (withdrawn)	250
69	Parlophone R 5773	The Beautiful Night/Above A Whisper (withdrawn; DJ copy)	200
69	Spark SRL 1035	(We Ain't Looking For) No Trouble/Springtime	100
70	Spark SRL 1040	White Dove/You Don't Have To Say Goodbye	12
72	Jay Boy BOY 67	Where There's A Will/Just Tryin' To Please You	6

(see also Sweet Dreams)

JOE THOMAS

| 72 | People PLE 015 | JOY OF COOKIN' (LP) | 15 |

KID THOMAS

| 79 | JSP 4503 | Rockin' This Joint Tonight/Cozy Lounge Blues | 5 |

KID THOMAS/EMANUEL BAND

| 64 | '77' LA 12/26 | VICTORY WALK (LP, with Barry Martyn's Band) | 30 |

LEON THOMAS

| 73 | Philips 6369 417 | BLUES & SOULFUL TRUTH (LP) | 30 |

NICKY THOMAS

70	Amalgamated AMG 863	Danzella/JOE GIBBS ALLSTARS: Kingstonians Reggae	25
70	Trojan TR 7750	Love Of The Common People/DESTROYERS: Compass	5
70	Trojan TR 7796	God Bless The Children/Red Eye	7
71	Trojan TR 7807	If I Had A Hammer/Lonely Feelin'	7
71	Trojan TR 7830	Tell It Like It Is/B.B.C.	5
70	Trojan TBL 143	LOVE OF THE COMMON PEOPLE (LP)	15
72	Trojan TRLS 25	TELL IT LIKE IT IS (LP)	20

(see also Joe Gibbs)

PAT THOMAS

| 62 | MGM 1194 | Home In The Meadow/Where There's Love There's Hope | 6 |
| 62 | MGM 1234 | Stranger On The Shore/C'est Si Bon | 6 |

PETER THOMAS SOUND ORCHESTRA

| 68 | Poydor 184171 | ORGANIC (LP) | 35 |
| 70 | Polydor 2418 074 | CHARIOTS OF THE GODS (LP) | 35 |

RAMBLIN' THOMAS

| 52 | Tempo R 51 | Jug Head Blues/Hard Dallas Blues (78) | 20 |

(see also Blind Blake, Blind Lemon Jefferson)

ROD THOMAS

| 72 | Fly BUG 19 | Timothy Jones/Arthur Smith | 7 |

RUDDY THOMAS

| 78 | Lightning LIG 526 | Loving Pauper/TRINITY: Judgement Time | 8 |

RUDY THOMAS

| 83 | Mobiliser MMLP 34 | VERY BEST OF (LP) | 15 |

RUFUS THOMAS

63	London HLK 9799	Walking The Dog/Fine And Mellow	25
64	London HLK 9850	Can Your Monkey Do The Dog/I Want To Get Married	15
64	London HLK 9884	Somebody Stole My Dog/I Want To Be Loved	15
64	Atlantic AT 4009	Jump Back/All Night Worker	18
66	Atlantic 584 029	Willy Nilly/Sho' Gonna Mess Him Up	12
67	Atlantic 584 089	Jump Back/Walking The Dog	10
67	Stax 601 013	Greasy Spoon/Sophisticated Sissy	8
68	Stax 601 028	Down Ta My House/Steady Holding On	8
68	Stax 601 037	The Memphis Train/I Think I Made A Boo-Boo	15
68	Stax STAX 105	Funky Mississippi/So Hard To Get Along With	8
70	Stax STAX 144	Do The Funky Chicken/Turn Your Damper Down	8
71	Stax 2025 060	The Breakdown (Parts 1 & 2)	6
71	Stax 2025 080	Do The Funky Penguin (Parts 1 & 2)	6
64	Atlantic AET 6001	DO THE DOG (EP)	50
65	Atlantic AET 6011	JUMP BACK WITH RUFUS (EP)	50
64	London HA-K 8183	WALKING THE DOG (LP)	80
70	Stax SXATS 1033	FUNKY CHICKEN (LP)	35
71	Stax 2363 001	FUNKY CHICKEN (LP, reissue)	15
71	Stax 2362 010	DOING THE PUSH AND PULL LIVE AT P.J.'s (LP)	25
72	Stax 2362 028	DID YOU HEAR ME? (LP)	20
74	Stax STX 1004	CROWN PRINCE OF DANCE (LP)	30

SANDRA THOMAS

| 76 | Angen ANG 113 | It Should Have Been Me/Loving Arms | 5 |

TERRY-THOMAS ESQUIRE

| 56 | Decca F 10804 | A Sweet Old Fashioned Boy (with Rock 'N' Roll Rotters)/Lay Down Your Arms | 12 |
| 61 | Decca LK 4398 | STRICTLY T-T (LP) | 40 |

TIM THOMAS

| 66 | Polydor BM 56052 | Walking/Fever | 8 |
| 71 | Decca F13235 | Silver Morning/Gravy Train | 10 |

TIMMY THOMAS
73	Mojo 2956 002	WHY CAN'T WE LIVE TOGETHER (LP)	20

VAUGHAN THOMAS
70	Page One POF 167	Need You Girl/Come Together	12
70	Page One POF 178	Is This What I Get For Loving You Baby/Since You've Been Mine	10
71	DJM DJS 238	I Wanna Be Famous Like My Dad/Love	15
72	Jam JAM 9	Gotta Be You, Gotta Be Me/Woman	6
72	Jam JAM 26	Giant/Good Old Sam	6
72	Jam JAL 101	VAUGHAN THOMAS (LP, textured sleeve, white/red/black label)	40

WAYNE THOMAS
67	Coral Q 72491	I've Never Known A Lady/My Life's Gonna Change	6

ANDREAS THOMOPOULOS
70	Mushroom 100 MR 1	SONGS OF THE STREET (LP)	80
71	Mushroom 150 MR 4	BORN OUT OF THE TEARS OF THE SUN (LP)	90

(see also Secondhand)

BARBARA THOMPSON
74	Explosion EX 2087	Single Girl/DANDY & COUNT PRINCE MILLER: Version	5

BOBBY THOMPSON
69	Columbia Blue Beat DB 113	That's How Strong My Love Is/Trouble In Town	6
69	Jolly JY 001	That's How Strong My Love Is/Trouble In The Town	30

(see also Dandy)

CHERYLE THOMPSON
64	Stateside SS 291	Teardrops/Black Night	15

CHRIS THOMPSON
73	Village Thing VTS 21	CHRIS THOMPSON (LP, allegedly 101 sold and 899 destroyed)	150

DONNEY THOMPSON
79	Third World TWDIS 20	Rocking Time/PAGET KING: Close Encounter (12")	60

EDDIE THOMPSON
55	Jazz Today JTE 101	THE FABULOUS EDDIE THOMPSON (EP)	60
57	Nixa NJE 1030	PIANO MOODS VOLUME 6 (EP)	60
60	Ember EMB 3303	PIANO MOODS (LP)	100
60	Tempo TAP 24	HIS MASTER'S JAZZ (LP)	250
69	77 LEU 12/39	BY MYSELF (LP)	40

ERIC THOMPSON
68	CBS EP 6398	THE MAGIC ROUNDABOUT NO. 1 (EP)	8
68	CBS EP 6399	THE MAGIC ROUNDABOUT NO. 2 (EP)	8

HANK THOMPSON (& BRAZOS VALLEY BOYS)
56	Capitol CL 14517	Honey, Honey Bee Ball/Don't Take It Out On Me	5
56	Capitol CL 14668	I'm Not Mad, Just Hurt/The Blackboard Of My Heart	5
58	Capitol CL 14869	Li'l Liza Jane/How Do You Hold A Memory	5
58	Capitol CL 14945	Gathering Flowers/Squaws Along The Yukon	5
58	Capitol CL 14961	I've Run Out Of Tomorrows/You're Going Back To Your Old Ways Again	5
60	Capitol CL 15114	A Six Pack To Go/What Made Her Change	10
76	Capitol CL 15877	Rockin' In The Congo/I Was The First One	5

JACKIE THOMPSON
69	Direction 58-4521	Bad Women A Dime A Dozen/Games People Play	6

JOHNNY THOMPSON & ONE-EYED JACKS
65	Ember EMB S 206	For Us There'll Be No Tomorrow/Soul Chant (in p/s)	20
65	Ember EMB S 206	For Us There'll Be No Tomorrow/Soul Chant	6

KAY THOMPSON
56	London HLA 8268	Eloise/Just One Of Those Things	50
56	London HLA 8268	Eloise/Just One Of Those Things (78)	10

LEROY THOMPSON
78	Noel DN 005	Hard Times Criminal Times/Since You Left Me & Gone (12")	30

LINVAL THOMPSON
75	Ackee ACK 541	Kung Fu (Vocal)/Kung Fu (Instrumental)	6
75	Action ACT 103	Natty Dread Girl/AGGROVATORS: Natty Dread Girl (Version)	10
75	Attack ATT 8101	Don't Cut Off Your Dreadlocks/KING TUBBYS: Version	10
75	Faith FA 010	Girl You Got To Run/Run Come Feel	5
75	Faith FA 018	Jah Redder Than Red/Version	8
78	Attack ATT 8135	I Love Marijuana/Jamaican Calley (Version)	8
78	Star PTP 1007	If I Follow My Heart/THOMPSON ALL STARS: Rocking version (12")	20
79	Burning Rockers BRD 003	Follow My Heart/THOMPSON ALL STARS: Rockers Version (12")	20
79	Burning Sounds BSD 023	Rocking Vibration/Natty Dread (12')	20
79	Burning Sounds BSD 031	Bound To Surrender/Dub Version (12")	20
79	GG's GG 056	Mad Dog (with Ranking Trevor)/REVOLUTIONARIES: Kevin At The Controls (12")	30
79	Greensleeves GRED 024	One More Chance/Long Time Me Na Rub You In A Dance (12", with Trinity)	20
80	Attack TACK 19	Here With Me/ROOTS RADICS BAND: Come On Baby Dub Style (12")	15
80	Attack TACK 22	Pop No Style/SCIENTIST: Second Hand Girl (12")	15
80	Black Joy DH 804	Brown Skin Girl/RANKING TREVOR: Brown Skin Girl Rub A Dub (12")	15
80	Strong Like Sampson SLSD 04	Mr Boss Man (with Trevor Ranking)/BARNABOUS: Stop Push Me Around (12")	22
80	Strong Like... SLSD 012	I'm Sorry/My Little Honey (12")	10
82	A1 A1 004	Poor People (with U Brown)/Reggae Dub (12")	12
78	Burning Sounds BSD 1014	LOVE IS THE QUESTION (LP)	25
78	Burning Sounds BS 1027	ROCKING VIBRATION (LP)	40
79	Burning Sounds BS 1035	I LOVE JAH (LP)	35
79	Trojan TRLS 153	NEGREA LOVE DUB (LP)	20
80	Burning Rockers BR 1006LP	FOLLOW MY HEART (LP)	30
83	Greensleeves GREL 51	BABY FATHER (LP)	15

LUCKY THOMPSON
56	Vogue V 2388	But Not For Me/East Of The Sun	10

MIKE THOMPSON JNR.
67	Island WI 3090	Rocksteady Wedding/Flower Pot Bloomers (both with Lyn Taitt & Jets) 25

MOLLIE THOMPSON
66	Asteroid JH 101	SONG NOTES SINGS FROM WORLDS AFAR (LP, private pressing)..........................40

OWEN THOMPSON
72	Camel CA 103	Must I Be Blue/Version 8

PETER THOMPSON & NTH DEGREE
65	Fontana TF 656	For Me It's All Over/The Way You Used To Do 20

RICHARD THOMPSON
72	Island ILPS 9197	HENRY THE HUMAN FLY (LP, 'pink rim palm tree' label)..25

RICHARD & LINDA THOMPSON
74	Island WIP 6186	I Want To See The Bright Lights Tonight/When I Get To The Border 5
75	Island WIP 6220	Hokey Pokey/I'll Regret It All In The Morning 5
73	Island ILPS 9266	I WANT TO SEE THE BRIGHT LIGHTS TONIGHT (LP, palm tree label)....................30
74	Island ILPS 9305	HOKEY POKEY (LP, blue rim palm tree label with lyric inner sleeve).....................25
75	Island ILPS 9348	POUR DOWN LIKE SILVER (LP, 'palm tree' label with lyrics)..................................20
75	Island	OFFICIAL LIVE TOUR 1975 (LP, unreleased, test pressings may exist).................100
76	Island ICD 8	GUITAR/VOCAL (2-LP, gatefold sleeve, blue rim/palm tree label)........................25
78	Chrysalis CHR 1177	FIRST LIGHT (LP)..12
76	Island ILPS 9305	HOKEY POKEY (LP, pink rim palm tree label with lyric inner sleeve) 12

(see also Fairport Convention, Richard Thompson, Sandy Denny, Marc Ellington, Nick Drake, Bunch, Gary Farr, Paul McNeill & Linda Peters)

ROBERT THOMPSON
75	Pinnacle P 8408	A Look At The Sun/You Can't See Me 12

ROY THOMPSON
67	Columbia DB 8108	Sookie Sookie/Love You Say...30

SIR CHARLES THOMPSON
53	Vogue LDE 032	SIR CHARLES THOMPSON'S ALL STARS WITH CHARLIE PARKER (10" LP) 20
56	Vanguard PPT 12011	AND HIS BAND FEATURING COLEMAN HAWKINS (10" LP) 15

SONNY THOMPSON & HIS RHYTHM & BLUES BAND
52	Vogue V 2143	Real, Real Fine (Parts 1 & 2) (78) 45
53	Esquire 10-320	House Full Of Blues/Creepin' (78) 45
53	Esquire 10-339	Screamin' Boogie/The Fish (78)..45
60	Starlite ST45 008	Screamin' Boogie/The Fish...250
56	Parlophone GEP 8562	SONNY THOMPSON INSTRUMENTALS (EP, as Sonny Thompson Orchestra).........60

(see also Claude Cloud & Thunderclaps, Swallows)

SUE THOMPSON
61	Polydor NH 66967	Sad Movies/Throwing Kisses 10
62	Polydor NH 66973	Norman/Never Love Again...5
62	Polydor NH 66976	Two Of A Kind/It Has To Be Me 5
62	Polydor NH 66979	Have A Good Time/If The Boy Only Knew 5
63	Polydor NH 66987	What's Wrong Bill/I Need A Harbour..5
62	Fontana 267 244TF	James (Hold The Ladder Steady)/My Hero 5
63	Fontana 267 262TF	Willie Can/Too Much In Love 5
64	Hickory 45-1240	Big Daddy/I'd Like To Know You Better 5
64	Hickory 45-1255	Bad Boy/Toys 5
65	Hickory 45-1284	Paper Tiger/Mama Don't Cry At My Wedding 6
65	Hickory 45-1328	It's Break Up Time/Afraid...8
65	Hickory 45-1340	Just Kiss Me/Sweet Hunk Of Misery 8
65	Hickory 45-1359	I'm Looking For A World/Walkin' My Baby 6
65	Hickory 45-1381	What Should I Do/After The Heartache 10
67	London HLE 10142	Ferris Wheel/Don't Forget To Cry 7
72	London HLE 1040	How I Love Them Old Songs/That's Just Too Much 7
73	London HLE 10440	Oh, Johnny, Oh Johnny, Oh/Just Pain Country 7
65	Hickory LPE 1507	INTRODUCING KRIS JENSEN AND SUE THOMPSON (EP, 2 tracks each) 10
64	Hickory LPM 102	PAPER TIGER (LP) 20

(see also Kris Jensen)

SUE THOMPSON & BOB LUMAN
63	Polydor NH 66989	I Like Your Kind Of Love/Too Hot To Dance 10
63	Hickory 45-1221	I Like Your Kind Of Love/Too Hot To Dance (reissue)..5

(see also Bob Luman)

COLIN THOMPSON
80	Fellside FE 021	THREE KNIGHTS (LP) 15

GUNILLA THORN
63	HMV POP 1239	Merry-Go-Round/Go On Then..90

TRACEY THORN
82	Cherry Red CHERRY 53	Plain Sailing/Goodbye Joe (p/s) 5
82	Cherry Red MRED 35	A DISTANT SHORE (LP) 15

(see also Marine Girls, Everything But The Girl, Grab Grab The Haddock)

DAVID THORNE
62	Stateside SS 141	The Alley Cat Song/The Moon Was Yellow 6
63	Stateside SS 190	One More Fool, One More Broken Heart/Don't Let It Get Away 6
64	Stateside SE 1020	WHAT WILL I TELL MY HEART (EP)...25
63	Stateside SL 10036	THE ALLEY CAT SONGSTER (LP)..35

KEN THORNE ORCHESTRA
63	HMV POP 1176	The Legion's Last Patrol Film Theme/Kisses In The Night 5
68	United Artists ULP 1201	INSPECTOR CLOUSEAU (LP, soundtrack)..30
69	Stateside S(S)L 10271	THE TOUCHABLES (LP, with Nirvana, Wynder K. Frog, et al.) 50

WOODY THORNE
62	Vogue Pop V 9202	Sadie Lou/Teenagers In Love 400

CLAUDE THORNHILL & HIS ORCHESTRA
54	London HL 8042	Pussy-Footin'/Adios 40

MINT VALUE £

54	London RE-P 1009	CLAUDE THORNHILL GOES MODERN (EP)	20
54	London H-ABP 1019	CLAUDE THORNHILL GOES MODERN (10" LP)	20
54	London H-ABP 1021	DREAM MUSIC (10" LP)	20

WILLIE MAE 'BIG MAMA' THORNTON

54	Vogue V 2284	Hound Dog/Mischievous Boogie (78) (as Willie Mae 'Big Mama' Thornton)	130
65	Sue WI 345	Tom Cat/Monkey In The Barn (as Willie Mae Thornton)	250
69	Mercury SMCL 20176	STRONGER THAN DIRT (LP)	40
78	Vanguard VPC 40001	MAMA'S PRIDE (LP)	25

EDDIE THORNTON OUTFIT

| 69 | Instant IN 003 | Baby Be My Gal/SONNY BURKE OUTFIT: All You | 120 |

CLIFFORD THORNTON

| 76 | JCOA/Virgin J2004 | GARDENS OF HARLEM (LP, with Jazz Composers Orchestra) | 15 |

GEORGE THOROGOOD & DESTROYERS

| 77 | Sonet SON 2148 | Can't Stop Lovin'/Homesick Boy | 5 |
| 77 | Sonet SNTF 760 | GEORGE THOROGOOD AND THE DESTROYERS (LP) | 12 |

PETER THOROGOOD

| 68 | Pye 7N 17597 | Haunted/If No One Sang | 100 |

BILLY THORPE & AZTECS

| 65 | Parlophone R 5381 | Twilight Time/Over The Rainbow | 7 |

THOR'S HAMMER

66	Parlophone DP 565	Once/A Memory (export issue)	200
66	Parlophone DP 567	If You Knew/Love Enough (export issue)	185
66	Parlophone CGEP 62	THOR'S HAMMER (EP, export issue, gatefold p/s, with bonus 45 "If You Knew"/"Love Enough" [CGEP 62])	1200

LINDA THORSON

68	Ember EMB S 257	Here I Am/Better Than Losing You (p/s)	40
68	Ember EMB S 257	Here I Am/Better Than Losing You	15
70	Ember EMBS 284	Wishful Thinking/You Will Want Me	20
70	Ember LT 1	Bad Time To Stop Loving Me/Pick Up My Heart (promo)	25

THOSE ATTRACTIVE MAGNETS

| 83 | Tavern AD MAG 10 | Nightlife/Love Chimes (p/s) | 60 |

THOSE HELICOPTERS

| 80 | State Of The Art STATE 1 | Shark/Eskimo (p/s) | 6 |
| 81 | Lavender LAVENDER 001 | Dr. Janov/Technical Smack (p/s) | 5 |

THOSE INTRINSIC INTELLECTUALS

| 80 | Fault Line CPS 040 | Do The Executive/Radio Iceland (fold out p/s in printed bag, insert) | 12 |

THOSE NAUGHTY LUMPS

| 79 | Zoo CAGE 002 | Iggy Pop's Jacket/Pure And Innocent (foldout p/s) | 6 |

THOUGHT POLICE

| 79 | Wessex WEX 263 | Mr Sad/You Tell Me Lies/Pictures (p/s) | 25 |

THOUGHTS

| 66 | Planet PLF 118 | All Night Stand/Memory Of Your Love | 100 |

(see also Tiffany [& Thoughts], Paul Dean & Soul Savages)

THOUGHTS & WORDS

| 69 | Liberty LBF 15187 | Morning Sky/Give Me A Reason | 10 |
| 69 | Liberty LBL 83224 | THOUGHTS & WORDS (LP) | 20 |

THOUGHTS OF DES COX

| 69 | Morgan MR 4S | Isn't It Nice/It's All Very Strange | 12 |

THREADBARE CONSORT

| 80s | private pressing | WEARING THIN (LP) | 15 |

THREADS

| 86 | Unicorn PHZ 2 | Step Back/UNDERGROUND ARROWS: Backbeat Of Life (p/s) | 10 |

THREADS OF LIFE

| 72 | Alco ALC 530 | THREADS OF LIFE (LP, actually by Alco) | 800 |

THREATS

82	Rondelet ROUND 22	GO TO HELL (EP)	15
82	Rondelet ROUND 29	Politicians & Ministers/Writing's On The Wall/Deep End Depression (p/s)	20
82	Rondelet ROUND 1229	POLITICIANS & MINISTERS (12" EP)	18

THREE BARRY SISTERS

59	Decca F 11099	Little Boy Blue/My Sweetie's Coming To Call	10
59	Decca F 11118	Tall Paul/Till Then	7
59	Decca F 11141	Jo Jo - The Dog Faced Boy/I-Aye Ove-Lay Oo-Yay	5
60	Decca F 11201	Spoilsport/Bonnie Prince Charlie	5

(see also Barry Sisters)

THREE BELLS

60	Pye 7N 15252	Steady Date/In Between (Wishing I Was Sweet Sixteen)	8
61	Pye 7N 15335	You/Melody Of Love	8
64	Columbia DB 7399	Softly In The Night/He Doesn't Love Me	10
65	Columbia DB 7570	Someone To Love/Over And Over Again	7
66	Columbia DB 7980	Cry No More/He Doesn't Want You	15

(see also Satin Bells)

THREE CAPS

66	Atlantic 584 004	Cool Jerk/Hello Stranger	15
66	Atlantic 584 043	I Got To Handle It/Zig-Zagging	12
69	Atlantic 584 251	Cool Jerk/Hello Stranger	10
71	Atlantic 2091 105	Cool Jerk/Hello Stranger (reissue)	5

(see also Capitols)

THREE CHUCKLES

55	HMV 7M 292	Runaround/At Last You Understand	40
55	HMV 7M 292	Runaround/At Last You Understand (78)	15
56	HMV 7M 333	Still Thinking Of You/Times Two I Love You	35
56	HMV 7M 333	Still Thinking Of You/Times Two I Love You (78)	15
57	HMV POP 292	We're Gonna Rock Tonight/Want You Give Me A Chance	80
57	HMV POP 292	We're Gonna Rock Tonight/Want You Give Me A Chance (78)	25

(see also Teddy Randazzo)

THREE CITY FOUR

65	Decca LK 4705	THREE CITY FOUR (LP)	160
67	CBS 63039	SMOKE AND DUST WHERE THE HEART SHOULD HAVE BEEN (LP)	100

(see also Martin Carthy, Leon Rosselson)

THREE COINS

70	Sugar SU 106	Come And Do The Right Thing/It's So Long	6

THREE DEGREES

65	Stateside SS 413	Gee Baby I'm Sorry/Do What You're Supposed To Do	60
65	Stateside SS 459	Close Your Eyes/Gotta Draw The Line	70
65	Stateside SS 459	Close Your Eyes/Gotta Draw The Line (DJ copy)	100
71	Mojo 2092 001	Maybe/There's So Much Love Around Me	6
71	Mojo 2092 002	You're The One/Rose Garden	6
71	Mojo 2092 009	There's So Much Love Around Me/Maybe (reissue)	6
71	Mojo 2092 009	There's So Much Love Around Me/Yours (different B-side)	6
75	Pye International 7N 25671	Sugar On Sunday/Maybe	6
71	Mojo 2916 002	THE THREE DEGREES (LP)	20

THREE DOG NIGHT

69	Stateside SS 8041	It's For You/Feelin' Alright	6
69	Stateside SS 8030	Eli's Coming/Circle For A Landing	6
69	Stateside-Dunhill SS 8008	Nobody/It's For You	6
70	Stateside-Dunhill SS 8052	Mama Told Me Not To Come/Rock And Roll Widow	7
71	Probe PRO 523	Joy To The World/I Can Hear You Calling	6
71	Probe PRO 536	Liar/Can't Get Enough Of It	6
69	Stateside-Dun. (S)SL 5006	THREE DOG NIGHT (LP)	15
69	Stateside-Dun. (S)SL 5013	SUITABLE FOR FRAMING (LP, laminated front cover)	12
70	Stateside-Dunhill SSL 5023	CAPTURED LIVE AT THE FORUM (LP)	12
70	Probe SPBA 6251	IT AIN'T EASY (LP, laminated gatefold sleeve)	12
73	Probe SPBA 6278	CYAN (LP, gatefold)	12

(see also Danny Hutton)

THREE DOLLS

57	MGM MGM 958	The Living End/The Octopus Song	10

THREE GOOD REASONS

65	Mercury MF 883	Build Your Love/Don't Leave Me Now	10
65	Mercury MF 899	Nowhere Man/Wire Wheels	18
65	Mercury MF 929	The Moment Of Truth/Funny Kind Of Loving	10

THREE JOHNS

82	CNT CNT 003	English White Boy Engineer/Secret Agent (p/s)	8
83	CNT CNT 011	Pink Headed Bug/Lucy In The Rain (p/s)	7
83	CNT CNT 013	Men Like Monkeys/Two Minute Ape!/Windolene/ Marx's Wife/Paris 1941 (12", p/s)	8
96	Dojo DOJOCD 255	THE BEST OF THE THREE JOHNS (CD)	20

THREE KAYES (SISTERS)

56	HMV 7M 401	Ivory Tower/Mister Cuckoo (Sing Your Song)	12
56	HMV POP 251	Lay Down Your Arms/First Row Balcony (as Three Kaye Sisters)	10

(see also Kaye Sisters, Frankie Vaughan)

THREE MAN ARMY

72	Pegasus PGS 1	What's Your Name/Travellin'	10
74	Reprise K 14292	Polecat Woman/Take Me Down From The Mountain	5
71	Pegasus PEG 3	A THIRD OF A LIFETIME (LP, gatefold)	60
74	Reprise K 54015	THREE MAN ARMY TWO (LP)	30

(see also Gun, Baker Gurvitz Army, Andy Newman, Spooky Tooth)

3 MINUTES

80	Rocket XPRES 40	Automatic Kids/Future Fun (p/s)	8

THREE PEOPLE

66	Decca F 12473	Have You Ever Been There/Good Times	10
66	Decca F 12514	Suspicions/Easy Man To Find	10
67	Decca F 12581	Got To Find A Reason/Simple Thing Would Be For You To Start Loving Me	10

(see also John Bromley)

THREE PIECES

75	Fantasy FTC 116	I Need You Girl/Short'nin' Bread	8

3PM

92	Busted Loop 3	Better Late Than Never (12")	20

3 PM

91	Alma Vale ALMA 1	Out Of Control (12")	15
91	Alma Vale ALMA 2	ST.P/3PM/Lynx (12")	20

THREE QUARTERS

65	Columbia DB 7467	People Will Talk/Love Come A-Tricklin' Down	15
65	Columbia DB 7576	The Pleasure Girls/Little People	6

THREE SOUNDS

68	Liberty LBF 15062	Makin' Bread Again/Still I'm Sad	8

3 THIEVES AND A LIAR

92	3 Thieves And A Liar 3TAL	In The House/I Get A Chill/You Bring Me Joy/Tonight (12")	25

THREE TONES

70	Bamboo BAM 32	Good Ways/Everything We Do	150

THREE TOPS

67	Doctor Bird DB 1101	Miserable Friday/This World Has A Feeling	30
67	Studio One SO 2023	Moving To Progress/Love And Inspiration	80
67	Trojan TR 003	It's Raining/Sound Of Music	40
67	Treasure Isle TI 7008	Do It Right/You Should Have Known	30
68	Coxsone CS 7033	A Man Of Chances/HORTENSE ELLIS: A Groovy Kind Of Love	120
68	Coxsone CS 7051	Great Train In '68/You Should Have Known	80
73	Bullet BU 527	Take Time Out/Just Like A Log	12

(see also Dion Cameron & Three Tops, Sir Lord Comic, King Rocky)

THREE WISE MEN

83	Virgin VS 642	Thanks For Christmas/Countdown To Christmas Partytime (p/s)	10

(see also XTC)

THREE DANCERS

87	Dilletante Disques 007	Seventeen/It Doesn't Matter (p/s)	40

THREE'S A CROWD

66	Fontana TF 673	Look Around The Corner/Living In A Dream	20

(see also Embers, Writing On The Wall)

THRESHOLD OF PLEASURE

68	Decca F12785	Rain Rain Rain/He Could Never Love You Like I Do	40

THRILLERS

68	Blue Cat BS 128	The Last Dance/DELTA CATS: Unworthy Baby	60

(see also Phil Pratt)

PERCY 'THRILLS' THRILLINGTON

77	Regal Zono. EMI 2594	Uncle Albert - Admiral Halsey/Eat At Home	100
77	Regal Zono. EMC 3175	THRILLINGTON (LP, with inner sleeve)	200
77	Regal Zono. TC-EMC 3175	THRILLINGTON (cassette)	25

(see also Paul McCartney)

THRILLS (1)

66	Capitol CL 15469	No One/What Can Go Wrong	100
66	Capitol CL 15469	No One/What Can Go Wrong (DJ copy)	200
79	Grapevine GRP 126	Show The World Where It's At/What Can Go Wrong	5

THRILLS (2)

03	Virgin VSDJ 1855	Last Night I Dreamt That Somebody Loved Me (1-sided gig issue, p/s, 500 only)	20

THROBBING GRISTLE

78	Industrial IR 0003	United/Zyklon B Zombie (p/s)	20
78	Industrial IR 0003/U	United/Zyklon B Zombie (p/s, white or clear vinyl, 1,000 only of each)	25
80	Industrial IR 0003	United/Zyklon B Zombie (longer version) (p/s, reissue, 'Memorial Issue' scratched in matrix)	15
80	Industrial IR 0013	Subhuman/Something Came Over Me (in polythene camouflage bag)	20
80	Industrial IR 0015	Adrenalin/Distant Dreams (Part Two) (in polythene camouflage bag)	20
81	Fetish FET 006	Discipline (live, Berlin)/Discipline (live, Manchester) (12", p/s)	20
77	Industrial IR 0002	SECOND ANNUAL REPORT (LP, 785 only, white sleeve, xerox strip & 2 stickers)	150
78	Industrial IR 0004	D.O.A. THE THIRD AND FINAL REPORT (LP, 1st 1,000 with calendar & postcard)	100
78	Industrial IR 0004	D.O.A. THE THIRD AND FINAL REPORT (LP)	25
78	Fetish FET 2001	SECOND ANNUAL REPORT (LP, 2,000 only, T.G. 'lightning flash' sleeve, with questionnaire & insert, "Coom" mispelling)	40
79	Fetish FET 2001	SECOND ANNUAL REPORT (LP, reissue, glossy sleeve with inserts, with correct "Coum" spelling)	15
79	Industrial IR 0004	D.O.A. THE THIRD AND FINAL REPORT (LP, re-pressing, 1,000 only, banded as 16 equal length tracks)	60
79	Industrial IR 0008	20 JAZZ FUNK GREATS (LP, 5,000 only, 1st 2,000 with b&w poster)	80
79	Industrial IR 0008	20 JAZZ FUNK GREATS (LP, 5,000 only)	40
80	Industrial IR 0009	HEATHEN EARTH (LP, gatefold sleeve, 785 on blue vinyl)	100
80	Industrial IR 0009	HEATHEN EARTH (LP, gatefold sleeve)	20
81	Fetish FET 2001	SECOND ANNUAL REPORT (LP, backwards version, 1st 2,000 in T.G. 'flash' sleeve)	40
81	Fetish FET 2001	SECOND ANNUAL REPORT (LP, backwards version, later issue in black & white sleeve)	15
81	Fetish FX 1	A BOXED SET (5-LP box set with 28-page booklet & badge, 5,000 only)	160
82	Death 01	MUSIC FROM THE DEATH FACTORY, MAY '79 (LP, 50 only)	350
82	Power Focus 001	ASSUME POWER FOCUS (LP, 500 only, numbered)	90
82	T.G. 33033	LIVE AT THE DEATH FACTORY, MAY '79 (LP, reissue picture disc, 1,355 only)	40
82	Karnage/Illuminated KILL 1	THEE PSYCHICK SACRIFICE (2-LP)	30
84	Illuminated JAMS 35	IN THE SHADOW OF THE SUN (LP, soundtrack)	20
84	Illuminated JAMS 39	THE INDUSTRIAL RECORDS STORY 1976-1981 (LP)	35
84	Casual Abandon CAS 1J	ONCE UPON A TIME (LP)	15
84	Mental Decay 01-1	SPECIAL TREATMENT (LP)	15
80s	Sprut 001	VERY FRIENDLY - THE FIRST ANNUAL REPORT OF T.G. (LP)	25
80s	Industrial IRC 1-IRC 24	24 HOURS (box set of cassettes with total of 24 hours playing time; every set is unique)	300
03	Grey Area	TG+ (10-CD box set)	100

(see also Psychic TV, Coil, Sabres Of Paradise)

THROWING MUSES

89	4AD BADD 903	Dizzy/Santa Claus/Mania (live)/Downtown (live) (10", gatefold p/s)	8
91	4AD CAD 1002	THE REAL RAMONA (LP)	12
93	4AD CADD 2013	RED HEAVEN (LP, with free live Kristin Hersh LP)	20
95	4AD CAD 5002	UNIVERSITY (LP)	12
96	4AD CAD 6014	LIMBO (LP)	15

(see also Belly, Kristin Hersh)

THE THRUST

80	Ellie Jay EJSP 9341	THE THRUST EP	100

THUNDER

89	EMI EMS 11	She's So Fine/Girl's Going Out Of Her Head (p/s, with free patch)	5
90	EMI EMPD 126	Dirty Love/Fired Up (logo-shaped picture disc with insert in PVC sleeve)	10
90	EMI EMPD 126	Dirty Love/Fired Up (uncut picture disc with insert in PVC sleeve)	15
90	EMI EMS 137	Back Street Symphony/No Way Out Of The Wilderness (box set with postcards, some also with badge)	10

| 90 | EMI 12 EMPD 137 | Back Street Symphony/No Way Out Of The Wilderness/An Englishman On Holiday (live) (12", picture disc with insert in PVC sleeve) ....8 |

(see also Terraplane, Nuthin' Fancy)

JOHNNY THUNDER

63	Stateside SS 149	Loop De Loop/Don't Be Ashamed 10
63	Stateside SS 168	Rock-A-Bye My Darling/The Rosy Dance 10
63	Stateside SS 200	Jailer, Bring Me Water/Outlaw 15
63	Stateside SS 229	Hey Child/Everybody Likes To Dance With Johnny..............................10
64	Stateside SS 337	More, More, More Love, Love, Love/Shout It To The World....................10
65	Stateside SS 370	Send Her To Me/Everybody Likes To Dance With Johnny 20
65	Stateside SS 454	Dear John I'm Going To Leave You/Suzie-Q..10
65	Stateside SS 476	Everybody Do The Sloopy/Beautiful..10
66	Stateside SS 499	My Prayer/A Broken Heart 10
63	Stateside SL 10029	LOOP DE LOOP (LP)..75

JOHNNY THUNDER & RUBY WINTERS

| 67 | Stateside SS 2005 | Make Love To Me/Teach Me Tonight ....15 |

THUNDERBIRDS

| 66 | Polydor 56710 | Your Ma Said You Cried (In Your Sleep Last Night)/Before It's Too Late ....70 |

(see also Chris Farlowe & Thunderbirds)

THUNDERBIRDS (AUSTRALIA)

| 61 | Oriole CB 1610 | Wild Weekend/Rat Race ....20 |
| 61 | Oriole CB 1625 | New Orleans Beat/Delilah Jones ....20 |

THUNDERBIRDS (U.S.)

| 55 | London HL 8146 | Ayuh, Ayuh/Blueberries..70 |
| 55 | London HL 8146 | Ayuh, Ayuh/Blueberries (78) ....15 |

(see also Bert Convy & Thunderbirds, Midnighters)

THUNDERBOLTS

| 62 | Decca F 11522 | Fugitive/Feelin' In A Mood ....15 |

THUNDERBOYS

| 80 | Recent EJSP 9339 | Fashion/Someone Like You (p/s) ....40 |

THUNDERCLAP NEWMAN

69	Track 604031	Something In The Air/Wilhemina 6
70	Track 2094 001	Accidents/I See It All 5
70	Track 2094 002	Wild Country/Hollywood 7
70	Track 2094 003	The Reason/Stormy Petrel 7
79	Track 2095 002	Wild Country/Hollywood (reissue, p/s) 8
70	Track 2406 003	HOLLYWOOD DREAM (LP, gatefold sleeve, lyric insert) 80
70	Track 2406 003	HOLLYWOOD DREAM (LP, gatefold sleeve, without lyric insert) 30

(see also Stone The Crows, One In A Million, Paul McCartney & Wings, Speedy Keen, Andy Newman)

THUNDER COMPANY

| 70 | Columbia DB 8706 | Ridin' On The Gravy Train (5.03)/Bubble Drum..40 |
| 70 | Columbia DB 8706 | Ridin' On The Gravy Train (2.35 Edit)/Bubble Drum (demo only) ....50 |

(see also Brian Bennett, Shadows)

THUNDERHEAD

| 93 | Thunderhead TH 01 | Lost In Time/Untitled (12") ....20 |

THUNDERMUG

| 73 | London HLZ 10411 | Africa/Will They Ever ....6 |
| 72 | Axe AXS 502 | STRIKES (LP) ....15 |

THUNDER ROAD

| 73 | Buddah Records 2011-163 | Peter Gunn/Holly Golly ....5 |

JOHNNY THUNDERS (& THE HEARTBREAKERS)

78	Real ARE 1	Dead Or Alive/Downtown (p/s) 15
78	Real ARE 3	You Can't Put Your Arms Around A Memory (Edit)/Hurtin' (p/s) 12
78	Real ARE 3T	You Can't Put Your Arms Around A Memory/Hurtin' (12", p/s, blue or pink vinyl, die-cut company sleeve) 12
83	Jungle JUNG 5	VINTAGE '77 (12" EP) 12
84	Jungle JUNG 14P	Get Off The Phone/All By Myself (picture disc).....................................10
84	Jungle JUNG 14T	GET OFF THE PHONE EP (12") 8
85	Jungle JUNG 18T	CHINESE ROCKS (12" EP) 8
85	Jungle JUNG 23P	Crawfish/Tie Me Up (with Patti Palladin, picture disc) 8
87	Jungle JUNG 33T	QUE SERA SERA (12" EP) 8
99	Jungle JUNG 62	Chinese Rocks/Born To Lose (p/s, pink vinyl)..5
77	Real RAL 1	SO ALONE (LP, with inner sleeve) 20
82	Jungle FREUD 1	LIVE AT THE SPEAKEASY (LP)..12
86	Jungle JT BOX 1	ALBUM COLLECTION (3-LP & 12" box set with poster and badge)..............30

(see also New York Dolls, Heartbreakers)

SAM THUNDER

| 84 | Bullet BOLT 8 | Don't Take Forever/Piece Of the Night/You Set My Heart On Fire (12", p/s) ....8 |
| 84 | Bullet BULP 5 | MANOUEVRES (Lp, picture disc) ....18 |

THUNDERSTICK

83	Thunderbolt THBE 1002	FEEL LIKE ROCK'N'ROLL (12" EP, p/s, with patch) 12
83	Thunderbolt THBE 1002	FEEL LIKE ROCK'N'ROLL (12" EP, p/s) 8
83	Thunderbolt THBL 008	BEAUTY AND THE BEASTS (LP)...12

(see also Samson, Gillan)

THUNDERTRAIN

| 77 | Jelly JPLP 1 | TEENAGE SUICIDE (LP)..12 |

THURSDAY'S CHILDREN

| 66 | Piccadilly 7N 35276 | Just You/You Don't Believe Me..25 |
| 66 | Piccadilly 7N 35306 | Crawfish/Come Softly To Me ....15 |

(see also Phil Cordell)

MINT VALUE £

THYRDS
64	Oak RGJ 133	Hide 'N' Seek/I've Got My Mojo Working	300
64	Decca F 12010	Hide 'N' Seek/No Time Like The Present	60

TIAMAT
90	CMFT CMFT 6	SUMERIAN CRY (LP)	40
90	Metalcore CORE 9	SUMERIAN CRY (LP, reissue)	30

TIARAS
63	Warner Bros WB 92	You Told Me/I'm Gonna Forget You	15

TIBET & STAPLETON
96	United Dairies UDOR 1	MUSICALISCHE KÜRBS HÜTTE (LP, clear vinyl, with insert)	30

(see also Current 93, Steven Stapleton & David Tibet)o

TICH - TED TAYLOR FOUR WITH CORONA KIDS
65	Oriole CB 1980	Santa Bring Me Ringo/Santa's Got Such A Terrible Cold/Tich & Quackers	10

(see also Ted Taylor)

TICKAWINDA
75	Pennine PSS 153	ROSEMARY LANE (LP)	450

KATHRYN TICKELL
84	Saydisc SDL 343	ON KIELDER SIDE (LP)	20

TICKETS
79	Bridgehouse BHS 3	I'll Be Your Pin Up/Guess I Have To Sit Alone (p/s)	6

(see also Wasted Youth)

TICKLE
67	Regal Zonophone RZ 3004	Subway (Smokey Pokey World)/Good Evening	500

(see also Junior's Eyes, Outsider, Bunch Of Fives)

TIC TAC TOE
92	Tic Tac Toe TTT 456	456/Ephemerol (12", stamped white label)	30
92	Tic Tac Toe TTT 457	456/(Remix)/Ephemerol (Mickey Finn Remix) (12")	10

TIDAL WAVE
69	Decca F 22973	With Tears In My Eyes/We Wanna Know	10

TIDBITS
71	Fly BUG 12	Jean Harlow/Vietnam/Six O'Clock Blues (p/s)	8

PETER TIERNEY & NIGHTHAWKS
65	Fontana TF 547	Oh How I Need You/That's Too Bad (p/s)	15

ROY TIERNEY
61	Philips BF 1159	Cupid/The Lonely One (in p/s)	15
61	Philips BF 1159	Cupid/The Lonely One	7
61	Philips BF 1194	Just Out Of Reach (Of My Two Empty Arms)/Casanova	10

TIERNEY'S FUGITIVES
65	Decca F 12247	Did You Want To Run Away?/Morning Mist	25

TIFFANIES
67	Chess CRS 8059	It's Got To Be A Great Song/He's Good For Me	100
67	Chess CRS 8059	It's Got To Be A Great Song/He's Good For Me (DJ copy)	150

TIFFANY (WITH THOUGHTS)
65	Parlophone R 5311	I Know/Am I Dreaming	20
66	Parlophone R 5439	Find Out What's Happening/Baby Don't Look Down (as Tiffany with Thoughts)	50

(see also Thoughts)

TIFFANY SHADE
68	Fontana (S)TL 5469	TIFFANY SHADE (LP)	90

JIMMY & LOUISE TIG
69	Deep Soul DS 9105	A Love That Never Grows Cold/Who Can I Turn To	40

TIGER
75	United Artists UP 35848	I Am An Animal/Stop That Machine	20
76	Retreat RTL 6006	TIGER (LP, with lyric inner sleeve)	15
76	EMI EMC3153	GOIN' DOWN LAUGHING (LP, lyric inner sleeve)	12

(see also Hackensack, Samson, Brinsley Schwarz, Big Jim Sullivan)

TIGER ASHBY
80	T&A Records TA 1	Jet Free/Burning Cross (p/s)	20

TIGER (JAMAICA)
70	New Beat NB 052	Soul Of Africa/Dallas Texas	10
70	New Beat NB 064	Musical Scorcher/Three Dogs Night	10
71	Camel CA 70	Guilty/United We Stand	7
71	New Beat NB 075	African Beat/Black Man Land	7
71	New Beat NB 088	Have You Ever Been Hurt/Our Day Will Come	7

TIGER LILY
75	Gull GULS 12	Monkey Jive/Ain't Misbehavin'	8
77	Gull GULS 54	Monkey Jive/Ain't Misbehavin' (reissue, p/s)	10
77	Gull GULS 54	Monkey Jive/Ain't Misbehavin' (reissue)	5
80	Dead Good DEAD 11	Monkey Jive/Ain't Misbehavin' (2nd reissue, different p/s)	5

(see also Ultravox)

TIGERMOTH
84	Rogue FMSL 2006	TIGERMOTH (LP)	15

TIGERS
69	Polydor 56339	Rain Falls On The Lonely/Smile For Me	10
79	Strike KIK 1	Kidding Stops/Big Expense, Small Income (p/s)	8

TIGER TAILS
80	Snotty Snails NELCO 2	Words Without Conviction/Norman/Fashion Fool (p/s)	20

TIGHT LIKE THAT
72	Village Thing VTS 12	HOKUM (LP)	40

TIGHTS
78	Cherry Red CHERRY 1	Bad Hearts/It/Cracked (p/s)	20
78	Cherry Red CHERRY 2	Howard Hughes/China's Eternal (p/s)	10

TIKKI, TAKI, SUZI, LIES
70	UPC UPC 102	Welcome To My House/I Believe In Love	8
70	UPC UPC 109	Ba-Da-Da-Dum/Dream Stealer	25

TILLER BOYS
79	New Hormones ORG 3	Big Noise From The Jungle/Slaves And Pyramids/What Me Worry? (p/s)	6

(see also Buzzcocks, Pete Shelley, Eric Random)

TILLERMEN
71	Duke DU 109	Be Loving To Me/Judgement Rock	7

(see also Greyhound)

DEREK JOHN TILLEY
70	Decca F 13043	Sunny Day/Living For Love	30

MEL TILLIS
67	London HLR 10141	Life Turned Her That Way/If I Could Only Start Over	5
68	London HA-R 8345	MR. MEL (LP)	12

BERTHA TILLMAN
62	Oriole CB 1746	Oh, My Angel/Lovin' Time	80

JOHNNY TILLOTSON
59	London HLA 8930	True True Happiness/Love Is Blind (78 rpm £25)	50
60	London HLA 9048	Why Do I Love You So/Never Let Me Go	25
60	London HLA 9101	Earth Angel/Pledging My Love	30
60	London HLA 9231	Poetry In Motion/Princess, Princess	5
61	London HLA 9275	Jimmy's Girl/His True Love Said Goodbye	10
61	London HLA 9412	Without You/Cutie Pie	15
62	London HLA 9514	Dreamy Eyes/Much Beyond Compare	6
62	London HLA 9550	It Keeps Right On A-Hurtin'/She Gave Sweet Love To Me	8
62	London HLA 9598	Send Me The Pillow You Dream On/What'll I Do	7
62	London HLA 9642	I Can't Help It/I'm So Lonesome I Could Cry	7
63	London HLA 9695	Out Of My Mind/Judy, Judy, Judy	7
63	London HLA 9811	Funny How Time Slips Away/A Very Good Year For Girls	7
63	MGM MGM 1214	Talk Back Trembling Lips/Another You	7
63	MGM MGM 1225	Worried Guy/Please Don't Go Away	6
63	MGM MGM 1235	I'm Watching My Watch/I Rise, I Fall	6
64	MGM MGM 1247	Suffering From A Heartache/Worry	6
64	MGM MGM 1252	She Understands Me/Tomorrow	8
64	MGM MGM 1266	Angel/Little Boy	7
65	MGM MGM 1275	Then I'll Count Again/One's Yours, One's Mine	8
65	MGM MGM 1281	Heartaches By The Number/Your Memory Comes Along	8
65	MGM MGM 1290	Our World/(Wait 'Til You See) My Gidget	8
66	MGM MGM 1300	Hello Enemy/I Never Loved You Anyway	8
66	MGM MGM 1311	Me Myself And I/Country Boy, Country Boy	8
66	MGM MGM 1319	No Love At All/What Am I Gonna Do	8
68	MGM MGM 1393	Cabaret/If I Were A Rich Man	8
69	London HLU 10281	Tears On My Pillow/Remember When	5
62	London RE-A 1345	JOHNNY TILLOTSON (EP)	40
63	London RE-A 1388	J.T. (EP)	40
63	MGM MGM-EP 788	JOHNNY TILLOTSON (EP)	25
64	MGM MGM-EP 790	JOHNNY TILLOTSON'S HIT PARADE (EP)	25
61	London HA-A 2431	JOHNNY TILLOTSON'S BEST (LP)	60
62	London HA-A 8019	IT KEEPS RIGHT ON A-HURTIN' (LP)	40
64	MGM MGM-C 972	ALONE WITH YOU (LP)	15
65	MGM C/CS 1002	SHE UNDERSTANDS ME (LP)	15
65	MGM MGM-C(S) 8005	JOHNNY TILLOTSON SINGS OUR WORLD (LP)	15
66	MGM MGM-C(S) 8025	NO LOVE AT ALL (LP)	15

TILSLEY ORCHESTRA
66	Fontana TF 783	Thunderbirds Theme/Theme From "The Power Game"	20
67	Polydor 56150	Mr. Aitch Theme/Cotton Reed	8
67	Fontana (S)TL 5411	TOP T.V. THEMES (LP)	20

(see also Electric Banana)

STEVE TILSTON
71	Village Thing VTS 5	AN ACOUSTIC CONFUSION (LP)	35
72	Transatlantic TRA 252	COLLECTION (LP, textured gatefold sleeve)	18
77	Cornucopia CR 1	SONGS FROM THE DRESS REHEARSAL (LP, with Rupert Hine/John Renbourn)	25
83	TM PROP 4	IN FOR A PENNY IN FOR A POUND (LP, with Peter Bardens)	15

TIMBER
71	Elektra K 12022	Bring America Home/Splinters From Timber	6
72	Elektra K 12042	Outlaw/Song For Two Signs	6
71	Elektra K 42093	BRING AMERICA HOME (LP)	12

TIMBER TIMBRE
11	Full Time Hobby FTH 114LP	CREEP ON CREEPING ON (LP)	18

TIME
65	Pye 7N 17019	Take A Bit Of Notice/Every Now And Then	60
66	Pye 7N 17146	The First Time I Saw The Sunshine/Annabel	30

TIME
75	B.U.K. BULP 2005	TIME (LP)	60

(see also Spontaneous Combustion)

T.I.M.E. (TRUST IN MEN EVERYWHERE)
69	Liberty LBF 15082	Take Me Along/Make It Alright	10

MINT VALUE £

TIME UK

68	Liberty LBL/LBS 83144	T.I.M.E. (LP)	50
69	Liberty LBL/LBS 83232	SMOOTH BALL (LP)	70

TIME UK

83	Red Bus TIM 123	The Cabaret/Remember Days (gatefold p/s)	10

(see also the Jam)

TIMEBOX

67	Piccadilly 7N 35369	I'll Always Love You/Save Your Love	100
67	Piccadilly 7N 35379	Soul Sauce/I Wish I Could Jerk Like My Uncle Cyril	180
67	Deram DM 153	Walking Through The Streets Of My Mind/Don't Make Promises	25
68	Deram DM 194	Beggin'/A Woman That's Waiting	45
68	Deram DM 219	Girl Don't Make Me Wait/Gone Is The Sad Man	35
69	Deram DM 246	Baked Jam Roll In Your Eye/Poor Little Heartbreaker	25
69	Deram DM 271	Yellow Van/You've Got The Chance	30

(see also Bo Street Runners, [Mike] Patto, V.I.Ps)

TIME CODE

86	Jive LOUT 1	Village House Stomp/Louie Louie (12")	8

TIME CRYSTALS

91	Talisman TAL 1	The Fool/Geve Me Back What's Mine	10

TIMELORDS

88	KLF 003GG	Gary In The Tardis (Radio)/(Minimal) (white label promo, 500 only)	15
88	KLF 003GG	Gary In The Tardis (Radio)/(Minimal) (12", p/s)	10
88	KLF 003P	Doctorin' The Tardis (Radio)/(Minimal) (car-shaped picture disc)	15
88	KLF 003R	Doctorin' The Tardis (Radio)/Doctorin' The Tardis (Minimal)/ Gary Glitter Joins The JAMs (12", 4,000 only, this price for those in full 'Gary Glitter' p/s)	30
88	KLF 003R	Doctorin' The Tardis (Radio)/Doctorin' The Tardis (Minimal)/ Gary Glitter Joins The JAMs (12", 4,000 only, in stickered black die-cut sleeve)	8
88	KLF TCD 003	Doctorin' The Tardis (12" mix)/What Time Is Love? (KLF original) (CD)	10
88	KLF CD 003	Doctorin' The Tardis (Radio)/Doctorin' The Tardis (Minimal)/Doctorin' The Tardis (Club Mix)/Doctorin' The Tardis (Video) (CD Video)	30

(see also KLF, Disco 2000, JAMs, Bill Drummond, Orb, Space)

TIME MACHINE

72	Play PLAY 41	Railroad/Going Down Down Down	30

TIMEPIECE

70	Dolphin 4759	Hitchin To Miami/Mad Dan The Romeo Man	8

TIMES (1)

65	EMI 7ES 24	Ooh Wee/Shepherd Blues/Suzie/Running And Hiding (EP, demo only)	70
66	Columbia DB 7804	Think About The Times/Tomorrow Night	35
66	Columbia DB 7904	(She Can't Replace) The Love We Knew/Reconciled	35
68	Pye 7N 17647	What's Made Milwaukee Famous/Follw The Times	10
70	Parlophone R 5855	Looking Thru' The Eyes Of A Beautiful Girl/Flyin' High Feelin' Low	10

TIMES (2)

81	Whaam! WHAAM 2	Red With Purple Flashes/Biff! Bang! Pow! (p/s)	90
82	Art Pop POP 50	Here Come The Holidays (Voici Les Vacances)/Three Cheers For The Sun (A-side as Joni Dee & Times, p/s, with 'Times' sticker)	18
82	Art Pop POP 50	Here Come The Holidays (Voici Les Vacances)/Three Cheers For The Sun (A-side as Joni Dee & Times, p/s)	12
83	Art Pop POP 49	I Helped Patrick McGoohan Escape/The Theme From "Danger Man" (p/s)	20
84	Art Pop POP 46	Boys Brigade/Power Is Forever (p/s)	7
84	Art Pop POP 45	Blue Fire/Where The Blue Begins (p/s)	6
85	Unicorn PHZ 1	London Boys/(Where To Go) When The Sun Goes Down (p/s)	5
90	Caff CAFF 13	Extase/BIFF BANG POW!: Sleep (p/s, with insert)	20
85	Art Pop 43DOZ	BOYS ABOUT TOWN (12", EP)	10
81	Whaam! BIG 1	POP GOES ART (LP, hand-sprayed sleeve)	40
82	Art Pop ART 20	POP GOES ART! (LP, reissue, hand-sprayed sleeve, with magazine cuttings taped to plain white cover)	25
82	Art Pop ART 20	POP GOES ART! (LP, reissue, hand-sprayed sleeve, without magazine cuttings taped to plain white cover)	20
83	Art Pop ART 19	THIS IS LONDON (LP, white label with blue print)	25
83	Art Pop ART 19	THIS IS LONDON (LP, black label with white print)	18
83	Art Pop No. 1	I HELPED PATRICK McGOOHAN ESCAPE (mini-LP)	18
84	Art Pop ART 17	HELLO EUROPE (LP, purple or blue sleeve)	18
85	Art Pop ARTPOP 2	BLUE PERIOD (mini-LP, grey sleeve)	12
86	Art Pop ART 16	UP AGAINST IT (LP)	12
86	Art Pop ART 15	ENJOY! (LP, gatefold sleeve)	12
90	Art Pop ART 20	POP GOES ART (LP, 'hand-painted' picture disc reissue, signed)	15
91	Creation CRELP 091	PURE (LP)	12
92	Creation CRELP 123	AT THE ASTRADOME LUNAVILLE (LP)	12
93	Creation CRELP 137	ALTERNATIVE COMMERCIAL CROSSOVER (LP, with inner)	12

(see also Television Personalities, Teenage Filmstars, O Level, Biff Bang Pow!, L'Orange Mechanik)

BOBBY TIMMONS

61	Riverside RLP 334	SOUL TIME (LP, with Art Blakey, also stereo [RLP 9334])	20
60	Riverside 12-317	THIS HERE IS (LP)	20

SALLY TIMMS & DRIFTING COWGIRLS

87	T.I.M. 12 MOT 6	This House Is A House Of Trouble! (Extended) (with Marc Almond)/ The Anchor Of Love/Heavenly Gates (12", p/s)	10

(see also Marc Almond, Mekons)

TIMON

68	Pye 7N 17451	Bitter Thoughts Of Little Jane/Ramblin' Boy	100
70	Threshold TH 3	And Now She Says She's Young/I'm Just A Travelling Man	8

(see also Tymon Dogg)

TIMONEERS

76	WHM WHM 1919	ROASTED LIVE (LP)	20

AL TIMOTHY & HIS BAND

55	Decca F 10558	Gruntin' Blues/You Mad Man!	10

TIM TAM & TURN ONS
67	Island WIP 6007	Wait A Minute/Ophelia	50

TINA
61	Piccadilly 7N 35022	What I Want For Christmas (Is Six More Years)/My Brother Wants A Doll For Christmas	6

TINA & MEXICANS
68	Pye 7N 17525	One Love Two/Longing To Hold You	8

TIN BISCUIT
70	Fontana TF 1077	The Last Time You Go/I'd Give My Life To You	5

TINDERBOX
68	Polydor 56296	Farewell Britannia/Rainsong	60

TINDERSTICKS
92	Tippy Toe 1	Patchwork/Milky Teeth (p/s, hand-coloured inner sleeve & insert; 1,000 only, numbered in positive or negative figures [from -500 to 500])	60
93	Tippy Toe/Ché TIPPY-CHE 2	Marbles/Joe Stumble/For Those.../Benn (10", p/s, stickered PVC sleeve, innersleeve & insert, 2,000 only)	25
93	Rough Trade 45rev16	A Marriage Made In Heaven/A Marriage Made In Heaven (Instrumental) ('singles club' release, p/s, 5,000 only)	12
93	Domino RUG 006	UNWIRED EP: Feeling Relatively Good/Rotweilers And Mace/She/Kooks (EP, numbered p/s; 1 copy in 10 with 'Domino' stamp, 1,500 only)	20
93	This Way Up WAY 1811	City Sickness/Untitled/The Bullring (p/s, 1,500 only)	15
93	This Way Up WAY 1899	City Sickness/Untitled/The Bullring (CD)	15
93	Clawfist XPIG 21	We Have All The Time In The World/GALLON DRUNK: Known Not Wanted ('singles club' release, p/s, 1,400 only)	15
93	Tippy Toe 003	LIVE IN BERLIN: Raindrops/Tyed (in stamped brown paper bag, mail-order/tour release, 1,500 only)	20
94	This Way Up WAY 2811	Kathleen/Summat Moon/Sweet, Sweet Man/E Type Joe (33 rpm 7", 5000 only)	5
94	This Way Up WAY 2899	Kathleen/Summat Moon/Sweet, Sweet Man/E Type Joe (CD)	15
95	Sub Pop SP 297	THE SMOOTH SOUND OF TINDERSTICKS: Here/Harry's Dilemma (p/s, 3,000 only)	15
95	This Way Up 2888	KATHLEEN (10")	15
08	Lucky Dog LD 05	What Are You Fighting For? (one-sided 7", die cut sleeve, 200 only)	15
93	This Way Up 518306	TINDERSTICKS (1st album) (2-LP, first 1000 with 4 postcards)	80
93	This Way Up 518306	TINDERSTICKS (1st album) (2-LP, without postcards)	45
95	This Way Up THIS 1.1	TINDERSTICKS (2nd album) (LP,with free 7")	40
94	This Way Up WAY 3288	LIVE IN AMSTERDAM (10" LP, brown sleeve)	15
94	This Way Up WAY 3299	LIVE IN AMSTERDAM (CD, numbered brown paper sleeve)	25
95	This Way Up	THE BLOOMSBURY THEATRE 12/3/95 (LP, 2-10" LP)	40
96	This Way Up 5243002	NENETTE ET BONI (LP)	40
97	This Way Up 5243441	CURTAINS (2xLP)	60
98	Island ILPS 8074	DONKEYS 92-97 (LP)	40
99	Simply Vinyl SVLP 112	SIMPLE PLEASURE (LP)	60
01	Beggars Banquet BBQLP 222	CAN OUR LOVE... (LP, gatefold)	25
01	Beggars Banquet BBQLP 225	TROUBLE EVERY DAY (LP, soundtrack, with booklet)	25
03	Beggars Banquet BBQLP 232	WAITING FOR THE MOON (LP)	18

(see also Asphalt Ribbons)

TING TINGS
07	Switchflicker SWALF 11	That's Not My Name/Great DJ (p/s)	15
07	No label or cat no	Fruit Machine/Impacilla Carpisung (4 x 100 7" given away at 4 live shows, customized blank sleeve)	50

TINGA (STEWART) & ERNIE (WILSON)
69	Explosion EX 2009	She's Gone/Old Old Song	8

TIN KAN
79	White Dove WD103A	A Thousand Miles Of White/Girl I'd Never Let You Down	10

TINKERBELL'S FAIRYDUST
67	Decca F 12705	Lazy Day/In My Magic Garden	70
68	Decca F 12778	Twenty Ten/Walking My Baby	70
69	Decca F 12865	Sheila's Back In Town/Follow Me Follow	100
69	Decca LK/SKL 5028	TINKERBELL'S FAIRYDUST (LP, unreleased; finished copies in laminated front sleeve with mono/stereo 'peephole' on rear, machine etched matrix number, blue/silver label with large unboxed Decca logo)	3000
69	Decca LK/SKL 5028	TINKERBELL'S FAIRYDUST (LP, unreleased; test pressings in sleeve)	800

TINKERS
69	Fontana SFJL 935	TIL THE WILD BIRDS (LP)	18
72	Argo ZFB 35	SPRING RAIN (LP)	25

BABS TINO
62	London HLR 9589	Forgive Me/If I Didn't Love You So Much	30
63	London RE-R 1377	FORGIVE ME (EP)	100

TINOPENERS
79	Logo GO 375	Set Me Free/I'm Not Your Type	150

TIN PAN SKIFFLE GROUP
57	Nestles NR 06	Poor Howard (1-sided card flexi 78)	12

MICK TINSLEY
67	Decca F 12544	Let It Be Me/How're You Gonna Tell Me	6

(see also Hedgehoppers Anonymous)

TIN SOLDIERS
93	Detour DR 002	A New Beat/Girlfriend/Get Up And Go! (p/s, insert 1,000, only 100 on clear vinyl)	12

TINTERN ABBEY
67	Deram DM 164	Beeside/Vacuum Cleaner	1000

TIN TIN
69	Polydor 56332	Only Ladies Play Croquet/He Wants To Be A Star	10
70	Polydor 2058 023	Toast And Marmalade For Tea/Manhattan Woman	12
70	Polydor 2058 076	Come On Over Again/Back To Winona	10
71	Polydor 2001 146	Shana/Rocky Mountain	10
71	Polydor 2058 114	Is That The Way/Swans On The Canal	10
72	Polydor 2058 232	Toast And Marmalade For Tea/Cavalry's Coming/Ships On The Starboard	10

TINY ALICE

72	Polydor 2058 238	Talking Turkey/Cavalry's Coming	10
69	Polydor 2384 011	TIN TIN (LP)	25
72	Polydor 2382 080	ASTRAL TAXI (LP)	20

(see also Steve & Stevie)

TINY ALICE

72	Kama Sutra 2013 043	Doctor Jazz/The Chocolate Dandies Of 1932/15¢ Hamburger Mama	5
72	Kama Sutra 2319 015	TINY ALICE (LP)	12

TINY TIM

68	Reprise RS 20760	Bring Back Those Rockabye Baby Days	6
68	Reprise RS 23258	Tiptoe Through The Tulips/I Got You Babe	6
68	Reprise RS 20769	Hello Hello/The Other Side	10
69	Reprise RS 20802	Great Balls Of Fire/As Time Goes By	6
69	Reprise RS 20855	Mickey The Monkey/Neighbourhood Children	6
71	Reprise RS 27004	There Will Always Be An England/Bless 'Em All/It's A Long Way To Tipperary/ Have You Seen My Little Sue	6
71	Reprise RS 27004	There Will Always Be An England/Bless 'Em All/It's A Long Way To Tipperary/ Have You Seen My Little Sue (78 rpm with union jack/plain label)	10
72	Wand WN 33	Am I Just Another Pretty Face/Movies	7
74	Polydor 2058 485	Happy Wanderer/My Nose Always Gets In The Way	6
68	Reprise RSLP 6292	GOD BLESS TINY TIM (LP)	20
69	Reprise RSLP 6323	TINY TIM'S SECOND ALBUM (LP)	20
69	Reprise RSLP 6351	FOR ALL MY LITTLE FRIENDS (LP)	15

TINY TOPSY (& CHARMS)

58	Parlophone R 4397	Come On, Come On, Come On/A Ring Around My Finger (with Charms)	90
58	Parlophone R 4397	Come On, Come On, Come On/A Ring Around My Finger (with Charms) (78)	30
58	Parlophone R 4427	You Shocked Me/Waterproof Eyes (solo)	120
58	Parlophone R 4427	You Shocked Me/Waterproof Eyes (solo) (78)	25
61	Pye International 7N 25104	After Marriage Blues/Working On Me Baby (solo)	30

DIMITRI TIOMKIN

54	Vogue Coral Q 2016	The High And The Mighty/Dial M For Murder	15

KEITH TIPPETT

69	Polydor 2384 004	YOU ARE HERE, I AM THERE (LP)	85
71	Vertigo 6360 024	DEDICATED TO YOU BUT YOU WEREN'T LISTENING (LP, gatefold sleeve, large swirl label)	120
72	RCA SF 8290	BLUEPRINT (LP)	75
76	Steam SJ 104	TNT (LP, with Stan Tracey)	15
77	Vinyl VS 101	WARM SPIRITS, COOL SPIRITS (LP)	12
78	Ogun OGD 003/4	FRAMES (2-LP)	20
78	Ogun OGUN 003/004	ARK (2-LP)	20

(see also Centipede, King Crimson, Ovary Lodge, Nicra)

JULIE TIPPETTS

76	Utopia UTS 601	SUNSET GLOW (LP)	22

(see also Julie Driscoll, Brian Auger, Centipede, Keith Tippett, Elton Dean, Ninesense, Mark Charig)

TIPPIE & THE CLOVERS

63	Stateside SS 160	My Heart Said/Bossa Nova Baby	25

LESTER TIPTON

80	Grapevine GRP 138	This Won't Change/MASQUERADERS: How	20

TIP TOPS

63	Cameo Parkway P 868	He's Braggin'/Oo-Kook-A-Boo	35

TÍR NA NOG

72	Chrysalis CHS 2001	The Lady I Love/Heidi	7
73	Chrysalis CHS 2016	Strong In The sun/The Mountain And I	6
71	Chrysalis ILPS 9153	TÍR NA NOG (LP, laminated gatefold sleeve)	25
72	Chrysalis CHR 1006	A TEAR AND A SMILE (LP, gatefold sleeve)	20
73	Chrysalis CHR 1047	STRONG IN THE SUN (LP)	15

TITAN

83	After Hours AFT 09	Imaginary Lady/Tooty Flutey	30
80	Wild Dog DOG 26	East Wind West Wind/Losing The Fight	200

TITANIC

72	CBS 7278	Sante Fe/Half Breed	5
72	CBS 8185	Rain 2,000/Blond	20
73	CBS 1670	Richmond Express/Heia Valenga	5
71	CBS 64104	TITANIC (LP)	20
72	CBS 64791	SEA WOLF (LP, gatefold sleeve)	20
73	CBS 65661	EAGLE ROCK (LP, gatefold sleeve)	15

TITANS

58	London HLU 8609	Don't You Just Know It/Can It Be	100
58	London HLU 8609	Don't You Just Know It/Can It Be (78)	35

TITUS GROAN

70	Dawn DNX 2503	Open The Door Homer/Woman Of The World/Liverpool (p/s)	20
70	Dawn DNLS 3012	TITUS GROAN (LP, gatefold sleeve)	300

CAL TJADER

65	Verve VS 529	Soul Sauce/Naked City Theme	50
65	Verve VS 529	Soul Sauce/Naked City Theme (DJ copy)	80
58	Vocalion LAE 556	RITMO CALIENTE (LP, as Cal Tjader Quintet)	20
62	HMV/Verve CLP 1587	IN A LATIN BAG (LP, as Cal Tjader Sextet, also stereo [CSD 1454])	15
64	Verve V8585	WARM WAVE (LP)	12
65	Vocalion LAE-F 599	GREATEST HITS (LP)	15
65	Verve (S)VLP 9136	SOUL BIRD: WHIFFENPOOF (LP)	15
66	Verve (S)VLP 9155	SOUL BURST (LP)	15
68	Verve (S)VLP 9192	THE BEST OF CAL TJADER (LP)	15
68	Verve (S)VLP 9215	HIP VIBRATIONS (LP)	20
69	Fontana STL 5527	SOLAR HEAT (LP)	12
61	Vogue SEA 568	CONCERT BY THE SEA (LP)	15

60	Vocalion LAE 560	THE WEST SIDE STORY (LP)	15

TMR

92	Pirate Club PCR 001	Pirate Toon (Moose Mix)/Pirate Toon (Pirate Excursion)/Pirate Toon (Pirate Dub) (12", white stamped label)	60

TNT

84	Neat NEAT 39	Back On The Road/Rockin' The Night (p/s)	12

T.N.T.

72	Jam JAM 4	Big Trouble (Part One)/Big Trouble (Part Two)	40

TOAD

72	RCA Victor SF 8241	TOAD (LP)	150

TOAD THE WET SPROCKET

79	Sprockets BRS 004	Pete's Punk Song/Feel It (fold out p/s)	40
80	Sprockets BRS 008	Reaching For The Sky/One Glass Of Whiskey (foldout stapled p/s)	70

TOAST

70	CBS 4768	Flowers Never Bend With The Rainfall/Summer Of Miranda	10

TOASTERS

87	Unicorn PHZA-5	POOL SHARK (LP)	18
90	Unicorn PHZA-60	FRANKENSKA (LP)	15

TOBA

82	Connection CONT 8203	Moving Up/Moving UP (Instrumental) (12", red or blue vinyl)	30

RUTH TOBI

69	Concord CON 002	Lazy/That's When I Cry	5

AMON TOBIN

94	Ninja Tune Zen 48	SUPERMODIFIED (2-LP)	30
97	Ninja Tune ZEN 29	BRICOLAGE (2-LP, gatefold sleeve)	25
97	Ninja Tune ZEN 29	BRICOLAGE (2-LP, single sleeve)	15
98	Ninja Tune ZEN 36	PERMUTATION (2-LP)	35
02	Ninja Tune ZEN 70	OUT FROM NOWHERE (2-LP)	18

TOBRUK

83	Neat NEAT 32	Wild On The Run/The Show Must Go On (p/s)	8
85	Parlophone 12R 6093	Falling/Like Lightning/Under The Gun (12", p/s)	10
85	Parlophone R 6101	On The Rebound/Poor Girl (p/s)	10
88	FM WKFMLP 105	PLEASURE AND PAIN (LP)	15

TOBY JUG

69	private pressing	GREASY QUIFF (LP, with insert)	175

TOBY TWIRL

68	Decca F 12728	Harry Faversham/Back In Time	30
68	Decca F 12804	Toffee Apple Sunday/Romeo And Juliet 1968	200
69	Decca F 12867	Movin' In/Utopia Daydream	40

(see also Shades Of Blue)

TODAY'S WITNESS

72	Emblem TDR 345	TODAY'S WITNESS (LP)	35

ART & DOTTY TODD

58	London HLB 8620	Chanson D'Amour (Song Of Love)/Along The Trail With You	18
59	London HLN 8838	Straight As An Arrow/Stand There, Mountain	18
59	London HLN 8838	Straight As An Arrow/Stand There, Mountain (78)	10

DIANE TODD

58	Decca F 10993	It's A Wonderful Thing To Be Loved/You Are My Favourite Dream	8

GARY TODD & ROGER TURNER

79	Incus INCUS 79	SUNDAY BEST (LP)	50

NICK TODD

57	London HLD 8500	Plaything/The Honey Song	40
58	London HLD 8537	At The Hop/I Do	15
59	London HLD 8902	Tiger/Twice As Nice	30

PATSY TODD

66	Doctor Bird DB 1086	Pitta Patta Rocky Steady (with Count Ossie)/COUNT OSSIE: Nyah Bongo	20
68	High Note HS 007	Fire In Your Wire/AL & VIBRATORS: Move Up Calypso	8
69	High Note HS 012	We Were Lovers/Give Me A Chance (B-side with Delano Stewart)	35

(see also Patsy, Stranger & Patsy, Derrick & Patsy)

SHARKEY TODD & MONSTERS

59	Parlophone R 4536	Cool Gool/The Horror Show	25
59	Parlophone R 4536	Cool Gool/The Horror Show (78)	20

(see also Wally Whyton, Vipers [Skiffle Group])

WILF TODD COMBO

64	Blue Beat BB 240	He Took Her Away/Have You Ever Been Lonely	12

WILF TODD & HIS MUSIC

66	Oak WT 101	WILF TODD AND HIS MUSIC (LP)	15

CAMY TODOROW

85	Virgin VS 816	Bursting At The Seams/Don't Stop It, I Like It (with Roger Taylor) (p/s)	30
85	Virgin VS 816-12	Bursting At The Seams (Backroom Version)/Bursting At The Seams (Instrumental)/Don't Stop It, I Like It (12", p/s, with Roger Taylor)	50

(see also Roger Taylor)

TOE-FAT

70	Parlophone R 5829	Working Nights/Bad Side Of The Moon	15
72	Chapter One SCH 175	Brand New Band/Can't Live Without You	10
70	Parlophone PCS 7097	TOE-FAT (LP, black/silver label with boxed logo)	150
70	Regal Zono. SLRZ 1015	TOE-FAT TWO (LP, red/silver label)	150

(see also Cliff Bennett, Uriah Heep, Glass Menagerie)

TOGETHER
68	Columbia DB 8491	Henry's Coming Home/Love Mum And Dad	70
69	Aurora 4278	Memories Of Melinda/Good Morning World	50
91	Thumbs Up Magic GH 002	FREE AT LAST EP (12")	10

(see also Keith Relf)

TOGETHER
90	Thumbs Up Magic GH 001	Hardcore Uproar (12", white label)	250
91	Thumbs Up Magic TUM002	The Luv Bug (12")	70
92	Thumbs Up Magic GH003	The House Sound Vol 2/Coming On Strong (12", with CYBERTEC)	60

TOGGERY FIVE
64	Parlophone R 5175	Bye Bye Bird/I'm Gonna Jump	45
65	Parlophone R 5249	I'd Much Rather Be With The Boys/It's So Easy	40

TOKALON
81	EDM Champagne BUBL 701	Coming To Get You/Dance Version	10

TOKENS
61	Parlophone R 4790	Tonight I Fell In Love/I Love My Baby	30
62	RCA RCA 1313	I'll Do My Crying Tomorrow/Dream Angel Goodnight	10
62	RCA RCA 1322	Wishing/A Bird Flies Out Of Sight	6
64	Fontana TF 500	He's In Town/Oh Kathy	10
66	Fontana TF 683	I Hear Trumpets Blow/I Could See Me Dancing With You	5
67	Stateside SS 598	Green Plant/Saloogy	5
67	Warner Bros WB 5900	Portrait Of My Love/She Comes And Goes	5
67	Warner Bros WB 7056	It's A Happening World/How Nice?	5
68	Warner Bros WB 7169	Till/Poor Man	5
70	Buddah 2011 011	Don't Worry Baby/Some People Sleep	5
62	RCA RD 27256	THE LION SLEEPS TONIGHT (LP, mono)	35
62	RCA SF 5128	THE LION SLEEPS TONIGHT (LP, stereo)	45
62	RCA RD 7535	WE THE TOKENS SING FOLK (LP)	20
70	Buddah 2359 007	BOTH SIDES NOW (LP)	12

(see also U.S. Double Quartet, We Ugly Dogs, Cross Country)

TOKYO BLADE
83	Powerstation OHM 2	Powergame/Death On Main Street (p/s)	8
85	Powerstation LEG 1T	THE CAVE SESSIONS (12" EP)	15
85	Tokyo Blade TBR 1	BLACKHEARTS AND JADED SPADES (LP, gatefold sleeve)	15

TOKYO OLYMPICS
83	Ritz 031	Shot By Love (Part 1)/(Part 2) (p/s)	5
83	Ritz 12 031	Shot By Love (Part 1)/(Part 2) (12", p/s)	8
83	Ritz 050	Radio (Turns Her On)/(Mix Version) (p/s)	5
83	Ritz 12 050	Radio (Turns Her On)/(Mix Version) (12", p/s)	8
83	Polydor 2078 143	One Step From Paradise/Paradise Disco Mix (p/s, Ireland-only)	5
82	Polydor 2908 046	RADIO (LP, Ireland-only, produced by Francis Rossi & Bernie Frost)	12

(see also Rossi & Frost)

TOKYO ROSE
83	Guardian GRC 270	Dry Your Eyes/This Is Tokyo Rose (p/s)	120

ISRAEL 'POPPER STOPPER' TOLBERT
70	Stax STAX 157	Big Leg Woman/I Got Love	7
71	Stax 2362 020	POPPER STOPPER (LP)	18

TOLL
86	Broken Flag BF V7	CHRIST KNOWS (LP, featuring Tim Gane)	20

(see also Ramleh, McCarthy)

GARY DALE TOLLETT & THE CRICKETS
01	Rollercoaster RRCT 1001	Go Boy Go/Gone (78 rpm, 250 only)	15

TOM & JERRIO
65	HMV POP 1435	Boo-Ga-Loo/Boomerang	30

TOM & JERRY
59	Gala GSP 806	Baby Talk/PAUL SHELDON: Thank You Pretty Baby (picture labels)	45
63	Pye International 7N 25202	I'm Lonesome/Looking At You	95

(see also Simon & Garfunkel)

TOM & JERRY (CARTOON CHARACTERS)
58	MGM MGM-EP 688	JOHANN MOUSE (EP)	15

TOM & MICK
69	Olga OLE 014	Somebody's Taken Maria Away/Pandemonium	15

TOM CATS
61	Starlite ST45 054	Tom Tom Cat/Big Brother	25

TOMCATS
97	Essex ESSEX 1018LP	THE TOMCATS (LP, with bonus 7": "Seventh Son"/"Walking"/"You Gotta Help"/Looking For My Baby by Second Thoughts [10187])	12

(see also July)

GARY TOMS EMPIRE
75	Epic S EPC 3611	Drive My Car/Love Me Right	12

TOMITA
77	RCA Red Seal RL1 1919	THE TOMITA PLANETS SUITE (LP, withdrawn after 1 day)	15

LEE TOMLIN
66	CBS 202455	Sweet Sweet Lovin'/Save Me	10

ALAN TOMLINSON
81	Bead Records BEAD 17	STILL OUTSIDE (LP)	25

ALBERT TOMLINSON
68	Giant GN 28	Don't Wait For Me/LLOYD EVANS: Losing You	150

ROY TOMLINSON
68	Coxsone CS 7056	I Stand For I/MARTIN: I Second That Emotion (actually by Martin Riley)	120

TOMMI & THE SPELLBINDERS
76	Target TQT 107	I Can't Get Away From You/Love Bandit	10

TOMMY (COWAN)
72	Dynamic DYN 433	Geraldine/Reverend Leroy	5

(see also Jamaicans)

TOMMY (MCCOOK) & UPSETTERS
69	Trojan TR 7717	Lock Jaw (actually by Dave Barker)/YARDBROOMS: My Desire	15

(see also Tommy McCook, Upsetters)

TOMORROW
67	Parlophone R 5597	My White Bicycle/Claramont Lake	60
67	Parlophone R 5627	Revolution/Three Jolly Little Dwarfs	70
69	Parlophone R 5813	My White Bicycle/Claramont Lake (reissue)	50
68	Parlophone PMC	TOMORROW (LP, mono, yellow/black label with "Sold in U.K..." text)	250
68	Parlophone PCS 7042	TOMORROW (LP, stereo, yellow/black label with "Sold in U.K..." text)	175
76	Harvest SHSP 2010	TOMORROW (LP, reissue)	25

(see also Keith West, Steve Howe, Twink, Four + One, In Crowd, Syndicats, Aquarian Age, Fairies, Bodast)

TOMORROW COME SOME DAY
69	SNB 97	TOMORROW COME SOME DAY (LP)	500

(see also Ithaca, Friends, Agincourt, Alice Through The Looking Glass, BBC Radiophonic Workshop/Peter Howell)

TOMORROW'S CHILDREN
70	Plexium PXM 17	You're My Baby/Maybe Today	5
71	Plexium PXM 25	Sing A Song/Don't Believe	5
71	Plexium PXM 26	Keep A Little Love In Your Life/My Way Of Living	5
72	Plexium PXM 31	We Can Make Funtime/If It Could Be	5

TOMORROW'S CHILDREN (JAMAICA)
67	Island WI 3073	Bang Bang Rock Steady/Rain Rock Steady (some w/same label on both sides)	150

TOMPALL & GLASER BROTHERS
68	MGM MGM-C 8082	THROUGH THE EYES OF LOVE (LP)	25

TOM TOM CLUB
81	Island ILPS 9686	TOM TOM CLUB (LP)	20

(see also Talking Heads)

TONE DEAF & THE IDIOTS
80s	Lyntone BLI 1/Angel BL 12	Why Does Politics Turn Men Into Toads/Repatriate The National Front (flexi)	10

(see also Idiots)

ELEANOR TONER
65	Decca F 12119	All Cried Out/A Hundred Guitars	8
65	Decca F 12192	Will You Still Love Me Tomorrow/Between The Window And The Phone	15
65	Decca F 12267	Danny Boy/It Hurts So Much (To See You Go)	6
66	Decca F 12454	Black Rose/Time To Spare Darling	6

TONES ON TAIL
82	4AD BAD 203	A Bigger Splash/Means Of Escape/Copper/Instrumental (12", p/s)	10

(see also Bauhaus, Love & Rockets)

TONETTES
62	Island WI 064	Love That Is Real/Pretty Baby	12

(see also Marlene Webber, Lyrics, Don Drummond)

OSCAR TONEY JR.
67	Stateside SS 2033	For Your Precious Love/Ain't That True Love	20
67	Stateside SS 2033	For Your Precious Love/Ain't That True Love (DJ Copy)	50
67	Stateside SS 2046	Turn On Your Love Light/Any Day Now	20
67	Stateside SS 2061	You Can Lead Your Woman To The Altar/Unlucky Guy	20
68	Bell BLL 1003	Without Love There Is Nothing/Love That Never Grows Cold	10
68	Bell BLL 1011	No Sad Songs/Never Get Enough Of Your Love	10
69	Bell BLL 1057	Down In Texas/Just For You	10
72	Capricorn K 17505	Thank You, Honey Chile/I Do What You Wish	6
73	Contempo C 6	Kentucky Bluebird/Everything I Own	6
73	Contempo CS2075	Chicken Heads/Everybody's Needed	15
74	Contempo CS 2002	Is It Because I'm Black/Make It Easy On Yourself	10
75	Contempo CS 2043	I've Been Loving You Too Long/For Your Precious Love	6
67	Stateside (S)SL 10211	FOR YOUR PRECIOUS LOVE (LP)	40

TONGUE & GROOVE
69	Fontana STL 5528	TONGUE & GROOVE (LP)	45

(see also Charlatans)

TONIGHT
78	TDS 1	Drummerman/Stroll On By (p/s)	8
78	TDS 2	Money, That's Your Problem/No Sympathy (p/s)	5
78	TDS 4	Wheels/I Can Play Faster Than You Can (p/s)	5
78	TDS 5	Jealousy Kills/Second Hand Man	5

(see also Andy Arthurs, Celia & Mutations)

TERRY TONIK
80	Posh TOFF 1	Just A Little Mod/Smashed And Blocked (some with die-cut p/s)	110
80	Posh TOFF 1	Just A Little Mod/Smashed And Blocked (with die-cut p/s, promo A4 booklet)	70
80	Posh TOFF 1	Just A Little Mod/Smashed And Blocked)	30

TONTO
74	Polydor 2383 308	IT'S ABOUT TIME (LP)	12

(see also Tonto's Expanding Head Band)

TONTON (MACOUTE)
72	RCA 2190	Summer Of Our Love/Greyhound Lady (as Tonton)	20
71	RCA Neon NE 4	TONTON MACOUTE (LP, gatefold sleeve, black inner)	250

MINT VALUE £

TONTO'S EXPANDING HEAD BANDO

71 Atlantic 2400 150 ZERO TIME (LP, gatefold sleeve) 18
(see also Tonto)

TONY & CHAMPIONS

70 Duke DU 90 Eye For An Eye/CHAMPIONS: Broke My Heart - Version 6
(see also Errol & Champions, Domino Johnson)

TONY & DENNIS

67 Trojan TR 002 Folk Song/TOMMY McCOOK & SUPERSONICS: Starry Night 35

TONY FIELD

66 Pye 7N 17020 Dale Ann/Dial My Number..10

TONY & GRADUATES

60s Hit HIT 13 The Statue 50
68 Pye 7N 17578 I Wanna Live/Angel...10
66 Pye 7N 17077 Just My Baby And Me/Another You 10

TONY & HIPPY BOYS

69 Gas GAS 121 Janet/HARMONIANS: Believe Me 20

TONY & HOWARD WITH DICTATORS

65 Oriole CB 307 Just In Case/Walk Right Out Of The Blues...30

TONY & HOWIE

72 Banana BA 371 Fun It Up/Fun Version 65

TONY & JOE

58 London HLN 8694 The Freeze/Gonna Get A Little Kissin' Tonight 45
58 London HLN 8694 The Freeze/Gonna Get A Little Kissin' Tonight (78) 25

TONY (TOMAS) & LOUISE

62 Island WI 059 Ups And Downs/TONY TOMAS: Brixton Lewisham 12
(see also Tony Washington)

TONY & TANDY

69 Atlantic 584 262 Two Can Make It Together/The Bitter And The Sweet (with Fleur De Lys) 20
71 Atlantic 2091 075 Two Can Make It Together/Look And Find 8
(see also Sharon Tandy, Fleur De Lys)

TONY & THE VELVETS

63 Decca F 11637 Sunday/One More Once 10

TONY & TYRONE

70 Ember EMBS 290 Everyday Fun/Whip Your Loving On Me (p/s) 10

TONY, CARO & JOHN

72 private pressing ALL ON THE FIRST DAY (LP, with insert)..300

TONY'S ALLSTARS

72 Green Door GD 4041 Rub Up A Daughter/DENNIS ALCAPONE: Daughter Version 15
72 Bullet BU 509 Dub Up A Daughter (as Prince Tony's Allstars)/ DENNIS ALCAPONE: Daughter Version 8
72 Big Shot BI 601 Must Care/L. SPARKS: You Don't Care...6
73 Downtown DT 508 You Don't Say/DENNIS ALCAPONE: Version 12

TONY'S DEFENDERS

66 Columbia DB 7850 Yes I Do/It's Easy To Say Hello 35
66 Columbia DB 7996 Since I Lost You Baby/Waiting For A Call From You 35
(see also Mike Stuart Span)

TOO FUNK

95 Ferox FER 008 THE RETURN OF TOO FUNK (12" EP)..15
95 Ferox FER 011 STORM THE FUNK (12" EP, plain sleeve) 8
96 Ferox FER 024 HOTEL IBIS (12" EP) 8

TOOL

94 Zoo-RCA 74321 19432-1 Prison Sex (LP Version)/Prison Sex (Edit Version)/Opiate (Live)/Undertow (Live) (12", grey vinyl) 30

TOOLS

79 Oily SLICK 2 Gotta Make Some Money Somehow/TV Eyes (p/s) 8

TOOMORROW

70 RCA RCA 1978 You're My Baby Now/Goin' Back (in custom RCA sleeve)....................................60
70 Decca F 13070 I Could Never Live Without Your Love/Roll Like A River 60
70 RCA LSA 3008 TOOMORROW (LP, soundtrack, with insert) 80
(see also Olivia Newton-John)

TOO MUCH

78 Lightning GIL 513 Who You Wanna Be/Another Time Another Place (in p/s).................................35
78 Lightning GIL 513 Who You Wanna Be/Another Time Another Place...10
78 Lightning GIL 552 Kick Me One More Time//Be Mine/It's Only For Me (p/s)...............................25

DAVID TOOP

75 Obscure OBS 48 NEW AND REDISCOVERED MUSICAL INSTRUMENTS (LP, with Max Eastley & Brian Eno) 25
79 Quartz 003 WOUNDS (LP, with Paul Burwell) 30
(see also Brian Eno)

TOOTS (ACTUALLY LEE PERRY)

70 Upsetter US 327 Do You Like It/UPSETTERS: Touch Of Fire..12

TOPO D. BILL

70 Charisma CB 116 Witchi Tai To/Jam (in p/s) 20
70 Charisma CB 116 Witchi Tai To/Jam...7
(see also Bonzo Dog [Doo Dah] Band, Roger Ruskin Spear)

TOPPERS

57 Brunswick 05678 Stash Pandowski (She's Not Very Much Good For Pretty)/Pots And Pans......................6

TOPPICKS

78 Basilick BVK 001 Can't Let You Go/Version 10

TOP SECRET
81	Cheapskate CHEAP 35	She's So Ugly/I Love Me (no p/s)	5

TOP TOPHAM
69	Blue Horizon 57-3167	Christmas Cracker/Cracking Up Over Christmas	25
70	Blue Horizon 7-63857	ASCENSION HEIGHTS (LP)	90

(see also Fox, Yardbirds)

TORA TORA
80	Mancunian Metal TT 5000	Red Sun Setting/Highway (Shooting Like A Bullet) (p/s)	15
80	Tora TT 5001	Don't Want To Let You Go/Sorry I Broke Your Heart	40

STEVE TORCH
70s	Redball RR 005	Live In Fear/Smoke Your Own (p/s)	5

(see also Gillan, Split Knee Loons, Girl)

(BERNIE) TORMÉ (BAND)
78	Jet JET 126	I'm Not Ready/Free (p/s, as Bernie Tormé Band, orange vinyl)	6
78	Jet JET 126	I'm Not Ready/Free (p/s, as Bernie Tormé Band, black vinyl)	5
79	Jet JET 137	Weekend/Secret Service/All Night/Instant Impact (as Bernie Tormé Band, p/s)	5
70s	Peter Collins PC 1	The Hunter/Soul Sister	8
80	Island WIP 6586	The Beat/I Want/Bony Maronie (p/s, pink vinyl, promos on black vinyl)	8
81	Fresh FRESH 7	All Day And All Of The Night/What's Next (p/s, also listed as Parole PURL 5)	12
82	Kamaflage KAMLP 2	TURN OUT THE LIGHTS (LP, white vinyl)	12
85	Zebra ZEB6	BACK WITH THE BOYS (LP, red vinyl)	12
87	Heavy Metal HMRLP94	DIE PRETTY DIE YOUNG (LP + bonus 12", stickered sleeve)	12

MEL TORME (& MEL-TONES)
SINGLES
56	Vogue Coral Q 72150	Mountain Greenery/Jeepers Creepers	10
56	Vogue Coral Q 72159	Blue Moon/That Old Black Magic	5
56	Vogue Coral Q 72185	Love Is Here To Stay/Goody Goody	5
56	London HLN 8305	Lulu's Back In Town/The Lady Is A Tramp	10
56	London HLN 8322	Lullaby Of Birdland/I Love To Watch The Moonlight	7
56	Vogue Coral Q 72202	All Of You/It Don't Mean A Thing	5
56	Decca F 10800	Walkin' Shoes/The Cuckoo In The Clock (with Ted Heath & His Music)	5
56	Decca F 10809	Waltz For Young Lovers/I Don't Want To Walk Without You	5
57	Vogue Coral Q 72217	My Rosemarie/How (as Mel Torme & Mel-Tones)	5
60	Philips PB 1045	The White Cliffs Of Dover/I've Got A Lovely Bunch Of Coconuts	5
61	HMV POP 859	Blue Moon/The Moon Song	5
61	MGM MGM 1144	The Christmas Song/Shine On Your Shoes	5
62	London HLK 9643	Comin' Home Baby/Right Now	20
62	London HLK 9643	Comin' Home Baby/Right Now (DJ copy)	40
64	Verve VS 505	Yes Indeed!/Her Face	5
66	CBS 202065	(You Got) The Power Of Love/Dominique's Discotheque	8

EPs
56	Decca DFE 6384	WALKIN' SHOES (EP)	8
56	MGM MGM-EP 562	VOICE IN VELVET (EP)	8
57	MGM MGM-EP 591	VOICE IN VELVET NO. 2 (EP)	8
58	Philips BBE 12181	TORME MEETS THE BRITISH (EP)	12

ALBUMS
55	Vogue Coral LVA 9004	MEL TORME AT THE CRESCENDO	12
56	Vogue Coral LVA 9032	MUSICAL SOUNDS ARE THE BEST SONGS	12
56	London Jazz LTZ-N 15009	MEL TORME AND THE MARTY PAICH "DEK-TETTE"	12
56	London HA-N 2016	IT'S A BLUE WORLD	12
57	London Jazz LTZ-N 15076	MEL TORME SINGS FRED ASTAIRE	12
57	Philips BBL 7205	TORME MEETS THE BRITISH	20
58	HMV CLP 1238	MEL TORME	12
59	Parlophone PMC 1096	GENE NORMAN PRESENTS MEL TORME AT THE CRESCENDO	12
60	Parlophone PMC 1114	SONGS FOR ANY TASTE	12
60	HMV CLP 1315	OLÉ TORMÉ (with Billy May)	12
60	HMV CLP 1382	BACK IN TOWN (with Mel-Tones)	12
60	HMV CLP 1405/CSD 1330	SWINGS SCHUBERT ALLEY (with Marty Paich Orch., mono/stereo)	12
61	HMV CLP 1449/CSD 1349	SWINGIN' ON THE MOON (mono/stereo)	12
62	HMV CLP 1584/CSD 1442	MY KIND OF MUSIC (mono/stereo)	12
63	London HA-K/SH-K 8021	MEL TORME AT THE RED HILL (with Jimmy Wisner Trio, mono/stereo)	15
63	London HA-K 8065	COMIN' HOME BABY	25
60s	Atlantic 590008	RIGHT NOW (LP)	12
66	CBS 62809	RIGHT NOW (LP)	12

TORNADOS
62	Decca F 11449	Love And Fury/Popeye Twist	15
62	Decca F 11494	Telstar/Jungle Fever	5
63	Decca F 11562	Globetrotter/Locomotion With Me (some B-sides credit "Locomotion With You")	6
63	Decca F 11606	Robot/Life On Venus	8
63	Decca F 11662	The Ice Cream Man/Theme From "The Scales Of Justice"	8
63	Decca F 11745	Dragonfly/Hymn For Teenagers	12
64	Decca F 11838	Hot Pot/Joystick	10
64	Decca F 11889	Monte Carlo/Blue Blue Beat	20
64	Decca F 11946	Exodus/Blackpool Rock	20
65	Columbia DB 7455	Granada/Ragunboneman	25
65	Columbia DB 7589	Early Bird/Stompin' Through The Rye (as Tornados '65)	25
65	Columbia DB 7687	Stingray/Aqua Marina	50
66	Columbia DB 7856	Pop-Art Goes Mozart/Too Much In Love To Hear	40
66	Columbia DB 7984	Is That A Ship I Hear/Do You Come Here Often	50
62	Decca DFE 8510	THE SOUNDS OF THE TORNADOS (EP)	20
62	Decca DFE 8511	TELSTAR (EP)	20
63	Decca DFE 8521	MORE SOUNDS FROM THE TORNADOS (EP)	30
63	Decca DFE 8533	TORNADO ROCK (EP)	40
63	Decca LK 4552	AWAY FROM IT ALL (LP)	50
72	Decca SPA 253	THE WORLD OF THE TORNADOS (LP)	12

MINT VALUE £

| 76 | Decca REM 4 | REMEMBERING...THE TORNADOS (LP) | 12 |

(see also Heinz, Billy Fury, Clem Cattini Ork, Saints, Original Tornados, Roger LaVern & Microns, Saxons, George Bellamy, Gemini, Roger La Vern & Microns)

MITCHELL TOROK
54	London HL 8004	Caribbean/Weep Away (with Louisiana Hayride Band) (gold tri label)	40
54	London HL 8004	Caribbean/Weep Away (with Louisiana Hayride Band) (round centre)	20
54	London HL 8048	Hootchy Kootchy Henry (From Hawaii)/Gigolo	50
54	London HL 8083	The Haunting Waterfall/Dancerette (with Louisiana Hayride Band)	50
55	Brunswick 05423	The World Keeps Turning Around/A Peasant's Guitar	15
56	Brunswick 05586	When Mexico Gave Up The Rhumba/I Wish I Was A Little Bit Younger	25
56	Brunswick 05626	Red Light, Green Light (with Tulane Sisters)/Havana Huddle	25
57	Brunswick 05642	Drink Up And Go Home/Take This Heart	15
57	Brunswick 05657	Pledge Of Love/What's Behind That Strange Door	15
57	Brunswick 05718	Two Words (True Love)/You're Tempting Me (with Anita Kerr Quartet)	10
60	London HLW 9130	Pink Chiffon/What You Don't Know (Won't Hurt You)	12
54	London RE-P 1014	LOUISIANA HAYRIDE (EP, with Louisiana Hayride Band)	40
60	London HA-W 2279	CARIBBEAN (LP)	50

TORPEDO (& THE CARIBBEANS)
| 55 | Parlophone MP 143 | Montego Bay/Lazy Jane (export 78) | 10 |
| 56 | Parlophone MP 148 | Pretty Woman/War Man Power Man (export 78) | 10 |

MICHELLE TORR
| 66 | Fontana TF 676 | Only Tears Are Left For Me/I Love That Man | 15 |
| 77 | Sonet SON 2104 | I'm Just A Simple Country Girl From France/Une Petite Française (p/s) | 5 |

DONALD TORR
| 69 | CBS 4383 | My Cherie Amour/Never Will I Be | 20 |
| 70 | CBS 4769 | Way Of The World/Green Green Yesterday | 10 |

GEORGE TORRENCE & NATURALS
| 68 | London HLZ 10181 | Lickin' Stick/So Long Goodbye | 15 |
| 71 | Jay Boy BOY 48 | Lickin' Stick/So Long Goodbye (reissue) | 6 |

CLARE TORRY
67	Fontana TF 852	The Music Attracts Me/It Takes One To Make The Other Cry (as Claire Terry)	6
67	Fontana TF 878	Unsure Feelings/The End Of A Lifetime (as Claire Terry)	6
69	Decca F 12945	Love For Living/Love Tomorrow, Love Today (as Clare Torry)	6

TORTOISE
96	Duophonic D-UHF-D 12	Yaus/STEREOLAB: Speedy Car (gig freebie, blue vinyl, p/s, 3,000 only)	20
96	Duophonic D-UHF-D 12	Yaus/STEREOLAB: Speedy Car (orange vinyl export issue, p/s, 3,000 only)	20
01	Duophonic Super 45s DS 33 09	Gamera/Cliff Dweller Society (12", 1500 on red vinyl, 1500 on clear vinyl, 1500 on black vinyl)	20
01	Duophonic Super 45s DS 33 09	Gamera/Cliff Dweller Society (12", 1000 on fluorescent yellow vinyl)	25
96	City Slang EFA 04971	RHYTHMS, RESOLUTIONS & CLUSTERS (LP, clear vinyl)	30
00	Warp WARPLP 81	STANDARDS (LP)	25

(see also Sea & Cake)

TORTURE
| 81 | Wildebeest WILD 1 | Last Post/Lucky/Finding My Way Home | 50 |

PETER TOSH
69	Unity UN 525	The Return Of Al Capone/LENNEX BROWN: O Club (B-side actually by Lennon Brown)	25
69	Unity UN 529	Sun Valley (as Peter Touch)/HE(A)DLEY BENNETT: Drums Of Fu Manchu	25
70	No label T 1023	No Sympathy/Boy Named Tom (actually Soulettes) (white label only)	40
71	Bullet BU 486	Maga Dog/THIRD & FOURTH GENERATION: Bull Dog	12
72	Pressure Beat PR 5509	Them A Fe Get A Beatin' (as Peter Touch)/ THIRD & FOURTH GENERATION: Version	18
79	Rolling Stones RSR 103	I'm The Toughest/Toughest Version (p/s)	5
79	Rolling Stones RSR 104	Buck In Hamm Palace/The Day The Dollar Die	5
76	Virgin V 2061	LEGALIZE IT (LP)	15
77	Virgin V 2081	EQUAL RIGHTS (LP, red "mirror" girl sleeve)	15

(see also Peter Touch, Bob Marley & Wailers, Cat & Nicky Campbell, Glen Adams)

TOTAL CHAOS
82	Volume VOL 1	There Are No Russians In Afghanistan/Primitive Feeling/ Revolution Part 10 (p/s, lyric insert, original copies have "50p" onl front)	20
83	Volume VOL 2	Factory Man/Brixton Prison/She Don't Care/Die (p/s)	7
83	Volume VOLM 6	FIELDS AND BOMBS EP(12")	15

TOTAL CONTRAST
| 84 | Total Contrast TCR 2 | Next Time I'll Know Better/Sunshine (12") | 35 |

TOTAL FIASCO
| 89 | White TF001 | See How They Run/Method To The Madness | 120 |

(see also Killa Instinct)

TOTAL OUTPUT AND KILLERHERTZ
| 92 | FX FXUKT 11 | Acid Mind/Monolithic/Analog Xpression/Digital Kiss (12") | 12 |

(see also Killerhertz)

TOTALLY OUTTA HAND BAND
| 78 | Kilgaron KIL 1 | Teenage Revolution/Too Much Trouble By Far (p/s) | 8 |

TO THE FINLAND STATION
| 81 | Melodia | DOMINO THEORY (7" EP) | 6 |

TOTNAMITES
| 61 | Oriole CB 1615 | Danny Boy/The Spurs Song | 15 |

TOTO
78	CBS S 11-6784	Hold The Line/Takin' It Back (picture disc)	5
82	CBS A 11-2079	Rosanna/It's A Feeling (picture disc)	5
82	CBS A 11-2510	Africa/We Made It (Africa-shaped picture disc)	6
83	CBS A 11-3392	I Won't Hold You Back/Afraid Of Love (picture disc)	5
84	Polydor 422 8237-7	DUNE (LP, soundtrack, 1 track by Brian Eno)	15

TOTS
74	Philips 6006 408	Please Yourself/Time To Go Home (p/s)	7

TINA TOTT
69	Pye 7N 17823	Take Away The Emptiness Too/Burning In The Background Of My Mind	30

TOTTENHAM HOTSPUR F.C.
67	Columbia SEG 8532	THE SPURS GO MARCHING ON: SINGALONG SPURS (EP)	20

(see also Terry Venables)

DAVE TOTTERDELL
77	Cottage COT 711	WHITBY BELLS (LP)	20

PETER TOUCH
65	Island WI 211	Hoot Nanny Hoot (actually by Peter Tosh & Wailers)/ BOB MARLEY: Do You Remember (actually by Peter Tosh & Wailers)	100
65	Island WI 215	Shame And Scandal (with Wailers)/WAILERS: The Jerk	60
67	Island WI 3042	I Am The Toughest (actually by Peter Tosh & Wailers)/ MARCIA GRIFFITHS: No Faith	60
67	Coxsone CS 7012	Dancing Time/Treat Me Good	150
69	Jackpot JP 706	The Crimson Pirate/Moon Duck	20
69	Unity UN 525	Return Of A Capone/LENEX BROWN : Q Club	25
69	Unity 529	Sun Valley/Headley Bennett - Drums Of Fu Man Chu	20

(see also Peter Tosh, Bop & The Beltone, Glen Adams)

TOUCH (1)
69	Deram DM 243	Miss Teach/We Feel Fine	12
69	Deram DML/SML 1033	THIS IS TOUCH (LP, with poster)	150
69	Deram DML/SML 1033	THIS IS TOUCH (LP, without poster)	65

(see also Don & Goodtimes, Kingsmen)

TOUCH (2)
80	Ariola ARO 209	When The Spirit Moves You/My Life Depends On You (p/s)	5
80	Ariola ARO 243	Don't You Know What Love Is/My Life Depends On You (in p/s)	20
80	Ariola ARO 243	Don't You Know What Love Is/My Life Depends On You	6
80	Ariola ARO 250	Love Don't Fail Me Now (p/s)	6
80	Ariola ARL 5036	TOUCH (LP)	12

TOUCH (3)
88	Touch T7:45	Departing Platform 5/Touch Ritual (Radio Cut-Up) (p/s)	5

TOUCHDOWN
83	Record Shack	Ease Your Mind (Remix)/Aquadance (12")	15

ALI FARKA TOURE
87	World Circuit WCB 007	ALI FARKA TOURE (LP)	20
94	World Circuit WCB 040	TALKING TIMBUKTU (LP)	25

TOURS
79	Tours T 1	Language School/Foreign Girls (paper p/s)	15
79	Tours T 1	Language School/Foreign Girls (printed PVC sleeve)	12
79	Virgin VS 307	Tourist Information/You Knew (p/s)	6

AL TOUSAN
61	London HLU 9291	Naomi/Indinna (some copies miscredited to 'Al Pousan')	8

(see also Allen Toussaint)

ALLEN TOUSSAINT
69	Soul City SC 119	We The People/Tequila	25
72	Reprise K 14200	Soul Sister/She Once Belonged To Me	6
72	Reprise K 44202	LIFE, LOVE AND FAITH (LP)	22
75	Reprise K 54021	SOUTHERN NIGHTS (LP)	12
85	Kent KENT 036	FROM A WHISPER TO A SCREAM (LP)	15

(see also Al Tousan)

CALINE & OLIVER TOUSSAINT
78	Epic S EPC 6334	The Gardens Of Monaco/Les Jardins De Monaco	12

ROBERTA TOVEY
65	Polydor BM 56021	Who's Who/Not So Old (in p/s)	45
65	Polydor BM 56021	Who's Who/Not So Old	25

TOWER OF POWER
73	Reprise K 16278	So Very Hard To Go/Clean Slate	8
73	Reprise K 16211	You're Still A Young Man/Skating On Thin Ice	8
74	Reprise K 16389	Don't Change Horses/Time Will Tell	5
75	Reprise K 16543	It's Not The Crime/Only So Much Time On The Ground	8

JOHNNY TOWERS
62	Philips 326554 BF	The Lonely Man Theme/There's No Place Like Rome	8
63	Philips 326570 BF	This Kind Of Love/My First Romance	7

COLIN TOWNS
78	Virgin VS 204	Full Circle (Main Theme)/Olivia (p/s)	10
80	MCA MCA 643	Breakdown/Working Man (p/s)	15
78	Virgin V 2093	FULL CIRCLE (LP, soundtrack)	12

(see also Gillan, Samson, Split Knee Loons)

TOWNSEL SISTERS
60	Polydor NH 66954	Will I Ever/I Know	12

DEVIN TOWNSEND
98	USG/East West USG 1028-4	Christeen/Wild Colonial Boy/Night (CD, withdrawn)	12

(see also Wildhearts)

ED TOWNSEND (& TOWNSMEN)
58	Capitol CL 14867	For Your Love/Over And Over Again	10
58	Capitol CL 14927	When I Grow Too Old To Dream/You Are My Everything	10
59	Capitol CL 14976	Richer Than I/Getting By Without You	7
59	Capitol CL 15020	Don't Ever Leave Me/Lover Come Back To Me	7
59	Capitol CL 15072	This Little Love Of Mine/Hold On	7

60	Capitol CL 15141	Don't Get Around Much Anymore/Do Nothin' Till You Hear	7
60	Warner Bros WB 21	Stay With Me (A Little While Longer)/I Love Everything About You	40
59	Capitol EAP1 1091	ED TOWNSEND (EP)	20
59	Capitol T 1140	NEW IN TOWN (LP)	25
76	Curtom K 56180	NOW (LP)	20

JOHN TOWNSEND

| 70s | Sweet Folk All SFA 002 | NO MUCKING ABOUT (LP) | 18 |

PETE TOWNSHEND

80	Atco K 11486	Let My Love Open The Door/Classified/Greyhound Girl (p/s, with sticker)	5
82	Atco K 11751P	Uniforms/Dance It All Away (picture disc)	5
82	Atco K 11751PT	Uniforms/Dance It All Away (12", picture disc)	8
82	Eva-Tone 623827XS	My Generation/Pinball Wizard (U.S. square flexidisc sewn into U.K. copies of Richard Barnes' Maximum R&B book; with book)	20
89	Virgin VSCD 1198	A Friend is A Friend (3.30)/Man Machines (Extended Mix)/Real World (Can You Really Dance?)/A Friend is A Friend (Album Version 4.45) (3" CD, card p/s)	10
89	Virgin VSCD 1209	I Won't Run Anymore/A Fool Says/Dig (Original Demo Version Recorded November 1987) (3" CD, card sleeve)	10
72	Track 2408 201	WHO CAME FIRST (LP, gatefold sleeve with poster)	25
72	Track 2408 201	WHO CAME FIRST (LP, laminated gatefold sleeve without poster)	15

(see also The Who, Meher Baba, Billy Nicholls, Elton John)

PETE TOWNSHEND & RONNIE LANE

77	Polydor 2058 944	Street In The City/RONNIE LANE: Annie (limited issue)	20
77	Polydor 2058 944	Street In The City/RONNIE LANE: Annie (12", p/s)	12
77	Polydor 2442 147	ROUGH MIX (LP, gatefold sleeve)	12

(see also Who, Ronnie Lane)

TOXIC

| 92 | D-Zone DANCE 26 | Simple Warnin' (Ruffneck Mix)/Simple Warnin' (Riffist Mix)/Simple Warnin' (Hi Power Version)Kik The Break (12", company sleeve) | 60 |

TOXIC EPHEX

| 89 | One Up | THE ADVENTURES OF NOBBY PORTHOLE - THE COCK OF THE NORTH (LP) | 20 |

TOXIC REASONS

| 84 | T-REASON HANG 1 | God Bless America/Can't Get Away/Destroyer (p/s) | 6 |
| 84 | Alt. Tentacles VIRUS 42 | KILL BY REMOTE CONTROL (LP) | 15 |

TOYAN

81	Greensleeves GREL 20	HOW THE WEST WAS WON (LP)	25
83	Vista STLP 1023	MURDER (LP, as Toyan with Tippa Lee)	45
83	Upfront UPFLP 11	DJ DADDY (LP)	15

TOY DOLLS

81	GBH SSM 005	Tommy Kowey's Car/She Goes To Finos (500 only)	60
81	GRC GRC 104	Tommy Kowey's Car/She's A Working Ticket/Everybody Jitterbug/ Teenager In Love/I've Got Asthma (yellow paper p/s, with insert)	60
82	Zonophone Z 31	Everybody Jitterbug/(She's A) Working Ticket (p/s)	30
83	Volume VOL 3	Nellie The Elephant/Dig That Groove Baby (p/s)	15
83	Volume VOL 5	Cheerio And Toodle Pip/H.O. (p/s)	10
83	Volume VOL 7	Alfie From The Bronx/Hanky Panky (p/s)	10
84	Volume VOL 10	We're Mad/Deirdre's A Slag (p/s)	6
84	Volume VOLT 10	We're Mad/Deirdre's A Slag/Rupert The Bear (12", p/s)	10
85	Volume VOL 12	She Goes To Fino's/Spiders In The Dressing Room (p/s)	5
85	Volume VOL 17	James Bond (Lives Down Our Street)/Olga... I cannot! (p/s)	8
85	Volume VOLT 17	James Bond (Lives Down Our Street)/Olga... I cannot! / Griefsville (12", p/s)	8
86	Volume VOL 21	Geordie's Gone To Jail/Idle Gossip (p/s)	8
82	WOWLP 1	THE TOY DOLLS ALBUM (LP)	15
84	Volume VOLP 1	DIG THAT GROOVE, BABY (LP)	15
85	Volume VOLP 2	A FAR OUT DISC (LP)	12
86	Volume VOLP 3	IDLE GOSSIP (LP)	12
94	Toy Dolls NIT 2	TEN YEARS OF TOYS (LP, with inner)	12

(see also Showbiz Kids)

TOY DOLLS (U.S.)

| 63 | London HLN 9647 | Little Tin Soldier/Fly Away | 30 |

TOYS

| 79 | SRT SRTS/79/CUS 345 | My Mind Wanders/The Girl On My Wall/Toytime/I'd Do Anything For You (p/s) | 10 |
| 79 | Toy TOYS 2 | STILL DANCING (EP, hand-stamped white label, foldaround p/s) | 20 |

TOYS

| 80 | Red Bus RBUS 54 | Go To The Police/Breakdown | 50 |

TOYS (U.S.)

65	Stateside SS 460	A Lover's Concerto/This Night	8
66	Stateside SS 483	Attack/See How They Run	8
66	Stateside SS 502	May My Heart Be Cast Into Stone/On Backstreet	20
66	Stateside SS 519	Silver Spoon/Can't Get Enough Of You Baby	22
66	Stateside SS 539	Baby Toys/Happy Birthday Broken Heart	10
67	Philips BF 1563	Ciao Baby/I Got Carried Away	10
67	Philips BF 1581	My Love Sonata/I Close My Eyes	10
69	Bell BLL 1053	A Lover's Concerto/Baby Toys	7
66	Stateside SL 10175	THE TOYS SING "A LOVER'S CONCERTO" AND "ATTACK" (LP, mono)	40
66	Stateside SSL 10175	THE TOYS SING "A LOVER'S CONCERTO" AND "ATTACK" (LP, stereo)	50

TOYSHOP

| 69 | Polydor 56317 | Say Goodbye To Yesterday/Send My Love To Lucy | 12 |

T.P.I.

| 79 | SRT SRTS 79 CUS 489 | She's Too Clever For Me/You Rool Me (no p/s, 1000 only) | 60 |

TRACE

| 74 | Vertigo 6360 852 | TRACE (LP) | 20 |
| 75 | Vertigo 6413 080 | BIRDS (LP) | 20 |

(see also Curved Air)

TRACER
83	Mouse Hole TRA 1	CHANNELLED AGGRESSION EP (p/s)	125

MARK TRACEY
62	Parlophone R 4944	Caravan Of Lonely Men/Never Ending (with John Barry & His Orchestra)	10

STAN TRACEY
58	Vogue LA 160130	STAN TRACEY SHOWCASE (LP)	70
59	Vogue LA 160155	LITTLE KLUNK (LP, as Stan Tracey Trio)	130
65	Columbia 33SX 1774	JAZZ SUITE (LP, as Stan Tracey Quartet, also stereo SCX 3589)	100
66	Columbia S(C)X 6051	ALICE IN JAZZLAND (LP, as Stan Tracey Big Band)	40
67	Columbia S(C)X 6124	STAN TRACEY... IN PERSON (LP)	40
68	Columbia S(C)X 6205	WITH LOVE FROM JAZZ (LP)	50
69	Ace Of Clubs ACL 1259	LITTLE KLUNK (LP, reissue)	30
69	Columbia S(C)X 6320	WE LOVE YOU MADLY (LP, as Stan Tracey Big Brass)	50
69	Columbia SCX 6358	THE LATIN AMERICAN CAPER (LP, with Big Brass & Woodwind)	40
70	Columbia SCX 6385	FREE AN' ONE (LP, as Stan Tracey Quartet)	70
70	Columbia SCX 6413	SEVEN AGES OF MAN (LP, as Stan Tracey Big Band)	35
72	Columbia SCX 6485	PERSPECTIVES (LP as Stan Tracey Trio)	40
74	Cadillac SGC 1003	ALONE AT WIGMORE HALL (LP)	15

(see also New Departures Quartet, Mike Osborne, Neil Ardley, Laurie Johnson)

ZEN TRACEY
62	Decca F 11492	Shamrocker (Phil The Fluter's Ball)/Two By Two	8

TRACK
66	Columbia DB 7987	Why Do Fools Fall In Love?/Cry To Me	18

TRACK 4
82	Track 4 TR4 001	Mr Charisma (p/s, with insert)	100

TRACTOR
72	Dandelion 2001 282	Stone Glory/Marie/As You Say	15
78	UK UK 93	Roll The Dice/Vicious Circle	8
81	Cargo CRS 002	No More Rock & Roll/Northern City	10
81	Roach RR 2	Average Man's Hero/Big Big Boy (p/s)	5
72	Dandelion 2310 217	TRACTOR (LP)	120

(see also Way We Live)

TRACY
66	Columbia DB 7802	Don't Hold It Against Me/These Four Walls	8
69	Columbia DB 8569	Life's Like That/Let Me Love You	7
69	Columbia DB 8637	Follow Me/A City Called Soul	12
71	Columbia DB 8750	Rock Me In The Cradle/Strange Love	10

ARTHUR TRACY
67	Decca F 12656	Marta/Wanderer	6

GRANT TRACY & SUNSETS
61	Ember EMB S 126	Say When/Please Baby Please	20
61	Ember EMB S 130	Pretend/Love Me	20
62	Ember EMB S 148	The Great Matchmaker/Tears Came Rolling Down	20
62	Ember EMB S 155	Taming Tigers/The Painted Smile	20
63	Decca F 11741	Everybody Shake/Turn The Lights Down, Jenny	20
64	Ember EMB 3352	TEENBEAT (LP)	80

(see also Pete Dello, Honeybus)

WENDALL TRACY
58	London HLM 8664	Who's To Know/Corrigidor Rock	15
58	London HLM 8664	Who's To Know/Corrigidor Rock (78)	10

TRADER HORNE
69	Pye 7N 17846	Morning Way/Sheena	40
70	Dawn DNS 1003	Here Comes The Rain/Goodbye Mercy Kelly	40
70	Dawn DNLS 3004	MORNING WAY (LP, gatefold, with photo & insert)	150
70	Dawn DNLS 3004	MORNING WAY (LP, gatefold, without photo & insert)	80

(see also Them, Fairport Convention, Jackie McAuley)

TRADEWINDS
59	RCA RCA 1141	Crossroads/Furry Murray	20
59	RCA RCA 1141	Crossroads/Furry Murray (78)	25

TRADE WINDS
65	Red Bird RB 10020	New York Is A Lonely Town/Club Seventeen	22
66	Kama Sutra KAS 202	Mind Excursion/Little Susan's Dreaming	20

TRAD GRADS (WITH LEN, HERB, KIKO & RICHARD)
61	Decca F 11403	Runnin' Shoes/Rag-Day Jazz-Band Ball	8

(see also Quarry Men)

TRADITION
76	Venture VEN 7705	Movin On/Movin Rocker	10
77	Venture VNLP 8877	MOVIN' ON (LP)	25
77	Venture CUT 6	IN DUB (LP)	45
78	RCA PL 25169	TELL YOUR FRIENDS ABOUT DUB (LP)	20
78	RAC PL 25186	ALTERNATIVE ROUTES (LP)	30

TRAFFIC
67	Island WIP 6002	Paper Sun/Giving To You (in p/s)	12
67	Island WIP 6002	Paper Sun/Giving To You	5
67	Island WIP 6017	Hole In My Shoe/Smiling Phases (in p/s)	12
67	Island WIP 6017	Hole In My Shoe/Smiling Phases	5
67	Island WIP 6025	Here We Go Round The Mulberry Bush/Coloured Rain (1st 100,000 in p/s)	15
67	Island WIP 6025	Here We Go Round The Mulberry Bush/Coloured Rain	12
68	Island WIP 6030	No Face, No Name, No Number/Roamin' In The Gloamin' With 40,000 Headmen	12
68	Island WIP 6041	You Can All Join In/Withering Tree (unissued in U.K.)	0
68	Island WIP 6041	Feelin' Alright/Withering Tree	10
68	Island WIP 6050	Medicated Goo/Shanghai Noodle Factory	10

MINT VALUE £

71	Island No Cat No	Welcome To The Canteen (promo 7" with blank labels in mini LP sleeve)	40
71	Island TIM 1	Gimme Some Lovin Part One (live)/Gimme Some Lovin Part Two (live) (p/s, white label only)	25
74	Island WIP 6207	Walking In The Wind/Walking In The Wind (Instrumental)	10
78	Island IEP 7	HOLE IN MY SHOE (EP, picture disc)	10
67	Island ILP 961	MR FANTASY (LP, gatefold sleeve internal flipbacks, 1st pressing pink label with black 'circle' logo, mono)	250
67	Island ILPS 9061	MR FANTASY (LP, gatefold sleeve internal flipbacks, 1st pressing pink label with black 'circle' logo, stereo)	200
68	Island ILPS 9081T	TRAFFIC (LP, gatefold sleeve with stapled-in booklet; pink label with black 'circle' logo)	120
68	Island ILPS 9081T	TRAFFIC (LP, gatefold sleeve with stapled-in booklet; pink rim label with 'palm tree' logo)	20
69	Island ILP(S) 9097	LAST EXIT (LP, pink label with black 'circle' logo)	120
69	Island ILP(S) 9097	LAST EXIT (LP, pink rim label with 'palm tree' logo)	20
69	Island ILP(S) 9112	THE BEST OF TRAFFIC (LP, 1st pressings with pink 'i' label)	30
69	Island ILP(S) 9112	THE BEST OF TRAFFIC (LP, subsequent pressings with pink rim label with 'palm tree' logo)	12
70	Island ILPS 9081	MR. FANTASY (LP, 2nd pressing, pink rim label with 'palm tree' logo)	20
70	Island ILPS 9116	JOHN BARLEYCORN MUST DIE (LP, gatefold sleeve, 1st pressings with pink 'i' label)	50
71	Island ILPS 9142	LIVE - NOVEMBER '70 (LP, unreleased, may exist as test pressing)	0
71	Island ILPS 9166	WELCOME TO THE CANTEEN (LP, 'sniped' spine edges, pink rim palm tree label)	20
71	Island ILPS 9180	THE LOW SPARK OF THE... (LP, laminated sleeve, pink rim/palm tree label)	20
73	Island ILPS 9224	SHOOT OUT AT THE FANTASY FACTORY (LP, pink rim/palm tree label)	15
73	Island ISLD 2	ON THE ROAD (2-LP, laminated gatefold sleeve)	18

(see also Spencer Davis Group, Stevie Winwood, Revolution, Hellions, Dave Mason, Gordon Jackson)

TRAFFIC JAM
67	Piccadilly 7N 35386	Almost But Not Quite There/Wait Just A Minute	275
67	Piccadilly 7N 35386	Almost But Not Quite There/Wait Just A Minute (demo copy)	300

(see also Status Quo, Spectres)

JIM TRAGAS
72	Buddah 2011 157	White Buffalo/Mama Took Me From The Jungle	6

TRAGEDY
10	Diggers With Gratitude DWG 009	THE BLACK RAGE DEMOS (EP, 175 only, black vinyl)	30
10	Diggers With Gratitude DWG 009	THE BLACK RAGE DEMOS (EP, 75 only, red vinyl)	80

TRAGICIAN
79	Look LKSP 6411	The Wild The Scared And The Timid/Traces Of Impact (numbered gatefold p/s)	35

PHIL TRAINER
73	BASF 05 19573-5	Beautiful Jim/No No No (p/s)	5
77	Splash CP17	Carousel/Rose Coloured Sky	8
73	BASF BAG 22 29107-3	TRAINER (LP, gatefold)	35

(see also Trees)

TRAIN SET
80s	Play Hard DEC 11	She's Gone (12", p/s)	35
80s	Play Hard DEC 17	Hold On (12", p/s)	35

TRAITOR
81	Airship APP 377	That's Life/Stone Cold Sober	100

TRAITOR'S GATE
85	Bullet BOLT 12	DEVIL TAKES THE HIGH ROAD (EP)	10

TRAITS
67	Pye International 7N 25404	Harlem Shuffle/Strange Lips (Start Ole Memories)	35

(see also Roy Head)

ALAN TRAJAN
69	MCA MK 5002	Speak To Me, Clarissa/This Might Be My Last Number	50
69	MCA MKPS 2000	FIRM ROOTS (LP, laminated front sleeve)	100

TRAMLINE
68	Island ILPS 9088	SOMEWHERE DOWN THE LINE (LP, pink label black/orange circle)	200
69	Island ILPS 9095	MOVES OF VEGETABLE CENTURIES (LP, pink label)	200

(see also Whitesnake)

BOBBY LEE TRAMMELL
64	Sue WI 326	New Dance In France/Carolyn	40

TRAMMY (RON WILSON)
72	Techniques TE 920	Horns Of Paradise/TECHNIQUES ALL STARS: Grass Root	30

TRAMP
69	Young Blood SBY 4	Vietnam Rose/Each Day	12
74	Spark SRL 1107	Put A Record On/You've Gotta Move	8
69	Music Man SMLS 603	TRAMP (LP, laminated front, flipbacks, white/black label)	150
73	Spark Replay SRLM 2001	TRAMP (LP, reissue)	30
74	Spark SRLP 112	PUT A RECORD ON (LP)	30

(see also Dave Kelly, Jo-Ann Kelly, Brunning Hall Sunflower Blues Band, Fleetwood Mac)o

TRAMWAY
91	Sarah SARAH 52	Technical College/Balla (p/s, insert)	12
91	Sarah SRH 43	Maritime City/Boathouse/Star (p/s, with insert)	10

TRANE
71	Penny Farthing PEN 773	Still Burning Bright/Misty Lady	5
71	BBC RESL 5	Wagoner's Walk/Jenny's Song/Ragged Bird/Mansion Of Cards (p/s)	15

TRANQUILITY
72	Epic EPC 64729	TRANQUILITY (LP, yellow label)	20
72	Epic EPC 65418	SILVER (LP, lyric insert, yellow label)	15

TRANS AM
95	Thrill Jockey THRILL 024	TRANS AM (LP)	15

TRANSATLANTICS

65	Fontana TF 593	Many Things From Your Window/I Tried To Forget	35
65	Fontana TF 638	Stand Up And Fight Like A Man/But I Know	20
65	Mercury MF 948	Don't Fight It/Look Before You Leap	50
65	King KG 1033	Run For Your Life/It's All Over	15
66	King KG 1040	Louie Go Home/Find Yourself Another Guy	30

TRANSCARGO

01	Trunk TTT 003	OH BOY (12" EP)	8

TRANSCRIPT CARRIERS

93	Transcript Carriers TC998	THE HAEMORRHOID FRY UP (EP)	8
93	Transcript Carriers TC999	ALL FEAR IS BONDAGE (EP)	10

TRANSIENT WAVES

98	Fat Cat 12FAT 011	Born With A Body And Fucked In The Heads/(2 Lone Swordsmen Mix)/ (Skye [Stasis] Mix) (12", custom embossed sleeve)	10

TRANSISTORS

81	Open Circuit	RIOT SQUAD (EP)	20

TRANSIT

09	Third Man TMR 012	Come On And Ride/After Party (100 only, luminous vinyl)	40

TRANSMISSION

84	PMP PMP 001	Mystery Lady/Bouncing Ball (12")	40

TRANSMITTERS

78	Ebony EYE 11	Party/0.5 Alive (p/s)	5
78	Ebony EYE 12	Nowhere Train/Uninvited Guest/Persons Unknown (die-cut p/s)	5
79	Step Forward SF 1212	The Ugly Man/The One That Won The War/Free Trade/Curious (12", p/s)	8
78	Ebony EBY 1002	24 HOURS (LP)	15
81	Heartbeat MB 4	AND WE CALL THIS LEISURE TIME (LP)	12

TRANSPARENT ILLUSION

81	Vortex VEX 001/002	Vortex/Nuclear Release (p/s)	20
82	Vortex VEX 5	Guilty Rich Men (p/s)	10
81	Vortex VEX 3	STILL HUMAN (LP)	35
82	Vortex VEX 4	CHAGRIN RECEIVER (LP)	20

TRANSPORTER

70s	Mother Truck MT 1	Kids On The Run/Intoxicating	6

TERRY TRANZ & THE VESTITES

81	Go Round TOUCH 1	State Hand Out/We Had It Here (2 different home-made sleeves)	100

TRAPEZE

69	Threshold TH 2	Send Me No More Letters/Another Day	10
72	Threshold TH 11	Coast To Coast/Your Love Is Alright	10
75	Warner Bros K 16606	Sunny Side Of The Street/Monkey	8
79	Aura AUS 114	Don't Ask Me How I Know/Take Good Care (p/s)	15
80	Aura AUS 116	Running Away/Don't Break My Heart (p/s)	15
69	Threshold THS 2	TRAPEZE (LP, gatefold sleeve)	60
70	Threshold THS 4	MEDUSA (LP)	50
73	Threshold THS 8	YOU ARE THE MUSIC ... WE'RE JUST THE BAND (LP)	20
74	Warner Bros K 56064	HOT WIRE (LP)	12
81	Aura AUL 717	LIVE IN TEXAS ... DEAD ARMADILLOS (LP)	12

(see also Finders Keepers, Montanas, Deep Purple, Glenn Hughes, Judas Priest, Whitesnake)

TRASH

69	Apple APPLE 6	Road To Nowhere/Illusions (initial copies as White Trash)	200
69	Apple APPLE 6	Road To Nowhere/Illusions (later copies as Trash)	60
69	Apple APPLE 17	Golden Slumbers - Carry That Weight/Trash Can	30

(see also Poets, Pathfinders)

TRASHCAN SINATRAS

89	Go! Discs GODX 34	Obscurity Knocks/The Best Man's Fall/Drunken Chorus/Who's He? (12", p/s)	12
89	Go! Discs GODCD 34	Obscurity Knocks/The Best Man's Fall/Drunken Chorus/Who's He? (CD)	12
90	Go! Discs GOD 41	Only Tongue/Useless Begins With You/Tonight You Belong To Me (p/s)	6
90	Go! Discs GODX 41	Only Tongue/Useless Begins With You/Tonight You Belong To Me (12", p/s)	10
90	Go! Discs GOD 46	Circling The Circumference/My Mistake (p/s)	8
90	Go! Discs GODX 46	Circling The Circumference/My Mistake (12", p/s)	12
93	Go! Discs GODX 98	Hayfever/Say/Kangaroo Court/Skin Diving (12", p/s)	8
93	Go! Discs GODCD 98	Hayfever/Say/Kangaroo Court/Skin Diving (CD, in box)	12
93	Go! Discs GOD 100	I've Seen Everything/Houseproud/I'm The One Who Fainted (p/s)	6
96	Go! Discs GOD 151	How Can I Apply?/Save Me (p/s)	6
90	Go! Discs 828 2011	CAKE (LP)	15

TRASHMEN

64	Stateside SS 255	Surfin' Bird/King Of The Surf	35
64	Stateside SS 276	Bird Dance Beat/A-Bone	35

TRAVELING WILBURYS

88	Warner Bros W 7732W	Handle With Care/Margarita (gatefold p/s with sticker, sealed)	10
88	Warner Bros W 7732W	Handle With Care/Margarita (gatefold p/s with sticker, unsealed)	8
88	Warner Bros W 7732TE	Handle With Care (Extended)/Margarita (10", p/s)	10
88	Warner Bros W 7732T	Handle With Care (Extended)/Margarita (12", p/s)	10
88	Warner Bros W 7732CD	Handle With Care (LP Version)/Margarita/Handle With Care (Extended Version) (3" CD, with adaptor, 5" case)	10
89	Warner Bros W 7637TW	End Of The Line (Extended)/Congratulations (12", p/s, with sheet of stickers)	15
89	Warner Bros W 7637TW	End Of The Line (Extended)/Congratulations (12", p/s, without sheet of stickers)	10
89	Warner Bros W 7637CD	End Of The Line (Extended Version)/Congratulations (3" CD, gatefold card p/s in PVC sleeve)	12
90	Warner Bros W 9773T	Nobody's Child/DAVE STEWART: Lumière/RINGO STARR: With A Little Help From My Friends (12", p/s)	12
90	Warner Bros W 9773CD	Nobody's Child/DAVE STEWART: Lumière/RINGO STARR: With A Little Help From My Friends (CD)	10
90	Warner Bros W 9523	She's My Baby/New Blue Moon (Instrumental Version) (p/s)	6
90	Warner Bros W 9523T	She's My Baby (LP Version)/New Blue Moon (Instrumental Version)/ Runaway (12", p/s)	10

90	Warner Bros W 9523CD	She's My Baby (LP Version)/New Blue Moon (Instrumental Version)/ Runaway (CD)..........10
91	Warner Bros W 0019	Wilbury Twist/New Blue Moon (Instrumental) (p/s) 6
91	Warner Bros W 0018W	Wilbury Twist/New Blue Moon (Instrumental) (card p/s with 4 postcards).....................15
91	Warner Bros W 0019T	Wilbury Twist/New Blue Moon (Instrumental)/Cool Dry Place (12", p/s)......................12
91	Warner Bros W 0019CD	Wilbury Twist/New Blue Moon (Instrumental)/Cool Dry Place (CD, silver or black print).....10
88	Warner Bros WX 224W	VOLUME ONE (LP, some with stickered sleeve & sticker inserts)...........................22
88	Warner Bros WX 224CD	VOLUME ONE (CD) 20
90	Warner Bros WX 7799-2 324-2	VOLUME THREE (CD) 20

(see also George Harrison, Bob Dylan, Roy Orbison, Jeff Lynne, Tom Petty)

TRAVELLERS
77	Paradise PDS 001	Jah Give Us The World (feat. U Brown)/Girl I Left Behind (12").........................15

TRAVELLING FOLK
70s	Cuchulainn CCHS 1017	TRAVELLING FOLK (LP) 15

MARY TRAVERS
72	Warner Bros K 16191	Morning Glory/That's Enough For Me 7

(See also Peter, Paul & Mary)

PAT TRAVERS
76	Polydor SFI 221/2814 040	Makes No Difference (1-sided flexidisc, promo only, black & white p/s) 10
77	Polydor Super 2383 436	MAKIN' MAGIC (LP with inner sleeve) 12
77	Polydor Super 2383 471	PUTTING IT STRAIGHT (LP) 12
79	Polydor POLS 1011	GO FOR WHAT YOU KNOW (LP, red vinyl) 12

(see also Nicko McBrain)

MERLE TRAVIS
53	Capitol CL45 13985	Gamblers Guitar/Shut Up And Drink Your Beer 40
56	Capitol EAP1 032	MERLE TRAVIS GUITAR (EP) 20
57	Capitol EAP2 650	MERLE TRAVIS GUITAR NO. 2 (EP) 18
59	Capitol EAP1 891	BACK HOME (EP) 15
63	Capitol EAP1 1391	WALKIN' THE STRINGS (EP) 15
57	Capitol T 891	BACK HOME (LP) 30
63	Capitol (S)T 1664	TRAVIS! (LP) 20
65	Capitol T 2102	MERLE TRAVIS & JOE MAPHIS (LP) 20

(see also Brown's Ferry Four)

PAUL TRAVIS
75	A&M AMLS 68290	RETURN OF THE NATIVE (LP, with lyric inner) 15

(see also Travis)

TRAVIS (1)
73	A&M AMS 7081	Band Of Heroes/Out In The Country 8
73	A&M AMLS 68120	SHINE ON ME (LP) 50

(see also Paul Travis)

TRAVIS (2)
96	Red Telephone Box PHONE 001	All I Want Do Is Rock/Line Is Fine/Funny Thing (10", numbered, stickered p/s, 750 only) 30
97	Independiente ISOM 1S	U16 Girls/Hazy Shades/Good Time Girls (p/s) 5
97	Independiente ISOM 3S	All I Want Do Is Rock/Blue On A Black Weekend (p/s) 8
97	Independiente ISOM 5S	Tied To The 90s/Me Beside You (p/s) 5
97	Independiente GOODT 1	The Line Is Fine/All I Want To Do Is Rock/More Than Us/ Tied To The 90s (12", promo only) 8
99	Independiente ISM 4946249	THE MAN WHO (CD, with bonus CD [Driftwood/Slide Show/More Than Us]).............20
99	Independiente ISOM 9 LP	THE MAN WHO (LP, with bonus remix 12") 50
99	Independiente ISOM 9 LP	THE MAN WHO (LP) 35
01	Independiente ISOM 25 LP	THE INVISIBLE BAND (LP) 30
03	Independiente ISOM 40LP	12 MEMORIES (LP) 20

TRAVIS & BOB
59	Pye International 7N 25018	Tell Him No/We're Too Young 15
59	Pye International 7N 25018	Tell Him No/We're Too Young (78) 10
61	Mercury AMT 1142	Baby Stay Close To Me/Give Your Love To Me 7

TRAX FOUR
66	Ace Of Clubs S/ACL 1216	WINGDING PARTY!!! (LP, mono/stereo) 55

JACK TRAYLOR & STEELWIND
73	Grunt FTR 0194	CHILD OF NATURE (LP) 20

TREASURE BOY
67	Trojan TR 010	Love Is A Treasure (actually by Freddie McKay)/ TOMMY McCOOK: Zazuka..............25

TREATMENT
81	Private Pressing	Stamp Out Mutants/Doncha Know (p/s) 15
87	Number NUMB 001	Feeling Like A Ghost/Rowing Boat 8
89	Number TAO 1	LIVE (LP) 18
93	Delerium DELEC 026	CIPHER CAPUT (LP) 20

TREBLETONES
61	Butlin CP 2424	Butlin Holiday/Butlin Holiday...8
63	Oriole CB 1838	In Real Life/Dream Of A Lifetime 12

TREDEGAR
86	Aries CEP 0001	Duma/The Jester (p/s) 75
86	Aries CEP LP 001	TREDEGAR (LP, gatefold sleeve, embossed) 18

(see also Budgie)

HERBERT BEERBOHM TREE
65	OMY 69	KEEP THOSE DOGS AWAY (EP) 25

TREEBOUND STORY
86	Fon ELM 1	I REMEMBER EP (12", p/s) 8

TREES
70	CBS 5078	Nothing Special/Epitaph 25
70	CBS 63837	THE GARDEN OF JANE DELAWNEY (LP) 300

71	CBS 64168	ON THE SHORE (LP)	350
87	Decal LIK 12	ON THE SHORE (LP, reissue)	15
87	Decal LIK 15	THE GARDEN OF JANE DELAWNEY (LP, reissue)	15

(see also Casablanca, Juliet Lawson, Trainer)

TREETOPS
67	Parlophone R 5628	Don't Worry Baby/I Remember	15
68	Parlophone R 5669	California My Way/Carry On Living	12
70	Columbia DB 8727	Mississippi Valley/Man Is A Man	12
71	Columbia DB 8799	Without The One You Love/So Here I Go Again	15
73	Columbia DB 9013	Gypsey/Life Is Getting Better	15

TREKKAS
65	Planet PLF 105	Please Go/I Put A Spell On You	90

TREMBLING BLUE STARS
96	Shinkansen SHINKANSEN 1	Abba On The Jukebox/She's Always There (p/s, 1,000 only)	10

TREMELOES
66	Decca F 12423	Blessed/The Right Time	20
66	CBS 202242	Good Day Sunshine/What A State I'm In	15
67	CBS 202519	Here Comes My Baby/Gentlemen Of Pleasure	6
67	CBS 2723	Silence Is Golden/Let Your Hair Hang Down (p/s)	6
67	CBS 2930	Even The Bad Times Are Good/Jenny's Alright (p/s)	6
67	CBS 3043	Be Mine/Suddenly Winter	10
68	CBS 3234	Suddenly You Love Me/As You Are	6
68	CBS 2889	Helule Helule/Girl From Nowhere	6
68	CBS 3680	My Little Lady/All The World To Me	6
68	CBS 3873	I Shall Be Released/I Miss My Baby	7
69	CBS 4065	Hello World/Up Down All Around	7
69	CBS 4582	(Call Me) Number One/Instant Whip	5
68	CBS Special Products WB 728	Here Comes My Baby/SIMON & GARFUNKEL: The 59th Street Bridge Song (p/s, mail-order only with Pepsi Cola tokens)	6
70	CBS 4815	By The Way/Breakheart Motel	6
70	CBS 5139	Me And My Life/Try Me	8
71	CBS 7294	Hello Buddy/My Woman	8
72	Epic EPC 5S 1019	Blue Suede Tie/Yodel Ay	5
73	Epic EPC 1399	Ride On/Hands Off	5
73	CBS 1139	Here Comes My Baby/Silence Is Golden (p/s, 'Hall Of Fame Hits' series)	5
84	Meteor MTS 002	Silence Is Golden (Acappella version)/The Last Word	5
75	SJM DJS 406	Be Boppin' Boogie/Asct Cowboys	7
68	CBS EP 6402	MY LITTLE LADY (EP)	18
67	CBS (S)BPG 63017	HERE COME THE TREMELOES (LP)	18
68	CBS (S)BPG 63138	THE TREMELOES: CHIP, RICK, ALAN AND DAVE (LP)	18
69	CBS 63547	THE TREMELOES 'LIVE' IN CABARET (LP)	15
70	CBS 64242	MASTER (LP)	15

(see also Brian Poole & Tremeloes, Trems, Chip Hawkes)

TREMORS
80s	Redball RR 0002	Modern World/Smashed Reality (p/s)	15

TREMS
73	Epic EPC 1660	Make It Break It/Movin' On	5

(see also Tremeloes)

TREND
80	MCA MCA 583	Polly And Wendy/Family Way (p/s)	20
80	MCA MCA 629	This Dance Hall Must Have A Back Way Out/Fiction, Love & Romance (p/s)	15

TREND (1)
67	Page One POF 004	Boyfriends And Girlfriends/Shoot On Sight	60

TREND (2)
70	Trendy TREND 1	Teenage Crush/Cool Johnny (with press sheet)	50
70	Trendy TREND 1	Teenage Crush/Cool Johnny	40

TRENDS
63	Piccadilly 7N 35171	All My Loving/Sweet Little Miss Love	15
64	Pye 7N 15644	You're A Wonderful One/The Way You Do The Things You Do	20

(see also Tammy St. John, Freddie Self, Freddie Ryder)

TRENDSETTERS
64	Silver Phoenix 1001	You Don't Care/My Heart Goes	65

TRENDSETTERS
60s	Oak RGJ 999	AT THE HOTEL DE FRANCE (EP)	30

TRENDSETTERS LTD
64	Parlophone R 5118	In A Big Way/Lucky Date	20
64	Parlophone R 5161	Hello Josephine/Move On Over	20
64	Parlophone R 5191	Go Away/Lollipops And Roses	15
65	Parlophone R 5324	You Sure Got A Funny Way Of Showing Your Love/I'm Coming Home	12

(see also King Crimson, Giles Giles & Fripp, Brain)

CHARLES TRENET
57	Columbia SEG 7319	BOUM (EP)	8
60	Columbia 33SX 1376	TRENET OF FRANCE (LP)	12

TRENIERS
58	Coral Q 72319	Ooh-La-La/Pennies From Heaven	25
58	Coral Q 72319	Ooh-La-La/Pennies From Heaven (78)	10
58	Fontana H 137	Go! Go! Go!/Get Out Of The Car (featuring Don Hill, Alto Sax)	100
58	Fontana H 137	Go! Go! Go!/Get Out Of The Car (featuring Don Hill, Alto Sax) (78)	20
59	London HLD 8858	When Your Hair Has Turned To Silver/Never, Never	45
59	London HLD 8858	When Your Hair Has Turned To Silver/Never, Never	35

JACKIE TRENT
61	Oriole CB 1711	Pick Up The Pieces/In Your Heart	15

MINT VALUE £

62	Oriole CB 1749	The One Who Really Loves You/Your Conscience Or Your Heart	40
63	Piccadilly 7N 35121	Melancholy Me/So Did I	15
64	Piccadilly 7N 35165	If You Love Me/Only One Such As You	40
64	Pye 7N 15692	Somewhere In The World/I Heard Somebody Say	5
64	Pye 7N 15742	Don't Stand In My Way/How Soon	5
65	Pye 7N 15865	When Summertime Is Over/To Show I Love Him	6
65	Pye 7N 15949	It's All In The Way You Look At Life/Time After Time	6
66	Pye 7N 17047	You Baby/Send Her Away (DJ Copy)	40
66	Pye 7N 17047	You Baby/Send Her Away	6
66	Pye 7N 17082	Love Is Me Love Is You/This Time	30
66	Pye 7N 17158	If You Ever Leave Me/There Goes My Love, There Goes My Life	6
67	Pye 7N 17249	Open Your Heart/Love Can Give	15
67	Pye 7N 17323	Your Love Is Everywhere/It's Not Easy Loving You	6
67	Pye 7N 17415	That's You/Stop Me And Buy One	6
67	Pye 7N 17437	Bye Bye Love (German Version)/Alles Okay (Send Her Away)	6
69	Pye 7N 17693	I'll Be There/Close To You	10
78	Casino Classics CC 4	You Baby/Send Her Away/FAMILY AFFAIR: Love Hustle	6
65	Pye NEP 4225	WHERE ARE YOU NOW (EP)	15
65	Pye NPL 18125	THE MAGIC OF JACKIE TRENT (LP)	25
67	Pye NPL 18173	ONCE MORE WITH FEELING (LP)	15
67	Pye NSPL 18201	STOP ME AND BUY ONE (LP)	20
69	Pye NSPL 18315	THE LOOK OF LOVE (LP)	20

JACKIE TRENT & TONY HATCH

67	Pye 7N 17300	The Two Of Us/I'll Be With You	6
68	Pye 7N 17604	Our Little Boat/Play It Again	5
74	Pye 7N 45392	Together/Going Our Own Sweet Way	6
75	Pye 7N 45490	Mr And Mrs (Be Nice To Each Other)/Positive Thinking	7
68	Pye NPL 18214	THE TWO OF US (LP)	20
68	Pye NSPL 18229	LIVE FOR LOVE (LP)	20
68	Pye NSPL 18304	TOGETHER AGAIN (LP)	15
74	Pye NSPL 18422	OPPOSITE YOUR SMILE (LP)	15

TRESPASS

79	Trial CASE 1	One Of These Days/Bloody Moon (p/s)	25
80	Trial CASE 2	Jealousy/Live It Up! (p/s)	18
81	Trial CASE 3	Bright Lights/The Duel/Man And Machine (p/s)	20

TREVOR (SHIELD)

64	Blue Beat BB 228	Down In Virginia/Hey Little Schoolgirl (with Caribs)	15
68	Blue Cat BS 129	Tender Arms (with Joe White & Glen Brown)/DERMOTT LYNCH: Something Is Worrying Me	25
68	Blue Cat BS 130	Pretty Girl (with Joe White & Glen Brown)/DERMOTT LYNCH: You Went Away	25
69	Blue Cat BS 153	Everyday Is Like A Holiday/Have You Time (by Trevor & Maytones)	80

TREVOR & KEITH

70	Punch PH 41	The Ark/MINNA BOYS: False Reador (actually titled "Got To Move")	7

(see also Carl Bryan)

TRIARCHY

79	SRT/79/CUS 599	Save The Khan/Juliet's Tomb (in p/s, 1,000 only)	80
79	SRT/79/CUS 599	Save The Khan/Juliet's Tomb (1,000 only)	30
79	Direct NEON 1	Save The Khan/Juliet's Tomb (reissue, p/s)	35
80	Direct NEON 2	Metal Messiah/Sweet Alcohol/Hell Hound On My Trail (in p/s)	70
80	Direct NEON 2	Metal Messiah/Sweet Alcohol/Hell Hound On My Trail	30

TRIBAN

69	Cambrian CSP 707	Leaving On A Jet Plane/Night In The City	6
71	Decca F 13115	Black Paper Roses/One Way Mirror	5
69	Cambrian MCT 592	TRIBAN (LP)	15
72	Cambrian MCT 218	RAINMAKER (LP, laminated cover)	18

TRIBE

73	Probe PRO 597	Koke Parts 1 & 2	15

TONY TRIBE

69	Downtown DT 419	Red Red Wine/RECO & RUDIES: Blues (some miscredited to Tony Tripe)	15
69	Downtown DT 439	Gonna Give You All The Love/HERBIE GREY: Why Wait	10

TRIBE (U.K.)

66	Planet PLF 108	The Gamma Goochie/I'm Leavin'	75
67	RCA RCA 1592	Love Is A Beautiful Thing/Steel Guitar	25

TRIBE (U.S.)

66	Polydor 56510	Dancin' To The Beat Of My Heart/Woofin'	50

TRIBESMAN

79	Boa BOA 102-12	Finsbury Park/The Tribe (12", p/s)	20
79	Boa BOA 001	STREET LEVEL (LP)	20

TRIBUTE

73	Jam JAM 48	Bobby Charlton/City Summer	12

TRICKS

70	CBS 4867	Wham! Bam! Ala Cazam!/Lucy Brown	8

TRICKSTER

79	Jet 165	Falling For The Wrong Guy/Tomorrow Belongs To Me	5

TRICKY

95	Island/4th & Broadway BRLP 610	MAXINQUAYE (LP, gatefold, inner)	30
96	Island/4th & Broadway BRLP 623	PRE-MILLENIUM TENSION (LP)	20
98	Island ILPSD 8071	ANGELS WITH DIRTY FACES (2-LP)	20

TRICKY DISCO

91	Warp WAP 11	HOUSEFLY EP (12")	10

TRI-CORE
92	Underground UNR 001T	BELFAST SAYS EP (12")	80

TRIDENT
84	SRT TRI 1	Destiny/Power Of The Trident	50

(see also Filthy Rich)

TRIFFIDS
65	Fontana TL 5231	THE TRIFFIDS ARE REALLY FOLK (LP)	12
63	Columbia DB 7084	Lookin Around/She's No Longer Your Girl	12

TRIFLE
69	United Artists UP 2270	All Together Now/Got My Thing	10
70	Dawn DNS 1008	Old-Fashioned Prayer Meeting/Dirty Old Town	10
71	Dawn DNLS 3017	FIRST MEETING (LP, textured gatefold sleeve)	120

(see also George Bean)

PANDIT KANWAR SAIN TRIKHA
71	Mushroom 100 MR 7	THREE SITAR PIECES (LP)	45

TRILOGY
71	Mercury 6338 034	I'M BEGINNING TO FEEL IT (LP)	20

TOMMY TRINDER & THE GANG
59	Fontana H 204	La Plume De Ma Tante/On The Sunny Side Of The Street	10

TRINIDAD ALL STARS
56	Parlophone DP 524	Trouble In Arima/Stone Cold Dead In De Market (78, export issue)	12

TRINIDAD OIL COMPANY
77	Harvest SHSP 4070	THE CALENDAR SONG (LP)	20

TRINIDAD STEEL BAND
52	Vogue V 9017	Mango Walk/Take Me (78)	10
52	Vogue V 9018	Ramadin/Johnny (78)	10

TRINITY
77	Burning Sounds BS 011	Natty Tired To Carry Load/Dubwise	10
77	Caribbean CBN 314	Natty On De Banking/Banking Dub	8
77	Carib Gems CG 005	Three Meals A Day/Version	8
77	Conflict CON 303	Up-Town Girl/PRINCE JAMMY & AGGROVATORS: Channel One A Boy	10
79	Attack TACK 2	Follow My Heart/Pope Paul Dead And Gone (12")	30
70s	Burning Vibrations BVD 002	Roots Man Party/Healing The Nation (12", with Mystic EMP Group)	20
80	Spectrum SP 01	Jamaican People A Nice People/Heaven And Hell/LLOYD CLARKE SPARROW: The Young Ones (12")	35
79	Burning Sounds BDS 012	SHOWCASE EP (12")	30
77	Magnum DERD 1003	UPTOWN GIRL (LP)	30
79	Trojan TRLS 170	ROCK IN THE GHETTO (LP)	20
81	JB JBLP 006	FULL HOUSE (LP)	20

TRINITY HOUSE
77	Profile GMOR 146	FLASHBACK THROUGH HISTORY (LP, private pressing, with insert)	40

TRIO
71	Dawn DNLS 3022	CONFLAGRATION (LP)	60
76	Dawn DNLS 3072	LIVE AT WOODSTOCK TOWN HALL (LP, with Stu Martin)	25

(see also John Surnam)

TRIPLE ELEMENT
88	Tam Tam TTT002	What's That Sound? (12")	8

TRIPLETS
69	President PT 245	When Lovers Say Goodbye/You Won't See Me Leaving	10

TRIPPERS
66	Pye International 7N 25388	Dance With Me/Keep A-Knockin'	20

TRIPTI DAS
67	Flowers FL 001	Kat Put Li {Puppet On A String)/Lagta Mahi Dil	20

TRISHA
65	CBS 201800	The Darkness Of My Night/Confusion	8

TRISTAR AIRBUS
72	RCA RCA 2170	Travellin' Man/Willie Morgan On The Wing	10

(see also Wimple Winch, 10cc, Hotlegs)

TRITONS
73	Bradley BAR 24	I Can't Get Not Satisfaction/Drifter	50

TRIUMVIRAT
74	Harvest SHSP 4030	ILLUSION ON A DOUBLE DIMPLE (LP, 1st pressing normal green label)	15
74	Harvest SHSP 4030	ILLUSION ON A DOUBLE DIMPLE (LP, 2nd pressing, more yellow green label)	12
75	Harvest SHSP 4048	SPARTACUS (LP)	15

TRIXIE'S BIG RED MOTORBIKE
82	Chew CH 9271	A Splash Of Red/Invisible Boyfriend (white label, stapled foldover p/s)	15
82	Ram RAM 51	TRIXIE'S BIG RED MOTORBIKE (EP, plain sleeve with stapled strip)	10
84	Lobby Ludd L 100001	Norman And Narcissus/In Timbuktu (p/s)	10
84	Lobby Ludd L 100002	A Splash Of Red/Invisible Boyfriend (reissue, different p/s)	8
84	Lobby Ludd L 100003	TRIXIE'S BIG RED MOTORBIKE (EP, reissue, stapled p/s)	8
95	Accident DENT 1	THE INTIMATE SOUND OF... (LP, handmade sleeve, numbered)	40
95	Accident DENT 1	THE INTIMATE SOUND OF... (LP, green vinyl, 500 only)	25

TRIXONS
69	Major Minor MM 665	Just Another Song/Sunny Side Sam	15

MARCUS TRO
65	Ember EMB S 203	Tell Me/What's The Matter Little Girl (in p/s)	18
65	Ember EMB S 203	Tell Me/What's The Matter Little Girl	10
65	Ember EMB 3365	INTRODUCING MARCUS TRO (LP)	40

MINT VALUE £

TROBWLL

| 79 | Buwch Hapus MW 1 | TAITH (EP) | 40 |

TROGGS
SINGLES

66	CBS 202038	Lost Girl/The Yella In Me	50
66	Fontana TF 689	Wild Thing/From Home	8
66	Fontana TF 717	With A Girl Like You/I Want You	7
66	Page One POF 001	I Can't Control Myself/Gonna Make You	7
66	Page One POF 010	Any Way That You Want Me/6-5-4-3-2-1	7
67	Page One POF 015	Give It To Me/You're Lyin'	7
67	Page One POF 022	My Lady/Girl In Black (withdrawn)	50
67	Page One POF 022	Night Of The Long Grass/Girl In Black	7
67	Page One POF 030	Hi Hi Hazel/As I Ride By	8
67	Page One POF 040	Love Is All Around/When Will The Rain Come	6
68	Page One POF 056	Little Girl/Maybe The Madman?	7
68	Page One POF 064	Surprise Surprise/Marbles And Some Gum?	8
68	Page One POF 082	You Can Cry If You Want To/There's Something About You	8
68	Page One POF 092	Hip Hip Hooray/Say Darlin'!	8
69	Page One POF 114	Evil Woman/Sweet Madeline	8
69	Page One POF 126	Wild Thing/I Can't Control Myself	6
70	Page One POF 164	Easy Lovin'/Give Me Something	8
70	Page One POF 171	Lover/Come Now	8
70	Page One POF 182	The Raver/You	10
71	DJM DJM 248	Lazy Weekend/Let's Pull Together	6
72	Jam JAM 25	Wild Thing/With A Girl Like You/Love Is All Around	5
72	Pye 7N 45147	Everything's Funny/Feels Like A Woman	5
73	Pye 7N 45244	Listen To The Man/Queen Of Sorrow	7
73	Pye 7N 45295	Strange Movies/I'm On Fire	15
75	Penny Farthing PEN 861	Good Vibrations/Push It Up To Me	6
75	Penny Farthing PEN 884	Wild Thing (Reggae Version)/Jenny Come Down	5
75	Penny Farthing PEN 889	Summertime/Jenny Come Down	5
75	Penny Farthing PEN 901	(I Can't Get No) Satisfaction/Memphis, Tennessee	5
76	Penny Farthing PEN 919	I'll Buy You An Island/Supergirl	5
77	Penny Farthing PEN 929	Feeling For Love/Summertime	5
78	Raw RAW 25	Just A Little Too Much/The True Troggs Tapes (p/s)	6
67	Page One POE 001	TROGGS TOPS (EP)	20
67	Page One POE 002	TROGGS TOPS VOLUME TWO (EP)	40
67	Page One	TRACK A TROGG (EP, unreleased)	0
81	DJM DJS 6	TROGGS TAPES (EP, double pack)	8

ALBUMS

66	Fontana TL 5355	FROM NOWHERE - THE TROGGS (LP, mono)	70
66	Fontana STL 5355	FROM NOWHERE - THE TROGGS (LP, stereo)	80
66	Page One POL 001	TROGGLODYNAMITE (LP, mono)	70
66	Page One POLS 001	TROGGLODYNAMITE (LP, stereo)	90
67	Page One FOR 001	THE BEST OF THE TROGGS (LP)	30
67	Page One POL 003	CELLOPHANE (LP, mono)	60
67	Page One POLS 003	CELLOPHANE (LP, stereo)	80
68	Page One POL 1	THE TROGGS ON TOUR (LP, export issue)	150
68	Page One FOR 007	THE BEST OF THE TROGGS VOLUME TWO (LP)	35
68	Page One POL(S) 012	MIXED BAG (LP)	150
69	Page One POS 602	TROGGLOMANIA (LP)	40
70	DJM Silverline DJML 009	CONTRASTS (LP, original issue)	25
76	Penny Farthing PELS 551	THE TROGG TAPES (LP)	20

(see also Reg Presley, Chris Britton, Ronnie Bond, Ten Feet Five)

CHUCK TROIS & AMAZING MAZE

| 68 | Action ACT 4517 | Call On You/Woodsman | 10 |

TROJAN

| 88 | GI GILP 444 | THE MARCH IS ON (LP) | 18 |

TROJANS

| 58 | Decca F 11065 | Man I'm Gonna Be/Make It Up | 15 |
| 58 | Decca F 11065 | Man I'm Gonna Be/Make It Up (78) | 10 |

TROLL BROTHERS

| 73 | SRT SRT 73316 | You Turn Me On/Turn Out The Lights (p/s) | 18 |

TROMBONES UNLIMITED

| 66 | Liberty LIB 55874 | Daydream/The Phoenix Love Theme (Senza Fine) | 5 |
| 66 | Liberty LBY 1350 | YOU'RE GONNA HEAR FROM ME (LP) | 12 |

TRONICS (1)

| 61 | Fontana H 348 | Cantina/Pickin' & Stompin' | 18 |

TRONICS (2)

78	Tronics T 001	Suzie (actually "Suzie's Vibrator")/Favourite Girls (plain sleeve with inserts)	8
79	Tronics T 002	Time Off/Goodbye (p/s)	8
81	Alien ALIEN 18	Shark Fucks/Time Off (p/s, with insert)	6
83	Red Rhino RED 3	Wild Cat Rock/Tonight (p/s)	5
82	Press PRESS 1	TRANZISTER SISTER (12" EP)	8
81	Alien BALIEN 3	LOVE BACKED BY FORCE (LP)	25

(see also Les Zarjaz)

TROOPERS

| 57 | Vogue V 9087 | Get Out/My Resolution | 700 |
| 57 | Vogue V 9087 | Get Out/My Resolution (78) | 150 |

TROOPS OF TOMORROW

| 82 | Troops TROOPS 1 | TROOPS OF TOMORROW (12" EP) | 8 |

(see also Vibrators, Fallen Angels)

TROPIC SHADOWS

72	Big Shot BI 603	Our Anniversary/Anniversary (Version)	6

ARCHIBALD TROTT

64	Black Swan WI 407	Get Together/Just Because	18

(see also Baba Brooks)

TROUBADORS DU ROI BAUDOUIN

69	Philips BF 1732	Sanctus (Missa Luba)/Kyrie	8

TROUBADORS/TROUBADOUR SINGERS

57	London HLR 8469	Fascination/Midnight In Athens	8
58	London HLR 8541	The Lights Of Paris/The Flaming Rose	12
58	London RE-R 1135	THE TROUBADORS (EP)	8
58	London HA-R 2095	THE TROUBADORS IN SPAIN (LP)	12

(see also Jane Morgan)

TROUBLE

88	Justice JTT002	I Get Hype/I Guess It's Dope (12")	50

BOBBY TROUP

55	Capitol CL 14219	Julie Is Her Name/Instead Of You	12
54	Capitol LC 6660	BOBBY TROUP (10" LP)	20

BOB TROW QUARTET

54	London HL 8082	Soft Squeeze Baby/I Went Along For The Ride	40
54	London HL 8082	Soft Squeeze Baby/I Went Along For The Ride (78)	10

ROBIN TROWER

78	Chrysalis CHS 2247	It's For You/My Love/In City Dreams (p/s, red vinyl)	5
81	Chrysalis CHS 2497	What It Is/Into Money (p/s, clear vinyl)	5
73	Chrysalis CHR 1039	TWICE REMOVED FROM YESTERDAY (LP)	12

(see also Paramounts, Procol Harum)

BENNY TROY

05	Atco 002	I Wanna Give You Tomorrow/OTIS REDDING: Loving By The Pound (promo, 500 only)	10

DORIS TROY

63	London HLK 9749	Just One Look/Bossa Nova Blues	35
64	Atlantic AT 4011	What'cha Gonna Do About It/Tomorrow Is Another Day	25
65	Atlantic AT 4020	Please Little Angel/One More Chance	18
65	Atlantic AT 4032	Heartaches/You'd Better Stop	18
65	Cameo Parkway C 101	I'll Do Anything (He Wants Me To)/But I Love Him	130
65	Cameo Parkway C 101	I'll Do Anything (He Wants Me To)/But I Love Him (DJ copy)	200
68	Atlantic 584 148	Just One Look/What'cha Gonna Do About It	12
68	Toast TT 507	I'll Do Anything (Anything He Wants Me To)/Heartaches	15
70	Apple APPLE 24	Ain't That Cute/Vaya Con Dios (with p/s)	22
70	Apple APPLE 24	Ain't That Cute/Vaya Con Dios	10
70	Apple APPLE 28	Jacob's Ladder/Get Back	12
71	Mojo 2092 011	I'll Do Anything (He Wants Me To)/But I Love Him (reissue)	15
73	Mojo 2092 062	Baby I Love You/To My Father's House	6
74	People PEO 112	Stretchin' Out/Don't Tell Your Mama	6
65	Atlantic AET 6007	WATCHA GONNA DO ABOUT IT (EP)	75
70	Apple SAPCOR 13	DORIS TROY (LP)	80
73	Mojo 2956 001	THE RAINBOW TESTAMENT (LP, with Gospel Truth)	35
74	Polydor 2464 001	JUST ONE LOOK (LP)	20
74	People PLEO 12	STRETCHIN' OUT (LP)	20
92	Apple SAPCOR 13	DORIS TROY (LP, reissue, gatefold sleeve with bonus 12" [SAPCOR 132])	20

TROY & THUNDERBIRDS

61	London HL 9476	Twistle/Take Ten	15

WILLIAM TRUCKAWAY

69	Reprise RS 20842	Bluegreens On The Wing/Besides Yourself	15
71	Reprise K 44165	BREAKAWAY (LP, with lyric insert)	20

TRUE ADVENTURE

74	Decca F 13528	Where The Roxy Use To Be/Outlaw Love	15

TRUE STYLE

91	Liberty Grooves LIB002	CODES OF CONDUCT (EP)	20

FRED TRUEMAN

69	NEMS 56-4293	Red Is Red/A Million Times A Day	6

TRUFFLE

81	Chesnut NUT 6	Round Tower/If You Really Want (p/s)	100
72	JAM 8	Poco Poco/Julie's Place	6

TRUK

71	CBS 57201	Winters Coming On/You	15

TRUMANS WATER

94	Clawfist CLAWFIST 25	New Kinda Radio/Do The Spazz/Bat Cave/Ride The No-Wave	8

JONNY TRUNK

01	Trunk TTT 001	The Snow It Melts/Scooby Don't (7", 300 only)	15
01	Trunk TTT 002	Sister Woo/Mr Hand (300 only)	15
03	Trunk TTT 004	Dead Soon/Dead MOuse Blues (7", 400 only)	15
04	Trunk JBH 008 LP	THE INSIDE OUTSIDE (LP, 500 only)	30

TRUTH

83	WEA TRUTH 1F	Confusion/Me And My Girl//Love A Go Go/From The Heart (p/s, doublepack)	8
84	IRS IRS 115	Exception Of Love/If You Ever Find Love (p/s)	5

TRUTH (1)

65	Pye 7N 15923	Baby Don't You Know/Come On Home	20
65	Pye 7N 15998	Who's Wrong/She's A Roller	25
66	Pye 7N 17035	Girl/Jailer Bring Me Water	8
66	Pye 7N 17095	I Go To Sleep/Baby You've Got It	30

66	Deram DM 105	Jingle Jangle/Hey Gyp (Dig The Slowness)	100
67	Decca F 12582	Walk Away Renee/Fly Away Bird	20
68	Decca F 22764	Seuno/Old Ma Brown	60

TRUTH & BEAUTY
| 74 | Rak RAK 181 | Tuff Little Surfer Boy/Touch-a Touch-a Touch Me | 25 |

TRUTH OF TRUTHS
| 71 | Oak OR 1001 | TRUTH OF TRUTHS (LP) | 25 |

TRUX
| 82 | Trux TRX 01 | Bad Luck (no p/s) | 200 |

TRYDAN
| 80 | Sain SAIN 77S | Mods A Rocers/Di-Waith, Di-'Fynedd | 5 |

TANIA TSANAKLIDOU
| 78 | EMI EMI 2797 | Charlie Chaplin (English)/Charlie Chaplin (Greek) | 12 |

TSD
| 96 | Avex AVEXCD 21 | Heart & Soul (Hyper Go Go 7" Edit)/Heart & Soul (Strike 12")/Heart & Soul (Hyper Go Go 12")/Heart & Soul (Dyme Brothers 12")/Heart & Soul (Johnny Versace 12") (CD) | 0 |

(see also STEPS)

T.S.O.L.
| 81 | Frontier FLP 1004 | DANCE WITH ME (LP) | 18 |
| 82 | Alt. Tentacles VIRUS 10 | WEATHERED STATUES (EP) | 10 |

T2
| 70 | Decca SKL 5050 | IT'LL ALL WORK OUT IN BOOMLAND (LP, blue/silver label/boxed logo) | 250 |
| 97 | Essex 1019LP | T2 (LP) | 12 |

(see also Flies, Cross & Ross)

ERNEST TUBB (& HIS TEXAS TROUBADORS)
50	Decca BM 31206	The Blues/Half A Mind (Export Issue)	15
56	Brunswick 05527	Thirty Days/Answer The Phone (triangular centre)	30
56	Brunswick 05587	So Doggone Lonesome/If I Never Have Anything Else	20
50s	Decca BM 31214	What Am I Living For/Goodbye Sunshine, Hello Blues (export issue)	15
56	Brunswick LA 8736	JIMMIE RODGERS SONGS (10" LP)	30
57	Brunswick LAT 8161	FAVOURITES (LP)	15
58	Brunswick LAT 8260	THE DADDY OF 'EM ALL (LP)	15
59	Brunswick LAT 8292	THE IMPORTANCE OF BEING ERNEST (LP)	15
60	Brunswick LAT 8313	THE ERNEST TUBB STORY VOLUME ONE (LP, mono)	15
60	Brunswick STA 3022	THE ERNEST TUBB STORY VOLUME ONE (LP, stereo)	12
60	Brunswick STA 3023	THE ERNEST TUBB STORY VOLUME TWO (LP, stereo)	12

(see also Red Foley & Ernest Tubb)

JUSTIN TUBB
67	RCA Victor RCA 1585	But Wait There's More/The Second Thing I'm Gonna Do	6
64	RCA RCX 7133	JUSTIN TUBB (EP)	30
63	Ember CW 100	STAR OF THE GRAND OLE OPRY (LP, pink & grey labels)	12
64	Ember CW 110	THE MODERN COUNTRY MUSIC SOUND OF JUSTIN TUBB (LP, pink & grey labels)	12

TUBES
| 79 | A&M AMS 7423 | Prime Time (promo box of 7 different coloured vinyl editions & picture disc) | 30 |

TUBEWAY ARMY
78	Beggars Banquet BEG 5	That's Too Bad/Oh! I Didn't Say (p/s)	10
78	Beggars Banquet BEG 8	Bombers/O.D. Receiver/Blue Eyes (p/s)	10
79	Beggars Banquet BEG 17	Down In The Park/Do You Need The Service?	5
(p/s)			
79	Beggars Banquet BEG 17T	Down In The Park/Do You Need The Service?/ I Nearly Married A Human 2 (12", p/s)	25
79	Beggars Banquet BEG 18	Are "Friends" Electric?/We Are So Fragile (p/s original semi-transparent sleeve)	18
79	Banquet Banquet BEG 18P	Are "Friends" Electric?/We Are So Fragile (picture disc, with insert)	10
79	Beggars Banquet BACK 2	That's Too Bad/Oh! Didn't I Say/Bombers/Blue Eyes/O.D. Receiver (double pack, gatefold p/s)	5
79	Beggars Banquet BACK 2	That's Too Bad/Oh! Didn't I Say/Bombers/Blue Eyes/O.D. Receiver (double pack, gatefold p/s, mispressed 2nd disc omits "O.D. Receiver")	15
81	Beggars Banquet SPC 4	Are "Friends" Electric/Down In The Park	8
83	Beggars Banquet BEG 92E	TUBEWAY ARMY VOL. 1 (12" EP, with "That's Too Bad [Alternate Mix]", yellow vinyl)	10
85	Beggars Banquet BEG 123 E	1978-1979 VOL. 2 (12", blue vinyl, p/s)	10
85	Beggars Banquet BEG 124E	1978-1979 VOL. 3 (12", red vinyl, p/s)	10
78	Beggars Banquet BEGA 4	TUBEWAY ARMY (LP, blue vinyl, g/fold stickered sleeve, some with badge)	70
78	Beggars Banquet BEGA 4	TUBEWAY ARMY (LP, blue vinyl, g/fold stickered sleeve)	60
79	Beggars Banquet BEGA 7	REPLICAS (LP, with large black & white poster)	25
08	VIN 180 LP 002	REPLICAS (LP, (LP, pressed on 180 gram vinyl, numbered with 8" x 6" print)	18

(see also Gary Numan, Paul Gardiner)

TUBILAH DOG
| 96 | S04 | IN SEARCH OF PLAICE (LP, gatefold with poster) | 20 |

TUB-THUMPER
| 74 | Alaska ALA 18 | Kick Out The Jams/Kahoutec | 25 |

TUCHWOOD
| 72 | Polydor 2058233 | Freedom For The Stallion/Morning Light | 8 |

BESSIE TUCKER
| 55 | HMV 7EG 8085 | BLUES BY BESSIE (EP) | 20 |

BILLY JOE TUCKER
| 61 | London HLD 9455 | Boogie Woogie Bill/Mail Train | 60 |

CY TUCKER
| 63 | Fontana TF 424 | My Prayer/High School Dance | 8 |
| 64 | Fontana TF 470 | Let Me Call You Sweetheart/I Apologise | 7 |

TERRY TUCKER'S ORANGE CLOCKWORK
| 70 | Warner Brothers K16337 | Overture To The Sun Part 1/Overture To The Sun Part II | 10 |

TOMMY TUCKER
64	Pye International 7N 25238	Hi-Heel Sneakers/I Don't Want 'Cha	20
64	Pye International 7N 25246	Long Tall Shorty/Mo' Shorty	25
64	London HLU 9932	Oh! What A Feeling/Wine Bottles	40
69	Chess CRS 8086	Hi-Heel Sneakers/I Don't Want 'Cha (reissue)	15
64	Pye Intl. NEP 44027	HI HEEL SNEAKERS (EP)	50

WINSTON TUCKER
73	Explosion EX 2083	I'm A Believer/You'll Be Mine	5

(see also Winston Groovy)

TUCKY BUZZARD
71	Capitol CL 15687	She's A Striker/Heartbreaker	5
73	Purple PUR 113	Gold Medallions/Fast Bluesy Woman	7
77	Purple PUR 134	Gold Medallions/Superboy Rock 'N' Roller '73'	7
71	Capitol E-ST 864	WARM SLASH (LP, laminated front sleeve, flipbacks)	60
73	Purple TPSA 7510	ALRIGHT ON THE NIGHT (LP, laminated gatefold sleeve)	25
73	Purple TPSA 7512	BUZZARD (LP)	20

(see also End)

HENRY TUDOR
67	Decca F12574	How Many Times/Another Name From Nowhere	25

TUDOR LODGE
71	Vertigo 6059 044	The Lady's Changing Home/Back To The Good Times We Had	75
71	Vertigo 6360 043	TUDOR LODGE (LP, foldout textured sleeve, swirl label)	1500

TUDOR MINSTRELS
66	Decca F 12536	Love In The Open Air/A Theme From "The Family Way"	22

TUDORS
83	Stiff BUY 172	Tied Up With Joe Cool/Cry Baby Cry (p/s)	7

TUESDAY
72	Pye 7N 45194	Big Mister Little Man/Sewing Machine	20

TUESDAY'S CHILDREN
66	Columbia DB 7978	When You Walk In The Sand/High And Drifting	20
66	Columbia DB 8018	High On A Hill/Summer Leaves Me With A Sigh	22
67	King KG 1051	A Strange Light From The East/That'll Be The Day	30
67	Pye 7N 17406	Baby's Gone/Guess I'm Losin' You	15
68	Pye 7N 17474	In The Valley Of The Shadow Of Love/Ain't You Got A Heart	12
68	Mercury MF 1063	She/Bright-Eyed Apples	12

(see also Warm Sounds)

T.U.F.F.
80s	SONO 001	We've Got A Hot One (Speed Mix) (unreleased, white label promos only)	10

(see also Hard Corps)

TUFF GONG ALLSTARS
72	Punch PH 114	You Should Have Known Better (actually by The Wailing Souls)/Known Better	12

(see also Wailing Souls)

TONY TUFF
79	Niagra NIADD 101	Ease Up Oppressor/JAH THOMAS: Answer The Phone (12")	15
79	King Sounds GMDM 26	You Wrong/TOMMY McCOOK: Sensimena (12")	25
80	Art & Craft 003	Look Ya/TONY TUFF & JAH STITCH: Rumours Of War (12")	50
80	Cha Cha CHAD 11	Deliver Me/Africa We Want To Go (12")	20
80	Grove ILPS 9619	TONY TUFF (LP)	40

SHANE TUFF
82	Roots Man Pro RMP 002	Can't Take No More/Yearning For Some Loving	40

TULIPS
74	Explosion EX 2091	Mocking Bird/DES ALL STARS: Version	7

LEE TULLY
57	London HL 8363	Around The World With Elwood Pretzel (Parts 1 & 2) (gold print label)	100
57	London HL 8363	Around The World With Elwood Pretzel (Parts 1 & 2) (silver print label)	60
57	London HL 8363	Around The World With Elwood Pretzel (Parts 1 & 2) (78)	25

TUMBLEWEEDS
70	Phoenix NIX 111	Making My Way Back To Louisiana/I Guess I'd Better Go	10

TUNDRA
70s	Greenwich Village GVR 208	THE KENTISH SONGSTER (LP)	15
78	Sweet Folk & C. SFA 078	A KENTISH GARLAND (LP, gatefold sleeve)	25
81	Greenwich Village GVR 218	SONGS FROM GREENWICH (LP, gatefold sleeve)	15

TUNE ROCKERS
58	London HLT 8717	The Green Mosquito/Warm Up	30
58	London HLT 8717	The Green Mosquito/Warm Up (78)	15

TUNEWEAVERS
57	London HL 8503	Happy Happy Birthday Baby/PAUL GAYTEN: Yo, Yo, Walk	200
57	London HL 8503	Happy Happy Birthday Baby/PAUL GAYTEN: Yo, Yo, Walk (78)	30

(see also Paul Gayten)

TUNJI WITH CHRIS McGREGOR
60s	Jika 001	Ko Gbele Oko/Lisabi Egba	8

TUNNEL RUNNERS
80	Sonic International SI 4282	Plastic Land/Drug (numbered p/s)	80

TUNNELVISION
81	Factory FAC 39	Watching The Hydroplanes/Morbid Fear (1st pressing, clear vinyl)	8
81	Factory FAC 39	Watching The Hydroplanes/Morbid Fear (later pressing, black vinyl)	5

PADDY TUNNEY
65	Topic 12T 139	A WILD BEES NEST (LP, blue label)	12
66	Topic 12T 153	IRELAND HER OWN (LP, with Arthur Kearney, Frank Kelly & Joe Tunney, blue label)	12

| 66 | Topic 12T 165 | THE IRISH EDGE (LP, blue label) ....12 |

TUNNG

04	Static Caravan VAN 72	Tales From Black/Pool Beneath The Pond (500 only) 15
05	Static Caravan VAN 73	Maypole Song/Suprize Me 44 (100 lathe cut only, p/s) 30
05	Nowhere Fast SLOW03	Magpie Bites/The Bonnie Black Hare (1000 only hand numbered poster sleeve) 5
05	Static Caravan VAN 94	Tunng Vs Dollboy Vs Dollboy Vs Tunng (1000 only, 200 with art sleeve) 5
05	Static Caravan VAN 94	Tunng Vs Dollboy Vs Dollboy Vs Tunng (1000 only) 5
05	Static Caravan VAN 88	MOTHER'S DAUGHTERS AND OTHER SONGS (LP, 300 only - withdrawn) 50

K.T. TUNSTALL

| 04 | Outcaste OUT 56 | Throw Me A Rope/Black & White (500 only) ....10 |

TURBO

| 80 | Cargo CRS 004 | STALLION (EP, p/s) ....100 |
| 82 | Turbo CUS 1261 | Charged For Glory/Race For The Dawn ....8 |

TURGID TOOL

| 01 | Stand STAND 11 | Terror In A Turgid Tool!/Stand Up For England (pop-up p/s) ....8 |

TURNBULL & ARKWRIGHT

| 72 | Peacock PEA 501 | Smuggling Man/Misty Roses ....15 |

BRUCE TURNER

54	Columbia SCMC 9	Falling Leaves/I Wished On The Moon (export issue) 6
60	Melodisc MEL 1551	Nuages/My Guy's Come Back 6
60s	CRD 1000	Jamaica Jump/Big Noise From Winetka 10
62	Storyville SXP 2025	BRUCE TURNER AND HIS JUMP BAND (EP) 8
63	Philips 433 627 BE	JUMPING FOR JOY NO. 1 (EP) 8
63	Philips 433 627 BE	JUMPING FOR JOY NO. 2 (EP) 8
63	77 EP/EU 1	LIVING JAZZ (EP) 10
64	Philips BL 7590	GOING PLACES (LP) 12

CHUCK TURNER

87	Stereo One STO 003	Youthman Struggling/FUNNY WONDER: Jollification (12") 70
87	Live & Love LLD 44	We Rule The Dance/We Rule The Dub (12") 30
88	Live & Love LALP 21	ON THE HARDWAY (LP) 15

DENNIS TURNER

| 62 | London HL 9537 | Lover Please/How Many Times ....25 |

FRANK TURNER

| 09 | Xtra Mile | Reasons Not To Be An Idiot/Thunder Road (p/s, 300 only, each with hand-written reason not to be an idiot by Frank Turner) ....30 |

GORDON TURNER

| 70 | Charisma CAS 1009 | MEDITATION (LP, 1st pressing laminated 'landscape' sleeve) ......40 |
| 70 | Charisma CAS 1009 | MEDITATION (LP, 2nd pressing non laminated 'blue room' sleeve) ......20 |

IKE TURNER

72	United Artists UP 35411	Lawdy Miss Clawdy/Tacks In My Shoes/Soppin' Molasses (with Family Vibes) 6
84	Fleetville FV 303	New Breed Part 1/New Breed Part 2 5
60s	Ember EMB 3395	IKE TURNER ROCKS THE BLUES (LP) 50
72	United Artists UAG 29362	BLUES ROOTS (LP) 18
75	DJM DJSLM 2010	FUNKY MULE (LP) 15

(see also Ike & Tina Turner)

IKE & TINA TURNER

SINGLES

60	London HLU 9226	A Fool In Love/The Way You Love Me 20
61	London HLU 9451	It's Gonna Work Out Fine/Won't You Forgive Me 20
64	Sue WI 306	Gonna Work Out Fine/Won't You Forgive Me (reissue) 20
64	Sue WI 322	The Argument/Poor Fool 20
64	Sue WI 350	I Can't Believe What You Say/My Baby Now 40
65	Warner Bros WB 153	Finger Poppin'/Ooh Poo Pah Doo 25
65	Sue WI 376	Please, Please, Please/Am I A Fool In Love 40
66	London HLU 10046	River Deep - Mountain High/I'll Keep You Happy 8
66	Warner Bros WB 5753	Tell Her I'm Not Home/Finger Poppin' 20
66	HMV POP 1544	Anything You Wasn't Born With/Beauty Is Just Skin Deep 30
66	London HLU 10083	A Love Like Yours (Don't Come Knockin' Every Day)/Hold On Baby 18
66	Stateside SS 551	Goodbye, So Long/Hurt Is All You Gave Me 18
66	Warner Bros WB 5766	Somebody (Somewhere) Needs You/(I'll Do Anything) Just To Be With You 100
66	Warner Bros WB 5766	Somebody (Somewhere) Needs You/(I'll Do Anything) Just To Be With You (DJ copy) 120
67	HMV POP 1583	I'm Hooked/Dust My Broom 70
67	HMV POP 1583	I'm Hooked/Dust My Broom (DJ copy) 100
67	London HLU 10155	I'll Never Need More Than This/Save The Last Dance For Me 20
68	London HLU 10189	So Fine/So Blue Over You 10
68	London HLU 10217	We Need An Understanding/It Sho' Ain't Me 15
69	London HLU 10242	River Deep - Mountain High/Save The Last Dance For Me 5
69	Minit MLF 11016	I'm Gonna Do All I Can/You've Got Too Many Ties That Bind 15
69	London HLU 10267	I'll Never Need More Than This/A Love Like Yours 8
69	Liberty LBF 15223	Crazy 'Bout You Baby/I've Been Lovin' You Too Long 10
70	Liberty LBF 15303	Come Together/Honky Tonky Women 6
70	A&M AMS 783	Make 'Em Wait/Everyday I Have To Cry 8
70	Harvest HAR 5018	The Hunter/Bold Soul Sister 8
70	Liberty LBF 15367	I Want To Take You Higher/Contact High 5
71	Liberty LBF 15432	Proud Mary/Funkier Than A Mosquito's Tweeter 15
71	A&M AMS 829	River Deep - Mountain High/Oh Baby 6
71	United Artists UP 35245	Ooh Poo Pah Doo/I Wanna Jump 5
72	United Artists UP 35373	Feel Good/Outrageous 5

EPs

64	Sue IEP 706	THE SOUL OF IKE AND TINA TURNER 200
65	Warner Bros WEP 619	THE IKE AND TINA TURNER SHOW 60
66	Warner Bros WEP 620	SOMEBODY NEEDS YOU 70
83	Sue ENS 1	SUE SESSIONS 15

ALBUMS

65	Warner Bros WM 8170	THE IKE AND TINA TURNER SHOW	60
65	London HA-C 8248	THE GREATEST HITS OF IKE & TINA TURNER	60
66	Ember EMB 3368	THE IKE AND TINA TURNER REVUE	40
66	Warner Bros W 1579	THE IKE AND TINA TURNER SHOW	40
66	London HA-U/SH-U 8298	RIVER DEEP MOUNTAIN HIGH	50
67	Warner Bros WB 5904	THE IKE AND TINA TURNER SHOW VOL. 2	35
69	London HA-U/SH-U 8370	SO FINE (with Fontella Bass)	30
69	Liberty LBS 83241	OUTTA SEASON	22
69	Minit MLS 40014	IN PERSON	25
69	Warner Bros ES 1810	GREATEST HITS	20
70	Liberty LBS 83350	COME TOGETHER	20
70	Harvest SHSP 4001	THE HUNTER	120
71	Liberty LBS 83455	WORKIN' TOGETHER	20
71	Liberty LBS 83468/9	LIVE IN PARIS	15
71	Capitol E-ST 571	HER MAN...HIS WOMAN	15
71	United Artists UAD 60005/6	WHAT YOU HEAR IS WHAT YOU GET	15
72	United Artists UAG 29256	NUFF SAID	12
73	Mojo 2916 020	PEACHES (with tracks by Ikettes)	12

(see also Ike Turner, Tina Turner, Ikettes)

JESSE LEE TURNER

59	London HLL 8785	The Little Space Girl/Shake, Baby, Shake	60
59	London HLL 8785	The Little Space Girl/Shake, Baby, Shake (78)	30
60	London HLP 9108	I'm The Little Space Girl's Father/Valley Of Lost Soldiers	20
60	Top Rank JAR 303	That's My Girl/Teenage Misery	20
60	Top Rank JAR 516	Do I Worry (Yes I Do)/All Right, Be That Way	15
62	Vogue V 9201	The Voice Changing Song/All You Gotta Do Is Ask	15

(see also Pete Johnson, Meade Lux Lewis, Pete Johnson, Albert Ammons, Sonny Terry & Brownie McGhee)

(BIG) JOE TURNER

51	Parlophone DP 265	Roll 'Em Pete/Goin' Away Blues (with Pete Johnson) (78, export only)	60
56	London HLE 8301	Corrine Corrina/Morning, Noon And Night (triangular or centre)	350
56	London HLE 8301	Corrine Corrina/Morning, Noon And Night (round centre)	100
56	London HLE 8301	Corrine Corrina/Morning, Noon And Night (78)	40
56	London HLE 8332	Boogie Woogie Country Girl/The Chicken And The Hawk	600
56	London HLE 8332	Boogie Woogie Country Girl/The Chicken And The Hawk (78)	45
57	London HLE 8357	Lipstick, Powder And Paint/Rock A While (gold label label print)	350
57	London HLE 8357	Lipstick, Powder And Paint/Rock A While (silver label print)	175
57	London HLE 8357	Lipstick, Powder And Paint/Rock A While (78)	40
60	London HLE 9055	Honey Hush/Tomorrow Night	60
60	London HLK 9119	My Little Honey Dripper/Chains Of Love	50
65	Atlantic AT 4026	Midnight Cannonball/Baby I Still Want You	20
57	London REE 1111	PRESENTING JOE TURNER (EP, initially tri-centre)	250
57	London REE 1111	PRESENTING JOE TURNER (EP, later round centre)	150
57	London Jazz LTZ-K 15053	BOSS OF THE BLUES (LP, mono)	80
57	London Jazz SAH-K 6123	BOSS OF THE BLUES (LP, stereo)	100
59	London HA-E 2173	ROCKIN' THE BLUES (LP)	120
60	London Jazz LTZ-K 15205	BIG JOE RIDES AGAIN (LP, mono)	75
60	London Jazz SAH-K 6123	BIG JOE RIDES AGAIN (LP, stereo)	90
60	London HA-E 2231	BIG JOE IS HERE (LP)	80
64	Realm RM 207	JOE TURNER SINGS THE BLUES VOL. 1 (LP)	20
64	Realm RM 229	JOE TURNER SINGS THE BLUES VOL. 2 (LP)	20
65	CBS 52229	JOE TURNER SINGS THE BLUES VOL. 2 (LP, reissue)	15
65	Fontana 688 802 ZL	JUMPIN' THE BLUES (LP)	25
67	Atlantic Special 590 006	BOSS OF THE BLUES (LP)	18
68	Stateside (S)SL 10226	SINGING THE BLUES (LP)	18
70	Philips SBL 7911	THE REAL BOSS OF THE BLUES (LP)	15
74	Atlantic K 40525	HIS GREATEST RECORDINGS (LP)	12

JOE TURNER/RUTH BROWN

56	London REE 1047	KING AND QUEEN OF R&B (EP, 2 tracks each)	200

(see also Ruth Brown, Big Joe Turner)

JOE TURNER & PETE JOHNSON GROUP

56	Emarcy ERE 1500	JOE TURNER & PETE JOHNSON GROUP (EP)	30

(see also Pete Johnson, Big Joe Turner)

MEL TURNER (& BANDITS)

61	Melodisc MEL 1580	Let Me Hold Your Hand/I'll Be With You In Apple Blossom Time (with Bandits)	20
62	Columbia DB 4791	Daddy Cool/Swing Low Sweet Chariot (with Bandits)	25
63	Columbia DB 4963	Don't Cry/I Need	10
63	Columbia DB 7076	I Can't Stand Up Alone/Doing The Ton (with Mohicans)	15
63	Carnival CV 7003	Mohican Crawl/White Christmas	10
66	Island WI 276	Welcome Home Little Darlin'/C'est L'Amour	40
64	Carnival CV 1005	The Hermit And The Rosetree/What's The Matter With Me	10

PRECIOUS CLARENCE TURNER

67	Saga SOC 1041	BOOGIE WOOGIE EXPLOSIONS (LP)	12

RUBY TURNER

86	Jive CHIP 1	WOMEN HOLD UP HALF THE SKY (CD)	25

SAMMY TURNER

59	London HLX 8918	Lavender Blue (Dilly, Dilly)/Sweet Annie Laurie	10
59	London HLX 8918	Lavender Blue (Dilly, Dilly)/Sweet Annie Laurie (78)	10
59	London HLX 8963	Always/Symphony	20
59	London HLX 8963	Always/Symphony (78)	20
60	London HLX 9062	Paradise/I'd Be A Fool Again	20
62	London HLX 9488	Raincoat In The River/Falling	25
60	London HA-X 2246	LAVENDER BLUE MOODS (LP)	90

SPYDER TURNER

67	MGM MGM 1332	Stand By Me/You're Good Enough For Me	20

TINA TURNER

| 74 | Kwanza K 19502 | Since I Don't Have You/Happy Days | 8 |

TINA TURNER

78	United Artists UP 36513	Sometimes When We Touch/Earthquakes And Hurricanes	5
82	Virgin VS 500	Ball Of Confusion/Ball Of Confusion (Instrumental) (with B.E.F.) (p/s)	8
83	Capitol 12CLP 316	Let's Stay Together/I Wrote A Letter (12", picture disc)	8
84	Capitol CLP 325	Help/Rock'n'Roll Widow (picture disc)	7
84	Capitol CLP 338	Better Be Good To Me/When I Was Young (picture disc)	5
85	Capitol CLP 364	We Don't Need Another Hero/(Instrumental) (picture disc)	5
86	Capitol CLP 338	Break Every Rule/Girls (picture disc)	5
85	Capitol TINAP 1	PRIVATE DANCER (LP, picture disc)	18

(see also Ike & Tina Turner, Eric Clapton)

TITUS TURNER

60	London HLU 9024	We Told You Not To Marry/Taking Care Of Business	25
61	Oriole CB 1611	Pony Train/Bla Bla Cha Cha Cha	20
61	Parlophone R 4746	Sound-Off/Me And My Lonely Telephone	25
61	Blue Beat BB 32	Miss Rubberneck Jones/Way Down Yonder	18

ZEB TURNER

| 51 | Vogue V 9002 | Chew Tobacco Rag/No More Nothin' (78) | 10 |

TURNING POINT

| 77 | Gull GULP 1022 | CREATURES OF THE NIGHT (LP) | 20 |
| 78 | Gull GULP 1027 | SILENT PROMISE (LP) | 15 |

TURNING SHRINES

| 86 | Temple TOPY 7 | FACE OF ANOTHER (12" EP) | 8 |

TURNPIKE

| 74 | Fontana 6007032 | Big Machine/Lazer Thereza | 6 |

TURNSTYLE

| 68 | Pye 7N 17653 | Riding A Wave/Trot | 325 |

TURQUOISE

| 68 | Decca F 12756 | 53 Summer Street/Tales Of Flossie Fillett | 70 |
| 68 | Decca F 12842 | Woodstock/Saynia | 100 |

(see also Ewan Stephens)

TURQUOISE DAYS

| 84 | Disques Strategie STRAT XX1 | Grey Skies/Blurred (p/s, 1000 only) | 70 |

STANLEY TURRENTINE

| 66 | Fontana TL 5300 | TIGER TAIL (LP) | 12 |

(see also Milt Jackson & Stanley Turrentine)

HENRY TURTLE

72	Columbia DB 8859	Do You Believe/You Turned Your Back And Walked Away	30
73	Bell 1318	When Eleanor Comes Around/One Of A Million Faces	8
81	Surrey Sounds HMS 6A	Hound Dog Man/All I Ever Need Is You	5

TURTLES

65	Pye International 7N 25320	It Ain't Me Babe/Almost There	20
66	Pye International 7N 25341	Let Me Be/Your Ma Said You Cried (In Your Sleep Last Night)	15
66	Immediate IM 031	You Baby/Wanderin' Kind	25
66	London HLU 10095	Can I Get To Know You Better/Like The Seasons	10
67	London HLU 10115	Happy Together/We'll Meet Again	5
67	Pye International 7N 25421	Let Me Be/Almost There	8
67	London HLU 10135	She'd Rather Be With Me/The Walking Song	5
67	London HLU 10153	You Know What I Mean/Rugs Of Woods And Flowers	8
67	London HLU 10168	She's My Girl/Chicken Little Was Right	12
68	London HLU 10184	Sound Asleep/Umbassa The Dragon	10
68	London HLU 10207	The Story Of Rock And Roll/Can't You Hear The Cows	10
68	London HLU 10223	Elenore/Surfer Dan	5
69	London HLU 10251	You Showed Me/Buzz-Saw	12
69	London HLU 10279	You Don't Have To Walk In The Rain/Come Over	12
69	London HLU 10291	Love In The City/Bachelor Mother	7
67	Pye Intl. NEP 44089	IT AIN'T ME BABE (EP)	45
67	London HA-U 8330	HAPPY TOGETHER (LP)	20
68	London HA-U/SH-U 8376	THE TURTLES PRESENT THE BATTLE OF THE BANDS (LP)	20

(see also Flo & Eddie, Frank Zappa)

GEOFF TURTON

| 68 | Pye 7N 17483 | Don't You believe It/I've Got To Tell Her | 10 |

RITA TUSHINGHAM & LYNN REDGRAVE

| 68 | Stateside SS 2081 | Smashing Time/Waiting For My Friend | 10 |

TUSKAN RAIDERS

| 95 | Clear CLR 410(X) | Bantha Trax (12", p/s, on clear vinyl) | 8 |

(see also -Ziq)

TUSKEN RAIDERS

| 99 | Planet Mu ZIQ 003 | BANTHA TRAX VOL. 2 EP (12", p/s) | 12 |

TUTCH

| 80 | Gargoyle GRGL 773 | The Battle/You Don't Care/Round And Round | 60 |

TU-TONES

51	London L 1079	Oh You Million Dollar Doll/Don't Fence Me In (78, as Lee Monti's Tu-Tones)	10
59	London HLW 8904	Still In Love WIth You/Saccharin Sally	125
59	London HLW 8904	Still In Love WIth You/Saccharin Sally (78)	30

WESLEY & MARILYN TUTTLE

| 55 | Capitol CL 14291 | Jim, Johnny And Jonas/Say You Do | 10 |

TUXEDOMOON

| 80 | Pre PRE 10 | Dark Companion/59 To One (p/s) | 5 |
| 80 | PREX 4 | DESIRE (LP, with art print insert) | 15 |

TV ON THE RADIO

04	4AD AD 2421	Staring At The Sun/Freeway/On A Train 10
04	4AD AD 2423	New Health Rock/Modern Romance 8
06	4AD 2606	Wolf Like Me/Snakes And Martyrs 8
07	4AD 2724	Province/Dumb Animal..8
06	4AD RTCM2	Province (with David Bowie, 200 only, green vinyl) 40
09	Parlophone LCO 299	TV ON THE RADIO : Heroes/DAVID BOWIE : Heroes..40
04	4AD CAD 2470	DESPERATE YOUTH, BLOODTHIRSTY BABES (LP, with free 12").......................................20
04	4AD CAD 2470	DESPERATE YOUTH, BLOODTHIRSTY BABES (LP)..18
06	4AD CAD 2607	RETURN TO COOKIE MOUNTAIN (LP)..18
08	4AD CAD 2821	DEAR SCIENCE (LP)..15

T.V. PRODUCTO

79	Limited Edition TAKE 3	Nowhere's Safe/Jumping Off Walls/PRAMS: Me/Modern Man (folded p/s) 12

(see also Mission)

T.V. & TRIBESMEN

66	Pye International 7N 25375	Barefootin'/Fat Man 30

TV 21

80	Powbeat AAARGH! 1	Playing With Fire/Shattered By It All (foldout p/s)..12
80	Powbeat AAARGH! 2	Ambition/Ticking Away/This Is Zero (foldout p/s)..15
81	Demon D 1004	On The Run/End Of A Dream (p/s) 8
82	Deram ATV 21	All Join Hands/A Journey Up The Zambezi (And Back) (p/s)..8

(see also DNV, Shake)

SHANIA TWAIN

95	Mercury MERCD 433	Any Man Of Mine/Raining On Our Love/God Ain't Gonna Getcha For That/Still Under The Weather (CD) 12
99	Mercury 562 264 2	Man! I Feel Like A Woman (Original Version) (CD, digipak, with lyrics, withdrawn).............12
99	NMC PILOT 54	ON THE WAY (CD, withdrawn)..18

TWELFTH NIGHT

73	Acorn CF 239	TWELFTH NIGHT (EP) 40
82	Revolution REV 009	Eleanor Rigby/East Of Eden (p/s) 10

TWELFTH NIGHT

80	Twelfth Night TN 001	THE FIRST 7" ALBUM ("The Cunning Man"/"Für Helene") (p/s) 30
86	Virgin/Charisma CB 424	Shame/Blue Powder Monkey (p/s) 5
86	Virgin/Charisma CBY 424	Shame/Blue Powder Monkey (picture disc)..8
86	Virgin/Charisma CB 424-12	Shame (Full Mix)/Shame (7")/Blue Powder Monkey (12", p/s)......................................8
86	Virgin/Charisma CBY 424-12	Shame (Full Mix)/Shame (7")/Blue Powder Monkey (12", picture disc) 10
86	Virgin/Charisma CB 425-12	Take A Look (Album Version)/Take A Look (Part 4)/ Blondon Fair (Extended) (12", p/s) 8
81	Twelfth Night TN 002	LIVE AT THE TARGET (LP) 12

TWELVE CUBIC FEET

82	Namedrop NR2	STRAIGHT OUT OF THE FRIDGE (10" EP, with Bumper Booklet)......................................15

20TH CENTURY FOX ORCHESTRA

65	Stateside SS422	Those Magnificent Men In Their Flying Machines/Arizona 15

(see also Ron Goodwin)

25 RIFLES

79	25 Rifles TFR 1	World War 3/Revolution Blues/Hey Little/Dance 'Bout Now (12") 15

22ND STREET

72	Polydor 2058 212	Sunny Sleeps Late/Home 8

23RD TURNOFF

67	Deram DM 150	Michael Angelo/Leave Me Here 90

(see also Kirkbys, Jimmy Campbell, Rockin' Horse)

23 JEWELS

79	Temporary TEMP 1	You Don't Know Me/Playing Bogart (white labels, plain sleeve with photocopied insert)....20
80	Temporary TEMP 2	WELTSCHMERZ A GO-GO! (EP, white label)..12

23 SKIDOO

81	Pineapple PULP 23	Ethics/Another Baby's Face (p/s) 8
81	Fetish FE 10	Last Words/Version (promo only) 12
81	Fetish FE 11	The Gospel Comes To New Guinea/Last Words (12", p/s) 12
82	Fetish FP 20	Tearing Up The Plans/Just Like Everybody/Gregouka (12", p/s) 10
85	Illuminated ILL 2812	Coup/Version (In The Palace) (12", p/s)..10
82	Fetish FM 2008	SEVEN SONGS (mini-LP) 15
83	Operation Twilight OPT 23	THE CULLING IS COMING (LP)...15
84	Illuminated JAM 40	URBAN GAMELAN (LP) 15

(see also Current 93)

22:20S

90s	Own label 2201	Such A Fool/Baby, You're Not In Love (1,000 only, die-cut sleeve) 8
04	Heavenly HVNLP51	22:20S (LP, gatefold)...12

TWICE AS MUCH

66	Immediate IM 033	Sittin' On A Fence/Baby I Want You..6
66	Immediate IM 036	Step Out Of Line/Simplified 12
66	Immediate IM 039	True Story/You're So Good 18
67	Immediate IM 042	Crystal Ball/Why Don't They All Go Away And Leave Me Alone 18
66	Immediate IMLP 007	OWN UP (LP, mono) 90
66	Immediate IMSP 007	OWN UP (LP, stereo) 100
69	Immediate IMCP 013	THAT'S ALL (LP) 60

TWIGGY

67	Ember EMB S 239	Beautiful Dreams/I Need Your Hand In Mine (in p/s)..20
67	Ember EMB S 239	Beautiful Dreams/I Need Your Hand In Mine...10
67	Ember EMB S 244	When I Think Of You/Over And Over (in p/s)..20
67	Ember EMB S 244	When I Think Of You/Over And Over...10
71	Bell BLL 1158	Zoo Do Zoo Song/Little Pleasure Acre (as Twiggy & Friends)..5
72	Columbia DB 8853	A Room In Bloomsbury (with Chistopher Gable)/You Are My Lucky Star/ All I Do Is Dream ...5
76	Mercury 6007 100	Here I Go Again/In Love Together (p/s) 5

78	Mercury 6007 175	Falling Angel/Virginia	5
72	Ember SE 8012	TWIGGY & THE GIRLFRIENDS (LP)	20

TWIGGY & ANNE
66	Columbia DB 7799	Some Do, Some Don't/With Open Arms	6

TWILIGHT
86	Lismor Folk LIFL 7014	MODERN FOLK ARRANGEMENTS (LP)	12

TWILIGHT ZONERS
79	ZIP/Dining Out ZEROZERO1	ZERO ZERO ONE (Hospital/The Wrap/Twister/The Film)(EP, various silk-screened in red & hand-coloured p/s, signed & numbered)	50
80	ZIP/Dining Out ZIP 002	Brighton Rock/Diversion (p/s)	6

(see also Occult Chemistry)

TWILIGHTS (AUSTRALIA)
66	Columbia DB 8065	Needle In A Haystack/I Don't Know Where The Wind Will Blow Me	30
67	Columbia DB 8125	What's Wrong With The Way I Live/It's Dark	20
68	Columbia DB 8396	Cathy, Come Home/The Way They Play	30

TWILIGHTS (U.S.)
65	London HLU 9992	Take What I Got/She's There	25

TWINK (& FAIRIES)
78	Chiswick SWT 26	Do It '77/Psychedelic Punkeroo/Enter The Diamonds (12", p/s, with Fairies)	12
86	Twink TWK 2	SPACE LOVER (EP)	12
90	Twink 12TWK 5	PSYCHEDELIC PUNKEROO (12" EP)	8
70	Polydor 2343 032	THINK PINK (LP, with pink lyric insert)	300
70	Polydor 2343 032	THINK PINK (LP, without pink lyric insert)	150
70	Polydor 2343 032	THINK PINK (LP, red vinyl with pink lyric insert)	350
90	Twink TWKLP 1	MR RAINBOW (LP)	12
91	Twink LP 2	ODDS & BEGINNINGS (LP, with insert, numbered & signed, some on red vinyl, 1,500 only)	15
91	Twink LP 2	ODDS & BEGINNINGS (LP, with insert, numbered & signed, 1,500 only)	12

(see also Pretty Things, Pink Fairies, Fairies, Tomorrow, Aquarian Age, Rings, Mick Farren, Magic Muscle)

TWINKLE (RIPLEY)
64	Decca F 12013	Terry/The Boy Of My Dreams	6
65	Decca F 12076	Golden Lights/Ain't Nobody Home But Me	10
65	Decca F 12139	Tommy/So Sad	12
65	Decca F 12219	Poor Old Johnny/I Need Your Hand In Mine	15
65	Decca F 12305	The End Of The World/Take Me To The Dance	15
66	Decca F 12464	What Am I Doing Here With You?/Now I Have You	15
69	Instant IN 005	Micky/Darby And Joan	15
74	Bradleys BRAD 7418	Days/Caroline (as Twinkle Ripley) (p/s)	15
74	Bradleys BRAD 7418	Days/Caroline (as Twinkle Ripley)	7
82	EMI 5278	I'm A Believer/For Sale (p/s)	15
65	Decca DFE 8621	TWINKLE - A LONELY SINGING DOLL (EP)	60

(see also Silkie Davis)

TWINKLE & HOT ROD ALL STARS
70	Torpedo TOR 3	Jook Jook/Graduate	5

TWINKLE BROTHERS
70	Jackpot JP 731	Shu Be Du/All My Enemies Beware	8
70	Jackpot JP 740	Miss World/Take What You've Got	8
70	Jackpot JP 741	Sweet Young Thing/Grandma	8
71	Jackpot JP 768	Do Your Own Thing/BOY WONDER: They Talk About Love	8
71	Green Door GD 4007	Miss Labba Labba/The Best Is Yet To Come	10
71	Big Shot BI 593	You Took Me By Suprise/You Took Me By Surprise - Version (both sides actually by Tony Brevitt)	12
71	Big Shot BI 600	It's Not Who You Know/I Need Someone	8
71	Tropical AL 002	Love Sweet Love/HERON ATTAR: Poor Man's Life	5
72	Sioux SI 003	Happy Song/Little Caesar	5
73	Camel CA 105	Room Full All Full/Version	6
73	Count Shelley CS 31	Mother Whiney/JACKIE BROWN: Fight My Way	6
73	Camel CA 106	Room Full All Full/Version	7
73	Magnet MG 033	Mother And Wife/Version	5
73	Pama PM 876	Village Ram/Push It Inna	10
75	Faith FA 007	Friends/No Big Thing	5
75	Faith FA 022	Mother And Wife/GENE RONDO: Impossible Dream	6
77	Carib Gems CG 009	Jah Army/Dub The Wicked	6
79	Virgin Front Line FLS 119 12	Keep On Trying/King Pharoah (12")	10
79	Virgin Front Line FLS 123 12	Jahoviah/Free Africa (12")	20
75	Grounation GROL 506	RASTA PON TOP (LP)	35
76	Carib Gems CGLP 1001	DO YOUR OWN THING (LP)	60
78	Front Line FCL 5001	LOVE (10" LP)	12
80	Virgin V2169	COUNTRYMEN (LP)	15

(see also Busty Brown, Sammy Jones)

TWINS
73	Downtown DT 511	Rastafari Ruler/TYRONE TAYLOR: Yesterday	8

TWINSET
67	Decca F 12629	Tremblin'/Sneakin' Up On You	25

TWIN-TONES
58	RCA RCA 1040	Jo Ann/Before You Go	50
58	RCA RCA 1040	Jo Ann/Before You Go (78)	15

TWIN TUNES QUINTET
58	RCA RCA 1046	The Love Nest/Baby Lover	12

TWIST
79	Polydor 2059 156	This Is Your Life/Life's A Commercial Break (p/s)	10
79	Polydor POSP 84	Ads/Rebound	10
79	Polydor 2383 552	THIS IS YOUR LIFE (LP)	20

TWIST

91	East West YZ 586	The Fat Lady Sings/Heavy Duty (p/s)	5

TWIST & SHOUT

79	Wessex WEX 268	Bounce Back/As It Happens (p/s)	20

TWISTED ACE

81	Heavy Metal HEAVY 9	Firebird/I Won't Surrender (in p/s)	10
81	Heavy Metal HEAVY 9	Firebird/I Won't Surrender	5

TWISTED SISTER

82	Secret SHH 137-12	RUFF CUTS (12" EP, p/s)	10
83	Atlantic A 9827P	The Kids Are Back/Shoot 'Em Down (shaped picture disc)	8
86	Atlantic A 9478D	Leader Of The Pack/I Wanna Rock (p/s, with free single)	5
86	Atlantic A 9478P	Leader Of The Pack/I Wanna Rock (shaped picture disc)	6
85	Atlantic 781 275-1P	COME OUT AND PLAY (LP, picture disc)	12

TWISTERS

60	Capitol CL 15167	Turn The Page/Dancing Little Clown	8
62	Aral/Windsor PSA 106	Peppermint Twist Time/Silly Chilli	12

TWISTING FERRARIS

80	Round TF 001	Our Favourite Photograph/Lipsticks (p/s)	12

CONWAY TWITTY

78s

57	Mercury MT 173	Shake It Up/Maybe Baby	30
59	MGM MGM 1003	The Story Of My Love/Make Me Know You're Mine	10
59	MGM MGM 1016	Hey Little Lucy! (Don'tcha Put No Lipstick On)/When I'm Not With You	15
59	MGM MGM 1029	Mona Lisa/Heavenly	20
59	MGM MGM 1047	Rosaleena/Halfway To Heaven	30

SINGLES

58	MGM MGM 992	It's Only Make Believe/I'll Try	10
59	MGM MGM 1003	The Story Of My Love/Make Me Know You're Mine	10
59	MGM MGM 1016	Hey Little Lucy! (Don'tcha Put No Lipstick On)/ When I'm Not With You	10
59	MGM MGM 1029	Mona Lisa/Heavenly	6
59	MGM MGM 1047	Rosaleena/Halfway To Heaven	6
60	MGM MGM 1056	Lonely Blue Boy/My One And Only You	10
60	MGM MGM 1066	What Am I Living For/The Hurt In My Heart	10
60	MGM MGM 1082	Is A Blue Bird Blue/She's Mine	15
60	MGM MGM 1095	What A Dream/Tell Me One More Time	6
60	MGM MGM 1108	Whole Lotta Shakin' Goin' On/The Flame	12
61	MGM MGM 1118	C'est Si Bon/Don't You Dare Let Me Down	12
61	MGM MGM 1129	The Next Kiss/Man Alone	6
61	MGM MGM 1137	It's Drivin' Me Wild/Sweet Sorry	10
62	MGM MGM 1152	Tower Of Tears/Portrait Of A Fool	12
62	MGM MGM 1170	Comfy An' Cozy/Unchained Melody	10
62	MGM MGM 1187	I Hope I Think I Wish/The Pick Up	12
63	MGM MGM 1201	Handy Man/Little Piece Of My Heart	10
63	MGM MGM 1209	She Ain't No Angel/Got My Mojo Workin'	12
63	HMV POP 1258	Go On And Cry/She Loves Me	8

EPs

58	MGM MGM-EP 684	IT'S ONLY MAKE BELIEVE	60
59	MGM MGM-EP 698	HEY LITTLE LUCY	60
60	MGM MGM-EP 719	SATURDAY NIGHT WITH CONWAY TWITTY	60
60	Mercury ZEP 10069	I NEED YOUR LOVIN'	150
60	MGM MGM-EP 738	IS A BLUEBIRD BLUE?	60
61	MGM MGM-EP 752	THE ROCK 'N' ROLL STORY	80

ALBUMS

59	MGM MGM-C 781	CONWAY TWITTY SINGS	100
60	MGM MGM-C 801	SATURDAY NIGHT WITH CONWAY TWITTY	100
60	MGM MGM-C 829	LONELY BLUE BOY	100
63	MGM MGM-C 950	R AND B '63	70
68	MCA MUP(S) 342	HERE'S CONWAY TWITTY (AND HIS LONELY BLUE BOYS)	18
68	MGM C/CS 8100	THE ROCK AND ROLL STORY	40
69	MCA MUPS 363	NEXT IN LINE	15
69	MCA MUPS 386	DARLING, YOU KNOW I WOULDN'T LIE	15
70	MCA MUP(S) 404	I LOVE YOU MORE TODAY	15
70	MCA MUP(S) 412	TO SEE MY ANGEL CRY	15
71	MCA MUPS 426	FIFTEEN YEARS AGO	15
71	MCA MUPS 429	WE ONLY MAKE BELIEVE (with Loretta Lynn)	15
72	MCA MUPS 443	I WONDER WHAT SHE'LL THINK ABOUT ME LEAVING	15

(see also Loretta Lynn)

TWIZZLE & HOT ROD ALLSTARS

70	Torpedo TOR 3	Jook Jook/The Graduate	10

TWO & A HALF

66	CBS 202248	Midnight Swim/Faith	10
66	CBS 202404	Questions/In Harmony	8
67	CBS 202526	The Walls Are High/Love You	8
67	Decca F 22672	Suburban Early Morning Station/Just Couldn't Believe My Ears	15
67	Decca F 22715	I Don't Need To Tell You/Christmas Will Be Round Again	18

TWO DARK TROOPERS

92	Basement BRSS 020	I Wanna Be Your Lover/Darkcore (12")	10

(see also Chemical, DJ Mayhem)

TWO FINGERED APPROACH

82	Virus 026	World War Album/Society Hooked/Family Traditions (p/s. 500 only)	60

TWO FOR THE ROAD

70s	Pastiche BJ 2929	TWO FOR THE ROAD (LP)	20

TWO KINGS
65	Island WI 240	Rolling Stone/SUFFERER: Tomorrow Morning (B-side act. by Frank Cosmo)	18
65	Island WI 249	Hit You Let You Feel It/Honey I Love You (both sides actually by Fugitives)	18

TWO MAN SOUND
74	Spark SRL 118	Amadeo/Somebody Is Ready To Love You	8
78	Miracle M12	Que Tal America/Brazil O Brazil (12")	15

TWO MINDS CRACK
84	Sedition EDIT 2	Enemies Of Promise/The Stealer (p/s)	6

TWO MUCH
67	Fontana TF 858	Wonderland Of Love/Mister Money	7
68	Fontana TF 900	It's A Hip Hip Hippy World/Stay In My World	10

TWO-NINETEEN (2.19) SKIFFLE GROUP
57	Esquire 10-497	Freight Train Blues/Railroad Bill (78)	15
57	Esquire 10-502	I'm A-Lookin' For A Home/When The Saints Go Marching In (78)	15
57	Esquire 10-509	In The Valley/Tom Dooley (78)	15
57	Esquire 10-512	Where Can I Go?/Roll The Union On (78)	20
57	Esquire 10-515	This Little Light Of Mine/Union Maid (78)	20
57	Esquire EP 126	TWO-NINETEEN SKIFFLE GROUP (EP)	40
57	Esquire EP 146	TWO-NINETEEN SKIFFLE GROUP (EP)	55
58	Esquire EP 176	TWO-NINETEEN SKIFFLE GROUP (EP)	55
58	Esquire EP 196	TWO-NINETEEN SKIFFLE GROUP (EP)	60

TWO OF CLUBS
64	Columbia DB 7371	The Angels Must Have Made You/True Love Is Here	15

TWO OF EACH
67	Decca F 12626	Every Single Day/I'm Glad I Got You	8
68	Pye 7N 17555	The Summer Of Our Love/Saturday Morning	7
78	Fast Products FAST 2	Where To Now?/All Time Low (p/s)	15

TWO PEOPLE
86	Polydor	Mouth Of An Angel (p/s)	20
80s	Polydor	This Is The Shirt (p/s)	10

2 SLICES OF JAM
92	White Label	Pressing On Ya Mind/Beat Like This (12" white label)	60

TWO SPARKS
72	Moodisc HM 113	Run Away Girl/When We Were Young	8

(see also Carl Bryan, Winston Wright)

2 THE TOP
89	Rhyme & Reason 12RNR2	The Rhythm I Give Em (12")	15
90	President PT12590	Score To Settle/The Matter At Hand (12")	60

(see also Kinetic Effect)

TWO TIMES DEF
92	Mendoza MEN016	First And Last (Vocal)/First And Last (Instrumental)/First And Last (Alternative Mix) (12", stamped white labels)	175

(see also Silent Eclipse)

TWO TONE COMMITTEE
91	Precinct PREC002	Beings From A Word Stuck Surface (12")	40

2-X-TREME
92	Empire E 001	X-TREMITY EP (12", white label stamped in red, beware of represses!)	60

TY
00	Big Dada BD023	Break The Lock/The Tale (12")	8
03	Big Dada BD049	We Don't Care (12")	8
03	Big Dada BD056	Groovement/Ha Ha (12")	8
06	Big Dada BD097	Don't Watch That (12" - Promo only 800 copies)	10
03	Big Dada BDLP057	UPWARDS (LP)	12

TYDE
02	Rough Trade RTRADES 056	Blood Brothers/Play It As It Lays (p/s)	6

ARLYNE TYE
59	London HLL 8825	The Universe/Who Is The One	25
59	London HLL 8825	The Universe/Who Is The One (78)	15

TYGERS OF PAN TANG
79	Neat NEAT 03	Don't Touch Me There/Burning Up/Bad Times (first pressing of around 1,000 in slightly oversized p/s giving it a 'home made' feel)	25
79	Neat NEAT 03	Don't Touch Me There/Burning Up/Bad Times (p/s)	12
80	MCA MCA 582	Don't Touch Me There/Burning Up/Bad Times (p/s, reissue)	10
80	MCA MCA 612	Rock'n'Roll Man/All Right On The Night/Wild Man (p/s)	5
80	MCA MCA 634	Suzie Smiled/Tush (p/s)	5
80	MCA MCA 634	Euthanasia/Straight As A Die (p/s)	5
81	MCA MCA 672	Hellbound/Bad Times//Bad Times/Don't Take Nothin' ('The Audition Tapes' double pack)	6
81	MCA MCA 692	The Story So Far/Silver And Gold/All Or Nothing (p/s)	5
81	MCA MCA 723	Don't Stop By/Slave To Freedom (p/s)	5
81	MCA MCAT 723	Don't Stop By/Slave To Freedom (12", p/s)	12
81	MCA MCA 755	Love Don't Stay/Paradise Drive (p/s)	8
81	MCA MCA 759	Do It Good/Slip Away (no p/s)	30
81	MCA MCA 769	Love Potion No. 9/The Stormlands (p/s)	5
81	MCA MCAP 769	Love Potion No. 9/The Stormlands (picture disc)	5
82	MCA MCA 777	Rendezvous/Life Of Crime (white vinyl, p/s)	6
82	MCA MCA 777	Rendezvous/Life Of Crime (red or blue vinyl, p/s)	5
82	MCA MCA 777	Rendezvous/Life Of Crime (poster p/s)	5
82	MCA MCA 777	Rendezvous/Life Of Crime (p/s)	5
82	MCA MCA 790	Paris By Air/Love's A Lie (standard p/s with earring)	10
82	MCA MCA 790	Paris By Air/Love's A Lie (poster p/s)	5
82	MCA MCA 798	Making Tracks/What You Saying (p/s)	5
82	MCA MCAT 798	Making Tracks (Extended Remix)/What You Saying (12", p/s)	10

80	MCA MCF 3075	WILD CAT (LP, with lyric insert)	12
81	MCA MCF 3104	SPELLBOUND (LP, with poster)	12
81	MCA MCF 3123	CRAZY NIGHTS (LP, stickered sleeve, insert, with bonus 12")	22
81	MCA MCF 3123	CRAZY NIGHTS (LP, stickered sleeve, insert)	12
85	MFN MFN 50	THE WRECK AGE (LP, lyric sleeve)	12
86	Neat 1037	FIRST KILL (LP, with inner)	12

(see also John Sykes)

TYLA GANG

76	Stiff BUY 4	Styrofoam/Texas Chainsaw Massacre Boogie (push-out centre, die-cut printed sleeve)	6
78	Beserkley BSERK 16	MOONPROOF (LP, yellow vinyl, with insert)	12

(see also Ducks Deluxe)

BIG 'T' TYLER

57	Vogue V 9079	King Kong/Sadie Green	200
57	Vogue V 9079	King Kong/Sadie Green (78)	100

JIMMY TYLER & HIS ORCHESTRA

56	Parlophone MSP 6215	Fool 'Em Devil/Stardust	18
60	Top Rank JAR 306	Junk Village/Happy Sax	12

T. TEXAS TYLER

59	Parlophone GEP 8788	COUNTRY ROUND-UP (EP)	30
67	London HA-B 8322	MAN WITH A MILLION FRIENDS (LP)	25

TERRY TYLER

61	Pye International 7N 25119	A Thousand Feet Below/Answer Me	15

TOBY TYLER

64	Emidisc no cat. no.	The Road I'm On (Gloria)/Blowin' In The Wind (acetate, 1 copy only)	3000
89	Archive Jive TOBY 1	The Road I'm On (Gloria) (mail-order issue, numbered p/s, 1-sided, 1,500 only)	15
93	Zinc Alloy ZAR CDS 9005	Blowin' In The Wind/The Road I'm On (Gloria)/Blowin' In The Wind (Take No. 6) (CD)	10
93	Zinc Alloy ZAR CD 9006	THE MAXIMUM SOUND SESSION (CD)	22

(see also Marc Bolan)

TYMES

63	Cameo Parkway P 871	So Much In Love/Roscoe James McClain	10
63	Cameo Parkway P 884	Wonderful Wonderful/Come With Me To The Sea (in p/s)	25
63	Cameo Parkway P 884	Wonderful Wonderful/Come With Me To The Sea	10
64	Cameo Parkway P 891	Somewhere/View From My Window	15
64	Cameo Parkway P 908	To Each His Own/Wonderland Of Love	15
64	Cameo Parkway P 919	The Magic Of Our Summer Love/With All My Heart	15
64	Cameo Parkway P 924	Here She Comes/Malibu	100
64	Cameo Parkway P 924	Here She Comes/Malibu (DJ copy)	200
69	Direction 58-3903	People/For Love Of Ivy	6
69	Direction 58-4450	If You Love Me Baby/Find My Way	10
71	CBS 7250	Someone To Watch Over Me/She's Gone (featuring George Williams)	6
63	Cameo Parkway P 7032	SO MUCH IN LOVE (LP)	70
69	Direction 8-63558	PEOPLE (LP, mono or stereo)	25
78	London HAU 8516	CAMEO PARKWAY SESSIONS (LP)	25

MCCOY TYNER

70s	Impulse IMPL 8043	INCEPTION (LP)	12

ROB TYNER & HOT RODS

77	Island WIP 6418	'Till The Night Is Gone (Let's Rock)/Flipside Rock (p/s)	5

(see also MC 5, Eddie & Hot Rods)

TYPHOONS (1)

63	Embassy WB 589	Surf City/I Want To Stay Here	7
65	Embassy WB 677	Tired Of Waiting For You/Baby Please Don't Go	7
65	Embassy WEP 1115	Hard Day's Night/And I Love Her/I Should Have Known Better/Tell Me Why (EP)	10
65	Embassy WT 2006	Ticket To Ride/Here Comes The Night/I'll Be There/I Can't Explain (EP)	15

(see also Bud Ashton, Ray Pilgrim, Mike Redway, Starlings)

TYPHOONS (2)

81	Bohemian BO 1	Telstar/In Fae A Brothin' (p/s)	5

(see also Ruts)

TYRANNOSAURUS REX

68	Regal Zonophone RZ 3008	Debora/Child Star (with promo only p/s)	400
68	Regal Zonophone RZ 3008	Debora/Child Star (with promo only p/s, with insert)	450
68	Regal Zonophone RZ 3008	Debora/Child Star (demo copy as above, but without promo only p/s)	375
68	Regal Zonophone RZ 3008	Debora/Child Star	35
68	Regal Zonophone RZ 3011	One Inch Rock/Salamanda Palaganda (promo only p/s)	375
68	Regal Zonophone RZ 3011	One Inch Rock/Salamanda Palaganda (promo only p/s, with insert)	425
68	Regal Zonophone RZ 3011	One Inch Rock/Salamanda Palaganda	40
69	Regal Zonophone RZ 3016	Pewter Suitor/Warlord Of The Royal Crocodiles	70
69	Regal Zonophone RZ 3022	King Of The Rumbling Spires/Do You Remember (with promo only p/s)	450
69	Regal Zonophone RZ 3022	King Of The Rumbling Spires/Do You Remember (demo, without promo only p/s)	400
69	Regal Zonophone RZ 3022	King Of The Rumbling Spires/Do You Remember	40
70	Regal Zonophone RZ 3025	By The Light Of A Magical Moon/Find A Little Wood	40
72	Magni Fly ECHO 102	Debora/One Inch Rock/The Woodland Bop/The Seal Of Seasons (p/s)	5
82	Old Gold OG 9234	Debora/One Inch Rock (1,000 mispressed with "Beltane Walk" on B-side)	5
91	Tyrannosaurus Rex TYR 1	Sleepy Maurice/1968 Radio Promos (Tyrannosaurus Rex Appreciation Society release, 2,000 only, p/s with card insert)	8
68	Regal Zonophone LRZ 1003	MY PEOPLE WERE FAIR AND HAD SKY IN THEIR HAIR BUT NOW THEY'RE CONTENT TO WEAR STARS ON THEIR BROWS (LP, mono, with lyric sheet & manuscript)	100
68	Regal Zonophone LRZ 1003	MY PEOPLE WERE FAIR AND HAD SKY IN THEIR HAIR BUT NOW THEY'RE CONTENT TO WEAR STARS ON THEIR BROWS (LP, mono)	50
68	Regal Zonophone SLRZ 1003	MY PEOPLE WERE FAIR AND HAD SKY IN THEIR HAIR BUT NOW THEY'RE CONTENT TO WEAR STARS ON THEIR BROWS (LP, stereo, with lyric sheet & manuscript)	60
68	Regal Zonophone SLRZ 1003	MY PEOPLE WERE FAIR AND HAD SKY IN THEIR HAIR BUT NOW THEY'RE CONTENT TO WEAR STARS ON THEIR BROWS (LP, stereo)	20
68	Regal Zonophone TA-LRZ 1003	MY PEOPLE WERE FAIR AND HAD SKY IN THEIR HAIR BUT NOW THEY'RE CONTENT TO WEAR STARS ON THEIR BROWS (reel-to-reel tape, mono)	35
68	Regal Zonophone LRZ 1005	PROPHETS, SEERS AND SAGES, THE ANGELS OF THE AGES (LP, with lyric sheet, textured sleeve, mono)	100

MINT VALUE £

68	Regal Zonophone SLRZ 1005	PROPHETS, SEERS AND SAGES, THE ANGELS OF THE AGES (LP, with lyric sheet, textured sleeve, stereo)	80
69	R. Zonophone LRZ 1007	UNICORN (LP, gatefold sleeve, original with blue/silver label mono)	120
69	R. Zonophone LRZ 1007	UNICORN (LP, gatefold sleeve, later issue with red/silver label mono)	60
70	R. Zonophone SLRZ 1007	UNICORN (LP, gatefold sleeve, original with blue/silver label, stereo)	100
70	R. Zonophone SLRZ 1007	UNICORN (LP, gatefold sleeve, later issue with red/silver label, stereo)	30
70	R. Zonophone SLRZ 1013	A BEARD OF STARS (LP, with lyric sheet)	60
70	R. Zonophone SLRZ 1013	A BEARD OF STARS (LP, without lyric sheet)	30

(see also Marc Bolan/T. Rex, John's Children, Dib Cochran & Earwigs, Shagrat)

TYRANT
83	SRTS 83 CUS 2046	Hold Back The Lightning/Eyes Of A Stranger	400

TYRONE & CARR
72	Jam JAM 7	I Want To Give You My Everything/I'm Still In Love With You	8
73	Jam JAM 36	Love Me Love You/Take Me With You	6

GORDON TYRRALL
78	Hill & Dale HD 002	FAREWELL TO FOGGY HILLS (LP)	18

TYSONDOG
83	Neat NEAT 33	Eat The Rich/Dead Meat (p/s)	10
85	Neat NEAT 46	Shoot To Kill/Hammerhead (p/s)	10
85	Neat NEAT 4612	Shoot To Kill/Hammerhead/Changeling/Back To The Bullet (12", p/s)	15
86	Neat NEAT 56	School's Out/Don't Let The Bastards Grind You Down (p/s)	12
86	Neat NEAT 1031	CRIMES OF INSANITY (LP, with inner)	18
84	Neat NEAT 1017	BEWARE OF THE DOG (LP, with insert)	20

TYTAN
82	Kamaflage KAM 6	Blind Men And Fools/The Ballad Of Edward Case (p/s)	18
82	Kamaflage KAMA 6	Blind Men And Fools/The Ballad Of Edward Case (12", p/s)	20
85	Metal Masters METALP 105	ROUGH JUSTICE (LP)	22

(see also Angel Witch)

JUDIE TZUKE
78	Rocket ROKN 541	For You/Sukarita	5

(see also Tzuke & Paxo, Zookie)

TZUKE & PAXO
76	Good Earth GD 12	These Are The Laws/It's Only Fantasies	15

U

U BROWN
77	Third World TWS 909	LONDON ROCK (LP)	30
78	Live & Love LALP 002	REVELATION TIME (LP)	30

UBX
80	Crazy Plane SP 002	Crazy Today/Mister Fix It (p/s)	150

U.F.O.
70	Beacon BEA 161	Shake It About/Evil	30
70	Beacon BEA 165	Come Away Melinda/Unidentified Flying Object	25
70	Beacon BEA 172	Boogie For George/Treacle People (with postcard)	30
70	Beacon BEA 172	Boogie For George/Treacle People	20
71	Beacon BEA 181	Prince Kajuku/The Coming Of Prince Kajuku	20
73	Chrysalis CHS 2024	Give Her The Gun/Sweet Little Thing (unreleased in U.K.)	0
74	Chrysalis CHS 2040	Doctor Doctor/Lipstick Traces	12
75	Chrysalis CHS 2072	Shoot Shoot/Love Lost Love (unissued)	0
77	Chrysalis CHS 2146	Alone Again Or/Electric Phase	10
77	Chrysalis CHS 2178	Gettin' Ready/Lights Out (unissued)	0
78	Chrysalis CHS 2241	Only You Can Rock Me/Cherry/Rock Bottom (p/s, red vinyl, with frisbee offer)	8
78	Chrysalis CHS 2241	Only You Can Rock Me/Cherry/Rock Bottom (p/, with frisbee offer)	6
79	Chrysalis CHS 2287	Doctor Doctor (live)/On With The Action (live)/Try Me (p/s, clear vinyl)	6
79	Chrysalis CHS 2287	Doctor Doctor (live)/On With The Action (live)/Try Me (p/s, mauve vinyl)	10
79	Chrysalis CHS 2318	Shoot Shoot (live)/Only You Can Rock Me (live)/I'm A Loser (live) (p/s, clear vinyl)	5
83	Lyntone LYN 12821	Blinded By A Lie (edit)/Diesel In The Dust (edit)/When It's Time To Rock (edit) (flexidisc with Metal Fury magazine, issue 12)	10
70	Beacon BEAS 12	U.F.O. 1 (LP)	70
72	Beacon BEAS 19	U.F.O. 2 - FLYING (ONE HOUR SPACE ROCK) (LP, with inner lyric sleeve)	70
72	Beacon BEAS 19	U.F.O. 2 - FLYING (ONE HOUR SPACE ROCK) (LP)	35
74	Chrysalis CHS 1059	PHENOMENON (LP, misprinted green label, matt sleeve)	15
76	Chrysalis CHR 1103	NO HEAVY PETTING (LP, 1st pressing, green labels, A1/B1 matrixes)	20
77	Chrysalis CHR 1127	LIGHTS OUT (LP, 1st pressing, etched matrix numbers CHR1127 A/B, TML-S stamped into dead wax on both sides, green label wih red text on outer rim, 'Chrysalis Records Ltd, Printed in U.K', on spine)	20
78	Chrysalis CDL 1182	OBSESSION (LP, with poster)	12

(see also Michael Schenker Group)

LESLIE UGGAME
59	Philips BBL 7370	THE EYES OF GOD (LP)	12

UGLY CUSTARD
70	Kaleidoscope KAL 100	UGLY CUSTARD (LP)	140

(see also Hungry Wolf, Alan Parker, Rock Machine)

UGLYS
65	Pye 7N 15858	Wake Up My Mind/Ugly Blues	30
65	Pye 7N 15968	It's Alright/A Friend	20
66	Pye 7N 17027	A Good Idea/A Quiet Explosion	30
66	Pye 7N 17178	End Of The Season/Can't Recall Her Name	40

| 67 | CBS 2933 | And The Squire Blew His Horn/Real Good Girl | 50 |
| 69 | MGM MGM 1465 | I See The Light/Mary Cilento (6 demo copies only, pink/silver labels) | 1500 |

(see also Steve Gibbons, Balls, Lemon Tree, Move, Trevor Burton)

UK
| 88 | Chain Reaction | UK (LP) | 12 |

(see also Business, Tank)

U.K. BONDS
| 65 | Polydor BM 56061 | The World Is Watching Us/I Said Goodbye To The Blues | 10 |
| 66 | Polydor BM 56112 | Anything You Do Is Alright/The Last Thing I Ever Do | 20 |

U.K. DECAY
79	Plastic PLAS 001	U.K. Decay/Car Crash/PNEUMONIA: Exhibition/Coming Attack (folded p/s)	25
80	Fresh 012	For My Country/Unwind (p/s)	8
81	Plastic PLAS 002	BLACK CAT EP (p/s)	8
81	Fresh FRESH 26	Unexpected Guest/Dresden (foldout p/s)	8
81	Fresh FRESH 33	Sexual/Twist In The Tale (poster p/s)	5
82	C. Christi CHRIST ITS 1	Rising From The Dread/Testament/Werewolf/Jerusalem Over (The White Cliffs Of Dover) (12", p/s with insert)	8
81	Fresh LP5	FOR MADMEN ONLY (LP)	18
80s	UK Decay DKLP1	FOR MADMEN ONLY (LP)	25

(see also Pneumonia)

UK PLAYERS
| 82 | A&M AMLH 68544 | NO WAY OUT (LP) | 20 |

U.K. SUBS
78	City NIK 5	C.I.D./Live In A Car/B.I.C. (p/s, clear, red, blue, green or orange vinyl)	8
78	City NIK 5	C.I.D./Live In A Car/B.I.C. (p/s, black vinyl)	5
80	Gem GEMS 30	Teenage/Left For Dead/New York State Police (p/s, pink or orange vinyl)	5
82	Ramkup CAC 2	Party In Paris (1-sided fan club single, no p/s, 500 only)	30
83	Fall Out FALL 017	Another Typical City (p/s)	5
84	Gem FALL 12024	SPELL EP (12")	10
79	Gem GEMLP 100	ANOTHER KIND OF BLUES (LP, blue vinyl, with inner sleeve)	12
80	Gem GEMLP 106	BRAND NEW AGE (LP, clear vinyl, with insert)	12
80	Gem GEMLP 111	CRASH COURSE LIVE (LP, purple vinyl, 15,000 with export 12" [GEMEP 1])	15
80	Gem GEMLP 111	CRASH COURSE LIVE (LP)	12
80	Stidd Records MAIL 1	LIVE KICKS (LP, brown card inner sleeve, mail order only)	12
81	Gem GEMLP 112	DIMINISHED RESPONSIBILITY (LP, red vinyl with inner sleeve)	12
82	Abstract AABT 300	RECORDED '79-'81 (LP, blue vinyl with free stencil)	12
82	Abstract AABT 300	RECORDED 1979-1981 (LP, red vinyl)	12
82	Abstract AABT 800	THE SINGLES 78-82 (LP, blue vinyl)	12
83	Scarlett FALLLP 018	FLOOD OF LIES (LP)	12

(see also Urban Dogs)

ANYAOGU UKONU & HIS AFRO-CALYPSOIANS
| 56 | London HA-U 2019 | AFRO U.S.A (LP) | 30 |

U.K.S
| 64 | HMV POP 1310 | Ever Faithful, Ever True/Your Love Is All I Want | 25 |
| 64 | HMV POP 1357 | I Will Never Let You Go/I Know | 25 |

TRACEY ULLMAN
83	Stiff BUY DJ 195	Move Over Darling/Bobby's Girl (pink promo, "A" label)	15
83	Stiff BUY DJ 232	Move Over Darling/Bobby's Girl (grey promo, "A" label)	5
85	Stiff BUY DJ 232	Shattered/Alone (light blue promo "A" label)	6

JAMES 'BLOOD' ULMER
| 81 | Rough Trade RT 045 | Are You Glad To Be In America?/T.V. Blues (p/s) | 5 |

PETER ULRICH
| 90 | Corner Stone PTD-001 | Taqaharu's Leaving/Evocation (12") | 10 |

ULTERIOR MOTIVES
| 79 | Motive Music MMR 1 | Another Lover (p/s) | 30 |

ULTIMATE SPINACH
| 68 | MGM MGM-C(S) 8071 | ULTIMATE SPINACH (LP) | 50 |
| 68 | MGM MGM-C(S) 8094 | BEHOLD AND SEE (LP) | 50 |

ULTRAFOX
| 71 | Deram DM339 | Nine By Nine/Stomping At Decca | 6 |

ULTRAFUNK
| 75 | Contempo CLP 509 | ULTRAFUNK (LP) | 15 |

ULTRA VIOLENT
| 83 | Riot City RIOT 25 | CRIME FOR REVENGE (EP) | 20 |

ULTRA VIVID SCENE
89	4AD BAD 906	Mercy Seat/Codeine/H Like In Heaven/Mercy Seat (LP Version) (12", uncut p/s [most copies die-cut])	22
89	4AD AD 908	Something To Eat/H Like In Heaven (freebie, 1,000 only)	10
90	4AD AD 0016	Special One/Kind Of Drag	7
90	4AD UVS 1	Staring At The Sun/Three Stars (12", promo only)	10
92	4AD UVS 2	Medicating Angels/Mirror To Mirror (12", promo only)	10

ULTRAVOX
77	Island WIP 6375	Dangerous Rhythm/My Sex (initially no p/s)	5
77	Island WIP 6375	Dangerous Rhythm/My Sex (later pressing with p/s)	8
77	Island WIP 6392	Young Savage/Slip Away (p/s)	6
77	Island IEP 8	LIVE RETRO (EP)	8
77	Island WIP 6404	Rockwrock/Hiroshima Mon Amour (p/s)	5
78	Island WIP 6454	Slow Motion/Dislocation (p/s)	5
78	Island 12WIP 6454	Slow Motion/Dislocation (12", p/s, translucent vinyl)	8
78	Island WIP 6459	Quiet Men/Cross Fade (p/s)	6
78	Island 12WIP 6459	Quiet Men/Cross Fade (12", p/s, white vinyl)	8
77	Island ILPS 9449	ULTRAVOX (LP, gatefold sleeve)	15

MINT VALUE £

77	Island ILPS 9505	HA! HA! HA! (LP, with 7" "Quirks"/"Modern Love" [WIP 6417] & inner sleeve)	15
78	Island ILPS 9555	SYSTEMS OF ROMANCE (LP, with inner sleeve)	15

(see also Tiger Lily, John Foxx, Midge Ure, Helden)

UMPS & DUMPS
80	Topic 12TS 416	THE MOON'S IN A FIT (LP)	15

UNANIMITY
69	Clementswood CC127	Loner/All Right	40

UNANIMOUS DECISION
92	Kold Sweat KSEP211	RAP SINGS THE BLUES (EP)	10
93	Kold Sweat KSMEP 301X	IT AIN'T CLEVER (DOUBLE PACK EP) (12")	12

UNAUTHORISED VERSION
69	CBS 4135	Hey Jude/Girl In A Bus Queue	20

UNCLE DOG
72	Signpost SGP 752	River Road/First Night	5
72	Signpost SG 4253	OLD HAT (LP)	200

(see also Carol Grimes)

UNCLE PO
78	Beeb BEEB 23	Use My Friends/15 Minutes	25

UNCLE SAM
78	Ariola ARO 116	Oh Pretty Woman/Do It For Love	6

UNCLE 22
92	U No Dat HN 08	Wonderful Life/Love Me Once/Calling All Cars (12")	10
93	Ram RAMM 008	SPICE OF LIFE EP: 6 Million Ways To Die (DJ Hype Remix)/6 Million Ways To Die (Uncle 22 Mix) (12")	20
93	Pure Energy PE 003	SUPER MARIO EP: Super Mario (In Darkness)/Take You High/Love Me Twice/Dark Forces (12")	10
93	Pure Energy PE 004	Choose One (Part 1)/Choose One (Part 2)/Crazy Kid (12", with Navigator)	15

UNCOMMUNITY
85	Black Dwarf BDBG 1	Brutality Of Fact/Wall Of Sleep (Soundtrack)/The Price Of Your Entry Is Sin (card sleeve, 525 only, numbered, hand-painted labels, with insert)	25

(see also McCarthy)

UNCOOL DANCEBAND
79	Polydor PB 30	Let Me Be Your Boyfriend/Heads I Win (no p/s)	100
81	Polydor POSP 253	Jacqueline/No. 17 (no p/s)	20

UNDEAD
82	Riot City RIOT 7	It's Corruption/Undead (p/s)	7
82	Stiff TEES 7	NINE TOES LATER EP	12
82	Riot City RIOT 15	VIOLENT VISIONS (EP)	10
84	City 006	KILLING OF REALITY (LP, lyric insert)	30

DUNDEEVILLE PLAYERS
65	Stateside SS451	Wheels/Woodpecker	7

UNDERCOVER ELEPHANT & SECRET SQUIRREL
92	Dance Bass DANCE BASS 03	VOLUME 3 EP (12", stamped white label)	30

(see also Secret Squirrel)

UNDERDOGS
83	Riot City RIOT 26	EAST OF DACHAU (EP)	12

UNDERGROUND
69	Major Minor SMCP 5014	BEAT PARTY (LP)	30

(see also Madeline Bell)

UNDERGROUNDS
72	High Note HS 061	Skavito/Savito	15

UNDERGROUND SET
70	Pantonic PAN 6302	UNDERGROUND SET (LP, laminated front sleeve, red/black label)	70

UNDERGROUND SUNSHINE
69	Fontana TF 1049	Birthday/All I Want Is You	10

UNDERGROUND WITH STYLE
92	UAR UAR001	Lyrics Of A Gangster/Unbound Rage/Words Of Reality (EP)	25

UNDERGROUND ZERO
83	(No cat no)	GROUND ZERO (Cassette EP)	10
83	(No cat no)	THE OFFICIAL BOOTLEG (Cassette)	10
84	Underground UNDER 001	Seven Light Years/Canes Venatici (12")	15
84	Flicknife SHARP 023	NEVER REACH THE STARS (LP)	12

UNDERNEATH
86	él GPO 17T	THE IMP OF THE PERVERSE (12" EP)	8
86	él ACME 9	LUNATIC DAWN OF THE DISMANTLER (LP)	12

(see also Karl Blake, Shock Headed Peters, Lemon Kittens)

UNDERTAKERS
63	Pye 7N 15543	Everybody Loves A Lover/Mashed Potatoes	25
63	Pye 7N 15562	What About Us/Money	25
64	Pye 7N 15607	Just A Little Bit/Stupidity	30

(see also 'Takers, Jackie Lomax)

UNDER THE SUN
79	Redball RR 010	UNDER THE SUN (LP)	45

UNDERTONES
78	Good Vibrations GOT 4	TEENAGE KICKS (EP, white poster p/s)	50
78	Good Vibrations GOT 4	TEENAGE KICKS (EP, pink p/s)	70
78	Sire SIR 4007 PRO	Teenage Kicks/True Confessions (specially mastered promo, no p/s)	10
79	Sire SIR 4015	Jimmy Jimmy/Mars Bars (green vinyl, printed PVC sleeve & insert)	5

79	Sire SIR 4022	Here Comes The Summer/One Way Love/Top Twenty (p/s)	5
79	Sire SIR 4024	You've Got My Number (Why Don't You Use It!)/Let's Talk About Girls (p/s)	5
79	No label	CRACKS 90 MANAGEMENT EP: Teenage Kicks/Get Over You/Jimmy Jimmy/ Here Comes The Summer (promo-only, numbered with typed insert, 250 only)	60
80	Sire SIR 4038	My Perfect Cousin/Hard Luck (Again) (p/s)	5
81	Ardeck 12 ARDS 6	My Perfect Cousin/Hard Luck (Again)/Don't Wanna See (You Again) (12", p/s)	8
81	Ardeck ARDS 9	Julie Ocean/Kiss In The Dark (p/s)	5
83	Ardeck ARDS 11	The Love Parade/Like That (p/s)	5
83	Ardeck 12 ARDS 11	The Love Parade/Like That/You're Welcome/Crises Of Mine/ Family Entertainment (12", p/s)	10
83	Ardeck ARDS 12	Got To Have You Back/Turning Blue (p/s)	8
83	Ardeck ARDS 13	Chains Of Love/Window Shopping For New Clothes (p/s)	10
86	Strange Fruit SFPS 016	PEEL SESSIONS (12" EP, p/s)	8
08	Salvo/Ardeck SALVOSV003	TEENAGE KICKS EP (30th Anniversary edition, stickered, no'd p/s, poster)	8
79	Sire SRK 6071	UNDERTONES (LP, black & white cover, without "Teenage Kicks" & "Get Over You" & different version of "Here Comes The Summer" to reissue)	12
80	Sire SRK 6088	HYPNOTISED (LP, with cardboard mobile)	12
83	Ardeck ARD 104	THE SIN OF PRIDE (LP, mispressing with different tracks: Bittersweet & "Stand So Close")	40
94	Dojo DOJOLP 192	HYPNOTISED (10" LP, numbered, 500 only)	12
94	Dojo DOJOLP 193	POSITIVE TOUCH (10" LP, numbered, 500 only)	12
94	Dojo DOJOLP 194	THE SIN OF PRIDE (10" LP, numbered, 500 only)	12

(see also Feargal Sharkey)

UNDERWORLD

92	Tomato PLUM 2001	Mother Earth/Mother Earth (FM Mix)/The Hump/The Hump (Groove Without A Doubt Mix) (12", p/s)	50
93	Boys Own BOIX 13	Mmm... Skyscraper I Love You/Mmm... Skyscraper I Love You (Telegraph 6.11.92)/Mmm... Skyscraper I Love You (Jam Scraper) (12", p/s)	20
93	Boys Own BOIXCD 13	Mmm... Skyscraper I Love You/Mmm... Skyscraper I Love You (Telegraph 6.11.92)/Mmm... Skyscraper I Love You (Jam Scraper) (CD)	20
93	Boys Own Collect 002	Rez/Cowgirl (12", company sleeve)	10
93	Boys Own Collect 002P	Rez/Cowgirl (12", glossy pink sleeve, pink vinyl, white label)	20
93	Junior Boy's Own JBOLP1	DUBNOBASSWITHMYHEADMAN (2-LP)	20
96	Junior Boy's Own LOC 187	SECOND TOUGHEST IN THE INFANTS (2-LP, gatefold)	15

(see also Lemon Interrupt)

UNDISPUTED TRUTH

71	Tamla Motown TMG 776	Save My Love For A Rainy Day/Since I Lost You	12
71	Parlophone TMG 776	Save My Love For A Rainy Day/Since I Lost You (mispress on Parlophone)	60
71	Tamla Motown TMG 789	Smiling Faces Sometimes/You Got The Love I Need	12
72	Tamla Motown TMG 818	Superstar/Ain't No Sun Since You've Been Gone	10
74	Tamla Motown TMG 897	Help Yourself/What It Is	8
76	Warner Bros K 16804	You + Me = Love Parts 1 & 2	8
76	Warner Bros K 16804	You + Me = Love Parts 1 & 2 (12")	10
72	Tamla Motown STMA 8004	FACE TO FACE WITH THE TRUTH (LP)	15
72	Tamla Motown STML 11197	THE UNDISPUTED TRUTH (LP)	20
73	Tamla Motown STML 11240	THE LAW OF THE LAND (LP)	15
75	Tamla Motown STML 11277	DOWN TO EARTH (LP)	15
75	Tamla Motown STMA 8023	COSMIC TRUTH (LP)	15
75	Tamla Motown STML 12009	HIGHER THAN HIGH (LP)	12

UNDIVIDED ATTENTION

99	Hairy Parents no matrix	A Change To The Scheduled Programme/Missed Treatment (12")	8

UNEXPLORED BEATS

95	Unexplored Beats UXB 001	Skool Beats/Inner Life (12")	30

(see also Black Dog)

UNFORGETTABLES

75	Angen ANG 108	Many A Call/Chosen Dub	8

UNICORN

71	Transatlantic BIG 138	P.F. Sloan/Going Back Home	6
72	Transatlantic BIG 509	Cosmic Kid/All We Really Want To Do	6
71	Transatlantic TRA 238	UPHILL ALL THE WAY (LP, gatefold, plastic inner)	35
74	Charisma CAS 1092	BLUE PINE TREES (LP, small 'Mad Hatter' logo)	12
76	Harvest SHSP 4054	TOO MANY CROOKS (LP, inner sleeve, EMI logo on label)	15

UNICORN (1)

70	Hollick & Taylor HT 1258	Going Home/Another World	250

UNIFICS

68	London HLR 10231	Court Of Love/Which One Should I Choose	10

UNION EXPRESS

73	Decca F 13408	Do You Love Me/Alligator Fix	12
71	Decca F 13230	Ring A Ring A Rosies/Emily Knows	10

UNIQUE (1)

83	Prelude TA 3707	What I Got Is What You Need/What I Got Is What YOu Need (Instrumental) (12")	10

UNIQUE (2)

08	Diggers With Gratitude DWG 003	THE DIE HARD (EP)	80

UNIQUES

80	Charly CTD 121	You Don't Miss Your Water/It's All Over Now/All These Things	5

UNIQUES

72	Trojan TR 7852	Mother And Child Reunion/Corner Hop	5
72	Trojan TR 7866	Lonely For Your Love/LIONS DEN: Chick-A-Bow	5

(see also Pioneers)

UNIQUES (FEATURING JOE STAMPLEY) (U.S)

65	Pye International 7N 25303	Not Too Long Ago/Fast Way Of Living	30
65	Pye International 7N 25303	Not Too Long Ago/Fast Way Of Living (DJ copy)	50
66	Pye Intl. NPL 28094	UNIQUELY YOURS (LP)	120

MINT VALUE £

UNIQUES (JAMAICA)

67	Collins Downbeat CR 002	Dry The Water/I'm A Fool For You	40
67	Island WI 3070	People Rock Steady/I'm Trying To Find A Home (credited to Roy Shirley)	60
67	Island WI 3084	Gypsy Woman/KEN ROSS: Wall Flower	70
67	Island WI 3086	Let Me Go Girl/SOULETTES: Dum Dum	30
68	Island WI 3087	Never Let Me Go/HENRY III: Won't Go Away	25
68	Island WI 3106	Speak No Evil/GLEN ADAMS: That New Girl	25
68	Island WI 3107	Lesson Of Love/DELROY WILSON: Til I Die	25
68	Island WI 3114	Build My World Around You/LLOYD CLARKE: I'll Never Change	70
68	Island WI 3117	Give Me Some More Of Your Loving/VAL BENNETT: Lovell's Special	35
68	Island WI 3122	My Conversation/SLIM SMITH: Love One Another	25
68	Island WI 3123	The Beatitude/KEITH BLAKE: Time On The River (actually "Time & The River")	40
68	Island WI 3145	Girl Of My Dreams/LESTER STERLING: Tribute To King Scratch	75
68	Trojan TR 619	Watch This Sound/Out Of Love	25
68	Trojan TR 645	A-Yuh/Just A Mirage	25
68	Blue Cat BS 126	Girls Like Dirt/GLEN ADAMS: She Is Leaving	30
69	Gas GAS 117	Too Proud To Beg/Love And Devotion	12
69	Nu Beat NB 034	Crimson And Clover/What A Situation	10
69	Nu Beat NB 037	I'll Make You Love Me/Lover's Prayer	30
69	Unity UN 527	The Beatitude/My Conversation	12
69	Trojan TRL 15	ABSOLUTELY THE UNIQUES (LP)	150

(see also Slim Smith, Melodians, Lloyd Charmers, Tommy McCook)

UNIT 4 + 2

64	Decca F 11821	The Green Fields/Swing Down Chariot	15
64	Decca F 11994	Sorrow And Pain/The Lonely Valley	12
65	Decca F 12071	Concrete And Clay/When I Fall In Love	6
65	Decca F 12144	(You've) Never Been In Love Like This Before/Tell Somebody You Know	8
65	Decca F 12211	Hark/Stop Wasting Your Time	7
65	Decca F 12299	You've Got To Be Cruel To Be Kind/I Won't Let You Down	7
66	Decca F 12333	Baby Never Say Goodbye/Rainy Day	12
66	Decca F 12398	For A Moment/Fables	12
66	Decca F 12509	I Was Only Playing Games/I've Seen The Light	10
67	Fontana TF 834	Too Fast, Too Slow/Booby Trap	20
67	Fontana TF 840	Butterfly/A Place To Go	15
67	Fontana TF 891	Loving Takes A Little Understanding/Would You Believe What I Say? (as Unit)	200
68	Fontana TF 931	You Ain't Goin' Nowhere/So You Want To Be A Blues Player	15
69	Fontana TF 990	I Will/3.30	50
65	Decca DFE 8619	UNIT 4 + 2 (EP)	60
65	Decca LK 4697	UNIT 4 + 2 - 1st ALBUM (LP)	60
69	Fontana SFL 13123	UNIT 4 + 2 (LP)	50
76	Decca REM 6	REMEMBERING (LP)	15

(see also Roulettes,Tom Sawyer, Capability Brown, Argent)

UNITED SONS OF AMERICA

71	Mercury 6338 036	GREETINGS FROM THE U.S. OF A. (LP)	18

UNITED SOUNDS OF LONDON

94	USL USL 6	Making Love/Making Dub (12")	15

UNITED STATES DOUBLE QUARTET

67	Stateside SS 590	Life Is Groovy/Split	20
67	BT Puppy BTS 45524	Life Is Groovy/Split (reissue)	15

(see also Tokens, Kirby Stone 4)

UNITED STATES OF AMERICA

68	CBS 3745	Garden Of Earthly Delights/Love Song For The Dead Che	16
68	CBS (S) 63340	UNITED STATES OF AMERICA (LP, laminated cover, mono/stereo)	50

UNITED STATES OF EXISTENCE

87	Bam Caruso OPRA 081	Gone/PAUL ROLAND: Madam Guillotine (jukebox issue, company sleeve)	5

UNITY ALL STARS

75	Nice N 001	Africa/BIG DREAD & UNITY ALL STARS: Africa Is Our Home	25

UNIVERSAL ENERGY

77	Harvest HAR 5138	Universal Energy/Christmas For Space	6
77	Harvest SHSP 4075	UNIVERSAL (LP)	12

UNIVERSAL INDICATOR

92	Rephlex TB-303	1-BLUE (12")	25
92	Rephlex TR-606	2-RED (12")	25
93	Rephlex MC-202	3-YELLOW (12")	20
95	Rephlex SH-101	4-GREEN (7", 10" + 12" in bag, all green vinyl)	50

(see also Kosmik Kommando)

UNIVERSAL PANZIES

98	Head Heritage HH4	TRANSCENDENTAL FLOSS (CD, mail order only)	30

(see also Julian Cope)

UNIVERSAL ROBOT BAND

84	Streetwave MKHAN 48	Barely Breaking Even (85 Club MIx)/Barely Breaking Even (Edit)/Barely Breaking Even (Instrumental) (12")	40

UNIVERSALS

67	Page One POF 032	I Can't Find You/Hey You	175
67	Page One POF 049	Green Veined Orchid/While The Cat's Away	35

(see also Chris Lamb & Universals, Gidian, Lace, Gary Walker & Rain, Plastic Penny)

U.N.K.L.E.

97	Mo' Wax MW 069L	Berry Meditation (Mixes) (12", clear etched vinyl stickered PVC sleeve)	8
97	Mo' Wax MW 069L	Berry Meditation (Mixes) (12", clear etched vinyl promo, unsealed poly sleeve)	20
99	Mo' Wax MW 108CD 2	Be There/Knock/Rabbit In Your Headlights (CD, 2 of 2-CD set, card sleeve)	12
95	Mo' Wax MW 028	THE TIME HAS COME EP (2 x 12" EP, picture disc)	15
94	Mo' Wax MWCD 028	THE TIME HAS COME EP (CD, picture disc, stickered card sleeve)	8
98	Mo' Wax MW 085DJ	PSYENCE FICTION SURVIVAL KIT (promo, 12" in pop-up gatefold p/s, 5" vinyl single in envelope, bag of stickers, press release, all in box mailer, 700 only)	35

98	Mo Wax 085	PSYENCE FICTION (2-LP)	15
98	Mo Wax 085	PSYENCE FICTION (2-LP, hardcover gatefold sleeve with booklet)	20
98	Mo' Wax MW 035CDX	PSYENCE FICTION (CD, gatefold card sleeve)	20
03	Mo Wax MWU 001	NEVER NEVER LAND (3-LP, gatefold sleeve)	20
03	Mo Wax MWU 001	NEVER NEVER LAND (3-LP, picture discs, gatefold sleeve, foldout inserts)	30
07	Surrender ALL SURR LPXX	WAR STORIES (2-LP, gatefold sleeve)	15
07	Surrender ALL SURR LPXX	WAR STORIES (4x12", gatefold sleeve in slipcase with book)	40
10	Surrender ALL SURR 017 LP	WHERE DID THE NIGHT FALL (3-LP box set with two books)	100
11	Vinyl Factory VF 029	THE HERETIC'S GATE SCORE (with Doug Foster) (1-sided LP. orange vinyl, sleeve signed and numbered by James Lavell and Doug Foster, 100 only)	100

(see also DJ Shadow)

UNKNOWN ARTIST

57	Woodbine Cigarettes	Big Beat (78, same track on both sides)	15
50s	Capstan Cigarettes	Capstan Go (1-sided flexi 78, promo)	15
50s	Capstan Cigarettes	Cha Cha (1-sided 78, promo)	15
50s	Strand Cigarettes	You're Never Alone With A Strand (78, p/s, same track on both sides)	35
66	Major MAJ 1	Roarin' 'N' Scorin'/The Toast Of Merseyside (p/s)	25

UNKNOWNS

66	London HLU 10082	Melody For An Unknown Girl/Peith's Song	7

UNLEASHED

03	Century Media 77544-0	AND WE SHALL TRIUMPH IN VICTORY (Numbered box set with 6 picture discs LPs and booklet, 2000 only)	75

UNSEEN TERROR

89	Strange Fruit SFPS 069	PEEL SESSIONS (12")	8

UNTAMED YOUTH

79	Hardcore HAR 001	Untamed Youth/Runnin' Wild (p/s, 1,000 only)	15

UNTAMED (1)

64	Decca F 12045	So Long/Just Wait	60
65	Parlophone R 5258	Once Upon A Time/I'm Asking You	100
65	Stateside SS 431	I'll Go Crazy/My Baby Is Gone	60
66	Planet PLF 103	It's Not True/Gimme Gimme Some Shade	100

(see also Lindsay Muir's Untamed)

UNTAMED (2)

88	Real World RWR 004	Next Please/Black Heart (p/s, with insert)	5

UNTOUCHABLES

80	Fried Egg EGG 2	Keep On Walking/Keep Your Distance (p/s)	5

UNTOUCHABLES (JAMAICA)

68	Blue Cat BS 137	Prisoner In Love/EDWARD RAPHAEL: True Love	30
68	Trojan TR 613	Tighten Up/ROY SHIRLEY: Good Ambition	30
70	Upsetter US 345	Same Thing All Over/UPSETTERS: It's Over	20
70	Upsetter US 350	Knock On Wood/UPSETTERS: Tight Spot	30
71	Bullet BU 460	Can't Reach You/CARL DAWKINS: Natural Woman	10
73	Bread BR 1113	Pay For The Wicked/Pay For The Wicked - Version (actually titled "Pray For The Wicked')	10
79	Sagittarius SUS 10	Help Us Jah/Sea Of Love (12")	20

(see also Inspirations, Dave Barker, Leroy Reid)

UNWANTED

77	Raw RAW 6	Withdrawal/1978/Bleak Outlook (p/s)	40
77	Raw RAWT 6	Withdrawal/1978/Bleak Outlook (12", reissue)	20
78	Raw RAW 15	Secret Police/These Boots Are Made For Walking (p/s)	20
78	Raw RAW 30	Memory Man/Guns Of Love (unissued)	0
85	Delorian No One	SECRET PAST (LP)	15

(see also Psychedelic Furs)

UPBEATS

58	London HLU 8688	Just Like In The Movies/My Foolish Heart	25
58	London HLU 8688	Just Like In The Movies/My Foolish Heart (78)	15
59	Pye International 7N 25016	You're The One I Care For/Keep Cool Crazy Heart	15
59	Pye International 7N 25028	Teenie Weenie Bikini/Satin Shoes	15
59	Pye International 7N 25028	Teenie Weenie Bikini/Satin Shoes (78)	12

PHIL UPCHURCH COMBO

61	HMV POP 899	You Can't Sit Down Parts 1 & 2	35
66	Sue WI 4005	You Can't Sit Down Parts 1 & 2 (reissue)	30
66	Sue WI 4017	Nothing But Soul/Evad	40
72	Blue Thumb ILPS 9219	DARKNESS, DARKNESS (LP)	20

ROBERT UPCHURCH

74	Phil. Intl. PIR 2652	The Devil Made Me Do It/Glad You're Mine	15
70s	Phil. Intl 82168 4ZP 2000	The Devil Made Me Do It/You're The Reason Why (12")	20

UPCOMING WILLOWS

65	Island WI 182	Jonestown Special/SHENLEY DUFFAS: La La La	40
65	Island WI 184	Red China/SHENLEY DUFFAS: You Are Mine	40

(see also Shenley Duffas)

UPFRONT RUDIES

92	Krazy Fly Recz RUDIE 9	REAL SKILLS (EP)	10

UPP

75	Epic EPC 80625	UPP (LP)	15
76	CBS EPC 81322	THIS WAY (LP)	12

(see also Clark-Hutchinson)

UPRISING

79	Tribesman TM 11	Come On Over/Try Me Girl (12")	18

UPROAR

82	Beat The System RAW 1	Rebel Youth/No More War/Fallen Angel/Victims (p/s)	12
83	Lightbeat RAW 2	DIE FOR ME (EP)	12

MINT VALUE £

| 83 | Volume VOL 9 | NOTHING CAN STOP YOU (EP) | 10 |
| 80s | Beat The System BTSLP 1 | AND THE LORD SAID LET THERE BE UPROAR (LP) | 30 |

UPSETTERS (1)

65	Island WI 223	Country Girl/Strange Country (both sides actually by Ossie & Upsetters)	35
65	Rio R 70	Walk Down The Aisle/So Bad	20
66	Doctor Bird DB 1034	Wildcat/I Love You So	40

(see also Ossie & Upsetters, Dave Barker)

UPSETTERS (2)

69	Duke DU 11	Eight For Eight/Stand By Me (B-side actually by Inspirations)	40
69	Camel CA 13	Taste Of Killing/My Mob	40
69	Punch PH 18	Return Of The Ugly/I've Caught You	25
69	Punch PH 19	Dry Acid/REGGAE BOYS: Selassie	50
69	Punch PH 21	Clint Eastwood/Lennox Mood	12
69	Upsetter US 300	Eight For Eight/You Know What I Mean (B-side actually by Inspirations)	15
69	Upsetter UP 301	Return Of Django/Dollar In The Teeth	12
69	Upsetter US 303	Ten To Twelve/LEE PERRY: People Funny Fi True	30
69	Upsetter US 305	Farmers In The Den/BUSTY BROWN : To Love Somebody	30
69	Upsetter US 307	Night Doctor/TERMITES: I'll Be Waiting	30
69	Upsetter US 309	Kiddyo/Endlessly (both sides actually by Silvertones)	18
69	Upsetter US 310	A Dangerous Man From MI5/WEST INDIANS: Oh Lord	18
69	Upsetter US 313	Live Injection/BLEECHERS: Everything For Fun	10
69	Upsetter US 315	Cold Sweat/Pound Get A Blow (B-side actually by Bleechers)	30
70	Upsetter US 317	Vampire/BLEECHERS: Check Him Out	25
70	Upsetter US 318	Soulful I/MILTON HENRY: Bread And Butter	15
70	Upsetter US 321	Drugs And Poison/Stranger On The Shore	18
70	Upsetter US 325	Kill Them All/Soul Walk	18
70	Upsetter US 326	Bronco/One More	22
70	Upsetter US 332	Na Na Hey Hey/Pick Folk Kinkyest	20
70	Upsetter US 333	Granny Show/Version	20
70	Upsetter US 334	Fire Fire/Jumper	20
70	Upsetter US 335	The Pillow/Grooving	20
70	Upsetter US 336	Self Control/The Pill	22
70	Upsetter US 338	Fresh Up/Toothaches	20
70	Upsetter US 342	Dreamland/BOB MARLEY: Version Of Cup	45
70	Upsetter US 343	Sipreano/Ferry Boat	20
70	Upsetter US 346	Bigger Joke/Return Of The Vampire	15
70	Upsetter US 349	Upsetting Station (actually plays "Did Your Grave" by Bob Marley & Wailers)/UPSETTERS: Justice (Instrumental)	40
70	Upsetter US 352	Heart And Soul/Zig Zag	18
70	Spinning Wheel SW 100	Haunted House/Double Wheel	85
70	Spinning Wheel SW 101	The Miser/CHUCK JUNIOR: Do It Madly	25
70	Spinning Wheel SW 102	The Chokin' Kind/CHUCK JUNIOR: Penny Wise	25
70	Spinning Wheel SW 103	Land Of Kinks/O'NEIL HALL: This Man	25
70	Trojan TR 7748	Family Man/Mellow Mood	12
70	Trojan TR 7749	Capo/Mama Look	15
70	Punch PH 27	The Result/Feel The Spirit	40
71	Bullet BU 461	All Combine Parts 1 & 2	10
71	Bullet BU 499	Beat Down Babylon/JUNIOR BYLES: Version	18
71	Upsetter US 353	Illusion/Big John Wayne (as Upsetters & King Teddy)	18
71	Upsetter US 361	Capasetic (actually "Copasetic" by Lord Comic)/All Africans (actually "Don't Cross The Nation" by Little Roy)	20
71	Upsetter US 365	Earthquake/JUNIOR BYLES: Palace Called Africa	20
71	Upsetter US 370	Dark Moon/DAVID ISAACS: You'll Be Sorry	15
72	Upsetter US 385	French Connection/Version	15
72	Upsetter US 387	Festival Da Da/JUNIOR BYLES: Version	18
72	Upsetter US 393	Crummy People/BIG YOUTH: Moving - Version	15
72	Upsetter US 394	Water Pump Parts 1 & 2	15
72	Randy's RAN 523	Nebuchadnezzer/JUNIOR BYLES: King Of Babylon	18
72	Punch PH 109	Hail To Power/JUNIOR BYLES: Pharaoh Hiding	18
73	Upsetter US 396	Puss Sea Hole/WINSTON GROOVY: Want To Be Loved	15
73	Upsetter US 397	Jungle Lion/Freak Out Skank	100
73	Upsetter US 398	Cow Thief Skank (with Charlie Ace)/7 3/4 Skank	20
73	Downtown DT 499	Black Ipa/Ipa Skank	18
73	Downtown DT 506	Sunshine Showdown/Sunshine Version	18
73	Downtown DT 512	Tighten Up Skank/Mid-East Rock	15
73	Downtown DT 513	Sucky Skank/Yucky Skank	18
74	Count Shelly CS 052	San-San/OSBOURNE GRAHAM: Baby Don't Go	8
74	Dip DL 5031	Enter The Dragon/JOY WHITE: Lady Lady	12
74	Dip DL 5032	Rebels Train/Rebels Dub	8
75	Dip DL 5054	Cane River Rock/Riverside Rock	12
75	Dip DL 5056	I Man Free/King Burnett: Version	12
75	Dip DL 5073	Key Card/Domino Game	8
75	Angen ANG 107	Stay Dread/Kingdom Of Dub	20
75	Attack ATT 8090	Kiss Me Neck/Da Ba Day	15
78	Island IPR 2010	Close Together/Dreadlocks In The Moonlight (12" as UPSETTERS REVIEW featuring JUNIOR MURVIN)	20
69	Pama Special PSP 1014	CLINT EASTWOOD (LP)	75
69	Trojan TRL 19	THE RETURN OF DJANGO (LP, orange/white label)	50
69	Trojan TTL 13	THE UPSETTER (LP)	40
70	Trojan TTL 28	SCRATCH THE UPSETTER AGAIN (LP)	50
70	Trojan TBL 119	THE GOOD, THE BAD AND THE UPSETTERS (LP)	30
70	Trojan TBL 125	EASTWOOD RIDES AGAIN (LP)	35
70	Pama SECO 24	THE MANY MOODS OF THE UPSETTERS (LP)	65
74	Trojan TRLS 70	DOUBLE SEVEN (LP, black sticker on rear cover showing song titles and marketed by B & C Records)	50
75	DIP DLPD 6002	RETURN OF THE WAX (LP, white-label only, plain sleeve)	45
76	Island ILPS 9417	SUPER APE (LP)	30
83	Pama PTLP 1026	BEST OF THE UPSETTERS VOL. 2 (LP)	30
90	Trojan PERRY 3	BUILD THE ARK (3-LP box set)	30

(see also Lee Perry, Ossie & Upsetters, Hippy Boys, Bob Marley/Wailers, Family Man, Tommy McCook, Max Romeo, Melodians, Lord Creator, Dennis Alcapone)

UPSETTING BROTHERS
71   Supreme SUP 229   Not You Baby/DREAD LOCK ALL-STARS: Baby (Version) 12

CHARLES UPTON
65   Ralph Tuck EP CU 01   SINGS (EP)..10

UPTOWNERS
64   London HLU 9877   If'n/Search Is Over 15

URBAN CLEARWAY (1)
70   Torpedo TOR 21   Open Up Wide Parts 1 & 2 6

URBAN CLEARWAY (2)
82   Bandit X 82 CUS 1609   Lost Memories/You've Always Known (12", p/s) 100

URBAN DISTURBANCE
79   Rok ROK V/VI   Wild Boys In Cortinas/V.I.P.S: Can't Let You Go (die-cut sleeve) 25

URBAN DOGS
82   Fallout FALL 008   New Barbarians/Speed Kills/Cocaine (p/s)..5
82   Fallout FALL 011   Limo Life/Warhead (p/s)...5
88   Fallout FALL LP 12   URBAN DOGS (LP) 12
     (see Hanoi Rocks, U.K. Subs, Vibrators)

URBAN MYTHS
98   Urban Myths MYTH 1   Lose You/Lose You (Dub)//Makin' Me Feel/No Man (12") 20

URBAN SHAKEDOWN
82   Respond RESP5   Wolves/Rap The Wolf 10

URBAN TRIBE
92   Sub Assertive CUE 6   THE UNKNOWN EP (12", white label)..20

URCHIN
77   DJM DJS 10776   Black Leather Fantasy/Rock & Roll Woman (in promo p/s) 275
77   DJM DJS 10776   Black Leather Fantasy/Rock & Roll Woman (no p/s) 100
78   DJM DJS 10850   She's A Roller/Long Time No Woman (in promo p/s)...275
79   DJM DJS 10850   She's A Roller/Long Time No Woman (no p/s) 100
     (see also A.S.A.P., Iron Maiden)

URCHINS
66   Polydor BM 56145   I Made Her That Way/Twas On A Night Like This 10

URGE
81   Consumer Discks CD 0861 Revolting Boy/Revolve (p/s)..10

URIAH HEEP
71   Bronze WIP 6111   Look At Yourself/Simon The Bullet Freak..7
72   Bronze WIP 6126   The Wizard/Gypsy 6
72   Bronze WIP 6140   Easy Livin'/Why 6
73   Bronze BRO 7   Stealin'/Sunshine..6
74   Bronze BRO 10   Something Or Nothing/What Can I Do 5
75   Bronze BRO 17   Prima Donna/Shout It Out 5
76   Bronze BRO 27   One Way Or Another/Misty Eyes 5
76   Bronze BRODJ 1   One Way Or Another/Misty Eyes (promo only p/s, 750 copies) 20
77   Bronze BRO 37   Wise Man/Crime Of Passion 5
77   Bronze BRO 47   Free Me/Masquerade (p/s) 6
78   Bronze BROP 62   Come Back To Me/Cheater...5
83   Bronze BROP 166   Lonely Nights/Weekend Warriors (picture disc) 8
83   Bronze BROG 168   Stay On Top/Playing For Time//Gypsy/Easy Livin'/Sweet Lorraine/ Stealin' (double
                              pack, gatefold p/s) 7
85   Portrait WA 6103   Rockerama/Back Stage Girl (shaped picture disc) 10
88   Legacy LGYT 65   Easy Livin' (live)/Corina (live)/Gypsy (live) (12", red vinyl) 8
88   Castle Comms. CD3-16   URIAH HEEP (CD EP, 5,000 only)..10
70   Vertigo 6360 006   VERY 'EAVY... VERY 'UMBLE (LP, gatefold sleeve, large swirl label) 300
71   Vertigo 6360 028   SALISBURY (LP, gatefold sleeve, large swirl label) 300
71   Bronze ILPS 9142   VERY 'EAVY... VERY 'UMBLE (LP, reissue) 30
71   Bronze ILPS 9152   SALISBURY (LP, reissue)..30
71   Bronze ILPS 9169   LOOK AT YOURSELF (LP, 'mirror' sleeve, inner sleeve) 100
72   Bronze ILPS 9193   DEMONS AND WIZARDS (LP, gatefold) 50
72   Bronze ILPS 9213   THE MAGICIAN'S BIRTHDAY (LP, gatefold with inner sleeve) 40
73   Bronze ILPS 9245   SWEET FREEDOM (LP, gatefold)..30
73   Bronze ISLD 1   LIVE (2-LP, laminated gatefold sleeve with booklet and inners) 20
89   Legacy LLP 120   RAGING SILENCE (LP, picture disc) 12
95   HTD LP 33   SEA OF LIGHT (LP, with inner) 15
     (see also Gods, Head Machine, Natural Gas, Spice, King Crimson, John Lawton, Grand Prix, Stratus)

URUSEI YATSURA
95   Modern Ind. MIR 001   Pampered Adolescent/BLISTERS: A Dull Thought In Itself (burgundy vinyl, p/s, 500
                              only)..12
95   Ché CHÉ 38   Siamese/Lo-Fi (orange & grey vinyl, p/s)...8
95   Love Train PUBE 08   Kernel/Teendream (p/s, 1,000 only)..10

US FOLK
65   Eyemark EMS 1001   Funny Old World/Dives...8

U.S. T-BONES
65   Liberty LIB 55836   No Matter What Shape/Feelin' Fine 12
66   Liberty LIB 55867   Sippin'n'Chippin'/Moment Of Softness 15
66   Liberty LIB 55951   The Proper Thing To Do/Tee-Hee-Hee 15

US (1)
70s Jeff Wayne Music SD 015 You're OK With Us/Tomorrow (p/s, promo for Johnson Wax)...............................10
     (see also David Essex, Randells)

US (2)
67   Polydor 56179   Barefoot In The Park/Four's A Crowd 8

USELESS UNICORN
74   Horny HORN 11   RUBBER HORN (LP, gatefold sleeve, with pop-up horn) 15

USERS

77	Raw RAW 1	Sick Of You/(I'm) In Love With Today (p/s, numbered on rear) 15
77	Raw RAW 1	Sick Of You/(I'm) In Love With Today (p/s) 10
77	Raw RAWT 1	Sick Of You/(I'm) In Love With Today (12", no p/s) 15
78	Warped WARP 1	Warped 45: Kicks In Style/Dead On Arrival (p/s, 5,000 only, numbered sleeve, some un-numbered) 25

PETER USTINOV

| 53 | Parlophone MSP 6012 | Mock Mozart (with Anthony Hopkins, Harpsichord)/Phoney Folk-Lore .... 8 |

(see also Peter Sellers)

UTOMICA

| 93 | Pro-One PRONE 9T | Rok A bye/Rok A Bye (12", stamped or hand-written white label) .... 50 |
| 93 | Pro-One PRONE 11T | Pumpkin/Pumpkin (12", white stamped label) .... 15 |

UTOPIA (GERMANY)

| 73 | United Artists UAG 29438 | UTOPIA (LP) .... 35 |

(see also Amon Duull)

UTOPIA (U.S.)

82	Epic XPS 166	Infrared And Ultra Violet/Forgotten But Not Gone/Private Heaven/Princess Of The Universe/Chapter And Verse (EP) 12
77	Bearsville K 55514	RA (LP, with lyric inner & pyramid insert) 12
82	Epic EPC 25207	UTOPIA (LP, with free 5-track EP) 20

U2

SINGLES : SINGLES: IRISH PRESSINGS

79	CBS 7951	U2: THREE (Out Of Control/Stories For The Boys/Boy-Girl) (p/s, black vinyl) (CBS 'Sunburst Label' with UK TM NoB81 809) on label (First Pressing)) 150
79	CBS 7951	U2: THREE (Out Of Control/Stories For The Boys/Boy-Girl) (p/s, black vinyl) 50
80	CBS 7951	U2: THREE (Out Of Control/Stories For The Boys/Boy-Girl) (p/s, white vinyl) 300
80	CBS 7951	U2: THREE (Out Of Control/Stories For The Boys/Boy-Girl) (p/s, orange vinyl) 150
80	CBS 7951	U2: THREE (Out Of Control/Stories For The Boys/Boy-Girl) (p/s, yellow vinyl) 100
80	CBS 7951	U2: THREE (Out Of Control/Stories For The Boys/Boy-Girl) (p/s, brown vinyl mispressing, fewer than 50 copies exist) 1000
81	CBS 12-7951	U2: THREE (12" EP, with numbered sticker, orange CBS sleeve, 1,000 only) 1500
81	CBS 12-7951	U2: THREE (12" EP, reissue, die-cut CBS sleeve) 60
81	CBS 12-7951	U2: THREE (12" EP, 2nd reissue, plain black sleeve, slightly different labels) 40
85	CBS 40-7951	U2: THREE (cassette, reissue) 50
80	CBS 8306	Another Day/Twilight (Demo Version) (p/s, yellow vinyl) 80
80	CBS 8306	Another Day/Twilight (Demo Version) (p/s, orange vinyl) 150
80	CBS 8306	Another Day/Twilight (Demo Version) (p/s, white vinyl) 350
80	CBS 8306	Another Day/Twilight (Demo Version) (p/s, black vinyl, with postcard designed by Bono) 200
80	CBS 8306	Another Day/Twilight (Demo Version) (p/s, black vinyl, without postcard designed by Bono) 40
80	CBS 8687	11 O'Clock Tick Tock/Touch (p/s, yellow vinyl) 60
80	CBS 8687	11 O'Clock Tick Tock/Touch (p/s, orange vinyl) 150
80	CBS 9065	I Will Follow/Boy-Girl (live) (p/s, yellow vinyl) 50
80	CBS 9065	I Will Follow/Boy-Girl (live) (p/s, orange vinyl) 100
80	CBS 9065	I Will Follow/Boy-Girl (live) (p/s, white vinyl) 300
80	CBS 9065	I Will Follow/Boy-Girl (live) (p/s, brown vinyl, fewer than 50 copies) 1500
82	CBS PAC 1	4 U2 PLAY (4 x 7", each in p/s, black vinyl) 120
82	CBS PAC 1	4 U2 PLAY (4 x 7", each in p/s, yellow vinyl) 300
82	CBS PAC 1	4 U2 PLAY (4 x 7", each in p/s, orange vinyl) 600
82	CBS PAC 1	4 U2 PLAY (4 x 7", each in p/s, white vinyl) 1000
80s	CBS PAC 2	PAC 2 (4 x 7" with p/s in plastic wallet) 60
80s	CBS PAC 3	PAC 3 (4 x 7" with p/s in plastic wallet) 50

SINGLES : SINGLES: UK PRESSINGS

95	Atlantic A 7131	Hold Me, Thrill Me, Kiss Me, Kill Me /ELLIOTT GOLDENTHAL: Themes From Batman 5
84	Island 12IS 202	Pride In The Name of Love/4th of July/Boomerang (12") 8
80	Island WIP 6601	11 O'Clock Tick Tock/Touch (p/s) 25
80	Island WIP 6630	A Day Without Me/Things To Make And Do (p/s) 20
80	Island WIP 6656	I Will Follow/Boy-Girl (live) (p/s) 15
81	Island WIP 6679	Fire/J. Swallo (p/s) 6
81	Island UWIP 6679	Fire/J. Swallo//11 O'Clock Tick Tock (live)/The Ocean (live)/Cry (live)/ The Electric Co. (live) (double pack, single p/s) 10
81	Island WIP 6733	Gloria/I Will Follow (live) (p/s) 10
82	Island WIP 6770	A Celebration/Trash, Trampoline And The Party Girl (p/s) 10
83	Island UWIP 6848	New Year's Day/Treasure (Whatever Happened To Pete The Chop)// Fire (live)/I Threw A Brick Through A Window (live)/A Day Without Me (live) (double pack, single p/s, black inners) 10
83	Island ISD 109	Two Hearts Beat As One/Endless Deep//New Year's Day (U.S.A. Remix)/ Two Hearts Beat As One (U.S.A. Remix) (p/s, double pack) 10
84	Island ISP 202	Pride (In The Name Of Love)/Boomerang 2 (Vocal) (picture disc) 20
84	Island ISD 202	Pride (In The Name Of Love)/4th Of July/Boomerang I (Instrumental)/ Boomerang 2 (Vocal) (double pack, gatefold p/s) 6
84	Island 12ISX 202	Pride (In The Name Of Love)/Boomerang I/ 11 O'Clock Tick Tock/Touch (Full Length Version) (12", blue p/s) 10
84	Island CIS 202	Pride (In The Name Of Love)/Boomerang I/4th Of July/Boomerang 2/ A Celebration (cassette) 8
85	Island ISD 220	The Unforgettable Fire/A Sort Of Homecoming (live)/Love Comes Tumbling/ Sixty Seconds In Kingdom Come/The Three Sunrises (double pack, gatefold p/s) 6
85	Island ISP 220	The Unforgettable Fire/A Sort Of Homecoming (live) (logo-shaped pic disc) 40
87	Island CID 319	With Or Without You/Luminous Times (Hold Onto Love)/ Walk To The Water (CD, gatefold card p/s) 15
87	Island 12IS 340	Where The Streets Have No Name/Race Against Time/Silver And Gold/ The Sweetest Thing (12", p/s with "Silver And Gold" lyric insert) 15
87	Island CID 340	Where The Streets Have No Name (edit)/Race Against Time/Silver And Gold/ The Sweetest Thing (CD, gatefold p/s) 15
88	Island IS 400	Desire/Hallelujah Here She Comes (non-gatefold p/s) 5
88	Island CIDP 400	Desire/Hallelujah Here She Comes/Desire (Hollywood Remix) (CD, picture disc) 8
88	Island CIDP 402	Angel Of Harlem (Remix)/A Room At The Heartbreak Hotel/Love Rescue Me (Live At "Smile Jamaica" Concert London Oct '88) (CD, picture disc) 8
88	Island CIDX 402	Angel Of Harlem (Remix)/A Room At The Heartbreak Hotel/Love Rescue Me (live) (3" CD, long box, U.S. import with stickered U.K. matrix number) 15

88	Island U2 PK 1	THE JOSHUA TREE SINGLES (4 x 7"s in PVC wallet with 'obi' band)	40
89	Island CIDP 411	When Love Comes To Town/Dancing Barefoot/When Love Comes To Town (Live From The Kingdom Mix) (with BB King)/God Part II (The Hard Metal Dance Mix) (CD picture disc)	15
89	Island CIDX 411	When Love Comes To Town/Dancing Barefoot/When Love Comes To Town (Live From The Kingdom Mix) (with Little Richard)/God Part II (The Hard Metal (as U2 with B.B. King) (3" CD, long box U.S. Import with stickered U.K. Matrix no)	15
89	Island ISB 422	All I Want Is You (Edit)/Unchained Melody (in numbered tin box)	15
89	Island 12 ISB 422	All I Want Is You (Full Version)/Unchained Melody/Everlasting Love (12", p/s, box set with 4 prints)	15
89	Island CIDP 422	All I Want Is You (4.14)/Unchained Melody/Everlasting Love/ All I Want Is You (Full Version) (CD, picture disc)	15
91	Island 12IS 509	Mysterious Ways (4.04)/(Solar Plexus Extended Club Mix 7.01)/(Apollo 440 Magic Hour Remix)/(Tabla Motown Remix)/(Solar Plexus Club Mix) (12" p/s, withdrawn)	15
92	Island 12IS 525	Even Better Than The Real Thing/Salomé/Where Did It All Go Wrong/ Lady With The Spinning Head (UVI) (Extended Dance Mix) (12" with giant 'Zoo TV' poster)	20
92	Island IS 550	Who's Gonna Ride Your Wild Horses (Temple Bar Edit)/Paint It Black (p/s)	5
92	Island CIDX 550	Who's Gonna Ride Your Wild Horses (Temple Bar Edit)/Paint It Black/Salomé (Zooromancer Remix)/Can't Help Falling In Love (Triple Peaks Remix) (CD, picture disc, tri-fold digipak with 4 prints)	15
95	Atlantic A 7131	Hold Me, Thrill Me, Kiss Me, Kill Me/ELLIOTT GOLDENTHAL: Themes From Batman Forever (p/s, red vinyl, black vinyl copies have correct/incorrect B side credits)	5
95	Atlantic A 7131	Hold Me, Thrill Me, Kiss Me, Kill Me/ELLIOTT GOLDENTHAL: Themes From Batman Forever (p/s, red vinyl, B-side miscredited to U2)	8
97	Island 12IST649	Discothèque (Howie B Hairy B Mix)/Discothèque (Hexidecimal Mix)// Discothèque (DM Deep Extended Club Mix)/Discothèque (DM Deep Beats Mix)/Discothèque (DM Tec Radio Mix)/Discotheque (DM Deep Instrumental Mix)/Discotheque (Single Version)/Discotheque (David	12
97	Island CID 649	Discothèque/Holy Joe (Garage Mix)/Holy Joe (Guilty Mix) (CD, jewel case, withdrawn)	10
97	Island 12IS 684	Mofo (Mother's Mix)/Mofo (House Flavour Mix)/Mofo (Romin Mix)/Mofo (Phunk Force Mix)/Mofo (Black Hole Dub) (12", die-cut p/s, 2,000 only)	10

ALBUMS

80	Island ILPS 9646	BOY (LP)	12
80	Island ICT 9646	BOY ('1+1' cassette)	12
81	Island ICT 9680	OCTOBER ('1+1' cassette, in plastic case or 'cigarette pack' card box)	12
83	Island ILPS 9733	WAR (LP, gatefold)	12
83	Island PILPS 9733	WAR (LP, picture disc, beware of counterfeits with ILPS cat. no.)	100
81	Island ILPS 9680	OCTOBER (LP)	12
83	Island ICT 9733	WAR ('1+1' cassette)	12
85	Island CID 112	WAR (LP, pink cover lettering)	20
85	Island CID 110	BOY (CD, with title rear sleeve; no bar code)	20
85	Island CID 102	THE UNFORGETTABLE FIRE (CD, no bar code)	30
87	Island U2 6	THE JOSHUA TREE (LP, gatefold)	15
88	Island U27	RATTLE AND HUM (LP)	18
91	Island U2-8	ACHTUNG BABY (LP, inner sleeve, lyric insert, 10 art prints)	40
93	Island U2-9	ZOOROPA (LP, inner sleeve, lyric insert)	30
95	Island MELONCD 1	MELON (REMIXES FOR PROPAGANDA) (CD, 9-track compilation, card sleeve, fan club issue, 20,000 only; sealed with Propaganda No. 21)	50
95	Island MELONCD 1	MELON (REMIXES FOR PROPAGANDA) (CD, 9-track compilation, card sleeve, fan club issue, 20,000 only; unsealed with Propaganda No. 21)	25
97	Island U2 10	POP (2-LP, gatefold sleeve)	35
98	Island U2 11	THE BEST OF 1980-1990 (2-LP, gatefold sleeve)	50
00	Island U2 12	ALL THAT YOU CAN'T LEAVE BEHIND (LP, with booklet)	60
02	Island U2 13	THE BEST OF 1990-2000 (2-LP, gatefold)	40
04	Island U2 14	HOW TO DISMANTLE AN ATOMIC BOMB (LP, with booklet)	30
04	Island CIDXU214	HOW TO DISMANTLE AN ATOMIC BOMB (CD & DVD set in numbered slipcase)	18
06	Island U2.COM2	U2 ZOO TV LIVE (2xCD & poster in card sleeve & outer card slipcase Issued to u2.com subscribers only)	50
07	Island U2.COM3	U2 GO HOME - LIVE FROM SLANE CASTLE (2xCD issued to u2.com subscribers only)	30
09	Island 1796038	NO LINE ON THE HORIZON (2-LP)	20
09	Island U2.COM 4	MEDIUM, RARE AND REMASTERED (2-CD, issued to u2.com subscribers only)	18

PROMOS : PROMOS - SINGLES

80	Island WIP 6601	11 O'Clock Tick Tock/Touch (p/s, 'A' label)	50
80	Island WIP 6630	A Day Without Me/Things To Make And Do (p/s, 'A' label)	50
80	Island WIP 6656 DJ	I Will Follow (Special Edited DJ Version) (1-sided, company sleeve)	80
81	WIP 6679	Fire (Radio Edit) (1-sided, p/s)	70
81	WIP 6733	Gloria (Radio Edit) (1-sided, p/s)	60
84	Island U2 2	Wire/Bad/The Unforgettable Fire (12", black die-cut sleeve)	70
87	Island ISJ 319	With Or Without You/Walk To The Water (jukebox issue, large centre hole)	10
87	Island ISJ 328	I Still Haven't Found What I'm Looking For/Spanish Eyes (jukebox issue, solid centre)	20
87	Island ISJ 328	I Still Haven't Found What I'm Looking For/Spanish Eyes (jukebox issue, large centre hole)	10
87	Island ISJB 340	Where The Streets Have No Name/Silver And Gold (jukebox issue, large centre hole)	10
88	Island 12ISX 400	Desire (9.23 Hollywood Remix) (12", 1-sided, custom black p/s, 800 only)	25
88	Island U2V 7	EXCERPTS FROM RATTLE AND HUM (In God's Country [live]/Hawkmoon 269/ Bad [live]/God Part II/With Or Without You [live]) (CD, card gatefold sleeve)	70
88	Island IS 319	With Or Without You/Luminous Times (Hold Onto Love)/Walk To The Water/ With Or Without You (Video) (CD Video, withdrawn, less than 100 copies)	350
89	Island 12 ISX 411	U2 3D DANCE MIXES: When Love Comes To Town (Live From The Kingdom Dance Mix)/God Part II (Hard Metal Dance Club Mix)/Desire (Hollywood Remix 5.23) (12" EP p/s)	25
90	Island RHB 1	Night And Day (Twilight Remix)/Steel String Mix) (12", p/s, numbered, 4,000 copies only)	50
91	Island U2-3	OCTOBER 1991: I Will Follow/Pride (In The Name Of Love)/God Part II/ Where The Streets Have No Name) (CD EP, 250 only)	400
92	Island 12IS 550DJ	Salomé (Zooromancer Remix 8.02)/Can't Help Falling In Love (Mystery Train Dub 8.20) (12", black die-cut sleeve, 1,000 only)	70
92	Island REAL 1	Even Better Than The Real Thing (The Perfecto Mix)/Even Better Than The Real Thing (Trance Mix)/Even Better Than The Real Thing (Sexy Dub Mix) (12", black die-cut sleeve with title sticker)	10
92	Island REAL 2DJ	Even Better Than The Real Thing (The Perfecto Mix-Radio Edit) (2-sided radio promo, some with p/s)	40
92	Island REAL 2DJ	Even Better Than The Real Thing (The Perfecto Mix-Radio Edit) (2-sided radio promo, some with p/s)	15
93	Island NUMJB 1	Numb (2-sided jukebox issue, large centre hole)	10

93	Island NUMCD 1	Numb (CD, 1-track, with lyric inner, 250 only) 80
93	Island 12LEM DJ 1	Lemon (Bad Yard Club)/(Momo Beats)/(Version Dub)/(Serious Def Dub)// (Perfecto Mix)/(Trance Mix) (12", double pack, p/s, 1,000 only, numbered with press sheets) 60
93	Island LEMCD 1	Lemon (Radio Edit) (CD, 1-track, with lyric inner) 30
95	Island 12 MELON 1	MELON (Salomé [Zooromancer Remix]/Lemon [Bad Yard Club Mix]/ Numb [The Soul Assassins Mix]/Numb [Gimme Some More Dignity Mix]) (12" EP, 800 only) 20
96	Island PRECD 1	U2 PREVIOUSLY: Lemon/Mysterious Ways/One/Desire/I Still Haven't Found What I'm Looking For (CD, card sleeve) 25
97	Island ISD(X) 649 D(J)	Discothèque (Howie B Hairy B Mix)/Discothèque (Hexidecimal Mix)// Discothèque (DM Deep Extended Club Mix)/Discothèque (DM Deep Beats Mix)/Discotheque (DM Tec Radio Mix)/Discotheque (DM Deep Instrumental Mix)/Discotheque (Single Version)/Discotheque (David 25
97	Island ISJB 649	Discotheque/Holy Joe (jukebox issue, large centre hole) 8
97	Island ISJB 658	Staring At The Sun/North And South Of The River (jukebox issue, large centre hole) 8
97	Island 12IS 658DJ	Staring At The Sun (Monster Truck Mix)/Staring At The Sun (Lab Rat Mix)/ Staring At The Sun (Sad Bastard's Mix) (12", p/s) 20
97	Island SUN CD 1	Staring At The Sun (Cd, 1-track promo) 10
97	Island ISJB 664	Last Night On Earth (Single Mix)/Last Night On Earth (First Night In Hell Remix) (jukebox issue, large centre hole) 10
97	Island 12IS 664DJ	Last Night On Earth (First Night In Hell Remix)/Happiness Is A Warm Gun (The Gun Mix)/Pop Muzik (Pop Mart Mix)/Happiness Is A Warm Gun (The Danny Sabre Mix)/ (12" p/s) 20
97	Island MUZIK 1	Pop Muzik (Pop Mart Mix - Radio Edit) (CD, 1-track, picture disc, jewel case, 250 only) 90
97	Island MART 1	Pop Muzik (Pop Mart Mix)/Last Night On Earth (First Night In Hell Mix) (12", plain black die-cut sleeve) 70
97	Island ISJB 673	Please/Where The Streets Have No Name (live) (jukebox issue, large centre hole) 10
97	Island CIDDJ 673	Please/Please (Call Out Hook) (CD) 15
97	Island PLEASE CD 1	Please (Single Edit)/Please (Single Version) (CD, 2-track, yellow graphics on disc, jewel case) 10
97	Island ISJB 684	If God Will Send His Angels (Single Version)/Sunday Bloody Sunday (live from Sarajevo) (jukebox issue, large centre hole) 15
97	Island 12MOFO 1	Mofo (Phunk Force Mix)/Mofo (Black Hole Dub)/Mofo (Romin Remix) (12", orange label, orange & silver die-cut title sleeve) 15
97	Island 12MOFO 2	Mofo (Mother's Mix)/Mofo (House Flavor Mix) (12", pink label, pink & silver die-cut title sleeve, 250 only) 15
97	Island 12MOFO 3	Mofo (Explicit Mix) (12", 1-sided, stamped white label, plain black die-cut sleeve, 200 only) 50
97	Island MOFOCD 1	Mofo (Album Version) (CD, 1-track, card sleeve, export issue [to Mexico]) 80
97	Island MOFOCD 2	Mofo (Phunk Force Mix) (CD, 1-track, jewel case, export issue [to Mexico]) 60
98	Island CIDDJ 727	Sweetest Thing/Twilight (Live)/An Cat Dubh (Live)/Stories For Boys Out Of Control (Live) (CD, die-cut sleeve) 50
00	Island GROUND CD 1	The Ground Beneath Her Feet/The Million Dollar Hotel Movie Trailer (CD-ROM, card sleeve, blue die-cut slipcase) 10
01	Island 12ISD 780	Beautiful Day (Quincy & Sonance Mix)/(The Perfecto Mix)/(David Holmes Remix)/Elevation (The Vandit Club Mix)/(Influx Remix)/(Escalation Mix)/Quincy & Sonance Remix) (2x12", p/s, inners) 15
00	Island 12 BEAUT 1	Beautiful Day (Quincey & Sonance Mix) (1-sided 12", in black die-cut title sleeve) 15
01	Island ISJB770	Stuck In A Moment You Can't Get Out Of/Big Girls Are Best (UK jukebox promo 7" with large centre) 10
01	Island 12 ELE 1	Elevation (Escalation Mix)/Elevation (Influx Mix) (12", red custom p/s, 250 only) 25
01	Island ELE CD 2	Elevation (Tomb Raider Mix) (1-track CD, Lara Croft sleeve, withdrawn) 20
01	Island 12 ELE 2	Elevation (Paul Vandyk Remix)/Elevation (The Vandit Club Mix) (12", blue custom p/s, 250 only, exclusive mixes) 10
02	Island CID 808	Electrical Storm (William Orbit Mix)/New York (Nice Mix)/New York (Nasty Mix)/ Bad (Live)/Where The Streets Have No Name (2-CD + DVD set in limited issue collectors' wallet, mail order only) 40
02	Island NEWCD U2 13	NEW SONGS AND MIXES FROM THE BEST OF 1990-2000 (CD sampler, black inner sleeve, silver outer sleeve) 25
03	Island HANDSCD 1	The Hands That Built America (promo only 1-track CD, card sleeve) 12
03	Island 12 Sun U2	Staring At The Sun (Brothers In Rhythm Club Mix)/Staring At The Sun (Brothers In Rhythm Ambient Mix) (12", black die-cut custom sleeve) 15
02	Island 12REMIX U2 13	U2 REMIXES FROM THE 1990S (2 x 12" sampler, black inner sleeves, silver outer sleeve) 20
04	Island U2PRO2	Vertigo (Jacknife Lee 7" mix) (7" vinyl promo, picture sleeve. Matt/gloss finish) 50
04	Island 10IS878DJ	Vertigo (Jacknife Lee 7" mix)/Vertigo (Jacknife Lee 10" mix) 10" vinyl promo 20
04	Island 12IS878DJ	Vertigo (Jacknife Lee 7" mix)/Vertigo (Jacknife Lee 12" mix) 12" vinyl p/s 8
04	Island CID878/X878/V878	Vertigo (CD1, CD2 & DVD set in wallet issued by U2.Com) 50
05	Island CID886/X/V	Sometimes You Can't Make It On Your Own (CD1, CD2 & DVD set in wallet, issued by U2.com) 25
05	Island 12IS890DJ	City Of Blinding Lights (Phones P.D.A in N.Y.C remix/City of Blinding Lights (Paradise Soul Vocal Mix)/All Because Of You (Killahurtz Fly Mix) (12" vinyl p/s 8
05	Island CID890/X/V	City Of Blinding Lights (CD1, CD2 & DVD set in wallet via U2.com) 20
05	Island CID906/X/V	All Because Of You (CD1, CD2 & DVD set in wallet in wallet via u2.com) 20

PROMOS : PROMOS - ALBUMS

83	Island U2 1	UNDER A BLOOD RED SKY - A DIALOGUE WITH U2 LIVE (LP, custom sleeve, with cue sheet, numbered, 1,000 only) 75
87	Island U2-6	THE JOSHUA TREE (CD, LP & cassette in black/gold 'pizza' box set) 250
87	Island U2 6-1 - U2 6-5	THE JOSHUA TREE COLLECTION Red Hill Mining Town/Where The Streets Have No Name//Trip Through Your Wires/Running To Stand Still//I Still Haven't Found What I'm Looking For/One Tree Hill/Exit//Mothers Of The Disappeared/In God's Country/Bullet The Blue Sky 500
87	Island U2 6-1 - U2 6-5	THE JOSHUA TREE COLLECTION (5 x 7" black box set, with U2 6-1 mispressed with "Red Hill Mining Town" both sides, less than 50 copies) 1000
87	Island U2CLP 1	THE U2 TALKIE: A CONVERSATION WITH LARRY, BONO, ADAM & THE EDGE (LP, music & interview with Dave Fanning for "The Joshua Tree") 30
87	Island U2CC 1	THE U2 TALKIE (cassette) 20
87	Island BOU2 1	CASSETTE SAMPLER (cassette, 17-track 'best of compilation) 30
88	Island U2-7	RATTLE AND HUM (CD, LP & cassette in flight case with leather tag, 250 only) 1000
89	Island U2 2D1	U2 2 DATE (LP, 8-track hits compilation) 25
91	Island U2-8	ACHTUNG BABY (CD, cassette in 'User's Kit', including map/poster, torch, key ring, spanner & screwdriver in printed green nylon kit bag) 500
91	Island CIDDJ U2-8	ACHTUNG (graphics CD, in jewel case marked "promo only - not for sale") 100
97	Island CID U2 10	POP (CD, in large cube-shaped picture box set, with prismatic pen & custom notepad) 200
97	Island POP 1	U2 TALK POP (CD, interview with Dave Fanning, card sleeve) 50
97	Island POP 2	U2 TALK POP (CD, interview with Dave Fanning, card sleeve, same tracks as POP 1) 50
97	Island POP 3	U2 TALK POP (CD, interview with Dave Fanning, card sleeve, same track as POP 1) 50

98	Island CIDDU211	THE BEST OF THE 'B' SIDES 1980-1990 (2-CD, discs marked 'A' and 'B', in card sleeves with gold slipcase)	50
98	Island BXU2 11	THE 'BEST OF' COLLECTION 1980-1990 (14 x 7" singles, 2-CDs, 16-page booklet, in gold box, 2000 copies only)	250
00	Island MDH CD1	THE MILLION DOLLAR HOTEL (CD, card sleeve)	15
00	Island CID U212	ALL THAT YOU CAN'T LEAVE BEHIND (promo pack, with 1-track CD Beautiful Day [BEAUT CD 1] in blue picture slipcase, booklet, window sticker, video tape, "playback" invitation, in laminated picture bag with rope handles; with signed print)	600
00	Island CID U212	ALL THAT YOU CAN'T LEAVE BEHIND (promo pack, with 1-track CD Beautiful Day [BEAUT CD 1] in blue picture slipcase, booklet, window sticker, video tape, "playback" invitation, in laminated picture bag with rope handles; without signed print)	200
00	no cat. no.	THE DAVE FANNING INTERVIEW (CD-R, dated 4.10.00, in white card sleeve, plastic outer sleeve)	20
00	no cat. no.	ALBUM INTERVIEW (CD-R, dated 25.10.00, in white card sleeve, plastic outer sl.)	20
00	Island HASTACD 1	HASTA LA VISTA BABY! LIVE FROM MEXICO CITY (CD, fan-club only p/s)	50
02	Island CIDDJ U2 13	THE BEST OF THE B-SIDES OF 1990-2000 (2-CD set card sleeves in card wallet)	30
02	Island BX U2 13	THE BEST OF COLLECTION 1990-2000 (15 x 7", with 2 CDs & 16-page booklet in silver fliptop card box)	200
02	Island REMIXCD U2 13	REMIXES FROM THE 90S (CD, 5-track album sampler in card sleeve, in silver card wallet)	25
02	Island REMIXCD U2 13	REMIXES FROM THE 90S (2 x 12", promo p/s) card wallet)	20
05	Island UCOMV1	U2 COMMUNICATION (CD & DVD fan club issue)	30
08	Island	U23D (Promo CD, audio press kit, DVD box)	35

(see also Bono & Gavin Friday, The Edge, Adam Clayton & Larry Mullen, Passengers)

U2 AND GREEN DAY
06	UNIVERSAL LC00268	The Saints Are Coming/The Saints Are Coming (Live From New Orleans) (p/s)	5

U.V. POP
85	Flow Motion FM 007	Anyone For Me/Hands To Me	30
85	Flow motion FM 12/007	ANYONE FOR ME (12" EP)	35
85	Native NTV4	SERIOUS EP (12")	30
86	Extra EXTRA T001	MUSIC TO YEAH TO EP (12")	30
83	Flow Motion FM 004	NO SONGS TOMORROW (LP)	30
86	Extra EXTRA LP1	BENDY BABY MAN (LP)	40

UXB 80
80	Crazy Plane SP 02	Crazy Today/Mr Fixit (p/s)	100

UZI
70	Beacon BEA 152	Morning Train/Where Were You Last Night	70

U-ZIQ
95	Planet Mu FLATDLP 20	IN PINE EFFECT (2-LP)	15
97	Planet Mu PULP 5	LUNATIC HARNESS (2-LP)	20

VACELS
65	Pye International 7N 25330	Can You Please Crawl Out Your Window/I'm Just A Poor Boy	35

VAGABONDS
63	Island ILP 916	PRESENTING THE FABULOUS VAGABONDS (LP)	250

(see also Jimmy James & Vagabonds, Jamaica's Own Vagabonds)

VAGINA DENTATA ORGAN
83	WSNS 001	VAGINA DENTATA ORGAN PRESENTS: MUSIC FOR HASHASINS, IN MEMORIAM OF HASSAN-I-SABBAH (LP, 500 copies)	50
84	WSNS 002	THE LAST SUPPER, THE REVEREND JIM JONES IN PERSON (LP, picture disc, 912 numbered, with transcript)	90
84	WSNS 002	THE LAST SUPPER, THE REVEREND JIM JONES IN PERSON (LP, picture disc, 912 numbered, without transcript)	80
84	WSNS 003	THE PAGAN DRUMS OF CALANDA (LP, picture disc, 12 copies adorned with 'real' blood and handpainted)	300
84	WSNS 003	THE PAGAN DRUMS OF CALANDA (LP, picture disc, 30 copies adorned with 'real' blood but not handpainted)	150
84	WSNS 003	THE PAGAN DRUMS OF CALANDA (LP, picture disc, adorned with 'fake blood')	100
84	WSNS 003	THE PAGAN DRUMS OF CALANDA (LP, 900 'bloodless' copies)	50
86	WSNS 004	COLD MEAT/EROS & THANATOS (LP picture disc, 4 copies with 1 black side with Elvis image missing)	150
86	WSNS 004	COLD MEAT/EROS & THANATOS (LP picture disc, 12 copies with hand drawings and personal dedications)	300
86	WSNS 004	COLD MEAT/EROS & THANATOS (LP picture disc, no drawings or dedications)	50
87	Temple TOPY 012	MUSIC FOR THE HASHISHINS (LP)	25
87	Temple TPY 013	THE LAST SUPPER (LP)	25
94	WSNS 001 CD	THE PERPIGNAN KILLINGS (CD)	20
94	WSNS 002 CD	UN CHIEN CATALAN (CD)	20
04	WSNS 003 CD	THE GREAT MASTURBATOR (CD)	20
07	WSNS 004	MUSIC FOR THE BLIND (CD)	20

VAGRANTS
66	Fontana TF 703	I Can't Make A Friend/Young Blues	60

VALADIERS
63	Oriole CBA 1809	I Found A Girl/You'll Be Sorry Someday	1100
63	Oriole CBA 1809	I Found A Girl/You'll Be Sorry Someday (DJ copy)	1000

RICKY VALANCE
60	Columbia DB 4493	Tell Laura I Love Her/Once Upon A Time	5
60	Columbia DB 4543	Movin' Away/Lipstick On Your Lips	10
61	Columbia DB 4586	Jimmy's Girl/Only The Young	10
61	Columbia DB 4592	Why Can't We/Fisherboy	10

61	Columbia DB 4680	Bobby/I Want To Fall In Love	10
61	Columbia DB 4725	I Never Had A Chance/It's Not True	10
62	Columbia DB 4787	Try To Forget Her/At Times Like These	10
62	Columbia DB 4864	Don't Play No. 9/Till The Final Curtain Falls	12
65	Decca F 12129	Six Boys/Face The Crowd	12
76	Valley VLY 001	RICKY VALANCE (EP, no p/s)	25
78	Tank BBS 324	RAINBOW (LP)	40

(see also Jason Merryweather)

JERRY VALE

59	Philips PB 963	Flame/The Moon Is My Pillow (78)	15
67	CBS 2682	Have You Seen The One I love Go By/Signs	5

RITCHIE VALENS

58	Pye International 7N 25000	Come On Let's Go/Dooby Dooby Wah	200
58	Pye International 7N 25000	Come On Let's Go/Dooby Dooby Wah (78)	150
59	London HL 8803	Donna/La Bamba	30
59	London HL 8803	Donna/La Bamba (78)	100
59	London HL 7068	Donna/La Bamba (export issue)	30
59	London HL 8886	That's My Little Suzie/Bluebirds Over The Mountains (tri centre)	40
59	London HL 8886	That's My Little Suzie/Bluebirds Over The Mountains (round centre)	25
59	London HL 8886	That's My Little Suzie/Bluebirds Over The Mountains (78)	150
62	London HL 9494	La Bamba/Ooh, My Head	20
79	London HLR 10571	La Bamba/Come On Let's Go/That's My Little Suzie (tri-centre)	10
59	London RE 1232	RITCHIE VALENS (EP, initial pressing with triangular centre)	200
59	London RE 1232	RITCHIE VALENS (EP, later round centre)	150
61	London HA 2390	RITCHIE (LP)	150
64	London HA 8196	HIS GREATEST HITS (LP)	60
67	President PTL 1001	I REMEMBER RITCHIE VALENS (LP)	25
79	London HA-R 8535	RITCHIE VALENS (LP)	15

DINO VALENTI

68	CBS 65715	DINO (LP)	45

(see also Quicksilver Messenger Service)

VALENTINE

72	Track 2094104	Time/Leader Of The Band	6

BILLY VALENTINE

55	Capitol CL 14320	It's A Sin/Your Love Has Got Me (Reelin' And Rockin')	10

DICKIE VALENTINE (& STARGAZERS)

SINGLES

54	Decca F 10346	Endless/I Could Have Told You	30
54	Decca F 10394	The Finger Of Suspicion (with Stargazers)/ Who's Afraid (Not I, Not I, Not I)	20
54	Decca F 10415	Mister Sandman/Runaround	40
55	Decca F 10430	A Blossom Fell/I Want You All To Myself (Just You)	15
55	Decca F 10484	Ma Cherie Amie/Lucky Waltz	10
55	Decca F 10493	I Wonder/You Too Can Be A Dreamer	10
55	Decca F 10517	Hello Mrs. Jones (Is Mary There?)/Lazy Gondolier	10
55	Decca F 10549	No Such Luck/The Engagement Waltz	10
55	Decca F 10628	Christmas Alphabet/Where Are You Tonight?	20
55	Decca F 10645	The Old Pi-Anna Rag/First Love	15
55	Decca F 10667	Dreams Can Tell A Lie/Song Of The Trees	7
56	Decca F 10714	The Voice/The Best Way To Hold A Girl	7
56	Decca F 10753	My Impossible Castle/When You Came Along	7
56	Decca F 10766	Day Dreams/Give Me A Carriage With Eight White Horses	8
56	Decca F 10798	Christmas Island/The Hand Of Friendship	15
56	Decca F 10820	Dickie Valentine's Rock 'N' Roll Party Medley (Parts 1 & 2)	10
57	Decca F 10874	Chapel Of The Roses/My Empty Arms	5
57	Decca F 10906	Puttin' On The Style/Three Sides To Every Story	5
57	Decca F 10949	Long Before I Knew You/Just In Time	5
57	Decca F 10950	Snowbound For Christmas/Convicted	5
58	Decca F 11005	Love Me Again/King Of Dixieland	12
58	Decca F 11020	In My Life/Come To My Arms	5
58	Decca F 11066	Take Me In Your Arms/An Old-Fashioned Song	5
59	Pye Nixa 7N 15192	Venus/Where? (In The Old Home Town)	10
59	Pye 7N 15202	A Teenager In Love/My Favourite Song	10
59	Pye 7N 15221	One More Sunrise (Morgen)/You Touch My Hand	5

EPs

55	Decca DFE 6236	SWING ALONG WITH DICKIE VALENTINE	15
56	Decca DFE 6279	PRESENTING DICKIE VALENTINE	15
56	Decca DFE 6363	ONLY FOR YOU	15
57	Decca DFE 6427	DICKIE GOES DIXIE	10
57	Decca DFE 6429	STANDARDS	10
58	Decca DFE 6529	WITH VOCAL REFRAIN BY DICKIE VALENTINE	10
59	Decca DFE 6549	BELONGING TO SOMEONE	10
59	Pye NPL 24120	DICKIE VALENTINE HIT PARADE	10

ALBUMS

58	Decca LK 4269	WITH VOCAL REFRAIN BY...	20

VALENTINE GUINNESS

80	RAK RAK 308	(Hey Hey) C.J.T./When Mandy Calls	50

JACK VALENTINE

55	MGM SPC 8	Dressing Up My Heart/Song Of The Bandit (export issue)	12

VALENTINES (JAMAICA)

67	Doctor Bird DB 1065	Blam Blam Fever/BABA BROOKS: The Scratch	50

VALENTINES (U.S.)

60	Ember EMB S 123	Hey Ruby/That's How I Feel	90

VALENTINO
| 75 | Gaiee GAE 101 | I Was Born This Way/Liberation ....6 |

ANNA VALENTINO
| 57 | London HLD 8421 | Calypso Joe/You're Mine........30 |
| 57 | London HLD 8421 | Calypso Joe/You're Mine (78)........12 |

DANNY VALENTINO
59	MGM MGM 1049	Stampede/(You Gotta Be A) Music Man 30
60	MGM MGM 1067	Biology/A Million Tears........20
60	MGM MGM 1109	Pictures From The Past/'Till The End Of Forever 15

MARK VALENTINO
63	Stateside SS 148	The Push And Kick/Walking Alone 25
63	Stateside SS 186	Do It/Hey You're Looking Good 15
63	Stateside SS 233	Jivin' At The Drive In/Part Time Job 25

VALENTINOS
68	Soul City SC 106	It's All Over Now/Tired Of Livin' In The Country 25
68	Stateside SS 2137	Tired Of Being Nobody/The Death Of Love........18
71	Polydor 2058 090	Don't Raise Up Your Hands In Anger/Stand Up And Be Counted 10
68	Soul City SCM 001	THE VALENTINOS/THE SIMS TWINS (LP, with Sims Twins)........70

(see also Bobby Womack)

VALERIE (THE ROCK 'N' ROLL YOUNGSTER)
| 56 | Columbia DB 3832 | Tonight You Belong To Me/The Man Who Owns The Sunshine ....20 |

DANA VALERY
| 64 | Decca F 11881 | This Is My Prayer/Would I Love You Again/T'en Va Pas ....7 |
| 64 | Decca F 11977 | I Wake Up Crying/Never Let Go........12 |

VALHALLA (1)
| 82 | Neat NEAT 22 | Coming Home/Through With You ....8 |
| 84 | Neat NEAT 36 | Still in Love With You/Jack ....6 |

VALHALLA (2)
| 81 | Asgard ASG 69151 | Lightning In The Sky/These Sunday Nights ....250 |

JOE VALINO (& GOSPELAIRES)
57	HMV POP 283	The Garden Of Eden/Caravan........25
58	London HLT 8705	God's Little Acre/I'm Happy With What I've Got (with Gospelaires) 15
58	London HLT 8705	God's Little Acre/I'm Happy With What I've Got (78, with Gospelaires) 10
60	Columbia DB 4406	Hidden Persuasion/Back To Your Eyes 5

VALJEAN (AT THE PIANO)
| 62 | London HLL 9593 | Till There Was You/The Eighteenth Variation ....6 |

VALKYRIES
| 64 | Parlophone R 5123 | Rip It Up/What's Your Name? ....40 |

DIORIS VALLADARES ORCHESTRA
| 64 | Island IEP 703 | AUTHENTIC MERINGUE (EP) ....12 |
| 64 | Island ILP 910 | LET'S GO LATIN (LP, withdrawn) ....30 |

MARCOS VALLE
| 68 | Verve VLP 9206 | SAMBA '68 (LP) ....20 |

VALLEY OF ACHOR
| 75 | Dovetail DOVE 18 | A DOOR OF HOPE (LP, gatefold sleeve) ....15 |

(see also Achor, Wine Of Lebanon)

FRANKIE VALLI
66	Philips BF 1467	(You're Gonna) Hurt Yourself/VALLI BOYS: Night Hawk........10
66	Philips BF 1512	You're Ready Now/Cry For Me 10
66	Philips BF 1529	The Proud One/Ivy........10
67	Philips BF 1556	Beggin'/Dody........10
67	Philips BF 1580	Can't Take My Eyes Off You/The Trouble With Me 7
67	Philips BF 1603	I Make A Fool Of Myself/September Rain 7
68	Philips BF 1634	To Give (The Reason I Live)/Watch Where You Walk 7
69	Philips BF 1795	The Girl I'll Never Know/A Face Without A Name 6
70	Philips 320 226 BF	You're Ready Now/Cry For Me (reissue) 10
74	Private Stock PVT 1	My Eyes Adored You/Watch Where You Walk 5
67	Philips (S)BL 7814	SOLO (LP) 25
69	Philips SBL 7856	TIMELESS (LP) 20
75	Mowest MWS 7007	INSIDE YOU (LP) 12
77	Private Stock PVLP 1029	LADY PUT THE LIGHT OUT (LP, withdrawn) 40

FRANKIE VALLI & THE FOUR SEASONS
71	Warner Bros K 16107	Whatever You Say/Sleeping Man (withdrawn, 300 only) 45
72	Tamla Motown TMG 819	You're A Song/Sun Country 10
72	Mowest MW 3002	The Night/When The Morning Comes 75
73	Mowest MW 3003	Walk On, Don't Look Back/Touch The Rainchild 8
75	Mowest MW 3024	The Night/When The Morning Comes (reissue) 5
72	Mowest MWSA 5501	CHAMELEON (LP) 20

(see also Four Seasons, Wonder Who)

JUNE VALLI
54	HMV 7M 245	I Understand (Just How You Feel)/Old Shoes And A Bag Of Rice 7
54	HMV 7M 259	Tell Me, Tell Me/Boy Wanted 7
55	HMV 7M 284	Wrong, Wrong, Wrong/Ole Pappy Time 7
56	HMV 7M 347	Por Favor (Please)/The Things They Say 7
59	Mercury AMT 1034	The Answer To A Maiden's Prayer/In His Arms 6
59	Mercury AMT 1048	An Anonymous Letter/Bygones 6
60	Mercury AMT 1091	Apple Green/Oh! Why 5
61	Mercury AMT 1130	I Guess Things Happen That Way/Tell Him For Me 7
62	HMV POP 1062	Hush Little Baby/Afraid 5

ANTON VALOTTI
| 75 | Rouge RMS 106 | BLACKOUT (LP)........80 |

VALUES
66	Ember EMB S 211	Return To Me/That's The Way (with p/s)	80
66	Ember EMB S 211	Return To Me/That's The Way	50

HUBERT THOMAS VALVERDE & THE HTS
68	S n B 55 3922	Genevieve/We Don't Care	25

VALVERDE BROTHERS
69	CBS 4519	River Of My Mind/I Wanna Love You	20

VALVES
77	Zoom ZUM 1	Robot Love/For Adolfs Only (p/s)	10
77	Zoom ZUM 3	Tarzan Of The Kings Road/Ain't No Surf In Portobello (p/s)	12
79	Albion DEL 3	I Don't Mean Nothing At All/Linda Vindalco (p/s)	12

VAL & V'S
67	CBS 2780	Do It Again A Little Bit Slower/For A Rainy Day	20
67	CBS 2956	I Like The Way/With This Theme	20
68	CBS 3316	This Little Girl/Dreamer	15

VAMP
68	Atlantic 584 213	Floatin'/Thinkin' Too Much	90
69	Atlantic 584 263	Green Pea/Wake Up And Tell Me (withdrawn)	150

(see also Sam Gopal, Viv Prince, Clark-Hutchinson)

VAMPIRE WEEKEND
07	Own Label	A Punk/Cape Cod Kwassa Kwassa (p/s, yellow vinyl, 500 only)	25
07	Own Label	A Punk/Cape Cod Kwassa Kwassa/Oxford Punk (CD, digipak, 500 only)	30

VAMPIRES (1)
59	Parlophone R 4599	Swinging Ghosts/Clap Trap	20

VAMPIRES (2)
68	Pye 7N 17553	Do You Wanna Dance/My Girl	20

VAMPS
79	Dental DK 001	She Edudes Sexuality/Love Letters/I Only Saw You (p/s, red vinyl, 1000 only)	15

VAN DER GRAAF GENERATOR
69	Polydor 56758	People You Were Going To/Firebrand	400
70	Charisma CB 122	Refugees/The Boat Of Millions Of Years (three prong centre)	45
72	Charisma CB 175	Theme One/W (with p/s, solid centre)	30
72	Charisma CB 175	Theme One/W (four prong centre)	5
76	Charisma CB 297	Wondering/Meurglys III	8
76	Charisma PRO 002	Wondering (Song)/Wondering (Heroics) (promo only)	25
11	Esoteric VDGS 101	Highly Strung/Elsewhere (die-cut sleeve)	6
69	Mercury SMCL 20177	THE AEROSOL GREY MACHINE (LP, unreleased, finished gatefold sleeve only)	400
70	Charisma CAS 1007	THE LEAST WE CAN DO IS WAVE TO EACH OTHER (LP, pink 'scroll' label, original mix, matrices read: CAS 1007 A/B, gatefold sleeve, with poster)	200
70	Charisma CAS 1007	THE LEAST WE CAN DO IS WAVE TO EACH OTHER (LP, pink 'scroll' label, original mix, matrices read: CAS 1007 A/B, gatefold sleeve, without poster)	60
70	Charisma CAS 1007	THE LEAST WE CAN DO IS WAVE TO EACH OTHER (LP, pink 'scroll' label, remix, matrices read: CAS 1007 A+G/B+G, gatefold sleeve; with poster)	100
70	Charisma CAS 1007	THE LEAST WE CAN DO IS WAVE TO EACH OTHER (LP, pink 'scroll' label, remix, matrices read: CAS 1007 A+G/B+G, gatefold sleeve; without poster)	50
70	Charisma CAS 1027	H TO HE, WHO AM THE ONLY ONE (LP, pink label, gatefold sleeve)	50
71	Charisma CAS 1051	PAWN HEARTS (LP, gatefold sleeve, pink 'scroll' label, with insert)	90
71	Charisma CAS 1051	PAWN HEARTS (LP, gatefold sleeve, pink 'scroll' label, without insert)	35
72	Charisma CS 2	1968-71 (LP, pink label)	25
75	Charisma CAS 1109	GODBLUFF (LP, with inner sleeve)	12
76	Charisma CAS 1116	STILL LIFE (LP, small 'Mad Hatter' logo)	15
76	Charisma CAS 1120	WORLD RECORD (LP)	12
76	Charisma CAS 1007	THE LEAST WE CAN DO IS WAVE TO EACH OTHER (LP, gatefold reissue, 'Mad hatter' label)	18
78	Charisma CVLP 101	VITAL (2-LP)	18
00	Virgin VDGGBOX 1	THE BOX (4-CD box set)	30

(see also Peter Hammill, Long Hello, Juicy Lucy, Misunderstood, Guy Evans)

HARRY VANDA
69	Polydor 56357	I Love Marie/Gonna Make It	10

(see also Easybeats)

MAMIE VAN DOREN
58	Capitol CL 14850	Something To Dream About/I Fell In Love (promos in p/s)	40
58	Capitol CL 14850	Something To Dream About/I Fell In Love	25

LINDA VAN DYCK
69	Gemini GM 004	The Seduction Song/Unlock My door	12

VANDYKE & BAMBIS
64	Piccadilly 7N 35180	Doin' The Mod/All I Want Is You	50

EARL VAN DYKE (& SOUL BROTHERS)
64	Stateside SS 357	Soul Stomp/Hot 'N' Tot	120
64	Stateside SS 357	Soul Stomp/Hot 'N' Tot (DJ copy)	200
65	Tamla Motown TMG 506	All For You/Too Many Fish In The Sea (as Earl Van Dyke & Soul Brothers)	125
65	Tamla Motown TMG 506	All For You/Too Many Fish In The Sea (as Earl Van Dyke & Soul Brothers)(DJ copy)	150
70	Tamla Motown TMG 759	Six By Six/All For You (matt black label, later shiny)	12
72	Tamla Motown TMG 814	I Can't Help Myself/How Sweet It Is (To Be Loved By You) (& Soul Brothers)	10
65	Tamla Motown TML 11014	THAT MOTOWN SOUND (LP)	110

LEROY VAN DYKE
61	Mercury AMT 1166	Walk On By/My World Is Caving In	5
62	Mercury AMT 1173	Big Man In A Big House/Faded Love	5
62	Mercury AMT 1183	I Sat Back And Let It Happen/A Broken Promise	5
65	Warner Bros WB 5650	It's All Over Now Baby Blue/Just A State Of Mind	8
66	Warner Bros WB 5807	You Couldn't Get My Love Back/Fool Such As I	8
67	Warner Bros WB 5777	Almost Persuaded/Less Of Me	10
62	Mercury MMC 14101	WALK ON BY (LP)	40
63	Mercury MMC 14118	MOVIN' VAN DYKE (LP)	40

VAN DYKES
66	Stateside SS 504	No Man Is An Island/I Won't Hold It Against You	25
66	Stateside SS 504	No Man Is An Island/I Won't Hold It Against You (DJ Copy)	40
66	Stateside SS 530	I've Gotta Go On Without You/What Will I Do	25

LON & DERREK VAN EATON
73	Apple APPLE 46	Warm Woman/More Than Words (in p/s)	90
73	Apple APPLE 46	Warm Woman/More Than Words	50
75	A&M AMS 7157	Wildfire/Music Lover	5
75	A&M AMS 7178	Dancing In The Dark/All You're Hungry For Is Love	5
73	Apple SAPCOR 25	BROTHER (LP, gatefold sleeve, with insert)	70
73	Apple SAPCOR 25	BROTHER (LP, gatefold sleeve, without insert)	50

NICK VAN EEDE
78	Barn 201 4128	Rock'n'Roll Fool/Ounce Of Sense	6
79	Barn BARN 003	All Or Nothing/Hold On To Your Heart	7
79	Barn BARN 008	I Only Want To Be Number One/Dicing	60

(see also Drivers)

VANGELIS
75	RCA RS 1025	HEAVEN AND HELL (gatefold sleeve)	12
76	Polydor 2489 113	L'APOCALYPSE DES ANIMAUX (LP, TV soundtrack)	18
83	Polydor BOX 1	CHARIOTS OF FIRE (LP, soundtrack, box set)	12
89	Polydor VGPK 1	THEMES (LP, 'display pack')	12

(see also Aphrodite's Child, Forminx, Cosmic Baby, Jon & Vangelis)

VAN HALEN
78	Warner Bros K 17107	You Really Got Me/Atomic Punk	5
78	Warner Bros K 17162	Runnin' With The Devil/Eruption.	5
79	Warner Bros K 17371	Dance The Night Away/Outta Love Again	7
79	Warner Bros K 17371P	Dance The Night Away/Outta Love Again (picture disc)	10
80	Warner Bros K 17645	And The Cradle Will Rock/Everybody Wants Some (p/s)	5
85	Warner Bros W 9199T	Hot For Teacher/Little Dreamer/Hear About It Later (12", p/s)	8
86	Warner Bros W 8740P	Why Can't This Be Love/Get Up (shaped picture disc with plinth, stickered PVC sleeve)	10
86	Warner Bros W 8642P	Dreams/Inside (car-shaped picture disc with stand, stickered PVC sleeve)	12
88	Warner Bros W 7816TW	When It's Love/Apolitical Blues (12", silver foldout p/s)	8
88	Warner Bros W 7816TP	When It's Love/Apolitical Blues (12", picture disc)	8

(see also David Lee Roth, Sammy Hagar)

ILA VAN
74	Pye Intl. DDS 108	Can't Help Loving Dat Man/I've Got The Feeling	6

CHERRY VANILLA
77	RCA PB 5053	The Punk/Foxy Bitch (title sleeve)	8
78	RCA PL 25122	BAD GIRL (LP)	12
79	RCA PL 25217	VENUS DE VINYL (LP)	15

VANILLA FUDGE
67	Atlantic 584 123	You Keep Me Hanging On/Take Me For A Little While	10
67	Atlantic 584 139	(Illusions Of My Childhood) Eleanor Rigby (Parts 1 & 2)	8
68	Atlantic 584 179	Where Is My Mind?/The Look Of Love	12
69	Atlantic 584 257	Shotgun/Good Good Lovin'	7
69	Atlantic 584 276	Some Velvet Morning/Thoughts	12
67	Atlantic 587/588 086	VANILLA FUDGE (LP, red & plum label)	45
68	Atlantic 587 100	THE BEAT GOES ON (LP, mono)	35
68	Atlantic 588 100	THE BEAT GOES ON (LP, stereo)	30
68	Atlantic 587 110	RENAISSANCE (LP, mono)	35
68	Atlantic 588 110	RENAISSANCE (LP, stereo)	30
69	Atco 228 020	NEAR THE BEGINNING (LP)	25
70	Atco 228 029	ROCK 'N' ROLL (LP)	25
84	Warner Bros. 7901 491	MYSTERY (LP)	12

(see also Beck Bogert & Appice, Cactus)

VANITY FARE
68	Page One POF 075	I Live For The Sun/On The Other Side Of Life	10
68	Page One POF 100	Summer Morning/Betty Carter	7
69	Page One POF 117	Highway Of Dreams/Waiting For The Downfall	7
69	Page One POF 142	Early In The Morning/You Made Me Love You	7
69	Page One POF 158	Hitchin' A Ride/Man Child	10
70	Page One POF 170	Come Tomorrow/Megowd (Something Tells Me)	12
70	Page One PDF 180	Carolina's Coming Home/On Your Own	8
71	DJM DJS 234	Where Did All The Good Times Go/Stand	6
71	DJM DJS 250	Better By Far/Rock 'N Roll Band	7
71	DJM DJS 526	Our Own Way Of Living/Nowhere To Go	6
72	Philips 6006237	I'm In Love With The World/At The End Of The Pier	6
69	Page One POLS 010	THE SUN, THE WIND AND OTHER THINGS (LP)	45
70	DJM DJSL 001	COMING HOME (LP)	20

(see also Avengers)

TEDDY VANN (ORCHESTRA)
60	London HLU 9097	Cindy/I'm Waiting	25
61	Philips PB 1160	The Lonely Crowd/I Was Born To Love You	6
78	Capitol CL 16012	Theme From 'Coloured Man'/Intro To 'Coloured Man' (as Teddy Vann Orchestra)	5

ORNELLA VANONI
67	Decca F 22703	Only Two Can Play/Can I?	10

DAVE VAN RONK
65	Stateside SL 10153	INSIDE (LP)	30

ROB VAN SPYK
70s	private pressing	FOLLOW THE SUN (LP)	60

(see also Stonefield Tramp)

TOWNES VAN ZANDT
99	Exile EX 7013	Riding The Range/Dirty Old Town (p/s, 2000 only)	6

69	RCA SF 8040	OUR MOTHER THE MOUNTAIN (LP)	25
73	United Artists UAS 29442	THE LATE GREAT TOWNES VAN ZANDT (LP, gatefold sleeve)	30
87	Heartland HLD 003	AT MY WINDOW (LP)	15
01	Charly SNAB 903 CD	TEXAS TROUBADOUR (4-CD, book-style box set)	35

PETER VARDAS
59	Top Rank JAR 173	He Threw A Stone/Checkerboard Love	6

VARDIS
79	Redball RR 017	100 MPH (EP)	120
80	Castle CQUEL 2/100MPH	Out Of The Way/If I Were King	7
81	Logo VAR3	Silver Machine/Come On (7", die cut p/s)	6
81	Logo VAR4	All You'll Ever Need/If I Were King/Jumping Jack Flash (p/s)	6
80	Logo MOGO4012	100MPH (LP + poster)	12
81	Logo LOGO1026	THE WORLD'S INSANE (LP + insert)	12
81	Logo LOGO1034	QUO VARDIS (LP + free 7")	12

VARIATION
72	Warner Bros K 16233	Snowbird/Nebula	6

VARIATIONS
65	Immediate IM 019	The Man With All The Toys/She'll Know I'm Sorry	20
69	Major Minor MM 638	Crimson And Clover/She Couldn't Dance	20

VARIATIONS (U.S.)
75	UK USA 10	Sayin' It And Doin' It Pts I & II	8

VARICOSE VEINS
78	Warped WARP 1	INCREDIBLE (EP, mail-order only, 200 only, beware of counterfeits)	60

(see also Orange Disaster)

PAUL VARNEY
91	PWL PWLT 201	If Only I Knew (On The Buses Piano Edit)/If Only I Knew (Hurley's House Mix)/ If Only I Knew (Silk's Answer)/If Only I Knew (Maurice's Underground Mix) 12" p/s)	12
91	PWL PWCD 201	If Only I Knew (7" Version)/If Only I Knew (12" Version)/ If Only I Knew (Dub)/If Only I Knew (On The Buses Piano Edit) (CD)	12

REG VARNEY
72	Columbia SCX 6518	THIS IS REG VARNEY (LP)	12

SYLVIE VARTAN
65	RCA Victor RCA 1490	One More Day/I Made My Choice	75
65	RCA Victor RCA 1495	Another Heart/Think About You	12
79	RCA PB 1578	I Don't Want The Night To End/Distant Shores (p/s, coloured vinyl)	6
65	RCA Victor RCX 7165	SYLVIE VARTAN (EP)	200

VARUKERS
81	Tempest/Inferno HELL 1	Protest And Survive/No Scapegoat (p/s)	10
83	Riot City RIOT 27	Die For Your Government/All Systems Fail (p/s)	7
83	Riot City RIOT 29	Led To The Slaughter/The End Is Nigh (p/s)	10
83	Riot City 005	BLOODSUCKERS (LP, with inner)	18
83	Riot City RIOT 31	ANOTHER RELIGION ANOTHER WAR (12" EP)	15
84	Rot ASS 16	MASSACRED MILLIONS (12" EP)	20
84	Attack ATTACK 001	PREPARE FOR THE ATTACK (LP, 1000 only)	18
85	Liberate 1	ONE STRUGGLE ONE FIGHT (LP)	15
87	Rot DUTCH 001	LIVE IN HOLLAND (LP)	15

VASALINES
92	Avalanche ONLYLP 013	ALL THE STUFF AND MORE (LP)	12

VASELINE TIGERS
80	Dance DANCE 513	I'm A Golliwog/Back In The Square (Again)	18

VASELINES
87	53rd & 3rd AGARR 10	Son Of A Gun/Rory Rides Away/You Think You're A Man (12", die-cut sleeve)	20
88	53rd & 3rd AGARR 17	Dying For It/Molly's Lips (p/s)	10
88	53rd & 3rd AGARR 17T	Dying For It/Molly's Lips/Teenage Superstars/Jesus Wants Me For A Sunbeam (12", p/s)	15
88	53rd & 3rd AGARR 17CD	Dying For It/Molly's Lips/Teenage Superstars/Jesus Wants Me For A Sunbeam (CD)	12
90	53rd & 3rd AGAS 7	DUM DUM (LP)	25

(see also Pastels, BMX Bandits)

VASHTI
65	Decca F 12157	Some Things Just Stick In Your Mind/I Want To Be Alone	80
66	Columbia DB 7917	Train Song/Love Song	60

(see also Vashti Bunyan)

FRANKIE VAUGHAN
57	Rainbow/Weekend 14140	The Truth About Me (78, 5", mail-order only, with mailer)	15
57	Rainbow/Weekend 14140	The Truth About Me (78, 5", mail-order only)	10
53	HMV 7M 167	Istanbul (Not Constantinople)/Cloud Lucky Seven	20
54	HMV 7M 182	The Cuff Of My Shirt/Heartless	10
54	HMV 7M 252	My Son, My Son/Cinnamon Sinner (Selling Lollipop Lies)	10
54	HMV 7M 270	Happy Days And Lonely Nights/Danger Signs	10
55	HMV 7M 298	Too Many Heartaches/Unsuspecting Heart	10
57	Philips JK 1002	Garden Of Eden/Priscilla (jukebox issue)	10
57	Philips JK 1014	What's Behind That Strange Door/Cold, Cold Shower (jukebox issue)	10
57	Philips JK 1022	These Dangerous Years/Isn't This A Lovely Evening (jukebox issue)	10
57	Philips JK 1030	Gotta Have Something In The Bank, Frank/Single (with Kaye Sisters, jukebox issue)	10
57	Philips JK 1035	Kisses Sweeter Than Wine/Rock-A-Chicka (jukebox issue)	15
57	Philips PB 775	Kisses Sweeter Than Wine/Rock-A-Chicka	10
58	Philips PB 793	We're Not Alone/Can't Get Along Without You	5
58	Philips PB 825	Kewpie Doll/So Many Women	5
58	Philips PB 834	Wonderful Things/Judy	5
58	Philips PB 865	Am I Wasting My Time On You/So Happy In Love	5
59	Philips PB 423	Give Me The Moonlight, Give Me The Girl/Happy Go Lucky	5
59	Philips PB 865	Am I Wasting My Time On You/So Happy In Love	5
59	Philips PB 895	That's My Doll/Love Is The Sweetest Thing	5
59	Philips PB 896	Honey Bunny Baby/The Lady Is A Square	5

59	Philips PB 913	Come Softly To Me/Say Something Sweet To Your Sweetheart (& Kaye Sisters)	6
59	Philips PB 930	The Heart Of A Man/Sometime Somewhere	6
59	Philips PB 931	Walkin' Tall/I Ain't Gonna Lead This Life	6
60	Philips PB 935	What More Do You Want/The Very Very Young	5
60	Philips PB 1054	Kookie Little Paradise/Mary Lou	5
62	Philips 326542 BF	Hercules/Madeleine (Open The Door)	10
65	Philips BF 1394	Someone Must Have Hurt You A Lot/Easter Time	10

(see also Kaye Sisters, Alma Cogan & Frankie Vaughan, Marilyn Monroe)

MALCOLM VAUGHAN

56	HMV 7M 338	With Your Love/Small Talk	25
56	HMV POP 250	St. Therese Of The Roses/Love Me As Though There Were No Tomorrow	10
57	HMV POP 303	The World Is Mine/Now	10
57	HMV POP 325	Chapel Of The Roses/Guardian Angel	10
56	HMV 7M 389	Only You (And You Alone)/I'll Be Near To You	10
57	HMV POP 419	My Special Angel/The Heart Of A Child	5
58	HMV POP 459	To Be Loved/My Young Arms	5
58	HMV POP 502	Ev'ry Hour, Ev'ry Day Of My Life/Miss You	5
58	HMV POP 538	More Than Ever (Come Prima)/A Night To Remember	5
59	HMV POP 590	Wait For Me (Ti Diro)/Willingly (Melodie Perdue)	5
60	HMV POP 700	Oh So Wunderbar/For Everyone In Love	5
60	HMV POP 739	Lady Of Spain/My Love For You	5
61	HMV POP 923	The Wedding/Guardian Angel	5
61	HMV POP 846	Dolce Vita/There's No Other Love	5
59	HMV CLP 1284	HELLO MALCOLM VAUGHAN (LP)	15

SARAH VAUGHAN
SINGLES

58	Mercury 7MT 198	My Darling, My Darling/Bewitched	10
58	Mercury 7MT 212	Padre/Spin Little Bottle	10
58	Mercury 7MT 222	Too Much, Too Soon/What's So Bad About It	10
59	Mercury AMT 1010	Everything I Do/I Ain't Hurtin'	8
59	Mercury AMT 1029	Cool Baby/Are You Certain?	10
59	Mercury AMT 1029	Cool Baby/Are You Certain? (78)	10
59	Mercury AMT 1044	Careless/Separate Ways	7
59	Mercury AMT 1057	Broken-Hearted Melody/Misty	10
59	Mercury AMT 1057	Broken-Hearted Melody/Misty (78)	15
59	Mercury AMT 1080	You're My Baby/Eternally	6
59	Mercury AMT 1087	Don't Look At Me That Way/Sweet Affections	6
60	Columbia DB 4491	Ooh! What A Day/My Dear Little Sweetheart	10
60	Columbia DB 4511	If I Were A Bell/Teach Me Tonight (with Count Basie & Joe Williams)	6
60	Columbia DB 4542	Serenata/Let's	5
63	Columbia DB 4990	My Favourite Things/Great Day	5
69	Mercury AMT 1107	The Boy From Ipanema/The Fever (p/s)	5

EPs

56	London RE-U 1065	SARAH VAUGHAN SINGS (with John Kirby's Orchestra)	20
57	Emarcy YEP 9507	SARAH VAUGHAN	10
60	Mercury ZEP 10054	SMOOTH SARAH	10
60	Mercury ZEP 10087	LIVE FOR LOVE (also stereo SEZ 19006)	12
62	Mercury ZEP 10115	NO COUNT BLUES (also stereo SEZ 19023)	12

ALBUMS

55	Oriole/Mercury MG 26005	IMAGES (10")	20
55	Mercury MG 25188	THE DIVINE SARAH	15
56	London HB-U 1049	SARAH VAUGHAN SINGS (10", with John Kirby & His Orchestra)	20
56	Emarcy EJL 100	IN THE LAND OF HI FI (10")	20
56	Philips BBL 7082	SARAH VAUGHAN	15
56	Mercury MPT 7503	MAKE YOURSELF COMFORTABLE (10")	20
57	Mercury MPT 7518	IMAGES (10", reissue)	15
57	Emarcy EJL 1258	SASSY	15
57	Mercury MPL 6522	SINGS GREAT SONGS FROM HIT SHOWS PART 1	15
57	Philips BBL 7165	LINGER AWHILE	15
57	Mercury MPL 6523	SINGS GREAT SONGS FROM HIT SHOWS PART 2	15
57	Mercury MPL 6525	SINGS GEORGE GERSHWIN VOL. 1	15
57	Mercury MPL 6527	SINGS GEORGE GERSHWIN VOL. 2	15
58	Mercury MPL 6532	WONDERFUL SARAH	15
58	Emarcy EJL 1273	SWINGIN' EASY	15
58	Mercury MPL 6540	IN ROMANTIC MOOD	15
58	Mercury MPL 6542	AT MISTER KELLY'S	15
59	Mercury CMS 18011	SINGS GEORGE GERSHWIN VOL. 1 (stereo reissue of MPL 6525)	15
59	Mercury CMS 18012	SINGS GEORGE GERSHWIN VOL. 2 (stereo reissue of MPL 6527)	15
59	Mercury MMC 14001	AFTER HOURS AT THE LONDON HOUSE	15
59	Mercury MMC 14011	VAUGHAN AND VIOLINS (also stereo CMS 18003)	15
60	Mercury MMC 14021	NO COUNT SARAH	15

SARAH VAUGHAN & BILLY ECKSTINE

59	Mercury AMT 1071	Passing Strangers/SARAH VAUGHAN: Smooth Operator	5
56	MGM MGM-EP 561	DEDICATED TO YOU (EP)	10
59	MGM MGM-EP 690	BILLY ECKSTINE AND SARAH VAUGHAN (EP)	10
59	Mercury 10025 MCE	PASSING STRANGERS (EP)	10
60	Mercury 10027 MCE	TOGETHER AGAIN (EP)	10
61	Mercury ZEP 10108	BEST OF BERLIN VOL. 1 (EP, mono)	10
61	Mercury SEZ 19016	BEST OF BERLIN VOL. 1 (EP, stereo)	10
58	Mercury MPL 6530	THE BEST OF IRVING BERLIN (LP)	12

(see also Billy Eckstine)

BILLY VAUGHN (& HIS ORCHESTRA)

55	London HL 8112	Melody Of Love/Joy Ride (gold label print)	15
55	London HLD 8205	The Shifting Whispering Sands (Parts 1 & 2) (with Ken Nordine) (gold print)	15
56	London HLD 8238	Theme From 'The Threepenny Opera'/I'd Give A Million Tomorrows (gold label print, later with silver label print)	20

MINT VALUE £

56	London HLD 8238	Theme From 'The Threepenny Opera'/I'd Give A Million Tomorrows (gold label print, later with silver label print)	5
56	London HLD 8319	When The Lilac Blooms Again/Autumn Concerto (gold label print)	20
56	London HLD 8319	When The Lilac Blooms Again/Autumn Concerto (later silver label print)	5
56	London HLD 8342	Petticoats From Portugal/La La Colette (gold label print)	20
56	London HLD 8342	Petticoats From Portugal/La La Colette (later silver label print)	5
57	London HLD 8417	The Ship That Never Sailed/Little Boy Blue (with Ken Nordine)	10
57	London HLD 8511	Johnny Tremain/Naughty Annetta (as Billy Vaughn's Orchestra & Chorus)	10
57	London HLD 8522	Raunchy/Sail Along Silvery Moon	15
58	London HLD 8612	Tumbling Tumbleweeds/Trying	8
58	London HLD 8680	Sail Along Silvery Moon/The Singing Hills	5
58	London HLD 8703	La Paloma/Here Is My Love	5
58	London HLD 8772	Cimarron (Roll On)/You're My Baby Doll	5
58	London HLD 8772	Cimarron (Roll On)/You're My Baby Doll (78)	10
61	London HLD 9423	Berlin Melody/Theme From Come September	5

(see also Hilltoppers, Ken Nordine)

MORRIS VAUGHN

69	Fontana TF 1031	My Love Keeps Growing/Make It Look Good	30

VAZZ

85	CRV 5401	Breath/Violent Silence (in folder & bag with postcards & inserts)	5

V.D.U.'S

79	Thin Sliced	Don't Cry For Me/Little White Lie/Holiday Romances (p/s)	15

(see also Boys Wonder)

VED BUENS ENDE

95	Misanthropy AMAZON 006	WRITTEN IN WATERS (2-LP, marbled purple vinyl)	60

CHUCK VEDDER

59	London HL 8951	Spanky Boy/Arriba	30
59	London HL 8951	Spanky Boy/Arriba (78)	20

BOBBY VEE

SINGLES

60	London HLG 9179	Devil Or Angel/Since I Met You, Baby	20
61	London HLG 9255	Rubber Ball/Everyday	5
61	London HLG 9316	More Than I Can Say/Stayin' In	5
61	London HLG 9389	How Many Tears/Baby Face	5
61	London HLG 9438	Take Good Care Of My Baby/Bashful Bob	5
61	London HLG 7111	Take Good Care Of My Baby/Bashful Bob (export issue)	10
61	London HLG 9459	Love's Made A Fool Of You/Susie-Q	12
61	London HLG 9470	Run To Him/Walkin' With My Angel	5
62	Liberty LIB 55388	Run To Him/Walkin' With My Angel (reissue)	10
62	Liberty LIB 55419	Please Don't Ask About Barbara/I Can't Say Goodbye	8
62	Liberty LIB 55451	Sharing You/At A Time Like This	5
62	Liberty LIB 10046	A Forever Kind Of Love/Remember Me, Huh?	5
63	Liberty LIB 10069	The Night Has A Thousand Eyes/Tenderly Yours	5
63	Liberty LIB 55530	Bobby Tomorrow/Charms	5
63	Liberty LIB 10124	Stranger In Your Arms/Yesterday And You	8
64	Liberty LIB 10141	She's Sorry/Buddy's Song	6
64	Liberty LIB 55700	Hickory, Dick And Doc/I Wish You Were Mine Again	6
65	Liberty LIB 10197	Keep On Trying/Cross My Heart	6
65	Liberty LIB 10213	True Love Never Runs Smooth/Hey Little Girl	6
65	Liberty LIB 55828	Run Like The Devil/Take A Look Around Me	8
66	Liberty LIB 55877	Look At Me Girl/Save A Love	6
67	Liberty LIB 10272	Like You've Never Known Before/Growing Pains	6
67	Liberty LIB 15016	Come Back When You Grow Up/Let The Four Winds Blow	6
67	Liberty LIB 15042	Beautiful People/I May Be Gone	6
68	Liberty LBF 15058	Maybe Just Today/You're A Big Girl Now	6
68	Liberty LBF 15096	Medley, My Girl - Hey Girl/Take Good Care Of My Baby	6
68	Liberty LBF 15134	Do What You Gotta' Do/Thank You	6
69	Liberty LBF 15178	(I'm Into Looking For) Someone To Love Me/Sunrise Highway	8
69	Liberty LBF 15234	I'm Gonna Make It Up To You/Let's Call It A Day	15
69	Liberty LBF 15305	Electric Trains And You/In And Out Of Love	15
70	Liberty LBF 15420	Sweet Sweetheart/Rock 'N Roll Music And You	15

EPs

61	London RE-G 1278	BOBBY VEE NO. 1	20
61	London RE-G 1299	BOBBY VEE NO. 2	20
61	London RE-G 1308	BOBBY VEE NO. 3	20
61	London RE-G 1323	BOBBY VEE NO. 4	25
61	London RE-G 1324	HITS OF THE ROCKIN' 50's	30
62	Liberty LEP 2053	SINCERELY	15
63	Liberty LEP 2084	JUST FOR FUN (2 tracks by Bobby Vee, 2 by Crickets)	15
63	Liberty LEP 2089	A FOREVER KIND OF LOVE	15
63	Liberty LEP 2102	BOBBY VEE'S BIGGEST HITS (mono)	15
63	Liberty SLEP 2102	BOBBY VEE'S BIGGEST HITS (stereo)	20
63	Liberty LEP 2116	BOBBY VEE MEETS THE CRICKETS (mono)	10
63	Liberty SLEP 2116	BOBBY VEE MEETS THE CRICKETS (stereo)	15
64	Liberty LEP 2149	BOBBY VEE MEETS THE CRICKETS VOL. 2	25
64	Liberty LEP 2181	NEW SOUNDS	35
65	Liberty LEP 2212	BOBBY VEE MEETS THE VENTURES (with Ventures)	25

ALBUMS

61	London HA-G 2320	BOBBY VEE SINGS YOUR FAVOURITES	50
61	London HA-G 2352	BOBBY VEE (mono)	25
61	London SAH-G 6152	BOBBY VEE (stereo)	35
61	London HA-G 2374	WITH STRINGS AND THINGS (mono)	25
61	London SAH-G 6174	WITH STRINGS AND THINGS (stereo)	35
61	London HA-G 2406	SINGS HITS OF THE ROCKIN' 50s (mono)	30
61	London SAH-G 6206	SINGS HITS OF THE ROCKIN' 50s (also stereo)	40
61	London HA-G 2428	TAKE GOOD CARE OF MY BABY (mono)	25

61	London SAH-G 6224	TAKE GOOD CARE OF MY BABY (stereo)	30
61	Liberty (S)LBY 1004	TAKE GOOD CARE OF MY BABY (reissue)	12
62	Liberty LBY 1084	BOBBY VEE RECORDING SESSION (mono)	12
62	Liberty SLBY 1084	BOBBY VEE RECORDING SESSION (stereo)	15
62	Liberty LBY 1086	BOBBY VEE MEETS THE CRICKETS (mono)	12
62	Liberty SLBY 1086	BOBBY VEE MEETS THE CRICKETS (stereo)	20
62	Liberty LBY 1112	BOBBY VEE'S GOLDEN GREATS (mono)	15
62	Liberty SLBY 1112	BOBBY VEE'S GOLDEN GREATS (stereo)	20
63	Liberty LBY 1139	THE NIGHT HAS A THOUSAND EYES (mono)	15
63	Liberty SLBY 1139	THE NIGHT HAS A THOUSAND EYES (stereo)	20
63	Liberty LBY 1147	BOBBY VEE MEETS THE VENTURES (with Ventures, mono)	25
63	Liberty SLBY 1147	BOBBY VEE MEETS THE VENTURES (with Ventures, stereo)	30
63	Liberty LBY 1188	I REMEMBER BUDDY HOLLY (mono)	12
63	Liberty SLBY 1188	I REMEMBER BUDDY HOLLY (stereo)	20
65	Liberty SLBY 1263	BOBBY VEE LIVE! ON TOUR (stereo)	15

(see also Crickets, Ventures)

ALAN VEGA

81	Celluloid WIP 6744	Jukebox Babe/Lonely (p/s)	6
81	Celluloid 12WIP 6744	Jukebox Babe/Lonely (12", p/s)	10
88	Sniffin' Rock SR 009	WACKO WARRIOR/(track by African Headcharge) (with Sniffin' Rock fanzine No. 12)	8
81	Ze/Island ILPS 9692	COLLISION DRIVE (LP)	12

(see also Suicide, Future Pilot AKA Alan Vega)

VEINS

| 80 | Redball RR 3 | Complete Control Rock 'n' Roll/Champagne | 25 |

VEJTABLES

| 65 | Pye International 7N 25339 | I Still Love You/Anything | 50 |

RUTH VELDON

| 66 | Decca F12436 | A Most Peculiar Man/Show Me The Way Back To My World | 15 |

MARTHA VELEZ

69	London HLK 10266	It Takes A Lot To Laugh/Come Here Sweet Man	10
69	London HLK 10280	Tell Mama/Swamp Man	25
69	London HLK 10280	Tell Mama/Swamp Man (DJ Copy)	40
72	Blue Horizon 2096 010	Boogie Kitchen/Two Bridges	20
69	London HA-K/SH-K 8395	FIENDS AND ANGELS (LP)	50
70	Blue Horizon 7-63867	FIENDS AND ANGELS AGAIN (LP)	75
76	Sire 9103 252	ESCAPE FROM BABYLON (LP)	15

CAETANO VELOSO

| 71 | Famous SFM 1002 | CAETANO VELOSO (LP) | 12 |

VELOURS

| 67 | MGM 2006 603 | I'm Gonna Change/Don't Pity Me | 10 |

(see also Fantastics)

VELVELETTES

64	Stateside SS 361	Needle In A Haystack/Should I Tell Them?	45
64	Stateside SS 361	Needle In A Haystack/Should I Tell Them? (DJ Copy)	100
65	Stateside SS 387	He Was Really Sayin' Something/Throw A Farewell Kiss	65
65	Stateside SS 387	He Was Really Sayin' Something/Throw A Farewell Kiss (DJ Copy)	125
65	Tamla Motown TMG 521	Lonely Lonely Girl Am I/I'm The Exception To The Rule	175
65	Tamla Motown TMG 521	Lonely Lonely Girl Am I/I'm The Exception To The Rule (DJ Copy)	300
66	Tamla Motown TMG 580	These Things Will Keep Me Loving You/Since You've Been Loving Me	55
65	Tamla Motown TMG 595	He Was Really Sayin' Something/Needle In A Haystack	20
67	Tamla Motown TMG 595	He Was Really Sayin' Something/Needle In A Haystack	30
71	Tamla Motown TMG 780	These Things Will Keep Me Loving You/Since You've Been Loving Me (reissue)	12
72	Tamla Motown TMG 806	Needle In A Haystack/I'm The Exception To The Rule	8

VELVET GLOVE

| 74 | Fresh Air 6370 502 | SWEET WAS MY ROSE (LP, laminated sleeve, lyric insert) | 15 |

VELVET HUSH

| 68 | Oak RGJ 648 | Broken Heart/Lover Please | 300 |

(see also Factory [Oak label])

VELVET OPERA

69	CBS 4189	Anna Dance Square/Don't You Realize	10
70	CBS 4802	Black Jack Davy/Statesboro' Blues	10
70	Spark SRL 1045	She Keeps Giving Me These Feelings/There's A Hole In My Pocket	7
69	CBS 63692	RIDE A HUSTLER'S DREAM (LP)	80

(see also Elmer Gantry's Velvet Opera, Stretch, Hudson-Ford, Johnny Joyce)

VELVETS

61	London HLU 9328	That Lucky Old Sun/Time And Time Again	30
61	London HLU 9372	Tonight (Could Be The Night)/Spring Fever	30
61	London HLU 9444	Laugh/Lana	40
61	London RE-U 1297	VELVETS (EP)	100

VEL-VETS

| 74 | Disco Demand DDS 109 | I Got To Find Me Somebody/What Now My Love | 10 |

VELVETTES

| 64 | Mercury MF 802 | He's The One I Want/That Little Boy Of Mine (in p/s) | 25 |
| 64 | Mercury MF 802 | He's The One I Want/That Little Boy Of Mine | 20 |

VELVETT FOGG

| 69 | Pye 7N 17673 | Telstar '69/Owed To The Dip | 25 |
| 69 | Pye NSPL 18272 | VELVETT FOGG (LP, laminated sleeve; beware of non-laminated counterfeits) | 120 |

(see also Ghost)

VELVET UNDERGROUND

71	Atlantic 2091 008	Who Loves The Sun/Sweet Jane	35
73	MGM 2006 283	I'm Waiting For The Man/Run Run Run/Candy Says (as Lou Reed & Velvet Underground)	15
73	Atlantic K 10339	Sweet Jane/Rock And Roll (as Velvet Underground featuring Lou Reed)	15

82	Polydor POSPX 603	Heroin/Venus In Furs/I'm Waiting For The Man/Run Run Run (12", p/s)	10
88	Old Gold OG 4049	I'm Waiting For The Man/Heroin (12", no p/s)	8
88	Old Gold OG 4051	Venus In Furs/All Tomorrow's Parties (12", no p/s)	8
67	Verve VLP 9184	THE VELVET UNDERGROUND AND NICO (LP, single sleeve, 'non-banana' cover, mono)	200
67	Verve SVLP 9184	THE VELVET UNDERGROUND AND NICO (LP, single sleeve, 'non-banana' cover, stereo)	150
68	Verve 2315 056	THE VELVET UNDERGROUND AND NICO (LP, UK pressing in stickered US peelable banana gatefold censored sleeve, stereo)	175
68	Verve VLP 9201	WHITE LIGHT WHITE HEAT (LP, 'skull' sleeve, mono)	150
68	Verve SVLP 9201	WHITE LIGHT WHITE HEAT (LP, 'skull' sleeve, stereo)	100
69	MGM MGM-CS 8108	THE VELVET UNDERGROUND (LP, 'Val Valentin mix', flapped laminated sleeve, with horizontal split of Lou Reed picture on rear sleeve)	150
71	MGM/Verve Super 2315 056	THE VELVET UNDERGROUND AND NICO (LP, reissue stereo, UK LP in US Verve stereo V6 5008 sleeve with peelable banana on front cover, UK sticker on back cover with 2315 056 covering US catalogue number, "Marketed by Polydor")	70
71	Atlantic 2400 111	LOADED (LP)	50
71	MGM 2315 056	THE VELVET UNDERGROUND AND NICO (LP, reissue, gatefold sleeve)	20
71	MGM Select 2353 022	THE VELVET UNDERGROUND (LP, reissue, gatefold sleeve)	20
71	MGM Select 2353 024	WHITE LIGHT WHITE HEAT (LP, reissue)	20
72	MGM Select 2683 006	ANDY WARHOL'S VELVET UNDERGROUND (2-LP)	30
72	Atlantic K 30022	LIVE AT MAX'S KANSAS CITY (LP)	25
73	Polydor 2383 180	SQUEEZE (LP)	30
79	Mercury 6641 900	1969 VOL. 1 (2-LP)	15
84	Polydor SPELP 73	WHITE LIGHT WHITE HEAT (LP, reissue, different sleeve)	15
84	Polydor SPELP 20	THE VELVET UNDERGROUND AND NICO (LP, reissue)	15
86	Polydor VUBOX 1	THE VELVET UNDERGROUND BOX SET (5-LP box set, with booklet)	40
88	HMV C88 1-15	THE VELVET UNDERGROUND AND NICO (LP or CD box set, with booklet, 1500 only)	25
95	Polydor 527887	PEEL SLOWLY AND SEE (5-CD box set)	35
99	Simply Vinyl SVLP 090	THE VELVET UNDERGROUND AND NICO (LP, reissue)	20
00	Simply Vinyl SVLP 200	WHITE LIGHT/WHITE HEAT (LP, reissue)	15

(see also Lou Reed, Nico, John Cale)

VENDETTA

| 88 | Plaza PZA 042 | Don't Let The World Drag You Under/Don't Let The World Drag You Under Pt.2 (p/s) | 6 |

VENDORS

| 64 | Domino Studios (no cat. no.) | Don't Leave Me Now/Twilight Time/Take Your Time/Peace Pipe (acetate, private pressing, 12 copies only) | 500 |

(see also 'N Betweens, Slade)

VENGERS

| 63 | Oriole CB 1879 | Shake And Clap/Shakedown | 25 |

VENIGMAS

| 79 | Graduate GRAD 2 | Red Revenge/Turn The Lights Out (P/S) | 10 |

VENOM

81	Neat NEAT 08	In League With Satan/Live Like An Angel, Die Like An Devil (p/s)	30
82	Neat NEAT 13	Bloodlust/In Nomine Satanas (p/s)	30
82	Neat NEAT 13	Bloodlust/In Nomine Satanas (purple vinyl)	80
83	Neat NEAT 27	Die Hard/Acid Queen (p/s, with poster)	25
83	Neat NEAT 27	Die Hard/Acid Queen (p/s)	15
83	Megaforce LOM 1/NEAT 27	Die Hard/Acid Queen (picture disc, export issue, 1,000 only)	25
84	Neat NEAT 38	Warhead/Lady Lust (p/s)	12
84	Neat NEATP 38	Warhead/Lady Lust (p/s, mauve vinyl)	20
84	Neat NEAT 3812	Warhead/Lady Lust/Gates Of Hell (12", p/s)	18
85	Neat NEATP 43	Manitou/Woman (picture disc)	18
85	Neat NEATSHAPE 43	Manitou/Woman (shaped picture disc)	20
85	Neat NEAT 4312	Manitou/Woman/Dead Of Night (12", p/s)	18
85	Neat NEATS 47	Nightmare/Satanarchist (shaped picture disc)	25
85	Neat NEAT 4712	Nightmare/Satanarchist/F.O.A.D./Warhead (live) (12", 'face' p/s)	20
85	Neat NEAT 4712	Nightmare/Satanarchist/F.O.A.D./Warhead (live) (12", p/s, withdrawn)	25
85	Neat NEATSP 4712	Nightmare/Satanarchist/F.O.A.D./Warhead (live) (12", picture disc, withdrawn)	40
06	Castle CMWSE 1333	Antechrist/Metal Black (p/s, signed by band)	10
06	Castle CMWSE 1333	Antechrist/Metal Black (p/s, not signed by band)	5
85	Neat 5312	HELL AT HAMMERSMITH EP (Witching Hour/Teacher's Pet/Poison) (12", 10,000 only)	25
81	Neat 1002	WELCOME TO HELL (LP, 1st issue, with poster and lyric insert)	30
82	Neat 1005	BLACK METAL (LP, 1st issue, textured sleeve, with poster, on coloured vinyl)	35
82	Neat 1005	BLACK METAL (LP, 1st issue, textured sleeve, with poster)	40
82	Neat NEAT 1005	BLACK METAL (LP, green marbled vinyl)	350
83	Neat NEATP 1002	WELCOME TO HELL (LP, reissue, purple vinyl)	50
84	Neat 1015	AT WAR WITH SATAN (LP, textured sleeve, 1st 19,000 with poster)	20
84	Neat 1015	AT WAR WITH SATAN (LP, textured sleeve)	15
85	Neat NEATP 1005	BLACK METAL (LP, reissue, picture disc)	40
85	Neat NEATP 1015	AT WAR WITH SATAN (LP, picture disc)	40
85	Neat NEATP 1024	POSSESSED (LP, picture disc)	20
85	Neat NEAT 1024	POSSESSED (LP, blue vinyl)	20
86	Demon APKPD 12	OBSCENE MATERIAL (LP, picture disc)	20
86	Raw Power RAWLP 001	FROM HELL TO THE UNKNOWN (2-LP)	25
86	A.P. APK 12	OFFICIAL BOOTLEG (LP, picture disc)	15
89	Under One Flag FLAG 36P	PRIME EVIL (LP, numbered picture disc, stickered clear sleeve)	20

CAROL VENTURA

65	Stateside SS 466	Please Somebody Help Me/The Old Lady Of Threadneedle Street	20
65	Stateside SL 10146	CAROL! (LP)	20
66	Stateside S(S)L 10180	I LOVE TO SING (LP)	20

CHARLIE VENTURA

| 55 | Vogue Coral Q 72048 | I Love You/Intermezzo | 7 |

DAVE VENTURA

| 64 | Mercury MF 805 | The Hurt Stays In The Heart/Is A Redbird Red? | 8 |
| 64 | Mercury MF 827 | I Forgot What It Was Like/I'll Never Love Again | 7 |

DAVE VENTURA & THE ORBITS

| 63 | Hardy Records 001 | Yo Yo Twist/Yo Yo Twist Story (Flexi) | 10 |

TOBY VENTURA

63	Decca F 11581	If My Heart Were A Storybook/Vagabond	40

VENTURES
SINGLES

60	Top Rank JAR 417	Walk Don't Run/Home	10
60	London HLG 9232	Perfidia/No Trespassing	8
61	London HLG 9292	Ram-Bunk-Shush/Lonely Heart	10
61	London HLG 9344	Lullaby Of The Leaves/Ginchy	10
61	London HLG 9411	Theme From 'Silver City'/Bluer Than Blue	10
61	London HLG 9465	Blue Moon/Wailin'	15
61	London HLG 7113	Lady Of Spain/Blue Moon (export issue)	30
62	Liberty LIB 60	Lolita Ya-Ya/Lucille	8
62	Liberty LIB 67	The 2,000 Pound Bee Parts 1 & 2	12
63	Liberty LIB 68	El Cumbanchero/Skip To M'Limbo	8
63	Liberty LIB 78	The Ninth Wave/Damaged Goods	10
64	Liberty LIB 91	Journey To The Stars/Walkin' With Pluto	10
64	Liberty LIB 96	Walk Don't Run '64/The Cruel Sea	12
64	Liberty LIB 10142	Penetration/Solar Race	10
65	Liberty LIB 300	Slaughter On Tenth Avenue/Rap City	10
65	Liberty LIB 303	Diamond Head/Lonely Girl	10
65	Liberty LIB 306	The Swingin' Creeper/Pedal Pusher	10
65	Liberty LIB 308	The Stranger/Bird Rockers	10
65	Liberty LIB 10219	Sleigh Ride/White Christmas	10
66	Liberty LIB 316	Secret Agent Man/007-11	15
67	Liberty LIB 10266	Theme From The Wild Angels/High And Dry	10
67	Liberty LIB 55967	Strawberry Fields Forever/Endless Dream	10
68	Liberty LBF 15075	Flights Of Fantasy/Pandora's Box	15
70	Liberty LBF 15221	Hawaii Five-O - Theme/Higher Than Thou	15
71	United Artists UP 36316	Theme From 'Shaft'/Tight Fit	7
72	United Artists UP 35326	Joy/Cherries Jubilee	5
73	United Artists UP 35574	Skylab/Little People	7
77	United Artists UP 36223	Starsky And Hutch/Charlie's Angels	7

EPs

61	London REG 1279	THE VENTURES	20
61	London REG 1283	THE VENTURES (export issue)	25
61	London REG 1288	RAM-BUNK-SHUSH!	25
62	London REG 1326	ANOTHER SMASH	25
62	London REG 1328	COLOURFUL VENTURES	25
62	Liberty LEP 2058	TWIST WITH THE VENTURES	20
62	Liberty LEP 2131	SMASH HITS	20
63	Liberty LEP 2104	THE VENTURES PLAY TELSTAR AND LONELY BULL	25
64	Liberty LEP 2174	THE VENTURES PLAY COUNTRY GREATS	25
65	Liberty LEP 2212	BOBBY VEE MEETS THE VENTURES (with Bobby Vee)	35
66	Liberty LEP 2250	SECRET AGENT MEN	35

ALBUMS

61	London HA-G 2340	THE VENTURES (mono)	40
61	London SAH-G 6143	THE VENTURES (stereo)	50
61	London HA-G 2376	ANOTHER SMASH (mono)	30
61	London SAH-G 6209	ANOTHER SMASH (stereo)	40
61	London HA-G 2409	THE COLOURFUL VENTURES (mono)	30
61	London SAH-G 6209	THE COLOURFUL VENTURES (stereo)	40
62	Liberty LBY 1002	WALK DON'T RUN	25
62	London HA-G 2429	TWIST WITH THE VENTURES (mono)	30
62	London SAH-G 6225	TWIST WITH THE VENTURES (stereo)	45
62	Liberty LBY 1072	TWIST PARTY	25
63	Liberty (S)LBY 1110	GOING TO THE VENTURES DANCE PARTY! (mono)	25
63	Liberty (S)LBY 1110	GOING TO THE VENTURES DANCE PARTY! (stereo)	30
63	Liberty (S)LBY 1147	BOBBY VEE MEETS THE VENTURES (with Bobby Vee, mono)	35
63	Liberty (S)LBY 1147	BOBBY VEE MEETS THE VENTURES (with Bobby Vee, stereo)	45
63	Liberty (S)LBY 1150	SURFING (mono)	22
63	Liberty (S)LBY 1150	SURFING (stereo)	30
64	Liberty (S)LBY 1169	LET'S GO! (mono)	18
64	Liberty (S)LBY 1169	LET'S GO! (stereo)	25
64	Liberty (S)LBY 1189	THE VENTURES IN SPACE (mono)	22
64	Liberty (S)LBY 1189	THE VENTURES IN SPACE (stereo)	30
65	Liberty (S)LBY 1228	WALK DON'T RUN - VOL. 2 (mono)	22
65	Liberty (S)LBY 1228	WALK DON'T RUN - VOL. 2 (stereo)	30
65	Liberty (S)LBY 1252	KNOCK ME OUT (mono)	20
65	Liberty (S)LBY 1252	KNOCK ME OUT (stereo)	20
65	Liberty (S)LBY 1270	ON STAGE (mono)	20
65	Liberty (S)LBY 1270	ON STAGE (stereo)	20
66	Liberty (S)LBY 1274	VENTURES A-GO GO (mono)	18
66	Liberty (S)LBY 1274	VENTURES A-GO GO (stereo)	20
66	Liberty (S)LBY 1285	THE VENTURES' CHRISTMAS ALBUM (mono)	22
66	Liberty (S)LBY 1285	THE VENTURES' CHRISTMAS ALBUM (stereo)	30
66	Liberty (S)LBY 1297	WHERE THE ACTION IS! (mono)	18
66	Liberty (S)LBY 1297	WHERE THE ACTION IS! (stereo)	20
66	Liberty (S)LBY 1323	GO WITH THE VENTURES (mono)	18
66	Liberty (S)LBY 1323	GO WITH THE VENTURES (stereo)	20
67	Liberty (S)LBY 1345	GUITAR FREAKOUT (mono)	18
67	Liberty (S)LBY 1345	GUITAR FREAKOUT (stereo)	20
67	Liberty (S)LBY 1372	SUPER PSYCHEDELICS (mono)	18
67	Liberty (S)LBY 1372	SUPER PSYCHEDELICS (stereo)	20
67	Liberty (S)LBY 1375	THE BEST OF THE VENTURES (mono)	18
67	Liberty (S)LBY 1375	THE BEST OF THE VENTURES (stereo)	20
68	Liberty LBL/LBS 83046E	GOLDEN GREATS (mono)	18
68	Liberty LBL/LBS 83046E	GOLDEN GREATS (stereo)	20
68	Liberty LBL/LBS 83085E	GREAT PERFORMANCES VOL. 1	18

68	Liberty LBL/LBS 83092E	$1,000,000 WEEKEND	18
68	Liberty LBL/LBS 83124E	LONELY BULL	15
68	Liberty LBX 2	VENTURES SAMPLER	15
68	Liberty LBL/LBS 83138E	FLIGHTS OF FANTASY	15
69	Liberty LBL/LBS 83164E	THE HORSE	15
69	Liberty LBL/LBS 83193E	UNDERGROUND FIRE	15
70	Liberty LBL/LBS 83279	SWAMP ROCK (mono)	15
70	Liberty LBL/LBS 83279	SWAMP ROCK (stereo)	12

(see also New Ventures, Bobby Vee, Nokie Edwards)

VENUS & RAZORBLADES
77	Spark SRL 1153	I Wanna Be Where The Boys Are/Dogfood (numbered p/s)	8
78	Spark SRL 1159	Workin' Girl/Midnight	8

BILLY VERA
68	Atlantic 584 196	With Pen In Hand/Good Morning Blues	10

BILLY VERA & JUDY CLAY
68	Atlantic 584 169	Country Girl City Man/Let It Be Me	7
68	Atlantic 584 164	Storybook Children/Really Together	8
69	Atlantic 584 293	Reaching For The Moon/Tell It Like It Is	8
68	Atlantic 588 158	THE STORYBOOK CHILDREN (LP)	20

(see also Judy Clay)

VIC VERGAT
81	Harvest HAR 5216	Down To The Bone/You Never Tell Me You Love Me (p/s)	5

JOHN VERITY BAND
74	Probe SPB 1087	JOHN VERITY BAND (LP)	35

(see also Argent)

TOM VERLAINE
80	Electric EM 342	The Twilight Zone - Psychotic Reaction/Wild Thing/Television - Poor Circulation (p/s)	10

TIM VERLANDER
72	Midas MR 007	TIM VERLANDER (LP, with booklet)	40

VERMILION
78	Illegal ILM 0010	Angry Young Women/Nymphomania/Wild Boys (p/s)	18
79	Illegal ILS 0015	I Like Motorcycles/The Letter (p/s)	10

(see also Menace)

VERN & ALVIN
69	Blue Cat BS 167	Everybody Reggae/Another Fool	25
69	Big Shot BI 525	Old Man Dead/G.G. RHYTHM SECTION: Reggae Me	15

(see also Maytones)

VERN & SON
71	G.G. GG 4523	Little Boy Blue/TYPHOON ALL STARS: Little Boy Blue - Version	6

(see also Maytones)

LARRY VERNE
60	London HLN 9194	Mr. Custer/Okeefenokee Two Step	8
61	London HLN 9263	Mr. Livingstone/Roller Coaster	7

LYN VERNON
60	Top Rank JAR 323	Woodchoppers Ball/Caravan	7

MIKE VERNON
72	Blue Horizon 2096 007	Let's Try It Again/Little Southern Country Girl	25
71	Blue Horizon 2931 003	BRING IT BACK HOME (LP, textured sleeve with insert)	250
71	Blue Horizon 2931 003	BRING IT BACK HOME (LP, textured sleeve without insert)	175

VERNON & THE G.I.S
79	Billy Goat BILL 004	Ghost Train Boogie/(I'm A) Teddy Boy	6
80	Billy Goat BILL 006	I Wanna Be A Ted/Banjo Baby (p/s)	7

VERNONS GIRLS
58	Parlophone R 4497	Lost And Found/White Bucks And Saddle Shoes	25
59	Parlophone R 4532	Jealous Heart/Now Is The Month Of Maying	20
59	Parlophone R 4596	Don't Look Now But/Who Are They To Say?	20
60	Parlophone R 4624	We Like Boys/Boy Meets Girl	15
60	Parlophone R 4654	Madison Time (with Jimmy Saville)/The Oo-We	15
61	Parlophone R 4734	Ten Little Lonely Boys/Anniversary Song	10
61	Parlophone R 4832	Let's Get Together/No Message	10
62	Decca F 11450	Lover Please/You Know What I Mean	7
62	Decca F 11495	The Loco-motion/Don't Wanna Go	10
62	Decca F 11549	Funny All Over/See For Yourself	10
63	Decca F 11629	Do The Bird/I'm Gonna Let My Hair Down	10
63	Decca F 11685	He'll Never Come Back/Stay-At-Home	5
63	Decca F 11781	Tomorrow Is Another Day/Why Why Why	10
64	Decca F 11807	We Love The Beatles/Hey Lover Boy	15
64	Decca F 11887	Only You Can Do It/Stupid Little Girl	10
64	Decca F 12021	It's A Sin To Tell A Lie/Don't Say Goodbye	10
62	Decca DFE 8506	THE VERNONS GIRLS (EP)	40
58	Parlophone PMC 1052	THE VERNONS GIRLS (LP)	50

(see also Krimson Kake, Wilde Three, Jimmy Saville, Lee Francis, Samantha Jones, Breakaways)

LILI VERONA
54	HMV 7MC 13	Massa Johnny/Hoggin' In The Cocoa (export issue)	15
56	Melodisc MEL 1383	French Lesson/Pica Now (78, with Gulf Stream Calypso Boys)	10
59	HMV DLP 1202	JAMAICA SINGS (10" LP)	22

VERSAILLES
80	MCA 595	White Sox/White Sox (p/s)	5

VERSATILE NEWTS
80	Shanghai No. 2	Newtrition/Blimp (p/s, stamped white label)	45

(see also Felt)

VERSATILES (JAMAICA)

68	Island WI 3142	Teardrops Falling/Someone To Love 28
68	Amalgamated AMG 802	Just Can't Win/LEADERS: Sometimes I Sit Down Down And Cry.......................25
68	Crab CRAB 1	Children Get Ready/Someone To Love 20
69	Amalgamated AMG 854	Lu Lu Bell/Long Long Time 40
69	Big Shot BI 520	Worries A Yard/VAL BENNETT: Hound Dog Special 8
69	Crab CRAB 5	Spread Your Bed/Worries A Yard...70
70	Nu Beat NB 060	Pick My Pocket/FREEDOM SINGERS: Freedom 8
71	Nu Beat NB 076	Give To Me/TIGER: With Hot..8
74	Dip DL 5039	Cutting Razor/UPSETTERS: Black Belt Jones 8

(see also Pioneers, Soul Sisters)

VERSATILITY

| 75 | President PT 435 | Tequila Madness/B Side Blues...10 |

VERTICAL HOLD

80	Vertical Hold VH 001	Rubber Cross/Injustice..40
84	Vertical Hold VH 002	Angel Dust/Four Years/Dub Years 15
85	Vertical Hold VH 003	The War That Time Won/Bio Hazard 15

VERVE

92	Hut HUT 12	All In The Mind/One Way To Go (p/s) 5
92	Hut HUTT 12	All In The Mind/Man Called Sun/One Way To Go (12" promo, white label) 15
92	Hut HUT 16	She's A Superstar (Edit)/Feel (p/s)...5
92	Hut HUTEN 21	GRAVITY GRAVE EP (Gravity Grave [Edit]/Endless Life/ She's A Superstar [Live at Clapham Grand]) (10", p/s) 10
92	Hut HUTT 16	She's A Superstar/Feel (12" promo, white label) 20
93	Hut HUTEN 29	Blue/Twilight/Where The Geese Go/No Come Down (10", p/s) 12
93	Hut HUT 35	Slide Away/Make It 'Til Monday (pink vinyl, p/s) 6
93	(no label) FLEXI 1	Make It 'Til Monday (Glastonbury '93) (clear vinyl stickered flexi with magazine)..12
95	Hut HUT 54	This Is Music/Let The Damage Begin (purple vinyl, p/s) 8
95	Hut HUT 55	On Your Own/I See The Door (green vinyl, p/s) 8
95	Hut HUT 55	On Your Own/I See The Door (green vinyl, p/s, mispressing, B-side plays 'Friends' by Daryll-Ann)..8
97	Hut HUTLH 82	Bitter Sweet Symphony/So Sister (Jukebox issue)..8
97	Hut HUTTR 82	Bitter Sweet Symphony (James Lavelle Remix)/(James Lavelle Instrumental Remix) (12", stickered plain die-cut sleeve, promo only) 8
97	Hut HUTTP 82	Bitter Sweet Symphony (Extended Version)/(M.S.G. Mix)/(Instrumental) (12", plain die-cut sleeve, promo only)...10
97	Hut HUTLH 88	The Drugs Don't Work/The Drugs Don't Work (Original Demo) (Jukebox issue) 7
98	Hut HUTTX 100	Sonnet/Stamped/So Sister/Echo Bass (12", title sleeve)....................................8
93	Hut HUTLP 3	A STORM IN HEAVEN (LP, gatefold)..60
95	Hut HUTLP 27	A NORTHERN SOUL (2xLP, mirrored sleeve) 60
97	Hut HUTLPX 45	URBAN HYMNS (2-LP) 40
97	Hut HUTLPX 45	URBAN HYMNS (2-LP, with inner sleeves, printed outer mailer, 5,000 only) 45
97	Hut CDPHUT 45	URBAN HYMNS (CD, ribbon-tied black gatefold sleeve, promo only) 20
93	Jolly Roger JOLLY ROGER 2	VOYAGER 1 (LP, official bootleg, blue vinyl, 1,000 only) 100
08	Parlophone 82075 2355841	FORTH (LP)...18

VETS

| 79 | SRT SRTS 79 | Flies/Contrix ....50 |

VEX

| 84 | Fight Back FIGHT 1 | SANCTUARY (12" EP, with insert)...10 |

VHF

| 80 | Lion PAW 1 | Heart Of Stone ....75 |
| 81 | Distill (NO Cat No) | First Impressions/In Stereo (no p/s, most labels signed by band) ....50 |

DANNY VIBES

| 00 | Jah Tubbys JT 006 | Want No Wickedness/Want No Dub ....20 |

VIBRASONIC

| 95 | Yep! YEPLP 01 | VIBRASONIC (LP)..15 |

VIBRATIONS

61	Pye International 7N 25107	The Watusi/Wallflower 25
64	London HLK 9875	My Girl Sloopy/Daddy Woo Woo 20
66	Columbia DB 7895	Canadian Sunset/The Story Of A Starry Night..25
67	Columbia DB 8175	Pick Me/You Better Beware 30
67	Columbia DB 8318	Talkin' 'Bout Love/One Mint Julep...25
68	Direction 58-3511	Love In Them There Hills/Remember The Rain 15
67	Columbia SX 6106	NEW VIBRATIONS (LP) 75
69	Direction 8-63644	GREATEST HITS (LP) 30
72	RCA SF 8254	THE VIBRATIONS (LP)...20

(see also Jayhawks)

VIBRATORS

76	RAK RAK 245	We Vibrate/Whips And Furs...10
76	RAK RAK 246	Pogo Dancing/The Pose (as Vibrators with Chris Spedding) 10
77	RAK RAK 253	Bad Times/No Heart (unreleased, this price is for acetates, of which 2 copies exist)......150
77	Epic EPC 5302	Baby Baby/Into The Future (p/s) 5
77	Epic EPC 5565	London Girls/Stiff Little Fingers (live) (p/s) 5
78	Epic EPC 6393	Judy Says (Knock You On The Head)/Pure Mania (p/s) 5
80	Rat Race RAT 2	Gimme Some Lovin'/Power Cry (live) (p/s, in slightly different colours)..............5
80	Rat Race RAT 4	Disco In Mosco/Take A Chance (p/s, with various coloured writing)...................5
77	Epic EPC 82097	PURE MANIA (LP) 18
78	Epic EPC 82495	V2 (LP, with inner lyric sleeve)..18

(see also Boyfriends, Chris Spedding, Nazis Against Fascism, Substitute, Troops Of Tomorrow, Urban Dogs)o

VIBRATORS (JAMAICA)

| 66 | Doctor Bird DB 1036 | Sloop John B/Amour ....18 |

(see also Al & Vibrators, Wilbert Francis & Vibrators)

VIBRONICS

| 04 | Jah Tubbys JT 10021 | Terror/African Stone (10")..20 |

VIC & JOHN
94	Kent 6T 10	Why Did She Lie/PHIL TERRELL: Love Has Passed Me By	35

VICE CREEMS
78	Tiger GRRRR 1	Won't You Be My Girl?/01-01-212 (gatefold p/s)	30
79	Zig Zag ZZ22 001	Danger Love/Like A Tiger (p/s)	25

VICE VERSA
80	Neutron NT 001/PX 1092	MUSIC 4 (EP, poster p/s)	10

(see also Liza Strike)

VICEROYS
67	Island WI 3095	Lip And Tongue/DAWN PENN: When Am I Gonna Be Free	100
67	Coxsone CS 7031	Magadown/RICHARD ACE: Don't Let The Sun Catch You Crying	50
67	Studio One SO 2016	Lose And Gain (as Voiceroys)/SOUL BROTHERS: Honey Pot	50
67	Studio One SO 2025	Shake Up/NORMA FRAZER: Telling Me Lies	30
68	Studio One SO 2064	Last Night/Ya Ho	25
68	Blue Cat BS 121	Fat Fish/OCTAVES: You're Gonna Lose	150
69	Studio One SO 2077	Things A-Come To Bump/LYRICS: Old Man Say	25
69	Punch PH 3	Jump In A Fire/Give To Get (as Voiceroys)	60
69	Crab CRAB 12	Work It/You Mean So Much To Me (B-side actually by Paragons)	30
69	Crab CRAB 27	Death A-Come (actually by Lloyd Robinson)/MATADOR ALLSTARS: The Sword	20
73	Harry J. HJ 6658	Chucky (Parts 1 & 2)	5
74	Harry J. HJ 6669	Wheel & Jig (Parts 1 & 2)	5
76	Angen ANG 112	Marcus Marcus Garvey/Change Your Style	8
84	Greensleeves GRED 146	New Clothes/New Clothes Rhythm/Bubblers Version (12")	15
82	Trojan TRLS 206	WE MUST UNITE (LP)	45
83	Csa CSLP 5	BRETHREN AND SISTREN (LP)	50

(see also Richard Ace, Interns [Jamaica], Derrick Morgan, Vincent Gordon, Hub)

VICEROYS (U.K.)
70	Bullet BU 441	Chariot Coming/SYDNEY ALLSTARS: Stackata	10
70	Bullet BU 444	Power Control/SLICKERS: Dip Dip	10
70	Bullet BU 450	Come On Over/SYDNEY ALLSTARS: Version	10
70	Bullet BU 453	Fancy Clothes/BIGGIE: Jack And Jill	10
71	Bullet BU 470	Rebel Nyah/Feel The Spirit	10

VICE SQUAD
80	Riot City RIOT 1	Last Rockers/Living On Dreams/Latex Love (p/s, with poster)	10
81	Riot City RIOT 2	Resurrection/Young Blood/Hurricane (p/s)	6
82	Riot City RIOT 12 1/2	SINGLES (12" EP)	8
82	Zonophone Z 26	Out Of Reach/Sterile/Out Of Reach (p/s)	5
82	Zonophone Z 30	Rock 'n' Roll Massacre/Stand Strong And Proud/Tomorrow	5
80s	Vice Squad Fan Club	EVIL (EP, flexidisc)	12
82	EMI ZEM 104	STAND STRONG STAND PROUD (LP, with inner)	15

(see also Sex Aids)

VICIOUS PINK (PHENOMENA)
82	Mobile Suit Corp. CORP 1	My Private Tokyo/Promises (p/s)	5
82	Mobile Suit Corp. CORP 12	My Private Tokyo (Long Version)/(Remix)/Promises (12", p/s)	8
83	Warehouse WARE 1T	Je T'Aime (Moi Non Plus) (12" Disco Version)/In The Swim (12", p/s)	8

(see also Soft Cell)

VICIOUS RUMOURS
87	Link LP 022	THE SICKEST MEN IN TOWN (LP)	12

SID VICIOUS
79	Virgin V 2144	SID SINGS (LP, picture inner, without poster)	15
79	Virgin V2144	SID SINGS (LP, picture inner, with poster)	45

(see also Sex Pistols)

MIKE VICKERS (ORCHESTRA)
65	Columbia DB 7657	On The Brink/The Puff Adder (as Mike Vickers & Orchestra)	50
65	Columbia DB 7657	On The Brink/The Puff Adder (as Mike Vickers & Orchestra) (DJ Copy)	100
66	Columbia DB 7825	Eleventy One/The Inkling	20
66	Columbia DB 7906	Morgan - A Suitable Case For Treatment/Gorilla Of My Dreams (as Mike Vickers Orchestra)	20
67	Columbia DB 8171	Air On A G-String/Proper Charles (as Mike Vickers Orchestra)	10
67	Columbia DB 8281	Captain Scarlet And The Mysterons/Kettle Of Fish	30
90s	Emidisc EMIDISC 101	On The Brink/SAINT ETIENNE: Emidisc Theme (promo only)	10
68	Columbia S(C)X 6180	I WISH I WERE A GROUP AGAIN (LP)	45

(see also Manfred Mann, Baker Street Philharmonic)

SUE VICKERS
72	Threshold TH 8	Loving You The Way I Do/Take Me With You	5

MACK VICKERY
60	Top Rank JAR 420	Fantasy/Hawaiian Stroll	12

VICKY
67	Philips BF 1565	Colours Of Love (Love Is Blue)/Who Can Tell	15
67	Philips BF 1599	Sunshine Boy/Tell Me	10
68	Philips BF 1631	Dance With Me Until Tomorrow/Give Me Your Hand	10

(see also Vicky Leandros)

VICKY & JERRY
60	HMV POP 715	Don't Cry/A Year Ago Tonight	20

VICTIM
78	Good Vibrations GOT 2	Strange Things By Night/Mixed Up World (wraparound p/s)	15
79	TJM TJM 13	THE VICTIM (EP, unreleased)	0
79	TJM TJM 14	Why Are Fire Engines Red/I Need You (p/s)	25
80	TJM TJM 15	The Teen Age/Junior Criminals/Hung On To Yourself (p/s)	25
80	Illuminated ILL 1	The Teen Age/Junior Criminals/Hung On To Yourself (p/s, reissue)	15

VICTIMIZE
79	I.M.E. IME 1	Baby Buyer/Hi Rising Failure (folded p/s)	70

80	I.M.E. IME 2	Wh?r? Did Th? Mon?y Go (p/s)	70

VICTIMS OF CHANCE
70	Stable SLE 8004	VICTIMS OF CHANCE (LP)	120

VICTIMS OF CIRCUMSTANCE
80s	Double Vision DV 1	Very Little Glory/OPPOSITION: Wires (p/s)	10

VICTIMS OF PLEASURE
80	P.A.M. VOP 1	When You're Young/If I Was/Sporting Pastimes (p/s)	10

VICTIMS OF VICTIMISATION
87	Death DEAD 2	Kill Or Be Killed/As A Doornail (p/s)	18

TONY VICTOR
62	Decca F 11459	Dear One/There Was A Time	25
63	Decca F 11626	Thinking Of You/Hokey Cokey	12
63	Decca F 11708	In The Still Of The Night/Money	12

VICTORIA
71	Atlantic 2091 084	Tule's Blues/Helplessly Hoping	6
71	Atlantic 2400 176	VICTORIA (LP)	30
71	Mojo 2466 008	SECRET OF THE BLOOM (LP)	45

VICTORIANS
64	Liberty LIB 55693	Oh What A Night For Love/Happy Birthday Blue	25

VICTORS (1)
65	Oriole CB 1984	Take This Old Hammer/Answer's No	15

VICTORS (2)
69	High Note HS 019	Reggae Buddy/Easy Squeeze	12
71	Escort ERT 846	Me A Tell Yuh/LLOYD'S ALL-STARS: More Echo	8

VICTORY
82	Rods HOT 3	TAKING THE FIGHT (LP, with lyric insert)	60

(see also Keith Howard)

VIDELS
60	London HLI 9153	Mister Lonely/I'll Forget You	80

VIDEOS
81	Guardian GRC 85	Beautiful People/Him Or Me	15

VIETNAM ALL STARS (ACTUALLY PRINCE BUSTER WITH UNKNOWN VOCALIST)
66	Rio R 109	The Toughest/ERROL DUNKLEY : Love Me Forever	100

VIGILANTES
61	Pye International 7N 25082	Eclipse/Man In Space	20

(PAUL) VIGRASS
68	RCA RCA 1755	New Man/Curly	10
69	RCA RCA 1800	Suzie/Funky Piano Joe (as Vigrass)	8
69	RCA RCA 1857	Free Lorry Ride/Flying	15
70	RCA RCA 1911	Stop/Like It Never Was	8

VIGRASS & OSBORNE
72	UNI UNS 544	Men Of Learning/Forever Autumn	10

VIKINGS (JAMAICA)
63	Island WI 035	Maggie Don't Leave Me/Henchmen (both actually with Victor Wong)	20
63	Island WI 065	Hallelujah/Helpin' Ages (actually by Maytals)	12
63	Island WI 075	Six And Seven Books Of Moses/Zacions (actually by Maytals)	25
63	Island WI 101	Never Grow Old/Irene (actually by Maytals)	30
63	Island WI 107	Just Got To Be/You Make Me Do (actually by Maytals)	20
63	Island WI 117	Fever/Cheer Up (actually by Maytals)	20
64	Island WI 167	Daddy/It's You (actually by Maytals)	20
64	Black Swan WI 423	Down By The Riverside/This Way	25
64	Black Swan WI 428	Treat Me Bad/Sitting On Top	25
64	Black Swan WI 430	Come Into My Parlour/I Am In Love	20

(see also Maytals, Flames [Jamaica], Bonnie & Skitto)

VIKINGS
66	Alp 595 011	Bad News Feeling/What Can I Do	30

VILENESS
90	Noisome STENCH 3	March Of The Vile/Sex Is Vile (12", vile-scented p/s)	10

VILLAGE
69	Head HDS 4002	Man In The Moon/Long Time Coming	60

(see also Peter Bardens, Quiver)

VILLAGE SOUL CHOIR
70	Direction 58-4969	Catwalk/Country Walk	8

VILLAGERS
88	Hole In One HOLEIN 1	Marie/Don't Try (p/s, 500 only)	35

VILLAGERS/PARCEL OF ROGUES
73	Deroy (no cat. no.)	PARCEL OF FOLK (LP, private pressing, with insert)	90

CATERINA VILLALBA
60	Ember EMB S 104	Quando La Luna/Amore Fantastico (p/s)	6

NICK VILLARD
62	Pye 7N 15418	High Noon/Sail Ho	10

VILLIERS & GOLD
68	Polydor 56235	Of All The Young Girls/This East	20

JOE VINA
59	Top Rank JAR 251	Marina/That's Alright	5

RAE VINCE & VINCENTS
64	Piccadilly 7N 35211	One Fine Day/Little Girl, I'm Sad	10

EDWARD J VINCENT
69	CBS 4388	Run To The Sun/I Never Thought I'd Fall In Love	15

GENE VINCENT (& BLUE CAPS)
78s
56	Capitol CL 14599	Be-Bop-A-Lula/Woman Love	15
56	Capitol CL 14628	Race With The Devil/Gonna Back Up, Baby	25
56	Capitol CL 14637	Bluejean Bop/Who Slapped John?	15
57	Capitol CL 14681	Jumps, Giggles And Shouts/Wedding Bells (Are Breaking Up That Old Gang Of Mine)	30
57	Capitol CL 14693	Crazy Legs/Important Words	30
57	Capitol CL 14722	Bi-I-Bickey-Bi, Bo-Bo-Go/Five Days, Five Days	30
57	Capitol CL 14763	Lotta Lovin'/Wear My Ring	25
57	Capitol CL 14808	Dance To The Bop/I Got It	25
58	Capitol CL 14830	Walkin' Home From School/I Got A Baby	35
59	Capitol CL 15053	Right Now/The Night Is So Lonely	150

SINGLES
56	Capitol CL 14599	Be-Bop-A-Lula/Woman Love	40
56	Capitol CL 14628	Race With The Devil/Gonna Back Up, Baby	100
56	Capitol CL 14637	Bluejean Bop/Who Slapped John?	60
57	Capitol CL 14681	Jumps, Giggles And Shouts/Wedding Bells (Are Breaking Up That Old Gang Of Mine) (promo copy in p/s)	125
57	Capitol CL 14681	Jumps, Giggles And Shouts/Wedding Bells (Are Breaking Up That Old Gang Of Mine)	100
57	Capitol CL 14693	Crazy Legs/Important Words (in p/s)	75
57	Capitol CL 14693	Crazy Legs/Important Words	50
57	Capitol CL 14722	Bi-I-Bickey-Bi, Bo-Bo-Go/Five Days, Five Days (in p/s)	150
57	Capitol CL 14722	Bi-I-Bickey-Bi, Bo-Bo-Go/Five Days, Five Days	75
57	Capitol CL 14763	Lotta Lovin'/Wear My Ring	50
57	Capitol CL 14808	Dance To The Bop/I Got It	50
58	Capitol CL 14830	Walkin' Home From School/I Got A Baby (in p/s)	70
58	Capitol CL 14830	Walkin' Home From School/I Got A Baby	50
58	Capitol CL 14868	Baby Blue/True To You	40
58	Capitol CL 14908	Rocky Road Blues/Yes I Love You, Baby	40
58	Capitol CL 14935	Git It/Little Lover	40
59	Capitol CL 14974	Say Mama/Be Bop Boogie Boy	30
59	Capitol CL 15000	Who's Pushin' Your Swing/Over The Rainbow	20
59	Capitol CL 15035	Summertime/Frankie And Johnnie	25
59	Capitol CL 15053	Right Now/The Night Is So Lonely	20
59	Capitol CL 15099	Wild Cat/Right Here On Earth	15
60	Capitol CL 15115	My Heart/I've Got To Get You Yet	15

(Credited to Gene Vincent & Blue Caps.)
60	Capitol CL 15136	Pistol Packin' Mama (as Gene Vincent & Beat Boys)/Weeping Willow	15
60	Capitol CL 15169	Anna-Annabelle/Ac-Cent-Tchu-Ate The Positive	15
61	Capitol CL 15179	Maybe/Jezebel	15
61	Capitol CL 15185	If You Want My Lovin'/Mister Loneliness	15
61	Capitol CL 15202	She She Little Sheila/Hot Dollar	15
61	Capitol CL 15215	I'm Going Home (To See My Baby)/Love Of A Man	15
61	Capitol CL 15231	Unchained Melody/Brand New Beat (with The Blue Caps)	15
62	Capitol CL 15243	Lucky Star/Baby Don't Believe Him (with Dave Burgess Band)	18
62	Capitol CL 15264	Be-Bop-A-Lula/The King Of Fools (with Charles Blackwell Orchestra)	15
63	Capitol CL 15290	Held For Questioning/You're Still In My Heart (with Charles Blackwell Orch.)	15
63	Capitol CL 15307	Rip It Up/High Blood Pressure (unissued, demo copies only)	250
63	Capitol CL 15307	Crazy Beat/High Blood Pressure	40
63	Columbia DB 7174	Temptation Baby/Where Have You Been All My Life	20
64	Columbia DB 7218	Humpity Dumpity/A Love 'Em And Leave 'Em Kinda Guy	20
64	Columbia DB 7293	La-Den-Da Den-Da-Da/The Beginning Of The End	20
64	Columbia DB 7343	Private Detective/You Are My Sunshine (as Gene Vincent & Shouts)	20
66	London HLH 10079	Bird Doggin'/Ain't That Too Much	30
66	London HLH 10099	Lonely Street/I've Got My Eyes On You	30
68	Capitol CL 15546	Be-Bop-A-Lula/Say Mama	15
69	Dandelion S 4596	Be-Bop-A-Lula '69/Ruby Baby	10
70	Dandelion S 4974	White Lightning/Scarlet Ribbons (For Her Hair)	10
71	Kama Sutra 2013 018	The Day The World Turned Blue/High On Life (some with large centre)	10
73	Spark SRL 1091	Story Of The Rockers/Pickin' Poppies (push-out or solid centre)	10
74	BBC BEEB 001	Roll Over Beethoven/Say Mama/Be-Bop-A-Lula '71 (push-out or solid centre)	5
77	Capitol CL 15906	Say Mama/Lotta Lovin'/Race With The Devil	5
81	Capitol CL 203	She She Little Sheila/Say Mama/Dance To The Bop (p/s)	5
87	Nighttracks SFNT 001	Nighttracks (Distant Drums/Be-Bop-A-Lula) (p/s, promo only with insert)	10

EPs
58	Capitol EAP 1-985	HOT ROD GANG	75
59	Capitol EAP 1-1059	A GENE VINCENT RECORD DATE	75
60	Capitol EAP 3-1059	A GENE VINCENT RECORD DATE PART 3	80
61	Capitol EAP 1-20173	IF YOU WANT MY LOVIN'	80
62	Capitol EAP 1-20354	RACE WITH THE DEVIL	80
63	Capitol EAP 1-20461	TRUE TO YOU	80
64	Capitol EAP 1-20453	THE CRAZY BEAT OF GENE VINCENT NO. 1	80
64	Capitol EAP 2-20453	THE CRAZY BEAT OF GENE VINCENT NO. 2	80
64	Capitol EAP 3-20453	THE CRAZY BEAT OF GENE VINCENT NO. 3	80
69	EMIdisc (no cat. no.)	LIVE & ROCKIN'! (fan club issue, mail-order, 99 only)	250
79	Rollin' Danny RD 1	RAINY DAY SUNSHINE (L.A. 1969 demos, 500 only)	12

ALBUMS : LPS
56	Capitol T 764	BLUEJEAN BOP! (original pressing with turquoise labels)	130
56	Capitol T 764	BLUEJEAN BOP! (later pressing with rainbow labels)	60
57	Capitol T 811	GENE VINCENT AND THE BLUECAPS (turquoise label)	125
57	Capitol T 811	GENE VINCENT AND THE BLUECAPS (rainbow label)	60
58	Capitol T 970	GENE VINCENT ROCKS! & THE BLUECAPS ROLL (turquoise label)	130
58	Capitol T 970	GENE VINCENT ROCKS! & THE BLUECAPS ROLL (later rainbow label)	60

59	Capitol T 1059	A GENE VINCENT RECORD DATE	70
59	Capitol T 1207	SOUNDS LIKE GENE VINCENT	70
60	Capitol T 1342	CRAZY TIMES! (mono)	60
60	Capitol ST 1342	CRAZY TIMES! (stereo)	100
63	Capitol T 20453	THE CRAZY BEAT OF GENE VINCENT	65
64	Columbia 33SX 1646	SHAKIN' UP A STORM (as Gene Vincent & The Shouts)	70
67	London HA-H 8333	GENE VINCENT	50
67	Capitol T 20957	THE BEST OF GENE VINCENT ('rainbow' label; reissue with pink label £12)	20
68	Capitol ST 21144	THE BEST OF GENE VINCENT VOL. 2 ('rainbow' label; reissue with pink label £12)	20
70	Dandelion 63754	I'M BACK AND I'M PROUD (gatefold sleeve)	30
71	Kama Sutra 2316 005	THE DAY THE WORLD TURNED BLUE	20
71	Kama Sutra 2316 009	IF YOU COULD ONLY SEE ME TODAY	20
87	Charly BOX 108	GENE VINCENT: THE CAPITOL YEARS '56-'63 (10-LP box set with 36-page booklet; later remastered and reissued with slimmer box, 1989)	50
90	EMI CDGV 1	THE GENE VINCENT BOX SET (Complete Capitol & Columbia Recordings, 1956-64) (6-CD set)	20

RORY VINCENT
| 73 | Columbia SCXA 9254 | SINGS THE MUSIC OF WLODEK GULGOWSKI (LP) | 20 |

CAROLE VINCI
| 78 | EMI EMI 2801 | Vivre/Souffire Et Sourire | 12 |

JOEY VINE
| 65 | Immediate IM 017 | Down And Out/The Out Of Towner | 30 |

VINEGAR JOE
72	Island WIP 6125	Never Met A Dog/Speed Queen Of Ventura	5
72	Island WIP 6148	Rock'n'Roll Gypsies/So Long	5
73	Island WIP 6174	Black Smoke From The Calumet/Long Way Round	5
72	Island ILPS 9183	VINEGAR JOE (LP)	25
72	Island ILPS 9214	ROCK 'N ROLL GYPSIES (LP, gatefold sleeve)	20
73	Island ILPS 9262	SIX STAR GENERAL (LP, gatefold sleeve)	20

(see also Dada, Robert Palmer, Elkie Brooks)

VINES
| 01 | RexRec REKD 195 | Factory/Ain't No Room/Drown The Baptists (p/s, 500 only) | 8 |

VINEYARD
| 74 | Decca F13518 | Ghost Train/Unicorns & Minotaurs | 8 |

LEROY VINNEGAR
| 63 | Contemporary LAC 570 | LEROY WALKS AGAIN! (LP) | 30 |
| 83 | Boplicity COP 011 | LEROY WALKS (LP, reissue) | 15 |

EDDIE 'MR. CLEANHEAD' VINSON
51	Vogue V 2023	Queen Bee Blues/Jump And Grunt (78)	25
64	Riverside RLP 3302	BACK DOOR BLUES (LP)	40
72	Philips 6369 406	THE ORIGINAL CLEANHEAD (LP)	18

(see also Wynonie Harris)

V. VINSTRICK & J.J. ALLSTARS
| 68 | Doctor Bird DB 1167 | Love Is Not A Game/CINDERELLA: The Way I See You | 30 |

IAN VINT
| 62 | Columbia DB 7514 | Long Lonely Nights/Satin | 7 |
| 64 | Columbia 33SX 1649 | TELL ME WHY (LP) | 25 |

BOBBY VINTON
61	Fontana H 307	Little Lonely One/Corrine Corrina	10
62	London HLU 9592	I Love You The Way You Are/CHUCK & JOHNNY: You Are My Girl	10
62	Columbia DB 4878	Roses Are Red/You And I	5
62	Columbia DB 4900	Rain Rain Go Away/Over Over	5
63	Columbia DB 4961	Trouble Is My Middle Name/Let's Kiss And Make Up	5
63	Columbia DB 7015	Over The Mountain/Faded Pictures	5
63	Columbia DB 7052	Blue On Blue/Those Little Things	5
63	Columbia DB 7110	Blue Velvet/Is There A Place	10
63	Columbia DB 7179	There! I've Said It Again/The Girl With The Bow In Her Hair	5
64	Columbia DB 7240	My Heart Belongs To Only You/Warm And Tender	5
64	Columbia DB 7303	Tell Me Why/Remembering	5
64	Columbia DB 7348	Clinging Vine/Imagination Is A Magic Dream	5
64	Columbia DB 7422	Mr Lonely/The Bell That Couldn't Jingle	15
68	CBS 3484	Take Good Care Of My Baby/Strange Sensations	5
68	CBS 3636	Halfway To Paradise/(My Little) Christie	5
69	CBS 4244	To Know You Is To Love You/The Beat Of My Heart	5
69	CBS 4451	The Days Of Sand And Shovels/So Many Lonely Girls	5
62	Columbia SEG 8212	YOUNG IN HEART (EP)	20
64	Columbia SEG 8363	SONGS OF CHRISTMAS (EP)	20
63	Columbia 33SX 1517	SINGS THE BIG ONES (LP)	25
62	Columbia 33SX1465	ROSES ARE RED (LP)	20
63	Columbia 33SX 1566	BLUE ON BLUE (LP)	20
63	Columbia 33SX 1611	MY HEART BELONGS TO ONLY YOU (LP)	20
65	Columbia 33SX1725	LAUGHING ON THE OUTSIDE (LP)	20

MATT VINYL
| 77 | Housewife's Choice | Useless Tasks (p/s) | 8 |

VIOLATORS
82	No Future OI 9	Gangland/Fugitive (p/s, with insert)	8
82	No Future OI 19	Summer Of '81/Live Fast Die Young (p/s)	8
83	Future FS 2	Life On The Red Line/Crossing The Sangsara (p/s)	6
80s	Oi 26	DIE WITH DIGNITY EP (12")	20

VIOLENT FEMMES
| 83 | Rough Trade RT 147 | Ugly/Gimme The Car (p/s) | 5 |

VIOLENTS
| 63 | HMV POP 1130 | Alpen Ros/Ghia | 18 |

MINT VALUE £

VIOLENT THIMBLE
| 67 | Polydor 56217 | Gentle People Parts 1 & 2 | 15 |

VIPERS (SKIFFLE GROUP)
56	Parlophone R 4238	Ain't You Glad/Pick A Bale Of Cotton	20
57	Parlophone R 4261	Don't You Rock Me Daddy-O/10,000 Years Ago	20
57	Parlophone R 4286	Jim Dandy/Hi Liley, Liley Lo	20
57	Parlophone R 4289	The Cumberland Gap/Maggie May	25
57	Parlophone R 4308	Streamline Train/Railroad Steam Boat	25
57	Parlophone R 4351	Homing Bird/Pay Me My Money Down	20
57	Parlophone R 4371	Skiffle Party Medley Parts 1 & 2	25
58	Parlophone R 4393	Baby Why?/No Other Baby (as Vipers)	25
58	Parlophone R 4393	Baby Why?/No Other Baby (as Vipers) (78)	10
58	Parlophone R 4435	Make Ready For Love/Nothing Will Ever Change (My Love For You)(as Vipers)	15
58	Parlophone R 4484	Summertime Blues/Liverpool Blues (as Vipers)	35
58	Parlophone R 4484	Summertime Blues/Liverpool Blues (as Vipers) (78)	20
57	Parlophone GEP 8615	SKIFFLE MUSIC VOL. 1 (EP)	20
57	Parlophone GEP 8626	SKIFFLE MUSIC VOL. 2 (EP)	25
57	Parlophone GEP 8655	SKIFFLING ALONG WITH THE VIPERS (EP)	30
57	Parlophone PMD 1050	COFFEE BAR SESSION (10" LP)	60

(see also Jet Harris & Tony Meehan, Shadows, Wally Whyton, Sharkey Todd & Monsters)

VIPERS
| 78 | Mulligan LUNS 718 | I've Got You/No Such Thing (p/s) | 10 |

VIPPS
| 66 | CBS 202031 | Wintertime/Anyone | 80 |

(see also VIPS)

VIPS
64	RCA RCA 1427	Don't Keep Shouting At Me/She's So Good	100
66	Island WI 3003	I Wanna Be Free/Don't Let It Go	50
67	Island WIP 6005	Straight Down To The Bottom/In A Dream	80

(see also Vipps, Art, Spooky Tooth, Felder's Orioles, Timebox, Patto, Baron & His Pounding Piano, Keith Emerson)

V.I.P.S
78	Bust SOL 3	MUSIC FOR FUNSTERS (EP)	20
79	Rok ROK V/VI	Can't Let You Go/URBAN DISTURBANCE: Wild Boys In Cortinas	25
80	Gem GEMS 25	Causing Complications/Run Run Belinda/Love Is A Golden Word (p/s)	6
80	Gem GEMS 39	The Quarter Moon/Hippy Hippy Shake (p/s)	5
80	Gem GEMS 43	I Need Somebody To Love (Could It Be You?)/One More Chance// Stuttgart Special/Who Knows/Janine (double pack, stickered p/s)	8
81	Gem GEMS 47	Things Aren't What They Used To Be/I Thought You Were My Friend (p/s)	6
90s	Tangerine	BEAT CRAZY (CD)	18

(see also Mood Six, Jed Dmochowski)

VIRGIL BROTHERS
| 69 | Parlophone R 5787 | Temptation 'Bout To Get Me/Look Away | 15 |
| 69 | Parlophone R 5802 | Good Love/When You Walk Away | 6 |

VIRGIN DANCE
| 84 | Spartan SP10 | Desire/Make Love (p/s) | 8 |

VIRGINIANS
| 63 | Pye International 7N 25175 | Limbo Baby/Greenback Dollar | 10 |

VIRGINIA TREE
| 75 | Minstrel 0001 | FRESH OUT (LP) | 50 |

(see also Shirley Kent, Ghost)

VIRGINIA WOLF
| 86 | Atlantic A 9459 | Waiting For Your Love/Take A Chance (p/s) | 10 |

VIRGINIA WOLVES
| 66 | Stateside SS 563 | Stay/B.L.T. | 50 |
| 66 | Stateside SS 563 | Stay/B.L.T. (DJ copy) | 100 |

VIRGIN PRUNES
81	Baby BABY 001	TWENTY TENS (EP)	15
81	Rough Trade RT 072	Moments Of Mine (Despite Straight Lines)/In The Greylight/War/Moments Of Mine (Despite Straight Lines) (1st issue in blue p/s with insert)	15
81	Rough Trade RT 072	Moments Of Mine (Despite Straight Lines)/In The Greylight/War/Moments Of Mine (Despite Straight Lines) (later issue in black p/s without insert)	10
81	Rough Trade RT 89	A New Form Of Beauty 1; Sandpaper Lullaby/Sleep Fantasy Dreams (p/s)	15
81	Rough Trade RT 090	A New Form Of Beauty Part Two: Come To Daddy/Sweet Home Under White Clouds/Sad World (10", p/s, 33rpm)	8
81	Rough Trade RT 091T	A New Form Of Beauty Part Three: The Beast (Seven Bastard Suck)/The Slow Children (Abbagal)/Brain Damage/No Birds To Fly (12", p/s)	8
82	Rough Trade TI COPY 007	A New Form Of Beauty 4:Din Glorious (cassette)	25
82	Rough Trade RT 106	Pagan Lovesong/Dave-id Is Dead (p/s)	8
82	Rough Trade 12 RT 106	Pagan Lovesong (Vibe Akimbo)/Pagan Lovesong/Dave-id Is Dead (12", p/s)	10
87	Baby BABY 011	HERESIE (10", double pack, gatefold p/s, 1st 1,000 on clear vinyl)	15
87	Baby BABY 011	HERESIE (10", double pack, gatefold p/s)	10

(see also Gavin Friday, Bono & Gavin Friday)

VIRGIN SLEEP
| 67 | Deram DM 146 | Love/Halliford House | 40 |
| 68 | Deram DM 173 | Secret/Comes A Time | 50 |

VIRGO
| 89 | Radical Records VIRG01 | VIRGO (LP) | 35 |

VIRTUE
| 85 | Other OTH 1 | We Stand To Fight/High Treason (p/s) | 20 |

VIRTUES (JAMAICA)
65	Island WI 196	Your Wife And Mother/Amen (actually with Ambassadors)	35
68	Doctor Bird DB 1164	High Tide/RUPIE EDWARDS & VIRTUES: Burning Love	25
68	Doctor Bird DB 1166	Sweet Nanny/RUPIE EDWARDS : Falling In Love	30

(see also Lloyd & Devon)

VIRTUES (U.S.)
59	HMV POP 621	Guitar Boogie Shuffle/Guitar In Orbit	20
59	HMV POP 637	Flippin' In/Shufflin' Along	20
59	HMV POP 637	Flippin' In/Shufflin' Along (78)	20

FRANK VIRTUOSO ROCKETS
56	Melodisc MEL 1386	Rollin' And A-Rockin'/Rock - Good Bye Mambo (78)	25
56	Melodisc MEL 1393	Toodle-Oo Kangaroo/Hop-Skip-Jump Mambo (78)	15
58	Melodisc MEL 1386	Rollin' And A-Rockin'/Rock - Good Bye Mambo (red label, tri centre, export issue)	30
58	Melodisc MEL 1386	Rollin' And Rockin'/Toodle-Oo Kangaroo (green label, round centre)	15

VISAGE
79	Radar ADA 48	Tar/Frequency 7 (p/s)	10
81	Polydor POSPX 194	Fade To Grey/The Steps (12", p/s)	15
81	Polydor POSPX 236	Mind Of A Toy (Dance Mix)/We Move (Dance Mix)/Frequency 7 (Dance Mix) (12", p/s)	10
82	Polydor POSPP 441	Night Train/I'm Still Searching (picture disc)	5
82	Polydor POSPP 523	Pleasure Boys (picture disc)	7
82	Polydor POSPX 523	Pleasure Boys (Dance Mix)/The Anvil (Dance Mix) (12", 800 only)	10
82	Polydor POSPV 523	Der Amboss/The Anvil (Mix) (12", stickered plain black sleeve & labels, promo only)	10

(see also Rich Kids, Steve Strange, Strange Cruise, Midge Ure, Ultravox)

TONY VISCONTI
79	Regal Zonophone RZ 3089	I Remember Brooklyn/Sitting In A Field Of Heather	10

(see also Dib Cochran & Earwigs)

VISCOUNTS
60	Pye 7N 15249	That's All Right/Rockin' Little Angel	5
60	Pye 7N 15287	Shortnin' Bread/Fee-Fi-Fo-Fum	7
61	Pye 7N 15323	Money Is The Root Of All Evil/One-Armed Bandit	5
61	Pye 7N 15344	Banned In Boston/Moonlight Promises	5
61	Pye 7N 15356	Joe Sweeney/Honey Come On And Dance With Me	5
61	Pye 7N 15379	Who Put The Bomp (In The Bomp Bomp Bomp)/What Am I saying	10
61	Pye 7N 15414	Mama's Doing The Twist/I'm Going - But I'll Be Back	5
62	Pye 7N 15431	One Of The Guys/Dear Mary Brown	5
62	Pye 7N 15445	Everybody's Got a Ya Ya/A Lot of Livin' To Do	8
63	Pye 7N 15479	That Stranger Used To Be My Girl/Silent Night	5
63	Pye 7N 15510	Don't Let Me Cross Over/I'm Coming Home	5
63	Pye 7N 15336	It's You/I'll Never Get over You	5
63	Columbia DB 7146	I Don't Care What People Say/Roll On Little Darlin'	6
60	Pye NEP 24132	VISCOUNTS' HIT PARADE (EP)	15

(see also Gordon Mills)

VISCOUNTS (U.S.)
59	Top Rank JAR 254	Harlem Nocturne/Dig	15
60	Top Rank JAR 388	The Touch (Le Grisbi)/Chug-A-Lug	15
60	Top Rank JAR 502	Night Train/Summertime	18
64	Columbia DB 7253	Where Do You Belong/Kiss Me	8
65	Stateside SS 468	Harlem Nocturne/Dig (reissue)	10
61	Top Rank JKP 3005	VISCOUNTS ROCK (EP)	60

VISIONS
69	Grape GR 3009	Captain Hook/The Girl	40

(see also King Horror)

VISIONS IN WINTER
84	VIW SRT4KS 226	The Calling /Secret Garden	10

VISITORS
78	NRG SRTS/NRG 002	Take It Or Leave It/No Compromise	25
79	Deep Heat DEEP ONE	Electric Heat/Moth/One Line (p/s)	10

VISITORS
87	Sha La La BA BA BA BA BA 8	Goldmining/MAGIC SHOP: It's True (flexidisc, p/s, free with Simply Thrilled & other fanzines. With magazine)	10

VITAL DUB
77	Virgin V 2055	WELL CHARGED (LP, green two virgins label)	20

VITAL FORCE
87	Buce BUCE 1	Roll The Dice/Poor Little Rich Boy (no p/s)	25

VITAL REMAINS
92	Deaf DEAF 9	LET US PRAY (LP)	25

VITAL DISORDERS
81	Lowther International VD 1	PRAMS EP: Snatcher/Tough TImes/'Prams (6 different p/s variations)	20

MIROSLAV VITOUS
79	Warner Bros. K 17448 T	New York City/Basic Laws (12")	40
76	Warner Bros. K56219	MAGIC SHEPHERD (LP)	15

AMOR VIVI
70	Big Shot BI 534	Dirty Dog/Round And Round The Moon	8

VIVIENNE
57	HMV 7EG 8290	VIVIENNE (EP)	8

VIXEN
88	EMI MTPD 48	Edge Of A Broken Heart/Charmed Life (shaped picture disc)	7
88	EMI MTL 1028	VIXEN (LP, early copies play extra track "Charmed Life", withdrawn)	12

VLADO & ISOLDA
84	Ariola 106 500	Ciao Amore (English)/Ciao Amore (Croatian)	10

CRISTIAN VOGEL
94	Ferox FER 004	NARCO SYNTHESIS EP (12", plain sleeve)	25
94	Mosquito MSQ 01	WE EQUATE MACHINES WITH FUNKINESS EP (12", custom sleeve)	25
95	Mosquito MSQ 03	ARTISTS IN CHARGE OF EXPERT SYSTEMS EP (12", custom sleeve)	20

VOGUES (U.K.)

95	Solid SOL 002	DEFUNKT EP (12". Three untitled tracks)	20
96	Solid SOL 004	The Visit/Spoke/Small Dogs (12")	30

(see also Blue Arsed Fly)

VOGUES (U.K.)

66	Columbia DB 7985	Younger Girl/Lies	18

(see also Llan)

VOGUES (U.S.)

65	London HLU 9996	You're The One/Some Words	20
66	London HLU 10014	Five O'Clock World/Nothing To Offer You	20
66	King KG 1035	Magic Town/Humpty Dumpty	25
68	Reprise RS 20766	My Special Angel/I Keep It Hid	6
68	Reprise RS 20686	Turn Around Look At Me/Then	6
69	Reprise SS 20788	Till/I Will	6
69	London HLG 10247	Five O'Clock World/You're The One	15
69	Reprise RS 20820	Earth Angel/P.S. I Love You	6
69	Reprise RS 23366	No, Not Much/You Were Too Good To Me	6
69	Reprise RS 20844	Green Fields/Easy To Say	5
66	King KGL 4003	MEET THE VOGUES (LP)	55
66	King KGL 4006	FIVE O'CLOCK WORLD (LP)	50
69	Reprise RSLP 6314	TURN AROUND, LOOK AT ME (LP)	25
69	Reprise RSLP 6326	TILL (LP)	18

VOICE

66	Mercury MF 905	Train To Disaster/Truth	250

(see also Karl Stuart & Profile, Profile, Miller Anderson)

VOICE OF PROGRESS

82	Negus Roots NERLP 003	MINI BUS DRIVER (LP)	30

VOICE OF THE PUPPETS

80	IS/VP/1044	I Don't Want To Know/You're All I Wanted (And A Car) (poster p/s)	50

STEVE VOICE

79	EMI RB 102	UFO/Radio Blue	6

VOICES

56	Beltona BL 2667	Rock And Roll Hit Parade Medley (Parts 1 & 2)	18
56	Beltona BL 2667	Rock And Roll Hit Parade Medley (Parts 1 & 2) (78)	12

VOICES IN LATIN

68	Morgan MR 104P	VOICE IN LATIN (LP)	60

VOIDS

66	Polydor BM 56073	Come On Out/I'm In A Fix	100

WES VOIGHT

59	Parlophone R 4586	I'm Movin' In/I'm Ready To Go Steady	80

(see also Chip Taylor)

VOIZ

77	Pilgrim/Grapevine GRA 110	BOANERGES (LP, with insert)	25

HOWARD VOKES COUNTRY BOYS

62	Starlite STEP 27	HOWARD VOKES COUNTRY BOYS (EP)	20
63	Starlite STEP 37	MOUNTAIN GUITAR (EP)	20
67	Starlite GRK 508	HOWARD VOKES COUNTRY BOYS (EP; reissue, with sleeve sticker over original catalogue number)	12

VOLCANOES

86	Hybrid HYB LP 8	INTO THE PSYCHE (LP)	12

VOLCANOS

61	Philips PB 1098	Ruby Duby Du/Redhead	20
61	Philips PB 1113	Tightrope/Great Imposter	20
62	Philips PB 1246	Polaris/Scotch Mist	20
60	Philips BBE 12432	THE VOLCANOS (EP)	100

VOLTZ

82	Airship PP 580	KNIGHT'S FALL (LP)	70

VOLUMES

62	Fontana 270 109TF	I Love You/Dreams	120
63	London HL 9733	Sandra/Teenage Paradise	75

VOLUNTEERS

63	Parlophone R 5088	Farther Along/Little David	8

(see also Karol Keyes)

VON BONDIES

03	Must Destroy DESTROYER 2	Tell Me What You See (p/s, 1-sided)	8

VON TRAP FAMILY

80	Woronzow W 001	Brand New Thrill/Dreaming/No Reflexes (p/s, 500 only)	18

(see also Bevis Frond)

VONTASTICS

66	Chess CRS 8043	Day Tripper/My Baby	25
67	Stateside SS 2002	Lady Love/When My Baby Comes Back Home	65
67	Stateside SS 2002	Lady Love/When My Baby Comes Back Home (DJ Copy)	85

VOOMINS

65	Polydor 56001	If You Don't Come Back/March Of The Voomins	35

VOXPOPPERS

58	Mercury 7MT 202	The Last Drag/Wishing For Your Love	30
58	Mercury 7MT 202	The Last Drag/Wishing For Your Love (78)	25
58	Mercury MEP 9533	VOXPOPPERS (EP)	150

VOYAGER

85	Fighting Cock	Run Away Heart/Don't Hold Back (p/s)	15

V2
78	Bent SMALL BENT 1	Speed Freak/Nothing To Do/That's It (800 only, later reissued on red vinyl)	30
79	TJM TJM 1	Man In The Box/When The World Isn't There (12", p/s)	20
79	TJM TJM 6	Is Anybody Out There? (unissued)	0
70s	Groove ZOE 1	Gee Whiz It's You/Face In The Crowd (p/s, stamped white labels)	30

VULCAN
73	Epic SEPC 1763	Much To Young/Action Man	6

VULCANS
72	Big Shot BI 612	Dr. Spock/Joe Kidd	5
73	Big Shot BI 615	Red Herring/Vulcanised	5
73	Trojan TRLS 53	STAR TREK (LP)	30

VULCAN'S HAMMER
73	Brown BVH 1	TRUE HEARTS AND SOUND BOTTOMS (LP, with insert)	450

VULTURES
79	Rubber Connection SP 522	Time Let's Go/Is This A Man (p/s, with insert & sticker)	6

PHIL WACHSMANN
85	Bead Records BEAD 23	WRITING IN WATER (LP)	20

PHILIPP WACHSMANN, ROCHARD BESWICK & TONY WREN
77	Bead Records BEAD 7	SPARKS OF THE DESIRE MAGNETO (LP, with insert)	30

WACKERS (1)
63	Oriole CB 1902	I Wonder Why/Why Can't It Happen To Me	25
64	Piccadilly 7N 35195	Love Or Money/Hooka Tooka	15
64	Piccadilly 7N 35210	The Girl Who Wanted Fame/You're Forgetting	15

WACKERS (2)
72	Elektra K12054	I Hardly Knew Her Name/Do You Know The Reason	5
72	Electra K12081	Day And Night/Last Night	5

ADAM WADE
60	HMV POP 787	Speaking Of Her/Blackout The Moon	5
60	HMV POP 807	In Pursuit Of Happiness/For The Want Of Your Love	5
60	Top Rank JAR 296	Tell Her For Me/Don't Cry My Love	5
60	Top Rank JAR 370	Ruby/Too Far	5
61	HMV POP 843	Take Good Care Of Her/Sleepy Time Gal	10
61	HMV POP 896	Point Of No Return/The Writing On The Wall	5
61	HMV POP 942	Tonight I Won't Be There/Linda	5
62	Columbia DB 4891	I'm Climbin' (The Wall)/They Don't Believe Me	5
63	Columbia DB 4986	Don't Let Me Cross Over/Rain From The Skies	70
63	Columbia DB 7045	Why Do We Have To Wait So Long/They Say	5
60	HMV 7EG 8620	AND THEN CAME ADAM (EP)	15
64	Columbia SEG 8316	FOUR FILM SONGS (EP)	15
61	HMV CLP 1451	ADAM AND EVENING (LP)	30

CLIFF WADE
69	Morgan Bluetown BT 1S	You've Never Been To My House/Sister	30

JOHNNY WADE
60	HMV POP 757	Funny Thing/Shadow Love	8

WAYNE WADE
77	Grove Music GMDM 2	Happy Go Lucky Girl/PRINCE POMPADO: Jamaican Girl/WAYNE WADE: I Kissed A Rose (12", p/s)	10
79	Cha Cha CHAD 34	Tell Me What Going On/WAILING COCKS: Rudeboy Say Him Bad (12")	15
80	Pirate PIR 003	African Monica/Down In Iran (12")	30
81	Greensleeves GRED 52	Poor And Humble/BUNNY LIE LIE: Babylonian (12")	25
78	Grove Music GMLP 3	DANCING TIME (LP)	20

WELLINGTON WADE
63	Oriole CB 1857	Let's Turkey Trot/It Ain't Necessarily So	40

(see also Ian & Zodiacs)

WADSWORTH MANSION
71	A&M AMS 842	Sweet Mary/What's On Tonight	6

DEREK WADSWORTH
00	Fanderson FANSP 8	SPACE 199: TEAR TWO (2-CD mail order)	25

WAGADU
79	Rokel ROK 12	Freetown Calypso/Easy Dancin'	25

WAGES OF SIN
70	CBS 4971	West Virginia/Hey Hey Hey (Well I'm On My Way)	10

ADRIAN WAGNER
74	Atlantic K 50082	DISTANCES BETWEEN US (LP, with Robert Calvert)	22
78	Charisma CAS 1135	THE LAST INCA (LP, with booklet)	12

(see also Robert Calvert)

ROBERT WAGNER
57	London HLU 8491	Almost Eighteen/So Young	10

CHUCK WAGON
79	A&M AMS 7450	Rock 'n' Roll Won't Go Away/The Spy In My Face (p/s, black vinyl)	10
79	A&M AMS 7450	Rock 'n' Roll Won't Go Away/The Spy In My Face (p/s, purple vinyl)	15

(see also Dickies)

PORTER WAGONER
67	RCA Victor RCA 1586	The Cold Hard Facts Of Life/You Can't Make A Heel Toe The Mark	5
64	RCA Victor RCX 7157	A LITTLE SLICE OF LIFE (EP)	10
64	RCA Victor RCX 7158	Y'ALL COME (EP)	10

WAH! (HEAT)
81	Inevitable INEV 001	Better Scream/Joe (wraparound p/s in poly bag)	5
81	Inevitable INEV 004	Seven Minutes To Midnight/Don't Step On The Cracks (p/s, different colour sleeves)	5

WAIKIKIS
61	Palette PG 9025	Hawaii Tattoo/Waikiki Welcome	7
65	Pye Intl. 7N 26286	Hawaii Tattoo/Waikiki Welcome (reissue)	12

WAILERS (U.S.)
59	London HL 8958	Tall Cool One/Road-Runner	25
59	London HL 8958	Tall Cool One/Road-Runner (78)	30
59	London HL 8994	Mau-Mau/Dirty Robber	150
59	London HL 8994	Mau-Mau/Dirty Robber (78)	70
64	London HL 9892	Tall Cool One/Road-Runner (reissue)	5

WAILING COCKS
78	Bird's Nest BN 116	Rockin' Youth/Stand Up For Peace	5
78	Bird's Nest BN 121	Listen To The Wailing Cocks/Listen To The Wailing Cocks	5

WAILING SOULS
70	Banana BA 305	Row Fisherman Row/Thou Shalt Not Steal	35
70	Banana BA 307	Back Out/Pack Your Things	25
71	Banana BA 335	Walk Walk Walk/KING SPORTY: Love Me - Version (B-side actually by Denis Alcapone)	40
71	Green Door GD 4014	Harbour Shark/Harbour Shark - Version	25
76	Conflict 301	Black Out/Dub	10
81	Cha Cha CHAD 34	Rudeboy Say Him Bad/WAYNE WADE: Tell Me What Going On (12")	40
81	Cha Cha CHAD 51	Grabbing And Running/Dub	20
82	Greensleeves GRED 111	They Don't Know Jah/Sticky Stay (12")	30
82	Upfront UPF 001	Take We Back (feat Ranking Trevor)/RANKING TREVOR: Yard Oh (12")	15
82	Upfront UPF 004	Take A Taste/JOHNNY RINGO: Don't Know Much (12")	15
79	Island ILPS 9523	WILD SUSPENSE (LP)	20

(see also Denis Alcapone, Tuff Gong All Stars)

CHERRY WAINER
58	Pye 7N 15161	Itchy Twitchy Feeling/Cerveza	10
59	Top Rank JAR 253	I'll Walk The Line/Saturday Night In Tia Juana	5
60	Columbia DB 4528	Happy Like A Bell (Ding Dong)/Money (That's What I Want)	20
63	Honey Hit TB 128	Sleepwalk/Red River Rock (with Red Price Combo, with p/s)	10
63	Honey Hit TB 128	Sleepwalk/Red River Rock (with Red Price Combo)	5
59	Pye NEP 24099	CHERRY WAINER (EP)	15

(see also Red Price Combo)

PHIL WAINMAN
65	Columbia DB 7615	Hear Me A Drummer Man/Hear His Drums	30
68	Fontana TF 978	Going Going Gone/Hey Paradiddle	300

LOUDON WAINWRIGHT III
71	Atlantic 2400 103	ALBUM I (LP)	22
72	Atlantic K 40107	ALBUM I (LP, reissue)	12
72	Atlantic K 40272	ALBUM II (LP)	15

WAITING FOR THE SUN
78	Profile GMOR 167	WAITING FOR THE SUN (LP, private pressing)	35

(see also After The Fire)

TOM WAITS
79	Asylum K 12347	Somewhere/Red Shoes By The Drugstore	8
86	Island ISD 260	In The Neighbourhood/Singapore//Tango Till They're Sore/Rain Dogs (double pack, p/s)	8
85	Island 12IS 260	In The Neighbourhood/Singapore//Tango Till They're Sore/Rain Dogs (12")	15
73	Asylum SYM 9007	CLOSING TIME (LP, with insert)	25
74	Asylum SYM 9012	THE HEART OF SATURDAY NIGHT (LP)	25
75	Asylum SYSP 903	NIGHTHAWKS AT THE DINER (2-LP, gatefold sleeve)	25
76	Asylum K 53030	CLOSING TIME (LP, reissue)	12
76	Asylum K 53035	THE HEART OF SATURDAY NIGHT (LP, 'door' label)	30
77	Asylum K 53050	SMALL CHANGE (LP, 'sky' label)	30
77	Asylum K 53068	FOREIGN AFFAIRS (LP, with inner sleeve)	30
79	Asylum K 53088	BLUE VALENTINE (LP, gatefold sleeve)	20
80	Asylum K 52252	HEARTATTACK AND VINE (LP, with inner sleeve)	20
81	Elektra K 52316	BOUNCED CHEQUES (LP)	15
82	Island ILPS 9762	SWORDFISHTROMBONES (LP)	20
83	Island TW1	A CONVERSATION WITH TOM WAITS (LP promo interview disc)	40
85	Island ILPS 9803	RAIN DOGS (LP)	30
86	Island ITW 3	FRANK'S WILD YEARS (LP, gatefold)	30
88	Island ITW4	BIG TIME (LP)	20
91	Island 212370	NIGHT ON EARTH (LP)	20
92	Island ILPS 9993	BONE MACHINE (LP)	60
93	Island ILPS 8021	BLACK RIDER (LP, with inner)	40

(see also Roy Orbison)

WAKE (1)
69	Pye 7N 17813	Angelina/So Happy	15
70	Carnaby CNS 4010	Live Today Little Girl/Days Of Emptiness	15
70	Carnaby CNS 4014	Boys In The Band/To Make You Happy	12
70	Carnaby CNS 4016	Noah/To Make You Happy	12
71	Carnaby 6151 001	Linda/Got My Eyes On You	12
70	Carnaby CNLS 6005	23.59 (LP, union jack flag label)	200

(see also Rubettes)

WAKE (2)
82	Scan SCN 01	On Our Honeymoon/Give Up (p/s in bag)	20
84	Scan 45/Factory FAC 88	Talk About The Past/Everybody Works So Hard (p/s)	7

84	Scan 45/Factory FAC 8812	Talk About The Past/Everybody Works So Hard (12", p/s)	12
87	Factory FAC12 178	Something No-one Else Can Bring/ Gruesome Castle	12
93	Sarah SARAH 48	Major John/Lousy Pop Group (p/s)	15
83	Factory FACT 60	HARMONY (LP)	25
91	Factory FACT 130	HERE COMES EVERYBODY (LP)	20
90s	Sarah SARAH 602	MAKE IT LOUD (LP)	15
90s	Sarah SARAH 618	TIDAL WAVE OF HYPE (LP)	15

JIMMY WAKELY

56	Vogue Coral Q 72125	Are You Mine? (with Ruth Ross)/Yellow Roses	15
56	Brunswick 05542	Are You Satisfied? (with Gloria Wood)/Mississippi Dreamboat	15
56	Brunswick 05563	Folsom Prison Blues/That's What The Lord Can Do	20
57	Brunswick LAT 8179	SANTA FE TRAIL (LP)	20

(see also Karen Chandler, Bob Hope, Margaret Whiting)

RICK WAKEMAN (BAND)

73	A&M AMS 7061	Catherine/Anne	5
75	A&M AMS 7206	Love's Dream/Orpheus' Song	6
75	A&M/Lyntone LYN 3176/7	Wagner's Dream/Love's Dream/Count Your Blessings (with 2 tracks by Roger Daltrey, flexidisc with 19 magazine)	10
79	A&M AMS 7435	Birdman Of Alcatraz (Theme From 'My Son My Son')/Falcons De Neige (p/s)	5
79	A&M AMS 7436	Animal Showdown/Sea Horses (p/s)	5
79	A&M AMSP 7436	Animal Showdown/Sea Horses (picture disc, in PVC sleeve)	6
79	A&M AMS 7497	Swan Lager/Woolly Willy Tango	5
80	A&M AMS 7510	I'm So Straight I'm A Weirdo/Do You Believe In Fairies? (p/s)	5
80	WEA K 18354	The Spider/Danielle (some with p/s, 2,000 only)	8
80	WEA K 18354	The Spider/Danielle (some with p/s, 2,000 only)	5
71	Polydor 2460 135	PIANO VIBRATIONS (LP, with John Schroeder Orchestra)	100
74	A&M QU-84361	THE SIX WIVES OF HENRY VIII (LP, gatefold sleeve, quadrophonic mix)	18
73	A&M AMLH 64361	THE SIX WIVES OF HENRY VIII (LP, gatefold sleeve)	15
75	A&M AMLH 64546	LISZTOMANIA (LP, soundtrack, with Roger Daltrey)	12
89	A&M RWCD 20	RICK WAKEMAN: 20TH ANNIVERSARY (4-CD box set, 1,000 only)	80

(see also Strawbs, Yes, Dib Cochran & Earwigs, Steve Howe, Jon Anderson)

LARRINGTON WALKER

| 77 | United Artists UP34210 | Joy/Trust In Me | 10 |

WALHAM GREEN EAST WAPPING CARPET CLEANING RODENT & BOGGIT EXTERMINATING ASSOCIATION

| 68 | Columbia DB 8426 | Sorry Mr. Green/Death Of A Kind | 250 |

HOWARD WALKER & BEACHCOMBERS

| 70 | Decca F12997 | Eat Me/Love Will Find A Way | 15 |

ANNA WALKER & CROWNETTES

| 69 | Pama PM 768 | You Don't Know/Billy Joe | 10 |

BILLY WALKER (U.K.)

| 65 | Columbia DB 7724 | A Certain Girl/I Don't Wanna Fall In love | 5 |

BILLY WALKER (U.S.)

| 60 | Philips PB 1001 | Forever/Changed My Mind | 6 |
| 66 | London HLU 10060 | Million And One/Close To Linda | 7 |

BOOTS WALKER

| 69 | London HLP 10265 | No One Knows/Geraldine | 15 |

CLINT WALKER

| 60 | Warner Bros WEP 6006 | INSPIRATION (EP, mono) | 12 |
| 60 | Warner Bros WSEP 2006 | INSPIRATION (EP, stereo) | 15 |

DAVID WALKER

| 68 | RCA RCA 1664 | Ring The Changes/Keep A Little Love | 120 |

(see also Paradox)

GARY WALKER (& RAIN)

66	CBS 202036	You Don't Love Me/Get It Right	20
66	CBS 202081	Twinkie-Lee/She Makes Me Feel Better	10
68	Polydor 56237	Spooky/I Can't Stand To Lose You (as Gary Walker & Rain)	20
69	Philips BF 1740	Come In You'll Get Pneumonia/Francis (as Gary Walker & Rain)	60
74	United Artists UP 35742	Hello How Are You/Fran	5
66	CBS EPS 5742	HERE'S GARY (EP)	45

(see also Walker Brothers, Paul & Ritchie & Cryin' Shames, Badfinger, Universals)

GRAHAM P WALKER

| 72 | Trojan GPW 62 | Love Of The Common People/Version (White label promo only) | 15 |

JACKIE WALKER

| 58 | London HLP 8588 | Oh Lonesome Me/Only Teenagers Allowed | 250 |
| 58 | London HLP 8588 | Oh Lonesome Me/Only Teenagers Allowed (78) | 60 |

JERRY JEFF WALKER

68	Atlantic 584 200	Mr Bojangles/Round And Round	8
68	Atco 228 006	MR BOJANGLES (LP)	20
71	Atlantic 2466 007	BEIN' FREE (LP)	18

JOHN WALKER

67	Philips BF 1593	Anabella/You Don't Understand Me	8
67	Philips BF 1612	If I Promise/I See Love In You	7
68	Philips BF 1655	I'll Be Your Baby Tonight/Open The Door Homer	7
68	Philips BF 1676	Kentucky Woman/I Cried All The Way Home	8
68	Philips BF 1724	Woman/A Dream	6
69	Philips BF 1758	Yesterday's Sunshine/Little One	6
69	Carnaby CNS 4004	Everywhere Under The Sun/Traces Of Tomorrow	6
70	Carnaby CNS 4009	True Grit/Sun Comes Up	7
70	Carnaby CNS 4012	Cottonfields/Jamie	7
70	Carnaby CNS 4017	Over And Over Again/Sun Comes Up	7
67	Philips (S)BL 7829	IF YOU GO AWAY (LP)	25

| 69 | Carnaby CNLS 6001 | THIS IS JOHN WALKER (LP) | 25 |

(see also Walker Brothers, John & Scott Walker, Johnny & Judy)

JOHN & SCOTT WALKER

| 66 | Philips BE 12597 | SOLO JOHN - SOLO SCOTT (EP, 2 tracks each) | 10 |

(see also Walker Brothers, Scott Walker, John Walker, Scott Engel)

JUNIOR WALKER & ALL STARS

65	Tamla Motown TMG 509	Shotgun/Hot'Cha	45
65	Tamla Motown TMG 509	Shotgun/Hot'Cha (DJ copy)	100
65	Tamla Motown TMG 520	Do The Boomerang/Tune Up	70
65	Tamla Motown TMG 520	Do The Boomerang/Tune Up (DJ copy)	150
65	Tamla Motown TMG 529	Shake And Fingerpop/Cleo's Back	50
65	Tamla Motown TMG 529	Shake And Fingerpop/Cleo's Back (DJ copy)	80
66	Tamla Motown TMG 550	Cleo's Mood/Baby You Know It Ain't Right	45
66	Tamla Motown TMG 550	Cleo's Mood/Baby You Know It Ain't Right (DJ copy)	80
66	Tamla Motown TMG 559	Road Runner/Shoot Your Shot	30
66	Tamla Motown TMG 559	Road Runner/Shoot Your Shot (DJ copy)	100
66	Tamla Motown TMG 571	How Sweet It Is (To Be Loved By You)/Nothing But Soul	25
66	Tamla Motown TMG 571	How Sweet It Is (To Be Loved By You)/Nothing But Soul (DJ copy)	60
67	Tamla Motown TMG 571	How Sweet It Is (To Be Loved By You)/Nothing But Soul (later pressing)	7
66	Tamla Motown TMG 586	Money (That's What I Want) Parts 1& 2	30
66	Tamla Motown TMG 586	Money (That's What I Want) Parts 1& 2 (DJ copy)	55
67	Tamla Motown TMG 596	Pucker Up Buttercup/Any Way You Wanna	30
67	Tamla Motown TMG 596	Pucker Up Buttercup/Any Way You Wanna (DJ copy)	60
68	Tamla Motown TMG 637	Come See About Me/Sweet Soul	18
68	Tamla Motown TMG 637	Come See About Me/Sweet Soul (DJ copy)	70
68	Tamla Motown TMG 667	Hip City Parts 1 & 2	25
68	Tamla Motown TMG 667	Hip City Parts 1 & 2 (DJ copy)	40
69	Tamla Motown TMG 682	Home Cookin'/Mutiny	20
69	Tamla Motown TMG 682	Home Cookin'/Mutiny (DJ copy)	30
69	Tamla Motown TMG 691	Road Runner/Shotgun	7
69	Tamla Motown TMG 691	Road Runner/Shotgun (DJ copy)	30
69	Tamla Motown TMG 712	What Does It Take (To Win Your Love)/Brainwasher	8
70	Tamla Motown TMG 727	These Eyes/I've Got To Find A Way To Win Maria Back	12
70	Tamla Motown TMG 727	These Eyes/I've Got To Find A Way To Win Maria Back (DJ copy)	30
70	Tamla Motown TMG 750	Do You See My Love (For You Growing)/Groove And Move	8
70	Tamla Motown TMG 750	Do You See My Love (For You Growing)/Groove And Move (DJ Copy)	30
72	Tamla Motown TMG 824	Walk In The Night/Right On Brothers And Sisters/ Gotta Hold On To This Feeling (maxi-single)	8
73	Tamla Motown TMG 840	Take Me Girl, I'm Ready/I Don't Want To Do Wrong	8
73	Tamla Motown TMG 857	Way Back Home (Vocal)/Way Back Home (Instrumental)	10
73	Tamla Motown TMG 857	Way Back Home (Vocal)/Way Back Home (Instrumental)/Country Boy (reissue)	20
73	Tamla Motown TMG 872	Holly Holy/Peace And Understanding (Is Hard To Find)	6
74	Tamla Motown TMG 889	Don't Blame The Children/Soul Clappin'	6
74	Tamla Motown TMG 894	Gotta Hold On To This Feeling/I Ain't Going Nowhere	10
74	Tamla Motown TMG 894	Gotta Hold On To This Feeling/I Ain't Going Nowhere (DJ copy)	25
76	Tamla Motown TMG 1027	I'm So Glad/Dancin' Like They Do On Soul Train (as Jr. Walker)	8
66	Tamla Motown TME 2013	SHAKE AND FINGERPOP (EP)	55
65	Tamla Motown TML 11017	SHOTGUN (LP)	55
66	T. Motown TML 11029	SOUL SESSION (LP, mono)	50
66	T. Motown STML 11029	SOUL SESSION (LP, stereo)	60
66	T. Motown TML 11038	ROAD RUNNER (LP, mono)	35
66	T. Motown STML 11038	ROAD RUNNER (LP, stereo)	45
69	T. Motown TML 11097	HOME COOKIN' (LP, mono)	30
69	T. Motown STML 11097	HOME COOKIN' (LP, stereo)	25
69	T. Motown (S)TML 11120	JUNIOR WALKER'S GREATEST HITS (LP, original with flipback sleeve)	15
70	T. Motown (S)TML 11140	THESE EYES (LP)	25
70	T. Motown STML 11152	LIVE (LP)	20
70	T. Motown STML 11167	A GASSSSSSSSSS! (LP)	20
72	T. Motown STML 11198	RAINBOW FUNK (LP)	20
72	T. Motown STML 11211	MOODY JR. (LP)	18
73	T. Motown STML 11234	PEACE AND UNDERSTANDING IS HARD TO FIND (LP)	12
76	T. Motown STML 12018	HOT SHOT (by Jr. Walker)	10
76	T. Motown STML 12033	SAX APPEAL (by Jr. Walker)	10
76	Motown STML 12048	WHOPPER BOPPER SHOW STOPPER (by Jr. Walker)	10

KARL WALKER & ALLSTARS

| 66 | Rymska RA 103 | One Minute To Zero/Don't Come Back (both sides actually featuring Tommy McCook & Supersonics) | 35 |

(see also Kent Walker, Ernel Braham)

KENT WALKER

| 68 | Fab FAB 53 | When You Going To Show Me How/Come Yah Come Yah | 8 |

(see also Karl Walker, Ernel Braham)

ROB WALKER

| 71 | Upsetter US 366 | Run Up Your Mouth (actually by Stranger Cole)/UPSETTERS: Mouth Version | 15 |
| 71 | Jackpot JP 761 | Hear My Heart/Puppet On A String | 15 |

(see also Stranger Cole, Tommy McCook)

RONNIE WALKER

69	Stateside SS 2151	It's A Good Feeling/Precious	30
69	Stateside SS 2151	It's A Good Feeling/Precious (DJ Copy)	50
75	Polydor 2066 578	Magic's In The Air/Just Can't Say Hello	8

SCOTT WALKER

67	Philips BF 1628	Jackie/The Plague	5
68	Philips BF 1662	Joanna/Always Coming Back To You	5
69	Philips BF 1793	Lights of Cincinnati/Two Weeks Since You've Gone	5
71	Philips 6006 168	I Still See You/My Way Home	6
73	Philips 6006 311	The Me I Never Knew/This Way Mary	6
73	CBS 1795	A Woman Left Lonely/Where Love Has Died	6
74	CBS 2521	Delta Dawn/We Had It All	6

66	Liberty LEP 2261	SCOTT ENGEL (WALKER) (EP)	40
67	Philips (S)BL 7816	SCOTT (LP, mono/stereo)	18
67	Philips (S)BL 7816	SCOTT (LP, mono/stereo)	25
68	Philips BL 7840	SCOTT 2 (LP, mono, with signed portrait)	25
68	Philips BL 7840	SCOTT 2 (LP, mono, without signed portrait)	15
68	Philips SBL 7840	SCOTT 2 (LP, stereo, with signed portrait)	35
68	Philips SBL 7840	SCOTT 2 (LP, stereo, without signed portrait)	20
68	Ember EMB LP 3393	LOOKING BACK WITH SCOTT WALKER (LP, mono or stereo)	30
69	Philips SBL 7882	SCOTT 3 (LP, gatefold sleeve)	35
69	Philips SBL 7900	SCOTT WALKER SINGS SONGS FROM HIS TV SERIES (LP)	18
69	Philips SBL 7910	THE BEST OF SCOTT WALKER VOL. 1 (LP)	18
69	Philips SBL 7913	SCOTT 4 (LP)	40
70	Philips 6308 035	'TIL THE BAND COMES IN (LP)	40
72	Philips 6382 007	THIS IS... SCOTT WALKER (LP)	12
72	Philips 6308 127	THE MOVIEGOER (LP)	25
73	Philips 6308 148	ANY DAY NOW (LP)	30
73	CBS 65725	STRETCH (LP)	20
73	Philips 6850 013	THE ROMANTIC SCOTT WALKER (LP, Audio Club issue)	30
73	Philips 6856 022	TERRIFIC (LP, Audio Club issue, reissue of "Scott 2" with different tracks)	40
73	Philips 6382 052	THIS IS SCOTT WALKER VOL. 2 (LP)	12
74	CBS 80254	WE HAD IT ALL (LP)	20
76	Philips 6625 017	SPOTLIGHT ON SCOTT WALKER (2-LP)	18
81	Zoo ZOO 2	FIRE ESCAPE IN THE SKY - THE GODLIKE GENIUS OF SCOTT WALKER (LP)	20
81	Philips 6359 090	SINGS JACQUES BREL (LP)	12
95	Fontana 526859-1	TILT (LP, limited edition)	50
06	4AD DRIFT 1	THE DRIFT (2-LP, 500 promo copies with 24 page booklet)	50

(see also Scott Engel, Scott Engel & John Stewart, John & Scott Walker, Walker Brothers, Routers)

STEWART WALKER
98	Mosquito MSQ 012	ARTIFICIAL MUSIC FOR ARTIFICIAL PEOPLE (12" EP)	15

SYLFORD WALKER
79	Art & Craft AC 002	Book Of The Old Testament/JAH STITCH: Jah Speak Unto Moses (12")	30
80	Art & Craft ACD002	I Love You (feat. Jah Stitch)/Version (12")	20
88	Greensleeves GREL 119	LAMBS BREAD (LP)	20

(see also Glen Brown)

T-BONE WALKER
54	London HL 8087	The Hustle Is On/Baby Broke My Heart (78)	40
65	Liberty LIB 12018	Party Girl/Here In The Dark	25
63	London REP 1404	TRAVELLIN' BLUES (EP)	70
54	Capitol LC 6681	CLASSICS IN JAZZ (10" LP)	40
63	Capitol T 1958	T-BONE WALKER (LP)	50
65	MFP MFP 1043	THE BLUES OF T-BONE WALKER (LP)	12
65	Liberty LBY 3047	SINGS THE BLUES (LP)	50
66	Liberty LBY 3057	SINGING THE BLUES (LP)	40
68	MCA MUPS 331	THE TRUTH (LP)	20
68	Stateside S(S)L 10223	STORMY MONDAY BLUES (LP)	30
69	Stateside S(S)L 10265	FUNKY TOWN (LP)	30
73	Reprise K 94001	VERY RARE (2-LP)	30
74	Atlantic K 40131	T-BONE BLUES (LP)	15

WENDY WALKER
63	Decca F 11573	Window Shopping/Ain't A Boy In The World	8
63	Decca F 11671	Boys Will Be Happy/Casanova	8

DEE WALKER
82	Arts Network DEE 1	DIAL 'L' FOR LOVE (mini-LP)	30

WALKER BROTHERS
65	Philips BF 1401	Pretty Girls Everywhere/Doin' The Jerk	15
65	Philips BF 1409	Love Her/The Seventh Dawn	10
65	Philips BF 1428	Make It Easy On Yourself/But I Do	6
65	Philips BF 1454	My Ship Is Coming In/You're All Around Me	6
66	Philips BF 1473	The Sun Ain't Gonna Shine Anymore/After The Lights Go Out	6
66	Philips BF 1497	(Baby) You Don't Have To Tell Me/My Love Is Growing	8
66	Philips BF 1514	Another Tear Falls/The Saddest Night In The World	8
66	Philips BF 1537	Deadlier Than The Male/Archangel	8
67	Philips BF 1548	Stay With Me Baby/Turn Out The Moon	8
67	Philips BF 1576	Walking In The Rain/Baby Make It The Last Time	8
76	GTO GT 42	No Regrets/Remember Me	5
76	GTO GT 67	Lines/First Day	6
77	GTO GT 78	We're All Alone/Have You Seen My Baby	6
66	Philips BE 12596	I NEED YOU (EP)	15
67	Philips BE 12603	THE WALKER BROTHERS (EP, probably unreleased)	0
65	Philips BL 7691	TAKE IT EASY WITH THE WALKER BROTHERS (LP)	18
66	Philips BL 7732	PORTRAIT (LP, with photo insert, mono)	20
66	Philips SBL 7732	PORTRAIT (LP, with photo insert, stereo)	30
67	Philips (S)BL 7770	IMAGES (LP)	20
67	Philips DBL 002	THE WALKER BROTHERS STORY (2-LP)	18
68	Wing WL 1188	THE FABULOUS WALKER BROTHERS (LP)	12
75	GTO GTLP 007	NO REGRETS (LP)	12
78	GTO GTLP 033	NITE FLIGHTS (LP, gatefold sleeve)	20

(see also Scott Walker, Scott Engel, John Walker, John & Scott Walker, Gary Walker [& Rain], Routers)

TREVOR WALKERS
82	Mutual Life MU 002	They'll Never Get Away/Version (12", blue vinyl)	20

WALKIE TALKIES
79	Sire SIR 4023	Rich And Nasty/Summer In Russia (p/s)	6

(see also Pauline Murray & Invisible Girls, Mission)

WALKING FLOORS
80s	My Death Telephone TEL 1	No Next Time/Removal (foldover p/s)	8

DENNIS WALKS

68	Amalgamated AMG 816	Having A Party/GROOVERS: Day By Day	20
68	Blue Cat BS 144	Belly Lick/DRUMBAGO & BLENDERS: The Game Song	50
69	Bullet BU 402	Heart Don't Leap/CLARENDONIANS: I Am Sorry	100
69	Bullet BU 408	Love Of My Life/Under The Shady Tree	12
71	Moodisc HM 101	Time Will Tell/Under The Shady Tree	7
74	Magnet MG 062	Don't Play That Song/Version	6
82	greensleeves GREL 77	Roast Fish And Cornbread/Wicked She Wicked (12", with Billy Boyo)	20

(see also I Roy)

SHELTON WALKS

73	Bullet BU 550	No Money No Friend/BOB MAC ALL STARS: Money Dub	6
74	Dip DL 5026	One Of Us Will Weep/KING EDWARDS ALL STARS: Version	6

WALL

79	Small Wonder SMALL 13	New Way/Suckers/Uniforms (p/s)	5
80	Fresh FRESHLP 2	PERSONAL TROUBLES AND PUBLIC ISSUES (LP)	15
80	Fresh FRESHLP 2	PERSONAL TROUBLES AND PUBLIC ISSUES LP, with insert, withdrawn "Crass style" stencil lettered sleeve)	30

(see also Ski Patrol)

MAX WALL

73	York YR 203	The Fiddley Foodle Bird/Story Of The Fiddley Foodle Bird	5
75	DJM DJS 10352	Why Should I Care/Devil Bomb	5
77	Stiff BUY 12	England's Glory/Dream Tobacco (glossy or matt p/s)	5

REM WALL & HIS GREEN VALLEY BOYS

60	Top Rank JAR 324	Heartsick And Blue/One More Time	10

ERROL WALLACE

69	Escort ES 817	Bandit/ASTON BORROT: Family Man Mood (actually by Aston "Family Man" Barrett)	12

GIG WALLACE & HIS ORCHESTRA

60	Philips PB 981	Rockin' On The Railroad/Show Me The Way To Go Home	10

JERRY WALLACE

58	London HL 8719	With This Ring/How The Time Flies	40
58	London HL 8719	With This Ring/How The Time Flies (78)	15
58	London HL 7062	With This Ring/How The Time Flies (export issue)	30
59	London HLH 8943	Primrose Lane/By Your Side	10
59	London HLH 8943	Primrose Lane/By Your Side (78)	15
60	London HLH 9040	Little Coco Palm/Mission Bell Blues	6
60	London HLH 9110	You're Singing Our Love Song To Somebody Else/King Of The Mountain	6
60	London HLH 9177	Swingin' Down The Lane/Teardrop In The Rain	5
61	London HLH 9264	There She Goes/Angel On My Shoulder	5
61	London HLH 9363	Life's A Holiday/I Can See An Angel	5
62	London HLH 9630	Shutters And Boards/Am I That Easy To Forget	5
64	London HLH 9914	Even The Bad Times Are Good/In The Misty Moonlight	5
65	Mercury MF 853	Time/Rainbow	5

MIKE WALLACE

70	Major Minor D570	Daffodil/Early Morning Bird	12
70	Polydor 2058065	Natural High/Mandrin	10

SIPPIE WALLACE

67	Storyville 671 198	SIPPIE WALLACE SINGS THE BLUES (LP)	15

WALLACE BROTHERS

64	Sue WI 334	Precious Words/You're Mine	40
65	Sue WI 355	Lover's Prayer/Love Me Like I Love You	40
67	Sue WI 4036	I'll Step Aside/Hold My Heart For A While	40
67	Sue ILP 950	SOUL CONNECTION (LP)	250

WALLACE COLLECTION

69	Parlophone R 5764	Daydream/Baby I Don't Mind	12
69	Parlophone R 5793	Fly Me To The Earth/Love	25
70	Parlophone R 5844	Serenade/Walk On Out	10
69	Parlophone PMC/PCS 7076	LAUGHING CAVALIER (LP)	12
70	Parlophone PCS 7099	WALLACE COLLECTION (LP)	12

GORDON (WALLER)

68	Columbia DB 8337	Rosecrans Boulevard/Red, Cream And Velvet	20
68	Columbia DB 8440	Every Day/Because Of A Woman	10
68	Columbia DB 8518	Weeping Analeah/The Seventh Hour	10
69	Bell BLL 1059	I Was A Boy When You Needed A Man/Lady In The Window	6
70	Bell BLL 1106	You're Gonna Hurt Yourself/Sunshine	6
72	Vertigo 6360 069	GORDON (LP, as Gordon, single sleeve, small swirl label)	700

(see also Peter & Gordon)

'FATS' WALLER (& HIS RHYTHM)

53	HMV 7M 128	My Very Good Friend The Milkman/Shortnin' Bread	5
53	HMV 7M 157	A Good Man Is Hard To Find/The Girl I Left Behind Me	5
53	HMV 7M 142	Honey Hush/You've Been Reading My Mail	5
54	HMV 7M 208	You've Been Taking Lessons In Love/I've Got A New Lease Of Life	5
54	HMV 7M 244	By The Light Of The Silvery Moon/Romance A La Mode (with Deep River Boys)	5
60	RCA RCA 1189	Dinah/When Somebody Thinks You're Wonderful	5

(see also Louisiana Sugar Babies, Deep River Boys, James P. Johnson)

GEORGE WALLINGTON

56	Columbia Clef 33C9035	THE WORK SHOP OF GEORGE WALLINGTON TRIO (10" LP)	50
57	Esquire 32-132	NEW YORK SCENE (LP)	70

BOB WALLIS & HIS STORYVILLE JAZZMEN

61	Pye Jazz 7NJ 2043	I'm Shy Mary Ellen I'm Shy/Three Live Wires	5
61	Pye Jazz 7NJ 2048	Come Along Please/Bobbin' Along	5
57	77 EP 10	NEW ORLEANS JAM SESSION VOLUME 1 (EP)	15
59	77 Records 77LE 12/2	THE RAVING SOUNDS OF BOB WALLIS (LP)	20
60	Top Rank BUY 023	EVERYBODY LOVES SATURDAY NIGHT (LP)	15

61	Pye Jazz NJL 27	OLE MAN RIVER (LP)	15
61	Pye Jazz NJL 30	TRAVELLIN' BLUES (LP)	15

LARRY WALLIS

77	Stiff BUY 22	Police Car/On Parole (with p/s)	7
77	Stiff BUY 22	Police Car/On Parole (die-cut company sleeve)	5

(see also Pink Fairies, Subs, Deviants, Shagrat, Peter Wyngarde, Motorhead)

SHANI WALLIS

60	Philips PB 1019	Sixteen Reasons (Why I Love You)/Forever Forever	5
63	Decca F11632	My Heart Cries For You/All Over Again	20
60	Philips BBE 12337	SHANI! (EP)	8

WALL OF SLEEP

95	Woronzow WOO 24	WALL OF SLEEP (LP, with insert)	12

WALL OF VOODOO

82	Illegal ILS 31	On Interstate 15/There's Nothing On This Side	5
83	Illuminated ILS 0036	Mexican Radio/Call Of The West (p/s)	5

WALL STREET DIVERSION

68	Concord CON 006	She's Mine/Joey The Lipstick Collector	25

WALLY

74	Atlantic K 50051	WALLY (LP, laminated sleeve)	12
75	Atlantic K 50180	VALLY GARDENS (LP)	12

WALLY BROTHERS

74	Explosion EX 2090	The Man Who Sold The World/Version	15

WALRUS

70	Deram DM 308	Who Can I Trust?/Tomorrow Never Comes	20
71	Deram DM 323	Never Let My Body Touch Ground/Why?	20
71	Deram SML 1072	WALRUS (LP)	200

JAMES WALSH GYPSY BAND

79	RCA PB 11403	Cuz It's You Girl/Bring Yourself Together	50
79	RCA PB 11403	Cuz It's You Girl/Bring Yourself Together (DJ copy)	100

SHEILA WALSH & CLIFF RICHARD

83	DJM SHEIL 100	Drifting/It's Lonely When The Lights Go Out (picture disc)	6
83	DJM SHEILT 100	Drifting/It's Lonely When The Lights Go Out (12", picture disc)	8
83	DJM DJF 20581	DRIFTING (LP, with inner sleeve, as Sheila Walsh)	12

(see also Cliff Richard)

JOHNNY WALSH

61	Warner Bros. WB 40	Girl Machine/Beautiful Obsession	10

BURT WALTERS

68	Trojan TR 636	Honey Love/KING CANNONBALL BRYAN: Thunderstorm	40

(see also Lee 'Scratch' Perry)

JULIE WALTERS

82	Deaville STL 7	Toy Boys/Bad Loser	6

DAVE WALTON

66	CBS 202057	Love Ain't What It Used To Be/Tell Me A Lie	8
66	CBS 202098	Every Window In The City/I've Left The Troubled Ground	15
67	CBS 202508	After You There Can Be Nothing/Can I Get It From You	30

(see also The First Gear)

TRAVIS WAMMACK

65	Atlantic AT 4017	Scratchy/Fire Fly	50
65	Atlantic AT 4017	Scratchy/Fire Fly (DJ copy)	100
72	United Artists UP 35412	Whatever Turns You On/Slip Away	6
73	United Artists UP 35468	So Good/Darling, You're All That I Need	6
75	Capricorn 2429 133	NOT FOR SALE (LP)	12

WANDERER

59	Top Rank JAR 183	The Happy Hobo/True True Happiness	6

WANDERERS

81	Polydor POSP 239	Ready To Snap/Beyond The Law	25
81	Polydor POSP 284	The Times They Are A'Changin'/Little Bit Frightening	6
81	Polydor POLS 1028	ONLY LOVERS LEFT (LP)	20

(see also Lords Of The New Church, Stiv Bators, Dead Boys)

WANDERERS (JAMAICA)

69	Trojan TR 7721	Wiggle Waggle/Jaga Jaga War	8

WANDERERS (U.S.)

60	MGM MGM 1102	I Could Make You Mine/I Need You More	50
61	MGM MGM 1169	As Time Goes By/There Is No Greater Love	20
64	United Artists UP 1020	Run Run Senorita/After He Breaks Your Heart	30

(see also Ray Pollard)

WANGLERS

79	Matchbox Classics MC 5	KICKIN' OUT FOR THE COAST (EP, white label, yellow or red stickered foldover p/s)	10

DEXTER WANSEL

85	Streetwave SWAVE 9	Life On Mars/WILLIE BOBO: Always There (12")	15

WAR

71	Liberty LBF 15443	Sun Oh Son/Lonely Feelin'	6
71	United Artists UP 35281	All Day Music/Get Down	6
72	United Artists UP 35327	Slippin' Into Darkness/Nappy Head	5
73	United Artists UP 35469	The World Is A Ghetto/Four Cornered Room	5
73	United Artists UP 35521	The Cisco Kid/Beetles In The Bog	5
73	United Artists UP 35576	Gypsy Man/Deliver The Word	5
74	United Artists UP 35623	Me And Baby Brother/In Your Eyes	8
71	Liberty LBG 83478	WAR (LP)	20

72	United Artists UAS 29269	ALL DAY MUSIC (LP)	15
73	United Artists UAS 29400	THE WORLD IS A GHETTO (LP)	15

(see also Eric Burdon & War)

JEAN WARD AND MICHAEL RAVEN
70	Roman Head RH 021	A COLLECTION OF FOLKSONGS AND GUITAR MUSIC (LP, 99 copies only)	80

BILL WARD
90	Chameleon 0174910	WARD ONE: ALONG THE WAY (LP, with innersleeve)	12

(see also Black Sabbath)

BILLY WARD & HIS DOMINOES
53	Parlophone R 3789	Don't Thank Me/Rags To Riches (78)	40
54	Parlophone MSP 6112	Three Coins In The Fountain/Lonesome Road	150
54	Parlophone MSP 6112	Three Coins In The Fountain/Lonesome Road (78)	25
56	Brunswick 05599	St. Therese Of The Roses/Home Is Where You Hang Your Heart	40
57	Brunswick 05656	Evermore/Half A Love (Is Better Than None)	30
57	London HLU 8465	Stardust/Lucinda	20
57	London HLU 8502	Deep Purple/Do It Again	20
58	London HLU 8634	Jennie Lee/Music, Maestro, Please	20
58	London HLU 8634	Jennie Lee/Music, Maestro, Please (78)	10
59	London HLU 8883	Please Don't Say 'No'/Behave, Hula Girl	20
59	London HLU 8883	Please Don't Say 'No'/Behave, Hula Girl (78)	10
58	London REU 1114	BILLY WARD & HIS DOMINOES (EP)	100
58	Parlophone PMD 1061	BILLY WARD & HIS DOMINOES FEATURING CLYDE McPHATTER (10" LP)	600
58	London HA-U 2116	YOURS FOREVER (LP)	60

(see also Dominoes, Clyde McPhatter, Jackie Wilson)

CHRISTIAN WARD
66	Decca F 12339	The Face Of Empty Me/Girl I Used To Know	35

CLARA WARD & HER SINGERS
65	Stateside SS 474	Gonna Build A Mountain/God Bless The Child	10

CLIFFORD T. WARD
72	Dandelion 2001 327	Carrie/Sidetrack	12
72	Dandelion 2001 382	Coathanger/Rayne	10
72	Charisma CB 205	Home Thoughts From Abroad/Game	7
73	Charisma CB 212	Wherewithal/Thinking Of Something To Do	7
74	Charisma CB 233	Jayne/Maybe I'm Right	7
75	Charisma CB 248	Jigsaw Girl/Cellophane	7
75	Philips 6006 490	No More Rock'n'Roll/Gandalf	7
76	Philips 6006 542	Ocean Of Love/Tomorrow Night	7
77	Mercury 6007 132	Up In The World/Not Waving, Drowning (Revisited)	7
77	Mercury 6007 149	I Got Lost Tonight/Detriment (p/s)	7
77	Mercury LUV 1	Someone I Know/If I Had Known (gatefold p/s)	8
80	WEA K 18294	Convertible/Taking The Long Way Round	7
81	WEA K 18426	The Best Is Yet To Come/Lost Again	7
81	WEA K 18486	Contrary/Climate Of Her Favour	7
84	Philips 880 550 7	Messenger/Where Do Angels Really Come From (p/s)	8
86	Tembo TML 114	Cricket/Computer	10
86	Tembo TML 123	Sometime Next Year/Turbo (p/s)	8
72	Dandelion 2310 216	SINGER SONGWRITER (LP)	25
73	Charisma CAS 1006	HOME THOUGHTS (LP, gatefold sleeve)	12
73	Charisma CAS 1077	MANTLE PIECES (LP, large "mad hatter" label, insert)	12
75	Charisma CAS 1098	ESCALATOR (LP)	15
75	Philips 9109 500	NO MORE ROCK'N'ROLL (LP, lyric inner sleeve)	12
75	Philips 9109 216	WAVES (LP)	12

(see also Secrets, Simon's Secrets, Martin Raynor & Secrets)

DALE WARD
64	London HLD 9835	Oh Julie/Letter From Sherry	20

DOUGLAS WARD
71	Forward FS1001	FROM AN ELEVATED PLATFORM (LP)	20

HEDLEY WARD TRIO
56	Melodisc MEL 1387	Steamboat Rock/My Baby's Got Such Lovin' Ways (78)	10

ROBIN WARD
63	London HLD 9821	Wonderful Summer/Dream Boy	25

TERRY WARD WITH BUMBLIES
65	Fontana TF 558	Gotta Tell/When I Come To You	10

SHEELAGH WARDE
59	Top Rank JAR 131	Let Mr. Maguire Sit Down/The Golden Jubilee	7

WARDENS
70s	SNO PEAS TIC 001	Lust Like This/Do So Well (with insert)	20

WARDS OF COURT
67	Deram DM 127	All Night Girl/How Could Say One Thing	60

WARD SINGERS
56	London Jazz EZ-C 19024	THE FAMOUS WARD SINGERS (EP)	20
56	London Jazz LZ-C 14013	THE FAMOUS WARD SINGERS (10" LP)	25

LEON WARE
77	Motown STML 12050	MUSICAL MASSAGE (LP)	15

WARFARE
83	Neat (No. cat. no.)	This Machine Kills/Burn Down The Kings Road (white label)	20
84	Neat NEAT 45-12	Two Tribes/Hell/Blown To Bits (12")	12
84	Neat NEAT 49-12	TOTAT DEATH (12", EP)	15
84	Neat NEAT 1021	PURE FILTH (LP)	15
85	Neat NEAT 1029	METAL ANARCH (LP)	12

WARHOLS
87	Zoot WAR 001	Fear Of Falling/Other Side	20

WARHORSE
71	Vertigo 6059 027	St. Louis/No Chance	15
70	Vertigo 6360 015	WARHORSE (LP, large swirl label, gatefold sleeve)	200
72	Vertigo 6360 066	RED SEA (LP, small swirl label, gatefold sleeve)	300

(see also Deep Purple, Nic Simper's Fandango)

RAY WARLEIGH
69	Philips (S)BL 7881	RAY WARLEIGH'S FIRST ALBUM (LP)	40

(see also John Mayall's Blues Breakers, Alexis Korner)

OZZIE WARLOCK & WIZARDS
59	HMV POP 635	Juke Box Fury/Wow!	12

(see also Tony Osbourne)

WARM
78	Warm 2001	It's The Kooler/Teenage Space Queen (p/s)	5
78	Warm SMS 001/2001/S	THE DEMO TAPES (EP, double pack)	8
78	Warm WARM 2003	Floosie/Chewing Gum Sue/Bye Bye It's Blues/Sometimes (p/s)	5
79	Warm AWMR 2007	007 (Shanty Town)/Just To Stay Ahead (promo only)	12
79	MHG GHM 208/PF 9002	Tired Of Waiting For You/Tired Dub	12

JOHNNY WARMAN
78	Ring O' 2017 112	Head On Collision/London's Burning/Mind Games (in p/s)	20
78	Ring O' 2017 112	Head On Collision/London's Burning/Mind Games	15

WARM DUST
71	Trend 6099 002	It's A Beautiful Day/Worm Dance	15
70	Trend TNLS 700	AND IT CAME TO PASS (2-LP, gatefold sleeve, grey label)	80
71	Trend 6480 001	PEACE FOR OUR TIME (LP, gatefold sleeve, grey label)	50

WARM GOLD
60s	Hurls 008	A TASTE OF CORNWALL (EP)	25

WARM JETS
78	Bridgehouse BHS 1	Sticky Jack/Shell Shock (p/s, some with sides reversed & small extra labels)	8
79	RSO RSO 47	Big City Boys/Mr Natural (p/s)	5

WARM SENSATION
69	Columbia DB 8568	I'll Be Proud Of You/The Clown	25

(see also Ivy League)

WARM SOUNDS
67	Immediate IM 058	Sticks And Stones/Angeline	20
67	Deram DM 120	The Birds And Bees/Doo-Dah	15
68	Deram DM 174	Nite Is A-Comin'/Smeta Mergaty	50

(see also Denny Gerrard, Tuesday's Children, Open Road)

FLORENCE WARNER
73	Epic EPC 1626	For No Good Reason/Remember	6
75	Epic EPC 3817	Anyway I Love You/Dreamer	6
74	Epic EPC 80077	FLORENCE WARNER (LP)	18

HERB & BETTY WARNER
59	Felsted AF 114	Slowly/'BUGS' BOWER GROUP: Slowly	7

JACK WARNER
71	President PT 360	You Have Got The Gear/ Somebody Asked Me	15
68	MFP MFP 1278	YER CAN'T 'ELP LAUGHIN' (LP)	15

JACK WARNER WITH TOMMY REILLY
58	Oriole CB 1426	An Ordinary Copper/On The Way Up	5

KAI WARNER'S ORIENTAL EXPRESS
77	Power Exchange PX 244	Fly Butterfly/Funky Harem	6

GALE WARNING
56	Pye N 15061	Heartbreak Hotel/Met Rock (78)	10
56	Oriole CB 1349	Rock Those Crazy Skins/I Need Your Love (78)	10

WARP NINE
75	Stax STXS 2030	Theme From 'Star Trek'/Para Song One	5

FRAN WARREN
59	MGM MGM 1008	Shame/As Long As You Believe Me	10

GUY WARREN OF GHANA
59	Brunswick 05791	Monkies And Butterflies/An African's Prayer (with Rod Saunders)	6
57	Brunswick LAJ 8237	AFRICA SPEAKS - AMERICA ANSWERS (LP)	35
64	Columbia 33SX 1584	EMERGENT DRUMS (LP)	100
69	Columbia SCX 6340	AFRO-JAZZ (LP, as Guy Warren Of Ghana)	75
72	Regal Zono. SLRZ 1031	THE AFRICAN SOUNDS OF GUY WARREN OF GHANA (LP)	100

SHORTY WARRENT & HIS WESTERN RANGE
52	London L 1125	I Thought She Was Local/You're Breaking The Only Heart (That Truly Loves You) (78)	10

WARRIÖR
80	Rambert RAM ONE	Don't Let It Show/The Lord's Prayer/Silver Lady (10", p/s)	120
80	Goodwood GM 12326	TROUBLE MAKER (LP)	150

WARRIOR (1)
72	Eden LP 27	INVASION! (LP, private pressing, plain white sleeve & label, some handwritten, 100 only)	160
80	Rainbow RSL 132	LET BATTLE COMMENCE (LP, private pressing, 500 only)	100

WARRIOR (2)
82	Neat NEAT 20	Dead When It Comes To Love/Kansas City/Stab In The Back	10
84	Warrior WOO 2	Breakout/Dragon Slayer/Take Your Chance (paper sleeve)	55
83	Warrior WOO 1	FOR EUROPE ONLY (mini-LP)	20

WARRIORS
| 64 | Decca F 11926 | Don't Make Me Blue/You Came Along | 40 |

(see also Hans Christian, Jon Anderson)

WARSAW PAKT
78	Island PAKT 1	Safe And Warm/Sick And Tired (with stamped sleeve)	30
78	Island PAKT 1	Safe And Warm/Sick And Tired	18
77	Island ILPS 9515	NEEDLE TIME (LP, numbered stamped mailer p/s, with insert)	25

WARWICK
| 75 | RAK RAK 211 | Let's Get The Party Going/How Does It Feel | 15 |

DEE DEE WARWICK
65	Mercury MF 860	Do It With All Your Heart/Happiness	20
65	Mercury MF 867	We're Doin' Fine/You Don't Know	20
65	Mercury MF 890	Gotta Get Hold Of Myself/Another Lonely Saturday	20
66	Mercury MF 909	A Lover's Chant/Worth Every Tear I Cry	75
65	Mercury MF 937	I Want To Be With You/Alfie	18
65	Mercury MF 953	Yours Till Tomorrow/I'm Gonna Make You Love Me	15
67	Mercury MF 974	When Love Slips Away/House Of Gold	40
68	Mercury MF 1061	I'll Be Better Off (Without You)/Monday, Monday	20
69	Mercury MF 1084	Foolish Heart/Thank God	10
69	Mercury MF 1125	That's Not Love/It's Not Fair	10
70	Atlantic 2091 011	She Didn't Know (She Kept On Talking)/Make Love To Me	8
70	Atlantic 2091 037	If This Was The Last Song/I'm Only Human	6
71	Atlantic 2091 057	Cold Night In Georgia/Searching	6
71	Atlantic 2091 092	Suspicious Minds/I'm Glad I'm A Woman	15
75	Private Stock PVT 13	Get Out Of My Life/Funny How We Change Places	20
66	Mercury 10036 MCE	WE'RE DOING FINE (EP)	80
71	Atco	TURNIN' AROUND (LP)	30

DIONNE WARWICK

SINGLES
76	Warner Bros SAM 61	Track Of The Cat/LIVERPOOL EXPRESS: You Are My Love (12", promo only)	15
63	Stateside SS 157	Don't Make Me Over/I Smiled Yesterday	22
63	Stateside SS 157	Don't Make Me Over/I Smiled Yesterday (DJ Copy)	50
63	Stateside SS 191	This Empty Place/Wishin' And Hopin'	22
63	Pye International 7N 25223	Please Let Him Love Me/Make The Music Play	8
64	Pye International 7N 25234	Anyone Who Had A Heart/The Love Of A Boy	10
64	Pye International 7N 25241	Walk On By/Any Old Time Of Day	8
64	Pye International 7N 25256	You'll Never Get To Heaven/A House Is Not A Home	8
64	Pye International 7N 25265	Reach Out For Me/How Many Days Of Sadness	8
65	Pye International 7N 25290	You Can Have Him/Don't Say I Didn't Tell You	8
65	Pye International 7N 25302	Who Can I Turn To/That's Not The Answer	6
65	Pye International 7N 25310	(Here I Go Again) Looking With My Eyes/Only The Strong, Only The Brave	6
65	Pye International 7N 25316	Here I Am/They Long To Be Close To You	6
65	Pye International 7N 25338	Are You There (With Another Girl)/If I Ever Make You Cry	6
66	Pye International 7N 25357	In Between The Heartaches/Long Day, Short Night	6
66	Pye International 7N 25368	A Message To Michael/Here Where There Is Love	6
66	Pye International 7N 25378	Trains And Boats And Planes/Don't Go Breaking My Heart	6
66	Pye International 7N 25395	Another Night/Go With Love	6
67	Pye International 7N 25424	Alfie/The Beginning Of Loneliness	6
67	Pye International 7N 25428	The Windows Of The World/Walk Little Dolly	6
67	Pye International 7N 25435	I Say A Little Prayer/Window Wishin'	7
68	Pye International 7N 25445	(Theme From) The Valley Of The Dolls/Zip-A-Dee-Doo-Dah	8
68	Pye International 7N 25457	Do You Know The Way To San Jose?/Let Me Be Lonely	7
68	Pye International 7N 25474	Who Is Gonna Love Me?/(There's) Always Something There To Remind Me	6
75	Warner Bros WB 16530	Take It From Me/Sure Thing	5
75	Warner Bros K 16595	Move Me No Mountain/We'll Burn Our Bridges Behind Us	5

EPs
64	Pye Intl. NEP 44024	IT'S LOVE THAT COUNTS	8
64	Pye Intl. NEP 44026	DON'T MAKE ME OVER	8
65	Pye Intl. NEP 44039	WISHIN' AND HOPIN'	8
65	Pye Intl. NEP 44044	DIONNE	8
65	Pye Intl. NEP 44046	FOREVER MY LOVE	8
65	Pye Intl. NEP 44049	WHO CAN I TURN TO?	8
66	Pye Intl. NEP 44051	HERE I AM	8
66	Pye Intl. NEP 44067	MESSAGE TO MICHAEL	8
66	Pye Intl. NEP 44073	WINDOW WISHIN'	8
66	Pye Intl. NEP 44077	I JUST DON'T KNOW WHAT TO DO WITH MYSELF	8
67	Pye Intl. NEP 44083	I LOVE PARIS	8
68	Pye Intl. NEP 44090	DO YOU KNOW THE WAY TO SAN JOSE?	8

ALBUMS
64	Pye Intl. NPL 28037	PRESENTING DIONNE WARWICK	20
64	Pye Intl. NPL 28046	MAKE WAY FOR DIONNE WARWICK	18
64	Pye Intl. NPL 28064	THE BEST OF DIONNE WARWICK (LP)	12
65	Pye Intl. NPL 28055	THE SENSITIVE SOUND OF DIONNE WARWICK	20
66	Pye Intl. NPL 28071	HERE I AM	20
66	Pye Intl. NPL 28076	DIONNE WARWICK IN PARIS	20
67	Pye Intl. NPL 28096	HERE WHERE THERE IS LOVE	15
67	Pye Intl. NPL 28101	ON STAGE AND IN THE MOVIES (LP)	20
67	Pye Intl. NPL 28105	THE WINDOWS OF THE WORLD (LP)	15
68	Pye Intl. N(S)PL 28114	VALLEY OF THE DOLLS (LP)	20

WASHBOARD RHYTHM KINGS
| 56 | HMV 7EG 8101 | WASHBOARD RHYTHM KINGS (EP) | 15 |

WASHBOARD SAM
| 72 | RCA RD 8274 | FEELING LOWDOWN (LP, with Big Bill Broonzy & Memphis Slim) | 15 |

(see also Big Bill Broonzy, Memphis Slim)

ALBERT WASHINGTON & KINGS

67	President PT 137	Doggin' Me Around/A Woman Is A Funny Thing	10
68	President PT 182	I'm The Man/These Arms Of Mine	50
68	President PT 227	Woman Love/Bring It On Up	10
69	President PT 242	Turn On The Bright Lights/Lonely Mountain	10
73	President PT 391	Rome, GA/Telling All Your Friends	10

BABY WASHINGTON

64	Sue WI 302	That's How Heartaches Are Made/Doodlin'	50
64	Sue WI 321	I Can't Wait Until I See My Baby/Who's Gonna Take Care Of Me	50
65	London HLC 9987	Only Those In Love/Ballad Of Bobby Dawn	25
68	United Artists UP 2247	Get A Hold Of Yourself/Hurt So Bad	70
69	Atlantic 584 299	I Don't Know/I Can't Afford To Lose Him	15
70	Atlantic 584 316	Breakfast In Bed/What Becomes Of A Broken Heart	15
73	People PEO 105	Just Can't Get You Out Of My Mind/You're Just A Dream	10
74	People PEO 107	I've Got To Break Away/Can't Get Over You	10
66	London HA-C 8260	THAT'S HOW HEARTACHES ARE MADE (LP)	50
66	London HA-C 8292	ONLY THOSE IN LOVE (LP)	50
68	United Artists SULP 1217	WITH YOU IN MIND (LP)	40

(see also Baby Washington/Wilbert Harrison)

BABY WASHINGTON & DON GARDNER

| 73 | People PEO 101 | Forever/Baby Let Me Get Close To You | 5 |
| 74 | People PLEO 13 | LAY A LITTLE LOVIN' ON ME (LP) | 20 |

(see also Don Gardner & Dee Dee Ford)

BABY WASHINGTON/WILBERT HARRISON

| 71 | Joy JOYS 191 | BATTLE OF THE GIANTS (LP) | 18 |

DELROY WASHINGTON

77	Virgin VDJ 22	Give All The Praise To Jah/Stand Up And Be Happy (12")	15
78	Burning Sounds BSD 006	Memories (with Jah Son)/ EVERARD THOMPSON & SUPERSTAR: Rasta roots (12")	15
76	Virgin V 2060	I-SUS (LP, with insert)	20
77	Virgin V 2088	RASTA (LP)	20

DINAH WASHINGTON

52	Oriole CB 1130	Mad About The Boy/I Can't Face The Music (78)	15
54	Oriole CB 1266	My Man's An Undertaker/Since My Man Has Gone And Went (78)	15
54	Oriole CB 1279	Fat Daddy/TV Is The Thing (78)	15
56	Mercury MT 124	Cat On A Hot Tin Roof/The First Time (78)	15
59	Mercury AMT 1051	What A Diff'rence A Day Made/Come On Home	10
59	Mercury AMT 1069	Unforgettable/Nothing In The World	5
60	Mercury AMT 1105	This Bitter Earth/I Understand	5
60	Mercury AMT 1119	Love Walked In/I'm In Heaven Tonight	5
61	Mercury AMT 1125	We Have Love/Looking Back	5
61	Mercury AMT 1162	September In The Rain/Wake The Town And Tell The People	10
62	Mercury AMT 1170	Tears And Laughter/If I Should Lose You	6
62	Mercury AMT 1176	Dream/Such A Night	8
63	Columbia DB 7049	Soulville/Let Me Be The First To Know	25
56	Emarcy EJT 501	AFTER HOURS WITH MISS D. (10" LP)	30
57	Emarcy EJL 1255	DINAH (LP)	25
57	Mercury MPL 6519	SINGS THE BEST IN BLUES (LP)	15
59	Top Rank RX 3006	THE BLUES (LP, with Betty Roche)	15
60	Mercury MMC 14030	WHAT A DIFF'RENCE A DAY MADE (LP)	15
60	Mercury MMC 14048	THE UNFORGETTABLE DINAH WASHINGTON (LP)	15
61	Mercury MMC 14063	I CONCENTRATE ON YOU (LP, mono)	18
61	Mercury CMS 18043	I CONCENTRATE ON YOU (LP, stereo)	20
61	Mercury MMC 14107	SEPTEMBER IN THE RAIN (LP)	15
62	Mercury MMC 14085	FOR LONELY LOVERS (LP)	15
62	Mercury MMC 14099	TEARS AND LAUGHTER (LP)	15

(see also Brook Benton & Dinah Washington)

ELLA WASHINGTON

| 69 | Monument MON 1030 | He Called Me Baby/You're Gonna Cry, Cry, Cry | 22 |

GENO WASHINGTON & RAM JAM BAND

66	Piccadilly 7N 35312	Water/Understanding	10
66	Piccadilly 7N 35329	Hi! Hi! Hazel/Beach Bash	12
66	Piccadilly 7N 35346	Que Sera Sera/All I Need	12
66	Piccadilly 7N 35359	Michael/Hold On To My Love	12
67	Piccadilly 7N 35392	She Shot A Hole In My Soul/I've Been Hurt By Love	15
67	Piccadilly 7N 35403	Tell It Like It Is/Girl I Want To Marry	8
67	Pye 7N 17425	Different Strokes/You Got Me Hummin'	7
68	Pye 7N 17570	I Can't Quit Her/Put Out The Fire Baby	7
68	Pye 7N 17649	I Can't Let You Go/Bring It To Me Baby	10
69	Pye 7N 17745	My Little Chickadee/Seven Eleven	7
71	Pye 7N 45019	Alison Please/Each And Every Part Me	7
71	Pye 7N 45085	Feeling So Good/Would You Believe My Little Chickadee	6
66	Piccadilly NEP 34054	HI (EP)	25
68	Pye NEP 24293	DIFFERENT STROKES (EP)	20
68	Pye NEP 24302	SMALL PACKAGE OF HIPSTERS (EP)	20
66	Piccadilly NPL 38026	HAND CLAPPIN', FOOT STOMPIN' FUNKY-BUTT . . . LIVE! (LP)	20
67	Piccadilly N(S)PL 38032	HIPSTERS, FLIPSTERS, FINGER-POPPIN' DADDIES! (LP)	20
68	Pye N(S)PL 38029	SHAKE A TAIL FEATHER! (LP)	15
68	Pye N(S)PL 18219	LIVE! - RUNNING WILD (LP)	15
75	DJM DJLPS 457	GENO'S BACK (LP)	12
76	DJM DJF 20486	LIVE (LP)	12

(see also Ram Jam Band, Ram John Holder, Ram Holder Brothers, Dave Greenslade)

GEORGE E. WASHINGTON

| 64 | Fontana TF 510 | Spare A Thought For Me/Words Of Love | 5 |

JERRY WASHINGTON

| 75 | Contempo CS 2040 | Right Here Is Where You Belong/In My Life I Haved Loved | 8 |
| 75 | Contempo CLP 517 | RIGHT HERE IS WHERE YOU BELONG (LP) | 20 |

KENNETH WASHINGTON (& CHRIS BARBER BAND)

| 67 | CBS 202494 | If I Had A Ticket/They Kicked Him Out Of Heaven (with Chris Barber & T-Bones) | 10 |
| 67 | CBS 202592 | Gimme That Old Time Religion (with Chris Barber Band)/Just A Closer Walk With Thee | 5 |

(see also Chris Barber)

NORMAN T. WASHINGTON

68	Pama PM 730	Same Thing All Over/You've Been Cheating	10
68	Pama PM 741	Tip Toe/Don't Hang Around	20
69	Punch PH 11	Oh Happy Day/Spinning	7
70	Gas GAS 159	It's Christmas Time Again/If I Could See You	8
70	Punch PH 26	Sweeter Than Honey/1,000 Pearls	7
70	Punch PH 31	Last Goodbye/Mother's Pride	7

SHERI WASHINGTON & BAND

| 57 | Vogue V 9070 | I Got Plenty/Ain't I Talkin' To You Baby | 500 |
| 57 | Vogue V 9070 | I Got Plenty/Ain't I Talkin' To You Baby (78) | 100 |

SISTER ERNESTINE B. WASHINGTON

| 50 | Melodisc MEL 1101 | God's Amazing Grace/Where Could I Go But To The Lord (78) | 10 |
| 55 | Melodisc EPM 7-52 | SISTER ERNESTINE WASHINGTON (EP) | 20 |

TONY WASHINGTON (& HIS D.C.S)

63	React EA 002	Crying Man/Please Mr. DJ	20
63	Island WI 068	Something Gotta Be Done/TONY & LOUISE: I Have Said	20
64	Sue WI 327	Show Me How (To Milk A Cow)/Boof Ska	50
64	Fontana TF 478	Surely You Love Me/Man To Man	15
65	Black Swan WI 459	But I Do/Night Train (as Tony Washington & His D.C.s)	25
65	Black Swan WI 460	Dilly Dilly/Night Train (as Tony Washington & His D.C.s)	25

(see also Tony & Louise)

WASHINGTON D.C.S

64	Ember EMB S 190	Kisses Sweeter Than Wine/Where Did You Go	15
66	CBS 202226	32nd Floor/Whole Lot More	15
67	CBS 202464	Seek And Find/I Love Gerald Chevin The Great (in p/s)	70
67	CBS 202464	Seek and Find/I Love Gerald Chevin The Great (no p/s)	50
69	Domain D 9	I've Done It All Wrong/Anytime	30

(see also Dave Clark Five, Freedom)

WASHINGTON FLYERS

| 74 | Dawn DNS 1076 | Another Saturday Morning/The Comets Are Coming | 6 |

WASP

| 75 | EMI EMI 2253 | Melissa/Little Miss Bristol | 20 |

(see also Brian Bennett, Shadows)

W.A.S.P.

84	Music For Nations PKUT 109	Animal (Fuck Like A Beast)/Show No Mercy (shaped picture disc, pig's head or codpiece designs)	20
84	Music For Nations 12KUT 109	Animal (Fuck Like A Beast)/Show No Mercy (12", gold vinyl, U.K. issue pressed in France)	35
84	Music For Nations 12KUT 109	Animal (Fuck Like A Beast)/Show No Mercy (12", white, vinyl, U.K. issue pressed in France)	15
84	Music For Nations 12KUT 109	Animal (Fuck Like A Beast)/Show No Mercy (12", clear vinyl, U.K. issue pressed in France)	20
84	Music For Nations 12KUT 109	Animal (Fuck Like A Beast)/Show No Mercy (12", red vinyl, U.K. issue pressed in France)	15
84	Capitol CLP 336	I Wanna Be Somebody/Tormentor (Rageways) (p/s)	5
84	Capitol 12 CLP 336	I Wanna Be Somebody/Tormentor (Rageways) (12", picture disc)	15
84	Capitol CL 344	Schooldaze/Paint It Black (poster p/s)	8
84	Capitol 12 CL 344	Schooldaze/Paint It Black (12", p/s)	8
85	Capitol CLP 374	Blind In Texas/Savage (shaped picture disc)	6
86	Capitol CLD 388	Wild Child/Mississippi Queen/On Your Knees/Hellion (double pack)	5
86	Capitol 12CL 388	Wild Child/Mississippi Queen (12", p/s)	8
89	Capitol CLPD 546	Forever Free (Eagle Edit)/L.O.V.E. Machine (Live '89) (die-cut pic. disc)	6
86	Capitol CLP 432	9.5 N.A.S.T.Y./Easy Living (shaped picture disc)	6

WASPS

77	4-Play FOUR 001	Teenage Treats/She Made More Magic (p/s)	25
77	NEMS NES 115	Can't Wait 'Til '78/MEAN STREET: Bunch Of Stiffs (p/s)	18
78	RCA PB 5137	Rubber Cars/This Time (p/s)	10

WASTE

| 86 | Morterhate MORT 21 | NOT JUST SOMETHING TO BE SUNG (EP, foldout p/s) | 25 |

WASTED YOUTH

80	Bridge House BHS 5	Jealousy/Baby (p/s, clear vinyl)	5
82	Bridge House BHFNEE 1	Caveman (1-sided, limited issue)	8
80	Bridge House BHLP006	WILD AND WANDERING (LP)	12
82	Bridge House BHLP007	THE BEGINNING OF THE END (LP, with free 'Caveman 7", 5000 only)	12

WASTELAND

| 79 | Ellie Jay/Disaster EJSP 9261 | WANT NOT EP (p/s, 2,000 only) | 30 |
| 80 | Invicta INV 014 | Friends, Romans, Countrymen/Leave Me Alone (p/s, 1,000 only) | 30 |

WATCH COMMITTEE

| 68 | Philips BF 1695 | Throw Another Penny In The Well/Now I Think The Other Way | 6 |

WATERBOYS

| 00 | Burning Airlines | THE LIVE ADVENTURES OF THE WATERBOYS (2xCD) | 20 |

WATERFALL

76	Bob FRR 001	FLIGHT OF THE DAY (LP, private pressing)	100
79	Avada AVA 104	THREE BIRDS (LP, with insert)	22
81	Gun Dog GUN 003LP	BENEATH THE STARS (LP, private pressing)	22

WATER FOR A THIRSTY LAND

| 74 | MRA P 100 | WATER FOR A THIRSTY LAND (LP, with insert) | 22 |

WATER INTO WINE BAND

| 73 | Myrrh MYR 1004 | HILL CLIMBING FOR BEGINNERS (LP, brown cover, with insert) | 150 |

| 73 | Myrrh MYR 1004 | HILL CLIMBING FOR BEGINNERS (LP, white cover, with insert) | 100 |
| 76 | CJT 002 | HARVEST TIME (LP, private pressing, 500 copies) | 100 |

WATER PISTOLS
| 76 | State STATE 38 | Gimme That Punk Junk/Soft Punk (p/s, with insert) | 10 |

WATERPROOF CANDLE
| 68 | RCA RCA 1717 | Electrically Heated Child/Saturday Morning Repentance | 15 |

ETHEL WATERS
| 66 | World Record Club T 949 | ETHEL WATERS (LP) | 12 |

(see also Ida Cox)

MUDDY WATERS
53	Vogue V 2101	Walkin' Blues/Rollin' Stone Blues (78)	80
54	Vogue V 2273	Hello Little Girl/Long Distance Call (78)	80
55	Vogue V 2372	Honey Bee/Too Young To Know (78)	80
65	Chess CRS 8001	My John The Conquer Root/Short Dress Woman	20
65	Chess CRS 8019	I Got A Rich Man's Woman/My Dog Can't Bark	15
69	Chess CRS 8083	Let's Spend The Night Together/I'm A Man	15
69	Python PKM 04	Country Boy/All Night Long (99 copies only)	85
55	Vogue EPV 1046	MUDDY WATERS WITH LITTLE WALTER (EP)	150
56	London RU-E 1060	MISSISSIPPI BLUES (EP)	175
63	Pye Intl. NEP 44010	MUDDY WATERS (EP)	40
65	Chess CRE 6006	I'M READY (EP)	55
66	Chess CRE 6022	THE REAL FOLK BLUES VOL. 4 (EP)	45
59	London Jazz LJZ-M 15152	THE BEST OF MUDDY WATERS (LP)	100
61	Pye Jazz NJL 34	AT NEWPORT (LP)	75
64	Pye Intl. NPL 28038	MUDDY WATERS - FOLK SINGER (LP)	55
64	Pye Intl. NPL 28040	THE BEST OF MUDDY WATERS (LP)	65
64	Pye Intl. NPL 28048	MUDDY SINGS BIG BILL (LP)	35
65	Chess CRL 4513	AT NEWPORT (LP, reissue)	40
66	Chess CRL 4515	THE REAL FOLK BLUES (LP)	30
67	Chess CRL 4525	MUDDY, BRASS AND THE BLUES (LP)	35
67	Chess CRL 4529	SUPER BLUES (LP, with Little Walter & Bo Diddley)	40
68	Chess CRL 4537	THE SUPER SUPER BLUES BAND (LP, with Howlin' Wolf & Bo Diddley)	50
68	Bounty BY 6031	DOWN ON STOVALL'S PLANTATION (LP)	35
69	Chess CRL 4542	ELECTRIC MUD (LP)	30
69	Chess CRL 4553	AFTER THE RAIN (LP)	25
69	Chess CRL 4556	FATHERS AND SONS (LP)	25
69	Polydor 236 574	BLUES MAN (LP)	25
69	Python PLP 12	MUDDY WATERS (LP, 99 copies only)	80
69	Python PLP 18	MUDDY WATERS VOLUME 2 (LP, 99 copies only)	80
69	Python PLP 19	MUDDY WATERS VOLUME 3 (LP, 99 copies only)	80
70	Syndicate Chapter SC 001/2	BACK IN THE EARLY DAYS (2-LP)	25
70	Syndicate Chapter SC 002	GOOD NEWS (LP)	20
70	Sunnyland KS 100	VINTAGE MUDDY WATERS (LP, gatefold sleeve with inserts, 99 copies only)	45
71	Chess 6671 001	McKINLEY MORGANFIELD AKA MUDDY WATERS (LP)	20
72	Black Bear LP 901	RARE LIVE RECORDINGS VOL. 1 (LP)	20
72	Black Bear LP 902	RARE LIVE RECORDINGS VOL. 2 (LP)	20
72	Black Bear LP 903	RARE LIVE RECORDINGS VOL. 3 (LP)	20
72	Chess 6310 121	THE LONDON SESSIONS (LP)	15
74	Chess 6310 129	CAN'T GET NO GRINDIN' (LP)	12
77	Blue Sky SKY 81853	HARD AGAIN (LP)	15

(see also Little Walter, Howlin' Wolf, Bo Diddley, Luther 'Georgia Boy Snake' Johnson)

ROGER WATERS
84	Harvest HAR 5228	5.01 AM (The Pros And Cons Of Hitch-Hiking)/ 4.30 AM (Apparently They Were Travelling Abroad) (p/s)	5
84	Harvest 12HAR 5228	5.01 AM (The Pros And Cons Of Hitch-Hiking)/4.33 AM (Apparently They Were Travelling Abroad)/4.33 AM (Running Shoes) (12", p/s)	8
84	Harvest HAR 5230	5.06 AM (Every Stranger's Eyes)/4.39 AM (For The First Time Today) (p/s)	15
87	EMI EM 6	Radio Waves/Going To Live In L.A. (Demo) (p/s)	6
87	EMI CDEM 6	Radio Waves (Remix)/Going To Live In L.A. (Demo)/ Radio Waves (7" Version) (CD)	10
87	EMI EM 20	Sunset Strip/Money (live) (withdrawn)	50
87	EMI EM 37	The Tide Is Turning (After Live Aid)/Money ('live') (p/s)	5
87	EMI CDEM 37	The Tide Is Turning (After Live Aid)/Money ('live')/Get Back To Radio (Demo Recording) (CD)	10
90	Mercury 878 147-2	PIECES FROM THE WALL: Another Brick In The Wall Part 2 (Edit)/Young Lust (Edit)/Run Like Hell/In The Flesh? (CD, promo only)	20
92	Columbia 658 139 9	What God Wants Part I (Video Edit)/What God Wants Part I (Album Version)/ What God Wants Part III (CD, box set with prints)	12
70	Harvest SHSP 4008	MUSIC FROM THE FILM "THE BODY" (LP, with Ron Geesin, green labels, with Waters/Geesin photos)	50
70	Harvest SHSP 4008	MUSIC FROM THE FILM "THE BODY" (LP, with Ron Geesin, black labels)	12
87	EMI KAOS DJ 1	RADIO KAOS (LP, 'banded' radio promo, custom sleeve)	30

(see also Pink Floyd, Ron Geesin)

LAL & MIKE WATERSON
72	Trailer LES 2076	BRIGHT PHOEBUS (LP, original pressing, red/black label)	40
73	Trailer LER 2076	BRIGHT PHOEBUS (LP, second pressing, yellow label)	35
82	Highway	BRIGHT PHOEBUS (LP, reissue)	20

LAL AND NORMA WATERSON
| 77 | Topic 12TS331 | A TRUE HEARTED GIRL (LP) | 20 |

(see also Watersons)

MIKE WATERSON
| 77 | Topic 12TS 332 | MIKE WATERSON (LP) | 20 |

(see also Waterson, Lal & Mike Waterson)

WATERSONS
65	Topic 12T 125	NEW VOICES (LP, blue label, with Harry Boardman & Maureen Craik)	18
65	Topic 12T 136	FROST AND FIRE (LP, blue label)	18
66	Topic 12T 142	WATERSONS (LP, blue label)	18
66	Topic 12T 167	A YORKSHIRE GARLAND (LP, blue label)	18

MINT VALUE £

60s	Topic TS 346	THE WATERSONS SOUND (LP)	15

GEORGE WATKINS
69	NEMS 56-3861	The Fly/Barrer Boy Blues	7

DILYS WATLING
64	Philips BF 1305	Don't Say You Love Me/Now's The Time	5
65	Philips BF 1393	I'm Over You/Act Like A Lady	5

DOC WATSON
64	Fontana TFL 6045	DOC WATSON (LP)	22
65	Fontana TFL 6055	DOC WATSON & SON (LP)	20
72	Vanguard VSD 9/10	ON STAGE (2-LP)	20

EARL WATSON
61	Ember EMB S 129	Nightmare/That Old Black Magic	10

JOHN L. WATSON (& HUMMELFLUGS)
64	Pye 7N 15746	Looking For Love/Dance With You	12
65	Piccadilly 7N 35233	Standing By/I'll Make It Worth Your While	10
70	Deram DM-R 285	A Mother's Love/Might As Well Be Gone (solo)	12
70	Deram SML 1061	WHITE HOT BLUE BLACK (LP)	40

(see also Web)

JOHNNY WATSON & KAMPAI KINGS
60	Oriole CB 1532	Moshi, Moshi, Anone!/ABDULLA & HIS LITTLE BAND: Fatima's Theme	5
60	Oriole CB 1532	Moshi, Moshi, Anone!/ABDULLA & HIS LITTLE BAND: Fatima's Theme (78)	30

PAULA WATSON
63	Oriole 45-CV1785	Love Me Forever/Tell All The World About You	20

ROGER WATSON
74	Tradition TSR 017	THE PICK AND THE MALT SHOVEL (LP)	15

WAH WAH WATSON
76	CBS 81582	ELEMENTARY (LP)	12

BEN WATT
81	Cherry Red CHERRY 25	Can't/Aubade/Tower Of Silence (p/s)	8
82	Cherry Red 12CHERRY 36	SUMMER INTO WINTER (12" EP, with Robert Wyatt, p/s)	10

(see also Everything But The Girl)

WATTS
73	Jam JAM 38	Girl You Make It Easy/Betsy Balou	5

CHARLIE WATTS
93	Continuum CDCTUM 103	My Ship/You Got To Me Head (CD)	12
86	CBS 450 253-1	LIVE AT FULHAM TOWN HALL (LP, as Charlie Watts & His Orchestra, with insert)	15
91	UFO UFO CD	FROM ONE CHARLIE (CD box set with book & Charlie Parker photo, signed)	40
91	UFO UFO CD	FROM ONE CHARLIE (CD box set with book & Charlie Parker photo, unsigned)	20
91	UFO UFO 2 LP	FROM ONE CHARLIE (10" LP, box set with book & Charlie Parker photo, signed)	50
91	UFO UFO 2 LP	FROM ONE CHARLIE (10" LP, box set with book & Charlie Parker photo, unsigned)	20

(see also Rolling Stones, People Band, Rocket 88)

NOBLE 'THIN MAN' WATTS (& HIS BAND)
57	London HLU 8627	Hard Times (The Slop)/Midnight Flight (with His Rhythm Sparks)	75
57	London HLU 8627	Hard Times (The Slop)/Midnight Flight (with His Rhythm Sparks) (78)	20
64	Sue WI 347	Noble's Theme/JUNE BATEMAN: I Don't Wanna	70
79	Flyright 547	BLAST OFF (LP, mono)	20

(see also Wild Jimmy Spurrill)

QUEENIE WATTS
66	Columbia SX 6047	QUEEN HIGH (LP)	30

TREVOR WATTS
78	Ogun OG 526	CYNOSURE (LP)	20

WATUSI WARRIORS
59	London HL 8866	Wa-Chi-Bam-Ba/Kalahari	15

ASHANTI WAUGH
80	Attack TACK 20	Babylon Wrong/BARRY BROWN: Cool Pun Yu Corner (12")	20

WAVING AT TRAINS
80s		WAVING AT TRAINS (EP)	30

(see also Playing At Trains)

WAX DOCTOR
92	Basement BRSS 011	A New Direction/Herbal Tekno/Protplasm (12")	15
93	Basement BRSS 018	Another Direction/The Stalker (12")	10
93	Basement BRSS 027	New Direction (93 Remix)/What's Goin' On (12", with Jack Smooth)	15
93	Basement BRSS 030	Unfriendly/Rock To The Groove (12", with Jack Smooth)	12
94	Face FACE 106	Logical Profession (Logical Mix)/Logical Progression (12")	8

(see also Kev Bird)

WAXIES DARGLE
69	Polydor S83080	HARBOUR FOLK (LP)	25

NANCY WAYBURN
65	Warner Bros WB 5646	The World Goes On Without Me/Listen To My Heart	15

WAYGOOD ELLIS
67	Polydor 56729	I Like What I'm Trying To Do/Hey Lover	50

(see also Fleur-De-Lys)

ALVIS WAYNE
63	Starlite ST45 104	Don't Mean Maybe, Baby/I'd Rather Be With You	600
73	Injun 113	I Gottum/Lay Your Head On My Shoulder	10

ARTIE WAYNE
52	London L 1164	Rachel/Tonight Or Never (78)	12

BOBBY WAYNE

51	London L 924	When The Wind Was Green/Buffalo Billy (78)	10
51	London L 968	Immaculate Mother/Mother At Your Feet Is Kneeling (78)	10
51	London L 972	Runnin' Around/Always You (78)	10
51	London L 973	Wild Card/Let Me In (78)	10
51	London L 1077	I Am Free/How Long Is Forever (78)	10
51	London L 1078	If You Turn Me Down/Let's Make Up Your Mind (78)	10

(see also Teresa Brewer)

BOBBY WAYNE

65	Pye International 7N 25315	Ballad Of A Teenage Queen/River Man	10

CARL WAYNE (& VIKINGS)

64	Pye 7N 15702	What's A Matter Baby/Your Loving Ways (as Carl Wayne & Vikings)	50
65	Pye 7N 15824	This Is Love/You Could Be Fun (as Carl Wayne & Vikings)	40
70	RCA RCA 2032	Maybe God's Got Something Up His Sleeve/Rosanna	6
72	RCA RCA 2177	Imagine/Sunday Kind Of Love	5
72	RCA RCA 2257	Take My Hands For A While/Sweet Seasons	5
73	Pye 7N 45290	You're A Star/Bluebird	5
75	Polydor 2058 527	Way Back In The Fifties/Candy (You Know That I'm In Love With You)	6
77	Target TGT 125	A Little Give, A Little Take/Home Lovin' Man	6
77	DJM DJS Weeken 10797	Hi Summer/My Girl And Me	6
72	RCA SF 8239	CARL WAYNE (LP)	20

(see also Move, Ace Kefford Stand, Cheetahs, Acid Gallery, Keith Powell [& Valets])

CHRIS WAYNE & ECHOES

60	Decca F 11231	Lonely/Counting Girls	15

JEFF WAYNE

69	Columbia S(C)X 6330	TWO CITIES (LP, soundtrack)	35

(see also Ran-Dells)

JERRY WAYNE

60	Vogue V 9169	Half-Hearted Love/Ten Thousand Miles	25

JOHN WAYNE

73	RCA PL 13484	AMERICA, WHY I LOVE HER (LP)	15

PAT WAYNE (& BEACHCOMBERS)

63	Columbia DB 7121	Go Back To Daddy/Jambalaya	20
63	Columbia DB 7182	Roll Over Beethoven/Is It Love?	25
64	Columbia DB 7262	Bye Bye Johnny/Strictly For The Birds	25
64	Columbia DB 7417	Brand New Man/Nobody's Child	20
65	Columbia DB 7603	Come Dance With Me/I Don't Want To Cry (solo)	12
65	Columbia DB 7739	My Friend/Tomorrow Mine (solo)	10
66	Columbia DB 7944	The Night Is Over/Hombre (solo)	12

RICK WAYNE

94	Pathway To Freedom R+R 002	Almighty Father/Bad Behaviour (12")	80

RICK(Y) WAYNE (& OFF-BEATS)

60	Triumph RGM 1009	Chick A'Roo/Don't Pick On Me (with Fabulous Flee-Rakkers)	50
60	Pye 7N 15289	Make Way Baby/Goodness Knows (as Ricky Wayne & Off-Beats)	45
65	Oriole CB 306	Say You're Gonna Be My Own/It's A Crying Shame (as Rick Wayne)	20
65	CBS 201764	In My Imagination/Don't Ever Share Your Love (as Rick Wayne)	15

(see also [Fabulous] Flee-Rekkers)

TERRY WAYNE

57	Columbia DB 4002	Matchbox/Your True Love	25
57	Columbia DB 4035	Plaything/Slim Jim Tie	25
57	Columbia DB 4035	Plaything/Slim Jim Tie (78 rpm = £10)	10
58	Columbia DB 4067	All Mama's Children/Forgive Me	25
58	Columbia DB 4067	All Mama's Children/Forgive Me (78 rpm = £10)	10
58	Columbia DB 4112	Oh! Lonesome Me/There's Only One You	20
58	Columbia DB 4112	Oh! Lonesome Me/There's Only One You (78 rpm = £12)	12
58	Columbia DB 4205	Little Brother/Where My Baby Goes	18
58	Columbia DB 4205	Little Brother/Where My Baby Goes (78 rpm = £15)	15
59	Columbia DB 4312	Brooklyn Bridge/She's Mine	20
58	Columbia SEG 7758	TERRIFIC (EP)	80

THOMAS WAYNE

59	London HLU 8846	Tragedy/Saturday Date	35
59	London HLU 8846	Tragedy/Saturday Date (78)	25
59	London HL 7075	Tragedy/Saturday Date (export issue)	20

WAYS & MEANS

66	Columbia DB 7907	Little Deuce Coupe/The Little Old Lady From Pasadena	25
66	Pye 7N 17217	Sea Of Faces/Make The Radio A Little Louder	25
68	Trend TRE 1005	Breaking Up A Dream/She	60

WAY WE LIVE

71	Dandelion DAN 8004	A CANDLE FOR JUDITH (LP, gatefold sleeve, label and sleeve DAN 8004)	125
71	Dandelion DAN 8004	A CANDLE FOR JUDITH (LP, gatefold sleeve, as K 49004)	60

(see also Tractor, Beau)

WAZMO NARIZ

78	Stiff BUY 33	Tele-tele-phone/Wacker Drive (blue label, push-out centre)	8
78	Stiff BUY 33	Tele-tele-phone/Wacker Drive (red label, push-out centre)	5

WBI RED NINJA

90	Red Ninja SRT90LS 2532	Danger Zone/This Mike's For Hire/Bad Testament (12")	15
91	Red Ninja RN002	HELLZ A PLACE I KNOW (EP)	8

WE'RE ONLY HUMAN

82	VC VC 002	I Wouldn't Treat A Dog/Hold Your Head Up High (no p/s, 500 only)	40

WEAPON

80	Weapon WEAP 1	It's A Mad Mad World/Set The Stage Alight (p/s)	30

MINT VALUE £

81   Virgin WEAPONE   It's A Mad Mad World/Set The Stage Alight (12", p/s, reissue) 40
(see also Wildfire)

WEASELSNOUT
72   Weaselsnout WUS 140   UNSUNG LIES (LP, private pressing) 150

WEATHER
69   Philips BF 1734   Look In My Eyes/Running Forward 35
69   Philips BF 1819   Jamboree Special/Two Peculiar People 10

WEATHER REPORT
85   Nimbus 80027   MYSTERIOUS TRAVELLER (LP, Nimbus Supercut, mail order only through Practical Hi Fi magazine) 40

ALFIE WEATHERBY
58   Columbia DC 729   49 Juke Boxes/Why Am I Crying? (78, export issue) 20

OSCAR WEATHERS
72   Mojo 2092 006   The Spoiler/You Want To Play 15

VIVIAN WEATHERS
79   Island 12WIP6529   Just A Game/Cheat Heart Dub/Married Woman/Wounded Dub (12", p/s).....................8

DENNIS WEAVER
77   DJM DJS 10758   Devil In My Arms/Flat Bed Truck (p/s, promo) 8

JANE WEAVER V DOVES
98   Manchester MANC 9   Seven Day Smile/ANDY VOTEL & JANE WEAVER: Gutter Girl (p/s) 6
(see also Doves)

WEAVERS
59   Top Rank JAR 120   Wild Goose Grasses/Meet The Johnson Boys 6
(see also Pete Seeger)

WEB (1)
68   Deram DM 201   Hatton Mill Morning/Conscience 25
68   Deram DM 217   Baby Won't You Leave Me Alone/McVernon Street...25
69   Deram DM 253   Monday To Friday/Harold Dubbleyew 25
68   Deram SML 1025   FULLY INTERLOCKING (LP) 90
70   Deram DAL-R 1058   THERAPHOSA BLONDI (LP, mono)...120
70   Deram SML-R 1058   THERAPHOSA BLONDI (LP, stereo)...90
70   Polydor 2383 024   I SPIDER (LP, gatefold sleeve, red label) 350
(see also John L. Watson [& Hummelflugs], Samurai, Greenslade)

WEB (2)
96   Fat Cat 12FAT 001   EVA EP (12", plain sleeve) 20

BARRY WEBB (O.P.M.C)
70   Decca F 23012   Live For Tomorrow Harry James/At The Hop 8

DEAN WEBB
59   Parlophone R 4549   Warm Your Heart/Hey Miss Fannie 50
59   Parlophone R 4587   The Rough And The Smooth/Streamline Baby...50

DON WEBB
60   Coral Q 72385   Little Ditty Baby/I'll Be Back Home 100

GEORGE WEBB DIXIELANDERS
56   Decca DFE 6351   AND HIS DIXIELANDERS (EP) 10
50s Melodisc EPM7 70   THE GEORGE WEBB DIXIELANDERS (EP) 10

JANET WEBB
71   Polydor 2058-131   I Cried For You/Mama (p/s)...10

JILLA WEBB
56   MGM SP 1180   You Gotta Love Me Now/What Do You Think It Does To Me? 10

JIM(MY) WEBB
68   CBS 3672   I Keep It Hid/I Need You (as Jim Webb) 25
71   Reprise RS 20978   P.F. Sloan/Psalm One-Five-O 10
73   Reprise K 14279   Campo De Encino/Once In The Morning 5
68   CBS (S) 63335   JIM WEBB SINGS JIM WEBB (LP, as Jim Webb, laminated front cover) 25
71   Reprise RSLP 6421   WORDS AND MUSIC (LP, with insert)...20
71   Reprise K 44101   WORDS AND MUSIC (LP, reissue) 15
72   Reprise K 44134   AND SO ON (LP) 18
72   Reprise K 44173   LETTERS (LP) 15
74   Asylum SYL 9014   LAND'S END (LP, with inner sleeve) 15
77   Atlantic K 50370   EL MIRAGE (LP, with inner sleeve) 15
(see also Strawberry Children, Glen Campbell)

JOHNNY WEBB
56   Columbia DB 3805   Dig/Glendora 10
60s Melodisc MEL 1617   Travelin' Man/Hold Back The Town (with p/s) 12
60s Melodisc MEL 1617   Travelin' Man/Hold Back The Town 5
(see also June Laverick)

PETA WEBB
73   Topic 12TS 223   I HAVE WANDERED IN EXILE (LP, blue label) 35
(see also Oak)

PETA WEBB & PETE COOPER
86   Heart   HEART IS TRUE (LP) 15

ROGER WEBB (& HIS TRIO)
67   RCA 1599   A Man And His Woman/The Spiderman 30
71   Columbia DB 8803   Strange Report/Summer Fancy 12
82   Chandos SBR 102   The Gentle Touch/Arthur's Theme 6
84   Chips CH 104   Hammer House Of Horror/Cover Theme (p/s) 12
64   Parlophone PMC 1233   JOHN, PAUL AND ALL THAT JAZZ (LP) 18

SKEETER WEBB
55	Parlophone CMSP 32	Was It A Bad Dream/Your Secret's Not A Secret Anymore (export issue)	15

SONNY WEBB & CASCADES
64	Oriole CB 1873	You've Got Everything/Border Of The Blues	45
64	Polydor NH 52158	You've Got Everything/Border Of The Blues (reissue)	15

A J WEBBER
80	Gundog GUN 002	OF THIS LAND (LP)	30

MARLENE WEBBER
70	Bamboo BAM 33	My Baby/BRENTFORD ALLSTARS: You Gonna Hold Me (Version)	20
71	Ackee ACK 120	Natengula/Natengula-Kera (as Merlin Webber)	8
71	Ackee ACK 122	Cumbaya/Hail-Hi Freedom (as Merlin Webber)	8
71	Smash SMA 2322	Hard Life/COLLINS ALL STARS: Version Life (as Merlene Webber)	10
71	Trojan TR 7815	Stand By Your Man/CLANCY ECCLES: Credit Squeeze	8

(see also Webber Sisters, Tonettes)

WEBBER SISTERS
67	Island WI 3109	My World/ALVA LEWIS: Lonely Still	60

(see also Delroy Wilson)

WEBBY JAY
79	Awawak DD 008	In The Rain/Rain Unlimited (12")	20

WEBS
68	London HLU 10188	This Thing Called Love/Tomorrow	25

WEBSPINNERS
73	Buddah 2011 150	Spider Man - Theme/Goin' 'Cross Town	6

BEN WEBSTER
55	Columbia CLEF 33CX 10014	MUSIC FOR LOVERS (LP)	20
59	HMV CLP 1336	BEN WEBSTER AND ASSOCIATES (LP)	20
65	Fontana FJL 126	INTIMATE! (LP)	20
69	Ember CJS 822	BEN WEBSTER AT EASE (LP)	12
70	Fontana FJL 316	BIG BEN TIME (LP)	18
72	Philips 6308 101	WEBSTER'S DICTIONARY (LP)	20

CHASE WEBSTER
64	Hickory 45-1283	Life Can Have Meaning/Where Is Your Heart	6

DEENA WEBSTER
68	Parlophone R 5699	You're Losing/Wish You Were Here	20
68	Parlophone R 5721	Your Heart Is Free Just Like The Wind/Queen Merka And Me	20
68	Parlophone R 5738	Scarborough Fair/The Water Is Wide	20
69	Parlophone R 5798	Joey/It's Alright With Me	20
68	Parlophone PMC/PCS 7052	TUESDAY'S CHILD (LP)	175

MAX WEBSTER (BAND)
78	Capitol EST 11776	MEETING UP MY SLEEVE (LP)	12
79	Capitol EST 11937	A MILLION VACATIONS (LP)	12
80	Mercury 6337 144	UNIVERSAL JUVENILES (LP)	12

(see also Rush)

WEDDING PRESENT
85	Reception REC 001	Go Out And Get 'Em Boy/(The Moment Before) Everything's Spoiled Again (p/s, 500 only, with poster & badge)	25
85	Reception REC 001	Go Out And Get 'Em Boy/(The Moment Before) Everything's Spoiled Again (p/s, 500 only, without poster & badge)	18
85	City Slang CSL 001	Go Out And Get 'Em Boy/(The Moment Before) Everything's Spoiled Again (reissue, different foldout p/s, 1,000 only)	10
86	Reception REC 002	Once More/At The Edge Of The Sea (p/s, 3,500 only)	8
86	Reception REC 002/12	DON'T TRY AND STOP ME MOTHER (12" EP, combines REC 001 & 002)	8
86	Reception REC 003	This Boy Can Wait/You Should Always Keep In Touch With Your Friends (p/s, matrix numbers: 003 A2 & 003 B1)	6
86	Reception REC 003	This Boy Can Wait/You Should Always Keep In Touch With Your Friends (p/s, mispress both sides play B-side, matrix numbers: 003 A1 & 003 A2)	5
86	Reception REC 003/12	This Boy Can Wait (Extended)/You Should Always Keep In Touch With Your Friends/Living And Learning (12", p/s)	8
87	Reception REC 005	My Favourite Dress/Every Mother's Son/Never Said (p/s, white vinyl, 3,000 only, 2,000 of which free with "George Best" LP)	6
87	Reception	A Million Miles/What Did Your Last Servant Die Of? (DJ promo, 200 only)	25
88	Reception REC 010X	Davni Chasy/Katrusya (promo only)	6
88	House Of Dolls HOD 004	Unfaithful (Peel Session)/TRUDY: Living On A Moon/HUNTERS CLUB: Little Sister/CLAYTOWN TROUPE: Real Life (free with House Of Dolls mag)	5
89	M'night Music DONG 39 CD	Pourquoi Es Tu Devenue Si Raisonable? (CD, unreleased)	0
89	RCA	Davni Chasy/Katrusya (promo only)	12
90	RCA PB 43403	Brassneck/Don't Talk, Just Kiss (custom hand-painted p/s, 3,000 only)	20
92	RCA PB 45185	Blue Eyes/Cattle And Cane (p/s)	7
92	RCA PB 45183	Go Go Dancer/Don't Cry No Tears (p/s)	6
92	RCA PB 45181	Three/Think That It Might (p/s)	6
92	RCA PB 45311	Silver Shorts/Falling (p/s)	6
92	RCA PB 45313	Come Play With Me/Pleasant Valley Sunday (p/s)	6
92	RCA No Cat. No.	HIT PARADE (12 x 7" in custom box)	40
87	Reception LEEDS 1	GEORGE BEST (LP, 2,000 only with white vinyl 7": My Favourite Dress/ Every Mother's Son/Never Said [REC 005] & inner sleeve; later with bonus black vinyl 7" or 12" edition, £10)	20
88	Reception LEEDS 2	TOMMY (LP, 1,000 signed by band, with poster & inner sleeve)	18
91	RCA PL 75012	SEAMONSTERS (LP, inner)	12
94	RCA 8014524-044-1	WATUSI (LP, inner)	25
96	Cooking Vinyl COOK 099	SATURNALIA (LP, 2 x 10")	20

WEDGE
69	Midas MD3904	Sleep Child/Fly Away	25

WEDGEWOODS
64	Pye 7N 15642	September In The Rain/Gone Gone Away	12
65	Pye 7N 15846	Peace/Summer Love	10

MINT VALUE £

68	Columbia DB 8459	Red Sky At Night/When Day Is Done	15

WEE CHERUBS
84	Bogaten	Dreaming /Waiting For My Man (p/s, 400 only)	175

WEE THREE
73	People PEO 104	Get On Board/Get On Board (Instrumental)	8

WEE WILLIE & WINNERS
74	Action ACT 4624	Get Some/A Plan For The Man	8
74	People PEO 116	I Don't Know What You Got But I Know What I Need (Parts 1 & 2)	8

BUDDY WEED & HIS ORCHESTRA
57	Vogue V 9075	The Kent Song/For Love	25

BERT WEEDON
56	Parlophone MSP 6242	The Boy With The Magic Guitar/Flannel-Foot	20
57	Parlophone R 4256	Theme From ITV's '$64,000 Question'/Twilight Time	20
57	Parlophone R 4315	The Jolly Gigolo/Soho Fair	20
57	Parlophone R 4381	Play That Big Guitar/Quiet, Quiet, Ssh!	10
58	Parlophone R 4446	Big Note Blues/Rippling Tango	10
59	Saga SAG 2906	Fifi/Cat On A Hot Tin Roof (as Bert Weedon & Rag Pickers)	5
59	Top Rank JAR 117	Guitar Boogie Shuffle/Bert's Boogie	5
59	Top Rank JAR 121	Sing Little Birdie/The Lady Is A Tramp	5
59	Top Rank JAR 122	Petite Fleur/My Happiness	5
59	Top Rank JAR 123	Charmaine/It's Time To Say Goodnight	5
59	Top Rank JAR 136	Teenage Guitar/Blue Guitar	5
59	Top Rank JAR 210	Jealousy/Tango, Tango	5
59	Top Rank JAR 211	Stardust/Summertime	5
59	Top Rank JAR 221	Nashville Boogie/King Size Guitar	5
60	Top Rank JAR 300	Big Beat Boogie/Theme From 'A Summer Place' (with p/s)	8
60	Top Rank JAR 300	Big Beat Boogie/Theme From 'A Summer Place'	5
60	Top Rank JAR 360	Twelfth Street Rag/Querida	7
60	Top Rank JAR 415	Apache/Lonely Guitar	7
60	Top Rank JAR 517	Sorry Robbie/Easy Beat	10
61	Top Rank JAR 537	Ginchy/Yearning	7
61	Top Rank JAR 559	Mr. Guitar/Eclipse	10
56	Esquire EP 56	WAXING THE WINNERS (EP)	25
59	Selmer Amplifiers	DEMONSTRATION RECORD WITH DAVID GELL (EP, with mailer)	20
59	Selmer Amplifiers	DEMONSTRATION RECORD WITH DAVID GELL (EP, without mailer)	10
61	Top Rank JKP 3008	WEEDON WINNERS (EP)	10
64	HMV 7EG 8856	GUITAR MAN (EP)	10
60	Top Rank BUY 026	KINGSIZE GUITAR (LP)	30
61	Top Rank 35/101	HONKY TONK GUITAR (LP)	30

(see also George Chisholm, Craig Douglas, Ragpickers)

WEEDS
86	In Tape IT 34	China Doll/Crazy Face (p/s)	12

WEEKENDERS
94	Blow Up (Blow UP BU 001)	All Grown Up/House Husband (mail-order only)	10

WEEN
94	Flying Nun FN31	CHOCOLATE & CHEESE (2-LP with free 7")	35
97	Mushroom MUSH 3LP	THE MOLLUSK (LP, inner)	40

WEENY BOPPERS
72	Pye 45203	David, Donny & Michael/Won't You Smile For Me	8

WEEZER
94	Geffen GFS 85	Undone: The Sweater Song/Mykel And Carli/Susanne/Holiday (blue vinyl, p/s)	20
94	Geffen GFSCD 85	Undone: The Sweater Song/Mykel And Carli/Susanne/Holiday (CD)	15
95	Geffen GFS 88	Buddy Holly/Jamie (p/s)	20
95	Geffen GFSV 95	Say It Ain't So (Remix)/No One Else (Live & Acoustic)/Jamie (10", p/s)	10
96	Geffen GFS 22167	El Scorcho/You Gave Your Love To Me Softly (p/s)	15
01	Geffen 497567-7	Hash Pipe/Teenage Victory Song (p/s)	10
01	Geffen 497616-7	Island In The Sun/Always (p/s, yellow vinyl)	10
02	Geffen 497771-7	Keep Fishin'/Photograph (live) (p/s)	8
05	Geffen 9881793	Beverley Hills/Butterfly (live) (picture disc, stickered PVC sleeve)	5
05	Geffen 9883498	We Are All On Drugs/Beverley Hills (Urbanix Mix) (p/s, pink vinyl)	5
95	Geffen GEF 24629	WEEZER (LP)	20

WE FIVE
65	Pye International 7N 25314	You Were On My Mind/Small World	12
66	Pye International 7N 25346	Let's Get Together/Cast Your Fate To The Wind	20
66	Pye Intl. NEP 44056	LET'S GET TOGETHER (EP)	60
65	Pye Intl. NPL 28067	YOU WERE ON MY MIND (LP)	60

WE 4
67	HMV POP 1603	Pretty Flowers/I'll Make You A Miracle	5
69	Major Minor MM 593	Candy Floss Man/Perry Park	6

BOB WEIR
72	Warner Bros WB 7611	One More Saturday Night/Cassidy	5
72	Warner Bros K 46165	ACE (LP)	12

(see also Grateful Dead, Kingfish, Bobby & Midnites)

FRANK WEIR & HIS ORCHESTRA
54	Decca F 10271	The Happy Wanderer/From Your Lips	10
60	Oriole CB 1559	Caribbean Honeymoon/Farewell My Love	10
62	Philips 326560 BF	Manhunt/Chant Of The Jungle	5
55	Decca DFE 6226	THE HAPPY WANDERER (EP)	10

(see also Bill Darnell, Vera Lynn, Janie Marden)

NORRIS WEIR (& JAMAICANS)
70	Duke DU 85	Hard On Me (with Jamaicans)/TOMMY COWAN & JAMAICANS: Please Stop The Wedding	6
74	Dragon DRA 1030	Reggay Revolution/Version	5
75	Horse HOSS 81	Dr. Honey/Honey Dub	5

(see also Jamaicans)

WEIRD STRINGS
80	Velvet Moon VM 1	Oscar Mobile/Ancient Square (foldover p/s)	10
80	Ace ACE 009	Criminal Cage/Mi££ionaire (p/s)	8

(see also Paul Roland, Midnight Rags)o

FRANK WEISS
71	Stax 2362 011	WEISS TO MEMPHIS (LP)	12

BRUCE WELCH
74	EMI EMI 2141	Please Mr. Please/Song Of Yesterday	50

(see also Marvin, Welch & Farrar; Shadows, Cliff Richard)

ED WELCH
71	United Artists UP35284	Clowns/The Bird Song	10
71	United Artists UAS 29248	CLOWNS (LP, with inner)	15

ELIZABETH WELCH
80	Industrial IR 0012	Stormy Weather/You're Blase (p/s)	8

HONEE WELCH
69	London HLU 10288	I'm Gonna Try/It's My Girl	7

KEN & MITZIE WELCH
62	London RE-R 1275	A PIANO, ICE BOX AND BED (EP)	15

LENNY WELCH
60	London HLA 9094	You Don't Know Me/I Need Someone	6
62	London HLA 9601	Taste Of Honey/Old Cathedral	6
63	London HLA 9810	Since I Fell For You/Are You Sincere	6
64	London HLA 9880	Ebb Tide/Congratulations Baby	6
64	London HLR 9910	If You See My Love/Father Sebastian	6
65	London HLR 9981	Darling Take Me Back/Time After Time	15
65	London HLR 9991	Two Different Worlds/I Was There	8
65	London HLR 10010	Run To My Lovin' Arms/Coronet Blue	20
66	London HLR 10031	Rags To Riches/I Want You To Worry	10
66	London HA-R/SH-R 8267	TWO DIFFERENT WORLDS (LP)	20
66	London HA-R 8290	RAGS TO RICHES (LP)	20

TIM WELCH
60	Columbia DB 4529	Weak In The Knees/A Boy And A Girl In Love	7

WELD OF LIQUOR
95	Weld Record WELD 05	We Are The Weld/For Manze's Sake (vinegar-scented p/s)	10

WELFARE STATE
78	Look LKLP 6347	WELFARE STATE SONGS (LP, with insert)	60

LAWRENCE WELK ORCHESTRA
56	Vogue Coral Q 72140	Chain Gang/The Poor People Of Paris	5
56	Vogue Coral Q 72141	The 'Threepenny Opera' Theme/Rock And Roll Waltz	5
57	Vogue Coral Q 72233	Pizzicato Waltz/Whispering Heart	5
57	Vogue Coral Q 72256	Around The World In 80 Days/Ten Little Trees	5
60	London HLD 9229	Last Date/Remember Lolita	5
61	London HLD 9261	Calcutta (Nicolette)/Melodie D'Amour	5
64	Dot DS 16697	The 'Addams Family' Theme/Apples And Bananas	10
59	Coral LVA 9117	T.V. WESTERN THEME SONGS (LP, as Welk & Champagne Music Makers)	12

PAUL WELLER
SINGLES
92	Go! Discs GOD 86	Uh Huh Oh Yeh/Fly On The Wall (7"; paper or plastic labels)	6
92	Go! Discs GODX 86	Uh Huh Oh Yeh/Arrival Time/Fly On The Wall/Always There To Fool You (12")	8
92	Go! Discs GOD 91	Above The Clouds/Everything Has A Price To Pay (7"; paper or plastic labels)	6
92	Go! Discs GODX 91	Above The Clouds/Everything Has A Price To Pay/All Year Round (Live at New York City The Ritz 25.7.92)/Feeling Alright (12")	8
93	Go! Discs GOD 102	Sunflower/Bull-Rush-Magic Bus (Live at RAH 10.92) (7")	6
93	Go! Discs GOD 104	Wild Wood/Ends Of The Earth (7")	6
93	Go! Discs GODT 104	Wild Wood/Ends Of The Earth (10", numbered with poster)	10
93	Go! Discs GODCD 104	Wild Wood/Ends Of The Earth (CD, Digipak with 5 prints; sealed)	12
93	Go! Discs GODCD 104	Wild Wood/Ends Of The Earth (CD, Digipak with 5 prints; unsealed)	10
93	Go! Discs GODT 107	THE WEAVER EP: The Weaver/This Is No Time/Another New Day/Ohio (Live at Royal Albert Hall 10.92) (10" EP, numbered sticker)	8
93	Go! Discs GODCD 107	THE WEAVER EP: The Weaver/This Is No Time/Another New Day/Ohio (Live at RAH 10.92) (CD EP + postcards, some sealed)	12
93	Go! Discs GODCD 107	THE WEAVER EP: The Weaver/This Is No Time/Another New Day/Ohio (Live at RAH 10.92) (CD EP + postcards, some sealed)	12
93	Matrix: WELLER+F1	The Loved (blank clear flexi with The Big Issue mag)	12
94	Go! Discs GOD 121	Out Of The Sinking/Sexy Sadie/Sunflower (Lynch Mob Dub) (7")	5
00	Island IS 760	He's The Keeper/Helioscentric/Bang-Bang (7", 3rd April 2000)	5
05	V2 VVR 5030597	Early Morning Rain/Come Together (7", red vinyl, die-cut sleeve, 4,000 only)	6
05	V2 VVR 5033410	From The Floorboards Up/From The Floorboards Up (Lynchmob Remix - Instrumental) (7", gatefold p/s, 4,000 only)	5
05	V2 VVR 5033417	From The Floorboards Up/Oranges And Rosewater (2nd 7", green & orange vinyl, stickered PVC sleeve)	5
09	Universal (No cat no)	7 & 3 Is The Striker's Name (one sided 7", screen printed sleeve, 1000 only)	50
10	V2	Aim High (Aim Higher)/Pieces Of A Dream (Dreams In Pieces)/Aim High (The Higher Aim)/Aim High (Like Water Needs A Flower) All The Amorphous Androgymous remixes (10", p/s, 500 only for 2010 Record Store Day)	25

ALBUMS
92	Go! Discs 828 343-1	PAUL WELLER (LP, gatefold sleeve, stapled-in lyric booklet)	40
93	Go! Discs 828 435-1	WILD WOOD (LP, gatefold sleeve with 'obi' band & poster)	22
94	Go! Discs 828 513-1	WILD WOOD (LP, gatefold sleeve with 'obi' band & poster; reissue with extra track 'Hung Up')	40
94	Go! Discs 828 561-1	LIVE WOOD (2-LP, single sleeve with picture inners)	25
95	Go! Discs 828 619-1	STANLEY ROAD (LP, gatefold sleeve with Excerpts booklet)	20
95	Go! Discs 850 070-7	STANLEY ROAD (6 x 7" singles in 7" box)	30
97	Island ILPS 8058	HEAVY SOUL (LP, gatefold sleeve with picture inner & insert)	20

Paul WELLER MOVEMENT

97	Island CID 8058	HEAVY SOUL ("unofficial" wooden box set, 1,000 only, incl.: hinged wooden box, numbered certificate, promo CD, 5 postcards, CD booklet, promo 7", 5 guitar plectrums & polo shirt) 125
98	Island ILPSD 8080	MODERN CLASSICS - THE GREATEST HITS (2-LP, gatefold sleeve with picture inners & insert) 18
98	Island IBX 8080	MODERN CLASSICS (box set, numbered 4 x 7" + 16-page photo book & colour print) 30
00	Island ILPS 8093	HELIOCENTRIC (LP, with foldout poster) 20
01	Independiente ISOM26LP	DAYS OF SPEED (2-LP, gatefold sleeve with pic inners) 70
02	Independiente ISOM33LP	ILLUMINATION (LP, rounded corners, gatefold sleeve with picture inner & booklet) 20
04	V2 VVR 1026902	STUDIO 150 (CD, autographed for competition) 18
04	V2 VVR 1026901	STUDIO 150 (LP, 2,000 only, with inner sleeve) 18
90s	(no label)	BOOT CUT (live CD, card sleeve, fan club issue) 20
90s	(no label)	ACOUSTIC EP (live DVD, with Gem Archer, features radio interview + 5 songs including U.S. TV appearance, fan club issue) 30
03	Universal 0635271	FLY ON THE WALL (3-LP, stickered sleeve) 35
06	V2 VVR 1039391	CATCH FLAME (2-LP, gatefold, 2 inners, free 7") 25

PROMOS

91	Freedom High FHP 1	Into Tomorrow/Here's A New Thing (7", white label promo, 1991) 25
91	Freedom High FHPT 1	Into Tomorrow/Here's A New Thing/That Spiritual Feeling/ Into Tomorrow (8-Track Demo) (12", white label promo, 1991) 35
92	Echantillon (no cat. no.)	Uh Huh Oh Yeh/Arrival Time/Fly On The Wall/ Always There To Fool You (12", yellow label test pressing) 50
92	Go! Discs KOSX 1	Kosmos (12", 1-sided) 25
92	Go! Discs GOXDJ 102	Kosmos (12", printed label) 25
93	Go! Discs GOPRO 102	Sunflower (12") 12
93	Go! Discs GOTDJ 104	Wild Wood/Ends Of The Earth (10") 20
93	Go! Discs GOXDJ 111	Hung Up/Foot Of The Mountain (Live Royal Albert Hall 23.11.93)/The Loved/ Kosmos (Lynch Mob Bonus Beats) (12", printed white labels) 10
94	Go! Discs PNME 1	Shadow Of The Sun (Live at Wolverhampton Civic Hall 9.3.94)/ Sunflower (Lynch Mob Dub Edit)/Wild Wood (Sheared Wood - Remixed by Portishead with A. Utley) (white label promo for NME cover mount) 35
94	Go! Discs PNPCD 2	Sexy Sadie (CD, 1-track, card sleeve, numbered, available by mail-order with 1st 500 copies of Highlights & Hang-Ups video) 12
94	Island GODJB 121	Out Of The Sinking/Sexy Sadie (7", jukebox issue) 5
95	Go! Discs LYNCH 1	Lynch Mob Beats (12", stamped 1-sided white label, 500 only) 60
95	Go! Discs STAN 1	A FEW STOPS FROM STANLEY ROAD (CD sampler, card p/s) 10
95	Go! Discs SPLINT 1	Walk On Gilded Splinters (12", white label test pressing, 1-sided, 1995) 70
95	Go! Discs (no cat. no.)	CD SAMPLER (CD, given away in queue for 100 Club gig, 200 only) 45
95	Disctronics matrix: WELLERSPEC 01	OUR PRICE PAUL WELLER SPECIAL (CD, in-store album, no inlay, PVC outer) 60
96	Go! Discs PSCD 1	Peacock Suit/Eye Of The Storm (CD, no inlay) 12
96	Go! Discs PWRT 1	PEACOCK SUIT (CD, 7-track, picture disc in cloth bag) 25
97	Island HEAVY 1	Heavy Soul (Pt 1)/Heavy Soul (Pt 2) (7", Island sleeve) 50
97	Island SOULCD 1	A PIECE OF HEAVY SOUL (CD sampler, card sleeve) 12
97	Island PAUL CD 1	WILD WOOD TO HEAVY SOUL (CD, in-store sampler, no inlay) 12
97	Island PWICD 1	HEAVY SOUL (box set: interview CD, EPK, 5 cards & insert) 45
97	Southern Songs WELLER 1	LIVE... FROM THE ROOF OF THE HAYWARD GALLERY (LP, finished sleeve, white labels) 25
97	Island KINGS 1	KINGS ROAD (CD sampler, 350 only) 45
98	Island 12IS 711DJ	Brand New Start/Right Underneath It (12") 12
99	Island 12IS 734DJ	Wild Wood (The Sheared Wood Remix)/Science (Lynch Mob Remix with Psychonauts) (12", white label, only 130 copies mailed out) 18
99	Island INTCD 3	IN CONVERSATION (interview CD, gatefold card p/s) 30
00	Island HELIO-1	Heliocentric (Two Lone Swordsmen 4UR Mix)/Heliocentric (Original Version)/There's No Drinking After You're Dead (Noonday Underground Mix) (12" white label) 30
01	Independiente DOSB 1	DAYS OF SPEED SELECTIONS (3-CD set, card outer sleeve with CDs in individual card inners) 50
02	Independiente PWICD 1	ILLUMINATION: SIX TRACK SAMPLER (CD, card sleeve with insert) 20
03	Universal CUFF 1	BUTTON DOWNS (LP, promo-only vinyl edition of third disc of cover versions from Fly On The Wall) 35
05	V2 VVR 5030593P	Come Together/Early Morning Rain (CD, card sleeve) 12
05	V2 VVR 5033488P	From The Floorboards Up (7", white label test pressing, stamped white sleeve) 25
05	V2 VVR 1033202P	SINGLES BOX (box set, mail-order only, houses all As Is Now 7"s; priced without singles) 20
05	Universal STAN 1	STANLEY ROAD - 10TH ANNIVERSARY EP (7") 10

(see also Jam, Style Council, Smokin' Mojo Filters, Andy Lewis & Paul Weller, Paul Weller Movement)

PAUL WELLER MOVEMENT

91	Freedom High FHP 1	Into Tomorrow/Here's A New Thing (7", with or without 'Paul Weller Movement' printed on label) 8
91	Freedom High FHPT 1	Into Tomorrow/Here's A New Thing/That Spiritual Feeling/ Into Tomorrow (8-Track Demo) (12") 12

ORSON WELLES

59	Top Rank TR 5001	The Courtroom Scene From The Film 'Compulsion' (both sides) (in p/s) 12
84	Splash SP 29	I Know What It Is To Be oung (But You Don't Know What It Is To Be Old)/ Love Is A Lovely Word (p/s) 8

(see also Manowar)

NICK WELLINGS & SECTION

77	The Label TLR 011	You Better Move On/Punk Funk 6

WELLINGTON

74	Concord CON 029	Alright I'll See You Tonight/How Would You Like To Rock With Me 8
74	Concord CON 031	Catch Us If You Can/Superstar 8

BOBBY WELLINS

78	Vortex VS1	LIVE JUBILATION (LP) 40
78	Vortex VS2	DREAMS ARE FREE (LP) 40

BOBBY WELLS

68	Beacon 3-102	Let's Copp A Groove/Recipe For Love (yellow label) 30
68	Beacon 3-102	Let's Copp A Groove/Recipe For Love (white label) 20
68	Beacon 3-102	Let's Copp A Groove/Recipe For Love (green label) 15
79	Grapevine GRP 124	Be's That Way Sometimes/Recipe For Love 10

BRIAN WELLS

72	Spark SRL 1082	Paper Party/Just A Summer High 6

COBY WELLS
67	Decca F 12560	My Feet Ache/Venus De Milo	12

HOUSTON WELLS (& MARKSMEN)
62	Parlophone R 4955	This Song Is Just For You/Paradise	10
62	Parlophone R 4980	Shutters And Boards/North Wind	10
63	Parlophone R 5031	Only The Heartaches/Can't Stop Pretending	8
63	Parlophone R 5069	Blowing Wild (The Ballad Of Black Gold)/Crazy Dreams	10
64	Parlophone R 5099	Anna Marie/Moon Watch Over My Baby	10
64	Parlophone R 5141	Galway Bay/Livin' Alone (as Houston Wells & Outlaws)	10
65	Parlophone R 5226	Blue Of The Night/Coming Home (solo)	7
68	CBS 3572	Teach Me Little Children/Does My Ring Hurt Your Finger	6
63	Parlophone GEP 8878	JUST FOR YOU (EP)	50
64	Parlophone GEP 8914	RAMONA (EP)	60
64	Parlophone PMC 1215	WESTERN STYLE (LP)	50

(see also Marksmen, Outlaws)

JEAN WELLS
71	Mojo 2092 023	After Loving You/Puttin' The Best On The Outside	10
70	Sonet SNTF 606	WORLD! HERE COMES JEAN WELLS (LP)	50

JOHNNY WELLS
59	Columbia DB 4377	Lonely Moon/The One And Only One	30

JOHNNY WELLS
67	Parlophone R 5559	Guess I'm Dumb/Wondering Why	20

JUNIOR WELLS
66	Delmark DS 9612	Hoodoo Man Blues (blue label)	30
66	Delmark DS 628	Southside Blues Jam (blue label)	20
68	Mercury MF 1056	Girl You Lit My Fire/It's A Man Down There	15
66	Delmark DJB 1	BLUES WITH A BEAT (EP)	35
68	Fontana (S)TFL 6084	IT'S MY LIFE BABY (LP)	40
68	Vanguard SVRL 19011	COMING AT YOU (LP, also stereo, VSD 79262)	30
68	Vanguard SVRL 19028	IT'S MY LIFE BABY (LP, reissue)	25
68	Mercury SMCL 20130	YOU'RE TUFF ENOUGH (LP)	45
71	Delmark DS 628	SOUTHSIDE BLUES JAM (LP)	22
75	Delmark DS 635	JUNIOR WELLS ON TAP (LP)	15

(see also Buddy Guy)

KITTY WELLS
64	Brunswick 05920	I Gave My Wedding Dress Away/I've Thought Of Leaving Too	7
55	Brunswick OE 9149	KITTY SINGS (EP)	12
61	Brunswick LAT 8361	KITTY'S CHOICE (LP)	12
64	Brunswick LAT 8575	QUEEN OF COUNTRY MUSIC (LP)	15
65	Brunswick LAT 8601	ESPECIALLY FOR YOU (LP)	15
65	Brunswick LAT 8621	LONESOME SAD AND BLUE (LP)	15
66	Brunswick STA 8646	SINGS SONGS MADE FAMOUS BY JIM REEVES (LP, stereo)	15
66	Brunswick LAT 8659	COUNTRY ALL THE WAY (LP, stereo)	15

MARY WELLS
62	Oriole CBA 1762	You Beat Me To The Punch/Old Love	70
63	Oriole CBA 1796	Two Lovers/Operator	50
63	Oriole CBA 1829	Laughing Boy/Two Wrongs Don't Make A Right	55
63	Oriole CBA 1847	Your Old Standby/What Love Has Joined Together	50
63	Stateside SS 242	You Lost The Sweetest Boy/What's Easy For Two Is So Hard For One	25
63	Stateside SS 242	You Lost The Sweetest Boy/What's Easy For Two Is So Hard For One (DJ Copy)	100
64	Stateside SS 288	My Guy/Oh Little Boy	12
64	Stateside SS 288	My Guy/Oh Little Boy (DJ Copy)	100
64	Stateside SS 316	Once Upon A Time (with Marvin Gaye)/What's The Matter With You, Baby	40
64	Stateside SS 316	Once Upon A Time (with Marvin Gaye)/What's The Matter With You, Baby (DJ Copy)	85
65	Stateside SS 372	Ain't It The Truth/Stop Takin' Me For Granted	30
65	Stateside SS 372	Ain't It The Truth/Stop Takin' Me For Granted (DJ Copy)	50
65	Stateside SS 396	Use Your Head/Everlovin' Boy	30
65	Stateside SS 396	Use Your Head/Everlovin' Boy (DJ Copy)	50
65	Stateside SS 415	Never Never Leave Me/Why Don't You Let Yourself Go	20
65	Stateside SS 415	Never Never Leave Me/Why Don't You Let Yourself Go (DJ Copy)	50
65	Stateside SS 439	He's A Lover/I'm Learnin'	25
65	Stateside SS 439	He's A Lover/I'm Learnin' (DJ Copy)	50
65	Stateside SS 463	Me Without You/I'm Sorry	25
65	Stateside SS 463	Me Without You/I'm Sorry (DJ Copy)	50
68	Stateside SS 2111	The Doctor/Two Lovers' History	20
66	Atlantic AT 4067	Dear Lover/Can't You See (You're Losing Me)	50
66	Atlantic 584 054	Me And My Baby/Such A Sweet Thing	18
67	Atlantic 584 104	Hey You Set My Soul On Fire/Coming Home	18
70	Direction 58-4816	Dig The Way I Feel/Love Shooting Bandit	15
72	Atlantic K 10254	Dear Lover/Can't You See (You're Losing Me) (reissue)	10
65	Tamla Motown TME 2007	MARY WELLS (EP)	100
63	Oriole PS 40045	TWO LOVERS (LP)	80
63	Oriole PS 40051	BYE BYE BABY (LP)	90
64	Stateside SL 10095	SINGS MY GUY (LP)	70
65	Stateside SL 10133	MARY WELLS (LP)	80
65	Tamla Motown TML 11006	MY BABY JUST CARES FOR ME (LP)	55
66	Stateside S(S)L 10171	LOVE SONGS TO THE BEATLES (LP)	50
66	Tamla Motown TML 11032	GREATEST HITS (LP)	35
68	Stateside S(S)L 10266	SERVIN' UP SOME SOUL (LP)	50
68	Atlantic 587 049	THE TWO SIDES OF MARY WELLS (LP)	30
69	T. Motown (S)TML 11102	VINTAGE STOCK (LP, unissued)	0

(see also Marvin Gaye)

ALEX WELSH & DIXIELANDERS
55	Decca F 10538	I'll Build A Stairway To Paradise/Eccentric	5
55	Decca F 10557	Blues My Naughtie Sweetie Gives To Me/Shoe Shiner's Blues	5
55	Decca F 10652	What Can I Say After I Say I'm Sorry/Hard-Hearted Hannah	5

MINT VALUE £

61	Columbia DB 4686	Tansy/Memphis March	10
55	Decca DFE 6254	DIXIELANDERS AT THE RFH (EP)	10

DANNY WELTON
60	Coral Q 72409	Boogie Woogie/To Each His Own	5

WENDY & LEMMY
82	Bronze BRO 151	Stand By Your Man/No Class/Masterplan (p/s)	7
(see also Motorhead)			

WE'RE TIRED
77	Deadline DEADS 8	My Life's On The Line/Against All Odds (p/s)	20
77	Deadline DEADS 11	Guide Me Through Hell/Time Is Against Me (p/s)	25
78	Deadline DEADS 15	Over The Edge/Anal Retentive (p/s, as We're Tired & We're Proud)	8
77	Deadline DEADLP 2	FIND THE PRICE IN TIME (LP)	50

WERLWINDS
61	Columbia DB 4650	Winding It Up/Dig Deep	22

HOWARD WERTH & MOONBEAMS
74	Charisma CB 225	Lucinda/Jonah	5
75	Charisma CAS 11004	KING BRILLIANT (LP, with inner sleeve)	12
(see also Audience)			

BRIAN WESKE
62	Oriole CB 1723	In The Midst Of The Crowd/All Mine Alone	15
62	Oriole CB 1776	24 Hours In A Day/Where Does The Clown Go	15

FRED WESLEY & J.B.S
73	Polydor 2066 322	Doing It To Death/Everybody Got Soul (with J.B.s)	5
74	Mojo 2093 025	J.B. Shout/Back Stabbers (with J.B.s)	5
80	RSO RSO 67	Houseparty/I Make Music (solo)	5
80	RSO RSO 67	Houseparty/I Make Music (12", solo)	10
74	Polydor 2391 125	DAMN RIGHT, I AM SOMEBODY (LP, with J.B.s)	20
74	Polydor 2391 161	BREAKIN' BREAD (LP, with J.B.s)	20
(see also James Brown, J.B.s)			

WES MINSTER FIVE
64	Carnival CV 7017	Shakin' The Blues/Railroad Blues	15
65	Carnival CV 7019	Sticks And Stones/Mickey's Monkey	20
(see also Maynell Wilson, Dave Greenslade)			

FRANK WESS
64	Fontana TL 5291	THE AWARD WINNER (LP)	12

ADAM 'BATMAN' WEST
76	Target TGT 111	Batman And Robin/The Story Of Batman	7

DODIE WEST
64	Decca F 12046	Goin' Out Of My Head/Is He Feeling Blue	15
65	Piccadilly 7N 35239	In The Deep Of The Night/Rovin' Boy (in p/s)	30
65	Piccadilly 7N 35239	In The Deep Of The Night/Rovin' Boy	20
65	Piccadilly 7N 35261	Thinking Of You/And Love Will Come	8
66	Piccadilly 7N 35287	Make The World Go Away/Who Does He Think He Is	8
68	Philips BF 1698	Living In Limbo/Birdie Told Me	7

HARRY & JEANIE WEST
60	Melodisc EPM 7-111	SOUTHERN MOUNTAIN FOLK SONGS (LP)	15

HEDY WEST
65	Topic 12T 117	OLD TIMES AND HARD TIMES (LP)	20
66	Topic 12T 146	PRETTY SARO (LP)	20
67	Topic 12T 163	BALLADS (LP, with Bill Clifton)	20
67	Fontana STL 5432	SERVES'EM FINE (LP)	20

KEITH WEST
67	Parlophone R 5623	Excerpt From "A Teenage Opera"/MARK WIRTZ ORCHESTRA: Theme From "A Teenage Opera"	8
67	Parlophone R 5651	Sam (From "A Teenage Opera')/MARK WIRTZ'S MOOD MOSAIC: Thimble Full Of Puzzles (promos in art sleeve)	30
67	Parlophone R 5651	Sam (From "A Teenage Opera')/MARK WIRTZ'S MOOD MOSAIC: Thimble Full Of Puzzles	12
68	Parlophone R 5713	On A Saturday/The Kid Was A Killer	65
72	Parlophone R 5957	Excerpt From "A Teenage Opera"/Sam (From "A Teenage Opera")	7
73	Deram DM 402	Riding For A Fall/Days About To Rain	7
74	Deram DM 410	Havin' Someone/Know There's No Livin' Without You	7
(see also Tomorrow, Four + One, In Crowd, Mark Wirtz)			

LESLIE WEST('S MOUNTAIN)
69	Bell BLL 1078	Dreams Of Milk And Honey/Wheels On Fire (as Leslie West's Mountain)	20
69	Bell SBLL 126	MOUNTAIN (LP, as Leslie West's Mountain)	25
75	RCA RS 1009	THE GREAT FATSBY (LP)	15
76	Phantom PHS 701	THE LESLIE WEST BAND (LP)	12
(see also Jolliver Arkansas, Mountain, West Bruce & Laing)			

MAE WEST
67	Stateside SS 2021	Twist And Shout/Day Tripper	15
73	MGM 2006 203	Great Balls Of Fire/Men	15
56	Brunswick LAT 8082	THE FABULOUS MAE WEST (LP)	65
67	Stateside (S)SL 10197	WAY OUT WEST (LP)	30
73	Polydor 2315 207	GREAT BALLS OF FIRE (LP)	15

SPEEDY WEST & JIMMY BRYANT
55	Capitol EAP1 520	TWO GUITARS COUNTRY STYLE PT. 1 (EP)	20
55	Capitol EAP2 520	TWO GUITARS COUNTRY STYLE PT. 2 (EP)	20
53	Capitol LC 6619	CAPITOL PRESENTS SPEEDY WEST & JIMMY BRYANT (10" LP)	25
55	Capitol LC 6694	TWO GUITARS COUNTRY STYLE (10" LP)	25

TABBY WEST
58	Capitol CL 14861	All That I Want/If You Promise Not To Tell	10

MIKE WESTBROOK (CONCERT BAND)

69	Deram DM 234	A Life Of Its Own/Can't Get It Out Of My Mind	20
70	Deram DM 286	Requiem/Hooray	20
70	Deram DM 311	Original Peter/Magic Garden (with Norma Winstone)	200
67	Deram DML 1013	CELEBRATION (LP, as Mike Westbrook Concert Band)	100
68	Deram DML/SML 1031	RELEASE (LP)	70
69	Deram SML 1047	MARCHING SONG VOL. 1 (LP)	70
69	Deram SML 1048	MARCHING SONG VOL. 2 (LP)	70
70	Deram SML 1069	LOVE SONGS (LP, as Mike Westbrook Concert Band with Norma Winstone)	70
71	RCA SER 5612	TYGER: A CELEBRATION OF WILLIAM BLAKE (LP, with insert)	100
72	RCA Neon NE 10	MIKE WESTBROOK'S METROPOLIS (LP, gatefold sleeve)	75
72	Cadillac SGC 1001	LIVE (LP, private pressing)	25
75	RCA SF 8433	CITADEL/ROOM 315 (2-LP, with John Surman)	30
75	Transatlantic TRA 323	LOVE/DREAM & VARIATIONS (LP)	20
76	Transatlantic TRA 312	PLAYS FOR THE RECORD (LP)	18
78	Original ORA 001	GOOSE SAUCE (LP)	18
78	Original ORA 002	PIANO (LP)	18
79	RCA PL 25252	MAMA CHICAGO (LP)	18
80	Original ORA 203	WESTBROOK BLAKE (LP)	25
82	Original ORA 309	THE CORTEGE (LP)	25
83	Westbrook LWN 1	A LITTLE WESTBROOK MUSIC (LP)	25
88	Venture VEB 13	LONDON BRIDGE IS BROKEN DOWN (LP)	12

(see also Solid Gold Cadillac, John Surman, Norma Winstone)

WEST, BRUCE & LAING

73	RSO 2090 113	Dirty Shoes/Backfire	6
72	CBS 65314	WHY DONTCHA (LP)	12
73	RSO 2394 107	WHATEVER TURNS YOU ON (LP)	12
74	RSO 2394 128	LIVE 'N' KICKIN' (LP)	12

(see also Jack Bruce, Leslie West, Mountain)

WEST COAST CONSORTIUM

67	Pye 7N 17352	Some Other Someday/Looking Back	20
68	Pye 7N 17482	Colour Sergeant Lillywhite/Lady From Baltimore	45

(see also Consortium)

WEST COAST DELEGATION

67	Deram DM 113	Reach The Top/Mr. Personality Man	20

WEST COAST KNACK

67	Capitol CL 15497	I'm Aware/Time Waits For No One	20

WEST COAST POP ART EXPERIMENTAL BAND

68	Reprise RSLP 6298	A CHILD'S GUIDE TO GOOD AND EVIL (LP)	250

WEST FIVE

65	HMV POP 1396	Congratulations/She Mine	40
65	HMV POP 1428	Someone Ain't Right/Just Like Romeo And Juliet	35
66	HMV POP 1513	If It Don't Work Out/Back To Square One	20

(see also Ferris Wheel)

WEST INDIANS

68	Doctor Bird DB 1121	Right On Time/Hokey Pokey	25
68	Doctor Bird DB 1127	Falling In Love/I Mean It	25
69	Camel CA 16	Strange Whisperings/CARL DAWKINS: Hard To Handle	15
71	Dynamic DYN 413	Never Gonna Give You Up/REBELLIOUS SUBJECTS: Never Give Up	10

(see also Eric Donaldson, Prunes, Kilowatts, Upsetters)

CLIVE WESTLAKE

68	Fontana TF 940	199 Days/From The Beginning To The End	6

JILL WESTLAKE

58	Columbia DB 4132	Sharin'/Over And Over Again	12

KEVIN WESTLAKE & GARY FARR

68	Marmalade 598 007	Everyday/Green	20
70	CBS	Born Under A Bad Sign/Missouri Train	10

(see also Gary Farr & T-Bones, T-Bones, Blossom Toes, B.B. Blunder)

WESTLAND STEAMBOAT

70	CBS	Born Under A Bad Sign/Missouri Train	10

WESTMORELITES

70	Clandisc CLA 217	Zion/CLANCY ECCLES & DYNAMITES: Revival	8

(see also Minstrels)

GLEN WESTON

67	Columbia DB8253	Pattern People/In The Still Of The night	20
68	Columbia DB 8328	With This Ring/Liane	5

KIM WESTON

64	Stateside SS 359	A Little More Love/Go Ahead And Laugh	100
64	Stateside SS 359	A Little More Love/Go Ahead And Laugh (DJ copy)	150
65	Tamla Motown TMG 511	I'm Still Loving You/Just Loving You	180
65	Tamla Motown TMG 511	I'm Still Loving You/Just Loving You (DJ copy)	300
65	Tamla Motown TMG 538	Take Me In Your Arms (Rock Me A Little While)/Don't Compare Me With Her	80
65	Tamla Motown TMG 538	Take Me In Your Arms (Rock Me A Little While)/Don't Compare Me With Her (DJ copy)	100
66	Tamla Motown TMG 554	Helpless/A Love Like Yours	100
66	Tamla Motown TMG 554	Helpless/A Love Like Yours (DJ Copy)	400
67	MGM MGM 1338	I Got What You Need/Someone Like You (DJ copy)	30
67	MGM MGM 1357	That's Groovy/Land Of Tomorrow	30
68	MGM MGM 1382	Nobody/You're Just The Kind Of Guy (DJ copy)	50
69	Major Minor MM 619	From Both Sides Now/We Try Harder	6
70	Major Minor MM 683	Danger, Heartbreak Dead Ahead/I'll Be Thinking	12
75	Tamla Motown TMG 1000	Do Like I Do/MARVELETTES: Finders Keepers, Losers Weepers	100
65	Tamla Motown TME 2005	KIM WESTON (EP)	110
66	Tamla Motown TME 2015	ROCK ME A LITTLE WHILE (EP)	450

Mark WESTON & THE TWO PART TARIFF

67	MGM MGM-C(S) 8055	FOR THE FIRST TIME (LP)	50
71	Stax 2362 021	KIM KIM KIM (LP)	30

(see also Johnny Nash & Kim Weston, Marvin Gaye & Kim Weston)

MARK WESTON & THE TWO PART TARIFF
69	Tepee TPR 1006	Standing At The Bus Stop/Portrait On The Blackboard	40

PETE WESTON
70	Gas GAS 146	Something Sweet/BIM & BAM: Love Letters	12
70	Punch PH 28	In The Mood (& His Band)/Slide Mongoose (actually "Sly Mongoose")	8
72	Ashanti ASH 402	Pup'n Temper/PETE'S ALL STARS: Version 2	8

(see also I Roy)

RANDY WESTON TRIO
55	London H-APB1040	RANDY WESTON PLAYS COLE PORTER IN A MODERN MOOD (10" LP)	20
55	London HB-U1046	THE RANDY WESTON TRIO (10" LP with Art Blakey)	20
56	London HA-U 2018	GET HAPPY WITH THE RANDY WESTON TRIO (LP)	20

WEST ONE
88	Que Q 9	California '69/Eurotrash (gig freebie, white label)	12

WEST POINT
70	Decca F 13050	Don't Know Why/Take What You Want	8

WEST POINT SUPERNATURAL
67	Reaction 591 013	Time Will Tell/Night Train	20

WESTWIND
70	Penny Farthing PEN 737	Love Is A Funny Sort Of Thing/Breakout	8
70	Penny Farthing PELS 505	LOVE IS (LP)	200

WE THE PEOPLE
66	London HLH 10089	He Doesn't Go About It Right/You Burn Me Up And Down	125

WE THREE TRIO
65	London HLA 9966	Baby The Rain Must Fall/Shine For Me	8
67	Fontana TL 5308	THE WE THREE TRIO (LP)	15

WET WILLIE
71	Atlantic 2091155	Dirty Leg/Rock And Roll Band	8

WE UGLY DOGS
67	BT Puppy BTS 45537	First Spring Rain/Poor Man	12

(see also Tokens, U.S. Double Quartet)

WHALE FEATHERS
71	Blue Horizon 2431 009	WHALE FEATHERS (LP)	150

WHALES
68	CBS 3766	Come Down Little Bird/Beachcomber	20
69	CBS 4126	Tell It To The Rain/Girl, Hey Girl	15

WHAM!
84	Epic (no cat. no.)	Merry Xmas From Wham (fan club Christmas single, no p/s)	5
86	Epic WHAM 2	THE FINAL (2-LP box, gold vinyl picture discs, with sealed T-shirt, calendar, pencil, note-pad and no'd certificate)	50

(see also George Michael, Pepsi & Shirley)

WHAT
79	Humber HREP 45	What Is The Cure?/Anything Goes/East Coast Kids	40

WHAT IS OIL
83	Oof BEAT 1	HUMAN SUFFERING EP	30

WHAT THE CURTAINS
84	Rideaux WTC 0042	Crime Of Passion/Words (Can't Tell)	20

WHAT TO WEAR
80	Basic And Typical BAT 1	CASUAL BUT SMART (EP)	25

PEETIE WHEATSTRAW
69	Matchbox SDR 191	THE DEVIL'S SON IN LAW (LP)	25
69	Matchbox SDR 192	THE HIGH SHERIFF FROM HELL (LP)	25

BILLY ED WHEELER
64	London HLR 9920	On The Outside (Lookin' In)/The Right Foot In His World	8
65	London HLR 9950	Ode To The Little Brown Shack Out Back/Sister Sara	8
65	London HAR/SHR 8221	MEMORIES OF AMERICA (LP)	20

KENNY WHEELER & JOHN DANKWORTH ORCHESTRA
68	Fontana STL 5494	WINDMILL TILTER (LP)	150
70s	Incus 10	SONG FOR SOMEONE (LP)	80

(see also Johnny Dankworth, Elton Dean)

WHEELER ST JAMES & JAMES
72	RCA 2233	My Impersonal Life/Lovely To See You	20

WHEELS OF TIME
67	Spin SP 62008	1984/So Long (not in company sleeves)	90
67	Spin SP 62008	1984/So Long (in company sleeve)	100

WHEELS (1)
65	Columbia DB 7682	Gloria/Don't You Know	120
66	Columbia DB 7827	Bad Little Woman/Road Block (mispressing, demos & a few issues play "Call My Name" on B-side)	150
66	Columbia DB 7827	Bad Little Woman/Road Block	375
66	Columbia DB 7981	Kicks/Call My Name	120

(see also James Brothers, Demick & Armstrong)

WHEELS (2)
71	Decca F13268	Take Me Home Country Roads/She Don't Mean It	30

WHICHWHAT

69	Beacon BEA 127	Gimme Gimme Good Lovin'/Wonderland Of Love	25
69	Beacon BEA 131	Why Do Lovers Break Each Other's Heart/When I See Her Smile	6
69	Beacon BEA 133	In The Year 2525/Parting	15
69	Beacon BEA 144	I Wanna Be Free/It's All Over Again	25
70	Beacon BEA 169	Vietnam Rose/Shame And Solution	6
70	Beacon BEAS 14	WHICHWHAT'S FIRST (LP)	50

OSCAR WHIFLEY

68	Dolphin DOS6	Tommy Jones/Creeque Alley (as The Oscar Whifley Sound)	8

WHIP

71	Mother MOT 6	Julie Ivory Towers/MUFF & BANKHOUSE ASSEMBLY: Funky Shoot Out	10

WHIRL

89	Sound Of Spasm 2	Bizarre Love Triangle/CROCODILE RIDE: Shimmer (1-sided flexi-disc, foldover p/s In poly bag with fanzine)	10

WHIRLWIND

78	Chiswick NS 25	Hang Loose/Together Forever (p/s)	10
78	Chiswick NS 42	I Only Wish (That I'd Been Told)/Ducktails (unissued)	0
78	Chiswick CHIS 103	I Only Wish (That I'd Been Told)/Ducktails (p/s)	10
79	Chiswick CHIS 117	You Got Class/Losing To You (unissued in U.K.; France-only)	0
79	Lyntone (No Cat. No)	On Wheels (flexi, originally promo for Isle Of Man TT races, repackaged in picture sleeve with 2 inserts for 1979 Earls Court Concert)	50
80	Chiswick CHIS 122	Heaven Knows/Cruisin' Around (p/s)	10
80	Chiswick CHIS 127	Stayin' Out All Night/Running Wild (unissued; p/s only)	0
80	Chiswick PSR 447	Midnight Blue/Honey Hush/Such A Fool/Stayin' Out All Night (promo only)	8
78	Chiswick CH 4	BLOWIN' UP A STORM (10" mini-LP)	12
78	Chiswick WIK 7	BLOWIN' UP A STORM (LP, with 2 extra tracks)	15
80	Chiswick CWK 3012	MIDNIGHT BLUE (LP)	15

WHIRLWIND HEAT

03	XL XL 163	Purple/Stunning Evaseev (with poster)	10

WHIRLWINDS

64	HMV POP 1301	Look At Me/Baby Not Like You	50

(see also Mockingbirds, Graham Gouldman, 10cc)

NANCY WHISKEY (& HER SKIFFLERS)

57	Oriole CB 1394	He's Solid Gone/Ella Speed (as Nancy Whiskey & Her Skifflers)	20
57	Oriole CB 1394	He's Solid Gone/Ella Speed (as Nancy Whiskey & Her Skifflers) (78)	10
58	Oriole CB 1452	Hillside In Scotland/I Know Where I'm Goin'	10
58	Oriole CB 1452	Hillside In Scotland/I Know Where I'm Goin' (78)	10
59	Oriole CB 1485	The Old Grey Goose/Johnny Blue	10
59	Oriole CB 1485	The Old Grey Goose/Johnny Blue (78)	10
65	Fontana TF 612	Bowling Green/I'm Leaving Today	5
67	CBS 3090	Freight Train/The Game	8
57	Topic 7T 10	NANCY WHISKEY SINGS (7" LP)	35
57	Oriole MG 10018	THE INTOXICATING MISS WHISKEY (10" LP, with Chas McDevitt Skiffle Group)	45

(see also Chas McDevitt Skiffle Group)

WHISTLE

74	York YR 209	When The Lights Go Out On Broadway/Lincoln Lullabies	12
73	York YR 201	The Party Must Be Over/Hideaway	20

WHISTLER

71	Deram SML 1083	HO-HUM (LP)	250

WHISTLING JACK SMITH

67	Deram DM 112	I Was Kaiser Bill's Batman/The British Grin And Bear	6
68	Deram DM 179	Ja Da/Sans Fairy Anne	7
68	Deram DM 189	Only When I Larf/Early One Morning	7
67	Deram DML 1009	AROUND THE WORLD WHISTLING JACK (LP)	15

WHISTLING WILLIE

68	Duke DU 8	Penny Reel/Soul Tonic	5

(see also Neville, Neville Willoughby)

SHARON WHITBREAD & FRED

72	RA RALP 6011	SPICE OF LIFE (LP)	25
72	Ralp 6011	SPICE OF LIFE (LP)	25

IAN WHITCOMB

65	Capitol CL 15382	This Sporting Life/Fizz	6
65	Capitol CL 15395	You Turn Me On/Poor But Honest	12
65	Capitol CL 15418	N-N-Nervous!/The End	6
66	Capitol CL 15431	Good Hard Rock/High Blood Pressure	6
66	Stateside SS 573	Where Did Robinson Crusoe Go With Friday/Poor Little Bird)	6
72	Ember EMBS 324	You Turn Me On/This Sporting Life (mono)	5
73	Ember NR 5065	YOU TURN ME ON (LP, with Jimmy Page & John Paul Jones)	40

BARRY WHITE

67	President PT 139	All In The Run Of A Day/Don't Take Your Love From Me	30

BERGEN WHITE

76	Private Stock PVT 69	Duke Of Earl/She Won't Let You Down	7

BRIAN WHITE & MAGNA JAZZ BAND

62	HMV CLP 1534	BRIAN WHITE AND THE MAGNA JAZZ BAND (LP)	80

(see also Magna Jazz Band)

BUKKA WHITE

66	Fontana 688 804 ZL	SKY SONGS (LP, with Big Willie)	40
66	CBS Realm 52629	BUKKA WHITE (LP)	35
69	Blue Horizon 7-63229	MEMPHIS HOT SHOTS (LP)	80
69	Sonet SNTF 609	THE LEGACY OF THE BLUES VOL. 1 (LP, with insert)	12

CHRIS WHITE
76	Charisma CB 272	Spanish Wine/She's Only Dancing	8
76	Charisma CB 282	Natural Rhythm/Another Little Miracle	7
76	Charisma CB 294	Don't Look Down/Summertime Summertime	8
77	Charisma CB 303	Don't Worry Baby/Child Of The Sun	15
76	Charisma CAS 1118	MOUTH MUSIC (LP)	15

(see also Joyce's Angels)

DANNY WHITE
67	Sue WI 4031	Keep My Woman Home/I'm Dedicating My Life	75
74	MCA MU 155	Cracked Up Over You/Taking Inventory	5

DUKE WHITE
63	Island WI 084	It's Over/Forever	15
64	Black Swan WI 442	Be Wise/BABA BROOKS: Musical Workshop	35
65	Black Swan WI 444	Sow Good Seeds/BABA BROOKS BAND: Bus Strike	35

ED WHITE (THE SOUNDS OF)
61	Pye 7N SR15320	Coral Reef/Tropical Blue (stereo only)	20

GEORGIA WHITE
54	Vocalion V 1038	Was I Drunk?/Moonshine Blues (78)	20

IAN WHITE
70	private pressing	IAN WHITE (LP)	20

JACK WHITE
09	Third Man Records TMR 013	Fly Farm Blues (luminous one-sided Halloween cover, 100-only)	150

(see also White Stripes, Raconteurs, Dead Weather)

JAMES WHITE
79	Ze ZE 3303	OFF WHITE (LP, as James White & The Blacks)	20
82	Animal CHR 1401	SAX MANIAC (LP, as James White & The Blacks)	20
83	Ze/Island ILPS 7023	JAMES WHITES FLAMING DEMONICS (LP)	12

JAY WHITE
56	London RE-F 1045	FAR-AWAY PLACES VOL. 1 (EP)	15

JEANETTE WHITE
69	A&M AMS 761	Music/No Sunshine	20
69	A&M AMS 761	Music/No Sunshine (Yellow DJ copy or brown label)	75

JOE WHITE
64	R&B JB 137	Sinners (as Joe White & Maytals)/ROLAND ALPHONSO: King Solomon	40
64	Ska Beat JB 180	Punch You Down (with Chuck)/TOMMY McCOOK: Cotton Tree	45
64	Island WI 145	When Are You Young/Wanna Go Home	15
64	Island WI 159	Hog In A Co Co/SKATALITES: Sandy Gully	30
64	Island WI 166	Downtown Girl/RICHARD BROS.: You Are My Sunshine (B-side is actually "Cool Smoke" by Don Drummond)	40
65	Island WI 201	Low-Minded People (as Chuck & Joe White)/Irene	15
66	Doctor Bird DB 1001	Every Night (with Chuck)/BABA BROOKS & HIS BAND: First Session	30
66	Doctor Bird DB 1024	My Love For You/SAMMY ISMAY & BABA BROOKS BAND: Cocktails For Two	25
66	Doctor Bird DB 1043	So Close (as Joe White & Della)/BABA BROOKS & HIS BAND: Eighth Games	25
67	Doctor Bird DB 1069	Rudies All Around/Bad Man	30
67	Doctor Bird DB 1080	Lonely Nights/I Need You	20
67	Doctor Bird DB 1090	I Need A Woman/Hot Hops	15
68	Blue Cat BS 108	Way Of Life (actually by Lyn Tait & Jets)/I'm So Proud	90
68	Blue Cat BS 119	Try A Little Tenderness/LYN TAITT & CARL BRYAN: Tender Arms	90
68	Blue Cat BS 130	Pretty Girl/DERMOTT LYNCH: You Went Away	80
69	Sugar ESS 102	My Guiding Star/If I Needed Someone	12
70	Sugar SU 103	Yesterday/I Am Free	12
70	Trojan TR 7742	So Much Love/Maybe Now	5
70	Trojan TR 7768	I'm Going To Get There/RUPIE EDWARDS ALLSTARS: Kinky Funky Reggae	10
70	Big BG 301	This Is The Time/The Other Day	8
71	Big BG 309	Baby I Care/Ain't Misbehavin'	5
72	Songbird SB 1072	Trinity/SCOTTY: Monkey Drop	12
72	Dynamic DYN 440	Kenyatta/RECORDING BAND: Version	15
73	Gayfeet GS 202	If It Don't Work Out/BABA BROOKS BAND: Ki Salaboca	12
73	Harry J. HJ 6648	Joe White (Mrs. Jones)/Joe White (Mrs. Jones) - Version (song actually titled "Me And Mrs Jones")	5
77	Ultra PFU 1002	Give And Take (On Both Sides)/Roots Dub	5
79	Splendor Heights SH 2	Forward To Zion/Only The Strong/Join Them/Are You Leavine Me (12" as Joe White Band)	20
77	Trench Town TRELP 002	LOVE FOR EVERY FAMILY (LP)	20
70s	Magnet MGT 006	SINCE THE OTHER DAY (LP)	20

(see also Chuck, Rue Lloyd)

JOSH WHITE
52	London L 1143	Call Me Darling/I Want You, I Need You (78)	10
52	London L 1144	Waltzing Landing/Apples, Peaches And Cherries (78)	10
52	London L 1161	Free And Equal Blues (Parts 1 & 2) (78)	10
54	London L 907	T.B. Blues/Molly Malone (78, silver label reissue)	10
58	Mercury YEP 9504	SOUTHERN BLUES (EP)	8
51	London H-APB 1005	A JOSH WHITE PROGRAM (10" LP)	12
52	Brunswick LA 8562	BALLADS AND BLUES (10" LP)	12
54	Brunswick LA 8653	BALLADS AND BLUES VOL. 2 (10" LP)	12
54	London H-APB 1032	JOSH WHITE SINGS - VOL. 2 (10" LP)	12
54	Mercury MG 25014	SONGS BY JOSH WHITE (10" LP)	12
55	London H-APB 1038	JOSH COMES A-VISITIN' (10" LP)	12
62	Golden Guinea GGL 0160	EMPTY BED BLUES (LP)	12

(see also Teddy Moss/Josh White)

JOSH & BEVERLEY WHITE
64	Realm REP 4003	BEVERLEY & JOSH WHITE JNR (EP)	12

JOY WHITE
79	Tribesman TM 25	Always Together (with Jerry Baxter)/Dubbing To Sir Coxsone Sound (12")	20

79	Fight FDD 4438	The First Cut Is The Deepest/ITALS : Rougher Yet (12")	20
78	Hawkeye HLP 002	SENTIMENTAL REASONS (LP)	25

K.C. WHITE
72	Dynamic DYN 434	Man No Dead/Man No Dead - Version	8
73	Green Door GD 4056	First Cut Is The Deepest/No Good Girl	10
73	Technique TE 929	Anywhere But Nowhere/Bush In Session	10

KITTY WHITE
54	London HL 8102	Jesse James/Scratch My Back (B-side with Dave Howard)	70
54	London HL 8102	Jesse James/Scratch My Back (78, B-side with Dave Howard)	20

LENNY WHITE
75	Atlantic K 50213	VENUSIAN SUMMER (LP)	12
78	Elektra K 12328	Lady Madonna/12 Bars From Mars	5
81	Elektra K 12500	Kid Stuff/Slipaway	5
83	Elektra ED 4921	My Turn To Love You (Special Mix)/(Dub Version) (12")	12

(see also Return To Forever)

LOUISA JANE WHITE
69	Philips BF 1810	When The Battle Is Over/Blue Ribbons	30
70	Philips BF 1834	How Does It Feel/Truth In My Tears	100

SHEILA WHITE
66	CBS 202465	Misfit/Switch Off The Night	15

TAM WHITE
67	Decca F 12711	World Without You/Someone You Should Know (unreleased)	0
68	Decca F 12723	Dancing Out Of My Heart/I'll Stay Loving You	10
68	Decca F 12849	Waiting Till The Night Comes Around/Girl Watcher	15
69	Deram DM 261	That Old Sweet Roll/Don't Make Promises	25
70	Middle Earth MDS 104	Lewis Carroll/Future Thoughts	50
70	Middle Earth MDLS 304	TAM WHITE (LP)	80

(see also Buzz, Boston Dexters)

TERRY WHITE & TERRIERS
59	Decca F 11133	Rock Around The Mailbags/Blackout	70
59	Decca F 11133	Rock Around The Mailbags/Blackout (78)	20

THOMAS WHITE
79	Hit Run HD 12	Ivory Girl/KEITH FRANCIS: Prejudice Country (12")	50

TONY JOE WHITE
68	Monument MON 1024	Soul Francisco/Whompt Out On You	8
69	Monument MON 1031	Polk Salad Annie/Aspen Colorado	15
69	Monument MON 1036	Willie And Laura Mae Jones/Baby Scratch My Back	10
69	Monument MON 1040	Roosevelt And Ira Lee/The Migrant	6
70	Monument MON 1043	Groupy Girl/High Sheriff Of Calhoun Parrish	7
70	Monument MON 1048	Save Your Sugar For Me/My Friend	6
71	Warner Bros WB 6129	A Night In The Life Of A Swamp Fox/The Daddy	6
68	Monument LMO/SMO 5027	BLACK AND WHITE (LP)	22
70	Monument LMO/SMO 5035	TONY JOE WHITE CONTINUED (LP)	20
70	Monument SMO 5043	TONY JOE (LP)	22
71	Warner Bros WS 1900	TONY JOE WHITE (LP)	18
71	Warner Bros K 46068	TONY JOE WHITE (LP, reissue)	12
72	Warner Bros K 46147	THE TRAIN I'M ON (LP)	15
73	Warner Bros K 46229	HOME-MADE ICE CREAM (LP)	18
73	Warner Bros K 56149	THE BEST OF TONY JOE WHITE (LP)	12

TREVOR WHITE
76	Island WIP 6291	Crazy Kids/Movin' In The Right Direction (with p/s)	20
76	Island WIP 6291	Crazy Kids/Movin' In The Right Direction	8

(see also Sparks, Radio Stars)

ANDY WHITE
85	Stiff BUY DJ 234	Religious Persuasion (Light blue promo "A" label)	7

WHITE DOOR
84	Clay 37	Flame In My Heart/Behind The White Door (p/s)	6

WHITE DUCK
72	Uni UN 541	Billy Goat/Really	8
73	Uni UN 555	Honey, You'll Be Alright/Carry Love	8
72	Uni UNLS 123	WHITE DUCK (LP)	22
73	Uni UNLS 129	IN SEASON (LP)	22

WHITE ELEPHANT
70s	White Elephant RIOCH 1	CITY WALLS (LP, with other artists)	12

RICK WHITEFIELD
71	Horse HOSS 10	Hey Mama/Ride Baby Ride	6

WHITEFIRE
78	Whitefire 98DB 001	SUZANNE (EP)	40

WHITE HART
79	Tradition TSR 033	IN SEARCH OF REWARD (LP)	50

WHITE HEAT (1)
79	Valium VAL 01	Nervous Breakdown/Sammy Sez (gatefold p/s)	25
80	Valium VAL 02	Finished With The Fashions/Ordinary Joe (p/s, with insert)	20
81	Valium VAL 03	City Beat/It's No Use (Young Ones) (p/s)	15
82	Valium VALP 101	IN THE ZERO HOUR (LP)	25

WHITE HEAT (2)
84	RSR 007	Soldier Of Fortune/Lovemaker	50
84	Rock Shop RSR 007	WHITE HEAT (LP)	20

WHITE HORN
75	Philips 6006 440	Making It Funky/Mama Said	8

WHITEHOUSE

90	Sue Lawley SLS 002	Still Going Strong/Ankles And Wrists	15
01	SLA-003	Cruise (Force The Truth)/Instrumental Version (12")	20
02	SLA-004	Wriggle Like A Fucking Eel/Instrumental Version (12")	18
80	Come Org. WDC 881004	BIRTHDEATH EXPERIENCE (LP, first pressing pink labels, 850 copies)	150
80	Come Org. WDC 881005	TOTAL SEX (LP, 400 on green vinyl)	120
80	Come Org. WDC 881005	TOTAL SEX (LP, 800 on black vinyl)	80
80	Come Org. WDC 883005	TOTAL SEX (cassette)	75
80	Come Org. WDC 883003	ULTRASADISM (cassette)	60
81	Come Org. WDC 881010	DEDICATED TO PETER KÜRTEN, SADIST AND MASS SLAYER (LP, some on coloured vinyl, some in custom sleeve)	120
80	Come Org. WDC 881007	ERECTOR (LP, different coloured vinyls)	100
81	Come Org. WDC 881013	BÜCHENWALD (LP, clear vinyl)	120
81	WDC 883013	BUCHENWALD (cassette)	60
81	Come Org. WDC 881017	NEW BRITAIN (LP, with insert)	125
82	Come Org. WDC 881027	PSYCHOPATHIA SEXUALIS (LP, clear vinyl, black is bootleg)	200
82	Come Org. WDC 883020	LIVE ACTION 1 (cassette)	45
83	Come Org. WDC 883027	PSYCHOPATHIA SEXUALIS (cassette)	70
83	Come Org. WDC 883033	RIGHT TO KILL - DEDICATED TO DENNIS ANDREW NEILSEN (LP, & inserts)	120
83	Come Org. WDC 883044048	USA I - V (5 cassettes documenting 1983 US tour, pice for each)	45
85	Come Org. WDC	GREAT WHITE DEATH (LP)	80

(Many Whitehouse LP's were issued in customised white card sleeves & were later available in a generic 'Peter Kürten' sleeve, originally used for the 2nd pressing of the 'Peter Kürten' LP. This latter design was also used for counterfeits. There may also be coloured vinyl variations which are worth the same)

80s	Come Org. WDC	150 MURDEROUS PASSIONS (LP, with Nurse With Wound)	75
80s	United Dairies UD 009	150 MURDEROUS PASSIONS (LP, with Nurse With Wound, reissue)	40
80s	United Dairies UD 009	150 MURDEROUS PASSIONS (LP, with Nurse With Wound, export issue, sealed in black vinyl)	125
80s	Susan Lawley 1	CREAM OF THE SECOND COMING (2-LP)	45
91	Susan Lawley SL 002	THANK YOUR LUCKY STARS (LP)	30
92	Susan Lawley SL 003	TWICE IS NOT ENOUGH (LP)	30

(see also Come, Nurse With Wound, New Order, Skullflower, Konstruktivits)

WHITE LIES

08	Fiction 1795718	To Lose My Life (6 x 7" box set with signed print)	50

WHITE LIGHTNING

84	Wild Party PP 1000	This Poison Fountain/Hypocrite (no p/s, 1,000 only)	50
90	Workshop JOB LP 2	AS MIDNIGHT APPROACHES (LP, with inner)	18

(see also Static)

WHITE LINING

70	Parlophone R 5868	Back In The Sun/Mon Amour	20

WHITE MULE

70	UNI UNS 523	Looking Through Cat's Eyes/Hundred Franc Blues	15

WHITE NOISE

75	Virgin VDJ 2	An Extract From White Noise 2 (promo only)	20
69	Island ILPS 9099	AN ELECTRIC STORM (LP, pink label black/orange circle logo)	125
69	Island ILPS 9099	WHITE NOISE (LP, repressing pink label with white 'i' logo)	50
75	Virgin V 2032	WHITE NOISE 2 (LP)	15

(see also BBC Radiophonic Workshop)

WHITE ON BLACK

74	Saydisc SDL 251	WHITE ON BLACK (LP, fully laminated sleeve)	30

WHITE PLAINS

70	Deram DM 280	My Baby Loves Lovin'/Show Me Your Hand	7
70	Deram DM 291	I've Got You On My Mind/Today I Killed A Man I Didn't Know	8
70	Deram DM 315	Julie Do Ya Love Me/I Need Your Everlasting Love	7
71	Deram DM 333	When You Are A King/The World Gets Better With Love	8
71	Deram DM 340	Gonna Miss Here Mississippi/I'll Go Blind	7
71	Deram DM 348	I Con't Stop/Julie Anne	7
73	Deram DM 371	Step Into A Dream/Look To See	8
73	Deram DM 388	Does Anybody Know Where My Baby Is/Just For A Change	10
70	Deram SML 1067	WHITE PLAINS (LP, laminated cover)	30
71	Deram SML 1092	WHEN YOU ARE A KING (LP)	25

(see also Edison Lighthouse, David & Jonathan, Kestrels, Brotherhood Of Man, Peter's Faces, Carter-Lewis & Southerners, Ivy League)

WHITE RABBIT

69	NEMS 56-4165	Ain't That Something/I'll Do The Rest	8

WHITESNAKE

78	EMI International INEP 751	SNAKEBITE (EP, white vinyl, p/s; later black vinyl with no p/s)	15
78	EMI International INT 568	Lie Down/Don't Mess With Me	6
79	EMI International INT 578	The Time Is Right For Love/Come On (live)	6
80	United Artists BP 352	Fool For Your Loving/Mean Business/Don't Mess With Me (in luminous p/s)	8
80	United Artists BP 352	Fool For Your Loving/Mean Business/Don't Mess With Me	5
82	Liberty BPP 416	Here I Go Again/Bloody Luxury (picture disc)	10
82	Liberty BP 418	Love An' Affection/Victim Of Love (withdrawn)	35
83	Liberty BPP 420	Guilty Of Love/Gambler (shaped picture disc)	10
84	Liberty BPP 423	Standing In The Shadows/All Or Nothing (US Mix) (picture disc)	6
87	EMI EMIW 5606	Still Of The Night/Here I Go Again (p/s, white vinyl with poster)	8
87	EMI 12 EMIP 5606	Still Of The Night/Here I Go Again/You're Gonna Break My Heart Again (12", picture disc)	8
87	EMI 10EMI 35	Here I Go Again '87 (US remix)/Guilty Of Love (10", p/s, white vinyl)	8
78	EMI Intl. INS 3022	TROUBLE (LP, grey or pink inner sleeve)	12
82	Liberty LBGP 30354	SAINTS AN' SINNERS (LP, picture disc)	15
84	Liberty LBGP 240 000 0	SLIDE IT IN (LP, picture disc, U.S. mixes)	15
87	EMI EMCP 3528	WHITESNAKE 1987 (LP, picture disc)	15
89	EMI EMCDJ 1013	SLIP OF THE TONGUE (LP, with track by track interview, promo only)	20

(see also David Coverdale, Deep Purple, Rainbow, Roger Glover, Bernie Marsden, Jon Lord, Phenomena, Cozy Powell, Young & Moody Band, Company, Snafu, Bogdon, Forcefield, Gogmagog, Tramline, National Health)

WHITE SOLES
76	Satril SAT 104	Beside You/Never Say Die	10

WHITE SPIRIT
80	Neat NEAT 05	Back To The Grind/Cheetah (p/s)	10
81	MCA MCA 638	Midnight Chaser/Suffragettes (p/s)	30
81	MCA MCA 652	High Upon High/No Reprieve/Arthur Guitar	15
80	MCA MCF 3079	WHITE SPIRIT (LP, with lyric insert)	18

(see also Gillan, Iron Maiden)

WHITE SS
78	White SS CIA 72	Mercy Killing/I'm Not One (live) (p/s)	25

WHITE STRIPES
01	XL XLS 139	Hotel Yorba (Live At The Hotel Yorba)/Rated X (p/s, 4000 only)	15
02	XL XLS 142	Fell In Love With A Girl/I Just Don't Know What To Do With Myself (p/s, 5000 only)	15
02	XL XLS 142 CD/2	Fell In Love With A Girl/Let's Shake Hands/Lafayette Blues/Fell In Love With A Girl (Live)/Lovesick (Live At The Forum)/I Just Don't Know What To Do With Myself/Fell In Love With A Girl (Video) (2-CD)	10
02	XL XLS 148	Dead Leaves And The Dirty Ground/Stop Breaking Down (Live) (p/s, 5000 only)	10
02	XL/MOJO no cat. no.	Red Death At 6:14 (1-sided, promo only, red vinyl, numbered label, 3000 only, mail order only via Mojo magazine, with letter)	35
02	XL XLS 162	Merry Christmas From The White Stripes: Candy Cane Children/The Reading Of The Story Of The Magi/The Singing Of Silent Night (1000 only, p/s)	18
03	XL XLS 166	I Just Don't Know What To Do With Myself/Who's To Say (p/s)	6
03	XL no cat. no.	I Just Don't Know What To Do With Myself/Who's To Say/Lafayette Blues (Live On Radio 1 Evening Session)/I'm Finding It Harder To Be A Gentleman (Live On The John Peel Show) (promo CD)	15
03	XL LP 162 DJ	Seven Nation Army/In The Cold, Cold Night (p/s, ELEPHANT SAMPLER)	8
03	XL XLS 162	Seven Nation Army/Good To Me (p/s)	6
03	XL no cat. no.	Seven Nation Army (1-sided 12" promo, stamped white label, no p/s)	30
04	XL XLS 207	Jolene (Live Under Blackpool Lights)/Do (Live Under Blackpool Lights) (p/s)	6
03	XL XLS173	Hardest Button To Button/St. Ides Of March (p/s)	6
04	XL XLS 181	There's No Home For You Here/I Fought Piranhas/Let's Build A Home (die-cut sleeve)	12
05	XL XLS 216	Blue Orchid/The Nurse	5
05	no. cat. No.	Blue Orchid (Michel Gondry Remix)/Blue Orchid (Jim Jarmusch Remix) (2000 only remix 12" - tour only product, p/s)	15
05	XL XLS 218	My Doorbell/Same Boy You've Always Known (live) (red/white vinyl, p/s)	10
05	XL (no. cat. No.)	DENIAL TWIST (10 x printed/stickered CD's in different artwork card wallets. One given away at each night of UK autumn tour. Each CD blank - 10 downloads were availiable online only, this price for complete set)	250
07	XL XL 277	Rag And Bone (with etched B-side of Jack and Meg's faces given away free with copies of NME, gatefold sleeve)	6
07	XL XLS293B	You Don't Know What Love Is (acoustic)/300 mph Torrential Outpour Blues	5
09	TMR017	Let's Shake Hands (alternate take)/Look Me Over Closely (alternate take)	40
01	XL XLLP 150	DE STIJL (LP)	25
01	XL XLLP151	WHITE BLOOD CELLS (LP, red vinyl)	25
01	XL XLLP 149	WHITE STRIPES (LP)	25
01	XL XLPD149	WHITE STRIPES (LP, picture disc)	30
03	XL XLLP 162	ELEPHANT (2-LP, promo, custom sleeve, 500 only)	70
05	XL XLLP 191 P	GET BEHIND ME SATAN (300 only worldwide. 2 x LP promo, different p/s)	200
07	XL XLLP271	ICKY THUMP (2-LP, red/white vinyl)	25

(see also Raconteurs)

WHITE TRASH
69	Apple APPLE 6	Road To Nowhere/Illusions (early copies as White Trash)	200
69	Apple APPLE 6	Road To Nowhere/Illusions (later copies as Trash)	60

(see also Trash, Poets, Stone The Crows)

WHITE ZOMBIE
89	Caroline CAROL 1457	God Of Thunder/Love Razor/Disaster Blaster 2 (12", withdrawn)	15

DAVID WHITFIELD
54	Decca F 10242	The Book/Heartless	10
54	Decca F 10327	Carla Mia/Love, Tears And Kisses	10
54	Decca F 10355	Smile/When Or Where	8
54	Decca F 10399	Santa Natale/Adeste Fideles	8
55	Decca F 10458	Beyond The Stars/Open Up Your Heart	8
55	Decca F 10515	Ev'rywhere/Mama	8
55	Decca F 10562	The Lady/Santa Rose Lea Rose	8
55	Decca F 10596	I'll Never Stop Loving You/Lady Of Madrid	8
55	Decca F 10627	When You Lose The One You Love/Angelus	8
56	Decca F 10690	My September Love/The Rudded And The Rock	8
56	Decca F 10769	My Son John/My Unfinished Symphony	5
57	Decca F 10833	The Adoration Waltz/If I Lost You	5
57	Decca F 10864	I'll Find You/I'd Give You The World	5
54	Decca LF 1165	YOURS FROM THE HEART (10" LP)	15
58	Decca LK 4242	FAVOURITES (LP)	15

WILBUR WHITFIELD
57	Vogue V 9078	P.B. Baby/The One I Love	600
57	Vogue V 9078	P.B. Baby/The One I Love (78)	150

(see also Little Wilbur & Pleasers)

LEONARD WHITING
65	Pye 7N 15943	The Piper/That's What Mama Says	40

MARGARET WHITING
55	Capitol CL 14213	My Own True Love (Tara's Theme)/Can This Be Love (triangular centre)	12
55	Capitol CL 14242	Heat Wave/Come Rain Or Shine (triangular centre)	12
55	Capitol CL 14307	Stowaway/All I Want Is All There Is And Then Some (triangular centre)	12
55	Capitol CL 14348	A Man/Mama's Pearls (triangular centre)	12
55	Capitol CL 14375	Lover, Lover/I Kiss You A Million Times (triangular centre)	12
56	Capitol CL 14527	I Love A Mystery/Bidin' My Time	10
56	Capitol CL 14591	Old Enough/Day In - Day Out	8
56	Capitol CL 14647	True Love/Haunting Love	8
57	Capitol CL 14685	The Money Tree/Maybe I Love Him	8

57	London HLD 8451	Kill Me With Kisses/Speak For Yourself, John	10
58	London HLD 8562	I Can't Help (If I'm Still In Love With You)/That's Why I Was Born	10
58	London HLD 8562	I Can't Help (If I'm Still In Love With You)/That's Why I Was Born (78)	10
58	London HLD 8662	Hot Spell/I'm So Lonesome I Could Cry	10
66	London HLD 10078	Nothing Lasts Forever/The Wheel Of Hurt	10
67	London HLD 10114	Just Like A Man/The World Inside Your Arms	5
68	London HLU 10196	Faithfully/Am I Losing You	6
68	London HLU 10227	Maybe Just Once More/Can't Get You Out Of My Mind	5
53	Capitol LC 6585	CAPITOL PRESENTS MARGARET WHITING (10" LP)	20
56	Capitol LC 6811	MARGARET WHITING (10" LP)	20
58	London HA-D 2109	GOIN' PLACES (LP)	20
61	HMV CLP 1418	SINGS THE JEROME KERN SONGBOOK VOL. ONE (LP, mono)	18
61	London HA-D 2321	JUST A DREAM (LP)	20

(see also Jimmy Wakely, Bob Hope, Dean Martin)

RAY WHITLEY

65	HMV POP 1473	I've Been Hurt/There Is One Boy	150
65	HMV POP 1473	I've Been Hurt/There Is One Boy (DJ copy)	250

BOBBY WHITLOCK

72	CBS 65109	BOBBY WHITLOCK (LP)	30
73	CBS 65301	RAW VELVET (LP)	20

(see also Derek & Dominoes)

SLIM WHITMAN
SINGLES

54	London L 1149	Indian Love Call/China Doll	20
54	London HL 1149	Indian Love Call/China Doll (re-pressing with different prefix)	15
54	London L 1214	There's A Rainbow In Every Teardrop/Danny Boy	20
54	London HL 1214	There's A Rainbow In Every Teardrop/Danny Boy (re-pressing)	15
54	London L 1226	North Wind/Darlin' Don't Cry	20
54	London HL 1226	North Wind/Darlin' Don't Cry (re-pressing with different prefix)	20
54	London HL 8018	Stairway To Heaven/Lord, Help Me To Be As Thou	20
54	London HL 8039	Secret Love/Why	25
54	London HL 8061	Rose Marie/We Stood At The Altar	15
54	London HL 8080	Beautiful Dreamer/Ride Away	15
54	London HL 8091	The Singing Hills/I Hate To See You Cry	15
54	London HL 8125	When I Grow Too Old To Dream/Cattle Call	12
55	London HL 8141	Haunted Hungry Heart/Roll On, Silvery Moon	10
55	London HLU 8167	I'll Never Stop Loving You/I'll Never Take You Back Again	10
55	London HLU 8196	Song Of The Wild/You Have My Heart	10
56	London HLU 8230	Tumbling Tumbleweeds/Tell Me	10
56	London HLU 8252	I'm A Fool/My Heart Is Broken In Three	10
56	London HLU 8287	Serenade/I Talk To The Waves	10
56	London HLU 8327	Dear Mary/Whiffenpoof Song	10
56	London HLU 8350	I'm Casting My Lasso Towards The Sky/There's A Love Knot In My Lariat	10
57	London HLP 8403	I'll Take You Home Again Kathleen/Careless Love	10

(The above 45's were originally issued with gold label print & tri-centres; later round-centre and/or silver label print copies are worth half these values.)

57	London HLP 8416	Curtain Of Tears/Smoke Signals (silver label print)	6
57	London HLP 8420	Gone/An Amateur In Love (gold label print)	15
57	London HLP 8434	Many Times/Warm, Warm Lips	6
57	London HLP 8459	Lovesick Blues/Forever	6
57	London HLP 8518	Unchain My Heart/Hush-A-Bye	6
58	London HLP 8590	A Very Precious Love/Careless Hands	6
58	London HLP 8642	Candy Kisses/Tormented	6
58	London HLP 8708	Wherever You Are/At The End Of Nowhere	6
59	London HLP 8835	I Never See Maggie Alone/The Letter Edged In Black	8
59	London HLP 8835	I Never See Maggie Alone/The Letter Edged In Black (78)	10
59	London HLP 8896	What Kind Of God (Do You Think You Are)/A Tree In The Meadow (unissued)	0
60	London HLP 9103	Roll, River, Roll/Twilla Lee	5
61	London HLP 9302	Vaya Con Dios/Ramona	5

EPs

54	London RE-P 1006	SLIM WHITMAN AND HIS SINGING GUITAR (at least 8 different colour sleeves, with matt finish & various label designs)	12
54	London RE-P 1006	SLIM WHITMAN AND HIS SINGING GUITAR (at least 8 different colour sleeves, gloss finish & various label designs)	8
55	London RE-P 1042	SONG OF THE WILD	10
56	London RE-P 1064	SLIM WHITMAN VOL. 2 PT. 1	10
56	London RE-P 1070	SLIM WHITMAN VOL. 2 PT. 2	10
57	London RE-P 1100	SLIM WHITMAN VOL. 2 PT. 3	10
59	London RE-P 1199	SLIM WHITMAN SINGS (triangular silver-top centre)	10
59	London RE-P 1199	SLIM WHITMAN SINGS (later round centre)	10
60	London RE-P 1258	SLIM WHITMAN SINGS No. 2	10
63	London RE-P 1360	THE WAYWARD WIND	10
64	Liberty LEP 4018	IRISH LOVE SONGS THE SLIM WHITMAN WAY	8
65	Liberty LEP 4027	SLIM WHITMAN SINGS MORE IRISH SONGS	8
66	Liberty LEP 4046	A SATISFIED MIND	10

ALBUMS

54	London H-APB 1015	SLIM WHITMAN & HIS SINGING GUITAR (10", gold label print)	40
54	London H-APB 1015	SLIM WHITMAN & HIS SINGING GUITAR (10", silver label print)	25
56	London HA-U 2015	SLIM WHITMAN & HIS SINGING GUITAR VOL. 2	30
59	London HA-P 2139	SLIM WHITMAN SINGS	20
59	London HA-P 2199	SLIM WHITMAN SINGS VOL. 2	20
60	London HA-P 2343	SLIM WHITMAN	20
61	London HA-P 2392	JUST CALL ME LONESOME	20
62	London HA-P 2443	SLIM WHITMAN SINGS VOL. 3 (Mono)	20
62	London HA-P 2443	SLIM WHITMAN SINGS VOL. 3 (also stereo SAH-P 6232)	25
62	London HA-P 8013	SLIM WHITMAN SINGS VOL. 4	12
63	London HA-P 8059	HEART SONGS AND LOVE SONGS	12
63	London HA-P 8093	I'M A LONELY WANDERER	12

MARVA WHITNEY
| 70 | Polydor 2001 036 | This Girl's In Love With You/He's The One | 10 |
| 69 | Polydor 583 767 | IT'S MY THING (LP) | 60 |

(see also James Brown)

JAKI WHITREN
| 73 | Epic EPC 65645 | RAW BUT TENDER (LP, with insert) | 45 |

TIM WHITSETT
| 64 | Sue WI 318 | Macks By The Tracks/Shine | 45 |

TIM WHITSETT/STICKS HERMAN
| 60s | Range JRE 7002 | RHYTHM & BLUES (EP) | 30 |

PAUL WHITSUN JONES & WALLAS EATON & HOLLAND
| 65 | Oriole CB 1991 | Shake It Baby/Instant Marriage | 20 |

WHITSUNTIDE EASTER
| 77 | Pilgrim/Grapevine GRA 109 | NEXT TIME YOU PLAY A WRONG NOTE...MAKE IT A SHORT ONE (LP, gatefold sleeve) | 100 |

ROGER WHITTAKER (& COMPANIONS)
62	Fontana H 358	The Charge Of The Light Brigade/Keep It A Secret	5
62	Fontana 267 217TF	Steel Men/After The Laughter	5
63	Fontana 267 258TF	Butterfly/Times Is Tough (as 'Rog' Whittaker)	6
63	Fontana TF 393	The Sinner/Settle Down (as Rog Whittaker & Companions)	6

(see also Hank & Mellowmen)

TOMMY WHITTLE (& HIS QUARTET)
57	HMV 45 POP 379	The Finisher/Cabin In The Sky	25
55	Esquire EP 37	TOMMY WHITTLE QUINTET (EP)	40
56	Esquire EP 37	TOMMY WHITTLE QUINTET (EP)	40
58	HMV 7EG 8325	TOMMY WHITTLE QUARTET (EP)	100
54	Esquire 20-028	WAXING WITH WHITTLE (LP)	50
55	Esquire 20-048	TOMMY WHITTLE QUINTET (LP)	60
56	Esquire 20-061	SPOTLIGHTING TOMMY WHITTLE (LP)	90
56	Esquire 20-068	LULLABY & RHYTHM (LP)	100
60	Tempo TAP 27	NEW HORIZONS (LP)	700
60s	Ember EMB 3305	EASY LISTENING (LP)	75
67	Masquerade MQ 2000	SAX FOR DREAMERS (LP)	100
77	Jam 648	WHY NOT? (LP)	20
82	Tee Jay 101	THE NEARNESS OF YOU (LP)	20
88	Esquire 334	MORE WAXING WITH WHITTLE (LP, reissue)	20

WHIZZ KIDS
| 79 | Dead Good DEAD SIX | P.A.Y.E./99% Proof/National Assistance/Cheek To Cheek (p/s, with insert) | 20 |
| 80 | Ovation OVS 1213 | Suspect No. 1/Coma Life (p/s) | 10 |

THE WHO
SINGLES
65	Brunswick 05926	I Can't Explain/Bald Headed Woman	40
65	Brunswick 05935	Anyway Anyhow Anywhere/Daddy Rolling Stone	35
65	Brunswick 05944	My Generation/Shout And Shimmy	20
66	Brunswick 05951	Circles/Instant Party Mixture (unreleased)	0
66	Reaction 591 001	Substitute/Circles (temporarily withdrawn)	40
66	Reaction 591 001	Substitute/Instant Party (temporarily withdrawn)	30
66	Brunswick 05956	The Kids Are Alright/The Ox (existence unconfirmed)	0
66	Brunswick 05956	A Legal Matter/Instant Party	40
66	Reaction 591 001	Substitute/WHO ORCHESTRA: Waltz For A Pig (B-side actually by Graham Bond Organisation)	25
66	Brunswick 05965	The Kids Are Alright/The Ox	60
66	Brunswick 05968	La-La-La-Lies/The Good's Gone	60
66	Reaction 591 004	I'm A Boy/In The City	12
66	Reaction 591 010	Happy Jack/I've Been Away	12
67	Track 604 002	Pictures Of Lily/Doctor, Doctor	12
67	Track 604 006	The Last Time/Under My Thumb	65
67	Track 604 011	I Can See For Miles/Someone's Coming	15
68	Track 604 023	Dogs/Call Me Lightning	25
68	Track 604 024	Magic Bus/Dr. Jekyll And Mr Hyde	12
69	Track 604 027	Pinball Wizard/Dogs Part Two	12
70	Track 604 036	The Seeker/Here For More	10
70	Track 2094 002	Summertime Blues/Heaven And Hell	10
70	Track 2094 004	See Me, Feel Me/Overture From 'Tommy' (withdrawn)	40
71	Track 2094 009	Won't Get Fooled Again/Don't Know Myself (p/s, large centre)	25
71	Track 2094 009	Won't Get Fooled Again/Don't Know Myself (p/s, with middle)	35
71	Track 2094 012	Let's See Action/When I Was A Boy (paper labels, solid centre)	5
73	Track 2094 115	5.15/Water	7
75	Polydor 2001 561	Overture/See Me Feel Me/Listening To You (from "Tommy" soundtrack, p/s)	10
76	Polydor 2058 803	Substitute/I'm A Boy/Pictures Of Lily (12", company sleeve)	8
79	Polydor WHO 2	Long Live Rock/I'm The Face/My Wife (withdrawn, blank run-off groove)	6
80	Polydor WHO 3	5.15/I'm One (p/s)	6
81	Polydor WHO 5	Don't Let Go The Coat/You	5
81	Polydor 2058 803	Substitute/I'm a Boy-Pictures Of Lily	5
81	Polydor WHO 004	You Better You Bet/The Quiet One	5
82	Polydor WHOP 6	Athena/A Man Is A Man (picture disc)	6
82	Polydor WHOPX 6	Athena/A Man Is A Man/Won't Get Fooled Again (12", picture disc)	8
82	Polydor WHOPX 6	Athena/A Man Is A Man/Won't Get Fooled Again (12", picture disc, mispressing, plays "Why Did I Fall For That")	10
89	Polydor POCD 907	My Generation/Substitute/Baba O'Riley/Behind Blue Eyes (CD, card sleeve)	10
89	Polydor POCD 917	Won't Get Fooled Again (Extended Version)/Bony Maronie/Dancing In The Street/Mary-Anne With The Shaky Hand (CD, card sleeve)	15

EXPORT SINGLES
66	Brunswick 05956	A Legal Matter/Instant Party (with Scandinavian p/s)	150
68	Decca AD 1001	My Generation/Shout And Shimmy	100
68	Decca AD 1001	My Generation/Shout And Shimmy (in p/s)	200

MINT VALUE £

| 68 | Decca AD 1002 | A Legal Matter/Instant Party | 100 |
| 72 | Track 2094 102 | Join Together/Baby Don't You Do It (p/s, for Spain) | 25 |

EPs

66	Reaction 592 001	READY STEADY WHO	100
70	Track 2252 001	EXCERPTS FROM "TOMMY" (33rpm)	25
83	Reaction WHO 7	READY STEADY WHO (reissue)	20

ALBUMS

65	Brunswick LAT 8616	MY GENERATION (laminated front sleeve, black/silver label)	800
66	Reaction 593 002	A QUICK ONE (laminated sleeve, blue/silver label)	200
67	Track 612 002	THE WHO SELL OUT (LP, mono)	150
67	Track 613 002	THE WHO SELL OUT (LP, stereo)	120
67	Track 612 002	THE WHO SELL OUT (mono, 500 with stickered sleeve & poster)	800
67	Track 613 002	THE WHO SELL OUT (stereo, 500 with stickered sleeve & poster)	800
68	Track 612 006	DIRECT HITS (mono)	40
68	Track 613 006	DIRECT HITS (stereo)	50
69	Track 613 013/014	TOMMY (2-LP, 1st issue fold-out laminated gatefold sleeve made by E.J. Day, A1/B1/C1/D1 matrixes, "double album" on labels and must not have catalogue number under 'ST33' on the right side (as this is a later pressing) with numbered 12-page booklet)	150
69	Track 613 013/014	TOMMY (2-LP, 2nd issue fold-out matt gatefold sleeve, no "double album" on labels with 12-page booklet, un-numbered)	40
70	Track 2406 001	LIVE AT LEEDS (1st issue with BLACK stamp on front, foldout sleeve with 12 inserts including poster)	250
70	Track 2406 001	LIVE AT LEEDS (with BLUE or RED stamp on front, foldout sleeve with 12 inserts including poster stating 'Tuesdays At The Marquee')	80
70	Track 2406 001	LIVE AT LEEDS (with BLUE or RED stamp on front, foldout sleeve with 12 inserts including poster stating 'Live At Leeds', A1/B1 matrix')	50
70	Track 2406 001	LIVE AT LEEDS (second pressing, BLUE or RED stamp on front, foldout sleeve with 12 inserts including poster stating 'Live At Leeds', A3/B3 matrix')	40
70	Track 2407 008	BACKTRACK 8: A QUICK ONE (mono budget reissue)	15
70	Track 2407 009	BACKTRACK 9: SELL OUT (stereo budget reissue)	15
70	Track 2407 014	BACKTRACK 14: THE OX	22
70	Track 2856 001	WHO DID IT? (mail-order only, withdrawn)	600
71	Track 2408 102	WHO'S NEXT (1st pressing with poly-lined inner sleeve with black and white Polydor artist photos on front and "HEAD HUNTERS - GET A HEAD" on rear. MATRIX: 2408 102 A1/B2) Pleated end spines)	45
71	Track 2408 102	WHO'S NEXT (later pressing, MATRIX: 2408 102 A4/B3)	25
71	Track 2406 006	MEATY, BEATY, BIG AND BOUNCY (gatefold sleeve)	20
71	Track 2406 006	MEATY, BEATY, BIG AND BOUNCY (gatefold sleeve, mispressed, plays "The Seeker" instead of "Magic Bus")	25
72	Track 2406 007	TOMMY PART ONE	12
72	Track 2406 008	TOMMY PART TWO (with lyric sheet)	15
73	Track 2657 013	QUADROPHENIA (2-LP, original with 22-page photo booklet, matt labels)	50
74	Track ACB 254	ODDS AND SODS (LP)	65
74	Track 2406 116	ODDS AND SODS (cut-away braille sleeve, with poster & lyric sheet)	20
75	Polydor 2490 129	THE WHO BY NUMBERS	15
80	Virgin V 2179	MY GENERATION (reissue)	20
81	Polydor 2675 216	PHASES (9-LP box set, stickered cover)	100
00	Polydor 5477271	BBC SESSIONS (2-LP)	20
02	POLYDOR 113 981-1	MY GENERATION - DELUXE EDITION (2-LP, reissue)	20
03	POLYDOR 076 176-1	WHO'S NEXT (3-LP, reissue)	30

PROMOS

69	Track PRO 1	The Acid Queen/We're Not Gonna Take It (existence unconfirmed)	0
69	Track PRO 2	Go To The Mirror!/Sally Simpson	80
69	Track PRO 3	I'm Free/1921	80
69	Track PRO 4	Christmas/Overture	80

(see also High Numbers, Pete Townshend, Roger Daltrey, John Entwistle, Keith Moon, Kenney Jones, Graham Bond Organisation, Rigor Mortis, McEnroe & Cash)

WHO THE HELL DOES JANE SMITH THINK SHE IS

| 87 | Influx FUX 1 | Use/Imagination (p/s) | 25 |
| 87 | Influx FUX 1T | Use/Imagination (12", p/s) | 60 |

WALLY WHYTON (& VIPERS)

59	Parlophone R 4585	Don't Tell Me Your Troubles/It's All Over You	5
60	Parlophone R 4630	All Over This World/Got Me A Girl	5
60	Pye 7N 15304	It's A Rat Race/Marriage Of Convenience/95% Of Me Loves You (with Sally Miles)/You're Going To Be Caught (as Wally Whyton & Vipers)	5
61	Piccadilly 7N 35089	Little Red Pony/Christmas Land	5
68	Fontana TF 960	Gentle On My Mind/Ballad Of The Bol Weevil	5
69	Fontana TF 994	Wichita Lineman/Leave Them A Flower	5
69	Fontana TF 1030	Jig Alone/Out On The Road	5
60	Parlophone GEP 8808	WILLUM AND ME (EP, stereo)	8
70	Fontana STL 5535	LEAVE THEM A FLOWER (LP)	12

(see also Vipers, Sharkey Todd & Monsters)

WI & HDEA

| 93 | Hype! VEN 001 | VENTURE F.M. PRESENTS SUMMER RUSH EP (12", stamped white label) | 20 |

WICHITA FALL

| 69 | Liberty LBS 83208 | LIFE IS BUT A DREAM (LP) | 25 |

WICHITA TRAIN WHISTLE

| 68 | Dot DOT 111 | Don't Cry Now/Tapioca Tundra (unissued) | 0 |
| 68 | Dot (S)LPD 516 | MICHAEL NESMITH PRESENTS THE WICHITA TRAIN WHISTLE SINGS (LP) | 40 |

(see also Michael Nesmith)

WIDERVISION

| 80 | Widermusic 001 | People/Truant (p/s) | 25 |

WIDOWMAKER

76	Jet JET 766	On The Road/Pin A Rose On Me	7
76	Jet JET 767	When I Met You/Pin A Rose On Me	5
76	Jet JET 782	Pin A Rose On Me/On The Road	5
76	Jet 2310 432	WIDOWMAKER (LP)	12

77	United Artists UAG 30038	TOO LATE TO CRY (LP, gatefold sleeve)..15

(see also Luther Grosvenor, Steve Ellis, Huw Lloyd Langton)

DAVID WIGG
66	CBS 202233	Life Is Complicated/Turning Around 10

WIGGANS
61	Blue Beat BB 29	Rock Baby/Let's Sing The Blues 25

PERCY WIGGINS
67	Atlantic 584 113	Book Of Memories/Can't Find Nobody (To Take Your Place) 10

SPENCER WIGGINS
67	Stateside SS 2024	Uptight Good Woman/Anything You Do Is Alright 25
70	Pama PM 794	I'm A Poor Man's Son/That's How Much I Love You 25

WIGWAM
75	Virgin V 2035	NUCLEAR NIGHTCLUB (LP)...15
76	Virgin V2051	LUCKY GOLDEN STRIPES AND STARPOSE (LP, "mirror" girl label, lyric insert, embossed sleeve) 15

LEO WIJNKAMP JR
75	Kicking Mule SNKF 108	RAGS TO RICHES (LP)..25
79	Kicking Mule SNKF 156	RETURN OF DR. HACKENBUSH (LP) 25

WIKKYD VIKKER
83	Boogie FUR 0235	Black Of The Night/Release (no p/s) 120

WILBURN BROTHERS
59	Brunswick 05799	That Silver-Haired Daddy Of Mine/A Boy's Faithful Friend 10
59	Brunswick LAT 8291	SIDE BY SIDE (LP)..20
61	Brunswick LAT 8501	CITY LIMITS (LP) 20
62	Brunswick LAT 8507	FOLK SONGS (LP)..15
67	Brunswick LAT 8686	COOL COUNTRY (LP) 15

JACK WILCE
69	Elektra EKSN 45068	Apple Pie, Mother & The Flag/Ballad Of Baby Browning 10

WILCO
04	Nonesuch 7559 79851	I'm A Wheel/Kicking Television (p/s)..6
11	dBpm 87162-7	I Might/I Love My Label (p/s, silver vinyl) 6
11	dBpm 87181-1	SPEAK INTO THE ROSE (10" red vinyl, Record Store Day release) 10
99	Reprise 9362 47282-1	SUMMERTEETH (2-LP)..30

WILD ANGELS
68	Major Minor MM 569	Nervous Breakdown/Watch The Wheels Go Round 25
69	B&C CB 114	Buzz Buzz/Please Don't Touch 12
70	B&C CB 123	Sally-Ann/Wrong Number, Try Again 12
71	B&C CB 145	Three Nights A Week/Time To Kill 8
72	Decca F 13308	Jo-Jo Ann/My Way 7
72	Decca F 13356	Beauty School Dropout/Midnight Rider 7
73	Decca F 13374	Running Bear/Sussin' 6
73	Decca F 13412	Greased Lightning/Born To Hand-Jive/Beauty School Dropout 6
73	Decca F 13456	Clap Your Hands And Stamp Your Feet/Wild Angels Rock'n'Roll 8
70	B&C BCM 101	LIVE AT THE REVOLUTION (LP)...15
70	B&C BCM 102	RED HOT'N'ROCKIN' (LP) 15
72	Decca SKL 5134	OUT AT LAST (LP) 12

WILD BOYS
78	Ring Piece CUS 886	Last One Of The Boys/We're Only Monsters...200

WILD BUNCH
84	Ariwa ARILP 15	THE WILD BUNCH (LP) 20

WILDCATS
59	London HLT 8787	Gazachstahagen/Billy's Cha Cha 25
59	London HLT 8787	Gazachstahagen/Billy's Cha Cha (78) 10

WILDCATS
80s	Wildbop WILDBOP 1	Talahassie Lassie/My Babe/Rip It UP 5

WILD COUNTRY
70	Trafalgar TRAF 01	Silent Village/Too Bad 65

JACK WILD(E)
69	Elektra EKSN 45068	Apple Pie Mother And The Flag/Ballad Of Baby Browning 6
70	Capitol CL 15635	Picture Of You/Some Beautiful...7
71	Buddah 2011-19	Punch & Judy/Takin It Easy 10
70	Capitol ST 22545	THE JACK WILD ALBUM (LP) 12

KIM WILDE
83	Rak 12 RAK 365	Dancing In The Dark (Extended)/Dancing In The Dark (Instrumental) (12", p/s, with poster) 8
84	MCA KIMP 1	The Second Time/Lovers On A Beach (picture disc) 10
84	MCA KIMP 2	The Touch/Shangri-La (shaped picture disc) 10
85	MCA KIMP 3	Rage To Love/Putty In Your Hands (shaped picture disc)................................10

MARTY WILDE (& WILDCATS)
78s
57	Philips PB 750	Honeycomb/Wild Cat (as Marty Wilde & Wildcats) 15
58	Philips PB 781	Love Bug Crawl/Afraid Of Love...30
58	Philips PB 804	Sing, Boy, Sing/Oh-Oh, I'm Falling In Love Again (with Wildcats) 20
58	Philips PB 835	Endless Sleep/Her Hair Was Yellow (as Marty Wilde & Wildcats) 10
58	Philips PB 850	My Lucky Love/Misery's Child (as Marty Wilde & Wildcats) 12
58	Philips PB 875	No One Knows/The Fire Of Love 25
59	Philips PB 902	Donna/Love-a, Love-a, Love-a 25
59	Philips PB 926	A Teenager In Love/Danny 30
59	Philips PB 959	Sea Of Love/Teenage Tears 40
59	Philips PB 972	It's Been Nice/Bad Boy...40
60	Philips PB 1002	Johnny Rocco/My Heart And I 50

SINGLES

57	Philips JK 1028	Honeycomb/Wild Cat (as Marty Wilde & Wildcats) (jukebox issue)	50
58	Philips PB 804	Sing, Boy, Sing/Oh-Oh, I'm Falling In Love Again (with Wildcats)	40
58	Philips PB 835	Endless Sleep/Her Hair Was Yellow (as Marty Wilde & Wildcats)	15
58	Philips PB 850	My Lucky Love/Misery's Child (as Marty Wilde & Wildcats)	12
58	Philips PB 875	No One Knows/The Fire Of Love	15
59	Philips PB 902	Donna/Love-a, Love-a, Love-a	10
59	Philips PB 926	A Teenager In Love/Danny	10
59	Philips PB 959	Sea Of Love/Teenage Tears	10
59	Philips PB 972	Bad Boy/It's Been Nice	10
60	Philips PB 1002	Johnny Rocco/My Heart And I	15
60	Philips PB 1022	The Fight/Johnny At The Crossroads	15
60	Philips PB 1037	I Wanna Be Loved By You/Angry	8
60	Philips PB 1078	Little Girl/Your Seventeenth Spring	8
61	Philips PB 1101	Rubber Ball/Like Makin' Love	8
61	Philips PB 1121	When Does It Get To Be Love/Your Loving Touch	7
61	Philips PB 1161	Hide And Seek/Crazy Dream	15
61	Philips PB 1191	Tomorrow's Clown/The Hellions	12
61	Philips PB 1206	Come Running/Ev'ryone	12
62	Philips PB 1240	Jezebel/Don't Run Away	10
62	Philips 326 546BF	Ever Since You Said Goodbye/Send Me The Pillow You Dream On	10
63	Columbia DB 4980	Lonely Avenue/Brand New Love	10
63	Philips 326 579BF	No! Dance With Me/Little Miss Happiness	7
63	Columbia DB 7145	Save Your Love For Me/Bless My Broken Heart	10
64	Columbia DB 7198	When Day Is Done/I Can't Help The Way I Feel	10
64	Columbia DB 7285	Kiss Me/My, What A Woman	10
64	Decca F 11979	The Mexican Boy/Your Kind Of Love	12
66	Philips PB 1490	I've Got So Used To Loving You/The Beginning Of The End	6
68	Philips BF 1632	By The Time I Get To Phoenix/Shutters And Boards	6
68	Philips BF 1669	Abergavenny/Alice In Blue	6
69	Philips BF 1753	All The Love I Have/Any Day	6
69	Philips BF 1783	Endless Sleep/Donna	5
69	Philips BF 1815	Shelley/Jump On The Train (with Deke Leonard)	6
70	Philips BF 1839	No Trams To Lime Street/Prelude To Old Age	7
71	Philips 6006 126	Busker/It's So Real	7
74	Magnet MAG 15	I Love You/She's A Mover	6

EPs

57	Philips BBE 12164	PRESENTING MARTY WILDE	60
58	Philips BBE 12200	MORE OF MARTY	50
59	Philips BBE 12327	SEA OF LOVE	50
60	Philips BBE 12385	VERSATILE MR. WILDE	55
60	Philips BBE 12422	MARTY WILDE FAVOURITES	50
62	Philips BBE 12517	COME RUNNING	40
63	Philips BE 433 638	MARTY	40

ALBUMS

59	Philips BBL 7342	WILDE ABOUT MARTY	60
60	Philips BBL 7380	MARTY WILDE SHOWCASE	50
60	Philips BBL 7385	THE VERSATILE MR. WILDE (mono)	50
60	Philips SBBL 570	THE VERSATILE MR. WILDE (stereo)	60
69	Philips SBL 7877	DIVERSIONS	15
70	Philips 6308 010	ROCK 'N' ROLL	12
74	Philips 6382 102	GOOD ROCKIN' - THEN AND NOW (LP)	12

(see also Wilde Three, Brian Bennett, Shadows, Keith Shields, Capricorn, Deke Leonard)

RICKY WILDE

73	UK 28	April Love/Round And Round	6
74	UK 59	Mrs Malinski/Cassette Blues	6
74	UK 63	Round And Round/Teen Wave	6

WILDER BROTHERS

57	HMV POP 365	I Want You/Teenage Angel	250
57	HMV POP 365	I Want You/Teenage Angel (78)	50

WILDERNESS ROAD

74	Dawn DNLS 3057	WILDERNESS ROAD (LP, unissued)	0

WILDE THREE

65	Decca F 12131	Since You've Gone/Just As Long	75
65	Decca F 12232	I Cried/Well Who's That?	75

(see also Marty Wilde, Justin Hayward, Vernons Girls)

WILDFIRE (1)

84	Mausoleum GUTS 8403	Nothing Lasts Forever/Blood Money	8
84	Mausoleum GUTS 8405	Jerusalem/Fight Fire With Fire (p/s)	5
83	Mausoleum SKUL 8307	BRUTE FORCE AND IGNORANCE (LP)	25
83	Mausoleum SKUL 8338	SUMMER LIGHTNING (LP, with insert)	15

(see also Weapon)

WILDFIRE (2)

80	Chrysalis CHR 1288	BURNING (LP)	12

WILDHEARTS

SINGLES

92	East West YZ 669T	MONDO AKIMBO A-GO-GO (12" EP, with inner sleeve)	25
92	East West YZ 669TX	MONDO AKIMBO A-GO-GO (12" EP, white vinyl, with inner sleeve, advance copies with artwork postcard & press sheet)	40
92	East West YZ 669TX	MONDO AKIMBO A-GO-GO (12" EP, white vinyl, with inner sleeve)	35
92	East West YZ 669CD	MONDO AKIMBO A-GO-GO (CD EP)	40
93	East West YZ 773	Greetings From Shitsville/The Bullshit Goes On (p/s, brown vinyl, with insert)	12
94	East West YZ 794	Caffeine Bomb/Girlfriend Clothes (p/s, green vinyl, with insert)	5
94	East West YZ 794CD	Caffeine Bomb/Girlfriend Clothes/Shut Your Fucking Mouth And Use Your Fucking Brain/And The Bullshit Goes On (CD, digipak)	12

94	East West YZ 828TE	Suckerpunch/Beautiful Thing You/Two-Way Idiot Mirror/29 x The Pain (10", p/s, 1-sided, etched) 12
94	East West YZ 874TEX	If Life Is Like A Lovebank I Want An Overdraft/Geordie In Wonderland/ Hate The World Day/Fire Up (10", gatefold sleeve with banknote)........................10
95	East West YZ 923TEX	I Wanna Go Where The People Go/Shandy Bang/Can't Do Right For Doing Wrong/Give The Girl A Gun (10", p/s)........................10
95	East West YZ 976TEX	Just In Lust/Mindslide/Friend For Five Minutes/S.I.N (In Sin) (10", p/s)........................10
97	Mushroom MUSH 6CD	Anthem/So Good To Be Back Home/Time To Let You Go (CD, mispressing, plays country music) 12
02	Round SMALP048	Vanilla Radio/Better Than Cable (picture disc, stickered PVC sleeve, 1500 only) 8

ALBUMS

92	East West 4509-91202-1	DON'T BE HAPPY... JUST WORRY (LP, as 2 x 12", with inner sleeves) 25
92	East West 4509-91202-2	DON'T BE HAPPY... JUST WORRY (2-CD, with bonus disc containing Anti-Dance Mixes of "Mondo Akimbo A-Go Go" tracks)........................25
93	East West 4509-93287-1	EARTH VS THE WILDHEARTS (LP, with exclusive uncredited track) 20
94	East West 4509-93039-2	FISHING FOR LUCKIES (CD, 6-track mini-album, fan club/mail-order only) 40
95	East West 0630-10404-1	P.H.U.Q. (LP, gatefold sleeve) 15
95	East West 0630-12850-1	FISHING FOR MORE LUCKIES (LP, reissue, with 3 extra tracks Underkill, "Saddened" & "I Wanna Go Where The People Go [Early Version]", unreleased, most copies destroyed) 100
95	East West 0630-12850-2	FISHING FOR MORE LUCKIES (LP, reissue, with 3 extra tracks Underkill, "Saddened" & "I Wanna Go Where The People Go [Early Version]", unreleased, most copies destroyed) 20
96	Round 0630-14888-1	FISHING FOR LUCKIES (2-LP, reissue, gatefold, Side 3 exclusive to vinyl)........................18
97	Mushroom MUSH13LP	ENDLESS, NAMELESS (LP, inner sleeve)........................15
98	Kuro Neko KNEKLP3	ANARCHIC AIRWAVES - THE WILDHEARTS AT THE BBC (2-LP, 200 mail-order copies only - 1000 copies made but 800 destroyed)........................25
98	Kuro Neko KNEK4LB	LANDMINES & PANTOMIMES - THE LAST OF THE WILDHEARTS...? (CD in square stickered metal tin in card box with insert, 1000 copies only) 30
03	Gut GUTLP25	THE WILDHEARTS MUST BE DESTROYED (LP, gatefold sleeve) 12
04	Gut GUTLP32	THE WILDHEARTS STRIKE BACK (2 x LP, gatefold)........................15
08	Round ROUND010LP	THE WILDHEARTS (2 x LP, white vinyl, photo insert, 1,000 only) 15

(see also Backyard Babies, Chasers, Energetic Krusher, Ginger, Honeycrack, Jellys, Quireboys, SilverGinger 5, SuperShit666, Devin Townsend, Yo-Yo's)

WILD HONEY
| 72 | Mam MAM 154 | Baby Don't You Know Anymore/He's My Sugar (featuring Tina Charles) ....5 |

(see also Tina Charles)

WILD HORSES
79	EMI International INTS 599	Criminal Tendencies/The Rapist (p/s) 5
80	EMI EMI 5047	Face Down/Dealer (p/s) 5
80	EMI EMI 5078	Fly Away/Blackmail (p/s, white vinyl; black vinyl demos £15) 6
80	EMI 12EMI 5078	Fly Away/Blackmail (12", p/s, white vinyl) 8
81	EMI EMI 5149	I'll Give You Love/Rocky Mountain Way (p/s) 5
81	EMI EMI 5149	I'll Give You Love/Rocky Mountain Way//The Kid/On A Saturday Night (double pack, gatefold p/s) 5
81	EMI EMI 5199	Everlasting Love/The Axe (no p/s) 5
80	EMI EMC 3326	WILD HORSES (LP, with inner sleeve)........................12
81	EMI EMC 3368	STAND YOUR GROUND (LP, with inner sleeve) 15

(see also Thin Lizzy, Motorhead, Rainbow, Dio)

WILD MAGNOLIAS
75	Barclay BAR 30	Smoke My Peace Pipe/Handa Wanda 5
75	Barclay BAR 34	They Call Us Wild/Jumalaka Boom Boom 5
75	Barclay 80 529	THE WILD MAGNOLIAS 1 (LP, gatefold sleeve) 20
75	Barclay 90 033	THEY CALL US WILD (LP, gatefold sleeve) 20

WILD OATS
| 63 | Oak RGJ 117 | WILD OATS (EP) ....750 |

WILD ONES (U.K.)
| 64 | Fontana TF 468 | Bowie Man/Purple Pill Eater ....75 |

WILD ONES (U.S)
| 65 | United Artsts ULP 1119 | THE ARTHUR SOUND (LP) ....40 |

WILD PUSSY
| 88 | Metallion | MECHANARCH (12", EP, wih insert) ....100 |

WILD SILK
68	Polydor 56256	Poor Man/Stop Crying 10
69	Columbia DB 8534	(Visions In A) Plaster Sky/Toymaker 30
69	Columbia DB 8611	Help Me/Crimson And Gold 20

WILD SWANS
82	Zoo CAGE 009	The Revolutionary Spirit/God Forbid (unissued, stamped white label) 12
82	Zoo CAGE 009	The Revolutionary Spirit/God Forbid (12", p/s) 10
82	Zoo CAGE 009	The Revolutionary Spirit/God Forbid (12", p/s, with 'The Lament Of Icarus' painting in top right of front sleeve, withdrawn) 15

(see also Lotus Eaters, Care)

WILD THING
69	Elektra EKSN 45076	Old Lady/Next To Me 6
70	Elektra EKS 74059	PARTYIN' (LP) 18
71	Elektra 2410 003	PARTYIN' (LP, reissue)........................12

WILD TURKEY
72	Chrysalis CHS 2004	Good Old Days/Life Is A Symphony 5
72	Chrysalis CHR 1002	BATTLE HYMN (LP, gatefold sleeve) 25
73	Chrysalis CHR 1010	TURKEY (LP, gatefold sleeve) 20

(see also Babe Ruth, Jethro Tull, Man, Gary Pickford-Hopkins, Whitesnake)

WILD UNCERTAINTY
| 66 | Planet PLF 120 | Man With Money/Broken Truth ....80 |

WILD WALLY
| 70 | Concord CON 1003 | I GO APE (LP) ....12 |

WILD & WANDERING
86 Iguana VYK 14 2,000 LIGHT ALES FROM HOME (12" EP, with insert) 25
(see also Pop Will Eat Itself)

WILDWEEDS
67 Chess CRS 8065 It Was Fun While It Lasted/Sorrow's Anthem 20

WILD WILL'S BLUE WASHBOARD BOYS
71 Flyright LP 4701 BABY YUM YUM (LP)..12

WILDY
76 Paladin PAL 12 No Smokin'/All The Children 10

WILFRED
70 Parlophone R5836 Candle In The WInd/Between The Lines 15

WILFRED & MILLICENT
65 Island WI 190 The Vow/I'll Never Believe In You 12
(see also Jackie [Edwards] & Millie [Small])

MIKE WILHELM
76 Zigzag/United Artists ZZ 1 MIKE WILHELM (LP, sold via Zigzag magazine) 45
(see also Charlatans, Flamin' Groovies)

JOHN BUCK WILKIN
70 LBF 15375 Apartment Twenty-One/Boy Of The Country 6

ROBERT WILKINS
60s Piedmont PLP 13162 REV ROBERT WILKINS (LP)..20
70 Spokane SPL 1002 BEFORE THE REVERENCE (LP) 40

C.T WILKINSON
76 DJM DJS 668 My Happiness/Monday Coming Up...8

WILLARDS LEAP
77 Wren CW 71010 ADIEU, JOHN BARLEYCORN 20

WILLETT FAMILY
62 Topic 12T 84 THE ROVING JOURNEYMAN (LP, blue label with booklet) 20

E WILLIAM
67 Polydor 56181 Lazy Life/Crazy How love Slips Away 50

AL WILLIAMS
80 Grapevine GRP 136 I Am Nothing/Brand New Love 30

ANDY WILLIAMS
56	London HLA 8284	Walk Hand In Hand/Not Any More...................................30
56	London HLA 8315	Canadian Sunset/High Upon A Mountain (gold label print) 40
56	London HLA 8315	Canadian Sunset/High Upon A Mountain (silver label print).......20
56	London HL 7013	Canadian Sunset/High Upon A Mountain (export issue)..............20
56	London HLA 8360	Baby Doll (From The Film)/Since I've Found My Baby (gold print) ..40
56	London HLA 8360	Baby Doll (From The Film)/Since I've Found My Baby (silver print) .20
57	London HLA 8399	Butterfly/It Doesn't Take Very Long...............................20
57	London HLA 8437	I Like Your Kind Of Love/Stop Teasin' Me..........................10
57	London HLA 8487	Lips Of Wine/Straight From My Heart 10
58	London HLA 8587	Are You Sincere/Be Mine Tonight 10
58	London HL 7034	Are You Sincere/Be Mine Tonight (export issue) 10
58	London HLA 8710	Promise Me, Love/Your Hand, Your Heart, Your Love 10
59	London HLA 8784	Hawaiian Wedding Song/House Of Bamboo 10
59	London HLA 8957	Lonely Street/Summer Love 7
59	London HLA 8957	Lonely Street/Summer Love (78)....................................10
59	London HLA 9018	The Village Of St. Bernadette/I'm So Lonesome I Could Cry..........6
59	London HLA 9018	The Village Of St. Bernadette/I'm So Lonesome I Could Cry (78).....10
60	London HLA 9099	Wake Me When It's Over/We Have A Date..............................5
60	London HLA 9241	Don't Go To Strangers/You Don't Want My Love 5
61	London HLA 9348	The Bilbao Song/How Wonderful To Know 5
67	CBS CBS 2675	Music To Watch Girls By/The Face I Love 5
67	CBS 3104	Holly/God Only Knows (B-side is Beach Boys cover) 8
57	London RE-A 1088	ANDY WILLIAMS' BIG HITS (EP).....................................12
57	London RE-A 1102	ANDY WILLIAMS' BIG HITS No. 2 (EP) 12
63	London RE-A 1394	ANDY WILLIAMS' BEST (EP) 8
57	London HA-A 2054	ANDY WILLIAMS SINGS STEVE ALLEN (LP) 30
58	London HA-A 2113	ANDY WILLIAMS SINGS RODGERS AND HAMMERSTEIN (LP)................30
59	London HA-A 2203	TWO TIME WINNERS (LP)...30
60	London HA-A 2238	LONELY STREET (LP)..12
62	London HA-A 8005	ANDY WILLIAMS' BEST (LP) 12
63	London HA-A 8090	UNDER PARIS SKIES (LP)..12

AUDREY WILLIAMS
56 MGM SP 1179 Ain't Nothing Gonna Be All Right No How/Livin' It Up And Havin' A Ball 25
(see also Hank Williams)

BIG JOE WILLIAMS
57	Jazz Collector JEN 3	A MAN SINGS THE BLUES (EP)....................................10
57	Jazz Collector JEN 4	A MAN SINGS THE BLUES VOLUME 2 (EP)...........................10
67	Delmark DJB 4	ON THE HIGHWAY (EP)..15
63	Esquire 32-191	BLUES ON HIGHWAY 51 (LP)...40
63	'77' LA 12-19	PINEY WOODS BLUES (LP)...30
64	CBS BPG 63813	CLASSIC DELTA BLUES (LP)...20
64	Storyville SLP 158	PORTRAITS IN BLUES VOLUME 4 (LP)..............................20
64	Storyville SLP 163	PORTRAITS IN BLUES VOLUME 7 (LP)..............................20
65	Fontana 688 800 ZL	TOUGH TIMES (LP) 25
66	Xtra XTRA 1033	BIG JOE WILLIAMS (LP)...30
66	Bounty BY 6018	BACK TO THE COUNTRY (LP) 40
66	Society SOC 1020	BIG JOE, SONNY, BROWNIE, LIGHTNIN' (LP, with Lightnin' Hopkins, Sonny Terry & Brownie McGhee) 15
69	Storyville 618 011	DON'T YOU LEAVE ME HERE (LP) 20

69	Liberty LBL/LBS 83207	HAND ME DOWN MY OLD WALKING STICK (LP)	20
69	Xtra XTRA 5059	LIVE AT FOLK CITY (LP)	15
70	RCA Intl. INTS 1087	CRAWLIN' KING SNAKE (LP)	18
72	Delmark DS 627	NINE STRING GUITAR (LP)	15

(see also Poor Joe Williams)

BILLY WILLIAMS (QUARTET)

54	Vogue Coral Q 2012	Sh'Boom/Whenever Wherever	15
54	Vogue Coral Q 2039	The Honeydripper/Love Me (as Billy Williams Quartet)	50
56	Vogue Coral Q 72149	A Crazy Little Palace/Cry Baby (as Billy Williams Quartet)	50
56	Vogue Coral Q 72180	Pray/You'll Reach Your Star	18
57	Vogue Coral Q 72222	Follow Me/Shame, Shame, Shame (as Billy Williams Quartet)	30
57	Vogue Coral Q 72222	Follow Me/Shame, Shame, Shame (as Billy Williams Quartet) (78)	15
57	Vogue Coral Q 72241	Butterfly/The Pied Piper	30
57	Vogue Coral Q 72266	I'm Gonna Sit Right Down And Write A Letter/Date With The Blues	25
57	Vogue Coral Q 72295	Got A Date With An Angel/The Lord Will Understand	40
58	Coral Q 72303	Don't Let Go/Baby, Baby (as Billy Williams Quartet)	40
58	Coral Q 72316	Steppin' Out Tonight/There I've Said It Again (as Billy Williams Quartet)	50
58	Coral Q 72331	I'll Get By/It's Prayin' Time	20
59	Coral Q 72359	Nola/Tied To The Strings Of Your Heart	10
59	Coral Q 72359	Nola/Tied To The Strings Of Your Heart (78)	10
59	Coral Q 72369	Goodnight Irene/Red Hot Love	30
59	Coral Q 72377	Telephone Conversation/Go To Sleep, Go To Sleep, Go To Sleep (with Barbara McNair)	25
60	Coral Q 72402	I Cried For You/Lover Of All Lovers	18
60	Coral Q 72414	Begin The Beguine/For You	5
58	Coral LVA 9092	BILLY WILLIAMS	100
60	Coral LVA 9120	HALF SWEET HALF BEAT	40
61	Coral LVA 9139	THE BILLY WILLIAMS REVUE	30

(see also Barbara McNair)

BOBBY WILLIAMS

68	Action ACT 4509	Baby I Need Your Love/Try It Again	10
73	Contempo C 17	Let's Jam/You're My Baby	8

CHRIS WILLIAMS & HIS MONSTERS

59	Columbia DB 4383	The Monster/The Eton Boating Song	35
60	Triumph RGM 1003	Kicking Around/Midnight Rocker (unissued; white label demo copies only)	250

CINDY WILLIAMS

67	Parlophone R 5648	They Talk About Us/Did He Call Today Mama	8

CLARENCE WILLIAMS (& HIS WASHBOARD BAND)

54	Columbia SCM 5134	High Society/Left All Alone With The Blues	20
58	Fontana TFE 17053	TREASURE OF NORTH AMERICAN MUSIC VOLUME 3 (EP)	15
59	Parlophone GEP 8733	CLARENCE WILLIAMS' WASHBOARD BAND (EP)	15
64	Jazz Collector JEL 18	JAZZ ORIGINATORS (EP)	10
54	London AL 3526	CLARENCE WILLIAMS AND HIS ORCHESTRA (10" LP)	20
55	Columbia 33S 1067	BACK ROOM SPECIAL (10" LP)	20
57	London AL 3561	CLARENCE WILLIAMS AND HIS ORCHESTRA VOL. 2 (10" LP)	20
60	Fontana TFL 5087	SIDNEY BECHET MEMORIAL (LP)	15
62	Philips BBL 7521	CLARENCE WILLIAMS VOL. 1: 1927-1935 (LP)	15

CLIVE WILLIAMS

69	Rock Steady Rev. REVR 6	Take Good Care Of My Baby/RICO: In Loving Memory Of Don Drummond	20

DAN WILLIAMS & HIS ORCHESTRA

55	London CAY 110	Donkey City/SHAW PARK CALYPSO BAND: Take Her To Jamaica	10

DANNY WILLIAMS

59	HMV POP 624	Tall A Tree/I Look At You	7
59	HMV POP 655	So High - So Low/My Own True Love	7
59	HMV POP 703	Youthful Years/It Doesn't Matter	7
60	HMV POP 803	A Million To One/Call Me A Dreamer	6
61	HMV POP 839	We Will Never Be As Young As This Again/Passing Breeze	5
61	HMV POP 885	The Miracle Of You/Lonely	5
63	HMV POP 1112	My Own True Love/Who Can Say?	8
63	HMV POP 1150	More/Rhapsody	6
63	HMV POP 1172	The Wild Wind/Once Upon A Time	8
63	HMV POP 1203	A Day Without You/Secret Love	6
63	HMV POP 1236	How Do You Keep From Crying?/Now The Day Is Over	6
63	HMV POP 1263	White On White/After You	8
64	HMV POP 1305	Today/Lonely In A Crowd	6
64	HMV POP 1325	The Seventh Dawn/The World Around Me	6
64	HMV POP 1372	Forget Her, Forget Her/Lollipops And Roses	30
65	HMV POP 1388	The Roundabout Of Love/I Wanna Be Around	5
65	HMV POP 1410	Go Away/Masquerade	30
65	HMV POP 1455	Lovely Is She/Gone And Forgotten	5
65	HMV POP 1487	And So We Meet Again/Violets For Your Furs	5
66	HMV POP 1506	I've Got To Find That Girl Again/Throw A Little Lovin' My Way	30
67	Deram DM 149	Never My Love/Whose Little Girl Are You (with inverted matrix)	30
67	Deram DM 149	Never My Love/Whose Little Girl Are You (re-pressing with matrix correct way up)	10
62	HMV 7EG 8748	HITS OF DANNY WILLIAMS (EP)	15
61	HMV CLP 1458	DANNY (LP, mono)	25
61	HMV CSD 1369	DANNY (LP, stereo)	20
61	HMV CLP 1521	MOON RIVER AND OTHER TITLES (LP)	20
62	HMV CLP 1605	SWINGING FOR YOU (LP, mono)	15
62	HMV CSD 1471	SWINGING FOR YOU (LP, stereo)	20
66	HMV CLP/CSD 3523	ONLY LOVE (LP)	30
66	Woman's Privilege AZ 3	ROMANCE WITH DANNY WILLIAMS (LP, mail-order via Woman magazine)	12
67	Deram DML 1017	DANNY WILLIAMS (LP)	20

DEL WILLIAMS

72	Grape GR 3027	Searching For Your Love/G.G. ALL STARS: Searching (Version)	5

DELROY WILLIAMS

71	Trojan TR 7813	Down In The Boondocks/Baby Make It	7

MINT VALUE £

| 76 | Treble C CCC 013 | Red, Green And Gold (In My Garden)/Let's Be People | 8 |

GEORGE WILLIAMS

| 69 | Bullet BU 405 | No Business Of Yours/Mast It Up (actually titled "Mash It Up") | 35 |

GEORGE WILLIAMS & HIS ORCHESTRA

| 55 | Vogue Coral Q 72053 | The Rompin' Stomper/Knock-Out Choo-Choo | 8 |
| 56 | HMV DLP 1140 | RHYTHM WAS HIS BUSINESS (10" LP) | 15 |

GINGER WILLIAMS

| 74 | Paradise PR 01 | I Can't Resist Your Tenderness/Little Boy | 12 |

GRANVILLE WILLIAMS ORCHESTRA

| 67 | Island WI 3062 | Hi-Life/More | 12 |
| 67 | Island ILP 971 | HI-LIFE (LP) | 60 |

(see also Silvertones)

HANK WILLIAMS (& HIS DRIFTING COWBOYS)

78s

50	MGM MGM 269	Lovesick Blues/Wedding Bells	10
51	MGM MGM 381	Moanin' The Blues/The Blues Come Around	10
51	MGM MGM 405	Dear John/Fly Trouble	10
51	MGM MGM 454	Hey, Good Lookin'/Howlin' At The Moon	10
51	MGM MGM 459	Cold, Cold Heart/I'm A Long Gone Daddy	10
52	MGM MGM 471	I Can't Help It (If I'm Still In Love With You)/Baby, We're Really In Love	10
52	MGM MGM 483	Why Don't You Love Me/I'd Still Want You	10
52	MGM MGM 505	Honky-Tonk Blues/I'm Sorry For You, My Friend	10
52	MGM MGM 527	Long Gone Lonesome Blues/Half As Much	10
52	MGM MGM 553	Nobody's Lonesome For Me/Mind Your Own Business	10
52	MGM MGM 566	Jambalaya (On The Bayou)/Settin' The Woods On Fire	10
53	MGM MGM 585	I'll Never Get Out Of This World Alive/I Could Never Be Ashamed Of You (as Hank Williams & His Drifting Cowboys)	10
53	MGM MGM 609	Kaw-Liga/Take These Chains From My Heart (& His Drifting Cowboys)	10
53	MGM MGM 630	I Saw The Light/ARTHUR 'GUITAR BOOGIE' SMITH: Recitation Sonny Smith: In Memory Of Hank Williams	10
53	MGM MGM 652	Ramblin' Man/I Won't Be Home No More	10
53	MGM MGM 666	My Bucket's Got A Hole In It/Let's Turn Back The Years	10
53	MGM MGM 678	Window Shopping/You Win Again	10
54	MGM MGM 704	Weary Blues (From Waitin')/I Can't Escape From You	10
54	MGM MGM 733	There'll Be No Teardrops Tonight/Crazy Heart	10
54	MGM MGM 768	I'm Satisfied With You/I Ain't Got Nothin' But Time	10
55	MGM MGM 799	I'm Gonna Sing/California Zephyr	10
56	MGM MGM 889	The First Fall Of Snow/Someday You'll Call My Name (withdrawn)	0
56	MGM MGM 896	Your Cheatin' Heart/A Teardrop On A Rose	10
56	MGM MGM 921	There's No Room In My Heart (For The Blues)/I Wish I Had A Nickel	10
56	MGM MGM 931	Blue Love (In My Heart)/Singing Waterfall	10
57	MGM MGM 942	Low Down Blues/My Sweet Love Ain't Around	10
57	MGM MGM 957	Rootie Tootie/Lonesome Whistle	10
57	MGM MGM 966	Leave Me Alone With The Blues/With Tears In My Eyes	10

SINGLES

53	MGM SP 1016	I'll Never Get Out Of This World Alive/I Could Never Be Ashamed Of You (as Hank Williams & His Drifting Cowboys)	50
53	MGM SP 1034	Kaw-Liga/Take These Chains From My Heart (& His Drifting Cowboys)	50
53	MGM SP 1049	Ramblin' Man/I Won't Be Home No More	45
53	MGM SP 1048	My Bucket's Got A Hole In It/Let's Turn Back The Years	40
54	MGM SP 1067	Weary Blues (From Waitin')/I Can't Escape From You	40
54	MGM SP 1085	There'll Be No Teardrops Tonight/Crazy Heart	40
54	MGM SP 1102	I'm Satisfied With You/I Ain't Got Nothin' But Time	40
56	MGM SP 1163	The First Fall Of Snow/Someday You'll Call My Name (unreleased)	0
56	MGM MGM 921	There's No Room In My Heart (For The Blues)/I Wish I Had A Nickel	30
56	MGM MGM 931	Blue Love (In My Heart)/Singing Waterfall	30
57	MGM MGM 942	Low Down Blues/My Sweet Love Ain't Around	30
57	MGM MGM 957	Rootie Tootie/Lonesome Whistle	30
57	MGM MGM 966	Leave Me Alone With The Blues/With Tears In My Eyes	30
66	MGM MGM 1309	You Win Again/I'm So Lonesome I Could Cry	12
66	MGM MGM 1322	Kaw-Liga/Let's Turn Back The Years	7

EPs

54	MGM MGM-EP 512	HANK WILLIAMS AND HIS DRIFTING COWBOYS (company sleeve)	25
54	MGM EPC 7	HANK WILLIAMS (export issue)	30
55	MGM MGM-EP 551	JUST WAITIN' (as Luke The Drifter, company sleeve)	20
55	MGM MGM-EP 551	JUST WAITIN' (as Luke The Drifter, later issue with p/s)	30
56	MGM MGM-EP 569	I SAW THE LIGHT (No. 1) (company sleeve)	15
56	MGM MGM-EP 569	I SAW THE LIGHT (No. 1) (later issue with p/s)	20
57	MGM MGM-EP 582	HONKY TONKIN'	20
57	MGM MGM-EP 608	I SAW THE LIGHT (No. 2)	20
57	MGM MGM-EP 614	HONKY TONK BLUES	20
58	MGM MGM-EP 639	SONGS FOR A BROKEN HEART (No. 1)	20
58	MGM MGM-EP 649	SONGS FOR A BROKEN HEART (No. 2)	20
58	MGM MGM-EP 675	HANK'S LAMENTS	20
60	MGM MGM-EP 710	THE UNFORGETTABLE HANK WILLIAMS	20
60	MGM MGM-EP 726	THE UNFORGETTABLE HANK WILLIAMS (No. 2)	20
60	MGM MGM-EP 732	THE UNFORGETTABLE HANK WILLIAMS (No. 3)	20
61	MGM MGM-EP 757	HANK WILLIAMS FAVOURITES	20
63	MGM MGM-EP 770	THE AUTHENTIC SOUND OF THE COUNTRY HITS	20

ALBUMS

52	MGM MGM-D 105	HANK WILLIAMS SINGS (10" LP, company sleeve)	40
52	MGM MGM-D 105	HANK WILLIAMS SINGS (10" LP, later issue in p/s)	50
53	MGM MGM-D 119	HANK WILLIAMS AS LUKE THE DRIFTER (10" LP, company sleeve)	30
53	MGM MGM-D 119	HANK WILLIAMS AS LUKE THE DRIFTER (10" LP, later issue in p/s)	40
55	MGM MGM-D 137	HANK WILLIAMS MEMORIAL ALBUM (10")	30
56	MGM MGM-D 144	MOANIN' THE BLUES (10")	40

58	MGM MGM-D 150	SING ME A BLUE SONG (10")	40
58	MGM MGM-D 154	THE IMMORTAL HANK WILLIAMS (10")	30
59	MGM MGM-C 784	THE UNFORGETTABLE HANK WILLIAMS	20
60	MGM MGM-C 811	THE LONESOME SOUND OF HANK WILLIAMS	30
60	MGM MGM-C 834	WAIT FOR THE LIGHT TO SHINE	20
62	MGM MGM-C 893	ON STAGE	20
63	MGM MGM-C 956	THE SPIRIT OF HANK WILLIAMS	20
66	MGM MGM-C 8019	MAY YOU NEVER BE ALONE	15
66	MGM MGM-C 8020	IN MEMORY OF HANK WILLIAMS	15
66	MGM MGM-C 8021	I'M BLUE INSIDE	20
66	MGM MGM-C 8022	LUKE THE DRIFTER	15
66	MGM MGM-C 8023	THE MANY MOODS OF HANK WILLIAMS	15
67	MGM MGM-C(S) 8031	THE LEGEND LIVES ANEW	15
67	MGM MGM-C(S) 8038	MORE HANK WILLIAMS AND STRINGS	15
67	MGM MGM-C 8040	LOVE SONGS, COMEDY AND HYMNS	15
79	World Records SM 551-556	THE LEGENDARY HANK WILLIAMS (6-LP box set)	20

(see also Audrey Williams)

HANK WILLIAMS & HANK WILLIAMS JR.

| 65 | MGM MGM-C 1008 | SINGING TOGETHER (LP) | 12 |

HANK WILLIAMS JR.

63	MGM MGM 1223	Long Gone Lonesome Blues/Doesn't Anybody Know My Name	6
63	MGM MGM 1242	Goin' Steady With The Blues/Guess What, That's Right, She's Gone	5
64	MGM MGM 1254	Endless Sleep/My Bucket's Got A Hole In It	7
65	MGM MGM 1276	Mule Skinner Blues/I Went To All That Trouble	5
66	MGM MGM 1294	You're Ruinin' My Life/Pecos Jail	5
66	MGM MGM 1299	Cold Cold Heart/Is It That Fun To Heart Someone	5
66	MGM MGM 1316	Standing In The Shadows/It's Written All Over Your Face	5
64	MGM C978	SINGS THE SONGS OF HANK WILLIAMS (LP)	15
64	MGM MGM-C 996	YOUR CHEATIN' HEART (LP)	15
67	MGM MGM-C(S) 8049	MY OWN WAY (LP)	15
70	MGM MGM-CS 8116	LIVE AT COBO HALL, DETROIT (LP)	15

(see also Connie Francis)

JEANETTE WILLIAMS

| 69 | Action ACT 4534 | Stuff/You Gotta Come Through | 8 |
| 70 | Action ACT 4557 | Hound Dog/I Can Feel A Heartbreak | 8 |

(see also Swamp Dogg, Brooks & Jerry)

(LITTLE) JERRY WILLIAMS

65	Cameo Parkway C 100	Baby You're My Everything/Just What Do You Plan To Do About It	85
65	Cameo Parkway C 100	Baby You're My Everything/Just What Do You Plan To Do About It (DJ copy)	120
74	Pye Disco Demand DDS 102	If You Ask Me/ Yvonne (as Jerry Williams)	8

JIMMY WILLIAMS

| 65 | Atlantic AT 4042 | Walking On Air/I'm So Lost | 25 |

JOE WILLIAMS

59	Columbia SCD 2116	Party Blues Parts 1 & 2	6
60	Columbia DB 4560	Somebody/One Is A Lonesome Number	6
58	Columbia SEG 7810	JOE WILLIAMS WITH COUNT BASIE (EP)	15
59	Columbia SEG 7984	BALLADS AND BLUES (EP)	10
59	Columbia/Clef SEB 10110	GROOVY JOE WILLIAMS (EP)	10
60	Columbia SEG 8001	EVERYDAY I HAVE THE BLUES (EP)	10
60	Columbia SEG 8016	JOE SINGS THE BLUES (EP)	10
56	London HB-C 1065	JOE WILLIAMS SINGS (10" LP)	25
57	HMV CLP 1109	THE GREATEST (LP)	20
58	Columbia 33SX 1087	A MAN AIN'T SUPPOSED TO CRY (LP)	25
60	Columbia 33SX 1229	JOE WILLIAMS SINGS ABOUT YOU (LP, mono)	12
60	Columbia SCX 3308	JOE WILLIAMS SINGS ABOUT YOU (LP, stereo)	15
60	Columbia 33SX 1253	THAT KIND OF WOMAN (LP, mono)	12
60	Columbia SCX 3325	THAT KIND OF WOMAN (LP, stereo)	15
61	Columbia SX 1392	TOGETHER (LP, with Harry "Sweets" Edison, also stereo SCX 3421)	15

(see also Count Basie)

JOHN WILLIAMS

67	Columbia DB 8128	She's That Kind Of Woman/My Ways Are Set	15
67	Columbia DB 8251	Flowers In Your Hair/Can't Find Time For Anything Now	10
67	Columbia SX 6169	JOHN WILLIAMS (LP)	100

(see also Maureeny Wishfull)

JOHN WILLIAMS

| 84 | Island IS 155 | Paul McCartney's Theme From 'The Honorary Consul'/Clara's Theme (p/s) | 7 |

JOHN WILLIAMS ORCHESTRA (U.S.)

66	Stateside S(S)L 10187	HOW TO STEAL A MILLION (LP, soundtrack)	25
83	MCA MCA 70000	E.T. - THE EXTRA TERRESTRIAL (LP, soundtrack, box set with booklet & poster)	30
83	MCA CAC 70000	E.T. - THE EXTRA TERRESTRIAL (cassette, soundtrack box set with booklet & poster)	30

KENNETH WILLIAMS

| 67 | Decca LK 4856 | ON PLEASURE BENT (LP) | 15 |

(see also Rambling Syd Rumpo, Tony Hancock)

LARRY WILLIAMS

57	London HLN 8472	Short Fat Fannie/High School Dance	40
58	London HLN 8532	Bony Moronie/You Bug Me Baby	20
58	London HLU 8604	Dizzy Miss Lizzy/Slow Down	25
58	London HLU 8604	Dizzy Miss Lizzy/Slow Down (78)	25
59	London HLU 8844	She Said "Yeah"/Bad Boy (silver top label)	30
59	London HLU 8844	She Said "Yeah"/Bad Boy (78)	30
60	London HLU 8911	I Can't Stop Loving You/Steal A Little Kiss	30
60	London HLU 8911	I Can't Stop Loving You/Steal A Little Kiss (78)	50
60	London HLM 9053	Baby, Baby/Get Ready	30
65	Sue WI 371	Strange/Call On Me	40
65	Sue WI 381	Turn On Your Lovelight/Dizzy Miss Lizzy	40

Larry WILLIAMS & JOHNNY 'GUITAR' WATSON

68	MGM MGM 1447	Shake Your Body Girl/Love, I Can't Seem To Find It	20
59	London RE-U 1213	LARRY WILLIAMS (EP)	100
65	Sue ILP 922	LARRY WILLIAMS ON STAGE (LP)	80
70s	Specialty SNTF 5025	SLOW DOWN (LP)	20
70s	Speciality SNTF 5008	ORIGINAL HITS (LP)	20

LARRY WILLIAMS & JOHNNY 'GUITAR' WATSON

65	Decca F 12151	Sweet Little Baby/Slow Down	20
67	Columbia DB 8140	Mercy, Mercy, Mercy/A Quitter Never Wins	50
67	Columbia DB 8140	Mercy, Mercy, Mercy/A Quitter Never Wins (DJ copy)	175
76	Epic EPC 4421	Too Late/Two For The Price Of One	20
65	Decca LK 4691	THE LARRY WILLIAMS SHOW (LP, with Stormsville Shakers)	80

(see also Johnny 'Guitar' Watson, Philip Goodhand-Tait [& Stormville Shakers])

LEONA WILLIAMS

| 74 | Fountain FB 303 | LEONA WILLIAMS AND HER DIXIE BAND (LP) | 12 |

LEVI WILLIAMS

| 75 | Locks LOX 5 | Come Me Breda/MIGHTY CLOUD BAND: Call Mi Sister | 5 |

LEW WILLIAMS

| 50s | London (no cat. no.) | Cat Talk (1-sided, orange label demo-only) | 50 |

LLOYD WILLIAMS

66	Doctor Bird DB 1051	Sad World/TOMMY McCOOK'S BAND: A Little Bit Of Heaven	30
68	Treasure Isle TI 7029	Funky Beat/Goodbye Baby	22
68	Doctor Bird DB 1135	Wonderful World (with Tommy McCook)/TOMMY McCOOK SUPERSONICS: Mad Mad World	35
70	Bamboo BAM 41	I'm In Love With You/Little Girl	30

LORETTA WILLIAMS

| 66 | Atlantic 584 032 | Baby Cakes/I'm Missing You | 50 |

LUCINDA WILLIAMS

| 89 | Rough Trade 130 | LUCINDA WILLIAMS (LP, with inner lyric bag) | 12 |

LUTHER WILLIAMS ORCHESTRA

| 61 | Limbo XL 101 | Early In The Morning/Little Vilma | 5 |
| 61 | Melodisc MLP 12-125 | TROPICAL RHYTHMS OF JAMAICA (LP) | 15 |

MARY LOU WILLIAMS

64	Sue WI 311	Chuck-a-Lunk Jug (Parts 1 & 2)	25
55	Vogue EPV 1042	DON CARLOS MEETS MARY LOU WILLIAMS (EP)	10
56	Parlophone GEP 8567	AT THE PIANO (EP)	10
56	Columbia SEG 7608	MARY LOU WILLIAMS (EP)	10
55	Esquire EP 66	MARY LOU WILLIAMS QUARTET (EP)	10
53	Vogue LDE 022	PLAYS IN LONDON (10" LP)	20
54	Esquire 20-026	PIANO PANORAMA (10" LP)	20
55	Felsted EDL 87012	IN PARIS (10" LP)	20

MASON WILLIAMS

| 68 | Warner Bros WB 7190 | Classical Gas/Long Time Blues | 6 |

MAURICE WILLIAMS (& ZODIACS)

60	Top Rank JAR 526	Stay/Do You Believe (as Maurice Williams & Zodiacs)	20
61	Top Rank JAR 550	I Remember/Always	20
61	Top Rank JAR 563	Come Along/Do I	30
61	Top Rank JKP 3006	STAY WITH MAURICE WILLIAMS & THE ZODIACS (EP)	175

(see also Gladiolas)

MIKE WILLIAMS

| 66 | Atlantic 584 027 | Lonely Soldier/If This Isn't Love | 25 |

MOON WILLIAMS

| 73 | DJM DJS10283 | Forever Kind Of Love/All For You | 200 |

OTIS WILLIAMS & HIS CHARMS

55	Parlophone CMSP 36	Ivory Tower/In Paradise (export issue)	300
56	Parlophone MSP 6239	Ivory Tower/In Paradise	400
56	Parlophone R 4175	Ivory Tower/In Paradise (78)	15
56	Parlophone R 4210	One Night Only/It's All Over	375
56	Parlophone R 4210	One Night Only/It's All Over (78)	25
57	Parlophone R 4293	Walkin' After Midnight/I'm Waiting Just For You	400
57	Parlophone R 4293	Walkin' After Midnight/I'm Waiting Just For You (78)	50
58	Parlophone R 4495	The Secret/Don't Wake Up The Kids	100
58	Parlophone R 4495	The Secret/Don't Wake Up The Kids (78)	70
62	Parlophone R 4860	The Secret/Two Hearts	60

(see also Charms)

PAUL WILLIAMS

| 73 | Sonet SNTF 654 | IN MEMORY OF ROBERT JOHNSON (LP) | 15 |

PAUL WILLIAMS

| 74 | A&M AMS 7125 | That's What Friends Are For/Born To Fly | 8 |
| 74 | A&M AMLS 63653 | PHANTOM OF THE PARADISE (LP, soundtrack) | 20 |

PAUL WILLIAMS

| 70s | Parry Music Library PML 168 | AQUARIUS (LP) | 18 |

PAUL WILLIAMS BIG ROLL BAND/SET

64	Columbia DB 7421	Gin House/Rockin' Chair (as Paul Williams Big Roll Band)	20
65	Columbia DB 7768	The Many Faces Of Love/Jumpback (as Paul Williams & Zoot Money Band)	30
68	Decca F 12844	My Sly Sadie/Stop The Wedding (as Paul Williams Set)	15

(see also Zoot Money's Big Roll Band, John Mayall's Bluesbreakers, Alan Price [Set], Juicy Lucy)

PAULINE WILLIAMS

| 73 | Explosion EX 2084 | My Island/My Island (Version) | 5 |

POOR JOE WILLIAMS

| 60 | Collector JEN 3 | A MAN SINGS THE BLUES (EP) | 10 |

60	Collector JEN 4	A MAN SINGS THE BLUES VOL. 2 (EP)	10

(see also Big Joe Williams)

PRINCE WILLIAMS
73	Atra ATRA 004	Action Wood Pt. 1/Action Wood Pt. 2	5

RANNY/RONNY WILLIAMS
69	Bullet BU 426	Summer Place (with Hippy Boys)/Big Boy	10
69	Gas GAS 120	Throw Me Corn (as Ronny Williams)/HIPPY BOYS: Temptation	25
69	Unity UN 526	Ambitious Beggar/Pepper Seed	18
70	Punch PH 32	Smile/Musical I.D.	10

(see also Winston Reed)

RITA WILLIAMS
58	Oriole CB 1417	Looking For Someone To Love/Love Me Forever	10
70	Gemini GMS 011	You're Nearer/With Love From Amsterdam	6

ROBBIE WILLIAMS
96	RCA FREELX 1	Freedom '96 (Radio Edit)/Freedom '96 (Full Length Version) (jukebox issue)	8
96	RCA PROPERDJ 1	Freedom '96 (Radio Edit)/Freedom '96 (Full Length Version) (CD, test pressing, no text on disc)	20
97	Chrysalis CHSLH 5055	Old Before I Die/Making Plans For Nigel (jukebox issue)	6
97	Chrysalis CDCHSDJ 5055	Old Before I Die (CD, withdrawn, different sleeve)	15
97	Chrysalis CHSLH 5063	Lazy Days/Teenage Millionaire (jukebox issue)	6
97	Chrysalis CHSLH 5068	South Of The Border/Cheap Love Song (jukebox issue)	6
98	Chrysalis 12CHSDJD 5080	Let Me Entertain You (remixes) (12", double-pack)	12
98	Chrysalis/HMV HMV 78	Millennium/ROYAL ALBERT HALL ORCHESTRA: Nimrod, Enigma Variations Op. 36 (78rpm, promo only, 1,000 only, numbered p/s)	25
99	Chrysalis CHSLH 5107	Strong/Antmusic (jukebox issue)	6
99	Chrysalis CDCHSLH 5112	It's Only Us/She's The One (jukebox issue)	6
00	Chrysalis CDCHSLH 5118	Rock DJ/She's The One (jukebox issue)	6
06	Chrysalis CDCHSDJX5162	Lovelight (CD, 9 remixes, promo, p/s)	12
97	Chrysalis RWEPK 01	THE EPK CD (interview and excerpts from "Life Thru A Lens")	25
98	Chrysalis CDPP 080	I'VE BEEN EXPECTING YOU (metal case with album CD, interview disc in digipak, EPK video in p/s, gold press release and photos)	150

(see also Take That)

ROBERT WILLIAMS
90	Blast First FU8	CHROME, FIRE AND SMOKE (2-LP, picture disc, 1000 only)	25

ROBERT PETE WILLIAMS
63	'77' LA 12-17	THOSE PRISON BLUES (LP)	35
70s	Blues Beacon 1932 101ST	SUGAR FARM (LP)	25
72	Saydisc AMS 2002	ROBERT PETE WILLIAMS (LP)	18
73	Sonet SNTF 649	LEGACY OF THE BLUES (LP)	12

ROBERT PETE WILLIAMS/ROOSEVELT SYKES
67	'77' LEU 12-50	BLUES FROM THE BOTTOM (LP)	25

(see also Roosevelt Sykes)

ROCKMORE WILLIAMS
73	Mooncrest Moon 15	Lady Rock/Junkyard Blues	10

ROGER WILLIAMS
55	London HLU 8214	Autumn Leaves/Take Care	10
56	London HLU 8341	Two Different Worlds (with Jane Morgan)/I'll Always Walk With You	8
57	London HLU 8379	Anastasia/A Serenade For Joy	6
58	London HA-R 2089	THE BOY NEXT DOOR (LP)	12

(see also Jane Morgan)

ROY WILLIAMS TRINITY
73	Hillside HIL LP 1013	A TOUCH OF CLASS (LP)	15
79	Hillside HIL LP 1016	GOOD NEWS IN TOWN (LP)	45

SAM WILLIAMS
78	Grapevine GRP 116	Love Slipped Thru' My Fingers/TOWANDA BARNES: You Don't Mean It	25

SID WILLIAMS
77	ATA ATA 1001	Don't Play That Rock 'N' Roll/Time To Spare	8

SIL WILLIAMS
69	Wolf WM 04	Reggae Moon Rising/People Get Ready	10

SMITTY WILLIAMS
62	MGM MGM 1167	The Cure/Oh Seymour	7

SONNY WILLIAMS
59	London HLD 8931	Bye Bye Baby Goodbye/Lucky Linda	45
59	London HLD 8931	Bye Bye Baby Goodbye/Lucky Linda (78)	20

SPARKIE WILLIAMS
58	Parlophone R 4475	Sparkie Williams/Sparkie the Fiddle	7

SYLVIAN WILLIAMS
69	Big Shot BI 532	Sweeter Than Honey/Son Of Reggae	35
69	Big Shot BI 533	This Old Man/When Morning Comes	7

TEX WILLIAMS
54	Brunswick 05327	River Of No Return/Dawn In The Meadow	10
54	Brunswick 05341	This Ole House (with Rex Allen)/They Were Doin' The Mambo	12
55	Brunswick 05393	Money/If You'd Believe Me	10
56	Brunswick 05516	Be Sure You're Right (And Then Go Ahead)/Old Betsy	5
57	Brunswick 05684	Talkin' To The Blues/Every Night (with Anita Kerr Singers)	5
60	Top Rank JAR 330	The Keeper Of Boothill/Bummin' Around	6

(see also Roberta Lee, Rex Allen)

TOMMY WILLIAMS
76	Free Reed FRR 008	SPRINGTIME IN BATTERSEA (LP, gatefold sleeve)	18

TONY WILLIAMS
61	Reprise RS 20019	Sleepless Nights/Mandolino Mandolino	10

MINT VALUE £

61	Reprise RS 20030	My Prayer/Miracle	10
63	Philips BF 1282	How Come/When I Had You	100
60	Mercury MMC 14027	A GIRL IS A GIRL IS A GIRL (LP)	40
61	Reprise R 6001	SINGS HIS GREATEST HITS (LP, mono)	20
61	Reprise ST R9 6006	SINGS HIS GREATEST HITS (LP, stereo)	30

(see also Platters, Linda Hayes)

TONY WILLIAMS' LIFETIME
69	Polydor 583 574	EMERGENCY! (2-LP, gatefold sleeve)	50
70	Polydor 2425 019	TURN IT OVER (LP)	25
71	Polydor 2425 065	EGO (LP, textured gatefold sleeve)	35

(see also Lifetime, John McLaughlin)

TREVOR WILLIAMS
| 75 | Virgin VS 122 | Lucy Brown/We Slowed Down | 5 |

WILLIE WILLIAMS, JACKIE MITTOO & MARSHAL COUSINS
| 79 | Ziggy FDP 001 | Rocking Universally/JACKIE MITTOO & BONGO GENE: Universal rock (12") | 30 |

WILLY WILLIAMS
| 81 | Black Roots BR 017 | Come Mek We Rally/YABBY YOU: Thirty Pieces Of Silver (12") | 45 |
| 83 | WLN WLN 004 | Repatriation/Come Along/Armagideon Time/Justice Tonight (12") | 10 |

WINSTON WILLIAMS
70	Jackpot JP 733	D.J.'s Choice/SLIM SMITH: Can't Do Without It (B-side actually titled "Lesson/Story Of Love" by Uniques)	12
70	Jackpot JP 743	The People's Choice/BOBBY JAMES: Let Me Go Girl	12
71	Jackpot JP 757	Love Version/SLIM SMITH: Ball Of Confusion	12

HARVEY WILLIAMS
| 94 | Sarah SARAH 406 | REBELLION (10" LP) | 15 |

BOBBY WILLIAMSON
| 54 | HMV 7MC 26 | Sh-Boom/Love March (export issue) | 20 |

DUDLEY WILLIAMSON
| 67 | Doctor Bird DB 1117 | Coming On The Scene/Anything You Want | 60 |

(see also Dudley & Attractions)

MARK WILLIAMSON
| 70s | Myrrh MYR 1154 | MISSING IN ACTION (LP) | 15 |

ROBIN WILLIAMSON
| 72 | Island HELP 2 | MYRRH (LP, textured sleeve, black label with pink 'i' logo, lyric inner sleeve) | 35 |
| 78 | Criminal STEAL 4 | AMERICAN STONEHENGE (LP) | 12 |

(see also Incredible String Band, Vashti Bunyan)

SONNY BOY WILLIAMSON (I)
| 69 | Matchbox SDR 169 | SONNY BOY AND HIS PALS (LP) | 30 |
| 70 | RCA Intl. INTS 1088 | BLUEBIRD BLUES (LP) | 15 |

SONNY BOY WILLIAMSON (I)/BIG BILL BROONZY
| 65 | RCA Victor RD 7685 | BIG BILL BROONZY/SONNY BOY WILLIAMSON (LP) | 30 |

SONNY BOY WILLIAMSON (II)
63	Pye International 7N 25191	Help Me/Bye Bye Bird	25
64	Pye International 7N 25268	Lonesome Cabin/The Goat	20
65	Sue WI 365	No Nights By Myself/Boppin' With Sonny Boy	40
66	Chess CRS 8030	Bring It On Home/Down Child	20
66	Blue Horizon 45-1008	From The Bottom/Empty Bedroom	80
64	Pye Intl. NEP 44037	SONNY BOY WILLIAMSON (EP)	25
65	Chess CRE 6001	HELP ME (EP)	35
66	Chess CRE 6013	IN MEMORIAM (EP)	35
66	Chess CRE 6018	REAL FOLK BLUES VOL. 2 (EP)	30
64	Pye Intl. NPL 28036	DOWN AND OUT BLUES (LP)	60
64	Storyville SLP 158	PORTRAITS IN BLUES, VOL. 4 (LP)	40
65	Chess CRL 4510	IN MEMORIAM (LP)	50
66	Storyville SLP 170	THE BLUES OF SONNY BOY WILLIAMSON (LP)	22
66	Fontana 670 158	PORTRAITS IN BLUES, VOL. 4 (LP, reissue)	30
67	Storyville 671 170	THE BLUES OF SONNY BOY WILLIAMSON (LP, reissue)	25
68	Marmalade 607/608 004	DON'T SEND ME NO FLOWERS (LP, with Brian Auger & Jimmy Page)	80
74	Rarity RLP 1	THE LAST SESSION - 1963 (LP)	25

(see also Ottilie Patterson)

SONNY BOY WILLIAMSON (II) & YARDBIRDS
65	Fontana TL 5277	SONNY BOY WILLIAMSON & THE YARDBIRDS (LP)	175
68	Fontana SFJL 960	SONNY BOY WILLIAMSON & THE YARDBIRDS (LP, reissue, different sleeve)	30
71	Philips 6435 011	SONNY BOY WILLIAMSON & THE YARDBIRDS (LP, 2nd reissue)	18

(see also Yardbirds, Brian Auger)

STU WILLIAMSON
| 56 | London Jazz LZ-N 14030 | SAPPHIRE (10" LP) | 20 |

WILLIE AND THE RED RUBBER BAND
| 69 | RCA 1842 | Mary Jane/Chicky Chicky Boom Boom | 12 |

WILLIE (FRANCIS) & LLOYD (LINDSAY)
| 71 | Camel CA 80 | Marcus Is Alive/GLADIATORS: Freedom Train | 12 |

(see also Willie Francis)

WILLIE & WHEELS
| 77 | ABC ABC 4184 | Skateboard Craze/Do What You Did (p/s, label states "illie & The Wheels") | 10 |

(see also P.F. Sloan, Grass Roots, Fantastic Baggys')

DORIS WILLINGHAM
| 69 | Jay Boy BOY 1 | You Can't Do That/Lost Again | 15 |

CHUCK WILLIS
| 57 | London HLE 8444 | C.C. Rider/Ease The Pain | 80 |
| 57 | London HLE 8444 | C.C. Rider/Ease The Pain (78) | 30 |

57	London HLE 8489	That Train Has Gone/Love Me Cherry...80
57	London HLE 8489	That Train Has Gone/Love Me Cherry (78)..20
58	London HLE 8595	Betty And Dupree/My Crying Eyes...80
58	London HLE 8595	Betty And Dupree/My Crying Eyes (78)..20
58	London HLE 8635	What Am I Living For/Hang Up My Rock And Roll Shoes....................................50
58	London HLE 8635	What Am I Living For/Hang Up My Rock And Roll Shoes (78)...........................25
58	London HL 7039	What Am I Living For/Hang Up My Rock And Roll Shoes (export issue)...........30
59	London HLE 8818	My Life/Thunder And Lightning..45
59	London HLE 8818	My Life/Thunder And Lightning (78)..30
59	Fontana TFE 17138	CHUCK WILLIS WAILS (EP)...300
65	Atlantic ATL 5003	I REMEMBER CHUCK WILLIS (LP)...80
69	Atlantic 588 145	I REMEMBER CHUCK WILLIS (LP, reissue)..20

DOUG WILLIS
| 97 | Z Records ZEDD 12029 | Get Your Own (12")...10 |

HAL WILLIS
| 68 | President PT 197 | The Lumberjack/Klondike Mike...12 |

LARRY WILLIS
| 74 | People PLEO 2 | INNER CRISIS (LP)..20 |

LLOYD WILLIS
| 70 | Pressure Beat PR 5502 | Mad Rooster (Parts 1 & 2)/As Far As I Can See (actually "The Wicked Must Survive" by Reggae Boys)..15 |
| 70 | Unity UN 543 | Ivan Hitler The Conqueror/The Splice...30 |

(see also Dynamic Gang, Urie Aldridge)

RALPH WILLIS
54	Esquire 10-370	Lazy Woman Blues/Goodbye Blues (78)...20
54	Esquire 10-380	Old Home Blues/Salty Dog (78)..20
61	Esquire EP 241	RALPH WILLIS (EP)...40

SLIM WILLIS
| 65 | R&B MRB 5004 | Running Around/No Feeling For You...30 |

TIMMY WILLIS
| 72 | United Artists UP 35352 | Mr. Soul Satisfaction/I'm Wondering...5 |

WILL-O-BEES
| 67 | CBS 3263 | It's Not Easy/Looking Glass...15 |

NEVILLE WILLOUGHBY
| 72 | Duke DU 140 | Wheel And Tun Me/Hey Mama...5 |

(see also Neville, Whistling Willie)

WILLOWS
| 56 | London HLU 8290 | Church Bells May Ring/Baby Tell Me...600 |
| 56 | London HLU 8290 | Church Bells May Ring/Baby Tell Me (78)..80 |

(see also Tony Middleton)

BOB WILLS & HIS TEXAS PLAYBOYS
| 51 | MGM MGM 455 | 'Tater Pie/Ida Red Likes The Boogie (78)...10 |
| 53 | MGM MGM 613 | Snatchin' And Grabbin'/I Want To Be Wanted (78)...10 |

BOB WILLS WITH TOMMY DUNCAN
| 60 | London HL 7102 | Heart To Heart Talk/What's The Matter With The Mill (export issue)..................20 |

MICK WILLS
| 88 | Woronzow WOO 9 | FERN HILL (LP)..15 |
| 97 | Acme AC 8013LP | THE MAGIC GARDEN (LP, foldover gatefold sleeve in poly bag)........................12 |

VIOLA WILLS
68	President PT 108	Lost Without The Love Of My Guy/I Got Love..10
68	President PT 150	Together Forever/Don't Kiss Me Hello And Mean Goodbye...............................10
68	President PT 152	I've Got To Have All Of You/Night Scene..8
68	President PT 154	You're Out Of My Mind/Any Time..8

WILMER & DUKES
| 68 | Action ACT 4500 | Give Me One More Chance/Get It...10 |

SUE WILSHAW
| 69 | SNB 55-3957 | Empty Sunday/My My My..15 |

ADA WILSON
| 79 | Ellie Jay EJSP 9288 | In The Quiet Of My Room/I'm In Control Here (p/s)..12 |
| 80 | Barn BARN 012 | In The Quiet Of My Room/I'm In Control Here (reissue, no p/s)..........................6 |

(see also Strangeways)

AL WILSON
68	Liberty LBF 15044	Do What You Gotta Do/Now I Know What Love Is...20
68	Liberty LBF 15121	The Snake/Who Could Be Lovin' You..20
69	Liberty LBF 15236	Shake Me Wake Me/I Stand Accused..8
69	Liberty LBF 15257	Lodi/By The Time I Get To Phoenix..8
75	Bell BLL 1436	The Snake/Willoughby Brook...10
02	Soul City	The Snake/Now I Know What Love Is...12
69	Liberty LBS 83173	SEARCHING FOR THE DOLPHINS (LP)...20

BRIAN WILSON
66	Capitol CL 15438	Caroline, No/Summer Means New Love...50
88	Sire W 7814 CD	Love And Mercy (LP Version)/One For The Boys (LP Version)/ He Couldn't Get His Poor Old Body To Move (3" CD)...15
88	Sire W 7787 CD	Night Time (LP Version)/One For The Boys/Being With The One You Love (3" CD)...............15
88	Sire W 7814 B	LOVE AND MERCY (7" box set, with interview and postcards, limited edition)......40
98	Giant/Mojo 74321 58760 2	INTERVIEW/IMAGINATION (promo CD, with Peter Buck)..................................40
04	Nonesuch 7559-79869-7	Wonderful/Wind Chimes (three different coloured vinyl - blue, yellow,green).....18
04	Nonesuch 7559-79885-7	Good Vibrations/Our Prayer/Good Vibrations (live)(p/s) (Ltd edition)................10
05	Nonesuch 7559-798957	Our Prayer (Freeform Reform) (10" one sided clear vinyl in clear plastic sleeve)...12

(see also Beach Boys, Date With Soul, American Spring)

MINT VALUE £

BRIAN WILSON & MIKE LOVE

67	Capitol CL 15513	Gettin' Hungry/Devoted To You (as Brian Wilson & Mike Love)	30

CARL WILSON

81	Caribou CRB 84840	CARL WILSON (LP, with lyric insert)	12
82	Caribou CRB 25225	YOUNGBLOOD (LP, with lyric Insert)	12

(see also Beach Boys)

CLIVE WILSON

64	R&B JB 144	Mango Tree/Midnight In Chicago	20

COLIN WILSON

75	Tabitha TAB 101	CLOUDBURST (LP)	30

DELROY WILSON

63	Island WI 097	Naughty People/I Shall Not Remove	25
63	Island WI 103	One, Two, Three/Back Biter	20
63	Island WI 116	You Bend My Love/Can't You See	20
63	R&B JB 108	Lion Of Judah/Joe Liges	30
63	R&B JB 128	Prince Pharoah/Don't Believe Him	30
63	R&B JB 132	Squeeze Your Toe/Sugar Pie	30
64	Black Swan WI 405	Spit In The Sky/Voodoo Man	25
64	Black Swan WI 420	Goodbye/Treat Me Good	20
64	R&B JB 148	Lover Mouth/Every Mouth Must Be Fed	25
64	R&B JB 168	Sammy Dead/CYNTHIA & ARCHIE: Every Beat	25
65	Island WI 205	Pick Up The Pieces/Oppression	18
66	Doctor Bird DB 1022	Give Me A Chance/(It's) Impossible	25
66	Island WI 3013	Dancing Mood/SOUL BROTHERS: More And More	30
67	Island WI 3033	Riding For A Fall/Got To Change Your Ways	25
67	Island WI 3037	Ungrateful Baby/ROY RICHARDS: Hopeful Village Ska	35
67	Island WI 3039	Close To Me/SOUL BROTHERS: Hi-Life	25
67	Island WI 3050	Get Ready/ROY RICHARDS: Port-O-Jam	45
67	Studio One SO 2009	Won't You Come Home Baby/PETER & HORTENSE: I've Been Lonely	50
67	Studio One SO 2014	Mother Word/HEPTONES: Fat Girl	30
67	Studio One SO 2019	Never Conquer/Run For Your Life	80
67	Studio One SO 2031	I'm Not A King/HEPTONES: Take Me (B-side actually by Soul Vendors)	50
68	Island WI 3099	This Old Heart Of Mine/GLEN ADAMS: Grab A Girl	50
68	Island WI 3127	Once Upon A Time/I Want To Love You (B-side actually with Stranger Cole)	80
68	Coxsone CS 7064	True Believer/MARSHALL WILLIAMS: College Girl	25
68	Studio One SO 2040	Mr. D.J./HEPTONES: Tripe Girl	60
68	Studio One SO 2046	Rain From The Skies/How Can I Love Someone	40
68	Studio One SO 2057	Feel Good All Over/I Like The Way You Walk	40
69	Studio One SO 2074	Easy Snappin'/WEBBER SISTERS: Come On	25
69	High Note HS 011	Put Yourself In My Place/It Hurts	12
69	High Note HS 015	I'm The One Who Loves You/AFROTONES: If I'm In A Corner	20
69	High Note HS 022	Your Number One/I've Tried My Best	20
69	High Note HS 028	Good To Me/What Do You Want Me To Do	12
69	Camel CA 15	Sad Mood (actually by Ken Parker)/STRANGER COLE: Give It To Me	30
70	Trojan TR 7740	Show Me The Way/BEVERLEY'S ALLSTARS: Version	10
70	Trojan TR 7769	Gave You My Love/BEVERLEY'S ALLSTARS: Version	10
70	Summit SUM 8503	Got To Get Away/BEVERLEY'S ALLSTARS: Version	8
70	Unity UN 559	Drink Wine, Everybody/Someone To Call My Own	6
71	Smash SMA 2317	I Am Trying/COLLINS ALLSTARS: Version	6
71	Smash SMA 2318	Satisfaction/Satisfaction Version (B-side with Alton Ellis)	40
71	Smash SMA 2323	What It Was/LLOYD CLARKE: Chicken Thief	7
71	Jackpot JP 763	Better Must Come/BUNNY LEE'S ALLSTARS: Better Must Come - Version	10
71	Jackpot JP 769	Cool Operator/I'm Yours	10
71	Jackpot JP 770	Try Again/AGGROVATORS: Try Again - Version	10
71	Jackpot JP 780	Keep Your Love Strong/Nice To Be Near	10
71	Jackpot JP 781	Peace And Love/JEFF BARNES: Who's Your Brother	12
71	Banana BA 333	Just Because Of You/I Love You Madly	25
72	Banana BA 367	You Keep On Running (& U Roy)/LARRY'S ALL STARS: Running Version	15
72	Bullet BU 520	Hear Come The Heartaches (actually "Here Come The Heartaches")/ You'll Be Sorry	8
72	Jackpot JP 792	Who Cares/HUGH ROY JUNIOR: Who Cares - Version	10
72	Jackpot JP 795	The Same Old Song/Stay By Me	10
72	Jackpot JP 804	Cheer Up/Loving You	10
72	Spur SP 2	Adis Ababa/KEITH HUDSON: Rudie Hot Stuff	40
73	Downtown DT 501	Pretty Girl/JOE GIBBS & PROFESSIONALS: Face Girl	8
73	Grape GR 3038	Can I Change My Mind/Just Because	10
73	Green Door GD 4060	Ain't That Peculiar/What Is Man	8
73	Smash SMA 2336	Trying To Wreck My Life/Live And Learn	10
73	Count Shelley CS 024	Never Give Up/I ROY: Problem Of Life	8
73	Count Shelley CS 047	Dum Dum/HORACE ANDY: Rasta Saw Them Coming	8
74	Faith FA 006	Love Got Me Doing Things/PHIL PRATT ALL STARS: Version	5
74	Harry J. HJ 6667	What Will Happen To The Youth Of Today/Baby Don't Do It	5
75	Fab FAB 266	Dancing Mood/Version	12
75	Attack ATT 8111	Seven Letters/Version	8
75	Attack ATT 8120	Honey Child/Time Is Running Out	6
76	Black Wax WAX 20	Mother Nature/CHANNEL ONE: Natural Version	6
77	Tribesman TM 002	What Is Man/Version	10
78	Burning Sounds BSD 017	All In This Together/Because I Am Black (12")	25
78	Burning Sounds BSD 018	Love Got Me Doing Things/Go Away Little Girl (12")	25
79	Cha Cha CHAD 10	Money Love/I Want To Love You (12")	20
79	E & J EJD1	Sharing The Night Together/I Won't Take You Back (12")	10
88	Conqueror LD 045	I Have Been In Love/NAGG MORRIS AND THE HEPTONES: You Want To Get I Out (12")	40
64	R&B JBL 1112	I SHALL NOT REMOVE (LP)	250
68	Coxsone CSL 8016	GOOD ALL OVER (LP)	100
72	Trojan TRLS 44	BETTER MUST COME (LP)	30
73	Big Shot BILP 102	CAPTIVITY (LP)	40
78	Burning Sounds BS 1020	LOVERS ROCK (LP)	20
79	Groundnation GROL 501	FOR I AND I (LP)	25

(see also Hortense & Delroy, Joe Liges, Roy Richards, Soul Brothers, Dennis Alcapone, Stranger Cole, Uniques, Soul Vendors)

DENNIS WILSON (& RUMBO)

70	Stateside SS 2184	Sound Of Free/Lady (as Dennis Wilson & Rumbo)	70
77	Caribou CRB 5663	River Song/Farewell My Friend	15
77	Caribou CRB 81672	PACIFIC OCEAN BLUE (LP, gatefold sleeve, lyric insert, on blue vinyl)	45
77	Caribou CRB 81672	PACIFIC OCEAN BLUE (LP, gatefold sleeve, lyric insert)	40

(see also Beach Boys)

THE DIERDRE WILSON TABAC

69	RCA RCA 1880	Get Back/Angel Baby	15

DOYLE WILSON WITH JIMMY LACEY & BAND

58	Vogue Pop V 9117	Hey-Hey/You're The One For Me	600
58	Vogue Pop V 9117	Hey-Hey/You're The One For Me (7)	150

EDDIE WILSON

69	Action ACT 4536	Shing-A-Ling Stroll/Don't Kick The Teenager Around	15
70	Action ACT 4555	Get Out On The Street/Must Be Love	15

EDITH WILSON

60s	Fountain FB 302	1921-1922 WITH JOHNNY DUNN'S JAZZHOUNDS (LP)	15

ERNEST WILSON

78	Cha Cha CC 001	I Know Myself/REVOLUTIONARIES: I Know Myself Dub	12

ERNEST WILSON & FREDDY (MCGREGOR)

70	Crab CRAB 45	Sentimental Man/It's A Lie	8
70	Unity UN 564	Love Makes The World Go Round/Love (Version Instrumental)	8
71	Gas GAS 168	What You Gonna Do About It/DOBBY DOBSON: Halfway To Paradise	8
71	Jackpot JP 765	Let Them Talk/The Truth Hurts	6

ERNEST ('SOUL') WILSON

67	Studio One SO 2032	Money Worries/SOUL VENDORS: Pe Da Pa	40
68	Studio One SO 2058	If I Were A Carpenter/SOUL VENDORS: Frozen Soul	40
68	Coxsone CS 7044	Storybook Children (as Ernest 'Soul' Wilson)/LITTLE FREDDIE: After Laughter (B-side actually by Freddie McGregor)	30
68	Coxsone CS 7059	Undying Love/SOUL VENDORS: Tropic Isle	30
69	Amalgamated AMG 837	Private Number/GLEN ADAMS: She's So Fine	50
69	Crab CRAB 9	Private Number/Another Chance	12
69	Crab CRAB 17	Freedom Train/STRANGER COLE: You Should Never Have To Come	25
69	Crab CRAB 21	Just Once In My Life (with Freddy)/GLEN ADAMS: Mighty Organ	25
76	Fab FAB 280	Storybook Children/SOUND DIMENSION: Version	10

(see also Tinga & Ernest)

FRANK WILSON

79	Tamla Motown TMG 1170	Do I Love You (Indeed I Do)/Sweeter As The Days Go By	30
79	Tamla Motown TMG 1170	Do I Love You (Indeed I Do)/Sweeter As The Days Go By (DJ copy)	60
04	Tamla Motown 982 153 0	Do I Love You (Indeed I Do)/CHRIS CLARK: Do I Love You (Indeed I Do) (die-cut p/s)	25

FRANK WILSON & CAVALIERS

64	Fontana TF 505	Last Kiss/That's How Much I Love You	12

GADDY WILSON

60	Philips PB 980	Nothin' At Night/I'll Never Be Myself Again (78)	10

GARLAND WILSON

53	HMV 7M 122	Just You, Just Me/Sweet Georgia Brown	6

GARY WILSON

80	Sourgrape SG 115	Movie Queen/Movie Queen (p/s)	6

JACK WILSON QUARTET

64	London HA-K/SH-K 8170	THE JACK WILSON QUARTET (LP, featuring Roy Ayers)	20
66	Vocalion LAE-L 603	RAMBLIN' (LP)	20

(see also Roy Ayers)

JACKIE WILSON

78s

57	Vogue Coral Q 72290	Reet Petite/By The Light Of The Silvery Moon	10
57	Coral Q 72290	Reet Petite/By The Light Of The Silvery Moon (2nd pressing)	10
58	Coral Q 72332	I'm Wanderin'/As Long As I Live	15
58	Coral Q 72338	We Have Love/Singing A Song	15
58	Coral Q 72347	Lonely Teardrops/In The Blue Of The Evening	40
59	Coral Q 72366	That's Why/Love Is All	40
59	Coral Q 72372	I'll Be Satisfied/Ask	50
59	Coral Q 72380	You Better Know It/Never Go Away	75
59	Coral Q 72384	Talk That Talk/Only You, Only Me	80

SINGLES

57	Vogue Coral Q 72290	Reet Petite/By The Light Of The Silvery Moon	25
57	Coral Q 72290	Reet Petite/By The Light Of The Silvery Moon (2nd pressing)	15
58	Coral Q 72306	To Be Loved/Come Back To Me	25
58	Coral Q 72332	I'm Wanderin'/As Long As I Live	25
58	Coral Q 72338	We Have Love/Singing A Song	22
58	Coral Q 72347	Lonely Teardrops/In The Blue Of The Evening	25
59	Coral Q 72366	That's Why/Love Is All	20
59	Coral Q 72366	That's Why/Love Is All (mispressing, B-side plays "You Better Know It")	15
59	Coral Q 72372	I'll Be Satisfied/Ask	15
59	Coral Q 72380	You Better Know It/Never Go Away	15
59	Coral Q 72384	Talk That Talk/Only You, Only Me	15
60	Coral Q 72393	Doggin' Around/The Magic Of Love	15
60	Coral Q 72407	A Woman, A Lover, A Friend/(You Were Made For) All My Love	15
60	Coral Q 72412	Alone At Last/Am I The Man	25
61	Coral Q 72421	The Tear Of The Year/My Empty Arms (withdrawn B-side, demos only)	65
61	Coral Q 72424	The Tear Of The Year/Your One And Only Love	15
61	Coral Q 72430	Please Tell Me Why/(So Many) Cute Little Girls	15
61	Coral Q 72434	I'm Comin' On Back To You/Lonely Life	15
61	Coral Q 72439	You Don't Know What It Means/Years From Now	15

61	Coral Q 72444	The Way I Am/My Heart Belongs To Only You	15
62	Coral Q 72450	The Greatest Hurt/There'll Be No Next Time	15
62	Coral Q 72453	Sing (And Tell The Blues So Long)/I Found Love (B-side with Linda Hopkins)	15
62	Coral Q 72454	I Just Can't Help It/My Tale Of Woe	15
63	Coral Q 72460	Baby Workout/What Good Am I Without You	15
63	Coral Q 72464	Shake A Hand/Say I Do (as Jackie Wilson & Linda Hopkins)	15
63	Coral Q 72465	Shake! Shake! Shake!/He's A Fool	15
63	Coral Q 72467	Baby Get It/The New Breed	15
64	Coral Q 72474	Big Boss Line/Be My Girl	15
64	Coral Q 72476	Squeeze Her - Tease Her (But Love Her)/Give Me Back My Heart	15
65	Coral Q 72480	Yes Indeed!/When The Saints Go Marching In (with Linda Hopkins)	18
65	Coral Q 72481	No Pity (In The Naked City)/I'm So Lonely	20
65	Coral Q 72481	No Pity (In The Naked City)/I'm So Lonely (DJ copy)	45
65	Coral Q 72482	I Believe I'll Love On/Lonely Teardrops	15
66	Coral Q 72484	To Make A Big Man Cry/Be My Love	20
66	Coral Q 72484	To Make A Big Man Cry/Be My Love (DJ copy)	45
66	Coral Q 72487	Whispers/The Fairest Of Them All)	40
66	Coral Q 72487	Whispers/The Fairest Of Them All (DJ copy)	85
67	Coral Q 72493	(Your Love Keeps Lifting Me) Higher And Higher/I'm The One To Do It	20
67	Coral Q 72493	(Your Love Keeps Lifting Me) Higher And Higher/I'm The One To Do It (DJ copy)	85
67	Coral Q 72496	Since You Showed Me How To Be Happy/The Who-Who Song	30
67	Coral Q 72496	Since You Showed Me How To Be Happy/The Who-Who Song (DJ copy)	75
68	MCA MU 1014	For Your Precious Love/Uptight (Everything's Alright) (with Count Basie)	10
68	Decca AD 1008	For Your Precious Love/Uptight (Everything's Alright) (export issue)	25
69	MCA Soul Bag BAG 2	(Your Love Keeps Lifting Me) Higher And Higher/Whispers (Gettin' Louder)	10
69	MCA Soul Bag BAG 7	Since You Showed Me How To Be Happy/Chain Gang	10
69	MCA MU 1104	Since You Showed Me How To Be Happy/The Who-Who Song (reissue)	10
69	MCA MU 1105	Helpless/Do It The Right Way	10
70	MCA MU 1131	(Your Love Keeps Lifting Me) Higher And Higher/Whispers (Gettin' Louder) (reissue)	6
72	MCA MU 1160	I Get The Sweetest Feeling/Soul Galore	6
73	Brunswick BR 3	Beautiful Day/What'cha Gonna Do About Love	6
75	Brunswick BR 18	I Get The Sweetest Feeling/(Your Love Keeps Lifting Me) Higher And Higher	5
75	Brunswick BR 23	Whispers (Gettin' Louder)/Reet Petite	5
75	Brunswick BR 28	Don't Burn No Bridges/Don't Burn No Bridges (Instrumental) (with Chi-Lites)	5
77	Brunswick BR 43	It Only Happens When I Look At You/Just As Soon As The Feeling's Over	80

EPs

59	Coral FEP 2016	JACKIE WILSON (triangular centre)	100
59	Coral FEP 2016	JACKIE WILSON (round centre)	70
60	Coral FEP 2043	THE DYNAMIC JACKIE WILSON (triangular centre)	100
60	Coral FEP 2043	THE DYNAMIC JACKIE WILSON (round centre)	70

ALBUMS

58	Coral LVA 9087	HE'S SO FINE	150
59	Coral LVA 9108	LONELY TEARDROPS	150
60	Coral LVA 9121	SO MUCH	110
60	Coral LVA 9130	JACKIE SINGS THE BLUES	125
60	Coral LVA 9135	MY GOLDEN FAVOURITES	90
61	Coral LVA 9144	A WOMAN, A LOVER, A FRIEND	100
61	Coral LVA 9148	YOU AIN'T HEARD NOTHIN' YET	85
62	Coral LVA 9151	BY SPECIAL REQUEST (mono)	75
62	Coral SVL 3018	BY SPECIAL REQUEST (stereo)	90
62	Coral LVA 9202	BODY AND SOUL	65
63	Coral LVA 9209	JACKIE (mono)	70
63	Coral SVL 9209	JACKIE (stereo)	80
63	Coral LVA 9214	THE WORLD'S GREATEST MELODIES (mono)	55
63	Coral SVL 9214	THE WORLD'S GREATEST MELODIES (stereo)	65
66	Coral LVA 9231	SPOTLIGHT ON JACKIE WILSON	70
66	Coral LVA 9232	SOUL GALORE (mono)	70
66	Coral SVL 9232	SOUL GALORE (stereo)	80
67	Coral LVA 9235	WHISPERS	75
68	MCA MUP(S) 304	HIGHER AND HIGHER	20
68	MCA MUP(S) 333	TWO MUCH (with Count Basie & His Orchestra)	20
69	MCA MUPS 361	I GET THE SWEETEST FEELING	20
70	MCA MUPS 405	DO YOUR THING	25
73	Brunswick BRLS 3001	YOU GOT ME WALKIN'	25
73	Brunswick BRLS 3004	GREATEST HITS	15
75	Brunswick BRLS 3016	THE VERY BEST OF JACKIE WILSON	15

(see also Billy Ward & Dominoes, Clyde McPhatter, Count Basie, Chi-Lites, Linda Hopkins)

JACKIE WILSON/CLYDE MCPHATTER

62	Ember JBS 705	Tenderly/CLYDE McPHATTER: Harbour Lights	250
62	Ember NR 5001	MEET BILLY WARD & THE DOMINOES (LP, 1 side each)	200

(see also Clyde McPhatter)

JOANNE WILSON

81	Red Stripe 2222	Gotta Have You Back/Part 2	12

JOE WILSON

71	Pye International 7N 25550	Sweetness/When A Man Cries	10

MARTY WILSON & STRAT-O-LITES

58	Brunswick 05750	Hey! Eula/Hedge-Hopper	20

MAYNELL WILSON (ACTUALLY WILSON MAYNELL) & WESTMINSTER FIVE

64	Carnival CV 7014	Hey Hey Johnny/Baby	10
67	CBM CBM 001	Motown Feeling/Mean Ole World (with p/s)	20
67	CBM CBM 001	Motown Feeling/Mean Ole World	10

(see also Wes[t]minster Five)

MURRY WILSON

67	Capitol CL 15525	Plumber's Tune/Love Won't Wait	8
67	Capitol (S)T 2819	THE MANY MOODS OF MURRY WILSON (LP)	20

(see also Beach Boys)

NANCY WILSON

64	Capitol CL 15343	The Best Is Yet To Come/Never Let Me Go	5
64	Capitol CL 15352	(You Don't Know) How Glad I Am/Never Less Than Yesterday	10
65	Capitol CL 15378	Don't Come Running Back To Me/Love Has Many Faces	10
65	Capitol CL 15412	Where Does That Leave Me/Gentle Is My Love	20
66	Capitol CL 15443	Power Of Love/Rain Sometimes	12
66	Capitol CL 15466	You've Got Your Troubles/Uptight (Everything's Alright)	20
67	Capitol CL 15508	Don't Look Over Your Shoulder/Mercy, Mercy, Mercy	15
68	Capitol CL 15536	You Don't Know Me/Ode To Billie Joe	10
68	Capitol CL 15547	Face It Girl It's Over/The End Of Our Love	40
68	Capitol CL 15547	Face It Girl It's Over/The End Of Our Love (DJ copy)	80
75	Capitol CL 15810	You're Right As Rain/There'll Always Be Forever	5
77	Capitol CL 15547	End Of Our Love/Face It Girl, It's Over (white logo, reissue)	12
62	Capitol EAP1 20604	SECOND TIME AROUND (EP)	10
64	Capitol EAP4 2082	TODAY, TOMORROW, FOREVER (EP)	10
62	Capitol (S)T 1767	HELLO YOUNG LOVERS (LP, mono/stereo)	18
63	Capitol (S)T 1828	BROADWAY - MY LOVE (LP, mono/stereo)	18
63	Capitol (S)T 1934	HOLLYWOOD - MY WAY (LP, mono/stereo)	18
63	Capitol (S)T 2012	YESTERDAY'S LOVE SONGS (LP, mono/stereo)	18
64	Capitol (S)T 2082	TODAY, TOMORROW, FOREVER (LP)	18
65	Capitol (S)T 2136	THE NANCY WILSON SHOW (LP)	18
65	Capitol (S)T 2155	HOW GLAD I AM (LP)	18
65	Capitol (S)T 2321	TODAY- MY WAY (LP)	18
65	Capitol (S)T 2351	GENTLE IS MY LOVE (LP)	18
66	Capitol (S)T 2433	FROM BROADWAY WITH LOVE (LP)	18
66	Capitol (S)T 2495	A TOUCH OF TODAY (LP)	30
66	Capitol (S)T 2555	TENDER LOVING CARE (LP)	20
67	Capitol (S)T 2634	NANCY - NATURALLY (LP)	20

NANCY WILSON & CANNONBALL ADDERLEY

62	Capitol T 1657	NANCY WILSON & CANNONBALL ADDERLEY (LP, mono)	12
62	Capitol ST 1657	NANCY WILSON & CANNONBALL ADDERLEY (LP, stereo)	15

(see also Cannonball Adderley)

PEANUTS WILSON

58	Coral Q 72302	Cast Iron Arm/You've Got Love	500
58	Coral Q 72302	Cast Iron Arm/You've Got Love (78)	150
76	MCA MCA 240	Cast Iron Arm/DON WOODY: Barking Up The Wrong Tree	6

PHIL WILSON

87	Creation CRE 036D	Waiting For A Change/Even Now/Down In The Valley/Love In Vain (double pack)	5
89	Caff CAFF 3	Better Days/You Won't Speak (p/s, with insert, handwritten label)	12

(see also June Brides)

REUBEN WILSON

76	Chess 6078 700	Got To Get Your Own Parts 1 & 2	20

RON WILSON

68	Island WI 3112	Dread Saras/DAVID BROWN: All My Life	40

(see also Winston Scotland, Douglas Brothers)

SHARK WILSON & BASEMENT HEATERS

71	Ashanti ASH 400	Make It Reggae/Version	12

SMILEY WILSON

60	London HLG 9066	Running Bear/Long As Little Birds Fly	50

TOMY WILSON

64	Decca F12033	Yes I Do/Lost Without You	10

TONY WILSON

67	Columbia DB 8153	Can't Waste A Good Thing/What Did I Do?	30
69	Bell BLL 1081	Baby, I Love, Love I Love You/Come Back To My Lonely World	6
76	Bearsville K 55513	I LIKE YOUR STYLE (LP)	12

(see also Hot Chocolate)

TREVOR WILSON

65	Ska Beat JB 207	You Couldn't Believe/You Told Me You Care	30

STEVEN WILSON

09	Kscope KSCOPE 804	Harmony Korine (edit)/The 78 (p/s, 1000 only)	10
09	Kscope KSCOPE 804	Harmony Korine (edit)/The 78 (p/s, red vinyl, 1000 only)	10
09	Kscope KSCOPE 804	Harmony Korine (edit)/The 78 (p/s, white vinyl, 1000 only)	10
09	Kscope KSCOPE 809	NSRGNTS RMXS (12" EP, p/s, 1000 only)	10
11	Kscope LOTSCOPE 001	Stone Age Dinosaurs/OCEANZIZE: Fear (white vinyl, p/s, 2000 only)	8
09	Kscope KSCOPE 808	INSURGENTES (2-LP, gatefold sleeve, 2000 only)	40

(see also Porcupine Tree)

GABY WILTON & CHARLIE ACE

72	Bullet BU 511	Babylon Falling/CHARLIE ACE: Make It Love	8

JOHNNY WILTSHIRE & HIS TREBLETONES

59	Oriole CB 1494	If The Shoe Fits/Cha Cha Choo Choo	10

TEACHO WILTSHIRE

57	Oriole CB 1376	Coffee Break/Shut-Eye (78)	10

(see also Annie Ross)

WIMPLE WINCH

66	Fontana TF 686	What's Been Done/I Really Love You	350
66	Fontana TF 718	Save My Soul/Everybody's Worried 'Bout Tomorrow	500
67	Fontana TF 781	Rumble On Mersey Square South/Typical British Workmanship	300
67	Fontana TF 781	Rumble On Mersey Square South/Typical British Workmanship (mispressing, B-side plays "Atmospheres")	600
91	Bam Caruso KIRI 108	THE PSYCHEDELIC YEARS VOLUME 2 (LP)	20

(see also Just Four Men, Four Just Men, Pacific Drift, Tristar Airbus)o

WIMPS
79	Sniff Records SNORT 1	Hamburger Radio/New Girl At School/Modern Girl (numbered p/s)	10
79	Sniff Records SNORT 2	At The Discoteque/Blind Minds/Gonna Lose (p/s)	10

WIN
87	Swamplands	UH! TEARS BABY (CD)	30

LEM WINCHESTER & BENNY GOLSON
59	Esquire 32-142	WINCHESTER SPECIAL (LP)	25
61	Esquire 32-172	ANOTHER OPUS (LP)	15

KAI WINDING
65	Verve VS 512	Comin' Home Baby/More	15
55	London LTZ-N 15003	K AND J.J. (LP, with J.J. Johnson Quintet)	15
59	Philips SBBL 515	TROMBONES (LP)	18
61	Parlophone PMC 1138	SLIDE RULE (LP, with J.J. Johnson Quintet)	20
63	Verve VLP 9049	SOUL SURFIN' (LP)	30

(see also Dizzy Gillespie, J.J. Johnson Quintet)

WIND IN THE WILLOWS
68	Capitol CL 15561	Moments Spent/Friendly Lion	25
68	Capitol ST 2956	WIND IN THE WILLOWS (LP)	30

(see also Debbie Harry, Blondie)

WINDMILL
69	MCA MU 1090	Big Bertha/Hey, Drummer Man	5
70	MCA MK 5024	Such Sweet Sorrow/I Can Fly	10
70	MCA MK 5045	Wilbur's Thing/Two's Company, Three's A Crowd	5

WINDMILLS
88	S.T.S. 2	The Day Dawned On Me/Dolphins (p/s)	20
90	Wasteful SRT 90s 2734	Nothing At All/Secrets (p/s)	20

BARRY WINDOW
69	BAF BAF 7	I Thank You/End Of Our Road	50

WINDOWS (1)
72	Polydor 2058 206	How Do You Do/Nobody's Baby	18

WINDOWS (2)
78	Skeleton SKL 008	Re-Arrange/Over Dub (p/s)	7
81	Skeleton SKULP 2	UPPERS ON DOWNERS (LP, with inserts)	12

(see also Mutants)

BARBARA WINDSOR
61	HMV POP 883	Ten Gallon Hat/Funny Face	7
62	HMV POP 1104	It Has Better Be A Wonderful Life/ I'm Not That Sort Of Girl (with Harry Fowler & Kenny Lynch)	7
63	HMV POP 1128	Sparrows Can't Sing/On Mother Kelly's Doorstep	7
67	Parlophone R 5629	Don't Dig Twiggy/Swinging London	7
70	UPC UPC 101	When I Was A Child/What A Right Carry On	12
72	Decca F 13323	Grin And Bare It/Cheeky Sorta' Bird	7

WINDY & CARL
95	Enraptured RAPT 4501	Emerald/Fragments Of Time And Space (500 in hand-painted p/s)	12
95	Enraptured RAPT 4501	Emerald/Fragments Of Time And Space (300 in tracing paper sleeve)	10
96	Enraptured RAPT 4509	Christmas Song/GRIMBLE GRUMBLE: Odyssey And Oracle (no'd p/s, coloured vinyl, 350 only)	20

WINDY CORNER
73	Deroy DER 977	THE HOUSE AT WINDY CORNER (LP, private pressing)	300

AMY WINEHOUSE
03	Island 12 IS 830 DJ	Stronger Than Me (Curtis Lynch Jnr Vocal Remix)/(Curtis Lyinch Jnr Dub Remix) (12" Promo)	20
03	Island 12 IS 830	Stronger Than Me (Album Version/(Curtis Lynch Jnr Remix featuring Blackout Ja and Isha Sesay)/(Harmonic 33 Remix)/Acapella Version) (12")	15
03	Island 12 ISX 840 DJ	Take The Box (Seiji's Buggin' Mix)/(Seiji's Buggin' Rub)/(The Headquarters MIx) (Promo 12")	18
04	Island 12 IS 840	Take The Box (Seiji's Buggin' Mix)/(The Headquarters MIx)/(Acapella) (12")	10
03	Island 12 IS 840 DJ	In My Bed (1-sided promo 12")	12
03	Island ISX 852 DJ	In My Bed (Bass Gangsta Mix)/(CJ Mix)/(Full Length Version) (Promo 12")	18
03	Island 12 IS 852 DJ	In My Bed (Bugz In The Attic Vocal Mix)/(Bugz In The Attic Dub)/(Full Length Version) (Promo 12")	18
04	Island 12 IS 852	In My Bed (Bugz In The Attic Vocal Mix)/You Sent Me Flying/In My Bed (Bad Gangsta/In My Bed (Radio Edit) (12")	10
03	Island 12 IS 865 DJ	Pumps (MJ Cole Remix)/Pumps (Mylo Remix)/Pumps (Promo 12")	18
04	Island IS 865	Pumps (MJ Cole Remix)/Pumps (Mylo Remix)/Pumps (Album Version) (12")	10
06	Island 3789621 0 1	Rehab - Amy Vs Pharoahe (Promo 12" stickered white label)	10
06	Island AMY 12 PRO 1	Rehab (Hot Chip Remix)/(Hot Chip Instrumental)/(Desert Eagle Discs Remix)/(Desert Eagle Discs Instrumental)/(Original Version) (Promo 12")	25
05	Universal Island AMY 12PRO 1	Rehab (Hot Chip Remix)/(Hot Chip Instrumental)/(DED Instrumental)/(Original Version) (promo 12")	10
06	AMY/AMX 12 PRO	Love Is A Losing Game (Moody Boyz Dubstep Remix)/(Moody Boyz Dubland Version) (Promo 12", 300 only)	25
06	Island AMY 7 PRO 2	Love Is A Losing Game/(Moody Boys Dubstep Remix) promo, 300 only	40
06	Island AMYLPPRO 1	Back To Black (The Rumble Strips Remix)/Back To Black (p/s, clear vinyl promo)	20
07	Island 1732327	Back To Black (Steve Mac Vocal 6:12)/(Steve Mac Smack Dub 6:15)/(Original Version 4:00)/(Mushtaq Vocal Remix 4.03) (12")	8
07	Island 1732326	Back To Black/Back To Black (Rumble Strips Remix) (p/s, white vinyl)	6
07	Island 1744792	Tears Dry On Their Own/Tears Dry On Their Own (NYPC's Fucked MIx) (p/s, clear vinyl)	10
07	Island 1744793	Tears Dry On Their Own (Alix Alvarez Sole Channel MIx)/(Al Usher Remix)/Tears Dry On Their Own (12")	8
07	Universal 1755180	Love Is A Losing Game (Kardinal Beats Remix)/(Album Version)/(Moody Boyz Original Ruffian Badboy Remix)/(Truth & Soul Remix) (12")	8
03	Iniversal Island FRANK LP 3	FRANK (ALBUM SAMPLER) EP (promo 12", p/s)	20
04	Isand/Universal (No Cat No)	FRANK (ALBUM SAMPLER) EP (5-track, promo CD, p/s)	25
03	Island 9812918	FRANK (LP)	20
07	Island 1735948	FRANK - REMIXES (2 x 12", gatefold)	12
07	Island/Universal 1734128	BACK TO BLACK (LP)	20

08   Island ILPS 8148   FRANK (LP, reissue, 180gm includes free download, sealed, stickered) 20
(see also Mark Ronson)

WINE OF LEBANON
76   Dovetail DOVE 46   WINE OF LEBANON (LP) 20
(see also Achor)

WINKIES
75   Chrysalis CHR 1066   THE WINKIES (LP)..12

PETE WINSLOW & KING SIZE BRASS
73   BBC 103S   GIRL ON THE TESTCARD (LP)...20

WINSTON
74   York YR 212   I Wanna Let Anna Go/Brother Jim..15
60s   Holyground   WINSTON SINGS (EP) 10
73   Bradley BRAD 306   Mona/Rockerdile (p/s)...20

WINSTON (RICHARDS) & BIBBIE (SEATON)
63   R&B JB 115   Lover Man/LESTER STIRLING: Gravy Cool 30

WINSTON (FRANCIS) & CECIL (LOCKE)
70   Banana BA 306   United We Stand/SOUND DIMENSION: Sweet Message 20

WINSTON & ERROL
64   Blue Beat BB 272   Fay Is Gone/MONARCHS : Sadler 10
71   Punch PH 74   There Is A Land/Goodnight My Love 6

WINSTON & FAY
64   Blue Beat BB 272   Fay Is Gone (Winston & Errol)/MONARCHS: Sauce And Tea............................22

WINSTON & GEORGE
66   Pyramid PYR 6002   Denham Town/Keep The Pressure On 20

JIMMY WINSTON (& HIS) REFLECTIONS
66   Decca F 12410   Sorry She's Mine/It's Not What You Do (But The Way That You Do It) 300
76   Nems NEMS 12   Sun In The Morning/Just Wanna Smile (solo) 8
(see also Small Faces, Winston's Fumbs, Spheres)

WINSTON (GROOVY) & PAT (RHODEN)
68   Trojan TR 605   Pony Ride/Baby You Send Me 8
71   Bullet BU 475   The Same Thing For Breakfast/Sweeter Than Honey 8
(see also Winston Tucker)

WINSTON (RICHARDS) & TONETTES
65   Ska Beat JB 225   You Make Me Cry/CHECKMATES: Invisible Ska 35

WINSTON & ROY
62   Blue Beat BB 80   Babylon Gone/COUNT OSSIE ON AFRICAN DRUMS: First Gone.....................25

WINSTON & RUPERT
70   Bullet BU 425   Come By Here/Somebody 10
70   Moodisc HM 106   Musically Beat/Let Me Tell You Girl 10
(see also Eternals)

ERIC WINSTONE (& HIS) ORCHESTRA
64   Pye 7N 15603   Dr. Who Theme/Pony Express 18
73   Avenue AVINT 1005   PLAYS 007 (LP) 12

NORMA WINSTONE
72   Argo ZDA 148   EDGE OF TIME (LP) 120
(see also Mike Westbrook, Michael Garrick)

WINSTONS
69   Pye International 7N 25493   Colour In Father/Amen, Brother 20
69   Pye International 7N 25500   Love Of The Common People/Wheel Of Fortune..7

WINSTON'S FUMBS
67   RCA RCA 1612   Real Crazy Apartment/Snow White...600
(see also Small Faces, Jimmy Winston & His Reflections, Yes, Spheres, Federals)

WINSTONS & M-SQUAD
71   Green Door GD 4003   Carroll Street/Carroll Street - Version (B-side act. by Ansel Collins/M-Squad)............6

EDGAR WINTER (GROUP)
70   CBS 64083   ENTRANCE (LP, as Edgar Winter) 15
71   CBS 64298   EDGAR WINTER'S WHITE TRASH (LP)...15
72   CBS 67244   ROAD WORK (2-LP) 15
73   CBS EQ 31584/Q 65074   THEY ONLY COME OUT AT NIGHT (LP, quadrophonic) 12

JOHNNY WINTER
69   CBS 4386   I'm Yours And I'm Hers/I'll Drown In My Tears...6
69   Liberty LBF 15219   Rollin' And Tumblin'/Bad Luck And Trouble 7
70   CBS 4794   Johnny B. Goode/I'm Not Sure 6
70   CBS 5358   Rock 'N' Roll Hoochie Koo/21st Century Man 5
71   CBS 7227   Jumping Jack Flash/Good Morning Little School Girl 5
69   CBS 63619   JOHNNY WINTER (LP) 25
69   Liberty LBL/LBS 83240E   THE PROGRESSIVE BLUES EXPERIMENT (LP) 20
70   Buddah 2359 011   FIRST WINTER (LP) 20
70   CBS 66231   SECOND WINTER (2-LP, 3-sided) 18
70   CBS 64117   JOHNNY WINTER AND... (LP)...15
71   CBS 64289   JOHNNY WINTER AND... LIVE (LP) 12
73   CBS 65484   STILL ALIVE AND WELL (LP) 12
74   CBS CQ 32188/Q 65484   STILL ALIVE AND WELL (LP, quadrophonic) 15
(see also Johnny & Jammers)

DON WINTERS
60   Brunswick 05827   Someday Baby/That's All I Need 15

JONATHAN WINTERS
61   HMV CLP 1482   HERE'S JONATHAN (LP) 12

Liz WINTERS & BOB CORT SKIFFLE GROUP

LIZ WINTERS & BOB CORT SKIFFLE GROUP

57	Decca F 10878	Freight Train/Love Is Strange	20
57	Decca F 10878	Freight Train/Love Is Strange (78)	10
57	Decca F 10899	Maggie May/Jessamine	20
57	Decca F 10899	Maggie May/Jessamine (78)	10
57	Decca DFE 6409	LIZ WINTERS AND BOB CORT (EP)	25

(see also Bob Cort Skiffle Group)

LOIS WINTERS

56	London HLD 8266	Japanese Farewell Song/JAN GARBER & HIS ORCHESTRA: My Dear	35

WINTERS REIGN

84	Scoff DTO33	Save It/Keep Trying	8
87	Link LOPL 501	THE BEIGNNING (LP, with free 7")	15

RON WINTERS

63	Colpix PX 11022	Snow Girl/In The Middle Of The Morning	20

RUBY WINTERS

68	Stateside SS 2090	I Want Action/Better	100
68	Stateside SS 2090	I Want Action/Better (DJ copy)	150

WYOMA WINTERS

54	HMV 7M 222	Where Can I Go Without You?/Won't You Give A Repeat Performance	7
54	HMV 7M 260	Toy Balloon/Shish Kebab	7

STEVIE WINWOOD

77	Island WIP 6394	Time Is Running Out/Penultimate Zone (12", pre-release sleeve)	10
80	Island IPR 2040	While You See A Chance/Vacant Chair (12", pre-release sleeve)	8
80	Island WIP 6655	While You See A Chance/Vacant Chair (p/s)	5
81	Island WIP 6747	There's A River/Two Way Stretch (p/s)	5
86	Island IS 294	Freedom Overspill/Spanish Dancer (p/s, with bonus cassette of LP highlights & interview [SW 2])	6
86	Island 12 ISD 294	Freedom Overspill (Liberty Mix)/(LP Version)/Spanish Dancer (12", stickered g/fold p/s & t/p 7" "Low Spark Of High-Heeled Boys"/"Gimme Some Lovin' ")	10
88	Virgin VST 1085	Roll With It (12" Mix)/The Morning Side/Roll With It (7" Version) (12", g/fold p/s)	8
86	Island SWCLP 1	A CONVERSATION WITH (LP, promo interview on "Back In The High Life" LP)	12
87	Island SWWLP 1	IN CONVERSATION (LP, promo interview on "Chronicles" LP)	12
87	Island SW 1/2/3	BACK IN THE HIGH LIFE (3 x 7" set, each in p/s, promo only)	20
87	Island	CHRONICLES (5 x 7" box set, promo, 500 only)	30

(see also Winwood Kabaka Amoa, Anglos, Spencer Davis Group, Traffic, Blind Faith.)

WINWOOD/KABAKA/AMAO

73	Island HELP 14	AIYE-KETA THIRD WORLD (LP)	15

(see also Stevie WInwood)

WIPEOUT

82	M&L MNL 2/ACE 37	Baby Please Don't Go/Two-O-Five/Crawdaddy/Should A' Known Better (p/s)	15
83	Out OUT 1A/B1	NO SWEAT (LP)	15

WIPEOUT

90s	Deluxe DELUX 002	Snowflake/Confusion Bee (12")	10

WIPERS

84	Psycho PSYCHO 22	IS THIS REAL? (LP, with lyric insert)	15
84	Psycho PSYCHO 23	YOUTH OF AMERICA (LP)	15

WIRE

77	Harvest HAR 5144	Mannequin/Feeling Called Love/12XU (p/s)	20
77	Harvest HAR 5144	Mannequin/Feeling Called Love/12XU (no p/s)	10
78	Harvest HAR 5151	I Am The Fly/Ex-Lion Tamer (p/s)	15
78	Harvest HAR 5151	I Am The Fly/Ex-Lion Tamer (no p/s)	10
78	Harvest HAR 5161	Dot Dash/Options R (p/s)	12
78	Harvest HAR 5161	Dot Dash/Options R (no p/s)	8
79	Harvest HAR 5172	Outdoor Miner/Practice Makes Perfect (p/s, white vinyl)	12
79	Harvest HAR 5172	Outdoor Miner/Practice Makes Perfect (p/s)	7
79	Harvest HAR 5187	A Question Of Degree/Former Airline (p/s)	10
79	Harvest HAR 5192	Map Ref 41° N 93° W/Go Ahead (p/s)	10
79	Harvest SPSLP 299	154 (12", p/s, white label sampler with insert & press release; beware of counterfeits)	35
81	Rough Trade RT 079	Our Swimmer/Midnight Bahnhof Cafe (p/s)	8
83	Rough Trade RTT 123	Crazy About Love/Second Length (Our Swimmer)/Catapult 30 (12", p/s, 2 different sleeve colours)	8
88	Mute MUTE 67	Kidney Bingos/Pieta (p/s)	5
89	Mute MUTE 87	Eardrum Buzz/The Offer (p/s, clear vinyl, withdrawn)	8
77	Harvest SHSP 4076	PINK FLAG (LP, with lyric inner)	40
78	Harvest SHSP 4093	CHAIRS MISSING (LP, 1st 10,000 with lilac lyric inner sleeve)	30
79	Harvest SHSP 4105	154 (LP, with inner lyric sleeve & bonus 7" EP: "Song 2"/"Get Down [Parts I & II]"/"Let's Panic"/"Later"/"Small Electric Piece" [PSR 444])	35
79	Harvest SHSP 4105	154 (LP, without 7")	20
84	Rough Trade ROUGH 29	DOCUMENT AND EYEWITNESS (LP, with free 12" EP [ROUGH 2912])	20
87	Mute STUMM 42	THE IDEAL COPY (LP)	12
89	Harvest SHSP 4127	ON RETURNING (LP)	15
89	Strange Fruit SFRLP 108	PEEL SESSIONS (LP)	12
96	WMO 4LP	TURNS AND STROKES (LP)	20
03	PF456REDUX	PF456 REDUX (LP)	20
	Harvest SHSP 4076	PINK FLAG (LP, reissue)	15
00s	Harvest SHSP 4093	CHAIRS MISSING (LP, reissue)	15

(see also Dome, Cupol, Colin Newman.)

MARK WIRTZ (ORCHESTRA & CHORUS)

68	Parlophone R 5668	(He's Our Dear Old) Weatherman (From "A Teenage Opera")/Possum's Dance	30
68	Parlophone R 5683	Mrs. Raven/Knickerbocker Glory	25
69	CBS 4306	My Daddie Is A Baddie/I Love You Because	15
69	CBS 4539	Caroline/Goody, Goody, Goody	18
64	World Record Club T 452	TEN AGAIN (LP, by Belle Gonzalez & Russ Loader, Wirtz as producer)	30

(see also Mood Mosaic, Keith West, Sweet Shop, Philwit & Pegasus, Mark Rogers & Marksmen, Belle Gonzalez, Russ Loader, Zion De Gallier, Elmer Hockett's Hurdy Gurdy, Steve Flynn, Fickle Finger, Matchmaker)

NORMAN WISDOM

56	Columbia SCM 5222	Two Rivers/Boy Meets Girl (with Ruby Murray)	10
57	Columbia DB 3864	Up In The World/Me And My Imagination	10
57	Columbia DB 3903	The Wisdom Of A Fool/Happy Ending	10
59	Top Rank JAR 246	Follow A Star/Give Me A Night In June	5
61	Columbia SCD 2160	Narcissus (The Laughing Record)/I Don't 'Arf Love You (with Joyce Grenfell)	6
61	Columbia DB 4601	If You Believe In Me/Yer Gotta Get Aht	6
64	Columbia DB 7352	The Joker/Who Can I Turn To	6
80	HMV POP 2001	The Wisdom Of A Fool/Don't Laugh At Me ('Cause I'm A Fool)	5
69	CBS 4569	Where Do I Go From Here?/Just Like The Day	5
56	Columbia SEG 7612	NORMAN WISDOM (EP)	10
57	Columbia SEG 7687	NORMAN AND RUBY (EP, with Ruby Murray)	10
58	Columbia SEG 7856	NORMAN WISDOM (EP)	10
59	Top Rank JKP 2052	FOLLOW A STAR (EP)	10
58	Columbia 33SX 1085	NORMAN WISDOM IN "WHERE'S CHARLEY?" (LP)	12

(see also Ruby Murray)

WISE BLOOD

85	Wise 1-12	Motorslug/Death Rape 2000 (12", p/s)	12
86	Wise 2-12	Someone Drowned In My Pool/Stumbo (12", p/s)	12
91	Wise 003	DISHDIRT (LP, with sticker)	15
91	Big Cut 030X	PEDAL TO THE METAL (mini LP)	12

(see also Foetus)

WISE BOYS

60	Parlophone R 4693	Why, Why, Why/My Fortune	10

WISE GUYS

60	Top Rank JAR 271	(Little Girl) Big Noise/As Long As I Have You	10

MAC WISEMAN

55	London HLD 8174	The Kentuckian Song/Wabash Cannon Ball	40
56	London HLD 8226	My Little Home In Tennessee/I Haven't Got The Right To Love You	40
56	London HLD 8259	Fireball Mail/When The Roses Bloom Again	40
56	London HLD 8259	Fireball Mail/When The Roses Bloom Again (78)	15
57	London HLD 8412	Step It Up And Go/Sundown	400
57	London HLD 8412	Step It Up And Go/Sundown (78)	40
59	London HL 7084	Jimmy Brown The Newsboy/I've Got No Use For Woman (export issue)	20
56	London RE-D 1056	SONGS FROM THE HILLS (EP)	20
58	London RE-D 1147	SONGS FROM THE HILLS VOL. 2 (EP)	20
60	London RE-D 1242	SONGS FROM THE HILLS VOL. 3 (EP)	20
56	London HB-D 1052	SONGS FROM THE HILLS (10" LP)	30
60	London HA-D 2217	GREAT FOLK BALLADS (LP)	20

TREVOR WISHART

78	private pressing	RED BIRD: A POLITICAL PRISONER'S DREAM (LP, with insert)	20
79	private pressing	BEACH SINGULARITY AND MENAGERIE (LP, with insert)	20

WISHBONE ASH

70	MCA MK 5061	Blind Eye/Queen Of Torture	8
72	MCA MKS 5097	No Easy Road/Blowin' Free	6
73	MCA MUS 1210	So Many Things To Say/Rock'n'Roll Widow	5
74	MCA MCA 165	Hometown/Persephone	5
75	MCA MCA 176	Silver Shoes/Persephone	6
76	MCA/SFI 263	Outward Bound/Runaway/Mother Of Pearl/You Rescue Me (flexidisc, with "New England" tour programme)	12
77	MCA MCA 291	Phoenix/Blowin' Free/Jail Bait (p/s)	5
78	MCA MCA 392	You See Red/Bad Weather Blues (live) (p/s)	5
79	MCA MCA 518	Come On/Fast Johnny (p/s)	5
80	MCA MCA 549	Living Proof/Jail Bait (live) (p/s)	5
80	MCA MCA 577	Helpless (live)/Blowin' Free (live) (p/s)	5
81	MCA MCA 695	Underground/My Mind Is Made Up (p/s)	5
81	MCA MCA 726	Get Ready/Kicks On The Street (p/s, with patch)	8
81	MCA MCA 726	Get Ready/Kicks On The Street (p/s)	5
70	MCA MKPS 2014	WISHBONE ASH (LP, gatefold sleeve, red/pink 'dogbone' label)	75
71	MCA MDKS 8004	PILGRIMAGE (LP, gatefold sleeve, purple/red 'dogbone' label)	50
72	MCA MDKS 8006	ARGUS (LP, gatefold sleeve, black/blue 'hexagon' label)	100
73	MCA MDKS 8011	WISHBONE FOUR (LP, gatefold sleeve, black label, with poster & lyrics)	30
74	MCA MCSP 254	LIVE DATES (2-LP, gatefold sleeve, pink label)	15
78	MCA MCG 3528	NO SMOKE WITHOUT FIRE (LP, with stickered sleeve & inner, with bonus live single "Come In From The Rain"/"Lorelei" [PSR 431])	12
80	MCA MCG 4012	LIVE DATES II (LP, textured gatefold sleeve, with live bonus LP)	15
82	AVM ASH 1	TWIN BARRELS BURNING (LP)	12
85	Neat NEAT 1027	RAW TO THE BONE (LP)	18

(see also Home, Big Daisy)

WISHFUL THINKING

66	Decca F 12438	Turning Round/V.I.P.	20
66	Decca F 12499	Step By Step/Looking Around	7
67	Decca F 12598	Count To Ten/Hang Around Girl	8
67	Decca F 12627	Peanuts/Cherry Cherry	12
67	Decca F 22673	Meet The Sun/Easier Said Than Loving You	10
68	Decca F 22742	Alone/Vegetables (export issue)	10
68	Decca F 12760	It's So Easy/I Want You Girl	15
72	B&C CB 169	Lu La Le Lu/We're Gonna Change All This	7
72	B&C CB 184	Clear White Light/Hiroshima	10
67	Decca SKL 4900	LIVE VOL. 1 (LP)	50
71	Charisma CAS 1038	HIROSHIMA (LP)	25

WISHING STONES

86	Head HEAD 2	Beat Girl/Two Steps Take Me Back (p/s)	6
87	Head HEAD 6	New Ways/House Is Not A Home (p/s)	5

87	Head HEAD 612	New Ways/Wildwood/Hold Up/A House Is Not A Home (12", p/s)	8

(see also The Loft)

WITCHCRAFT

06	Rise Above RISE 7/089	If Crimson Was Your Colour/I Know You Killed Someone... (P/s, clear, red, green or black vinyl)	10
04	Rise Above RISELP 47	WITCHCRAFT (LP)	25
04	Rise Above RISEPD 47	WITCHCRAFT (LP, picture disc)	30
07	Rise Above RISELP 103	THE ALCHEMIST (LP, green, clear, purple or suitably gold vinyl)	20

WITCHES BREW

80s	Pussy PU 016	Angeline (p/s)	20

WITCHFINDER GENERAL

81	Heavy Metal HEAVY 6	Burning A Sinner/Satan's Children (p/s)	40
82	Heavy Metal 12HM 17	Soviet Invasion/Rabies/R.I.P. (live) (12", p/s)	35
83	Heavy Metal HEAVY 21	Music/Last Chance (p/s)	12
83	Heavy Metal HMPD 21	Music/Last Chance (picture disc)	8
82	Heavy Metal HMRLP 8	DEATH PENALTY (LP, red, blue or clear vinyl, with inner)	30
82	Heavy Metal HMRPD 8	DEATH PENALTY (LP, picture disc)	18
83	Heavy Metal HMRLP 13	FRIENDS OF HELL (LP, red, silver or clear vinyl)	20
83	Heavy Metal HMRPD 13	FRIENDS OF HELL (LP, picture disc)	18

WITCHFYNDE

79	Rondelet ROUND 1	Give 'Em Hell/Getting' Heavy (p/s)	6
80	Rondelet ROUND 4	In The Stars/Wake Up Screaming (p/s)	5
83	Expulsion OUT 3	I'd Rather Go Wild/Cry Wolf (p/s)	20
80	Rondelet ABOUT 1	GIVE 'EM HELL (LP)	25
80	Rondelet ABOUT 2	STAGE FRIGHT (LP)	15
83	Expulsion EXIT 5	CLOAK AND DAGGER (LP)	12
83	Expulsion PEXIT 5	CLOAK AND DAGGER (LP, picture disc)	18
84	Mausoleum SKULL 8352	LORDS OF SIN (LP, gatefold sleeve, with bonus 12" [Cloak & Dagger/ I'd Rather Go Wild/Moon Magic/Give 'Em Hell])	15

BILL WITHERS

71	A&M AMS 845	Everybody's Talkin'/Harlem	5
71	A&M AMS 858	Ain't No Sunshine/Harlem	5
72	A&M AMS 7004	Lean On Me/Better Off Dead	5
72	A&M AMS 7038	Use Me/Let Me In Your Life	5
73	A&M AMS 7055	Kissing My Love/I Don't Know	5
73	A&M AMS 7068	Look What I Found/The Lady Is Waiting	5
73	A&M AMS 7080	Ain't No Sunshine/Harlem/Grandma's Hands	5
72	A&M AMLH 68107	STILL BILL (LP)	20
71	A&M AMLS 65002	JUST AS I AM (LP)	15
73	A&M AMLD 3001	LIVE AT CARNEGIE HALL (2-LP)	15
74	A&M AMLH 68230	'JUSTMENTS	15

BRIAN WITHERS

66	RCA RCA 1536	For No One/Here There And Everywhere	8

JIMMY WITHERSPOON

78s

54	Parlophone R 3914	It/Highway To Happiness	40
54	Parlophone R 3951	Oh Boy/I Done Told You	40
54	Vogue V 2261	Failing By Degrees/New Orleans Woman	40
54	Vogue V 2295	Who's Been Jivin' With You/Rain, Rain, Rain	40
56	Vogue V 2060	Big Fine Girl/No Rollin' Blues	40
56	Vogue V 2356	Jump, Children/Take Me Back Baby	40

SINGLES

54	Parlophone MSP 6125	It/Highway To Happiness	100
54	Parlophone MSP 6142	Oh Boy/I Done Told You	100
56	Vogue V 2060	Big Fine Girl/No Rollin' Blues	75
62	Vogue V 2420	When The Lights Go Out/All That's Good	75
64	Stateside SS 304	Evenin'/Money Is Getting Cheaper	15
64	Stateside SS 325	I Will Never Marry/I'm Coming Down With The Blues	15
64	Stateside SS 362	You're Next/Happy Blues	15
65	Stateside SS 429	Come Walk With Me/Oh How I Love You	15
65	Stateside SS 461	Love Me Right/Make My Heart Smile Again	15
66	Stateside SS 503	If There Wasn't Any You/I Never Thought I'd See The Day	15
66	Verve VS 538	It's All Over But The Crying/If I Could Have You Back Again	8
67	Verve VS 553	Past Forty Blues/My Baby's Quit Me	6
71	Probe PRO 526	Handbags And Gladrags/It's Time To Live	5
75	Capitol CL 15828	Fool's Paradise/Reflections	5

EPs

61	Vogue EPV 1269	JIMMY WITHERSPOON AT MONTEREY	30
61	Vogue EPV 1270	JIMMY WITHERSPOON AT MONTEREY No. 2	30
64	Vocalion EPVH 1278	JIMMY WITHERSPOON	20
65	Vocalion EPVH 1284	OUTSKIRTS OF TOWN	20
66	Vocalion VEH 170158	FEELING THE SPIRIT VOL. 1	20
66	Vocalion VEH 170159	FEELING THE SPIRIT VOL. 2	20

ALBUMS

59	London Jazz LTZ-K 15150	NEW ORLEANS BLUES (with Wilbur de Paris)	40
60	Vogue LAE 12218	SINGIN' THE BLUES	40
61	Vogue LAE 12253	AT THE RENAISSANCE (with Gerry Mulligan)	35
64	Society SOC 968	SINGS THE BLUES	12
64	Stateside SL 10088	EVENIN' BLUES	35
65	Stateside SL 10105	BLUES AROUND THE CLOCK	40
65	Fontana 688 005 ZL	THERE'S GOOD ROCKIN' TONIGHT	30
65	Stateside SL 10114	SOME OF MY BEST FRIENDS ARE BLUES	25
65	Stateside SL 10139	BLUE SPOON	22
65	Vogue VRL 3005	JIMMY WITHERSPOON IN PERSON	22
66	Ember EMB 3369	JIMMY WITHERSPOON	20

67	Fontana (S)TL 5382	'SPOON SINGS AND SWINGS	20
67	Verve (S)VLP 9156	BLUE POINT OF VIEW	18
67	Transatlantic PR 7300	EVENIN' BLUES (reissue)	15
68	Transatlantic PR 7356	SOME OF MY BEST FRIENDS ARE THE BLUES (reissue)	15
68	Stateside (S)SL 10232	LIVE	20
68	Verve (S)VLP 9181	BLUES IS NOW (with Brother Jack McDuff)	15
68	Verve (S)VLP 9216	SPOONFUL OF SOUL	18
68	Transatlantic PR 7418	SPOON IN LONDON	15
68	Transatlantic PR 7475	BLUES FOR EASY LIVERS	15
69	Stateside SSL 10289	THE BLUES SINGER	18
69	Ember CJS 820	SINGS THE BLUES AT THE RENAISSANCE (reissue, with Gerry Mulligan)	12
69	Polydor Intl. 623 256	BACK DOOR BLUES	20
71	Probe SPB 1031	HANDBAGS AND GLADRAGS	15

(see also Eric Burdon & Jimmy Witherspoon, Brother Jack McDuff)

JIMMY WITHERSPOON/HELEN HUMES

| 60 | Vogue EPV 1198 | RHYTHM AND BLUES CONCERT (EP, 2 tracks each) | 80 |

(see also Helen Humes)

BITTER WITHY

| 69 | Nevis NEVIS R005 | SAMPLER (LP) | 20 |

WITNESSES

| 60s | Herald ELR 1076 | THE WITNESSES (EP) | 70 |

D WITTER

| 78 | D-Roy DRLP 1001 | MAWAMBA DUB (WARRIOR) (LP) | 50 |

(See also World Sound & Power Band)

WIZARD'S CONVENTION

| 76 | RCA RS 1085 | WIZARD'S CONVENTION (LP, with insert) | 15 |

(see also Deep Purple, Roger Glover, Jon Lord, David Coverdale, Ray Fenwick,Tony Ashton, Glenn Hughes, ELP, Hardin & York))

WIZZARD

73	Harvest SHSP 4025	WIZZARD BREW (LP, with lyric insert)	15
74	Harvest SHSP 4034	SEE MY BABY JIVE (LP)	12
74	Warner Bros. K 56029	INTRODUCING EDDY AND THE FALCONS (LP, with poster)	25

(see also Roy Wood, Balls, Idle Race, Grunt Futtock)

WJW & ROOTS TRUNKS & BRANCHES

| 79 | Splendour Heights WJWX 1945 | THE WEAK WILL BE STRONG (LP) | 25 |

WKGB

| 79 | Fetish FET 002 | Non-Stop/Ultra Marine (p/s) | 8 |

W.L.S.

| 77 | Cancer CAND 001 | Dub Punk/Simply Funky (12") | 15 |

JEZZ WODROFFE

| 80 | Graduate GRAD LP 1 | OPPOSITE DIRECTIONS (LP) | 50 |

CHARLES WOLCOTT

| 60 | MGM 1115 | Leatherjacket Cowboy/Ruby Duby Do | 15 |

DARRYL WAY'S WOLF

73	Deram DM 378	Wolf/Spring Fever	8
73	Deram DM 395	A Bunch Of Fives/Five In The Morning	8
73	Deram DM 401	Two Sisters/Go Down	8
73	Deram SDL 14	CANIS LUPUS (LP, as Darryl Way's Wolf, gatefold sleeve)	18
73	Deram SML 1104	SATURATION POINT (LP, laminated sleeve, as Darryl Way's Wolf)	15
74	Deram SML 1116	NIGHT MUSIC (LP)	18

(see also Curved Air, King Crimson, Marillion)

WOLF

| 81 | Gremlin GREM 72 | See Them Running/Creatures Of The Night (no p/s) | 75 |
| 84 | Mausoleum 8323 | EDGE OF THE WORLD (LP) | 18 |

WOLF

| 82 | Chrysalis CHS 2592 | Head Contact/Rock'n'Roll (p/s, clear vinyl, with sticker) | 15 |
| 82 | Chrysalis CHS 2592 | Head Contact/Rock'n'Roll (p/s, clear vinyl, without sticker) | 6 |

PATRICK WOLF

| 02 | Faith & Industry FAI 001 | THE PATRICK WOLF EP: Bloodbeat/Empress/A Boy Like Me/Pumpkin Soup (12", 1000 only) | 60 |

WOLFETONES

| 65 | Fontana STL 5244 | THE FOGGY DEW (LP) | 12 |

WOLFGANG

| 70 | Bell BLL 1120 | Sandman/You | 12 |

WOLFGANG PRESS

| 83 | 4AD (no cat. no.) | Kings Of Soul (Crowned Mix)/(De-Throned Mix)/(7" Mix) (12", same both sides, promo only, 50 copies pressed) | 15 |

(see also Mass, Models)

WOLFMAN

| 04 | Rough Trade RTRADS177 | For Lovers/Back From The Dead (with Pete Doherty, p/s) | 8 |

WOLFRILLA

| 71 | Concord CON 015 | Song For Jimi/Come Tomorrow | 7 |

WOOLLY WOLSTENHOLME

| 80 | Polydor 2374 165 | MAESTOSO (LP) | 12 |

(see also Barclay James Harvest)

WOLVES

64	Pye 7N 15676	Journey Into Dreams/What Do You Mean	20
64	Pye 7N 15733	Now/This Year Next Year	30
65	Pye 7N 17013	At The Club/Distant Dreams	35
66	Parlophone R 5511	Lust For Life/My Baby Loves Them	70

BOBBY WOMACK

68	Minit MLF 11001	Broadway Walk/Somebody Special	8
68	Minit MLF 11005	What Is This?/What You Gonna Do	15
68	Minit MLF 11010	Fly Me To The Moon/Take Me	8
69	Minit MLF 11012	California Dreamin'/Baby You Oughta Think It Over	10
72	United Artists UP 35339	That's The Way I Feel About 'Cha/Come, L'Amore	7
72	United Artists UP 35375	Woman's Gotta Have It/If You Don't Want My Love	5
73	United Artists UP 35456	I Can Understand It/Harry Hippie (in p/s)	12
73	United Artists UP 35456	I Can Understand It/Harry Hippie	8
73	United Artists UP 35512	Across 110th Street/Hang On In There (as Bobby Womack & Peace)	10
73	United Artists UP 35565	Nobody Wants You When You're Down And Out/I'm Through Trying To Prove My Love For You	6
74	Jay Boy BOY 75	What Is This?/I Wonder	15
75	United Artists UP 35859	Check It Out/Interlude No. 2	6
76	United Artists UP 36042	Where There's A Will There's A Way/Everything's Gonna Be Alright	6
76	United Artists UP 36098	Daylight/Trust Me	8
77	CBS 4827	Home Is Where The Heart Is/We've Only Just Begun	10
79	Arista ARIST 284	How Could You Break My Heart/I Honestly Love You	15
82	Tamla Motown TMG1267	So Many Sides of You/Just My Imagination (7", p/s)	30
87	Arista RIS 17	How Could You Break My Heart/Give It Up (p/s)	20
87	Arista RIST 17	How Could You Break My Heart/Give It Up/Mr. D.J. Don't Stop The Music (12", p/s)	20
72	United Artists UAS 29365	UNDERSTANDING (LP)	15
73	United Artists UAS 29451	ACROSS 110TH STREET (LP, soundtrack, with J.J. Johnson)	20
79	Arista ARTY 165	ROADS OF LIFE (LP)	20

(see also Valentinos, Ted Wood)

WOMB

| 69 | Dot DLP 25933 | WOMB (LP) | 25 |
| 70 | Dot DLP 25959 | OVERDUB (LP) | 30 |

WOMBATS

| 06 | Kids KIDS 005 | Lost In The Post/Patricia The Stripper (in stickered mailer, 500 only) | 10 |
| 07 | No Label | Moving To New York/Happily Screwed/The Barman's Fault/Ba Ba Song (EP) | 20 |

ALISON WONDER

| 70 | Columbia DB 8667 | Once More With Feeling/Black Paper Roses | 6 |

(see also Cheryl St. Clair)

(LITTLE) STEVIE WONDER

63	Oriole CBA 1853	Fingertips (Parts 1 & 2)	40
63	Oriole CBA 1853	Fingertips (Parts 1 & 2) (DJ copy)	85
63	Stateside SS 238	Workout, Stevie, Workout/Monkey Talk	50
63	Stateside SS 238	Workout, Stevie, Workout/Monkey Talk (DJ copy)	100
64	Stateside SS 285	Castles In The Sand/Thank You (For Loving Me All The Way)	80
64	Stateside SS 285	Castles In The Sand/Thank You (For Loving Me All The Way) (DJ copy)	100
64	Stateside SS 323	Hey, Harmonica Man/This Little Girl	55
64	Stateside SS 323	Hey, Harmonica Man/This Little Girl (DJ copy)	85

(The above 45's are credited to Little Stevie Wonder.)

65	Tamla Motown TMG 505	Kiss Me Baby/Tears In Vain	50
65	Tamla Motown TMG 505	Kiss Me Baby/Tears In Vain (DJ copy)	100
65	Tamla Motown TMG 532	High-Heel Sneakers/Music Talk	40
65	Tamla Motown TMG 532	High-Heel Sneakers/Music Talk (DJ copy)	100
66	Tamla Motown TMG 545	Uptight (Everything's Alright)/Purple Raindrops	25
66	Tamla Motown TMG 545	Uptight (Everything's Alright)/Purple Raindrops (DJ cop)	200
66	Tamla Motown TMG 558	Nothing's Too Good For My Baby/With A Child's Heart	45
66	Tamla Motown TMG 558	Nothing's Too Good For My Baby/With A Child's Heart (DJ copy)	150
66	Tamla Motown TMG 570	Blowin' In The Wind/Ain't That Asking For Trouble	25
66	Tamla Motown TMG 570	Blowin' In The Wind/Ain't That Asking For Trouble (DJ copy)	75
66	Tamla Motown TMG 588	A Place In The Sun/Sylvia	20
66	Tamla Motown TMG 588	A Place In The Sun/Sylvia (DJ copy)	50
67	Tamla Motown TMG 602	Travelin' Man/Hey Love	18
67	Tamla Motown TMG 602	Travelin' Man/Hey Love (DJ copy)	50
67	Tamla Motown TMG 613	I Was Made To Love Her/Hold Me	10
67	Tamla Motown TMG 613	I Was Made To Love Her/Hold Me (DJ copy)	40
67	Tamla Motown TMG 626	I'm Wondering/Every Time I See You I Go Wild	12
67	Tamla Motown TMG 626	I'm Wondering/Every Time I See You I Go Wild (DJ copy)	40
68	Tamla Motown TMG 653	Shoo-Be-Doo-Be-Doo-Da-Day/Why Don't You Lead Me To Love	12
68	Tamla Motown TMG 653	Shoo-Be-Doo-Be-Doo-Da-Day/Why Don't You Lead Me To Love (DJ copy)	30
68	Tamla Motown TMG 666	You Met Your Match/My Girl	15
68	Tamla Motown TMG 666	You Met Your Match/My Girl (DJ copy)	35
68	Tamla Motown TMG 679	For Once In My Life/Angie Girl	6
68	Tamla Motown TMG 679	For Once In My Life/Angie Girl (DJ Copy)	30
69	Tamla Motown TMG 690	My Cherie Amour/I Don't Know Why I Love You	6
69	Tamla Motown TMG 690	My Cherie Amour/I Don't Know Why I Love You (DJ copy)	25
69	Tamla Motown TMG 717	Yester-Me, Yester-You, Yesterday/I'd Be A Fool Right Now	6
69	Tamla Motown TMG 717	Yester-Me, Yester-You, Yesterday/I'd Be A Fool Right Now (DJ copy)	25
70	Tamla Motown TMG 731	Never Had A Dream Come True/Somebody Knows, Somebody Cares	7
70	Tamla Motown TMG 731	Never Had A Dream Come True/Somebody Knows, Somebody Cares (DJ copy)	25
70	Tamla Motown TMG 744	Signed, Sealed, Delivered, I'm Yours/I'm More Than Happy (I'm Satisfied)	6
70	Tamla Motown TMG 744	Signed, Sealed, Delivered, I'm Yours/I'm More Than Happy (I'm Satisfied) (DJ copy)	25
70	Tamla Motown TMG 757	Heaven Help Us All/I Gotta Have A Song	6
70	Tamla Motown TMG 757	Heaven Help Us All/I Gotta Have A Song (DJ copy)	20
71	Tamla Motown TMG 772	We Can Work It Out/Don't Wonder Why (in p/s)	30
71	Tamla Motown TMG 772	We Can Work It Out/Don't Wonder Why	6
71	Tamla Motown TMG 772	We Can Work It Out/Don't Wonder Why (DJ copy)	25
71	Tamla Motown TMG 779	Never Dreamed You'd Leave Me In Summer/If You Really Love Me	8
71	Tamla Motown TMG 779	Never Dreamed You'd Leave Me In Summer/If You Really Love Me (DJ copy)	25
72	Tamla Motown TMG 798	If You Really Love Me/Think Of Me As Your Soldier	7
64	Stateside SE 1014	I CALL IT PRETTY MUSIC BUT THE OLD PEOPLE CALL IT THE BLUES (EP)	120
65	Tamla Motown TME 2006	LITTLE STEVIE WONDER (EP)	90

(Credited to Little Stevie Wonder.)

| 63 | Oriole PS 40049 | TRIBUTE TO UNCLE RAY (LP) | 325 |
| 63 | Oriole PS 40050 | THE TWELVE-YEAR-OLD GENIUS - LIVE (LP) | 110 |

64	Stateside SL 10078	THE JAZZ SOUL OF LITTLE STEVIE WONDER (LP)..................160

(The above LP's are Credited to Little Stevie Wonder.)

65	Stateside SL 10108	HEY, HARMONICA MAN (LP)..................160
66	T. Motown TML 11036	UPTIGHT (EVERYTHING'S ALRIGHT) (LP, mono)..................35
66	Tamla Motown TMG STML 11036	UPTIGHT (EVERYTHING'S ALRIGHT) (LP, stereo)..................45

(Originally came with flipback sleeves)

67	T. Motown TML 11045	DOWN TO EARTH (LP, mono)..................30
67	Tamla Motown STML 11045	DOWN TO EARTH (LP, stereo)..................40
68	T. Motown STML 11059	I WAS MADE TO LOVE HER (LP, stereo)..................25
68	T. Motown TML 11059	I WAS MADE TO LOVE HER (LP, mono)..................20
68	Tamla Motown (S)TML 11075	GREATEST HITS (LP, mono/stereo)..................15
68	T. Motown (S)TML 11085	SOMEDAY AT CHRISTMAS (LP, mono/stereo)..................35
69	T. Motown (S)TML 11098	FOR ONCE IN MY LIFE (LP, mono/stereo)..................20
69	T. Motown (S)TML 11128	MY CHERIE AMOUR (LP, mono/stereo)..................18

(The LP's listed above originally came with flipback sleeves.)

70	Tamla Motown STML 11150	STEVIE WONDER LIVE..................15
70	T. Motown STML 11164	LIVE AT THE TALK OF THE TOWN..................12
70	T. Motown STML 11169	SIGNED SEALED AND DELIVERED..................15
71	T. Motown STML 11183	WHERE I'M COMING FROM (LP)..................15
71	T. Motown STML 11196	GREATEST HITS VOL 2..................12

WONDER WHO

65	Philips BF 1440	Don't Think Twice, It's Alright/Sassy..................20
66	Philips BF 1504	On The Good Ship Lollipop/You're Nobody Till Somebody Loves You..................10
67	Philips BF 1600	Lonesome Road/FOUR SEASONS: Around And Around..................20

(see also Four Seasons, Frankie Valli)

WONDER BOY

69	Jackpot JP 703	Sweeten My Coffee (actually by Slim Smith)/MISTER MILLER: Cherry Pink..................12
69	Jackpot JP 705	Love Power (actually by Slim Smith)/PAT KELLY: Since You Are Gone..................12
71	Jackpot JP 764	Just For A Day/He Ain't Heavy..................8
71	Concord CON 015	Just For A Day/He Ain't Heavy..................5
75	Ackee ACK 546	Pressure Parts 1 & 2..................6

(see also Slim Smith, Pat Kelly)

GIRL WONDER

66	Doctor Bird DB 1015	Mommy Out Of The Light/Cutting Wood..................18

WONDERLAND

68	Polydor 56539	Poochy/Moscow..................15

ALICE WONDERLAND

63	London HLU 9783	He's Mine/Cha Linde..................20

WONDER STUFF

87	Far Out GONE ONE	It's Not True.../A Wonderful Day/Like A Merry-Go-Round/Down Here (EP, p/s)..................25
87	Far Out GONE 002	Unbearable/Ten Trenches Deep (with p/s)..................6
87	Far Out GO BIG 002	Unbearable/Ten Trenches Deep/I Am A Monster/Frank (12", p/s)..................8
88	Polydor GONE 3	Give Give Give Me More More More/A Song Without An End (p/s)..................6
89	House Of Dolls HOD 011	Who Wants To Be The Disco King? (King Of Disco Megamix)/PRUDES: Christmas/SANDKINGS: Colourblind/WORLD MUSIC: Stop Playing With My Heart (no p/s, free with House Of Dolls magazine)..................6
87	Far Out	A HANDFUL OF SONGS (private cassette)..................20
87	Polydor	A HANDFUL OF SONGS (cassette, promo only, different to above)..................20
88	Polydor GONECD 1	THE EIGHT-LEGGED GROOVE MACHINE (CD, mispressed with 'Wish Away' printed on front cover)..................20

(see also Vic Reeves)

ROYCE WONG

65	Blue Beat BB 301	Everything's Gonna Be Alright/Hang Your Head And Cry..................20

WONKY ALICE

92	Pomona POM 004	SIRIUS EP (12", p/s)..................12

WOOB

93	Woob	WOOB WOOB WOOB (Cassette demo tape)..................20
94	Em:t	WOOB 1194 (CD)..................40
95	Em:t	WOOB 4495 (CD)..................40

ANITA WOOD

62	London HLS 9585	I'll Wait Forever/I Can't Show You How I Feel..................25
64	Sue WI 328	Dream Baby/This Happened Before..................40

BOBBY WOOD

64	Pye International 7N 25264	I'm A Fool For Loving You/My Heart Went Boing! Boing! Boing!..................15

BRENTON WOOD

67	Philips BF 1579	Oogum Boogum Song/I Like The Way You Love Me..................8
67	Liberty LBF 15021	Gimme Little Sign/I Think You Got Your Fools Mixed Up..................8
68	Liberty LBF 15065	Baby You Got It/Catch You On The Rebound..................8
68	Liberty LBF 15103	Some Got It, Some Don't/Me And You..................8
70	Pye International 7N 25522	Great Big Bundle Of Love/Can You Dig It..................15
67	Liberty LBL/LBS 83088E	GIMME A LITTLE SIGN (LP)..................20

WOOD CHILDREN

88	Cat & Mouse ABB 05	Happens Everyday/2 Red Buses..................8

CHUCK WOOD

67	Big T BIG 104	Seven Days Too Long/Soul Shing-A-Ling..................20
67	Big T BIG 104	Seven Days Too Long/Soul Shing-A-Ling (DJ Copy)..................50
68	Big T BIG 107	I've Got My Lovelight Shining/Baby You Win..................10
71	Mojo 2092 010	Seven Days Too Long/Soul Shing A Ling (reissue)..................5
75	Pye Disco Demand DDS 111	Seven Days Too Long (in p/s)..................10
75	Pye Disco Demand DDS 111	Wigan's Chosen Few/Seven Days Too Long..................5

DEL WOOD

54	London HL 8036	Ragtime Annie/Backroom Polka..................50
54	London RE-P 1007	RAGTIME PIANO (EP)..................15

57	RCA RD 27011	DOWN YONDER (LP)	12

RONNIE WOOD

74	Warner Bros K 16463	I Can Feel The Fire/Breathe On Me (as Ron Wood)	5
75	Warner Bros K 16618	If You Don't Want Me Love/I've Got A Feeling	5
76	Warner Bros K 16679	Big Bayou/Sweet Baby Mine	5
92	Continuum 12210-2	Show Me/Breathe On Me (CD, with Ronnie Wood print, signed & numbered, in black card case tied with ribbon, 600 only)	50
74	Warner Bros K 56065	I'VE GOT MY OWN ALBUM TO DO (LP, with insert)	12
75	Warner Bros K 56145	NOW LOOK (LP)	12

(see also Faces, Rolling Stones, Jeff Beck, Ted Wood)

ROY WOOD

72	Harvest HAR 5048	When Gran'ma Plays The Banjo/Wake Up	5
75	Jet JET 754	Oh What A Shame/Bengal Jig (cartoon p/s)	5
75	Jet JET 761	Look Thru' The Eyes Of A Fool/Strider (copies miscredited as "Looking Thru' The Eyes Of A Fool")	5
76	Jet JET 785	Any Old Time Will Do/The Rain Came Down On Everything	5
77	Warner Bros K 16961	The Stroll/Jubilee (p/s, by Wizzo Band)	5
77	Warner Bros K 17028	I Never Believed In Love/Inside My Life (as Roy Wood & Annie Haslam)	5
78	Warner Bros K 17094	Dancin' At The Rainbow's End/Waiting At This Door (p/s, as Wizzo Band)	5
78	Warner Bros K 17248	Keep Your Hands On The Wheel/Giant Footsteps	5
79	Automatic K 17459P	(We're) On The Road Again/Saxmaniacs (picture disc)	5
73	Harvest SHVL 803	BOULDERS (LP, textured sleeve with EMI logo on label)	12
76	Harvest SHDW 408	THE ROY WOOD STORY (LP)	15

(see also Wizzard, Gerry Levine & Avengers, Mike Sheridan, Danny King['s Mayfair Set], Move, ELO, Renaissance [UK], Rockers, Birds)

TED WOOD

76	Penny Farthing PEN 891	Am I Blue/Shine (B-side features Rod Stewart, Ronnie Wood, Gary Glitter & Bobby Womack)	8

(see also Temperance Seven)

WOODEN HORSE

72	York SYK 526	Pick Up The Pieces/Wake Me In The Morning	20
73	York SYK 543	Wooden Horses/Typewriter And Guitar	20
72	York FYK 403	WOODEN HORSE (LP)	250
73	York FYK 413	WOODEN HORSE II (LP, withdrawn, with sleeve, blue/silver label)	900
73	York FYK 413	WOODEN HORSE II (LP, withdrawn, without sleeve, blue/silver label)	500

(see also Fox)

WOODEN O & GUESTS

69	Middle Earth MDLS 301	A HANDFUL OF PLEASANT DELITES (LP)	125

(see also 'Middle Earth Sampler' in Various Artists section)

WOODEN SHJIPS

09	Great Pop Supplement GPS 50	I Believe It/SPACEMEN 3: Big City (demo) (red marbled vinyl, insert & sticker)	10

GEORGE WOODHOUSE

79	Milestone M 001	Thanks/HOPETON JURNER: Living In The Ghetto (12")	150

KEN WOODMAN & HIS PICCADILLY BRASS

66	Strike JLH 101	THAT'S NICE (LP)	40

WOODMARK

83	Ooze S83 CUS 1692	When You're Gone/Life Is Cruel	20

WOODPECKERS

64	Decca F 11835	The Woodpecker/You Can't Sit Down	10
65	Oriole CB 311	Hey Little Girl/What's Your Name	20

STANLEY WOODRUFF & U.S. TRIO

70	Ember EMB S 288	If I Let You/Will You Still Love Me Tomorrow	7
77	Grapevine GP 102	What Took You So Long/Now Is Forever	10

CAROL WOODS

70	Ember EMB S 288	If I Let You/Will You Still Love Me Tomorrow (p/s)	10
72	Ember NR 5059	OUT OF THE WOODS (LP)	15

CORA WOODS

56	Parlophone DP 505	Rocks In Your Head/I Don't Want To Cry (export 78)	10

DONALD WOODS & EARL PALMER BAND

58	Vogue V 9107	Memories Of An Angel/That Much Of Your Love	650
58	Vogue V 9107	Memories Of An Angel/That Much Of Your Love (78)	150

GAY & TERRY WOODS

77	Polydor 2058 810	Save The Last Dance For Me/One More Time	10
78	Rockburgh ROCS 202	We Can Work This One Out/Piece Of Summer (p/s)	10
75	Polydor 2383 322	BACKWOODS (LP)	50
76	Polydor 2383 375	THE TIME IS RIGHT (LP, with lyric insert)	60
76	Polydor 2383 406	RENOWNED (LP, with lyric insert)	50
78	Rockburgh ROC 104	TENDER HOOKS (LP, with lyric insert)	20

(see also Woods Band, Gay Woods, Steeleye Span, Sweeney's Men)

NICK WOODS

62	London HLU 9621	Ballad Of Billy Budd/Don't Let Me Down	8

PHIL WOODS

57	Esquire EP 168	THE YOUNG IDEAS (EP)	12
55	Esquire 20-055	NEW JAZZ QUINTET (10" LP)	35
57	Esquire 32-020	WOODLORE (LP)	50

TONY WOODS

71	Spiral DIT 2	I'm Only A Man/Blues	6

JIMMY WOODS

63	Contemporary LAC 571	CONFLICT (LP)	20

PEGGY WOODS

88	Kent 6T 4	Love Is Gonna Get You/ZZ: You Just Cheat And Lie	20

TED WOODS
71	Spiral DIT 2	I'm Only A Man/Blues	10

TERRY WOODS
81	Chiswick CHIS 142	Tennessee Stud/I Don't Know About Love	30

WOODS BAND
71	Greenwich GSLP 1004	THE WOODS BAND (LP, gatefold sleeve)	150
77	Rockburgh CREST 29	THE WOODS BAND (LP, reissue in different sleeve)	20

(see also Gay & Terry Woods)

MAGGIE WOODWARD
59	Vogue V 9148	Ali Bama/Zulu Warrior	15
59	Vogue V 9148	Ali Bama/Zulu Warrior (78)	20

WOODY KERN
69	Pye 7N 17672	Biography/Tell You I'm Gone (demo)	100
69	Pye NSPL 18273	THE AWFUL DISCLOSURES OF MARIA MONK (LP)	140

WOOL
69	Stateside SS2153	Love Love Love Love Love/If They Left Us Alone Now	25

BRIAN WOOLEY
58	Esquire EP 170	BRIAN WOOLEY'S JAZZMEN (EP)	10
58	Esquire EP 190	WILD 'N WOOLEY (EP)	10

SHEB WOOLEY
51	MGM MGM 439	Hoot Owl Boogie/Country Kisses (78)	20
54	MGM MGM 757	Panama Pete/Blue Guitar (78)	10
55	MGM SP 1130	38-24-35/I Flipped	25
55	MGM SPC 5	Hill Billy Mambo/I Go Outa My Mind (export issue)	30
58	MGM MGM 981	The Purple People Eater/I Can't Believe You're Mine	15
58	MGM MGM 981	The Purple People Eater/Recipe For Love (2nd pressing, different B-side)	6
58	MGM MGM 997	Santa And The Purple People Eater/Star Of Love)	5
59	MGM MGM 1017	Sweet Chile/More	8
60	MGM MGM 1081	Luke The Spook/My Only Treasure	7
61	MGM MGM 1132	The Wayward Wind/Bars Across The Windows	6
61	MGM MGM 1147	That's My Pa/Meet Mr. Lonely	6
62	MGM MGM 1162	Laughing The Blues/Somebody Please	5
65	MGM MGM 1257	Hootenanny Hoot/Old Joe Rag	5
65	MGM MGM 1263	Blue Guitar/Natchez Landing	5
56	MGM MGM-EP 540	JEST PLAIN, WILD AND WOOLEY (EP)	40
61	MGM MGM-C 859	SONGS FROM THE DAY OF RAWHIDE (LP)	20
62	MGM MGM-C 903	THAT'S MY MA AND THAT'S MY PA (LP)	20
63	MGM MGM-C 945	SPOOFING THE BIG ONES! (LP)	15

(see also Ben Colder)

CHARLIE WOOLFE
68	NEMS 56-3675	Dance Dance Dance/Home	20

(see also At Last The 1958 Rock & Roll Show)

WOOLIES
67	RCA RCA 1602	Who Do You Love?/Hey Girl	50

JOHN WOOLLEY & JUST BORN
71	Decca 23134	Ruby Baby/Make Love Not War	10

WOOLLY FISH
70	Plexium PXM 16	Way You Like It/Sound Of Thick	6

BRENDA WOOTTON
71	Sentinel SENS 1006	PASTIES & CREAM (LP, with John The Fish)	12
73	Sentinel SENS 1016	CROWDY CRAWN (LP, with Richard Gendall)	12
74	Sentinel SENS 1021	NO SONG TO SING? (LP, with Robert Bartlett, private pressing with lyric inner sleeve)	12
76	Sentinel SENS 1031	STARRY-GAZEY PIE (LP, with Robert Bartlett)	12

WORD
83	Word WORD 001	Colour It!/Recurring	5

WORDBUG
91	Boss Tuneage BOSSTAGE6	LOSING IT ALL (LP, also listed as Home 4, with insert)	12

WORK
81	Woof WOOF 2	I Hate America/Fingers & Toes/Duty (p/s, clear vinyl)	5
82	Recommended	SLOW CRIMES (LP, with insert)	12

(see also Art Bears)

JIMMY WORK
56	London HLD 8270	When She Said "You All"/There's Only One You	60
56	London HLD 8270	When She Said "You All"/There's Only One You (78)	20
56	London HLD 8308	You've Gotta Heart Like A Merry-Go-Round/Blind Heart	45
56	London HLD 8308	You've Gotta Heart Like A Merry-Go-Round/Blind Heart (78)	20
55	London RE-D 1039	COUNTRY SONGS - WORK STYLE (EP)	30

WORKFORCE
80s	WF WF 1	The Right To Work/Holy Moses (p/s)	5

WORKS
72	London HLU 10360	Orange Medley (Music Inspired By "A Clockwork Orange")/Sweet Charity	5

WORLD
70	Liberty LBF 15402	Angelina/Come Out Into The Open	10
70	Liberty LBG 83419	LUCKY PLANET (LP, textured gatefold sleeve)	50

(see also Neil Innes, Bonzo Dog [Doo-Dah] Band)

WORLD COLUMN
76	Capitol CL 15852	So Is The Sun/It's Not Right	8

WORLD OF OZ
68	Deram DM 187	The Muffin Man/Peter's Birthday (Black And White Rainbows)	15

68	Deram DM 205	King Croesus/Jack	15
69	Deram DM 233	Willow's Harp/Like A Tear	25
69	Deram DML/SML 1034	THE WORLD OF OZ (LP)	100

(see also David Kubinec)

WORLD OF TWIST
| 91 | Circa CIRCD 17 | QUALITY STREET (CD) | 18 |

WORLD SOUND & POWER BAND
| 80 | D Roy DRLP 1006 | MAWAMBA DUB (WARRIOR) CHAPTER TWO (LP) | 55 |

(See also D Witter)

WORMS
| 78 | Ice GUY 21 | London Bus (I Can't Take My Eyes Off You/Okay At Christmas (500 only) | 15 |

BIMBI WORRICK
| 69 | Polydor 56321 | Long Time Comin'/Tomorrow Is My Day | 8 |

WORRYING KYNDE
| 67 | Piccadilly 7N 35370 | Call Out The Name/Got The Blame | 80 |

WORTH
| 70 | CBS 5309 | Shoot 'Em Up Baby/Take The World In Your Hands | 5 |

JOHNNY WORTH
| 57 | Columbia DB 3962 | Let's Go/Just Because | 6 |
| 60 | Oriole CB 1545 | Nightmare/Hold Me, Thrill Me, Kiss Me | 40 |

MARION WORTH
| 60 | London HL 7089 | Are You Willing, Willie/This Heart Of Mine (export issue) | 25 |
| 60 | London HL 7097 | That's My Kind Of Love/I Lost Johnny (export issue) | 25 |

STAN WORTH ORCHESTRA
| 63 | London HLU 9703 | Roman Holiday/Wiggle Wobble Walkers | 8 |

WRANGLERS
| 64 | Parlophone R 5163 | Liza Jane/It Just Won't Work | 70 |

(see also Kenny Bernard, Kenny & Wranglers)

LINK WRAY (& HIS RAY MEN)
58	London HLA 8623	Rumble/The Swag (as Link Wray & His Ray Men)	50
58	London HLA 8623	Rumble/The Swag (as Link Wray & His Ray Men) (78)	30
63	Stateside SS 217	Jack The Ripper/The Black Widow	30
64	Stateside SS 256	The Sweeper/Weekend	20
65	Stateside SS 397	Good Rockin' Tonight/I'll Do Anything For You	20
71	Polydor 2066 120	Fire And Brimstone/Jukebox Mama	6
73	Polydor 2066 320	Lawdy Miss Clawdy/Shine The Light	6
73	Virgin VS 103	I'm So Glad, I'm So Proud/Shawnee Tribe	6
76	Virgin VS 142	I Know You're Leaving Me Now/Quicksand	6
64	Stateside SE 1015	MR. GUITAR (EP, sleeve credits Link Ray)	100
71	Polydor 2489 029	LINK WRAY (LP)	30
71	Union Pacific UP 002	THERE'S GOOD ROCKIN' TONIGHT (LP)	25
73	Virgin V 2006	BEANS & FATBACK (LP)	15
74	Polydor 2391 128	THE LINK WRAY RUMBLE (LP)	15
88	Hangman HANG 31 UP	64 (THE SWAN DEMOS) (LP)	30
88	Hangman HANG 33 UP	JACK THE RIPPER (LP)	30

(see also Robert Gordon with Link Wray)

RAY WRAY QUARTET
| 62 | Salvo SLO 1808 | When Your Lover Has Gone/A Song Is Born | 20 |

WRECKERS
| 64 | Granta GR 7EP 1010 | THE WRECKERS' SOUND (EP) | 120 |

WRECKLESS ERIC
77	Stiff BUY 16	Whole Wide World/Semaphore Signals (p/s)	7
78	Stiff BUY 25	Reconnez Cherie/Rags And Tatters ("Factory sample" sticker on label)	10
78	Stiff SEEZ 9	THE WONDERFUL WORLD OF... (LP, picture disc in LP sleeve)	15
93	Hangman HANG 50 UP	THE DONOVAN OF TRASH (LP)	18

(see also Len Bright Combo)

JENNY WREN
| 66 | Fontana TF 672 | Chasing My Dreams All Over Town/A Thought Of You | 130 |
| 66 | Fontana TF 772 | The Merry-Go-Round (Is Slowing You Down)/Take A Walk Bobby | 15 |

BIG JOHN WRENCHER
| 75 | Big Bear BB 4 | BIG JOHN'S BOOGIE (LP) | 12 |

WRETCHED
| 81 | Wretched Music GRC 102 | DNR/Souls In Torment (500 only) | 50 |

WRIGGLERS
| 68 | Giant GN 26 | The Cooler/You Cannot Know | 150 |
| 68 | Blue Cat BS 106 | Get Right/If I Did Look | 35 |

BETTY WRIGHT
68	Atlantic 584 216	Girls Can't Do What The Guys Do/Sweet Lovin' Daddy	10
72	Atlantic K 10143	Clean Up Woman/I'll Love You Forever	10
72	Atlantic K 10190	Is It You Girl/Cryin' In My Sleep	5
75	RCA RCA 2548	Where Is The Love/My Baby Ain't My Baby Any More	5

BILLY WRIGHT
| 61 | Parlophone R 4852 | Sing Song For Kicks Part 1/Part 2 | 10 |

CHARLES WRIGHT & WATTS 103RD STREET RHYTHM BAND
69	Warner Bros WB 7250	Do Your Thing/A Dance, A Kiss And A Song	8
69	Warner Bros WB 7298	Till You Get Enough/Light My Fire	8
70	Warner Bros WB 7365	Love Land/Sorry Charlie	8
70	Warner Bros WB 7417	Express Yourself/Living On Borrowed Time	20
72	Jay Boy BOY 71	Spreadin' Honey/Charley (as Watts 103rd Street Rhythm Band)	10

70s	Warner Bros	EXPRESS YOURSELF (LP)	20

DALE WRIGHT
58	London HLD 8573	She's Neat/Say That You Care (as Dale Wright & Rock-Its)	175
58	London HLD 8573	She's Neat/Say That You Care (as Dale Wright & Rock-Its) (78)	40
59	Pye International 7N 25022	That's Show Biz/That's My Gal (as Dale Wright & Wright Guys)	80
59	Pye International 7N 25022	That's Show Biz/That's My Gal (as Dale Wright & Wright Guys) (78)	50

EARL WRIGHT
75	Capitol CL 15825	Thumb A Ride/Like A Rolling Stone	8
75	Capitol CL 15825	Thumb A Ride/Like A Rolling Stone (DJ Copy)	15

GARY WRIGHT('S WONDERWHEEL)
72	A&M AMS 888	I know/Tonight It's Right	12
71	A&M AMLS 2004	EXTRACTIONS (LP, poster sleeve)	30
72	A&M AMLS 64296	FOOTPRINT (LP)	12
72	A&M AMLH 64362	RING OF CHANGES (LP, as Wright's Wonderwheel; unissued, test pressings only)	50

(see also Spooky Tooth, Magic Christians, Thomas F. Browne)

GEORGE WRIGHT/NEVILLE MITCHELL
82	Kingdom KV 8026	GEORGE WRIGHT - You Are The One I Love/ROOTS RADICS - I Done It Dub/NEVILL MITCHELL - Get Out Of Hand/ROOTS RADICS - Hand Made Dub	25

GINNY WRIGHT (& TOM TALL)
55	London HL 8119	Indian Moon/Your Eyes Feasted Upon Her (solo)	50
55	London HL 8119	Indian Moon/Your Eyes Feasted Upon Her (solo) (78)	12
55	London HL 8150	Are You Mine?/Boom Boom Boomerang (with Tom Tall)	30
55	London RE-U 1035	COUNTRY SONGS VOL. 2 (EP, with Tom Tall)	30

(see also T. Tommy Cutrer & Ginny Wright, Tom Tall)

MILTON WRIGHT & TERRA SHIRMA STRINGS
77	Grapevine GRP 103	I Belong To You/The Gallop	5

NAT WRIGHT
59	HMV POP 629	Anything/For You My Love	75

OTIS WRIGHT
69	High Note HS 033	Man Of Galilee/Take Up The Cross	6
67	Doctor Bird DLM 5005	PEACE PERFECT PEACE (LP)	50
67	Doctor Bird DLM 5006	IT WILL SOON BE DONE (LP)	50
69	High Note BSL5003	SACRED SONGS (LP)	30
60s	Coxsone TLP 1001	OVER IN GLORYLAND (LP)	40
73	Tabernacle BSLP 5021	SOUL STIRRING GOSPEL SONGS (LP)	40

O.V. WRIGHT
65	Vocalion VP 9249	You're Gonna Make Me Cry/Monkey Dog	20
66	Vocalion VP 9255	Poor Boy/I'm In Your Corner	20
66	Vocalion VP 9272	Gone For Good/How Long Baby	20
67	London HLZ 10137	8 Men 4 Women/Fed Up With The Blues	15
68	Sue WI 4043	What About You/What Did You Tell This Girl Of Mine	50
68	Action ACT 4505	Oh Baby Mine/Working Your Game	15
69	Action ACT 4527	I Want Everyone To Know/I'm Gonna Forget About You	15
65	Vocalion VEP 170165	CAN'T FIND TRUE LOVE (EP)	100
68	Island ILP 975	8 MEN, 4 WOMEN (LP)	120

OWEN WRIGHT
70	Banana BA 310	Wala Wala (actually by Burning Spear)/JERRY & FREEDOM SINGERS: Got To Be Sure (B-side actually by Horace Andy)	20

RICHARD WRIGHT
78	Harvest SHVL 818	WET DREAM (LP, gatefold stickered sleeve)	12

(see also Pink Floyd, Zee)

RITA WRIGHT
68	Tamla Motown TMG 643	I Can't Give Back The Love I Feel For You/Something On My Mind	25
68	Tamla Motown TMG 643	I Can't Give Back The Love I Feel For You/Something On My Mind (DJ copy)	40
71	Tamla Motown TMG 791	I Can't Give Back The Love I Feel For You/Something On My Mind (reissue)	10
78	Jet UP 36382	Love Is All You Need/Touch Me, Take Me	100

RUBEN WRIGHT
66	Capitol CL 15460	Hey Girl/I'm Walking Out On You	30
66	Capitol CL 15460	Hey Girl/I'm Walking Out On You (DJ copy)	75

RUBY WRIGHT
53	Parlophone MSP 6025	Till I Waltz Again With You/When I Gave You My Love (with Charlie Gore)	20
54	Parlophone MSP 6073	Bimbo/Boy, You Got Yourself A Gal	25
54	Parlophone MSP 6133	Santa's Little Sleigh Bells/Toodle-oo To You	10
55	Parlophone MSP 6150	What Have They Told You?/I Had The Funniest Feeling	15
56	Parlophone MSP 6209	I Fall In Love With You Ev'ry Day/Do You Believe?	15
59	Parlophone R 4556	Three Stars/I Only Have One Lifetime	5
59	Parlophone R 4589	You're Just A Flower From An Old Bouquet/Sweet Night Of Love	5
59	Parlophone GEP 8785	THE THREE STARS GIRL (EP)	30

SAMUEL E. WRIGHT
73	Paramount PARA 3035	There's Something Funny Going On/300 Pounds Of Hunger	15

STEVE WRIGHT
59	London HLW 8991	Wild, Wild, Woman/Love You	250
59	London HLW 8991	Wild, Wild, Woman/Love You (78)	125

STEVEN WRIGHT
93	Reggae On Top ROT 001	Vision Of Jah/Dub Versions (12")	25

STEVIE WRIGHT
74	Polydor 2121246	Evie - Let Your Hair Down/Evie	8
74	Polydor 2480 249	HARD ROAD (LP)	20

SYREETA WRIGHT
72	Mowest MWS 7001	SYREETA (LP)	20

WINSTON WRIGHT

69	Doctor Bird DB 1308	Five Miles High/CARL DAWKINS: Only Girl	40
69	Camel CA 32	Power Pack/TWO SPARKS: Throwing Stones	30
69	Explosion EX 2003	Barefoot Brigade/Slippery	20
69	Trojan TR 7701	Moonlight (Lover) Groover/SENSATIONS: Everyday Is Just A Holiday	20
69	Trojan TR 7715	Moon Invader (with Tommy McCook)/RADCLIFF RUFFIN: You Got To Love Me	20
70	Trojan TR 7775	Meshwire (with Tommy McCook)/BARONS: Darling Please Return	20
70	Explosion EX 2011	Flight 404/LLOYD & ROBIN: Gawling Come Down (B-side actually Higher Than The Highest Mountain by Monty Morris)	20
70	Explosion EX 2015	Funny Girl/Funny Girl Version II	20
70	Duke DU 62	Poppy Cock (with J.J. All Stars)/CARL DAWKINS: This World And Me (B-side actually "Satisfaction")	20
70	Bamboo BAM 60	Reggae Feet/DON DRUMMOND: Royal Flush (B-side act. titled "The Rocket")	30
70	High Note HS 040	Soul Pressure/Seed You Sow (with Gaytones)	12
70	Moodisc MU 3501	Musically Red (with Maudie's Allstars; actually also with Count Sticky)/ RHYTHM RULERS: Bratah	20
70	G.G. GG 4504	It's Been A Long Time/PAULETTE & GEE: Feel It More And More	8
70	Techniques TE 907	Top Secret/Crazy Rhythm	10
71	Upsetter US 378	Example (with 3rd & 4th Generation)/UPSETTER: Version	25
71	Duke DU 111	Silhouettes/That Did It	10
71	Camel CA 71	Silhouettes/That Did It	12
71	Green Door GD 4011	Heads Or Tails/THE ROASTERS: Raunchy	6
77	Third World TWS 923	JUMP THE FENCE (LP)	20

(see also Ethiopians, John Holt, J.J. Allstars, Slickers)

ZACHARIAH WRIGHT

| 70s | Bamboo BAM 403 | Lumumba Limbo/Green, Red and Gold | 10 |

WRIGHTSOUND

| 75 | Peacock AT 842 | Dance Apache/Jelly | 18 |

BERNARD WRIGLEY

| 74 | Topic 12TS 241 | ROUGH AND WRIGLEY (LP) | 12 |
| 76 | Transatlantic TRA 327 | SONGS, STORIES AND ELEPHANTS (LP) | 12 |

WRIGLEYS

| 69 | Page One POF 118 | A Little Bit/Come Down Little Bird | 10 |

WRINKLE

| 01 | Mook MKCDS | LA LUMINOL EP: La Luminol/Wool Box DC/The Source Of The Flood/Canada Cool (CD single) | 30 |

WRIT

| 66 | Decca F 12385 | Did You Ever Have To Make Up Your Mind/Solid Golden Teardrops | 20 |

WRITING ON THE WALL

69	Middle Earth MDS 101	Child On A Crossing/Lucifer Corpus	50
73	Pye 7N 45251	Man Of Renown/Buffalo	20
69	Middle Earth MDLS 303	THE POWER OF THE PICTS (LP, textured sleeve)	350
95	Pie & Mash PAM 003	RARITIES FROM THE MIDDLE EARTH (LP, 500 copies only)	12
95	Tenth Planet TP 017	CRACKS IN THE ILLUSION OF LIFE (LP, gatefold sleeve)	12
96	Tenth Planet TP 018	BURGHLEY ROAD (LP, 1,000 copies only)	12

(see also 'Middle Earth Sampler' in Various Artists; Three's A Crowd)

W12 SPOTS

| 70s | Shepherds Bush SB 1 | Sid Never Did/COSMIC PUNKS: 99 Years | 12 |

WUGGERY

| 98 | Wuggery WUG 1 | Wuggery Muggery/Wugwats Weekend (p/s) | 8 |

WURZEL

| 87 | GWR GWR 4 | Bess/People Say I'm Crazy (p/s) | 8 |
| 87 | GWR GWT 4 | Bess/People Say I'm Crazy/Midnight In London/E.S.P. (12", p/s) | 15 |

(see also Motorhead)

WURZELS

| 77 | EMI EMI 2686 | One For The Bristol City/Cheddar Cheese (p/s) | 6 |
| 05 | Rough Trade RTRADS302 | Remember Me/I Am A Cider Drinker (British Sea Power) (7" ltd ed. 1,966 copies) | 10 |

JOHNNY WYATT

68	President PT 109	This Thing Called Love/To Whom It May Concern (DJ Copy)	50
68	President PT 109	This Thing Called Love/To Whom It May Concern (horizontal)	30
68	President PT 109	This Thing Called Love/To Whom It May Concern (vertical artist credit)	10

ROBERT WYATT

74	Virgin VS 114	I'm A Believer/Memories	5
77	Virgin VS 115	Yesterday Man/Sonia	6
81	Rough Trade RT 081	Grass/Trade Union/Dishari (p/s)	8
82	Rough Trade	Shipbuilding/Memories of You (This 7" came in 4 different multi-fold art sleeves. Most common are 'Blanket' and 'Rope' covers, 'Metal Rings' and 'Hot Coals' are less common)	6
97	Hannibal TRDSC 010	Free Will And Testament/The Sight Of The Wind	6
87	Strange Fruit SFPS 037	PEEL SESSIONS (12")	15
70	CBS 64189	THE END OF AN EAR (LP)	40
74	Virgin V 2017	ROCK BOTTOM (LP, 1st pressing, coloured "girl and dragon" labels)	25
75	Virgin V 2034	RUTH IS STRANGER THAN RICHARD (LP)	35
82	Rough Trade ROUGH 35	NOTHING CAN STOP US (LP, early pressing without "Shipbuilding", insert)	15
81	Virgin VGD 3505	ROCK BOTTOM/RUTH IS STRANGER THAN RICHARD (2-LP reissue)	35
85	Rough Trade ROUGH 69	OLD ROTTENHAT (LP, gatefold)	20
08	Domino REWIGLP 47	CUCKOOLAND (2-LP)	18
08	Domino REWIGLP 45	SHLEEP (2-LP)	18

(see also Soft Machine, Matching Mole, Centipede, Ben Watt)

RICHARD ('POPCORN') WYLIE

| 63 | Columbia DB 7012 | Brand New Man/So Much Love In My Heart (as Richard Wylie) | 40 |
| 77 | Grapevine GRP 100 | Rosemary What Happened (Parts 1 & 2) (as Richard 'Popcorn' Wylie) | 8 |

BILL WYMAN

| 74 | Rolling Stones RS 19112 | Monkey Grip Glue/What A Blow | 5 |

74	Rolling Stones RS 19115	White Lightning/Pussy	7
76	Rolling Stones RS 19119	A Quarter To Three/Soul Satisfying	5
76	Rolling Stones RS 19120	Apache Woman/Soul Satisfying	8
81	A&M AMS 8144	(Si Si) Ju Suis Un Rock Star/Rio De Janeiro	6
81	Polydor POSP 259	Tenderness (Maria Muldaur)/Noche De Amor	7
81	Polydor POSP 291	Green Ice Theme/Cloudhoppers (p/s)	12
83	Ripple (no cat. no.)	DIGITAL DREAMS (LP, soundtrack, promo only)	50

(see also Rolling Stones, End)

WYNDER K. FROG

66	Island WI 280	Turn On Your Lovelight/Zooming	30
66	Island WI 3011	Sunshine Superman/Blues For A Frog	30
67	Island WIP 6006	Green Door/Dancing Frog	45
67	Island WIP 6014	I Am A Man/Shook Shimmy & Shake	55
68	Island WIP 6044	Jumping Jack Flash/Baldy	35
67	Island ILP 944	SUNSHINE SUPERFROG (LP, white label, mono)	90
67	Island ILPS 9044	SUNSHINE SUPERFROG (LP, white label, stereo)	125
68	Island ILP 982/ILPS 9082	OUT OF THE FRYING PAN (LP, pink label)	50

(see also Keef Hartley Band, Miller Anderson, Fair Weather, Grease Band)

KES WYNDHAM

71	Pye 7N 45082	Honey Call Me Home/Broken Bicycle	10

MARTYN WYNDHAM-READ

70	Trailer LER 2009	NED KELLY AND THAT GANG (LP, white label)	18
70	Trailer LER 2009	NED KELLY AND THAT GANG (LP, later 'highway' label)	12
71	Trailer LER 2028	MARTYN WYNDHAM-READ (LP)	12
73	Argo ZFB 82	HARRY THE HAWKER IS DEAD (LP)	15
75	Trailer LER 2092	MAYPOLES TO MISTLETOE (LP)	12
77	Broadside BRO 128	ENGLISH SPORTING BALLADS (LP, 1 side by High Level Ranters, 2000 only)	15

(see also A.L. Lloyd)

WYNDRUSH

72	Wealden WS 116	LET IT SHINE (LP)	300

PETER WYNGARDE

70	RCA Victor RCA 1967	La Ronde De L'Amour/The Way I Cry Over You	30
70	RCA Victor PW 1	Commits Rape/The Way I Cry Over You (LP sampler, promo only)	45
70	RCA Victor SF 8087	PETER WYNGARDE (LP, gatefold sleeve)	50

(see also Larry Wallis, Tyrannosaurus Rex)

PETER WYNNE

59	Parlophone R 4597	Twilight Time/Chapel Of Dreams	7
60	Parlophone R 4668	Ask Anyone In Love/I Need You Close Again	6
60	Parlophone R 4705	Our Concerto/Your lover	6

SANDY WYNNS

65	Fontana TF 550	Touch Of Venus/Lovers' Quarrel	250

MARK WYNTER

60	Decca F 11263	Image Of A Girl/Glory Of Love	7
60	Decca F 11279	Kickin' Up The Leaves/That's What I Thought	10
61	Decca F 11323	Dream Girl/Two Little Girls	5
61	Decca F 11354	Exclusively Yours/Warm And Willing	5
61	Decca F 11380	Girl For Ev'ry Day/The Best Time For Love	5
62	Decca F 11434	Heaven's Plan/In Your Heart	5
62	Decca F 11467	Angel Talk/I Love Her Still	6
62	Pye 7N 15466	Venus In Blue Jeans/Please Come Back To Me	5
62	Pye 7N 15492	Go Away Little Girl/That Kinda Talk	5
63	Pye 7N 15511	Aladdin's Lamp/It Can Happen Any Day	6
63	Pye 7N 15525	Shy Girl/Because Of You	5
63	Pye 7N 15554	Running To You/Don't Cry	6
65	Pye 7N 15771	Can I Get To Know You Better/Am I Living A Dream	5
66	Pye 7N 17122	We'll Sing In The Sunshine/Pencil And Paper	8
60	Decca DFE 6674	MARK TIME (EP)	10
63	Pye NEP 24176	IT'S MARK TIME (EP)	8
64	Pye NEP 24185	WYNTER TIME (EP)	8
61	Decca LK 4409	THE WARMTH OF WYNTER (LP)	25
65	Ace Of Clubs ACL 1141	MARK WYNTER (LP)	15

(see also Joe Brown & Mark Wynter)

GAIL WYNTERS

67	London HLE 10144	Snap Your Fingers/Find Myself A New Love	12

WYOMING

72	MAM MAMR 76	Seven Days/Two Faced Woman	12

JOHNNY X & THE SINGIN' SWINGIN' EIGHT

63	Fontana TF 408	Lemonade/Come Closer Melinda	12

X-CALIBURS

65	CBS 201805	We Will Love/Swing That Chariot	10
65	Mercury MF 941	You'll Find Out/That's What Happens (possibly as Xcalibres)	10

X-CELLS

81	Snotty Snail NEL COL 4	Freedom Man/SCHIZOID: Nowhere To Go (p/s)	20

X-CERTS

78	Zama	Feeling The Groove (p/s)	15

| 81 | Recreational PLAY 1 | Together/Untogether (p/s, with lyric insert)...6 |

X-DREAMYSTS

78	Good Vibrations GOT 5	Right Way Home/Dance Away Love (p/s) 12
79	Polydor 2059 129	Bad News/Money Talks (p/s) 10
80	Polydor 2059 235	I Don't Wanna Go/Silly Games (p/s)..10
80	Polydor 2059 252	Stay The Way You Are/Race Against Time (p/s) 10
80	Polydor	XDREAMYSTS (LP)..25

X-E-CUTORS

| 80 | Rok ROK 13/14 | Too Far To Look Inside My Head/X-FILMS: After My Blood (die-cut co. sleeve) ....10 |

XENTRIX

| 90 | Roadracer RO 2435 2 | Ghost Busters/Nobody's Perfect/Interrogate (CD)..10 |

XERO

83	Brickyard XERO 1	Oh Baby/Hold On (2-track issue, p/s, Moon Williams on vocals) 15
83	Brickyard XERO 1	Oh Baby/Hold On/Lone Wolf (3-track limited issue, p/s) 8
83	Brickyard XERO 1T	Oh Baby/Hold On/Lone Wolf (12", plain card sleeve with sticker, withdrawn)..........15
83	Brickyard XERO 1T	Oh Baby/Hold On/Killer Frog (12", reissue)..8

(see also Bruce Dickinson, Iron Maiden)

XILES

| 64 | Xiles 80-XIL-1 | THE XILES (EP, home-made p/s)...40 |
| 65 | Xiles XIL 004 | Our Love Will Never End/The Only People In This World ....25 |

XIT

72	Rare Earth RES 107	I Was Raised/End 5
73	Rare Earth RES 111	Reservation Of Education/Young Warrior 5
72	Rare Earth SREA 4002	PLIGHT OF THE RED MAN (LP) 15

XL5

| 63 | HMV POP 1148 | XL5 (Zero G)/Caviare ....20 |
| 63 | HMV 7EG 8802 | FIREBALL AND OTHER TITLES (EP, 2 tracks by Don Spencer) ....70 |

XL5'S

| 80 | Fourplay FOUR 004 | Fireball/Misirlou ....8 |

X-MAL DEUTSCHLAND

| 83 | 4AD AD 311 | Incubus Succubus II/Vito (12" p/s, with "Vito" listed as A-side)..............................10 |
| 83 | 4AD CAD 302 | FETISCH (LP, inner) ....12 |

X-MEN

| 84 | Creation CRE 006 | Do The Ghost/Talk (foldaround p/s in bag, orange/blue or yellow/green p/s) ....5 |
| 85 | Creation CRE 013 | Spiral Girl/Bad Girl (foldaround p/s in polyester bag) ....5 |

X-O-DUS

| 79 | Factory FAC 11 | English Black Boys/See Them A-Come (12", dark-grey textured p/s, later light grey p/s)...15 |

XPANSIONS

| 90 | Optimisim 613 683 | Move Your Body (12")...8 |

XPOZEZ

81	Retaliation FIGHT 1	SYSTEMS KILL EP (photocopied sleeve with insert stating that if you want a proper sleeve to send the band a SAE) 25
82	Red Rhino RED 15	1,000 Marching Feet/Terminal Case (p/s)...5
83	Sexual Phonograph SPH 2	(Be My) New York Doll/It's All Been Done Before (p/s)..5
84	Retaliation/Bearded Viking FIGHT 2	BURNOUT YOUTH EP (folded poster p/s with lyrics and photos)............................10
85	Children Of The Revolution COR 2	FORCEFED THE TRUTH DRUG (EP) 10

X-PRESS

| 80 | Express 1 | Junked Up Judy/Stop Start ....60 |

X PRESS

| 75 | A Rover AR 03 | Tell Me Baby/High Road...8 |

X-RAY SPEX

77	Virgin VS 189	Oh Bondage, Up Yours/I Am A Cliche (in p/s) 30
77	Virgin VS 189	Oh Bondage, Up Yours/I Am A Cliche 5
77	Virgin VS 189-12	Oh Bondage, Up Yours/I Am A Cliche (12", company sleeve)..................................12
78	EMI International INT 553	The Day The World Turned Day-Glo/Lama Poseur (p/s, 15,000 orange vinyl).............8
78	EMI International INT 563	Identity/Let's Submerge (p/s, on pink vinyl) 8
78	EMI International INT 573	Germ Free Adolescents/Age (p/s) 5
79	EMI International INT 583	Highly Inflammable/Warrior In Woolworths (p/s, on red vinyl)................................8
78	EMI Intl. INS 3023	GERM FREE ADOLESCENTS (LP, with lyric inner sleeve)..30
01	Earmark 640005	GERM FREE ADOLESCENTS (LP, reissue, clear vinyl) 15

(see also Poly Styrene, Essential Logic)

X-RAYS

| 59 | London HLR 8805 | Chinchilla/Out Of Control ....35 |
| 59 | London HLR 8805 | Chinchilla/Out Of Control (78) ....20 |

XS DISCHARGE

| 80 | G. Marxist COMMINIQUE 3 | Across The Border/Frustration (p/s) ....15 |
| 80 | Groucho Marxist WH 3 | Life's A Wank (p/s) ....20 |

XS ENERGY

78	World WRECK 1	Eighteen/Jenny's Alright/Horrorscope! (numbered foldover yellow or green p/s, stamped white labels)..18
79	Dead Good DEAD 1	Eighteen/Jenny's Alright/Horrorscope! (reissue, 'National Souvenir Issue', different foldover p/s, stamped white labels)..10
79	Dead Good DEAD 1	Eighteen/Jenny's Alright/Horrorscope! (stamped white sleeve & yellow printed labels)...10
79	Dead Good DEAD 3	Use You/Imaginary (p/s) 15

XTC

77	Virgin VS 188	Science Friction/She's So Square (unreleased, in picture sleeve) 2500
77	Virgin VS 188	Science Friction/She's So Square (unreleased, no picture sleeve) 80
77	Virgin VS 188-12	3D EP (12" version of the above, p/s)..8

78	Virgin VS 201	Statue Of Liberty/Hang On To The Night (p/s) 5
78	Virgin VS 209	This Is Pop?/Heatwave (p/s) 5
78	Virgin VS 231	Are You Receiving Me/Instant Tunes (p/s)...5
79	Virgin VS 259	Life Begins At The Hop/Homo Safari (30,000 clear vinyl, PVC sleeve & insert)..................5
79	Virgin VS 282	Making Plans For Nigel/Bushman President (Homo Safari Series No. 2)/ Pulsing, Pulsing (with game-board p/s with playing pieces)..5
80	Virgin VS 365	Generals And Majors/Don't Lose Your Temper//Smokeless Zone/ The Somnambulist (double pack)...6
81	Virgin VS 372	Towers Of London/Set Myself On Fire (live)//Battery Brides (live)/ Scissor Man (double pack)...6
81	RSO RSO 71	Take This Town/RUTS: Babylon's Burning (p/s)..6
81	Virgin VS 384	Sgt. Rock (Is Going To Help Me)/Living Through Another Cuba/Generals And Majors (1st 20,000 in poster p/s, with stickered PVC sleeve) 5
82	Virgin VS 490	No Thugs In Our House/Chain Of Command/Limelight/ Over Rusty Water (9" die-cut gatefold p/s)..6
92	Virgin VS 1426	Wrapped In Grey (p/s, withdrawn, 2,000 only)..60
92	Virgin VSCDT 1426	WRAPPED IN GREY (CD EP, withdrawn, 2,000 only) 80
78	Virgin V 2095	WHITE MUSIC (LP, with black inner sleeve) 12
78	Virgin V 2108	GO 2 (LP, with insert, 1st 15,000 with bonus 12" EP: "Go +")......................................15
79	Virgin V 2129	DRUMS AND WIRES (LP, with gatefold insert, 1st 15,000 with free 7": Chain Of Command/"Limelight" [VDJ 30])...12
80	Virgin V 2173	BLACK SEA (LP, with green paper outer sleeve & lyric insert) 12
84	Virgin V 2251	WAXWORKS (LP, with bonus LP, "Beeswax") 12
84	Virgin V 2325	THE BIG EXPRESS (LP, circular sleeve & lyric inner)...12
99	Cooking Vinyl COOK 172	APPLE VENUS (LP, inner)..30
00	Cooking Vinyl COOK 194	WASP STAR (2-LP, gatefold, inners)..30

(see also Mr Partridge, Barry Andrews, Three Wise Men, Dukes of Stratosphere)o Colonel, Spys)

XTRACT
| 83 | Pax PAX 10 | Blame It On The Youth/War Heroes/Iron Lady/Boys In Blue (p/s).................................25 |

XTRAVERTS
78	Spike SRTS SP 001	Blank Generation/A-Lad-In-Sane 90
78	Rising Sun RS 1	Police State/PLASTIC PEOPLE: Demolition (p/s, multi-coloured vinyl) 60
81	Xtraverts XTRA 001	Speed/1984 (white labels, 'photo' foldout poster p/s) 35
81	Xtraverts XTRA 001	Speed/1984 (white labels, 'no photo' foldout poster p/s)...............................50

XX
| 10 | Young Turks YT 041 | Do You Mind?/Hot Like Fire/Teardrops/Blood Red Moon (die-cut p/s with inner p/s, tour issue)..25 |
| 09 | Young Turks YT 023 | Crystalised/Hot Like Fire (p/s)..8 |

Y

YACHTS
77	Stiff BUY 19	Suffice To Say/Freedom (Is A Heady Wine) 5
78	Radar ADA 23	Look Back In Love (Not In Anger)/I Can't Stay Long (p/s, blue vinyl) 6
79	Radar RAD 19	THE YACHTS (LP, with live 7" "Suffice To Say"/"On And On" [SAM 98, p/s]) 12
80	Radar RAD 27	YACHTS WITHOUT RADAR (LP) 12

(see also Big In Japan)

YADS
| 92 | Fairfields YAD 2 | Yippee For Shtonk/It's There, You Mong (p/s) ....7 |

YA HO WA 13
| 83 | Psycho PSYCHO 2 | GOLDEN SUNRISE (LP, 319 copies only, different coloured vinyls, some on black vinyl without sleeve)..60 |

(see also Seeds)

YAKS
| 65 | Decca F 12115 | Yakety Yak/Back In '57 ....15 |

YAMASUKI
| 05 | Finders Keepers FKR 002LP | LE MONDE FABULEUX DES (LP, insert) ....25 |

YAMASUKIS
| 71 | Dandelion DAN 7004 | Yamasuki/Aieada (p/s)..15 |

YAMI BOLO
| 86 | Greensleeves GREL 140 | JAH JAH MADE THEM ALL (LP)...20 |

YANA
56	HMV POP 252	Climb Up The Wall/If You Don't Love Me..20
57	HMV POP 340	Mr. Wonderful/Too Close For Comfort 15
58	HMV POP 481	I Need You/I Miss You Mama 10
58	HMV POP 546	Papa And Mama/In The Morning 10

YANCEY
| 79 | Octane WS 302 | Standing Waiting/Woman (no p/s)..20 |
| 79 | Hammer HS 302 | Standing Waiting/Woman (reissue) ....8 |

JIMMY YANCEY
54	HMV 7EG 8062	JIMMY YANCEY (EP) 20
55	HMV 7EG 8083	JIMMY YANCEY (EP) 20
58	Vogue EPV 1203	YANCEY'S PIANO (EP) 20
54	London AL 3525	JIMMY YANCEY - A LOST RECORDING DATE (10" LP) 25
56	Vogue LDE 166	JAZZ IMMORTALS VOLUME 2 (10" LP) 30
68	Atlantic 590 018	LOWDOWN DIRTY BLUES (LP)...15

MAMA YANCEY/DON EWELL
| 57 | Tempo LAP 7 | MAMA YANCEY-DON EWELL (10" LP) ....30 |

(see also Don Ewell)

ZALMAN YANOVSKY
67	Kama Sutra KAS 209	As Long As You're Here/Ereh Er'uoy Sa Gnol Sa (unreleased)	0
67	Pye International 7N 25438	As Long As You're Here/Ereh Er'uoy Sa Gnol Sa	8
71	Kama Sutra 2316 003	ALIVE AND WELL IN ARGENTINA (LP)	18

(see also Mugwumps, Lovin' Spoonful)

GLENN YARBOROUGH
65	RCA 1449	Baby The Rain Must Fall/I've Been To Town	7
66	RCA 1555	Everybody's Rich But Us/Walk On Little Baby	6

(see also Limeliters)

YARDBIRDS
64	Columbia DB 7283	I Wish You Would/A Certain Girl	35
64	Columbia DB 7391	Good Morning Little Schoolgirl/I Ain't Got You	35
65	Columbia DB 7499	For Your Love/Got To Hurry	10
65	Columbia DB 7594	Heart Full Of Soul/Steeled Blues	10
65	Columbia DB 7706	Evil Hearted You/Still I'm Sad (some copies with A-side miscredited to Samwell-Smith & McCartney)	7
66	Columbia DB 7848	Shapes Of Things/You're A Better Man Than I	7
66	Columbia DB 7848	Shapes Of Things/Still I'm Sad (mispressing)	45
66	Columbia DB 7928	Over, Under, Sideways, Down/Jeff's Boogie	15
66	Columbia DB 8024	Happenings Ten Years Time Ago/Psycho Daisies	35
67	Columbia DB 8165	Little Games/Puzzles	35
64	Columbia SEG 8421	FIVE YARDBIRDS (EP)	100
67	Columbia SEG 8521	OVER UNDER SIDEWAYS DOWN (EP)	225
64	Columbia 33SX 1677	FIVE LIVE YARDBIRDS (LP, 1st pressing, blue/black label, flipback sleeve)	250
69	Columbia 33SX 1677	FIVE LIVE YARDBIRDS (LP, 2nd pressing, black/silver label, flipback sleeve)	25
60s	Columbia TA SX 6063	FIVE LIVE YARDBIRDS (reel-to-reel tape)	20
66	Columbia SCXC 28	HAVING A RAVE UP WITH THE YARDBIRDS (LP, export issue)	200
66	Columbia SX 6063	THE YARDBIRDS (LP, 1st pressing, blue/black label, flipback sleeve, mono)	70
66	Columbia SCX 6063	THE YARDBIRDS (LP, 1st pressing, blue/black label, flipback sleeve, stereo)	60
69	Columbia S(C)X 6063	THE YARDBIRDS (LP, 2nd pressing, black/silver label, flipback sleeve)	25
70	Columbia S(C)X 6063	THE YARDBIRDS (LP, 3rd pressing, black/silver label, non-flipback sleeve; misprinted without front cover illustration)	18
70	Columbia S(C)X 6063	THE YARDBIRDS (LP, 3rd pressing, black/silver label, non-flipback sleeve)	15
84	Charly BOX 104	SHAPES OF THINGS (LP, box set)	50

(see also Eric Clapton, Jeff Beck, Jimmy Page, Keith Relf, Reign, Stairway, Sonny Boy Williamson & Yardbirds, Shoot)

PER YARROH
88	HMV PY 1	Laughing Inside/Laughing Inside (p/s, promo only; actually by Roy Harper)	7

(see also Roy Harper)

TOM YATES
67	CBS BPG 63094	SECOND CITY SPIRITUAL (LP, as Thomas Yates)	90
72	President PTLS 1053	LOVE COMES WELL ARMED (LP, with booklet)	25
77	Satril SATL 4007	SONG OF THE SHIMMERING WAY (LP, with insert)	20

TOMMY YATES
65	Pye 7N 15980	Rattle Of A Toy/Long Time Gone	10

YA-YA
83	Buzz BUZZ 2	What Can I Say/Maybe Tomorrow	6

Y BLEW
67	Qualiton QSP 7001	Maes 'B'/Beth Sy'n Dod Rhyngom Ni (p/s)	50

Y DILFOR
73	Westwood WSR 002	Y DILFOR (LP)	30

YE ASCOYNE D'ASCOYNES
92	Hangman GIBBET 1	JUST THE BIGGEST THING (EP)	8

(see also Dentists, Claim)

YEAH YEAH YEAHS
01	Wichita WEBB 029T	YEAH YEAH YEAHS EP: Bang/Mystery Girl/Art Star/Miles Away/Our Time (12", p/s)	10
03	Polydor 981 141-4	Maps/Countdown/Miles Away (p/s)	10
06	Polydor 170 687-5	Cheated Hearts/Cheated Hearts (Peaches Remix) (Heart-shaped picture disc)	10
07	Polydor 1741099	IS IS EP (2 x 7")	20
10	Polydor 2734679	Skeletons/Skeleton (no'd, 500 only)	5
03	Dress Up 0760611	FEVER TO TELL (LP picture disc with bonus travk 'Poor Song')	40
06	Polydor 985 295-6	SHOW YOUR BONES (LP)	15
09	2702576	IT'S BLITZ! (LP)	15

YEAR ONE
69	Major Minor MM 660	Eli's Comin'/Will You Be Staying After Sunday	12

YEARS
79	Tuff Going TGF 123	TUFF GOING EP (p/s, 500 only)	80

(see also Chameleons, Sun And The Moon)

YEH YEH
85	Berlin BRS 001	You Will Pay/7 Bells (1st pressing in grey p/s)	5

YELLO
81	Do It DUN 11	Bimbo/I.T. Splash (p/s)	6
82	Do It DUN 13	Bostich/She's Got A Gun (Instrumental) (p/s)	5
82	Do It DUNIT 13	Bostich/Downtown Samba/She's Got A Gun/Daily Disco (12", p/s)	10
82	Do It DUN 18	She's Got A Gun/Glue Head (p/s)	5
82	Do It DUNIT 18	She's Got A Gun/The Evening's Young/There Is No Reason (12", p/s)	8
82	Do It DUN 23	Pinball Cha Cha/Smile On You (p/s)	5
82	Do It DUNIT 23	Pinball Cha Cha/Smile On You (12", p/s)	12
83	Stiff PBUY 176	I Love You/Rubber West (3-D picture disc, with glasses)	5
83	Stiff BUY 191	Lost Again/Base For Alec (p/s)	5
83	Stiff DBUY 191	Lost Again/Base For Alec//Let Me Cry/She's Got A Gun (double pack)	6
86	Mercury MERDP 218	Goldrush/She's Got A Gun (live at Palladium N.Y.)//I Love You/ Desire (double pack, unreleased)	0
87	Mercury MERXR 253	The Rhythm Divine (Version Two)/Dr. Van Steiner (Instrumental)/The Rhythm Divine (Original 7" Version) (12", p/s, as Yello featuring Billy MacKenzie)	15

83	Stiff SEEZ 48	YOU GOTTA SAY YES TO ANOTHER EXCESS (LP, with bonus white label 12": "I Love You"/"Lost Again"/"You Gotta Say To Another Excess [Remix]"Pumping Velvet")	15
87	Mercury MERH 100	ONE SECOND (LP, with bonus 12" in p/s: "Call It Love (Trego Snare Version 2)"/"Santiago [live at Roxy New York]")	12
88	Mercury 836 778-1	FLAG (LP, HMV competition issue, 100 only)	40

(see also Associates)

YELLOTONE
03	Ai AI 004	GREEN MAYO EP (12", p/s)	8

YELLOW
70	CBS 4869	Roll It Down The Hill/Living A Lie	40

YELLOW BALLOON
67	Stateside SS 2008	Yellow Balloon/Noollab Wolley	20
68	Stateside SS 2124	Stained Glass Window/Can't Get Enough Of Your Love	20

YELLOW BELLOW ROOM BOOM
68	CBS 3205	Seeing Things Green/Easy Life	30

(see also 10cc, Frabjoy & Runcible Spoon)

YELLOW BIRD
74	Magnet MAG 16	Attack Attack/Right On	12

YELLOW MAGIC ORCHESTRA
80	A&M JAPAN 2	Nice Age/Rydeen (p/s, yellow vinyl)	5

(see also Ruichi Sakamoto)

YELLOW PAGES
68	Page One POF 090	Here Comes Jane/Ring-A-Ding	25

(see also Mirage)

YELLOW PAYGES
70	UNI UNS 516	Follow The Bouncing Ball/Little Woman	8
71	UNI UNS 534	Birds Of A Feather/Lady Friend	5

YELLOW 6
90s	Enraptured RAPTLP 36	OVERTONE (2-LP, clear vinyl, numbered, handprinted sleeve, 300 only)	20

YELLOW TAXI
70	President PT 296	Anna Laura Lee/Mary Ann	15

YELLOWMAN
82	Arrival ALP 004	FOR YOUR EYES ONLY (LP, as Yellowman And Fathead)	15
84	Pama PMLP 3215	OPERATION RADICATION (10" LP)	15
84	Greensleeves GREL 57	ZUNGGUZUNGGUGUZUNGGUNZENG!!! (LP)	15
84	Arrival ARLP 013	UNDER ME FAT THING (LP)	15

YELLOWSTONE & VOICE
72	Parlophone R5965	Philosopher/The Flying Dutchman	12
72	Regal Zono. SRZA 8511	YELLOWSTONE & VOICE (LP)	20

YEMM & YEMEN
66	Columbia DB 8022	Black Is The Night/Do Blondes Really Have More Fun?	35

YES
69	Atlantic 584 280	Sweetness/Something's Coming	50
69	Atlantic 584 298	Looking Around/Everydays (unreleased; demos may exist)	175
70	Atlantic 584 323	Time And A Word/The Prophet	150
70	Atlantic 2091 004	Sweet Dreams/Dear Father	45
71	Atlantic 2814 003	I've Seen All Good People (a) Your Move/Starship Trooper (a) Life Seeker (promo only)	75
72	6-A1/-B1	Siberian Khatru/And You And I (white label promo)	50
74	Atlantic K 10407	And You And I/Roundabout	5
77	Atlantic K 10985	Going For The One/Parallels (unreleased, copies may exist)	60
77	Atlantic K 10985T	Going For The One (Extended)/Parallels (12", unreleased, copies may exist)	40
70s	Lyntone LYN 2535	Interview/Five Songs (flexidisc or vinyl, with 80-page Yes songbook)	70
70s	Lyntone LYN 2535	Interview/Five Songs (flexidisc or vinyl)	35
69	Atlantic 588 190	YES (LP, gatefold, red/plum label with lyric insert)	150
70	Atlantic 2400 006	TIME AND A WORD (LP, red/plum label, with lyric insert)	80
71	Atlantic 2400 101	THE YES ALBUM (LP, red/plum label, gatefold sleeve)	50
71	Atlantic 2401 019	FRAGILE (LP, red/plum label, gatefold sleeve with booklet)	70
72	Atlantic K 50012	CLOSE TO THE EDGE (LP, 1st pressing with A1/B1 matrix numbers, no "W" logo at 3 O'clock, textured sleeve inside and outside, green inner sleeve, darker with lyric insert)	40
73	Atlantic K60045	YESSONGS (2-LP, wide spine, 'book opening' gatefold sleeve printed by 'Robor Ltd', no 'W' logo on labels, outline 'Yes' on inner sleeves, all matrixes end in '1')	25
73	Atlantic K 80001	TALES FROM TOPOGRAPHIC OCEANS (2-LP)	25
77	Atlantic DSK 50379	GOING FOR THE ONE (LP, as 3 x 12" singles, promo only)	100
80	Atlantic K 50842	CLASSIC YES (LP, with bonus 7" "Roundabout"/"Your Move" [SAM 141])	15
80	Atlantic K 50842	CLASSIC YES (LP, promo, with different sleeve)	30

(see also Jon Anderson, Hans Christian, Syn, Syndicats, Winston's Fumbs, Warriors, Federals, Peter Banks, Flash, Asia, Rick Wakeman, Steve Howe, Refugee, Chris Squire)

YETTIES
74	Argo AFW 113	Dorest Is Beautiful/Fling It Here! (Fling It There!)	6
69	Acorn CF 203	FIFTY STONE OF LOVELINESS (LP)	12
72	Argo ZBF 38	DORSET IS BEAUTIFUL (LP)	18
73	Argo ZBF 86	ALL AT SEA (LP)	18
74	Argo ZDA 168	OF YETMINSTER (LP)	15

JOHN YLVISAKER
68	Avantgarde AV 107	COOL LIVIN' (LP)	75

YOBS
77	NEMS NES 114	Run Rudolph Run/The Worm Song (p/s)	10
78	Yob YOB 79	Silent Night/Stille Nacht (p/s)	7
81	Safari YULE 1	Rub-A-Dum-Dum/Another Christmas (p/s)	7
82	Fresh FRESH 41	Yobs On 45/The Ballad Of Warrington (p/s)	7
80	Safari RUDE 1	CHRISTMAS ALBUM (LP)	12

MINT VALUE £

(see also Boys)

MAHARISHI MAHESH YOGI
67	Liberty LBS 83075E	MAHARISHI MAHESH YOGI (LP)	25

SUSUMU YOKOTA
99	Leaf BAY 9	IMAGE 1983-1998 (LP)	15
00	Leaf BAY 13	SAKURA (2-LP)	25

YO LA TENGO
95	Duophonic Super 45s DS 45-10	Evanescent Psychic Pez Drop/STEREOLAB: Long Hair Of Death (gig single, fluorescent yellow vinyl,	0
96	Earworm WORM 4	Blue - Green Arrow/Watching The Sun Set On Johnny Carson (2,000 only, 100 in handmade p/s)	12
96	Earworm WORM 4	Blue - Green Arrow/Watching The Sun Set On Johnny Carson (2,000 only)	8

YOLANDA
60	Triumph RGM 1007	With This Kiss/Don't Tell Me Not To Love You	40

(see also Kenny Graham & His Satellites)

STEVE YORK'S CAMELO PARDALIS
73	Virgin V 2003	MANOR LIVE (LP)	20

(see also Elkie Brooks, Boz Scaggs, Lol Coxhill, Graham Bond, Mike Patto)

NOLA YORK
64	HMV POP 1326	I Don't Understand/Here I Stand	5
66	Philips BF 1527	A Whole Lotta Lovin'/You Just Didn't Wanna Know	5
67	Philips BF 1558	I Can Hear You Calling/Clown Face	6
67	Philips BF 1582	Photographs/He's Looking At Her	5
67	Philips BF 1606	There's So Much Love All Around Me/Sleeping Boutique	5
68	Philips BF 1714	Ciao Baby/We'll Get To Heaven	6

(see also Bow Bells)

PETE YORK PERCUSSION BAND
73	Decca TXS 109	PERCUSSION BAND (LP, with Ian Paice, gatefold sleeve)	50

(see also Spencer Davis Group, Hardin & York, Deep Purple)

RUSTY YORK
58	Parlophone R 4398	Peggy Sue/Shake 'Em Up Baby (unissued, demos only)	1500

(see also Bonnie Lou & Rusty York)

YORK BROTHERS
54	Parlophone CMSP 5	Why Don't You Open The Door?/You're My Every Dream Come True (export issue)	20
54	Parlophone CMSP 22	Strange Town/Three O'Clock Blues (export issue)	20
58	Parlophone GEP 8736	COUNTRY AND WESTERN (EP)	40
58	Parlophone GEP 8753	COUNTRY AND WESTERN NO. 2 (EP)	40

THOM YORKE
07	XL XLT238P	Harrowdown Hill/The Drunkk Machine/Jetstream, (12" promo)	12
08	XL XLT 335	Eraser Rmxs 1 (12", 2000 only)	10
08	XL XLT 336	Eraser Rmxs 2 (12", 2000 only)	10
08	XL XLT 337	Eraser Rmxs 3 (12", 2000 only)	10
09	_Xurbia _Xendless XX002	Feelingpulledapartbyhorses/Thehollowearth (12", 8000 only)	10
11	Text 10	Ego/Mirror (12", with Burial and Four Tet, black labels on both sides)	15
06	XL XLLP 200	THE ERASER (LP, 3D effect on embossed sleeve)	20

(see also Radiohead)

YOU
80	Ram RAMYOU2	THE NIGHT AND MUSIC (EP)	20

YOU & I
73	Grape GR 3055	Morning Has Broken/Don't Take Love For A Game	5

YOU KNOW WHO GROUP
65	London HLR 9947	Roses Are Red My Love/Playboy	20

CHRIS YOULDEN
73	Deram DM 377	Nowhere Road/Standing On The Corner	12
73	Deram SML 1099	NOWHERE ROAD (LP, lyric insert)	60
74	Deram SML 1112	CITY CHILD (LP)	50

(see also Savoy Brown)

BARRY YOUNG
65	Dot DS 16756	One Has My Name (The Other Has My Heart)/Show Me The Way	10

BILLY YOUNG
72	Atlantic K 10277	The Sloopy/Same Old Thing Again	8
72	Jay Boy BOY 55	I'm Available/Sweet Woman	8

BILLY YOUNG/LIZZIE MILES
56	HMV 7EG 8178	THE BLUES THEY SANG (EP, with Jelly Roll Morton)	20

BOB YOUNG
86	Making Waves SURF 115	Mean Girl/Living On An Island (p/s)	5

(see also Status Quo, Young & Moody Band)

BRETT YOUNG (& GHOST SQUAD)
63	Pye 7N 15578	Guess What/It Just Happened	12
64	Pye 7N 15641	Never Again/You Can't Fool Me (as Brett Young & Ghost Squad)	12

COLIN YOUNG
71	Trend 6099 005	Anytime At All/You're No Good	8

DARREN YOUNG
63	Parlophone R 4919	My Tears Will Turn To Laughter/I've Just Fallen For Someone	20

(see also Johnny Gentle)

DESI YOUNG
70	Pressure Beat PB 5504	News Flash/JOE GIBBS & DESTROYERS: News Flash - Version	25

EDDY YOUNG
71	Beacon BEA 178	A Little On The Heavy Side/Give'Em A Hand	12

FARON YOUNG

55	Capitol CL 14336	Live Fast, Love Hard, Die Young/Forgive Me, Dear	30
55	Capitol CL 14336	Live Fast, Love Hard, Die Young/Forgive Me, Dear (78)	10
56	Capitol CL 14574	If You Ain't Lovin' (You Ain't Livin')/All Right	20
56	Capitol CL 14655	I've Got 5 Dollars And It's Saturday Night/You're Still Mine	30
57	Capitol CL 14735	The Shrine Of St. Cecilia/He Was There	8
57	Capitol CL 14762	Love Has Finally Come My Way/Moonlight Mountain	8
57	Capitol CL 14793	Honey Stop! (And Think Of Me)/Vacation's Over	15
58	Capitol CL 14822	Snowball/The Locket	6
58	Capitol CL 14860	I Can't Dance/Rosalie (Is Gonna Get Married)	15
58	Capitol CL 14891	Every Time I'm Kissing You/Alone With You	15
58	Capitol CL 14930	I Hate Myself/That's The Way I Feel	5
59	Capitol CL 14975	Last Night At A Party/A Long Time Ago	15
59	Capitol CL 15004	That's The Way It's Gotta Be/We're Talking It Over	5
59	Capitol CL 15050	I Hear You Talkin'/Country Girl	25

GEORGIE YOUNG & ROCKIN' BOCS

58	London HLU 8748	Nine More Miles/The Sneak	15
58	London HLU 8748	Nine More Miles/The Sneak (78)	15

HARRY YOUNG

65	Dot DS 16756	Show Me The Way/One Has My Name	10

YOUNG JESSIE

58	London HLE 8544	Shuffle In The Gravel/Make Believe	300
58	London HLE 8544	Shuffle In The Gravel/Make Believe (78)	50

JIMMY YOUNG

54	Decca F 10232	A Baby Cried/Remember Me	10
54	Decca F 10406	Give Me Your Word/Lonely Nightingale	10
55	Decca F 10444	These Are The Things We'll Share/Don't Go To Strangers	8
55	Decca F 10483	If Anyone Finds This, I Love You/The Sand And The Sea	8
55	Decca F 10502	Unchained Melody/Help Me Forget	15
55	Decca F 10597	The Man From Laramie/No Arms Can Ever Hold You	15
55	Decca F 10640	Someone On Your Mind/I Look At You	15
56	Decca F 10694	Chain Gang/Capri In May	10
56	Decca F 10736	Rich Man, Poor Man/The Wayward Wind	10
56	Decca F 10774	More/I'm Gonna Steal You Away	10
57	Decca F 10842	Lovin' Baby/My Faith, My Hope, My Love	5
57	Decca F 10875	Round And Round/Walkin' After Midnight	6
57	Decca F 10925	Man On Fire/Love In The Afternoon	5
57	Decca F 10948	Deep Blue Sea/Harbour Of Desire	5
63	Columbia DB 7119	Miss You/Take Care Of Yourself	5
64	Columbia DB 7234	Unchained Melody/There's Always Me	5
55	Pye NEP 24004	JIMMY YOUNG SINGS (EP)	8
56	Decca DFE 6277	PRESENTING JIMMY YOUNG (EP)	10
57	Decca DFE 6404	JIMMY YOUNG (EP)	8
55	Decca LF 1200	PRESENTING JIMMY YOUNG (10" LP)	20
57	Decca LK 4219	THE NIGHT IS YOUNG (LP)	15
58	Columbia 33SX 1102	YOU (LP)	12

JOE E. YOUNG & TONIKS

68	Toast TT 502	Life Time Of Lovin'/Flower In My Hand	20
69	Toast TT 514	Good Day Sunshine/Life Time Of Lovin'	20
68	Toast (S)TLP 1	SOUL BUSTER! (LP)	40

JOHNNIE YOUNG

67	Polydor 56199	Every Christian/Epitath To Mr Simon Sir	20
67	Polydor 56186	Craise Finton Kirk/I Am The World	20

JOHNNY YOUNG

67	Decca F 22548	Step Back/Cara Lyn (as Johnny Young & Kompany)	15
67	Decca F 22636	Lady/Good Evening Girl	10
68	RCA RCA 1826	Always Thinking Of You/Dreaming Country (as Johnny Young Four)	10
70	Blue Horizon 7-63852	FAT MANDOLIN (LP)	90

KAREN YOUNG

65	Mercury MF 943	I'm Yours, You're Mine/Are You Kidding	8
65	Pye 7N 15956	We'll Start The Party Again/Wonderful Summer	8
68	Major Minor MM 584	Too Much Of A Good Thing/You Better Sit Down	50
70	Major Minor MM 691	One Tin Soldier/Que Sera Sera (B-side arranged by Paul McCartney)	12
69	M. Minor MMLP/SMLP 66	SINGS NOBODY'S CHILD AND 13 OTHER GREAT SONGS (LP)	20

KATHY YOUNG & INNOCENTS

61	Top Rank JAR 534	A Thousand Stars/Eddie My Darling	40
61	Top Rank JAR 554	Happy Birthday Blues/Someone To Love	30

(see also Innocents)

K.G. YOUNG

69	CBS 4302	Spider/Spider Woogie 9th Movement	30

LEON YOUNG STRINGS

64	Pye 7N 15646	This Boy/Glad All Over	40

LESTER YOUNG (QUINTET)

56	Vogue V 2362	New Lester Leaps In/She's Funny That Way	6
56	Vogue V 2384	You're Driving Me Crazy/East Of The Sun	6
56	Vogue EPV 1127	LESTER YOUNG (EP)	10
53	Mercury MG 25015	KANSAS CITY 7/THE LESTER YOUNG QUARTET (LP, 1 side each)	15
55	Felsted EDL 87014	BATTLE OF THE SAXES (10" LP)	15
55	Columbia Clef 33C 9001	LESTER YOUNG WITH THE OSCAR PETERSON TRIO (10" LP)	15
56	Columbia Clef 33C 9015	LESTER YOUNG (10" LP)	15
56	Columbia Clef 33CX 10031	THE PRESIDENT, LESTER YOUNG (LP)	15
56	Columbia Clef 33CX 10054	THE JAZZ GIANTS '56 (LP)	15
57	Columbia Clef 33CX 10070	PRES (LP)	15
58	London Jazz LTZ-C 15132	BLUE LESTER (LP)	18

MINT VALUE £

59	HMV CLP 1302	PRES AND TEDDY (LP, with Teddy Wilson)	12

(see also Count Basie, Coleman Hawkins & Lester Young, Oscar Peterson)

LESTER YOUNG & CHARLIE PARKER, ET AL.

50	Melodisc 8003	JAZZ AT THE PHILHARMONIC, VOL. 2: BLUES FOR NORMAN, PARTS 1 & 2 (12" 78)	10

LLOYD YOUNG

72	Bullet BU 500	Bread And Butter/SHALIMAR ALLSTARS: Version	8
72	Duke DU 135	Soup/J.J. ALLSTARS: Version	12
72	Green Door GD 4037	Shalimar Special/G. MAHTANI ALLSTARS: Version	8
72	Techniques TE 917	High Explosion/ANSELL COLLINS: Version	8

(see also Carey & Lloyd)

YOUNG MARBLE GIANTS

80	Rough Trade RT 043	Final Day/Radio Silents/Cakewalking/Colossal Youth (p/s)	6
81	Rough Trade RT 059	TESTCARD (EP)	12
80	Rough Trade ROUGH 8	COLOSSAL YOUTH (LP)	30
84	Rough Trade ROUGHL8	COLOSSAL YOUTH (LP, reissue)	15
07	Domino REWIGLP 32	COLOSSAL YOUTH (LP, reissue)	18

YOUNG MC

88	Delicious Vinyl BRW 120	KNOW HOW (12", EP)	20

MIGHTY JOE YOUNG

69	Parlophone 5794	Why Don't You Follow Me/By My Side	25
72	Sonet SNTF 633	THE LEGACY OF THE BLUES VOL. 4 (LP)	12
72	Delmark DS 629	BLUES WITH A TOUCH OF SOUL (LP, blue label)	22

YOUNG & MOODY (BAND)

77	Magnet MAG 87	Chicago Blue/Warm Winds	5
79	Fabulous JC 1	The Devil Went Down To Georgia/You Can't Catch Me	5
79	Fabulous JC 3	All The Good Friends/Playing Your Game (p/s)	5
77	Magnet MAG 5015	YOUNG AND MOODY (LP, with lyric insert, as Young & Moody)	12

(see also Bob Young, Whitesnake, Snafu, Cozy Powell, Motorhead, Nolan Sisters)

NEIL YOUNG

69	Reprise RS 23405	The Loner/Everybody Knows This Is Nowhere	25
70	Reprise RS 20861	Oh Lonesome Me (Long Version)/Sugar Mountain	12
70	Reprise RS 23462	Down By The River (edit)/Cinnamon Girl (alternate mix)	12
70	Reprise RS 20958	Only Love Can Break Your Heart/Birds	6
71	Reprise RS 23488	When You Dance I Can Really Love/After The Goldrush	6
72	Reprise K 14167	Old Man/The Needle And The Damage Done	6
73	Reprise SAM 15	Don't Be Denied/Love In Mind/Last Dance (p/s, 1-sided, promo only sampler for "Time Fades Away" LP)	20
74	Reprise K 14350	Southern Man/Till The Morning Comes/After The Goldrush/Heart Of Gold (special sleeve)	5
76	Reprise K 14431	Don't Cry No Tears/Stupid Girl	5
74	Reprise K 14360	Walk On/For The Turnstiles	20
93	Geffen NYCD 1	LUCKY THIRTEEN ALBUM SAMPLER (Ain't It The Truth/Depression Blues/This Note's For You) (CD, promo only)	15
69	Reprise RSLP 6317	NEIL YOUNG (LP, with name on front of sleeve)	60
69	Reprise RSLP 6317	NEIL YOUNG (LP, without name on front of sleeve)	100
69	Reprise RSLP 6349	EVERYBODY KNOWS THIS IS NOWHERE (LP)	60
70	Reprise RSLP 6383	AFTER THE GOLDRUSH (LP, gatefold sleeve with lyric insert)	50
71	Reprise K 44059	NEIL YOUNG (LP, reissue)	15
71	Reprise K 44073	EVERYBODY KNOWS THIS IS NOWHERE (LP, reissue)	15
71	Reprise K 44088	AFTER THE GOLDRUSH (LP, reissue, gatefold sleeve with lyric insert)	15
72	Reprise K 54005	HARVEST (LP, thick cardboard gatefold sleeve with insert)	40
72	Reprise K 64015	JOURNEY THROUGH THE PAST (2-LP, soundtrack, fold-out sleeve & inners)	35
73	Reprise K 54010	TIME FADES AWAY (LP, with lyric insert)	20
74	Reprise K 54014	ON THE BEACH (LP, with inner sleeve)	50
75	Reprise K 54040	TONIGHT'S THE NIGHT (LP, gatefold sleeve with inner sleeve & insert)	20
75	Reprise K 54057	ZUMA (LP, with inner sleeve & lyric insert)	25
77	Reprise K 54088	AMERICAN STARS AND BARS (LP, with inner sleeve)	15
77	Resprise K 64037	DECADE (3-LP)	25
79	Reprise K 54105	RUST NEVER SLEEPS (LP, with inner sleeve & lyric insert)	12
79	Reprise K 64041	LIVE RUST (2-LP, with inner sleeves)	15
80	Reprise K 54109	HAWKS & DOVES (LP, with inner sleeve)	12
85	Geffen GEF 26377	OLD WAYS (LP, inner sleeve)	12
93	Geffen GEF24452	LUCKY THIRTEEN (LP)	50
93	Reprise 9362-4 5310-1	UNPLUGGED (LP)	50

(see also Buffalo Springfield, Crosby Stills Nash & Young, Stills-Young Band, Crazy Horse)

RALPH YOUNG

55	Brunswick 05466	The Man From Laramie/The Bible Tells Me So	7
55	Brunswick 05500	Bring Me A Bluebird/A Room In Paris	5
56	Brunswick 05605	The Legend Of Wyatt Earp/Do You Know?	5

(see also Jack Pleis)

ROBERT YOUNG

71	CBS 7350	Rosemary Blue/When Time Began	7

ROGER YOUNG

66	Columbia DB 7869	Sweet, Sweet Morning/Whatcha Gonna Give Me?	60
66	Columbia DB 8092	No Address/It's Been Nice	250

ROY YOUNG (BAND)

59	Fontana H 200	Just Keep It Up/Big Fat Mama	25
59	Fontana H 200	Just Keep It Up/Big Fat Mama (78)	10
59	Fontana H 215	Hey Little Girl/Just Ask Your Heart	20
59	Fontana H 215	Hey Little Girl/Just Ask Your Heart (78)	15
60	Fontana H 237	I Hardly Know Me/Gilee	20
60	Fontana H 247	Taboo/I'm In Love	15
61	Fontana H 290	You Were Meant For Me/Plenty Of Love (as Roy Young & Hunters)	10
61	Ember EMB S 128	Four And Twenty Thousand Kisses/Late Last Evening	12
71	MCA MKS 5071	Wild Country Wine/New Sun New Horizon (p/s)	8
70	RCA SF 8161	ROY YOUNG BAND (LP)	20

ROY YOUNG
73	MCA MUS 1214	Dig A Hole/I'm A Loner	12

SUSANNAH YOUNG
67	Philips BF 1559	Lazy Afternoon/Here's That Rainy Day	5
67	Philips BL 7728	SWEETEST SOUNDS (LP)	12

TERRY YOUNG
61	Pye 7N 15321	Maverick/Partners	7
61	Pye 7N 15353	Someone New/Now Forever And A Day	12
62	Pye 7N 15416	Joe's Been A-Gittin' There/They Took John Away	6

TOMMIE YOUNG
73	Contempo C 12	Everybody's Got A Little Devil In Their Soul/Do You Still Feel The Same Way	10
73	Contempo C 23	She Don't Have To See You/That's All Part Of Loving Him	10
74	Contempo CLP 501	DO YOU STILL FEEL THE SAME WAY (LP)	75

VICKI YOUNG
55	Capitol CL 14228	Hearts Of Stone/Tweedlee Dee (triangular centre)	40
55	Capitol CL 14228	Hearts Of Stone/Tweedlee Dee (78 rpm)	10
55	Capitol CL 14281	Live Fast, Love Hard, Die Young/Zoom, Zoom, Zoom(triangular centre)	25
56	Capitol CL 14528	Steel Guitar/Bye Bye For Just A While	12
56	Capitol CL 14653	Spanish Main/Tell Me In Your Own Sweet Way (with Joe 'Fingers' Carr)	12
56	Capitol CL 14653	Spanish Main/Tell Me In Your Own Sweet Way (with Joe 'Fingers' Carr)(78)	10
56	Capitol EAP1 593	VICKI YOUNG (EP)	35

(see also Joe 'Fingers' Carr)

YOUNG AL CAPONE
71	Green Door GD 4012	Girl Called Clover/Girl Called Clover (Version)	8

YOUNG AND MOODY BAND
81	Bronze BRO 130	Don't Do That/How Can I help You Tonight	6

YOUNG BLOOD
68	Pye 7N 17495	Green Light/Don't Leave Me In The Dark	25
68	Pye 7N 17588	Just How Loud/Masquerade	20
68	Pye 7N 17627	Bang-Shang-A-Lang/I Can't Stop	20
69	Pye 7N 17696	The Continuing Story Of Bungalow Bill/I Will	20

(see also Cozy Powell, Ace Kefford Stand, Big Bertha)

YOUNG BLOOD
84	Landslide LAND 1	FIRST BLOOD (12" EP, p/s)	18

YOUNGBLOODS
69	RCA RCA 1821	Darkness, Darkness/On Sir Francis Drake	10
69	RCA RCA 1877	Get Together/Beautiful	10
69	RCA SF 8026	ELEPHANT MOUNTAIN (LP)	22
70	Warner Bros WS 1878	ROCK FESTIVAL (LP)	15

YOUNG BROTHERS
68	MCA MU 1042	I've Always Wanted Love/Mirror Mirror	15

YOUNG BUCKS
77	Blueport BLU 1	Get Your Feet Back On The Ground/Cold, Cold Morning (p/s)	6

YOUNG DISCIPLES
90	Talkin' Loud TLKX 2	Get Yourself Together/Young Disciples Theme (12", p/s)	8

COLE YOUNGER
74	ABC ABC 4009	Don't Stop/Call Me	10
77	Magnet MAG 112	She's Not My Lover/Don't Use Me	8
80	Ariola AHA 555	Candy/I'd Rather Be Me	6

YOUNGFOLK
68	President PT 136	Lonely Girl/Joey	20

YOUNG FOLK
72	Midas MR 001	RIBBLE VALLEY DREAM (LP)	50

YOUNG FREDDIE
70	Camel CA 38	Drink And Gamble/LENNOX BROWN & HUE ROY: King Of The Road	15

(see also Freddie McGregor)

YOUNG GROWLER & CALYPSO RHYTHM KINGS
66	Columbia DB 7870	Amy The Sunbather/Sweet Trinidad	7
66	Columbia DB 7958	V For Victory/Be Nice To Women (in 'Test Match' p/s)	12
66	Columbia DB 7958	V For Victory/Be Nice To Women	7
66	Columbia SEG 8502	V FOR VICTORY (EP)	12

YOUNG-HOLT TRIO
67	Coral Q 72489	Wack Wack/This Little Light Of Mine	15
67	Coral Q 72489	Wack Wack/This Little Light Of Mine (DJ copy)	40

YOUNG-HOLT UNLIMITED
69	MCA MU 1053	Soulful Strut/Country Slicker Joe	5
72	MCA MU 1159	Just Ain't No Love/Love Makes A Woman	5
73	Contempo COLP-R 1004	PLAYS SUPERFLY (LP)	15
69	MCA MUP(S) 368	SOULFUL STRUT (LP)	15

(see also Ramsey Lewis Trio)

YOUNG IDEA
66	Columbia DB 7961	The World's Been Good To Me/It Can't Be	10
66	Columbia DB 8067	Gotta Get Out Of The Mess I'm In/Games Men Play	5
67	Columbia DB 8132	Peculiar Situation/Just Look At The Rain	5
67	Columbia DB 8205	With A Little Help From My Friends/Colours Of Darkness	12
67	Columbia DB 8284	Mister Lovin' Luggage Man/Room With A View	8
68	Music For Pleasure MFP 1225	WITH A LITTLE HELP FROM MY FRIENDS (LP)	20

YOUNG LIONS
78	Discovery D-DISC 001	Take Five (12", p/s)	30

YOUNG ONES (1)
63	Decca F 11705	How Do I Tell You/Baby That's It	8

YOUNG ONES (2)
78	Virgin VS 205	Rock 'N' Roll Radio/Little Bit Of Loving (p/s)	6

YOUNG RASCALS
65	Atlantic AT 4059	I Ain't Gonna Eat My Heart Out Anymore/Slow Down	15
66	Atlantic AT 4082	Good Lovin'/Mustang Sally	12
66	Atlantic 584 024	You Better Run/Love Is A Beautiful Thing	18
66	Atlantic 584 050	Come On Up/What Is The Reason	18
66	Atlantic 584 067	Too Many Fish In The Sea/No Love To Give	15
67	Atlantic 584 081	I've Been Lonely Too Long/If You Knew	15
67	Atlantic 584 085	I Ain't Gonna Eat My Heart Out Anymore/Good Lovin'	12
67	Atlantic 584 111	Groovin'/Sueno	10
67	Atlantic 584 128	A Girl Like You/It's Love	12
67	Atlantic 584 138	How Can I Be Sure/I Don't Love You Anymore	7
68	Atlantic 584 161	It's Wonderful/Of Course	10
67	Atlantic 587/588 012	THE YOUNG RASCALS (LP)	30
67	Atlantic 587/588 060	COLLECTIONS (LP)	20
67	Atlantic 587/588 074	GROOVIN' (LP)	25

(see also Rascals, Joey Dee & Starlighters)

RICHARD YOUNGS
88	No Fans NFR01	ADVENTS (LP)	35

YOUNG SISTERS
62	London HLU 9610	Casanova Brown/My Guy	25

YOUNG SOULS
69	Amalgamated AMG 844	Why Did You Leave/Main A Wail	100

YOUNG TRADITION
74	Argo AFW 115	The Shepherd's Hymn/The Boar's Head Carol	6
68	Transatlantic TRAEP 164	CHICKEN ON A RAFT (EP)	25
66	Transatlantic TRA 142	THE YOUNG TRADITION (LP)	22
67	Transatlantic TRA 155	SO CHEERFULLY ROUND (LP)	18
68	Transatlantic TRA 172	GALLERIES (LP, with Dave Swarbrick)	18
68	Transatlantic TRASAM 13	THE YOUNG TRADITION SAMPLER (LP)	12

(see also Dave Swarbrick, Peter Bellamy)

YOUNG TURKS
66	CBS 202353	Duel At Diablo/Our Lady From Maxim's	12

YOUNG WORLD SINGERS
64	Brunswick 05916	Ringo For President/A Boy Like That	6

YOUR FAVOURITE HORSE
00s	Endorphin ENDORLP 010	EVERYDAY MAGIC (LP, orange vinyl)	12

JOHNNY YOUTH
69	Grape GR 3002	Darling It Won't/HIP CITY BOYS: Moon Train	10

YOUTH VALLEY CHORALE
63	London HLU 9818	Do You Hear What I Hear/Little Bell	5

YOUTH (1)
66	Polydor 56121	As Long As There Is Your Love/Your One And Only Love	20

YOUTH (2)
69	Deram DM 226	Meadow Of My Love/Love Me Or Leave Me	20

YOU'VE GOT FOETUS ON YOUR BREATH
81	Self Immolation WOMB 07	Wash It All Off/333 (p/s)	10
80s	Self Immolation	Tell Me, What Is The Bane Of Your Life?	15
81	Self Imm. WOMB OYBL-1	DEAF (LP)	30
81	Self Imm. WOMB OYBL-2	ACHE (LP)	30

(see also Foetus etc., Philip & His Foetus Vibrations, Scraping Foetus Off The Wheel)

LES YPER SOUND
67	Fontana TF 880	Too Fortiche/Psyche Rock	60

(see also Pierre Henry)

YR HWNTWS
82	Loco LOCO 1001	YR HWNTWS (LP)	80

Y TRWYNAU COCH
70s	Record. Sqwar RSROC 1	WASTOD AR Y TU FAS (BANANAS) (EP, around 1,000 only)	50
78	Recordian Sqwar RSROC 002	Merched Dan 15 (I Often Think Of Girls Under 15)/Byw Ar Arian Fy Rhieni/ Mynd I'r Capel Mewn Levis/Ail Ddechre (around 1,000 only)	50
80s	Record. Coch OCHR 2198	RHEDEG RHAG Y TORPIDOS (LP)	30

JOHNNY YUKON
60	Top Rank JAR 347	Made To Be Loved/Magnolia	7

YUNGUN/MR THING
03	White (Janomi) JACKIT0001	STRAIGHT JACK IT (EP)	20

TIMI YURO
61	London HLG 9403	Hurt/I Apologise	20
62	London HLG 9484	Smile/I Believe (B-side with Johnnie Ray)	15
62	Liberty LIB 55410	Let Me Call You Sweetheart/Satan Never Sleeps	10
62	Liberty LIB 55469	What's A-Matter Baby (Is It Hurting You)/Thirteenth Hour	30
63	Liberty LIB 55519	The Love Of A Boy/I Ain't Gonna Cry No More	30
63	Liberty LIB 55519	The Love Of A Boy/I Ain't Gonna Cry No More (DJ Copy)	60
63	Liberty LIB 55587	Make The World Go Away/Look Down	12
64	Liberty LIB 10177	Hurt/Be Anything (But Be Mine)	10
64	Mercury MF 826	If/I'm Afraid The Masquerade Is Over	20
65	Mercury MF 848	You Can Have Him/Could This Be Magic	12
65	Mercury MF 859	Get Out Of My Life/Can't Stop Running Away	60

65	Mercury MF 903	Once A Day/Pretend	5
65	Mercury MF 949	Turn The World Around The Other Way/Just A Ribbon	5
66	Mercury MF 978	Cuttin' In/Why Not Now	6
68	Liberty LBF 15092	Something Bad On My Mind/Wrong	30
68	Liberty LIB 15142	I Must Have Been Out Of My Mind/Interlude	25
68	Liberty LIB 15182	It'll Never Be Over For Me/As Long As There Is You	700
65	Liberty LEP 2214	TIMI YURO: SOUL! (EP)	30
66	Liberty LEP 2253	MAKE THE WORLD GO AWAY (EP)	25
62	London HA-G 2415	TIMI YURO (LP)	75
62	Liberty LBY 1042	SOUL! (LP)	35
63	Liberty LBY 1154	WHAT'S A-MATTER BABY (LP, mono)	25
63	Liberty SLBY 1154	WHAT'S A-MATTER BABY (LP, stereo)	30
64	Liberty LBY 1192	MAKE THE WORLD GO AWAY (LP)	25
64	Mercury 20032 MCL	THE AMAZING TIMI YURO (LP)	22
65	Liberty LBY 1247	HURT (LP)	30
66	Liberty LBY 1275	LET ME CALL YOU SWEETHEART (LP, mono)	20
66	Liberty SLBY 1275	LET ME CALL YOU SWEETHEART (LP, stereo)	30
66	Liberty (S)LBY 1290	THE BEST OF TIMI YURO (LP)	20
68	Liberty LBL/LBS 83115	GREAT PERFORMANCES (LP)	15
68	Liberty LBL/LBS 83128	TIMI IN THE BEGINNING (LP)	20
69	Liberty LBS 83198E	SOMETHING BAD ON MY MIND (LP)	50
69	Mercury SMWL 21010	TALENTED TIMI (LP)	15

(see also Johnnie Ray)

HELMUT ZACHARIAS
65	Polydor 236 809	PLAYS THE HITS OF THE BEATLES (LP)	12

JOHN ZACHERLE
58	London HLU 8599	Dinner With Drac Part 1/Dinner With Drac - Conclusion	20
58	London HLU 8599	Dinner With Drac Part 1/Dinner With Drac - Conclusion (78)	25

(see also Dave Appell & Applejacks)

ZAFTIG MADEL
84	Shine SHTUP 3	Dori Duz/Curvy 'N' Creamy (p/s)	6

ZAGER & EVANS
69	RCA SF 8056	2525 (LP)	20

ZAKARRIAS
71	Deram SML 1091	ZAKARRIAS (LP, white/red label, small logo)	800

ZAKATEK
73	Bell 1289	I Gotcha Now/So Good To You	7

GEORGE ZAMBETAS & THE GROUP TEN PLAYERS
66	Pye 7N 17180	Moussaka/Monlight Over The Acropolis (p/s)	6
69	RCA RCA 1860	In The Year 2525 (Exordium Terminus)/Little Kids	5

ALEX ZANETIS
71	Moodisc HM 102	Guilty/JOLLY BOYS: Do Fe Do	5

TOMMY ZANG
59	HMV POP 611	Break The Chain/I'll Put A String On Your Finger	10
62	Polydor NH 66955	I'm Gonna Slip You Offa My Mind/Every Hour, Every Day	10
62	Polydor NH 66957	Hey, Good Lookin'/With Love (For You)	20
62	Polydor NH 66960	Take These Chains From My Heart/Truly, Truly	10
62	Polydor NH 66977	I Can't Hold Your Letters (In My Arms)/She's Getting Married	10
62	Polydor NH 66980	Just Call My Name/I Love You Because	10

WILLY ZANGO
73	Jam JAM 58	Hot Rod/Goom	8
74	DJM DJS 312	Hot Rod/The Voice Of Melody	7

ZANTI MISFITZ
82	Clay 9	Kidz Songs/Alice Liddle's Bad Trip (p/s)	10

FRANK ZAPPA/MOTHERS OF INVENTION
SINGLES
66	Verve VS 545	It Can't Happen Here/How Could I Be Such A Fool (as Mothers Of Invention)	50
67	Verve VS 557	Big Leg Emma/Why Don't You Do Me Right (as Mothers Of Invention)	50
71	Reprise K 14100	Tears Began To Fall/Junier Mintz Boogie (as Mothers Of Invention)	40
71	United Artists UP 35319	What Will This Evening Bring Me This Morning?/Daddy, Daddy, Daddy	35
74	Discreet K 19201	Cosmic Debris/Uncle Remus	10
74	Discreet K 19202	Don't Eat The Yellow Snow/Camarillo Brillo	10
79	CBS 7261	Dancin' Fool/Baby Snakes	5
80	CBS 7950	Joe's Garage/Catholic Girls	6
80	CBS 7950	Joe's Garage/BOB DYLAN: When You Gonna Wake Up (mispressing)	30
80	CBS 8652	I Don't Wanna Get Drafted/Ancient Armaments (p/s)	6
81	CBS A 1622	You Are What You Is/Harder Than Your Husband (p/s)	6
81	CBS A 12-1622	You Are What You Is/Pink Napkins/Harder Than Your Husband/Soup 'N Old Clothes (12", picture disc)	15
81	CBS XPS 147	Shut Up 'N' Play Yer Guitar/Variation On The C. Santana Secret (p/s, issued free with "Ship Arriving Too Late To Save A Drowning Witch" LP)	6
82	CBS A 2412	Valley Girl/Teenage Prostitute (p/s)	6
84	EMI EMI 5499	Baby Take Your Teeth Out/Stevie's Spanking (p/s)	8

ALBUMS : VERVE ORIGINALS
66	Verve VLP 9154	FREAK OUT! (as Mothers Of Invention, mono, single disc)	100

66	Verve SVLP 9154	FREAK OUT! (as Mothers Of Invention, stereo, single disc)	80
67	Verve VLP 9174	ABSOLUTELY FREE (as Mothers Of Invention, mono)	100
67	Verve SVLP 9174	ABSOLUTELY FREE (as Mothers Of Invention, stereo)	70
68	Verve VLP 9199	WE'RE ONLY IN IT FOR THE MONEY (as Mothers Of Invention, gatefold sleeve, mono)	100
68	Verve SVLP 9199	WE'RE ONLY IN IT FOR THE MONEY (as Mothers Of Invention, gatefold sleeve, stereo)	90
68	Verve VLP 9223	LUMPY GRAVY (gatefold sleeve, mono)	100
68	Verve SVLP 9223	LUMPY GRAVY (gatefold sleeve, stereo)	60
69	Verve VLP 9237	CRUISING WITH RUBEN AND THE JETS (as Mothers Of Invention, mono)	100
69	Verve SVLP 9237	CRUISING WITH RUBEN AND THE JETS (as Mothers Of Invention, stereo)	60
69	Verve VLP 9239	MOTHERMANIA - THE BEST OF THE MOTHERS (as Mothers Of Invention, mono)	40
69	Verve SVLP 9239	MOTHERMANIA - THE BEST OF THE MOTHERS (as Mothers Of Invention, stereo)	30

ALBUMS : VERVE REISSUES

71	Verve/Polydor 2683 004	FREAK OUT (2-LP)	30
72	Verve/Polydor 2317 034	WE'RE ONLY IN IT FOR THE MONEY (gatefold sleeve)	30
72	Verve/Polydor 2317 035	ABSOLUTELY FREE (gatefold sleeve)	25
72	Verve/Polydor 2317 046	LUMPY GRAVY (gatefold sleeve)	30
72	Verve/Polydor 2317 047	MOTHERMANIA - THE BEST OF THE MOTHERS	25
73	Verve/Polydor 2352 017	MOTHERMANIA - THE BEST OF THE MOTHERS (2nd reissue)	25
73	Verve/Polydor 2317 069	CRUISIN' WITH RUBEN AND THE JETS (gatefold sleeve)	25
75	Verve/Polydor 2352 057	ROCK FLASHBACKS (LP)	15

ALBUMS : ORIGINAL REPRISE/WARNER/DISCREET ISSUES

70	Reprise RSLP 6356	HOT RATS (1st pressing, pink, gold & green 'riverboat' label, gatefold sleeve)	40
70	Reprise RSLP 6356	HOT RATS (2nd pressing, tan 'riverboat' label, gatefold sleeve)	20
70	Reprise RSLP 6370	BURNT WEENY SANDWICH (as Mothers Of Invention, 1st pressing, pink, gold & green 'riverboat' label, gatefold sleeve)	30
70	Reprise RSLP 2028	WEASELS RIPPED MY FLESH (as Mothers Of Invention, tan 'riverboat' label)	25
70	Reprise RSLP 2030	CHUNGA'S REVENGE (tan 'riverboat' label, green gatefold sleeve)	45
70	Reprise RSLP 2030	CHUNGA'S REVENGE (tan 'riverboat' label, red gatefold sleeve)	20
71	Reprise K 44150	FILLMORE EAST, JUNE 1971 (as Mothers Of Invention)	15
72	Reprise K 44179	JUST ANOTHER BAND FROM L.A. (as Mothers Of Invention, gatefold sleeve)	18
72	Reprise K 44203	WAKA/JAWAKA (HOT RATS)	15
72	Reprise K 44209	THE GRAND WAZOO (gatefold sleeve)	15
73	DiscReet K 41000	OVER-NITE SENSATION (as Mothers Of Invention, gatefold sleeve)	15
74	DiscReet K 69201	ROXY AND ELSEWHERE (2-LP, as Mothers Of Invention, gatefold sleeve)	15
74	DiscReet K 49201	APOSTROPHE (') (no lyric insert)	12
75	DiscReet K 59207	ONE SIZE FITS ALL (as Mothers Of Invention, gatefold sleeve)	12

(First pressings issued without Warner Bros logo on label or sleeve; copies with Warners logos are post-1975 pressings worth £6-£8 each.)

76	Warner Bros K 56298	ZOOT ALLURES (LP)	12
77	DiscReet K 69204	ZAPPA IN NEW YORK (LIVE) (2-LP, with & without reference to Punky's Whips)	20
77	DiscReet K 69204	ZAPPA IN NEW YORK (LIVE) (2-LP, "Punky's Whips" listed on sleeve but not on label or LP)	20
77	DiscReet K 69204	ZAPPA IN NEW YORK (LIVE) (2-LP, plays "Punky's Whips", listed on sleeve but not on label)	60
78	DiscReet K 59210	STUDIO TAN	12
78	DiscReet K 59211	SLEEP DIRT	12
78	DiscReet K 59212	ORCHESTRAL FAVORITES	12
71	Reprise K 44078	HOT RATS (tan 'riverboat' label, gatefold sleeve)	15
71	Reprise K 44083	BURNT WEENY SANDWICH (tan 'riverboat' label)	15
71	Reprise K 44019	WEASELS RIPPED MY FLESH (tan 'riverboat' label)	15
71	Reprise K 44020	CHUNGA'S REVENGE (tan 'riverboat' label, gatefold sleeve)	15

ALBUMS : CBS/EMI/OTHER LABELS

69	Transatlantic TRA 197	UNCLE MEAT (2-LP, as Mothers Of Invention)	70
71	United Artists UDF 50003	200 MOTELS (2-LP, with booklet & poster, as Frank Zappa & Mothers Of Invention)	35
79	CBS 88339	SHEIK YERBOUTI (2-LP, gatefold sleeve printed with lyrics)	15
79	CBS 86101	JOE'S GARAGE ACT 1 (gatefold sleeve, lyric insert)	12
79	CBS 88475	JOE'S GARAGE ACTS 2 & 3 (2-LP, gatefold sleeve, lyric insert)	15
81	CBS 88560	YOU ARE WHAT YOU IS (2-LP, gatefold sleeve, lyric insert)	15
81	CBS 88516	TINSELTOWN REBELLION (2-LP, gatefold sleeve with lyrics)	15
81	CBS 66368	SHUT UP 'N' PLAY YER GUITAR (3-LP box set, with inner sleeves)	25
82	CBS 85804	SHIP ARRIVING TOO LATE TO SAVE A DROWNING WITCH (LP, with bonus 7" Shut Up 'N' Play Yer Guitar/"Variation On The C. Santana Secret" [XPS 147])	12
84	EMI EL 2701531	BOULEZ CONDUCTS ZAPPA: 'THE PERFECT STRANGER'	12
84	EMI EJ2702561	FRANCESCO ZAPPA (with inner sleeve)	15
84	EMI 2402943	THING-FISH (3-LP, box set, with libretto)	20
84	EMI EMC 3500	THE MAN FROM UTOPIA	12
84	EMI EMC 3501	SHIP ARRIVING TOO LATE TO SAVE A DROWNING WITCH (with inner sleeve)	12
84	EMI FZAP1	JOE'S GARAGE ACTS 1, 2 & 3 (3-LP, box set, inner sleeves only, with libretti)	25
84	EMI E5 0021	TINSELTOWN REBELLION (2-LP, gatefold sleeve, printed with lyrics)	15
84	EMI no cat. no.	SHEIK YERBOUTI (2-LP, gatefold sleeve, printed with lyrics)	15
84	EMI no cat. no.	SHUT UP 'N' PLAY YER GUITAR (3-LP box set, with inner sleeves)	25
86	EMI EN 352	JAZZ FROM HELL	12
86	EMI EC 3507	FRANK ZAPPA MEETS THE MOTHERS OF PREVENTION (European version)	12
95	Simply Vinyl SLVP 0024	WEASELS RIPPED MY FLESH (180gm vinyl)	20
95	Simply Vinyl SLVP 0025	BURNT WEENY SANDWICH (gatefold sleeve, 180 gm vinyl)	12

ALBUMS : ZAPPA LABEL

84	Zappa Records ZAPPA 1	FREAK OUT (2-LP, gatefold sleeve, some in single sleeve £35)	18
80s	Zappa Records ZAPPA 5	LONDON SYMPHONY ORCHESTRA VOLUME II	12
88	Zappa Records ZAPPA 6	GUITAR (2-LP, gatefold sleeve)	18
88	Zappa Records ZAPPA 7	YOU CAN'T DO THAT ON STAGE ANY MORE SAMPLER (2-LP, gatefold sleeve)	15
88	Zappa Records ZAPPA 14	BROADWAY THE HARD WAY (gatefold sleeve with inner sleeve)	12
90	Zappa Records ZAPPA 30	THEM OR US (2-LP, gatefold sleeve, printed with lyrics)	15
90	Zappa Records ZAPPA 20	JOE'S GARAGE ACTS 1, 2 & 3 (3-LP, box set, original sleeves, with libretti)	22
91	Zappa Records ZAPPA 28	SHEIK YERBOUTI (2-LP, gatefold sleeve without lyrics)	15
91	Zappa Records ZAPPA 35	BURNT WEENY SANDWICH (gatefold sleeve)	12
91	Zappa Records ZAPPA 37	ZAPPA IN NEW YORK (LIVE) (2-LP, plays "Punky's Whips", listed on label, but not on sleeve)	15
91	Zappa Records ZAPPA 42	SHIP ARRIVING TOO LATE TO SAVE A DROWNING WITCH	12
92	Zappa Records ZAPPA 39	ROXY AND ELSEWHERE (2-LP, as Mothers Of Invention, gatefold lyric sleeve)	20

(see also Flo & Eddie, Jeff Simmons, Wild Man Fischer, Captain Beefheart, John Lennon, Geronimo Black)

ZAPPO
| 73 | Magnet MAG 2 | Rock And Roll Crazy/Right On! | 12 |

ZAP POW
72	Harry J HJ 6650	Lottery Spin/Lottery Spin - Version	8
73	Trojan TR 7741	This Is Reggae Music/Break Down The Barriers	7
73	Blue Mountain BM 1027	This Is Reggae Music/Break Down The Barriers	6
74	Island WIP 6181	This Is Reggae Music/Break Down The Barriers	6
76	Vulcan VUL 1010	Jungle Beat/Rock Your Bones	8
78	Island IPR 2028	Roots Man Reggae/Let's Fall In Love (12")	12
76	Vulcan VULP 004	NOW (LP)	15

LES ZARJAZ
| 85 | Creation CRE 014 | One Charming Nyte/My Baby Owns A Fallout Zone (foldover p/s, poly bag) | 8 |

(see also Tronics)

PETE ZEAR
| 80 | (no label) matrix: 22-1 | Tomorrow's World/Fast Food (stamped white label, with insert, numbered) | 10 |

(see also Ruts, Rat Scabies)

ZEBEDEE
| 71 | Decca F13144 | So Long Marianne/She Couldn't Make Gravy | 30 |

ZEE
84	Harvest HAR 5277	Confusion/Eyes Of A Gypsy (p/s)	5
84	Harvest HAR 125277	Confusion (Extended Mix)/Eyes Of A Gypsy (Dub) (12", p/s)	8
84	Harvest SHSP 2401 018	IDENTITY (LP, with inner sleeve)	12

(see also Rick Wright)

ZEITGEIST
| 80 | Enchaine ENC 1 | Shake-Rake/Sniper (p/s) | 6 |
| 82 | Jamming CREATE 4 | Stop (p/s) | 5 |

ZEN
| 68 | Philips BF 1746 | Hair/Aquarius | 20 |

ZENITH
| 86 | ZENITH 5001 | Heavy Heavy Heart (p/s) | 75 |

SI ZENTNER ORCHESTRA
| 64 | Liberty LIB 10169 | The James Bond Theme/Bond's 007 Theme | 7 |
| 63 | Liberty LBY 1164 | RHYTHM PLUS BLUES (LP) | 15 |

ZEPHYR
| 70 | Probe SPB 1006 | ZEPHYR (LP) | 60 |

(see also Tommy Bolin)

ZEPHYRS
63	Decca F 11647	What's All That About/Oriental Dream	40
64	Columbia DB 7199	I Can Tell/Sweet Little Baby	50
64	Columbia DB 7324	A Little Bit Of Soap/No Message	35
64	Columbia DB 7410	Wonder What I'm Gonna Do/Let Me Love You Baby	35
65	Columbia DB 7481	She's Lost You/There's Something About You	35
65	Columbia DB 7571	I Just Can't Take It/She Laughed	35

ZERO
| 75 | BEEB 014 | Angels Theme/Truckin' | 5 |

EARL ZERO
78	Studio 16 WE 401	Rough And Tough/PRINCE JAZZBO: Suffer Must Live (12")	30
79	Sufferers Height SUF004	Please Officer/PABLO: Moonlight City (12")	50
79	Greensleeves GRED 23	City Of The Wicked/Rightous Works (12")	40

ZERO FIVE
| 65 | Columbia DB 7751 | Dusty/Just Like A Girl | 6 |

ZERO LE CRECHE
| 84 | Flicknife FLS 029 | Last Year's Wife/Women Say (p/s) | 6 |

ZERO 7
00	Ultimate Dilemma UDR	EP VOL. 1 (12")	18
00	Ultimate Dilemma UDR 040	EP VOL. 2 (12")	18
01	Ultimate Dilemma UDRLP	SIMPLE THINGS (2-LP)	25
04	Ultimate Dilemma 5050467 0987 1 8	WHEN IT FALLS (2-LP)	25
06	Ultimate Dilemma 5015011 2857 1 4	THE GARDEN (2-LP, gatefold, inners)	30

ZERO TWENTY ONE
| 81 | UK UK 201 | Pop Song (p/s) | 100 |

ZERO ZERO
| 79 | Interference INT 00 | Chinese Boys/Coup De Ville Dawn (p/s, 1000 only) | 8 |

ZEROS
| 77 | Small Wonder SMALL 2 | Hungry/Radio Fun | 20 |
| 79 | Rok ROK XV/XVI | What's Wrong With A Pop Group/ACTION REPLAY: Decisions (die-cut co. sleeve) | 20 |

MONICA ZETTERLUND
58	Columbia DB 4246	There's No You/Don't Be That Way	15
59	Columbia SEG 8015	SWEDISH SWEET (EP)	60
58	Columbia 33CSX 20	SWEDISH SENSATION (LP, export only)	200
64	Philips BL 7647	MAKE MINE SWEDISH STYLE (LP)	100

Z'EV
| 82 | Fetish FE 13 | Wipeout!/Element L. (p/s) | 10 |
| 88 | Coercion COERCIONLP 001 | THE INVISIBLE MAN (LP) | 25 |

ZIMBO TRIO
| 68 | Page One FORS 017 | INTRODUCING THE ZIMBO TRIO (LP) | 12 |

ZIMM & DEE DEE
71   Green Door GD 4006   You've Got A Friend (actually by Winston Francis & Donna Hinds)/GROOVERS: Cheep 7
(see also Winston Francis)

TUCKER ZIMMERMAN
69   Regal Zonophone RZ 3020   The Red Wind/Moondog 25
69   Regal Zono. (S)LRZ 1010   TEN SONGS BY TUCKER ZIMMERMAN (LP) 120
72   Village Thing VTS 13   TUCKER ZIMMERMANN (LP) 70

ZION TRAIN
99   Universal Egg WWLP030   LOVE REVOLUTIONARIES (2-LP) 25

ZIOR
71   Nepentha 6129 002   Za Za Za Zilda/She's A Bad Bad Woman 25
71   Nepentha 6129 003   Cat's Eyes/I Really Do 20
71   Nepentha 6437 005   ZIOR (LP, gatefold sleeve) 250
(see also Monument, Cardboard Orchestra)

ZIPPER
74   Youngblood YB 170   Streak Up And Down/Funk 74 30

RB ZIPPER
76   Alaska ALA 2004   Cruisin With The Fonz/Superstream 6
77   Alaska ALA 2006   Come On Marriane/Lamplight Lady 8

ZIPPERS
64   Hickory 45-1252   My Sailor Boy/Pretend You're Still Mine 15

ZIPPS
79   Rip Off RIP 12   Friends/Don't Tell The Detectives (p/s) 60

ZIPS
79   Black Gold ZIPS1   Take Me Down/Don't Be Pushed Around/I'm In Love Over and Over (500 only with A4 insert & 2 stickers) 150
80   Tenement Toons TEN 01   Radioactivity/I'm Not Impressed (p/s) 25

ZIPZ
80   Voyage VOY 14   As I Pass You By/Tonight (p/s) 8

ZNR
81   Recommended RR 7   BARRICADE 3 (LP) 18

ZODIAC
68   Elektra EKL 4009   COSMIC SOUNDS (LP, also stereo EKS 74009) 45

ZODIACS
57   Oriole CB 1383   Why Don't They Understand/The Game Of Love 18
58   Oriole CB 1432   The Yum-Yum Song/Secrets 10

EMIL DEAN ZOGHBY
70   Polydor 2058 032   Won't You Join Me/Misery Lane 5

ZAC ZOLAR & ELECTRIC BANANA
84   Butt FUN 5   Take Me Home/James Marshall 5
(see also Pretty Things, Phil May, Fenmen, Electric Banana)

ZOMBIES
64   Decca F 11940   She's Not There/You Make Me Feel Good 10
64   Decca F 12004   Leave Me Be/Woman 12
65   Decca F 12072   Tell Her No/What More Can I Do 12
65   Decca F 12125   She's Coming Home/I Must Move 15
65   Decca F 12225   Whenever You're Ready/I Love You 15
65   Decca F 12296   Is This The Dream/Don't Go Away 15
66   Decca F 12322   Remember You/Just Out Of Reach 20
66   Decca F 12426   Indication/How We Were Before 25
66   Decca F 12495   Gotta Get A Hold Of Myself/The Way I Feel Inside 30
67   Decca F 12584   Goin' Out Of My Head/She Does Everything For Me..........25
68   Decca F 12798   I Love You/The Way I Feel Inside 15
67   CBS 2960   Friends Of Mine/Beechwood Park 60
67   CBS 3087   Care Of Cell 44/Maybe After He's Gone 50
68   CBS 3380   Time Of The Season/I'll Call You Mine 60
73   Epic EPC 3380   Time Of The Season/I'll Call You Mine (reissue)..........8
65   Decca DFE 8598   THE ZOMBIES (EP) 110
65   Decca LK 4679   BEGIN HERE (LP) 500
65   RCA RD 7791   BUNNY LAKE IS MISSING (LP, soundtrack) 65
68   CBS BPG 63280   ODESSEY AND ORACLE (LP, mono) 700
68   CBS SBPG 63280   ODESSEY AND ORACLE (LP, stereo) 500
70   Decca SPA 95   THE WORLD OF THE ZOMBIES (LP) 18
73   Epic EPC 65728   TIME OF THE ZOMBIES (2-LP) 25
(see also Unit Four Plus Two, Argent, Neil MacArthur, Colin Blunstone)

ZONES
78   Zoom ZUM 4   Stuck With You/No Angels (p/s) 5
78   Arista ARTIST 205   Sign Of The Times/Away From It All (p/s).........5
79   Arista SPART 1095   UNDER INFLUENCE (LP) 12
(see also PVC 2)

ZOO
70   Major Minor SMLP 74   ZOO (LP) 30
71   Barclay 521172   ZOO (LP) 20

ZOO BOUTIQUE
82   Lightbeat LIGHT 006   Forgive And Forget/Happy Families (p/s, clear vinyl) 6

ZOOKIE
77   DJM DJS 10796   Judie Judie Hold On/I Couldn't Be You 8
78   DJM DJS 10866   Bubbles/Don't Rock Me 8
(see also Judie Tzuke, Tzuke & Paxo)

ZOOT ALORS
79	Decca FR 13874	Send Me A Postcard/It's A Crime	40

ZORN
01	City Centre Offices BLOCK 11	Eckerman (plain sleeve with inserts, 1000 only)	6

ZORRO
79	Bridgehouse BHEP 1	'Arrods Don't Sell 'Em/Soldier Boy/Starflight (with p/s)	30
79	Bridgehouse BHEP 1	'Arrods Don't Sell 'Em/Soldier Boy/Starflight	10

ZORRO FIVE
70	Decca F 23042	Reggae Shhh!/Reggae Meadowlands	5

ZOSKIA
84	All The Madmen MAD 8	Rape/Thank You (p/s)	8
85	Temple TOPY 005	Be Like Me (12", p/s, transparent vinyl)	12
86	All The Madmen MADT 8	Rape/Black Action (12", p/s)	8

ZOSKIA MEETS SUGARDOG
84	Temple TOPYS 021	J.G. /`That's Heavy Baby	10

ZOUNDS
81	Crass 4219844/3	Can't Cheat Karma/War/Subvert (gatefold paper p/s, with poster)	15
81	Rough Trade RT 069	Demystification/Great White Hunter (p/s)	10
82	Rough Trade RT 094	Dancing/True Love (p/s)	8
82	Not So Brave NSB 001	LA VACHE QUI RIT (EP, with poster)	12
82	Rough Trade RT 098	More Trouble Coming Every Day/Knife (p/s)	8
84	Rough Trade ROUGH 31	THE CURSE OF ZOUNDS (LP, inner)	20

ZOVIET-FRANCE
82	Red Rhino RED 12	ZOVIET-FRANCE (12" EP, printed hessian sleeve)	60
83	Red Rhino RED 23	NORSCHE (LP)	35
84	Red Rhino RED 40	MOHNOMISCHE (LP)	35
84	Red Rhino REDLP 45	ELSTRE (LP)	35

ZOWLAS
67	Amusicon SLE 12	Honest I Do/Gonna Love My Baby	12

ZUIDERZEE
66	CBS 202062	(You're My) Soul And Inspiration/Please Don't Call Me	10
66	CBS 202235	Peace Of Mind/Provocative Child	10

TAPPA ZUKIE
78	Music Of The Most High MER 602	Viego/Archie The Rednose (p/s)	8
73	Count Shelly CSLP 04	MAN A WARRIOR (LP)	50
75	Locks LOX 8	Judge I O' Lord/LLOYDIE SLIM AND KING TUBBY: State Dub	10
75	Attack ATT 8110	Natty Dread Don't Cry (as Topper Zukie)/TOMMY McCOOK : The Meducia	8
77	New Star DNEW 1	What's Yours/Make Faith (12")	25
77	Achilles ACHILLES 54	Liberation Struggle/Double Struggle	10
76	Stars (No. Cat. No.)	TAPPA ZUKIE IN DUB (LP)	100
76	KLIK 9022	M.P.L.A. (LP)	12
79	Virgin Frontline FL 1029	TAPPA ZUKIE IN DUB (LP)	20
79	Virgin Frontline FL 1032	TAPPER ROOTZ (LP)	12
95	Blood & Fire BAFLP 008	TAPPA ZUKIE IN DUB (LP, reissue)	12

ZULU
77	Big Bear BB9	Red Red Libanon/Okavanga Swamp	15

ZUM ZEAUX
70s	Black Pig PUG1	WOLF AT THE DOOR (LP)	40

ZUTONS
02	Deltasonic DKTCD 007	Devil's Deal/Six Foot Man/Zutonkhamuun (CD)	20

ZYGOAT
74	Polydor 2058 124	Catching A Thief/Letitia's Song	5
74	Polydor 2383 270	ELECTROPHON (LP)	20

ZZ
88	Kent 6T3	PEGGY WOODS: Love Is Gonna Get You/ZZ: You Just Cheat And Lie	20

ZZEBRA
74	Polydor 2058 446	Zardoz/Amusofi	20
75	Polydor 2058 579	Mr. J/Put The Light On Me	6
74	Polydor 2383 296	ZZEBRA (LP)	15
75	Polydor 2383 326	PANIC (LP, with insert)	18

(see also John McCoy, Gillan)

ZZ TOP
72	London HLU 10376	Francene/Down Brownie	15
74	London HLU 10458	Beer Drinkers And Hell Raisers/La Grange	12
75	London HLU 10475	La Grange/Just Got Paid	10
75	London HLU 10495	Tush/Blue Jean Blues	10
76	London HLU 10538	It's Only Love/Asleep In The Desert	8
77	London HLU 10547	Arrested For Driving While Blind/Neighbour, Neighbour	8
77	London HLU 10547	Arrested For Driving While Blind/Neighbour, Neighbour (mispressing, B-side plays Ray Charles' "I Can See Clearly Now")	12
79	Warner Bros K 17647	Cheap Sunglasses/Esther Be The One	5
80	Warner Bros K 17576	I Thank You/A Fool For Your Stockings (p/s)	7
83	Warner Bros W 9693T	Gimme All Your Lovin'/If I Could Only Flag Her Down (car-shaped picture disc)	8
85	Warner Bros W 2001F	Sleeping Bag/Party On The Patio//Sharp Dressed Man/I Got The Fix (p/s, sealed, stickered double pack)	10
85	Warner Bros W 2001P	Sleeping Bag/Party On The Patio ('sphinx'-shaped picture disc)	8
85	Warner Bros W 2001P	Sleeping Bag/Party On The Patio (shaped pic-disc, part 1 of interlocking set)	12
86	Warner Bros W 2002BP	Stages/Hi-Fi Mama (shaped pic-disc, part 2 of interlocking set)	8
86	Warner Bros W 2003FP	Rough Boy/Delirious (shaped pic-disc, part 3 of interlocking set, shrinkwrapped with bonus 12")	30
86	Warner Bros W 2003FP	Rough Boy/Delirious (shaped pic-disc, part 3 of interlocking set)	20
71	London PS 584	ZZ TOP (LP, with inner sleeve)	30

72	London SH-U 8433	RIO GRANDE MUD (LP, original issue)	25
73	London SH-U 8459	TRES HOMBRES (LP, original issue)	25
75	London SH-U 8482	FANDANGO! (LP, original issue)	18
76	London LDU 1	TEJAS (LP, original foldout sleeve)	12
83	Warner Bros W 3774	ELIMINATOR (LP, with bonus stickered p/s 12" "Legs [Metal Mix]")	15
83	Warner Bros W3774P	ELIMINATOR (LP, picture disc)	15

Various Artists

VARIOUS ARTISTS EPs 50s/60s
(alphabetical by title)

A

56	Decca F 10752	ALL STAR HIT PARADE (Dickie Valentine/Joan Regan/Winifred Atwell/ Dave King/Lita Roza/David Whitfield)	10
57	Decca F 10915	ALL STAR HIT PARADE No. 2 (Johnston Bros/Bill Cotton/Jimmy Young/ Max Bygraves/Beverley Sisters/Tommy Steele)	10
63	Pye NEP 24168	ALL STAR HIT PARADE (Kenny Ball/Chris Barber Jazz Band/Joe Brown/ Lonnie Donegan Skiffle Group/Mary Wynter)	10
64	Pye NEP 24172	ALL STAR HIT PARADE VOL. 2 (Joe Brown/Petula Clark/Julie Grant/ Benny Hill/Mark Wynter)	10
64	Decca DFE 8571	AMERICAN COUNTRY JUBILEE NO. 1 (Ray Phillips/Audrey Inman/ Marvin McCullough/Billy Parker)	10
62	MGM MGMEP 768	A VERY PRIVATE AFFAIR (includes Brigitte Bardot: Sidonie)	80

B

63	Concert Hall BPC 712	BEAT TIME (Timebeats/Charlie Young/Heartbeats)	15
63	Concert Hall BPC 717	THE BIG BEAT (Bob Miller & Millermen/Al Saxon/Roy Young/Duffy Power)	20
66	Fontana TF 17469	THE BIG FOUR (Dave Dee Dozy Beaky Mick & Tich/Spencer Davis Group/ Mindbenders/Pretty Things)	10
56	Philips BBE 12021	THE BIG FOUR (Roy Hamilton/Frankie Laine/Mitch Miller Orchestra/ Something Smith & Redheads)	10
56	Philips BBE 12040	THE BIG FOUR NO. 2 (Mindy Carson/Don Cherry/Frankie Laine/Jo Stafford)	10
56	Philips BBE 12088	THE BIG FOUR NO. 3 (Shirley Bassey/Ronnie Carroll/David Hughes/ Anne Shelton)	10
57	Philips BBE 12114	THE BIG FOUR NO. 5 (Shirley Bassey/Ronnie Carroll/Anne Shelton/ Frankie Vaughan)	10
57	Philips BBE 12139	THE BIG FOUR NO. 6 (Shirley Bassey/Ronnie Carroll/Kaye Sisters/ Frankie Vaughan)	10
57	Philips BBE 12158	THE BIG FOUR NO. 8 (Shirley Bassey/Robert Earl/Kaye Sisters/Steve Martin)	10
58	Philips BBE 12165	THE BIG FOUR NO. 9 (Robert Earl/Anne Shelton/Joyce Shock/ Frankie Vaughan & Kaye Sisters)	10
58	Philips BBE 12190	THE BIG FOUR NO. 10 (Jimmy Lloyd/Robert Earl/Kaye Sisters/Anne Shelton)	10
59	Philips BBE 12288	THE BIG FOUR NO. 11 (Shirley Bassey/Kaye Sisters/Frankie Vaughan/ Marty Wilde)	10
59	Philips BBE 12336	THE BIG FOUR NO. 12 (Frankie Laine/G. Mitchell/Johnnie Ray/Leslie Uggams)	10
66	Philips BBE 12593	THE BIG FOUR (Roger Miller/Four Seasons/Dusty Springfield/Walker Bros)	10
64	Fontana TFE 18010	BLOWIN' IN THE WIND (withdrawn; Bob Dylan/Joan Baez/Pete Seeger)	100
59	Fontana TFE 17081	THE BLUES (Danny Barker/Jimmy Giuffre/Jo Jones/Pee Wee Russell)	10
61	Pieces Of 8 PEP 605	THE BLUES (Big Bill Broonzy/Josh White)	10
64	Pye Intl. NEP 44029	THE BLUES VOL. 1 PT. 1 (John Lee Hooker/Muddy Waters/Sonny Boy Williamson/Jimmy Witherspoon)	35
64	Pye Intl. NEP 44035	THE BLUES VOL. 1 PT. 2 (Howling Wolf/Buddy Guy/Little Walter/Muddy Waters)	25
66	Chess CRE 6011	THE BLUES VOL. 2 PT. 1 (Otis Rush/Chuck Berry/John Lee Hooker/ Little Walter)	25
64	Pye Intl. NEP 44038	BLUES FESTIVAL (Sugar Pie De Santo/Willie Dixon/Sonny Boy Williamson/ Howlin' Wolf)	30
63	Columbia SEG 8226	BLUES ON PARADE NO. 1 (Jimmy Cotton/Brownie McGhee/ Roosevelt Sykes/Sonny Terry)	25
56	HMV 7EG 8178	THE BLUES THEY SANG (Lizzie Miles/Billy Young & Jelly Roll Morton)	20
61	Pye NEP 24142	BYE BYE BIRDIE (Brook Brothers/Patti Brook/Joe Brown/Jimmy Justice/ Kids/Viscounts)	8
61	RCA RCX 205	BREAKFAST AT TIFFANY'S (Henry Mancini)	18
61	Philips BBE 12472	BYE BYE BIRDIE NO. 1 (original cast; Marty Wilde et al.; stereo SBBE 9064)	8
61	Philips BBE 12473	BYE BYE BIRDIE NO. 2 (original cast; Marty Wilde et al.; stereo SBBE 9065)	8
61	Philips BBE 12474	BYE BYE BIRDIE NO. 3 (original cast; Marty Wilde et al.; stereo SBBE 9066)	8
61	Philips BBE 12475	BYE BYE BIRDIE NO. 4 (original cast; Marty Wilde et al.; stereo SBBE 9067 = £10)	8
63	Fontana TFL 6037	BLUES AT NEWPORT (LP)	20

C

63	Cameo Parkway CPE 552	CAMEO BIG FOUR (Bobby Rydell/Chubby Checker/Dovells/Orlons)	20
60	Top Rank JKP 2055	COUNTRY AND WESTERN EXPRESS VOL. 1 (Bill Alex Dixie Drifters/ Jenny Herrill/Elmer Snodgrass/Musical Pioneers)	10
60	Top Rank JKP 2056	COUNTRY AND WESTERN EXPRESS VOL. 2 (Jack Chambers & Rainbow Boys/Ralph Hodge & Hodges Brothers Band)	10
60	Top Rank JKP 2063	COUNTRY AND WESTERN EXPRESS VOL. 4 (Claude Gray/Eddie Noack)	15
60	Top Rank JKP 2065	COUNTRY AND WESTERN EXPRESS VOL. 6 (Tony Douglas/James O'Gwynn)	15
63	CBS AGG 20033	COUNTRY AND WESTERN HITS VOL. 1 (Carl Butler/Lester Flatt & Earl Scruggs/Lefty Frizzell/Stonewall Jackson/Ray Price)	8
64	CBS AGG 20041	COUNTRY AND WESTERN HITS VOL. 2 (Johnny Cash/Lester Flatt & Earl Scruggs/Lefty Frizzell/Marty Robbins)	10
65	Hickory LPE 1505	COUNTRY AND WESTERN SHOWCASE VOL. 2 (Roy Acuff/Wilma Lee/ Stoney Cooper)	8
57	Philips BBE 12149	COUNTRY AND WESTERN SPECTACULAR (George Morgan/Ray Price/ Mel Tillis/Marty Robbins)	8
59	Mercury ZEP 10038	COUNTRY AND WESTERN TRAIL BLAZERS NO. 1 (Connie Hall/ James O'Gwynn/Jimmy Skinner/Charlie Walker)	8
60	Mercury ZEP 10052	COUNTRY AND WESTERN TRAIL BLAZERS NO. 2 (Bill Clifton & Dixie Mountain Boys/George Jones)	8
60	Mercury ZEP 10080	COUNTRY AND WESTERN TRAIL BLAZERS NO. 3 (James O'Gwynn/ Connie Hall)	8
60s	Heritage 105	THE COUNTRY BLUES (99 only)	80
58	RCA RCX 107	COUNTRY GUITAR VOL. 1 (Bonnie, Jim Edward & Maxine Brown/ Hank Locklin/Jim Reeves/Hank Snow)	8
58	RCA RCX 110	COUNTRY GUITAR VOL. 2 (Skeeter Davis/Don Gibson/Jim Reeves/Hank Snow)	10

59	RCA RCX 127	COUNTRY GUITAR VOL. 5 (Eddy Arnold/Browns/Skeeter Davis/ Johnny & Jack/Hank Snow/Porter Wagoner)	8
59	RCA RCX 141	COUNTRY GUITAR VOL. 6 (Hank Locklin/Eddy Arnold/Browns/Hank Snow/ Porter Wagoner/Johnny & Jack)	8
59	RCA RCX 147	COUNTRY GUITAR VOL. 8 (Browns/Don Gibson/Hawkshaw Hawkins/ Johnny & Jack/Jim Reeves)	8
59	RCA RCX 159	COUNTRY GUITAR VOL. 9 (Hank Locklin/Gail Davis/Skeeter Davis/Jimmy Driftwood/Jim Reeves)	10
59	RCA RCX 176	COUNTRY GUITAR VOL. 10 (Hank Locklin/Skeeter Davis/Hawkshaw Hawkins/Johnny & Jack/Sons Of The Pioneers/Hank Snow)	10
59	RCA RCX 177	COUNTRY GUITAR VOL. 11 (Browns/Eddy Arnold/Jack Clement/Hank Snow)	10
60	RCA RCX 185	COUNTRY GUITAR VOL. 12 (Eddy Arnold/Hawkshaw Hawkins/Jim Reeves/ Hank Snow/Porter Wagoner)	8
62	RCA RCX 7105	COUNTRY GUITAR VOL. 16 (Bill Monroe & Blue Grass Boys/Monroe Bros)	10

D

60s	XX MIN 706	DARK MUDDY BOTTOM (Jimmy Slim/Good Jelly Bess/Lightning Leon/ Little Red Walters/Willie B.)	20
50s	Poydras 102	DEPRESSION BLUES	25
63	Decca DFE 8520	DISCS-A-GO GO (Karl Denver/Billy Fury/Jet Harris/Vernons Girls)	50
60s	Jan & Dil JR 450	DOWN HOME BLUES - SIXTIES STYLE (Lightning Leon/Jerry McCain/ Little Red Walters)	30
60s	XX MIN 709	DOWNHOME HARP (Kid Thomas/Eddie Hope/Jerry McCain)	15
59	Fontana TFE 17146	DRUMBEAT (Lana Sisters/Adam Faith/Bob Miller & Millermen/ Sylvia Sands/Roy Young)	40

E

65	Edinburgh S.C. ESC 02	EDINBURGH STUDENTS CHARITIES APPEAL (33rpm, die-cut paper p/s; Athenians/Avengers/Ray & Archie Fisher/Lynn & Kathy)	50
66	Edinburgh S.C. ESC 03	EDINBURGH STUDENTS CHARITIES APPEAL (33rpm, Athenians/Gear System/Old Bailey's Jazz Advocates)	60
67	Philips P 160E	EXQUISITE FORM (freebie; Dave Dee, Dozy, Beaky, Mick & Tich/Herd/ Walker Brothers/Dusty Springfield)	12

F

59	Jazz Collector JEL 12	THE FEMALE BLUES VOL. 1 (Ida Cox/Ma Rainey)	10
60	Jazz Collector JEL 14	THE FEMALE BLUES VOL. 2 (Bertha Henderson/Rosa Henderson)	10
64	Jazz Collector JEL 22	THE FEMALE BLUES VOL. 3 (Ma Rainey/Trixie Smith)	10
64	Pye Intl. NEP 44030	FESTIVAL OF THE BLUES NO. 1 (Willie Dixon/Buddy Guy/Muddy Waters/ Sonny Boy Williamson)	20
58	Parlophone GEP 8694	FLUTE COCKTAIL (Bill Doggett/Johnny Pate Quartet)	10
63	Ember EMB EP 4530	FOOL BRITANNIA (Peter Sellers/Dan Massey/Anthony Newley/Joan Collins/ Maureen Lipton)	12
57	Philips BBE 12140	FOUR GREAT MOVIE THEMES (Vic Damone/Hi-Lo's/Frankie Laine/Jerry Vale)	12
63	Decca DFE 8538	FROM A LONDON HOOTENANNY (Davy Graham/Thamesiders)	25

G

59	MGM MGM-EP 703	GIRLS AND MORE GIRLS (June Allyson/Ava Gardner/Judy Garland/ Kathryn Grayson)	10
67	Down with the Game 202	GOD DON'T LIKE IT (99 only)	40
67	Down with the Game 203	GOD DON'T LIKE IT VOLUME 2 (99 only)	40
60s	XX MIN 707	GOING TO CALIFORNIA (Little Sonny Willis/Eddie Williams)	15
59	Philips BBE 12318	GREAT COUNTRY AND WESTERN HITS (Johnny Cash/Johnny Horton/ Stonewall Jackson/Carl Smith)	10
66	Pye Intl. NEP 45054	THE GREATEST ON STAGE (Maxine Brown/Chuck Jackson/Shirelles/ Dionne Warwick)	25
63	London RE-U 1393	GROUP OF GOODIES (Marcie Blane/Kokomo/Bill Black's Combo/ Ernie Maresca)	50
59	Mercury ZEP 10010	GROUPS GALORE (Del Vikings/Mark IV/Diamonds/Hi-Liters)	150

H

64	Hickory LPE 1500	HICKORY SHOWCASE VOL. 1 (Roy Acuff/Wilma Lee/Stoney Cooper)	10
57	Capitol EAP1 852	HIT CALYPSOS (Andrews Sisters/Nat 'King' Cole/Stan Kenton/ Lord Flea Calypsonians)	10
65	Pye NEP 24213	THE HITMAKERS NO. 1 (Searchers/Kenny Ball Jazzmen/Dixie Cups/ Dionne Warwick)	15
65	Pye NEP 24214	THE HITMAKERS NO. 2 (Honeycombs/Tony Jackson/Kinks/Shangri-La's)	18
65	Pye NEP 24215	THE HITMAKERS NO. 3 (Chuck Berry/Julie Grant/Rockin' Berries/ Sandie Shaw)	15
66	Pye NEP 24241	THE HITMAKERS VOL. 1 (Ivy League/Tommy Quickly/Sandie Shaw/ Sounds Orchestral)	10
66	Pye NEP 24242	THE HITMAKERS VOL. 2 (Chuck Berry/Kinks/Sue Thompson/Shangri-La's)	30
66	Pye NEP 24243	THE HITMAKERS VOL. 3 (Kinks/Lancastrians/Rockin' Berries/Searchers)	12
66	Piccadilly NEP 34100	THE HITMAKERS (Petula Clark/Kenny Ball/Anita Harris/Honeycombs)	10
66	Pye Intl. NEP 44065	HITMAKERS INTERNATIONAL (Fontella Bass/James Brown/Petula Clark/ Lovin' Spoonful)	25
55	Mercury MEP 9003	HIT PARADE VOL. 1 (Georgia Gibbs/Platters/Crew Cuts/Patti Page)	15
56	Mercury MEP 9510	HIT PARADE VOL. 2 (Sarah Vaughan/Ralph Marterie/Patti Page/Crew Cuts)	15
57	Brunswick OE 9340	HIT PARADE (Rex Allen/Peggy Lee/Jeri Southern/Victor Young Orchestra)	10
58	Brunswick OE 9450	HIT PARADE NO. 2 (Carmen Cavallaro/Four Aces/Grandpa Jones/ Jack Pleis & His Orchestra)	10
65	Decca DFE 8648	HITS VOL. 1 (Chris Andrews/Fortunes/Hedgehoppers Anonymous/ Jonathan King)	10
65	Decca DFE 8649	HITS VOL. 2 (Lulu/Chris Andrews/Marianne Faithfull/Fortunes)	10
65	Decca DFE 8653	HITS VOL. 3 (Pinkerton's Assorted Colours/St. Louis Union/Mexicans/ Paul & Barry Ryan)	10
66	Decca DFE 8662	HITS VOL. 4 (Dave Berry/Val Doonican/Joy Marshall/Crispian St. Peters)	10
66	Decca DFE 8663	HITS VOL. 5 (Animals/Los Bravos/Alan Price Set/Small Faces)	10
66	Decca DFE 8667	HITS VOL. 6 (Jonathan King/Lulu/Alan Price Set/Small Faces)	10
67	Decca DFE 8675	HITS VOL. 7 (Ronnie Aldrich/Val Doonican/Bachelors/Small Faces)	10
62	Mercury ZEP 10133	HITSVILLE! (Brook Benton/Crew Cuts/Phil Philips/Diamonds)	30
59	Coral FEP 2034	HITSVILLE VOL. 1 (Buddy Holly/McGuire Sisters/Betty Madigan/Billy Williams)	60
59	Coral FEP 2035	HITSVILLE VOL. 2 (Lennon Sisters/Art Lund/Teresa Brewer/Jackie Wilson)	50
65	Tamla Motown TME 2001	HITSVILLE U.S.A. NO. 1 (Marvin Gaye/Brenda Holloway/Carolyn Crawford/ Eddie Holland)	110
66	Post War Blues 100	HOBOS AND DRIFTERS	50

I

65	Chess CRE 6010	IN CROWD (Radiants/Ramsey Lewis Trio/Little Milton/Billy Stewart)	30
56	Mercury MEP 9503	ITEMS FROM GUYS AND DOLLS (Richard Hayes/Kitty Kallen/Frankie Laine/ David Le Winter)	12
62	Pye Jazz NJE 1083	IT'S TRAD, DAD - FILM SOUNDTRACK (Bob Wallis/Kenny Ball & His Jazzmen)	12

J

| 64 | Columbia SEG 8337 | JUST FOR YOU (Peter & Gordon/Freddie & Dreamers)......................................15 |

K

63	Lyntone LYN 347/348	KEELE RAG RECORD (flexidisc; Rhythm Unlimited & Halettes/Keele Quintet)......................18
64	Lyntone LYN 508/509	KEELE RAG RECORD NO. 2 (flexidisc; Escorts/Lance Harvey & Kingpins/ Keele Row; some in die-cut sleeve) 35
65	Lyntone LYN 765/766	KEELE RAG RECORD (flexidisc; Bob Wilson/Changing Times/ Lance Harvey & Kingpins/Incas) 40
61	RCA Victor RCX 203	KINGS OF THE BLUES VOL. 2 (Jazz Gillum/Big Maceo/Washboard Sam/ Sonny Boy Williamson).................20
61	RCA Victor RCX 204	KINGS OF THE BLUES VOL. 3 (Arthur Big Boy Crudup/Furry Lewis/ Poor Joe Williams).........25
59	Top Rank 45-TR 5004	KING SIZE (maxi-single; Craig Douglas/Sheila Buxton/Bert Weedon) 10
60	Warner Bros WEP 6010	KOOKIE STARS OF SEVENTY SEVEN SUNSET STRIP (Joannie Sommers/Eddie Byrne/Connie Stevens).................10
66	Holyground HG 111	THE LAST THING ON MY MIND (EP, 99 copies only) 90
59	Top Rank JKR 8008	LET'S GO NO. 1 (Jimmy Lee/Johnny Hines/Treetoppers) 35
59	Top Rank JKR 8012	LET'S GO NO. 2 (Johnny Hines/Billy Mack/Victors/Ted & Ray) 35
60	Philips BBE 12414/	LET'S MAKE LOVE - FILM SOUNDTRACK (Yves Montand/Marilyn Monroe/ Frankie Vaughan; stereo)......................40
63	Embassy WEP 1104	LIVERPOOL BEAT (Typhoons/Mike Redway/Ray Pilgrim/Bobby Stevens) 10
57	London RE-D 1075	LONDON HIT PARADE NO. 1 (Tab Hunter/Hilltoppers/Pat Boone/Fontane Sisters).........25
57	London RE-P 1096	LONDON HIT PARADE NO. 2 (Fats Domino/Slim Whitman/Ken Copeland/ Roy Brown) .. 100
58	London RE-D 1097	LONDON HIT PARADE NO. 3 (Pat Boone/Gale Storm/Tab Hunter/Jim Lowe) 25
58	London RE-D 1130	LONDON HIT PARADE NO. 4 (Pat Boone/Nick Todd/ Bonnie Guitar/Hilltoppers) 25
58	London RE-D 1136	LONDON TOPPERS NO. 2 (export issue; Pat Boone/Nick Todd/Tab Hunter/ Jim Lowe).........25
58	London RE-P 1137	LONDON TOPPERS NO. 3 (export issue; Slim Whitman/Fats Domino/ Ricky Nelson/Ernie Freeman) 60
58	London RE-D 1145	LONDON HIT PARADE NO. 5 (Pat Boone/Fontane Sisters/Frank De Rosa) 20

M

59	Jazz Collector JEL 2	THE MALE BLUES VOL. 1 (Georgia Slim/Walter Roland) 25
59	Jazz Collector JEL 4	THE MALE BLUES VOL. 3 (Blind Blake/Ramblin' Thomas) 25
59	Jazz Collector JEL 5	THE MALE BLUES VOL. 4 (Tall Tom/Pinewood Tom) 25
59	Jazz Collector JEL 8	THE MALE BLUES VOL. 5 (Blind Lemon Jefferson/Buddy Boy Hawkins) 25
60	Jazz Collector JEL 10	THE MALE BLUES VOL. 6 (Hound Head Henry/Frankie Jaxon) 25
60	Jazz Collector JEL 13	THE MALE BLUES VOL. 7 (Blind Lemon Jefferson/Ed Bell) 25
61	Jazz Collector JEL 24	THE MALE BLUES VOL. 8 (Blind Lemon Jefferson/Leadbelly) 25
67	Piccadilly NEP 34100	MAXWELL HOUSE PRESENTS HITMAKERS (Kenny Ball/Petula Clark/Honeycombs/Anita Harris).................10
57	Decca DFE 6408	MERRY CHRISTMAS (Dave King/Mantovani Orchestra/Dickie Valentine/ David Whitfield) .. 10
60	MGM MGM-EP 749	MGM EVERGREENS (Billy Eckstine/Tommy Edwards/Lennie Hayton/ Sam 'The Man' Taylor & Catmen) 10
69	Middle Earth MDE 201	MIDDLE EARTH SAMPLER (WRITING ON THE WALL: Aries/WOODEN O: Overture/ ARCADIUM: Poor Lady) (promo only, 33rpm, no p/s) 80
65	RCA RCX 7159	MONTH'S BEST FROM THE COUNTRY AND WEST (Eddy Arnold/Bobby Bare/George Hamilton IV/Connie Smith).................10
64	RCA RCX 7162	MONTH'S BEST FROM THE COUNTRY AND WEST VOL. 2 (Skeeter Davis/Bobby Bare/Don Gibson/Jim Reeves/Hank Snow) 10
64	RCA RCX 7171	MONTH'S BEST FROM THE COUNTRY AND WEST VOL. 3 (Eddy Arnold/Archie Campbell/Porter Wagoner/Dottie West) 10
65	RCA RCX 7172	MONTH'S BEST FROM THE COUNTRY AND WEST VOL. 4 (Bobby Bare/Jim Edward Brown/Willie Nelson/Connie Smith) 10
65	RCA RCX 7178	MONTH'S BEST FROM THE COUNTRY AND WEST VOL. 5 (Bobby Bare/Norma Jean/Porter Wagoner/Connie Smith) 10
65	RCA RCX 7181	MONTH'S BEST FROM THE COUNTRY AND WEST VOL. 6 (Don Gibson/ Bobby Bare/Carl Belew/George Hamilton IV/Hank Locklin/Dottie West) 10
67	RCA RCX 7186	MONTH'S BEST FROM THE COUNTRY AND WEST VOL. 7 (Waylon Jennings/Stu Phillips/Connie Smith/Dottie West) 10
60s	Jan & Dil TR 451	MORE DOWN HOME BLUES (Good Jelly Boss/Juke Boy Bonner/ Papa Lightfoot/Snooky Prior) 30
64	Stateside SE 1021	MOVIE MUSIC (John Barry/Artie Butler/Eddie Heywood/Bill Ramal Combo)......................0

N

56	Vogue EPV 1106	NEGRO SPIRITUALS (Original Five Blind Boys/Sensational Nightingales) 18
64	Vocalion EPVP 1271	NEGRO SPIRITUALS (Dixie Hummingbirds/Sensational Nightingales)......................18
64	Vocalion EPVP 1276	NEGRO SPIRITUALS (Five Blind Boys/Spirits Of Memphis) 18
66	Tamla Motown TME 2014	NEW FACES FROM HITSVILLE (Jimmy Ruffin/Chris Clark & Lewis Sisters/ Tammi Terrell/Monitors).................350
57	Pye NEP 24052	NIXA HIT PARADE NO. 1 (Gary Miller/Pet Clark/Lonnie Donegan/John Frazer) 15
58	Pye NEP 24064	NIXA HIT PARADE NO. 2 (Pearl Carr & Teddy Johnson/Petula Clark/ Lonnie Donegan Skiffle Group/Colin Hicks & Cabin Boys) 20
58	Pye NEP 24071	NIXA HIT PARADE NO. 3 (Marion Ryan/Gary Miller/Lonnie Donegan/ Edmund Hockridge) .10
58	Pye NEP 24078	NIXA HIT PARADE NO. 4 (Marion Ryan/Pet Clark/Joe Henderson/Gary Miller) 10
58	Pye NEP 24082	NIXA HIT PARADE NO. 5 (Petula Clark/Lonnie Donegan Skiffle Group/ Marion Ryan/Bill Shepherd Orchestra) 10
58	Pye NEP 24090	NIXA HIT PARADE NO. 6 (Lita Roza/Petula Clark/Lonnie Donegan Skiffle Group/Joe Henderson) 10
59	Pye NEP 24100	NIXA HIT PARADE NO. 7 (Lita Roza/Petula Clark/Lonnie Donegan Skiffle Group/Edmund Hockridge) 10

O

65	Columbia SEG 8413	ON THE SCENE (Downliners Sect/Animals/Cherokees/Cheynes/ Georgie Fame/ Yardbirds) 150
63	MGM MGM-EP 787	ORIGINAL HITS (Tommy Edwards/Johnny Ferguson/Jimmy Jones/ Conway Twitty) 35
63	London RE-K 1390	THE ORIGINAL HITS (Drifters/Ritchie Barrett/Coasters/Ben E. King) 55
65	Atlantic AET 6006	ORIGINAL HITS VOL. 2 (Barbara Lewis/Coasters/Solomon Burke/Drifters) 50
62	Ember EMB 4522	ORIGINAL RHYTHM AND BLUES HITS (Jesse Belvin/Ray Charles/ Linda Hayes/Jimmy McCracklin/Johnny Moore Blazers) 75
55	Pye Jazz NJE 1043	ORIGINS OF SKIFFLE (Isla Cameron/Guy Carawan/Peggy Seeger) 20

P

58	Pye NSEP 85000	POPS GO STEREO (Marion Ryan/Tony Osborne Orch./Bill Shepherd Orch.)	20
70	Harvest SHSS 1	PICNIC (LP)	35
91	Jumpin' & Pumpin' 12TOT 14	PULSE TWO (Future Sound Of London, Smart Systems Indo Tribe, 12" p/s)	8
91	Jumpin' & Pumpin' 12 TOT 16	PULSE THREE (Smart Sytems, Indo Tribe, Tage, 12", p/s)	12

R

67	Action ACT 002 EP	RAG GOES MAD AT THE MOJO (33rpm: Joe Cocker's Blues Band/ Tangerine Ayr Band/Pitiful Souls/Delroy Good Good Band)	50
56	Vogue EPV 1113	RHYTHM AND BLUES (Dominoes/Swallows)	350
60s	Range JRE 7002	RHYTHM AND BLUES (Sticks Herman/Tim Whitsett)	15
60s	Range JRE 7006	RHYTHM AND BLUES (Harry Lewis/Tommy Wills)	15
63	Stateside SE 1008	RHYTHM AND BLUES (Jimmy Reed/John Lee Hooker)	40
64	Stateside SE 1009	R&B CHARTMAKERS (Martha/Vandellas/Miracles/Marvin Gaye/Marvelettes)	100
64	Stateside SE 1018	R&B CHARTMAKERS NO. 2 (Miracles/Kim Weston/Supremes/Marvelettes)	125
64	Stateside SE 1022	R&B CHARTMAKERS NO. 3 (Marvin Gaye/Darnells/Eddie Holland/ Martha & Vandellas)	125
64	Stateside SE 1025	R&B CHARTMAKERS NO. 4 (Supremes/Eddie Holland/Temptations/ Contours)	120
60	Vogue EPV 1198	RHYTHM AND BLUES CONCERT (Helen Humes/Jimmy Witherspoon)	80
64	Pye Intl. NEP 44021	RHYTHM AND BLUES SHOWCASE VOL. 1 (Don & Bob/Dale Hawkins/ Clarence Henry/Larry Williams)	30
64	Pye Intl. NEP 44022	RHYTHM AND BLUES SHOWCASE VOL. 2 (Jimmy McCracklin/ Muddy Waters/Little Walter/Howlin' Wolf)	30
57	Vogue VE 170111	ROCK AND ROLL (Mister Google Eyes August/Louis Jones Rock & Roll Band/Walter Price Rock & Roll Band/Clarence Gatemouth Brown)	170
62	Capitol EAP1 20197	ROUND-UP (Tommy Collins/Farmer Boys/Ferlin Husky/Texas Bill Strength)	15
60	Top Rank JKP 2060	RUSHING FOR PERCUSSION (Preston Epps/Sandy Nelson)	20

S

60s	S.A.U.C.C. PR 5462	ST. ANDREWS UNIVERSITY CHARITIES CAMPAIGN (20th Century Sounds/ Steve Hall & Roosters/Black Ring; no p/s)	35
64	Lyntone LYN 738/739	SHEFFIELD UNIVERSITY RAG RECORD (flexidisc; Vantennas/Dave Allen Band/ Addy Street Five/Los Caribos; die-cut sleeve)	40
55	Columbia SEG 7528	SHOUT FOR JOY (Pete Johnson/Albert Ammons/Meade Lux Lewis)	30
63	London RE-P 1403	SINGING THE BLUES (Ernie K-Doe/Showmen/Jesse Hill/Chris Kenner)	100
58	Decca DFE 6485	SIX FIVE SPECIAL (Jackie Dennis/Joan Regan/Diane Todd/Dickie Valentine)	40
66	Lyntone LYN 995	THE SOUND OF THE STARS (flexidisc with Disc And Music Echo; with/without mag & envelope/stamp)	20
65	Keele Rag/Lyntone	SOUNDS OF SAVILE (flexidisc; Hipster Image/London Apprentices/ Tom & Brennie; some in die-cut title sleeve)	80
55	Decca DFE 6147	STAR PARADE (Stargazers/Edmundo Ros Orchestra/Joan Regan & Squadronaires/Dickie Valentine)	10
60s	208 Radio Luxembourg	STAR SOUVENIR GREETINGS (flexidisc)	12
60	Mercury ZEP 10088	SURPRISE PACKAGE (Ben Hewitt/Diamonds)	140
59	Top Rank JKR 8007	SWEET BEAT (Lee Allen Band/Fred Parris/Cindy Mann/Mellokings)	50

T

63	Oriole EP 7080	TAKE SIX (Mark Peters' Silhouettes/Ian & Zodiacs/Faron's Flamingos/Earl Preston & T.T.s/Rory Storm & Hurricanes/Sonny Wade & Cascades)	70
59	Mercury ZEP 10015	TEAR IT UP (Boyd Bennett Orchestra/Red Prysock/Hi-Liters)	160
57	Mercury MEP 9522	TEEN-AGE ROCK (Red Prysock/Rusty Draper/Chuck Miller/Crew Cuts)	125
58	RCA RCX 111	TEENAGE TOPS (Ray Peterson/Jimmy Dell/Marlin Greene/Barry De Vorzon)	40
64	Ember EMB 4540	TEEN SCENE '64 (Dave Clark Five/Ray Singer/Washington D.C.s)	50
60	Heritage RE 102	THAT COUNTRY ROCK (with Walter Hawkins & William Moore, 99 copies only)	50
58	Brunswick OE 9425	THEY SOLD A MILLION NO. 9 (Bobby Helms/Four Aces/Jerry Lewis/ Kitty Kallen)	25
59	Brunswick OE 9426	THEY SOLD A MILLION NO. 10 (Andrews Sisters/Four Aces/Ink Spots/ Mills Brothers)	10
59	Brunswick OE 9427	THEY SOLD A MILLION NO. 11 (Ink Spots/Louis Jordan & His Tympany Five/ Mills Brothers/Weavers)	25
59	Brunswick OE 9431	THEY SOLD A MILLION NO. 15 (Four Aces/Bill Haley & His Comets)	20
60s	Argo EAF 66	THROUGH THE LOOKING GLASS (SCENES FROM) (soundtrack)	10
59	Decca DFE 6583	TOPS IN POPS NO. 7 (Beverley Sisters/Ted Heath & His Music/ Lord Rockingham's XI/Tommy Steele)	10
63	Stateside SE 1004	TOP TEEN DANCES (Johnnie Morisette/Huey 'Piano' Smith & Clowns/ Al Brown's Tunetoppers/Spartans)	20
57	Parlophone R 4356	TOP TEN SPECIAL (Jim Dale/King Brothers/Vipers Skiffle Group)	15
67	Pye NEP 24276	TOP T.V. THEMES (Cyril Stapleton/Ron Grainer Orchestra/Barry Gray Orchestra/Eliminators/Johnny Keating & Z Men)	10
60	Fontana TFE 17265	TREASURES OF NORTH AMERICAN NEGRO MUSIC VOL. 6 (Reverend J.C. Burnett/Reverend J.M. Gates/Reverend W. Mosley)	15
65	Century 21 MA 105	T.V. CENTURY 21 THEMES (David Graham/Sylvia Anderson/Peter Dyneley/ Barry Gray Orchestra/Gary Miller/Eric Winstone Orchestra)	15
64	Decca DFE 8585	T.V. THEMES (Andrew Oldham Orchestra/Ted Heath Music/ Ron Grainer Music/Cyril Stapleton Orchestra)	40
62	Starlite STEP 31	TWIST OFF (Wayne Farmer/Medallions/Charles Perrywell/Piano Slim/ Teenbeats/ Dellos)	200
62	Starlite STEP 29	TWIST ON (Mighty Trojans/Dee Dee Gaudet/Dixie Lee/ Percy & The Rocking Aces)	125

V

65	Vogue VRE 5002	VOGUE SURPRISE PARTIE (Petula Clark/Jean Jacques Debout/ Francoise Hardy/Michel Paje)	10

W

69	Apple CT 1	WALLS ICE CREAM PRESENTS (Mary Hopkin/Iveys/Jackie Lomax/ James Taylor; with/without p/s)	50
65	Liberty LEP 4036	WE SING THE BLUES (Jesse Hill/Ernie K. Doe/Aaron Neville/Benny Spellman)	65
64	Fontana TFE 18009	WITH GOD ON OUR SIDE (withdrawn; Bob Dylan/Joan Baez/Pete Seeger)	100
66	Chess CRE 6009	WITH THE BLUES (Eddie Boyd Blues Combo/Buddy Guy)	40

Y

64	Fontana TFE 18011	YE PLAYBOYS AND PLAYGIRLS (withdrawn; Bob Dylan/Joan Baez/ Pete Seeger)	100
68	Chess CRE 6026	YOUR CHESS REQUESTS (Fontella Bass/Tony Clarke/Mitty Collier/ Billy Stewart)	65
57	Mercury MEP 9525	YOUR CHOICE (Hal Mooney Orchestra/Chuck Miller/Sarah Vaughan/ Florian Zabach)	15

| 58 | Mercury MEP 9532 | YOUR CHOICE NO. 2 (Ralph Marterie Orchestra/Patti Page/ Platters/Myoshi Umeki) ....15 |

VARIOUS ARTISTS SINGLES & EPs 70s/80s/90s/00s

A

87	SAM 4	ADONIS: No Way Back (Club Mix)/ADONIS : No Way Back (Mix)/HERCULES: 7 Ways To Jack/MR. FNGERS: Can You Feel It (12", Promo only) 30
91	ART 1	APPLIED RHYTHMIC TECHNOLOGY (12" EP)...25
92	ART 2.1	THE PHILOSOPHY OF SOUND AND MACHINE EP 1 (12")...............................12
92	ART 2.1	THE PHILOSOPHY OF SOUND AND MACHINE EP 2 (12")...............................15
98	Twisted Nerve TN 003	ALL OAR NOTHING (10", p/s; Badly Drawn Boy/Mum & Dad/Dakota Oak/ Sirconical/Andy Votel)..15
56	Decca F 10752	ALL STAR HIT PARADE (EP, credited to the Lord's Taverners) 12
57	Decca F 10915	ALL STAR HIT PARADE NO. 2 (EP, credited to the Lord's Taverners).........12
84	Relegated	ARISTOCRAP (p/s; Pulex Irritans/Seventh Plague/Vendetta) 10
80	Deleted DEP 002	ANGST IN MY PANTS (2x7", fold-out numbered sleeve, Instant Automatons/Door & The Window/Mic Woods/Midnight Circus/012/Digital Dinosaurs/Missing Persons, etc) 50

B

82	Secret SHH 138	BACK ON THE STREETS EP 10
83	Secret SHH 138	BACK ON THE STREET (p/s; Skin Disease/Angela Rippon's Bum/Venom/ Strike/East End Badoes) 12
92	Rhythmic Tech. ART 1	NORT ROUTE (12")...20
87	Other OTH 6	BATTLEAXE (p/s; Black Riders/Holosade/Kes/Teacher's Pet).....................30
78	Good Vibrations GOT 7	BATTLE OF THE BANDS (double pack, no'd p/s; Idiots/Rudi/Outcasts/Spider) 25
95	Ka-boom KA-BOOM 1	BIG BOLLOCKED BONFIRE BLOW-UP (Hood, et al.).....................................12
80	Vinyl Drip DRIP 001	BLACKPOOL ROX (p/s; Membranes/Section 25/Syntax/Kenneth Turner Set) 8
79	Skeleton SKL 002	THE BLANK TAPES VOL. 1 (folded p/s; Attempted Moustache/Junk Act/ Geisha Girls/Zorkie Twins)...8
81	Secret SHH 126	BOLLOCKS TO CHRISTMAS (p/s; Business/4-Skins/Gonads/Max Splodge) 30
80s	Secret	BRITANNIA WAIVES THE RULES (12", p/s; Exploited/Chron Gen/Infa Riot) 12
80	Crass 421984/5	BULLSHIT DETECTOR (12", p/s; A.P.F. Brigade/Alternative/Amebix/ Clockwork Criminals/Counter Attack/Crass/Frenzy Battalion/Fuck The CIA/ 0

C

95	Orange ORANGE 001	CARMIHOOD (Hood/Carmine) 8
98	Twisted Nerve TNXMS 1	CHRISTMAS STOCKING FILLER (Badly Drawn Boy/Dakota Oak/Sirconical/Mum & Dad/Elbow) (green vinyl in green wraparound sleeve or red vinyl in red sl.)..................25
98	Twisted Nerve TNXM 025	CHRISTMAS STOCKING FILLER 2 (10", p/s; Andy Votel/D.O.T./Lost Children's Desk/Misty Dixon/Cherrystones)...8
80s	No Future	A COUNTRY FIT FOR HEROES (12", p/s) 12
80s	No Future	A COUNTRY FIT FOR HEROES VOL. 2 (12", p/s) 20
94	Fierce Panda NING 02	CRAZED AND CONFUSED (p/s; Supergrass/Ash et al.)...............................15

D

71	Dandelion DS 7001	DANDELION (die-cut sleeve; Principal Edwards Magic Theatre/Stackwaddy/ Siren/The Way We Live)...15
92	Delirious DELIS 6	DELIRIOUS PRIME CUTS VOL. 1 (12"; The Moog/Hardcore Rhythm Team/Justice And Mercy) 40
86	BBC ZRSL 193	DOCTOR WHO (cassette, holographic inlay; Dominic Glynn/Mankind/ BBC Radiophonic Workshop)...8
86	BBC 12RXL 193	DOCTOR WHO (12", holographic p/s; Dominic Glynn/Mankind/ BBC Radiophonic Workshop)...8
87	BBC RESL 193	DOCTOR WHO (p/s, reissue; Dominic Glynn/Mankind) 6
01	Trunk WWW 1	DIRTY FAN MAIL (7", white vinyl) 15

E

79	Fast Products FAST 9B	EARCOM 2 (12", p/s; Joy Division/Thursdays/Basczax)................................35
97	Fat Cat 12FAT 003	8. 8.5, 9 (12", custom sleeve) 10
99	Lowlife LOW8	EASTER ISLAND (EP, 750 only) 15
78	Stiff FREEBIE 2	EXCERPTS FROM STIFF'S GREATEST HITS (promo only sampler, 33rpm) 10
96	Mo' Wax MWEX 001-010	EXCURSIONS (10 x 12", box set; the Prunes/IO/Olde Scottish/David Caron/DJ Solo & DJ Aura/Midnight Funk Assoc./Stasis/Solo feat. JT/Twig Bud/DJ Shadow) 30
99	AI AI 001	EXPERIMENTS IN COLOUR (12"; Normal/Cell/Fil) 20

F

78	Factory FAC 2	A FACTORY SAMPLE (double pack, p/s, in plastic bag, with 5 stickers; Joy Division/Cabaret Voltaire/Durutti Column/John Dowie;.....................................200
95	555 5X555	5x555 (5x7" box set; Boyracer/Mike Nichols And His Excellency/Amy Linton & Stewart Anderson/Father/Hood) 30
91	Fontana FONT 1	THE FONTANA SINGLES BOX SET VOLUME 1 - HITS AND RARITIES (12-single box set, with 12 inserts)..30
91	Fontana FONT 2	THE FONTANA SINGLES BOX SET VOLUME 2 - HITS AND RARITIES (12-single box set, with 12 inserts)..30
79	Heartbeat PULSE 4	4 ALTERNATIVES (p/s; 48 Hours/Joe Public/Numbers/X-Certs) 15
80	Con (no cat. no.)	THE FOUR EPs (cassette; Mark Perry et al.)...15
96	Ché CHE 059	4 TRACK 3 BAND TOUR EP (p/s, Mogwai/Urusei Yatsura/Backwater, 50 only) 25
96	Mosquito MSQ 05	FRESH AS YOU FUCKIN' LIKE (12"; Paul Hannah/Russ Gabriel/Steve Patton/ Cristian Vogel/Si Begg) 15

G

| 83 | Mouth MOUTH 1 | G-FORCE (Shady Deal/Dead Loss/Blythe Rocket/Egypt) ....20 |
| 70 | Village Thing VTSX 1000 | THE GREAT WHITE DAP (Wizz Jones/Sun Also Rises/Ian A. Anderson/ Pigsty Hill Light Orchestra) ....20 |

H

80	Groucho Marxist	HA! HA! FUNNY POLIS (PAISLEY ROCKS AGAINST RACISM) (p/s; Defiant Pose/Fegs/Urban Enemies/XS Discharge) 20
71	Abreaction ABR 001	HART ROCK (Brass Alley/Yellow/Trilogy/Lucas Tyson) (no p/s) 20
90s	Sub Pop	HELTER SHELTER (box set, 4 x 7", Elastica/Gene) 8

I

97	B. Banquet Random 2.2	I DIE, YOU DIE (12", green vinyl promo, die-cut sleeve, 1200 only; Greenhaus/ Mike Dearborn/Dave Clarke)	8
78	Radar SAM 88	INTERNATIONAL ARTISTS (13th Floor Elevators/Red Crayola/ Lost & Found/Golden Dawn; Red Crayola Hope & Anchor gig freebie)	0
74	Galbraith POT 1	It's A Gas/Put In A Potterton (features 'The Goodies' on B-side)	6

L

80	Stiff BUY DJ 111	Oklahoma!/Oh what A Beautiful Morning (by The London Cast)	80
79	Decca FR 13864	THE LONDON BOYS (p/s; David Bowie/Small Faces/Birds/Dobie Gray)	10
73	Ronco MR EP 001	LONG LIVE ROCK (no p/s; Billy Fury/Eugene Wallace/Wishful Thinking)	15

M

88	Record Mirror SURE 1	Megablast Rap Version	6
71	Track 2094 011	MAXI TRACK RECORD (John's Children/Crazy World Of Arthur Brown/ Thunderclap Newman/Jimi Hendrix; withdrawn blue sleeve crediting	0
71	Track 2094 011	MAXI TRACK RECORD (John's Children/Crazy World Of Arthur Brown/ Thunderclap Newman/Jimi Hendrix; red & white sleeve with press pack,	0
97	Begg. Banquet Random 2.1	METAL (12", red vinyl promo, die-cut sleeve, 1200 only; Robert Armani)	10
97	V/VM VVMT4	MISSINGTOE & WHINE (EP, 500 only)	15
99	Twisted Nerve TN 009	MODERN MUSIC FOR MOTORCYCLES (10" EP, some on yellow vinyl; Dakota Oak/Alfie/Sirconical & Andy Votel/Mum & Dad/Badly Drawn Boy)	15
99	Twisted Nerve TNC 009	MODERN MUSIC FOR MOTORCYCLES (cassette; Dakota Oak/Alfie/Sirconical & Andy Votel/Mum & Dad/Badly Drawn Boy)	8
79	JSP JSP 4504	MORE BANDERA ROCKABILLIES (p/s)	12
95	Fierce Panda NING 15	MORTAL WOMBAT (double pack, p/s; Super Furry Animals/Baby Bird/ Panda/Mexican Pets/Harvey's Rabbit/Spare Snare)	8
75	Happy Time HT12	MUSIC FROM THUNDERBIRDS AND DOCTOR WHO (p/s)	8
80	EMI 12EMI 5074	MUTHA'S PRIDE (12", p/s; Wildfire/Quartz/White Spirit/Baby Jane)	20

N

98	Lowlife LOW6	98 Series Vol. 1 (EP)	15
98	Lowlife LOW7	98 Series Vol. 2 (EP)	20
80	Neutron NT 003	1980! THE FIRST FIFTEEN MINUTES EP (gatefold p/s with inserts; Vice Versa/Clock DVA/I'm So Hollow/Stunt Kites)	15

O

| 82 | Neat NEAT 25 | ONE TAKE NO DUBS (12", p/s; Black Rose/Hellanbach/Alien/Avenger) | 12 |

P

90s	Fierce Panda NING 12CD	PANDEMONIUM (Easyworld, et al.) (250 only)	10
80s	A&M A&M PARTY 1/2/3/4/5/6	THE PARTY PARTY PACK (6 x 7", with picture sleeves, in PVC outer sleeve; Sting/Pauline Black/Dave Edmunds/Midge Ure/Modern Romance/Bad Manners/	20
80s	Pink & Black	PINK 'N' BLACK VOL 1 (p/s, re-issue of 1950's Rock 'n' Roll	10
97	V/VM VVMT4	PRIVILEGED FRAMES FOR REFERENCE (12" EP, p/s, 450 only)	15

R

93	Raptor RAP 1	RAPTOR PRESENTS . . . (12", p/s, 500 only; Ash/Buttlip/Marrow Bone/Fat)	40
91	Ptolemaic Terrascope POT 8	RED FLIPPER (no p/s, Nurse With Wound/The Underworlde/Caravan Of Dreams)	20
94	Fierce Panda NING 03	RETURN TO SPLENDOUR (double pack in foldover p/s with insert in poly bag, 1,000 only; Bluetones et al.)	12
77	Rollercoaster RRCEP 00002	ROCKABILLY HOP (test pressings only)	12
83	Consett Music Project RD 1	ROCK AND DOLE (Obnoxious Tartus/Decade Waltz/Task Force/Hot Banana)	25
92	Melody Maker MMI	ROLLERCOASTER EP (CD, Blur/Jesus & Mary Chain/Dinosaur Jr./ My Bloody Valentine; 2,000 only)	12

S

95	Atol ATOL 02	S4C MAKES ME WANT TO SMOKE CRACK VOL. 1 (500 only, Catatonia et al.)	15
80	Sonic Int. S14283	SEX, VIOLENCE & ETERNAL TRUTH (Lost Boys/What To Wear/The Venom/The Dodos, oversized poster sleeve, 4 A5 inserts, 250 only, stickered white labels, stamped plain white inner sleeve)	125
94	Fierce Panda/	SHAGGING IN THE STREETS (double pack, wraparound p/s in poly bag, 1,000 only; SMASH/Blessed Ethel/Mantaray/Done Lying Down)	0
93	Duophonic DS 45-05/06	SHIMMIES IN SUPER 8 (double pack, 1 disc green vinyl, other white vinyl, numbered in poly bag, 800 with tri-foldout p/s, 400 also with sticker)	0
95	Enraptured RAPT 4502	SILVER APPLES TRIBUTE (10", 12 in hand-drawn sleeve; Windy & Carl/Scaredycat/Third Eye Foundation/Flowchart/Sabine	25
86	Broken Flag BF F1	THE SOFT VOLCANO ERUPTS (flexidisc; Controlled Bleeding/Kehamas Curse/ Uncommunity/Nails Of Christ/Cananes/Ramleh)	10
79	Groucho Marxist WH 1	SPECTACULAR COMMODITY (p/s; Mental Errors/Mod Cons/ Poems/Sneex/XS Discharge)	10
70s	Stiff BUY 1-10	STIFF BOX SET NO. 1 (10 x 7" box set)	35
70s	Stiff BUY 11-20	STIFF BOX SET NO. 2 (10 x 7" box set)	35
01	Edel 0128655ERESA	SUBSTITUTE EP : THE SONGS OF THE WHO (white vinyl, promo)	60

T

90s	Enraptured RAPT 4513	TERRASCOPE/TERRASTOCK (Bevis Frond/Damon & Naomi/Flying Saucer Attack/Silver Apples)	12
83	White Noise WN 3	THIS IS WHITE NOISE (p/s; Skrewdriver/Brutal Attack/Die Hards/A.B.H.)	40
02	Warner Bros 50466 13441	TOP-DECK SKA 45'S BOX (8 x 7"s, coloured vinyl in cardboard box)	25
82	Total Noise TOT 1	TOTAL NOISE # 1 (Business/Blitz/Dead Generation/Gonads)	10
93	2 Tone CHSTT31	2 TONE EP	8
01	Trunk JBH 01	Theme To Screen Test (Marching There & back) (1-sided 7", 500 only)	20

U

80s	Fierce FRIGHT/SFTRI 38	AN UNHOLY MONTAGE (200 only [100 U.K./100 U.S.], coloured vinyl with numbered insert)	25
98	Wurlitzer JUKEBOX 37	UNITED IN THE HATRED OF (676 only, 176 in embossed sleeve)	6
96	V/VM VVMT1	UPLINK DATA TRANSMISSIONS (12" EP, with 'data sheets', 250 only)	20

MINT VALUE £

W

80	Fuck Off FEP 001	WEIRD NOISE (p/s, white labels; Danny & Dressmakers/The Door & The Window/Instant Automatons/012/Sell-Outs)	10
82	Bluurg FISH 1	WESSEX '82 (Subhumans/Pagans/Organized Chaos/The Heads)	12
77	MPL MPL 1	WE'VE MOVED! (Wings/Gene Vincent/Frank Sinatra et al., promo only excerpts sampler, some with press pack)	175
84	Rather/Seventeen	WHAT A NICE WAY TO TURN SEVENTEEN NO. 2 (p/s; Swell Maps & others; with magazine)	12

Y

80s	Wonderful World Of WOW 1	YOU ARE NOT ALONE (p/s, with insert; Oi Polloi/Hex/Stalag 17/Symbol Of Freedom)	15

UNTITLED EPs & SINGLES 50s-00s

60	Triumph RGM 1008	Green Jeans/You Are My Sunshine (as Fabulous Flee-Rakkers)	35
60	Top Rank JAR 431	Green Jeans/You Are My Sunshine (reissue, as Fabulous Flea-Rakkers)	50
60	Pye 7N 15288	Sunday Date/Shiftless Sam	20
60	Pye 7N 15326	Blue Tango/Bitter Rice	12
61	Piccadilly 7N 35006	Lone Rider/Miller Like Wow	20
62	Piccadilly 7N 35048	Stage To Cimarron/Twistin' The Chestnuts	20
62	Piccadilly 7N 35081	Sunburst/Black Buffalo	20
63	Piccadilly 7N 35109	Fireball/Fandango	20
61	Pye NEP 24141	THE FABULOUS FLEE-REKKERS (EP)	75
91	C5 C5 564	JOE MEEK'S FABULOUS FLEE REKKERS (LP)	15
60s	Coxsone SCE 1	(no p/s, 33rpm; Gaylads/Hugh Godfrey/Glen & Dave/Roy Richards/Cables/Richard Ace)	75
63	Embassy WEP 1086	(p/s; Mike Redway/Bud Ashton Group/Rory Pilgrim)	15
69	De Wolfe	(Lemon Dips, et al.)	30
73	Buddah 2011 164	(Shangri-La's/Tradewinds/Ad Libs)	6
94	Kennel Club VTDOG 10	(Strangelove/Tindersticks/God Machine/Breed (10", numbered, 1,500 only, free with Purr magazine issue 2)	10
98	Fat Cat 12FAT 008	REMIXES (12", custom sleeve; remixes of Fat Cat 12FAT 003 by Autechre et al.)	12
94	Kennel Club VTDOG 10	TINDERSTICKS: Girl On Death Row/STRANGELOVE: Wolf's Story/GOD MACHINE: The Devil Song/BREED: Diamonds Are Forever (10", numbered p/s, free with	0
96	SKAM MASK 1	UNTITLED (12", custom sleeve, 100 only; Freeform/Funkstorung/ Boards Of Canada/Jega)	150
97	SKAM MASK 2	UNTITLED (12", custom sleeve, 350 only; Hellinterface/Funkstorung/Bola/ Jega/Intron)	75
98	Mosquito MSQ 012.5	(10"; Si Begg/Blue Arsed Fly)	0

VARIOUS ARTISTS LPs & COMPILATIONS
(alphabetical by title)

A

70	ATP 102	THE ABBEY TAVERN	20
88	Woronzow WOO 6	ACID JAM (with insert)	18
89	Popdy POPDY 101	(0222) A COMPILATION OF CARDIFF BANDS (LP)	50
02	Topic TSFCD4001	THE ACOUSTIC FOLK BOX (4-CD)	40
69	Action ACLP 6005	ACTION PACKED SOUL	50
70s	Jem JEM	A DEAL A DAY	25
96	Ferox FERLP 1	ADVENTURES IN TECHNO SOUL (2-LP; Too Funk/Paul Hannah/Carl Craig et al.)	20
85	United Dairies UD 012	AN AFFLICTED MAN'S MUSICA BOX (3 different editions, 1st in gatefold sleeve)	75
75	Leader LEE 4056	A FINE HUNTING DAY - SONGS OF THE HOLME VALLEY BEAGLES (with book)	15
70	Pama PMP 2004	AFRICAN MELODY	70
71	Trojan TBL 166	AFRICA'S BLOOD (Lee Perry, et al.) (orange/white label)	20
70s	Contempo 2870 311	AFRO ROCK FESTIVAL	15
64	Decca LK 4606	AFTER SUNSET	150
66	Stateside SL 10172	AN ALBUM FULL OF SOUL	50
69	Key KL 002	ALIVE!	20
84	Creation CRELP 001	ALIVE IN THE LIVING ROOM	12
70	Talisman STAL 5013	ALL FOLK TOGETHER	20
84	Whaam! BIG 8	ALL FOR ART... AND ART FOR ALL	30
71	Utd. Artists UDX 201/202	ALL GOOD CLEAN FUN (2-LP)	15
83	Neat NEAT 102A/B	ALL HELL LET LOOSE	20
61	Blue Beat BBLP 801	ALL STARS - JAMAICAN BLUES	300
70	Speciality SPE 6609	ALL THE BLUES ALL THE TIME	22
58	Pye Nixa NJT 509	ALL THE WINNERS (10")	20
76	Riva RVLP 2	ALL THIS AND WORLD WAR TWO (2-LP, box set with booklet)	15
58	Parlophone PMD 1064	ALL TIME COUNTRY AND WESTERN HITS (10")	30
73	Polydor 2460 186	AMERICAN BLUES LEGENDS '73	15
63	Polydor LPHM 46 397	AMERICAN FOLK BLUES FESTIVAL (also stereo SLPHM 237 597)	15
70s	Rare Records 2	AMERICAN FOLK BLUES FESTIVAL 1962	25
64	Fontana TL 5204	AMERICAN FOLK BLUES FESTIVAL 1963	25
65	Fontana TL 5225	AMERICAN FOLK BLUES FESTIVAL 1964	25
66	Fontana TL 5286	AMERICAN FOLK BLUES FESTIVAL 1965	25
66	Fontana (S)TL 5389	AMERICAN FOLK BLUES FESTIVAL 1966 (mono/stereo)	22
70	CBS 63912	AMERICAN FOLK BLUES FESTIVAL 1969	20
80s	Pleasantly Surprised PS 2	THE ANGELS ARE COMING (2-cassette, with booklet)	25
83	No Future MPUNK 8	ANGELS WITH DIRTY FACES	18
60s	77' 77LA 12/13	ANGOLA PRISON SPIRITUALS	18
69	Immediate IMAL 03/04	ANTHOLOGY OF BRITISH BLUES VOLUME 1 (2-LP, gatefold sleeve)	30
69	Immediate IMAL 05/06	ANTHOLOGY OF BRITISH BLUES VOLUME 2 (2-LP, gatefold sleeve)	30
64	London HA-K/SH-K 8174	APOLLO SATURDAY NIGHT (mono/stereo)	60
93	Art ART 2CD	APPLIED RHYMIC TECHNOLOGY (CD)	30
93	Art ART 4CD	APPLIED RHYMIC TECHNOLOGY (CD)	20
91	Delerium DELP 005D	A PSYCHEDELIC PSAUNA (2-LP)	30
80s	Ram RAMLP 001	THE ART OF SOLVING PROBLEMS (with poster & insert)	18
74	Ashanti SHAN 106	ASHANTI SHOWCASE	12
69	Atco 228 021	ATCO BLOCKBUSTERS	18
69	Atlantic 587/588 180	ATLANTIC BLOCKBUSTERS	20
65	Atlantic ATL 5020	ATLANTIC DISCOTHEQUE	40

60s	Atlantic AP 2	ATLANTIC IS SOUL	15
60s	Atlantic AC 3	ATLANTIC CLASSICS	25
67	Pye NPL 18198	AT LAST THE 1948 SHOW	15
90	Dover/PWL CCD 19	A TON OF HITS - THE HIT FACTORY VOL. 4 (2-CD)	25
64	Decca LK 4597	AT THE CAVERN	80
63	London HA-R 8133	AT THE HOOTENANNY - VOLUME 3	15
70	Beacon SBEAB 9	AUTHENTIC CHICAGO BLUES	20
72	Windmill WMD 124	AUTHENTIC CHICAGO BLUES	12
66	RCA RD 7776	AUTHENTIC COWBOYS & THEIR WESTERN FOLKSONGS	12
57	London WB 91034	AUTHENTIC CARIBBEAN CALYPSOS (10" LP)	30
64	Stateside SL 10107	AUTHENTIC SKA	70
64	Stateside SL 10068	AUTHENTIC R & B.	40
79	Heartbeat HB 1	AVON CALLING - THE BRISTOL COMPILATION (with poster)	25
95	Ministry Of Sound/AWOL LP 1	A.W.O.L: A WAY OF LIFE (3-LP, stickered sleeve)	40
80	K-Tel NE 1100	AXE ATTACK (early copies with demo of Iron Maiden's "Running Free")	15
85	Steeltrax JCI 7102	AXE ATTACK (LP)	18
80s	Flaccid FLAC 1	AYLESBURY GOES FLACCID	15
74	Deroy DER 1052	AYRSHIRE FOLK (LP, private pressing)	50

B

92	Chrysalis CHR TT 5012	BEST OF 2 TONE (LP)	40
70	Track 2407 001	BACKTRACK ONE	25
70	Track 2407 002	BACKTRACK TWO	12
70	Track 2407003	BACKTRACK THREE	15
70	Track 2407005	BACKTRACK FIVE	15
70	Track 2407 006	BACKTRACK SIX	15
70	Track 2407 007	BACKTRACK SEVEN	12
54	London AL 3535	BACKWOODS BLUES (10")	50
73	Incus INCUS 11	BALANCE (Ian Brighton, et al.)	60
62	Fontana 688 200 ZL	BALLIN'	18
79	JSP 1005	BANDERA ROCKABILLIES	15
68	Pama PMLP 4	BANG BANG LULU	30
69	Pama Economy ECO7	BANGARANG (LP)	45
73	BBC/Roundabout 17	BANG ON A DRUM	18
60	Melodisc 12-115	BANJO BREAKDOWN	15
64	Storyville 670 155	BARRELHOUSE BLUES AND BOOGIE-WOOGIE VOLUME 1	15
65	Storyville 670 183	BARRELHOUSE BLUES AND BOOGIE-WOOGIE VOLUME 2	15
65	Storyville SLP 213	BARRELHOUSE BLUES AND BOOGIE-WOOGIE VOL. 3	15
59	Fontana TFR 6018	BARRELHOUSE, BOOGIE WOOGIE AND BLUES (10")	25
58	Vogue Coral LRA 10022	BARRELHOUSE PIANO (10" LP)	25
59	Vogue Coral LRA 10023	BARRELHOUSE PIANO VOLUME 2 (10" LP)	25
83	London CAVE 1	THE BATCAVE - YOUNG LIMBS AND NUMB HYMNS	12
95	Sarah SARAH 359	BATTERY POINT (LP)	15
71	Trojan TBL 167	BATTLE AXE	30
52	Capitol LC 6510	BATTLE OF THE BANDS (10" LP)	18
71	B&C BCM 103	BATTLE OF THE BANDS VOL. 1	15
64	Melodisc MLP 12-192	BATTLE OF THE GIANTS	20
53	MGM MGM-D 115	A BATTLE OF JAZZ: HOT VERSUS COOL (10")	30
71	BBC REC 118	BBC's FOLK ON TWO PRESENTS NORTHUMBRIAN FOLK	20
69	Beacon BEAB 1	BEACON BRINGS IT TO YOU	18
71	Revival RVS 1004	BEALE STREET MESS AROUND	15
84	Well Suspect SUSS 1	THE BEAT GENERATION AND THE ANGRY YOUNG MEN	20
86	Mercury WILD 1	BEAT RUNS WILD (Wet Wet Wet et al.)	25
87	Pink PINKY 15	BEAUTY (McCarthy et al.)	12
77	Impulse IS/BED/123	BEDROCK - ALTOGETHER BEDROCK LP (private pressing)	12
68	Elektra EUK 262	BEGIN HERE (also stereo EUKS 7262)	20
78	Rip Off ROLP 1	BELFAST ROCKS	35
71	Delmark DS 622	BELL'S BLUES HARP	15
68	Bell MBLL 102	BELL'S CELLAR OF SOUL VOLUME 1	30
69	Bell MBLL 107	BELL'S CELLAR OF SOUL VOLUME 2	30
69	Bell MBLL 117	BELL'S CELLAR OF SOUL VOLUME 3	30
69	Bell MBLL/SBLL 111	THE BEST FROM BELL	20
69	Bell MBLL/SBLL 124	THE BEST FROM BELL VOLUME 2	20
78	Stiff ODD 2	BE STIFF (TOUR '78 OFFICIAL RELEASE) (promo only)	15
78	Stiff DEAL 1	BE STIFF ROUTE '78 (with 16-page booklet & biographies, etc.)	15
70s	Storyville 671 188	THE BEST OF THE BLUES	15
96	Universal Sounds US LP 2	BEST OF BLACK JAZZ RECORDS (2-LP)	25
65	Xtra XTRA 1031	THE BEST OF BRITISH FOLK	15
69	Pama SECO 18	THE BEST OF CAMEL	150
72	Paramount SPFL 286	BEST OF FILM MUSIC	15
76	Epic EPC 81224	THE BEST OF OKEH VOL. I	15
76	Epic EPC 81532	THE BEST OF OKEH VOL. II	15
69	President PTL 1016	THE BEST OF PRESIDENT VOLUME 1	12
69	President PTL 1036	THE BEST OF PRESIDENT VOLUME 2	12
67	Xtra XTRA 1053	BEST OF SCOTTISH FOLK	12
83	Statik STATLP 14	THE BEST OF YOUR SECRET'S SAFE WITH US (This LP came with a free 7". The tracks were 'Sub Dub' by Sun Ya and on Side Two 'The Fools by Anthony Lindo. Cat. number was STAT26A/26B)	20
86	Plastic Head PLASLP 008	BEYOND THE FENCE BEGINS THE SKY (LP)	40
73	Attack ATLP 1011	BIG BAMBOO	30
60	Fontana TFL 5080	THE BIG BEAT!	55
85	Big Beat WIKM39	BIG BEAT BEACH PARTY	15
64	London HA-B 8199	THE BIG 'D' JAMBOREE	25
78	Giorno GPS	BIG EGO	15
69	Fontana SFXL 55	THE BIG FOLK	12
69	Minit MLL/MLS 40007E	THE BIG ONE	22
64	Capitol ST 2146	BIG SOUNDS OF THE DRAGS Vol 2	30
72	CBS 64844	THE BIG SUR FESTIVAL	18
70	Pama SECO 32	BIRTH CONTROL	30
80	Black Ark Intl. BALP 4001	BLACK ARK VOLUME 2	30
70	Matchbox SDX 207/8	BLACK DIAMOND EXPRESS TO HELL (2-LP)	25

Year	Label/Cat No	Title	Value
60	Columbia 33SX 1244	BLACKPOOL NIGHTS	35
80	Form BB 1003	BLACK MAGIC DUB (LP)	100
58	HMV CLP 1167	BLACK SLACKS AND BOBBY SOCKS (LP)	300
70	Ember SE 8009	BLACK SOUL EXPLOSION	18
70	CBS 52796	BLACK WHITES AND BLUES	20
83	Quiet QLP 3	BLOOD ON THE ROQ! (withdrawn)	15
68	Coxsone CSP 1	BLUE BEAT SPECIAL	50
66	RCA Victor RD 7786	BLUEBIRD BLUES	20
63	Stateside SL 10021	THE BLUEGRASS HALL OF FAME	15
65	London HA-B 8227	BLUEGRASS HALL OF FAME VOL. 2	18
64	London HA-B 8118	BLUEGRASS SPECTACULAR	12
62	Columbia 33SX 1417	THE BLUES	60
64	Pye Intl. NPL 28030	BLUES VOL. 1	18
64	Pye Intl. NPL 28035	BLUES VOL. 2	18
64	Pye Intl. NPL 28045	BLUES VOL. 3	18
64	Chess CRL 4003	BLUES VOL. 4	18
65	Chess CRL 4512	BLUES VOL. 5	18
68	Immediate IMLP 014	BLUES ANYTIME VOL. 1	18
68	Immediate IMCP 015	BLUES ANYTIME VOL. 2	18
68	Immediate IMLP 019	BLUES ANYTIME VOL. 3	18
65	Fontana TFL 6048	THE BLUES AT NEWPORT 1964 PART 1	22
69	Saga FID 2165	BLUES AT SUNRISE	12
66	London HA-S 8265	THE BLUES CAME DOWN FROM MEMPHIS	80
73	Flyright LP 504	BLUES CAME TO CHAPEL HILL	15
65	Storyville SLP 176	BLUESCENE USA: VOLUME 1 - CHICAGO	18
65	Storyville SLP 177	BLUESCENE USA: VOLUME 2 - LOUISIANA BLUES	18
65	Storyville SLP 181	BLUESCENE USA: VOLUME 3 - BLUES ALL AROUND MY BED	18
67	Storyville SLP 180	BLUESCENE USA: VOLUME 4 - MISSISSIPPI BLUES	18
71	Python PLP-KM 17	BLUES - CHICAGO STYLE (LP)	45
60	Philips BBL 7369	BLUES FELL THIS MORNING	40
73	Polydor 2383 257	BLUES FOR MR. CRUMP	18
72	Transatlantic TRASAM 25	BLUES FOR YOUR POCKET	12
69	Chess CRLS 4558	BLUES FROM BIG BILL'S COPACABANA	35
69	Python PLP 6	BLUES FROM CHICAGO (99 copies only)	80
70	Python PLP 9	BLUES FROM CHICAGO VOL. 2 (99 copies only)	80
71	Python PLP 15	BLUES FROM CHICAGO VOL. 3 (99 copies only)	80
60s	Heritage 1004	BLUES FROM MAXWELL STREET (99 copies only)	80
71	Pye Intl. NPL 28142	BLUES FROM THE BAYOU	22
72	Saydisc SDM 226	BLUES FROM THE DELTA	25
71	Python PLP 21	BLUES FROM THE WINDY CITY (99 copies only)	80
77	Flyright LP 4713	BLUES FROM THE WINDY CITY	15
80	Kicking Mule SNKF 159	BLUES GUITAR WORKSHOP	15
63	Stateside SL 10076	BLUES HOOT (Lightning Hopkins)	35
57	Pye Nixa NJL 8	(ALAN LOMAX PRESENTS) BLUES IN THE MISSISSIPPI NIGHT	35
60s	Sunflower (no cat. no.)	BLUES IS MY COMPANION (99 copies only)	42
60s	Sunflower (no cat. no.)	BLUES KEEP FALLING (99 copies only)	80
69	Blue Horizon 7-66227	BLUES JAM AT CHESS (2-LP)	60
69	Immediate IMLP 024	BLUES LEFTOVERS	12
67	Saydisc Match. SDM 142	BLUES LIKE SHOWERS OF RAIN	70
68	Saydisc Match. SDM 167	BLUES LIKE SHOWERS OF RAIN VOLUME 2	70
65	Decca LK 4681	BLUES NOW	60
72	Blues Obscurities BOV 1	BLUES OBSCURITIES VOL. 1: SOUTHERN BLUES/DARK MUDDY BOTTOM (plain cover with photocopied inserts)	40
72	Blues Obscurities BOV 2	BLUES OBSCURITIES VOL. 2: LONESOME HARMONICA	25
72	Blues Obscurities BOV 3	BLUES OBSCURITIES VOL. 3: WEST COAST BLUES	25
72	Blues Obscurities BOV 4	BLUES OBSCURITIES VOL. 4: ONE RAINY MORNING	25
72	Blues Obscurities BOV 5	BLUES OBSCURITIES VOL. 5: SOMETHING'S GONE WRONG	25
72	Blues Obscurities BOV 6	BLUES OBSCURITIES VOL. 6: COMING BACK HOME	25
72	Blues Obscurities BOV 7	BLUES OBSCURITIES VOL. 7	25
72	Blues Obscurities BOV 8	BLUES OBSCURITIES VOL. 8	25
72	Blues Obscurities BOV 9	BLUES OBSCURITIES VOL. 9	25
72	Blues Obscurities BOV 10	BLUES OBSCURITIES VOL. 10	25
74	London HA-U 8454	BLUES OBSCURITIES VOL. 1: DARK MUDDY BOTTOM (reissue)	15
74	London HA-U 8455	BLUES OBSCURITIES VOL. 2: LONESOME HARMONICA (reissue)	15
74	London HA-U 8456	BLUES OBSCURITIES VOL. 3: STRETCHIN' OUT	15
69	Mercury SMXL 77	BLUES PACKAGE '69	15
69	Highway 51 H 102	BLUES PEOPLE	40
68	Matchbox SDR 146	BLUES PIANO	20
72	Atlantic K 40404	BLUES PIANO - CHICAGO PLUS	20
68	Kokomo K 1001	A BLUES POTPOURRI (99 copies only)	60
71	Rarities (Tony's Records)	BLUES RARITIES VOL. 1 (2-LP)	25
69	Atlantic Special 590 019	THE BLUES ROLL ON (reissue of "Southern Folk Heritage: The Blues Roll On")	12
69	Poppy PYM 11001	BLUES ROOTS VOLUME ONE	25
66	Decca LK 4748	BLUES SOUTHSIDE CHICAGO	55
71	Python PLP 16	BLUES TODAY - SOUTHERN STYLE (99 copies only)	40
71	Polydor 2675 007	BOMBERS	12
65	Topic 12T 128	BONNY LASS COME O'ER THE BURN	12
73	Storyville SLP 229	BOOGIE WOOGIE BOYS	12
70s	Milestone MLP 2009	BOOGIE WOOGIE RARITIES	12
60s	Storyville 670184	BOOGIE WOOGIE TRIO	12
55	London AL 3544	BOOGIE WOOGIE WITH THE BLUES (10")	50
69	Pama SECO 17	BOSS REGGAE	100
74	Eron 002	BOTH SIDES OF THE DOWNS (with insert)	25
80	Aardvark STEAL 2	BOUQUET OF STEEL (blue vinyl with 27-page booklet)	15
81	Bristol Recorder BR 002	THE BRISTOL RECORDER VOL. 2 (with magazine booklet)	15
68	Island ILP 966/ILPS 9066	BRITISH BLUE-EYED SOUL	75
67	Tamla Motown TML 11055	BRITISH MOTOWN CHARTBUSTERS (mono, flipback sleeve)	20
69	T. Motown STML 11055	BRITISH MOTOWN CHARTBUSTERS (stereo reissue, flipback sleeve)	20
68	T. Motown (S)TML 11082	BRITISH MOTOWN CHARTBUSTERS VOL. 2 (mono/stereo, flipback sleeve)	18
83	Royal Records JBLP 306	BRITISH MUSIC SCENE (LP)	80
93	Hammer (no catalogue no.)	BRITISH OI! - WORKING CLASS ANTHEMS	12

87	See For Miles SEE 66	BRITISH PSYCHEDELIC TRIP 1	12
87	See For Miles SEE 206	BRITISH PSYCHEDELIC TRIP 4	12
70	Trojan TBL 106	BRIXTON CAT	35
64	Decca LK 4598	BRUM BEAT	85
64	Dial DLP 1	BRUM BEAT	50
79	Big Bear BRUM 1	BRUM BEAT - LIVE AT THE BARREL ORGAN (2-LP, with inserts)	20
80	MCA MCF 3074	BRUTE FORCE	20
70	Buddah 2349 008	BUDDAH IN MIND	12
72	Flyright LP 106	BULL CITY BLUES	15
69	Pama Economy SECO 18	BULLET : A WORLD OF REGGAE, SKA, ROCK STEADY, BLUE BEAT (LP)	150
81	Crass 421984/4	BULLSHIT DETECTOR 1	15
84	Crass 1984/3	BULLSHIT DETECTOR THREE (2-LP)	15
82	Crass 221984/3	BULLSHIT DETECTIVE 2	15
83	Crass	BULLSHIT DETECTIVE 3	15
66	Decca LK 4734	BUMPER BUNDLE 16 HITS	25
77	Stiff SEEZ 2	A BUNCH OF STIFF RECORDS	15
79	Cherry Red ARED 2	BUSINESS UNUSUAL (with Zig Zag small labels catalogue)	30
81	Autumn AU 2	BUSTED AT OZ	20
84	Dambusters DAM 003	BUTTONS AND BOWS VOLUME 1 (2-LP)	30
84	Dambusters DAM 006	BUTTONS AND BOWS VOLUME 2 (2-LP)	30
69	BBC REB 39M	BRITISH PRIME MINISTERS 1924-1964 (LP)	15
98	Trunk BARKED 3	THE BATTLE OF BOSWORTH (LP)	20

C

50s	Melodisc MLP 507	CALYPSO CARNIVAL (10" LP)	18
72	Topic 12TS 219	CANNY NEWCASSEL (with booklet, blue label)	20
67	Bounty BY 6035	CAN'T KEEP FROM CRYING (TOPICAL BLUES ON THE DEATH OF PRESIDENT KENNEDY)	20
78	Capitol CAPS 1025	CAPITOL SOUL CASINO	20
50s	Parlophone CPMD 13	CARIBBEAN CALYPSO (10" LP, export issue)	25
71	Trojan TBL 171	CARIBBEAN DANCE FESTIVAL (wraparound paper sleeve)	50
73	Flyright LP 505	CAROLINA COUNTRY BLUES	12
81	Secret SEC 2	CARRY ON OI!	15
73	Nottingham Festival FEST 2	CASTLE ROCK	50
78	Nice NICE 1	CATCH A WAVE (2 x 10", gatefold sleeve)	30
80	Island IRSP7	CATCH THIS BEAT	15
77	CBS 82401	CBS ROCKABILLY CLASSICS VOL. 1	12
78	CBS 82993	CBS ROCKABILLY CLASSICS VOL. 2	12
79	CBS 83911	CBS ROCKABILLY CLASSICS VOL. 3	12
90	Cerne CERNE 001/002/003	THE CERNE BOX SET (3-LP box set; Nurse With Wound/ Current 93/Sol Invictus; with 3 inserts)	125
80	Quality QP 32/80	CHAMPIONS AGAIN: HIGHLIGHTS OF 1979-80 SEASON	20
71	Chess 6671 102	CHARLIE PARKER MEMORIAL CONCERT	12
60s	Columbia	CHARTBUSTERS USA	45
73	Checker 6445 150	CHESS GOLDEN DECADE VOL. 1: THE EARLY 50s	12
73	Checker 6445 151	CHESS GOLDEN DECADE VOL. 2: 1956 TAKE IT EASY GREASY	12
73	Checker 6445 152	CHESS GOLDEN DECADE VOL. 3: 1957 DIMESTORE PONYTAIL	12
74	Chess 6445 153	CHESS GOLDEN DECADE VOL. 4: 1958-1959 BOOK OF LOVE	12
74	Chess 6445 154	CHESS GOLDEN DECADE VOL. 5: 1959-1961 GOOD MORNING LITTLE SCHOOLGIRL	12
74	Chess 6445 202	CHESS GOLDEN DECADE VOL. 6: 1961-1962 TALKIN' TRASH	12
74	Chess 6445 203	CHESS GOLDEN DECADE VOL. 7: 1963-1965 HIGH HEEL SNEAKERS (gatefold sleeve)	15
74	Chess 6445 204	CHESS GOLDEN DECADE VOL. 8: 1965-1966 THE IN CROWD	12
78	Chess 9124 213	CHESS ROCKABILLIES	12
64	Chess CRL 4004	CHESS STORY VOL. 1	25
65	Chess CRL 4516	CHESS STORY VOL. 2	25
71	Vanguard VSD 79217	CHICAGO BLUES VOLUME 2	15
66	Fontana TFL 6068	CHICAGO/THE BLUES/TODAY	18
66	Fontana TFL 6069	CHICAGO/THE BLUES/TODAY VOLUME 2	18
66	Fontana TFL 6070	CHICAGO/THE BLUES/TODAY VOLUME 3	18
69	Vanguard SVRL 19020	CHICAGO/THE BLUES/TODAY VOLUME 1	20
69	Vanguard SVRL 19021	CHICAGO/THE BLUES/TODAY VOLUME 2	20
69	Vanguard SVRL 19022	CHICAGO/THE BLUES/TODAY VOLUME 3	18
68	Sunflower ET 1401	THE CHICAGO HOUSE BANDS (99 copies only)	40
69	Kokomo K 1005	CHICAGO SESSIONS VOLUME 1 (99 copies only)	50
70	Flyright LP 4700	CHICKEN STUFF	15
80	Relics LSD 1	CHOCOLATE SOUP FOR DIABETICS VOL. 1	15
81	Relics ACID 1	CHOCOLATE SOUP FOR DIABETICS VOL. 2 (gatefold sleeve)	15
83	Relics CSFD 3	CHOCOLATE SOUP FOR DIABETICS VOL. 3	12
84	MCA CHUNK 1	CHUNKS OF FUNK	20
58	Philips BBR 8112	CHRISTMAS (10")	12
73	United Artists UDX 205/6	CHRISTMAS AT THE PATTI (2 x 10", gatefold sleeve)	22
68	Chess CRLS 4541	CHRISTMAS DEDICATION	25
81	Ze/Island ILPS 7017	A CHRISTMAS RECORD (LP, initially white vinyl, then black)	12
63	London HA-U 8141	A CHRISTMAS GIFT FOR YOU (plum label, later black label)	100
78	Incus INCUS 33	CIRCADIAN RHYTHM	50
72	Specialty SNTF 5015	CITY BLUES	12
80s	White Elephant RIOCH 1	CITY WALLS - A SOUTHAMPTON COMPILATION (with insert)	12
70	Charisma CAS 1008	CLASSICAL HEADS	12
55	London AL 3559	CLASSIC JAZZ PIANO (10")	25
69	Atlantic 587 167	CLASSIC RHYTHM AND BLUES	12
70s	Waldo's DS 005	CLEANING UP THE MUSIC BIZ	12
85	Pusmort 0012-02	CLEANSE THE BACTERIA	20
72	Pegasus PS 1	CLOGS (FOLK SAMPLER) (with insert)	15
90s	Distronics ITCD 3	THE CLOSING PARTY - IN THE CITY LIVE UNSIGNED (CD)	50
72	Pegasus PS 2	CLUB FOLK VOLUME ONE	15
72	Pegasus PS 3	CLUB FOLK VOLUME TWO	15
71	Trojan TRLS97	CLUB REGGAE	12
72	Trojan TBL178	CLUB REGGAE 3	10
70	Trojan TTL 54	CLUB ROCK STEADY	25
68	W.I.R.L. ILP 965	CLUB ROCK STEADY '68	45
67	W.I.R.L. ILP 948	CLUB SKA '67	30
67	W.I.R.L. ILP 956	CLUB SKA '67 VOL. 2	35

70	Trojan TTL 48	CLUB SKA VOLUME ONE	20
70	Trojan TTL 51	CLUB SKA VOLUME TWO (Existence unconfirmed)	30
68	Island ILP 964	CLUB SOUL	50
84	Kent 022	CLUB SOUL	15
67	Elektra EUK 253	A COLD WIND BLOWS	15
65	Tamla Motown TML 11001	A COLLECTION OF 16 TAMLA MOTOWN HITS	30
67	Tamla Motown TML 11043	A COLLECTION OF 16 ORIGINAL BIG HITS VOL. 4	40
67	Tamla Motown TML 11050	A COLLECTION OF 16 ORIGINAL BIG HITS VOL. 5	40
68	T. Motown (S)TML 11074	A COLLECTION OF 16 ORIGINAL BIG HITS VOL. 6 (mono/stereo)	30
69	T. Motown (S)TML 11092	A COLLECTION OF 16 ORIGINAL BIG HITS VOL. 7 - THE MOTOWN SOUND	30
70	T. Motown (S)TML 11130	A COLLECTION OF 16 ORIGINAL BIG HITS VOL. 8	25
75	Chicago 202	COLLECTORS BLUES SERIES VOL. 1	15
75	Chicago 205	COLLECTORS BLUES SERIES VOL. 2	15
75	Chicago 210	COLLECTORS BLUES SERIES VOL. 3	15
75	Chicago 212	COLLECTORS BLUES SERIES VOL. 4	15
75	Chicago 213	COLLECTORS BLUES SERIES VOL. 5	15
54	London AL 3514	COLLECTORS' ITEMS VOLUME ONE (10")	18
54	London AL 3533	COLLECTORS' ITEMS VOLUME TWO (10")	18
56	London AL 3550	COLLECTORS' ITEMS VOLUME THREE (10")	18
86	Color Disc COLORS 4	COLOR SUPPLEMENT (400 only)	15
93	2-Tone CDCHRTT 5013	THE COMPACT 2-TONE STORY (4-CD, box set with book)	40
76	Incus INCUS 21	COMPANY 1	40
77	Incus INCUS 29	COMPANY 6	40
77	Incus INCUS 30	COMPANY 7	40
72	Apple STCX 3385	THE CONCERT FOR BANGLA DESH (3-LP box set, orange inside with BMI/ASCAP label credits, with booklet, featuring Bob Dylan)	70
64	Decca LK 4664	CONVERSATION WITH THE BLUES	70
57	Tempo TAP 10	COOL MUSIC FOR A HOT NIGHT - MOOD MUSIC IN THE MODERN MANNER	150
72	Wicksteed WCKLP 02	CORBY CATCHMENT AREA (private pressing)	200
78	ABC ABCL 5247	COTTON PICKIN' ROCK	12
80s	Third Mind TMLP 09	COULD YOU WALK ON THE WATER	15
64	London HA-B 8145	COUNTRY & WESTERN GOLDEN HIT PARADE VOL. 1	18
64	London HA-B 8146	COUNTRY & WESTERN GOLDEN HIT PARADE VOL. 2	18
60	Philips BBL 7410	COUNTRY AND WESTERN REQUESTS	12
62	Philips BBL 7552	COUNTRY AND WESTERN REQUESTS VOL. 2	12
63	Mercury 20015 MCL	COUNTRY AND WESTERN ROUND UP	12
60	Storyville SLP 129	THE COUNTRY BLUES	20
73	Specialty SNTF 5014	COUNTRY BLUES	15
60s	Saydisc Roots RL 334	COUNTRY BLUES OBSCURITIES VOLUME 1	20
66	Stateside SL 10170	COUNTRY COUSINS	18
56	Brunswick LA 8729	COUNTRY FAVOURITES VOL. ONE (10")	30
81	No Future OI 3	COUNTRY FIT FOR HEROES	15
82	No Future 12 OI 23	COUNTY FIT FOR HEROES 2	18
65	London HA-B 8243	COUNTRY GUITAR HALL OF FAME	15
64	London HA-B 8198	THE COUNTRY MUSIC FESTIVAL	12
66	London HA-B 8263	COUNTRY MUSIC FESTIVAL VOL. 2	12
66	London HA-B 8287	COUNTRY MUSIC FESTIVAL VOL. 3	12
63	Stateside SL 10017	THE COUNTRY MUSIC HALL OF FAME	18
63	London HA-B 8076	COUNTRY MUSIC HALL OF FAME VOL. 1	15
63	London HA-B 8077	COUNTRY MUSIC HALL OF FAME VOL. 2	15
64	London HA-B 8156	COUNTRY MUSIC HALL OF FAME VOL. 3	15
64	London HA-B 8157	COUNTRY MUSIC HALL OF FAME VOL. 4	15
62	Stateside SL 10003	COUNTRY MUSIC SPECTACULAR	15
63	Starlite STLP 15	COUNTRY MUSIC U.S.A. (reissued as GRK 605)	15
64	London HA-B 8185	COUNTRY MUSIC U.S.A.	15
65	London HA-B 8224	COUNTRY MUSIC WHO'S WHO	15
59	Capitol T 1179	THE COUNTRY'S BEST	12
69	Pama ECO 2	CRAB - GREATEST HITS	100
80	Rabid/Absurd LAST 1	THE CRAP STOPS HERE	25
87	Supreme CDSU 1	THE CREAM OF SUPREME (CD)	25
60	Fontana TFL 5103	THE CREAM OF 'TAKE IT FROM HERE' (also stereo SFL 534)	12
60s	Saydisc Roots RL 332	CREAM OF THE CROP	12
74	Eron 005	CRYPTADIA	15
79	Trojan TRLS 185	CREATION ROCKERS 5	15
79	Trojan TRLS 183	CREATION ROCKERS 3	18
77	Carib Gems CGDD 301	CARIB GEMS DISCO DISC	25

D

81	Two Tone CHRTT 5004	DANCE CRAZE	15
68	H. Note/B. Shot BSLP 5002	DANCING DOWN ORANGE STREET	80
84	Kent KENT 026	DANCING 'TIL DAWN	15
76	Dark Horse DH 1 (DHSAM 1)	DARK HORSE RECORDS '76 (promo only sampler, stickered sleeve & inner)	40
86	EMI EQ 5003	DAVE CLARK'S TIME (2-LP, with brochure and lyric inner, some with hologram)	30
90s	Nuphonic NUX 136LP	DAVID MANCUSO PRESENTS THE LOFT VOL. 1 (4 x 12" with booklet)	40
90s	Nuphonic NUX 154LP	DAVID MANCUSO PRESENTS THE LOFT VOL. 2 (4 x 12")	30
71	Dawn DNLB 3024	DAWN TAKEAWAY CONCERT	12
79	Dead Good DEAD 4	DEAD GOOD'S DEAD GOODS (unissued)	0
78	Virgin VD 2508	DEAD ON ARRIVAL (glow-in-the-dark vinyl with poster, export copies to US have "EXPACK 001" sticker on sleeve))	20
66	Highway 51 H 100	DECADE OF THE BLUES - THE 1950's (99 copies only)	75
66	Highway 51 H 104	DECADE OF THE BLUES - THE 1950's VOLUME 2 (99 copies only)	50
54	Decca LF 1160	DECCA SHOWCASE VOL. 3 (10")	15
55	Decca LF 1265	DECCA SHOWCASE VOL. 5 (10")	18
65	London HA-B 8249	DECK OF CARDS	12
71	United Artists UAS 29153	DEEPER INTO THE VAULTS	12
70	Polydor 2673 001	DEEP OVERGROUND POP	20
70	Stax SXATS 1037	THE DEEP SOUL OF STAX	22
71	Flyright LP 102	DEEP SOUTH COUNTRY BLUES	15
86	Decal LIK 9	DERAM DAYZE	15
68	Deram SML 1027	THE DERAM GOLDEN POPS SAMPLER	80
67	Island ILP 955	DERRICK HARRIOTT'S ROCK (SKA) STEADY PARTY	225

72	Trojan TTL 54	DERRICK HARRIOTT'S ROCKSTEADY PARTY (reissue - existence unconfirmed)......................50
85	Yangki 01	DEVASTATE TO LIBERATE 15
89	Blast First BFDJ 1	DEVIL'S JUKEBOX (10 x 7" in numbered box, with booklet, 3,000 only)...........................20
79	Topic 12TS 349	DEVON TRADITION - AN ANTHOLOGY FROM TRADITIONAL SINGERS 12
73	London ZGU 131	DIMENSION DOLLS...15
70	Mercury 6641 006	DIMENSION OF MIRACLES...15
80	DinDisc DONE 1	DINDISC 1980 (with free 20"x 20" game)..12
74	DIP DLP 5026	D.I.P. PRESENTS THE UPSETTER (Lee Perry et al.)...70
69	Minit MLL/MLS 40005	DIRT BLUES 25
70	BBC REC 65M	DISC A DAWN..20
57	RCA RC 2400	DICTIONARY OF JAZZ (10")..12
67	Island ILP 943	DOCTOR SOUL 90
82	BBC 2-LP-22001	DOCTOR WHO COLLECTOR'S EDITION (2-LP, with poster) 30
80s	Pleasantly Surprised PS 12	DOCUMENT (cassette) 18
84	Hope Springs HOP 1	DON'T LET THE HOPE CLOSE DOWN 15
70	Python PLP	DOWNHOME BLUES (99 copies only)..90
94	React REACT LP 55	DOPE ON PLASTIC! (2-LP) 20
94	React REACT LP 65	DOPE ON PLASTIC 2 (2-LP) 20
96	React REACT LP 073	DOPE ON PLASTIC 3 (2-LP) 20
96	React REACT LP 97	DOPE ON PLASTIC 4 (3-LP) 20
98	React REACT LP 118	DOPE ON PLASTIC 5 (4-LP) 20
99	React REACT LP 147	DOPE ON PLASTIC 6 (4-LP) 20
00	React REACT LP 169	DOPE ON PLASTIC 7 (3-LP) 20
01	React REACT LP 195	DOPE ON PLASTIC 8 (3-LP) 20
70	Python PLP 14	DOWNHOME BLUES VOLUME 2 (99 copies only) 90
71	Python PLP 22	DOWNHOME BLUES VOLUME 3 (99 copies only) 90
71	Flyright LP 4703	DOWN IN HOGAN'S ALLEY 15
67	Down With The Game 200	DOWN WITH THE GAME VOLUME 1 (99 copies only)..55
67	Down With The Game 201	DOWN WITH THE GAME VOLUME 2 (99 copies only)..55
68	Down With The Game 203	DOWN WITH THE GAME VOLUME 3 (99 copies only)..55
68	Down With The Game 204	DOWN WITH THE GAME VOLUME 4 (99 copies only)..55
68	Down With The Game 205	DOWN WITH THE GAME VOLUME 5 (99 copies only)..55
68	Down With The Game 206	DOWN WITH THE GAME VOLUME 6 (99 copies only)..55
67	Island ILP 954	DR. KITCH 60
85	Capitol EG 26 0573 1-4	DREAM BABIES 15
72	Ember EMB 3413	A DROP OF THE HARD STUFF...12
59	Parlophone PMC 1101	DRUMBEAT (Adam Faith et al.) 55
60	Columbia SCX 3359	DRUM NIGHT AT BIRDLAND 12
68	Island ILP 976	THE DUKE AND THE PEACOCK 90
69	Trojan TTL 8	DUKE REID'S GOLDEN HITS 40
67	Island ILP 958	DUKE REID'S ROCK STEADY 350
70	Trojan TTL 53	DUKE REID'S ROCK STEADY (reissue, existence unconfirmed) 30
69	BBC REC 35S	DUNGEON FOLK 12
87	Manic Ears ACHE 3	DIGGING IN WATER (LP, featuring Disorder/Chaos UK/Oi Polloi..)...............................12
01	Trunk DFM 001 LP	DIRTY FAN MAIL (LP) 20

E

70	Matchbox SDR 199	EARLY BLUES VOLUME 1: SKOODLE-UM-SKOO 20
70	Matchbox SDR 206	EARLY FOLK BLUES VOLUME 2: HOMETOWN SKIFFLE 15
70	Middle Earth MDLS 20	EARTHED 30
80	Dead Good GOOD 1	EAST (with inner & stickered sleeve) 25
73	Southern Sound SD 200	EAST VERNON BLUES 30
63	Decca LK 4546	EDINBURGH FOLK FESTIVAL VOLUME 1 30
63	Decca LK 4563	EDINBURGH FOLK FESTIVAL VOLUME 2 30
55	Philips BBR 8046	EIGHT EVERGREENS (10")..15
75	Island/Transatlantic	ELECTRIC MUSE - THE STORY OF FOLK INTO ROCK (4-LP box set with booklet)............40
64	Turnabout TV340465	ELECTRONIC MUSIC 25
73	YES 2-4	ELECTRONIC MUSIC FROM YORK (3-LP, box set, with insert)...................................250
85	Push PUSH 001	ELEGANCE, CHARM AND DEADLY DANGER 15
80s	Master BBSLP 007	ELEMENTALS 20
83	Extract XX 001	THE ELEPHANT TABLE ALBUM (2-LP) 18
57	Philips BBR 8115	ELLA, LENA, BILLIE AND SARAH (10") 15
71	Island IDLP 1	EL PEA (pink rim label) 15
77	EMI PSPL 209	EMI INTRODUCES THE NEW BRONZE AGE (LP)...20
83	Psycho PSYCHO 1	ENDLESS JOURNEY VOL. 1 (numbered)..20
83	Psycho PSYCHO 3	ENDLESS JOURNEY VOL. 2 (numbered)..15
83	Psycho PSYCHO 19	ENDLESS JOURNEY VOL. 3 (numbered)..15
76	Topic 12T 296	ENGLISH COUNTRY MUSIC 12
88	MEK MEK 006	THE ENGLISH REBELS (with insert)..20
84	Street Sounds HBOX 1	ESSENTIAL ELECTRO (9 LP box set, 5000 only)..100
67	Speciality SPE 6601	EVERY DAY I HAVE THE BLUES...15
72	Blue Horizon 2683 007	THE EXCELLO STORY (2-LP) 120
68	Amal. AMGLP 2002	EXPLOSIVE ROCKSTEADY 85
87	Rot ASS 100	THE END OF AN ERA (LP) 15

F

80	fACTORY fact 24	A FACTORY QUARTET (2-LP, featuring Durutti Column, Kevin Hewick, Blurt & Royal Family And The Poor) 20
67	Elektra EUK 259	FANTASTIC FOLK...15
64	Topic 12T 110	FAREWELL NANCY (blue label) 18
(Each of the above 10 LPs came with blue labels and a booklet.)		
76	Lightning LIP 2	FAREWELL TO THE ROXY (LP)...20
76	Polydor 2475 605	A FEAST OF IRISH FOLK..12
68	Zeus CF 201	FESTIVAL AT TOWERSEY 50
63	Pye Intl. NPL 28033	FESTIVAL OF THE BLUES...30
67	Marble Arch MAL 724	FESTIVAL OF THE BLUES (reissue) 12
61	Melodisc 12-116	FIDDLIN' COUNTRY STYLE..12
60s	Melodisc MS 4	15 OLDIES BUT GOODIES 18
65	Sue ILP 920	50 MINUTES & 24 SECONDS OF RECORDED DYNAMITE! 100
85	L.A.Y.L.A.H. LAY 10	THE FIGHT IS ON (Nurse With Wound, Organum, et al.) 30

MINT VALUE £

| 72 | Warner Bros K 66013 | FILLMORE: THE LAST DAYS (3-LP box set with poster & booklet) | 35 |
| 72 | CBS 63816 | FILLMORE WEST | 12 |

(Each of the above 10 LPs came with blue labels and a booklet.)

88	Re-Elect The President NIXON 4	THE FINAL COUNTDOWN (LP)	25
65	London HA-B 8205	FINGERS ON FIRE	15
60	HMV CLP 1358/CSD 1298	FINGS AIN'T WOT THEY USED TO BE	20
64	London HA-B 8117	FIRE ON THE STRINGS	15
69	Music Man	FIREPOINT - A COLLECTION OF FOLK BLUES	100
73	Spark SRLM 2003	FIREPOINT - A COLLECTION OF FOLK BLUES (reissue)	30
71	CBS 66311	THE FIRST GREAT ROCK FESTIVALS OF THE 70s: ISLE OF WIGHT AND ATLANTA (3-LP)	30
58	Esquire 20-091	THE FIRST MODERNS (10")	20
57	Esquire 20-089	THE FIRST NATIONAL SKIFFLE CONTEST (10")	80
56	Mercury MPT 7512	FIRST ROCK 'N' ROLL PARTY (10")	130
89	Confection LC 7871	FLAIR: THE OTHER WORLD OF BRITISH FOOTBALL (2-LP)	20
75	Chrysalis CHR 1081	FLASH FEARLESS V THE ZORG WOMEN PARTS 5 & 6 (Alice Cooper, Elkie Brooks, et al.)	12
80s	Alt. Tentacles VIRUS 22	FLEX YOUR HEAD	15
83	Kent KENT 007	FOR DANCERS ONLY	15
64	Blue Beat BBLP 803	FLY FLYING SKA	300
69	Atlantic 588 184	FLYING HIGH (record club edition)	15
76	Flams/Wounded WR 1068	FOLK AT THE CHEQUERS (private pressing)	15
64	Ember NR 5015	FOLK BLUES SONG FEST	20
69	World Rec. Club ST 890	FOLK FESTIVAL	15
76	Transatlantic TRA 324	FOLK FESTIVAL (2-LP)	15
60	Top Rank 35/070	FOLK FESTIVAL AT NEWPORT 1959 VOLUME 1	15
60	Top Rank 35/071	FOLK FESTIVAL AT NEWPORT 1959 VOLUME 2	15
60	Top Rank 35/072	FOLK FESTIVAL AT NEWPORT 1959 VOLUME 3	15
62	Fontana TFL 6000	FOLK FESTIVAL AT NEWPORT (VOL. 1)	18
62	Fontana TFL 6004	FOLK FESTIVAL AT NEWPORT (VOL. 2)	18
62	Fontana TFL 6009	FOLK FESTIVAL AT NEWPORT (VOL. 4)	18
63	Pye Intl. NPL 28033	FOLK FESTIVAL OF THE BLUES	20
73	Counterpoint CPT 3994	FOLK FROM McTAVISH'S KITCHENS	30
73	Windmill WMD	FOLK HERITAGE	30
73	Nottingham Festival FEST 1	FOLK NOTTINGHAM STYLE	200
65	Decca LK 4783	FOLK NOW	25
70	BBC REC 955	FOLK ON FRIDAY	18
71	Talisman STAL 5019	FOLK PHILOSOPHY	20
63	Golden Guinea GGL 0265	THE FOLK SCENE	15
66	Folkscene FSP 001	FOLK SCENE (LP, private pressing)	100
61	Topic 12T 157	THE FOLK SONGS OF BRITAIN - SONGS OF COURTSHIP	15
61	Topic 12T 158	THE FOLK SONGS OF BRITAIN VOL. 2 - SONGS OF SEDUCTION	15
61	Topic 12T 159	THE FOLK SONGS OF BRITAIN VOL. 3 - JACK OF ALL TRADES	15
61	Topic 12T 160	THE FOLK SONGS OF BRITAIN VOL. 4 - CHILD BALLADS 1	15
61	Topic 12T 161	THE FOLK SONGS OF BRITAIN VOL. 5 - CHILD BALLADS 2	15
61	Topic 12T 194	THE FOLK SONGS OF BRITAIN VOL. 6 - SAILORMEN AND SERVINGMAIDS	15
61	Topic 12T 195	THE FOLK SONGS OF BRITAIN VOL. 7 - FAIR GAME AND FOUL	15
61	Topic 12T 196	THE FOLK SONGS OF BRITAIN VOL. 8 - A SOLDIER'S LIFE FOR ME	15
61	Topic 12T 197	THE FOLK SONGS OF BRITAIN VOL. 9 - SONGS OF CEREMONY	15
61	Topic 12T 198	THE FOLK SONGS OF BRITAIN VOL. 10 - SONGS OF ANIMAL	15

(Each of the above 10 LPs came with blue labels and a booklet.)

69	Topic	THE FOLK SONGS OF BRITAIN VOLS. 1-10 (10 x LP box set)	80
61	Topic TPS 201	TOPIC SAMPLER No. 6 - FOLK SONGS	12
57	HMV DLP 1143	FOLK SONG TODAY (SONGS AND BALLADS OF ENGLAND AND SCOTLAND) (10")	25
65	HMV CLP 1910	FOLKSOUND OF BRITAIN	18
71	Nicro K 220971	FOLK UPSTAIRS	80
63	Ember CEL 902	FOOL BRITANNIA	20
65	Decca LK 4695	FOURTEEN - THE LORD'S TAVERNERS' ALBUM	20
78	Harvest SHSM 2024	FOUR ROCK N ROLL LEGENDS RECORDED IN LONDON (LP, featuring Jack Scott, Charlie Feathers, Buddy Knox & Warren Smith)	18
79	Pickwick PLD 8013	40 FOLK FAVOURITES (2-LP, limited edition)	18
70	Bamboo BLP 205	FREEDOM SOUNDS	50
81	Fresh FRESHLP 8	A FRESH SELECTION	12
81	BBC REH 426	FRIDAY NIGHT ROCK SHOW (LP)	12
72	Trojan TRL 51	FROM BAM BAM TO CHERRY OH BABY	15
81	Alternative ALT 007A	FROM BROMLEY WITH LOVE (LP)	120
70	Liberty LBS 83321	FROM THE BAYOU	15
70	Liberty LBS 83278	FROM THE VAULTS	15
83	New European BADVC 666	FROM TORTURE TO CONSCIENCE (with insert)	80
77	Caroline C 1521	THE FRONT LINE (LP)	12
78	Virgon/Caroline C1521	FRONTLINE	12
71	Cutty Wren	FROST LANE	50
89	Sub Pop DAMP 104	FUCK ME, I'M RICH!	15
89	Unrest UNREST 14	FULL FORCE VOL. 3	15
70	Trojan TBL 137	FUNKY CHICKEN	18
70	Bamboo BLP 206	FUNKY REGGAE	40
82	Come Org. WDC 881021	FÜR ILSE KOCH (some on red vinyl)	120
70	Ember	FUTURE STAR EXPLOSION	12
70	RCA Victor SF 8118	49 GREEK STREET (LP, featuring Synanthesia, Nadia Cattouse, Tin Angel & Keith Christmas)	50
76	Burning Sounds BS 1024	FUNNY FEELING (LP)	30
83	Greensleeves GREL 60	FORWARD	20
03	Trunk JBH 004 LP	FLEXI SEX (LP)	40
06	Trunk JBH 018 LP	FUZZY FELT FOLK (LP)	25
73	Eron ERON 001	FOLK IN SANDWICH (LP)	40

G

69	Pama ECO 4	GAS - GREATEST HITS	75
66	Doctor Bird DLM 5001	GAYFEET (Jamaican sleeve and UK pressed LP)	300
84	Kent KENT 021	GEMS	15
55	HMV DLP 1039	GENE NORMAN PRESENTS JUST JAZZ (10")	20
72	Chess 6641 047	GENESIS - THE BEGINNINGS OF ROCK (4-LP box set with booklet)	60
73	Chess 6641 125	GENESIS - MEMPHIS TO CHICAGO (4-LP box set with booklet)	60

75	Chess 6641 174	GENESIS - SWEET HOME CHICAGO (4-LP box set with booklet).............................60
69	Kokomo K 1004	GEORGIA GUITARS 1927-1938 (99 copies only)...60
67	Coxsone CSL 8007	GET READY ROCK STEADY 130
69	Pama SECO 20	A GIFT FROM PAMA 40
71	Wand WCS 1003	THE GIRLS WITH SOUL..15
80s	Sarah	GLASS ARCADE (The Field Mice/The Sea Urchins, et al.)..............................30
72	Revelation REV 1/2/3	GLASTONBURY FAYRE REVELATIONS - A MUSICAL ANTHOLOGY (3-LP, poster sleeve with booklets, pyramid & printed polythene bag)...................................200
66	Columbia SX 6062	GO!...70
80s	Touch & Go TG 11	GOD'S FAVOURITE DOG...20
95	Lissy's LISS 5	GODZ IS NOT A PUT ON (500 only, in hand-pressed sleeve; some with free 7").........30
72	Flyright LP 103	GOIN' AWAY WALKING..15
70	Python LP 1	GOIN' BACK TO CHICAGO (99 copies only)..80
70	Warner Bros WS 1874	GOING HOME 12
60s	Heritage 1003	GOING TO CALIFORNIA (99 copies only)...80
68	Decca LK 4931	GOIN' UP THE COUNTRY 20
69	Oliver & Boyd SBN 05 002118/9	THE GOLDEN BIRD (2-LP)..30
64	Columbia 33SX 1664	GOLDEN GOODIES VOL. 1...60
64	Columbia 33SX 1672	GOLDEN GOODIES VOL. 2...60
69	Roulette RCP 1000	GOLDEN GOODIES VOL. 1...20
69	Roulette RCP 1001	GOLDEN GOODIES VOL. 2...20
59	Philips BBL 7331	GOLDEN HITS 15
60	Philips BBL 7422	GOLDEN HITS VOL. 2...12
61	Philips BBL 7581	GOLDEN HITS VOL. 3...15
68	Allegro ALL885	GOLDEN HITS OF SOUL...20
57	Capitol T 830	THE GOLD RECORD (blue label) 15
03	Dust To Digital DTD 01	GOODBYE BABYLON (6-CD box set) 60
75	Eron 004	GOOD FOLK OF KENT (with insert) 40
65	Atlantic ATL 5004	GOOD OLD FIFTIES 55
68	Elek. EUK 260/EUKS 7260	GOOD TIME MUSIC (U.K. version of "What's Shakin' ", gold or red label)...............40
72	CBS 67234	GOSPEL SOUND (2-LP)...20
59	Brunswick LAT 8290	GOSPEL TRAIN 20
64	London HA-B 8172	GRAND OLE OPRY SPECTACULAR VOL. 1..18
64	London HA-B 8173	GRAND OLE OPRY SPECTACULAR VOL. 2..18
73	Greasy Truckers GT 4997	GREASY TRUCKERS - LIVE AT DINGWALLS DANCE HALL (2-LP with insert) 18
73	United Artists UDX 203/4	GREASY TRUCKERS PARTY (2-LP, gatefold sleeve).....................................20
72	Vanguard VSD 25/26	GREAT BLUESMEN (2-LP)..18
54	London AL 3530	THE GREAT BLUES SINGERS (10")..45
60s	Riverside RLP 12-121	THE GREAT BLUES SINGERS 25
70	Trojan TBL 111	GREATER JAMAICA 20
75	Brunswick BRLS 3006	GREATEST HITS 15
64	Stateside SL 10075	THE GREATEST GOSPEL SONGS OF OUR TIME 25
67	Doctor Bird DLM 5009	GREATEST JAMAICAN BEAT 150
70	Transatlantic TRASAM 17	GREAT SCOTS SAMPLER..20
70	Transatlantic TRASAM 21	GREAT SCOTS SAMPLER VOL. 2..20
54	HMV DLP 1054	GREAT TRUMPET SOLOISTS (10") 25
85	Crashed METALPS 107	GREEN METAL...30
89	Earache MOSH 12	GRINDCRUSHER (with free 7") 15
71	Bamboo BDLP 215	GROOVING WITH BAMBOO 50
69	Direction 8-63452	GROOVY BABY 15
63	Realm RM 149	GROUP BEAT '63 40
63	London HA-U 8086	GROUP OF GOODIES 55
64	World Record Club TP 444	GROUP '64 20
78	Virgin VCL 5001	GUILLOTINE (10" mini-LP, with inner sleeve) 18
60s	Storyville SLP 166	GUITAR BLUES 20
73	Transatlantic TRA 271	GUITAR WORKSHOP (2-LP)...15
71	Sunnyland KS 102	GULF COAST BLUES (99 copies only)...40
69	Trojan TTL 16	GUNS OF NAVARONE 12
69	Liberty LBX 3	GUTBUCKET 20
68	Island ILP 977	GUY STEVENS' TESTAMENT OF ROCK AND ROLL 60
71	Wand WCS 1002	THE GUYS WITH SOUL...20
69	BBC RESR 4	GANDHI - MAN ON TRIAL (LP) 15
84	Fashion FAD LP 001	GREAT BRITISH MCS..15
79	Bead Records BEAD 15	GROUPS IN FRONT OF PEOPLE (LP) 25
79	Bead Records BEAD 15	GROUPS IN FRONT OF PEOPLE 2 (LP) 25

H

77	Harvest SHSM 2020	HARVEST HERITAGE : 20 GREATS 15
88	Strange Fruit SFRLP 101	HARDCORE HOLOCAUST 15
90	Strange Fruit SFRLP 113	HARCORE HOLOCAUST 2 20
80	Hackney Music Coll LP1	HACKNEY MUSIC COLLECTIVE...25
58	Oriole MG 20033	HAIL VARIETY!..15
70	Probe PSS 1	HANDLE WITH CARE...12
88	Hangman HANG 22-UP	HANGMAN SAMPLER 20
88	HandMade (no cat. no.)	HANDMADE FILMS MUSIC - THE 10TH ANNIVERSARY (CD, promo only) 100
85	Anagram GRAM 23	HANG 11 (MUTANT SURF PUNKS) 20
68	Immediate IMLYIN 2	HAPPY TO BE PART OF THE INDUSTRY OF HUMAN HAPPINESS 18
88	BPM BPLP2	HARDCORE ONE (LP) 40
77	VJM VLP 40	HARD LUCK BLUES 18
74	Decca DPA 3009/10	HARD UP HEROES 1963-68 (2-LP, gatefold sleeve) 20
57	London TKL 93119	HARLEM CONGREGATION 30
56	London AL 3553	HARLEM PIANO ROLL (10") 20
72	Carnival 2941 001	HARPIN' ON IT 12
71	Harvest SHSS 3	HARVEST BAG 15
69	Harvest SPSLP 118	HARVEST SAMPLER OF THE INITIAL FOUR JUNE RELEASES (promo only) 150
63	Reprise R 50001	HAVE YOURSELF A MERRY LITTLE CHRISTMAS 15
71	Sunnyland KS 101	HAVIN' A GOOD TIME - CHICAGO BLUES ANTHOLOGY (99 copies only)..................50
66	Polydor 582 701	HEADLINE NEWS 15
71	Vertigo 6360 045	HEADS TOGETHER, FIRST ROUND (gatefold sleeve, swirl label).........................18
94	Mo' Wax MWLP 026	HEADZ: A SOUNDTRACK OF EXPERIMENTAL BEATHEAD JAMS (3-LP) 25

96	Mo' Wax MW 061LP	HEADZ VOLUME 2A (4-LP)	25
90	Imaginary ILLUSION 016	HEAVEN AND HELL VOLUME 1: A TRIBUTE TO THE VELVET UNDERGROUND	70
81	Heavy Metal HMR LP 1	HEAVY METAL HEROES	30
82	Heavy Metal HMR LP 7	HEAVY METAL HEROES VOLUME 2	25
84	Heavy Metal HMR LP 24	HEAVY METAL RECORDS (blue, clear & white vinyl, round sleeve)	15
68	Trojan TRL 6	HERE COMES THE DUKE	30
65	Pye NPL 18121	HERE COME THE GIRLS	15
85	Rock 'N' Dole RDR 2	HEROES	15
80s	Temps Modernes LTMV:XI	HEURES SANS SOLEIL	20
69	Pama PSP 1002	HEY BOY HEY GIRL	40
58	Capitol T 926	HI-FI DRUMS	15
58	Melodisc MLP 518	HIGHLIFE: AUTHENTIC WEST AFRICAN MUSIC VOL. 1 (10")	12
58	Melodisc MLP 519	HIGHLIFE: AUTHENTIC WEST AFRICAN MUSIC VOL. 2 (10")	12
59	Parlophone PMD 1085	HIGHWAY TO HEAVEN (10")	20
52	Capitol LC 6508	THE HISTORY OF JAZZ - THE SOLID SOUTH	20
52	Capitol LC 6527	THE HISTORY OF JAZZ - THIS MODERN AGE	12
68	Atlantic 587 094	HISTORY OF RHYTHM AND BLUES - VOL. 1, THE ROOTS 1947-52	15
68	Atlantic 587 095	HISTORY OF RHYTHM AND BLUES - VOL. 2, THE GOLDEN YEARS 1953-55	15
68	Atlantic 587 096	HISTORY OF RHYTHM AND BLUES - VOL. 3, ROCK 'N' ROLL 1956-57	15
68	Atlantic 587 097	HISTORY OF RHYTHM AND BLUES - VOL. 4, THE BIG BEAT 1958-60	15
68	Atlantic 587 140	HISTORY OF RHYTHM AND BLUES - VOL. 5	15
68	Atlantic 587 141	HISTORY OF RHYTHM AND BLUES - VOL. 6	15
69	Bamboo BDLP 203	HISTORY OF SKA VOLUME ONE	200
87	Stylus/PWL SMD 740	HIT FACTORY - THE BEST OF STOCK, AITKEN & WATERMAN VOL. 1 (CD)	25
87	Fanfare/PWL HFCD 4	HIT FACTORY - THE BEST OF STOCK, AITKEN & WATERMAN VOL. 2 (CD, with exclusive mix of Kylie Minogue's "I Should Be So Lucky", etc)	30
64	Pye NPL 18108	THE HITMAKERS	20
65	Pye NPL 18115	THE HITMAKERS VOL. 2	20
65	Pye NPL 18116	THE HITMAKERS VOL. 3	20
66	Pye NPL 18144	THE HITMAKERS VOL. 4	20
57	Pye Nixa NPT 19015	HIT PARADE OF 1956 (10")	18
59	Pye Nixa NPT 19032	HIT PARADE OF 1958	15
66	Marble Arch MAL 650	HITS FROM THE IVY LEAGUE, THE ROCKIN' BERRIES & THE SORROWS	12
77	Stiff FIST 1	HITS - GREATEST STIFFS (with 7", Max Wall's "England's Glory" [BUY 12])	12
65	Tamla Motown TML 11019	HITSVILLE U.S.A.	35
67	Stax 589 005	HIT THE ROAD STAX	30
81	United Dairies UD 05	HOISTING THE BLACK FLAG	35
55	Philips BBR 8048	HOLLYWOOD DANCE DATE (10")	12
62	Golden Guinea GGL 0129	HONEY HIT PARADE	12
74	Melodisc 12-216	HONEYS	35
52	Capitol LC 6544	HONKY TONK PIANO (10")	15
60s	Riverside RLP 8806	HONKY TONK TRAIN (with booklet)	22
65	Summit ATL 4150	HOOTENANNY AT THE BARGE	15
64	Stateside SL 10079	HOOTENANNY AT THE TROUBADOUR	18
63	Decca LK 4544	HOOTENANNY IN LONDON	15
63	Fontana 688 009ZL	HOOTENANNY SATURDAY NIGHT	15
64	Waverley ZLP 2025	HOOT'NANNY SHOW VOLUME 1	15
64	Waverley ZLP 2032	HOOT'NANNY SHOW VOLUME 2	15
84	Kent KENT 023	HOT CHILLS AND COLD THRILLS	15
71	Pama PMP 2006	HOT NUMBERS	40
71	Pama PMP 2009	HOT NUMBERS VOLUME TWO	30
77	WEA M 100	HOT PLATTER CORDON BLEU (available via Melody Maker)	20
70	Trojan TBL 128	HOT SHOTS OF REGGAE	12
72	Hot Wax SHW 5008	HOT WAX GREATEST HITS	15
69	Track 613 016	THE HOUSE THAT TRACK BUILT (gatefold sleeve)	30
80	Stark ST1	HOUSEHOLD SHOCKS	40
69	Blue Horizon PR 45/46	HOW BLUE CAN WE GET (2-LP, gatefold sleeve with insert)	40
84	Rot ASS 18	HAVE A ROTTEN CHRISTMAS (LP)	25
08	Jonny JBH 025 LP	HEAR O ISRAEL (LP)	15

I

88	Idea IDEALP 003	IDEA COMPENDIUM (LP)	35
81	TJM TJML 1	IDENTITY PARADE (LP)	15
95	Dig The Fuzz DIG 001	INCREDIBLE SOUND SHOW STORIES VOL 1: THE TECHNICOLOUR MILKSHAKE (LP)	20
96	Dig The Fuzz DIG 004	INCREDIBLE SOUND SHOW STORIES VOL 2: WHEN THE TANGERINE STRIKES TWELVE (LP, gatefold sleeve, orange vinyl)	20
96	Dig The Fuzz DIG 007	INCREDIBLE SOUND SHOW STORIES VOL 3: 200 FEEL DEEP IN A PURPLE IDEA (LP)	20
96	Dig The Fuzz DIG 008	INCREDIBLE SOUND SHOW STORIES VOL 4: A TRIP ON THE MAGIC FLYING MACHINE (LP)	20
96	Dig The Fuzz DIG 009	INCREDIBLE SOUND SHOW STORIES VOL. 5: YELLOW STREET BOUTIQUE (LP)	20
97	Dig The Fuzz DIG 010	INCREDIBLE SOUND SHOW STORIES VOL. 6: PLASTIC & OTHER RUBBERS OF LIFE (LP)	20
97	Dig THe Fuzz DIG 013	INCREDIBLE SOUND SHOW STORIES VOL. 7: ILLUSIONS OF ALICE IN BLACK (LP, with booklet)	20
99	Dig The Fuzz DIG 016	INCREDIBLE SOUND SHOW STORIES: VOL. 8: PROFESSOR POTTS PORNOGRAPHIC PROJECTOR (LP, with booklet)	30
99	Dig The Fuzz DIG 036	INCREDIBLE SOUND SHOW STORIES VOL. 9: CLAP HANDS DADDY COME HOME! (LP, with booklet)	20
99	Dig THe Fuzz DIG 039	INCREDIBLE SOUND SHOW STIRIES VOL. 10: A HIDDEN SECRET GARDEN FOUND (LP, with booklet)	20
99	Dig The Fuzz DIG 033	INCREDIBLE SOUND SHOW STORIES: VOL. 11: CRIMSON VALLET CREATURES IN YOUR ZOO (LP, with booklet)	20
01	Dig THe Fuzz DIG 043	INCREDIBLE SOUND SHOW STORIES VOL. 12: FUZZ PUDDING FACTORY (LP)	15
01	Buzz With Fuzz FUZZLP 3301	INCREDIBLE SOUND SHOW STORIES VOL. 13: FAR AWAY ROUNDABOUT (LP, 500 only)	15
00	Dig The Fuzz DIG 042	INCREDIBLE SOUND SHOW SPORIES VOL. 14: CANDY COLOURED DAYDREAMS (LP, with gatefold insert)	20
03	Dig THe Fuzz DIG 046	INCREDIBLE COUND SHOW STORIES VOL. 16 : SECOND GLANCE THROUGH THE LOOKING GLANCE (LP)	20
02	Dig THe Fuzz DIG 045	INCREDIBLE SOUND SHOW STORIES VOL. 17 CLAP HANDS DADDY COME HOME1 PART 2 (LP, with inner sleeve, 400 only)	20
02	Universal 0647491	IMPRESSED (2-LP, Gilles Peterson compilation)	30
02	Universal 982 197 0	IMPRESSED 2 (2-LP, Gilles Peterson compilation)	25
69	Liberty LBL/LBS 83252	I ASKED FOR WATER ... AND SHE GAVE ME GASOLINE	80
88	Bam Caruso MARX 085	ILLUSIONS FROM THE CRACKLING VOID	15
90s	Dig The Fuzz DIG 013	ILLUSIONS OF ALICE IN BLACK (650 only, with booklet)	20

69	Immediate IMLYIN 1	IMMEDIATE LETS YOU IN	20
70	Highway 51 H-104	I'M YOUR COUNTRY MAN (99 copies only)	40
77	United Artists UAS 30101	IMPERIAL ROCKABILLIES	12
66	CBS/Denson Shoes	THE IN CROWD (shoe offer compilation)	25
69	Trojan TTL 15	INDEPENDENT JAMAICA	12
67	Fontana TL 5426	INDIAN MUSIC	12
79	Object Music OBJ 002	INDISCRETE MUSIC - DUBIOUS COLLABORATION (500 only)	15
84	Illuminated JAMS 39	THE INDUSTRIAL RECORDS STORY 1976-1981	35
84	United Dairies UD 015	IN FRACTURED SILENCE	35
69	T. Motown (S)TML 11124	IN LOVING MEMORY (TRIBUTE TO MRS LOUCYE G. WAKEFIELD)	55
70	Blue Horizon PR 37	IN OUR OWN WAY (OLDIES BUT GOODIES)	20
70	Ember EMB 34111	IN REGGAE TIME	15
80	Island IRSP3	INTENSIFIED VOLUME 2	12
66	Ember FA 2034	IRELAND'S GREATEST SOUNDS: FIVE TOP GROUPS FROM BELFAST'S MARITIME CLUB	70
64	Decca LK 4633	IRISH FOLK NIGHT	12
63	Topic 12T 86	THE IRON MUSE (blue label with lyric insert)	15
79	Rationale RATE 8	IRRATIONALE (cassette, in bag with booklet)	20
61	Oriole MG 20046	IT'S ALL HAPPENING HERE	35
64	Philips BL 7609	IT'S ALL OVER TOWN	15
63	Pye Golden Guinea GGL 0249	IT'S DANCE TIME	0
85	Kent KENT 046	IT'S TORTURE	15
84	Sain 002	IT'S UNHEARD OF	150

J

69	Amalgamated CSP 3	JACKPOT OF HITS	35
74	Atra ALP 001	JAH GUIDE - JAMAICA'S GREATEST HITS	20
71	Ashanti SHAN 102	JAMAICAN FOLK SINGERS	20
68	Blue Cat BCL 1	JAMAICAN MEMORIES	100
64	Atlantic 587 075	JAMAICA SKA (colour 'Dancers' sleeve)	50
67	Atlantic 587 075	JAMAICA SKA (reissue, orange sleeve)	30
60s	Whirl WHIRL 1	JAMAICA'S AMBASSADORS OF SONG	70
60s	Melodisc MLP 12-158	JAMAICA'S GREATEST	30
68	Flyright LP 3502	JAMBALAYA ON THE BAYOU - VOLUME 1	15
69	Flyright LP 3503	JAMBALAYA ON THE BAYOU - VOLUME 2	15
72	Utd. Artists UAS 60027/8	THE JAMES BOND COLLECTION (2-LP, with booklet)	25
72	Rolling Stones COC 39100	JAMMING WITH EDWARD	15
55	Columbia Clef 33CX 10008	JAM SESSION	15
61	HMV/Utd Artists CSD 1381	JAZZ ALIVE - A NIGHT AT THE HALF NOTE	12
56	Tempo TAP 5	JAZZ AT THE FLAMINGO	120
55	Columbia 33CX 10078	JAZZ AT THE PHILHARMONIC, 1955 VOL. 1	12
55	Columbia 33CX 10079	JAZZ AT THE PHILHARMONIC, 1955 VOL. 2	12
68	Columbia SLJS 1	JAZZ EXPLOSION	15
72	Decca ECS 2114	JAZZ IN BRITAIN 1968-1969	50
62	Parlophone PMC 1195	JAZZ IN THE MAKING	12
84	Streetsounds MUSIC 1	JAZZ JUICE	25
85	Streetsounds SOUND 1	JAZZ JUICE (reissue)	15
86	Streetsounds SOUND 4	JAZZ JUICE 2	15
86	Streetsounds SOUND 5	JAZZ JUICE 3	15
86	Streetsounds SOUND 6	JAZZ JUICE 4	15
57	London AL 3562	JAZZ OF THE ROARING TWENTIES VOL. 2 (10")	12
58	Philips BBL 7184	JAZZ OMNIBUS	12
63	VJM LC 6	JAZZ PANORAMA OF THE SIXTIES	12
58	Vogue LAE 12097	JAZZ PIANISTS GALORE	12
57	London AL 3565	JAZZ PIANO RARITIES (10")	12
55	Columbia Clef 33C 9007	JAZZ SCENE (10")	12
55	Columbia Clef 33C 9008	JAZZ SCENE VOL. 2 (10")	12
62	Parlophone PMC 1177	JAZZ SOUNDS OF THE 20s VOL. 4: BLUES SINGERS & ACCOMPANISTS	12
56	Vogue LAE 12038	JAZZ WEST COAST	12
57	Vogue LAE 12061	JAZZ WEST COAST VOLUME 2	12
58	Vogue LAE 12115	JAZZ WEST COAST VOLUME 3	12
61	Vogue LAE 12235	JAZZ WEST COAST VOLUME 5	12
77	Decca DPA 3035/3036	THE JOE MEEK STORY (2-LP)	40
60	Top Rank 35/064	JOHN HAMMOND'S SPIRITUALS TO SWING VOLUME 1	15
60	Top Rank 35/065	JOHN HAMMOND'S SPIRITUALS TO SWING VOLUME 2	15
72	Vanguard VRS 8523/4	JOHN HAMMOND'S SPIRITUALS TO SWING: LEGENDARY CARNEGIE HALL CONCERTS OF 1938/9 (2-LP)	18
69	BBC REC 52S	JOHN PEEL PRESENTS TOP GEAR	40
70	BBC REC 68M	JOHN PEEL'S ARCHIVE THINGS	35
60	HMV CLP 1327	A JUG OF PUNCH (also issued as XLP 50003)	25
67	Ace Of Hearts AH 163	JUGS AND WASHBOARDS	15
67	RCA Victor RD 7893	JUGS WASHBOARDS AND KAZOOS	15
70s	Eric's ERICS 008	JUKEBOX AT ERIC'S	15
62	Embassy WLP 6052	JUKE BOX FAVOURITES	12
76	RCA RS 1066	JUMPING AT THE GO GO	18
77	Policy Wheel PW 459-1	JUMPING ON THE HILL	12
64	R&B JBL 1111	JUMP JAMAICA WAY	400
69	RCA Intl. INT 1014	JUST A LITTLE BIT OF SOUL	22
79	Kick KK 1	JUST FOR KICKS	35

K

59	Capitol T 1057	K.C. IN THE 30's	20
56	Vogue LAE 12028	KENTON'S SIDEMEN (Don Rendell, et al.)	60
81	White Witch	KENT ROCKS (200 only, white cover)	180
71	Jay Boy JSX 2009	KERBSIDE ENTERTAINERS	12
54	HMV DLP 1048	KEYBOARD KINGS OF JAZZ (10")	20
72	Key	KEY COLLECTION (with insert)	15
70	Trojan TBL 140	KING SIZE REGGAE	15
72	Sioux SLX 7502	KING OF THE ROAD	25
68	Polydor 623 273	KINGS OF RHYTHM AND BLUES	15
60s	Gryphon 13159	KINGS OF THE TWELVE STRING GUITAR	20

60s	Saydisc Roots RL 333	KINGS OF MEMPHIS TOWN 1927-1930	20
94	Mercury 522 476-1	KISS MY ASS (red, white or blue vinyl)	12
85	Rot ASS 21	KICK UP THE ARSE (LP)	15

L

83	Fetish FR 2011	THE LAST TESTAMENT (with inner, stickered sleeve)	18
87	Other OTH 10	LAST WARRIOR	18
68	Island ILP 986	LEAPING WITH MR LEE (by Bunny Lee All Stars)	300
80	Atra ATRA LP 1003	THE LEGENDS (Augustus Pablo et al.)	15
03	Ai AILP 004	LEISURE (100 copies only)	15
99	Jazzman 1	LE JAZZBEAT!	20
66	Blue Horizon LP 2	LET ME TELL YOU ABOUT THE BLUES (99 copies only)	1000
63	Polydor SLPHM 237 622	LET'S DO THE TWIST, HULLY GULLY, SLOP, SURF, LOCOMOTION, MONKEY	30
66	Neshoba N 11	LET'S GO DOWN SOUTH (99 copies only)	55
84	Cult 1	LET'S GET PISSED IT'S CHRISTMAS	15
58	Brunswick LAT 8271	LET'S HAVE A PARTY	30
73	Bell DUBL 9002/3	LET THE GOOD TIMES ROLL	15
81	Alt. Tentacles VIRUS 4	LET THEM EAT JELLYBEANS (with lyric poster)	20
74	Sonet SNTX 1	LEGACY OF THE BLUES SAMPLER	12
80s	Third Mind/Abstract	LIFE AT THE TOP	20
85	Riot City CITY 019	LIFE'S A RIOT WITH RIOT CITY RECORDS	20
68	Transatlantic TRASAM 2	LISTEN HERE!	12
81	NEMS NEL 6020	LIVE AND HEAVY	12
80	BUN 01	LIVE AT BUNJIES (gatefold sleeve with insert)	30
74	Key KL 021	LIVE AT SPREE	15
77	NEMS NEL 6013	LIVE AT THE VORTEX	15
65	Fontana TL 5240	LIVE AT THE WHISKEY A-GO-GO	40
68	Big Shot BBTL 4000	LIVE IT UP	75
64	Embassy WLP 6065	LIVERPOOL BEAT	15
65	Ember NR 5028	LIVERPOOL TODAY - LIVE AT THE CAVERN	40
64	CBS Realm RM 209	LIVIN' WITH THE BLUES	15
08	Honest Hard HJRLP 33	LIVING IS HARD - WEST AFRICAN MUSIC IN BRITAIN 1927-29 (2-LP)	20
70	Trojan TBL 135	LOCH NESS MONSTER	15
87	4AD CAD 703D	LONELY IS AN EYESORE (cardboard pack with book)	30
87	4AD CADX 703	LONELY IS AN EYESORE (CD, LP & cassette, in wooden box with etching, screen print & video, 100 only)	1000
71	Count Shelly SSLP 03	LOOK BEFORE YOU LEAP	60
91	Holyground HG 121	LOOSE ROUTES (2-LP, gatefold foldover sleeve)	30
65	Storyville 616002	LOUISIANA PRISON BLUES	15
69	Pama PSP 1001	A LOVELY DOZEN	40
96	Earth EARTHLP 001	LTJ BUKEM PRESENTS EARTH VOLUME 1 (5 LP box set, stickered box, 5 picture sleeves, 5000 only)	35
97	Earth EARTHLP 002	LTJ BUKEM PRESENTS EARTH VOLUME 2 (5 LP box set, 5 picture sleeves)	25
98	Good Looking EARTH LP 003	LTJ BUKEM PRESENTS EARTH VOLUME 3 (5 LP box set)	25

M

76	Cornish Legend CLM 1	MADE IN CORNWALL (with insert)	25
58	Pye Nixa Jazz NJL 13	(LEONARD FEATHER PRESENTS) MAD THAD	12
79	Object Music OBJ 003	A MANCHESTER COLLECTION	25
70	Trojan TBL 129	MAN FROM CAROLINA	15
53	Brunswick LA 8567	MAN WITH A HORN (10" LP)	12
70	CBS 52798	MA RAINEY AND THE CLASSIC BLUES SINGERS	20
69	Marmalade 643 314	MARMALADE - 100% PROOF	15
72	Village Thing VTSAM 16	MATCHBOX DAYS	25
68	President PTL 1002	MAR-V-LUS SOUND OF R&B AND SOUL MUSIC	40
60s	Wudwink ISMF 107	MARY'S FOLK	200
78	CBS 82670	MAX'S KANSAS CITY	12
66	CBS Special Prod. WSR 853	McDONALDS ALL-STAR FAVOURITES	12
69	Liberty LBL/LBS 83190	ME AND THE DEVIL	75
88	Hangman HANG 15-UP	THE MEDWAY POETS (LP)	20
87	Hangman HANG 4 UP	MEDWAY POWER HOUSE 1	20
87	Hangman HANG 8 UP	MEDWAY POWER HOUSE 2	20
88	Hangman HANG 17 UP	MEDWAY POWER HOUSE 3	25
78	Topic 12T 376	MELODEON GREATS - A COLLECTION OF MELODEON MASTERPIECES	15
64	London HA 8129	MEMORIES ARE MADE OF HITS VOL. 1	25
64	London HA 8130	MEMORIES ARE MADE OF HITS VOL. 2	25
64	London HA 8131	MEMORIES ARE MADE OF HITS VOL. 3	25
64	London HA 8138	MEMORIES ARE MADE OF HITS VOL. 4	25
64	London HA 8148	MEMORIES ARE MADE OF HITS VOL. 5	25
64	London HA 8171	MEMORIES ARE MADE OF HITS VOL. 6	25
64	London HA 8189	MEMORIES ARE MADE OF HITS VOL. 7	25
65	London HA 8213	MEMORIES ARE MADE OF HITS VOL. 8	25
69	Stax 589001	MEMPHIS GOLD	15
54	Vogue Coral LVC 10008	MERRY CHRISTMAS (10")	15
69	T. Motown (S)TML 11126	MERRY CHRISTMAS FROM MOTOWN (mono/stereo)	40
67	Capitol T 9030	MERRY CHRISTMAS TO YOU	15
85	Neat NEAT 1014	METAL BATTLE	15
80	BBC REH 397	METAL EXPLOSION	20
82	Ebony EBON 1	METAL EXPLOSION	12
80	EMI EMC 3318	METAL FOR MUTHAS	20
80	EMI EMC 3337	METAL FOR MUTHAS VOL. 2	12
97	Metalheadz METBOX 001	METALHEADZ (5 discs in circular tin, booklet)	30
82	Ebony EBON 8	METAL MANIAXE	15
83	Ebony EBON 14	METAL PLATED	15
87	Other OTH 9	METAL WARRIOR	50
83	Ebony EBON 11	METAL WARRIORS	15
60	RCA/Camden CDN 122	METRONOME ALL STARS	12
80	MGM 2315 394	THE MGM ROCKABILLY COLLECTION	12
56	Nixa Jazz Today NJL 3	MIDNIGHT AT NIXA	20
66	Atlantic 587 021	MIDNIGHT SOUL	20
69	Storyville 616 009	MIDNIGHT SPECIAL	15

62	Brunswick LAT 8401	MIDNIGHT JAMBOREE (also stereo STA 3061)	12
56	London AL 3554	MIDWESTERN JAZZ (10")	15
66	Xtra XTRA 1047	THE MIKE RAVEN BLUES SHOW	12
69	Transatlantic TRASAM 5	THE MIKE RAVEN BLUES SAMPLER	12
72	Polydor	MILL VALLEY JAM SESSION	12
60	Coral LVA 9126	MILLION-AIRS	18
80	Pipe PIPE 2	MINIATURES (with poster insert, 500 only)	15
80	Pipe PIPE 2	MINIATURES (cassette with mini-booklet insert, 100 only)	30
71	Trojan TBL 174	MISS LABBA LABBA REGGAE	30
60	Top Rank BUY 028	MR. BLUE	40
60s	Bounty BY 6025	MODERN CHICAGO BLUES	30
53	Capitol LC 6561	MODERN IDIOM (10")	15
55	HMV DLP 1022	MODERN JAZZ PIANO (10")	15
56	Tempo TAP 2	MODERN JAZZ SCENE 1956	100
53	Esquire 20-011	MODERN MIXTURE VOLUME ONE (10")	20
79	Bridge House BHLP 003	MODS MAYDAY '79 (original issue)	20
80	Polydor 2488810	MONSTERS OF ROCK	15
73	Stax STX 1029	MONTREUX FESTIVAL 1973	15
70	Trojan TTL 31	MOONLIGHT GROOVER	15
70	Liberty LBS 83377	MORE FROM THE VAULTS	15
62	HMV CLP 1583	MORE OF YOUR FAVOURITE TV AND RADIO THEMES	20
67	Atlantic 587088	MORE MIDNIGHT SOUL	15
68	Marble Arch MAL 813	MORE RHYTHM AND BLUES	12
65	private pressing	MORE SINGING AT THE COUNT HOUSE	30
72	Island HELP 5	MORRIS ON (black label with pink 'i')	18
80	Conventional CON 013	MOTHER OF A PUNK (cassette)	12
86	Iguana VYK LP 11	MOTOR CITY 9 (with booklet)	15
65	Tamla Motown TML 11007	THE MOTORTOWN REVUE LIVE	80
66	Tamla Motown TML 11027	THE MOTORTOWN REVUE IN PARIS	70
70	T. Motown (S)TML 11127	THE MOTORTOWN REVUE LIVE (mono/stereo)	20
69	T. Motown (S)TML 11121	MOTOWN CHARTBUSTERS VOL. 3 (original with flipback sleeve)	12
70	T. Motown STML 11162	MOTOWN CHARTBUSTERS VOL. 4 (original with flipback sleeve)	12
71	T. Motrown STML 11181	MOTOWN CHARTBUSTERS VOL. 5	12
74	T. Motown STML 11270	MOTOWN CHARTBUSTERS VOL. 9 (green vinyl)	12
72	Tamla Motown STMA 8005	MOTOWN DISCO CLASSICS VOL. 2	15
66	Tamla Motown TML 11030	MOTOWN MAGIC	35
68	Tamla Motown TML 11064	MOTOWN MEMORIES (flipback sleeve)	60
68	Tamla Motown TML 11077	MOTOWN MEMORIES VOL. 2	60
70	T. Motown STML 11143	MOTOWN MEMORIES VOL. 3	50
72	Tamla Motown STML 11200	MOTOWN MEMORIES	12
80	Tamla Motown ZL 72032	MOTOWN MOD CLASSICS VOL. 1	12
80	Tamla Motown STML 12133	MOTOWN MOD CLASSICS VOL. 2	12
72	Tamla Motown TMSP 1130	THE MOTOWN STORY (5-LP box set)	20
83	Tamla Motown TMSP 6019	THE MOTOWN STORY - THE FIRST 25 YEARS (box set)	20
77	Mountain PSLP 200	MOUNTAIN ROCKS INTO '77 (Mountain label sampler, promo only)	20
84	Kent 013	MOVING ON UP	15
53	London AL 3503	MUGGY, TESCH AND THE CHICAGOANS (10")	15
57	Pye NJL 11	MURDERER'S HOME	20
71	Mushroom 100 MR 16	THE MUSHROOM FOLK SAMPLER	40
57	Brunswick LAT 8201	MUSIC FOR THE BOYFRIEND - HE REALLY DIGS ROCK'N'ROLL	100
57	Brunswick LAT 8202	MUSIC FOR THE BOYFRIEND - HE REALLY DIGS JAZZ	30
57	Brunswick LAT 8205	MUSIC FOR THE BOYFRIEND - THE FEMININE TOUCH	35
67	Argo RG 533	MUSIC FROM THE FAR NORTH (with foldout inner)	15
73	Charisma CADS 101	MUSIC FROM FREE CREEK (2-LP)	15
72	Trojan TBL 177	MUSIC HOUSE 2	18
72	Trojan TBL 192	MUSIC HOUSE 3	20
70	Disques Vogue VRLS 3043	LA MUSIQUE PROGRESSIVE	12
81	Ze ISSP 4001	MUTANT DISCO (3 x 12" box set, numbered, 2,000 only)	20
77	EMI NUT 4	MY GENERATION	15
89	Hangman HANG 35 UP	MEDWAY POWERHOUSE (LP)	30
78	Tartone TTL 010	MASTER MIX (LP)	25

N

73	Enterprise ESAM 100	THE NAME OF THE GAME	15
71	Eden LP 43	NAPTON FOLK CLUB (private pressing, 100 only)	35
62	London HA-B 8003	NASHVILLE SATURDAY NIGHT	18
63	London HA-B 8028	NASHVILLE STEEL GUITAR	18
69	Bamboo BLP 201	NATURAL REGGAE VOLUME ONE	50
70	Bamboo BLP 204	NATURAL REGGAE VOLUME TWO	100
81	4AD CAD 117	NATURES MORTES - STILL LIVES (export issue)	60
85	Musique Brut BRV 002	NECROPOLIS, AMPHIBIANS AND REPTILES: THE MUSIC OF ADOLF WOLFLI	20
70s	Bounty BY 6012	NEGRO FOLKLORE FROM TEXAS STATE PRISON	20
57	Vogue LAE 12033	NEGRO SPIRITUALS	28
61	World Records LH 12	NEGRO SPIRITUALS	15
83	Pax PAX 14	NEVER MIND THE GONADS - HERE'S THE TESTICLES	15
87	Broken Flag BF V8	NEVER SAY WHEN	40
72	Atlantic K 20024	THE NEW AGE OF ATLANTIC	12
80	Logo MOGO 4011	NEW ELECTRIC WARRIORS	12
53	London AL 3509	NEW ORLEANS HORNS (10")	15
56	London AL 3557	NEW ORLEANS HORNS VOLUME 2 (10")	15
67	Ace Of Hearts AH 140	NEW ORLEANS MEMORIES	12
74	Flyright LP 4708	NEW ORLEANS R&B VOLUME 1	15
74	Flyright LP 4709	NEW ORLEANS R&B VOLUME 2	15
60s	77' 77LA 12/16	NEW ORLEANS TODAY	20
60s	77' 77LA 12/29	NEW ORLEANS TODAY VOL. 2	20
65	Fontana TFL 6038	NEWPORT BROADSIDE - TOPICAL SONGS AT THE NEWPORT FOLK FESTIVAL 1963	20
65	Fontana TFL 6041	NEWPORT FOLK FESTIVAL EVENING CONCERT VOL. 1	20
65	Fontana TFL 6050	NEWPORT FOLK FESTIVAL VOL. 1	12
57	Philips BBL 7147	NEWPORT JAZZ FESTIVAL	12
57	Philips BBL 7152	NEWPORT JAZZ FESTIVAL	12
58	London Jazz LTZ C15155	NEWPORT SPIRITUAL STARS	20

77	Vertigo 6300 902	NEW WAVE	20
72	Flyright LP 4706	NEW YORK CITY BLUES	12
55	London AL 3541	NEW YORK JAZZ OF THE ROARING TWENTIES (10")	15
72	Flyright LP 4707	NEW YORK RHYTHM AND BLUES	12
69	Island IWP(S) 6	NICE ENOUGH TO EAT (pink label)	12
57	Vanguard PPL 11004	A NIGHT AT THE APOLLO	15
69	Blue Horizon 7-63210	THE 1968 MEMPHIS COUNTRY BLUES FESTIVAL	25
83	DEL 306	19TH CAMBRIDGE FOLK FESTIVAL VOLUME 1	20
81	NMX	NMX: LIVE AT SHEFFIELD (cassette)	20
68	Spark SRLM 107	NO INTRODUCTION	30
69	Trojan TTL 14	NO MORE HEARTACHES	20
70	Polydor 545 017	NON STOP SOUL	30
69	Regal Starline SRS 5013	NO ONE'S GONNA CHANGE OUR WORLD	18
64	Concert Hall AM 2339	NORTHUMBRIAN MINSTRELS	15
60	Fontana TFL 5123	NOTHIN' BUT THE BLUES (gatefold sleeve)	60
71	CBS 66278	NOTHING BUT THE BLUES (2-LP, Blue Horizon pressings may also exist (£75))	60
82	See For Miles CM 112	NOT JUST BEAT MUSIC, 1965-70	12
79	Giorno GPS	THE NOVA CONVENTION	20
70	Decca Nova SPA 72	NOVA SAMPLER	20
70s	Warm PFLP 201	NOVA-VAGA	15
79	A&M AMLE 68505	NO WAVE (orange, mauve or blue vinyl)	12
84	Virgin/EMI CDP 26 0408 2	NOW THAT'S WHAT I CALL MUSIC 4 (CD)	200
86	Virgin/EMI CDNOW 8	NOW THAT'S WHAT I CALL MUSIC 8 (CD)	35
87	Virgin/EMI CDNOW 9	NOW THAT'S WHAT I CALL MUSIC 9 (CD)	35
69	Pama ECO 6	NU BEAT - GREATEST HITS	60
73	Elektra K 62012	NUGGETS (Original Artyfacts From The First Psychedelic Era 1965-1968) (2-LP, gatefold sleeve)	45
86	Numa NUMA 1004	NUMA RECORDS YEAR 1 (with bonus Italian 12" "My Dying Machine")	15
90s	NWOBHM CD 002	NWOBHM - VOLUME 2 (CD)	30
90s	NWOBHM CD 003	NWOBHM - VOLUME 3 (CD)	30
81	Guardian Records	N E 1 (LP)	40

O

69	Liberty LBS 83234	OAKLAND BLUES	30
80	Object Music OBJ 006	THE OBJECT SINGLES ALBUM (LP)	12
79	Rok ROK LP 001	ODD BODS, MODS AND SODS	75
85	Micro MIC 15001	OFFERING OF ISCA (LP, features 2 tracks by Circuit 7)	100
58	Parlophone PMC 1072	OH BOY!	40
78	Raw RAWLP 2	OH NO IT'S MORE FROM RAW (Users/Killjoys et al.)	20
72	Music F. Pleasure MFP 1416	OH! WHAT A CARRY ON	15
98	MPO IRL 01	OH YEAH (CD, 'Heineken Rock Awards' issue free with Hot Press magazine, with Neil Hannon/Ash et al.)	18
80	EMI ZIT 1	OI! - THE ALBUM (initially mail-order only from Sounds magazine)	30
87	Link LP 23	OI! GLORIOUS OI!	15
84	Syndicate SYNLP 4	OI! OF SEX	15
83	Secret SEC 5	OI! OI! THAT'S YER LOT	15
60s	Melodisc MS 4	OLDIES BUT GOODIES	50
64	Stateside SL 10094	OLDIES R & B	70
60	Parlophone PMC 1127	OLD TIME MUSIC HALL	15
69	Transatlantic XTRA 1076	O LIVERPOOL WE LOVE YOU (Stan Kelly/Bill Shankley/Jimmy Tarbuck et al.)	40
68	Big Shot BBTL 4001	ONCE MORE	70
69	Marmalade 643 314	100% PROOF	15
86	Stateside/EMI SSL 6002	ONE MINIT AT A TIME	18
73	Charisma CLASS 3	ONE MORE CHANCE	20
63	Columbia 33SX 1536	ONE NIGHT STAND	40
63	Stateside SL 10065	ON STAGE LIVE!	65
69	Atco 228 009/010	ON STAGE - LIVE (2-LP)	25
73	Xtra XTRA 1133	ON THE ROAD AGAIN	20
83	Kent KENT 006	ON THE SOUL SIDE	15
64	Columbia 33SX 1662	ON THE SCENE	90
84	Kent KENT 20	ON THE UP BEAT	15
63	Stateside SL 10024	OPRY TIME IN TENNESSEE	18
65	Allegro ALL 778	ROY ORBISON SINGS (some tracks by Jerry Lee Lewis, Tommy Roe; black or blue label)	12
65	Ember FA 2005	ROY ORBISON AND OTHERS (with 4 tracks by Orbison)	12
67	Polydor 236 216	ORIGINAL AMERICAN FOLK BLUES FESTIVAL	18
64	Rio RLP 1	THE ORIGINAL COOL JAMAICAN SKA	130
70	Mercury SMCL 20182	ORIGINAL GOLDEN HITS OF THE GREAT BLUES SINGERS	20
73	Prince Buster PB 10	ORIGINAL GOLDEN OLDIES VOLUME 2	12
70	Mercury SMCL 20183	ORIGINAL GOLDEN RHYTHM AND BLUES HITS VOLUME 1	20
60	London HA-G 2308	THE ORIGINAL HITS	50
61	London HA-G 2339	THE ORIGINAL HITS VOL. 2	50
63	Golden Guinea GGL 0240	THE ORIGINAL HOOTENANNY	15
67	Ember SPE 6602	THE ORIGINAL SOUND OF DETROIT	18
68	United Artists ULP 1182	ORIGINAL SOUNDTRACKS OF HITS MUSIC	15
64	Vocalion VA 8017	ORIGINAL SURFIN' HITS	65
52	Vogue LDE 006	ORIGINATORS OF MODERN JAZZ (10")	15
75	Trailer LET SAM 2087	OUR FOLK MUSIC HERITAGE	12
62	London HA-U 2404	OUR SIGNIFICANT HITS	70
65	Ace Of Hearts AH 72	OUT CAME THE BLUES	15
67	Ace Of Hearts AH 158	OUT CAME THE BLUES VOLUME 2	15
83	Peninsula	OUT OF THE UNKNOWN	70

P

70	Golden Guinea GGL 0451	PADDY IS DEAD AND THE KIDS KNOW IT (LP)	150
64	Golden Guinea GGL 0268	PACKAGE TOUR	22
65	Blue Beat BBLP 804	PAIN IN MY BELLY	250
55	London HA-A 2001	THE PAJAMA GAME	15
67	Island ILP 945	PAKISTANI SOUL SESSION	75
90	Factory FACT 400	PALATINE - THE FACTORY STORY (4-LP)	80
61	Parlophone PMC 1134	PARADE OF THE POPS	15
85	LIL LP2	PARKSIDE STEELWORKS	60

73	Charisma CAS 1078	THE PARLOUR SONG BOOK (LP)	15
68	Studio One SOL 9009	PARTY TIME IN JAMAICA	120
66	Decca LK 4824	PENTHOUSE MAGAZINE PRESENTS THE BEDSIDE BOND	40
83	Psycho PSYCHO 6	THE PERFUMED GARDEN	20
84	Psycho PSYCHO 15	THE PERFUMED GARDEN II	20
81	Cherry Red BRED 15	PERSPECTIVES AND DISTORTION (gatefold sleeve)	15
86	Streetsounds PHST 1986	THE PHILADELPHIA YEARS (14-LP box set)	80
72	Apple APCOR 24	PHIL SPECTOR'S CHRISTMAS ALBUM (reissue of "A Christmas Gift For You")	30
75	Warner Bros K 59010	PHIL SPECTOR'S CHRISTMAS ALBUM (2nd reissue, some with poster)	18
80	Phil Spector Intl. 2307 015	PHIL SPECTOR '74/'79	25
67	Riverside RLP 8809	PIANO BLUES 1927-1933	20
56	Vogue Coral LVA 9069	PIANO JAZZ - BARRELHOUSE AND BOOGIE WOOGIE	12
72	Flyright LP 104	PIEDMONT BLUES	15
60	HMV CLP 1362/XLP 50004	A PINCH OF SALT - BRITISH SEA SONGS OLD AND NEW	20
53	London AL 3506	PIONEERS OF BOOGIE WOOGIE (10")	40
54	London AL 3537	PIONEERS OF BOOGIE WOOGIE VOLUME TWO (10")	40
73	Trojan TBL 203	PIPELINE	15
80	Incus INCUS 37	PISA 1980: IMPROVISOR'S SYMPOSIUM	50
81	K-Tel NE 1134	THE PLATINUM ALBUM	12
70s	Flyright LP 4711	PLAY MY JUKEBOX	12
81	P. Surprised KLARK 002	PLEASANTLY SURPRISED - AN HOUR OF ELOQUENT SOUNDS (cassette)	20
71	Argo ZPR 264/5	POETRY AND JAZZ IN CONCERT 250	15
56	Mercury MPT	POP PARADE VOL. 1 (10")	15
56	Mercury MPT	POP PARADE VOL. 2 (10")	15
57	Mercury MPT 7519	POP PARADE VOL. 3 (10")	15
57	Mercury MPT 7523	POP PARADE VOL. 4 (10")	15
57	Mercury MPT 7525	POP PARADE VOL. 5 (10")	25
68	Polydor 236 517/8/9	POP PARTY! (3-LP in box)	20
83	Fall Out FALL 032	POSH HITS VOL. 1	15
65	Post War Blues PWB 1	POST WAR BLUES: CHICAGO (99 copies only)	45
66	Post War Blues PWB 2	POST WAR BLUES: MEMPHIS ON DOWN (99 copies only)	45
67	Post War Blues PWB 3	POST WAR BLUES: EASTERN AND GULF COAST STATES (99 copies only)	45
68	Post War Blues PWB 4	POST WAR BLUES: TEXAS (99 copies only)	45
68	Post War Blues PWB 5	POST WAR BLUES: DETROIT (99 copies only)	45
60s	Post War Blues PWB 6	POST WAR BLUES: WEST COAST (99 copies only)	45
60s	Post War Blues PWB 7	POST WAR BLUES: THE DEEP SOUTH (99 copies only)	45
69	Python PWBC 1	POST WAR COLLECTOR SERIES VOL. 1 (99 copies only)	80
63	Stateside SL 10046	PREACHIN' THE BLUES	25
80	4AD BAD 11	PRESAGES (mini-LP, green/pink or brown sleeve)	15
79	Preseli PRE 001	PRESELI FOLK (private pressing with insert)	30
70	Kokomo K 1006	PRE-WAR TEXAS BLUES (99 copies only)	45
60s	Jazz Collector JGN 1001	PRIMITIVE PIANO	20
87	A&M AMA 3906	PRINCE'S TRUST 10TH ANNIVERSARY BIRTHDAY PARTY (2-LP, some stickered, with Paul McCartney 7": "Long Tall Sally"/"I Saw Her Standing There"	0
63	London HA-B 8062	PRISONERS' SONGS	20
70	Lyntone LYN 2745	PRIVATE EYE'S GOLDEN YEARS OF SOUND 1964-70	20
90	United Dairies UD 134	PSILOTRIPITAKA (3-LP [UD 01, 03 & 04], with bonus LP "Registered Nurse" [UD 00], 1,000 only, some possibly in leather bag)	400
90	United Dairies UD 134CD	PSILOTRIPITAKA (3-CD [UD 01, 03 & 04], with bonus CD "Registered Nurse" [UD 00CD], 1,000 only, 30 in 'leather bondage bag')	400
91	Delerium DELP 005	PSYCHEDELIC SAUNA (2-LP, 500 numbered on multi-coloured vinyl)	18
81	Abstract AABT 100	PUNK AND DISORDERLY (red vinyl)	15
82	Anagram GRAM 001	PUNK AND DISORDERLY 2 (blue vinyl)	15
82	Anagram GRAM 005	PUNK AND DISORDERLY 2 (Multi-coloured vinyl)	20
82	Pax 7	PUNK DEAD?...NAH MATE	20
65	Sue ILP 919	PURE BLUES VOLUME ONE	60
83	Guardian GRC 2162	PURE OVERKILL	18
73	Purple TPSS 1	PURPLE PEOPLE	12
85	Color Disc COLORS 2	PURPLE TWILIGHT (400 only)	20
68	Island ILP 978	PUT IT ON, IT'S ROCK STEADY	40
71	Pye PSA 6	PYE SALES SAMPLER (sampler for Pye & Dawn releases; 99 copies only, with release sheet)	20
91	Sink Below SINK 2	PUNK'S NOT DREAD (LP, with inner)	15
88	On U Sound 37	PAY IT ALL BACK VOL 1	15
88	On U Sound 42	PAY IT ALL BACK VOL 2 (with booklet)	20
77	Uptempo UTLP 001	PRESENTING THE POSSE	30

Q

68	Stateside S(S)L 10209	A QUARTET OF SOUL	50
70	Trojan TBL 136	QUEEN OF THE WORLD	20
59	Vogue LAE 12031	THE QUINTET OF THE YEAR	15

R

54	London AL 3515	RAGTIME PIANO ROLL (10")	15
54	London AL 3523	RAGTIME PIANO ROLL VOLUME 2 (10")	15
55	London AL 3542	RAGTIME PIANO ROLL VOLUME 3 (10")	15
57	London AL 3563	RAGTIME PIANO ROLL VOLUME 4 (10")	15
81	Island ILPS 9705	RAIDERS OF THE LOST DUB (LP, withdrawn)	12
76	Phil Spector Intl. 2307 008	RARE MASTERS VOL. 1	15
76	Phil Spector Intl. 2307 009	RARE MASTERS VOL. 2	15
79	Harvest SHSM 2028	THE RARE STUFF	12
69	United Artists (S)UX 1214	RAVE	25
74	Mooncrest CREST 17	RAVE ON	12
73	Attack ATLP 1012	RAVE ON BROTHER	35
67	Ace Of Clubs ACL 1220	RAW BLUES (also stereo SCL 1220)	20
77	Raw RAWLP 1	RAW DEAL (black & white sleeve & red/blue label)	20
61	Pye NPL 18069	RAZZAMATAZZ AND ALL THAT JAZZ	30
83	Mean MNLP 82	READING ROCK VOL. 1 (2-LP)	20
64	Decca LK 4577	READY, STEADY, GO!	45
68	Pama PMLP 3	READY STEADY GO ROCKSTEADY	45
64	Decca LK 4634	READY, STEADY, WIN	75

65	Stateside SL 10112	THE REAL R & B..40
82	Recommended 104	RECOMMENDED SAMPLER..15
79	Destiny DS 10001	THE RECORD COLLECTOR..20
81	Recorder BR 003	RECORDER THREE..20
70	CBS 52797	RECORDING THE BLUES..22
65	Red Bird RB 20-102	RED BIRD GOLDIES..65
81	WEA K 58344	RED HOT ROCKABILLIES (with inner sleeve)....................12
70	Downtown TBL 116	RED RED WINE VOLUME 2..15
69	Trojan TBLS 105	REGGAE CHARTBUSTERS..20
70	Trojan TBL 115	REGGAE FLIGHT 404..12
70	Pama Economy ECO 34	REGGAE FOR DAYS (LP)..100
68	Big Shot BIL 3000	REGGAE GIRL..100
69	Pama ECO 3	REGGAE HITS '69 VOL. 1...25
69	Pama ECO 11	REGGAE HITS VOL. 2..25
69	Pama PTP 1001	REGGAE HIT THE TOWN..25
68	Studio One SOL 9007	REGGAE IN THE GRASS..95
71	Trojan TBL 181	REGGAE JAMAICA..15
71	Trojan TBL 193	REGGAE JAMAICA VOL. 2...18
71	Bamboo BDLP 208	REGGAEMATIC SOUNDS..70
70	Trojan TBL 144	REGGAE MOVEMENT...15
72	Trojan TBL 189	REGGAE POWER 2..15
72	Trojan TBL	REGGAE REGGAE 2..30
70	Trojan TBL 130	REGGAE REGGAE REGGAE..12
69	Coxsone CSP 2	REGGAE SPECIAL..30
70	Trojan TBL 151	REGGAE STEADY GO..18
73	Trojan TRLS 54	REGGAE STRINGS..20
68	Coxsone CSL 8017	REGGAE TIME..100
72	Ashanti ANB 201	REGGAE TIME..15
71	Pama PMP 2012	REGGAE TO REGGAE..32
69	Pama PSP 1004	REGGAE TO UK WITH LOVE...150
86	Rot HELL 36	RELIGION AS HELL (LP)..20
80s	Ré 0101	RE RECORDS QUARTERLY VOL. No. 1 (with book)...........15
72	Count Shelly CSLP 01	RETURN TO ME REGGAE..25
73	Count Shelly CSLP 02	RETURN TO ME REGGAE 2...25
64	Decca LK 4616	RHYTHM AND BLUES..80
67	Marble Arch MAL 726	RHYTHM AND BLUES..12
64	Golden Guinea GGL 0280	RHYTHM AND BLUES VOL...20
64	Golden Guinea GGL 0351	RHYTHM AND BLUES VOL. 2...12
69	Liberty LBL 83216	RHYTHM AND BLUES VOLUME 1: END OF AN ERA..........20
70	Liberty LBL 83328	RHYTHM AND BLUES VOLUME 2: SWEET 'N' GREASY.....20
64	Golden Guinea GGL 0293	RHYTHM AND BLUES ALL STARS.......................................12
69	Minit MLL/MLS 40008E	RHYTHM AND BLUES CLASSICS...22
69	Minit MLL/MLS 40009E	RHYTHM AND BLUES CLASSICS VOL. 2.............................22
63	CBS Realm RM 101	R&B GREATS VOLUME 1..20
64	CBS Realm RM 175	R&B GREATS VOLUME 2..22
64	Mercury MCL 20019	RHYTHM AND BLUES PARTY..70
76	Philips 6436 028	RHYTHM AND BLUES PARTY (reissue)...............................15
89	Performance PFP 1004	RHYTHM OF THE RAIN - 16 HITS OF THE 60s....................12
70	Moodisc TBL 132	RHYTHM RULERS - MUDIES MOODS...................................20
73	Tamla Motown STML 11232	RIC TIC RELICS..20
68	Coxsone CSL 8015	RIDE ME DONKEY..110
69	Trojan TTL 18	RIDE YOUR DONKEY..20
85	Kent KENT 039	RIGHT BACK WHERE WE STARTED FROM..........................15
03	Dig The Fuzz DIG048	RIOT OF THE AMPHETAMINE GENERATION (400 copies only, with booklet)...............40
82	Riot City ASSEMBLY 1	RIOTOUS ASSEMBLEY (red vinyl).....................................18
55	Vogue Coral LRA 10023	RIVERBOAT JAZZ (10" LP)..15
71	London SHU 8245	RIVERTOWN BLUES...20
61	London HA-A 2338	ROCK-A-HITS..95
57	London HB-C 1067	ROCK 'N' ROLL (10")...110
59	London HA-E 2180	ROCK AND ROLL FOREVER..95
60	HMV DLP 1204	ROCKET ALONG - NEW BALLADS ON OLD LINES (10").....20
70s	Flynight FLY 662	ROCKIN' ACCORDION...12
58	Decca LF 1300	ROCKIN' AT THE '2 I'S' (10")...60
59	London HA-E 2167	ROCKIN' TOGETHER..80
63	Philips BL 7583	ROCKING GUITARS (LP)..30
69	Decca LK 5002	ROCK STEADY..30
69	Pama PMLP 7	ROCKSTEADY COOL...60
68	Coxsone CSL 8013	ROCKSTEADY COXSONE STYLE...130
80	Guardian GRC 80	ROKSNAX...50
68	Atlantic Special 590 019	ROOTS OF THE BLUES...15
83	Cha Cha CHALP 016	ROOTS AND CULTURE...20
82	Guardian GRC 130	ROXCALIBUR..70
77	Harvest SHSP 4069	THE ROXY LONDON W.C.2 (JAN - APR 77) (with inner bag)...25
94	Mo' Wax MWLP 003	ROYALTIES OVERDUE (2-LP, coloured vinyl)....................60
84	Bam Caruso KIRI 024	RUBBLE 1: THE PSYCHEDELIC SNARL (with 8-page insert; first 2000with inner sleeve and lightshow labels)..................20
86	Bam Caruso KIRI 025	RUBBLE 2: POP-SIKE PIPE DREAMS (with inner sleeve) ...20
86	Bam Caruso KIRI 026	RUBBLE 3: NIGHTMARES IN WONDERLAND (with inner sleeve)...20
86	Bam Caruso KIRI 027	RUBBLE 4: THE 49 MINUTE TECHNICOLOUR DREAM (some with 4-page insert; first 2000 with inner sleeve and lightshow labels)..............20
86	Bam Caruso KIRI 044	RUBBLE 5: THE ELECTRIC CRAYON SET (with inner sleeve) ...15
86	Bam Caruso KIRI 049	RUBBLE 6: THE CLOUDS HAVE GROOVY FACES (with inner sleeve)...15
88	Bam Caruso KIRI 083	RUBBLE 7: PICTURES IN THE SKY (with inner sleeve)........15
91	Bam Caruso KIRI 051	RUBBLE 8: ALL THE COLOURS OF DARKNESS....................15
85	Bam Caruso KIRI 065	RUBBLE 9: FROM THE HOUSE OF LORDS (1000 copies only)...18
91	Bam Caruso KIRI 079	RUBBLE 9: PLASTIC WILDERNESS......................................15
88	Bam Caruso KIRI 098	RUBBLE 10: PROFESSOR JORDAN'S MAGIC SOUND SHOW (with inner sleeve)...15
86	Bam Caruso KIRI 069	RUBBLE 11: ADVENTURES IN THE MIST (with inner sleeve) ...20
86	Bam Caruso KIRI 070	RUBBLE 12: STAIRCASE TO NOWHERE (with inner sleeve) ...20
89	Bam Caruso KIRI 102	RUBBLE 13: FREAK BEAT FANTOMS....................................20
88	Bam Caruso KIRI 106	RUBBLE 14: THE MAGIC ROCKING HORSE (with inner sleeve)...20

91	Bam Caruso KIRI 084	RUBBLE 15: 5000 SECONDS OVER TOYLAND	20
91	Bam Caruso KIRI 096	RUBBLE 16: GLASS ORCHID AFTERMATH	15
91	Bam Caruso KIRI 099	RUBBLE 17: A TRIP IN A PAINTED WORLD	20
92	Bam Caruso KIRI 101	RUBBLE 18: RAINBOW THYME WINDERS (unreleased, 25 test pressings only)	200
92	Bam Caruso KIRI 109	RUBBLE 19: EIDERDOWN MINDFOG (unreleased, 25 test pressings only)	200
90s	Bam Caruso KIRI 110	RUBBLE 20: THRICE UPON A TIME - NOTHING IS REAL (unreleased)	0
07	Fallout FALLBOX001	RUBBLE COLLECTION (10-CD)	30
92	Forty NME 40 LP	RUBY TRAX (3-LP, box set)	40
92	Forty NME 40 CD	RUBY TRAX (3-CD)	30
81	Naive 002	RUPERT PREACHING AT A PICNIC (LP)	100
74	Cactus CTLP 104	RUPIE'S GEMS	20
69	Xtra XTRA 1035	RURAL BLUES (2-LP)	25
69	Liberty LBL 83213	RURAL BLUES VOLUME 1: GOIN' UP THE COUNTRY	20
69	Liberty LBL 83214	RURAL BLUES VOLUME 2: SATURDAY NIGHT FUNCTION	20
70	Liberty LBL 83329	RURAL BLUES VOLUME 3: DOWN HOME STOMP	20
01	Trunk/Second Coming SEC 001	RESURRECTION: THE AMPLIFIED BIBLE OF HEAVENLY GROOVES (LP)	30

S

70	Transworld SPLP 101	SAMANTHA PROMOTIONS (orange cover, private pressing, a few with poster)	500
70	Transworld SPLP 102	SAMANTHA PROMOTIONS (purple cover, private pressing, a few with poster)	500
78	Live And Love LAP 005	SATISFACTION IN DUB	50
60	Parlophone PMC 1130	SATURDAY CLUB	50
64	Decca LK 4583	SATURDAY CLUB	40
67	Atlantic Special 590 007	SATURDAY NIGHT AT THE APOLLO (reissue of "Apollo Saturday Night")	20
63	Brunswick LAT/STA 8520	SATURDAY NIGHT AT THE GRAND OLE OPRY	15
70	CBS 52799	SAVANNAH SYNCOPATORS	15
81	Suspect SU S3	SCENE OF THE CRIME	60
65	Columbia 33SX 1730	SCENE '65	125
74	Polydor 2383 282 A	SCOTLAND SCOTLAND (Scottish World Cup Squad/Rod Stewart/Dennis Law)	10
69	Bamboo BDLP 202	A SCORCHA FROM BAMBOO	60
68	CBS 63288	SCREENING THE BLUES	20
95	Blue Eyed Dog VTDOG 12	SEARCH AND DISOBEY (2-LP, 10")	20
81	Airship AP 342	SEASIDE ROCK (2-LP, with insert)	20
81	Come Org. WDC 881008	THE SECOND COMING (various coloured vinyls)	30
87	Cherry Red BRED 74	SEEDS I: POP (TV Personalities/Marine Girls, et al.)	20
68	Elektra EUK 261	SELECT ELEKTRA (also stereo EUKS 7261)	30
80	Kathedral KATH 1	SENT FROM COVENTRY (with booklet)	15
88	Sarah SARAH 587	SHADOW FACTORY (The Sea Urchins/14 Iced Bears, et al.)	30
68	Atlantic 587 109	SHAKE, RATTLE AND ROCK	25
74	Topic 12TS 234	SEA SHANTIES	12
78	GVR 201	THE SHANTY MEN	18
74	Eron 003	SHEPWAY FOLK (with insert)	30
84	Kent KENT 015	SHOES	15
78	Virgin VCL 5003	SHORT CIRCUIT - LIVE AT THE ELECTRIC CIRCUS (10"; orange, yellow or blue vinyl)	120
78	Virgin VCL 5003	SHORT CIRCUIT - LIVE AT THE ELECTRIC CIRCUS (10"; black vinyl with free John Dowie EP [VED 1004])	20
90	Horaces HRH 101	SHRINE - THE RAREST SOUL LABEL	12
87	ABC NOSE 15	SICK SICK SICK	12
76	Topic 12TS 281	THE SILVER BOW - SHETLAND FOLK FIDDLING VOL. 1	15
66	Chess CRL 4519	SING A SONG OF SOUL	40
57	RCA Camden CDN 147	SINGIN' THE BLUES	12
73	Sir Collins SCMW 001	SIR COLLINS MUSICAL WHEEL (LP)	40
79	Sire SMP 1	THE SIRE MACHINE TURNS YOU UP	12
57	Parlophone PMC 1047	SIX-FIVE SPECIAL	50
76	BBC REB 252	SIX-FIVE SPECIAL	12
72	Trojan TBL 191	16 DYNAMIC REGGAE HITS	18
73	Trojan TBL 209	16DYNAMIV HITS 2	20
71	Pama PMP 2015	16 DYNAMIC REGGAE HITS	30
66	Island ILP 930	SKA AT THE JAMAICA PLAYBOY CLUB (gatefold sleeve)	400
67	Coxsone CSL 8003	SKA-A-GO-GO	200
66	Doctor Bird DLM 5000	SKA-BOO-DA-BA	250
67	Studio One SOL 9000	SKA TO ROCKSTEADY	250
60s	Page One FOR 006	SKA'S THE LIMIT	15
68	Ace Of Clubs ACL 1250	SKIFFLE	30
80s	Kent KENT 052	SMART! 16 IMMACULATE CUTS TAILORED FOR STYLE	12
81	RSB 1	THE SNOOPIES ALBUM (THE LAST REMAINS OF A RICHMOND VENUE) (numbered, with booklet, 1,000 only)	20
83	Kent KENT 003	SLOW 'N' MOODY BLACK 'N' BLUESY	15
87	Countdown NXON 1	SMASHING TIME	15
67	Polydor 583 064	SOCK IT TO 'EM	15
60s	Solar	THE SOLAR BOX SET	40
70s	United Artists LBR 1007	SOLD ON SOUL	15
71	Bamboo BDLP 212	SOLID GOLD	50
66	Atlantic ATL 5048	SOLID GOLD SOUL	20
67	Atlantic 587 058	SOLID GOLD SOUL VOL. 2	20
75	Disco Demand DDLP 5002	SOLID SOUL SENSATIONS	18
81	Some Bizzare BZLP 1	THE SOME BIZZARE ALBUM	12
72	South. Preservation SPR 1	SOME COLD RAINY DAY	15
75	Flyright LP 114	SOME COLD RAINY DAY (reissue)	12
65	Lestar LLP 101	SOME FOLK IN LEICESTER (private pressing)	20
58	Decca LK 4292	SOMETHING NEW FROM AFRICA	18
70	Pama PMP 2003	SOMETHING SWEET FROM THE LADY	100
60	Topic 12001	SONGS AGAINST THE BOMB	12
72	Argo ZDA 147	SONGS AND MUSIC OF THE REDCOATS	15
77	Topic 12T 317	SONGS & SOUTHERN BREEZES - COUNTRY SINGERS FROM HAMPSHIRE & SUSSEX	15
77	private pressing	SONGS AT A SUSSEX FEAST	12
79	EMI NUT 18	SONGS LENNON AND McCARTNEY GAVE AWAY	12
67	Fontana STL 5436	SONGS OF GRIEF AND GLORY	12
69	Liberty LBX 4	SON OF GUTBUCKET	20
76	Harvest SHSM 2012	SON OF MORRIS ON	25
83	Syndicate SYNLP 3	SON OF OI!	15

72	Probe SPB 1061	SOUL BIBLE	15
84	Kent KENT 011	SOUL CLASS OF '66	15
69	Direction (S)PR 28	SOUL DIRECTION	25
69	Page One POS 608	SOULED AGAIN	20
69	Polydor 584 163	SOUL FEVER	20
60s	Minit MLL 40011E	SOUL FOOD	40
69	Soul City SCB 1	SOUL FROM THE CITY	45
70	Specialty SPE 6606	SOUL FROM THE VAULTS	15
74	Trojan TRL 65	SOULFUL REGGAE	12
70	Polydor 583 757	SOUL GOLD	18
72	Avco 6467 251	SOUL - IN THE BEGINNING	12
68	Trojan TRL 3	SOUL OF JAMAICA	35
68	Polydor Special 236 213	SOUL PARTY	20
69	Pama PMLP 8	SOUL SAUCE FROM PAMA	70
69	Polydor 236 554	SOUL SELLER	18
70s	United Artists UAL 229018	SOUL SENSATION	15
85	Kent KENT 041	SOUL SERENADE	15
66	Stateside SL 10186	SOUL SIXTEEN	45
66	Sue ILP 934	SOUL '66	60
67	CBS BPG 62965	SOUL SOUNDS	25
67	HMV CLP 3619	SOUL SOUNDS OF THE 60s	45
67	Stateside SL 10203	SOUL SUPPLY	50
86	SMP/Inferno SIMLP 4	SOUL TIME	12
69	Atlantic 218005	SOUL TOGETHER	15
73	Trojan TRLS 74	SOUL TO SOUL DJ CHOICE	20
65	Pye Intl. NPL 28061	THE SOUND OF BACHARACH	20
95	EMI EMI 8322 801	THE SOUND GALLERY	25
58	Fontana TFL 5025	THE SOUND OF JAZZ	15
68	President PTL 1008	THE SOUND OF SOUL	30
72	United Artists UAS 29215	SOUND OF THE CITY	12
79	Grapevine GRAL 1001	SOUND OF THE GRAPEVINE	20
64	Stateside SL 10077	THE SOUND OF THE R&B HITS	65
69	Joy JOY 125	SOUNDS LIKE SKA	12
70	Sentinel SENS 1001	SOUNDS LIKE WEST CORNWALL	20
78	Sonet SNTF 806	SOUTHEND ROCK	12
69	London HAK 8405	SOUTHERN COMFORT	125
83	Spectrum ASPEC 001	SOUTHERN COMFORT	75
80s	Spectrum ASPEC 003	SOUTHERN COMFORT 3	50
60s	Saydisc Roots RL 328	SOUTHERN SANCTIFIED SINGERS	15
61	London Jazz LTZ-K 15209	SOUTHERN FOLK HERITAGE VOLUME 1: SOUNDS OF THE SOUTH	20
61	London Jazz LTZ-K 15210	SOUTHERN FOLK HERITAGE VOLUME 2: BLUE RIDGE MOUNTAIN MUSIC	20
61	London Jazz LTZ-K 15211	SOUTHERN FOLK HERITAGE VOLUME 3: ROOTS OF THE BLUES	20
61	London Jazz LTZ-K 15209	SOUTHERN FOLK HERITAGE VOLUME 7: THE BLUES ROLL ON	20
54	London AL 3529	SOUTHSIDE CHICAGO JAZZ (10")	18
71	Python PLP 10	SOUTHSIDE CHICAGO (99 copies only)	80
70	CBS Special Prod. WSR 932	SPARKLING COLOUR (multicoloured vinyl)	12
58	Tempo TAP 17	SPEAK LOW - MORE MUSIC IN THE MODERN MANNER	150
85	Music For Nations MFN 54	SPEED KILLS (with inner)	12
69	BAF BAF001	SPECIAL BAF SOUNDS VOL. 1	30
73	Tempo TMP 9001	SPIN A MAGIC TUNE	20
57	Pye Nixa NPT 19019	SPIN WITH THE STARS - SELECTION NO. 2 (10")	18
57	Pye Nixa NPT 19021	SPIN WITH THE STARS - SELECTION NO. 3 (10")	18
65	Fontana TL 5243	SPIRITUAL AND GOSPEL FESTIVAL	20
59	Top Rank 35/064	SPIRITUALS TO SWING VOLUME 1	15
59	Top Rank 35/065	SPIRITUALS TO SWING VOLUME 2	15
82	WEA K 58415	A SPLASH OF COLOUR	15
62	Liberty LBY 1001	THE STARS OF LIBERTY	30
57	Decca LF 1299	STARS OF THE 6.5 SPECIAL (10")	50
84	Broken Flag BF V5	STATEMENT	40
85	Statik POL 274	STATIK COMPILATION ONE (2-LP)	20
04	Ai AILP 006	STATION (2-LP, clear vinyl, 1000 copies only)	15
69	Stax XATS 1007	STAX SOUL EXPLOSION	18
70s	Stax STXH 5004	THE STAX STORY (VOL. 1)	20
70s	Stax STXH 5005	THE STAX STORY (VOL. 1)	15
67	Stax 589 010	THE STAX/VOLT SHOW VOL. 1	20
67	Stax 589 011	THE STAX/VOLT SHOW VOL. 2	20
07	Step Forward CMXBX 1509	STEP FORWARD - I WANNA PUNK ROCK - SINGLES COLLECTION (10x7")	25
78	Stiff GET 1	STIFFS LIVE STIFFS	12
60	Topic 10T 59	STILL I LOVE HIM	12
69	CBS 66218	THE STORY OF THE BLUES (2-LP)	20
70	CBS 66232	THE STORY OF THE BLUES VOLUME 2 (2-LP)	20
94	Tenth Planet TP 010	THE STORY OF OAK RECORDS	25
94	Wooden Hill WHCD 007	THE STORY OF OAK RECORDS (CD)	20
70	Pama PMP 2002	STRAIGHTEN UP	50
71	Pama PMP 2007	STRAIGHTEN UP VOLUME TWO	20
71	Pama PMP 2014	STRAIGHTEN UP VOLUME THREE	20
72	Pama PMP 2017	STRAIGHTEN UP VOLUME FOUR	15
77	Beggars Banquet BEGA 1	STREETS	15
80s	Streetsounds	STREETSOUND ELECTRO (box set)	70
83	Streetsounds ELCST 1	STREETSOUND ELECTRO 1	12
83	Streetsounds ELCST 2	STREETSOUND ELECTRO 2	12
84	Streetsounds ELCST 3	STREETSOUND ELECTRO 3	12
84	Streetsounds ELCST 4	STREETSOUND ELECTRO 4	12
79	Open Eye OE LP 501	STREET TO STREET - A LIVERPOOL ALBUM	20
81	Open Eye OE LP 502	STREET TO STREET - A LIVERPOOL ALBUM VOL. 2	12
81	Decca SKIN 1	STRENGTH THROUGH OI!	50
85	Wonderful World WOWLP 3	STRENGTH THROUGH OI! (reissue)	20
80s	Private Pressing CFCEPI	STUFF THE NEIGHBOURS, PLAY IT LOUD (p/s, in poly bag, with fanzine)	12
86	Sub Pop SP 0010	SUB POP 100	20
81	Chick CHR 001	SUBWAY (clear vinyl)	15
73	Vertigo 6499 386	SUCK IT AND SEE (2-LP, spaceship label)	20

98	Sorted SRLP 04	SUCTION PRINTS (handpainted or wraparound sleeve)	35
65	Sue ILP 919	SUE SAMPLER RECORD FOR CLUBS (promo, no sleeve, typed labels with detail sheet)	120
65	London HA-C 8239	THE SUE STORY	60
65	Sue ILP 925	THE SUE STORY!	55
69	United Artists UAS 29028	THE SUE STORY (reissue)	18
66	Sue ILP 933	THE SUE STORY VOL. 2	55
66	Sue ILP 938	THE SUE STORY VOL. 3	55
76	Giorno GPS	SUGAR, ALCOHOL & MEAT	20
82	CBS 22139	SUMMER MEANS FUN (2-LP)	20
75	Island ISS 1	SUMMER '75 (promo-only sampler)	15
66	Reprise R 5031	THE SUMMIT	30
02	Sun FBUBX 002	SUN RECORD COMPANY 50 GOLDEN YEARS 1952-2002 (8-CD + 7")	50
86	Sun/Charly BOX 105	SUN RECORDS: THE BLUES YEARS (9-LP box with booklet)	60
81	Sunset Gun	SUNSET GUN (cassette with Sunset Gun fanzine)	15
68	Ember NR 5038	SUNSTROKE	20
73	Philips 6369 416	SUPER BLACK BLUES	20
69	Blue Horizon (S)PR 31	SUPER DUPER BLUES	15
68	Pye Intl. NPL 28107	SUPER SOUL	25
68	Chess SRL 4537	SUPER SUPER BLUES BAND	25
74	People PLEO 24	SUPER SWEET SOUL	15
64	Vocalion VA 8018	SURF BATTLE	60
86	Capitol EMS 1180	SURF CITY/DRAG CITY	25
88	Decal LIK 39	SURFERS STOMP	25
73	Pye/Disques Vogue HEN 1	SURPRISE PARTIE TOUS LES JEUNES	18
71	Blue Horizon 7-66263	SWAMP BLUES (2-LP)	75
68	Stateside S(S)L 10243	SWEET SOUL SOUNDS	50
68	Coxsone CSL 8018	SWING EASY	125
68	Saga FID 2136	SWINGING SAGA	15
58	Tempo TAP 21	SWINGIN' THE BLUES	25
93	Tenth Planet TP 002	SYDE TRYPS ONE (numbered, 500 only, with insert)	40
93	Tenth Planet TP 004	SYDE TRYPS TWO ... FROM THERE TO UNCERTAINTY (numbered, 500 only, with insert)	30
93	Tenth Planet TP 006	SYDE TRYPS THREE (numbered, 500 only, with insert)	30
94	Tenth Planet TP 008	SYDE TRYPS FOUR (numbered, 500 only, with insert)	60
96	Tenth Planet TP 024	SYDE TRYPS SIX (numbered, gatefold sleeve, 1,000 only)	30
82	EBONY 2 S82 CUS 1362	SYNTHETIC ROMANCE (LP)	450
71	BBC RED 67 M	SINGING ALONG WITH THE GIRL GUIDES (LP)	15
72	BBC RESR 28M	SOME BRITISH ACCENTS AND DIALECTS (LP)	15
78	BBC REC 303	SCRAPBOOK OF 1977 (LP)	15
96	Trunk BARKED 1	THE SUPER SOUNDS OF BOSWORTH (LP)	50
96	Trunk BARKED 2	THE SUPER SOUNDS OF BOSWORTH 2 (LP, 750 only)	50

T

72	Rubber RUB 001	TAKE OFF YOUR HEAD AND LISTEN	15
71	A&M Mayfair AMLB 51029	TAKE ONE	12
78	Grapevine GRAL 1000	TALK OF THE GRAPEVINE	25
65	London HA-B 8250	THE TALL 12	12
67	London HA-B 8315	THE TALL 12 VOL. 2	12
85	Kent KENT 045	TEAR IN MY EYES	30
58	Capitol T 1009	TEENAGE ROCK (turquoise or 'rainbow' label)	55
90	Sarah SARAH 376	TEMPLE CLOUD - A SARAH COMPILATION (LP)	30
63	Stateside SL 10020	TENNESSEE GUITAR	20
56	Nixa Jazz Today NJL 4	TENORAMA	200
77	Talisman STAL 1051	10 YEARS ON - THE UNIVERSAL FOLK CENTRE (LP)	20
70s	Fountain FV 205	TEXAS BLUES	18
69	Highway 51 H 103	TEXAS-LOUISIANA BLUES (99 copies only)	60
62	Ace Of Clubs ACL 1108	THANK YOUR LUCKY STARS	25
63	Golden Guinea GGL 0190	THANK YOUR LUCKY STARS	15
63	Decca LK 4554	THANK YOUR LUCKY STARS VOLUME 2	35
82	No Future PUNK 9	THERE IS NO FUTURE	18
72	Dandelion 2485 021	THERE IS SOME FUN GOING FORWARD (with poster)	18
82	Big Beat NED 3	THESE CATS AIN'T NOTHING BUT TRASH	20
69	Action ACLP 6009	THESE KIND OF BLUES VOL. 1	80
82	MCA MCA 6111	THE THING (LP)	20
81	TTFTC 001	THE THING FROM THE CRYPT (I NEARLY DIED LAUGHING)	15
87	Kent KENT 066	THINK SMART SOUL STRINGS	15
57	Tempo TAP 11	THIRD BRITISH FESTIVAL OF JAZZ	50
80s	Come Org. WDC 881021	33 FÜR ILSE KOCH (some on red vinyl)	70
68	Minit MLL/MLS 40002	THIRTY-THREE MINITS OF BLUES AND SOUL	45
83	2-Tone CHR TT 5007	THIS ARE 2-TONE (with free poster, green or pink sleeve)	15
64	Island ILP 910	THIS IS BLUE BEAT (unreleased, white labels may exist)	200
69	Island IWP 5	THIS IS THE BLUES	15
69	Chess CRL 4540	THIS IS CHESS	22
76	Loma/Warners K 56265	THIS IS LOMA VOL. 1	20
76	Loma/Warners K 56266	THIS IS LOMA VOL. 2	20
76	Loma/Warners K 56267	THIS IS LOMA VOL. 3	20
76	Loma/Warners K 56268	THIS IS LOMA VOL. 4	20
76	Loma/Warners K 56269	THIS IS LOMA VOL. 5	20
76	Loma/Warners K 56270	THIS IS LOMA VOL. 6	20
63	Oriole PS 40047	THIS IS MERSEYBEAT VOL. 1	50
63	Oriole PS 40048	THIS IS MERSEYBEAT VOL. 2	50
80	Grapevine GRAL 1002	THIS IS NORTHERN SOUL	30
69	Pama PSP 1003	THIS IS REGGAE	20
71	Pama PMP 2005	THIS IS REGGAE VOLUME TWO	20
71	Pama PMP 2008	THIS IS REGGAE VOLUME THREE	15
72	Pama PMP 2016	THIS IS REGGAE VOLUME FOUR	15
60s	Island IWP 3	THIS IS SUE!	25
60	Philips BBL 7356	THIS WONDERFUL WORLD OF JAZZ	12
63	RCA RD/SF 7608	THE THREE GREAT GUYS (Paul Anka, Sam Cooke & Neil Sedaka)	30
70	Saydisc Matchbox SDR182	THOSE CAKEWALKIN' BABIES FROM HOME	22
66	Allegro ALL 807	THUNDERBALL AND OTHER SECRET AGENT THEMES	15
69	Trojan TTL 7	TIGHTEN UP VOLUME TWO (pink Island label with different track listing & sleeve)	40

69	Parlophone PMC 7072	THAT TODDLIN' TOWN - CHICAGO (1926-1928)	12
71	CBS SPR 52	TOGETHER!	12
92	Too Pure SFRLP 119	TOO PURE - THE PEEL SESSIONS (LP, limited issue, custom sleeve)	20
64	Ember FA 2018	TOPS OF THE POPS	12
64	Golden Guinea GGL 0277	TOP 10 HITS, ORIGINAL ARTISTS	15
72	Studio 2 TWO 391	TOP TV THEMES AND COMMERCIALS	30
82	Zoo ZOO 4	TO THE SHORES OF LAKE PLACID (gatefold sleeve with 4-page booklet)	18
64	Topic TPS 114	TOPIC SAMPLER NO. 1 - FOLK SONGS (blue label)	15
66	Topic TPS 145	TOPIC SAMPLER NO. 2 - FOLK SONGS (blue label)	15
66	Topic TPS 166	TOPIC SAMPLER NO. 3 - MEN AT WORK (blue label)	15
66	Topic TPS 168	TOPIC SAMPLER NO. 4 - FROM ERIN'S GREEN SHORE (blue label)	15
66	Topic TPS 205	TOPIC SAMPLER No. 7 - SEA SONGS & SHANTIES (blue label)	15
72	Topic TPSS 221	TOPIC SAMPLER NO. 8 - ENGLISH GARLAND (blue label)	15
56	Tempo TAP 4	TOP TRUMPETS	50
90s	Acid Jazz JAZIDLP 13	TOTALLY WIRED	12
90s	Acid Jazz JAZIDLP 16	TOTALLY WIRED VOLUME TWO	12
90s	Acid Jazz JAZIDLP 22	TOTALLY WIRED VOLUME THREE	12
90s	Acid Jazz JAZIDLP 103	TOTALLY WIRED SWEDEN	12
55	Decca LK 4088	TRADITIONAL JAZZ AT THE ROYAL FESTIVAL HALL	15
55	Decca LK 4100	TRADITIONAL JAZZ AT THE ROYAL FESTIVAL HALL VOL. 2	15
60s	Fishers Music	TRANSAFRICK MUSICMAKERS	25
77	Free Reed FRRD 021/022	THE TRANSPORTS (2-LP, with book)	60
76	Eron 006	TRAVELLING FOLK (with insert)	25
70	RCA Intl. INTS 1175	TRAVELLING THIS LONESOME ROAD	12
61	77' LA 12-2	A TREASURY OF FIELD RECORDINGS VOLUME 1.	35
61	77' LA 12-3	A TREASURY OF FIELD RECORDINGS VOLUME 2	35
61	Embassy WLP 6041	TRIBUTE TO CLIFF	15
60	Embassy WLP 6034	TRIBUTE TO ELVIS	15
64	Columbia 33SX 1635	TRIBUTE TO MICHAEL HOLLIDAY	25
72	CBS 64861	A TRIBUTE TO WOODY GUTHRIE PART 1 (gatefold sleeve)	12
69	Key KL 003	A TRIBUTE TO YOUTH PRAISE	20
80	Skeleton SKL LP 1	A TRIP TO THE DENTIST (with insert)	15
61	Parlophone PMC 1139	TRIPLE TREAT	25
71	Trojan TALL 1	TROJAN STORY (3xLP in fold-over sleeve)	20
50s	Esquire 32-036	TROMBONE BY THREE	12
71	Revival RVS 1007	TROUBLE IN MIND... (GEORGIA BLUES)	15
67	Riverside RLP 8802	TUB JUG WASHBOARD BANDS	15
74	Melodisc 12-193	12 BIG HITS	15
74	Melodisc 12-217	12 CARAT GOLD	20
60s	Envoy VOY 9159	12 STRING STORY	12
63	Fontana 688 0082L	12 STRING GUITAR: THE FOLK SINGERS	15
66	London HA-F/SH-F 8285	THE TWELVE-STRING STORY - GUITAR SOLOS	18
76	Lucky LYLP 5004	TWELVE TRIBES OF ISRAEL (LP)	200
73	Dragon DRLS 5003	20 DRAGON HITS	18
73	Trojan TRLS 81	20 EXPLOSIVE REGGAE HITS	18
79	Polydor POLS 1006	20 OF ANOTHER KIND	12
65	Ember EMB 3359	25 YEARS OF RHYTHM & BLUES HITS	45
89	WEA 241 690-1	TWIST & SHOUT - 12 ATLANTIC TRACKS PRODUCED BY PHIL SPECTOR (gatefold sleeve)	35
63	Philips BL 7578	TWIST AT THE STAR-CLUB, HAMBURG	80
89	2-TONE CHR TT 5009	THE 2 TONE STORY (2-LP)	30
82	Beat The System BTSLP 1	TOTAL ANARCHY (LP)	15

U

68	BBC REC 28M	ULSTER'S FLOWERY VALE	15
69	Island ILP 993/ILPS 9093	THE UNFOLDING OF THE BOOK OF LIFE VOL. 1	45
72	Nevis NEV R 007	UNITY CREATES STRENGTH	25
69	Pama ECO 7	UNITY'S GREATEST	80
88	Unicorn PHZA 17	UNSUNG HEROES (red vinyl)	15
80	Safari UPP 1	UPPERS ON THE SOUTH DOWNS (original issue without Purple Hearts)	12
68	Atlantic 588 122	UPTOWN SOUL	20
77	Specialty SNTF 5023	URBAN BLUES	20
69	Liberty LBL 83215	URBAN BLUES VOLUME 1: BLUES UPTOWN	20
70	Liberty LBL 83327	URBAN BLUES VOLUME 2: NEW ORLEANS BOUNCE	20
72	Village Thing VTSAM 15	US	20

V

50s	Audubon AAM	VAUDEVILLE (10")	20
70	VJM VLP 30	VAUDEVILLE BLUES	15
78	Attrix RB 03	VAULTAGE '78 (TWO SIDES OF BRIGHTON) (originally hand-screened sleeve, later with insert)	20
71	Trojan TBL 175	VERSION GALORE VERSION TWO	15
73	Trojan TBL 200	VERSION GALORE VERSION THREE	12
72	Trojan TBL 182	VERSION TO VERSION	18
73	Trojan TBL 206	VERSION TO VERSION VOLUME THREE	12
70	Vertigo 6499 407/8	VERTIGO ANNUAL 1970 (2-LP, set no.: 6657 001)	30
87	BB BBLP 02	VINYL FRONTIER	12
55	Philips BBR 8071	VISIT TO JAZZLAND (10")	12
55	Philips	VISIT TO JAZZLAND NO. 2 (10")	12
56	Philips BBR 8098	VISIT TO JAZZLAND NO. 3 (10")	12

W

70s	Object Music OBJ 007	WAITING ROOM	15
62	Columbia 33SX 1385	WAKEY WAKEY	20
85	Psycho PSYCHO 35	THE WAKING DREAM	15
64	Pye Intl. NPL 28041	WALKING BY MYSELF	40
64	Pye Intl. NPL 28044	WALKING THE BLUES	35
81	Phil Spector Intl. WOS 001	WALL OF SOUND (9-LP box set)	60
78	CBS WOW 100	THE WAR OF THE WORLDS (boxed 2-LP, book & poster)	18
63	Ace Of Hearts AH 55	WASHBOARD RHYTHM	15
70s	Polydor 218 006	WAY INTO THE 70'S	12

78	Bridgehouse BHLP 001	A WEEKEND AT THE BRIDGEHOUSE E16 (with bonus 12" EP)	30
85	Music For Nations MFN 49	WELCOME TO THE METAL ZONE (2-LP)	18
59	Coral LVA 9096	WE LIKE GIRLS	25
59	Coral LVA 9098	WE LIKE GUYS	25
63	London HA-P 8061	WE SING THE BLUES	60
65	Liberty LBY 3051	WE SING THE BLUES	45
65	Sue ILP 921	WE SING THE BLUES!	45
84	Rot ASS 4	WET DREAMS (LP)	20
72	Syndicate Chapter SC 005	WE THREE KINGS	15
70	Trojan TTL 34	WHAT AM I TO DO	30
68	Elektra EKS 7304	WHAT'S SHAKIN' (reissue of "Good Time Music")	15
80	S & T	WHERE THE HELL IS LEICESTER? (with bonus single & booklet)	25
86	Sunrise A40 111M	WHERE WOULD YOU RATHER BE TONIGHT?	25
83	Kamera KAM 14	THE WHIP (with insert)	20
79	London Bomp DHS-Z 3	WHO PUT THE BOMP? (2-LP, gatefold sleeve)	25
70	Trojan TBL 131	WHO YOU GONNA RUN TO	50
72	private pressing	WHOLLY GRAIL	25
74	Topic 12TS 227	WILD HILLS O'WANNIE - THE SMALL PIPES OF NORTHUMBRIA	12
61	Philips BBL 7430	WINNERS OF DOWNBEAT'S INTERNATIONAL CRITICS' POLL 1960	12
66	Dot DLP 3535	WIPE OUT	25
76	RCA RS 1085	WIZARD'S CONVENTION (with insert)	12
82	Womad WOMAD 001	WOMAD: RAINDROPS CLATTERING ON BANANA LEAVES	15
67	RCA Victor RD 7840	WOMEN OF THE BLUES	20
81	Stiff FREEB 3	WONDERFUL TIME OUT THERE (Xmas freebie)	12
81	Glass GLASS 010	THE WONDERFUL WORLD OF GLASS	15
87	Black Crow CRO 217 A	WOODY LIVES: A TRIBUTE TO WOODY GUTHRIE	15
96	Magna Carta MA 9010/2	WORKING MAN	15
63	London HA-P 8099	A WORLD OF BLUES	40
69	Decca (S)PA-R 14	THE WORLD OF BLUES POWER	12
70	Decca (S)PA 63	THE WORLD OF BLUES POWER VOL. 2	12
73	Decca SPA 263	THE WORLD OF BLUES POWER VOL. 3	12
69	Pama SECO 19	A WORLD OF BULLET	50
71	Decca SPA 156	WORLD OF CONTEMPORARY FOLK	12
71	Argo SPA-A 132	THE WORLD OF FOLK	15
73	Argo SPA-A 307	THE WORLD OF FOLK VOLUME 2	15
78	Yuk NE 1023	THE WORLD'S WORST RECORD SHOW (multi-coloured vinyl)	20
69	Decca (S)PA 34	WOWIE ZOWIE! - THE WORLD OF PROGRESSIVE MUSIC	15
09	Warp WARP 20	WARP 20 (5 x 10", 5-CD, booklet, box set)	150
73	Myrrh MST 6510	WHAT IS MYRRH? (LP)	12

Y

85	Cathexis/Pleasantly Surprised PS 014	YOU BET WE'VE GOT SOMETHING AGAINST YOU	15
69	Island IWPS 2	YOU CAN ALL JOIN IN (pink label)	12
70	Trojan TBL 142	YOU CAN'T WINE	40
69	Trojan TTL 9	YOU LEFT ME STANDING	25
84	Peninsula PENCV 1002	YOUNG BLOOD (LP)	50
69	Young Blood SBYB 1	YOUNGBLOOD VOL. 1	15
71	Youngblood SBYB4	YOUNBLOOD VOL. 2	18
70	Pama ECO 35	YOUNG GIFTED AND BLACK	200
71	Bamboo BDLPS 211	YOUNG JAMAICAN GIRL	30
78	Stiff DEAL 1	YOU'RE EITHER ON THE TRAIN OR OFF THE TRAIN (promo only, with booklet)	12
62	HMV CLP 1565	YOUR FAVOURITE TV AND RADIO THEMES	20
63	HMV CLP 1676	YOUR FAVOURITE TV AND RADIO THEMES (VOL. 3)	20
63	HMV CLP 1762	YOUR FAVOURITE TV AND RADIO THEMES (VOL. 4)	20
66	HMV CLP 3521	YOUR FAVOURITE TV AND RADIO THEMES (VOL. 5)	20
71	Bamboo BDLP 211	YOUR JAMAICAN GIRL	80
82	Statik STATLP 7	YOUR SECRET'S SAFE WITH US (2-LP)	20

Z

84	Zulu ZULU 6	THE ZULU COMPILATION	20

FILM & TV SOUNDTRACK LPs

(alphabetical by title, composers/artists in brackets)

(Only the first issue of soundtracks by the Beatles and Elvis Presley are listed below: for later repressings see their entries)

A

73	United Artists UAS 29451	ACROSS 110TH STREET (J.J. Johnson & Bobby Womack)	15
70	Paramount SPFL 260	THE ADVENTURERS (Antonio Carlos Jobim)	12
62	RCA RD 7512	ADVISE AND CONSENT (Jerry Fielding)	15
64	Parlophone PMC 1230	A HARD DAY'S NIGHT (Beatles) (LP, mono, 1st pressing, with The Parlophone Co. Ltd label rim copy & "Sold In The UK..." text)	80
64	Parlophone PCS 3058	A HARD DAY'S NIGHT (Beatles) (LP, stereo, 1st pressing, with "The Parlophone Co. Ltd" label rim copy & "Sold In The UK..." text; stereo, with mid-sized "stereo"	200
67	United Artists (S)ULP 1172	AFRICA ADDIO (Riz Ortolani/Jimmy Roselli)	20
66	United Artists (S)ULP 1151	AFTER THE FOX (Burt Bacharach/Hollies)	25
56	Nixa NPT 19010	ALEXANDER THE GREAT (Mario Nascimbene) (10"; beware of counterfeits)	40
69	MGM CS 8112	ALFRED THE GREAT (Ray Leppard)	150
72	Warner Bros K 56009	ALICE'S ADVENTURES IN WONDERLAND (John Barry) (gatefold sleeve)	12
79	20th Century T 593	ALIEN (Jerry Goldsmith)	12
65	Reprise R 6151	AMERICANIZATION OF EMILY (Johnny Mandel)	20
65	RCA RD 7732	THE AMOROUS ADVENTURES OF MOLL FLANDERS (John Addison)	35
57	Brunswick LAT 8175	ANASTASIA (Alfred Newman)	15
60	Philips SBBL 514	ANATOMY OF A MURDER (Duke Ellington)	25
76	BBC REB 236	ANGELS AND 15 OTHER BBC TV THEMES (Alan Parker, et al.)	15
72	Polydor 2383 109	ANTONY AND CLEOPATRA (John Scott) (foldout sleeve)	20

60	London HA-T 2287	THE APARTMENT (Adolph Deutsch)..18
79	Elektra K 62025	APOCALYPSE NOW (2-LP, music & dialogue) 20
69	CBS 70054	APRIL FOOLS (Marvin Hamlisch)..15
66	RCA Victor RD 7817	ARABESQUE (Henry Mancini)..15
66	Fontana FJL 135	L'ASCENSEUR POUR L'ECHAFAUD/FEMME DISPARAISSANTE (Miles Davis/Art Blakey [1 side each])...30
54	HMV DLPC 1	AS LONG AS THEY'RE HAPPY (Jack Buchanan) (10")......................................50
87	Illegal ILP 017	ATHENS, GA. - INSIDE/OUT (R.E.M.)...12
67	Pye NPL 18198	AT LAST THE 1948 SHOW (TV soundtrack)..25
67	Marble Arch MAL 695	THE AVENGERS AND OTHER FAVOURITES (Laurie Johnson)..........................35
61	Fontana TFL 591	ALL NIGHT LONG (LP, mono, Dave Brubeck, Tubby Hayes, Johnny Dankworth et al.) 30
61	Fontana STFL 591	ALL NIGHT LONG (LP, stereo, Dave Brubeck, Tubby Hayes, Johnny Dankworth et al.)..........20

B

66	Fontana TL 5306	BABY, THE RAIN MUST FALL (Elmer Bernstein) 15
62	Pye Intl. NPL 28020	BARABBAS (Mario Nascimbene) 15
68	Stateside (S)SL 10260	BARBARELLA (Bob Crewe/Charles Fox)..75
67	London HA-D 8337	BAREFOOT IN THE PARK (Neal Hefti) 30
75	Warner Bros K 56189	BARRY LYNDON (Leonard Rosenman)..12
66	Stateside S(S)L 10179	BATMAN (Nelson Riddle) (TV show music)..50
66	Warner Bros W 1617	BATTLE OF THE BULGE (Benjamin Frankel) 25
60	Columbia 33SX 1225	BEAT GIRL (John Barry/Adam Faith) 50
57	London HAP 2056	BEAU JAMES (Joseph Lilley)..25
64	RCA Victor RD 7679	BECKET (dialogue only) 15
68	Decca LK 4923	BEDAZZLED (LP, mono, Peter Cook/Dudley Moore) 120
70	Island ILPS 9140	BE GLAD FOR THE SONG HAS NO ENDING (Incredible String Band)..............15
60	Capitol W/SW 1435	BELLS ARE RINGING (André Previn) (mono/stereo)......................................15
73	Ronco RR 2006	THE BELSTONE FOX (Laurie Johnson) (gatefold sleeve) 12
60	MGM MGM-C(S) 802	BEN HUR (Miklos Rozsa) (box set with hardback book; mono/stereo) 15
70	Stateside SSL 10311	BEYOND THE VALLEY OF THE DOLLS (Stu Phillips/Strawberry Alarm Clock)......................100
59	London HA-T 2142	THE BIG COUNTRY (Jerome Moross) ('sun' cover)..12
68	MGM MGM-C(S) 8066	BIGGEST BUNDLE OF THEM ALL (Riz Ortolani/Eric Burdon)...........................20
86	MCA MCF 3328	BIGGLES (Stanislas/Deep Purple/Motley Crue et al.)......................................15
69	United Artists (S)ULP 1228	THE BIG GUNDOWN (Ennio Morricone)..15
67	United Artists (S)ULP 1183	BILLION DOLLAR BRAIN (Richard Rodney Bennett)..30
73	Polydor 2490 117	BLACK CAESAR (James Brown)...35
62	Stateside SL 10026	BLACK NATIVITY (Alex Bradford) 12
72	Pye NSPL 18376	BLOOMFIELD 15
66	MGM MGM-C(S) 8039	BLOW-UP (Herbie Hancock/Yardbirds) 80
68	Dot (S)LPD 508	BLUE (Manos Hadjidakis) 30
61	RCA RD 27238	BLUE HAWAII (Elvis Presley) (black/silver label, mono)................................15
66	RCA RD 7795	BOEING BOEING (Neal Hefti) 20
62	RCA RD 7520	BONANZA (L.Greene, M. Langdon)...20
69	MCA MUPS 360	BOOM! (John Barry/Georgie Fame)..60
68	Warner Bros W 1742	BONNIE AND CLYDE (Charles Strouse) 20
70	Paramount SPFL 263	BORSALINO (Claude Bolling) 15
58	RCA RD 27054	BOTH ENDS OF THE CANDLE (Gogi Grant)...15
57	Brunswick LAT 8193	BOY ON A DOLPHIN (Hugo Friedhoffer)...30
80	MCA MCF 2013	BUCK ROGERS IN THE 25th CENTURY (Stu Phillips) 12
71	Capitol E-SW 621	THE BUGALOOS (LP)...18
72	Bell BELLS 209	THE BURGLARS (Ennio Morricone) 30
66	RCA RD 7791	BUNNY LAKE IS MISSING (Paul Glass/Zombies) 65
65	Liberty LBY 1246	BURKE'S LAW (Herschel/Burke/Gilbert) (TV series music).............................15
63	RCA Victor RD 7580	BYE BYE BIRDIE (musical) (Charles Strouse; mono)......................................12
61	RCA SF 5115	BLUE HAWAII (Elvis Presley) (black/silver label, stereo)...............................20
63	RCA Victor SF 7580	BYE BYE BIRDIE (musical) (Charles Strouse; stereo) 20
80	Chrysalis CHR 1294	BABYLON (blue/white label) 20
05	Trunk JBH 016LP/PD	BOD: WORDS & MUSIC (LP 1-sided picture disc) 20
07	Trunk JBH 023 LP	BLOOD ON SATAN's CLAW (LP, 500 only) 25

C

56	Philips BBR 8104	CALAMITY JANE (Doris Day/Howard Keel) (10") 15
66	RCA Victor SF 7820	CALIFORNIA HOLIDAY (Elvis Presley) (black/red dot labels, stereo)................30
69	Stateside (S)SL 10276	CANDY (Dave Grusin/Steppenwolf, et al.) 30
69	MCA MUPS 380	CAN HIERONYMUS MERKIN EVER FORGET MERCY HUMPPE AND FIND TRUE HAPPINESS? (Anthony Newley)..15
64	Philips SBL 7634	CAPTAIN FROM CASTILE (Robert Farnon) 12
60	Delyse DL 3057/DLS 6057	CAPTAIN HORATIO HORNBLOWER (Robert Farnon) (mono)..........................40
86	Virgin V 2401	CAPTIVE (The Edge et al.)...12
67	RCA Victor RD/SF 7874	CASINO ROYALE (Burt Bacharach/Herb Alpert/Dusty Springfield) (mono/stereo)......30
66	United Artists (S)ULP 1140	CAST A GIANT SHADOW (Elmer Bernstein/Vince Hill)..................................18
65	Columbia SX 1756	CATCH US IF YOU CAN (Dave Clark Five)..45
62	Fontana TFL 5170/STFL 585	CHANNEL THRILL: THE T.V. THRILLER THEMES (Johnny Gregory) 15
62	Warner Bros WS 8177	THE CHAPMAN REPORT (Leonard Rosenman) 15
63	RCA SF 7620	CHARADE (Henry Mancini)...20
63	MGM MGM-C 969	THE CHARGE IS MURDER (John Green) 20
68	United Artists SULP 1189	THE CHARGE OF THE LIGHT BRIGADE (John Addison/Manfred Mann)............18
83	Polydor BOX 1	CHARIOTS OF FIRE (Vangelis) (box set) 20
66	CBS (S)BPG 62665	THE CHASE (John Barry) (mono) (stereo copy is £30) 20
69	Polydor 583 736	CHE! (Lalo Schifrin) 20
67	Fontana TL 5417	CHIMES AT MIDNIGHT (Angelo Lavagnino) 30
74	ABC ABCL 5068	CHINATOWN (Jerry Goldsmith) 20
68	United Artists (S)ULP 1200	CHITTY CHITTY BANG BANG (Sherman Brothers) (gatefold sleeve)................12
68	RCA Victor RD/SF 7917	CLAMBAKE (Elvis Presley) (black/red dot labels, mono/stereo).....................20
01	Trunk SOUP 001LP	THE CLANGERS (Vernon Elliot) (TV soundtrack, with knitted sleeve, 26 only)..100
74	Buddah BDLP 4010	CLAUDINE (Curtis Mayfield/Gladys Knight) 12
63	Stateside S(S)SL 10044	CLEOPATRA (Alex North) 15
72	Warner Bros K 46127	A CLOCKWORK ORANGE (Walter Carlos) 20
65	Fontana (S)TL 5259	THE COLLECTOR (Maurice Jarre)...25
78	MGM 2315 398	COMA (Jerry Goldsmith) 12

67	MGM MGM-C(S) 8058	THE COMEDIANS (Laurence Rosenthal) 15
72	Pye NSPL 18389	CONCERTO FOR HARRY - SOMETHING TO HIDE (Roy Budd) 35
75	Polydor 2383 350	CONFESSIONS OF A POP PERFORMER (Three's A Crowd/Ed Welch) 30
71	Philips 6332 033	CONTINENTAL CIRCUS (Gong) 20
62	Parlophone PMC 1194	THE COOL MIKADO (John Barry Seven/Frankie Howerd, et al.)...................................25
67	Brunswick AXA 4544	COUNTESS FROM HONG KONG (Charles Chaplin) (with booklet) 15
70	Capitol E-ST 640	CROMWELL (Frank Cordell) 15
70	Word WST 5550	THE CROSS & THE SWITCHBLADE (Ralph Carmichael) 25
77	EMI EMA 782	CROSS OF IRON (Ernest Gold) (gatefold sleeve) 15
80	CBS 70182	CRUISING (John Hiatt/Willy DeVille/Germs) 18
73	Buddah 2318 091	CURTIS IN CHICAGO (Curtis Mayfield/Impressions/Jerry Butler, Gene Chandler, Leroy Hutson) (TV soundtrack, gatefold sleeve) 15
68	Stateside (S)SL 10222	CUSTER OF THE WEST (Bernardo Segall) 20
66	RCA Victor RD 7820	CALIFORNIA HOLIDAY (Elvis Presley) (black/red dot labels, mono) 20
01	Trunk SOUP 001LP	THE CLANGERS (Vernon Elliot) (TV soundtrack, without knitted sleeve) 20

D

81	2-Tone CHR TT 5004	DANCE CRAZE (with poster) 20
62	Fontana TFL 5184	DANGEROUS FRIENDSHIPS (Art Blakey, et. al.) 18
70	RCA SF 8138	DARLING LILI (Henry Mancini) (gatefold sleeve) 12
63	MGM MGM-C 952	DAVID AND LISA (Mark Lawrence/Victor Feldman All Stars) 15
04	Trunk JBH0011LP	DAWN OF THE DEAD (LP) 15
74	Phase 4 Stereo PFS 4339	THE DAY OF THE LOCUST (John Barry) 12
67	Stateside (S)SL 10217	THE DAY THE FISH CAME OUT (Mikis Theodorakis) 15
68	Stateside (S)SL 10263	DEADFALL (John Barry/Shirley Bassey) 35
73	Columbia SCX 6550	DEAF SMITH AND JOHNNY EARS (Daniele Patucchi) 35
74	CBS 80546	DEATH WISH (Herbie Hancock)...15
68	Stateside (S)SL 10259	DECLINE AND FALL... OF A BIRDWATCHER (Ron Goodwin) 80
55	MGM MGM-C 755	DEEP IN MY HEART (Howard Keel/Vic Damone, et al.) 12
58	London HA-D 2111	DESIRE UNDER THE ELMS (Elmer Bernstein) 20
63	Colpix PXL 440	DIAMOND HEAD (John Williams) 15
76	Pye Intl. NSPL 28219	DIAMOND MERCENARIES (Georges Garvarentz) 15
76	Bradley BRADS 8002	DIAMONDS (Roy Budd) 50
71	United Artists UAS 29216	DIAMONDS ARE FOREVER (John Barry/Shirley Bassey) 30
59	Top Rank RX 3016	THE DIARY OF ANNE FRANK (Alfred Newman) 30
83	Ripple (no cat. no.)	DIGITAL DREAMS (Bill Wyman) (promo only) 50
68	MGM MGM-C(S) 8048	DIRTY DOZEN (Frank de Vol/Trini Lopez) (yellow label) 18
67	Stateside S(S)L 10214	DOCTOR DOLITTLE (Lionel Newman) (foldout sleeve) 12
65	United Artists ULP 1097	DOCTOR NO (Monty Norman) (momo) 40
62	Columbia 33SX 1446	DON'T KNOCK THE TWIST (Chubby Checker/Gene Chandler, et al.) 25
67	RCA Victor SF 7892	DOUBLE TROUBLE (Elvis Presley) (black/red dot labels, stereo) (Mono version RD7892 = £20) 20
67	CBS S 63189	DR. FAUSTUS (Mario Nascimbene) 75
65	United Artists (S)ULP 1097	DOCTOR NO (Monty Norman) (stereo) 50
69	Capitol EST 672	THE DOUBLE DECKERS (TV soundtrack) 30
87	Crammed MTM 14	DOWN BY LAW (John Lurie) 20
74	Studio Two TWO 500	DRACULA (HAMMER PRESENTS...) (Christopher Lee) (gatefold sleeve) 12
70	President PTLS 1068	DRAKE'S DREAM (Paul Jones) 20
90	Adventure ADVTCD 1001	THE DREAMSTONE (CD, Mike Batt, Ozzy Osbourne, Bonnie Tyler, Joe Brown, etc) 20
59	Parlophone PMCL 1101	DRUMBEAT (Adam Faith/John Barry Seven, et al.) 50
66	United Artists (S)ULP 1141	DUEL AT DIABLO (Neal Hefti) 18
58	Decca LF 1308	THE DUKE WORE JEANS (Tommy Steele) (10") 15
84	Polydor 422 8237-7	DUNE (Toto, 1 track by Brian Eno) 12
00	Trunk/Bonk XXX 1 LP	DEEP THROAT (LP) 40
04	Trunk JBH 011 LP	DAWN OF THE DEAD (LP, 500 only) 30

E

58	HMV DLP 1088	EDDIE FOY AND THE SEVEN LITTLE FOYS (10", Bob Hope/James Cagney) 30
54	Brunswick LAT 8040	THE EGYPTIAN (Alfred Newman) 25
67	Columbia S(C)X 6155	EL DORADO (Nelson Riddle)...25
63	Colpix PXL 459	ELIZABETH TAYLOR IN LONDON (John Barry) (stereo) (Mono = £30) 35
69	RCA Victor RD 8011	ELVIS ("TV Special", mono)..15
74	Warner Bros K 56084	EMMANUELLE (Pierre Bachelet) 15
76	Warner Bros K 56231	EMMANUELLE 2 (Francis Lai) 12
57	Vogue Coral LVA 9063	END AS A MAN (Kenyon Hopkins) 30
74	DJM DJLPS 431	ENGLAND MADE ME (John Scott) 12
74	Warner Bros K 46275	ENTER THE DRAGON (Lalo Schifrin) 20
84	Alt. Ten. VIRUS 30	ERASERHEAD (Fats Waller/Peter Ivers/et al.) (with insert) 40
76	EMI EMC 3148	ESCAPE FROM THE DARK (Ron Goodwin) 15
63	Parlophone PMC 1198	THE ESTABLISHMENT (Peter Cook, et al.)..20
83	MCA MCA 70000	E.T. - THE EXTRA TERRESTRIAL (John Williams) (box set, with booklet & poster) 30
83	MCA CAC 70000	E.T. - THE EXTRA TERRESTRIAL (John Williams) (cassette, box set, with booklet & poster) 15
67	Brunswick LAT 8678	AN EVENING WITH BORIS KARLOFF AND FRIENDS 30
74	Warner Bros K 56071	THE EXORCIST (Jack Nitzsche, et al.) 20
71	Ember NR 5057	EXPERIENCE - THE ORIGINAL SOUNDTRACK (Jimi Hendrix) (g/fold sleeve)..............12
72	Deram SML 1095	EXTREMES (Tony Klinger & Michael Lyons) 50

F

57	Capitol LCT 6139	A FACE IN THE CROWD (Tom Glazer) (10") 20
64	CBS (S)BPG 62277	FALL OF THE ROMAN EMPIRE (Dimitri Tiomkin) 20
67	Decca LK 4847	THE FAMILY WAY (Paul McCartney/George Martin) (mono).................................70
67	Decca SKL 4847	THE FAMILY WAY (LP, stereo, soundtrack) 90
60	Top Rank 30/003/4/5	FANTASIA (various classical pieces) (3-LP, with book) 30
58	Capitol LCT 6162	A FAREWELL TO ARMS (Mario Nascimbene) 15
67	MGM MGM-C(S) 8053	FAR FROM THE MADDING CROWD (Richard Rodney Bennett) 20
68	London HA-U/SH-U 5047	THE FASTEST GUITAR ALIVE (Roy Orbison) 20
67	Stateside S(S)L 10213	FATHOM (Johnny Dankworth) 40
73	Pye NSPL 18398	FEAR IS THE KEY (Roy Budd) 50
70	United Artists UAS 29118	FELLINI-SATYRICON (Nino Rota) 20

65	Columbia 33SX 1693	FERRY CROSS THE MERSEY (Gerry & Pacemakers/Cilla Black/Fourmost) (also stereo SCX 3544 = £35)	25
63	CBS SBPG 62148	55 DAYS AT PEKING (Dimitri Tiomkin/Andy Williams)	18
66	Columbia SX 6079	FINDERS KEEPERS (Cliff Richard) (with inner sleeve, mono) (stereo SCX 6079 = £15)	15
57	Brunswick LAT 8194	FIRE DOWN BELOW (Arthur Benjamin)	25
84	MCA MCF 3233	FIRESTARTER (Tangerine Dream)	12
78	United Artists UAS 30181	F-I-S-T (Bill Conti)	12
67	RCA Victor RD/SF 7875	A FISTFUL OF DOLLARS (Ennio Morricone)	20
72	United Artists UAS 29345	A FISTFUL OF DYNAMITE (Ennio Morricone)	40
71	CBS 70091	FIVE EASY PIECES (Tammy Wynette, et al.)	12
65	RCA Victor RD 7723	FLAMING STAR AND SUMMER KISSES (Elvis Presley) (mono only, black labels)	75
85	Heavy Metal HMXD 29	FLASHPOINT (Tangerine Dream) (CD, playable [most copies faulty])	50
68	Stateside SSL 10253	A FLEA IN HER EAR (Bronislau Kaper)	12
71	Decca SKL 5093	FLIGHT OF THE DOVES (Roy Budd/Dana)	12
61	Golden Guinea GGL 0092	THE FLINTSTONES (TV soundtrack)	15
62	Brunswick LAT 8392	FLOWER DRUM SONG (Nancy Kwan, et al.) (also stereo STA 3054)	15
64	Ace Of Clubs ACL 1166	FLYING CLIPPER (Riz Ortolani)	15
73	York BYK 715	FOLLYFOOT (LP)	20
62	MGM MGM-C 882	THE 4 HORSEMEN OF THE APOCALYPSE (André Previn)	12
65	Ember NR 5029	FOUR IN THE MORNING (John Barry) (mono)	35
74	T. Motown STML 11269	FOXY BROWN (Willie Hutch)	15
66	RCA Victor RD 7793	FRANKIE AND JOHNNY (Elvis Presley) (black/red dot labels, mono) (Stereo SF 7793 = £30)	20
64	Fontana TL 5208	FREEDOM ROAD (Madeleine Bell, et al.) (TV production)	15
71	Paramount SPFL 269	FRIENDS (Elton John)	12
63	United Artists (S)ULP 1052	FROM RUSSIA WITH LOVE (John Barry/Matt Monroe) (mono/stereo)	25
60	London HA-T 2257	THE FUGITIVE KIND (Kenyon Hopkins)	30
67	RCA RD 7860	FUNERAL IN BERLIN (Konrad Elfers/Puppets)	20
63	RCA Victor RD/SF 7609	FUN IN ACAPULCO (Elvis Presley) (black/silver label, mono/stereo)	20

G

65	Liberty (S)LBY 1261	GENGHIS KHAN (Dusan Radic) (mono/stereo)	20
56	Vogue Coral LVA 9003	GENTLEMEN MARRY BRUNETTES (Robert Farnon)	30
53	MGM MGM-D 116	GENTLEMEN PREFER BLONDES (Marilyn Monroe, et al.) (10")	75
65	Mercury 20061 MCL	GENTLE RAIN (Luis Bonfa & Deodato)	15
98	Stella STELP 2	GET CHISHOLM! (David Beaumont, et al.)	12
70	RCA SF 8137	GETTING STRAIGHT (Ronald Stein)	20
57	Capitol LCT 6122	GIANT (Dimitri Tiomkin)	15
60	RCA RD 27192	G.I. BLUES (Elvis Presley) (black/silver label, mono) (stereo SF 507 = £25)	20
66	MGM MGM-C(S) 8034	GIRL FROM U.N.C.L.E. (Jerry Goldsmith & Teddy Randazzo)	40
65	RCA Victor RD 7714	GIRL HAPPY (Elvis Presley) (black/red dot labels, mono) (stereo SF 7714 = £30)	20
68	Polydor 583 714	GIRL ON A MOTORCYCLE (Les Reed)	40
63	RCA Victor RD 7534	GIRLS! GIRLS! GIRLS! (Elvis Presley) (black/silver labels, mono) (Stereo SF 7534 = £35)	15
66	United Artists SULP 1120	THE GLORY GUYS (Riz Ortolani)	30
72	Paramount SPFA 7003	THE GODFATHER (Nino Rota) (gatefold sleeve)	15
75	ABC ABCL 5128	THE GODFATHER - PART 2 (Nino Rota) (gatefold sleeve)	15
58	London HA-T 2125	GOD'S LITTLE ACRE (Elmer Bernstein)	20
72	Mother MO 4001	GOLD (MC5/David McWilliams, et al.)	35
73	United Artists UAS 29576	THE GOLDEN VOYAGE OF SINBAD (Miklos Rozsa)	15
64	United Artists ULP 1076	GOLDFINGER (John Barry/Shirley Bassey) (mono) (Stereo, SULP 1076 = £30)	25
67	MGM CS 8056	GONE WITH THE WIND (Max Steiner)	12
64	Decca LK 4673	GONKS GO BEAT (Lulu/Nashville Teens/Graham Bond, et al.)	100
68	United Artists (S)ULP 1197	THE GOOD, THE BAD AND THE UGLY (Ennio Morricone)	15
61	HMV CSD 1386	GOODBYE AGAIN (Georges Auric)	12
65	Stateside SL 10126	GOODBYE CHARLIE (André Previn)	12
69	Warner Bros W(S) 1786	GOODBYE COLUMBUS (Charles Fox/Association)	18
70	DJM DJLPS 408	GOODBYE GEMINI (Christopher Gunning/Peddlers/Jackie Lee)	50
66	MGM MGM-CS 8037	GRAND PRIX (Maurice Jarre)	12
53	HMV ALP 1071	THE GREAT CARUSO (Mario Lanza)	12
63	United Artists (S)ULP 1041	THE GREAT ESCAPE (Elmer Bernstein) (mono/stereo)	20
77	Arista SPARTY 1013	THE GREATEST (Michael Masser/George Benson)	12
65	United Artists SULP 1093	THE GREATEST STORY EVER TOLD (Alfred Newman)	12
65	RCA RD 7759	THE GREAT RACE (Henry Mancini)	12
71	Pye NSPL 18373	GREAT SONGS AND THEMES FROM GREAT FILMS (Roy Budd)	40
75	MCA MCF 2707	THE GREAT WALDO PEPPER (Henry Mancini)	15
68	United Artists SULP 1220	GREAT WESTERN FILM THEMES (Various Artists)	15
70	Polydor 2384 021	GROUPIE GIRL (Opal Butterfly/English Rose, et al.)	40
67	RCA RD/SF 7899	GUNN (Henry Mancini)	18
69	RCA SF 8025	THE GURU (Ustad Vilayet Khan)	12
09	Trunk JBH 032 LP	G SPOTS (LP)	20

H

65	United Artists SULP 1106	THE HALLELUJAH TRAIL (Elmer Bernstein)	15
75	Contour 2870 437	THE HANGED MAN (Bullet) (TV soundtrack)	30
68	United Artists SULP 1204	HANG 'EM HIGH (Dominic Frontiere) (stereo/mono)	15
69	United Artists SULP 1231	HANNIBAL BROOKS (Francis Lai)	30
70	United Artists UAS 29084	THE HAPPY ENDING (Michel Legrand)	20
56	Philips BBL 7100	HAPPY HOLIDAY (Jo Stafford)	15
65	RCA Victor RD 7767	HAREM HOLIDAY (Elvis Presley) (black/red dot labels, mono) (stereo SF 7767 = £25)	20
65	Warner Bros W 1599	HARLOW (Neal Hefti)	25
66	United Artists (S)ULP 1154	HAWAII (Elmer Bernstein)	12
80s	PRT/Chips CHILP 1	HAWK THE SLAYER (Harry Robertson) (gatefold sleeve)	15
68	RCA RD/SF 8051	HEAD (Monkees) (mono/stereo)	60
73	Fantasy FT 516	HEAVY TRAFFIC (Chuck Berry/Sergio Mendes/et al.)	12
72	Reprise K 44168	THE HEIST (Quincy Jones/Little Richard)	15
74	Tamla Motown STML 11260	HELL UP IN HARLEM (Edwin Starr)	15
65	Parlophone PMC 1255	HELP! (Beatles) (1st pressing, with "The Gramophone Co. Ltd" & "Sold In The UK..." label text; mono, with "mono" in outline type on front cover)	90

65	Parlophone PCS 3071	HELP! (Beatles) (1st pressing, with "The Gramophone Co. Ltd" & "Sold In The UK..." label text; stereo, with "stereo" in outline type on front cover)......................120
67	United Artists ULP 1186	HERE WE GO ROUND THE MULBERRY BUSH (Spencer Davis/Traffic/Andy Ellison) (mono) (stereo SULP 1186 = £35)......................40
59	Capitol T 1160	HEY BOY! HEY GIRL! (Louis Prima/Keely Smith, et al.) 25
62	Columbia 33SX 1421	HEY, LET'S TWIST (Joey Dee, et al.) 20
83	A&R FILM 001	HIGH ROAD TO CHINA (John Barry) 15
70	Columbia SCX 6443	HIS LAND (Cliff Richard/Cliff Barrows) 20
67	United Artists ULP 1161	THE HONEY POT (John Addison) 15
59	London HA-T 2197	THE HORSE SOLDIERS (David Buttolph) 15
59	Philips BBL 7292	HOUSEBOAT (George Duning) 25
87	Silva Screen FILM 041	HOW TO GET AHEAD IN ADVERTISING/WITHNAIL & I......................20
87	Silva Screen FILMCD 041	HOW TO GET AHEAD IN ADVERTISING/WITHNAIL & I (CD) 18
65	United Artists (S)ULP 1098	HOW TO MURDER YOUR WIFE (Neal Hefti) 25
72	Atlantic K 40371	HOW TO STEAL A DIAMOND IN FOUR UNEASY LESSONS (Quincy Jones) 15
66	Stateside S(S)L 10187	HOW TO STEAL A MILLION (John Williams) 25
61	Golden Guinea GGL 0069	HUCKLEBERRY HOUND (TV soundtrack) 12
67	RCA Victor RD/SF 7877	HURRY SUNDOWN (Hugo Montenegro) 20

I

69	MGM MGM-C(S) 8101	ICE STATION ZEBRA (Michel Legrand) 12
70	United Artists UAS 29044	IF IT'S TUESDAY THIS MUST BE BELGIUM (Walter Scharf) 15
67	Brunswick LAT/STA 8689	I'LL NEVER FORGET WHAT'S 'ISNAME (Francis Lai) 25
65	United Artists ULP 1105	I'LL TAKE SWEDEN (Bob Hope/Frankie Avalon, et al.) 15
68	RCA Victor RD/SF 7931	IN COLD BLOOD (Quincy Jones) 45
71	RCA RD 7707	IN HARM'S WAY (Jerry Goldsmith) 25
67	Stateside S(S)L 10207	IN LIKE FLINT (Jerry Goldsmith) 50
68	United Artists ULP 1201	INSPECTOR CLOUSEAU (Ken Thorne) 20
69	RCA Victor RD/SF 7990	INTERLUDE (Georges Delarue/Timi Yuro) 15
62	Colpix PXL 427	THE INTERNS (Leith Stevens) 18
67	United Artists (S)ULP 1181	IN THE HEAT OF THE NIGHT (Quincy Jones/Ray Charles) 25
65	CBS BPG 62530	THE IPCRESS FILE (John Barry) (mono only) 60
84	Illuminated JAMS 35	IN THE SHADOW OF THE SUN (Throbbing Gristle) 20
63	United Artists SULP 1051	IRMA LA DOUCE (Andre Previn) 12
66	CBS (S)BPG 62843	IS PARIS BURNING? (Maurice Jarre) 18
69	Paramount SPFL 256	THE ITALIAN JOB (Quincy Jones/Matt Monro) 75
63	RCA Victor RD 7565	IT HAPPENED AT THE WORLD'S FAIR (Elvis Presley) (black/silver label, mono) (stereo SF 7565 = £35)......................18
63	Columbia 33SX 1533	IT'S ALL HAPPENING (Tommy Steele/Shane Fenton, et al.) (also stereo SCX 3486)......................15
63	United Artists (S)ULP 1053	IT'S A MAD MAD MAD MAD WORLD (Ernest Gold) 15
62	Columbia 33SX 1412	IT'S TRAD, DAD! (Helen Shapiro/Gene Vincent, et al.) 12
65	Decca LK 4677	I'VE GOTTA HORSE (Billy Fury/Bachelors, et al.) 40
71	CBS 70083	I WALK THE LINE (Johnny Cash) 15
59	London LTZ-T 15160	I WANT TO LIVE (Johnny Mandel) 12
07	Trunk JBH 027 LP	IVOR THE ENGINE & POGLES WOOD (LP)......................20

J

57	Capitol LCT 6140	THE JAMES DEAN STORY (Leith Stevens) 25
54	Brunswick LA 8671	JAZZ THEMES FROM "THE WILD ONE" (Leith Stevens) (10") 30
62	HMV CLP 1582	JESSICA (Mario Nascimbene) 15
77	Pye NSPH 28504	JESUS OF NAZARETH (Maurice Jarre) (gatefold sleeve) 15
73	Reprise K 64017	JIMI HENDRIX - SOUNDTRACK RECORDINGS FROM THE FILM (2-LP) 18
71	Mercury 6338 029	JOE (Bobby Scott/Jenny Butler) 20
64	United Artists ULP 1060	JOHNNY COOL (Billy May/Sammy Davis Jr.) 25
72	Reprise K 64015	JOURNEY THROUGH THE PAST (Neil Young) (2-LP, fold-out cover with inner sleeves) 25
77	Polydor/EG 2302 079	JUBILEE (Adam & Ants/Brian Eno, et al.) 20
61	HMV CLP 1545	JUDGEMENT AT NUREMBURG (Ernest Gold) 15
66	RCA RD 7788	JUDITH (Sol Kaplan) 12
67	Fontana (S)TL 5317	JULIET OF THE SPIRITS (Nino Rota) 30
63	Decca LK 4524	JUST FOR FUN (Tornados/Karl Denver, et al.) 25
64	Decca LK 4620	JUST FOR YOU (Applejacks/Merseybeats, et al.) 40
70	Monument LMO/SMO 5031	JUSTINE (Jerry Goldsmith)......................20

K

71	MGM 2315 019	KELLY'S HEROES (Lalo Schifrin/Mike Curb)......................25
66	United Artists (S)ULP 1139	KHARTOUM (Frank Cordell) 30
72	Polydor 2383 102	KIDNAPPED (Roy Budd/Mary Hopkin) 25
58	RCA RD 27088	KING CREOLE (Elvis Presley) (black/silver labels) 40
76	Reprise K 54090	KING KONG (John Barry) (with poster) 15
61	MGM MGM-CS 6043	KING OF KINGS (Miklos Rozsa) 20
58	Capitol LCT 6165	KINGS GO FORTH (Elmer Bernstein) 15
66	Fontana (S)TL 5302	KING RAT (John Barry) 18
64	RCA Victor RD 7645	KISSIN' COUSINS (Elvis Presley) (black/red dot labels, mono) (stereo SF 7645 = £30)......................18
54	MGM MGM-C 753	KISS ME KATE (Howard Keel, et al.) 15
65	United Artists ULP 1104	THE KNACK (AND HOW TO GET IT) (John Barry) 50
54	Brunswick LA 8668	KNOCK ON WOOD (Danny Kaye) (10") 12
69	Stateside (S)SL 10277	KRAKATOA: EAST OF JAVA (Frank De Vol) 12
74	Warner Bros K 46271	KUNG FU (TV soundtrack) (with inner sleeve) (Jim Helms) 20
01	Trunk KES 001 LP	KES (LP - 1-sided) 40

L

61	RCA RD 27202	LA DOLCE VITA (Nino Rota) (gatefold sleeve) 50
63	Ace Of Hearts AH 70	THE LADY AND THE TRAMP (Peggy Lee) 20
69	Stateside S(S)L 10267	LADY IN CEMENT (Hugo Montenegro) 40
71	United Artists UAS 29120	THE LANDLORD (Al Kooper) 20
72	MGM 2315 072	THE LAST RUN (Jerry Goldsmith/Steve Lawrence) 25
80	Charisma CDS 4020	LARK RISE TO CANDLEFORD (A COUNTRY TAPESTRY) 12
73	United Artists UAS 29440	LAST TANGO IN PARIS (Gato Barbieri) 15
71	Probe SPB 1027	THE LAST VALLEY (John Barry) (mono, with insert) (stereo = £25) 18

85	United Artists 86002	LEGEND (Jerry Goldsmith)	25
71	M. F. Pleasure MFP 50034	THE LEGEND OF FRENCHIE KING (Francis Lai)	12
74	Warner Bros K 56085	THE LEGEND OF THE 7 GOLDEN VAMPIRES (James Bernard/Peter Cushing)	18
64	Stateside S(S)L 10058	THE LEOPARD (Nino Rota)	30
70	Apple PXS 1	LET IT BE (Beatles) (LP box set, 1st pressing, dark green label, red Apple logo on LP rear sleeve & white inner, with Get Back book housed in black card tray ['PXS1'] not listed on package)	800
70	Apple PCS 7096	LET IT BE (Beatles) (2nd pressing, green Apple logo on rear sleeve, plain white inner)	40
60	Philips BBL 7414/SBBL 592	LET'S MAKE LOVE (Marilyn Monroe/Yves Montand/Frankie Vaughan)	40
79	Warner Bros K 56751	LIFE OF BRIAN (Monty Python) (with inner sleeve)	12
64	Columbia SX 1626	LILIES OF THE FIELD (Jerry Goldsmith)	20
66	MGM MGM-CS 8029	THE LIQUIDATOR (Lalo Schifrin/Shirley Bassey)	40
73	United Artists UAS 29475	LIVE AND LET DIE (George Martin/Wings) (gatefold sleeve)	25
87	Warner Bros 925 616-1	THE LIVING DAYLIGHTS (John Barry)	12
76	MGM 2315 376	LOGAN'S RUN (Jerry Goldsmith)	25
62	MGM MGM-C 896	LOLITA (Nelson Riddle)	25
67	Polydor 583 014	LONG DUEL (Patrick John Scott/Vince Hill)	20
63	Stateside S(S)L 10045	THE LONGEST DAY (dialogue only)	20
83	CES CES 1001	THE LONG GOOD FRIDAY (Francis Monkman) (numbered sleeve with insert, black label print, 2,000 only)	50
83	CES CES 1001	THE LONG GOOD FRIDAY (Francis Monkman) (re-pressing, with insert, blue label print, 500 only)	40
84	CES CES 1001	THE LONG GOOD FRIDAY (Francis Monkman) (3rd pressing, with insert, blue label print, 5,000 only)	40
89	Silva Screen FILM 020	THE LONG GOOD FRIDAY (Francis Monkman) (reissue)	20
89	Silva Screen FILM 020	THE LONG GOOD FRIDAY (Francis Monkman) (CD)	25
70	CBS 70073	LOOT (Keith Mansfield/Steve Ellis)	50
65	Colpix PXL 521	LORD JIM (Bronislau Kaper)	15
69	Uni UNLS 103	LOST MAN (Quincy Jones)	25
70	CBS 70067	LOVE CIRCLE (Ennio Morricone)	50
57	RCA RC 24001	LOVING YOU (Elvis Presley) (10", silver spot label)	90

M

73	Tamla Motown STMA 8003	THE MACK (Willie Hutch)	15
69	RCA Victor SF 8017	MACKENNA'S GOLD (Quincy Jones/Jose Feliciano)	15
69	Warner Bros WS 1805	THE MADWOMAN OF CHAILLOT (Michael Lewis)	15
70	Pye Intl. NSPL 28133	THE MAGIC CHRISTIAN (Ken Thorne/Badfinger, et al.)	40
54	Brunswick LAT 8045	MAGNIFICENT OBSESSION (Frank Skinner)	20
65	MGM MGM-C 995	THE MAGNIFICENT SHOWMAN (Dimitri Tiomkin)	25
76	Atlantic K 50308	MAHONEY'S LAST STAND (Ronnie Lane & Ron Wood)	15
63	Ace Of Clubs ACL 1135	MAIGRET (Ron Grainer) (TV series music)	15
66	CBS SBPG 62525	MAJOR DUNDEE (Daniele Amfitheatrof/Mitch Miller)	15
66	Brunswick LAT/STA 8651	A MAN COULD GET KILLED (Bert Kaempfert)	15
67	RCA RB 6712/3	A MAN FOR ALL SEASONS (2-LP, dialogue only)	15
59	Top Rank 35/043	MAN FROM INTERPOL (Tony Crombie) (TV series music)	15
69	RCA Victor RD 7758	THE MAN FROM U.N.C.L.E. (Hugo Montenegro)	40
64	Stateside S(S)L 10087	MAN IN THE MIDDLE (Lionel Bart & John Barry)	30
56	Brunswick LAT 8101	THE MAN WITH THE GOLDEN ARM (Elmer Bernstein)	20
74	United Artists UAS 29671	THE MAN WITH THE GOLDEN GUN (John Barry/Lulu)	15
63	Stateside S(S)L 10048	MARILYN (Marilyn Monroe) (mono/stereo)	20
72	MCA MUPS 441	MARY QUEEN OF SCOTS (John Barry)	20
70	United Artists UAS 29122	MASTER OF THE ISLANDS (Henry Mancini)	15
69	Philips SBL 7876	MAYERLING (Francis Lai)	20
64	United Artists SULP 1059	McLINTOCK (Frank De Vol)	35
80	Polydor POLD 5034	McVICAR (Roger Daltrey) (some on clear vinyl)	15
71	Polydor 2383 043	MELODY (Bee Gees, Richard Hewson, et al.)	15
69	CBS 70061	ME, NATALIE (Henry Mancini/Rod McKuen)	12
57	London HA-P 2076	MEN IN WAR (Elmer Bernstein)	15
69	Bell BELL 6053	MERRY CHRISTMAS (David Frost/Billy Taylor)	20
65	MGM MGM-C 8001	MICKEY ONE (Stan Getz & Eddie Sauter) (with booklet, mono) (stereo MGM-CS 8001 = £25)	20
66	Mercury 20072 (S)MCL	MIRAGE (Quincy Jones)	25
61	HMV CLP 1481	THE MISFITS (Alex North)	25
68	Dot (S)LPD 503	MISSION: IMPOSSIBLE - MUSIC FROM THE TV SERIES (Lalo Schifrin)	40
54	Mercury 25181	MISS SADIE THOMPSON (George Duning) (10")	20
66	Fontana TL 5347	MODESTY BLAISE (Johnny Dankworth)	40
70	Paramount SPFL 259	THE MOLLY MAGUIRES (Henry Mancini)	15
80	BBC REB 384	MONKEY (Godiego) (TV soundtrack)	25
69	Paramount SPFL 255	MONTE CARLO OR BUST! (Ron Goodwin)	40
79	United Artists UAG 30247	MOONRAKER (John Barry/Shirley Bassey)	15
69	Columbia SCX 6346	MORE (Pink Floyd) (laminated flipback sleeve, 'couple facing west' photo on green-tinted rear sleeve)	50
70s	Columbia SCX 6346	MORE (Pink Floyd) (laminated non-flipback sleeve, 'couple facing west' photo on black-tinted rear sleeve)	45
70s	Columbia SCX 6346	MORE (Pink Floyd) (laminated non-flipback sleeve, 'couple facing east' photo on black-tinted rear sleeve)	50
72	Ember NR 5061	MORE EXPERIENCE (Jimi Hendrix)	12
69	Paramount SPFL 252	MORE 'MISSION: IMPOSSIBLE' (Lalo Schifrin)	40
60	MGM MGM-C(S) 857	MORE MUSIC FROM BEN-HUR (Miklos Rozsa)	15
66	RCA Victor RD 7832	MORE MUSIC FROM 'THE MAN FROM U.N.C.L.E.' (Hugo Montenegro)	45
62	MGM	MORE MUSIC FROM 'MUTINY ON THE BOUNTY' (Bronislau Kaper)	20
68	MGM CS8063	MORE THAN A MIRACLE (Piero Piccioni)	15
65	Columbia SX 6303	MRS BROWN YOU'VE GOT A LOVELY DAUGHTER (Hermans Hermits, mono, some with manuscript) (stereo SCX 6303 = £15)	12
67	RCA RD 7847	MURDERERS' ROW (Lalo Schifrin)	50
80	Unicorn Kachana KPM 7009	MUSIC FROM THE AVENGERS, THE NEW AVENGERS AND THE PROFESSIONALS	20
70	Harvest SHSP 4008	MUSIC FROM THE BODY (Ron Geesin & Roger Waters) (photos/green labels)	50
62	MGM MGM-CS 6060	MUTINY ON THE BOUNTY (Bronislau Kaper)	20
85	Cloud Nine CN 4002	MYSTERIOUS ISLAND (Bernard Herrman)	25

N

| 70 | United Artists UAS 29108 | NED KELLY (Shel Silverstein/Mick Jagger/Waylon Jennings) | 35 |

72	Bell BELLS 202	NICHOLAS AND ALEXANDRA (Richard Rodney Bennet)	15
67	RCA RD 7848	NIGHT OF THE GENERALS (Maurice Jarre)	30
65	MGM MGM-C 994	NIGHT OF THE IGUANA (Benjamin Frankel)	15
69	United Artists (S)ULP 1235	THE NIGHT THEY RAIDED MINSKY'S (Charles Strouse)	20
62	Decca LK 4527	NINE HOURS TO RAMA (Malcolm Arnold)	70
68	Dot (S)LPD 507	NO WAY TO TREAT A LADY (American Breed)	20

O

72	Harvest SHSP 4020	OBSCURED BY CLOUDS (Pink Floyd) (rounded sleeve)	25
76	Phase 4 Stereo PF5 4381	OBSESSION (Bernard Herrman)	15
83	A&M AMLX 64967	OCTOPUSSY (John Barry/Rita Coolidge)	12
83	A&M 394 967-2	OCTOPUSSY (John Barry) (CD, withdrawn)	75
68	Dot (S)LPD 514	THE ODD COUPLE (Neal Hefti)	30
60	London HA-T 2220	ODDS AGAINST TOMORROW (John Lewis)	20
64	Stateside S(S)L 10056	OF LOVE AND DESIRE (Ronald Stein)	12
69	Paramount SPFL 251	OH! WHAT A LOVELY WAR (Alfred Ralston, et al.) (gatefold sleeve)	12
70	Starline SRS 5019	OLIVER IN THE OVERWORLD (Freddie Garrity)	12
57	Brunswick LAT 8226	OMAR KHAYYAM/THE MOUNTAIN (Victor Young/Daniele Amfitheatrof)	30
75	Fantasy FTA 3004	ONE FLEW OVER THE CUCKOO'S NEST (Jack Nitzsche) (gatefold sleeve)	15
69	United Artists UAS 29020	ON HER MAJESTY'S SECRET SERVICE (John Barry) (foldout sleeve)	40
59	Columbia 33SX 1208	ON THE BEACH (Ernest Gold)	12
70	Fontana SFJL 950	ORFEU NEGRO (BLACK ORPHEUS) (Luis Bonfa/Antonio Carlos Jobim)	15
69	RCA SF 8014	OTLEY (Stanley Myers/Don Partridge)	25
66	Stateside S(S)L 10174	OUR MAN FLINT (Jerry Goldsmith)	50
76	Warner Bros K 56286	THE OUTLAW JOSEY WALES (Jerry Fielding)	25

P

58	Philips BBL 7197	THE PAJAMA GAME (Doris Day, et al.)	12
63	Warner Bros WM 8141	PALM SPRINGS WEEKEND (Frank Perkins)	20
74	EMI EMC 3020	PAPILLON (Jerry Goldsmith)	12
66	RCA Victor SF 7810	PARADISE, HAWAIIAN STYLE (Elvis Presley) (black/red dot labels, mono) (stereo SF 7810 = £30)	20
61	HMV CLP 1499	PARIS BLUES (Duke Ellington)	15
61	Warner Bros WS 8044	PARRISH (Max Steiner/George Creely)	20
70	Stateside SSL 10302	PATTON (Jerry Goldsmith)	12
65	Mercury 20063 SML	THE PAWNBROKER (Quincy Jones)	30
66	Philips (S)BL 7782	THE PEKING MEDALLION (Georges Garvarentz/Dusty Springfield)	20
67	Ember NR 5040	THE PENTHOUSE (John Hawksworth)	40
71	Pye NSPL 18365	PERCY (Kinks)	40
70	Warner Bros WS 2554	PERFORMANCE (First pressing, orange label, Mick Jagger/Jack Nitzsche/Randy Newman, et al.)	45
59	RCA RD 27123/SF 5033	PETER GUNN (Henry Mancini)	15
55	Philips BBL 7059	PETE KELLY'S BLUES (Sammy Cahn, Matty Matlock, et al.)	12
61	Ace Of Hearts AH 26	PETE KELLY'S BLUES (Peggy Lee, Ella Fitzgerald)	12
79	Gem GEM 102	PHANTASM (Fred Myrow & Malcolm Seagrave)	20
62	United Artists ULP 1016	PHAEDRA (Mikis Theodorakis)	12
56	Brunswick LAT 8120	PICNIC (George Duning)	20
68	Philips SBL 7858	PLAYTIME (Jacques Tati, Yan Tatore, Leo Petit)	35
70	Paramount SPFL 258	POOKIE (Fred Karlin/Sandpipers)	15
57	Capitol LCT 6141	THE PRIDE AND THE PASSION (Georges Antheil)	15
86	Bam Caruso WEBA 066	THE PRISONER (Ron Grainer, et al.) (fan club issue, gatefold sleeve with inner sleeve, booklet, membership form, map & poster)	40
66	HMV CLP/CSD 3623	PRIVILEGE (Paul Jones & Mike Leander)	30
69	RCA SF 8072	THE PRODUCERS (John Morris)	15
69	United Artists UAS 29005	A PROFESSIONAL GUN (Ennio Morricone)	25
67	RCA Victor RD/SF 7876	THE PROFESSIONALS (Maurice Jarre)	50
60	Contemporary LAC 12293	THE PROPER TIME (Shelly Manne)	15
68	Stateside S(S)L 10248	PRUDENCE AND THE PILL (Bernard Ebbinghouse)	25
75	Unicorn RHS 336	PSYCHO (Bernard Herrmann)	20
02	Trunk JBH002LP	PSYCHOMANIA	40
70	Warner Bros WS 2554	PERFORMANCE (Second pressing, green label, Mick Jagger/Jack Nitzsche/Randy Newman, et al.)	35

Q

71	Sonet SNTF 622	QUIET DAYS IN CLICHY (Country Joe McDonald)	15
66	CBS (S)BPG 62869	THE QUILLER MEMORANDUM (John Barry/Matt Monro) (mono)	15

R

88	Silva Screen FILM 033	THE RAGGEDY RAWNEY (Michael Kamen)	12
71	Reprise K 44159	RAINBOW BRIDGE (Jimi Hendrix) (matt gatefold sleeve, 'steamboat' label)	20
75	Dart ARTS 65376	RANSOM (Jerry Goldsmith)	40
60	London HAD 2288	THE RAT RACE (Sam Butera & The Witnesses)	25
67	United Artists (S)ULP 1184	RED AND BLUE (Vanessa Redgrave)	40
72	Paramount SPFL 275	THE RED TENT (Ennio Morricone)	15
70	CBS 70068	THE REIVERS (John Williams)	12
85	Big Beat WIK 38	RETURN OF THE LIVING DEAD	12
76	United Artists UAS 30007	THE RETURN OF A MAN CALLED HORSE (Laurence Rosenthal)	12
75	RCA Red Seal RS 1010	THE RETURN OF THE PINK PANTHER (Henry Mancini)	15
69	United Artists UAS 1226	REVOLUTION (Quicksilver Messenger Service/Steve Miller, et al.)	20
70	United Artists UAS 29137	RIDER IN THE RAIN (Francis Lai)	25
68	MGM MGM-C(S) 8079	THE RISE AND FALL OF THE THIRD REICH (Lalo Schifrin)	20
53	Brunswick LA 8578	ROAD TO BALI (Bob Hope, Bing Crosby) (10")	30
62	Decca LKR 4427	THE ROAD TO HONG KONG (Robert Farnon/Bob Hope & Bing Crosby)	20
54	Brunswick LAT 8031	THE ROBE	15
67	Decca LK/SKL 4892	ROBBERY (Johnny Keating/Jackie Lee)	30
64	Reprise R 2021	ROBIN AND THE SEVEN HOODS (Nelson Riddle)	20
61	RCA RD 27233	ROCCO AND HIS BROTHERS (Nino Rota)	20
57	Mercury MPT 7527	ROCK ALL NIGHT (Platters, Norah Hayes, et al.) (10")	175
67	Polydor 583 013	JULES VERNE'S ROCKET TO THE MOON (John Scott)	100
57	Brunswick LAT 8162	ROCK, PRETTY BABY (Henry Mancini/Rod McKuen)	80

87	Ode RHVX 1	ROCKY HORROR BOX SET (Richard O'Brien) (4-LP box, with inserts, numbered) 20
87	Ode RHBXLP 1	ROCKY HORROR BOX SET (Richard O'Brien) (4-LP box, with different inserts to above) 20
75	Ode ODE 78332	THE ROCKY HORROR PICTURE SHOW (Richard O'Brien) (Original Soundtrack)....................12
83	Ode OSVP 78332	THE ROCKY HORROR PICTURE SHOW ALBUM (picture disc) 15
90	Ode RHBXCD 1	THE ROCKY HORROR PICTURE SHOW - 15TH ANNIVERSARY (Richard O'Brien, et al.) (4-CD box) 40
77	MCA MCF 2813	ROLLERCOASTER (Lalo Schifrin/Sparks) 12
68	Dot (S)LPD 519	ROSEMARY'S BABY (Kryzstophe Komeda) 40
65	Parlophone PMC 1262	ROTTEN TO THE CORE (New Jazz Voices) 20
64	RCA Victor RD 7678	ROUSTABOUT (Elvis Presley) (black/red dot labels, mono) (stereo SF 7678 = £25) 15
64	Capitol (S)T 1771	ROUTE 66 AND OTHER GREAT T.V. THEMES (Nelson Riddle) (TV show) 15
66	United Artists ULP 1147	THE RUSSIANS ARE COMING THE RUSSIANS ARE COMING (Johnny Mandel) 15

S

72	RCA SF 8211	SACCO AND VANZETTI (Ennio Morricone/Joan Baez)..20
53	Brunswick LA 8604	SALOMÉ (George Duning) (10")..30
68	United Artists SULP 1202	SALT AND PEPPER (Johnny Dankworth/Sammy Davis Jr) 15
67	Stateside S(S)L 10198	THE SAND PEBBLES (Jerry Goldsmith) 12
65	Mercury MCL 20065	THE SANDPIPER (Johnny Mandel) 15
78	Polydor 2480 429	SCOUSE THE MOUSE (Ringo Starr/Adam Faith, et al.) (some w/stickered sleeve & printed [not photocopied] competition insert)...100
78	Polydor 3194 429	SCOUSE THE MOUSE (Ringo Starr/Adam Faith, et al.) (cassette) 30
70	CBS 70077	SCROOGE (Leslie Bricusse) (musical, gatefold sleeve) 12
80	EMI EMC 3340	THE SEA WOLVES (Roy Budd/Matt Monroe) 12
62	Reprise R 2013	SERGEANTS 3 (Billy May) 20
73	Paramount SPFL 296	SERPICO (Mikis Theodorakis) 25
64	United Artists ULP 1072	THE 7th DAWN (Riz Ortolani) 15
74	United Artists UAS 29763	THE SEVENTH VOYAGE OF SINBAD (Bernard Hermann) 20
71	Stax 2659 007	SHAFT - ORIGINAL SOUNDTRACK (Isaac Hayes) (2-LP, gatefold sleeve) 15
73	Probe SPB 1077	SHAFT IN AFRICA (Johnny Pate/Four Tops) 30
72	MGM 2315 115	SHAFT'S BIG SCORE! (Gordon Parks/O.C. Smith/Isaac Hayes) 35
66	CBS BPG 62755	SHAKESPEARE WALLAH (Satyajit Ray) 15
68	Philips SBL 7867	SHALAKO (Robert Farnon) 20
80	Warner Bros K 56827	THE SHINING (Bela Bartok et al.) 25
69	MGM MGM-CS 8103	SHOES OF THE FISHERMAN (Alex North) 12
70	Stateside SSL 10307	THE SICILIAN CLAN (Ennio Morricone)...40
72	MCA MUPS 458	SILENT RUNNING (Pete Schikele/Joan Baez) 18
66	RCA RD 7792	THE SILENCERS (Elmer Bernstein/Vikki Carr) 30
58	Capitol T 929	SING, BOY, SING (Tommy Sands) 50
56	MGM D 140	SINGIN' IN THE RAIN/EASTER PARADE (Gene Kelly/Judy Garland) (10") 12
66	MGM MGM-C(S) 8011	THE SINGING NUN (Debbie Reynolds) 15
78	Charisma CAS 1139	SIR HENRY AT RAWLINSON END (Vivian Stanshall) (with insert) 20
64	United Artists ULP 1071	633 SQUADRON (Ron Goodwin) 20
69	RCA SF 8010	SKIDOO (Nilsson) 20
74	Polydor 2442 126	SLADE IN FLAME (Slade) 12
73	Polydor 2391 084	SLAUGHTER'S BIG RIP-OFF (James Brown) 30
66	Mercury MCL 20080	THE SLENDER THREAD (Quincy Jones) 20
73	CBS 70127	SLEUTH (John Addison) 12
69	NEMS 6-70059	THE SMASHING BIRD I USED TO KNOW (Bobby Richards) 20
68	Stateside S(S)L 10224	SMASHING TIME (John Addison) 20
73	PRT FBLP 8085	SMIKE 15
56	Pye Disneyland DPL 39003	SNOW WHITE AND THE SEVEN DWARFS (Disney Orchestra) 30
61	Philips BBL 7504	SNOW WHITE AND THE THREE STOOGES (Harry Harris)......................................12
70	Pye NSPL 18348	SOLDIER BLUE AND OTHER THEMES (Roy Budd) 40
60	London HA-T 2221	SOLOMON AND SHEBA (Mario Nascimbene)..75
59	Capitol LCT 6180	SOME CAME RUNNING (Elmer Bernstein) 15
59	London HA-T 2176	SOME LIKE IT HOT (Marilyn Monroe) (also stereo SAH-T 6040 = £60) 50
67	RCA RD 7845	SONGS FROM THE SWINGER (Marty Paich/Ann-Margret) 30
74	Rapple/RCA APL1-0220	SON OF DRACULA (Ringo Starr/Harry Nilsson, fold-out sleeve) 15
65	CBS (S)BPG 62558	THE SONS OF KATIE ELDER (LP, stereo, Elmer Bernstein/Johnny Cash) (Mono, BPG 62558 = £10) 12
73	CBS 70123	SOUNDER (Taj Mahal) 12
69	RCA Victor SF 8024	THE SOUTHERN STAR (Matt Monro/Georges Garvarentz)......................................15
58	London HA-D 2079	SPANISH AFFAIR (Daniele Amfitheatrof)..50
61	Brunswick LAT 8363	SPARTACUS (Alex North) (gatefold sleeve) 20
68	RCA Victor SF 7957	SPEEDWAY (Elvis Presley/Nancy Sinatra) (black/red dot labels, mono) (stereo SF 7957 = £25) 30
53	Capitol CCL 7505	SPELLBOUND/THE RED HOUSE (Miklos Rozsa) (10")..25
66	RCA RD 7787	THE SPY WHO CAME IN FROM THE COLD (Sol Kaplan) 20
77	United Artists UAG 30098	THE SPY WHO LOVED ME (Marvin Hamlisch/Carly Simon) (gatefold sleeve) 12
68	CBS 62919	THE SPY WITH THE COLD NOSE (Riz Ortolani) 35
66	Fontana TL 5354	STAGECOACH (Jerry Goldsmith)..25
79	CBS 70174	STAR TREK - THE MOTION PICTURE (Jerry Goldsmith) 12
77	20th C. BTD 541	STAR WARS (John Williams) (2-LP, with insert) 20
69	CBS 70062	STILETTO (Sid Ramin)..30
52	Capitol LC 6542	A STREET CAR NAMED DESIRE (Alex North) (10") 50
61	MGM MGM-C 864	THE SUBTERRANEANS (André Previn)...12
63	Columbia 33SX 1472	SUMMER HOLIDAY (Cliff Richard) (with inner sleeve, mono) 12
63	Columbia SCX 3462	SUMMER HOLIDAY (Cliff Richard) (first pressing, stereo, with inner sleeve, with green labels) 25
57	London HA-R 2077	THE SUN ALSO RISES (Hugo Friedhofer) 25
70	Avco Embassy 6466 002	SUNFLOWER (Henry Mancini) 12
55	HMV DLP 1104	SUN VALLEY SERENADE (Glenn Miller) 15
62	Golden Guinea GGL 0106	SUPERCAR - FLIGHT OF FANCY (Barry Gray/Edwin Astley) 50
68	Buddah 2318 065	SUPERFLY (Curtis Mayfield) (gatefold sleeve) 15
73	Buddah 2318 087	SUPER FLY T.N.T. (Osibisa) 15
64	Stateside SL 10089	SURF PARTY (Astronauts, Routers, et al.)...50
79	EMI EMC 3222	SUSPIRIA (Goblin)..40
57	Brunswick LAT 8195	SWEET SMELL OF SUCCESS (Elmer Bernstein) 20
68	Stateside S(S)L 10250	THE SWEET RIDE (Pete Rugolo/Dusty Springfield) 15
68	CBS 70043	THE SWIMMER (Marvin Hamlisch) 25
65	MGM MGM-C 8012	THE SWINGIN' SET (Dave Clark Five/Animals, et al.)..30

| 66 | Mercury 20057 SMCL | SYLVIA (David Raksin) | 15 |
| 63 | Columbia SCX 3462 | SUMMER HOLIDAY (Cliff Richard) (second pressing, stereo, with blue/black labels) | 18 |

T

70	Pye NSPL 18353	TAKE A GIRL LIKE YOU (Stanley Myers/Foundations)	30
73	EMI EMC 3016	TAKE ME HIGH (Cliff Richard) (some with poster)	12
67	RCA RB 6711	THE TAMING OF THE SHREW (dialogue only) (with insert)	12
57	Vogue Coral LVA 9070	TAMMY/INTERLUDE (Frank Skinner/Debbie Reynolds) (1 film per side)	30
63	United Artists ULP 1025	TARAS BULBA (Franz Waxman)	25
76	Arista ARTY 132	TAXI DRIVER (Bernard Herrman)	25
69	T. Motown (S)TML 11110	T.C.B. (Supremes/Temptations, et al.) (laminated gatefold sleeve)	12
58	London HA-D 2074-5	THE TEN COMMANDMENTS (Elmer Bernstein) (2-LP)	15
71	RCA Victor SF 8162	THAT'S THE WAY IT IS (Elvis Presley) (glossy or matt sleeve)	15
63	Parlophone PMC 1197	THAT WAS THE WEEK THAT WAS (Millicent Martin, et al.) (also stereo PCS 3040)	15
59	Coral LVA 9102	THEMES FROM HORROR MOVIES (Dick Jacobs)	15
70	United Artists UAS 29128	THEY CALL ME MISTER TIBBS (Quincy Jones)	60
69	Philips SBL 7898	THEY CAME TO ROB LAS VEGAS (Georges Gavarentz)	60
70	Stateside SSL 10305	THEY SHOOT HORSES, DON'T THEY? (John Green)	15
73	Elektra K 46239	THE THIEF WHO CAME TO DINNER (Henry Mancini)	15
82	MCA MCF 3148	THE THING (Ennio Morricone)	30
66	Verve VLP 9147	THIS PROPERTY IS CONDEMNED (Kenyon Hopkins)	35
68	United Artists SULP 1218	THE THOMAS CROWN AFFAIR (Michel Legrand/Noel Harrison)	35
68	Sunset SLS 50519	THE THOMAS CROWN AFFAIR (Michel Legrand, reissue)	20
65	Stateside SL 10136	THOSE MAGNIFICENT MEN IN THEIR FLYING MACHINES (Ron Goodwin)	20
54	Capitol LC 6665	THREE SAILORS AND A GIRL (Gordon MacRae, et al.) (10")	30
61	Golden Guinea GGL 0065	THREE WORLDS OF GULLIVER (Bernard Herrmann)	20
85	Cloud Nine CN 4003	THREE WORLDS OF GULLIVER (Bernard Herrmann) (reissue)	15
65	United Artists (S)ULP 1110	THUNDERBALL (John Barry) (mono/stereo)	25
67	United Artists (S)ULP 1159	THUNDERBIRDS ARE GO! (Barry Gray/Cliff Richard & Shadows) (mono) (stereo = £120)	100
66	NPL 18154	TILL DEATH US DO PART (Warren Mitchell et al.)	15
69	Polydor 583 717	TILL DEATH DO US PART (Wilfred Burns)	15
72	RCA SF 8253	TIME FOR LOVING (Michel Legrand/Dusty Springfield, et al.)	12
63	MGM MGM-C 934	TO KILL A MOCKINGBIRD (Elmer Bernstein)	20
64	United Artists SULP 1062	TOM JONES (John Addison)	12
59	MGM MGM-C 772	TOM THUMB (Russ Tamblyn)	15
68	Instant INLP 002	TONITE LET'S ALL MAKE LOVE IN LONDON (Pink Floyd/Chris Farlowe, et al.)	100
70	RCA LSA 3008	TOOMORROW (with insert)	80
67	Fontana (S)TL 5446	TO SIR, WITH LOVE (Ron Grainer/ Lulu/Mindbenders)	35
69	Stateside S(S)L 10271	THE TOUCHABLES (Ken Thorne/Nirvana/Wynder K. Frog, et al.)	35
66	Polydor 582 004	THE TRAP (Ron Goodwin)	40
60	Pye Nonesuch PPLD 206	THE TRIAL OF LADY CHATTERLEY (drama/documentary)	12
96	EMI EMC 3789	TRAINSPOTTING (2-LP)	40
67	United Artists ULP 1176	TRIPLE CROSS (Georges Garvarentz/Tony Allen)	25
82	CBS 70223	TRON (Wendy Carlos/Journey)	15
73	T. Motown STML 11225	TROUBLE MAN (Marvin Gaye)	20
74	Stax STXD 4001/2	TRUCK TURNER (Isaac Hayes) (2-LP)	15
69	Polydor 583 728	TWISTED NERVE/LES BICYCLETTES DE BELSIZE (Les Reed/Barry Mason, Bernard Herrman)	80
69	Columbia S(C)X 6330	TWO CITIES (Jeff Wayne)	30
67	RCA RD/SF 7891	TWO FOR THE ROAD (Henry Mancini)	15
63	United Artists ULP 1027	TWO FOR THE SEESAW (André Previn)	15
71	United Artists UDF 50003	200 MOTELS (Frank Zappa) (2-LP, with booklet & poster)	35
70	MCA MKPS 2013	TWO MULES FOR SISTER SARA (Ennio Morricone)	30
62	Columbia 33SX 1482	TWO TICKETS TO PARIS (Joey Dee)	20
06	Trunk JBH 017 LP	THE TOMORROW PEOPLE (LP)	20

U

04	Trunk JBHO10LP	UFO (500 black/500 clear vinyl)	50
60	London HA-T 2258	THE UNFORGIVEN (Dimitri Tiomkin)	18
68	Fontana (S)TL 5460	UP THE JUNCTION (Manfred Mann)	50
70	Fontana 6852 005	UP THE JUNCTION (Manfred Mann) (reissue)	25
69	Stax (S)XATS 1005	UPTIGHT (Booker T & MGs)	15

V

73	Philips 6303 075	THE VALACHI PAPERS (Riz Ortolani)	25
68	Stateside (S)SL 10228	VALLEY OF THE DOLLS (André Previn/John Williams)	20
71	London SH-U 8420	VANISHING POINT (Delaney & Bonnie/Sam & Dave, et al.)	20
82	MGM 2315 437	VICTOR, VICTORIA (Henry Mancini)	15
63	Colpix PXL 516	THE VICTORS (Sol Kaplan/Frank Sinatra)	15
59	RCA SF 5092	VICTORY AT SEA (Richard Rogers)	12
85	Parlophone BOND 1	A VIEW TO A KILL (John Barry/Duran Duran)	12
58	London HAT 2118	THE VIKINGS (Mario Nascimbene)	40
68	Dot (S)LPD 515	VILLA RIDES (Maurice Jarre)	15
63	MGM MGM-C 951/CS 6074	THE VIPs (Miklos Rozsa)	20
66	United Artists (S)ULP 1126	VIVA MARIA! (Georges Delerue) (mono/stereo)	30
67	United Artists (S)ULP 1185	VIVRE POUR VIVRE (LIFE FOR LIFE) (Francis Lai)	12

W

60	Mercury MMC 14033	WAGON TRAIN (Stanley Wilson, et al.)	25
62	MGM MGM-C 891	WALK ON THE WILD SIDE (Elmer Bernstein)	15
66	Brunswick STA 8636	THE WAR LORD (Jerome Moross)	35
85	London YEAR 2	WATER	12
78	Satril SATL 4009	THE WATER MARGIN (Godiego) (TV soundtrack)	20
67	United Artists ULP 1173	THE WAY WEST (Bromislaw Kaper/Serendipity Singers)	12
67	Virtuoso TPLS 13010	WELLES RAISES KANE (Bernard Herrman)	30
64	Piccadilly N(S)PL 38011	WHAT A CRAZY WORLD (Joe Brown/Susan Maughan/Marty Wilde; mono/stereo)	22
64	Golden Guinea GGL 0272	WHAT A CRAZY WORLD (Joe Brown/Susan Maughan/Marty Wilde) (reissue)	12
64	Stateside SL 10090	WHAT A WAY TO GO! (Nelson Riddle)	12
66	RCA SF 7818	WHAT DID YOU DO IN THE WAR, DADDY? (Henry Mancini)	15

65	United Artists ULP 1096	WHAT'S NEW PUSSYCAT? (Burt Bacharach/Tom Jones/Manfred Mann, et al.)	20
66	MGM MGM-C(S) 8006	WHEN THE BOYS MEET THE GIRLS (Connie Francis/Herman's Hermits) (mono/stereo)	15
66	United Artists (S)ULP 1166	WHIPLASH WILLIE (André Previn)	15
67	United Artists (S)ULP 1168	THE WHISPERERS (John Barry)	20
67	Warner Bros W 1656	WHO'S AFRAID OF VIRGINIA WOOLF? (Alex North)	25
98	Trunk BARKED 4	THE WICKER MAN (Giovanni) (2nd pressing, red vinyl with inserts)	60
90	London 845128	WILD AT HEART	20
57	London HA-N 2023	WILD BILL HICKOCK AND JINGLES ON THE SANTA FE TRAIL (TV s/track)	18
69	Warner Bros WS 1814	THE WILD BUNCH (Jerry Fielding) (orange label original)	25
71	Warner Bros K 46035	THE WILD BUNCH (Jerry Fielding) (reissue)	15
78	A&M AMLH 64730	THE WILD GEESE (Roy Budd/Joan Armatrading)	15
68	Capitol (S)T 5099	WILD IN THE STREETS (Les Baxter/Gurus) (original issue, black label, rainbow rim)	25
71	MGM 2315 062	WILD ROVERS (Jerry Goldsmith)	20
83	Chrysalis CHR 1453	WILD STYLE (various artists)	20
71	Paramount SPFL 274	WILLY WONKA AND THE CHOCOLATE FACTORY (Leslie Bricusse)	25
75	Arista ARTY 111	THE WIND AND THE LION (Jerry Goldsmith)	15
87	Filmtrax MOMENT 110	WITHNAIL AND I (David Dundas)	30
57	MGM MGM-C 757	THE WIZARD OF OZ (Judy Garland, et al.)	40
67	Capitol (S)T 2800	WOMAN TIMES SEVEN (Riz Ortolani)	18
64	Columbia SX 1628	WONDERFUL LIFE (Cliff Richard) (gatefold sleeve with inner, also stereo SCX 3515 = £20)	12
63	Elstree Extra Range	SUMMER HOLIDAY (2-LP, full soundtrack recording, 80 copies only)	300
64	Elstree Extra Range	WONDERFUL LIFE (2-LP, full soundtrack recording, 150 copies only)	200
68	Apple (S)APCOR 1	WONDERWALL MUSIC (George Harrison) (with insert & black inner sleeve, mono/stereo)	250
70	Atlantic 2663 001	WOODSTOCK (Jimi Hendrix/Who/Joe Cocker, et al.) (3-LP in foldout sleeve with inners)	18
60	RCA RD 27198	THE WORLD OF SUZIE WONG (George Duning)	15
57	Brunswick LAT 8174	WRITTEN ON THE WIND/FOUR GIRLS IN TOWN (Frank Skinner)	25
98	Trunk BARKED 4	THE WICKER MAN (Giovanni) (1 st pressing, black vinyl)	50

Y

65	MGM MGM-C 997	THE YELLOW ROLLS-ROYCE (Riz Ortolani)	12
69	Apple PMC 7070	YELLOW SUBMARINE (Beatles) (1st pressing, laminated flipback sleeve with red lines above & below rear liner note & black inner; with "Sold In The UK..." label text, mono	225
69	Apple PCS 7070	YELLOW SUBMARINE (Beatles) (1st pressing, laminated flipback sleeve with red lines above & below rear liner note & black inner; with "Sold In The UK..." label text, stereo)	80
79	Warwick WW 5075	YESTERDAY'S HERO	12
61	Golden Guinea GGL 0081	YOGI BEAR TV SERIES (TV soundtrack)	12
69	CBS (S) 70045	YOU ARE WHAT YOU EAT (Tiny Tim/Electric Flag, et al.)	18
71	Ember NR 5055	YOU CAN'T HAVE EVERYTHING (Joe Parnello/Bobby Scott)	12
79	MCA MCF 2804	YOUNGBLOOD (War)	15
66	Philips (S)BL 7792	YOUNG GIRLS OF ROCHEFORT (Michel Legrand)	25
57	Brunswick LAT 8252	THE YOUNG LIONS (Hugo Friedhofer)	35
61	Columbia 33SX 1384	THE YOUNG ONES (Cliff Richard) (with inner sleeve, also stereo SCX 3397 = £30)	15
67	United Artists (S)ULP 1171	YOU ONLY LIVE TWICE (John Barry/Nancy Sinatra)	20
65	MGM MGM-CS 6081	YOUR CHEATIN' HEART (Hank Williams Jr.)	15
67	Kama Sutra KLP 402	YOU'RE A BIG BOY NOW (Lovin' Spoonful)	18

Z

70	MGM MGM CS 8120	ZABRISKIE POINT (Pink Floyd/Jerry Garcia/Kaleidoscope, et al.)	30
71	Probe SPB 1026	ZACHARIAH (Country Joe & Fish/James Gang, et al.)	12
69	Philips 600-287	ZITA	40
64	Ember NR 5012	ZULU (John Barry) (yellow/orange label, flipback sleeve)	20
65	Stateside SL10127	ZORBA THE GREEK (Nikis Theodoratis)	12

ORIGINAL STAGE SHOW & RADIO CAST RECORDING LPs

A-Z

60	Columbia SX 1211	ALADDIN (Bob Monkhouse)	15
70	Argo ZTA 501-2	ALICE IN WONDERLAND (2-LP, Jane Asher)	15
71	RCA SER 5618	AMBASSADOR (Howard Keel)	12
70	CBS 70053	ANNE OF GREEN GABLES	12
70	CBS 70052	ANN VERONICA (Arthur Lowe)	12
59	Decca SKL 4136	BELLE - OR THE BALLAD OF DOCTOR CRIPPEN	15
65	Parlophone PMC 1238	BEYOND OUR KEN	15
61	Parlophone PMC 1145	BEYOND THE FRINGE (Kenneth Williams etc.)	12
62	HMV CSD 1441	BLITZ! (stereo)	12
63	Decca LK 4564	THE BOYS FROM SYRACUSE (Bob Monkhouse)	12
63	Parlophone PMC 1190	BRIDGE ON THE RIVER WYE (also stereo PCS 3036)	15
56	HMV CLP 1064	BUCCANEER (Kenneth Williams)	30
61	Philips ABL 3383	BYE BYE BIRDIE - LONDON CAST (Marty Wilde) (also stereo SABL 205 = £15)	12
61	HMV CSD 1366	BYE BYE BIRDIE (Studio cast including Sid James)	35
69	CBS (S)BRG 70039	CABARET (Judi Dench)	12
64	Melodisc MLP 12-146	CALYPSO CARNIVAL	12
60s	Encore	CAN CAN	30
65	Pye N(S)PL 18408	THE CARD	12
58	Decca LK 4303	CINDERELLA (Tommy Steele)	12
67	Columbia S(C)X 6103	CINDERELLA (Cliff Richard/Shadows)	20
64	Decca LK 4559	CINDY-ELLA (Cleo Laine)	12
66	Decca LK/SKL 4810	COME SPY WITH ME (Barbara Windsor)	20
56	HMV CLP 1082	CRANKS (Anthony Newley)	40
60	HMV CLP 1375	NEW CRANKS (Bernard Cribbins)	40
75	Warner Bros K 56186	DAD'S ARMY	12
70	CBS 70063	DAMES AT SEA	12
58	Pye NPL 18016	EXPRESSO BONGO (Millicent Martin)	20
60	HMV CLP 1366	FOLLOW THAT GIRL (Susan Hampshire)	12
57	Oriole MG 20016	FREE AS AIR	12
64	Parlophone PCS 3065	FUNNY GAME POLITICS	12

63	HMV CLP 1685	A FUNNY THING HAPPENED ON THE WAY TO THE FORUM (Frankie Howerd)	18
71	Columbia SCXA 9252	GONE WITH THE WIND (gatefold sleeve)	12
57	Oriole MG 20014	HARMONY CLOSE (Bernard Cribbins)	18
64	Pye NPL 18100/NSPL 83022	HIGH SPIRITS	15
70	CBS BRG 70027	HOUDINI - MAN OF MAGIC	12
64	Oriole PS 40062	INSTANT MARRIAGE	25
75	MCA MCF 2726	JEEVES	40
74	RSO 2394 141	JOHN, PAUL, GEORGE, RINGO AND BERT (with London cast)	20
58	Decca LK 4352	JOHNNY THE PRIEST	50
83	TER S1044	JOHNNY THE PRIEST (Limited Edition reissue)	20
73	Reflection RL 306	LONESOME STONE	20
64	Decca LK/SKL 4643	MAGGIE MAY (mono/stereo)	12
60	HMV CLP 1333	MAKE ME AN OFFER (Daniel Massey)	12
61	Oriole MG 20054	MINE FAIR SADIE	15
60	World Record Club TP 151	OLIVER! (mono/stereo) (cast includes Steve Marriot)	12
61	HMV CLP 1459/CSD 1370	OLIVER! (mono/stereo) (Alma Cogan)	40
61	Decca LK 4393/SKL 4133	ONE OVER THE EIGHT (mono/stereo) (Kenneth Williams)	20
63	CBS 60005	ON THE TOWN	15
65	CBS BPG 62598	PASSION FLOWER HOTEL (mono only)	12
63	Parlophone PMC 1198	PETER COOK PRESENTS THE ESTABLISHMENT	15
69	Philips SBL 7916	PHIL THE FLUTER	15
59	Decca LK 4337	PIECES OF EIGHT (Kenneth Williams)	15
59	Decca SKL 4084	PIECES OF EIGHT (stereo) (Kenneth Williams)	20
60	Melodisc MLP 12-117	PREACHIN', PRAYIN', SINGIN' AND SHOUTIN' GOSPEL	12
64	London HA-U/SH-U 8201	THE PRINCE AND THE PAUPER	12
75	UK UKAL 1015	THE ROCKY HORROR SHOW (London Cast)	12
58	Pye NPL 18011	SHARE MY LETTUCE (Kenneth Williams)	15
60s	Philips 632 303 BL	SPACE IS SO STARTLING	15
60	Fontana TFL 5103	TAKE IT FROM HERE (excerpts from radio show, also stereo STFL 534)	20
63	Parlophone PMC 1197	THAT WAS THE WEEK THAT WAS (also stereo PCS 3040)	12
72	Decca SKL 5137	TOM BROWNE'S SCHOOLDAYS	12
69	Columbia S(C)X 6330	TWO CITIES (Jeff Wayne)	15
66	United Artists (S)ULP 1116	TWANG! (Lionel Bart)	25
65	HMV CLP 1834/CSD 1587	THE WAYWARD WAY	20
56	HMV DLP 1125	WILD GROWS THE HEATHER (10")	15
68	RCA SB 6792	THE YOUNG VISITORS	12

SPORT RECORDINGS

77	Quality QP 23/77	BATTLE OF THE GIANTS: 1977 FA CUP FINAL - MANCHESTER UNITED V LIVERPOOL	12
78	Quality QP 26/78	BOBBY'S DAZZLERS: 1978 FA CUP FINAL - IPSWICH V ARSENAL	12
71	Quality QP 8/71	CHELSEA KINGS OF EUROPE: 1971 EUROPEAN CUP WINNERS CUP FINAL - CHELSEA V REAL MADRID	15
70	Quality QP 4/70	CHELSEA'S CUP:1970 FA CUP FINAL - CHELSEA V LEEDS	15
73	Quality QP 12/73	EUROPEAN CUP: THE MATCH 1968 - MANCHESTER UNITED V BENFICA	25
79	Quality QP 28/79	FOREST ARE MAGIC: 1979 LEAGUE CUP FINAL - FOREST V SOUTHAMPTON	12
80	Quality QP 33/80	FOREST'S EURO DOUBLE: 1979 EUROPEAN CUP FINAL V MALMÖ/1980 EUROPEAN CUP FINAL V HAMBURG	12
84	Quality HM 2	THE FRIENDLY FINAL: EVERTON V LIVERPOOL MILK CUP 1984	12
75	Quality QP 17/75	HAIL TO THE HAMMERS: 1975 FA CUP FINAL - WEST HAM V FULHAM	12
80	Quality QP 31/80	HAMMERS HEROES: 1980 FA CUP FINAL OFFICIAL SOUVENIR	12
76	Quality QP 18/76	LEAGUE CUP FINAL 1976: MANCHESTER CITY V NEWCASTLE UNITED	12
72	Quality QP 9/72	LEAGUE CUP FINAL 1972: CHELSEA V STOKE CITY	15
74	Quality QP 15/74	LIVERPOOL'S CUP: 1974 FA CUP FINAL - LIVERPOOL V NEWCASTLE	12
82	Quality QP 38/82	LIVERPOOL'S 1982 LEAGUE CUP DOUBLE: LIVERPOOL V SPURS	12
79	Quality QP 29/79	MATCH OF THE CENTURY: 1979 FA CUP FINAL - ARSENAL V MANCHESTER UNITED	15
71	Quality QP 7/71	1971 FA CUP FINAL: ARSENAL V LIVERPOOL	15
71	Quality QP 6/71	1971 LEAGUE CUP FINAL: SPURS V ASTON VILLA	15
72	BBC REC 122M	1972 FA CUP FINAL: LEEDS V ARSENAL	12
69	Quality QP 37/81	1969 FA CUP FINAL: MANCHESTER CITY V LEICESTER CITY	12
69	Quality QP 2/69	1969 HOME INTERNATIONAL TOURNAMENT: ENGLAND V SCOTLAND	12
73	Quality QP 15/74	SUNDERLAND'S CUP: 1973 FA CUP FINAL - SUNDERLAND V LEEDS	12
76	Quality QP 19/76	SUPER SAINTS: 1976 FA CUP FINAL - SOUTHAMPTON V MANCHESTER UNITED	15
81	Quality QP 37/81	VIVA EL KOP: THE STORY OF LIVERPOOL'S 1981 EUROPEAN CUP VICTORY	12
75	Quality QP 16/75	VIVA THE VILLA: 1975 FOOTBALL LEAGUE CUP FINAL	12
80	Quality QP 30/80	WOLVES CUP: 1980 FOOTBALL LEAGUE CUP	12
74	Quality QP 14/74	WONDERFUL WOLVES: 1974 LEAGUE CUP FINAL - WOLVERHAMPTON WANDERERS V MANCHESTER CITY	15
66	Centaur CPC 1234	WORLD CUP '66	40
81	Quality QP 35/81	YEAR OF THE COCKEREL: 1981 CENTENARY CUP FINAL	12

MUSIC LIBRARY LPs

At one point in time little was known about the mysterious and often forgotten sub genre of music known as library, or rather non-commercial music pressed just for use in film, TV and radio. Thankfully, the internet has allowed light to be shined into the darkest nooks and crannies of this genre and labels like Trunk have reissued many wonderful examples of this music. Since the mid 1990s collecting interest has peaked, dropped away and is now well on the rise again, as are prices for some of the rarer and more important pieces. Collectors either favour early recordings by famous artists such as Jimmy Page or Tubby Hayes or those of a more funky persuasion that can be mined for breakbeats. Original pressing numbers and distribution still remain mysterious, although most people guestimate that 500 to 1,000 copies for each library pressing is about the average, especially as we move towards the mid 1970s. Older and larger music companies such as De Wolfe originally issued recordings on ten inch (throughout the late 1960s) in incredibly short runs - maybe only 200 - 300 copies, and if these recordings proved commercially successful they were repressed later on twelve inch. Obviously the original smaller pressings are more desirable. But still

pressing numbers and habits remain shrouded in mystery. It has to be noted that many international and desirable labels distributed their
library recordings over here and these do turn up from time to time, however we only list original UK pressings in this price guide. Also, it is
worth noting that for libraries such as Chappell and Conroy, not all LPs have titles, they simply list the artist names and track titles. In these
cases we have just put own the LP catalogue numbers. One final note, all library records are still the property of the libraries companies that
issued them and they can, at any time, ask for them back. Like promos for pop and rock artists this is all a little unlikely, but you have been
warned.

MUSIC LIBRARY AMPHONIC
| 73 | AMPSLP1001 | Moodsetter/Pacesetter | 20 |

MUSIC LIBRARY APOLLO SOUNDS
| 71 | APP 5012 | Robin Jones - DENGA (blue label) | 40 |
| 71 | APP 5016 | Robin Jones - EL MAJA (blue label) | 50 |

MUSIC LIBRARY BOSWORTH
66	BLP 102	ELECTRONIC MUSIC (10")	40
67	BLP 104	ATONAL JAZZ STRUCTURES (10")	25
68	BLP 108	JAZZ DRAMATICS (10")	20
69	BLP 109	MODERN RHYTHM (10")	20
70	BLP 116	INDUSTRIAL ROCK (10")	15
70	BLP 118	MODERN DRAMATICS (10")	25
70	BLP 120	HARD AND FAST (10")	25
71	BLP 121	MISCELLANEA (10")	25
72	BLP 126	RHYTHMIC MOODS (10")	15
73	BLP 130	KEYBOARD PLUS	20
74	BLP 135	RHYTHM AT RANDOM	40
75	BLP 141	AMERICA '76	40
75	BLP 142	LET'S GO SOLO	15
75	BLP 143	MUSICAL COCKTAIL	20

MUSIC LIBRARY BRUTON
78	Bruton BRL 1	Auturbine	20
78	Bruton BRK 2	High Adventure	40
78	Bruton BRI 1	Terrestrial Journey	15
78	Bruton BRH2	Heavy Rock	30
78	Bruton BRI 2	Tempus Fugit	15
78	Bruton BRJ 2	Drama Montage	40
78	Bruton BRJ 8	Drama Montage Volume 2	40
78	Bruton BRC 4	Percussion Volume 1	12
78	Bruton BRC 4	Percussion Volume 2	12
78	Bruton BRN 8	Expanding Horizons	15
78	Bruton BRI 10	Fantasia	15
78	Bruton BRJ 12	Wildlife	15
78	Bruton BRJ 17	Theme Sets	12
78	Bruton BRJ 22	Theme Sets	12
78	Bruton BRJ 22	Interpol	30
78	Bruton BRJ 24	Earth	15
78	Bruton BRI 23	Forcefield	15
78	Bruton BRK 9	High Tension	20
78	Bruton BRJ 9	Web Of Intrigue	20
78	Bruton BRJ 4	Thriller	12
79	Bruton BRM 1	Menace	15
79	BRS 3	Small Band Jazz	15
79	Bruton BRM 3	Darkside	12
79	BRI 4	Energism	12
79	Bruton BRD 10	Relax	12
79	Bruton BRK 5	Contemporary Motion	20
79	Bruton BRL 4	Futurama	15
79	Bruton BRI 8	Kinetics	12
79	Bruton BRG 7	Spread Your Wings	15
79	Bruton BHR 5	Light My Fire	15
79	Bruton BRJ 25	Espionage	15
80	Bruton BRK 1	Driving Force	15
80	Bruton BRK 3	Speed Fever	15
80	Bruton BRK 4	Dramatic Action	15
80	Bruton BRM 5	House Of Horror	12
80	Bruton BRM 6	Building Tension	12
80	Bruton BRL 6	Undergroove	15
80	Bruton BRM 8	Watchful Eye	12
80	Bruton BRM 13	String Tension	15
80	Bruton BRH 10	Blow Out	12
80	Bruton BRI 12	Gyroscope	15

MUSIC LIBRARY CHAPPELL
70	CIS 5001	BIG BAND SOUNDS VOL 1	12
70	CIS 5003	INDUSTRIAL SOUNDS VOL 2	25
70	CIS 5007	LIGHT ATMOSPHERE VOL 2	40
70	CIS 5008	MUSIC FOR DRAMA VOL 1 (John Barry etc)	30
70	CIS 5009	MUSIC FOR DRAMA VOL 2	25
70	CIS 5013	DANCE MUSIC VOLUME 1 (Night Club)	25
70	CIS 5023	JAZZ (SMALL GROUP) (John Barry etc)	30
70	CIS 5024	MUSIC FOR DRAMA VOL 3 (Robert Farnon)	30
75	CIS 5047	POP SOUNDS	40
70	672-677	672-677	25
70	678-682	678-682	20
71	1040	1040	15
72	LPC 1045	Lee Mason	100
72	LPC 1051	Lee Mason	75
72	LPC 1052	Mark Duval	60

72	LPC 1053	Pop Sounds	30
73	LPC 1055	Electronic Music	25
73	LPC 1056	Cacavas / Hawksworth - Mark Duval	50
73	LPC 1058	Mark Duval	50
73	LPC 1059	Lee Mason	75
73	LPC 1060	Robert Farnon	20
73	LPC 1063	Roger Webb	30
73	LPC 1065	Rhythm'n'Brass - Mark Duval	80
73	LPC 1068	Dave Holland	30
73	LPC 1069	Light And Bright - Mark Duval	40
74	LPC 1070	Mark Duval	60
74	LPC 1711	Mark Duval	30
74	LPC 1075	Mark Duval	20
74	LPC 1076	Mark Duval	80
74	LPC 1077	Mark Duval	40

MUSIC LIBRARY CONROY

70	BMLP070	BMLP070	15
70	BMLP071	BMLP071	20
70	BMLP072	Electronic Percussion Points	25
70	BMLP074	Theme And Variation	20
70	BMLP080	Electroscope	30
71	BMLP089	BMLP089	20
72	BMLP090	BMLP090	25
72	BMLP092	London's Underground	75
73	BMLP093	BMLP093	80
73	BMLP097	BMLP097	30
74	BMLP101	Happy Moog	15
74	BMLP103	Clap Trap	25
74	BMLP114	Soft Sounds	30
75	BMLP115	Londons Underground 2	20
75	BMLP117	Sounds And Percussion	20
75	BMLP123	Electronic Sounds	30
75	BMLP124	Dramatic Tempi	75
75	BMLP128	Chromozones	35
75	BMLP131	On The Road	40
75	BMLP132	Sounds Funky	20
75	BMLP143	Feelings	250

MUSIC LIBRARY CONROY EUROBEATS SERIES

73	EURO 1	Silly Synthesisers	15
73	EURO 2	Ethnic / India	40
73	EURO 3	Modern baroque	20
73	EURO 4	Romantic backgrounds	50
73	EURO 5	Dramatic backgrounds	50
73	EURO 10	World At Work	50
73	EURO 11	Colla Voce	80

MUSIC LIBRARY DE WOLFE

65	DW LP2949	Band 8 (10")	60
65	DW LP2950	High Speed Jazz (10")	30
65	DW/LP2966	Mind On The Run (10")	60
66	DW/LP2968	Journey Into Sound (10")	40
66	DW LP2973	Abstractions Of The Industrial North (10")	80
66	DW LP2974	The Wild One (10") - (features Jimmy Page)	60
67	DW/LP2975	Town Beat (10")	20
67	DW/LP3022	Checkpoint (10")	20
67	DWL/LP 3033	Chapter 2 - Beat Groups (10" LP)	25
67	DW/LP3040	Electric Banana (10")	100
67	DW/LP 3046	Young Friends (10" LP)	20
67	DW/LP3066	Don't Lose Your Cool (10")	30
68	DW/LP3069	More Electric Banana (10")	80
68	DWL LP 3084	Electroshake (10" LP)	30
68	DW/LP 3097	On The Button (10" LP)	20
68	DW/LP3088	Quietly With Johann (10")	20
69	DW/LP3114	Who's Gonna Buy? (The Lemon Dips) (10")	75
66	DW LP3115	Caribbean Sound (10")	20
69	DW/LP3123	Even More Electric Banana (10")	40
69	DW/LP3135	Electroshake Vol 2 (10")	25
69	DW/LP3136	Pop Sounds by The Cool (10")	40
70	DW/LP3154	Heavy Gravy (10")	25
71	DW/LP3182	Vocal Patterns	40
71	DW/LP3212	Moonshade	30
71	DW LP3214	Anglo Amercan Jazz	100
71	DW/LP3220	Afro-Rock	50
71	DW/LP3224	Little Bossa	30
71	DW/LP3227	Vocal Shades And Tones	100
72	DW/LP3243	Hogan, The Hawk And Dirty John Crown	40
73	DW/LP3285	Big Beat	60
74	DW/LP3318	Hard Hitter	40
75	DW/LP3324	Bite Hard	40
75	DW/LP3328	Rhythmes	80
76	DW/LP3347	A Rose For Dracula	25

MUSIC LIBRARY DE WOLFE "IN EDITIONS" SERIES

76	Timing 12	Conversations Between East And West	60
76	Timing 14	Cradle Of Time	30

MUSIC LIBRARY FRANCIS, DAY & HUNTER

68	FDH 1018	Diplomatic Immunity	70

MUSIC LIBRARY HARMONIC

68	CBL618	Fonteyns Folk Jazz (10")	30
69	CBL621	More Beat (10")	20

MINT VALUE £

69	CNW 598	Ronnie Ross Plays (no 1)	100

MUSIC LIBRARY HUDSON

71	501 HMC	Rocking Tempo (Peter Merrick)	12
72	506 HMC	Mindbender (peter Merrick)	15
81	527 HMC	Headline (Barbara Moore)	12

MUSIC LIBRARY KPM

66	KPM/ACW1	Music For Your Movies	20
69	KPM1021	Light Jazz Feeling	30
69	KPM1027	Soul Organ Showcase (Alan Hawkshaw)	50
69	KPM1029	Colours In Rhythm	30
69	KPM1037	Flamboyant Themes	20
69	KPM1038	Flamboyant Themes 2	25
69	KPM1042	Jazz Graphics/Spy Set	25
69	KPM1043	Beat Incidental (Alan Hawkshaw/Keith Mansfield)	50
69	KPM1044	The Big Beat (Mohawks & Alan Hawkshaw)	80
69	KPM1046	Sounds In Percussion	20
69	KPM1049	Chorus And Orchestra (Syd Dale)	100
69	KPM1054	Native Africa	25
70	KPM1055	Dramatic Background	40
69	KPM1061	Impact And Action	20
69	KPM1063	Contemporary Colour (Syd Dale)	20
70	KPM1067	The Big Beat - Volume 2 (Alan Moorhouse)	80
70	KPM1070	Bugaloo In Brazil (Les Baxter)	40
70	KPM1071	The Brazillian Suite (Roger Duprat)	40
71	KPM1076	Speed And Excitement (Mansfield, Hawkshaw, Pearson)	35
72	KPM1079	Beat Industrial	40
72	KPM1080	Beat Incidental (Alan Hawkshaw)	50
72	KPM 1080	Flute For Moderns (with Alan Hawkshaw, Alan Parker and Joe Hailer)	35
72	KPM1084	Mediterranean Intrigue (Neil Ardley)	60
71	KPM1085	Electronic Music	50
71	KPM1086	Music For A Young Generation (Alan Hawkshaw)	50
71	KPM1087	Technical Viewpoint	50
71	KPM1088	Bass Guitar And Percussion - Volume 1	50
71	KPM1089	Bass Guitar And Percussion - Volume 2 (Herbie Flowers)	30
71	KPM1090	Bass Guitar And Percussion - Volume 3	30
71	KPM1091	Vibraphone Jazz Quartet	20
71	KPM1094	Accent on Percussion/Construction In Jazz	40
71	KPM1095	Theme Suites / Mustang (John Cameron/Keith Mansfield)	60
71	KPM1097	Jazzrock (John Cameron)	45
71	KPM1100	The Big Screen (Johnny Pearson)	20
72	KPM1102	Electrosound (Ron Geesin)	30
72	KPM1103	Electromusic	25
72	KPM1104	Electrosonic (Delia Derbyshire)	60
72	KPM1111	Brass Plus Moog	40
72	KPM1122	Move With The Times	25
72	KPM1124	Big Business (Keith Mansfield)	35
72	KPM1125	Voices In Harmony (John Cameron/Keith Mansfield)	40
73	KPM1126	Summer Songbirds	40
73	KPM1128	Counterpoint In Rhythm	40
73	KPM1130	Afro Rock (John Cameron/Alan Parker)	100
73	KPM1131	Trendsetters	25
74	KPM1136	Industrial Panorama (Johnny Pearson/Keith Mansfield)	35
75	KPM1160	Friends anf Lovers (Brian Bennett, David Lindup, Duncan Lamont etc)	30
74	KPM1161	Industry Volume 1	40
74	KPM1163	Rock Spectrum	30
74	KPM1165	Jazz Inclination	30
74	KPM1166	Piano Vibrartions	30
74	KPM1168	Drama	40
74	KPM1170	Sounds Of The Time	20
74	KPM1171	Impact (Keith Mansfield/Brian Bennett)	30
74	KPM1177	Hot Wax (Alan Hawkshaw/Brian Bennett)	30
77	KPM1183	Middle East Suite	40
77	KPM1191	Landscapes	15
77	KPM1196	Rock On	30
77	KPM1214	Pulse Of The City	15

MUSIC LIBRARY PEER INTERNATIONAL

70	PIL9006	My Thing	60
71	PIL9009	BIG HAMMER	60
72	PIL9013	Mindbender	200
73	PIL9023	Reggae For Real	75
74	PIL9026	Solar Flares	60
74	PIL9027	Electric Bazaar	40
75	PIL9028	Scoop!	25
76	PIL9029	5+4	25
77	PIL9037	Hit Man	25
77	PIL9038	Hangover	40
78	PIL9039	Lost Star	75

MUSIC LIBRARY PROGRAMME MUSIC

75	PM8	On The Side Of Angels	35
75	PM11	Music To Varnish Owls By	20
75	PM18 -	Ad-Version Therapy!	20

MUSIC LIBRARY REGENCY LINE

75	RL1001	Light Background Vol. 1	15
75	RL1002	Themes	15
75	RL1003	Rock	15
75	RL1004	Rock	15
75	RL1008	Synthesiser Spots	15
76	RL1013	Dramatic Moods	20

| 76 | RL1019 | The Detectives ....25 |

MUSIC LIBRARY ROUGE

75	RMS 101	Skyboat 35
75	RMS 102	Sweet Soul 30
75	RMS 103	Interlace 35
75	RMS 104	The King And The Clown 40
75	RMS 105	Hi-Fly 40
75	RMS 106	Blackout 70
76	RMS 107	Return To Base 30
76	RMS 108	Cobra 35
77	RMS 109	Meal Ticket 25
77	RMS 110	Music Report 20
77	RMS 111	Kites "Electronic Music" 20
77	RMS 112	Let The Music Play 20
78	RMS 113	Hard As A Rock 20
78	RMS 114	Soft And Tender 20
78	RMS 115	Do It (Wally Waller Band - ex Pretty Things) 25
78	RMS 116	Faded Jeans 20
78	RMS 117	All About The Sea 15
78	RMS 118	Discos Like This 40
79	RMS 119	Pulses "Electronic Music"...25
79	RMS 120	Candover 25
79	RMS 121	Friday Girl 30
79	RMS 122	Robot Dancer..20
81	RMS 124	Country Grass 20
81	RMS 125	Making Tracks 20
81	RMS 126	Patterns 20
81	RMS 127	Dancing Grass 15
81	RMS 128	Impetus 15
81	RMS 129	Play On (by Patchwork) 20
81	RMS 130	Glass-Head..25
81	RMS 131	Superdoup 20
81	RMS 132	Sliced Apple 20
81	RMS 133	Pipsqueek 15
81	RMS 134	Whisper To The Moon 20
81	RMS 135	History Of Jazz 15
82	RMS 136	Telletext "Electronic" Music 30
82	RMS 137	Voyage Of Discovery 20
82	RMS 138	Movement...30
82	RMS 140	Instant Reggae (by Roots) 15
82	RMS 141	Hercules 12
82	RMS 142	Red Kite 20
82	RMS 143	New-Age..15
82	RMS 144	Remember...25
82	RMS 145	Dramatics 20
82	RMS 146	Eight Orchestral Sketches 15
83	RMS 147	Cutaway...20
83	RMS 148	Solarium 20
83	RMS 149	Some Shufflin' 15
83	RMS 150	Bass Moods Vol 1 15
83	RMS 151	Bass Moods Vol 2 15
83	RMS 152	Undercover..30
84	RMS 156	Frontrunner 15
84	RMS 157	Breakdance 15
84	RMS 158	Topsy Turvy 15
85	RMS 160	New-Outlook 15
85	RMS 165	Sound On Sound 15
86	RMS 166	Music Break 15
86	RMS 168	Audiotronics 15
86	RMS 169	Highlights (by Darryl Way) 15
87	RMS 173	Pace-Age..15
87	RMS 174	Breaking Ground...15
87	RMS 175	Changing Seasons 25
87	RMS 178	Kinetics (Alan Parker)..20

MUSIC LIBRARY SOUNDS OF NOW

71	Sounds of Now 1	Sounds Of Now 1 (LP) 50
71	Sounds Of Now 2	Sounds Of Now 2 (LP) 75
72	Sounds Of Now 3	Sounds Of Now 3 (LP) 100

MUSIC LIBRARY STANDARD

| 00 | ESL 103 | Solo Guitar (Michael Chapman) ....40 |
| 00 | ESL 104 | Electronic Music ....100 |

MUSIC LIBRARY STUDIO G

70	LPSG1001	Beat Group 75
70	LPSG1002	Big Jazz & Big Beat 40
70	LPSG1008	Dramatic And Horror..20
80	LPSG4004	Abstract 15

MUSIC LIBRARY STUDIO ONE

| 71 | SO7 | MAURICE POP ....15 |
| 73 | SO14 | PIERRE LAVIN POP BAND ....30 |

MUSIC LIBRARY SYLVESTER

67	SMC/LP501	Jazz Waves (10") 15
67	SMC/LP502	Voices In The Wind (10")..20
67	SMC/LP503	Striptease (10")...15
67	SMC/LP504	Aquaplane (10") 15
67	SMC/LP505	And So On (10") 15
67	SMC/LP506	Tutti Flutti (10") 15
67	SMX/LP507	Go (10")...15
68	SMX/LP511	Rhythm For Ursula (10") 20

MUSIC LIBRARY THEMES

68	SMX/LP512	Exchanges (10")	80
68	SMX/LP516	Racing Tempo (10")	15
70	SMC/LP525	Jazz For Action	15
71	SMC/LP526	Post Combustion	15
71	SMC/LP527	Blue Cylinder	30
71	SMC/LP528	Chronoradial	20
71	SMC/LP529	Ultra Pop-Op	15

MUSIC LIBRARY THEMES

74	TIM1012	Synthesizer And Percussion	25
74	TIM1013	Breath Of Danger	40
74	TIM1015	Mystery Movie	20
75	TIM1018	The All American Powerhouse	20
76	TIM1021	The Voice Of Soul	40
76	TIM1022	The Sound Of Soul	50
76	TIM1024	Drama Suite - Part 1	100
76	TIM1025	The Drama Suite - Part II	100
76	TIM1025	Things To Come	0

MUSIC LIBRARY TIMING

76	Timing No 12	Conversations Between The East And The West	35
76	Timing No 13	Brazil	40
76	Timing No 14	Cradle Of Time	50

Sleeve Type A: coloured wavy lines with small box on front (left), large box on reverse (right).

Sleeve Type B: coloured wavy lines without box on front (left), with large box on reverse (right).

Sleeve Type C: multicoloured shapes on front (left) and LP details on reverse (right).

Green sleeve Type 1: straight cut at top (left) and '6/- to 50/- record tokens' on reverse (right).

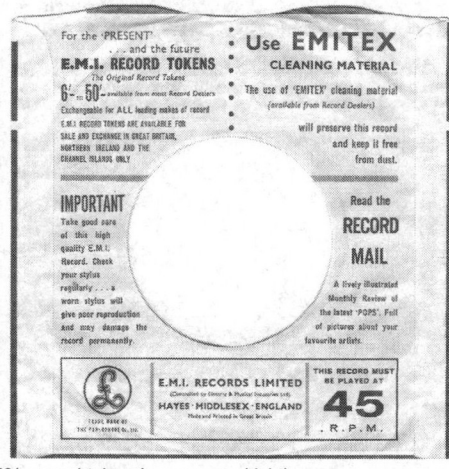

Green sleeve Type 1B: wavy cut at top (left) and '6/- to 50/- record tokens' on reverse (right).

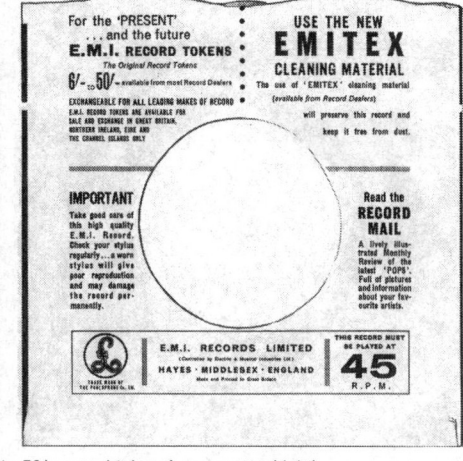

Green sleeve Type 2: rectangular box on front (left),'6/- to 50/- record tokens' on reverse (right).

Green sleeve Type 3: wavy cut at top (left) and 'Fran The Fan' advert on reverse (right).

Green sleeve Type 4: wavy cut at top (left) and 'Morphy-Richards offer' advert on reverse (right).

Green sleeve Type 5: straight cut at top (left), 'Fran The Fan, Dear Miss Brown' ad. on reverse (right).

Green sleeve Type 6: top wavy cut, front rectangular box (left), '6/- to 50/-' on reverse (right).

Green sleeve Type 7: wavy cut at top (left) and 'Big M' advert on reverse (right).

Green sleeve Type 8: wavy cut at top (left) and 'Hit make-up' advert on revesre (right).

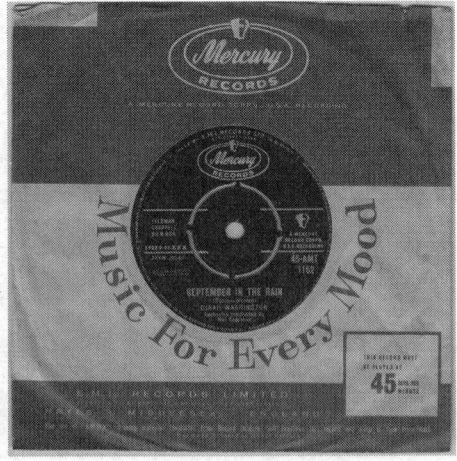

MANUFACTURED AND DISTRIBUTED BY FONTANA RECORDS

RECORD COLLECTOR'S
GRADING SYSTEM

In order to assist everyone who buys and sells rare discs, *Record Collector* magazine has originated a set of standards for the condition of second-hand records, cassettes and CDs. Anyone buying or selling records through the magazine must use our conditions to state what amount of wear and tear the disc, its sleeve and/or contents have been subject to. The seven standard condition categories, and a description of what each one means, are listed below:

MINT: The record itself is in brand new condition with no surface marks or deterioration in sound quality. The cover and any extra items such as the lyric sheet, booklet or poster are in perfect condition. Records advertised as Sealed or Unplayed should be Mint.

EXCELLENT: The record shows some signs of having been played, but there is very little lessening in sound quality. The cover and packaging might have slight wear and/or creasing.

VERY GOOD: The record has obviously been played many times, but displays no major deterioration in sound quality, despite noticeable surface marks and the occasional light scratch. Normal wear and tear on the cover or extra items, without any major defects, is acceptable.

GOOD: The record has been played so much that the sound quality has noticeably deteriorated, perhaps with some distortion and mild scratches. The cover and contents suffer from folding, scuffing of edges, spine splits, discoloration, etc.

FAIR: The record is still just playable but has not been cared for properly and displays considerable surface noise; it may even jump. The cover and contents will be torn, stained and/or defaced.

POOR: The record will not play properly due to scratches, bad surface noise, etc. The cover and contents will be badly damaged or partly missing.

BAD: The record is unplayable or might even be broken, and is only of use as a collection-filler.

CDs & CASSETTES: As a general rule, CDs and cassettes either play perfectly — in which case they are in Mint condition — or they don't, in which case their value is minimal. Cassette tape is liable to deteriorate with age, even if it remains unplayed, so care should be taken when buying old tapes. CDs are difficult to grade visually: they can look perfect but actually be faulty, while in other cases they may appear damaged but still play perfectly. Cassette and CD inlays and booklets should be graded in the same way as record covers and sleeves. In general, the plastic containers for cassettes and CDs can easily be replaced if they are broken or scratched, but card covers and digipaks are subject to the same wear as record sleeves.

RECORD COLLECTOR'S
GRADING READY RECKONER

This Ready Reckoner will help you work out the value of a record in any condition. For example, if you see a disc which is valued at £10 in Mint condition, but which you consider to be in only Very Good condition, then you can consult the Ready Reckoner and find out the appropriate price for the record — in this case, £5. As very few collectors are interested in records in Poor or Bad condition, we consider that any disc worth less than £10 in Mint condition is effectively worthless in Poor or Bad condition.

MINT	EX	VG	Good	Fair	Poor	Bad
1,000	800	500	300	150	80	25
500	400	250	150	75	40	12
300	240	150	90	45	25	8
250	200	125	75	38	20	6
200	160	100	60	30	15	5
150	120	75	45	25	13	4
125	100	60	38	18	12	3
100	80	50	30	15	8	2.50
75	60	35	22	10	6	2
50	40	25	15	8	4	1.50
40	32	20	12	6	3	1
30	25	15	9	4.50	2.50	—
25	20	12	7.50	3.50	2	—
22	18	11	6.50	3	1.75	—
20	16	10	6	2.50	1.50	—
15	12	8	4.50	2	1	—
12	10	6	3.50	1.75	0.75	—
10	8	5	3	1.50	—	—
8	6	4	2.50	1	—	—
7	5	3.50	2	0.75	—	—
6	4.50	3	1.75	—	—	—
5	4	2.50	1.50	—	—	—
4	3.25	2	1.25	—	—	—
3	2.50	1.50	1	—	—	—
2	1.75	1	—	—	—	—